P9-EDU-925

THE OXFORD DICTIONARY OF ENGLISH ETYMOLOGY

THE OXFORD DICTIONARY OF ENGLISH ETYMOLOGY

EDITED BY

C. T. ONIONS

WITH THE ASSISTANCE OF

G. W. S. FRIEDRICHSEN

AND

R. W. BURCHFIELD

OXFORD

AT THE CLARENDON PRESS

Oxford University Press, Walton Street, Oxford OX2 6DP
London Glasgow New York Toronto
Delhi Bombay Calcutta Madras Karachi
Kuala Lumpur Singapore Hong Kong Tokyo
Nairobi Dar es Salaam Cape Town
Melbourne Auckland
and associated companies in
Beirut Berlin Ibadan Mexico City Nicosia

Oxford is a trade mark of Oxford University Press

ISBN 0 19 861112 9

Published in the United States by
Oxford University Press, New York

First published 1966
Reprinted 1966
Reprinted 1967 (with corrections), 1969 (with corrections)
1974, 1976, 1978, 1979, 1982 (twice), 1983

Printed in Great Britain
at the University Press, Oxford
by Eric Buckley
Printer to the University

INTRODUCTION

Etymology

ETYMOLOGY has been briefly defined in this book as 'the origin, formation, and development (of a word)'. Some of the words going back to OE. are as old as time, and are represented in many of the Indo-European languages; *acre*, for instance, in OE. *æcer*, has cognates in all the Germanic languages, and can be recognized in Latin *ager*, Greek *agrós*, and Sanskrit *ájras*, which go back to an Indo-European original **agros*, which is based on a root **ag* to drive, do, ACT.

Other words commence their documented life not before the Middle English period, such as *Lent*, in ME. *lenten*, which is traced to a West Germanic form cognate with LONG, whilst many others appear in written works much later, or derive from or are compounded with words already long in use, such as *handicap* (XVII, = 'hand in cap'), *landslide* (XIX: see LAND).

Acre, *Lent*, *handicap*, *landslide* are native words by descent through a long ancestry of Germanic stock. Other words have come into English from a foreign language such as Greek or Latin, (Old) French or Low Dutch and, later, from many non-Indo-European languages of the East, South, and West.

The forms from which English words are derived, whether by descent or by adoption, are traced to their ultimate source so far as this is known or reasonably to be presumed. Words whose cognates are within the Germanic group of dialects are traced back to the inferred Germanic originals, with mention of any Indo-European collaterals as may be thought expedient. It often happens that a Germanic word is represented in West and North Germanic, but not in Gothic as, e.g., OAK, OE. *āc*, OHG. *eih*, ON. *eik*:– CGerm. (exc. Gothic) **aiks*. Here '(exc. Gothic)' means that no Gothic cognate appears in the extant Gothic fragments, not that the word in question did not exist in Gothic, although that may have been the case, as it seems to be with the West and North Germ. STARK, STRONG, where the notion is expressed in known Gothic by *swinþs* = ἰσχυρός, *swinþei* = κράτος: similarly, s.v. BREAK[I], 'CGerm. (exc. ON.) **brekan*'.

For words derived from French, the ultimate source is given where possible, and the same treatment is given to many Latin originals from which the English has directly or mediately been derived. The etymology of Greek words is usually given in detail, as, for instance, under COMET.

Derivation directly from French or from Latin

One of the permanent difficulties that beset the etymologist is to determine whether a word such as *evident*, which has its counterpart in (O)F. *évident* as well as in L. *ēvident-* f. *ēvidēns*, is to be derived from the French or the Latin. Since literate Englishmen have been acquainted with both French and

Latin throughout the Middle Ages and down to our own times, either channel, or both, could be assumed as the means of entry into English, other things being equal.

This is especially true of the flood of new words of French-Latin form that came into English during the late xvth and the xvith centuries in the wake of the renaissance. The reader will see that '– (O)F. or L.' has been predicated of a very large number of words from this period. In this connexion 'French or Latin' is to be understood as 'French and/or Latin', or even 'French and Latin', according to circumstances.

There was a comparable period during the xivth/xvth centuries when many words were adopted from Latin, especially in translations of scientific and theological works, among which may be mentioned the writings of Trevisa (xiv), Lanfranc (xiv), Arderne (xv), the anonymous translation of Guy de Chauliac's *Grande Chirurgie* (xv), and the writings of Wyclif (xiv).

For the earlier period, in ME. of the xiith and xiiith centuries, the source is more likely to be Anglo-Norman or Old French, and this is often revealed by the earliest spelling of the English adoptions, which point conclusively to their French origin. Liturgical terms and words relating to the Church or to monasticism are likely to have come into English from the 'Anglo-Norman of the cloisters', yet even there the Clerks were conversant with Latin also.

These and other factors have to be taken into consideration, and each word needs to be judged on its own merits, from its form and context. It is hoped that the conclusions arrived at will be as correct as probability and human wit can make them.

Words from Low Dutch

Many words have been adopted into English from Low Dutch, that is from (Middle) Dutch and (Middle) Low German, and that from quite early times, from the xiiith century at least, since when there has been constant traffic between England and the adjacent Continent. Where the *O.E.D.* tentatively refers to MDu. and MLG. forms as 'probably' being the source of the English word, or with 'cf.', these words will in the present work be more often found given as the actual source of the English, see e.g., BOWSPRIT (xiii), DECK[1] (xv).

Development of individual words in English

The etymologist might be content to give the earliest recorded date of each word, with its previous history, whether of English or Germanic descent or admitted to citizenship from other languages, thus accounting for their 'origin and formation'. There remains, however, the 'development' of the word, that is, its progressive development in form and sense in English. This is every whit as important, and to many whose interests are the history of words in English rather than their remoter ancestry, the more useful and important function of etymology.

In the present work the development of spelling, pronunciation, and sense has been considered, so far as this does not usurp the functions of lexicography. Thus, under ACRE is explained the source of *God's acre*, and under LENT is the added information 'the eccl. sense of the word is peculiar to English', whilst MERRY includes a reference to *merry England*.

The account of individual words includes, where useful or necessary, pronunciation and spelling. Thus under DIE[1] the reader will find 'For the development of *die* from ME. *dēȝe*, cf. *dye*, *eye*, *high*, *nigh*, *thigh*', and under JOIST 'The development (of ME. *giste*) to *joist* is paralleled by *foist*, *hoist*'; s.v. JOLLY, 'Final *f* was lost as in *hasty*, *tardy*'; s.v. HARBINGER, 'The intrusive *n* occurs XV; cf. *celandine*; *messenger*, *ostringer*, *passenger*, *porringer*, *scavenger*, *wharfinger*; *nightingale*; *popinjay*'; and s.v. ANCIENT[1], 'The addition of homorganic *t* to final *n* (XV) is paralleled in *pageant*, *pheasant*, *tyrant*'. Under MOB[2] we are reminded that it is 'one of a group of shortened forms (as *cit*, *rep*, *pos*, *incog*.) in Addison's "Spectator" ', and comments on the pronunciation and spelling will be found wherever necessary, as, e.g., under ANTHEM and ANTIPODES.

Earlier forms are recorded, as under HIPPOPOTAMUS, 'Earlier forms (from XIV) were *ypotam(e)*, *hippotame*, *ypotamos*, *-anus*, – OF. *ypotame*'. Contemporary, now obsolete, synonyms are given, as under DIGEST: 'In XVI–XVII *disgest*, *disgestion* were also current'.

Words common and current in earlier stages of the language are sometimes replaced by other words. Thus OE. *niman* (see NIM), which was in general literary use until XV, was replaced by *take*, which had been in concurrent use since late OE. times, into which it had been taken from ON. 'In OE. the words for "die" were *steorfan*, *sweltan*, or *wesan dēad*.' OE. *capellān*, from medL. *cappellānus*, was superseded in early ME. by *capelein*, from AN., and that by *chapelain* from Central French (see CHAPLAIN). ACCLIMATIZE (XIX) superseded *acclimate* (XVIII) which was a direct adoption from French.

Then there are words which come into political history, the connexion being explained in addition to their more general history. Thus under HOLD[1] reference is made to *copy-*, *free-*, *lease-*, *house-*, *stronghold*. Less known words such as *floruit* are referred to the similar forms *habitat*, *tenet*, †*tenent*. Among many items of more general interest are such as the origin of *psychological moment*, *lushington*, *quack*, *tantivy*, etc.

Order and arrangement of articles

The word heading each article is printed in bold type, e.g., **depose**, and any related words which may be grouped under this are printed in the same type; if any of these end in a suffix which is treated in a separate article, this is printed in small capitals, thus **depose** . . . **deposit** . . . **deposit**ARY . . . **depos**ITION . . . **deposit**ORY[1] . . . **depot**. References to other articles are printed in small capitals, e.g. under BUSY, 'cf. BUILD; contrast BURY'. These words are arranged in alphabetical order, except when a word is selected to head the article because it best or most conveniently illustrates the etymology of the other words which are associated with it: thus *astrologer*, *astrological* are treated under the catchword *astrology*. The catchword is followed by the pronunciation, the key to which is given below.

After this comes a selection of the senses in order to illustrate the general trend of the sense-development. The meanings are given in their chronological order, which often involves a re-grouping of the uses of the word as given in the *Oxford English Dictionary*. The century in which any word or sense is first recorded is indicated by roman numerals. Thus, under ESTEEM: A. †value, assess XV (Love); hold in (such-and-such) estimation XVI; B. †judge of XV (Fortescue); account, consider XVI. Similarly under FRANK: †free XIII; bounteous, generous; †of superior quality (see FRANKINCENSE) XV; ingenuous, candid XVI. The semicolon serves to separate a sense, or group of senses, from what precedes or follows: thus in the second example the senses 'free' and 'of superior quality' are obsolete, the other two are not.

For dates earlier than those recorded in the *Oxford English Dictionary* this work is indebted especially to the published parts (A–F) of the *Middle English Dictionary*, and for the later period to Craigie and Hulbert's *Dictionary of American English* and M. M. Mathews's *Dictionary of Americanisms*, and for Scottish words to Craigie's *Dictionary of the Older Scottish Tongue*. Some earlier dates have also been obtained from publications of the Early English Text Society and from miscellaneous sources.

Spelling of Germanic words

In Germanic words, long vowels are distinguished by the macron (¯), except in ON., for which the traditional diacritic (′) has been retained; thus OE., OFris., OS., OHG. *hūs*, ON. *hús* HOUSE.

In Germanic inferred forms (*ȝ*) is employed for the palatal and the voiced guttural spirants, as in **ȝeƀan* GIVE, **ȝōðaz* GOOD. The unvoiced guttural spirant is represented by (*χ*), as in **doχtēr* DAUGHTER, **χorsam, -az* HORSE. The voiced dental spirant is denoted by the barred *d* (*ð*), the unvoiced by the 'thorn' (*þ*), thus **brūðiz* BRIDE, **brōþar* BROTHER.

In OE. words the voiceless palatal stop, which in manuscripts is written *c*, is in this work printed *ć*, as in *ćild* CHILD, *cyćene* KITCHEN, *bićće* BITCH, similarly after *s* as in *sćield* SHIELD, *blysćan* BLUSH. The palatal spirant (*g*) is distinguished as (*ġ*), as in *gaġel* GALE[I], *ēaġe* EYE, *reġn* RAIN, *ġiefan* GIVE; after *n*, and in gemination, as (*ǵ*), thus *swenǵan* SWINGE, *crinǵan* CRINGE; *bryćǵ* BRIDGE[I], *byćǵan* BUY (but *byġest*, *byġeþ*, etc.). The letter *g* without diacritic is used for both voiced guttural spirant and voiced stop, as in *lagu* LAW[I], *fugol* FOWL; *gōd*, GOOD.

The corresponding spirants in ME. are represented by the 'yogh' (*ȝ*), as in *deȝen* DIE[I], *laȝe* (*lawe*) LAW[I], *Laȝamon* (personal name).

Dating of Latin words

In Latin words it is important to indicate their age and status, and for this purpose L. is used for words recorded as being in use down to *c.* A.D. 200, late L. covers the period *c.* A.D.200–*c.* A.D. 600, medL. from then to *c.* 1500, and modL. after 1500.

KEY TO THE PRONUNCIATION

Vowels

The incidence of main stress is shown by a raised point (·) after the vowel, and a secondary stress by a double point (:) as in **chu:rch**WA·RDEN, me:ditərei·niən.

à *chant* (tʃànt), *enhance* (ėnhà·ns), *bath* (bàþ)
ā *arm* (āɹm), *calm* (kām), *bravado* (brəvā·dou)
ă *Marathi* (mărā·ti), *alamode* (æ·lămoud), *loofah* (lū·fă)
æ *man* (mæn), *access* (æ·kses), *detach* (ditæ·tʃ)
æ̆ *accessary* (æ̆kse·səri), *borax* (bō·ræ̆ks)
ai *bind* (baind), *rely* (rilai·)
au *allow* (əlau·), *bough* (bau)

e equity (e·kwĭti), *correct* (kəre·kt)
ė *estate* (ėstei·t), *endow* (ėndau·)
ĕ *accent* (æ·ksĕnt), *Moslem* (mɔ·zlĕm)
ɛ (with glide-vowel) *bare* (bɛəɹ), *declare* (diklɛə·ɹ)
ə *accept* (əkse·pt), *measure* (me·ʒəɹ), (as glide-vowel before ɹ) *desire* (dizaiə·ɹ)
ə̄ *bird* (bə̄ɹd), *occur* (əkə̄·ɹ)
ei *delay* (dilei·), *rain* (rein)

i *bid* (bid), *naked* (nei·kid), *Monday* (mʌ·ndi), *acme* (æ·kmi), *depart* (dipā·ɹt), *gatling* (gæ·tliŋ), (with glide-vowel) *beer* (biəɹ), *career* (kəriə·ɹ)
ĭ *clarity* (klæ·rĭti), *discrepant* (di·skrĭpənt), *bulletin* (bu·lĭtin)
ī *equal* (ī·kwəl), *deviate* (dī·vieit)

ɔ *moral* (mɔ·rəl), *priority* (praiɔ·rĭti)
ɔ̀ *oft* (ɔ̀ft), *broth* (brɔ̀þ)
o *boreen* (borī·n), *cocotte* (kokɔ·t)
ŏ *bodega* (bŏdī·gə), *bolero* (bŏlɛə·rou), *obedient* (ŏbī·diənt), *diplomatic* (diplŏmæ·tik)
ɔ̄ *awful* (ɔ̄·fəl), (with glide-vowel) *board* (bɔ̄əɹd), *four* (fɔ̄əɹ)
oi *boy* (boi), *destroy* (distroi·)
ou *hero* (hiə·rou), *zoology* (zouɔ·lədʒi)

u *look* (luk), *bulbul* (bu·lbul), (with glide-vowel) *poor* (puəɹ), *cure* (kjuəɹ)
ŭ *opulent* (ɔ·pjŭlənt), *monument* (mɔ·njŭmənt)
ū *moon* (mūn), *boudoir* (bū·dwāɹ). *few* (fjū), *endue* (ėndjū·)
ʌ *blood* (blʌd), *butter* (bʌ·təɹ), *frustum* (frʌ·stəm)

The stressed vowels a, æ, e, i, o, u become obscured with loss of stress, and the indeterminate sounds thus arising, and approximating to the 'neutral' vowel ə, are normally printed ă, æ̆, ĕ, ĭ, ŏ, ŭ. Examples: *loofah* (lū·fă), *acclivity* (æ̆kli·vĭti), *accent* (æ·ksĕnt), *elegy* (e·lĭdʒi), *brocade* (brŏkei·d), *opulent* (ɔ·pjŭlənt).

KEY TO THE PRONUNCIATION

Vowels in French Words

a *Marseillaise* (marsɛjɛ̄z)
e *écarté* (*e*karte)
ɛ *gourmet* (gurmɛ)
ɛ̄ *Gruyère* (grüjɛ̄r)
ə *fleur-de-lis* (flördəlis)
i *lingerie* (lɛ̃ʒr*i*)
o *margaux* (marg*o*)
ö, *ö* *œillade* (ö·jad), *morbleu* (mɔ̄ɹblö·)
ȫ *hauteur* (otȫr)
u *bouts-rimés* (b*u*rime)
ū *bourg* (būr)
ü *curé* (küre)

Nasal Vowels

ã *enjamb(e)ment* (ãjãbmã)
ɛ̃ *lingerie* (lɛ̃ʒri)
ɔ̃ *feuilleton* (föjtɔ̃)

Consonants and Semi-Consonants

b, d, f, h, k, l, m, n, p, s, t, v, z *have their usual values*
ɹ *her* (hɔ̄ɹ), *farther* (fā·ɹðəɹ)
r *run* (rʌn), *harrow* (hæ·rou)
þ *thin* (þin), *bath* (bàþ)
ð *bathe* (beið), *father* (fā·ðəɹ)
ʃ *shop* (ʃɔp), *dish* (diʃ), *vicious* (vi·ʃəs)
tʃ *chop* (tʃɔp), *ditch* (ditʃ), *butcher* (bu·tʃəɹ)
ʒ *incision* (insi·ʒən), garage (gæ·rāʒ)
dʒ *judge* (dʒʌdʒ), *gender* (dʒe·ndəɹ), *pigeon* (pi·dʒin)
j *allure* (əljuə·ɹ), *junker* (ju·ŋkəɹ), *yes* (jes)
ŋ *bring* (briŋ), *hanger* (hæ·ŋəɹ), *finger* (fi·ŋgəɹ)
ʍ *what* (ʍɔt), *wheat* (ʍīt), *whether* (ʍe·ðəɹ)
w *wen* (wen), *away* (əwei·)
χ Sc. *loch* (lɔχ), *Sassenach* (sæ·sənàχ)
lj, nj repr. *gl, gn* in Italian words: *imbroglio* (imbrou·ljou), *bagnio* (bæ·njou)

The reversed r and small 'superior' letters (l[j]ūt, frin[d]ʒ, nɔstæ·ldʒ[i]ə) are used to denote elements that may or may not be present in a local or an individual pronunciation.

Special symbols

* indicates a hypothetical etymological form
† = obsolete
f. = formed on, as L. *discipulus*, f. *discere* learn
– = adoption of, as OE. *discipul* – L. *discipulus*
:– = normal development of, as ME. *mesel* leper – OF. *mesel* :– L. *misellus*, f. *miser* wretched
)(as in *concave*)(*convex*, means 'contrary to, the opposite of'
|| = alien, or not naturalized

The printing of a word in SMALL CAPITALS indicates that further information will be found under the word so referred to.

ABBREVIATIONS

a.	ante
abbrev.	abbreviation, -ated
abl.	ablative
abstr.	abstract
acc.	according
acc., accus.	accusative
act.	active
add.	addition
adj.	adjective
adv., advb.	adverb
Aeol.	Aeolic
Afr.	African
agric.	agriculture
AL.	Anglo-Latin
Alb.	Albanian
alch.	alchemy
alt.	altered, -ation
Amer.	American
AN.	Anglo-Norman
anat.	anatomy
AncrR	'Ancrene Riwle'
Angl.	Anglian
Anglo-Ind.	Anglo-Indian
Anglo-Ir.	Anglo-Irish
anthrop.	anthropology
antiq.	antiquities, -quarian
aor.	aorist
Apocr.	Apocrypha
app.	apparently
Arab.	Arabic
Aram.	Aramaic
arch.	archaic
archaeol.	archaeology
archit.	architecture
arith.	arithmetic
Arm.	Armenian
assim.	assimilation, -ated
assoc.	association, -iated
astrol.	astrology
astr., astron.	astronomy, -ical
attrib.	attributive
augm.	augment(ation, -ative
Austral.	Australia(n
Av.	Avestan, Avestic
A.V.	Authorized Version
biol.	biology
bot.	botany
Braz.	Brazilian
Bulg.	Bulgarian
c.	circa
Cat.	Catalan
Cath. Angl.	'Catholicon Anglicum'
Celt.	Celtic
cent.	century
CEur.	Common European
cf.	*confer*, 'compare'
CGerm.	Common Germanic
Ch.	Chaucer
chem.	chemistry
CIE.	Common Indo-European
classL.	classical Latin
cogn.	cognate(s
coll.	collective
colloq.	colloquial
comb.	combining
comp.	compound(s
compar.	comparative
concr.	concrete
conj.	conjugation
conj.	conjunction
cons.	consonant
contemp.	contemporary
contr.	contraction
Corn.	Cornish
corr.	corresponding
correl.	correlative
Cotgr.	Cotgrave
CRom.	Common Romanic
cryst.	crystallography
CSl.	Common Slavonic
Cursor M.	'Cursor Mundi'
d.	dative
Da.	Danish
dat.	dative
decl.	declension
dem., demonstr.	demonstrative
deriv.	derivative
dial.	dialect(al
dim.	diminutive
dissim.	dissimilation
dissyll.	dissyllable
Du.	Dutch
eccl.	ecclesiastical
EFris.	East Frisian
e.g.	*exempli gratia*, 'for example'
el.	element
electr.	electricity
ellipt.	elliptical(ly
emph.	emphatic
Eng.	English
entom.	entomology, -ical
equiv.	equivalent
Ernout & Meillet	A. Ernout et A. Meillet, *Dictionnaire étymologique de la langue latine*
erron.	erroneous
esp.	especially
etym., etymol.	etymology, -ical

euph., euphem.	euphemistic(ally
Eur.	European
ex., exx.	example(s
exc.	except
exclam.	exclamation
expl.	explained
ext.	extended
F.	French
f.	formed on
fem.	feminine
fig.	figurative(ly
Finn.	Finnic, Finnish
Flem.	Flemish
fortif.	fortification
freq.	frequent(ly
Fris.	Frisian
fut.	future
G.	German
g.	genitive
Gael.	Gaelic
Gallo-Rom.	Gallo-Roman
Gamillscheg	E. Gamillscheg, *Etymologisches Wörterbuch der französischen Sprache*
Gaul.	Gaulish
gen.	general(ly
gen.	genitive
geol.	geology
geom.	geometry
Germ.	Germanic
Goth.	Gothic
Gr.	Greek
gram.	grammar
Heb.	Hebrew
her.	heraldry
HG.	High German
Hind.	Hindustani
hist.	history, -ical
ib., ibid.	*ibidem*, 'in the same book or passage'
Icel.	Icelandic
id.	*idem*, 'the same'
i.e.	*id est*, 'that is'
IE.	Indo-European
imit.	imitative
immed.	immediate(ly
imper.	imperative
imperf.	imperfect
impers.	impersonal
ind.	indicative
indef. art.	indefinite article
Indo-Iran.	Indo-Iranian
inf., infin.	infinitive
infl.	influence(d
instr.	instrumental
int.	interjection
intr.	intransitive
Ir.	Irish
irreg.	irregular(ly
It.	Italian
J.	(Dr. S.) Johnson
Jap.	Japanese
joc.	jocular(ly
L.	Latin
Laȝ.	Laȝamon
lang.	language(s
law-L.	law-Latin
LDu.	Low Dutch
leg.	legal
Lett.	Lettic, -ish
LG.	Low German
lit.	literal(ly, literary
Lith.	Lithuanian
liturg.	liturgy, -ical
Lydg.	Lydgate
LXX	Septuagint
m.	masculine
math.	mathematics
Maund.	Maundeville
MDu.	Middle Dutch
ME.	Middle English
med.	medicine, -ical
med.	mediaeval
metaph.	metaphysics
metath.	metathetic
meteor.	meteorology
Mex.	Mexican
Meyer-Lübke	W. Meyer-Lübke, *Romanisches etymologisches Wörterbuch*
MHG.	Middle High German
midl.	midland
mil.	military
min.	mineralogy
MIr.	Middle Irish
MLG.	Middle Low German
mod.	modern
modL.	modern Latin
monosyll.	monosyllable
MSc.	Middle Scottish
mus.	music
myth.	mythology
N.	North
n.	neuter
nat. hist.	natural history
N. & Q.	*Notes and Queries*
naut.	nautical
NEF.	north-eastern French
neg.	negative
Nhb.	Northumbria(n
nom.	nominative
north.	northern
Norw.	Norwegian
n. pl.	nominative plural
N.T.	New Testament
N.Z.	New Zealand
obj.	object
obl.	oblique
OBret.	Old Breton
obs.	obsolete
occas.	occasional(ly
ODa.	Old Danish

OE.	Old English
OF.	Old French
(O)F.	Old and modern French
OFris.	Old Frisian
OHG.	Old High German
OIr.	Old Irish
OL.	Old Latin
OLG.	Old Low German
OLith.	Old Lithuanian
ON.	Old Norse
ONF.	Old Northern French
ONhb.	Old Northumbrian
OPers.	Old Persian
opp.	opposed to
orig.	origin(al
OS.	Old Saxon
OScand.	Old Scandinavian
OSl.	Old Slavonic
OSp.	Old Spanish
OSw.	Old Swedish
O.T.	Old Testament
OW.	Old Welsh
palaeogr.	palaeography
Palsgr.	Palsgrave
pass.	passive
path.	pathology
perf.	perfect
perh.	perhaps
pers.	person
Pers.	Persian
pert.	pertaining
Peruv.	Peruvian
Peterb. Chron.	'Peterborough Chronicle'
Pg.	Portuguese
pharm.	pharmacy
philol.	philology
philos.	philosophy, -ical
phon.	phonetics
photogr.	photography
phr.	phrase
phys.	physics
physiol.	physiology
pl.	plural
P.L.	'Paradise Lost'
poet.	poetic(al
pop.	popular
popL.	popular Latin
poss.	possessive
poss.	possible, -ly
pp.	past participle, -ial
ppl.	participial
PPl.	'Piers Plowman'
Pr.	Provençal
prec.	preceding
pref.	prefix
prep.	preposition
pres.	present
prob.	probably
Promp. Parv.	'Promptorium Parvulorum'
pron.	pronoun

pronunc.	pronunciation
prop.	proper(ly
pros.	prosody
prp.	present participle
Prud.	Prudentius
Ps.	Psalm
psych., psychol.	psychology
pt.	past (tense)
q.v.	*quod vide*, 'which see'
R.C.Ch.	Roman Catholic Church.
redupl.	reduplicating
ref.	reference
refash.	refashioned, -ing
refl.	reflexive
rel.	related (to)
rel.	relative
repl.	replacing, -ed
repr.	representing, -ed, -ation
RGlouc.	Robert of Gloucester
rhet.	rhetoric(al
Rom.	Roman, -ic, -ance
Rum.	Rumanian
Russ.	Russian
S.	South
SAfr.	South African
Sandahl	B. Sandahl, *Middle English Sea Terms*, I (1951), II (1958)
sb.	substantive
sc.	*scilicet*, 'understand' or 'supply'
Sc.	Scottish
Scand.	Scandinavian
scholL.	scholastic Latin
Sem.	Semitic
S.Eng.Leg.	'South English Legendary'
Serb.	Serbian
sg.	singular
Sh.	Shakespeare
sing.	singular
Sinh.	Sinhalese
Skr.	Sanskrit
Sl., Slav.	Slavic, Slavonic
sl.	slang
south.	southern
Sp.	Spanish
sp.	spelling, spelt
spec.	specific(ally
str.	stress, -ed
str.	strong
subj.	subject
subseq.	subsequent(ly
superl.	superlative
surg.	surgery
s.v.	*sub voce*, 'under the word'
Sw.	Swedish
s.w.	south-western
syll.	syllable
syn., synon.	synonym, -ous
Syr.	Syrian
techn.	technical
theol.	theology, -ical

Tokh.	Tokharian
tr.	translating, -ion
tr., trans.	transitive
transf.	transferred
trissyll.	trissyllable
Turk.	Turkish
typogr.	typography
ult.	ultimate(ly
unexpl.	unexplained
unkn.	unknown
unstr.	unstressed
U.S.	United States
usu.	usual(ly
var., varr., vars.	variant(s
vb.	verb
vbl.	verbal
viz.	*videlicet*, 'namely'
Vulg.	Vulgate
W.	Welsh
W.	West
w.	with
WF.	western French
WGerm.	West Germanic
WIE	western Indo-European
wk.	weak
wk. vb.	weak verb
WS.	West Saxon
Wycl.	Wyclif
zool.	zoology

PUBLISHERS' NOTE

DR. C. T. ONIONS, whose lifetime of learning this dictionary harvests, died while it was still going through the press. He was the last of the editors of the original *Oxford English Dictionary* and for many years the doyen unquestioned of English lexicography. The publishers would like to take this last opportunity of saluting the man to whom this etymological dictionary will be an enduring monument.

They also wish to acknowledge the part played in the enterprise by Dr. G. W. S. Friedrichsen, once his collaborator on the *Oxford English Dictionary* and Mr. R. W. Burchfield who is now editing that dictionary's new Supplement. In 1962 they undertook the task of helping him to see the book through the press. The text was already in galley and some of the earlier sheets were in revise. Although Dr. Onions had decided the main points of policy and drafted nearly all the entries, Dr. Friedrichsen and Mr. Burchfield still had much exacting work to do in the way of reading proof and settling knotty points. The publishers would like to thank both of them for their scrupulous diligence and to thank Dr. Friedrichsen not only for his labours in dealing with the revises but for contributing the Introduction.

The publishers are also indebted to the late Professor D. P. Costello and to Mr. I. P. Foote for verifying the Slavonic forms and Professor Norman Davis for checking the spellings of the Lithuanian words.

A

A, first letter of the alphabet, used in the symbol *A1*, applied in Lloyd's Register to ships in first-class condition in respect of hull and stores, *A* denoting ships new or renewed, *1* and *2* the state of the stores. Hence *A1* adj. first-class; in U.S. *A No. 1*.

a[1] ə, (emph.) ei reduced form of AN[1] used since XII immed. before a word beginning with a cons. For the loss of *n* cf. MY, THY, NO[1], and *i'*, *o'* for IN, ON.

a[2] ə ME. *o*, *a* (XII), in a distributive sense, e.g. *twice a day*, reduced form of ON, as in OE. *on dæġe*; cf. Icel. *á dag*. Formerly used widely in other idiomatic phrases and surviving in comps. of A-[1], and NOWADAYS; linked with a gerund, as *go a-begging* XIV.

a[3] a, ə prefixed to proper names in war-cries rallying men to a leader, e.g. *a Warwick*. XIV. – (O)F. *a* to :– L. *ad* (see AT).

a[4] ə appended to lines 'in burlesque poetry, to lengthen out a syllable, without adding to the sense' (J.), as in *And merrily hent the Stile-a .. Your sad tyres in a Mile-a* (Sh. 'Winter's Tale' IV iii 133, 135); prob. originating in ME. inflexional *-e*; e.g. *sonnë/yronnë* would be treated as *sun-a/run-a*. XVI.

a-[1] ə reduced form of ON prep., occurring in late OE., but not general before XII, and varying in ME. with *o*; the first el. of many predicative adjs. and advs. arising from phrases consisting of the prep. and a sb., e.g. *aback*, *abed*, †*aknee*, *alive*, *aright*, *asleep*, *asunder*, *away*, all of which have OE. antecedents. Early ME. formations directly modelled on these are *afire*, *afoot*, *aland* (in imitation of which were formed later *aflame*, *a-horseback*, *ashore*); some were modelled on or influenced by Scand. expressions, as *afloat*, *alee*, *aloft*, *amiss*; some depend upon French, as *aboard*, *abroach*, *across*, *agog*, *around*, in which the preps. *à*, *en* have been assim. to or replaced by the Eng. prefix. In XIII appear formations on adjs. used ellipt. or as sbs., as *abroad*, *ahigh*, *alow*; later are *adry*, *aloud*, *awry*. Partly as a result of analogous formations (e.g. *adrift* after *afloat*), partly in consequence of the identity of many vbs. and their allied sbs. (e.g. *brood*, whence *abrood* sitting on eggs XIII–XVII), the prefix came to be combined in XVI with a vb.-stem to express the meaning of its present participle, as †*alack* lacking, *agape* gaping, *asoak*, *astride*; such formations increased in the foll. centuries, esp. in XIX, when many occasional comps. appear, such as *a-chatter*, *adrip*, *adroop*, *agasp*, *agush*, *a-riot*, *asmoke*, *asprawl*, *awaste*.

Some adjs. of a prob. different origin came to be apprehended as comps. of this prefix, e.g. *acold* (XIV), from OE. *ācōlod*, pp. of *ācōlian* become COOL.

The analysis of some naut. terms that appear to have this prefix is obscure, e.g. †*abackstays*, *a-burton*, *a-hull*, †*aluff* (see ALOOF, LUFF), *a-trip*, *a-try*; in some of them *a-* may repr. *at*, while others may be modelled on *abaft*, *athwart*.

In some instances the orig. form with *on* persisted after the comp. had been established, e.g. *on side* (XIV–XVI) beside ASIDE.

a-[2] ə reduced form of OF prep., as in *adown*, *afresh*, *akin*, †*alate* (XIV), *anew*; blended with A-[1] in AFAR. Cf. †*a clock* (XV–XVIII), now O'CLOCK. Not in living use since the ME. period. (In comps. with verbs the prefix *of-* is repr. in *ahungered*, *athirst*.)

a-[3] ə prefix of verbs, OE. *ā-*, orig. *ar-*, *or-* = OS. *ur-*, *ar-*, OHG. *ar-*, *ir-*, *ur-* (G. *er-*), Goth. *us-*, *ur-*, meaning 'away, out', and hence used as an intensive, as in OE. *ābīdan* ABIDE, *ālihtan* ALIGHT[1], *ārīsan* ARISE, *āmasod* AMAZED, *āsċamod* ASHAMED; *āgān* AGO. New formations are ACCURSE, AGHAST.

a-[4] ə, ei, (stressed) æ prefix of negation and privation, repr. Gr. *a-* (before a vowel AN-[2]) = UN-[1]. Occurs in (i) words repr. Gr. comps., mostly adopted through French or Latin, and in which the significance of the prefix is wholly or partially obscured, as *abyss*, *adamant*, *amethyst*, *amorphous*, *atom*, *atrophy*, *azote*; (ii) terms of the arts and sciences, having Gr. bases, but coming mainly through late L., medL., or modL., as *abranchiate*, *aboulia*, *acatalectic*, *acephalous*, *agamic*, *alogical*, *apetalous*, *aphasia*, *aseptic*, *asymmetry*, *athematic*, *atonal*; (iii) such terms derived from other bases, as *acaulous*, *asexual*; (iv) gen. terms modelled on these, as *amoral*, *asocial*.

-a[1] ə repr. Gr. and L. *-a* of fem. sgs.; cf. -IA[1].

-a[2] ə repr. Gr. and L. *-a* of n. pls.; cf. -IA[2].

aardvark ā·ɹdvāɹk S. African insectivorous quadruped. XIX. Afrikaans (now *erdvark*), f. *aarde* EARTH + *varken* pig (see FARROW[1]).

aasvogel ā·svougəl S. African vulture. XIX. Afrikaans (now *aasvoël*), f. *aas* carrion (rel. to EAT) + *vogel* bird, FOWL.

ab- æb, əb L. prefix, being the adv.-prep. *ab* (*ā*) away, off (= Skr. *apa*, Gr. *apó*, etc., OF), used in composition with vb.-stems, as in *abdicāre*, *abicere*, *abrādere*, *abrumpere*, *absorbēre*, *abūtī* (see ABDICATE, ABJECT, ABRADE, ABRUPT, ABSORB, ABUSE). Some scientific formations, as *abactinal*, *aboral* (XIX) away from the actinal/oral area, have been partly suggested by ABNORMAL. The var. *abs-* appears in ABSCESS, ABSCOND, ABSTAIN, etc.

ab(b)a æ·bə Arabian sleeveless outer garment. XIX. – Arab. ʿ*abā*. Also **abaya** əbā·jə.

aback əbæ·k at or to the back. ME. *abec, abak, o bak,* late OE. *on bæc,* i.e. ON prep., A-[1] and BACK[1]; reinforced in ME. by ON. *á bak.* From XVII esp. in naut. lang. of the sails of a ship being laid back against the mast by a headwind; hence the phr. (of the ship) *be taken aback* XVIII, fig. (of persons) be discomfited XIX. Aphetic BACK[2].

abacus æ·bəkəs calculating frame; (archit.) upper member of the capital of a column. XVI. – L. *abacus,* f. Gr. *abak-, ábax* table (of various kinds) – Heb. *'ābāq* dust; the orig. sense of the Gr. word was 'drawing-board covered with dust' (for the use of mathematicians).

Abaddon əbæ·dən Apollyon, 'the angel of the bottomless pit' (Rev. ix 11) XVI; hell XVII (Milton). – Heb. *ābaddōn* destruction, f. *ābad* perish.

abaft əbà·ft (esp. naut.) in or to the rear (of). XIII (Cursor M.). ME. *o(n) baft,* i.e. ON prep., A-[1] and *baft,* OE. *beæftan,* f. *be* BY+*æftan* behind (see AFTER).

abalone æbəlou·ni (U.S.) mollusc of the genus Haliotis. XIX. – Sp., of unkn. origin.

abandon[1] əbæ·ndən †subjugate; give up, orig. to the control of another XIV; †banish XVI. – OF. *abandoner* (mod. *abandonner*), f. phr. *a bandon* (whence ME. adv. *abandon* under control, at one's will, entirely), i.e. *a* to (AD-), *bandon* jurisdiction, control :– Rom. **bandōnem* (cf. Pr. *bandó* permission, freedom), f. **bandum,* var. of medL. *bannum* BAN[1]. In pa. ppl. adj. **aba·ndon**ED[1] given over to evil XVII. Hence, or – (O)F. *abandonnement,* **aba·ndon**MENT. XVII.

abandon[2] əbæ·ndən, ‖abã·dɔ̃ freedom from restraint. XIX. F., f. *abandonner* (see prec.).

abase əbei·s lower, depress, humiliate. XIV (Gower). Late ME. *abesse, abasse* – OF. *abaissier* (mod. *abaisser*), f. *a* to, AD-+*baissier* lower :– Rom. **bassiāre,* f. late L. *bassus* BASE[3], by direct assoc. with which the present form *abase* (XVI) has arisen. Hence, or – F. *abaissement,* **aba·se**MENT. XV.

abash əbæ·ʃ confound, discomfit. XIV. ME. *abaiss(e)* – AN. *abaiss-,* for OF. *e(s)baïss-,* lengthened stem (see -ISH[2]) of *e(s)baïr* (mod. *ébahir*) astound, dumbfound = Pr. *esbahir,* f. *es-* EX-+(acc. to some) *ba,* int. of astonishment, (acc. to others) OF. *baer* (mod. *bayer*) yawn, with alteration of conjugation after OF. *baïf* astounded.

abate əbei·t beat down, put or bring down (in various applications) XIII; deduct XIV. – OF. *abatre* (mod. *abattre*) = Pr. *abatre,* It. *abbattere,* etc. :– Rom. **abbatt(u)ere,* f. *ad* AD-+L. *batt(u)ere* beat. Cf. BATE[2]. So **aba·te**MENT. XV. – OF.

abatis, abbatis əbæ·ti(s) (fortif.) defence of felled trees. XVIII. – F. *abatis,* OF. *abateïs,* f. *abatre* fell (see prec.)+*-eïs* :– Rom. **-āticium,* f. L. *-ātus* -ATE[2]+*-īcius* (cf. GLACIS).

abattoir əbæ·twāɹ public slaughterhouse. XIX. F. (1806), f. *abattre* fell (see ABATE)+*-oir* :– L. *-ōrium* -ORY[1].

abba æ·bə father (Mark xiv 36, Rom. viii 15, Gal. iv 6). XIV. ecclL. *abba,* NT.Gr. *abbâ* – Aramaic (Syriac) *abbā.*

abbacy æ·bəsi position of abbot or abbess. XV (Wyntoun). – ecclL. *abbācia,* var. of *abbātia,* f. *abbāt-* ABBOT; see -ACY. **abbatial** əbei·ʃəl pertaining to an abbot, abbess, abbey. XV. – F. **abbé** æ·bei gen. title for men wearing clerical dress. XVIII. – F. (OF. *abe, abet*) :– L. *abbātem.* **abbess** æ·bis female superior corr. to abbot. XIII (RGlouc.). – OF. *ab(b)esse* (= Pr. *abadesa*) :– ecclL. *abbadissa, -tissa* (whence OE. *abbodisse, -esse*), f. *abbāt-*; see -ESS[1]. **abbey** æ·bi monastery presided over by an abbot. XIII (Laȝ.). – OF. *ab(b)eie* (mod. *abbaye*) = Pr. *abadia* :– ecclL. *abbādia, -tia* abbacy; see -Y[3]. **abbot** æ·bət superior of an abbey. OE. *abbud, -od, -ad, -ot,* corr. to MDu. *abbet,* OHG. *abbăt* (Du., G. *abt*) – ecclL. *a·bbatem,* for *abbā·tem* (whence Pr. *abat,* F. *abbé,* It. *abate*), nom. *abbās* – Gr. *abbâs* – Syriac *abbā* ABBA; the word was formerly applied in the East gen. to monks. The var. sp. *abbat* (XII) was especially freq. XV–XVII.

abbreviate əbrī·vieit cut short, abridge. XV. f. pp. stem of late L. (Vulg.) *abbreviāre,* f. L. *ab* or *ad* (see AB-, AD-)+*breviāre,* f. *brevis* BRIEF; see ATE[3] and cf. ABRIDGE. So **abbrevia**·TION. XV. – F. or late L. (Vulg.).

abc eibīsī· alphabet. XIII. ME. *abece* (as in OF.), with vars. *apece, apsie,* early mod. *abce, abcie* (cf. *absey booke* in Sh. 1st Folio); f. first three letters of the (Roman) alphabet. Cf. OE. *ābēcēdē* alphabet, and ABECEDARIAN.

abdicate æ·bdikeit disown, renounce. XVI. f. pp. stem of L. *abdicāre* lit. 'announce away' (i.e. as not belonging to one), f. *ab* AB-+*dicāre* proclaim (as in INDICATE). So **abdica**·TION. XVI. – L.

abdomen æ·bdəmen, æbdou·men belly. XVI. – L. *abdōmen.* The variation in pronunc. has obtained since XVIII. So **abdomin**AL[1] ǽbdɔ·minəl XVIII. – modL. *abdōminālis,* f. L. stem *abdōmin-*; **abdo·min**OUS big-bellied. XVII.

abduct ǽbdʌ·kt carry off feloniously. XIX. f. *abduct-,* pp. stem of L. *abdūcere* (whence rare **abdu·ce** XVI), f. *ab* AB-+*dūcere* lead, carry (cf. DUKE). So **abdu·c**TION. XVII. – late L. **abdu·ct**OR (anat.). XVII. modL. (sc. *musculus* muscle); see -OR[2].

abeam əbī·m (naut.) at right angles to a ship's length (the beams of a ship being at right angles to the keel). XIX. f. A-[1]+BEAM, after ATHWART.

abear əbɛə·ɹ endure, tolerate. OE. *āberan,* ME. *abere,* f. *ā-* A-[3]+*beran* BEAR[2]. The mod. dial. and vulgar use is a new formation (perhaps XIX in Cockney dial.) after *abide* ('can't abide' having suggested 'can't abear').

abecedarian eiːbīsīdɛə·riən alphabetical; (one) occupied in learning the alphabet. XVII. f. late L. *abecedārius*, f. first four letters of the alphabet, *abcd*; see -ARIAN. So **abece·dARY** XVI; also (XV) spelling-book, primer (medL. *abecedārium*, sb. use of n.adj. sc. *manuāle* manual). Cf. ABC.

abed əbe·d in bed. ME. *abedde* (XIII), OE. *on bedde*; see A-[1], BED.

abele əbī·l, ei·bəl white poplar. XVI (*abeel*, Gerarde). – Du. *abeel* – OF. *abel*, *aubel* :– medL. *albellu-s*, dim. of *albus* white (cf. ALBUM).

aberdevine æ·bəɹdĭvain siskin. XVII. Of unkn. origin.

aberglaube ā·bərglaubə superstition. XIX (M. Arnold). G., f. pejorative or negative prefix *aber-*+*glaube* BELIEF.

Abernethy æbəɹnī·þi kind of hard biscuit. XIX. f. name of John *Abernethy*, surgeon (1764–1831).

aberration æbərei·ʃən straying, deviation. XVI. – L. *aberrātiō(n-)* (in classL. only in Cicero, relief, diversion), f. *aberrāre*, f. *ab* AB-+*errāre* ERR. So **aberrANT** æbe·rənt going astray XVI (Sc.; rare before XIX); deviating from the normal XIX.

aberuncator see AVERRUNCATOR.

abet əbe·t incite (now, to wrongdoing). XIV. – OF. *abeter*, f. *a* to, AD-+*beter* BAIT. So **abe·tMENT**. XIV. – AN. *abetement*. **abe·ttor.** XVI. – AN. *abettour* (OF. *abetere*); see -OR[1].

abeyance əbei·əns (leg.) state of expectancy XVI; suspension XVII. – AN. *abeiance*, OF. *abeance*, f. *abeer* aspire after, f. *a-* AD-+*beer*, *baer* gape (mod. *bayer*, *béer*) = Pr., Sp. *badar*, It. *badare* :– medL. *batāre* gape (cf. BAY[3]), perh. of imit. origin; see -ANCE. ¶ In OF. *abeance* was applied to the condition of the aspirant in whose appetence a property stands; in Eng. law the term was transferred to the condition of the property.

abhor əbhō·ɹ regard with horror or loathing. XV. – L. *abhorrēre* shrink in dread, be far from or inconsistent with, f. *ab* AB-+*horrēre* stand with hair on end, stand aghast, shudder (cf. HORRID); F. *abhorrer* (XVI) prob. influenced the Eng. word. So **abhorrENCE** əbhɔ·rəns XVII, superseding earlier **abho·rrENCY** (Bacon), which succeeded to †*abhorment* (XVI). **abho·rrENT**. XVII.

abide əbai·d wait, stay; wait for OE.; endure, bear XVI. OE. *ābīdan* = Goth. *usbeidan*; see A-[3], BIDE.

abiet- æ·biət comb. form of L. *abiet-*, *abies* fir, in chem. terms.

abigail æ·bigeil waiting-woman, female domestic servant. XVII ('a cousin Abigail to wait upon his lady', Eachard, 1671; 'tawdry Abigails', Oldham, 1678; earlier as vb. 'they did Abigail it each to others', Gayton, 1654). Appellative use of the name of the waiting gentlewoman in Beaumont and Fletcher's play 'The Scornful Lady' (1610), prob. so named in allusion to the expression 'thine handmaid' freq. applied to herself by *Abigail* the Carmelitess in 1 Sam. XXV 24–31.

ability əbi·lĭti †fitness; sufficient power XIV; faculty of mind XVI. ME. *ablete*, *abilite* – OF. *ablete*, *(h)abilite*, the first form being :– L. *habilitātem*, *-tās* (f. *habilis* ABLE), the second a later latinization of it (in modF. *habileté*). Forms with *hab-* were common XV–XVII, but the conflict between *hab-* and *ab-* was over before 1700.

abiogenesis ăbaiodʒe·nĭsis origination of living organisms from lifeless matter. XIX. modL., f. Gr. *ábios* lifeless (f. *a-* A-[4]+*bíos* life, BIO-)+*génesis* birth, GENESIS.

abject æ·bdʒekt †pp. rejected XV; adj. degraded, despicable, downcast XVI; sb. outcast, castaway XVI (More). – L. *abjectus*, pp. of *abicere* (corr. to Gr. ἀφιέναι) cast away, reject, f. *ab* AB-+*jacere* cast, throw, f. base repr. also by Gr. *híēmi* I send, cast (cf. the relation of L. *facere* make, and Gr. *títhēmi* I put, place).

abjure əbdʒuə·ɹ †cause to forswear XV (Caxton); renounce on oath XV. – (O)F. *abjurer* or L. *abjūrāre* deny on oath, f. *ab* AB-+*jūrāre* swear (see JUROR).

ablactation æblæktei·ʃən weaning XV; grafting XVII. – late L. *ablactātiō(n-)*, f. *ablactāre* wean, f. *ab* AB-+*lactāre* suckle; see LACTATION.

ablation æblei·ʃən removal. XV. – F. *ablation* or late L. *ablātiō(n-)*, f. *ablāt-*, used as pp. stem of *auferre* take away, remove, f. *ab* AB-+*ferre* BEAR[2]; see -ATION.

ablative æ·blətiv (gram.) of a case expressing removal, distance, source, cause, agent, etc. XV. – (O)F. *ablatif*, *-ive* or L. *ablātīvus* (in *casus a.*, so called from its prominent function of expressing direction away from a place), f. *ablāt-*; see prec. and -IVE.

ablaut æ·blaut (philol.) vowel-gradation, as in *sing*, *sang*, *sung*. XIX. G. (Jacob Grimm, 1819), f. *ab* OFF+*laut* sound (see LOUD).

ablaze ablei·z in a flame. XIX. f. A-[1]+BLAZE, after *afire*, *aflame*. (Gower had *on blase*.)

able ei·bl having sufficient power; †apt, fit. XIV. – OF. *able* :– L. *habili-s*, f. *habēre* have, hold (see -ILE), lit. 'easy to hold, handy'; the later F. sp. *hable* (mod. *habile* clever) was reflected in Eng., and similar conditions prevailed to those in ABILITY. *Able-bodied* (XVII), f. *able body* (cf. Sh. 'All's Well' IV v 86), perpetuates the gen. obs. sense 'physically strong' (XIV). Hence **a·bly** XIV; see -LY[2].

-able əbl – (O)F. *-able* – L. *-ābilis*, produced orig. by the addition of *-bilis* -BLE to vbs. with *a*-stem, as *amāre*, *amābilis*, but extended to vbs. with other stems, e.g. *capere*, *capābilis* CAPABLE, and to sbs., as *amīcābilis* AMICABLE, *favōrābilis* FAVOURABLE, *voluptābilis* pleasurable. In Rom. this extension went further; so F. *concevable* CONCEIVABLE, *périssable* PERISHABLE. Eng. formations on sbs. are *actionable* (XVI), *clubbable* (Johnson), *pleasurable* (XVI), *saleable* (XVI). The meaning in new formations is now always passive, but the active meaning, always formerly possible, is seen in *agreeable*, *answerable*, *capable*, *comfortable*, *companionable*, *durable*, *equable*, *favourable*, *serviceable*, *suitable*; in some, e.g. *fashionable*, both uses were current from the outset, but only the active survives. The wide application of the suffix in Eng. is largely due to assoc. with ABLE, *eatable* (e.g.) being analysed as *eat*+*able* 'able to be eaten'; hence its use in *come-at-able* (XVII), *get-at-able* (XVIII). Alternation between *-able* and *-ible* occurs; e.g. †*feasable* and *feasible*, *negligeable* and *negligible*. For phonetic reasons and for ease of recognition the retention of *e* before *-able* is necessary in (e.g.) *changeable*, *peaceable*, and *nameable*, *saleable*; but variation occurs in such words as *mov(e)able*, *siz(e)able*. Notable formations are *knowledgeable and* RELIABLE. The corr. advs. end in **-ably** əbli.

ablution əblū·ʃən washing. XIV (Ch.). – (O)F. *ablution* or eccl. L. *ablūtiō(n)-*, f. L. *abluere* wash off, f. *ab* AB-+*luere* wash, LAVE; see -TION.

abnegate æ·bnigeit renounce. XVII. f. pp. stem of L. *abnegāre*, f. *ab-* AB-+*negāre*; see -ATE[3]. So **ab**NEGA·TION. XIV. – F. or late L.

abnormal ǣbnō·ɹməl deviating from the ordinary. XIX. refash., after †*abnormous* (XVIII–XIX) or its source L. *abnormis*, of earlier †*anormal* – (O)F. *anormal* – medL. *anormālis*, *anormalus*, resulting from blending of late L. *anōmalus* ANOMALOUS and *abnormis*; see AB-, NORM, -AL[1].

aboard əbɔə·ɹd adv. and prep. on or on to a ship. XIV (Gower). var. of *on board*, partly after (O)F. *à bord*; see A-[1], BOARD.

abode əbou·d †delay, stay; dwelling-place. XIII. ME. *abād*, *abōd*, f. *abīden* ABIDE, after OE. *bād* waiting, expectation, f. *bīdan* BIDE.

abolish əbɔ·liʃ do away with. XV. – (O)F. *aboliss-*, lengthened stem of *abolir* – L. *abolēre* destroy, f. *ab* AB-+**ol-*, perh. rel. to Gr. *ollúnai* destroy, *ólethros* destruction; see -ISH[2]. So **aboli**TION æbəli·ʃən. XVI. – F. or L. Hence **aboli·tion**ISM, -IST (early XIX), with ref. to the abolition of slavery.

abominable əbɔ·minəbl offensive, loathsome. XIV. – (O)F. *abominable* – L. *abōminābilis* deserving imprecation or abhorrence, f. *abōminārī* deprecate as an ill omen, f. *ab* AB-+*ōmin-*, OMEN; see -ABLE. In medL., OF., and Eng. (XIV–XVII) commonly spelt *abhom-*, being regarded as f. *ab* and *homin-*, *homō* man, quasi 'away from man, inhuman'; no other sp. occurs in Sh. 1st Folio (cf. 'Love's Labour's Lost' v i 27). So **abo·minate.** XVII. f. pp. stem of *abōminārī*; see -ATE[3]. **abomin**A·TION. XIV. – (O)F. – L.

aborigines æbɔ̆ri·dʒinīz original inhabitants. XVI. – L. *aborīginēs* pl. the first inhabitants of Latium and Italy; usu. explained as f. *ab orīgine* from the beginning (see OF, ORIGIN)+pl. suffix *-ēs*; but perh. a proper name altered by pop. etym. Naturalized in It. *aborigeni*, Sp., Pg. *aborigenes*. Singularized forms *aborigin(e)*, *aborigen* have been used in Eng.; cf. F. *aborigène* sb. and adj., Sp. *aborigen* adj. Hence **abori·gin**AL[1]. XVII.

abortion əbɔ̄·ɹʃən untimely birth (spec. artificially produced) XVI; fig. XVII. – L. *abortiō(n-)*, f. *abort-*, pp. stem of *aborīrī* miscarry, f. *ab* AB-+*orīrī* arise, appear; see ORIENT, -TION. So **abo·rt**IVE (first as sb.). XIII (Cursor M.). – (O)F. – L.

abound əbau·nd overflow, be plentiful. XIV (Ch., Wyclif). – OF. *abunder*, (also mod.) *abonder* – L. *abundāre* (whence also It. *abbondare*, Sp. *abundar*, and in pop. form Pr. *aondar*), f. *ab* AB-+*undāre* flow, f. *unda* wave (see WATER); by assoc. with L. *habēre* possess, spelt with *hab-* in late OF. and in Eng. (XIV–XVI). Cf. ABUNDANCE.

about əbau·t adv. round, round the outside OE.; afoot, astir; †(with inf.) busy or engaged in XIII; going *to* XVI; prep. in corr. senses; (also) near, approximating to XII; concerning XIII. OE. *onbūtan*, *abūtan* (cf. OFris. *abūta*), ME. *abuten* (XII–XIII), *aboute*; f. *on* in, ON+*būtan* outside (of); see BUT.

above əbʌ·v overhead; higher up. ME. *abufan* XII, *abuve-n* XIII, *aboven* XIII–XV (surviving as *aboon*, *abune* in Sc. and north. dial.), f. *a-* (repr. OE. *on*, as in ABOUT)+ OE. *bufan*, ME. *buven* = OS. *biob̄an* (Du. *boven*), f. *be* BY + *ufan* = OS. *ob̄an*, OHG. *oban*, *obana* (G. *oben*) from above, above :- WGerm. **ufana*, **ub̄ana*, f. **uf*, **ub̄* UP+ **-ana*, suffix expressing motion from.

abracadabra æ:brəkədæ·brə charm, spell. XVI. orig. a cabalistic word of the gnostic sect of Basilides, first found in a poem by Q. Serenus Sammonicus (III), used as a charm or amulet – (perh. through F.) Gr. *ΑΒΡΑϹΑΔΑΒΡΑ*, in which *Ϲ* (i.e. *S*) was read as *C* (i.e. *K*); rel. to *abrasax*, ABRAXAS.

abrade əbrei·d rub away. XVII. – L. *abrādere*, f. *ab*+*rādere* scrape; see AB-, ERASE. So **abras**ION əbrei·ʒən. XVII. – L., f. *abrās-*, pp. stem of *abrādere*.

abraxas əbræ·ksæs cabalistic word used like *abracadabra*. XVIII. Also **abrasax** æ·brəsæks. (*Ἀβρασάξ* or *Ἀβραξάς*, name of the supreme god of the Basilidans, contains the number 365, which is the number of heavens, with their spirits, emanating from him.

abreaction æbriæ·kʃən cathartic process induced by living again emotions associated with forgotten or repressed ideas. XX. f. AB-+REACTION, tr. G. *abreagierung*.

abreast əbre·st with breasts or fronts in line. XVI. Earlier †*on a brest* (XV), also †*of (a) breast* (XVI–XVII), †*in a breast* (XVII); see A-[1], BREAST, and cf. F. *de front* (Froissart).

abridge əbri·dʒ shorten. XIV. ME. *abreg(g)e* – OF. *abregier* (mod. *abréger*) = Pr. *abrevjar* :– late L. *abbreviāre* ABBREVIATE. So **abri·dg(e)**MENT. XV. – (O)F. *abrègement.*

abroach əbrou·tʃ broached. XIV (Gower). – AN. *abroche*, f. OF. *abrochier*, f. *a* AD-+ *brochier* BROACH[1]; see A-[1].

abroad əbrɔ̄·d †widely, at large XIII; out of doors XIV; in or into foreign lands XV. f. A-[1]+BROAD; prob. suggested by ME. **a brēde, on brēde* (OE. *brǣd* BREADTH).

abrogate æ·brŏgeit repeal. XVI. f. pp. stem of L. *abrogāre*, f. *ab*+*rogāre* propose (a law); after earlier pp. †*abrogate* (XV); see AB-, ROGATION, -ATE[3].

abrupt əbrʌ·pt †broken away or off; marked by sudden change XVI (Sh.); steep XVII. – L. *abruptus* precipitous, disconnected, adj. use of pp. of *abrumpere* break off, sever, f. *ab*+*rumpere*; see AB-, RUPTURE.

abs- æbs, əbs var. of AB- before *c, t.*

abscess æ·bsės collection of pus in a cavity. XVI. – F. *abcès* – L. *abscessus* going away, abscess (Celsus, rendering Gr. ἀπόστημα *aposteme*, IMPOST(H)UME), f. *abscess-*, pp. stem of *abscēdere* depart, f. *abs* ABS-+*cēdere* go (CEDE).

abscissa æbsi·sə (math.) segment of a line intercepted between a point therein and an ordinate drawn to it. XVII. – modL. (Stefano degli Angeli), sb. use (sc. *linea* line) of fem. pp. of *abscindere* cut off, f. *ab* AB-+*scindere* cut asunder (see SCISSORS). Also anglicized †*absciss(e)* XVII–XVIII.

abscond əbskɔ·nd hide away (now only intr.), depart hurriedly and secretly. XVI. – L. *abscondere*, f. *abs* ABS-+*condere* put together, stow (see CONDITION).

absence æ·bsəns a being away. XIV (Ch., Gower). – (O)F. *absence* – L. *absentia*, f. *absent-, absēns*, functioning as prp. of *abesse* (*ab* away, *esse* be; see AB-, ESSENCE, and cf. PRESENCE). The stem *sent-* corr. to Skr. *sant-*, Gr. *ont-* being, prob. rel. to L. *sons* guilty and Germ. **sonta-* true, SOOTH. So **a·bs**ENT. XIV (Wycl. Bible). – (O)F. – L. **abse·nt** vb. XV. – (O)F. *absenter.* Hence **absentee** æbsəntī· one who absents himself. XVI. Earlier also †*absentie*; of obscure origin; see -EE[1].

absinthe æ·bsinþ wormwood XV; liqueur orig. flavoured with this XIX (Thackeray). – F. *absinthe* – L. *absinthium* – Gr. *apsínthion* wormwood, of alien origin.

absolute æ·bsəlʲūt free from imperfection, restriction, or qualification XIV; (gram.; based ult. on Gr. ἀπολελυμένος) XV. – L. *absolūtus* freed, free, separated, completed, pp. of *absolvere* ABSOLVE; infl. partly by F. †*absolut* (mod. *absolu*), which superseded earlier †*asolu.* As sb. (*the a.*) XIX (Coleridge, 1809–10).

absolution æbsəlʲū·ʃən remission of sins. XII. – (O)F. *absolution* – L. *absolūtiō(n-)* legal acquittal, (eccl.) forgiveness of sins, f. *absolūt-*, pp. stem of *absolvere* free, acquit (whence **absolve** æbsɔ·lv, əbz- †solve, resolve XV; acquit, remit XVI), f. *ab* AB-+ *solvere* loose, SOLVE, rendering Gr. ἀπολύειν; see -TION.

absorb əbsɔ̄·ɹb, əbz- swallow up. XV. – (O)F. *absorber*, refash. after L. of †*asorber* :– L. *absorbēre*, f. *ab* AB-+*sorbēre* swallow, which has a wide range of cogns. in IE. (Gr. *rhopheîn* :– **srobh-* swallow, and Lett., Lith., and Arm. forms). So **abso·rp**TION. XVI. – L. *absorptiō(n-)*, f. *absorpt-*, pp. stem of *absorbēre.* **abso·rb**ENT. XVIII. **abso·rp**TIVE. XVII. – medL.

absquatulate æbskwɔ·tjŭleit (U.S.) decamp. XIX. joc. formation with reminiscence of *abscond, squattle* decamp, *perambulate*; said to have been first used in Bernard's play 'The Kentuckian', 1833.

abstain əbstei·n withhold oneself *from.* XIV (Wycl. Bible). Late ME. *abstene, -eine* repr. tonic stem of (O)F. *abstenir* (AN. *abstener*), refash. after L. of *astenir* :– L. *abstinēre*, f. *abs* ABS-+*tenēre* hold, keep (cf. TENURE). The same phonetic conditions are seen in *attain, contain, detain, maintain, obtain, pertain, retain, sustain.* So **absten**TION əbste·nʃən. XVI. – F. *abstention*, f. L. *abstent-*, pp. stem of *abstinēre.*

abstemious ǽbstī·miəs temperate in food, drink, etc. XVII. f. L. *abstēmius*, f. *abs* ABS- +base of *tēmētum* intoxicating drink, *tēmulentus* intoxicated; see -IOUS.

absterge ǽbstɔ̄·ɹdʒ wipe away. XVI. – F. *absterger* or L. *abstergēre*, f. *abs* ABS-+*tergēre* wipe (cf. TERSE).

abstinence æ·bstinəns forbearance, self-restraint. XIII. – (O)F. *abstinence*, refash. of OF. *astenance* :– L. *abstinentia*, f. *abstinent-, -ēns*, prp. of *abstinēre* ABSTAIN; see -ENCE.

abstract æ·bstrækt †derived XIV; †withdrawn;)(*concrete* XVI; sb. compendium, epitome XV. – F. †*abstract* or L. *abstractus* drawn away, withdrawn, (in Isidore) adj. abstract, pp. of *abstrahere*, f. *abs* ABS-+ *trahere* draw (see TRACT). So **abstract** əbstræ·kt take away, withdraw. XV. Partly f. pp. †*abstract*, partly f. *abstract-*, pp. stem of *abstrahere.* **abstra·c**TION. XV. – F. or late L.

abstruse əbstrū·s †hidden; recondite. XVI. – F. *abstrus, -use*, or L. *abstrūsus, -a*, pp. of *abstrūdere* conceal, f. *abs* ABS-+*trūdere* thrust (cf. THREAT). 'An uncouth and unusual word' (P. Heylin, 1656).

absurd əbsɔ̄·ɹd irrational, stupid. XVI. – F. *absurde* or L. *absurdus* incongruous, senseless, f. *ab* AB-+a base perh. identical with that of L. *susurrus* murmur, whisper, Skr. *svárati* make a sound, and ANSWER, SWEAR (cf. for the meaning L. *absonus* discordant, incongruous). So **absu·rd**ITY. XV. – F. or late L.

abuna abū·na patriarch of the Abyssinian church. XVII. – Arab. *abūna* 'our father'.

abundance əbʌ·ndəns overflowing state or amount. XIV. – OF. *abundance*, (also mod.) *abondance* – L. *abundantia*, f. *abundant-*, *-āns* (whence **abu·ndant** XIV), prp. of *abundāre* ABOUND; see -ANCE, -ANT.

abuse əbjū·s wrong use; †deceit; injurious speech. XV. – (O)F. *abus* (= Sp., It. *abuso*) or L. *abūsus*, f. *abūs-*, pp. stem of *abūtī* use up, misuse, f. *ub* AB- + *ūtī*, *ūs-* USE; superseded †*abusion* (XIV) – OF. *abusion* – L. *abūsiō(n-)*. So **abuse** əbjū·z †misrepresent, impose upon; misuse, ill-use; malign. XIV. – (O)F. *abuser* – Rom. **abūsāre* (cf. Pr., Sp. *abusar*, It. *abusare*), f. *abūs-* (as above). **abu·s**IVE əbjū·siv. XVI. – F. or L.

abut əbʌ·t A. border *upon* XV; B. end *on* or *against* XVI. In A, – AL. *abuttāre*, f. *a-* AD- + *butta* BUTT[2]; in B, – (O)F. *abouter*, †*abuter*, f. *à* AD- + *bouter* BUTT[1]. Hence **abu·t**MENT lateral support of a building. XVII.

aby əbai· (arch.) pay the penalty for. XII. OE. *ābyćġan* redeem, atone for (= Goth. *usbugjan*), f. *ā-* A-[3] + *byćġan* BUY. (Used confusedly by Spenser for *abide*.)

abysm əbi·zm (arch.) abyss. XIII. ME. *abime*, *-yme*, later *abisme*, *-ysme* – OF. *abime*, *abisme* (mod. *abîme*) = Pr. *abisme*, Sp. *abismo* – medL. *abysmus*, alteration of *abyssus* ABYSS by assim. to Gr. suffix *-ismós* -ISM. Hence **aby·sm**AL. XIX.

abyss əbi·s bottomless pit or gulf, void XVI; deep chasm XVII. – late L. *abyssus* (whence also OF., Pr. *abis*, It. *abisso*) – Gr. *ábussos* fem., sb. use (sc. *límnē* lake) of *ábussos* unfathomable, f. *a-* A-[4] + *bussós*, Ionic var. of *buthós* depth. *Abyssus*, *abissus* were formerly in Eng. use.

ac- ək assim. form of AD- before *c* and *q*. In OF., L. *acc-* was reduced to *ac-*, which appears consequently in ME. adoptions, e.g. OF. *acorder*, ME. *acorde* ACCORD; in later F., and hence in Eng., *acc-* was restored by latinization; the process accounts also for the sp. of *accurse*, *acknowledge*, *acquaint*.

-ac æk suffix primarily of adjs. denoting 'pertaining to', formerly *-aque*, *-ack(e)*, *-ak(e)*, repr. ult. (through L. *-acus*), Gr. *-akós*, as in *kardiakós* CARDIAC, *demoniakós* DEMONIAC, *elegeiakós* ELEGIAC, on the model of which others were formed at various periods, e.g. *iliacus* ILIAC, *maniacus* MANIAC. These were the immed. source of or model for many learned F. words in *-aque*, whence, or directly from L. or Gr., many adoptions in Eng., e.g. *aphrodisiac*, *hypochondriac*. Many of these adjs. were used as sbs., as their originals or models were in Gr. and L. Cf. -ACAL.

acacia əkei·ʃə leguminous shrub or tree of the Mimosa group XVI. N. Amer. locust-tree (false acacia) XVII. – L. *acacia* – Gr. *akakíā*, prob. f. base of *akḗ* point (cf. ACID), with allusion to the thorns of the acacia.

academy əkæ·dəmi place where the arts and sciences are taught; university, etc. XVI; society for their cultivation XVII. – F. *académie* or L. *acadēmīa* – Gr. *akadēmíā* and *akadḗmeia* (orig. fem. of adj. *akadḗmeios*) name of a gymnasium (called after the hero Academus) in the suburbs of Athens, where Plato taught, and hence applied to the Platonic school of philosophy (Caxton has *achadomye*, after medL. *achademia*, for Plato's school); see -Y[3]. The application to societies and institutions came ult. from Italy (It. *accademia*), via France. Formerly str. *acade·my*. 'Dr. Johnson seems to have decided justly in saying the word *academy* ought to have the accent on the first syllable; though present usage, it must be confessed, seems to lead to the contrary pronunciation' (Walker, 1828). So **academ**IC ækəde·mik, -ICAL. XVI. – (O)F. *académique* or L. *acadēmicus* (cf. Gr. *Akadēmeikós*, *-aikós*). **academi·**CIAN. XVIII. – F. *académicien* (XVI).

Acadian əkei·diən pert. to Nova Scotia. XVIII. f. *Acadia*, latinized form of *Acadie* name (of unkn. origin) given by the French in 1603 to part of the mainland of N. America; see -IAN.

-acal əkəl suffix compounded of -AC and -AL, forming adjs., some merely alternative to those in -AC, some with differentiated use, some serving as adjs. to sbs. in *-ac*; e.g. *ammoniacal*, *demoniacal*, *heliacal*, *hypochrondriacal*, *zodiacal*.

acanthus əkæ·nþəs plant of the genus so named; conventional figure of its leaf. XVII. – L. – Gr. *ákanthos*, f. *ákantha* thorn, prob. adaptations of alien words which became assoc. with the base **ak-* be sharp (see ACID).

acarus æ·kərəs (zool.) mite. XVII. modL. – Gr. *ákari*, f. *akarḗs* minute, f. *a-* A-[4] + **kar-* **ker-*, base of *keírein* cut.

acatalectic æ:kætəle·ktik ei:- (pros.) not wanting a syllable in the last foot. XVI. – late L. *acatalēcticus* – Gr. *akatalēktikós*; see A-[4].

Accadian, Akkadian əkei·diən name of a Semitic language preserved in cuneiform inscriptions. XIX ('the newly discovered Accadian language', *c.* 1855). f. *Accad*, *Akkad*, name of a city in the 'land of Shinar' or Babylonia (Gen. x 10), prob. to be identified with Agade; see -IAN and cf. F. *accadien*, G. *akkadisch*.

accede æksī·d approach, arrive XV; agree *to* XVIII (one early ex. in XV). – L. *accēdere* approach, be added, assent, resemble, f. *ad* AC- + *cēdere* go (CEDE[1]); cf. (O)F. *accéder*. So **access**ION ǽkse·ʃən addition XVI; approach; coming to the throne XVII. – L. *accessiō(n-)*, f. *access-*, pp. stem of *accēdere*,

accelerate ǣkse·lǝrẹit increase speed. XVI. f. pp. stem of L. *accelerāre*, f. *ad* AC-+*celer* swift; see CELERITY, -ATE[3]. So **acceler-A·TION**. XVI. – (O)F. or L. **acce·leRATOR**. 1900.

accent æ·ksĕnt prominence of pitch or stress given to a syllable XIV (Trevisa; rare before XVI); diacritic mark indicating this; peculiar mode of utterance XVI. – (O)F. *accent* or L. *accentus* (f. *ad* AC-+*cantus* song, CHANT), lit. rendering of Gr. *prosōidiā* PROSODY, lit. 'song added (sc. to speech)'. So **accent** æksе·nt accentuate. XVI. – OF. *accenter*, f. *accent*. **acce·ntuAL[1]**. XVII. f. L. *accentus*. **acce·ntuate** mark with an accent; emphasize. XVIII. f. medL. *accentuāre*; see -ATE[3] and cf. F. *accentuer* (XVI). **accentuA·TION**. XIX. – medL.

accentor æksе·ntǭɹ one of a genus of passerine singing-birds, e.g. hedge-sparrow. XIX. Late L. (Isidore) one who sings with another, f. *ad*+*cantor* singer; see AC-, CANTOR.

accept ǝkse·pt receive willingly or with approval. XIV (Wycl., Ch.). – (O)F. *accepter* or L. *acceptāre*, f. *accept-*, pp. stem of *accipere*, f. *ad* AC-+*capere* take (cf. HEAVE). So **acce·ptABLE**. XIV. – (O)F. – late L. **acce·ptANCE**. XVI. – OF. **accepta·TION** †acceptance XV; †(Sc.) purport, tenor XVI; received meaning XVII. – (O)F. – lateL. ('acceptance', 'meaning').

access æ·kses approach, admission, entrance; attack of disease, †ague XIV; addition XVI. – OF. *aces*, (also mod.) *accès* :- L. *accessus* approach, attack (of disease, *morbi*), f. *access-*, pp. stem of *accēdere* ACCEDE. The earliest use appears to be 'attack, fit'. The stressing *a·ccess* is attested from the beginning, but *acce·ss* was prevalent XVI–XVIII; spellings of the type *axces, axes, axis* were common XIV–XVI. So **acce·ss-IBLE**. XV. – (O)F. or late L. **acce·SSION** a coming to, esp. as an addition. XVI. – (O)F. – L.

accessary ǣkse·sǝri, (formerly) æ·ksisǝri adherent, assistant, participant in an offence XV; †adjunct, accompaniment XV; adj. XVI. – medL. *accessārius*, f. L. *access-*; see prec. and -ARY. So **acce·ssory** that is an accession, additional; also sb. adjunct; participant. XV. – medL. *accessōrius*; see -ORY. The two words have been often confused. (Also †*accessoire* XV, and in Sc. form *accessor* XVI – F. *accessoire*.)

accidence æ·ksidǝns part of grammar dealing with inflexions (the changes to which words are subject), morphology. XV – L. *accidentia* (tr. Gr. παρεπόμενα 'accompanying things'), n.pl. of *accidēns* ACCIDENT, taken as fem. sg.; see -ENCE. The L. word was used as a title of books containing the rudiments of Latin grammar (e.g. 'Accidentia Stanbridgiana', 1534); *accidents* was occas. so used XVI–XVII, but *accidence* is earlier.

accident æ·ksidǝnt something that happens XIV (Ch.); (philos.) attribute of a subject XIV (Wyclif). – (O)F. *accident* – late L. *accident-, -ēns*, sb. use (sc. *rēs* thing) of prp. of *accidere* happen, f. *ad*+*cadere* fall; see AC-, CASE, -ENT. In the philos. use based on τὸ συμβεβηκός (Aristotle). Hence **accide·ntAL**. XIV. – F. *accidentel*, †*-al* – late L. *accidentālis* (Augustine).

accidie æ·ksidi sloth (the fourth of the seven deadly sins). XIII. – AN. *accidie* = OF. *accide* (whence ME. by-form *accide*) – medL. *accīdia*, alteration of late L. *acēdia* – Gr. *akēdīā* heedlessness, torpor, f. *a-* A-[4]+ **kēd-*, base of *kêdos* care, *kḗdesthai* be concerned. Revived after long desuetude by Bishop F. Paget, 1891.

accinge æksi·ndʒ gird *oneself*. XVII. – L. *accingere*, f. *ad-* AC-+*cingere* gird (see CINCTURE).

accipitral æksi·pitrǝl hawk-like. XIX. f. L. *accipiter* (*-tr-*) hawk (cf. Gr. *ōkúpteros*, Skr. *āçupatvan-* swiftly flying)+-AL[1]. So **acci·pitrine**. XIX; after F. *accipitrin-e*.

acclaim ǝklei·m applaud. XVII. – L. *acclāmāre*, f. *ad* AC-+*clamāre*, with sp. assim. to CLAIM. So **acclamATION** æklǝmei·ʃǝn. XVI. – L. (An earlier *acleime, acclame* was – medL. *acclāmāre* make a claim for.)

acclimatize ǝklai·mǝtaiz inure to a climate. XIX. f. F. *acclimater* (f. *à* to, AC-+*climat* CLIMATE)+-IZE; has superseded older **acclimate** (XVIII), which was a direct adoption from F. Hence **accli:matizA·TION** XIX; also **acclima·tion, acclimata·tion** (– F.).

acclivity ǣkli·vĭti ascending slope. XVII. – L. *acclīvitās*, f. *acclīvis* sloping upward, f. *ad* AC-+*clīvus* slope; see INCLINE, -ITY.

accolade ækŏlei·d, -ā·d salutation on the bestowal of knighthood. XVII. – F. *accolade* – Pr. *acolada* (= OF. *acolée*), f. Rom. **accollāre* (OF. *acoler*, Pr. *acolar*) embrace about the neck, f. L. *ad*+*collum* neck; see AC-, COLLAR, -ADE[1].

accommodate ǝkǫ·mǝdeit adapt, adjust; furnish *with* something convenient. XVI. – pp. stem of L. *accommodāre*, f. *ad*+*commodus*; see AC-, COMMODIOUS, -ATE[3]. So **accommodA·TION**. XVII. – F. or L.

accompany ǝkʌ·mpǝni †associate, conjoin; go in company with XV; (mus.) XVI. Earlier *accompa(i)gne* – (O)F. *accompagner*, f. *a-* AC-+*compaing* COMPANION; later assim. to COMPANY. Hence **acco·mpaniMENT**. XVIII; after F. *accompagnement*.

accomplice ǝkǫ·mplis associate in guilt. XV (Caxton). prob. alteration, by assoc. with prec., of †*complice* (XV, Caxton) – (O)F. *complice* – late L. *complicem*, nom. *complex* confederate, f. *com-*+*plic-* (cf. *complicāre* COMPLICATE and *simplex* SIMPLE).

accomplish ǝkǫ·mpliʃ, ǝkʌ·mpliʃ fulfil, perform. XIV (Ch.). OF. *acompliss-*, lengthened stem (see -ISH²) of *acomplir* (mod. *acc-*), f. *a* AC-+†*complir* (L. *complēre* fill, COMPLETE). Hence **acco·mplish**MENT accomplishing, thing accomplished XV; †equipment, accoutrement XVII (Bacon); ornamental attainment(s) XVIII; after F. *accomplissement*.

accord əkɔ̄·ɹd †reconcile; agree XII (pt. *acordede*, pp. *acordad*, Peterborough Chron.). – OF. *acorder* (mod. *acc-*) :– Rom. **accordāre* (Sp. *acordar*, It. *accordare*), f. L. *ad* AC-, after *concordāre* (see CONCORD). So **acco·rd** agreement. XIII. – OF. *acord*, f. *acorder*. **acco·rd**ANCE. XIV. – OF. **acco·rd**ANT agreeing, consonant. XIV. – OF. prp. of *acorder*. The use of the prp. **acco·rding** as adv. 'in a manner answering (*to*)' dates from XV.

accordion əkɔ̄·ɹdiən musical hand-instrument with bellows and keys. XIX. – G. *akkordion*, f. It. *accordare* tune (an instrument)+-*ion*, as in *orchestrion*; cf. F. *accordéon* after *odéon*, etc.).

accost əkɔ·st †lie or go alongside; approach; make up to and address. XVI. – F. *accoster* – It. *accostare* :– Rom. **accostāre* (cf. OF. *acoster*, F. *acoter*, Sp. *acostar*), f. L. *ad*+*costa* rib, side; see AC-, COAST. In early use, by assim. to *coast*, often spelt *accoast*.

accouchement ækū·ʃmã lying-in. XIX. – F., f. *accoucher*, f. *à* AC-+*coucher* put to bed (see COUCH). So **accoucheur** ækū·ʃɔ̄ɹ man-midwife. XVIII.

account əkau·nt reckoning, a rendering of this XIII; estimation XIV; relation, report XVII. ME. *acunt*, *acount* – AN. *acunt*, OF. *acont*, later *ac(c)ompt*, f. *acunter*, *aconter* (f. *a-* AC-+*conter* COUNT²), whence **accou·nt** vb. make a reckoning XIV. Formerly often *a(c)compt*. Hence **accou·nt**ABLE XIV; cf. *unaccountable* (XVII). **accou·nt**ANT one who renders or is liable to render an account XV, takes charge of accounts XVI. – Law F. use of prp. of OF. *aconter*.

accoutre əkū·təɹ furnish with proper equipment. XVI (Bellenden). – (O)F. *accoutrer*, earlier *acoustrer* orig. equip gen. (later, with clothing), f. *a-* AC-+*cousture* (mod. *couture*) sewing :– Rom. **consūtūra*, f. L. *consūt-*, pp. stem of *consuere* sew together (see CON-, SEW). So **accou·tre**MENT -təɹ-, -trə-. XVI.

accredit əkre·dit vouch for. XVII. – F. *accréditer*, f. *a-* AC-+*crédit* CREDIT, after phr. *mettre à crédit*, lit. 'put to credit'.

accretion əkrī·ʃən growth by (external) enlargement, extraneous addition. XVII. – L. *accrētiō(n-)*, f. *accrēt-*, pp. stem of *accrēscere* be enlarged (whence **accre·sce** accrue XVI), f. *ad*+*crēscere* grow; see AC-, CRESCENT, -TION.

accrue əkrū· come by way of addition. XV. prob. f. AN. *accru(e)*, OF. *accreu(e)*, pp. of *acreistre* :– L. *accrēscere* (see prec.).

accumulate əkjū·mjŭleit heap together. XVI. f. pp. stem of L. *accumulāre*, f. *ad*+*cumulus* heap; see AC-, CUMULUS, -ATE³. So **accumula·**TION. XV. – L. Cf. (O)F. *accumuler*, *-ation*. **accu·mul**ATOR. XVII. – L.

accurate æ·kjŭrət exact, correct. XVI. – L. *accūrātus* performed with care, f. *accūrāre* apply care to, f. *ad*+*cūrāre* care for, f. *cūra* care; see AC-, CURE, -ATE². Hence **a·ccur**ACY. XVII.

accurse əkɔ̄·ɹs place under a curse. Late OE. *ācursian* (in pp. *-od*). Now only in pp.; f. A-³+CURSE vb. For the sp. with *-cc-* see AC-.

accusative əkjū·zətiv (gram.) case expressing chiefly destination or the goal of motion. XV. –(O)F. *accusatif* or L. *accūsātīvus* (sc. *cāsus* case), f. pp. stem of *accūsāre* ACCUSE. L. *cāsus accūsātīvus* (Varro, Quintilian) renders Gr. *ptôsis aitiātikḗ* case of accusing, f. *aitiâsthai* accuse, *aitiân*, *aitíā* cause, but was interpreted also as 'pert. to what is caused', whence the alternative L. tr. *causātīvus* (Priscian); see -ATIVE.

accuse əkjū·z charge with a fault or crime. XIII (RGlouc.). – OF. *acuser*, (also mod.) *accuser* :– L *accūsāre* call to account, f. *ad* AC-+*causa* CAUSE. So **accusa·**TION. XIV. – (O)F. – L.

accustom əkʌ·stəm make used (*to*). XV. – AN. *acustumer*, OF. *acostumer* (mod. *accoutumer*), f. *a-* AC-+*costume* CUSTOM.

ace eis throw of one at dice XIII; playing-card bearing one pip (reckoned as of the highest value) XVI; the highest or best XVIII (Burns). ME. *as*, *aas* – (O)F. *as* :– L. *assem*, nom. *ās* unity, unit, AS².

-acean ei·ʃ ⁱən f. L. *-āceus* -ACEOUS+-AN. In sb. use supplying an Eng. form for names of groups in **-acea** (n.pl., sc. *animālia* animals), e.g. *Crustacea*, *crustaceans*.

-aceous ei·ʃ ⁱəs f. L. *-āceus* (f. *-āc-* -AC)+-OUS (cf. -EOUS); in nat. hist. it supplies adjs. for names of groups in **-acea, -aceæ,** e.g. *crustaceous* pert. to the Crustacea, *rosaceous* pert. to the Rosaceæ.

acephalous eise·fələs headless. XVIII. f. late L. *acephalus* – Gr. *aképhalos* (*kephalḗ* head); see A-⁴, CEPHALIC, -OUS. (In ecclL. *Acephali* was applied to various Christian sects or bodies who acknowledged no leader or superior.)

acerbity əsɔ̄·ɹbĭti bitter sourness. XVI. – F. *acerbité* or L. *acerbitās*, f. *acerbus* bitter, sour (whence **ace·rb** XVII) :– **akridhos*, f. **akro-*; cf. ACID and see -ITY.

acetic əsī·tik, əse·tik name of the acid of vinegar. XIX. – F. *acétique*, f. L. *acētum* vinegar, f. *acēre* be sour; see ACID, -IC.

ache eik pain. OE. *ǣće*, also *eće*, early ME. *eche* (:– **akiz*), f. base of *acan* str. vb.; OE. pt. *ōc*, ME. *ok*, *ook*, *oke*, and pp. *acen*, early ME. *aken*, were replaced by weak forms *akede*, *aked* in XIV; mod. **ached** eikt. The normal repr. of the OE. sb. was *ache* eitʃ, and this pronunc. was prevalent until *c.* 1820; traces of the influence of the vb., which was normally repr. by *ake* eik, but has now the sp. proper to the sb., appear XV ('ake or ache . . *dolor*', Promp. Parv.).

acherontic ækərɔ·ntik infernal, gloomy. XVII. – lateL. *acheronticus*, f. *Acheront-*, nom. *-ōn* – Gr. *Akhérōn* fabulous river of the Lower World; see -IC.

achieve ətʃī·v finish, accomplish. XIV (Ch., Gower). – (O)F. *achever* come or bring to an end, f. OF. phr. *a chief* 'to (a) head', to an end, repr. L. *ad* and Rom. **capum*, for L. *caput* head; see AD-, CHIEF. Hence, or – (O)F. *achèvement*, **achie·ve**MENT. XV (Caxton).

achromatic ækromæ·tik free from colour. XVIII. – F. *achromatique*, f. Gr. *akhrṓmatos*; see A-[4], CHROMATIC.

acid æ·sid sour, tart. XVII (Bacon). – F. *acide* or L. *acidus*, f. IE. **ak-* be pointed or sharp, as in *acēre* be sharp, *aciēs* sharpness, point, *acus* needle (cf. ACETIC, ACRID, ACUTE), rel. to Gr. *ákros* ACRO-, *ákris*, *akís*, *akḗ* point, *akmḗ* ACME, Skr. *áçris* corner, sharp edge, Lith. *aštrùs* sharp, OSl. *osŭtŭ* thistle, Gr. *oxús* sharp (see OXY-, OXYGEN, OXYTONE), and Germ. **ag-* (repr. by EDGE); see -ID[1]. As sb. first applied (XVII) to 'sharp salts', after modL. *acidum*, F. *acide*. *Acid drop* is short for *acidulated drop* (Dickens). So **acid**ITY əsi·dĭti. XVII. – F. – late L. **aci·dulated**. XVII. f. L. *acidulus* sourish (whence **aci·du**LOUS XVIII); see -ATE[3].

-acious ei·ʃəs suffix repr. F. *-acieux*, as in *astucieux*, *audacieux*, †*contumacieux*, †*mendacieux*, based on L. sbs. *astūtia*, *audācia*, *contumācia*, *mendācium*+*-eux* -OUS; *capacious*, *fugacious*, *loquacious*, *rapacious* are immed. f. L. adjs. in *-āc-*, *-āx*. The earliest Eng. exx. are *audacious* and *contumacious*. *Froudacious* (f. name of the historian J. A. *Froude*) is a joc. formation after *mendacious*.

acknowledge əknɔ·lidʒ admit knowledge of, recognize. XV (Caxton). prob. f. †*knowledge* (XIII) on the analogy of the relation of †*aknow* (OE. *oncnāwan*) and KNOW; see AC-. Hence **acknow·ledg(e)**MENT. XVI.

acme æ·kmi highest point, culmination. XVII (written earlier and later in Gr. letters ἀκμή). – Gr. *akmḗ* point, top, sharp edge, f. **ak-* be pointed (see ACID).

acne æ·kni skin eruption. XIX. – modL. *acnē*, deduced from a misreading ἀκνάς for ἀκμάς, acc. pl. of Gr. ἀκμή eruption on the face (ACME) in Aetius of Amida's works (cf. 'De uaris faciei, qui tum ionthi, tum acnæ Græcis uocantur' IV xiii, tr. J. B. Montanus, 1533).

acolyte æ·kəlait (eccl.) member of one of the minor orders of the Church XIV; minor attendant XVI. – OF. *acolyt* (mod. *-yte*) or ecclL. *acolytus*, *-itus*, *-ithus* – Gr. *akólouthos* following, follower (cf. ANACOLOUTHON). The aphetic deriv. *colet* (XIV) survives in the surname *Colet*, *Collett*.

aconite æ·kənait poisonous plant Aconitum Napellus. XVI. – F. *aconit* or L. *aconītum* – Gr. *akóniton*.

acorn ei·kɔ̄ɹn fruit of the oak. OE. *æcern* = MLG. *ackeren*, Du. *aker* acorn, MHG. *ackeran* oak or beech mast (G. *ecker* is from LG.), ON. *akarn*, Goth. *akran* fruit, produce; connected through its gen. sense with OE. *æcer*, etc. ACRE, as if meaning 'produce of uncultivated land', 'wild fruit', and so ult. with OIr. *áirne* sloe, W. *aeron* fruits. OE. *æcern* is regularly repr. by ME. and mod. dial. *achern* æ·tʃəɹn, but forms with unambiguous *k* are found XIV, and association with *corn* (and *oak*), which is shown by sp. such as *akecorn*, *okecorn*, had established the present standard form by XVI; *acorn*, beside *ocorn*, is in Promp. Parv. (XV).

acotyledon ei:kɔtilī·dən (bot.) plant having no distinct cotyledons. XIX. f. modL. pl. (*-ones*); see A-[4], COTYLEDON.

acoustic əkau·stik, əkū·stik pert. to hearing. XVII (Bacon). – Gr. *akoustikós*, f. *akoúein* HEAR; cf. F. *acoustique* (XVIII); see -IC. Being direct from Gr., it has normally the Eng. pronunc. of Gr. *ou*, viz. au, as in NOUS. Also sb. pl. (see -ICS) XVII.

acquaint əkwei·nt †refl. and intr. become known *to*; give knowledge to, inform. XIII (earliest in pp.). ME. *aqueynte*, *aquointe*, *acointe* – OF. *acointer* :– medL. *accognitāre* make known, f. L. *accognitus*, f. *ad* AC-+*cognitus*, pp. of *cognōscere* know (see COGNITION, QUAINT). So **acquai·nt**ANCE personal knowledge; person(s) known. XIV. – OF. *acointance*, f. *acointer*. For the sp. with *ac-* cf. *acknowledge*.

acquiesce ækwie·s †remain quiet; †submit; agree tacitly. XVII. – L. *acquiēscere*, f. *ad*+*quiēscere* rest; see AC-, QUIET. So **acquie·sc**ENCE, **acquie·sc**ENT. XVII. Cf. F. *acquiescer*, etc.

acquire ækwaiə·ɹ gain, obtain. XV. Late ME. *acquere* – OF. *acquerre* :– Rom. **acquærere*, for L. *acquīrere* get in addition, f. *ad* AC-+*quærere* seek (cf. QUERY); superseded *c.* 1600 by the latinized form *acquire*. So **acquisi**TION ækwizi·ʃən. XIV. – L. *acquīsītiō(n-)*, f. *acquīsīt-*, pp. stem of *acquīrere*.

acquit əkwi·t settle, discharge; deliver, release; exculpate. XIII. ME. *acwite*, *aquite* – OF. *acuiter*, *a(c)quiter* = Pr. *aquitar* – Rom. (medL.) **acquitāre*, f. *ad* AC-+**quitāre* QUIT. Hence **acqui·ttal**. XV (Lydg.); see -AL[2]. **acqui·tt**ANCE settlement, discharge. XIV. – OF. *aquitance* (cf. QUITTANCE).

acre ei·kəɹ †piece of tilled or arable land, field; unit of square measure of land OE.; (dial.) linear measure XIV. OE. *æcer* = OFris. *ekker*, OS. *akkar* (Du. *akker*), OHG. *acchar*, *ackar* (G. *acker*), ON. *akr*, Goth. *akrs* :– CGerm. **akraz* :– IE. **agros*, repr.

also by L. *ager* (cf. AGRICULTURE), Gr. *agrós*, Skr. *ájras* field; prob. orig. 'pasture land' and f. **ag-* drive, do, ACT. The sense 'piece of tilled land' is original in proper names such as *Long Acre*, *Black Acre*, *Whittaker* (i.e. *White Acre*). *God's acre* churchyard (Longfellow) is tr. G. *Gottesacker*. The sp. *acre*, which superseded *aker* (current till XVII) is due to medL. *acra*, (O)F. *acre*. Hence **acre**AGE ei·kəridʒ. XIX.

acrid æ·krid bitterly pungent. XVIII. f. L. *ācri-*, *ācer* sharp (f. **ăc-* as in ACID, ACUTE); irreg. formation with suffix -ID[1], prob. after *acid*; an earlier attempt to anglicize L. *ācris* was †*acrious* (XVII only).

acrimony æ·kriməni bitter pungency. XVI. – F. *acrimonie* or L. *ācrimōnia*, f. *ācris*; see ACRID, -MONY. So **acrimon**IOUS -mou·niəs. XVII. – F. *acrimonieux* – medL. *ācrimōniōsus*.

acro- æ·krou, əkrɔ· repr. Gr. *akro-*, comb. form of *ákros* terminal, outmost, topmost (see ACID) as in *akrṓmion* outer extremity of the shoulder-blade (*ômos* shoulder), whence Eng. *acromion* (XVII); in mod. techn. terms XIX.

acroamatic æːkroəmæ·tik communicated by oral teaching, esoteric. XVII. – Gr. *akroāmatikós*, f. *akróāma*, *-mat-* what is heard, f. *akroâsthai* hear; see -IC.

acrobat æ·krəbæt rope-dancer, tumbler. XIX. – F. *acrobate* – Gr. *akrobátēs*, f. *akróbatos* walking on tiptoe, f. *ákros* ACRO- + *-batos*, f. base of *baínein* walk (see COME).

acropolis əkrɔ·pəlis citadel of a Greek city, esp. that of Athens. XVII. – Gr. *akrópolis*, f. *ákros* topmost + *pólis* city; see ACRO-, POLITIC.

acrospire æ·krouspaiəɹ first leaf-shoot. 1674. MSc. *acherspire*, *akyrspire*, f. *acher* :– Nhb. OE. *æhher*, *eher* (Sc. †*echir*, *icker*) EAR[2] + *spīr* shoot, SPIRE[1]; through the vars. *akerspire*, *acrespire*, assim. to words in ACRO-, and prob. assoc. with SPIRE[2]. (Modern dial. vars. are *acrespire*, *ackersprit*.) Hence **a·crospire** vb. throw out the first leaf-shoot. 1609.

across əkrɔ̀·s adv. †in the form of a cross, crosswise XIII; transversely, from side to side XVI; prep. XVI. ME. *a creoix*, *o(n) croice* (XIII) was succeeded by *acros*, *acrosse* (XV), with occas. vars. *in* or *on crosse* (XV–XVI). – OF. *a croix*, *en croix*; later assim. to native formations in A-[1] and the sb. CROSS. Aphetic *cross* was formerly in gen. use (e.g. 'waft me safely crosse the Channell', Sh.).

acrostic əkrɔ·stik short poem, etc. in which the initial letters taken in order spell a word, etc. – F. *acrostiche* – Gr. *akrostikhís*, f. *ákros* endmost, ACRO- + *stíkhos* row, line of verse, rel. to *steíkhein* go (cf. STILE, STIRRUP); the etymol. sp. *acrostich* (as in *distich*) has been superseded through assoc. with -IC, as in *acrostic verses*.

act ækt deed, transaction XIV (Ch., Gower); legislative decree XV; (hist.) academic thesis; large section of a drama XVI. Mainly – L. *āctus* doing, playing a part, dramatic action, act of a piece, *āctum* public transaction, (pl.) records, register, f. *āct-*, pp. stem of *agere* (see AGENT); but partly through F. *acte* (XV) – L. So **act** vb. †(Sc.) enact, record; †put in motion, bring into action or being; carry out, perform. XVI. f. L. *āct-*. Cf. ACTION, ACTOR.

actinism æ·ktinizm property of the sun's rays. XIX. f. Gr. *aktīn-*, *aktís* ray + -ISM. So **acti·n**IC.

action æ·kʃən doing, thing done; legal process. XIV. – (O)F. *action* – L. *āctiō(n-)*, f. *āct-*, pp. stem of *agere*; see AGENT, -TION. Hence **a·ction**ABLE subject to action at law. XVI. So **a·ct**IVE given to (outward) action XIV; (gram.) connoting action (XIV); full of action, lively XVI. First applied to *active*)(*contemplative* life – L. *āctīvus* (in *vita activa*), f. *āct-*, *agere* ACT; partly through (O)F. *actif*, *-ive*. **acti·v**ITY. XV. – F. or late L. **a·ctivate.** XVII (Bacon). f. pp. stem of medL. *āctivāre*; in more recent use influenced by F. *activer*, G. *aktivieren*; see -ATE[3].

acton æ·ktən (arch.) stuffed jerkin worn under mail. XIII. – OF. *auqueton* (later, with *h* from *huque* hooded mantle), *hocqueton*, *hocton* (mod. *hoqueton*) prob. – Pr. *alcoton* – Arab. *alquṭun* 'the COTTON' (see AL-[2]).

actor æ·ktəɹ †agent XIV (in Wycl. Bible Gal. iv 2 a literalism; later Sc. XV–XVII); †pleader XV (Lydg.); stage-player; doer XVI. – L. *āctor* doer, actor in a play, speaker, prosecutor, agent, f. *āct-*, pp. stem of *agere* do; see AGENT, -OR[1]. Cf. (O)F. *acteur* †author XIII (so in Sc. XVI), play-actor XVII. Not freq. in genuine Eng. use before late XVI. Hence **a·ctress** †female doer XVI; female stage-player XVII; see -ESS[1]. Cf. late L. *āctrix*, F. *actrice* (app. from Eng.).

actual æ·ktʃuəl exhibited in acts, spec. of *actual*)(*original* sin; existing in act or fact XIV. orig. *actuel* – (O)F. *actuel*; later assim. to the source, late L. *āctuālis* (Macrobius), f. *āctus* ACT; see -AL. So **actua·l**ITY †activity XIV; reality, objectivity XVII. – (O)F. or medL. **a·ctually** †actively XV; in act or fact XVI; in truth XVIII; partly after F. *actuellement*, L. *āctuāliter*.

actuary æ·ktjuəri registrar, recorder XVI; insurance company's official who compiles statistics of mortality, accidents, etc. XIX. – L. *āctuārius* shorthand-writer, keeper of accounts, f. *āctus* ACT; see -ARY. Hence **actuar**IAL -ɛə·riəl. XIX.

actuate æ·ktjueit †make active; communicate motion to. XVI. f. pp. stem of medL. *āctuāre*, f. *āctus* ACT; see -ATE[3].

acuity əkjū·īti sharpness. XV. – F. *acuité* or medL. *acuitās*, f. *acuere*; see ACUTE, -ITY.

aculeate əkjū·lieit (nat. hist.) furnished with a sting or prickle. XVII. – L. *aculeātus*, f. *aculeus*, dim. of *acus* needle, f. **ak-*; see ACID, -ATE[2].

acumen əkjū·men sharpness of intellect. XVI. – L. *acūmen* point, acuteness, f. *acuere* sharpen (see ACUTE). So **acu·minate** pointed, tapered. XVII (Sir T. Browne). – L. *acūminātus*, f. *acūmin-*, *acūmen*; see -ATE[2]. **acu·min**OUS. XVII.

acushla əku·ʃlə darling. XIX. Short for Ir. *a cushla* (*cuisle*) *mo chroidhe* O pulse of my heart.

acute əkjū·t sharp, keen. XIV. – L. *acūtus*, pp. of *ecuere* sharpen (see ACID); as applied to accent (*accentus acutus*, Priscian), a lit. rendering of Gr. *oxeîa*, fem. (sc. *prosōidíā* accent) of *oxús* sharp.

-acy əsi suffix repr. (i) L. *-ācia*, forming nouns of quality on adjs. in *-āci-*, *-āx*, as *fallācia* fallacy, *contumācia* contumacy (the corr. Eng. adjs. ending in -ACIOUS); (ii) L. *-ātia*, in medL. often *-ācia*, as *abbātia* abbacy, *pāpātia* papacy, *prīmātia* primacy, on which was modelled *supremacy*; (iii) medL. *-ātia*, forming nouns of state on sbs. in *-ātus*, as *advocātia* advocacy, *legātia* legacy, *prælātia* prelacy, on the analogy of which the suffix was extended to sbs. in *-ate*, as *confederacy*, *curacy*, *magistracy*, and to adjs. in *-ate*, as *accuracy*, *delicacy*, *obstinacy*, *privacy*; (iv) Gr. sbs. in *-áteia*, as *peiráteia* piracy; cf. -CRACY. *Lunacy* (XVI) was f. *lunatic*, perh. after *frenetic*, *frenesy* (FRENZY).

ad æd L. prep. 'to, towards, in the direction of' (see AT) in many phr., as *ad eundem* (sc. *gradum* degree) to the same degree, i.e. in another university), *ad hoc*, *ad hominem*, *ad interim*, *ad lib*(*itum*), (*usque*) *ad nauseam*, *ad rem*, *ad valorem*.

ad- æd, əd prefix repr. L. *ad* (see AT) to express motion to or direction towards, addition, adherence, increase, as *advenīre* arrive (see ADVENT), *adversus* turned towards or against, hostile, ADVERSE, *addere* put to, ADD, *administrāre* give service to, ADMINISTER; the *d* was assim. to following *c*, *f*, *g*, *l*, *n*, *q*, *r*, *s*, *t*, producing AC-, AF-, AG-, etc.; *ad-* was reduced to *a-* before *sc*, *sp*, *st* (see e.g. ASCEND, ASPIRE, ASTRINGENT) and *gn* (as in AGNATE); see also ABBREVIATE. In OF. the double cons. of *acc-*, *add-*, *agg-*, etc. were reduced to single ones, and *adv-* became *av-*, and OF. words were adopted with such forms in Eng.; but in XIV these began to be latinized (as some had been in French) by the resumption of the second cons., as in *address*, *affirm*, *allow*, *announce*, *arrest*, *assault*, *attend*; note *advowson*)(*avow*.

-ad[1] æd, əd repr. L. – Gr. *-ad-*, nom. *-as*, pl. *-ades*, in (i) coll. numerals, as MONAD, DYAD, etc., CHILIAD, MYRIAD, and similarly OLYMPIAD; (ii) fem. patronymics, as DRYAD, NAIAD (cf. -ID[2]); (iii) the name of the epic celebrating the Trojan war, ILIAD, which has been imitated in *Columbiad*, *Dunciad*, *Lusiad*, *Rosciad*; (iv) names of orders of plants used by Lindley, as *asclepiad*, *liliad*. (In *decade* the F. form is retained; in *ballad*, *salad* the ending was orig. -ADE.)

-ad[2] æd suffix invented by J. Barclay in 'A new anatomical nomenclature', 1803, in the sense 'towards' (the part denoted), as *caudad* toward the tail (L. *cauda*), *laterad* towards the side (L. *later-*, *latus*); presumably intended to repr. L. prep. *ad* to (see AT).

-ada ei·də, ā·da repr. Sp., Pg. suffix *-ada* (:– L. *-āta*), fem. pp. ending of vbs. in *-ar*, which has been replaced in several Eng. adoptions by -ADO.

adage æ·didʒ maxim, proverb. XVI. – F. *adage* – L. *adagium*, f. *ad* AD- + **agjō* (*aiō*) I say. The L. form was directly anglicized as †*adagy* (XVI–XVII).

adagio ədā·dʒiou (mus.) slowly. XVIII. It., i.e. *ad agio* at EASE.

Adam æ·dəm name of the first man (Gen. ii), Heb. *ādām*; *the Old Adam* (cf. *the old man* of Rom. vi 6, etc.), also formerly simply *Adam* (XVI), unregenerate nature; *Adam's ale* water (XVII); *Adam's apple* (i) applied to various plants (XVI); (ii) cartilaginous projection in the throat (XVIII); after modL. *pomum Adami*, tr. Heb. *tappuach hā'ādām*; cf. Da. *Adamsæble*, G. *Adamsapfel*, F. *pomme d'Adam*.

adamant æ·dəmænt hard rock or mineral, now only as a symbol of extreme hardness (cf. Ezek. iii 9); †diamond; †loadstone XIV (Wycl. Bible, Ch., Gower, Trevisa, Maund.). – OF. *adamaunt*, *ademaunt* – L. *adamant-*, nom. *adamāns*, *adamās* – Gr. *adamant-*, *adámās* hardest iron or steel, diamond, orig. adj. 'invincible', f. *a-* A-[4] + *damân* TAME. The sense 'magnet, loadstone' arose from assoc. of medL. *adamās* with L. *adamāre* have a strong liking for. Cf. DIAMOND. So **adaman·tine**. XIII (H. Meith.; rare before XVI). – L. *adamantīnus* – Gr. *adamántinos*; see -INE[1].

Adamite æ·dəmait one of a sect claiming to follow Adam, e.g. in nudity; child of Adam, human being. XVII. – ecclL. *Ādāmīta*; see ADAM, -ITE.

adapt ədæ·pt make suitable. XVII. – F. *adapter* – L. *adaptāre*, f. *ad* + *aptāre*, f. *aptus* fit; see AD-, APT. So **adapt**A·TION ædəp-. XVII. – F. – medL.

add æd join, unite (Ch.); say in addition (Wycl. Bible) XIV; perform the arithmetical process of addition XVI. – L. *addere* (cf. Gr. προσδιδόναι, προστιθέναι), f. *ad* AD- + base of *dare* put (see DO[1]). So **addendum** əde·ndəm pl. **-a** addition to be made. XVII. sb. use of gerundive of L. *addere*. **addi·ta**MENT. XV. – L. *additāmentum*, f. *addit-*, *addere*. **addi**TION ədi·ʃən. XV. – F. or L. Hence **addi·tion**AL[1]. XVII; cf. F. *additionnel*. **a·ddit**IVE subject to addition. XVII. – late L. *additīvus*, tr. Gr. ἐπιταγματικός.

adder æ·dəɹ †serpent; viper. OE. *nǣd*(*d*)*re*, corr. to OS. *nādra* (MDu. *nadre*, Du. *adder*), OHG. *nātara* (G. *natter*), and (with a different vowel-grade) ON. *naðr*, *naðra*, Goth. *nadrs*; rel. to L. *natrix* water-snake, OIr. *nathir*, W. *neidr* snake, viper. As in *apron*, *auger*, *eyas*, *ouch*, *umpire*, orig. *n* has been lost by coalescence with a preceding indef. art., *a nadder* becoming *an adder* (XIV). For the reverse process see NEWT, etc.

addict ədi·kt devote or apply habitually. XVI. At first and still mainly in pp. *addicted*, which superseded †*addict* (XVI) – L. *addictus* assigned by decree, made over, pp. of *addīcere*, f. *ad* AD-+*dīcere* appoint, allot (see DICTION). Hence **addict** sb. æ·dikt one addicted to drugs, etc. XX.

addle æ·dl (of an egg) rotten, putrid. XIII. ME. *adel* (in *adel eye* 'addle egg'), adj. use of OE. *adela* stinking urine or other liquid filth (surviving dial. in *addle*) = MLG. *adele*, MDu. *adel* (Du. *aal*), G. *adel* mire, puddle, OSw. *adel* in *ko|adel* cow's urine. *Addle egg* tr. medL. *ōvum ūrīnæ* 'egg of urine', which is a perversion of L. *ōvum ūrīnum*, repr. Gr. *oúrion ōón* wind-egg. Used fig. in *addle-head(ed)*, *-pate(d)* XVII. Hence **addled** æ·dld XVII (see -ED), whence **a·ddle** vb. XVIII.

address ədre·s †make straight or right (Barbour); †accoutre, dress (Gower); †direct the aim of (Ch.) XIV; refl. apply oneself *to* XIV (Gower); direct (words or speech) *to* XV (Caxton). – (O)F. *adresser* = Pr. *adreisar*, Sp. *aderezar*, It. *addirizzare* :– Rom. **addrictiāre*, f. *ad* AD-+**drictum*, for L. *dīrēctum* straight, DIRECT. Cf. DRESS. Hence, or partly – (O)F. *adresse*, f. the vb. **addre·ss** sb. XVI. **address**EE[1]·. XIX.

adduce ədjū·s bring forward for consideration. XV. – L. *addūcere*, f. *ad* AD-+*dūcere* lead, bring (cf. DUKE). So **adduct**OR ædʌ·ktɔ̄ɹ (anat.) muscle which draws a part of the body towards the main axis. XVIII. modL. use (sc. *musculus* muscle) of L. *adductor* bringer-to, f. *adduct-*, pp. stem of *addūcere*.

-ade eid repr. F. *-ade* in adoptions of (i) Pr., Sp., Pg. words in *-ada* or It. words in *-ata*, as *ambuscade*, *barricade*, *cavalcade*, *crusade*, *marmalade*, *palisade*, *parade*, *tirade*; (ii) new F. formations, as *balustrade*, *cannonade*, *colonnade*, *fusillade*, *harlequinade*, *lemonade*, *promenade*. (In *ballad* and *salad* reduced to *-ad*.) Of limited use in Eng. as a living suffix, e.g. *blockade* (prob. after *ambuscade*), *gingerade* (after *lemonade*, *orangeade*); but several words formerly current with -ADO survive only with -ADE.

ademption əde·mᵖʃən (leg.) revocation of a grant, etc. XVI. – L. *ademptiō(n-)*, f. *adempt-*, pp. stem of *adimere* take away, whence **adeem** ədi·m XIX, by assim. to REDEEM; see -TION.

adenoid æ·dīnoid glandular; sb. pl. glandular growths. XIX. – Gr. *adenoeidḗs*, f. *aden-*, *adḗn* acorn, gland = L. *inguen* swelling, groin (cf. *inguinal*), rel. to ON. *økkr* swelling, *økkuinn* swollen; see -OID.

adept əde·pt, (sb.) æ·dept well skilled. XVII. – L. *adeptus* having attained, f. *adept-*, pp. stem of *adipīscī* attain, acquire, f. *ad* AD-+**ap-* bind (cf. APT, COPULA).

adequate æ·dikwət commensurate, fully sufficient. XVII. – L. *adæquātus*, pp. of *adæquāre* equalize, f. *ad* AD-+*æquus* EQUAL; see -ATE[2].

adhere ədhiə·ɹ stick fast, cleave. XVI. – (O)F. *adhérer* or L. *adhærēre*, f. *ad* AD-+*hærēre* stick. So **adhe·r**ENT attached XIV; sb. supporter XV. – (O)F. *adhérent* – L. *adhærent-*, *-ēns*. **adhes**ION ədhī·ʒən. XVII. – F. *adhésion* or L. *adhæsiō*, f. *adhæs-*, pp. stem of *adhærēre*.

Adiantum ædiæ·ntəm (bot.) genus of ferns. XVIII. L. – Gr. *adíanton* maidenhair, sb. use of n. adj. 'unwetted' (sc. *phutón* plant), f. *a-* A-[4]+*diaínein* moisten; so named from the resistance of the surface of the fronds to moisture.

adiate æ·dieit (leg.) accept as heir or beneficiary under a will. XIX. irreg. f. L. *adīre* approach (see ADIT)+-ATE[3].

adieu ədjū· good-bye. XIV (Ch., Gower). Late ME. *adew(e)* – AN. *adeu*, (O)F. *adieu*, f. *à* to+*Dieu* God :– L. *deu-s* (see DEITY); the early sp. *adew*, *adue* was remodelled after F.

adipose æ·dipous fatty. XVIII. – modL. *adipōsus*, f. L. *adip-*, *adeps* fat; see -OSE. An earlier form was †**a·dip**OUS XVII; cf. F. *adipeux*.

adit æ·dit approach (spec. to a mine). XVII. – L. *aditus*, f. *adit-*, pp. stem of *adīre* approach, f. *ad* AD-+*īre* go (IE. base **ei-* **i-*); cf. EXIT, INTROIT, OBIT, TRANSIT.

adjacent ədʒei·sənt lying near. XV. – L. *adjacent-*, *-ēns*, prp. of *adjacēre*, f. *ad* AD-+*jacēre* lie down, intr. of *jacere* throw, lay (cf. DEJECT, INJECT, etc.); see -ENT.

adjective æ·dʒiktiv (gram.) designating an attribute. XIV. – (O)F. *adjectif*, *-ive* – late L. *adjectīvus*, *-īva*, f. *adject-*, pp. stem of *adicere* to add, f. *ad*+*jacere*; see prec. and -IVE. First in *noun adjective*, rendering L. *nōmen adjectīvum* (Priscian), tr. Gr. *ὄνομα ἐπίθετον* (NOUN, EPITHET).

adjoin ədʒoi·n join on (to). XIV. – OF. *ajoin-*, *ajoign-*, stem of *ajoindre* (mod. *adjoindre*) :– L. *adjungere*, f. *ad* AD-+*jungere* JOIN.

adjourn ədʒɔ̄·ɹn †appoint a day for XIV (R. Mannyng); defer, put off XV (Lydg.). – OF. *ajorner* (mod. *ajourner*), f. phr. *à jorn* (*nomé*) to an (appointed) day, i.e. *à* AD-, *jorn* :– late L. *diurnum* day (whence F. *jour*, Pr. *jorn*, It. *giorno*), n. of L. *diurnus* daily (cf. DIURNAL).

adjudicate ədʒū·dikeit assess judicially. XVIII. f. pp. stem (see -ATE[3]) of L. *adjūdicāre* (f. *ad* AD-+*jūdic-*, *jūdex* JUDGE), whence OF.

ajuger (mod. *adjuger*), the source of **adjudge** ədʒʌ·dʒ XIV (Ch.). So **adjudic**A·TION. XVII. – F. or L.

adjunct æ·dʒʌŋkt subordinate, auxiliary, or incidental (person or thing), adj. and sb. XVI (Sh.; earlier Sc.). – L. *adjunctus, -um*, pp. of *adjungere* ADJOIN.

adjure ədʒuə·ɹ †put (one) to his oath XIV (Wycl. Bible); charge solemnly XV (Caxton). – L. *adjūrāre* swear to, (later) put to an oath, conjure, f. *ad* AD-+*jūr-*, *jūs* oath (cf. JURY). So **adjur**A·TION. XIV (Ch.; rare before XVII). – F. or L.

adjust ədʒʌ·st arrange suitably. XVII. – F. †*adjuster* (now *ajuster*), refash., after *juste* JUST, of OF. *ajoster* (mod. *ajouter* add) :– Rom. **adjuxtāre* (cf. Sp. *ajustar*, It. *aggiostare*), f. L. *ad* AD-+*juxtā* close to, rel. to *jugum* YOKE. So **adju·st**MENT. XVII. – OF. *adjustement* (mod. *aj-*).

adjutage, ajutage æ·dʒutidʒ, ədʒū·tidʒ mouthpiece of a fountain. XVIII. – F. *ajutage, ajoutage*, f. *ajouter* (see prec.); see -AGE.

adjutant æ·dʒŭtənt †assistant; (mil.) officer in the army assisting superior officers. XVII. – L. *adjūtant-, -āns*, prp. of *adjūtāre*, frequent. of *adjuvāre*, f. *ad* AD-+*juvāre* help; see -ANT. In the mil. sense corr. to G. *adjutant* (1667), F. *adjudant* (1721), †*ayudant* (1701) – Sp. *ayudante*, f. *ayudar* help, assist. *Adjutant bird* large stork so named from its 'military' gait.

ad libitum æd li·bitəm; abbrev. **ad lib.** XVII. L. phr., i.e. *ad* according to, *libitum* pleasure, sb. use of n. pp. of *libet* it pleases (cf. LOVE).

adminicle ædmi·nikl auxiliary means. XVI. – L. *adminiculum* prop, support, f. *ad* AD- and dim. *-culum* -CLE, on an obscure base.

administer ədmi·nistəɹ manage, dispense. XIV. ME. *amynistre* – OF. *aministrer* – L. *administrāre*, f. *ad* AD-+*ministrāre* MINISTER; later refash. on latinized (O)F. *administrer* (XIV). So **administr**A·TION. XIV. – F. or L. **admi·nistr**ATIVE. XVIII. – L. **admi·nistr**ATOR. XVI; cf. F. *administrateur*. **admi·nistra**TRIX. XVII.

admiral æ·dmərəl †emir XIII–XV; †naval commander-in-chief; highest naval officer XV. ME. *amyrayl, amyral(l), admira(i)l* – (O)F. *amiral*, †*admira(i)l* – (through medL. *a(d)mirālis, -allus, -ālius*) Arab. *'amīr a'ālī* (or *a'lā*) high (or higher) commander (see AMEER, EMIR). In medL. and Rom. the initial and final sylls. were altered on various analogies, e.g. with L. prefix *ad-* and suffixes *-ābilis, -andus, -ātus*, and (since Arab. *'amīr* was often followed by *al* AL-[2], as in *'amīr-al-mā* commander of the sea) with forms in *-aldus*, and (in Sp.) with sbs. in which the initial syll. repr. Arab. AL-[2]. Hence such forms as OF. *amiré(t), amirauble, amirant, amiralt, almiral*, OSp. *almiralle*, It. *ammiraglio*, medL. *admirābilis, -aldus, -antus, -ātus, almirallus*, Sp., Pg. *almirante*, some of which are repr. in ME., e.g. *admirald, almeral, ameraunt*. So **a·dmiral**TY office of admiral; branch of the executive superintending the navy. XV. – OF. *admiral(i)té* (mod. *amirauté*); cf. AL. *admirālitās*.

admire ədmaiə·ɹ †wonder, wonder at; regard with pleased surprise. XVI (late). – F. *admirer* (OF. *amirer*) or L. *admīrārī*, f. *ad* AD-+*mīrārī* wonder (see MIRACLE). So **a·dmir**ABLE æ·dmĭrəbl. XV. **admir**A·TION. XV. – (O)F. or L.

admit ədmi·t let come or go in XIV; allow the truth of XV. – L. *admittere*, f. *ad* AD-+*mittere* send (see MISSION); but some early forms (*amitte*) reflect the semi-pop. OF. *amettre*. Hence **admi·tt**ANCE. XVI. So **admiss**ION ədmi·ʃən XV. – L. *admissiō(n-)*, f. *admiss-*, pp. stem of *admittere*. So **admi·ss**IBLE. XVII.

admixture ədmi·kstʃəɹ. XVII. f. *admixt-*, pp. stem of L. *admiscēre*, f. *ad* AD-+*miscēre* MIX (cf. MIXTURE); replaced earlier †*admixtion* (XV) – L.

admonish ədmɔ·niʃ put in mind of a duty XIV; give warning or cautionary notice to XVI. ME. *amoneste* – OF. *amonester* – Rom. **admonestāre*, unexpl. deriv. of L. *admonēre*, f. *ad* AD-+*monēre* advise (cf. MONITION); the final *t*, esp. in pt. and pp. forms, was taken as an inflexion, and the initial syll. was latinized to *ad-*, whence such inf. forms as *amonace, admonase, -monyss*; the final syll. became *-ish* by assoc. with -ISH[2]. So **admo·nish**MENT XIV (earlier *a(d)monestement* – OF.). **admon**ITION ædməni·ʃən. XIV (earlier *amonicion* – OF.).

adnate æ·dneit (nat. hist.) attached congenitally. XVII. – L. *adnātus*, var. of *agnātus* AGNATE, due to assoc. with AD-.

ado ədū· (arch., dial., first in northern and eastern areas) dealings, concern, trouble, labour, fuss. XIV. f. phr. *at do*, f. adoption of ON. *at* (see AT)+DO[1]; corr. to the native formation TO-DO.

-ado ei·dou, ā·dou repr. Sp., Pg. *-ado* (:– L. *-ātu-s* -ATE[2]), m. pp. ending of vbs. in *-ar*, as in DESPERADO, RENEGADO, TORNADO. This suffix was also freq. used irreg. in late-XVI and XVII adoptions of F. words in -ADE, Sp. words in -ADA, and It. words in -ATA; e.g. *ambuscado, armado, barricado, bastinado, bravado, carbonado, crusado, gambado, palisado, strappado*, some of which have survived as the regular form, while in others *-ado* has been superseded by -ADE.

adobe ədou·bi, ədou·b unburnt brick dried in the sun. XIX. Sp., f. vb. *adobar* plaster, f. Arab. *aṭṭōb*, i.e. *al-ṭōb* the brick, f. *al* AL-[2]+*ṭōb, ṭūb*, of Egypt. origin. In U.S. also *adob(e)y, -ie*, and shortened *dobie, doby, dobe*.

adolescent ædŏle·sənt sb. a youth XV; adj. XVIII. – (O)F. *adolescent* – L. *adolēscent-, -ēns*, prp. of *adolēscere*, f. *ad*+*alēscere* grow up, f. *alēre* nourish; see AD-, ALIMENT, -ESCENT. So **adole·scENCE**. XV (Lydg.). – (O)F. – L.

Adonis ədou·nis, ədɔ·nis youth beloved by Venus for his beauty, (gen.) beautiful youth. XVI. L. – Gr. *Ádōnis*, *Ádōn* – Phœnician *adōni* my lord, *adōn* lord, title of the god Tammuz, in Heb. a name of God.

adopt ədɔ·pt take (up) as one's own. XVI. – (O)F. *adopter* or L. *adoptāre* choose for oneself, f. *ad*+*optāre* choose. So **ado·pTION** XIV (Ayenb., Trevisa), **ado·ptIVE** XV (Lydg.). – (O)F. – L.; see AD-, OPTION.

adore ədɔə·ɹ pay divine honours to, worship XV (Caxton); reverence or honour highly XVI. – (O)F. *adourer*, (mod.) *adorer*, refash., after L., of OF. *ao(u)rer* (whence ME. *aoure* XIV) = Pr. *azorar*, Sp. †*aorar*, It. *adorare* :– L. *adōrāre* address, salute, reverence, (eccl.) worship, f. *ad*+*ōrāre*; see AD-, ORATE. So **adorA·TION** ædərei·ʃən. XVI. – (O)F. – L. **ado·rABLE**. XVII. – F. or L.

adorn ədɔ̄·ɹn beautify, embellish. XIV (Ch.). – (O)F. *adorner*, refash., after L., of OF. *ao(u)rner* (whence ME. *aourne*) = Pr. *azornar*, It. *adornare* :– L. *adornāre*, f. *ad*+*ornāre* furnish, deck; see AD-, ORNAMENT. So **ado·rnMENT**. XV (Caxton). – OF. *adournement*.

adown ədau·n (dial., poet.) down(ward). OE. *adūn(e)*, reduced form of *ofdūne*, i.e. *of* from (A-[2]) and dative of *dūn* hill, DOWN[1]. Aphetic DOWN[3].

adrift ədri·ft drifting. XVII (Capt. Smith). f. A-[1]+DRIFT.

adroit ədroi·t dexterous. XVII. – (O)F. *adroit*, f. adv. phr. *à droit* 'according to right', rightly, properly, i.e. *à* to+*droit* :– Rom. **d(e)rictum*, for L. *dīrēctum*; see AD-, DIRECT, and cf. DRESS.

adscititious ædsiti·ʃəs added from outside. XVII. f. *adscit-*, pp. stem of L. *adscīscere* admit, adopt, f. *ad*+*scīscere* acknowledge, inceptive of *scīre* know, after *adventitious*; see AD-, SCIENCE, -IOUS.

adscript see ASCRIPT.

adulation ædjulei·ʃən servile flattery. XV (Lydg.). – (O)F. *adulation* or L. *adūlātiō(n-)*. f. *adūlāt-*, *adūlārī* fawn upon, whence **a·dulate**. XVII; see -ATE[3], -ATION.

adult æ·dʌlt, ədʌ·lt grown up XVI (Elyot); sb. XVII. – L. *adultus*, pp. of *adolēscere* (see ADOLESCENT); cf. F. *adulte* (late XVI).

adulterate ədʌ·ltəreit †commit adultery; †debauch; falsify, debase. XVI. f. pp. stem of L. *adulterāre* debauch, corrupt, explained by Festus as from *ad alterum (-am) sē conferre* betake oneself to another; see -ATE[3]. Superseded early modE. †*adulter* (– L. inf. or F. *adultérer*), which itself replaced ME. *avoutre* (XIV – OF. *avoutrer*; cf. next). So **adulterA·TION**. XVI.

adulterer ədʌ·ltərəɹ one guilty of adultery (violation of the marriage-bed). XVI. Used XVI–XVIII beside synon. †*adulter*, but finally established as the more congruent form in the series *adulterate* †commit adultery, *adulterer*, *adulteress*, *adulterous*, **adu·lterY**[3]. These had emerged in XV or XVI and finally superseded the ME. forms (XIV) derived from OF., viz. *avouter* adulterer, *avoutrer* commit adultery, *avout(e)rer* adulterer, *avoutres* adulteress, *avoutrous* adulterous, *avoutrie* adultery, all of which were from regular phonetic derivs. in OF. of L. *adulterāre* (see prec.). The forms in *avout-* had vars. in *advout-* (after later OF.), which facilitated adoption of forms in *adult-* (in Law F. *adulterie* is as early as XIII, being preceded by *avult-* in XII).

adulterine ədʌ·ltərain spurious XVI; illegal, unlicensed XVII. – L. *adulterīnus*, f. *adulter* adulterous, adulterer; see ADULTERATE, -INE[1].

adumbrate æ·dəmbreit represent as a shadow or in outline, shadow forth, prefigure XVI; overshadow XVII. f. pp. stem of L. *adumbrāre*, f. *ad*+*umbrāre* shadow, f. *umbra*; see AD-, UMBRA, -ATE[3]. So **adumbrA·TION**. XVI (earlier than the vb.). – L.

adust ədʌ·st atrabilious XIV (Lanfr.); scorched; brown, sunburnt XVI. – F. *aduste* or L. *adūstus*, pp. of *adūrere*, f. *ad* AD-+*ūrere* burn (cf. COMBUSTION). ¶ A conspicuous term in the medical nomenclature of the Middle Ages, applied to a supposed state of the body and its humours characterized by dryness, heat, and black or burnt colour of the blood.

advance ədvà·ns trans. and intr. move forward (or upward) in place, time, or condition (first in the sense 'promote'). XIII (AncrR.). ME. *ava(u)nce* – (O)F. *avancer* = Pr. *avansar* (Sp. *avanzar*), It. *avanzare* :– Rom. **abantiāre*, f. late L. *abante* (whence F. *avant* before, Pr. *avan*, *aban*, It. *avanti*), f. L. *ab* OFF, away+*ante* before (see ANTE-). The forms with *adv-*, recorded XV and established XVI, were anticipated in OF. and arose from assoc. with the *av-* which originated in *adv-*, as in *aventure*, ADVENTURE. Hence **adva·nce** sb. XVII. So **adva·nceMENT**. XIII (RGlouc.). – (O)F. *avancement*.

advantage ədvà·ntidʒ superior position; benefit. XIV (R. Mannyng). ME. *avantage* – (O)F. *avantage* (whence It. *vantaggio*, etc.), f. *avant* before; see prec. and -AGE. Aphetic VANTAGE. Hence or – (O)F. *avantager* **adva·ntage** vb. XV (†add to the amount of). **advantageOUS** ædvəntei·dʒəs XVI (in XVI–XVII often *-ious*). – (O)F. *avantageux*. For the form with *adv-* cf. prec.

advent æ·dvĕnt Church season preceding Christmas XII; the Coming of Christ XV; arrival XVIII. – OF. *advent*, refash. after L. of *auvent* (mod. *avent*) – L. *adventu-s* arrival,

f. *advent-*, pp. stem of *advenīre* arrive, f. *ad* AD-+*venīre* COME.

adventitious ædventi·ʃəs coming from without, accidental, casual. XVII. f. *adventitius*, medL. sp. of L. *adventīcius*, f. *advent-*, pp. stem of *advenīre*; see prec. and -ITIOUS[1]. (Cf. F. *adventice*.)

adventure ədve·ntʃəɹ †chance, luck; †hazard, venture; †risk, peril XIII; hazardous enterprise XIV. – (O)F. *aventure* = Pr., Sp. *aventura*, It. *avventura* :– Rom. **adventūra*, sb. use (sc. *rēs* thing) 'something about to happen', of fut. part. of *advenīre*; see ADVENT, -URE. The form *adv-* is due to refash. in late OF. after L. So **adve·nture** vb. XIV. – (O)F. *aventurer*. **adve·nturer**. XV. – F. *aventurier*; see -ER[2]. **adve·nturous**. XIV. – OF. *aventureus*. In XIV–XV *aventure* and *aventurous* appear often in the contr. forms *aunter*, *auntrous*, which were due to initial stress. Aphetic VENTURE.

adverb æ·dvɜ̄ɹb word that qualifies an adjective, a verb, or another adverb. XV. – F. *adverbe* (earlier †*averbe*) or L. *adverbium*, f. *ad* AD-+*verbum* word, VERB; lit. rendering of Gr. ἐπίρρημα (f. *epí* denoting addition, EPI-+*rhēma* word). So **adverbIAL** ədvɜ̄·ɹbiəl XVII. – late L. or F. **adve·rbially**. XV; rendering L. *adverbiāliter* (Charisius).

adversaria ædvəɹsɛə·riə miscellaneous collection of notes, etc. XVIII (occas. earlier anglicized †*adversaries*). L., sb. use of n. pl. (sc. *scripta* writings) of *adversārius* lying before one (see next), in mercantile use, collection of items as they occur (Cicero), waste-book, day-book.

adversary æ·dvəɹsəri opponent, enemy. XIV. – OF. *adversarie* (mod. *adversaire*) – L. *adversārius* opposed, opponent, f. *adversus* against (cf. *contrārius* contrary, f. *contrā*); see next and -ARY. ME. and later Sc. had such forms as *adversere*, *-aire*, *-air*, *-ar(e)* – AN. *adverser*, OF. *adversier* (replacing pop. *aversier*), *adversaire*.

adverse æ·dvɜ̄ɹs hostile, opposing, unfavourable. XIV (Ch.). – later OF. *advers*, *-se*, refash. after L. of *avers* :– L. *adversu-s* standing opposite, hostile, pp. of *advertere* turn towards; see AD-, VERSE.

adversity ədvɜ̄·ɹsĭti adverse fortune. XIII (AncrR.). – (O)F. *adversité*, refash. after L. of *aversité* – L. *adversitās* opposition (Pliny), misfortune (Cassiodorus), f. *adversus* ADVERSE; see -ITY.

advert ǣdvɜ̄·ɹt (obs. or arch.) turn one's attention (L. *animum advertere* ANIMADVERT). XV. Earlier *avert* – (O)F. *avertir* (now only) admonish, warn :– Rom. **advertīre*; see prec. and for sp. cf. ADVERSE, ADVERTISE. The rel. **adve·rtENCE** (XIV, Ch.), -ENCY (XVII), -ENT (XVII) are now mainly repr. in the neg. INADVERTENCE, etc.

advertise æ·dvəɹtaiz (formerly, and still Sc. and U.S.) ædvəɹtai·z, in XVI–XVII adve·rtis †take note of, notice XV (Lydg.); †direct the attention of; give notice of XV. f. *advertiss-*, lengthened stem (see -ISH[2]) of F. †*advertir*, refash. of *avertir* warn :– Rom. **advertīre*, for L. *advertere* (see ADVERSE). The F. forms *avertir*, †*advertir* are repr. by †*avert*, ADVERT. The current form has been infl. by **adve·rtiseMENT** †warning, attention; notification, notice XV; earlier *avertisement* – F. *avertissement*, †*advert-*, f. the above vb.

advice ədvai·s †opinion XIII (RGlouc.); †consideration, deliberation; counsel XIV; information given XV (Caxton). ME. *avis*, *avys* – (O)F. *avis* = Pr. *avis*, Sp. *aviso*, It. *avviso* :– Rom. **advīsum*, f. L. *ad* AD-+*vīsum* (as in *mihi vīsum est* it has seemed good to me, it is my opinion; cf. OF. *ce m'est vis* or *avis*), n. pp. of *vidēre* see (*vidērī* seem); cf. WIT. So **advise** ədvai·z †observe, consider; †refl. take thought, reflect (cf. F. *s'aviser*); counsel, warn XIV; inform XVI (Sh.). ME. *avise*, *avyse* – (O)F. *aviser* (refash. after L. †*adviser*) = Pr. *avizar*, Sp. *avisar*, It. †*avvisare* :– Rom. **advīsāre*, f. L. *ad* AD-+-*vīsāre*, for L. *vīsere*, f. *vīs-*, *vidēre*. **advisedly** ədvai·zidli †warily; †judiciously; deliberately. XV. Superseded ME. †*avisely*, *-ily* (XIV), f. *avisy* – *avisé*, pp. of (O)F. *aviser*, by substitution of pp. *advised*.

advocate æ·dvəkət counsellor, counsel; intercessor XIV; maintainer XVIII. ME. *avocat* – (O)F. *avocat* – L. *advocātus* legal witness or counsellor, (later) advocate, attorney, (eccl.) of Christ as intercessor, sb. use of pp. of *advocāre* call in as witness or counsellor, f. *ad*+*vocāre* call; see AD-, VOCATION, -ATE[3]. The mod. form with *ad-* (XIV) is due to latinization, first in OF. Aphetic †*vocate*, †*voket* (XV). The pop. F. repr. of L. *advocātus* is *avoué*, AN. *avowé*, *advowé*, whence legal Eng. **advowEE·** patron of a benefice (XVII). So **a·dvocate** -eit vb. †intr. plead *for* XVII; trans. plead in favour of XVII.

advowson ədvau·zən patronage of an ecclesiastical office, etc.; right of presentation to a benefice. XIII (also aphetic *voweson*). – AN. *a(d)voweson*, *a(d)voeson*, OF. *avoeson* :– L. *advocātiōnem*, f. *advocāre*; see prec. and -ATION. The direct repr. of the L., *advocation* (XV), formerly current in various senses, survives in Sc. law for the calling of an action before itself by a superior court.

adytum æ·ditəm innermost shrine. XVII (occas. anglicized †*adyt* XVI). – Gr. *áduton*, sb. use of n. sg. of *ádutos* impenetrable, f. *a-* A-[4]+*dúein* enter.

adze ædz tool for cutting away the surface of wood. OE. *adesa*, whence ME. *adese*, later *adys*, *addis*, *add(e)s*; *adz(e)* dates from XVIII; peculiarly Eng.; of unkn. origin.

ædile ī·dail ancient Roman magistrate superintending municipal works. XVI. L. *ædīlis*, sb. use of adj., prop. 'having to do with buildings', f. *ædēs, -is* building (cf. EDIFICE); see -ILE.

ægis ī·dʒis defence, protection. XVIII. – L. – Gr. *aigís* shield of Zeus (in L. of Jupiter or Minerva), pop. assoc. with *aig-*, *aíx* goat, as if 'shield of goatskin'.

ægrotat ī·groutæt, īgrou·tæt (in Eng. universities) certificate of illness. XIX. 3rd pers. sg. pres. indic. of L. *ægrōtāre* be sick, f. *ægr-*, *æger* sick, ill. ¶ *Æger* ī·dʒəɹ has been similarly used.

Æneid ī·niid, īnī·id Virgil's epic. XVII. f. *Æneid-*, stem of L. *Æneis*, f. *Æneās* name of the hero of the poem; cf. F. *Énéide*, It. *Eneide*. Before the mod. period most freq. in genitive form *Eneydos* (XIV–XVI), *-idos* (XVI) – L. *Æneidos* (sc. *libri* books); from XVI the L. nom. *Æneis* has been often used; in XVI–XVII *Æneas*, *Ænead* occurred; sporadic exx. of anglicized forms (e.g. *eneyde*) are found in XV; the anglicized pl. denoting the whole poem appears in XVI, whence the sg. form (XVIII) used for a single book.

Æolian iou·liən pert. to Æolis (Aiolis) or Æolus (Aiolos). XVIII. f. L. *Æolius* f. (i) Æolis or Æolia, ancient district of Asia Minor, (ii) Æolus, mythical god of the winds; see -IAN. So **Æol**IC iɔ·lik of Æolis. XVII. – L. *Æolicus* – Gr. *Aiolikós*.

æon ī·ɔn age of the universe. XVII (H. More). – ecclL. *æōn* – Gr. *aiṓn* age, rel. to L. *ævum* (cf. AGE, AY[1]).

aerate ei·əreit, ɛə·reit expose to or supply with air. XVIII. f. L. *āēr* AIR + -ATE[3], after F. *aérer*, itself a learned formation on the L. sb. So **aer**A·TION. XVI (rare before XIX).

aerial ɛə·riəl, (formerly) eiiə·riəl pert. to or resembling air or the atmosphere. XVII (*eriall*, Sh.). f. L. *āerius* (– Gr. *āérios*, f. *āer-*, *āēr* AIR) + -AL; occas. †*aereal* (XVI–XVII) is f. L. *āereus*. Also †*aereous*, *-ious* (XVI–XVII), *aerian* (XVII); cf. F. *aéreux*, *aérien*.

aerie see EYRIE.

aero- ɛə·rou ei·ərou, comb. form of Gr. *āēr* AIR, in many techn. terms, some of which are – F. terms in *aéro-*; Gr. had *āerometreîn* measure the air, *āeroskopíā* divination by observation of the atmosphere. **ae·rodrome,** †(i) aeroplane XIX; (ii) course for flying-machines XX; in (i) – Gr. *aerodrómos* traversing the air; in (ii) f. Gr. *drómos* course (cf. HIPPODROME). **ae:ro**DYNA·MIC, -ICS; cf. F. *aérodynamique*. **ae·ro**MANCY divination by air. XIV (*-ance* Gower). – OF. **ae·ronaut** navigator in the air XVIII. – F. *aéronaute*, f. Gr. *naútēs* sailor (cf. NAUTICAL). **ae·roplane,** †(i) plane of a flying-machine; (ii) heavier-than-air flying-machine XIX; in (i) f. PLANE[3]; in (ii) – F. *aéroplane*, f. Gr. *-planos* wandering (see PLANET). **ae·rostat** balloon, etc. XVIII. – F. *aérostat*, f. Gr. *statós* standing, f. **sta-* STAND.

aery[1] ei·əri, ɛə·ri aerial; etherial. XVI (in later use poet.; a favourite with Milton). – L. *āerius*, f. *āēr* AIR; the suffix has been assoc. with -Y[1].

aery[2] see EYRIE.

æruginous iərū·dʒinəs like copper-rust. XVII. – L. *ærūginōsus*, f. *ærūgin-*, nom. *ærūgō* verdigris, f. *ær-*, *æs* brass; see -OUS.

Æsculapian īskjulei·piən medicinal, medical. XVII. f. *Æsculāpius*, ancient Roman god of medicine; see -IAN.

æsthetic īsþe·tik, U.S. **es-** XIX (but used occas. before 1800 in the Kantian sense 'pert. to the philosophy of sensuous perception'). The current sense 'pert. to the criticism of the beautiful or to the theory of taste' is derived ult. (through F. *esthétique* – G. *ästhetik*) from the title of A. T. Baumgarten's 'Æsthetica' (1750), which treats of the criticism of taste considered as a philosophical theory. – Gr. *aisthētikós*, f. *aisthētá* things perceptible by the senses, f. *aisthesthai* perceive (**aɹisth-*, rel. to L. *audiō* I hear :– **awizdiō*); see -IC. Also sb. **æsthe·**TICS. XIX (Crabb Robinson, Carlyle). Hence **æsthete** ī·sþīt XIX; prob. after *athlete*, *athletic*, but cf. Gr. *aisthētḗs* one who perceives.

æstival īstai·vəl pert. to the summer or the summer solstice. XIV. Also, as in early use, *estival* – (O)F. *estival* – L. *æstīvālis*, f. *æstīvus*, f. *æstus* heat; see -IVE, -AL. The analogical pronunc. is e·stivəl, but *esti·val* is evidenced XVI (cf. *autu·mnal*); the sp. with æ- is now prevalent, exc. in U.S.

ætiology ītiɔ·lədʒi doctrine of cause or causation. XVI. – late L. *ætiologia* (Isidore) – Gr. *aitiologíā*, f. *aitíā* cause + *-logíā* -LOGY.

af- assim. form of AD- before *f*; cf. AC-.

afar əfā·ɹ from or at a distance. XII. ME. *of feor*, *on ferr*, later *a fer*, *a far*, i.e. OF from, ON, FAR; phrasal substitute for OE. *feorran* far off, from far, perh. after late L. *dē longē*, *ā longē*, (O)F. *de loin*, *au loin*.

afeard əfiə·ɹd (dial., arch.) afraid. OE. *āfǣred*, pp. of *āfǣran* frighten; see A-[3] and FEAR. Superseded in gen. use by AFRAID (cf. 'nat afered nor affrayed', Ch.).

affable æ·fəbl complaisant of manner. XVI. – (O)F. *affable* – L. *affābilis* easy to be spoken to, f. *affārī* address, f. *ad* + *fārī* speak; see AF-, FABLE, -ABLE. So **affa**BI·LITY. XV. – (O)F.

affair əfɛə·ɹ business, concern. XIII (Cursor M.). ME. *afer(e)*, *affer(e)* – AN. *afere*, OF. *afaire* (mod. *affaire*), f. phr. *à faire* do (repr. L. *ad*, *facere*; see AD, FACT). For the formation and meaning cf. ADO, TO-DO.

affect[1] əfe·kt †aim at XV; have a liking for XVI; display or assume openly XVI (Sh.); assume or pretend falsely XVII. – F. *affecter* or L. *affectāre* aim at, aspire to, endeavour or pretend to have, f. *affect-*, pp. stem of *afficere* put to, (refl.) apply oneself to; see next. So **affect**A·TION. XVI. – F. *affectation* or L. *affectātiō(n-)*, f. *affectāre*.

affect[2] əfe·kt lay hold of, attack; impress, influence, move. XVII. – F. *affecter* or f. L.

affect-, pp. stem of *afficere* act upon, influence, f. *ad* AF-+*facere* do. Like the F. vb., has been infl. by the earlier AFFECTION.

affected əfe·ktid (i) †sought after, cherished; assumed; full of affectation, artificial XVI; pp. of AFFECT[1]. (ii) having (a certain) disposition or affection XVI; f. L. *affectus* disposed, pp. of *afficere* (see prec.)+-ED[1]. (iii) laid hold of, attacked, infected XVII; pp. of AFFECT[2].

affection əfe·kʃən emotion, feeling XIII (AncrR.); disposition XIV (R. Mannyng); bodily state, spec. abnormal XVI. – (O)F. *affection* – L. *affectiō(n-)* (favourable) disposition or inclination, f. *afficere* AFFECT[2]. So **affe·ctionate** †affected, esp. unduly or wilfully; †kindly inclined; fond, loving. XVI. – medL. *affectionātus* devoted, or its deriv. F. *affectionné*, which was itself anglicized as †*affectioned* (XVI); see -ATE[2]. Earlier synonyms were †*affectual* XV (– OF. *affectuel*), †*affectuous* XIV (– OF. *affectueux*, late L. *affectuōsus*). **affective** əfe·ktiv pert. to the emotions. XV. – F. *affectif*, *-ive* – late L. *affectīvus*, f. L. *affect-*; see AFFECT[2] and -IVE.

affiance əfai·əns (arch.) trust, confidence. XIV. – OF. *afiance*, f. *afier* (whence †*affy* XIV–XVII) :– medL. *affīdāre* bind oneself in loyalty, f. L. *ad* AF-+*fīdāre* trust, f. *fīdus* trusty, rel. to *fides* FAITH; see -ANCE.

affiche æfi·ʃ placard. XVIII. F., f. *afficher* :– Rom. **affīgicāre*, f. L. *ad* AF-+*fīgere* FIX.

affidavit æfidei·vit statement confirmed by oath. XVII (Jonson). 3rd sg. pt. of medL. *affīdāre* declare on oath (see AFFIANCE).

affiliate əfi·lieit adopt; fix the paternity of. XVIII. f. pp. stem of medL. *affīliāre*, f. *ad* AF-+*fīlius* son (see FILIAL); prob. after F. *affilier*; see -ATE[3]. So **affili**A·TION. XVIII. – F. – medL.; cf. FILIATION.

affinity əfi·nĭti relationship (spec. by marriage) XIV; (nat. hist., chem.) structural likeness XVIII. – OF. *afinité* (mod. *affinité*) – L. *affīnitās*, f. *affīnis* related, lit. bordering on, f. *ad* AF-+*fīnis* border; see FINIS, -ITY.

affirm əfɔ̄·ɹm assert strongly, make solemn declaration. XIV. ME. *afferme* – OF. *afermer* (mod. *affirmer*) :– L. *affirmāre*, f. *ad* AF-+*firmus* FIRM. In XVI the sp. was assim. to L., as in F. So **affirm**A·TION. XV. – F. or L. Earlier †**affi·rm**ANCE. XIV. – OF. **affi·rm**ATIVE. XV. – (O)F. – late L.

affix ǽfi·ks fix or fasten *to*, *on*. XV (first in Sc. pp. *affix(i)t*). – (O)F. *affixer* or medL. *affixāre*, f. *ad* AF-+*fixāre* FIX. So **affix** æ·fiks sb. PREFIX or SUFFIX. XVII.

afflatus əflei·təs rush of prophetic or poetic inspiration. XVII. – L. *afflātus*, f. *afflāt-*, pp. stem of *afflāre* blow upon, f. *ad* AF-+*flāre* BLOW[1].

afflict əfli·kt †dash down XIV; trouble grievously XVI. – L. *afflictāre* or f. *afflict-*, pp. stem of *afflīgere* dash against, throw down, distress, f. *ad* AF-+*flīgere* strike; partly after pp. †*afflict* (in XIV–XV *aflight*) orig. – OF. *aflit* :– L. *afflictu-s*. So **affli·c**TION. XIV. – (O)F. – L. (esp. eccl.).

affluent æ·fluənt flowing in abundance XV; wealthy XVIII; sb. feeder of a river XIX. – (O)F. *affluent* – L. *affluent-*, *-ēns*, prp. of *affluere* flow towards, f. *ad* AF-+*fluere* flow (see FLUENT). So **a·ffLu**ENCE profusion XIV; wealth XVII. – F. – L.

afflux æ·flʌks flowing of humours, etc. towards a point. XVII. – medL. *affluxus*, f. *afflux-*, *affluere*; see prec. Cf. F. *afflux*.

afford əfɔ̄·ɹd †set forward, carry out OE.; manage, provide the means XV; grant, yield XVI. Late OE. *ġeforþian* advance, promote, accomplish, f. *ġe-* Y-+*forþian* further, promote, f. *forþ* forward, FORTH. Typical ME. forms were *iforðen*, *aforth(e)*; after the reduction of the prefix to *a-*, the sp. was assim. to words of L. origin in *aff-*; for the change of *th* to *d* cf. *burden*, *murder*.

afforest ǽfɔ·rist convert into forest. XV. – medL. *afforestāre* (Charter of Forests, temp. Henry III), f. *ad* AF-+*foresta* FOREST. So **afforest**A·TION. XVII. – medL.

affray əfrei· (arch.) alarm, startle, frighten. XIV. – AN. *afrayer*, OF. *effreer*, *esfreer* (mod. *effrayer*) = Pr. *esfredar* :– Rom. **exfridāre*, f. L. *ex* EX-[1]+Rom. **fridus*, – Germ. **friþuz* peace (whence OE. *friþ* FRITH[1]); lit. 'remove from peace'. The pp. *af(f)rayed* alarmed, in a state of fear, has become a distinct word, AFRAID. So **affray·** sb. †attack, alarm, disturbance XIV; violent breach of the peace XV. – AN. *affrai*, for OF. *effrei*, *esfrei*, f. the vb. Aphetic FRAY[1].

affright əfrai·t (arch.) frighten. XVI. f. †*affright* frightened, ME. *affriȝt*, OE. *āfyrhted*, pp. of **āfyrhtan*, collateral with *offyrhtan*. Hence **affri·ght** sb. XVI (Spenser).

affront əfrʌ·nt insult (one) openly to his face; put to the blush. XIV. – OF. *afronter* strike in the face (mod. *affronter*) = Pr., Sp. *afrontar*, It. *affrontare* :– Rom. **affrontāre*, f. L. phr. *ad frontem* to the face; see AF-, FRONT. Hence **affro·nt** sb. XVI; cf. F. *affront*.

affusion əfjū·ʒən pouring water on the body in baptism. XVII. – late L. *affūsiō(n-)*, f. *affūs-*, *affundere*; see AF-, FUSION.

afield əfī·ld on or to the field OE.; abroad XV. ME. *o felde*, *a felde*, OE. *on felda*; i.e. ON, A-[1], and dative of FIELD.

afire əfaiə·ɹ (arch., dial.) on fire. XIII. ME. *afüre*, *o füre*, i.e. *a*, ON, A-[1], and dative of FIRE.

aflame əflei·m ablaze, glowing. XVI. f. A-[1]+FLAME, after AFIRE.

afloat əflou·t on the water or the sea. ME. *on flote* (XII), *o flote* on the sea, at sea, i.e. ON, A-[1], and dative of OE. *flot* sea (see FLOAT[1]); in ME. partly after ON. *á flot*, *á floti* and OF. *en flot*; from XVI prob. a new formation.

afoot əfu·t on foot (lit. and fig.). XIII. ME. *afote*, i.e. ON, A-[1], and dative of FOOT; partly after ON. *á fótum*.

afore əfɔ̄ə·ɹ (arch.) in front, in advance. OE. *onforan*, ME. *on-*, *aforen*, reinforced by XIV *afore*, f. ON+obs. *fore* adv. and prep. Hence †**afo·rehand, afo·retime(s), afo·resaid** (XIV), modelled on BEFOREHAND, -TIME, †*beforesaid* (XIII). **afo·rethought** premeditated (leg. phr. *malice a.*) XVI; *thought*, pp. of THINK; after †*prepensed* (see PREPENSE).

afraid əfrei·d in fear. XIV (R. Mannyng). ME. *af(f)raied*, *-ayed*, pp. of AFFRAY used as adj. after AN. *afrayé*; superseded AFEARD. The sp. *-aid* dates from XVI; cf. STAID.

afreet, afrit æ·frīt (also *efreet*) evil demon of Mohammedan mythology. XVIII. – Arab. *'ifrīt* – Pers. *āfarīd* creature, f. *āfrīdan* create.

afresh əfre·ʃ anew. XV. Earlier *of fresh* (XV–XVI), after ANEW; see A-[2], FRESH, and cf. OF. *de frais* recently.

African æ·frikən pert. to Africa. XIII (Laȝ.). – L. *Āfricānus* (Cicero), f. *Āfrica*, sb. use of fem. (sc. *terra* land) of *Āfricus*, f. *Āfrī* (sg. *Āfer*) ancient people of N. Africa; see -AN and cf. F. *africain*, etc.

Afrikaner (older **Africander, -kander**) æfrikā·nəɹ (-kændəɹ) white native of S. Africa. XIX. – Afrikaans, earlier (Cape) Du. *Afrikaander*, f. *Afrikaan* (sb.) African+*-d)er*, pers. suff., after *Hollander* Dutchman. So **Afrikaans** æfrikā·ns Cape Dutch, the taal. XX. var. of *Afrikaansch*.

aft àft (prop. naut.) in or near the hinder part. XVII (*fore and aft*). prob. alteration of earlier *abaft*, *baft*, after LG., Du. *achter* abaft, AFTER; there is no historical connexion with OE. *æftan* behind.

after à·ftəɹ behind in place or time. OE. *æfter* adv. and prep. = OFris. *efter*, OS., OHG. *aftar*, *-er* (Du. *achter*), ON. *aptr* adv. (*eptir* prep.), Goth. *aftra* back, again; CGerm. adv., prob. compar. deriv. of **af-* in OE. *æftan* from behind, OS. *at|aftan*, ON. *aptan*, Goth. *aftana*; perh. to be referred to IE. **op-* in Gr. *opísō* behind, again, or **ap-* in Gr. *apó* OF. Hence **a·fter** adj., in OE. *æfter(r)a*; later the adv. in attrib. use (cf. next).

after- à·ftəɹ the adv.-prep. AFTER in comb., fixed or transitory, with sbs., adjs., and vbs., in various relations and senses, 'hinder', 'subsequent(ly)', 'eventual(ly)', 'subordinate(ly)'. (OE. had e.g. *æfterboren* posthumous, *æfterfolgere* successor, *æfterġield* additional payment, *æfterrāp* crupper.)

after-birth à·ftəɹbɔ̄ɹþ placenta. XVI (also †*after-burthen*). perh. directly – G. *afterbürde* (Luther, Deut. xxviii 57), also *aftergeburt*; cf. Icel. *eftirburðr*, OSw. *efterbörd*, Da. *efterbyrd*; see AFTER-, BIRTH.

aftermath à·ftəɹmæþ second crop of grass XVI; esp. fig. XVII. f. AFTER-+MATH.

aftermost à·ftəɹmŏst most aft. XVIII. f. AFTER (in naut. use, as *after sails*)+-MOST. (There is no historical connexion with OE. *æftemest*, Goth. *aftumists* last, latest, or the occas. early ME. *aftermest*.)

afternoon àftəɹnū·n time between midday and evening. XIII. f. AFTER-+NOON; cf. late L. *postmeridiem* adv. (medL. *postmeridies* afternoon meal), F. *après-midi*.

afterward à·ftəɹwəɹd †behind OE.; subsequently XIII. Late OE. *æfterwearde* (see AFTER, -WARD), to which corr. an adj. *æfterweard* latter part of, of which *æftan-*, *æfteweard* are collateral forms.

ag- assim. form of AD- before *g*; cf. AC-.

aga, agha ā·gă Ottoman title of distinction. XVI. – Turk. *āghā* master, lord.

again əge·n, əgei·n adv. †in the opposite direction, back OE.; †in return XIII; once more, anew XIV; †prep. towards, opposite, against. OE., WS. *onġēan*, *onġēn*, later *aġēn*, Anglian *onġæġn*, *onġeġn*, whence typical ME. forms *aȝen*, *ayen*, and *aȝain*, *aȝein*; corr. to OS. *angegin*, OHG. *ingagan*, *ingegin(i)*, MHG. *engegene*, *engein* (G. *entgegen* opposite), ON. *í gegn* against (Sw. *igen*, Da. *igjen* again, anew); CGerm. (exc. Goth.) phr. f. ON (varying with IN)+**gagan-*, **gagin-* direct, straight (cf. OE. *ġeġn*, ON. *gegn* straight), the orig. meaning being 'in a direct line (with)'; the Germ. base **gag-* is of unkn. origin.

The native forms in *aȝ-*, *ay-* did not survive beyond XVI, being superseded universally by forms in *ag-*, derived from Scand. and appearing first in northern and eastern texts XIII. Aphetic *gain* survives in GAINSAY.

against əge·nst, əgei·nst opposite (now only in *over against*); in resistance to XII; in opposition to; in return for XIII. ME. *aȝænes*, *aȝeines*, *aȝaines*, *aȝens*, f. *aȝein*, etc.+*-es*; see AGAIN, -S. For the parasitic *-t* cf. AMIDST. Aphetic *gainst* (XVI, Spenser), often sp. *'gainst*.

agamous æ·gəməs (biol.) non-sexual. XIX. f. late L. *agamus* – Gr. *ágamos* unmarried, f. *a-* A-[4]+*gámos* marriage; see GAMO-, -OUS.

agape[1] əgei·p gaping. XVII (Milton). f. A-[1]+GAPE.

agape[2] æ·gəpi love-feast. XVII (used earlier and later in Gr. letters ἀγάπη). – Gr. *agápē* brotherly love, f. *agapân* vb. love. Hence (irreg. formed) **agapemone** ægəpī·məni 'abode of love' (Gr. *monḗ* abode). XIX.

agar-agar ei·gārei·gāɹ East Indian seaweed. XIX. Malay.

agaric æ·gərik, əgæ·rik kind of fungus. XV. – L. *agaricum* (Pliny) – Gr. *agarikón*, said by Dioscorides to be named from *Agaria* in Sarmatia; see -IC.

agate æ·gət variety of chalcedony. XVI. – (O)F. *agate*, also †*agathe* (cf. It. *agata*) – L. *achātēs* – Gr. *akhátēs*. The older F. form *ac(h)ate* was adopted in ME. (XIII).

agave əgei·vi American aloe. XVIII. – modL. adoption as generic name of L. *Agavē* – Gr. *Agauḗ*, mythological name (daughter of Cadmus and Harmonia), prop. fem. of *agauós* illustrious.

age eidʒ period of existence or of time; time of life. XIII. – OF. *age*, earlier *aäge*, *eäge* (mod. *âge*) = Pr. *atge* :– Gallo-Rom. **ætāticum*, f. L. *ætāt-*, *ætās*, earlier *ævitās*, f. *ævum* age of time; see ÆON. Hence **age** grow old XIV; make old XVII. **aged**[1] ei·dʒid having lived long XV; eidʒd of the age of (so-and-so) XVII; after F. *âgé*; see -ED[1].

-age -idʒ suffix repr. (O)F. *-age* = Pr. *-atge*, It. *-aggio* :– L. *-āticu-s*, -ATIC. (For the Rom. extended use of *-āticum* see AGE, COURAGE.) The meanings are typified by *baggage, carriage, cartage, damage, dotage, hermitage, homage, language, luggage, marriage, passage, tillage, tonnage, vicarage, village*. In *badinage, barrage, camouflage, entourage, garage, sabotage* the suffix is pronounced āʒ.

agenda ədʒe·ndə things to be done, e.g. items of business to be considered. XVII. – L., pl. of *agendum* (also current), sb. use of n. gerundive of *agere* (see next).

agent ei·dʒənt one who (that which) acts or operates. XV. – L. *agent-*, *agēns*, sb. use of prp. of *agere* do; perh. through It. *agente*, whence (acc. to R. Étienne) F. *agent* (XVI); see -ENT. So **a·gency**. XVII. – medL. *agentia*, whence also F. *agence*.

L. *agere* drive, pursue, occupy oneself with, carry on, perform, act (a play), do, is f. IE. **ag-* drive, lead, whence also Skr. *ájati*, Av. *azaiti* drives, Arm. *acem* I bring, OIr. *-aig* leads, Gr. *ágein* lead, ON. *aka* drive a vehicle, carry. ¶For other derivs. of the base see ACT, AGILE, AGITATE, AGONY, AMBIGUOUS, COAGULATE, COGENT, COGITATE, EXACT, EXAMINE, EXIGENT, EXIGUOUS, PRODIGAL.

agglomerate ǎglɔ·məreit gather into a mass. XVII. f. pp. stem of L. *agglomerāre*, f. *ad* AG-+*glomus* ball, mass, partly through F. *agglomérer*; see -ATE[3]. So **agglomera·tion**. XVIII. – F. or L.

agglutinate əglʲū·tineit fasten as with glue. XVI. f. pp. stem of L. *agglūtināre*, f. *ad* AG-+ *glūten* GLUE; see -ATE[3]. So **agglutina·tion**. XVI. **agglu·tinative** (of languages, first used by Max Müller, 1861).

aggrandize æ·grəndaiz make or make to appear greater. XVII. f. *agrandiss-*, lengthened stem (see -ISH[2]) of (O)F. *agrandir* prob. – It. *aggrandire*, f. *a-* AG-+*grandire* – L. *grandīre*, f. *grandis* GRAND; the ending was assim. to verbs in *-ise*, -IZE. So **aggrandizement** əgræ·ndizmənt. XVII. – F. *agrandissement*.

aggravate æ·grəveit †load, burden; add weight or gravity to XVI; incense, provoke XVII. f. pp. stem of L. *aggravāre*, f. *ad* AG-+ *gravis* heavy, GRAVE; prob. through F. *aggraver*; see -ATE[3]. So **aggrava·tion**. XV. †oppression (Caxton); (eccl.) censure XVI; increasing in gravity XVII. – F. – medL.

aggregate æ·grigeit collected into one body (now techn.) XV; sb. -ət sum total, entire mass XV. – L. *aggregātus*, pp. of *aggregāre*, f. *ad* AG-+*greg-*, *grex* flock (cf. GREGARIOUS). So **a·ggregate** -eit vb. (see -ATE[3]), **aggrega·tion** XV.

aggression əgre·ʃən unprovoked assault. XVII. – F. *agression* or L. *aggressiō(n-)*, f. *aggress-*, pp. stem of *aggredī* attack, f. *ad* AG-+*gradī* walk, step, f. *gradus* step, GRADE; see -ION. So **aggre·ssive**. XIX; perh. after F.

aggrieve ə·grīv bear heavily upon. XIV. ME. *agreve* – OF. *agrever* make heavier :– L. *aggravare* AGGRAVATE. The sp. was assim. to L. (with *agg-*) from XV, the F. word being latinized to *aggraver*. (A Rom. by-form **aggreviāre* gave OF. *agregier*, whence Eng. †*aggrege* XIV–XVII.)

aghast əgā·st dumbfounded. XIII. ME. *agast*, short form of pp. of †*agaste* frighten, strengthened form (with A-[3]) of †*gaste*, app. :– OE. *gǣstan*, which is, however, recorded only once and with the sense 'torment'. The sp. with *gh*, established from XVIII, is due to assoc. with GHASTLY.

agile æ·dʒail nimbly active. XV (Wyntoun). – (O)F. *agile* – L. *agilis*, f. *agere*; see AGENT, -ILE. So **agility** ədʒi·lĭti. XIV. – (O)F. – L.

agio æ·dʒiou percentage of charge for exchange. XVII. – It. *aggio*, of unkn. origin; so F., Du. *agio*. So **a·giotage** speculation in stock. XIX. – F. *agiotage*, f. *agioter* speculate, f. *agio*, with connective *t*.

agist ədʒi·st take in live stock at a certain rate XVI; subject to a charge XVII. – OF. *agister* (mod. *agîter*), f. *a* AD-+*gister* lodge :– Rom. **jacitāre*, frequent. of *jacēre* (cf. ADJACENT). So **agi·stment**. XVI. – OF.

agitate æ·dʒiteit excite, disturb; †act as agent; discuss. XVI. f. pp. stem of L. *agitāre* move to and fro, frequent. of *agere* (see AGENT, -ATE[3]); cf. (O)F. *agiter*. So **agita·tion**. XVI. – F. or L. (Public 'agitation' first in 1828.) **a·gitator**. XVII. – L. *agitātor*. (First used in 1647 in the sense of 'agent' for the delegates of private soldiers in the Parliament of 1647–9; political agitator in the present sense dates from XVIII.)

aglet, aiglet æ·glit, ei·glit tag; catkin. XV. – (O)F. *aiguillette*, dim. of *aiguille* needle :– late L. *acūcula* pine-needle, dim. of *acus* needle (cf. ACID). Cf. AIGUILLE.

agley, agly əglai·, əglī· (Sc.) crooked, awry. XVIII (Burns). f. A[1]- †*gley*, *gly* (XIII) squint; cf. Sc. *aglied* (XVII) squintingly.

agnail æ·gneil †corn on the foot OE.; whitlow XVI; sore piece of skin at the root of a nail XVIII. OE. *angnæġl*, corr. to OFris. *ongneil*, OHG. *ungnagel* (G. dial. *anneglen*, *einnegeln*); f. **aŋg-* compressed, tight, painful (cf. ANGUISH)+*næġl* NAIL, in the sense of 'hard excrescence in the flesh' (cf. L. *clavus* and F. *clou* used of a metal nail and a corn on the foot). The two later senses have arisen from assoc. of *-nail* with the finger-nail; in the last sense also dial. *hang-nail* (XVII) and Sc. *anger-nail*.

agnate æ·gneit kinsman by the father's side; kinsman by descent from a common male ancestor. XV. – L. *agnātus*, f. *ad* AD- + *(g)nātus* born (cf. NATURE). See also ADNATE.

agnize æ·gnaiz recognize. XVI. f. L. *agnōscere* (f. *ad* AG- + *(g)nōscere* KNOW), after *cognize, recognize*.

agnomen ægnou·men second cognomen. XVIII. – L. *agnōmen*, f. *ad* AG- + *(g)nōmen* NAME.

agnostic ǽgnɔ·stik holding that nothing is knowable beyond material phenomena. 1869. f. A-[4] + GNOSTIC; invented by Thomas Henry Huxley (1825–95) when a member of the Metaphysical Society to express his attitude of mind in contrast with that of contemporary 'gnostics'; see his own account in 'Agnosticism' and 'Agnosticism and Christianity' in Collected Essays (1900), vol. v, pp. 239, 309. There was no allusion to the use of Gr. *ágnōstos* (unknown) in Acts xvii 23 (*Ἀγνώστῳ Θεῷ* to an unknown god).

Agnus Dei æ·gnəs dī·ai, a·gnus dē·ī part of the canon of the mass beginning with these words. XIV. L., 'Lamb of God'.

ago əgou·, (arch. and dial.) **agone** əgɔ·n gone by, past. XIV. pp. of ME. †*ago*, OE. *āgān* pass away, corr. to OS. *āgangan*, OHG. *irgangan, irgān* (G. *ergehen*), Goth. *usgaggan*; see A-[3], GO. Used first to qualify an expression of time in adv. phr., e.g. *ago fif yer* five years passed, *longe tyme agoo*; later as an adv. in *long ago* at a time long distant.

agog əgɔ·g in eager expectation. XV. prob. modelled (with assim. to formations with A-[1]) on late OF. *en gogues* (cf. '*Estre en ses gogues*, to be frolicke, lustie . . . all a-hoit, in a pleasant humour', Cotgr.), i.e. *en* IN, pl. of *gogue* merriment, pleasantry, of unkn. origin.

agony æ·gəni anguish of mind XIV (Ch., Wycl. Bible); death struggle XVI; extreme bodily suffering XVII. – (O)F. *agonie* or late L. *agōnia* – Gr. *agōniā* contest, mental struggle, f. *agṓn* contest, struggle, rel. to *ágein*; see AGENT, -Y[3]. So **a·gon**IZE torment XVI; suffer agony XVII; contend XVIII. – F. *agoniser*, late L. *agōnizāre* (after Gr. *agōnizesthai*).

agoraphobia æ:gərəfou·biə morbid dread of public places. XIX. modL., irreg. f. Gr. *agorá* (place of) assembly, market-place, rel. to L. *grex* flock; see GREGARIOUS, -PHOBIA.

agouti əgū·ti W. Indian animal of the cavy family. XVII (Purchas). – F. *agouti* or Sp. *aguti* – Tupi *aguti*.

agrarian əgrɛə·riən pert. to the land. XVII. f. L. *agrārius*, f. *agr-, ager* land; see ACRE, -ARIAN. Used first with ref. to the *lex agraria* of ancient Rome (cf. *the law agrarie*, Bellenden's 'Livy', 1533).

agree əgrī· †please, become favourable, accede XIV (Ch.); be in harmony or accord XVI. – (O)F. *agréer* = Pr., Sp. *agradar*, It. *aggradare* :- Rom. **aggrātāre*, f. L. *ad* AG- + *grātus* pleasing, agreeable (cf. GRACE). So **agree·**ABLE pleasing, harmonious, suitable. XIV (Ch.). – (O)F. *agréable*. Hence **agree·ably**. XIV (Ch.); see -LY[2]. **agree·**MENT accord, covenant; concord. XIV.

agriculture æ·grikʌltʃəɹ cultivation of the soil. XVII. – F. *agriculture* or L. *agricultūra*, i.e. *agrī cultūra* tillage of the land; see ACRE, CULTURE. Hence **agricu·ltur**AL XVIII, **agricu·ltural**IST (cf. *naturalist*) XIX, **agricu·lturist** XVIII.

agrimony æ·griməni plant of the genus Eupatoria. Earlier *egre-, egrimoigne, -moine* (XIV, Ch.). – (O)F. *aigremoine*; the later *agrimony* (XV), with var. †*egri-*, is based directly on *agrimōnia*, misreading for L. *argemōnia* (Pliny, Celsus) – Gr. *argemṓnē* poppy (Dioscorides), f. *árgemon* white spot on the eye (which the plant was reputed to cure), f. *argḗs, argós* white, shining (cf. ARGENT).

agro- æ·grou comb. form of Gr. *agrós* field, ACRE.

agrostis əgrɔ·stis genus of grasses. XVIII. late L. – Gr. *ágrōstis*, f. *agrós* (see prec.).

aground əgrau·nd †on or to the ground XIII; on or to the bottom of shallow water XVI. f. A-[1] + GROUND; cf. ON. *á grunn* into the shallows.

ague ei·gju †acute fever XIV (PPl.); malarial fever XIV (Ch.). – OF. *ague* :- medL. *acūta*, sb. use (sc. *febris* fever) of fem. of L. *acūtus* ACUTE. Earlier ME. †*fever agu* – OF. *fievre ague* – L. *febris acūta* (Celsus).

ah ā int. XIII. Earliest form *a* – OF. *a* (later and mod. *ah*); cf. It., Sp. *ah*, and similar forms in various langs., as L. *ā, āh*, Gr. *â, aá*, OHG. *ā* (G. *ah*), Lith. *à, aà*, Skr. *ā*. (OE. had *ǣ, ēa*, ON. *æ*.) Combination with HA produced **aha** ahā· XIII (Cursor M.); so in L., (M)HG., etc.

ahead əhe·d (orig. naut.) at the head; in front (of); forward, onward. XVII. Earlier †*on head* (XVI); see A-[1], HEAD.

ahem (ə)hm excl. to attract attention, or used in hesitating speech. XVIII. var. of HEM with the 'indeterminate' vowel ə prefixed.

ahoy əhoi· (naut.) call used in hailing. XVIII. f. *a*, AH + HOY[1].

ahungered əhʌ·ŋgəɹd (arch.) hungry. XIV. prob. repr. a var. of ME. *ofhungred, offingred*, OE. *ofhyngrod*, pp. of *ofhyngran*, f. *of-*, A-[2] + *hyngran* be hungry, f. HUNGER; by confusion of A-[2] (of) and A-[1] (on) altered to **anhu·ngered** XIV (as in Tindale, Matt. xii 1, whence in A.V.); so †*a(n)hungry* XVII.

ai ā·i S. American sloth. XVII. – native Brazilian word repr. the animal's cry, prob. through F. *aï* (†*hay*, †*haiit*).

aid eid help, assistance. XV. – OF. *aïde* (mod. *aide*) = Pr. *ajud(h)a*, Sp. *ayuda* :– Rom. **adjūta*, sb. use of fem. pp. of *adjuvāre*. So **aid** vb. XV. – OF. *aïdier* (mod. *aider*) = Pr. *ajudar* :– L. *adjūtāre*, frequent. of *adjuvāre*, f. *ad* AD-+*juvāre* help, assist.

aide-de-camp eid də kã officer who assists a general. XVII. F., lit. 'camp assistant' (*aide*, f. *aider* AID, *de* of, *camp* CAMP).

aigrette ei·gret spray of gems, etc.; feathery tuft, bundle of rays, etc. XVII (*ægret*, *egrette*). – F. *aigrette*; see EGRET.

aiguille ei·gwī(l) slender sharp-pointed rock. XIX. – F., needle (= It. *aguglia*, etc.) :– Rom. **acūcula*, dim. of *acus* needle (cf. ACID). So **aiguillette** eigwile·t ornamental tag. XIX. F., dim. of *aiguille*; see -ETTE.

ail eil (arch.) trouble, afflict; be ill (now in prp. *ailing*). OE. *eġlan*, *eġlian*, f. *eġle* troublesome, rel. to Goth. *agls* disgraceful, *aglo* oppression, *us|agljan* oppress; further connexions doubtful. Hence **ai·l**MENT. XVIII.

ailanto eilæ·ntou large E. Indian tree. XIX. – Native name in Amboyna, whence modL. *ailantus*, *-thus* (after Gr. *ánthos* flower).

aileron ei·lərɔn small hinged flap on an aeroplane. XX. – F. *aileron*, dim. of *aile* wing (see ALATE[2]).

aim eim †estimate; calculate a course or direction XIV; direct (a missile, blow) XIV. ME. *ame*, later *ayme*, *aime*; partly – OF. *amer*, dial. var. of *esmer* (= Pr. *esmar*, It. *stimare*) :– L. *æstimāre* (see ESTIMATE); partly – OF. *aesmer*, *aemer*, Pr. *azesmar*, OSp. *a(e)smar* :– L. **adæstimāre* (see AD-). Hence (or – OF. *aesme*, *aeme*, *esme*, *aime*) **aim** sb. XIV. f. the vb.

air ɛəɹ A. fluid enveloping the earth XIII (AncrR.); B. outward appearance, manner XVI (Sh.); C. melody, tune XVI (Sh.). prop. three words, but, as in F., the earliest has absorbed the others. In A, ME. *eir*, later *air*, *ayr* – (O)F. *air* = Pr. *air(e)*, Sp. *aire*, Pg. *ar*, It. *aere*, †*aire*, Rum. *aier* – L. *āerem*, nom. *āēr* – Gr. *āḗr*, rel. to *áēmi* I blow, *aúrā* breeze (cf. AURA). In B, – F. *air* (XVI, Montaigne), prob. repr. OF. *aire* place, site, race, stock, disposition, quality (cf. *de bon aire* DEBONAIR) = Pr. *aire*, *agre* nest, family, stock (cf. EYRIE) :– L. *agrum*, nom. *ager* territory (cf. ACRE), infl. by L. *ārea* AREA. In C, like later F. *air* (XVII), repr. It. *aria*, orig. :– L. (Gr.) *āera*, acc. of *āēr*, but later infl. by OF. *aire*, from which it derived the meanings 'quality', 'nature', 'manner', whence was developed that of 'tune' (perh. after G. *weise* (i) manner, (ii) tune). Hence **air** vb. XVI. **ai·ry** XIV; see -Y[1].

Airedale ɛə·ɹdeil name of a district in the W. Riding of Yorkshire, epithet of a breed of terrier. XIX.

airt ɛəɹt (Sc.) point of the compass, direction. XIV (*art*, Cursor M.). – Gaelic *aird*, *ard* (= OIr. *aird*, Ir. *ard*) height, top, quarter of the compass, cogn. with Gr. *árdis* point.

air-tight ɛə·ɹtait impermeable to air. XVIII. f. AIR+TIGHT, after *water-*, *wind-tight*; cf. G. *luftdicht*.

airwood see HAREWOOD.

aisle ail lateral section of a church XIV; passage-way in a church XV. ME. *ele*, later *ile*, *yle*, *isle* (XVI–XVIII), *aile*, *aisle* (from XVIII) – OF. *ele* (mod. *aile*) :– L. *āla* wing of bird, army, or building :– **akslā* (cf. OE. *eaxl*, G. *achsel* shoulder); the var. forms of the F. word (partly confused with *isle* island, as if 'detached part of a building', whence medL. *insula* aisle) were repr. in Eng., the common early modF. form *aisle* being finally established.

ait, eyot eit islet. OE. *iġġaþ*, *iġ(e)oþ*, *īġ(e)þ*, ME. *yȝet* (XII), *eigt*, *eyt*, *eit* (XIII), later *eight*, *aight*, *ait* (XVII), *eyot* (XIX). The ME. and later history suggest an Angl. var. **ēġaþ* of WS. **īeġaþ* (of which the extant OE. forms repr. late vars.), f. *īeġ* ISLAND+ dim. suffix *-aþ*. The final *t* may be due to AN. habits of pronunciation.

aitch-bone ei·tʃboun the bone of the buttock. XIX (also *H-bone*), orig. *nache*-BONE (XV), *natch-* (XVII), earlier *nage* (XIV) – OF. *nache*, *nage*, pl. *naches* (cf. Pr. *naggas*, Sp. *nalga*, Pg. *nadega*, It. *natica*) :– late L. *naticas*, acc. pl. of *naticæ*, f. L. *natis* (usu. pl. *-es*) buttock. (*Hach boon* in 'The Boke of St. Albans' f. iij[v] must be a mispr. for *nach boon*.) The forms *ice-*, *izebone* (XVII) are – (M)LG. *īsbēn*, Du. *ijsbeen*, whence also G. *eisbein*. Cf. ADDER, etc.

ajar ədʒā·ɹ slightly open. XVIII. Alteration of Sc. and n. dial. *achar*, *a char* (XVI), earlier *on char-e* (Dunbar, G. Douglas), i.e. ON, *char* :– OE. *ċerr* (*ċierr*) turn (see CHARE); cf. late ME. *char up* lit. '(on the) turn open'. Parallel forms are MLG. *enkare*, MDu. *aenkerre*, (also WFlem.) *akerre*; cf. Du. *op een kier* 'on a turn', WFlem. *met eene kerre*, WFris. *yn 't kier* (*tsjier*) half-open. The earliest records of the *j*-form (XVII) are in the analytical var. *at jar*, which was further modified to *on the jar*, *on a jar*, *on jar*; *a jarr* is in Bailey's dict. 1721.

ajar[2] ədʒā·ɹ out of harmony. XIX. Reduction of earlier *at jar* (XVI–XVIII), of which there was a var. *at a jar*; see JAR[1].

akimbo əki·mbou with hands on hips and elbows turned outwards. XV. Late ME. *in kenebowe*, later (by assim. to A-[1], ON) *a* or *on kenbow*, *a kenbol(d)* or *kembol*, *a kembo* (*kimbow*), *akimbo* (XVIII), mod. dial. (*a-*)*king-bow*; prob. – ON. phr. **í keng boginn* 'bent in a curve' (cf. *kengboginn* crooked, *beygja sik í keng* crouch, *beygja kenginn* arch the back); see IN, BOW[2]. Some vars., e.g. *a cannebow*, may show blending with CAM[2] crooked.

al-[1] assim. form of AD- before *l*; cf. AC-.

al-² Arab. def. art. *al* the, forming an essential el. of many words of Rom. (esp. Sp. and Pg.) origin adopted in Eng., as *alcohol, alcove, algebra, alkali, almagest*.

-al¹ (ə)l suffix repr. L. *-ālis* forming adjs. from sbs. with the sense 'of the kind of, pertaining to'. It became *-el* in OF., with which many F. words were adopted, e.g. *actuel, mortel*; this form, to some extent in F. and gen. in Eng., was refash. after L. as *-al*, whence L. adjs. in *-ālis* and F. adjs. in *-el* have been adopted with *-al* unrestrictedly. The L. adjs. were primarily f. sbs., as *ōrālis* ORAL, f. *ōr-, ōs* mouth, and varied sometimes with *-āris*, as *lineālis* LINEAL, *lineāris* LINEAR (when the stem ended in *l*, *-āris* was used, as *stellāris* STELLAR). This type was greatly increased in medL. and modL. and consequently in the Rom. langs. by formations not only on L. but on Gr. stems (after L. *boreālis, hebdomadālis, theātrālis*), e.g. *baptismālis, cathedrālis*, etc. In L. itself *-ālis* was added to existing adjs., as *annuālis* (f. *annuus*), *infernālis* (f. *infernus*); hence the suffix is added freely in the mod. langs. to many classes of formations, including those with suffixes of Gr. origin, *-ac, -ic, -oid* (see -ACAL, -ICAL, -OIDAL). The corr. advs. end in *-ally*, nouns of quality in **-ality** æ·lĭti, as *liberality* (– F. – L.). The comp. suffixes *-alize, -alization* appear orig. in adoptions from F. *-aliser, -alisation*.

In L. some adjs. in *-ālis* were used sb. in various genders and in sg. or pl., as *animal, annāles, rīvālis, tribūnal, Bacchānālia, Saturnālia, penetrālia*; the number was much enlarged in later L. and in the mod. langs., whence e.g. *cardinal, canonicals, mammalia, morals, oval, principal, signal, terminal, urinal*; see also -AL².

-al² əl earlier *-aile, -ayle*, repr. F *-aille, -ail, -al*, which was generalized from such words as *bataille* BATTLE, *(e)spousaille-s* (E)SPOUSAL, *funeraille* FUNERAL, where the orig. L. was a sb. use of the n.pl. of an adj. in *-ālis* -AL¹. Among the earliest exx. are *acquittal* (XV), *arrival* (XIV); from XVI onwards many derivs. of L. or F. vbs. came into use, e.g. *trial*; a few have been made on native end-stressed vbs., as *beheadal, bestowal, betrothal, withdrawal*. ¶*Bridal* and *burial* simulate this ending, though their origin is different.

alabaster æ·ləbàstəɹ fine variety of carbonate or sulphate of lime. XIV (Ch.). – OF. *alabastre* (mod. *albâtre*) – L. *alabaster, -trum* – Gr. *alábastos, -tros*, prob. of foreign origin. The most freq. form in XVI and XVII was *alablaster*, surviving dial.; the early Sc. form (XIV–XVI) was *alabast*.

alack əlæ·k (arch.) excl. of dissatisfaction, (hence) of surprise or regret. XV. prob. f. *a*, AH+LACK loss, after ALAS. Hence **alack-a-day**; cf. LACKADAISICAL.

alacrity əlæ·krĭti briskness. XV. – L. *alacritās*, f. *alacr-, alacer* brisk (whence †*alacrious* XVII); see AMBLE, -ITY.

alamode æ·lămoud adv. phr. in the fashion; adj. phr. fashionable; sb. glossy black silk XVII; cooked beef (attrib., after F. *bœuf à la mode*). – F. phr. *à la mode*, i.e. *à* according to (AD), *la* the, *mode* manner, fashion, MODE.

alar ei·ləɹ pert. to wings. XIX. – L. *ālāris*, f. *āla* wing (cf. AISLE); see -AR.

alarm əlā·ɹm †(excl.) to arms! XIV; call to arms, warning; †surprise attack; state of surprise with fear XVI. ME. *alarme, alarom*, later *alarum* (XVI) – (O)F. *alarme* – It. *allarme*, i.e. *all' arme* 'to the arms' (see ARM²) orig. a call. Hence **ala·rm** vb. XVI.

alarum əlæ·rəm var. of ALARM, formerly current in all senses but now restricted in prose usage to the note of a warning bell or clock, or the mechanism producing this. Aphetic †*larum* (c. 1530; in XIX arch.).

alas əlà·s excl. of grief. XIII (Cursor M.). – OF. *a las(se)* (also *helas*, mod. *hélas*) 'ah! weary (that I am)!', i.e. *a* AH+*las(se)* :– L. *lassu-s*, fem. *lassa* weary (cf. LASSITUDE); corr. to Pr. *ai las* (*lasa*), It. *ahi lasso* (*lassa*); the adj. was orig. in concord with the gender of the subject.

alate ei·leit (nat. hist.) winged. XVII. – L. *ālātus*, f. *āla* wing (rel. to OE. *eaxl* shoulder); see -ATE². Also **ala·ted**. XVII.

alb ælb (eccl.) long tunic with sleeves. OE. *albe* – ecclL. *alba*, sb. use (sc. *tunica* tunic, *vestis* garment) of L. *albus* white; some ME. forms show adoption of (O)F. *aube*, and later forms show blending of the two types, e.g. *aulbe*.

albacore, albicore æ·lbəkōɹ large tunny. XVI. – Pg. *albacor, -ora* (whence Sp. *albacora*, F. *albicore*), f. Arab. *al* AL-², *bukr*, pl. *bakārat* young camel, heifer.

Albanian ælbei·niən pert. to Albania, a Balkan state, the native name of which is Shqipnija; sb. a native of this; the language of Albania. XIX. f. medL. *Albania*+-IAN; the Gr. names for the inhabitants are *Albánoi, Al-, Arbanêtes* (cf. ARNAOUT).

albatross æ·lbətrɔs bird of the petrel family, esp. Diomedea exulans. XVII (1672). Usually taken to be alteration, by assoc. with L. *albus* white, of †*alcatras* pelican, gannet, sea-mew, frigate-bird (XVI) – Sp., Pg. *alcatraz*, var. of Pg. *alcatruz* orig. bucket of an irrigating water-wheel, corr. to Sp. *alcaduz, arcaduz* – Arab. *alqādūs* 'the pitcher', i.e. *al* AL-², *qādūs* – Gr. *kádos* jar, itself of Sem. origin (cf. Heb. *kad* bucket). The orig. ref. is held to have been to the pelican's large pouch, in which it was supposed to carry water. The changes of sense and form are a serious difficulty. Hence Du., G., F. *albatros* (XVIII), whence Pg. *albatroz*.

albeit ōlbī·it even though. XIV (Ch.). Conjunctive phr. *al be it*, fuller form of *albe*, i.e. ALL adv., *be* 3rd sg. pres. subj. of the vb. BE, with a clause following (introduced or not by *that*), the orig. meaning being 'let it entirely be (that)', 'let (what is expressed by the clause) be fully so'; formerly with corr. pt., †*al were it*. Cf. HOWBEIT.

albert æ·lbəɹt kind of watch-chain. XIX. In full *Albert chain*, named after Prince *Albert* (d. 1861), Consort of Queen Victoria.

albino ælbī·nou man or animal distinguished by absence of colouring pigment in the skin, etc. XVIII. – Sp., Pg. *albino*, f. *albo* white + *-ino* (see -INE[1]). First applied by the Portuguese to the white negroes (*negros albinos*) of W. Africa. Hence **a·lbin**ISM. XIX; so F.

Albion æ·lbiən Britain. XIII (Laȝ.). – F. *Albion*, L. *Albiōn* (Pliny), Gr. *Alouīōn* (Ptolemy) – Celtic **Albio*, g. **Albionos*, whence Ir.-Gael. *Alba*, g. *Alban* Scotland (cf. medL. *Albānus* Scottish); usu. referred to **albho-* (L. *albus*) white, the allusion being to the white cliffs of Britain (cf. ALP).

album æ·lbəm blank book for the insertion of collected items. XVII ('his Album of Friends'; earlier in L. abl. form 'in his *Albo*', 1651). – L. *album* (in classical use, white tablet on which records or notices were inscribed, register, list), sb. use of n. of *albus* white (cf. prec.); first in G. use as *album amicorum* 'album of friends', in which the owner collected the signatures of fellow scholars (cf. 'a dull Dutch [i.e. German] fashion, their *album amicorum*', Fuller, 1642; 'what the Germans call an *Album*', Ld. Chesterfield, 1748).

albumen ælbjū·men, æ·lbjumen white of egg. XVI. – L. *albūmen*, f. *albus* white; cf. prec. Hence **albu·min**OUS. XVIII. f. L. stem *albūmin-*; cf. F. *albumineux*.

alcaic ælkei·ik (pros.) form of Gr. and L. verse. XVII. – late L. *alcaicus* – Gr. *alkaikós*, f. *Alkaîos* name of a lyric poet of Mytilene (c. 600 B.C.), who used the metre; see -IC.

alcalde ælkæ·ldi magistrate in Spain and Portugal. XVII. – Sp. *alcalde*, *alcaide*, Pg. *alcaide* – Arab. *al-qāḍī* 'the judge' (see AL-[2], CADI). Cf. F. *alcade*.

alcayde ælkai·di governor of a fortress. XVI. – Sp. *alcaide* – Arab. *al-qā'id* 'the leader', f. *qāda* lead.

alcazar ælkəzā·ɹ, alkā·þar fortress, spec. of Seville, Spain. XVII. – Sp. *alcazar* – Arab. *al-qaçr* 'the castle' – L. *castra* fortified camp (see AL-[2], CASTLE).

alchemy æ·lkĭmi chemistry of the Middle Ages. XIV. ME. *alkamye* (with vars. assim. to *astronomy*, e.g. *alknamye*, *alconomye*) – OF. *alkemie*, *alkamie* (mod. *alchimie*) = Pr. *alkimia*, Sp. *alquimia*, It. *alchimia* – medL. *alchimia*, *-chemia* – Arab. *alkīmiā*, i.e. *al* AL-[2], *kīmiā* – Gr. *khēmiā*, *khēmeiā* art of transmuting metals (Suidas), e.g. as practised by the Egyptians (whence the suggestion that the word is the same as *Khēmiā* the old name for Egypt, *Khmi*, lit. 'black land'). By assoc. with Gr. *khūmeiā* infusion (f. *khu-*, *kheîn* pour) arose the modL. *alchymia*, whence the frequent XVI–XVIII Eng. sp. *alchymy* (cf. *chymistry*, var. of CHEMISTRY). So **alche·mi**CAL. XVI. **a·lchem**IST. XVI. – OF. *alkemiste* or medL. *alchemista* (It. *alchimista*, etc.). †**alchemister**. XIV–XVI. †**alchemist**RY. XIV.

alcohol æ·lkŏhɔl fine metallic powder, esp. as produced by sublimation XVI; distilled or rectified spirit, e.g. *a. of wine* (after Paracelsus) XVII; spec. rectified spirit of wine XVIII; (chem.) compound of the type of this XIX. – F. (now *alcool*) or medL. *alcohol* – Arab. *alkoḥ'l* collyrium (fine powder used in the East to stain the eyelids), i.e. *al* AL-[2], KOHL. Hence **alcohol**IC ælkŏhɔ·lik. XVIII. **a·lcohol**ISM. XIX. – modL. (Magnus Huss, 1852).

alcoran æ·lkoræn, ælkorā·n XIV (Maund., Ch.). – (O)F. *alcoran* – Arab. *al-qorān*; see AL-[2], KORAN.

alcove æ·lkouv recess (vaulted or arched). XVII. – F. *alcôve* – Sp. *alcoba* – Arab. *al-qobbah*, i.e. *al* AL-[2], *qobbah* vault, vaulted chamber, f. *qubba* to vault. Formerly stressed *alco·ve*, as by Addison, Pope, and Cowper, and in Walker's dict.

Aldebaran ælde·bərən the star α Tauri. XIV (Ch.). – medL. – Arab. *aldabarān* 'the follower', f. *dabara* follow; so called because it follows the Pleiades; see AL-[2].

aldehyde æ·ldihaid (chem.) fluid obtained by oxidation of alcohol; compound of this type. XIX. f. *al. dehyd.*, abbrev. of *alcohol dehydrogenatum* dehydrogenated alcohol.

alder ɔ̄·ldəɹ the tree Alnus glutinosa. OE. *alor*, *aler*, rel. to MLG. *aller*, *alre*, *elre*, *else* (LG. *eller*), MDu. *else* (Du. *els*), OHG. *elira*, *erila* (G. *erle*), ON. *ǫlr* (*alr-*), *elrir*, *elri*, Goth. **aliza* (whence Sp. *aliso*), and outside Germ. to L. *alnus* (:- **alsnos*), Lith. *alksnis*, *elksnis*, Lett. *àlksnis*, Pol. *olcha*, Russ. *ol'khá*. Several varieties of form are repr. in earlier and dial. Eng., or are preserved in proper names: *aller*; *oller*, *owler*; *eller* (from Scand.); *Aldershot*, *Aller*, *Alresford*, *Arle*, *Ellershaw*, *Ollerton*, *Orleton*, *Oldershaw*. The deriv. adj. *aldern* (OE. *ælren* = OFris. *elren*, MLG. *ellern*, OHG. *erlīn*) is repr. in *Ollerenshaw*; it was in gen. Eng. use till XVII, and in Sc. (*alron*) XV–XVII. Forms with glide-*d* appear XIV.

alder-, later form of ME. *aller*, *alre*, OE. *alra*, g.pl. of ALL, as in *alderbest* (Ch.), *alderliefest* (Sh.) best of all, dearest of all, most dear, which was an arch. survival in XVI.

alderman ɔ̄·ldəɹmən †man of noble or high rank OE. (after XIII only hist. from XVI onwards); †warden of a guild, (hence) magistrate of a borough XII. OE. *aldormann* (= OFris. *aldermann*), f. *aldor* (*ealdor*) chief, prince (f. *ald* OLD + *-or* as in OE. *baldor* prince) + MAN. Hence **alderman**IC -mæ·nik XVIII; †**-ma·n**ICAL XVII; replacing earlier *aldermanlike*.

Aldine æ·ldain, ɔ̄·ldain designation of editions of Gr. and L. classics printed or published by Aldo Manuzio and his family (1450–1597). XIX. – modL. *Aldīnus*, f. *Aldus*, latinized form of *Aldo*; see -INE[1].

ale eil liquor made from an infusion of malt. OE. *alu* (*ealu*), g., d. *aloþ* (*ealoþ*), g. pl. *ealeþa* = OS. *alo-* and OHG. *al-* (each in rare comps.), ON. *ǫl* :– Germ. **aluþ-* (*t*-stem); dubiously connected with L. *alūmen* ALUM, *alūta* leather prepared with alum. OSl. *olŭ*, Lith. *alùs* may be from Germ. Only Eng. retains both *ale* and *beer*, the Scand. langs. only *ale*, and the other Germ. langs. only *beer*.

aleatory ei·liətəri depending on a throw of the dice. XVII. – L. *āleātōrius*, f. *āleātor* dicer, f. *ālea* die, dice; see -ORY[2].

alecost ei·lkɔst the plant Chrysanthemum Balsamita, formerly used for giving a flavour to ale. XVI. f. ALE+*cost* – L. *costum* – Gr. *kóstos* plant used as a spice.

alee əlī· (naut.) on or to the lee side. XIV. f. A-[1]+LEE[1], partly after ON. *á hlé*.

alegar æ·ligəɹ, ei·ligəɹ malt vinegar. XIV. f. ALE+*-eger*, *-egar* (see EAGER) of *vinegar*. Cf. †*beeregar* (XV) vinegar made from beer.

alehoof ei·lhūf ground-ivy, Nepeta Glechoma. XIV. prob. alteration of *hayhove*, f. *hay* hedge, OE. *heġe*+*hōfe* (also in *tūnhōfe* 'garden hove'); there appears to be an allusion to its alleged use in brewing instead of hops.

Aleman(n)ic, Alle-, Ala- ælĭmæ·nik. XVIII. – late L. *Alemannicus*, f. *Alemannī* pl. (Gr. *'Alamanoí*), Germanic tribe first mentioned by Dio Cassius s.a. 213 – Germ. **Alamanniz* (cf. ON. *almanna-* general, public, Goth. *alamannam* d. pl. mankind), prob. f. ALL+MAN and so denoting a wide alliance of peoples; see -IC.

alembic əle·mbik distilling apparatus. XIV (Ch.). Late ME. *alambic*, *alembike* – OF. *alembic* (mod. *alambic*; cf. Sp. *alambique*, It. *lambicco*) – medL. *alembicus* – Arab. *al-anbīq*, i.e. *al* AL-[2], *anbīq* still – Gr. *ambīk-*, *ámbix* cup, beaker, cap of a still. Almost superseded by the aphetic *limbeck* (earlier *lembik*) from XV to XVII, when the full form again came into vogue. So **ale·mbicated**, over-refined or subtilized. XVIII. – F. *alembiqué*; see -ATE[3], -ED[1].

alerion əliə·riən (her.) footless and beakless eagle. XVII. – F. *alérion* (cf. medL. *alario*) – (with L. suffix *-iōn-*) OHG. *adelare* (G. *adler*), f. *adel* noble (see ATHELING)+*ar* (G. *aar*) eagle (see ERNE).

alert əlɔ̄·ɹt on the look-out; lively, nimble. XVII. – F. *alerte*, earlier *allerte*, *à l'airte* – It. *all' erta* on the watch or look-out, i.e. *alla* at the, *erta* look-out (tower), sb. use (sc. *torre* tower) of fem. pp. of *ergere* :– L. *erigere* ERECT; orig. an adv. phr., it became an adj. used predicatively, then a sb. (*on the alert* is etymologically pleonastic).

alexandrine æligzà·ndrain, -ks- pert. to verse of twelve syllables (the F. *vers héroïque*). XVI. – F. *alexandrin* (XV), f. *Alexandre*, title of a famous OF. romance (XII–XIII) concerning Alexander the Great, in which the metre is used; see -INE[1].

alexin əle·ksin (biol. chem.) substance having the property of destroying bacteria. XIX. – G. *alexin* (Buchner, 1888), f. Gr. *aléxein* ward off; see -IN.

alexipharmic əleksifā·ɹmik (that is) an antidote to poison. XVII. Alteration, by assim. to -IC, of †*alexipharmac* – F. *alexipharmaque* – modL. *alexipharmacum* – Gr. *alexiphármakon*, n. sg. of adj. f. *aléxein* ward off +*phármakon* poison (cf. PHARMACY).

alfalfa ælfæ·lfə variety of lucerne. XIX. – Sp. *alfalfa*, formerly *alfalfez* – Arab. *al-façfaçaḥ* 'the best sort of fodder'.

al fresco æl fre·skou in the open air. XVIII. It. phr. *al fresco* 'in the FRESH'. Cf. FRESCO.

alga æ·lgə pl. **algæ** æ·ldʒī seaweed. XVI. L.

algebra æ·ldʒibrə †bone-setting (as in obs. Sp.) XIV; department of mathematics using general symbols. XVI. – It., Sp., medL. *alge·bra* – Arab. *aljebr*, i.e. *al* AL-[2], *jebr* reunion of broken parts, f. *jabara* reunite, redintegrate. The full Arabic term for algebraic computation was *'ilm aljebr wa'lmuqābalah* science of redintegration and equation, the first part of which was taken into It. in XIII, the second, *almucabala*, being used by some medL. writers in the same sense. The str. *a·lgebra* is shown in Butler's 'Hudibras' (I i 126), 1663. Recorde, the earliest user of the math. term, has the form *algeber*, directly repr. the Arabic; Billingsley, Dee, and Digges have *algebra*. Hence **algebra**IC -brei·ik XVII, -ICAL XVI; **a·lgebra**IST XVII, which was preceded by †**algebri**·CIAN XVI–XVII. The retention of *-a* in the derivs. is abnormal, but is paralleled by Sp. *algebraico*; more regular forms are seen in F. *algébrique*, It. *algebrico*, Sp., It. *algebrista*.

-algia æ·ldʒ[i]ə terminal el. repr. Gr. *-algiā*, comb. deriv. of *álgos* pain, rel. to *alégein* be anxious, as in *kephalalgiā* headache, *neuralgiā* NEURALGIA. The corr. adj. ends in **-a·lg**IC.

algid æ·ldʒid cool, chill. XVII. – L. *algidus*, f. *algēre* be cold; see -ID[1].

Algonkin, -quin ælgɔ·nkin N. Amer. Indian tribal name. XVII. – F. *Algonquin*, †*Algonkain*, contr. of †*Algoumequin*; cf. Micmac *algoomeaking* at the place of spearing fish and eels, f. *algoome* spear fish. Hence **Algo·nk**IAN, **-qu**IAN applied to a large family including the Algonquins, and to the languages spoken by any member of it. XIX.

algorism æ·lgərizm Arabic system of numeration, arithmetic. XIII. Earliest form *augrim*, later *algorisme* – OF. *augori(s)me*, *algorisme* – medL. *algorismus* (cf. Sp. *guarismo* cypher), f. (with assim. to *-ismus*

-ISM) Arab. *al-Khowārazmī* the man of Khwārazm (ancient name of Khiva), surname of the Arab mathematician Abu Ja'far Mohammed Ben Musa (IX), through the European translation of whose work on algebra the Arabic numerals became generally known. Cf. the use of *Euclid* for plane geometry. (By contamination with Gr. *árithmos* number, a form *algorithm* became current XVII–XIX.)

alguazil ælgwazi·l, Sp. algwaþi·l justiciary; sergeant; minion. XVI. Early Sp. *alguazil* (now *alguacil*) – Arab. *al-wazīr*, i.e. *al* AL-², *wazīr* minister, officer, VIZIER.

algum æ·lgəm tree of the Bible (2 Chron. ii 8, erron. *almug* 1 Kings x 11), variously identified. XVI. Heb. *algūm*.

Alhambra ǽlhæ·mbrə ancient royal Moorish palace at Granada. XVII. – Sp. – Arab. *al-hamra'* 'the red', i.e. *al* AL-² and fem. of *ahmar*, named after Muhammad Ben al Ahmar, who built it in 1273.

alias ei·liǣs otherwise named XVI; another (assumed) name XVII. – L. *aliās* at another time, otherwise, f. *alius* (cf. ELSE).

alibi æ·libai (leg.) †elsewhere; plea of having been elsewhere. XVIII. – L. *alibī*, f. *alius* other (see ELSE), with loc. ending after *ibī* there, *ubī* where.

alidad æ·lidæd index of an astrolabe, etc. XV. orig. in medL. forms *allidatha*, *alhidada* (cf. Sp. *alhi-*, *alidada*) – Arab. *al-ʿiḍādah* revolving radius of a graduated circle, f. *ʿaḍd*, *ʿaḍid* upper arm, radius; later – F. *alidade*.

alien ei·liən not one's own, foreign. XIV (R. Rolle). – OF. *alien* – L. *aliēnus* belonging to another person or place, f. *alius* other (see ELSE). For the freq. ME. forms in *-nt*, e.g. *aliente*, *alia(u)nt*, cf. *ancient*. So **a·lien** vb. XIV (Ch.) – (O)F. *aliéner*; earlier synon. of **a·lienate** estrange (XVI), which was preceded by the pp. †*alienate* (XV) – L. *aliēnātus*, pp. of *aliēnāre*; see -ATE³. **a·lien**ABLE. XVII. – F. **alien**A·TION. XIV (Wycl. Bible). – (O)F. or L. **a·lien**IST. XIX. – F. *aliéniste*.

alight¹ əlai·t come or get down, dismount OE.; settle *on* XIII. OE. *ālīhtan*; see A-³, LIGHT⁴.

alight² əlai·t lighted, on fire. XVIII. prob. evolved from phr. †*on* (also *of*, *in*) *a light fire* (XVI–XVIII) ablaze, where *light* appears to be pp. of LIGHT³ kindle, ignite.

align, aline əlai·n place in line. XVII. – (O)F. *aligner*, f. phr. *à ligne*, repr. L. *ad lineam* in a straight line (see AD-, LINE²). So **ali·gn**MENT. XVIII. – (O)F. *alignement*.

alike əlai·k (adj. used predic., rarely otherwise) like one another. OE. *ġelīċ* (ME. *ilich-e*, *ilik-e*; *a-* forms from XIV) = OFris. *gelīk*, OS. *gelīc* (Du. *gelijk*), OHG. *galīh* (G. *gleich*), ON. *glíkr*, Goth. *galeiks* :– CGerm. **galīkaz*, f. **ga-* Y-+**līkam* form, body (see LYCHGATE); for the development of OE. *ġe-* to *a-* cf. AFFORD, AWARE. See LIKE. So **ali·ke** adv. OE. *ġelīċe*, f. *ġelīċ* with adv. ending *-e*. In ME. both words were prob. reinforced, or superseded in certain areas, by ON. adj. *álíkr*, adv. *álíka*, which corr. to OE. *anlīċ*, *onlīċ*, *anlīċe*, OHG. *analīh*, Goth. *analeiks*, in which the prefix is Germ. **ana-* (see ON).

aliment æ·limĕnt nourishment, food. XV (rare before XVII). – F. *aliment* or L. *alimentum*, f. *alere* nourish, f. **al-* grow (cf. OLD); see -MENT. So **alime·nt**ARY. XVII. – L.

alimony æ·liməni maintenance, spec. of a separated wife by her husband. XVII. – L. *alimōnia*, f. *alere*; see prec. and -MONY.

aliquot æ·likwɔt (math.) of a quantity contained exactly in another. XVI (Billingsley). – F. *aliquote* (*les parties aliquotes* XV), medL. *aliquota* fem. (in AL. *partes aliquotæ* XIII), f. L. *aliquot* some, several, f. *alius* one of two (cf. ALIEN)+*quot* how many (cf. QUOTIENT).

-ality æ·lĭti comp. suffix – (O)F. *-alité* – L. *-ālitāt-*, *-tās*; see -AL¹, -ITY.

alive əlai·v living. OE. phr. *on līfe*, ME. *on livë*, *olive*, *alive*; i.e. ON (cf. A-¹) and *līfe*, d. sg. of *līf* LIFE. *On live* is found as late as XVII.

alkahest, alc- æ·lkəhest universal solvent of alchemists. XVII. First used by Paracelsus, and believed to have been arbitrarily invented by him with a form simulating Arabic (*al* AL-²).

alkali æ·lkəlai †soda ash XIV; saltwort, Salsola Kali XVI; gen. applied to substances having the properties of soda XVII; (mod. chem.) hydroxide of sodium, potassium, etc. XIX. Late ME. *alcaly* – medL. *alkali* – Arab. *al-qalīy* calcined ashes of Salsola and Salicornia, f. *qalay* fry, roast; see AL-², KALI. Cf. F. *alcali* (XVI). So **a·lka**LINE XVII; see -INE and cf. F. *alcalin* (1700). **a·lkal**OID. XIX. – G. *alkaloid*.

alkanet æ·lkənet (plant, Anchusa or Alkanna tinctoria, yielding) a dye. (XIV) XV. – Sp. *alcaneta*, f. *alcana* (medL. *alchanna*), corr. to OF. *alchanne*, *arcanne* – Arab. *al-ḥennā*; see AL-², HENNA.

alkekengi ælkike·ndʒi winter cherry, Physalis Alkekengi. XIV. – medL. – Arab. *al-kākanj*, *-kenj*, i.e. *al* AL-², Pers. *kākanj* kind of medicinal resin, (also) nightshade.

all ɔ̄l every; entire; the whole of; also adv. OE. *all*, (*eall*) = OFris. *al*, *ol*, OS., OHG. *al* (Du. *al*, G. *all*), ON. *allr*, Goth. *alls*, prob. :– CGerm. **alnaz*, ppl. formation on **al-*, which is found also in OS., OHG. *alung* completely, and the prefix **ala-* of Goth. *alaniuwi* quite new, *alawāri* quite true, *alamannam* (see ALEMANIC), and has been referred to IE. **ol-*, repr. by (O)Ir. *uile* all (:– **oljo-*), W. *oll* (:– **oljod*) wholly.

Allah æ·lə the deity among the Mohammedans. XVI. – Arab. *allāh*, for *al-ilāh*, i.e. *al* AL-², *ilāh* god = Aram. *elāh*, Heb. *elōah* (see ELOHIST). (Early forms in Eng. writers are *Alla, Allah, Ala, Alà, Allough, Alha.*)

allantois əlæ·ntouis (anat.) fœtal membrane lying between amnion and chorion. XVII. modL., spurious form evolved from *allantoīdes* – Gr. *allantoeidḗs* sausage-shaped (Galen), f. *allanto-, allâs* sausage; see -OID.

allay əlei· †lay aside OE.; put down, repress, quell; appease, assuage XIV; dilute, temper XV; mitigate XVIII. OE. *alecġan*, pt. *aleġde, alēde*, pp. *aleġd, alēd*, ME. *alegge* (*aleide, aleid*), superseded by *aleie, alay* (cf. LAY[1]). The sense-development has been infl. by formal assoc. with OF. *aleger*, lighten (:– L. *alleviāre* ALLEVIATE) and *aleier, alier* (:– L. *alligāre*) ALLOY, temper, qualify.

allegation æligei·ʃən charge or matter to be proved XV; affirmation of a thing to be proved XV; assertion without proof XVII. – (O)F. *allégation* or L. *allēgātiō(n-)*, f. *allēgāre* depute, bring forward, adduce, f. *ad* AL-+*lēgāre* dispatch, commission (cf. LEGATE); see -ATION. Used as the noun of action of next.

allege əle·dʒ †declare before a tribunal, plead; cite, quote; advance as a reason; assert without proof. XIV. – AN. *alegier*, for OF. *esligier* :– Rom. **exlītigare* clear at law, f. L. *ex* EX-+*līt-, lis* lawsuit (see LITIGATE); used in the senses of L. *allegāre* (see prec.), whence F. *alléguer* (which cannot be the source of *allege*).

allegiance əlī·dʒəns relation of a liege man to his lord; obligation of a subject. XIV. – AN. **alligeance* (AL. *alligantia*), f. OF. *ligeance* (AL. *ligantia*), f. *lige* LIEGE (see -ANCE); so contemp. †*ligeance* – OF.; the prefixing of *al-* was perh. due to assoc. with *alligantia* ALLIANCE.

allegory æ·ligəri figurative description or narrative. XIV. – (O)F. *allégorie* – L. *allēgoria* – Gr. *allēgoríā* 'speaking otherwise', f. *állos* other (cf. ALLO-)+*agor-*, as in *agoreúein* speak, *agorā́* public assembly; see -Y[3]. So **allegor**IC æligɔ·rik XIV, **allego·r**ICAL XVI. **a·llegor**IZE. XV. F. *allégoriser* – late L. *allēgorizāre* (Jerome).

allegro ælei·grou (mus.) lively. XVII (Purcell). It., repr. L. *alacer* brisk (see ALACRITY). ¶ Familiar from the title of Milton's poem 'L'Allegro', 1632, 'the cheerful one'.

alleluia ælilū·jə XIV. – eccl. L. *allēluia* – Gr. *allēloúïa*, the LXX repr. of Heb. HALLELUJAH. As applied in medL. (and It.) to the wood-sorrel, Oxalis Acetosella, it may be a perversion of some vernacular name.

allergy æ·ləɹdʒi sensitiveness to certain foods, emanations, etc. XX. – G. *allergie* (Pirquet, 1906), f. Gr. *állos* other, ALLO-+*érgon* WORK+-Y[3] (cf. *energy*); orig. denoting a changed condition brought about by an injection. Hence **alle·rg**IC hypersensitive (hence, antipathetic) *to*. So **allergen** ælə̄·ɹdʒin substance to which a body is allergic; with *-en* after *pollen*.

alleviate əlī·vieit lighten, mitigate. XV. f. pp. stem of late L. *alleviāre*, f. *ad* AL-[1]+*levis* LIGHT[2]; see -ATE[3]. The L. verb was repr. earlier by †*allege* (XIV–XVI) – OF. *alegier* (mod. *alléger*) = Pr. *aleujar*, It. *alleggiare*; cf. ALLAY.

alley[1] æ·li walk, passage; enclosure for bowls, etc. XIV. – OF. *alee* (mod. *allée*) walking, passage, f. *aller* walk, go (:– L. *ambulāre* walk; cf. AMBLE).

alley[2], **ally** æ·li toy marble. XVIII. Familiar dim. (see -Y[6]) of ALABASTER. Cf. the similar use of LG., Du. *albast*.

all fours ōl fōəɹz In the sense 'all four extremities' orig. *all four* XVI; the name of the card-game has always been *all-fours* XVIII.

All Hallows ōl hæ·louz (feast of) All Saints, 1 November. OE. *ealra hālgena dæġ* day of all saints; hence, with retention of the g. pl. inflexion, ME. *alle halewene day* (XIII), *alhalwen* (XIV), *all halown* (XV), *all holland, allhollondaye* (XVI), etc.; with loss of this, *al halow, al hal* (XIV), *alhalwgh* (XV), etc.; with substitution of *-s* from XV. See HALLOW, HALLOWE'EN, HALLOWMAS.

alliaceous æliei·ʃəs (bot.) of the genus Allium (garlic, onion, etc.). XVIII. f. modL. *alliāceus*, f. L. *allium* garlic; see -ACEOUS.

alliance əlai·əns union by marriage; confederation. XIII. – OF. *aliance* (mod. *alliance*), f. *alier* ALLY[2]; see -ANCE.

alligator æ·ligeitəɹ reptile of the crocodile family, cayman. XVII. Earlier forms *lagarto, aligarto, alagarto* (XVI) – Sp. *el lagarto* the lizard (repr. **lacarto* for L. *lacerta* LIZARD), which was applied spec. to the large saurians of the New World. The 1st Folio (1623) edition of Sh. 'Romeo & Juliet' v i 43 has *Allegater*, the 1st Quarto (1597) *Aligarta*. ¶ *Alligator pear* (XVIII) is a corruption of AVOCADO *pear*.

alliteration əlitərei·ʃən commencement of words in a passage with the same letter, prop. with the same or the same kind of sound. XVII. – modL. *alliterātiō(n-)* rhet. repeating and playing upon the same letter, f. *ad* AL-[1]+*litera* LETTER, after L. *agnōminātiō* paronomasia; see -ATION. Hence **alli·terate(d), alli·ter**ATIVE. XVIII.

allo- æ·lo, ælɔ· comb. form of Gr. *állos* other (see ELSE).

allocate æ·lŏkeit allot to a place. XVII (before XIX only Sc.). f. pp. stem of medL. *allocāre*, f. L. *ad* AL-[1]+*locāre* place, LOCATE, after pp. †*allocat* (XVI). So **alloca·**TION. XV. – F. – medL.

allocution ælŏkjū·ʃən address, exhortation. XVII. – L. *allocūtiō(n-)*, f. *allocūt-, alloquī* address, f. *ad* AL-[1]+*loquī* speak (see LOCUTION).

allodium əlou·diəm estate held in absolute ownership. XVII. – medL. *allōdium* (Domesday Book), f. Frankish **allōd-* 'entire property' (in latinized forms *alodis, alaudes*), f. *all* ALL+*ōd* (OHG. *ōt*, OE. *ēad*, ON. *auðr*) estate, property, wealth. Also (anglicized) **al(l)od** æ·lɔd. XVII. So **allo·dIAL**. XVII. – medL.

allopathy ælɔ·pəþi)(*homœopathy*. XIX. – G. *allopathie*, f. Gr. *állos* other+*-pátheia*, *páthos* suffering. So **allopath** æ·lopæþ – F. *allopathe*, back-formation from *allopathie*. **allopa·thIC**. – F. See ALLO-, PATHOS.

allot əlɔ·t assign, orig. by lot. XVI. – OF. *aloter* (repl. by mod. *allotir*), f. *a* AD-, AL-[1]+ *lot* (of Germ. origin); see LOT. Hence **allo·t-MENT** action of allotting XVI; portion of land allotted XVII.

allotropy əlɔ·trəpi variation of physical properties without change of substance. XIX. – modL. *allotropia* – Gr. *allotropíā* variation, f. *allótropos* of another form, f. *állos* ALLO-+*trópos* manner (cf. TROPE); see -Y[3].

allow əlau· A. (arch.) commend; admit, accept; permit; B. assign, allot. XIV. – OF. *alouer*, later *all-* :– (i) L. *allaudāre*, f. *ad* AL-[1]+*laudāre* praise, LAUD, (ii) medL. *allocāre*, f. *ad* AL-[1]+*locāre* place, stow, ALLOCATE. The phonetic identification in OF. of the orig. distinct forms involved semantic conflation and the development of a variety of meanings in which the two main senses were blended, e.g. assign with approval, grant, concede, permit. So **allow·ABLE** (aphetic †*lowable*) – OF. *allouable*. XIV. **allow·ANCE**. XIV. – OF. *alouance*.

alloy əloi·, æ·loi admixture of metals; inferior metal of a mixture; quality, standard. XVI. – (O)F. *aloi* (orig. in phr. *de bon aloi* of good mixture), f. OF. *aloier*, earlier *aleier* = Pr. *aliar*, Sp. *allegar*, It. *allegare* :– L. *alligāre*, f. *ad* AL-[1]+*ligāre* bind (cf. ALLY[2], LIEN). So **alloy·** vb. XVII. – F. *aloyer*, f. *aloi*; superseded †*allay* sb. and vb. (XIV) – (O)F. *alei, aleier*.

allspice ɔ̄·lspais Jamaica pepper. XVII. f. ALL+SPICE, so called because supposed to combine the flavour of cinnamon, nutmeg, and cloves.

allude əlʲū·d †'play' with or upon; refer indirectly (*to*). XVI. – L. *allūdere* play or dally with, touch lightly upon, f. *ad* AL-[1]+ *lūdere* engage in play, f. *lūdus* play, game (cf. LUDICROUS). So **allu**SION əlʲū·ʒən. XVI. – F. *allusion* or late L. *allūsiō(n-)*, f. pp. of *allūdere*.

allure əljuə·ɹ attract strongly, entice. XV. – OF. *alurer*, f. *a-* AD-, AL-[1]+*lure* falconer's bait, LURE.

alluvion əlʲū·viən wash of sea against shore; flood; alluvium. XVI. – F. *alluvion* – L. *alluviō(n-)*, f. *ad* AL-[1]+*-luviō*, f. *luere* (see ABLUTION).

alluvium əlʲū·viəm deposit left by water flowing over land. XVII. L., n. of *alluvius* washed against, f. *ad* AL-[1]+*luv-* of *luere* (cf. prec.). Hence **allu·vIAL** XIX, earlier **allu·vIAN**, **allu·vIOUS** XVIII.

ally[1] æ·lai, əlai· A. †kindred, kinsman XIV; B. allied person or people XV. In A, – (O)F. *allié*, sb. use of pp. of *allier* (see next). For the loss of final *é* cf. ASSIGN[2], COSTIVE, TAIL[2], TROVE. In early Sc. repr. by *allya, alye* (3 syll.), which are used for 'ally', 'allies', and 'alliance'. In B, f. next; the str. *a·lly* is found XVII.

ally[2] əlai· join as associate or confederate. XIII. – OF. *alier*, analogical alteration of *aleier* (see ALLOY).

alma(h) æ·lmə Egyptian dancing-girl. XIX (Byron). – Arab. *'ālimat* adj. fem. learned (i.e. instructed in music and dancing), f. *'alama* know. (In F. *almée*.)

almacantar ælməkæ·ntāɹ (pl.) parallels of altitude. XIV (Ch.). – OF. *almicantarat* or medL. *almicantarath* – Arab. *almuqanṭarāt* pl. sundial, f. *qanṭarah* bridge, arch; see AL-[2].

almagest æ·lmədʒest orig. the great astronomical treatise of Ptolemy (II), 'Mathēmatikē súntaxis'. XIV. – OF. *almageste*, ult. – Arab. *al-majisṭī* – (with *al*, AL-[2]) Gr. *megístē* greatest (sc. *súntaxis* composition), superl. fem. of *mégas* great (see MAGNITUDE).

Alma Mater æ·lmə mei·təɹ. XVII. L., 'bounteous mother' (*alma*, fem. of *almus*, f. *alere* nourish; cf. ALIMENT); title given by the Romans to Ceres, Cybele, and other bounteous goddesses, transf. to universities and schools as the fostering mothers of their alumni.

almanac ɔ̄·lmənæk annual table containing essentially a calendar of days and months with astronomical data and computations. XIV (*almenak*, Ch.). – medL. *almanac(h)* (Roger Bacon, 1267); the only authenticated antecedent form with which this may be connected is late Gr. *almenikhiaká* (Eusebius, IV), described as containing the names of the lords of the ascendant and their properties; the formal relation of *almanac* to this is obscure; a supposed Arab. *al-manākh*, invented to account for the medL. and Rom. forms (It. *almanacco*, Sp. *almanaque*, F. *almanach*), is non-existent.

almandine ælmæ·ndin, -ain variety of garnet. XVII (in XIX poet.). – F. †*almandine*, alteration of †*alabandine* (in ME. *alabaundryne* XIV) – late L. *alabandīna* (sc. *gemma* gem), f. *Alabanda* city of Caria; see -INE[1].

almighty ɔ̄lmai·ti. OE. *ælmihtiġ*, corr. to OFris. *elmachtich*, OS. *alomahtig*, OHG. *alamahtīc*, ON. *almáttigr*; f. prefix form of ALL + MIGHTY, rendering L. *omnipotens* OMNIPOTENT.

almoign, almoin, AN. var. of ALMS.

almond ā·mənd (fruit of) the tree Amygdalus communis. XIII (Cursor M.). – OF. *alemande, a(l)mande* (mod. *amande*), for **almandle* – medL. *amandula* (cf. Sp. *almendra*, Pg. *amendoa*, It. *mandola, mandorla*, OHG. *mandala*, G. *mandel*), alteration of L. *amygdala* – Gr. *amugdálē*; initial *al-*

appears to be due to assoc. with Rom. words having AL-[2] prefixed.

almoner ā·mənəɹ, æ·lmənəɹ official distributor of alms. XIII (Cursor M.). – AN. *aumoner*, OF. *aumonier*, earlier *au-*, *a(u)lmosnier* (mod. *aumônier*) :– Rom. **almosināriu-s*, for medL. *eleēmosynārius* ELEEMOSINARY, used sb.; see -ER[2] and cf. ALMS.

almost ɔ̄·lmoust, -məst OE. *ælmǣst* nearly all, for the most part (cf. *mǣst eall* 'for the most part entirely'); see ALL and MOST; substitution of -MOST for the regularly developed *-mest* was established XIV.

alms āmz charitable gift. OE. *ælmysse*, *-messe*, whence *almes* (XIII–XVII; so in A.V.), reduced to *alms* XVII; corr. to OFris. *ielmisse*, OS. *alamosna* (MDu. *aelmoese*, Du. *aalmoes*), OHG. *alamuosan* (G. *almosen*), ON. *ǫlmusa* :– Germ. **alemos(i)na* – popL., Rom. **alimosina* (Pr., OSp. *almosna*, OF. *almosne*, modF. *aumône*, It. *limosina*), alteration, prob. through L. *alimōnia* ALIMONY, of Christian L. *eleēmosyna* (Tertullian) – Gr. *eleēmosúnē* compassionateness, f. *eleḗmōn* compassionate, f. *éleos* mercy. In OE. the orig. *-n* was treated as if inflexional and disappeared from the nom.; ME. vars. are †*almose* XIII, *almoin* (AN.) XIV, Sc. *almous*, *awmous* (– ON. *ǫlmusa*); †*almosna*, †*almoise* XV (cf. AN. *almosne*, *almoisne*). ¶ Treated as a pl. like *eaves*, *riches*, which are orig. sgs.

almuce see AMICE.

almug æ·lmʌg XVII (A.V.) erron. form of ALGUM.

aloe æ·lou †lignaloes XIV; liliaceous genus of plants with a bitter juice, whence is made a drug XIV (Trev.). OE. *al(e)we* – L. *aloē* – Gr. *alóē* plant and drug, (also) lignaloes (used in LXX tr. Heb. *akhalōth*); in late ME. reinforced by OF. *aloes* (mod. *aloès*) or its source, *aloēs*, g. sg. of L. *aloē*, as in LIGNALOES; whence the frequent use of the word in pl. form.

aloft əlɔ̀·ft on high. XII (Orm). ME. *o loft(e)* – ON. *á lopt* (of motion), *á lopti* (of position), i.e. *á* in, on, to, A-[1], *lopt* air, sky (rel. to OE. *lyft*, OHG. *luft*, Goth. *luftus* air; cf. LOFT, LIFT).

alone əlou·n by oneself, itself, themselves. XIII. ME. *al ane*, *al one*, i.e. OE. *all* entirely (ALL), *āna* by oneself (f. *ān* ONE). In ME. sometimes written *a lone* (whence LONE); also with pron. inserted, as *al him one* he quite by himself. The pronunc. with oun is as in ATONE and ONLY, as opp. to WʌN in ONE (cf. ONCE).

along[1] əlɔ·ŋ (dial.) *along of* belonging or owing to. OE. *ġelang* (with preps. *on*, *æt*) depending, belonging = OS. *gilang* ready, OHG. *gilang* neighbouring; WGerm. f. **gi-* Y- + **laŋg-*; cf. next and BELONG.

along[2] əlɔ·ŋ through the length of OE.; lengthwise, in a line forward XIV; in company *with* XVI (Sh.). OE. *andlang*, advb. use (with genitive) of adj. meaning 'extending in same direction', 'continuous' = OS. *antlang*, f. **and-* opposite (see ANTI-) + **laŋg-* extend (cf. LONG[1]). For the assim. of *nl* to *ll* and ult. simplification to *l* cf. *eleven*; the stages were *andlong*, *anlong*, *allong*, *along* (assim. appears early in OE. *ollung*, but was not gen. before XIV). Hence **alo·ng**SHORE, **alo·ng**SIDE XVIII.

aloof əlū·f (naut.) †order to the steersman to go to windward; to or at a distance. XVI. Early forms are *a luf*, *aloufe*, *alowfe*, *on luffe*, i.e. *a*, ON, A-[1], LUFF, prob. after Du. *te loef*.

alopecia æloupī·ʃ[1]ə (med.) mangy baldness. XIV. – L. *alōpecia* – Gr. *alōpekíā*, f. *alōpek-*, *-pēx* fox; so named from the resemblance to mange in foxes.

aloud əlaud with a loud voice. XIV (PPl., Ch.). f. A-[1] + LOUD. (An earlier syn. was †*ahigh*, opp. to †*alow*.)

Alp ælp (pl.) proper name of a mountain system in Switzerland, etc. XIV. – F. *Alpes* – L. *Alpēs* = Gr. *Álpeis*, variously explained as (i) 'white' (snow-capped) and so rel. to ALBION, Ir. *Alba* Scotland, and (ii) 'high' (cf. the Italic names of towns in high positions). So **Alp**INE[1]. XV. – L.

alpaca ælpæ·kə Peruvian llama, its wool, fabric made from this. XVIII. – Sp. *alpaca* (also *paco*) – Quichua *alpako* (also *pako*, *pakollama*), f. *pako* reddish-brown.

alphabet æ·lfəbet letters used in a language. XV. – late L. *alphabētum* (Tertullian), f. Gr. *álpha* + *bêta*, first two letters of the Gr. alphabet taken to repr. the whole, like ABC; cf. F. *alphabet*, It. *alfabeto*, etc. Hence **alphabet·**IC XVII, -ICAL XVI; cf. F. *alphabétique*, It. *alfabetico*, etc. **a·lphabet**IZE XIX.

already ɔ̄lre·di by this or that time. XIV. orig. two words, ALL adv. and READY, used predic. 'fully prepared', passing into adv. (e.g. *He is al redy heere* 'He is here just at hand', Ch. 'Clerk's Tale' 299, shows the possibility of transition). Cf. MLG. *al(ge)rede* (where *gerede* corr. to OE. *ġerǣde*), whence OSw. *alla* or *alt redho* (Sw. *allaredan*), Da. *allerede*.

Alsatian ælsei·ʃ[1]ən *A. wolfhound* (also sb.), German sheepdog XX. f. *Alsatia* Elsasz, Alsace.

alsike æ·lsik the clover Trifolium hybridum. XIX. f. *Alsike* name of a town near Uppsala, Sweden, its habitat.

also ɔ̄·lsou in addition, besides. OE. *alswā* (*ealswā*) = OFris. *alsa*, Du. *alzoo* thus, consequently, OHG. *alsō* even so, as (G. *also* therefore); i.e. ALL + SO, lit. 'altogether or even so or thus'. See AS[1].

Altaic æltei·ik Ugro-Finnish (group of languages). XIX. – F. *altaïque*, f. *Altai*, a mountain range in Central Asia; see -IC.

altar ɔ̄·ltəɹ table for sacrificial offering. OE. *altar*, *alter*, corr. to OFris. *altare*, *alter*, OS., OHG., ON. *altari*, *alteri*; Germ. adoption of late L. *altar*, *altāre*, *altārium* for L. *altāria* n. pl. burnt offerings, altar, prob. rel. to *adolēre* burn in sacrifice, *adolēscere* burn (cf. *olēre* smell, and ODOUR). Forms repr. OF. *auter* appear XIII; finally the present form, infl. by L., was established XVI. ¶ The native OE. word was *wēofod*, *wēobed*, *wīgbēod* 'idol-table'; the alien word was applied spec. to the Christian altar.

altazimuth æltæ·zimʌþ (astron.) instrument for determining the altitude and azimuth. XIX (Airy). f. ALT|ITUDE + AZIMUTH.

alter ɔ̄·ltəɹ make different, change. XIV (Ch.). – (O)F. *altérer* – late L. *alterāre*, f. *alter* other (orig. one of two), f. **al-* (see ELSE) + compar. suffix **-tero-* -THER. So **alter**A·TION. XIV. – (O)F. or late L. **a·lter**ATIVE adj. and sb. (med.) XIV. – medL.

altercation ɔ̄ltəɹkei·ʃən wordy strife. XIV (Ch.). – (O)F. *altercation* – L. *altercātiō(n-)*, f. *altercāt-*, *-āre* wrangle (whence **a·ltercate** XVI), f. **altercus*, parallel formation to *alternus*; see next and -ATION.

alternate ɔ̄ltɔ̄·ɹnət occurring in turn. XVI. – L. *alternātus*, pp. of *alternāre* do things by turns, f. *alternus*, f. *alter* one or other of two, second (see ALTER). So **alternate** ɔ̄·ltəɹneit XVI; cf. F. *alterner*; see -ATE[2] and [3]. **alterna**·TION. XV. – F. or L. **alte·rn**ATIVE. XVII. – medL.

althæa ælþī·ə genus of plants. XVII. L. – Gr. *althaíā* marsh-mallow, f. *álthein* heal (base **al-* grow, nourish, as in L. *alere* nourish).

althing ɔ̄·lþiŋ general parliament of Iceland. XIX. Icel. *alþing*, ON. *alþingi* general assembly; see ALL, THING.

although ɔ̄lðou·, (Sc.) ɔ̄lþo· even if. XIV. ME. *al þah*, *þa(u)ȝ*, *þo(u)ȝ*, i.e. ALL adv., THOUGH; varying with *þouȝ al* (XIV), which presumably descends from OE. *þēah . . eal* (recorded once in 'Beowulf' 680); ME. *al (ȝ)if*, *(ȝ)if al* were similarly used; for the use of *al* cf. ALBEIT.

altitude æ·ltitjūd height. XIV (Ch., in astron. sense). – L. *altitūdō*, f. *altus* high; see OLD, -TUDE.

alto æ·ltou highest male voice, countertenor. XVIII. – It. *alto* high (sc. *canto* song) :– L. *altu-s* high (cf. prec.)

altogether ɔ̄ltəge·ðəɹ †the whole together (now usu. *all together*); in every respect, entirely. XII. Early ME. *al togedre*, i.e. ALL (sb. the whole, adv. in every way), TOGETHER.

altruism æ·ltruizm devotion to the welfare of others. XIX. – F. *altruisme* (A. Comte, 1830), f. It. *altrui* somebody else, what is another's (cf. F. *autrui*) :– Rom. **alterī huic* 'to this other'; prob. suggested by the legal use of F. *l'autrui* for *le bien* or *le droit d'autrui* the welfare or the rights of others. Hence **a·ltru**IST, **altru**I·STIC.

aludel æ·ljudel sublimating vessel. XVI (*alutel* XIV). – F. *aludel* – Sp. – Arab. *al-'uthāl* 'the apparatus' (pl. of *athla* utensil); see AL-[2].

alum æ·ləm astringent whitish mineral salt, used (e.g.) in dressing skins. XIV. – OF. *alum* (mod. *alun*) :– L. *alūmen*, rel. to *alūta* tawed leather.

aluminium æljŭmi·niəm (chem.) metallic element. XIX. Alteration (in imitation of *potassium*, *sodium*, etc.) of *aluminum*, Humphrey Davy's modification (1812) of the form first suggested by him, viz. *alumium* (1808). *Aluminum* is parallel to *alumina* (XVIII), modL. formation on the type of *magnesia*, *potassa*, *soda*, for the 'earth of alum', aluminium oxide; f. L. *alūmin-*, *alūmen* ALUM, whence L. *alūminōsus* (F. *alumineux*), the source of **alumin**OUS əljū·minəs XVI.

alumnus əlʌ·mnəs pupil of a school, etc. XVII. L., f. *alere* nourish, bring up (cf. ALIMENT), with ending rel. to Gr. pp. suffix *-ómenos*.

alveolus ælvī·ələs small cavity, tooth-socket, etc. XVIII. L., dim. of *alveus* cavity (cf. *alvus* belly, beehive, rel. to Gr. *aulós* long narrow channel, flute, *aulṓn* valley, canal, OSl. *ulij*, Lith. *aulȳs* beehive). Hence **alveol**AR ælvī·ŏləɹ, æ·lviŏləɹ XVIII. So **alvine** æ·lvain pert. to the belly. XVIII. – modL. *alvīnus*, f. *alvus*; see -INE[1].

alway ɔ̄·lwei, (formerly) ɔ̄lwei· all the time, every time. OE. *alne weġ*, acc. of *all* ALL and *weġ* WAY, prob. orig. denoting extent of space or distance, but at its first appearance already transf. to extent of time. Superseded in ordinary prose by **always** ɔ̄·lweiz, ɔ̄·lwiz, ME. *alles weis* XIII (see -S), later *alleweyes*, *alway(e)s*.

alyssum əli·səm, æ·lisəm genus of cruciferous plants. XVI. modL., for L. *alysson* (Pliny) – Gr. *álusson*.

am see BE.

amadavat æ:mədəvæ·t; also **avadavat**. Indian song-bird, waxbill. XVIII. f. name of the city of *Ahmadabad* (Gujerat, India), whence the birds were orig. brought; the place-name is found in Pg. as *Amadava* (XVI), in Du. as *Amadabat* (XVII), in Eng. as *Amidavad* (XVII).

amadou æ·mədū German tinder prepared from fungus. XVIII. – F. *amadou* – modPr. *amadou* lit. 'lover' (so called from its quick kindling) :– L. *amātōrem* (see AMATEUR).

amain əmei·n (arch.) with main force; at full speed; exceedingly. XVI. f. A-[1] + MAIN[1], replacing earlier †*with main*.

amalgam əmæ·lgəm mixture of a metal with mercury XV; intimate mixture or combination XVII. – F. *amalgame* or medL. *amalgama*, prob. ult. f. Gr. *málagma* emollient, f. *malássein* soften, through some Arab. form with prefixed AL-[2]. So **ama·lgam**ATE[3] XVII; †**ama·lgam** vb. XIV (Ch.). – medL. *amalgamāre*. **amalgam**ATION. XVII; so F.

amanuensis əmænjue·nsis clerk who writes from dictation. XVII. – L. *āmanuensis*

(Suetonius), f. *ā manū* in *servus ā manū* 'slave at hand', secretary + *-ēnsis* belonging to (cf. -ESE). (Cf. MANUAL.)

amaranth æ·mərænþ mythical fadeless flower; genus of ornamental plants with coloured foliage. XVII (earlier in L. form). – F. *amarante* or modL. *amaranthus*, alteration after names in *-anthus* (Gr. *ánthos* flower) of L. *amarantus* – Gr. *amárantos*, f. *a-* A-[4] + *maran-*, stem of *maraínein* to wither (f. base **mar- *mor-*; see MORTAL). So **amaranthine** æməræ·nþain. XVII (*amarantin* Milton). – modL.; see -INE[1].

amaryllis æməri·lis genus of bulbous plants. XVIII. modL. (Linnæus) use of L. *Amaryllis*, Gr. *Amarullís* typical name for a pretty country girl in Theocritus, Virgil, and Ovid.

amass əmæ·s collect in a mass, heap up. XV. – (O)F. *amasser* :– Rom. **admassāre*, f. L. *ad* AD- + *massa* MASS[2].

amateur æ·mətjuəɹ, -tʃuəɹ, æ·mətə̄ɹ one who is fond *of*; one who is not a specialist or professional. XVIII. – F. – It *amatore* – L. *amātōrem*, nom. *-ātor*, f. *amāre*, love.

amatory æ·mətəri pert. to love-making. XVI. – L. *amātōrius*, f. *amātor* lover, f. *amāt-*, pp. stem of *amāre* love; see -ORY. So **a·mat**IVE disposed to loving. XVII. – medL.

amaurosis æmōrou·sis (med.) loss of sight. XVII. modL. – Gr. *amaúrōsis*, f. *amauroûn* darken, f. *amaurós* dark, dim.

amaze əmei·z †stun, bewilder OE.; overwhelm with wonder XVI. OE. *āmasian*, pp. *āmasod*, whence ME. *amased*; not frequent till XVI; f. A-[3] + base **mas-*, perh. as in Norw., Da. *mase* be busy or active (Norw. dial. *masast* lose consciousness), Sw. *masa* warm, refl. bask. Aphetic MAZE.

Amazon æ·məzən one of a race of female warriors. XIV. – L. *Amāzon* – Gr. *Amazṓn*, *-ónos*, expl. by the Greeks as meaning 'breastless' (as if f. *a-* A-[4] + *mazós* breast), but prob. of foreign origin. Hence **Amazon**IAN æməzou·niən. XVI. f. L. *amazonius*.

ambassador æmbæ·sədəɹ official messenger of a sovereign or state. XIV. ME. *ambass(i)atour*, *embassatour*, *-dour*, later with different combinations of the vars. of the initial and final sylls. (*am-*, *em-*, *im-*, and *-tour*, *tor*, *-dour*, *-dor*) and alternations between *-ss-*, *-s-*, *-x-* followed by *a*, *e*, or *i*; the present sp. *ambassador*, U.S. *embassador*, date from XVI. orig. – various Rom. forms, (O)F. *ambassadeur*, †*ambaxateur*, Pr. *ambaissador* – It. *ambasciator*, Sp. *ambajador*; all ult. resting on Rom. **ambactiātōrem* (*-or*), f. **ambactiāre* go on a mission, f. medL. *ambactia*, *ambaxia* (Salic and Burgundian Laws), f. Germ. **ambaχtaz* (Goth. *andbahts*, OE. *ambeht* servant, messenger, OHG. *ambaht*, G. *amt*) – L. *ambactus* servant, vassal (Ennius, Cæsar), a Gaulish word, **ambactos* (cf. W. *amaeth* husbandman, serf), prob. f. **amb-* around + **ag-* drive; see AMBI-, ACT, -OR[1]. Cf. EMBASSY. Hence **amba·ssadress** XVI; see -ESS[1]; forms in *-drice*, *-trix*, *-trice* occur in XVII.

amber æ·mbəɹ yellow fossil resin. XIV. ME. *aumber* – (O)F. *ambre* = Pr., It. *ambra*, Sp. *ambar*, medL. *ambar(e)*, *ambrum* – Arab. *'anbar* (orig.) AMBERGRIS, (later) amber. In ME., OF. *l'ambre*, with def. art. prefixed, was adopted as †*lamber* (XIV).

ambergris, -grease æ·mbəɹgrīs wax-like ashy-coloured substance. XV. – (O)F. *ambre gris* 'grey amber'; this is the orig. sense of *amber*, which was later used by some confusion for the yellow resin; this latter being afterwards distinguished in F. as *ambre jaune* yellow amber, ambergris received its distinctive designation of 'grey'. Various early sp. show assim. to *grease*. (Milton has *gris-amber*.)

ambi- æmbi L. *ambi-*, comb. form of *ambō* both = Gr. *ámphō*, corr., with variation of initial syll., to OSl. *oba*, Lith. *abù*, Skr. *ubhau*, the second el. being repr. also in BOTH.

ambidexter æ·mbidekstəɹ able to use both hands equally. XVI. – late L. *ambidexter*, f. *ambi-* on both sides (see prec.) + *dexter* right-handed (cf. DEXTEROUS). (In XVII often *ambo-*, after L. *ambō* both.) So **ambide·xtr**OUS. XVII.

ambient æ·mbiənt moving or lying round. XVI. – F. *ambiant* or L. *ambient-*, *-ēns*, prp. of *ambīre* go round, f. *amb-*, AMBI- + *īre* go; see -ENT. Cf. ITINERANT.

ambiguous æmbi·gjuəs of double meaning. XVI. f. L. *ambiguus* shifting, doubtful (whence F. *ambigu*), f. *ambigere* go round, wander about, argue, f. *amb-* both ways + *agere* drive; see AMBI-, ACT, -UOUS. So **ambigu**ITY -jū·ĭti. XV. – (O)F. or L.

ambit æ·mbit circuit, precincts, bounds. XVI. – L. *ambitus* circuit, compass, f. *ambīre* (see AMBIENT).

ambition æmbi·ʃən ardent desire to attain distinction or success. XIV. – (O)F. *ambition* – L. *ambitiō(n-)* going round to canvass citizens for votes, excessive desire to please, adulation, desire for honour or power, ostentation, f. *ambit-*, *ambīre* go round (cf. AMBIENT, AMBIT); see -ITION. So **ambi·t**IOUS. XIV. – (O)F. or L.

amble æ·mbl sb. and vb. denoting distinctive pace of a horse. XIV. – (O)F. *amble* sb. and its source *ambler* vb. – Pr. *amblar* (It. *ambiare*, Rum. *umbla*) :– L. *ambulāre* (pop. word) walk, f. *amb-* AMBI- + base **el-* go, repr. also in L. *ex|ul* EXILE, *al|acer* (see ALACRITY), W. *el* that he may go; cf. PERAMBULATE.

ambo æ·mbou pulpit, reading-desk. XVII. – medL. *ambō(n-)* – Gr. *ámbōn* ridge, rim, (medGr.) pulpit (Paulus Silentiarius VI).

ambrosia æmbrou·ziə, -ʒiə (Gr. myth.) fabled food of the gods. XVI. – L. *ambrosia* – Gr. *ambrosíā* immortality, elixir of life, f. *ámbrotos* immortal, f. *a-* A-[4]+ **mbrotós* (*brotós*) MORTAL. So **ambro·**SIAL immortal, divine. XVI. f. L. *ambrosius* – Gr. *ambrósios*.

ambs-ace, ames-ace æ·mzeis, ei·mzeis double ace (the lowest throw at dice). XIII. – OF. *ambes as* :– L. *ambo* both, *as* ACE; see AMBI-, ACE.

ambulance æ·mbjŭləns moving hospital accompanying an army; vehicle to convey injured. XIX. – F. *ambulance* (1796), replacing *hôpital ambulant* (1762) 'walking hospital', earlier *hôpital ambulatoire* (1637); F. *ambulant* – prp. of L. *ambulāre* walk; see AMBLE, -ANCE, -ANT.

ambulatory æ·mbjŭlətəri pert. to or adapted for walking; sb. a place (covered way) to walk in. XVII. – L. *ambulātōrius* (in medL. *ambulātōrium* as sb.), f. *ambulāt-*, *ambulāre* walk; see AMBLE, -ORY.

ambuscade æmbʌskei·d ambush. XVI. – F. *embuscade* – It. *imboscata* or Sp. *emboscada*, Pg. *embuscada*, pp. deriv. of *imboscare*, etc.; in XVI–XVIII also †*ambuscado*; see AMBUSH, -ADE, -ADO.

ambush æ·mbuʃ dispose troops, etc. so as to take an enemy by surprise. XIV. – OF. *embuschier* = It. *imboscare*, Sp. *embuscar* :– Rom. **imboscāre* lit. 'put in a wood', f. *in* IM-[1]+ **boscus* wood, BUSH. So **a·mbush** sb. XV. – OF. *embusche*, f. the vb. Earlier **a·mbush**MENT. XIV. – OF. *embuschement*.

ameer, amir ămiə·ɹ, æ·miəɹ ruler of Scinde and Afghanistan. XIX. – (through Pers. and Urdu) Arab. *amīr* commander, f. *amara* tell, command. Formerly used for EMIR.

amelcorn æ·məlkɔ̄ɹn the larger spelt, French rice. XVI. – Du., G. *amelkorn*, f. L. *amylum* (– Gr. *ámulon*) starch+*korn* CORN.

ameliorate əmī·liəreit improve. XVIII. Alteration of earlier MELIORATE after F. *améliorer*, refash. after L. *melior* of OF. *ameillorer*, f. *a-* AD-+*meillorer*, f. *meilleur* better.

amen eime·n, āme·n. XIII. – ecclL. *āmēn* – Gr. *āmḗn* – Heb. *āmēn* certainty, truth, f. *āman* strengthen, confirm; used advb. as in affirmation or ratification of what is said by another, 'certainly', 'verily', and taken into Christian liturgical use from the Bible (cf. Deut. xxvii 15–26, 1 Kings i 36) as a conclusion to prayers or confessions of faith.

amenable əmī·nəbl liable to be brought before any jurisdiction; answerable or responsive (*to*). XVI. Earliest form *amesnable*, presumably – legal AN. **ame(s)nable*, f. (O)F. *amener* bring to, f. *a-* AD-+*mener* bring, lead :– (pop.) L. *mināre* drive (animals), for L. *minārī* threaten, f. *minæ* threats; see MENACE, -ABLE.

amend əme·nd †mend (clothes) XIII (AncrR.); correct, reform, improve. XIII. – (O)F. *amender* = Pr., Cat. *amendar*, It. *ammendare* :– Rom. **admendāre*, alteration by prefix-substitution of *ēmendāre* EMEND. Aphetic MEND. So **ame·nd**MENT. XIII (RGlouc.). – OF. *amendement*. **ame·nds** compensation for loss, etc. XIII (Cursor M.). – OF. *amendes* pecuniary fine, penalties, pl. of *amende* reparation, f. *amender*.

amenity əmī·nĭti, -en- pleasantness. XIV. – (O)F. *aménité* or L. *amœnitās*, f. *amœnus* pleasant, rel. to *amāre* love.

amerce əmɔ̄·ɹs impose a fine on. XIV. ME. *amercy* – AN. *amercier*, orig. in *estre amercié* be placed at the mercy of another (as to the amount of a fine), f. phr. *à merci* at (the) MERCY. So **ame·rce**MENT. XIV. – AN. *amerciment*. **ame·rciament**. XV. – medL. *amerciāmentum*, f. *amerciāre*, latinization of AN. *amercier*.

American əme·rikən pert. to America. XVI. – modL. *Americānus*, f. *America*, which appears first, as an alternative suggestion to *Amerige*, in 'Cosmographiae Introductio ... Insuper quattuor Americi Vespucii nauigationes', 1507; f. L. form, *Americus* Vesputius, of the name of the It. navigator *Amerigo* Vespucci (XV); see -AN. Hence **Ame·rican**ISM, **Ame·rican**IZE XVIII. **A·merind, Ameri·**NDIAN XIX.

ames-ace var. of AMBS-ACE.

amethyst æ·mĭþist precious stone. XIII. ME. *amatist(e)*, *ametist* – OF. *amatiste*, *ametiste* – L. *amethystus* – Gr. *améthustos*, sb. use (sc. *líthos* stone) of adj. f. *a-* A-[4]+ **méthustos*, f. *methúskein* intoxicate, f. *méthu* wine, MEAD[1]; the stone was so named because it was supposed to prevent intoxication. In XVI the sp. was remodelled with *-th-* after later F. and L. So **amethy·stine**. XVII. – L. – Gr.; see -INE[1].

amiable ei·miəbl friendly (now only of temper, etc.) XIV; †lovable XIV; likeable XVIII. – (O)F. *amiable* :– L. *amīcābilem*, *-is* friendly, AMICABLE. Later infl. in sense by F. *aimable* lovable, likeable (OF. *amable*) :– L. *amābilem*, f. *amāre* love; see -BLE. Hence **amia**BI·LITY XIX. ('It is quite painful to look at such terms as *womanized*, *amiability* ...', 'Edinburgh Review', 1807, p. 439.)

amianthus æmiæ·nþəs variety of asbestos. XVII. – L. *amiantus* – Gr. *amíantos*, f. *a-* A-[4] +*miaínein* defile; so called because it is freed from all stains by being thrown into fire. For the sp. with *th* cf. AMARANTH. (Earlier †*amiant* – F. *amiante*.)

amicable æ·mikəbl friendly. XV. – late L. *amīcābilis*, f. L. *amīcus* friend (rel. to *amāre* love); see -ABLE, AMIABLE.

amice æ·mis (eccl.) linen vestment covering neck and shoulders. XV (XIV in Wycl. Bible tr. Vulg. *amictus*). Earlier *amis*, *ames(s)* – medL. *amicia*, *-isia*, of obscure formation; superseding the var. †*amit* (XIV) – OF. *amit* (mod. *amict*) :- L. *amictu-s* outer garment, cloak, sb. use of pp. of *amicīre* wrap round, f. *am-*, shortd. form of *ambi-*, *amb-*+**-ic-* throw (cf. INJECT). Formally not distinct from the word denoting the tippet or hood, usually furred, worn in choir (XV *amisse of gris*) – OF. *aumusse*, corr. to Pr. *almussa*, Sp. *almucio* (cf. MOZZETTA) – medL. *almūcia*, *-ium*, which has the appearance of a formation with Arab. AL-² (but no such Arab. form is known). The latter word is now often dist. as **almuce** æ·lmjūs with assim. to medL.

amid əmi·d in the middle or midst of. OE. *on middum*, *on middan*, *on midre*, i.e. ON (in) with obl. case of MID in concord with a sb. ME. *amidde* (XIII) was later extended with -s to *amiddes*, whence **ami·dst** (XVI), by addition of parasitic *t*, as in *against*.

amide æ·maid (chem.) XIX. f. AM|MONIA+-IDE. The present application, dating from 1863, differs from the original. So **amine** æ·main 1863; see -INE⁵. Cf. VITAMIN.

amir see AMEER.

amidships əmi·dʃips in the middle of the ship. XVII. Alteration, by assoc. with AMID, of *midships* (XVII), prob. of LG. origin (Du. *midscheeps*, f. *mid* MID, *scheeps*, g. of *schip* SHIP; cf. G. *mittschiffs*).

amiss əmi·s erroneously, badly. XIII. ME. *a mis*, *on mis*, prob. – ON. *á mis*, so as to miss or not to meet, i.e. *á* ON, A-¹, *mis*, identical in form with the prefix *mis-* MIS-¹ and rel. to *missa*, *missir* loss, *missa* lose, MISS¹. Hence adj.

amity æ·mĭti friendliness. XV. – (O)F. *amitié* = Pr., Cat. *amistat*, It. *amistà*, Pg. *amizade* :- Rom. **amīcitātem*, *-tās*, f. *amīcus* friend; see AMICABLE, -ITY.

ammonia əmou·niə nitrogen hydride XVIII; aqueous solution of this XIX. – modL. *ammōnia* (Bergman, 1782), so named as being obtained from sal ammoniac, L. *sal ammōniacus*. So **ammo·ni**AC. XIV. Earliest form *armoniak* – medL. *armōniacus*, *-um*, alteration of *ammōniacus*, *-um* – Gr. *ammōniakós*, *-kón*, applied as sb. to a salt and a gum obtained from a region in Libya near the temple of Jupiter *Ammon* (*Ammōn*, Gr. form of the name of the Egyptian deity *Amūn*). Also **ammoni**ACAL æmŏnai·əkəl XVIII. **ammonium** əmou·niəm radical of salts of ammonia. XIX. – modL. *ammōnium* (Berzelius, 1808), f. AMMONIA; see -IUM.

ammonite æ·mənait fossil genus of cephalopods. XVIII. – modL. *ammōnītēs* (Bruguière), f. medL. name *cornu Ammonis* 'horn of Ammon' given to these fossils from their resemblance to the involuted horn of Jupiter *Ammon*; see prec. and -ITE.

ammunition æmjuni·ʃən military supplies, formerly gen., now only of offensive missiles. XVII. Earliest forms *amunition*, *am(m)onitioune* – F. † *am(m)unition*, resulting from a wrong analysis of *la munition* the supplies (see MUNITION) as *l'amunition*.

amnesia æmnī·siə, -ziə (path.) loss of memory. XIX. – modL. – Gr. *amnēsíā*, f. *a-* A-⁴+ **mnē-* (base **men-* **mon-*; see MIND).

amnesty æ·mnĭsti act of oblivion, authoritative pardon of offences. XVI. – F. *amnestie* or L. *amnēstia* – Gr. *amnēstíā* oblivion, f. *ámnēstos* not remembering, f. *a-* A-⁴+ **mnē-*; see prec. and -Y³.

amnion æ·mniən (anat.) caul. XVII. – modL. – Gr. *amníon*, dim. of *amnós* lamb.

amœba əmī·bə (zool.) microscopic animalcule of the class Protozoa, the shape of which is perpetually changing. XIX. – modL. – Gr. *amoibḗ* change, alternation.

amœbæan æmibī·ən alternately answering. XVII. f. late L. *amœbæus* – Gr. *amoibaîos* interchanging, f. *amoibḗ*; see prec. and -AN.

among əmʌ·ŋ in the midst of. OE. *onġemang*, *-mong*, i.e. ON, *ġemang* mingling, assemblage, crowd (cf. *ġemengan* MINGLE), prop. a phr. used as a prep. with dative; later *onmang*, *-mong*, whence *amang*, *among*; cf. A-¹. The simple OE. *ġemang* was also used as a prep., later †*imong*, aphetic *mong*, which was freq. spelt *'mong* as if for *among*. Extended with advb. -s to *amonges* XIII, whence *amongest*, **amongst** (XVI); cf. AMIDST, AGAINST.

Amontillado əmɔntilʲā·dou variety of sherry. XIX. Sp., f. *Montilla* town in Spain, after *afrancescado* Frenchified, etc.

amoral æmɔ·rəl, eimɔ·rəl non-moral. XIX (R. Stevenson). f. A-⁴+MORAL.

amorce əmɔ̄·ɹs cap for a toy pistol. XX. – (O)F. *amorce*, orig. *amorse*, sb. use of fem. pp. of †*amordre* bite on, attract, f. *a-* AD-+*mordre* (cf. MORDANT).

amorous æ·mərəs inclined to love; enamoured. XIV. – OF. *amorous* (mod. *amoureux*) – medL. *amōrōsus*, f. *amor* love; see -OUS.

amorphous əmɔ̄·ɹfəs shapeless. XVIII. f. modL. *amorphus* – Gr. *ámorphos*, f. *a-* A-⁴+ *morphḗ* shape (cf. MORPHIA); see -OUS.

amort əmɔ̄·ɹt (arch.) lifeless, spiritless. XVI. orig. *all amort* – (with assim. to ALL) F. *à la mort* to the death; the unqualified *amort* (XVII) has the appearance of being – F. *à mort*.

amortize əmɔ̄·ɹtiz (leg.) alienate in mortmain XIV; extinguish (a debt) XIX. f. *amortiss-*, lengthd. stem of (O)F. *amortir* = Pr. *amortir*, It. *ammortire* :- Rom. **admortīre*, f. *ad* AD-+*mort-*, *mors* death (see MORTAL); the sp. with *-ize* is due to medL. *admortizāre*, which is formed on the Rom. forms with *-izāre* -IZE. Hence **amortiza·**TION. XVII; in medL. *admortizātiō*.

amount əmau·nt †go up, ascend; rise to a certain level. XIII. – OF. *amunter*, *amo(u)nter*, f. *amont* upward, i.e. *à mont* :- L. *ad montem* to the hill, upward; see MOUNT¹ and cf.

PARAMOUNT. Hence **amou·nt** sb. XVIII.

amour əmuə·ɹ †love XIII; (illicit) love-affair XVI (pl., Barbour). – (O)F. *amour* :– L. *amōrem*, nom. *amor* love, rel. to *amāre* vb. love. The F. word was reintroduced in XVI, when the early anglicized *amour* had become obs. or was replaced (temporarily) by the L. form *amor* (XVI—XVII). Cf. PARAMOUR.

ampère æ·mpɛəɹ unit of electric current. XIX. f. name of André Marie *Ampère*, French physicist (d. 1836); adopted by the Congrès Électrique at Paris, 1881. abbrev. **amp.**

ampersand æmpəɹsæ·nd XIX. For *and per se and*, name of the character & as it appears at the end of the alphabet in a primer or hornbook; 'and (standing) by itself, and'; see PER. Current dial. in many var. forms, e.g. *ampussy (and), ampusand, amsiam.* ('Of all the types in a printer's hand Commend me to the Amperzand', Punch, 17 April 1869.)

amphi- æ·mfi repr. Gr. *amphi-*, prefix used in the senses of *ámphō* BOTH, of both kinds, and *amphí* on both sides (of.)

amphibium æmfi·biəm creature that lives in water or on land. XVII. modL. (sc. *animal*) – Gr. *amphíbion* (sc. *zôion*), sb. use of n. of adj. *amphíbios* (*bíos* life; see QUICK); pl. **Amphi·bia** division of animals variously defined since Linnæus XVIII. So **amphi·bIAN**, -IOUS XVII.

amphibole æ·mfiboul †ambiguity XVII; (min.) hornblende, so named by Haüy, 1801, on account of the protean variety of its composition. – F. – L. *-bolum* – Gr. *-bolon* (*bállein* throw). **amphibo·**LOGY amphiboly. XIV (Ch.). – (O)F. – late L. (*-bologia*, for L. *-bolia*, whence **amphi·boly** XVI).

a·mphibrach -bræk metrical foot ⏑ – ⏑. XVI. – L. *-ys*, *-us* 'short at both ends' – Gr. *amphíbrakhus* (cf. BRACHY-).

amphimacer æmfi·məsəɹ (pros.) metrical foot – ⏑ –. XVI. – L. *amphimacrus* – Gr. *amphímakros* (sc. *poús* foot) long at both ends (*makrós* long; cf. MAGNITUDE).

amphisbæna æmfisbī·nə fabled serpent with a head at each end. XVI. L. – Gr. *amphísbaina*, f. *amphís* at both ends, AMPHI- + base of *baínein* go (cf. COME).

amphitheatre æ·mfiþiətəɹ oval or circular building built round an arena XIV. – L. *amphitheātrum* – Gr. *amphithéātron*; see AMPHI-, THEATRE. So F. *amphithéâtre*.

amphora æ·mfərə two-handled vessel; liquid measure XVII (cited earlier as L.; and anglicized †*amfor*, †*amfer*, or – F. *amphore*). L. – Gr. *amphoreús*, for **amphiphoreús* lit. 'borne on both sides', f. *amphí-* AMPHI- + **phor-* **pher-* BEAR[2].

ample æ·mpl spacious, copious, quite enough. XV. – (O)F. *ample* – L. *amplus*. So **ampli**A·TION enlargement XVI. **a·mpli**FY XV. **a·mplific**A·TION. XVI; (rhet.) tr. Gr. αὔξησις. **a·mpli**TUDE. **amp**LY[2] æ·mpli. XVI.

ampulla æmpu·lə vessel for holy oil, etc. XVI (earlier *ampul(le)* XII – (O)F.). L., two-handled big-bellied flask or pot, dim. of *ampora*, var. of AMPHORA.

amputate æ·mpjuteit lop or cut off. XVII. f. pp. stem of L. *amputāre*, f. *am-* for *amb-* around, AMBI- + *putāre* prune, lop; see -ATE[3]. So **amput**A·TION. XVII. – F. or L.

amuck, amok əmʌ·k in frenzied thirst for blood; also fig. XVII. – Malay *āmoq* fighting furiously, in homicidal frenzy. Appears first in XVI in forms (pl. *amochy, amocchi, amouchi*) repr. Pg. *amouco, amuco*, in the sense of 'frenzied Malay'; otherwise chiefly in phr. *run amuck*, also (wrongly divided) *a muck*, whence the treatment of *muck* as a sb., e.g. 'to run an Indian muck' (Dryden).

amulet æ·mjŭlĕt object worn as a charm. XVII. – F. *amulette* – L. *amulētum* (Varro); a proposed Arabic origin is unsupported.

amuse əmjū·z †beguile, delude XV; †distract, bewilder; divert with entertaining matter XVII. – (O)F. *amuser* †deceive, entertain, f. *à* AD- + *muser* MUSE[1] (which is earlier); recorded only occas. before 1600 (not in Sh.). **amu·se**MENT. XVII. – F.

amygdaloid əmi·gdəloid almond-shaped; rock containing almond-shaped nodules. XVIII. f. Gr. *amugdálē* ALMOND + -OID.

amyl- æ·mil (chem.) f. L. *am|ylum* starch (– Gr. *ámulon*) + -YL.

an[1] ən, (emph.) æn reduced form of OE. *ān* ONE, due to loss of stress; now a var. of A[1] retained before vowel sounds and before unstressed syllables having initial (h) (e.g. *an histo·rical*) and occas. before (j), as *an unique*, and arch. in *such an one.*

an[2] ən reduced form of AND, recorded from XII and in colloq. use since then. For for sense 'if' (XIII) see AND.

an-[1] ən assim. form of AD- before *n*; cf. AC-.

an-[2] ən, æn repr. Gr. privative *an-* not, without, lacking, orig. form of A-[4] retained before vowels, as in words taken from Gr., e.g. *anarchy, anonymous*, and hence in mod. technical terms, e.g. *analgesic, anallagmatic, analphabetic, anharmonic, anhydrous, anisomerous.*

-an ən repr. L. *-ānus, -āna, -ānum* of or belonging to, as in *urbānus* URBAN, f. *urbs* city, *silvānus* SILVAN, f. *silva* wood. The F. form *-ain, -aine* was at first retained in some adoptions, but was later superseded by *-an*. In *german, germane, human, humane, urban, urbane*, there is differentiation of meaning by the use of different forms of the suffix. See also -EAN, -IAN.

ana[1] æ·nə XIV. medL. – Gr. *aná* ANA-, used in recipes for 'of each, of every one alike'.

ana[2] ei·nə, ā·nə collection of miscellaneous writings or sayings of or concerning a person. XVIII. A detached use (prob. after F.) of L. *-āna*, n. pl. of *-ānus* -AN, used in titles of such collections, more usu. in *-iana*, e.g. 'Scaligeriana, sive excerpta ex ore Josephi Scaligeri' (1666).

ana- æ·nə, ənæ·, before a vowel **an-** æn, ən repr. Gr. *aná* up (in place or time), back, again, anew (see ON), as in *Anabaptist*, *analysis*, *anatomy*.

Anabaptist ænəbæ·ptist one who rebaptizes (German sect); Baptist XVI. – F. *anabaptiste* or modL. *anabaptista*, f. ecclL. *anabaptismus* (Augustine), ecclGr. *anabáptisma*, f. *anabaptizāre*, *anabaptizein*; see ANA-, BAPTIZE, -IST.

anabasis ənæ·bəsis military advance (spec. that of Cyrus the Younger into Asia, related by Xenophon). XVIII. – Gr. *anábasis* ascent, f. *anabaínein* walk up; see ANA-, BASIS.

anachronism ənæ·krənizm chronological error or discrepancy. XVII. – F. *anachronisme* or Gr. *anakhronismós*, f. *anakhronízesthai* refer to a wrong time, f. *aná* back + *khrónos* time; see ANA-, CHRONIC, -ISM.

anacoluthon ænəkŏlʲū·þən lack of grammatical sequence. XVIII. – late L. – Gr. *anakólouthon*, n. sg. of adj. 'lacking sequence', f. AN-[2] + *akólouthos* following (cf. ACOLYTE).

anaconda ænəkɔ·ndə large S. American boa. XVIII. First applied to an alleged large snake of Ceylon, app. as an (unexpl.) alteration of *anacandaia* (Ray 1693), which is for Sinhalese *henacandāya* 'lighting-stem', whip-snake; by some blunder transf. by Daudin to the aquatic boa Eunectes murinus (Boa anacondo).

anacreontic ənækriɔ·ntik resembling the poems of the Greek lyric poet Anacreon (VI B.C.); also sb. XVII (Cowley). – late L. *anacreonticus*, f. Gr. *Anacreont-*, *Anacréōn*; see -IC.

anacrusis ænəkrū·sis (pros.) introductory syllable(s) at the beginning of a line. XIX. – modL. – Gr. *anákrousis* prelude, f. *anakroúein*, f. *aná* up, ANA- + *kroúein* strike.

anadem æ·nədem wreath. XVII (Drayton). – L. *anadēma* – Gr. *anádēma* head-band, f. *anadeîn*, f. *aná* up, ANA- + *deîn* bind (cf. DIADEM).

anadromous ənæ·drəməs (zool.) ascending rivers to spawn. XVIII. f. Gr. *anádromos*, f. *aná* up, ANA- + *drom-*, as in *drómos* course (*drameîn*, corr. to Skr. *drámati* run); see -OUS.

anæmia ənī·miə morbid lack of blood. XIX. – modL. – Gr. *anaimíā*, f. *an-* A-[4] + *haîma* blood (cf. HÆMATO-). Hence **anæ·mic**. XIX.

anæsthesia ænīsþī·ziə loss of feeling or sensation. XIX. – modL. – Gr. *anaisthēsíā*, f. *an-* A-[4] + *aísthēsis* sensation, f. base of *aisthánesthai* feel, perceive, rel. to *aíein* hear, L. *audīre* (see AUDIENCE). So **anæsthetic** -þe·tik. XIX. f. Gr. *anaisthētós* insensible (cf. ÆSTHETIC). Both introduced by Oliver Wendell Holmes in 1846. Hence **anæsthetist**, -IZE ænī·sþitist, -aiz. XIX.

anaglyph æ·nəglif embossed ornament. XVII. – Gr. *anagluphḗ* work in low relief, f. *aná* ANA- + *glúphein* carve (cf. CLEFT).

anagogic ænəgɔ·dʒik mystical. XIV (Wycl. Bible; rare before XVII) (of biblical exegesis). – medL. *anagōgicus* – Gr. *anagōgikós*, f. *anagōgḗ* (religious or ecstatic) elevation, mystical sense, f. *anágein* lift up, elevate, f. *an-* ANA- + *ágein* lead (cf. ACT); see -IC. So **anago·gical**. XVI (Tindale).

anagram æ·nəgræm transposition of the letters of a word or phrase to make a new one. XVI. – F. *anagramme* – modL. *anagramma*, f. Gr. *aná* ANA- + *grámma* letter (see GRAMMAR), after *anagrammatízein* transpose letters.

anal ei·nəl see ANUS.

analects æ·nəlekts literary gleanings. XVII. – L. *analecta* – Gr. *análekta* (n. pl.) things gathered up, f. *analégein*, f. *aná* up, ANA- + *légein* gather (cf. COLLECT).

analogue æ·nəlɔg analogous word, thing, etc. XIX. – F. *analogue* – Gr. *análogon* (used in Eng. somewhat earlier), sb. use of n.sg. of *análogos* (f. *aná* + *lógos* ratio, proportion), whence, through L. *analogus*, **analogous** ənæ·ləgəs similar, parallel. XVII. See ANA-, LOGIC.

analogy ənæ·lədʒi proportion XV; similarity, parallelism XVII. – (O)F. *analogie* or L. *analogia* – Gr. *analogíā* equality of ratios, proportion (orig. math.), f. *análogos* ANALOGOUS. So **analogic** ænəlɔ·dʒik XVII, **analo·gical** XVI. f. F. *analogique* or L. *analogicus* – Gr. *analogikós*.

analyse æ·nəlaiz †dissect; ascertain the elements of; examine minutely. XVII. First recorded in the title 'The Phœnix Analysde' (1601), by B. Jonson: perh. orig. f. †*analyse*, †*analise* (XVII–XVIII), anglicized form of ANALYSIS, and later infl. by F. *analyser*. Early forms such as *analize*, *analyze* show assimn. to verbs in -IZE; the second of these forms prevails in U.S. So **analyst** æ·nəlist. XVII. – F. *analyste*, f. *analyser*, by assocn. with pairs in *-iser*, *-iste* (-IZE, -IST). **analysis** ənæ·lĭsis resolution into elements. XVI. – medL. *analysis* – Gr. *análusis*, f. *analúein* unloose, undo, f. *aná* up, back, ANA- + *lúein* LOOSE. **analytic** ænəli·tik. XVI. – late L. *analyticus* – Gr. *analutikós*, f. *analúein*; earliest use as sb. pl. (title of Aristotle's treatise on logic). Also **analy·tical**. XVI.

ananas ənā·næ̆s pine-apple, Ananassa sativa. XVI. – F. or Sp. *ananas*, *anana* – Guarani *anānā* fruit of the tree, under which name it was first described by André Thevenet in 1555.

anapæst æ·nəpĭst (pros.) the foot ◡◡–. XVII (earlier in L. form). – L. *anapæstus* – Gr. *anápaistos* reversed, lit. 'struck back' (sc. *poús* foot), f. *aná* ANA- + *paíein* strike; so called because it is the dactyl (–◡◡) reversed. So **anapæ·stic**. XVII. – late L. – Gr.

anaphora ənæ·fərə (rhet.) repetition XVI; (liturg.) Eucharistic canon XVIII. – L. – Gr. *anaphorá* carrying back, repetition (Longinus), offering (LXX), f. *anaphérein* carry up or back, f. *aná* ANA- + *phérein* BEAR[2].

anarchy æ·năɹki absence of government. XVI. – medL. *anarchia* – Gr. *anarkhíā*, f.

ánarkhos without a chief or head, f. *an-* A-[4]+*arkhós* leader (cf. ARCH-); so (O)F. *anarchie.* Hence **ana·rch**IC XVIII, -ICAL XVI; cf. F. *anarchique.* **anarch** æ·nāɹk leader of revolt. XVII (Milton). – Gr. *ánarkhos.* **a·narch**ISM, -IST. XVII; in more recent use dependent on F. *anarchisme, -iste.*

anarthrous ænā·ɹþrəs (gram.) used without the article. XIX. f. Gr. *an-* A-[4]+*árthron* joint, definite article (see ARM[1]) + -OUS.

anastatic ænəstæ·tik printed from plates in relief. XIX. f. Gr. *anástatos,* ppl. formation on *anasta-, anistánai* set up, f. *aná* up, ANA-+**sta-* (cf. STAND, STATIC).

anastomosis ənæstŏmou·sis cross connexion of arteries, etc. XVI. modL. – Gr. *anastómōsis,* f. *anastomoûn* furnish with a mouth or outlet, f. *aná* ANA-+*stóma* mouth (cf. STOMACH); see -OSIS.

anathema ənæ·þimə curse; accursed thing. XVI. – ecclL. *anathema* excommunicated person, sentence of excommunication – Gr. *anáthema* thing offered or devoted, (later spec.) thing devoted to evil, accursed thing (see Rom. ix 3); orig. var. of *anáthēma* offering, f. *anathe-, anatithénai* set up, f. *aná* up, ANA-+*tithénai* place (see DO[1]). So **ana·themat**IZE. XVI. – F. – ecclL. – Gr.

anatomy ənæ·təmi dissection of the body; science of organic structure; †skeleton. XIV (in early use often *anath-, anoth-*). – F. *anatomie* – late L. *anatomia* – Gr. *anatomíā,* f. *aná* up, ANA-+**tom-* cut (cf. -TOMY). Through identification of *an-* with the indef. art. A[1], AN[1], aphetic forms *natomy, atomy, otamy* came into use, esp. in the sense 'skeleton'; e.g. 'Thou atomy, thou!' (Sh. '2 Hen. IV' v iv 33), 'withered atomies of teaspoons' (Dickens). So **ana·tom**IST. XVI. – F. *-iste* or medL. **anatomista,* f. **anatomizāre,* whence **ana·tom**IZE. XVI.

anbury, ambury æ·n-, æ·mbəri tumour in cattle; disease of turnips, etc. XVI. perh. f. *ang-* in OE. *angnægl* AGNAIL, *angseta* carbuncle, pimple+BERRY in the sense of red mark or pustule; cf. Sc. †*angilberry* (XVI), north. dial. *angleberry.*

-ance əns suffix repr. F. *-ance* :– L. *-antia,* f. *-ant-* -ANT+*-ia* -Y[3]. Through such pairs as *appear, appearance,* it became to some extent a living suffix and was appended to vbs. of non-Rom. origin, e.g. *forbear, forbearance, hinder, hindrance, rid, riddance, utter, utterance.* Cf. -ANCY.

ancestor æ·nsĭstəɹ, -ses- forefather. XIII. Early forms are of three types: (i) *auncetre,* surviving XVII in latinized sp. *auncitor;* (ii) *ancestre,* antecedent of the present form through *ancestour,* by assim. to *-tour,* -TOR; (iii) *ancessour* (rare). – OF. *ancestre* (mod. *ancêtre*) orig. nom. :– L. *antecēssor,* and OF. *ances(s)our* acc. :– L. *antecēssōrem* predecessor (cf. Pr. *ancestre, ancessor*), f. *antecēdere* precede, f. *ante* before + *cēdere* go (cf. CEDE). MF. *antécesseur* was also repr. by †*antecessor* (XV–XIX). So **a·ncest**RY descent, line of ancestors. XIV. Modification, after *ancestre,* of OF. *ancesserie,* f. *ancessour;* see -Y[3], -RY.

anchor[1] æ·ŋkəɹ appliance for mooring a vessel to the bottom. OE. *ancor, -er, ancra* – L. *ancora* – Gr. *ágkūra* (see ANGLE[2]). The L. word was adopted early in the LG. area, hence it passed eastwards and northwards; cf. OFris., (M)LG., (M)Du. *anker,* late OHG. *anchar* (G. *anker*), ON. *akkeri.* The OE. word was reinforced in ME. by (O)F. *ancre* (= It., Pr., etc. *ancora*). The present sp. follows corrupt L. *anchora.* So **a·nchor** vb. XIII. – (O)F. *ancrer,* medL. *ancorāre.* Hence **a·nchor**AGE XVII; after F. *ancrage.*

anchor[2] æ·ŋkəɹ (arch.) anchorite. OE. *ancra, ancor, -er* – OIr. *anchara,* shortened – ecclL. *anachorēta* ANCHORITE; used by Sh. ('Hamlet' III ii 229). Hence *anchor-hold* anchorite's retreat XVII; see HOLD[2]. Hence **a·nchoress, a·ncress** XIV; see -ESS[1].

anchorite, anchoret æ·ŋkərait, -et religious recluse occupying a cell. XV. – medL. *anc(h)orīta,* ecclL. *anchorēta* – ecclGr. *anakhōrētés,* f. *anakhōreîn* retire, retreat, f. *ană* back, ANA-+*khōreîn* give place, withdraw, f. *khôrā, khôros* space, place. (Cf. F. *anachorète.*) Superseded ANCHOR[2].

anchovy æ·ntʃouvi, æ·ntʃəvi small fish of the herring family. XVI (Sh.). Earlier forms usu. pl. *anchoves, anchovas, anchioves,* later *anchovees.* – Sp., Pg. *anchova, anchoa* (It. *acciuga,* dial. *anciova*); has been supposed to be :– Rom. **apiu(v)a* – Gr. *aphúē* some small fish; but G. *anschovis* (– Du. *ansjovis*) has been referred to Basque *anchu.* (F. *anchois* is – modPr. *anchoio* – Sp.)

anchusa ænkjū·zə, æntʃū·zə boraginaceous plant alkanet. – L. *anchūsa* (Pliny) – Gr. *ágkhousa* (Theophrastus), *égkhousa* (Aristophanes).

anchylosis æŋkilou·sis formation of a stiff joint. XVIII. – modL. – Gr. *agkúlōsis,* f. *agkuloûn* crook, f. *agkúlos* crooked; see -OSIS. The normal repr. of the Gr. form would be **ancylosis; h* has been inserted to denote the *k*-sound (cf. F. *ankylose*). Hence, by back-formation, **a·nchylose** vb. XVIII; prob. after F. *ankyloser.*

ancient[1] ei·nʃənt of times long past, very old XIV; sb. XIV. ME. *auncien, -ian* – AN. *auncien,* (O)F. *ancien,* corr. to Pr. *ancian,* Sp. *anciano,* It. *anziano,* repr. Rom. **antiānu-s, *anteānu-s,* f. *ante* before, ANTE-+*-ānus* -AN. The addition of homorganic *t* to final *n* (XV) is paralleled in *pageant, pheasant, tyrant,* and the pronunc. of the first syll. in *angel, chamber, change, manger.* Hence **a·ncient**RY. XVI. †**ancienty.** XIV. – AN. *auncienté,* (O)F. *ancienneté;* see -Y[3].

ancient[2] ei·nʃənt. XVI. (arch.) corruption of ENSIGN by assocn. of such forms as *ensyne* with *ancien,* ANCIENT[1]; in senses (i) standard

XVI and (ii) standard-bearer XVI (Sh.), for †*ancient-bearer*.

ancillary æ·nsiləri subsidiary. XVII. – L. *ancillāris*, f. *ancilla* handmaid, fem. dim. of *anculus* servant; see -ARY. Cf. CAPILLARY.

ancona ænkou·nə altar-piece consisting of panels. XIX. – It., medL. *ancona*, prob. – Gr. *eikóna*, acc. of *eikṓn* image, ICON, perh. blended with Gr. *ankṓn* (modGr. *ankṓnē*) corner, sacred images being often at street corners in Italy.

-ancy ənsi repr. L. *-antia* -ANCE.

and ənd, ən, n, (emph.) ænd along with, in addition to. OE. *and*, *ond*, corr. to OFris. *and*(*a*), *ande*, *end*(*a*), *en*, OS. *ande*, *endi* (Du. *en*), OHG. *anti*, *enti*, *inti*, *unti* (G. *und*), and Skr. *átha* (:- **n̥tha*) thereupon, also. (OE. *ænd*, *end*, showing mutation, if it survived, would, owing to lack of stress, coincide with *and*; see AN[2].) Connexion with OE. *and-* (as in *andswaru* ANSWER), ON. *and-*, Goth. *anda-*, and Skr. *antí* over against, Gr. *antí* against, L. *ante* before, and OE. *ende* END, etc. is no longer gen. accepted.

A special development of meaning is that of 'if' (XIII), which was a common use also of MHG. *unde*; it may have arisen out of such constructions as OE. *ġeliċe and* just as if, and have been reinforced from Scand. (cf. ON. *enda* and if, even if, *en* if). Now usu. spelt *an*, *an'* in this sense; formerly often coupled with *if*, whence dial. *nif*, for *an if*.

andante ændæ·nti (mus.) moderately slow. XVIII. It., prp. of *andare* go :- **ambitāre*, alteration of L. *ambulāre* (cf. AMBLE). So **andantino** -ī·nou. XIX.

andiron æ·ndaiəɹn fire-dog. XIV. ME. *aundyre*, *aundyrne*, *-erne* – OF. *andier* (mod. *landier* for *l'andier*) with assimn. of the second syll. to IRON (ME. *ire*, *iren*); ult. origin unkn. Cf. †*landiron* (XV–XVII).

androgynous ændrɔ·dʒinəs hermaphrodite; spec. in bot. XVII. f. L. *androgynus* – Gr. *andrógunos* male and female in one, f. *andro-*, *anḗr* man, male (f. base meaning 'strong')+*gunḗ* woman, female (cf. QUEAN); see -OUS. Also **androgyne** æ·ndrodʒain hermaphrodite XVI; androgynous plant XVIII. – (O)F. *androgyne* – L.

-ane[1] see -AN.

-ane[2] ein (chem.) in the systematic nomenclature of Hofmann (1866), the termination for names of the hydrocarbons called paraffins, e.g. *ethane*; devised to introduce with *a* the vowel series already in vogue, *-ene*, *-ine*, *-one* (repr. Gr. *-ēnē*, *-īnē*, *-ōnē*), in the nomenclature of other classes of hydrocarbons.

anecdote æ·nikdout † (pl.) secret history XVII; story of a detached incident XVIII. orig. pl. – modL. *anecdota* (or its deriv. F. *anecdotes*) – Gr. *anékdota* things unpublished, n. pl. of *anékdotos*, f. *an-* A-[4]+*ékdotos*, f. *ekdidónai* publish, f. *ek* out+*didónai* give (see DONATION). Derived primarily from the title *Anékdota* of Procopius' unpublished memoirs (VII) of the private life of the Emperor Justinian and Theodora. Hence **a·necdot**AGE anecdotes collectively XIX (De Quincey); garrulous old age XIX (attributed to John Wilkes) assoc. with DOTAGE.

anele ənī·l (arch.) anoint. XIV. f. *an-*, OE. *on-* + ME. *elien*, f. OE. *ele* – L. *oleum* OIL. Preserved in *unaneled* not having received extreme unction (Sh. 'Hamlet' I v 77).

anemo- æ·nimou, ænimɔ· repr. *anemo-*, comb. form of Gr. *ánemos* wind, rel. to ANIMUS; e.g. **anemo·**METER XVIII.

anemone əne·məni genus of ranunculaceous plants (the flowers were said to open under the influence of wind) XVI; name of certain bright-coloured zoophytes with expanded disks XVIII. – L. *anemōnē* – Gr. *anemṓnē*, f. *ánemos* wind (cf. ANIMATE) + suffix *-ōnē*. It has been suggested that the Gr. word is an etymologizing perversion of Heb.-Aram. *Naʿamān*, name of Adonis, from whose blood the plant was fabled to have sprung.

anent əne·nt †in company with OE.; †facing, towards; concerning XIV. OE. phr. *on efen*, *efn*, or *emn*, ME. *onevent*, *anont*, *anentes*, (dial.) *anenst*, from XIV *anent*; i.e. ON, *efen* EVEN, on a level (with), side by side (with), beside, opposite, against, towards, in view of; = OS. *an eban*, MHG. *eneben*, *nebent*, (also mod.) *neben*. The suffix *-es*, -S and parasitic *t* appear *c.* 1200.

aneroid æ·nərɔid kind of barometer. XIX. – F. *anéroïde*, f. Gr. *a-* A-[4]+*nērós* wet, damp + *-oïde* -OID (used arbitrarily); so called because the pressure of the air is not measured by means of a column of fluid.

aneurysm, **aneurism** æ·njurizm morbid dilatation of an artery. XV. – Gr. *aneúrusma* dilatation, f. *aneurúnein* widen out, f. *aná* ANA-+*eurúnein* widen, f. *eurús* wide. Cf. F. *anévrisme*. The unetymological sp. with *i* is the commoner.

anew ənjū· †lately, recently; afresh. XIV. ME. *of newe*, *of the newe*, *o newe*, i.e. OF, A-[2], NEW, prob. after OF. *de neuf*, *de nouveau*, L. *dē novō*; replacing OE. *niwe*, *niwan*, *edniwe*, *edniwan* newly, recently (OMercian *ofniowe*, tr. L. *dēnuō*, is isolated). The form *anew* was established XVI.

anfractuosity æ:nfræktjuɔ·sĭti circuitousness, intricacy. XVI. – F. *anfractuosité*, f. late L. *anfractuōsus* winding, f. L. *anfractus* bending, f. *anfract-*, pp. stem of *anfringere*, f. *amb-* AMBI-+*frangere* BREAK. So **anfra·c**TUOUS circuitous XVII; cf. F. *anfractueux*.

angary æ·ŋgəri right of a belligerent to use or destroy neutrals' property. XIX. – F. *angarie* – It. *angaria* – late L. *angaria* forced service – Gr. *aggareíā* office of an *ángaros* (Persian word, perh. rel. to *ággelos* ANGEL) mounted courier liable to be impressed for carrying royal dispatches; see -Y[3].

angel ei·ndʒəl messenger of God; guardian spirit XII; in full *angel noble*, gold coin with a figure of the archangel Michael XV. – OF. *angele* = Pr. *angel*, It. *angelo* – ecclL. *angelus* – Gr. *ággelos* messenger. Superseded OE. *engel* e·ŋgl (which survived till XIII) = OFris. *angel, engel*, OS. *engil*, OHG. *angil, engil* (Du., G. *engel*), ON. *engill*, Goth. *aggilus*; CGerm. – ecclL. *angelus* (in Goth. perh. immed.–Gr.); one of the earliest Germ. adoptions from L. Hence **angel**IC ændʒe·lik XV. – (O)F. – late L. – Gr. **ange·l**ICAL. XVI.

angelica ændʒe·likə aromatic plant used in cooking, etc. XVI. – medL., short for *herba angelica* 'angelic plant', so named on account of its reputed efficacy against poison and pestilence.

angelus æ·ndʒĭləs devotional exercise commemorating the Incarnation. XVII. Named from the first word of the first sentence, 'Angelus Domini nuntiavit Mariæ' the angel of the Lord brought tidings to Mary.

anger æ·ŋgəɹ †distress, vex XII (Orm); excite to wrath XIV. – ON. *angra* grieve, vex, f. *angr* grief, f. base **aŋg*- narrow, repr. also by ON. *ǫngr*, Goth. *aggwus*, and OE. *enge*, OS., OHG. *engi* (Du., G. *eng*) narrow; rel. to L. *angere* (see ANGUISH). Hence **anger** sb. †trouble, affliction; hot displeasure. XIII. (Rare ME. *ange* (Orm) was a direct adoption of ON. *angr*.) Hence **a·ngry** †troublesome; †troubled; enraged XIV; see -Y[1].

angina (prop.) æ·ndʒinə, (usu.) ændʒai·nə †quinsy XVI; short for *angina pectoris* 'spasm of the chest' XVIII. – L. *angina* quinsy – Gr. *agkhónē* strangling, with assim. to *angere* (see ANGUISH).

angio-, first el. in many scientific terms, repr. Gr. *aggeîon* vessel, receptacle, dim. of *ággos* (*agge-*) chest, box.

angle[1] æ·ŋgl fishing-hook. OE. *angul* = OS., OHG. *angul* (G. *angel*), ON. *ǫngull*; f. Germ. **aŋg*- (whence OE. *anga* sting, goad, MHG. *ange* fish-hook, hinge); cf. next. Hence **a·ngle** vb. fish for. XV. **a·ngl**ER[1] XVI.

angle[2] æ·ŋgl space between two meeting lines or planes. XIV (Ch.). – (O)F. *angle* or L. *angulu-s* corner, dim. of **angus* (cf. Gr. *ágkos* bend, *agkúlos* bent, arched, *ágkūra* ANCHOR[1]).

Angle æ·ŋgl one of a LG. tribe that settled in Britain. XVIII. – L. *Anglus*, pl. *Anglī*, in Tacitus *Angliī* – Germ. **Aŋgli*- (whence OE. *Engle*; cf. ENGLISH) the people of *Angul* district of Slesvig so called from its shape (mod. *Angeln*), the same word as ANGLE[1]. Hence **A·ngl**IAN. XVIII.

Anglican æ·ŋglikən pert. to the Church of England. XVII. – medL. *Anglicānus* (*Anglicana ecclesia* in 'Magna Carta'), f. *Anglicus*, f. *Anglus* ANGLE; see -IC, -AN. Hence F. *anglican*.

anglicism æ·ŋglisizm English feature or idiom. XVII. f. L. *Anglicus*; see prec. and -ISM. Hence F. *anglicisme*. So **a·nglic**IZE XVIII; earlier (rare) †*anglize* XVII (Fuller).

Anglo- æŋglou mod. comb. form of L. *Anglus* ENGLISH, as in modL. *Anglo-Americanus* XVIII, *Anglo-puritanus* XVI; so **Anglo**MA·NIA mania for what is English XVIII, after F. *anglomanie*; **Anglo**PHO·BIA XIX; *Anglo-American, Anglo-Catholic, Anglo-Irish, Anglo-Norman* or *-French* variety of French current in England in the Middle Ages, ANGLO-SAXON.

Anglo-Saxon æŋglousæ·ksən. XVII (P. Holland, tr. Camden's 'Britannia'). – modL. *Anglo-Saxones* pl. (see prec.), for medL. *Angli Saxones* (Paulus Diaconus, VIII) designation of Continental origin for the 'English Saxons' in distinction from the 'Old Saxons' of the Continent; after OE. *Angulseaxe, -seaxan*, in hybrid form *Angulsaxones*.

angostura æŋgəstjuə·rə bark used as a febrifuge and tonic. XVIII (also *angustura*). f. name of a town on the Orinoco, S. America, now called Ciudad Bolivar.

angry æ·ŋgri see ANGER.

anguish æ·ŋgwiʃ severe bodily or mental suffering. XIII. – OF. *anguisse* (mod. *angoisse*) = Pr. *angoisa*, It. *angoscia* :– L. *angustia* straitness, pl. straits, distress, f. *angustus* narrow, tight, f. **aŋgh*- in L. *angere*, Gr. *ágkhein* squeeze, strangle, OE. *enge*, OS., OHG. *engi* (G. *enge*), ON. *ǫngr*, Goth. *aggwus* narrow, and ON. *angr* (see ANGER). For the development *-ish* cf. -ISH[2].

angular æ·ŋgjŭləɹ sharp-cornered, pert. to an angle. XV. – L. *angulāris*, f. *angulus* ANGLE[2]; see -AR and cf. F. *angulaire*.

anhungered ənhʌ·ŋgəɹd (arch. or obs.) hungry. XIV. Alteration of AHUNGERED by substitution of *an-* A-[1] for *of-* A-[2]. Hence †**anhu·ngry**. XVII (Sh.).

anhydrous ænhai·drəs (chem.) having no water in its composition. XIX. f. Gr. *ánūdros*, f. *an-* A-[4]+*hudr-*, *húdōr* WATER; see -OUS.

anigh ənai· (arch.) near. XVIII. f. NIGH, after AFAR; cf. ME. *aneh*.

anight ənai·t (arch.) at or by night. XIII. ME. *a niht*, OE. *on niht*, i.e. ON, NIGHT; cf. A-[1]. So **ani·ghts**. XV.

anil æ·nil indigo plant; indigo dye. XVI (*anele, -ile, anill*). – F. or Pg. *anil* – Arab. *an-nīl*, i.e. *al* AL-[2], Arab.-Pers. *nīl* – Skr. *nīlī* indigo (*nīla* dark blue) NIL[1]. Cf. LILAC.

anile ei·nail, æ·nail old-womanish. XVII. – L. *anīlis*, f. *anus* old woman; see -ILE.

aniline æ·nilain chemical base, the source of many dyes. XIX. – G. *anilin* (C. J. Fritzsche, 1841); see ANIL, -INE[4].

animadvert æ:nimæ̆dvə̄·ɹt to observe XVI; pass criticism *on* XVII. – L. *animadvertere*, i.e. *animum advertere* turn the mind to (*ad* AD-, *vertere* turn; see -WARD. So **a:nimadve·r**SION. XVI. – L. or F. The unfavourable meaning seems to be due to assoc. with L. *adversus* ADVERSE.

animal æ·nimǝl now)(*vegetable, mineral.* (i) As adj. of limited use before XVI as with *virtue, spirit*; first in late ME. (XIV, Ch., Trev.) and applied to the faculties of sensation and intelligence)(*vital* and *natural*, a use fossilized in phr. *animal spirits* (orig.) principle of sensation or volition, (now) healthy vivacity, natural gaiety. – (O)F. *animal*, or L. *animālis*, in medL. bestial, f. *anima* vital breath; see ANIMATE and -AL[1]. (ii) As sb. (XIV, Trev.) ult. – L. *animal*, for *animāle*, sb. use of n. of the adj. In *animal kingdom*, after F. *règne animal*, the word is felt to be rather an attrib. use of the sb. Hence **a·nimal**ISM. XIX (Carlyle).

animalcule ænimæ·lkjūl †tiny animal; (biol.) microscopic animal. XVI. – modL. *animalculum* (whence also F. *animalcule*), dim. of *animal*; see prec. and -CULE. The L. form was formerly in Eng. use, with pl. *animalcula*, often irreg. *animalculæ*.

animate æ·nimeit give life to. XVI. f. pp. stem (see -ATE[3]) of L. *animāre* quicken, f. *anima* air, breath, life, soul, rel. to *animus* spirit, Gr. *ánemos* wind, Skr. *ániti* breathe, and in Germ. to ON. *andi, ǫnd* soul, spirit, Goth. *us|anan* breathe out. So **a·nim**ATE[2] endowed with life XV;)(INANIMATE. **animа**·TION. XVI. – L.

animosity ænimɔ·sĭti †spiritedness XV; active enmity XVII. – F. *animosité* or late L. *animōsitās*, f. *animōsus* spirited, f. *animus* spirit, mind; see prec. and -OSITY.

animus æ·nimǝs hostile spirit. XIX. – L. *animus* spirit; see ANIMATE.

anion æ·naiǝn (electr.) electro-negative element. XIX (Faraday). – Gr. *aniṓn*, n. prp. of *aniénai* go up.

anise æ·nis umbelliferous plant with aromatic seeds. XIII. – (O)F. *anis* :– L. *anīsum* – Gr. *ánīson*, prob. of foreign origin. Hence **a·niseed** seed of this. XIV (*annes, aneys sede*).

ankle, ancle æ·ŋkl joint connecting the foot with the leg. XIV (*ankel*). – ON. **ankul-* (OSw. *ankol*, OIcel. *ǫkkla*), corr. to OFris. *ankel*, MLG. *enkel*, MDu. *ankel* (Du. *enkel*), OHG. *anchal, enchil* (G. *enkel*); f. **aŋk-* :– IE. **aŋg-*, as in L. *angulus* ANGLE[2]. (Superseded OE. *anclēow*, whence ME. *anclow, anclee* (Ch.) = MDu. *anclau*, OHG. *anchlāo*; perh. f. Germ. **aŋkal-*+**klāwa-* CLAW.) Hence **anklet** æ·ŋklit ring for the ankle XIX; after *bracelet*.

ankylosis see ANCHYLOSIS.

anlace æ·nlǝs (hist.) short two-edged knife. XIII. ME. *aunlaz, anla(a)s*, of unkn. origin; recorded by Matthew Paris (XIII) as a vernacular word, in latinized form *anelacius*.

anna æ·nǝ $\frac{1}{16}$ of a rupee. XVIII. – Hind. *ānā* (Panjabi *ānnā*); cf. Skr. *áṇus* small.

annals æ·nǝlz pl. chronicle of events year by year. XVI. – F. *annales* or L. *annālēs* m. pl. (sc. *librī* books) of *annālis* yearly, f. *annus* (see ANNUAL). Hence **a·nnal**IST XVI; after F. *annaliste*.

annates æ·neits first year's revenue of benefice or see. XVI (in Sc. use in sg. form *annat, -et*). – pl. of F. *annate* – medL. *annāta* year's space, work, or proceeds (whence F. *année* year), f. *annus* year (see ANNUAL)+*-āta*, pp. fem. ending used to form sbs.

anneal ǝnī·l †kindle OE.; †fuse, fire XIV; burn in colours, temper, etc. with fire XV. OE. *onǣlan*, f. *on*+*ǣlan* kindle, burn, bake, f. *āl* fire, burning; rel. to *ǣl(e)d* fire, burning = OS. *ēld*, ON. *eldr* :– **ailiðaz*. Aphetic (dial.) *neal* (XVI).

annelid a·nǝlid (zool.) red-blooded worm. XIX. – F. *annélide* or modL. *annelida*, n. pl. f. F. *annelés* 'ringed animals' (Lamarck, 1801), pp. of *anneler*, f. OF. *annel* (mod. *anneau*) ring :– L. *annellu-s* for *ānellu-s*, dim. of *ānulus*; see ANNULAR, -ID.

annex[1] æ·neks something annexed XVI; supplementary building (usu. **annexe**) XIX. – F. *annexe* – L. *annexum*, sb. use of pp. of *annectere* (see next).

annex[2] ǝne·ks join, add, attach. XIV. – (O)F. *annexer*, f. *annex-*, pp. stem of L. *annectere*, f. *ad* AN-+*nectere* bind (cf. NEXUS). So **annex**A·TION. XV (first in Sc.). – medL.

annihilate ǝnai·(h)ileit bring to naught. XVI. Superseded †*annihil* – (O)F. *annihiler* – late L. *annihilāre* (f. *ad* AD-+*nihil* nothing, NIL), from the pp. of which was derived the pp. †*annihilate* (XIV), whence the inf. form; see -ATE[3]. So **annihil**A·TION. XVII. – F.

anniversary ænivǝ̄·ɹsǝri sb. yearly return of a date, or its celebration XIII (AncrR.); adj. XV. – L. *anniversārius*, f. *annus* year+*versus* turning+*-ārius*; used sb. in medL. *anniversāria* (sc. *diēs* day) and *anniversārium* (sc. *festum* feast); cf. (O)F. *anniversaire* and see ANNUAL, VERSE, -ARY.

Anno Domini æ·nou dɔ·minai in the year of the Lord, i.e. of the Christian era XVI; (joc.) advancing age XIX. L., abl. of *annus* year, and g. of *dominus* lord; see ANNUAL DOMINICAL.

annotate æ·nŏteit furnish with notes. XVIII. f. pp. stem of L. *annotāre*, f. *ad* AN-[1]+*nota* mark, NOTE. So †**annote** XV. **annot**A·TION. XV. – F. or L.

announce ǝnau·ns make publicly known. XV (Caxton; rare before XVIII). – (O)F. *anoncer* :– L. *annuntiāre*, f. *ad* AN-[1]+*nuntius* message, messenger (cf. ANNUNCIATION, NUNCIO). Hence **annou·nce**MENT. XVIII. For the vocalism cf. *denounce, enounce, pronounce, renounce*, and *ounce*.

annoy ǝnoi· vexation, annoyance. XIII (AncrR.). ME. *anui, anuy, anoy* – OF. *anui, anoi, enoi* (mod. *ennui*) = Pr. *enoi, enoc*, Cat. *enutg*, Sp. *enojo*, OIt., Pg. *nojo* :– Rom. **inodio*, from the L. phr. *mihī in odiō est* it is hateful to me (cf. ODIUM). So **annoy·** vb. XIII (Laȝ.). – OF. *anuier, anoier* (mod. *ennuyer*) = Pr. *enojar*, Cat. *enujar*, It. *an-*

noiare; cf. late L. *inodiāre* make loathsome, f. **inodio*. So **annoy**·ANCE. XIV (Ch.). – OF. *anoiance*, f. *anoier*.

annual æ·njuəl yearly. XIV (Wycl. Bible). Earlier *annuel* – (O)F. *annuel* – late L. *annuālis*, for L. *annuus* and *annālis*, f. *annus* year :– **atnos* (cf. Oscan g. pl. *acunum*, Umbrian *acnu* solemn festival), rel. to synon. Goth. (d. pl.) *aþnam*, (g. sg.) *at|aþnjis*, and prob. to Skr. *átati* go, wander; see -AL[1].

annuity ənjū·ĭti yearly grant XV; investment securing annual payment XVII. – F. *annuité* – medL. *annuitās*, f. *annuus* ANNUAL; see -ITY. Hence **annu·it**ANT one who holds an annuity. XVIII.

annul ənʌ·l reduce to nothing, make null. XIV. – OF. *anuller*, *adnuller* (mod. *annuler*) :– late L. (Vulg.) *annullāre*, f. *ad* AN-+ *nullum* nothing, n. sg. of *nullus* none, NULL, after Gr. *exoudeneîn*, f. *oudén* nothing.

annular æ·njŭləɹ ring-shaped, ringed. XVI. – F. *annulaire* or L. *annulāris*, f. *annulus*, late form of *ānulus*, dim. of *ānus* ring; see ANUS, -ULE, -AR.

annunciation ənʌnsiei·ʃən announcement (spec. of the Incarnation). XIV. – (O)F. *annonciation* – late L. *annuntiātiō(n-)*, f. *annuntiāre* ANNOUNCE; see -ATION.

anode æ·noud (electr.) positive pole. XIX (Faraday). – Gr. *ánodos* way up, f. *aná* up, ANA-+*hodós* way (cf. HODOMETER); applied orig. to the path by which an electric current leaves the positive pole. Cf. *cathode*, *electrode*.

anodyne æ·nŏdain (medicine) assuaging pain. XVI. – L. *anōdynus* (Celsus) – Gr. *anṓdunos* free from pain, f. *an-* A-[4]+*odúnē* pain. Cf. F. *anodin*, *-ine*, perh. the immed. source.

anoint ənoi·nt apply ointment to. XIV (R. Mannyng). f. *anoint* anointed – OF. *anoint*, *enoint*, pp. of *enoindre* :– L. *inungere*, f. *in* IN-[1]+*ungere* anoint (cf. OINTMENT). Aphetic †*noint* (XIV–XVII). Replaced OE. *smerian* SMEAR in special senses. **The (Lord's) Anointed**, the CHRIST. XVI.

anomalous ənɔ·mələs irregular, abnormal. XVII. f. late L. *anōmalus* – Gr. *anṓmalos* uneven, f. *an-* A-[4]+*homalós* even, f. *homós* SAME; see -OUS. So **ano·maly.** XVI. – L. *anōmalia* – Gr. *anōmalíā*; see -Y[3].

anon ənɔ·n †into or in one body, state, course, etc.; †at once OE.; soon, shortly; now again XVI. OE. *on ān* into one, *on āne* in one, i.e. ON, and acc. and dat. of *ān* ONE.

anonymous ənɔ·nimǝs nameless, unnamed. XVII. f. late L. *anōnymos*, *-us* – Gr. *anṓnumos*, f. *an-* A-[4]+*ónuma*, *ónoma* NAME. The earliest exx. are in Gr. or L. form. Cf. *paronymous*, *synonymous*. Hence **anony·mi**TY ænəni·mĭti. XIX.

another ənʌ·ðəɹ an additional (one). XIII. ME. *an other* (in two words as late as XVI), i.e. AN[1], OTHER second, remaining, different; superseded the simple *ōþer* of OE.

anserine æ·nsərain goose-like. XIX. – L. *anserīnus*, f. *anser* GOOSE; see -INE[1].

answer à·nsəɹ reply. OE. *andswaru*, corr. to OFris. *ondser*, OS. *antswōr*, ON. *andsvar* :– Germ. **andswarō*, f. **and-* against, opposite (see ANTI-)+**swar-*, base of OE. *swerian* SWEAR, ON. *svara*, Goth. *swaran* answer; orig. a solemn affirmation in rebutting a charge (cf. Gr. *apokrínesthai* answer, f. *apó* off+*krínein* judge, lit. get oneself off from judgement, L. *respondēre* RESPOND). Hence **a·nswer** vb. OE. *andswarian* = OFris. *ondswera*, ON. *andsvara*. **a·nswer**ABLE responsible, accountable; suitable, agreeable XVI; that can be answered (cf. *unanswerable*) XVII.

ant ænt emmet, pismire. OE. *æmet(t)e* = MLG. *āmete*, *ēmete*, OHG. *ā̆meiʒa* (G. *ameise*) :– WGerm. **ā̆maitjōn*, **aimaitjōn*, f. **ai-* off, away+**mait-* cut, hew (OHG. *meiʒan*, ON. *meita*, Goth. *maitan*). The OE. forms gave two ME. types, (i) *am(e)te*, whence *ampte* (cf. the place-name *Ampthill*), *ante*, *ant* (the prevailing standard form), and (ii) *emete*, EMMET (widespread dial. var., occurring also as a surname).

ant- ænt var. of ANTI- used before vowels, as *antacid* (XIX), earlier *antiacid* (XVIII).

-ant ənt repr. (O)F. *-ant* :– L. *-antem*, nom. *-āns*, under which all prps. were levelled in French; rarely used as a living suffix and only on some spec. analogy, as in *anæsthesiant*, *annuitant*.

antagonist æntæ·gənist opponent, adversary. XVI (Jonson). – F. *antagoniste* or late L. *antagōnista* (Jerome) – Gr. *antagōnistḗs*, f. *antagōnízesthai* struggle against, vie with; see ANTI-, AGONIZE. So **anta·gon**ISM XIX; prob. after F. **anta·gon**IZE oppose, counteract XVII (rare before XIX); make hostile XIX. – Gr. *antagōnízesthai*.

Antarctic æntā·ɹktik opposite to the Arctic. XIV (Maund., Ch.). Late ME. *antartik*, later conformed (like the F.) to the Gr. form – OF. *antartique* (mod. *-arctique*) = Pr. *antartic*, It. *antartico* or their source L. *antarcticus* – Gr. *antarktikós* opposite to the north; see ANTI-, ARCTIC.

ante æ·nti (in poker) stake put up by the player before drawing new cards. XIX. – L. *ante* before (see next).

ante- æ·nti repr. L. adv.-prep. *ante* in comps., corr. to Gr. acc. *ánta* over against, and loc. *antí* ANTI-, Skr. *ánti* opposite (adv.), with the sense 'before' in place or time, as in ANTECEDENT, etc. below; also *a·nte-chapel* XVIII, *anteda·te* XVI, *antena·tal* XIX, *a:nte-penu·ltimate* XVIII, *a·nte-room* XVIII.

antecedent æntisī·dənt a thing preceding another, orig. in grammar and logic. XIV (PPl.). – (O)F. *antécédent* or L. *antecēdent-*, *-ēns* (used sb. in n. pl.), prp. of *antecēdere*. f. *ante* ANTE-+*cēdere* go, CEDE.

antechamber æ·ntitʃeimbəɹ chamber leading to the chief apartment. XVII (before XIX usu. *anti-*). – F. *antichambre* – It. *anticamera*; see ANTE-, CHAMBER.

antediluvian æ:ntidil^jū·viən before the Flood. XVII. f. *ante* ANTE- + L. *dīluvium* DELUGE + -AN. Cf. F. *antédiluvien* (XVIII).

antelope æ·ntiloup †savage horned beast of Asia Minor XV (Lydg.); deer-like ruminant of the genus Antilope XVII. – OF. *antelop* (once, Brunetto Latini) or medL. *ant(h)alopus* – medGr. *anthólops*, of which the source and orig. meaning are unkn. ¶ The generic name *Antilope* is due to Pallas, *c.* 1775; F. *antilope*, used by Buffon, is from Eng.

antenna ænte·nə horn or feeler of insects. XVII. – L. *antenna*, prop. *antemna* sail-yard, used in pl. to tr. Aristotle's κεραῖοι 'horns' of insects.

antependium æntipe·ndiəm altar frontal. XVII (earlier †*antepend* XVI). medL., f. *ante* ANTE-+*pendēre* hang (see PENDENT).

anterior æntiə·riəɹ earlier, prior. XVII. – F. *antérieur* or L. *anterior*, f. *ante* before, after *posterior*; see ANTE-, -IOR.

anthelion ænþī·liən, ænthī·liən luminous ring surrounding the shadow of an observer's head projected opposite to the sun. XVII. – Gr. *anthḗlion*, n. of *anthḗlios*, earlier *antḗlios* opposite to the sun, f. *antí* ANTI-+ *hḗlios* SUN.

anthem æ·nþəm (hist.) antiphon OE.; composition in unmeasured prose to be sung; song of praise, etc. XVI. OE. *antefn*, *antifne* – late L. *anti·phona*, for *antiphō·na* ANTIPHON. The forms indicate the foll. development of pronunc.: ante·vne, ante·m(ne), a·ntem, a·nthem (the last from XV; cf. OF. *anthaine*; perh. infl. by *hymne* hymn); the sp. with *th* finally affected the pronunc., as in *author*.

anther æ·nþəɹ (bot.) part of a stamen containing the pollen. XVIII (earlier in L. form). – F. *anthère* or modL. *anthēra*, in cl. L. medicine extracted from flowers – Gr. *anthērá*, fem. of *anthērós* of flowers, f. *anthe-*, *ánthos* flower. As these medicines often consisted of the internal organ of flowers (e.g. saffron was the stigma), *anthera* was applied to these parts by early pharmacists, and was later by herbalists restricted to the pollen-bearing organs, a use sanctioned by Linnæus.

anthology ænþɔ·lədʒi collection of literary 'flowers'. XVII. – F. *anthologie* or medL. *anthologia* (cf. L. *anthologica*) – Gr. *anthología*, f. *ánthos* flower.

anthracite æ·nþrəsait non-bituminous coal. XIX (Davy). – Gr. *anthrakîtis* kind of coal, f. *anthrak-*, *ánthrax*, see next and -ITE b.

anthrax æ·nþræks carbuncle; splenic fever of sheep and cattle; malignant pustule. Hardly in naturalized use before XIX. – late L. – Gr. *ánthrax* coal, carbuncle.

anthropo- ænþrou·pou, æ·nþrŏpŏ, -pɔ· comb. form of Gr. *ánthrōpos* man; e.g. Gr. *anthrōpológos* (Aristotle) treating of man, whence modL. *anthrōpologia*, Eng. **anthropo·logy** (XVI), the science of man; ecclGr. *anthrōpomorphîtai* sect ascribing human form to God, whence Eng. **anthropomo·rph**ITE (XVI); so **anthropomorph**ISM (XVIII), -IST (XVII), -IC; Gr. *anthrōpophagoi* man-eaters, whence L. *unthrōpophagi*; and in many mod. formations on these models.

anti- æ·nti before a vowel **ant-,** before *h* **anth-,** repr. Gr. *anti-*, *antí* opposite, against, instead of, rel. to OE. *and-* (as in ALONG², ANSWER), OS. *and-*, *ant-*, OHG. *ant-*, *int-*, *ent-*, ON. *and-*, Goth. *and* along, above, OLith. *anta* on, towards, L. *ante* before (ANTE-), Skr. *ánti* before, in the presence of, near. Used in many words adopted from Gr. comps. and in words modelled on these, and, as a gen. living formative, very freely prefixed to (i) sbs., on the pattern of ANTICHRIST, *antipope* (XVI; medL. *antipāpa*), (ii) adjs., the prefix governing the sb. implied, as *anti-national*, *anti-Semitic*; (iii) sbs. in attrib. phr., as *anti-aircraft* (defences), *anti-church* (politics), *anti-slavery* (committee).

antic æ·ntik (arch.) grotesque or fantastic (form, gesture, person); sb. †fantastic or grotesque figure; †clown, buffoon; ludicrous gesture or posture. XVI (freq. *antike*, *antique* XVI–XVII). – It. *antico* ancient, ANTIQUE, used as synon. with *grottesco* GROTESQUE; orig. applied to the fantastic figures found in ancient Roman remains, and subsequently to anything grotesque.

Antichrist æ·ntikraist opponent of Christ or Christianity. XII (Vesp. D. Hom.). ME. *ante-*, *anticrist* (later assim. to L. and Gr.) – OF. *antecrist* (mod. *antéchrist*) – ecclL. *antichrīstus* – Gr. *antíkhrīstos* (1 John ii 18), f. *antí* ANTI-+*Khrīstós* CHRIST. Hence **antichri·stian.** XVI; now treated only as *anti-*+ *Christian.*

anticipate ænti·sipeit take up beforehand. XVI. f. (partly after F. *anticiper*) pp. stem of L. *anticipāre*, f. *ante* ANTE-+*cip-*, var. of base of *capere*; see CAPTURE, -ATE³.

antidote æ·ntidout medicine to counteract poison. XV. – F. *antidote* or L. *antidotum* – Gr. *antídoton*, sb. use of n. of *antídotos*, f. *antí* ANTI-+*do-*, stem of *didónai* give (see DONATION). XVI also in Gr. or L. form.

antimacassar æ:ntiməkæ·səɹ covering for chair-backs, etc., orig. to protect them from grease in the hair. XIX. f. ANTI-+MACASSAR.

antimony æ·ntiməni trisulphide of antimony XV; (chem.) metallic element (Sb) XIX (earlier *regulus of a.* XVI). – medL. *antimōnium* (Constantinus Africanus of Salerno, XI), of unkn. origin. Conjectured to be latinization of Arab. *uthmud*, *ithmid*, perh.

– Gr. *stimmid-*, *stimmi* (whence L. *stibium*); cf. Egyptian *śdm* powder used for the eyes.

antinomian æntinou·miən. XVII. f. medL. *Antinomī* German sect which denied obligation of the moral law upon Christians, f. Gr. *antí* ANTI- + *nómos* law; see NOMAD, -IAN.

antinomy æ·ntinəmi contradiction. XVI. – L. *antinomia* – Gr. *antinomíā*, f. *antí* ANTI- + *nómos* law; cf. prec., see -Y[3].

antipathy ænti·pəþi feeling against, aversion. XVII. – F. *antipathie* or L. *antipathīa* – Gr. *antipátheia*, f. *antipathḗs* opposed in feeling, f. *anti* ANTI- + *pathe-*, *páthos*; see PATHOS, -Y[3]. So **a:ntiPATHE·TIC**. XVII.

antiphon æ·ntifən (liturg.) short verse of Scripture recited responsively in connexion with a psalm. XV. – ecclL. *antiphōna* – Gr. (*tà*) *antíphōna*, n. pl. of *antíphōnos* responsive, f. *antí* ANTI- + *phōnḗ* sound (cf. PHONETIC); see ANTHEM. So **antiphoner** ænti·fənəɹ book of antiphons. XIV (Wycl., Ch.). – OF. *antifenier*, *-phonier* – ecclL. *antiphōnārium*, anglicized as **anti·phonARY**. XV.

antiphrasis ænti·frəsis (rhet.) use of a word in a sense opposite to its proper meaning. XVI (More). – late L. – Gr. *antíphrasis*, f. *antiphrázein* express by the opposite; see ANTI-, PHRASE.

antipodes ænti·pədīz †people inhabiting the opposite side of the globe; places on the earth exactly opposite to each other. XVI. – F. *antipodes* or late L. *antipodes* – Gr. *antípodes*, pl. of *antípous* having the feet opposite, f. *antí* ANTI- + *poús* FOOT. Formerly 3 syll. *a·ntipodes*, with sg. *antipode*; the 4-syll. form shows reversion to L. and Gr.

antiquary æ·ntikwəri official custodian or recorder of antiquities (title bestowed by Henry VIII on John Leland), whence gen. student or collector of these. XVI. – L. *antīquārius*, f. *antīquus*; see next and -ARY. So **antiquARIAN** -kwɛə·riən. XVII.

antique æntī·k ancient; old-fashioned; also sb. XVI. – F. *antique* or L. *antīquus*, *antīcus* (whence pop. OF. *antif*, Pr. *antic*, etc.), f. *ante* before, ANTE- + *-īcus* (as in *postīcus*, f. *post*); orig. identical in form and pronunc. with ANTIC, but finally differentiated after 1700. So **antiquity** ænti·kwĭti. XIV. – OF. – L. **a·ntiquated**. XVII, orig. pp. of *antiquate* (XV).

antirrhinum æntirai·nəm snapdragon. XVI. – L. – Gr. *antírrhīnon*, f. *antí* opposite, counterfeiting, ANTI- + *rhīn-*, *rhī́s* nose (cf. RHINOCEROS), from the resemblance of the flower to an animal's mouth.

antiseptic æntise·ptik counteracting putrefaction. XVIII. – modL. *antisēpticus*, f. Gr. *antí* ANTI- + *sēptikós* SEPTIC.

antistrophe ænti·strəfi answer to the strophe in a Gr. chorus. XVII. – late L. – Gr. *antistrophḗ*, f. *antistréphein*; see ANTI-, STROPHE.

antithesis ænti·þisis opposition of ideas. XV. – late L. – Gr. *antíthesis*, f. *antithénai*, f. *antí* ANTI- + *tithénai* set, place (cf. THESIS). So **antithetIC** -þe·tik XVII, -ICAL XVI. ult. – Gr. *antithetikós*.

antler æ·ntləɹ branch of deer's horn. XIV. Late ME. *auntelere* – AN. var. of OF. *antoillier*, later *ondoillier*, *endoulier* (mod. *andouiller*), with early vars. *endoillee*, *andouillee*, of unkn. origin; deriv. from popL. **antoculāre* (L. *ante* before, *oculus* eye) is not phonologically tenable.

antonomasia æntŏnŏmei·ziə (rhet.) substitution of an epithet for a person's proper name; use of proper name generically. XVI. L. – Gr. *antonomasíā*, f. *antonomázein*, f. *antí* ANTI- + *onomázein* name, f. *ónoma* NAME.

antonym æ·ntŏnim antithetical term)(*synonym*. XIX. – F. *antonyme*, f. Gr. *antí* ANTI-, after *synonyme* SYNONYM.

anus ei·nəs fundament. XVI. – L. *ānus* orig. ring (cf. ANNULAR). So **a·NAL**[1]. XVIII. – modL.

anvil æ·nvil block on which a smith shapes metal. OE. *anfilte* (earlier *onfilti*) m. or n., also *anfealt* fem., corr. to MDu. *aenvilte*, OHG. *anafalz* (G. dial. *afilts*, *amfilt*, *anefilt*), to which are parallel MLG. *anebelte*, *-bolt*, MDu. *aen-*, *anebelt*, *-bilt* (Du. *aanbeald*, *aambeeld*), and OHG. *anabōʒ* (G. *amboss*); all based on Germ. **ana* ON + vb.-stem meaning 'beat' (cf. FELT) and perh. all modelled on L. *incūs* anvil, f. *in* IN-[1] + *cūd-*, stem of *cūdere* beat (cf. HEW).

anxious æ·ŋkʃəs troubled in mind. XVII. f. L. *anxius*, f. pp. stem *anx-* of *angere* choke, oppress; see ANGUISH, -IOUS. So **anxieTY** æŋzai·ĭti uneasiness of mind XVI; (med.) distressful pain in the region of the heart XVII (so F. *anxiété* XVI). – F. or L. *anxietās*.

any e·ni OE. *ǣniġ* = OFris. *ēnich*, OS. *ēnig*, MLG. *einich*, MDu. *ēnich* (Du. *eenig*), OHG. *einag* (G. *einig*), ON. *einigr*, Goth. *ainah-* :– CGerm. **ainagaz*, *-igaz*, f. **ain-* ONE + **-ig-* -Y[1]; parallel formations are L. *ūnicus* UNIQUE, OSl. *inokŭ* monk, wild boar. In ME. two types were current, *ani* and *eni*; the present sp. continues the first, the pronunc. the second (cf. dial. æ·ni). **anybody**. XIII. **anyhow**. XVIII. **anything**. OE. **anywhere**. XIII (Cursor M.).

Anzac æ·nzæk Australasian. 1915. Made up of the initials of *A*ustralian and *N*ew *Z*ealand *A*rmy *C*orps.

aorist ɛə·rist (gram.) tense denoting past time (simply, without limitation). XVI. – Gr. *aóristos* undefined (sb. sc. *khrónos* time, Dionysius Thrax), f. *a-* A-[4] + *horistós* delimited, f. *horízein* define (cf. HORIZON).

aorta eiɔ̄·ɹtə (anat.) the great artery. XVI. modL. – Gr. *aortḗ*, by Hippocrates used pl. for the branches of the windpipe, by Aristotle for the great artery, f. **aor-*, var. of **aer-* of *aeírein* (:– **aerj-*) raise; cf. ARTERY.

ap- assim. form of AD- before *p*; cf. AC-.

apace əpei·s with speed. XIV. – OF. *a pas* at (a considerable) pace, i.e. *a* (:– L. *ad* AT), *pas* step, PACE.

apache ǽpæ·ʃ ruffian of a type infesting Paris. XX (1902). – F. *apache*, a use of the name of a warlike tribe of N. American Indians. Cf. MOHOCK.

apart əpā·ɹt to one side, aside, separately. XIV (PPl.). – OF. *apart* (now *à part*) = It. *a parte* :– L. *ā parte* at the side, i.e. *ā* AB-+ abl. of *pars* side, PART. **apa·rtheid** -heit racial segregation as in S. Africa XX.

apartment əpā·ɹtmənt self-contained portion of a house, etc. XVII. – F. *appartement* – It. *appartamento*, f. *appartare* separate, f. *a parte* APART; see -MENT.

apathy æ·pəþi insensibility XVII; indolence of mind XVIII. – F. *apathie* – L. *apathīa* – Gr. *apátheia*, f. *apathḗs* without feeling, f. *a-* A-[4]+*pathe-*, PATHOS; see -Y[3]. So **apathe·tic** XVIII; after PATHETIC.

apatite æ·pətait (min.) native phosphate of lime. XIX. – G. *apatit* (Werner 1786), f. Gr. *apátē* deceit; so named from its diverse and deceptive forms; see -ITE[1].

ape eip tailless monkey. OE. *apa* m., *ape* fem. = OS. *apo* (Du. *aap*), OHG. *affo* m., *affe* fem. (G. *affe*), ON. *api* :– CGerm. (exc. Goth.) **apan-*, which with ORuss. *opica* and OBoh. *opice* may have been collateral adoptions of an alien word along trade-routes (possibly through Celtic regions; cf. Hesychius' *ἀβράνας· Κελτοὶ τοὺς κερκοπιθήκους*). There is no CIE. or CWEur. word for 'ape'. Ir. *apa*, *napa*, Gael. *apa*, W. *epa*, †*āb* are from Eng. Hence **a·pery**. XVII. **a·pish**[1]. XVI.

apeak əpī·k (naut.) vertical(ly). XVI. orig. *a pike* – F. *à pic*, i.e. *à* AT, on+*pic* PEAK (to which the second syll. was assim.).

apepsy eipe·psi (med.) lack of digestive power. XVII. – modL. *apepsia* – Gr. *apepsíā*, f. *a-* A-[4]+*péptein* digest; see PEPTIC, -Y[3].

aperient əpiə·riənt laxative (medicine). XVII. f. L. *aperient-*, *-ēns*, prp. of *aperīre* open)(*operīre* cover, hide; see -ENT. So **aperitive** əpe·ritiv. XVI (*-ative*). – F. *apéritif* (used sb. for appetizing drink) – medL. *aperitīvus*, var. of late L. *apertīvus* (Cælius Aurelianus), f. *apertus*, pp. of *aperīre*.

apert əpə̄·ɹt (arch.) open, manifest; †outspoken, forward. XIV. – OF. *apert* – L. *apertu-s* open (see prec.). Aphetic PERT.

aperture æ·pəɹtʃuəɹ opening. XV (Sc. *-ore*; in Eng. use from XVII). – L. *apertūra*, f. *apert-*, pp. stem of *aperīre*; see prec., -URE.

apex ei·peks pl. *apices* ei·pisīz tip, peak. XVII. – L. *apex*. Hence **a·pical**[1] XIX.

aphæresis ǽfiə·rīsis suppression of an initial syllable. XVII. – late L. – Gr. *aphaíresis*, f. *aphaireîn* take away, f. *apó* APO-+*haireîn* take (cf. HERESY).

aphasia əfei·ziə (med.) loss of speech. XIX. – modL. – Gr. *aphasíā*, f. *áphatos* speechless, f. *a-* A-[4]+*phánai* speak (cf. PHASE); see -IA[1].

aphelion ǽfī·liən (astron.) point of a planet's or comet's orbit at which it is farthest from the sun. XVII. Græcized form (Kepler) of modL. *aphēlium*, f. Gr. *apó* APO-+*hḗlios* SUN, after L. *apogæum* APOGEE.

aphesis æ·fīsis (philol.) loss of a short initial unaccented syllable as in *(a)lone*, *(e)squire*. 1880 (suggested by J. A. H. Murray). – Gr. *áphesis* letting go, f. *aphiénai*, f. *apó* APO-+*hiénai* let go, send. So **aphetic** əfe·tik. f. Gr. *áphetos*, verbal adj. of *aphiénai*.

aphis ei·fis, æ·fis pl. *aphides* -idīz, *aphises* -isiz plant-louse, green-fly. XVIII. – modL. *aphis*, first used by Linnæus, and based on *ἄφις* (*áphis*) in Aldrovandi's 'De animalibus insectis' (1602). The Gr. form appears first (with the L. gloss *cimex*) in Gulielmus Rainus' 'Lexicon Græcum' (1523); it is relegated to the appendix of aberrant forms in Stephanus' Thesaurus of 1562; it is prob. an error for *κόρις* bug, *κορ* having been misread as *αφ*. The pl. *aphides* was poss. made on the model of *kórides*, pl. of *kóris*.

aphorism æ·fərizm concise pithy maxim. XVI. – F. *aphorisme*, or late L. *aphorismus* – Gr. *aphorismós* definition, f. *aphorízein* to define, f. *apó* APO-+*horízein* (cf. HORIZON).

aphrodisiac æfrodi·ziæk (drug) exciting sexual desire. XVIII. – Gr. *aphrodīsiakós*, f. *aphrodísios*, f. *Aphrodítē* goddess of love ('foam-born'; *aphrós* foam).

apiary ei·piəri place for keeping bees in. XVII. – L. *apiārium*, f. *apis* bee; see -ARY. **a·piculture** XIX.

apiece əpī·s for each piece, unit, or one of a set. XIV. orig. two words, viz. A[1], PIECE sb.

aplomb æplɔ̃· perpendicularity, steadiness XVIII; self-possession XIX. F., f. phr. *à plomb* according to the plummet (see PLUMB).

apo- æ·pou, əpɔ· before a vowel **ap-**, before *h* **aph-** prefix repr. Gr. *apo-*, comb. form of prep. *apó* away, OFF, in many words adopted ult. from Gr. and denoting removal, departure, completion, cessation, return, or reversion.

Apocalypse əpɔ·kəlips Revelation of St. John the Divine. XIII (AncrR.). – (O)F. *apocalypse* – ecclL. *apocalypsis* – Gr. *apokálupsis*, f. *apokalúptein* uncover, disclose, f. *apó* APO-+*kalúptein* cover (IE. base **kel-*, etc.; cf. CONCEAL). So **apocaly·ptic**, -ICAL. XVII. – F. *-ique* (Rabelais). – Gr. *apokaluptikós*, f. the vb.

apocope əpɔ·kəpi (gram.) cutting off the end of a word. XVI. – late L. – Gr. *apokopḗ*, f. *apokóptein* cut off, f. *apó* APO-+*kóptein* cut (*kopḗ* incision, etc.). So **apo·copate** XIX, **apocopa·tion** XVIII; see -ATE[2] and [3].

Apocrypha əpɔ·krifə †adj. of unknown authorship, uncanonical XIV–XVII; sb. writings of doubtful authorship (also in n. sg. *apocryphon* and †pl. *apocryphas*) XIV; (spec.)

uncanonical books of the O.T. XVI. – n. pl. (sc. *scripta* writings) of ecclL. *apocryphus*, Gr. *apókruphos* hidden, f. *apokrúptein* hide away; see APO- and CRYPT. Hence **apo·cryph**AL. XVI.

apod æ·pɔd (animal) without feet or ventral fins. XVII. f. Gr. *apod-*, *ápous*, f. *a-* A-[4]+*poús* FOOT. So **a·pod**AL[1] XVIII, **a·pod**OUS XIX.

apodeictic, -dictic æpodai·ktik, -di·ktik demonstratively clear. XVII. – L. *apodīcticus* – Gr. *apodeiktikós*, f. *apodeiknúnai* demonstrate, f. *apó* APO- + *deiknúnai* show, f. **deik-*, as in L. *dīcere* (cf. DICTION); see -IC.

apodosis əpɔ·dəsis (gram.) consequent clause answering to the protasis; †application of a parable. XVII. – late L. (Donatus) – Gr. *apódosis* 'a giving back', f. *apodidónai*, f. *apó* APO-+*didónai* give (see DONATION).

apogee æ·podʒī (astron.) point of a planet's orbit at which it is farthest from the earth. XVII (in XVI and XVII the L. forms were current). – F. *apogée* or modL. *apogæum*, *-eum* – Gr. *apógaion*, *-eion*, sb. use (sc. *diástēma* distance) of n. of adjs. *apógaios*, *-eios* far from the earth, f. *apó* APO-+*gai-*, *gei-*, stems of *gê* (*gaîa*) earth. ¶ A term of the Ptolemaic astronomy which viewed the earth as the centre of the universe.

apolaustic æpolɔ̄·stik self-indulgent. XIX. – Gr. *apolaustikós*, f. *apolaúein* enjoy, f. *apó* APO-+**law-*, connected by some with L. *lucrum* gain, LUCRE; see -IC.

Apollyon əpɔ·liən the Devil. XIV. – L. (Vulg.) *Apollyōn* – Gr. (N.T.) *Apollúōn* (Rev. ix 11), sb. use of prp. of *apollúnai* intensive (see APO-) of *ollúnai* destroy (cf. ABOLISH).

apologue æ·pŏlɔg moral fable. XVII. – F. *apologue* or L. *apologus* – Gr. *apólogos* story, account, f. *apó* APO-+*lógos* discourse (see LOGOS). Earlier †*apology* (XVI–XVII).

apology æpɔ·lədʒi defence, justification (T. More); acknowledgement of offence given XVI; poor substitute XVIII. – F. *apologie* or late L. *apologia* – Gr. *apologiā* speech in defence, f. *apologeîsthai* speak in one's own defence, f. *apó* APO-+**log-* **leg-* speak (see LOGOS, -LOGY). So **apologe·t**IC vindicatory XVII; self-excusing XIX; sb. XV. – F. *apologétique* – late L. *apologēticus* – Gr. *apologētikós* (Aristotle). **apo·log**IST. XVII. – F. *apologiste*, f. Gr. *apologízesthai* render an account (f. *apólogos*; see prec.), whence **apo·log**IZE XVI; now assoc. with *apology*.

apo(ph)thegm æ·pŏþem pithy saying or maxim. XVI (often *apothegm*, as now regularly in U.S.). – F. *apophthegme* or modL. *apophthegma* – Gr. *apóphthegma*, f. *apophthéggesthai* speak one's opinion plainly, f. *apó* APO-+*phthéggesthai* utter, speak, f. **phthegg-* **phthogg-* sound (cf. DIPHTHONG).

apophysis əpɔ·fisis (anat.) protuberance of a bone XVII; (bot.) XVIII. – modL. – Gr. *apóphysis*, f. *apó* APO-+*phýsis* growth (cf. PHYSIC).

apoplexy æ·pŏpleksi sudden loss of powers of sensation and motion. XIV. – (O)F. *apoplexie* – late L. *apoplēxia* – Gr. *apoplēxiā*, f. *apoplḗssein* disable by a stroke, f. *apó* APO-+*plḗssein* strike (cf. PLECTRUM). So **apople·c**TIC(AL). XVII. – F. *apoplectique* – late L. *apoplēcticus*, Gr. *apoplēktikós*.

aport əpɔ̄·ɹt (naut.) to the port or larboard side. XVII. f. A-[1]+PORT[4], after ALEE.

aposiopesis æ:posaiəpī·sis (gram.) sudden breaking-off in the middle of speech. XVI. – L. (Quintilian) – Gr. *aposiṓpēsis*, f. *aposiōpân* be silent, f. *apó* off, APO-+*siōpḗ* silence.

apostate əpɔ·stət one who abjures his faith. XIV (often in L. form from XIV–XVII). – (O)F. *apostate* or ecclL. *apostata* – late Gr. *apostátēs*, f. *apostênai*, f. *apó* APO-+*stênai* STAND. So **apo·stasy**. XIV. – ecclL. *apostasia* – late Gr. *apostasíā*, for *apóstasis* defection. **apo·stat**IZE. XVI. f. ecclL. *apostatāre*.

apostle əpɔ·sl any of the Twelve commissioned by Jesus Christ to preach the Gospel. OE. *apostol* (whence ME. *apostel*, *-yl*) – ecclL. *apostolus* – Gr. *apóstolos* one sent forth, messenger, f. *apostéllein*, f. *apó* APO-+*stéllein* place, make ready (rel. to L. *locus* LOCALITY); the early forms were reinforced or superseded by adoption of OF. *apostle* (mod. *apôtre*). So **apostol**IC(AL) -ɔ·lik(əl). XV. – F. *apostolique* – ecclL. – Gr.

apostrophe[1] əpɔ·strəfi (rhet.) exclamatory address. XVI. – L. *apostrophē* – Gr. *apostrophḗ* turning away to one in particular, f. *apostréphein*, f. *apó* away, APO-+*stréphein* turn (cf. STROPHE). Hence **apo·stroph**IZE. XVIII (Pope).

apostrophe[2] əpɔ·strəfi †omission of a sound or letter; the sign ' denoting this. XVII. – F. *apostrophe* or late L. *apostrophus* (also formerly used) – late Gr. *apóstrophos* mark of elision, sb. use (sc. *prosōidiā* accent) of adj. 'turned away', f. *apó* away, APO-+*stroph-* (as in prec.); prop. of 3 sylls., but erron. assim. to prec.

apothecary əpɔ·þikəri druggist, pharmaceutical chemist. XIV. ME. *apotecarie* – OF. *apotecaire*, *-icaire* – late L. *apothēcārius* store-keeper, f. *apothēca* – Gr. *apothḗkē* store-house, f. *apotithénai* put away; cf. BODEGA, THESIS, and see -ARY. Aphetic *pot(h)ecary* (XIV—mod. dial.).

apotheosis əpɔþiou·sis deification. XVII. – ecclL. *apotheōsis* (Tertullian) – Gr. *apothéōsis*, f. *apotheoûn* deify, f. *apó* APO-+*theoûn* make a god of, f. *theós* god (cf. THEO-). Formerly stressed *apothe·osis*, in dependence on the Gr. accent. Hence **apotheos**IZE æpɔ·þiŏsaiz, æpoþiə·saiz deify. XVIII.

appal əpɔ̄·l †grow or make pale XIV; dismay XVI. – OF. *apal(l)ir*, grow pale, languish, waste away, be dismayed, also trans., f. *a-* AD-+*pâlir* PALE[2].

appanage æ·pənidʒ provision made for younger children of princes, etc.; accessory, adjunct XVII; dependency XIX. – (O)F. *apanage*, f. OF. *apaner* dower (a daughter) = Pr. *apanar* – medL. *appānāre* provide with means of subsistence, f. L. *ad* AP- + *pānis* bread (cf. PABULUM); see -AGE.

apparatus æpərei·təs equipment or mechanical requisites; materials for a process. XVII. (Somewhat earlier in anglicized form †*apparate*, perh. after F. *apparat*.) – L. *apparātus*, f. *apparāre* make ready, f. *ad* AP- + *parāre* PREPARE.

apparel əpæ·rəl †prepare, equip XIII; array, attire XIV. ME. *aparaile* – OF. *apareiller* (mod. *app-*) = Pr. *aparelhar*, Sp. *aparejar*, Pg. *apparelhar*, It. *apparecchiare* :– Rom. **adpariculāre* make equal or fit, f. *ad* AP- + **pariculum* (F. *pareil* like, Pr. *parelh*, etc.), dim. of L. *pār* equal. So **appa·rel** sb. †apparatus, equipment; attire. XIV. – OF. *apareil* (mod. *app-*), f. the above vb. Aphetic PARREL.

apparent əpɛə·rənt, əpæ·rənt manifest, obvious XIV (*ayre aparant*, Wycl.); seeming XVII. – OF. *aparant*, *-ent* (mod. *apparent*) – L. *appārent-*, *-ēns*, prp. of *appārēre* APPEAR; see -ENT.

apparition æpəri·ʃən action of appearing XV; something appearing XV; phantom, ghost XVII (Sh.). – (O)F. *apparition* (in OF. the Epiphany) or L. *appāritiō(n-)* attendance, service, f. *appārēre* spec. appear at a summons, attend; see prec. and -ITION.

apparitor əpæ·ritɔ̄ɹ Roman magistrate's servant; officer of a court; herald. XV (Henryson). – L. *appāritor* public servant (lictor, etc.), f. *appārēre* APPEAR; see -OR[1].

appeal əpī·l †charge, accuse; call to a higher tribunal for deliverance from the decision of a lower; call *to* a witness for testimony. XIV. ME. *apele* – OF. *apeler* (mod. *appeler*) call :– L. *appellāre* accost, address, appeal to, impeach, f. *ad* AP- + *pell-* of *pellere* drive (see PULSE[1]). So **appea·l** sb. XIII. – OF. *apel* (mod. *appel*), f. *ap(p)eler*.

appear əpiə·ɹ become or be visible or manifest XIII; seem *to be* XIV. ME. *apere* – *aper-* (as in *il apert* it appears), tonic stem of OF. *apareir* (= Pr. *aparer*) :– L. *appārēre*, f. *ad* AP- + *pārēre* come into view. So **appea·r**ANCE becoming visible; apparent form; seeming, semblance XIV; apparition XV; phenomenon XVII. ME. *aparaunce* – OF. *aparance*, *aparence* (mod. *apparence*) :– late L. *appārentia*, f. prp. of *appārēre*, assim. in form to the vb.

appease əpī·z pacify, assuage. XVI. ME. *apese* – AN. *apeser*, OF. *apaisier* (mod. *apaiser*), f. *a* AD- + *pais* PEACE. Hence **appea·se**MENT. XV. – OF. *apaisement*.

appellant əpe·lənt adj. appealing XIV; sb. one who appeals XV – (O)F. *appellant*, prp. of *appeler* APPEAL. So **appell**ATION æpělei·ʃən †appeal; designation. XV. – (O)F. – L. The sequence of meanings was developed in L. thus: address, appeal, naming, name, (gram.) substantive. **appell**ATIVE əpe·lətiv adj. designating a class XV; sb. descriptive name. XVI. – late L. (gram., pert. to a species).

append əpe·nd attach. XV (Sc.; in Eng. XVII). – L. *appendere*, f. *ad* AP- + *pendere* hang (see PENDENT). Hence **appe·nd**AGE. XVII.

appendix əpe·ndiks pl. *-ices*, *-ixes* subsidiary addition. XVI. – L. *appendix* (*-ic-*), f. *appendere* APPEND. Hence **appendic**ITIS əpendisai·tis inflammation of vermiform appendix of intestine. 1886.

apperception æpəɹse·pʃən (philos.) the mind's perception of itself. XVIII. – F. *aperception* – modL. *apperceptiō* (Leibnitz); see AD-, AP-, PERCEPTION.

appertain æpəɹtei·n belong (in various applications). XIV (Ch.). Late ME. *apertene* – OF. *apertenir* (mod. *appartenir*), corr. to Pr. *apertener*, It. *appartenere* :– Rom. **appartenēre* alteration of late L. *appertinēre*, f. *ad* AP- + *pertinēre* PERTAIN. Cf. APPURTENANCE.

appetence æ·pitəns longing desire. XVII. – F. *appétence* or L. *appetentia*, f. *appetere*; see next and -ENCE. So **a·ppet**ENT XV.

appetite æ·pitait desire, spec. for food. XIV (R. Mannyng). ME. *apetyte* – OF. *apetit* (mod. *appétit*) – L. *appetītus*, f. *appetere* seek after, f. *ad* AP- + *petere* seek (see PETITION). So **a·ppetizing** stimulating the appetite. XVII. – (O)F. *appétissant*, with ending assim. to -IZE, -ING[2].

applaud əplɔ̄·d clap the hands in approval, express approval (of). XV. – L. *applaudere*, f. *ad* AP- + *plaudere* clap (see PLAUDIT), partly after F. *applaudir*. So **applause** əplɔ̄·z. XV. – L. *applausus*, f. *applaus-*, pp. stem of *applaudere*.

apple æ·pl fruit of the apple-tree, Pyrus Malus. OE. *æppel*, corr. to OFris., OS., (M)Du. *appel*, OHG. *apful* (G. *apfel*), ON. *epli* (n.), Crim-Goth. *apel* :– CGerm. **aplu-*, rel. to **ab(a)la-*, **ablu-*, repr. by OIr. *ubull* (Ir. *ubhall*), W. *afal*, *afall* apple(-tree), and **ōb(ō)l-*, repr. by OSl. *ablŭko*, Lith. *óbuolas* apple, *obelìs* apple-tree, Lett. *ābuols*, OPruss. *woble*, Pol. *jabłko*. These point to a NEur. base **abl-*, which has been plausibly connected with the It. place-name *Abella*, called *malifera* 'apple-bearing' by Virgil ('Æn.' VII 740). With *apple of the eye* (in OE. simply *æppel*) cf. Du. *oogappel*, G. *augapfel*. ¶ OE. *apuldor* apple-tree (corr. to OHG. *apholtra*, ON. *apaldr*) survives in the place-names *Apperknowle*, *Apperley*, *Appledore*, *Appledram*, *Appuldurcomb* (the ON. form appearing in *Applegarth*, repr. *apaldgarðr* apple-orchard).

applicable æ·plikəbl †pliable XVI; capable of being applied XVII; pertinent XIX. f. L. *applicāre* APPLY + -ABLE; cf. F. *applicable*, It.

applicabile. Superseded †*appliable* (XIV) in all senses. So **applic**A·TION. XIV (Trev.). – (O)F.– L.; the noun of action of APPLY.

appliqué æplī·kei applied ornament. XVIII. F., pp. of *appliquer* – L. *applicāre* APPLY.

apply əplai· bring into contact; devote, direct. XIV (Ch., Trev., Wyclif, Gower). – OF. *aplier* :– L. *applicāre*, f. *ad* AP-+ *plicāre* fold (see PLY²). Hence **appli·**ANCE application, apparatus. XVI (Sh.).

appoggiatura əpɔ:dʒiətjuə·rə (mus.) grace-note prefixed to a principal note. XVIII. It., f. *appoggiare* cause to lean (cf. APPUI).

appoint əpoi·nt fix by arrangement, prescribe, ordain; equip. XIV (Ch., Gower). – OF. *apointer*, f. *à point* to a point, into condition (see POINT). **appoi·nt**MENT † agreement; engagement; ordinance XV; equipment XVI. – OF. *apointement.*

apport æpɔ̄·ɹt in spiritualism, thing produced at a séance. XIX. f. AP-+-*port* of IMPORT.

apportion əpɔ̄·ɹʃən assign proportionally. XVI. – (O)F. *apportionner*; see AP-, PORTION.

appose æpou·z apply. XVI. Formed to repr. L. *appōnere*; see APPOSITE and cf. POSE¹. ¶ Another vb. *appose* confront with objections or questions (current XIV–XVII), repr. *aposer*, var. of OF. *oposer* OPPOSE. Aphetic POSE².

apposite æ·pəzit well applied, aptly put. XVII. – L. *appositus*, pp. of *appōnere* apply, f. *ad* AP-+*pōnere* place (see POSITION). So **appos**ITION æpəzi·ʃən placing in close contact. XV (first in gram.). – F. *apposition* or late L. *appositiō(n-)*, f. *apposit-*, *appōnere.* ¶ *Apposition* speech-day at St. Paul's School, London (XVII, Pepys), is another word, orig. an OF. var. of OPPOSITION used in the sense 'public disputation', 'formal examination by question and answer'; cf. prec.

appraise əprei·z fix a price for XV; estimate the amount or quality of XIX. Alteration, by assim. to PRAISE, of arch. *apprize*, †*apprise* – OF. *aprisier*, f. *à* AP-+*pris* PRICE. Hence **apprai·s**AL XIX, **apprai·se**MENT XVII.

appreciate əprī·ʃieit estimate duly; esteem highly XVII; raise or rise in value (orig. U.S.) XVIII. f. pp. stem of late L. *appretiāre* set a price on, f. *ad* AP-+*pretium* PRICE; see -ATE³ and cf. (O)F. *apprécier.* (A rare *appreciate* pp. 'valued' occurs in Sc. XVI.) Cf. APPRAISE. So **appreci**A·TION estimation XVII (an isolated early instance occurs *c.* 1400 in sense 'recognition, notice'). – (O)F. – late L. **appre·ci**ABLE (once XV), -ATIVE XIX; after F.

apprehend æprihe·nd †learn; †lay hold of XIV; seize, arrest; recognize, understand; anticipate, esp. with fear. XVI. – F. *appréhender* or – L. *apprehendere*, f. *ad* AP-+ *prehendere* seize (cf. PREHENSILE). The contr. L. form *apprendere* (whence F. *apprendre* learn, teach) is repr. in Eng. by a rare †*apprend* (XVI–XVII). So **apprehe·n**SION, **apprehe·n**SIVE in corr. senses, from XIV. –(partly through F.) late L. *apprehensiō(n-)*, medL. *apprehensīvus.*

apprentice əpre·ntis learner of a craft. XIV; adj. or attrib. XV. – OF. *aprentis* (mod. *apprenti*), nom. of *aprentif*, f. *aprendre* learn (see prec.)+-*tis*, -*tif* :– L. -*tīvu-s* (see -IVE). Aphetic PRENTICE.

apprise əprai·z inform. XVII. f. *appris*, fem. -*ise*, pp. of F. *apprendre* teach (causative of the sense 'learn'); see APPREHEND.

apprize see APPRAISE.

appro æ·prou abbrev. of APPROBATION.

approach əprou·tʃ come near. XIV. – OF. *aproch(i)er* (mod. *approcher*) = Pr. *apropchar*, OIt. *approciare* :– late L. (Vulg.) *appropiāre*, f. *ad* AP-+*propius* nearer, compar. of *prope* near, nigh (cf. PROPINQUITY). Hence **approa·ch** sb. XV.

approbation æprŏbei·ʃən †proof XIV; sanction, approval XV. – (O)F. *approbation* – L. *approbātiō(n-)*, f. *approbāre* APPROVE; see -ATION.

appropriate əprou·prieit make one's own, take to oneself. XV. f. *appropriate* -iət, pp. and adj. (XV), or pp. stem of late L. *appropriāre* (whence F. *approprier*), f. *ad* AP-+*proprius* own, PROPER; superseded earlier †*appropre*, -*ie* XIV–XVIII (from F.); see -ATE³. So **appropri**A·TION. XIV. – (O)F. – late L.

approve¹ əprū·v †prove, demonstrate; sanction, commend. XIV. – OF. *aprover* (mod. *approuver*) :– L. *approbāre* make good, assent to as good, f. *ad* AP-+*probus* just, good (cf. PROBE). The tonic stem *appreuv-* of the OF. vb. gave ME. *appreve.* Hence **appro·val** XVII (rare before XIX); see -AL²; earlier syns. were †*approof* (XV), †*approvance* (XVI), †*approvement* (XVII).

approve² əprū·v (leg.) make profit out of (land) by raising the rent. XV (but implied earlier in *apprower*, *aprouer* XIV, Ch.). Lawyer's form (in XVII) of *approue*, var. of *approwe* – OF. *apprower*, *appro(u)er*, f. *à* AP- + *pro*, *prou* advantage, profit (see IMPROVE).

approximate əprɔ·ksimət very near in position or nature XV (Chauliac); nearly exact XIX. – *approximātus*, pp. of late L. *approximāre* (Tertullian) draw near to, f. *ad* AP-+*proximus* very near, next, PROXIMATE. Hence or directly f. *approximāt-*, pp. stem (see -ATE³) **appro·ximate** -eit vb. XV. **approxim**A·TION. XV.

appui æpwī· support. XVI. F., f. *appuyer* support, OF. *apuyer* (= It. *appoggiare*; cf. APPOGGIATURA) :– Rom. **appodiāre* lean on, f. L. *ad* AP-+*podium* support – Gr. *podíon* base , f. *pod-*, *poús* FOOT.

appurtenance əpɔ̄·ɹtĭnəns adjunct, accessory. XIV (Ch., PPl.). – AN. *apurtenaunce*, OF. *apart-*, *apertenance* (= Pr. *apartenensa*, It. *appartenenza*) :– Rom. **appertinentia*, f. late L. *appertinēre* APPERTAIN; see -ANCE. The second vowel has been variously rendered *a, e, o, u*. So **appu·rten**ANT belonging, appertaining. XIV (Gower, Ch.). – OF. *apartenant*, prp. of *apartenir* APPERTAIN.

apricot ei·prikɔt (stone-fruit of) tree allied to the plum, Prunus armeniaca. XVI. Earliest forms *abrecock, apricock*, pl. *ab-, aprecox* – Pg. *albricoque* or Sp. *albaricoque* (cf. It. *albercocco, albicocco*, dial. *barkokka, berikokla*) – Arab. *al-barqūq, -birqūq*, i.e. *al* AL-[2], *birqūq* – late Gr. *praikókion* (Dioscorides), Byz. Gr. *berikokkon* – L. *præcoquum, -cocum*, n. (sc. *mālum*) of var. of *præcox* early-ripe (see PRECOCIOUS); this name succeeded to the earlier L. *prūnum* or *mālum Armeniacum* 'Armenian plum or apple'. The later Eng. forms show assim. to F. *abricot* (whence Sc. *abrico* XVI), and subsequent alteration of *abr-* to *apr-*, perh. by connecting the name with L. *aprīcus* sunny (cf. Minsheu's baseless etym. *in aprīcō coctus* ripened in a sunny place).

April ei·pril fourth month of the year. XIV (Ch.). – L. *Aprīlis* prop. adj. (sc. *mensis* month), whence (O)F. *avril* (= Pr., Sp. *abril*, It. *aprile*, Rum. *prier*), which was adopted earlier in Eng. *averil* XIII (RGlouc.), a form continuing long in Sc.

apron ei·prən outer garment covering the front of the body. XVI (Coverdale, Gen. iii 7). Evolved by misdivision of *a napron* as *an apron* (cf. ADDER, AUGER, UMPIRE); ME. *napron, -(o)un* (XIV) – OF. *naperon* (mod. *napperon*), f. *nape, nappe* table-cloth (cf. NAPERY, NAPKIN) :– L. *mappa* napkin (see MAP). ¶ For Rom. initial *n* repr. L. *m* cf. F. *natte* :– L. *matta*, F. *nèfle* :– L. *mespilus*.

apropos æprəpou· to the point or purpose. XVII (Dryden). – F. *à propos*, i.e. *à* to (AD), *propos* plan, purpose (L. *prōpositum*, sb. use of n. pp. of *prōpōnere* PROPOSE).

apse æps arched or domed recess in a church, etc. XIX. – L. *apsis, absis* – Gr. *apsís*, var. of *hapsís* fastening, felloe, wheel, arch, vault, perh. f. *háptein* join, fit. The L.-Gr. form **a·psis** was used earlier in this sense, and in astron. (apogee or perigee, aphelion or perihelion). XVII. Hence **apsid**AL[1] æ·psidəl. XIX. f. L. *apsīd-, apsis*.

apt æpt suited, fitted *for* XIV (Trev.); suited to its purpose; ready to learn XVI. – L. *aptus*, pp. of *apere* fasten, attach (cf. ADAPT, ADEPT, INEPT, COPULA), pt. **ēpī*, repr. by *coēpī, cœpī* I begin, began, rel. to Vedic pf. *ā́pa*, aor. *ā́pat* (has) reached, obtained, Skr. *āpnoti* reaches, attains. So **a·pti**TUDE. XV. – (O)F. – late L.; cf. ATTITUDE.

apteryx æ·ptəriks N.Z. bird, the kiwi, having rudimentary wings. XIX. modL., f. Gr. *a-* A-[4] + *ptérux* wing (cf. *pterón*, rel. to FEATHER).

aqua æ·kwə L. *aqua* water (rel. to OE. *ēa*; see ISLAND) occurring in certain much-used phr.: **aqua fortis** 'strong water', nitric acid XV; **aqua regia** rī·dʒiə 'royal water', mixture of nitric and hydrochloric acids, which dissolves the 'noble metals', gold and platinum XVII (Jonson); **aqua vitæ** vai·tī 'water of life' (cf. WHISKY) ardent spirits, spec. brandy (F. *eau-de-vie*) XV (sometimes semi-anglicized as *aqwavyte, -wyte, aqwowyte*).

aquamarine æ:kwəmərī·n bluish-green (beryl). XIX. – L. *aqua marīna* sea-water, whence also F. (also formerly in Eng. use) *aigue-marine*, i.e. *aigue* :– L. *aqua, marīna*, fem. of *marīnus*; see AQUA, MARINE.

aquarelle ækwəre·l painting with Indian ink and thin water-colours. XIX. F. – It. *acquerella* water-colour, f. *acqua* :– L. *aqua* water.

aquarium əkwɛə·riəm tank for live aquatic animals and plants. XIX. sb. use of n. sg. of L. *aquārius* (see next), after VIVARIUM. ¶ L. *aquārium* meant 'watering-place for cattle'.

Aquarius əkwɛə·riəs zodiacal constellation. XIV. L., water-carrier, sb. use of *aquārius* of water, f. *aqua* water; see -ARY.

aquatic əkwæ·tik †watery XV (Caxton); living in water XVII. – (O)F. *aquatique* or L. *aquāticus* (varying with *aquātilis*, whence †*a·quatile* XVII); see AQUA, -ATIC.

aquatint æ·kwətint, also **aquati·nta** engraving on copper with nitric acid. XVIII. – F. *aquatinte*, It. *acquatinta*, repr. L. *aqua* water, *tinta* dyed (see TINT).

aqueduct æ·kwidʌkt conduit for water. XVI. – L. *aquæductus*, i.e. *aquæ*, g. of *aqua*, *ductus* conveyance (see DUCT). Cf. F. *aqueduc* (XVI), †*aqueduct* (XVI–XVII), perh. the immed. source.

aqueous ei·kwiəs watery. XVII. f. L. *aqua* water + -EOUS as if modelled on L. **aqueus* (like *terreus*, f. *terra* earth); perh. suggested by the form of F. *aqueux* (– L. *aquōsus*).

aquiline æ·kwilain eagle-like, hooked. XVII. – L. *aquilinus*, f. *aquila* EAGLE, prob. after F. *aquilin*; see -INE[1].

ar- assim. form of AD- before *r*; cf. AC-.

-ar əɹ repr. L. *-āris* belonging to, of the kind or form of, as in *ālāris* ALAR, *globulāris* GLOBULAR, *lūnāris* LUNAR, *stellāris* STELLAR, f. *āla* wing, etc.; synon. with -AL[1], but replacing it after an *l*-stem. The regular F. descendant of L. *-āri-* is *-ier* (AN. *-er*), whence *-er* in Eng. adoptions, which was often assim. to L. with *-ar*; e.g. L. *scholāris*, AN. *escoler*, ME. *scoler*, later *scholar*. Learned F. formations have *-aire*, e.g. *angulaire* ANGULAR, *militaire* MILITARY. In *beggar, burglar, liar, pedlar*, -ER[1] has been assim. to this suffix.

Arab æ·rəb one of a branch of the Semitic race XIV (Trev.); (from the nomadic character of the Arabs) wandering child of the streets XIX. – F. *Arabe* (= Sp., It. *Arabo*, etc.) – L. *Arab-s* – Gr. *A'raps, Arab-* – Arab. *'arab*. **Arab**IAN ərei·biən. XIV (first as sb.

arabiens, Ch.). f. OF. *arabi* (see below) or L. *Arabus* or *Arabius* – Gr. *Arábios* (Herodotus). **Arab**IC æ·rəbik. XIV (first as sb., Ch.). – (O)F. *arabique*, †*arabic* – L. *Arabicus* – Gr. *Arabikós*. *Gum arabic* (*c.* 1400), OF. *gomme arabic*, etc., exudation of an African species of acacia. **Araby** æ·rəbi †Arab horse XII; †native of Arabia, Arab; †adj. Arabian, Arabic XV. – OF. *ar(r)abi*, prob. – Arab. *'arabī*, adj. of *'arab*. ¶ As the name of the country *Araby* is a different word – (O)F. *Arabie* – L. *Arabia* – Gr. *Arabíā*.

arabesque ærəbe·sk Arabian or Moorish in design; sb. such a design or style. XVIII. – F. *arabesque* – It. *arabesco*, f. *arabo* ARAB; see -ESQUE. ¶ †*Rebesk* is used by Cotgr. 1611 in defining *arabesque*; cf. It. †*rabesco*, Florio.

arabis æ·rəbis genus of crucifers. XVIII. – medL. *arabis* – Gr. *arabís* (Dioscorides), sb. use of fem. of *Araps* Arabian.

arable æ·rəbl fit for tillage. XV (M. Game). – (O)F. *arable* or L. *arābilis*, f. *arāre* plough; see EAR[3] and -ABLE.

arachnid əræ·knid (zool.) any of the class comprising spiders, scorpions, and mites. XIX. – F. *arachnide* or modL. *arachnida*, n. pl. f. Gr. *arákhnē* spider; see -ID.

Aramaic ærəmei·ik pert. to the northern Semitic languages. XIX. f. Gr. *Aramaîos*, f. *Aram*, Heb. name of Syria; see -IC. Also **Aramæ**·AN. XIX. f. L. *Aramæus*. Formerly *Aramites language* (XVI), *Aramitish* (XVII).

araucaria ærɔ̄kɛə·riə genus of lofty coniferous trees (esp. monkey-puzzle). XIX. modL., fem. sg. (sc. *arbor* tree) f. *Arauco* name of a province of Chile; cf. -ARY.

arbalest ā·ɹbəlest cross-bow. XI. ME. *arblast*, *arbelest*, later *alblast*, and (with assim. to *arrow*) *arwe-blast*, *arowblast*, *ar(e)blast* – OF. *arbaleste*, *arbeleste* (mod. *arbalète*) = Pr. *arbalesta*, *albaresta* :– late L. *arcuballista*, f. *arcus* bow, ARC+BALLISTA.

arbiter ā·ɹbitəɹ judge, umpire. XV. – L. *arbiter* (whence F. *arbitre*). So **a·rbitr**AGE arbitration, arbitrament XV (Caxton); (from modF. arbitrāʒ, and so usu. pronounced) traffic in bills of exchange or stocks XIX. – F., f. *arbitrer* (whence †*arbitre* XV–XVI, an earlier syn. of *arbitrate*). **arbi·tra**MENT, **-ement** †free choice XIV; decision XV. – OF. *arbitrement* – medL. *arbitrāmentum*, f. L. *arbitrārī*. **a·rbitr**ARY †at one's discretion; (leg.) pert. to the discretion of an authorized arbitrator XV; depending on mere opinion or uncontrolled power XVII. – L. *arbitrārius*, perh. after F. *arbitraire*. **a·rbitrate** give an authoritative decision, act as formal arbitrator XVI. f. pp. stem of L. *arbitrārī* examine, give judgement, f. *arbiter*; see -ATE[3]. **arbitr**A·TION. XIV. – (O)F. – L. **a·rbitr**ATOR. XIV. – late L.

arbor[1] ā·ɹbəɹ main beam of a machine; axle of wheel in clocks. XVII. – F. *arbre* tree, principal axis; assim. in sp. to L. *arbor*.

arbor[2] ā·ɹbɔ̄ɹ L., 'tree', attrib. in (U.S.) *Arbor Day* day set apart for planting trees. XIX.

arboreal āɹbɔ̄·riəl pert. to trees. XVII. f. L. *arboreus*, f. *arbor* tree; -AL[1]. Also **arbo·r**EOUS XVII, **a·rbor**OUS XVII (Milton), **arbor**E·SCENT tree-like XVII (Grew). So **ar·boric**U:LTURE.

arbour ā·ɹbəɹ †plot of grass, flower-garden, fruit-garden; †trees on trellis work; bower of which the side and roof consist of trees. XIV. orig. *erber* – AN. *erber*, OF. *erbier* (early vars. have *h*-; mod. *herbier* bank of herbage, grass-shed, herbarium, herbal), f. *erbe* HERB+*-ier* :– L. -ARIUM. Normal phonetic change gave *(h)arber*, *(h)arbour*, and the prevalence of the sp. *arbour* was furthered by assoc. with L. *arbor* tree.

arbutus āɹbjū·təs, ā·ɹbjutəs strawberry-tree, Arbutus Unedo. XVI. L. Also anglicized *a·rbute* (XVI).

arc āɹk part of a circle. XIV (earliest form *ark*, the present latinized sp. dating from XVI). – (O)F. *arc* :– L. *arcu-s* bow, arch, curve, prob. rel. to ARROW.

arcade āɹkei·d arched passage. XVIII (earlier in spurious Sp. form *arcado*, Evelyn). – F. *arcade* – Pr. *arcada* or It. *arcata*, f. Rom. **arca* ARCH[1]; see -ADE.

Arcadian āɹkei·diən. XVI. f. L. *Arcadius*, f. Gr. *Arkadiā* mountainous district in the Peloponnesus, taken as the ideal region of rural contentment; see -IAN.

arcana āɹkei·nə (rarely sg. **arca·num**) mysterious secrets. XVI. – L., n. pl. (secret decrees or rites) of *arcānus* hidden, secret, f. *arca* chest, ARK; see -AN.

arch[1] āɹtʃ †arc XIV (Ch.); curved overhanging structure XIV. – (O)F. *arche* = Pr. *arca* :– Rom. **arca* n. pl. taken as fem. sg., f. L. *arcus* ARC. *Court of Arches* ecclesiastical court of appeal formerly held at the church of St. Mary-le-Bow, London (*Sancta Maria de Arcubus* 'of the Arches', so named from the arches supporting the steeple). Hence **arch** vb. furnish with an arch XV; curve XVII.

arch[2] āɹtʃ chief, pre-eminent XVI; (passing, through *arch impostor*, *rogue*, *thief*, etc. into) cunning, crafty, waggish XVII. The prefix ARCH- used independently as adj.

arch- āɹtʃ (but āɹk in *archangel*) repr. ult. Gr. *arkh(i)-* chief, comb. form f. base of *arkhós* chief, *árkhein* begin, take the lead, *arkhḗ* beginning, rule, as in *arkhággelos* archangel, *arkhidiákonos* archdeacon, *arkhiepískopos* archbishop, whence L. *archangelus*, *archidiāconus*, *archiepiscopus*, OF. *arc(h)-angele*, *arc(h)ediacre*, *arc(h)evesque*. In OE. at first tr. by *hēah* HIGH, as *hēahengel*, but later adopted from L. as *ærće-*, *arće-*, *erće-*, as in *ærćebisćop*, etc. The OE. forms gave ME. *erche-*, *arche-*, the latter coinciding with OF. *arche-*. From such comps. the prefix was generalized, and freely used in the senses 'chief', 'principal', 'pre-eminent in his or its kind', 'extreme, out-and-out' (cf. ARCH[2] and the use of F. *archi-*, It. *arci-*, as in *archifou* extremely mad, *arcibenissime* extremely well), occas. 'first in time, original'. Cf. ARCHI-.

-arch, repr. Gr. *-arkhos* ruling, rel. to *arkhḗ* (see prec.), as in *mónarkhos* MONARCH, *tétrarkhos* TETRARCH. The corr. abstract sbs. end in -ARCHY.

archæology āɹkiɔ·lədʒi ancient history, antiquities XVII; study of prehistoric matters XIX. – modL. *archæologia* – Gr. *arkhaiologíā*, f. *arkhaîos*; see ARCHIVES, -LOGY.

archaic āɹkei·ik old-fashioned, (of language) belonging to an earlier period but retained or revived in individual or special use. XIX. – F. *archaïque* – Gr. *arkhaïkós*, f. *arkhaîos*; cf. prec. and see -IC. So **a·rcha**ISM. XVII. – modL. *archaismus* – Gr. *arkhaïsmós*, f. *archaïzein*.

archangel ā·ɹkeindʒəl (repl. OE. *hēahengel*). XII. – AN. *archangele* – ecclL. *archangelus* – ecclGr. (LXX) *arkhággelos*; see ARCH-, ANGEL.

archer ā·ɹtʃəɹ bowman. XIII (RGlouc.). – AN. *archer*, OF. *archier* (mod. *archer*) :– Rom. **arcārius*, f. L. *arcus* bow, ARC; see -ER[2]. So **a·rch**ERY. XIV. – OF.

archetype ā·ɹkitaip original pattern. XVII (earlier in L. form; Bacon has *arch-tipe*). – L. *archetypum* – Gr. *arkhétupon*, sb. use of n. of adj. 'first moulded as a model', f. *arkhe-* (var. of *arkhi-*)+*túpos* model, TYPE. Cf. F. *archétype* (OF. *arquetipe*).

archi- ā·ɹki repr. L. *archi-*, Gr. *arkhi-*, rel. to *arkhḗ* beginning, reign, *árkhein* begin, reign, *árkhos* guide, head (sometimes through F. *archi-* arʃi, or It. *arci-* artʃi, but pronounced nevertheless with k); some adjs. with this prefix have corr. sbs. with ARCH-, e.g. *archidiaconal* (XV), *archdeacon* (OE.).

archil var. of ORCHIL.

archimandrite āɹkimæ·ndrait (Gr. Ch.) superior of a monastery. XVII. – F. *archimandrite* or ecclL. *archimandrīta* – ecclGr. *arkhimandrítēs*, f. *arkhi-* ARCHI- + *mándrā* enclosure, stable, (eccl.) monastery (cf. Skr. *mandurá* stable); see -ITE.

archipelago āɹkipe·ləgou Ægean Sea; sea with numerous islands, group of many islands. XVI. – It. *arcipelago* (XIII), f. Gr. *arkhi-* ARCHI- + *pélagos* sea (cf. PELAGIC); medL. *archipelagus* was frequent in Eng. XVI–XVII; forms modelled on F. †*archipélague* (now *archipel*) occas. occur. ¶ It is possible that the It. word was an alteration of It. *Egeopelago* Ægean Sea.

architect ā·ɹkitekt designer of buildings. XVI. – F. *architecte* – It. *architetto*, or their source, L. *architectus* – Gr. *arkhitéktōn*, f. *arkhi-* ARCHI- + *téktōn* builder, craftsman, rel. to *tékhnē* (cf. TECHNICAL). So **a:rchitecto·n**IC pert. to building. XVII. – L. – Gr. **a·rchitect**URE art of building. XVI. – F. *architecture* or L. *architectūra*, f. *architectus*.

architrave ā·ɹkitreiv (archit.) lowest division of an entablature XVI; (coll.) parts surrounding a doorway or window XVII. – F. *architrave* – It. *architrave*, f. *archi-* ARCHI- + *trave* :– L. *trabe-*, *trabs* beam.

archives ā·ɹkaivz (rarely sing.) repository of public records; the records themselves. XVII. – F. *archives* – L. *archīva*, *archīa* – (with *v* as in OLIVE) Gr. *arkheîa* magisterial residence, public office, n. pl. of adj. *arkheîos* governmental, f. *arkhḗ* government. So **a·rchiv**IST. XVIII. – F.

archivolt āɹ·kivoult under-curve of an arch. XVIII. – F. *archivolte* or It. *archivolto* (whence medL. *archivoltum*), f. *arco* :– L. *arcu-s* ARC+*volto*, pp. of †*volvere*, *volgere* turn (cf. VAULT).

archon ā·ɹkən chief magistrate in ancient Athens. XVII. – Gr. *árkhōn* ruler, sb. use of prp. of *árkhein* rule (cf. ARCH-).

-archy āɹki terminal el. of abstract nouns corr. to words in -ARCH, repr. Gr. *-arkhíā* sovereignty, rule, rel. to ARCH-, ARCHI-; e.g. *monarchy*, *tetrarchy*.

Arctic ā·ɹktik pert. to the north pole. XIV. Earliest forms *artik*, *-ic(k)* – OF. *artique* – L. *ar(c)ticus* – Gr. *arktikós*, f. *árktos* bear, the Great Bear, pole-star; from XVII refash. after L. *arct-*; see -IC. ¶ Gr. *árktos* is rel. to L. *ursus*; cf. URSINE.

Arcturus āɹktjuə·rəs the brightest star of the constellation Bootes. XIV. L. – Gr. *arktoûros*, f. *árktos* (see prec.) + *oûros* guardian; so called from its situation at the tail of the Great Bear.

arcuation āɹkjuei·ʃən arching. XVII. – F. *arcuation* or L. *arcuātiō(n-)*, f. *arcuāre* curve, f. *arcus* ARC; see -ATION.

-ard əɹd suffix repr. (O)F. *-ard*, †*-art* = It. *-ardo*, etc. – OHG. *-hart*, being the adj. *hart* bold, hardy, HARD, often forming part of personal names, as OHG. *Reginhart* REYNARD; in MHG. and Du. a formative of common nouns, gen. pejorative; in Eng. orig. in adoptions of F. sbs., as *bastard*, *coward*, *haggard*, *mallard*; the depreciatory sense of some of these led to its being used to form similar words on various stems, as *dastard*, *dotard*, *drunkard*, *dullard*, *laggard*, *niggard*, *sluggard*, *stinkard*, *wizard*; in names of things it is sometimes augm. or of vague import, as *billiard*, *bollard*, *placard*, *poniard*, *standard*. ¶ In several words it conceals endings of a different origin, as *bustard*, *custard*, *hazard*, *leopard*, *steward*, *tankard*.

ardent ā·ɹdənt burning (lit. and fig.). XIV (*ardaunt*, Ch.). – OF. *ardant* (mod. *ardent*) :– L. *ārdent-*, *-ēns*, prp. of *ārdēre* burn, f. *āridus* ARID; see -ANT, -ENT. So **a·rd**OUR[2], U.S. **a·rdor** fierce heat. XIV (Ch.). – OF. *ardour* (mod. *ardeur*) :– L. *ārdōrem*, *-or*, f. *ārdēre*. Cf. ARSON.

arduous ā·ɹdjuəs difficult, laborious XVI; (arch.) lofty, steep XVIII. f. L. *arduus* high, steep, rel. to Gaulish **arduo-* in *Arduenna silva* the Ardennes, OIr. *ard* high, big, ON. *ǫrðugr* steep, Av. *ərəðwa-* high, and further to Gr. *orthós* (Doric *borthós* :– **ϝorthϝos*), Skr. *ūrdhvás* upright, *várdhate* cause to grow; cf. ORTHO- and see -UOUS.

are[1] āɹ French unit of superficial measurement. XIX. F. – L. *ārea* AREA.

are[2] āɹ see BE.

area ɛə·riə clear open space; superficial extent XVI; enclosed court XVII. – L. *ārea* vacant piece of level ground, threshing-floor. So **areola** (anat.) əri·ŏlə small area XVII; see -OLE.

areca æ·rikə tree and fruit of a genus of palms. XVI. Early forms *arreca, ar(e)cha, arrequa, arracca, arec* – Pg. *areca* – Malayalam *áḍekka* = Canarese *áḍike*, Tamil *áḍaikāy*, f. *aḍai* denoting close arrangement of the cluster + *kāy* nut, fruit.

arena ərī·nə centre of an amphitheatre. XVII; scene of conflict or strong action XVIII. – L. *arēna*, prop. *harēna* (Sabine *fasēnā*) sand, sandy place, spec. sand-strewn place of combat. So **arena·ceous** ærīnei·ʃəs. XVII. f. L. *arēnāceus*.

arête arei·t sharp ridge. XIX. F., fish-bone, sharp edge or ridge :– L. *arista* ear of corn, fish-bone or spine. Cf. ARRIS.

argand ā·ɹgænd lamp with cylindrical wick (and gas-burner). XVIII. f. name of the inventor, Aimé *Argand* (1755–1803), of Geneva.

argent ā·ɹdʒənt silver; (her.) white. XV. – (O)F. *argent* – L. *argentum* silver, f. IE. base **arg-* be white or bright (cf. OIr. *a(i)rget*, Arm. *arcatʻ*, Skr. *rajatám* silver; Gr. *árguros* silver; Gr. *argḗs, argós* shining, bright, Skr. *árjunas* white; and see ARGILLACEOUS, ARGUE).

argillaceous āɹdʒilei·ʃəs clayey. XVIII. f. L. *argillāceus*, f. *argilla* – Gr. *árgillos* clay, f. *argḗs*; see prec. and -ACEOUS.

argle ā·ɹgl (dial.) dispute, bandy words. XVI. prob. alteration of ARGUE, with *-le* as in *haggle*. Also in jingling comp. **a·rgle-ba·rgle.**

argol ā·ɹgəl tartar deposited from wines. XIV (*argoile*, Ch.). – AN. *argoil*, of unkn. origin.

argon ā·ɹgɔn (chem.) inert gas of the atmosphere. XIX. – Gr. *argón*, n. of *argós* idle, inert, for *aergós*, f. *a-* A-[4] + *érgon* WORK.

argosy ā·ɹgəsi large merchant vessel. XVI. Earliest forms *ragusye, argose, argosea, arguze* – It. *ragusea*, fem. adj. used sb. (sc. *nave* or *caracca*) vessel or carrack of Ragusa, a port of Sicily, the name of which occurs XVI in an Eng. context as *Aragouse* (attrib. in *Arag(o)usey shippes*).

argot ā·ɹgou cant, slang. XIX. F., of unkn. origin.

argue ā·ɹgju debate, discuss; †bring evidence against; †prove. XIV. – (O)F. *arguer* :– L. *argūtāre*, frequent. of *arguere* make clear, prove, assert, accuse, f. base **arg-* (see ARGENT). So **a·rgufy** XVIII (Smollett), **a·rgument** XIV (Seven Sages, Ch.). – (O)F. *argument*, L. *argūmentum*. **argumenta·tion.** (XV, Pecock). – F. – L.

Argus ā·ɹgəs mythological person with a hundred eyes; vigilant guardian XIV; genus of pheasants XVIII. L. – Gr. *Argós*; used as adj. in sense 'vigilant' in *Argus eyes* (XVI), *Argus-eyed* (Ch.).

argute āɹgjū·t sharp, keen. XV. – L. *argūtus*, pp. of *arguere* make clear (see ARGUE).

aria ā·riə, ɛə·riə (mus.). XVIII. It.; see AIR.

Arian ɛə·riən (adherent) of Arius (IV), a presbyter of Alexandria, who denied the consubstantiality of Jesus Christ with God the Father. XIV. – ecclL. *Ariānus*, f. *Arius*, *Arīus* – Gr. *'Arīos, Areîos*.

-arian ɛə·riən suffix f. L. *-ārius* -ARY + -AN, first appearing in late XVI in *disciplinarian*, *quinquagenarian*, later (XVII) becoming common in designations of religious bodies and their tenets, e.g. *millenarian, predestinarian, sectarian, Trinitarian, Unitarian*, on the analogy of which were formed *humanitarian, necessitarian, parliamentarian, utilitarian*, and joc. *anythingarian, nothingarian* (XVIII).

arid æ·rid dry. XVII. – F. *aride* or L. *āridus*, f. *ārēre* be dry or parched, perh. rel. to ASH[2]; cf. ARDENT and see -ID. So **aridity** əri·dĭti. XVI. – F. or L.

ariel ɛə·riəl. XIX. – Arab. *aryil* (var. of *ayyil* stag), applied in Syria to the gazelle.

Aries ɛə·riīz zodiacal constellation. XIV (Ch., Gower). L., 'ram'.

aright ərai·t (arch.) rightly. OE. *on riht, ariht*, i.e. ON, A-[1], *riht* RIGHT[1].

-arious ɛə·riəs comp. adj. suffix based on L. *-āris* -AR, or *-ārius* -ARY + -OUS.

arise ərai·z gen. superseded by *rise*, exc. in sense 'come into existence, originate'. OE. *ārīsan* (Nhb. *arrīsa*) = OS. *ārīsan*, OHG. *ur-, ar-, irrīsan*, Goth. *us-, urreisan*; see A-[3], RISE.

aristocracy æristɔ·krəsi government by 'the best' citizens; political supremacy of a privileged order XVI; patrician order, nobles XVII. – (O)F. *aristocratie* – (through medL. translations of Aristotle) Gr. *aristokratíā* (Plato, Aristotle), f. *áristos* best. So **aristocrat** æ·ristŏkræt, əri·s- member of an aristocracy. XVIII. – F. *aristocrate* (a word of the French Revolution). **aristocratic** æ:ristŏkræ·tik XVII, -ICAL XVI. – (O)F. *aristocratique* – Gr. *aristokratikós*. See -CRACY, etc.

arithmetic əri·þmĭtik science of numbers. XIII. Earliest forms *arsmetike, -metrike, arismetrik* – OF. *arismetique* – Rom. **arismetica* (so Pr., OSp.), for L. *arithmētika* – Gr. *arithmētikḗ* (sc. *tékhnē* art) 'art of counting', f. *arithmeîn* count, reckon, f.

arithmós number; assoc. with L. *ars metrica* 'measuring art' led to forms of the type *ar(i)smetrik*, which were later (XVI) conformed, through the stage *arithmetrik*, to the orig. L. and Gr. So **arithmet**ICAL æriþme·tikəl. XVI. f. L. *arithmēticus*, Gr. *arithmētikós*. **arithmeti**·CIAN. XVI. – F. *arithméticien*.

-arium ɛə·riəm L. n. sg. of *-ārius* -ARIOUS, -ARY, in sb. uses of adjs., e.g. *auctarium, frigidarium, honorarium, sacrarium*, and the group *aquarium, herbarium, vivarium*.

ark āɹk †chest, coffer; floating vessel built by Noah (Gen. vi 14–16). OE. *ærc* (*earc*), corr. to OFris. *erke*, OHG. *archa* (G. *arche*), ON. *ǫrk, ark-*, Goth. *arka*; CGerm. – L. *arca* (whence also F. *arche*, which was adopted in Eng. and current XIII–XVI), rel. to L. *arx* citadel, *arcēre* enclose, ward off.

arm[1] āɹm upper limb of the body. OE. *arm* (*earm*) = OFris. *arm, erm*, OS., OHG. (Du., G.) *arm*, ON. *armr*, Goth. *arms* :- CGerm. **armaz* (whence Finn. *armas*). Like several other names of parts of the body, e.g. *eye, foot, heart, knee, nail, tooth*, common to a large area of the IE. stock; cf. L. *armus*, OSl. *ramo*, OPruss. *irmo*, Av. *arəma-*, Pers. *arm*, Skr. *īrmás*, all meaning 'shoulder' or 'arm'; f. base **ar-* fit, join (cf. ART, ARTICLE).

arm[2] āɹm (pl.) weapons for fighting XIII; employment of these; heraldic insignia XIV; sg. (after F. *arme*) any kind of troops, e.g. infantry XVIII. – (O)F. *armes* = Pr. *armas*, fem. pl., Sp., It. *arme*, Rum. *armă*, repr. L. *arma* n. pl. (no sg.), f. base **ar-* fit, join (see prec.). So **arm** vb. furnish with arms. XIII. – (O)F. *armer* = Pr., etc. *armar* :- L. *armāre*, f. *arma*.

armada āɹmei·də, -ā·də fleet of ships of war. XVI. Early forms *armado* (see -ADO), *armada*, and *-ade, -ata* – Sp. *armada* :- Rom. *armāta* ARMY.

armadillo āɹmədi·lou S. Amer. burrowing animal with a body cased in bony armour. XVI. – Sp. *armadillo*, dim. of *armado* armed man :- L. *armātu-s*, pp. of *armāre* (see ARM[2]).

Armageddon āɹməge·dən place of the last decisive battle at the Day of Judgement (see Rev. xvi 16 A.V.; R.V. *Harmagedon*); (allusively) any final conflict on a grand scale XIX (Shelley). Taken to be the Gr. equivalent of Heb. *har megiddōn* mountain region of Megiddo, which had been a site of great battles (e.g. Judges iv 6, etc.).

armament ā·ɹməmənt force equipped for war XVII; military equipment XVIII. – L. *armāmentum*, class. only pl., f. *armāre*; see ARM[2], -MENT, and cf. F. *armement*.

armature ā·ɹmətjuəɹ †arms, armour XV; piece of iron placed in contact with the poles of a magnet, which preserves and increases the magnetic power XVIII. – F. *armature* – L. *armātūra*, f. pp. stem of *armāre*; see ARM[2], -URE.

Armenian āɹmī·niən pert. to Armenia, a country east of Asia Minor, the inhabitants of which use a language of the IE. group. XVI. f. L. *Armenia*, Gr. *Armeniā*, f. OPers. *Arminà* (the Armenian name is Hayasdan or Hayq); see -IAN.

armiger ā·ɹmidʒəɹ esquire. XVI. – L. *armiger* bearing arms, f. *arma* ARM[2]+*-ger, gerēre* bear, carry (cf. -GEROUS, GERUND).

armillary ā·ɹmiləri, āɹmi·ləri formed with (metal) rings or hoops. XVII (*a. sphere*). f. modL. *armillāris*, f. *armilla* bracelet, hoop, dim. f. *armus* shoulder; see ARM[1], -ARY.

Arminian āɹmi·niən. XVII. f. *Arminius*, latinized form of the surname of Jakob *Hermanns* or *Harmensen*, Du. Protestant theologian (d. 1609); see -IAN.

armistice ā·ɹmistis cessation of fighting. XVIII. – F. *armistice* or modL. *armistitium*, f. *arma* arms (ARM[2])+*-stitium* stoppage, after L. *jūstitium* cessation of legal business (for the formation cf. INTERSTICE, SOLSTICE).

Armorican āɹmɔ·rikən pert. to Brittany. XV. f. medL. *Armoricus* (in Cæsar *Armoricæ* northern provinces of Gaul), f. Gaulish *Aremorici* 'people living by the sea', f. *are-* (= L. *præ* in front of)+*mor* sea (rel. to L. *mare*); see -IC, -AN.

armory ā·ɹməri heraldry. XV. – (O)F. *armoirie*, f. *armoier* (= It. *armeggiare*) blazon, f. *arme* ARM[2]; see -Y[3]. Hence **armor**IAL āɹmō·riəl heraldic. XVI; cf. F. *armorial* (XVII).

armour, U.S. **-or** ā·ɹməɹ defensive covering (also †offensive arms) used in fighting. XIII (RGlouc.). – (O)F. *armure*, earlier *armëure* :- L. *armātūra* ARMATURE. The present form shows assim. to words of a different type, ending in -OUR.

armoury ā·ɹməri †armour XIV (R. Mannyng); place for keeping arms XVI. prob. orig. – OF. *armoirie* ARMORY, with assim. to ARMOUR (cf. the early forms *armurie, armery*); see -Y[3].

army ā·ɹmi †armed expedition XIV (Ch.); armed force; (transf. and fig.) host XV; (coll.) organized military forces of a state XVII. – (O)F. *armée* = Pr., Sp. *armada* (cf. ARMADA), It. *armata* :- Rom. *armāta* (x), sb. use of pp. fem. of *armāre* ARM in the senses 'armed force', 'army', 'navy', 'fleet'; see -Y[5].

arnaout āɹnau·t Albanian soldier, esp. in the Turkish army. XIX. – Turk. – medGr. *Arbanêtes*, var. of *Albanêtes*, f. *Albaniā*; see ALBANIAN.

arnica ā·ɹnikə genus of composite plants; medicine prepared therefrom. XVIII. – modL., of unkn. origin, but conjectured to be an alteration of modL. *ptarmica* – Gr. *ptarmikḗ* sneezewort, sb. use of fem. of *ptarmikós* causing to sneeze, f. *ptárein* sneeze.

aroma ərou·mə spicy odour, sweet smell. XVIII. – L. *arōma* – Gr. *árōma* (-*at*-). There was an earlier †*aromat* (XIII–XVII) spice(s) – OF. *aromat* (mod. -*ate*) – L. pl. *arōmata*. So **aromat**IC æromæ·tik. XIV. – F. – late L. – Gr.

around ərau·nd adv. and prep. in a circle (about), along the circuit (of). XIV. Not frequent before XVI; prob. of mixed origin; in earliest use perh. after OF. *à la reonde* round about, lit. 'in the round' (fem.); later f. A-[1]+ROUND; cf. F. *en rond* in a circle, *au rond de* round about (XVI).

arouse ərau·z stir up. XVI (Sh.). f. A-[3]+ROUSE, after *rise, arise, wake, awake*.

a-row ərou· †in succession; (dial.) in a row. XIII. ME. *on* or *a rawe* or *rewe, areawe*, repr. OE. *on ġerǣwe*; later *arowe*; see A-[1], ROW[1].

arpeggio āɹpe·dʒiou (mus.) notes of a chord played in rapid succession. XVIII. It., f. *arpeggiare* play on the harp, f. *arpa* HARP.

arquebus see HARQUEBUS.

arrack æ·rək Eastern name for native spirituous liquor. XVII. Like F. *arak*, †*arach*, Sp. *arac*, etc. derived from forms in Indian vernaculars, which are ult. – Arab. *ʿaraq* sweat, juice, esp. in *ʿaraq at-tamr* (fermented) juice of the date. Aphetic *rack* (XVII).

arrah æ·rə Anglo-Ir. int. expressing emotion. XVIII (Farquhar). – Ir. *ara*.

arraign ərei·n †call to account; indict XIV. – AN. *arainer, areiner*, OF. *arais-, areisner* – Rom. **adratiōnāre*, f. *ad* AR-+*ratiō(n-)* account, REASON. Hence **arrai·gn** sb. indictment (now in *clerk of arraigns*) XVII.

arrange ərei·ndʒ †draw up in battle array XIV; put in order XVIII. In XIV–XV in Eng. and Sc.; occas. in XVI (e.g. Spenser); not frequent before late XVIII (Burke), when it was prob. readopted (cf. the date of *derange*); orig. – OF. *arangier, arengier* (mod. *arranger*), f. *a*- AD- + *rangier* RANGE. So **arra·nge**MENT. XVIII. – (O)F.

arrant æ·rənt notorious, downright, thorough. XVI. First in *knight arrant, arrant thief*, in which *arrant* is a later form of ERRANT vagabond, wandering; in the collocation *arrant thief* it acquired the sense 'public, common', and hence, when transf. to other nouns, 'manifest, undisguised, notorious'.

arras æ·rəs rich tapestry fabric; hanging of this. XV. – *arras* in AN. *draps d'arras* 'cloths of *Arras*', name of a town in Artois, France; cf. It. *(a)razzo*.

array ərei· (arch.) attire XIII (Cursor M.); arrangement, order XIV (*battle array* XVI); arming of a force, military force XVII. – AN. *arai*, OF. *arei* (mod. *arroi*) = Pr. *arrei*, It. *arredo*; f. AN. *araier*, OF. *areer* = Pr. *arezar*, Sp. *arrear*, It. *arredare* :– Rom. **arrēdāre* put in order, f. L. *ad* AR-+Germ. **rǣð*- prepare (see READY and cf. CURRY[1]). So **array·** vb. (arch.) attire, dress XIII (RGlouc., Cursor M.); make ready, place in order XIV. – AN. *araier*.

arrear əriə·ɹ phr. *in arrear* behindhand; sb. (chiefly pl. **arrears**) duty or liability overdue, debts unpaid. XVIII. The phr. *in arrear* superseded the adv. †*arrear* behind, behindhand. – OF. *arere, ariere* (mod. *arrière*) = Pr. *areire*, Sp. *arredro*, It. *addietro* :– medL. *adretrō*, f. L. *ad* to (AT)+*retrō* backward, behind (cf. REAR[2]). As sb. *arrear(s)* took the place of **arrea·**RAGE**(s)** XIV (now U.S.) – OF. *arerage-s* (mod. *arrérage*), f. *arere*; cf. AN. sb. *areres* XIV.

arrest əre·st cause to stop; capture, seize XIV (Barbour, Ch.); catch the attention XIX. – OF. *arester* = Pr. *arestar*, Sp. *arrestar*, It. *arrestare* :– Rom. **arrestāre*, f. *ad* AR-+*restāre* stop behind, REST. (Formerly used also intr. 'stop, stay', as in OF.) So **arre·st** sb. stoppage (in intr. and trans. sense), legal restraint. XIV. – OF. *areste* delay, and *arest* (mod. *arrêt*) act of arresting, f. the vb.

arrière-ban æ·riəɹbæn, ‖ arjɛ̄rbã order summoning vassals to military service; body of vassals. XVI. – F. *arrière-ban*, OF. *ariereban*, alteration of *arban, herban* – Germ. **hariban* (OHG. *heriban*), f. *hari, heri* army +*ban* proclamation, BAN.

arrière-guard see REARGUARD.

arris æ·ris sharp edge formed by the angular contact of two surfaces. XVII. Corruptly – early modF. *areste* sharp ridge, ARÊTE.

arrival ərai·vəl †coming to land XIV (Ch.); act of arriving XVI. – AN. *arrivaile*, f. *arriver*; see next and -AL[2].

arrive ərai·v †bring or come to shore, land XIII; come to the end of a journey, a goal, etc. XIV; †reach (a port, etc.) XVI; †come to pass XVII. – OF. *ariver* (mod. *arriver* arrive, happen) = Pr. *aribar*, Sp. *arribar* :– Rom. **arripāre* come to land, f. *ad* AR-+*rīpa* shore (cf. RIVER). Formerly sometimes inflected †*arove*, †*ariven*; cf. STRIVE.

arroba ərou·bə weight used in Spain and Portugal. XVI. – Sp. *arroba* – Arab. *arrubʿ*, i.e. *al-rubʿ* 'the quarter', the weight being ¼ of the Sp. quintal; see AL-[2].

arrogance æ·rəgəns aggressive presumption. XIV (R. Mannying). – (O)F. *arrogance* – L. *arrogantia*, f. *arrogant-, -āns*, prp. of *arrogāre*; see -ANCE. So **a·rrog**ANT. XIV (Ch.). – (O)F. **arrogate** æ·rŏgeit lay undue claim to. XVI. f. pp. stem of L. *arrogāre* claim for oneself, f. *ad* AR-+*rogāre* ask; see ROGATION, -ATE[3]. So **arroga·**TION. – L. In the spec. legal sense of adopting a person who is *sui juris*, the forms **a·drogate, adroga·tion** (XVI) are used.

arrow æ·rou missile to be shot from a bow. Late OE. *ar(e)we* – ON. **arw-*, nom. *ǫr* (g. sg., pl. *ǫrvar*), rel. to Goth. *arhwazna* arrow; the native OE. form was *earh* (recorded once, the usual names being *strǣl, flā, flān*); Germ. base **arχw-* :– IE. **arkw-*, whence also L. *arcus* bow, ARC (OL. g. *arquī*; *arquitenēns* bowman).

arrowroot æ·rŏrūt herb of the W. Indies, Maranta arundinacea, the tubers of which were used to absorb poison from wounds, esp. those made by poisoned arrows XVII; starch made from this XIX. Perversion of Aruak *aru-aru* 'meal of meals', by assim. to ARROW and ROOT.

arse āɹs fundament. OE. *ærs* (*ears*) = OFris. *ers*, MLG. *ars*, *ers*, MDu. *aers*, *e(e)rs* (Du. *aars* and *naars*), OHG. *ars* (G. *arsch*), ON. *ars* and *rass* :– CGerm. (exc. Goth.) **arsaz* :– IE. **órsos*, whence also Gr. *órros*, Arm. *or* rump, rel. to Gr. *ourá* (:– **orsā*) tail.

arsenal ā·ɹsənəl †naval dock (in early use, of Venice); establishment for storage of weapons and ammunition XVI. Early forms *arse-*, *arzenale*, *archynale* – F. *arsénal*, †*archenal* or its source It. †*arzanale*, (mod.) *arsenale* (whence also Sp., Pg. *arsenal*), f. Venetian It. *arzanà*, ult. (with unexpl. loss of *d*) – Arab. *dār-aççinā'ah*, f. *dār* house, *al* AL-², *çinā'ah* art, mechanical industry, f. *çana'a* make, fabricate (cf. OIt. *tarcenale*, whence F. †*tarcenal*; Sp. *atarazana*, *-al*, Pg. *taracena*; Genoese It. *darsena*, whence OF. *darse*, *darsine* dock).

arsenic ā·ɹs(ə)nik †orpiment (*yellow a.*, Pers. *zirnīkhi aṣfar*) XIV (Ch.); †realgar (*red a.*, Pers. *zirnīkhi qirmiz*) XV; white mineral substance (*white a.* trisulphide of arsenic) XVII; (chem.) semi-metallic element XIX. – (O)F. *arsenic* – L. *arsenicum* – Gr. *arsenikón*, var. of *arrenikón* yellow orpiment, lit. male (f. *árrēn* male) – (with etymologizing alteration, to express its powerful properties) Arab. *azzernīkh*, i.e. *al* AL-², *zernīkh* – Pers. *zarnī(k)*, *zirnīkh*, f. *zar* gold. Also **arsenic** aɹse·nik XIX, **arsenical** XVII. adjs.

arsis ā·ɹsis (pros.) unemphatic syllable XVIII; strong syllable XIX. – late L. – Gr. *ársis* lifting, raising, f. *aírein* (:– **árjein*) raise; opposed to THESIS. By Gr. writers applied to the raising of the foot in beating time, which marked the unaccented syllable, by later L. writers (followed by Bentley) referred to the raising of the voice, which marked the accented syllable; there is consequently the same opposition of meaning in *thesis*.

arson ā·ɹsən wilful setting fire. XVII. – legal AN., OF. *arson* :– medL. *arsiōnem*, f. *ars-*, pp. stem of *ardēre* burn (see ARDENT).

arsy-versy āːɹsivə̄·ɹsi back-foremost, upside-down. XVI. f. ARSE+L. *versus* turned (cf. -WARD), with -Y¹ added to both elements to make a jingle.

art āɹt skill or its application XIII (in relation to poetry, music, painting, etc. XVII); learning of the schools (e.g. *terms of art*); pl. branches of learning (*the seven arts, the liberal arts*) XIII/XIV; *magic art*, etc. XIV (Gower); artifice XVI (Sh.). – (O)F. *art* = Pr. *art*, Sp., It. *arte* :– L. *artem*, nom. *ars*, f. base **ar-* put together, join, fit (cf. ARM¹ and ², ARTICLE). Phr. *art and part* (orig. Sc. law XV), skill in contriving and active participation. Hence **a·rtful** †skilful, dexterous; †artistic XVII; wily, craftily ingenious XVIII; see -FUL¹.

art see BE.

artefact, also **arti-** ā·ɹtifækt product of human art. 1821 (*artéfact*, Coleridge). f. *arte*, abl. sg. of L. *ars* ART+*factum*, n. pp. of *facere* make, DO¹; cf. It. *artefatto*.

artery ā·ɹtəri any of the tubes conveying blood from the heart; †trachea (L. *artēria aspera*). XIV (Trev.). – L. *artēria* – Gr. *artēría*, prob. f. base **ar-* raise, repr. in AORTA, ARSIS. Cf. F. *artère*, whence Eng. †*arter(e)*, †*artir(e)* (XVI–XVII). Hence **arter**IAL aɹtiə·riəl. XV. – F. †*arterial* (mod. *artériel*). (Referred by the ancients to *aḗr* AIR in accordance with their notions of arterial functions.)

artesian āɹtī·ziən, āɹtī·ʒən. XIX. – F. *artésien*, f. OF. *Arteis* (mod. *Artois*) name of an old French province; applied orig. to wells made there, in which water rises spontaneously when a small hole is bored into the water-bearing strata; see -IAN.

arthritis āɹþrai·tis inflammation of a joint. XVI. – L. *arthrītis* – Gr. *arthrîtis*, f. *árthron* joint, f. **ar-* fit (cf. L. *artus* limb, ARTICLE); see -ITIS. So **arthrit**IC -i·tik. XV. orig. *artetik* – OF. *artetique* – medL. *arteticus*, alteration of *arthrīticus* – Gr. *arthrītikós*; assim. later (through *arthetick*) to the L.-Gr. form. The comb. form **arthro-** of Gr. *árthron* is repr. in various scientific terms, e.g. *a·rthropod* (modL. *Arthro·poda*).

artichoke ā·ɹtitʃouk plant allied to the thistle, having edible parts XVI; *Jerusalem a.* species of sunflower with edible tuberous roots XVII. Earliest forms *archicokk*, *-choke*, *artechock*, *artichaugh* – northern It. *arti-*, *arciciocco*, for *arcicioffo*, alteration of **alcarcioffo* (cf. modIt. *carciofo*) – OSp. *alcarchofa* (mod. *alcachofa*, Pg. *alcachofra*) – Arab. *al-kharshōf*, i.e. *al* AL-², *kharshōf* artichoke. (F. *artichaut*, G. *artischocke*, Du. *artisjok* are also ult. – It.) The form *artichoke* (from XVI) shows dissim. of *ch . . ch* to *t . . ch*, and assim. of the final syll. to *choke*.

article ā·ɹtikl clause of the Creed XIII; head or point of a contract, item XIII; †nick of time, moment XIV; †piece of business XV; detail, particular XVIII; commodity, chattel XIX. – (O)F. *article* – L. *articulus*, dim. of *artus* joint, f. base **ar-* join (cf. ARM, ART). In gram. sense (XVI) repr. the use of L. *articulus* by Quintilian, etc., tr. Gr. *árthron* joint, which was applied by the Stoic grammarians to (i) the personal pronouns ('definite articles') and (ii) other pronouns, and demonstratives ('indefinite articles').

articulate ā.ti·kjŭlət divided into distinct parts, jointed; of distinct utterance. XVI. – L. *articulātus* jointed, f. *articulus* ARTICLE. So **arti·culate** -eit vb. †formulate in articles (intr. capitulate); utter (vocal sounds) with distinctness XVI; joint XVII; see -ATE[2] and [3]. **articul**A·TION jointing, joint XV; utterance XVII. – F. – L., f. *articulāre* joint.

artifice ā·ɹtifis †workmanship XVI; skill, address; expedient, contrivance XVII. – (O)F. *artifice* – L. *artificium*, f. *arti-*, *ars* ART+*fic-*, var. of *fac-* of *facere* make, DO[1]. So **artifici**AL āɹtifi·ʃəl)(*natural* XIV (Wyclif, Ch.); †skilful XV. – (O)F. *artificiel* or L. *artificiālis*. **artificer** aɹti·fisəɹ craftsman. XIV. – AN. *artificer* (cf. medL. *artificiārius*), prob. after OF. *artificien*; see -ER[2].

artillery āɹti·ləri †munitions XIV (Ch.); engines for discharging missiles XV. – (O)F. *artillerie* (whence It. *artiglieria*, Sp. *artilleria*), f. *artiller* alteration (after *art*) of OF. *atillier* (= Pr. *atilhar*) equip, arm, prob. by-form of *atirier*, f. *à* AD-+*tire* order; see TIER, -ERY.

artisan āɹtizæ·n handicraftsman; †artist. XVI. – F. *artisan* – It. *artigiano* :– Rom. **artītiānu-s*, f. L. *artītus*, pp. of *artīre* instruct in the arts, f. *art-*, *ars* ART; see -AN and cf. *courtesan*, *Parmesan*, *partisan*.

artist ā·ɹtist †one skilled in the (learned, useful) arts XVI; one who cultivates any of the fine arts XVI. – (O)F. *artiste* – It. *artista*, f. *arte* ART; see -IST. Hence **arti·st**IC. XVIII. **a·rtist**RY. XIX (Browning).

artiste āɹtī·st public singer, dancer, etc. XIX. F. (see prec.); superseded *artist* in this use (XVIII–XIX).

arum ɛə·rəm cuckoo pint, Arum maculatum. XVI (in form *aron* XVI–XVIII, whence mod. dial. *aaron*). – L. *arum* – Gr. *áron*.

arundinaceous ərʌ:ndinei·ʃəs reedy. XVII. f. L. *arundināceus*, f. *(h)arundin-*, *(h)arundō* reed; see -ACEOUS.

-ary əri suffix repr. L. *-ārius* 'pertaining to, connected with': formed on sbs., as *elementārius* elementary, *honōrārius* honorary, *voluntārius* voluntary; on adjs., as *primārius* primary; on advs., as *contrārius* contrary, *necessārius* necessary. Many of these adjs. were used as sbs.: in the masculine, as *adversārius* adversary, *commentārius* (sc. *liber*) commentary, *Januārius* (sc. *mēnsis*) January, *secrētārius* secretary; in the neuter, as *aviārium* aviary, *salārium* salary; and occas. in the feminine, as *Calvāria* Calvary. Since in French L. *-ārius* and *-āris* were repr. by *-aire*, it came about that, when F. words in *-aire* were adopted in modEng., they received the ending *-ary*, as *capillaire* capillary, *militaire* military (but in ME. and esp. in Sc. such adjs. commonly took *-air*, *-ar*, as *contrair*, *contrar*).

Aryan, Arian ɛə·riən, ā·riən Indo-European; also (restrictedly) Indo-Iranian. XIX (Max Müller). f. Skr. *āryas* (Vedic *āria*) noble, applied earlier as a national name. Cf. L. *Ariāna*, *-ē* eastern region of the Persian kingdom (*Ariānī*, *-ēnī* its inhabitants), Gr. *A'rioi* Medes (Herodotus), *Ariānē* (Strabo), *Ariānoi*; cf. Av. *Airyana*, whence mod. *Iran*. Cf. F. *arien*, G. *arisch*, sb. pl. *Arier*. See -AN.

arytenoid æriti·noid (anat.) epithet of two pyramidal cartilages of the larynx. XVIII. – modL. *arytænoīdēs* – Gr. *arutainoeidḗs*, f. *arútaina* funnel, f. *arú(t)ein* draw (off, etc.); see -OID.

as[1] əz, (emph.) æz to that or such a degree; in the manner or to the extent in which. ME. reduced form (XII) of *ase* or *als*, which are divergent developments of *alse* :– OE. *alswā* (*ealswā*) ALSO. Cf. OFris. *asa*, *as(e)*, *is*, and G. *als* as, than, reduced form of *also* (which survives in the sense 'therefore').

as[2] æs ancient Roman coin. XVII. – L. *ās*, of foreign (perh. Etruscan) origin. Cf. ACE.

as- assim. form of AD- before *s*; cf. AC-.

asafœtida, assa- æsəfī·tidə resinous gum with a strong smell of garlic. XIV. – medL. ('stinking asa'), i.e. *āsa* (– Pers. *āzā* mastic), *fœtida*, fem. of *fœtidus* FETID.

asbestos ǽzbe·stəs †fabulous unquenchable stone XIV; fibrous mineral made into an incombustible fabric XVII. The earliest exx. *asbeston*, *abiston*, *albestone* are – OF. *abeston*, *albeston* – L. – Gr. *ásbeston*, acc. of *ásbestos*, f. Gr. *a-* A-[4]+*sbestós*, f. *sbennúnai* quench. The present form dates from XVII.

ascend əse·nd go or come up. XIV (Ch.). – L. *ascendere*, f. *ad* AS- + *scandere* climb (see SCANSION). So **asce·nd**ANT first in astron. sense (XIV, Ch.); in the sense 'superiority' (XVI–) superseded by **asce·nd**ANCY XVIII. – (O)F. *ascendant* – prp. used sb. of L. *ascendere*. See -ENT, -ENCY.

ascension əse·nʃən ascent of Jesus Christ to Heaven XIV; rising of a celestial body XIV (Ch.). – (O)F. – L. *ascensiō(n-)*, f. *ascens-*, pp. stem of *ascendere*. So **asce·nt** upward movement, rise. XVII (Sh., AV.). f. ASCEND, after the pair *descend*, *descent*.

ascertain æsəɹtei·n make certain XV; learn, find out XVIII. – OF. *acertain-*, tonic stem of *acertener* (later *ass-*, *asc-*, and so in Eng.), f. *a* AD- + *certain* CERTAIN; stressed *asce·rtain* till XVII.

ascetic əse·tik exercising rigorous self-discipline. XVII (Sir T. Browne). – medL. *ascēticus* or Gr. *askētikós*, f. *askētḗs* monk, hermit (Philo), f. *askeîn* exercise; see -IC.

ascititious var. of ADSCITITIOUS.

asclepiad ǽsklī·piæd (pros.) specific verse-form. XVII. – late L. *asclēpiadēus* – Gr. *asklēpiádeios*, f. *Asklēpiádēs* name of a Gr. poet. (Earlier in *asclepiadics* XVI (Sidney), *asclepiadical* XVI.)

ascribe əskrai·b assign, attribute. XV. – L. *ascrībere* enter in a list, enrol, impute, f. *ad* AS- + *scrībere* write. Preceded by †*ascrive* (XIV–XVII) – OF. *ascriv-*, stem of *ascrire* = It. *ascrivere* – L. *ascrībere*. So **ascript**ION əskri·pʃən. XVI. – L.

aseptic eise·ptik non-putrefying. XIX. f. A-⁴+SEPTIC.

ash¹ æʃ well-known forest-tree (family Fraxineæ). OE. *æsć* = OS. *ask* (Du. *esch*), OHG. *ask* (MHG. *asch*; G. *esche* is from the adj. *eschen*), ON. *askr* :– CGerm. (exc. Goth.) **askiz*. An IE. base **ŏs-*, with various extensions, is repr. also by L. *ornus* elm, Gr. *oxúē*, Alb. *ah* beech, Lith. *úosis*, OSl. *jasenĭ*, OPruss. *woasis*, W. *onnen* ash.

ash² æʃ powdery residue of combustion. OE. *æsće*, *æxe* = MLG. *asche*, Du. *asch*, OHG. *asca* (G. *asche*), ON. *aska*; cf. Goth. *azgo*; perh. rel. to ARID. *Ash Wednesday* first day of Lent XIII; after ecclL. *dies cinerum* 'day of ashes'; cf. F. *jour* or *mercredi des cendres*, G. *aschermittwoch*.

ashamed əʃei·md affected with shame. OE. *āsćamod*, pp. of *āsćamian* feel shame, f. *ā-* A-³ + *sćamian* (same sense), f. *sćamu* SHAME; cf. OE. *ofsćamod*.

ashlar æ·ʃləɹ squared stone for building (which succeeded the wooden shingle). XIV. ME. *as(s)heler* – OF. *aisselier* – L. *axilla*, dim. of L. *axis*, *assis* board, plank (whence F., Pr. *ais*, It. *asse*).

ashore əʃɔə·ɹ on or on to the shore. XVI. f. A-¹+SHORE¹, on the model of the earlier *aland* (XII).

Asian ei·ʃⁱən, ei·ʒⁱən XIV (Trev.). – L. *Asiānus* – Gr. *Asiānós*; see -IAN. So **Asi**ATIC eiʃiæ·tik, eiʒ-. XVII. – L. *Asiāticus* – Gr. *Asiātikós*.

aside əsai·d to one side. XIV. ME. *on syde*, *a syde*, i.e. ON, A-¹, SIDE.

asinine æ·sinain ass-like. XVI. – L. *asinīnus*, f. *asinus* ASS; see -INE¹.

-asis əsis repr. L. *-āsis*, Gr. *-āsis*, forming names of diseases, prop. nouns of state or process derived from verbs in *-dein*, *-ân*; as *elephantiasis*, *phthiriasis*, *psoriasis*.

ask àsk call upon for information, inquire. OE. *āscian*, *ācsian*, *āhsian*, *āxian* = OFris. *āskia*, OS. *ēscōn*, OHG. *eiscōn* (MHG. *eischen*, G. *heischen*, with *h* after *heissen*) :– WGerm. **aiskōjan*; cogns. are found in OSl. *iskati*, Lith. *ieškóti*, Skr. *iccháti* seek. Various types of development are repr. in ME. and later; *āscian* gave *asche*, *asshe*, beside *esche*, *esse* from an OE. by-form *ǣscian*; retention of *ā* with metathesis to *ācsian* gave local ME. *oxy*; shortening of *ā* before *cs*, *x* gave *axy*, *axe*, whence widespread mod. dial. *ax*. The standard form *ask* (*c.* 1200) resulted from metathesis of *aks-*, *ax-*. The var. *asse* persists dial., with pt. and pp. *ast*.

askance əskà·ns sideways, obliquely. XVI. Early forms are *a scanche*, *a sca(u)nce*, *a sconce*, which suggest a F. origin; but cf. It. *a*, *di*, and *per scancio* obliquely. The source, which has been much disputed, remains unkn., as also that of the more or less synon. †*askie* (Gower), †*askile* (XVI rare), †*askoye*, †*askoyne* (XV–XVI). ¶ The adv. †*ascaunse(s)* as if, as much as to say (XIV–XVI) is unrelated.

askari æ·skarī native soldier of W. Africa. XX. – Arab. *'askarī* soldier, f. *'askar* army.

askew əskjū· obliquely, awry. XVI. f. A-¹+SKEW.

aslant əslà·nt oblique, slanting XIII (Cursor M.); prep. XVII (Sh.). Early ME. *o slant*; a later var. is †*on slent*, Sc. *asklent*, *esklent*, continued in mod. dial. *on the slent*; the relation of the forms is obscure (see SLANT).

asleep əslī·p sleeping. OE. *on slǣpe*, ME. *o slæpe*, *o slepe*, *aslepe*; see A-¹, SLEEP.

aslope əslou·p sloping, obliquely. XIV. Earlier than SLOPE (XVI); of uncertain origin. On formal grounds a proposed deriv. from OE. **āslopen*, pp. of *āslūpan* slip away, disappear, is appropriate; but there are chronological difficulties, and transference in sense from obliquity of motion to obliquity of position must be assumed.

asp¹ æsp tree of the poplar family, Populus tremula. OE. *æspe* = OHG. *aspa* (MHG. *aspe*; G. *espe* is from the adj. *espen*) :– Germ. **aspōn*; and OE. *æps* (for **æsp*) = ON. *ǫsp* :– CGerm. (exc. Goth.) **aspō*; rel. to OPruss. *abse*, Lith. *āpušė*, *ēpušė*, Lett. *apsa*, *-e*, Russ. *osína*, Pol. *osika*. Superseded by ASPEN.

asp² æsp small venomous hooded serpent of N. Africa. XV. – OF. *aspe* or its source L. *aspis* – Gr. *aspís*, *aspid-*. The L. form was formerly current in Eng., as well as *aspic* (poet. in Addison, Tennyson) – F. *aspic* – Pr. *aspic* (prob. assim. to *basilic* basilisk); also †*aspide* – OF. *aspide* (cf. Sp. *aspid*, Pg., obs. It. *aspide*).

asparagus əspæ·rəgəs liliaceous plant cultivated for its vernal shoots. XV. – L. *asparagus* – Gr. *aspáragos*, Attic *aspháragos*. In polite use the L. form has supplanted the various altered or deriv. forms that have been current: (i) *sparagus*, a medL. form, whence It. *sparagio*, G. *sparge(n)*, *spargel*, MF. *esperage*, *esparge* (mod. *asperge*), Eng. (ii) *(a)sperage*, ***sparage*** (XV–XVII); (iii) *sparrow-grass* (XVII), formerly *sparagras*, alteration of *sparagus* by assoc. with *grass* (which is the usual term with cooks and greengrocers). 'The corruption of the word into *sparrow-grass* is so general that *asparagus* has an air of stiffness and pedantry' (Walker, 1791).

aspect æ·spekt way of looking; appearance. XIV (Ch., in astron. sense; Gower, Trevisa). – L. *aspectus* (whence F. *aspect*, It. *aspetto*, etc.), f. *aspect-*, pp. stem of *aspicere* look at, f. *a-* AD-+*specere* look (cf. SPY). The orig. stressing *aspe·ct* continued till the time of Swift, but *a·spect* is found in early XVII.

¶ L. *spec-* and its var. *spic-* are repr. by many derivs., as (i) *special, species, specious, spectacle, spectre, speculate*; *aspect, circumspect, conspectus, expect, inspect, introspection, prospect, respect, suspect*; (ii) *auspice, conspicuous, despicable* (cf. DESPISE), *perspicacious, perspicuous, suspicion.*

aspen æ·spən adj. of an asp-tree XIV; sb. aspen tree XVI. f. ASP[1]+-EN[1]. The sb. arose from apprehending the adj., in such collocations as *aspen leaf* (Ch.), as a sb. used attrib.

asperges æ̆spə̄·ɹdʒīz (liturg.) (antiphon accompanying) the sprinkling of holy water before the principal mass on Sunday; first word of '*Asperges* me hyssopo et mundabor' Thou shalt purge me with hyssop and I shall be clean (Ps. l[i] 9).

asperity æ̆spe·rĭti roughness, harshness. XVI. – L. *asperitās*, f. *asper* rough; see -ITY. Earlier †*asprete* (XV) – OF. *asprete* (mod. *âpreté*).

asperse əspə̄·ɹs besprinkle XV; calumniate XVII. f. *aspers-*, pp. stem of L. *aspergere*, f. *a-* AD-+*spargere* sprinkle (cf. SPARSE). So **asper**SION əspə̄·ɹʃən sprinkling; calumniation. XVI. – L.

asphalt æ·sfælt, (formerly) æsfæ·lt mineral pitch XIV; composition for paving made from bituminous limestones XIX. The earliest exx. show adoption from various sources; *aspaltoun, aspalt* (XIV) from OF., *aspallto* from It. *aspalto*; later the Gr. and L. forms were used, till more recent times, when *asphalt(e)* reproduces the F. *asphalte*; ult. – L. *asphalton, -um* – Gr. *ásphalton, -os*, of alien origin.

asphodel æ·sfŏdel liliaceous plant, Asphodelus ramosus XVI (*asphodil*); used poet., after Homer's ἀσφοδελὸς λειμών asphodel-covered mead haunted by the heroes XVII (Milton). – L. *asphodilus, -elus* – Gr. *asphódelos*; the medL. var. *affodilus* was repr. by †*affodil* (XIV–XVII); cf. DAFFODIL.

asphyxia æsfi·ksiə stoppage of the pulse, (hence) suffocation. XVIII. modL. – Gr. *asphuxíā*, f. *a-* A-[4] + *sphúxis* pulse (cf. SPHYGMO-). Hence **asphy·xiate** (-ATE[3]), -A·TION XIX.

aspic[1] æ·spik savoury meat jelly. XVIII. – F. *aspic*, a use of *aspic* serpent (see ASP[2]), due to comparison of the various colours of the jelly with those of the serpent (F. *sauce* or *ragoût à l'aspic*).

aspic[2] see ASP[2].

aspidistra æspidi·strə plant of the liliaceous genus so named. XIX. – modL., f. Gr. *aspid-, aspís* shield (with ref. to the shape of the leaves)+-*istra*, after *tupistra*.

aspire əspaiə·ɹ have a desire for something above one XV; rise up, mount XVI. – (O)F. *aspirer* or L. *aspīrāre* breathe upon, favour, have an ambition, aspirate (cf. Gr. προσπνεῖν), f. *ad* AS-+*spīrāre* breathe, prob. of imit. origin. So **aspi·r**ANT one who aspires to high position XVIII. – F. or L. prp. **aspirate** æ·spĭrət adj. aspirated XVII; sb. consonant diphthong consisting of a stop followed by *h*; sound of *h* XVIII. – pp. of L. *aspīrāre*; see -ATE[2]. **a·spirate** -eit pronounce with an aspirate XVIII; see -ATE[3]. **aspir**A·TION action of aspirating, aspirated sound XIV; †favour, inspiration XV; drawing breath; aspiring thought XVII. – (O)F. – L.

aspirin æ·spĭrin acetylsalicylic acid chemically prepared, used as a sedative drug. XIX. – G.; invented by Heinrich Dreser ('Pflüger's Archiv' 1899); f. A-[4]+*Spiræa*+-IN (i.e. without the aid of Spiræa) and so named to distinguish it from the natural acid found in Spiræa ulmaria.

asquint əskwi·nt (arch.) *to look* to one side XIII (AncrR.); obliquely through a defect in the eyes, cross-eyed XIV (Trev.); with an unfavourable or furtive glance XV. perh. f. A-[1]+a LG. or Du. form now repr. by Du. *schuinte* obliquity, slant, f. *schuin* oblique = Fris., LG. *schüns*. ¶ The source of SQUINT.

ass æs donkey OE.; stupid person XV. OE. *assa, asa* – OCeltic **as(s)in* (W. *asyn* = MIr. *assan*, Corn. *asen*, Bret. *azen*) – L. *asinus* (whence F. *âne*, Pr. *ase*, Sp. *asno*, It. *asino*), which has been referred, together with Gr. *ónos* and Arm. *eš*, to Sumerian *anšu*. The pronunc. ās is now old-fashioned or affected. With its vars. the word is CEur. Germ. **asiluz* (for *asinus*, repr. by ON. *asni*) is repr. by OE. *esol, eosol*, OS., OHG. *esil*, (M)LG., MDu. *esel* (Du. *ezel* EASEL, G. *esel*), Goth. *asilus*. ¶ From Germ. were adopted OSl. *osĭlŭ* (Russ. *osël*), Lith. *ãsilas*.

assail əsei·l make a violent attack on. XIII. – OF. *asalir*, tonic stem *asaill-* (mod. *assaillir*) :- medL. *assalīre* (for L. *assilīre*), f. *ad* AS- + *salīre* to leap (see SALIENT). Hence **assai·l**ANT XVI; after F. *assaillant*; superseded **assai·ler** (XIV), orig. – OF. *assaileor* (see -ER[2]).

assart əsā·ɹt grub up trees from forest land. XVI. – AN. *assarter, -ier, -ir*, OF. *essarter* :- medL. *ex(s)artāre*, f. *ex* EX-[1]+*sart-* (as in L. *sartūra* for *sarritūra* weeding), pp. stem of *sar(r)īre* hoe, weed (cf. *sarculum* hoe). Hence **assa·rt** sb. land converted into arable. XV. – AN. *assart*, f. the vb.

assassin əsæ·sin (hist.) pl. Moslem fanatics engaged to murder Christians; one who kills another treacherously. XVII. – F. *assassin* or medL. *assassīnus* (whence also Pr. *assassin*, It. *assassino*, Sp. *asesino*) – Arab. *ḥashshāshīn*, pl. of *ḥashshāsh* HASHISH-eater, Ismaili sectaries who intoxicated themselves with hashish when preparing to dispatch their victim. For the adoption of the pl. form cf. BEDOUIN; formerly stressed *a·ssassin*. Hence **assa·ssin**ATE[3], **assassin**A·TION XVII (Sh.).

assault əsǭ·lt hostile onset XIII; unlawful attack on the person XV. ME. *asaut* (later with *l* as in *fault*; cf. AN. *assalt*, Gower) – OF. *asaut* (mod. *assaut*) = Pr. *asalt*, Sp. *asalto*, It. *assalto* :– Rom. **assaltu-s* (replacing L. *assultus*), f. **assalīre* ASSAIL. So **assau·lt** vb. XV. – OF. *assauter* = Pr., Sp. *asaltar*, It. *assaltare* :– Rom. **assaltāre* (replacing L. *assultāre*), f. *ad* AS- + *saltāre*, frequent. of *salīre* leap (see SALIENT).

assay əsei· trial (gen. and spec., now only of metals). XIV (R. Mannyng). – OF. *assai*, *assay*, var. of *essai* ESSAY. So **assay·** vb. XIV (R. Mannyng). – OF. *assaier*. Aphetic †*say* (XIV, R. Mannyng).

assegai æ·sigai (orig.) Moorish lance, (now) spear of S. African tribes. XVII. Also (now less freq.) *assagai* – F. †*azagaie* (Rabelais; mod. *zagaie*, *sagaie*) or its source Pg. *azagaia* (Sp. *-aya*) – Arab. *azzaghāyah*, i.e. *al* AL-², *zaghāyah* Berber word for 'spear'. Earlier in the form †*zagaie* (XVI) – F. *zagaie* (cf. Pg., It. *zagaia*, It. *zagaglia*); still earlier evidence of the penetration of the Arab. word into Europe is shown by OF. *archegaie*, *arcigaye* (whence Sp. *arsagaya* and rare Eng. *archegaye*, used by Berners, 1523, and perverted by W. Morris to *archgay*), and by OF. *lancegaye* (blended with LANCE), whence late ME. *launcegay* (Ch., Gower), which was continued in arch. use.

assemble əse·mbl bring or come together. XIII. ME. *asemle* – OF. *asembler* (mod. *ass-*) = Pr. *asemblar* :– Rom. **assimulāre*, f. L. *ad* AS-+*simul* together (cf. SAME, SIMILAR, HOMO-). So **asse·mbly**. XIV (R. Mannyng). – OF. *asemblée*, sb. use of fem. pp., with ending assim. to -Y⁵.

assent əse·nt give agreement or concurrence *to*. XIII (RGlouc.). – OF. *as(s)enter* = Pr. *asentar* :– Rom. **assentare*, L. *-ārī*, f. *ad* AS-+*sent-*, of *sentīre* feel, think (cf. SENTENCE, SENTIENT). So **asse·nt** sb. XIII (Cursor M.). – OF. *asent*, *-e*, f. the vb.

assert əsɔ̄·ɹt maintain, claim; declare formally, state firmly. XVII (with a considerable variety of applications, some only temporary). f. L. *assert-*, pp. stem of L. *asserere* (i) declare one's slave free by laying one's hands on him, (hence) set free, (ii) declare to be one's slave, (hence) appropriate, claim, (further) maintain, affirm, f. *ad* AS-+ *serere* join (cf. SERIES). So **asser**TION əsɔ̄·ɹʃən in various senses. XV (declaration, averment). – F. or L. **asse·rt**IVE. XVII (the corr. adv. is XV). – F. *assertif*.

assess əse·s settle the amount of; rate for taxation. XV. – OF. *assesser*, f. L. *assess-*, pp. stem of *assidēre* sit by, etc. (cf. ASSIDUOUS), in medL. levy, tax, f. *ad* AS-+*sedēre* SIT. Hence **asse·ss**MENT. XVI. **asse·ss**OR assistant judge XIV; rater of taxes XV. – OF. *assessour* (mod. *-eur*) – L. *assessor*.

assets æ·sets sufficient estate, spec. as applicable to the discharge of debts. XVI. – legal AN. *assets*, earlier *asetz* (Britton), OF. *asez* (mod. *assez* enough) = Pr. *asatz*, OSp. *asaz*, Pg. *assaz*, It. *assai* :– Rom. **assatis*, i.e. L. *ad* to, *satis* enough, sufficiency (cf. SATISFY); orig. in legal phr. *aver asetz* have sufficient (sc. to meet claims); prop. sg., but taken as pl. on account of its ending; the new sg. *asset* dates from XIX. ¶ In OF. *asez* was taken as a nom. and an obl. case *aset* was formed thence; this, with pronunc. ase·þ and the sense 'satisfaction, amends', was adopted in Eng. and was current XIV–XV; the north. and Sc. var. of this was *as(s)yth* XIV–XVI, with a corr. vb., and a deriv. *assythment* XVI.

asseveration əsevərei·ʃən emphatic assertion. XVI. – L. *asseverātiō(n-)*, f. *asseverāre*, f. *ad* AS-+*sevērus* grave, SEVERE; see -ATION. So **asse·verate** (see -ATE³) XVIII; preceded by †*asse·ver* (XVI).

assibilate əsi·bileit make SIBILANT. XIX. f. pp. of L. *assibilāre*; see -ATE³.

assiduous əsi·djuəs unremittingly diligent. XVI. f. L. *assiduus*, f. *assidēre* sit by the side of, attend or apply oneself to, f. *ad* AS-+*sedēre* SIT; see -OUS. So **assidu**ITY æsidjū·iti. XVII. – L.

assign¹ əsai·n allot, appoint, designate XIV; ascribe XV. – OF. *asi(g)ner* (mod. *assigner*) :– L. *assignāre*, f. *ad* AS-+*signāre* SIGN. So **assign**A·TION æsig-. XIV. – (O)F. – L. **assign**EE æsainī· ASSIGN². XV. – (O)F. *assigné*, pp. of *assigner*, used sb. **assi·gn**MENT. XIV. – OF. *assignement* – medL. *assignāmentum*.

assign² əsai·n one to whom a property or right is assigned. XIV. – AN., (O)F. *assigné*; see ASSIGNEE, from which it is differentiated by the muted final syll. (cf. ASTRAY, COSTIVE, DEFILE², TAIL², TROVE).

assimilate əsi·mileit make like; absorb and incorporate. XV. f. pp. stem of L. *assimilāre*, f. *ad* AS-+*similis* like, SIMILAR; see -ATE³. So **assimil**A·TION. XV. **assi·milative**. XIV. – F. or L.

assist əsi·st †give help *to* XV (Sc.); help; †stand near XVI; be present *at* XVII. – F. *assister* – L. *assistere*, f. *ad* AS-+*sistere* take one's stand (cf. STAND, STATION). So **assi·st**ANCE †presence, persons present XV; aid XIV. – F. *assistance* – medL. *assistentia*. **assist**ANT †(one who is) present; helper. XV. – F. *assistant* – medL. *assistēns*, prp. of *assistere*.

assize əsai·z (arch.) judgement (spec. the Last Judgement); legal inquest or trial XIII; sessions of a court; ordinance; assessment; regulation (spec. of weights, measures, prices); standard measure; †size XIV. – OF. *as(s)ise* sitting, seat, settlement, assessment, regulation, regular mode, sb. use of fem. of *assis*, pp. of *asseeir* (mod. *asseoir*) sit, settle, assess :– L. *assidēre* (see ASSESS). See also SIZE.

associate əsou·ʃieit pp. joined in function or status XIV; sb. (-ət) companion, confederate, colleague XVI. – L. *associātūs*, pp.

of *associāre*, f. *ad* AS-+*socius* sharing, allied (cf. SOCIAL). So **asso·ciate** vb. XV (pt. *associat*). See -ATE², -ATE³. **associa·TION**. XVI. – F. or medL.

assoil əsoi·l (arch.) absolve XIII; acquit XIV. – AN. *as(s)oilier*, *-ir*, f. OF. *assoil-*, tonic stem of *asoldre* (mod. *absoudre*) :– L. *absolvere* ABSOLVE. A latinized var. †*absoil* (XV–XVI) partly paved the way for the prevalence of *absolve*.

assonance æ·sənəns form of rhyme consisting in agreement of the stressed or tonic vowel. XVIII. – F. *assonance*, f. L. *assonāre* (of Echo) answer to, f. *ad* AS-+*sonāre* SOUND².

assort əsɔ̄·ɹt arrange in sorts. XV (Caxton; rare before late XVIII, when it was prob. readopted). – OF. *assorter*, mod. *assortir*, f. *à* AD- + *sorte* SORT. So **asso·rtMENT** proper agreement XVII; arrangement into sorts XVIII; after F. *assortiment*.

assuage əswei·dʒ mitigate, soothe. XIV. – OF. *as(s)ouagier* = Pr. *asuaviar* :– Rom. **assuāviāre*, f. *ad* AS- + *suāvis* SWEET. Aphetic SUAGE.

assume əsjū·m take to or upon oneself XV; claim, take for granted XVI. – L. *assūmere* take up, adopt, usurp, f. *ad* AS-+*sūmere* take, f. *sub* SUB-+*emere* take (cf. EXEMPT). So **assumpsit** əsʌ·mpsit (leg.) promise, contract. XVII. 3rd sg. pt. of *assūmere*.

assumption əsʌ·mʃən A. (feast of) the reception of the Virgin Mary into Heaven XIII (RGlouc.); B. (Sc.) levy XVI; adoption; taking for granted, postulate XVII. – OF. *asompsion* (mod. *assomption*) or L. *assūmptiō(n-)*; in B a re-adoption. See -TION. **assu·mptIVE**. XVII.

assure əʃuə·ɹ make sure. XIV (Barbour, Ch., Gower). – (O)F. *assurer*, earlier *aseurer* = Pr. *asegurar*, It. *assecurare* :– Rom. **assēcūrāre*, f. *ad* AS-+*sēcūrus* SECURE. So **assu·rANCE**. XIV (Barbour, Ch.). – (O)F.

Assyrian əsi·riən pert. to Assyria or its language. XV. f. L. *Assyrius*, Gr. *Assúrios*; see -IAN. sb. XIV (Wycl. Bible).

aster æ·stəɹ genus of plants with radiated flowers. XVIII. – modL. use of L. *astēr* – Gr. *astḗr* STAR.

-aster æstəɹ repr. L. *-aster* or *-āster* (whence F. *-âtre*), suffix of sbs. and adjs. expressing incomplete resemblance, and hence gen. of pejorative force; e.g. *philosophaster* petty philosopher, *oleaster* wild or bastard olive, *surdaster* somewhat deaf, *filiaster* stepson, *patraster* father-in-law. The best-known comp. in Eng. is POETASTER, on which was modelled *criticaster*.

asterisk æ·stərisk star-shaped object; sign *. XVII. – late L. *asteriscus* – Gr. *asterískos*, dim. of *astḗr* STAR.

asterism æ·stərizm (astron.) group of stars. XVI. – Gr. *asterismós*, f. *astḗr* STAR; see -ISM.

astern əstɔ̄·ɹn in, at, or towards the stern. XVII. f A-¹+STERN¹, after AHEAD.

asteroid æ·stəroid (astron.) minute planetary body. XIX. – Gr. *asteroeidḗs*, f. *astḗr* STAR; see -OID.

asthma æ·s(þ)mə (formerly also æ·stmə) disease of respiration. XIV. Earliest form (after medL.) *asma* – Gr. *âsthma* hard breathing, f. *ázein* breathe hard, rel. to *áein* blow (cf. AIR, WIND).

asthore əstɔ̄ə·ɹ (Anglo-Ir.) darling. XIX. – Ir. *a stóir* (– ME. *stōr*, STORE) O treasure. ¶ In Sh. 'Henry V' IV iv 4 *calmie custure me* appears to be intended for Ir. *cailín óg a stóir* 'young girl, O treasure'; see COLLEEN.

astigmatism əsti·gmətizm defect in the eye preventing exact focusing. XIX. f. Gr. *a-* A-⁴+*stigmat-*, STIGMA+-ISM. So **astigmatIC** æstigmæ·tik. XIX.

astir əstɔ̄·ɹ stirring, up and about. XIX. First in north. writers, e.g. Lockhart, Scott (Wordsworth has *on the stir*, 1805); anglicization of Sc. *asteer* (Burns, Scott), earlier *asteir* (XVI), *on steir* (XIV), f. ON, A-¹+Sc. form of STIR. A rare †*astirbroad* (XVII, once) is of obscure formation.

astonish əstɔ·niʃ †shock, dumbfound, stun XV; amaze XVII. First in (Sc.) pp. *astonist*, prob. extension, with -ISH², of pp. of †*astonie*, †*astony* (XIV–XVII), obscure var. of †*astone*, the pp. of which is the source of ASTOUND.

astound əstau·nd †shock, stun; amaze. XVII. prob. f. pp. †*astound*, †*astouned*, earlier †*astoned*, †*astuned* (XIII), f. AN. **astoné*, **astuné*, for OF. *estoné*, pp. of *estoner* (mod. *étonner*), corr. to Pr. *estonat*, pp. of Gallo-Rom. **extonāre*, f. L. *ex* EX-²+ *tonāre* THUNDER. See also STUN.

astragal æ·strəgæl architectural moulding of semicircular section. XVII. – L. *astragalus* (partly through F. *astragale*) – Gr. *astrágalos* huckle-bone, (pl.) dice, moulding of a capital. Used earlier in L. form XVI.

astrakhan æ·strəkæn, æstrəkæ·n. XVIII. f. name of an eastern province of Russia, to the north of the Caspian Sea, applied to the skin of unborn or young lambs.

astral æ·strəl of the stars, starry, star-like. XVII. – late L. *astrālis*, f. *astrum* STAR; see -AL¹.

astray əstrei· wandering, orig. of horses. XIII. ME. *o strai*, *astraie* – AN. **astraié*, OF. *estraié*, pp. of *estraier* (= Pr. *estraguar*) :– Rom. **extrāvagāre*, f. L. *extrā* out of bounds + *vagārī* wander (cf. VAGUE); the first syll. has been assoc. with A-¹. For the loss of *-é* cf. ASSIGN², etc.

astrict əstri·kt bind closely. XVI. f. *astrict-*, pp. stem of L. *astringere* ASTRINGE; in Sc. law *astrict(ed)* (XVI–XVII) was applied to lands held on such terms that the tenant was obliged to have grain grown thereon ground at a particular mill. So **astri·cTION**. XVI. – F. or L.

astride əstrai·d with the legs stretched apart. XVII. f. A-¹+STRIDE.

astringe əstri·ndʒ bind closely. XVI. – L. *astringere*, f. *ad* AD- + *stringere* bind, draw tight (see STRICT). So **astri·ngENT**. XVI. – F. *astringent*, L. *astringēns*.

astringer see OSTRINGER.

astro- æ·strou repr. comb. form of Gr. *ástron* STAR.

astrolabe æ·strəleib instrument used for taking altitudes and solving astronomical problems. XIII (corruptly *ars table*). – OF. *astrelabe* – medL. *astrolabium* – Gr. *astrólabon*, sb. use of n. of adj. *astrólabos* 'star-taking', f. *ástron* STAR + **lab-*, base of *lambánein* take. In XIV–XVI forms in *-labie* after medL. are frequent.

astrology əstrɔ·lədʒi practical application of astronomy to human uses; in the sense 'divination by the stars' (now the only use) more spec. *judicial a.*)(*natural a.*, which related to the prediction of natural phenomena. XIV (Barbour, Ch., Gower). – (O)F. *astrologie* – L. *astrologia* astronomy – Gr. *astrologíā*, f. *astrológos* telling of the stars, astronomer; see STAR, -LOGY. So **astro·loger** †practical astronomer XIV (Wycl. Bible); one who divines by the stars XVII. contemp. with and finally superseding †*astrolog* (Barbour) and †*astrologien* (Ch.) – OF. *astrologue* and *astrologien*, based on L. *astrologus* astronomer, star-diviner – Gr. *astrológos*; see -ER[1]. **astrolo·gICAL**. XVI. f. F. *-ique* or late L. *-icus* – Gr. *astrologikós*.

astronomy əstrɔ·nəmi science which treats of the stars XIII (Laȝ.); †astrology XIV. – (O)F. *astronomie* – L. *astronomia* (Seneca; the earlier term was *astrologia* ASTROLOGY) – Gr. *astronomíā*, f. *astronómos* astronomer, *astronomeîn* observe the stars, f. *ástron* STAR + *nom-*, *némein* (see -NOMY). So **astro·nomer** student of astronomy, †astrologer. XIV. Late ME. *astronomyer*, f. *astronomy*, after earlier †*astronomyen* – OF. *astronomien*, f. *astronomie*; see -ER[1]. **astrono·mICAL**. XVI. f. F. *-ique* or L. *-icus* – Gr. *astronomikós*.

astute əstjū·t of keen discernment. XVII. – F. †*astut* or L. *astūtus*, f. *astus* craft, cunning. (Cf. rare Sc. (XVI) †*astuce* adj. – OF. *astus*, *-uce*, and sb. – OF. *astuce* – L. *astūtia*.)

asunder əsʌ·ndəɹ apart. ME. *asundre* (XII), *o sunder* (XIII), OE. phr. *on sundran*, *-um*, i.e. *on* ON, A-[1] + obl. forms of *sundor*; see SUNDER.

aswoon əswū·n (arch.) in a swoon. XIV (Ch.). Late ME. *aswowne*, alteration of *iswown*, OE. *ġeswōgen*, pp. of *swōgan*; see SWOON.

asylum əsai·ləm inviolable sanctuary for criminals, etc. XV (Lydg.); place of refuge XVII; institution for the afflicted XVIII. – L. *asȳlum* – Gr. *ásūlon* refuge, sb. use of n. of *ásūlos* inviolable, f. *a-* A-[4] + *súlē*, *sûlon* right of seizure. Formerly also †*asile* (XIV–XVIII) – (O)F. *aisle*, *asyle*.

asymptote æ·simtout (geom.) line which approaches nearer and nearer to a curve without meeting it. XVII. – modL. *asymptōta* (sc. *linea* line) – Gr. *asúmptōtos*, sb. use (sc. *grammḗ* line) of adj. 'not falling together', f. *a-* A-[4] + *sún* with, SYN- + *ptōtós* apt to fall (**pt-* **pet-*, *píptein* fall).

asyndeton əsi·ndətən (gram.) construction in which a conjunctive element is omitted. XVI. – modL. – Gr. *asúndeton*, n. of *asúndetos* unconnected, f. *a-* A-[4] + *súndetos*, vbl. adj. of *sundeîn*, f. *sun-* SYN- + *deîn* bind.

at æt, ət CGerm. (and to some extent IE.) prep. denoting position and motion towards. OE. *æt* = OFris. *et*, OS. *at*, OHG. *az*, ON., Goth. *at*; CGerm. prep. and verbal prefix, further rel. to L. (and Osco-Umbrian) *ad* to, at, AD-, OIr. *ad-*, as in *ad|con|dare* I have seen. Lost in sw. Eng. dial., as in modDu. and G., and replaced by *to*; in Scand., on the other hand, *to* was lost and its place taken by *at* (e.g. with the inf.; whence the use in north. Eng. dial.; cf. ADO). In ME. in combination with the dative of the def. art. (OE. *æt þǣm* m., n., *æt þǣre* fem.) it made a single word, *atten*, later *atte*, *ate*, *atter(e)*; e.g. *atten ende*, *attende* at the end, *attere dure*, *ate dure*, whence early mod. Eng. reduced forms *at end*, *at door* (Sh.), *at first*, *at last*, and the like.

at- assim. form of AD- before *t*; see AC-.

atabal æ·təbæl Moorish kettle-drum. XVII. – Sp. *atabal* – Arab. *aṭ-ṭabl*, i.e. *al* AL-[2], *ṭabl* drum.

ataghan, **ataman** vars. of YATAGHAN, HETMAN.

ataunt ətɔ̄·nt (naut.) with all sails set. XVII. See TAUNT[2].

atavism æ·təvizm tendency to reproduce the ancestral type. XIX. – F. *atavisme*, f. L. *atavus* great-grandfather's grandfather, f. *at-* 'farther beyond' + *avus* grandfather (cf. OPruss. *awis*, Lith. *avýnas* uncle, Goth. *awō* grandmother); see -ISM.

ataxy æ·təksi †disorderliness; (path.) functional irregularity (see LOCOMOTOR). XVII. – modL. *ataxia* (also used) – Gr. *ataxíā*, f. *a-* A-[4] + *táxis* order; see TACTIC, -Y[3].

-ate[1] eit, ət repr. F. *-at* (= Sp. -ADO, It. *-ato*) – L. *-ātus*, comp. suffix orig. f. stems of verbs in *-āre* + *-tus* (cf. *juventus* YOUTH), but later added directly to sbs. to form abstract sbs. (i) denoting action or state, as *cōnātus* endeavour, *plōrātus* weeping, *ululātus* howling; *cōnsulātus* consulship, *magistrātus* magistracy, *pontificātus*, *primātus* PRIMACY; similarly ChrL. *diaconātus*, *episcopātus*, *presbyterātus*; (ii) in coll. sense, as *comitātus* escort, retinue, *equitātus* cavalry, *senātus* SENATE; (iii) in concr. sense, as *magistrātus* MAGISTRATE, *matrōnātus* matron's dress, *potentātus* POTENTATE; corr. to Gr. *-ētús* in *boētús* shouting, *edētús* food, *pothētús* longing = OE. *-oþ*, *-aþ* (as in *fiscóþ* fishing, *drugoþ* DROUGHT), OHG. *-ōd*, Goth. *-ōþu-*. On the model of *cardinalate* (– F.), *-ate* has been suffixed to native words, e.g. *aldermanate*.

-ate[2] (in adjs.) ət, (in some sbs.) eit suffix of pps., ppl. adjs., and sbs., repr. (partly through OF. *-at*, *-ate*) L. *-ātus*, *-āta*, *-ātum*, ending of the pps. of verbs in *-āre*, f. *-ā-*+ *-tus*, gen. ppl. suffix, as in *doctus*, *monitus*, *rectus*, *auditus*, pps. of *docēre*, *monēre*, *regere*, *audīre*, and corr. to Gr. *-tos*, as in *ágnōstos* unknown, *gnōtós* known, *mathētós* (that may be) learnt, *siteutós* fatted. There are many adjs. of this origin, as *desolate*, *desperate*, *inchoate*, *moderate*, *separate*; *situate* survives as a pp. **a.** Added to sbs. with the sense 'provided with', it produced many adjs., as *dentātus* toothed, *foliātus* leaved, leafy, *insensātus* INSENSATE, *litterātus* LITERATE, *togātus* wearing a toga, *tessellātus* tiled; on this model were made numerous adjs. in nat. hist., etc., as *angustifoliate* narrow-leaved, *lunulate* crescent-shaped. **b.** L. pps. were used as sbs., in all three genders, as (i) *legātus* one sent as a deputy, LEGATE, (medL.) *prælātus* PRELATE, *curātus* one provided with a cure of souls, CURATE (cf. -ADO); (ii) medL. *carucāta* CARUCATE, *virgāta* VIRGATE, and numerous sbs. in the Rom. langs. (repr. by F. *-ée*, Sp. *-ada*, It. *-ata*; cf. -ADE); (iii) L. *mandātum* command, MAUNDY, modL. *præcipitātum* PRECIPITATE; in chem. (through uses like modL. *plumbum acetatum* salt produced by the action of acetic acid on lead) extended to the nomenclature of salts of acids denominated by adjs. in *-ic*. Cf. -Y[5].

-ate[3] eit suffix of verbs formed on pp. stems (*-āt-*) of L. verbs in *-āre*, orig. on the basis of existing pp. forms in -ATE[2], which were at first often used concurrently with the infs. as their pps., e.g. inf. *consecrate*, pp. *consecrate* (later *consecrated*); it consequently became possible to form an Eng. verb in *-ate* on any L. verb in *-āre*. Many F. verbs in *-er* (:– L. *-āre*) have been anglicized by the addition of this suffix to their stems, e.g. FELICITATE.

atelier æ·təliei, atəlje workshop, artist's studio. (XVII), XIX (Greville, Thackeray). (O)F., f. (with *-ier* :– L. *-ārium* -ARIUM) OF. *astelle* splinter, thin board :– late L. *astella*, for L. *astula*, alteration of *assula*, dim. of *assis* board, plank.

Athanasian æþənei·ʃiən pert. (traditionally) to *Athanasius* (A.D. 293–373), bishop of Alexandria. XVI. – ecclL. *Athanasiānus* (Augustine); see -IAN.

atheism ei·þiizm disbelief in God. XVI. – F. *athéisme* (XVI), f. Gr. *átheos* without God, denying God, f. *a-* A-[4]+*theós* god. (A rare †*atheonism* XVI was perh. f. It. *atheo*; Coverdale refers to 'the Italian *atheoi*'.) So **a·theist.** XVI. – F. *athéiste* or It. *atheista*; see -ISM, -IST; hence **athei**·STIC, -I·STICAL. XVII. (Other attempts to adopt Gr. *átheos*, viz. †*atheal*, †*athean*, were short-lived. Cf. F. *athée* atheist.)

atheling æ·ðəliŋ (hist.) prince. OE. *æþeling* = OFris. *etheling*, *edling*, OS. *eðiling* (MLG., MDu. *edelinc*), OHG. *adaling* (whence medL. *adal-*, *adelingus*) :– WGerm. **aþeliŋga*, f. **aþal-* race, family (cf. OE. *æþele* noble, etc.)+patronymic suffix -iŋ-.

athematic æþimæ·tik (philol.) formed without a thematic vowel. XIX. f. A-[4]+ THEMATIC.

athenæum æþinī·əm temple of Athene at Athens, in which professors taught, etc.; literary or scientific club; literary club-room. XVIII. – late L. *Athēnæum* – Gr. *Athēnaîon*, sb. use of n. of adj. 'pert. to *Athēnē*', goddess of wisdom.

athetize æ·þitaiz reject (a passage) as spurious. XIX. f. Gr. *áthetos* set aside; formed to render Gr. *atheteîn*; see -IZE.

athirst əþə̄·ɹst (arch.) thirsting. OE. *ofþyrst*, short form of *ofþyrsted*, pp. of *ofþyrstan* suffer thirst, f. *of-* A-[2]+*þyrst* THIRST; ME. vars. were *ofþurst*, *athurst*, *afurst*, *athrist*. Cf. AHUNGERED.

athlete æ·þlīt competitor in public games of ancient Greece and Rome; one trained or expert in physical exercises. XVIII (once XV). – L. *āthlēta* – Gr. *athlētḗs*, f. *athleîn* contend for a prize, f. *áthlos* contest, *áthlon* prize; before *c.* 1750 the L. form was in use. (Not in J.) So **athlet**IC æþle·tik. XVII. – F. *athlétique* (Rabelais) or L. *athlēticus* – Gr. *athlētikós*, f. *athlētḗs*; sb. pl. **athlet**ICS XVIII; **athle·t**ICAL XVI.

athwart əþwō·ɹt across. XV (first in Sc.). f. A-[1]+THWART, prob. after ON. *um þvert* 'over in a transverse direction'.

-atic æ·tik repr. F. *-atique* – L. *-āticus*, orig. f. pp. stems in *-āt-* (see -ATE[3])+*-icus* -IC, as *errāticus* of a wandering nature, ERRATIC, *volāticus* of the flying kind, later extended to sbs., e.g. *aquāticus* AQUATIC, *Asiāticus*, *fānāticus* FANATIC, *umbrāticus* shady. The neuter of such adjs. was used as sb., e.g. *viāticum* provision for a VOYAGE, whence the extended use of the suffix in Rom. repr. by -AGE. ¶ In AROMATIC, AXIOMATIC, PROBLEMATIC, and the like, *-atic* repr. Gr. *-atikós*, f. n. stems in *-at-*.

-atile ətail repr. F. *-atile* – L. *-ātilis*, in formation (see -ILE) and sense similar to -ATIC, e.g. *volātilis* VOLATILE, f. *volāt-*, *volāre* fly, (with sbs.) *fluviātilis*, *umbrātilis*, f. *flūvius*, *umbra*.

atilt əti·lt tilted; at the tilt (in jousting). XVI. f. A[1]-+TILT[1].

-ation ei·ʃən – OF. *-acioun*, *-aciun* (mod. *-ation*) – L. *-ātiōnem*, nom. *-ātiō*, the form resulting from the addition of *-tiō* -TION to verb-stems in *ā*. The great majority of Eng. words in *-ation* have corr. vbs. in -ATE[3], as *creation*, *moderation*, *saturation*, beside *create*, *moderate*, *saturate*; some have no such corr. vb., as *capitation*, *constellation*, *duration*, *lunation*; others are formed directly on vbs. in -IZE, as *civilization*, *organization*. A large number, by the circumstances of their origin, have corr. vbs. of other forms, as *apply* and *application*, *modify* and *modification*, *publish* and *publication*, *prove* and *probation*. Others have the appearance of being formed on Eng. vbs., as *alteration*, *causation*, *formation*, *notation*, *vexation*; hence the practice (from XVI) of adding the suffix to miscellaneous vbs., as †*blindation*, *botheration*, *flirtation*, †*foolation*, †*schoolation*, *starvation*, and occas. to other parts of speech, as *backwardation* (in stock exch. lang.).

-ative ətiv – F. *-atif*, *-ative* – L. *-ātīvus*, *-īva*, formed by the addition of *-īvus* -IVE to pp. stems in *-āt-*, as *demonstrātīvus* DEMONSTRATIVE; the number of such adjs. was increased in late and med. L. (among them several techn. terms, as *ablātīvus*, *affirmātīvus*, *figūrātīvus*, *putātīvus*) and were the models for many more in the Rom. langs. Such pairs as *affirm* and *affirmative* furnished an analogy for *talkative* (XV). In medL. *quālitātīvus* and *quantitātīvus* were formed on the sbs. *quālitās*, *quantitās*; hence *authoritative*, f. *authority*. The neut. of a few L. adjs. was used sb., e.g. *donātīvum* DONATIVE. In Eng. several adjs. have been so used, as *narrative*, *purgative*.

Atlantic ətlæ·ntik. XV (Higden). – L. *Atlanticus* – Gr. *Atlantikós*, f. *Atlant-*, *A'tlās* name of (i) the Titan who was supposed to hold up the pillars of the universe, and (ii) the mountain in Libya which was held to support the heavens, whence the application of the adj. to the sea near the west coast of Africa, from which it was extended to the ocean lying between Europe and Africa on the east and the Americas on the west; see -IC and cf. F. *atlantique*. ¶ Trevisa has 'þe sea of occean of athlant', rendering L. *oceanus Atlanticus*.

atlas æ·tləs supporter, mainstay XVI; volume of maps XVII. The Titan Atlas (see prec.) was often figured with the terrestrial globe on his shoulders, whence the application of the name to a collection of maps.

atmosphere æ·tməsfiəɹ gaseous envelope of a body, spec. the mass of air enveloping the earth. XVII. – modL. *atmosphæra*, f. Gr. *atmós* vapour + *sphaîra* ball, SPHERE. Hence **atmospheric** -sfe·rik XVIII, -ICAL XVII.

atoll ətɔ·l, æ·tɔl coral island XVII; lagoon belt (Darwin, 1842). – Maldive *atoḷu*, said to be rel. to Cingalese *ätul* interior; the Maldive name for the islands, which are typical examples of coral structure.

atom æ·təm (hist.) body so small as to be incapable of division XVI; supposed ultimate particle of matter XVII; hence in mod. physics and chem. XIX. – (O)F. *atome* – L. *atomus* smallest particle, smallest medieval division of time – Gr. *átomos*, sb. use of adj. 'indivisible' (as in ἄτομοι φύσεις atoms), f. *a-* A-[4] + **tom-* (cf. ANATOMY, TOME). Hence **atomic** ətɔ·mik XVII. – modL. *atomicus*.

atomy[1] æ·təmi skeleton (lit. and fig.). XVI (Sh.). Aphetic of ANATOMY.

atomy[2] æ·təmi atom, mote, tiny being, mite. XVI (Sh.). prob. f. *atomī*, pl. of L. *atomus* ATOM, but assoc. with prec.

at once ətwʌ·ns with one grasp, step, act. ME. *at ōnes* (XIII), phr. f. AT + g. of ONE (cf. NONCE).

atone ətou·n reconcile, appease. XVI (once XV be reconciled). Back-formation from **ato·nement** (XVI, More, Tindale), f. phr. *at one* in harmony (XIII) + -MENT, after medL. *adūnāmentum* (VIII), f. *adūnāre* unite, and earlier *onement* (in Wycl. Bible tr. L. *ūniō* union), as used in *make an onement* be reconciled, *set at onement* reconcile. The pronunc. oun of *-one* is as in *alone* and *only*.

atonic ətɔ·nik lacking tone XVIII; (philol.) unaccented XIX. f. *a-* A-[4] + TONIC, infl. (esp. philol.) by F. *atonique*; cf. Gr. *átonos*.

-ator eitəɹ repr. L. *-ātor*, suffix combining -TOR with vb.-stems in *-ā-* and forming agent-nouns, e.g. *creātor*, *dictātor*, *mediātor*, *spectātor*, *translātor*; a few others were formed in L. on *-ātus* -ATE[1], e.g. *senātor*. The earliest of such sbs. were adopted in OF. form with *-atour* (mod. *-ateur*), and later accommodated to the L. originals. From XVI modL. formations such as *denominator* and *numerator* appear. From XVII the suffix began to be used for names of instruments, e.g. *perambulator*, and in anat., e.g. *levator*, *rotator*; but such formations were not common till early XIX, since when they have become fairly numerous as names of implements and machines, e.g. *accumulator*, *detonator*, *elevator*, *escalator*, *generator*, *incubator*, *indicator*, *percolator*, *refrigerator*, *regulator*, *separator*, *ventilator*.

atrabilious ætrəbi·liəs hypochondriac. XVII. f. L. *ātra bīlis* black BILE, tr. Gr. *melagkholíā* MELANCHOLY; see -IOUS. The deriv. medL. adj. *ātrabīlārius* has been repr. by †*atrabilar*, *-aire* (so F.), *atrabilarian*, *-arious*, †*atrabilary*, *-biliar*, *-iary*.

atrip ətri·p (naut.) applied to things in raised positions. XVII. f. A-[1] + TRIP.

atrium ei·triəm central court of an ancient Roman house XVII; (anat.) chamber of an organ of the body XIX. – L.

atrocious ətrou·ʃəs excessively cruel or wicked. XVII. f. L. *atrōci-*, *atrōx* fierce, cruel, prob. orig. 'of black aspect', f. *āter* black, dark + *oc-*, stem of *oculus* EYE; see -IOUS and cf. F. *atroce*. So **atrocity** ətrɔ·siti. XVI. – (O)F. or L.

atrophy æ·trəfi wasting away of the body. XVII. – late L. *atrophia* – Gr. *atrophíā*, f. *átrophos* ill-nourished, f. *a-* A-[4] + *trophḗ* nourishment, *tréphein* nourish. So **a·trophied** -fid. XVI. – F. *atrophié* (Paré).

atropine æ·trŏpīn alkaloid poison from belladonna. XIX. f. modL. *atropa* deadly nightshade, fem. f. Gr. *Átropos* ('Inflexible') name of one of the Fates, f. *a-* A-[4]+**trop-* **trep-* turn (cf. TROPIC); see -INE[5].

attach ətæ·tʃ A. seize, arrest XIV; B. fasten, join XV; adhere XVIII. In A. – OF. *atachier* (mod. *attacher*) = It. *attaccare*, Sp. *atacar*; in B. – alteration, by prefix-substitution, of OF. *estachier* fasten, fix = Pr., Sp. *estacar*; – Germ. **stakōn*, f. **stak-* STAKE[1]. In B – modF. So **atta·chMENT** leg. (writ of) apprehension XV; fastening XVIII. – (O)F.; in legal AL. *attachiāmentum*.

attaché ætæ·ʃei, ||ataʃe one attached to the suite of an ambassador. XIX. F., pp. of *attacher* ATTACH.

attack ətæ·k assail, assault. XVI (Holland). – F. *attaquer* – It. *attaccare*, as in *attaccare battaglia* join battle (see ATTACH). Hence, or – F. *attaque* (– It. *attacco*) **attack** sb. XVII (once in Milton's poems).

attain ətein †strike, attaint; reach (*to*). XIV. – AN. *atain-*, *atein-*, OF. *ataign-*, *ateign-*, stem of *ataindre*, *-eindre* (mod. *atteindre*) :– L. *attingere* touch on, reach, f. *ad* AT- + *tangere* touch (cf. TANGENT). Hence **attai·nMENT** personal accomplishment (now chiefly pl.). XVII. Cf. CONTAIN.

attainder ətei·ndər process of attainting. XV. – AN. *attainder*, *atteinder* (XIV), sb. use of inf. *atteinder*, (O)F. *atteindre* ATTAIN; see -ER[4].

attaint ətei·nt †convict; subject to attainder XIV; (arch.) affect, infect XVI. f. *attaint* pp. convicted, attainted, infected (XIV) – OF. *ataint*, *ateint*, pp. of *ataindre* ATTAIN; infl. later in meaning by TAINT. (Cf. the origin of *convict* vb.). Hence †**attai·nt** sb. conviction XIV; blow, wound; taint. XVI.

attar æ·təɹ fragrant essence (of roses). XVIII. – Pers. *'atar* perfume essence (*'atar-gul* essence of roses) – Arab. *'uṭūr*, *'oṭōr*, pl. of *'iṭr* aroma, f. *'aṭara* exhale perfume. Earlier OTTO.

attempt əte·mᵖt make an effort, try. XIV (Gower). – OF. *attempter*, latinized form of *atenter* (mod. *attenter*) = Pr. *attentar*, It. *attentare*: – L. *attemptāre*, f. *ad* AT-+ *temptāre* TEMPT. Hence **atte·mpt** sb. XVI.

attend əte·nd A. direct the mental or physical faculties, apply oneself to XIII (Cursor M.). B. take care of, wait upon XV; be present at XVII; †C. wait for, expect XV. – OF. *atendre* (mod. *attendre* wait for) :– L. *attendere*, f. *ad* AT- + *tendere* stretch, TEND[1]. Aphetic TEND[2]. So **atte·ndANCE**. XIV (Ch.). – OF. *attendance*. **atte·ndant** adj. XIV (Gower); sb. XV. – OF. *attendant*. **atte·nTION**. XIV (Ch., tr. L.; thereafter rare before XVI, Sh.). – L. *attentiō(n-)*; cf. F. *attention* (XVI). **atte·ntIVE**. XIV (Sc.). – (O)F. *attentif*.

attenuate əte·njueit make thin or weak. XVI. f. pp. stem of L. *attenuāre*, f. *ad* AT-+ *tenuāre*, f. *tenuis* THIN; see -ATE[3].

attest əte·st bear witness to; call as witness. XVI (Spenser, Sh.). – F. *attester* – L. *attestārī*, f. *ad* AT-+*testārī* witness (cf. TESTAMENT). So **attestA·TION**. XV. – F. – late L.

attic æ·tik (archit.) decorative structure placed above an order (usu. Attic) of much greater height; (orig. *attic storey*) top storey of a building, prop. one enclosed by such a structure. XVIII. spec. use of ATTIC as applied to a square column of any of the five orders. (Cf. 'Nous appellons aussi *Attique* dans nos bastimens un ordre que l'on met sur un autre beaucoup plus grand. . . . Ce petit ordre n'a ordinairement que des Pilastres d'une façon particuliere, qui est à la maniere Attique dont le nom luy a esté donné', Félibien, 1676.)

Attic æ·tik of Attica, Athenian. XVI. – L. *Atticus* – Gr. *Attikós*. *A. salt* or *wit* (L. *sal atticum*). So **AtticISM** æ·tisizm Greek idiom as used by Athenians; elegant Greek. XVII. – Gr. *Attikismós*. **A·tticIZE**. XVII. – Gr.

attire ətaiə·ɹ †put in order, equip XIII; dress XIV. – OF. *atir(i)er* arrange, equip, dress, deck = Pr. *atieirar*, f. phr. OF. *a tire*, Pr. *a tieira* in succession or order, of unkn. origin. See TIRE[2]. Hence **atti·re** sb. †equipment; dress. XIII.

attitude æ·titjūd †disposition of a figure in statuary or painting XVII; posture XVIII. – F. *attitude* – It. *attitudine*, Sp. *actitud* fitness, disposition, posture :– late L. *aptitūdinem*, *-ūdō* APTITUDE; prop. a techn. term of the arts of design; see -TUDE.

attorney[1] ətə̄·ɹni legal agent. XIV. – OF. *atorné*, *aturné*, sb. use of pp. of *atorner* assign, appoint (whence law L. *attornāre*), f. *a* AD-+*torner* TURN.

attorney[2] ətə̄·ɹni legal agency (in *letter*, *power of attorney*). XV. – OF. *atornée*, sb. use of fem. pp. of *atorner* (see prec.).

attract ətræ·kt draw to oneself or itself. XV. f. *attract-*, pp. stem of L. *attrahere*, f. *ad* AT-+*trahere* draw (cf. TRACT). So **attra·cTION**. XV. – F. *attraction* or L. *attractiō(n-)*. **attra·cTIVE**. XIV. – F. *attractif*, *-ive* (= Pr. *atractiu*, It. *attrattivo*) – late L.

attribute æ·tribjūt quality or character ascribed, appropriate, or characteristic. XV. – (O)F. *attribut* or L. *attribūtum*, sb. use of n. pp. of *attribuere*, f. *ad* AT-+*tribuere* allot (cf. TRIBUTE). So **attribute** ətri·bjūt assign, ascribe. XVI. f. the pp. stem; formerly str. *a·ttribute*, *attribu·te*. **attribu·TION**. XV. – (O)F. – L. **attri·butIVE**. XVII. – F. *attributif*, *-ive*.

attrition ətri·ʃən (theol.) imperfect contrition XIV (Ch.); rubbing away XV. – late L. *attrītiō(n-)*, f. *attrīt-*, pp. stem of *atterere*,

f. *ad* AT- + *terere* rub; see TRITE, -ITION, and cf. F. *attrition* (XVI).

atwo ətū· (dial.) in or into two parts. OE. *on twā, on tū*, i.e. ON, TWO; cf. OFris. *ontwa, atwa*.

aubade oubā·d, || obad song or salute at dawn. XIX. F. – Sp. *albada*, f. *alba* (= F. *aube*, etc.) :– CRom. **alba* dawn, sb. use of fem. of *albus* white (cf. ALB); see -ADE.

aubergine ou·bəɹʒīn, -ʒī·n fruit of the egg-plant, Solanum esculentum, BRINJAL. XVIII. – F. *aubergine* – Cat. *alberginia* – Arab. *albādinjān* – (with AL-²) Pers. *bādingān* – Skr. *vātiṃgaṇa* (whence Hind. *baingan, began*).

aubrietia ōbriī·ʃə (erron. *aubretia*) cruciferous plant. XIX. – modL., f. name of Claude *Aubriet*, after whom it was named by Adanson in 1763; see -IA¹.

auburn ō·bəɹn (orig.) yellowish-white, (now) golden-brown. XV (*aborne, alborne*). XV (Lydg.). – OF. *alborne, auborne* :– medL. *alburnus* whitish, f. *albus* white (rel. to Gr. *alphós*); in XV–XVII often *abrun, -o(u)n, abrown*, and so assoc. with *brown*.

auctarium ōktɛə·riəm architectural enlargement of a library. XVII (also anglicized †*auctary*, and in gen. sense). – mod. use of L. *auctārium* surplus weight or charge, f. *auct-*, pp. stem of *augēre* increase, AUGMENT; see -ARIUM.

auction ō·kʃən public sale in which articles are sold to the highest bidder. XVI. – L. *auctiō(n-)* increase, public sale in which bids are increased, f. *auct-*, pp. stem of *augēre* increase; see AUGMENT, -TION. Hence **auctionEE·R**¹. XVIII.

audacious ōdei·ʃəs daring; presumptuously defiant. XVI. f. L. *audāci-, audāx* bold, f. *audēre* dare, f. **audus*, contr. of *avidus* AVID; see -IOUS. So **audacITY** ōdæ·sĭti. XV. f. medL. *audācitās*; see -ITY.

audible ō·dĭbl that can be heard. XVI. – late L. *audībilis*, f. L. *audīre* hear, f. base **awiz-*, found also in Gr. *aisthánesthai* (**aϝis-*) perceive; see -IBLE. So **audiENCE** ō·diəns hearing, esp. formal, judicial, etc. XIV (PPl., Ch.); assembly of hearers XV. – (O)F. *audience*, refash. after L. of †*oiance* :– L. *audientia*, f. prp. of *audīre*. **audit** ō·dit examination of accounts; settlement of accounts between landlord and tenant XV; †hearing XV. – L. *audītus* hearing, f. *audīt-*, pp. stem of *audīre*; cf. AN. *audit* hearing (Gower). (Auditing was performed by oral recitation of the accounts.) Hence **au·dit** vb. XV. **audi·TION**. XVI. – L. **au·ditOR**¹. XIV (Shoreham). – AN. *auditour*, (O)F. *auditeur* – L. *audītōrem*. **audito·rium** XVII, earlier **au·ditORY**² XIV (Wyclif). – L.

Augean ō·dʒiən abominably filthy. XVI. f. L. *Augēās*, Gr. *Augeíās* name of a fabulous king of Elis whose stable of 3,000 oxen, uncleansed for 30 years, was purged by Hercules; see -EAN.

auger ō·gər carpenter's boring-tool. OE. *nafogār*, f. *nafu* NAVE¹ + *gār* javelin, spear, piercer, borer (GORE²), i.e. orig. pointed tool for boring the naves of wheels; corr. to OS. *nabugēr* (Du. *avegaar, eveger, egger*), OHG. *nabugēr* (G. *näber*, †*neber*), ON. *nafarr*; the CGerm. word was adopted in Finn. as *napakaira*. Forms showing loss of initial *n*, as in *adder, apron, umpire*, occur XV; cf. the Du. forms.

aught ōt (arch.) anything. OE. *āwiht, āwuht, āuht, āht*; corr. to OFris. *āwet, āet*, OS. *ēowiht*, MDu. *iet* (Du. *iets* :– **ietwes*), OHG. *eowiht, iewiht* (MHG. *ieht, iewet, iet*); WGerm. comp. of AY¹ (ever) and WIGHT (creature, thing). The sp. *aught* reflects a var. of OE. *āht* (ME. *auht, auȝt*) with shortened vowel)(OUGHT². Cf. NAUGHT.

augment ō·gmənt †increase XV; (gram.) prefixed syllable in past tenses of IE. verbs XVIII. – (O)F. *augment* or late L. *augmentum*, f. *augēre* increase; see -MENT. So **augme·nt** vb. XV (Lydg.) – (O)F. *augmenter* or late L. *augmentāre*. **augmentA·TION**. XV. **augme·ntATIVE**. XV.

augur ō·gəɹ one who divines by the flight, etc. of birds. XIV. – L. *augur*, earlier *auger*, prob. f. *avis* bird (cf. AUSPICE) + *gerere* perform (see GESTURE). Hence **au·gur** vb. XVI (Sc.; in Eng. use XVII, Jonson), after L. *augurārī*. So **augury** ō·gjŭri the augur's art XIV (Ch.); omen, prognostic XVII. – OF. *augurie* or L. *augurium*; see -Y⁴. Cf. INAUGURAL, -ATE³.

august ōgʌ·st of stately dignity. XVII (Wither). – (O)F. *auguste* or L. *augustus*, prob. f. base of *augēre* increase, AUGMENT.

August ō·gəst eighth month of the year. OE. *August* – L. *Augustus*, so named after the first Roman emperor, *Augustus* Cæsar.

auk ōk northern sea-bird. XVII (prob. earlier in local use). – ON. *álka* (Sw. *alka*, Da. *alke*).

auld ōld, (Sc.) āld Sc. form repr. OE. (Anglian) *ald* OLD; familiar in England in *auld lang syne* 'old long ago' (see SYNE), *Auld Reekie* 'Old Smoky', Edinburgh.

aumbry, ambry ō·mbri, ɑ·- (dial.) cupboard, press, locker XIV (Ch., PPl., Wycl. Bible, Trevisa); (in church use) XV. Late ME. *almarie*, passing to *aumery, aumbry* (XVI) – OF. *almarie*, var. of *armarie* (mod. *armoire*) – L. *armārium* closet, chest, f. *arma* in the transf. sense 'utensils' (see ARM²).

aunt ānt father's or mother's sister. XIII (RGlouc.). – AN. *aunte*, OF. *ante* (mod. *tante*) = Pr. *amda* :– L. *amita*, extension of a hypocoristic form **am(m)a* mother (cf. Gr. *ammâs*, G. *amme* nurse, ON. *amma* grandmother). In XIII–XVII by coalescence of *n* in *myn aunt, thyn aunt, naunt* was established and survives dial. (cf. NEWT). Hence **au·ntie, -y** XVIII (Burns); see -Y⁶.

aunter, auntrous see ADVENTURE.

aura ɔ̄·rə exhalation. XVIII. – L. – Gr. *aúrā* breath, breeze (cf. AIR, WIND).

aural ɔ̄·rəl pert. to the organ of hearing. XIX. f. L. *auris* EAR + -AL. So **au·r**IST specialist in diseases of the ear. XVII.

aureate ɔ̄·riət golden (lit. and fig.). XV (Lydg.). – late L. *aureātus*, f. *aureus* golden, f. *aurum* gold; see -ATE².

aurelia ɔ̄rī·liə chrysalis. XVII (Topsell, Boyle). – It. *aurelia* silkworm in its cocoon, sb. use of fem. of *aurelio* golden (Florio).

aureole ɔ̄·rioul saint's crown of glory XIII; halo XIX. – (O)F. *auréole* – L. *aureola*, sb. use (sc. *corōna* crown) of adj. *aureolus* golden, f. *aurum* gold.

auri- ɔ̄·ri, ɔ̄ri· comb. form of L. *aurum* gold, e.g. *auri·*FEROUS (XVIII), f. L. *aurifer*. Also irreg. **auro-** (see -O-).

auricle ɔ̄·rikl external ear; lobe; cavity of the heart. XVII. – L. *auricula* (see next).

auricula ɔ̄ri·kjŭlə species of primula. XVIII (earlier †*auriculus*). – L., dim. of *auris* EAR; so named from the shape of the leaves.

auricular ɔ̄ri·kjŭləɹ spoken into the ear. XV. – late L. *auriculāris*, f. *auricula*; see prec. and -AR.

aurochs ɔ̄·rɔks wild ox; European bison. XVIII. G., early var. of *auerochs* (OHG. *ūrohso*, f. *ūr* = OE. *ūr*, etc., of unkn. origin +*ohso* ox). The Germ. word is the source of L. *ūrus*.

aurora ərɔ̄·rə dawn XIV (Trev.); luminous atmospheric phenomenon near the poles, 'northern lights' XVII; also **aurora borealis** bɔ̄riei·lis (see BOREAL), so named by Pierre Gassendi in 1621. – L. *aurōra*, for **aurōs*, *-ōris* (cf. FLORA and *flōs*); see EAST.

auscultation ɔ̄skʌltei·ʃən listening (spec. med.). XVII. – L. *auscultātiō(n-)*, f. *auscultāre*, f. **aus-*, base of *auris* EAR+an obscure el.; see -ATION.

auspice ɔ̄·spis usu. pl. divination by birds XVI; propitious token; favourable influence XVII. – F. *auspice* or L. *auspicium* action of an *auspex* observer of the flight of birds for omens (cf. AUGUR), f. *avi-s* bird (rel. to synon. Gr. and Indo-Iranian words) + **spic-* look (cf. SPY). Hence **auspic**IOUS ɔ̄spi·ʃəs. XVII (Sh.).

austere ɔ̄stiə·ɹ stern; severe in self-discipline. XIV. – (O)F. *austère* – L. *austērus* – Gr. *austērós* making the tongue dry and rough, (hence) harsh, severe, f. *aúein*, f. *(h)aûos* dry (see SERE). So **auster**ITY əste·rĭti. XIV.

Austin ɔ̄·stin Augustinian (friar), following the so-called Rule of St. Augustine. XIV (Wyclif). Reduction of *Au·gustin* – (O)F. *Augustin*, transf. use of the proper name *Augustin*, L. *Augustīnus*, St. Augustine (354–430), bishop of Hippo.

autarchy ɔ̄·tāɹki absolute sovereignty; self-government. XVII. – Gr. *autarkhíā*, f. *aútarkhos*, f. *autós* AUTO- + *árkhein* rule, *-arkhos* ruling; see -Y³.

autarky ɔ̄·tāɹki self-sufficiency. XVII (*-archie*). – Gr. *autárkeia*, f. *autárkēs* self-sufficient, f. *autós* AUTO- + *arkeîn* suffice; see -Y³.

authentic ɔ̄þe·ntik †authoritative XIV (R. Rolle); entitled to acceptance or belief as being reliable XIV (Ch.); actual, not imaginary XV; genuine, not counterfeit; (mus.) of modes XVIII. ME. *au(c)tentik* – OF. *autentique* – late L. *authenticus* (whence also Sp., It. *autentico*) – Gr. *authentikós* principal, genuine, f. *authentíā* original authority, *authéntēs* doer, perpetrator, master, f. *autós* AUTO- + *-hentēs* (as in *sunéntēs* fellow-worker); see -IC. Hence **authe·nticate** (see -ATE³), **authenti·c**ITY. XVII.

author ɔ̄·þəɹ originator, inventor; composer of a book, etc. XIV (Wyclif, Ch.). ME. *autour* – AN. *autour*, OF. *autor* (mod. *auteur*) – L. *auctōrem* (*-or*), f. *auct-*, *augēre* increase, promote, originate (cf. AUGMENT). The latinized spellings *auctour*, *auctor* were usual XV–XVI; *aucthor*, *authour*, *author* appear XVI, with the graphic variant *th* for *t* (cf. *rethour* for *rhetor*), which finally influenced the pronunc. Hence **au·thor**ESS¹. XV (earliest forms *aucteuresse*, *auctorice*, *auctrice*). So **author**ITY ɔ̄þɔ·rĭti. XIII (AncrR.). ME. *autorite* – (O)F. *autorité* – L. *auctōritās*. Hence **autho·rit**ATIVE. XVII. **au·thor**IZE give authority to or for. XIV (Wyclif, Gower). – (O)F. – medL.

au·to¹ short for AUTO-DA-FÉ. XVIII.

au·to² short for AUTOMOBILE, after F. XIX.

auto- ɔ·tou, ɔ̄tɔ· repr. comb. form of Gr *autós* self, meaning 'of or by oneself, independently, self-', used in the foll. and in others ult. based on Gr. comps., and in many scientific words: **au:to**BIO·GRAPHY. XIX (Southey). **autoce·phal**OUS. XIX. – Gr.; see CEPHALIC. **autochthon** ɔ̄tɔ·kþən, -þoun one sprung from the soil. XVII (Sir T. Browne); pl. aborigines. XVIII. – Gr. *autókhthōn* (*khthṓn* earth); hence **auto·chthon**OUS. XIX.

autocrat ɔ̄·təkræt absolute ruler. XIX. – F. *autocrate* (a word of the French Revolution) – Gr. *autokratḗs*, f. *autós* AUTO-+ *krate-*, *krátos* power (cf. HARD). So **auto**CRACY ɔ̄tɔ·krəsi †independent power XVII; absolute government XIX. – Gr. *autokrateíā*; in mod. use after *autocrat*. **autocra·t**IC. XIX.

auto-da-fé ɔ̄:toudafei· sentence of the Inquisition, and (esp.) its execution. XVIII. – (through F.) Pg. *auto-da-fé* 'act (i.e. judicial sentence) of the faith' (the Sp. form is *auto de fe*); see ACT, FAITH.

autograph ɔ̄·təgrȧf author's own manuscript XVII or signature XVIII. – F. *autographe* or L. *autographum* – Gr. *autógraphon*, sb. use of n. of *autógraphos*; see AUTO-, -GRAPH. Hence vb. XIX.

automaton ɔ̄tɔ·mətən a thing viewed as self-acting. XVII. – L. *automaton,-um.* – Gr. *autómaton*, sb. use of n. of *autómatos*, f. *autós* AUTO-+ **mn̥tós*, ppl. adj. f. base **men-* think (cf. MIND, MENTAL). So **automa·**TIC. XVIII. **automa·**TION. XX.

automobile ɔ̄təmou·bīl, ɔ̄:təmŏbī·l adj. self-propelling; sb. (chiefly U.S.) motor-car. 1887. – F. *automobile* adj. (1876); see AUTO-, MOBILE.

autonomy ɔ̄tɔ·nəmi right of self-government. XVII. – Gr. *autonomíā*, f. *autónomos* (f. *autós* AUTO-+*nómos* law), whence **auto·nom**OUS XIX; see -Y[3].

autopsy ɔ̄·tɔpsi post-mortem examination. XVII. – F. *autopsie* or modL. *autopsia* – Gr. *autopsíā*, f. *autóptēs* eye-witness; see AUTO-, OPTIC, -Y[3].

autumn ɔ̄·təm third season of the year. XIV (*autumpne*, Ch.; rare before XVI). – OF. *autompne* (mod. *automne*), later directly – L. *autumnus*. (For the omission of final *n* cf. *column, condemn, damn, hymn, limn, solemn.*) So **autu·mn**AL[1]. XVII. – L. *autumnālis*.

auxiliary ɔ̄gzi·ljəri affording help; subsidiary. XVII (Bacon; †*auxiliar* is earlier XV). – L. *auxiliārius*, f. *auxilium* help, f. base **aug-* increase, AUGMENT, with *s*-extension as in Gr. *aúxein, auxánein*; see -ARY.

avadavat var. of AMADAVAT.

avail əvei·l be of service, profit, or advantage XIII (Cursor M.); refl. with *of* XVII. Native formation on †*vail* vb. (of equal date) – OF. *vail-*, tonic stem of *valoir* :– L. *valēre* be strong or worth (cf. VALOUR); prob. on analogy of pairs like *amount, mount.* So **avai·l** sb. advantage XV; cf. AN. *avail.* Hence **avai·l**ABLE †of advantage XV; at one's disposal XIX.

avalanche æ·vəlānʃ mass of descending or fallen snow. XVIII. – F. *avalanche*, of Roumansch origin (*avalantze, vallantze*), alteration, by blending with *avaler* descend, of Alpine F. dial. *lavanche* (cf. Pr. *lavanca*, It. *valanga*), of unkn. origin. ¶ Occas. †*valanche* (Smollett), †*vollenge* (XIX).

avarice æ·vəris inordinate desire for wealth. XIII (Cursor M.). – (O)F. *avarice* – L. *avāritia*, f. *avārus* greedy, rel. to AVE, AVID, AUDACIOUS. So **avar**ICIOUS ævəri·ʃəs. XIV (Ch.). – (O)F. *avaricieux*; preceded by †*avarous* (XIV–XVI) – OF. *averos* wealthy, f. *aver* possessions (:– L. *habēre* have, hold), later assoc. with *avare* greedy, miser(ly).

avast əvà·st (naut.) stop! XVII. – Du. *hou' vast, houd vast* 'hold fast' (see HOLD[1], FAST[1]); the first syll. has been assim. to A-[1].

avatar ævətā·ɹ (Hindu myth.) descent of a deity in incarnate form XVIII; manifestation in human form, etc. XIX. – Skr. *avatāra* descent, f. *áva* off, away, down + *tar-* pass over.

avaunt əvɔ̄·nt (arch.) begone! XV. – AN. *avaunt*, (O)F. *avant* before, onward :– Rom. *abante*, f. L. *ab* from, OFF + *ante* before (cf. ANTE-).

ave ei·vi short for *Ave Maria!* Hail, Mary! XIII, partially anglicized *Ave Mary* XIV (Ch.); hail! welcome! farewell! XIV. As sb. XIII (A. Riwle). – L. *avē*, taken as imper. sg. of *avēre* be or fare well.

avenge əve·ndʒ take vengeance for. XIV. – OF. *avengier*, f. *a-* AD-+*vengier* :– L. *vindicāre* VINDICATE.

avens æ·vənz species of Geum. XV. – OF. *avence* = medL. *avencia*, of unkn. origin.

aventurine əve·ntjurin brownish glass interspersed with golden spangles, first made at Murano, near Venice; (min.) variety of quartz. XIX. – F. *aventurine* – It. *avventurino*, f. *avventura* chance; so called from its accidental discovery; see ADVENTURE, -INE[1].

avenue æ·vənju approach; broad roadway. XVII. – F. *avenue*, sb. use of fem. pp. of *avenir* :– L. *advenīre* approach, f. *ad* AD-+ *venīre* COME; cf. VENUE.

aver əvɔ̄·ɹ †declare to be true XIV (Wyclif); justify, prove XV; assert as a fact XVI. –(O)F. *avérer* (corr. to Pr. *averar*, It. *avverare*), f. *a-* AD-+OF. *veir, voir* :– L. *vērus* true (cf. VERITY, VERY). So **ave·r**MENT. XV. – AN., OF. *aver(r)ement.*

average æ·vəridʒ †charge over and above the shipment freight (XV ?); loss to owners arising from damage at sea; incidence of such loss or its equitable distribution among interested parties XVI; (arithmetical mean obtained by) distribution of the aggregate irregularities of a series among all the members of the series XVIII. Earlier forms *auerays, averi(d)ge* – F. *avarie* (pl. *-ies*) damage to ship or cargo – It. *avaria* (first known from Genoa and Pisa) – Arab. *ʽawārīya* damaged goods, pl. of *ʽawār* damage at sea, loss, f. *ʽāra* mutilate; perh. the use of the F. pl. (cf. also '*avaris* decay of wares, or merchandise, leakage of wines', Cotgr.) induced phonetic assoc. with -AGE (through *-i(d)ge*) and esp. with *damage.* The word has spread over most of Europe; cf. Pr. *avarias* expenses, Sp. *averia*, Du. *(h)averij*, G. *havarie, haferei*, Sw. *haveri* average, sea damage, Da. *havari* damage, break-down, Russ. *avāriya.* ¶ Distinct from (hist.) *average* feudal service involving horse-transport (XV) – medL. *averāgium*, f. OE. *aferian* (*au-*) supply with horse-transport, f. **afor, eafor* nag.

Avernus əvɔ̄·ɹnəs Lago Averno in Campania, the poisonous effluvium from which was said to kill birds, whence the name was used by Virgil ('Aen.' VI 126) to denote the mouth of Hades, and so by moderns for the infernal regions. XVI. L. (sc. *lacus* lake) – Gr. *áornos* (sc. *límnē*) 'the birdless (lake)', f. *a-* A-[4]+*órnis* bird (see ERNE).

Averroism æverou·izm doctrine of a peripatetic sect embracing the tenet of the mortality of the individual soul. XVIII. f. *Averr(h)oes*, latinization of *Ibn Rushd*, name of an Arabian philosopher of Cordova (d. 1225).

averruncator æ:vərʌŋkei·təɹ branch-lopping instrument (shears or knife-blade) mounted on a pole. XIX. f. *averruncate* (XVII) prop. avert, ward off, transf. prune, weed, f. pp. stem of L. *āverruncāre* (f. *ā*, AB- + *verruncāre* turn), which was falsely interpreted as f. *ab*+*ēruncāre* (f. *ē* EX- + *runcāre* weed); see -ATOR. ¶ Bailey (1731) invented a supposedly correct *aberuncate*, perpetuated by J.

averse əvə̄·ɹs turned away (mentally). XVI. – L. *āversus*, pp. of *āvertere* AVERT. So **ave·rSION**. XVI. – F. or L. So **avert** əvə̄·ɹt turn away. XV. Partly – OF. *avertir* :– Rom. **avertīre*, for L. *āvertere* (f. *ā* AB-+ *vertere* turn); partly direct from L.

Avesta see ZEND-AVESTA.

aviary ei·viəri large cage for keeping birds. XVI (Harrison). – L. *aviārium*, f. *avis* bird (cf. AUGUR, AUSPICE); see -ARY[1] 3.

aviation eiviei·ʃən aerial navigation. XIX (1887). – F. *aviation* (1869), irreg. f. L. *avis* bird+-ATION. So **aviator** ei·vieitəɹ †flying-machine; pilot of an aeroplane. late XIX. – F. *aviateur*. Hence **a·viate**.

avid æ·vid greedy. XVIII. – F. *avide* or L. *avidus*, f. *avēre* long for; see AVARICE, -ID. Earlier (rare) †*avidious* XV, †*avidous* XVI. So **avidITY** əvi·dĭti. XV. – F. or L.

avizandum, avis- ævizæ·ndəm (Sc. law) consideration of a case out of court. XVII. – medL., n. gerund (sc. *est*; 'it is to be considered') of *avizāre*, *avisāre* consider; see ADVISE.

avocado ævoukā·dou fruit of Persea gratissima. XVII (*avogato*). – Sp. *avocado* advocate (whence F. *avocat*), substituted by popular perversion for Aztec *ahuacatl* testicle, more closely repr. by Sp. *aguacate*; further corrupted, through *avigato*, to *alligator* (*pear*) XVIII.

avocation ævŏkei·ʃən †distraction from an occupation; task to which one is called away; minor occupation XVII; transf. to ordinary occupation XVIII. – L. *āvocātiō(n-)*, f. *āvocāre* call away, f. *ā* AB- + *vocāre*; see VOCATION.

avocet, avoset æ·voset wading bird Recurvirostra. XVIII. – F. *avocette* (Buffon) – It. *avosetta*, of unkn. origin.

avoid əvoi·d †empty; †make void; †withdraw, retire XIV; leave alone, evade XVI. – AN. *avoider* = (with prefix-substitution) OF. *esvuidier*, *evuider*, f. *es-* EX-+*vuide* empty, VOID. Hence **avoi·dANCE**. XIV.

avoirdupois æ:vəɹdjupoi·z †merchandise sold by weight; British system of weights. XIV. ME. *aver-*, *avoirdepeis*, *-pois* (later often *hauer-*, *haber-*) – OF. *aveir de peis* 'goods of weight', i.e. *aveir*, *avoir*, ME. *aver* possession, estate (:– L. *habēre* have), *de* of, *peis*, later *pois* (mod. *poids*) weight (see POISE). The substitution of meaningless *du* for *de* was established XVII.

avouch əvau·tʃ in various senses of VOUCH. XVI. – OF. *avochier* – L. *advocāre* ADVOCATE vb.; cf. next.

avow əvau· acknowledge, own. XIII (Cursor M.). – (O)F. *avouer* (prop.) acknowledge as one's own, (hence) recognize as valid – L. *advocāre* appeal to, invoke (see ADVOCATE). Hence **avow·al.** XVIII; see -AL[2].

avulsion əvʌ·lʃən forcible separation or removal. XVII. – L. *āvulsiō(n-)*, f. *āvuls-*, *āvellere*, f. *ā-* AB-+*vellere* pluck (cf. VELLICATE); see -SION.

avuncular əvʌ·ŋkjŭləɹ pert. to an uncle. XIX. f. L. *avunculus* UNCLE+-AR.

await əwei·t †watch for XIII (AncrR.); wait upon; wait for XIV (Gower). – AN. *awaitier* = OF. *aguaitier*, f. *a-* AD-+*waitier* (mod. *guetter*) WAIT.

awake əwei·k be roused from sleep OE.; rouse from sleep XIII. OE. str. pt. *onwōc*, *āwōc*, pp. *āwacen*; wk. pt. *āwacode*; see WAKE[1]. Hence **awa·ke** adj. XIII; clipped form of pp. *awaken*. So **awa·ken** cease to sleep OE.; rouse from sleep XVI. OE. *onwæcnan*, *āwæcnan*, *āwæcnian*; see WAKEN.

award əwɔ̄·ɹd †decide, determine XIV (Gower); determine upon, assign judicially, adjudge XVI. – AN. *awarder*, var. of ONF. *eswarder*, OF. *esguarder* consider, ordain = Pr., Pg. *esguardar*, It. *sguardare* :– Rom. **exwardāre*, f. L. *ex* EX-[1]+**wardāre* WARD[2]. So **awa·rd** sb. XIV (Ch.). – AN. *award*, f. the vb.

aware əwɛə·ɹ †on one's guard; cognizant *of*. XIII. ME. *awar*, for earlier *iwar*, OE. *ġewær* = OS. *giwar* (MDu. *ghewāre*), OHG. *ga-*, *giwar* (G. *gewahr*); WGerm. formation f. **ga-* Y-+**war-* WARE[2].

awash əwɔ·ʃ flush with or washed by waves, washing about. XIX. f. A-[1]+WASH.

away əwei· Late OE. *aweġ*, for earlier *onweġ*, orig. two words, 'on (the or one's) way', (hence) 'from such-and-such place'; out of existence XII; see ON, A-[1], WAY. In ME. (XIII) and mod. dial. reduced to *way* (e.g. in phr. †*do way* 'put away', have done!); cf. MHG. *enwec* (for *in wec*), whence G. *weg* away, used as an adv. and as a separable prefix (e.g. *wegtun* remove; *tut die hände weg!* hands off!).

awe ɔ̄ dread. XIII. ME. *aȝe* – ON. *agi* :– **agon*, f. Germ. **ag-* :– IE. **agh-*, repr. by Gr. *ákhesthai* be grieved, OIr. *-āgor* (in *adāgor*, etc.) fear, Goth. *agis* fear, *unagands* fearless, *afagjan* frighten off. The Scand. word displaced the native *eie*, *eȝe*, OE. *eġe* :– **agiz*), first in the north and east, and finally elsewhere. Hence **awe** vb. XIV, **aw**FUL[1] ɔ̄·fəl XIII, **awfully** ɔ̄·fəli XIV. **awe-struck** ɔ̄·strʌk. XVII (Milton).

awhile əʍai·l for a time. OE. *āne hwīle*, ME. *ōne hwīle*, obl. case of A and WHILE, reduced to *a while* and finally written as one word. XIV. ¶ *Awhile* is often by confusion written for *a while*, as *after awhile*.

awkward ɔ̄·kwəɹd †adv. in the wrong direction, with a back stroke XIV; adj. †froward XV; †untoward; clumsy or ungainly XVI; embarrassing, difficult XVIII. orig. north. and Sc.; f. †*awk* perverse, untoward (– ON. *afugr*, *ǫfugr* turned the wrong way, back foremost)+-WARD. The ON. word is rel. to OS. *aƀich*, *aƀoch*, OHG. *apuh*, *apah* (MHG. *ebech*, *ebich*, G. dial. *äbich*), f. **aƀ* OFF, away.

awl ɔ̄l small tool for piercing holes. OE. *æl* = OHG. *ala* (MHG. *ale*, G. *ahle*), ON. *alr*, of unascertained origin; on the analogy of *small* (OE. *smæl*), the present sp. would be *all*, which was current XVI–XVII; *au-* and *aw-* sps. are found as early as XVI; in Exodus xxi 6 A.V. has *aule*. Cf. BRADAWL. ¶ To be distinguished from OE. *āwel*, *ōwel*, **ǣwel*, giving ME. *owel*, *eawel* flesh-hook.

awn ɔ̄n 'beard' of grain. XIV. – ON. *agn-*, obl. stem of *ǫgn* (Sw. *agn*, Da. *avn*), corr. to late OE. *æġnan* (pl.), also *eġenu* husk, chaff (whence dial. *ain*, *ane*), NFris. *ein*, OHG. *agana* (MHG. *agene*, *agne*, *ane*, G. *ahne*), Goth. *ahana* chaff; cf. OL. *agna* (:– **acnā*) ear of corn, Gr. *ákhnē* chaff, and, with other suffixes, Gr. *ákhuron*, Lith. *akúotas* awn; all based on IE. **ak-* be sharp or pointed (cf. ACUTE).

awning ɔ̄·niŋ roof-like shelter (prop. naut.). XVII (Capt. John Smith of Virginia). Of unkn. origin.

awry ərai· obliquely, askew. XIV. Late ME. *on wry* (Barbour), *awrie*, *-y* (Ch., Gower), f. *on*, *a* A-[1]+WRY.

axe, U.S. **ax** æks hewing implement. OE. *æx* (*eax*), *æces* = OS. *akus* (Du. *aaks*), OHG. *ackus* (MHG. *ackes*, mod. *axt*), OFris. *axa*, ON. *øx* (obl. *ex-*), Goth. *aqizi* :– CGerm. **akwisjō*, **akusjō*, repr. IE. **agwesī*, **akusī*; cf. also Gr. *axínē* axe, L. *ascia* (:– **acsiā*) plane, trowel, hoe, pick.

axil æ·ksil (bot.) upper angle between leaf and stem or branch and trunk. XVIII. – modL. use of L. *axilla* arm-pit, dim. of **acslā*, *āla* wing. So **a·xill**AR, **a·xill**ARY. XVII; after F. *axillaire*.

axiology æksiɔ·lədʒi (philos.) value theory. XX. f. Gr. *axia*+-LOGY.

axiom æ·ksiəm universally accepted proposition. XV (Caxton). – F. *axiome* or L. *axiōma* – Gr. *axíōma* that which is thought fitting, decision, self-evident principle (Aristotle), f. *axioûn* hold worthy, f. *áxios* worthy. Hence **axiom**A·TIC XVIII, -A·TICAL, *-a·tically* XVI.

axis[1] æ·ksis pl. *axes* æ·ksīz straight line about which a thing revolves or is symmetrically arranged. XIV (Trev.). – L. *axis* axle, pivot, axis of the earth, rel. to Skr. *ákshas*, Gr. *áxōn*, OSl. *osĭ*, Lith. *aszìs*, and OE. *eax*, *æx* axle (cf. †*axtree* XIII–XVII) = OFris. *axe*, MLG., MDu. *asse* (Du. *as*), OHG. *ahsa* (G. *achse*) :– Germ. **aχsō* fem.; cf. AXLE.

axis[2] æ·ksis hog-deer of India. XVIII. Named by Buffon; a use of L. *axis*, recorded by Pliny as the name of an Indian quadruped.

axle æ·ksl bar on the ends of which opposite carriage-wheels revolve XVII; but earlier (first in Cursor M. XIII) in **a·xle**-TREE – ON. *ǫxultré*, f. *ǫxull* :– **aχsulaz*, f. **aχsō*, ult. replacing the native *ax-tree*; see AXIS[1]).

axolotl æ·ksŏlətl batrachian reptile of Mexico. XVIII. Nahuatl, f. *atl* water, *xolotl* servant.

axunge æ·ksʌndʒ fat of the kidney. XVI. – F. †*axunge* (mod. *axonge*) – L. *axungia* axle-tree grease, f. *axis* axle, AXIS[1]+*ung-* of *ungere* grease, ANOINT.

ay[1] ei ever. XII. ME. *ai*, *ei* (*agg*, Orm) – ON. *ei*, *ey* = OE. *ā* (ME. *ā*, *ō*, *oo*), OS. *eo*, OHG. *eo*, *io* (MHG. *ie*, G. *je*), Goth. *aiw*; acc. of *aiws* age, eternity :– CGerm. **aiwaz*, rel. to L. *ævum* age, Gr. *aeí*, *aiϝeí* ever, *aiϝṓn* ÆON.

ay[2] ei ah! alas! XIV (*ey*). (dial.) natural excl. of surprise, sorrow, or pity; *ay me* (XVI) is prob. modelled on OF. *aimi* or It. *ahimè*, Sp. *ay de mi*.

ayah ā·jă Hindu nurse. XVIII. – Indo-Pg. *aia*, fem. of *aio* (= Sp. *ayo*, It. *ajo* tutor).

aye ai yes. XVI (c. 1575). In earliest use spelt *I* (XVI–XVIII), later *ai*, *ay*, and *ey*; *aye* not common before XIX. prob. the pron. *I* used as a formula of assent in answer to a question; cf. OE. *nić* 'not I', used as a negative answer, whence the vb. *niććan* deny, ME. *nicke*, freq. in phr. *nicke* (*with*) *nay*; also the use of OF. *je* I, as in *oje*, for *o je* 'that (say) I', yes, beside *na|je* no.

aye-aye ai·ai quadrumanous squirrel-like animal. XVIII. – F. *aye-aye* – Malagasy *aiay*.

azalea əzei·liə flowering shrubby plant allied to the rhododendron. XVIII. – modL. *azalea* (Linnæus) – Gr. *azaléa*, sb. use of fem. of *azaléos* dry (cf. ARID, ASH[2]), so called because it flourishes in dry soil.

azarole æ·zəroul Neapolitan medlar. XVII. – F. *azerole* (†*azarole*) – Sp. *acerola* (cf. It. *azzeruolo*, *lazzeruolo*) – Arab. *az-zu'rūr*, i.e. *al-zu'rūr* (AL-[2]).

azedarac əze·dəræk E. Indian tree, Melia Azedarach XVIII; bark of this XIX. – F. *azédarac* – Sp. *acedaraque* – Arab. *azād-dirakht*, i.e. Pers. *azād* free, *dirakht* tree; said to be so named because Medjnoun, the lover of Leila, saved a specimen from the gardener's axe because of the resemblance he saw in it to his beloved.

azimuth æ·zimʌþ arc extending from zenith to horizon. XIV (Ch.). – (O)F. *azimut*, corr. to It. *azzimutto*, Pg. *azimuth* – Arab. *assumūt*, i.e. *al* AL-², *sumūt*, pl. of *samt* way, direction, point of the compass (see ZENITH).

azote æ·zout (chem.) nitrogen. – F. *azote* (Lavoisier and de Morveau, 1787), improperly f. Gr. *a-* A-⁴+*zōḗ* life (cf. BIO-, QUICK); so called from its inability to support life. In comb. form shortened to **azo-** æ·zou, e.g. *azo-compound, azo-yellow*.

Aztec æ·ztek Indian of the Nahuatlan tribe; their language. XVIII. – F. *Aztèque* or Sp. *Azteca* – Nahuatl *aztecatl* 'north- men', f. *aztlan* north, the Mexican tradition being that the Nahuatl-speaking peoples came from the north.

azure æ·ʒəɹ, ei·ʒəɹ, -ʒuə †lapis lazuli; bright or clear blue colour. XIV (Ch.). ME. *asur(e)*, *azur(e)*, *azer* – OF. *asur*, (also mod.) *azur*, corr. to Pr., OSp., Rum. *azur*, Sp., Pg. *azul*, It. *azzurro*, *azzuolo* – medL. *azzurum*, *azolum* – Arab. *allazward*, f. (with *al* AL-²) Pers. *lāzhward*, *lājward* LAPIS LAZULI, blue. ¶ The word has become CEur. (with or without initial *l*).

B

baa bā bleat. XVI. mit. ¶ G. *bäh*, L. *bē*, Gr. *bê*, and vbs. L. *bālāre*, *bēlāre* (F. *bêler*, etc.), W. *beichio*, Skr. *békati*.

baas bās (S. Africa) master. XVII. Du.; see BOSS².

babacoote bæ·bəkūt largest species of lemur. XIX. – Malagasy *babakoto*.

babble bæ·bl chatter, prattle XIII (AncrR.); utter indistinct sounds XIV. prob. – MLG. (Du.) *babbelen* (whence Sw. *babbla*, Da. *bable*), if not a parallel native imit. formation; cf. F. *babiller* prattle, L. *babulus* fool; see -LE².

babe beib XIV; contemp. and synon. with BABY; also (dial.) **bab** XIV.

babel bei·bl Name in Gen. xi 9 of the city and tower where the confusion of languages is related to have taken place; Heb. *bābel* Babylon (perh. for Ass. *bābilu* gate of God, or *bābili* gate of the gods, tr. Akkadian *Cadimira*); (hence) city of confusion XVI; confusion, confused noise XVII.

babiana bæbiā·nə, -ei·nə S. African iris. XIX. – modL. – Du. *babianer*, f. *baviaan* (earlier *babiaen*) baboon; so called because the stems are fed upon by baboons.

babiroussa bābirū·sə Asiatic wild hog. XVII. Malay, f. *bābi* hog+*rūsa* deer.

baboo, babu bā·bū Mr., Esq.; Hindu gentleman. XVIII. Hind. (– Hindi) *bābū*.

baboon bəbū·n †grotesque figure; one of a subdivision of monkeys. XIV. ME. *baboyne*, *babewyn(e)* – OF. *babuin* gaping figure, manikin, baboon (mod. *babouin*) or medL. *babewynus* (cf. It. *babbuino*, Sp. *babuino*). These forms have been plausibly connected with (O)F. *baboue* muzzle, grimace, but there are difficulties of chronology; some recognize a base **bab-* grimace, which may be the common source.

babouche babū·ʃ Oriental slipper. XVII. – F. *babouche* = It. *babuccia*, Sp. *babucha* – Arab. *bābūsh* – Pers. *pāpōsh*, f. *pā* FOOT+ *pōsh* covering.

baby bei·bi infant in arms XIV; †doll XVI. *Babe* and *baby* appear about the same time and are prob. both derivs. of a redupl. form **baba* (cf. ME. †*baban* XIII and later †*babbon* XVI) similar to MAMA, PAPA. Also **ba·bby** (XVI), which, like *bab*, is first recorded from the north. See -Y⁶.

baccalaureate bækəlɔ̄·riət bachelor's status or degree in a university. XVII. – F. *baccalauréat* or medL. *baccalaureātus*, f. *baccalaureus* BACHELOR; see -ATE¹.

baccara(t) bæ·kəra gambling card game. XIX. – F., of unkn. origin.

bacchanal bæ·kənəl pert. to Bacchus XVI; riotously drunken XVIII. – L. *bacchānālis*, f. *Bacchus*, Gr. *Bákkhos* god of wine; cf. F. *bacchanal*. So **Bacchanalia** bækənei·liə n. pl. festival in honour of Bacchus, drunken revelry. XVI; see -AL¹. Hence **bacchana·lIAN** XVI. **Bacchante** bəkæ·nti female votary of Bacchus. XVII; formerly **Ba·cchANT** – F. *Bacchante* (= It. *Baccante*) – L. *Bacchantem*, *-āns*, prp. of *bacchārī* – Gr. *Bakkhân* celebrate the feast of Bacchus. **Ba·cchIC**. XVII. – F. or L. – Gr. **bacchius** bækai·əs (pros.) foot ⏑ – – or – – ⏑. XVI. L. – Gr. *bakkheîos* frenzied.

bachelor bæ·tʃələɹ young knight XIII; university graduate (PPl., Ch.); unmarried man (Ch.) XIV. ME. *bacheler* – OF. *bacheler* young man aspiring to knighthood = Pr. *bacalar*, It. *baccalaro* squire :– Rom. **baccalāris* (It. *baccelliere*, Sp. *bachiller*, Pg. *bacharel* are from F.). The ult. source and connexions are doubtful. ¶ There is close formal correspondence to medL. *baccalāria* area of plough-land, *baccalārius* labourer on an estate (which have been plausibly derived from *bacca*, late form of L. *vacca* cow), but the sense-development offers serious difficulties. A proposed deriv. from a Celtic **bakalākos* in OIr. *bachlach* shepherd, peasant (f. *bachall* staff – L. *baculum*) is equally unsatisfactory. The later Eng. sp. *bachelour*, *bachelor* has been infl. by the suffixes -OUR¹, -OR¹; cf. *ancestor*. In the academic use the medL. form was *baccalārius*, later altered by assoc. (perhaps joc.) with *bacca lauri* (laurel berry) to *baccalaureus* (see BACCALAUREATE).

bacillus bəsi·ləs rod-shaped vegetable organism. XIX. mod. use of late L., dim. of *baculus* rod, stick. Cf. earlier BACTERIUM.

back[1] bæk hinder surface. OE. *bæc* = OFris. *bek*, OS. *bak*, (M)LG., MDu. *bak*, OHG. *bah*, ON. *bak* :- CGerm. (exc. Goth.) **bakam*; not surviving in Du. (exc. in comps.), German, or the Scand. langs. (see RIDGE). Hence **back** vb. XIV; adj. XV, with superl. **ba·ck**MOST XVIII. **backside**. XIV; prob. Scand.; cf. Sw. *baksida*, Norw. *bakside*.

back[2] adv. to the back XIV; aphetic of ABACK.

back-bite bæ·kbait detract from the character of. XII. - MSw. *bakbīta*, f. *bak* BACK+*bīta* BITE. (MSw. has also *bakbītari* back·biter, *bakbītilse* detraction.)

back-formation bækfɔ̄ɹmei·ʃən formation of a word from a longer word which has the appearance of being derived from it, e.g. *edit* from *editor*. XIX (J. A. H. Murray). Hence G. *rückbildung*.

backgammon bæ·kgæmən game played with draughtsmen on two tables, the moves being determined by throws of the dice. XVII. f. BACK[2]+an earlier form of GAME[1] (see GAMMON[2]); the origin of the name is obscure; it may have been first applied to a particular kind of victory in the game.

backward bæ·kwəɹd towards the back or rear. XIII. Aphetic of †*abackward* (Laȝ.), f. ABACK+-WARD. Cf. OFris. *bekward*.

bacon bei·kən cured flesh of the pig. XII (*an bacun*, glossing *i flicce* a flitch). - OF. *bacon*, *-un* = Pr. *bacon* - Frankish *bako* ham, flitch = OHG. *bahho* :- Germ. **bakkon*, rel. to **bakam* BACK[1].

bacterium bæktiə·riəm rod-shaped vegetable organism. XIX. - modL. - Gr. *baktḗrion*, dim. of *báktron* stick, staff. Cf. BACILLUS.

bad bæd)(*good*; first applied to worthless or contemptible persons. XIII (RGlouc.). ME. *badde* (2 syll.), perh. repr. OE. *bǣddel* hermaphrodite (cf. *bǣdling* sodomite), with loss of *l* as in *much(e)*, *wench(e)*, for OE. *myčel*, *wenčel*; there have been other, more dubious conjectures. Formerly (XIV–XVIII) and still dial. compared *badder*, *baddest*.

badge bædʒ distinctive device or emblem. XIV. In AN. *bage* (XIV), OF. (XV), AL. *bagia* (cf. Eng. *bagy* XV; Sc. *bawgy*, *badgie*, *bagie* XVI); of unkn. origin.

badger bæ·dʒəɹ quadruped, Meles taxus, which burrows and lives in earths. XVI (also *bageard* XVI, *badgerd* XVI–XVII). perh. f. BADGE+-ARD, with allusion to the white mark on the animal's forehead (but *badge* is not recorded in this sense). Identity in form with (dial.) *badger* middleman, huckster (XV) has suggested that the latter was the original and that the animal was so named because it hoards corn (which it does not), a supposed analogy being found in F. *blaireau* badger, which was derived from *blé* corn, but may be f. OF. *bler* (prob.) spotted with white. ¶ Earlier names were *bauson*, *brock*, and *gray*.

badinage bæ·dināʒ banter. XVII. F., f. *badiner* 'play the foole, or Vice . . trifle it in any way' (Cotgr.), f. *badin* - modPr. *badin* fool, f. *badar* :- Rom. **batāre* gape; see -AGE.

badmash, budmash bædmā·ʃ rascal. XIX. Urdu - Pers., f. *bad* evil+*ma'āsh* means of livelihood.

badminton bæ·dmintən ball-game played with nets, rackets, and shuttlecock. XIX. Name of the Duke of Beaufort's country seat, in Gloucestershire.

bael, bel bel Bengal quince. XVII. - Hindi *bel*, Marathi *bail* :- Skr. *bilvas*, *vilvas*.

baffle bæ·fl A. †disgrace (spec. a perjured knight; cf. Spenser 'F.Q.' VI vii 27) XVI; B. †hoodwink XVI; †confound; foil the plans of XVII. The earliest exx. in A refer to Sc. usage and suggest alteration of Sc. *bauchle* (XV) disgrace, of unkn. origin. In B we have perh. a word of different origin rel. in some way to F. *bafouer* (XVI) 'to hoodwinke; to deceiue; to besmeare; also to baffle, abuse, reuile, disgrace' (Cotgr.), which is held to be an alteration of OF. *beffer* (= Sp. *befar*, It. *beffare* mock); cf. also F. †*beffler* (Rabelais) mock, deceive.

baffy bæ·fi kind of golf-club. XIX. f. Sc. *baff* sb. stroke or vb. strike (of imit. origin; cf. G. *baff*, Du. *baffen*)+-Y[1].

bag bæg small receptacle of the sack kind. XIII (AncrR.). The locality of the earliest exx. (from AncrR., PPl., Promp. Parv.) is consistent with a Scand. origin, but it is not certain that ON. *baggi* is a native word; similar forms are found in Rom., OF. *bague*, Pr. *bagua* baggage (whence medL. *baga* sack, chest), but the source of these is not known, nor their relation to WFlem. *bagge* pannier carried on the back. Hence **ba·g**PIPE. XIV (Ch.); prob. tr. LG. *sakpīpe*, Du. †*sack-*, *zakpijpe*.

bagatelle bægəte·l A. trifle XVII; B. table ball-game XIX. - F. - It. *bagatella*, dim. of (dial.) *bagata* little property, prob. f. *baga* (see BAG, BAGGAGE); formerly in anglicized form *bagatel(l)* in sense A. Sense B is purely Eng. in origin and use.

baggage bæ·gidʒ portable property (orig. in packages), impedimenta XV; †rubbish, refuse; worthless woman XVI (Sh.); (saucy, silly, flighty) young woman XVII. - (O)F. *bagage* (= Pr. *bagatge*, Sp. *bagage*), f. *baguer* tie up, or f. *bagues* (pl.) bundles, packs; see BAG and -AGE. The sense of 'rubbish, refuse', which is found in Sp. *bagage*, leads to that of 'worthless woman', for which there is no need to assume infl. from F. *bagasse*.

bagnio bæ·njou †Turkish bath; Oriental prison; brothel. XVI. – It. *bagno* :– L. *balneum* (whence also F. *bain*, Sp. *baño*).

bah bā int. XIX; after F. *bah*. A synon. but independent form *baw* occurs in PPl. (XIV); *baw* in Goldsmith 'Goodnatured Man' IV ii may, however, repr. F. *bah* (cf. *baugh*, *baw* for F. *bât*, in *bawman* BATMAN[2]).

bahadur bəhɔ̄·dəɹ great personage. XVIII. (Hind. – Nepali) – Pers. *bahādur* brave, warlike, sb. soldier, knight (f. *bahā* price, value), whence Russ. *bogatýr'* hero, valiant knight.

baignoire bei·nwāɹ box on a level with stalls in a theatre. XIX. F., prop. bathing-vessel, f. *baigner* :– L. *balneāre* bathe, f. *balneum* (cf. BAGNIO); so called from its shape.

bail[1] beil †charge, custody XIV; †temporary release from custody; security for such release XV; person(s) providing such security XVI. – OF. *bail* power, custody, jurisdiction, delivery (in modF. lease), f. *baillier* take charge of, receive, hand over, deliver = Pr. *bailar* :– L. *bājulāre* bear a burden, (later) manage, rule, be guardian, f. *bājulus* carrier. The chronology of the sense-development is uncertain. Hence **bail** vb. admit to bail, be bail for. XVI.

bail[2] beil (cricket) orig. single cross-piece of wood resting on two stumps. XVIII. prob. of local origin and identical with (dial.) *bail* (recorded early once XVI, but prob. much older), having the gen. sense of 'bar', perh. – OF. *bail* cross-beam, possibly from a transf. use of L. *bājulus* (see prec.). ¶ An earlier synon. *cricket-bar* (Littleton's Latin Dict. s.v. *vibia*, 1678) had prob. no currency, like *cricket-staffe* for the bat (Cotgr. s.v. *crosse*, 1611).

bail[3] see BALE[2].

bailey bei·li external wall of a precinct, circuit of defences. XIII (Cursor M.). ME. *bail(l)y*, var. *baile*, prob. – OF. *bail*, *baille*, enclosed court (whence medL. *ballium*, *ballia*), f. *bailler* enclose, of unkn. origin. The Old Bailey (medL. *Vetus Ballium*) in London is so called from the ancient 'bailey' of the city wall between Lud Gate and New Gate, within which it was situated.

bailie bei·li (now only) municipal magistrate in Scotland. XIII. ME. *bail(l)i* – OF. *bailli*, later form of *baillis* (nom.), *bailif* (see next). Hence **bailiwick** bei·liwik jurisdiction or office of a bailiff XV; see WICK[2].

bailiff bei·lif public administrator of a district; sheriff's officer XIII; landholder's steward XVI. ME. *baillif* – OF. *baillif*, obl. case of *baillis* (mod. *bailli*) :– medL. **bājulīvus* (*ballivus*), adj. deriv. of L. *bājulus* carrier, (hence) manager, administrator (cf. BAIL[1]).

bain-marie bɛ̄marī· vessel containing hot water for heating saucepans. XIX. F., tr. medL. *balneum Mariæ*, tr. medGr. *káminos Mariās* furnace of Maria, an alleged Jewish alchemist. Also rare †*balne Mary* (XVII) from L., and earlier in semi-anglicizations, as *in balneo of Mary* (XV), the common usage from XVI to XVIII being the full L. form, or the simple *balneum*.

bairn bɛəɹn, bɛrn child. XVI. Sc. form of ME. *barn* (as *airm*, *wairn* of *arm*, *warn*), repr. OE. *bearn* = OS., OHG., ON., Goth. *barn* :– CGerm. **barnam*, f. **bar-*, var. of stem of **beran* BEAR[2].

bait beit A. set on dogs; harass persistently XIII (*beȝȝtenn*, Orm); B. provide provender for; C. furnish with bait XIII (Cursor M.). – ON. *beita* pasture, hunt or chase with dogs or hawks, deal (badly) with (= OE. *bǣtan* bridle, restrain, hunt, worry, OHG. *beiȥen*, G. *beizen* soak, corrode, hawk), causal of *bíta* BITE; this origin applies to senses A and B; C is prob. f. **bait** sb., which is partly (i) in the sense 'enticing morsel' (XIII) – ON. *beit* pasture, *beita* bait for fish, and partly (ii) in the sense of 'provender' (XVI), f. the vb. (B).

baize beiz coarse woollen stuff. XVI (*baies*). – F. *baies* fem. pl., sb. use of *bai* reddish-brown, BAY[5]; so named presumably from its orig. colour. The pl. form was early taken as a sg.; the sp. with *z* was not established before XIX.

bake beik cook by dry heat. OE. *bacan*, pt. *bōc*, pp. *bacen* str. vb. = OHG. *bachan*, ON. *baka*, f. Germ. **bak-* :– IE. **bhog-*, whence Gr. *phṓgein* roast, parch. Weak inflexions (*baked*) began to appear before 1400, and were established by XVI; *boke* pt. survives dial., and *baken* is the more freq. form of the pp. in AV.; ME. *bake* pp. remained in †*bake-meat* pastry, pie (Ch., Sh., AV.).

bakelite bei·kəlait synthetic resin used as a plastic. XX. – G. *bakelit* (1909), f. name of L. H. *Baekeland*, its inventor; see -ITE.

baksheesh bæ·kʃīʃ gratuity. XVII (*bac(s)-cheese*), XVIII (*buxie*, *bac-shish*, etc.). ult. – Pers. *bakhshīsh*, f. *bakhshīdan* give, chiefly through Arabic, Turk., or Hind. Cf. BUCKSHEE.

balalaika bæləlai·kə guitar-like instrument. XVIII. Russ., of Tatar origin.

balance bæ·ləns †uncertainty, doubt, risk XIII (RGlouc.); weighing-scales XIV; adjustment of accounts XVI; sum remaining over XVII (remainder in gen. sense first Amer. XVIII). – (O)F. *balance* = Pr., Cat. *balansa*, It. *bilancia*, Sp. *balanza* :– Rom. **bilancia*, f. late L. *bilanc-*, *bilanx* (in *lībra bilanx* balance having two scales), f. *bi-* BI- + *lanx* scale. So **ba·lance** vb. XVI. – (O)F. *balancer*, f. *balance*.

balas bæ·ləs variety of spinel ruby. XV. – (O)F. *balais* (= Pr. *balais*, Sp. *balax*, It. *balascio*) – medL. *balascus*, *-cius*, f. Arab.

balakhsh, f. Pers. *Badakhshān*, name of a district of Persia near Samarcand, where it is found. Cf. G. *ballasrubin*.

balbriggan bælbri·gən epithet of a make of hose. XIX. Name of a seaport in co. Dublin, Ireland.

balcony bæ·lkəni balustraded platform on the outside of a house. XVII (*balcone*). – It. *balcone* (whence also F. *balcon*, Sp. *balcón*, etc.), prob. f. Germ. **balkon* beam, BALK, with augm. suffix; but the transf. of meaning is not clear, while the proposed deriv. from Pers. *bālākhāneh* (f. *bālā* high, *khāneh* house) is not satisfactory phonologically. Regularly str. *balco·ny* till early XIX, as in Cowper 'John Gilpin' 142, Byron 'Beppo' xi (r. w. *Giorgione*); Swift in 'Tom Clinch' has *ba·lconies*, but Samuel Rogers (d. 1855) says: '"cóntemplate" is bad enough, but "balcŏny" makes me sick'.

bald bōld hairless; bare. XIV. ME. *balled(e)*, MSc. *bellyde, beld, bellit* hairless, having a white blaze, prob. an OE. formation (**bællede, *beallede*) with suffix *-ede* (as in *healede* ruptured, *hoferede* hunch-backed) on a base **ball-* meaning orig. 'white patch' (cf. dial. *ball* white-faced horse, and *bald* white-faced), perh. developed from 'shiny round surface'. (For a parallel sense-association cf. MDu. *blaer* bald, Du. *blaar* white patch on the forehead, MHG. *blas* bald, *blasse* white patch, Gr. *phálios* white, *phalakrós* bald-headed.) Cf. also PIEBALD, SKEWBALD, and *ballard* (XIV) bald, which survives as a surname. Among the earlier exx. of *bald* is *balled cote* bald-coot, the coot Fulica atra, glossing OF. *blarye*.

baldac(c)hino bældəkī·nou canopy for an altar, throne, etc. XVII (*baldaquino*, Evelyn). – It. *baldacchino*, f. (with suffix *-ino* -INE[1]) *Baldacco*, It. form of *Bagdād* name of a city on the Tigris, in Asia Minor, place of origin of the embroidered stuff or rich brocade of which canopies were made. The It. word was formerly used also for the stuff, in which sense it is the source of OF. *baldekin, baudequin*, whence ME. *baudekin* (XIII/XIV), later *baldakin* (XVI); the It. word has passed into most Eur. langs.

balderdash bō·ldəɹdæʃ †froth XVI (Nashe); †mixture of drinks XVII (Chapman); nonsense, trash spoken or written XVII (Marvell). Of unkn. origin; cf. medL. *balductum* posset, *-a* pl. curd, used in Eng. for 'balderdash', 'trashy' XVI (Holinshed, Stanyhurst, Harvey). (Various continental forms f. *balder-* expressing loud noise or clatter are not relevant in sense).

baldric bō·ldrik belt worn pendent from one shoulder under the opposite arm. XIII (*baudry, bauderyk*; forms with *l* from XVI). The earliest ex. ('King Alisaunder' 4698 r. w. *amy*) is – OF. *baudrei*; the later forms corr. to early MHG *balderich*, of obscure origin, which has been doubtfully referred to L. *balteus* BELT.

bale[1] beil evil, mischief, woe. (Almost entirely poet.) OE. *balu* (*bealu*) = OFris., OS. *balu*, OHG. *balo*, ON. *bǫl* :– CGerm. **balwam*, n. of adj. **balwaz* (OE. *balu* evil, wicked), repr. also in Goth. *balwawesei* wickedness, *balwjan* torment, *balweins* punishment; the base has been connected with OSl. *bolŭ* sick person, *bolěti* be sick, grieve. The OE. word was reinforced in ME. by ON. *bal-*, *bǫl*. Hence **ba·leful** OE. *baluful* (see -FUL[1]); until XIX chiefly poet., and still only literary.

bale[2] beil bundle, package. XIV. prob. – MDu. *bale* (Du. *baal*) – OF. *bale* (later and mod. *balle*) = Pr., Sp. *bala*, It. *balla*, medL. *bal(l)a* ball, rolled or rounded package; ult. identical with BALL[1].

bale[3] beil lade out. XIII. Later sp. of *bail* (XVII), f. †*bail* sb. vessel for lading water (XV) – OF. *baille* bucket, prob. :– Rom. **bajula*, fem. f. L. *bājulus* BAIL[1].

baleen bəlī·n whalebone. XIV (*balene, -eyne, -ayne*). – OF. *baleine* whale (so in ME.) :– L. *ballæna*.

balefire bei·lfaiəɹ (arch.) great fire. XIV. In Sc. use XIV–XVII and revived by Scott for 'beacon fire'. f. north. *bale* large fire, bonfire – ON. *bál* = OE. *bǣl* (also *bǣlfȳr*), which has been referred to a base meaning 'white', 'shining' and so connected with BALD.

balibuntal bælibʌ·ntəl fine straw for hats. XX. Short for *Baliuag buntal*, buntal originating from *Baliuag* in Bulacan, Philippine Islands.

balk bōk (in billiards **baulk**) A. ridge, esp. between furrows OE.; ridge in the way, obstacle, hindrance XVI; B. beam of timber XIII (Cursor M.). Late OE. *balc* – ON. *bálkr* partition :– **balkuz*, rel. to OFris. *balca*, OS., OHG. *balco* (Du. *balk*, G. *balken*), ON. *bjálki* :– Germ. **balkon*, **belkon* beam, another grade of which may be repr. by OE. *bolca* gangway of a ship. IE. **bhalg-* is referred by some to the **bhalŋg-* of PHALANX, by others to the base of L. *sufflāmen* (:– **subflagmen*) wheel-drag. Hence **balk**, usu. **baulk** vb. A. †plough in ridges XIV (Gower); B. †pass by or over, avoid; stop at an obstacle XV; C. hinder, frustrate XVI.

ball[1] bōl round body; (earliest use) globular body to play with. XIII (Laȝ.). ME. *bal*, inflected *balle, balles* – ON. *ball-*, *bǫllr* (OSw. *baller*, Sw. *båll*) :– Germ. **balluz*, rel. to **ballōn* (whence OHG. *balla*, MHG. *balle*, the source of It. *palla*, whence prob. F. *balle*); the base is repr. also by OE. *bealluc* BALLOCK.

ball[2] bōl assembly for dancing. XVII. – (O)F. *bal* dance (= Pr. *bal*, It. *ballo* dancing), f. †*baler*, †*baller* dance (= Pr.

balar, It. *ballare*) – late L. *ballāre* – Gr. (Sicily and Magna Græcia) *ballizein* dance.

ballad bæ·ləd song; narrative poem in short stanzas. XV (in Sc. forms *ballat, ballet*). (O)F. *ballade* – Pr. *balada* dance, song or poem to dance to, f. *balar* dance; see BALL[2].

ballade bælā·d specific verse-form. XIV (Ch.). Early (and modF.) form of BALLAD differentiated in application.

ballast bæ·ləst material placed in a ship's hold to give stability. XVI. A word now common to countries of the northern seaboards of Europe from England to Russia; in early XVI Eng. prob. directly from LG. (where it appears a. 1400), but possibly from Scand. (a. 1400), in OSw. and ODa. *ballast,* also *barlast,* which last has been assumed to be the orig. form and derived from (i) *bar* 'bare', mere, or (ii) *barm* hull (of a ship) + *last* burden. (In XVI–XVII also *ballace, -asse, -esse,* as if *ballast* vb. were analysed as *ballass*+*-ed*; cf. 'The Shipes were balissed with great coble stone', Leland 1538.)

ballerina bælerī·nə female ballet dancer. XVIII. – It., fem. of *ballerino* dancing-master, f. *ballare* (see BALL[2]); see -INE[1].

ballet bæ·lei combined performance of professional dancers. XVII (*balette, ballat*). – F. *ballet* – It. *balletto,* dim. of *ballo* BALL[2].

ballista bəli·stə, also **balista** ancient missile engine. XVI (earlier anglicized *balist* XIV). L., f. (ult.) Gr. *bállein* throw. Hence **balli·stic** pert. to projectiles. XVIII (sb. -ICS).

ballock (dial.) bæ·lək, bo·l- testicle. OE. **balluc* (*bealluc*), dim. f. Germ. **ball-* BALL[1]; see -OCK.

balloon bəlū·n ball, ball-game XVI; lighter-than-air round or pear-shaped air-vessel XVIII. – F. *ballon* or It. *ballone,* augm. of *balla* BALL[1]; see -OON.

ballot bæ·lət (hist.) ball, ticket, etc. used in secret voting; method of such voting, orig. by dropping a ball into a box. XVI (the earliest exx. refer to Venice). – It. *ballotta,* dim. of *balla* BALL[1]. So vb. XVI. – It. *ballottare.*

bally bæ·li. XIX. (sl.) euphem. alteration of BLOODY, perh. suggested by the writing *bl—y.*

ballyhoo bælihū· (U.S.) publicity; blarney, humbug. XIX. Said to be orig. the name of a Central Amer. wood, of which some schooners were made that were failures, and hence applied to badly rigged vessels.

ballyrag var. of BULLYRAG.

balm bām aromatic resinous product of certain trees XIII; (gen.) aromatic oil or ointment XIII; healing or soothing agency XV. ME. *basme, bame,* later *baume* – OF. *basme, bame,* later refash. after L. to *bausme, baume* = Pr. *basme,* It. *balsamo* :– L. *balsamum* BALSAM. Further assim. to L. produced *balsme, baulme,* whence (from XV) *balm*; for the mod. pronunc. cf. *calm, palm, psalm.* Hence **balmy** bā·mi. XV; see -Y[1].

ba·lm-cri:cket cicada. XVIII. Earlier *baum-cricket,* partial tr. of G. *baumgrille* 'tree-cricket', altered after BALM.

balmy var. of BARMY.

balsam bō·lsəm in senses of *balm* XV; plant of the genus Impatiens XVIII. – L. *balsamum* – Gr. *bálsamon*; perh. of Semitic origin (cf. Arab. *balasān*). Taken into many Eur. langs.: e.g. OE. *balsam, -zam, -zama* or *-e,* OHG. *balsamo* (MHG., G. *balsam*), MDu. *balseme,* OIcel. *balsamr,* Goth. *balsan*; for the Rom. forms see BALM.

baltimore bō·ltimōəɹ N. Amer. bird of the starling family. XVIII. f. name of Lord *Baltimore,* governor of Maryland (d. 1647). ('The Baltimore Bird hath its Name from being of the same Colour with Lord Baltimore's Coat of Arms', Phil. Trans. XXVI 432.)

baluster bæ·ləstəɹ one of a series of short moulded shafts supporting a coping or rail. XVII. – F. *balustre* – It. *balaustro,* ult. f. L. *balaustium* – Gr. *balaústion* blossom of the wild pomegranate, one feature of the pillar or column resembling the double-curving calyx tube of this. See BANISTER. **balustrADE** bæləstrei·d. XVII. – F. *balustrade,* after It. *balaustrata,* Sp. *balaustrada.*

bambino bæmbī·nou image of the Infant Jesus. XVIII. It., dim. of *bambo* silly, f. base **bamb-* as in late L. *bambalō* stammerer, Gr. *bambaínein, bambalízein* stammer.

bamboo bæmbū· giant grass, Bambusa. XVI (*bambus, -os, -ous*). In early forms – Du. *bamboes* (whence G. *bambus*), modL. *bambusa,* alteration, with unexpl. *b-* and *-s,* of Pg. (– Malay) *mambu* (also in Eng. use XVII–XVIII). *Bamboo* (= F. *bambou,* Sp., Pg. *bambu,* It. *bambù*) was deduced from *bambos,* which was taken as a pl.

bamboozle bæmbū·zl hoax, humbug. XVIII (Cibber, 1703). Included by Swift in 'Tatler' No. 230 among slang terms recently come into vogue; prob. of cant origin; cf. Sc. *bum-, bombaze* perplex (XVII) and the contemp. short form *bam* (*bamb*).

ban[1] bæn. In the earliest uses 'proclamation, summons to arms', 'body of vassals summoned' (XIII), partly aphetic of ME. *iban,* OE. *ġebann* (cf. OHG. *pan, ban,* ON. *bann*), partly – OF. *ban* – Germ. **bann-* of **bannan* BAN[2], whence late L. *bannus, bannum*; in the sense 'proclamation of marriage' only pl. BANNS; the later senses 'anathema, curse' and 'denunciation, prohibition' (XV) are prop. a separate word, f. BAN[2].

ban[2] bæn †summon; curse, denounce. OE. *bannan,* pt. *bēonn,* pp. *bannen* = OFris. *banna,* MLG., MDu. *bannen,* OHG. *bannan,*

ON. *banna* :- CGerm. (exc. Goth.) **bannan*; IE. **bhă-* is repr. also by Gr. *phánai* speak, *phásis* PHASE, L. *fārī* speak, *fāma* FAME. The weak inflexion is recorded XIII.

ban[3] bæn governor of military district in Hungary, etc. XVII. – Pers. *bān* lord, master; brought to Europe by the Avars.

banal bæ·nəl, bei·nəl, bənā·l pert. to all the tenants of a feudal jurisdiction XVIII; open to all, (hence) commonplace XIX. – (O)F. *banal* (in mod. sense XVIII), f. *ban* BAN[1]; see -AL.

banana bənā·nə (fruit of) the tree Musa sapientum, bearing finger-like berries. XVI. – Sp., Pg. *banana* (the fruit; the tree is *banano*), given by De Orta (1563) and Pigafetta (1591) as the native name in the Congo; referred by some to Arab. *banān* fingers, *banāna* finger or toe, but the coincidence of form may be fortuitous.

band[1] bænd that with or by which a person or thing is bound. XIII (Orm). – ON. *band* = OFris., OS. *band*, OHG. *bant* (Du., G. *band*) :- Germ. **bandam*, f. base **band-* of **bindan* BIND; superseded OE. *bend* BEND[1] in the sense 'fetter' and replaced mainly by BOND in the fig. sense 'restraint, binding agreement'. Now assoc. with BAND[2].

band[2] bænd strip, stripe. XV. – (O)F. *bande*, earlier *bende* (cf. BEND[1]) = Pr., It., medL. *benda* – Germ. **bendōn* (OHG. *binda*), f. **bendan*, **bindan* BIND.

band[3] bænd company XV; company of musicians XVII. – (O)F. *bande* = Pr., Sp., It., medL. *banda*, prob. of Germ. origin and assoc. with medL. *banda* scarf, *bandum* banner (cf. Goth. *bandwa* sign), also company, crowd. The var. *bende* (– OF. *bende*) was in regular use from late XV to early XVII. Hence **band** vb. XVI. Cf. DISBAND.

bandage bæ·ndidʒ strip of material for binding. XVI. – F. *bandage*, f. *bande* BAND[1]; see -AGE.

bandalore bændəlɔ̄ə·ɹ toy containing a coiled spring, which caused it when thrown down to rise again to the hand. XIX. Of unkn. origin.

bandanna bændæ·nə coloured handkerchief with spots left white or yellow. XVIII (*bandanno*). prob. through Pg. *bandana* from Hind. (cf. *bāndhnū* mode of dyeing in which the cloth is tied in different places to prevent parts of it from receiving the dye).

bandeau bændou· head- or hair-band. XVIII (also †*bandore*). – F. *bandeau*, OF. *bandel*, dim. of *bande* BAND[2].

banderole bæ·ndəroul narrow flag, streamer. XVI (*banaroll*, *bannerol*, *-all*). – F. *banderole*, earlier *banerolle* – It. *banderuola*, dim. of *bandiera* BANNER.

bandicoot bæ·ndikūt large Indian rat. XVIII. corruption of Telugu *pandikokku* 'pig-rat'.

bandit bæ·ndit pl. **bandits, banditti** bændi·ti lawless marauder. XVI (Sh., Nashe). The earliest forms are *bandito*, pl. *banditi*, also *bandetto*, pl. *-oes*, *bandittoes*; sg. *bandit* (cf. F. *bandit* XVII), pl. *bandits*, *banditti* all date from XVII. ult. – It. *bandito*, pl. *-iti*, sb. use of pp. of *bandire* ban = medL. *bannīre* proclaim, prescribe, BANISH. The later currency is largely due to literature concerning organized gangs of marauders in southern Europe. The word has become CEur.

bandog bæ·ndɔg chained dog; mastiff. XV (*band dogge*). f. BAND[1] (fetter, chain) + DOG; cf. *tie-dog*.

bandoleer bændŏliə·ɹ broad belt worn over one shoulder and across the breast. XVI. – Du. *bandelier*, or its source F. *bandoulière*, dial. *bandroulière*, prob. f. *banderole* BANDEROLE; cf. It. *bandoliera*, Sp. *bandolera*.

bandore bændɔ̄ə·ɹ stringed lute-like instrument. XVI (also *bandora* XVI–XVII; Gascoigne, 1563, has *bandurion*). immed. origin doubtful; the nearest forms are Du. *bandoor*, Sp. *bandurria*, It. *pandora*, *-ura* – late L. *pandūrium* – Gr. *pandoûra* PANDORA. Cf. MANDOLIN, BANJO.

bandy[1] bæ·ndi. XVI. Formerly (i) a special form of tennis, (ii) a stroke with a racket; later, the game of hockey, hockey-stick; obscurely rel. to next.

bandy[2] bæ·ndi throw, toss; exchange (blows, etc.); †band together; †contend. XVI. contemp. with synon. †*band* (XVI–XVIII); both may be – F. *bander* 'to bandie at Tennis', 'to bandy or oppose himself against' (Cotgr.), corr. to It. *bandare* 'to side or bandy' (Florio), and Sp. *bandear* 'to bandy, follow a faction, . . to become factious' (Minsheu), perh. f. *bande*, *banda* side (BAND[3]). If the immediate source is F., the extension of the stem by means of *-y* may be paralleled in OCCUPY, F. *occuper*.

bandy[3] bæ·ndi curved inwards. XVII. perh. adj. use of *bandy* hockey-stick (see BANDY[1]).

bane bein †murderer; poison (surviving in names of poisonous plants, *dogbane*, *fleabane*, *henbane*, *leopard's bane*, *ratsbane*, *wolf's bane*); murder, destruction, ruin. OE. *bana* = OFris. *bona*, OS., OHG. *bano*, ON. *bani* (Sw., Da. *bane* death, murder) :- Germ. **banon*; cf. Goth. *banja*, ON., OE. *ben* :- Germ. **banjō*; the ulterior connexions are uncertain.

bang bæŋ sb., vb., int. XVI. imit.; perh. immed. – Scand. (cf. ON. *bang* hammering, *banga* hammer); LG. has *bangen*, *bangeln* beat.

bang var. of BHANG.

bangle bæ·ŋgl bracelet, anklet. XIX. – Hind. *bangrī*, *bangrī* orig. coloured glass bracelet.

banian, banyan bæ·njən Hindu trader, esp. one from Guzerat settled in an Arabian port (the caste abstains from animal food, whence the nautical use of *banian day* for a meatless day) XVI; Indian fig-tree, Ficus indica XVII. – Pg. *banian* or Arab. *banyān* – Gujarati *vāṇiyo* (pl. *vāṇiyān*) man of the trading caste :– Skr. *vāṇija* merchant. The application of the name to the tree was first made by Europeans to an individual tree of the species growing near Gombroon on the Persian Gulf, under which the Hindu traders of the port had built a pagoda.

banish bæ·niʃ compel to leave the country. XIV (Barbour, Ch.; but earlier in comp. pp. *forbannuste*, after OF. *forbannir*). – OF. *baniss-*, lengthened stem (see -ISH²) of *banir* (mod. *bannir*) :– Rom. *bannīre – Germ. *bannjan, f. *bann- BAN¹. Hence **ba·nish-MENT**. XV.

banister bæ·nistəɹ (usu. pl.) posts and handrail(s) guarding the side of a staircase. XVII. Also *bannister*, later form of †*barrister* (XVII), alteration of BALUSTER, partly by assoc. with BAR. ¶ Regarded as improper or vulgar by writers of the early XIX long after its acceptance in good usage.

banjo bæ·ndʒou, bændʒou· instrument of the guitar type with a resonating back of parchment. XVIII (*banjer*, *-jore*, earlier *banshaw*). – Negro slave pronunc. *banjō·*, *banjo·re* of BANDORE. Hence **banjulele** bændʒulei·li XX, by conflation with *ukulele*.

bank¹ bæŋk raised ridge XII (*bannke*, Orm); bordering slope XIII. – ON. *banki (OIcel. *bakki* ridge, bank; ODa. *banke*; Sw. *backe*, Da. *bakke* hillock, ascent) :– Germ. *baŋkon, rel. to *baŋkiz BENCH.

bank² bæŋk †bench XIII; tier of oars XVII. – (O)F. *banc* bench (= Pr. *banc*, Sp., It. *banco*), Rom. deriv. of Germ. *baŋk- BANK¹, BENCH.

bank³ bæŋk †counter or shop of a money-changer XV; sum or stock of money (surviving in the *bank* of the gaming-table) XVI; establishment for the custody of money XVII. – F. *banque*, or its source It. *banca*, also *banco* = Pr. *banc*, *banca*, Sp. *banco*, *banca*, medL. *bancus*, *banca* – Germ. *baŋk- (OHG., MHG. *banc* is both masc. and fem.); cf. BANK¹ and ². So **ba·nker** †money-changer, usurer XVI; proprietor of a bank XVII. – (O)F. *banquier* (cf. It. *banchiere*, AL. *bancārius*), f. *banque*; see -ER².

bankrupt bæ·ŋkrəpt. XVI (*banke rota*, *banque-*, *banckrou(p)t*, *-route*). The orig. meaning 'bankruptcy' is found esp. in phr. †*make bankeroute* (= F. *faire banqueroute*, Du. *een bankroet maken*); like F. *banqueroute*, G. *bankerott* (earlier *banca-*, *banckorotta*), and Du. *bankroet* (earlier *bamkeroet*) – It. *banca rotta* lit. 'bench or table broken', said to be the sign of a money-changer's insolvency. The forms in Eng. were infl. later by F. *banqueroute*, and further by L. *ruptus* broken, in medL. ruined, broken, or insolvent man. See BANK³, RUPTURE. The transference of the word from the action or state to the person is paralleled in Du. *bankroet zijn*, G. *bankerott werden* be bankrupt. Hence as vb. XVI. **bankruptcy** bæ·ŋkrəpᵗsi. c. 1700; preceded by †*bankrupting*, †*-ism*, †*-ship*, †*bankrupture*.

Banksian bæ·ŋksiən XIX. f. name of Sir Joseph and Lady *Banks*, designating a Chinese species of climbing rose, and the Labrador pine, Pinus banksiana; see -IAN.

banner bæ·nəɹ royal, knightly, ecclesiastical, etc., standard, ensign, or flag. XIII. – AN. *banere*, OF. *baniere* (mod. *bannière*) for *bandiere (= Pr. *bandieira*, *banieira*, It. *bandiera*, Sp. *bandera*, Pg. *bandeira*) :– Rom. *bandāria, f. medL. *bandum* standard, f. Germ. base repr. in Goth. *bandwa*, *bandwō* sign; some Rom. forms are due to crossing with medL. *bannum*, *bannīre* BAN¹ and ².

banneret bæ·nəret knight entitled to bring vassals into the field under his own banner; order of knights extinct after 1611. XIII. ME. *baneret*, f. OF. *baneret*, f. *banere* BANNER + *-et* :– L. *-ātu-s* -ATE².

bannock bæ·nək flat round cake. XV. OE. *bannuc* (recorded once); XV in north. Eng.; XVI in Sc. (whence prob. Gael. *bannach*, *bonnach*); perh. orig. – OBrit. word repr. by Bret. *bannach*, *banne* drop, bit, Cornish *banna* drop.

banns bænz proclamation (of marriage). XIV (*bane*, pl. *banes*, later *baines*, from XVI *bann(e)s*). pl. of BAN¹, after medL. pl. *banna*.

banquet bæ·ŋkwit (ceremonial) feast. XV. – (O)F. *banquet* (whence also G., Du. *banket*), dim. of *banc* bench (BANK²), corr. to It. *banchetto*, dim. of *banco*; the orig. application seems to have been to a slight meal taken on the domestic bench (cf. the obs. Eng. senses 'slight repast between meals', 'course of sweetmeats or dessert').

banshee bæ·nʃī spirit whose wail portends death. XVIII (*benshi*, *ben-shie*). – Ir. *bean sidhe*, OIr. *ben side*, i.e. *ben* woman (see QUEAN), *side* fairies.

bant bænt reduce by the Banting method. Back-formation from *Banting* (taken as vbl. sb.), name of a London cabinet-maker who published (1864) a method of reducing corpulence.

bantam bæ·ntəm small variety of domestic fowl. XVIII. app. f. name of a district (*Bāntān*) of n.w. Java, but the fowls are not native there.

banter bæ·ntəɹ ridicule good-humouredly; also sb. XVII (the vb. is used by Pepys, 'Diary' 24 Dec. 1667). Of unkn. origin; its introduction and vogue are referred to by Locke ('An Essay concerning Human Understanding' III ix § 7) and Swift ('Tale of a Tub, Apol.', and 'Tatler' No. 230).

bantling bæ·ntliŋ young child, formerly with implication of 'bastard'. XVI. perh. corruptly – G. *bänkling* bastard (f. *bank* bench, BANK[2]), lit. 'child begotten on a bench' (cf. BASTARD); see -LING[1].

Bantu bæ·ntu designation of an extensive group of Negro languages of Africa south of the Equator. XIX. – pl. of Bantu *muntu* man, in which *-ntu* orig. signified 'object' or 'person'.

banxring bæ·ŋksriŋ squirrel-like insectivorous animal. XIX. – Javanese *bangsring*.

banzai bænzai·. XX. Jap. cheer, lit. 'ten thousand years'.

baobab bā·obæb Ethiopian sour gourd. XVII. acc. to Prosper Alpinus (1592) an Ethiopian tree; prob. the name is from some dialect of Central Africa.

baptise, -ize bæptai·z christen. XIII (RGlouc.). – (O)F. *baptiser* – ecclL. *baptizāre* – Gr. *baptízein*, f. *báptein* dip; see -IZE. So **baptism** bæ·ptism ceremony or rite of baptising. XIII (Cursor M.). ME. *baptem(e)* (in Sc. till XVII) – OF. *ba(p)teme, -esme* (now *baptême*), semi-pop. – ecclL. *baptismus* – Gr. *baptismós*, f. *baptízein*; assim. later to the Gr.-L. form. **Baptist** bæ·ptist name of John, forerunner of Jesus Christ; XII (*seint iohan baptiste*); – (O)F. *baptiste* – ecclL. *baptista* – ecclGr. *baptistḗs*; see -ISM, -IST. One of a Protestant body known earlier as Anabaptists (perh. originating in the appellation '*Baptized* Churches', etc.) XVII. **baptistery** bæ·ptistri. XIII. – OF. *baptisterie* – ecclL. *baptistērium* – ecclGr. *baptistḗrion*, f. *baptízein*.

bar bāɹ A. rod; B. barrier. XII. – (O)F. *barre* = Pr., Sp., It. *barra* :– Rom. **barra*, of unkn. origin. The earliest sense recorded in Eng. is 'rod of metal or wood for fastening a gate or the like'; the application to the barrier of courts of justice dates from XIV, to the bar of inns of court and the counter of an inn, etc. from XVI. So **bar** vb. XIII, cf. BARRISTER – (O)F. *barrer*, f. *barre*.

barb[1] bāɹb beard-like appendage, etc.; recurved process (of arrow). XIV. (O)F. *barbe* :– L. *barba* BEARD.

barb[2] bāɹb Barbary horse and pigeon. XVII. – F. *barbe* – It. *barbero* of Barbary, a country of northern Africa (cf. BERBER).

Barbado(e)s bāɹbei·douz name of a British island in the W. Indies, said to be f. Pg. *las barbadas* fem. pl. 'the bearded', epithet applied by the Portuguese to the Indian fig-trees growing there.

barbaresque bāɹbəre·sk pert. to Barbary; barbarous. XIX. – F. *barbaresque* – It. *barbaresco*, f. *Barbaria* (ult. f. Arab. *Barber*, BERBER), which was identified with L. *barbaria, barbariēs* land of barbarians, MGr. *barbariā* (cf. next); see -ESQUE.

barbaric bāɹbæ·rik uncivilized XV (Caxton); not Greek or Roman, foreign XIX. (Once as sb. in Wycl. Bible.) – F. *barbarique* or L. *barbaricus* – Gr. *barbarikós*, f. *bárbaros* foreign (esp. non-Greek-speaking), rude, prob. orig. referring to unintelligible speech, rel. to Skr. *barbaras* stammering (cf. L. *balbus*). So **barbar**IAN -bɛə·riən adj. and sb. XV (first in Sc.). – F. *barbarien* or L. **barbariānus*, extended forms (after *chrétien, christiānus* CHRISTIAN) of (O)F. *barbare*, L. *barbarus* – Gr. *bárbaros*. **ba·rbar**ISM. XVI. – (O)F. – L. – Gr. **barbar**OUS bā·ɹbərəs. XV. f. L. *barbarus*. Earlier are †*barbar* adj. and sb. (XIV, Wycl. Bible), †*barbary* barbarian nationality, etc. (XIII). – OF. *barbarie* or L. *barbaria, -iēs* land of barbarians, barbarity; see -Y[3].

barbecue bā·ɹbikjū framework for sleeping on or roasting a carcass; animal roasted whole; entertainment at which animals are roasted whole, etc. XVII. – Sp. *barbacoa* – Haitian *barbacòa* framework of sticks set on posts. Also vb. (XVII), dry flesh, cook an animal whole, on a barbecue; var. **barbecute** (XVII), app. after F. *babracot*.

barbed bāɹbd (arch.) caparisoned. XVI. Alteration of †*barded* (XVI), f. BARD[2], after F. *bardé*; see -ED.

barbel bā·ɹbəl freshwater fish. XIV (Ch.). – OF. *barbel* (mod. *barbeau*) :– late L. *barbellus* (cf. medL. *barbulus*), dim. of *barbus* barbel (It., Sp. *barbo*), f. *barba* BEARD; so named from the flesh filaments depending from its mouth.

barber bā·ɹbəɹ hairdresser. XIII. – AN. *barber, barbour*, OF. *barbeor* :– medL. *barbātōrem*, f. *barba* BEARD; see -ER[1], -ER[2].

barberry bā·ɹbəri (fruit of) shrub of the genus Berberis. XV (*barbere, barbaryn*). – OF. *berberis*, corr. to It. *berberi*, Sp. *berberis*, medL. *barbaris*; assim. early to BERRY.

barbette bāɹbe·t platform or mound within a fortification. XVIII. F., dim. of *barbe* beard; see -ETTE.

barbican bā·ɹbikæn outer fortification. XIII. – (O)F. *barbacane* = Pr., Sp. *barbacana*, Pg. *barbacão*, It. *barbacane*, medL. *barbacana*, of unkn. origin.

barcarolle bā·ɹkəroul Venetian boat-song. XVIII. – F. *barcarole* – Venetian It. *baracruola*, rel. to *barcaruolo* gondolier, f. *barca* BARQUE.

bard[1] bāɹd. XIV (Sc., as a personal designation). – Gael., Ir. *bárd*, W. *bardd* :– OCelt. **bardos* (whence Gr. *bárdos*, L. *bardus*). Until late XVI found only in Sc. writings or in forms repr. W. *bardd*, and applied to Celtic minstrel poets or strolling minstrels; the application to poets gen. (XVII) is after Lucan, 'Pharsalia' I 449 ('Plurima securi fudistis carmina, bardi').

bard[2] bāɹd horse armour. XV. – (O)F. *barde*, corr. to Pr., It., Pg. *barda*, Pr. *aubarda*, Sp., Pg. *albarda* used in various senses connected with the furniture of a horse – Arab. (*al*)*barda'ah* stuffed pack-saddle. Corruptly *barb* (XVI–XVII), whence BARBED.

bare bɛəɹ uncovered. OE. *bær* = OFris., OS., (O)HG. *bar*, MDu. *baer* (Du. *baar*), ON. *berr* :– CGerm. (not in Goth.) **bazaz* :– IE. **bhosós* (whence Lith. *bãsas*, OSl. *bosŭ* barefoot); cf. Arm. *bok* naked (:– **bhosko-*).

barège barei·ʒ woollen fabric. XIX. F., f. *Barèges*, name of a village of Hautes-Pyrénées, France, the place of origin.

bareserk var. of BERSERK.

bargain bā·ɹgin chaffering, etc. XIV. – OF. *bargaignier* trade, dispute, hesitate (mod. *barguigner* hesitate) = Pr. *barganhar*, It. *bargagnare*, medL. *barcaniāre*, prob. – Germ. **borganjan*, extended form of **borgan* (OHG. *borgēn* look after, in MHG., G. give or take on loan, borrow); but the vowel *-a-* of the first syll. is not explained. So **ba·rgain** sb. XIV. – OF. *bargaine*, *-ga(i)gne* fem., *bargaing* m. (cf. Pr. *barganha*, *barganh*, It. *bargagno*, Pg. *barganha*). Sc. (from XIV to XVII) has the particular sense of 'struggle, fight' for vb. and sb.

barge bāɹdʒ long heavy boat. XIII (Cursor M.). – (O)F. *barge*, possibly :– medL. **barica*, f. Gr. *bâris* Egyptian boat; cf. BARQUE. Hence **bargee** bāɹdʒī· barge-man. XVII. f. BARGE + -EE[2] (used irregularly).

barilla bəri·lʲə impure alkali. XVII. – Sp. *barrilla*, dim. of *barra* BAR.

baritone bæ·ritoun (mus.) male voice of a compass intermediate between tenor and bass; †deep-toned instrument XVII; baritone singer; kind of saxhorn XIX. – It. *baritono* – Gr. *barútonos* BARYTONE. Formerly also *barytone*; cf. F. *baryton* (XIX).

barium bɛə·riəm (chem.) metallic element. 1808 (H. Davy). f. BARYTA; see -IUM.

bark[1] bāɹk utter the sharp explosive cry characteristic of a dog. OE. *beorcan*, pt. **bearc*, pp. *borcen* :– **berkan*, perh. metathetic var. of Germ. **brekan* BREAK (for the sense-development cf. L. *fragor* crackling noise, din, f. **frag-* BREAK). Strong forms of the pt. survived till XV; str. pp. *borken* occurs once in Ch. Hence **bark** sb. XVI; preceded by OE. (*ġe*)*beorc*, *bercæ*, *byrce*, and ME. *berk*.

bark[2] bāɹk outer rind of a tree. XIII. – ON. **barkuz*, OIcel. *bǫrkr* (Sw., Da. *bark*), perh. rel. to BIRCH. The native word is RIND[1]. Hence **bark** vb. tan with bark. XV.

bark[3] see BARQUE.

Barker's mill bā·ɹkəɹz mil mechanical contrivance for producing rotary motion. The alleged inventor, a Dr. *Barker*, is assigned to XVII, but has not been identified.

barley[1] bā·ɹli the cereal Hordeum sativum. OE. *bærlic*, of adj. form and so used in *bærlice croft* field of barley, ME. *barrliȝ lafess* (Orm) barley loaves; first as a sb. in 'Peterborough Chronicle' an. 1124; f. OE. *bære*, *bere* barley (cf. BARN) + *-lic* -LY[1]; other Germ. forms are ON. *barr* barley, Goth. *barizeins* of barley. The IE. base **bhar-* is widespread; cf. L. *far*, *farr-* spelt, whence *farīna* (:– **farsīnā*) flour (cf. FARINACEOUS), OSl. *brašŭno* food, Russ. *bórošno* rye flour.

barley[2] bā·ɹli (dial.) call for a truce in games. XVI (? XIV). First recorded in Sc. *barlafumill*, unless *barlay* in 'Gawain and the Green Knight' l. 296 is an instance; of unkn. origin. It is perh. the first el. of **barley-break** (also Sc. *breaks*) XVI, a game resembling prisoner's base, and of Sc. †*barlacheis*, *-chois*.

barm[1] bāɹm (dial.) bosom, lap. OE. *barm* (*bearm*) = OFris., OS., OHG. *barm*, ON. *barmr*, Goth. *barms* :– CGerm. **barmaz*, f. **bar-*, rel. to **beran* BEAR[2].

barm[2] ·bāɹm yeast. OE. *beorma* :– **bermon*, prob. orig. a CLG. word (cf. Fris. *berme*, *barm*, LG. *barm*, *barme*, *borme*), whence G. *bärme*, Sw. *barma*, Da. *bärme*; ult. rel. to L. *fervēre* boil, *fermentum* FERMENT.

barmy bā·ɹmi frothy XV; flighty, empty-headed, daft XVII. f. BARM[2] + -Y[1]. In the fig. sense also BALMY.

barn bā·ɹn building for storing grain. OE. *bern*, *beren*, earlier *berern*, f. *bere* (BARLEY[1]) + *ern*, *ærn* (= OFris. *ern*, ON. *rann*, Goth. *razn*) house, f. base **ras-* of REST[1].

barnacle[1] bā·ɹnəkl A. wild goose Anas leucopsis XII (Neckam); B. pedunculate cirriped XVI. orig. *bernak*, *-ek*(*ke*), corr. to medL. *bernaca*, *-eca*, the apparent source of F. *bernaque*, mod. Pr., Pg. *bernaca*, Sp. *berneca*; *barnacle* dates from XV and is paralleled by F. *barnacle*, *bernacle*, †*bernicle*, but may be of independent origin: ult. source unkn. ¶ The two meanings depend upon an early belief that the goose was generated from a shellfish, which acc. to some accounts grew on a tree.

barnacle[2] bā·ɹnəkl bit for horse, etc. XIV (Wycl. Bible, Trevisa); pl. spectacles XVI. ME. *bernacle*, *barnackle*, alteration of AN. *bernac* (also in Eng. glossaries XV), of unkn. origin; perh. after OF. *bernicles* (Joinville) Saracen instrument of torture. The sense 'spectacles' may perh. be due to assocn. with another word; cf. F. *besicles*, formerly *bericles*.

barometer bərɔ·mitəɹ instrument for measuring atmospheric pressure. XVII (Boyle). f. Gr. *báros* weight + *métron* measure (-METER). Hence **barometr**IC bærŏme·trik XIX, **-me·tr**ICAL XVII. So **ba·ro**GRAPH XIX, †**ba·ro**SCOPE XVII.

barometz bæ·rəmets woolly fern, Cibotium barometz, called also Scythian Lamb.

XVII (*bonarets, boraneth, boranez*). – Russ. *barānets*, dim. of *barán* ram.

baron bæ·rən (hist.) man holding from the king or other superior; one of the lowest grade of nobility XII; judge of the exchequer XIV. – AN. *barun*, (O)F. *baron*, acc. of *ber* = Pr. *bar*, acc. *baron* (whence Sp. *baron*, It. *barone*), Sp. *varon*, Pg. *varão* man :– medL. *barō, -ōnem* man, male, warrior, in the sense 'mercenary' fantastically derived by Isidore from Gr. *barús* 'gravis', and identified by scholiasts and others with L. *bārō* simpleton, dunce (Cicero, etc.), but of unkn. origin. The sense 'undivided double sirloin of beef' (XVIII) is prob. a joc. elaboration of *Sir Loin* XVII (see SIRLOIN). So **ba·ronAGE** body of barons. XIII. ME. *barnage* – OF. *barnage*, medL. *barōnāgium*. **ba·roness.** XV (*barnesse*). – OF. *baronesse, barronnesse* (AL. *baronissa*); see -ESS[1]. **ba·ronET** †lesser baron (sometimes synon. with BANNERET) XIV; man of the rank below baron, instituted 1611. – AL. *barōnettus*. **ba·ronRY** XV, **ba·rony** XIII domain or rank of a baron. – OF. *baronie*, AL. *baronia* (XII); see -Y[3].

baroque, barrok bərɔ·k, -ou·k whimsical, odd XVIII; spec. of (i) irregular pearls, (ii) a florid style of Renaissance architecture XIX. – F. *baroque* (in earliest use of pearls) – Pg. *barroco*, Sp. *barrueco*, of unkn. origin; as applied to architecture (orig. that of Francesco Borromini) – It. *barroco*.

barouche bərū·ʃ four-wheeled carriage. XIX. – G. dial. *barutsche* – It. *baroccio* (Sp. *barrocho*), for **biroccio* 'two-wheeled' – late L. **birotium* (*birodium*), f. L. *birotus*, f. *bi-* BI- + *rota* wheel (see ROTATION).

barque, bark bāɹk small sailing-vessel XV; boat XVI; three-masted vessel XVII. – (O)F. *barque*, prob. – Pr. *barca* :– late L. *barca* (so Sp., It.), of which a collateral form **barica* may be repr. by BARGE. The sp. *barque* is now regular in techn. use.

barquentine bā·ɹkəntīn small barque. XVII. f. BARQUE, after BRIGANTINE.

barrack[1] bæ·rək soldiers' quarters. XVII (*barraque*). – F. *baraque* – It. *baracca* or Sp. *barraca* soldier's tent, of unkn. origin.

barrack[2] bæ·rək banter, chaff. Also vb. XIX. Alteration of native (New South Wales) *borak* (phr. *to poke borak*).

barrage bā·ridʒ, bæ·ridʒ, bæ·rāʒ bar in a watercourse XIX; curtain of artillery fire XX. – F. *barrage*, f. *barrer* BAR.

barrator bæ·rətōɹ †fraudulent dealer; †fighter; mover of litigation. XIV. – AN. *baratour*, OF. *barateor* cheat, trickster, f. *barater* (= Pr., OSp., Pg. *baratar*, It. *barattare*) :– Rom. **prattāre* exchange, cheat – Gr. *prắttein* do, perform, manage, practise (sometimes dishonestly); the deriv. OF. *barat, barate* (whence ME. *barat, baret* deception, trouble, distress, strife) corr. to Pr. *barat*, It. *baratto*, etc.; ON. *barátta* contest, fighting (from Rom.) perh. influenced the ME. word. So **ba·rratRY** purchase of preferment or office XV; fraud or criminal negligence by a ship's master XVII. – OF. *bar(a)terie* = Pr. *barataria, baratteria*.

barrel bæ·rəl A. cask XIV; B. applied to various cylindrical objects XVI. – (O)F. *baril* = Pr. *baril*, It. *barile* (medL. *barriclus, barillus, barile*); plausibly taken by Diez to be a deriv. of *barra* BAR. ¶ W. *baril*, Gael. *baraill*, etc. are from Eng.

barren bæ·rən incapable of offspring. XIII (*barain*). – AN. (fem.) *barai(g)ne*, OF. *barhaine, brahai(g)ne, brehai(g)ne* (mod. *bréhaigne*), of unkn. origin.

barricade bærikei·d hastily constructed obstruction to stop an enemy. XVII. Earlier *barricado* (XVI) – F. *barricade* (whence Sp. *barricada*, It. *barricata*), f. *barrique* – Sp. *barrica* cask, f. stem of *barril* BARREL; the first barricades in Paris (*la journée des barricades* 1588) were composed of barrels filled with earth, paving-stones, etc. Hence **barrica·de** vb. XVI, after F. *barricader*. See -ADE, -ADO.

barrier bæ·riəɹ fence barring passage. XIV (*barere*). – AN. *barrere*, (O)F. *barrière* = Pr., It. *barriera*, Sp. *barrera* :– Rom. **barrāria*, coll. deriv. of *barra* BAR; see -IER. The sp. was later conformed to that of Continental French.

barring bā·riŋ excepting. XV. prep. use of prp. of BAR vb. exclude, except; see -ING[2].

barrister bæ·ristəɹ lawyer practising as an advocate in courts of law. XVI (Act 2 Hen. VIII c. 13 s. 3). Earliest form *barrester*, obscurely f. BAR, perh. after †*legister* lawyer, or *minister*. ¶ A student of the law when admitted a barrister is technically 'called to the bar', which orig. had reference to the bar or barrier separating the seats of benchers or readers from the rest of the hall, and to which students were 'called' from the body of the hall to take part in moots.

barrow[1] bæ·rou †mountain; grave-mound. OE. *beorg* = OFris., OS., OHG. (Du., G.) *berg* :– Germ. **bergaz* (cf. ON. *berg, bjarg* n. rock, precipice, Goth. *bairgahei* hill country); IE. **bhergh-* is repr. also by OSl. *brěgŭ* overhanging bank, Av. *barəzan-* height, Arm. *berj*; for another var. of the base see BOROUGH. In gen. literary use obs. before 1400; survived locally, in the north as *bargh*, in the west and south as *barrow*, whence the use of the latter by archæologists, being generalized from the barrows of Salisbury Plain, etc.

barrow[2] bæ·rou castrated boar. OE. *barg* (*bearg*) = OFris., MDu. *barch* (Du. *barg*), OHG. *barug, barc* (G. dial. *barch*), ON. *bǫrgr* :– CGerm. (exc. Goth.) **barguz* or **bargwaz*; not known outside Germ.

barrow[3] bæ·rou frame on which a load can be carried, in early use including bier and stretcher, later restricted to *wheelbarrow* (XIV) and *handbarrow* (XV). OE.

bearwe :– **barwōn*, f. **bar-* **ber-* BEAR². Cf. EFris. *barve*; MHG. *rade-ber(e)* handbarrow :– **barjō*; also ON. fem. pl. *barar* handbarrow, stretcher, funeral bier, and BIER.

barry bā·ri (her.) divided by bars of colours laid alternately. XV. – F. *barré* barred, striped, f. *barre* BAR. So **ba·rrulé, ba·rruly** bæ·rjŭli. XVI; see -Y⁵.

barsac bā·ɹsæk white wine manufactured at *Barsac*, Gironde, France. XIX.

barter bā·ɹtəɹ give in exchange for an equivalent. XV. Form and meaning suggest deriv. from OF. *barater* (see BARRATOR), but connecting links are wanting.

bartizan bā·ɹtizæn battlemented parapet. 1801 (Scott). orig. pseudo-arch. use of Sc. var. (*bartisane*) of BRATTICING.

baryta bərai·tə (chem.) monoxide of barium. XIX. f. BARYTES, with final *a* after *soda*, etc.

barytes bərai·tīz (chem.) native sulphate of barium. XVIII. f. Gr. *barús* heavy, after mineral names in *-ites*; named in ref. to its great weight.

barytone bæ ritoun (Gr. gram.) not having the acute accent on the last syllable. XIX. – Gr. *barútonos*, f. *barús* heavy, (of sound) deep)(*oxús* (cf. OXYTONE), rel. to L. *gravis* GRAVE³ + *tónos* TONE. Cf. BARITONE.

basalt bæ·sōlt, -ɔlt hard trap-rock. XVIII (earlier in L. form). – L. *basaltēs*, in MSS. and editions of Pliny's 'Natural History' var. of *basanītēs* – Gr. *basanítēs* (sc. *líthos* stone), f. *básanos* touchstone.

basan, bazan bæ·zən bark-tanned sheepskin. XVIII. – (O)F. *basane* – Pr. *bazana* – Sp. *badana* (cf. medL. *bedana*) – Arab. *biṭānah* lining, f. *baṭāna* be hidden.

bascule bæ·skjūl apparatus on the lever principle. XVII. – F. *bascule*, earlier *bacule* see-saw, f. stem of *battre* beat + *cul* posteriors.

base¹ beis bottom, foundation. XIV. – (O)F. *base* or L. *basis*; see BASIS. Hence **bas**AL¹ bei·səl, **ba·s**IC XIX; cf. F. *basal*, *basique*. Hence **ba·seball** (BALL¹) national field-game of the U.S.A. XIX; the *base* is the term for each of four stations at the angles of the square called the diamond.

base² beis the game of 'prisoner's base'. XV. prob. for *bars* (bars), pl. of BAR; cf. 'Bace . . . *barri*' (Promp. Parv.). Cf. BASS¹.

base³ beis of low quality or status. XIV. – (O)F. *bas*, fem. *basse* = Pr. *bas*, It. *basso* :– medL. *bassu-s*, *bassa* (expl. by Isidore as 'thick, fat', by Papias as 'short, low'), found in classical times as a cognomen. Hence **ba·se**BORN XVI; cf. *low-born*, ME. *loh iboren* (XIII).

basement bei·smənt foundation, fundamental structure; lowest storey below ground level. XVIII. prob. – Du. †*basement* foundation (Kilian), in WFlem. *bazement*, perh. – It. *basamento* base of a column, etc., f. *basare*, f. *base* BASE¹; see -MENT and cf. (O)F. *soubassement*.

bash bæʃ strike heavily. XVII. ult. imit., perh. a blend of *bang* and ending of *dash*, *smash*, etc.

bashaw bəʃɔ· early form of PASHA.

bashful bæ·ʃfŭl shy. XVI (Udall). f. †*bash* aphetic of ABASH + -FUL¹; for a similar formation on a vb. stem cf. *mournful* (XVI).

bashi-bazouk bæ:ʃibəzū·k mercenary irregular Turkish soldier. XIX. – Turk. *bāshi bōzuk* 'wrong-headed' (*bāsh* head, *bōzuk* turned).

basil bæ·zĭl aromatic plant Ocymum. XV (Caxton). – OF. *basile* – medL. *basilicum* – Gr. *basilikón*, n. of adj. 'royal'.

basilar bæ·silāɹ pert. to the base. XVI. – modL. *basilāris*, irreg. f. *basis* BASE¹.

basilica bəzi·likə church built on the model of a royal palace, oblong with colonnades and an apse. XVI. – L. – Gr. *basilikḗ*, sb. use of fem. of *basilikós* royal, f. *basileús* king.

basilisk bæ·zilisk, bæ·s- fabulous reptile, cockatrice XIV; large cannon XVI. – L. *basiliscus* – Gr. *basilískos*, dim. of *basileús* king; acc. to Pliny, the name is due to a crown-like spot on the reptile's head. In the sense of 'cannon' the Sp. form *basilisco* was also used.

basin bei·s'n hollow circular vessel XIII; deep depression XVIII. ME. *ba(s)cin*, also *-ine* – OF. *bacin* (mod. *bassin*) = Pr., Sp. *bacin*, It. *bacino* :– medL. **bac(c)hinu-s* (cf. *bacchinon* wooden vessel, Gregory of Tours, VI), f. *bacca* 'vas aquarium' (Isidore), perh. of Gaulish origin.

basinet bæ·sinet, **basnet** bæ·snit small headpiece of armour. XIV. – OF. *bacinet*, dim. of *bacin* BASIN; see -ET.

basis bei·sis foundation, support. XIV (Trev.). – L. *basis* – Gr. *básis* stepping, step, pedestal, BASE¹ :– IE. **gwm̥tis* (whence also G. *kunft* coming), f. **gwm̥-* COME.

basistan bæzistā·n, **bezesteen** bezistī·n clothes-market. XVI. – Turk. – Pers. *bazzāzistān*, f. Arab. *bassaz* clothes-dealer (f. *bazz*, Turk. *bez* clothing) + *-istān* place.

bask bàsk A. †bathe (esp. in blood) XIV; B. expose to the heat of the sun, etc. XVI (Sh.); intr. for refl. XVII (Cowley, Dryden). In A mainly in eastern writers (Gower, Lydg., Skelton); of doubtful origin, but usu. referred to ON. **baðask* (later *baðast*), refl. of *baða* BATHE. Cf. BUSK¹.

basket bà·skit vessel of wicker-work with a handle. XIII. In AL. as *baskettum* (XIII–XV), in AN. and OF. as *basket* (gloss on Neckam XIII, 'Roman d'Alexandre', MS. Bodl. 264, an. 1338), of unkn. origin. It has been referred to L. *bascauda* (Juvenal,

Martial), said by Martial to be British (but no OCeltic forms are extant, and the mod. forms are from Eng.) and expl. by Papias as 'washing-tub', 'brazen vessel'; but *bascauda* was repr. by OF. *baschoe*, from which *basche* was a back-formation.

Basque bàsk member of a race inhabiting the slopes of the western Pyrenees; their language. XIX. – F. *Basque* – L. *Vascō* (in pl. *Vascones*, Juvenal, Pliny), which has also given *Gascon*. The Basques' name for themselves is *Eskualdunak*.

bas-relief bāsrilī·f carving in low relief. XVII. Earlier *basse relieve* – It. *basso rilievo* (basso riljē·vo); altered later after F. *bas-relief*.

bass[1] bæs fish of the perch family. XVII. Late ME. (XV) alteration of (dial.) *barse*, OE. *bærs* (*bears*) = MDu., MHG. *bars* (Du. *baars*, G. *barsch*), f. **bars-*, rel. to **bors-* (whence OHG. *burst*, OE. *byrst* bristle); cf. (dial.) *bace*, *base* (XV), and DACE.

bass[2] bæs inner bark; fibre. XVII. Alteration of BAST by suppression of *t*, as in *bast mat*, *bast tree*.

bass[3] beis deep-sounding; (mus.) of the lowest part. XV. orig. identical in form and still in pronunc. with BASE[3]; from XVI assim. in form to It. BASSO.

bass[4] bæs. XIX. Name of manufacturers of the ale and beer so designated, Messrs. *Bass* & Co. of Burton-on-Trent.

basset bæ·sit short-legged breed of dog. XVII. – F. *basset*, f. *bas* low, BASE[3]; see -ET.

basset-horn bæ·sithɔ̄ɹn tenor clarinet. XIX. – G., partial tr. of F. *cor de bassette* – It. *corno di bassetto* (*bassetto* dim. of BASSO BASS[3]).

bassinette bæsine·t baby's cradle with hood at one end. XIX. Earlier sp. *bassinet*, identical in form with F. *bassinet* (see BASINET), which is applied to various basin-shaped objects; in its later sp. *bassinette* infl. by spurious F. *berceaunette* (in Eng. use c. 1860–70), alteration of F. *bercelonnette* (*bar-*) after *berceau* cradle.

basso bæ·sou (mus.) bass. XIX. It.; see BASE[3].

bassoon bəsū·n, bəzū·n bass instrument of the oboe family. XVIII. – F. *basson*, augm. f. *bas* BASS[3]; see -OON.

bast bæst inner bark of the lime. OE. *bæst*, corr. to (M)Du., (O)HG., ON. *bast* :- CGerm. (exc. Gothic) **bastaz*, *-am*, of unkn. origin.

bastard bà·stəɹd illegitimate child. XIII. – OF. *bastard* (mod. *bâtard*) = Pr. *bastard*, It., Sp., Pg. *bastardo* :- medL., Rom. *bastardus*, commonly held to be f. *bastum* BAT[3] + *-ardus* -ARD, which appears to be confirmed by OF. *fils de bas(t)* 'pack-saddle son' (mule-drivers and others using the pack-saddle for a pillow), whence ME. *bast* bastardy, bastard (also in phr. †*abast ibore* borne in bastardy, †*sone abast* bastard son); cf. the origin of such synons. as OF. *coitrart* (f. *coite* QUILT), G. *bankert*, f. (*bank* bench), *bänkling* (see BANTLING), LG. *mantelkind* 'mantle child', ON. *hrísungr* (f. *hrís* brushwood). As a term of legal status *bastardus* was applied to the acknowledged son of a prince or nobleman not born of the lawful wife; cf. *William the Bastard*, a title of William the Conqueror. (The Rom. word passed into all the Continental Germ. langs.) Hence **ba·stardize** XVI. **ba·stard**RY XV, the regular Sc. form for **ba·stardy** XV (cf. AN. *bastardie* XIII); see -IZE, -Y[3].

baste[1] beist sew loosely. XIV (Ch.). – OF. *bastir* = Pr. *bastir* build, prepare, equip, compose, Sp. *bastir*, It. *bastire* build – Germ. **bastjan* (cf. OHG. *besten* lace, sew), f. **bastaz* BAST, the orig. sense being 'put together (as) with bast', hence 'construct, build'. For the sense cf. Sp. *bastear*, *embastar*, It. *imbastire*. A Sc. var. *bais* (XVI) survives as *beass*.

baste[2] beist pour fat over (roasting meat). XV (pp. †*baast*, Sc. inf. *bais*). prob. orig. *base*, the past inflexions being later incorporated as part of the stem. Two F. vbs. in this sense are given by Du Guez (1530), *bastir* 'to cast butter upon rost', and *basser* 'to bast the roste', but these are not corroborated; cf. 'bastyng of meate, *bastiment*, baysting of clothe, *bastiment*' (Palsgr. 1530). The vb. meaning 'beat' (XVI) is prob. identical with this; for a similar transference of sense cf. *anoint*, and G. *schmieren* (i) anoint, (ii) thrash.

bastille bæstī·l bastion, fortress. XIV. – (O)F. *bastille*, prob. refash. of OF. *bastide* (Cotgr. has a mixed form, *bastilde*) – Pr. *bastida*, sb. use of fem. pp. of *bastir* build (cf. BASTE[1]).

bastinado bæstinā·dou beating with a stick (esp. on the soles of the feet). XVI. – Sp. *bastonada* (= It. *bastonata*, OF. *bastonnée*), f. *baston* stick, BATON; see -ADO. The sp. has varied, *-tan-* and *-ton-* being formerly frequent.

bastion bæ·stiən projecting part of a fortification. XVI. – F. *bastion*, earlier *bastillon*, f. *bastille* (see above); cf. It. *bastione*, held by some to be the source of the F. word.

bat[1] bæt A. club, stout stick OE.; B. lump (as in *brickbat*) XIV. Late OE. *batt* 'clava' (whence Ir., Gael. *bat*, *bata* staff, cudgel); some uses may be due to (O)F. *batte* (f. *battre* beat); the source of sense B is entirely obscure and it may belong to a different word. Hence, or directly – (O)F. *battre*, **bat** vb. strike XV; in the sense 'wink' the eyelids perh. a var. of BATE[2].

bat[2] bæt mouse-like winged quadruped. XVI (*a Backe, some call it a Bat*). Alteration of ME. *backe*, *bakke* (surviving till XVII in gen. use, and later dial., also in Sc. *backie*) – Scand. word repr. in MSw. *aftan|bakka*, *nat|bakka* evening or night bat, MDa. *nat(h)|bakke*, beside which is a var. **blaka*, as in ON. *leðrblaka* 'leather-flapper', Sw. *nattblaka*, whence rare ME. *blak*; the change of *k* to *t* (cf. Sw. dial. *nattbatta*) may have been due to assoc. with medL. *blatta*, *blacta*, *batta*.

¶ The native name was *rearmouse* (OE. *hrēremūs*); cf. *flittermouse* (XV) – Du. *vledermuis* = G. *fledermaus* (OHG. *fledarmūs*) 'flutter-mouse', (dial.) *flindermouse* (– Du. *vlinder* butterfly), F. *chauve-souris*, L. *calva sorex* 'bald mouse'.

bat[3] bæt, bā pack-saddle. XV–XVI (only in *bat-needle* packing-needle); XVIII (in *bat-horse*, *-mule*; *bat-money*; BATMAN[2]). – OF. *bat*, earlier *bast* (mod. *bât*) :– medL. *bastum*, perh. f. **bastāre*, ult. based on Gr. *bastázein* bear.

bat[4] bæt colloquial speech of a foreign country (*sling the bat* speak the lingo). XIX (Kipling). Hindi, 'speech, language, word'.

batata bətā·tə sweet potato, Ipomæa Batatas, Batatas edulis. XVI. – Sp. *batata* – Taino *batata*. See POTATO.

batch bætʃ baking. XV. ME. *bac(c)he* :– OE. **bæċċe*, f. *bacan* BAKE; cf. OE. *ġebæċ* baking, thing baked, G. *gebäck*, and for the formation *wæċċe* WATCH, *wacan* WAKE[1].

bate[1] beit †fight; beat the wings. XIII (Cursor M.). – OF. *batre* (mod. *battre*) beat, fight :– Rom. **batere* for L. *batuere* (cf. BATTLE).

bate[2] beit lower, reduce, (now only) moderate, as in *bated breath*; (arch.) except, as in *bating* excepting. XIV. Aphetic of ABATE.

bateau bæ·tou Canadian boat. XVIII. F. :– OF. *batel* (whence It. *battello*, Sp. *batel*), f. OE. *bāt*, ON. *bátr* BOAT.

batells see BATTEL.

bath[1] bàþ bathing, water for bathing in OE.; vessel for bathing in XVI. OE. *bæþ* = OFris. *beth*, OS. *bað*, (O)HG. *bad*, ON. *bað* :– CGerm. (exc. Goth.) **baþam*, perh. f. **ba-* FOMENT (cf. OHG. *bājan*, *bāen*, G. *bähen*). Hence **bath** vb. (XV), a new formation distinct from BATHE, now restricted to the sense 'give a bath to'. The place-name *Bath* was orig. *æt þǣm* (*hātum*) *baþum* at the (hot) baths, *æt Baþum*, whence the indeclinable *Baþum*, *Baþon* (cf. G. *Baden*, orig. d. pl.); in XVIII it was commonly known as 'the Bath'. There are many spec. attrib. uses, as *Bath bun*, *chap* (CHAP[1]), *brick*, *chair* (orig. used at Bath for invalids), *Oliver* (a biscuit named after William Oliver, a physician of Bath, 1695–1764), *stone*. *Bathon* was latinized as *Bathonia*, whence **Bathonian** bāþou·niən. XVIII.

bath[2] bæþ Hebrew liquid measure. XVI. Heb. (in L. *batus*, Gr. *bátos*).

bathe beið immerse in a bath; take a bath. OE. *baþian* = Du. *baden*, OHG. *badōn* (G. *baden*), ON. *baða* :– Germ. **baþōn*, f. **baþam* BATH[1].

bathos bei·þɔs, bæ·þɔs ludicrous descent from the elevated to the commonplace. XVIII (Pope; earlier in Gr. letters). – Gr. *báthos*, f. *bathús* deep (as in *bathymetry* measurement of depths). Hence **bathetic** bəþe·tik. XIX; after *pathos*, *pathetic*.

bathybius bəþi·biəs (zool.) flocculent precipitate of gypsum in the ocean. XIX (Huxley, who at first regarded it as protoplasm). modL., f. Gr. *bathús* deep + *bíos* life (cf. BIO-).

batik bæ·tik decoration on silk, etc. XIX. – Javanese *'mbatik* writing, drawing.

batiste bæti·st cambric. XVII (*baptist cloth*, tr. F. *toile de Batiste*). – F. *batiste*, for *Baptiste*, name of the first maker, who lived at Cambrai.

batman[1] bæ·tmən Oriental weight. XVI. – Turk. *bātmān*, *baṭmān*, *-man* (whence also Russ. *batmán*).

batman[2] bæ·tmən army officer's servant. XVIII. f. BAT[3], as used in *bat-horse*, *-mule* for carrying officers' baggage (F. *cheval de bât*), *bat-money* allowance for carrying baggage; formerly also *baugh-*, *baw-*, repr. the pronunc. ba of F. *bât*.

baton bæ·tn staff, stick (now spec.). XVI (*batton*). – F. *bâton* (earlier †*baston*, which was adopted in Eng. XIII) = Pr., Sp. *baston*, It. *bastone* :– Rom. **bastō(n-)*, f. **bastāre* drive with a stick (cf. L. *burdu|basta* donkey-driver, Petronius), f. late L. *bastum* stick.

batrachian bətrei·kiən (zool.) frog-like. XIX. f. modL. *batrachia* bətrei·kiə, prop. bætrəkai·ə – Gr. *batrákheia* (sc. *zôia* animals), n. pl. of *batrákheios*, f. *bátrakhos* frog; after F. *batracien* (1811); see -IAN.

batta[1] bæ·tə agio, discount. XVII. – Hind. *baṭṭa*, *bāṭṭa*.

batta[2] bæ·tə (military) allowance. XVIII. – Indo-Pg. *bata* – Canarese *bhatta* rice.

battalion bətæ·ljən division of an army. XVI. – F. *battaillon* – It. *battaglione*, augm. of *battaglia* BATTLE. The present sp. was established XVII.

battel, batell bæ·tl † (perh.) provision of commons XV; (pl.) accounts of sums due for provision of board and lodging in colleges of the university of Oxford XVI. In medL. *batellī*, *-illī*, *batellæ* (pl.), of unkn. origin; perh. connected with †*battle* vb. feed, nourish, †*battle* adj. (Sc. and north.) feeding, nourishing, which may be derivs. (with -LE[2]) of *bat-* in BATTEN[2]. Hence **battel** vb. XVI.

batten[1] bæ·tn strip of wood. XV. Earliest forms *batant*, *-ent* (cf. '*batant* .. a batant; the piece of wood, that runnes all along vpon the edge of the lockeside of a doore, gate, or window', Cotgr.) – OF. *batant*, sb. use of prp. of *batre* beat (see BATTERY). For the loss of final *t* cf. *batten* movable bar in a silk-loom (XIX) – F. *battant*.

batten[2] bæ·tn †improve in condition XVI, grow fat, thrive (*on*) XVII (Sh., Jonson); prob. earlier in dial. use. – ON. *batna* improve, get better, f. **bat-* (cf. OE. *ġebatian* get BETTER); see -EN[5].

batter[1] bæ·təɹ beat with repeated blows. XIV. – AN. *baterer*, f. OF. *batre* (mod. *battre*) beat; cf. BAT[1] and see -ER[3].

batter[2] bæ·teɹ paste used in cooking. XV (*bater*, *-our*, *-ure*). prob. f. BATTER[1], but cf. OF. *bat(e)ure* beating, beaten metal.

battery bæ·təri beating (as in *assault and battery*); †battering (as of fortifications by guns); unit of artillery. XVI. – (O)F. *batterie*, f. *battre* beat (= Pr. *batre*, Sp. *batir*, It. *battere*) :– L. *battuere*, later *battere*; see -ERY and cf. Pr. *bataria*, etc.

battle bæ·tl combat XIII (RGlouc., Cursor M.); †battle array, battalion XIV (R. Mannyng). ME. *batai·le* – (O)F. *bataille* = Pr. *batalha*, Cat. *batalla* (whence Sp. *batalla*, Pg. *batalha*), It. *battaglia*, Rum. *bătaie* :– Rom. **battālia*, for late L. *battuālia* military or gladiatorial exercises, f. *battuere* beat (cf. prec.); like other n. pls., e.g. *biblia* BIBLE, *mirābilia* MARVEL, *battalia* was treated as fem. sg. In the sense 'order of battle', 'host' *battalia* (– It. *battaglia*) was current from late XVI (Sh.) to early XIX. So **ba·ttle** vb. XIV. – (O)F. *batailler*.

battledore bæ·tldɔəɹ washing-beetle XV (*batyldo(u)re*, *batyndore*, *badildore*); bat used with a shuttlecock XVI. perh. – Pr. *batedor* beater (cf. Sp. *batidor*), f. *batre* beat (cf. BATTERY), infl. by †*battle* vb. (XVI), f. BAT vb. (see BAT[1]); but the history is obscure.

battlement bæ·tlmənt indented parapet in fortification. XIV. contemp. with †*battled* – pp. of OF. *batailler* fortify with *batailles* fixed or movable turrets of defence (the sense-development from 'battle' is not clear); some forms show assoc. with OF. *bastillement* (f. *bastilier*, *-iller*; cf. BASTILLE). See -MENT.

battleship bæ·tlʃip. 1884. Short for *line-of-battle ship* (XVIII) ship designed to fight in line of battle.

battology bætɔ·lədʒi vain repetition. XVII. – modL. *battologia* – Gr. *battologiā*, f. *battólogos*, f. *báttos* stammerer (cf. the proper name *Battos* in Herodotus IV clv); see -LOGY.

battue bæ·tju beat-up of game. XIX. F. (= Pr. *batuda*, It. *battuta*) :– Rom. **battūta*, sb. use of fem. pp. of L. *battuere* beat (cf. BATTLE).

batty bæ·ti (sl.) crazy, 'balmy'. XX. f. phr. *to have bats in the belfry* to be crazy; see BAT[2], -Y[1].

bauble bɔ̄·bl trinket; jester's baton XIV; trifling matter, 'toy' XVI. ME. *babel*, *babulle* – OF. *babel*, *baubel* child's toy, plaything, of unkn. origin (cf. AL. *baubellum* XII–XIII). The ME. forms are repr. normally by *bable* (XVI–XVII); *bauble* appears first c. 1600.

baudekin bɔ̄·dikin rich brocade. XIV. – OF. *baudekin* – medL. *baldachīnus*; see BALDACCHINO.

baulk var. of BALK.

bauson bɔ̄·sən (dial.) badger. XIV. sb. use of *bausand* – OF. *bausant* having white spots on a dark ground, piebald (sb. piebald horse) = Pr. *bausan* (whence It. *balzano*, whence modF. *balzan*) :– Rom. **balteānus* 'belted', striped, f. L. *balteus* BELT. For the application to the animal cf. the development of F. *blaireau* (see BADGER).

bauxite, beauxite bɔ̄·ksait hydrous oxide of silicon and iron. XIX. – F. *bauxite*, f. Les *Baux*, near Arles, France; see -ITE.

bavin bæ·vin bundle of brushwood. XIV. Of unkn. origin.

bawbee bɔ̄·bi (Sc.) coin equivalent to the Eng. halfpenny. XVI. Named after the laird of Sille*bawby*, mint-master under James V (mentioned in a Treasurer's account of 1541 as Alexander Orok de Sillebawby).

bawd bɔ̄d pander, procuress. XIV (PPl., Ch.). The fuller form *bawdstrot*, Sc. *bald(e)strod* (XIV–XVI) suggests ult. deriv. from OF. *baudetrot*, *baudestroyt* 'pronubus', 'pronuba' (XIII), which seems to be f. *baud* lively, gay (– Germ. **bald-* BOLD) + the word repr. by AN. *trote* old woman, hag (Gower); but the history is obscure and the relation with †*bawdy* dirty, filthy (XIV, PPl.) and †*bawdy* befoul, defile (XIV, Trevisa) is undetermined. ¶ Against a proposed deriv. as an aphetic reduction of *ribald* must be set the prevalent stressing *ri·bald* in the texts in which *bawd* first occurs. Hence **baw·d**RY. XIV (Ch.). **baw·dy** XVI, sb. XVII; see -Y[1].

bawl bɔ̄l †bark; cry vociferously. XV (Promp. Parv.). corr. in form and meaning to medL. *baulāre* bark, of imit. origin; but cf. Icel. *baula* (Sw. *böla*) low, as an ox.

bawn bɔ̄n fortified enclosure; cattlefold. XVI (Spenser). – Ir. *bábhún*, MIr. *bódhún*, f. *bó* cow + *dún* fortress (see TOWN).

bay[1] bei †berry XIV; bay-tree, Laurus nobilis; pl. leaves of this made into a garland XVI. – (O)F. *baie* (= Pr., Sp. *baga*) :– L. *bāca* berry. See also BAYBERRY.

bay[2] bei indentation of the sea. XIV. – (O)F. *baie* – (O)Sp. *bahia*, recorded first as *baia* by Isidore of Seville (VII) and perh. of Iberian origin. See also BAY-SALT.

bay[3] bei opening between columns, etc. XIV; recess XV. – (O)F. *baie*, f. *bayer*, earlier *baer*, *beer* gape, stand open (mod. *béant* wide open) = Pr. *badar*, It. *badare* :– medL. *batāre* (c. 800), of unkn. origin. Hence *bay-window* (XV); cf. *bow-window* (BOW[1]).

bay[4] bei barking of dogs in company XIII; chiefly (now only) in phr. (*hold*, *keep*) *at bay*,

†*at a bay*, (*turn*, *bring*, etc.) to bay XIV. – OF. *bai*, or aphetic deriv. of ME. *abay* (*at abay* being apprehended as *at a bay*) – OF. *abai* (mod. *aboi* in phr. *être* and *mettre aux abois* be and bring to bay; cf. OF. *tenir a bay*, It. *stare* and *tenere a bada*); the F. sbs. are f. *bayer*, *abayer* BAY⁶. The phrases refer to the position of a hunted animal when, driven to extremity, he faces his barking pursuers. ¶ In the sense 'deep bark' (XVI) a new formation on BAY⁶.

bay⁵ bei reddish-brown. XIV (Ch.). –(O)F. *bai* :– L. *badiu-s* (Varro) chestnut-coloured (only of horses), rel. to OIr. *buide* yellow.

bay⁶ bei bark with a deep voice. XIV. Aphetic of †*abaye* – OF. *abaiier* (mod. *aboyer*) = It (*ab*)*baiare*, f. imit. base **bai*-; infl. by BAY⁴.

bayadère bājadɛə·ɹ Hindu dancing-girl. XVIII. F. – Pg. *bailadeira*, f. *bailar* dance, obscurely rel. to medL. *ballāre* (see BALL²).

bayard bei·āɹd bay horse, spec. the magic steed given by Charlemagne to Renaud; a type of blind recklessness. XIV. – OF. *baiard*, f. *bai* BAY⁵; see -ARD.

bayberry bei·be:ri (fruit of) the bay-tree XIV; (fruit of) Pimenta acris XVIII; (fruit of) Myrica cerifera XIX. f. BAY¹+BERRY. Hence **bay rum** bei rʌm (see RUM²); cf. G. *baiöl* 'oleum myricæ'.

bayonet bei·ənet, beiəne·t †short dagger XVII; stabbing instrument for fixing to the muzzle of a rifle XVIII. – F. *baïonnette*, earlier *bayonnette*, said to be f. *Bayonne*, France, the orig. place of manufacture (cf. *bayonnettes de Bayonne*, Tabourot Des Accords, d. 1590); see -ET. The early vars. (XVII; later U.S. dial.) *bagnet*, *bagonet* are not accounted for.

bayou bai·ju outlet of river or lake, etc., in N. America. XVIII. – Amer. F. – Choctaw *bayuk*.

bay-salt bei·sɔ̀:lt salt in large crystals. XV. f. BAY²+SALT; prop. salt obtained by evaporation of water in bays of the sea, orig. in the *Baie* de Bourgneuf, south of the river Loire, France (called *la Baye*, *le Bay* in ref. to salt production in documents of XIV–XV). So G. *baisalz*, MLG. *bayesout*, Du. *baaizout*, Da. *baisalt*.

bazaar bəzā·ɹ Oriental market-place XVI; fancy fair XIX. Early forms are *bazarro*, *basar*, *buzzar(d)*, *bazar*; prob. – It. – Turk. – Pers. *bāzār* market, which has passed into various Eastern and Eur. langs.

bdellium de·liəm (tree yielding) a gum resin. XVI. – L. *bdellium* (Pliny, Vulg.) – Gr. *bdéllion* (Dioscorides), used in versions of the O.T. later than LXX to render Heb. *b'dhōlaḥ*, of uncertain meaning and origin.

be bī, (unstressed) bi. The 'substantive' and 'copulative' verb expressing (i) simple existence, and (ii) existence in a defined state (whence its use with participles as an auxiliary of tense and voice). Conjugational forms: pres. ind. 1st pers. sg. **am,** 2nd (arch. and dial.) **art, beest,** 3rd **is**; pl. **are,** (arch. and dial.) **be**; pt. **was,** pl. **were**; pres. subj. **be,** pt. subj. **were**; pp. **been.** The forms are derived from four bases as follows.

A. IE. **es*- **s*-. 1st pers. sg. OE. *eam*, *am*, WS. *eom* (with *eo* after *bēo*(*m*); see below) = ON. *em*, Goth. *im*, OIr. *am*, Lith. *esmì*, OSl. *jesmi*, L. *sum* (for **esem*; infl. by *sumus* we are), Gr. *eimi*, Skr. *asmi*, OPers. *amiy*, Arm. *em*, Alb. *jam* :– IE. **ésmi*.

3rd pers. sg. OE. *is* = OFris., OS. *ist* (Du. *is*), (O)HG., Goth. *ist*, ON. *es* (later *er*), OIr. *is*, W. *ys*, L. *est*, Gr. *esti*, OSl. *jestĭ*, Skr. *ásti* :– IE. **ésti*.

pl. OE. *sind*, *sindon*, surviving in ME. till c. 1200 = OFris. *send*, OS. *sind*, *sindan*, OHG. 3rd pl. *sint* (G. *sind*), Goth. 3rd pl. *sind*, OIr. *it*, OW. *int*, L. *sunt*, Gr. *eisi* (Dor. *enti*), Skr. *sánti* :– IE. **sénti*.

pres. subj. OE. *sīe*, pl. *sīen*, later *sī*, *sīn*, surviving till c. 1200 = OS., OHG. *sī*, *sīn* (Du. *zij*, *zijn*, G. *sei*, *seien*) = L. *siēm*, *sim*, *sint*, Gr. *eiē̃n*, etc., Skr. *syát* :– IE. **s*(*i*)*jḗm*, **s*(*i*)*jénti*.

B. Germ. **ar*- (:– **or*-), of unkn. origin. 2nd pers. sg. OE. *eart*, pl. *aron*, *earon* are; these are old perfect formations.

C. IE. **bheu*- **bhu*-. 1st pers. sg. *bēo*, earlier *bīo* (:– **biju*) = OFris. *bim*, OS. *bium*, *biom* (Du. *ben*), OHG. *bim* (G. *bin*), corr. to L. *fīo* I become (:– **bhwijō*), rel. further to L. *fuī* I was, *futūrus* FUTURE, Gr. *phúein* bring forth, cause to grow, *éphūn*, *péphūka* I was, *phúesthai* grow, come into being (see PHYSIC), Lith. *búti*, OSl. *byti* (Russ. *bytʹ*), OIr. *buith*, W. *bod* be, Skr. *bhávati* becomes, is, Pers. *būd* was, *būdan* be, become, exist. So OE. *bist* wilt be, art = OS., OHG. *bis*(*t*) (G. *bist*), OE. *biþ* will be, is, corr. to L. *fīs* becomest, *fit* becomes; cf. W. *bydd* will be); OE. *bēoþ* pl. will be, are, inf. *bēon* (a new formation on *bēo*). The orig. meaning of this base is 'grow'; the derived sense 'become' led to its adoption as an appropriate el. in the paradigm of the verb 'to be', esp. for expressing the future; for another sense-development see BOWER¹, BUILD.

D. IE. **wes*- **wēs*-. OE. inf. *wesan* = OFris. *wesa*, OS., OHG. *wesan* (Du. *wezen*; G. *wesen*, surviving as sb.), ON. *vesa*, *vera*, Goth. *wisan* remain, continue, rel. to Skr. *vásati* dwells, remains. The orig. meaning is 'dwell, remain', and the use of this base is therefore appropriate to the imper. (OE. *wes*, pl. *wesaþ*) and the pt. (OE. 1st and 3rd sg. *wæs* was, 2nd sg. *wǣre* wast, pl. *wǣron* were, in which latter alone it survives).

Of the three types of the pres. ind. pl. in OE., *bēoþ*, *aron*, and *sind*(*on*), the first continued in gen. ME. as *beth*, *ben*, and finally *be* (surviving till XVII, as in A.V. *the powers that be*, and in mod. dial.), the second, orig. confined to the Anglian area, had become the standard form by XVI (regularly used by Tindale), and the third became obs. soon after c. 1200. In the pt. ind. the 2nd pers. sg. *wēre* (OE. *wǣre*) became obs. in XVI, and new forms, *wast*, †*werst*, and *wert*, were introduced, the two last esp. for the subjunctive. There was orig. no pp. of the verb *am, was, be* in OE.; a new formation *ġebēon*, on the inf. *bēon*, appears c. 1100, which completed the conjugation *am-was-been* as it now stands.

be- bi prefix, OE. *be-*, weak var. of *bī* BY, varying in cognate comps. with *bī-*, e.g. *begān* surround, practise, *begang* and *bīgeng* circuit, practice; = OFris., OS. *be-*, *bĭ* (Du. *be-*, *bij-*), OHG. *bi-*, *bī* (G. *be-*, *bei-*). The main uses, developed from the orig. and gen. sense of 'about', are: (1) with verbs, meaning 'around, all round, on all sides', 'from side to side, to and fro, in all ways', as in OE. *besettan* BESET, *besmierian* besmear, *bestrēowan* BESTREW, so *bedaub* (xvi), *besmirch* (Sh.); (2) 'thoroughly, soundly, to the full, extremely, excessively', as BESEECH (early ME.), after OE. *befriġnan*, etc., passing into a mere intensive as in BEFALL, BEFIT; (3) 'off, away', marking deprivation, as in OE. *behēafdian* BEHEAD; so *bedǣlan* bereave, deprive, *beceorfan*, *besċeran* cut off; (4) 'about, over' (lit. and fig.) as in OE. *beġēotan* sprinkle, *beþenċan* BETHINK, *bewēpan* bewail; (5) with sbs. and adjs. 'so as to make what is expressed by them', as *becalm* (XVI), *bedim* (XVI), *befoul* (XIV); hence, 'call by the name of', as *beblockhead*, *berascal*; (6) with sbs. used in an instr. relation, 'surround or envelop with', hence (gen.) 'affect with', as in *befog* (XVII), *benight* (XVI); (7) with ppl. adjs., often combining uses 2 and 6 with vague meaning or rhetorical force, as in *beblubbered* (XVI), *bedabbled* (Sh.), *bemused* (Pope), and so, with derogatory implication, in such adjs. as *becloaked*, *beribboned*, *beturbaned*.

beach bītʃ (dial.) shingle, pebbles of the seashore; seashore. XVI. Early forms also *bache*, *bayche*, *baich*. The first sense remained in the local usage of Sussex and Kent; it is difficult to determine the date of the emergence of the present sense (see, e.g., Sh. 'Merch. V.' IV i 71, 'Lear' IV vi 17, 'Cor.' V iii 58; cf. the development of F. *grève*); perh. identical with OE. *bæċe*, *beċe* brook, stream (cf. BECK[1]), with transf. meaning '(pebbly) river valley', a word surviving in many place-names, as *Bache*, *Betch*ton, Cole*batch*, Sand*bach*, Wis*bech*. Hence **bea·ch-co:mber** U.S. (1) ocean-roller; (2) settler on a Pacific island XIX; *comber* breaker (f. COMB vb. in the sense 'roll over as a wave, break with foam').

Beach-la-mar bītʃ la māɹ jargon English used in the Western Pacific. XX (also *biche-*). Alteration of Pg. *bicho do mar* BÊCHE-DE-MER.

beacon bī·kn †sign, standard OE.; signal-fire; lighthouse. XIV. OE. *bēacn* sign, portent, ensign = OFris. *bēcen*, *bācen* (hence MLG. *bāke*, LG. *bāken*, and MDu. *bāken*, Du. *baak*), OS. *bōkan*, OHG. *bouhhan* (G. *bake* is from LG.) :- WGerm. **baukna* (cf. BECKON), of unkn. origin.

bead bīd prayer; (pl.) prayers XIII; rosary (†*pair of beads*); ornamental perforated object XIV. ME. *bede*, pl. *bedes*, partly aphetic of *ibede* (OE. *ġebed* prayer, pl. *ġebedu*), partly generalized from OE. *bedhūs* house of prayer (whence W. *bettws* church); rel. sbs. are OFris. *bede*, OS. *beda* (Du. *bede*), *gibed*, OHG. *beta*, *gibet* (G. *gebet*), Goth. *bida*; f. CGerm. **beð-* BID. Hence **beadsman, bedesman** bī·dzmən one who offers prayers for another's welfare. XIII (AncrR.). ME. *beode-*, *bed(e)man*, f. BEAD, repl. by *beadsman* (prob. after *almsman*) in XVI.

beadle bī·dl †herald, crier; †messenger; apparitor, parish constable, etc. XIII (Cursor M.). – OF. *bedel* (mod. *bedeau*) = Pr. *bedel*, It. *bidello* :- Rom. **bidellu-s*, of Germ. origin. The adopted F. word ousted the native OE. *bydel*, ME. *büdel*, *bidel* = MDu. **bödel* (Du. *beul*), OHG. *butil* (G. *büttel*) :- Germ. **buðilaz*, f. **buð-*, base of **beuðan*, OE. *bēodan* (see BID).

beagle bī·gl small hound having a loud musical bark. XV. perh. – OF. *beegueule* noisy person, prob. f. *beer* open wide (cf. BAY[3])+*gueule* throat (cf. GULES). F. *bigle* (XVII) is from Eng.

beak bīk bird's bill XIII; beak-shaped object XV. ME. *bec*, *bek* (*beck* continuing till XVIII; the form with lengthened vowel arose from obl. form *beke*) – (O)F. *bec* = Pr. *bec*, Sp. *bico*, It. *becco* :- L. *beccu-s* (Suetonius), of Celtic origin (but the mod. Celtic words are from Eng. or F.), repl. L. *rostrum*. In the slang sense of 'magistrate' prob. orig. thieves' cant (cf. *harman beck* constable XVI).

beaker bī·kəɹ open goblet XIV; open-mouthed glass vessel XIX. – ON. *bikarr* = OS. *bikeri*, (M)Du. *bēker*, OHG. *behhāri*, *behhar* (G. *becher*) – pop. L. **bicārium* (whence It. *bicchiere*), perh. f. Gr. *bîkos* drinking-bowl (cf. medGr. *bíkion*); see PITCHER. The orig. ME. *biker* (repr. by Sc. *bicker* bowl, cup) was superseded by *bēker*, perh. by assoc. with MDu.

beak iron (XVII) see BICKERN.

beam bīm †tree (cf. *hornbeam*, *quickbeam*, *whitebeam*); plank; ray of light. OE. *bēam* = OFris. *bām*, OS. *bām*, *boom*, (M)Du. *boom* (see BOOM[2]), OHG. *boum* (G. *baum*) :- WGerm. **bauma*; rel. obscurely to Goth. *bagms*, ON. *baðmr* tree. The WGerm. forms have been referred to IE. **bhou-* **bheu-* **bhu-* grow (see BE), but the uncertainty whether the orig. sense was 'wooden stem or block' or 'growing tree' makes the ult. origin doubtful. The sense 'beam of light' is found in OE. *byrnende bēam*, *fȳren bēam* pillar of fire (tr. **Vulg.**

columna lucis), *lēohtbēamed* having bright rays, *sunnebēam* sunbeam; for the sense development cf. L. *radius* RAY[1], SHAFT.

bean bīn (seed of) leguminous plants Faba (OE.) and Phaseolus (XVI). OE. *bēan* = MDu. *bōne* (Du. *boon*), OHG. *bōna* (G. *bohne*), ON. *baun* :- CGerm. (exc. Goth.) **baunō*; connexion with L. *faba* bean, OSl. *bobŭ*, OPruss. *babo*, is phonetically improbable. Hence **bea·n**FEAST XIX, whence **beano** bī·nou orig. printers' colloq.; see -O.

bear[1] bɛəɹ quadruped of the genus Ursus. OE. *bera* = MDu. *bere* (Du. *beer*), OHG. *bero* (G. *bär*) :- WGerm. **bero*; rel. to ON. *bjǫrn* :- **bernuz*; possibly sb. use of an IE. **bheros* brown (Lith. *bėras*, Lett. *bērs*) (in stock exchange sl. correl. to BULL[1]). ¶ The earliest IE. name of the bear, **ṛksos* (Skr. *ṛkšas*, L. *ursus*, Gr. *árktos*, W. *arth*) is not repr. in Germ. or Slav. Hence **bea·r-lea:der** tutor accompanying a young man on travel XVIII; after G. *bärenführer*, *-treiber*.

bear[2] bɛəɹ A. carry; B. bring forth. OE. *beran* (pt. *bær*, *bǣron*, pp. *boren*) = OFris. only pp. *beren*, *boren*, OS., OHG. *beran* (in modG. only *gebären* bring forth, OHG. *gaberan* = OE. *ġeberan*, OS. *giberan*, Goth. *gabairan*), ON. *bera*, Goth. *bairan*, f. Germ. **ber-* :- IE. **bher-*, as in Skr. *bhárati*, Arm. *berem*, Gr. *phérein*, L. *ferre* (cf. -FEROUS, FERTILE), OIr. *berim*, W. *cymryd* (:- **kom|bhṛt-*) take, OSl. *bĭrati* (Russ. *brat'* take, seize). Since both main groups of meaning are repr. in the IE. langs. it is not certain which was prior. The mod. pt. **bore** dates from c. 1400, but did not gen. supersede **bare** (OE. *bær*) till after 1600; for the pp. see BORN, BORNE.

beard biəɹd hair on the face. OE. *beard* = OFris. *berd*, MDu. *baert* (Du. *baard*), OHG., G. *bart* :- WGerm. **barđa*, rel. to OSl. *brada* beard (Russ. *borodá*), Lith. *barzdà*, OPruss. *bordus*, and L. *barba* (:- **bhardhā*).

beast bīst animal; domesticated animal of the cattle kind; brute, savage. XIII. - OF. *beste* (mod. *bête*) :- pop. L. *besta*, for L. *bēstia*, referred by some to a base **dhewes-* breathe (cf. the basic sense of ANIMAL), which is widespread in Slav., and hence rel. to Goth. *dius*, OE. *dēor* DEER. *Beast* displaced *deer* and was itself displaced by *animal*, in the gen. sense, but is retained in dial. and techn. use, in special phr., as 'man and beast', 'wild beast', and fig. Hence **bea·stly** XIII; see -LY[1].

beat[1] bīt strike repeatedly. OE. *bēatan* (pt. *bēot*, pp. *bēaten*) = OHG. *boȥan* (cf. *anabōȥ*, mod. *amboss* ANVIL), ON. *bauta* :- Germ. **bautan*, the base of which may be rel. to **fu-* of L. *confutāre* strike down, CONFUTE. The OE. pt. *bēot*, orig. a redupl. form, was repl. first by *bĕt(t)* and later by *beated*, which gave place to **beat**; the pp. **beaten** survives, by the side of a new formation *beat* (now chiefly dial. or vulgar, and in *dead-beat*), which superseded *bĕt(t)*. Cf. BEETLE[1]. Hence **beat** sb. action of beating XVII; course traversed by a watchman, policeman, etc. XVIII.

beat[2] bīt strive against a contrary wind or current at sea. XVII. perh. a use of BEAT[1]; but poss. repr. an earlier **bait* - ON. *beita* sail, cruise (see BAIT), unless it may be referred to nearly synon. rare OE. *bǣtan*, with noun of action *bǣting* (Alfred's tr. of Boethius xli § 3); but, in either case, the late appearance of the word is a difficulty.

beatific biəti·fik making blessed or happy. XVII (earlier *-ical*). - F. *béatifique* or L. *beātificus*, f. *beātus* blessed, pp. of *beāre* make happy, f. the same base as *bellus*; see BEAUTY, -FIC. So **beati**FY biæ·tifai make or pronounce blessed. XVI. - (O)F. *béatifier* or late L. *beātificāre*. **beati**TUDE biæ·titjūd blessedness. - (O)F. or L. (Cicero).

beau bou pl. *beaux* bouz dandy XVII; lady's suitor XVIII. F. *beau* :- L. *bellu-s* :- **dwenolos*, dim. of **dwenos*, OL. *duenos*, *duonos*, L. *bonus* good. Cf. BELLE.

beau ideal bou aidī·əl †the ideally beautiful; perfect type of beauty. XIX. F.; *beau* sb., *idéal* adj.; see BEAU, IDEAL; often apprehended as meaning 'beautiful ideal'.

Beaujolais bou·ʒəlei ‖ boʒolɛ light red burgundy. XIX. F., name of an ancient district of France.

beaumontague boumɔntei·g composition for filling cracks, etc. XIX. Said to be named from Élie de *Beaumont* (1798–1874), French geologist.

Beaune boun red burgundy. XIX. F., name of a town in Côte d'Or, France.

beauty bjū·ti perfection affording great pleasure to the senses or other faculties. XIII. ME. *bealte*, *beute*, *beaute* - AN. *beute*, OF. *bealte*, *beaute* (mod. *beauté*) = Pr. *beltat*, *beutat*, Sp. *beldad*, It. *beltà* :- Rom. **bellitātem*, f. L. *bellus*; see BEAU, -TY. Hence **beau·ti**FUL[1] XV, **beau·ti**FY XVI.

beaver[1] bī·vəɹ large amphibious rodent. OE. *beofor*, *befor* = (M)LG., (M)Du. *bever*, OHG. *bibar* (G. *biber*), ON. *bjórr* :- CGerm. (not in Goth.) **bebruz* :- IE. **bhebhrús*, **bhibrús* (whence also Skr. *babhrús* brown, great ichneumon, L. *fiber*, OSl. *bebrŭ*, Lith. *bebrùs*, Czech *bobr*), redupl. deriv. of **bhru-* brown (see BEAR[1], BROWN). ¶ CIE. animal-name, like *cow*, *ewe*, *hound*, *mouse*, *wolf*. Hence (after *velveteen*) **bea·verteen** cotton twilled cloth with the pile left uncut XIX; cf. WFlem. *bevertein*.

beaver[2] bī·vəɹ movable face-guard of a helmet. XV (*baviere*, *bavoure*). - OF. *baviere* (whence Sp. *babera*, Pg. *baveira*, It. *baviera*), f. *baver* slaver, f. Rom. **baba* (OF. *beve*) slaver. The form with *ea*, recorded XVI, is difficult to account for.

because bikɔ·z, -kō·z for the reason *that*; on account *of*. XIV. ME. *bi cause*, i.e. *bi* BY, CAUSE, after OF. *par cause de* by reason of.

beccafico bekəfī·kou small migratory warbler. XVII. It., f. *beccare* peck+*fico* FIG; forms corr. to Pr. *beccofigo*, F. *becfigue* have also been used.

bechamel bei·ʃəmel white cream sauce. XVIII. – F. *béchamel*, f. name of the Marquis de *Béchamel*, steward of Louis XIV.

bêche-de-mer beiʃdəmɛə·ɹ sea-slug, trepang. XIX. quasi-F. of Eng. origin, for *biche de mer* – Pg. *bicho do mar* 'worm of the sea' (*bicho* :– late L. *bēstulus*, dim. of L. *bēstia* BEAST; *mar* :– L. *mare* sea).

beck[1] bek (arch. and dial.) brook. XIV (in place-names XI). – ON. *bekkr* :– **bakkiz*, rel. to **bakiz*, whence OE. *beće*, OS. *beki* (Du. *beek*), OHG. *bah* (G. *bach*); referred to IE. **bheg-* **bhog-* run, whence Lith. *bégti*, OSl. *běžati* flee (Russ. *begat'*), Gr. *phébesthai* flee, *phóbos* flight, fear.

beck[2] bek (arch. exc. in phr. *at one's beck and call*) significant gesture, as a nod; (chiefly north.) obeisance, curtsy. XIV. f. (dial.) *beck* vb. (XIV), shortening of ME. *bekene* BECKON, the *-(e)n-* of the stem being taken for the inf. ending (cf. *open, ope*).

becket be·kit (naut.) loop or rope with a knot at one end and an eye at the other. XVIII. Of unkn. origin.

beckon be·kn make a mute signal (to). OE. *bēcnan*, **bīecnan* = OS. *bōknian*, OHG. *bouhnen* :– WGerm. **bauknian*, f. **baukna* BEACON.

become bikʌ·m †come, arrive; come to be; befit. OE. *becuman* = OFris. *bikuma*, MLG., (M)Du. *bekomen*, OHG. *biqueman* (G. *bekommen*) obtain, receive, Goth. *biquiman* come upon suddenly (ἐφίστασθαι 1 Thess. v 3); f. **bi-* BE-+**kweman* COME. For the sense development cf. OE. *ġecwēme* fitting, pleasant, MDu. *bequāme* (Du. *bekwaam*), OHG. *biquāmi* (G. *bequem*) suitable, Goth. *gaqimiþ* it is fitting; F. *devenir* turn out to be, become (L. *dēvenīre* arrive); F. *convenir*, L. *convenīre* (see CONVENIENT), Gr. *proshḗkein* be fitting (*prós* to, *hḗkein* come).

bed bed OE. *bed(d)* = OFris. *bed(d)*, OS. *bed, beddi*, MDu. *bedde* (Du. *bed*), OHG. *betti* (G. *bett*), Goth. *badi* :– CGerm. (exc. ON.) **baðjam*, rel. to **baðjaz*, whence ON. *beðr* bolster, bedding. The ult. origin and primary sense are uncertain; the Germ. base has been referred to IE. **bhodh-*, as in L. *fodere* dig, *fossa* grave, ditch; but uncertainty as to the priority of the chief Germ. senses, 'sleeping-place' and 'growing-place for plants', invalidates conjecture; for the sense 'bolster' of ON. *beðr* cf. Finnish *patja* cushion, bolster, a very early adoption from Germ. Hence **be·dspread**. c. 1845. orig. U.S. – Du. *beddesprei* (in LG. *bedspreed*, EFris. *beddspreet*).

bedad bidæ·d Anglo-Ir. int. XVIII (Swift). For *by dad*, substituted for *by Gad* (see BEGAD), after earlier †*adad* (XVII–XVIII).

bedeguar be·digāɹ moss-like growth in rose-bushes. XVI. – F. *bédegar* – Arab., Pers. *bādāwar(d)* lit. 'wind-brought', later interpreted as Pers. *bād* wind, breath + Arab. *ward* rose.

bedel(l) bide·l old forms of BEADLE retained in the universities of Oxford and Cambridge. XVI.

bedesman see *beadsman* s.v. BEAD.

bedevil bide·vl treat diabolically; play the devil with. XVIII. f. BE- 5, 6+DEVIL.

bedew bidjū· cover with dew. XIV (Ch., Trevisa). f. BE- 6+DEW; cf. MHG. *betouwen*, MLG. *bedauwen*.

bedight bidai·t (poet.) array, deck. XIV. f. BE- 2 +DIGHT.

bedim bidi·m make dim. XVI. f. BE- 5+ DIM.

bedizen bidai·zn, (U.S.) bidi·zn dress up. XVII. f. BE- 2 +DIZEN. 'A low word' (J.).

Bedlam, bedlam be·dləm Hospital of St. Mary of Bethlehem, orig. for the entertainment of the bishop and canons of the church of St. Mary at *Bethlehem*; (later) hospital, esp. for lunatics; †inmate of this XV; lunatic asylum (gen.); scene of uproar XVII. (Early forms of the town name are OE. *Betleem*, ME. *Beth(e)leem, Bedlem*.)

Bedlington be·dliŋtən Name of a town in Northumberland applied to a breed of short-haired terrier. XIX.

Bedouin be·duīn Arab of the desert. XIV (*Bedoyn*). – OF. *beduin* (mod. *bédouin*), ult. (through medL.) – Arab. *badāwīn, badawīn*, pl. of *badāwīy, badawīy*, f. *badw* desert. First adopted in Eur. langs. in the pl. (medL. *bedewīnī*, etc.), whence new sg. forms were made; for the retention of the pl. inflexion of Arab. or Heb. cf. *assassin, cherubim, fellahin, rabbin, seraphim*.

bedridden be·dridn permanently confined to bed. XIV. ME. *bedreden*, extension (with -EN[6]) of *bedred(e)*, later *bedrid* (XVI), repr. OE. *bedreda, -rida, -ryda* sb. and adj. paralysed (man), agent-noun f. *bedd* BED+ **rid-*, short base of *rīdan* RIDE; cf. synon. LG. *bedderēde, -rēdig*.

bee bī hymenopterous insect (Apis, Bombus). OE. *bēo* = OFris. *bē*, MLG., MDu. *bīe* (Du. *bij*), OHG. *bīa* (G. dial. *beie*), ON. *bý* :– CGerm. (exc. Gothic) **bīōn*. The *n* of the wk. declension in coalescence with the base produced OHG. *bini* (G. *biene*) and OHG. *bīna* (G. dial. *bein*); derivs. with other formatives exist in OPruss. *bitte*, Lith. *bitìs*, OSl. *bičela*, Ir. *bech* (:– **bhikos*), L. *fūcus* drone (:– **bhoikos*); all plausibly referred to a base **bhi-* tremble, quiver (whence OE. *bifian*, G. *beben*), as if 'the quivering insect'.

beech bītʃ forest tree of the genus Fagus. OE. *bēće* = MLG. *bōke*, *bȫke* (wk. fem.) :– Germ. **bōkjōn*, rel. to **bōkō* (str. fem.), whence OE. *bōc* (as in *bōctrēow* beech-tree, *bōcwudu* beech-wood, and surviving with shortened vowel in BUCKMAST, BUCKWHEAT and the proper name *Buckhurst*), OHG. *buohha* (G. *buche*), MDu. *boeke* (Du. *beuk*), ON. *bók*; all cogn. with IE. **bhāgos*, whence Gr. *phāgós*, *phēgós* edible oak, L. *fāgus* beech, perh. rel. to Gr. *phageîn* eat, as if 'tree with edible fruit'. Cf. BOOK.

beef bīf flesh of the ox. XIII. ME. *boef*, *beef* – AN., OF. *boef*, *buef* (mod. *bœuf*) = Sp. *buey*, It. *bove* :– L. *bovem*, nom. *bōs* ox (see COW[1]). Hence **bee·feater** eater of beef; Yeoman of the Guard. XVII.

Beelzebub bie·lzibʌb the Devil; a devil. OE. *Belzebub*, ME. *Beelzebub*, *Belsabub* – L. (Vulgate) *Beelzebūb*, rendering (i) Heb. *ba'al-z'būb* 'fly-lord' (2 Kings i 2) and (ii) Gr. *Beelzeboúb* of the N.T. (Matt. xii 24).

been bīn, bin see BE.

beer biəɹ malt beverage; from XVI the proper designation of hopped malt liquor, as dist. from ALE. OE. *bēor* = OFris. *biār*, *bier*, MLG., MDu. *bēr*, OHG. *bior* (Du., G. *bier*), a WGerm. word (whence prob. ON. *bjórr*) – monastic L. *biber* drink, f. L. *bibere* (see IMBIBE). Until XV rarely found exc. in verse (not in PPl. or Ch.); prob. reinforced from LG. on the introduction of hopped liquor (cf. Beere .. *hummuli potus*, *cervisia hummulina*, 'Promp. Parv.').

beeregar biə·rigāɹ sour beer. XV. f. BEER + *eger* sour (EAGER), after *alegar*, *vinegar*.

beest bī·ist, bīst see BE.

beestings bī·stiŋz first milk from a cow after calving. OE. **bēsting* (late WS. *bȳsting*), f. synon. *bēost* = NFris. *bjast*, *bjüst*, (M)Du. *biest*, OHG. *biost* (G. *biest*, as in *biestmilch*): of unkn. origin.

beet bīt plant having a succulent root, red or white. OE. *bēte* = MLG. *bēte* (LG. *beete*, whence G. *beete*), MDu. *bēte* (Du. *beet*), OHG. *bieza* (G. dial. *biessen*); early CWGerm. – L. *bēta*, perh. of Celtic origin. Unrecorded between OE. and late ME., when its currency was prob. due to LG.

beetle[1] bī·tl beating implement. OE. (Anglian) *bētel*, (WS.) *bīetel* :– Germ. **bautilaz*, f. **bautan* BEAT + *-il-* -LE[1]; cf. OHG. *bōzil* cudgel, (M)LG. *bōtel*, ON. *beytill* penis.

beetle[2] bī·tl coleopterous insect. OE. *bitula*, *bitela* (glossing 'blatta', 'mordiculus'), f. **bit-*, short base of *bītan* BITE (cf. early ME. *bitel* biting); see -LE[1]. ME. *ĭ* is repr. by ī as in *evil*, *weevil*.

beetle[3] bī·tl. XIV. First in *bytell browet* ('Destruction of Troy'), *bitelbrowed* (PPl.) having bushy, shaggy, or prominent eyebrows; later (XVI, More) *betle browes*, *beetil brow* was used of the human brow and the brow of a mountain ('high hills lifted up their beetil-browes', Sidney); *beteled* is somewhat earlier (Hawes). Whence **beetle** vb. overhang threateningly (Sh. 'Hamlet' I iv 71). Of unkn. origin.

befall bifɔ̄·l fall (chiefly fig.) OE.; pertain, belong XII; fall out, happen XIII. OE. *befeallan*, corr. to OFris. *befalla*, OS. *bifallan* (Du. *bevallen* please), OHG. *bifallan* (G. *befallen* pass. be seized or taken); see BE- 2, FALL.

befit bifi·t be fit for or proper to, become. XV. f. BE- 2 + FIT vb.; replaced earlier *besit* (XV), intensive of synon. *sit* (XIV).

before bifɔə·ɹ adv., prep. OE.; conj. XII (Orm). OE. *beforan* = OFris. *befara*, OS. *biforan*, OHG *bifora* (G. *bevor*), f. Germ. **bi-* BY + **forana* from the front (f. **fora* FOR). Hence **befo·reHAND.** XIII; cf. AN. *avant main*, OF. *avant la main* (*les mains*).

beg[1] beg ask as alms or as a favour. XIII. ME. *begge-n*, occurring along with *beggare*, and fem. *beggild* in AncrR., and in prp. *beg(g)and* in Cursor M.; prob. :– OE. *bedecian*, deriv. (cf. Goth. *bidagwa* beggar) of **beð-*, base of BID; for the same development of *c* after *d* cf. **Badecan tūn*, *Badechitone*, Baginton, **Badecan healh*, *Badegenhall*, Bagnall. ¶ Derivation from OF. *begard* or *beguine* (see BEGHARD, BEGUINE) has been gen. favoured, but it is not confirmed, in spite of certain coincidences, e.g. alternation of the vbs. *begger* and *beguigner* in texts of Britton, 1292, of *beggild* and *begenild* in PPl., the concurrent use by Gower of AN. *begant* begging, *beggerie*, *begyner*, and *beguinage*, and the rendering of F. *Béguin* by *beggar*, *begger* in the ME. translation of the 'Roman de la Rose'.

beg[2] beg. XVII. Osmanli *beg* = BEY; cf. BEGUM.

begad bigæ·d. XVIII. f. *be* BY + minced form of GOD; cf. †*agad* (XVIII), EGAD, GAD[3].

beget bige·t pt. *begot*, arch. *begat*, pp. *begotten* †acquire XII; procreate XIII (Laȝ.). First in north. texts (Orm, Cursor M.) with *g* repl. *ġ*, *ȝ* of the native forms OE. *beġietan*, ME. *biȝete*, corr. to OS. *bigetan* seize, OHG. *pigezzan* receive = Goth. *bigitan* find; see BE-, GET (XIII in the sense 'procreate', after ON. *geta*).

Beghard be·gāɹd name of a lay brotherhood modelled on the Beguines. XVII. – medL. *Beghardus*, f. OF. *Bégard*, *-art*, MDu. *Beggaert*, MHG. *Beghart*, f. stem of *Beguina*, etc. BEGUINE; see -ARD.

begin bigi·n pt. *began*, pp. *begun* enter upon, set oneself *to do* something. OE. *beġinnan*, pt. *began*, *begunnon*, pp. *begunnen* = OFris. *biginna*, *biienna*, OS., OHG. *biginnan* (Du., G. *beginnen*), CWGerm. f. *bi-* BE- + **ginnan* (of unkn. origin), in comps. meaning 'begin': OE. *āġinnan*, *onġinnan* (much commoner than *beginnan*), MDu. *ontghinnen*, OHG. *inginnan*, Goth. *duginnan*. (The arch. *gin*, sp. also *'gin*, is an aphetic deriv. of *agin, ongin, begin.*) *Begun* as pt. was widespread XVI–XIX; Sc. pt. *begouth* prob. arose from assoc. with *couth*, pt. of *can*, which in Sc. was a var. of *gan* (aux. of pt.) did.

beglerbeg be·glɘɹbeg governor of a province of the Ottoman empire. XVI. Turk., 'bey of beys' (*begler* is pl. of BEG[2]).

begone[1] bigɔ·n depart! XIV. imper. *be gone* treated as one word, like BEWARE.

begone[2] bigɔ·n pp. of †*bego*; see WOEBEGONE.

begonia bigou·niɘ genus of mostly tropical plants. XVIII. modL., named by Charles Plumier (d. 1706), French botanist, after Michel *Begon* (d. 1710), French patron of botany; see -IA[1].

beguile bigai·l delude, cheat XIII; charm or wile away XVI (Sh.). f. BE-2+*guile* vb., f. GUILE sb.; cf. MDu. *begīlen*, AN. *degiler*.

Beguine begi·n member of a lay sisterhood. XV. – (O)F. *béguine* (MDu., MHG. *begīne*), in medL. *Beguina*, said to be f. name of Lambert (le) *Bègue* (i.e. the Stammerer), a priest of Liège (XII), founder of the community; but this is disputed. Cf. BEGHARD.

begum bī·gɘm Indian lady of high rank. XVIII. – Urdu (Pers.) *begam* – E. Turk. *bigim* princess, fem. of *big* prince, of which the Osmanli form is BEG[2].

behalf bihā·f. XIV. orig. and mainly in phr. with genitive, as *on God's, my*, etc. *behalf* on the part of or in the name of God, etc. *On goddes, my*, etc. *behalve* replaced earlier ME. *on goddes halve, on min halve* (in late OE. *on mīnre healfe* for my part), with which cf. ON. *af e-s hálfu.*

behave bihei·v conduct oneself. XV. orig. refl., lit. hold oneself in a certain respect; f. BE- 2+HAVE (with the early pronunc. of the stressed form preserved); cf. MHG. *sich behaben* maintain oneself, (now) conduct oneself, behave. Hence **behaviour**, U.S. **-ior** bihei·vjɘɹ deportment, manners XV (Caxton); conduct of life XVI. Early forms *behavour, behaver*, later *-your, -iour*, on the anal. of *haver, havour, haviour*, vars. of *aver* possession (OF. *aveir, avoir* :– L. *habēre* have, used sb.) infl. by *have*; cf. *demeanour.*

behead bihe·d remove the head of. OE. *behēafdian*, f. BE- 3+*hēafod* HEAD; cf. MHG. *behoubeten* (G. *behaupten*).

behemoth bihī·mɔþ, -ouþ prob. hippopotamus (Job xl 15). XIV. – Heb. *b'hēmōth* (pl. of dignity, 'great or monstrous beast') of *b'hēmāh* beast, held to be – Egyptian *p-ehe-mau* water-ox. Cf. Russ. *begemót* hippopotamus.

behest bihe·st †promise; (arch.) command. OE. *behǣs*+parasitic *t* :– Germ. **biχaissi-*, abstr. sb. f. **biχaitan*, f. **bi-* BE- 2+**χaitan* bid, call (see HIGHT).

behind bihai·nd adv., prep. OE. *bi-, behindan* = OS. *bihindan*; lit. at a place in the rear; f. *bi* BY+*hindan* (see HIND[2]). Hence **behi·ndhand** XVI; after BEFOREHAND.

behold bihou·ld look upon. OE. *bihaldan* (*-healdan*) = OFris. *bihalda*, OS. *bihaldan*, (Du. *behouden*), OHG. *bihaltan* (G. *behalten*); see BE- 2 and HOLD. Eng. alone has the sense 'watch, look', the cogn. langs. having only the applications derived from 'hold, occupy, keep', viz. 'maintain, retain'.

beholden bihou·ldn (arch.) obliged. XIV. repr. OE. *behealden* cautious, assiduous (cf. *behealdennes* observance, regard), pp. of *behealdan*, in the senses 'guard', 'keep', 'observe' (see prec.). An altered form †**beho·lding** (XV–XVIII) is due to suffix-substitution (-ING[2]) to express active meaning.

behoof bihū·f (arch.) use, advantage. OE. *behōf*, in phr. *tō* . . *behōfe* for (one's) use or needs (cf. *behōflic* useful, necessary) = OFris. *bihōf*, (M)Du. *behoef*, MHG. *behuof* (G. *behuf*), WGerm. f. **bi-* BE-+**χōf-*, var. of the base of **χafjan* HEAVE. For final *f* instead of *v* cf. *behalf.*

behove bihou·v (arch.) †need OE.; be needful or fitting. XII. OE. *behōfian* = OFris. *bihōvia*, MLG. *behōven*, (M)Du. *behoeven*; f. prec.

beige beiʒ woollen fabric orig. left in its natural colours; yellowish-grey. XIX. – F. *beige* (OF. *bege*), of unkn. origin.

bejan bī·dʒɘn freshman in a Sc. university. XVII. – F. *béjaune*, for *bec jaune* 'yellow-beak', i.e. fledgeling.

beknown binou·n (dial. exc. as in UNBEKNOWN) known, familiar. XV. pp. of †*beknow* acknowledge, recognize (XIII), f. *be-* BE- 2+KNOW.

belabour bilei·bɘɹ †labour at; lay heavy blows on. XVI. f. BE- 4+LABOUR vb., which it superseded in these senses.

belated bilei·tid overtaken by lateness of the night; that is too late. XVII. f. BE- 5 +†*lated* (XVI), f. LATE+-ED.

belay bilei· A. beset, surround OE. B. (naut.) fasten a running rope round a pin, etc. XVI. OE. *beleċġan* = OFris. *bilega*, Du. *beleggen*, OHG. *bileggen* (G. *belegen*) cover, surround, invest, survived sporadically in ME. *bilegge*, pt. *bileide*; from XVI *belay* appears as a new formation; the naut., now the only current, sense seems to be modelled on Du. *beleggen.*

belch belᵗʃ void wind noisily from the stomach. XV. perh. shortening of OE. *belċettan, bylċettan,* **bielċettan* (:– **balikatjan*), varying with *bealċettan*, if not repr. an OE. **belċan*, **bielċan*, rel. to *bealcan*, *bælcan* 'eructare', repr. in ME. by *balke, belk-e* (XIV–XVII and mod. dial.); there is also a rare ME. *bolke* (XV). A Germ. base **balk-* **belk-* **bulk-* is repr. also by vbs. meaning 'bray, bellow, low', e.g. Fris. *balkje*, MLG., MDu. *belken*, LG. (whence G.) *bölken*, Du. *balken, bulken*, MG. *bülken*.

belcher beˈlᵗʃəɹ spotted handkerchief. XIX. f. name of the pugilist Jim *Belcher* (1781–1811).

beldam beˈldəm †grandmother; old woman; hag. XV. f. *bel* (OF. *belle* fair, fem. of *bel* BEAU) as in †*belfather*, †*belsire* grandfather, †*belmoder* grandmother+DAME; cf. the use of *good* in †*goodsire*, †*gooddame*, and F. *bon-papa, bonne-maman*.

beleaguer bilīˈgəɹ besiege, invest. XVI. – Du. *belegeren*, f. *be-* BE- 1+*leger* camp, LEAGUER.

belemnite beˈləmnait (geol.) fossil cuttle-fish. XVII. – modL. *belemnītēs*, f. Gr. *bélemnon* dart (see -ITE); so called from the pop. notion that the fossils were thunder-bolts.

belfry beˈlfri †movable siege-tower XIII; bell-tower XV; bell-chamber XVI. ME. *berfrey* – OF. *berfrei*, later *belfrei, be(l)froi* (mod. *beffroi*)–Frankish **bergfriđ-* (repr. by MDu. *bergfret*, MHG. *bercfrit, berfrit* siege-tower), prob. f. **bergan* protect (OE. *beorgan*, OHG. *bergan*, G. *bergen*, etc.)+**friþuz* peace, shelter (see FRITH[1]); the etymol. meaning being 'defensive place of shelter'. Dissimilation of *r* . . *r* gave medL. *belfredus* (cf. PALFREY), OF. *belfrei*, whence by assim. or fall of *l*, *befroi, beffroi*; pop. assoc. with BELL[1] established the Eng. forms with *bel-* (XV).

belga beˈlgă Belgian monetary unit. XX. Use of fem. of L. *Belgus* Belgian, sc. *pecūnia* money or *monēta* coin.

Belgravia belgreiˈviə fashionable district of London, south of Knightsbridge. XIX (Thackeray). f. *Belgrave* (as in *B. Square*), title of the viscounty of the marquess of Westminster; see -IA.

Belial bīˈliəl spirit of evil personified; the Devil. XIII. – Heb. *b'liya'al* worthlessness, destruction, f. *b'li* not, without+*ya'al* use, profit.

belie bilaiˈ tell lies about; be false to. OE. *belēogan* = OFris. *biliuga*, OHG. *biliugan*; see BE- 1, LIE[2].

believe bilīˈv have faith (in). Late OE. *belȳfan, belēfan*, replacing, by prefix-substitution, earlier *ġelēfan*, (WS. *ġelīefan*) = OFris. *gelēva*, OS. *gilōƀian* (Du. *gelooven*), OHG. *gilouben* (G. *glauben*), Goth. *galaubjan* :– CGerm. (exc. ON.) **galauƀjan* hold dear, cherish, trust in, f. **ga-* Y-+**lauƀ-* dear, lief. So **belieˈf.** XII (*bileafe*), replacing OE. *ġelēafa*; the loss of the final syll. resulted in unvoicing of the final cons.

belike bilaiˈk (arch.) probably. XVI. orig. *by like* (varying with *of like*, i.e. BY, LIKE adj. used as sb. 'probability, likelihood', prob. after the earlier *by* or *of liklyhode* XV.

belittle biliˈtl make small; disparage. XVIII (orig. Amer.). f. BE- 5+LITTLE.

bell[1] bel hollow cup-shaped metal body producing a resonant musical sound when struck. OE. *belle* (also in *belhring* bell-ringing, *belhūs* bell-chamber) = MLG., MDu. *belle* (Du. *bel*); a word of the LG. area (Icel. *bjalla* is – OE.); perh. rel. to BELL[2]. Hence **bell** vb. put a bell on. XVIII.

bell[2] bel (techn.) bellow, roar. OE. *bellan*, corr. to OHG. *bellan* (G. *bellen*) bark, bray; cf. ON. *belja* and BELLOW.

belladonna belədɔˈnə deadly nightshade XVI; drug prepared from this XVIII. modL. – It. *bella donna* lit. 'fair lady'; said to be so named because in Italy a face cosmetic was made from it.

bellarmine beˈlāɹmin large drinking-jug with capacious belly and narrow neck, orig. designed by the Protestants of Holland in ridicule of their opponent Cardinal *Bellarmine* (Roberto Francesco Romolo Bellarmino 1542–1621). XVIII.

belle bel handsome woman. XVII. F., fem. of *bel*, BEAU.

belles-lettres bɛl lɛtr polite literature. XVII. F., lit. 'fine letters or literature', parallel to *beaux arts* fine arts; see BELLE, LETTER. Hence **belleˈtr**IST (cf. G. *belletrist* XVIII), **belletriˈst**IC(AL) XIX.

bellicose beˈlikous warlike. XV. – L. *bellicōsus*, f. *bellicus* warlike, f. *bellum* (:– *duellum* DUEL); see -OSE.

belligerent biliˈdʒərənt waging war. XVI. Earlier *belligerant* – L. *belligerant-*, prp. stem of *belligerāre*, f. *belliger* waging war, f. *bellum* war+*-ger* (see GERENT).

Bellona belouˈnə Roman goddess of war, personification of war or warlike spirit. XVI. L., f. *bellum* war.

bellow beˈlou roar as a bull. XIV. ME. *belwe*, of uncertain origin; possibly OE. (Anglian) **belgan*, (WS.) **bielgan* (:– **balgjan*), late *bylgan* (but this form may be :– **bulgjan*), rel. to OE. *bellan* BELL[2].

bellows beˈlouz instrument used to blow a fire. ME. *belwes, belows*, pl. of *belu, below*, prob. repr. OE. pl. *belga, belgum*, of *bel(i)ġ, bæl(i)ġ* BELLY, which in late OE. occurs as abbrev. of earlier *blǣstbel(i)ġ* 'blowing-bag' = ON. *blástrbelgr*; see BLAST, BELLY and cf. Sw. *blåsbälg*, Da. *blæsebælg*, G. *blasebalg*. ME. *belies*, later *bellies*, Sc. *bell(e)is*, retained the meaning 'bellows' till XVI. The traditional pronunc. is (dial.) beˈlis (cf. bɔˈdis, repr. ME. *bodies*); the present standard pronunc. is based on the spelling.

belly beˈli A. †bag, pod; †bellows OE.; †body XIII; abdomen, paunch, stomach XIV. OE. *beliġ*, var. of *bæl(i)ġ*, WS. *biel(i)ġ, byl(i)ġ* = MDu. *balch*, OHG. *balg*, ON.

belgr, Goth. *balgs* :- CGerm. **balgiz* bag, sack, f. **balg-* **belg-* be inflated, swell (cf. BILLOW); the same word as that of which the pl. appears as BELLOWS.

belong bilɔ·ŋ be appropriate *to* or connected (with). XIV. prob. intensive (see BE-), f. ME. *longen* (OE. *langian*; see LONG); cf. (M)Du. *belangen* concern, be of importance (to). Hence **belo·ngings** connecting circumstances, relations XVII (Sh.); possessions, effects XIX; see -ING[1].

beloved bilʌ·vid, -lʌ·vd much loved. XIV. First with qualifying adv. *well*, *best*; pp. of (arch.) *belove* (XIII), f. BE- 2+LOVE[2]. Cf. G. *beliebt* favourite, f. *belieben* be pleased with, like.

below bilou· beneath, low or lower down. XIV (*bilooghe*; rare before XVI). f. *be*, BY+LOW[2], on the model of *alow*, †*on lau*, and BENEATH.

belt belt girdle. OE. *belt*, corr. to OHG. *balz*, ON. *belti* (Sw. *bälte*, Da. *bælte*) :- Germ. **baltjaz*, **baltjon* – L. *balteus*, *-um*, of Etruscan origin acc. to Varro.

Beltane be·ltən (Sc.) May-day. XV. – Gael. *bealltainn* (= OIr. *belltaine*, Manx *boaltinn*, *boaldyn*), Celtic name of the First of May, on which the heathen Irish lit fires and drove cattle through them; referred to OCeltic **belōte(p)niā* 'bright fire'.

beluga bilū·gə great sturgeon; white whale. XVIII (in XVII *bieluga*; in XVI *bellougina*; Hakluyt). – Russ. *belúga* in the former sense, and *belúkha* in the latter, f. *bélyĭ* white+*-uga*, *-ukha*, augm. suffixes.

belvedere belvīdiə·ɹ turret on a building commanding a view. XVI. – (partly through F. *belvédère*) It. *belvedere* lit. 'fair sight', f. *bel*, *bello* beautiful+*vedere* (sb. use of inf.) sight; see BEAU, WIT[2]. The F. etymol. equiv. *belvoir* bī·vəɹ is current in England as a proper name (surnames *Beevor*, *Bever*).

bema bī·mə raised platform; chancel. XVII. – Gr. *bêma* step, pace, f. **ba-* go, walk (cf. BASIS).

bemean bimī·n lower in dignity. XVII. f. BE- 5+MEAN[2], prob. after *demean*.

bemoan bimou·n moan or lament for. XVI. repl. ME. *bemene*, OE. *bemǣnan*; see BE- 4, MOAN.

bemuse bimjū·z stupefy. XVIII (Pope). f. BE- 2+MUSE[2].

ben[1] ben within XIV; inner; inner room XVIII. Sc. and north. Eng. var. (unexpl.) of ME. *bin*, *binne* :- OE. *binnan* (= OFris. *binna*, (M)LG., (M)Du., (M)G. *binnen*), f. *be* BY+*innan* within; see IN and cf. BUT.

ben[2] ben winged seed of the horse-radish tree. XV. – dial. var. *bēn* of Arab. *bān*.

ben[3] ben mountain peak (as in Ben Nevis, etc.). XVIII. – Gael. *beann* = OIr. *benn* (Ir. *beann*), W. *ban* prominence, peak, height, Gaul. *canto|bennicus* white peak.

bench benᵗʃ long seat; justice's seat (XIII, RGlouc.). OE. *benć* = OFris. *benk*, OS. *banc*, OHG. *banch* (Du., G. *bank*), ON. **benkr* (Icel. *bekkr*) :- CGerm. (exc. Goth.) **baŋkiz*; cf. BANK[1]. Hence **be·ncher** one who sits on a bench, esp. officially XV; senior member of the Inns of Court XVI; see -ER[1].

bend[1] bend †ribbon, band OE.; (her.) ordinary formed by two parallel lines XV. OE. *bend* :- Germ **bandjō*, f. **band-* **bend-* BIND; later coinciding with *bende* – OF. *bende* (mod. *bande*) BAND[2].

bend[2] bend bow, curve. OE. *bendan* (also, bind, fetter) = MHG. *benden*, ON. *benda* :- Germ. **bandjan*, f. **band-* BAND[1].

bene bīn (arch.) prayer. OE. *bēn* = ON. *bæn* :- **bōniz*; see BOON[1].

beneath binī·þ adv. in a low or lower position; prep. under, underneath. OE. *biniþan*, *bineoþan* (= OFris. *binetha*), f. *bi* BY+*niþan*, *neoþan* below, down, orig. from below, in fuller form *neoþane*, *-one* = OS. *nithana*, MLG. *neddene*, MDu. *neden(e)*, Du. *be|neden*, *nieden*, ON. *neðan*; f. Germ. **niþ-* (as in NETHER); for the formation cf. BEN[1], BUT, and HENCE, etc.

benedicite benidai·siti †int. bless us! bless you! XII (Laȝ.); sb. blessing at meat; †blessing, deliverance XIII; (gen.) invocation of a blessing; the canticle beginning 'Benedicite omnia opera Domini Domino', 'O all ye works of the Lord, bless ye the Lord', the Song of the Three Children, Dan. iii 57–90 XVII. 2nd pl. imper. of L. *benedīcere* wish well to, bless, f. *bene* well+*dīcere* say (cf. DICTION). In ME. abbrev. to *benste*.

benedick be·nidik newly married man. Name of a character in Sh. 'Much Ado about Nothing' (see esp. v iv 100). Also erron. *Benedict* (Scott).

Benedictine benidi·ktin (monk or nun) of the order of St. Benedict, founded by him c. 529. XVII. – F. *bénédictin* or modL. *benedictīnus*, f. *Benedictus*; see -INE[1]. So **benedi·ctine** liqueur made by these monks. XIX. – F. *bénédictine* (sc. *liqueur*), fem. of above adj.

benediction benidi·kʃən blessing. XV. – (O)F. *bénédiction* – L. *benedictiō(n-)*, f. *benedict-*, *benedīcere* bless, f. *bene* well+*dīcere* speak; see DICTION and cf. BENISON.

Benedictus benidi·ktəs. XVI. First word, L. *benedictus* blessed (see prec.), used as the title, of (i) the canticle of Zacharias (Luke i 68) beginning 'Benedictus Dominus Deus Israel', (ii) 'Benedictus qui venit in nomine Domini' (Matt. xxi 9, etc.) in the Mass, used as the title of either of these and of the settings to which they are sung.

bene esse bī·ni e·si state of well-being. XVII. L. phr., 'well to be', used sb.; *bene* well, f. **dwenos*, L. *bonus* good; *esse*, f. **es-* (see BE).

benefaction benifæ·kʃən doing good; endowment. XVII. – late L. *benefactiō(n-)*, f. *benefact-*, *beneficere*; see BENEFICE, BENEFIT, -TION. So **benefac**TOR be·nifæktəɹ. XV. – late L.

benefice be·nifis †kindness, favour, benefit; ecclesiastical living. XIV. – OF. *benefice* (mod. *bénéfice* profit, perquisite) – L. *beneficium* favour, support, (military) promotion, f. (after *beneficus* BENEFICENT) *bene* well (rel. to *bonus* good; cf. BOON²)+*fic-*, var. of stem of *facere* do, make; see FACT and cf. OFFICE. So **benefici**AL benifi·ʃəl. XV. – F. or late L. **benefi·ci**ARY holding (holder of) a benefice XVII. – L.; cf. F. *bénéficiaire*. From the L. stem *benefic-* are also **benefic**ENCE bine·fisəns XVI, **bene·fic**ENT XVII. – F. – L. *beneficentia*, **-ficent-*.

benefit be·nifit †good or kind deed XIV; advantage XV. Late ME. *benfe(e)t* – AN. *benfet*, OF. *bienfet*, *-fait* :– L. *benefactum* good deed, kind service, f. *bene facere* do well; assim. of the first syll. to L. *bene-* appears XV, and the change of *-fet* t *-fit* XVI. Hence **be·nefit** vb. XVI.

benevolence bine·vələns disposition to do good XIV (Ch.); enforced gift of money XV. – OF. *benivolence* – L. *benevolentia* well-wishing, f. *benevolent-*, *-ēns*, prp. stem of *bene velle* wish well (cf. WILL). So **bene·vol**ENT. XV. – OF. *benivolent*.

Bengali beŋgɔ̄·li pert. to Bengal, a province of India; native or language of B. XIX. An Eng. formation (also sp. *-ee*) on *Bengal* (in early Eur. use *Bangala*, *Bemgala*, *Bengala*). The native name of the language is *baŋgabhāṣā* language of Baŋga, i.e. Bengal.

benight binai·t (pass.) be overtaken by the darkness of night. XV. f. BE- 6+NIGHT.

benign binai·n kindly. XIV (R. Mannyng). – (O)F. *bénigne* fem., *bénin* m. :– L. *benigna*, *-us*, prob. for *benigenus*, f. *bene* well+*-genus* (see -GENOUS). For the formation cf. MALIGN and for the sense-development cf. L. *gentilis* GENTLE, Gr. *gennaîos*, L. *generōsus* GENEROUS and KIND². So **benignant** bini·gnənt gracious, favourable. XVIII. f. BENIGN or L. *benignus*, after *malignant*. Not in dicts. before 1800, though used by Burke and Boswell. **beni·gn**ITY. XIV (Ch., Wyclif). – OF. or L.

benison be·nizən, -sən (arch.) blessing, benediction. XIII (Cursor M.). ME. *bene(y)sun* – OF. *beneiçun*, *beneis(s)on* :– L. *benedictiōnem* BENEDICTION.

benjamin be·ndʒəmin. XVI. Alteration of early var. *benjoin* of BENZOIN, by assoc. with the name *Benjamin*.

bent¹ bent (arch.) grassy plain, field XIV; reedy or rush-like grass XV. repr. OE. *beonet*, found as an el. of place-names, e.g. *Beonetlēah* (Bentley), perh. 'meadow of stiff grass'; corr. to OS. *binet*, OHG. *binuʒ* (G. *binse*, orig. pl., rush, reed, stout grass of marshland) :– WGerm. **binut-*, of unkn. origin.

bent² bent †curved position; inclination, tendency; extent to which a bow may be bent (fig. in 'to the top of my bent', Sh.). XV. prob. f. BEND² on the analogy of pairs like *descend*, *descent*, *extend*, *extent*.

benthos be·nþɔs (zool.) flora and fauna of the sea-bottom. XIX (Haeckel). – Gr. *bénthos* depth of the sea.

benumb binʌ·m render insensible. XV. f. †*benombe*, †*benomme*, earlier †*benomen*, pp. of †*benim*, OE. *beniman* take away (= OFris. *benima*), f. *be-* BE- 3+*niman* take; see NIM, NUMB.

benzene benzī·n (chem.) the hydrocarbon C_6H_6. f. BENZOIC acid, whence it is derived; earlier *benzine* (now used for a mixture of petroleum hydrocarbons), after Mitscherlich (1833), *benzene* being due to A. W. Hofmann. The name was changed by Liebig in 1834 to **be·nz**OL, whence **be·nzoline** (-INE⁵), impure benzene, etc. The comb. form is **benz(o)-**.

benzoin be·nzoᵘin resin obtained from the tree Styrax benzoin XVI; genus of trees (Benjamin tree); (chem.) bitter almond oil, camphor XIX. Early forms also *belzoin*, *bengewine*, *benjoine*, etc. – F. *benjoin*, repr. Sp. *bengui*, Pg. *beijoim*, It. *benzoi*, for **lobenzoi*, **lobenjui* (*lo-* being taken for the definite article) – Arab. *lubān-jāwī* 'frankincense of Java'. Forms with *z*, seemingly from It., prevailed in Eng. and in Du., G. *benzoe*. Hence **benzo·ic** *acid* $C_7H_6O_2$. XVIII.

bequeath bikwī·ð †utter, declare; assign (property), esp. by will. OE. *becweþan*, f. BE- 4+*cweþan* say (see QUOTH); a term of the traditional language of wills; orig. a str. vb. (*becweþan*, *becwæþ*, *becweden*), it acquired weak inflexions in XV.

bequest bikwe·st act of bequeathing, legacy. XIV (R. Mannyng). ME. *bequeste*, *-quyste*, f. (after BEQUEATH) BE-+†*quiste* (Havelok), repr. OE. *-cwiss* (only in comps.), repl. *cwide* saying, decree, sentence, will, testament; OE. *-cwiss*=Goth. *-qiss* :– Germ. **kweþtiz*, f. **kweþ-* say (see QUOTH); for the parasitic *t* cf. BEHEST.

berate birei·t rate severely. XVI. f. BE- 4+RATE vb.; appears to have become obs. in England, but to have survived in U.S.A.

Berber bɔ̄·ɹbəɹ. XIX. Ancient Arabic name of the aboriginal people to the west and south of Egypt; applied to one of the three great subdivisions of the Hamitic group of languages.

bereave birī·v despoil, leave destitute, etc. OE. *berēafian* = OFris. *birāvia*, OS. *birōbon* (Du. *beroven*), OHG. *biroubōn* (G. *berauben*), Goth. *biraubōn* :– CGerm. (exc. ON.) **biraubōjan*, f. *bi-* BE- 3+**raubōjan* REAVE.

Pt. and pp. *bereft* is developed normally from OE. *berēafode, berēafod*; *bereaved* is a new formation.

beret be·rei round flat peakless cloth cap. XIX. – F. *béret* Basque cap – s.w. F. dial. *berret*, Pr. *berret* (see BIRETTA).

bergamot[1] bɔ̄·ɹgəmɔt A. the tree Citrus Bergamia XVII; aromatic oil derived therefrom; †snuff scented therewith XVIII; kind of mint, Mentha citrata XIX. B. kind of tapestry XIX. Presumably both uses derive from *Bergamo*, a town of Lombardy, Italy; but the early sp. *burg-*, *bourg-* in A raises doubts.

bergamot[2] bɔ̄·ɹgəmɔt kind of pear. XVII. – F. *bergamotte* – It. *bergamotta* – Turk. *begarmūdi*, f. *beg* prince, BEG[2]+*armūdi* pear (cf. synon. G. *fürstenbirne* 'prince's pear').

beriberi be·riberi disease marked by paralytic weakness prevalent in India. XIX. Sinhalese; redupl. of *beri* weakness. So F. *béribéri* (*-berii* XVIII).

berlin, berline bɔ̄·ɹlin, bəɹlī·n four-wheeled carriage. XVIII (Swift). – F. *berline* (whence in G.), f. *Berlin*, name of the capital of Prussia; introduced (XVII) by an architect of the Elector of Brandenburg.

berm bɔ̄ɹm (fortif.) narrow space between rampart and ditch. XVIII. – F. *berme* – Du. *berm*, prob. rel. to ON. *barmr* brim.

berry be·ri small globular or ovate fruit. OE. *beri(ġ)e*; cognates are in all the Germ. langs., with variation in form and gender, viz. OS. *beri* (in *wīnberi* grape), MDu. *bēre*, (M)Du. *bezie* (Du. *bes*), OHG. *beri* (G. *beere*), ON. *ber* (Da. *bær*), Goth. *basi* (only in acc. pl. *weinabasja*), f. Germ. **basj-*, **bazj-*, perh. rel. ult. to OE. *basu* red.

berserker bɔ̄·ɹsɔ̄ɹkəɹ; also **be·rserk** Norse warrior who fought with frenzied fury. XIX (Scott). – Icel. *berserkr*, acc. *berserk*, prob. f. *bern-*, *bjǫrn* BEAR[1]+*serkr* coat, SARK, but otherwise expl. as f. *berr* BARE, whence Eng. *baresark* (Carlyle, etc.).

berth bɔ̄ɹþ (naut.) convenient sea-room (hence fig. phr. *give a wide berth to*) XVII; situation or office on board ship; appointment, job; sleeping-place on board ship XVIII. Early vars. *birth, byrth*; prob. f. BEAR[2]+-TH[1], with ref. to the nautical sense of the vb. 'sail in a certain direction' (cf. 'When a ship sailes with a large wind towards the land . . we say she beares in with the land . . . And when she would not come neere the land, but goeth more Roome-way than her course, wee say she beares off'. Capt. Smith, 1627).

bertha bɔ̄·ɹþə, **berthe** bɔ̄ɹþ deep falling collar. XIX. – F. *berthe*, anglicized as *bertha*, a use of the fem. proper name F. *Berthe*, Eng. *Bertha*.

beryl be·rīl precious stone. XIII. – (O)F. *beryl, beril* (mod. *béryl*) :– L. *bēryllu-s* – Gr. *bḗrullos*, prob. of foreign origin. (The deriv. Rom. vb. **bērillāre* gave F. *briller*; see BRILLIANT.) ¶ The use of the beryl in reliquaries and monstrances led to its use by opticians, whence (O)F. *berille, bericle*, modF. *besicles*, and G. *brille* spectacles.

beseech bisī·tʃ beg earnestly, supplicate. XII. f. BE- 2+*seche*, SEEK; cf. OFris. *besēka*, pp. *-socht*. Forms repr. by the type *beseek* were current XIII–XVII (e.g. Sh., First Folio); the normal pt. and pp. form is *besought* (ME. *bisohte, bisoht*), but *beseeched* has been current since XVI.

beseem bisī·m †seem; (arch.) suit, befit. XIII. f. BE- 2+SEEM.

beset bise·t A. surround, invest, besiege OE.; B. †bestow XII. OE. *besettan* = OFris. *bisetta*, OS. *bisettian* (Du. *bezetten*), OHG. *bisezzan* (G. *besetzen*), Goth. *bisatjan*; CGerm. (exc. ON.), f. **bi-* BE- 1, 4+**satjan* SET[1].

beshrew biʃrū· †deprave, corrupt; (arch.) curse. XIV. f. BE- 2+SHREW.

beside, besides bisai·d(z) †by the side (of); outside (of), apart (from); in addition (to). XIII (Laȝ.). Early ME. *biside, bisides*, repr. OE. *be sīdan*, i.e. *be* BY, d. sg. of *sīde* SIDE; for the *-es* form see -S. Cf. Du. *bezijden*, MHG. *besīt, besīte(n)*.

besiege bisī·dʒ lay siege to. XIII (RGlouc.). f. (by substitution of prefix BE-) ME. *assiege* (XIII) – OF. *asegier* (mod. *assiéger*) = Pr. *assetjar*, Sp. *asediar*, It. *assediare* :– Rom. **assedicāre*, f. L. *ad* AS-+**sedicum* SIEGE.

besmirch see BE- 2, SMIRCH. XVI (Sh.).

besom bī·zəm broom. OE. *besema, besma* = OFris. *besma*, OS. *besmo* (Du. *bezem*), OHG. *besamo* (G. *besen*) :– WGerm. **besmo*, of unkn. origin. For the dial. application to women cf. *malkin* and G. *besen* servant-girl, wench.

bespeak bispī·k †speak or call out OE.; speak for, order; speak to, address XVI; tell of, indicate XVII. OE. *bisprecan* = OFris. *bispreka*, OS. *besprekan* (Du. *bespreken*), OHG. *bisprehhan* (G. *besprechen*); CWGerm. f. **bi-* BE- 1+**sprekan* SPEAK. There seems to be little historical connexion between the Eng. groups of senses, which have prob. arisen independently from different uses of the prefix. In ordinary colloq. use surviving only in pp. *bespoke* (of work commissioned).

besprent bispre·nt (arch.) sprinkled. XIV. pp. of ME. *besprenge*, OE. *besprenġan*, f. BE- 1+*sprenġan* sprinkle :– Germ. **spraŋgjan*, causative of **spreŋgan* SPRING[2]. So **bespri·nkle.** XVI (earlier †*besprengil* XV).

Bessemer (*steel, iron*) be·siməɹ f. name of inventor of an iron and steel process, Sir Henry *Bessemer*, in 1856.

best best most good or well. OE. *betest* inflected *betsta*, etc., adv. *betost, betst* = OFris., OS. (Du.) *best*, OHG. *beȥȥist-o*

(G. *best*), ON. *bezt-r, bazt-r*, Goth. *batist-s* :- CGerm. **batist-az*, superl. of **bat-*; see BETTER, -EST. *Best man* groomsman, and *best maid* bridesmaid, are of Sc. origin (XVIII). Hence **best** vb. get the better of XIX; of dial. origin; cf. *worst* (XVII).

bested, bestead biste·d (arch.) situated, circumstanced. XIII. ME. *bistad*, f. *bi-* BE- 2 +*stad* - ON. *staddr*, pp. of *steðja* place, with later assim. to native *sted*, STEAD.

bestial[1] be·stiəl (chiefly Sc.) cattle. XIV. - OF. *bestial* - late L. *bēstiālis*, used sb. (Earlier ME. *bestaile* - OF. *bestaille* - medL. *bēstiālia*, n. pl. of *bēstiālis* used as fem. sg.) See next.

bestial[2] be·stiəl of beasts, like a beast. XIV(Gower). - (O)F. *bestial* - late L. *bēstiālis*, f. *bēstia* BEAST; see -IAL. So **bestia·lity**. XIV (Ch.). - (O)F. *bestialité*.

bestiary be·stiəri treatise about beasts. XIX. - medL. *bēstiārium*, f. *bēstia* BEAST; see -ARY. Cf. (O)F. *bestiaire*.

bestir bistə̄·ɹ rouse to activity. XIV. f. BE- 2+STIR. (Not continuous with OE. *bestyrian* heap up.)

bestow bistou· place or stow away; apply. XIV. ME. *bistowen*, f. BE- 2+OE. *stow* place (see STOW). Hence **bestow·al** XVIII; see -AL[2].

bestrew bistrū· strew *with*. OE. *bistrēowian* (cf. Du. *bestroojen*, MHG. *beströuwen*), f. BE- 1+STREW.

bestride bistrai·d sit upon with legs astride. OE. *bistrīdan*; see BE- 4 and STRIDE, and cf. MDu., MLG. *bestrīden*.

bet bet lay a wager. XVI. The sb. and vb. appear in the last decade of XVI, and it is uncertain which is prior; perh. aphetic of ABET in the sense 'instigation, support (of a cause)', the vb. being then derived from the sb.

beta bī·tə second letter of the Gr. alphabet, *bêta*; applied techn. to things of a second order or rank. XIX.

betake bitei·k †hand over, commit, commend XIII (Laȝ., RGlouc.); refl. commit oneself XVI; refl. resort, go XVII. f. BE- 2+ TAKE; in ME. functioning as a var. of †*beteach*, OE. *betǣċan* (f. *be-*+*tǣċan* show, TEACH).

betel bī·təl leaf of the plant Piper betle, chewed by Indians with areca nut. XVI. - Pg. *betel* - Malayalam *veṭṭila*.

bête noire beit nwāɹ object of aversion. XIX. F. 'black beast', fig. insufferable person or thing.

Bethel be·þəl hallowed spot (Gen. xxviii 17) XVII; Nonconformist chapel XIX. - Heb. *bēthēl*, f. *bēth* house+*ēl* God.

bethink biþi·ŋk think about; (refl.) †collect one's thoughts OE.; reflect, recollect XIII. OE. *biþenċan* = OFris. *bithanka, bithenzia*, OS. *bithenkian*, OHG. *bidenken* (Du., G. *bedenken*), Goth. *biþagkjan*; CGerm. (exc. ON.), f. **bi-* BE- 4+**þaŋkjan* THINK.

betide bitai·d happen. XIII. f. BE- 2+ *tide(n)* (see TIDE). Surviving mainly in *woe betide . . !*

betimes bitai·mz at an early time, in good time. XIV. f. *betime* (XIII), f. *be* BY+TIME; see -S.

betoken bitou·kn signify, be a token of. XII. OE. **bitācnian* = OFris. *bitēknia*, Du. *beteekenen*, OHG. *bizeichanōn* (G. *bezeichnen*); see BE- 2, TOKEN.

beton be·tən kind of concrete. XIX. - F. *béton*, OF. *betun* = Pr. *betun* cement :- L. *bitūmen* mineral pitch, BITUMEN.

betony be·təni purple-flowered labiate plant. XIV. - (O)F. *betoine* - popL. **betonia* for *betonica*, in Pliny *vettōnica*, said by him to be a Gaulish name of a plant discovered by a Spanish tribe named Vettones.

betray bitrei· give up treacherously XIII; reveal involuntarily XVI; show signs of XVII. f. BE- 2+†*tray* (XIII) - OF. *traïr* (mod. *trahir*) = Pr. *traïr*, It. *tradire* - L. *tradere* deliver up (see TRADITION, TREASON). Hence **betray·al** XIX; see -AL[2].

betroth bitrou·ð engage with promise to marry. XIV. ME. *betrouþe, betreuþe*, f. BE- 6+*trouþe, treuþe*, TRUTH, later assim. to TROTH. Hence **betro·thal** XIX; after *espousal*.

better be·təɹ compar. of *good* (OE.) and of *well* (XIII). OE. *betera* (m. adj.) = OFris. *betera*, OS. *betiro* (Du. *beter*), OHG. *beȥiro* (G. *besser*), ON. *betri*, Goth. *batiza* :- CGerm. **batizon*, f. **bat-*, rel. to OE. *bōt* remedy, compensation, BOOT[2], *bētan* improve, remedy. The OE. compar. adv. was *bet*, which survived till XVII = OFris., OS. *bet* (Du. *bet-*), ON. *betr* :- Germ. **batiz* (cf. also OS., OHG. *bat*, G. *bass*). Hence **be·tter** vb. XIV. (Not continuous with OE. *ġebeterian*, corr. to OFris. *beteria*, etc.) **be·tter-**MENT. XVIII (orig. U.S.).

Betty be·ti dim. of *Bet*, abbrev. of *Elizabet, -beth*, applied like many other hypocoristic forms to various instruments or implements (e.g. burglar's jemmy XVII). ¶ The allusion in *all my eye and Betty Martin* is unkn.

between bitwī·n in the space which separates two points; (in wider sense) amid, amongst. OE. *betwēonum* (beside *betwēon* and *betwēonan*), f. Germ. **bi* BY+**twēon* :- **twiχnai* (cf. OFris. *twine* two each, Goth. *tweihnai* two together, two each), formation with *n*-suffix (cf. L. *bīnī* two at a time, and TWIN) on **twīχ-* (whence OE. *twēo*, OS. *tweho*, OHG. *zweho* doubt, difference, any adv. *twīh* in OE. *mid unc twīh* between us two) :- IE. **dweik-* **dwik-* (repr. by Skr. *dvikás* consisting of two, Russ. *dvóĭk.ɹ* pair), f. **dwō* TWO.

In OE. *twēonum* occurs in concord with a sb. in the dative pl. governed by *be*, as several times in *be sǣm twēonum* 'between seas', and once in *be werum twēonum* among men; cf. Goth. *miþ tweihnaim markom* between two borders. So **betwixt** bitwi·kst ME. *bitwixte* (Laȝ., later text), OE. *betwēohs, betwēox, betwux, betwyx*, also *betwēoxn*, corr. to OFris. *bituischa, bituiskum*; f. Germ. **bi* BY+**twisk-*, repr. also by OFris. *twiska*, OS. *twisc*, OHG. *zwiski* two each, twofold, (M)HG. *zwischen* adv.-prep. between (short for OHG. *in* and *untar zwiskēn* in the midst of two), Du. *tisschen*, f. **twa* TWO+**-isk-* -ISH[1].

beurré bö·rei mellow variety of pear. XVIII. F. 'buttered, buttery', f. *beurre* butter :- L. *būtyrum* – Gr. *boúturon*.

bevel be·vəl adj. having two equal acute alternate angles XVI; oblique XVII; sb. joiner's tool for setting off angles; obtuse angle XVII. – OF. **bevel* (whence Sp. *baivel*), F. *béveau, biveau, buveau, beauveau* (XVI), f. OF. *baif* open-mouthed, f. *baer* (see BAY[3]); cf. OF. *bever* give bias to.

bever bī·vəɹ (obs. or dial.) snack between meals. XIV. – AN. *bever*, OF. *beivre* drinking, drink, sb. use of *beivre* (mod. *boire*) :- L. *bibere* drink (cf. IMBIBE).

beverage be·vəridʒ drink. XIII (*beverech, -ege*). – OF. *bevrage, beuvrage* (mod. *breuvage*) = Pr. *beuratje*, Sp. *bebrage*, It. *beveraggio* :- Rom. **biberāticum*, f. L. *bibere* drink; see prec. and -AGE.

bevy be·vi company of ladies, birds, etc. XV. Of unkn. origin.

bewail biwei·l wail over. XIII. f. BE- 4+ WAIL; after synon. OE. *begrētan, besorgian, bewēpan* BEWEEP.

beware biwɛə·ɹ take care. XIII (RGlouc.). orig. *be war*, i.e. BE imper., inf., or pres. subj., and *war* WARE[2]; used mostly only where *be* (not *am*, etc.) is the appropriate verbal form, but formerly also inflected †*bewared*, †*bewaring*. Cf. BEGONE.

beweep biwī·p (arch.) weep for or over. OE. *bewēpan* (= OFris. *biwēpa*, OS. *biwōpian*), f. BE- 4+*wēpan* WEEP.

bewilder biwi·ldəɹ confuse. XVII. f. BE- 2+†*wilder* lose one's way, cause to lose one's way, perh. back-formation from WILDERNESS.

bewitch biwi·tʃ affect by witchcraft or magic. XIII. f. BE- 2+WITCH (OE. *wiććian*).

bewray birei· (arch.) betray. XIII. f. BE- 2+ ME. *wreie*, OE. *wrēġan* accuse = OFris. *wrēia*, OS. *wrōgian*, OHG. *ruogen* (G. *rügen*), ON. *rœgja* :- CGerm. **wrōgjan* (in Goth. *wrohjan*), of unkn. origin.

bey bei Turkish governor. XVI. – Osmanli *bey*, mod. pronunc. of BEG[2].

beyond bijɔ·nd at or to the farther side. OE. *beġ(e)ondan*, f. *be* BY+*ġ(e)ondan* from the farther side :- Germ. **jandana*, f. **jand-* YOND.

bezant be·zənt gold coin. XIII (*beȝȝsannt*, Orm). – OF. *besant*, nom. *besanz* :- L. *Bȳzantius* (sc. *nummus* coin), adj. of *Bȳzantium*, Gr. *Būzántion*, the modern Istanbul (Constantinople), where it was first coined. So **bezanty** be·zənti (her.) charged with or formed of bezants. XVII (earlier anglicized *besauntid* 'Book of St. Albans'). – AN. *besanté*; see -Y[5].

bezantler bei·zæntləɹ second branch of a deer's horn. XVI. – AN. **besantouiller*, f. OF. *bes-* BIS-+*andouiller* ANTLER.

bezel be·zəl sloping edge or side. XVII. – OF. **besel* (mod. *béseau, bizeau*; cf. Sp. *bisel*), of unkn. origin. Early synon. forms are *basil, bazil* – F. *basile* angle of inclination in a carpenter's plane.

bezique bəzī·k card-game. XIX. – F. *bésigue* also *bésy*, perh. – Pers. *bāzīchi, bazi* sport, play.

bezoar bī·zouəɹ, be·zouəɹ †antidote; intestinal calculus (orig. that obtained from the wild goat of Persia) supposed to act as an antidote. XV. Attested in a great variety of forms repr. F. *bezahar(d)*, OF. *bezar* (mod. *bézoard*), Sp. *bezár*, modL. *beza(h)ar* – Arab. *bēzahr*, var. of *bāzahr, bādizahr* – Pers. *pādzahr*, f. *pād* protector + *zahr* stone.

bezonian bĭzou·niən raw recruit; ruffian. XVI. f. It. *bisogno* need, want, needy recruit +-IAN. The It. and F. forms, *bi-, besognio, besogne*, were also in use XVI–XVII.

bhang, bang bæŋ Indian variety of hemp chewed or smoked. XVI. orig. – Pg. *bangue*, afterwards assim. to Pers. *bang* (whence Arab. *banj*), and Urdu, etc. *bhāng, bhang, bhung* :- Skr. *bhaṅgā* hemp.

bheesty bī·sti Indian servant who supplies water. XVIII. – (Urdu –) Pers. *bihishtī*, f. *bihisht* paradise.

bi- bəi repr. L. *bi-* (earlier *dui-* = Gr. *di-*, Skr. *dvi-*) twice, doubly, two-, in L. chiefly in adj. formations on sb. stems, as BICEPS, *bicolor* of two colours, *biformis* of two forms, *bisulcus* two-furrowed, also with pp. ending, as *bicamerātus* (cf. BICAMERAL), *biformātus* of two forms; in a few, e.g. BIFID, the formation is on a vb.-stem. The prefix appears in Eng. first in adoptions from F., as *bigam* XIII (cf. BIGAMOUS), later in adoptions or adaptations of L. words, as *biforked* XVI, BIFURCATE, *biformed* XVI (L. *biformis*), *bifront* two-faced XVI (L. *bifrons*), *bipartite* XVI (L. *bipartītus*); from XVII the L. analogy was widely extended and the prefix used with any adj. to express that a quality or property is doubled or repeated; in mod. scientific terminology forms in *-ate, -ated* are most freq. employed.

On the model of BIENNIAL, *bi-monthly, by-yearly* (XIX) are used for 'occurring every two months/years'; but in U.S.A. formations of this type are used for 'occurring or appearing twice in a ——' (otherwise expressed by *semi-*).

In chem. *bi-* denotes the presence in a compound of twice the amount of acid, etc. that is indicated by the simple term.

bias bai·əs oblique; sb. oblique line, inclination; adv. XVI. – (O)F. *biais* = Pr. *biais* (whence It. *biescio*), Cat. *biax*, *biaix*, referred by Diez to late L. *bifacem*, *-fax* looking two ways, f. L. *bi-* BI-+*faciēs* FACE, after Gr. *διπρόσωπος*. Hence **bi·as** vb. XVII.

bib bib drink, tipple. XIV. poss. – L. *bibere* drink (cf. IMBIBE); but perh. independently imit. (cf. the var. *beb* XV, surviving in Yorks dial.); preserved in arch. *winebibber* (Prov. xxiii 30, etc.; *wyne bebber*, Coverdale, who was a Yorks man). Hence perh. **bib** sb. cloth to protect the front of a child's dress XVI; also, front upper part of dress or apron XVII; whence in phr. *best band and bib* (XVIII), *best bib and tucker*.

bibelot bi·bəlou small curio. XIX. F., alteration of earlier *bimbelot*, OF. *beubelot*, dim. of **belbel*, redupl. of *bel* beautiful (see BEAU, BELLE; cf. *bonbon*).

Bible bai·bl the Holy Scriptures XIII (Cursor M.). – (O)F. *bible* = Pr. *bibla*, Sp. *biblia*, It. *bibbia* – ecclL. *biblia*, n. pl. taken in Rom. as fem. sg. – Gr. (*tà*) *biblía* 'the books'. The Gr. sg. *biblíon*, dim. of *bíblos*, *búblos* papyrus, scroll, roll, book (of Sem. origin) lost its dim. sense and became the ordinary word for 'book' before its application (as in LXX) to the Hebrew and Christian sacred scriptures.

biblio- bi·bliou, biblio· repr. Gr. *biblio-*, stem of *biblíon* (see prec.), as in **biblio·-GRAPHY** – F. or modL. (*bibliographia* list or account of books on a particular subject) – Gr. *bibliographíā* writing of books; **biblio·GRAPHER**, **bi:blioGRA·PHICAL**; **bi:blio-MA·NIA**, after F. *bibliomanie*; **bi·bliOPHILE** (– F.); all used by Dibdin.

bibulous bi·bjŭləs given to much drinking, tippling. XVII. f. L. *bibulus*, f. *bibere* drink; see IMBIBE, -ULOUS.

bicameral baikæ·mərəl having two legislative chambers. XIX. f. BI- + L. *camera* CHAMBER+-AL[1].

bice bais †brownish-grey XIV; shade of blue obtained from smalt XV; pigment yielding this XVI. – (O)F. *bis* dark-grey = Pr. *bis*, It. *bigio*, of unkn. origin. From the F. collocations *azur bis* dark blue, *vert bis* dark green, erron. transferred in Eng. to blue and green pigments, and the colours yielded by them.

biceps bai·seps (anat.) muscle of upper arm and thigh. XVII. – L. *biceps* (*-cipit-*) two-headed, f. BI-+*-ceps*, rel. to *caput* (*capit-*) HEAD.

bicker[1] bi·kəɹ †skirmish XIII (RGlouc.); altercation XIV. ME. *biker*, *beker*, of unkn. origin; the termination suggests a frequent. formation (-ER[5]) on a base **bik-* or **bek-*, perh. that of *beak* vb. (XIII) strike with the beak, peck. So **bi·cker** vb. XIII (*bikering*, RGlouc.).

bicker[2] bi·kəɹ Sc. form of BEAKER. XV.

bickern bi·kəɹn anvil with two taper ends. XVI (*bycorne*). – F. *bigorne* – Pr. *bigorna* (cf. Sp. *vigornia*, It. *bicornia*), f. L. *bicornis* two-horned, f. *bi-* BI-+*cornu* HORN. Altered to *beak-iron* (XVII) by assim. to BEAK and IRON.

bicycle bai·sikl two-wheeled velocipede. XIX. – F. *bicycle*, f. BI-+Gr. *kúklos* circle, wheel, CYCLE.

bid bid pt. (in D) *bade* bæd, beid, (in B) *bid*; pp. (in D) *bidden*, (in B and C) *bid*. A. ask, pray; B. offer; C. announce; D. command. The present forms repr. OE. str. vb. *biddan*, pt. *bæd*, *bǣdon*, pp. *beden* ask, entreat, demand = OFris. *bidda*, *bidia*, OS. *biddian*, MDu. *bidden*, OHG. (G.) *bitten*, ON. *biðja*, Goth. *bidjan* :– CGerm. **biðjan*, f. base **beð-*, repr. by OE. *ġebed*, *bed|hūs* (see BEAD), of which the ultimate connexions are unkn.

The present meanings combine those of this vb. with those of OE. *bēodan*, pt. *bēad*, *budon*, pp. *boden* offer, proclaim, announce, command, decree = OFris. *biada*, OS. *biodan*, (M)Du. *bieden*, OHG. *biotan* (G. *bieten*), ON. *bjóða*, Goth. *biudan*, repr. IE. **bheudh-* **bhudh-* (whence Gr. *peúthesthai*, *puthésthai* inform oneself, ascertain, and many forms in Aryan, Slavonic, and Celtic). OE. *biddan* had already acquired the sense 'command', and the similarity of several of the ME. forms of the two vbs. furthered the unification of the two words. The sense 'announce, proclaim' is obs. unless it survives in the phr. *bid the banns*.

Bidding prayer (XVII), which is now apprehended as meaning 'prayer in which the supplications of the people are asked or enjoined' is a perversion of *bidding prayers*, *bidding of the* (*common*) *prayers*, of which earlier forms were *bidding of the beads*, *beads bidding* (see BEAD), i.e. praying of (the) prayers, the shift of meaning being assisted by the obsolescence of the sense 'pray' of *bid*.

The origin of the pp. *bidden*, superseding ME. *beden*, *bēden*, is obscure; it reacted upon the pt., producing the var. *bid*.

biddy bi·di chicken, fowl. XVII (Sh.). perh. a use of *Biddy*, pet-form of *Bridget*; cf. the dial. use of *Betty* and *Molly* for the hedge-sparrow, and *Jenny* for the wren. See also CHICKABIDDY.

bide baid remain; wait; wait for OE.; endure, suffer XIII. OE. *bīdan*, pt. *bād*, *bidon*, pp. *biden* = OS. *bīdan* (MDu. *bīden*), OHG. *bītan* (G. dial. *beiten*), ON. *bíða*, Goth. *beidan* :– CGerm. **bīðan*; formally identical with Gr. *peíthō*, etc. (see BID), but the connexion of sense is not clear; the corr. short base is repr. by OE. *and|bidian* and ON. *biða* wait.

bield bīld †boldness OE; †confidence, comfort, resource XIII; †protector XIV; (Sc. and north. Eng.) refuge, shelter XV. OE. *beldu* (WS. *bieldu*) = OHG. *baldī*, Goth. *balþei* boldness, confidence :- Germ. **balþjōn*, f. **balþaz* BOLD.

biennial baie·niəl lasting two years; recurring every two years. XVII. f. L. *biennis* of two years, *biennium* space of two years; see BI- and ANNUAL. ¶ So *triennial, quadrennial, quinquennial, sexennial, septennial, octennial, decennial*, all of similar date exc. *quinquennial* (XV, Fortescue).

bier biəɹ stand for a corpse. OE. *bēr* (WS. *bǣr*) = OFris. *bēre*, OS., OHG. *bāra* (G. *bahre*) :- WGerm. **bērō* (whence (O)F. *bière*, Pr. *bera*), f. **beran* BEAR; the sp. with *ie* dates from c. 1600.

biestings var. of BEESTINGS.

biff bif (sl.) sb. and vb. hit. XIX. imit. Cf. earlier (dial.) *beft, beff, baff* (XVI).

biffin bi·fin variety of apple XVIII; baked apple XIX. Also *beefin*, dial. pronunc. of *beefing*, f. BEEF, in ref. to the deep-red colour of the apple; for the suffix cf. *golding, jenneting, sweeting, wilding*.

bifid bai·fid cleft in two XVII. – L. *bifidus*, f. *bi-* BI- + **fid-*, base of *findere* cleave (see FISSILE).

bifurcate bai·fəɹkeit fork into two. XVII. f. medL. *bifurcātus*, f. L. *bifurcus* two-forked, f. *bi-* BI-+*furca* FORK; see -ATE[3]. Hence **bifurca·tion**. XVII. Cf. earlier *biforked* (XVI).

big big †strong, stout XIII; advanced in pregnancy; of great bulk XVI. The earliest exx. are from northerly texts; of unkn. origin, possibly Scand. The existence of the gen. current sense before XVI is doubtful.

bigamy bi·gəmi marriage during the lifetime of an existing husband or wife XIII; (hist.) marriage of or with a widow or widower XVI. – (O)F. *bigamie*, f. *bigame* (whence ME. *bigam*) – late L. *bigamus*, f. L. *bi-* BI-+Gr. *-gamos* married. Hence **bi·gamous** XIX, **bi·gamist** XVII.

bigaroon bigərū·n large whiteheart cherry. XVII (*bigarreau, bigarro, biguar*). – F. *bigarreau* – modPr. *bigarreu*, f. *bigarra* variegate. The form in *-oon* is of Eng. origin.

biggin[1] bi·gin child's cap, nightcap. XVI. – F. *béguin*, f. *Béguine* BEGUINE.

biggin[2] bi·gin kind of coffee-pot. XIX. f. name of inventor.

bight bait bend, angle OE.; as a geographical feature XV; loop of a rope XVII; bay XVI. OE. *byht* :- **buχtiz*; cf. (M)LG. *bucht* (whence Du. *bocht*, G. *bucht*, Sw., Da. *bugt*) :- **bug-*, short stem of **beug-*, see BOW[2].

bigot bi·gət †hypocritical or superstitious professor of religion XVI; obstinate adherent of a creed or opinion XVII. – F. *bigot* (XV), of unkn. origin. Found (XII) as the proper name of a people of S. France, whence it has been referred by some to medL. *Visigothi* (the Visigoths of the region were Arians); it is used in Wace's 'Roman du Rou' (XII) as an abusive term by French to Normans, and it became a Norman family name. The gap between these early references and the much later use of the word as a common noun has not been bridged. ¶ A story relating the refusal of Rollo of Normandy to kiss the foot of Charles the Simple with the Eng. phr. *Nese bi god* 'No, by God', and the interpretation of *bi god* by Charles as the name of Rollo's people, is not credible. Hence **bi·goted** XVII (Evelyn), **bi·gotry** XVII (Clarendon).

bigwig bi·gwig man of note or importance. XVIII (Southey). f. BIG+WIG, with ref. to the large wigs worn by men of distinction.

bijou bī·ʒu trinket. XIX. F. – Breton *bizou* finger-ring, f. *biz* (cf. W. *bys*), finger.

bike[1] baik (n. dial.) nest of wasps, etc. XIII (Cursor M.). Of unkn. origin; cf. AL. *bigrus* hive, apiary (XII).

bike[2] baik. XIX. sl. abbrev. of BICYCLE, said in 1890 to be in use in Washington, U.S.A.

bilander bi·ləndəɹ, bai·- two-masted merchant vessel used for coast and canal traffic XVII. – Du. *bijlander* (Flem. *billander*), f. *bij* BY+*land* LAND; adopted in F. as *bélandre*; see -ER[1].

bilberry bi·lbəri fruit of Vaccinium Myrtillus. XVI. prob. of Norse origin; cf. Da. *bøllebær*, f. *bølle* bilberry+*bær* BERRY.

bilbo bi·lbou sword of fine temper. XVI (Greene, Sh.). orig. *Bilbo blade*, f. *Bilboa*, Eng. form of *Bilbao* name of a town in Spain, famous for its swords.

bilboes bi·lbouz (pl.) iron bar with sliding shackles. XVI. Of unkn. origin; commonly referred to *Bilbao* (see prec.) but without evidence.

bile bail bitter fluid secreted by the liver. XVII. – F. *bile* – L. *bīlis* :- **bislis* (cf. W. *bustl*, Corn. *bistel*, Bret. *bestle* :- **bistl-*). So **bilious** bi·ljəs. XVI. – F. *bilieux* – L. *bīliōsus*, f. *bīlis*.

bilge bildʒ bottom of a ship's hull XV (1496 in Sandahl) (in early use Sc.); filth collecting there XIX (cf. *bilge water* XVIII). prob. obscure var. of BULGE, used in the same senses.

bilk bilk spoil an adversary's score at cribbage; defraud; elude. XVII. perh. alteration of BALK, with symbolic 'thinning' of the vowel.

bill[1] bil weapon of war (sword or halberd); pruning-hook. OE. *bil* = OS. *bil*, OHG. *bill* (MHG. *bil*; but G. *bille* fem. axe) :- WGerm. **bilja*, perh. :- **bhidliam*, f. IE. **bhid-* cleave (see BITE).

bill[2] bil beak. OE. *bile*, not elsewhere in Germ.; perh. f. same base as prec. Hence

bill vb.[1] peck XIII; stroke or caress with the bill XVI.

bill[3] bil †written document; †legal statement of a case; †list, catalogue XIV; note of charges, account; poster XV; draft of an act of parliament XVI. – AN. *bille* or AL. *billa* (XIII), prob. unexpl. alteration of medL. *bulla* BULL[2]. Hence **bill** vb.[2] enter in a bill XIV; announce by bill XVII.

billabong bi·ləbɔŋ (Austral.) affluent of a river forming a backwater. XIX. Native name, *billa* river + *bong* dead.

billet[1] bi·lit A. †short document XV. B. (f. the vb.) military order to provide board and lodging XVII; place of such lodging; situation, job XIX. – AN. *billette* or AL. *billetta*, dim. of *billa* BILL[3]. Hence **bi·llet** vb. assign quarters to. XVI.

billet[2] bi·lit thick piece of wood. XV. – (O)F. *billette* and *billot*, dims. of *bille* tree-trunk, length of round timber – medL. *billa*, *billus* branch, trunk, prob. of Celtic origin (cf. Ir. *bile* sacred tree, large tree); see -ET.

billet-doux bilĭdū· love-letter. XVII (Dryden). F., 'sweet note'; see BILLET[1], DULCET.

billiards bi·ljeɹdz cue-and-ball game played on a table. XVI. – F. *billard* name of the game and the cue, f. *bille*; see BILLET[2] and -ARD. In Eng. only the name of the game, and made pl. like *bowls*, etc.; in early Sc. (XVI) *bilȝeart* was applied also to the cue.

Billingsgate bi·liŋzgeit proper name (ME. *Billingesgate* (Ekwall), f. personal name) of one of the gates of London and of the fish-market there; hence (XVII) abusive or foul language (such as that used by fishwives).

billion bi·ljən a million millions. XVII (Locke). – F. *billion*, arbitrarily f. *million* MILLION, by substitution of BI- for the initial *mi*; in later French use and in U.S.A. denoting 1,000 millions. Hence **bi·llionth** XVIII; see -TH[2]. ¶ So *trillion, quadrillion, quintillion, sextillion, septillion, octillion, nonillion* (third power of a million or 1,000 billions, etc.); all XVII.

billon bi·lən alloy of gold or silver with a baser metal. XVIII. – (O)F. *billon* (orig.) ingot, (now) bronze or copper money, f. *bille* (see BILLET[2]); cf. -OON.

billow bi·lou †swell, surge; great wave. XVI. – ON. *bylgja* billow (Sw. *bölja*, Da. *bölge*), f. Germ. **bulg-* **belg-* swell; cf. (M)HG. *bulge* †billow, leather bag, and BELLY.

billy bi·li (Sc.) fellow, comrade XVI; various machines and implements XVIII. Familiar form of *Willy*, pet-form of WILLIAM. Hence **bi·lly-goat** he-goat XIX; cf. *nanny-goat*.

billycock bi·likɔk hard felt hat. XIX. Said to be f. name of *William Coke*, nephew of Thomas William Coke, Earl of Leicester (1752–1842), to whose order the first hat of the kind was made (still called *coke* in the hat trade). For *billy-* see prec.

biltong bi·ltɔŋ sun-dried meat in strips. XIX. Afrikaans, f. Du. *bil* buttock + *tong* tongue, so called from being cut chiefly from the buttock and resembling smoked tongue.

bimbashi, -ee bimbā·ʃi Turkish commander; English officer under the khedive of Egypt. XIX. Turk. 'head of a thousand', f. *bīm* thousand, *bāsh* head (cf. BASHAW).

bimetallism baime·təlizm unrestricted currency of gold and silver. XIX. f. **bimeta·llic** – F. *bimétallique*, first used in an address, 5 Jan. 1869, and in Eng. form at Liverpool in 1876; see BI-, METAL, -IC, -ISM.

bin bin †manger OE.; receptacle for corn, etc. XIV. OE. *bin(n)*, *binne* – OBrit. **benna* (W. *ben* cart) :– **bhendhnā*, f. IE. **bhendh-* weave, BIND (cf. Gr. *phátnē, páthnē* manger :– **bhn̥tnā*); or – medL. *benna* (Festus, recording a Gaul. word), which is the source of F. *banne*, It. dial. *benna* hamper, Du. *ben*, G. *benne* body of a cart. ¶ For other names of vessels or conveyances which passed from the Celtæ to the Germani, partly through the Romans, cf. *bushel, car, carpenter*.

binary bai·nəri dual, based on the number two XVI; combination of two XV. – late L. *bīnārius*, f. *bīnī* two together (cf. BI-); see -ARY.

bind baind make fast with a band, tie up. OE. *bindan*, pt. *band, bundon*, pp. *bunden* = OFris. *binda*, OS. *bindan* (M)Du. *binden*, OHG. *bintan* (G. *binden*), ON. *binda*, Goth. *bindan* :– CGerm. **bindan*, f. IE. base **bhendh-* (Skr. *bandh* bind, Gr. *peîsma* cable :– **bhendhsma*). Hence **bi·nd**ER[1]. *OE. bindere*; (of books) XVI (the vb. is found in this sense XIV); whence **bi·nd**ERY bookbinding establishment XIX (orig. U.S.), after Du. *binderij*.

bindweed bai·ndwīd convolvulus. XVI. f. BIND + WEED[1].

bine bain flexible (climbing) stem. XIX. Adoption as a literary form of a var. of synon. dial. *bind* (XIV), rel. to BIND.

binge bin^{d}ʒ drinking-bout; also as vb. XIX. prob. sl. use of dial. *binge* vb. soak (a wooden vessel).

bingo bi·ŋgou (sl.) brandy. XIX. prob. f. *b* of BRANDY + ST|INGO.

binnacle bi·nəkl box containing ship's compass. XV. Earlier forms *bitakle, biticle, bittacle* (still in Marryat 1839) – Sp. *bitácula, bitácora*, or Pg. *bitácola* (corr. to Pr. *abitacle*, It. *abitacolo*, F. *habitacle*) – L. *habitāculum* habitation, f. *habitāre* inhabit (cf. HABITATION); the change from *tt* to *nn* may have been bridged by such a form as *biddikil* (XVII).

binocular bainɔ·kjŭləɹ adapted to both

eyes XVIII; sb. pl. field-glass, opera-glass XIX. f. L. *bīnī* two together (cf. TWIN)+ *oculus* EYE, after OCULAR.

binomial bainou·miəl (math.) having two terms. XVI. f. F. *binôme* or modL. *binōmius*, f. L. BI-+Gr. *nómos* part, portion; see -IAL.

bio- bai·ou, baiɔ· comb. form of Gr. *bios* life (cf. QUICK, VITAL, ZOO-), as in **bio·**GRAPHY. XVII (Dryden). – F. *biographie* or modL. *biographia*, medGr. *biographía*; so **bio·**GRAPHER. XVIII (Addison). **bio·**LOGY. XIX. – F. *biologie* (Lamarck, 1802) – G. *biologie* (Gottfried Reinhold, 1802). **bi·o-**GRAPH, **bi·o**SCOPE (1897), early names of the cinematograph.

biped bai·ped two-footed (animal). XVII. – L. *biped-*, *bipēs*, f. *bi-* BI- + *pēs* FOOT.

biplane bai·plein two-winged aeroplane. XX. f. BI-+PLANE[3].

birch bɜ̄ɹtʃ hardy northern forest tree, Betula. OE. *birće*, *bierće* = MLG. *berke*, OHG. *birihha*, *birka* (G. *birke*) :– Germ. **berkjōn*; rel. to synon. OE. *berc*, *beorc* = Du. *berk*, ON. *bjǫrk* :– Germ. **berkō*; one of the few IE. tree-names, repr. also by Skr. *bhūrjas*, Lith. *béržas*, OSl. *brěza* (:– **bhergā-*) and L. *farnus*, *fraxinus* ash-tree.

bird bɜ̄ɹd (obs. or dial.) young bird OE.; feathered animal (in this sense superseding *fowl*); maiden, girl XIII (Cursor M.). OE. *brid* (surviving dial.), late Nhb. *bird*; of unkn. origin and without cognates. In the sense 'maiden' there may have been blending with ME. *bürde* young woman, lady (prob. orig. 'embroideress'). Hence †**bird-**BOLT[1] arrow for shooting birds. XV. **bird-cage.** XV. **bird-**LIME[1]. XIV. vb. XVI. **bird's-eye** name of certain plants. XVI (*birds eine*, primula). **bird's-nest.** XVI.

bireme bai·rīm (galley) having two banks of oars. XVII. – L. *birēmis*, f. BI-+*rēmus* oar (cf. ROW[2]).

biretta bire·tə clerical square cap. XVI. – It. *berretta*, †*bar(r)etta* (cf. F. *barrette*) or Sp. *birreta*, fem. dims. corr. to Pr. *berret* BERET, based on late L. *birrus* and *-um* hooded cape or cloak, perh. of Celtic origin.

birth bɜ̄ɹþ bringing forth of offspring; nativity XII; lineage XIII. ME. *bürþ*, *birþ* – ON. *byrð* birth, descent (OSw. *byrdh*, Da. *byrd*), corr. to Goth. *ga|baurþs* :– EGerm. **gaburþiz*, f. **ga-* Y-+**bur-* **ber-* BEAR[2]; see -TH[1] and cf. ON. *burðr* bearing, carriage, birth, offspring, *byrðr* burden, load (whence †Sc. *birth*). The adoption of the ON. word was assisted by OE. *beorþor*, *byrþor*, etc. child-birth, offspring, *byrþ-þiġenu* midwife. For the development of meaning cf. also OIr. *brith* birth, Goth. *bērusjos* parents, OHG. *berd* child, and BAIRN. (WGerm. forms with *d* against EGerm. *þ* are OE. *ġebyrd*, OFris. *berd*, OS. *giburd*, OHG. *giburt*, G. *geburt*.) Hence **bi·rth**DAY XIV; cf. OE. *ġebyrddæġ*, ON. *burðardagr*, G. *geburtstag*.

Biscayan biskei·ən pert. to Biscay (native name *Vizcaya*), maritime province of N. Spain; sometimes equiv. to *Basque* XVII; sb. (after F. *biscaïen*) musket, first used in Biscay, a bullet used in this XIX; see -AN.

biscuit bi·skit crisp dry bread in thin flat cakes. XIV. Early forms *besquite*, *byscute*, *bisket* (XVI–XVIII) – OF. *bescoit*, *-cuit*, *biscut* (mod. *biscuit*) = Pr. *bescueit*, Sp. *bizcocho*, Pg. *biscuto*, It. *biscotto* :– medL. **biscoctu-s* twice-baked (sc. *panis* bread), f. *bis* twice+ *coctus*, pp. of *coquere* COOK.

bisect baise·kt cut into two equal parts. XVII. f. BI-+*sect-*, pp. stem of L. *secāre* cut, after INTERSECT. So **bise·c**TION. XVII.

bishop bi·ʃəp clergyman consecrated for the rule of a diocese. OE. *bisćop*, corr. to OFris., OS. *biskop*, (M)Du. *bisschop*, OHG. *biscof* (G. *bischof*), ON. *biskup* – popL. **biscopus*, for ecclL. *episcopus* (whence OF., Pr. *evesque*, F. *évêque*, Sp. *obispo*, Pg. *bispo*, It. *vescovo*) – Gr. *epískopos* overseer (whence Goth. *aipiskaupus*), f. *epí* EPI-+*-skopos* looking (see SCOPE). Celtic and Sl. adoptions of the L. are repr. by OIr. *epscop*, W. *esgob*, OSl. *jepiskupŭ*, Russ. *jepískop*, Ir. *easbog*, Gael. *easbuig*.

bisk, bisque bisk rich (esp. crayfish) soup. XVII. – F. *bisque*, of unkn. origin.

bismuth bi·zməþ metallic element. XVII (*bismute*, *-muto*, *-mutum*). – modL. *bisemutum* (Georg Agricola, 1530), latinization of G. *wismut*, of doubtful origin.

bison bai·sən species of wild ox. In the present form first recorded from A.V. (Deut. xiv 5 margin), earlier in L. pl. *bisontes* of *bison* (whence F. *bison*) – Germ. **wisand-*, **wisund-* (OE. *wesend*, OHG. *wisant*, *-unt*, ON. *visundr*); familiar in recent times in connexion with the American bison.

bisque bisk term at tennis. XVII. F., of unkn. origin.

bissextile bise·kstail leap-year. XVI. – late L. *bi(s)sextilis* (sc. *annus* year) year of the *bissextus* intercalary day inserted in the Julian calendar every fourth year after the *sixth* day before the calends of March (24 Feb.), f. *bis* twice+*sextus* SIXTH.

bisson bi·sən (dial.) blind, purblind. OE. (late Nhb.) *bisene*; later forms are *byson*, *bysom* (XV), *beason*, *beesome* (Sh. 1st Folio), north. dial. *beesen*; of unkn. origin.

bistoury bi·stəri scalpel. XVIII. – F. *bistouri* (Paré), earlier *bistorit* dagger, of unkn. origin.

bistre bi·stəɹ brown pigment from soot. XVIII. – F., of unkn. origin.

bit[1] bit A. †biting, bite OE.; †cutting edge XIV; boring-piece, borer XVI; B. mouthpiece of a bridle XIV. OE. *bite* = OFris. *bit*, *bite*, OS. *biti* (MDu. *bēte*, Du. *beet*), OHG. *biʒ* (G. *biss*), ON. *bit* (Sw. *bett*, Da. *bid*) :– CGerm. (exc. Goth.) **bitiz*, f. **bītan* BITE.

The origin of sense B is not clear; OE. has *bitol* bridle, ON. *bitill, -ull*, Du. *gebit*, G. *gebiss*, Sw. *bett*, Da. *bidsel* horse's bit.

bit[2] bit portion bitten off; morsel of food OE.; small piece XVI. OE. *bita* = OFris. *bita*, OS. **bito* (MDu. *bēte*, Du. *beet*), OHG. *bizzo* (MHG. *bizze*, G. *bissen*), ON. *biti* (see BITT) :- Germ. **biton*, f. **bit-*, **bītan* BITE.

bitch bitʃ female dog OE.; bad woman XV. OE. *bićće*, rel. obscurely to ON. *bikkja* (connected by some with Lappish *pittja*), of which there is a syn. *grey|baka*; G. *petze* (which is modern) may be an adoption of the Eng. word; there has been no contact with (O)F. *biche*, †*bisse* hind, doe.

bite bait pt. *bit*, pp. *bitten*, *bit* cut with the teeth or as a sharp-edged weapon. OE. *bītan*, pt. *bāt*, *biton*, pp. *biten* = OFris. *bīta*, OS. *bītan* (Du. *bijten*), OHG. *bīzan* (G. *beissen*), ON. *bíta*, Goth. *beitan* :- CGerm. **bītan*; the corr. short base is repr. by Skr. *bhidyáté* is split, L. *fid-*, *findere* cleave (cf. FISSION). The orig. pt. *bāt* is still repr. dial. by *bote*, but in gen. Eng. was superseded by *bit* in XVII (cf. *writ*, former pt. of *write*); pp. *bit*, surviving in 'the biter bit' dates from XVIII. Hence **bite** *sb.* XV.

bitt bit (naut.) usu. pl. pair of posts on deck for fastening cables. XIV (in Sandahl). prob. orig. a LG. sea term; cf. synon. LG., Du. *beting*, †*beeting* (whence G. *beting*, Sw. *beting*, Norw. *beiting*, Da. *beding*), f. Germ. **bit-*, repr. also by MHG. *bizze* wooden peg, ON. *biti* cross-beam, rel. to **bait-* BOAT. medL. *bitus* whipping-post, F. *bitte*, It. *bitta*, Sp. *bita* bitt are - Germ.

bitter[1] bi·təɹ)(*sweet* OE. *biter*, corr. to OS., OHG. *bittar* (Du., G. *bitter*), ON. *bitr*, Goth. (with variation of vowel) *baitrs*; prob. f. **bit-*, base of **bītan* BITE, and orig. meaning 'cutting', 'biting', hence 'cruel', 'harsh', 'violent', later 'biting to the tongue'. Hence **bi·tter**-SWEE·T mixture of bitter and sweet XIV (Ch.); kind of apple XIV (Gower); adj. XVII. Cf. F. *aigre-doux*, *amer-doux*, L. *dulcamārum*. So **bi·tter** adv. OE. *bitere*. **bi·tterly.** OE. *biterlīce*; see -LY[2]. **bi·tter**-NESS. OE. *biternes*.

bitter[2] bi·təɹ 'a Bitter is but the turn of a Cable about the Bits . . And the Bitters end is that part of the Cable doth stay within boord' (1627, Capt. Smith). f. BITT+-ER[1]. Hence prob. phr. *to the bitter end* to the last extremity (now assoc. with BITTER[1]).

bittern bi·təɹn marsh bird with booming note. XIV. Earliest forms *botor*, *butor*, *bitoure*, *bittor*, *bitter* - OF. *butor* - Rom. **būtitaurus*, f. L. *būtiō* bittern + *taurus* bull (used by Pliny of a bird that bellows like an ox; cf. synon. F. *taureau d'étang*, *bœuf de marais* 'marsh-ox', G. *meerochs*, *meerrind* 'sea-ox'). Forms with final *n* (XVI) are perh. due to assoc. with *hern* HERON.

bitumen bitjū·men, bi·tjŭmen mineral pitch. XV. - L. *bitūmen* (-*min*-), of which the first syll. has been referred to **gwet-*, base of OE. *cwidu*, *cwudu* CUD, mastic. So **bitu·min**OUS. XVII. - F. *bitumineux* - L. *bitūminōsus*.

bivalve bai·vælv (mollusc) having two valves. XVII. f. BI- + VALVE.

bivouac bi·vuæk (orig.) night-watch under arms; (hence) temporary encampment without tents. XVIII (recorded only from dicts. until the Napoleonic campaigns). - F. *bivouac* (†*bivac*, †*biwacht*), prob. - Swiss-G. *beiwacht* lit. 'extra watch' (BY, WATCH), said to have been used in Aargau and Zürich to denote a patrol of citizens added to assist the ordinary town watch. Hence as vb. 1809.

biz sl. shortening (orig. U.S., c. 1860) of BUSINESS bi·znis.

bizarre bizā·ɹ eccentric, odd. XVII. - F. *bizarre* (formerly) handsome, brave - Sp., Pg. *bizarro* handsome, brave (cf. It. *bizzarro* angry) - Basque *bizarra* beard; (cf. Sp. *hombre de bigote* lit. 'moustached man', man of spirit).

blab blæb tell-tale, tatler; loose chatter. XIV (Ch.). contemp. with †*blabber* babble, chatter (PPl., Wyclif) and synon. †*lab* (PPl., Ch.). *Blab*, *blabber* and the foll. forms point to an imit. Germ. base **blab-*; OHG. *blabbizōn* (MHG. *blepzen*), Icel. *blabbra* (Da. *blabbre*). Hence **blab** vb. XV.

black blæk absorbing all light (in fig. uses from XVI). OE. *blæc*, *blac-*, corr. to OS. *blac* ink, OHG. *blah-*, *blach-* (in comps.); cf. ON. *blakkr* dusky, black, dun; of unkn. origin. (In ME. confused with *blāc* pale, wan; cf. BLEAK[2].) *Black* has superseded SWART in gen. use as a colour-name. As sb. XIII. Hence **black** vb. XIII; **bla·cken** XIII (Cursor M.); see -EN[5]. **Blackamoor** blæ·kəmōəɹ, -muəɹ Ethiopian, Negro. XVI. orig. *black More* (*Blak moir*, Dunbar), also *black morian*; see MOOR. Forms with inserted *-a-*, which is unexpl., appear XVI. **black art** XVI; prob. after LG. *swarte kunst*, G. *schwarze kunst*; cf. L. *niger* black, fig. wicked, and medL. var. *nigromantia* of *necromantia* NECROMANCY. **black-ball** black ball recording an adverse vote; hence vb. XVIII (whence F. *blacbouler*). **bla·ck**BERRY. OE. (pl.) *blaceberian*. **Black Death**, the Great Pestilence of 1348–9, adaptation by 'Mrs. Markham' (1823) of some foreign term applied to similar plagues (cf. Icel. *svarti dauði*, G. *der Schwarze Tod*, Du. *de zwaarte dood*, F. *la peste noire*). **black**GUARD blæ·(k)gāɹd A. †(coll.) company or band of menials, camp-followers, etc. XVI; †vagrants or criminals as a body XVII; B. †man in black, †boot-black, etc. XVI; low worthless character XVIII. orig. meaning and application unkn. **bla·ck**LEG turf swindler XVIII; workman taking the place of one on strike XIX; of unkn. origin. **blackmail** blæ·kmeil (hist., orig. Sc.) tribute (see MAIL[2]) exacted by freebooting chiefs in return for protection XVI; (gen.) payment extorted by intimidation or pressure XIX. **Black** ROD, short for *Gentleman Usher of the Black Rod*, so called from the symbol of his office. XVII. **bla·ck**SMITH one who works in 'black metal' (i.e. iron). XV.

bladder blæ·dəɹ membranous bag. OE. *blǣdre*, later *blæddre* = OS. *blādara*, MLG., MDu. *blāder* (Du. *blaar*), OHG. *blātara* (G. *blatter*), ON. *blaðra* :- CGerm. (exc. Goth.) **blǣdrōn*, f. **blǣ-* BLOW[1] + **-dro-*, instr. suffix corr. to L. *-trum*, Gr. *-trā*, *-tron*, Skr. *-tram*.

blade bleid A. leaf OE.; spathe of grass XIV. B. broad flattened part of an implement OE.; flattened part of a bone (after ON.) XIII; thin cutting edge, sword XIV. OE. *blæd*, pl. *bladu* = OFris. *bled*, OS. (Du.) *blad*, OHG. *blat* (G. *blatt*), ON. *blað* leaf, blade of rudder, knife, etc. :- CGerm. (exc. Goth.) **blaðam*, perh. pp. formation (IE. **-tos*) on the base **blō̆-* BLOW[2]. Literary exx. are not recorded between OE. and XIV; in OE. the more usual sense is 'flattened part', the sense 'leaf' being rare and its later prevalence prob. due to ON. The application to a brave fellow or gallant appears XVI (Sh.); its origin is obscure; perh. the notion is 'wielder of a sword' (cf. F. *bonne épée* good sword, i.e. swordsman). The present form derives from OE. obl. cases.

blae blē, blī (dial.) blackish blue, livid. XIII (*blaa*, *blo*). – ON. *blár*; see BLUE. Hence **blae·**BERRY bilberry XV; after ON. *bláber*.

blague blāg humbug, bunkum. XIX. F., prob. of LG. origin (cf. LG. *blagen* blow oneself out).

blah blā (sl.) nonsense, silly talk. XX. imit. of aimless or nerveless utterance.

blain blein blister, pustule. OE. *blegen* = MDu. *bleine* (Du. *blein*), LG. *bleien* :- Germ. **blegen* (cf. OHG. *blehinougi* blear-eyed). Surviving in gen. use in CHILBLAIN; otherwise mainly in echoes of 'a boil breaking forth with blains' (Ex. ix 10).

blame bleim find fault with. XII. – OF. *blamer*, earlier *blasmer* (mod. *blâmer*) = Pr. *blasmar*, Cat. *blastemar*, Sp. *lastimar* (wound, injure, offend, etc.), Rum. *blestema* (It. *biasimare* is – F.) :- popL. *blastēmāre*, for ecclL. *blasphēmāre* revile, reproach – Gr. *blasphēmeîn* (dial. *blast-*) BLASPHEME. So **blame** sb. XIII. – (O)F. *blâme*, f. the vb.

blanch blānʃ whiten (orig. in cookery). XIV. – (O)F. *blanchir*, f. *blanc*, fem. *blanche* white, BLANK.

blancmange bləmɔ·nʒ, -mā·nʒ, -mɔ̃·ʒ, -mã·ʒ †dish of white meat with dressing XIV (PPl., Ch.); (orig. white) jelly made with milk XVI. Earliest form *blancmanger* – (O)F. *blancmanger*, f. *blanc* white, BLANK + *manger* food, sb. use of *manger* eat (cf. MANGER); the second el. was shortened to *mange* in XVIII; the progress of the pronunc. of the first syll. is seen in the forms *blawe-* (XV), *blow-* (XVI), *bla-* (XVII), *blo-* (XVIII).

bland blænd pleasing; smooth and suave. XV (only Sc.), XVII (Pepys, Milton). – L. *blandus*.

blandish blæ·ndiʃ flatter gently. XIV. – OF. *blandiss-*, lengthened stem (see -ISH[2]) of *blandir* :- L. *blandīrī*, f. *blandus* BLAND. Hence **bla·ndish**MENT. XVI (Spenser).

blank blæŋk †white XV; (of paper, etc.) 'empty of all marks' (J.); looking as if deprived of speech, etc.; (verse) 5-stress without rhyme XVI. – (O)F. *blanc* = Pr. *blanc*, Sp. *blanco*, Pg. *branco*, It. *bianco* :- CRom. **blancus* – Germ. **blaŋkaz* (OHG. *blanc* white, shining, corr. to OE. *blanca* steed, ON. *blakkr* pale, sb. horse).

blanket blæ·ŋkit †white woollen stuff XIII (*ȝwijt blaunket*) sheet of soft woollen cloth XIV. – OF. *blancquet* (AL. *blanchettum*, *-ketum*, *-chetta* XIII), var. of *blanchet*, f. *blanc* white; see BLANK, -ET.

blare blɛəɹ roar, bellow XIV; trumpet XVIII. Late ME. *blere*, early mod. *blear*, *blare*, Sc. *bleir* (XVI) – (M)Du. *bleren* (whence prob. MHG. *blēren*, *blerren*, G. *plärren*) and MLG., MDu. *blaren*; of imit. origin.

blarney blā·ɹni cajoling talk. XIX. f. *Blarney*, name of a village near Cork, Ireland, in the castle of which there is an inscribed stone difficult of access; the popular saying is that anyone who kisses or licks this 'Blarney stone' will ever after have a flattering tongue and the capacity for shameless lying.

blasé blā·zei weary and disgusted with enjoyment, success, etc. XIX (Byron). F., pp. of *blaser* exhaust by enjoyment or indulgence – Pr. *blazir*, of unkn. origin. Cf. G. *blasiert* (XVIII).

blaspheme blàsfī·m utter profane words (about). XIV. – OF. *blasfemer*, modF. *-ph-* (= Pr., Sp. *blasfemar*) – ecclL. *blasphēmāre* revile, blaspheme – Gr. *blasphēmeîn*, f. *blásphēmos* evil-speaking (**pha-* speak; *phēmí* I say). Cf. BLAME. So **blasphem**OUS blà·sfiməs. XV. **bla·sphemy.** XIII. – OF. *blasfemie* – ecclL. *blasphēmia*; see -Y[3].

blast blàst gust of wind or air. OE. *blǣst* = OHG. *blāst*, ON. *blástr* (perh. the immed. source in ME.) :- Germ. **blǣstaz*, f. **blǣs-* (see BLAZE[3]). Hence **blast** vb. †blow XIV; blow upon perniciously, blight XVI.

-blast blæst terminal el. in biol. terms such as *mesoblast* in the sense 'germ', 'bud'; so **blasto-** blæ·stou as in *blastoderm*; Gr. *blastós* sprout, germ.

blatant blei·tənt. First used by Spenser in *the blat(t)ant beast* ('F.Q.' v xii 37, etc.) to describe the thousand-tongued monster produced by Cerberus and Chimæra and symbolizing calumny 1596; offensively noisy or clamorous XVII. perh. alteration, after adjs. in -ANT (e.g. *rampant*), of Sc. *blatand* (G. Douglas), prp. of *blate*, BLEAT, and assoc. with *blatter* speak volubly (XVI) – L. *blat(t)erāre* babble, f. imit. base like the synon. *blat(t)īre*.

blather, blether blæ·ðəɹ, ble·ðəɹ talk nonsense. XV (*blether*), XVI (*bledder, bladder*). orig. Sc. – ON. *blaðra*, f. *blaðr* nonsense. For the var. *blether* cf. Sc. *gether* for *gather*. Hence as sb. XVIII (Burns). **ble·ther-, bla·therskate, -skite** (dial. and U.S.) noisy talkative fellow (Sc. *skate* used as a term of contempt); the song 'Maggie Lauder' by F. Sempill (XVII), containing the line 'Jog on your gait, ye bletherskate', was a favourite in the American camps during the War of Independence.

blay blei bleak (fish). OE. *blæġe* = MLG., MDu. *bleie* (Du. *blei*), G. *blei(h)e* :- WGerm. **blaijjōn*, of unkn. origin.

blaze[1] bleiz †torch; bright flame or fire. OE. *blæse, blase* :- Germ. **blasōn*; cf. MHG. *blas* torch; rel., through the gen. sense 'shining', to BLAZE[2]. Hence **blaze** vb. XIII. **bla·zer** thing that blazes or shines bright XVII; (orig. univ. sl.) bright-coloured jacket for sports wear XIX; see -ER[1].

blaze[2] bleiz white spot. XVII. Of uncertain origin, but identical in meaning with ON. *blesi* white spot on a horse's forehead, MDu. *blesse* (Du. *bles*), G. *blässe, blesse*; cf. synon. OHG. *blassa* (MHG. *blasse*) and OHG. *blas|ros*, MLG. *blasenhengst* horse with a blaze; also MHG. *blas* bald, G. *blass* pale, and parallel formations with *r*, as MLG. *blare*, Du. *blaar* cow with a blaze, MDu. *blaer* bald. Hence **blaze** vb. mark a tree with white by stripping the bark, indicate (a trail) in this way XIX.

blaze[3] bleiz †blow (a trumpet, etc.) XIV; proclaim, publish; blazon XV. – MLG., MDu. *blāzen* blow = OHG. *blāsan* (G. *blasen*), ON. *blása*, Goth. *uf|blēsan* puff up :- Germ. **blǣsan* (cf. BLAST), extension of **blǣ-*; see BLOW[1].

blazon blei·zn (her.) shield XIII; heraldic description XVI. – (O)F. *blason* orig. shield (whence Sp. *blason*, Pg. *brasão*, It. *blasone*) = Pr. *blezon, blizon*; of unkn. origin. Hence vb.

-ble bl –(O)F. *-ble* – L. *-bili-s*, adj. suffix denoting tendency, fitness, ability, or capability of doing or being something, added to vb.-stems, as *flēbilis* lamentable, tearful (see FEEBLE), *(g)nōbilis* renowned, of high birth, NOBLE, *mōbilis* easily moved, MOBILE, *stabilis* steadfast, STABLE; with vb.-stems in *a, i*, and *u* it combined to form the compound suffixes repr. in Eng. by -ABLE, -IBLE, and *-uble*, of which the first is by far the most common and the only one in living use, and so capable of being compounded with any verb; the last is repr. only in *soluble, voluble*. The corr. abstract nouns end in *-bility* and advs. in *-bly*.

bleaberry see BLAEBERRY.

bleach blīʃ whiten. OE. *blǣċan* = ON. *bleikja* :- Germ. **blaikjan*, f. **blaik-* shining, white, pale (cf. BLEAK[2]).

bleak[1] blīk small river-fish. XV. prob. – ON. *bleikja* = OHG. *bleicha* :- Germ. **blaikjōn*, f. **blaik-* white (see next); for the phonology cf. *steak, weak*. The OE. word was *blǣġe* BLAY.

bleak[2] blīk †pale, wan; bare of vegetation, exposed; cold from bareness. XVI. Obscurely rel. to †*blake* pale, yellow, †*bleach* pale, bare, †*bleike, blayke* pale, yellow – ON. *bleikr* shining, white = OE. *blāc* (ME. *blāke, blōke*), OS. *blēk*, OHG. *bleih*; for the phonology cf. *weak* (– ON. *veikr*). Variants of the base are seen in OE. *blǣċan* BLEACH and *blīcan* shine = OS. *blīkan* (Du. *blijken* look, appear), ON. *blíkja* and *blika* gleam, twinkle; cf. Gr. *phlégein* burn (see PHLEGM, PHLOX).

blear bliəɹ (of the eyes) dim. XIV (Trevisa). Now chiefly in *blear-eyed*, with which cf. LG. *blarroged, blerroged*, and MHG. *blerre* blurred vision; the vb. is recorded earlier XIII; immed. source and ult. origin unkn. Hence **blea·ry** XIV (PPl.); see -Y[1].

bleat blīt cry as a sheep. OE. *blǣtan* = OHG. *blāzan*, Du. *blaten*; of imit. origin. ¶ Various synon. forms in *bl-*, *b . . l-* are (dial.) *blea* (XVI); MHG. *blæjen*, MDu. *bloiken*, LG. *bleken, blöken* (whence G. *blöken*); Gr. *blēkhâsthai*, OSl. *blějati*, Russ. *bleyát'*, L. *bālāre, bēlāre*.

bleb see BLOB.

bleed blīd emit blood OE.; let (a person) blood XV. OE. *blēdan* = OFris. *blēda*, MLG. *blōden*, ON. *blœða* :- Germ. **blōðjan*, f. **blōðam* BLOOD.

blemish ble·miʃ †hurt, damage; mar, impair. XIV. – OF. *blemiss-*, extended stem (see -ISH[2]) of *blemir, blesmir* render pale, injure (also †*blesmer* = Pr. *blesmar, blasmar* cause to faint), prob. of Germ. origin. Hence **ble·mish** sb. XVI.

blench blentʃ †deceive OE.; start aside. XIII. OE. *blenċan* = ON. *blekkja* impose upon :- Germ. **blaŋkjan*, which has the form of a causative vb. corr. to †*blenk*, BLINK. A common var. XVI–XVII was *blanch*, which survives in hunting parlance for heading back a deer. Hence †**blench** sb. trick (ME.); side-glance XVI (Sh.).

blend blend mix, mingle. XIII (Cursor M.). In its earliest use predominantly north.; prob. of Scand. origin and due to *blend-* pres. stem, *blĕnd-* pt. stem, of ON. *blanda* mix = OE., OS., Goth. *blandan*, OHG. *blantan*; the formally corr. OE. *blendan* blind, deceive, survived till XVI. Cf. BLIND.

blende blend native sulphide of zinc. XVII. – G. *blende* (cf. *blendendes erz* 'deceptive ore'), f. *blenden* deceive (see BLIND); so called because, while often resembling galena (hence its name *pseudogalena*), it yielded no lead.

Blenheim ble·nəm name of the Duke of Marlborough's palace at Woodstock, Oxfordshire, so called after the first duke's victory in 1704 at *Blenheim* (Bavaria); applied to a variety of spaniel, and in *Blenheim Orange* a golden-coloured apple.

blenny ble·ni genus of spiny fishes. XVIII. – L. *blennius*, var. of *blendius* (Pliny) – Gr. *blénnos*, so called from *blénnos* slime, in ref. to the mucous coating of its scales.

blesbok ble·sbɔk S. African antelope. XIX. Afrikaans, f. Du. *bles* BLAZE[2] + *bok* goat (BUCK[1]). ¶ Other comps. of *bok* more or less naturalized are *bontebock, gemsbok, grysbok, kleenebok, reebok, springbok, waterbok*.

bless bles make holy, hallow; hold or call holy; pronounce or make happy. A purely Eng. formation. OE. *blētsian, blēdsian, blǣdsian* :- **blōðisōjan*, f. *blōðam* BLOOD; the etymol. meaning being 'mark so as to hallow with blood'; the sense-development was influenced by its being used to translate L. *benedīcere* and Gr. *eulogeîn* in Christian use (orig. speak well of or to, but used to render Heb. *bārak* bend the knee, worship, bless God, etc.), and by its formal assoc. with *bliss*. The pp. is current in two forms and pronunciations, *blessed* (ble·sid or blest) and *blest*; the former is used in verse and in liturgical reading, and in titular phr. such as *The Blessed Trinity, the blessed dead*, and in the euphemistic sense (e.g. *every blessed thing*); the latter is mainly poetical in the sense 'blissful', 'beatified', but is also used trivially, e.g. *I'm blessed (blest)*.

blight blait disease in plants, as mildew; baleful influence, orig. on plants. XVII (also *blite*). perh. for earlier **blěht*, repr. formally OE. *blǣċþu, blǣċþ|rust*, rel. to *blǣċe* (all applied to skin diseases), and further to BLEACH.

blighter blai·təɹ contemptible fellow. XIX. f. *blighted*, euph. substitute for *blasted* (see BLAST) as an epithet of reprobation; see -ER[1].

blighty blai·ti (army sl.) England, home. XX. contr. form, originating in the Indian army, of Hind. *bilāyatī* foreign, (esp.) European, f. Arab. *wilāyat* inhabited country, district, VILAYET, in Hind. esp. foreign country. Cf. *bilayutee pawnee*, Hind. *bilāyatī pānī* ('European water'), soda-water.

blimp blimp small non-rigid dirigible airship. XX. Said to have been coined by the aviator Horace Shortt, and to have been based on the adj. LIMP.

blim(e)y blai·mi. XIX. (vulg.) short for GORBLIMY.

blind blaind sightless; unperceiving; dark, obscure OE.; secret, privy XIV; having no opening XVII. OE. *blind* = OFris. (in *stareblind*), OS. (Du.) *blind*, OHG. *blint* (G. *blind*), ON. *blindr*, Goth. *blinds* :- CGerm. **blindaz* :- IE. **bhlendhos* wandering, erring, confused, obscure, dark; cf. Lith. *blendžiùs* become dark, Lett. *blendu* see dimly, OSl. *blędą* go blindly, and BLUNDER. Hence **blind** vb. XIII (Cursor M.); repl. †*blend*, OE. *blendan* = OHG. *blentan* (G. *blenden*) :- **blandjan*. **blind** sb. screen (in earliest use fortif.); misleading pretext. XVII. **blind-man's-buff** (earlier *-man-*) game in which a player is blindfolded and struck (see BUFF[1]). XVI. **blind-nettle** dead-nettle; OE. *blindnetle*. **blind-worm** slow-worm XV; cf. Du. *blindworm*.

blindfold blai·ndfould cover the eyes of, with a bandage. XVI. Superseded †*blindfelle* (XIII–XVI), OE. *ġeblindfellian* strike blind, f. BLIND + FELL[4]; the pt. and pp. *blindfelled, -feld* (*blindfield, -fielded* XVI), was altered to *blindfold* by assoc. with FOLD[2].

blink bliŋk †A. deceive; start aside XIV; B. twinkle with the eyes or eyelids, †glance, peep XVI (Sh.); cast a momentary gleam XVIII. prob. of mixed origin; partly later form of synon. †*blenk* (XIV), var. of BLENCH; partly – (M)Du. *blinken* shine, glitter, which may be based on a nasalized var. of **blik-* shine (see BLEAK[2]); cf. Da. *blinke*, Sw. *blinka* wink, twinkle. Hence **blink** sb. †glance, twinkling gleam, etc. XVI. **bli·nker** one who blinks XVII; pl. spectacles for directing the vision; leather screens at the side of a bridle to make a horse look straight ahead XVIII; see -ER[1].

bliss blis joy, happiness. OE. *bliss, blīþs* = OS. *blīzza, blīdsea, blītzea* :- Germ. **blīþsjō*, f. **blīþiz* BLITHE + *-sjō*, for *-tjō* (cf. -CY). Contact with BLESS prob. infl. the sense in the direction of 'heavenly joy'. Hence **bli·ssful** XII; see -FUL[1].

blister bli·stəɹ vesicle caused by injury. XIII (Cursor M.). ME. *blister, blester*, early Sc. *blistar, bleistir* (XVI), in Eng. occas. †*bluster* (XVI), of unkn. origin; possibly – OF. *blestre, blostre, bloustre* swelling, pimple, app. vars. of a word meaning 'clod of earth'; connexion with ON. *blástr* swelling is formally out of the question. Hence **bli·ster** vb. XV.

blithe blaið joyous. OE. *blīþe* = OFris. *blī(d-)*, OS. *blīði* (Du. *blijde, blij*), OHG. *blīdi* cheerful, friendly, ON. *blíðr*, Goth. *bleiþs* :- CGerm. **blīþiz*, the orig. sense of which, 'mild, gentle, merciful', is shown in ON. and Goth.; of unkn. origin. Cf. BLISS.

blither bli·ðəɹ (colloq.) talk nonsense. XIX. Alteration of BLETHER; esp. in *blithering* prp.

blitz blits shortening of G. *blitzkrieg* 'lightning-war'. XX.

blizzard bli·zəɹd (U.S.) sharp blow or knock 1829; furious blast of wind and snow 1870. Of unkn. origin.

bloat blout *bloat herring*, herring smoked and half-dried. XVI–XIX (dial.). Hence

bloa·ted in the same sense XVII–XIX; whence **bloa·ter,** for *bloated herring* XIX; see -ED[1], -ER[1]. Identical in form are *bloat* adj. and vb. and *bloated* ppl. adj., which are used of a puffed, swollen, or inflated condition (lit. and fig.) XVII (*bloat face, bloatfac'd*, G. Daniel; *bloated looks*, H. More); but it is doubtful whether the two groups have the same ultimate origin, since the adj. meaning 'puffed' may be an altered form of an earlier †*blout* (XIII), later *blowt* (Sh. 'Ham.' III iv 182 Qq), meaning 'soft', 'flabby', the form of which indicates adoption from ON. *blautr* soft, wet, soaked (cf. BLOT[2]), rel. to *blotna* become soft or moist (whence rare ME. *blotne*; cf. rare ME. *blot*, app. synon. with *blout*). The available evidence is insufficient to determine whether there is any connexion with OE. (poet.) *blāt* pale, livid, the mod. repr. of which would be *bloat*.

blob blɔb bubble XV (Wyntoun); blister; small round mass XVI. In early use north.; like the earlier *bluber, blober*, BLUBBER, and the later synon. *bleb* (XVII), containing the symbolical consonant-combination *bl . . b*; cf. BUBBLE.

block blɔk solid piece or mass (orig. of wood) XIV; mould for a hat, etc. XVI; group of buildings XVIII. – (O)F. *bloc* – (M)Du. *blok*, (M)LG. *block*, of unkn. orig. (whence G. *block*, superseding *bloch* = OHG. *bloh*). Hence (or – F. *bloquer*) **block** vb. impede XV (Wyntoun); mark *out* roughly XVI; whence **blocka·de** XVII; prob. after *ambuscade*, contemp. with G. *blockade* (which was preceded by †*blocquada*). **blo·ckhouse** †detached fort blocking a passage; timber building loopholed for firing XV. – (M)Du. *blokhuis*, whence in F. *blocquehuys* (mod. *blocus*).

bloke blouk (sl.) man, fellow. XIX. Shelta.

blond blɔnd light-coloured. XV. Only occas. in gen. sense before XIX; *blond(e) lace* and simply *blond(e)* – F. *blonde* (sc. *dentelle* lace) is XVIII. – (O)F. *blond*, fem. *blonde* (= Pr. *blon*, It. *biondo*, Sp. *blondo*) :– medL. *blundu-s, blondu-s* yellow, perh. of Germ. origin (but no forms are extant). Most freq. in fem. form *blonde*, esp. as sb.

blood blʌd red liquid in the veins of animals. OE. *blōd* = OFris., OS. *blōd* (Du. *bloed*), OHG. *bluot* (G. *blut*), ON. *blóð*, Goth. *blōþ* (Crim-Goth. *plut*) :– CGerm. **blōðam*, of unkn. origin. (There is no CIE. word for 'blood'.) Hence **bloo·dhound** dog used for tracking. XIV; cf. Du. *bloedhond*. **bloo·dshed** XVI; superseded *bloodshedding* (XIII). **bloo·dshot** XVII; for earlier †*blood-shotten* (XVI); see SHOOT. **bloo·dthirsty**. XVI (Coverdale, after Luther's *blutdürstig*).

bloody blʌ·di sanguinary. OE. *blōdiġ* = OFris. *blōdich*, etc.; see BLOOD, -Y[1]. The expletive use, orig. adv. as in *bloody drunk* (XVII), *bloody hot, bloody sick* (Swift), was prob. f. the int. *blood, 'sblood* (for *God's blood*), as *woundy*, similarly used, was f. *wounds, 'swounds* (ZOUNDS); cf. the parallel use of *woundily afraid* (Smollett, 1749) and *bloodily drunk* (Fielding, 1749). ¶ Some earlier superficially similar uses mean 'cruel(ly)', 'savage(ly)', 'murderous(ly)'.

bloom[1] blūm blossom, flower XIII (Orm); powdery deposit on fruits XVII. ME. (north. and n.midl.) *blom, blome* – ON. *blóm* flower, blossom, and *blómi* prosperity, pl. flowers, corr. to OS. *blōmo*, MDu. *bloeme* (Du. *bloem*), OHG. *bluomo, -ma* (MHG. *bluome*, G. *blume*), Goth. *blōma* :– CGerm. (exc. OE.) **blōmon -ōn*, f. **blō̆-* BLOW[2]. For the OE. syn. see BLOSSOM. Hence **bloom** vb. XIII (Orm); cf. ON. *blómandi* blooming, flourishing. The prp. **bloo·ming** (-ING[2]) is used as one of the many sl. euph. substitutes for *bloody* XIX; whence **bloo·mer** (cf. -ER[1]), prob. for *blooming error* XIX.

bloom[2] blūm mass of iron brought into the form of a thick bar. OE. *blōma*, identical in form with BLOOM[1], but prob. a different word. Hence **bloo·mery** first forge in an ironworks. XVI; in AL. *blomeria* (XIV).

bloomer blū·məɹ (chiefly pl.) women's trouser costume. 1851. f. name of Mrs. Amelia *Bloomer*, who advocated the use of the dress, which was invented c. 1850 by Mrs. Elizabeth Smith Miller of New York.

blossom blɔ·səm flower OE.; mass of flowers on a tree XIII. OE. *blōstm, blōs(t)ma*, corr. to WFris. *blossum*, (M)Du. *bloesem*, MLG. *blōs(s)em*; cf. ON. *blómstr*; gen. referred to the same base as BLOOM[1], viz. **blō̆-*, of which **blō̆s-* appears to be an extended form (cf. L. *flōrēre* FLOURISH for **flōsēre*, and *flōs, flōr-* FLOWER). Hence **blo·ssom** vb. OE. *blōstmian*; cf. Du. *bloesemen*. **blo·ssomy.** XIV (Ch.); see -Y[1].

blot[1] blɔt spot, stain. XIV. The local distribution of the earliest exx. is consistent with a Scand. origin, but no suitable form is known; cf., however, Icel. *blettr* blot, stain, Da. dial. *blat* spot, blot. Hence **blot** vb. spot, stain. XV (*blotting-paper* XVI).

blot[2] blɔt (in backgammon) exposed piece. XVI. prob. – Du. *bloot* naked, exposed = OE. *blēat* wretched, OFris. *blāt* miserable, MLG., MDu. *bloot* naked, poor, OHG. *blōʒ*, G. *bloss* bare, mere, ON. *blautr* soft, wet :– CGerm. (exc. Gothic) **blautaz*, of unkn. origin.

blotch blɔtʃ inflamed patch on the skin XVII; blot (as of ink) XVIII. Partly alteration of synon. †*plotch* (XVI–XVII), by assoc. with BLOT and BOTCH, partly blending of these. Cf. contemp. SPLOTCH.

blouse blauz light loose upper body garment. XIX. – F. *blouse* blūz, of unkn. origin.

blow[1] blou intr. produce a current of air; puff air (into). OE. str. vb. *blāwan*, pt. *blēow*, pp. *blāwen* = OFris. **blā* (pt. *blē*),

OHG. *blā(h)an* (pp. *blāhan, blān*), replaced by wk. OHG. *blājan* (MHG. *blæjen*, G. *blähen* blow up, swell); IE. base **bhlā-*, repr. also by L. *flāre* (see INFLATE).

blow[2] blou (arch.) bloom, flourish. OE. str. vb. *blōwan*, pt. *blēow*, pp. *blōwen*, corr. to wk. vbs. in the other Germ. langs., OFris. *blōia*, OS. *blōjan* (MDu., Du. *bloeien*), OHG. *bluojan, bluoen* (G. *blühen*); all f. Germ. **blō̆-*, repr. also by BLADE, BLOOM[1], BLOSSOM.

blow[3] blou hard stroke with fist or weapon. XV (first in north. texts as *blaw*). Of unkn. origin; neither formal nor chronological contact can be established with OS. *ūt|bliuwid* 'excudit', (M)Du. *blouwen* beat, brake hemp, or OHG. *bliuwan* (G. *bläuen, bleuen*) beat, batter, Goth. *bliggwan* beat :- Germ. **blewwan*.

blowzy blau·zi bloated or red-faced; dishevelled. XVIII. f. (dial.) *blowze* beggar wench, trull, slattern XVI (Sh.), of unkn. origin, perh. LG.; see -Y[1]. Also *blowzed*, †*blowzing*, in same sense (XVIII).

blub blʌb (colloq.) weep effusively. XIX. Shortening of next vb.

blubber blʌ·bəɹ †foam, bubble (XII), XIV; †pustule; entrails (of fish) XV; jelly-fish; fat of whales XVII. Late ME. *blober, bluber*, perh. of imit. origin; cf. LG. *blubbern* babble, G. *blubbern* bubble, splutter. Early exx. of the form are found in proper names, viz. *Bluberhusum* (XII), Blubberhouses, in Yorkshire, *Blubure, -er* as a surname in Oxfordshire (XIII). Hence **blu·bber** vb. †bubble; weep copiously. XIV.

blucher blū·kəɹ, blū·tʃəɹ leather half-boot. XIX (*Blücher boots*, Carlyle). f. name of Gebhard Leberecht von *Blücher* blṻ·χər, general field marshal in command of the Prussians at the battle of Waterloo (1815).

bludgeon blʌ·dʒən heavy-headed stick. XVIII. Of unkn. origin; perh. orig. cant.

blue blū of the colour of the clear sky or the deep sea. XIII (Cursor M.). ME. *bleu, blew(e)* – (O)F. *bleu, -e* = Pr. *blau, blava*, OSp. *blavo*, It. dial. *biavo* :- Rom. **blāvus* – CGerm. (exc. Goth.) **blǣwaz* (whence OE. *blǣ|hǣwen, blǣwen* 'perseus', OFris. *blāw*, MDu. *blā(u)*, Du. *blaauw*, OHG. *blāo*, G. *blau*, ON. *blár* dark-blue, livid, BLAE), prob. rel. to L. *flāvus* yellow. In *blue blood* tr. Sp. *sangre azul*, applied to Spaniards claiming freedom from Moorish, Jewish, or other admixture. As sb. in various uses from XIII; *the blues* (orig. U.S.) fit of depression, for earlier *the blue devils*.

blue-stocking blū·stɔːkiŋ attrib. wearing blue stockings XVII; applied from c. 1780 to the intellectuals who met in London at the houses of Mrs. Montague and others, where blue worsted stockings were worn by some instead of black silk. ¶ Hence F. *bas-bleu*, G. *blaustrumpf*.

bluff[1] blʌf nearly vertical or perpendicular XVII; rough, blunt XVIII; good-naturedly curt or abrupt XIX. orig. naut., perh. of LDu. origin, but no suitable form is known and Du. †*blaf* (Kilian, 1599) broad and flat (of the face) appears to be isolated. As sb. broad precipitous headland XVII (first in N. America).

bluff[2] blʌf (orig. U.S. in poker) impose on an opponent by heavy betting on a weak hand, etc.; also sb. XIX. – Du. *bluffen* brag, boast, and *bluf* bragging, boasting. The obs. dial. *bluff* blindfold (superseded by *bluft*) appears to be unrelated.

blunder blʌ·ndəɹ †confuse XIV; move blindly or stupidly XIV (Ch.); make a stupid mistake XVIII (Swift). prob. of Scand. origin; cf. MSw. (Norw.) *blundra* shut the eyes, frequent. of the base found in ON. (Sw.) *blunda*, ODa. *blunde*, rel. to BLIND; but the sense-development is not clear.

blunderbuss blʌ·ndəɹbʌs short gun with large bore. XVII (also *-bush*). Alteration, by assoc. with BLUNDER, of Du. *donderbus*, f. *donder* THUNDER + *bus* gun (orig. BOX, tube).

blunt blʌnt †dull, stupid XII (Orm); not physically sharp XIV; †rude, unrefined XV; abrupt of speech XVI. The earliest evidence suggests a Scand. source and a possible neuter formation (as in SCANT, THWART, WIGHT[2]) on the base of ON. *blundr* dozing, sleep (used as a nickname), *blunda* close the eyes (Norw. *blunde* doze). Cf. BLUNDER.

blur blǝ̄ɹ smear, stain. XVI. The priority of sb. or vb. cannot be determined; poss. rel. to BLEAR, but Levins's 'Manipulus Vocabulorum' (1570) has 'blirre, *deceptio*, blirre, *fallere*'.

blurb blǝ̄ɹb (orig. U.S.) publisher's commendatory advertisement. XX. Of unkn. origin.

blurt blǝ̄ɹt utter abruptly. XVI. prob. imit. of the discharge of breath after an effort to retain it; formerly used of snorting and puffing, and as int. ('pooh!'); now dial. of a burst of weeping (also in Sc. *blirt*).

blush blʌʃ become red, spec. with shame or confusion. OE. *blyśċan* (glossing L. *rutilāre* glow red), corr. to MLG. *bloschen*, LG. *blüsken*; rel. in meaning and no doubt ult. in form to MDu. *blōzen, blōzen* (Du. *blozen*) blush; cf. OE. *āblysian* blush, *āblysnung* redness of confusion, and *blysa* torch, *blysian* blaze. ¶ For the vowel-development cf. *burden, cluster, crutch, cudgel, flush, much, rush* sb., *shut, thrush*.

bluster blʌ·stəɹ be boisterous, rage. XV. ult. imit.; there is a formal analogue in LG. *blustern, blistern* flutter. *Bluster*, used in alliterative verse (XIV) of the blind or aimless wandering or rushing of animals, may be a different word.

bo, boh bou int. XV. A combination of consonant and vowel esp. suited to surprise or startle. Cf. BOO.

boa bou·ə large S. American snake. XIX. – modL. use by Linnæus ('Systema Naturæ' I iii 1083) of L. *boa* (Pliny), of unkn. origin. **boa constrictor** bou·ə kənstri·ktəɹ largest Brazilian serpent of the genus Boa; modL. *constrictor* squeezer (f. L. *constrict-* CONSTRAIN), was Linnæus's specific name (1788).

Boanerges bouənə̄·ɹdʒīz two sons of Zebedee (see Mark iii 17); hence, as sg. vociferous orator (XVII). – Gr. *boanergés*, prob. repr. Heb. *b'nēy regesh*, expl. as 'sons of thunder'.

boar bɔ̄əɹ male swine. OE. *bār* = OS. *bēr|swīn*, (M)Du. *beer*, OHG. *bēr* (G. *bär*) :– WGerm. **bairaz* (cf. Lombardic *sonor|pair* boar of the sounder).

board bɔ̄əɹd flat piece of wood; table (now only as used for meals); border, edge (now only in *seaboard*); ship's side. OE. *bord* in its uses combines two orig. distinct CGerm. words: (i) a str. n. = OFris., OS. *bord* (Du. *boord* board, *bord* shelf, plate), MHG., G. *bort* board, ON. *borð* board, plank, table, maintenance (Sw., Da. *bord* table), ON. *fót|borð*, Goth. *fōtu|baurd* footstool) :– CGerm. **borðam*, f. gradation-var. of **breð-* (OE., OS. *bred*, MLG., OHG. *bret*, G. *brett* board, plank); (ii) a str. m. = OS. *bord*, MDu. *bort* (Du. *boord*) border, edge, ship's side, ON. *borð* margin, shore, shipboard (Sw., Da. *bord* shipboard) :– Germ. **borðaz*; the further connexions of both are doubtful. The OE. words were reinforced in ME. by the uses of F. *bord* edge, rim, side of a ship (= Sp., It. *bordo* :– Rom. **bordu-s* – Germ. **borðaz*), and by the uses of the ON. words, prob. in this group of senses, as well as in that of 'table' (barely evidenced in OE.) and the derived sense of 'maintenance at table', 'supply of provisions' (XIV). Hence **board** vb. come alongside (a ship) XV; cover with boards; provide with board or provisions XVI.

boast boust In their earliest occurrences both sb. (XIII) and vb. (XIII) denote or imply clamorous or threatening utterance; the senses 'threat', 'threaten' continued in Sc. till XVIII; it is difficult to determine the date of the transition to vainglorious speaking, for which OE. had *ġielp*, *ġielpan* (see YELP), early north. ME. *rōs*, *rōse*, dial. *roose* (– ON. *hrós*, *hrósa*) and later ME. *glory*. – AN. *bost* and **boster*, of unkn. origin; W. *bost*, Ir., Gael. *bósd* are from Eng.

boat bout small open oared or sailing vessel. OE. *bāt*, str. m., corr. to ON. *beit*, str. n. (:– **bait-*, not repr. elsewhere, but perh. rel. to BITT). ON. *bátr* was from Eng.; from Eng. or Scand. the word was adopted into LG. and Du., and thence into G. (*boot*); from Eng. is also OW. *bat*, W. *bad*. OF. *batel* (mod. *bateau*) is a dim. formation on OE. and early ME. *bāt*; thence Pr., Sp. *batel*, It. *battello*. Hence **boa·tMAN**, in Sc. *bat(e)man* (XIV–XV), *boytman* (XVI), *bot(e)man* (XV–XVII); cf. ON. *bátmaðr*. **boa·tSWAIN** bou·sn (denoted by Dryden's sp. *boson*, which was preceded by *boatsonne*, and is now commonly *bosun*); late OE. *bātsweġen*.

bob¹ bɔb bunch, knob, knot (of hair). XIV. First recorded from north. texts in the sense 'bunch or cluster of flowers, fruit, etc.', which survives in north. dial.; used gen. later for various roundish objects, e.g. grub, larva (XV), knot or bunch of hair or the like (XVII). Hence **bob** vb. make into a bob, cut short, dock XVI; fish with a bob or bunch of worms XVII. Of unkn. origin.

bob² bɔb A. (dial.) pummel, buffet, rap XIII; B. move with a jerk up or down or to and fro XIV ('a litel toun, which that ycleped is Bobbe vp and doun', Ch.); curtsy XVIII. prob. of symbolic origin; cf. BUFFET¹. Hence **bob** sb. (dial.) blow, rap XVI; method of change-ringing XVII; curtsy XIX. (Cf. †*bobet* blow with the fist XV.)

bob³ bɔb pet-form of the name *Robert*, perh. the source of various phr. in which it means 'man', as *Cheapside bob* (XVIII), *dry/wet bob* one who devotes himself to land/river sports, *light bob* light infantryman, and of *bob* (also formerly *bobstick*) shilling (XIX). Cf. BOBBY.

bobbery bɔ·bəri noisy disturbance. XIX. Of Anglo-Indian origin acc. to the literary evidence (from 1816), and taken by Yule to repr. Hindi *bāp re!* O father! excl. of surprise or grief; but in gen. dial. use and recorded for East Anglia in 1825.

bobbin bɔ·bin reel, spool. XVI. – F. *bobine*, †*bobin*, of unkn. origin.

bobbish bɔ·biʃ (colloq.) brisk. XIX (Scott). f. BOB² + -ISH.

bobby bɔ·bi dim. (see -Y⁶) of *Bob* (BOB³), pet-form of *Robert*, used as a slang nickname for a policeman, in allusion to *Robert* Peel, Home Secretary when the Metropolitan Police Act was passed in 1828.

bobolink bɔ·bəliŋk N. Amer. song-bird. XVIII. Fuller forms are *boblinco(l)n*, *bob-a-lincum*, imit. of the bird's note. Cf. *labalinkin* (Purchas). ¶ Similar imit. names are *katydid*, *mopoke*, *morepork*, *whippoorwill*.

bobtail bɔ·bteil having the tail cut short XVI (implied in the vb. *bobtail*); as adj. (Sh.) and sb.; in *tag rag and bobtail* XVII. f. BOB¹ or *bobbed* pp., but the corr. uses of the simple *bob* are not recorded so early.

bocardo bŏkā·ɹdou A. (logic) mnemonic word repr. by the vowels the 5th mood of the 3rd figure. B. †prison, spec. that formerly situated at the North Gate of Oxford. XVI. The transference to sense B may have been a university joke.

Boche bɔʃ (sl.) German. XX. F. (sl.) 'bad lot', 'rascal', 'German', held to be shortening of *tête* (*de*) *boche*, in which *boche* is for *caboche* hard skull (see CABBAGE[1]).

bock bɔk variety of German beer; glass of this. XIX. – F. *bock* – G. *bock*, in full *bockbier*, short for *Eimbockbier*, now *Einbecker bier*, f. *Einbeck*, *Eimbeck*, town in Hanover, Germany.

bocking bɔ·kiŋ coarse woollen drugget. XVIII. f. name of *Bocking*, village in Essex, formerly renowned for the manufacture of baize.

bode boud †announce, proclaim OE.; betoken, portend XIV. OE. *bodian* (= OFris. *bodia*), f. *boda* messenger = OFris. *boda*, OS. *bodo*, OHG. *boto* (G. *bote*), ON. *boði* :- CGerm. (exc. Gothic) **buðon*, f. **buð-*, weak grade of **beuðan* BID.

bodega bŏdī·gə wine-shop. XIX. Sp. :- L. *apothēca* (whence also F. *boutique* shop) – Gr. *apothḗkē* store (see APOTHECARY).

bodge see BOTCH[2].

bodice bɔ·dis woman's body garment. XVI (earliest in Sc. use, *bodeis and slevis*). orig. *bodies*, pl. of BODY in the sense 'part of a woman's dress above the waist', formerly often in *a pair of bodies*, i.e. stays, corsets. For the retention of the unvoiced pronunc. (s) of the pl. ending cf. *dice*, *pence*.

bodkin bɔ·dkin †dagger XIV (Ch.); small pointed instrument XV; long pin XVI; instrument with eyes for drawing tape, etc. XVIII. orig. *boidekyn* (three syll.), possibly of Celtic origin (cf. W. *bidog*, Gael. *biodag* dagger); *-kin* suggests a dim. formation; adopted in W. as *bwdcin*. The phonetic development of the first syll. to *bod-* is obscure.

bodle, boddle bɔ·dl (Sc.) copper coin (two pennies Scots). XVII. 'Said to have been denominated from a mint-master of the name of *Bothwell*' (Jamieson).

body bɔ·di frame of an animal; main portion, trunk OE.; person XIII. OE. *bodiġ* str. n., corr. to OHG. *potah* str. m. (MHG. *botich*, mod. Bavarian dial. *bottech* body of a chemise), superseded in G. by *leib* (see LIFE) and *körper* (– L. *corpus*); perh. an alien word in OE. and OHG. *Bodyguard* (XVIII), tr. F. *garde du corps*. Hence **bo·dy** vb. provide with a body or shape. XV (Pecock).

Bœotian biou·ʃən. XV. f. L. *Bœōtia*, Gr. *Boiōtía*, name of a district of ancient Greece proverbial for the stupidity of its inhabitants; see -IAN.

Boer buəɹ, bou·əɹ Dutch-descended S. African. XIX (earliest form *boor*). Du.; see BOOR.

bog bɔg wet spongy land. XIII. orig. Sc. – Gael. (and Ir.) *bogach*, f. *bog* soft (in comps. 'bog', as *bogbhuine*, *bogluachair* bulrush); in early modEng. adopted from Irish (cf. *bog-trotter* wild Irishman XVII); the base is **bhugh-* of BOW[2]. Hence **bog** vb. XVII. **bo·ggy** XVI; see -Y[1].

bogey, bogy bou·gi person or thing much dreaded. XIX. orig. as proper name (*Bogey* and *Old Bogey* the Devil), presumably rel. to synon. †*bog*, north. dial. *boggard*, *-art*, Sc. *bogle*, north. Eng. *boggle* (all recorded from XVI), and further to BUG[1], but the connexions of the group are uncertain.

Bogey, U.S. **Bogie** bou·gi in golf, the number of strokes a good player may be supposed to need for each hole. XIX. Said to be from an imaginary partner 'Colonel Bogey'.

boggle bɔ·gl start with fright (often of horses) XVI; demur, hesitate XVII. prob. f. dial. *boggle* (see BOGEY) as if orig. 'to see a boggle or spectre'.

bogie bou·gi (north. dial.) low truck on four wheels; (hence gen.) revolving undercarriage. XIX. Of unkn. origin.

bogle bou·gl see BOGEY. XVI (*bogill*, Dunbar); its use by Burns, Scott, and Hogg brought it into Eng. literature.

bogus bou·gəs (orig. U.S.) counterfeit, sham. XIX. Appears first in 1827 applied to an apparatus for coining false money; of unkn. origin.

Bohairic bouhai·rik standard form of the Coptic language. XIX. f. *Bohairah*, Arabic name of Lower Egypt, f. *buḥair* lake; see -IC.

bohea bouhī· finest kinds of black tea. XVIII. – Fuhkien Chinese *Bu-i*, local var. of *Wu-i*, name of hills in northern Fuhkien, whence black tea was first brought to England.

Bohemian bouhī·miən gipsy XVII; socially unconventional person XIX. f. *Bohemia* a state of Central Europe + -(I)AN; after F. *bohémien* gipsy (XV) orig. one who has passed through Bohemia, (later) in the transf. sense 'vagabond', 'adventurer', which was introduced into Eng. by Thackeray.

bohunk bou·hʌŋk (U.S.) South-European of inferior class. XX. Of unkn. origin.

boil[1] boil hard inflamed tumour. OE. *bȳl* and *bȳle* = OFris. *bēle*, *beil*, OS. *būla* (Du. *buil*), OHG. *būlla* bladder (G. *beule*) :- WGerm. **būlja*, *-jon*, f. **bŭl-* (cf. Goth. *ufbauljan* puff up, and Icel. *beyla* hump :- **baulj-*). The normal repr. of the OE. forms is the gen. mod. dial. *bile* bail, which remained in literary Eng. till XVIII (cf. '*Bile*, this is generally spelt *boil*; but, I think, less properly', J.); the form *boil* dates from XV (in PPl. C. XXIII 84 the MSS. have *Bules*, *Byles*, *Belis*, and *Boilus*).

boil[2] boil bubble up with heat. XIII. – AN. *boiller*, OF. *boillir* (mod. *bouillir*) :-

L. *bullīre* bubble, boil, f. *bulla* bubble, BULL². Hence **boil** sb. XV.

boisterous boi·stərəs †stout, stiff, bulky; violent and rough in manner. XVI. var. of †*boisteous*, later by-form of †*boistous*, *-uous* (XIII), of unkn. origin. ¶ The formally identical AN. *boistous*, OF. *boisteus* (mod. *boiteux*) lame, does not give a suitable sense.

bolas bou·ləs missile used by S. Amer. peoples consisting of balls or stones connected by cord. XIX. Sp., Pg., pl. of *bola* ball, BULL².

bold bould stout-hearted OE.; audacious XII (Orm). OE. *bald* (*beald*) = OS. *bald*, MDu. *bout* (Du. *boud*), OHG. *bald* (MHG. *balt*, surviving in G. adv. *bald* soon), ON. *ballr* dangerous, fatal :- CGerm. **balþaz* (repr. in Gothic by *balþei* boldness, *balþata* boldly, *balþjan* venture, with which cf. OE. *bieldan* encourage); perh. pp. formation (IE. *-*tos*) on the base **bhel*- swell.

bole¹ boul tree trunk. XIV. – ON. *bolr*; cf. MHG. *bole* (G. *bohle*) plank; poss. rel. to BALK.

bole² boul kind of compact clay. XIII. – late L. *bolus*; see BOLUS. First in *bole armeniac* or *armoniac* astringent earth brought from Armenia.

bolection boule·kʃən (archit.) moulding projecting from the face of a work. XVIII. Other forms are *ba-*, *be-*, *bilection*; of unkn. origin.

bolero bŏlɛə·rou lively dance XVIII; short jacket XIX. Sp., presumably f. *bola* ball.

boletus boulī·təs genus of fungi. XVII. L. – Gr. *bōlítēs*, perh. f. *bôlos* lump, BOLUS.

bolide bo·laid large meteor. XIX. – F. *bolide* – L. *bolid-*, *bolis* – Gr. *bolís* missile, f. **bol-* **bel-* **bl-* throw (cf. BALLISTA).

boll¹ boul †vesicle, bubble XIII; rounded seed-vessel XV. – MDu. *bolle*, Du. *bol* (gen.) round object, introduced in connexion with the medicinal use of poppy-heads and flax-cultivation (cf. Du. *bolzaad* poppy-seed, flax-knop); corr. to OE. *bolla* BOWL¹.

boll² boul (north. Eng. and Sc.) measure of capacity for grain, etc. XIV – ON. *bolli* (cf. *blótbolli* sacrificial bowl) = OE. *bolla* BOWL¹ (cf. prec.).

Bollandist bo·ləndist any of the compilers of the 'Acta Sanctorum'. XVIII. f. name of Jean *Bolland*, Belgian Jesuit who carried on the work from 1629 onwards; see -IST.

bollard bo·ləɹd (naut.) post in a ship, etc. XIV (in Sandahl). Perh. f. ON. *bolr* BOLE¹ + *-ard* -ARD. ¶ Not recorded XV–XVIII.

Bolshevik bo·lʃivik. 1917. – Russ. *Bol'shevík*, f. *ból'she*, compar. of *bol'shóy* big; first applied to the section favouring a maximum socialist programme at the Second Congress of the Russian Social Democratic Party in 1903, later interpreted as denoting the section which formed the majority; cf. MENSHEVIK.

bolster bou·lstəɹ long stuffed pillow OE.; in many techn. uses from XVI. OE. *bolster* cushion = (M)Du. *bolster*, OHG. *bolstar* (G. *polster*), ON. *bolstr* :- Germ. **bolstraz*, perh. for **bolχstraz*, f. **bolg-* **belg-* swell (cf. BELLY, etc.). Hence **bo·lster** vb. (chiefly fig.) prop up XVI; cf. OE. *ġebolstrod* supported on pillows.

bolt¹ boult stout arrow OE.; stout pin for fastening XIII (in Sandahl); (from LG.) bundle XV. OE. *bolt* arrow = MLG. *bolte*, *-en* bolt, fetter, piece of rolled-up linen, (M)Du. *bout* bolt, leg or quarter (of a beast), OHG. *bolz* (G. *bolzen*) arrow, bolt for a door, of unkn. origin; Lith. *baldas* 'tongs' has been compared. Hence **bolt** vb. (in many and various uses derived ult. from the two main senses of the sb. 'missile' and 'fastening') spring, dart, break away XIII; fasten with a bolt XVI; whence a secondary sb. *bolt* †start XVI; act of bolting or breaking away XIX. **bolt** adv. 'as straight as a bolt', as in *bolt* UPRIGHT. XIV (Ch.).

bolt², boult boult sift. XIII (*bulltedd* pp., Orm). – OF. *bulter* (mod. *bluter*), earlier *buleter*, presumably for **bureter* (cf. *buretel*, mod. *bluteau* sieve) = It. *burattare*; of unkn. origin. The sp. *bolt* has arisen by assoc. with prec. (Survives in the surname *Boulter*.)

boltel, bowtel bou·(l)təl (archit.) plain round moulding. XV. Of unkn. origin.

bolter bo·ltəɹ clog, clot (esp. in pp.). XVII. chiefly midl. dial.; also *baulter* (XVII), mod. *bawter*, *bolter*; in Sh. 'Macbeth' IV i 123 *blood-bolter'd* matted with blood; perh. frequent. f. BALL.

bolus bou·ləs large pill. XVII. – medL. *bōlus* – Gr. *bôlos* clod, lump of earth. Cf. HOLUS BOLUS.

bomb bom, (formerly) bʌm hollow explosive projectile. XVII. – F. *bombe* – It. *bomba*, prob. f. L. *bombus* – Gr. *bómbos* booming, humming, of imit. origin. Hence (or – F.) **bomb** vb. XVII. So **bomb**ARD bo·m-, bʌ·mbāɹd early kind of cannon XVI; †leather jug XVII (Sh.); mortar-carrying vessel XVIII. – (O)F. *bombarde*, medL. *bombarda*, prob. f. L. *bombus* BOMB. **bombard** bombā·ɹd vb. XV. – F. *bombarder*; hence **bomba·rd**MENT. XVIII. **bombard**IE·R †artilleryman XVI; non-commissioned officer of artillery XIX. – F.

bombasine bombəzī·n †cotton; twilled dress-material of silk and worsted. XVI. – (O)F. *bombasin* – medL. *bombacīnum*, for *bombȳcinum* (Isidore), n. of *bombȳcinus* (Pliny), f. *bombȳc-*, *-byx* – Gr. *bómbux* silkworm, silk; see -INE¹.

bombast bo·mbæst, (formerly) bʌ·mbæst †cotton-wool, esp. as used for padding; turgid language. XVI. var., with parasitic *t*, of †*bombace* – OF. *bombace* – medL. *bombācem, -bax,* alteration of L. *bombyx* silk (see prec.). The pp. *bombast* of the derived vb. was formerly used in the sense 'bombastic' (XVII, Sh. 'Othello' I i 13). Hence **bomba·st**IC XVIII, -ICAL XVII.

bombinate bɔ·mbineit make a buzzing noise. XIX. f. pp. stem of late L. *bombināre*, medL. also *bombilāre* (cf. *bombus* buzzing, *bombīre* buzz); used chiefly in echoes of Rabelais' 'chimæra in vacuo bombinans'. So **bombin**A·TION. XIX (cf. Sir T. Browne's *bombilation*, 1646).

bona fide bou·nə fai·di genuine(ly). XVI (as adj. XVIII). L., 'with good faith', abl. of *bona fidēs* (see BONNE, BENE-, FAITH).

bonanza bonæ·nzə (U.S.) good luck, prosperity. XIX. – Sp. *bonanza* fair weather, prosperity = (O)F. *bonace, -asse*, Cat., Pr. *bonansa*, It. *bonaccia* :– Rom. **bonacia*, f. L. *bonus* good, after L. *malacia* (analysed as if containing *malus* bad) – Gr. *malakiā* softness, f. *malakós* soft.

bona-roba bɔ·na rɔ·ba (arch.) fine wench. XVI (Sh.). – It. *buonaroba* 'as we say good stuffe, that is a good wholesome plum-cheeked wench' (Florio), f. *buona* good, *roba* dress, stuff, gear.

bonbon bɔ·nbɔn sweetmeat. XIX. – F. *bonbon* lit. 'good-good' (see BONNE); cf. GOODY.

bond[1] bɔnd fetter; band; binding force XIII; covenant XIV; deed binding a person to pay money XVI; debenture XVII (cf. F. *bon*). var. of BAND[1], and at first interchangeable with it, but later restricted in ordinary prose use to the sense 'binding agreement'.

bond[2] bɔnd in bondage or servitude. XIV (R. Mannyng). adj. use of ME. *bonde*, late OE. *bonda* – ON. *bóndi* occupier and tiller of the soil, husbandman, HUSBAND, for *bóandi*, sb. use of prp. of East Norse *bóa* = OIcel. *búa*, f. **bū-* (see BOWER[1]). Forming permanent comps. in *bondmaid, -maiden* (XVI), *-man* (XIII; cf. AL. *bondemannus* XI), *bondservant, -slave* (XVI), *bondwoman* (XIV, Trevisa), which are assoc. in sense with BOND[1].

bonduc bɔ·ndʌk (nut of) tropical shrub called also *nicker*. XVII. – F. *bonduc* – Arab. *bunduq* – Pers. *bundūq* (see BUNDOOK).

bone[1] boun any of the parts of a vertebrate skeleton. OE. *bān* = OFris., OS. *bēn* (MDu., LG. *been*), OHG. (G.) *bein*, ON. *bein* :– CGerm. (exc. Goth.) **bainam*, of which no further cogns. are recognized (contrast *arm, eye, foot, heart, knee, nail, tooth*). The continental langs. have also the spec. sense of 'shank', 'leg', for which OE. had *sćeanca* SHANK, which was partly superseded by LEG (of Scand. origin). Hence **bone** vb. XV. **bo·ny** XVI; see -Y[1].

bone[2] boun (sl.) lay hold of, seize. XIX (Vaux). Of unkn. origin; perh. f. BONE[1], as if with ref. to a dog seizing a bone.

boneen bənī·n (Anglo-Ir.) young pig. XIX. – Ir. *banabhín* sucking-pig, f. *banbh*+*-ín* -EEN[2].

bonfire bɔ·nfaiəɹ †fire of bones XIV; open-air fire in celebration or as a display XV. f. BONE[1]+FIRE. In the north. 'Catholicon Anglicum' (1483) *banefyre* is glossed by L. 'ignis ossium'; descriptions of and allusions to fires of bones occur XV–XVII, and locally old bones were collected and stored for the purpose down to c. 1800.

bonhomie bɔ·nŏmi good nature. XVIII (Walpole). – F., f. *bonhomme* 'good man' (L. *bonus, homō*), good-natured fellow.

Boniface bɔ·nifeis. XIX. Name of the jovial innkeeper in Farquhar's 'The Beaux Stratagem', 1707, taken as a generic proper name of innkeepers.

bonito bənī·tou striped tunny. XVI (Hakluyt). Early forms also *-eto, -eta* – Sp. *bonito*, of unkn. origin.

bonne bɔn, formerly bʌn French nursemaid. XVIII. – F., fem. of *bon* :– L. *bonus* good.

bonnet bɔ·nit head-dress; various techn. uses. XIV. – OF. *bonet* (mod. *bonnet*), short for *chapel de bonet* hat made of 'bonet', in medL. *bonetus, -um*, of unkn. origin.

bonny bɔ·ni comely, fine. XV (*bonie, bony*). orig., and still in vernacular use, Sc. and north. Eng.; of doubtful origin, perh. to be referred to OF. *bon*, fem. *bone* good.

bonny-clabber bɔ·niklæ·bəɹ (Anglo-Ir.) clotted milk. XVII (B. Jonson). – Ir. *bainne clabair* (*bainne* milk, *clabair* thick sour milk).

bonspiel bɔ·nspīl (Sc.) †match, contest; curling match. XVI. prob. of LG. origin; cf. WFlem. *bonespel* child's game.

bontebok bɔ·ntibɔk S. African antelope. XVIII. Afrikaans, f. *bont* pied+*bok* BUCK[1].

bonus bou·nəs addition to normal pay. XVIII. prob. joc. or ignorant application of L. *bonus* m., for *bonum* n. good thing. (Cf. circus and thieves' sl. *bono* for 'good'.)

bonze bɔnz Buddhist priest in Japan, etc. XVI. – F. *bonze* or Pg. *bonzo* (modL. *bonzus, bonzius*), prob. – Jap. *bonzō* or *bonzi* – Chinese *fan seng* religious person, or Jap. *bo-zi* – Chinese *fa-sze* teacher of the law. Early forms in Eng. works are *bonso, bonzi* pl., *boze*.

boo bū (dial.) lowing, as of a cow; utterance of 'boo' in derision; also as vb. XIX. imit.

booby bū·bi silly fellow; gannet. XVII. prob. (with -Y[6]) – Sp. *bobo* (used in both senses) :– L. *balbu-s* stammering, stuttering (ult. imit.). Connexion with MHG. *buobe* (G. *bube* boy, lad, knave), MDu. *boeve* (Du. *boef* rogue, knave) seems to be impossible.

boodle bū·dl (U.S.) counterfeit money; money, esp. acquired or spent improperly;

the whole boodle, the whole lot or number. XIX. – Du. *boedel* the whole of one's possessions (*de heele boel*), disorderly mass, corr. to OFris. *bōdel* moveable goods, LG. *bödel* (*de ganse bödel*). Cf. CABOODLE.

boohoo buhū· imit. of loud laughter or weeping. XIX. (An isolated ex. of *bo ho* is in Skelton's 'Replycacion'.)

book buk †written document or record; written or printed literary composition; ***the Book***, the divine writings (cf. OE. *on Godes bōcum, Crīstes bōc*); main division of a work XIII; volume of accounts, notes, etc. XV. OE. *bōc* fem., pl. *bēċ*, corr. to OFris., OS. *bōk* fem. and n. (Du. *boek*), OHG. *buoh* mostly n., pl. *buoh* fem. (G. *buch*), ON. *bók*, pl. *bœkr* fem. :– Germ. **bōks*, pl. **bōkiz* (the stem is repr. in Goth. by *bōka* fem. letter of the alphabet, a writing, pl. *bōkōs* book, letter); usu. taken to be a deriv. of **bōkā* BEECH, the wood of the tree being the material of the tablets on which runes were inscribed (cf. 'Barbara fraxineis pingatur runa tabellis', Venantius Fortunatus, VI, and the use of the pl. in the phr. Goth. *gakunnan ana bōkum*, OHG. *lesan ana buohhum*, ON. *ríta á bókum*).

bookie bu·ki. XIX. (sl.) f. first syll. of *bookmaker* maker of a betting-book + -IE, -Y[6].

boom[1] būm give out a deep humming note XV (*bombe, bumbe, bumme*); sail with great speed XVII. ult. imit. (cf. BOMB); perh. orig. – Du. *bommen*. Hence **boom** sb. XVI.

boom[2] būm (naut.) long spar; floating timber barrier. XVI (Sc. *boume*). – Du. *boom* tree, pole, BEAM.

boom[3] būm (orig. U.S.) sudden activity in commerce. XIX. prob. application of BOOM[1], with ref. to the notion of a ship booming along. Also as vb.

boomerang bū·mərӕŋ Australian missile. XIX. Native name (*wo-mur-rāng* is recorded as a Port Jackson word, *būmarin* as Kamilaroi).

boon[1] būn †prayer, request; thing prayed for; favour XII; benefit, blessing XVIII. – ON. *bón* (Sw., Da. *bön*) :– Germ. **bōniz*, whence also OE. *bēn* BENE: ult. relations doubtful.

boon[2] būn good, gracious XIV; surviving in *boon companion* (XVI) in the sense 'jolly', 'convivial'. – (O)F. *bon* :– L. *bonus* (cf. BENE ESSE). In early use freq. in partly anglicized F. phr., e.g. *bone chere, bon sire, bone order, bon voiage, bone fortune*.

boor buəɹ husbandman XV; Dutch or German peasant XVI (Dutch colonist, BOER XIX); rustic, clownish fellow XVI. – LG. *būr* or Du. *boer* (which was adopted from a dialect that preserved the old ū-sound); the word is repr. in Germ. by OE. *ġebūr* (also *nēahġebūr* NEIGHBOUR), MDu. *ghebuer, buer* (Du. *buur* neighbour), MLG. (*ge*)*būr*, OHG. *gibūr, gibūro* (G. *bauer*) :– WGerm. **gibūr-*, f. **gi-* Y- + **būram* dwelling, BOWER[1], the orig. meaning being, therefore, 'fellow-occupier of a dwelling', hence 'neighbour', and finally by assoc. with **bū-* cultivate, 'peasant, rustic'. ¶ Du. distinguishes *boer* peasant, farmer, *buur* neighbour, *bouwer* builder; in G. *bauer* the words meaning 'builder' and 'rustic' have coalesced. Hence **boo·rish** XVI; see -ISH[1] and cf. Du. *boersch*.

boost būst (U.S.) hoist up, assist over obstacles, give a lift to, 'puff'. XIX (defined as 'raise up, lift up, exalt' in 1815). Of unkn. origin.

boot[1] būt (arch.) advantage (in phr. *to boot* †to advantage, in addition); †making good, repair, remedy, amends. OE. *bōt* = OFris. *bōte*, OS. *bōta*, (M)Du. *boete*, OHG. *buoȥa* (G. *busse*), ON. *bót*, Goth. *bōta* :– CGerm. **bōtō* remedy, advantage, f. **bōt-* **bat-* (see BETTER, BEST). Hence **boot** vb. profit, avail. XIV. **boo·tLESS** irremediable (OE. *bōtlēas* = OFris. *bōtelas, bōtlos*, ON. *bótalauss*); useless XVI.

boot[2] būt A. covering for the foot and (lower part of) the leg XIV; B. †space for attendants on the outside of a coach XVII; receptacle for luggage on a coach XVIII. ME. *bote* – ON. *bóti* or its source, OF. *bote* (mod. *botte*) = Pr. *bota*; in AL. *bota* (XII), *botta*; of unkn. origin. The senses under B appear to derive from modF. (Identity with F. *botte* butt, cask, leathern vessel (XV) cannot be entertained on account of the discrepancy of form and date.) W. *botasen*, Gael. *bot* are from Eng. or F. *Boot and saddle* (XVII), order for cavalry to mount; alteration, by partial translation, of †*boutesel*, †*bot et sel* – F. *boute-selle* 'put-saddle' (see BUTT[1]). Hence **boo·tle:gger** (orig. U.S.) one who carries (illicit) liquor in his boot-legs. XIX.

booth būð temporary dwelling; covered stall. XII (Orm). ME. *bōþ* (cf. AL. *botha, bothus* XII) – OEast Norse **bóð* (Sw., Da. *bod* stall, shop) = OIcel. *búð* dwelling, f. East Norse *bóa* = OIcel. *búa* dwell (see BOWER[1]).

booty bū·ti plunder. XV. First recorded from Caxton, who has *botye, buty*, beside *butyn, butin* (which was current in Eng. XV–XVIII). – (O)F. *butin* (cf. Sp. *botin*, It. *bottino*) – MLG. *būte, buite* exchange, distribution (whence G. *beute*), rel. to ON. *býta* deal out, exchange, of doubtful origin.

booze, boose būz (sl. or colloq.) drink. XIII. ME. *bous* sb., *bouse* vb. (each recorded once); these gave normally *bouse* baus, and *bouse* bauz (cf. Browning's rhyming of *bowsed* with *caroused* and *drowzed*); but this pronunc. appears to have been gen. arrested by re-adoption in XVI (Skelton, Harman) of the orig. etymon, MDu. *būsen* (Du. *buizen*) drink to excess.

bo-peep boupī·p game played by peeping from behind a hiding-place and crying bo! XVI. f. BO int. + PEEP[1].

borage bɔ·ridʒ, bʌ·ridʒ genus of plants, Borago. XIII. – (O)F. *bourrache* = Pr. *borraga*, It. *borragine*, Sp. *borraja*, Pg. *borragem* – medL. *bor(r)āgo*, *-āgin-*, perh. – Arab. *abū ʿāraq* 'father of sweat', the Arabian physicians using the plant as a diaphoretic. Cf. G. *bor(r)etsch*.

borax bō·ræks biborate of sodium. XIV (*boras*, Ch.; *borace*; *borax*, after medL., from XVI). – OF. *boras* – medL. *borax* (so modF.; in Sp. *borrax*, It. *borrace*) – Arab. *būraq* – Pers. *būrah*. So **boracic** bŏræ·sik. XIX. f. *borac-*, stem of medL. *borax*.

Bordeaux bōɹdou·. XVI (in earliest use Sc., of skins and wine). Formerly *b(o)urdeaux*, *burdeous* – OF. *b(o)urdeaux*, appellative use of the name of a city in S. France :– *Burdigalis*, f. L. *Burdigala*, chief town of the Bituriges Vivisci, a people of Gallia Aquitania.

border bō·ɹdəɹ edge, boundary. XIV (*bordure*, Ch.). – OF. *bordure*, earlier *bordeure*, corr. to Pr., Sp. *bordadura*, It. *bordatura* – CRom. deriv. of **bordāre* (F. *border*, etc.), f. **bordus*; see BOARD, -URE. The suffix *-ure* was weakened to *-er* as in BRACER; but the orig. form is retained in techn. use (e.g. her.). Hence **bo·rder** vb. XIV. **bo·rderer** dweller on the borders of a country XV (in earliest use Sc.); see -ER[1].

bore[1] bɔəɹ pierce. OE. *borian* = MLG., MDu. *boren*, OHG. *borōn* (G. *bohren*), ON. *bora* :– CGerm. (exc. Goth.) **borōn*, f. **boraz* (whence OE., ON. *borr* auger, gimlet); the IE. base **bhor-*, **bhr̥-* is repr. by L. *forāre* pierce, Gr. *pháros* plough, ploughing, *phárynx* PHARYNX. Hence **bore** sb. XIV; in earliest use prob. – ON. *bora* bore-hole = OHG. *boro* auger :– Germ. **borōn*.

bore[2] bɔəɹ extraordinary tidal wave. XVII. The absence of earlier evidence makes the origin very doubtful, but deriv. from ON. *bára* wave, billow, is appropriate for form and meaning.

bore[3] bɔəɹ †ennui; †annoyance, nuisance; tiresome thing XVIII; (early U.S.) hoax; tiresome person XIX. Of unkn. origin; some of the earliest exx. (1766, 1767, 1768) make reference to *French bore* (connoting dullness or lack of interest), which has not been explained.

boreal bō·riəl northern. XV. – (O)F. *boréal* or late L. *boreālis*, f. L. *boreās* – Gr. *boréās* north wind; see -AL. Cf. AURORA BOREALIS.

borecole bɔə·ɹkoul variety of cabbage. XVIII. – Du. *boerenkool* 'peasants' cabbage', f. *boer* BOOR + *kool* COLE.

boreen borī·n (Anglo-Ir.) lane. XIX. –Ir. *bóithrín* dim. of *bóthar* bōhər road; see -EEN[2].

born, borne bōɹn var. forms of the pp. (OE. *boren*) of BEAR[2], differentiated since c. 1600; *born* is now no longer assoc. with *bear*, the phr. *to be born* being an independent intr. vb. equiv. to F. *naître*, L. *nāscī*; *borne* is retained in literary use for 'carried', 'endured'.

boron bɔə·rɔn (chem.) non-metallic element, extracted from borax and resembling carbon in some of its properties. XIX (Davy). f. BOR|AX + *-on* of CARBON.

borough bʌ·rə †fortress; town (orig. fortified) OE.; town of a certain (political) status XVI. OE. *burg*, *burh* = OFris. *burch*, OS. *burg* (MDu. *burch*, Du. *burg*; see BURGOMASTER), OHG. *burug* (G. *burg*), ON. *borg*, Goth. *baurgs* :– CGerm. **burgs*, str. fem. (hence medL. and Rom. *burgus*; see BOURG), rel. to **bergan* protect, shelter (cf. BORROW, BURY). The sense of 'town', 'civil community' may have been developed in early Germ., but in German and the Scand. langs. the word is recorded chiefly in the sense 'fortress', 'castle'. The OE. dative sg. *byrġ* (early ME. *büri*, *biri*, *beri*) is preserved in place-names ending in *-bury* bəri, and in *Bury* be·ri.

borrow bɔ·rou take on pledge or credit. OE. *borgian* = OFris. *borgia*, MLG., MDu. *borgen*, OHG. *borgēn* (G. *borgen*), f. Germ. **borg-*, whence OE., OFris., OS. *borg*, MHG. *borc* pledge, rel. to OE. *beorgan* = OS., OHG. *bergan* (Du., G. *bergen*), ON. *bjarga*, Goth. *bairgan* :– Germ. **bergan* (see prec.).

OE. *borg* survived in Sc. legal use; it was continued in ME. in the phr. *to borrow* (e.g. *seint John to borwe*, Ch.) orig. in appealing to God or a saint 'as security' for one's honour, hence as a mere asseveration.

borzoi bō·ɹzoi Russian wolf-hound. XIX. – Russ. *bórzyj* swift (the Russ. word for the dog is *borzája*).

bosh bɔʃ nonsense. XIX. – Turk. *bosh* empty, worthless; gained currency from its frequent use in James Justinian Morier's novel 'Ayesha', 1834.

bosky bɔ·ski (arch.) grown with bushes or thickets. XVI. f. *bosk* (ME. XIII–XIV, but in mod. literary use a back-formation from *bosky*), var. of *busk*, BUSH[1] + -Y[1].

bosom bu·zəm breast. OE. *bōsm* = OFris. *bōsm*, OS. *bōsom* (Du. *boezem*), OHG. *buosam* (G. *busen*) :– WGerm. **bōsm-*, perh. for **bōχsm-*, f. **bōg-* (see BOUGH), the primary meaning being the space embraced by the arms (cf. *fathom*).

boss[1] bɔs protuberance, round prominence. XIII. ME. *boce*, *bose*, *boos* (the earliest recorded sense is 'hump') – OF. *boce* (mod. *bosse*) = Pr. *bosa*, It. *bozza*, *boccia* (whence Sp. *bocha*) :– Rom. **bokja* or **botja*, of unkn. origin.

boss[2] bɔs (orig. U.S.) master, employer. XIX (W. Irving). – Du. *baas* master, gen.

held to be rel. to OHG. *basa* aunt (G. *base* aunt, niece), of unkn. origin.

boston bɔ·stən card-game allied to whist. XIX (*Boston whist*, 1805). – F. *boston*, said to be named from the siege of *Boston* (Massachusetts, U.S.A.) in the American War of Independence, to which the technical terms of the game refer; but other accounts are given.

bosun bou·sn see BOATSWAIN.

bot(t) bɔt parasitic worm or maggot. XV. prob. of LDu. origin and introduced as a farming term; cf. Du. *bot*, WFris. *botten* (pl.), WFlem. *botse*, NFris. *galboten* liver-worm, WFris. *botgalle* disease caused by these; further relations unkn.

botanic bŏtæ·nik pert. to the study of plants. XVII. – F. *botanique*, or its source, late L. *botanicus* – Gr. *botanikós*, f. *botánē* plant; see -IC. So **bota·nical.** XVII. Hence **botany** bɔ·təni the scientific study of plants XVII; on the analogy of *astronomic*, *astronomy*; see -Y[3]. **bo·tan**IZE collect or study plants. XVIII. – modL. *botanizāre* – Gr. *botanízein* gather plants. **bo·tan**IST. XVII. – F.

botargo boutā·ɹgou relish of mullet or tunny roe. XVI (*botarge*; Capt. Smith has *buttargo* and *puttargo*, 1616). – It. *botargo*, *botarga* (now *bottarga*) – Arab. *buṭarkhah* preserved mullet roe – Coptic *outarakhon*, f. *ou-* indef. article + Gr. *taríkhion* pickle.

botch[1] bɔtʃ †hump, tumour, boil; plague of boils, etc. XIV (PPl., Wyclif, Trevisa). – ONF. *boche*, var. of OF. *boce* BOSS[1].

botch[2] bɔtʃ put a patch on (now, clumsily) XIV (Wycl. Bible); fig. XVI. Of unkn. origin; poss. transf. use of BOTCH[1], or rel. obscurely to synon. dial. *bodge* (XVI).

both bouþ the one and the other. XII (*baþe*, Orm). ME. *bāþe*, *bōþe* (g. *bāþre*, *bāþer*, *bōther*) – ON. *báðir* m., *báðar* fem., *báði* and *bæði* n. = OFris. *be(i)the*, *be(i)de*, OS. *bēðia* m., fem., *bēðiu* n., OHG. *bēde*, *beide* m., *bēdo*, *beido* fem., *bēdiu* n. (G. *beide*); extended form of the base found in OE. *bēġen* m., *bā*, *bū* fem. and n. (ME. *beie-n*, *bō*), Goth. *bai* m., *bā* n., and as the second el. of L. *ambō*, OSl. (Russ.) *oba*, Skr. *ubhāu*, Av. *uva* both. Also adv. (conj.) XII (Peterborough Chron.). It is doubtful how far rare late OE. *bā þā* both the (corr. to Goth. *bā þō* n.) contributed to the establishment of this word.

bother bɔ·ðəɹ (dial.) bewilder, confuse; pester, worry. XVIII (also *bodder*, Swift). First recorded from the writings of Irishmen (T. Sheridan, Swift, Sterne), and doubtless of Anglo-Ir. origin, but no plausible Ir. source can be adduced; poss. an Ir. pronunc. of POTHER. Hence **bo·ther** sb. XIX. (For sb. and vb. there is a local sense 'humbug', 'blarney'.) **bother**A·TION. XIX (*boderation*, Southey).

bothy, bothie bɔ·þi hut, cottage. XVIII (Pennant). rel. obscurely to Ir., Gael. *both*, *bothan*, perh. cogn. with BOOTH.

bo-tree bou·trī pipal tree. XIX. repr. Sinhalese *bogaha*, f. *bo* (:– Pali, Skr. *bodhi* perfect knowledge), more fully *bodhitarū* (*taru* tree) + *gaha* tree; under such a tree Gautama attained the enlightenment which constituted him the Buddha.

botryo- bɔ·triou comb. form of Gr. *bótrus* bunch of grapes.

bottle[1] bɔ·tl narrow-necked vessel for liquids. XIV (Wyclif). – OF. *botele*, *botaille* (mod. *bouteille*), whence Sp. *botella*, It. *bottiglia* :– medL. *butticula*, dim. of late L. *buttis* BUTT[5].

bottle[2] bɔ·tl bundle of hay, etc. XIV (Ch.). – OF. *botel*, dim. of *botte* bundle – MLG., MDu. *bote* bundle of flax, prob. f. Germ. **but-* strike (cf. BUTT[1]).

bottom bɔ·tm A. lowest surface or part OE.; valley, dell (surviving in place-names); foundation XV; B. keel of ship, hull XVI. OE. *botm* (*boþm*) = OS. *bodom* (Du. *bodem*), corr. with variation of suffix (cf. OE. *bytme*, *byþme*, *byþne* bottom, keel) to ON. *botn*, and parallel to OE. *bodan*, corr. to OHG. *bodam* (G. *boden* ground, earth) :– Germ. **buþm-*, **buþn-* :– IE. **bhudhm(e)n-*, f. **bhudh-* (also **bhundh-*), whence also L. *fundus*, Gr. *puthmḗn* (:– **phuthmḗn*), OIr., Gael. *bond*, *bonn*, W. *bon*, Skr. *budhnás*, the orig. sense being 'foundation', 'base'. Sense B is from Du.

bottomry bɔ·təmri borrowing on the security of a ship. XVI. – Du. *bodemerij* (also *bomerij*; cf. *bummary*, Pepys), f. *bodem* BOTTOM in the sense 'ship's hull, ship'; see -RY.

botulism bɔ·tjulizm poisoning from eating decomposed foods (the bacillus is Bacillus botulinus). XIX. f. L. *botulus* sausage (cf. BOWEL) + -ISM, after G. *botulismus*.

boucherize bū·ʃəraiz impregnate timber with copper sulphate. XIX. f. name of *Boucherie*, French chemist + -IZE.

boudoir bū·dwāɹ lady's private room. XVIII (Chesterfield). – F. *boudoir* prop. 'place to sulk in', f. *bouder* pout, sulk, of imit. origin; see -OIR.

bougainvillæa būgeinvi·liə, -vilī·ə genus of tropical plants. XIX. f. name of Louis Antoine de *Bougainville*, French navigator (1729–1811).

bough bau †shoulder; †(Sc.) limb; limb of a tree. OE. *bōg*, *bōh* = MLG. *bōch*, *būch* (LG. *boog*), MDu. *boech* (Du. *boeg* shoulders, chest of a horse, bows of a ship), OHG. *buog* shoulder, forearm (G. *bug* horse's hock or point of shoulder, bow of a ship), ON. *bógr* shoulder :– CGerm. (exc. Gothic) **bōguz* :– IE. **bhāghús*, repr. also by Gr. *pâkhus*, *pêkhus* (:– **phâkhus*) forearm, cubit,

Skr. *bāhús* arm, forearm, forefoot. The basic meaning is unkn.; the sense 'limb of a tree' is a purely Eng. development. See also BOW[3].

bougie bū·ʒī wax candle. XVIII. – (O)F. *bougie* (orig. the wax itself, as in *chandeles de bougie*), f. name of a town *Bougie* (Arab. *Bujīyah*) in Algeria, where a trade in wax was carried on; so Sp., It. *bugia*.

bouillabaisse būjabei·s dish of stewed fish. XIX. F. – modProv. *bouiabaisso*.

bouilli bū·ji boiled or stewed meat. XVII (*buollie*, Butler's 'Hudibras'). – F. *bouilli*, sb. use of pp. of *bouillir* BOIL[2]; cf. BULLY[3].

bouillon bū·jɔ̃ broth. XVIII. F., f. *bouillir* BOIL[2].

boulder bou·ldəɹ large rounded water-worn stone. XIII. First in 'Havelok' l. 1790 as *bulder ston*, of Scand. origin; cf. Sw. dial. *bullersten*, *buldurstajn*; perh. orig. a stone that causes a rumbling noise in water (cf. Sw. *buller* sb., *bullra* vb. rumble).

boule see BUHL.

boulevard būl(i)vāɹ, -vāɹd broad tree-lined walk. XVIII. – F. *boulevard* (whence It. *baluardo*, Sp. *baluarte*), †*boullewerc* – G. *bollwerk* BULWARK; orig. applied to a promenade laid out on the horizontal portion of a rampart in a demolished fortification.

bounce bauns First in the vb. (*bunsen* †beat, thump XIII); the application to loud explosive noise, blustering, and bounding like a ball appears in vb., sb., and int. in early XVI; possibly of LDu. origin (cf. LG. *bunsen* beat, thwack, Du. *bons* thump, which are, however, not recorded early), but perh. of independent imit. origin.

bound[1] baund †landmark XIII; boundary; pl. territory; limit of action XIV. – AN. *bounde*, OF. *bun(n)e*, *bone*, *bunde*, *bonde*, earlier *bodne* :– medL. *bodina*, earlier *butina*, of unkn. origin. Cf. BOURN. Hence **bound** vb. †limit XIV; form the boundary of XVII. **bou·nd**LESS. XVI.

bound[2] baund †ready XIII (Orm); prepared to go, destined XIV. ME. *būn*, *boun* – ON. *búinn*, pp. of *búa* prepare (cf. BOOR, BOWER[1]); the final *d* of *bound* (XVI) may be purely phonetic, as in SOUND[3], but is prob. in part due to assoc. with BOUND[3].

bound[3] baund shortened form of BOUNDEN; in the senses 'obliged', 'fated, destined', (U.S.) 'determined', functioning as an adj. XIV.

bound[4] baund †rebound; spring upwards. XVI (Sh.). – (O)F. *bondir* resound, (later) rebound = Pr. *bondir* :– Rom. **bombitīre*, for late L. *bombitāre*, var. of *bombilāre* (see BOMBINATE). So **bound** sb. XVI. – F. *bond*, f. *bondir*.

boundary bau·ndəri limiting line. XVII (Bacon). Alteration of (dial.) *bounder* (XVI), f. *bound* vb. (see BOUND[1])+-ER[1]; perh. after *limitary*.

bounden bau·ndn pp. (OE. *bunden*) of BIND, formerly used in various senses of the vb., in mod. times mainly in the sense 'beholden, indebted' (XVI), and in echoes of the phr. *bounden duty* (XVI).

bounder bau·ndəɹ (sl.) A. †four-wheeled dog-cart or trap; B. ill-bred fellow. XIX. f. BOUND[4]+-ER[1]; in A. with ref. to springiness; in B perh. assoc. with *bounce* and *bumptious*.

bounteous bau·ntiəs generously liberal. XIV (Ch.). Late ME. *bountevous* (later *bounteous* XV), f. OF. *bontif*, *-ive* benevolent (f. *bonté* BOUNTY), after *plentevous* PLENTEOUS.

bounty bau·nti †goodness, excellence; gracious liberality XIII; gift, gratuity XVIII. – (O)F. *bonté* :– L. *bonitātem*, f. *bonus* good (cf. BOON[2]); see -TY. Hence **bou·ntiful** XVI; see -FUL[1].

bouquet bu·kei nosegay XVIII; aroma of wine XIX. – F. *bouquet* (earlier, clump of trees), f. dial. var. of OF. *bos*, *bois* wood (cf. BUSH[1]); see -ET.

bourdon buə·ɹdən †undersong XIV; (from mod F.) bass stop in an organ XIX.– (O)F. *bourdon* drone = Sp. *bordon*, It. *bordone* :– Rom. **burdō(n-)*, of imit. origin.

bourg buəɹg, ‖ būr (hist.) town. XV. – (O)F. *bourg* = Pr. *borc*, Sp. *burgo*, It. *borgo* :– medL. *burgus* BOROUGH.

bourgeois[1] buə·ɹʒwa French citizen of the trading middle class. XVI. – (O)F. *bourgeois*, earlier *burgeis*; see BURGESS; adj. XVIII (Walpole).

bourgeois[2] bəɹdʒoi·s (typogr.) size of type between long primer and brevier. XIX. Conjectured to be f. the name of a printer; but perh. referring to its intermediate size.

bourn[1] buəɹn, bɔəɹn boundary, bound, limit. XVI. – (O)F. *borne*, earlier *bodne*; see BOUND[1]. Recorded early only from Ld. Berners (*boundes and bornes*) and Sh. (seven times); to the latter is due its modern currency (since XVIII), esp. in echoes of 'Hamlet' III i 79; assim. in form to *bourn*, BURN[2].

bourn[2] var. of BURN[2].

bourse buəɹs, ‖ burs money exchange, spec. (*B-*) French stock exchange. XIX. F., 'purse'; see BURSE.

bouse, bowse[1] baus haul with tackle. XVI. Of unkn. origin.

bouse, bowse[2] see BOOZE.

boustrophedon baustrəfī·dən alternately from right to left and from left to right. XVII. Gr., f. *boustrophos* 'ox-turning' (with ref. to ploughing), f. *boûs* ox (see COW)+ *stroph-* (cf. STROPHE).

bout baut †circuit; (dial.) length of a furrow and back again; round of exercise, fighting. XVI. var. of †*bought* (XV) bend, fold, turn, prob. – LG. *bucht* (see BIGHT); assoc. with *bout*, aphetic form of ABOUT.

bouts-rimés būrī·mei, ‖ burime versification to set rhymes. XVIII. F.; *bouts* ends, *rimés* rhymed.

bovate bou·veit oxgang. XVII. – medL. *bovāta*, f. L. *bov-*, *bōs* ox; see COW[1], -ATE[1].

bovine bou·vain ox-like. XIX. – late L. *bovīnus*, f. *bov-*; see COW[1], -INE[1].

bow[1] bou weapon for shooting arrows OE.; transf. to various bent objects XIV. OE. *boga* bow, rainbow, arch = OFris. *boga*, OS. *bogo* (Du. *boog*), OHG. *bogo* (G. *bogen*), ON. *bogi* :– CGerm. (exc. Goth.) **bugon*, f. **bug-*, short stem of **beugan* (cf. BOW[2]). In *bow legs*, and the earlier *bow-back*, *-backed* (XV), now assoc. with this sb., *bow* may be orig. *bowe* ppl. adj. :– OE. *bogen*, pp. of BOW[2]. Hence **bo:w-**WI·NDOW curved bay window. XVIII (Richardson).

bow[2] bau bend (esp. the body) OE.; cause to bend XIII; incline the head in salute XVII. OE. *būgan*, pt. *bēah*, *bugon*, pp. *bogen*, corr. to MLG. *būgen*, MDu. *būghen* (Du. *buigen*) and (with a different grade in the pres. stem) OHG. *biogan* (G. *biegen*), ON. **bjúga* (pt. pl. *bugum*, pp. *boginn*). Goth. *biugan*, *baug*, *bugum*, *bugans* :– CGerm. **beugan* (cf. BOW[1]). The obvious connexions outside Germ. have *-g-* (to which Germ. *-k-* should corr.), viz. L. *fugere* flee (a sense found in OE. *būgan*), Gr. *pheúgein* flee, Skr. *bhuj* bow, bend. Weak inflexions appear before 1300 (Cursor M.). Hence **bow** sb. bend of the head or body XVII (Cowley).

bow[3] bau fore-end of a boat. XV (in Sandahl). – LG. *boog*, Du. *boeg* (whence Sw. *bog*, Da. *boug*); see BOUGH and cf. BOWLINE, BOWSPRIT, which are earlier. Not related to BOW[1] or BOW[2], but pop. assoc. with the latter and infl. by its pronunc.

bowdlerize bau·dləraiz expurgate. XIX. f. the name of Dr. T. *Bowdler*, who in 1818 published an edition of Shakespeare's works 'in which those words and expressions are omitted which cannot with propriety be read aloud in a family'; see -IZE.

bowel bau·əl intestine, gut. XIII (Cursor M.). ME. *buel*, *bouel* – OF. *buel*, *boel*, *bouel*, *boiel* (mod. *boyau*) = Pr. *budel*, It. *budello* :– L. *botellus* pudding, sausage (Martial), small intestine, dim. of *botulus* sausage, prob. of alien origin.

bower[1] bau·əɹ †dwelling; inner apartment, lady's apartment OE.; arbour XVI. OE. *būr*, corr. to OS. *būr* (LG. *buur*), OHG. *būr* (G. *bauer* birdcage), ON. *búr* :– CGerm. (exc. Gothic) **būraz*, **būram*, f. **bū-* dwell (see BE, BOOR). For the present sp., which appeared XV and superseded *bour*, cf. *flower*, *tower*.

bower[2] bau·əɹ either of two anchors carried at the bows. XVII. In full *bower anchor*; f. BOW[3]+-ER[1].

bower[3] bau·əɹ knave of trumps and knave of the same colour at euchre. XIX. – G. *bauer* (see BOOR) knave at cards.

bowery bau·əri (hist.) Dutch farm in New York State XVII; (*B-*) region of New York City orig. occupied by Governor Stuyvesant's country seat XVIII. – Du. *bouwerij* husbandry, farm, f. *bouwen* cultivate; see BOOR, -ERY.

bowie bou·i, bū·i large slightly-curved knife. XIX (1838). In full *bowie-knife*; f. name of Colonel James *Bowie* (killed 1836), who possessed a hunting-knife which served as a pattern.

bowl[1] boul round vessel to hold liquids, etc. OE. *bolla*, *bolle*, corr. to OS. *bollo* cup (Du. *bol* round object; see BOLL[1]), OHG. *bolla* (MHG. *bolle*) bud, round pod, globular vessel (cf. OE. *hēafodbolla*, OHG. *hirnibolla* skull, OE. *þrotbolla* Adam's apple), f. **bul-* **bel-* **bal-* swell (cf. BALL[1], BULWARK).

bowl[2] boul †ball; globular body used in games; (pl.) game with bowls. XV. – (O)F. *boule* = Pr. *bola*, Sp. *bolla* ball, It. *bolla* bubble, pustule:– L. *bulla* (see BULL[2]).

bowler bou·ləɹ low-crowned stiff felt hat. XIX. f. name of John *Bowler*, hat-manufacturer of Nelson Square, London.

bowline bou·lin (naut.) rope connecting the weather side of a sail with the bow. XIII. (In ONF. and AN. *boeline* XII–XIII) – MLG. *bōlīne*, MDu. *boechlijne*, f. *boeg* BOW[3]+*lijne* LINE[1]; cf. OSw. *boghline*, G. *buline*, F. *bouline*, Sp., It. *bolina*, all of like origin. So **bowsprit** bou·sprit spar running out from the stem of a vessel. XIII (in Sandahl). – (M)LG. *bōgsprēt*, MDu *boechspriet* (Du. *boeg-*), whence also G. *bugspriet*, Sw. *bogspröt*, Da. *bogspryd*, F. *beaupré*, Sp. *baupres*, It. *bompresso*; see SPRIT.

bow-wow bau·wau· imit. of a dog's bark. XVII (*bowgh wawgh*, *bough wough*), earlier *baugh baw* (XV), *bough* (XVI), *baw waw* (XVI); cf. †*baffe* vb (XV), (dial.) *waff*, *waugh* (XVII), and G. *wau wau*, Du. *boubou*, *bafbaf*, WFlem. *bauwbauw*, L. *baubārī*, Gr. *baù baú*, F., Pr. *baubau*.

box[1] bɔks evergreen tree Buxus. OE. *box* – L. *buxus* – Gr. *púxos*.

box[2] bɔks receptacle with a lid, of wood, etc., in earliest use for medicaments OE.; for money XIV (Ch.); so *Christmas box* orig. of earthenware, used for collecting money for Christmas, when it was broken and the contents shared out XVII; various transf. and techn. uses from XVII. Late OE. *box*, prob. – **buxem*, for late L. *buxidem*, acc. of *buxis*, var. of L. *pyxis*, prop. box of boxwood (cf. '*pixis*, bixen [i.e. of boxwood] **box**',

Ælfric); see PYX. Cf. OF. *boiste* (mod. *boîte*) box :– med. L. *buxida*, and MDu. *busse*, *bosse* (Du. *bus*, *bos*), OHG. *buhsa* (G. *büchse*) :– WGerm. **buχsja* – L. *pyxis*. *Boxing-day* 26 December, the day for giving Christmas boxes XIX. Hence **box** vb. enclose in a box XV.

box[3] bɔks blow, buffet (now usu. on the ear). XIV. Of unkn. origin. Hence **box** vb. beat, esp. with the fist; fight with fists XVI; whence **bo·xer**[1] pugilist XVIII, from 1900 designating a member of a Chinese nationalist secret society, *i ho chuan* or *chuen* 'righteous harmony boxers (fists)'. ¶ The words have passed into many Eur. langs.

box[4] bɔks phr. *box the compass* repeat the points of the compass in order and backwards; (fig.) make a complete revolution; (in full *box-haul*) veer a ship round on her keel. XVIII. prob. – Sp. *bojar* (*boxar*) sail round (e.g. *bojar el mundo, la isla*) – MLG. *bōgen* to bend, bow, f. base of BOW[1], BOW[2]. ¶ Other naut. terms of Sp. origin are *buoyant* and *capsize*.

box-calf bɔ·kskāf Named c. 1890 by Edward L. White, of White Bros. & Co., Massachusetts, U.S.A., after Joseph *Box*, bootmaker, of London.

boy boi †male servant; †youth or man of low estate; †'fellow', 'knave' XIII; young male child XIV; native servant, negro slave XVII. ME. *boie*, *boy*(*e*), also *bay*, *bey*(*e*), *bye*, *bwey*, in which the variation of vowel suggests an OF. original with *-ui-*, and aphetic – AN. **abuié*, **embuié*, pp. of OF. *embuier* fetter :– L. **imboiāre*, f. *in* IM-[1] + *boia*, chiefly pl. *boiæ* fetters – Gr. *boeîai* (*doraí*) ox-hides, f. *boûs* ox, cow. The primary meaning would be 'man in fetters', hence 'slave', 'serf'. For the loss of *é* cf. ASSIGN[2]. ¶ Contact cannot be proved with MDu. *boye*, which appears to be :– *bode* messenger, servant, and is of later date than *boy*; the MDu. word is prob. the source of LG. and Fris. *boi*.

boyar, boyard boujā·ɹ, boi·āɹd member of an old Russian aristocracy. XVI (*boiaren*). – Russ. *boyárin*, pl. *boyáre* :– **bolyárin*, prob. f. *bol-* great (cf. BOLSHEVIK); cf. Byzantine Gr. *boïládai*, *boliádai*, Bulg. *bolerin*, Serb. *bolyar*.

boycott boi·kɔt refuse to have social or business relations with. 1880 (first used of the action of the Irish Land League against those who incurred its hostility). f. name of Captain C. C. *Boycott* (1832–1897), who was a victim of such treatment as agent for the estates of the earl of Erne, Co. Mayo, Ireland, at the hands of the tenants. ¶ The word has passed into other Eur. langs.

brabble bræ·bl (dial.) dispute captiously, squabble. XVI. prob. ult. imit., but perh. immed. – (M)Du. *brabbelen* jabber (cf. *brabbeltaal* gibberish); cf. G. *brabbelen* babble, (of the sea) boil; possibly, however, a blend of BRAWL[1] and BABBLE.

brace[1] breis †guard for the arm XIV; pair, couple XV (Lydg.); clasp, clamp, thong; strap XIV; (archit.) strengthening band; clasp, etc. XV; carpenter's tool to hold a bit XVI; (typogr.) bracket XVII. – OF. *brace* two arms or their extent (mod. *brasse* fathom) :– L. *bracchia*, pl. of *bracchium* arm (whence F. *bras*) – Gr. *brakhī̆ōn*. Some senses depend upon BRACE[2].

brace[2] breis †embrace; encircle, gird XIV; make tense or firm XV. – OF. *bracier* embrace, f. *brace* (see prec.); but the later sense is direct from the sb.

bracelet brei·slit ornamental ring for arm or wrist. XV. – (O)F. *bracelet*, dim. of *bracel* (= Sp. *brazal*, It. *bracciale*) :– L. *bracchiāle*, f. *bracchium* arm (see BRACE[1]).

bracer brei·səɹ armour or guard for the arm. XIV (Ch.). – OF. *brasseüre*, f. *bras* arm (:– L. *bracchium*; see BRACE[1]) + *-eüre* -URE; for change of suffix cf. BORDER.

brach brætʃ (arch.) hunting-dog; bitch-hound. XIV. ME. *braches* pl. – OF. *braches*, *-ez*, pl. of *brachet*, dim. of *brac*, acc. *bracon* (= Pr. *brac*, Sp. *braco*, It. *bracco*) :– CRom. **bracco* – Frankish **brak* (cf. OHG. *brakko*, G. *bracke*); the sg. *brach* is a back-formation.

brachiopod bræ·kiŏpɔd (zool.) bivalve mollusc having a long spiral arm. XIX. – modL. *brachiopoda* n.pl. (see -A[2]), f. Gr. *brakhī̆ōn* arm + *pod-*, *poús* FOOT.

brachy- bræ·ki comb. form of Gr. *brakhús* short (see MEGAL(O)), as in **bra:chy**CEPHA·LIC (of skulls) XIX; **brachy**·GRAPHY shorthand XVI – F. *brachygraphie*; **brachy**·LOGY conciseness of speech XVII. – late L. – Gr.

bracken bræ·kn fern, spec. Pteris aquilina. XIV (earlier in Sc. place-name *Brakanwra* XIII). north. ME. *braken* – ON. **brakni* (whence Sw. *bräken*, Da. *bregne*).

bracket bræ·kit projection serving as a support XVI; (typogr.) one of the marks ( ) [ ] { } XVIII (earlier *brace*). Earliest forms *brag*(*g*)*et* – F. *braguette* codpiece, or Sp. *bragueta* codpiece, bracket, corbel, dim. of F. *brague* mortice, pl. breeches, lashing – Pr. *braga*; Sp. *braga* swaddling-clothes, pl. breeches, cf. Pg. *braga* chain for galley-slaves, pl. breeches, It. *braca* leg of breeches, baby's napkin, lashing, clamp, pl. *brache* breeches. The source is L. *brāca*, pl. *brācæ* breeches, long hose, of Gaulish origin. It has been suggested that the bracket of architecture and of shipbuilding was so called from its resemblance to a codpiece or a pair of breeches. See -ET.

brackish bræ·kiʃ saltish. XVI. f. (dial.) *brack* salty, brine (XVI) – MLG., MDu. *brac* (LG., Du. *brak*, whence G. *brackwasser* salt water), of which the source and orig. meaning are unkn.; see -ISH[1].

bract brækt (bot.) small modified leaf. XVIII. – L. *bractea*, var. of *brattea* thin plate of metal, gold leaf. So **bra·cteate.** XIX. – L. *bracteātus*; see -ATE[2].

brad bræd thin flattish headless nail. XV. Later var. of (dial.) *brod* shoot, spike, prick (XII) – ON. *broddr* spike, sting, prick = OE. *brord* point, spike, blade of grass, OHG. *brort* edge, margin :- Germ. **brozdaz*, rel. to OCeltic **brott-* (whence OIr. *brot* sting, prick, Ir., Gael. *brod*). For the vowel cf. *strap*. Hence **bra·d**AWL. XIX.

Bradbury bræ·dbəri (colloq.) currency note of £1. 1917. f. name of John Swanwick *Bradbury*, Secretary to the Treasury 1913–19.

Bradshaw bræ·dʃɔ̄ colloq. designation of 'Bradshaw's Railway Guide', first issued in 1839 by George *Bradshaw*, printer and engraver, and discontinued in 1961.

brae brei, brē steep bank. XIII. Sc. and north. ME. *brā* – ON. *brá* eyelash = OE. *brǣw* eyelid, OFris. *brē*, OS., OHG. *brāwa* (G. *braue*) eyebrow; the sense-development is parallel to that of BROW.

brag bræg sb., adj., vb. The earliest member of the group is the adj. (XIII–XVII), which means (i) coupled at first with *bold*, 'spirited, brisk, mettlesome', and (ii) 'boastful'; sb. and vb. (XIV), in the earliest exx. often with *boast*, denote arrogant, boastful, or pompous behaviour. Of unkn. origin; the similar F. words, *braguer* vaunt, brag, *brague* ostentation, are recorded only some three centuries later than the Eng. words. So **braggart** bræ·gəɹt vain bragger. XVI. – F. *bragard*, f. *braguer*; var. of -ARD.

braggadocio brægədou·tʃiou, -ou·ʃiou idle boaster or swaggerer XVI; boasting XVIII. Spenser's name for his personification of vainglory (F.Q. II iii Argt.); f. *r*-less form of BRAGGART (as in *Bragadisme*, Sh. 'Two Gent.' II iv 164)+*-occio*, It. augm. suffix. Spenser's sp. was with *-cch-*, and perh. pronounced with k; cf. the sp. *braggodokean* adj. (recorded from 1631).

bragget bræ·git drink made of honey and ale. XIV (*bragot*, *braket*, Ch.). – early W. *bragaut*, *bracaut* (mod. *bragawd*) = Ir. *bracát* :- OCeltic **bracātā*, f. **brac-*, repr. by L. acc. *bracem* (Pliny, Columella), pl. *braces*, OCeltic name for a kind of grain (whence W. *brag*, OIr. *brac*, Ir. *braich* malt).

brahma, short for **brahmaputra** brāmə-pū·trə breed of domestic fowl said to have been first brought from Lakhimpur, on the river *Brahmaputra*, India, in 1846.

Brahman, Brahmin brā·mən, -in member of the priestly or learned caste of Hindus. XIV (*bragman*, Trevisa; cf. AL. *Bragmannus* XIII). Early forms reflect mainly late L. pl. *Brachmānæ* (Tertullian), *Brachmānī*, *-mānes*, corr. to Gr. *Brakhmânes*, – Skr. *brā́hmaṇas* one of the caste, f. *brahmaṇ* (nom. *brahmā́*) priest; forms in *-in* are as early as XVI.

braid breid †move with a sudden jerky movement; interweave, plait OE.; (from the sb.) bind or ornament with braid XVIII. OE. *breġdan*, pt. *bræġd*, *brugdon*, pp. *brogden* = OFris. *breida*, *brīda*, OS. *bregdan* (Du. *breien*), OHG. *brettan*, ON. *bregða* :- CGerm. (exc. Goth.) **bregðan*, of unkn. origin. Hence **braid** sb. †sudden movement XIII; plait XVI; plaited fabric XVIII.

brail breil (naut.) pl. small ropes for trussing up sails. XV. – OF. *brail*, *braiel* :- med. L. *brācāle* waist-belt, f. *brāca* (see BRACKET). Hence **brail** vb. XVII.

braille breil embossed printing for the blind, named after the inventor, Louis *Braille* (1809–52).

brain brein mass of nervous substance contained in the skull. OE. *bræġen* = MLG. *bragen*, *bregen*, (M)Du. *brein* :- Germ. **bragnam*, a word of the LG. area, prob. ult. rel. to Gr. *brekhmós*, *bregmós* forehead. ¶ A syn. of wider Germ. and IE. distribution is *harns* (now Sc.), of ON. origin in Eng. (XII). Hence **brain** vb. dash out the brains of. XIV.

braise breiz cook in a closed pan, properly with a charcoal fire above and below. XVIII. – F. *braiser*, f. *braise* hot charcoal (cf. BRAZIER[2]), in OF. *brese* = Pr. *brasa* – Germ. **brasa*, rel. to OHG. *brātan* (G. *braten*) roast = OE. *brǣdan*, etc. (cf. BREATH, BROOD).

brake[1] breik thicket. OE. *bracu* (recorded in g. pl. *fearnbraca* beds of fern, in ME. *fernebrake*), corr. to MLG. *brake* branch, twig, tree-stump (whence OF. *bracon* branch); prob. f. **brak-* **brek-* BREAK, the orig. sense being 'broken wood'; perh. reinforced in ME. from LG. (cf. *busk unde brake* 'bush and brake').

brake[2] breik fern, bracken. XIV. perh. shortening of BRACKEN, through the apprehension of this as a pl. form.

brake[3]**, break** breik apparatus for retarding the motion of a wheel. XVIII. prob. spec. use of †*brake* bridle, curb (XV–XVIII) – MDu. *braeke* applied to various breaking or crushing instruments and app. adopted in Eng. at different periods with different applications, rel. to *braken* break (hemp) and *breken* (see BREAK).

brake[4] see BREAK[2].

Bramah brā·mă, bræ·mă name of Joseph *Bramah* (1749–1814), designating machines invented by him, as *Bramah key*, *lock*, *press*. ('Their patent Bramahs over the street-door locks', Dickens.)

bramble bræ·mbl blackberry bush. OE. *bræmbel*, later form of *brǣmel*, *brēmel*, f. the base repr. in OE. *brōm* BROOM; cf. OS. *brāmalbusc* and see -LE[1].

bran bræn (ground) husk of wheat, etc. XIII. ME. *bran, bren* – (O)F. *bran* bran, (now) excrement, muck, filth, †*bren* (whence F. *breneux* soiled with fæces) = Pr., OSp., It. dial. *bren*, of unkn. origin; W., Ir., Gael. *bran*, Bret. *brenn* are from Eng. or F.; AL. forms are *brenn(i)um, brannum* (XIII–XIV).

branch brànᵗʃ limb of a tree; offshoot. XIII (RGlouc., Cursor M.). – (O)F. *branche* = Pr., Sp. *branca* claw, It. *branca* claw, paw, Rum. *brîncă* hand, paw :– late L. *branca* (*branca ursina* 'bear's foot', acanthus), of unkn. origin.

branchio- bræ·ŋkiou comb. form of Gr. *brágkhia* gills, sg. *brágkhion* (latinized as *branchia*, pl. *-iæ*), as in **bra·nchiopod** having gills on the feet – modL. *branchiopoda* (sc. CRUSTACEA), f. Gr. *pod-, poús* FOOT.

brand[1] brænd piece of burning wood OE.; mark made with a hot iron; stigma XVI; trade-mark; class of goods XIX. OE. *brand* = OFris., (M)Du. *brand*, OHG. *brant* (G. *brand*), ON. *brandr* :– CGerm. (exc. Goth.) **brandaz*, f. **bran-* **bren-* BURN[2]+abstr. suffix **-þa-* (:– IE. **-to-*). Hence **brand** vb. to burn XIV.

brand[2] brænd (poet.) sword. OE. *brand* = MHG. *brant*, ON. *brandr*; perh. a use of prec., with ref. to the gleaming blade. ¶ From Germ. are OF. *brand* blade of a sword, It. *brando* sword.

brandish bræ·ndiʃ wave about, flourish. XIV. – (O)F. *brandiss-*, lengthened stem of *brandir* = Pr. *brandir* (whence Sp. *blandir*, Pg. *brandir, blandir*), It. *brandire* :– Rom. **brandīre*, f. **brandaz* sword, BRAND[2]; see -ISH[2].

brandling bræ·ndliŋ red worm with bright bands. XVII. f. BRAND[1]+-LING[1]; so named with ref. to its markings.

brand-, bran-new bræ·nᵈnjū quite new. XVI (*brande newe*). perh. f. BRAND[1]+NEW, as if meaning orig. 'fresh from the furnace'; cf. *fire-new* (Sh.).

brandreth bræ·ndriþ (dial.) gridiron, trivet XIV; framework of wood XV. – ON. *brandreið* grate, f. *brandr* BRAND[1]+*reið* carriage, vehicle (f. *ríða* RIDE); cf. OE. *brandrod, -red* (for *-rād*), *-rida*, MLG. *brantrēde*, OHG. *brantreita*. (The OE. *brandīsen* is repr. by w. dial. *brandize* XVII, *brandis*; cf. dial. *brandiron, brander*, ME. *brandhirne, brandern*; see IRON.)

brandy bræ·ndi ardent spirit distilled from wine. XVII. Earlier *brand(e)wine*, altered later to *brandy wine*, whence ellipt. *brandy* – Du. *brandewijn* (whence also G. *branntwein*, etc.), f. *branden* burn, roast, char, distil (f. *brand* fire, BRAND[1])+*wijn* WINE.

branks bræŋks (Sc.) bridle with wooden side-pieces; scold's bridle. XVI. perh. alteration of *bernaks*, pl. of ME. *bernak* (– OF. *bernac*) bridle; see BARNACLE[2].

brankursine bræŋkɔ̄·ɹsīn acanthus. XVI. – F. *branche* (dial. *branque*) *ursine* 'bear's claw'; see BRANCH, URSINE.

brant-goose see BRENT.

brash[1] bræʃ †attack, bout XV; (slight or short) bout of sickness XVII (surviving gen. in *water-brash* eructation of liquid from the stomach). orig. Sc. and still mainly Sc. and n. dial., perh. of imit. origin.

brash[2] bræʃ brittle XVI; rash, impetuous XIX; 'raw', showy XX; of unkn. origin.

brass bràs alloy of copper with tin or zinc (formerly incl. BRONZE) OE. (sepulchral tablet of this metal XVII); (sl.) money XVI; effrontery XVII (from *face of brass* XVI). OE. *bræs* = OFris. *bres* (*bras-penning* copper penny), MLG. *bras* metal; of unkn. origin.

brassage bræ·sidʒ mint charge to cover the expense of coining money. XIX. – F. *brassage*, f. *brasser* mix, stir (melted metals), brew :– popL. **braciāre*, f. L. *brace*.

brassard bræ·sāɹd armour for the upper arm; armlet. XIX. – F. *brassard*, f. *bras* arm; see BRACE[1], -ARD.

brasserie bræ·səri beer-saloon. XIX. F., prop. 'brewery', f. *brasser* brew, OF. *bracier*, f. *brace* (mod. *brasse*) :– L. *brace*, of Gaulish origin, acc. to Pliny; see -ERY.

brassiere bræ·siɛəɹ woman's underbodice to support the breasts. XX. F. *brassière*, f. *bras* arm (see BRACE[1]).

brassy brà·si wooden golf-club shod with brass. XIX. f. BRASS+-Y[1].

brat bræt child (contemptuous). XVI. perh. shortening of Sc. *bratchart* (mod. *bratchet*), possibly f. *brat* ragged garment, OE. (late Nhb.) *bratt* cloak – OIr. *bratt* (Ir., Gael. *brat*) mantle. Cf. BASTARD and the parallel formations given there.

brattice bræ·tis †breastwork or parapet of wood XIII; wooden partition XIX. In early use there are several types, *brutaske, brutage, bretage, bretais, -ise* – AN. *breteske, brutesche, bretesche, -asce*, OF. *bretesque, -esche* (mod. *bretèche*) = Pr. *bertresca*, whence OIt. *bertesca, beltresca*; cf. medL. *bretachia, bertescha*; perh. Rom. deriv. of Germ. **breð-* (OE. *bred*, G. *brett*), var. of **borð-* BOARD+**-isca* -ISH[1]. The mod. use is local and connected with coal-mining; the current forms are *brettis, brattice, brattish*. Hence **bra·tticing** †parapet, rampart XIV; brattice work in a coal-pit XIX. var. **bra·ttishing** open work on the top of a shrine. XVI. See -ING[1] and cf. BARTIZAN.

bravado brəvā·dou ostentatious or simulated boldness. XVI. – Sp. *bravada, -ata*, f. *bravo* BRAVO[1], with alteration of suffix (see -ADO). Cf. F. *bravade* (– It. *bravata*), whence Eng. †*bravade* (XVI).

brave[1] breiv stout-hearted XV (Caxton); finely dressed, grand; fine, excellent XVI. – F. *brave* – It. *bravo* bold, accomplished, expert, untamed, or Sp. *bravo* courageous, bullying, savage, fine (= Pr. *brau* savage) :- Rom. ***brabu-s**, for L. *barbarus* BARBAROUS, through ***brabarus**.

brave[2] breiv challenge, defy XVI; †boast XVI; meet bravely XVIII. – F. *braver*, f. *brave* (see prec.), after It. *bravare*. So **bra·VERY** †bravado; brave conduct or temper; show, splendour; finery. XVI. – F. *braverie* or It. *braveria*.

bravo[1] brā·vou, (formerly) brei·vou daring villain, hired assassin. XVI. – It. *bravo* BRAVE[1].

bravo[2] brāvou· capital! well done! XVIII. – F. – It. *bravo* fine, splendid (BRAVE[1]); introduced into France with It. music. The superl. **bravi·ssimo** is also used.

bravura brəvʲuə·rə spirit, dash; (mus.) passage requiring great spirit in execution. XVIII. It., f. *bravo* BRAVE[1]; see -URE.

braw brɔ̄ (Sc.) fine, excellent. XVI. var. of *brawf*, BRAVE[1].

brawl brɔ̄l 'quarrel noisily and indecently' (J.). XIV (Barbour, PPl.). Late ME. *brawle, braule, bralle*, of unkn. origin, perh. imit.

brawn brɔ̄n fleshy part, muscle; flesh of the boar or swine, now esp. as collared, boiled, etc. XIV. – AN. *braun*, OF. *braon* fleshy part, esp. of the hind leg = Pr. *brazon, bra(z)ó* upper arm – Germ. ***brādon** (OHG. *brāto*, G. *braten* roast flesh; cf. synon. OE. *brǣde*, and *brǣdan* roast); prob. ult. related to BREATH, BROOD.

bray[1] brei †cry out XIII; of animals, now esp. of the ass; similarly of a trumpet, etc. XIV. – (O)F. *braire* cry (now only of the ass) = Pr. *braire* cry, sing, weep, resound :- Rom. ***bragere**, perh. of Celtic origin.

bray[2] brei crush small. XIV. – AN. *braier*, OF. *breier* pres. stem *bri-* (mod. *broyer*) = Pr., Sp. *bregar*, It. *brigare* – Germ. ***brekan** BREAK.

brazen brei·zn made of brass. OE. *bræsen*, f. *bræs* BRASS; see -EN[3]. Hence **bra·zen** vb. face impudently. XVI.

brazier[1] brei·ziəɹ, brei·ʒⁱəɹ worker in brass. XIV. prob. f. BRASS on the model of *glass, glazier*.

brazier[2], **brasier** brei·ziəɹ, brei·ʒⁱəɹ pan for holding burning charcoal, etc. XVII. – F. *brasier*, f. *braise* hot coals (see BRAISE).

brazil brəzi·l wood of an East India tree yielding a red colour; †dye produced therefrom. XIV. Late ME. *brasile* – medL. *brasilium, -illum*; in F. *brésil*, Pr. *bresil*, Sp., Pg. *brasil*, It. *brasile*; of unkn. origin. An allied species of tree, of S. America, also yielding a dye, gave its name to Brazil, Sp. *Brasil*, short for *tierra de brasil* 'red-dye-wood land'. Brazil nuts (XIX) were named from the country. Formerly and still dial. pronounced bræ·zĭl.

breach brītʃ breaking or the result of it XIV; gap in a fortification XV. – (O)F. *brèche* = Pr. *breca* :- Germ. ***brecho**, cf. OHG. *brecha*, f. *brechan* BREAK. Superseded ME. *brüche*, OE. *bryċe* (ult. connected), with which there is no continuity.

bread bred article of food made with flour. OE. *brēad* = OFris. *brād*, OS., (M)LG. *brōd*, OHG. *brōt* (G. *brot*), ON. *brauð* :- CGerm. (exc. Goth.) ***brauðam** n., of unkn. origin. The proper Germ. word for 'bread' is seen in LOAF, the orig. meaning of *bread* being perh. 'fragment, piece, morsel' (as in OE. pl. *brēadru*); but before 1200 *bread* had displaced *loaf* as the name of the substance, the latter being restricted to the shaped and baked article. (Its use for a food-substance is, however, seen in OE. *bēobrēad* bee-bread.) For the shortening of the vowel before a point-consonant cf. *ate*, **breath**, *dead, lead* (sb.), *red, thread, threat*.

breadth bredþ, bretþ measure from side to side. XVI. f. †*brēde* breadth (OE. *brǣdu* = OFris. *brēde*, OHG. *breitī*, ON. *breidd*, Goth. *braidei* :- Germ. ***braidjōn**, abstr. sb. f. ***braid-** BROAD) + -TH[1]; the new formation provided a parallel to *length*; cf. WIDTH.

break[1] breik sever into parts. OE. *brecan*, pt. *bræc, brǣcon*, pp. *brocen* = OFris. *breka*, OS. *brekan* (Du. *breken*), OHG. *brehhan* (G. *brechen, brach, gebrochen*), Goth. *brikan, brak, brēkum, brukans* :- CGerm. (exc. ON.) ***brekan**; IE. base ***bhreg-** ***bhrg-**, whence also L. *frangere* (*frēgī, fractum*) break. *Brake*, repr. OE. pt. *bræc*, persisted in arch. use, mainly through its being the only form in A.V. (cf. *spake*); in ordinary use it began to be displaced in XV by **broke**, which was based on the pp. **broken**, of which the var. *broke* (XIV) remains in the spec. sense of 'bankrupt', 'out of funds' (XVIII).

break[2], **brake** breik carriage-frame; large waggonette. XIX. perh. identical with *brake* cage, rack (XVI), frame (XVII), of unkn. origin.

break[3] see BRAKE[3].

breaker[1] brei·kəɹ one who or that which breaks XII; heavy ocean-wave breaking on the shore XVII. f. BREAK[1] + -ER[1].

breaker[2] brei·kəɹ (naut.) small keg or cask. XIX (Marryat). – Sp. *bareca*, var. of *barrica*, f. stem repr. in BARREL. For the perversion of form cf. GROUPER.

breakfast bre·kfəst first meal of the day. XV (*brekfast, breke-*). f. phr. *break one's fast* (XIV); see BREAK[1], FAST[2]. So vb. intr. XVII, trans. XVIII.

bream[1] brīm fresh-water fish Abramis brama. XIV. – OF. *breme, bresme* (mod. *brème*) – WGerm. ***brexsmo** beside ***braxsmo** (OS. *bressemo*, MDu. *bressem*, Du. *brasem*,

OHG. *brahsema*, MHG. *brahsem*, *brasme*, G. *brassen*, dial. *brachsme*); perh. f. base of **breχwan* (OHG. *brehan*) glitter.

bream[2] brīm clean a ship's bottom. XV. prob. of LG. origin and rel. to BROOM (cf. Du. *brem* broom, furze).

breast brest front of the thorax (spec. the mamma), regarded as the seat of the affections. OE. *brēost* (freq. in pl.) = OFris. *briast*, OS. *briost*, ON. *brjóst* :- Germ. **breustam*; parallel to a fem. cons.-stem **brusts*, prob. orig. inflected as a dual, and repr. by (M)LG., (M)Du. *borst*, OHG., G. *brust*, Goth. *brusts* (only in pl.). There is no CIE. word for the breast, but the assumed base of this word, **bhrus-* **bhreus-*, is repr. by OS. *brustian* bud, MHG. *briustern* swell up, (O)Ir. *brú* abdomen, womb, bosom, Gael. *brù*, Russ. *bryúkho* belly. Sc. and north. Eng. pronunc. brīst repr. the normal development of OE. *brēost* (cf. *priest*); evidence of shortening appears in XVI, with *brest* beside *breast*. Hence **breast** vb. oppose the breast to. XVI (Sh.). **brea·st-**PLATE. XIV (Ch.). **breastsummer, bressummer** bre·səməɹ beam extending horizontally over an opening XVII; see SUMMER[2].

breath breþ †odour OE.; †vapour; respiration XIII; air from the lungs XIV. OE. *brǣþ* odour, exhalation :- Germ. **brǣþaz* :- IE. **bhrētos*, f. **bhrē-* burn, heat, as in OE. *brǣdan* roast, and BROOD. The sense 'air in the lungs or mouth' was taken over from OE. *ǣþm* and *anda* (ME. *ethem* and *ande*, *onde*). The orig. long vowel is preserved dial. (cf. *breath/beneath*, Clare 1821); for the shortening cf. BREAD. Hence **breathe** brīð. XIII; cf. *sheath*, *sheathe*. **brea·th**ER[1] XIV.

breccia bre·tʃiə composite rock of angular fragments. XVIII. It., = F. *brèche*, Sp. *brecha* – Germ. **breka-* breach (cf. OHG. *brecha*), f. **brekan* BREAK[1].

brede brīd plaiting, embroidery; interweaving of colours, colouring. XVII (Milton, Dryden). Early var. of BRAID used arch. by modern poets.

breech brītʃ usu. pl. **breeches** bri·tʃiz garment covering the loin and thighs; buttocks. OE. *brēć* (pl. only), 'femoralia', 'lumbare', corr. to OFris. *brōk*, pl. *brēk*, OS. *brōk* (Du. *broek*), OHG. *bruoh* (G. *bruch*), ON. *brók*, pl. *brœkr* :- CGerm. (exc. Goth.) **brōks*, monosyll. fem. The further relations are obscure; some favour the early adoption of pre-Germ. **bhrāg-* in Gaulish *brāca*, whence L. *brāca*, *bracca*.

breed brīd hatch, produce young. OE. *brēdan* = OHG. *bruotan* (G. *brüten*) :- WGerm. **brōdjan*, f. **brōd-* BROOD. Hence *breed* sb. stock, strain, †offspring. XVI.

breeks brīks (Sc. and north. Eng.) formerly also sg. breeches. XIII (*breke*, Cursor M.). var. of BREECH affected by ON. *brœkr*, pl. of *brók* BREECH.

breeze[1] brīz gad-fly. OE. *briosa*, of unkn. origin.

breeze[2] brīz †north or north-east wind XVI; †cool wind from the sea on tropical coasts; light wind XVII. prob. – OSp., Pg. *briza* (Sp. *brisa*) north-east wind (cf. It. *brezza*, dial. *brisa* cold wind), whence also F. *brise*; the relation to F. *bise* north-east wind is obscure.

breeze[3] brīz small cinders. XVIII. – F. *braise*, earlier *brese* burning charcoal, hot embers, half-burnt coal (*braise de boulanger* baker's breeze); cf. BRAISE.

Brehon brī·hən in *Brehon law* the law prevailing in Ireland before the English occupation. XVI. – Ir. *breathamb* ancient Ir. judge, in OIr. *brithem*, f. *breth* judgement.

brent brent, in full *brent-goose*, also *brant-goose* kind of wild goose, Bernicla brenta, formerly often identified with the barnacle goose. XVI (*brant*, *brend*, and latinized *branta*). perh. rel. (with ref. to variegation of colour) to *branded*, *brended*, *brinded* (all XVI), for which see BRINDLED. ¶ The corr. ON. *brandgás*, Sw. *brandgås*, G. *brandgans* are applied chiefly to the sheldrake.

brer brōɹ Negro pronunc. of BROTHER, perh. due partly to Du. *broer*, familiar pronunc. of *broeder*. 1800 (*Brer Fox*).

bressummer var. of BREASTSUMMER.

brethren pl. of BROTHER.

Breton bre·tən pert. to (native or language of) Brittany. XVII (earlier *Britain*, *-on*). – F. *breton* (see BRITON).

Bretwalda bre·twəldə ruler of Britons (L. *Brettonum dux*, Bede). OE. (Parker MS. of Anglo-Saxon Chronicle, an. 827), varying with *Brytenwalda*, f. *Brettas* (see BRITISH), *Bryten* (see BRITAIN) + **wald-* WIELD.

breve brīv ME. *breve* (XIII), var. of BRIEF in various senses; (mus.) orig. the shortest note of the series *large*, *long*, *breve* (XV), after medL. *brevis*; in mod. usage (XVII), after It. *breve*, note equal to two semibreves, the longest now used.

brevet bre·vit official document granting privileges XIV; (in the army) XVII. – (O)F. *brevet*, f. *bref*, *brief* BRIEF[1]; see -ET.

breviary brī·viəri, bre·viəri †epitome XVI; (eccl.) book containing the Divine Office for the year XV (also Sc. *breviar* XV). – L. *breviārium* summary, abridgement, f. *breviāre* abridge ABBREVIATE. The eccl. use (in medL. *c.* 800) originated in the gathering together into one book of the contents of the various manuals necessary for the recitation of the office, viz. the psalter, antiphoner, legendary, etc.

brevier brīviə·ɹ (typog.) size of type. XVI. – Du. or G. *brevier* – L. *breviārium* BREVIARY. Cf. *canon*, *pica*, *long primer*, and G. *missal* canon (type), similarly derived from the names of liturgical books or formularies, of which the types so named were orig. characteristic.

brevity bre·vĭti shortness. XVI. – AN. *breveté*, (O)F. *brièveté*, f. *bref*, fem. *briève* BRIEF[2]; see -ITY.

brew brū make ale, beer, etc. OE. *brēowan*, pt. *brēaw*, *bruwon*, pp. *browen* = OFris. **briuwa* (pp. *browen*), OS. *breuwan* (Du. *brouwen*), OHG. *briuwan*, *brūwan* (G. *brauen*), ON. *brugga* :– CGerm. (exc. Goth.) **breu(w)an*, f. IE. **bhreu-*, **bhru-*, whence have been derived Thracian Gr. *broûtos* beer, L. *dēfrutum* boiled must, *fervēre* boil (cf. FERVENT), OIr. *bruthe* broth, *berbaim* cook, boil, melt, and (by some) BREAD and BROTH. Hence **brew·**ERY. XVIII. prob. – Du. *brouwerij* (whence G. *brauerei*); earlier **brew·**HOUSE XIV; cf. OHG. *brūhūs* (G. *brauhaus*). **brew**STER brū·stəɹ brewer XIV; survives in *Brewster Sessions* licensing sessions, and as a surname; also *Browster* XIII–XVII.

brewis see BROSE.

briar[1], **brier** braiəɹ white heath, Erica arborea, the root of which is used for tobacco pipes. XIX. In earliest exx. *bruyer* (1868) – (O)F. *bruyère* heath = Pr. *bruguieira* :– Gallo-Rom. **brūcaria*, f. **brūcus* – Gaulish **brūko*; assim. in form to BRIER[1], BRIAR.

bribe braib †purloin, steal XIV (Ch.); corrupt by means of gifts XVI. – OF. *briber*, also *brimber* beg, be a mendicant = Sp. *bribar* beg; of unkn. origin. So **bri·ber** †thief XIV (PPl., Trevisa); †vagabond, scoundrel XIV; †one who levies blackmail or accepts bribes; one who gives bribes XVI. orig. – AN. *bribour*, OF. *bribeur* beggar, vagabond; later f. the vb.; see -ER[1]. **bri·b**ERY †theft (Ch., Trevisa); †exaction of money; offer or acceptance of bribes XVI. – OF. *briberie*. Hence **bribe** sb. XV.

bric-à-brac bri·kəbræk old knick-knacks. XIX (Thackeray). F., f. phr. †*à bric et à brac* at random; cf. *de bric et de broc* by hook or crook.

brick brik moulded and baked clay used in building. XV. Late ME. *brik(e)*, *breke*, prob. introduced by Flemish workmen and so – MLG., MDu. *bricke*, *brike* (also *bricsteen*; cf. occas. †*brick-stone*), Du. dial. *brik*, WFlem. *brijke*; whence also (O)F. *brique*, which prob. reinforced the adoption from LG.; of unkn. origin. Replaced *waltyle* 'wall-tile')(*thaktyle* 'thatch-tile'.

bricole bri·koul military engine or catapult; rebound of a tennis ball from the wall of the court. XVI. – (O)F. *bricole* – Pr. *bricola* or It. *briccola*, of unkn. origin.

bridal brai·dəl (arch. except in attrib. use, which from late XVI has been furthered by assoc. with adjs. in -AL[1]) wedding feast, (later) wedding. Late OE. *brȳdealu*, f. *brȳd* BRIDE (in attrib. use equiv. to 'marriage') + *ealu* ALE, i.e. ale-drinking.

bride braid woman about to be married or recently married. OE. *brȳd* = OFris. *brēd*, *breid*, *breyd*, OS. *brūd* (Du. *bruid*), OHG. *brūt* (G. *braut*), ON. *brúðr*, Goth. *brūþs* :– CGerm. **brūðiz*, of unkn. origin. Hence **bri·degroom.** OE. *brȳdguma* = OS. *brūdigomo* (Du. *bruidegom*), OHG. *brūtigomo* (G. *bräutigam*), ON. *brúðgumi*; altered by assim. to GROOM (Sc. *brydgromen* XIV). **bri·des**MAID brai·dzmeid XVIII, earlier *bridemaid* XVI.

bridewell brai·dwəl house of correction. XVI. f. *Bride Well*, i.e. St. Bride's Well, a holy well in London, near which Henry VIII had a lodging, given by Edward VI for a hospital, afterwards converted.

bridge[1] bridʒ elevated structure (often arched over water) forming a passage way between two points. OE. *bryćġ* = OFris. *brigge*, *bregge*, OS. *bruggia*, MDu. *brugghe* (Du. *brug*), OHG. *brucca* (G. *brücke*), ON. *bryggja* (whence north. Eng. dial. *brig* XII) :– CGerm. (exc. Goth.) **brugjō*. The sense 'landing-stage, gangway' of the ON. word points to a wider meaning for the orig. base **bruw-*, such as 'log-road'; cf. OSl. *brŭvĭno* beam. Hence vb. OE. *bryćġian*.

bridge[2] bridʒ card game based on whist. XIX. Said to have been played in Constantinople and the Near East, c. 1870, and the name may be, therefore, of Levantine origin; the source of the earliest (seemingly Russ.) form *biritch* is unkn.

bridle brai·dl headgear of a horse's harness. OE. *brīdel* (:– **briġdel*; cf. *briġdils* VIII), corr. to OFris. *brīdel*, (M)Du. *breidel*, OHG. *brittil*; WGerm. deriv. of **bregd-*; see BRAID, -LE. Hence **bri·dle** vb. put a bridle on (OE. *brīdlian*); draw in the chin as a gesture XV.

bridoon bridū·n snaffle and rein of a military bridle. XVIII. – F. *bridon*, f. *bride*, a bridle; see -OON.

brief[1] brīf letter of authority XIV (R. Mannyng); letter patent from the sovereign as head of the Church XVI; (leg.) summary of the facts of a case for the instruction of counsel XVII. – AN. *bref*, OF. *brief* = Pr. *breu* document, It. *breve* amulet, device :– L. *breve* (in late L., summary), n. of *brevis* (see next).

brief[2] brīf of short duration. XIV. Late ME. *bref* – (O)F. *bref* = Pr. *breu*, It. *breve* :– L. *brevis*. ¶ The vowel has been lengthened as in *chief*, *relief*. Cf. BREVITY.

brier[1], **briar**[2] braiəɹ prickly bush OE.; species of wild rose XVI (Spenser). OE. (Anglian) *brēr*, (WS.) *brǣr*, of unkn. origin; for the vocalism cf. *friar*, *quire*.

brier[2] see BRIAR[1].

brig brig. XVIII. Shortening of BRIGANTINE, but applied to a ship of a different rig.

brigade brigei·d division of troops, spec. subdivision of an army. XVII (in Milton *bri·gad*). – (O)F. *brigade* – It. *brigata* troop, company, f. *brigare* be busy with, f. *briga* strife, contention, which has been referred to Germ. **brekan* BREAK; see -ADE. Hence **briga·de** vb. XIX; cf. F. *embrigader* (1795), It. *brigatare*. So **brigadIER** brigədiə·ɹ. XVII. – F. *brigadier*.

brigand bri·gənd †light-armed irregular foot-soldier XIV; freebooter, bandit XV. – OF. *brigand* – It. *brigante*, sb. use of prp. of *brigare* contend, intrigue for (see prec.). Hence **bri·gandAGE** XVI; after F.

brigandine, brigantine bri·gəndīn, -tīn chain or body armour. XV. – OF. *brigandine*, f. *brigand* BRIGAND (in the earlier sense); see -INE[3].

brigantine bri·gəntīn †small vessel attending on larger ships XVI; two-masted vessel XVII. – F. †*brigandin* (mod. *-tin*) – It. *brigantino*, f. *brigante*; see BRIGAND, -INE[3].

bright brait shining OE.; 'resplendent with charms' (J.) XIII; of vivid colour XIV; animated XVII (Sh.). OE. *beorht*, Anglian *berht*, late Nhb. *breht* = OS. *ber(a)ht*, OHG. *beraht*, *-eht*, ON. *bjartr*, Goth. *bairhts* :- CGerm. **berχtaz*, f. IE. **bhereg-*, repr. also by words denoting brightness, dawn, whiteness, and the like, in Indo-Iranian, Balto-Slav., and Celtic (e.g. Skr. *bhrājate* shine, Lith. *brė̃kšta* dawns, W. *berth* beautiful).

brigue brīg †strife, contention XIV; intrigue XVIII. –(O)F. *brigue* – It. *briga*; see BRIGADE.

brill bril flat-fish, Rhombus vulgaris, having brilliant spots. XV. Also *brell*, *prylle* (XV), *prill* (XVII), *pearl* (XVII–XIX), of which the connexions are obscure and the origin unkn.

brilliant bri·ljənt brightly shining XVII; illustrious, strikingly talented XVIII. Not freq. before XVIII, but current XVII in sb. use †(i) brilliancy, varying with †*brillant*, (ii) diamond of the finest cut and brilliancy. – F. *brillant*, prp. of *briller* shine – It. *brillare* (i) shine, (ii) flutter (whence also Sp. *brillar*, Pg. *brilhar*), of unkn. origin.

brim brim †border, margin, brink XIII (Laȝ.); edge of a cup, etc.; projecting rim of a hat (Sh.) XVI. Of obscure history, but corr. in sense to MHG. *brem* (G. *bräme*, *brähme*), ON. *barmr* edge; cf. MLG. *vorbrēmen*, G. *verbrämen* provide with a border or edge. The basic meaning of a Germ. **berm-* **barm-* was perh. 'raised border', f. **ber-* carry, BEAR[2]; cf. Du. *berm* (*baerm*, *barm*, *berm* 'agger', Kilian; see BERM), *barmte* heap of earth. Hence **bri·mful** XVI; see -FUL[2]; succeeded to †*bretful*, OE. *brerdfull*.

brimstone bri·mstən sulphur. XII. The earliest forms are *brynstan*, *brünston*, continued as *brinston* and *brunsto(o)n*, north. *-stane*, till XVI; prob. f. OE. *bryne* (= ON. *bruni*) burning (f. **burn-* BURN[2])+STONE; a common ME. var. *brenston* (also *brem-*) is due to ON. *brennisteinn*; forms in *brim-*, due to dissimilation of *n* . . *n* to *m* . . *n*, appear *c*. 1300. ¶ A parallel formation in MLG. *bornstēn*, MDu., Du. *barnsteen*, etc. means 'amber'.

brindled bri·ndld brown with streaks of other colour. XVII. Alteration (prob. by assoc. with *grizzled*, *speckled*) of (arch.) *brinded* (XVI), earlier †*brended* (XV), f. †*brende* (Lydg.), prob. of Scand. origin (cf. ON. *bröndóttr* brindled, f. *brandr* burning, BRAND, and *brandkrossóttr* brindled with a white cross on the forehead).

brine brain water saturated with salt. OE. *brīne* = MDu. *brīne* (Du. *brijn*), of unkn. origin.

bring briŋ pt., pp. **brought** brɔ̄t convey or carry with one. OE. *bringan*, pt. *brōhte*, pp. (*ġe*)*brōht* = OFris. *bringa*, OS., OHG. *bringan* (Du. *brengen*, G. *bringen*), Goth. *briggan* :- CGerm. (exc. ON.) **breŋgan*, pt. **braŋχta*, pp. **braŋχtaz*. (Cf. OE. *brenġan* = OS. *brengian*, OHG. *brengen*, also OE. str. pp. *ġebrungen*, mod. dial. *brung*.) IE. **bhreŋk-* **bhroŋk-* is repr. otherwise only in Celtic (W. *he|brwng* accompany, convey, OCorn. *he|brenchiat*, MBret. *ham|brouk*, in which the prefix means 'with').

brinjal bri·ndʒɔ̄l egg-plant Solanum Melongena. XVIII (preceded by *pallingenie*, *berenjaw* XVII). ult. – Pg. *beringela* = Sp. *berengena*; see AUBERGINE.

brinjarry brindʒā·ri travelling grain and salt merchant in the Deccan. XVIII. – Urdu *banjārā*, prob. based on Skr. *vaṇij* (*baṇij*) trader, trade.

brink briŋk edge or border of a steep place, river, etc. XIII (K. Horn, Cursor M.). ME. also *brenk* – ON. **brenkōn* (in OIcel. *brekka* slope), corr. to MLG. *brink* edge of a field, grassland, (brow of) a hill (whence G. *brink* hill), MDu. *brinc* (Du. *brink* grassland), of unkn. origin.

brio brī·ou liveliness, vivacity. XIX (Thackeray). – It. *brio* = OF. *brif*, Pr. *briu* – Celtic **brīgos* (cf. Ir. *brig* strength, W. *bri* dignity, worth).

briony see BRYONY.

briquette brike·t block of compressed coal-dust. XIX. – F., dim. of *brique* BRICK; see -ETTE.

brisk brisk †smart, spruce XVI (Marlowe, Sh.); quick and active; sharp (in various senses; as applied to beverages cf. F. †*vin brusque* and It. *brusco*) XVI (Sh.). prob. (with unrounding of the vowel) – F. *brusque* (see BRUSQUE), but the connexion of sense is not clear. ¶ W. *brysg*, Gael. *brisg*, Ir. *brisc* are from Eng.

brisket bri·skit breast of a beast. XIV (*brusket*). prob. – AN. **brusket*, **brisket*, vars. of OF. *bruschet*, **brischet*, *bruchet*, *brichet* (mod. *bréchet*), poss. f. ON. *brjósk* (Norw., Da. *brusk*) cartilage, gristle; see -ET.

¶ There are vars. in Sc. *birsket* XVI–XVII, and †*bisket* XVII–XVIII.

bristle bri·sl stiff hair. XIII. ME. *brüstel, bristel, brestel,* pointing to OE. **brystel,* **byrstel,* corr. to OS. **brustil,* (M)Du. *borstel,* deriv. of the base repr. by OE. *byrst* bristle (surviving in ME. *brüst,* Sc. *birse*), OS. *brusta,* OHG. *burst* (in MHG., G. *borste*), ON. *burst, bursti,* and outside Germ. by L. *fastīgium* top, summit, Skr. *bhṛshṭís* spike, top.

Bristol bri·stəl city and seaport on the Lower Avon famous from early times for maritime trade; attrib., e.g. in *Bristol diamond* (XVI), *gem* (XVIII), *stone* (XVII) rock crystal found in Clifton limestone near Bristol; *Bristol milk* (XVII) sherry. OE. *Bryćġstow* site of the BRIDGE (cf. STOW).

Britain bri·tn the island containing England, Scotland, and Wales. XIII (RGlouc.). ME. *Bretayne* – OF. *Bretaigne* (mod. *-agne*) :– L. *Brittānia, -annia,* f. *Brit(t)annī* = Gr. *Bret(t)anoí, Pret(t)anoí.* (OE. *Breoten, Breten, Bryten* – L. *Brittonēs*; cf. BRITISH.)

British bri·tiʃ pert. to ancient Britons OE.; pert. to Great Britain XIV (Trevisa). OE. *Brettisć, Brittisć, Bryttisć,* f. *Bret,* pl. *Brettas,* etc., based on L. *Britto* (pl. *Brittonēs*) or OCeltic **Britto* or **Brittos*; see -ISH[1]. Hence **Bri·tish**ER[1] native of Great Britain. XIX (1829, Marryat); with *-er* as in *foreigner* or *stranger.* 'The American origin or currency of this word has sometimes been questioned by American writers' ('Dict. American English').

Briton bri·tn inhabitant or native of Britain. XIII (RGlouc.). – (O)F. *Breton* – L. *Brittōnem* (nom. *Britto*), prop. *Brittonem,* with pl. *Brittones,* corr. to OCeltic **Britto,* **Brittones,* whence W. *Brython,* prop. coll. pl. (cf. BRYTHONIC).

brittle bri·tl liable to break. XIV (Wyclif). The variation in ME. *britil, bretil, brütil* points to deriv. from *bryt-* (as in OE. *brytsen* fragment, *ġebryttan* break in pieces, *brytta* distributor), f. mutated form of Germ. **brut-*, wk. grade of **breutan* (OE. *brēotan* = ON. *brjóta*) break up, of unkn. origin. The somewhat earlier (Kentish and eastern) synon. *brotel* is f. OE. *broten,* pp. of *brēotan* (cf. *ġebrot* fragment). See -LE[2].

britzka bri·tskə, bri·tʃka open carriage with calash top. XIX. – Pol. *bryczka,* dim. of *bryka* goods waggon. Cf. G. *britschka.*

broach broutʃ A. †pointed rod or pin; roasting-spit XIV, church spire XVI; tapered boring-bit XVIII. B. (f. the vb.) †perforation with a tap XV; cf. ABROACH. – (O)F. *broche* spit = It. *brocca* split cane, Sp., Pg. *broca* drill, auger :– Rom. **brocca* spike (cf. AL. *brocha* skewer, brooch), sb. use of fem. of L. *brocc(h)us* (as in *brocchī dentes* projecting teeth); cf. BROOCH. So **broach** vb. pierce XIV; give vent to XVI. – (O)F. *brocher* = Pr. *brocar,* etc. :– Rom. deriv. of the sb.

broad brɔ̄d extended in measurement from side to side. OE. *brād* = OFris., OS. *brēd* (Du. *breed*), (O)HG. *breit,* ON. *breiðr,* Goth. *braiþs* :– CGerm. **braiðaz,* of which no cogns. are known. Hence **broa·d**CAST adj. scattered abroad, widely disseminated XVIII; f. *broad* adv. abroad, widely + *cast* pp.; also used as adv.; whence as vb. XIX, from which a sb. (e.g. *wireless broadcast*) was formed XX. **broa·d**CLOTH. XV. **broa·d**SIDE of a ship; of the discharge of artillery on one side of a ship; synon. with *broadsheet.* XVI.

Brobdingnagian brɔbdiŋnæ·giən of huge dimensions, gigantic. XVIII. f. *Brobdingnag,* name given by Swift in 'Gulliver's Travels' to an imaginary country where everything is on a gigantic scale; see -IAN.

brocade brŏkei·d textile fabric with raised figures. XVII. Earlier *brocardo, brocado* (XVI) – Sp., Pg. *brocado,* with blending of F. *brocart* – It. *broccato,* lit. 'embossed stuff', f. *brocco* twisted thread; see -ADE.

brocard brou·kāɹd elementary principle or maxim. XVII. – F. *brocard* or medL. *brocardus,* appellative use of the latinized form of Burchard, name of a bishop of Worms (XI), author of 'Regulæ Ecclesiasticæ' in 20 books.

brocatelle brɔkəte·l imitation of brocade. XVII (Evelyn). F., earlier *brocatel* – It. *broccatello* gold tinsel, dim. of *broccato* (see BROCADE).

broccoli brɔ·kəli kind of cauliflower. XVII ('the Broccoli from Naples', Evelyn). – It. *broccoli,* pl. of *broccolo* cabbage sprout or head, dim. of *brocco* shoot (see BROACH).

broch brɔχ, brʌχ (archæol.) prehistoric tower-like structure in north. Scotland. XVII (*brugh, brogh, burgh*). var. of BURGH.

broché brou·ʃei (fabric) woven with a pattern on the face. XIX. F., pp. of *brocher* stitch, f. *broche* knitting-needle (see BROACH).

brochure brou·ʃuəɹ pamphlet. XVIII. – F. *brochure* lit. 'stitching', f. *brocher* stitch; see -URE.

brock brɔk (dial.) badger. OE. *broc(c)* – OBrit. **brokkos* (W., Corn., Bret. *broch,* Ir., Gael. *broc,* OIr. *brocc*).

brocket brɔ·kit stag in its second year with its first horns, which resemble a short dagger. XV. – AN. **broquet* (cf. AL. *brokettus* XIII), f. *broque,* dial. var. of *broche* BROOCH; cf. F. *brocard* young roe (XV) and synon. *daguet,* †*dagard* (f. *dague* dagger, stag's first antler).

brogue[1] broug rude shoe of Ireland and the Scottish Highlands XVI; pl. †hose, trousers XVII; strong outdoor shoe XIX. – Ir., Gael. *brōg* (OIr. *bróc*) – ON. *brók* (see BREEKS).

brogue[2] broug strongly marked provincial (esp. Irish) accent. XVII ('Irish Hudibras', 1689). perh. the same word as prec. used in playful allusion to the foot-gear of Ir. or

Sc. speakers; in XVIII freq. in phr. *have the brogue on his tongue*. Improbably connected by some with Ir. *barróg* hold, grip (*barróg teangan* 'grip of the tongue', lisp).

broil[1] broil turmoil, quarrel. XVI. Earliest forms *breull, bruill*, f. †*broil* vb. confuse, disturb (cf. EMBROIL) – AN. *broiller*, (O)F. *brouiller*, earlier *brooillier* :– Rom. **brodiculāre*, f. **brodicāre* (cf. Bergamo dial. *brodigar* defile), f. **brodum*, whence OF. *breu* (see BROSE); cf. IMBROGLIO.

broil[2] broil †burn XIV (Barbour); grill XIV (Ch.). Earliest forms (Sc.) *brulȝe, broille, brule, bruyle* – OF. *bruler, bruller*, earlier *brusler* (mod. *brûler*) burn :– Rom. **brustulāre*, perh. f. Germ. **brun*- **bren*- BURN[2] + L. *ūstulāre* burn up, whence Pr. *usclar*, It. *ustolare* long for (cf. COMBUSTION).

broke(n) brou·k(n) see BREAK[1].

broker brou·kəɹ †pedlar, small trader; second-hand dealer (cf. *pawnbroker*); middleman; †go-between XIV; appraiser or seller of distrained goods XIX. Late ME. *broco(u)r* (PPl.) – AN. *brocour*, beside *abrocour* (cf. AL. *brocātor, abrocātor*), corr. to Pr. *abrocador* broker, *abrocatge* brokerage, beside *brocatge* charge on wine; of unkn. origin, but the existence of vars. with *a*- has suggested connexion with Sp. *alboroque* drinking on the conclusion of a bargain, Pg. *alborque* truck, exchange, *alborcar* barter, in which *al*- is AL-[2], and the root is held to be of Sem. origin. Hence **bro·ker**AGE XV; repl. †*brokage* (XIV, PPl., Wyclif, Ch.) – AN. *brocage* (AL. *brocāgium*).

brolly brɔ·li (colloq.) unexpl. alteration of UMBRELLA, said to have been first used at Winchester College, and later at the universities of Oxford and Cambridge. XIX (1874).

bromine brou·mīn (chem.) non-metallic element. 1827. f. F. *brome* (formerly also used in Eng.), f. Gr. *brômos* stink + -INE[5]; so named from its strong irritating smell. Hence **bro·m**IDE XIX; the sl. sense of 'common place or person', 'trite remark', derives from the use of potassium bromide as a sedative XX.

bronchia brɔ·ŋkiə branches of the bronchi. XVII. late L. – Gr. n.pl. *brógkhia*, f. *brógkhos* windpipe, whence late L. **bronchus**, pl. **-i** the branches of the windpipe. Hence **bro·nchi**AL. XVIII. – modL. **bronchi·**TIS. XIX. – modL., f. *bronchī, bronchia*. **bro·nch(o)**-, comb. form of *bronchus*, as in *bronchocele* goitre (XVII) – modL. – Gr. *brogkhokḗlē* lit. 'tumour of the throat'.

bronco brɔ·ŋkou (California and New Mexico) half-tamed horse. XIX. – Sp. *bronco* rough, rel. to OF. *bronche*, It. *bronco* block, lump.

brontosaurus brɔntousɔ̄·rəs huge dinosaurian reptile. XIX. modL. (1879), f. Gr. *brontḗ* thunder + *saûros* lizard.

bronze brɔnz alloy of copper and tin (formerly included under BRASS); prob. first used of objects of antiquity made of this. XVIII. – F. *bronze* – It. *bronzo* (whence medL. *bronzium, brontium*, in It. documents), prob. – Pers. *birinj, pirinj* copper. ¶ The vocalism is difficult to account for, but a similar difficulty attaches to Berthelot's deriv. from MGr. *brontḗsion* – medL. *æs brundisium* 'brass of Brindisi', where, acc. to Pliny, bronze mirrors were produced. The word has passed into the Germ. and Slav. langs.

brooch broutʃ ornamental (safety-)pin. XIII. – (O)F. *broche* spit, long needle = Sp. *broca*, It. *brocca* :– Rom. **brocca* spike, sb. use of fem. of L. *brocc(h)us* projecting (see BROACH).

brood brūd progeny, offspring. OE. *brōd*, corr. to MDu. *broet* (Du. *broed*), OHG. *bruot*, MHG. heat, warmth, hatching, brood (G. *brut*), f. Germ. **brōd*-, dental deriv. of **brō*- warm, heat, whence MDu. *broeyen* warm up, hatch, MHG. *brüejen* (G. *brühen* scald). Hence **brood** vb. sit on eggs XV; hover *over* XVI; meditate intensely XVIII. **broo·dy** inclined to sit OE.; †prolific. OE. *brōdiġ*; see -Y[1].

brook[1] bruk small stream. OE. *brōc*, corr. to LG. and HG. words meaning 'marsh, bog', MLG. *brōk*, (M)Du. *broek*, OHG. *bruoh* (G. *bruch*); of unkn. origin. Hence **broo·klime** the plant speedwell XV; orig. *brokelemk* (OE. *hleomoce* = MLG. *lömeke*), whence *brooklem, -lyme* (XVI).

brook[2] bruk (Sc. or arch.) enjoy, use OE.; (arch.) put up with, endure XVI. OE. *brūcan*, pt. *brēac*, pp. *ġebrocen* = OFris. *brūka*, OS. *brūkan* (Du. *bruiken*), OHG. *brūhhan* (G. *brauchen* use, want, need), Goth. *brūkjan* (cf. *brūks* useful); CGerm. (exc. ON.) deriv. of **brūk*- make use of :– IE. **bhrug*-, whence L. *fruī* enjoy (see FRUIT). Weak inflexions occur XIV. The vowel of the present pronunc. is abnormal, modern *u* answering usu. to ME. *ō*; the date of the appearance of the sense 'endure' may point to literary adoption from a dialect, whence perh. the unusual vocalism.

broom brūm, brum yellow-flowered shrub Cytisus scoparius OE.; sweeping implement, orig. one of broom twigs XV. OE. *brōm*, corr. to MLG. *brām*, MDu. *brāme* (Du. *braam*), OHG. *brāmo, brāma* (comp. OHG. *brāmberi*, G. *brombeere* hip), OS. *hiop|brāmio* hawthorn bush, MLG. *brēme, brumme*. MDu. *bremme*, OHG. *brāmma* brier, and forms s.v. BRAMBLE.

brose brouz dish of oatmeal made with boiling water. XVII. modSc. form of ME. *broys, browis, browes* (XIII–XVII), also *brewes, brewis* (XVI–) – OF. *broez, brouez* (mod. *brouet*), f. *breu* = Pr. *bro*, It. *brodo* :– Rom. **brodo* – Germ. **broþam* BROTH.

broth brɔþ liquid in which meat, etc. has been boiled. OE. *broþ* = OHG. *brod*, ON. *broð* :- Germ. **broþam*, f. (**bro-*) **bru-*, base of BREW.

brothel brɔ·ðl, brɔ·þl †worthless fellow XIV (Gower); †prostitute XV; bawdy-house XVI. Late ME. *broþel*, f. OE. *ā|broþen* gone to ruin, pp. of *brēoþan* deteriorate, degenerate (cf. *brīeþel* worthless), of unkn. origin; for a similar formation cf. *brotel* s.v. BRITTLE. In the present sense, short for †*brothel-house* (Sh.), †*brodel-*, †*brothelles house* (XVI), by assoc. with earlier †*bordel* (- OF. *bordel* = Pr. *bordel* hut, brothel, f. *bord* BOARD), which it superseded.

brother brʌ·ðəɹ CGerm. and CIE. term of relationship, like *daughter*, *father*, *mother*, *sister*. OE. *brōþor*, pl. *brōþor*, *brōþru*, dial. *brǣþre* = OFris. *brōther*, *brōder*, OS. *brōthar*, (M)Du. *broeder*, (M)LG. *brōder*, OHG. *bruodar* (G. *bruder*), ON. *bróðir*, Goth. *brōþar* :- Germ. **brōþar* :- IE. **bhrāter*, whence Skr. *bhrātr̥*, Gr. *phrā́tēr*, *-ōr*, L. *frāter*, OSl. *bratrŭ*, OCeltic **brāter* (Ir., Gael. *brathair*, W. *brawd*, Breton *breur*). The arch. pl. **brethren** bre·ðrĭn.

brougham brou·əm, bru·əm, brūm one-horse closed carriage. XIX. f. name of Henry Peter, Lord *Brougham* (1778–1868).

brough var. of BROCH.

brow brau †eyelash, eyelid; arch of hair above the eye OE.; projecting edge of a hill, etc. XV; forehead XVI. OE. *brū* :- Germ. **brūs* :- IE. **bhrūs*, whence also Gr. *ophrús*, Lith. *bruvìs*, OIr. acc. pl. *for|bru*, Pers. *(a)brū*, Skr. *bhrūs*; ON. *brú* bridge is perh. the same word, but the ON. word for 'eyebrow' is *brún*. ¶ Not allied to OE. *brǣw*; see BRAE. Hence **brow·**BEAT. XVI; the etymol. meaning is perh. 'beat by frowning', but this is uncertain.

browis see BROSE.

brown braun (arch.) dusky, dark OE.; of the colour produced by mixing orange and black XIII. OE. *brūn* = OFris., OS. *brūn* (Du. *bruin*; see BRUIN), OHG. *brūn* (G. *braun*), ON. *brúnn* :- CGerm. (exc. Goth.) **brūnaz* (adopted in Rom., as F., Pr. *brun*, It. *bruno*, and in Lith. *brúnas*). Reinforced in ME. from (O)F. *brun* - Germ. The base of the Germ. word appears in Lith. *bėras* brown (cf. BEAR[1]), and with redupl. in Skr. *babhrús* reddish-brown (cf. BEAVER); cf. also Gr. *phrū́nē*, *phrū́nos* toad. OE. *brūn*, ME. *broun*, ON. *brúnn*, OHG. *brūn*, were applied to burnished or glistening surfaces; see BURNISH. *Brown Bess* flint-lock musket (XVIII; earlier *brown musket*); *Bess*, pet-form of *Elizabeth*. In *brown study* (XVI) the sense appears to have been orig. 'dark', 'overcast', 'gloomy'.

brownie brau·ni benevolent sprite. XVI. f. BROWN + *-ie*, -Y[6]. (Hence Gael. *brúinidh*.)

browning brau·niŋ automatic pistol. XX. Name of John M. *Browning* of Ogden, Utah, U.S.A.

Brownist brau·nist follower of Robert *Brown*, English puritan and nonconformist, who advocated (*c.* 1580) a system of church government of the congregationalist pattern. XVI. Hence **Brow·n**ISM. XVII.

brown-jolly brau·ndʒəli W. Indian perversion of BRINJAL. XVIII.

browse brauz sb. young shoots and twigs, cattle-fodder; vb. crop and eat, feed ***on*** leaves, etc. XV. Both sb. and vb. are first recorded from Fitzherbert's 'Husbandry', 1523, and are ult. - early modF. *broust* (earlier *brost*, now *brout*) bud, young shoot, *brouster* (now *brouter*) crop, prob. of Germ. origin; but the loss of *t* in Eng. is difficult to account for.

Bruin, bruin brū·in common or brown bear. XVII. - Du. *bruin*, with spelling-pronunc. (in Butler's 'Hudibras' r.w. *ruine*), the Du. form of BROWN used as a proper name in 'Reynard the Fox', whence its isolated early occurrence in 1481 in Caxton's transl. of the Flemish.

bruise brūz (orig.) crush, mangle, (now) injure by a blow or pressure without breaking skin. OE. *brȳsan* (whence ME. *brüse*, *brise*, *bryse*, *brese*) rel. to OE. *brosnian* crumble, decay, and further to L. *frustum* piece, fragment (see FRUSTUM). With this coalesced *brüse*, *broyse*, *brose*, later *bruise* - AN. *bruser*, OF. *bruisier* (mod. *briser*) break, smash, of unkn. origin. Hence **bruise** sb. †breach XV; contusion XVI.

bruit brūt noise, clamour; report, rumour. XV. (O)F. *bruit*, sb. use of pp. of *bruire* roar :- Rom. **brūgere*, alteration of L. *rugīre* roar by assoc. with **bragere* BRAY[1]. Hence **bruit** vb. noise, rumour. XV.

brumal brū·məl wintry. XVI (G. Douglas). - L. *brūmālis*, f. *brūma* winter, for **brevima* (sc. *diēs*) 'shortest (day)', f. *brevis* BRIEF. So **brumous** brū·məs foggy. XIX. - F. *brumeux* - late L. *brūmōsus* rainy (Isidore), f. *brūma*; see -AL, -OUS.

brumby brʌ·mbi (Austral.) wild or unbroken horse. XIX. Of unkn. origin.

Brummagem brʌ·midʒəm counterfeit, sham. XVII. Local pronunc., now vulgar, of the name of *Birmingham*, England, used allusively, orig. with ref. to the counterfeit groats made there *c.* 1680, more recently to the cheap plated and lacquer ware manufactured there. The form depends on an old var. of the name, *Bromwichham*, *Bromecham* XVI, *Bromegem* XVII, earlier *Burmincham*, *Burmingeham* XIII.

brunette brune·t dark-complexioned (girl or woman) XVII (anglicized *brunet*, Dryden), XVIII. - (O)F. *brunette*, fem. of *brunet*, dim. of *brun* BROWN; see -ETTE. (Earlier †*brownetta* XVI - It. *brunetta*, with assim. to ***brown***.) Cf. BURNET.

Brunswick brʌ·nzwik name of a city of Germany, used attrib. in *Brunswick black* (kind of varnish). – LG. *Brunswīk* (G. *Braunschweig*), f. g. of *Brūn* Bruno (the founder) + *wīk* WICK[1].

brunt brʌnt †blow, onset, attack XIV–XVII; shock; (chief) stress XVI. Of unkn. origin.

brush[1] brʌʃ (dial.) loppings of trees XIV (R. Mannyng); (U.S., etc.) thicket XVI. ME. *brusche* – AN. *brousse*, OF. *broce, brosse* (whence F. *broussaille*) = Pr. *brosa*, Sp. *broza* :– Rom. **bruscia*, perh. f. L. *bruscum* excrescence on the maple (Pliny).

brush[2] brʌʃ utensil for sweeping or scrubbing dirt away XIV; for painting XV. – OF. *broisse*, (also mod.) *brosse*, perh. to be identified with prec.; cf. *broom*. Hence vb. XV.

brush[3] brʌʃ †rush with speed XIV; (sl.) decamp; move briskly *by, past*, etc. XVII. poss. – OF. *brosser* go through brushwood, f. *brosse* BRUSH[1]. Hence sb. forcible rush or encounter. XIV.

brusque brusk, brʌsk, brüsk blunt, offhand. XVII (*brusk*). – F. *brusque* lively, wild, fierce, harsh – It. *brusco* sour, tart, sour-looking, a use of the sb. = Sp., Pg. *brusco* butcher's broom (a spiny bush) :– Rom. *bruscum*, perh. blend of L. *rūscum* butcher's broom with **brūcus* heather (see BRIAR). Cf. BRISK.

Brussels brʌ·səlz name (Flem. *Brussel*, F. *Bruxelles*) of the capital of Belgium, as in *Brussels carpet* (XIX), *Brussels sprouts* (XVIII).

Brut brūt chronicle of British history. XIV (*brout*). – MW. *brut* (W. *brud*) in the titles of Welsh chronicles of British history; transf. use (in French or in Welsh) of *Brutus* name of the legendary eponymous founder of Britain, reputed grandson of Æneas.

brutal brū·təl †animal XV (Sc. *brutal beist*); inhuman, brutish XVI. – (O)F. *brutal* or med. L. *brūtālis*, f. L. *brūtus* BRUTE + -AL. Hence **bruta·lITY** XVI, **bru·talIZE** XVIII. – F. *brutaliser*. So **brute** brūt adj. (esp. in *brute beast*) of the lower animals XV; brutish; irrational XVI; sb. lower animal XVII. – F. *brut, brute* = Sp., It. *bruto* – L. *brūtus* heavy, stupid, dull, held to be from an Italic dial. in which *b-* :– **gw-*, and so rel. to L. *gravis* heavy, GRAVE[3], Lett. *grūts* heavy. Hence **bru·tish** XV; see -ISH[1].

brutus brū·təs rough short-haired wig. XIX. – F., f. cognomen of two ancient Romans famous for their patriotism and merciless virtue.

bryology braiɔ·lədʒi branch of botany concerning mosses. XIX. f. Gr. *brúon* mossy seaweed + -LOGY.

bryony brai·əni cucurbitaceous plant. XVI. – L. *bryōnia* (Pliny) – Gr. *bruōniā* (Dioscorides). Earlier †*brione* (XIV) – OF. *brione*.

Brythonic briþɔ·nik pert. to the Celts of South Britain. XIX (J. Rhŷs). f. W. *Brython* Britons (:– Celtic **Brittones*, pl. of **Britto* BRITON) + -IC. Cf. GOIDELIC.

bubble bʌ·bl sb. globule of liquid enclosing air, etc.; vb. form bubbles. XIV. prob. imit. like the parallel Du. *bobbel, bobbelen*, G. dial. *bobbel, bubbel, -en*, Sw. *bubla*, Da. *boble*; perh. in part a modification of the earlier BURBLE.

bubbly-jock bʌ·blidʒɔk (Sc.) turkey. XIX (Scott). The first el. is imit. of the bird's cry (cf. *gobbler*), the second is *jock* JACK.

bubo bjū·bou inflamed swelling in groin or armpits. XIV (Trevisa). – L. *bubō(n-)* owl, medL. swelling – Gr. *boubṓn* groin, swelling in groin. Hence **bubonIC** bjubɔ·nik. XIX.

buccal bʌ·kəl pert. to the cheek(s). XIX. f. L. *bucca* cheek, mouth, familiar syn. of *ōs* (see ORAL); see -AL.

buccaneer bʌkəniə·ɹ †curer of flesh on a barbecue; sea-rover. XVII. – F. *boucanier*, f. *boucaner* cure flesh on a *boucan* or barbecue (Tupi *mukem, mocaém*, whence Pg. *moquém*). The sb. and vb. *boucan, buccan* (from the F. sb. and vb.) appear earlier in XVII. The orig. application was to French and English hunters of oxen and swine in San Domingo and Tortugas, who dried the flesh of their prey on a wooden framework called by a name reported by De Léry (16..) as *boucan*, the Haitian equiv. of which is *barbacóa* BARBECUE. The name was transf. to the pirates of the Spanish Main whose habits were similar.

buccinator bʌ·ksineitəɹ (anat.) cheek muscle used in blowing. XVII. – L. *buccinātor*, f. *buccināre* blow the *buccina, būcina*, or crooked trumpet; see -ATOR.

bucellas bjuse·ləs Portuguese white wine. XIX. f. name of a village near Lisbon, Portugal.

bucentaur bjuse·ntɔ̄ɹ papal or ducal state barge adorned with gilding and paintings. XVII. – F. *bucentaure* (simulating *centaure* CENTAUR) – It. *bucentoro*, f. (Venetian) **bucio int' oro* 'barge in gold' (†*bucio* – Germ. **buk-* paunch; †*into* :– L. *intus* within; *oro* :– L. *aurum* gold).

Bucephalus bjuse·fələs pompous name for a riding-horse. XVII. L. – Gr. *Bouképhalos* name of Alexander the Great's charger, f. *boûs* ox (see COW[1]) + *kephalḗ* HEAD[1].

buck[1] bʌk A. male of deer; †he-goat OE; B. †fellow (? from ON. *bokki*) XIV; gay, dashing man XVIII. (i) OE. *buc* male deer = MDu. *boc* (Du. *bok*), OHG. *boc* (G. *bock*), ON. *bukkr, bokkr* :– Germ. **bukkaz* (whence, only in the sense 'he-goat', (O)F. *bouc*, Pr. *boc*); (ii) OE. *bucca* he-goat = ON. *bokki* my good fellow, old buck :– **bukkon*; prob., like *cow, ewe, goat, mouse, wolf*, of prim. IE. origin (cf. OIr. *bocc* he-goat, Arm. *buc* lamb, Av. *būza-*, Skr. *bukka* he-goat), but the connexions are doubtful. *Buckbean* (XVI), tr. Flem. *bocks boonen* 'goat's beans'. Hence **buck** vb. **(dial.)**

dress *up* (i.e. like a 'buck' or smart fellow); (sl.) cheer *up*; hurry *up* XIX.

buck[2] bʌk (obs. or dial.) lye for washing; quantity of clothes washed. XVI. f. †*buck* vb. steep in lye (XIV, *bouken*, PPl.) :- OE. **būcian*, corr. to MHG. *būchen* (G. *beuchen*), LG. *büken*, Sw. *byka*, Da. *byge*, f. Germ. **būk-* (whence F. *buer* wash, *buée* lye).

buckeen bʌkī·n (Anglo-Ir.) young man of the inferior or poorer gentry. XVIII. f. BUCK[1] B+-EEN[2].

bucket bʌ·kit pail-shaped vessel for holding liquid. XIII. Also *bouket, buket, boket* – AN. *buket, buquet* tub, pail (cf. AL. *bo-, bukettum* XIII), perh. f. OE. *būc* belly, pitcher = OFris., MLG. *būk*, OHG. *būh* (Du. *buik*, G. *bauch* belly, paunch, bulge), ON. *búkr* body; see -ET. Hence **bu·cket-**SHOP (U.S.) place where liquor was obtainable in buckets, etc. supplied by customers; (hence) establishment orig. for smaller gambling transactions in grain, (later gen.) for miscellaneous gambling on the markets.

buckle bʌ·kl clasp with a hinged tongue, for securing a belt, etc. XIV. – (O)F. *boucle* metal ring, boss of shield :- L. *buccula* cheek-strap of a helmet, boss of a shield, dim. of *bucca* cheek. (The common F. sense 'curl of hair' was current in Eng. XVIII.) Hence **bu·ckle** vb. fasten with a buckle XIV (Ch.); (after F. *boucler*) bend under stress XVI. See -CLE.

buckler bʌ·klər small round shield. XIII. ME. *boc(e)ler* – OF. *bocler, boucler, bucler* (mod. *bouclier*), orig. adj. in *escu boucler* shield having a boss, f. *boucle* boss (see prec.)+*-er* -ER[2].

buckra bʌ·krə white man. XVIII. – Surinam *bakra* master (cf. Efik *mbākara, mākara* encompass, master).

buckram bʌ·krəm †fine linen or cotton fabric XIV; coarse linen or cloth stiffened XV. ME. *boker(h)am* – AN. *bukeram*, OF. *boquerant* (mod. *bougran*), corr. to Pr. *bocaran*, Sp. *bucaran*, It. *bucherame*, obscurely f. *Bukhara*, name of a town in Turkestan, whence a fine fabric was exported to Europe. (So MDu. *bocraen*, MHG. *buggeram, -an*, from French.) ¶ For the change of final *n* to *m* cf. *grogram, megrim, vellum*.

buckshee bʌ·kʃī (sl.) extra rations; adj., adv. gratuitous(ly). XIX. Alteration of BAKSHEESH.

buckthorn bʌ·kþɔ̄ɹn shrub Rhamnus catharticus. XVI (Lyte). f. BUCK[1]+THORN; tr. modL. *cervi spina* 'stag's thorn'.

buckwheat bʌ·kʍīt the cereal Polygonum Fagopyrum. XVI (Turner). – MDu. *boecweite* (Du. *boekweit*), MLG. *bōkwēte* (LG. *bookweten*), f. *boek, bōk* (see BEECH)+*weite* WHEAT; so named from its triquetrous seeds resembling those of the beech. (The LG. word has been adopted in F. as *bou-, bucail(le), bouquette*, and *beaucuit*.)

bucolic bjukɔ·lik pastoral, rustic; sb. pl. pastoral poems. XVI. – L. *būcolicus* – Gr. *boukolikós*, f. *boukólos* herdsman, f. *boûs* ox (see COW)+**kol-*, perh. rel. to HOLD; see -IC.

bud[1] bʌd flower or leaf not opened. XIV (Trevisa). Late ME. *bodde, budde*, of unkn. origin. (The synon. MDu. *botte*, Du. *bot* cannot be connected.) Hence **bud** vb. XIV (Trevisa).

bud[2] bʌd (U.S.) infantile or negro alteration of BROTHER. Also **bu·ddy** (-Y[6]). XIX.

Bude bjūd f. name of a town in Cornwall, place of residence of Sir Goldsworthy Gurney (1793–1875), inventor of a burner and a light so named.

budge[1] bʌdʒ lambskin with the wool dressed outwards. XIV. Early forms (disyll.) *bugee, bugeye, buggy, bog(e)y*, in AL. *buggetum*, of unkn. origin. From Milton's *budge doctors of the Stoic fur* ('Comus' 707), where the reference seems to be to the wearing of gowns trimmed with budge, the word was freq. used XVII–XVIII for 'stiff, formal, pompous'.

budge[2] bʌdʒ stir. XVI (*bouge*). – (O)F. *bouger*, prob. = Pr. *bolegar* disturb oneself, It. *bulicare* bubble up :- Rom. **bullicāre* bubble, f. L. *bullīre*, f. *bulla* bubble (BULL[2]).

budgerigar bʌ·dʒərigā:ɹ love-bird. XIX (many vars.). XIX. Native Australian (Port Jackson), f. *budgeri* good+*gar* cockatoo.

budgerow bʌ·dʒərou Indian keelless barge. XVIII (earlier †*bazara* XVI). – Hindi, Bengali *bajrā*.

budget bʌ·dʒit †pouch, wallet XV; bundle, stock XVI; annual estimate made by the Chancellor of the Exchequer (who was formerly said to 'open his budget') XVIII. – OF. *bougette*, dim. of *bouge* leather bag :- L. *bulga*, said by Festus to be Gaulish (cf. Ir. *bolg* belly, bag, pouch, etc.); see -ET.

budmash see BADMASH.

buff[1] bʌf blow, stroke, buffet (surviving only in BLIND-MAN'S-BUFF). – OF. *buffe* BUFFET[1]; cf. Du. *bof*.

buff[2] bʌf A. †buffalo, wild ox XVI; B. (earlier *buff leather*) leather of buffalo hide, hence of ox hide; military attire (orig. of this leather) XVI; the bare skin XVII; C. light-brownish yellow (hence as adj.) XVIII. prob. – F. *buffle* BUFFALO.

buffalo bʌ·fəlou species of ox, orig. Indian. XVI. prob. immed. – Pg. *bufalo* (mod. *bufaro*), corr. to It. *bufalo* (whence F. *buffle*), Sp. *búbalo, búfalo* :- late L. *būfalu-s*, L. *būbalu-s* – Gr. *boúbalos* antelope, wild ox. (F. *buffle* was adopted earlier in XVI and continued in use till *c.* 1800; cf. BUFF[2].)

buffer[1] bʌ·fəɹ fellow. xviii. prob. ult. from an imit. base **buff-* blow, puff, make the sound of a soft blow, whence the meanings 'stammerer' (xiv), 'soft fellow' (dial.); see next. Cf. OE. *ābyffan* mutter.

buffer[2] bʌ·fəɹ device for deadening the force of concussion. xix. prob. f. *buff* vb. sound as a soft body when struck, (earlier) stutter, splutter (as with laughter); if so, ult. identical with prec.

buffet[1] bʌ·fit blow. xiii. – OF. (now dial.) *buffet*, dim. of *buffe*, of imit. origin. So **bu·ffet** vb. xiii. – (O)F. *buffeter*.

buffet[2] bu·fei, || büfɛ sideboard, cupboard in a recess xviii; refreshment bar xix. F., of unkn. origin.

buffo bu·fou comic actor; adj. comic. xviii (Foote). – It. *buffo* puff of wind, buffoon, f. *buffare* (see next).

buffoon bʌfū·n clown. xvi. – F. *bouffon*, – It. *buffone*, f. *buffare* puff (prob. with allusion to puffing out the cheeks as a comic gesture), of imit. origin; see -OON.

bug[1] bʌg object of dread. xiv. The earliest of several words, mostly evidenced from xvi, of similar form and meaning ('goblin', 'spectre', 'bugbear', 'bogey'), the connexions of which are obscure; viz. †*bog*, †*boggard*, (dial.) *bogle* (Dunbar), *bogle-bo*, BUGABOO, BUGBEAR, and the more recent BOGEY. Comparison with W. *bwg*, *bwgan* ghost, hobgoblin, *bwgwl* fear, threat, is inevitable, but it is uncertain how these forms are related. The phr. *big bug*, meaning 'important person', is presumably an example of this word; but cf. (dial.) *bug* swaggering, pompous (xvi), and 'one whom no big, nor bugs wordes can terrifie' (Cotgr. s.v. Cheval).

bug[2] bʌg insect, beetle (as still in U.S.); bed-bug, Cimex lectularius. xvi (in *turd bug* dung-beetle). Origin unascertained; poss. alteration of *budde*, OE. *budda*, as in *sćearn-budda* dung-beetle, (dial.) *shorn-bug* (xvii); but conjectured to be identical with BUG[1] through assoc. with *fly* in the sense of 'familiar demon', *Baalzebub* (*Beelzebub*) 'the prince of devils' being interpreted by some as 'lord of flies'.

bugaboo bʌgəbū· bogey, bugbear. xviii (*buggybow*; earlier *bugboy* may be a corruption). prob. of dial. origin; cf. W. *bwcibo* the Devil (*bwci* hobgoblin, *bo* scarecrow), Corn. *buccaboo*; the OF. demon-name *Bugibus* may be of Celtic origin.

bugbear bʌ·gbɛəɹ †hobgoblin; object of dread. xvi. app. f. BUG[1]+BEAR[1]. (ME. *bokeberet*, glossing OF. *escarrie*, as an alternative to ME. *skerlis* scarecrow, is isolated and obscure, but is remarkably like in form and sense.) A former syn. was †*scare-bug* (xvi–xvii); also †*bull-bear*, †*bull-beggar* (xvi).

bugger bʌ·gəɹ sodomite xvi (*bouguer*, *bowgard*); (vulgar and dial.) coarse term of abuse; also, fellow, chap xviii. – MDu. *bugger* – (O)F. *bougre* †heretic, (arch.) sodomite, (colloq.) 'chap' :– medL. *Bulgarus* BULGARIAN, heretic (the Bulgarians being so regarded as belonging to the Greek Church), spec. Albigensian. So **bu·gg**ERY. xiv. – MDu. *buggerie* (OF. *bouguerie*); cf. MLG. *buggernie*.

buggy bʌ·gi light horse-vehicle. xviii. Of unkn. origin; taken into F. as *boghei* (Lamartine spells it *boguey*).

bugle[1] bjū·gl †buffalo, bull; kind of horn (short for **bugle horn** horn of a wild ox used as a drinking-vessel and as a musical instrument). xiv. – OF. *bugle* :– L. *būculu-s*, dim. of *bōs* ox (see COW[1]).

bugle[2] bjū·gl plant of the genus Ajuga. xiii. – late L. *bugula* (whence F. *bugle*, Sp. *buġula*, It. *bugola*).

bugle[3] bjū·gl tubular glass bead. xvi (also *buegle*, *beaugle*). Of unkn. origin.

bugloss bjū·glɔs boraginaceous plant. xv. – F. *buglosse* or L. *būglōssus* – Gr. *boúglōssos* lit. 'ox-tongued', f. *boûs* ox (see COW[1])+ *glôssa* tongue (cf. GLOSS).

buhl būl material prepared for inlaid work. xix. f. name of André *Boule*, designer of marqueterie, who lived in France in the reign of Louis XIV; the sp. *buhl* appears to be a Germanized form.

build bild construct, orig. for a dwelling. OE. *byldan* (cf. *bylda* builder), f. *bold* dwelling, house, var. of *botl* (surviving in proper names, as *Newbolt*, *Newbould*, *Harbottle*, *Bootle*) = OFris. *bōdel*, OS. *bodl*, ON. *ból* :– Germ. **buþlam*, f. **bu-* dwell (see BOWER[1]). The present sp. reflects a southern and western development, the pronunc. a northern and midland; cf. BUY.

bukshee bʌ·kʃī paymaster. xvii (*buxy*). – Urdu, Pers. *bakhshī*, f. *bakhshīdan* give (see BAKSHEESH). Cf. BUCKSHEE.

bulb bʌlb †onion xvi; 'root' of onion, etc. xvii; roundish dilatation, spec. of a glass tube xviii. – L. *bulbus* = Gr. *bólbos* onion, bulbous root, with Baltic cogns. Hence **bu·lb**OUS xvi; cf. F. *bulbe* (xvi), *bulbeux*.

bulbul bu·lbul Eastern song-thrush. xviii. – Pers. – Arab. *bulbul*, of imit. origin.

Bulgarian bʌlgɛə·riən pert. to (a native of) Bulgaria. xvi. f. medL. *Bulgaria*, f. *Bulgarus* Bulgarian – OSl. *Blŭgarinŭ*; see -IAN. (In OE. *Bulgarisć*.) *Old Bulgarian*, the oldest extant form of the Slavonic group of languages, also called Old Church Slavonic. So **Bu·lgar.** xviii. – F. *Bulgare*, G. *Bulgar*, or medL. *Bulgarus*.

bulge bʌldʒ †wallet, pouch xiii; bottom of a ship's hull xvii; (f. the vb.) protuberance xviii. – (O)F. *bouge* – L. *bulga* leathern sack, bag, of Gaulish origin; the second sense is of obscure origin (cf. BILGE). Hence **bulge**

vb. stave in the bottom of a ship; also intr. XVI; protrude XVII.

bulimy bjū·limi morbid hunger, (fig.) voracity. XVII. – modL. *bulīmia* – Gr. *boulīmiā*, f. *boû-s* ox, cow[1], used as an intensive el. + *līmós* hunger; cf. F. *boulimie*. (Gr. synon. *boúlīmos* was adopted in medL. as *bolismus*, whence OF. *bolisme*, later *boulime*; Trevisa has *bolisme*, Sylvester, tr. Du Bartas, *boulime*.)

bulk[1] bʌlk A. cargo (*in bulk*, in large unbroken quantities) XIV; †heap XV; B. †belly, trunk, body XIV; large body, huge frame XVI; C. magnitude, volume, mass XV. prob. orig. three separate words but subsequently identified by assoc. of sense; in A – OIcel. *búlki* cargo; in B perh. at first an alteration of †*bouk*, OE. *būc* belly = OS. *būk* (Du. *buik*), OHG. *būh* (G. *bauch*), ON. *búkr* :– CGerm. (exc. Goth.) **būkaz*; in C prob. transf. use of either A or B. Hence **bulk** vb. (in several unconnected uses). XVI. **bu·lky**[1] XV.

bulk[2] bʌlk stall XV; framework projecting from a shop-front XVI. Also earlier †*bolk*, perh. – ON. *bálkr* partition, low wall; but cf. OE. *bolca* gangway of a ship; poss. rel. to BALK. Hence **bu·lk**HEAD upright partition in a ship XV (in Sandahl); roof of a stall XVIII.

bull[1] bul male of the ox, etc. Late OE. *bula* (in place-names), ME. *bole* – ON. *boli*, corr. to MLG. *bulle*, MDu. *bulle*, *bolle* (Du. *bul*), f. a base whence the OE. dim. *bulluc* BULLOCK. (In stock exchange sl. correl. to BEAR[1] XVIII.)

bull[2] bul papal edict XIII; official seal XIV. – (O)F. *bulle* – L. *bulla* bubble, round object (whence F. *boule*; see BOWL[2]), in medL. seal, sealed document, spec. papal letter with the pontifical seal, rel. to *bullīre* BOIL.

bull[3] bul A. †jest XVII only (1630); B. statement so expressed as to imply an absurdity XVII (1638–40). Origin unascertained; connexion with ME. *bul* deceit (XIII), *bulle* deceive, cheat (XV–XVII), has been suggested, but there are chronological difficulties and the meaning is remote. The association of sense B with the Irish is late and obscure.

bullace bu·ləs species of wild plum. XIV. –OF. *buloce*, (also mod.) *beloce* sloe :– Rom. **bullucea*, f. **bulluca* (perverted to *bellicum* in Corpus Glossary B 75), perh. of Gaulish origin.

bullamacow bu·ləməkau cattle; tinned meat. XIX. Said to be Fiji combination of BULL[1] and COW[1].

bullate bu·leit having vesicles, inflated. XIX. – medL. *bullātus*, f. *bulla*; see BULL[2], -ATE[2].

bulldose, -doze bu·ldouz (U.S.) intimidate (orig. Negroes) by violence. XIX. f. BULL[1] + DOSE (as if to give a dose fit for a bull, but ?); **-dozer** XIX (person), XX (machine).

bullet bu·lit †cannon-ball (as F. *boulet*); ball for small fire-arms. XVI. – F. *boulette*, dim. of *boule* ball (BULL[2]).

bulletin bu·lĭtin †note, warrant, etc. XVII; short account or report XVIII. – F. *bulletin* – It. *bulletino*, *boll-* safe-conduct, pass, f. *bulletta* passport, lottery ticket, dim. of *bulla* BULL[2].

bullfinch[1] bu·lfintʃ finch of the genus Pyrrhula. XIV. f. BULL[1] + FINCH; so called from its large head and squat form; cf. F. *bouvreuil*, based on *bœuf* ox.

bullfinch[2] bu·lfinʃ high quickset hedge with a ditch. XIX. The first el. is presumably BULL[1]; second el. may be a corruption of *fence*.

bullion bu·ljən precious metal in the mass. XIV. – AN. *bullion* (XIV), which appears to mean 'mint', var. of (O)F. *bouillon* :– Rom. **bulliōnem* boiling, f. L. *bullīre* BOIL[2]. The history is obscure.

bullock bu·lək young bull. Late OE. *bulluc*, dim. of BULL[1]; see -OCK.

bully[1] bu·li †sweetheart; fine fellow XVI; bravo, swashbuckler, (hence) tyrannical coward XVII; †hired ruffian; †protector of prostitutes XVIII. prob. – (M)Du. *boele* (MHG. *buole*, G. *buhle*) used as a term of endearment or reproach, of which the dims. *boelekijn* and *boeltje* appear to be repr. in Eng. by synon. †*bulcking* (XVI, rare), †*bulchin* (XVII), and †*bulch* (XVII, rare).

bully[2] bu·li (now esp. U.S.) fine, capital, first-rate. XVII. perh. arising from attrib. use of prec.

bully[3] bu·li (also *bully beef*) tinned beef. XVIII (Smollett). – F. *bouilli* boiled beef, sb. use of pp. of *bouillir* BOIL[2]; used as a label of tinned army rations of beef in the Franco-Prussian war of 1870–1.

bullyrag bu·liræg, **ballyrag** bæ·liræg (orig. U.S.) †bully; use abusive language of. XVIII. Also *bulrag*, *balrag*.

bulrush bu·lrʌʃ tall rush, Scirpus lacustris. XV. perh. f. BULL[1], used, as later in BULLFINCH, *bull-frog*, *bull-trout*, in the sense 'large' or 'coarse' (cf. the similar use of *cow* and *horse*) + RUSH[1].

bulwark bu·lwəɹk rampart, fortification XV; raised side of a ship XIX. immed. source doubtful, but prob. ult. a comp. of the words repr. by BOLE[1] and WORK. Late MHG. *bolwerk* meant (1) ballista, (2) fortification, whence Du. *bolwerk*, Sw. *bolverk*, Da. *bulværk*. The Germ. word was adopted in Russ. *bolverk*, F. †*boullewerc*, BOULEVARD.

bum bʌm fundament, buttocks. XIV (Trevisa). Late ME. *bom*, of unkn. origin; unconnected with synon. Sc. †*bun* (XVI), which may be – Gael. *bun* root, bottom. Hence **bu·m-**BAI·LIFF bailiff employed to make arrests or distraints. XVII (Sh.). So called because he attacks from the rear; cf. F. *pousse-cul* 'push-bum', which is shortened to *cul*, as *bum-bailiff* is to *bum* (XVII).

bumble-bee bʌ·mblbī large hairy bee. XVI. f. †*bumble* frequent. of ME. *bumme, bumbe, bombe* boom, buzz (see -LE[3])+BEE. Cf. HUMBLE-BEE.

Bumbledom bʌ·mbldəm official pomposity and stupidity, esp. as displayed in petty corporations. XIX. f. *Bumble* (prob. to be assoc. with prec.) name of the consequential domineering beadle in Dickens's 'Oliver Twist'; see -DOM.

bumble-puppy bʌ·mblpʌ:pi nine-holes; unscientific whist; game in which a ball on a string is wound round a post. XIX. Of unkn. origin.

bumbo bʌ·mbou drink made of rum, sugar, and water. XVIII (Smollett). perh. – It. *bombo* child's word for drink. (But *bombo* is somewhat earlier in U.S. and said to be so called from an admiral of that name.)

bumboat bʌ·mbout †scavenger's boat on the Thames XVII; boat for the carriage of small merchandise XVIII. prob. f. Du. *bom* (also in *bomschuit*) bluff-bowed fishing-boat.

bumf bʌmf (sl.) paper. XIX. Short for *bumfodder* 'anitergium' (XVII), trashy literature (XVIII); see BUM, FODDER.

bummalo bʌ·məlou small fish, Harpodon nehereus, of S. Asia. XVII. Also *bumbalo, -eloe*, which has been referred to Marathi *bombīl(a)*.

bummaree bʌmərī· middleman in the fish trade at Billingsgate. XVIII. Of unkn. origin.

bummer bʌ·məɹ (U.S. sl.) idler. XIX. perh. based on G. *bummler*, f. *bummeln* loaf about.

bump[1] bʌmp imit. of a somewhat heavy dull blow; its result, swelling, protuberance (Sh.). XVI. The sb. and vb. appear about the same time; perh. of Scand. origin; cf. MDa. *bumpe* strike with fist. Hence **bump** vb. †swell, bulge XVI; strike heavily XVII. **bu·mper** [-ER[1]] full glass of drink XVII; anything unusually large XIX; f. *bumping* prp. adj. huge, 'thumping' (cf. 'bumping bignes', 1566).

bump[2] bʌmp (of the bittern) make a booming sound. XVII (Sir T. Browne, Dryden). imit. Cf. BUTTERBUMP.

bumpkin bʌ·mᵖkin country lout. XVI. The earliest ex., with the gloss *Batavus* Batavian (Levins 1570), suggests that it was orig. applied joc. to Dutchmen; perh. – Du. *boomken* little tree, or MDu. *bommekijn* little barrel, used fig. for 'squat figure'.

bumptious bʌ·mᵖʃəs offensively self-assertive. XIX (Mme D'Arblay). joc. f. BUMP, after FRACTIOUS; cf. the fig. uses of *bounce* and *bounder*.

bun[1] bʌn kind of cake (in England usu. small, round, and sweet). XIV. Late ME. *bunne*, of unkn. origin. ¶ Words to some extent analogous in form and sense are OF. *bunette, bugnete*, Sp. *buñuelo* fritter.

bun[2] bʌn (now U.S.) squirrel XVI; (dial.) rabbit XIX. Cf. BUNNY. Of unkn. origin.

bunch bʌnᵗʃ †hump, swelling XIV; †bundle XIV; collection or cluster of similar things XVI. Of unkn. origin; *hunch* and dial. *clunch* have similar meanings.

bunco bʌ·ŋkou (U.S. sl.) swindle by card or confidence trick. XIX. Said to be – Sp. *banca* (BANK[3]) card-game similar to monte.

buncombe early var. of BUNKUM.

bundle bʌ·ndl †A. bandage XIV (Wycl. Bible, tr. Vulg. L. *fascia*); B. collection of things bound together XIV (Wycl. Bible, tr. Vulg. L. *fasciculus*). orig. perh. repr. OE. *byndelle* binding, taken in concr. sense = OS. *bundilin* (Du. *bundel* bundle, sheaf of arrows, papers, etc.), OHG. *gi|buntili* (G. *bündel*), but reinforced later by (if not wholly due to) LG., Du. *bundel*; f. **bund-* (**bend-* **band-*) BIND, BOND.

bundobust, bandobast bʌ·ndobʌst arrangement, settlement. XVIII. – Hind. – Pers. *band o bast* tying and binding.

bundook bʌ·ndūk musket, match-lock. XIX. – Hind. *bandūq* – Pers. *bundūq* filbert, musket or cannon ball, firearm – Gr. *Pontikón*, sc. *káruon* 'Pontic hazel nut'.

bung bʌŋ stopper, esp. for a cask. XV (Promp. Parv.). – MDu. *bonghe*, varying with *bomme* and *bonde*, whence MDu. *bonne*, beside Du. *bom*, of doubtful origin.

bungalow bʌ·ŋgəlou one-storied lightly built house. XVII (*bungale*). – Gujarati *bangalo* – Hind. *banglā* belonging to Bengal.

bungle bʌ·ŋgl make or act unskilfully. XVI. prob. of symbolic formation, like synon. and contemp. †*bumble* (cf. BUMBLE-BEE).

bunion bʌ·njən inflamed swelling on the foot. XVIII. Formerly also *bunnian, -on, bunyan, -on*; rel. to dial. (E. Anglian) *bunny* swelling, earlier *bony* (XV, Promp. Parv.), and obs. dial. (Essex) *boine* (cf. †*boin* vb., swell, used by Golding, who was of Essex parentage) – OF. *buigne, buyne* (mod. *bigne*) bump on the head, perh. of Germ. origin (cf. MHG. *bunge* lump).

bunk[1] bʌŋk sleeping-berth in a ship, etc. XIX. Of unkn. origin; perh. rel. to BUNKER.

bunk[2] bʌŋk (sl.) be off, make off. XIX. Of unkn. origin.

bunk[3] bʌŋk (sl.) short for BUNKUM. XX.

bunker bʌ·ŋkəɹ chest or box often serving as a seat XVI (Sc. *boncure, bonkcar, bonker*; *bunker* XVII); sandy hollow on a golf course XIX (Scott); storage room for coal or oil fuel XIX. Not Eng. before XIX; of unkn. origin.

bunkum bʌ·ŋkəm political chicanery or clap-trap; humbug. XIX (*c.* 1845). f. *Buncombe* name of a county in North Carolina, U.S.A., the member for which, it is said, in a debate in Congress persisted in speaking, declaring that he was bound to 'make a speech for Buncombe'; hence applied to vaporous political talk; but *talking to Bunkum* is recorded as early as 1828.

bunny bʌ·ni †term of endearment for a woman or child; rabbit. XVII. f. synon. BUN[2]+-Y[6].

bunodont bjū·nodɔnt pert. to or having tuberculate molars. XIX. f. Gr. *bounós* mound+*odont-, odoús* TOOTH. So **bu·noid**.

bunsen bʌ·nsən. XIX. f. name of R. W. von *Bunsen* (1811–99), German chemist, applied to a gas-burner, lamp, etc., invented by him.

bunt[1] bʌnt baggy part of a sail, net, etc. XVI. Of unkn. origin.

bunt[2] bʌnt push, butt. XIX. Of dial. origin.

buntal bʌ·ntəl straw from the fibres of the talipot. XX. Native name in the Philippine Islands.

bunter bʌ·ntəɹ (geol.) lower stage of triassic rocks. XIX. – G. *bunter* in *bunter sandstein* varicoloured or mottled sandstone.

bunting[1] bʌ·ntiŋ bird of the genus Emberiza. XIII. Of unkn. origin; perh. f. a base meaning 'short and thick', *buntin(g)* being used in this sense from *c.* 1600. (The recorded syns. *buntyle, bunkin, buntlin* are of doubtful authenticity.)

bunting[2] bʌ·ntiŋ open-made woollen stuff for flags; flags collectively. XVIII (also *-ine*). Of unkn. origin; connexion with (dial.) *bunt* sift, boult (*bonte* XIV), as if orig. 'boulting-cloth', is suggested by the fact that F. *étamine* means both boulting-cloth and bunting.

bunyip bʌ·njip aboriginal name of a fabulous monster of the interior of Australia; fig. impostor. XIX.

buoy boi floating body marking navigable limits. XIII. Earlier forms *boy(e), buy, buie, bwoy*; prob. – MDu. *bo(e)ye, boeie* (Du. *boei*), perh. – OF. *boie, buie* chain, fetter :– L. *boia*, esp. pl. *boiæ* – Gr. *boeîai* (sc. *doraí*) straps of ox-leather, f. *boûs* (see COW[1]). *Buoy-rope* (XIV) corr. to Du. *boeireip*. Formerly pron. bwoi. ¶ The word has become CEur. (F. *bouée*, Sp. *boya*, It. *boia*, Russ. *buĭ*, Sw. *boj*).

buoyant boi·ənt having the power of floating XVI; keeping bodies afloat XVII; fig. easily recovering from depression XVIII. – OF. *bouyant* or Sp. *boyante* light-sailing, prp. of *boyar* float, f. *boya* BUOY; see -ANT. Hence **buoy·ancy**. XVIII. ¶ For the prob. Sp. origin cf. BOX[4], CAPSIZE.

bur, burr bəːɹ rough or prickly seed-vessel or flower-head XIV; obstacle in the throat XIV (PPl.). perh. of Scand. origin; cf. Da. *burre* bur, burdock, Sw. *kard|borre* burdock, which may depend on **bhr̥s-*, the base of BRISTLE. Cf. BURR.

burberry bəː·ɹbəri trade-name of cloth and clothing made by *Burberrys* Ltd. 1903.

burble bəː·ɹbl †form bubbles, flow with bubbling sound XIV (R. Mannyng); (revived or formed afresh by Kipling) talk with a continuous murmur XIX. Of imit. origin; there are similar and synon. forms in Rom., e.g. Sp. *borbollar* bubble, gush, *barbullar* talk loud and fast, It. *borbugliare*.

burbot bəː·ɹbət freshwater fish, Lota vulgaris. XIV. – F. *bourbotte*, earlier *bourbet(t)e*, prob. f. *bourbe* slime, mud; see -ET.

burden[1] bəː·ɹdn, (arch.) **burthen** bəː·ɹðn load. OE. *byrþen* = OS. *burthinnia* :– WGerm. **burþinnja*, f. **burþi-* (see BIRTH) +**-innja* -EN[2]; cf., with different suffix, OHG. *burdi* (G. *bürde*), Goth. *baúrþei*. Forms with *d* appear XII; cf. MURDER and dial. *farden* FARTHING, *furder* FURTHER; for *u* repr. OE. *y* cf. *blush*. Hence **bu·rden** vb. †**bu·rdenous**, **bu·rdensome**. XVI.

burden[2] bəː·ɹdn †bass, 'undersong'; refrain XVI (Sh.); chief theme XVII. Later form of BOURDON, assim. to prec. as if with the notion that the bass or the refrain was 'carried' by the melody or the song.

burdock bəː·ɹdɔk weed, Arctium Lappa, having prickly flower-heads. XVI (Gerarde). f. BUR+DOCK[1].

bureau bjurou· writing-desk with drawers; office. XVII. – F. *bureau* orig. woollen stuff, baize (used for covering writing-desks), earlier *burel*, prob. f. *bure*, var. of OF. *buire* dark-brown = It. *buio* dark :– Rom. **būriu-s* dark-red (cf. Pr. *burel* brownish-red), alteration of L. *burrus* fiery-red – Gr. *purrhós* red, f. *pur-, pûr* FIRE. So **bureaucracy** bjuərɔ·krəsi, bjuərou·krəsi XIX. – F. *bureaucratie* (Gournay, d. 1759).

burg bəːɹg (hist.) fortress, walled town XVIII; (U.S. sl.) town, city XIX. – (i) medL. *burgus*; (ii) G. *burg*; see BOROUGH.

burgage bəː·ɹgidʒ †freehold property in a borough XIV (PPl.); tenure whereby lands in a town were held of the king or other lord XVI. – medL. *burgāgium*, f. *burgus* BOROUGH; see -AGE.

burgee bəːɹdʒī· (naut.) small three-cornered flag, yacht flag. XVIII. perh. for **burgee's flag*, i.e. owner's flag; – F. *bourgeois* (see BURGESS) in the sense of 'master', 'owner' (cf. '*Le Bougeois d'un navire*, the owner of a ship', Cotgr., and occas. †*burgees caution*, equiv. to F. *caution bourgeoise*).

burgeon bəː·ɹdʒən (arch.) bud. XIII (Cursor M.). – OF. *bor-, burjon* (mod. *bourgeon*) :– Rom. **burriōnem*, f. late L. *burra* wool (whence F. *bourre* tag-wool, flock-wool, or long-haired stuff, down covering buds, Pr., Sp., It. *borra*). So **bu·rgeon** vb. bud. XIV. – (O)F. *bourgeonner*.

burgess bəː·ɹdʒis inhabitant of a borough XIII; parliamentary representative XV. ME.

burgeis, burges, borges – OF. *burgeis* :– Rom. **burgensis*, f. late L. *burgus* BOROUGH + -*ensis* (cf. -ESE), after **pagensis*, f. *pagānus* PAGAN.

burg(g)rave bə̄·ɹgreiv hereditary ruler of a town in Germany. XVI. – G. *burggraf*, f. *burg* BOROUGH + *graf* (OHG. *grav(i)o*) count.

burgh bʌ·rə Sc. form of BOROUGH since XIV, var. of *burch* XIV (Barbour); there is a local variant *bruch* (cf. BROCH), *brugh*; early exx. are in place-names, e.g. *Edenesburg, Rokesburgh* (XII).

burgher bə̄·ɹgəɹ citizen. XVI. – G. or Du. *burger*, f. *burg* BOROUGH. Cf. BURGOMASTER.

burglar bə̄·ɹgləɹ one who feloniously breaks into a house, spec. at night. XV (implied in adv. *burgular[l]ie*, after AL. *burgulāriter*). – legal AN. *burgler* = AL. *burg(u)lātor* (XII), varying with AN. *burge(y)sour, -issour*, and AL. *burgātor, -isor*, with corr. vb. AL. *burg(u)lāre* and noun of action AN. *burglarie* (whence **bu·rglary** XVI; see -Y[3]); these appear to be all derivs. of a base **burg*-, which is repr. in its simple form by OF. *burgier* pillage, plunder, agent-noun *burgur* (coupled with *larron* robber), whence rare ME. *burgur* (XIII), beside AL. *burgāria, -ēria, -ātio* burglary. Hence **burglar**IOUS -ɛə·riəs. XVIII (Blackstone). **bu·rgle** vb. XIX; joc. back-formation.

burgomaster bə̄·ɹgəmàstəɹ chief magistrate of a Dutch or Flemish town. XVI (also *burg(h)m-, bourgm-* XVI, *burghermaster* XVII–XVIII). – Du. *burgemeester*, f. *burg* BOROUGH, with assim. to MASTER. (Cf. G. *bürgermeister*, earlier *bürgem-*, Da. *borgermester*, Sw. *borgemästere* – MLG. *borge(r)mēster*; F. *bourgmestre*, †*bourgamaistre*.)

burgonet bə̄·ɹgənet light casque. XVI. – F. *bourguignotte*, perh. fem. of *bourguignot* Burgundian, f. *Bourgogne* Burgundy; with ending assim. to -ET.

burgoo bəɹgū· thick oatmeal gruel. XVIII (also *burgle*). – Arab. *burghul* (recorded as *burgu, borgu* in XVII) – Pers. ('bruised grain').

burgundy bə̄·ɹgəndi kind of (usu. red) wine of *Burgundy*, ancient province (formerly, kingdom and duchy) of eastern France. XVII. – medL. *Burgundia* (whence F. *Bourgogne*), f. (late) L. *Burgundiī, -iōnes* (in OE. *Burgendas*) tribe extending from the Main to the Vistula; see -Y[3].

burial be·riəl †grave XIII; interment XV. ME. *buriel, biriel*, spurious sg. of *buriels*, OE. *byrġels* = OS. *burgisli* :– Germ. **burgisli*-, f. **burg*- (see BURY) + *-*isli*-, as in OE. *græfels* quarry (f. *grafan* dig), *rǣdels* RIDDLE; the ending has been assim. to -AL[2].

burin bjuə·rin graving-tool. XVII (Evelyn). – F. *burin*, rel. to It. *burino* (*bulino*), which has been referred to OHG. *boro* auger (see BORE[1]).

burke bəɹk suffocate, stifle; 'smother', hush up. XIX. f. name of William *Burke*, executed at Edinburgh in 1829 for smothering people in order to sell their bodies for dissection.

burl bə̄ɹl dress (cloth) by removing knots and lumps. XV (Cath. Angl.). f. *burl* sb. knot or lump in cloth or wool – OF. *bourle* tuft of wool, corr. to Sp., Pg. *borla* tuft, tassel, dim. f. (O)F. *bourre*, Sp., Pg. *borra* coarse wool :– late L. *burra* wool.

burlesque bəɹle·sk †droll; derisively imitative; sb. burlesque composition. XVII. – F. *burlesque* – It. *burlesco*, f. *burla* ridicule, joke, fun = Cat., Sp., Pg. *burla*, of unkn. origin; see -ESQUE.

burly bə̄·ɹli †comely, imposing, stately XIII (Bestiary, Cursor M.), hence as a conventional epithet in ME. 'noble'; massively built, corpulent XIV. ME. *borli, burli, -lich*, Sc. *buyrli*, prob. :– OE. **būrlić* 'fit for the bower' = OHG. *būrlīh* exalted, lofty, excellent, stately; see BOWER[1], -LY[1]. The word with first el. unchanged is recorded as *bowerly* from XVI and survives dial.

burn[1] bəɹn stream, brook. OE. *burna* wk. m., *burne* wk. fem., *burn* str. fem., corr. to OFris. *burna*, MLG. *borne, born*, MDu. *borne* (Du. *born*), G. *born*, repr. a metathetic form of Germ. **brunnon*, **brunnaz*, appearing as OS., OHG. *brunno* (Du. *bron*, G. *brunne*), ON. *brunnr*, Goth. *brunna*; of unkn. origin.

burn[2] bəɹn pt., pp. **burned, burnt** A. be on fire. B. consume with fire. In meaning repr. two OE. verbs, viz. (i) an intr. str. vb. *birnan, beornan*, pt. *barn, born, burnon*, pp. *burnen*, (ii) a trans. wk. vb. *bærnan*, pt. *bærnde*, which became obs. in early ME., so that in form *burn* repr. only the intr. vb. Both verbs contain metathesized forms of the Germ. **bren*- **bran*- (**brun*- is repr. by OE. *bryne* burning); OE. *birnan*, var. of *brinnan* = OS., OHG. *brinnan*, Goth. *brinnan*, pt. *brann, brunnum*, pp. *brunnans*; OE. *bærnan* = OS., OHG. *brennan* (G. *brennen* trans. and intr.), ON. *brenna* (intr. and trans.), Goth. *brannjan*, pt. *brannida*, pp. *brannips*. (Similar phonetic conditions are found in RUN[1].) Connexions have been sought with MIr. *bruinnim* bubble forth, L. *fervēre* boil (cf. FERMENT), and BRAN. Hence **burn** sb. XVI.

burnet bə̄·ɹnit gen. name for plants of the genera Sanguisorba and Poterium. XIV. sb. use of ME. *burnet* (XII) dark-brown – OF. *burnete* BRUNETTE, with ref. to the brownish-red colour of the flowers.

burnish bə̄·ɹniʃ polish (metal) by friction. XIV. f. *burniss*-, lengthened stem (see -ISH[2]) of OF. *burnir* (= Pr. *bornir*), var. of *brunir*, f. *brun* BROWN. ¶ ME. *burn* burnish, immed. – OF. *burnir*, occurs in Ch., Gower, and Lydg.

burnous, burnouse bəɹnū·s, -nū·z hooded mantle worn by Arabs. XVII. – F. *burnous*

– Arab. *burnus* – Gr. *bírros*. Sp., Pg. *albornoz*.

burr[1] bɜ̄ɹ A. broad ring on a spear XVI; washer for a rivet, etc. XVII; B. disk round the moon XVII. var. of *burrow* (as †*fur* of *furrow*), which is recorded in XV as a gloss on L. *orbiculus*, and in sense B, in the latter sense varying with *brough*.

burr[2] bɜ̄ɹ uvular pronunciation of r, characteristic of Northumberland. XVIII ('with the Newcastle bur in her throat'); rough whirring sound XIX. prob. imit., but perh. transf. application of BUR to a 'rough' sound.

burrow bʌ·rou rabbit's, fox's (etc.) hole. XIII (Laȝ.). Late ME. *borwȝ*, *borow*, prob. var. of BOROUGH in the sense of 'fortified or inhabited place'. Hence **bu·rrow** vb. make a burrow XVIII; fig. XIX.

bursa bɜ̄·ɹsə (path.) synovial sac. XIX. – medL. *bursa* bag, PURSE – Gr. *búrsa*.

bursar bɜ̄·ɹsəɹ A. treasurer XIII; B. (Sc.) endowed student, exhibitioner XVI. In A – medL. *bursārius*, f. *bursa* PURSE; in B – F. *boursier*, f. *bourse* PURSE; see -AR. So **bu·rsary** treasury, bursar's office XVI; student's endowment XVIII. – medL. *bursāria*; see -ARY, -ERY.

burse bɜ̄ɹs (eccl.) case to contain the corporal. XIX. – medL. *bursa* PURSE – Gr. *búrsā*. ¶ Formerly used for 'exchange', 'bourse', and 'bursary', 'scholarship' XVI–XVIII.

burst bɜ̄ɹst break or be broken suddenly. OE. *berstan*, pt. *bærst*, *burston*, pp. *borsten* = OFris. *bersta*, OS., OHG. *brestan* (Du. *bersten*, *barsten*; G. *bersten* from LG.), ON. *bresta*, pt. *brast*, *brustum*, pp. *brostinn* :– CGerm. (exc. Goth.) **brestan*; IE. **bhrest-* is repr. also in OIr. *brissim* I break, Gael. *bris*. In the LG. and Anglo-Fris. areas the metathesized forms are typical, but in ME. there was much mixture of types aggravated by ON. influence. The form **burst** for all parts prevailed by the end of XVI (e.g. in Sh.). Hence **burst** sb. act of bursting. XVII (Sh.). Distinct from ME. *bürst*, *byrst*, *berst* :– OE. *byrst* damage, injury = OHG. *brust* :– Germ. **brustiz*, rel. to **brestan*.

burthen var. of BURDEN.

burton bə·ɹtn (naut.) tackle block used to tighten rigging. XV. orig. in *Breton* or *Brytton takles* ('Naval Accounts', 1495); presumably a use of BRETON.

bury be·ri put underground. OE. *byrgan* (ME. *bürie*, *birie*, *berie*) :– WGerm. **burʒjan* (cf. BURIAL), f. **burg-* **berg-*, base of OE. *beorgan* shelter, protect (see BORROW). ¶ The retention of southern and western sp. with *u* together with the south-easterly pronunc. e is unique; contrast *busy*.

bus, 'bus bʌs. XIX (*buss*, Harriet Martineau). Short for OMNIBUS.

busby bʌ·zbi †large bushy wig XVIII; tall fur cap of hussars, etc. XIX. Of unkn. origin; cf., however, *buzz wig* (XVIII–XIX), and the local use of *buzz* for various hairy or downy objects. ¶ Connexion cannot be assumed with the surname *Busby*, borne e.g. by the famous headmaster of Westminster School, who died 1695.

bush[1] buʃ shrub, esp. one with close foliage near to ground XIII; branch of ivy as vintner's sign XVI. Early forms are *busse*, *busshe*, also *boysche*, *boisshe*, *buysche*, pointing to an OE. **byść*, which has been dubiously assumed for the place-name *Bushey*; beside this, in northern and eastern areas there was a form *busk* (from XIII) – ON. *buski*, which survives in north. dial., with the Sc. by-form *bus*. There were also ME. forms with *-o-*, viz. *bosk* (from XIII), surviving dial. (cf. BOSKY), beside *bosh*, *bossche* (XIV–XV); these were perh. – OF. *bos*, *bosc*, vars. of *bois* wood. The ult. basis is Germ. **busk-*, repr. by OS. *busc* (Du. *bos*, MDu. *bosch*, *busch*), OHG. *busc* (G. *busch*), which was taken into Gallo-Rom. (Pr. *bosc*, whence It. *bosco*).

As applied to wooded or uncleared land in British colonies (from XVIII), prob. originating in S. Africa and derived immed. from Du. *bosch* (which has also been used). So **bu·sh**MAN, (i) after Afrikaans *bos(ch)jeman* native, one of a tribe of aborigines in S. Africa (*boshees-men* XVIII), (ii) dweller in the Australian bush.

bush[2] buʃ metal lining of a hole, etc. XV. – MDu. *busse* (Du. *bus*) bush of a wheel (see BOX[2], and cf. G. *büchse*, *rad|büchse*, Sw. *hjul|bössa* 'wheel-box'); for the form with *-sh* cf. the earlier forms of *blunderbuss*, *harquebus*. Hence **bush** vb. XVI.

bushel bu·ʃl dry measure of capacity. XIV. – OF. *buissiel*, *boissiel* (mod. *boisseau*) = Pr. *boissel*; perh. of Gaulish origin (cf. Celtic-derived BIN). ¶ For the repr. of F. *ss* by *sh* cf. -ISH[2], and *crush*, *cushion*, *leash*, *parish*, *usher*.

bushido bū·ʃidou in feudal Japan, the ethical code of the Samurai. XIX. Jap., 'military-knight-ways'.

business bi·znis †solicitude OE.; †industry, diligence XIII; occupation, pursuit XIV; affair XVI. OE. *bisignis* (late Nhb., once), f. *bisiġ* BUSY + -NESS. The disyll. pronunc. is shown in the sp. *bus'ness* (Wither, 1634), *buis'ness* (Dryden, 1697).

busk[1] bʌsk (arch., dial.) prepare. XIII (Cursor M.). – ON. *búask*, refl. of *búa* prepare (see BOUND[1]); for the ending cf. *bask*.

busk[2] bʌsk strip of rigid material in a corset to stiffen it. XVI. – F. *busc* – It. *busco* splinter, rel. to OF. *busche* (mod. *bûche*) log – Germ. **būsk-* piece of wood.

buskin bʌ·skin half-boot; high thick-soled boot (*cothurnus*) worn in Attic tragedy. XVI.

prob. – late OF. *bouzequin*, var. of *bro(u)sequin* (mod. *brodequin*), corr. to Cat., Sp. *borceguí*, Pg. *borzeguim*, It. *borzacchino*; of much disputed origin.

buss[1] bʌs †freight-vessel XIV; vessel of the kind used in the Du. herring-fishery XV. orig. – OF. *busse, buce*, later influenced by MDu. *buisse* (mod. *buis*), parallel to which are OHG. *būzo* (MHG. *būze*), MLG. *butze*, OE. *būtse* in *būtsecarlas* sailors, ON. *búza*, medL. *bucia*; the origin is unkn.

buss[2] bʌs (arch., dial.) sb. and vb. kiss. XVI. poss. alteration of earlier †*bass* (XV). ¶ The similar Sp. *buz* kiss of respect (– Arab. *būs*) and G. *buss, butsch* are unconnected.

bust[1] bʌst sculpture representing head, shoulders, and breast XVII; female bosom XVIII. – F. *buste* – It. *busto* (= Sp. *busto*); the Rom. word is of unkn. origin. (Used earlier in It. form XVII.)

bust[2] bʌst vulgar and dial. pronunc. of BURST (cf. *cussed* cursed, *fust* first, *nuss* nurse). XVIII.

bustard bʌ·stəɹd bird of the genus Otis. XV (earlier as a surname). perh. – AN. **bustarde*, blending of OF. *bistarde* and *oustarde* (mod. *outarde*) = Pr. *austarda*, Sp. *ave-*, *avutarda*, Pg. *(a)betarda* :– L. *avis tarda* 'slow bird', given by Pliny as Sp.; but the bustard is a swift bird, and the L. term may be a perversion of a foreign word.

bustle[1] bʌ·sl bestir oneself busily. XVI. perh. alteration of †*buskle*, frequent. of BUSK[1]; see -LE. Not certainly identical with ME. *bustele* (XIV) wander blunderingly (cf. BLUSTER).

bustle[2] bʌ·sl frame or pad thrusting out a woman's skirt behind. XVIII. Of unkn. origin.

busy bi·zi constantly or fully occupied OE.; curiously or officiously active XIV (cf. *busybody*, Tindale); marked by activity XVI. OE. *bisiġ*, later *bysiġ* (ME. *büsi, besy, bisy*) = MLG., MDu. *besich* (Du. *bezig*), of unkn. origin. For the retention of southern and western sp. with *u* along with the pronunc. i cf. BUILD; contrast BURY.

but bʌt, bət adv. outside (surviving dial., as in *but and ben*); prep. (dial.) outside; except; unless, if . . not OE.; adversative conj. XIII. OE. *būtan* (*beūtan, būton, būta, būte*) = OS. *biūtan, būtan*, OHG. *biūʒan* (MG. *būʒen*); WGerm. comp. of **be*, **bi* BY and **ūtana* from without (see OUT). The OE. form was continued as ME. *būte, boute, bout* in stressed positions; unstressed the prep. and conj. became *bŭte, but*.

butcher bu·tʃəɹ slaughterer of animals for the market, dealer in meat. XIII. ME. *bocher, boucher* – AN. var. of OF. *bo(u)chier* (mod. *boucher*) = Pr. *bochier*; f. OF., Pr. *boc* (F. *bouc*) he-goat, prob. – OCelt. **bukkos* (cf. OIr. *bocc*, Ir., Gael. *boc*, W. *bwch*); see BUCK[1], -ER[4]. For the sense-development cf. It. *beccaio* butcher, f. *becco* he-goat. Hence **bu·tcher** vb. slaughter (brutally). XVI. So **bu·tchERY** slaughter-house, butcher's shop XIV; butcher's trade XV; (brutal) slaughter XVI. – (O)F. *boucherie*.

butler bʌ·tləɹ servant having charge of the wine-cellar. XIII. – AN. *buteler*, OF. *bouteillier*, f. *bouteille* BOTTLE[1]; see -ER[4].

butt[1] bʌt intr. strike, thrust XII (Orm); trans. XVI. – AN. *buter*, OF. *boter* (mod. dial. *bouter* put) – Germ. **buttan*, repr. by MDu. *botten* strike, sprout (cf. BUTTON). The vb.-stem is used advb. with a vb. of motion, esp. with *full* adv., to express head-on meeting or violent collision (XIV); cf. OF. *de plein bout*.

butt[2] bʌt ridge between furrows, strip of land. XIII (in local designations, as *Shorte* and *Long Buttes, Suthebuttes*). perh. repr. OE. **butt* (whence BUTTOCK), in AL. *butta, buttis* (XII), rel. to LG. *butt*, MDu. *botte*, MHG. *butze*, ON. *butr*, and OE. *bytt* small piece of land.

butt[3] bʌt (locally) applied to various flat-fish. XIII (Havelok). – MLG. *but*, MDu. *but(te), bot(te)*, whence also G. *butt, butte*, Sw. *butta* turbot, Da. *bot* flounder; prob. rel. to LG. *but*, MDu. *bot* stumpy. Cf. HALIBUT.

butt[4] bʌt mark for archery practice (orig. embankment holding targets) XIV; †goal, object XVI; target for ridicule, etc. XVII. prob. – (O)F. *but*, of unkn. origin; perh. infl. by F. *butte* rising ground, knoll, (also) target.

butt[5] bʌt cask for wine, etc. XIV. In AL. *butta* (XIII), *bota* (XIV) – AN. *but* (e.g. *but de malmesie*, 1483), var. of OF. *bot, bout* = Pr. *bot*, Sp. *bote*, It. *botte* (whence F. *botte* butt) :– late L. *buttis*, perh. based on Gr. *būtínē*, var. of *pūtínē* osier-covered flask. (Cf. BOTTLE.)

butt[6] bʌt thicker end of a thing; (dial.) buttock XV; base of a tree trunk XVII. rel. to the base of which BUTTOCK seems to be a deriv. and which is repr. by words meaning 'short and stumpy', as Du. *bot* (BUTT[3]).

butte bʌt, (earlier) bjūt (U.S.) isolated hill or peak. XIX. – F. *butte* (cf. BUTT[4]).

butter bʌ·təɹ fatty substance obtained from cream. OE. *butere*, corr. to OFris., OHG. *butera* (Du. *boter*, G. *butter*); CWGerm. – L. *būtȳrum* (Celsus, Pliny) – Gr. *boútūron*, prob. of alien origin. The L. word is repr. in Rom. by OF. *burre* (mod. *beurre*), Pr. *buire*, It. *butirro*.

butterbump bʌ·təɹbʌmp (dial.) bittern. XVII. f. *butter*, var. of BITTERN + BUMP[2].

buttercup bʌ·təɹkʌp yellow-flowered ranunculus. XVII (Ray; in early use *-cups*). prob. blending of †*butterflower* (XVI, after Du. *boterbloeme*) with *goldcup* or *kingcup*.

butterfly bʌ·təɹflai diurnal erect-winged insect. Late OE. *buttorflēoġe*, f. BUTTER+FLY[1]; cf. Du. *botervlieg* (earlier *-vlieghe*), G. *butterfliege* and *buttervogel* (-bird). The reason for the name is unkn.; an early Du. syn. *boterschijte* suggests an allusion to the colour of its excrement; on the other hand, allusion to milk (or whey) is seen in the G. names *milchdieb, molkendieb* 'milk-', 'whey-thief'.

buttersco·tch kind of toffee. XIX (dial. *-scot*); perh. orig. of *Scotch* manufacture.

buttery bʌ·təri (orig.) store-room for liquor, (hence) for provisions in general. XIV (*boteri*). – AN. *boterie, *buterie* (AL. *buteria* XIII, *butria* XV), prob. f. *but* BUTT[5]; see -ERY. An earlier term was †*botelery* (XIII) – OF. *butelerie, bouteillerie*, f. *bouteille* BOTTLE.

buttock bʌ·tək (chiefly pl.) rump. XIII. Formally identical with OE. *buttuc* (once) prob. end ridge of land, rounded slope, dim. of **butt*; see BUTT[2], -OCK.

button bʌ·tn small knob or stud used as a fastening or for ornament; bud, (later) young mushroom. XIV. – (O)F. *bouton* (whence Sp. *boton*, Pg. *botão*, It. *bottone*) :- Rom. **bottōne*, rel. to **bottāre* thrust, put forth (see BUTT[1]). *Button-hole* hole through which a button passes XVI; as vb. detain (a person) in conversation, superseding *button-hold* take hold of by a button (XIX), which was a back-formation from *button-holder*. Hence **bu·tton** vb. XIV (in pp. *ibotened*; cf. AL. *botonātus* XIV).

buttress bʌ·tris structure built against a wall to support it. XIII (Sir Orfeo). ME. *butras, -es, boterace, -as* (cf. AL. *boteracium* XIII) – OF. *bouterez*, short for *ars bouterez* 'thrusting arch' (cf. F. *arc-boutant*), inflexional form of *bouteret*, f. *bouter* BUTT[1]; the ending was assim. first to *-ace*, and thence in XVI to *-ess*.

butty bʌ·ti (dial.) confederate, partner, mate; middleman in mining. XIX. prob. evolved from the phr. *play* BOOTY (XVI) join with confederates to share 'plunder' with them.

butyric bjuti·rik pert. to butter. XIX. f. L. *būtȳrum* BUTTER+-IC. So **butyra·ceous**. XVII.

buxom bʌ·ksəm †obedient, compliant XII; †flexible; †blithe, gay; plump and comely XVI. ME. *buhsum, ibucsum, buxum, bowsom*, repr. OE. **(ġe)būhsum*, f. (*ġe*)*būgan* bend, BOW[2]+SOME; cf. MDu. *būchsam* (Du. *buigzaam*), G. *biegsam* pliant.

buy bai **bought** bōt pt., pp. get possession of by giving an equivalent (in money) OE.; †redeem, ransom XII; †expiate XIII. OE. *byċġan*, pt. *bohte*, pp. *ġeboht*=OS. *buggian*, pp. *giboht*, ON. *byggja*, pt. *bygða* let out, lend, Goth. *bugjan*, pt. *baúhta*, pp. *-bauhts*; CGerm. (exc. HG.) wk. vb., of unkn. origin. OE. pres. ind. *byċġe, byġest, byġeþ*, pl. *byċġaþ*, pres. subj. *byċġe, byċġen*, imper. *byġe, byċġaþ*, were repr. by typical ME. forms thus: pres. *bügge, bigge, begge, büȝeþ, buyeþ, biȝeþ, beȝeþ*, pl. *büggeþ, biggeþ, beggeþ*; the existing present-stem form was generalized (in the north, as *bi-*, before 1300) from the 2nd and 3rd pres. ind. and imper. sg.; the sp. *buy* repr. the southern and western type, the pronunc. a midland and northern type; cf. BUILD, BUSY.

buzz[1] bʌz make a sibilant humming sound. XVI. Earlier *busse* (XIV); hence as sb. XVII; of imit. origin.

buzz[2] bʌz epithet of a large bushy wig. XVIII. abbrev. of BUSBY; cf. the name of Serjeant *Buz*fuz in Dickens's 'Pickwick Papers'.

buzzard bʌ·zəɹd inferior kind of hawk, genus Buteo XIII; fig. stupid person XIV (PPl.). – (O)F. *busard* (whence also Du. *buizert*, G. *bussard*), corr. to Pr. *buzart*, It. *bozzagro, abuzzago*, based like OF. *buson* (whence F. *buse*) on L. *būteō(n-)*, of unkn. origin; see -ARD.

by bai (dial. or arch. bi, as prep.) alongside; in the course of; according to; in relation to; marking the means or instrument (ult. superseding *from, through, of*) OE.; marking the agent (ult. superseding *of, from*) XIV. OE. *bī*, unstressed *bi, be* = OFris., OS., OHG. *bī, bi* (Du. *bij*, G. *bei*), Goth. *bi* :- CGerm. (exc. ON.) **bi*, prob. identical with the second syll. of Gr. *amphí*, L. *ambi-* (see AMBI-, AMPHI-), OE. *ymb(e)-* around. If the disyll. forms were the original, there seems to have been the same loss of the first syll. as in OE. *bā, bū*, beside Gr. *ámphō*, L. *ambō*, etc. BOTH. Cf. BE-, BEFORE, BEHIND, BESIDE, BETIMES, BY-, BY AND BY.

by- bai the adv. BY used attrib. and entering into composition with a sb. in the senses 'lying or situated at one side', 'out of the way', 'running alongside and apart', 'devious', as *by-path* (Ch.), *by-street* (Dryden), *by-way* (R. Mannyng), 'collateral', 'side-', as *by-play, by-product* (XIX), 'additional', 'subsidiary', as *by-name* (Ch.), *by-election, by-term*.

by-and-by bai·ən[d]bai· (adv. phr.) †one by one, in succession, on and on XIV; †straightway XV; shortly, before long XVI. prob. originating in the use of BY to denote succession, as in *by two and two, by little and little*, ME. *bi sixti and bi sixti*. For the development of the last sense cf. *anon, presently*, and F. *bientôt*.

bye bai †second or subsidiary object or course XVI; phr. *by the bye* (i) as a subsidiary matter XVII, (ii) 'by the way' XVIII. The usual sp. of *by* when used subst., but varying with *by*; ellipt. use of the adj. BY(E) meaning 'secondary', 'subsidiary', e.g. as opp. to *main* in dicing, referring to stake, throw, or chance, and in various sports.

bye-bye[1] bai·bai sounds to lull a child to sleep xv (*byby byby by*); (nursery colloq.) sleep xix. Cf. ON. *bí bí* and *bíum bíum*.

bye-bye[2] baibai·. xviii. colloq. and child's var. of GOOD-BYE.

bygone bai·gɔn past xv; sb. pl. things past; arrears xvi. orig. Sc., and, though used once by Sh., hardly naturalized in England before xviii. f. BY adv. 'past'+pp. of GO.

by-law, bye-law bai·lɔ̄ A. †local law or custom established by common consent xiii; B. ordinance regulating internal matters made by a local authority or corporation xiv. In A orig. varying with *birlaw* (xiii) – ON. **býjarlagu*, f. g. sg. of *býr* habitation, village, town (f. **bū-*; cf. BOWER)+ **lagu* LAW; in B alteration of this by substitution of *by* sb. town (preserved in Scand. place-names, as *Whitby*) and by assoc. with BY-. (*Birlaw*, with many vars., survived in Sc. and north. dial.)

byon bjoun ruby-bearing clay of Upper Burma. xix. – Burmese *brun* refuse of grain, matrix earth of rubies and rejected stones, app. rel. to *prun, phrun* be worn out or exhausted.

byre baiəɹ (dial.) cow-house. OE. *bȳre*, prob. :– **būrjom*, rel. to **būrom* BOWER[1].

byrnie bə̄·ɹni (arch.) coat of mail. xiv (Barbour). Sc. var. of ME. *brinie* (xii–xv) – ON. *brynja* = OE. *byrne*, OS. *brunnia*, OHG. *brunna* (G. *brünne*), Goth. *brunjō* :– CGerm. **brunjōn*, perh. of Celtic origin (cf. OIr. *bruinne*, OW., Bret. *bronn* breast). ¶ From Germ. were adopted OSl. *bronja*, OF. *broigne*, Pr. *bronha*.

byssus bi·səs fine textile fabric. xvii. L. – Gr. *býssos*, of Sem. origin (Heb. *būts*). Anglicized as *bysse* (xvi–xvii) esp. with ref. to Luke xvi 19 and earlier repr. by ME. *biis, bys* – OF. *bysse*.

byword bai·wə̄ɹd proverb xii (Peterborough Chron.); object of scorn xvi (Coverdale). Early ME. *biword*, preceded by late OE. *bīwyrde* = OHG. *pīwurti*, rendering L. *prōverbium*; see BY- and WORD.

Byzantine baizæ·ntain, bi·zəntain pert. to (inhabitant of) Byzantium or Constantinople (Istanbul) xviii (earlier *Byzantian* xvii); bezant xvi. – F. *byzantin* or L. *Bȳzantīnus*; see -INE[1] and cf. BEZANT.

C

Caaba kā·əbə sacred edifice at Mecca, Holy of Holies of Islam. xviii (earlier *Alcaaba* xvii). – Arab. *ka'bah* square or cubical house.

cab[1] kæb Heb. dry measure. xvi. – Heb. *qab* (prop.) vessel, f. *qabab* hollow out.

cab[2] kæb. xix. Shortening of CABRIOLET. Hence **ca·bby** cab-driver; see -Y[6].

cabal kəbæ·l †cabbala; private intrigue; junta, clique. xvii. – F. *cabale* – medL. *cab(b)ala* (It., Sp. *cabala*); see CABBALA. (Applied in the reign of Charles II to the Committee for Foreign Affairs, and hence applied (1673) to the junta consisting of Clifford, Arlington, Buckingham, Ashley, and Lauderdale, the initials of whose names so arranged chanced to spell the word.) Hence **caba·l** vb. conduct an intrigue xvii; cf. F. *cabaler*. ¶ A widespread Eur. word.

caballero kæbalʲɛə·rou Spanish gentleman. xix. Sp., = F. *chevalier*, It. *cavaliere* CAVALIER.

caballine kəbæ·lain pert. to horses; mainly in *Caballine fountain* the Hippocrene of Greek poetry, and *caballine aloes*, which is given to horses. xv. – L. *caballīnus*, f. *caballus*; see CAVALCADE, -INE[1].

cabaret kæ·bərei French tavern. xvii. – (O)F., prob. of Walloon origin and orig. denoting a structure of wood.

cabbage[1] kæ·bidʒ green vegetable with a round heart. xiv. Earliest forms *cabache, -oche* – (O)F. *caboche* head, Picard var. of OF. *caboce*, of unkn. origin. For the development of the final cons. cf. *knowledge, partridge, sausage, spinach*, and *Greenwich* gri·nidʒ, *Harwich* hæ·ridʒ, *Woolwich* wu·lidʒ. ¶ The Germ. word is COLE.

cabbage[2] kæ·bidʒ shreds of cloth cut off by tailors and kept as a perquisite. xvii. Of unkn. origin. (Herrick has *carbage* and *garbage* in the same sense, 1648.) Hence **ca·bbage** vb. pilfer, crib. xviii. (Strikingly similar forms are OF. *cabas* deceit, theft, Du. *kabassen* pilfer.)

cabbala kæ·bələ oral tradition handed down from Moses to the Rabbis; tradition of mystical interpretation of the O.T. xvi. – medL. *cabbala* – Rabbinical Heb. *qabbālāh* tradition, f. *qibbēl* receive, accept, admit. Hence **ca·bbal**IST, **cabbal**I·STICAL.

caber kei·bəɹ (Sc.) pole, spar. xvi. – Gael. *cabar* = Ir. *cabar*, W. *ceibr* beam, rafter.

cabin kæ·bin †hut, tent, booth; †cell; †cave, den; compartment in a ship xiv; rude habitation xv; †political cabinet (only xvii). Late ME. *cabane* – (O)F. *cabane* – Pr. *cabana* = It. *capanna*, Sp. *cabaña* – late L. *capanna* (according to Isidore, a rustic word), *cavanna*; spellings with *-in* appear xvi.

cabinet kæ·binĭt †cabin, hut, lodging; †small chamber, boudoir; †room for exhibiting works of art, etc.; case with compartments for keeping valuables xvi; †council room (cf. F. *cabinet du roi* king's private room); body of councillors (orig.

cabinet council) XVII. Early forms *cabanet, cab(b)onet*, f. *cabane, cabon*, CABIN, after F. *cabinet* (XVI), occas. †*gabinet* – It. *gabbinetto*, perh. dim. of *gabbia* :– L. *cavea* CAGE; see -ET.

cable kei·bl strong thick rope for towing, etc. XIII (Laȝ.). – AN., ONF. **cable*, var. of OF. *chable* (mod. *câble* – Pr. *cable* = Cat., Sp. *cable*, Pg. *cabo*, It. *cappio*) :– late L. *cap(u)lum* halter – Arab. *ḥabl*, assoc. with L. *capere* seize, hold (cf. HEAVE); perh., however, immed. – Pr. *cable*, and in any case reinforced by (M)LG., (M)Du. *kabel* (whence G. *kabel*, Icel. *kabill*), of Rom. origin. Applied *c.* 1850 to a rope-like line used for submarine telegraphy; hence **cable** vb. send a message by cable; **ca·blegram** message so sent (1868, New York), formed by superficial analogy with *telegram*.

cabob kəbɔ·b Oriental meat-dish. XVII. – Urdu (Pers.) – Arab. *kabāb*.

caboceer kæbosiə·ɹ headman of a W. African tribe. XIX. – Pg. *cabociero*, f. *cabo* head :– L. *caput* HEAD; cf. -EER[1].

caboched kəbɔ·ʃt (her.) borne full-faced and cut off just behind the ears. XVI. – F. *caboché* (see -ED), pp. of *cabocher* decapitate just behind the ears, f. *caboche* head, var. of OF. *caboce*, of unkn. origin.

cabochon kabɔʃɔ̃ convex precious stone polished and not cut. XVI. – (O)F. *cabochon*, dim. of *caboche* (see prec.).

caboodle kəbū·dl (orig. U.S.) often *whole caboodle* whole lot; varying with *whole kit and* BOODLE, of which it may be a contraction. XIX.

caboose kəbū·s cook-house of a ship. XVIII. – early modDu. *cabūse*, var. *combūse* (now *kabuis, kombuis*) = (M)LG. *kabūse*, of unkn. origin, whence also G. *kabuse, kombüse*, Sw. *kabysa*, Da. *kabys*, F. *cambuse*.

cabotage kæ·bŏtidʒ coasting trade. XIX. – F. *cabotage*, f. *caboter* coast along, perh. f. †*cabo* (XVI) – Sp. *cabo* CAPE[2].

cabriole kæ·brioul curved leg in Queen Anne and Chippendale furniture, its form suggesting a quadruped's front leg in a caper. XVIII. – F. *cabriole*, f. *cabrioler*; see next.

cabriolet kæ:bri̯ŏlei· (hist.) light two-wheeled one-horse vehicle. XVIII. – F. *cabriolet*, f. *cabrioler*, later form of *caprioler* – It. *capriolare* leap into the air, f. *capriola* CAPRIOLE; see -ET; so named from its springiness. Cf. CAB[2].

ca'canny kākæ·ni 'going slow' at work. XIX. f. Sc. and north. Eng. phr. *ca' canny* (i.e. CALL vb., in Sc. from XIV 'drive', CANNY used adv. 'warily') drive cautiously, go warily or carefully.

cacao kəkei·ou, kəkā·ou seed from which cocoa is prepared. XVI. – Sp. *cacao* – Nahuatl *cacauatl* (*uatl* tree). See also COCOA.

cachalot kæ·ʃələt sperm-whale having an enormous head. XVIII. – F. *cachalot* – Sp., Pg. *cachalote*, of unkn. origin. ¶ The word has become CEur.

cache kæʃ hiding-place; secret hoard XIX. – F. *cache*, f. *cacher* hide (see next).

cachet kæ·ʃei (Sc.) seal XVII; stamp, mark XIX. – F. *cachet*, f. *cacher* (in the sense of 'press' repr. now in *écacher* crush) :– Rom. **coacticāre*, for L. *coactāre* constrain, f. *coact-*, pp. stem of *cōgere* compel, f. *co-* CON- + *agere* drive (see ACT).

cachexy kæke·ksi, kæ·keksi depraved condition or habit. XVI. – F. *cachexie* or late L. *cachexia* – Gr. *kakhexíā*, f. *kakós* bad + *-hexíā* = *héxis* habit, state, f. *ékhein* have, be (in a certain state). So **cache·ctic**. XVII. ult. – Gr. *kakhektikós*, through F. or L. *cachecticus* (Pliny).

cachinnation kækinei·ʃən immoderate laughter. XVII. – L. *cachinnātiō(n-)*, f. *cachinnāre*, of imit. origin, whence **ca·chinnate** vb. XIX. See -ATE[3], -ATION.

cachou kæ·ʃū †CATECHU XVIII; sweetmeat for sweetening the breath XIX. – F. *cachou* – Pg. †*cacho, cachu* – Malay *kāchu*.

cacique kəsī·k chief in the W. Indies. XVI. – Sp. *cacique, cazique*, of Carib origin; so in F.

cack kæk (dial.) void excrement. XV. prob. – MLG., MDu. *cacken* (Du. *kakken*), corr. to G. *kacken*, etc. – L. *cacāre* (whence F. *chier*, Pr., etc. *cagar*), f. IE. **kak-* (cf. Gr. *kakkân*, Czech *kakati*, Ir. *cacaim*; Icel. shows another vowel in *kúka* vb., *kúkr* sb.).

cackle kæ·kl make a noise as a hen. XIII. prob. CLG., though unrecorded in OE.; otherwise prob. – (M)LG., (M)Du. *kākelen* (whence Sw. *kackla*, Da. *kagle*), of imit. origin, but partly f. *kāke* jaw (CHEEK). See -LE[3].

caco- kæ·kou, kĕkɔ· repr. Gr. *kako-* stem of *kakós* bad, as in **ca·cochymy** XVI (F. *cacochymie*, Gr. *kakokhūmíā*) unhealthy state of the 'humours', **caco**DÆ·MON XVI (Gr. *kakodaímōn*) evil spirit, CACOETHES, **caco**·GRAPHY XVI (F. *cacographie*, medGr. *kakographía*) bad writing or spelling, **caco**·PHONY XVI (F. *cacophonie*, Gr. *kakophōníā*) discordant sound.

cacoethes kækouī·þiz evil habit. XVI. – L. *cacoēthes* – Gr. *kakóēthes*, sb. use of n. of *kakoḗthēs* ill-disposed, f. *kakós* bad + *êthos* disposition, character, ETHOS. Its currency is due mainly to Juvenal's *insanabile scribendi cacoethes* incurable itch for writing ('Satires' vii 52).

cacomistle kæ·komisl animal (Bassariscus) of the bear tribe, allied to the raccoon. XIX. – Sp. *cacomixtle, -miztle* – Nahuatl *tlacomiztli*.

cactus kæ·ktəs †cardoon XVII; prickly plant with thick fleshy stems XVIII. – L. *cactus*

– Gr. *káktos* cardoon or Spanish artichoke (of Sicily); the name was adopted by Linnæus for a genus of entirely different prickly plants.

cacuminal kǽkjū·minəl (phon.) articulated with the point of the tongue turned upwards and backwards. XIX. f. L. *cacūmin-*, *-men* summit; see -AL.

cad kæd †unbooked passenger on a coach; †assistant to coachman or waggoner XVIII; †omnibus conductor (Hood, Dickens, Thackeray); †confederate, familiar; (dial.) youngest of a litter; (dial.) odd-job man; †townsman)(collegian; ill-bred fellow XIX. Shortening of *cad(d)ee*, CADDIE.

cadastre kədæ·stəɹ register of property, etc. XIX. – F. *cadastre* – modPr. *cadastro* – It. *catast(r)o*, earlier *catastico* – late Gr. *katástikhon* list, register, prop. *katà stíkhon* line by line (cf. CATA-, STICHIC). So **cada·stral**[1]. XIX. – F.

cadaver kədei·vəɹ dead body. XVI. – L. *cadāver*, prop. 'fallen thing', f. *cadere* fall (see CASE[1]); cf. Gr. *ptôma* fall, corpse.

cadaverous kədæ·vərəs corpse-like. XV. – L. *cadāverōsus*, f. *cadāver*; see prec. and -OUS.

caddie kæ·di †army cadet XVII; †errand boy, porter, commissionaire XVIII; golfer's attendant XIX. orig. Sc. (earliest form *caudie*) – F. *cadet*; see CADET[1]. The form *cadee* was in gen. use XVII–XVIII beside *cadet*. See CAD.

caddis kæ·dis larva of may-fly (used as angler's bait). XVII. contemp. with synon. (dial.) *cadbait*, *codbait*, *cadew*, of unkn. origin; identical in form with *caddis* wool, silk, etc. used as padding (XIV), worsted, serge (XVI) – (O)F. *cadis* serge – Pr. *cadis*, also of unkn. origin.

caddy kæ·di small box for holding tea. XVIII. unexpl. alteration of CATTY.

cade[1] keid cask, barrel. XIV. – L. *cadus* wine-jar, measure for liquids – Gr. *kádos* cask, jar, of Semitic origin (cf. Heb. *kad* pail).

cade[2] keid young of animal brought up by hand; pet lamb. XV (*kad*; *kod lomb*). Of unkn. origin.

cadence keidəns rhythm XIV (Ch.); fall of the voice; close of a musical phrase, etc. XVI. OF. **cadence* (first recorded XV). – It. *cadenza* – popL. **cadentia*, f. *cadent-*, prp. stem of *cadere* fall; see CASE[1] and cf. CHANCE. So **ca·dency** †cadence XVII; (her.) descent of a younger branch from the main line XVIII; see -Y[3]. **cadenza** kəde·nzə (mus.) flourish at a cadence. XIX. It. (see above).

cadet[1] kəde·t younger son, brother, or branch of family; gentleman in the army without a commission XVII; junior officer XVIII. – F. *cadet*, earlier *capdet* – Gascon dial. *capdet* (= Pr. *capdel*) :– Rom. **capitellu-s*, dim. of *capit-*, *caput* head, CHIEF; orig. applied to Gascon officers (younger sons of noble families) at the French court.

cadet[2] kəde·t (in Russian politics). XX. – Russ. *kadét*, pl. *kadétȳ*, fr. Russ. names of letters *KD* (initials of *Konstitutsiónnȳe Demokrátȳ* Constitutional Democrats) plus *-t* through assim. to CADET[1].

cadge kædʒ †carry (a pack) XVII; go about begging XIX. Origin obscure; connexion with ME. and dial. *cagge* fasten, tie, is improbable; perh. back-formation from **cadger** kæ·dʒəɹ orig. carrier, itinerant dealer XV (first in Sc.), of unkn. origin.

cadi kei·di, kā·di judge in Oriental countries. XVI. ult. – Arab. *qāḍī*, f. *qaḍā* judge. Also †*casi* (XVII), *kazi*, repr. the Pers. and Indian pronunc. Cf. F., Sp., Pg. *cadi*, G., etc. *kadi*, and see ALCALDE.

cadmium kæ·dmiəm (chem.) metallic element. XIX. f. †*cadmia* calamine (XVII) – L. *cadmīa* – Gr. *kadmeíā* or *kadmíā gê* Cadmean earth; see -IUM, CALAMINE.

cadre kādr frame, framework (Scott); permanent establishment of a regiment XIX. – F. – It. *quadro* :– L. *quadru-s* square (cf. QUADRATE).

caduceus kədjū·siəs wand borne by Hermes. XVI. L. *cādūcĕus* (also *-ĕum*) – Doric Gr. *kārúkeion*, *kārúkion* = Attic *kērúkeion*, sb. use of n. of adj., f. *kēruk-*, *kêrux* herald = Skr. *kārúś* singer, poet.

caducity kədjū·sĭti perishableness, frailty, infirmity. XVIII. – F. *caducité*, f. *caduque* – L. *cadūcus* (f. *cadere* fall), whence **caducous** kədjū·kəs †epileptic XVII; deciduous, fleeting, transitory XIX. (Cf. earlier †*caduke* XIV.)

cæcum sī·kəm (anat.) first part of the large intestine, which terminates in a cul-de-sac. XVIII. L., short for *intestinum cæcum* blind gut, tr. Gr. *tuphlòn énteron* (cf. TYPHLITIS); n. sg. of *cæcus* blind (see CECITY).

cærulean var. of CERULEAN.

Cæsar sī·zəɹ cognomen of Caius Julius *Cæsar*, Roman dictator; hence applied to the Roman emperors. XIV (Ch.). ME. *Cesar*, which gave way later to the sp. *Cæsar*. ¶ In the sense 'emperor, monarch' L. *Cæsar* was adopted in Germ. as OE. *cāsere* (which disappeared in ME.), OFris. *kaiser*, *keiser*, OS. *kēsar*, OHG. *keisar*, G. *kaiser* (see KAISER), ON. *keisari* (adopted in ME. as *caysere*, etc.), Goth. *kaisar*. See also CZAR.

Cæsarean, -ian sīzɛə·riən pert. to the delivery of a child by cutting through the walls of the abdomen, as was done, according to legend, at the birth of Julius *Cæsar* (see prec.). XVII. – L. *Cæsariānus* or f. *Cæsareus*; see -EAN, -IAN.

cæsium sī·ziəm (chem.) metallic element. XIX. – modL., n. of L. *cæsius* bluish-grey; after names in -IUM.

cæstus var. of CESTUS.

cæsura, U.S. **cesura** sīzjuə·rə, sīʒ-, sīsj- (pros.) division of a foot between two words. XVI. – L. *cæsūra* lit. cutting, f. *cæs-*, pp. stem of *cædere* cut; see -URE. (Early forms †*cesure*, †*ceasure* may be – F. *césure*.)

café kæ·fei coffee-house. XIX. F. – It. *caffè* COFFEE.

cafeteria kæfītiə·riə, kæfītərī·ə (orig. U.S.) restaurant in which customers serve themselves. XX. Amer. Sp. 'coffee shop', f. Sp. *cafetero* maker or seller of coffee, f. *café* COFFEE.

caffeine kæ·fiīn (chem.) alkaloid found in the coffee and tea plants. XIX. – F. *caféine*, f. *café* COFFEE; see -INE[5].

Caffre, Caffer kæ·fəɹ early forms of KAFFIR XVI (*Caphar*, *Caf(f)ar*).

cafila kā·filə caravan. XVI. – Arab. *qāfilah* company journeying together, f. *qafala* return from a journey.

caftan kæ·ftæn kæftā·n Oriental under-tunic. XVI. – Turk. *qaftān*, partly through F. *cafetan*.

cage keidʒ box or place for the confinement of birds, etc. XIII. – (O)F. *cage* = Pr. *gabia*, Sp. *gavia* prison, It. *gabbia* :– L. *cavea* stall, cage, coop, hive, spectators' seats in a theatre (the senses do not favour Varro's deriv. from *cavus* hollow). Cf. GAOL.

caiman see CAYMAN.

cainozoic kainozou·ik (geol.) Tertiary. XIX. f. Gr. *kainós* recent (connected by some with L. *re|cēns* RECENT)+*zôion* animal (see ZOO-)+-IC. (Also rarely *cæno-* sī·no.)

caique kaī·k light boat used in the Mediterranean. XVII. – F. *caïque* – It. *caicco* – Turk. *qaiq*.

cairn kɛəɹn pile of stones. XV (in designations of persons, e.g. *Iohannes del Carnys*, XIV). Earlier *carn* (cf. *barn* BAIRN) – Gael. *carn* heap of stones, corr. to OIr., W. *carn*. So **cai·rngorm** precious stone used for ornaments by the Highlanders of Scotland, named from a mountain (Gael. *Carngorm* 'blue cairn') where it is found.

caisson keisū·n, kei·sən chest for ammunition, etc.; watertight vessel used in deep water. XVIII. – F. *caisson*, †*casson* – It. *cassone*; afterwards assim. to *caisse* CASE[2]; see -OON.

caitiff kei·tif †prisoner; †poor wretch; base fellow, villain. XIII. ME. *caitif* (Cursor M.), occas. *chaitif* – OF. *caitif* captive, var. of *chaitif* (mod. *chétif* wretched) = Pr. *caitiu*, *captiu*, Sp. *cautivo* prisoner, It. *cattivo* bad :– Rom. **cactivu-s*, alteration of L. *captīvus* CAPTIVE by assoc. with OCeltic **cactos* (= L. *captus*); cf. late L. sense 'wretched' of *captīvus*, in Christian use, 'in bondage to sin', (hence) 'wicked'.

cajole kədʒou·l delude by flattery. etc. XVII (Milton). – F. *cajoler*, perh. a blend of two or more words (cf. *cageoller*, *cajoller* XVI chatter like a jay, prate, babble, and *enjôler* put in GAOL, inveigle, allure). So **cajo·l**ERY. XVII (Evelyn). – F.

cajuput kæ·dʒəput (oil obtained from) species of Melaleuca. XVIII. ult. – Malay *kayuputih*, i.e. *kayu* wood, *puteh* white. The sp. with *j*, as also in F. *cajeput*, and the consequent pronunc., are due to Du. transliteration of the Malay word as *kajoepoetih* (whence modL. *kajuputi*).

cake keik (arch.) flat sort of loaf XIII; confectionery made with flour, flavoured more or less richly XV; (Sc.) thin hard-baked oaten bread XVI (*Land of Cakes*, Scotland). prob. – ON. *kaka* (Icel., Sw. *kaka*, Da. *kage*), f. **kak-*, rel. to **kōk-*, repr. by G. *kuchen*, etc. (see COOKIE). Hence **cake** vb. form into a cake. XVII.

calabar, -ber kæ·ləbəɹ kind of squirrel fur. XIV (PPl.). ME. *calabre* – medL. *calabris*, *-ebrum*, presumably f. *Calabria* name of a province of Italy; cf. medL. *scuriolus calabrinus*.

calabash kæ·ləbæʃ gourd, gourd-shell. XVII (*calibasse*, *-bash*). – F. *calebasse*, †*cala-* – Sp. *calabaza*, corr. to Cat. *car(a)bassa* and other Rom. forms with *r*; prob. of Oriental origin (cf. Pers. *kharbuza* water-melon).

calaboose kæləbū·z (U.S.) prison. XVIII. – Negro F. *calabouse* – Sp. *calabozo* dungeon.

calamanco kæləmæ·ŋkou glossy woollen stuff of Flanders. XVI (Lyly). In Du. *kal(a)mink*, G. *kalmank*, F. *calmande*; of unkn. origin. Connexion with medL. *calamancus* kind of cap cannot be made out.

calamary kæ·ləməri squid, pen-fish. XVI. – medL. *calamārium* pen-case, n. of L. *calamārius*, f. *calamus* pen – Gr. *kálamos*, rel. to *culmus* HAULM; see -ARY.

calambac kæ·ləmbæk aloes wood, eagle wood. XVI. – Sp. *calambac* (so F., also *-bouc*).

calamine kæ·ləmain ore of zinc. XVII (Holland). – (O)F. *calamine* – medL. *calamīna*, alteration of L. *cadmīa* – Gr. *kadmīá*, *kadmeiā* (sc. *gê* earth), fem. of the adj. of Cadmus; cf. G. *galmei*, †*kalmei*, †*gadmey*.

calamint kæ·ləmint aromatic herb. XIV. – (O)F. *calament* – medL. *calamentum*, for late L. *calaminthe* – Gr. *kalaminthē*.

calamity kəlæ·mīti grievous affliction or distress XV; grievous disaster XVI. – F. *calamité* – L. *calamitās*, prob. rel. to *in|columis* intact, safe; see -ITY. So **cala·mit**OUS. XVI. – F. *calamiteux* or L. *calamitōsus*.

calash kəlæ·ʃ light carriage with folding hood XVII; woman's hood XVIII. Early forms *caleche*, *galeche* (Dryden), *calleche* – F.

calèche, †*galeche* (Molière) – G. *kalesche*, – Pol. *kolaska* or Czech *kolesa*, f. *kolo* WHEEL.

calcareous kælkɛə·riəs of the nature of lime. XVII. f. L. *calcārius*, f. *calc-*, CALX + -*ārius* -ARY; the orig. etymol. sp. with -*ious* was altered by assoc. with words in -EOUS.

calceolaria kæ:lsiŏlɛə·riə genus of plants having slipper-shaped flowers. XVIII. modL., f. L. *calceolus*, dim. of *calceus* shoe (f. *calx* heel) + -*āria*, fem. of -*ārius* -ARY.

calcine kælsai·n reduce to quicklime. XIV (Ch.). – (O)F. *calciner* or medL. *calcīnāre* (a term of alchemy), f. late L. *calcīna* lime, quick-lime, f. L. *calc-*, CALX. So **calcin**A·TION. XIV (Ch.). – (O)F. – medL.

calcium kæ·lsiəm (chem.) metallic element. XIX (H. Davy). f. L. *calc-*, CALX; see -IUM.

calculate kæ·lkjŭleit reckon, compute. XVI. f. pp. stem of late L. *calculāre*, f. *calculus* stone (see next); superseded †**calcule** (XIV–XVI) – (O)F. *calculer* (= It. *calcolare*, Sp. *calcular*); see -ATE[3]. So **calcul**A·TION. XIV (Gower). – (O)F. – late L.

calculus kæ·lkjŭləs stone in an animal body; †gen. (system of) calculation XVII; spec. in *differential*, *integral* (etc.) *calculus* XVIII. – L. *calculus* pebble, stone in the body, stone used in counting, calculation, the relation of which to L. *calx* counter, limestone, lime, goal, and Gr. *khálix* pebble, is undetermined.

Caledonian kælidou·niən. XVII. f. *Calēdonia* (Tacitus) Roman name of part of northern Britain, now assoc. with the Scottish Highlands or Scotland in general; rel. to *Dunkeld* 'fort of the Caledonians', earlier *Duni-Callen*, *Dun-Callden*, referred by some to **kald-* (Gael. *coille*) wood (cf. HOLT); see -IAN.

calefaction kælifæ·kʃən heating. XVI. – (O)F. *caléfaction* or late L. *calefactiō(n-)*, f. *calefacere*, f. *calēre* be warm + *facere* make, DO; see -TION.

calendar, kalendar kæ·lĭndəɹ system of divisions of the civil year XIII; table showing these XIV. ME. *kalender* – AN. *calender*, OF. *calendier* (mod. *calendrier*) – L. *calendārium* account-book, f. *calendæ* CALENDS, the day on which accounts were due. The final -*ar* is due to assim. to L.

calender kæ·ləndeɹ machine for calendering. XVII. – F. *calandre* (whence prob. Prov. *calandra*, Du. *kalander*), presumably f. the vb. So **ca·lender** vb. pass material between rollers for glazing, etc. XV. – (O)F. *calandrer*, of unkn. origin; hence **ca·lender**ER[1], in shortened form †*calender* (XVI–XVIII, as in Cowper's 'John Gilpin').

calends, kalends kæ·ləndz. XIV. – (O)F. *calendes* – L. *kalendæ*, acc. -*as*, first day of the month, when the order of days was proclaimed, f. **kal-* call, proclaim, as in L. *calāre* (cf. INTERCALATE), Gr. *kaleîn*.

calenture kæ·ləntjuəɹ tropical disease incident to sailors. XVI. – F. *calenture*, – Sp. *calentura*, f. *calentar* be hot :– Rom. **calentāre*, f. prp. stem of L. *calēre* be warm (cf. LEW).

calf[1] kāf, pl. *calves* kāvz young of the cow. OE. *cælf* (*ċealf*), pl. *calfru* (*ċealfru*) = OS. *calf* (Du. *kalf*), OHG. *chalb* (G. *kalb*) :– WGerm. **kalƀam* n., beside ON. *kálfr* m. and Goth. *kalbō* fem. = OHG. *chalba* (G. *kalbe* female calf). WS. *ċealf* continued in Kentish dial. as *chalf* (XII), *chawlfe* (XVI), and in place-names, as *Chawleigh*, *Chawton*, *Chalvey*, *Chelvey*. The descendant of the OE. g. sg. *cælfes* is preserved in *calves-foot*, and of the OE. g. pl. *calfra* in *Calverton*.

calf[2] kāf, pl. *calves* kāvz fleshy hinder part of the shank of the leg. XIV. – ON. *kálfi*, of unkn. origin, whence also Ir., Gael. *calpa*. ¶ Note that LEG also is of ON. origin.

Caliban kæ·libæn name of 'a saluage and deformed slaue' in Sh. 'Tempest'. XVII (Butler, 'Hudibras'). perh. a var. of CANNIBAL or derived from a form of CARIB.

calibogus kælibou·gəs (U.S.) mixture of rum and spruce beer. XVIII. Of unkn. origin.

calibre kæ·libəɹ, kəlī·bəɹ †diameter of a projectile; bore of a gun (also CALIVER); (fig.) XVI. – F. *calibre* – It. *calibro* or Sp. *calibre* (also †*calibo*) – Arab. *qālib* mould for casting metal, f. *qalaba* turn, convert. See also CALIVER, CALLIPER.

calico kæ·likou cotton cloth. XVI. Earliest exx. have *Callicut*, *kalyko*, *Calocowe cloth*; f. name of a city and port on the coast of Malabar, India; relevant forms are Arab. *Qaliqūt*, medL. *Collicuthia*, Malayalam *Kōḷikōḍu*, Pg. *Qualecut*, *Calecut*, Eng. *Calȝecot* (Dunbar), *Calyco* (Boorde, 1547). ¶ F. *calicot* is from Eng.

caligraphy, calisthenics vars. of CALLIGRAPHY, -STHENICS.

calipash kæ·lipæʃ, **calipee** kælipī· correl. words denoting (i) upper/lower shell of the turtle, (ii) gelatinous substance next to these. XVII. Earliest forms of the first are *galley patch*, *calapatch*; perh. of native W. Indian origin, unless a native alteration of Sp. *carapacho* CARAPACE.

caliph, calif, khalif kæ·lif, kei·lif Mahommedan chief ruler (successor of Mahommed). XIV (Gower). – (O)F. *caliphe* (medL. *calīpha*, -*es*) – Arab. *khalīfa*, f. *khalafa* succeed. Hence **ca·liphate.** XVIII. – F. *caliphat* (medL. *caliphātus*); see -ATE[1]. This word penetrated into Europe as a result of the Crusades.

caliver kæ·livəɹ, kəlī·vəɹ light musket or harquebus. XVI (also *kalyver*, *qualivre*, *caleever*). var. of CALIBRE, prob. first in phr. *harquebuze* or *piece de calibre*, which was misunderstood, *calibre* being taken for the name of the piece.

calix, calyx kæ·liks, kei·liks pl. *calices* cup-like cavity. XVIII. – L. *calix* cup, rel. to Gr. *kúlix*.

calkin kō·kin, kæ·lkin turned edge of a horse-shoe. XV (*kakun*). – (M)Du. *kalkoen* or its source OF. *calcain* (cf. Pr. *calcanh*, It. *calcagno*) :– L. *calcāneum* heel, f. L. *calc-*, *calx* heel (cf. RECALCITRANT).

call kōl cry out OE.; summon with a shout; name XIII; drive XIV (Sc.; cf. CA'CANNY). Late OE. *ceallian* (once) – ON. *kalla* cry, summon loudly, name, claim = MLG., (M)Du. *kallen*, OHG. *challōn* talk, chatter :– **kallōjan*, f. CGerm. (exc. Gothic) **kal-* (which appear to be repr. in OE. *hilde|calle* 'war-herald') :– IE. **gol-*, repr. also by W. *galw* call, OSl. *glasŭ* voice, *glagolŭ* word (cf. GLAGOLITIC).

callant kæ·lənt (Sc.) customer; lad, youth. XVI (*-and*). – Flem. *kalant* 'customer', 'chap' – north. F. dial. *caland*, superseding earlier *calland*, var. of *chaland* customer, †friend, acquaintance, protector, prp., with change of suffix, of *chaloir* be warm, in impers. use, be the concern of :– L. *calēre* be warm, heated, ardent (cf. NONCHALANT). For the sense cf. CHAP[3].

caller kæ·ləɹ, ka·lər (Sc. and north. dial.) fresh. XIV (*caloure*). var. (with assim. of *lv* to *ll*, as in *siller* from *silver*) of ME. *calver*, *-ur*, *calwar*, presumably adj. use of OE. *calwer* (*ćealer*, *ćealre*) curds, surviving in *caluer of saulmon* 'escume de saulmon' (Palsgr.), rel. to MLG. *keller*, and f. Germ. base **kal-* be COLD. 'This term appears to denote the state of the fish [i.e. salmon] freshly taken, when its substance appears interspersed with white flakes like curd' (Way in 'Promp. Parv.', ed. 1865, p. 59).

calli-, cali- kæ·li, kəli· repr. Gr. *kalli-* (the var. sp. *cali-* is unetymological), used as comb. form of *kalós* beautiful (cf. *kállos* beauty), e.g. *kallipais* having beautiful children: **calli**GRAPHY kəli·grəfi handwriting, prop. elegant penmanship. XVII – modL. *calligraphia* – Gr. *kalligraphiā*, f. *kalligráphos*. So **calli**·GRAPHER (cf. F. *calligraphe*), **calli**GRA·PHIC XVIII. **callipyg**IAN kælipi·dʒiən 'largely composed behinde' (Sir T. Browne). XVIII. f. Gr. *kallipūgos* designation of a famous statue of Venus, f. *pūgḗ* buttocks. **callisthen**ICS kælisþe·niks exercises for developing strength with beauty. XIX. f. Gr. *sthénos* strength.

callidity kǽli·dǐti cunning, craftiness. XVI. – L. *calliditās*, f. *callidus* skilful, cunning, crafty; see -ITY.

calliper kæ·lipəɹ (usu. pl.) compasses for measuring diameters. XVI. orig. *calliper compasses* compasses used for measuring the calibre of a bullet or piece of ordnance; presumably var. of CALIBRE.

callous kæ·ləs hardened. XVI. – (partly through F. *calleux*) L. *callōsus*, f. **ca·llus** hardened skin, which has been used in Eng. since XVI. So **callos**ITY kǽlɔ·sǐti. XVI. – F. or L.

callow kæ·lou †bald OE.; unfledged. XVI. OE. *calu* (*calw-*) = MLG. *kale*, MDu. *kale* (Du. *kaal*), OHG. *chalo* (G. *kahl*) :– WGerm. **kalwaz*, prob. – L. *calvus* bald (whence F. *chauve*), rel. to OSl. *golŭ* bare, naked, Skr. *kulvas*, Av. *kaurva* bald. ¶ The treatment of the hair was a matter of interest between the Romans and the Germans; cf. WGerm. adoption of L. *crispus* (CRISP) and Goth. *kapillōn* (f. L. *capillus* hair) cut hair.

calm kām still, quiet. XIV. The sb., adj., and vb. appear about the same time, and earlier than the corr. F. words (XV), which are presumed to be – It. *calma*, *calmo*, *calmare*; these are referred to popL. **calma*, alteration of late L. *cauma* (Vulgate) – Gr. *kaûma* heat (of the day or the sun), by assoc. with L. *calēre* be hot; the sense-development may have been 'heat of the day', 'rest during this', 'quiet, stillness'. The Eng. words may have been taken direct from popL. (cf. medL. *calmacio*, *calmus* adj.). Hence **calm**ATIVE kæ·lmətiv, kā·m- sedative. XIX.

calomel kæ·ləmel mercurous chloride. XVII. – modL. *calomel*, *calomeles* (so in F. XVIII), said to be f. Gr. *kalós* beautiful + *mélas* black, because in its first preparation a black powder turned into a white one.

caloric kǽlɔ·rik supposed elastic fluid, the source of heat. XVIII. – F. *calorique* (Lavoisier . . .), f. L. *calor* heat + *-ique* -IC.

calorie, -y kæ·ləri unit of heat. XIX. – F. *calorie* (Guillemin), arbitrarily f. L. *calor* heat; cf. -Y[3]. **calori-**, stem of L. *calor* heat, as in *calori*·FIC (F. *calorifique*, L. *calōrificus*), *calori*·METER (F. *calorimètre*, Lavoisier).

calotte kəlɔ·t skull-cap. XVII. – F. *calotte*, – Pr. *calota* or It. *callotta*, referred by some to Gr. *kalúptra* hood, by others to Arab. *kalūta* cap; cf. also L. *calautica* woman's head-dress.

calotype kæ·lotaip patent name of a photographic process. XIX (Fox Talbot). f. Gr. *kalós* beautiful + *túpos* TYPE.

caloyer kæ·lojəɹ Greek monk. XVII. – F. *caloyer* – It. *caloiero* – ecclGr. *kalógēros*, f. *kalós* beautiful + *gêras*, *gḗrōs* old age.

calpack kæ·lpæk Oriental cap. XVI (*colepecke*, *colpack*). – Turki *qalpāq*, *qālpāq*.

caltrop[1] kæ·ltrəp (usu. pl.) name of various plants that entangle the feet; (later) star-thistle, Trapa natans. OE. *calcatrippe*, ME. *calketrappe* – medL. *calcatrippa*, whence also OF. *cachatrepe*, *cauche-*, AN. *calketrappe*, Pr. *calcatrepa*.

caltrop[2] kæ·ltrəp †trap, snare XIII; (mil.) iron ball with sharp spikes XVI. ME. *calketrap* – OF. *kauketrape*, dial. var. of *cauche-*, *chauchetrape*, later (mod.) *chaussetrape*, f. *chauchier* (mod. *côcher*) tread + *trappe* trap; ult. identical with prec.

calumet kæ·ljŭmet Amer.-Indian pipe of peace. XVIII. – F. *calumet*, dial. var. (with suffix-substitution) of *chalumeau* – late L. *calamellus*, dim. of *calamus* reed – Gr. *kálamos* HAULM.

calumny kæ·ləmni malicious misrepresentation. XV. – L. *calumnia* false accusation (whence F. *calomnie*); cf. CHALLENGE and CAVIL. So **calumniate** kəlʌ·mnieit XVI. f. pp. stem of L. *calumniārī*, f. *calumnia*; see -ATE[3]. **calumni**A·TION. XVI (cf. F. *calomniation*). **calu·mni**ATOR. XVI. – late L. **calu·mn**IOUS. XV. – (O)F. *calomnieux* or L. *calumniōsus*.

calvary kæ·lvəri outdoor (life-size) representation of the Crucified Christ. XVIII. – L. *calvāria* skull (f. *calva* scalp, *calvus* bald, rel. to Skr. *kulvas*), tr. in Matt. xxvii 33, etc. of Aram. *gogulthō*, *gogoltha* skull (= Heb. *gulgōleth*), rendered in Gr. by *golgothá*; cf. F. *calvaire*; see -ARY.

calve kāv give birth to a calf. OE. *calfian* (*ćealfian*), f. *cælf* CALF; cf. Du. *kalven*, MHG. *kalben*, etc.

calvered kæ·lvəɹd applied to salmon that is cut up alive. XVII (Jonson). f. *calver* (see CALLER) + -ED.

Calvinism kæ·lvinizm adherence to Calvin's doctrine. XVI. – F. *calvinisme* or modL. *calvinismus*, f. name of Jean *Calvin*, French Protestant reformer (1509–64); see -ISM. So **Ca·lvin**IST. XVI; after F.

calx kælks (alch. and early chem.) powder resulting from calcination of a mineral. XV. – L., 'lime', 'limestone', prob. – Gr. *khálix* pebble, limestone. Cf. CALCINE, CALCULATE, CALCULUS, and CHALK.

calyx kei·liks, kæ·liks outer envelope of a flower. XVII. – L. *calyx* – Gr. *kálux* shell, husk, pod, f. base of *kalúptein* hide. ¶ Confused with CALIX.

cam[1] kæm projection on a wheel. XVIII. – Du. *kam* COMB, as in *kamrad* toothed wheel, cog-wheel; G. *kammrad*, Sw., Da. *kamhjul*, and F. *came* are also of Du. origin.

cam[2] kæm (dial.) crooked XVI; but implied in *cammed(e)* XIV. The base is Celtic **kambos* (as in *Cambodunum* 'crooked town', Yorkshire), whence W., Gael., Manx, Ir. *cam* crooked, bent, wrong, false.

camaraderie kæməræ·d(ə)ri goodfellowship. XIX. F., f. *camarade* COMRADE; see -ERY.

camarilla kæməri·lə private cabinet, cabal. XIX. Sp., dim. of *camara* CHAMBER.

camber kæ·mbəɹ arched surface or line. XVII. – OF. *cambre*, f. dial. var. of OF. *chambre* arched :- L. *camurus* curved inwards. So **ca·mber** vb. XVII. – F. *cambrer*, f. *cambre*.

cambist kæ·mbist one skilled in monetary exchange. XIX. – F. *cambiste* – It. *cambista*, f. *cambio* CHANGE.

cambium kæ·mbiəm (physiol.) †one of the alimentary humours; (bot.) fluid between the wood and the bark of trees. XVII. – medL., 'exchange', used in the physiological sense by Arnaldus de Villa Nova (XIII–XIV): 'cambium humiditas manifeste alterata membri continentis complexione.'

Cambrian kæ·mbriən Welsh. XVII (preceded by *Camber* XVI). f. *Cambria*, var. of *Cumbria*, latinization of W. *Cymry* Wales :- OCeltic **Kombroges*, f. **kom-* together, COM- + **brog-* border, region, MARCH[1]; see -IAN.

cambric kei·mbrik fine white linen. XVI (*cameryk*; Sc. forms have unexpl. *-eche*, *-age*, *-ige*, *-oche*). f. *Kamerijk*, Flemish form of *Cambrai* a town of northern France, famous for fabrics :- medL. *Camaracum*.

camel kæ·ml humped hornless ruminant. OE. *camel*, reinforced in ME. by OF. *cameil*, *chameil*, later *camoil*, *camel*, *chamel* (mod. *chameau*); two L. types are repr. in OF., *camēlus* and **camellus* (cf. Pr. *camel*, Sp., It. *cammello*) – Gr. *kámēlos*, of Semitic origin (Heb., Phœnician *gāmāl*). ¶ The L. word is repr. in other Germ. langs., e.g. Du. *kameel*, G. *kamel*; but the earlier CGerm. name (presumably based on L. *elephantus* elephant) is seen in OE. *olfend*, OS. *olbundeo*, OHG. *olbenta*, ON. *ulfaldi*, Goth. *ulbandus*; cf. OSl. *velĭbǫndŭ* camel.

camellia kəmī·liə, -e·liə genus of shrubs of the tea family. XVIII. – modL. (Linnæus), f. name of Josef *Kamel* (latinized *Camellus*), a Moravian jesuit who described the botany of Luzon; see -IA[1].

came see COME.

camelopard kæ·məlopā:ɹd, kəme·l- giraffe. XVI. – L. *camēlopardus*, *-pardalis* – Gr. *kamēlopárdalis*, f. *kámēlos* CAMEL + *párdalis* PARD.

Camembert kæ·mãbɛəɹ small soft rich cheese originating from *Camembert*, village of Normandy, France. XIX.

cameo kæ·miou precious stone having two layers of different colours. XV (*cameu*). – OF. *came(h)u*, *camahieu* (mod. *camaïeu*), corr. to Sp., Pg. *camafeo*, pointing to a type **camahæus* (cf. medL. *camahutus*, etc.); later – It. *cam(m)eo*, corr. to medL. *cammæus*, whence also F. *camée*; prob. ult. of Oriental origin.

camera kæ·mərə CHAMBER, in several spec. uses. XVIII. – L. *camera* vault, arched chamber – Gr. *kamárā* object with arched cover. In photography, short for *camera obscura* darkened chamber or box, orig. an optical instrument. ¶ *In camera*, (leg.) in the judge's private chamber)(in open court.

camerlingo kæməɹli·ŋgou pope's or cardinal's chamberlain. XVII. It.; see CHAMBERLAIN.

cami- kæ·mi shortening of CAMISOLE, as in *cami-knickers* XX.

camisado kæmisā·dou (mil.) night attack. XVI. – Sp. *camisada* lit. 'attack in one's shirt', f. *camisa* shirt; see CHEMISE, -ADO.

camisole kæ·misoul (formerly) woman's jacket, (now) underbodice. XIX. – F. *camisole* – It. *camiciola* or Sp. *camisola*, dim. of *camicia*, *camisa* shirt (see CHEMISE).

camlet kæ·mlit fabric of which the nature has varied much. XIV. Early forms *chamlett*, *-lot*, Sc. *cammeloit*, prob. – OF. *chamelot*, *camelot*, perh. ult. from Arab. *khamlat*, f. *khaml* pile carpet, but pop. assoc. with camel's hair.

camomile ka·məmail plant of the genus Anthemis. XIV. – (O)F. *camomille* – late L. *c(h)amomilla*, alteration of *chamæmēlon* – Gr. *khamaímēlon* 'earth-apple' (*khamaí* on the ground, *mêlon* apple), so called from the apple-like smell of the blossoms.

camorra kəmɔ·rə secret society in Naples. XIX. It., of doubtful origin, but perh. – Sp. *camorra* dispute, quarrel.

camouflage kæ·muflāʒ disguise of appearance. XX. F., f. *camoufler* (thieves' sl.), – It. *camuffare* disguise, deceive, perh. assoc. with *camouflet* whiff of smoke in the face; see -AGE.

camp kæmp place where troops are lodged in tents, etc.; temporary quarters. XVI. – (O)F. *camp* – It. *campo* (= (O)F. *champ* field, battlefield, Pr. *camp*, Sp. *campo*) :– L. *campu-s* level field, place for games and military exercises, field of battle, whence CGerm. (exc. Gothic) **kampaz* fight, battle, repr. by OE., OFris., MDu. *camp* (Du. *kamp*), OHG. *champf* (G. *kampf*), ON. *kapp*. So **camp** vb. XVI. – F. *camper*; cf. ENCAMP.

campaign kæmpei·n army's operations in the field. XVII (Clarendon). – F. *campagne* – It. *campagna* (used in the mil. sense XVI) = (O)F. *champagne* CHAMPAIGN, in the other senses of which *campaign* was also formerly used (XVII). The military application arose in those conditions of warfare according to which an army remained in quarters during the winter and on the approach of summer went into the country (*nella campagna*, *dans la campagne*) to conduct operations. Hence as vb. XVIII.

campanile kæmpənī·li bell-tower (usu. lofty and detached). XVII (Evelyn). – It. *campanile* (whence F. *campanile*), f. *campana* – late L. *campāna*.

campanology kæmpənɔ·lədʒi art of bell-ringing. XIX. – modL. *campānologia*, f. late L. *campāna*; see prec. and -LOGY.

campanula kəmpæ·njŭlə plant of a large genus so named with bell-shaped flowers. XVII (Evelyn). – modL. dim. of *campāna*; see prec. and -ULE. So **campa·nulate** bell-shaped. XVII. – modL.; see -ATE².

Campeachy kæmpī·tʃi epithet of a red dye-wood, also called *logwood*. XVII (*Cam-*, *Compeche wood*, *tree*). Name of a southern state of Mexico, whence the wood was orig. exported; in Sp. *campeche*, in F. *campêche*.

campestral kæmpe·strəl pert. to fields or open country. XVIII. f. L. *campester*, *-tri-*, f. *campus*; see CAMP, -AL. Also †**campe·strial.** XVII.

camphor kæ·mfəɹ white translucent vegetable oil. XV. Early forms are various, both disyll. and trisyll., *camphire* prevailing from XV to *c.* 1800. – OF. *camphore*, later and mod. *camphre* (AN. *caumphre*) or medL. *camphora* – (prob. through Sp. *alcanfor*) Arab. *kāfūr* (whence medGr. *kaphourá*) – Prakrit *kappūra*, Skr. *karpūra*. ¶ Has become a CEur. word. Hence **ca·mphorated** XVII; see -ATE³.

campion kæ·mpiən plant of the genus Lychnis. XVI. First recorded from Lobel and Lyte and applied to Lychnis Coronaria; tr. of Gr. *lukhnìs stephanōmatikḗ* (i.e. 'used for garlands'), on which has been based a derivation from †*campion* (– OF. (north.) *campion* CHAMPION).

campshed kæ·mᵖʃed facing of piles and boarding to protect a bank. XVI. prob. f. CANT¹+SHIDE; this deriv. is suggested by the earliest forms with *-shide*, *-shed*, *-shead*, of which the later *-shot*, *-shut*, *-sheet*, *-sheath* in var. spellings of the coll. *campshedding* (XIX) appear to be corruptions.

campus kæ·mpəs (U.S.) college or university grounds. XVIII (first at Princeton, New Jersey). – L. *campus* field.

camwood kæ·mwud hard red wood of W. Africa. XVII (Dampier). Said to be – native dial. word *kambi*.

can¹ kæn vessel for liquid. OE. *canne*, corr. to MDu. *kanne* (Du. *kan*), OHG. *channa* (G. *kanne*), ON. *kanna*; it is uncertain whether the word is orig. Germ. or – late L. *canna* (VI), whence OF. *channe*, Pr. *cana*. OE. *canne* is recorded only once, in a gloss, after which there is no Eng. evidence till XIV, when the word was prob. introduced from the Continent.

can² kæn, (unstressed) kən, kn pt. **could** kud, kəd know, (with inf.) know how, (passing into) have power, be able. One of the group of Germ. preterite-present verbs (see DARE, MAY, SHALL, WIT²); the primary meaning was 'have learned', 'come to know'. OE. *cunnan*, pres. ind. *can(n)*, *con(n)*, pl. *cunnon*, pt. *cūþe* (:– **cunþa*) = OFris. *kunna*, *kan*, *kunda*, OS. *cunnan*, *can*, *consta* (Du. *kunnen*, *kan*, *konde*), OHG. *kunnan*, *kan*, *kunda* or *kunsta* (G. *können*, *kann*, *konnte*), ON. *kunna*, *kann*, *kunna* (:– **kunða*), Goth. (and CGerm.) *kunnan*, *kann*, *kunþa*. The second *n* of the pres. stem is formative; e.g. OE. pl. *cunnon*, Goth. *kunnum*, etc. = Skr. *jānīmas* (:– **gn̥nəmós*) we know. The IE.

base **gn-*, **gnē-*, **gnō-* appears also in Lith. *žinóti* know, and OIr. *ath|gnin* recognizes. Cf. KNOW. The pt. *could*, with analogical *l* after *should* and *would*, appeared in early XVI, and superseded *coude* (XIV–XVI), which was an alteration of ME. *couþe* by assim. to regular wk. pt. forms in *-de*. See also CON[1], CUNNING, UNCOUTH.

canaille kænai· rabble, mob. XVII. F. – It. *canaglia* (= Sp. *canalla*, Pg. *canalha*), f. *cane* dog :– L. *cani-s* (see HOUND). The It. form was in earlier use (B. Jonson).

canal kənæ·l †pipe to convey liquid XV; tubular cavity in the body, duct XVII; artificial watercourse XVII. – (O)F. *canal*, refash. of earlier *chanel* CHANNEL, after L. *canālis* or It. *canale*. So **canalize** kæ·nəlaiz, -A·TION. XIX. – F. *canaliser*, *-isation*.

canard kæ·nāɹ(d) cock-and-bull story. XIX. F., lit. 'duck'; the sense of 'hoax' is said to have arisen from the phr. *vendre un canard à moitié* 'half-sell a duck' (cf. '*vendeur de canards à moitié*, a cousener, guller, cogger; foister, lyer' Cotgr. 1611; *bailleur de canards* lit. 'deliverer of ducks', 1612 in Littré's dict.).

Canarese kænərī·z Dravidian language of *Canara* or *Kanara* (S.W. India), the native form of which is *Kannāda*, f. *kan* black + *nādu* country; see -ESE.

canary kənɛə·ri name of a dance, a wine, and a singing-bird derived from the Canary Islands. XVI. – F. *Canarie* – Sp. *Canaria*, in L. *Canāria insula* 'Isle of Dogs', one of the Fortunate Isles, so named from its large dogs (L. *canārius* pert. to dogs, f. *canis* dog, HOUND). As the name of the bird modelled on F. *canari*, †*-ie* – Sp. *canario*.

canaster kənæ·stəɹ kind of tobacco, so called from the rush basket in which it was imported. XIX. – Sp. *canastro* – medL. **canastrum* – Gr. *kánastron* CANISTER.

cancan kæ·nkæn extravagant dance. XIX. – F. *cancan* kãkã noise, disturbance (XVI), vulgar noisy dance (XIX), said to be L. *quanquam* (with contemp. pronunc. of Latin) although, taken as the typical beginning of a wrangle in the Schools.

cancel kæ·nsl cross out, obliterate; annul. XIV. – (O)F. *canceller* – L. *cancellāre* make lattice-wise, cross out (a writing), f. *cancellus*, pl. *cancellī* cross-bars (see CHANCEL).

cancer kæ·nsəɹ zodiacal constellation of the Crab XIV (Ch.); malignant tumour XVII. – L. *cancer* crab, creeping ulcer, after Gr. *karkínos* crab, *karkínōma* CARCINOMA, the tumour being so called, acc. to Galen, on account of the resemblance to a crab's limbs of the swollen veins about the part affected. Cf. CANKER, CHANCRE.

candelabrum kændīlei·brəm, -lā·brəm candlestick, chandelier. XIX. – L. *candēlābrum*, f. *candēla* CANDLE; the pl. *candelabra* has been often used as sg., with pl. in *-as*.

candid kæ·ndid †white; free from bias or malice; frank. XVII. – F. *candide* or L. *candidus*, f. *candēre* be white, glisten (cf. INCANDESCENT, INCENSE); see -ID.

candidate kæ·ndidət aspirant to an office. XVII. – (O)F. *candidat* or L. *candidātus* clothed in white, candidate for office (who appeared in a white toga), f. *candidus*; see prec. and -ATE[1]. Hence **ca·ndidat**URE. XIX. prob. after F.

candle kæ·ndl cylinder of tallow or wax with a wick enclosed. OE. *candel* – L. *candēla*, later *-della*, f. *candēre* glisten. One of the L. words introduced into Eng. after the Conversion of A.D. 597; reinforced in ME. by AN. *candele*, OF. *candeile*, var. of *chandeile*, *-oile* (= Pr., Sp., It. *candela*, Pg. *candeia*) :– L. *candēla*, and OF. *candelle* (mod. *chandelle*) :– L. *candella*. Hence **Ca·ndlemas** -məs 2 February; OE. *candelmæssedæġ*; see MASS[1]. **ca·ndle**STICK (formerly including candelabra); OE. *candelsticca*.

candour kæ·ndəɹ †purity; freedom from bias or malice XVII (Jonson); outspokenness XVIII. – F. *candeur* or L. *candor*, f. *cand-* of *candēre* and *candidus* CANDID; see -OUR.

candy kæ·ndi sugar-candy XVIII; (U.S.) sweetmeats XIX. – F. *candi* in *sucre candi* SUGAR-CANDY.

candytuft kæ·nditʌft the plant Iberis umbellata, orig. brought from Candia. XVII. f. *Candy*, the island Candia (Crete) + TUFT.

cane kein hollow stem of giant reeds, etc. XIV (Trevisa); used as a walking-stick or rod XVI. ME. *canne*, *cane* – OF. *cane*, (also mod.) *canne* = Pr. *cana*, Sp. *caña*, It. *canna*. :– L. *canna* reed, cane, tube, pipe – Gr. *kánna*, *kánnē* – Ass. *ḳanū* (Heb. *ḳaneh*) – Sumerian *gin*. Hence **cane** vb. beat with a cane. XVII.

cangue kæŋ wooden frame worn about the neck as a punishment. XVIII. – F. *cangue* – Pg. *canga* – Annamite *gong*.

canicular kəni·kjŭlər of the days preceding or following the heliacal rising of the dog-star. XIV (Trevisa). – late L. *canīculāris*, f. *canīcula* dog-star, dim. of *canis* dog.

canine kæ·nain, kei·nain pert. to a dog. XVII. – F. *canin*, *-ine*, or L. *canīnus*, *-īna*, f. *canis* dog, HOUND; see -INE[1].

canister kæ·nistəɹ †basket XVII; small case or box for tea, etc. XVIII. – L. *canistrum* basket for bread, fruit, etc. – Gr. *kánastron* wicker basket, f. *kánnā* reed, CANE.

canker kæ·ŋkəɹ gangrenous affection. OE. *cancer*, reinforced or superseded by – ONF. *cancre*, var. of (O)F. *chancre* :– L. *cancrum*, nom. *cancer*; see CANCER, CHANCRE. Applied from XV to larvæ destructive to plants; so *canker-worm* (XVI).

cannel kæ·nl bituminous coal burning with a very bright flame. XVI (*canel*, Leland).

Since XVIII currently expl. as standing for *candle* (north. dial. *cannle*) *coal*; but it is not clear that the orig. form was *cannel coal* and not simply *can(n)el*.

cannelure kæ·nəljuəɹ grooving. XVIII. – F. *cannelure*, f. *canneler*, f. *cannel* CHANNEL. (Also *channelure*, in adj. *-ed* XVI.)

cannibal kæ·nibəl man-eating man. XVI. First in pl. *Canibales* – Sp. *Canibales*, one of the forms (recorded by Columbus) of the ethnic name *Caribes* (see CARIB) of a fierce man-eating nation of the West Indies; according to Oviedo ('La historia general de las Indias' II viii) *caribe* means 'brave and daring'. Cf. CALIBAN.

cannon[1] kæ·nən piece of ordnance. XVI. – (O)F. *canon* – It. *cannone*, augm. of *canna* tube, CANE; see -OON. So **cannon**A·DE. XVII. – F. *canonnade* – It. *cannonata*. **cannon**EE·R. XVI. – F. *canonnier* – It. *cannoniere*.

cannon[2] kæ·nən stroke at billiards. XIX. Perversion, by assoc. with CANNON[1], of *car(r)om* (XVIII; still in U.S.A. as vb. 're-bound', 'bounce'), shortening of CARAMBOLE. Also as vb. XIX.

canny kæ·ni (Sc.) sagacious, cautious XVI; clever, cunning; careful, quiet, gentle XVIII; (north. Eng.) agreeable, comely XIX; advb. cautiously, gently XVIII (cf. CA'CANNY). Presumably f. CAN[2]+-Y[1]; corr. to *cunning* in its primary sense.

canoe kənū· primitive boat of savage races XVI; light boat propelled by paddling XVIII. The native name, Haytian (whence Sp.) *canoa*, is recorded by Eden, 1555, and continued in use till XVIII; in later XVI a var. *canow* (cf. Carib *canaoua*) appeared and was continued as *canoo*, to which the present pronunc. corresponds, the present sp. (XVIII) being due to F. *canoë*; forms based on Du. *cano* were also current.

canon[1] kæ·nən rule, law (of the Church) OE.; central portion of the Mass XIII; list of books of the Bible accepted as authentic XIV; (mus.) XVI; size of type (cf. *brevier*, *pica*) XVII. OE. *canon* – L. *canōn* – Gr. *kanṓn* rule; reinforced or superseded by ME. *cano(u)n* – AN. *canun*, (O)F. *canon*. So **canon**IC(AL) -ɔ·nikəl based on ecclesiastical law or rule XV (Caxton); f. F. *canonique* or L. *canonicus* – Gr. *kanonikós*. **ca·non**IST professor of canon law XV. – F. – medL. **ca·non**IZE place in the canon of saints, -IZA·TION. XIV (Wyclif). – medL.

canon[2] kæ·nən clergyman living according to the 'vita canonica', i.e. religious life based on rule. XIII. ME. *canun*, *canoun*, also *chanun*, *chanoun* – OF. *canonie*, *chanoine* (with ending assim. to *cano(u)n* CANON[1]) – ecclL. *canonicus* (repr. in OE. *canonic*, MHG. *kanunich*), sb. use of adj. (see CANONICAL). Hence **ca·non**ESS. XVII; after F. *chanoinesse*, in medL. *canonica*. **ca·non**RY. XV.

cañon, canyon kæ·njən deep gorge. XIX. – Sp. *cañon* tube, pipe, conduit, augm. of *caña* CANE. The specific application was given by the Spaniards of New Mexico.

canoodle kənū·dl (U.S. sl.) indulge in caresses. XIX (Sala). Of unkn. origin.

canopy kæ·nəpi covering over a throne, etc. XIV (Wycl.). Late ME. *canope*, *canape* – medL. *canopeum* baldacchino, for L. *cōnōpēum*, *-eum*, *-ium* net over a bed, pavilion – Gr. *kōnōpeîon* Egyptian bed with mosquito curtains, f. *kṓnōps* gnat, mosquito.

canorous kənɔ̄ə·rəs melodious. XVII. f. L. *canōrus*, f. *canor* song, f. *canere* sing; see CHANT, -OUS.

cant[1] kænt †edge, border (?) XIV; nook, corner XVII; oblique line or face XIX. prob. – MLG. *kant* point, creek, border, *kante* side, edge (whence G. *kante*), (M)Du. *cant* border, side, corner – Rom. **canto* (as in OF. *cant*, F. *chant*, *champ*, Sp., It. *canto* edge, corner, side), for L. *cant(h)us* iron tire, said by Quintilian to be a barbarism of Sp. or African origin. (Connexion, if any, with W. *kant* circumference, Breton *kant* circle, OSl. *kątŭ* corner, Gr. *kanthós* corner of the eye, is obscure.) Cf. CANTON. Hence **cant** vb. bevel, slant, toss, tilt XVI; whence a new sb. **cant** toss, throw, slope, tilt XVIII.

cant[2] kænt (sl.) speak, talk, esp. in the whining fashion of beggars XVI (Harman); use the particular jargon of a class or set; affect religious or pietistic phraseology XVII. prob. – L. *cantāre* sing (see CHANT), which was applied contemptuously as early as XII to the singing in church services and perh. later to the speech of religious mendicants. Hence **cant** sb. †whining speech; peculiar phraseology or jargon of a class, esp. of pedlars, gipsies, thieves, and vagabonds XVII; affected use of (religious) language XVIII. (An obscure *cantum* 'something sung' in Caxton's 'Reynard the Fox' xxvii may be somehow connected.) So **canting** vbl. sb. (often attrib.) and ppl. adj., esp. of beggars' cant (*peddelars Frenche or Canting*, Harman; *an old Canting Beggar*, Jonson; *canting speech*, 1592; *Canting Crew*, Beggers, Gypsies, 1690). *Canting arms* (her.) those in which the figures bear a punning allusion to the name of the family.

Cantab kæ·ntæb XVIII. Short for **Cantabrig**IAN kæntəbri·dʒiən (XVII), f. *Cantabrigia*, L. form of *Cambridge* name of an Eng. university town.

cantaloup kæ·ntəlūp variety of musk-melon. XVIII. – F. *cantaloup* – It. *Cantaluppi*, name of a former summer residence of the popes near Rome, where it was cultivated on its introduction from Armenia.

cantankerous kæntæ·ŋkərəs quarrelsome. XVIII (Goldsmith, Sheridan). Said by Grose to be a Wiltshire word, but the earliest literary evidence suggests an Ir. origin;

perh. blending of Ir. *cant* auction, outbidding, with *rancorous* (cf. also Ir. *cannrán* contention, grumbling).

cantata kæntā·tə choral composition, formerly a recitative. XVIII. – It. (sc. *aria* AIR), fem. pp. of *cantare* sing; see CHANT, -ADE.

canteen kæntī·n sutler's shop in a camp, etc.; outfit of cooking and table vessels or utensils. XVIII. – F. *cantine* – It. *cantina* cellar, perh. f. *canto* corner (see CANT[1]).

canter kæ·ntəɹ easy gallop. XVIII. Short for *Canterbury gallop, pace, trot* (XVII), a pace such as mounted pilgrims to Canterbury were supposed to have ridden. Hence vb. XVIII; cf. occas. †*canterbury* vb. (XVII).

canterbury kæ·ntəɹberi stand with partitions to hold music portfolios, etc. XIX. prob. named after Charles Manners-Sutton, first viscount *Canterbury*, Speaker of the House of Commons, elder son of Charles Manners-Sutton, archbishop of Canterbury.

Canterbury bells kæ·ntəɹbəri belz plant of the genus Campanula. XVI (Lyte, Gerarde). The flowers were fancifully assoc. with the small bells worn by horses ridden by pilgrims to Canterbury.

cantharides kænþæ·ridīz Spanish fly; this dried and used medicinally. XV. L., pl. of *cantharis* – Gr. *kantharís* blister fly.

canticle kæ·ntikl song, hymn, spec. liturgical hymn in the Divine Office XIII; (pl.) Song of Solomon, Canticum Canticorum XVI. – OF. *canticle*, var. of *cantique* – L. *canticum*, f. *cantus* CHANT; prob. reinforced by L. dim. *canticulum* (cf. -CLE).

cantilever kæ·ntilīvəɹ bracket of stone, etc. XVII; projecting support in bridge-building XIX. Earliest forms *cantlapper, candilever*, of which the formal significance is doubtful. The first syll. has been connected with Sp. *can* dog, (transf.) bracket, modillion, corbel; but the formation is altogether obscure.

cantle kæ·ntl †corner; (arch. or dial.) section, segment. XIV. – AN. *cantel* = OF. *chantel* (mod. *chanteau*) = Pr. *cantel* :- medL. *cantellu-s*, dim. of *cantus* CANT[1].

canto kæ·ntou division of a poem. XVI (Spenser). – It. (Dante), lit. 'song' :- L. *cantus* CHANT.

canto fermo kæ·ntou fɔ̄·ɹmou plain-song melody as adopted for contrapuntal treatment. XVIII. It., 'fixed song'; see CHANT, FIRM.

canton kæ·ntən, kæntə·n †corner; (her.) ordinary of a shield XVI; subdivision of a country XVII. – (O)F. *canton* – Pr. *canton* (= It. *cantone*) :- Rom. **cantōnem*, f. L. *cantus* CANT[1]. Hence **ca·nton** vb. quarter (in various senses). XVI. – F. *cantonner*, It. *cantonare*. **canton**MENT kǝ̆ntū·nmənt quarters. XVIII. – F. *cantonnement*.

cantor kæ·ntɔ̄ɹ leader of a church choir. XVI. – L., 'singer', f. *cant-, canere* (see CHANT). So **cantoris** kæntɔ̄·ris north (sometimes south) side of the choir of a church, being the precentor's side. XVIII; g. sg. used absol. (cf. *decani*).

cantrip kæ·ntrip (Sc.) spell, charm (phr. *cast cantrips*); trick. XVI. Also *cantrap, -ep, -op*, of unkn. origin.

Canuck kənʌ·k native or inhabitant of Canada. XIX. Also *Kanu(c)k* and (occas.) *Canack, Cannacker*, f. *Can|ada*, perh. after *Polack* Pole.

canvas kæ·nvəs strong hemp or flax cloth. XIV. ME. *canevas* – ONF. (and mod.) *canevas*, var. of OF. *chanevaz* = Pr. *canabas* or It. *canavaccio* :- Rom. **cannapāceum*, f. **cannapum*, for L. *cannabis* HEMP.

canvass kæ·nvəs A. †toss in a canvas sheet, (hence) criticize destructively; discuss (a matter) XVI; B. solicit votes or support *for* XVI; †sue for (a thing) XVIII; solicit (person, etc.) for votes XIX. f. CANVAS; the emergence of sense B is difficult to account for.

canyon var. of CAÑON.

canzone kæntsou·ni song, ballad. XVI. – It. 'song' = (O)F. *chanson*, Pr. *cansó*, Sp. *canción* :- L. *cantiōnem*, f. *cant-, canere*; see CHANT, -ION. Also **canzon**ET kænzǒne·t short song. XVI. – It. *canzonetta*, dim. of *canzone*.

caoutchouc kautʃū·k indiarubber. XVIII. – F. *caoutchouc* – Carib *cahuchu*; in G. *kautschuk*.

cap kæp close head-covering OE.; many techn. senses from OE. *cæppe* – late L. *cappa* (whence OF. *cape*, F. *chape*, Pr., Sp. *capa*), possibly a deriv. of *caput* head; cf. CAPE[1]. (For the medL. var. *cāpa* see COPE[1].) Hence **cap** vb. put a cap on XV; take off the cap XVI; (north. dial.) overtop, excel XIX.

capable kei·pəbl †able to hold; able to be affected (by); having capacity. XVI. – F. *capable* – late L. *capābilis*, f. *capere* take (see HEAVE), prob. after *capāci-*; see next and -ABLE. Hence **capa**BI·LITY. XVI. ¶ Among derivs. of the same base are: *capacious, caption, captious, captive, capture*; *accept, concept, except, precept*; *inception, reception, susception*; *conceive, deceive, perceive, receive*; *conceit, deceit, receipt*; *anticipate, municipal, participate, precipitate*; *nuncupation, occupy, recuperate*; CASE[1]; *prince, principal*.

capacious kəpei·ʃəs able to hold or receive (so much). XVII. f. L. *capāci-, capāx*, f. *capere* take; see HEAVE and -ACIOUS. So **capac**ITY kəpæ·sīti. XV. – F. – L.

cap-a-pie kæpapī· from head to foot. XVI (Berners). – OF. *cap a pie* (now *de pied en cap*); i.e. *cap* – Pr. *cap* head (see CHIEF), *a* to, *pie* (:- L. *pedem* FOOT).

caparison kəpæ·risən trappings of a horse. XVI. – F. †*caparasson* (mod. *-açon*) – Sp.

caparazón saddle-cloth (cf. Pr. *caparasso* hooded cloak, and medL. *caparo* old woman's cloak), f. *capa* CAPE¹. So as vb. XVI (Sh.). – F. *caparaçonner*.

cape¹ keip tippet of a cloak XVI; sleeveless cloak XVIII. – F. *cape* – Pr. *capa* (= (O)F. *chape*) :– late L. *cappa* (Isidore); see CAP.

cape² keip promontory. XIV (Ch.). – (O)F. *cap* – Pr. *cap* = Sp. *cabo* :– Rom. **capo*, for L. *caput* head (cf. CHIEF).

capelin kæ·pəlin small smelt-like fish. XVII. – F. *capelan* – Pr. *capelan* CHAPLAIN.

caper¹ kei·pəɹ flower-buds of Capperis spinosa XV; the shrub itself XVI. Late ME. *capres* – F. *câpres* – L. *capparis* (whence also It. *cappero*) – Gr. *kápparis*. The final *s*, being apprehended as the pl. sign, was dropped to form a new sg. (XVI); cf. G. *kaper*, from earlier pl. *kappren, cappres*.

caper² kei·pəɹ frisky leap. XVI (Greene, Sh.). Shortening of CAPRIOLE. Also vb. (Sh.).

capercailzie kæpəɹkei·lzi, -kei·lji wood-grouse. XVI (Bellenden). – Gael. *capull coille* ka·pəl kɔ·lje great cock (lit. horse) of the wood. The sp. *lz*, deriving from MSc. *lȝ*, which repr. the pronunc. lj, has influenced the Eng. pronunc., as in *Menzies*.

capias kei·piæs (leg.) writ authorizing arrest. XV. L., 'you are to seize' 2nd sg. pres. subj. of *capere* take (see HEAVE).

capillary kəpi·ləri of hair, hair-like. XVII. – L. *capillāris*, f. *capillus* hair (prob. deriv. of *caput* HEAD); after F. *capillaire*; see -ARY.

capital¹ kæ·pitəl †pert. to the head XIII (AncrR.); affecting the head or life (now in *capital crime, punishment*); (of letters) standing at the head, of the largest size XIV (Trev.); chief XV; first-rate XVIII. – (O)F. *capital* – L. *capitālis*, f. *capit-, caput* HEAD; see -AL. The sense 'punishable by death' rests ult. on L. *res* or *causa capitalis, crimen capitale*, and the like, as also that of 'pre-eminent', 'first-rate'. The sb. uses, 'chief city' (XVII, Milton), 'capital fund, accumulated wealth' (XVII), derive ult. from medL. *capitale* (n. of adj. used as sb.), but are prob. immed. from F. *capital*. So **capitalist** kæ·pitəlist, kəpi·t- possessor of capital. XVIII (A. Young). – F. *capitaliste* (a Revolution word of derogatory implication); hence **capital**ISM. XIX. So **capital**IZE. XIX. – F. *capitaliser*.

capital² kæ·pitəl head of a column. XIV. – OF. *capitel* (mod. *chapiteau*) – L. *capitellum*, secondary dim. of *caput* HEAD. In XVI–XVII often *capitel(l)* after It. *capitello*; the present form in *-al* is mainly due to assocn. with prec.

capitan kæ·pitæn chief admiral of the Turkish fleet, esp. in *capitan* (earlier †*captain*) *pasha*. XVIII. – Sp. *capitan* CAPTAIN.

capitation kæpitei·ʃən charge or payment per head. XVII. – F. *capitation* or late L. *capitātiō(n-)*, f. *capit-, caput* HEAD; see -ATION.

Capitol kæ·pitəl temple in ancient Rome on the Tarpeian hill dedicated to Jupiter. XIV (*capitolie, -oile*). In ME. – OF. *capitolie, -oile*, later assim. to the source, L. *Capitōlium*, f. *capit-, caput* HEAD.

capitular kəpi·tjŭləɹ (eccl.) pert. to a chapter. XVII. – late L. *capitulāris*, f. *capitulum* CHAPTER; cf. F. *capitulaire* and see -AR.

capitulate kəpi·tjŭleit †specify as under heads; †propose terms, make terms about XVI; make terms of surrender XVII. f. pp. of medL. *capitulāre* draw up under distinct heads, f. *capitulum* head of a discourse, CHAPTER; see -ATE³. So **capitul**A·TION. XVI. – late L.

capon kei·pən castrated cock. Late OE. *capun* – AN. *capun*, var. of (O)F. *chapon* = Pr., Sp. *capon*, It. *cappone* :– Rom. **cappone* (whence OHG. *kappo*), for L. *capō(n-)*, prob. to be referred to a base meaning 'cut' (cf. Gr. *kóptein*; see COMMA).

caponier kæpŏniə·ɹ (fortif.) covered passage across a ditch. XVII. – Sp. *caponera* (whence F. *caponnière*) prop. capon-pen (see prec.).

caporal kæ·pŏræl superior kind of tobacco. XIX. F., short for *tabac de caporal* corporal's tobacco, so called because superior to *tabac de soldat* private soldier's tobacco; *caporal* is – It. *caporale*, f. *capo* head (CHIEF), after *corporale* (f. *corpo*), *pettorale* (f. *petto*).

capot kəpɔ·t winning of all the tricks at piquet by one player. XVII. – F. *capot*, perh. f. *capoter*, dial. form of *chapoter* castrate (cf. CAPON). So **capo·t** vb. XVII. ¶ The F. word is the source of G. *kaput* done for.

capote kəpou·t long cloak or mantle; close-fitting hat. XIX. – F. *capote* rain-cloak, dim. of *cape* CAPE.

caprice kəprī·s sudden unaccountable turn of mind XVII; work of art of lively or sportive character XVIII. – F. *caprice* – It. *capriccio* (dial. *capurriccio*) orig. horror (the mod. sense being due to assoc. with *capra* goat), f. *capo* head (:– L. *caput*) + *riccio* hedgehog (:– L. *ericeu-s* URCHIN), lit. 'head with the hair standing on end'. Earlier forms were †*capricchio, -iccio* (XVII–XIX) and †*caprich*, based immed. on It. *capriccio* or Sp. *capricho*. So **capric**IOUS -i·ʃəs. XVI. – F. *capricieux* – It. *capriccioso*.

Capricorn kæ·prikɔ̄ɹn zodiacal constellation. XIV. – (O)F. *Capricorne* – L. *capricornus*, f. *capr-, caper* goat (= OE. *hafr* he-goat) + *cornu* HORN, 'goat-horn', after Gr. *aigó|kerōs*.

capriole kæ·prioul leap, caper. XVI. – F. *capriole* (now *cabriole*) – It. *capriola*, f. *capriolare* leap, f. *capriolo* roebuck :– L. *capreolus*, dim. of *caper* goat (see prec.).

capsicum kæ·psikəm seed-pod of Guinea pepper. XVIII. – modL. (Tournefort), perh. f. *capsa* CASE².

capsize kæpsai·z upset (on the water). XVIII. orig. a sailor's word; earlier form *capacise*, perh. to be referred ult. to Sp. *capuzar* sink (a ship) by the head, perh. alteration (by assoc. with *cabo* head) of *chapuzar* dive, duck :– Rom. **subputeāre*, f. L. *sub* SUB-+*puteus* well, PIT. Cf. BOX[4].

capstan kæ·pstən mechanism for weighing the anchor, etc. XIV. – Pr. *cabestan*, earlier *cabestran* (whence F. *cabestan*, Sp. *cabestrante*, Sp., Pg. *cabrestante*), f. *cabestre* halter :– L. *capistrum*, f. *capere* seize (see HEAVE). (There have been many vars., due to pop. attempts to interpret the second syll., e.g. *capstang*, *-stand*, *-stall*, *-stern*, *-storm*, *-string*.)

capsule kæ·psjūl membranous envelope; dry seed-vessel. XVII. – F. *capsule* – L. *capsula*, dim. of *capsa* box, CASE[2]; see -ULE.

captain kæ·ptĭn chief, leader; head officer of a company. XIV (Barbour, Wyclif, Ch., Gower). ME. *capitain* – late OF. *capitain* (mod. *capitaine*), superseding earlier *chevetaigne* CHIEFTAIN and *chataigne*, *catanie* – late L. *capitāneus* chief, f. *capit-*, *caput* HEAD; cf. It. *capitano*, Sp. *capitan*, which may have influenced the F. word. Hence **ca·ptain**CY. XIX.

caption kæ·pʃən (arch.) seizure, arrest XIV; †cavilling objection XVII; (orig. U.S.) heading, title XVIII. – L. *captiō(n-)*, f. *capt-*, *capere* take, seize; see HEAVE, -TION.

captious kæ·pʃəs catching at faults, fault-finding XIV (Wyclif); ensnaring in argument, sophistical XV. – (O)F. *captieux* or L. *captiōsus*, f. *captiō* deception, fallacious argument; see CAPTION, -IOUS.

captivate kæ·ptiveit †make captive, capture; enthrall. XVI. f. pp. stem of late L. *captivāre* (after *captivate* pp. XIV), f. *captīvus*; see next and -ATE[3]. Finally superseded **captive** vb. XIV (orig. *capti·ve*, as still in Milton). – (O)F. *captiver* – late L. So **captive** kæ·ptiv taken prisoner. XIV. – L. *captīvus*, f. *capt-*, pp. stem of *capere* take; see HEAVE and -IVE. Also sb. So **capti·**VITY. XIV. **ca·ptor**[1], XVII. – L. **ca·pt**URE taking captive XVI; one captured XVIII. – F. – L.; hence as vb. XVIII, superseding †*captive*. ¶ L. *captus* corr. to OE. *hæft* prisoner = OS., OHG. *haft* (cf. G. *häftling*), ON. *haptr*, Goth. *hafts*, (O)Ir. *cacht* bondmaid, W. *caeth* serf.

capuchin kæ·puʃin (*C-*) Franciscan friar of the new order of 1528 XVI; hooded cloak of feminine wear XVIII. – F. *capuchin* (now *capucin*) – It. *cappuchino*, f. *cappuccio* hood, augm. of *cappa* CAPE[1]; so named from the pointed hood adopted by the order.

capybara kæpibā·rə largest extant rodent, Hydrochærus capybara. XVIII. Native name of S. America.

car kāɹ wheeled vehicle (of various kinds). XIV. ME. *carre* – AN., ONF. *carre* :– Rom. **carra* (whence OHG. *karra*, G. *karre*, MDu. *carre*, Du. *car*), pl. or parallel fem. form of L. *carrum* n., *carrus* m. (whence F. *char*, It. *carro*, etc.; cf. CHARIOT) – OCeltic **karrom* (**karros*), repr. by (O)Ir. *carr*, OW. *carr* (W. *car*), rel. to L. *currus* chariot.

carabineer kærəbiniə·ɹ mounted soldier armed with a carbine. XVII. – F. *carabinier*, f. *carabine* CARBINE; see -EER[1].

caracal kæ·rəkæl feline animal of N. Africa. XVIII. – F. or Sp. *caracal* – Turk. *qarahqulaq*, f. *qarah* black+*qulak* ear.

caracole kæ·rəkoul half-turn executed by a horse. XVII. – F. *caracole*, f. *caracoler* wheel.

carafe kəræ·f glass water-bottle. XVIII. – F. *carafe* – It. *caraffa*, prob. (through Sp. *garrafa*) – Arab. *gharrāfa*, f. *gharafa* draw water. ¶ The word has become CEur.

carageen kæ·rəgīn kind of seaweed. XIX. f. *Carragheen*, place near Waterford, Ireland, where it is abundant.

carambole kæ·ræmboul CANNON[2]. XVIII. – Sp. *carambola* (whence F. *carambole* red ball at billiards), obscure comp. of *bola* ball = (O)F. *boule* :– L. *bulla* BULL[2].

caramel kæ·rəmel sugar melted and browned. XVIII. – F. *caramel* – Sp. *caramelo*, of unkn. origin.

carapace kæ·rəpeis body-shell of tortoises, etc. XIX. – F. *carapace* – Sp. *carapacho*, of unkn. origin.

carat kæ·rət measure of weight for precious stones; measure of $\frac{1}{24}$ used in stating the fineness of gold. XVI. – F. *carat* – It. *carato* – Arab. *qīrāṭ* weight of 4 grains (cf. Sp., Pg. *quilate*, Pg. *quirate*) – Gr. *kerátion* fruit of the carob, f. *kéras* horn. ¶ The word has become CEur.

caravan kæ·rəvæn, kærəvæ·n company travelling through the desert; fleet of ships XVI; covered carriage or cart XVII. Mainly – F. *caravane* – Pers. *kārwān* (latinized *carvana*, *caravanna* XII–XIII); but some early forms (e.g. *carouan*) repr. the Pers. directly. So **carava·nserai** -sərai Eastern inn. XVI. ult. – Pers. *kārwānsarāī* (*sarāī* and *sarā* palace, inn), but the various early forms repr. more or less closely F. *caravansérai*, *-sérail*, †*car(a)vansera*, Pg. *caravançara*.

caravel see CARVEL.

caraway kæ·rəwei 'seed' of the umbelliferous plant Carum Carui. XIV. The form corr. most closely to OSp. *al|carahueya* (mod. *alcaravea*) = Pg. *alcaravia* – Arab. *alkar(a)wiyā* (see AL-[2]); medL., F., It., Sp. *carvi* is repr. by Sc. *carvy*; the ult. source may be Gr. *káron*, *káreon* (L. *carum*, *careum*) cummin.

carbine kā·ɹbain kind of fire-arm. XVII. Earlier *carabine* – F. *carabine*; in It., Sp., Pg. *carabina*; orig. the weapon of the †*carabin* (– F.) mounted musketeer.

carbolic kāɹbɔ·lik a powerfully antiseptic acid, phenol or phenyl alcohol. XIX. f. CARB|ON + -OL + IC.

carbon kā·ɹbən (chem.) non-metallic element. XVIII. – F. *carbone* (de Morveau, 1787), f. L. *carbō(n-)* coal, charcoal, prob. f. base **qar-* heat, fire. Hence **carbon**A·CEOUS. XVIII. **ca·rbonate.** XVIII. – F. *carbonate* (de Morveau, 1787) – modL. *carbōnātum*; see -ATE[1]. **carbon**IC kaɹbɔ·nik. XVIII.

carbonado kāɹbənei·dou piece of meat scored and grilled. XVI. – Sp. *carbonada* (see -ADO), f. *carbon* coal, CARBON. Hence as vb. score, slash. XVI (Nashe, Sh.).

Carbonari kāɹbŏnā·ri secret society of Italian republicans. XIX (Byron). It., pl. of *carbonaro* collier, charcoal-burner, f. *carbone* coal :– L. *carbō* CARBON; the name was arbitrarily chosen by the members.

carboy kā·ɹboi large wicker-covered bottle for chemicals. XVIII. ult. – Pers. *qar(r)ābah* large flagon.

carbuncle kā·ɹbʌŋkl fiery-coloured precious stone XIII; inflammatory tumour XVI. The early forms present several types – OF. *charbucle, -buncle, carboucle, -buncle* (now repl. by *escarboucle*) = Pr., Sp. *carbuncle*, It. *carbonchio* :– L. *carbunculus* small coal, carbuncle stone, red tumour, dim. of *carbō* coal (cf. CARBON); assim. to the orig. L. determined the final form.

carburet kā·ɹbjŭret (chem.) compound of carbon with another element. XVIII. Superseded earlier †*carbure* – F. *carbure* (1795), f. L. *carbō* CARBON; see -URET; in turn superseded by **ca·rb**IDE. XIX. Survives in **ca·rburetted** adj., whence **ca·rburett**OR[1].

carcajou kā·ɹkədʒū wolverine. XVIII (Goldsmith). – F. *carcajou* – some native name not identified.

carcanet kā·ɹkənet ornamental collar. XVI. f. †*carcan* (XVI) – F. *carcan* (earlier †*quercant*, †*charchant*) = Pr. *carcan*, medL. *carcannum*, It. *carcame* – Germ. **querkbann* (cf. ON. *kverkband* string of a cap going below the chin, f. *kverk* angle below the chin, pl. throat + *band* BAND[2]); see -ET. Revived in XIX by archaistic writers (Moore, Scott).

carcase, carcass kā·ɹkəs (dead) body of man or beast (XIV), XVI; spherical shell or bomb XVII. The present forms are immed. – F. *carcasse* (XVI), whence prob. It. *carcassa*, Sp. *carcasa*. They were preceded by the type *carcays, -as, carkeis, -ois* (XIV), which survived till XVII (e.g. *carkeis* in A.V. Judges xiv 8) and is prop. a distinct word – AN. *carcois* = OF. *charcois* (still dial.); AL. forms are *carcasium, -osium, -oisum*, in Sc. use *carcagium* (all XIII). The ult. origin of the several forms is unkn. The sp. *carcase* may be due to CASE[2], which was applied to the body or its skin XVI–XVII.

carcinoma kāɹsinou·mə cancer. XVIII. – L., – Gr. *karkínōma* (*-mat-*), f. *karkínos* crab; cf. CANCER. So **carcino·mat**OUS. XVII.

card[1] kāɹd implement orig. consisting of teasel heads set in a frame, for raising the nap on cloth; toothed instrument for combing out fibre. XV. – (O)F. *carde* – Pr. *carda*, f. *cardar* tease, comb :– popL. **caritāre*, f. L. *car(r)ere* card (cf. *caritor* carder, *carmen* wool-card, *carmināre* card). So **card** vb. XIV (PPl.). – (O)F. *carder* – Pr. *cardar*.

card[2] kāɹd piece of pasteboard XV; †map, chart XVI. – (with unexpl. *d*) (O)F. *carte* – L. *charta* papyrus leaf, paper (whence F. *charte* CHART) – Gr. *khártēs* leaf of papyrus, metal plate, written work, supposed to be of Egyptian origin. The earliest use in Eng. (as in F.) is of playing-cards; there are many fig. phrases arising from this use, of which *sure card* (XVI) in the sense of 'a person whose agency will ensure success' may be the source of the slang use of *card* for an eccentric, unusual, etc., person (XIX).

cardamom kā·ɹdəməm spice used medicinally and as a flavouring. XV. – (O)F. *cardamome* or L. *cardamōmum* – Gr. *kardámōmon*, f. *kárdamon* cress + *ámōmon* Indian spice.

cardiac kā·ɹdiæk pert. to the heart. XVII. – F. *cardiaque* or L. *cardiacus* – Gr. *kardiakós*, f. *kardíā* HEART; see -AC.

cardigan kā·ɹdigən woollen over-waistcoat. XIX. Named after James Thomas Brudenell, seventh earl of *Cardigan*, who led the famous charge of the Light Brigade in the Crimean war, 1854.

cardinal kā·ɹdinəl chief, principal. XIII. – (O)F. *cardinal* or L. *cardinālis*, f. *cardin-*, *cardō* hinge; in Eng. first applied to the four virtues of justice, fortitude, temperance, prudence (XIII, Cursor M.), on which conduct 'hinges', later to the chief winds (the earliest use in L.), and to numbers)(*ordinal* (from Priscian); see -AL[1]. So **ca·rdinal** sb. any of the seventy princes (cardinal bishops, priests, and deacons) of the Roman Church that constitute the Pope's council or the Sacred College. XII (Peterborough Chron.). – (O)F. – medL.; ecclL. *cardinalis* was orig. of wider application, designating clergy attached to their particular church in a stable relation, as a door to a building by its hinges.

cardio- kā·ɹdiou, -diə· comb. form of Gr. *kardíā* HEART, as in *ca·rdiograph, cardio·meter.*

cardoon kāɹdū·n plant allied to the artichoke. XVII. – F. *cardon*, f. *carde* edible part of the artichoke – modPr. *cardo* :– Rom. **carda*, for L. *cardus, carduus* thistle, artichoke (rel. to *car(r)ere*; see CARD[1]); see -OON.

care kɛəɹ †grief; burdened state of mind; serious attention OE.; charge, oversight XIV; object of concern XVI. OE. *caru* (*ċearu*) =

OS. *kara*, OHG. *chara* grief, lament, ON. *kǫr* (gen. *karar*) bed of sickness, Goth. *kara* :- CGerm. **karō*; the IE. base **gǎr-* is repr. by Gr. *gêrus* voice, L. *garrīre* (see GARRULOUS), OIr. *gāir*, *gairm*, Gael. *gàir*, *gairm* (cf. OE. *ćearm* CHARM[2] and SLOGAN), W. *gawr* cry. So **care** vb. †grieve, be troubled OE; take thought *for* XIII; have affection or liking *for* XVI. OE. *carian* = OS. *karōn*, OHG. *charōn*, *-ēn*, Goth. *karōn* :- CGerm. (exc. ON.) **karōjan*, *-ǣjan*; in later uses re-formed on the sb. Hence **ca·reful.** OE. *carful*; see -FUL[1]. Cf. CHARY.

careen kərī·n position of a ship heeled over. XVI. - F. *carène*, †*carine* - It. *carena* (whence also Sp. *carena*, Pg. *querena*), dial. (prob. Genoese) repr. of L. *carīna* keel, also nutshell, rel. to Gr. *káruon* nut, Skr. *kárakas* coco-nut, water-vessel made of a nutshell. Hence **caree·n** vb. XVI (F. *caréner* is later).

career kəriə·ɹ †racecourse; †gallop at full speed; course (of action) XVI; (a re-adoption from F.) course of life or employment XIX. - F. *carrière* - It. *carriera* - Pr. *carreira* (= Sp. *carrera*, Pg. *carreira*) :- Rom. **carrāria* (sc. *via*) carriage-road, road (whence OF. *charrière* road, way), f. *carrus* CAR. Hence **caree·r** vb. XVI. **caree·rIST.** XX. - F. *carriériste*.

caress kəre·s fondling action. XVII. - F. *caresse* - It. *carezza* :- Rom. **cāritia*, f. *cārus* dear; see CHARITY, -ESS[2]. Hence, or - F. *caresser* - It. *carezzare*, **care·ss** vb. XVII.

caret kæ·rit mark indicating omission. XVII. L., 3rd sg. pres. ind. of *carēre* be without, taken to mean 'is lacking'.

carfax kā·ɹfæks place where four roads meet, esp. as a proper name. XIV. - AN. *carfuks* (XIV), for **carrefurkes* = OF. *carrefurc-s* (mod. *carrefour*), Pr. *carreforc-s* :- popL. **quadrifurcu-s*, f. *quadri-* comb. form of *quatuor* FOUR+*furca* FORK.

cargo kā·ɹgou ship-load. XVII. - Sp. *cargo* (also *carga*), corr. to (O)F. *charge* load, Pr. *carc* (*carga*), It. *carico* (*carica*), medL. *carricum* (*carrica*), f. Rom. **carricāre* CHARGE.

Carib kæ·rib name of (i) a native race of the southern West Indies, (ii) a large group of West Indian languages. XVI. - Sp. *caribe*; according to Oviedo, 'Historia General' II viii, *caribe* means 'brave and daring'; formerly often synon. with CANNIBAL.

caribou kæribū· N. Amer. reindeer. XVIII. - Canadian F. *caribou*, presumably from a N. Amer. Indian dialect.

caricature kæ·rikətʃuəɹ grotesque representation in which characteristic features are exaggerated. XVIII. - F. *caricature* - It. *caricatura*, f. *caricare* load, burden, exaggerate (see CHARGE). The It. form was formerly in use (XVII–XIX). So vb. XVIII.

caries kɛə·riīz (med.) decay of bones, etc. XVII. L., 'rottenness, decay', perh. f. a base **kr- kĕr-* ravage, ruin (in Skr., Ir., and Gr.). So **ca·rious** decayed. XVI. - L. *cariōsus*.

carillon kəri·ljən (tune played on) a set of bells. XVIII. - F. *carillon* (†*quarellon* XIV), alteration of OF. *car(e)ignon*, *quarregnon* :- Rom. **quatriniō(n-)* peal of four bells, alteration of *quaterniō* (see QUATERNION) after late L. *trīniō* number three, f. *trīnus* TRINE, whence Pr. *trinho*, dial. *trilho*.

carina kərai·nə (nat. hist.) keel-like structure. XVIII. L. 'keel'; cf. CAREEN.

cark kāɹk †charge, burden XIII (Cursor M.); load of trouble XIV. - AN. *karke*, repr. northern var. of OF. *carche*, *charche*, f. *carchier*, *charchier* (:- Rom. **carcāre*, for **carricāre* CHARGE), the corr. var. of which, *carkier*, appears in **cark** vb. (XIII), now surviving mainly in arch. phr. *carking* (i.e. distressing, grieving) *care*.

carl kāɹl churl XIII (Cursor M.); (later) fellow. - ON. *karl* man, male, freeman, man of the people (found in late OE. only in comps., viz. *hūscarl* man of the king's bodyguard, *carlman* man, male, *carlfugol* male bird, all - ON.) = OHG. *charal*, *karl*, beside *charlo* :- Germ. **karlaz*, **karlon*; as a proper name the Germ. word was latinized as *Carolus*, whence F. (and Eng.) *Charles*. Another grade of the base is repr. by CHURL. Hence **carl hemp** female hemp. XVI. f. CARL in the sense of 'male', the name being applied to the robuster and coarser plant, which is now known to be the female (the popular error was pointed out by Ray and Linnæus).

carline[1], -ing[1] kā·ɹlin, -iŋ (dial.) old woman. XIII (Cursor M.). ME. *kerling* - ON. *kerling*, fem. of *karl* CARL (*-ing* = -EN[1]).

carline[2] kā·ɹlin genus of composite plants, allied to thistles. XVI. - F. *carline* = Sp., It. *carlina*, medL. *carlina*, perh. alteration of *cardina* (f. L. *cardō* thistle) by assoc. with *Carolus* Charles, it being said that Charlemagne received a revelation of the plant's efficacy (it was used as a sudorific).

carling[2] kā·ɹliŋ (naut.) timbers lying fore and aft under the deck of a ship. XIV. - ON. *kerling* CARLINE[1].

Carlist kā·ɹlist Spanish legitimist. XIX. - F. *carliste* - Sp. *carlista*, f. name of Don *Carlos*, second son of Carlos IV, regarded as the legitimate successor of Fernando VII (d. 1833); see -IST.

Carlovingian kāɹlovi·ndʒiən pert. to the French dynasty founded by Charlemagne (Carolus Magnus). XVIII (Gibbon). - F. *carlovingien*, f. *Karl* Charles (see CARL) after *mérovingien* MEROVINGIAN; largely superseded by **Carolingian** (XIX) kærəli·ndʒiən, a re-formation on *Carolus* Charles.

carmagnole kaɹmænjou·l song and dance popular among French revolutionists;

revolutionist soldier. XVIII (Burns, applying it to Satan). – F. *carmagnole* orig. jacket which became popular during the first Revolution in France, prob. from name of a town in Piedmont, *Carmagnola*, which was occupied by the Revolutionists in 1792.

Carmelite kā·ɹməlait one of an order of mendicant friars originating from Mount Carmel, a White Friar. XV. – F. *carmélite* or medL. *carmēlīta* (cf. late L. *Carmēlītēs* inhabitant of Mount *Carmel*, Vulg.).

carminative kā·ɹminətiv expelling flatulence. XV. – (O)F. *carminatif, -ive*, or medL. *carminātīvus*, f. *carmināt-*, *carmināre* CHARM, (hence) heal, or card wool, (hence) purify; see -ATE[3], -IVE.

carmine kā·ɹmain crimson pigment obtained from cochineal. XVIII. – (O)F. *carmin* or medL. *carminium*, perh. conflation of *carmesīnum* (see CRIMSON) and *minium* cinnobar.

carnac kā·ɹnæk elephant-driver. XVIII. – F. *cornac*, Pg. *cornaca*, perh. – Sinhalese **kūrawanayaka* (cf. the form *cournakeas*, reported by a Du. traveller XVII) elephant-tamer.

carnage kā·ɹnidʒ great slaughter. XVI (Holland). – F. *carnage* – It. *carnaggio* (cf. Pr. *carnatge* heap of slain) :– medL. *carnāticum*, f. L. *carn-*, *carō* flesh; see -AGE.

carnal kā·ɹnəl †bodily; fleshly; secular XV; not spiritual XVI. – ChrL. *carnālis* (Tertullian), f. *carn-*, *carō* flesh, prop. piece of flesh such as was distributed at sacrifices and warriors' feasts, f. **kar-*, as in Umbrian *karu*, Oscan *carneis* (g.) part, Gr. *keírein* cut. *Carnālis* tr. Gr. *sárkinos* (f. *sark-*, *sárx* flesh); see -AL[1] and cf. CHARNEL. So **carna·lity**. XIV. – ChrL. *carnālitās* (Augustine).

carnation[1] kāɹnei·ʃən flesh-colour, flesh tints; rosy pink or crimson, as of the carnation. XVI. – F. *carnation* – It. *carnagione* – late L. *carnātiō(n-)* fleshiness, corpulence, f. *carn-*, *carō* flesh; see prec. and -ATION.

carnation[2] kāɹnei·ʃən clove-pink, Dianthus Caryophyllus. XVI (Lyte). In early use varying with *coronation*.

carnival kā·ɹnivəl season of revelry immediately preceding Lent. XVI (*carnoval*, later *-aval*, *-ival*). – It. *carne-*, *carnovale* (whence F. *carnaval*), with dial. vars. *carnelevare*, *karlevá* – medL. *carnelevāmen*, *-levārium* Shrovetide, f. L. *carn-*, *carō* flesh (see CARNAL) + *levāre* lighten, raise (cf. LIGHT[2]); lit. 'cessation of flesh-eating' (for the same notion cf. synon. It. *carnelasciare*, dial. † *carlassare*, Rum. *lăsăr de carne*, medL. *carnemlaxāre*, and Cat. *carnes toltes*, Sp. *carnes tolendas*).

carnivorous kāɹni·vərəs flesh-eating. XVII (Sir T. Browne). f. L. *carnivorus* (the modL. n. pl. *Carnivora* is the name of an order of mammals), f. *carni-*, *carō* flesh; see CARNAL, -VOROUS.

carob kæ·rɔb (fruit of) the leguminous tree Ceratonia siliqua. XVI (Turner). – F. †*car(r)obe* (mod. *caroube*), superseding OF. *carouge* :– medL. *carrūbia*, *-ium* – Arab. *kharrūba*, whence also Sp. *(al)garroba*, Pg. *alfarroba*, It. *carruba*, G. *karobe*, *-ube*.

carol kæ·rəl †ring-dance accompanied by song XIII (Cursor M.); †the song itself XIV; hymn of joy for Christmas, etc. XVI. – OF. *carole* (surviving dial. in senses '(round) dance', 'dance-song', 'merrymaking') = Pr. *carola*, *corola* (whence It. *carola*), of doubtful origin; the prevalence of old and mod. dial. forms with *cor-* seems to point to a Rom. sb. **choreola*, f. L. *chorus* (see CHORUS) or to a vb. **chorаulāre*, f. L. *choraulēs* (Gr. *khoraúlēs*) one who accompanies a dance on the flute; but the gen. sense of 'ring, circle' of OF. *carole* and medL. *carola*, recorded also for ME., may indicate a wider sense, of which 'round-dance' was a particular application, and therefore some entirely different source. So **ca·rol** vb. †dance in a ring XIII (Cursor M.); sing XIV. ¶ The W. and Bret. forms are from Eng. and F. respectively.

Caroline kæ·rəlain pert. to Charles. XVII. – med. or modL. *Carolīnus*, f. *Carolus*; see CARL, -INE[1]. Also sb. name of certain coins (XVI); cf. medL. *carlinus*, F. *carlin*, It. *carlino*, G. *karolin*.

Carolingian see CARLOVINGIAN.

carolus kæ·rələs gold coin bearing 'Carolus' as the monarch's name, e.g. of Charles VIII of France, Charles I of England. XVI. – *Carolus*; see CARL.

carom kæ·rəm XVIII. See CANNON[2].

carotid kərɔ·tid (anat.) name of the two great arteries supplying blood to the head. XVII. – F. *carotide* or modL. *carōtides* – Gr. *karōtídes*, pl. of *karōtís*, f. *karoûn* stupefy; so named (as stated by Galen) because compression of these arteries produces stupor.

carouse kərau·z drinking a bumper; full draught XVI; drinking-bout XVII. From the phr. *drink* or *quaff carouse* (XVI), repr. G. *garaus trinken* drink completely (lit. 'quite out'; cf. the similarly used phr. †*all out*; Rabelais has *voire* (i.e. *boire*) *carous et alluz*); cf. F. †*carrousse*.' So **carou·se** vb. XVI; cf. F. †*carrousser*. (The form *garouse* is found in Eng. XVI.) Aphetic ROUSE[2]. Hence **carou·sal.** XVIII (Sterne); see -AL[2]; a superfluous formation.

carp[1] kāɹp †talk, speak XIII; †sing, recite XV; talk censoriously XVI. In its earlier history mainly a poetic word of the Scandinavianized areas. – ON. *karpa* brag, with generalization of sense; in the mod. sense, dating from XVI, either infl. by, or a new formation on, L. *carpere* pluck (see HARVEST), fig. slander, calumniate.

carp[2] kāɹp freshwater fish, Cyprinus carpio. XIV. – (O)F. *carpe* – Pr. *carpa*

(= Sp., Pg. *carpa*) or the common source late L. *carpa*, given by Cassiodorus (VI) as the name of a fish of the Danube; perh. of Germ. origin (cf. (M)LG. *karpe*, (M)Du. *karper*, OHG. *karpfo*, G. *karpfen*, ON. *karfi*). ¶ Not IE., but the word has become widespread in Europe, and there has been much interadoption.

carpal kā·ɹpəl (anat.) pert. to the wrist. XVIII. – modL. *carpālis*, f. *carpus* (used in Eng. from XVII) – Gr. *karpós* wrist, f. IE. **kwrp-* **kwerp-* be mobile, whence Germ. **χwerƀan* (cf. WHIRL); see -AL[1].

carpel kā·ɹpəl (bot.) division of a compound pistil or fruit. XIX. – F. *carpelle* or modL. *carpellum* (Dunal, 1817), f. Gr. *karpós* fruit (cf. HARVEST); see -EL.

carpenter kā·ɹpĭntəɹ artificer in wood. XIV. – AN. *carpenter*, OF. *carpentier*, (also mod.) *charpentier* = Pr. *carpentier* (whence Sp. *carpintero*, It. *carpentiere*) :– late L. *carpentāriu-s* (sc. *artifex*) carriage-maker, f. *carpentum* two-wheeled carriage, like *carrus* CAR, of Gaulish origin (cf. *carpentis Gallicis*, Livy XXXI xxi), beside OCeltic **carpentos* (whence (O)Ir. *carpat*, Gael. *carbad*, W. *cerbyd* chariot); see -ER[2]. So **ca·rpent**RY. XIV (PPl.). – AN. *carpentrie* = (O)F. *charpenterie*, f. *charpentier*, after late L. *carpentāria* (sc. *fabrica*) carriage-maker's workshop.

carpet kā·ɹpit †thick fabric for covering tables, etc. XIV; (piece of) fabric for covering a floor or stairs XV. – OF. *carpite* or medL. *carpīta* – It. †*carpita* woollen counterpane, corr. to (O)F. *charpie* lint, sb. use of pp. of *charpir* = Sp. *carpir* scratch, It. *carpire* snatch, tear :– Rom. **carpīre*, for L. *carpere* pluck, pull to pieces (see HARVEST). ¶ F. *carpette* is from Eng.

carpo- kā·ɹpou repr. comb. form of Gr. *karpós* fruit (see HARVEST). XIX. ¶ As a terminal el. in *endocarp*, *mesocarp*, *pericarp*.

carrack kæ·rək (hist.) large ship of burden. XIV (*carryk*, Ch.). – (O)F. *caraque*, prob. (like It. *caracca*) – Sp. *carraca* – Arab. *qarāqīr*, pl. of *qurqūr* merchant ship.

carraway var. of CARAWAY.

carrel kæ·rəl study in a monastic cloister. XV (used hist. XVIII–XIX and more recently revived for a study in a library). – OF. *carole*, medL. *carola*, of unkn. origin.

carriage kæ·ridʒ conveyance, transport XIV (Ch., Wycl. Bible); †baggage, luggage XIV (Barbour, Trevisa); means of conveyance, vehicle XV; manner of carrying oneself, bearing, deportment XVI (Sh.). – ONF. *cariage*, f. *carier* CARRY; see -AGE.

carriole kæ·rioul small carriage, light cart; Canadian sledge. XIX. – F. *carriole* – It. *carriuola* (whence Sp. *carriola*), f. *carro* CAR.

carrion kæ·riən †corpse; dead putrefying flesh. XIII. ME. *charoine* (AncrR.), *caroyne* (RGlouc.), *-oigne* (Cursor M.) – AN., ONF. *caroine*, *-oigne*, OF. *charoigne* (mod. *charogne*) = Pr. *caronha*, Sp. *carroña*, It. *carogna* :– Rom. **carōnia*, f. L. *carō* flesh (cf. CARNAGE); antecedents of the present form appear XIV (*carion*), alongside *careyne*, *caren*, later *carren* (XVI–XVII); their development is obscure.

carronade kærənei·d short piece of ordnance. XVIII. f. *Carron*, near Falkirk, Scotland, famous for a large iron foundry, where it was first cast + -ADE, prob. by assoc. with *cannonade* or *grenade*.

carrot kæ·rət (edible root of) the umbelliferous plant Daucus Carota. XVI. – (O)F. *carotte* – L. *carōta* – Gr. *karōtón*.

carry kæ·ri bear or take from place to place, transport; convey while bearing up; support, sustain, bear. XIV (R. Mannyng, PPl., Wyclif). – AN., ONF. *carier*, var. of *charier* (mod. *charrier* cart, drag), corr. to Pr. *carrejar*, f. *car* CAR + *-ier*, *-eier* (:– **-idiāre*). Hence **ca·rrier** XIV (*veyne* .. *carier of blode* Trevisa); see -ER[1].

cart kāɹt †carriage XIII (Orm); strong two-wheeled vehicle XIII; light sprung two-wheeled vehicle XIX. ME. *carte* (disyll.; so, e.g., in Chaucer and Gower), in Ormulum *karrte*, and *cart*, *kart*; (i) partly metathetic repr. of OE. *cræt* carriage, chariot, (once, late) *cert*; in comps. *cræt-* (e.g. *crætwæġn*) and *cræte-* (e.g. *crætehors* 'veredus'); cf. ME. *cartelode* (Havelok), *carte weie* (Gower), *cart(e) wheel* (Ch.); (ii) partly – cogn. ON. *kartr* cart; and prob. infl. by AN., ONF. *carete* (mod. *charrette* cart) dim. of *car*, *char* CAR. ¶ Whether OE. *cræt* is immed. or ult. connected with Germ. words cited s.vv. CRADLE, CRATE is doubtful.

carte kāɹt var. sp. of QUARTE. XVIII (*cart*).

carte blanche kart(ə) blānʃ blank paper to be filled in at one's discretion; full discretionary power. XVIII. F. (formerly *charte blanche*) 'blank paper'. **carte de visite** də vizī·t 'visiting card', small photographic portrait. XIX (patented 1854).

cartel kā·ɹtəl written challenge XVI; written agreement as to exchange of prisoners XVII; after G. *kartell*, combination for business or political purposes XX. – F. *cartel* – It. *cartello* placard, challenge, dim. of *carta* paper, letter (cf. CHART); see -EL. ¶ Now a CEur. word.

Cartesian kāɹtī·ʒiən, -ziən. XVII. – modL. *Cartesiānus*, f. *Cartesius*, latinized form of the surname of René *Descartes*, French philosopher and mathematician (1596–1650); see -IAN.

Carthusian kāɹþjū·ziən one of an order of monks founded by St. Bruno in 1084. XVI. – medL. *Carthusiānus*, f. *Cart(h)ūsia* Chartreuse, near Grenoble, France (cf. CHARTREUSE). The earlier form of the place-name was *Charteuse*, whence ME. *Chart(h)ous* (XIV); the altered form *Chartreuse*, AN.

Chartrous, was adopted in later ME. and, by assim. to HOUSE[1], became *Charterhouse* (i) Carthusian monastery XVI, (ii) hospital founded 1611 on the site of the C. monastery in London, which became one of the foremost public schools. Cf. MLG. *Karthuiser*, *-euser*, MHG. *Kartūser* (G. *Kartäuser*) occas. Eng. †*Cartusier* (XVII). See -IAN.

cartilage kā·ɹtĭlidʒ (anat.) firm elastic tissue. XVI. – F. *cartilage* – L. *cartilāgō* (*-āgin-*), prob. rel. to *crātis* wicker-work. So **cartilagin**OUS -æ·dʒinəs. XVI. – (O)F. or L. (*-ōsus*).

cartography kāɹtɔ·grəfi map-making. XIX. – F. *cartographie*, f. *carte* map – L. *charta* CHART; see -O-, -GRAPHY.

carton kā·ɹtən white disk within the bull's-eye of a target XIX; pasteboard container XX. – F. *carton* pasteboard, cardboard, f. *carte* CARD[2] + augm. *-on*.

cartoon kāɹtū·n drawing made as a design for a painting XVII (Evelyn); illustration in a periodical as a comment on current events XIX. – F. *carton* – It. *cartone*, augm. of *carta* paper (cf. CHART); see -OON.

cartouche kāɹtū·ʃ cartridge; (archit.) corbel, tablet, etc. XVII. – F. *cartouche* cornet of paper, cartridge – It. *cartoccio*, f. *carta* paper (cf. CHART).

cartridge kā·ɹtridʒ case containing a charge of powder for fire-arms. XVI. Earliest forms *cartage*, *cartrage*, later *cartruce*, *cartrouche*, *-edge*, *-idge*; alteration of prec., but actually recorded earlier.

cartulary, chartulary kā·ɹt-, tʃā·ɹtjŭləri (hist.) place where records are kept; collection or register of records. XVI. – medL. *c(h)artulārium*, f. *c(h)artula*, dim. of *c(h)arta* paper; see CHART, CHARTER, and -ARY. Cf. (O)F. *cartulaire*.

carucate kæ·rʲukeit (hist.) as much land as can be tilled with one plough in one year. XV. – medL. *car(r)ūcāta*, f. *car(r)ūca* orig. coach, chariot, in Gaul early applied to the wheel-plough, rel. to *carrus* CAR; see -ATE[1].

caruncle kæ·rʌŋkl (anat., etc.) fleshy excrescence. XVII. – F. †*caruncle* (mod. *caroncule*) – L. *caruncula*, dim. of *carō* flesh.

carve kāɹv †cut; cut artistically or ornamentally OE.; cut up meat at table XIII. OE. *ċeorfan* pt. *ċearf*, *curfon*, pp. *corfen* = OFris. *kerva*, (M)Du. *kerven*, MHG. *kerben* :- WGerm. **kerfan*, pt. **karf*, **kurƀum*, pp. **kurƀan-*; other grades of the base appear in Sw. *karfwa*, Da. *karve*, Icel. *kyrfa*; prob. cogn. with Gr. *gráphein* write, orig. scratch, engrave (cf. WRITE). The weak conjugation is found as early as XV; a new analogical pp. *carven* (XVI) survives arch. The normal repr. of OE. *ċeorfan* would be **charve*, but initial k had established itself by *c.* 1200 in the pres. stem through the infl. of other parts of the vb. or of the Scand. forms.

carvel kā·ɹvəl, **caravel** kæ·rəvəl light fast ship, esp. of Spain and Portugal. XV. – OF. *carvelle* – Pg. *caravela* (whence also F. *caravelle*, Sp. *carabela*, It. *caravella*), dim. of Pg. *caravo* :- late L. *carabus* (Isidore), – Gr. *kárabos* horned beetle, crayfish, light ship. The later form *caravel* (XVI) is due to F. *caravelle* or It. *caravella*.

caryatid kæriæ·tid (archit.) orig. and usu. pl. female figure used as a column. XVI. – F. *cariatide* – It. *cariatide*, or their source, L. *caryatides* (Vitruvius) – Gr. *karuátides* (pl.) priestesses of Artemis at Karuai (Caryæ) in Laconia (*Karuâtis* was an epithet of Artemis).

caryophyllaceous kæ:riɔfilei·ʃⁱəs (bot.) pert. to the family Caryophyllaceæ. XIX (earlier *-phy·lleous* XVIII, after F. *-phyllée*). f. modL. *caryophyllus* – Gr. *karuóphullon* clove-pink; see -ACEOUS.

caryopsis kæriɔ·psis pl. *-ides* (bot.) small one-seeded dry indehiscent fruit. XIX. modL., f. Gr. *káruon* nut + *ópsis* appearance (cf. OPTIC).

cascabel kæ·skəbel knob at the rear end of a cannon. XVII. – Sp. *cascabel* – Cat. (Pr.) *cascavel* :- medL. *cascabellu-s* little bell, of unkn. origin.

cascade kæskei·d waterfall. XVII (Evelyn). – F. *cascade* – It. *cascata*, f. *cascare* fall :- Rom. **cāsicare*, f. L. *cāsus* fall; see CASE[1], -ADE. Hence vb. XVIII.

cascara kæ·skərə (pop. pron. kæskā·rə in *casca·ra sagra·da* 'sacred bark', a laxative drug) bark canoe in Sp. America. XIX. Sp., 'rind', 'peel', f. *cascar* crack, burst :- Rom. **quassicāre*, f. L. *quassāre*, intensive f. *quass-*, *quatere* shake (cf. CONCUSSION).

case[1] keis †event, chance; instance, example XIII; state, condition XIV; (gram.) inflexional form of noun, adjective, pronoun XIV; (leg.) state of the facts, cause, suit XIV. ME. *cas*, *caas* – (O)F. *cas* – L. *cāsus* fall, chance, occasion, misfortune, (tr. Gr. πτῶσις lit. fall) grammatical case, f. base of *cadere* fall, rel. to Skr. *çad* fall away. *Case of conscience* (XVI), F. *cas de conscience*, medL. *casus conscientiæ*, so called because involving the particular application of ethics to circumstances. ¶ From the same base are derived *cadence*, *cadenza*, *decadent*; *occasion*; *accident*, *incident*, *occident*; *deciduous*.

case[2] keis receptacle, holder XIII (Cursor M.); protective covering XIV; chest; frame XVI, as in *staircase* (XVII). ME. *case*, *caas*, *cass* – OF. *casse*, dial. var. of *chasse* (mod. *châsse* reliquary, frame) = Pr. *caisa*, It. *cassa* :- L. *capsa* box, bookcase, f. base of *capere* hold (see HEAVE).

casein kei·siin (chem.) proteid constituent of milk. XIX. f. L. *caseus* CHEESE; see -IN.

casemate kei·smeit vaulted chamber in the ramparts of a fortress. XVI (*casamate*). Orig. – It. *casamatta* or Sp. *casamata*; later assim. to F. *casemate*, which is itself – It., as are also G. *kasematte*, Du. *kazemat*. The earlier form of the It. word is *camata*, which is perh. – Gr. *khásma*, pl. *khásmata* gap, CHASM (cf. Rabelais' form †*chasmate*); the word was presumably remodelled on It. *casa* house.

casement kei·smĕnt (archit.) hollow moulding, cavetto XV (Lydg.); window frame opening on hinges XVI (*caze-*, *-mund*). f. unidentified el. + -MENT. ¶ No connexion can be made out with medL. *cāsamentum* (i) fee, property, (ii) tenement, dwelling, or OF. *casement*, *chasement* holding, property, or It. *casamento* large house, house divided into flats.

caseous kei·siəs of cheese. XVII. f. L. *caseus* CHEESE + -OUS.

cash[1] kæʃ †money-box; money. XVI (Nashe, Sh.). – F. †*casse*, or its source It. *cassa* :– L. *capsa* CASE[2].

cash[2] kæʃ name for various Eastern coins of low value. XVI. ult. – Pg. †*caxa*, *caixa* – Tamil *kāsu* :– Skr. *karsha* weight of silver or gold equal to $\frac{1}{400}$ of a tulā.

cashew kæ·ʃū, kăʃū· large W. Indian tree, Anacardium occidentale. XVIII (Dampier). – Pg. *caju*, var. of *acaju* (whence F. *acajou* mahogany) – Tupi *caju*, *acaju*.

cashier[1] kæʃiə·ɹ one who pays out and receives money. XVI (Nashe). – Du. *cassier*, or its source, F. *caissier*, f. *caisse* CASH[1]; see -IER.

cashier[2] kăʃiə·ɹ disband (troops); dismiss from office. XVI. Early forms *casseer*, *casseir*, *-ier* – early Flem. *kasseren* disband (soldiers), revoke (a will) – F. *casser* break, dismiss, rescind = It. *cassare* cancel :– L. *quassāre* QUASH. Its currency was prob. orig. due to the Netherlands campaign of 1585.

cashmere kæʃmiə·ɹ (in full *Ca·shmere shawl*), shawl made of fine wool obtained from the Cashmere goat; the material itself. XIX. *Cashmere* (*Kashmīr*) name of a province in the W. Himalayas. Cf. CASSIMERE.

casino kəsī·nou public room for social meetings. XVIII (Mrs. Piozzi). – It. *casino*, dim. of *casa* house :– L. *casa* cottage (prob. f. base **kat-* cover, protect, as in *cassis* helmet, *castrum* fort).

cask kȧsk hooped wooden vessel formed of curved staves; †casket, case; †helmet. XV. – F. *casque* or Sp. *casco* helmet, CASQUE. The earliest and prevailing sense was prob. imported with the wine trade and depended on provincial uses of the S. French or Sp. region, where, however, the only recorded sense is 'helmet'.

casket kȧskit small box or chest for precious articles. XV. Of obscure origin; poss. – AN. alteration of synon. (O)F. *cassette* – It. *cassetta*, dim. of *cassa* :– L. *capsa* (see CASE[2], CASH[1]); see -ET.

casque kȧsk helmet. XVII. – F. *casque* – Sp. *casco*; cf. CASK.

cassation kæsei·ʃən annulment. XV. – (O)F. *cassation*, f. *casser* QUASH; see -ATION.

cassava kăsā·və plant also called mandioc; starch obtained from this (tapioca). XVI. The earliest forms *cazibi*, *cas(s)avi*, *-vie*, *-via*, repr. original Taino (Hayti) *casavi*, *caçabi*; the present form is an alteration of these after F. *cassave* (cf. Sp. *casabe*, Pg. *cassave*); a common var. was *cassada* (XVII), after F. †*cassade*.

casserole kæ·səroul stew-pan; edible casing of a made dish. XVIII. – F. *casserole*, extension of *cassole* (= Pr. *casola*, It. *cazzuola*), dim. of *casse* – Pr. *casa* (= It. *cazza*) :– Rom. (late L.) *cattia* 'trulla, panna' (whence OHG. *chazzi*) – Gr. *kuáthion*, *kuátheion*, dim. of *kúathos* cup.

cassia kæ·siə kind of cinnamon. OE. and ME. (biblical), but not naturalized till XVI, when its poetical use for 'fragrant plant', derived partly from Psalm xlv 8, partly from Latin poets, begins. – L. *cassia*, *casia* – Gr. *kasiā* – Heb. *q'tsī'āh* bark resembling cinnamon, f. *qātsa'* strip off.

cassimere kæ·simiəɹ fine twilled woollen cloth. XVIII. Early var. of CASHMERE; *Cassimer* occurs as the name of the country in Herbert's Travels (1665). Cf. F. *casimir*, It. *casimirra*, Du. *kasjmier*, KERSEYMERE.

cassock kæ·sək soldier's or rider's cloak; long loose coat or gown XVI; long (esp. black) tunic worn by ecclesiastics XVII. – F. *casaque* – It. *casacca*, prob. – Turk. *quzzāk* vagabond, nomad (see COSSACK); the application was presumably transf. from the light horsemen to the riding-coat worn by them. ¶ The word has spread over a great part of Europe.

cassowary kæ·səwəri bird related to the ostrich, Casuarius. XVII (*cassawar(a)way*). – Malay *kasuārī*, *kasavārī*; in modL. (Linnæus) *casuaris*, Du. *kasuaris*, F. *casoar*, It. *casuario*.

cast kȧst superseded OE. *weorpan* WARP in the sense of THROW, but is now largely itself superseded by the latter in the ordinary physical sense, though used extensively in many transf. and techn. applications. XIII (earliest in the West, but current over a wide area before 1300). – ON. *kasta*, rel. to *kǫs* (:– **kasu*), *köstr* (:– **kastuz*) heap thrown up, pile (for the formation of the last, cf. L. *gestus* pile, rel. to *gerere* heap together; cf. CONGERIES). Hence **cast** sb. throw XIII; in many derived uses, e.g. †design, device XIII; assignment of parts in a play; twist, turn XVI; tinge, hue XVII (Sh.); style, sort XVII. ¶ For comps. see BROADCAST, CASTAWAY, DOWNCAST, FORECAST, OUTCAST, OVERCAST, ROUGHCAST.

Castalian kæstei·liən pert. to the spring *Castalia* on Mount Parnassus, sacred to the Muses. XVII. f. L. *Castalius*; see -IAN.

castanet kæstəne·t instrument consisting of a small concave shell, used by Spaniards, etc. to produce a rattling noise. XVII (the earliest exx. reflect the Sp. form). – Sp. *castañeta* (with later assim. to F. *castagnette*), dim. of *castaña* :– L. *castanea* CHESTNUT; see -ET.

castaway kà·stəwei rejected, reprobate; and as sb. XVI (Tindale). f. pp. of CAST + AWAY. Its currency is orig. due to the rendering of L. *reprobus*, Gr. *ἀδόκιμος* in 1 Cor. ix 27, 2 Cor. xiii 5; its assoc. with the sea ('shipwrecked man') to Cowper's poem 'The Castaway' (1799).

caste kāst race, stock XVI; hereditary class in Indian society XVII (*cast*; the present sp., modelled on F., is rare before 1800). – Sp., (and particularly in its Indian application) Pg. *casta*, sb. use (sc. *raza*, *raça* race) of fem. of *casto* pure, unmixed (see CHASTE). Formerly identified with CAST sb. in the sense 'stamp, type, sort'.

castellated kæ·stĭleitid built like a castle, as with battlements XVII; furnished with castles XIX. f. medL. *castellātus*, f. L. *castellum* CASTLE; see -ATE², -ED. So **castellA·-TION**. XIX. – medL.

castigate kæ·stigeit correct by punishment or discipline. XVII (Sh.). f. pp. stem of L. *castīgāre* correct, reprove, CHASTISE, f. *castus* pure, CHASTE; see -ATE³. So **castigA·TION**. XIV (Ch.). – L.

castle kà·sl large fortified dwelling; (hence) large mansion of the feudal type XI; tower borne on an elephant's back; tower on the deck of a ship XIV. – AN., ONF. *castel*, var. of *chastel* (mod. *château*) = Pr. *castel*, Sp. *castillo*, It. *castello* :– L. *castellum*, dim. of *castrum* entrenchment, fortified place, fort. In late OE. and ME. biblical use *castel* appears as – L. *castellum* in the sense 'village' (Gr. *kṓmē*) and as tr. of L. *castra* camp. (L. *castrum* is the source of OE. *cæster*, *ċeaster*, repr. by *-caster*, *-chester*, etc. in place-names, and *Caister*, *Caistor*.) As a name of the rook in chess (XVII, Drummond of Hawthornden), after F. *tour* tower, it is based ult. on Vida's poem 'Scacchia Ludus' (XVI).

castor¹ kà·stəɹ beaver XIV; unctuous substance obtained from the beaver, castoreum (used as a drug) XIV. – (O)F. or L. *castor* – Gr. *kástōr*. The history of the present use of *castor oil* (XVIII) for the pale-yellow oil obtained from the seeds of Palma Christi (Ricinus communis) is obscure; it is supposed that this oil took the place in medical use of the drug castoreum (called *huile de castor* by Paré XVI).

castor² kà·stəɹ perforated vessel for sprinkling pepper, sugar, etc. XVII (*Sugar Castar*, *Pepper Caster*); swivel wheel on legs of furniture XVIII. var. of *caster*, agent-noun f. CAST + -ER¹. The sp. *-or* for *-er* (still current) may have been favoured as being more appropriate to an instrument; cf. *razor*, *mirror*, and words in -ATOR.

castrametation kæ:strəmĭtei·ʃən laying out a camp. XVII. – F. *castramétation*, f. L. phr. *castra mētārī* measure or mark out a camp (*mēta* boundary, prop. pillar, post).

castrate kæ·streit remove the testicles of. XVII. f. pp. stem of L. *castrāre*, perh. f. **castrum* knife (= Skr. *çastram*, f. *ças-* cut); see -ATE³. So **castrA·TION**. XV. – F. or L.

casual kæ·ʒuəl, -zj- accidental XIV (Ch.); occurring uncertainly XV; occurring without design XVII. Late ME. *casuel*, *-all* – (O)F. *casuel* and L. *cāsuālis* (in its late and med. uses), f. *cāsus* CASE¹; see -AL¹. Hence **ca·sually.** XIV (Ch.); after medL. *cāsuāliter*. **ca·sualTY** casual occurrence, loss, etc. XV; casual charge XV; after medL. *cāsuālitās*.

casuist kæ·ʒⁱuist student of cases of conscience. XVII. – F. *casuiste* – Sp. (modL.) *casuista*, f. L. *cāsus* CASE¹; see -IST. Hence **ca·suistRY**. XVIII (Pope); prob. after *sophistry*, and so at first derogatory.

cat kæt the quadruped Felis domesticus. OE. *catt* m. (= ON. *kǫttr*), *catte* fem. (= OFris., MDu. *katte*, Du. *kat*, OHG. *kazza*, G. *katze*); reinforced in ME. by *cat*, *kat* – AN., ONF. *cat*, var. of (O)F. *chat* = Pr., Cat. *gat*, Sp., Pg. *gato*, It. *gatto* :– late L. *cattu-s* (Palladius, IV), which superseded the older *fēlēs* (cf. FELINE) on the introduction of the domestic cat into Rome. A CEur. word, repr. also by Ir., Gael. *cat*, W. *cath* :– Celtic **kattos* (in Gaulish as a proper name *Cattos*; in OIr. *Cenn Cait* 'cat-head', name of a prince), Sl. *kotŭ* (Russ. *kot*) tomcat, Lith. *katẽ* cat; the mutual relations and ult. source are doubtful; perh. ult. of African origin (cf. Nubian *kadīs*). Hence **ca·t-HEAD** beam projecting from the bows of a ship for raising the anchor from the water to the deck; said to be so called because orig. the anchor was drawn up to a ring depending from a lion mask XVII (*Cats head*, Capt. Smith); nodule of limestone XVII. **cat** vb. (naut.) raise (an anchor) to the cat-head XVIII; (sl.) vomit (f. phr. *shoot*, earlier *jerk*, or *whip*, *the cat*, of unkn. origin) XIX. Hence **ca·ttish** XVI; **ca·tty** XIX; see -ISH¹, -Y¹.

cata- kæ·tə, kətæ· before a vowel **cat-,** combining with *h* **cath-,** repr. Gr. adv.-prep. *katá* down, down from, according to, used with the senses (1) down, in position, (2) down, in quantity or degree, (3) amiss, mis-, (4) against, alongside, (5) thoroughly, entirely.

catachresis kætəkrī·sis improper use (of word). XVI. – L. *catachrēsis* – Gr. *katákhrēsis*, f. *katakhrêsthai* use amiss, f. *katá* CATA- 3 + *khrêsthai* use, rel. to *khrḗ* it is necessary. So **catachre·stIC(AL)** adjs. XVII. – Gr. (*-ēstikós*).

cataclysm kæ·təklizm deluge; great upheaval. XVII. – F. *cataclysme* – L. *cataclysmos* – Gr. *kataklusmós*, f. *kataklúzein*, f. *katá* CATA- 1 + *klúzein* wash (see CLOACA).

catacombs kæ·təkoumz subterranean cemeteries in Rome, and hence gen. XVII. – F. *catacombes* (cf. Pr. *cathacumbas*, etc.) – late L. *catacumbas*, specific name from *c.* 400 of the cemetery of St. Sebastian on the Appian Way, *Cœmetērium Catacumbas*, or simply *Catacumbas*; the word seems to be orig. invariable, but later was treated as acc. pl., from which a sing. *catacumba* was formed, whence the occas. use of the sg. in modern langs.; the ult. origin is unkn.

catadromous kətæ·drəməs (zool.) descending a river to spawn. XIX. f. Gr. *katádromos*, f. *katá* CATA- 1 + *drómos* running (*drameîn* run) + -OUS. Cf. ANADROMOUS.

catafalque kæ·təfælk erection in a church to receive the coffin of a deceased person; also an imitation of this. XVII (Evelyn; the It. form was sometimes used). – F. *catafalque* – It. *catafalco* (= Pr. *cadafalcs*, Sp. *cadafalso*, *cadahalso*, OF. *escafaut*, mod. *échafaud* SCAFFOLD).

Catalan kæ·tælæn of Catalonia, the most north-easterly province of Spain; the language of this region, the most nearly allied to Spanish of the Romance languages. XV. – F. *Catalan* – Pr., Sp. *Catalan* = Cat. *Cataló* (fem. *Catalane*), adj. of Sp. *Cataluña*, Cat. *Catalunya*. So **Catalon**IAN kætəlou·niən. XVIII. f. *Catalōnia*, L. form of *Cataluña*.

catalepsy kæ·təlepsi disease characterized by a seizure or trance. XVI. – F. *catalepsie* or late L. *catalēpsia*, f. Gr. *katálēpsis*, f. *katalambánein* seize upon, f. *katá* CATA- 5 + *lambánein* take. See -Y[3]. So **catale·p**TIC. XVII.

catalogue kæ·təlɔg list or register, now usu. one methodically arranged. XV. – (O)F. *catalogue*, †*cathalogue* – late L. *catalogus* – Gr. *katálogos*, f. *katalégein* pick out, enlist, enroll, f. *katá* CATA- 5 + *légein* collect, choose, enumerate (see LECTION, LEGION).

catalpa kətæ·lpə plant of the family Bignoniaceæ. XVIII (Catesby). From the language of the Indians of Carolina, U.S.A.

catalysis kətæ·lisis †dissolution. XVII; (chem.) Berzelius's name for chemical actions brought about by a substance that remains unchanged. 1836. – modL. – Gr. *katálusis*, f. *katalúein* dissolve, f. *katá* CATA- 2 + *lúein* loosen (see LOOSE). Hence **ca·talyse**; **cataly·t**IC XIX; **ca·talyst** substance influencing the rate of chemical reaction XX; after *analyse, analysis, analyst, analytic*.

catamaran kæ:təməræ·n raft or float made up of logs tied together side by side. XVII (Dampier). – Tamil *kaṭṭumaram* 'tied wood', f. *kaṭṭu* tie, bond + *maram* wood.

catamite kæ·təmait sodomite's subject. XVI. – L. *catamītus* – (through Etruscan *catmite*) Gr. Γανυμήδης GANYMEDE, Jupiter's cup-bearer.

catamount kæ·təmaunt †catamountain XVII; puma XVIII. Short for **ca·tamountain** leopard, panther, ocelot, tiger-cat XVI (Sh.): earlier *cat of the mountain* (XV–XVI), which was first used to render L. *pardus*, Gr. *párdos* PARD[1].

cataplasm kæ·təplæzm poultice, plaister. XVI. – (O)F. *cataplasme* or late L. *cataplasma*, – Gr. *katáplasma*, f. *kataplássein* plaster over, f. *katá* CATA- 5 + *plássein* fashion, mould (cf. PLASMA).

catapult kæ·təpʌlt (mil.) missile engine XVI; shooting instrument consisting of a forked stick with elastic band XIX. – (O)F. *catapulte* or L. *catapulta* – Gr. *katapéltēs*, f. *katá* CATA- 1 + **pel-*, var. of base of *pállein* hurl.

cataract kæ·tərækt †(pl.) floodgates of heaven (cf. Gen. vii 11, viii 2) XV (Lydg.); †waterspouts; (sg.) waterfall; opacity of the crystalline lens of the eye (prob. fig. use of the sense 'portcullis'; cf. 'cataracte ou coulisse', Paré, *c.* 1550) XVI. – L. *cataracta* (whence F. *cataracte* XVI) – Gr. *katar(r)ákt̄ēs* down-rush, waterfall, portcullis, sb. use of adj. down-rushing, f. *katá* CATA- 1 + (prob.) *rássein* beat, strike.

catarrh kətā·ɹ †running at the nose; inflammation of the mucous membrane. XVI. – F. *catarrhe*, †*catarre*, †*caterre* = Pr. *catar*, Sp., It. *catarro* – late L. *catarrhus* – Gr. *katárrhous* rheum, f. *katarrheîn* run down, f. *katá* CATA- 1 + *rheîn* flow (cf. STREAM).

catarrhine kæ·tərain (zool.) one of a division of the Quadrumana, having the nostrils close together and pointed downwards. XIX. f. Gr. *katá* CATA- 4 + *rhin-*, *rhī́s* nostril.

catastrophe kətæ·strəfi dénouement of a drama XVI (Spenser); disastrous end XVII (Sh.); event subversive of fortune XVII; sudden disaster XVIII. – L. *catastropha* (Petronius) – Gr. *katastrophḗ* overturning, sudden turn, f. *katastréphein* overturn, f. *katá* CATA- 1 + *stréphein* (cf. STROPHE). Cf. F. *catastrophe* (Rabelais). Hence **catastro·ph**IC. XIX.

catawampous, catawamptious kætəwɔ·mpəs, -wɔ·mpʃəs (U.S.) fierce, destructive. XIX. Humorous coinage symbolical of its meaning.

catawba kətɔ̄·bə American grape and the wine made therefrom. XIX. f. name of the river *Catawba*, South Carolina, U.S.A., named after the *Katahba* Indians.

catch kætʃ †chase; capture, grasp, seize; take, get, receive XIII. ME. *cac(c)he-n* – AN., ONF. *cachier*, var. of OF. *chacier* (mod. *chasser*) = Pr. *cassar*, Sp. *cazar*, It. *cacciare* :- Rom. **captiāre*, repl. L. *captāre* try to catch, lie in wait for, (hence) hunt, CHASE (the sense in all the Rom. langs.). *Catch* took over the sense 'seize' and its conjugational forms from the native *latch* (OE. *læććan*), e.g. *ca(u)hte, caught* and *cachte, catched,* beside *la(u)hte, laught* and *lachte, latched.* Hence **catch** sb. act of catching, something caught XV; contrivance for checking a mechanism XIV; (mus.) round (each singer 'catching up' his part at the right moment) XVII; **ca·tch**MENT collection of rainfall XIX.

catchpoll kæ·tʃpoul †tax-gatherer OE.; sheriff's officer XIV, late OE. *kæćepol* (XI) – AN., OF. **cachepol*, var. of OF. *chacepol*, or – AL. *cacepollus* (x, Laws of Æthelred, Quadripartitus 3, 3), also *chassipullus*, etc.; f. Rom. **captiāre* CHASE, CATCH+L. *pullus* fowl.

catchup, catsup see KETCHUP.

catechize kæ·tĭkaiz give systematic oral instruction XV; question systematically (from the question-and-answer form of the Church Catechism) XVII (Sh.). – ChrL. *catēchīzāre* (Tertullian), in medL. also *cath-* (whence (O)F. *catéchiser*, Pr. *cathezizar*, etc.) – eccl.Gr. *katēkhízein*, f. *katēkheîn* sound through, instruct orally, spec. in N.T. in the elements of religion, f. *katá* CATA-+ *ēkheîn* sound; see ECHO, -IZE. So **ca·tech**ISM †catechetical instruction; manual of religious instruction in the form of question and answer. XVI. – ChrL. *catēchismus* (Augustine) – Gr. **ca·tech**IST. XVI. – ChrL. *catēchista* (Jerome) – Gr.; cf. (O)F. *catéchisme, -iste.* **catechet**ICAL -ke·tikəl. XVII.

catechu kæ·tiʃū astringent substance obtained from various Eastern barks, etc. XVII. – modL. *catechu*, defined as 'terra japonica' (Japanese earth) on account of its appearance, unexpl. deriv. of Malay *kachu*; see CACHOU.

catechumen kætikjū·mĕn convert under instruction. XV. – (O)F. *catéchumène* or ecclL. *catēchūmenus* – Gr. *katēkhoúmenos* being instructed, prp. pass. of *katēkheîn* (see CATECHIZE). The present form is of doubtful occurrence before 1600; the early pl. *cathecumynys* is prob. an anglicization of L. pl. *catēchūmenī.*

category kæ·tigəri classification, 'predicament' XV; class, division XVII. – F. *catégorie* (Rabelais) or its source, late L. *catēgoria* (Augustine) – Gr. *katēgoriā* accusation, assertion, predication, f. *katḗgoros* accuser, etc., *katēgoreîn*, f. *katá* CATA- (4)+ *agorā́* assembly, harangue, rel. to *ageírein* assemble; see -Y³. The proper L. equiv. is *prædīcāmentum* PREDICAMENT. So **categor**IC kætigɔ·rik XVII, **catego·r**ICAL XVI. – F. *catégorique* (Rabelais) or late L. *catēgoricus* (Sidonius).

catena kətī·nə series of excerpts or quotations in support of a thesis, etc. XVII (Milton). Short for ecclL. *catēna patrum* 'chain of the Fathers' (viz. of the Church); see CHAIN. So **cate·n**ARY (math.) curve formed by a chain hanging from two points. XVIII. – medL. *catēnāria*, sb. use of fem. of L. *catēnārius.* **catena**A·TION linking into or as with a chain. XVII. – L. *catēnātiō(n-)*, f. *catēnāre* chain together f. *catēna.*

cater kei·təɹ provide food *for.* XVI (Sh.). f. †*cater* (XIV) buyer of provisions, caterer, aphetic form of †*acater* purchaser, purveyer – AN. *acatour*, var. of OF. *achatour*, agent-n. of *achater* (mod. *acheter*) = Pr. *acaptar*, OIt. *accattare* :– Rom. **accaptāre*, f. *ad* AC-+*captāre* catch, f. *capt-*, *capere* take (see HEAVE); cf. CATES. Hence **ca·terer.** XVI; see -ER¹.

cateran kæ·tərən (Sc.) Highland marauder. XIV (*ketharine*), XVI (*catherein*, Dunbar). – medL. *caterānus, kethernus*, and its source Gael. *ceathairne* peasantry, corr. to Ir. *ceithern* KERN.

cater-cousin kei·təɹkʌzn (arch.) intimate friend. XVI (Latimer). Of unkn. origin; poss. f. †*cater* caterer (see CATER)+COUSIN, as if the orig. notion was of persons being catered for or boarded together; cf. *foster-brother*, etc.

caterpillar kæ·təɹpiləɹ larva of butterfly or moth XV; †rapacious person XVI. The earliest recorded form, *catyrpel* (Prompt. Parv.) is prob. – AN. var. (cf. Norman-Picard *katplöz, ka(r)plüz, -plöz*) of OF. *chatepelose* 'hairy cat' (popL. **catta pilōsa*); assoc. in XVI with †*piller* ravager, plunderer (see PILLAGE), prob. brought about the extended form in *-piller, -pillar*, the latter form becoming prevalent after Johnson. ¶ For the application to caterpillars of words meaning 'cat', cf. It. dial. *gat(a), gatin(a), gatola*, G. dial. *teufelskatz* 'devil's cat'; similarly synon. F. *chenille* :– L. *canīcula*, dim. of *canis* dog.

caterwaul kæ·təɹwōl make the characteristic cry of cats at rutting time. XIV (Ch.). One of a group of cogn. formations of which the earliest is *caterwawed* caterwauling ('Wife of Bath's Prologue' 354, where some MSS. have *-wrawet*), a noun of action with *-ed*, repr. OE. *-aþ.* The first el. is to be identified with CAT, but it is doubtful whether it is rel. to or – LG., Du. *kater* male cat, or whether the *-er-* is merely an arbitrary connective syll.; the second el. appears variously as *-wawe, -wrawe, -wall, -waul* (XVI), *-wrall* (cf. the use of *waw, waul* XVI, and *wraw, wraul* XV as independent vbs., all of which are imit. formations with some Continental analogues); immed. connexion with an identical LG. dial. *katterwaulen* is dubious.

cates keits †provisions, victuals XV; (arch.) delicacies XVI. pl. of *cate*, aphetic form of *acate* – AN. *acat*, var. of (O)F. *achat*, f. *achater* (see CATER).

catgut kæ·tgʌt dried intestines of sheep, etc. used for the strings of musical instruments. XVI. f. CAT+GUT; cf. synon. *catling* XVI (see -LING); the reason for the use of *cat* is unkn., but cf. synon. Du. *kattedarm.*

cathartic kăþā·ɹtik cleansing, purgative. XVII. – late L. *catharticus* – Gr. *kathartikós*, f. *kathairein* cleanse, f. *katharós* clean. So

catharsis kǽþā·ɹsis purgation. XIX. – modL. – Gr. *kátharsis*.

Cathay kəþei· (Northern) China. XIV (also *Chatay*, Maund.). – medL. *Cataia, Cathaya*, f. *Kitai*, name of the inhabitants (still the Russ. name for China), f. name of the alien dynasty *Khitán*. Hence **Cathay·an** Chinese, also †*Cataian* (sl.) sharper, rascal XVI (Sh.); see -AN.

cathedral kəþī·drəl pert. to an episcopal see. XIII (*chyrche cathedral*). – (O)F. *cathédral* – late L. *cathedrālis*, f. L. *cathedra* – Gr. *kathédrā* seat, f. *katá* down, CATA- (1) + **hed-* :– **sed-* SIT; as sb. (cf. F. *cathédrale*), short for *cathedral church*. XVI.

catheter kæ·þitəɹ (surg.) tubular instrument for passing into the bladder. XVII. – late L. *cathetēr* – Gr. *kathetḗr*, f. **kathe-, kathiénai* send or let down, f. *katá* down, CATA- (1) + *hiénai* send (base **je-*, as in L. *ja|cere* throw) + agent-suffix *-tēr*.

Catherine kæ·þərin name of a female saint (of Alexandria) martyred by beheading after having been condemned to be broken on the wheel; *Catherine wheel*, (esp. her.) figure of a wheel with spikes projecting from its circumference XVI; firework that rotates while burning XVIII; lateral somersault XIX.

cathode kæ·þoud (electr.) opp. to ANODE. XIX (Faraday). – Gr. *káthodos* going down, way down, f. *katá* CATA- (1) + *hodós* way (cf. HODOMETER).

catholic kæ·þəlik universal (spec. of the Christian Church) XIV; sb. member of the Catholic Church XV. – (O)F. *catholique* or its source ChrL. *catholicus* – Gr. *katholikós* general, universal, f. *kathólou* (i.e. *kath' hólou*) in general, generally, f. *katá* in respect of (cf. CATA-), *hólos* whole, rel. to L. *salvus* SAFE. Hence **catholic**ISM kəþɔ·lĭsizm, -IZE. XVII. **catholic**ITY kæþəli·sĭti. XIX.

cation kæ·taiən (electr.) electro-positive element. XIX (Faraday). – Gr. *katión*, sb. use of n. of *katiṓn*, prp. of *katiénai*, f. *katá*, CATA- (1) + *iénai* go (rel. to L. *īre* go); cf. ANION.

catkin kæ·tkin downy (pendent) inflorescence. XVI (Lyte, tr. Dodoens). – Du. †*katteken* lit. kitten, dim. of *katte* CAT; so modL. *catulus* and many Rom. forms (e.g. F. *chats de saule* willow catkins, and *chaton* catkin, dim. of *chat*), G. *kätzchen*.

catling see CATGUT.

catmint kæ·tmint the plant Nepeta Cataria, which attracts cats. XIII (*kattesminte*). f. CAT + MINT². after medL. *herba catti, h. cataria*; so F. *herbe du chat*, G. *katzenminze*, Du. *kattekruid*.

catoptric kætɔ·ptrik relating to optical reflexion. XVIII (Goldsmith); sb. XVI (Dee). – Gr. *katoptrikós*, f. *kátoptron* mirror, f. *katá* CATA- (4) + **op-* see (cf. OPTICS) + *-tron*, instrumental suffix; see -IC.

catsup var. of CATCHUP.

cattle kæ·tl †property; live stock XIII (Laȝamon, later version; Cursor M.). ME. *catel(l)* – AN., ONF. *catel*, var. of *chatel*, which is directly repr. by CHATTEL, q.v. The orig. gen. sense 'wealth, property' became narrowed to 'movable property', esp. as typified by live stock, which has been the only application in modern times, except in the legal phr. †*goods and cattels* (cf. AL. *bona et catalla*). The sp. *cattle* is found *c.* 1600, but did not supersede *cattel(l)* till *c.* 1700.

catty kæ·ti weight of $1\frac{1}{3}$ lb. avoirdupois. XVI. – Malay-Javanese *kātī, katī*; cf. CADDY.

catydid see KATYDID.

Caucasian kōkei·ziən XIX. f. *Caucasus* or *Caucasia*, f. Sl. *Kavkaz*; formerly applied (after Blumenbach) to the white race of mankind as being supposed to derive from the Caucasus; see -IAN.

caucus kō·kəs (U.S.) private meeting of the chiefs of a political party XVIII; in Eng. use applied from 1878 to organizations for managing political elections, etc. Plausibly referred to Algonkin *cau-cau-as-u*, which appears in Capt. John Smith's 'Virginia' (16..) as *caw-cawaassough* adviser, from a vb. meaning 'talk to, advise, urge'; but there is an earlier reference to a place 'West-Corcus in Boston'.

caudal kō·dəl pert. to a tail. XVII. – medL. *caudālis*, f. L. *cauda* tail; see -AL¹. So **cau·date** tailed. XVII. – modL.; see -ATE².

caudle kō·dl thin gruel sweetened and spiced. XIII. – ONF. *caudel*, var. of *chaudel* (mod. *chaudeau*) :– medL. **caldellum*, dim. of L. *caldum* hot drink, sb. use of n. of *cal(i)dus* hot (cf. LEE¹, LUKEWARM).

caul kōl (hist.) woman's close-fitting cap, hairnet; investing membrane, e.g. omentum, amnion. XIII. ME. *calle*, of doubtful origin; perh. – (O)F. *cale* head-covering, f. *calotte* (see CALOTTE) by back-formation; but the Eng. word is recorded earlier. Cf. KELL.

cauldron kō·ldrən large kettle. XIII. ME. *caudroun* – AN., ONF. *caudron* (mod. *chaudron*) = Sp. *calderón*, It. *calderone*, augm. of Rom. **caldario*, L. *caldārium* hot bath (cf. late *caldāria* pot, whence F. *chaudière*), f. *cal(i)dus* hot, ult. rel. to LEE¹, LEW. The etymologizing sp. with *l* appeared XV and subseq. infl. the pronunc.

cauliflower kɔ·liflauəɹ variety of cabbage, the inflorescence of which forms a white head. XVI (Gerarde). Earlier *cole flory, colliflory*, alteration (by assim. to COLE) of F. †*chou fleuri* (*flori*), prob. – It. *cavolfiore*, pl. *cavoli fiori* (cf. Sp. *coliflor*) or modL. *cauliflōra* 'flowered cabbage' (cf. G. *blumenkohl*, Du. *bloemkool* 'flower-cole'). The second el. was assim. to *flower* XVII, as in F. *chou-fleur*.

caulk kɔ̄k stop the seams of (a ship). XV. – OF. *cauquer, caukier*, north. var. of OF. *cauchier* tread, press with force (mod. *côchier* tread, of birds) = Pr., Sp., Pg. *calcar*, It. *calcare* :– L. *calcāre* tread, press, f. *calc-, calx* heel.

cause kɔ̄z ground or reason of action XIII; that which produces an effect XIV; legal case or suit XIII. – (O)F. *cause* (= Pr., Sp., It. *causa*) – L. *caus(s)a* reason, motive, lawsuit (whence in the sense of 'thing', developed from 'business, matter, subject', Pr., Sp., It. *cosa*, F. *chose*). So **cau·**SAL[1]. XVI. – late L. *causālis*; so in F. **causa·**LITY XVII, **causa·**TION XVII, **cau·sat**IVE XV; all – late L. or F. **cause** vb. be the cause of. XIV. – (O)F. *causer* or medL. *causāre*, f. *causa*.

causerie kou·zəri, || kōzri informal talk. XIX. F., f. *causer* talk – L. *causārī* plead a CAUSE.

causeway kɔ̄·zwei raised road XV; (paved) highway XVII. Early forms are *cawce, cawcy*, and *causey way*, reduced to *caus(e)way* XVI; f. *cauce, cauci*, early forms (XIV) of *causey* + WAY. *Causey* is – AN. **caucé(e)* = ONF. *caucíée* (mod. *chaussée*) = Pr. *calsada* (whence Sp., Pg. *calzada*) :– Rom. **calciāta* (sc. *via* way, road), fem. pp. f. L. *calcis, calx* lime, CHALK.

caustic kɔ̄·stik corrosive XIV; fig. bitter XVIII. – F. *caustique* or L. *causticus* – Gr. *kaustikós* capable of burning, f. *kaustós* combustible, f. **kaϝ-*, base of *kaíein* burn; see -IC.

cautelous kɔ̄·tiləs artful, wily XIV; cautious XVI. – (O)F. *cauteleux*, f. L. *cautēla* precaution, f. *caut-*; see CAUTION, -OUS.

cauterize kɔ̄·təraiz sear as with a caustic. XIV. – (O)F. *cautériser* – late L. *cautērizāre*, altered – Gr. *kautēriázein*, f. *kautḗrion*, whence (through L. *cautērium*), **cau·tery** XIV searing instrument, caustic drug, cauterizing operation, beside which †*cau·ter* was formerly used for the instrument – (O)F. *cautère* (= Pr. *cauteri*, etc.); ult. from Gr. *kaíein*; see CAUSTIC, -IZE.

caution kɔ̄·ʃən security, bail XIII; taking heed; word of warning XVII. orig. – (O)F. *caution* – L. *cautiō(n-)*, f. pp. stem of *cavēre* take heed; a re-adoption from L. took place *c.* 1600; see -TION. Hence **cau·tion** vb. warn. XVII. So **cautious** kɔ̄·ʃəs XVII; on the model of *ambition, ambitious*, etc.; see -TIOUS.

cavalcade kævəlkei·d †ride XVI; procession on horseback XVII. – F. *cavalcade*, earlier †*-cate* – It. *cavalcata* (corr. to F. *chevauchée*), f. *cavalcare* :– Rom. **caballicāre* ride, f. L. *caballus* pack-horse, nag, in Rom. (VI) soldier's word for 'horse' (F. *cheval*, Sp. *caballo*, It. *cavallo*, etc.), which, like Gr. *kabállēs*, is an alien word; see -ADE.

cavalier kævəliə·ɹ horseman; courtly gentleman, gallant XVI; seventeenth-century Royalist XVII (1642). – F. *cavalier* or its source It. *cavaliere* (cf. Pr. *cavalier*, Sp. *caballero*, Pg. *cavalleiro*), deriv. of L. (Rom.) *caballus* horse (see prec.); cf. late L. *caballārius* rider, ostler, and see -IER. In XVI–XVII forms of Sp. or Pg. origin were in use. As adj. off-hand, supercilious XVII.

cavallo, cavally kəvæ·lou, -æ·li horse-mackerel. XVII (Capt. Smith). – Sp. *caballo*, for *caballa*; forms in *-ally*, pl. *-allies* perh. depend on It. *cavalli*, pl. of *cavallo* mackerel.

cavalry kæ·vəlri horse-soldiers. XVI (*cavallerie*). – F. *cavallerie* – It. *cavalleria* (corr. to F. *chevalerie* CHIVALRY), f. *cavallo*; see CAVALCADE and -ERY, -RY.

cavatina kævətī·nə short simple song. XIX (M. Edgeworth, Dickens). It. 'air sung by an actor on his first appearance in an act', f. *cavata* production of sound from an instrument, f. *cavare* extract, f. *cavo* hollow :– L. *cavus* (see CAVE[1]).

cave[1] keiv underground hollow. XIII. – (O)F. *cave* (now 'cellar') – L. *cava*, sb. use of fem. sg. or n. pl. of *cavus* hollow (cf. It. *cava* ditch, mine, quarry).

cave[2] keiv fall *in* over a hollow. XVIII. The earliest evidence is from Amer. sources; prob. of East Anglian origin and a var. of dial. (esp. eastern) *calve* (XVIII), *cauve*, which may have been a LG. word introduced by workmen from the Low Countries engaged in the drainage of the Lincolnshire fens; cf. WFlem. *inkalven* fall in, Du. *afkalven* fall away, *uitkalven* fall out.

caveat kei·viæt, kæ·viæt warning, caution. XVI. L., 3rd sg. pres. subj. of *cavēre* beware (see CAUTION).

cavendish kæ·vəndiʃ kind of tobacco. XIX. Said to be named after an American manufacturer.

cavern kæ·vəɹn subterranean cavity. XIV (Ch.). – (O)F. *caverne* or L. *caverna*, f. *cavus* hollow; cf. CAVE[1] and, for the suffix, CISTERN, TAVERN. So **ca·vern**OUS. XV. – (O)F. *caverneux*, L. *cavernōsus*.

cavesson kæ·visən horse's nose-band. XVI. – F. *caveçon* – It. *cavezzone*, augm. of *cavezza* halter :– Rom. **capitia*, f. medL. *capitium* head-covering, f. *capit-, caput* HEAD.

cavetto kəve·tou (archit.) hollow moulding. XVII. It., dim. of *cavo* hollow (see CAVE[1]).

caviare kæ·viāɹ roe of sturgeon. XVI. In its earliest use with a variety of forms repr. It. *caviale* (whence F. †*cavial*), Sp. *cabial*, Pg. *caviar*, †*cavial*, F. *caviar*, all based on Turk. *khāvyār*. The pronunc. has varied; orig. four syll. as in *cauiarie* (Sh. 'Hamlet' II ii 457), *caueary* (Bacon), *cavialy* (XVII), it was commonly reduced in XVII to three or two; in XVIII r.w. *prepare* or *cheer* (Swift); the more recent pronunc. kæ·viāɹ or kæviā·ɹ may be due to the F. ¶ The comestible is of Russ. origin, but the Russ. name is *ikrá*.

cavil kæ·vĭl raise captious objections. XVI. – (O)F. *caviller* – L. *cavillārī*, f. *cavilla* scoffing, mockery, prob. for **calvilla* and rel. to *calvārī* use artifice, *calumnia* CALUMNY. So **cavilla·tion**. XIV. – (O)F. – L.

cavity kæ·vĭti hollow place. XVI. –F. *cavité*, for earlier † *caveté*, or late L. *cavitās* (cf. Sp. *cavidad*, It. *cavità*), f. *cavus* hollow; see CAVE[1], ITY.

cavort kəvɔ̄·ɹt (orig. U.S.) prance or caper about, orig. of a horse or rider. XIX. perh. perversion of CURVET suggested by *vault* (cf. *cavaulting* in 'Slang Dict.' 1874).

cavy kei·vi rodent of the genus Cavia or family Caviidæ, including the guinea-pig and the capybara. XVIII. – modL. *cavia*, f. Galibi (French Guiana) *cabiai*. Cf. F. *cavié*. ¶ Goldsmith has *cabiai*, following Buffon.

caw kɔ̄ imit. of the cry of rooks and the like. XVI (Sh.). Cf. Du. *kauw* jackdaw.

cay kei, kī low insular bank of sand, etc. XVIII (Sloane's 'Jamaica'). – Sp. *cayo* shoal, sandbank, barrier reef – F. *quai*, †*cay* QUAY. (The proper name of several islands off Central America.)

cayenne keie·n, (with *pepper*) kei·en very pungent kind of pepper. XVIII. Early forms *kayan*, *kian* (whence a former pronunc. kaiæ·n); orig. – Tupi *kyynha*, *quiynha*, later assim. to *Cayenne*, chief town of French Guiana.

cayman, caiman kei·mən American alligator. XVI. – Sp., Pg. *caiman* (whence also F. *caïman*) – Carib *acayuman*, *cay(e)man*.

cease sīs bring or come to an end. XIV (Cursor M.). ME. *cesse*, beside *cese* – (O)F. *cesser* (= Pr., Pg. *cessar*, Sp. *cesar*, It. *cessare*) :– L. *cessāre* stop, f. *cess-*, pp. stem of *cēdere* yield, CEDE. The lengthening of the stem-vowel is paralleled in *appeal*, *lease*, *prease*, ME. form of *press*.

cecity sī·sĭti blindness. XVI. – L. *cæcitās*, f. *cæcus* blind; see -ITY.

cedar sī·dəɹ evergreen conifer, Cedrus Libani. XIII (*cedre*, Cursor M.). – OF. *cedre* (mod. *cèdre*) – L. *cedrus* – Gr. *kédros*, juniper, cedar, rel. to Lith. *kadagỹs*, OPruss. *kadegis* juniper. (OE. had *ceder* from L.) The sp. with *-ar* dates from XVI. Hence **ce·darn** of cedar. XVII (Milton, whence in later poets); see -EN[3].

cede sīd †give way XVII; give up, yield XVIII. – F. *céder* or L. *cēdere* go, go away, retire, yield (acc. to some, combining two distinct words). ¶ Compound derivs. of the L. vb. are repr. by *accede, concede, intercede, precede, recede*; *exceed, proceed, succeed*; *abscess, excess, process, success*; *accession, concession, intercession, precession, procession, succession; processional, recessional*; *ancestor*; cf. CEASE, CESSATION, CESSION.

cedilla sidi·lə the mark ̧ written under *c*. XVI. – Sp. *cedilla*, now *zedilla*, dim. of *zeda* letter *z*. ¶ The Sp. var. *cerilla* has also been used; cf. F. *cérille*.

cee sī name of the letter C. OE. *cē* (Ælfric); cf. F. *cé*, L. *cē*. attrib. in **cee-spring, C-spring** carriage spring shaped like C.

ceiling sī·liŋ †lining of the inside of roof or walls XIV; †screen of tapestry, curtain XV; (naut.) inside planking of a ship's bottom XVII; plaster covering the top of a room XVI. Late ME. *celynge*, *sil-*, *syling*, early modEng. *syll-*, *seel-*, *ciel-*, *seyl-*, appearing contemp. with *celure*, *selure*, *sil(l)our*, later *seller* canopy, hangings, tapestry (XIV–XVI), and somewhat earlier than *ceil* vb. line with woodwork, etc. (XV–XVII); these correspond in use to medL. *cēlum* (XII), *cēlātūra* (XIII), *cēlūra* (XIV), and vb. *cēlāre* (XIII), but the meaning in particular instances is freq. uncertain; possible OF. connexions are rare (e.g. *celé* perh. ceiling, panelling), and it remains doubtful whether L. *cælum* heaven, vault of the sky, is the ult. base, and how far L. *cælāre* engrave, *cælātūra* engraving, carving, are concerned.

celadon se·lədɔn pale shade of green. XVIII. – F. *céladon*, name of a languorous gallant in the 'Astrée' of d'Urfé (1610), who took it from Ovid's 'Metamorphoses'.

celandine se·ləndain name of two (distinct) plants bearing yellow flowers regarded by the ancients as species of the same plant. XIII–XIV. Earliest form *celidoine*, the intrusive *-n-* being recorded XV. – OF. *celidoine* – medL. *celidonia*, for L. *chelidonia* (sc. *herba* plant), *-onium* – Gr. *khelidónion*, f. *khelidṓn* swallow; the ancients associated the plant in various ways with the swallow and its habits.

-cele sīl, as the final el. in various medical terms in the sense 'tumour', repr. modL. *-cēlē* – Gr. *kḗlē* swelling, rel. to OE. *hēala* rupture.

celebrate se·libreit perform or observe publicly and duly XV; proclaim XVI. f. †*celebrate*, pp. (XV) – L. *celebrātus*, pp. of *celebrāre*, f. *celebr-*, *celeber* frequented, frequent, renowned; see -ATE[3]. Hence **ce·lebrated** famous, renowned XVII. So **celebra·tion**. XVI. – L.

celeriac sĭle·riæk turnip-rooted celery. XVIII. f. CELERY, with arbitrary use of the suffix -AC.

celerity sĭle·rĭti swiftness. XV. – (O)F. *célérité* – L. *celeritās*, f. *celer* swift, prob. rel. to Gr. *kéllein* drive, *kélēs* runner; see -ITY.

celery se·ləri the plant Apium graveolens. XVII (Evelyn). – F. *céleri* (*sceleri d'Italie* XVII) – dial. It. (Lombard) *selleri* :– L. *selīnon*, *-selīnum* – Gr. *sélinon*. ¶ The native name of the wild form is SMALLAGE.

celestial sile·stiəl heavenly. XIV (Ch.). – OF. *celestial* (= Sp. *celestial*, It. *celestiale*) – medL. **cælestiālis*, f. L. *cælestis*, f. *cælum* heaven; see -IAL.

celibacy se·libəsi unmarried state, devotion to the single life. XVII. f. L. *cælibātus*, f. *cælib-*, *-ebs* unmarried, bachelor; see -ACY. This superseded †**celibate**[1] (XVII) – F. *célibat* or its L. source as above; see -ATE[1]. Hence, after such pairs as *magistracy*, *magistrate*, **celibate**[2] se·libət unmarried (man) XIX; for this F. has *célibataire*, whence **ce:libat**A·RIAN XIX.

cell sel dependent religious house XII; small dwelling or apartment; cavity in an organism XIV; compartment of honeycomb XVI; of a plant XVII; various scientific uses (electr., etc.) XIX. – OF. *celle*, or its source L. *cella* store-room, chamber, small apartment, 'chapel' in a temple, in medL. in the first two senses above, rel. to L. *cēlāre*, *occulere* CONCEAL (cf. OCCULT).

cellar se·ləɹ †store-room XIII; underground room XIV (?). ME. *celer* – AN. *celer* = OF. *celier* (mod. *cellier*) :– late L. *cellārium* set of cells, storehouse for food, f. *cella* CELL; see -ARY.

'cello tʃe·lou colloq. shortening of VIOLONCELLO. XIX.

cellular se·ljŭləɹ characterized by cells. XVIII. – F. *cellulaire* – modL. *cellulāris*, f. *cellula*, dim. of *cella* CELL; see -AR. ¶ In F. *cellule* has superseded the simple †*celle*.

cellulose se·ljŭlous adj. consisting of cells XVIII; sb. lignin, essential part of the solid substance of plants XIX. As adj. – modL. *cellulōsus*; as sb. – F. *cellulose* (Payen, 1863); see prec. and -OSE. Hence **ce·lluloid** artificial substitute for ivory, etc. invented in America by the brothers Hyatt in 1869 and patented in Great Britain 1871; the use of -OID is arbitrary.

Celt, Kelt selt, kelt †a Gaul XVII; one who speaks a Celtic language XVIII. In the earliest use – L. *Celtæ* pl. – Gr. *Keltoí* (later *Kéltai*, perh. from L.); in the mod. use – F. *Celte* (Pezron 1703), applied first to the Bretons as representatives of the ancient Gauls. So **Ce·ltic** of the ancient Celtæ XVII; epithet of the IE. group of languages consisting of Breton, Cornish, Welsh, Irish, Manx, and Gaelic XVIII. – L. *Celticus* and F. *celtique*.

celt selt prehistoric implement with chisel edge. XVIII. – modL. *celtes* (Beger, 'Thesaurus Brandeburgicus', 1696), based on *celte*, which occurs in the Clementine text of Vulg., Job xix 24 ('stylo ferreo et plumbi lamina vel *celte* sculpantur in silice'), where some MSS. read *certe* 'surely' (corr. to 'for ever' of A.V.); the adoption of the term as a technical term of archæology was prob. assisted by a supposed connexion with *Celt*.

cement sime·nt strong mortar. XIII. ME. *si·ment* – (O)F. *ciment* = Pr. *cimen*, Sp. *cimiento* foundation, It. *cimento* experiment, test :– L. *cæmentum* quarry stone, pl. chips of stone, for **cædmentum*, f. *cædere* hew (cf. -CIDE, DECIDE); see -MENT. The meaning of the L. word appears to have passed from 'broken stone' to 'pounded stone, etc. mixed with lime, etc. to make a strong setting mortar'. The forms *ciment*, *cyment* continued till XVII, and the stressing on the first syll. till XIX. So **ceme·nt** vb. XIV. – (O)F. *cimenter*.

cemetery se·mĭt(ə)ri burial-ground. XIV. –late L. *cœmētērium* (whence also F. *cimetière*) – Gr. *koimētḗrion* dormitory, (in Christian writers) burial-ground, f. *koimân* put to sleep (cf. *keîsthai* lie down, rel. to HOME.)

cenobite var. of CŒNOBITE.

cenotaph se·nŏtàf sepulchral monument to a person buried elsewhere. XVII (Holland). – F. *cénotaphe* – late L. *cenotaphium* – Gr. *kenós* empty + *táphos* tomb.

censer se·nsəɹ vessel in which incense is burnt ceremonially. XIII (*senser*). – AN. *censer*, *senser*, OF. *censier*, aphetic of *encensier*, f. *encens* INCENSE[1]. So **cense** sens vb. burn incense to, fumigate with incense. XIV (Ch.). – (O)F. *encenser*, f. *encens*.

censor se·nsəɹ supervisor of morals, etc. XVI. – L. *cēnsor*, f. *cēnsēre* pronounce as an opinion, declare the status of, assess, rate, judge, think, f. **kens-* make known with authority (cf. Skr. *çáṁsati* recite, OPers. *θātiy* speak, proclaim). Hence **ce·nsor** vb. late XIX. So **censure** se·nʃəɹ †judgement XIV; adverse judgement XVII (Sh.). – (O)F. *censure* – L. *cēnsūra*; see -URE. **ce·nsure** vb. give judgement upon. XVI. – F. *censurer*.

census se·nsəs registration of citizens in ancient Rome XVII; enumeration of population XVIII (Gibbon). – L. *cēnsus*, f. *cēns-*; see prec.

cent sent A. in phr. *per cent* for every hundred XVI, prob. orig. as a financial term – It. *per cento*, with partial assim. to F. *pour cent*, and perh. infl. by pseudo-L. *per centum* (see PER, HUNDRED); B. as independent sb. (U.S., etc.) $\frac{1}{100}$ of a dollar XVIII (first applied in 1782 to a proposed unit of coinage of which 100 should make a coin equal to $\frac{5}{72}$ of a dollar; in 1786 the present use was adopted); French centime XIX.

cental se·ntəl weight of 100 lb. avoirdupois. 1859. f. L. *centum* 100, perh. after *quintal*.

centaur se·ntɔ̄ɹ fabulous creature, half man, half horse. XIV (Ch.). – L. *centaurus* – Gr. *kéntauros*, of unkn. origin; in early Gr. literature the name of a savage people of Thessaly.

centaury se·ntɔ̄ri plant the medicinal properties of which were said to have been discovered by Chiron the centaur. XIV (Ch.).

– late L. *centauria, -ea*, for L. *centaurion, -ēum* – Gr. *kentaúreion, -taúrion*, f. *kéntauros* CENTAUR.

centenary sentī·nəri, se·ntinəri adj. of a hundred years XVII; sb. †100 pounds XVI; century XVII; centennial anniversary XVIII. – L. *centēnārius* containing a hundred, f. *centēnī* hundred each, f. *centum*; see HUNDRED and -ARY. Cf. F. *centenaire*. So **centenARIAN** -ɛə·riən (one) 100 years old. XIX. **centennial** sente·niəl of 100 years. XVIII. f. L. *centum*, after *biennial*. **centesimal** sente·siməl hundredth (part). XVII. f. L. *centēsimus* hundredth, f. *centum*.

centi- senti- comb. form of L. *centum* HUNDRED, used in the F. metric system to denote the 100th part of a unit, as *centi*-GRAMME (1795), -LITRE, -METRE; also in **centigrade** se·ntigreid pert. to Celsius's thermometer in which the space between the freezing and boiling points of water is divided into 100 degrees. 1812. – F. *centigrade* (in *thermomètre centigrade*), f. L. *gradus* step, GRADE; **centipede** se·ntipīd vermiform articulated animal having many feet. XVII (Holland). – F. *centipède* or L. *centipeda* (*ped-, pēs* FOOT).

centime sãtī·m $\frac{1}{100}$ of a franc. – F. *centime* (1795), f. L. *centum* HUNDRED, after F. *décime* – L. *decima* (sc. *pars*) tenth (part).

cento se·ntou †patchwork; composition made up of scraps. XVII. – L. *centō* patchwork garment, poem made up of verses from other sources (as the 'cento nuptialis', 13th idyll, of Ausonius), rel. to Gr. *kenteîn* stitch, *kéntrōn* patchwork garment, Skr. *kanthā* patched garment.

centre, U.S. **center** se·ntəɹ middle point of an object. XIV (Ch.). – (O)F. *centre* or its source L. *centrum* – Gr. *kéntron* goad, peg, stationary point of a pair of compasses, f. base of *kenteîn* prick, rel. to W. *cethr* nail, OHG. *hantag* sharp. From XVI to XVIII the prevalent sp. was *center*; *centre* appeared in Bailey's Dict. 1727 and was adopted by Johnson. As a designation of the moderate party of a political body its use originated in the French National Assembly of 1789, in which the nobles and the Third Estate sat on the right and left respectively of the president. Hence **centre** vb. XVII. So **ce·ntrAL**[1] XVI, **ce·ntralIZE** XIX. – F. or L.

centri-, comb. form of L. *centrum* CENTRE in *centri·fugal, centri·petal* XVIII, f. modL. *centrifugus, -petus* (Newton's 'Principia' 1687), f. stems of L. *fugere* flee, *petere* seek. In some other mod. techn. terms *centro-*, repr. Gr. *kéntron*, has been used.

centuple se·ntjupl hundredfold. XVII. – F. *centuple* or ecclL. *centuplus*, var. of *centuplex*, f. *centum* HUNDRED + **plek-* **pl-* -FOLD.

century se·ntʃəri group of 100 XVI; 100 years XVII. – L. *centuria* assemblage of 100 things, division of the Roman army (orig. 100 horsemen), f. *centum* HUNDRED; see -Y[3]. So **centurion** sentjuə·riən commander of a century. XIV. – L. *centuriō(n-)*, f. *centuria*.

ceorl tʃɛəɹl (hist.) Anglo-Saxon freeman of the lowest status; see CHURL. By historians of XVII–XVIII sp. *ceorle*.

cephalic sifæ·lik of the head. XVI. – (O)F. *céphalique* – L. *cephalicus* – Gr. *kephalikós*, f. *kephalḗ* head (cf. GABLE); see -IC. So **cephalo-** se·fəlou, sefəlo· comb. form of Gr. *kephalḗ*, as in *ce·phalopod* one of the *Cephalopoda* (Gr. *pod-, poús* FOOT) class of molluscs comprising cuttle-fishes, nautilus, etc. and having a distinct head with arms or tentacles attached.

ceramic siræ·mik pert. to pottery. XIX. – Gr. *keramikós*, f. *kéramos* potter's earth, pottery (cf. CREMATE); see -IC.

cerastes siræ·stīz horned viper. XVI. L. – Gr. *kerástēs*, f. *kéras* HORN.

Cerberus sə̄·ɹbərəs many-headed watchdog of Hades; also fig. L. – Gr. *Kérberos*.

cere siəɹ wax-like membrane at the base of a bird's beak. XV (Bk. of St. Albans). – medL. use of L. *cēra* wax (Gr. *kērós*).

cereal siə·riəl of edible grain; also sb. XIX. – L. *cereālis* pert. to the cultivation of grain, f. *Cerēs* goddess of agriculture; see -AL[1].

cerebral se·ribrəl of the brain; (tr. Skr. *mūrdhanya* 'produced in the head', f. *mūrdhan* head) of consonants formed with the tip of the tongue on the soft palate. XIX. f. L. *cerebrum* (:– **kerasrom*), rel. to Skr. *çiras* head, point, Gr. *kéras* horn, ON. *hiarni* (whence ME. *hernes*, mod. dial. *harns* brains). Cf. F. *cérébral*; see -AL[1]. So **cerebrA·TION** action of the brain. XIX (W. B. Carpenter, 1853). L. **cerebe·llum** little or hinder brain, dim. of *cerebrum*, is used anat. (XVI).

cerecloth siə·ɹklɔ̀þ waxed cloth used as a winding-sheet, etc. XV (*sirecloth*). Also *cered cloth* with pp. of *cire, cere* vb. (XIV) – (O)F. *cirer* assim. to L. *cērāre* wax, f. *cēra* wax (Gr. *kērós*). So **ce·rements** waxed wrappings for the dead (Sh. 'Hamlet' I iv 48; whence taken up by Scott and later writers); see -MENT.

ceremony se·rīməni outward observance. XIV. – (perh. through (O)F. *cérémonie*) L. *cærimōnia* religious worship, (pl.) ritual observances, which is not found earlier than Cicero; see -MONY. So **ceremo·niAL**[1] -mou·-. XIV (Wyclif). – late L.; cf. F. *cérémonial*. **ceremo·niOUS**. XVI. – F. or late L.

ceriph see SERIF.

cerise sirī·z light clear bright red. XIX. adj. use of F. *cerise* :– Rom. **ceresea* CHERRY.

cerium siə·riəm (chem.) metallic element. XIX. – modL. (Hisinger and Berzelius, 1804), named, along with its source *cerite*, after the planet *Ceres*, discovered 1801; see -IUM.

cero- siə·rou comb. form of L. *cēra*, more prop. of Gr. *kērós* wax.

cert sə̄ɹt colloq. abbrev. of CERTAINTY. XIX.

certain sə̄·ɹtĭn fixed; sure XIII; established as truth; fully confident XIV; some (particular or definite) XIII; *a certain* XVIII; *a certain age* (after F. *d'un certain âge* rather elderly) XIX. – (O)F. *certain* (= Pr. *certain*, Sp., †It. *certano*) :– Rom. **certānus*, extension of L. *certus* settled, sure, pp. formation on *cernere* sift, separate, decide, decree, rel. to Gr. *krī́nein* (see CRISIS); cf. Gr. *kritós* chosen, choice. So **ce·rtain**TY. XIV. – AN. *certainté*, OF. *certaineté*.

certes sə̄·ɹtiz (arch.) assuredly. XIII. – (O)F. *certes*, corr. to Pr., OSp. *certas*, Cat. *certes*, prob. :– Rom. *(*ad*) *certās* (sc. *rēs*) for a certainty, used in the sense of late L. *ad certum*, *ex certō*, etc. Sometimes a monosyll., as in Sh. 'Henry VIII' I i 48.

certify sə̄·ɹtifai make certain. XIV (R. Mannyng, Rolle). – (O)F. *certifier* – ChrL. *certificāre* (Vulgate), f. *certus* CERTAIN; see -FY. So **ce:rtifica·**TION. XV. – (O)F. **certificate** səɹti·fikət document certifying something. XV. – F. *certificat* or medL. *certificātum*, sb. use of pp. of *certificāre*; see -ATE[1].

certiorari səɹʃiŏrɛə·rai (leg.) writ from a higher court for the production of records from a lower. XV. pass. of late legal L. *certiōrāre* inform ('certiorem facere'), f. *certior*, compar. of *certus* CERTAIN.

certitude sə̄·ɹtitjūd certainty. XV. – ChrL. *certitūdō* (Augustine), f. *certus* CERTAIN; see -TUDE and cf. F. *certitude* (XVI).

cerulean, cærulean sirū·liən of a deep blue. XVII. f. L. *cæruleus* sky-blue, sea-blue (or -green), prob. :– **cælolos*, f. *cælum* sky, heaven. Cf. the earlier *ce·rule* (*cærule*, Spenser); see -EAN.

ceruse siə·rūs, sĭrū·s white lead. XIV (Ch.). – (O)F. *céruse* (cf. Pr. *ceruza*, etc.) – L. *cērussa*, perh. – Gr. **kēróessa*, f. *kērós* wax (cf. CERE).

cervical sə̄·ɹvikəl, səɹvai·kəl pert. to the neck. XVII. – F. *cervical* or modL. *cervīcālis* (cf. L. *cervīcal* pillow, bolster), f. *cervīc-*, *cervīx* neck; see -AL[1].

cervine sə̄·ɹvain pert. to deer. XIX. – L. *cervīnus*, f. *cervus* deer, prob. rel. to HART; see -INE[1].

Cesarevitch sizā·rĭwitʃ, sī·zəɹwitʃ long-distance handicap run at Newmarket, named in 1839 after the Russian prince (see CZAREVITCH) who became Alexander II.

cespitose, cæs- se·spitous turfy. XVIII. – modL. *cæspitōsus*, f. *cæspit-*, *cæspes* turf; see -OSE.

cess ses local rate (in Ireland still the official term); †in Ireland spec. applied to military exactions. XVI. var. of *sess*, aphetic form of *assess*. ¶ The Ir. imprecation *bad cess to* (XIX) may contain this word, or is perh. aphetic of *success*.

cessation sesei·ʃən stoppage. XIV. – L. *cessātiō*(*n-*), f. pp. stem of *cessāre*; see CEASE, -ATION.

cesser se·səɹ (leg.) cessation. XVI. sb. use of (O)F. *cesser* CEASE; see -ER[4].

cession se·ʃən action of ceding or surrendering. XIV. – (O)F. *cession* or its source L. *cessiō*(*n-*), f. *cess-*, *cēdere* CEDE; see -ION.

cesspool se·spūl excavation in the bottom of a drain to retain solid matter XVII; well to receive soil from privies, etc. XVIII. perh. alteration, with assim. to POOL[1], of *cesperalle*, *susprall*, *suspirel* settling tank, cesspool (XVI), vars. of †*suspiral* vent, esp. of a conduit, water-pipe – OF. *souspirail* (mod. *soupirail*) air-hole f. *sou*(*s*)*pirer* (L. *suspīrāre*) SUSPIRE + L. *spiraculum* air-hole. Hence **ce·sspit.** XIX.

cestui se·stwi (leg.) in *cestui que* a or the person that. XVI. – AN., OF. *cestui*, f. *cest* (mod. *cet*, *ce*) :– Rom. **eccistui*, i.e. L. *ecce* lo! + **istui*, f. *iste* that (one), after *celui* :– **ecce illuī* (modelled on L. *cuī* to whom).

cestus[1] se·stəs belt, girdle. XVI. – L. *cestus* – Gr. *kestós*, sb. use of ppl. adj. 'stitched', f. **kent-*, base of *kenteîn* stitch (cf. CENTRE).

cestus[2], **cæstus** se·stəs Roman boxer's protection of thongs for the hand. XVIII. – L. *cæstus*, f. *cædere* strike (cf. -CIDE).

cesura see CÆSURA.

cetaceous sĭtei·ʃəs of the whale kind. XVII (Sir T. Browne). f. modL. *cētacea* (used zool. as the name of an order), f. L. *cētus* – Gr. *kêtos* whale; see -ACEOUS.

ceterach se·tərӕk genus of ferns. XVI (Turner, Lyte). – medL. *ceterach* (cf. F. *céterac*, It. *cetracca*, *citracca*, modGr. *kitarák*) – Arab. *shītarakh*.

chabazite kӕ·bəzait (min.). XIX. Earlier *chabazie* – F. *chabazie* (1780), from *khabázie*, erron. reading in pseudo-Orpheus, 'Lithiká' (III), for *khalázie*, voc. of *khalázios* (var. *khalazías*, *khalazítēs líthos*), f. *khálaza* hail; the mineral is so called from its form and colour; see ITE[1].

Chablis ʃӕ·bli French white wine. XVII. F., f. name of a town in Yonne, France.

chabouk tʃā·buk whip. XVII (*chawbuck*). – Urdu, Pers. *chābuk* horse-whip. Cf. SJAMBOK.

chaconne ʃəko·n old stately dance. XVII (Dryden). – F. *chaconne* – Sp. *chacona*, which has been improbably derived from Basque *chukun* pretty.

chafe tʃeif †heat, inflame; ruffle, vex XIV; rub so as to warm XV; rage, fret XVI. Late ME. *chaufe* – OF. *chaufer* (mod. *chauffer*) = Pr. *calfar* (whence It. †*caleffare*) :– Rom. **calefāre*, for *calefacere* make warm (see CALEFACTION). For the vowel cf. *Ralph* reif, *safe*, *wafer*, and *angel*, *chamber*, *gauge*, *manger*.

chafer tʃei·fəɹ beetle (now chiefly in COCKCHAFER). OE. *ćeafor* 'bruchus' :– Germ. **kaƀraz*, *-uz*, parallel to *ćefer* = OS., (M)Du. *kever*, OHG. *chevar*, *chevaro* (G. *käfer*) :– Germ. **keƀraz*; cf., with a different suffix, MLG. *kevel*, LG. *kavel*; prob. lit. 'the gnawer', and rel. to next and OE. *ćeafl* CHAWL, JOWL.

chaff[1] tʃàf husks of grain OE.; refuse XIII; cut hay and straw XVIII. OE. *ćæf*, *ćeaf* = MLG., (M)Du., MHG. *kaf* (G. dial. *kaff*), corr. to OHG. *cheva* husk; prob. f. Germ. base **kaf-* **kef-* gnaw, chew.

chaff[2] tʃàf banter lightly; also as sb. XIX. Of slang origin; perh. a var. of CHAFE, for which spellings with *-ff-* occur from XVI in the sense of 'scolding'.

chaffer tʃæ·fəɹ traffic, trade; merchandise. XIII. ME. *chaffare*, *cheffare*, *ch(e)apfare* :– OE. **ćēapfaru*, f. *ćēap* bargain, sale+*faru* going, journey, proceedings (prob. after ON. *kaupfǫr* trading journey); see CHEAP and FARE. The orig. word became obs. in XVII; a new sb. meaning 'bargaining' f. the vb. appeared XIX. Hence **cha·ffer** vb. †trade; bargain, haggle XIV.

chaffinch tʃæ·fintʃ the finch Fringilla cælebs. OE. *ćeaffinć*, f. CHAFF[1]+FINCH; so named from its habit of haunting domestic dwellings to pick amongst chaff and barn-refuse; cf. its late L. name *furfuriō* (Isidore), f. *furfur* bran, and G. *buchfink* 'beech-finch' (as feeding on beech-mast). (A northern and eastern *caffynche*, *cafinche* occurs XV–XVI; but a mod. dial. *caffincher* is recorded for Surrey and Sussex.)

chagrin ʃægrī·n, ʃæ·grin †anxious care, melancholy XVII; vexation XVIII (Pope); also †adj. grieved, mortified XVII (Pepys). – F. *chagrin* sb. (implied in earlier *chagrineux*), *chagrin* adj. (XIV), of unkn. origin. ¶ For chronological, if for no other reasons, not to be referred to *chagrin*, SHAGREEN.

chain tʃein series of links forming a continuous line XIII; as a lineal measure, 66 feet XVII. – OF. *chaine*, for earlier *chaeine* (mod. *chaîne*) = Pr., Sp. *cadena*, Pg. *cadea*, It. *catena* :– L. *catēna*, referred by some to the same base as *cassis* hunting-net, snare. Hence, or – (O)F., **chain** vb. XIV.

chair tʃɛəɹ seat for one person, spec. of authority. XIII (*chaere*, *chaier*). – AN. *chaere*, OF. *chaiere* (mod. *chaire* bishop's throne, see, pulpit, professorial chair; the ordinary word for 'chair' being *chaise*) = Pr. *cadiera*, Sp. *cadera* :– L. *cathedra* – Gr. *kathédrā* (see CATHEDRAL). The old disyll. pronunc. remains dial., as in Sc. tʃē·jər. In the sense of 'seat cocupied by the president of a meeting' first recorded 1647 (Clarendon); so **chai·r**MAN 1654. Replaced OE. *stōl* STOOL in certain applications. For †*chair organ* see CHOIR *organ*.

chaise ʃeiz pleasure or travelling carriage. XVIII. – F. *chaise* (XV, Villon), var. of *chaire* CHAIR, the substitution of z for r being specially characteristic of Parisian speech in XV–XVII. Also *post-chaise* XVIII (F. *chaise de poste*); see SHAY.

chalcedony, cal- kælse·dəni precious stone; in early use of vague application as a traditional name with many fabulous and legendary associations; now, a subspecies of quartz. The present forms, dating from XV–XVI, are – L. *c(h)alcēdonius* – Gr. *khalkēdṓn* (Rev. xxi 19, stone forming the third foundation of the New Jerusalem), assumed to mean 'stone of Chalcedon' in Asia Minor, but var. L. forms *carc(h)edonia*, *-ius* led to assoc. with Carthage (Gr. *Karkhēdṓn*), alleged to be the medium of export of a N. African stone. Earlier forms, *cassidoine*, *calcidoine*, etc. (from XIII) were – OF. (XII), semi-learned – L.

chalcography kælkɔ·grəfi engraving on copper. XVII (Evelyn). – Gr. **khalkographíā*, f. **khalkográphos*, f. *khalkós* copper. **chalco·grapher** (Evelyn); see -GRAPHER, -GRAPHY.

Chaldaic XVII, **Chaldean -æan** XVI, **Chaldee** XIII kældei·ik, -ī·ən, -ī· gen. equiv. to 'Babylonian'; as the name of a language often used for 'Aramaic'. Earliest forms are *Caldeis* (Wycl. Bible), *Caldeez* (Maund.), *Chaldey* (Tindale), *C(h)aldees* (Coverdale, A.V.), repr. L. *Chaldæī* (pl. of *Chaldæus* – Gr. *Khaldaîos*, f. Ass. *Kaldū*), freq. used for the name of the country *Chaldæa* (anglicized in Maund. as *Caldee*), the forms *Caldey* (XIII), *Caldie* (XVII), *Chaldee* being also formerly used for Chaldæan.

chaldron tʃɔ̄·ldrən dry measure (32 bushels). XVII. – OF. *chauderon* (mod. *chaudron*) CAULDRON. Superseded †*chalder* XVI–XVIII (– (O)F. *chaudière*), a northern word brought to London with the coal trade.

chalet ʃæ·lei Swiss hut or cottage. XIX (Byron). – (Swiss) F. *chalet*, introduced into literature by Rousseau. dim. of OF. *chasel* farmstead, dairy = Pr., Sp., Pg. *casal* :– Rom. **casāle*, f. L. *casa* hut, cottage. (Often miswritten *châlet*.)

chalice tʃæ·lis drinking-cup, spec. that used in the Eucharist. XIII (Cursor M.). – OF. *chalice* – L. *calicem*, *calix* cup, rel. to Gr. *kálux* CALYX, *kúlix* CYLIX. The form *chalice* superseded *caliz*, *calice* (XIII) – dial. var. *calice* (also modF.) of *chalice*; this had itself superseded OE. *cæliċ*, *caliċ*, an adoption of the Latin word in the Christian period, which had in turn succeeded to *cælċ*, *celċ* (early ME. *calch*), repr. a pre-Christian WGerm. adoption (= OS. *kelik*, Du. *kelk*, OHG. *chelih*, G. *kelch*).

chalk tʃɔ̄k white soft earthy limestone. OE. **ċælc*, *ċealc* = OS. *calc* (Du. *kalk*), OHG. *kalk*, *chalch* (G. *kalk*, dial. *kalch*), CWGerm. (like *tile* and *street*, an early adoption of a building term) – L. *calc-*, CALX lime, which sense has remained in the Germ. langs. except Eng., where it has taken over that of L. *crēta* (whence F. *craie*; cf. CRAYON). Hence **chalk** vb. XVI. **cha·lky**. XIV; see -Y[1].

challenge tʃæ·lənᵈʒ †accusation XIII (Cursor M.); †claim; invitation to a contest XIV; legal exception taken XVI. ME. *calenge*, *chalange* – OF. *ca-*, *chalenge* = Pr. *calonja*, :– L. *calumnia* false accusation, malicious action at law (see CALUMNY). So **cha·llenge** vb. XIII. ME. *chalange*, earlier *ca-*, *kalenge*, *calange* – OF. *ca-*, *chalengier*, *-anger*, *-onger* = Pr. *calonjar* :– L. *calumniārī* accuse falsely, CALUMNIATE.

challis tʃæ·lis fine silk and worsted fabric. XIX. perh. f. Eng. surname *Challis*; in F. *challis*, *chaly(s)*.

chalybeate kəli·biət impregnated with iron. XVII. – modL. *chalybeātus*, f. L. *chalybs* – Gr. *khálups* steel; see -ATE[2].

Cham tʃæm ruler of Tartars and Mongols. XVI (earlier *Cane*, *Chane*). – F. *cham*, *chan* – Turki *khān* lord, prince; see KHAN.

chamade ʃəmā·d drum or trumpet signal to a parley. XVII. – F. – Pg. *chamada*, f. *chamar* :– L. *clāmāre* call (see CLAIM).

chamber tʃei·mbəɹ room XIII; enclosed space in a body; deliberative body or assembly XIV; †charge piece in old ordnance XV; †small piece of ordnance XVI; part of the bore of a gun in which the charge is placed XVII. – (O)F. *chambre* = Pr. *cambra*, Sp., Pg. *cámara*, It. *camera* :– L. *camera*, *camara* – Gr. *kamárā* vault (cf. CAMERA). ¶ The L.-Rom. word became CEur., e.g. OLG., OHG. *kamara* (Du. *kamer*, G. *kammer*) room, ON. *kamarr* privy, OIr. *camra* privy, sewer, Russ. *kámera* chamber, office, cell. Cf. COMRADE.

chamberlain tʃei·mbərlin attendant on a royal or noble chamber XIII; steward of a king, etc. XV. ME. *cha(u)mberleyn*, *-laine*, occas. *-ling* – OF. *chamberlain*, *-lenc* (mod. *chambellan*) – Frank. **kamarling* (= Pr. *camarlenc*, Sp. *camarlengo*, It. *camarlingo*, *camerlingo*, medL. *camerlingus*), f. *kamara* CHAMBER; see -LING[1].

chameleon kəmī·liən saurian reptile that varies the colour of its skin XIV; applied to certain plants having variable-coloured leaves XVI. – L. *chamæleōn* – Gr. *khamailéōn*, f. *khamaí* on the ground (rel. to HUMUS) + *léōn* LION.

chamfer tʃæ·mfəɹ make a groove in XVI; bevel off a square edge XVII. Back-formation from *chamfering* – (with assim. to -ING[1]) F. *chamfrain*, f. *chant* edge (CANT[1]) + *fraint*, pp. of OF. *fraindre* :– L. *frangere* BREAK.

chamfrain, chamfron tʃæ·mfrən (arch.) frontlet of an armed horse. XIV. – (O)F. *chamfrein*, perh. for **chafrein*, f. OF. *chafresner* (= Pr. *capfrenar*) put on a bridle, f. *chef* head (cf. CHIEF) + *frein* :– L. *frēnum* bridle, bit (perh. rel. to *frendere* gnash).

chamois ʃæ·mwa European antelope; soft pliable leather orig. from this. XVI. First recorded from the Geneva Bible (1560), Deut. xiv 5 (Coverdale has *camelion*), where the Vulgate has *camēlopardus*, LXX *kamēlopárdalis*, Luther *elend* elk. – (O)F. *chamois*, which, with Pr. *camos*, Rhæto-Romansch *kamuotsch*, *kyamorto*, It. dial. *kamus*, *kamužu*, *kamots* (in literary It. *camozza*), Sp. *camuza*, *gamuza*, Pg. *camurça*, the earliest Rom. form medL. *camox* (v), and OHG. *gamiza* (G. *gemse*), prob. all derive ult. from a pre-Rom. name current in the Alpine areas. Cf. SHAMMY.

champ tʃæmp chew noisily; bite on (something hard). XVI. prob. imit.

champac tʃʌ·mpʌk Indian species of magnolia. XVIII. – Hind. *champak* (Skr. *champaka*).

champagne ʃæmpei·n wine of *Champagne*, a province of E. France XVII; see next.

champaign tʃæ·mpein level open country. XIV. ME. *champayne* – OF. *champagne* = Pr. *campanha*, Sp. *campaña*, It. *campagna* (see CAMPAIGN) :– late L. *campānia*, fem. sg. and n. pl., sb. uses of adj. f. *campus* level field (cf. CAMP), particularized as proper names of regions in France (*Champagne*) and Italy (*Campagna*). In XVI–XVII a very frequent var. was *champion*, *-ian*.

champart ʃãpā·r form of tenure (as in the Channel Islands) in which the landlord receives a fixed share of the produce. XVII. (O)F. *champart* :– legal L. *campī partem* (see next).

champerty tʃæ·mpəɹti †partnership in power XIV (Ch.); (leg.) illegal proceeding in which an outside party engages to help a party in a suit XV. – AN. *champartie*, f. (O)F. *champart* division of the produce of land :– L. *campī pars* 'part of the field or land' (see CAMP and PART, PARTY).

champion tʃæ·mpiən fighting man; one who fights on behalf of another. XIII. – (O)F. *champion* = Pr. *campio*, Sp. *campion*, It. *campione* :– medL. *campio* ('*campiones* gladiatores, pugnatores', Isidore), f. *campus* field, CAMP (as *tabellio* scrivener, f. *tabella* writing-tablet). Hence **cha·mpion** vb. †challenge XVII (Sh.); fight on behalf of XIX (Scott).

chance tʃāns fortune, accident; opportunity. XIII (RGlouc., Cursor M.). ME. *chea(u)nce*, *chaunce* – AN. *ch(e)aunce*, OF. *cheance* (mod. *chance*), f. *cheoir* fall, befall :– Rom. **cadēre* (whence also Pr. *cazer*, Sp. *caer*, It. *cadere*), for L. *cadere* fall (cf. CADENCE). Hence **chance** vb. XIV. **cha·ncy** †Sc. lucky XVI; risky XIX; see -Y[1].

chancel tʃà·nsəl part of a church reserved for clergy and choir. XIV. – OF. *chancel* (now in latinized form *cancel*) :– L. *cancellī* lattice, grating (the pl. form being extended to the part screened off became sg.), dim. of *cancer* lattice, perh. dissimilated form of *carcer* barrier, prison (cf. INCARCERATE).

chancellor tʃà·nsələɹ *Chancellor of England*, the highest officer of the Crown XI; *Chancellor of the Exchequer* (AL. *cancellarius de scaccaria*, AN. *chanceller del escheqer*), the highest finance minister XIV; head of a university XIV; diocesan vicar-general XVI; (Sc.) foreman of a jury XVIII. The earliest forms *canceler, cancheler*, were succeeded by *chanceler*, later (XVI) by forms with the substituted suffix *-our, -or* (cf. ANCESTOR). – AN. *canceler, chanceler*, OF. *cancelier*, (and mod.) *chancelier*, semi-learned – late L. *cancellārius* porter, secretary, f. *cancellī* (see CHANCEL) + *-ārius* -ER[2]; the L. word was orig. applied to an officer whose position was *ad cancellos* at the bars (e.g. of a court); in medieval times its application varied, but continually rose in dignity and importance. The term was introduced into England in the reign of Edward the Confessor.

chance-medley tʃà·ns me·dli (leg.) accident not purely accidental XV; inadvertence XVI. – AN. *chance medlee*, i.e. the sb. CHANCE and *medlee*, fem. pp. of *medler* mix (see MEDDLE); sometimes misunderstood as 'accidental mixture' or 'pure chance'.

chancery tʃà·nsəri court of the Lord Chancellor; since 1873, a division of the High Court of Justice. XIV. Late ME., reduced form of *cha(u)ncel(e)rie* – (O)F. *chancellerie*, f. *chancelier* CHANCELLOR; for the reduction cf. ME. *constorie* CONSISTORY.

chancre ʃæ·ŋkəɹ venereal ulcer. XVI. – F. *chancre* – L. *cancr-, cancer*; see CANCER.

chandelier ʃændəliə·ɹ (mil.) wooden framework to protect sappers in trenches XVII; branched support to hold lights XVIII ('as we now modishly call them', Stukeley, 1736). – F. *chandelier*, f. *chandelle* CANDLE; see -IER. ¶ In the sense 'candlestick, candelabrum' the AN., OF. form was adopted as ME. *chaundeler* (XIV), remaining dial. till XVIII.

chandler tʃà·ndləɹ maker or seller of candles XIV; retail dealer (now in *corn-chandler, ship-chandler*) XVI. – AN. *chaundeler*, OF. *chandelier*, f. *chandelle* CANDLE; see -ER[2].

change tʃeindʒ alteration; substitution of one for another; †exchange XIII; place of meeting for merchants XIV; money given in exchange XVIII. – AN. *chaunge*, OF. *change*, f. *changer* (whence **change** vb. XIII) = Pr. *cambiar*, Sp. *cangear*, It. *cambiare*:– late L. (Rom.) *cambiāre*, f. L. *cambīre* exchange, barter, prob. of Celtic origin (cf. Ir. *gaimbim* tax). In the phr. *on change* often treated as aphetic of *exchange* and written *'change*. Hence (f. the vb.) **cha·ngeling** †waverer, turncoat; person, esp. an infant, substituted for another XVI; see -LING[1].

channel[1] tʃæ·nəl bed of running water XIII (Cursor M.); tubular passage XIV; course, direction XVI; groove XVII. – OF. *chanel*, partly latinized var. of *chenel* = Pr., Sp. *canal*, It. *canale* :– L. *canālem*, *-ālis* pipe, groove, channel, f. *canna* pipe, CANE; see -EL[2]. Cf. CANAL.

channel[2] tʃæ·nəl (naut.) plank projecting horizontally from a ship's side. XVIII. Alteration of *chain-wale* (XVII), f. CHAIN (in the sense 'contrivance used to carry the lower shrouds of a mast outside the ship's side') + WALE. Cf. *gunnel*, var. of GUNWALE.

chanson ʃã·sɔ̃ song. XVII (Sh.). – (O)F. *chanson* = Pr. *cansó*, OSp. *canzón*, It. CANZONE :– L. *cantiōnem*, f. *cant-*; see next.

chant tʃànt sing XIV (Ch.); sing as to a chant XV. – (O)F. *chanter* = Pr., Sp. *cantar*, It. *cantare*, Rum. *cîntà* :– L. *cantāre*, frequent. of *canere* sing (cf. HEN); in Rom. *cantāre* entirely superseded *canere*. Hence **chant** sb. song XVII (Milton); tune to which the psalms, etc. are sung XVIII; cf. (O)F. *chant* (:– L. *cantu-s*); see also PLAIN-CHANT.

chantarelle, -erelle tʃà·ntərel yellow kind of edible fungus. XVIII. – F. *chanterelle*, modL. *cantharellus*, dim. of *cantharus* drinking-vessel; so called from its shape.

chanticleer tʃæntikliə·ɹ cock, orig. as a proper name. XIII. – OF. *chantecler* (mod. *chanteclair*), proper name of the Cock in the fabliau of Reynard the Fox, f. *chanter* CHANT + *cler* CLEAR; the sp. with *-i-* occurs in MSS. of Chaucer's works.

chantry tʃà·ntri endowment for a priest to pray for the departed XIV; chapel, etc., so endowed XV. – OF. *chanterie*, f. *chanter* sing, CHANT; see -ERY, -RY.

chanty var. of SHANTY[2].

chaos kei·ɔs †chasm, abyss (as in Luke xvi 26) XV; primordial formless void XVI; utter confusion XVII (Sh.). – F. *chaos* or L. *chaos* – Gr. *kháos* vast chasm, void, f. IE. base **ghəw-* hollow. Hence **chaot**IC keiɔ·tik. XVIII; after *erotic, hypnotic*; cf. F. *chaotique*.

chap[1] tʃæp open fissure, spec. in the skin. XIV (Trevisa). rel. to *chap* vb. (north. dial. and Sc.) strike XIV; crack in fissures XV; similar in meaning to (M)LG., (M)Du. *kappen* (whence G. *kappen* chop off) and to CHOP, but initial *ch* cannot be explained.

chap[2] tʃæp jaw, chiefly pl. XVI. Somewhat later in appearance than the synon. CHOP[1] (occurring in Dunbar as *choip*); of unkn. origin.

chap[3] tʃæp (dial.) purchaser, customer XVI; 'fellow', (young) man XVIII. abbrev. of CHAPMAN; for the sense-development cf. *callant, customer*. Hence **cha·ppie, -y** XIX; see -Y[6]; orig. Sc.

chaparejos tʃæpăreiˑhous stout leather trousers. XIX. Mex. Sp.

chaparral ʃæpəræˑl (U.S.) dense brushwood. XIX. – Sp. *chaparral*, f. *chaparro* evergreen oak+-*al* (denoting a plantation, as in *almendral*).

chap-book tʃæˑpbuk collector's name for specimens of popular literature formerly hawked by itinerant dealers. XIX (Dibdin). f. *chap* in CHAPMAN+BOOK.

chape tʃeip metal plate covering an object. XIV. – (O)F. *chape* cope, hood (whence Sp., Pg. *chapa*) in techn. uses; see CAPE[1].

chapel tʃaˑpəl oratory in a large house, etc. XIII; compartment (with an altar of its own) of a church XIV; parochial place of worship dependent upon a church XV; nonconformist place of worship XVII; printing office, association of journeyman printers XVII. – OF. *chapele* (mod. *chapelle*) = Pr., Pg. *capella*, Sp. *capilla*, It. *cappella* :– medL. *cappella* (dim. of *cappa* CAPE[1]), orig. the sanctuary devoted to the preservation of the cloak (*cappella*) of St. Martin of Tours, later (*c.* 800) extended to oratories attached to palaces or the like, and to parochial places of worship other than churches; cf. CHAPLAIN. Hence **chaˑpel**RY. XVI.

chaperon ʃæˑpəroun A. †hood, cap XIV; B. woman who accompanies a young unmarried woman as protector (often spelt -*one*, as if a fem. ending were required) XVIII (Mrs. Delany). – (O)F. *chaperon*, f. *chape* cope, CAPE[1]. Sense B appears to have arisen from the application of the sb. and of the vb. *chaperonner* (whence **chaˑperon** vb. XVIII, Jane Austen) to protection of various kinds.

chaplain tʃæˑplĭn clergyman (orig.) serving a chapel. XII. Early ME. *capelein*, superseding OE. *capellān* and superseded by *chapelein* – AN., OF. *capelain*, *chapelain* = Pr., Sp. *capellan*, It. *cappellano* :– medL. *cappellānus* orig. custodian of the cloak of St. Martin, f. *cappella* CHAPEL; see -AN. Hence **chaˑplain**RY. XVI.

chaplet tʃæˑplit wreath for the head XIV (*ane rose of his chaplet*, Barbour); string of beads in the rosary XVII. – (O)F. *chapelet* orig. a crown of roses, dim. of *chapel* (mod. *chapeau* hat) = Pr. *capell*, It. *cappello*, etc. :– Rom. **cappellu-s*, dim. of *cappa* hood, CAPE[1]; see -ET. The application to the rosary arises from the orig. rose form of the beads.

chapman tʃæˑpmən (arch.) trader, dealer OE.; †purchaser, customer (CHAP[3]) XIII. OE. *ćēapman* = (M)Du. *koopman* (cf. COPER), OHG. *koufman* (G. *kaufmann*); WGerm. comp. of **kaup-* (see CHEAP) and MAN.

chapter tʃæˑptəɹ main section of a book XIII; general assembly of members of a religious community or collegiate church (orig. with ref. to the reading of a chapter of Scripture or of the Rule, e.g. *ad capitulum convenire* orig. to meet for the reading of the chapter) XIV; members of this XV. ME. *chapiter*, later *chapter* (XIV) – (O)F. *chapitre*, earlier *chapitle* (which was also adopted in ME.), corr. to Pr. *capitol*, Sp. *cabildo*, It. *capitolo* – L. *capitulum* small head, CAPITAL of a column, section of a law, (in Christian use) chapter of a book, dim. of *caput* HEAD.

char[1] tʃāɹ small fish of the trout kind. XVII. Of unkn. origin; appears to be specially assoc. with the n.w. Midlands; perh. of Celtic origin.

char[2] tʃāɹ reduce to charcoal, scorch. XVII. Presumably the first syll. of CHARCOAL apprehended as a verbal element; cf. synon. and contemp. *chark*, which arose from the analysis of *charcoal* as †*chark coal* (XVI).

char[3] tʃāɹ (i) var. of CHARE sb. from XIII; (ii) short for CHARWOMAN XIX. Hence as vb.

char-a-banc ʃæˑrəbæŋ long vehicle with transverse seats looking forward. XIX (Lady Morgan, Byron). – F. *char-à-bancs* lit. 'carriage with seats' (see CAR, BANK[2]), in its earlier form a long light carriage open or only curtained at the sides. Colloq. abbrev. **chara** ʃæˑrə **charry** ʃæˑri. XX.

character kæˑrĭktəɹ distinctive mark XIV; graphic symbol XV; sum of mental and moral qualities XVII; personage, personality XVIII. ME. *caracter* – (O)F. *caractère* – (mostly late) L. *charactēr* – Gr. *kharaktḗr* instrument for marking, impress, distinctive nature, f. *kharássein* (:– **kharakj-*) sharpen, furrow, scratch, engrave, prob. f. base meaning 'scratch'. So **cha:racter**IˑSTIC. XVII. – F. *caractéristique* – late Gr. *kharaktēristikós*; †*characterical* and -*istical* were earlier. **chaˑracter**IZE. XVI. – F. or medL. – late Gr.

charade ʃərāˑd riddle in which a word is enigmatically described or represented in action. XVIII. – F. *charade* – modPr. *charrado* conversation, f. *charra* chatter, perh. of imit. origin.

charcoal tʃāˑɹkoul solid residue of the imperfect combustion of wood, etc. XIV. The second element, COAL, orig. meant 'charcoal'; the first el. is obscure, but has been referred to CHARE, as if the comp. meant 'turn-coal'. Cf. CHAR[2] (†*chark*).

chard tʃāɹd central leaf-stalk of artichoke, midrib of white beet. XVII (Evelyn, who uses *card* also). – F. *carde*, or alteration of this by assoc. with *chardon* thistle :– late L. *cardō(n-)*, for L. *carduus*.

chare, char tʃɛəɹ, tʃāɹ †turn (in various senses) OE.; turn of work, odd job, esp. of household work (cf. CHORE) XIV. OE. *ćerr*, WS. *ćierr*, (late) *ćyrr*, rel. to *ćierran* turn away or aside, whence **chare, char** vb. †turn OE.; †do or accomplish (a job) XVI; (from the sb.) do odd turns of work XVIII.

charge tʃɑ̄ɹdʒ †load, burden (material or immaterial) XIII; task or duty laid upon one, custody of affairs; precept, official instruction XIV; burden of expense; accusation XV; (from modF.) impetuous onset XVI; (f. the vb.) quantity loaded (cf. CARGO) XVII. – (O)F. *charge*, corr. to Pr., Sp. *carga*, It. *carica* :– Rom. **carrica*, f. late L. *car(ri)cāre* load (whence (O)F. *charger*, Pr., Sp. *cargar*, Cat., Pg. *carregar*, It. *car(i)care*), f. L. *carrus* wagon, CAR (cf. *caballicāre* ride, f. *caballus* horse); cf. CARRY. So **charge** vb. †load, burden XIII; lay a duty or command upon; put to expense; lay blame or accusation upon XIV; (from modF. put (a weapon) in position for offence; make a powerful onset (upon) XVI. – (O)F. *charger*.

chargé d'affaires ʃā·ɹʒei dæfɛə·ɹ official representative of a country abroad of lower grade than ambassador or minister. XVIII (Chesterfield). F. 'one in charge of (charged with) affairs'.

chariot tʃæ·riət †cart, waggon; stately vehicle for the conveyance of persons. XIV. – (O)F. *chariot* waggon, augm. of *char* CAR. (The form *charet(te)* – (O)F. *charrette* two-wheeled carriage was in concurrent use XVI–XVII.) Hence **chariot**EE·R[1]. XVII (Milton); superseded †*charieter*, *-oter* (XIII–XVII) – OF. *charieter*, *charioteur*.

charisma kəri·zmə (theol.) free gift of God's grace. XVII. – Gr. *khárisma*, f. *kharízesthai* show favour, f. *kháris* favour, grace (cf. YEARN). Also anglicized **cha·rism**. XVII.

charity tʃæ·rĭti Christian love; benevolence, charitableness; alms. The earliest forms were *carited*, *karitep* (XI), repr. AN. vars.; these were succeeded by the immed. antecedent of the present form, ME. *charite* (XIII) – (O)F. *charité* (dial. *carité*) = Pr. *caritat*, Sp. *caridad*, It. *carità* – L. *cāritātem*, *cāritās*, whence F. *cherté* dearness, dearth, f. *cārus* dear; see -ITY.

charivari ʃārivā·ri serenade of 'rough music', in derision of unpopular persons, babel of noise. XVII. – F. (earlier *chalivali*, *-vari*); many vars. in F. and medL.; of unkn. origin, perh. echoic. ¶ From its use as the title of a satirical journal in Paris it was adopted in that of 'Punch, or the London Charivari', 1841.

charlatan ʃā·ɹlətən †mountebank, cheap jack; quack XVII; pretentious impostor XIX. – F. *charlatan* – It. *ciarlatano*, f. *ciarlare* = Sp., Pg. *charlar* to babble, patter, f. imit. base **char-* (cf. Pr. *charra* s.v. CHARADE). Some early forms (e.g. *ciarlatan*, Coryat) are based immed. on It.; B. Jonson has pl. *ciarlatani*.

Charles's Wain tʃā:ɹlziz wei·n the seven bright stars of the Great Bear. In OE. *Carles wæġn*, ME. *C(h)arlewayn*, later *Charles (his) wain*, *Carols waine*, etc. 'the waggon (WAIN) of Charles', i.e. Charlemagne (see CARL); the name appears to have arisen through assoc. of the star-name *Arcturus* with *Arturus* (Arthur) and the legendary connexion of Arthur with Charlemagne. †*Charlemagne(s)* (var. †*Charlmons*) *wain* was used XIV–XVII.

charley, charlie tʃā·ɹli night watchman; vandyke beard (from portraits of Charles I). XIX. Proper name, dim. (see -Y[6]) of *Charles* (see CARL); the origin of the first sense is unknown.

charlock tʃā·ɹlɔk field mustard. OE. *ċerlic*, *ċyrlic* 'mercurialis', synon. with *ċedelc* (cf. dial. *kedlock*, †*cadlock*); the var. *carlock* is found as early as XV; of unkn. origin.

charlotte ʃā·ɹlət (usu. *apple charlotte*) dish consisting of apple marmalade baked in bread XIX; also *charlotte russe* (i.e. Russian), custard in a mould of sponge cake. F.; an unexpl. use of the female proper name.

charm[1] tʃāɹm incantation, enchantment XIII; amulet XVI; attractive quality XVII. – (O)F. *charme* :– L. *carmen* song, verse, oracular response, incantation. So **charm** vb. enchant XIV; fascinate, bewitch XV. – (O)F. *charmer*, f. the sb.

charm[2] tʃāɹm (arch.) blended noise of many voices. XVI. Later var. of *cherme* (XV), in mod., chiefly western and southern, dial. *chirm*; repr. OE. *ċirm*, *ċyrm*, *ċerm*, **ċierm* clamour, cry :– Germ. **karmjaz*, **kermjaz*, f. **karm-* **kerm-* (as in OE. *ċearm*, *ċeorm*, OS. *karm*), f. imit. base **kar-* **ker-* :– IE. **gar-* **ger-*; cf. CARE, GARRULOUS. In its literary use, as by Milton, prob. assoc. with prec.

charnel tʃā·ɹnəl mortuary XIV; now only *charnel house* (XVI). – OF. *charnel* :– medL. *carnāle* (glossed by OE. *flǣsċhūs*, i.e. 'flesh-house'), sb. use of n. of late L. *carnālis* CARNAL.

charpoy tʃā·ɹpoi light Indian bedstead. XIX. – Hind. *chārpāī* – Pers. *chahārpāī*, lit. four-footed (*chahārpā* quadruped, bedstead; see FOUR, FOOT).

charqui tʃā·ɹki jerked beef. XVIII. – Quichua *echarqui* dried slice of flesh or hung beef. Cf. JERK[2].

chart tʃāɹt map (now in restricted sense). XVI (Digges). – L. *charta* (whence F. *charte*) – Gr. *khártēs*, perh. of Egyptian origin.

charter tʃā·ɹtəɹ document conveying a privilege or right. XIII. – OF. *chartre* :– L. *chartula*, dim. of *charta* CHART (cf. the phonology of *chapitre* CHAPTER).

charter-party tʃā·ɹtəɹpā:ɹti deed between owners and merchants for hire of a ship and delivery of the cargo. XV. Earliest forms *chartwrpartte*, *chart parte*, *chartipartie* – F. *charte partie* – medL. *charta partīta* 'divided charter', i.e. deed written out in duplicate and then divided like an indenture. The first part of the term was assim. to CHARTER.

Charterhouse see CARTHUSIAN.

Chartist tʃā·ɹtist (hist.) one of the body of Eng. political reformers who upheld 'the People's *Charter*' of 1837. f. L. *charta* (used in the sense of 'charter') + -IST.

chartreuse ʃāɹtrǭ·z liqueur made at La Grande *Chartreuse*, near Grenoble. XIX. F., fem. of *chartreux* CARTHUSIAN. ¶ *Chartreux* was used for *Carthusian* by Lydgate, Shakespeare, Cowley, and Pope, and for *Charterhouse* by Johnson.

chartulary see CARTULARY.

charwoman tʃā·ɹwu:mən woman hired to do household jobs. XVI (also *charewoman* XVII). f. CHAR, CHARE + WOMAN.

chary tʃɛə·ri †sorrowful OE.; †dear, precious XIV; careful, frugal XVI. OE. *ċeariġ*, **cæriġ* = OS. *carag* (in *mōdcarag* sorrowful at heart), OHG. *charag* :- WGerm. **karagaz*, f. **karō* CARE; see -Y[1].

Charybdis kəri·bdis whirlpool on the coast of Sicily opposite the It. rock Scylla, with which it is proverbially coupled. XVI (Tottel's Miscellany, Ascham, Baxon, Sh.).

chase[1] tʃeis hunting, pursuit. XIII (RGlouc.). - OF. *chace* (mod. *chasse*) = Pr. *cassa*, Sp. *caza*, It. *caccia* :- Rom. **captia*, f. **captiāre*. So **chase** vb. pursue, drive away XIII (Cursor M.); hunt XIV. - OF. *chacier* (mod. *chasser*) = Pr. *cassar*, Sp. *cazar*, It. *cacciare* :- Rom. **captiāre*, for L. *captāre*, frequent. of *capere* take (cf. HEAVE). See CATCH.

chase[2] tʃeis adorn (metal) with engraving. XIV. contemp. with synon. *enchase*, of which it may be an aphetic deriv.; perh. - (O)F. *enchâsser* enclose in a reliquary, put a gem in a setting (of which the Eng. use may be a spec. development), f. *en* EN- + *châsse* casket, reliquary :- L. *capsa* CASE[2].

chase[3] tʃeis A. (typogr.) frame in which composed type is locked up XVII; B. cavity of a gun-barrel XVII. perh. - F. *chas* enclosure, *châsse* setting, casing, case :- L. *capsus* enclosed receptacle (cf. It. *casso* chest), and *capsa* repository, box, CASE[2]; but it is doubtful whether A and B should be coupled.

chasm kæ·zm deep cleft or fissure (earlier in Gr.-L. form); intervening blank or hiatus. XVII. - L. *chasma* - Gr. *khásma* yawning hollow, rel. to *khaínein* gape.

chassé ʃæ·sei perform the gliding step called *chassé*. XIX (also *chassez*, *-ey*). - imper. of F. *chasser* CHASE[1], or some other part of the vb. similarly pronounced.

chassis ʃæ·si †window-frame, SASH XVII (Evelyn); base-frame of a carriage XIX. - F. *châssis* :- Rom. **capsīcium*, f. L. *capsa* CASE[2].

chaste tʃeist sexually pure. XIII. - (O)F. *chaste*, semi-pop. - L. *castus*. So **cha·stITY**. XIII. ME. *chastete* - (O)F. *chasteté* - L. *castitās*; later assim. to L. spelling.

chasten tʃei·sn discipline, chastise XVI (Tindale); restrain from excess XIX. Extension (with -EN[2]) of †*chaste* vb. XIII (- OF. *chastier* :- L. *castigāre* CASTIGATE), which it superseded.

chastise tʃæstai·z †correct the faults of; inflict punishment on. XIV. Of doubtful origin; prob. (like CHASTEN) a new formation on †*chaste* vb., or its var. †*chasty* (both XIII), after vbs. in *-iser* or *-iss-* (*-ir*); see IZE, -ISH[2]. Formerly pronounced also *cha·stise*. Hence **chastise**MENT tʃæ·stizmənt. XIV.

chasuble tʃæ·zjŭbl (eccl.) sleeveless vestment with a hole to put the head through. XIII. ME. *chesible* - OF. *chesible* (cf. AL. *cassibula* XIII); vars. of this were in use till XVI; from XVII superseded by *chasuble* - (O)F. *chasuble* :- late L. *casubla*, obscure alteration of L. *casula* little cottage, hut, hooded cloak (Isidore, Augustine), dim. of *casa* house.

chat[1] tʃæt †chatter XIV–XV; converse easily and familiarly XVI. Shortening of CHATTER. So **chat** sb. XVI. Hence **cha·tty**; see -Y[1].

chat[2] tʃæt small bird, esp. of the warbler kind. XVII. prob. imit. of their note. Also in *furze-chat*, *gorse-chat*, *whinchat*.

chatelaine ʃæ·tĭlein mistress of a castle, etc.; chains on girdle bearing articles of domestic use. XIX. - F. *châtelaine*, fem. of *châtelain* lord of a castle (earlier *chastelain*, with var. *cast-*, both adopted in Eng. XIV) = Pr., Sp. *castellan*, It. *-ano* :- L. *castellānus*, f. *castellum* CASTLE (see -AN).

chattel tʃæ·tl †property XIII (in pl. *chateus*); movable possession; property other than real estate XVI. - OF. *chatel* (the var. is repr. by *catel* CATTLE) = Pr. *captal* :- medL. *capitāle*; see CAPITAL[1].

chatter tʃæ·təɹ (of birds and men) utter a rapid succession of vocal sounds. XIII. imit., of frequent. formation; see -ER[5]. Hence sb. XIII. **chatterbox** tʃæ·təɹbɔks habitual chatterer. XIX. f. prec., after †*prattle-box* (XVII–XVIII), which itself was prob. modelled on *sauce-box* (XVI; cf. 'Why sauceboxes must you be pratling?' 1588).

chatty tʃæ·ti Indian water-pot. XVIII. - Hindi *chāṭī*.

chauffeur ʃou·fǝ̄ɹ driver of a motor-car. XX. F. 'stoker', 'fireman', f. *chauffer* heat up, CHAFE = Pr. *calfar* :- Gallo-Rom. **calefāre*, for L. *calefacere* (see CALEFACTION).

chauvinism ʃou·vinizm exaggerated bellicose patriotism, jingoism. 1870. - F. *chauvinisme* (1843), f. name of Nicolas *Chauvin*, a veteran of the First Republic and Empire, noted for demonstrative patriotism, and popularized as the name of a character in 'La Cocarde tricolore', 1831, by the brothers Cogniard; see -ISM.

chavender tʃæ·vĭndəɹ chub. XV. rel. to CHEVIN (*cheueyne*, XV).

chaw-bacon tʃɔ̄·beiːkn country bumpkin. XIX. f. *chaw*, var. of CHEW+BACON.

chawbuck tʃɔ̄·bʌk whip (in India). XVII. f. Pers. and Urdu *chābuk* horse-whip. Hence vb. XVII. Cf. CHABOUK.

cheap tʃīp adj. low-priced; adv. at a low price. XVI. ellipt. for †*good cheap* (compar. †*better cheap*) XIV–XVII, for earlier †*to greate cheape*, †*at good cheape* XIV–XV 'as a great or good bargain', phr. formed, after (O)F. *à bon marché* 'at good market', on ME. *chēp*, OE. *ćēap* barter, bargain, price, market = OFris. *kāp*, OS. *kōp* (Du. *koop*), OHG. *kouf* (G. *kauf*) :- WGerm. **kaupa* (cf. ON. *kaup* :- **kaupam*); rel. to OE. *ćīepan* (:- **kaupjan*) and *ćēapian* trade, bargain (ME. *chēpe*) = Du. *koopen* (cf. COPER), G. *kaufen*, Goth. *kaupōn*; all based on an early Germ. adoption of L. *caupō* small tradesman, innkeeper (cf. *caupōnārī* traffic) and so belonging to the same stratum of adoptions as MONGER. ¶ OE. *ćeap* survives in the proper names *Cheapside, East Cheap, Chepstow* (OE. *ćēapstōw* market-place), *Chapman* (OE. *ćēapmann* CHAPMAN), and the verb in *Chipping* (*Campden, Norton*, etc.). Cf. also CHAP[3].

cheat tʃīt †escheat XIV; †booty, spoil; †(thieves' cant) stolen thing, (gen.) thing, article XVI; fraud; deceiver, impostor XVII. Aphetic of ESCHEAT. The two last senses are from the vb., which appears XV with the sense 'escheat', and from XVI with the sense 'defraud, deceive'; but **chea·ter** is earlier (XIV) – AN. *chetour*, for *eschetour*, and had the specific sense 'dishonest gamester' (XVI–XVII).

chebec see XEBEC.

check[1] tʃek threat to the king at chess XIV; †attack, reprimand XIV; (from the vb.) arrest, stoppage, restriction XVI; counterfoil, identifying token (cf. CHEQUE) XVIII. Aphetic – OF. *eschec* (mod. *échec*), alteration of **eschac* (pl. *-as*) = Pr. *escac*, Sp. *jaque*, Pg. *xaque*, It. *scacco* :- Rom. (medL.) *scaccu-s* – Arab. – Pers. *shāh* king, SHAH; cf. CHECKMATE, CHESS, EXCHEQUER. So **check** vb. put in check, arrest, stop. XIV. Aphetic – OF. *eschequier*, f. *eschec*.

check[2] tʃek pattern of cross lines forming squares. XIV; also vb. XV. prob. short for *checker*, CHEQUER.

checkmate tʃe·kmeiːt call at chess at the move which puts the king into inextricable check. XIV. Aphetic – OF. *eschec mat* = Pr. *escac mat*, It. *scaccomatto*, etc. – Pers. *shāh māt* the king is helpless; see CHECK[1] and MAT[2]. Hence as vb. XIV.

Cheddar tʃe·dəɹ epithet of a cheese named after a Somerset village. XVII.

chee-chee, chi-chi tʃī·tʃī minced English of half-breeds in India. XVIII. perh. – Hindi *chhīchhī* fie! excl. attrib. to Eurasians, if not merely imit. of affected pronunc.

cheek tʃīk †jaw, jawbone; fleshy side of the face OE.; side, side-piece (in techn. uses) XIV; (colloq.) insolence, cool assurance XIX. OE. *ćēoce* = OFris. *ziāke* :- WGerm. **keukōn*; varying with OE. *ćēace, ćēce* = (M)LG. *kāke, kēke*, MDu. *kāke* (Du. *kaak*) :- WGerm. **kǣkōn*; there are no known cogns. outside WGerm. Hence **chee·ky**[1] XIX.

cheep tʃīp utter shrill feeble sounds. XVI. In early use only Sc. (Dunbar, G. Douglas, Lyndesay); of imit. origin; cf. PEEP[2].

cheer tʃiəɹ †face, visage; disposition, mood (only arch. in *What cheer?, be of good cheer*, etc.); kindly reception XIII; fare, provisions XIV; (from the vb.) shout of encouragement or welcome XVIII ('We gave them a cheer, as the seamen call it', Defoe). ME. *chere* – AN. *chere*, OF. *chiere* face (mod. *chère* in phr. *faire bonne chère* give a welcome, feed well) = Pr., Sp. *cara* face (not in It. or Rum.) :- late L. *cara* face – Gr. *kárā* head. Hence **cheer** vb. make cheerful XIV; encourage by word or deed XV. **chee·rFUL**[1] tʃiə·ɹfl, tʃɔ̄·ɹfl. XIV; the second pronunc. is given by Sheridan and Walker. **chee·rly** adv. XVI.

cheese[1] tʃīz food made of pressed curds OE. *ćēse*, **ćiese, ćȳse* = OS. *kāsi, k(i)ēsi* (Du. *kaas*), OHG. *chāsi* (G. *käse*) :- WGerm. **kāsjo* – L. *cāseus*, which is continued in the Rom. langs., exc. in the Gallo-Rom. area, where **formāticus* (F. *fromage*, Pr. *formatge*) 'cheese made in a form' was substituted. (The L. word was adopted also in Celtic, as (O)Ir. *cáise*, Gael. *càise*, W. *caws*.) ¶ A native Germ. word is repr. by ON. *ostr* (Sw., Da. *ost*) :- **justaz* (adopted in Finn. as *juusto*), rel. to L. *jūs* JUICE; this denoted orig. a liquid kind, the firm kind, introduced into Germ. areas from the South, carrying with it the L. name.

cheese[2] tʃīz *the* correct thing. XIX. – Hind. – Pers. *chīz* thing.

cheese[3] tʃīz (thieves' sl.) *cheese it*, stop, have done. XIX. Of unkn. origin.

cheetah tʃī·tə the hunting leopard, Felis jubata. XVIII. – Hind. *chītā* – Skr. *chitraka* speckled, variegated, f. *chitra* spot, mark (cf. CHIT[2]).

chef ʃef head cook. XIX. F., for *chef de cuisine* 'head of cooking or kitchen'; see CHIEF.

chef d'œuvre ʃei-, ʃedō̃·vr masterpiece. XVII. F., orig. work qualifying for mastery in a craft (lit. 'principal piece of work').

cheffonier ʃefəniə·ɹ. XVIII. Formerly *chiffonier* and earlier *chiffon(n)ière* – fem. of F. *chiffonnier* rag-picker (cf. CHIFFON), applied to a piece of furniture with drawers in which needlework materials, scraps of cloth, etc. are put away.

cheir(o)- kaiə·rou, kairə· comb. form of Gr. *kheir* hand (which has immed. cognates only in Arm., Alb., and Tokh.). Also CHIRO-.

Cheka tʃe·kă Soviet organization superseded by Ogpu. XX. Russ. *che* and *ka*, names of the initial letters of *chrezvýchǎínaya komíssiya* extraordinary commission.

chela kī·lə (zool.) prehensile claw. XVII (*chely*, Sir T. Browne). modL. alteration of L. *chēlē* or its source Gr. *khēlḗ*.

chemic ke·mik †alchemical XVI; †pert. to Paracelsian medicine (based on chemical doctrines); pert. to chemistry XVII. Earlier form *chymick* – F. *chimique* or modL. *chi-, chymicus*, for *alchimicus* ALCHEMIC. So **che·mical**. XVI (earlier than *chemic* in the last sense). The sp. *che-*, dating from mid-XVII, is based on Gr. *khēmíā, khēmeíā* (cf. ALCHEMY).

chemise ʃimī·z woman's linen body undergarment. XIX (Byron). – (O)F. *chemise* = Pr., Pg., Sp. *camisa*, It. *camicia* :– late L. *camīsia* shirt, nightgown (Jerome). ¶ Casual adoptions of the F. word in other senses are found earlier (from XIII), and the L. word was adopted in OE. *cemes*, whence ME. *kemes*.

chemist ke·mist †alchemist XVI; one versed in chemistry XVII; dealer in medicinal drugs XVII. Earlier form *chymist* – F. *chimiste*, †*chymiste* – modL. *chimysta, chimista*, for *alchimista* ALCHEMIST. Cf. CHEMIC. Hence **che·mistry** †alchemy; branch of science dealing with natural elementary substances. XVII (*chymistry*). The sp. has been assim. to *chemical*.

chenille ʃənī·l kind of velvety cord. XVIII. – F. *chenille* hairy caterpillar = Pr. *canilha* :– L. *canīcula* small dog, dim. of *canis* dog (cf. CANICULAR).

cheque, U.S. **check** tʃek (banking) †counterfoil; written order to a banker to pay out money. XVIII. Spec. use of CHECK in the sense 'device for checking the amount of an item', with Eng. sp. perh. after *exchequer*. ¶ F. *chèque* is from Eng.

chequeen see SEQUIN, ZECCHIN.

chequer tʃe·kəɹ chess, chess-board XIII; †exchequer XIV; chess-board or chequered pattern XVII. Aphetic of EXCHEQUER. Hence **che·quer** vb. diversify as with a chess-board pattern. XIV.

chequy, chequee tʃe·ki (her.) chequered. XV. Aphetic – AN. *eschekee*, OF. *eschequé*, marked with chess-board pattern, f. *eschec*; see CHESS, -Y[5].

cherimoya tʃerimoi·ə (pulpy fruit of) a Peruvian tree, Anona Cherimolia. XVIII. (Also *-oyer*; cf. F. *chérimolier*) – modL. *cherimolia* – native name.

cherish tʃe·riʃ hold dear, entertain, cheer; guard carefully, harbour fondly. XIV. – (O)F. *chériss-*, extended stem of *chérir*, f. *cher* dear :– L. *cāru-s* (cf. CHARITY); see -ISH[2].

cheroot ʃərū·t cigar with the ends cut off square. XVII. – F. *cheroute* – Tamil *shuruṭṭu* roll of tobacco.

cherry tʃe·ri (stone fruit of) the tree Prunus Cerasus, not indigenous to W. Europe. XIV. ME. *cheri(e), chiri(e)* – ONF. *cherise* (which was apprehended as pl.), mod. *cerise* = Pr. *cereisa*, Sp. *cereza*, It. *ciliegia* :– medL. *ceresia*, for **cerasia*, perh. orig. n. pl. of adj. *ceraseus*, f. L. *cerasus* – Gr. *kérasos* (whence late Gr. *kerásion, kerasíā, -éā* cherry-tree). ¶ The L. form is repr. by OE. *ċiris* (in comps.; cf. ME. *chirritre* XII), *ċyrse*, MDu. *kerse* (Du. *kers*), OHG. *kirsa* (G. *kirsche*) :– WGerm. **kirissā* :– **keresjā*.

chersonese kə·ɹsənīs (arch.) peninsula. XVII. – L. *chersonēsus* – Gr. *khersónēsos*, f. *khérsos* dry (cf. HIRSUTE) + *nêsos* island.

chert, chirt tʃəːɹt flint-like variety of quartz. XVII (Plot). Local (n. midl.) name of unkn. origin, taken up by geologists.

cherub tʃe·rəb, (as †sg. and pl.) **che·rubim** †(*cherubim*) seat or dwelling of the Deity (after biblical use) OE.; (*cherub, -im, -in*) angel(s) of the second order of the pseudo-Dionysian hierarchy XIII (Orm); †(*cherubin*) beautiful or beloved woman (Sh.); (*cherub*) beautiful innocent child XVIII. OE. and ME. *cherubin, -im*, ult. (through L. and F.) from O.T. Heb. *kerūbīm*, pl. of *kerūb* – Accadian *karūbu* gracious, *kirūbu* propitious, f. *karābu* incline graciously. The currency of the word is due primarily to renderings of Vulgate L. *cherūb, cherūbīn*, LXX Gr. *kheroúb, kheroubī́m, -ī́n, -eín*. The forms *cherubin, -im* when applied to angels were pluralized in Eng. as *cherubins* (XIII), *-ims* (XVI), which were ousted through scholarly reaction by *cherubim* (XVII, Bacon, Milton); sg. *cherub* occurs in the Wycl. Bible; pl. *cherubs* is used by Tindale and Coverdale.

chervil tʃə̄·ɹvil garden pot-herb, Anthriscus Cerefolium. OE. *ċerfille, -felle*, corr. to (M)LG., (M)Du. *kervel*, OHG. *kervela* (G. *kerbel*) – L. *chærephylla, -phyllum* – Gr. *khairéphullon*, perh. f. *khaírein* greet + *phúllon* leaf. ¶ F. *cerfeuil*, It. *cerfoglio*, are – L. var. *cærefolium*.

chess tʃes game played on a chequered board of 64 squares. XIII (Cursor M.). Aphetic – OF. *esches* (mod. *échecs*), pl. of *eschec* CHECK[1]. Hence **che·ssmen** the pieces and pawns with which the game is played. XV (Caxton). Partly alteration of *chessemeyne* (also in Caxton), 'chess-company' (see MEINIE, which was used for the men in XIV); partly comp. of *chess* with the pl. of MAN (which was used for a piece *c.* 1400, after AN. *home* and medL. *homo*; cf. Icel. *skákmaður*). ¶ For *chessemeyne* cf. W. *gwerin* body of persons, in *gwerin y wyddbwyll* chessmen.

chess-tree tʃe·strī (naut.) either of two pieces of wood having holes for attaching the lower corners of the mainsail. XIV (Sandahl). f. unidentified el. + TREE ('wood').

chest tʃest box, coffer OE.; thorax XVI. OE. *ćest*, **ćiest*, *ćist*, corr. to OFris., MDu. *kiste* (Du. *kist*), OHG. *chista* (G. *kiste*), ON. *kista* (whence ME. *kiste*) :- Germ. **kistō*, *-ōn* - L. *cista* (whence also W., Gael. *cist*, Ir. *ciste*; cf. CISTERN) - Gr. *kístē* box, chest.

Chesterfield tʃe·stəɹfīld applied to an overcoat (XIX) and a sofa (XX), presumably named after an earl of *Chesterfield*.

chestnut tʃe·snʌt (edible nut of) the tree Castanea vesca XVI (*chesten nut*); short for HORSE *chestnut* XIX. The first element is ME. *chesteine*, *chasteine* (XIV) - OF. *chastaine* (mod. *châtaigne*) = Pr. *castanha*, Sp. *castaña* (cf. CASTANET), It. *castagna* :- L. *castanea* - Gr. *kastanéā* chestnut, also *kastáneion*, short for *kastáneion káruon* nut of Castanæa (Pontus) or Castana (Thessaly). The L. word was adopted in WGerm. as **kastinjā* (for **kastanjā*), whence OE. *ćisten(bēam)* chestnut tree, OHG. *chestinna*.

cheval-glass ʃəvæ·lglàs long mirror swung on a frame. XIX (Dickens, Thackeray). f. F. *cheval* horse, (hence) support (cf. EASEL) + GLASS.

chevalier ʃevəliə·ɹ horseman, knight XIV; cavalier, gallant XVII. ME. *chevaler* - AN. *chevaler*, (O)F. *chevalier* = Pr. *cavalier*, Sp. *caballero*, It. *cavaliere* :- medL. *caballārius*, f. L. *caballus* horse; refash. after modF. in XVI. Cf. CAVALIER.

chevaux-de-frise ʃəvoudəfrī·z spiked contrivance for obstructing cavalry. XVII. F., lit. 'horses of Friesland', so called because they were first used by the Frisians to compensate for their lack of cavalry; called in Du. *Vriesse ruyters* Frisian cavalry.

chevelure ʃəvlū·r head of hair (XV), XVII. In late ME. naturalized as †*chevaler* - OF. *cheveleure* (mod. *-elure*) = Pr., Sp. *cabelladura*, It. *capellatura* (now usu. *capigliatura*) :- L. *capillātūra*, f. *capillātus* haired, f. *capillus* hair; in XVII - modF.; see -URE.

chevin tʃe·vin chub. XV. - OF. *chevenne*, *chevesne* (mod. *chevanne*) :- Rom. **capitinem*, f. L. *capitō* orig. big-head, f. *capit-*, *caput* HEAD. Cf. CHAVENDER.

Cheviot, cheviot tʃe·viət name of the mountain range on the borders of England and Scotland and of a breed of sheep thriving there, noted for their fine thickset wool, from which a cloth is made. XIX.

chevron ʃe·vrən (her.) charge of this shape ^ XIV: mark of officer's rank XIX. - (O)F. *chevron* = Pr. *cabrion*, Sp. *cabrio* rafter, chevron, long-service stripe :- Rom. **capriōne*, f. *caper* goat, corr. to ON. *hafr* he-goat; cf. Sp. *cabriol* rafter :- L. *capreolus* (dim. of *caper*), the pl. of which was applied to two pieces of wood inclined like rafters.

chevrotain, chevrotin ʃe·vroutein, -tin small musk deer. XVIII. - F. *chevrotain*, *-tin*, dim. of OF. *chevrot*, dim. of *chèvre* goat :- L. *capra*, fem. of *caper* (see prec.).

chew tʃū grind to pulp with the teeth. OE. *ćēowan*, pt. *ćēaw*, *cuwon*, pp. *cowen*) = MLG. *keuwen* (Du. *kauwen*), OHG. *kiuwan* (G. *kauen*) :- WGerm. **kewwan* (cf. ON. *tyggva*, *tyggja*, with *j-* stem and dissimilation of *k*), rel. to OSl. *žĭvati* chew, Arm. *kiv*, L. *gingīva* gum. Conjugated wk. from XIV. The var. *chaw* is now dial. or vulgar exc. in CHAW-BACON.

Chian kai·ən pert. to Chios, island in the Ægean Sea, famous for its wine. XVII. f. L. *Chīus* - Gr. *Khîos*, adj. of *Khíos* + -AN.

chianti kiæ·nti Italian wine. XIX. Named from the *Chianti* Mountains, Tuscany, the place of its production.

chiaroscuro kiāroskū·rou †painting in light and shade; disposition of light and shade. XVII. It., f. *chiaro* CLEAR + *oscuro* dark, OBSCURE.

chiasmus kaiæ·zməs figure of speech in which the order of parallel words in phrases is inverted. XIX. - modL. - Gr. *khiasmós* crossing, diagonal arrangement, f. *khiázein* mark with the letter *X* (*khī*).

chiaus tʃaus Turkish messenger. XVI (Hakluyt). - Turk. *chāush* messenger, herald, sergeant. Cf. F. *chiaoux*.

chibouk tʃibū·k Turkish tobacco-pipe. XIX (*chibouque*, Byron). - Turk. *chibūk* small stick, tube of pipe, pipe, partly through F. *chibouque*.

chic ʃik good style; stylish. XIX. - F. *chic* (in artist's slang XIX), perh. identical with *chic* (XVI) trickery in legal matters, (in Walloon) skill in conducting legal cases (- MLG. *schick* order, skill), or joc. shortening of *chicane* (see next).

chicanery ʃikei·nəri legal trickery, quibbling. XVII (Overbury). - F. *chicanerie*, f. *chicaner* pursue at law (XV, Villon), quibble, wrangle, of unkn. origin; see -ERY. So **chica·ne** sb. XVII (Locke). - F., f. the vb.; **chica·ne** vb. use chicanery, quibble. XVII. - F. *chicaner*. ¶ 'We have hardly any words that do so fully expresse the French *clinquant*, *naïveté*, *ennui*, *bizarre*, *concert*, *façonier*, *chicaneries*, *consommé*, *emotion*, *defer*, *effort*, *chocq*, *entours*, *débouche*' (Evelyn, Letter to Sir P. Wyche, 20 June 1665).

chicha tʃi·tʃə fermented liquor of S. America. XVII. Amer. Sp.

chick tʃik chicken. XIV. Shortening of CHICKEN, which prob. lost the final *n*, like pps. and such words as *seven*, in southern dialects (in some of which *chick* is now sg., with pl. *chicken*). Hence **chi·ckabiddy** child's name for a fowl XVIII; †*biddy* fowl (Sh.), with connecting vowel.

chicken tʃi·kin young fowl. OE. *ćicen*, *ćȳcen* (late WS.), **ćiecen* :– Germ. **kiukīnam*, f. **keuk-*, gradation-var. of **kuk-* COCK, with dim. suffix characteristic of animal-names (cf. SWINE); corr. synon. forms are (M)Du. *kieken*, Du. *kuiken*, (M)LG. *küken*, MHG. *kūchelīn* (G. *küchlein*), ON. *kjúklingr*. Shortening of the stem-vowel was due to its position in OE. syncopated inflexional forms, as **cĭcnes*, **cĭcnu*; cf. *weapon*. See CHICK. Hence **chi·cken-pox** varicella XVIII; perh. so named because of the mildness of the disease, but by some an allusion to *chick-pea* has been assumed.

chick-pea tʃi·kpī dwarf species of pea. XVI. orig. *ciche pease(n)*, later (to XVIII) *chich peas* – F. (*pois*) *chiche* (earlier †*ciche*) – L. *cicer* chick-pea. The form *chick-pea*, perh. originating in a misprint, occurs in Lisle's 'Husbandry', 1752, along with *chickling* (cultivated vetch), which was orig. *c(h)ichling* (XVI, W. Turner).

chickweed tʃi·kwīd small weedy plant, Stellaria media, etc. XVI. Earlier (and still Sc.) *chickenweed* (XV), so called from being eaten by chickens.

chicory tʃi·kəri the plant Cichorium Intybus XV; ground root of this used with or instead of coffee XIX. Late ME. *cicoree* – F. †*cicoree*, mod. *chicorée* (Norman-Picard form) endive – medL. *cic(h)orēa*, for L. *cichorēum*, *cichorium* – Gr. *kikhóreia*, *kíkhora* n. pl., *kikhórion*. Cf. SUCCORY.

chide tʃaid †wrangle; dispute angrily with OE.; scold, reprove XIII. OE. *ćīdan*, of unkn. origin; pt. *ćīdde*, pp. *ćidd*, whence mod. *chid*. From XVI the conjugation was assim. to that of *ride* in *chode* (Coverdale), *chidden*; in recent times *chided* and *chidded* have also been used, beside the normal *chid*.

chief tʃīf head man; (feudal law) *in chief* (OF. *en chief*, medL. *in capite*) holding or held immediately from the lord paramount XIII; †head, top XIV; (her.) *in chief* on the upper part of the shield XV. – (O)F. *chef*, †*chief* = Pr. *cap*, Sp. *cabo*, It. *capo* :– Rom. **capum*, for L. *caput* HEAD. As adj. XIII (*chef chyrche*, *chef cite*, *chef conseler*), as in OF. (e.g. *chef baillif*, *chef sire*, *chieve seignurie*); cf. the attrib. and adj. use of *head*. Hence **chie·f**LY[2]. XIV.

chieftain tʃī·ftən chief; captain. XIV. Late ME. *cheftain*, alteration, by assim. to prec., of earlier †*chevetaine* – OF. *chevetaine*, semi-pop. – late L. *capitāneus* (see CAPTAIN).

chield tʃīld, **chiel** tʃīl †child XIV; servant (as in †*chalmer chiel(d)* valet) XV; young man, lad, fellow XVI. Sc. var. of CHILD.

chiff-chaff tʃi·ftʃæf one of the warblers, Phylloscopus rufus. XVIII (Gilbert White). imit. of the bird's note.

chiffon ʃi·fən, ʃi·fɔ̃ (pl.) fallals, finery XVIII; diaphanous silky muslin XIX (late). – F., f. *chiffe* scrap of paper, rag, of unkn. origin.

chignon ʃinjɔ̃·, ʃinɔ·n coil of hair worn at the nape of the neck. XVIII. – F. *chignon* orig. nape of the neck, earlier *chaaignon* :– Rom. **catēniōne*, f. L. *catēna* CHAIN; cf. -OON.

chigoe tʃi·gou W. Indian and S. American flea. XVII. Earliest in F. form *chique*; later *chego(e)*, *chig(g)er*, *jigger*; presumably a native name.

chilblain tʃi·lblein inflammatory swelling of hands and feet. XVI. f. CHILL + BLAIN, or reduction of **chilled blain* (*child-blane* is recorded XVII).

child tʃaild young human being OE.; youth of gentle birth (OE.). A word peculiar to English. OE. *ćild* :– **kilþam*, rel. to Goth. *kilþei* womb, *inkilþo* pregnant, quasi 'fruit of the womb'; OSw. *kulder*, *kolder* (Sw. *kull*), ODa. *kol(l)* (Da. *kuld*) young of a litter, child, have been compared. The orig. nom. pl. of OE. *ćild* was uninflected; later OE. has nom. pl. *ćildru*, g. *ćildra*, whence ME. *childre* (mod. dial. *childer*), the addition to which of the weak pl. ending *-(e)n* produced the surviving standard pl. *children* (XII). OE. g.pl. *ćildra* is repr. in *Childermas* Holy Innocents' Day (see MASS[1]). As a title often sp. *Childe*, as in Byron's *Childe Harold* (cf. *Horn Childe* XIII/XIV). See also CHIELD.

chiliad ki·liæd 1,000, esp. 1,000 years. XVI. – late L. *chīliad-*, *-ās* – Gr. *khīliad-*, *khīliás*, f. *khī́lioi* 1,000 (perh. rel. to L. *mīlle* 1000, if this is :– **smi|gheslī* 'one thousand'; cf. Skr. *sa|hásram* 'one thousand'); see -AD[1].

chill tʃil sb., adj., and vb. The earliest recorded member of this group is the verb ('grow cold'), which appears in late XIV. Its origin is obscure; in the pp. †*child* ('Piers Plowman' C. XVIII 49) it may repr. an OE. **ćieldan*, **ćildan* (:– Germ. **kalþjan*, f. **kalþaz* COLD). The adj. *chill* (XVI) may be an alteration of †*child* on the analogy of *cool*, *cold*; the sb. *chill* (XVII) is f. the vb. and is not a continuation of ME. †*che(e)le* :– OE. *ćele*, *ćiele* (:– **kaliz*, f. **kalan* be COLD). Hence **chi·lly** XVI; see -Y[1]. Cf. CHILBLAIN.

chilli, chilly tʃi·li dried pod of capsicum. XVII. – Sp. *chile*, *chili* – Aztec *chilli*.

chimæra kaimiə·rə, kim- (Gr. myth.) fire-breathing monster; horrible phantasm; wild fancy. XVI. – L. *chimæra* – Gr. *khímaira* she-goat, monster, f. *khímaros* he-goat. Preceded XIV–XVI by an anglicized form †*chimere* (cf. F. *chimère*). So **chimer**ICAL[1] kime·rikəl. XVII; after F. *chimérique*.

chime[1] tʃaim †cymbal XIII; †apparatus for striking bells XV; set of bells or of sounds produced by them XVI; (musical) concord, harmony XVII. ME. *chimbe*, *chymbe*, *chim(e)*, prob. arose from *chym(b)e bell* (XIII–XV), which may have been an analysis of a ME. **chimbel* :– OE. *ćimbal* – L. *cymbalum* CYMBAL. So **chime** vb. †make a musical sound XIV; accord or join in harmoniously XVII. The relation of sb. and vb. is not clear.

chime², **chimb** tʃaim projecting rim of a cask. XIV (Ch.). prob. identical with the sb. occurring in OE. *ċimstān* base, pedestal, *ċimīren* clamp-iron, *ċimbing* joint, corr. to MDu. *kimme* (Du. *kim*) edge of a cask, MLG. *kimme*, *kimm* (whence G. *kimme*), perh. rel. to COMB.

chimere tʃimiə·ɹ, ʃi- kind of tabard, spec. that worn over the rochet by bishops. XIV (Barbour). The earliest evidence is Sc., with varying stress (cf. †*chimmer*); in AL. *chimera* (XIV); obscurely rel. to Sp. *zamarra* (whence F. †*samarre*, †*chamarre*) sheepskin cloak, It. *zimarra*, *cimarra* long robe (whence F. *simarre*, †*chimarre* loose gown XVII), prob. to be ult. referred to Arab. *sammūr* Siberian weasel.

chimney tʃi·mni †fireplace; †stove; smoke-flue. XIV. – (O)F. *cheminée* fireplace, chimney, corr. to It. *camminata* – late L. *camīnāta*, perh. orig. for *camera camīnāta* room with a fireplace, f. *camīnus* – Gr. *káminos* oven, furnace, rel. to *kamárā* (see CHAMBER).

chimpanzee tʃimpænzī· African ape, Anthropopithecus. XVIII. – F. *chimpanzé*, – native name in Angola, W. Africa.

chin tʃin extremity of the lower jaw. OE. *ċin(n)*, corr. (with variation of gender and declension) to OFris. *kin*, OS. *kinni* (Du. *kin*), OHG. *chinni* (G. *kinn*), ON. *kinn* chin, lower jaw, Goth. *kinnus* cheek; CGerm. **kinn-* :– **kenw-* :– IE. **genw-*, whence Gr. *génus* lower jaw, Skr. *hánus* jaw (with aberrant *h*-), L. *gena* cheek, OIr. *gin* mouth, W. *gen* jaw, chin (cf. further Gr. *gnáthos*, Lith. *žándas* jaw).

china tʃai·nə fine semi-transparent earthenware. Short for *china ware*, i.e. ware from China. The Pers. form *chīnī* (prop. adj.), widely diffused in the East, gave rise to Eng. *chiny* (XVI), *chen(e)y*, *chenea* (XVII), whence the former pronunc. tʃei·ni, tʃī·ni.

chinch tʃintʃ bed-bug. XVII. – Sp. *chinche* = It. *cimice* :– L. *cimicem*, nom. *cimex*.

chinchilla tʃintʃi·lə small S. Amer. rodent. XVII. – Sp. *chinchilla*, dim. of *chinche* (see prec.).

chin-chin tʃi·ntʃin (colloq.) phr. of salutation. XVIII. – Chinese *t'sing t'sing*.

chine¹ tʃain †cleft, chink OE.; (generalized from place-names in Hampshire and the Isle of Wight) deep narrow ravine cut by a stream. XIX. OE. *ċinu* = MDu. *kēne* (Du. *keen*), f. Germ. base **kī*- burst open, repr. also by OE. *ċīnan* = OS., OHG. *kīnan*, Goth. *keinan* sprout, shoot forth, CHIT¹.

chine² tʃain spine, backbone. XIV. Aphetic – OF. *eschine* (mod. *échine*) = Pr. *esquina*, Sp. *esquena*, It. *schiena* :– Rom. **skīna*, blending of Germ. **skin-* (in OHG. *scina*, G. *schiene*) and L. *spīna* SPINE.

chine³ tʃain projecting rim. XV. Unexpl. var. of CHIME².

Chinese tʃainī·z pert. to (native of) China. XVII. f. *China* (Indian name) + -ESE. Earlier *Chinnish* and *Chinian* (XVI) were used; and in XVII *Chinenses* pl. (Burton), *Chinensian*, *Chinesian*, *Chino* (– OSp.), *Chinois* (Purchas) (– F.). *Chinese* is now invariable for the pl.; formerly *Chineses* was regular; a new sg. **Chinee** tʃainī· (XIX, Bret Harte 1870) is of U.S. origin, as is also **Chink** tʃiŋk (XX), an irreg. formation.

chink¹ tʃiŋk fissure, cleft; slit. XVI. prob. of dial. origin; rel. in some way, as yet undetermined, to CHINE¹.

chink² tʃiŋk make a sharp ringing sound. XVI. imit.; cf. Du. *kinken*. Hence as sb. the sound; (sl.) money XVI.

Chinook tʃinu·k jargon based on English used by N. Amer. Indians. XIX. Name of an Indian tribe on Columbia River, N. America, with which intercourse was carried on by the Hudson Bay Company.

chintz tʃints varicoloured cotton cloth with floral designs. XVII. Fanciful sp. of *chints*, orig. pl. of *chint* – Hindi *chīṇt* (also Marathi *chīt*, whence F. *chite*, Pg. *chita*) :– Skr. *chitra* variegated (cf. CHIT²).

chip tʃip small thin piece of wood, stone, etc. XIV. repr. OE. *ċipp*, *ċyp* beam, corr. to OS. *kip* post, *kipa* stave (Du. *kip* beam of a plough), OHG. *chipfa* (G. dial. *kipf*, *kipfe*) axle, stave, ON. *keppr* stick, staff. The transference of sense in Eng. is remarkable; the basic sense seems to be 'piece hewn or cut'. So **chip** vb. †chap XIV; pare the crust from (bread) XV; crack and break open XVI; cut with an axe or adze XVII; cf. OE. **ċippian* (in *forċypped* 'præcisus') = (M)LG., (M)Du. *kippen* hatch out by chipping the shell. Hence **chi·ppy** pert. to chips XVIII; dry as a chip, (hence) 'off colour' XIX; see -Y¹.

chipmunk, -muck tʃi·pmʌŋk, -mʌk N. Amer. ground-squirrel, Tamias. XIX (J. F. Cooper). Of Algonquin origin.

chippendale tʃi·pəndeil f. name of Thomas *Chippendale*, which belonged to three English cabinet-makers of XVIII.

chir(o)- kaiə·r|ou, kaiərɔ· more usual var. of CHEIRO-, as in **chi·ro**GRAPH †obligation, bond XV (*cirographe*, Caxton); papal expression of will in writing XVI; indenture XVII. – F. *chirographe* – L. *chirographum* – Gr. *kheirógraphon*; **chi·ro**MANCY divination by the hand. XV (Lydg.). – F. or L. – Gr. **chiro·podist** one who treats the hands and the feet. 1785 (D. Low 'Chiropodologia'). f. Gr. *kheír* hand, *pod-*, *poús* FOOT + -IST.

chirp tʃɜ̄ɹp utter a short sharp thin sound. XV. Symbolical modification of earlier *chirk* (XIV, Ch.; cf. OE. *ċearcian* 'stridere') or *chirt* (XIV, Ch.). Hence **chirrup** tʃi·rəp XVI; a modification due to strong trilling of the r.

chirurgeon, etc., see SURGEON, etc. So **chirurgical** kaiərə̄·ɹdʒikəl surgical. XVI. – F. *cirurgical* or medL. *cirurgicālis*, f. *cirurgicus*.

chisel tʃi·zl cutting tool with the edge transverse to the axis. XIV. – ONF. *chisel* (mod. *ciseau*, in pl. scissors) = Pr. *cizel*, Cat. *sisell* (whence Sp. *cincel*, Pg. *cinzel*) :– Rom. **cīsellum*, for **cæsellum* (whence It. *cesello*) after late L. *cīsōrium* (see SCISSORS), f. *cīs-*, var. of *cæs-*, stem of *cædere* cut (cf. CÆSURA).

chit[1] tʃit young of a beast XIV (Wycl. Bible); very young person; (potato) shoot XVII. perh. repr. obscurely OE. *ćīþ*, ME. *chithe* shoot, sprout, seed, mote (in the eye), corr. to OS. **kīð* (in *cidlek* tax on fagots), MDu. *kijt*, OHG. *-kīdi* (MHG. *kīde*, *kīt*) sprout; f. Germ. **kī-* split (cf. CHINE[1]).

chit[2] tʃit letter, note, certificate, pass. XVIII. Shortening of †**chitty** (XVII) – Hindi *chiṭṭhi*, Marathi *chiṭṭī* :– Skr. *chitra* spot, mark; see CHINTZ.

chit-chat tʃi·ttʃæt. XVIII. Reduplication on CHAT[1].

chitin kai·tin (zool., chem.) substance of the elytra of insects, etc. XIX. – F. *chitine*, irreg. f. Gr. *khitṓn* tunic, coat of mail, of Sem. origin; see -IN. ¶ *Chiton* kai·tən is the name of a genus of molluscs whose shell consists of a series of plates.

chittagong tʃi·təgəŋ breed of domestic fowls. XIX. f. *Chittagong* in Bengal, India.

chitterlings tʃi·təɹliŋz smaller intestines of beasts used as food. XIII (*cheterlingis*). orig. form uncertain; perh. OE. **ćieter-*, f. Germ. **keut-* **kut-*, whence synon. MHG. *kutel* (G. *kutteln*); see -LING[1]. The widespread dial. vars. *chidling*, *chitling* seem to be merely contr. forms.

chivalrous ʃi·v-, (arch.) tʃi·vəlrəs †knightly, valorous XIV; (in mod. revived use) pert. to the Age of Chivalry XVIII (Warton 1774); having the virtues of the ideal knight XIX. Late ME. *chevalrous*, *chiv-* – OF. *chevalerous*, f. *chevalier*; see CHEVALIER, -OUS. In its orig. use obs. before 1600, its occurrence in Sh. and Spenser being merely traditional; entered in Bailey's dict. as a word of Chaucer and Spenser, in J. as a Spenserian word 'now out of use'. So **chi·valRY** †mounted men-at-arms, cavalry; †knighthood, knightliness XIII; knightly system of feudal times XVIII (Percy 1765, Warton 1774); chivalrous character XVIII. – (O)F. *chevalerie*, †*chivalerie* = Pr. *cavaleria*, Sp. *caballeria*, It. *cavalleria* knighthood, horse soldiery; Rom. deriv. of medL. *caballerius*, for medL. *caballārius* CAVALIER. The pronunc. with ʃ depends on mod. assim. to F. Hence **chivalrIC** -æ·lrik. XVIII (Mrs. Radcliffe). ¶ Forms in *chiv-* were characteristic of ONF. and AN.

chive tʃaiv smallest species of Allium. XIV (*cive*, *chive*). – dial. var. **chive* (cf. Picard *chivot* green onion) of (O)F. *cive* = Pr. *ceba* :– L. *cēpa* onion.

chivy tʃi·vi chase, harass. XIX. var. of *chevy*, of dial. origin; formerly used as a hunting cry ('With a hey, ho, chivy, Hark forward, hark forward, tantivy' XVIII), prob. arising out of *Chevy Chase*, name of a ballad celebrating a Border skirmish at *Chevy* or *Chevyat Chase*.

chloral klɔ̄·rəl (chem.) trichloraldehyde. XIX. – F. *chloral* (Liebig, 1831), f. CHLOR|INE + AL|COHOL, after *ethal*.

chlorine klɔ̄·rīn, -ain. 1810. Named by Sir H. Davy from its colour; f. Gr. *khlōrós* yellowish or pale green + -INE[5].

chloro-[1] klɔ̄·rou comb. form of Gr. *khlōrós* pale green, as in **chlo·rophyll** (XIX) – F. *chlorophylle* (Gr. *phúllon* leaf).

chloro-[2] klɔ̄·rou comb. form of CHLORINE.

chloroform klɔ·rəfɔ̄ɹm liquid of which the vapour is anæsthetic. XIX. – F. *chloroforme* (J. Dumas, 1834), f. *chloro-* (see prec.) + *form|yl*, as being a chloride of formyl (in its obs. sense of methenyl, CH).

chlorosis klɔ̄rou·sis (path.) green-sickness XVII; (bot.) disease of plants in which green parts become yellow XIX. modL., f. Gr. *khlōrós* green; see -OSIS.

chock tʃɔk (dial.) block, log XVII; piece of wood, etc. for holding an object in position, etc. XIV (Sandahl). With its var. CHUCK[3] (which is now partly differentiated in usage), prob. – ONF. **choque*, **chouque* (mod. Picard *choke* big log, Norman *chouque*), var. of OF. *çoche*, *çouche* (mod. *souche*) log, block of wood = Pr. *soca* stump, trunk, of unkn. origin.

chock-full tʃɔ·kfu·l (colloq.) full to the utmost. The rare ME. (XIV) forms *chokkefulle*, *chekefull* ('Morte Arthure') are of doubtful status because of the uncertainty of the tradition; but, if genuine, they may repr. differentiated forms of OE. *cēoce* or *cēace* CHEEK, according as the diphthong was rising or falling. The modern *chokefull* dates from XVII, *chock-full* from XVIII, with a var. *chuck-full*, which may be due to the gen. variation between CHOCK and CHUCK. Hence prob. **chock** adv. (XVIII) close (*up*) *to*, and in *chock-a-block* (i) naut., said of a tackle with the two blocks run close together, (ii) gen., crammed close together.

chocolate tʃɔ·kələt beverage made from seeds of the cacao tree; paste made from these ground. XVII. – F. *chocolat*, or its source Sp. *chocolate* – Aztec *chocolatl* article of food made from cacao seeds; this seems to have been confounded by Europeans with *cacaua-atl*, which was actually a drink made from cacao.

Choctaw tʃɔ·ktɔ̄ name of a tribe of Amer. Indians XVIII; step in skating (cf. MOHAWK). XIX. perh. alteration of Sp. *chato* flat (:– Rom. **plattu-s* – Gr. *platús* broad, PLATY-), the tribe being so named from their custom of flattening their heads.

choice tʃois act of choosing XIII; thing chosen XIV (Gower). ME. *chois* – OF. *chois* (mod. *choix*), f. *choisir* choose = Pr. *causir* :– Gallo-Rom. **causīre* – Germ. **kausjan* (so in Gothic), f. **kaus-* **keus-* CHOOSE. Superseded ME. *kire, cüre*, OE. *cyre* :– Germ. **kusiz*, f. wk. grade **kus-*. Hence as adj. chosen, selected. XIV.

choir, quire kwaiəɹ †cathedral or collegiate church clergy; body of singers in a church; part of a church appropriated to them XIII; (transf. and gen.) organized body of singers XVI. ME. *quer(e)* – OF. *quer* (mod. *chœur*) – L. *chorus* (see CHORUS). The development of *quere* to *quire* is paralleled by *briar, friar, umpire*; the sp. *choir*, with assim. to F. and L., was established XVII. *Choir organ* (XVIII) is a perversion of *chair organ* (XVII), which may have been so called because it often formed the back of the organist's seat.

choke tʃouk stop the aperture of the throat. XIV. ME. *cheke, choke*, aphetic of *acheke, achoke* (Ch.) :– late OE. *āċēocian* (once), f. *ā-* A-[3] + *ċēoce, ċēce* jaw, CHEEK (cf. the formation of late ME. *athrote* throttle, f. *throte* THROAT). For the twofold ME. development of OE. *-ċēocian* cf. ME. *chese, chose*, CHOOSE from *ċēosan*. Hence **choke** sb. constriction. XVI. ¶ The application to the centre of an artichoke head is due partly to a pop. analysis of *artichoke*.

chokee, choky tʃou·ki toll station in India; (sl.) police station. XVII (*chukey, chowkie*). – Hindi *chaukī* shed, watch-house, station, lock-up.

choler kɔ·ləɹ bile XIV; anger XVI. ME. *coler(e)* – (O)F. *colère* – L. *cholera*; see next. In late L. *cholera* took over the meanings of Gr. *kholḗ* bile, anger, and became the techn. name for one of the four 'humours' of the old physiologists (cf. MELANCHOLY). So **cho·leric** †bilious XIV; irascible, angry XVI. – (O)F. *colérique* – L. *cholericus* – Gr. *kholerikós*.

cholera kɔ·lərə †bile XIV; disorder attended with bilious diarrhoea, etc. XVII; disease endemic in India, so named from the resemblance of its symptoms to those of European cholera XIX. – L. *cholera* – Gr. *kholérā*. The L. word was orig. applied, like the Gr., only to the disease, but later took over the sense 'bile', 'anger' from Gr. *kholḗ* (see GALL). Cf. COLIC.

choliambic kouliæ·mbik (pros.) iambic line with spondee or trochee in the last foot. XIX. – Gr. *khōliambikós*, f. *khōlíambos*, f. *khōlós* lame + *íambos* IAMBUS.

chondro- kɔ·ndrou comb. form of Gr. *khóndros* cartilage, for **khrondros*, rel. to GRIND.

choose tʃūz take by preference. OE. *ċēosan*, pt. *ċēas, curon*, pp. *coren* = OFris. *kiāsa, ziāsa*, OS. *kiosan* (Du. *kiezen*), OHG. *chiosan*, ON. *kjósa*, Goth. *kiusan* :– CGerm. **kiusan*, **kaus*, **kusum*, **kusanaz*. The IE. base **geus-* **gaus-* **gus-* is repr. also by L. *gustāre* taste (cf. OE. *costian*), *gustus* (cf. Goth. *kustus* taste), Gr. *geúein* give a taste of, OIr. *asa|gussim* I wish, Skr. *júṣtis* favour, satisfaction, *juṣátē* enjoy, Av. *zušta-* loved, desired, OPers. *dauš-* take pleasure in.

The normal ME. development of the OE. forms was: inf. *chēse* (XII–XVI); pt. *chēs* (XII–XV), *chās-e* (XIII–XVI), pl. *curen* (XIII); pp. *i-corn, core* (XIII–XV). These were superseded by: inf. *chōse* (from the treatment of *ċeósan* as with a rising diphthong), the antecedent of *choose*; pt. pl. (from the new pp.) *chosen*, whence sg. *chōse* (from XVI); pp. *chosen* (from XIII), partly after ON. *kosinn*; later also *chose*, which was in common literary use in XVIII. The frequent sp. *chuse* (XVI–XVIII) is unexpl.; the sp. *choose* was established by Bailey and Johnson. Weak inflexions date from XIV and survive dial.

chop[1] tʃɔp cut, hew; (dial.) strike, knock; †crack; (dial.) thrust. XVI. var. of CHAP[1]. Hence **chop** sb. cutting blow XIV; slice of meat with bone XV. For the alteration of vowel cf. *strap*.

chop[2] tʃɔp barter, exchange XIV; phr. *chop and change* bargain (XV), make frequent changes (XVI); hence, change as the wind, veer XVII. First evidenced in †*choppe-church*, trafficker in ecclesiastical benefices, and in phr. *chop and change* ('I .. choppe and chaunge with symonye, and take large yiftes', Digby Myst.); perh. var. of ME. *chappe*, which appears to have been evolved from OE. *ċēapian* (*ċeápian*) with influence from *chapman* (see CHEAP). A sense 'exchange or bandy words' (from XVI) survived in †*chop-logic* sophistical argument or disputant.

chop[3] tʃɔp (usu. pl.) jaws XV; opening, entrance (as in *Chops of the Channel* the entrance into the English Channel from the Atlantic) XVII. var. of CHAP[2]. Hence **chop** vb. †snap *up* XVI; (in hunting) kill in lair or covert before the quarry has time to get away fairly XVII.

chop[4] tʃɔp seal, stamp; licence, passport XVII; trademark, brand; (in *first*, etc., *chop*) rank, quality XIX. – Hindi *chhāp* impression, print, stamp, seal.

chopsticks tʃɔ·pstiks pair of 'sticks' used by the Chinese in eating. XVII. f. Chinese and Pidgin English *chop* quick + STICK[1]; tr. Chinese *k'wâi-tsze* nimble boys, nimble ones.

chop suey tʃɔp sū·i Chinese dish. XIX. Chinese, 'mixed bits'.

choragus koreiˑgəs at the University of Oxford, a functionary presiding over musical exercises XVII; (Gr. drama) leader of a chorus XIX. – L. *chorāgus* – Gr. *khorāgós*, var. of *khorēgós*, f. *khorós* CHORUS + **ag-* lead (see AGENT).

choral[1] kōˑrəl pert. to a choir, e.g. *vicar choral* XVI; pert. to a chorus XVII (Milton). – medL. *chorālis*; see CHORUS and -AL.

choral[2] kōrāˑl (often *choraˑle* and mistakenly pron. as three sylls.) German choral song on a devotional theme. XIX. – G. *choral*, from *choralgesang*, tr. medL. *cantus choralis*.

chord[1] kōɹd †harmony XV; (mus.) concord, note of a chord XVI; combination in harmony of simultaneous notes XVIII. orig. *cord*, aphetic of ACCORD.

chord[2] kōɹd †tendon; line joining extremities of an arc XVI; string of musical instrument XVII. refash. of CORD, after L. *chorda*.

chore tʃōəɹ little job. XIX. In gen. use derived immed. from U.S.; in Eng. dial. use characteristic of the south-western area: unexpl. var. of CHARE.

chorea kŏrīˑə convulsive disorder of the body. XIX. Short for earlier *chorea sancti Viti* St. Vitus's dance; L. *chorēa* – Gr. *khoreíā*, f. *khorós* CHORUS.

choreography koriɔˑgrəfi designing of ballet. XVIII.

choriamb kɔˑriæmb, **choriambus** kɔriæˑmbəs metrical foot – ◡ ◡ –. XIX. – late L. *choriambus* – Gk. *khoríambos*, f. *khoreîos* trochee, f. *khorós* CHORUS + *íambos* IAMBUS. So **choriaˑmb**IC. XVII.

choric kɔˑrik pert. to a chorus. XIX. – late L. *choricus* – Gr. *khorikós*, f. *khorós* CHORUS. So rare †**choˑrical** XVII. See -IC, -ICAL.

chorion kɔəˑriɔn (anat.) outermost membrane of the fœtus. XVI. – Gr. *khórion*. So **choˑroid** epithet of certain membranes. XVIII. – Gr. *khoroeidḗs*, for *khorioeidḗs* (χοριοειδὴς χιτών choroid coat of the eye, Galen).

chorister kɔˑristəɹ member of a choir. XIV. ME. *queristre* – AN. **cueristre*, var. of OF. *cueriste*, f. *quer* CHOIR; refashd. (XVI) after †*chorist* or its source (O)F. *choriste*, medL. *chorista* (see CHORUS, -IST). Formerly pronounced *quiˑrister*.

chorography korɔˑgrəfi description or delineation of particular regions. XVI. – F. *chorographie* or L. *chōrographia* – Gr. *khōrographíā*, f. *khṓrā*, *khôros* country; see -GRAPHY.

chortle tʃōˑɹtl Invented by 'Lewis Carroll' (C. L. Dodgson) in 'Through the Looking-glass', 1871; a 'portmanteau' word combining *chuckle* and *snort*. Cf. GALUMPH.

chorus kōˑrəs in Gr. drama and dramatic pieces modelled thereon XVI; band of singers XVII; musical composition to be sung by this; refrain or burden XVIII. – L. *chorus* – Gr. *khorós* dance, band of dancers (in Attic drama forming a body of interested spectators who danced and sang), choir.

chough tʃʌf bird of the crow family, Pyrrhocorax. XIV. ME. *choȝe*, *choghe*, *chouȝe*, *chow(e)*, not repr. directly synon. OE. *ćēo*, *ćīo*. Some ME. forms, e.g. *co*, *cowe*, *chowe* may be – OF. *cauwe*, *choue* = Pr. *cava* – Frank. *cava* (Meyer-Lübke); but the type *cho(u)ȝe*, *chough* remains unexpl.; an aberrant form *schoha* (*c.* 1200) may anticipate it. No doubt orig. imit.; cf. Gael. *cadhag*, MIr. *caog*, Ir. *cág*, *cabhóg* jackdaw, 'the ca-er'.

chouse tʃaus cheat, swindle. XVII. Earliest forms *chiause*, *chiauze*; f. *chiause* sb., later *chouse* swindler, dupe; the forms suggest identity with CHIAUS, but connexion of meaning has not been made out.

chow tʃau dog of Chinese breed usu. black or brown, with a black tongue. XIX. Short for next.

chow-chow tʃauˑtʃau A. mixture; mixed; B. Chinese dog, CHOW. XIX. Used in India and China; perh. Pidgin English, of unkn. origin.

chowder tʃauˑdəɹ in Newfoundland and adjacent regions, stew of fish, bacon, etc. XVIII (Smollett). perh. – F. *chaudière* pot, CAULDRON, in phr. *faire la chaudière*, said to be used in fishing villages of Brittany for supplying, with savoury condiments, a pot in which a mess of fish, etc., is cooked.

chrematistic krīmətiˑstik pert. to the acquisition of wealth XVIII (Fielding); sb. science of the wealth of nations XIX. – Gr. *khrēmatistikós*, f. *krēmatízein* make money, f. *khremat-*, *khrêma* money, rel. to *khrêsthai* need, use, *khrḗ* there is need.

chrestomathy krestɔˑməþi collection of choice passages. XIX. – F. *chrestomathie*, or its source Gr. *khrēstomátheia*, f. *khrēstós* useful (cf. prec.) + *-matheia* learning.

chrism kriˑzm consecrated oil OE.; Holy Unction; chrisom cloth XIII. OE. *crisma* – medL. *crisma*, ecclL. *chrisma* – Gr. *khrîsma*, f. *khríein* anoint (cf. CHRIST); refash. (like F. *chrême*) in XVI after L. See CREAM.

chrisom kriˑzəm (orig. *chrisom cloth*) white cloth put on a child at baptism, perh. orig. to protect the chrism. Differentiated form of prec. (cf. *alarm*, *alarum*) first appearing in XIII (*crisum*).

Christ kraist the Lord's Anointed, title of Jesus of Nazareth. OE. *Crīst* = OS., OHG. *Crīst*, *Krīst* – L. *Chrīstus* – Gr. *Khrīstós*, sb. use of *khrīstós* anointed, f. *khríein* anoint; tr. Heb. *māshīaχ* MESSIAH. So **christen** kriˑsn †make Christian OE.; baptize XII (Orm). OE. *crīstnian*, f. *crīsten* Christian (see -EN), whence **Christen**DOM kriˑsndəm †Christianity OE.; Christians collectively XII; †baptism XIII. OE. *crīstendōm*. So **Christ**IAN kriˑstʃən adj. and sb. XVI. – L. *Chrīstiānus* (Tacitus), f. *Chrīstus*;

superseding †*christen*, OE. *crīsten* = OS., OHG. *crīstin* – L.; cf. OF. *crestien* (mod. *chrétien*), etc. **Christian**ITY kristiæ·nĭti †Christendom; the Christian religion XIV. ME. *cristianite*, superseding (by assim. to L.) earlier *cristiente*, *cristente* – OF. *crestienté* (mod. *chrétienté*), f. *crestien*, after late L. *chrīstiānitās*.

Christadelphian kristəde·lfiən pert. to a religious sect founded in 1833 by John Thomas (1805–71). f. late Gr. *khristádelphos* in brotherhood with Christ, f. *Khristós* CHRIST+*adelphós* brother; see -IAN.

Christmas kri·sməs festival of the nativity of Jesus Christ, 25 Dec. Late OE. *Crīstes mæsse*, ME. *cristes masse* ('Owl & N.'), *cristesmesse* ('Ayenbite'), *cristmasse* ('Sir Gawain'); i.e. 'mass', i.e. festival (MASS[1]) of CHRIST.

chromatic kroumæ·tik (mus.) including notes not contained in the diatonic scale XVII; pert. to colour XIX. – F. *chromatique* or L. *chrōmaticus* – Gr. *khrōmatikós*, f. *khrōmat-*, *khrôma* colour, fig. modification (chromatic music involving modifications of the diatonic); see -IC.

chrome kroum †chromium; hence applied to pigments obtained from chromate of lead. XIX. – F. *chrome* (Vauquelin, 1797) – Gr. *khrôma* colour (see prec.); so named from the brilliant colours of its compounds. Hence **chro·m**IUM (metallic element). XIX.

chromo- kroumou used as comb. form of Gr. *khrôma* colour, as in *chromo(litho)graph*, *chromosome* [Gr. *sôma* body].

chronic krɔ·nik long-continued, inveterate XV; continuous, constant XIX. – F. *chronique* – L. *chronicus* (in late L., of disease) – Gr. *khronikós*, f. *khrónos* time; see -IC.

chronicle krɔ·nikl register of events in order of time. XIV (R. Mannyng). ME. *cronikle* – AN. *cronicle*, var. of OF. *cronique* (mod. *chronique*) – L. *chronica* – Gr. *khronikà* annals, sb. use (sc. *bíblia* books) of *khronikós* pert. to time (see prec.).

chrono- krənɔ· comb. form of *khrónos* time, as in *chronology*, *chronometer*.

chrysalis kri·səlis form taken by an insect in the stage between larva and imago. XVII (occas. with *-ll-*). – L. *chrȳsal(l)is* (Pliny) – Gr. *khrūsallís* gold-coloured sheath of butterflies, f. *khrūsós* gold (see CHRYSO-).

chrysanthemum krisæ·nþĭməm (orig.) corn marigold, (now) cultivated species of the genus so named by Linnæus. – L. *chrȳsanthemum* (Pliny) – Gr. *khrūsánthemon*, f. *khrūsós* (see CHRYSO-)+*ánthemon*, rel. to *ánthos* flower.

chryselephantine kri:selifæ·ntain overlaid with gold and ivory. XIX. – Gr. *khrūselephántinos*, f. *khrūsós* (see CHRYSO-)+*elephant-*, *eléphās* ELEPHANT, ivory; see -INE[1].

chrys(o)- kri·s(ou) comb. form of Gk. *khrūsós* gold, of Semitic origin (cf. Heb. *ḥarūz*, Ass. *ḥurāšu*); chiefly in chem. terms. XIX.

chrysolite kri·sŏlait (in early use) applied to various green gems. XIII. ME. *crisolite* – OF. *crisolite* – medL. *crisolitus*, for L. *chrȳsolithus* – Gr. *khrūsólithos* perh. topaz, f. *khrūsós*+*líthos*; see CHRYSO-, -LITE.

chrysoprase kri·sopreiz, krai·so-, -preis (in early use) golden-green gem, perh. beryl, (in mod. min.) apple-green chalcedony. XIII. ME. *crisopace*, *-pase* – OF. *crisopace* = It. *crisopasso* – L. *chrȳsopassus*, var. of *chrȳsoprasus* – Gr. *khrūsóprasos*, f. *khrūsós* gold (see CHRYSO-)+*práson* leek = L. *porrum*. The L. form **chrysoprasus** krisɔ·prəsəs is familiar as the form used in A.V. (after the Geneva Bible), Rev. xxi 20. (*Chrysopass* is found as late as Bp. Ken.)

chub tʃʌb river fish of the carp family, Cyprinus or Leuciscus cephalus, 'the worst fish that swims' (Izaak Walton). XV (Bk. of St. Albans). Of unkn. origin; also called CHEVIN (XV) and CHAVENDER, †*chevender* (XV).

Chubb tʃʌb in full *Chubb's (detector) lock*; name of Charles *Chubb*, who patented locks and safes 1824–33, and his son John *Chubb*.

chubby tʃʌ·bi †thickset XVII; round-faced XVIII. f. CHUB+-Y[1], presumably from the shape of the fish.

chuck[1] tʃʌk kind of clucking noise; also as vb. XIV (Ch.). imit. Cf. CHUCKLE[1].

chuck[2] tʃʌk term of endearment XVI; (dial.) chick, fowl XVII. Alteration of CHICK, infl. by prec.

chuck[3] tʃʌk (dial.) lump XVII; contrivance for holding work in a lathe XIX. var. of CHOCK. Cf. CHUNK.

chuck[4] tʃʌk 'give a gentle blow under the chin' (J.); throw with the hand XVI. Also (dial.) *chock* (XVI). perh. – OF. *chuquer*, earlier form of *choquer* knock, bump, of unkn. origin.

chuckle[1] tʃʌ·kl †laugh vehemently XVI; cluck, cackle XVII; laugh in a suppressed manner XIX. perh. *chokelyng* (*c.* 1400) repr. an early form; f. CHUCK[1] (vb.)+-LE[2].

chuckle[2] tʃʌ·kl big and clumsy, blockish. XVIII. prob. rel. to CHUCK[3]; now repr. mainly by *chuckle-head(ed)* XVIII.

chum tʃʌm one who shares rooms with another, (hence) intimate associate. XVII. prob. short for *chamber-fellow* (XVI), orig. a word of Oxford univ. sl., corr. to the Cambridge *crony*. Hence **chum** vb. share rooms XVIII (Wesley); *chum* (one) *on another* XIX (Dickens).

chump tʃʌmp short thick lump of wood XVIII; thick end-piece; blockhead XIX. perh. blending of CHUNK and LUMP or STUMP.

chunk tʃʌŋk thick lump. XVII (Ray). Of dial. origin; prob. alteration of dial. *chuck* (XVII), var. of CHOCK.

chupatty tʃəpā·ti small cake of unleavened bread. XIX. – Hindi *chapātī*.

chuprassy tʃəprā·si wearer of an official badge. XIX. – Hindi *chaprāsī*, f. *chaprās* official badge.

church tʃə̄ɹtʃ building for public Christian worship; body of the Lord's faithful people. OE. *ćiriće*, *ćirće*, *ćyr(i)će* = OFris. *szereke*, *szurka*, *tzierka*, OS. *kirika*, *kerika* (Du. *kerk*), OHG. *chirihha*, *kiricha* (G. *kirche*) :- WGerm. **kirika* (ON. *kirkja* KIRK is – OE.) – medGr. *kūrikón*, for *kūriakón*, sb. use (sc. *dôma* house) of n. of *kūriakós* pert. to the Lord, f. *kūrios* master, lord. The word is widely repr. in Slav. langs.: OSlav. *crĭky*, *cirkovĭ*, Russ. *tsérkov'*, Serb. *crkva*, Pol. *cerkiew* (of the Greek church), OPruss. *kīrkis*. The threefold development in ME. *churche*, *chirche*, *cherche* is evidence that the late OE. form *ćyrće* indicates a rounding of the vowel i to ü. Hence **church** vb. present or receive in church. XIV. **chu·rch**MAN ecclesiastic XVI (earlier XIV *kirkman*); male member of the church (of England) XVII. **chu:rch**WA·RDEN XV; earlier terms were †*churchman* XVI, †*church master* (†*kyrkmaster*) XV, †*church reve* (XIV, Ch.). **chu·rchyard.** late OE. (XII *cyrceiærd*, Peterborough Chron.); see YARD[2].

churl tʃə̄ɹl †man, husband; free man without rank OE.; †serf; (arch.) peasant, rustic; low base fellow XIII; niggard, miser XVI. OE. *ćeorl* = OFris. *tzerl*, *tzirl*, MLG., MG. *kerle* (whence G. *kerl* fellow), (M)Du. *kerel* :- WGerm. **kerlaz*, rel. by gradation to **karlaz* CARL. So **chu·rlish.** OE. *ćeorlisć*, *ćierlisć*; see -ISH[1].

churn tʃə̄ɹn butter-making machine. late OE. *ćyrin*, var. of **ćirn*, **ćiern* = MLG. *kerne*, *kirne*, MDu. *kerne*, ON. *kirna* :- Germ. **kernjōn*, of unkn. origin. Hence **churn** vb. XV (also transf. and fig. XVII); cf. Du. *karnen*, MG. (G. dial.) *kernen*, *kirnen*.

chut tʃʌt, tʃt excl. of impatience. XIX (Lytton, Dickens).

chute ʃūt rapid fall in a river; steep slope or channel down which stuff is shot. XIX. – F. *chute* fall, refash. of OF. *cheoite*, fem. sb. f. pp. of *cheoir* :- popL. **cadēre*, for L. *cadere* fall; often extended to senses which originated with SHOOT or are still commonly so spelt.

chutney tʃʌ·tni hot relish of fruits, chillies, etc. XIX. – Hindi *chaṭnī*.

chyle kail milky fluid into which the chyme is converted. XVII (earlier *chilus*, *chylus* XVI). – late L. *chȳlus* – Gr. *khūlós* animal or plant juice, f. **khū-* (cf. CHYME); cf. F. *chyle*, †*chile*. ¶ The distinction between *chyle* juice produced by decoction or digestion, and *chyme* juice in its raw or natural state, was made by Galen.

chym- see CHEM-.

chyme kaim semi-fluid matter into which food is converted in the stomach. XVII. – late L. *chȳmus* – Gr. *khūmós* animal or plant juice, f. **khŭ* **kheu-* pour (see FUSION, GUT).

ciborium səibɔ̄·riəm A. (eccl.) canopy, baldacchino; B. cup-shaped vessel for the Eucharistic bread. XIX. – medL. *cibōrium* vessel for the reserved sacrament, in classL. drinking-cup – Gr. *kibṓrion* cup-shaped seed-vessel of the Egyptian water-lily, drinking-cup made from this; sense B above was prob. assoc. with L. *cibus* food. ¶ Evelyn has the form *cibarium*.

cicada sikei·də insect, the male of which makes a shrill chirping sound. XIX (rarely anglicized †*cicade* XV; cf. OF. *cigade*). – L. *cicāda*, also *cicāla*. The following forms have also been used: It. **cicala** sikā·lə, ‖tʃ- XIX (Byron), Pr. **cigala** sigā·lə XVIII (H. Walpole), F. (– Pr.) **cigale** sigā·l XVII.

cicatrice si·kətris scar remaining from a wound. XIV. – (O)F. *cicatrice* or L. *cicātrīc-*, *cicātrīx* (also used in Eng. from XVII).

cicerone tʃitʃərou·ni, sisərou·ni guide who shows antiquities, etc. XVIII (Addison, Pope). – It. *cicerone* :- L. *Cicerōnem* cognomen of the Roman orator Marcus Tullius *Cicero*; orig. applied to learned It. antiquaries, later appropriated by the ordinary professional guide. So also in F.

cicisbeo tʃitʃizbei·ou recognized gallant of a married woman. XVIII. – It. (also, sword-knot, walking-stick), of unkn. origin; in Sp. *chichisbeo*, in F. *sigisbée*.

Cid sid, as Sp. þið title of Ruy Diaz, Christian champion against the Moors. XVIII. Sp. *cid* chief, commander – Arab. *sayyid* lord.

-cide[1] said repr. F. *-cide*, L. *-cīda* -killer, -slayer, f. *cædere* (in compounds *-cīdere*) cut down, kill, as in *homicīda* HOMICIDE[1], *parricīda* PARRICIDE[1].

-cide[2] said repr. F. *-cide*, L. *-cīdium* (see prec.), as in *homicīdium* HOMICIDE[2], *parricīdium* PARRICIDE[2].

cider sai·dəɹ †(in biblical use) strong drink (esp. in forms *ciser*, *sicer*); beverage made from apples. XIV. ME. *sither(e)*, *cidre* – OF. *sidre*, earlier *cisdre* (mod. *cidre*), whence Sp. *sidra*, It. *sidro* :- ecclL. *sīcera* (medL. *cisera*) – ecclGr. *sīkéra* – Heb. *shēkār* intoxicating liquor, f. *shākar* drink heavily.

cigar sigā·ɹ compact roll of tobacco-leaf for smoking. XVIII (often *segar* till early XIX). – F. *cigare* or its source Sp. *cigarro*, supposed, but without direct evidence, to be f. *cigarra* cicada, the roll of tobacco-leaf being compared to the insect. So **cigar**ETTE sigəre·t. 1842. – F.

cilia si·liə (anat.) eyelids, eyelashes. XVIII. L., pl. of *cilium* (cf. SUPERCILIOUS). So **ci·li**ARY. XVII.

Cimmerian simiə·riən pert. to the Cimmerii, fabled to live beyond the Ocean in perpetual darkness. XVI. f. L. *Cimmerius*, – Gr. *Kimmérios* ('Odyssey' XI 14); see -IAN.

cinch sinʃ saddle-girth (U.S., from Mexican use); (fig.) sure hold, dead certainty. XIX. – Sp. *cincha* = F. *sangle*, It. *cinghia*, etc. :– L. *cingula* girdle, f. *cingere* gird (cf. CINCTURE).

cinchona siŋkou·nə Peruvian bark or the tree from which it is derived. XVIII. – modL. *cinchona* (Linnæus), named after the Countess of *Chinchon*, who in 1638, when vice-queen of Peru, was cured of a fever by the use of the bark, and introduced the drug into Europe. ¶ Not rel. to *quinine*.

cincture si·ŋktʃəɹ †girding XVI; girdle XVII. – L. *cinctūra*, f. *cinct-*, pp. stem of *cingere* gird; see -URE.

cinder si·ndəɹ scoria, slag OE. residue of burnt substance XIV. OE. *sinder* = MLG. *sinder*, OHG. *sintar* (G. *sinter*), ON. *sindr*, rel. to OSl. *sędra* stalactite, Serb. *sedra* calc-sinter; respelt with *c* from XVI after unrelated F. *cendre* (L. *cinerem*, *cinis* ashes).

Cinderella sindəre·lə young and beautiful maiden in a fairy-tale who is the object of a stepmother's and sisters' jealousy. f. CINDER+fem. ending *-ella*, after F. *Cendrillon* (transf. household drudge of a family), f. *cendre* CINDER+dim. ending *-illon*.

cinematograph sinimæ·təgràf. 1896. – F. *cinématographe* (brothers Lumière), f. Gr. *kīnēmato-*, *kī́nēma* movement, f. *kīneîn* move (cf. CITE); see -GRAPH. Abbrev. **cinema** si·nĭmə 1910; after F. *cinéma*; comb. form **cine-** si·ni 1897; cf. F. *ciné*. Variants with *k-* have been used by reversion to the orig. Gr.

cineraria sinĭrɛə·riə genus of composite plants. XVI. modL., fem. (sc. *herba* plant) of L. *cinerārius* (see next); so called from the ash-coloured down on the leaves.

cinerary si·nərəri pert. to ashes. XVIII. – L. *cinerārius*, f. *ciner-*, *cinis* ashes; see -ARY.

Cingalese siŋgəlī·z pert. to Ceylon. XVII. – F. *Cing(h)alais*, Pg. *Singhalez*, f. Skr. *Siṅhalam*; see SINHALESE.

cinnabar si·nəbāɹ vermilion XV; red sulphide of mercury XVI. – L. *cinnabaris* – Gr. *kinnábari*, of Oriental origin; cf. (O)F. *cinabre*.

cinnamon si·nəmən (bark of) an E. Indian tree. XV. late ME. *sinamome* – (O)F. *cinnamome* – L. *cinnamōmum* – Gr. *kinnámōmon*; later refash. after L. *cinnamon*, *cinnamum* – Gr. *kínnamon*, of Semitic origin (cf. Heb. *qinnāmōn*).

cinquecento tʃiŋkwitʃe·ntou sixteenth century. XVIII (Goldsmith). It. 'five hundred', short way (by omitting *mil* thousand) of denoting the century beginning with 1501. So **quattrocento** kwa·tro- fifteenth century, **seicento** se·i- seventeenth century.

cinquefoil si·ŋkfoil plant Potentilla reptans, the leaves of which have each five leaflets. XIII. repr. L. *quinquefolium*, f. *quinque* FIVE+*folium* leaf, FOIL².

Cinque Ports si·ŋkpɔ̄ɹts group of (orig. five) seaports on the SE. coast of England and having jurisdiction there. XIII (*sink pors*). – OF. *cink porz*, repr. L. *quinque portus* (see FIVE, PORT¹).

cipher, cypher sai·fəɹ A. (arith.) symbol by itself denoting 'nothing' XIV; nonentity; Arabic numeral XVI; B. secret manner of writing; †hieroglyph XVI; literal device, monogram XVII; C. continuous sounding of a note on an organ due to mechanical defect XVIII. late ME. *siphre*, *sipher* – OF. *cif(f)re* (mod. *chiffre*) – medL. *cif(e)ra*, partly through It. *cifra*, †*cifera*, corr. to Sp., Pg. *cifra* (whence also MLG., MDu. *cifer*, *sipher*, G. *ziffer*), f. Arab. *çifr* ZERO, sb. use of adj. 'empty', and orig. transl. Skr. *sūnya* empty, f. *çafara* be empty. Transference of meaning to 'secret writing' was due to the fact that older systems of cryptography consisted in the use of numerals for letters. Hence **ci·pher, cy·pher** vb. work sums; write in cipher XVI. Cf. DECIPHER.

cipolin si·pəlin an Italian marble. XVIII. – F. *cipolin* or its source It. *cipollino*, f. *cipolla* onion (L. *cēpa*); so called from the resemblance of its foliated structure to the coats of an onion.

circle sɜ̄·ɹkl perfectly round figure. XIV. ME. *cercle* – (O)F. *cercle* = Pr., Cat. *cercle*, It. *cerchio* :– L. *circulus*, dim. of *circus* ring (see CIRCUS); later respelt after L. ¶ OE. *circul* was an independent adoption of the L. word, which did not survive; cf. Du., Sw., Da. *cirkel*, OHG. *zirkil* (G. *zirkel*). So **ci·rcle** vb. XIV (Ch.). – L. *circulāre*, or f. the sb.; cf. F. *cercler* (XVI).

circuit sɜ̄·ɹkit distance round XIV; journey through an area, as of judges XV; area of this XVI. – (O)F. *circuit* – L. *circuitus* (Cicero uses it to tr. Gr. *περίοδος* PERIOD), f. *circu(m)īre*, f. *circum* round, CIRCUM-+*īre* go. So **circu**ITION sɜ̄ɹkjui·ʃən. – L. **circuit**OUS səɹkjū·itəs XVII; cf. medL. *circuitōsus*.

circular sɜ̄·ɹkjŭləɹ of the form of a circle XV; affecting a 'circle' of persons XVII (*circular letter*); sb. for 'circular note' XVIII. – AN. *circuler*, OF. *circulier* (mod. *-aire*), learned alteration of *cerclier* :– late L. *circulāris*, f. *circulus* CIRCLE; further latinized in Eng. (XVI). See -AR. So **ci·rculate** †subject to repeated distillation XV; †encircle XVI; move or turn round; pass continuously from place to place XVII. f. pp. stem of L. *circulāre*, f. *circulus*; see -ATE³. **circul**A·TION. XVI. – F. or L.

circum- sɜ̄·ɹkəm repr. L. *circum-*, being the adv. and prep. *circum* round (about), around (orig. acc. of *circus* circle, CIRCUS), used as the first el. of many comp. vbs. and sbs., several of which are direct renderings of Gr. words in *περι-* PERI- (see below). The (O)F. equiv. is *circon-*; this form is occas. repr. by *circoun-* in Eng.

circumbendibus sə̄ɹkəmbe·ndibəs roundabout process, periphrasis. XVII (Dryden). joc. f. CIRCUM- and BEND[2] with L. abl. pl. ending *-ibus*; perh. modelled on †*recumbentibus* (*-endibus*) knock-down blow (*c.* 1400–XVII).

circumcise sə̄·ɹkəmsaiz cut the foreskin of. XIII. – OF. *circonciser*, or f. *circoncis-*, stem of *circoncire* – L. *circumcīdere* (tr. Gr. περιτέμνειν), f. *circum* CIRCUM-+*cædere* cut (see CÆSURA). So **circumcis**ION -si·ʒən. XII. – (O)F. – late L. (tr. Gr. περιτομή).

circumference səɹkʌ·mfərəns encompassing boundary, esp. of a circular form. XIV (Gower). – (O)F. *circonférence* – L. *circumferentia*, tr. Gr. περιφέρεια PERIPHERY; see CIRCUM-, -FEROUS.

circumflex sə̄·ɹkəmfleks accent mark ^ ^ ~. XVI. – L. *cirumflexus* (pp. of *circumflectere* bend round; cf. FLEXURE), tr. Gr. περισπώμενος *perispṓmenos* drawn round, f. *perí* PERI-+*spân* draw (cf. SPASM).

circumincession -inse·ʃən (theol.) reciprocal inexistence and compenetration of the Three Persons of the Trinity. XVII. – medL. *circumincēssiō(n-)*, f. L. *circum* CIRCUM-+*incēdere*, move, PROCEED; rendering Gr. περιχώρησις rotation, circuition, used by John Damascene to express the doctrine involved in the passage 'I am in the Father and the Father in me' (John xiv 10). Often altered to **circuminsession,** for 'reciprocal indwelling' (see SESSION), because of the difficulty of connecting the required sense with the proper form.

circumjacent sə̄ɹkəmdʒei·sənt lying around. XV (Caxton). – L. *cirumjacent-*, *-ēns*, prp. of *circumjacēre*; see CIRCUM-, ADJACENT.

circumlocution sə̄:ɹkəmlŏkjū·ʃən roundabout speech. XV. – F. *circumlocution* or L. *circumlocutiō(n-)*, literal rendering of Gr. περίφρασις PERIPHRASIS; see CIRCUM-, LOCUTION. Hence **circumlo·cut**ORY. XVII.

circumscribe sə̄·ɹkəmskraib draw a line round; describe (a figure) about another; delimit. XV. – L. *circumscrībere* (used in the various senses of Gr. περιγράφειν), f. *circum* around+*scrībere* draw lines, write (see CIRCUM-, SCRIBE, SCRIPTURE). So **circumscri·p**TION. XV. – L.

circumspect sə̄·ɹkəmspekt cautious, watchful. XV. – L. *circumspectus* (of things) well considered, (of persons) considerate, cautious, pp. of *circumspicere* look round, f. *circum* CIRCUM-+*specere* look (cf. SPECIES). So **circumspe·c**TION circumspect action. XIV (Trevisa; rare before XVI). – L.

circumstance sə̄·ɹkəmstəns (pl.) adjuncts of an action XIII; condition of affairs XIV (Wyclif); formality, ceremony XIV (Ch.); accessory matter, detail XIV (R. Mannyng). – (O)F. *circonstance*, †*circun-* or L. *circumstantia* (tr. Gr. περίστασις and περιοχή), f. prp. of *circumstare* stand around, surround; see CIRCUM-, STAND. Hence **circumsta·n**TIAL. XVI (Sh.); cf. F. *circonstanciel* (XVIII). **circumsta·ntiate** set forth the circumstances of. XVII; cf. F. *circonstancier* (Cotgr.).

circumvallation sə̄:ɹkəmvælei·ʃən (construction of) a rampart or entrenchment round a place. XVII. – late L. *circumvallātiō(n-)*, f. *circumvallāre*, f. *circum* CIRCUM-+*vallum* rampart, WALL; see -ATION.

circumvent sə̄ɹkəmve·nt encompass with evil or hostility; overreach, outwit. XV. f. *circumvent-*, pp. stem of L. *circumvenīre* surround, beset, deceive, f. *circum* CIRCUM-+*venīre* COME. So **circumve·n**TION. XV. – late L.

circumvolution sə̄:ɹkəmvŏlʲū·ʃən revolution, rotation XV; winding or rolling round XVI. f. L. *circumvolvere*, after *revolution*.

circus sə̄·ɹkəs building surrounded with rising tiers of seats XVI; circular area for equestrian and acrobatic feats; circular range of houses XVIII. – L. *circus* circle, circus = Gr. *kírkos, kríkos* ring, circle, prob. rel. to L. *curvus* CURVE.

cirque sə̄ɹk circus XVII (Holland); (poet.) circle, ring XVII; natural amphitheatre XIX. – F. *cirque* – L. CIRCUS.

cirrhosis sirou·sis (path.) disease of the liver occurring in spirit-drinkers, orig. so called from the presence of yellow granules. XIX. modL. (Laennec), f. Gr. *kirrhós* orange-tawny; see -OSIS.

cirrus si·rəs (bot.) tendril; (zool.) filamentary process or appendage XVIII; form of cloud having the appearance of filaments or wisps XIX. L., 'curl, fringe'; comb. form **ci·rro-** (see -O-), as in *cirro-cumulus*, *-stratus* (L. Howard, 1803).

cissoid si·soid (math.) curve of the second order, the cusp of which resembles the re-entrant angles of an ivy-leaf. XVII. – Gr. *kissoeidḗs*, f. *kissós* ivy; see -OID.

Cistercian sistə̄·ɹʃən pert. to (a monk of) the Benedictine order of Cîteaux, founded 1098. XVII. – F. *Cistercien*, f. L. *Cistercium* Cîteaux, near Dijon, France (cf. medL. *Cisterciensis*); see -IAN.

cistern si·stəɹn reservoir or tank for water. XIII. – OF. *cisterne* (mod. *citerne*) = Pr., It. *cisterna* :– L. *cisterna*, f. *cista* CHEST, prob. of Etruscan origin, with suffix as in *caverna* CAVERN, *taberna* TAVERN.

cistus si·stəs genus of shrubs (rock rose, etc.). XVI. modL. – Gr. *kístos, kísthos*.

cistvaen see KISTVAEN.

cit sit (arch.) 'a pert low townsman; a pragmatical trader' (J.). XVII. Shortening of CITIZEN. Cf. FAN[2], MOB[2].

citadel si·tədəl fortress commanding a city. XVI (Sidney). – F. *citadelle* or It. *citadella*, dim. of *cittade*, obs. var. of *città* :– L. *civitātem* CITY.

cite sait summon officially XV; quote, adduce as an authority XVI. – (O)F. *citer* – L. *citare*, frequent. of *ciēre*, *cīre* set in motion, call (cf. EXCITE, INCITE, SOLICIT), rel. to Gr. *kíō* I go, *kīneîn* move, OE. *hātan* call (see HIGHT). So **cita·tion** summons XIII; quotation XVII. – (O)F. – L.

cither si·þəɹ zither. XVII. – (O)F. *cithare* or G. *zither* (cf. ZITHER) – L. *cithara* – Gr. *kithárā* lyre-like instrument, prob. of Eastern origin.

cithern, cittern si·þəɹn, -ð-, si·təɹn instrument of the guitar kind. XVI (*cythren, cithron, cittarn, -ern*). – L. *cithara* (see above), crossed with GITTERN. One of the earliest known Eng. forms derived ult. from *cithara* is *citole* (XIV), which is immed. – OF. *citole* (= Pr. *citola*), whence also MHG. *zitōl(e)*.

citizen si·tizən inhabitant of a city, member of a state. XIV (*citisein, citizein*). – AN. *citesein, citezein*, alteration of OF. *citeain* (mod. *citoyen*) = Pr. *ciutadan*, Sp. *ciudadano*, It. †*cittadano* (now *-ino*), Rum. *cetățean* :– Rom. **cīvitātānu-s*, f. *cīvitās* CITY. The intrusion of *s, z* in the AN. form was prob. due to assoc. with *deinsein* DENIZEN.

citra- si·trə repr. L. *citrā* on this side (see HITHER).

citric si·trik derived from the citron. XVIII. – F. *citrique* (de Morveau, 1787), f. L. *citrus*; see next and -IC. So **ci·trate** XVIII; see -ATE[4].

citron si·trən (tree bearing) ovate fruit like a lemon but larger and less acid. XVI. – (O)F. *citron*, f. (after *limon* lemon) L. *citrus* (i) thuya, (ii) citron-tree, prob., like Gr. *kédros* CEDAR, an adoption from a non-IE. lang.; from F. is also It. *citrone*, whence G. *zitrone*.

city si·ti †town (often in biblical and derived use; a more dignified substitute for OE. *burh* BOROUGH) XIII; town of ecclesiastical or political importance XIV. ME. *cite* – (O)F. *cité* = Pr., Cat. *ciutat*, Sp. *ciudad*, Pg. *cidade*, It. *città*, Rum. *cetate* (castle, fortress) :– L. *cīvitātem*, nom. *cīvitās* condition (see -TY) of a citizen, citizenship, body of citizens, body politic, state, (later, an equivalent of *urbs*) city, f. *cīvis* (see CIVIC).

civet si·vit (quadruped yielding) the musky secretion called by the same name. XVI. – F. *civette* – It. *zibetto* – medL. *zibethum* (cf. medGr. *zapétion*) – Arab. *qaṭṭ azzabād* 'cat producing the secretion *zabād*'. Also *civet-cat* XVII; cf. It. *gatto zibetto*, Du. *civet(kat)*, G. *zibetkatze*.

civic si·vik pert. to a citizen or citizens XVI; of a city XVII; of citizenship, civil XVIII. – F. *civique* or L. *cīvicus*, f. *cīvis* citizen; see HIDE[2], and -IC. As sb. pl. (after *politics*) XIX (orig. U.S. 1886).

civies, civvies si·viz (colloq.) civilian clothes. 1889. f. CIVI|LIAN + pl. suffix *-(e)s*.

civil si·vĭl A. of citizens XIV (*batayle ciuile*); befitting a citizen; civilized; refined, 'polite' XVI; courteous XVII; B. non-ecclesiastical XVI; non-military XVII; opp. to (i) *criminal*, (ii) *natural* XVII. – (O)F. *civil* – L. *cīvīlis*, f. *cīvis* citizen; see CIVIC and -ILE. So **civi·lity**. XIV. – (O)F. *civilité* – L. *cīvīlitās*, orig. used to render Gr. *polītikḗ* civil government, POLITICS, *polīteiā* citizenship, POLITY. **ci·vilize**. XVII. – F. *civiliser*; hence **civiliza·tion**. XVIII.

civilian sivi·ljən student or professor of civil law XIV (Wycl. Bible); †follower of civil (i.e. natural, unregenerate) righteousness (*justitia civilis*) XVII; non-military man XVIII. – OF. *civilien* in *droit civilien* civil law, f. *civil*; see CIVIL, -IAN. ¶ *Civilist* was formerly used (XVI–XVIII) – medL. *cīvīlista*.

civism si·vizm devotion to the order established by the French Revolution of 1789. XVIII. – F. *civisme*, f. L. *cīvis* citizen; see CIVIC and -ISM. So **i·ncivism**. XVIII. – F. *incivisme*; see IN-[2].

clack klæk chatter XIII; make a clattering noise XVI. prob. – ON. *klaka* twitter, (of birds) chatter; of imit. origin; cf. Du. *klakken* crack, F. *claquer*. Hence **clack** sb. clatter of talk XV; clapping or clacking noise XVI; pump-valve XVII. Cf. ON. *klak* chirping of birds, Du. *klak*, MHG. *klac*.

clad see CLOTHE.

claim kleim demand or assert as one's own. XIII (Cursor M.). – OF. *claim-*, tonic stem of *clamer* cry, call, appeal = Pr. *clamar*, Sp. *llamar*, Pg. *chamar*, It. *chiamare*, Rum. *chemà* :– L. *clāmāre* cry, call, proclaim, call upon, rel. to *clārus* CLEAR. So **claim** sb. XIII. – OF. *claime*, f. *clamer*. Hence **clai·mant**. XVIII; primarily a legal term, after *appellant, defendant*.

clairvoyance klɛəɹvoi·əns mental perception, esp. of things concealed from sight. XIX (Mrs. Carlyle, Emerson). – F., f. *clairvoyant* (in Eng. also XIX), f. *clair* CLEAR + *voyant*, prp. of *voir* see (see VISION). In F. used of visual and mental clearsightedness.

clam klæm clamp XIV; bivalve shell-fish (orig. *clam-shell*) XVI. OE. *clam* bond, fetter, corr. to OHG. *chlamma* (G. dial. *klamm*), and MHG., G. *klemme*, Du. *klemme, klem*, f. Germ. **klam-* press or squeeze together. The application to shell-fish may refer to their shutting like a pair of clamps or to their tenacious clinging to rocks.

clamant klei·mənt clamorous XVII; crying, urgent XVIII. – L. *clāmant-*, *clāmāns*, prp. of *clāmāre* cry out; see CLAIM, -ANT.

clamber klæ·mbəɹ climb with hands and feet. XV. Of frequent. form, prob. f. *clamb*, obs. pt. of CLIMB (cf. the equiv. dial. *climber* XVI); see -ER[4].

clamjamphrie klæmdʒæ·mfri (Sc.) trumpery people, rabble. XIX (Scott). Of unkn. origin; Scott's form *clanjamphrie* suggests a contemptuous ref. to a Highland clan.

clammy klæ·mi sticky with moisture. XIV. f. (with -Y[1]) *clam* (XIV) smear, daub, choke, (dial.) parch, benumb, a new formation on *clammed*, pt. and pp. of OE. *clǣman* (*clǣmde, clǣmd*) smear, anoint, daub = MDu. *klēmen*, OHG. *chleimen*, ON. *kleima* daub, plaster :- Germ. **klaimjan*, f. **klaimaz* clay, f. base repr. by CLAY. An earlier form was †*claymy* (XIV), with which cf. †*cleymows* (XV), both f. *cle(i)me*, OE. *clǣman*, ON. *kleima*.

clamour klæ·məɹ loud outcry. XIV (Ch., Gower). – AN. *clamur*, OF. *clamour* – L. *clāmōrem, clāmor*, rel. to *clāmāre*; see CLAIM and -OUR. Hence **cla·mour** vb. XIV.

clamp[1] klæmp brace or band of metal. XIV. prob. of LG. origin; cf. Du., LG. *klamp*, †*klampe* (whence G. *klampe*), f. **klamp-*, by-form of **klamb-* (cf. CLIMB), **klamm-* (cf. CLAM). Hence **clamp** vb. XVII.

clamp[2] klæmp stack of bricks XVI; (agric.) stack of earth, turf, etc. XVIII. prob. as a brick-making term – (M)Du. *klamp* heap, rel. to CLUMP.

clan klæn group of associated families in Scotland bearing the same name. XIV (Sc. *clen*). – Gaelic *clann* offspring, family, stock, race, corr. to OIr. *cland*, (mod.) *clann* – L. *planta* sprout, scion, PLANT (for the sense cf. *stirps* stock, stem, race).

clandestine klænde·stin secret, underhand. XVI. – F. *clandestin* or L. *clandestīnus*, f. *clam* secretly, rel. to *celāre* CONCEAL. ¶ For the L. formation cf. *cælestīnus, intestīnus*.

clang klæŋ resonant ringing sound. XVI. imit. formation parallel to OHG. *chlang* (G. *klang*). Also as vb. XVI; perh. partly – L. *clangere* resound (as a trumpet).

clangor klæ·ŋgəɹ loud clanging. XVI (Sh.). – L. *clangor*, f. *clangere*, rel. to Gr. *klaggḗ* loud cry. Hence **cla·ngor**OUS XVIII; cf. medL. *clangōrōsus*.

clank klæŋk sound as of heavy pieces of metal struck together. XVII. imit. formation parallel to MLG., (M)Du. *klank*, OHG. *chlanch*. Cf. prec. and CLINK. Also as vb. XVII.

clap[1] klæp make a sharp, forcible, or resounding noise. OE. *clappian* throb, beat = OFris. *klappia*, MLG. *klappen*, OHG. *klapfōn*, ON. *klappa*, beside OE. *clæppan* = OFris. *kleppa*, MLG. *kleppen*, OHG. *kleppfen*; also OE. *clæpp-*, *cleppet(t)an*; of imit. origin (cf. *flap, rap, slap, tap*).

clap[2] klæp (sl.) gonorrhœa. XVI. Of uncertain origin; but cf. OF. *clapoir* venereal bubo, obs. Du. *klapoore* 'botch or Soare in the Groin, gotten from a whore' (Hexham).

clapboard klæ·pbɔəɹd split oak for barrel staves. XVI. Partial tr. of †*clapholt* (XV) – LG. *klappholt* = Du. *klaphout*, f. *klappen* crack + *holt* wood (see HOLT).

clapperclaw klæ·pəɹklō (arch., dial.) claw with open hand, beat, thrash. XVI. Obscurely f. *clapper* + CLAW vb. (perh. with iron. ref. to the sense 'flatter', from the phr. *claw the back of*).

claque klæk organized body of hired applauders. XIX. – F. *claque*, f. *claquer* clap (cf. CLACK), of imit. origin.

Clare klɛəɹ nun of the Second Order of St. Francis, founded by St. *Clara* of Assisi, *c.* 1212. Cf. F. *Clarisse*, Du. *Klarisse*.

clarence klæ·rəns four-wheeled four-seated carriage. XIX. Named after the Duke of *Clarence*, afterwards William IV.

Clarenc(i)eux klæ·rənsjū king-of-arms of England south of the Trent, formerly also called *Surroy*. XV. – AN. *Clarenceux* (in AL. *Clarencius*), f. *Clarence*, an English dukedom named from *Clare* in co. Suffolk, the first duke being Lionel, second son of Edward III, whose wife brought with her the Honour of *Clare*.

clarendon klæ·rəndən (typogr.) thick-faced type. XIX. Named after the *Clarendon* Press, which was first housed in the *Clarendon* Building at Oxford, erected with funds partly provided by the profits of the sale of the Earl of *Clarendon*'s history of 'the Rebellion and Civil Wars in England' (1647).

claret klæ·rət †epithet of light red wines, (later) red wine gen., (now) red wine of Bordeaux. XIV. orig. qualifying *wine*, after OF. *vin claret* (mod. *clairet*), which superseded OF. *claré* (whence Eng. †*clary* mixture of wine, honey, etc. XIII) :- medL. *clārātum* (sc. *vīnum*) 'clarified wine', n. pp. of *clārāre*, f. L. *clārus* CLEAR.

clarify klæ·rifai †illumine, make illustrious XIV; make clear XV. – (O)F. *clarifier* – late L. *clārificāre*, f. *clārus* CLEAR; see -FY.

clarion klæ·riən kind of trumpet. XIV. – medL. *clāriō(n-)*, f. L. *clārus* CLEAR; cf. OF. *claron* (mod. *clairon*). Hence **clarione·t**. XVIII; partly alteration of *clarinet* – F. *clarinette*, f. *clarine*, sb. use of fem. of †*clarin*, f. *clair* CLEAR.

clarity klæ·rĭti †lustre, splendour XVI; clearness XVII. – L. *clāritās*, f. *clārus* CLEAR; see -ITY. (Superseded †*clar(e)te, clerte* XIV – OF. *clarté*, †*clerté*.)

clary klɛə·ri the plant Salvia Sclarea. XIV. app. – F. †*clarie*, repr. medL. *sclarea* (whence OE. *slarie*, OHG. *scar(a)leia*), but the loss of initial *s* is unexpl.

clash klæʃ loud sound of collision followed by a confusion of lesser sounds. XVI. imit.; rel. to *clack*, as *crack* to *crash*, *smack* to *smash*, dial. *swack* to *swash*; cf. also the series *clack, clap, clash* and *swack, swap, swash*. Also as vb. XVI.

clasp klàsp sb. fastening consisting of interlocking parts; vb. secure with this. XIV. perh. f. CLIP[1] after the pair *grasp, grip*; for the terminal sounds cf. HASP and MLG., MDu. *gaspe, gespe* (Du. *gesp* clasp, buckle).

class klàs division of persons or things. XVII (earlier Sc. in senses 'division of the Romans', 'class in a university', 'fleet' XVI, when the L. word was current in Eng.). Prob. first in gen. use in the sense 'division of pupils in a school', and immed. – L. *classis* each of the six ancient divisions of the Roman people, body of citizens under arms, spec. fleet, prop. levy :– **qladtis*, f. extended form of **qel-* call (cf. L. *calāre*, Gr. *kaleîn* call, *clāmor* CLAMOUR). Cf. (O)F. *classe*. Hence **class** vb. XVIII (earlier than *classify*). So **cla·ssi**FICA·TION. XVIII (Burke, 1790). – F. (1787); whence **cla·ssi**FY.

classic klæ·sik of the first rank; of the standard authors of ancient Greece and Rome; hence more widely, of others XVII; sb. (esp. pl.) ancient Gr. or L. writer XVIII; classical scholar XIX. – F. *classique* or L. *classicus*, f. *classis* CLASS; see -IC. So **cla·ssi**CAL. XVI. The application to the ancient 'classics' may have been due in part to the notion that the ancient Greek and Roman literatures were superior to the modern, and in part to their predominant use in the *classes* of schools.

clatter klæ·təɹ make the noise of repeated collision of hard bodies (in ME. earliest use 'be shattered' XIII); †chatter, rattle through XIV. OE. **clatrian*, implied in *clatrung*, corr. to (M)Du. *klateren* rattle, chatter, frequent. formation (see -ER[5]) on imit. base **klat-*.

clause klōz short sentence XIII; article or proviso XIV (Ch.). – (O)F. *clause* = Pr. *clauza* – Gallo-Rom. **clausa*, for L. *clausula* close of a rhetorical period, (later) conclusion of a legal formula, section of a law, fem. dim. f. *claus-*, pp. stem of *claudere* CLOSE.

claustral klō·strəl of a cloister. XV. – late L. *claustrālis*, f. *claustrum* CLOISTER; see -AL.

claustrophobia klōstrəfou·biə (path.) morbid dread of enclosed places. XIX. f. *claustro-*, taken as comb. form (see -O) of L. *claustrum* CLOISTER + -PHOBIA.

clavate klei·veit (nat. hist.) club-shaped. XIX. – modL. *clāvātus*, f. *clāva* staff, club; see -ATE[2].

clavichord klæ·vikōɹd string-and-key instrument. XV. – medL. *clāvichordium* (whence It. *clavicordio*, G. *klavichord*), f. L. *clāvis* key (rel. to *claudere* CLOSE) + *chorda* string, CHORD.

clavicle klæ·vikl collar-bone. XVII. – L. *clāvicula* small key, door-bolt, applied in modL. to the bone because of its shape, dim. of *clāvis* key (cf. prec.).

clavier klæ·viəɹ, kləviə·ɹ keyboard XVIII; keyboard instrument XIX. – F. *clavier*, or its deriv. G. *klavier* – L. **clāviārius* (see -ARY), f. *clāvis* key.

claw klō sharp horny toe-nail. OE. *clawu* (new formation on the obl. cases, the orig. nom. being repr. by *clēa*, whence ME. and dial. *clee*) = OFris. *klē*, *klāwe*, OS. *clāuua* (Du. *klauw*), OHG. *chlāwa* (G. *klaue*) :– WGerm. **klawō*; another type is repr. by OHG. *chlōa*, ON. *kló*. Hence **claw** vb. OE. *clawian* = MLG. *klāwen*, OHG. *klāwēn*.

clay klei stiff viscous earth. OE. *clǣġ* = OFris. *klāy*, (M)LG., (M)Du. *klei* :– WGerm. **klaijō-*, f. **klai-* **klei-* **kli-*, repr. also by OE. *clām*, mod. dial. *cloam* mud, clay, OE. *clǣman* (see CLAMMY); IE. **gloi-* **glei-* **gli-* smear is widely repr., e.g. by Gr. *gloiós*, *glínē*, *glía*, L. *glūs*, *glūten* (see GLUE, GLUTINOUS), OIr. *glenaid* remains sticking, OSl. *glĕnŭ*, Lith. *glitùs* slippery. Hence **clay·ey.** late OE. *clǣġiġ*. See -Y[1].

claymore klei·mōəɹ Highlander's two-edged broadsword. XVIII. f. Gaelic *claidheamh* klai·əv sword + *mór* (= W. *mawr*, Ir. *már*) great.

-cle kl terminal el. repr. F. *-cle* – L. *-culus*, *-a*, *-um* -CULE, as in †*animalcle*, *article*, *corpuscle*, *follicle*, *versicle*.

clean klīn †clear; free from dirt or filth. OE. *clǣne* = OFris. *klēne*, *kleine*, OS. *klēni*, *cleini* (Du. *kleen*, *klein* small), OHG. *chleini*, MHG. *kleine* clear, pure, delicate, fine, neat, small, puny (G. *klein* small) :– WGerm. **klainiz*, usu. supposed to be formed (with *-n-*; cf. *green*) on **klai-* (see CLAY), as if the prim. meaning were 'shining with oil'. The historically orig. sense 'clear, pure' is most nearly preserved by Eng. among the mod. langs. Hence **cleanly** kle·nli adj. and adv. OE. *clǣnlīċ*, *-līċe*: see -LY[1], -LY[2]. **cleanse** klenz. OE. *clǣnsian*; the mod. sp., replacing †*clense*, is due to assim. to the adj.

clear kliəɹ free from obscurity, murk, or impurity. XIII. ME. *clēr* – OF. *cler* (mod. *clair*) = Pr. *clar*, Sp. *claro*, It. *chiaro* :– L. *clāru-s* bright, clear, manifest, illustrious, famous, poss. rel. to *calāre* call (cf. INTERCALATE, COUNCIL). Hence **clear** vb. XIV (R. Rolle, Ch., Wyclif). **clea·r**ANCE. XVI.

cleat klīt wedge (spec. naut.). XIV. repr. OE. **clēat* = MLG. **klōt* (Du. *kloot*) ball, sphere, OHG. *chlōz* clod, lump, pommel of sword, wedge (G. *kloss*) :– WGerm. **klautaz*, rel. to **klūt-* CLOT, CLOUT, and OE. *clēot* 'pittacium'.

cleave[1] klīv hew or cut asunder, split. OE. *clēofan* (*clēaf*, *clufon*, *clofen*) = OS. *kliobhan* (Du. *klieven*), OHG. *chliuban* (G. *klieben*), ON. *kljúfa* :– Germ. **kleuƀan* (**klauƀ*, **kluƀum*, **kluƀanaz*) :– IE. base **gleubh-* (cf. Gr. *glúphein* hollow out, as in HIEROGLYPH, and perh. L. *glūbere* peel). The forms of the pt. have followed similar lines of development to those of *choose*; since *c.* 1800 the pp. *cloven* has been mainly limited to adj. use, e.g. *cloven hoof*; pt. and pp. *cleaved* (from XIV) are mainly in geol. use; *cleft* dates from XIV.

cleave[2] klīv stick fast, adhere. The present form repr. OE. *cleofian, clifian* = OS. *clibon* (Du. *kleven*), OHG. *chlebēn* (G. *kleben*) :– WGerm. wk. vb. **klibōjan, -ǣjan*, f. **klib-*, the strong form of which is repr. by OE. *clīfan* (**clāf, clifon, clifen*), ME. *clive*, pt. *clāf*, later *clave* (A.V.) = OS. *biklīban* (Du. *beklijven*), OHG. *chlīban*, ON. *klífa*; f. **klī-* stick, adhere (cf. CLAY, CLIMB). *Cleft* dates from XVII; cf. *bereft, left*. The sp. with *ea* for this and prec. is abnormal.

cleavers klī·vəɹz, **clivers** kli·vəɹz goose-grass, Galium Aparine, which adheres to objects by its minute hooked bristles. XV. Earliest forms *cliure, clyure*, superseding OE. *clīfe* = OS. *klība*, OHG. *chlība*, f. base of CLEAVE[2]; presumably apprehended as an agent-noun.

cleek klīk (Sc.) large hook XV; kind of golf club XIX. f. *cleek*, var. of *cleech, cleach*, repr. OE. **clǣćan* (**clǣhte*) clutch.

clef klef (mus.) character indicating the name and pitch of a note. XVI. – F. *clef* :– L. *clāvi-s* key, rel. to or – Doric Gr. *klāîs* (:– **klāϝís*), f. **klau-* (cf. L. *claudere* CLOSE).

cleft kleft fissure, split. XIII. Earliest form *clift*; the present form, due to assim. to *cleft*, pp. of CLEAVE[1], dates from XVI.

clematis kle·mətis wild twining shrub (Old Man's Beard). XVI (Gerarde). – L. *clēmatis* – Gr. *klēmatís*, f. *klēma* vine-branch.

clement kle·mənt mild and humane. XV. – L. *clēment-, -ēns*, assoc. by the ancients with *clīnāre* incline, LEAN[2]. So **cle·m**ENCY. XV. – L. *clēmentia*.

clench klentʃ fix firmly; grasp firmly XIII; close tightly (the fist, etc.) XVIII. OE. *-clenćan* (in *beclenćan*) = OHG. *chlankhan, klenken* :– Germ. **klaŋkjan*, f. **klaŋk-* **kleŋk-* **kluŋk-*, parallel to **klaŋg-*, etc. (see CLING). Cf. CLINCH.

clepsydra klepsi·drə instrument to measure time by the discharge of water. XVII (Sir T. Browne). – L. – Gr. *klepsúdrā*, f. *kleps-*, comb. form of *kléptein* steal + *húdōr* WATER.

clerestory kliə·ɹstōri row of lights above the arches or triforium of a church. XV. f. *clere*, CLEAR ('light, lighted') + STOREY.

clergy klə̄·ɹdʒi A. body of ordained men in the Church XIII; B. learning (survived in legal phr. *benefit of clergy*) XIII. repr. two F. words, which were both used in sense A, (O)F. *clergé* :– ecclL. *clēricātu-s*, f. *clēricus* (see CLERK, -ATE[1]), and (O)F. *clergie*, f. *clerc* + *-ie* -Y[3], with *-g-* after *clergé*.

cleric kle·rik adj. clerical; sb. clergyman. XVII. – ecclL. *clēricus* (Jerome) – Gr. *klērikós* (eccl.) belonging to the Christian ministerial order, f. *klêros* lot, heritage, as used (e.g.) in Acts i 17 'the lot (*klêros*) of this ministry'. So **cle·r**ICAL of the clergy XVI; of a clerk or penman XVIII. – ecclL. *clēricālis*, f. *clēricus*; the second meaning is due to assoc. with the later sense of CLERK.

clerk klāɹk, (dial., vulgar, and U.S.) klə̄ɹk ordained minister of the Church XI; learned man, scholar XIII; lay officer of a church (e.g. *singing c., parish c.*); one having charge of records, correspondence, or accounts XVI. Late OE. *cleric, clerc* – ecclL. *clēricus* CLERIC; this merged with ME. *clerc* – (O)F. *clerc* (= Pr. *clerc*, It. *chierico*), of the same origin. The sp. *clark* appears XV. Learning in the Middle Ages being mainly confined to the clergy, the word came to express 'scholar', and to denote any one engaged in a notarial or secretarial occupation. Hence **cle·rkly** adj. XVI; modelled on **cle·rkly** adv. XV, which is after late L. *clēricāliter*; see -LY[1], -LY[2].

cleugh klʲūχ Sc. form of CLOUGH. XIV.

clever kle·vəɹ adroit, dexterous (XIII ?) XVI; (dial.) nimble, active; lithe, handsome XVII; (dial.) convenient, agreeable, nice XVIII. prob. long in local use before it became gen. established, and still recorded as provincial in XVII, as by Sir Thomas Browne (E. Anglia) and Ray ('South and East Country Words', 1674). The earliest ex., in the form *cliuer*, if identifiable with this word, is from the ME. 'Bestiary' (prob. E. Anglian) and its context suggests etymol. connexion with †*cliver* claw, as if 'sharp to seize'; rare Sc. *cleverous* apt to seize (Dunbar), similarly assoc. with *cluik* claw, precedes the earliest ex. of *clever* in the mod. period. Correspondence in form and sense to LG. *klöver, klever*, MDu. *klever* sprightly, brisk, smart, suggests that the word may belong to the LG. area.

clew klū (arch.) ball, esp. of thread OE.; (naut.) corner of a sail to which tacks and sheets are made fast XVI (Nashe). OE. *cliwen, cleowen* = MLG., Du. *kluwen*, f. base of OHG. *chliuwi, chliuwa*, MHG. *kliuwel, kliuwelīn*, by dissimilation *kniuwel(īn)*, whence G. *knäuel* ball of wool; prob. ult. rel. to CLAW (cf. ON. *kló* claw, clew of sail). For the loss of final *-en* cf. *eve, game, maid*. See the differentiated var. CLUE.

cliché kli·ʃei stereotype block; stereotyped phrase, literary tag. XIX. F., sb. use of pp. of *clicher* stereotype (fig., as in *discours cliché* stereotyped speech), said to be imit. of the sound produced by the dropping of the matrix on the molten metal (cf. G. *klitsch* slap, clash, perh. the immed. source).

click klik slight sharp hard sound XVII; catch, latch XVIII; non-vocal suction-sound in some languages XIX. Also vb. XVII. ult. imit.; cf. OF. *clique* tick of a clock, *cliquer* click (whence modF. *cliqueter, cliquetis*), Du. *klik* tick, MDu. *klikken*. Cf. CLIQUE.

client klai·ənt one under the protection of a patron XIV (Gower); one for whom an advocate pleads XV; customer XVII. – L. *client-, cliēns*, earlier *cluēns*, sb. use of prp. of *cluere, cluēre* hear, listen; lit. 'one who is at another's call'; see LISTEN. So **clientele** kliãtei·l orig. (XVI) – L. *clientēla*, but obs. in XVII and readopted from F. *c.* 1850.

cliff klif steep face of rock OE.; steep slope (now local) XII. OE. *clif* = OS. (Du.) *klif*, OHG. *klep*, ON. *klif* :– Germ. **klibam*; beside MDu. *klippe* (whence G. *klippe*) :– **klibn-*, and ON. *kleif*; of unkn. origin.

climacteric klaimækte·rik, -æ·ktərik pert. to a critical period (in human life); also sb. XVI (formerly often *climateric*). – F. *climatérique* or L. *clīmactēricus* – Gr. *klīmaktērikós*, f. *klīmaktḗr* critical period, f. *klīmak-*, *klîmax* ladder (CLIMAX) + *-tēr* agent-suffix. Also **climacte·RICAL**. XVI.

climate klai·mət belt of the earth's surface between two parallels of latitude XIV (Barbour, Ch., Gower); region having certain atmospheric conditions; these conditions themselves XVII. – (O)F. *climat* or late L. *clīma*, *clīmat-* – Gr. *klíma*, *klímat-* in the sense 'zone or region of the earth occupying a particular elevation on the supposed slope of the earth and sky from the equator to the poles', which had developed from the gen. sense 'slope of ground'; f. **klī̆-*, as in *klī́nein* slope, LEAN². (†*Climature* XVII was a former syn., as in Sh.; see also CLIME.) Hence **climatIC** klaimæ·tik. XIX.

climax klai·mæks (rhet.) ascending series of expressions XVI; (transf., by misuse) culmination, highest point XVIII. – late L. *clīmax* – Gr. *klîmax* ladder, hence in rhet., f. **klī-* (see LEAN²).

climb klaim raise oneself or ascend by means of some hold or footing. OE. *climban*, pt. *clamb*, *clumbon*, pp. *clumben* = (M)LG., (M)Du. *klimmen*, OHG. *chlimban* (G. *klimmen*) :– WGerm. **klimban*, nasalized var. of **kliban* (see CLEAVE²), the orig. sense being 'hold fast'. Now inflected wk. *climbed* klaimd XIII, except for an arch. pt. *clomb* kloum. In many dialects *clim* is the surviving form, and in Sc. the orig. conjugation is preserved, *clim*, *clam*, *clum*.

clime klaim. XVI (now arch.). – late L. *clīma* CLIMATE.

clinch klinᵗʃ later var. of CLENCH, now differentiated for certain meanings. XVI.

cling kliŋ †coagulate, congeal; †shrink, wither OE.; adhere, stick, cleave XIII. OE. *clingan*, pt. *clang*, pp. *clungen*, corr. to MDu. *klingen* stick, adhere, MHG. *klingen* climb: f. Germ. **klaŋg-* **kliŋg-* **kluŋg-* (cf. OE. *clengan*, ME. *clenge* adhere, cling, MHG. *klengel* swinging object, ON. *klengjast* interfere, OHG. *klungilīn*, G. *klüngel* clew), parallel to **klaŋk-*, etc. (cf. CLENCH).

clinic kli·nik pert. to the sick-bed. XVII. sb. bedridden person. XVII. – L. *clīnicus* – Gr. *klīnikós*, f. *klī́nē* bed (see LEAN²); cf. F. *clinique* and see -IC. So **cli·NICAL**. XVIII.

clink¹ kliŋk make a sharp metallic sound. XIV (Ch.). prob. – (M)Du. *klinken* sound, ring, tinkle, rel. to MLG., (M)Du. *klank* sound (cf. CLANK), and parallel to OHG. *chlanch* (G. *klang*); cf. CLANG. Hence **clink** sb. XIV.

clink² kliŋk proper name of a prison in Southwark; (gen.) prison. XVI. Of unkn. origin.

clinker¹ kli·ŋkəɹ very hard kind of brick XVII; mass of slag or lava XVIII. Earlier *klincard*, *clincart* – early modDu. *klinckaerd* (now *klinker*), f. *klinken* sound, ring, CLINK¹; so called because the brick rings when struck.

clinker² kli·ŋkəɹ applied to boats of which the planks are overlapped and secured with clinched nails. XVI. f. *clink*, var. of CLINCH + -ER¹; prob. infl. by LG., Du. *klinken* rivet. *Clincher-built* has varied with *clinker-built* from XVIII.

clinometer klainɔ·mitəɹ instrument for measuring slopes. XIX. f. *clino-*, used as comb. form of stem of Gr. *klī́nein* slope (see LEAN²) + -METER.

clinquant kli·ŋkənt glittering (lit. and fig.). XVI. – F. prp. of †*clinquer* to ring, glitter (*clinquant d'or* XVI) – LG. *klinken* CLINK.

clip¹ klip embrace, grip, clutch. OE. *clyppan* = OFris. *kleppa* :– WGerm. **kluppjan*, with cogns. outside Germ. in OSl. *raz|globiti* press, Lith. *glóbti* embrace. Hence **clip** sb.¹ instrument that clips or grips. XV.

clip² klip cut, shear. XII (Orm); mutilate (coin) XIV; cut short (words) XVI; move rapidly XVII. – ON. *klippa*, prob. imit. of the sound produced; cf. LG., Fris. *klippen*.

clipper kli·pəɹ fast-sailing vessel. XIX. f. CLIP² in the sense 'move quickly', said of vessels taking the water, and formerly of the flight of birds; prob. infl. by CUTTER. (In gen. sense 'one who or that which clips' from XIV.)

clique klīk small exclusive set. XVIII. – (O)F. *clique*, f. OF. *cliquer* make a noise – MDu. *klikken* (see CLICK); for the sense-development cf. CLAQUE.

clitoris klai·təris (anat.) female homologue of the penis. XVII. modL. – Gr. *kleitorís*.

cloaca klouei·kə sewer XVIII; (anat.) excretory canal XIX. – L. *cloāca*, *cluāca*, earlier *clovāca*, rel. to *cluere* cleanse, f. IE. **klu-* **kleu-* **klou-*, repr. also by OE. *hlūt(t)or* pure, Gr. *klúzein* wash, bathe (see CATACLYSM, CLYSTER). So **cloa·CAL**. XVII. – L.

cloak klouk loose outer garment. XIII. – OF. *cloke*, *cloque*, dial. var. of *cloche* (i) bell, (ii) cloak = OIt. dial. *ciocca*, Pg. *choca* cow-bell :– medL. *clocca* (VII), perh. of Ir. origin (cf. CLOCK). Hence **cloak** vb. XVI.

clock klɔk instrument for measuring and recording time by a pendulum. XIV. Introduced by Flemish clockmakers imported by Edward I. – MLG., MDu. *klocke* (LG., Du. *klok*), corr. to OE. *clucge*, OFris. *klokke*, OHG. *glocka* (G. *glocke* bell), ON. *klokka*, *klukka*; Germ. – medL. *clocca* bell (whence F. *cloche*, etc.; cf. CLOAK).

clod klɔd †clot of blood XIV; lump of earth, etc. XV. In OE. in *clodhamer* (cf. YELLOWHAMMER) fieldfare, *Clodhangra* (place-name); corr. to (M)HG. *klotz*. Hence **clo·dho:pper** †ploughman, country lout. XVII; + agent-noun of HOP.

clog klɔg (dial.) block of wood XIV; wooden-soled shoe XV. Of unkn. origin. Hence **clog** vb. fetter, hamper, encumber. XIV.

cloisonné klwazɔ·nei (of enamels) divided into compartments. XIX. pp. of F. *cloisonner*, f. *cloison* partition = Pr. *clauzó* :– Rom. **clausiō(n-)*, f. *claus-* (see CLOSE).

cloister kloi·stəɹ enclosure, close XIII; convent; covered walk, esp. round a court XIV. – OF. *cloistre* (mod. *cloître*), earlier *clostre* = Pr. *claustre*, It. *chiostro* :– L. *claustrum*, *clōstrum* lock, bar, enclosed place, f. *claud-*, stem of *claudere* CLOSE, + *-trum*, instr. suffix.

Clootie klū·ti the Devil. XVIII (Burns). f. *cloot* hoof + -IE.

close klous sb. enclosed place, enclosure XIII; adj. closed, shut up XIV. – (O)F. *clos* :– L. *clausu-s*, pp. of *claudere* shut, close, rel. to *clāvis* key, *clāvus* nail, Gr. *kleis* key, *kleíein* shut, Ir. *cló* nail, W. *clo* lock. So **close** klouz vb. stop an opening. XIII. f. *clos-*, ppl. stem of (O)F. *clore* :– L. *claudere*; superseded OE. *clȳsan*, *beclȳsan*, ME. *(be)clüsen* (early XIII), f. *clūse* bar, enclosure, cloister – medL. *clūsa*, var. of *clausa*, sb. use of fem. pp. of L. *claudere*.

closet klɔ·zit private room XIV; cabinet, cupboard; privy XVII. – OF. *closet*, dim. of *clos*; see prec. and -ET.

closure klou·ʒəɹ †barrier, fence XIV (Ch.); †ENCLOSURE XV; conclusion, close XVI. – OF. *closure* :– late L. *clausūra*, f. *claus-*; see CLOSE, -URE. In the last sense a new formation on CLOSE, and in parliamentary use (*c.* 1880) superseding earlier *cloture* (*c.* 1870) – F. *clôture* :– Rom. **clausitura*, f. *claus-* + *-tura* -TURE.

clot klɔt lump, esp. one formed by coagulation. OE. *clot(t)* = MHG. *kloz* (G. *klotz*) :– WGerm. **klutt-*, f. **klut-* **kleut-* **klaut-*; cf. CLEAT, CLOUT.

cloth klɔ̄þ A. piece of woven or felted stuff OE.; the stuff or material itself (in these two uses with mod. pl. *cloths*) XIV; B. †(coll.) clothing, raiment XII, equivalent to **clothes** klouðz, klouz, OE. *clāþas*, ME. *clāþes*, *clōþes*, later †*cloaths*, also †*close*, north. *clāþis*, modSc. *claes*. OE. *clāþ* = OFris. *klāth*, *klēth*, MDu. *kleet* (Du. *kleed*), MHG. *kleit* (G. *kleid*); ON. *klæði* is of different origin, and the distribution of the word in Germ. is irregular; of unkn. origin. So **clothe** klouð pt., pp. **clothed** klouðd and arch. **clad** klæd provide with clothes. XII. ME. *clāþen*, pointing to OE. **clāþian*, f. *clāþ*. Late Nhb. OE. had *clǣþde*, pt. of *clǣþan*, and pp. *ġecladed*, which appear to have been the source of ME. pt. *cladde*, pp. *clad*; but ON. *klædda*, *klæddr*, pt. and pp. of *klæða*, were partly the source; ME. *yclad* (XIV) was revived as an archaism XVI (Spenser).

cloud klaud †hill, rock OE.; visible mass of watery vapour in the air XIII. OE. *clūd*, prob. rel. to CLOD. In the second sense it superseded OE. *wolcen* WELKIN and ME. *skie* SKY. The orig. sense survives in place-names. Hence **cloud** vb. XVI.

clough klʌf ravine. OE. *clōh* (in place-names) :– Germ. **klaŋχ-*, rel. to OHG. *klinga* (G. dial. *klinge*) ravine.

clout klaut †patch; metal plate OE.; piece of cloth XIII; (from the vb.) blow with the hand XIV. OE. *clūt*, corr. to (M)LG., MDu. *klūt(e)* (Du. *kluit* lump, clod), ON. *klútr* kerchief; rel. to CLEAT, CLOT. Hence **clout** vb. patch OE.; OE. *clūtian* (in pp. *ġeclūtod*) cuff heavily. XIV.

clove[1] klouv one of the divisions of the bulb of garlic, etc. OE. *clufu*, pl. *clufe*, also in comps. *clufeht* bulbous, *clufþung* crow-foot, *clufwyrt* buttercup, corr. to the first el. of OS. *cluflōc* 'clove-leek', garlic, OHG. *klobolouch* (MHG. *klobelouh*, *knobelouh*, G. *knoblauch*), f. weak grade of Germ. **kleuƀ-* (see CLEAVE[1]).

clove[2] klouv dried flower-bud of Caryophyllus aromaticus used as spice. XIV. orig. *clow (of) gilofer* – (O)F. *clou de girofle* (*gilofre*) 'nail of clove-tree', so called from its shape; see GILLYFLOWER. The change from *clow* to *clove* is difficult to account for; it may have taken place in AN., *clou de* giving **clov|de*, perh. with the same change as in *lieutenant*.

cloven see CLEAVE[1].

clover klou·vəɹ species of trefoil. OE. *clāfre* = (M)LG., Du. *klāver* :– Germ. **klaiƀrōn*, the first syll. of which corr. to OS. *klē*, OHG. *klēo* (G. *klee*) :– WGerm. **klaiwaz*, *-am* clover. From XV–XVII a common var. was *claver*, which may repr. OE. *clǣfre*, with shortening of the stem-vowel, or may be of LDu. origin.

clown klaun rustic, ill-bred man; fool or buffoon, esp. on the stage. XVI. perh. of LG. origin; cf. NFris. *klönne*, *klünne* clumsy fellow, *klünj* clod, lump, and the like. The earliest forms (setting aside an obscure reference to *Sanct Cloun* in Dunbar, which may be unconnected) are *cloine*, *cloyne*, the diphthong of which may point to an orig. *ü*. Some favour the deriv. suggested by Ben Jonson in 'Tale of a Tub' I iii [Latin] '*Colonus* is an Inhabitant: A Clowne originall', 'An ancient Colon (as they say) a Clowne of Midlesex'; but evidence is wanting.

cloy kloi †nail, prick (a horse) with a nail XIV; †clog, obstruct; surfeit, satiate XVI. Aphetic of †*acloy* – AN. *acloyer*, var. of OF. *encloyer* (mod. *enclouer*) :– Rom. **inclāvāre*, f. L. *in* EN-¹+*clāvus* nail, rel. to *clāvis* key (cf. CLAVICLE, CONCLAVE), *claudere* CLOSE.

club klʌb heavy stick XIII; stick used in ball-games XV; (tr. It. *bastone*, Sp. *baston* BATON) suit at cards XVI; combination or association of persons XVII. – ON. *klubba*, assim. form of *klumba* club (cf. *klumbu-*, *klubbufótr* club-footed), rel. to CLUMP. The last sense appears to have been derived from the sense 'form into a club-like mass' (XVII) of the vb., which was itself derived from the orig. meaning of the sb. Hence **clu·bb**ABLE. XVIII (Johnson).

cluck klʌk make the peculiar sound of a broody hen. XVII (Cotgr.). corr. to MHG. *klucken*, (also mod.) *glucken*, Da. *klukke*, Sw. *klucka*, imit. formation to which there are parallel forms with the vowel *o*, OE. *cloccian* (dial. *clock*), MDu. *clocken* (Du. *klokken*), Sw. dial. *klokka*; cf. synon. L. *glōcīre*, Gr. *klṓssein* (:– **klōkj-*).

clue klū later form (XV) of CLEW, now restricted mainly to the sense 'fact, etc., leading (through a difficulty) to a solution or discovery'.

clumber klʌ·mbəɹ breed of spaniel. XIX. f. *Clumber*, name of a seat of the duke of Newcastle, in Nottinghamshire.

clump klʌmp compact mass of trees XVI; transf. of other things XVII. – MLG. *klumpe* (LG. *klump*, whence Norw. *klump*, etc.), rel. to MDu. *klompe* (Du. *klomp*) lump, mass, and OE. *clympre* (mod. dial. *clumper*) lump of metal, and further to CLAMP²; cf. CLUB.

clumsy klʌ·mzi †benumbed; moving as if benumbed, awkward in action. XVI. perh. of dial. origin (Marston's use of it is ridiculed by Ben Jonson in 'Poetaster' v iii). f. (dial.) *clumse* benumb (XIII, Cursor M.), prob. of Scand. origin (cf. Norw. dial. *klumsen* strike dumb, clog, hamper, *klumst* clumsy, Icel. *klumsa* lock-jawed, Sw. dial. *klumsen* benumbed, dazed, *klumsig* numb, clumsy); the base **klum-* is repr. also by Norw. dial. *kluma*, *klumra*, Du. *kleumen*, *kleumsch*, cf. *clem*.

Cluniac klū·niæk pert. to (a monk of) the monastery of Cluny. XVII. – medL. *Cluniacus*, f. *Clun(i)æum* Cluny or Clugny, France; see -AC.

cluster klʌ·stəɹ collection of things close together. OE. *clyster*, (rare) *cluster*, also *ġeclystre* bunch of grapes, prob. f. **klut-* (see CLOT). For the vocalism cf. BLUSH.

clutch¹ klʌtʃ †crook, bend; seize with claws, seize eagerly. XIV. ME. *clucche*, pp. *clought*, varying with *clicche*, pt. *clihte*, pp. *cliht*, repr. late OE. *clyććan*, pp. *gecliht* crook, clench, also in *forclyććan* stop up (the ears), *ymbclyććan* enclose :– **klukjan*. (A synon. dial. *cleach*, ME. *cleche*, pt. *clahte*, pp. *claht*, *cleȝt*, points to OE. **clǣćan*, pt. **clǣhte*.) Hence **clutch** sb. claw; grasp XVI; earlier synon. forms are (dial.) *cloke*, †*cloch* (XIII), Sc. *cluk*, *cleuk* (XIV), †*clouch* (XV), †*clooch* (XVI). The interrelation and history of the series of forms is obscure.

clutch² klʌtʃ laying or sitting of eggs, brood of young birds. XVIII. prob. of southern dial. origin like synon. north. *cletch* (XVII), rel. obscurely to *cleck* hatch (XV; chiefly Sc.) – ON. *klekja* assoc. with CLUTCH¹.

clutter klʌ·təɹ †clotted mass XVI; confused mass or crowd; noisy turmoil; confused noise XVII. var. of †*clotter* (Ch.), †*clodder* (XV), f. CLOT, CLOD; and see -ER⁴; has been assoc. to some extent with *cluster* and *clatter*. So **clu·tter** vb. in similar senses (XVI); appears to have been introduced into literature from dial. use, to which it has largely reverted.

Clydesdale klai·dzdeil breed of horse reared in the neighbourhood of the river *Clyde* in Scotland. XIX.

clypeus kli·piəs (ent.) shield-shaped part of the head of insects. XIX. var. of L. *clipeus*, *clupeus* shield; comb. form *cly·peo-*.

clyster kli·stəɹ injection, enema. XIV. – (O)F. *clystère* or L. *clystēr* – Gr. *klustḗr* syringe, rel. to *klúzein* wash, rinse, f. IE. **klud-* **kleud-* (whence also OE. *hlūttor* pure), further rel. to OL. *cluere* purify, *cluāca*, *cloāca* sewer (cf. CLOACA).

co- kou var. of COM- used before vowels, *h*, and *gn*, as in L. *coadjūtor*, *coalescere* COALESCE, *coæquālis* CO-EQUAL, *cognātus* COGNATE, *cohērēs* CO-HEIR, *cooptāre* CO-OPT; in very extensive use from XVII as a living formative in the senses 'together', 'in common', 'joint(ly)', 'reciprocally'. In math. repr. *complement*, in the sense '. . . of the complement', 'complement of . . .', as in COSINE, etc.

coacervation kou:æsəɹvei·ʃən heaping together. XIV. – L. *coacervātiō(n-)*, f. *coacervāre*, f. *com-* CO-+*acervus* heap; see -ATION.

coach koutʃ large carriage XVI; private tutor (orig. university slang), instructor in sport and athletics XIX. immed. – F. *coche* (Ronsard). A Common European word since XVI, e.g. G. *kutsche*, Du. *koets*, Sp., Pg. *coche*, It. *cocchio*, Pol. *kocz*; ult. – Magyar *kocsi* ko·tʃi, current from the reign of Matthias Corvinus (1458–90), adj. f. *Kocs* name of a town near Raab in Hungary, the full form being *kocsi szeker* 'Kocs cart', whence modL. *cocius currus*, *currus kotsi*, G. †*cotschiewagen*, †*gutschiwagen*, Du. †*koetsiwaghen*, etc.; occas. †*cochee* in Eng. (XVI).

coadjutor kouədʒū·təɹ fellow-helper. XV.

– (O)F. *coadjuteur*, †*-tor* – late L. *coadjūtor*, f. CO- + *adjūtor* helper (see ADJUTANT).

coagulate kouæ·gjŭleit curdle, form into a mass. XVII. f. pp. stem of L. *coāgulāre*, f. *coāgulum* rennet, f. **coagere* drive together; see COGENT, -ATE[3]. So **coagul**A·TION. XV (?).

coaita kou·aitā red-faced spider monkey. XVIII. Tupi.

coal koul †glowing piece of wood OE.; †charcoal XIII; black mineral used for fuel XIII (orig. *seacoal*, perh. because orig. derived from beds exposed by marine denudation). OE. *col*, corr. with variation of form and gender to OFris., MLG. *kole*, (LG. *kale*), MDu. *cole* (Du. *kool*), OHG. *kol, kolo* (G. *kohle*), ON. *kol* :– CGerm. (exc. Goth.) **kolam*, **kolon*, referred by some to Skr. *jval* glow, by others to OIr. *gūal*, W. *glo* coal. The present standard form derives from OE. obl. cases.

coalesce kouəle·s unite in one body. XVI. – L. *coalēscere*, f. *com* CO- + *alēscere* grow up, f. *alere* nourish (see ALIMENT). So **coali**·TION. XVII. – medL.

coalmouse, colemouse kou·lmaus the bird Parus ater. OE. *colmāse*, corr. to MDu. *koolmēze* (Du. *koolmees*), MHG. *kolemeise* (G. *kohlmeise*), f. *col* COAL (with allusion to its black cap) + *māse* (see TITMOUSE).

coaming kou·miŋ (naut.) raised edges of hatches and scuttles. XVII. Of unkn. origin.

coarse kɔəɹs †ordinary, common XIV; wanting in fineness or delicacy XVI (later in various lit. and fig. uses). Earliest forms *cors(e), course*; the present form appears XVII, but is anticipated by †*cowarce* (XVI); the earliest application is to cloth or clothes; of unkn. origin; that it should be based on the phr. *of course* customary, usual (XVI) seems to be chronologically impossible.

coast koust †tract, region XIII (Cursor M.); †quarter, direction; †side; sea-shore XIV; (Canada and U.S.) hill-slope XVIII. ME. *cost(e)* – OF. *coste* (mod. *côte*) = Pr., Pg., It. *costa*, Sp. *cuesta* :– L. *costa* rib, flank, side. So **coast** vb. †keep or move by the side or coast of; †border *upon* XIV; †traverse, scour XV; (U.S.) slide down a slope in a sled; hence in cycling XIX. In early use *costay, -ey, -ie* – OF. *costeier* (mod. *côtoyer*), f. *coste* (cf. It. *costeggiare*); later assim. to the form of the sb.

coat kout tunic, (later) man's outer garment; (dial.) petticoat; natural covering. XVI. ME. *cote* – OF. *cote* (mod. *cotte* petticoat), corr. to Pr., Sp. *cota*, It. *cotta* (cf. COTTA) :– Rom. **cotta* – Frank. **kotta* (cf. OHG. *kozzo* (G. *kotze*) coarse woollen garment or stuff, OS. *cot* woollen coat or cloak), of unkn. origin. Hence **coat-armour** †tabard with heraldic device; †heraldic bearings XIV; blazonry XV. prob. – OF. **cotte d'armure* (cf. *coat-of-arms* XV – F. *cotte d'armes*). †**coat-card**; see COURT-**card**.

coati kou·ti Amer. mammal resembling civet and racoon. XVII. – Tupi *coati, coatim*, f. *cua* cincture + *tim* nose.

coax kouks †fool, take in; pet, fondle XVI; wheedle XVII. orig. 'make a *cokes* [i.e. fool] of', of unkn. origin; 'a low word' (J.).

cob[1] kɔb in many applications which can be mostly grouped under the headings 'head' and 'roundish object, round clump', among the earliest being 'great man, leader' (XV), *cob-iron* (XV) one of the irons on which a spit turns (also †*cobbard*), *cob-nut* (XVI), earlier †*cobble-nut*; *cob-loaf* loaf with a round head (XVII); the application to a stout short-legged horse (XIX) has been referred to dial. *cobs* testicles. Of obscure origin; in AL. *cobus* cob-loaf (XIII); cf. WFlem. *kobbe* tuft of feathers, head of hair, dome of the head, WFris. *kobbe* drop.

cob[2] kɔb gull. XVI (*sea cobbe*). perh. of LG. origin; cf. Du. *kobbe, kobmeeuw*, EFris. *sē|kobbe*.

cobalt kɔbɔ̄·lt, kou·bɔ̄lt (chem.) metallic element. XVII (*cobolt*). – G. *kobalt, -old*, †*-olt*, †*-elt*, disparaging application of MHG. *kobolt* (mod. *kobold*) fairy or demon of the mine, from the miners' belief that cobalt ore was deleterious to the silver ores in which it occurred; for similar applications cf. *nickel, wolfram*.

cobble[1] kɔ·bl rounded stone XV (in earliest exx. *c.-stone*, also †*cobled stone*); pl. small coal XIX. f. COB[1] + -LE[1].

cobbler kɔ·bləɹ maker or mender of shoes. XIII (as a surname), XIV (PPl.), of unkn. origin. Hence **cobble**[2] vb. mend roughly, patch up. XV.

coble kou·bl (Sc.) boat used esp. for salmon-fishing XIII; (north. Eng.) sea fishing-boat XIII. In AL. *cobellum* (XIII), *cobla* (XIV); poss. of Celtic origin (cf. W. *ceubal* ferry-boat, skiff, lighter, Breton *caubal*).

cobra kou·brə. XIX; short for *cobra (de) capello* (XVII) hooded snake; Pg. *cobra* (:– L. *colubra*) snake, *de* with, *capello* hood (:– medL. *cappellus*, dim. of *cappa* CAPE).

coburg kou·bɔ̄ɹg name of a dress fabric and a fancy bread. XIX. f. name of Prince Albert of Saxe-*Coburg*, consort of Queen Victoria of England.

cobweb kɔ·bweb spider's web. XIV. ME. *cop(pe)web*, f. *coppe*, short for *attercop(pe)* :– OE. *āt(t)ōrcoppe*, f. *āt(t)ōr* poison + *coppe* = MDu. *koppe*, prob. rel. to †*cop*; see WEB.

coca kou·kə shrub, Erythroxylon coca, of which the dried leaves are used as a masticatory, etc. XVI. – Sp. *coca* – Quichua *cuca*. **cocaine** kŏkei·n, prop. kou·keiain alkaloid occurring in the leaves of the coca; see -INE[3].

coccagee kɔkəgī· cider apple. XVIII. – Ir. *cac a' ghéidh* 'dung of goose'; so called from its greenish-yellow colour.

coccus kɔ·kəs pl. *cocci* kɔ·ksai insect of the genus so named XVIII; (bot.) carpel of a dried fruit XIX (earlier *coccum*); (med.) rounded form of bacterium XIX. modL. – Gr. *kókkos* berry, seed, pippin.

coccyx kɔ·ksiks (anat.) terminal bone of the spinal column. XVII. – L. *coccyx* – Gr. *kókkux* CUCKOO, used by Galen for the *os coccygis* 'cuckoo's bone' because it was supposed to resemble a cuckoo's bill. So **coccyge**AL[1] kɔksi·dʒiəl. XIX. f. medL. *coccȳgeus*.

cochin-china koutʃintʃai·nə breed of poultry. XIX. f. name of a country in the Annamese empire, the place of origin.

cochineal kɔtʃinī·l dye-stuff consisting of the dried bodies of a S. American insect, which was at first supposed to be a berry. XVI. – F. *cochenille* or Sp. *cochinilla*, which is gen. referred to L. *coccinus* scarlet (Gr. *kókkos* kermes), but its orig. application is doubtful.

cochlea kɔ·kliə spiral cavity of the internal ear. XVII. – L. *coc(h)lea* snail-shell, screw, – Gr. *kokhlías*, prob. rel. to *kógkhē* CONCH.

cock[1] kɔk male domestic fowl OE.; male bird XIV; in various transf. applications, the earliest (XV) being 'spout, tap', the origin of which is not clear, but is paralleled by G. *hahn* cock; the latter, like Du. *haan*, is also used, as *cock* is (XVI), for the discharging mechanism of fire-arms. OE. *cocc*, *kok* = ON. *kokkr*, prob. – medL. *coccus* (Salic Laws), of imit. origin (cf. the cry *cok cok* in Ch., 'Nun's Priest's Tale' 457); reinforced in ME. by (O)F. *coq*. ¶ The native Germ. word is repr. by OE. *hana*, OS., OHG. *hano* (Du. *haan*, G. *hahn*), ON. *hani*. Hence **cock** vb. set or stick up (assertively) XVII; prob. from the attitude of fighting cocks; whence a new sb. upward turn XVIII.

cock[2] kɔk heap of hay. XIV. immed. source uncertain; perh. Scand. (cf. Norw. *kok* heap, lump, Da. dial. *kok* haycock, Sw. *koka* clod), but an OE. **cocc* hill has been assumed for the place-names *Cockhampstead*, *Cookham* (*Coccham* VIII), *Coughton* (*Cocton* XIII). Hence as vb. XIV.

cockabondy kɔkəbɔ·ndi angler's fly. XIX. – W. *coch a bon ddu* 'red with black (*du*) trunk or stem (*pon*)'.

cockade kɔkei·d rosette, etc., worn in the hat as a badge. XVII (in *cockared cap*), XVIII (*cockard*, *cockade*). – F. *cocarde*, orig. in phr. *bonnet à la coquarde* (Rabelais) cap worn assertively on one side; fem. of †*coquard* proud, saucy, as sb. coxcomb, f. *coq* COCK[1]; see -ARD. The ending was assim. to -ADE.

cock-a-doodle-doo kɔ:kədū:dldū· crow of a cock. XVI (*-too*). imit.; cf. F. *cocorico*, G. *kikeriki*, late L. *cūcūrīre* crow, and ME. *cok cok* (see COCK[1]).

cock-a-hoop kɔkəhū·p in phr. *set cock a hoop*, denoting some action preliminary to hard drinking XVI; in a state of elation XVII. Of doubtful origin; the explanation of the literal meaning as 'set the spigot on the hoop of the cask' (Blount's 'Glossographia', 1670) is unconvincing; the problem is complicated by the occurrence (from XV), in tavern-signs, of a hoop and of figures (a bell, angel, mitre, swan, hart, cock, etc.) on a hoop.

Cockaigne, Cockayne kɔkei·n imaginary country of luxury and idleness. XIV. – OF. *cocaigne*, as in *pais de cocaigne* fool's paradise (mod. *cocagne*), corr. to Sp. *cucaña*, Pg. *cucanha*, It. *cuccagna* – MLG. *kōkenje* small very sweet cake sold to children at fairs, dim. f. *kōke* CAKE; in the ME. poem called 'The Land of Cokayne' the buildings of the country are described as being built of pasties, cakes, and puddings.

cock-a-leekie kɔkəlī·ki (Sc.) soup made from a fowl boiled with leeks. XVIII. f. COCK[1] + LEEK, with connecting vowel and suffix *-ie*, -Y[6].

cockalorum kɔkəlɔ̄·rəm self-important little man XVIII; *hey cockalorum* cry in certain games XIX. f. COCK[1] in the sense 'leader' (XVI), with fanciful termination simulating L. g.pl. ending *-orum* (cf. G. *buckelorum* hunchback, f. *buckel* hump).

cock-and-bull kɔkənᵈbu·l applied to an idle story. XVIII. orig. in phr. *talk of (a story of) a cock and a bull* (XVII), said of rambling or misleading talk; parallel to F. *coq-à-l'âne* (anglicized as †*cockalane* XVII), orig. in phr. *saillir du coq en l'âne* 'jump from the cock to the ass'.

cockatiel kɔkətī·l crested grass parrakeet of S. Australia. XIX. – Du. *kaketielje* assim. to COCK[1].

cockatoo kɔkətū· large bird of the parrot kind. XVII (*cacatoe*). – Du. *kaketoe* (whence G. *kakadu*, F. *cacatoès*) – Malay *kakatua*, whence Pg. also *cacatua*; infl. by COCK[1].

cockatrice kɔ·kətrais basilisk XIV (Wycl. Bible); (her.) hybrid of cock and serpent XVI. – OF. *cocatris* = Pr. *calcatriz*, It. *calcatrice* (Sp. *cocotriz* is from F.) – medL. *calcātrix*, *caucātrix* (fem. agent-noun f. *calcāre* tread, (later) track, f. *calx* heel) used to render Gr. *ikhneúmōn* ICHNEUMON, lit. 'tracker'. Through a complicated series of erroneous identifications OF. *cocatris* came to denote the crocodile; by a further (obscure) transference *cockatrice* was applied in Eng. translations of the Bible to the basilisk, rendering Vulgate *basiliscus* and *regulus*, LXX *basilískos* and *aspís*; assoc. with COCK[1] produced the her. sense.

cockboat kɔ·kbout small ship's BOAT. XV. Formerly also simply *cock*, which was partly synon. with †*cog* (XIII). *Cock* (in AL. *cocha*, *coqua*, *cocco*) was – OF. *coque*, dial. var. of *coche* = Pr. *coca*, OIt. *cocca* :– medL. *caudica* (cf. *caudiceus*, *cōdicārius* applied to boats as being carved out of trunks, f. *caudex, cōdex* block of wood; see CODE). *Cog* (in AL. *coga, cogo*) was – MLG., MDu. *kogge* (Du. *kog*), whence also OF. *cogue, koge*.

cockchafer kɔ·ktʃeifəɹ coleopterous insect, Melolontha vulgaris. XVIII. The second el. is (dial.) *chafer, chaffer* :– OE. *ćeafor*, prob. f. Germ. **kab̄*- gnaw, parallel to **keb̄*-, repr. by OE. *ćefer* (whence dial. *cheever*) = OS. *kevera* (Du. *kever*), OHG. *chevaro, kevar* (G. *käfer* beetle); if the first el. is COCK¹, the reference is obscure.

cocker¹ kɔ·kəɹ pamper, indulge, humour. XV. rel. obscurely to synon. †*cock* and †*cockle* (both XVI); the status of Flem. *kokelen, keukelen* 'nutrire sive fovere culina' (Kilian) and F. *coqueliner* 'to dandle, cocker, pamper' (Cotgr.) is doubtful.

cocker² kɔ·kəɹ spaniel of a breed trained to start woodcock, etc. XIX. f. *cocking* (XVII) shooting of woodcock, f. COCK¹+-ING¹; see -ER¹.

Cocker kɔ·kəɹ name of Edward *Cocker* (1631–75), arithmetician, reputed author of a popular 'Arithmetick', used in phr. *according to Cocker* by strict rule or calculation. XIX.

cockerel kɔ·kərəl young cock. XV (Promp. Parv.). f. COCK¹+-EREL.

cocket kɔ·kit seal of the king's custom house XIII; custom-house certificate XIV. In AN *cokete*, AL. *coketa, coketum*; poss. from the concluding phr. of the document, *quo quietus est* by which he is QUIT.

cockle¹ kɔ·kl plant growing among corn; 'tares'. OE. *coccul, -el*, perh. – medL. **cocculus*, f. late L. *coccus*, earlier *coccum* kermes – Gr. *kókkos*.

cockle² kɔ·kl edible bivalve mollusc. XIV. – (O)F. *coquille* shell (whence It. *cocchiglia*) :– medL. **cochilia* – medGr. *kokhúlia*, pl. of *kokhúlion*, for Gr. *kogkhúlion*, f. *kógkhē* CONCH. In phr. *the cockles of the heart* a reference has been supposed to the spiral conformation of the fibres of the heart.

cockle³ kɔ·kl go into rucks, pucker. XVI. – F. *coquiller* blister (bread) in cooking (cf. *recoquiller* turn or curl up, dog's-ear), f. *coquille* shell, shell-like object, blister on head (see prec.).

cockloft kɔ·klɔ̀ft small upper loft. XVI. prob. f. COCK¹+LOFT, as being orig. a place where fowls roosted.

cockney kɔ·kni †hen's egg, perh. small or mis-shapen egg, 'cock's egg'; †petted or cockered child, mother's darling, milksop XIV; †townsman, as a type of effeminacy; one born in the city of London XVI. ME. *cokeney, cokenay*, prob. f. *cokene*, g.pl. of *cok* COCK¹+*ey, ay* (OE. *ǽġ*) egg; cf. the formation of G. *hahnenei* 'cocks' egg'. The second sense was assoc. with COCKER¹; cf. 'I coker *je mignotte*; I bring up like a cocknaye *je mignotte*' (Palsgrave).

cockpit kɔ·kpit pit or enclosure to be used for cock-fighting XVI; (naut.) after part of the orlop deck of a man-of-war XVIII. f. COCK¹+PIT.

cockroach kɔ·kroutʃ dark-brown beetle-like insect. XVII (*cacarootch* Capt. Smith; *cockroche*). – Sp. *cucaracha* (cf. Pg. *caroucha*), whence Creole F. *coquerache*; unaccountably assim. to *cock* and *roach*.

cocksure kɔkʃūəɹ (with variable stress) †(objectively) quite secure or certain XVI; (subjectively) feeling quite sure or certain XVII. The formation suggests that the orig. sense was 'sure as a cock', with COCK¹ perh. in the sense of 'tap', which would agree with the earlier objective meaning; but evidence is lacking.

cocktail kɔ·kteil A. 'cock-tailed' horse, i.e. one with the tail docked and so sticking up like a cock's tail; beetle that cocks up its 'tail'; B. (orig. U.S.) mixed drink with a spirit as basis. XIX. f. COCK¹ vb.+TAIL; the origin of B is obscure. ¶ An early ex. of the comp. is in *cock-taile proude*, 1600.

cocky kɔ·ki (sl.) arrogantly pert. XVIII. f. COCK¹+-Y¹; also *cocksy* (XIX), cf. *tricksy* (?).

coco, cocoa¹ kou·kou †nut of the coco-palm, Cocos nucifera, and the tree itself XVI; now only in *coco-, cocoa-, coker-nut* kou·kə XVII. – Sp., Pg. *coco* (whence also F. *coco*), orig. playful use of *coco* grinning face, grin, grimace, with allusion to the monkey-like appearance of the base of the shell of the nut. Appears first in latinized form †*cocus*, later †*cocos* (as in botany), used for sg. and pl.; cf. Du. *kokosboom, -noot*, G. *kokosbaum, -nuss*. The sp. *cocoa* is due to an error in Johnson's dictionary, in which this word and COCOA² were combined under one heading; *coker*, †*cocar* (– Du. †*koker|noot*) dates from XVII and is established in commercial use.

cocoa² kou·kou †seed of a tropical American tree; powder produced by grinding the seed, and beverage made from this. XVIII. Alteration of *cacao* kəkā·ou, -ei·ou (XVI), also †*cacoa* – Sp. *cacao* – Aztec *kakaua-*, comb. form of *kakaua-atl* (see CHOCOLATE).

cocoon kəkū·n silky case spun by insect-larva. XVII. – F. *cocon*, †*coucon* – modPr. *coucoun* egg-shell, cocoon, dim. of *coca* shell.

cocotte kokɔ·t fast woman. XIX. F., (also) child's word for a fowl, ult. f. *coc* COCK¹.

cod¹ kɔd husk OE. (surviving dial., as in *peascod* pea-shell); scrotum; (pl.) testicles XIV; hence **co·d**PIECE XV. OE. *cod(d)* bag, scrip, husk, corr. to ON. *koddi*, ODa. *kodde*, Sw. *kudde* cushion, pillow, pad, Norw. *kodd* testicle, scrotum; f. Germ. **kud-* **keud-* (whence OE. *ćēod* pouch).

cod² kɔd sea-fish, Gadus morrhua. XIII. Of unkn. origin; possibly a use of COD¹, as if 'bag-fish', from its appearance; connexion with Gr. *gádos* (modL. *gadus*) is phonetically impossible. *Cod's head* was sl. for 'blockhead' (XVI); hence prob. (sl.) *cod* fool, simpleton (XVII), whence **cod** vb. (sl.) hoax, humbug. XIX.

coda kou·də (mus.) concluding passage. XVIII. It. :- L. *cauda* tail.

coddle kɔ·dl treat as an invalid. XIX. prob. of dial. origin and a var. of *caudle* (XVII Sh.) administer a caudle to; but perh. a fig. use of *coddle* (XVI) parboil, stew, (dial.) roast. Cf. MOLLYCODDLE. ¶ 'How Dr. Johnson could be guilty of so gross an oversight as to spell this word and its compounds with one *d* is inconceivable' (Walker).

code koud systematic collection of laws. XIV. – (O)F. *code* – L. *cōdex, cōdic-* block of wood, block split into leaves or tablets, book. The L. word **codex** kou·deks was formerly (XVI–XVIII) in Eng. use in the same sense, but is now used only for 'manuscript volume').

codger kɔ·dʒəɹ stingy (old) fellow; familiar appellation for an elderly man; (hence) fellow, chap. XVIII. perh. var. of CADGER.

codicil kɔ·dĭsil supplement to a will. XV. – L. *cōdicillus*, dim. of *cōdex* (see CODE).

codling, codlin kɔ·dliŋ, -lin variety of apple. XV. Earliest form *querd(e)lynge*, later *quodling, quadlin*; but *codlyng* occurs XVI, when it appears to be already assoc. with *coddle* vb. cook. The forms correspond to those of the surname *Codlin*, earlier *Querdelioun, Querdling*, surviving in Norfolk as *Quadling, Quodling* (cf. *querdlynge appulle* in Promp. Parv., which was written in Norfolk). – AN. *Quer de lion* (F. *Cœur-de-lion*) 'lion-heart'.

co:-educa·tion (orig. U.S.) education of the sexes together. XIX. See CO-. Hence **co-e·d** co-educated person. XIX.

coefficient kouifi·ʃənt co-operating to produce a result. XVII. – modL. *coefficiens*; see CO- and EFFICIENT. As sb. in math. ('multiplier') introduced by the French mathematician Franciscus Vieta (1540–1603).

co(e)horn kou·hɔ̄ɹn small mortar invented by a Dutch engineer, Baron van Menno *Coehoorn* (1641–1704). XVIII.

cœlenterata sīlentərei·tə (zool.) primary group of the animal kingdom established by Leuckart. modL., f. Gr. *koîlos* hollow + *énteron* intestine (cf. ENTERIC) + *-āta* -ATE².

cœliac sī·liæk pert. to the abdomen. XVII. – L. *coeliacus* – Gr. *koiliakós*, f. *koiliā́* belly, bowels, f. *koîlos* hollow, rel. to L. *cavus* (see CAVE¹); see -AC.

cœnobite sī·nŏbait, sen- member of a religious order living in a community. XVII. – (O)F. *cénobite* or ecclL. *cœnobīta*, f. *cœnobium* – Gr. *koinóbion* community life, (eccl.) convent, f. *koinós* common + *bíos* life (cf. QUICK); see -ITE.

coerce kouə̄·ɹs constrain by superior force. XVII. – L. *coercēre* shut up, restrain, f. *com* CO- + *arcēre* restrain, ward off, resembling in form Gr. *arkeîn* keep off, defend, suffice, avail, but not altogether in meaning. An early syn. was *cohert* (XV–XVI) – *coert-*, pp. stem of L. *coercēre*, with *h* as in next. Cf. EXERT. So **coercion** kouə̄·ɹʃən control by force XV; government by force XVIII. Early form *cohercion* – OF. *cohercion, -tion* – L. *coer(c)tiō(n-)* (medL. *coerciōnem*), var. of *coercitiō(n-)*, f. *coercit-*, pp. stem of *coercēre*; the sp. *-cion* is an exceptional var. of *-tion*.

coeval kouī·vəl contemporary. XVII. f. late L. *coævus*, f. *com* CO- + *ævum* AGE; see -AL¹.

coffee kɔ·fi drink made by infusing the berries of a shrub, Coffea arabica, native to Arabia and Abyssinia. (XVI) XVII. The present form is first recorded in XVII, with vars. *coffe, cauphe, cophee*; ult. – *kahveh*, Turkish pronunc. of Arab. *qahwah*, through Du. *koffie*. Earlier forms in Eng. writings repr. more closely the Arab. and Turk. forms, viz. *chaoua, coffa, cahve, caffa, kauhi*; cf. Russ. *kófe*, G. †*chaube*. Supposed to be ult. f. *Kaffa*, name of a part of Abyssinia, the native home of the coffee plant. ¶ F., Sp., Pg. *café* (cf. CAFÉ), G. *kaffee*, Sw., Da. *kaffe* are from It. *caffè* – Turk.

coffer kɔ·fəɹ box, chest. XIII. – (O)F. *coffre* :- L. *cophinu-s* basket; see next.

coffin kɔ·fin †chest, box, basket XIV; box for a corpse XVI. – OF. *cof(f)in* little basket, case – L. *cophinus* – Gr. *kóphinos* basket, perh. of Mediterranean origin. Cf. prec.

cog¹ kɔg projecting tooth on a wheel. XIII. ME. *cogge* (in AL. *coggus* XIII), of unascertained origin, but prob. Scand. (cf. synon. Sw. *kugge, kughjul* cog-wheel, Norw. *kug*).

cog² kɔg practise (fraudulent) tricks in throwing dice (often incorrectly taken to mean 'load the dice'); cheat, feign, etc. XVI. Appears first, with the corr. sb., in 'Dice Play' (1532); prob. a canting term, of unkn. origin.

cogent kou·dʒənt constraining, convincing. XVII. – L. *cogent-, -ēns*, prp. of *cōgere* drive together, compel, f. *com* CO- + *agere* drive; see ACT, -ENT.

cogitation kɔdʒitei·ʃən thinking. XIII. – OF. *cogitacioun* – L. *cogitātiō(n-)*, f. *cogitāre* to think, f. *com* CO- + *agitāre* put in motion, spec. turn over in the mind; see AGITATE, -ATION. So **co·gitate** think, devise. XVI. f. L. *cogitāt-*; see -ATE³.

cognac kɔ·njæk prop. French brandy distilled from Cognac wine. XVI (*Coniacke wine*) – F., f. name of a town in the department of Charente, France.

cognate kɔ·gneit akin, descended from a common ancestor; also sb. XVII. – L. *cognātus* (cf. Gr. συγγενής), f. *com, co-* + *gnātus* born, f. *gn- *gen- produce; see CO-, KIN, -ATE². So **cogna·tion**. XIV. – L.

cognition kɔgni·ʃən action or faculty of knowing. XV. – L. *cognitiō(n-)*, f. *cognit-*, pp. stem of *cognōscere* get to know, investigate, f. *co-*+*gnōscere*, inchoative of **gnō-*; see CO-, GNOSTIC, NOTION, KNOW, -TION.

cognizance kɔ·gnizəns, kɔ·n- knowledge (now *take c. of*); device by which one is known XIV; taking legal notice, jurisdiction; acknowledgement, admission XVI. – OF. *conis(s)aunce, conus(s)aunce*, vars. of *conois(s)ance* (mod. *connaissance*) = Pr. *conoisenza*, etc. – Rom. **connōscentia*, f. *cognōscent-*, prp. stem of L. *cognōscere* (see prec.). Latinization of the sp. by the insertion of *g* has infl. the pronunc., but in legal use the older pronunc. survives. Hence **co·gniz**ANT. XIX.

cognomen kɔgnou·men third name of a Roman citizen; distinguishing epithet; surname; name, appellation. XIX. L., f. *com* CON-+**gnōmen* NAME.

cognoscente kɔnjoʃe·nti connoisseur. XVIII. It., latinized form of *conoscente* :- L. *cognōscentem* (see COGNITION and -ENT).

cognovit kɔgnou·vit (leg.) acknowledgement by defendant that plaintiff's cause is just. XVIII. Short for L. formula *cognovit actionem* he has acknowledged the charge; 3rd sg. pt. of *cognōscere* (see COGNITION).

cohabit kouhæ·bit live together (as husband and wife). XVI. – late L. *cohabitāre*. So **cohabita·**TION. XV. Cf. (O)F. *cohabiter, -ation*, and see CO-, HABITATION.

co-heir kouɛə·ɹ joint heir. XVI. – L. *cohērēs*; see CO-, HEIR, and cf. OF. *cohoir*.

cohere kouhiə·ɹ cleave together, combine. XVI. – L. *cohærēre*, f. *com* CO-+*hærēre* stick. So **cohe·r**ENT XVI, **cohe·**SION XVII; cf. F. *cohérent, cohésion*.

cohort kou·hɔ̄ɹt body of infantry in the ancient Roman army; also transf. XV. – (O)F. *cohorte* or L. *cohort-, cohors* enclosure, company, crowd, f. *com* CO-+**hort-*, as in *hortus* garden; see YARD[1], and cf. COURT.

coif koif close-fitting cap. XIV. – OF. *coife* (mod. *coiffe*) head-dress, also *escoife*, corr. to Pr., Pg. *coifa*, Sp. *(es)cofia*, It. *(s)cuffia*, Rum. *coif* :- late L. *cofia* helmet (VI, Venantius Fortunatus).

coign koin obs. sp. of COIN (corner) derived from Sh. 'Macbeth' I vi 7 (1st Folio) Coigne of Vantage; popularized by Scott.

coil[1] koil (arch.) disturbance, confusion, fuss. XVI. Of unkn. origin; now familiar mainly in *mortal c.* (from Sh. 'Hamlet' III i 67).

coil[2] koil lay up (a cable) in concentric rings XVI; twist or twine *up* XVII. (Also †*quoil.*) – OF. *coillir* (mod. *cueillir* gather) = Pr. *colhir*, Sp. *coger*, Pg. *colher* (also) furl, coil (rope) :- L. *colligere* COLLECT. So and (partly) hence **coil** sb. length of rope coiled up XVI (*quille*); series of concentric rings XVII. – F. **cueille*.

coin koin A. †corner-stone XIV; †corner, angle, wedge; B. †die for stamping money XIV (PPl.); piece of money XIV (Ch.); coined money XIV (Gower). – (O)F. *coin*, †*coing*, wedge, corner, †stamping-die = Pr. *conh, cunh*, Sp. *cuño* die, stamp, It. (semi-learned) *conio* wedge, Rum. *kuĭu* nail :- L. *cuneu-s* wedge. See COIGN, QUOIN. So **coin** vb. make (money) from metal, make (metal) into money. XIV. – OF. *coignier* mint, f. *coin*. **coi·n**AGE coining money XIV; money coined XV. – OF. *coigniage*, f. *coignier*.

coincide kouinsai·d be identical in area, etc. XVIII. – medL. *coincidere* (in astrol.), f. *com* CO-+*incidere* fall upon or into, f. *in* IN-[1]+*cadere* fall (see CASE); cf. (O)F. *coïncider*, Sp. *coincidir*, It. *coincidere*. In XVII the L. inf. was used in Eng. contexts. So **coincid**ENCE koui·nsidəns XVII (Bacon), after **coi·ncid**ENT XVI; cf. medL. *coincidentia*, F. *coïncidence* (XV), *-ent*.

coir koiəɹ prepared coco-nut fibre. XVI (*cairo, cayro*), XVII (*coire*). ult. – Malayalam *kāyar* cord, f. *kāyaru* be twisted; the earlier forms repr. Pg. *cairo* (whence F. *caire*), †*coyro*.

coition koui·ʃən †conjunction XVI; copulation XVII. – L. *coitiō(n-)*, f. *coit-, coīre*, f. *com* CO-+*-īre* go; see EXIT, -ITION. So **coitus** kou·itəs XVIII.

coke kouk solid residue of the dry distillation of coal. XVII. orig. a northern word (formerly often pl.); prob. identical with north. dial. *colk* (XIV) core, of unkn. origin.

coker-nut see COCO.

col kɔl depression in a mountain chain. XIX. – F., Pr. *col* :- L. *collum* neck (used by Statius of the middle part of Parnassus). Cf. the similar use of north. Eng. *hause* and *swire* neck, Afrikaans *nek*.

col- kɔl, kəl assim. form of COM-, CON- before *l*. In Rom., L. *coll-*, earlier *conl-*, was reduced to *col-*, and this form was preserved in early adoptions of F. words; the later *coll-* was due to assoc. with L.

colander kʌ·lindəɹ straining vessel. XIV (*colonur, colyndore, culdor(e), culatre*). perh. alteration of Pr. **colador* (whence modPr. *couladou*) = Sp. *colador* :- Rom. **cōlātōrem, -ātor*, f. *cōlāre* strain, f. *cōlum*, strainer; cf. medL. *cōlātōrium*, It. *colatojo*, F. *couloir, -oire*. ¶ For the parasitic *n* cf. *farthingale, messenger, muckender, nightingale*.

colchicum kɔ·ltʃikəm, kɔ·lkikəm genus of liliaceous plants (e.g. C. autumnale 'meadow-saffron'). XVI (Gerarde). – L. (Pliny) – Gr. *kolkhikón*, sb. use of n. of *Kolkhikós* pert. to Colchis, ancient name of a region east of the Black Sea; the name had reference orig. to the poisonous arts of Medea of Colchis, the plant being described by Dioscorides as a poison.

colcothar kɔ·lkoþāɹ red peroxide of iron. XVII. – Arab. *qolqotār*, perh. – Gr. *khálkanthos* 'copper flower', i.e. copper sulphate.

cold kould opposite of *hot*. OE. Anglian *cald* (WS. *ċeald*) = OFris., OS. *cald* (Du. *koud*), OHG. *chalt* (G. *kalt*), ON. *kaldr*, Goth. *kalds* :– CGerm. **kaldaz* prop. chilled, frozen; formation (as in DEAD, LOUD, OLD) with ppl. suffix (= L. *-tus*, Gr. *-tós*) on **kal-* :– IE. **gol-*, var. of **gel-*, as in L. *gelu* frost, *gelidus* GELID, Lith. *gelumà* severe cold (cf. OSl. *goloti* ice); see CHILL, COOL, and CONGEAL. ¶ The ME. vars. *cald*, *chald*, *chold* are repr. in the place-names *Caldecote*, *Calcott*, *Caldwell*, *Chadwell*, *Chatfield*, *Cholwell*.

cold-short kou·ldʃɔ̄ɹt (of iron) brittle in the cold state. Earlier *colsar*, *col(e)shire*, *coldshare*, *-shore*, *-shire* (XVII), later *coldshort* (XVIII). – Sw. *kallskör* (= Norw., Da. *koldskjør*), n. *kallskört* (sc. *jern* iron), f. *kallr* COLD + *skör* brittle. So **re·d-short** brittle when red-hot (XVIII), earlier †*red-sear*, †*-shire*, †*-share* (XVII) – Sw. *rödskör*, f. *röd* RED. The development of the form in *-short* was assisted by the prevalence of *short* in the sense of 'brittle'. Hence, by analogy, **ho·t-short** XVIII (late).

cole koul kind of cabbage (Brassica). XIV. Late ME. *cōl*, *coole* – ON. *kál* (see KALE, KAILYARD), corr. to OE. *cāwel*, *cāul*, MDu. *cōle* (Du. *kool*), OHG. *chōl(i)*, *chōlo*, *-a* (G. *kohl*), and Ir., Gael. *cál*, W. *cawl*, all adoptions, along with the Roman arts of gardening and cookery, of L. *caulis* (later *caulus*, *caula*) stem, stalk, cabbage, of which the basic meaning is 'hollow stem' (see HOLLOW), whence F. *chou*, Sp. *col*, It. *cavolo*. Surviving mainly as in **co·le**SEED (prob. – Du. *koolzaat*; cf. OE. *cāwelsǣd*), **co·le**WORT XIV (Wyclif).

colemouse see COALMOUSE.

coleoptera kɔliɔ·ptərə (zool.) the beetles. XVIII. modL. n. pl., f. Gr. *koleópteros* sheath-winged, f. *koleón* sheath + *pterón* wing (see FEATHER).

colibri kɔ·libri humming-bird. XVIII. – F., Sp. *colibri*, of Carib origin.

colic kɔ·lik sb. griping pains in the belly XV; adj. affecting the colon XVI. – (O)F. *colique* – late L. *cōlicus*, *collicus* (in medL. as sb. fem. for *colica passio* colic), f. *cōlon* COLON[1]; see -IC.

Coliseum see COLOSSEUM.

collaborate kəlæ·bəreit work in conjunction. XIX. f. pp. stem of late L. *collabōrāre*, f. *com* CON-, COL- + *labor* LABOUR. So **collabor**A·TION XIX, **colla·bor**ATOR (Bentham); after F. *collaborer*, *-ateur*, *-ation*.

collapse kəlæ·ps give way, fall in. XVIII. Back-formation f. pp. *collapsed* (XVII), f. L. *collāpsus*, pp. of *collābī*, f. *com* COL- + *lābī* fall; see LAPSE, -ED[1]. So **colla·pse** sb. XIX. – medical L. *collāpsus*.

collar kɔ·ləɹ band, etc. worn round the neck XIII (Cursor M.); various techn. uses ('ring', 'band') from XVII. ME. *coler* – AN. *coler*, OF. *colier* (mod. *collier*) = Pr. *colar*, Sp. *collar*, It. *collare* :– L. *collāre*, f. *collum* neck :– **kols-* (cf. HAWSE); see -AR[1]. The sp. was early assim. to the L. Hence **collared** kɔ·ləɹd wearing a collar XIV; (culin.) rolled up and tied with a string, pressed into a roll XVII. **collar** vb. lay hold on (first in wrestling) XVI; put a collar on XVII.

collard kɔ·ləɹd (dial., U.S.) variety of cabbage that does not heart. XVIII. Earlier *collart*, reduction of COLEWORT.

collate kəlei·t A. †confer XVI; appoint to a benefice XVII; B. compare critically XVII. f. *collāt-*, stem of the form used as pp. of L. *conferre* CONFER; see -ATE[3].

collateral kəlæ·tərəl lying, situated, or existing side by side. XIV (Ch., PPl., Barbour). – medL. *collaterālis*; see COL- and LATERAL.

collation kəlei·ʃən A. in renderings of Johannes Cassianus' 'Collationes Patrum in Scetico eremo commorantium' (Conferences of hermits in the Egyptian desert); reading of this at monastic meals XIII; light repast taken after such reading XIV; light meal (gen.) XVI; B. bringing together, esp. for comparison XIV (Ch.). C. bestowal, spec. of a benefice XIV (Wyclif). Occurs in sense A in AN. form *collatiun*, *c.* 1200, in 'Winteney Rule of St. Benedict' and thereafter in the same sense in 1340 in the form *collacion* – OF. *collacion*, *-tion* – L. *collatiō(n-)* contribution, collection, comparison, in medL. conference, repast, noun of action to *conferre* CONFER; see COLLATE, -ATION.

colleague kɔ·līg one who is associated with another, partner in work, etc. XVI. – F. *collègue* – L. *collēga* partner in office, f. *com* COL- + *lēg-* of *lēx* law, *lēgāre* depute (cf. LEGATION). Somewhat earlier in Sc. than in Eng.

collect[1] kɔ·lekt (liturg.) short prayer, varying with the season, said before the epistle in the mass, and at the divine offices. XIII (AncrR.). – (O)F. *collecte* (= Pr. *collecta*, Sp. *colecta*, It. *colletta*) – L. *collēcta* gathering, collection, (late) assembly, meeting, sb. use of fem. pp. of *colligere* COLLECT[2]. The meaning has been evolved from the use in ecclL. of *oratio ad collectam* prayer at the assembly of people (viz. at one of the regular stations made before the celebration of mass at a particular church), with which has blended the earlier use of *collecta* or *collectio* as a title of prayers that sum up the *rogationes* (biddings) preceding them. (Classical and late L. meanings have been sparsely represented in Eng.) An OF. semi-pop. *coleite* is repr. in late ME. *colett(e)*.

collect[2] kəle·kt gather together. XVI. – (O)F. *collecter* or medL. *collēctāre*, f. *collēct-*, pp. stem of *colligere* (tr. Gr. συλλέγειν), f. *com* COL- + *legere* collect, assemble, choose, read (cf. ELECT, etc., LECTION). So **collectanea** -ei·niə collected passages. XVIII. L. n. pl. of adj. as used in *dicta collēctānea* of Cæsar, and sb. in *collēctānea* of Solinus (III); see -ANEOUS. **colle·c**TION action of collecting XIV (Trevisa); things collected XV (Capgrave). – (O)F. – L. **col-le·ct**IVE earliest in gram. sense. XV. – F. or L.; hence **colle·ctiv**ISM, -IST XIX, after F. **colle·ctor** XIV. – AN. *collectour* – medL. *collēctor*; see -OR[1].

colleen kɔ·līn girl. XIX. – Ir. *cailín*, dim. of *caile* countrywoman, girl; see -EEN. (Cf. ASTHORE.)

college kɔ·lidʒ society or corporation of persons having common functions and rights XIV (Wyclif); building occupied by this XIV (Ch.). – (O)F. *collège* or its source L. *collēgium* association, partnership, guild, corporation, f. *collēga* COLLEAGUE. (*College pudding* was earlier *New College pudding*.) So **colleg**IAL kəlī·dʒiəl XIV, **colle·g**IAN XV, **colle·giate** [-ATE[2]] XV – F. *collégial* or late L. *collēgiālis*, medL. *collēgiānus*, late L. *collēgiātus* (in medL. as adj.).

collet kɔ·lĭt band, ring, collar; in jewellery, circle or flange in a ring, setting of a stone XVI; †neck of glass left on the end of a blowing-iron (cf. CULLET) XVII. – (O)F. *collet*, dim. of *col* :– L. *collum* (see COLLAR). The sense in glass-blowing is prob. – It. *colletto*.

collide kəlai·d bring or come into violent contact. XVII. – L. *collīdere* clash together, f. *com* COL- + *lædere* hurt by striking (see LESION). So **collis**ION kəli·ʒən. XV. – late L. *collīsio(n-)*, f. *collīs-*, pp. stem of *collīdere*.

collie kɔ·li shepherd's dog. XVII. orig. Sc., perh. f. *coll* COAL (from its black colour) + *-ie*, -Y[6].

collier kɔ·liəɹ †charcoal-burner XIV; coal-miner XVI. ME. *colyer*, f. *col* COAL; see -IER. Hence **colli**ERY kɔ·ljəri. XVII.

colligate kɔ·ligeit bind together. XVI. f. pp. stem of L. *colligāre*, f. *com* COL- + *ligāre* bind; see LIEN, -ATE[3].

collimation kɔlimei·ʃən adjustment of the line of sight of a telescope. XVII. – modL. *collimātiō(n-)*, f. *collimāre* (used by astronomical writers, e.g. Kepler), erron. reading in some editions of Cicero for *collīneāre* aim, f. *com* COL- + *līnea* LINE; see -ATION.

collocate kɔ·lŏkeit place side by side. XVI. f. L. *collocat-*, *-āre*, f. *com* COL- + *locāre* place, LOCATE. So **colloca·**TION. XVII. – L.

collodion kəlou·diən solution of gun-cotton in ether producing a gummy liquid. XIX. f. Gr. *kollṓdēs* glue-like, f. *kólla* glue, with Gr. termination.

collogue kəlou·g †speak with feigning or flattery, coax XVI (Nashe); (dial.) intrigue, conspire XVII; confer privately XIX (Scott). prob. alteration, by assoc. with L. *colloquī* converse (see COLLOQUY), of †*colleague* unite, ally, enter into alliance, conspire (XVI) – OF. *colleguer*, *colliguer* – L. *colligāre* combine, COLLIGATE.

collop kɔ·ləp †fried bacon and egg (later *collops and eggs*) XIV (PPl.); fried slice of meat XV; thick fold of flesh (Job xv 27) XVI. ME. *coloppe*, *colhoppe* – Scand. word repr. by OSw. *kolhuppadher* roasted on coals (f. *kol* COAL + *huppa* leap; cf. SAUTÉ), Sw. *kalops*, dial. *kollops* dish of stewed meat. ¶ Occurs as a proper name *Colop*, *Colhoppe* (XIII).

colloquy kɔ·ləkwi conversation. XVI. – L. *colloquium* (also used in Eng. XVII), f. *com* COL- + *loquī* speak (see LOCUTION).

collotype kɔ·lətaip process or print in which a thin sheet of gelatine is used. XIX. f. Gr. *kólla* glue + TYPE.

collusion kəlʲū·ʒən secret and fraudulent agreement. XIV (Ch.). – (O)F. *collusion* or L. *collūsiō(n-)*, f. *collūs-*, *collūdere* have a secret agreement (whence **collu·de** XVI), f. *com* COL- + *lūdere* play, f. *lūdus* play, sport.

Collyridian kəliri·diən member of a sect of heretics who are said to have offered cakes to the Queen of Heaven. XVI. – medL. *collȳridiānus*, f. late L. *collȳrida* – Gr. *kollūrís* (*-id-*) bread roll; see -IAN.

collyrium kəli·riəm eye-salve XVI; suppository XVIII. L. – Gr. *kollū́rion* poultice, eye-salve, f. *kollū́ra* roll of coarse bread. Anglicized, or – AN. **collirie*, OF. *colire*, in †*collyrie*, etc. (XIV–XVII).

collywobbles kɔ·liwɔblz (sl.) belly-ache. XIX. Fancifully f. COLIC and WOBBLE.

colocynth kɔ·losinþ bitter-apple (gourd family). XVII. – L. *colocynthis* – Gr. *kolokunthís* (Dioscorides). Also in medL. (Sp., Pg., It.) form **coloquintida** kɔlokwi·ntidə XVI; f. stem in *-id-*.

Cologne kəlou·n name of a German city on the Rhine, famous in the Middle Ages for its shrine of the Three Wise Men of the East (the Three Kings of Cologne). ME. *Coloyne*, *Coleyne* (from XIV), later (from *Co·leyne*) *Cullen* (XVI), *Collen*, as in *Cullins* or *Collins earth* a brown pigment. – OF. *Coleine* :– medL. **Colinia*, for *Colōnia* (sc. *Agrippīna*) prop. COLONY of Agrippa; superseded XIX by the modF. form *Cologne* (OF. *Coloigne*), as in *Cologne water* (U.S. simply *cologne*), tr. F. *eau de Cologne*. ¶ Cf. G. *Köln*, Du. *Keulen* :– **Co·l(i)nia*; and *Lincoln*, OE. *Lindcyl(e)ne* (:– medL. *Lindo-co·lina*), beside *Lindcolne*.

colon[1] kou·lɔn greater portion of the large intestine. XVI. – (O)F. *côlon* or L. *colon* – Gr. *kólon* (incorrectly *kôlon*) food, meat, colon.

colon[2] kou·lən member of a sentence; the punctuation mark (:). XVI. – L. *cōlon* – Gr. *kôlon* limb, clause.

colonel kə̄·nl superior officer of a regiment. XVI. In earliest use both *coronel* and *colonel*, but the first prevailed before mid-XVII. – F. †*coronel* (so also Sp.), later and mod. *colonnel* – (orig. with dissimilation of *l..l* to *r..l*) It. *colonnello*, f. *colonna* COLUMN, the officer being so named as leader of the first company of a regiment (It. *compagnia colonnella*, F. *compagnie colonnelle*). The present pronunc., which was established by the late XVIII, depends on the form †*coronel*; but kʌ·lnəl is the only pronunc. recorded by Johnson, 1755. Walker comments: 'This word is among those gross irregularities which must be given up as incorrigible.'

colonnade kɔlənei·d series of columns at regular intervals. XVIII. – F. *colonnade* (earlier †*-ate*), f. *colonne* COLUMN, after It. *colonnato* (cf. L. *columnātus* supported on columns); see -ADE.

colony kɔ·ləni settlement in a new country. XVI. – L. *colōnia* farm, landed estate, settlement, f. *colōnus* tiller, cultivator, planter, settler, f. *colere* cultivate; see WHEEL, -Y[3]. (An isolated early ex. in Wycl. Bible, Acts xvi 12, tr. Vulg. *colonia*, Gr. *kolōniā*, bears the ancient Roman sense.) Hence **colon**IAL kəlou·niəl XVIII (Burke); perh. after F. **co·lon**IZE XVII (Bacon), whence **co·lon**IST XVIII.

colophon kɔ·ləfən inscription containing title, date, etc., at the end of a book. XVIII. – late L. *colophōn* – Gr. *kolophṓn* summit, finishing touch.

colophony kɔlɔ·fəni dark or amber-coloured resin. XIV. – L. *colophōnia*, for *rēsīna Colophōnia* resin of Colophon, a town in Lydia.

coloquintida see COLOCYNTH.

coloration kʌlərei·ʃən, kɔl- colouring. XVII (Bacon). – F. *coloration* or late L. *colōrātiō(n-)*, f. L. *colōrāre* COLOUR; see -ATION. So **coloratura** kɔlŏrătuə·rə (mus.) XIX. It. (whence F. *colorature*, G. *koloratur*); see -URE. **colori**FIC kɔlŏri·fik producing colour(s). XVII. – F. or modL.

colosseum, coliseum kɔlə-, kɔlisī·əm amphitheatre of Vespasian at Rome. XVIII. – medL. *colisēum* (whence F. *colisée*, It. *coliseo*), sb. use of n. of L. *colossēus* gigantic, colossal, f. *colossus*; see next and -EAN. Anglicized as †*colossee* XVI.

colossus kəlɔ·səs gigantic statue, e.g. that at Rhodes. XIV. – L. *colossus* – Gr. *kolossós* applied by Herodotus to the statues of Egyptian temples (whence F. *colosse*, It. *colosso*, which were also adopted in Eng. XVI). So **colo·ss**AL[1] of vast size. XVIII; – F. *colossal*; superseding †*colossean* (Evelyn), †*colossian*, †*colossic* (Chapman), all XVII.

colour, U.S. **color** kʌ·ləɹ hue, tint XIII; the fig. senses 'semblance', 'pretext' are ME. – OF. *colur*, *colour* (mod. *couleur*) = Pr., Sp. *color*, It. *colore* :– L. *colōrem*, *color*, rel. to *cēlare* hide, CONCEAL, as if 'outside show'; supplemented OE. *hīw* HUE; see -OUR. So **co·lour** vb. XIII. – OF. *coulourer* (mod. *colorer*) – L. *colōrāre*.

colporteur kɔlpɔ̄ɹtə̄·ɹ hawker of books, etc. XVIII. – F., f. *colporter*, presumably alteration of *comporter* – L. *comportāre* transport, f. *com* COM-+*portāre* carry (cf. PORTER[1]).

colt koult young horse. OE. *colt*, applied to the young of the ass and the camel: of obscure origin, but cf. Sw. *kult*, *kulter*, *kulting*, applied to half-grown animals and boys. Hence **co·lts**FOOT name of various plants so named from the shape of their leaves. XV. tr. medL. *pēs pullī* 'colt's foot'.

Colt koult in full *Colt's revolver*, invented by Samuel *Colt* (1814–62) of Connecticut, U.S.A.

colubrine kɔ·ljubrəin snake-like. XVI. – L. *colubrīnus*, f. *coluber* snake; see -INE[1].

columbarium kɔləmbɛə·riəm dovecot; underground sepulchre with niches. XVIII. L., f. *columba* dove, pigeon; see -ARIUM.

columbiad kəlʌ·mbiæd (with *C-*) title of an epic by J. L. Moore on the discovery of America 1796; heavy cannon formerly used in the U.S. army XIX. f. modL. *Columbia*, poetical name of America, f. the name of *Columbus*, its discoverer; see -AD[1]. ¶ An epic entitled *La Colombiade* was written by Marie-Anne du Boccage (1710–1802).

columbine kɔ·ləmbəin dove-like. XIV (Ch.). – (O)F. *colombin*, *-ine* – L. *columbīnus*, f. *columba* dove (cf. OSl. *golǫbĭ* dove, OPruss. *golimban*, Russ. *golubói* blue, *gólub'* dove). As sb. name of plants of the genus Aquilegia. XIII. – OF. *colombine* – medL. *columbīna* (sc. *herba*) 'dove's plant', so called from the resemblance of the inverted flower to five pigeons clustered together.

Columbine kɔ·ləmbain (orig. in It. comedy) the mistress of Harlequin. XVIII. – F. *Colombine* – It. *Colombina*, sb. use of fem. of *colombino* dove-like in gentleness (cf. prec.). ¶ Words from a similar source are *Harlequin*, *pantaloon*, *Punch*, *scaramouch*, *zany*.

column kɔ·ləm vertical support of part of a building XV (Lydg.); vertical division of a page, etc. XV (Promp. Parv.). Partly – OF. *columpne* (mod. *colonne*, after It. *colonna*), partly – its source L. *columna* pillar, f. **col-*, as in *columen*, *culmen* (see CULMINATE), var. of **cel-*, as in **cellere* (see EXCEL), *celsus* high. So **column**AR kəlʌ·mnəɹ. XVIII. – late L.; earlier †*colu·mnary* (XVI–XVIII). **colu·mniated** XVIII, for earlier *co·lumnated*, f. L. *columnātus* supported on columns (see -ATE[2]). **columni**A·TION XVII, for *columna·tion* (– L.), by assim. to *intercolumniation* (f. L. *intercolumnium*).

colure kouljuə·ɹ, kou·ljuəɹ each of the great circles intersecting at right angles at the poles. XVI. – late L. *colūrī* pl. – Gr. *kólourai* (sc. *grammaí* lines), pl. of *kólouros* truncated, lit. dock-tailed, f. *kólos* docked + *ourá* tail (cf. ARSE); so called because their lower part is permanently cut off from view.

colza kɔ·lzə oil expressed from coleseed, Brassica campestris. XVIII. – F. (Walloon) *kolza*, earlier *kolzat* – LG. *kōlsāt*, Du. *koolzaad*; see COLE, SEED.

com- kəm, kɔm repr. L. *com-* (cf. SYN-), arch. form of the prep. *cum* with, used in comps. with the meanings 'together, in combination or union', 'altogether, completely'. *Com-* was retained before *b, p, m,* and some vowels (as in *comes* COUNT[1]), assim. before *r, l* (as in *corruptus* CORRUPT, *collātiō* COLLATION), and reduced to CO- before most vowels; elsewhere it became CON- (but before *f*, as in COMFIT, COMFORT, *com-* has replaced *con-* in Eng.). In OF. *comm-* was regularly reduced to *com-* as in *comandement*, but *-mm-* was restored later by assim. to the L. forms. Before *b, p* the orig. OF. form was *cum-*, which is reflected in the pronunc. kʌm of *comfort, company, compass*; but the altered sp. with *com-* has led to the prevalence of kɔm in *accomplish, combat*, though in these kʌm is preferred by some.

coma[1] kou·mə unnatural deep and prolonged sleep. XVII. – medical L. – Gr. *kôma* (*kōmat-*), rel. to *koítē* bed, *keîsthai* lie down. Hence **co·mat**OSE. XVIII.

coma[2] kou·mə (bot.) tuft XVII; (astron.) nebulous envelope of a comet XVIII. – L. *coma* – Gr. *kómē* hair of the head; cf. COMET.

comb koum toothed implement for straightening the hair; cock's crest, which is indented or serrated OE.; flat cake of cells of wax made by bees (an exclusively Eng. use, the origin of which is doubtful), late OE. in *huniġcamb* honeycomb. OE. *camb, comb* = OS. *camb* (Du. *kam*), OHG. *chamb* (G. *kamm*), ON. *kambr* :- CGerm. (exc. Goth.) **kambaz* :- IE. **gombhos*, whence also Gr. *gómphos*, Skr. *jámbhas*, Tocharian *kam*, OSl. *zǫbŭ* tooth. Hence **comb** vb. XIV; replacing *kemb*, OE. *cemban* (:- **kambjan*), which survives in UNKEMPT.

comb(e) see COOMB.

combat kɔ·mbæt, kʌ·mbət fight. XVI. – F. *combat*, f. *combattre* (whence **co·mbat** vb. XVI), OF. *cumbatre* = Pr. *combattre*, Sp. *combatir*, It. *combattere*, f. late L. *combattere*, f. L. *com-* COM- + **battere*, for *batuere* fight (cf. ABATE, DEBATE). So **co·mbat**ANT fighter. XV. – OF. *combatant*, prp. of *combattre*.

combine kəmbai·n couple or join together. XV. – (O)F. *combiner* or late L. *combīnāre* join two and two, f. *com* COM- + *bīnī* two together (see BINARY). So **combina·tion** kɔmbin-. XIV (Trev.). – OF. or late L. Hence **co·mbine** sb. †plot XVII (rare); commercial (etc.) combination XIX (orig. U.S.).

combustion kəmbʌ·stʃən burning. XV. – (O)F. *combustion* or late L. *combustiō(n-)*, f. *combust-*, f. pp. stem of *combūrere* burn up, f. *com* COM- + **būrere*, prob. evolved from *amb|ūrere* (rel. to Gr. *heúein*); see -TION.

come kʌm pt. **came** keim, pp. **come** elementary vb. of motion expressing movement towards an object. OE. *cuman*, pt. *cōm, cwōm, c(w)ōmon*, pp. *cumen* = OFris. *kuma*, OS. *cuman* (Du. *komen*), OHG. *queman, coman* (G. *kommen*), ON. *koma*, Goth. *qiman* :- CGerm. **kweman*, **kuman*, pt. **kwam*, **kwǣmum*, pp. **kumanaz*. Pt. *came*, orig. ME. *cam, cāme*, pl. *cāmen* (XIII, first in north and east, prob. after ON. *kvam*), finally repl. *come* (still dial.). The IE. base **gʷem-* **gʷm-* is repr. also by Skr., Av. *gam* come, Gr. *bainein* go (cf. BASIS), L. *venīre* come (cf. ADVENT, CONVENE, etc.).

comeatable kʌmæ·təbl accessible. XVII. f. phr. *come at* + -ABLE; prob. first in the negative *uncomeatable*.

comedy kɔ·mĭdi †narrative poem with a pleasant ending XIV (Ch.); †miracle play or interlude with a happy ending XVI; light and amusing play XVII. – (O)F. *comédie* – L. *cōmœdia* – Gr. *kōmōidíā*, f. *kōmōidós* comic actor, comic poet, f. *kômos* revel, merrymaking, wrongly derived by Dorian writers from *kṓmē* village. So **comed**IAN kəmī·diən comic writer XVI (Sidney); comic actor, †stage-player XVII (Sh.). – F. *comédien*, f. *comédie*; cf. It. *commediante*, which was also adopted (XVI–XVII).

comely kʌ·mli †decent, proper; pleasant to look at, fair XIII. ME. *cumelich, cumli*, prob. aphetic of †*becumelich* (XII), f. BECOME + -LY[1]; cf. MHG. *komlich* suitable (beside *bekōme* suitably; G. dial. *kommlich, kömmlich*), Du. †*komlick* 'conveniens'. So †**comely** adv. XIII; see -LY[2] and cf. MHG. *komlīche*. ¶ Not identical with OE. *cȳmlic* beautiful, which would have become **kimly* (cf. OE. *cȳme* beautiful, ME. *kime* weak, silly), rel. to OHG. *chūmīg* weak, delicate, *chūmo* with difficulty (G. *kaum* hardly).

comestible kŏme·stibl eatable; †adj. XV (Caxton); sb. XIX. – (O)F. *comestible* – medL. *comestibilis* (Isidore), f. *comest-*, pp. stem of L. *comedere* eat up, f. *com* COM- + *edere* EAT; see -IBLE.

comet kɔ·mit heavenly body with a 'tail'. XIII (XII in L. form). – (O)F. *comète* – L. *comēta* – Gr. *komḗtēs* long-haired, sb. comet (for *astḕr komḗtēs* 'long-haired star'), f. *komân* wear the hair long, f. *kómē* hair of the head, tail of a comet.

comfit kʌ·mfit sweetmeat. XV. ME. *confyt* – OF. *confit, confite* :- L. *confectum, confecta*, sb. uses of n. and fem. of *confectus*, pp. of *conficere* (see CONFECTION).

comfort kʌ·mfəɹt †encouragement, support; relief in distress XIII (AncrR.); cause of satisfaction or content XVI; material well-being XIX. – OF. *confort* (= OSp., It. *conforto*), Rom. sb. f. late L. *confortāre*, f. *com* CON-+*fortis* strong (cf. FORCE). So **co·mfort** vb. XIII (RGlouc.). – OF. *conforter* (= Pr., Sp. *confortar*, It. *confortare*) – L. **co·mfortABLE** †encouraging, reassuring, pleasant XIV; affording content; at ease XVIII. – AN. *confortable* (modF. is – Eng.). **co·mforter** consoler, as a title of the Holy Ghost, tr. L. *consolātor*, rendering of Gr. *παράκλητος* PARACLETE XIV; woollen scarf (*comfortable* was formerly so used and for a quilt) XIX. – AN. *confortour*; see -ER[1].

comfrey kʌ·mfri the plant Symphytum officinale, formerly esteemed as a vulnerary. XV (*confyrie*, *cowmfory*). – AN. *cumfirie*, OF. *confire*, *confiere* (mod. dial. *confier*, etc.), with var. *confierge*, Friulian *konfiervye* :– medL. **confervia*, for L. *conferva*, f. *confervēre* intr. heal, prop. boil together (see CON-, FERVENT). ¶ The medL. syns. *confirma*, *conserva*, *consolida* (whence OF. *consoude*, Eng. *consound*) also refer to the plant's healing properties, and all are renderings of Gr. *súmphuton* (*sumphúein* cause to grow together).

comic kɔ·mik pert. to comedy XVI; ludicrous, funny XVIII. – L. *cōmicus* – Gr. *kōmikós*, f. *kômos*; see COMEDY, -IC. So **co·mICAL**. (XV) XVI. **co·mico-**, comb. form of the L. and Gr. adjs. XVI (*comico-tragical*).

comitadji kɔmitæ·dʒi in Balkans, member of band of irregular soldiers. XX. – F. *comitadji* – Common Balkan form f. Turk. *komita* – F. *comité* COMMITTEE+*-ji*; lit. member of a (revolutionary) committee.

comitia kəmi·ʃiə legal assembly of the ancient Romans. XVII. L., pl. of *comitium*, f. *com* COM-+*-itium*, noun of action f. *it-*, *īre* go.

comity kɔ·miti courtesy XVI; friendly understanding. XIX. – L. *cōmitās*, f. *cōmis* courteous; see -ITY.

comma kɔ·mə phrase smaller than a colon; the punctuation mark (,); (mus.) minute interval. XVI. – L. *comma* – Gr. *kómma* piece cut off, short clause, f. **kop-*, stem of *kóptein* strike, cut, with various Slav. cogns.

command kəmà·nd give an order to XIII (Cursor M.); control, dominate XIV. ME. *com(m)a(u)nde* – AN. *comaunder*, OF. *comander* (mod. *comm-*) = Pr., Sp. *comandar*, Pg. *commandar*, It. *commandare* :– late L. *commandāre*, f. *com* COM- (intensive)+ *mandāre*; see MANDATE and cf. *demand*, *remand*, and *commend*. Hence **comma·nd** sb. XVI (Sh.). So **commandA·NT**. XVII. – F., or It., etc. *-ante*. **comma·nder**. XIII (Cursor M.). – OF. *comandere*, AN. *-dour* (mod. *-deur*) :– Rom. **commandātor*, *-ātōrem*; see -ER[2]. **comma·ndMENT**. XIII (Cursor M.). ME. *com(m)a(u)ndement* (4 syll.) – OF. *comandement* (mod. *comm-*). **commando** kəmà·ndou (orig. S. Africa) military party, expedition, raid. XIX. – Pg. *commando*, f. *commandar*.

commandeer kɔmən·diə·ɹ (orig. S. Africa) seize for military use. XIX. – Afrikaans *kommanderen* – F. *commander* (see prec.).

commandery kəmà·ndəri benefice held in commendam; estate, etc. belonging to an order of knights. XV. – F. *commanderie*, f. *commander*; see prec. and -ERY.

commemorate kəme·məreit call to remembrance. XVI. f. pp. stem of L. *commemorāre*, f. *com* COM- (intensive)+*memorāre* relate, f. *memor* (see MEMORY). So **commemorA·TION**. XIV. – (O)F. or L.

commence kəme·ns begin; take a degree of master or doctor in a faculty (medL. *incipere*) XIV (but the reduced form *comse*, *cumse* is XIII). ME. *comence* – OF. *com(m)encier* = Pr. *comesar*, Cat. *comensar*, It. *cominciare* :– Rom. **cominitiāre*, f. *com* COM- (intensive)+*initiāre* INITIATE. So **comme·nceMENT**. XIII. – (O)F. *commencement*.

commend kəme·nd A. give in trust or charge; B. approve conduct or character of. XIV. – L. *commendāre*, f. *com* COM- (intensive)+*mandāre* commit, entrust (see MANDATE and cf. COMMAND). In earlier ME. *command*, like OF. *comander*, was used in this sense. So **comme·ndABLE**. XIV (Ch.) – (O)F. *commendable* – L. *commendābilis*. Formerly *co·mmendable* (as in Sh.), earlier *commenda·ble*. **commendA·TION**. XIII (first in liturg. use). – (O)F. – L. **comme·ndaTORY**. XVI. – late L.

commendam kəme·ndæm temporary custody of a benefice. XVI. From ecclL. phr. (*dare*) *in commendam* (commit) in trust or as a deposit, *commenda* being f. L. *commendāre*; see prec.

commensal kəme·nsəl eating one who eats) at the same table. XIV. – medL. *commensālis*, f. *com* COM-+*mensa* table; see -AL.

commensurable kəme·nʃŭrəbl reducible to the same measure. XVI. – late L. *commensurābilis* (Boethius), f. *com* COM-+*mensurābilis* MEASURABLE. So **comme·nsurate** having the same or a corresponding measure or extent. XVII. – late L. *commensurātus* (Boethius); see MEASURE, -ATE[2].

comment kɔ·mĕnt †commentary XV; explanatory note XV. – L. *commentum* invention, contrivance, (in Isidore) interpretation, comment, f. *comment-*, pp. stem of *comminiscī* devise, contrive, f. *com* CON-+**men-*, base of *mēns* MIND. Hence (or – F. *commenter*) **co·mment** vb. (formerly kəme·nt). XVI. (An earlier verb meaning 'devise, invent' XV was – medL. *commentāre*, L. *-ārī*, frequent. f. *comment-*, *comminiscī*.) So **commentARY** kɔ·məntəri (hist.) memoir(s), as in Cæsar's Commentaries; systematic series of comments XV. – L. *commentārius*,

-ārium adj. used sb. (sc. *liber* book, *volūmen* volume), f. *commentārī*. **comment**ATOR kɔ·mənteitəɹ †chronicler XIV (Trev.); writer of a commentary XVII. – L.

commerce kɔ·mə̄ɹs intercourse; exchange of merchandise, trading. XVI. – F. *commerce* or L. *commercium* trading, merchandise, (earlier in actual evidence) intercourse, f. *com* COM-+*merc-*, *merx* merchandise (cf. MERCHANT). The stressing *comme·rce* is found as late as XVIII. Hence **commerc**IAL kəmə̄·ɹʃəl. XVII (F. *commercial* is later).

commination kəminei·ʃən denunciation of punishment. XV. – L. *comminātiō(n-)*, f. *comminārī* menace; see COM-, MINATORY, -ATION.

comminute kɔ·minjūt reduce to small particles. XVII. f. L. *comminūt-*, *comminuere*, f. *com* COM- (intensive)+*minuere* lessen (see MINUTE). So **comminu·**TION. XVI. – late L.

commiserate kəmi·zəreit show pity for. XVII. f. L. *commiserāt-*, *-ārī* and *-āre*, f. *com* COM-+*miserārī* lament, pity, f. *miser* wretched; see MISERY, -ATE[3]. So **commisera·**TION. XVI. – L.

commissar kəmisā·ɹ head of a government department in the U.S.S.R. XX. Russ. – F. *commissaire* – medL. *commissārius* COMMISSARY.

commissary kɔ·misəri (eccl.) officer representing another XIV; official having charge (esp.) of supplies XV. – medL. *commissārius* officer in charge, f. *commiss-*, pp. stem of L. *committere* COMMIT; see -ARY. So **commissariat** kəmisɛə·riət (Sc. law) commissary's court XVII; military department charged with providing supplies XVIII; partly – medL. *commissariātus*; partly – F. *commissariat*; see -ATE[1].

commission kəmi·ʃən authoritative charge; warrant of authority XIV; body charged with special authority XV. – (O)F. *commission* – L. *commissiō(n-)*, f. *commiss-*, pp. stem of *committere* COMMIT; see -ION. So **commi·ssioner** one deputed by commission for some work. XV. – medL. *commissiōnārius*; see -ARY, -ER[1] and [2]. **commission(n)aire** kəmiʃənɛə·ɹ messenger, light porter. XVIII. F., – medL. (as above).

commissure kɔ·misjuəɹ juncture, seam XV; (physiol.) bundles of nerve-substance XIX. – L. *commissūra*, f. *commiss-*, pp. stem of *committere* put together; see next and -URE.

commit kəmi·t A. entrust XIV (Ch.); B. perpetrate XV; C. engage, involve XVII. – L. *committere* join, join (battle), practise, perpetrate, place with another for safety, etc., entrust, (medL.) consign to custody, f. *com* COM-+*mittere* put, send (see MISSION). Hence **commi·t**MENT. XVII. **commi·tt**AL[2]. XIX.

committee kəmi·ti A. (surviving leg.; pron. kəmitī·) one to whom a charge is committed XV; B. body of persons appointed for a special business XVII. f. COMMIT+-EE, after legal terms such as *feoffee*. ¶ Hence F. *comité*.

commode kəmou·d †woman's tall head-dress XVII; chest of drawers, cheffonier XVIII; close-stool XIX. – F. *commode* (in first two senses), sb. use of *commode* convenient – L. *commodus* (see next). For the third sense cf. the use of *convenience* for 'urinal', 'W.C.'

commodious kəmou·diəs †advantageous, serviceable XV; conveniently roomy XVI. – F. *commodieux* or medL. *commodiōsus*, f. L. *commodus* of due measure, convenient, f. *com* COM-+*modus* measure (see MODE); for the L. form cf. *perfidiōsus* beside *perfidus*. So **commod**ITY kəmɔ·dĭti. XIV (Maund.). – (O)F. or L.

commodore kɔ·mədɔəɹ naval officer above captain and below rear-admiral. XVII. orig. *commandore* (temp. William III), later *commadore*, prob. – Du. *komandeur* – F. *commandeur* COMMANDER; but the form suggests Sp. or Pg. influence. ¶ Hence F. *commodore* (Voltaire).

common kɔ·mən belonging equally to two or more; in gen. use XIII (Cursor M.); (math. and gram.) XVI. ME. *comun* – OF. *comun* (mod. *commun*) = Pr. *comú*, Sp. *común*, It. *comune* :– L. *commūni-s*, OL. *comoinis*, cogn. with OE. *ġemǣne* (whence ME. *imene* MEAN[1], which *common* superseded in the sense 'general'), OHG. *gimeini* (G. *gemein*), Goth. *gamains*, f. IE. **ko(m)*-Y-+**moin-* **mein-* (cf. Lith. *mainýti* exchange, OSl. *mena* change), f. **moi-* **mei-*, another deriv. of which is seen in L. *mūtāre*, *mūtuus* (see MUTATE, MUTUAL); cf. IMMUNE, REMUNERATE. (sb. for common land.) **co·mmonal**TY †people of a nation, etc. XIII; general body of the community, common people XIV; †the commons XVI. – OF. *comunalté* (mod. *communauté*) = Pr. *cominaltat*, etc. – medL. *commūnālitās*; see -AL[1], -ITY. **co·mmon**ER[2] †burgess, citizen XIII; one of the common people XIV; member of the House of Commons; student or undergraduate not on the foundation of a college XVII. – medL. *commūnārius*.

commonplace kɔ·mənpleis, (formerly) kɔ·mən plei·s †passage of general application, leading text, theme; notable passage stored up for use in a *book of common places* or *commonplace-book*; ordinary topic, stock theme or subject. XVI. As adj. XVII. tr. L. *locus commūnis*, tr. Gr. *koinòs tópos* (cf. TOPIC).

commotion kəmou·ʃən public disturbance XV; (gen.) agitation, perturbation XIV. – (O)F. *commotion* or L. *commōtiō(n-)*; see COM-, MOTION.

commune[1] kə·mjūn, (formerly) kəmjū·n communicate, esp. orally, *with* XIII; hold spiritual intercourse *with* XVII. – OF. *comuner* share, f. *comun* COMMON. (The orig. form *comune*, with shifted stress, gave †*common* vb. XIV–XVI.)

commune[2] kə·mjūn in France, territorial division XVIII; (hist.) commonalty, corporation XIX. – F. *commune*, earlier †*comugne* – medL. *commūnia*, n. pl. of *commūnis* COMMON, taken as fem. sg. in sense 'group of people having a common life'. So **communAL** kə·mjunəl, kəmjū·nəl. XIX. – F. *communal*.

communicate kəmjū·nikeit give a share of, share in; receive, administer Holy Communion; hold intercourse *with* XVI; have a common channel of passage XVIII. f. pp. stem of L. *commūnicāre*, f. *commūnis* COMMON+*-ic-*, formative of factitive verbs; see -ATE[3]. So **communicA·TION**. XIV (Wycl. Bible). **commu·nicatIVE**. XIV (Trevisa; rare before XVII).

communion kəmjū·niən sharing, participation; spiritual fellowship XIV; sacrament of the Lord's Supper, participation in this XV (in religious uses earlier †*communing*). – (O)F. *communion* or L. *commūniō(n-)*, f. *commūnis* COMMON; see -ION. The religious uses depend on ChrL. *communio ecclesiæ catholicæ*, *c. sanctorum*, *c. carnis Christi*, *c. sancti altaris*, etc., and similar uses of Gr. *κοινωνία*.

communism kə·mjunizm state of society in which property is vested in the community. 1841. – F. *communisme* (1840, Estienne Cabet), f. *commun* COMMON; see -ISM. So **co·mmunIST**. 1841. – F. *communiste* (used in another sense XVIII). ¶ An earlier form was *communionist* 1827.

community kəmjū·nĭti A. body of people associated by common status, pursuits, etc. XIV (Barbour, Wycl.); B. common character XV. Late ME. *comunete* – OF. *comuneté* (mod. *communité*) – L. *commūnitātem*, f. *commūnis*; see COMMON, -ITY; later assim. to modF. and L.

commute kəmjū·t †exchange; change *for* something else. XVII. – L. *commūtāre* change altogether, exchange, f. *com* COM-+ *mūtāre* (see MUTATION). So **commutA·TION**. XV. – (O)F. or L. **commu·tER**[1] XIX.

comp.[1], abbrev. of COMPANY XVII; also †*compa*. XVII; cf. *Comp*[a] on currency notes; now usu. *Co.* (XVIII).

comp.[2] abbrev. of COMPOSITOR; said to be orig. for *companion*, i.e. one of a companionship of compositors. XIX.

compact[1] kə·mpækt covenant, contract. XVI (Sh.). – L. *compactum*, sb. use of n. of pp. of *compaciscī* make an agreement; see COM-, PACT. ¶ *Compaction* was earlier (Skelton).

compact[2] kəmpæ·kt closely packed or knit together. XIV (Trevisa). – L. *compactus*, pp. of *compingere* put closely together, f. *com* COM-+*pangere* fasten. Hence **co·mpact** sb. compact make-up powder, etc. XX; cf. F. *poudre compacte*, *fard compact*. So **compa·ct** vb. join firmly together. XVI. f. pp. stem of L. *compingere*.

compages kəmpei·dʒīz compacted whole, framework of conjoined parts. XVII (earlier anglicized †*compage*). – L. *compāges*, f. *com* COM-+*pag-*, as in *pangere*. So **compaginate** -pæ·dʒineit knit together. XVII. f. late L. *compāgināre*, f. *compāgin-*, *-pāgō*, syn. of *compāges*.

companion[1] kəmpæ·njən associate, mate XIII; (of an order of knighthood) XVI. ME. *compainoun* – OF. *compaignon* = Pr. *companhó*:– Rom. **compāniōnem*, acc. of **compāniō* (whence OF. *compain*, mod. *copain*, Pr. *companh*, Sp. *compaño*), f. L. *com* COM- + *pānis* bread, after Germ. **gaχlaiƀaz* (Goth. *gahlaiba*, OHG. *galeipo* messmate) 'one who eats bread with another', f. **ga*- Y-+**χlaiƀ*- LOAF. Hence **compa·nionABLE** fitted to be a companion. XVII. Alteration, by assoc. with this sb., of †*compan(i)able* (XIV) – OF. *compaignable*, f. *compaigner* accompany, f. *compainz* – Rom. **compāniō*. So **company** kʌ·mpəni. XIII (in the commercial sense orig. dependent on It. *compagnia*; in the spec. mil. sense on F. *compagnie*). ME. *compainie*, *compaignie* – AN. *compainie*, OF. *compa(i)gnie* = Pr. *companhia*, Sp. *compañia*, It. *compagnia*, alterations of OF. *compagne* (prob. repr. by ME. *compayne* XIV), Sp. *compaña*, It. *compagna* :– Rom. **compānia*, f. **compāniō*; see -Y[3].

companion[2] kəmpæ·njən (naut.) framed windows over a hatchway, hooded staircase to the captain's cabin. XVIII (Falconer). Alteration, by assoc. with prec., of Du. †*kompanje* (now *kam-*) – OF. *compagne* – It. *compagna* (for *camera della compagna* storeroom for provisions, caboose.

company see COMPANION[1].

compare kəmpɛə·ɹ represent as similar. XV (earlier *comper* XIV). – (O)F. *comparer* (earlier *comperer*) = Pr., Sp. *comparar*, It. *comparare* :– L. *comparāre* pair, match, f. *compar* like, equal, f. *com* COM-+*par* equal (see PEER). So **comparATIVE** kəmpæ·rətiv earliest in gram. use. XV. – L. *comparātīvus*, f. *comparāt-*, *-āre*. **compa·rison** action of comparing, capacity for being compared. XIV. – OF. *comparesoun* (mod. *-aison*) = Pr. *comparasó*, etc. :– L. *comparātiōnem* (see -ATION).

compartment kəmpā·ɹtmənt separate division or part. XVI (*-iment*, *-ement*). – F. *compartiment* – It. *compartimento*, f. *compartire* share – late L. *compartīrī*, f. *com* COM- (intensive)+*partīrī*, f. *part-*, *pars*; see PART and -MENT.

compass kʌ·mpəs †designing, ingenuity; †area, space XIII (Cursor M.); †circle, circuitous course; (pl.) two-legged measuring instrument XIV; mariner's instrument for determining position; bounds, limits XVI. – (O)F. *compas* †measure, rule, pair of compasses, corr. to Pr., Sp. *compas*, Pg., It. *compasso* (chiefly) compasses, but in some langs. also measure, time in music, rule, pattern, step, stride, derivs. of the vb. (see below). From Rom. are G. *kompass* mariner's compass, †sundial, Du. *kompas*, ON. *kompáss* circle, compass, Sw. *kompass*, Russ. *kómpas*, etc. The transference of sense to the mariner's instrument is held to have arisen in It. *compasso*, from the circular shape of the compass-box. So **co·mpass** vb. contrive, devise XIII (RGlouc.); go round, encircle, ENCOMPASS XIV; attain to XVI. – (O)F. *compasser* (now only) measure as with compasses, corr. to Pr., Sp. *compasar*, It. *compassare*, repr. Rom. **compassāre* measure, f. L. *com* COM- + *passus* step, PACE.

compassion kəmpæ·ʃən fellow-feeling in adversity. XIV. – (O)F. *compassion* – ecclL. *compassiō(n-)*, f. *compass-*, pp. stem of *compatī* suffer with, feel pity; see COM- and PASSION. So **compa·ssion**ATE[2] characterized by compassion. XVI. – F. *compassionné*, pp. of *compassionner* feel compassion; after *affectionate*.

compatible kəmpæ·tĭbl †sympathetic XV; mutually tolerant, congruous XV. – F. *compatible* – medL. *compatibilis* (as in *beneficium compatibile* benefice tenable with another), f. *compatī*; see prec. and -IBLE. Cf. INCOMPATIBLE.

compatriot kəmpæ·triət fellow-countryman. XVII. – (O)F. *compatriote* – late L. *compatriōta* (tr. Gr. συμπατριώτης); see COM-, PATRIOT.

compeer kəmpiə·ɹ companion, fellow XIII; peer, equal XV. ME. *comper* – OF. *comper*; see COM-, PEER[1].

compel kəmpe·l constrain XIV; drive or force together XV. – L. *compellere* (lit. and fig.), f. *com* COM- + *pellere* drive, rel. to Gr. *pállein* shake, *pelemizein* move violently, *pólemos* fighting, Arm. *halacem* I pursue. ¶ Other comps. of L. *pellere* give *dispel*, *expel*, *impel*, *propel*, *repel*, with sbs. in *-pulse*, *-pulsion*; cf. also *appeal*, *repeal*.

compendious kəmpe·ndiəs comprehensive but brief. XIV. – (O)F. *compendieux* – L. *compendiōsus* abridged, brief, f. **compe·ndium,** lit. 'that which is weighed together', saving, abbreviation, which has been used as Eng. since XVI. L., f. *compendere*, f. *com* COM- + *pendere* weigh (cf. POISE).

compensate kɔ·mpənseit, formerly kəmpe·nseit make up for. XVII. f. pp. stem of L. *compensāre* weigh (one) against another, counterbalance, f. *com* COM- + *pensāre*, frequent. of *pendere* weigh; see prec. and -ATE[3]. So **compens**A·TION. XIV. – (O)F. – L.

compère kɔ·mpɛəɹ sponsor of an entertainment. XX. F. 'godfather', 'accomplice', 'announcer' – Rom. **compater*, f. *com* COM- + *pater* FATHER. Also vb.

compete kəmpī·t vie, strive *with* another. XVII (not frequent before XIX; stigmatized as a Scotticism and as an Americanism, *c.* 1825). – L. *competere*, in its late sense of 'strive for (something) together with another', f. *com* COM- + *petere* aim at, seek. So **competi**·TION. XVII. – late L. (cf. PETITION). **competit**IVE kəmpe·tĭtiv. XIX. **compe·titor** fellow candidate, rival. XVI. – F. (*-eur*) or L.; see -OR[1].

competent kɔ·mpitənt suitable, proper, adequate XIV; legally qualified or sufficient XV. – (O)F. *compétent* or L. *competent-*, *-ēns*, prp. of *competere* in the sense 'be fit, proper, or qualified'; see prec. and -ENT. Hence **co·mpet**ENCE, -ENCY sufficiency (of qualification). XVI. Cf. L. *competentia* agreement; F. *compétence* jurisdiction, ability, Sp. *competencia* competition, rivalry, legal competence, aptitude, It. *competenza* ability, rivalry, (pl.) fees. ¶ Though originating from the same L. verb as the prec. group, this group of words has a different range of meanings.

compile kəmpai·l put together (literary materials). XIV (Trev.). – (O)F. *compiler* put together, collect, or its presumed source L. *compīlāre* plunder, (contextually) plagiarize, f. *com* COM- + *pīla* PILE[2]. So **compil**A·TION. XV. – (O)F. – L. **compi·ler.** XIV (R. Mannyng). – (O)F. *compileur* :– late L. *compilatōrem*; see -ER[1].

complacent kəmplei·sənt †pleasing XVII; satisfied, esp. with oneself XVIII. – L. *complacent-*, *-ēns*, prp. of *complacēre*, f. *com* COM- intensive + *placēre* PLEASE; see -ENT. (The current sense was formerly expressed by †*complacential* XVII.) So **compla·**CENCE (self-) satisfaction. XV. **compla·**CENCY. XVII. – medL. *complacentia*. Cf. COMPLAISANT.

complain kəmplei·n †bewail, lament XIV (Ch.); (intr. and †refl.) give vent to feelings of injury or discontent XIV (Gower). ME. *compleigne* – (O)F. *complaign-*, pres. stem of *complaindre* (orig. refl.) = Pr. *complanher*, Cat. *complanyer*, It. *compiangere* :– Rom. (medL.) *complangere*, f. *com* COM- intensive + *plangere* lament (see PLAINT). So **complai·nt** act of complaining. XIV (Ch.). – (O)F. *complainte*.

complaisant kɔ·mplizənt, kəmplei·zənt politely agreeable. XVII. – F. *complaisant* obliging: prp. of *complaire* acquiesce in order to please, repr. L. *complacēre* (see COMPLACENT). So **complais**ANCE. XVII. – F.

complement kɔ·mplimənt accomplishment, consummation XIV; something which completes a whole XVI; †adjunct; personal accomplishment; †observance of ceremony, tribute of courtesy XVI. – L. *complēmentum*, f. *complēre*; see next, and -MENT, and cf. COMPLIMENT. Hence **compleme·nt**AL¹, **-ment**ARY †accessory; †ceremonious, complimentary XVII; forming a complement XIX.

complete kəmplī·t entire, finished, perfect XIV (Ch., Wyclif); †accomplished, consummate XVI. – (O)F. *complet* or L. *complētus*, pp. of *complēre* fill up, finish, fulfil, f. *com* COM- (intensive)+ **plē-*, base of *plēnus* FULL. Hence **comple·te** vb. XVI; cf. F. *compléter*. So **comple·**TION, **comple·t**IVE. XVII. – late L.

complex kɔ·mpleks consisting of parts united or combined (later with notion of complication). XVII. – F. *complexe* or its source L. *complexus*, pp. of *complectere*, *complectī* encompass, embrace, comprehend, comprise; but sometimes analysed as COM- +*plexus* woven. Formerly str. *comple·x*. Hence **comple·x**ITY. XVIII; cf. F. *complexité*.

complexion kəmple·kʃən combination of the four humours of the body, (hence) bodily constitution and (further) habit of mind XIV; natural texture of the skin XV. – (O)F. *complexion* – L. *complexiō(n-)* combination, association, (late) bodily habit, f. *complex-*; see prec. and -ION.

compliant kəmplai·ənt disposed to comply, complaisant. XVII. f. COMPLY+-ANT, prob. after PLIANT. Hence **compli·**ANCE. XVII.

complicate kɔ·mplikeit †intertwine; mix up *with* XVII; make complex XIX. f. pp. stem of L. *complicāre*, f. *com* COM-+*plicāre* fold. So **complic**A·TION. XVII. – late L.

complicity kəmplı·sitı partnership in wrong. XVII (rare before XIX). – F. *complicité* or L. **complicitās*, f. *complic-*, COMPLEX; see -ITY and cf. *duplicity*, *simplicity*.

compliment kɔ·mplimənt ceremonious tribute of courtesy, esp. polite phrase of commendation XVII; pl. formal greetings XVIII. – F. *compliment* – It. *complimento* – OCat. *complimento*, Sp. *cumplimiento*, repr. Rom. **complimentum*, for L. *complēmentum* COMPLEMENT. The earlier sp. was *complement*, the occurrence of which has often been disguised, under the present form, in modern editions or reissues. The orig. sense of 'filling up, fulfilment, accomplishment' became specified as 'fulfilment or observance of the requirements of courtesy'.

compline kɔ·mplin last of the canonical hours. XIII (*compelin, complin*). Alteration, prob. after *matines, matins*, of (O)F. *complie* (now pl. *complies*; cf. Sp., Pg. *completas* pl.), sb. use of fem. pp. pl. of †*complir* complete = Pr. *complir*, etc. :- Rom. **complīre* (cf. ACCOMPLISH), for L. *complēre* fill up, COMPLETE. ¶ The medL. forms are *complētōrium* and *complendum* (abbrev. *compl'*, *complen'*).

comply kəmplai· A. †fulfil XVII (Sh.); B. †use compliments, observe formalities XVII (Sh.); †be complaisant *with*; act in accordance *with* circumstances, others' desires, etc. XVII. – It. *complire* – Cat. *complir*, Sp. *cumplir* (in which was developed the sense of 'satisfy', hence 'satisfy the requirements of courtesy') – L. *complēre* COMPLETE. Cf. COMPLEMENT, COMPLIMENT, and ACCOMPLISH(MENT). ¶ ME. *complien* fulfil, carry out (XIV) is f. OF. *complire*.

compo kɔ·mpou short for COMPOSITION. XIX.

component kəmpou·nənt composing, constituent; also sb. XVII. – L. *compōnent-*, *-ēns*, prp. of *compōnere* COMPOUND; see -ENT.

comport¹ kəmpɔ̄·ɹt †bear, endure; agree *with* XVI; behave *oneself* XVII. – L. *comportāre*, f. *com* COM-+*portāre* carry, bear (see PORT³); cf. F. *comporter*.

comport² kɔ·mpɔ̄ɹt dessert dish raised on a support. XVIII. perh. short for synon. **compo·rtier** (XVIII), unexpl. alteration of COMPOTIER.

composant, corrupt. of CORPOSANT. XVIII.

compose kəmpou·z A. put together, make up XV; set up (type); B. arrange, adjust; pacify, tranquillize XVII. – (O)F. *composer*, based on L. *compōnere*; see COMPOUND², POSE¹. Hence **compo·**SURE †composition, in various senses XVI; composed state XVII (Milton). Cf. EXPOSURE; modelled on *closure*. So **composite** kɔ·mpəzit (archit.) fifth of the classical orders XVI; of compound structure XVII. – F. *composite* or L. *compositus*, pp. of *compōnere*. **composi·**TION. XIV (Ch., Wycl. Bible). – (O)F. – L. **compositor** kəmpɔ·zitəɹ †(Sc.) arbiter XIV; type-setter XVI. – AN. – L.

compost kɔ·mpəst (cookery) compote XIV; prepared manure XVI; (arch.) composition XVII. – OF. *composte* and *compost* :- L. *composta*, *-tum*, sb. uses of fem. and n. of *compōnere* COMPOUND.

compote kɔ·mpout fruit preserved in syrup, (later) fruit salad. XVII (Evelyn). – F. *compote*, later form of OF. *composte* stew, dish consisting of fruit :- **composita*, sb. use of fem. of L. *compositus*, pp. of *compōnere* COMPOUND².

compotier kəmpɔ·tiei dish for dessert fruit. XVIII. F., f. *compote*; see prec.

compound¹ kɔ·mpaund compounded, composite. XIV. pp. of *compoune*; see next. Also sb. compound word XVI (Palsgr.); compound substance XVII (Sh.).

compound[2] kəmpau·nd put together, combine, compose XIV (Ch.); trans. and intr. settle differences, claims, or terms XV. ME. *compoune* – OF. *compo(u)n-*, pres. stem of *compondre* = Pr. *compon(d)re*, It. *comporre* :– L. *compōnere* (rendering Gr. συντιθέναι; cf. SYNTHESIS) put or bring together, arrange, devise; see COM-, POSITION. The orig. ME. form was superseded by the present form in XVI, on the model of EXPOUND.

compound[3] kɔ·mpaund in the East, enclosure within which a (European) residence or factory stands. XVII. – Pg. *campon* or Du. *kampoeng* – Malay *kampong*, *-ung* enclosure, fenced-in space, quarter occupied by a particular nationality.

comprador kɔmpradō·ɹ †native servant in the East XVII; in China, principal native servant XIX. – Pg. *comprador* buyer :– late L. *comparātōrem*, f. *comparāre* purchase, f. *com* COM-+*parāre* furnish, PREPARE, -OR[1].

comprehend kɔmprihe·nd grasp with the mind; comprise, include. XIV. – OF. *comprehender* or L. *comprehendere*, f. *com* COM-+*prehendere* seize (cf. GET). So **comprehe·ns**IBLE. XVI. **comprehe·n**SION inclusion; mental grasp. XV. **comprehe·n**SIVE. XV. All – F. or L.

compress kəmpre·s press together XIV (Trevisa); condense XVIII. – OF. *compresser* or late L. *compressāre*, or f. pp. *compress-* of *comprimere*; see COM-, PRESS. So **compress** sb. kɔ·mpres (surg.) mass of material formed into a pad. XVI. – F. *compresse* (Paré), f. *compresser*. **compress**ION -pre·ʃən. XIV. – (O)F. – L.

comprise kəmprai·z †lay hold of; comprehend, include. XV. In earliest use Sc.; f. F. *compris-e*, pp. of *comprendre* COMPREHEND, on the analogy of comps. of *prendre*, of which a sb. and vb. in *-prise* existed, as *enterprise* (†*emprise*), *surprise* (†*supprise*).

compromise kɔ·mprəməiz †joint agreement to abide by a decision XV; coming to terms by concessions on both sides XVI. – (O)F. *compromis* – juridical L. *comprōmissum*, sb. use of n. of pp. of *comprōmittere* consent to arbitration, f. *com* COM-+*prōmittere* PROMISE. Hence **co·mpromise** vb. XV. In part repl. †*compromit* (XV) – L. *comprōmittere*.

compter kau·ntəɹ var. of COUNTER[1], from XVII the official sp. in the name of certain prisons for debtors, etc.

comptometer kɔmptɔ·mitəɹ calculating-machine. XIX. f. F. *compte* COUNT[1]+-O-+-METER.

comptroller sp. of CONTROLLER, due to assoc. of *cont-* with COUNT[1] (L. *computus*), used in certain official designations. XVI.

compulsion kəmpʌ·lʃən action of compelling. XV. – (O)F. *compulsion* – late L. *compulsiō(n-)*, f. *compuls-*, pp. stem of *compellere* COMPEL; see -SION. So **compu·ls**ORY enforced, obligatory XVI; coercive XVII. Formerly also †*compulsative*, *-atory*, *compulsive* XVII (Sh.).

compunction kəmpʌ·ŋkʃən pricking of the conscience. XIV; in weakened sense XVIII. – (O)F. *componction* – ChrL. *compunctiō(n-)*, f. *compungere*, f. *com* COM- (intensive)+*pungere* prick (see PUNCTURE and -TION). Hence **compu·nct**IOUS remorseful. XVII (Sh.).

compurgator kɔ·mpəɹgeitəɹ witness who swears to the credibility of an accused person when he purges himself by oath. XVI. – medL. *compurgātor* (XIII), f. *com* COM-+*purgātor* purger (see PURGE). So **compurg**A·TION. XVII. – medL.

compute kəmpjū·t determine by mathematical reckoning. XVII. – F. *computer* or L. *computāre*, f. *com* COM-+*putāre* clear or settle (an account), reckon, think, rel. to *putus* unmixed (esp. in *argentum pūrum putum* pure silver without alloy). So **computa**·TION. XV. **compu·ter**[1]. XVII. – F. or L. Cf. PUTATIVE.

computus kɔ·mpjŭtəs set of tables for calculating astronomical occurrences and dates in the calendar. XIX. late L., 'computation', in medL. as above, rel. to prec. So **co·mput**IST one skilled in the computus. XVII. – medL. *computista*.

comrade kɔ·mrəd, kʌ·mrəd close companion. XVI. Earlier *camerade*, *camarade*, *com(m)erade*, *cumrade* – F. *camerade*, *camarade* (orig. fem.) – Sp. *camarada* (i) barrack-room, (ii) chamber-fellow, mate, f. *camara* CHAMBER; see -ADE. The stress was orig. on the final syll., as in Sh. (varying with *co·mrade*) and Milton.

comstockery kɔ·mstɔkəri opposition to realism in literature or art. XX (1905, G. B. Shaw). f. name of A. *Comstock*, an American who attacked the nude in art; see -ERY.

comtism kɔ̃·tizm positivism. XIX. – F. *comtisme*, f. name of Auguste *Comte* (1798–1857), French philosopher; see -ISM.

con[1] kɔn in the sense 'get to know, learn', hence 'get by heart, commit to memory', 'peruse, scan', and in (dial.) phr. *con thank(s)*, from OE. *þanc cunnan* (= ON. *kunna þǫkk*); differentiated var. of ME. *cunne*, OE. *cunnan* know (see CAN[2]); not clearly evidenced (with pt. and pp. *conned*) before XV, earlier instances of *conne*, *konne* being normal graphic vars. of *cunne*. A specially interesting ex. is 'I can konne more by herte in a day than he can in a weke' (Palsgr.).

con[2] kɔn, kʌn direct the steering of (a ship) from a commanding position. XVII (*cun*, *con*). Reduced form of †*cond*, †*cund* (XVII), shortening of †*condie*, †*condue* (XIV) – (O)F. *conduire* :– L. *condūcere* CONDUCT. Survives mainly in *conning-tower* pilot-house of a warship or submarine XIX.

con[3] see PRO[1].

con[4] (U.S.) short for CONFIDENCE (man, trick). XIX.

con- kən, kɔn comb. form of L. prep. *com* (later *cum*) with, used regularly before all consonants except *b, m, h, r*, and *l*; see COL-, COM-. In OF. *conv-* was reduced to *cov-*, e.g. COVENANT, COVET; many Eng. adoptions preserve this, but in some words *con-* was restored, e.g. CONVENT, the orig. form of which survives in the name of *Covent* Garden, London. For the meaning see COM-.

conacre kɔ·neikəɹ in Ireland, letting by a tenant of land prepared for a crop. XIX. orig. *corn-acre*, i.e. CORN[1], ACRE.

conation kounei·ʃən (philos.) faculty of volition. XIX. – L. *cōnātiō(n-)*, f. *cōnāt-*, *cōnārī* endeavour; see -ATION. So **con**ATIVE kou·nətiv. XIX.

concatenate kɔnkæ·tineit link together. XVI. f. pp. stem of late L. *concatēnāre*, f. *com* CON-+*catēna* CHAIN; see -ATE[3]. So **co:ncatena**·TION. XVII. – F. or L.

concave kɔ·nkeiv hollow)(*convex*. XV. – L. *concavus* (perh. through F. *concave*), f. *com* CON-+*cavus* hollow. So **conca·vity.** XIV. – F. or late L.; see CAVE, CAVITY.

conceal kənsī·l keep from being seen or known. XIV (Barbour). – OF. *conceler* – L. *concēlāre*, f. *com* CON-+*cēlāre* hide, f. base **kel-* (cf. CELL, CLANDESTINE, OCCULT). So **concea·l**MENT. XIV. – OF. *concelement*, f. *conceler*.

concede kənsī·d grant, yield. XVII. – F. *concéder* or its source L. *concēdere* withdraw, yield; see CON- and CEDE. So **concess**ION kənse·ʃən. XVI. – F. or L.

conceit kənsī·t †conception, thought; personal opinion XIV (Ch.); fanciful opinion, etc., fancy XV; for *self-conceit* XVII. f. CONCEIVE on the analogy of the pairs *deceive, deceit, receive, receipt*, which have F. originals. The sense-development was infl. by It. *concetto* (:– late L. *conceptus* CONCEPT), which the Eng. word was prob. designed to represent. Hence **conceit** vb. XVI. **concei·ted.** XVI. f. vb. or sb.; see -ED[2].

conceive kənsī·v become pregnant (with) XIII; take into the mind XIV; formulate in words XVI. – OF. *conceiv-*, tonic stem of *concevoir*, for **conceivre* = Pr. *concebre*, Sp. *concebir*, It. *concepire* :– L. *concipere* take to oneself, be pregnant, comprehend mentally, express, f. *com* CON-+*capere* take (cf. CAPTIVE). So **concei·**VABLE XVI.

concentrate kɔ·nsəntreit bring to a common centre. XVII. f. pp. stem of L. **concentrāre* (cf. F. *concentrer*, It. *concentrare*, Sp. *concentrar*), modelled on *concentricus*; see -ATE[3]. So **concentra**·TION. XVII. **conce·ntre.** XVI. – F. *concentrer* – L. **concentric** kənse·ntrik having a common centre. XIV (Ch.; rare before XVII; *concentrical* from XVI). – (O)F. *concentrique* or medL. *-icus*; see CON-, CENTRE, -IC.

conception kənse·pʃən action of conceiving in the womb XIII; apprehension, imagination XIV; notion XVII. – (O)F. *conception* – L. *conceptiō(n-)*; f. *concept-*, *concipere* CONCEIVE; see -TION. So **concept** kɔ·nsept †thought, opinion, etc. XVI; (philos.) XVII. – late L. *conceptus*, f. pp. stem of *concipere*. **conce·ptu**AL. XVII. – medL. *conceptuālis*, f. *conceptus*; hence **conce·ptual**IST (scholastic philos.) XVIII, -ISM XIX; cf. F. *conceptualisme*, G. *-ismus*.

concern kənsə̄·ɹn †discern; sc. relate to XV; engage the attention of XVI; pass. be interested, involved. XVII. – (O)F. *concerner* or late L. *concernere* sift, distinguish, in medL. have respect or reference to, f. *com* CON-+ *cernere* sift, f. base **ker-* (cf. CERTAIN). Somewhat earlier in prp. **conce·rning** (XV) in uses leading to its use as prep., prob. modelled on a similar use of F. *concernant*. Hence **conce·rn** sb. XVI.

concert[1] kɔ·nsəɹt harmony; musical performance. XVII. – F. *concert* – It. CONCERTO.

concert[2] kənsə̄·ɹt †unite XVI; arrange by agreement XVII. – F. *concerter* – It. *concertare* bring into agreement or harmony, of obscure origin (identity with L. *concertāre* contend, dispute is improbable). **concertina** kɔnsəɹtī·nə musical instrument with bellows and keys. XIX (invented by Sir Charles Wheatstone, 1829). f. CONCERT[1] + *-ina*, after *seraphina*.

concerto kəntʃə̄·ɹtou, kənsə̄·ɹtou musical composition for solo instruments accompanied by orchestra. XVIII. It., f. *concertare* (see CONCERT[2]).

concession kənse·ʃən conceding or thing conceded. XVI. – (O)F. *concession* or L. *concessiō(n-)*, f. *concess-*, pp. stem of *concēdere* CONCEDE; see -ION. So **conce·ss**IVE (chiefly gram.). XVIII. – late L.

concetto kɔntʃe·ttou literary conceit. XVIII. It. :– L. *conceptu-s* (in late L.) thought, purpose (see CONCEPT).

conch kɔŋk shell, shell-fish. XVI. – L. *concha* bivalve, mussel, pearl oyster, shell of snail, etc. – Gr. *kógkhē* (cf. Skr. *çaŋkhás* conch). The earliest Eng. form was perh. *conche*, pl. *conches*; cf. the surviving alternative pronunc. kɔntʃ.

conchy kɔ·nʃi colloq. shortening of *consci|entious objector* (sc. to military or other service). XX. Cf. -Y[6].

concierge kɔ̃siə̄·ɹʒ, ‖ kɔ̃sjɛrʒ janitor, caretaker. XVII. F., OF. *cumcerges* (whence medL. *consergius*) :– Rom. **conservius*, alteration of L. *conservus* fellow slave (see CON-, SERF), after *consocius* companion.

conciliar kənsi·liəɹ pert. to a council. XVII. f. L. *concilium* COUNCIL+-AR.

conciliate kənsi·lieit gain the goodwill of, win over; reconcile. XVI. f. pp. stem of L. *conciliāre* combine, unite, procure, gain, win, f. *concilium* meeting, union, COUNCIL; see -ATE[3]. So **concili**A·TION. XVI. – L. **conci·li**ATOR. XVI. – L. **conci·lia**TORY. XVI.

concinnity kənsi·nĭti congruity; elegance of literary style. XVI. – L. *concinnitās*, f. *concinnus* skilfully put together, well adjusted, elegant, neat; see -ITY.

concise kənsai·s expressed in few words. XVI. – F. *concis-e* or L. *concīsus* divided, broken up, brief, pp. of *concīdere* cut or divide up, f. *com* CON- (intensive)+*cædere* cut (cf. CÆSURA).

conclave kɔ·nkleiv †private chamber; private place of assembly of cardinals XIV (assembly of cardinals for election of pope XVII); (gen.) private assembly XVI. – F. *conclave* – L. *conclāve*, f. *com* CON-+*clāvis* key (cf. CLAVICLE).

conclude kənklū·d †enclose, include; bring or come to a close, settlement, decision; infer, prove. XIV. – L. *conclūdere* (in the above senses), f. *com* CON-+*claudere* shut (cf. CLOSE). So **conclus**ION kənklū·ʒən end, issue; inference; †proposition; †experiment; decision. XIV. – (O)F. *conclusion* or L. *conclūsiō(n-)*, f. *conclūs-*, *conclūdere*. So **conclus**IVE kənklū·siv. XVI. – late L.

concoct kənkɔ·kt †maturate (metals); †digest (food) XVI; compose, devise XVII. f. *concoct-*, pp. stem of L. *concoquere* digest, put up with, mature, consider, reflect upon, f. *com* CON-+*coquere* cook, f. *coquus* COOK. So **conco·c**TION. XVI. – L.

concomitant kənkɔ·mitənt accompanying or attendant (person or thing). XVII. – prp. of late L. *concomitārī* accompany, f. *com* CON-+*comitārī*, f. *comit-*, *comes* companion; see COUNT[2], -ANT. So **conco·mit**ANCE coexistence (spec. theol.). XVI. – medL.

concord kɔ·ŋkɔ̄ɹd, kɔ·nkɔ̄ɹd agreement, harmony. XIII (Cursor M.). – (O)F. *concorde* – L. *concordia*, f. *concord-*, *concors* of one mind, f. *com* CON-+*cor* HEART. So **concord**ANCE kənkɔ̄·ɹdəns A. alphabetical register with citations of words contained in a work (orig. and esp. the Bible) XIV; B. agreement XV. – F. *concordance* – medL. *concordantia*, f. prp. stem of *concordāre* agree, f. *concors*; the use in A was orig. pl. (medL. *concordantiæ*), each series of parallel passages being a *concordantia*. So **conco·rd**ANT agreeing. XV. **concordat** kənkɔ̄·ɹdæt agreement, compact. XVII. – F. *concordat* or L. *concordātum*, sb. use of n. pp. of *concordāre*, after the formula 'transactum, compositum, et concordatum est' (it has been concluded, arranged, and agreed).

concourse kɔ·ŋkɔ̄ɹs, kɔ·n- running or flowing together, meeting XIV; concurrence; assemblage XVII. ME. *concours* – (O)F. *concours* – L. *concursu-s*, f. *concurs-*, *concurrere* run together, CONCUR.

concrete kɔ·nkrīt, kɔ·ŋ-, (formerly) kənkrī·t †united, composite; opp. to *abstract* XIV (Trev.); sb. concreted mass XVII; composition of gravel or sand and cement XIX. – F. *concret* or L. *concrētus*, pp. of *concrēscere* grow together, f. *com* CON-+*crēscere* grow (see CRESCENT). So **concre·**TION. XVI. – F. – L.

concubine kɔ·ŋkjubain. XIII. – (O)F. *concubine* – L. *concubīna*, f. *com* CON-+*cub-* lie down (cf. CUBICLE). So **concubin**AGE kənkjū·binidʒ. XIV. – F. **concu·bin**ARY (one) living in concubinage. XVI. – medL. *concubīnārius*; cf. F. *concubinaire*.

concupiscence kənkjū·pisəns vehement desire; libidinous desire, lust. XIV. – (O)F. *concupiscence* – late L. *concupiscentia*, f. *concupiscent-*, prp. stem of *concupiscere*, inceptive of *concupere*, f. *com* CON-+*cupere* desire; see CUPIDITY, -ENCE. So **concu·pisc**IBLE vehemently to be desired XV; vehemently desirous XIV.

concur kənkɔ̄·ɹ †collide, converge XV; fall together, coincide; agree in action or opinion XV. – L. *concurrere*, f. *com* CON-+*currere* run (see COURSE). So **concurr**ENT kʌ·rənt. XIV (Trev.). **concu·rr**ENCE. XV; cf. medL. *concurrentia*.

concussion kənkʌ·ʃən violent agitation XV; injury due to the shock of a blow, etc. XVI. – L. *concussiō(n-)*, f. *concuss-*, pp. stem of *concutere* dash together, shake violently, f. *com* CON-+*quatere* shake (cf. QUASH); see -ION.

condemn kənde·m pronounce adverse judgement on. XIII (Cursor M.). – OF. *condem(p)ner* (mod. *condamner*) – L. *condem(p)nāre*, f. *com* CON-+*damnāre* DAMN. So **condemn**A·TION. XIV. – late L.

condense kənde·ns increase the density of XV; reduce from vapour to liquid XVII. – (O)F. *condenser* or L. *condensāre*, f. *condensus* very dense; see CON-, DENSE. So **condens**A·TION. XVII. – late L.

condescend kəndise·nd †settle down *to* XIV (Ch.); bend down *to*, †be complaisant, agree XV. – (O)F. *condescendre* – ecclL. *condēscendere* stoop (fig.), in medL. accede, agree to, f. *com* CON-+*dēscendere* DESCEND. So **condesce·n**SION. XVII. – ecclL.

condign kəndai·n †of equal worth XV; †worthy, deserving XV; deserved, fitting, esp. in *condign punishment*, a phr. derived from Tudor acts of parliament XV. – (O)F. *condigne* (XIV in *amende condigne* fitting fine) – L. *condignus* wholly worthy, f. *com* CON- (intensive)+*dignus* worthy (cf. DIGNITY).

condiment kɔ·ndimənt seasoning, relish. XV. – L. *condīmentum*, f. *condīre* preserve, pickle, embalm, by-form of *condere* preserve, prop. put together, prob. modelled on *salīre* season with salt (beside *sal(l)ere*).

condition kəndi·ʃən convention, stipulation; mode of being. XIV. – OF. *condicion* (mod. *condition*), corr. to Pr. *condicio*, It. *condizione*, etc. – L. *condiciō(n-)* agreement, compact, terms, situation, state, rel. to *condīcere* agree upon, promise, lit. talk over together, f. *com* CON- + *dīcere* declare, say (cf. DICTION); for the stem *dĭc-* cf. *diciō* authority, sway, ABDICATE, DEDICATE, INDICATE, PREDICATE. So **condi·tionAL**. XIV. – OF. *condicionel* (mod. *-tionnel*) or late L. *condiciōnālis* (juridical term).

condole kəndou·l †sorrow greatly; †trans. grieve with or over XVI; express sympathy *with* XVII. – ChrL. *condolēre*, f. *com* CON- + *dolēre* suffer pain, grieve (see DOLOUR). So **condo·lENCE** †sympathetic grief; outward expression of sympathy. XVII. f. the vb.; but in the second sense orig. in the form †*condoleance*, later modified to †*condolance*, – F. *condoléance* (f. *condouloir*, under the influence of *doléance*); hence the stress on the second syll.

condominium kəndəmi·niəm joint rule. XVIII (Burnet). modL., f. CON- + L. *dominium* lordship (cf. DOMINION).

condone kəndou·n overlook and forgive (an offence). XIX (dating from the Divorce Act of 1857; in dictionaries of XVII–XVIII merely an anglicization of the L. word without reference to use). – L. *condōnāre* deliver up, surrender, refrain from punishing as a favour, f. *com* CON- altogether + *dōnāre* give (cf. DONATION, PARDON), a term of canon law with spec. reference to violation of the marriage vow. So **condonA·TION**. XVII. – L.; adopted from casuistic use.

condor kɔ·ndɔ̄ɹ large S. American bird of the vulture kind. XVII. – Sp. *cóndor* – Peruvian *cuntur*.

condottiere kɔndɔtiɛə·ri leader of mercenary troops. XVIII (Mrs. Radcliffe). It., f. *condotto* leadership, CONDUCT + *-iere*, agent-suffix :- L. *-ārius* -ARY.

conduce kəndjū·s †lead XV; †engage, hire; contribute, lead, or tend *to* XVI. – L. *condūcere* bring together (and all the above senses), f. *com* CON- + *dūcere* lead (see DUCT). Hence **condu·CIVE** conducing *to*. XVII; after earlier *conductive* (XVI; cf. F. †*conductif*).

conduct kɔ·ndʌkt guiding, leading (surviving in *safe conduct*); management XV; manner of conducting oneself XVII. – L. *conductus*, f. *conduct-*, *condūcere* (see CONDUCE). Preceded by *conduit(e)*, *condut(e)*, *-dyt* (XIII–XVI) – OF. *conduit*, (also mod.) *conduite* – medL. *conductus*, Rom. **conducta* (cf. Pr. *conduch*, Sp. *conducto*, *-ducta*, It. *condotto*, *-dotta*). Cf. CONDUIT. So **conduct** vb. kəndʌ·kt lead, guide XV (Lydg.); command XVI; direct, manage XVII. Preceded by *conduite*, *-dyte* (XV), f. (O)F. *conduit*, pp. of *conduire*; later assim. to the L. pp. *conductus*. **conducTION** kəndʌ·kʃən †leading, leadership; †management; †hiring XVI; conducting (of liquid) XVII; transmission of heat, electricity, etc. XIX. – (O)F. or L. **condu·ctor** A. leader, commander XVI; manager XVII; director of singers and musicians XVIII; B. substance or object that conducts heat, etc. XVIII. – (O)F. *conducteur* – L.; see -OR[1]; earlier *conduitour*, *conditour* (XV) – OF.

conduit kʌ·ndit channel or pipe for the conveyance of liquid. XIV. ME. *condut*, *condit* – (O)F. *conduit* :- medL. *conductu-s*, f. *conduct-*, pp. stem of *condūcere* CONDUCE (cf. AQUEDUCT).

condyle kɔ·ndil rounded process at the end of a bone. XVII. – F. *condyle* (Paré, XVI) – L. *condylus* – Gr. *kóndulos* knuckle (f. base meaning 'round object').

Condy's fluid kɔ·ndiz flū·id disinfecting fluid named after Henry Bollmann *Condy*, English physician. XIX.

cone koun figure of which the base is a circle and the summit a point XVI (in earlier use her. †angular division of a shield XV). (Also in XVI–XVII *con*) – F. *cône* – L. *cōnus* – Gr. *kônos* pine-cone, geometrical cone, conical apex, spinning-top, rel. to HONE. So **conIC** kɔ·nik, -ICAL. XVI. – modL. *cōnicus* – Gr. *kōnikós*. **cono-** comb. form, as in *conocuneus* XVII, *conodont* XIX. **conOID** kou·noid XVII, **conoi·dAL** XVI. – mod. *cōnoidēs* – Gr. *kōnoeidḗs*.

confab kɔ·nfæb. XVIII. colloq. shortening of **confabulATION** kənfæbjŭlei·ʃən talk, chat. XV. – late L. *confabulātiō(n-)*, f. *confabulārī* converse (see CON- and FABLE), whence **confa·bulate** XVII, which was also formerly abbrev. *confab*.

confarreation kɔ·nfæriei·ʃən solemn form of marriage among the ancient Romans, marked by the offering of a cake of spelt. XVI. – L. *confarreātiō(n-)*, f. *confarreāre* unite in marriage in this way, f. *com* CON- + *farreum* spelt cake, sb. use of n. of *farreus*, f. *far* grain, spelt (cf. BARLEY[1]); see -ATION.

confection kənfe·kʃən compounded medicinal preparation; prepared dish, preparation of fruit, etc., conserve, sweetmeat. XIV. – (O)F. *confection* – L. *confectiō(n-)* preparation (abstr. and concr.), f. *confect-*, pp. stem of *conficere* prepare, f. *com* CON- + *facere* put, make; see CON-, FACT, -TION. Hence, through the vb. *confection* (XVI), **confe·ctioner** maker of sweetmeats, cakes, etc. XVI; see -ER[1]; whence **confe·ctionERY** XVIII.

confederate kənfe·dərət leagued, allied XIV; sb. accomplice XV; ally XVI. – late (eccl.) L. *confœderātus*; see CON-, FEDERATE. So **confederA·TION** league, alliance, †conspiracy XV; body of states leagued together XVII. – (O)F. or late L. (Jerome). **confe·derACY** (in same senses). XIV. – AN. *confederacie*.

confer kənfə̄·ɹ †bring together, collect; compare, collate; converse, take counsel; bestow. XVI. – L. *conferre* (in these senses), f. *com* CON-+*ferre* bring, BEAR[2]. The stress is as in other direct derivs. from L., *defe·r*, *infe·r*, as contrasted with *di·ffer*, *o·ffer*, *pro·ffer*, *su·ffer*, which came through French. So **confer**ENCE kɔ·nfərəns †collation, collection; taking counsel, discourse; meeting for consultation. XVI. – F. *conférence* or medL. *conferentia*.

confess kənfe·s own to, acknowledge, esp. guiltily; hear the confession of, shrive. XIV (Ch.). – (O)F. *confesser* = Pr. *confessar*, etc. :– Rom. **confessāre*, f. L. *confessus*, pp. of *confitērī* acknowledge, f. *com* CON-+*fatērī* declare, avow, rel. to *fārī* speak, *fābula* FABLE. So **confess**ION -fe·ʃən acknowledgement (of guilt) XIV (Wyclif); matter confessed XV; formulary of belief XVI. – (O)F. – L. **confe·ssion**AL place for hearing confessions. XVIII. – F. *confessional* – It. *confessionale* – medL. *confessionāle*, sb. use of n. sg. of adj. **confessor** kənfe·səɹ (eccl.) one who avows his religion in the face of danger but does not suffer martyrdom XII; (gen.) one who makes confession (of belief, guilt, etc.) XIII; (eccl.) one who hears confessions (in this sense often kɔ·nfesə̄ɹ, with normal stress-development from ME. *confessou·r*) XIV. – AN. *confessur*, OF. *confessour* (mod. *-eur*) – ecclL. *confessor*, f. *confess-*, *confitērī*; see -OR[1].

confetti kənfe·ti small sweets used as missiles at a carnival, small disks of paper so used at weddings. XIX. It., pl. of *confetto* COMFIT.

confide kənfai·d put faith *in*. XV. – L. *confīdere*, f. *com* CON- (intensive)+*fīdere* trust (see FAITH). So **confid**ENT kɔ·nfidənt trusting, self-assured XVI; †trusted, trusty XVII; sb. confidential friend or adviser XVII; in the earlier sense – L. *confīdent-*, *-ēns*; in the later, and as sb. – F. *confident* – It. *confidente*; in sb. use superseded by **confidant,** fem. **-ante** (XVII) kɔnfidæ·nt (XVIII) which are not regular F. forms, but were presumably adopted orig. to represent the pronunc. of F. *confidente* (a conventional character of the French stage). **confiden**TIAL -e·nʃəl †confident XVII; done in confidence, betokening intimacy XVIII.

configuration kɔnfigjurei·ʃən (astron.) relative position XVI; conformation, outline XVII. – late L. *configūrātiō(n-)*, f. L. *configūrāre* fashion after a pattern; see CON-, FIGURE, -ATION.

confine kənfai·n have a common boundary *with*, border; keep within bounds, imprison. XVI. – F. *confiner*, f. *confins* CONFINES, prob. after It. *confinare*. Hence (or – F. *confinement*) **confi·ne**MENT imprisonment XVII; childbed XVIII (so *to be confined*, i.e. to bed, XVIII).

confines kɔ·nfainz (pl.) †region XIV; boundaries, borders XVI. – F. *confins*, †*confines* – L. *confīnia*, pl. of *confīne* and *confīnium*, f. *confīnis* bordering, f. *com* CON-+*fīnis* end, limit (pl. *fīnes* territory). (†*Confine*, as in Sh., confinement, enclosure, is prob. f. the vb.)

confirm kənfə̄·ɹm settle, establish XIII; administer confirmation to (superseding †*bishop*, OE. *biscopian*); strengthen, fortify XIV. – OF. *confermer* (later *confirmer*) – L. *confirmāre*, f. *com* CON- (intensive)+*firmāre* strengthen, f. *firmus* FIRM. So **confirma·**TION eccl. rite conveying special grace for the strengthening of the baptized XIV; corroboration, ratification XIV. – (O)F. – L.

confiscate kɔ·nfiskeit (formerly) kənfi·skeit appropriate to the public treasury XVI; seize summarily XIX. f. L. *confiscāt-*, *-āre*, f. *com* CON-+*fiscus* chest, treasury; see FISCAL, -ATE[3]. Earlier †*confisk* XV; cf. (O)F. *confisquer*. So **confis**CA·TION. XVI. – L.

confiteor kənfi·tiə̄ɹ form of confession of sins. XIII. L., 'I confess', the first word of the formula *Confiteor Deo Omnipotenti* I confess to Almighty God, etc.; see CONFESS.

conflagration kɔnfləgrei·ʃən †consumption by fire XVI; great fire XVI. – L. *conflagrātiō(n-)*, f. *conflagrāre* burn up; see CON-, FLAGRANT, -ATION.

conflation kənflei·ʃən blowing or fusing together XVII (Bacon); fusion of textual readings XIX (Westcott & Hort). – ecclL. *conflātiō(n-)* fanning (of fire), fusion (of metals), f. *conflāre* kindle, effect, fuse; see CON-, BLOW[1], -ATION. ¶ Also XV (Pecock) conflation or harmony (of the Gospels).

conflict kɔ·nflikt encounter in arms, struggle. XV. – L. *conflīctus*, f. *conflict-*, pp. stem of *conflīgere*, f. *com* CON-+*flīgere* strike (cf. *afflict*, *inflict*; *profligate*). So **confli·ct** contend XV; be at variance, clash XVII. f. the pp. stem above.

confluence kɔ·nfluəns flowing together, junction of streams. XVI. – late L. *confluentia*, f. *confluent-*, *-ēns*, prp. of *confluere*; see CON-, FLUENT. So **co·nflu**ENT. XVII.

conform kənfə̄·ɹm bring into or act in accordance with a pattern, etc. XIV. – (O)F. *conformer* – L. *conformāre*; see CON-+FORM vb. Hence **confo·rm**ABLE. XVI. **confo·rm**IST. XVII; cf. NONCONFORMIST. So **conforma**·TION. XVI. – L. **confo·rm**ITY. XV. – (O)F. or late L.

confound kənfau·nd †overthrow XIII (Cursor M.); bring to perdition; throw into confusion XIV. – AN. *confundre*, *-foundre*, (O)F. *confondre* = Pr. *cofondre*, Cat. *confondre* :– L. *confundere* pour together, mix up, f. *com* CON-+*fundere* (see FUSION).

confraternity kɔnfrətə̄·ɹniti organized (religious) brotherhood. XV. – (O)F. *confraternité* – medL. *confrāternitās*, f. *confrāter*; see next and -ITY.

confrère kɔ·nfrɛəɹ †fellow member of a fraternity, etc. XV; fellow member of a learned body XVII. – (O)F. *confrère* = Pr. *confraire*, Sp. *confrade*, It. *confrate* – medL. *confrāter*; see CON- and FRIAR. The second sense is a mod. readoption from F.

confront kənfrʌ·nt stand in front of, face with hostility XVI; bring face to face XVII. – F. *confronter* = Pr., Sp. *confrontar*, It. *confrontare* – medL. *confrontāre*, f. L. *com* CON-+*front-*, *frons* forehead, face, FRONT.

Confucian kənfjū·ʃən pert. to the Chinese philosopher Confucius. XIX. f. *Confucius*, latinized form of Chinese *K'ung Fû tsze* K'ung the (our, your) Master; see -IAN.

confused kənfjū·zd †discomfited, confounded XIV; thrown into disorder, mixed XVI. f. (O)F. *confus* or its source L. *confūsus* (whence †*confuse* adj. XIV–XVIII), pp. of *confundere* CONFOUND+-ED. Hence **confu·se** vb. in corr. active senses, and in the sense 'mix up in the mind'. XVIII. So **confu·sion** †discomfiture XIII; throwing into disorder, result of this XIV. – (O)F. or L.; cf. FUSION.

confute kənfjū·t prove to be wrong or false. XVI. – L. *confūtāre* check, restrain, answer conclusively, f. *cum* CON-+**fūt-*, as in *refūtāre* REFUTE. Cf. F. *confuter*. So **confuta·tion** XV.

congé kɔ̃·ʒei leave, permission. XVI. – F. *congé*, adopted earlier (XV) as *congie*, CONGEE (lasting till XIX).

congeal kəndʒī·l make or become solid as by freezing. XIV (Gower, Maund.). – (O)F. *congeler* – L. *congelāre*, f. *com* CON-+*gelāre* (see GELID).

congee kɔ·ndʒi †leave to depart, passport XV; bow on taking leave XVI. – OF. *congié* (mod. *congé*) = Pr. *comjat*, Cat. *comiat*, It. *commiato* (It. *congedo* – F.) :– L. *commeātus* passage, leave to pass, leave of absence, furlough, f. *com* COM-+*meāre* go, pass. Since late XVII remodelled on modF. and spelt *congé*; in law F. *congé d'élire* (XVI) permission (to a cathedral chapter) to elect (to a vacant see).

congee see CONJEE.

congener kɔ·ndʒinəɹ member of the same class or group. XVIII. – L. *congener*, f. *com* CON-+*gener-*, GENUS.

congenial kəndʒī·niəl of the same disposition or temperament XVII; suited to one's taste XVIII. – modL. **congeniālis*, f. L. *com* CON-+GENIUS, after GENIAL.

congenital kəndʒe·nitəl dating from one's birth. XVIII. f. L. *congenitus* born along with, connate, f. *com* CON-+*genitus*, pp. of *gignere* produce (see GENITAL).

conger kɔ·ŋgəɹ large species of eel. XIV. – (O)F. *congre* :– L. *congrus*, also *conger*, – Gr. *góggros*.

congeries kəndʒiə·riīz, -dʒe·riīz massed collection. XVII. – L. *congeriēs* heap, pile, f. *congerere* (see next).

congestion kəndʒe·stʃən †accumulation XVI; (med.) of blood XV; overcrowded state XIX. – (O)F. *congestion* – L. *congestiō(n-)*, f. *congest-*, pp. stem of *congerere* heap together (whence **conge·st** XVI), f. *com* CON-+*gerere* carry; see GESTURE, -TION.

conglomerate kənglɔ·mərət †massed together XVI; (physiol.) of complex glands XVII; (geol.) formed of fragments cemented together (also sb.) XIX. – L. *conglomerātus*, pp. of *conglomerāre*, f. *com* CON-+*glomer-*, *glomus* ball, rel. to *globus* GLOBE; see -ATE[2]. So **conglomera·tion**. XVII (Bacon). – late L.

congou kɔ·ŋgu, -ou black tea. XVIII. – Chinese (Amoy) *kung hu tē*, for *kung fu ch'a* tea on which labour has been expended, f. *kung fu* work, workman, *ch'a* TEA.

congratulate kəngræ·tjŭleit †express sympathetic joy; address with expressions of satisfaction. XVI. f. pp. stem of L. *congrātulārī*, f. *com* CON- (intensive)+*grātulārī* manifest one's joy, f. *grātus* pleasing; see GRATEFUL, -ATE[3]. So **congratula·tion**. XV. – L.

congregation kɔŋgrigei·ʃən A. meeting, assembly XIV (Ch.); B. orig. in biblical language, in O.T. whole body or solemn assembly of Israelites XIV; in N.T. whole or a particular body of Christians; body of persons assembled for worship XVI; C. religious community)(*order* XV; special committee of the College of Cardinals XVII. – (O)F. *congrégation* or L. *congregātiō(n-)*, f. *congregāre*, whence **co·ngregate** collect together XV; see CON-, GREGARIOUS, -ATE[3], -ATION. Hence **congrega·tional** (spec. of a form of church polity). XVII.

congress kɔ·ŋgres meeting, union XVI; formal assembly of delegates, etc. XVII; legislative body of U.S.A. XVIII. – L. *congressus* (whence F. *congrès*), f. *congress-*, pp. stem of *congredī* go together, meet, f. *com* CON-+*gradī* step, walk (see GRADE).

congressional kəngre·ʃənəl pert. to the Congress of the United States. XVIII. f. CONGRESS with insertion of *-ion-* from L. *congressiō(n-)* to avoid the awkwardness of immed. derivation; see -ION, -AL.

congruent kɔ·ŋgruənt conforming, accordant, agreeable. XV. – L. *congruent-*, *-ēns*, prp. of *congruere* meet together, agree, correspond, f. *com* CON-+**gruere*, *ruere* fall, rush; see RUIN, -ENT. So **congruity** kəngrū·iti conformity, etc. XV. – F. or late L. **co·ngruous**. XVI. f. L. *congruus*.

conic see CONE.

conicopoly kɔnikɔ·pɔli native clerk in the Madras Presidency, India. XVII. – Tamil *kanokka-pillai* 'account-man'.

conifer kou·nifəɹ cone-bearing tree. XIX. – L. *cōnifer* (Virgil), f. *cōnus* CONE. So **coni·ferous** cone-bearing. XVII.

conjecture kəndʒe·ktʃəɹ †interpretation of signs, etc. XIV; (formation of) an opinion on grounds insufficient for proof XVI. – (O)F. *conjecture*, or L. *conjectūra* conclusion, inference, f. *conject-*, pp. stem of *conicere* throw together, put together in speech or thought (cf. Gr. συμβάλλειν), conclude; see CON-, ABJECT (etc.), -URE. So **conje·cture** vb. XIV (Wyclif). – (O)F. *conjecturer* – late L. *conjectūrāre*; superseding †*conject* XIV (Ch., Trevisa). **conje·ctur**AL XVI. – F. – L.

conjee, congee kɔ·ndʒi water in which rice has been boiled. XVII. – Tamil *kãnji*.

conjoin kəndʒoi·n join together. XIV (Ch.). Late ME. *conjoigne*, *-oyne* – (O)F. *conjoign-*, pres. stem of *conjoindre* – L. *conjungere* (see CONJUNCT). So **co·njoint** combined, united. XVIII (earlier in adv. *conjointly* Sh.). – F. *conjoint*, pp. of *conjoindre*.

conjugal kɔ·ndʒŭgəl pert. to husband and wife. XVI. – L. *conjugālis*, f. *conjug-*, *-ju(n)x* consort, spouse, f. *com* CON- + **jug-*, base of *jungere* JOIN; see -AL. So **co·njugate** joined together XV; joined in reciprocal relation XVII. – L. *conjugātus*, pp. of *conjugāre* (f. *jugum* YOKE), whence **co·njugate** -eit †couple, yoke; inflect (a verb) in its various forms XVI. See -ATE[2] and **conjuga**TION earliest in gram. sense XV. – L.

conjunct kɔ·ndʒʌŋkt joined together. XV. – L. *conjunctus*, pp. of *conjungere*, f. *com* CON- + *jungere* JOIN; cf. CONJOINT. So **conjunc**TION kəndʒʌ·ŋkʃən union, connexion (gen. and astron.) XIV (Ch., Barbour, Trevisa); (gram.) connecting particle XIV (Wyclif). – (O)F. *conjonction* – L. *conjunctiōnem*, f. *conjungere*; in gram. sense L. *conjunctiō* tr. Gr. σύνδεσμος **conju·nct**IVE. XV. – late L. **conju·nctivi**·TIS inflammation of the *membrana conjunctiva* 'conjunctive membrane' lining the inner surface of the eyeball.

conjure A. kəndʒuə·ɹ constrain by oath or by a sacred invocation XIII; B. kʌ·ndʒəɹ affect or effect by jugglery XVI. – (O)F. *conjurer* to plot, exorcise, adjure = Pr., Sp. *conjurar*, It. *congiurare* :– L. *conjurāre* band together by an oath, conspire, in medL. invoke, f. *com* CON- + *jūrāre* swear, f. *jūr-*, *jūs* right, law (cf. JURY). Hence **conjurer** kʌ·ndʒərəɹ one who conjures spirits XIV; one who practises legerdemain XVIII. Partly – AN. *conjurour*, OF. *conjurere*, *-eor* – medL. *conjurātor*, *-ōrem*; see -ER[1].

conk kɔŋk (sl.) nose. XIX. prob. an application of CONCH.

conkers kɔ·ŋkəɹz children's game played orig. with snail-shells, later with chestnuts on a string. XIX. f. dial. *conker* snail-shell, presumably f. CONCH; assoc. with *conquer*.

connate kɔ·neit existing from birth, congenital; cognate XVII; congenitally united XVIII. – late L. *connātus*, pp. of *connascī*, f. *com* CON- + *nascī* be born (see NATAL).

connect kəne·kt join together XVII; associate XVIII. – L. *connectere* (*cōnectere*), f. *com* CON- + *nectere* bind, fasten (cf. NEXUS). Hence **conne·ct**IVE. XVII; superseding †*connexive* (XVI) – L. *connexīvus*. So **connex**ION, **connec**TION kəne·kʃən joining or linking together XIV (Trev.); causal or logical relation XVII; personal relation, as by family; body of persons related by political or religious bonds XVIII. – L. *connexiō(n-)*, f. *connex-*, *connectere*; cf. (O)F. *connexion*.

conning-tower see CON[2].

connive kənai·v shut one's eyes to, wink *at*. XVII. – F. *conniver* (*à*) – L. *connivēre* (*cōnivēre*) shut the eyes, f. *com* CON- + **nivēre*, rel. to *nictāre* (see NICTITATION). So **conni·v**ANCE. XVI. orig. *connivence* – F. *connivence* or L. *connīventia*; the sp. *-ance* has prevailed since *c.* 1700.

connoisseur kɔnisȫ·ɹ critical judge of matters of taste. XVIII. F., earlier sp. of *connaisseur*, f. *connaiss-*, ppl. stem of *connaître*, f. *cognōscere* ascertain, learn, f. *com* CO- (intensive) + **gnōscere* KNOW.

connote kənou·t imply in addition or as a consequence. XVII. – scholastic L. *connotāre* mark in addition, f. *com* CON- + *notāre* NOTE. So **connot**A·TION. XVI. – medL.

connubial kənjū·biəl pert. to marriage. XVII. – L *connūbiālis*, f. *connūbium* marriage, wedlock, f. *com* CON- + *nūbere* marry; see NUPTIAL and -IAL.

conquer kɔ·ŋkəɹ †win, esp. by fighting; overcome by force. XIII. – OF. *conquerre* = Pr. *conquerre* :– Rom. **conquerere*, for L. *conquīrere* seek for, procure, gain, win (whence It. *conquidere*), f. *com* CON- + *quærere* seek (see QUERY). So **conqueror** kɔ·ŋkərəɹ. XIII (Cursor M.). – AN. *conquerour*, OF. *-eor*, nom. *-ere*, f. *conquerre*; see -OR[1]. **conquest** kɔ·ŋkwest acquisition by force of arms XIII (Cursor M.); (leg.) acquisition otherwise than by inheritance (Sc.) XV (earlier *conquese*). – OF. *conquest* (= Pr. *conquêst*, It. *conquisto*), *conqueste*, mod. *conquête* (= Pr. *conquesta*, Sp., Pg. *conquista*), repr. sb. uses of n. and fem. of Rom. **conquestus*, pp. of **conquerere*.

consanguinity kɔnsæŋgwi·nĭti blood-relationship. XIV (Wyclif). – L. *consanguinitās*, f. *consanguineus* of the same blood, f. *com* CON- + *sanguin-*, *sanguis* blood; see SANGUINE, -ITY.

conscience kɔ·nʃəns moral sense of right and wrong XIII; †consciousness, inmost thought; †conscientiousness XIV. – (O)F. *conscience* = Pr., Sp. *conciencia*, It. *coscienza* – L. *conscientia* privity of knowledge, consciousness, f. *conscīre* know or be privy with (another or oneself); see CON- and SCIENCE. (Superseded ME. *inwit*.) So **conscient**IOUS kɔnʃiə·nʃəs obedient to conscience, scrupulous. XVII. – F. *consciencieux* – medL. *conscientiōsus*. **co·nscion**ABLE kɔ·nʃənəbl conscientious, scrupulous. XVI.

f. †*conscion|s*, var. of *conscience*+-ABLE; cf. †-*conscioned* -conscienced (XVI–XVII), †*conscionless* (XVII). Now familiar in UNCONSCIONABLE. **consci**OUS kɔ·nʃəs †privy *to* a thing with another or within oneself (L. *conscius alicui rei, conscius sibi alicujus rei, de aliqua re*); aware *of*; known to oneself. XVII. f. L. *conscius*, f. *com* CON-+*sci-, base of *scīre* know.

conscript kɔ·nskript enrolled or elected as a senator (L. *patres conscripti* fathers elect) XV; enrolled by compulsory enlistment 1800 (as a sb. after F. *conscrit*). – L. *conscriptus*, pp. of *conscrībere* enrol, f. *com* CON- +*scrībere* write (cf. SCRIPTURE). So **conscri·p**TION †enrolment XIV; compulsory enlistment 1800 (after F. *conscription*, which was introduced in connexion with the law of the French Republic, 5 Sept. 1798, which dealt with this). – late L. Hence by back-formation **conscri·pt** vb. XIX (orig. U.S. 1813).

consecrate kɔ·nsikreit devote to a sacred purpose XV; dedicate XVI; make sacred XVII. f. (after †*consecrate* pp. XIV) L. *consecrāt-*, *-āre*, f. *com* CON- (intensive)+ *sacrāre* dedicate, f. *sacr-*, *sacer* SACRED; see -ATE³. So **consecr**A·TION. XIV (Wyclif, Trevisa). – (O)F. or L.

consecution kɔnsikjū·ʃən logical sequence XVI; succession XVII. – L. *consecūtiō(n-)*, f. *consecūt-*, *-sequī* follow closely; see CONSEQUENCE, and -TION. So **consecut**IVE kənse·kjŭtiv following continuously or successively XVII; (gram.) expressing consequence XIX. – F. *consécutif* – medL. *consecūtīvus*.

consensus kənse·nsəs general agreement, orig. physiol.. (of parts of the body), after Bausner, 'De consensu partium humani corporis', 1556. XIX. – L., f. *consens-*, pp. stem of *consentīre* CONSENT.

consent kənse·nt voluntary agreement or acquiescence XIII; agreement, accord XIV. – OF. *consente*, f. *consentir* (whence **conse·nt** vb. XIII) = Pr., Sp. *consentir*, It. *consentire* – L. *consentīre* agree, accord, f. *com* CON-+*sentīre* feel (see SENSE). ¶ The sb. when spelt *concent* was liable to confusion with *concent* (XVI) harmony, concord – L. *concentus*.

consequence kɔ·nsikwəns thing resulting, logical result XIV; importance, moment (orig. in phr. *of consequence* prop. having issues or results) XVI. – (O)F. *conséquence* – L. *consequentia*, f. *consequent-*, *consequī* follow closely; see SEQUENCE. So **co·nseque**NT resulting XV; earlier in **co·nsequently** (XV), based on L. *consequenter* or F. *conséquemment*. **conseque·nt**IAL. XVII.

conservancy kənsə̄·ɹvənsi control of, (hence) commission controlling, a port, river, etc. XVIII ('The Jurisdiction and Conservancy of the River Thames', R. Griffiths, 1746). Alteration, by assim. to -ANCY, of †*conservacy* (XV–XVIII) – AN. *conservacie* (*pur la conservacie de les ditz graundes rivieres* Act of 9 Henry VI c. 9) – AL. *conservātia* (see -ACY), by-form of L. *conservātiō* CONSERVATION.

conservatoire kɔ̃sɛrvatwār academy for instruction in music, dancing, declamation. (The earliest of these were the It. conservatorios, which originated in hospitals for orphans and foundlings at which a musical education was given.) XVIII. F., – It. *conservatorio* – modL. *conservātōrium*, sb. use of neut. of late L. *conservātōrius*, f. *conservāt-*, *-āre* to preserve, CONSERVE. So **conservat**ORY kənsə̄·ɹvətəri †preservative XVI; †storehouse; greenhouse for tender plants XVII (Evelyn); (U.S.) conservatoire XIX. – late L.

conserve kənsə̄·ɹv preserve safely. XIV (Ch.). – (O)F. *conserver* = Sp. *conservar*, It. *conservare* – L. *conservāre*; see CON- (intensive) and SERVE. So **conse·rve** sb. †preservative XIV (Gower); medicinal or confectionery preparation XVI. – (O)F. *conserve* = It., Sp., medL. *conserva*, f. the vb. **conserv**A·TION preservation in being XIV (Ch.); conservancy XV; *c. of energy*, etc. XIX. – (O)F. or L. **conse·rvat**IVE preservative XIV (Ch.); (in politics) 1830 (J. W. Croker); hence **conse·rvat**ISM 1835.

consider kənsi·dəɹ regard or contemplate attentively, take carefully into account. XIV (Barbour, Ch.) – (O)F. *considérer* = Pr. *cosirar*, Sp. *considerar*, etc., – L. *consīderāre*, f. *com* CON- (intensive)+base **sīder-*, found also in *dēsīderāre* DESIRE. **consi·der**ABLE †that can be considered XV; †that should be considered XVI; worthy of consideration, large in amount, etc. XVII. – medL. *considerābilis*; in F. XVI. **consider**A·TION †contemplation, survey XIV (Ch.); attentive thought XIV (Wycl. Bible); taking into account; thoughtfulness XV; estimation; recompense, equivalent XVI. – (O)F. – L.

consign kənsai·n †attest, confirm XV; †mark with the cross; hand or make over XVI. – F. *consigner* = Pr., Sp. *consegnar*, It. *consegnare* – L. *consignāre* attest with a seal, f. *com* CON- (intensive)+*signāre* SIGN.

consist kənsi·st have a certain existence, be composed *of* or comprised *in* XVI; be congruous with XVII. – L. *consistere* stand still, remain firm, exist, f. *com* CON- (intensive)+*sistere* place, stand firm or still, stop (see STATE). Cf. F. *consister*. So **consi·st**ENCE, -ENCY material coherence or solidity. XVI. – F. *consistance*, †-*ence* (corr. to Pr., Sp. *consistencia*, It. *consistenza*) or late L. *consistentia*. **consi·st**ENT †remaining still XVI; agreeing, esp. self-consistent XVII.

consistory kənsi·stəri †council-chamber; council; (eccl.) bishop's court, papal 'senate' XIV; court of presbyters XVI. – AN. *consistorie* = (O)F. *consistoire*, Pr. *consistori*, It. *consistorio* – late L. *consistōrium*; see CONSIST, -ORY. (The older pronunc. ME. *co·nsistorie* led to a contr. form †*co·nstorie*.) Hence **consisto·r**IAL. XV; after medL.

consolation kɔnsəlei·ʃən comfort in distress. XIV (Ch.). – (O)F. *consolation* – L. *consōlātiō(n)-*, f. *consōlāt-*, *-ārī*. Hence, or through F. *consoler*, **console**[1] kənsou·l XVII (Dryden), repl. †*co·nsolate* XV–XVIII (used by Sh.); see CON- (intensive), SOLACE, -ATION.

console[2] kɔ·nsoul (archit.) kind of bracket XVIII; ensemble of keyboards and stops in an organ XIX. – F. *console*, obscure deriv. of *consolider* CONSOLIDATE.

consolidate kənsɔ·lideit make firm or solid. XVI. f. pp. stem of L. *consolidāre*, f. *com* CON- (intensive)+*solidāre*, f. *solidus* SOLID; see -ATE[3]. So **consolida·tion** in various techn. uses, earliest (*c.* 1400) of the uniting of fractured or wounded parts. – late L.

consols kɔ·nsɔlz, (formerly) kənsɔ·lz. 1770. Short for *consolidated annuities*, the government securities of Great Britain, consisting orig. of a great variety of public securities, which were *consolidated* in 1751 (Act 25 Geo. II, c. 27) into a single stock.

consommé kɔ̃sɔ·mei strong meat soup. XIX (Byron). F., sb. use of pp. of *consommer* – L. *consummāre* CONSUMMATE; the nutriment of the meat is completely used up.

consonant kɔ·nsənənt alphabetic or phonetic element used with a vowel. XIV. – OF. *consonant* – L. *consonant-*, *-āns*, sb. use (sc. *littera* letter) of prp. of *consonāre* sound together (see CON-, SOUND[2]); so named because it can only be 'sounded with' a vowel. So **co·nsonant** adj. in harmony, concordant. XV. **co·nsonance**, XV (Lydg.), -ANCY XIV (Trevisa; rare before XVII). – (O)F. or L.

consort[1] kɔ·nsɔːt †partner, mate XV; ship sailing with another; partner in marriage, spouse. XVII. – F. *consort*, fem. *-sorte* = Sp., It. *consorte* – L. *consort-*, *-sors* sharing in common, partner, colleague, f. *com* CON-+ *sors* portion, lot (see SORT); orig. str. *conso·rt*.

consort[2] kənsɔ̄·ɹt †accompany, escort; associate or accord *with*. XVI (Sh.). In the first sense f. CONSORT[1]; in the second prob. a reinforcement of *sort* vb., which was commonly so used from *c.* 1570 onwards. So †**consort** sb. fellowship; accord; concert of music. XVI. Partly a deriv. of the verb, suggested by L. *consortium* partnership; partly early form of CONCERT.

conspectus kənspe·ktəs general view. XIX. – L. *conspectus*, f. *conspect-*, pp. stem of *conspicere* look attentively, f. *com* CON- (intensive)+*specere* (see ASPECT).

conspicuous kənspi·kjuəs clearly visible. XVI. f. L. *conspicuus*, f. *conspicere*; see prec. and -UOUS.

conspire kənspaiə·ɹ combine privily for unlawful purposes, plot. XIV (PPl., Gower). – (O)F. *conspirer* – L. *conspīrāre* agree, combine, f. *com* CON-+*spīrāre* breathe (see SPIRIT). So **conspiracy** kənspi·rəsi act of conspiring, plot. XIV (Ch.). – AN. *conspiracie*, alteration (cf. *conservacy* s.v. CONSERVANCY) of (O)F. *conspiration* (– L.), whence earlier ME. *conspiration* (XIII, Cursor M.), which was superseded by *conspiracy*. **conspi·rator**. XV. – (O)F. *-eur*.

constable kʌ·nstəbl chief officer of the household, etc. of a sovereign; governor of a royal castle XIII; officer of the peace XIV. ME. – OF. *cunestable*, *conestable* (mod. *connétable*) = Pr. *conestable*, Sp. *condestable*, It. *conestabile*, repr. late L. *comes stabulī* (v) lit. COUNT (i.e. head officer) of the STABLE; for the transition of application to the principal officer of the household and army of the Frankish kings, cf. the development of the senses of *marshal*. So **constabulary** kənstæ·bjŭləri †constable's office or district XVI; body of constables XIX preceded by †*constablery* XV–XVIII. – medL. *constabulāria*.

constant kɔ·nstənt steadfast XIV (Ch.); invariable XVI. – (O)F. *constant* – L. *constant-*, *-āns*, prp. of *constāre* stand firm; cf. COST, STAND, and see -ANT. So **co·nstancy**. XVI. – L. *constantia* (whence F. *constance*).

constantia kənstæ·nʃə wine produced on the *Constantia* farms near Cape Town, South Africa. XVIII.

constellation kɔnstəlei·ʃən †(astrol.) relative position of the stars XIV; (astron.) number of fixed stars artificially grouped together XIV (Trev.). – (O)F. *constellation* – late L. *constellātiō(n)-*, f. *com* CON-+*stella* STAR; see -ATION.

consternation kɔnstəɹnei·ʃən amazement. XVII. – F. *consternation* or L. *consternātiō(n-)*, f. *consternāre* lay prostrate, terrify, f. *com* CON-+*sternere* lay low (cf. STRATUM); see -ATION.

constipate kɔ·nstipeit †pack or bind close together; confine the bowels. XVI. f. pp. stem of L. *constīpāre*, f. CON-+*stīpāre* press, cram (cf. STIPULATE); see -ATE[3]. So **constipa·tion**. XV. – (O)F. or late L. Cf. COSTIVE.

constituent kənsti·tjuənt jointly constituting XVII; constituting or appointing a representative XVIII; having the power to frame a constitution (after F. *assemblée constituante*, 1789) XIX; sb. one who appoints a representative XVII; elector; constituent element XVIII. – (partly through F. *constituant*) L. *constituent-*, *-ēns*, prp. of *constituere*; see next and -ENT. Hence **consti·tuency** body of constituents. XIX (Macaulay).

constitute kɔ·nstitjūt set up, establish XV; make up, form XVI. f. L. *constitūt-*, pp. stem of *constituere* establish, appoint, f. *com* CON- (intensive)+*statuere* set up (see STATUTE). So **constitu·tion** decree, ordinance XIV (Wyclif); nature, disposition XVI; mode or principles of state organization XVII. – (O)F. – L. Hence **constitu·tional** XVII; cf. F. *constitutionnel* (1785). **co·nstitutive** constructive XVI; formative, component XVII; cf. F. *constitutif*.

constrain kənstrei·n force, compel, confine forcibly. XIV (Ch.). – OF. *constraindre*, pres. stem *constraign-* (mod. *contraindre*) = Pr. *costrenher*, It. *costringere* :– L. *constringere* bind tightly together; see CON- and STRINGENT. So **constrai·nt** †affliction XIV (Ch.); compulsion, confinement XVI; restraint of natural feelings XVIII. – OF. *constrainte*, fem. pp. sb. f. *constraindre*.

constriction kənstri·kʃən compression XV; constricted part XIX. – late L. *constrictiō(n-)*, f. *constrict-* (whence **constri·ct** vb. XVIII), pp. stem of *constringere* (whence **constri·nge** vb. XVII); see prec. and -TION. So **constri·ctor** (anat.) constricting muscle XVIII; large snake that crushes its prey (orig. specific name of *Boa* given by Linnæus 1788) XIX. – modL.; see -OR[1].

construct kənstrʌ·kt make by fitting parts together. XVII. f. *construct-*, pp. stem of L. *construere* pile up, build, f. *com* CON- + *struere* (see STRUCTURE). So **constru·ction** A. †construing XIV; interpretation XV; (gram.) syntactical arrangement XVI; B. building XV; mode of building, etc. XVI. – (O)F. – L. (in the gram. sense in Priscian, tr. Gr. *σύνταξις* SYNTAX). **constru·ctive** inferential XVII; pert. to construction XIX; cf. F. *constructif*, late L. *constructīvus*.

construe kɔ·nstru, kənstrū· (gram.) analyse the construction of; expound, interpret. XIV. – L. *construere* CONSTRUCT. In school use regularly *co·nster* (from XVI), which Walker, 1791, calls 'a scandal to our seminaries of learning'.

consubstantiation see TRANSUBSTANTIATION. XVI (Hooker).

consuetudinary kɔnswitjū·dinəri book of customs or usages. XV. – late L., sb. use (sc. *liber* book) of *consuētūdinārius*, f. *consuētūdin-*, *-tūdō* CUSTOM; see -ARY.

consul kɔ·nsəl supreme magistrate in the ancient Roman republic XIV (Wycl. Bible, Gower); applied to various magistrates or chief officials, spec. head of a merchant company resident in a foreign country XV; representative agent of a state in commercial relations with a foreign country XVI. – L. *consul* 'nominatus qui consularet populum et senatum' (Varro), rel. to *consultāre* (see next) and *consilium* COUNSEL. So **co·nsulate.** XIV. – L.; see -ATE[1].

consult kənsʌ·lt take counsel; provide for, take into consideration; seek counsel from. XVII. – (O)F. *consulter* – L. *consultāre*, frequent. f. *consult-*, pp. stem of *consulere* take COUNSEL. So **consulta·tion**. XV. – (O)F. or L.

consume kənsjū·m use up destructively or wastefully. XIV. – (partly through F. *consumer*) L. *consūmere*, f. *com* CON- + *sūmere* take, for **subsemere*, f. *subs-* up + *emere* take (see EMPTION). So **consumption** kənsʌ·mʃən using up, wasting away, spec. by disease. XIV. – (O)F. *consomption* – L. *consumptiō(n-)*, f. *consumpt-*, *consumere*. **consu·mptive**. XV. – medL. *consumptīvus*; cf. (O)F. *consomptif*.

consummate kənsʌ·mət pp. †completed XV; adj. complete, perfect XV. – L. *consummātus*. So **consummate** kɔ·nsəmeit bring to completion. XVI. f. L. *consummāt-*, *-āre*, f. *com* CON- + *summa* SUM, *summus* highest, utmost, supreme; see -ATE[2] and [3]. **consumma·tion** completion, perfection XIV; crowning end XVII (Sh. 'Hamlet' III i 63). – (O)F. *consommation* or L. *consummātiō*.

contact kɔ·ntækt mutual touch. XVII (Bacon). – L. *contāctus*, f. *contāct-*, pp. stem of *contingere* touch closely, border on, be CONTIGUOUS to, f. *com* CON- + *tangere* touch (cf. TANGENT). Cf. F. *contact*.

contadino kɔntədī·nou Italian peasant. XVII. It., f. *contado* COUNTY; cf. -INE[1].

contagion kəntei·dʒən contagious disease, infecting influence XIV (Ch., Trevisa). – L. *contāgiō(n-)*, f. *com* CON- + base of *tangere* touch (cf. TANGENT); cf. F. *contagion* (XVI). So **conta·gious**. XIV (Ch., Trevisa). – late L. *contāgiōsus* (Vegetius).

contain kəntei·n keep within certain limits XIII; have in it, comprise XIV. ME. *conteine*, *-tene* repr. tonic stem of (O)F. *contenir*, corr. to Pr. *contener*, *-ir*, Sp. *contener*, It. *contenere* :– L. *continēre*, f. *com* CON- + *tenēre* hold; cf. the ult. related TEND. ¶ From the same base are *abstain, detain, maintain, obtain, pertain, retain, sustain*; *tenable, tenacious, tenant, tenon, tenor*; *détenu*; *maintenance, sustenance*; *abstinence, continence, continent, pertinent, retinue*; *content, retention, sustentation.* For the diverse sense-development of L. *contin-* see CONTENT[1] and [2], CONTINENCE, CONTINUAL, COUNTENANCE.

contakion kɔntæ·kiən (Gr. Church) hymn or anthem occurring in an office. XIX. – medGr. *kontákion* roll, scroll, liturgical hymn, perh. dim. of *kóntax* shaft (on which a scroll is rolled), f. Gr. *kontós* pole.

contaminate kəntæ·mineit pollute by contact. XV. f. pp. stem of L. *contamināre*, f. *contāmin-*, *-āmen* contact, pollution, for **contagmen*, f. *com* CON- + **tag-*, base of *tangere* touch; see TANGENT and -ATE[3]. So **contamina·tion**. XV. – late L.

contango kəntæ·ŋgou percentage which a buyer of stock pays to the seller to postpone transfer. XIX. perh. arbitrary formation on the analogy of L. 1st pres. sg. in *-ō*, poss. with the notion '(I) make contingent'.

contemn kənte·m treat with contempt. XV. – OF. *contemner* or L. *contemnere*, f. *com* CON- (intensive) + *temnere* despise.

contemplate kɔ·ntəmpleit, (earlier) kənte·mpleit view with attention. XVI. f. L. *contemplāt-*, *-ārī*, f. *com* CON- + *templum* open space for observation, TEMPLE; see -ATE[3]. So **contempla·tion**. XIII (religious meditation). – (O)F. – L. **contemplative**

kənte·mplativ. XIV (*c. life*)(*active life*, repr. the antithesis of L. *vita activa* and *contemplativa*, which depends on Aristotle's distinction of *πρακτικός* and *θεωρητικός*).

contemporary kənte·mpərəri belonging to the same time. XVII. – medL. *contemporārius*, f. *com* CON- + *tempor-*, *tempus* time, after L. *contemporāneus* (whence **contempora·neous** XVII and †*contemporane*, *-anye* XV) and late L. *contemporālis* (whence †*contemporal* XVII). See TEMPORAL and -ARY. The var. form **cote·mporary,** which was of equal date, had equal currency until *c.* 1870.

contempt kənte·mpt act or attitude of despising. XIV (Gower). – L. *contemptus*, f. *contempt-*, pp. stem of *contemnere* CONTEMN. So **conte·mpt**IBLE. XIV. – (O)F. or late L. **conte·mpt**UOUS †contemptible; full of contempt. XVI. – medL. *contemptuōsus*.

contend kənte·nd strive. XV. – OF. *contendre* or L. *contendere*, f. *com* CON- + *tendere* stretch; see TEND[1]. So **conte·n**TION. XIV. – (O)F. *contention* or L. *contentiō*, f. *content-*, pp. stem of *-tendere*. **conte·n**TIOUS. XV. – (O)F. *contentieux* – L. *contentiōsus*.

content[1] kɔ·ntent, kənte·nt (usu. pl.) what is contained XV; containing capacity or extent XV. – medL. **contentum*, pl. *contenta* things contained, sb. use of n. of L. *contentus*, pp. of *continēre* CONTAIN. The second pronunc. is now somewhat old-fashioned and restricted to the pl. *contents*.

content[2] kənte·nt satisfied, gratified. XIV. – (O)F. *content* = Pr. *content*, Sp., It. *contento* :– L. *contentu-s* that is satisfied, pp. of *continēre* fig. repress, restrain (see CONTAIN). So **conte·nt** vb. satisfy, gratify. XV. – (O)F. *contenter* = Pr., Sp. *contentar*, It. *contentare* – Rom. (medL.) *contentāre*, f. *contentus*. **conte·nt**MENT. XV. – F. *contentement*.

content[3] kənte·nt satisfaction. XVI. immed. source obscure; perh. f. prec. as a shorter form equiv. to the earlier †*contentation* (XV) or *contentment* (XV), and corr. to Sp., Pg., It. *contento*.

conterminous kəntə̄·ɹminəs having a boundary in common. XVII. f. L. *conterminus*, f. *com* CON- + *terminus* boundary, TERM; see -OUS.

contest kənte·st †bear witness to XVI; contend for, dispute XVII. – L. *contestārī* call to witness, introduce (a suit) by calling witnesses, set on foot (an action), f. *com* CON- + *testārī* bear witness (cf. TESTAMENT). Hence, or – F. *conteste* (f. the corr. vb.), **co·ntest** sb. wordy strife, (gen.) conflict. XVII.

context kɔ·ntekst †construction, composition XV; connected structure of a composition or passage, parts immediately before and after a given passage XVI. – L. *contextus*, f. *context-*, pp. stem of *contexere* weave together, f. *com* CON- + *texere* weave (see TEXTURE). Hence **conte·xtu**AL[1]. XIX.

contiguous kənti·gjuəs touching, adjoining. XVII. f. L. *contiguus*, f. *contingere*; see CONTACT, CONTAGION, CONTINGENT, and -UOUS. So **contigu·**ITY. XVII. – late L.

continence kɔ·ntinəns (sexual) self-restraint. XIV (R. Rolle). – (O)F. *continence* or L. *continentia*, f. *continent-*, *-ēns*, prp. of *continēre* restrain, CONTAIN, whence **co·ntinent** self-restraining XIV (Wyclif, Trevisa); †cohering, continuous XV (†*continent land*); sb. †container; †summary; continuous land, mainland XVI (spec. of Europe, Asia, etc. XVII); in the last sense *continent* corr. to F. *continent*, It. *continente*, and repr. an ellipt. use of L. *terra continens* continuous land. Hence **contine·nt**AL[1]. XVIII.

contingent kənti·ndʒənt liable to happen XIV; dependent upon or subject to conditions XVI; sb. †accident, possibility XVI; †proportion falling to one; spec. of troops contributed to a force XVIII. – L. *contingent-*, *-ēns*, prp. of *contingere* be CONTIGUOUS, in connexion or in contact, befall, f. *com* CON- + *tangere* touch; see TANGENT. So **conti·ng**ENCY. XVI. – late L.

continual kənti·njuəl always going on XIV; †continuous in space, etc. XVI. – (O)F. *continuel*, f. *continuer*; see next and -AL[1]. So **conti·n**UOUS uninterrupted in space or time. XVII. f. L. *continuus*. **continu·**ITY. XV. – (O)F. – L. **continue** kənti·nju carry on; persist, last. XIV. – (O)F. *continuer* – L. *continuāre* make continuous, (less commonly) be continuous, f. *continuus* uninterrupted, f. *continēre* in its intr. sense of 'hang together' (cf. CONTINENT, the trans. use being repr. by CONTAIN). So **conti·nu**ANCE maintenance, prolongation; continued state, †duration. XIV (Ch.). – OF. **continu**A·TION †persistency XIV; prolongation XV; (pl.) gaiters, trousers XIX. – (O)F. – L. **conti·nuum** -juəm. XVII (Sir T. Browne). n. sg. of L. *continuus*.

conto kɔ·ntou a million reis. XVII. Pg. :– L. *computu-s* COUNT[1].

contort kəntɔ̄·ɹt twist. XV. f. *contort-*, pp. stem of L. *contorquēre*, f. *com* CON- (intensive) + *torquēre* twist; see TORT. So **conto·r**TION. XVII. – L.

contour kɔ·ntuəɹ outline. XVII (Evelyn). – F. *contour* – It. *contorno*, f. *contornare* draw in outline, f. *con-* CON- + *tornare* TURN.

contra kɔ·ntrə against; adv. on or to the contrary XIV; prep., esp. in absol. use in *pro and contra* (abbrev. CON[2]) for a motion, (etc.) and against it XV; sb. the contrary or opposite; now only in *per contra* on the opposite side of the account, as a set-off XVI; orig. an It. banking term. L. *contra* against (adv. and prep.), abl. fem. of a compar. f. *com, cum* with.

contra- kɔ·ntrə repr. L. prefix *contrā-* (see prec.), denoting opposition or the opposite side or direction, which, somewhat rare in classical L., became common in later L. and Rom. (in Sp., Pg., It. *contra-*, in F. *contre-* COUNTER-); see the foll. words. ¶ A L. var. *contrō-* occurs in CONTROVERSY. **b.** In It. terms of music *contra-* denotes a part additional to that denoted by the word with which it is compounded and written below or above it; first in *contrappunto* COUNTERPOINT, and thence transf. to voices, as *contrattenore* COUNTERTENOR, CONTRALTO. Applied to instruments it denotes an octave below the normal or standard, the notes for them being written an octave higher than they sound, e.g. *contrabbasso, contraffagotto.*

contraband kɔ·ntrəbænd illegal traffic; smuggled goods XVI; anything forbidden to be supplied by neutrals to belligerents XVIII; also adj. XVII. The present form was not current before XVII, the earlier forms being †*counterbande* (after F. *contrebande*) and *contrabanda* – Sp. *contrabanda* – It. *contrabando* (now *contrabb-*), f. *contra* (see prec.) and *bando* BAN[1].

contraceptive kɔntrəse·ptiv preventive of uterine conception. XIX. irreg. f. CONTRA- + CON|CEPT*ion* + -IVE. So **contrace·p**TION. XIX. Superseded earlier *anticonception, -tive, contraceptic.*

contract[1] kɔ·ntrækt mutual agreement. XIV. – OF. *contract* (mod. *contrat*) = Pr. *contract*, It. *contratto* – L. *contractu-s*, f. pp. stem of *contrahere*; see next.

contract[2] kəntræ·kt A. agree upon, make a contract; B. incur, be involved in; C. reduce in compass or limits. XVI. Based partly on earlier *contract* pp. (now used only of contracted grammatical forms) – OF. *contract* – L. *contractus*, pp. of *contrahere*, f. *com* CON- + *trahere* draw. So **contra·c**TION (now limited to the notions of decrease and abbreviation). XIV (Trev.). – (O)F. – L. **contra·c**TOR †contracting party XVI; undertaker of a work XVIII. – late L.; see -OR[1].

contradict kɔntrədi·kt †speak in opposition to; declare untrue. XVI. f. *contrādict-*, pp. stem of L. *contrādīcere*, orig. *contrā dīcere* speak against. So **contradi·c**TION. XIV. – (O)F. – L. **contradi·ct**ORY[2] adj. and sb. XIV. – late L. *contrādictōrius*. See CONTRA-, DICTION.

contralto kəntræ·ltou (mus.) part or voice next above the alto. XVIII (earlier *contrealt*). – It., f. CONTRA- b and ALTO; cf. COUNTERTENOR.

contraption kəntræ·pʃən colloq. (ingenious) device. XIX. Of western dial. and U.S. origin; perh. f. *contrive*, vaguely after *deceive/deception*, by assoc. with TRAP[1].

contrapuntal kɔntrəpʌ·ntəl (mus.). pert. to counterpoint. XIX. f. It. *contrappunto* COUNTERPOINT + -AL. So **contrapu·nt**IST. XVIII. – It. *contrappuntista.*

contrary kɔ·ntrəri opposed, opposite; †antagonistic. XIV (R. Rolle). – AN. *contrarie*, (O)F. *contraire* (whence ME., Sc. †*contrair*) = Sp., It. *contrario* – L. *contrāriu-s*, f. *contrā* against, opposite; see CONTRA, -ARY and cf. *adversary.* (*Contrarious* was earlier XIII – OF. *contrarious* – medL. *contrāriōsus.*) Regularly stressed *contra·ry* till XVIII, but this is stigmatized as 'illiterate and vulgar' by Walker, 1791; its use is perpetuated (in the sense of 'perverse, obstinate') dial. and by the nursery rhyme 'Mary, Mary, quite contrary'. So **contrari**ETY kɔntrərai·ĭti. XIV (Ch.). – (O)F. – late L.; *contrariosity* was earlier (R. Rolle). **co·ntrari**WISE. XV; earlier *on the contrary wise* XIV (R. Rolle).

contrast kɔ·ntràst A. †contention XVI; B. (in art) juxtaposition of varied forms, etc., to heighten effect; hence gen. XVIII. – F. *contraste* – It. *contrasto* (corr. to Pr. *contrast*, Sp. *contraste*) strife, opposition, f. *contrastare* withstand, strive :– medL. *contrāstāre*, i.e. *contrā* against, *stāre* STAND. So **contrast** kəntrà·st (in art) set in contrast. XVII (Dryden). – F. *contraster* – It. *contrastare.*

contravallation kɔ:ntrəvælei·ʃən (fortif.) works constructed by besiegers against sorties of the besieged. XVII. – F. *contrevallation* or It. *contravallazione*, f. L. *contrā* CONTRA + *vallātiō(n-)* entrenchment, f. late L. *vallāre* entrench, f. *vallum* rampart; see WALL, -ATION.

contravene kɔntrəvī·n go counter to. XVI. In earliest use Sc. – late L. *contrāvenīre* (Augustine), i.e. *contrā* against, CONTRA + *venīre* COME. Cf. F. *contrevenir.* So **contrave·n**TION. XVI. – (O)F. – medL.

contre-dance, ‖**-danse** kɔ̃·trədɑ̃s country-dance, esp. one of French origin. XIX. – F., alteration of COUNTRY-DANCE, by assoc. with *contre* against, opposite, which was furthered by the fact that in such dances the partners are arranged in two opposite lines; so It. *contraddanza*, Sp. *contradanza.*

contretemps kɔ̃·trətɑ̃ †(fencing) inopportune thrust XVII; inopportune occurrence XIX. F., orig. motion out of time, f. *contre* against, CONTRA- + *temps* (:– L. *tempus*) time.

contribute kəntri·bjūt give or pay jointly XVI; furnish along with others XVII. f. L. *contribūt-*, pp. stem of *contribuere* bring together, f. *com* CON- + *tribuere* bestow (see TRIBUTE). So **contribu·**TION. XIV. – (O)F. or late L. **contri·but**ORY. XV. – medL.

contrite kɔ·ntrəit broken in spirit. XIV. – (O)F. *contrit-e* – L. *contrītus, -a*, pp. of *conterere*, f. *com* CON- + *terere* rub, grind (see TRITE). The pronunc. *contri·te* persisted till XVIII. So **contri**TION kəntri·ʃən. XIII (Cursor M.). – (O)F. – late L.

contrive kəntrəi·v devise, invent XIV; †plot XV; effect XVI. ME. *controve, contreve* – OF. *controver* (with suffix stress), *contreuve* (with stem-stress), modF. *controuver* †imagine – medL. *contropāre* compare, prob. f. L. *com* CON- + *tropus* TROPE. For the ME. variation of vowel cf. †*meve*, MOVE, †*preve*, PROVE, and see RETRIEVE. The transition from *contreve* to *contrive* (XV) is unexpl.; poss. *contrive* was an approximation to Sc. *contrüve* (XV–XVI). Hence **contri·**VANCE. XVII.

control kəntrou·l check (accounts) by comparison with a duplicate register; exercise restraint or sway over. XV. – AN. *contreroller*, F. †*conteroller* (now *contrôler*) – medL. *contrārotulāre*, f. *contrārotulus*, f. *contrā* opposite + *rotulus* ROLL. Hence, or – F. *contrôle*, **contro·l** sb. restraint, check, sway. XVI (Sh.). So **contro·ller,** COMPTROLLER.

controvert kɔntrəvə̄·ɹt make the subject of verbal contention; dispute. XVII. First in pp. and ppl. adj. *controverted*, replacing †*controversed* disputed, called in question – F. *controversé*, for earlier †*controvers* – L. *contrōversus* disputed, questionable, f. *contrō-*, var. of CONTRA- + *versus*, pp. of *vertere* turn (see WORTH[3]). So **controversy** kɔ·ntrəvə̄ɹsi. XIV. – L. *contrōversia* (see -Y[3]); cf. F. †*controversie* (mod. *controverse*). **controve·rs**IAL. XVI. – late L. **controve·rsial**IST. XVIII; for earlier †*controvertist* (XVII).

contumacy kɔ·ntjŭməsi rebellious stubbornness. XIV (Ch.). – L. *contumācia*, f. *contumāc-*, *-āx*, perh. f. *com* CON- (intensive) + *tumēre* swell; see TUMOUR, -ACY. Hence **contum**A·CIOUS. XVI; superseding †*contumace* (XV–XVI), †*contumax* (XIV Ch.–XVII).

contumely kɔ·ntjum(i)lĭ insulting or offensively contemptuous treatment. XIV (Ch.). – OF. *contumelie* – L. *contumēlia*, f. *com* CON- + *tumēre*, as in prec. So **contumel**IOUS -ī·liəs. XV. – (O)F. – L. *contumēliōsus*.

contuse kəntjū·z bruise. XV. f. L. *contūs-*, pp. stem of *contundere*, f. *com* CON- + *tundere* beat, thump, f. *(*s*)*tud-* (cf. STUNT). So **contu·**SION. XIV. – F. or L.

conundrum kənʌ·ndrəm †whim, crotchet XVI; †pun XVII; riddle involving a pun, puzzling statement or question XVIII. In early use also *conimbrum, quinombrum, quonundrum, quadundrum*; of obscure origin, but prob. arising from a university joke based on some L. formula (involving *quoniam* or *quin*) current in the schools.

conurbation kənə̄ɹbei·ʃən urban aggregation. XX. f. CON- + L. *urb-*, *urbs* city (cf. URBAN) + -ATION.

convalesce kɔnvəle·s regain health. XV (Caxton; not in regular use before XIX). – L. *convalēscere*, f. *com* CON- (intensive) + *valēscere* grow strong, f. *valēre* be strong or well (cf. VALOUR). So **convale·sc**ENCE. XV (Caxton). – F. or late L.; hence **convale·sc**ENT. XVII.

convection kənve·kʃən (physics) transportation of heat or electricity. XIX (a casual instance of *conuexion* occurs XVII). – late L. *convectiō(n-)*, f. *convect-*, pp. stem of *convehere*, f. *com* CON- + *vehere* carry (see WAY).

convenance kɔ̃·vənãs pl. conventional proprieties. XIX. F., f. *convenir* be fitting, refash. of OF. *covenir* :– L. *convenīre*; see next and -ANCE.

convene kənvī·n come together XV; call together XVI; †agree XVI. – L. *convenīre* assemble, be fitting, agree, suit, f. *com* CON- + *venīre* COME. So **conve·ni**ENT †accordant, befitting, suitable XIV (Ch.); personally fitting, commodious XV. – L. *convenient-*, *-ēns*, pp. of *convenīre*. **conve·ni**ENCE. XV. – L. *convenientia*. **conven**TION kənve·nʃən A. †assembling XV; formal assembly XV; B. agreement, covenant XV; general agreement or consent; conventional usage XVIII. – (O)F. *convention* – L. *conventiō(n-)* meeting, covenant. **conve·ntion**AL. XV. – F. *conventionnel* or late L. *conventiōnālis*.

convent kɔ·nvənt company of religious persons living together XIII (since XVIII often restricted to nunneries); building housing this XVI. ME. *covent* (surviving in the name *Covent* Garden, London) – AN. *covent*, OF. *convent* (regularly with latinized sp., which finally prevailed in Eng.), mod. *couvent* = Pr. *coven*, (Sp., It. *convento*) :– L. *conventu-s* assembly, company, f. *convent-*, pp. stem of *convenīre* CONVENE. So **conventu**AL kənve·ntjuəl. XV (Wyntoun). – medL. *conventuālis*; cf. (O)F. *conventuel*.

conventicle kənve·ntikl †meeting, assembly, esp. of a clandestine or illegal kind, at first political, later religious XIV; meeting or meeting-place of Protestant Dissenters XVI. – L. *conventiculum* assembly, place of assembly, in form dim. of *conventus* meeting (see CONVENT), but not used with derogatory reference till medieval times, though the transitional diminutive sense appears in 'conventicula hereticorum non ecclesia sed conciliabula appellantur' (Fourth Council of Carthage, A.D. 254). In early use stressed on the first and third sylls., and so in Bailey's Dict. 1730–6, but *conve·nticle* was established before 1800 (cf. Cowper 'Task' ii 437 'Heard at conve·nticle', which was altered 1787 from 'At co·nventicle heard').

converge kənvə̄·ɹdʒ tend to one point. XVII. – late L. *convergere*; see CON- and VERGE[2]. Hence **conve·rg**ENT. XVIII.

conversation kɔnvəɹsei·ʃən †living, mode of living XIV (cf. A.V., Ps. l 23, Phil. iii 20); sexual intercourse XVI (surviving in *criminal conversation*, abbrev. *crim. con.*); familiar discourse XVI; †acquaintance; †company XVII. – (O)F. *conversation* = It. *conversazione*, etc. – L. *conversātiō(n-)* frequent use or abode, intercourse, f. *conversārī* CONVERSE[1]; see -ATION. Hence **conversa·tion**AL. XVIII. So **convers**ANT kɔ·nvəɹsənt †dwelling habitually; associating familiarly *with*; †occupied *in* XIV; exercised or versed *in*, familiar *with* XVI. – prp. of (O)F. *converser* CONVERSE[1].

conversazione kɔ:nvəɹsætsiou·ni assembly for conversation and social or intellectual recreation, orig. in Italy. XVIII (Gray). – It. (CONVERSATION). Anglicized as *conversation* by Walpole and Johnson.

converse[1] kənvə̄·ɹs †dwell, live XIV; †associate familiarly, have to do *with* XVI; talk *with* XVII. – (O)F. *converser* †pass one's life, exchange words = Pr., Sp. *conversar*, It. *conversare* :– L. *conversārī* live, have intercourse, middle use of *conversāre* turn round, f. CON- + *versāre*, frequent. of *vertere* turn (see WORTH[3]). Hence **co·nverse** sb. †intercourse; conversation; communion. XVII.

converse[2] kɔ·nvə̄ɹs proposition or relation turned round or upside down. XVI (math.). – L. *conversus*, pp. of *convertere* CONVERT.

convert kənvə̄·ɹt turn or change *into*. XIII (Cursor M.; with ref. to religious faith). – (O)F. *convertir* = Pr., Sp. *convertir*, It. *convertire* :– Rom. **convertīre*, for L. *convertere* turn about, transform, f. *com* CON- + *vertere* turn (see WORTH[3]). Hence **convert** kɔ·nvə̄ɹt sb. converted person. XVI; superseding and perh. suggested by syn. †*converse* (XIV) – (O)F. *convers* – L. *conversus*, pp. used sb. †**co·nvertite.** XVI; after F. *converti*, sb. use of pp.; see -ITE[1]. So **conve·rt**IBLE. XIV (Ch.). – (O)F. – L. **conve·r**SION. XIV (earliest in religious application, R. Rolle). – (O)F. – L.

convex kɔ·nveks curved like the outside of a circle)(*concave.* XVI. – L. *convexus* vaulted, arched, to be connected with *dēvexus* steep, *subvexus* sloping upwards, and prob. referred to *vehere* carry (see VEHICLE), as if lit. 'drawn together to a point' (cf. CONVECTION).

convey kənvei· †escort XIII (Cursor M.); †guide, conduct; transport; communicate XIV; transfer; steal XV. – OF. *conveier* (mod. *convoyer* CONVOY) = Pr. *conviar*, It. *conviare* accompany :– medL. *conviāre*, f. L. *com* CON- + *via* way. (Formerly often †*conveigh* by assoc. with unrelated L. *convehere.*) Hence **convey·**ANCE. XVI.

convict kənvi·kt prove guilty XIV (Ch., Wyclif); bring error home to; †convince XVIII. f. *convict-*, pp. stem of L. *convincere* CONVINCE; the pp. *convictus* was adopted earlier as *convi·ct* (also in AN.) pronounced or proved guilty, whence, with shift of stress, **convict** kɔ·nvikt sb. †convicted person XVI; condemned criminal XVIII.

convince kənvi·ns †overcome in argument; †convict; †prove XVI; bring to a belief XVII. – L. *convincere* convict of error, refute, prove clearly (guilt, etc.), f. *com* CON- (intensive) + *vincere* overcome (see VICTORY).

convivial kənvi·viəl of a feast, festive XVII. – L. *convīviālis*, f. *convīvium* feast, f. *com* CON- + stem of *vīvere* live; see QUICK, VIVID, -IAL.

convocation kɔnvəkei·ʃən assembly of persons, spec. for legislation, etc. XIV. – L. *convocātiō(n-)*, f. *convocāre*, whence **convoke** kənvou·k call together XVI; see CON-, VOCATION.

convolution kɔnvəl^j^ū·ʃən coiling, twisting. XVI. – medL. *convolūtiō(n-)*, f. pp. stem of *convolvere*, f. *com* CON- + *volvere* roll; see VOLUTE, -TION. So **convolvulus** kənvɔ·lvjŭləs. XVI. – L., 'bindweed' (Pliny).

convoy kənvoi· accompany, escort XIV (in early use Sc.); †convey, conduct XV. – (O)F. *convoyer*, var. and mod. form of *conveier* CONVEY. So **convoy** sb. kɔ·nvoi. XVI. – (O)F. *convoi*, f. the vb.

convulse kənvʌ·ls affect with violent shaking or agitation. XVII. f. *convuls-*, pp. stem of L. *convellere* pull violently, wrest, wrench, f. *com* CON- + *vellere* pluck, pull. So **convu·l**SION. XVI. – F. or L. (in medical use, 'cramp').

cony, coney kou·ni, kʌ·ni rabbit and its skin. XIII. Earliest forms *cunin*, *cuning*, *conyng*, repr. later by *cunning* (XVI Sc.), – AN. *coning*, OF. *conin* (whence Du. *konijn*, LG. *kanīn*, whence G. *kaninchen*), parallel form to OF. *conil* = Pr. *conil*, It. *coneglio*, Sp. *conejo*, Pg. *conelho* :– L. *cunīculu-s*, prob. of Iberian origin, since the rabbit became known to the Romans through the Spaniards. The form *cony* (XIV) is a back-formation from pl. *conyes* – AN. *con(i)ys*, pl. of *conil*. The pronunc. kʌ·ni is traditional, as in *honey*, *money*; kou·ni was introduced in XIX as the pronunc. 'proper for solemn reading' (Smart, 1836), the word remaining gen. familiar only from its occurrence in the Bible (see esp. Ps. civ. 18), where it translates a name of the hyrax. The earliest sense recorded in Eng. is 'skin or fur of rabbit'. In the cant sense of 'dupe' familiar XVI–XVII in *cony-catcher* cheat, swindler, *cony-catching*.

coo kū characteristic note of doves and pigeons. XVII (Dryden). imit.

cooee, cooey kū·i call used as a long-distance signal, orig. by Australian aborigines. XIX. (A vocabulary of 1790 has *cow-ee* come.)

cook kuk preparer of food by boiling, etc. OE. *cōc* – popL. *cōcus*, for L. *coquus*, which is directly repr., with short vowel, by OS. *kok* (Du. *kok*), OHG. *choh* (G. *koch*), Icel. *kokkr*. The IE. base of L. *coquus* is **quequo-* :– **pekwo-* (as in Gr. *péssein* ripen, boil, cook; see also PEPTIC and cf. OSl. *peką* I bake, roast, Skr. *páčati* cook, bake). Hence **cook** vb. XIV, which has parallels in other Germ. langs. **coo·k**ERY. XIV.

cookie ku·ki (Sc.) bun, (U.S.) small cake. XVIII. – Du. *koekje*, dim. of *koek* cake.

cool kūl moderately cold. OE. *cōl* = MLG., MDu. *kōl* (Du. *koel*) :- Germ. **kōluz*, f. **kōl-* **kal-* (see COLD); as sb. from XIV. (HG. has forms derived from a *-ja*-stem, OHG. *kuoli*, G. *kühl*.) Hence **cool** vb. OE. *cōlian* = OS. *cōlōn* :- Germ. **kōlōjan*, f. **kōluz*, from which also Germ. **kōljan* (OE. *cēlan* KEEL[2]). Hence **cool**TH[1] kūlþ (chiefly joc.) coolness XVI.

coolie, cooly kū·li hired native labourer (prop.) in India and China. XVII. Of uncertain origin; Urdu *qulī*, Bengali, etc., *kūlī*, perh. to be identified with the name *Kulī*, *Kolī* of an aboriginal tribe of Gujerat, India (in XVI *Colles*), the name being prob. conveyed by the Portuguese to S. India and China; the formal correspondence of Tamil *kūli* hire is prob. accidental.

coomb, combe kūm deep hollow, valley. OE. *cumb*, not found in OE. or ME. literature, but occurring from early times in charter place-names belonging to the south of England, many of which survive, e.g. *Batcombe*, *Salcombe*. Its present gen. use goes back to XVI.

coon kūn (U.S.) raccoon XVIII; fellow; negro XIX. Aphetic of RACCOON.

coop kūp †basket XIII; cage for poultry XV; place of confinement XVI. – MLG., MDu. *kūpe* (Du. *kuip* tub, vat), parallel with OS. *kōpa*, OHG. *kuofa* (G. *kufe*) cask – L. *cūpa*, also medL. *cōpa* tun, barrel. The forms and phonology (cf. *coupe* XIV–XVII) present the same features as *cooper*, *droop*, *stoop*. Hence vb. XVI.

cooper kū·pəɹ one who makes and repairs vessels formed with staves and hoops. XIV (earlier as a personal designation passing into a surname XIII; cf. AL. *cūperius* XIII). – MDu., MLG. *kūper*, f. *kūpe* COOP; see -ER[1]. For the phonology cf. COOP. ¶ An obs. sp. is preserved in the surname *Cowper*, pronounced like *Cooper* by those who bear it.

co-operate kouɔ·pəreit work together. XVII. f. pp. stem of late L. *cooperārī*, f. *com* CO-+ *operārī* work, OPERATE. So **co-opera**TION. XIV. – L., partly, in later use, through F. *coopération*. **co-o·perat**IVE. XVII. **co-o·per**ATOR. XV. – late L. (Vulg.).

co-opt kouɔ·pt elect as a colleague. XVII. – L. *cooptāre*, f. *com* CO-+*optāre* choose (see OPTION). So **co-o·ptate.** XVII. f. pp. stem of L. *cooptāre*. **co-opt**A·TION. XVI. – L.

co-ordinate kouɔ̄·ɹdinət of equal rank XVII; sb. (math.) each of two or more magnitudes used to define the position of other magnitudes XIX. f. CO-+L. *ordinātus*, pp. of *ordināre* arrange, ORDAIN, after the earlier SUBORDINATE. So **co-o·rdinate** -eit vb. XVII; cf. medL. *coordināre* ordain together, F. *coördonner*. **co-ordin**A·TION. XVII. – F. or late L.

coot kūt the bird Fulica atra, having a white spot on the head; formerly more widely used. XIV. ME. *cote*, *coote* (first in *balled cote* 'bald coot'), prob. of LG. origin (cf. Du. *koet* :- **kōte*).

cop kɔp (sl.) catch, capture. XVIII. Of north. dial. origin; prob. var. of *cap* arrest, seize (XVI) – OF. *caper* seize – L. *capere* take (see CAPTURE). Hence **cop** and **co·pper** (-ER[1]) policeman. XIX.

copaiba, -aiva kopai·bə, -ei·bə, -ai·və. a S. American balsam. XVIII. – Sp., Pg. *copaiba* – Guarani *cupauba*.

copal kou·pəl resin yielding varnish. XVI. – Sp. *copal* – Aztec *copalli* incense.

coparcener koupā·ɹsənəɹ co-heir(ess). XV. f. CO-+PARCENER. Also **copa·rcen**ARY, -ERY, **-pa·rceny** joint-heirship or -ownership; see -Y[3]. **co-**PA·RTNER. All XVI.

cope[1] koup long cloak or cape (esp. eccl.) XIII; 'canopy' or 'vault' of night, heaven XIV; outer mould in founding XIX. Early ME. *cāpe*, repr. OE. *cāp* (in *cantelcāp*) and **cāpe* = ON. *kápa* (Da. *kaabe*), – medL. *cāpa*, var. of *cappa* whence F. *chape*, Pr. *capa*, It. *cappa*; cf. CAP, CHAPEL, CHAPERON. Hence **cope-**STONE top stone of a building. XVI (Sc. *kaip-*, *cape stone*); whence prob. **cope** vb. cover (a wall) with a head stone XVII; **co·ping** kou·piŋ uppermost course of masonry or brickwork XVII; see -ING[1].

cope[2] koup †come to blows (*with*) XIV; meet or contend *with* XVI. – OF. *coper*, var. of *colper* (mod. *couper*) strike, (now) cut, f. *cop*, *colp* (mod. *coup*) blow :- Rom **colpu-s* :- L. *colaphus* – Gr. *kólaphos* blow with the fist, box on the ear.

cope[3] koup †buy XV (Lydg.); exchange, barter XVI. – MDu., (M)LG. *kōpen* (Du. *koopen*) = G. *kaufen*; see CHEAP. Hence **co·per**[1] dealer, esp. in *horse-coper* XVI; see -ER[1].

copeck kou·pek Russian coin. XVII. – Russ. *kopéjka*, dim. of *kopjë* lance (OSl. *kopije*, rel. to Gr. *kóptein*; cf. COMMA); so named from the substitution in 1535 of the figure of Ivan IV on horseback with a lance for that of his predecessor with a sword.

coper[2] kou·pəɹ (sl.) floating grog-shop for North Sea fishermen. XIX. – Du., Flem. *kooper* trader, dealer, f. *koopen* buy (see CHEAP).

Copernican koupə̄·ɹnikən. XVII. f. *Copernicus*, latinized form of Nicolas *Koppernik*, name of the founder of modern astronomical theory, a native of Thorn in Prussian Poland (d. 1543); see -AN.

copious kou·piəs †plentifully furnished; abundant. XIV. –(O)F. *copieux* or L. *cōpiōsus*, f. *cōpia* abundance, f. *com* CO-+*ops* wealth, OPULENCE)(*inopia* want; see -IOUS.

copper[1] kɔ·pəɹ metal distinguished by its peculiar red colour OE.; vessel made of this XVII; copper money XVIII. OE. *copor, coper,* corr. to MDu. *coper* (Du. *koper*), ON. *koparr* :- **kupar*, of which the var. **kuppar* gave MLG. *kopper*, OHG. *chuphar, kupfar* (G. *kupfer*) – late L. *cuprum* (Edict of Diocletian, 301), for L. *cyprium*, in full *cyprium æs* 'metal of Cyprus', so named from its most noted ancient source. ¶ Cf. OF. *cuevre*, Pr. *coure*, Sp., Pg. *cobre* :- Rom. **coprum*, late L. *cuprum*, and (O)F. *cuivre* :- Rom. **copreum*, sb. use of n. of L. *cupreus* of copper.

copper[2] see COP.

copperas kɔ·pərəs sulphate of copper, iron, or zinc; vitriol. XIV (*coperose*). – (O)F. *couperose*, corr. to It. *copparosa* – medL. *cup(e)rosa*, perh. orig. **aqua cuprosa* 'copper-water', but later assoc. with *rosa* rose, after Gr. *khálkanthon* vitriol, lit. 'flower of brass' (cf. Du. †*koperroose* and *koperwater*, G. †*kupferrose* and *kupferwasser*). Obscuration of the final syll. appears in XVI.

copper-nose kɔ·pəɹnouz red nose caused by drink, etc. XVI (implied in *copper-nosed*). perh. alteration of F. *couperose* (Paré) COPPERAS, after COPPER and NOSE; cf. G. *kupfernase*.

coppice kɔ·pis thicket of underwood and small trees. XIV (*copeys, copys*). – OF. *copeïz* :- Rom. **colpāticium* (for the suffix cf. CHASSIS, GLACIS), f. **colpāt-*, pp. stem of **colpāre* cut (F. *couper*), f. medL. *colpus* earlier *colapus* (Salic and Alemannic laws), for L. *colaphus* blow with the fist – Gr. *kólaphos* blow, buffet. As a result of the final syll. being regarded as the pl. ending, a new sg. *cop(p)y* arose, which survives dial.; an independent contr. form is †*cop(p)s*, COPSE.

copra kɔ·prə dried kernel of the coco-nut. XVI. – Pg. (and Sp.) *copra* – Malayalam *koppara* coco-nut.

coprolite kɔ·prəlait fossil resembling petrified excrement. XIX (Buckland). f. Gr. *kópros* dung; see -LITE.

copse, contr. of *coppis*, COPPICE. XVI.

Copt kɔpt native Egyptian (Jacobite) Christian. XVII. – F. *Copte* or modL. *Coptus*, also *Cophtus* – Arab. *Quft*, *Qubt* (coll.) Copts – Coptic *Gyptios* – Gr. *Aigúptios* EGYPTIAN. Hence **Co·ptic**. XVII. – modL. *Copticus*.

copula kɔ·pjŭlə (gram.) part of a proposition connecting subject and predicate, spec. the verb 'to be'; connexion. XVII. – L. *cōpula* tie, connexion, linking of words, f. *com* CO- + *apere* fasten; see APT, -ULE, and cf. COUPLE. So **co·pulate** †couple; unite sexually. XVII. f. pp. stem of L. *cōpulāre*, f. *cōpula*; see -ATE[3]. **copula·tion**. XIV. – (O)F. – L.

copy kɔ·pi transcript of an original XIV; individual specimen of a work; exemplar; matter prepared for printing (Caxton) XV. (The etymol. sense of 'abundance' occurs XIV–XVII.) – (O)F. *copie* = Pr., Sp., It. *copia* – L. *cōpia* abundance, plenty, pl. forces, ability, opportunity, means (see COPIOUS). The sense 'transcript', which is medL. and Rom., arose from such phr. as *copiam describendi facere* give permission to transcribe, whence the sense 'right of reproduction' and simply 'reproduction'. Hence **co·py**HOLD holding of lands by copy of the manorial court roll XV. **co·py**RIGHT right to print, publish, and sell copies of a work of literature or of art XVIII.

coquelicot kɔ·klikou colour of the red poppy. XVIII. – F. *coquelicot* (in OF. 'cock'), imit. formation on the cock's crow; the flower was so named from comparison with the red cock's comb.

coquette kouke·t girl or woman who trifles with a man's affections. XVII. – F., fem. of *coquet* gallant, amorously forward, f. *coqueter* flirt, prop. strut or show off like a cock before hens, f. *coq* COCK[1].

cor- assim. form of *com* CON- before *r*.

coracle kɔ·rəkl small wickerwork boat. XVI (*corougle*). – W. *corwgl, cwrwgl*, f. *corwc* coracle, †carcass (= Ir., Gael. *curach* CURRACH).

coracoid kɔ·rəkoid beaked like a crow. XVIII. – modL. *coracoīdēs* – Gr. *korakoeidḗs*, f. *korak-*, *kórax* raven, crow, ult. of imit. origin; see -OID. *Coraco-* is used as a comb. form.

coral kɔ·rəl calcareous substance secreted by marine polyps. XIV. – OF. *coral* (mod. *corail*) = Pr. *coralh*, Sp. *coral*, It. *corallo* :- L. *corallum, -alium* – Gr. *korállion, kourálion*, prob. of Semitic origin. So **co·ralline** genus of seaweeds once supposed to be of the nature of coral XVI; plant-like animal such as the Polyzoa XVIII. – It. *corallina*, f. *corallo*; adj. XVII. – F. *corallin, -e* or L. *corallinus*; see -INE[1].

coram kō·rəm L. prep. *cōram* (f. *com* CO- + *ōr-*, *ōs* face) in the presence of, used in legal and other phr., as *coram judice* before a judge, *coram publico* in public; as a sb. in colloq. phr. †*under coram* under discipline or correction. XVI. ¶ Misused for *quorum* in Sh. 'Merry Wives' I i 6, and in early Sc.

coranto koræ·ntou (hist.) dance in triple time. XVI (*couranto*). Alteration, by addition of an It. termination, of F. *courante* (sc. *danse* dance) 'running dance', prp. fem. of *courir* run (cf. CURRENT).

corban kō·ɹbæn offering given to God. XIV. – Vulgate L. – N.T. Gr. *korbân* – Heb. *qorbān* offering, f. *qārab* approach.

corbel kɔ̄·ɹbəl (archit.) projection jutting from a wall to support a weight. XV. – OF. *corbel* (mod. *corbeau*) raven, also archit., dim. of †*corp* :– L. *corvu-s* raven (cf. ROOK[1]). ¶ Chaucer has a var. *corbet*.

corbie kɔ̄·ɹbi (Sc.) raven. XV (Wyntoun, Henryson). – OF. *corb* (see prec.) + -IE, -Y[6].

cord kɔ̄ɹd string XIII (Cursor M.); cord-like structure, as in the body XV; measure of cut wood XVII. – (O)F. *corde* (vocal cords) = Pr., It., Pg. *corda*, Sp. *cuerda* :– L. *chorda* – Gr. *khordḗ* (see CHORD). With the third sense cf. the use in OIt., F., and Pr. for a superficial and cubic measure. Hence **co·rd**AGE. XVI; after F.

Cordelier kɔ̄ɹdəliə·ɹ Franciscan of the strict rule. XIV. – (O)F. *Cordelier*, f. †*cordele*, dim. of *corde* CORD; so named from their rope girdle.

cordial kɔ̄·ɹdiəl pert. to the heart XIV; stimulating to the heart; hearty XV; sb. XIV (Ch.). – medL. *cordiālis*, f. *cord-*, *cor* HEART; so F. (XV); see -IAL. Hence **cordia·l**ITY. XVII; cf. F. *cordialité*.

cordillera kɔ̄ɹdiljɛə·rə mountain chain or ridge. XVIII. Sp., f. *cordilla*, dim. of *cuerda* CORD, string, chain.

cordite kɔ̄·ɹdait smokeless explosive, so called from its cord-like appearance; introduced in 1889. f. CORD + -ITE.

cordon kɔ̄·ɹdən projecting course of stones XVI; line of military posts or police XVIII. – It. *cordone*, augm. of *corda* CORD; superseded by F. *cordon* (dim.).

cordovan kɔ̄·ɹdəvən Cordova leather. XVI. – Sp. *cordován* (now *-bán*); see CORDWAINER.

corduroy, corderoy kɔ̄·ɹdəroi, -djŭroi coarse thick-ribbed stuff. XVIII. prob. f. CORD (pl. *cords* is applied to a ribbed fabric in Woostenholme's patent, 1776) + †*duroy*, †*deroy* (XVII) coarse West-of-England woollen stuff, of unkn. origin; spelt *cord de roy*, *corde du roy* and interpreted as 'king's cords' in some books of XIX. There is no evidence to confirm the suggestion that it is an alteration of †*colour de* or *du roy* 'king's colour' (orig.) purple, (later) tawny, or to connect it with the surname *Corderoy*.

cordwainer kɔ̄·ɹdweinəɹ shoemaker, orig. maker of Cordovan leather. XI. – AN. *cordewaner*, OF. *cordoanier* (mod. *cordonnier*), f. *cordewan*, *cordoan* (whence ME. *cordewane*, mod. *cordwain* Spanish leather), f. *Cordoue* – Sp. *Cordoba*, †*Cordova* :– L. *Corduba* town in Spain where a goatskin (later, horsehide) leather was made. The Sp. adj. †*cordovano* and sb. †*cordován* were adopted in Eng. as CORDOVAN. The F. word passed also into It. and the Germ. langs.

core kɔ̄əɹ horny seed-capsule of apple, etc. XIV; unburnt centre of coal XV; hard centre of a boil XVI; central or innermost part XVII. ME. *core*, *coore*, of unkn. origin; poss. – (O)F. *cor* horn, CORN[2], but the orig. final *-e* is a difficulty; superseded earlier *colk* (see COKE); cf. the blended form †*corke* (XV).

corf kɔ̄ɹf basket, (later) spec. in mining. XIV. – (M)LG., (M)Du. *korf* = OHG. *chorp* (G. *korb*) – L. *corbis*; reintroduced in XVII by continental miners.

coriaceous kɔriei·ʃəs leathery. XVII. f. late L. *coriāceus*, f. *corium* skin, hide, leather; see -ACEOUS.

coriander kɔriæ·ndəɹ the plant Coriandrum sativum. XIV. – (O)F. *coriandre* – L. *coriandrum* – Gr. *koríannon*. ¶ From L. are also OE. *cellendre*, OHG. *chulluntar*, and OF. *coliandre*, whence ME. †*coliandre*.

cork kɔ̄ɹk bark of the tree Quercus Suber, the cork-oak XIV (*corktre* 'suberies', *corkbarke* 'cortex', Promp. Parv.); †cork sole or sandal XIV; stopper, prop. of cork XVI. prob. – Du., LG. *kork* (whence G. *kork*) – Sp. *alcorque* cork sole or shoe, perh. of Arab. origin (*al* is the def. article; cf. *alcornoque* cork-tree); the orig. application may have been to the cork-shoe, and transference to the material later (cf. earlier G. name for cork, *pantoffelholz* 'slipper-wood'). Hence **cork** vb. †furnish with a cork sole XVI; stop with a cork XVII; whence **co·rker** (sl.) something decisive, 'settler' (orig. U.S.) XIX; see -ER[1].

cormorant kɔ̄·ɹmərənt large voracious sea-bird, Phalacrocorax carbo. XIII (*cormerant*, *cormaraunt*). – OF. *cormaran* (mod. *cormoran*), earlier *cormareng*, for **corp mareng*, repr. (with assim. of adj. suffix to Germ. *-ing*) medL. *corvus marīnus* (VIII) 'sea raven', whence Pr. *corpmari(n)*, Pg. *corvo marinho*. For the final parasitic *t* cf. *pageant*, *parchment*, *peasant*, *pennant*, *pheasant*, *truant*, *tyrant*, *varmint*.

corn[1] kɔ̄ɹn grain, seed, fruit of a cereal. OE. *corn* = OFris., OS., OHG., ON. *korn*, Goth. *kaurn* :– CGerm. **kurnam* :– IE. **gṛnóm* 'worn-down particle', n. pp. of base **gṛ-*, **ger-* wear away, grow old, whence also L. *grānum* GRAIN, OIr. *grān*, OSl. *zrŭno* seed, Gr. *graûs* old woman, *gérōn* old man, Skr. *jīryati* wastes away, *jīrṇás* wasted, old; cf. KERNEL. Hence **corn** vb. †make or become granular; sprinkle with salt in grains, preserve with salt (as *corned beef*). XVI. **co·rn**CRAKE landrail, Crex pratensis. XV.

corn[2] kɔ̄ɹn horny hardening of the skin. XV. – AN. *corn* = (O)F. *cor* :– L. *cornū* HORN.

cornea kɔ̄·ɹniə (anat.) horny covering of the eyeball. XIV. modL., short for medL. *cornea tēla* or *tunica* horny tissue or coating; fem. of *corneus* (whence **co·rneous** XVII), f. *cornū* HORN.

cornel kɔ̄·ɹnəl tree of the genus Cornus. XVI (Turner). orig. in *cornel berry, cornel tree*, semi-tr. of G. *kornelbeere, kornelbaum* (OHG. *kornulberi, -boum*, the source of which is some medL. deriv. of L. *cornus* cornel tree = Gr. *krános*). ¶ OE. had *corntrēow*.

cornelian kɔ̄ɹnī·liən red or reddish variety of chalcedony. XIV (*corneline*). – OF. *corneline* (mod. *cornaline*), corr. to Pr. *cornelina*, Sp. *cornerina*, It. *cornalina*; refash. after medL. *cornelius*, var. of *corneolus*.

corner kɔ̄·ɹnəɹ projecting or hollow angle. XIII (Cursor M.). – AN *corner*, OF. *cornier* :– Rom. **cornārium*, f. L. *cornum, cornū* HORN, point, end; see -ER[2] 2. Hence **corner** vb. furnish with, place in, a corner XIV; (orig. U.S.) drive into a corner XIX. **corner-stone.** XIII (Cursor M.); after L. *lapis angularis* (Vulg., e.g. Job xxxviii 6, Eph. ii 20).

cornet[1] kɔ̄·ɹnit wind-instrument (now, the cornet à piston) XIV; conical twisted paper, and other transf. uses XVI. – (O)F. *cornet* = Pr. *cornet*, It. *cornetto*, dim. of Rom. **corno*, L. *cornum, cornū* HORN; see -ET.

cornet[2] kɔ̄·ɹnit woman's head-dress with horns or lappets; †cavalry standard, orig. with a pointed pennon; †company of cavalry; officer in this. XVI. – (O)F. *cornette*, dim. of *corne* horn (= Pr., Pg., It. *corna* antlers, Sp. *cuerna*) orig. coll. :– Rom. **corna*, for L. *cornua*, pl. of *cornū* HORN; see -ET.

cornice kɔ̄·ɹnis horizontal moulded projection on a building, etc. XVI (*cornish*). – F. *corniche*, †*-ice*, †*-isse* – It. *cornice*, perh. – L. *cornic-, cornix* crow (cf. the origin of CORBEL), but with blending of a deriv. of Gr. *korōnís* coping-stone.

Cornish kɔ̄·ɹniʃ pert. to Cornwall. XV (Boorde). f. first el. of *Cornwall*, OE. *Cornwēalas*, f. OCeltic **Kornovjos, -ja*, whence medL. *Cornubia* Cornwall; see WELSH, -ISH[1]. The native name was *Kernūak, Kernewec*, f. *Kernóu* (cf. W. *Cernyw* Cornwall, *Cernywaidd* Cornish (adj.), *Cernyweg* (sb.), and Breton *Kernéō* the district of Cornouailles in Brittany).

cornopean kɔ̄ɹnou·piən cornet à piston. XIX. Obscurely f. CORNET[1].

cornucopia kɔ̄ɹnjukou·piə (myth.) goat's horn overflowing with fruits, etc. XVI. – late L. *cornūcōpia*, earlier *cornū cōpiæ* 'horn of plenty', the horn of the goat Amalthæa placed in heaven, emblem of fruitfulness and abundance.

corolla kərɔ·lə †little crown, garland XVII; (bot.) whorl of petals XVIII. – L. *corolla*, used bot. by Linnæus, dim. of *corōna* CROWN. ¶ Called by Grew *foliation*.

corollary kərɔ·ləri (geom.) proposition appended to another as a self-evident inference XIV (Ch.); immediate deduction or consequence XVII. – L. *corollārium* money paid for a garland, present, gratuity, deduction (Boethius), f. *corolla*; see prec. and -ARY. ¶ A str. on the first syll. is indicated by ME. *corellari* (cf. medL. *corellārium*).

corona kərou·nə member of a cornice XVI; circle or halo of light XVII. L., CROWN.

coronach kɔ·rənaχ (Sc. and Ir.) funeral lament, dirge. XVI. – Ir. *coranach*, Gael. *corranach*, outcry, funeral cry, dirge, f. *comh-* together (CON-) + *rànach* roaring.

coronation kɔrənei·ʃən ceremonial crowning. XIV. – (O)F. *coronation* = Pr., Sp. *coronacion*, It. *coronazione* – medL. *corōnatiō(n-)*, f. L. *corōnāre* CROWN; see -ATION.

coroner kɔ·rənəɹ (hist.) officer orig. charged with maintaining the rights of crown property XIV; officer who holds inquests on bodies of persons who have died by violence or accident XV. – AN. *cor(o)uner*, f. *coro(u)ne* CROWN, after the L. title *custos placitorum coronæ* guardian of the pleas of the crown; latinized as *corōnārius, corōnātor* (XIII). From XV freq. in contr. form *crowner* (from *corou·ner*), as in Sh. 'Hamlet' v i 4.

coronet kɔ·rənet small crown. XV. – OF. *coronet(t)e*, dim. of *corone* CROWN; see -ET. Earlier †*crownet* (XIV), †*cronet* (XVI) – OF. *corounete, querounete*.

coronis kərou·nis (Gr. gram.) sign resembling an apostrophe placed over a vowel to denote contraction or crasis. XIX. L. – Gr. *korōnís* flourish at the end of a book or chapter, sb. use of adj. 'curved', rel. to *korṓnē* CROWN.

corozo korou·zou, ||-ōðo species of palm, Phytelephas, of S. America, the source of vegetable ivory. XVIII. Sp. – native name.

corporal[1] kɔ̄·ɹpərəl linen cloth on which the host and chalice are placed at the Eucharist. XIV. – (O)F. *corporal* or medL. *corporāle*, sb. use (sc. *pallium* PALL[1]) of *corporālis* CORPORAL[2]; the reference is to the use of the cloth for the 'Corpus Christi' (Body of Christ). The OF. nom. form *corporaus* was adopted earlier in ME. (XII), later **co·rporas**.

corporal[2] kɔ̄·ɹpərəl bodily XIV; †corporeal, material XIV (Trev.). – OF. *corporal* (mod. *corporel*) – L. *corporālis*, f. *corpor-*, CORPUS; see -AL[1]. So **corpora·lity**. XIV. – late L.

corporal[3] kɔ̄·ɹpərəl non-commissioned officer below a sergeant. XVI. – F. †*corporal*, var. of *caporal* – It. *caporale*, of which there appears to have been a Venetian form †*corporale* (latinized *corporalis* XV), f. *corpor-, corpus* body (of troops), the standard form being assim. to *capo* head. Cf. prec.

corporas see CORPORAL[1].

corporate kɔ̄·ɹpərət forming a corporation XV; corporeal, belonging to the body politic XVII (Sh.). – L. *corporātus*, pp. of *corporāre* fashion into or with a body, collect, f. *corpor-*, CORPUS; see -ATE[2]. So **corpora·**TION †incorporation XV; body of persons, esp. one formally incorporated XV; (large) abdomen XVIII (cf. the obs. use of *corporate* for 'corpulent', after late L.). – late L. ('corporeal nature', 'corporate body'). **co·rpor**ATIVE applied to the state as organized in Fascist Italy on the basis of collective labour relations. – It. (*stato*) *corporativo*.

corposant kɔ̄·ɹpəsænt ball of light observed on the masts and yards of a ship on stormy nights. XVII (earlier in foreign forms). – OSp., It. *corpo santo* (Sp. *cuerpo santo*) 'holy body', i.e. of a saint (cf. the synon. 'St. Elmo's fire').

corps kɔ̄ɹ portion of an army forming a tactical unit. XVIII. – F. *corps*, used as short for *corps d'armée* army corps; introduced during the Duke of Marlborough's campaigns; see next. ¶ Earlier in *corps de garde* 'body of guard', small body of troops stationed on guard, also the post occupied by them (XVI), perverted to †*court of guard* (XVI, Greene, Sh.).

corpse kɔ̄ɹps †body, person; (orig. *dead corpse*, as in 2 Kings xix 35, Isaiah xxxvii 36) lifeless body. XIV. ME. *corps*, orig. graphic var. of *cors* (XIII), later *corse* (XIV; still arch.) – OF. *cors* (mod. *corps*) = Pr. *cors* :– L. *corpus* body (see CORPUS). The inserted *p* had infl. the pronunc. before 1500; the sp. *corpse* (with final *e*), which differentiates this word from prec., though appearing as early as XVI, did not become general before XIX. The form *corps* at first functioned both as sg. and pl.; a new sg. *corp* appeared in Sc. XV.

corpulent kɔ̄·ɹpjŭlənt †material, gross XIV; bulky of body XIV (Trev.). – L. *corpulentus*, f. *corpus*; see next and -ULENT.

corpus kɔ̄·ɹpəs pl. *corpora* kɔ̄·ɹpərə body XIV; body of writings XVIII. L. 'body' (cf. MIDRIFF). In XIV–XVI perh. a var. of *corpes*, CORPSE. **Corpus Christi** kri·stai, -ti 'Body of Christ', feast of the Blessed Sacrament of Christ's Body and Blood, observed on the first Thursday after Trinity Sunday. XIV.

corpuscle kɔ̄·ɹpʌsl, kɔ̄ɹpʌ·sl minute particle of matter. XVII. – L. *corpusculum*, dim. of L. CORPUS. The L. form was formerly current, and **corpu·scule** (as in F.) has been used from early XIX. See -CLE.

corral kərā·l enclosure for cattle, etc. XVI (*corall*). – Sp., OPg. *corral*, Pg. *curral* (of Hottentot origin), whence KRAAL.

correct[1] kəre·kt set right; chastise XIV; counteract, neutralize XVI. f. *correct-*, pp. stem of L. *corrigere*, f. *com* COR- + *regere* lead straight, direct (see REGENT). So **corre·c**TION setting right, amendment, chastisement. XIV. – (O)F. – L. **corre·cti**VE adj. XVI; sb. XVII (Jonson). – F. **corre·ctor.** XIV (PPl.). – AN., OF. – L.; see -OR[1].

correct[2] kəre·kt that is in accordance with a standard XVII (Dryden); that is in accordance with truth XVIII. – F. *correct* – L. *correctus* amended, correct, pp. of *corrigere* (see prec.). Hence **corre·cti**TUDE correctness of conduct. XIX; after *rectitude*.

corregidor *koreyidō·r* Sp. magistrate. XVI. Sp., agent-noun f. *corregir* – L. *corrigere* CORRECT[1].

correlate kɔ·rīleit bring into or stand in mutual relation. XVIII (Fielding). Back-formation from **corr**ELA·TION, **corr**E·LATIVE. XVI. – scholL. *correlātiō*, *-ātīvus* (XIII); cf. F. *corrélation*, *-atif*, *-ive*.

correspond kɔrispɔ·nd be agreeable *to* or congruous *with*, answer *to* XVI; communicate by interchange of letters XVII. – (O)F. *correspondre* – medL. *correspondēre*; see COR-, RESPOND. So **correspo·nd**ENCE congruity XV; †(gen.) relation XVI; intercourse spec. by letters XVII (the letters themselves XVIII). – (O)F. – medL. **correspo·nd**ENT adj. XV; sb. XVII (spec. one who communicates by letter; so in F.) – (O)F. or prp. of medL. *correspondēre*.

corridor kɔ·ridɔ̄ɹ covered way XVI; outside gallery round a court, etc. XVII; passage running the length of a building, etc. XIX. – F. *corridor* – It. *corridore*, alteration, by assim. to *corridore* runner, of *corridojo* :– Rom. **curritōrium*, f. **currit-*, for *curs-*, pp. stem of L. *currere* run (see CURRENT); see -ORY.

corrie kɔ·ri (Sc.) circular hollow on a mountain side. XVIII. – Gael. *coire* ko·re cauldron, whirlpool, hollow, rel. to OE. *hwer* cauldron.

corrigendum, pl. **-da** kɔridʒe·ndəm, -də error(s) to be corrected. XIX. L., sb. use of n. of gerundive of *corrigere* CORRECT[1].

corroborate kərɔ·bəreit strengthen, confirm XVI; (an opinion) by concurrent evidence XVIII. f. pp. stem of L. *corrōborāre*, f. *com* COR- + *rōborāre* strengthen, f. *rōbur* strength; see ROBUST, -ATE[3]. So **corrobo-ra·**TION. XV. – F. or late L.

corroboree kərɔ·bəri native Australian dance. XIX. A word of Port Jackson dialect, New South Wales.

corrode kərou·d wear away. XIV. – L. *corrōdere*, f. *com* COR- + *rōdere* gnaw (see RODENT). So **corro·**SION. XIV. – OF. or late L. **corro·s**IVE adj. and sb. XIV (Ch.). – OF. *corosif* – medL. *corrōsīvus*; orig. str. on the first syll., whence the frequent vars. †*co·rsie* (XV), †*co·rsive* (XVI).

corrody kɔ·rədi (hist.) provision for maintenance. XV. – AN. *corodie*, AL. *corrōdium*, varying with *-rādium*, *-rēdium*, f. OF. *conrei*, *-roi* (mod. *corroi*) :– Rom. **conrēdo*, f. **conrēdāre* CURRY[1].

corrugated kɔ·rŭgeitid wrinkled XVII (also *corrugat* pa. pple. XIV); of iron, etc. XIX. f. pp. of L. *corrŭgāre*, f. *com* COR- (intensive)+ *rūgāre*, f. *rūga* wrinkle; see RUGOSE, -ATE[3], -ED[1].

corrupt kərʌ·pt †as pp. corrupted XIV; unsound, rotten, debased, venal XIV (Wyclif, Ch., Gower). – OF. *corrupt* or L. *corruptu-s*, pp. of *corrumpere* destroy, ruin, falsify, seduce, f. *com* COR-+*rumpere* break (see RUPTURE). Hence **corru·pt** vb. render unsound XIV; make venal XVI; alter (language) for the worse XVII; superseding †*corrump* (XIV, R. Rolle). **corru·pTION.** XIV. – (O)F. – L.

corsage kɔ̄ɹsā·ʒ †body XV; bodice XIX. – (O)F. *corsage*, f. *cors* body; see CORPSE, CORSE, -AGE.

corsair kɔ̄·ɹsɛəɹ privateer XV. Not in gen. use in this form before XVII, current early forms being *corsale*, *cursarie*, *corsario*, *cursaro*. – F. *corsaire*, †*coursaire*, †*cursaire*, Pr. *corsari*, Sp. *corsario*, It. *corsale*, *-are*, †*-aro*, †*-ario* :– Rom. (medL.) *cursārius*, f. *cursa* and *cursus* hostile inroad, plunder, a spec. use of L. *cursus* COURSE. See COURSER.

corse obs. and arch. form of CORPSE.

corset kɔ̄·ɹsit close-fitting body garment XIV; laced inner bodice, stays XVIII. – (O)F. *corset*, dim. of *cors* body; see CORPSE, -ET.

corslet kɔ̄·ɹslit garment, spec. defensive armour, covering the body. XV. – (O)F. *corselet*, dim. of *cors* body; see CORPSE, -LET.

cortège kɔ̄ɹtei·ʒ train of people. XVII. – F. *cortège* – It. *corteggio*, f. *corteggiare* attend court, keep a retinue, f. *corte* COURT.

Cortes kɔ̄·ɹtiz, -ez the two chambers of the legislative assembly of Spain and of Portugal. XVII. Sp., Pg. *cortes*, pl. of *corte* COURT.

cortical kɔ̄·ɹtikəl (bot.) of the bark or superficial investment. XVII. – modL. *corticālis*, f. L. *cortic-*, **cortex** bark (anglicized XVII), rel. to *corium* leather; see -AL.

corundum kərʌ·ndəm mineral allied to sapphire and ruby. XVIII. – Tamil *kurundam* = Telugu *kuruvindam* – Skr. *kuruvinda*, *-as* ruby.

coruscate kɔ·rəskeit sparkle, glitter. XVIII. f. pp. of L. *coruscāre* vibrate, glitter; see -ATE[3]. So **coruscA·TION.** XV. – L.

corvée kɔ̄·rvei forced labour XIV (isolated ex.); XVIII (with ref. to the French peasants' statute labour). – (O)F. *corvée* = Pr. *corroada* (cf. medL. *coruada*) :– Rom. **corrogāta* (sc. *opera*) requisitioned (works), n. pl. of pp. of L. *corrogāre* call together, collect, f. *com* (intensive) COR-+*rogāre* ask, request (see ROGATION).

corvette kɔ̄ɹve·t flush-decked war-vessel. XVII. – F. *corvette* (beside †*corvot*), dim. f. MDu. *korf* kind of ship; see -ETTE.

corvine kɔ̄·ɹvain of the crow kind. XVII. – L. *corvīnus*, *f*. *corvus* raven; cf. CORBEL and see -INE[1].

Corybant kɔ·ribænt priest of the worship of Cybele. XIV (*coribande*, Ch.). – L. *Corybant-*, *-bās* – Gr. *Korúbās*. Hence **Coryba·ntIC.** XVII.

corymb kɔ·rimb (bot.) species of raceme. XVIII. – F. *corymbe* or L. *corymbus* – Gr. *kórumbos* summit, cluster of fruit or flowers, close head of a composite flower.

coryphæus kɔrifī·əs leader (of a chorus). XVII. L. – Gr. *koruphaîos* chief, (in the Attic drama) leader of the chorus, f. *koruphḗ* head, top. Earlier anglicized †*coryphe(e)* XVII.

cos kɔs variety of lettuce introduced from the island of *Cos* (Gr. *Kôs*) in the Ægean Sea. XVII (Evelyn).

cosh[1] kɔʃ (sl.) stout stick, truncheon. XIX. Of unkn. origin.

cosh[2] kɔsei·tʃ (math.) abbrev. for h*yperbolic* cos*ine*. XIX.

cosher see KOSHER.

cosine kou·sain (math.) sine of the complement of an angle. XVII; see CO-, SINE. So **coSE·CANT**, **coTA·NGENT.** XVII. ¶ In modL. *cosecans* occurs in Rheticus' 'Opus Palatinum', *a.* 1576, *cosinus* and *cotangens* in Gunther's 'Canon Triangulorum' 1620.

cosmetic kɔzme·tik (preparation for) embellishing the personal appearance. XVII. – F. *cosmétique* – Gr. *kosmētikós*, f. *kosmeîn* adorn, f. *kósmos*; see next and -IC.

cosmos kɔ·zmɔs the universe as an ordered system. XVII (isol. ex. XII (Orm)). – Gr. *kósmos* order, ornament, order of the universe, (with the Pythagoreans) the world. Hence **co·smIC.** XIX; after F. *cosmique*. **cosmo-** kɔ·zmou, kɔzmɔ· comb. form, as in **cosmo·-GONY** creation of the world XVII, **cosmo·GRAPHY** description of the earth or the universe XV; **cosmo·LOGY** theory of the universe XVII; all ult. from Gr. forms through F. or (mod)L. **cosmopolitAN** kɔzmɔpɔ·litən, **cosmopolITE** kɔzmɔ·pəlait citizen of the world. XVII; as adjs. XIX. – F. *cosmopolitain*, *-polite* – It. *cosmopolitano*, *-polita* – Gr. *kosmopolī́tēs* (*polī́tēs* citizen; see POLITIC).

cos(s) kɔs measure of length in India. XVII. – Hindi *kos*, Pali *koss* :– Skr. *króças* measure of distance, orig. cry, shout, (hence) range of the voice in calling or hallooing.

Cossack kɔ·sək one of, or descendant of, early Russian people who sought free life on steppes, noted for warlike qualities, etc. XVI. – F. *Cosaque* (1578), varying in early use with *Casaque* (cf. CASSOCK) – Russ. *kazák*, †*kozák* – *Turkī quzzāq* vagabond, nomad, adventurer, guerrilla, f. *qaz* wander about.

cosset kɔ·sit pet, pamper. XVII. f. dial. *cosset* pet-lamb, plausibly regarded by Skeat as a transf. use of AN. *coscet*, *cozet* (Domesday Book) – OE. *cotsǣta* cottager (corr. to MLG. *kotsete*, whence G. *kossat* cottage-dweller), f. *cot* COT+**sǣt-*, var. of **set-*, base of **sitjan* SIT. ¶ For similar origins cf. It. *casiccio* pet lamb (Florio), f. *casa* house, and G. *hauslamm*, Du. *huislam*.

cossid kɔ·sid courier. XVII. – Arab. (Pers.) *qāçid* travelling, courier.

cost kɔ̀st price, pl. expenses. XIII. – AN. *cost*, OF. *coust* (mod. *coût*) = Pr. *cost*, Sp., It. *costo* :– CRom. sb. **costo*; f. OF. *coster*, *couster* (mod. *coûter*), the source of **cost** vb. XIV = Pr., Sp. *costar*, It. *costare* :– CRom. **costāre*, for L. *constāre* stand firm, be fixed, stand at a price, f. *com* CON- (intensive)+ *stāre* STAND. The L. idiom which is the source of present usage is repr. by *Hoc constat mihi tribus assibus* this 'stands me in' at three asses. Hence **co·stly.** XIV (Wyclif); see -LY[1].

costal kɔ·stəl pert. to the ribs. XVII. – F. *costal* – modL. *costālis*, f. *costa* rib (cf. COAST); see -AL[1].

costard kɔ·stəɹd large variety of apple XIV; (joc.) head XVI. – AN. *costard*, f. *coste* rib :– L. *costa*; see -ARD. So called from being prominently ribbed. Hence †*costardmonger*, **co·ster**MONGER (XVI) apple-seller, fruiterer, esp. one who sold this fruit in the open, in mod. use, a seller of fruit, vegetables, fish, etc., from a barrow in the street; abbrev. **coster** kɔ·stəɹ. XIX.

costive kɔ·stiv constipated. XIV. – AN. **costif*, for OF. *costivé* :– L. *constipātus* (see CONSTIPATE). For the loss of F. *-é* cf. ASSIGN[2].

costmary kɔ·stmɛəri aromatic plant Chrysanthemum (Pyrethrum, Janacetum) Balsamita. XV. f. *cost* (OE. *cost* – L. *costum*, *-os* – Gr. *kóstos* – Arab. *qust* – Skr. *kúṣṭhas*, *-am*)+the name of the Virgin *Mary*.

costume kɔ·stjūm †manners and customs proper to a time and place XVIII; mode of personal attire; complete set of outer garments, etc. XIX. – F. *costume* (first used of realistic portrayal in works of art) – It. *costume* custom, fashion, habit :– L. *consuetūdinem* CUSTOM. So **costu·mier** maker of costumes. XIX. – F.

cosy, cozy kou·zi comfortable from being sheltered and warm XVIII; sb. kind of hood put over a teapot, etc., to keep it warm XIX. orig. Sc. (Ramsay, Burns); earliest form *colsie*; of unkn. origin.

cot[1] kɔt cottage. OE. *cot* = MLG., MDu., ON. *kot* :– Germ. **kutam* (cf. ON. *kytja* hovel), rel. to COTE.

cot[2] kɔt light bedstead XVII; swinging bed for officers, the sick, etc., XVIII; small child's bed XIX. – Hindi *khaṭ* bedstead, couch, hammock :– Prakrit *khaṭṭa*, Skr. *khaṭvā* bedstead, couch, cot.

cote kout †cottage XI; small building for sheltering small animals, as *dovecot(e)*, *sheepcote* XIV. OE. *cote*, corr. to LG. *kote* (whence G. *kote*) :– Germ. **kutōn*, rel. to COT[1].

coterie kou·təri †society, club; exclusive set or clique. XVIII. – F. *coterie* (in OF. feudal tenure, tenants holding land together), f. **cote* hut (cf. †*cotin*) – MLG. *kote* COTE; see -ERY. Formerly pronounced with short initial syll., and so rhyming with *lottery* in Byron, 'Don Juan' IV cix.

cothurnus kəþə̄·ɹnəs buskin of ancient tragic actors. XVIII (earlier anglicized †*cothurn* XVII). L. – Gr. *kóthornos*.

cotill(i)on kouti·ljən one of several kinds of dance. XVIII. – F. *cotillon* petticoat, dance, dim. of *cotte* COAT.

cotoneaster kətouniæ·stəɹ genus of rosaceous trees. XVIII. modL., f. L. *cotōnium* QUINCE; see -ASTER.

cotta kɔ·tə short surplice. XIX. – It. *cotta*; see COAT.

cottage kɔ·tidʒ small humble dwelling-house XIV (Ch.); small country or detached suburban house XVIII (Walpole). – AN. **cotage*, AL. *cotāgium* (XII), f. COT[1], COTE; see -AGE. ¶ F. *cottage* is from Eng. Hence **co·ttager.** XVI; see -ER[1].

cotter[1], **cottar** kɔ·təɹ (Sc.) cottager paying rent-service. XIV (*cottar*, *cotar*). f. COT[1]+ -ER[1] (Sc. *-ar*); cf. medL. *cotārius* and COTTIER.

cotter[2] kɔ·təɹ pin, etc. for fastening a thing into its place. XIV. Earlier (dial.) *cotterel* XVI; perh. transf. uses of COTTER[1] and **cotterel* (cf. the surname *Cotterell* and AL. *coterellus* cottager).

cottier kɔ·tiəɹ cottager XIV; (in Ireland) peasant cultivating a small holding XIX. – (O)F. *cotier*, f. *cote*; see COTERIE, -IER.

cotton kɔ·tn white fibrous substance covering the seeds of the cotton plant, Gossypium XIV (Maund.). ME. *coto(u)n* – (O)F. *coton* = Pr. *coton*, It. *cotone* – Arab. *qutn*, in Sp. Arab. *qoton*. (From Arab. with prefixed article AL-[2] Sp. *algodon*, †*alcoton*; see ACTON. Sp. *coton* is now 'printed cotton fabric'.) Hence **co·tton** vb. furnish with or take on a nap XV; (prob. transf. from the production of a nap in the finishing of cloth) †prosper, get on XVI (orig. in *This gear* or *matter cottons*); get on *with* XVII; take *to* XIX.

cotyledon kɔtilī·dən (zool.) patch of villi on the chorion of ruminants XVI; (bot., after Linnæus, 1751) seed-leaf in phanerogams XVIII. – L. *cotylēdon* navelwort, pennywort (so used occas. in Eng.) – Gr. *kotulēdṓn* applied to various cup-shaped cavities, f. *kotúlē* hollow, cup, socket.

couch kautʃ bed; lair XIV; layer XVII. – (O)F. *couche*, f. *coucher* (whence **couch** vb. lay down, lie down XIV) = Pr. *colcar*, It. *colcare* :– L. *collocāre* lay in its place, lodge, COLLOCATE.

couch-grass kau·tʃgràs var. of QUITCH. XVI.

cougar kū·gaɹ puma. XVIII. – F. *couguar* (Buffon) – Marcgraf's name *cuguacu ara*, repr. Guarani *guaçu ara*.

cough kɔf expel air noisily from the lungs. XIV. ME. *coȝe, cowhe, co(u)we*, f. imit. base **koχ-* repr. by OE. *cohhetan* shout, (M)LG., (M)Du. *kuchen* cough, MHG. *kūchen* breathe, exhale. Hence **cough** sb. XIV (PPl., Ch.).

could pt. of CAN[1].

coulee kū·li in W. Canada and U.S.A., deep ravine. XIX. – F. *coulée* flow, lava flow, f. *couler* flow :– L. *cōlāre* filter, strain, in Rom. flow, f. *cōlum* strainer (cf. COLANDER).

coulisse kuli·s groove in which a partition slides; side-scene or wings of a stage. XIX. – F. *coulisse*, sb. use of fem. of *coulis*, orig. adj. sliding, f. *couler* flow, glide, slide; see prec. and cf. *glacis*. See CULLIS.

couloir kū·lwāɹ steep gorge. XIX. – F. *couloir* colander, lobby, steep incline down which felled wood is run, f. *couler* glide, slide + *-oir* (:– L. *-ōrium* -ORY).

coulomb kulɔ·m unit of electric quantity. 1881. f. name of C. A. de *Coulomb* (1736–1806), French physicist.

coulter kou·ltəɹ iron blade at the front of a ploughshare. OE. *culter* – L. *culter* knife, ploughshare. The sp. *culter* is familiar from Sh. 'Henry V' v ii 46; *colter* is the favoured sp. in U.S.A.

council kau·nsĭl legislative assembly of ecclesiastics XII; advisory or deliberative assembly; body of councillors XIII. – AN. *cuncile, concilie* – L. *concilium* convocation, assembly, meeting, f. *com* CON- + *calāre* call, summon, rel. to Gr. *kaleîn* call. In form and meaning (through the sense 'assembly for consultation') blended at an early date with *counsel*, but differentiation began XVI. So **cou·ncillor** member of a council. XIV; alteration of COUNSELLOR by assim. to *council*.

counsel kau·nsəl consultation, deliberation; advice, direction; plan, design XIII; body of legal advisers XIV; legal advocate XVIII. – OF. *cun-, counseil* (mod. *conseil*) = Pr. *conselh*, Sp. *consejo*, It. *consiglio* :– L. *consilium* consultation, plan, advice, judgement, prudence, deliberating body, f. *com* CON- + **sal-*; see CONSUL, CONSULT. Now restricted to the above senses; for the sense 'deliberating body' see COUNCIL. So **cou·nsel** vb. advise. XIII. – (O)F. *conseiller* = Pr. *cosselhar*, etc. :– L. *consiliārī*. **counsellor** kau·nsĭləɹ adviser. XIII. – (O)F. *conseiller*, †*conseillour* :– L. *consiliātor, -atōrem*; see -OR[1].

count[1] kaunt reckoning, ACCOUNT XIV; consideration, notice XV; particular of a legal charge XVI. – OF. *conte, counte* (mod. *compte* reckoning, *conte* tale) = It. *conto* account, tale, Sp. *cuento* tale :– late L. *computu-s* calculation, f. *computāre* COUNT[3].

count[2] kaunt used to repr. foreign titles of nobility (F. *comte*, G. *graf*, etc.). XVI. – OF. *conte* (mod. *comte*) = Pr. *comte*, Sp. *conde*, It. *conte* :– L *comitem* nom. *comes* companion, associate, partner, overseer, tutor, attendant on a distinguished private person, one of the imperial retinue, (late L.) occupant of a state office, in *comes Britanniæ* and *comes littoris Saxonici* designating two generals of the Roman province of Britain; for **comis* :– **comits* lit. 'one who goes with', f. *com* COM- + ppl. stem *it-* of *īre* go (cf. ITINERARY). So **countess** kau·ntĭs. XII (*cuntesse*). ¶ A form *countie, countee* denoting 'count' was in use XVI–XVII, which may be a modification due to disyll. It. *conte*.

count[3] kaunt tell over; reckon. XIV. – OF. *counter, cunter* reckon, relate (mod. *compter* count, *conter* relate) = Pr. *comtar*, Sp. *contar*, It. *contare* in both senses :– L. *computāre* calculate, COMPUTE. For the sense 'tell a story' see RECOUNT.

countenance kau·ntĭnəns †demeanour, conduct; 'calmness of look, confidence of mien' (J.) XIII; †aspect, appearance XIV (PPl.); facial look or expression XIV (R. Mannyng, Barbour); face, visage XIV (Gower); 'appearance of favour' (J.), support XVI. – AN. *c(o)untenaunce*, (O)F. *contenance* bearing, behaviour, mien, contents, f. *contenir* maintain (oneself), CONTAIN; cf. L. *continentia* CONTINENCE, (late) contents, (in medL.) demeanour, way of living; see -ANCE. Hence **cou·ntenance** vb. †make a show (of), pretend XV; †face *out*; †set off; give support to XVI.

counter[1] kau·ntəɹ object used in counting or keeping account XIV; desk for counting money, etc., (hence) money-changer's table, tradesman's table in his shop XIV. – AN. *count(e)our*, OF. *conteoir, -eor* (mod. *comptoir*) :– medL. *computātōrium*, f. L. *computāre* COMPUTE; see -ER[2].

counter[2] kau·ntəɹ A. †opposite direction to that taken by the game XVI; B. part of a horse's breast lying between the shoulders XVII; curved part of a ship's stern XVII (Capt. Smith). f. COUNTER[4] or [6].

counter[3] kau·ntəɹ in fencing, circular parry, the particular engagement being indicated by an addition, as *counter-seconde, -tierce, -quarte, -septime*. XVII; counterblow XIX. – F. *contre*, corr. to It. *contro*, sb. use of the prep. (see COUNTER[6]).

counter[4] kau·ntəɹ opposed, opposite. XVI. adj. use of the prefix COUNTER-, generalized from comps. such as *counterblast, countermine, counterpoise*.

counter[5] kau·ntəɹ go counter to, oppose, controvert XIV (Wyclif); give a counterblow XIX. orig. aphetic of †*acounter*, var. of ENCOUNTER; in later use a fresh formation on COUNTER- or COUNTER[6].

counter[6] kau·ntəɹ in the opposite direction, orig. in hunting, *hunt, run counter*. XV. – OF. *countre* :– L. *contrā* adv. and prep. against, in return, orig. fem. abl. with locative meaning; cf. CONTRA.

counter- kau·ntəɹ prefix, ME. *countre-* – AN. *countre-*, (O)F. *contre-* :– L. *contrā-* CONTRA-; denoting (i) against, opposite, in opposition to, (ii) in reversal of or parallelism with a former action, as *counter-reformation*, *-revolution*, (iii) in reciprocation or reply, as *countersign*, (iv) as the opposite member or constituent, as *counterfoil*, *-part*, (v) with a contrary action or movement, etc., in mutual opposition, as *counterchange*, (vi) mus., cf. CONTRA-; her., in the contrary direction, on opposite sides, with tinctures reversed, as *counter-compony*. **counter**BLAST kau·ntəɹblàst. XVI. **counterfeit** kəu·ntəɹfīt, -fit made in imitation, spurious, sham (Gower); also sb. (Maund.) XIV. OF. *countrefet*, *-fait* (mod. *contrefait*), pp. of *contrefaire*, corr. to Pr. *contrafar*, It. *contraffare* – Rom. (medL.) *contrāfacere* (cf. late L. *contrāfactiō* contrast), f. *contrā* COUNTER-+*facere* make (see FACT). So **cou·nterfeit** vb. make a fraudulent imitation (of). XIII. – AN. *countrefeter*, f. *countrefet* pp. **counterfoil** kau·ntəɹfoil complementary part of a cheque, receipt, etc. XVIII; FOIL[1] was used in the same sense XV. **cou·ntermand** revoke or annul a command or order XV; †go counter to, counteract XVI. – OF. *contremander* – medL. *contrāmandāre*; see MANDATE. **counterpane** kau·ntəɹpein outer bed-covering. XVII. Alteration, by assim. to PANE[1] in the same sense (XIV), which appears also in †*cover-pane* (XV), of †*counterpoint* XV (cf. Sh. 'Taming of the Shrew' II i 345) – OF. *contrepointe*, alteration of **coutrepointe*, *cou(l)tepointe* :– medL. *culcit(r)a puncta* 'quilted mattress', i.e. *culcit(r)a* cushion, mattress, and *puncta*, fem. pp. of *pungere* prick, stab (see POINT). **counterpart** kau·ntəɹpāɹt opposite part of an indenture, also gen. XV. f. COUNTER-+PART[1], after (O)F. *contre-partie*. **counterpoint** kau·ntəɹpoint melody added as an accompaniment to a given melody; art or practice of doing this. XV. – (O)F. *contrepoint* = It. *contrappunto* (cf. CONTRAPUNTAL), – medL. *contrāpunctum*, *cantus contrāpunctus* 'song pointed-against', the accompaniment being orig. noted by points or pricks set against those of the plainsong melody; see CONTRA- b. **cou·nter**POISE weight balancing another weight XV; equilibrium XVI. – OF. *countrepeis*, *-pois*. **cou·nter**SCARP (fortif.) outer wall of the ditch. XVI. – F. *contrescarpe* – It. *contrascarpa*. **cou·nter**SIGN sign used in response to another sign. XVI. – F. *contresigne* – It. *contrasegno*. **counter**TE·NOR part next above the tenor; alto. XIV. – OF. *contreteneur* – It. †*contratenore*; cf. medL. *contrātenens*; see CONTRA- b.

countervail kauntəɹvei·l match, counterbalance, compensate. XIV (Gower, Wyclif). – OF. *contrevaloir* (pres. stem *-vail-*) – L. phr. *contrā valēre* be effective or avail against (cf. VALID).

country kʌ·ntri tract of land; *one's* native land XIII (Cursor M.); territory of a nation; nation, people XIV; rural districts XVI. ME. *cuntre(e)*, *contre(e)* – OF. *cuntrée*, (mod.) *contrée* = Pr., It. *contrada* :– medL., Rom. *contrāta* (Leges Siciliæ), sb. use (sc. *terra* land) of fem. of adj. meaning 'lying opposite or facing one', hence 'the landscape spread out before one'; cf. Pr. *encontrada* in the same sense. ¶ G. *gegend* region, f. *gegen* against, opposite, was modelled on the F. word. Hence **cou·ntry** DA·NCE dance of rural origin. XVI; see CONTRE-DANSE. **cou·ntry**MAN native XIV; compatriot XV; husbandman XVI; so **cou·ntry**WO·MAN XV. **cou·ntry**SIDE particular region of a country; orig. Sc.

county kau·nti shire. XIV (first in the sense 'county court', R. Mannyng). – AN. *counté* (Laws of William I), OF. *cunté*, *conté* (mod. *comté*) = Pr. *comtat*, Sp. *condado*, It. *contado* :– L. *comitātu-s*, f. *comit-*, *comes* COUNT[1]. The L. word primarily meant 'body of companions, retinue'; when the *comes* became a state officer, *comitatus* became the name of his office, and when the 'count' became a territorial lord, 'county' became the designation of his territory; consequently AN. *counté* was used to render the native *shire*, the designation of a territory administered orig. by an 'earl' (OE. *eorl*) and later by a sheriff (AN. *viscounte*).

coup kū stroke, hit. XVIII (earlier in some phr., e.g. *coup d'état*, *coup de grâce* XVIII, *coup de théâtre* early XVIII). F. *coup* blow :– medL. *colpus* (see COPPICE).

coupé[1] kū·pei (her.) said of the head, etc., cut off clean. XVI. F., pp. of *couper* cut, f. *coup* (see prec.). Also anglicized with -ED **couped** kūpt. XVII.

coupé[2] kū·pei short four-wheeled closed carriage for two. XIX. F., short for *carrosse coupé* 'cut carriage', the body having the form of a berline from which the hind seat has been cut away; sb. use of pp. (see prec.).

couple kʌ·pl union of two, esp. male and female XIII (AncrR.); leash, usu. pl. (hence phr. *hunt in couples*) XIV. – OF. *cople*, *cuple* (mod. *couple*) :– L. *cōpula* tie, connexion (see COPULA). So **couple** vb. XIII (Cursor M.). – OF. *copler*, *cupler* (mod. *coupler*) :– L. *cōpulāre* COPULATE. **coupl**ET kʌ·plit pair of successive lines of verse. XVI. – (O)F. *couplet*, dim. of *couple*.

coupon kū·pɔn separable certificate or ticket. XIX. – F. *coupon*, earlier *colpon* piece cut off, slice (whence ME. *colpon*, Ch.), f. *colper*, *couper* cut, f. *coup* blow, cut; cf. COUP and -OON.

courage kʌ·ridʒ †heart as the seat of feeling, spirit, nature XIII; †intention, purpose; bravery, valour XIV. – OF. *corage*, *curage* (mod. *courage*) = Pr. *coratge*, Sp. *coraje*, It. *coraggio* :– Rom. **corāticum*, f. *cor* HEART; see -AGE. So **courage**OUS kərei·dʒəs. XIII. – AN. *courageous* OF. *corageus* (mod. *courageux*).

courier ku·riəɹ running messenger XVI; servant employed to make travelling arrangements XVIII. Earlier *currior*, *-ier* – F. †*courier*, (also mod. *courrier* – It. *corriere* (medL. *currerius*), f. *corre* :– L. *currere* run (see CURRENT). In the first sense the earlier word was †*cur(r)our* (XIV–XVII) – OF. *coreor* (mod. *coureur*) :– Rom. **curritōrem*.

course kɔ̄əɹs running, onward movement; path, line, direction; progress, procedure, order XIII; set of dishes placed for a meal, one of the successive parts of a meal XIV; series, serial succession; sail attached to lower masts or yards XV. – (O)F. *cours* = Pr. *cors*, Sp. *curso*, It. *corso* :– L. *cursu-s*, f. *curs-*, pp. stem of *currere* run (cf. CURRENT); reinforced XV by (O)F. *course* = Pr., It. *corsa* :– Rom. **cursa*, sb. use of corr. fem. form of ppl. (cf. ASSIZE, *venue*). Hence **course** vb. chase, hunt; cause to run; run about. XVI. ¶ From the same base are: *courier*, *concourse*, *discourse*, *recourse*, *courser*; *concur*, *incur*, *occur*, *recur*; *succour*; *current*, *recurrent*; *excursion*, *incursion*, *excursus*, *precursor*, *cursitor*, *cursive*, *cursory*.

courser kɔə·ɹsəɹ charger; in mod. times, a swift horse. XIII. – OF. *corsier* (mod. *coursier*) = Pr. *corsier*, It. *corsiere* :– Rom. **cursārius*, f. *cursus* COURSE; see -ER[2], CORSAIR.

court kɔ̄ɹt (place of residence of) royal household and retinue; assembly held by a sovereign XII; assembly of judges, etc.; place of such assembly; enclosed area, yard XIII; homage, courtly attention (after F. *faire la* or *sa cour*, It. *far la corte* pay court) XVI. ME. *curt*, *court* – AN. *curt*, OF. *cort* (mod. *cour*) = Pr. *cort*, Sp., It. *corte*, Rum. *curte* :– late L. (Rom.) *curtem*, earlier *cortem*, *cohortem* yard, enclosure, (enclosed) crowd, retinue, COHORT. **court-**BA·RON assembly of the freehold tenants of a manor under the presidency of the lord XVI. – AN. *court baron*, for earlier *court de baron* (medL. *curia baronis*). **cou·rt-**CARD picture card of a suit. XVII. Alteration, suggested by the personages depicted, of †*coat card* card bearing a 'coated' or habited figure (XVI–XVII). **cou·rt** HAND style of handwriting of the English law courts. XVI (Sh.). **court** LEET. XVI. **cou:rt-**MA·RTIAL. XVII, earlier †*martial court*. **cou·rt-**PLA:STER sticking-plaster used for wounds. XVIII; so called from being used for the black silk patches worn on the face by ladies at court. **court** vb. †frequent the court; pay court to, woo. XVI; after OIt. *corteare* (later *corteggiare*), OF. *courtoyer* (later *courtiser*), f. *corte*, *court*. **courtier** kɔ̄·ɹtiəɹ attendant at the court of a sovereign. XIII. ME. *courteour* – AN. *courte(i)our*, for OF. **cortoyeur*, f. *cortoyer*; suffix assim. to -IER, through *-e(y)er*. **cou·rtly.** XV; see -LY[1]. **cou·rt**SHIP. XVI (Sh.).

courteous kə̄·ɹtiəs, kɔ̄·ɹtiəs befitting the court of a prince, graciously polite or respectful. XIII. – OF. *corteis*, *curteis* (mod. *courtois*) = Pr. *cortes*, Sp. *cortés*, It. *cortese* :– Rom. **cortensis*, f. **corte* COURT + *-ensis* -ESE. The suffix -EOUS replaced *-eis* XVI.

courtesan kɔ̄·ɹtizən, (formerly) kə̄·ɹ- kept mistress, prostitute. XVI. – F. *courtisane* – It. †*cortigiana*, fem. of *cortigiano* COURTIER, f. *corte* COURT. Cf. ARTISAN.

courtesy kə̄·ɹtəsi, kɔ̄·ɹ- courteous behaviour or disposition. XIII (AncrR., RGlouc.). – OF. *cur-*, *co(u)rtesie* (mod. *courtoisie*) = Pr. *cortezia*, It. *cortesia*; f. *courteis*, etc., COURTEOUS; see -Y[3]. Cf. CURTSY.

couscous ku·skus spotted phalanger. XIX. – F. – Du. *koeskoes* – native Moluccas word.

cousin kʌ·zn †relative; son or daughter of one's uncle or aunt XIII; term of address from one sovereign to another, or to a peer XV. – OF. *cosin*, *cusin* (mod. *cousin*) = Pr. *cosin*, Cat. *cosí*, Rumansch *cus(d)rin* (cf. Sp. *sobrino*, *-a*, Pg. *sobrinho*, *-a* (chiefly) nephew, niece) :– L. *consobrīnus* mother's sister's child, pl. cousins german :– **conswesrinos*, f. *com* CON- + **swesōr* SISTER + *-*īnos* -INE[1].

couvade kuvā·d custom of 'man-childbed'. XIX (E. B. Tylor). – F., f. *couver* hatch :– L. *cubāre* lie down (cf. INCUBATION); see -ADE.

cove[1] kouv †bedchamber, storechamber; (Sc. and north.) hollow in a rock, etc. OE.; sheltered recess on a coast. XVI. OE. *cofa* chamber = MLG. *cove*, MHG. *kobe* (G. *koben*) stable, pigsty, ON. *kofi* hut, shed :– Germ. **kuƀon* (cf., with other suffix, OHG. *chubisi* hut).

cove[2] kouv (colloq.) fellow, chap. XVI. orig. thieves' cant (*gentry cofe* nobleman, gentleman, *bene cofe* good fellow), perh. identical with Sc. *cofe* chapman, pedlar (cf. the origin of CHAP[3], CUSS[2]).

covenant kʌ·vĭnənt mutual agreement; divine contract with mankind (Heb. *berīth*, LXX. *diathḗkē*, Vulgate L. *fœdus*, *pactum*, in N.T. always *testamentum*) XIII; legal agreement or contract XIV. – OF. *covenant* (later and mod. *convenant*), sb. use of prp. of *co(n)venir* agree (see CONVENE). Hence **co·venant** vb. XIV (Wycl. Bible, *couenauntide a boond of pees*, tr. Vulg. *pepigi fœdus*). **co·venanter** (leg. **-or**); spec. adherent of the National Covenant of 1638 or the Solemn League and Covenant of 1643.

cover kʌ·vəɹ put or lay something over; screen, shield, protect. XIII. – OF. *cuvrir*, *covrir* (mod. *couvrir*) = Pr. *cobrir*, Sp. *cubrir*, It. *coprire* :– L. *cooperīre*, f. *co-* CON- (intensive) + *operīre* cover (cf. *aperīre* open; see APERIENT). Hence **cover** sb. XIV; or partly variant of COVERT (OF. *couvert*, pl. *-ers*). For the ME. var. *keuer* cf. *meve* MOVE, *preve* PROVE, RETRIEVE.

coverlet kʌ·vəɹlĭt counterpane, quilt. XIII (Cursor M.). ME. *coverled*, *-lite* – AN. *covrelet*, *-lit*, f. *covre-*, pres. stem of OF. *covrir* COVER + *lit* bed (cf. LITTER). The var. *coverlid* (with assim. to LID) was current in literature till XIX, and persists dial.

covert kʌ·vəɹt covering XIV; woody shelter for game (pron. kʌ·vəɹ) XIV (Trev.); feathers covering the bases of larger feathers XVIII. – OF. *covert* (mod. *couvert*), pp. of *couvrir* COVER. So **co·vert** adj. covered, hidden, concealed. XIV. – OF. *covert-e*. **coverture** kʌ·vəɹtʃəɹ cover, covering XIII; position of a woman during her married life XVI. – OF. *coverture* (mod. *couverture*) :- Rom. **coopertūra*.

covet kʌ·vit desire, spec. culpably. XIII (AncrR.). ME. *cuveite, coveite* – OF. *cu-, coveitier* (mod. *convoiter*) = Pr. *cobeitar*, It. *cubitare* :- Rom. **cupiditāre*, f. *cupiditās* CUPIDITY. So **co·vetous**. XIII (Cursor M.). – OF. *coveitus*, *-os* = Pr. *cobeitos* :- L. **cupiditōsus*.

covey kʌ·vi brood of partridges, etc. XIV. – OF. *covee* (mod. *couvée*) = It. *covata* :- Rom. **cubāta* hatching, f. L. *cubāre* lie (cf. INCUBATION).

covin kʌ·vin †company; private agreement; collusion, fraud. XIV. – OF. *covin, covine* :- medL. *convenium*, pl. or fem. sing. *-ia*, f. *convenīre* come together, agree (see CONVENE).

cow[1] kau female of a bovine animal. OE. *cū* = OFris. *kū*, OS. *kō* (Du. *koe*), OHG. *chuo* (G. *kuh*), ON. *kýr* :- CGerm. (exc. Gothic) **kōuz*, **kōz*, fem. :- IE. **gʷōus*, whence also Skr. *gāús* (*gav-, go-*), Arm. *kov*, Gr. *boûs* (*boϝ-, bo-*), L. *bōs* (*bov-, bo-*), OIr. *bó*, Lett. *gùovs*. The normal descendant of the mutated OE. pl. *cȳ* (cf. G. *kühe*) is north. *kye*; the form *kine* (now arch.) descends from a ME. (XIII) extension of this with *-n* from the weak declension, which was mainly due to late OE. g.pl. *cȳna* (for *cūa*).

cow[2] kau depress with fear. XVII (Sh.). prob. in dial. use long before its appearance in literature (cf. *dwindle*), and – ON. *kúga* oppress, tyrannize over (Norw. *kue*, MSw. *kufwa*, Sw. *kuva*).

cowage, cowitch kau·idʒ hairs of the pod of Mucuna pruriens. XVII. – Hindi *kiwāṅch, kawāṅch, kawāch*.

coward kau·əɹd ignobly faint-hearted person. XIII. ME. *cu(e)ard* – OF. *cuard*, later *couard* = Pr. *coart*, It. *codardo*, f. Rom. **cōda*, L. *cauda* tail; see -ARD. The reference to 'tail' is obscure; in the OF. 'Roman de Renart', 'Reynard the Fox', *coart* is the name of the hare. So **cow·ardice** XIII. – OF. *couardise*; an earlier OF. syn. was *couardie*, whence ME. (XIV) *cowardy* (see -Y[3]).

cower kau·əɹ crouch for shelter or in fear. XIII (*koure*). – MLG. *kūren* lie in wait (whence also Icel. *kúra*, Sw. *kura*, Da. *kure* squat, G. *kauern*); Gr. *gurós* round, curved, *gûros* circle, have been compared.

cowl kaul hooded garment worn by religious OE.; hood of the habit or of a cloak XVI; hood-shaped top of chimney XIX. OE. *cug(e)le, cūle*, corr. to MLG., MDu. *cōghel*, OHG. *cucula, cugula, chugela* (G. *kugel, kogel*) – ecclL. *cuculla*, f. L. *cucullus* hood of a cloak. In ME. reinforced by *kuuele* :- OE. *cufle* = MLG., MDu. *cōvele* (Du. *keuvel*), ON. *kofl, kufl*, and prob. by (O)F. *coule* = Pr. *cogolla*, Sp. *cogulla*, It. *cocolla* :- ecclL. *cuculla*.

cowrie kau·ri shell of a small gastropod, Cypræa moneta. XVII. – Urdu, Hindi *kauṛī* :- Skr. *kaparda, kapardika*.

cowslip kau·slip the wild plant Primula veris. OE. *cūslyppe*, f. *cū* cow[1]+*slyppe* viscous or slimy substance, i.e. 'cow-slobber' or 'cow-dung'; cf. OXSLIP. The OE. var. *cūsloppe* continued into mod. dial.; cf. dial. *bull-slop* and see SLOP.

cox kɔks shortening of COXSWAIN; hence as vb. XIX.

coxal kɔ·ksəl pert. to the coxa or hip. XIX. f. L. *coxa* hip (with cogns. denoting various bones in Indo-Iran., Celtic, and Germ.)+-AL. Cf. CUISSE.

coxcomb kɔ·kskoum cap worn by a professional fool (in shape and colour like a *cock's comb*); (arch.) †head (Sh.); †fool; fop. XVI.

coxswain kɔ·kswein helmsman of a boat. XV. f. COCK[3] ship's boat+SWAIN. Formerly also †*coxon, coxen*; cf. BOATSWAIN, BOSUN.

coy koi †quiet, still; shyly reserved. XIV. – (O)F. *coi*, earlier *quei* = Pr. *quet*, Sp. *quedo*, It. *cheto*, Rum. *cet* :- Rom. **quētu-s*, for L. *quiētus* QUIET.

coyote koi·out, koiə·ti prairie wolf of N. America. XIX. – Mex. Sp. – Aztec *coyotl*.

coz kʌz abbrev. of †*cozen*, COUSIN. XVI.

cozen kʌ·zn cheat, defraud. XVI (Tusser, Stubbes). prob. orig. vagrants' cant, and perh. to be assoc. with COUSIN, through OF. *cousin* dupe, or *cousiner* 'to clayme kindred for aduantage, or particular ends' (Cotgr.); but the frequent sp. with *-on* has suggested deriv. from It. *cozzonare* 'to play the horse-breaker, to play the craftie knaue' (Florio), f. *cozzone* middleman, broker = OF. *cosson* dealer :- L. *coctiō(n-)*. Hence **co·zenage** XVI (Stubbes, Nashe), **co·zener** XVI (Awdeley).

crab[1] kræb crustacean of the tribe Brachyura. OE. *crabba* = (M)LG., (M)Du. *krabbe* (whence F. *crabe*), ON. *krabbi*, rel. to OS. *krēbit*, MLG. *krēvet*, (M)Du. *kreeft*, OHG. *chrebiz, chrebazo* (G. *krebs*, whence F. *écrevisse* CRAYFISH), and to MLG. *krabben*, ON. *krafla* scratch, claw, OHG. *krapho* hook; the creature may have been named from its claws.

crab[2] kræb wild apple. XIV. contemp. with north. *scrab* (prob. of Scand. origin; cf. Sw. dial. *skrabba* wild apple), of which it may be an alteration by assoc. with prec. or CRABBED.

crab[3] kræb (of hawks) scratch, claw XVI (Turbervile); (sl.) find fault with, 'pull to pieces' XIX. – (M)LG. *krabben* (see CRAB[1]).

crab[4] kræb alteration of *carap*, the S. Amer. tree *Carapa guianensis*, as in *crab nut, oil, tree, wood.* XVIII.

crabbed kræ·bid †froward, wayward XIII (Cursor M.); out of humour; †harsh, rugged XIV; difficult to deal with or make sense of; cross-tempered XVI. f. CRAB[1]+-ED, with orig. ref. to the gait and habits of the crab, which suggest cross-grained or fractious disposition; cf. for meaning LG. *krabbe* cantankerous man, *krabbig* contentious, cross-grained, and for formation *dogged.* There has been later assoc. with CRAB[2] with connotation of sourness.

crack kræk A. make a sharp short noise OE.; break with a sudden sharp report XIII; B. utter loudly or sharply XIV; (dial.) boast XV (whence *crack up* eulogize XIX). OE. *cracian* sound, resound = (M)Du. *krāken*, OHG. *chrahhōn* (G. *krachen*). The normal repr. of the OE. word, i.e. *crake* (now dial.), has been superseded by the short form by assoc. with (i) **crack** sb. (ME. *crak*) XIV, corr. to MDu. *crak*, OHG. *chrac* (G. *krach*), or with (ii) F. *craquer* (XVI), of Germ. origin. **crack** adj. pre-eminent, first-class XVIII; attrib. use of *crack* sb. in the sense 'that which is cracked up or highly commended' (XVII). Hence **cracked** krækt crazy (cf. F. *fêlé*), earlier *brain-cracked* XVII. **cra·ck**ER[1] †boaster, liar; kind of firework XVI; instrument for cracking or crushing XVII. **cra·ckle** XVI; see -LE[3]; whence **cra·ckling** crisp skin of roast pork XVIII.

cracknel kræ·knəl light crisp biscuit. XV (Promp. Parv.). Alteration of F. *craquelin* (whence dial. *crackling* XVI) – MDu. *krākelinc*, f. *krāken* CRACK.

cracksman kræ·ksmən house-breaker. XIX. f. CRACK sb. in the sense 'house-breaking' (XIX), on the analogy of *craftsman.*

-cracy krəsi repr. F. *-cratie* krasi, medL. *-cratia*, Gr. *-kratiā* power, rule (f. *krátos* strength, might, authority) in Gr. originals of ARISTOCRACY, DEMOCRACY, OCHLOCRACY, PLUTOCRACY, THEOCRACY. The suffix has in mod. times acquired the sense of 'ruling body or class' of the kind denoted by the first element. Many joc. or contemptuous formations are or have been used, such as *beerocracy, clubocracy, mobocracy, snobocracy*; for the connecting el. see -O-.

cradle krei·dl child's light bed or cot OE.; framework of bars, cords, etc. XIV. OE. *cradol*, of which an unattested var. **crædel* was prob. the source of north. ME. *credel*, dial. *craddle, creddle*; perh. f. the same base as OHG. *kratto*, MHG., G. *kratte* basket.

craft kràft A. †strength, power OE.; B. skill, deceit OE.; C. art, trade OE.; D. structure, work XII; E. vessels, boats XVII. OE. *cræft* = OFris. *kraft*, OS. *kraft* (Du. *kracht*), OHG. *chraft* (G. *kraft*), ON. *kraptr*, with no cogns. outside Germ. As a second el. of comps. in the sense 'art', in *handicraft, statecraft, witchcraft.* Hence **cra·fts**MAN. XIV (PPl., Wycl. Bible). f. g.sg. **cra·fty** †strong; †skilful OE; cunning, wily XIII. OE. *cræftiġ* = OS. *kraftag, -ig*, OHG. *chreftig* (G. *kräftig*), ON. *krǫptugr*; see -Y[1].

crag kræg steep rugged rock. XIII (Cursor M.; also in Cumberland place-names *Blakrag, Buckecrag*). Of Celtic origin; not, however, from a form repr. by Ir., Gael. *creag*, W. *craig* rock (:– **krakjo-*) but prob. from an OBritish **crag* (:– **krako-*). Hence **cra·ggy** XV; see -Y[1].

crake kreik (dial.) crow, raven XIV; CORN-CRAKE XV. – ON. *kráka, krákr*, of imit. origin (cf. CROAK).

cram kræm fill to repletion or excess. OE. (*ġe*)*crammian*, corr. to MLG. *kremmen*, ON. *kremja* squeeze, pinch; Du. *krammen* cramp, clamp, MHG. *krammen* claw; f. **kram-* **krem-*; cf. OE. (*ġe*)*crimman* cram, stuff, and further L. *gremium* bosom (cf. GREMIAL), OSl. *gramada*, Lett. *grãmatas* heap, Skr. *grā́mas* group of men.

crambo kræ·mbou rhyming game; (contemptuously) rhyme, rhyming. XVII. Modification, on an It. or Sp. model, of †*crambe* (two syll.) used XVI–XVIII in phr. echoing Juvenal's *crambe repetita* (VII 154) cabbage served up again, and hence for '(distasteful) repetition', and spec. of repetition of identical sounds in rhyme (XVII) – L. *crambē* – Gr. *krámbē* kind of cabbage.

cramoisy kræ·moizi, -əzi chiefly Sc.; see CRIMSON. XV.

cramp[1] kræmp violent contraction of the muscles. XIV (Ch.): – OF. *crampe* – MLG., MDu. *krampe* = OHG. *krampfo*, rel. to OS. *kramp*, OHG. *chrampf* (G. *krampf*), sb. uses of an adj. meaning 'bent' (OHG. *krampf*, ON. *krappr* narrow, and OE. *crampiht*); cf. next and CRIMP. Hence **cramp** vb. affect with cramp; (in applications infl. by CRAMP[2]) compress, confine narrowly XVI.

cramp[2] kræmp metal bar with bent end(s). XV. – MDu. *krampe* (whence G. *krampe*, F. *crampe*) = OHG. *chrampho*, MHG. *kramphe*, of the same ult. origin as prec.

cranberry kræ·nbəri fruit of the shrub Vaccinium Oxycoccos. XVII. First used in England for the imported American species, Vaccinium macrocarpon, and thence transf. to the native European kind. Adopted by the colonists of N. America from G. *kranbeere* or LG. *kranebere* 'CRANE-berry' (cf. G. *kranichbeere*, and Sw. *tranbär*, Da. *tranebær*, f. *trana, trane* CRANE).

crane krein large grallatorial bird OE.; machine for raising and lowering weights (so Gr. *géranos*, L. *grūs* battering-ram, F. *grue*, G. *kran*, etc.). XIV. OE. *cran*, corr. to MLG. *krān*, *krōn*, and MDu. *crāne* (Du. *kraan*), OHG. *krano* (G. *kran* machine), also (with *k*-suffix; cf. *hawk*, *lark*) OE. *cranoc*, *cornuc*, MLG. *krānek*, OHG. *chranuh*, *-ih* (G. *kranich* bird); IE. bird-name f. imit. base **ger-*, repr. also by L. *grūs*, Gr. *géranos*, Arm. *krunk*, Lith. *garnŷs* heron, stork, *gérvė* crane, OSl. *žeravĭ*, W. *garan*; the Scand. forms have *tr-*, e.g. ON. *trani*. The present form depends on OE. obl. cases. Hence **crane** vb. hoist or lower with a crane XVI; stretch one's neck XVIII.

cranesbill krei·nzbil species of Geranium (the ref. is to the long slender beak of the fruit). XVI (Turner, Gerarde); cf. Du. †*craenhals*, MLG. *krāneshals* 'crane-neck', so called from resemblance to the long neck of the bird.

cranium krei·niəm skull. XVI. – medL. *crānium* – Gr. *krānion*, rel. to *kárā* head, and hence to the group of *kéras*, L. *cornū* HORN. The comb. form is **cranio-** (see -O-), as in **cranio·**LOGY, **cranio·**SCOPY. XIX. Hence **cra·ni**AL. XVIII.

crank[1] kræŋk portion of an axis bent at right angles. OE. *cranc* in *crancstæf* weaver's implement (cf. *crencestre* female weaver), rel. to *crinćan* (rare), parallel to *cringan* fall in battle, of which the prim. meaning appears to have been 'bend up, crook, curl up', hence 'shrink, give way, become weak'; cf. (M)HG., Du. *krank* sick, ill, (formerly) weak, slight, small, implied in OHG. *chrancholōn* be weak, stumble; the latter adj. is the source of thieves' cant *crank* rogue who feigned sickness (XVI). Cf. CRINGE, CRINKLE.

crank[2] kræŋk †bend, crook; fanciful turn of speech XVI; crotchet, whim (now usu. in *quips and cranks*, after Milton's 'L'Allegro' 25) XVI; (orig. U.S., back-formation from CRANKY) eccentric or crotchety person XIX (1881). prob. ult. identical with prec.

crank[3] kræŋk (naut.) liable to capsize. XVII (also *cranke sided*). perh. to be connected with *crank* adj. crabbed, awkward (XVIII), infirm, shaky (XIX), and CRANK[1].

cranky kræ·ŋki (dial.) sickly XVIII; out of order; wayward, cross-tempered; (colloq.) crotchety XIX (Dickens). perh. orig. f. cant †*crank* (see CRANK[1]), but infl. later by assoc. with CRANK[2]; see -Y[1].

crannog kræ·nəg ancient lake-dwelling. XIX. – Ir. *crannog*, Gael. *crannag* timber structure, f. *crann* tree, beam.

cranny kræ·ni chink, crevice. XV (Promp. Parv.). Earliest form *cranye*; poss. based on (O)F. *cran*, *cren*, *crenne*, dial. *crain*, *cren* notch, corr. to It. *crena* :– late popL. *crēna* notch (see CRENATE).

crape kreip thin gauze-like fabric. XVII (earliest ex. have *crispe*, *crespe*). – F. †*crespe*, *crêpe*, sb. use of OF. *crespe* curled, frizzed (see CRISP).

crapulous kræ·pjŭləs grossly excessive in drink or food XVI; suffering from such excess XVIII. – late L. *crāpulōsus*, f. *crāpula* intoxication – Gr. *kraipálē* result of a drunken debauch; see -OUS.

crash[1] kræʃ dash to pieces XIV; make the noise of this XVI. imit. formation, perh. partly suggested by *craze* and *dash*. Hence **crash** sb. (noise of) crashing XVI; financial collapse XIX (Coleridge).

crash[2] kræʃ coarse linen. XIX. – Russ. *krashenína* dyed and glossed linen. ¶ Hakluyt (1598) and Purchas (1625) have *craska*, *crasko* for a kind of stuff.

crasis krei·sis blending of elements XVII; combination of two vowels in one XIX. – Gr. *krâsis* mixture, combination, f. base of *kerannúnai* mix (cf. CRATER).

crass kræs coarse, gross XVI; grossly stupid XVII. – L. *crassus* solid, thick, fat. So **cra·ssi**TUDE †thickness XV; gross ignorance XVII. – L.

-crat kræt terminal el. repr. F. *-crate*, Gr. *-kratēs* in *aristocrate*, *démocrate* partisan of an aristocracy or democracy, (at the time of the French Revolution, passing into) member of the aristocracy, etc.; modelled on these are *plutocrat* and many nonce or joc. formations, as *cottonocrat*. See also AUTOCRAT. The corr. abstr. sbs. end in -CRACY, the adjs. in *-cratic(al)*.

cratch krætʃ (dial.) crib, manger XIII; wooden grating, hurdle XIV. ME. *crecche* (mod. dial. *cretch*) – OF. *creche* (mod. CRÈCHE) = Pr. *crepcha*, It. *greppia* :– Rom. **creppja* – Germ. **krippja* (whence OE. *cribb* CRIB).

crate kreit large case or hamper, box of open bars or slats. XVII. Earliest forms *creat* (XVII), *crade* (XVIII); poss. introduced with imports from Holland; cf. Du. *krat* tailboard of a wagon, skeleton case, †basket, †box of a coach (Kilian), of unkn. origin. ¶ An ex. of *crate* meaning 'hurdle' (XVI) is presumably – L. *crātis*.

crater krei·təɹ mouth of a volcano XVII; hole made in the ground by an explosion XIX. – L. *crātēr* bowl, basin, aperture of a volcano – Gr. *krātḗr* bowl, lit. mixing-vessel, f. **k(e)rā-* mix (cf. CRASIS).

cravat krəvæ·t kind of necktie. XVII (*crabat*, *crevatt*, *cravatt*). – F. *cravate*, appellative use of *Cravate* – G. *Krabate* – Serbo-Croatian *Hrvat* CROAT. ¶ The early form of the cravat was copied from the linen scarf worn round the neck by Croatian mercenaries in France.

crave kreiv †demand OE.; beg for XII; yearn for XIV. OE. *crafian* (:– **kraƀōjan*), rel. to ON. *krǫf* request, *krefja* (:– **kraƀjan*); the base is perh. that of CRAFT, with the radical sense of 'force, exact'.

craven krei·vn defeated (arch. in *cry craven*) XIII; poor-spirited, pusillanimous XIV; sb. XVI. ME. *crauaunt*, later *crauaunde*, *cravand*, perh. – clipped AN. form (cf. ASSIGN[2]) of OF. *cravanté* overcome, vanquished, pp. of *cravanter* crush, overwhelm = Pr. *crebantar*, Sp. *quebrantar* :– Rom. **crepantāre*, f. *crepant-*, prp. stem of L. *crepāre* rattle, burst (see CREPITATION); the ME. form was later assim. to pps. in -EN.

craw krɔ̄ pouch-like enlargement of the gullet in birds. XIV. – or orig. cogn. with MLG. *krage* (whence Icel. *kragi*), MDu. *crāghe* (Du. *kraag*) neck, throat, gullet = MHG. *krage* (G. *kragen*), of unkn. origin. The limitation of sense is peculiar to Eng.

crawfish see CRAYFISH.

crawl[1] krɔ̄l move along in a prone position XIV; be alive *with* creeping things XVI. Late ME. *crawle*, superseding earlier *creule*, *croule*, of unkn. origin (but cf. Sw. *kravla*, Da. *kravle*).

crawl[2] krɔ̄l †hog-pen XVII; pen or reservoir for fish, etc. XVIII. – colonial Du. *kraal* – Sp. CORRAL.

crayfish krei·fiʃ †crustacean XIV; freshwater crustacean Astacus fluviatilis XV; spiny lobster, langouste XVIII. ME. *crevis(se)*, *-es(se)* – OF. *crevice*, *crevis*, *crevesce* – OHG. *krebiz* (G. *krebs*) CRAB. Stressed orig. on the final syll., the word developed two types, (i) *crevis*, whence *crevish*, which by lengthening of the first syll. and assim. to *fish*, became *crayfish* (XVI), and (ii) *cravis*, which, through *cravish*, *crafish* (XVI), became **craw·fish** (XVII), which survives as the U.S. form. ¶ OF. var. *escrevisse* gave ME. *scrafisse* (XIV), *skrafysch* (XIV–XV).

crayon krei·ən stick of coloured chalk. XVII (Evelyn, Pepys, Dryden). – F. *crayon*, f. *craie* chalk = Pr. *greda* :– L. *crēta* chalk, clay; see -OON.

craze kreiz †shatter, batter, crack XIV (Ch.); †break down in health; impair in intellect (cf. *cracked*) XV. perh. – ON. **krasa* (cf. Sw. *krasa* crunch, *kras* in phr. *gå i kras* fly into pieces, *slå i kras* dash to pieces). Hence **craze** sb. †crack, flaw XVI; †crack-brain XVII; insane fancy, mania XIX. **cra·zy** unsound, liable to fall to pieces; †failing in health XVI; of unsound mind XVII; see -Y[1].

creak krīk †croak XIV; †speak stridently or querulously XV; make a shrill grating noise XVI. orig. synon. with †*crake* (XIV) and CROAK, and of similar imit. origin; the change of the ME. vowel ē to ī may have assisted the sense development.

cream krīm oily part of milk XIV; best or choice part XVI; applied to purified preparations XVII. ME. *creme* (*creym*, *craym*) – OF. *creme*, *craime*, *cresme* (mod. *crème*), repr. blending of late L. *crāmum* (Venantius Fortunatus), *crāma*, which is perh. of Gaulish origin, with late L. *chrisma* CHRISM (modF. *chrême*). ¶ The OE. word *rēam* survives dial.

crease krīs mark produced by folding; also vb. XV; (cricket) lines marked on the ground to define positions XVIII. In XVI–XVII also *creast*, which was a frequent var. of CREST (cf. *beast*); orig. *crĕst*, which was reduced to *crease* by assimn. to the var. *cress* (XVI–XVII) of the vb., the mark of a fold being looked at as a ridge in the material. Cf. OF. *cresté* wrinkled, furrowed.

create kriei·t bring into being. The inf. is not attested before late XV, but is anticipated in early XV by the pp. *created*, which was an extension (see -ED) of †*creat* (XIV, Ch., Trevisa) – L. *creātus*, pp. of *creāre* bring forth, produce, cause to grow, prob. rel. to *crēscere* grow (cf. CRESCENT). The sense 'form out of nothing', and the consequent applications of *creation*, *creator*, etc., are of Christian origin. So **crea·TION**. XIV (Gower). – (O)F. – L. In gen. senses first recorded from Sh.; in the sense 'created world' first in A.V., Rom. viii 22. **crea·tive**. XVII (Cudworth). **crea·TOR** one who creates; in earliest use of God (replacing early ME. *sheppend*, OE. *sċieppend*). XIII. – OF. *creatour*, *-ur* (mod. *créateur*) – L. *creātōrem*, *creātor*. **creatURE** krī·tʃəɹ created thing. XIII (Cursor M.). orig. *creātu·rē* – (O)F. *créature* – late L. *creātūra*, f. *creāt-*, *creāre*.

crèche kreiʃ, ||krɛʃ public nursery for infants. XIX. F., 'manger, crib', 'day nursery' = Pr. *crepcha*, It. *greppia* :– Rom. **creppia* – OHG. *kripja*, *krippa* CRIB.

credence krī·dəns A. †trust, confidence, credit XIV (*letter of credance*, R. Mannyng); belief XIV (Wycl. Bible, Gower). B. †assaying of food XV; †sideboard for dishes, etc. XVI; (eccl.) in full *credence table*, side table near an altar for holding vessels XIX. – (O)F. *crédence* – medL. *crēdentia* (whence It. *credenza*, the source of F. *crédence* in the senses under B above), f. *crēdent-*, *-ēns*, prp. of L. *crēdere*; see CREED, -ENCE. So **cre·de·nda** things to be believed. XVII. n. pl. of gerundive of L. *crēdere*. **cre·dENT** believing; †credible, creditable. XVII (Sh.). **credential** kride·nʃəl recommending or entitling to credit, esp. in *letters c.*, *c. letters* (in medL. *litteræ credentiales*) XVI; sb. pl. XVII (Clarendon). – medL. *crēdentiālis*, f. *crēdentia* CREDENCE; see -IAL. **credible** kre·dibl believable, reliable. XIV (Ch., Gower). – L. *crēdibilis*, f. *crēdere*; see CREDIT, -IBLE. So **crediBI·LITY**. XVI (Hooker). – medL. **credit** kre·dit faith, trust; (favourable) repute; power based on confidence; acknowledgement of merit; confidence in a buyer's ability to pay, reputation of solvency XVI; sum at one's disposal in a bank XVII; acknowledgement of payment (hence fig. phr. *give* a person *credit for*) XVIII. – F. *crédit* – It. *credito* or L. *crēditum* (thing entrusted to one, loan),

n. pp. of *crēdere*. Hence, or f. pp. *crēdit-* of *crēdere*, **cre·dit** vb. put trust in; †do credit to XVI; enter on the credit side of an account XVII; ascribe *to* XIX. So **cre·ditor** one who gives credit or to whom money is owing. XV. – AN. *creditour*, OF. *créditeur* – L. *crēditor*; see -OR[1].

credo krī·dou creed. XII. 1st pers. pres. sg. indic. of L. *crēdere* believe. ¶ So used also in Rom. and other Germ. langs.

credulous kre·djŭləs ready (now always, over-ready) to believe. XVI. f. L. *crēdulus*, f. *crēdere* believe; see CREED, -ULOUS. So **credul**ITY kridjū·lĭti †belief, credence XV; over-readiness to believe XVI. – (O)F. – L.

creed krīd authoritative form of words setting forth the articles of belief. OE. *crēda* – L. *crēdō* I believe (with cogns. in Indo-Iranian and Celtic), the first word of the Apostles' and the Nicene Creeds in the Latin versions.

creek krīk A. narrow inlet in a coast XIII; arm or branch of a river (now esp. in U.S. and British dominions) XVI; B. cleft, chink, corner, nook XIII. (i) ME. *crike* – ON. *kriki* chink, nook (in *handarkriki* armpit; cf. Norw., Sw. dial. *krik* corner, etc.), whence also (O)F. *crique*, which may be partly a source of the Eng. word; (ii) ME. *crēke*, either – MDu. *krēke* (Du. *kreek* creek, bay), or by lengthening of *ĭ* in *crike*; cf. AL. *crica* and *creca*; ult. origin unkn. (a stem with *ī* occurs in ON. *krīkar* m. pl. groin).

creel krīl large wicker basket. XV (Wyntoun). orig. Sc., of unkn. origin.

creep krīp move with the body prone and close to the ground OE.; move forward cautiously or slowly XII; grow along the ground, a wall, etc. XVI. OE. *crēopan*, pt. *crēap*, *crupon*, pp. *cropen* = OFris. *kriapa*, OS. *criopan*, ON. *krjúpa* :– Germ. **kreupan*, **kraup*, **krupun*, **krupanaz*; cogn. forms have *ū* in the pres. stem, as OS. *krūpan* (Du. *kruipen*), MLG. *krūpen*, MHG. *krūfen*; rel. to CROP, CRIPPLE. Weak forms of the pt. are found as early as *c.* 1300 and of the pp. in XV; these replaced ME. *crope* and *crop(p)en* respectively, which survived dial.

creese krīs, **kris** kris Malay dagger. XVI. ult. – Malay *kirīs*, *krīs*, *kris*, but immed. – such forms as Du. *kris* (so in G.), Sp., Pg. *cris*, F. *criss*; there have been numerous vars.

cremate krimei·t consume (esp. a corpse) by fire. XIX. f. pp. stem of L. *cremāre*, or back-formation from **crem**A·TION. XVII (Sir T. Browne). So **cremat**ORIUM krem-, krīmətɔ̄·riəm establishment for cremation; superseding *cre·matory* XIX; see -ORY.

cremona[1] krimou·nə violin made at *Cremona*, in Lombardy, Italy. XVIII (Sterne).

cremona[2] krimou·nə 8-foot organ reed-stop. XVII. Alteration of *cromorne* – F. CROMORNE.

crenate krī·neit (nat. hist.) notched, finely scalloped. XVIII. – modL. *crēnātus*, f. L. *crēna* notch (occurring once as a gloss on Gr. γλυφίς notched end of an arrow, but established in Rom. from XII); cf. next and see -ATE[2].

crenellate kre·nĭleit provide with embattlements or embrasures. XIX (first in pp.). f. (O)F. *créneler* (in OF. pp. only), f. *crenel* embrasure = Pr. *crenel* :– popL. **crenellu-s*, (medL. *kernellus*), dim. of late L. *crēna* (see CRANNY). So **crenell**A·TION. XIX (Lytton). – F. ¶ The OF. sb. and vb. have been repr. by †*kernel* sb. (XIII–XVII), vb. (XIV–XVIII), †*crenelle* (her.) embattled (XVI–XVII), *crenelled* notched (XVIII), embattled (XIX).

Creole krī·oul (descendant of) European or Negro settler in the W. Indies, etc. XVII (*criole*). – F. *créole*, earlier *criole* – Sp. *criollo*, prob. – Pg. *crioulo* negro born in Brazil, home-born slave, formerly of animals reared at home, f. *criar* nurse, breed :– L. *creāre* CREATE.

creosote krī·əsout oily liquid distilled from wood tar. XIX. – G. *kreosote* (1832, Reichenbach), f. Gr. *kreo-*, *kreō-*, comb. form of *kréas* flesh (rel. to L. *crūdus* CRUDE) + *sōt|ḗr* saviour, *sōt|eríā* safety; intended to mean 'flesh-saving' with ref. to the antiseptic properties.

crêpe kreip transparent dress material, esp. in *crêpe de chine* kreip də ʃīn 'China crape'. XIX. F.; see CRAPE.

crepitation krepitei·ʃən crackling noise XVII; (path.) sound accompanying breathing in lung disease, etc. XIX. – F. *crépitation* (Paré) – late L. *crepitātiō(n-)*, f. *crepitāre*, frequent. of *crepāre* crack, creak, of imit. origin. So **cre·pitate.** XVII; see -ATE[3].

crepitus kre·pitəs (path.) crepitation. XIX. L., f. *crepāre*.

crepuscular kripʌ·skjŭləɹ pert. to twilight. XVII. f. L. *crepusculum*, f. (evening) twilight, f. (prob. after *dīlūculum* dawn) **crepus*, *creper* dark, obscure; see -AR.

crescendo kriʃe·ndou (mus.) direction for increase in loudness. XVIII. It., prp. of *crescere* INCREASE.

crescent kre·sənt convexo-concave figure, as of the waxing (or waning) moon XIV; row of buildings in the form of an arc of a circle (first applied to the Royal Crescent at Bath) XVIII. ME. *cressa(u)nt* – AN. *cressaunt*, OF. *creissant* (mod. *croissant*) :– L. *crēscentem*, *-ēns*, prp. of *crēscere* grow, INCREASE. In XVII assim. to the L. form, which was already current in **crescent** adj. XVI. See -ENT. ¶ L. *luna crescens* waxing moon (Columella) has no reference to shape, which was developed in Rom.

cress kres any kind of cruciferous plants with pungent edible leaves. OE. *cressa*, *cresse*, *cærse*, *cerse* = MLG. *kerse*, MDu. *kersse*, *korsse* (Du. *kers*), OHG. *chresso*, *chressa* (G. *kresse*) :– WGerm. **krasjŏn*.

cresset kre·sit vessel containing oil or other fuel to give light. XIV. – OF. *cresset, craisset*, f. *craisse*, var. of *graisse* oil, GREASE; see -ET.

crest krest tuft or plume of feathers XIV; top, ridge XIII; ridge of an animal's neck XVI. – OF. *creste* (mod. *crête*) = Pr., Sp., It. *cresta*, Rum. *creastă* :– L. *crista* tuft, plume, prob. rel. to *crīnis* hair.

cretaceous krītei·ʃəs chalky. XVII. f. L. *crētāceus*, f. *crēta* chalk; see -ACEOUS.

Cretan krī·tən pert. to the island of *Crete* in the Mediterranean. XVI (Sh.). – L. *Crētānus*; see -AN. ¶ The forms used in early translations of the Bible are, in Acts ii 11 *Cretes* (Geneva and A.V.) – Vulg. *Crētēs*, in Titus i 12 *Cretayns* (Tindale and Coverdale), *Cretyans* (Cranmer), *Cretians* (Geneva and A.V.); Rheims and Douay have *Cretensians* (– Vulg. *Cretenses*) in both places.

cretic krī·tik (pros.) amphimacer (– ᴗ –), verse consisting of such feet. XVI. – L. *crēticus* – Gr. *krētikós* Cretan, f. *Krētē* Crete; see -IC. For the pronunc. cf. *stratēgic*.

cretin krī·tin deformed idiot of the Alpine valleys. XVIII. – F. *crétin* – Swiss F. *creitin, crestin* :– L. *Chrīstīanu-s* CHRISTIAN, the reprs. of which in Rom. langs. mean 'human being' as dist. from the brutes (cf. F. *parler chrétien* speak an intelligible language). The implication in this word is that these beings are human, although dwarfed and deformed.

cretonne kre·tən, krĭto·n figured cotton cloth. XIX. – F. *cretonne*, f. *Creton* village in Normandy famous for linen manufacture.

crevasse krĭvæ·s fissure in a glacier. XIX. – F. *crevasse* (OF. *crevace*); see next.

crevice kre·vis small crack in a surface. XIV. ME. *crevace, crevisse*, later *creves(se), -ice* – OF. *crevace* (mod. *crevasse*), f. *crever* burst, split :– L. *crepāre* rattle, crack, break with a crash; the suffix is L. *-ācea* fem. (see -ACEOUS).

crew krū †military reinforcement XV; (armed) company XVI; ship's company XVII. Late ME. *crue* – OF. *creue* increase, augmentation, reinforcement, sb. use of fem. pp. of *croistre*, mod. *croître* :– L. *crēscere* grow, INCREASE.

crewel krū·əl thin worsted yarn. XV. orig. *crule, crewle, croole* (monosyll.); of unkn. origin.

crib krib rack for fodder in a cow-shed, manger OE.; ox-stall; †wicker basket XIV; cabin, hovel XVI; child's bed XVII. OE. *crib(b)* = OFris. *cribbe*, OS. *kribbia* (Du. *kribbe, krib*), OHG. *chrippa* (G. *krippe*); beside OE. *crybb* (also repr. by *crib* in standard Eng.) = MLG. *krübbe*, Du. *krub*; cf. MHG. *krēbe* basket; no further cogns. are known. Hence **crib** vb. †feed as at a manger XV; confine narrowly XVII (Sh.); **pilfer, thieve** XVIII (prob. orig. thieves' cant from the sense 'basket' of the sb.); from the latter sense is derived a new sb. theft, plagiarism; translation, esp. illegitimately used XIX.

cribbage kri·bidʒ card-game, a characteristic feature of which is the *crib*, which consists of cards thrown out from each player's hand and belonging to the dealer. XVII. Of unkn. origin.

crick krik painful stiffness in the neck. XV (Promp. Parv.). Of unkn. origin.

cricket[1] kri·kit chirping house-insect. XIV. – (O)F. *criquet* †grasshopper, cricket, f. *criquer* crackle, of imit. origin; cf. (M)Du. *krekel* cricket, f. imit. base **krik-*.

cricket[2] kri·kit game played with ball, bat, and wicket. XVI. Of uncertain origin; perh. – OF. *criquet* bat used in a ball-game, with which cf. Flem. *krick(e)* stick.

crikey krai·ki dial. and sl. excl. of astonishment. XIX. euphem. alteration of CHRIST used to avoid the appearance of profanity; also dial. *crikes* and *becrike* ('by Christ'). So **criminy** kri·mĭni, earlier †*crimine*. XVII (Otway, Congreve); also *criminy jiminy* (XIX, Byron), for *Christ Jesus*. **crimes** kraimz (dial. *crimy, crimons*) XIX, **cripes** kraips XX.

crim. con. see CONVERSATION. XVIII.

crime krəim act punishable by law. XIV. – (O)F. *crime*, †*crimne* :– L. *crīmen* judgement, accusation, offence, f. reduced form of base of *cernere* (cf. pp. *crētus*) decide, give judgement; cf. DISCERN. **crimin**AL kri·minəl. XV. – late L. *crīminālis*, f. *crīmin-, crīmen*. **cri·min**OUS (now in *c. clerk*). XV. – AN. *criminous*, OF. *crimineux* – L. *crīminōsus* **crimino·**LOGY. XIX (1890).

crimp krimp crumple, wrinkle. Sparsely evidenced before XVII, its currency being prob. due to – (M)LG., (M)Du. *krimpen* shrink, wrinkle, shrivel = OHG. *chrimphan* (MHG. *krimpfen*), rel. distantly to OE. *(ġe)crympan* curl, with which, though it would be repr. now by *crimp*, there appears to be no continuity. Cf. CRAMP.

crimson kri·mzən deep red. XIV. Late ME. *cremesin, crimesin*, corr. in form to Sp. †*cremesin*, It. †*cremesino*, medL. *cremesīnus*, metathetic var. of *kermesīnus, carmesīnus*, Sp. *carmesin*, It. *chermesino*, f. Sp. *carmesí*, It. *chermesi, cremesi* (whence F. *cramoisi* CRAMOISY) – Arab. *qirmazī*, f. *qirmaz* KERMEZ. For the sp. with *-son* cf. DAMSON.

cringe krin^{d}ʒ shrink, cower XIII; bend the body timorously or servilely XVI. ME. *crenġe*, varying with *crenche*, corr. to OE. *crinġan, crinċan* fall in battle, OFris. *krenza*, Du. *krengen* heel over, and rel. to ON. *krangr* weak, frail, *kranga* creep along, and MLG., Du., MHG. *krenken* weaken, injure, OFris., (M)LG., (M)HG. *krank* sick, ill, slight (see CRANK[1]); cf. OSl. *po|gręznąti* sink down underneath, Lith. *gręžiù*.

cringle kri·ŋgl ring or eye of rope. XVII. – LG. *kringel*, dim. of *kring* circle, ring, f. **kriŋg-*, parallel to **kriŋk-* (cf. CRANK[1], CRINKLE).

crinite krai·nait hairy. XVI. – L. *crīnītus*, f. *crīnis* hair (cf. CREST); see -ITE.

crinkle kri·ŋkl form short turns or twists. XIV (in pp. *krynkeled*, *crenkled*, Ch.). frequent. f. base of OE. *crinćan* yield, orig. weaken, rel. to OFris., MLG., (M)HG. *krank* weak, sickly, OFris. *krenza*, MLG., MHG. *krenken* weaken; see CRANK[1], -LE[2], CRINGE.

crinkum-crankum kri·ŋkəm kræ·ŋkəm fancifully elaborated object. XVII. Formation with variation of vowel intended to symbolize intricacy.

crinoid kri·noid, krɔi- lily-shaped. XIX. – Gr. *krinoeidēs*, f. *krínon* lily; see -OID.

crinoline kri·nəlin, -īn stiff fabric of horsehair, etc.; stiff petticoat made of this. XIX. – F. *crinoline*, irreg. f. L. *crīnis* hair (F. *crin* horsehair) + *līnum* thread (F. *lin* flax), the intention being to denote the woof of horsehair and the weft of thread.

cripple kri·pl lame person. OE. (Nhb.) *crypel*, also *eorþcrypel* 'paralyticus', ME. (s.w.) *crüpel*, corr. to OLG. *krupil*, f. **krup-*; also OE. *crēopel*, ME. *crēpel*, corr. to MLG., MDu. *krēpel*, rel. to forms cited s.v. CREEP. Hence **cripple** vb. XIII.

crisis krai·sis turning-point of a disease XV; vital or decisive stage in events XVII. – medical L. *crisis* (Seneca) – Gr. *krísis* decision, judgement, event, issue, turning-point of a disease (Hippocrates, Galen), f. *krínein* decide (cf. DISCERN).

crisp krisp curly OE.; wrinkled, rippled XIV; brittle but hard or firm XVI. OE. *crisp*, *crips* – L. *crispus* curled (whence OF. *crespe*; see CRÊPE). The development of the last sense may be due to symbolic interpretation of the sound of the word.

crispin kri·spin (arch.) shoemaker. XVIII. f. name of St. *Crispin*, patron saint of shoemakers (cf. F. *lance de saint Crispin* awl).

criss-cross kri·skrɔ̀s A. †figure of a cross; †alphabet XVI; B. transverse crossing (also adj., adv., and vb.) XIX. Early modEng. *c(h)ris(se)-crosse*, for *Christscrosse* figure of a cross, esp. as used in front of the alphabet in hornbooks and primers, called *Chris(t)-cross row* (XVI–XIX); in later sense usu. regarded as a redupl. formation on CROSS[1] with variation of vowel.

cristate kri·steit (nat. hist.) crested. XVII. – L. *cristātus*, f. *crista* CREST; see -ATE[2].

criterion kraitiə·riən standard of judgement. XVII. – Gr. *kritḗrion* means of judging, test, f. *kritḗs* judge. (Often in XVII written in Gr. letters; occas. in latinized form *criterium*, as in F.)

critic kri·tik †one who passes censure XVI (Sh.); one who judges a work of art XVII (Bacon). – L. *criticus* (also used in Eng. XVI–XVII) – Gr. *kritikós*, sb. use of adj. f. *kritḗs* judge, rel. to CRISIS; see -IC. So **†cri·tic** adj. (med.) relating to a crisis in a disease; faultfinding; skilful in judging. XVI. – F. *critique* – late L. **cri·t**ICAL censorious XVI (Sh.); pert. to a crisis; pert. to criticism or critics; †nice, precise XVII. f. L. *criticus*. **cri·tic**ISM act or art of criticizing XVII (Dekker); critical science concerned with literary documents; †nice point, subtlety XVII. **cri·tic**IZE play the critic XVII (Milton); discuss critically XVII. (†*Critism* and †*critize* were used XVII.) **critique** kritī·k criticism, esp. a critical review XVII. Later form of †*critic(k)* XVII, altered after F. *critique*, the orig. source, which is based on Gr. (*hē*) *kritikḗ* the critical art. Cf. G. *kritik*.

croak krouk utter a deep hoarse cry, as of a rook, etc. XVI. Preceded by synon. †*crok* (XIII), with similar imit. formations, viz. OE. *crakettan*, *cræccettan*, ME. †*crake* (XIV) and †*creke* (see CREAK), †*crouk* (XIV), †*craik* (XV, Henryson).

Croat krou·æt native of Croatia, formerly with Slavonia forming a kingdom of the Hungarian monarchy, now part of Yugoslavia. XVIII. – modL. (pl.) *Croatæ* (F. *Croate*, G. *Kroate*) – Serbo-Croatian *Hrvat*, formerly pronounced χr̥wât; cf. CRAVAT. So **Croat**IAN krouei·ʃən. XVI.

crochet krou·ʃei knitting with a hooked needle. XIX. – F. *crochet*, dim. of *croc*, with *-ch-* from *crochié*, *crochu* hooked.

crocidolite krosi·dŏlait (min.) fibrous silicate of iron and sodium. XIX. f. Gr. *krokid-*, *krokís* nap of woollen cloth; see -LITE.

crock[1] krɔk earthen pot, jar, etc. OE.; (dial.) metal pot. XV. OE. *croc* and *crocca*, rel. to synon. Icel. *krukka*, and prob. further to OE. *crōg* (= OHG. *chruog*, G. *krug*), OE. *crūce* (= OS. *krūka*, Du. *kruik*, MHG. *krūche*), Ir. *crogán*, Gael. *crog(an)*, W. *crochan*, Gr. *krōssós* (:– **krōkjos*).

crock[2] krɔk old ewe XV; old broken-down horse; decrepit person or thing XIX. In earliest use Sc.; perh. of Flem. origin, but appropriate words have a different vowel, as MDu. *kraecke* (Du. *krak*), Flem. *krake*; presumably rel. to CRACK.

crocket krɔ·kit †curl; (archit.) small ornament (bud, curled leaf, etc.) on the inclined side of a pinnacle, etc. XVII; bud of a stag's horn XIX. – var. of (O)F. *crochet* CROTCHET.

crocodile krɔ·kədail large amphibious saurian reptile. XIII. ME. *coko-*, *cokadrille* – OF. *cocodrille* (mod. *crocodile*) = Pr. *cocodrilh*, Sp. *cocodrilo*, It. *coccodrillo* :– medL. *cocodrillus*, which occurs together with many other vars. in MSS. of ancient Latin writers for *crocodīlus* – Gr. *krokódīlos* (later *-eilos*), for **krokódrīlos* 'worm of the stones', f. *krókē* pebbles, shingles + *drîlos* worm, with allusion to its basking habits. The present form, assim. to L., appears XVI.

crocus krou·kəs (flower of) bulbous plant of the iridaceous genus so named; yellow or red powder obtained from metals by calcination. XVII. – L. *crocus* crocus plant, saffron (whence OE. *croh*, Gael., Ir. *croch*) – Gr. *krókos*, of Sem. origin (cf. Heb. *karkōm*, Arab. *kurkum*).

croft krɔft enclosed piece of land OE.; small agricultural holding. XVIII. OE. *croft*, of unkn. origin.

cromlech krɔ·mlek prehistoric erection of large unhewn stones. XVII. – W. *cromlech*, f. *crom*, fem. of *crwm* bowed, arched + *llech* flat stone. Cf. DOLMEN.

cromorne krəmɔ̄·ɹn reed-stop in an organ. XVII. – F. *cromorne* – G. *krummhorn* cornet, lit. 'crooked horn'. Another perversion is CREMONA².

crone kroun withered old woman XIV (Ch.); old ewe XVI. prob. – MDu. *croonje*, *caroonje* carcass, (in Kilian) old useless ewe – ONF. *carogne* CARRION (also, cantankerous or mischievous woman), which may be the immed. source of the first sense.

crony krou·ni intimate associate. XVII. Earliest form *chrony* – Gr. *khrónios* long-lasting, long-continued, f. *khrónos* time (see CHRONIC); orig. university slang word ('vox academica', Skinner 1671), the Gr. word being perverted to the sense 'contemporary'. Pepys, who uses the word, and Skinner were Cambridge men. ¶ The corr. Oxford term was *chum*.

crook kruk trick, wile XII (Orm); hooked instrument; †claw XIII; shepherd's staff, bishop's pastoral staff XIV; bend, curve XV. ME. *crōc*, *crōk*, north. *crūk* – ON. *krókr* hook, barb, peg, bend, curve, winding, corner (Sw. *krok*, Da. *krog*). Hence **crook** vb. bend, curve XII.

crooked kru·kid not straight (lit. and fig.). XIII. f. CROOK sb. + -ED², prob. after ON. *krókóttr* crooked, winding, cunning, wily.

croon krūn (dial.) bellow, roar, rumble XIV; utter a low murmuring sound XVIII. north. Eng. and Sc. *croyne*, *crune* – MLG., MDu. *krōnen* lament, mourn, groan (Du. *kreunen* groan, whimper), of imit. origin; cf. OHG. *chrōnnan*, *chrōnan* chatter, prattle.

crop krɔp A. bird's craw OE.; B. †head of a plant OE.; top of an object XV; upper part of a whip XVI (hence, whipstock with a handle and loop XIX); C. produce of plants used for food XIII (also in AL. *croppus*, *cropa*). OE. *crop(p)*, corr. to MLG., MDu. *kropp*, (O)HG. *kropf*, ON. *kroppr*; further relations uncertain. Hence **crop** vb. lop, poll XIII; pluck, pull XIV; raise a crop on, bear a crop XVI; come *up* to the surface XVII; whence a new sb. **crop** cropping (in various uses) XVII.

croquet krou·kei, -ki game played on a lawn with wooden balls which are driven through hoops with mallets, introduced from Ireland into England in 1852: Supposed to be – var. of F. *crochet* hook; see CROCHET, CROTCHET. Hence in F. (1877).

croquette kroke·t ball of potato, etc., or mince fried crisp. XVIII (occas. *croquet*). F., f. *croquer* crunch, of imit. origin; see -ETTE.

crore krɔ̄əɹ ten millions (of rupees). XVII. – Hindi *k(a)rōṛ* :– Prakrit *kroḍi*, Skr. *koṭi* end, top, highest point, spec. highest number in the older system (viz. 10,000,000).

crosier, crozier krou·ʒⁱəɹ †cross-bearer to an archbishop XIV (PPl.); bearer of a bishop's pastoral staff, hence (through the phr. *crosier('s) staff*) the staff itself XIV; (erron.) archbishop's cross XVIII. Two words have blended here, (i) – OF. *croisier* (medL. *cruciārius*) cross-bearer, f. *crois* CROSS, (ii) – OF. *crocier*, *crossier* bearer of a bishop's *crosse* or crook (OF. *croce* = Pr. *crossa*, It. *croccia* :– Rom. **croccia*, f. **croccus* CROOK).

cross¹ krɔ̀s gibbet consisting of a vertical post with transverse bar; sign or symbol representing this, esp. in Christian use. Late OE. *cros* – ON. *kross* – OIr. *cros* (corr. to Gael. *crois*, W. *croes*) – L. *crucem* (nom. CRUX), whence also OF. *croiz* (mod. *croix*), Pr. *crotz*, Sp. *cruz*, It. *croce*, Rum. *cruce*; OF. *croiz* was adopted in ME. as *cr(e)oiz*, later *crois*, *croice* (XIII–XV). ¶ The L. word was adopted (with lengthened vowel) in Germ. as OE. *crūć*, ME. *crouch* (whence *crouched* adj. wearing a cross, esp. in *Crouched*, later *Crutched*, *Friars*, earlier †*crossed freres*), OS. *crūci*, OHG. *crūzi* (G. *kreuz*). Hence **cross** vb. †crucify; set or lie in a cross-position XIV (draw a line across XVIII); mark with a cross; put, pass, come, go across or athwart XV; thwart, oppose XVI.

cross² krɔ̀s adj. lying or passing athwart; contrary, opposite; †contentious XVI; out of humour, peevish XVII. Partly attrib. use of CROSS¹, partly ellipt. use of CROSS³ adv.

cross³ krɔ̀s †adv. crosswise, and prep. across. XVI. Aphetic of ACROSS; the prep. survives in *cross-country* adj. (XVIII).

crotalus krɔ·tələs genus of serpents containing the rattlesnakes. XIX. modL. – Gr. *krótalon* rattle, rel. to *krótos* clapping, tapping.

crotch krɔtʃ fork or fork-shaped stake, branch, etc., fork of a tree where it branches. XVI. perh. identical with ME. *croche* crook, crozier – OF. *croche* hook, etc., f. *crocher*, f. *croc* hook – ON. *krókr* CROOK.

crotchet krɔ·tʃit A. †crocket XIV; hook (latterly techn.) XV; B. (mus.) note in the form of a stem with a black head ♩ 𝄽 XV ('crochett of songe, *semiminima*', Promp. Parv.); C. whimsical fancy XVI. – (O)F. *crochet*, dim. of *croc* hook, CROOK; see -ET. The origin of sense C is doubtful, but cf. '*Crochue*, a Quauer in Musicke; whence *Il a des crochues en teste*, (we say) his head is full of crochets' (Cotgr.).

croton krouˑtən genus of Euphorbiaceæ, mostly tropical XVIII; an allied plant, Codiæum pictum XIX. – modL. – Gr. *krótōn* sheep-tick, castor-oil plant (Ricinus communis).

crouch krautʃ bend low with general compression of the body. XIV. Late ME. *cruche, crouche*, poss. – OF. *crochir* be bent, f. *croc* hook (cf. *crochu* hooked, crooked) – ON. *krókr* CROOK; the vocalism would be paralleled in *pouch, vouch*.

croup[1] krūp hindquarters. XIII. –(O)F. *croupe* (whence G. *kruppe*) = Pr. *cropa* :– Rom. **croppa* – Germ. **kruppō*, rel. to CROP.

croup[2] krūp throat-disease with a sharp cough. XVIII. f. *croup* vb. (dial.) XVI, of imit. origin.

croupier krūˑpiəɹ †second standing behind a gamester; raker-in of money at a gaming-table; assistant chairman at a dinner. XVIII. – F. *croupier* orig. one who rides behind on the croup, f. *croupe* CROUP[1].

crow[1] krou black carrion-feeding bird, Corvus OE.; bar of iron with beak-like end XIV. OE. *crāwe*, corr. to OS. *krāia* (Du. *kraai*), OHG. *chrāwa, chrāja, krā* (G. *krähe*); f. next.

crow[2] krou utter the cry of a cock. OE. *crāwan*, pt. *crēow*, pp. *crāwen*, corr. to OS. **krāian* (Du. *kraaien*), OHG. *chrājan, crāwan, krāen* (G. *krähen*); WGerm. vb. of imit. origin. The str. pt. is still prevalent in the proper sense, but *crowed* is used in the sense 'utter joyful cries'; the str. pp. is now dial. Hence **crow** sb. act of crowing XIII (*cockes crow*; cf. *cockcrow* XV).

crowd[1] kraud press on OE.; †push; press in a throng XIV; fill up with compression XVI; (naut.) *crowd sail* XVII. OE. *crūdan*, pt. *crēad*, **crudon*, **croden*) intr. push forward, orig. str. vb. corr. to MLG., MDu. *krūden* (Du. *kruien* push in a wheelbarrow); cf. OE. *croda* crowd, MLG. *krōden*, MHG. *kroten* oppress. Hence **crowd** sb. dense multitude. XVI.

crowd[2] kraud fiddle. XIII (*crouth*). – W. *crwth* fiddle, also swelling body, rel. to *croth* swelling, belly (cf. Gael. and Ir. *cruit* harp, violin, hump, OIr. *crot* harp, cithara, whence in late L. *crotta* British musical instrument mentioned by Venantius Fortunatus, *c*. 600).

crown kraun circlet, wreath, etc., worn on the head XII; †tonsure; vertex of the skull XIII; top, summit XVI; various coins, orig. bearing the figure of a crown XV. ME. *crune, corune* (superseding OE. *corona*) – AN. *corune*, OF. *corone* (mod. *couronne*) = Pr., Sp., It. *corona* :– L. *corōna* wreath, chaplet – Gr. *korṓnē* anything bent (*korōnís* crown), rel. to *curvus* bent (see CURVE). So **crown** vb. XII. – AN. *coruner*, OF. *coroner* (mod. *couronner*) :– L. *corōnāre*; cf. CORONATION.

crowner see CORONER.

croydon kroiˑdən two-wheeled carriage. XIX. f. *Croydon* in Surrey; cf. SURREY.

crozier see CROSIER.

crucial krūˑʃəl cross-shaped XVIII; that decides between rival hypotheses, decisive XIX. – F. *crucial* (XVI in medical use), f. *cruci-, crux* CROSS; see -IAL. The second sense (as in *crucial instance, experiment*) is based on Francis Bacon's phr. *instantia crucis* 'instance, i.e. of the cross', a metaphor from the *crux* or finger-post at cross-roads, and on Boyle's and Newton's *experimentum crucis*.

crucible krūˑsĭbl vessel for fusing metals. XV (early forms *corusible, kressibulle*). – medL. *crucibulum* night-lamp, crucible (cf. It. *cruciuolo*, OF. *croiseul, crusol*, from a by-form **cruceolus*), f. L. *cruc-, crux* CROSS; perh. orig. lamp hanging before a crucifix; for the suffix cf. *tūribulum* THURIBLE.

crucifer krūˑsifəɹ cross-bearer XVI; cruciferous plant XIX. – ChrL. *crucifer* (applied to Christ by Prudentius), L. *cruci-, crux*; see CROSS, -FEROUS. So **cruciˑ**FEROUS bearing or wearing a cross XVII; (bot.) belonging to the Cruciferæ (having petals crosswise) XIX. **cruciˑ**FORM cross-shaped. XVII. – modL.

crucifix krūˑsifiks figure of Christ on the cross XIII; †the Crucified One XV. –(O)F. *crucifix* – late L. *crucifixus*, i.e. *crucī fixus* fixed to a cross. So **crucifiˑx**ION. XVII. – late L. **cruˑci**FY put to death on a cross. XIII (Cursor M.). –(O)F. *crucifier* = Pr., Sp. *crucificar* – Rom. **crucificāre*, replacing ChrL. *crucifigere*, i.e. *crucī figere* FIX to a CROSS.

crude krūd in a raw state XIV (Ch.); ill-digested, not matured XVI; (gram.) without inflexion XIX. – L. *crūdus* raw, rough, cruel; see RAW. So **cruˑd**ITY XV.

cruel krūˑəl disposed to inflict or causing suffering. XIII. –(O)F. *cruel* = Pr., Sp. *cruel*, It. *crudele* :– L. *crūdēli-s*, rel. to *crūdus* CRUDE. So **cruˑel**TY[1]. XIII. – OF. *crualté* (mod. *cruauté*) :– Rom. **crūdālitās*, for L. *crūdēlitās*.

cruet krūˑit small bottle or vial. XIII. – AN. **cruet*, **cruete*, dim. of OF. *crue* – OS. *krūka* (Du. *kruik*) = OE. *crūce*, MHG. *krūche* (G. *krauche*), rel. to CROCK[1].

cruise krūz sail to and fro over the sea. XVII. prob. – Du. *kruisen* cross, f. *kruis* CROSS; cf. Sp., Pg. *cruzar*, F. *croiser* in the same sense. So **cruiˑ**SER. XVII. – Du. *kruiser*; so F. *croiseur*.

crumb krʌm small particle of bread. OE. *cruma*, corr. with variation of vowel to MDu. *crūme* (Du. *kruim*), MLG., MDu. *crōme*, (M)HG. *krume*, Icel. *krumr, kraumr*; rel. to L. *grūmus* mound, Gr. *grūméā*, Alb. *grimë* crumb. The parasitic *b* appears XVI; cf. *thumb*, in which it is much earlier Hence **crumb** vb. superseding †*crim* (XV)

:- OE. *ġe|crymman* :- **krumjan*. **cru·mble** vb. break into crumbs or little bits. XVI. Earlier forms †*kremele* (XV), †*crimble* (XVI) repr. an OE. type **crymelan* (:- **krumilōn*); cf. Du. *kruimelen*, LG. *krömeln*, G. *krümeln*.

crump krʌmp imit. of the sound of eating moderately firm substances, walking over slightly compressed snow, etc., the soft fall of a shell. XVII; contrast *crunch, crush*.

crumpet krʌ·mpit †thin griddle cake XVII; soft cake made of flour, etc., mixed into a batter XVIII. Of doubtful origin; perh. to be connected with †*crompid cake* (Wycl. Bible; tr. Vulgate *laganum*) lit. 'curled up cake', and so rel. to MDu. *cromp* = OE. *crumb*, etc., bent, crooked.

crumple krʌ·mpl become or make creased or wrinkled. XVI. f. †*crump* curve, curl up (XIV), rel. to CRAMP; see -LE[2].

crunch krʌnʃ crush with the teeth. XIX. var. of *craunch* (XVII), assim. to *munch*.

crupper krʌ·pəɹ leather strap passing under a horse's tail XIII; horse's hindquarters XVI. – AN. *cropere*, OF. *cropiere* (mod. *croupière*) = Pr. *cropiera*, Sp. *gropera*, It. *groppiera* :- Rom. **croppāria, -ēria*, f. **croppa* (whence F. *croupe*, etc.) – Germ. **krupp-* CROP; see -ER[2].

crural kruə·rəl pert. to the leg. XVI. – L. *crūrālis*, f. *crūr-*, *crūs* leg; see -AL[1].

crusade krūsei·d military expedition for the recovery of the Holy Land from the Mohammedans XVI; gen. XVII. The earlier forms were (i) *croisade* (XVI) – F. *croisade* (Rabelais), an alteration of earlier *croisée* by assim. to the Sp. form (see -ADE); (ii) *crusado, -ada* (XVI) – Sp. *cruzada*; (iii) *croisado, -ada* (XVII) which are blends of (i) and (ii). Earlier still synon. OF. *croisiée* and *croiserie* had been adopted as *croysie* (XV–XVII) and *croiserie* (XIII–XV). The current form is first recorded XVIII (in Phillips' 'World of Words', 1706, and by Johnson, 1755, as a by-form); it was generally familiarized by Goldsmith and Gibbon.

cruse krūz, (formerly) krūs pot, jar, bottle. XIII. OE. *crūse*, repr. normally by (occas.) *crowce, crowse* (XV), *crouse* (XVI); evidence is lacking between OE. and XV, whence *cruse* and *crewse* are found, perh. – (M)LG. *krūs*; cf. OHG. (dim.) *krūselīn*, MHG. *krūse* (G. *krause*), MDu. *cruyse*, Icel. *krús*, beside (M)LG. *krōs*, Du. *kroes*; ult. relations unkn.

crush krʌʃ †crash, clash; compress with violence XIV; break down the power of XVI. – AN. *crussir, corussier*, OF. *croissir, cruissir* gnash (the teeth), crash, crack = Pr. *croisir, cruisir*, Cat. *cruxir* (Sp. *crujir*, It. *crosciare* are derived) :- Rom. **cruscīre*, of unkn. origin. For *sh* cf. BUSHEL, etc.

crust krʌst hard outer part of a loaf, etc. XIV. ME. *crouste* – OF. *crouste* (mod. *croûte*) :- L *crusta* rind, shell, incrustation, referred to **kru-*, repr. also by Gr. *krúos* frost, *krústallos* CRYSTAL, L. *crūdus* CRUDE, OHG. *hrosa* crust, ice, OE. *hruse* earth, ON. *hrúðr* crust, scab. Hence **cru·st**ED. XIV (Wycl. Bible 'crustid cake', tr. Vulg. *crustula*); of wine XVIII. Hence **cru·sty** encrusted XIV; short of temper XVI; see -Y[1].

crustaceous krʌstei·ʃəs that is or having a hard integument; of the crustacea. XVII. f. modL. *crustāceus*, f. L. *crusta* CRUST; see -ACEOUS. **crusta·cea.** XIX. modL. n. pl. of the adj. (Lamarck, 1801, after Cuvier's *les insectes crustacées*, 1798).

crutch krʌtʃ staff with crosspiece for an infirm person OE.; (naut.) forked or crooked timber, etc. OE. *cryċ(ċ)* = OS. *krukka* (Du. *kruk*), OHG. *chrucha, chruchja* (G. *krücke*), ON. *krykkja* :- CGerm. (not in Goth.) **krukjō*, **krukjōn*; see CROOK. For the vocalism cf. BLUSH.

Crutched Friars see CROSS[1].

crux krʌks pl. *cruxes, cruces* krū·sīz † conundrum, riddle XVIII (Sheridan, Swift); difficulty the solution of which perplexes XIX. L., 'CROSS'; short for *crux interpretum, crux philosophorum* torment of interpreters or commentators, of philosophers; G. *kreuz* cross (XVIII) is similarly used. Cf. CRUCIAL.

cry krai call out for; call loudly; announce publicly; shout in lamentation XIII; weep XVI. – (O)F. *crier* = Pr. *cridar*, Sp., Pg. *gritar*, It. *gridare* :- L. *quirītāre* cry aloud, wail, orig., acc. to Varro, call upon the *Quirītēs*, or Roman citizens, for help. So **cry** sb. loud utterance. XIII. – (O)F. *cri* = Pr. *crit*, Sp., Pg. *grito*, It. *grido*; CRom. f. the vb.

cryo- krai·ou, kraiə· comb. form of Gr. *krúos* frost, icy cold (cf. CRYSTAL).

crypt kript underground chamber. XVIII (from XVI to XVIII the L. form was current). – L. *crypta* – Gr. *krúptē* vault, sb. use of fem. of *kruptós* hidden. See GROT, GROTTO.

cryptic kri·ptik hidden, secret. XVII (Bacon). – late L. *crypticus* – Gr. *kruptikós*, f. *kruptós*; see prec. and -IC. So **crypto-** kri·ptou, kriptə· used as comb. form of Gr. *kruptós* hidden, as in **cryptogamia** -gæ·miə (bot.) division of plants having no stamens or pistils and therefore no flowers. XVIII. modL. (Linnæus), f. Gr. *gámos* marriage + *-ia* -Y[3]; so **crypto·gam**OUS. XVIII. **crypto·**GRAPHY secret manner of writing. XVII (Sir T. Browne). – modL. *cryptographia*; so **crypto·**GRAPHER. XVII.

crystal kri·stəl †ice; pure quartz (resembling ice) OE.; piece of rock crystal, etc., XIV; highly transparent glass XVI; mineralogical form XVII. – (O)F. *cristal* = Pr., Sp. *cristal*, It. *cristallo* – L. *crystallum* – Gr. *krústallos* ice, f. *krustaínein* freeze, *krúos* frost. **cry·stall**INE. XIV (*crystalline heaven, crystalline humour*) – (O)F. *cristallin* – L. *crystallinus* – Gr. *krustállinos*; see -INE[1]. Formerly *crysta·lline*, as in Milton, Gray, Shelley. **cry·stall**IZE. XVI.

cteno- (k)tī·nou, (k)tinə· comb. form of Gr. *ktenós*, nom. *kteís* comb. :– **pktens*, rel. to L. *pecten*, Gr. *pékein* comb, shear.

cub kʌb young of the fox, bear, etc. XVI. Of unkn. origin.

cubby-hole kʌ·bihoul snug place, small room or closet. XIX. orig. dial., f. *cub* (XVI) cattle-pen, coop, crib, prob. of LG. origin (cf. COVE[1]).

cube kjūb regular 6-sided figure; third power of a quantity. XVI. – (O)F. *cube* or L. *cubus* (Vitruvius) – Gr. *kúbos* solid square, 6-sided die, cubic number, iliac cavity (see HIP). So **cu·bIC**. XV. – (O)F. or L. – Gr. **cu·bICAL**. XV. **cu·bISM** form of pictorial art in which the design is based on cubes. 1912. – F. *cubisme* (1908).

cubeb kjū·beb berry of the shrub Piper Cubeba or Cubeba officinalis. XIV (*quibibe*). – (O)F. *cubèbe*, †*quibibe* :– Rom. **cubēba* (so Pr., Sp., It.), – Arab. *kabābah*.

cubicle kjū·bikl †bedchamber XV; one of a series of sleeping-rooms XIX. – L. *cubiculum*, f. *cubāre* recline, lie in bed; see CONCUBINE, -CLE.

cubit kjū·bit †forearm; measure of length derived from this (so in L., corr. to Gr. *pêkhus*, Heb. *ammah*). XIV.– L. *cubitum* elbow, distance from the elbow to the finger-tips (whence F. *coude*, Sp. *codo*, It. *cubito*), popularly assoc. with *cubit-*, pp. stem of *cubāre*, *-cumbere* lie down, recline, but prob. rel. directly to Gr. *kúbos* (see CUBE).

cucking-stool kʌ·kiŋstūl instrument of punishment consisting of a chair (sometimes in the form of a close-stool) in which the offender was exposed or ducked. XIII. orig. varying with †*cuck*-STOOL (XIII); presumably f. †*cuck* void excrement (not recorded before XV, but doubtless earlier) – ON. (mod. Icel.) **kúka*, rel. to *kúkr* excrement (cf. CACK). Rendered in medL. *cathedra stercoris* 'chair of excrement'.

cuckold kʌ·kəld husband of an unfaithful wife. XIII (*cukeweld*, 3 syll.; later *cokewold*, *cokwald*, *kukwold*, *cocold*). – AN. **cucuald*, var. of OF. *cucuault* (recorded XV), f. *cucu* CUCKOO + pejorative suffix *-ald*, *-aud*, *-ault*. The pronunc. of the first syll. with *kuk-* (cf. CUCKOO) has been preserved because there has been no conscious assoc. with the bird name.

cuckoo ku·kū the bird Cuculus canorus, whose well-known voice the name echoes. XIII (*cuccu*). – OF. *cucu* (mod. *coucou*); imit., like most names of the bird, as L. *cucŭlus* (whence It. *cuculo*, Pg. *cogul*), Gr. *kókkūx*, Skr. *kokilás*. The normal pronunc. would be kʌ·kū, which was current till *c.* 1800 (cf. CUCKOLD); ku·kū has prevailed as the supposed echo of the bird's cry. The fig. sense 'fool' of the word cuckoo is found in many langs., in Eng. XVI. ¶ Superseded OE. *ġēac* (ME. *ȝeke*), which, though orig. imit., ceased, through normal phonetic development, to suggest the bird's cry; it corr. to OFris., OS. *gāk*, OHG. *gouh* (G. *gauch*, itself superseded as the bird's name by *kuckuck*, from LG.; cf. MDu. *cuccūc*, Du. *koekoek*), ON. *gaukr* (see GOWK); cf. OHG. *guckōn* cry cuckoo; also Ir. *cuach*, W. *cog*, OSl. *kukavica* cuckoo, Russ. *kukúshka*.

cucumber kjū·kʌmbəɹ creeping plant, Cucumis sativus, with long fleshy fruit. Late ME. *cucumer* (XIV–XVII) was superseded by *cucumber* (XV, 'Palladius' Husbandry'), †*cocomber*, by assim. to OF. *co(u)combre* (mod. *concombre*), corr. to Pr. *cogombre*, Sp. *cohombro*, It. *cocomero* – L. *cucumer*, *cucumis* (-*er*-), prob. of Mediterranean origin. The pronunc. of the first syll. has been infl. by the sp.; the development *cowcumber* (XVI) is still preserved in illiterate speech. ¶ 'In some counties of England, especially in the west, this word is pronounced as if written *Coocumber*. . . But . . it seems too firmly fixed in its sound of *Cowcumber* to be altered, and must be classed with its irregular fellow esculent *Asparagus*' (Walker, 1798); 'No well-taught person, except of the old school, now says *cow-cumber* . . although any other pronunciation . . would have been pedantic some thirty years ago' (Smart, 1836).

cud kʌd half-digested food of a ruminant. OE. *cudu*, earlier *cwudu*, *cwidu* what is chewed, mastic, corr. to OHG. *quiti*, *chuti* glue (G. *kitt* cement, putty) and rel. ult. to L. *bitūmen* BITUMEN, pitch, Skr. *játu* resin, gum, and further to ON. *kváða* (Sw. *kåda*) resin, the source of ME. *code* pitch.

cudbear kʌ·dbɛəɹ dyeing powder prepared from lichen, esp. Lecanora tartarea; this lichen. XVIII. f. var. *Cudber(t)* of the christian name of Dr. *Cuthbert* Gordon, who patented the powder; cf. CUDDY[2].

cuddle kʌ·dl fondle in close embrace. XVIII. Of dial. origin; perh. f. dial. *couth* comfortable, snug + -LE[2]; cf. *fondle* (f. *fond*). But cf. †*cull* (XVI) fondle, var. of †*coll* (XIV) aphetic – OF. *acoler* embrace (see ACCOLADE).

cuddy[1] kʌ·di cabin in a large ship. XVII (Pepys). prob. – early modDu. *kajute*, *kaiuyte* (now *kajuit*, whence F. *cajute*) – (O)F. *cahute*, of unkn. origin.

cuddy[2] kʌ·di donkey. XVIII. Of lowly origin, like *donkey*; perh. a use of *Cuddy* (XVI), pet form of *Cuthbert* (cf. CUDBEAR); cf. similar applications of *dicky*, *neddy*.

cudgel kʌ·dʒəl short thick stick. OE. *cyćġel*, of unkn. origin; for the phonetic development cf. BLUSH.

cue[1] kjū actor's word(s) serving as a signal for another to enter or speak; (hence) hint. XVI (*q*, *qu*, *quew*, *kew*, *cue*). Of unkn. origin; the supposition that it is a use of F. *queue* tail, is not based on evidence.

cue[2] kjū pigtail; billiard-player's stick. XVIII. var. of QUEUE.

cuff[1] kʌf †glove, mitten XIV (PPl.); band at the bottom of a sleeve XVI; fetter for the wrist XVII (cf. HANDCUFF). Of unkn. origin.

cuff[2] kʌf strike with the fist or open hand. perh. imit. of the sound; cf. G. sl. *kuffen* thrash, Sw. *kuffa* thrust, push. Hence **cuff** sb. XVI; cf. FISTICUFF.

cui bono kai bou·nou Who benefits by it? XVII. L. phr., 'To whom (is it) for good?' (attributed by Cicero to one Lucius Cassius Longinus, 'pro Roscio' xxx); pop. taken to mean 'What is the good of it?

cuirass kwiræ·s armour for the body orig. of leather. XV (Lydg.). – F. *cuirasse*, †*curas*, †*-ace*, perh. – It. *corazza* = Pr. *coirassa*, Sp. *coraza* :– Rom. **coriācia*, sb. use of fem. of L. *coriāceus*, f. *corium* leather (see -ACEOUS); in F. *cuirasse* repl. OF. *cuiriée*, *quiriée* :– Rom. **coriāta*. A frequent var. in XVI–XVII was †*curats* (XVI–XVII), whence a spurious sg. †*curat*; cf. MLG. *koritz*, ODa. *körritz*, *kyrritz*. So **cuirass**IE·R. XVII. – F.

cuisine kwizī·n cookery. XVIII. – F. *cuisine* kitchen, cookery :– L. *coquīna* (cf. KITCHEN), f. *coquere* COOK.

cuisse, cuish kwis, kwiʃ thigh-piece of armour. XV. pl. *cus(c)hes*, *cushies*, *cuisses*, later forms of ME. *cussues*, *quyssewes* (XIV) – OF. *cuisseaux*, pl. of *cuissel* = It. *cosciale* :– late L. *coxāle*, f. *coxa* hip.

Culdee kʌldī member of a Scoto-Irish religious order. XVI (preceded by *Kylde*, Wyntoun). – medL. *Culdeus* (Hector Boece, 1526), alteration (after L. *cultor Deī* worshipper of God) of *Kel(e)deus* – OIr. *céle dé* (Ir. *ceilede*) anchorite, lit. associate or servant of God (*dé*, g. of *dia* God).

cul-de-sac kuldəsæ·k, ‖küdsak (anat.) vessel, etc., open at only one end XVIII; blind alley XIX. F., lit. 'bottom of sack' (*cul* :– L. *cūlus* posteriors = Gael., (O)Ir. *cúl*, W. *cil* back).

-cule kjūl terminal el. (varying with -CLE) repr. F. *-cule*, L. *-culus*, *-a*, *-um*, dim. suffix of all three genders, as in *animalcula* †*animalcle*, *articulus* ARTICLE, *fasciculus* FASCICLE, *masculus* MALE, *versiculus* VERSICLE; *auricula* (see AURICULAR); *corpusculum* CORPUSCLE, -CULE.

culet kjū·lit horizonal face forming the bottom of a diamond cut as a brilliant. XVII. Earlier form *collet*, altered – OF. *culet*, dim. of *cul* bottom (cf. CUL-DE-SAC).

culinary kjū·linəri, kʌ·l- pert. to the kitchen or to cooking. XVII. – L. *cūlīnārius*, f. *culīna* kitchen; see KILN, -ARY.

cull kʌl select, pick XV (Promp. Parv.); gather XVII (Milton). Earlier *cole* (XIV, R. Mannyng), and varying with *coile* and (rare) *cuyl*, both of late XIV. – OF. *coillier*, *-ir*, *cuiller*, *collier*, *coillir*, *quillir*, (also mod.) *cueillir*, repr. L. *colli·gere* (see COLLECT), Rom. **cólgere*, which, in various parts of the Rom. domain, took different inf. endings, as *-ĕre* in It. *cogliere*, *-ēre* in Sp. *coger*, Pg. *colher*, *-īre* in Pr. *coillir*, *cu(e)lhir*, Cat. *cullir*, and *-āre* in OF. *cueiller*.

cullender see COLANDER.

cullet kʌ·lit refuse glass with which crucibles are replenished. XVII. Earlier *collet* neck of glass left on the end of a blowing-iron – (O)F. *collet*, dim. of *col*, *cou* :– L. *collum* neck (cf. COLLAR); but cf. F. *cueillette* rags collected for making paper.

cullion kʌ·ljən †testicle XIV (Ch.); †base fellow XVI. – OF. *coillon* (mod. *couillon*) = Pr. *colho*, Sp. *cojon*, It. *coglione* :– Rom. **cōleone*, f. L. *cōleus*, *culleus* bag, testicle – Gr. *koleós* sheath.

cullis kʌ·lis (archit.) gutter, channel. XIX. – F. *coulisse*; see COULISSE and cf. PORTCULLIS.

cully kʌ·li (sl.) dupe, gull, simpleton; man, fellow, mate. XVII. prob. orig. rogues' cant; of unkn. origin.

culm[1] kʌlm (dial.) coal dust XIV; soot XV (Promp. Parv.); anthracite XVIII (hence geol. series of shales containing anthracite XIX). repr. earlier in *colmie* (XIII), *culmy* (XIV) sooty, now Sc. *coomy*; of unkn. origin, but presumably based on *col* COAL.

culm[2] kʌlm (bot.) stalk of a plant. XVII. – L. *culmus*; cf. HAULM.

culminate kʌ·lmineit reach its greatest altitude. XVII. f. pp. stem of late L. *culmināre* exalt, extol, f. *culmin-*, *culmen* summit, acme; see -ATE[3]. So **culmin**A·TION. XVII; so F.

culpable kʌ·lpəbl guilty XIV; blameworthy XVII. ME. *coupable* – (O)F. *coupable* :– L. *culpābilis*, f. *culpāre* blame, censure, f. *culpa* blame; see -ABLE. The sp. and pronunc. were later assim. to L. Hence **culpabi**·LITY. XVII. ¶ The base appears also in *inculpate*.

culprit kʌ·lprit in the formula 'Culprit, how will you be tried?', formerly said by the Clerk of the Crown to a prisoner who pleaded Not Guilty to high treason or felony; the accused XVII; (by assoc. with L. *culpa* guilt) offender XVIII. According to legal tradition (Blount's Law Dict. 1717), compounded of *cul*, short for AN. *culpable* guilty (see prec.), and *pri(s)t* (= OF. *prest*, F. *prêt*) ready; it is supposed that, when the prisoner had pleaded Not Guilty, the Clerk replied with *Culpable: prest daverrer notre bille*, i.e. 'Guilty: ready to aver our indictment', and that this was noted in the form *cul. prist*, which was later mistaken for a formula addressed to the accused.

cult kʌlt worship XVII; devotion, homage XVIII. – F. *culte* or L. *cultus*, noun of action f. *colere* inhabit, cultivate, protect, honour with worship, f. **kwel-* be or move habitually (in or with), whence also *colōnus* (see COLONY); cf. WHEEL. Also in L. form **cultus** kʌ·ltəs. XVII (rare before XIX).

cultivate kʌ·ltiveit till; improve and refine. XVII. f. medL. *cultīvāt-*, *-āre* (cf. (O)F. *cultiver*, Pr. *coltivar*, etc.), f. medL. *cultīvus*, in *cultiva terra* arable land (cf. OF. *teres cultives*), f. *cult-*, pp. stem of *colere* cultivate; see prec. -IVE, -ATE[3]. So **cultiva·tion**. XVIII. **cu·ltivator**. XVII.

culture kʌ·ltʃəɹ piece of tilled land XV; cultivation XV; cultivating *of* the mind, manners, etc., XVI; intellectual training and refinement XIX. – F. *culture* (repl. earlier †*couture*) or its source L. *cultūra*, f. *cult-*; see prec. and -URE. Hence **cu·ltural**[1]. XIX.

culver kʌ·lvəɹ (arch.) dove, (local) wood-pigeon. OE. *culfre, culufre, -efre, culfer* – **columbra*, for L. *columbula*, dim. of *columba* dove, pigeon.

culverin kʌ·lvərin gun and cannon formerly in use. XV. – (O)F. *coulevrine* (cf. medL. *colu-*, *colobrīna*, It. *colubrina*), f. *couleuvre* snake :– Rom. **colobra*, for L. *colubra*, beside *coluber* (whence It. *colubro*) snake; see -INE[1].

culvert kʌ·lvəɹt tunnel drain for water crossing a road, etc. XVIII. Of unkn. origin; there appears to be no historical point of contact with OF. *coulouere* channel, gutter (Cotgr.), of similar form and meaning.

cum kʌm L. *cum* with, as in *cum div.* with dividend.

cumber kʌ·mbəɹ †harass, overwhelm XIII (Cursor M.); burden, load XIV. prob. aphetic of †*acumber*, ENCUMBER, but there are difficulties of chronology. Hence **cu·mbersome** †obstructive, harassing XIV; inconveniently bulky or heavy XVI; see -SOME[1]. **cu·mbrous**. XIV (Barbour, Maund.).

Cumbrian kʌ·mbriən pert. to Cumberland, England, or to its rocks, or to the ancient British kingdom of Cumbria. XVIII. f. medL. *Cumbria*, f. W. *Cymry* (cf. CYMRIC) :– OW. **kombrogī*, pl. of **kombrogos* fellow countryman, f. **kom-* COM- + **mrog-* (W. *bro*) region (cf. MARCH[1], MARGIN); see -IAN.

cummer, kimmer kʌ·məɹ, ki·məɹ godmother XIV (R. Mannyng); female intimate XVI; woman XVIII. – (O)F. *commère* = Pr. *comaire*, Sp., It. *comare* :– ecclL. *commātrem*, *-māter*; see COM-, MOTHER. From XVI only Sc.

cummerbund kʌ·məɹbʌnd waist-belt. XVII. – Hind. – Pers. *kamarband* 'loin-band'.

cummin, cumin kʌmi·n plant cultivated in the Levant for its aromatic seed. XII. – OF. *cumin, comin* (whence Du. *komijn*) = Sp., It. *comino* :– L. *cumīnum* – Gr. *kúminon*, prob. of Semitic origin (cf. Heb. *kammōn*, Arab. *kammūn*). Superseded OE. *cymen* (which would have yielded **kimmen*) corr. to OHG. *cumin, cumil* (G. *kümmel*) – L.

cumquat kʌ·mkwət small variety of orange. XVII. – Cantonese var. of Chinese *kin kü* 'gold orange'.

cumulate kjū·mjŭleit heap up. XVI. f. pp. stem of L. *cumulāre*, f. *cumulus* heap; see -ATE[3]. So **cu·mulative**. XVII. **cumulus** kjū·mjŭləs heap, pile, accumulation XVII; (meteor.) cloud of rounded masses heaped one on the other XIX; comb. form **cu·mulo-**, as in *cumulo-stratus* (L. Howard, 1803).

cuneiform kjū·niifɔ̄ɹm wedge-shaped, spec. of the elements of Assyrian and other inscriptions. XVII (*cuneoform*, *cuneform*). – F. *cunéiforme* or modL. *cuneiformis*, f. *cuneus* wedge (cf. COIN); see -FORM.

cunning kʌ·niŋ †learning, wisdom XIV; (arch.) ability, skill XIV (Ch.); skilful deceit, craftiness XVI. perh. – ON. *kunnandi*, f. *kunna* know (see CAN[2]). So **cu·nning** adj. †learned XIII; able, skilful XIV; crafty, artful XVI. – ON. *kunnandi*. Both words appear first in northerly texts, and in both the ON. suffix has been assim. to the native -ING; the adj. was prob. the earlier and the sb. perh. modelled on it rather than derived immed. from ON. ¶ There appears to be no historical contact with OE. *cunning* carnal knowledge, *cunnung* trial.

cup kʌp small open drinking-vessel OE.; various transf. uses XIV. OE. *cuppe* – medL. *cuppa*, presumably differentiated var. of L. *cūpa* tub, vat (whence F. *cuve*, etc.). ME. by-forms *cupe, coupe, coppe, cope* repr. partly OF. *cupe*, etc. (mod. *coupe*), but there was some blending with the descendant of OE. (late Nhb.) *copp* = MLG., Du. *kop*, OHG. *chopf* (MHG., G. *kopf* head). **cupboard** kʌ·bəɹd †sideboard (to hold cups, etc.) XIV; cabinet or closet with shelves for crockery, food, etc. XVI.

cupel kjū·pəl circular vessel for assaying gold and silver. XVII. orig. – F. *coupelle* – late L. *cūpella*, dim. of *cūpa* (see CUP); ult. assim. to the L. form.

Cupid kjū·pid god of love; beautiful young boy. XIV. – L. *Cupīdō*, personification of *cupīdō* desire, f. *cupere* desire, long for. So **cupidity** kjupi·dĭti inordinate desire for gain. XV. – F. *cupidité* or L. *cupiditās*, f. *cupidus* eagerly desirous, f. *cupere*; see -ID, -ITY, and cf. CONCUPISCENCE, COVET.

cupola kjū·pələ rounded dome XVI (in XVII–XVIII often *-olo, -ulo, -elo*); furnace for melting metals, orig. with a dome leading to the chimney XVIII. – It. *cupola* (whence F. *coupole*) – late L. *cūpula* little cask, small burying-vault, dim. of *cūpa* (see CUP).

cupreous kjū·priəs of copper. XVII. f. late L. *cupreus*, f. *cuprum* COPPER; see -EOUS.

cupro- kjū·prou used as comb. form (see -O-) of late L. *cuprum* COPPER[1].

cur kɔ̄ɹ watch-dog, shepherd's dog; now always, low-bred dog. XIII (AncrR.). prob. orig. in *cur-dog* (which was formerly frequent XIII–XIX; the simple word is as early as Ch.), perh. f. ON. *kurr* grumbling, *kurra* murmur, grumble, as if 'growling dog'.

curaçao kjuərəsou· liqueur flavoured with rind of bitter oranges. XIX. – F. name of one of the Antilles that produces the oranges so used.

curare kjurā·ri substance obtained from plants, used by S. Amer. Indians to poison arrows. XVIII. Also *woorara* (XVIII), *oorali, urali, urari, woorali, wourali* (all XIX). Macuchi.

curassow kjuə·rəsou gallinaceous bird of Central and S. America. XVII (*corrosou, -eso*). Anglicized sp. of *Curaçao*; see CURAÇAO.

curate kjuə·rət one having a cure of souls (now familiar only in 'bishops and curates' of the Book of Common Prayer) XIV (R. Rolle); assistant to a parish priest (in the Church of England and the R.C. Church in Ireland) XVI. – medL. *cūrātus*, f. *cūra* CURE[1]; see -ATE[1]. Hence **cu·r**ACY. XVII.

curative kjuə·rətiv pert. to the curing of disease XV; promoting cure XVII. – F. *curatif, -ive* – medL.; see -ATIVE.

curator kjuərei·təɹ †one having a cure of souls XIV (PPl.); guardian of a minor, lunatic, etc., XV (Lydg.); manager, governor, spec. as member of an academic body XVII. – AN. *curatour* = (O)F. *curateur*, or the source L. *cūrātōr, -ōrem*, agent-noun f. *cūrāre*; see CURE[1], -ATOR.

curb[1] kɔ̄ɹb chain or strap passing under a horse's lower jaw and fastened to the branches of a bit. XV. Early forms *courbe, corbe*, prob. f. †*courbe*, †*corbe* vb. bend, bow, curve (XIV) – (O)F. *courber* :– L. *curvāre* CURVE.

curb[2] kɔ̄ɹb enclosing framework or border. XVI. f. CURB[1]. See also KERB.

curb[3] kɔ̄ɹb put a curb on (a horse); (hence) restrain, check. f. CURB[1].

curcuma kɔ̄·ɹkjŭmə turmeric. XVII. – medL. or modL. – Arab. *kurkum* (Pers. *karkam*) – Skr. *kuṅkuma*^{m} saffron.

curd kɔ̄ɹd coagulated substance formed from milk. XIV (PPl.). Late ME. *crud(de), crod(de)*; the present metathesized form dates from XV; of unkn. origin, but Gael., (M)Ir. *gruth* curds, have been plausibly compared. Hence **curd** vb. curdle XIV (Trevisa, Wycl. Bible). **cu·rdle** form into curd(s). XVI (in pp. *crudled*, Spenser; *cruddled*, A.V., Job x 10); see -LE[2].

cure[1] kjuəɹ A. †care, charge, office XIII; spiritual charge, as of a parish XIV; B. (successful) medical treatment XIV (Gower). – (O)F. *cure* = Pr., Sp., It. *cura* :– L. *cūra* :– **koisā* (cf. Pælignian *coisatens* = L. *cūrauerunt*, OL. *coirauit*). So **cure** vb. A. †take care or charge of XIV (PPl., Wycl. Bible); B. †treat medically; heal XIV (Trevisa, Wycl. Bible); preserve for keeping XVII. – (O)F. *curer* take care of, clean = Pr., Sp. *curar*, It. *curare* :– L. *cūrāre* care for, cure, f. *cūra*. **cu·r**ABLE. XIV (Trevisa). – (O)F. or L. ¶ The same base is repr. in *accurate, curious, procure, secure*.

cure[2] kjuəɹ eccentric person. XIX. Shortening of CURIOUS; popularized by a music-hall song of 1862, with the chorus 'The cure, the cure, the perfect cure'.

curé kjuə·rei, ‖ *küre* parish priest in a French-speaking country. XVII. F. = It. *curato* – medL. *cūrātus* CURATE.

curette kjure·t surgeon's small scraping instrument. XVIII. – F. *curette*, f. *curer* (see CURE[1]) in the sense 'clear, cleanse' + -ETTE -ET.

curfew kɔ̄·ɹfju ringing of an evening bell for the covering or extinction of domestic fires in a town, camp, etc.; also transf. and gen. XIII. – AN. *coeverfu*, OF. *cuevrefeu* (mod. *couvrefeu*), f. tonic stem of *couvrir* COVER + *feu* fire :– L. *focus* hearth (see FOCAL).

curia kjuə·riə (Rom. antiq.; see below) XVI (Holland); *the Curia* the Papal Court XIX. – L. *cūria* division of the Roman people, its place of assembly, (hence) senate; of unkn. origin, but, if repr. **kowirīyā*, cf. Volscian *couehriu*, f. **ko-* CO- + **wiro-* man (see VIRILE). So **cu·ri**AL pert. to a (royal, papal, etc.) court. XV. – F. – L.

curio kjuə·riou curious or rare object of art. XIX. Shortening of *curiosity*, prob. suggested by the form of It. words, e.g. *cameo, intaglio*.

curious kjuə·riəs A. †careful, studious; †ingenious, skilled; eager to know or learn; B. †carefully or skilfully wrought XIV; †interesting XVII; exciting attention by being strange or odd XVII. – OF. *curios* (mod. *curieux*) = Pr. *curios*, Sp., It. *curioso* :– L. *cūriōsu-s* (only in subjective sense) careful, assiduous, inquisitive, f. *cūra* care; see CURE[1], -IOUS. The objective sense (B) is found in F. in XIV (*robes curieuses*). So **curi**OSITY -ɔ·sĭti †carefulness, attention XIV; eager desire to know, inquisitiveness XVI. – OF. *curiouseté* (mod. *curiosité*) – L.

curl kɔ̄ɹl twist or form into ringlets. First recorded (XIV) in pp. *crolled, crulled*, extended form with -ED of ME. *crolle, crulle* – MDu. *krul* (= MHG. *krol*) curly, prob. :– **krusl-*, and rel. to MLG. *krūs*, MDu. *kruis*, MHG. *krūs* crisp, curly (G. *kraus* curled, fig. crabbed, sullen), of which the LG. form was the source of northern ME. *crūs* irate, crabbed (still in mod. dial. *crouse*), bold, daring, brisk, lively. Hence **curl** sb. XVII (Sh.); whence **cu·rly** (see -Y[1]) XVIII.

curlew kɔ̄·ɹlju †quail; wading bird with musical cry. XIV. ME. *cor-, curlu(e)* – (O)F. *courlieu*, var. of *courlis* (cf. Rum. *corlă*, It. *chiurlo*, Pr. *correli*), orig. imit. of the bird's cry, but prob. assim. to OF. *courliu* courier, messenger, f. *courre* run (cf. CURRENT), *lieu* place :– L. *locus* (cf. LOCAL). By-forms †*cor-, curlure, -lowyr* corr. to F. dial. *corleru*, etc.

curling kə̄·ɹliŋ Sc. game played on the ice with large rounded stones which are hurled along towards a tee. XVII. perh. f. CURL with ref. to the motion given to the stone; see -ING[1]. Also **cu·rl**ER[1]; whence prob. **curl** vb. XVIII. Cf. Flem. *krullebol* 'curl-bowl' wooden ball used in *bolspel* 'bowl-play'.

curmudgeon kə̄ɹmʌ·dʒən 'avaricious churlish fellow' (J.). XVI (Stanyhurst, Nashe). Early vars. are *cormogeon, curmuggion, curre-megient*; Holland's *cornmudgin* is an alteration for the nonce by assim. to *corn* to render L. *frumentarius* corn-dealer; of unkn. origin, as is also the rare syn. †*cormullion* (XVI). ¶ A remarkably similar form is seen in the personal name 'Boselinus *Curmegen*' (Cartulary of Ramsey, temp. Henry I).

currach kʌ·rə(χ) (Sc. and Anglo-Ir.) small wicker boat. XV (*currok*). – Ir., Gael. *currach* boat; cf. CORACLE.

currant kʌ·rənt dried fruit prepared from a dwarf seedless grape of the Levant; the name was transf. (XVI) to species of Ribes imported from N. Europe, which were popularly supposed to be the source of the Levantine currant. orig. (XIV) in pl. phr. *raysons of coraunce* (see RAISIN) – AN. *raisins de corauntz* (cf. AL. *racemi de corenc* or *coraunt*), for OF. *raisins de Corinthe* grapes of Corinth, in Greece (their original place of export); later reduced to *coraunce, corans, currans* (surviving dial. as coll. pl.); a sg. form *coren, coran* appear XVI, and *currant* XVII; the final *t* appears to have arisen from forms like *corinthes, corints, cor(r)ants* (XVI), which are due to direct assim. to *Corinth.*

current kʌ·rənt flowing XIII; in circulation or vogue XV; in progress XVII. ME. *cora(u)nt* – OF. *corant*, prp. of *courre* :– L. *currere* run, f. **qers-* (cf. COURSE); see -ENT. Also sb. stream XIV (Wyclif); course, progress (of time, etc.) XVI (Hooker); (electr.) XVIII. Hence **cu·rr**ENCY circulation, vogue XVII; medium of exchange XVIII.

curricle kʌ·rikl two-wheeled carriage. XVIII. – L. *curriculum* racing-chariot, dim. f. *currere* (see prec.). In the orig. sense of 'course' the L. word **curri·culum** has been adopted (XIX) for 'course of study or training' (orig. in Sc. universities).

currier kʌ·riəɹ leather-dresser. XIV. ME. *corier* – OF. *corier* :– L. *coriāriu-s*, f. *corium* leather (cf. CUIRASS, EXCORIATE); see -ER[2].

curry[1] kʌ·ri rub down with a comb and brush XIII; dress (tanned leather) XV. – OF. *correier* arrange, equip, curry (a horse) = Pr. *conrear* arrange, Sp. *correar* prepare (wool) for use, It. *corredare* equip :– CRom. **conrēdāre* (cf. CORRODY), modelled on Germ. **garǣðjan*, f. **ga-* Y- + **raiðjō* READY. ¶ The phr. *curry favour* seek to ingratiate oneself (†hence, by extension, with other sbs., e.g. *acquaintance, friends, pardon*) XVI, was an etymologizing alteration of †*curry favel* (XIV), partial tr. of OF *estriller* or *torcher fauvel* rub down the fallow or chestnut horse, which, for some obscure reason, was taken as a type of perfidy or duplicity (see esp. the OF. 'Roman de Fauvel', 1310). Hence **cu·rry**-COMB. XVI (Tusser).

curry[2] kʌ·ri dish (esp. of rice) cooked with a preparation of turmeric. XVI (*carriel*), XVII (*carree*). – Tamil *kari* relish with rice, Canarese *karil* (whence Pg. *caril*).

curse kə̄ɹs utterance consigning an object to evil; formal ecclesiastical censure OE.; evil inflicted by supernatural power XVI. *Not worth a curse* (XVIII); see CUSS[1] and cf. DAMN sb. Late OE. *curs*. Hence **curse** vb.; late OE. *cursian*. Of unkn. origin; it has been referred to OIr. *cūrsagim* I censure, chastise.

cursitor kə̄·ɹsitəɹ clerk of the Court of Chancery, whose office (abolished 1835) it was to make out writs *de cursu*, i.e. of common official course or routine. XVI. – legal AN. *coursetour* – medL. *cursitor*, f. *cursus* COURSE.

cursive kə̄·ɹsiv written in a 'running' (i.e. not formal) hand. XVIII. – medL. *cursīvus* (in *scriptura cursiva*), f. *curs-*, pp. stem of *currere* run; see CURRENT, -IVE.

cursory kə̄·ɹsəri passing rapidly or hurriedly. XVII. – L. *cursōrius*, f. *cursor* runner: see prec., and -ORY. So **cu·rsorily** adv. XVI; after L. *cursōriē*; see -LY[2].

curt kə̄ɹt short, shortened, brief, terse XVII; so brief as to be lacking in courtesy XIX. – L. *curtus* cut short, mutilated, abridged, ppl. formation on IE. **kur-*; see SHORT.

curtail kəɹtei·l †dock; cut short. XVI. orig. *curtal(l)*, f. †*curtal* horse with docked tail, short cannon (XV) – F. *courtault, -auld* (mod. *courtaud*), f. *court* short (see CURT) + suffix *-ald* (of Germ. origin, earlier *-wald*, assoc. at an early date with TAIL.

curtain kə̄·ɹtin piece of cloth suspended as a screen. XIII (Cursor M.). ME. *cortine, curtine*, later *curtain(e), -ein(e)*, – OF. *cortine* (mod. *courtine*) = Sp., It. *cortina*, Rum. *cortină* :– late L. *cortīna*, used in the Vulgate (Exodus xxvi 1) to render Gr. *aulaía* curtain (f. *aulḗ* court), as if it was regarded as a deriv. of L. *co(ho)rt-* COURT, whereas in classical L. it meant 'cauldron' and was hence applied to circular or arched objects. *Curtain-raiser*, tr. F. *lever de rideau*. Hence **cu·rtain** vb. XIII; cf. Anglo-L. *cortināre*.

curtal-axe kə̄·ɹtəlæks cutlass. XVI. Alteration, by assim. to AXE, of †*curtelace* (XVI), itself an alteration (by assimn. to *court* short) of *coutelace* CUTLASS. (¶ Spenser has a further altered form *curtaxe*.

curtana kəɹtei·nə pointless sword used at English coronations. XIII. – Anglo-L. *curtāna* fem. (sc. *spatha* sword) – AN. *curtain*, OF. *cortain* name of Roland's sword, so called because it had broken at the point when thrust into a block of steel, f. *cort, curt* short (see CURT).

curtilage kɔ̄·ɹtilidʒ area attached to and enclosing a dwelling-house. XIV. – AN. *curtilage*, OF. *co(u)rtillage*, f. *co(u)rtil* small court (= Pr. *cortil*, It. *cortile*), f. *cort* COURT; see -AGE.

curts(e)y kɔ̄·ɹtsi obeisance. XVI. var. of COURTESY, formerly used in various senses of this, but restricted since *c.* 1700. ¶ The formerly common form *curchy* (XVII) remains dial. (cf. Burns' 'Holy Fair' iii). Hence as vb. XVI.

curule kjuə·rul epithet of a chair (orig. mounted on a chariot) used by the highest magistrates in ancient Rome. XVI (Holland). – L. *curūlis*, f. *currus* chariot, f. *currere* run (cf. COURSE).

curve kɔ̄ɹv †curved XV; sb. short for *curve line* XVII. – L. *curvus*, app. rel. to Gr. *kurtós* curved, and further to *circus* CIRCLE, *corōna* CROWN. So **curve** vb. XVII. – L. *curvāre*. Cf. CURB. **cu·rva**TURE. XV. – OF. or L. **curvi-** kɔ̄·ɹvi comb. form of L. *curvus*, as in *curvilineal* XVII, *-linear* XVIII.

curvet kɔ̄ɹve·t special leap of a horse in the manège. XVI. – It. *corvetta*, dim. of *corva*, early form of *curva* curve :– L. *curva*, fem. of *curvus*: see prec. and -ET. Hence **curve·t** vb. XVI (Sh.).

cushat kʌ·ʃət (dial.) wood-pigeon. OE. *cūsćute*, *-sć(e)ote*, of unkn. origin. The present sp. (a modification of *cuschate*, XVI, Montgomerie) appears to be due to Burns and Scott.

cushion ku·ʃən stuffed case of cloth, etc. used as a support in reclining, etc., XIV; various techn. uses since XVI. Two types are repr. in ME. by (i) *quisshon*, (ii) *cushin* – OF. (i) *coissin*, *cuissin*, (ii) *cossin*, *cussin*, (also mod.) *coussin* (whence Pr. *coissin*, Sp. *cojin*, It. *cuscino*) :– a Gallo-Rom. form based on L. *culcita* mattress, cushion; the somewhat earlier forms with *qui-* remained in full use till XVII; for the phonology cf. *ambush*, *bushel*, *crush*, *usher*.

cushy ku·ʃi (sl.) easy, comfortable. XX (orig. used in the British army in India). f. Hind. (– Pers.) *khūsh* excellent, charming, healthy, happy + -Y[1].

cusp kʌsp (astrol.) entrance of a house XVI; point, apex XVII. – L. *cuspis*, *-id-* point, pointed weapon. So **cu·spidate, -ated** sharp-pointed. XVII. – pp. of L. *cuspidāre*; see -ATE[2].

cuspidor kʌ·spidɔ̄ɹ (U.S.) spittoon. XVIII. – Pg. *cuspidor* spitter, f. *cuspir* spit :– **conspuīre*, for L. *conspuere*, f. *com* CON- (intensive) + *spuere* spit (see SPEW).

cuss[1] kʌs. XIX (orig. U.S.) vulgar disguising of CURSE; for the loss of *r* cf. *bust* burst, *fust* first. So **cussed** kʌ·sid pp. used as adj.

cuss[2] kʌs (sl.) person or thing regarded as an affliction or a nuisance; (humorously) fellow, chap. XVIII. prob. orig. identical with CUSS[1], but later regarded as short for *customer* (cf. CHAP[3], COVE[2]).

custard kʌ·stəɹd †open meat or fruit pie, thickened with eggs, etc. XV; dish or sweet made from eggs beaten up with milk XVII. In early recipes varying with †*crustade*, also †*crustarde* – AN. **crustade*, f. *cruste*, OF. *crouste* CRUST; see -ADE.

custody kʌ·stədi safe-keeping XV; keeping of an officer of justice XVI. – L. *custōdia*, f. *custōd-*, *custōs* guardian, keeper; see -Y[3]. Hence **custod**IAN kʌstou·diən. XVIII; after *guardian*.

custom kʌ·stəm habitual practice XII; established usage; tribute, impost XIV; business patronage. – OF. *custome*, *co(u)stume* (mod. *coutume*) :– **costumne*, for **costudne* :– L. *consuētūdinem*, *-tūdō*, f. *consuēscere* accustom, accustom oneself, f. *com* CON- + *suēscere* become accustomed, f. *suī* g. sg. of refl. pron. 'oneself' (cf. Skr. *svadhā́* habit, custom, Gr. *eiōtha* was accustomed :– **seswōdha*); see CONSUETUDINARY, COSTUME. So **cu·stom**ARY liable to customs or dues, holding by custom XVI; accustomed XVII (Sh.). – medL. *custumārius*, f. *custuma*, – AN. *custume*; superseding †*customable* (XIV) – OF. *customable*. **cu·stomer** †customary tenant; †collector of customs XIV; customary purchaser XV; (colloq.) person (to have to do with) XVI. orig. – AN. *custumer*, medL. *custumārius*; in some senses newly f. *customary*; see -ER[1].

custos kʌ·stɔs keeper, guardian. XV (pl. *custoses*). L. *custōs*; cf. CUSTODY.

custumal kʌ·stjuməl collection of customs of a city, etc. XVI. – medL. *custumāle*, n. of *custumālis*, f. *custuma* – OF. *custome* CUSTOM; see -AL[1].

cut[1] kʌt lot, in phr. *draw cuts* formerly *cut*. XIII (Cursor M.). Of unkn. origin; the absence of variation in the vowel in the earliest usage, and the chronological evidence, are against identification with CUT[2] vb. and sb.

cut[2] kʌt make a way with an edged instrument into (an object). XIII (Laȝ., later text; Havelok). The early dial. vars. *cutte*, *kitte*, *kette* point to an OE. **cyttan*, f. **kut-* (cf. Norw. *kutte*, Icel. *kuta* cut with a little knife, *kuti* sb. little blunt knife). Hence **cut** sb. XVI. ¶ The obscure phr. †*keep (one's) cut* is earlier (XIV), but it is doubtful whether it involves the same word.

cutaneous kjūtei·niəs of the skin. XVI. – modL. *cutāneus*, f. *cutis* skin; see HIDE[1], -AN, -EOUS.

cutch kʌtʃ catechu. XVIII (*cotch*). – Malay *kachu*.

cutcha kʌ·tʃə temporary, makeshift; sb. sun-dried brick. XIX. – Hindi *kachchā* raw, crude.

cutcher(r)y kʌtʃe·ri, kʌ·tʃəri business office. XVII. – Hindi *kachachrī, kachērī.*

cute kjūt clever XVIII; (U.S.) attractive XIX. Aphetic of ACUTE.

Cuthbert kʌ·þbəɹt the OE. name *Cūþbeorht* (*cūþ* famous, *beorht* BRIGHT), notable as the name of a great Northumbrian saint (d. 687), which appears in (*St.*) *Cuthbert's beads* detached and perforated joints of encrinites found in Northumbria (XVII), and (*St.*) *Cuthbert's duck, Cuthbert duck* eider duck, which breeds on the Farne Islands XVII (cf. *avis beati Cuthberti* XII and *Cuthbert doun* XIV). Cf. CUDBEAR, CUDDY[2].

cuticle kjū·tikl epidermis. XVII. – L. *cutīcula*, dim. of *cutis*; see CUTANEOUS.

cutlass kʌ·tləs short broad-bladed sword. XVI. – F. *coutelas*, corr. to It. *coltellaccio*, repr. Rom. **cultellāceum*, f. L. *cultellus*, dim. of *culter* COULTER. Perverted to †*cutleax*, †*cuttleaxe, cutlash,* CURTAL-AXE.

cutler kʌ·tləɹ maker of or dealer in knives. XIV (*le cotiler, la cutiller* occur as personal designations XIII). – AN. *cotillere*, (O)F. *coutelier*, f. *coutel* (mod. *couteau*) knife :– L. *cultellu-s*, dim. of *culter* COULTER; see -ER[2]. So **cu·tl**ERY. XIV. – (O)F. *coutellerie.*

cutlet kʌ·tlit slice of meat, esp. from the short ribs. XVIII. – F. *côtelette*, OF. *costelette*, dim. of *coste* (mod. *côte*) rib :– L. *costa*; assim. to CUT sb. (s.v. CUT[2]) and -LET.

cutter kʌ·təɹ ship's rowing and sailing boat; small one-mast vessel sloop-rigged XVIII. perh. f. CUT[2]+-ER[1]; but deriv. from Indo-Pg. *catur* (XVI) narrow vessel cannot be excluded.

cuttle kʌ·tl now usu. *cuttle-fish* (XVI), cephalopod of the genus Sepia, which ejects a black fluid from a sac. Late OE. *cudele*, ME. (XV) *codel*, corr. to OLFrankish *cudele*, Norw. dial. *kaule* (:– **kodle*), f. base of COD[1], with allusion to its ink-bag. Forms with orig. *-d-* remain dial.; the unexpl. change to *-t-* appears XV (*cotul*); a by-form *scuttle* is found from XVI.

cutty kʌ·ti (Sc. and north.) cut short, stumpy, as in *cutty pipe, cutty sark* (Burns); also sb. XVIII. f. *cut*, pp. of CUT[2]+-Y[6].

cwt symbol for *hundredweight*, *c* standing for L. *centum* HUNDRED, *wt.* for WEIGHT; formerly simply *c* or *C*.

-cy si suffix corr. to F. *-tie*, †*-cie*, originating in L. *-cia, -tia*, Gr. *-kíā, -keíā, -tíā, -teíā*, f. *-k-, -t-*+*-íā*, etc. -Y[3]; occurs chiefly in -ACY, -ANCY, -ENCY, -CRACY, -MANCY. On the model of *prophet/prophecy* was formed *idiocy* from *idiot*, and thence *secrecy* from *secret*. The correspondence of *agent* and *agency* and consequently of *lieutenant* and *lieutenancy* gave rise, through phonetic proximity, to *captaincy, chaplaincy,* from *captain, chaplain,* whence, by further extention, *colonelcy* from *colonel*. The suffix is added to some words ending in *t*, as *bankruptcy, baronetcy, paramountcy*; cf. the variation *idiocy/idiotcy.*

cyan(o)- sai·ən(ou), saiæ·n(ou) comb. form of Gr. *kúanos* dark-blue mineral, *kuáneos* dark-blue, in designations of certain bluish salts and minerals, as **cya·no**GEN – F. *cyanogène* (Gay-Lussac, 1815); so named from its entering into the composition of Prussian blue. So *cya·nic, cy·anide*, etc. So **cyano**·SIS (path.) blueness of the skin. XIX. – modL., – Gr. *kuánōsis* dark-blue colour. Hence **cy·anosed** affected with cyanosis.

cybernetics saibəɹne·tiks theory of control and communication in the animal or the machine. XX. f. Gr. *kubernḗtēs* steersman, f. *kubernân* steer, GOVERN; see -ICS.

cycad sai·kæd (bot.) palm-like plant of the genus Cycas. XIX. – modL. *cycad-, cycas* – spurious Gr. *kúkas*, scribal error in Theophrastus for *koîkas*, acc. pl. of *koîx* Egyptian doum-palm; see -AD[1].

cyclamen si·kləmen (plant of a) genus of Primulaceæ. XVI. – medL. *cyclamen*, for L. *cyclamīnos, -on* – Gr. *kukláminos*, perh. f. *kúklos* circle, CYCLE, ref. its bulbous roots.

cycle sai·kl recurrent period of years XIV (only occas. before XVII); recurrent succession of things XVII; series of poems, etc., relating to a central event or epoch (after Gr. ὁ ἐπικὸς κύκλος the epic cycle, scil. of poems written to supplement Homer) XIX. – F. *cycle* or late L. *cyclus* – Gr. *kúklos* circle (see WHEEL). As a form generalized from *bicycle, tricycle*, to include all machines of the kind XIX (whence **cy·cl**IST), it is prop. a separate word. So **cycl**IC si·klik. XVIII. – F. *cyclique* or L. *cyclicus* or Gr. *kuklikós.*

cyclo- sai·klou, saiklə· comb. form of Gr. *kúklos* CYCLE, in: (i) scientific terms denoting circular or coiled forms or parts, e.g. *cyclosto·matous, cyclo·stomous* having a round sucking mouth, as the lamprey, (ii) names of inventions having circular parts or concerned with circles, e.g. *cyclo·meter*, instrument for measuring arcs, apparatus for registering distance traversed by a vehicle. XIX.

cyclone sai·kloun orig. storm in which the wind takes a circular course (H. Piddington, 1848); (hence) tornado; system of rotating winds. prob. intended to repr. Gr. *kúklōma* wheel, coil of a snake, f. *kúklos* CYCLE; *cyclome* occurs as an early variant.

cyclopædia saiklǒpī·diə. XVII. Clipped form of ENCYCLOPÆDIA (in Gr. form in the title of 'Lucubrationes vel potius absolutissime κυκλοπαιδεία' by Joachim Fortius Ringelbergius, 1541), perh. intended to express more obviously the notion 'circle of learning': but the result is an etymologically meaningless word, and it is stigmatized as an inferior form by G. J. Vossius in 'De vitiis sermonis' 1645. As the title of an English work it appears first in Ephraim Chambers's 'Cyclopædia, or General Dictionary of Arts and Sciences' 1728.

Cyclops sai·klɔps (Gr. myth.) one of a race of one-eyed giants. XV. – L. *Cyclōps* – Gr. *Kúklōps* 'round-eyed', f. *kúklos* (see CYCLE)+*ṓps* EYE. In F. *Cyclope*, Sp., It. *Ciclope*, whence Eng. *Cyclop* sg. (XVI). So **Cyclope·**AN, **Cyclo·pi**AN. XVII. f. L. *Cyclōpēus* – Gr. *Kuklṓpeios* and L. *Cyclōpius* – Gr. *Kuklṓpios*.

cyder var. of CIDER.

cygnet si·gnit young swan. XV (*signett*). prob. – AN. **cignet*, f. OF. *cigne* (mod. *cygne*), latinized form of earlier †*ci(s)ne* = Sp. *cisne*, OIt. *cecino*, *cecero* :– medL. (Rom.) *cīcinus*, for L. *cycnus* (in late MSS. *cygnus*) – Gr. *kúknos*; see -ET.

cylinder si·lindəɹ roller-shaped figure or body. XVI. – L. *cylindrus* – Gr. *kúlindros* roller, f. *kulíndein* roll. So **cyli·ndr**ICAL. XVII. f. modL. *cylindricus* – Gr. *kulindrikós*.

cyma sai·mə (archit.) moulding of cornice. XVI. – modL. *cȳma* – Gr. *kûma* billow, wave, waved moulding, f. *kueîn* be pregnant, f. **ku-* be curved, swell. Also **cymatium** simei·ʃiəm. XVI. – L. *cȳmatium* – Gr. *kūmátion*. **cymar** simā·ɹ woman's light undergarment XVII (Dryden); chimere XVII. var. of SIMAR.

cymbal si·mbəl (mus.) one of a pair of metal plates which are clashed together. XIV (*symbal*). – (O)F. *cymbale* – L. *cymbalum* – Gr. *kúmbalon*, f. *kúmbē* cup, hollow vessel. ¶ The L. word was adopted in OE. as *cimbal*, but this did not survive; see, however, CHIME[1].

cyme saim (bot.) kind of inflorescence. XVIII. – F. *cyme*, var. of *cime* summit, top :– **cīma*, pop. form of L. *cȳma* – Gr. *kûma* in the special sense of young cabbage-sprout (see CYMA).

Cymric ki·mrik pert. to the Welsh or their language. XIX. f. W. *Cymru* Wales, *Cymry* the Welsh (:– **kombrogī* fellow-countrymen, f. COM-; cf. *Allobroges* men of another country), CUMBRIAN; see -IC.

cynegetic sainidʒe·tik relating to hunting. – Gr. *kunēgetikós*, f. *kunēgétēs* hunter, f. *kun-*, *kúōn* dog (HOUND)+*hēgétēs* leader; see HEGEMONY, -IC.

cynic si·nik sect of ascetic philosophers in ancient Greece; sneering critic. XVI. – L. *cynicus* – Gr. *kunikós* dog-like, currish, churlish, Cynic (the application being derived from the gymnasium (*Κυνόσαργες*) where they taught or from certain dog-like qualities), f. *kun-*, *kúōn* dog (HOUND); see -IC. So **cy·ni**CAL. XVI. **cy·nic**ISM. XVII (Sir T. Browne; once before XIX, when it was preceded by *cynism* – F. *cynisme* – late L. *cynismus* – Gr. *kunismós*).

cynocephalus sainouse·fələs dog-faced baboon. XVI. – L. – Gr. *kunoképhalos*, f. *kuno-*, *kúōn* dog (HOUND)+*kephalḗ* head (cf. CEPHALIC).

cynosure sai·nŏʃuəɹ, si·nŏ-, -ʒuəɹ constellation Ursa Minor; 'guiding star' XVI; centre of interest XVII. (Also in L. form XVI–XVII). – F. *cynosure* or L. *cynosūra* – Gr. *kunósoura*, f. *kunós*, g. of *kúōn* dog (HOUND)+*ourá* tail (cf. ARSE).

cypher see CIPHER.

cy pres sī prei (leg.) as nearly as possible. Law-F. sp. (XV) of F. *si près* 'as near' (L. *sīc*, *pressē* closely, concisely, exactly; cf. It. *presso* near).

cypress[1] sai·prəs dark-foliaged coniferous tree. XIII (Cursor M.). ME. *cipres* (assim. later to L.) – OF. *cipres* (mod. *cyprès*) = Pr. *cypres*, It. *cipresso* – late L. *cypressus* – Gr. *kupárissos*, of alien origin.

cypress[2] sai·prəs name of several textile fabrics, (in later use) a lawn or crape. XIV. – AN. *cipres*, *cypres*, a use of OF. *Cipre*, *Cypre* (now *Chypre*) the island of Cyprus, from which various fabrics were brought during and after the Crusades.

Cyprian si·priən of Cyprus; (transf.) licentious, lewd. XVI. f. L. *Cyprius* of Cyprus, island of the Mediterranean, famous in ancient times for the worship of Aphrodite or Venus (called Cypria, Cypris); see -IAN. So **Cypriot, -ote** si·priət, -out inhabitant of Cyprus. XVIII. – Gr. *Kupriṓtēs*. See -OT[2], -OTE.

Cyrillic siri·lik of the alphabet used by Slavonic peoples in the Eastern Church, the invention of which is traditionally attributed to the Greek missionary *Cyril* (IX). XIX; see -IC.

cyst sist sac, esp. of morbid matter. XVIII. – modL. *cystis* (formerly used in Eng.) – Gr. *kústis* bladder, rel. to various words denoting 'hole', 'cavity', 'convexity'. So **cysti-** sisti comb. form of Gr. *kústis*, **cy·sto-** comb. form of Gr. *kústē* bladder.

cytisus si·tisəs fodder plant of ancient writers; Linnæan leguminous genus (broom, laburnum, etc.). XVI. L. – Gr. *kútisos*.

czar, tzar, tsar zāɹ, tsāɹ emperor of Russia. XVI (Eden, G. Fletcher). – Russian *tsar'* (= Bulg., Serb., Pol. *tsar*) :– **tsĭsari* :– OSl. *tsēsarĭ*, ult. repr. L. CÆSAR through the medium of Germ., in which the word meant 'emperor' (cf. OLG. *kēsar*, OHG. *keisar*, ON. *keysari*, Goth. *kaisar*; whence Finnish *keisari*). The sp. *cz-*, which is non-Slavonic, is due to Herberstein, 'Rerum Muscovitarum Commentarii', 1549, the chief early authority on Russia in Western Europe. So **czarevitch** zā·-, tsā·rĭvitʃ, Russ. tsarē·vitʃ czar's son; the eldest son had the differentiated title CESAREVITCH. **czarevna** zāre·vnə daughter of a czar. XIX. **czarina** zārī·nə czar's wife. XVIII. – It., Sp. *czarina*, *zarina* (= F. *czarine*) – G. (*c*)*zarin*, f. *czar*+native fem. suffix *-in* as in *königin* queen; the Russ. title was *tsarítsa*, which was in Eng. use from XVIII.

Czech tʃek Polish sp. of the native name *Čech* of the people of Bohemia (Czech *Čechy*, adj. *Česk*). XIX. Cf. F. *tchèque*, G. *Tscheche*, *tschechisch*.

D

dab[1] dæb (dial.) strike with a sharp blow XIV; strike with soft pressure XVI. Rare before XVI, when there may have been a fresh formation, but perh. in continuous dial. or colloq. use from early times; of imit. origin, but cf. DABBLE.

dab[2] dæb small flatfish. XV. Of unkn. origin.

dab[3] dæb adept, expert. XVII. Of unkn. origin. Hence synon. **da·bSTER**. XVIII.

dabble dæbl make or become wet by splashing or dipping. XVI. – Du. †*dabbelen*, or f. DAB[1] + -LE[2].

dabchick dæ·btʃik little grebe. XVI. The early forms *dap-*, *dopchick*, and (later) *dipchick* suggest connexion with OE. *dufe|doppa* 'pelicanus', ME. *doue|doppe*, *dyve|dap* (later *divedopper*, *-dapper*), OE. *dop|ened*, *dop|fugol* moorhen, and hence with the base **deup-* **dup-* (see DEEP, DIP).

daboya dəboi·ə large East Indian viper. XIX. – Hindi *daboyā* 'lurker', f. *dabnā* lurk.

dabster dæ·bstəɹ see DAB[3].

da capo da kā·pou (mus.) direction to repeat from a certain point. XVIII. It., *da* from (:– Rom. **dē ā*), *capo* beginning (:– Rom. **capum*, for L. *caput* head; see CHIEF).

dace deis small fresh-water fish, Leuciscus vulgaris. XV (*darce, darse, dace*). – OF. *dars*, nom. of *dart* dace (identical with DART), whence also †*dare* (XIV–XVIII). For the loss of *r* cf. BASS[1].

dachshund dæ·kshund German short-legged long-bodied dog. XIX. – G., lit. 'badger-dog', so called from its shape.

dacoit dəkoi·t class of robber in India and Burma. XIX. – Hindi *ḍakait*, orig. *ḍākait*, f. *ḍākā* gang-robbery :– Skr. *dashṭaka* compressed, crowded.

dactyl dæ·ktil †date (fruit); (pros.) the foot –◡◡. XIV. – L. *dactylus* – Gr. *dáktulos* finger, date, dactyl (so called from its three 'joints'). So **dacty·lIC**. XVI. – L. – Gr.

dad dæd (colloq.) father; also **da·ddy** (see -Y[6]) XVI; **da·d(d)a** XVII; in early Sc. *dade*, *daid*, *dadie* (XVI). Cf. the series *bab*, *babby*, *baby*, *baba* and *mam*, *mammy*, *mam(m)a*, and synon. Gr. *táta* Skr. *tatás*, W. *tad*, etc.; perh. of infantile origin.

dado dei·dou cubical block of a pedestal XVII (Evelyn); lining along the lower part of a wall XVIII. – It. *dado* die, cube (= Pr. *dat*, OF. *det*, mod. *dé* DIE[2]).

dædal dī·dəl skilful; varied. XVI (Spenser). – L. *dædalus* – Gr. *daidalos* skilful, variegated (whence *Dædalus* 'the cunning one', name of the mythical constructor of the Cretan labyrinth). So **dædalIAN**, -EAN dīdei·liən. XVII. f. L. *dædalius*, Gr. *daidáleos* cunningly wrought.

dæmon(ic) see DEMON, DEMONIC.

daff dæf †put off; (arch.) turn *aside*. XVI (Sh.). var. of DOFF.

daffodil dæ·fədil †asphodel; plant of the genus Narcissus; Lent lily, Narcissus pseudonarcissus. XIV. Alteration (with unexpl. *d-*) of †*affodil* (XV–XVII) – medL. *affodillus*, prob. a book-perversion of **asfodillus*, var. (simulating a dim. formation) of late L. *asphodelus*, *-ilus* – Gr. *asphódelos* ASPHODEL. ¶ Evidence is lacking for a proposed deriv. from Du. *de affodil* the daffodil; but Cotgr. s.v. *Affrodille* has *Th' Affodill*. The extended forms *daffodilly*, *daffadowndilly* date from XVI.

daffy dæ·fi children's medicine to which gin was often added; (hence) gin. XIX. orig. *Daffy's elixir* (XVIII), named after Thomas *Daffy*, an English clergyman (XVII).

daft dȧft †mild, meek XIII; stupid XIV; crazy XVI. ME. *daffte* (Orm), repr. OE. *ġedæfte* mild, gentle, meek :– Germ. **gaðaftjaz*, f. **gaðafti*, f. stem **dab-* of Goth. *gadaban* become, be fit (cf. OE. *ġedæftlīċe* fitly, suitably, *ġedæftan* make fit, prepare). The transition to the sense 'stupid' may have been assisted by ME. †*daff* (of unkn. origin) simpleton, fool; but cf. the development of *silly*. See DEFT.

dag[1] dæg (hist.) heavy pistol or hand-gun. XVI. Of unkn. origin; in earliest use Sc.

dag[2] dæg (dial., sl.) feat of skill, esp. in *doing (one's) dags*. XIX. prob. alteration of (Sc. and north.) *darg* task, earlier *dawark* (XV), *daurk* (XVIII), contr. of *daywark*, etc., OE. *dæġweorc* (DAY, WORK).

dagesh dā·gēʃ dot placed within a Heb. letter. XVI. – med. Heb. *dāghēsh*, f. Syriac *d'ghash* prick.

dagger dæ·gəɹ short sword-like weapon for thrusting and stabbing. XIV (*dagge·re*, *da·ggere*, Ch.). Has the form of an agent-noun in -ER[1], and perh. f. ME. *dagge* (XIV) pierce, stab; but infl. by (O)F. *dague* (XIII) – Pr. or It. *daga*, which has been referred to Rom. **daca* 'Dacian knife', sb. use of fem. of *Dacus* Dacian.

dago dei·gou American Spaniard; Southern Latin. XIX. Earlier form *dego* (1832); alteration of *Diego*, Sp. equivalent of the name JAMES. Cf. *Dandego*, i.e. Don Diego, and *Diego* for 'Spaniard' (XVII, Dekker).

dagoba dā·gobə Buddhist monument containing relics. XIX. – Sinhalese *dāgaba* :– Pali *dhātugabbha* :– Skr. *dhātugarbha*, f. *dhātu* ashes, relics of a body + *gárbha* inner chamber.

daguerreotype dăge·rotaip one of the earliest photographic processes. XIX. – F. *daguerréotype*, f. name of Louis-Jacques-Mandé *Daguerre* (1789–1851) the inventor; see -O- and TYPE.

dahabeeya dahabī·jə sailing-boat of the Nile. XIX. – Arab. *ðahabīyah* lit. 'the golden' (f. *ðahab* gold), name of the gilded state barge of the Moslem rulers of Egypt.

dahlia dei·liə genus of showy composite plants. XIX. Named 1791 in honour of Andreas *Dahl*, Swedish botanist, a pupil of Linnæus; see -IA[1].

daily see DAY.

dainty dei·nti † honour, esteem; †liking, pleasure; choice or delightful thing, delicacy. XIII. – AN. *dainté*, OF. *daintié, deintié* :– L. *dignitātem*, nom. *-tās* worthiness, worth, beauty, DIGNITY. Hence **dai·nty** adj. †choice, excellent; pleasing to the taste, of delicate beauty XIV; fastidious XVI; for the sense cf. *nice*, and for the adj. use of the sb. cf. *choice, plenty*.

dairy dɛə·ri place for treating milk and its products. XIII. ME. *deierie, dayerie*, f. *deie, daye* female servant, (later) farm servant, dairy-woman :– OE. *dǣġe* kneader of bread = ON. *deigja* :– Germ. **daigjōn*, f. base of Goth. *deigan* (pt. *daig, digun*, pp. *digan*) knead, whence also Goth. *daigs*, OE. *dāh* DOUGH, and the second el. of OE. *hlǣfdiġe* LADY. See -RY.

dais deis, dei·is †high table in a hall; raised platform for this. XIII. ME. *deis* – OF. *deis* (mod. *dais*, from Picard dial.) = Pr. *desc*, It. *desco* :– L. *discu-s* quoit, DISH, DISC, in medL. table. Obsolete in Eng. use before 1600, but surviving in Sc. in the sense 'bench against a wall, settle, pew'; the present Eng. use is due to revival by antiquarian and historical writers since 1800. The disyllabic pronunc. is based on an interpretation of the written word, and is due in part to the notion that it is Greek.

daisy dei·zi composite plant, Bellis perennis. OE. *dæġes ēaġe* 'day's eye'; so named from its covering the yellow disk in the evening and disclosing it in the morning.

dak see DAWK.

dal dāl kind of pulse. XVII. – Hindi *dāl* split pulse :– Skr. *dala*, f. *dal* split.

dale deil valley. OE. *dæl* n., g. *dæles*, nom. pl. *dalu*, corr. to OFris. *del*, OS. (Du.) *dal*, OHG. *tal* m. and n. (G. *tal* n.), ON. *dalr* m., Goth. *dals* m. or *dal* n. :– CGerm. **dalam*, **dalaz*, the relations of which are doubtful. Reinforced in ME. from ON. The present form derives from OE. obl. cases (cf. *whale*).

dally dæ·li talk lightly XIV; sport, esp. amorously XV; trifle, spend time idly XVI. – OF. *dalier* converse, chat (frequent in AN.), of unkn. origin. Hence **da·lli**ANCE talk; sport, amorous play XIV; frivolous action XVI.

dalmatic dælmæ·tik (eccl.) wide-sleeved tunic slit up the sides. XV. – (O)F. *dalmatique* or late L. *dalmatica*, sb. use (sc. *vestis* robe, prop. made of Dalmatian wool) of *Dalmaticus* pert. to Dalmatia; see -IC.

Daltonism dɔ̄·ltənizm colour-blindness. XIX. – F. *daltonisme* (P. Prevost, of Geneva), f. name of John *Dalton* (1766–1844), English chemist, who was afflicted with this; see -ISM.

dam[1] dæm barrier checking the downward flow of water, expanse of water thus held up XII (in *mulnedam* 'mill-dam'; Sc. *dam|dik* XIII). – (M)LG., (M)Du. *dam* (whence Icel. *dammr*, etc.) = OFris. *dam, dom*, MHG. *tam* (G. *damm* from LG.), f. a base repr. also by OE. *for|demman* (ME. *demme*), OFris. *demmen*, Goth. *faur|dammjan* dam up, close up; of doubtful origin. Hence **dam** vb. XVI.

dam[2] dæm †dame, lady XIII; female parent XIV. var. of DAME, due to lack of stress.

damage dæ·midʒ (arch.) loss, detriment; injury, harm XIV; money value of something lost XV. – OF. *damage* (mod. *dommage*), f. *dam, damme* loss, damage, prejudice (= Pr. *dan*, Sp. *daño*, It. *danno*, Rum. *daună*) – L. *damnum* loss, hurt; see DAMN and -AGE. So **da·mage** vb. XIV. – OF. *damagier*.

damascene dæməsī·n pert. to the city of Damascus, capital of Cœle-Syria, famous for its steel and its silk fabrics; also sb. XIV. – L. *Damascēnus* – Gr. *Damaskēnós*, f. *Damaskós* – Semitic name (Heb. *Dameseq*, Arab. *Dimashq*). Hence **damasce·ne** vb. ornament (steel) by inlaying XIX; earlier (XVI) in the form *damaskine*, later *-keen* – F. *damasquiner*, f. *damasquin* – It. *damaschino*. Cf. next and DAMSON.

damask dæ·məsk in various names of natural and artificial products reputed to derive from *Damascus* (see prec.); orig. attrib. uses of the name (in ME. *Damaske*), in some uses absol. as sb., e.g. *damask (cloth)* XIV; *damask plum* (L. *prunum Damasci*), *damask rose* XVI; †*damask water* (cf. medL. *aqua rosata de Damasco*); *damask (steel)* XVII; the colour of the damask rose XVI (Sh.). Cf. F. *damas* (orig. *drap de damas*) silk stuff, steel blade, It. *dam(m)asco, dommasco* silk, Sp. *damasco* silk, Brussels apricot, DAMSON, Du., G. *damast*. ¶ *Baldacchino* and *muslin* are also derived from Arabic place-names.

dame deim †female head or superior; as a form of address or title; †mother, dam XIII; (arch., dial.) lady of the house XIV; – (O)F. *dame*, earlier †*damme* = Pr. *domna*, Sp. *dueña* (see DUENNA), *doña* (see DONA), Pg. *dona*, It. *donna* Rum. *doamnă* :– L. *domina* fem. corr. to *dominus* lord (cf. DAN, DOM[1], DON[2]).

dammar dæm·əɹ resin of the East Indies, etc. XVII. – Malay *damar*.

damn dæm †condemn XIII (Cursor M.); doom to eternal perdition XIV; (in imprecations) XVI. – (O)F. *damner* (= Pr. *damnar*, Sp. *dañar*, It. *dannare*) – L. *damnāre* orig. inflict loss upon, f. *damnum* loss, damage, expenditure. Cf. CONDEMN. The oath *God damn!* is preserved in F. *godon* Englishman (†*goddem* XV). The int. **damme** dæ·mi, also †*dammee*, †*dammy* (XVII), is for (*God*) *damn me*. Hence **damn** sb. the imprecation 'damn!' XVII; *not to care a damn, not worth a damn* (cf. *curse* similarly used) XVIII. **damnABLE** dæ·mnəbl XIV (R. Mannyng, R. Rolle, Wyclif; rare before XVI). – (O)F. – late L. **damnA·TION**. XIII (Cursor M.). – (O)F. – L. **damnaTORY**[2] dæ·mnətəri condemnatory XVII; consigning to damnation XVIII. – L.

damned dæmd in imprecatory use XVI; in clipped form *damn* from XVIII; *damn all*, nothing (XX).

Damnonian dæmnou·niən pert. to (the ancient inhabitants of) Devon and Cornwall. XIX. f. L. *Damnoniī*, var. of *Dumnoniī* (see DEVONIAN).

damp dæmp vapour, (noxious) gas (surviving in *choke-damp, fire-damp*) XIV; fog, mist; humidity; depression, discouragement, †stupor XVI. – (M)LG. *damp* vapour, steam, smoke (so in modDu.) = (O)HG. *dampf* steam; rel. to OHG. *dempfan* (G. *dämpfen*) cause to smoke, smother, suffocate = OS. *bi|thempian*; f. Germ. **þamp-*, of which the var. **þump-* appears to be repr. by (O)HG. *duft* (:– **þunft*) vapour, odour, (earlier) dust, cloud, dew, frost. Hence **damp** adj. †dazed XVI (Greene); †noxious (Milton); slightly wet XVIII; so Fris. *damp*. **damp** vb. XIV. **da·mpen** XVII; see -EN[5].

damsel dæ·mzəl young unmarried lady XIII; young unmarried woman (without implication of rank or respect) XIV; female attendant XIV. ME. *dameisele, damisel* – OF. *dameisele, damisele* (mod. *demoiselle*), alteration (after *dame*) of *danzele, donsele* = Pr. *donsela* (whence Sp. *doncella*, It. *donzella*) :– Gallo-Rom. **dominicella*, dim. of *domina* lady, DAME. The arch. var. **damosel, -zel** dæ·mozel is a later form (XVI–XVII, and poet. in XIX) of *damoisel* – arch. F. *damoiselle*.

damson dæ·mzən small blackish plum, Prunus communis or domestica. XIV. ME. *dama(s)cene, damesene* – L. *damascēnum* (sc. *prunum*) plum of Damascus (see DAMASCENE); cf. G. *damaszenerpflaume*.

Dan dæn master (title); esp. latterly in *Dan Chaucer*, after Spenser. XIV (R. Mannyng). – OF. *dan* (nom. *dans, danz*), also *dam* (whence ME. †*dam, damp*), mod. *dom* = Pr. *don, dompn*, Sp. *don* (see DON[2]), It. *donno* :– L. *dominu-s* master, lord (cf. DOMINICAL).

dance dàns leap, hop, or glide with measured steps. XIII. – OF. *dancer*, (also mod.) *danser* = Pr. *dansar*, Sp. *danzar*, It. *danzare* :– Rom. **dansāre*, of unkn. origin. So **dance** sb. XIII. – OF. *dance*, (also mod.) *danse*, f. the vb.

dancetté dà·nseti (her.) deeply indented. XVII. Alteration of F. *danché, denché*, earlier †*dansié* :– late L. **denticātus*, f. *dent-*, *dēns* TOOTH.

dandelion dændiləi·ən composite plant, Leontodon Taraxacum. XV *dent de lyon*, – F. *dent-de-lion*, rendering medL. *dēns leōnis* 'lion's tooth'; so called from the toothed leaves.

dander dæ·ndəɹ (U.S. and dial.) ruffled temper. XIX. perh. fig. use of *dander* ferment in working molasses, var. of DUNDER.

Dandie Dinmont dæ·ndi di·nmənt terrier from the Scottish Border. XIX. Name of a character in Walter Scott's 'Guy Mannering' (ch. xxii 'Dandy Dinmont's Pepper and Mustard Terriers').

dandiprat dæ·ndipræt †small coin; (arch.) insignificant fellow; young urchin. XVI. Of unkn. origin.

dandle dæ·ndl toss (a child) lightly up and down. XVI. Of unkn. origin; presumably f. a symbolic base **dand-* **dond-* denoting from-side-to-side motion (cf. F. *se dandiner* waddle, It. *dondolare* waggle).

dandruff dæ·ndrəf scurf on the scalp. XVI. Also early or dial. *-riff, -raff*, and †*dandro*, (dial. and U.S.) *dander*; the first el. is obscure; the second el., *-ruff*, may be identical with late ME. *rove*, later *rofe, roufe* scurfiness, scab – ON. *hrufa* or MLG., MDu. *rōve* (Du. *roof*) = (M)HG. *rufe*, rel. to OE. *hrēof*, OHG. *riob*, ON. *hrjúfr* scabby, leprous; cf. dial. *reef* skin eruption, dandruff.

dandy[1] dæ·ndi beau, fop; *the dandy* the correct thing XVIII; applied to various trim or handy objects XIX. First recorded from the Scottish Border; in vogue in London in Byron's day ('a Dandy Ball', Letter to Moore, 1813; 'a Dandy's dandiest chatter', Don Juan v cxliii); perh. a shortening of *jack-a-dandy* pert fellow (XVII); the source of *dandy* remains unkn., but it may be ult. identical with *Dandy*, pet-form of *Andrew*.

dandy[2] dæ·ndi var. of DENGUE in the West Indies. XIX.

Dane dein native of Denmark XIII (Cursor M.); breed of dog (after F. *danois*) XVIII (Goldsmith, after Buffon). – ON. *Danir* pl. (late L. *Danī*); superseding OE. *Dene*, which is repr. in *Denmark* (OE. *Denemearc*). So **danegeld** dei·ngeld tax imposed *c.* 1000, the origin of which is disputed. XI (Domesday Book). – ON. **Danagjald* (ODa. *Danegjeld*), f. g.pl. of *Danir* Danes + *gjald* payment, tribute (cf. YIELD). **danehole** see DENE-HOLE. **DaneLAW** dei·nlɔ̄ the Danish laws anciently in force over the part of England occupied by the Danes, (hence) the region itself. Late OE. *Dena lagu* 'Danes' law', ME. *Denelawe*, was modernized by Lambarde (1576) as *Dane lawe*, and taken up by historians of XIX in the forms *Danelage, -lagh, -law*.

dang dæŋ. XVIII. euphem. alteration of DAMN suggested by *hang!* (which was in use XVI).

danger deiˑndʒəɹ †power of a master, dominion XIII; (hence) †liability to punishment, etc.; †hesitation, reluctance XIII; liability to injury XIV (Ch.). – AN. *da(u)nger*, OF. *dangier* :– Rom. **domniārium*, f. *dominus*, *dominus* lord, master (cf. DAN). So **daˑngerous** †difficult to deal with or please XIII; †reluctant to comply XIV (Ch.); fraught with danger XV. – AN. *da(u)ngerous*, OF. *dangereus* (mod. *-eux*). ¶ For the vocalism cf. *chamber*, *change*, *strange*.

dangle dæˑŋgl hang or carry loosely with swaying movement. XVI. Of symbolic formation; cf. NFris. *dangeln*, Sw. *dangla*, Da. *dangle*, parallel to Icel., Sw. *dingla*, Da. *dingle*, of similar meaning; see -LE[2].

Danish deiˑniʃ pert. to the Danes or Denmark. XIII (Cursor M.). ME. *danais*, *danis* (in *danisax* 'Danish axe') – AN. *danes*, OF. *daneis* (mod. *danois*) :– medL. *Danēnsis*; later (XIV) assim. to adjs. in -ISH[1]; superseded the native †*densh* :– OE. *Denisć* = ON. *Danskr* :– Germ. **daniskaz*; see DANE, -ISH[1].

dank dæŋk †wet, watery XIV; (injuriously) damp XVI. Implied earlier in the deriv. *dank* vb. (XIII); prob. of Scand. origin (cf. Sw. *dank* marshy spot, Icel. *dökk* pit, pool (:– **daŋku-*).

danseuse dãˑsōz professional female dancer. XIX. F., fem. of *danseur*, f. *danser* DANCE.

dapper dæˑpəɹ neat, trim. XV ('dapyr or praty, *elegans*', Promp. Parv.). – MLG., MDu. *dapper* heavy, powerful, strong, stout (Du. *dapper* bold, valiant) = OHG. *tapfar* heavy, weighty, firm (late MHG., G. *tapfer* brave), ON. *dapr* sad, dreary. The transf. of sense in Eng. from 'bold, energetic' to 'smart, trim' is similar to that in BRAVE[1]. The basic meaning is 'heavy'; cogns. outside Germ. are recognized in Russ. *debélȳi* plump, OPruss. *debīkan* large, OSl. *debelŭ* thick.

dappled dæˑpld marked with roundish spots. XIV (Maund.). contemp. with *dapple-grey* (Ch.), whence **dapple** sb., adj., and vb. (all XVI; the verb first in Sh.). Of unkn. origin; *dappled* varies in Maund. with *pomelee* (– OF. *pommelé* 'appled'; cf. *pomely grey* in Ch. 'Canterbury Tales', prol. 616 – F. *gris pommelé*), and the notion 'apple-grey' is expressed in ON. *apalgrár*, OHG. *aphelgrāo* (G. *apfelgrau*), Du. *appelgrauw*; cf. also Russ. *v yablokakh* dappled, f. *yábloko* APPLE; the problems raised by these correspondences seem to be insoluble (the comp. *apple-grey* has no standing).

darbies dāˑɹbiz (sl.) pl. handcuffs, †fetters. XVII. app. evolved from phr. (*Father Darby's bands* some kind of rigid bond binding a debtor XVI). *Darby* is a southern (not the local) pronunc. of *Derby*, name of an Eng. town and county and a personal name. *Darby and Joan* (prov.) strongly attached husband and wife XVIII.

dare dɛəɹ pt. *durst* dəɹst, pt. and pp. *dared* dɛəɹd have boldness or courage (*to dar*) OE. Trans. senses with a plain object appear XVI. A preterite-present vb. (cf. CAN[2]), OE. *durran*, pres. *dearr*, *durron*, pt. *dorste*, corr. to OFris. *dūra*, *dar*, *dor*, *dorste*, OS. *gidurran*, *-dar*, *-durrum*, *dorsta*, OHG. *giturran*, *-tar*, *-turrun*, *-torsta*, pp. *gitorran*, Goth. *ga-daursan*, *-dars*, *-daursun*, *-daursta*; f. the Germ. series **ders-* **dars-* **durs-* (not ON.) :– IE. **dhers-* **dhors-*, **dhṛs-*, whence Skr. *dhṛsh*, perf. *dadārsha* be bold, Gr. *tharseîn* be bold, *thrasús* bold, OSlav. *drŭzate* be bold. The orig. 3rd pers. sg. pres. (*he*) *dare* and pt. (*he*) *durst* remain in idiomatic usage, but *durst* is obsolescent and even so is restricted; *dareth*, *dares*, and *dared* appeared in XVI; there has been considerable crossing of forms, *dare* being used for the pt. (XVIII–) and *durst* for the present (XVII–).

dark dāɹk marked by lack of light. OE. *deorc*, prob. f. Germ. base **derk-* **dark-*, whence also OHG. *tarchanjan*, *terchinen* conceal, hide (:– **darknjan*). Hence **daˑrken** XIII (Cursor M.; rare in ME.); see -EN[5]. **daˑrkling** in the dark XV; being, lying, etc., in darkness XVIII; see -LING[2]. Whence as a back-formation **daˑrkle.** XV.

darling dāˑɹliŋ dear or beloved person. OE. *dēorling*; see DEAR and -LING[1]. The present form is developed normally from ME. *derling*; a new formation on DEAR appeared in ME. and *dearling* continued in use till XVIII.

darn[1] dāɹn mend (clothes) with yarn or thread. XVI. poss. a use of *darn*, later form of †*dern* conceal, hide (OE. *diernan*, f. *dierne* DERN); cf. MDu. *dernen* stop holes in (a dike).

darn[2], **darned, darnation.** Earliest in *darn* adv. (late XVIII), used as an intensive, which Noah Webster identified with DERN in its later senses of 'dark, drear, dim', as in the phr. *dern and dismal*, which presumably became *darn(ed) dismal*; cf. the vars. *dern*, *durn*. When *darn(ed)* had become a mild substitute for *damn*, *darnation* would readily follow. Cf. U.S. *tarnation* sb., adj., adv. (XVIII), which is prob. to be assoc. with the similarly used and somewhat earlier *tarnal*, aphetic form of *etarnal*, *eternal*.

darnel dāˑɹnəl the grass Lolium temulentum. XIV. prob. of NEF. origin, e.g. Walloon *darnelle* (var. *-ette*), which has been connected with words denoting giddiness, reeling, and the like, the plant being so named from its stupefying properties (cf. F. *ivraie* tares – L. *ēbriāca* fem. 'drunken', and the epithet *temulentum* 'drunken' of the bot. name).

dart dāɹt pointed missile to be hurled through the air. XIV. – OF. *dart* (mod. *dard*) = Pr. *dart* (whence Sp., It. *dardo*) :– Germ. **daroðaz* spear, lance, repr. by OE. *daroþ*, OHG. *tart*, ON. *darraðr*. Hence **dart** vb. cast as a dart XIV; move swiftly XVII.

dartre dā·ɹtəɹ herpes, etc.; tetter, scab. XIX. – (O)F. *dartre*, corr. to Pr. *derti, derbi*, It. dial. *derbi, derbga, derbeda* :– medL. *derbita*, of Gaulish origin (cf. Breton *dervoed*); earlier adopted as †*dartars, -ers* disease of sheep (XVI–XVIII).

dash[1] dæʃ strike with violence (with many transf. and fig. uses) XIII (RGlouc.); move violently XIV; euph. for 'damn' (partly from the use of a dash — in place of this word) XIX. ME. *dasche, dasse*, prob. of imit. origin; an appropriate base **dask-* is repr. by Sw. *daska*, Da. *daske* beat, but no older Scand. forms are recorded. Hence **dash** sb. act of dashing XIV; stroke made with a pen, etc. XVI.

dash[2] dæʃ present, gratuity. XVIII. prob. alteration of *dashee, dasje* (XVIII), *dache* (Purchas), by taking the pl. *dashees* as *dashes*; native word of Guinea.

dastard dæ·stəɹd †dullard, sot (Promp. Parv.); despicable coward. XV. Of obscure origin; prob. to be referred ult. to ME. *dase*, DAZE, but perh. immed. based on ME. †*dasart* (XIV) dullard (cf. MDu. *dasaert* fool) and †*dasiberd* (XIV), f. †*dasi* inert, dull + *berd*, BEARD (cf. LG. *dösbārt*), with infl. from DOTARD.

dasyure dæ·sijuəɹ brush-tailed opossum. XIX. – F. *dasyure* (H. E. Geoffroy St-Hilaire) – modL. *dasyūrus*, f. Gr. *dasús* rough, hairy (rel. to L. *dēnsus* DENSE) + *ourá* tail (cf. ARSE).

data dei·tə pl. of DATUM.

date[1] deit fruit of the palm Phœnix dactylifera. XIII. – OF. *date* (mod. *datte*) :– L. *dactylu-s* – Gr. *dáktulos* finger, toe, date (see DACTYL). The application to the date-palm has reference to the finger-like shape of its leaves. ¶ Continental forms are: OHG. *dahtilboum* date-tree (MHG. *tahtel*), MHG. *datel* (G. *dattel*) after It. *dattilo*, OF. whence MDu. *dade* (– Rom. **dada* for *data*), Du. *dadel*, after G.

date[2] deit time or period of an event. XIV. – (O)F. *date* – medL. *data* (cf. Pr., Sp., It. *data*), sb. use of fem. of *datus*, pp. of *dare* give. Derived from the L. formula used in dating letters, e.g. *Data* [sc. *epistola*] *Romæ*, [letter] given or delivered (and so, written) at Rome, i.e. by the writer to the bearer. So **date** vb. XV. – (O)F. *dater* – medL. *datāre*, f. *data*.

dative dei·tiv (Sc.) appointed by the king or the commissary; (gram.) case denoting 'to' or 'for'. XV. – L. *datīvus* pert. to giving (gram. *casus dativus*, rendering Gr. *πτῶσις δοτική*; see CASE[1]), f. *dat-*, pp. stem of *dare* give (cf. DONATION); see -IVE.

datum dei·təm thing given or granted; chiefly pl. **data** dei·tə. XVII. L., n. pp. of *dare* give; cf. prec.

datura dətjuə·rə genus of poisonous plants (Datura Stramonium, thorn apple). XVI. – modL. – Hindi *dhatūra* :– Skr. *dhattura*. Earlier repr. by †*dewtry* (vars. *deutroa* XVI, *doutro, doutry* XVII) – Marathi *dhutrā, dhutrō*.

daub dōb coat with a layer of mortar, etc. XIV; lay on colours crudely XVII. – OF. *dauber* :– L. *dēalbāre* whiten, whitewash, plaster, f. *dē* DE- 3 + *albus* white (cf. ALBUM). Hence **daub** sb. mortar, plaster XV; coarsely executed painting XVIII.

daughter dō·təɹ female child. OE. *dohtor* = OFris. *dochter*, OS. *dohtar* (Du. *dochter*), OHG. *tohter* (G. *tochter*), ON. *dóttir*, Goth. *dauhtar* :– CGerm. **doχtēr*, earlier **dhuktēr* :– IE. **dhughətēr*, whence also Skr. *duhitár-*, Av. *duγδar*, Gr. *thugátēr*, Arm. *dustr*, OSl. *dŭšti*, g. *dŭštere* (Russ. *doč'*, g. *dóčeri*); of unkn. origin. ¶ Like *son*, not repr. in Italic or Celtic. The normal repr. of the OE. is †*doughter* (to XVI), Sc. *dauchter* dau·χtər, north. Eng. *dowter* dau·təɹ. The standard pronunc., which is shown XVI, is of dial. origin; cf. early modE. and dial. *dafter*.

daunt dōnt †overcome, tame XIII; dispirit, abash XV. – AN. *daunter*, OF. *danter*, var. of *donter* (mod. *dompter*) = Pr. *domtar* :– L. *domitāre*, frequent. of *domāre* TAME. ¶ For the vowel in OF. cf. DAME, DAN, DANGER.

dauphin dō·fin title of the King of France's eldest son (1349–1830). XV (*daulphyn, dolphyn*). – F. *dauphin*, earlier †*daulphin* – Pr. *dalfin* :– medL. *dalphīnus* (VIII), for L. *delphīnus* – Gr. *delphís, delphīn-* (see DOLPHIN); orig. a title attached to certain seigneuries, e.g. Viennois, the lords of which are said to have borne the name. Hence **dau·phiness** XVI; see -ESS[1].

davenport dæ·vənpōɹt writing-table with drawers. XIX. Supposed to be f. the maker's name.

davit dæ·vit (naut.) piece of timber or iron at a ship's stern used as a crane. XIV (*daviottes, devettes, dyvettes*; also *dauyd, -id* XVI–XVII). – AF, OF. *daviot*, later *daviet* (now *davier*), dim. of *Davi* David.

davy[1] dei·vi, in full *Davy lamp, Davy's lamp*, miner's safety-lamp invented by Sir Humphry *Davy* (1778–1829), natural philosopher. XIX (1817).

davy[2] dei·vi oath. XVIII. (sl.) clipped form of AFFIDAVIT.

Davy Jones dei·vi dʒounz (naut. slang) spirit of the sea, sailor's devil; *Davy Jones's locker*, grave of those who perish at sea. XVIII (Smollett). The allusion is unkn. (*Jonas*, var. of *Jonah* name of O.T. prophet, Jonah i 17 and ii, has been suggested, but *David* appears to be an essential element); vars. are *David Jones, Old Davy*, and simply *Davy*.

daw dō jackdaw; †simpleton; (Sc.) sluggard, slut. XV. prob. to be referred to an OE. **dāwe*, rel. to OHG. *tāha* (G. dial. *tach*), beside MHG. *dāhele, tāle* (G. *dahle, dohle*), whence It. *taccola*, medL. *tacula*. Also in contemp. compound †*cadaw*, †*caddow*, the first el. of which is *ca* (Sc. *kae*), *co* – ON. *ká* (Da. *kaa*), of imit. origin.

dawdle dɔ̄·dl waste time. XVII. prob. of dial. origin (there are vars. *daddle, daidle, doddle*); see -LE[2].

dawk dɔ̄k post-relay. XVIII. – Hindi, Marathi *ḍāk* :– Skr. *drāk* quickly.

dawn dɔ̄n begin to grow light. XV. Back-formation from *dawning*, ME. *dai(ȝ)ening, da(i)ning* (XIII), *dawenyng* (XIV Ch.), alteration of *daiing, dawyng* (OE. *dagung*, f. *dagian* grow light) after Scand. (OSw. *daghning*, Sw., Da. *dagning*); see DAY, -ING[1]; repl. ME. †*day*. Hence **dawn** sb. XVI (Sh.).

day dei time of sunlight)(*night*; 24 hours OE; daylight XIV. OE. *dæġ* = OFris. *dei*, OS. (Du.) *dag*, OHG. *tac* (G. *tag*), ON. *dagr*, Goth. *dags* :– CGerm. **dagaz*, beside which a wk. form **dagan* is repr. by OE. *ān|daga* appointed time, OS. *ēn|dago* death-day, OHG. *giburt|tago* birthday, ON. *ein|dagi* term, and a gradation-var. **dǒg*- by OE. *dōgor* (*s*-stem), Nhb. *dœg* day, ON. *dœgr* 12 hours, Goth. *fidur|dōgs* of four days. On the assumption of a basic meaning 'time when the sun is hot', connexion is made out with Skr. *ni dāghás* heat, summer, Lith. *dãgas* harvest time, OPruss. *dagis* summer, and with a base **dhegh*- burn, which is recognized in Skr., Gr., L., Balto-Slav., and Celtic. Hence **daily** dei·li adj. and adv. XV; see -LY[1] and [2]; the equiv. OE. words were *dæġhwamlić, -līće*.

daze deiz benumb the senses of. XIV (R. Rolle). First in pp. *dased* – ON. pp. *dasaðr* weary or exhausted from cold or exertion (cf. Icel. *dasask* refl. become exhausted, *dusi* lazy fellow, Sw. *dasa* lie idle). Cf. †*adased* (XVI).

dazzle dæ·zl †lose distinctness of vision XV; confuse the vision of XVI. Late ME. *dasele*, f. *dase*, DAZE + -LE[3].

de dī L. prep. *dē* of, (down) from, off, concerning (corr. to Ir. *di, de*), occurring in commonly used phrases, e.g. *de facto, de fide, de jure, de novo*. Cf. DE-.

de- repr. (often through F. *dé-*) L. *dē-*, which is the prep. *dē* down from, away from, off, aside (with cogns. only in Celtic, e.g. Ir., Gael. *de*), used in verbal comps., as *dēcrēscere* DECREASE, *dēfendere* DEFEND, *dēsīderāre* DESIRE. The earliest adoptions of such vbs. in Eng. were through French, as AN. *decreisser, defender*, OF. *decreistre, defendre, desirer*; later adoptions were direct from L. infins. or pps. The meanings denoted are (1) down (from or to a place or state), as in *depend, depose, depress, descend*; (hence) down from (a vehicle), as *debus, detrain*; (2) off, away, aside, as in *decline, deduce, defend, deport, design, desist, deter*; spec. away from oneself, as in *delegate, deprecate*; (3) down to the bottom or dregs, (hence) completely, thoroughly, as in L. *dēcoquere* (see DECOCTION), *dēliquēscere* DELIQUESCE; sometimes merely strengthening vbs., as in L. *dēclāmāre* DECLAIM, *dēclārāre* DECLARE, *dēnudāre* DENUDE, *dērelinquere* (see DERELICT), *dēsiccāre* DESICCATE; (4) with pejorative sense, as in L. *dēcipere* take in, DECEIVE, *dērīdēre* laugh to scorn, DERIDE, *dētestārī* DETEST; (5) by late L. grammarians used uniquely in *dēcompositus* derived from a compound word, further compounded; whence *decomposite, decompound* in chem., bot., etc.; (6) with the sense of undoing or reversing what is expressed by a vb., as in L. *dēarmāre* disarm, *dēvēlāre* unveil, whence the formation of similar vbs. from sbs. to denote removal, as in *dēcollāre* (see DECOLLATION), *dēflōrāre* DEFLOWER, *dēsquāmāre* (see DESQUAMATION); a similar notion was expressed by L. *dis-*, as in *disjungere* DISJOIN, and the use of this prefix, repr. in Rom. by *des-*, was widely extended, and through F. *dé-* (OF. *des-*) it became in Eng. adoptions identical with *dé-* (cf. DEBATE, DEFY, DERANGE, DEVELOP). Hence (7) as a living formative *de-* forms vbs., with corr. sbs., (*a*) denoting removal or riddance, as *de-bark* (XVIII), †*debowel* (XIV) disembowel, *de-frost* (XX), *de-husk* (XVI), *dehydrate* (XIX), *delouse*, also *debag* (f. *bags* trousers); (*b*) with privative or reversive force mainly from late XVIII (but *decanonization* XVII), as *decasualize, decentralize, decontrol, de-Italianize, demagnetize, denazification, de-rate, devolatilize*.

deacon dī·kən one of an order of Christian ministers. OE. *diacon* – ecclL. *diāconus* – Gr. *diā́konos* servant, waiting man, messenger, eccl. Christian minister (cf. *diākoneîn* serve, *egkoneîn* be active). Hence **dea·coness**[1]. XVI; after late L. *diāconissa*.

dead ded no longer living OE.; (in various transf. uses) without animation, motion, or some vital quality OE. or ME.; inactive, quiet, still; unrelieved, absolute, complete XVI. OE. *dēad* = OFris. *dād*, OS. *dōd* (Du. *dood*), OHG. *tōt* (G. *tot*), ON. *dauðr*, Goth. *dauþs* :– CGerm. **dauðaz* :– **dhautós*, pp. of base **dhau-*, repr. also in OS. *dōian*, OHG. *touwen*, ON. *deyja* DIE[1]. There are many special comps. involving transf. and fig. uses (as above), e.g. *dead-eye* (for earlier †*dead man's eye* XV), *dead hand* (tr. MORTMAIN), *dead heat* (XIX), *dead letter, dead level, deadlock* (metaphor from wrestling), *dead nettle* (non-stinging), *dead reckoning* (a proposed etym. *ded.*, for *deduced*, has no justification), *dead weight*. Hence **deaden** de·dn. XVII; see -EN[5]. **dea·dly** adj. and adv. OE. *dēadlić, -līće*; see -LY[1], -LY[2], and cf. OHG. *tōtlich*, MDu. *doodlick* adjs.

deaf def lacking in the sense of hearing. OE. *dēaf* = OFris. *dāf*, OS. *dōf* (Du. *doof*), OHG. *toup* (G. *taub*), ON. *daufr*, Goth. *daufs* (*-b-*) :– CGerm. **dauƀaz* (cf. also Goth. *af|daubnan* grow dull. The IE. base **dhoubh-* **dheubh-* **dhubh-* is repr. also by Gr. *tuphlós* (:– **thuphlós*) blind; cf. DUMB. The pronunc. with a long vowel (dīf) was still gen. current in XVIII, and remains widely diffused dial. and in U.S. Hence **dea·fen**. XVI (Sh.); superseding †*deaf* vb. (XIV); see -EN[5].

deal[1] dīl †part, portion; quantity, amount. OE. *dǣl* = OFris., OS. *dēl* (Du. *deel*), OHG., G. *teil*, Goth. *dails* :– CGerm. (exc. ON.) **dailiz*, f. **dail-*; see DOLE[1]. So **deal** vb. A. †divide; distribute, bestow among a number OE.; deliver (blows) XIII (Laȝ.); B. †take part *in* XII; have to do *with* XIII. OE. *dǣlan* = OFris. *dēla*, OS. *dēljan* (Du. *deelen*), OHG. *teilen* (G. *teilen*), ON. *deila*, Goth. (CGerm.) *dailjan*. Hence **deal** sb. distribution of cards XVII; transaction (orig. U.S.) XIX.

deal[2] dīl plank, board of fir or pine XIV; wood of these XVII. Introduced through the Baltic trade in timber. – MLG., MDu. *dēle* plank, floor (Du. *deel* plank), corr. to OHG. *dil*, *dilo*, *dillo*, *dilla* (G. *diele* deal board, dial. floor), ON. *þilja*, OE. *þille* :– Germ. **þelaz*, **þeliz*, **þeljōn* (cf. Finnish *teljo*); see THILL.

dean[1], **dene** dīn (dial. and surviving in local names) valley. OE. *denu* (:– **dani-*), rel. to DEN (:– **danjam*).

dean[2] dīn head of cathedral or collegiate chapter XIV (R. Mannyng); supervisor of conduct and studies in a college; president of a university faculty XVI. ME. *deen*, *den(e)* – AN. *deen*, *den*, OF. *deien*, *dien* (mod. DOYEN) = Pr. *degan*, Cat. *degá*, Sp., It. *decano* :– late L. *decānu-s* – Gr. *dekānós* one set over ten, chief of a division of ten, (eccl.) of ten monks, f. *déka* TEN. Hence **dea·nERY**. XV; after AN. *denrie*.

dear diəɹ †glorious, noble; regarded with esteem and affection; †precious OE.; high-priced, costly XI. OE. *dēore*, WS. *dīere* = OFris. *diore*, OS. *diuri* (Du. *dier* beloved, *duur* high-priced), OHG. *tiuri* distinguished, worthy, costly (G. *teuer*), ON. *dýrr* :– CGerm. (exc. Gothic) **deurjaz*, of unkn. origin. ¶ To be distinguished from *dear* hard, severe, grievous; OE. *dēor*, of unkn. origin, surviving poet., as in Spenser, Sh., and Milton, by whom it may have been regarded as merely a special sense of the ordinary adj. *dear*.

dearborn diə·ɹbɔ̄ɹn (U.S.) light four-wheeled waggon. XIX. f. name of the inventor.

dearth dɔ̄ɹþ condition of scarcity. XIII. ME. *derþ*, f. *dēr* DEAR + -TH[1]; cf. OS. *diuriða*, MDu. *dierte*, Du. *duurte*, MHG. *tiurde* honour, value, costliness, ON. *dýrð* glory.

death deþ end of life, state of being dead. OE. *dēaþ* = OFris. *dāth*, OS. *dōð* (Du. *dood*), OHG. *tōd* (G. *tod*), ON. *dauðr*, Goth. *dauþus* :– CGerm. **dauþuz*, f. **dau-* (cf. ON. *deyja* DIE[1]) + **-þuz* :– **-tus* -TH[1].

débâcle deibā·kl breaking up of ice, sudden deluge; sudden downfall or rout. XIX. – F. *débâcle*, f. *débâcler* unbar, remove a bar, f. *dé* DE- 6 + *bâcler* bar – modPr. *baclar* prop. bar a door – medL. **bacculāre*, f. **bacculum*, for L. *baculum* stick (cf. BACILLUS, BACTERIUM).

debar dibā·ɹ bar out, exclude XV; prohibit, prevent XVI. – F. *débarrer*, OF. *desbarer*, f. *des-* DE- 6 + *barrer* BAR.

debark dībā·ɹk disembark. XVII. – F. *débarquer*, f. *dé-*, *des-* (see DE- 6) + *barque* BARK[2]. ¶ Later than *disembark*.

debase dibei·s †abase; †decry, vilify; lower in quality or character. XVI. f. DE- 1, 3 + BASE[3].

debate dibei·t contention XIII (Cursor M.); dispute, discussion XIV. – (O)F. *débat*, corr. to Pr. *debat*, It. *dibatto*; Rom. deriv. of the vb. So **deba·te** vb. XIV. – (O)F. *débattre* = Pr. *de(s)batre*, Sp. *debatir*, It. *dibattere* :– Rom. **desbattere* (see DE- 6, BATTLE).

debauch dibɔ̄·tʃ †seduce from allegiance XVI; seduce from virtue or chastity XVII. – F. *débaucher*, OF. *desbaucher*, f. *des-* DE- 6 + an uncertain el. of unkn. origin. Hence **debau·ch** sb. XVII. – F. *débauche*, f. the vb. **debauchEE** debɔ̄tʃī·. XVII. – F. *débauché*, pp. of the vb. Cf. DEBOSHED. **debau·chERY**. XVII (Milton); earlier †*debauchment*.

debenture dibe·ntʃəɹ voucher for a sum due XV; †certificate of a loan made to a government XVIII; bond issued by a corporation acknowledging indebtedness for interest XIX. – mod. use of L. *dēbentur* are owing or due, 3rd pres. ind. pl. pass. of *dēbēre* owe (see DEBT, DUE), occurring as the first word of a certificate of indebtedness (XIV); cf. legal F. *bille de debentour* (XV); there has been assim. of the final syll. to -URE.

debility dibi·lĭti weakness. XV (Wyntoun, Caxton). – (O)F. *débilité* – L. *dēbilitās*, f. *dēbilis* weak, f. *dē-* DE- 4 + IE. base repr. by Skr. *bálam* strength, power, OSl. *bolij* greater (cf. BOLSHEVIK), OIr. *ad|bal* powerful. See -ITY. So **debi·litate** weaken, enfeeble. XVI (Elyot). f. pp. stem of L. *dēbilitāre*, f. *dēbilitās*; see -ATE[3]. **debilitA·TION**. XV – (O)F. – L.

debit de·bit †debt XV; entry of a sum owing, left-hand side of an account XVIII. – L. *dēbitum* DEBT; in the later sense – F. *débit*.

debonair de:bŏnɛə·ɹ †gracious, courteous; genial. XIII (*debonere*). – OF. *debonaire* (mod. *débonnaire*), prop. phr. *de bon aire* of good disposition (see BONNE, AIR).

deboshed dibɔ·ʃt var. (XVI) of DEBAUCHED, to repr. mod. pronunc. of F. *débauché*; mainly Sc. (but used by Sh. and J. Heywood); revived by Scott.

debouch dibau·tʃ, dibū·ʃ emerge from a narrow into a wider space. XVIII. – F. *déboucher*, f. *dé-* DE- 6 + *bouche* mouth (:– L. *bucca*), after synon. It. *sboccare*.

debris de·brī, dei·brī broken remains. XVIII. – F. *débris*, f. †*débriser* break down or up, f. *dé-* DE- 1 + *briser* break (see BRUISE).

debt det what is owed. XIII. ME. *det*, *dette* (till XVI) – (O)F. *dette* :– Rom. **dēbita*, femininized pl. of L. *dēbitum*, pp. n. of *dēbēre* owe, f. *dē-* DE- 6+*habēre* (cf. HABIT). From XIII to XVI spelt *debte* in F., whence *debt* in Eng. from XVI onwards. So **debtor** de·təɹ one who owes. XIII (in A.V. *detter, debter, debtor, -our* all occur). – OF. *det(t)or, -our* :– L. *dēbitōrem*, nom. *dēbitor*; see -OR[1].

debunk dībʌ·ŋk (orig. U.S. sl.) remove the humbug or pretence from. XX. f. DE- 7+ BUNK[3], abbrev. of BUNKUM.

debus dībʌ·s unload from or get off a bus. XX. f. DE- 1+BUS, after DETRAIN.

début dei·bü entry into society. XVIII. F., f. *débuter* make the first stroke in a game, f. *dé-* DE-+*but* goal, BUTT.

deca- de·kə, dėkæ· repr. Gr. *déka* TEN, as in **de·cagon** ten-sided figure (XVII) – modL. *decagōnum* – Gr. *dekágōnon* (*gōníā* angle); **de·castyle** (portico or colonnade) of ten columns (Gr. *stûlos*). XVIII; **decas**Y·LLABLE. XIX; cf. F. *décasyllabe*. ¶ In the F. metric system designating measures and weights ten times the standard unit of the particular series (cf. DECI-).

decade de·kəd, -eid group of ten, esp. of ten years. XV (of the books of Livy). – (O)F. *décade* – late L. *decad-, decas* – Gr. *dekás*, f. *déka* TEN.

decadence de·kədəns state of decay. XVI. – F. *décadence* – medL. *dēcadentia*, f. *dēcadēre* DECAY. So **de·cad**ENT. XIX. – F. *décadent* (used spec. 1884 by Maurice Barrès to designate a French literary movement).

decalogue de·kələg the Ten Commandments. XIV (Wycl. Bible). – (O)F. *décalogue* or ecclL. *decalogus* – Gr. *dekálogos*, orig. fem. adj. sc. *bíblos* book (after *hoi dekalógoi* 'the ten behests', LXX), f. *déka* TEN+*lógos* saying (see LOGOS).

decamp dikæ·mp break up a camp XVII; make off XVIII. – F. *décamper*, earlier †*descamper*, f. *dé-* DE- 6+*camp* CAMP, after It. *scampare*.

decanal dikei·nəl pert. to a dean; of the decani side. XVIII. f. late L. *decānus* DEAN[2]+ -AL. So **decani** dikei·nai dean's side of the choir)(CANTORIS. XVIII. g. sg. of L. *decānus*.

decant dikæ·nt pour off (liquid) so as not to disturb the sediment. XVII. – medL. *dēcanthāre* (whence also F. *décanter*), f. L. *dē-* DE- 1+*canthus* angular lip of a jug – Gr. *kanthós* corner of the eye. Hence **deca·nter** vessel to receive decanted liquor. XVIII; see -ER[1].

decapitate dikæ·piteit behead. XVII. f. pp. stem of late L. *dēcapitāre*, f. *dē* DE- 6+ *capit-, caput* head; see -ATE[3]. Cf. (O)F. *décapiter*.

decay dikei· fall off or away in quality or quantity; fall into ruin. XV. – OF. *decair*, by-form of *decaoir*, var. of *dechaoir, decheoir* (mod. *déchoir*), corr. to Pr. *decaire, decazer*, Sp. *decaer*, Pg. *decahir*, It. *decadere* :– CRom. **dēcadere*, **dēcadēre*, for L. *dēcidere*, f. *dē* DE- 1+*cadere* fall (see CASE[1]). Hence **decay·** sb. XV.

decease disī·s death. XIV (R. Rolle). – (O)F. *décès* – L. *dēcessus* departure, death, f. pp. stem of *dēcēdere* go away, depart, f. *dē* DE- 2+*cēdere* go. Hence vb. XV.

deceit disī·t act or practice of deceiving. XIII. – OF. *deceite*, f. pp. *deceit* (:– L. *deceptu-s*) of *decevoir* DECEIVE. The variation between *ai* (*ay*) and *ei* (*ey*), *c* and *s*, *de-* and *des-*, *dis-*, and the etymologizing insertion of *p*, brought about a great variety of forms. So **deceive** disī·v †ensnare, betray XIII (Cursor M.); lead into error XIV. – OF. *deceivre, deçoivre* = Pr. *decebre*, Sp. *decebir* :– L. *dēcipere*, f. *dē-* DE- 4+*capere* to take, seize (see HEAVE); or – *deceiv-*, tonic stem of OF. *deceveir* (mod. *décevoir*) :– Rom. **dēcipēre*. **dece·p**TION. XIV. – (O)F. or late L. (*dēcept-*, pp. stem of *dēcipere*).

decelerate dīse·ləreit reduce the speed of. XIX. f. DE- 7, after ACCELERATE.

December dise·mbəɹ last month of the year. XIII. – (O)F. *décembre* – L. *December*, f. *decem* TEN, this being the tenth month of the ancient Roman year; the origin of the element *-ber*, as in the three other names of months, is unkn.

decemvir dise·mvə̄ɹ pl. (Roman antiq.) body of ten men acting as a commission, etc. – L. *decemvirī*, i.e. *decem* TEN, *virī* men, pl. of *vir* (see VIRILE).

decennial dise·niəl pert. to a period of 10 years. XVII. f. L. *decennium* decade, f. *decennis*, f. *decem* TEN+*annus* year (cf. ANNUAL); see -IAL.

decent dī·sənt †becoming, fitting; modest, in good taste XVI; respectable; fair, tolerable XVIII. – F. *décent* or L. *decent-, decēns*, pp. of *decēre* be fitting, rel. to *decōrus* DECOROUS, *dignus* worthy (see DIGNITY). So **de·c**ENCY. XVI. – L. *decentia*; see -Y[3]; cf. F. *décence*.

deci- de·si in the F. metric system, short for L. *decimus* tenth, f. *decem* TEN, designating weights and measures that are one tenth of the standard unit (cf. DECA-).

decide disəi·d determine XIV; settle a question XVIII. – F. *décider* or L. *dēcīdere* cut off, cut the knot, determine, f. *dē* DE- 2+*cædere* cut (with no direct cogns.). So **decis**ION disi·ʒən. XV. – (O)F. *décision* or L. *dēcīsiō*, f. *dēcīs-*, pp. stem of *decīdere*. **decis**IVE disəi·siv. XVII. – F. – medL.

deciduous disi·djuəs falling off at a particular season. XVII. f. L. *dēciduus*, f. *dēcidere* fall down or off, f. *dē* DE- 2+*cadere* fall (see CASE[1]).

decimal de·siməl proceeding by powers of 10, as in the Arabic notation; also sb. XVII. – modL. *decimālis*, f. *decimus* tenth, f. *decem* TEN; see -AL[1].

decimate de·simeit exact tithe from; put to death one in ten of a number. XVII. f. pp. stem of L. *decimāre*, f. *decimus* tenth; see prec. and -ATE[3]. So **decim**A·TION exaction of tithe XV; destruction of one in ten. XVI. – late L.

decipher disəi·fəɹ reduce to ordinary writing, make out (a writing in cipher, etc.). XVI. f. DE- 7+CIPHER, after F. *déchiffrer*.

deck[1] dek †covering XV; platform extending from side to side of a ship XV; pack of cards XVI (Sh.; now dial. and U.S.). – MDu. *dec* roof, covering, cloak :– Germ. **þakjam* THATCH; the nautical sense (of which the primary notion was rather 'covering', 'roof' than 'floor') appears to be an Eng. development, since it does not appear for the Du. word till late XVII, and then as a syn. of *verdek* (whence G. *verdeck*).

deck[2] dek †cover; clothe richly, array. XVI. – (M)Du. *dekken* cover = OE. *þeććan* cover, roof over, THATCH.

deckle de·kl in paper-making, contrivance to limit the size of the sheet. XIX. – G. *deckel* cover, lid, tympan, dim. of *decke* covering (OHG. *decki*, f. base of *decken* DECK[2]); cf. -LE[2].

declaim diklei·m speak or utter aloud. XIV (Ch.) (*declame*). – F. *déclamer* or L. *dēclāmāre*; see DE- 3 and CLAIM. So **declamATION** dekləmei·ʃən. XV (Lydg.). – F. or L. **declamatORY** diklæ·mətəri. XVI. – L.

declare diklɛə·ɹ †manifest; state publicly or explicitly. XIV. – L. *dēclārāre* make clear, f. *dē* DE- 3+*clārāre*, f. *clārus* CLEAR. (Cf. F. *déclarer* (XV), which superseded OF. *desclairier*.) So **declarATION** deklərei·ʃən. XIV. – L.; so F. (XV). **declaratORY** diklæ·rətəri. XV. – medL.

declension dikle·nʃən (gram.) case-inflexion, class of sbs., etc., depending on this XV; declining, deviation XVI (Sh.). repr. (O)F. *déclinaison*, f. *décliner* DECLINE, after L. *dēclīnātiō* DECLINATION; retraction of the stress to the second syll. (cf. COMPARISON) produced *declynsone* (Promp. Parv., Winchester MS.), which was modified to †*declenson* (XV–XVI), with aphetic var. †*clenzon*, †*clensone* (XV, Promp. Parv.), the termination being subsequently assim. to -SION.

decline diklai·n turn aside, deviate (trans. and intr.); bend or go down; (gram.) inflect XIV; turn aside or away from XV. – (O)F. *décliner* – L. *dēclīnāre*, f. *dē* DE- 2+*clīnāre* bend, cogn. with Gr. *klínein* bend, Germ. **χlinōjan* LEAN[2]. (Preceded by an occas. adoption in OE. *declīnian*.) Hence **decli·ne** sb. falling off or away. XIV. So **declinA·TION** dek- (astron.) XIV (Ch.); †(gram.) declension XV (Capgrave); turning aside or down XVI. – L.

declivity dikli·vĭti downward slope. XVII. – L. *dēclīvitās*, f. *dēclīvis* sloping downwards, f. *dē* DE- 1+*clīvus* slope :– IE. **kloiwos*, whence (Germ. **χlaiw-*) OE. *hlāw* grave-mound, OS., OHG. *hlēo*, ON. *hlaiwa*, Goth. *hlaiw* grave; cf. LEAN[2] and see -ITY.

decoction dikɔ·kʃən liquor in which a substance has been boiled. XIV. – (O)F. *décoction* or late L. *dēcoctiō(n-)*, f. *dēcoct-*, pp. stem of *dēcoquere* boil down, f. *dē* DE- 3+*coquere* COOK; see -TION. Hence **deco·ct** †pp. adj. and vb. XV.

decode dīkou·d convert (a coded message) into ordinary language. XIX. f. DE- 7+CODE.

decollation dīkəlei·ʃən beheading (spec. of St. John Baptist). XIV. – (O)F. *décollation* or late L. *dēcollātiō(n-)*, f. *dēcollāre* behead, f. *dē* DE- 6+*collum* neck; see COLLAR, -ATION.

decolleté deikɔ·ltei cut low at the neck. XIX. F., pp. of *décolleter*, f. *dé-* DE- 6+*collet*, collar, dim. of *col* collar :– L. *collum* (cf. prec.).

decompose dīkəmpou·z separate into its parts; decay. XVIII. – F. *décomposer*, f. *dé-* DE- 6+*composer* COMPOSE. So **de**:COMPOSI·TION XVII, after **de**COMPOU·ND XVII. See also DE- 5.

décor deikɔ̄·ɹ theatre scenery. XIX. F., f. *décorer* DECORATE.

decorate de·kəreit †adorn XVI; deck with ornamental accessories XVIII; invest with an honour XIX. f. *decorate* pp. (XV) or its source L. *decorātus*, *-āre* beautify, f. *decor-*, *decus*; see DECOROUS and -ATE[3]. So **decorA·TION**. XV. – (O)F. or late L. **de·corATIVE**. XV. – F. **decorous** de·kərəs, dikɔ̄·rəs †seemly XVII; marked by propriety XVIII. f. L. *decōrus*, rel. to *decēns* DECENT. **decorum** dikɔ̄·rəm what is proper, propriety of behaviour. XVI. – L. *decōrum*, sb. use of n.sg. of *decōrus*.

decorticate dikɔ̄·ɹtikeit strip the bark from. XVII. f. pp. stem of L. *dēcorticāre*, f. *dē* DE- 6+*cortic-*, CORTEX; see -ATE[3].

decoy dikoi· pool with netted approaches for the capture of wildfowl. XVII. Evidence for the corr. vb. is earlier in Sc. (XVI) and in the gen. sense 'entice, allure'; but the sb. was no doubt prior, and perh. – Du. *de kooi* 'the decoy' (whence also contemp. Eng. syn. †*coy*), with assim. to †*decoy* gambling card-game (XVI), of unkn. origin; the forms †*duck(c)oy* (XVII–XVIII) are due partly to substitution of DUCK for the first syll., partly to tr. of Du. *eendenkooi* 'duck-decoy'; cf. †*coy-duck* (XVII), tr. Du *kooieend*. ¶ Du. *kooi*, †*koye* is a parallel development to MDu. *kouwe* (Du. dial. *kouw* cage), MLG. *kaue* – L. *cavea* CAGE.

decrease dikrī·s grow less. XIV (Wyclif, Gower, Trevisa). – OF. *de(s)creiss-*, pres. stem of *de(s)creistre* (mod. *décroître*) = Pr. *descreisser*, Sp. *descrecer*, It. *discrescere* – Rom. **discrēscere*, for L. *dēcrēscere*, f. *dē* DE- 6+*crēscere* grow (see CRESCENT). So **decrea·se** sb. XIV (Gower). – OF. *de(s)creis*, f. the above vb.

decree dikrī· ordinance, edict. XIV (R. Mannyng). – OF. *decré*, var. of *decret*, corr. to Pr. *decret*, Sp., It. *decreto* – L. *dēcrētum*, sb. use of n. of *dēcrētus*, pp. of *dēcernere*, f. *dē* DE- 2+*cernere* separate, distinguish, decide (cf. DISCERN). So **decree** vb. XIV.

decrement dī·krimənt decrease, lessening. XVII. – L. *dēcrēmentum*, f. *dēcrē-*, stem of *dēcrēscere* DECREASE; see -MENT.

decrepit dikre·pit old and feeble. XV. – (partly through F. *décrépit* XVI, earlier *descrepy*) L. *dēcrepitus*, f. *dē* DE- 3 + *crepitus*, pp. of *crepāre* rattle, creak, of imit. origin (cf. CREPITUS). Forms in *-id* show assim. to adjs. in -ID. Hence **decre·pi**TUDE. XVII; after (O)F. *décrépitude*; superseding †*decrepity* (XVI–XVII) – F. †*décrepité*, medL. *dēcrēpitās*. (Florio has both words.)

decretal dĭkrī·təl adj. of a decree or decretal XV; sb. papal decree XIV (R. Mannyng). – (O)F. *décrétal* – late L. *dēcrētālis* (medL. *dēcrētālēs*, sc. *epistolæ*, papal letters containing decrees, *dēcrētāle* decree), f. *dēcrēt-*, pp. stem of *dēcernere* DECREE.

decry dikrəi· denounce by proclamation; disparage openly. XVII. f. DE- 4 + CRY vb., after (O)F. *décrier*, in the senses of *cry down* (XV, XVI).

decuman de·kjumən (of a wave) very large. XVII. – L. *decumānus*, var. of *decimānus* of the tenth part, f. *decimus* tenth (cf. DECIMAL); see -AN. ¶ The application to waves (L. *decumani fluctus*) rests on the belief that every tenth wave is greater than the others.

decurion dikjuə·riən (Rom. antiq. and hist.) cavalry officer in command of ten horse; member of the senate of a colony or town. XIV (Wycl. Bible). – L. *decuriō(n-)*, f. *decem* TEN after *centuriō* CENTURION.

decussate dī·kʌseit cross at an acute angle. XVII (Sir T. Browne). f. *decussāt-*, pp. stem of L. *decussāre*, f. *decussis* number 10, 10-as piece, intersection of lines crosswise (×), f. *decem* TEN + *as* AS². So **decuss**A·TION. XVII.

dedicate de·dikeit devote to the service of a deity XV; assign to an end or purpose XVI. f. pp. stem of L. *dēdicāre* proclaim, devote, consecrate, f. *dē* DE- 2 + *dic-*, weak var. of *dīc-* say (cf. DICTION); after †*dedicate* pp. (XIV, Ch.) or the foll. sb.; see -ATE³. So **dedic**A·TION. XIV. – (O)F. or L.

deduce didjū·s †bring, convey; †derive; trace the course of; draw as a conclusion XV; †deduct XVI. – L. *dēdūcere*, f. *dē* DE- 2 + *dūcere* lead (cf. DUCT). So **deduct** didʌ·kt take away, subtract XV; †derive; †trace out; †deduce by reasoning XVI. f. *dēduct-*, pp. stem of L. *dēdūcere* DEDUCE; prob. after earlier †*deduct* pp. **dedu·c**TION subtraction, abatement XV; †detailed account; deducing a conclusion, inference by reasoning XVI. – (O)F. – L.

dee dī A. name of the letter D applied to a D-shaped object. XVIII. B. euphem. (like *d* and *d*—) put for *damn*; so *deed* for *damned*, and *deedeed* for *d—d*, i.e. damned. XIX.

deed dīd that which is done OE.; legal instrument in writing XIV. OE. (Anglian) *dēd*, (WS.) *dǣd* = OFris. *dēd(e)*, OS. *dād* (Du. *daad*), OHG. *tāt* (G. *tat*), ON. *dáð*, Goth. *-dēþs* (in *gadēþs*, *missadēþs* MISDEED) :– CGerm. **dǣdiz* :– **dhēti·s*, f. IE. **dhē-* **dhō-* (see DO¹). **deed poll** deed made by one party only, so called because it is 'polled' or cut even, not indented. XVI (*polle dede*, *deede pole*).

deem dīm †give judgement, judge; think, consider. OE. *dēman* = OFris. *dēma*, OS. *dōmian* (Du. *doemen*), OHG. *tuomen*, ON. *dœma*, Goth. (CGerm.) *dōmjan*, f. **dōmaz* DOOM. Hence **deemster** dī·mstəɹ either of the two judges of the Isle of Man. XVII; see -STER. ¶ With regularly shortened stem-vowel, †*dem(p)ster* (i) judge XIII (Cursor M.); (ii) Sc. officer of a court who pronounced judgement XVI.

deep dīp having great extension downwards; fig. profound OE.; penetrating XIII; (of colour) intense; subtle, crafty XVI. OE. *dēop* = OFris. *diāp*, OS. *diop*, *diap* (Du. *diep*), OHG. *tiuf* (G. *tief*), ON. *djúpr*, Goth. *diups* :– CGerm. **deupaz*, f. **deup-* **dup-* (see DIP). The normal ME. compar. *depper* (:– OE. *dēoppra*) was repl. by the new formation *deeper*. As sb. deep water OE.; *the deep* the ocean (XIV); cf. (M)Du. *diep*. Hence **deep**EN⁵. XVI, **dee·p**LY². OE.

deer diəɹ †animal OE.; antlered ruminant (Cervus) XII. OE. *dēor* = OFris. *diār*, OS. *dior* (Du. *dier*), OHG. *tior* (G. *tier*), ON. *dýr*, Goth. **dius* (in d.pl. *diuzam*) :– CGerm. **deuzam* :– IE. **dheusóm* orig. 'breathing creature' (cf. the sense-development in ANIMAL), if rel. to OSl. *duchŭ*, *duša* breath, Lith. *dùsti* sigh.

deface difei·s mar the face or appearance of; blot out. XIV. – F. †*defacer*, earlier *deffacer*, for *desfacer*, f. *des-*, *dé-* DE- 6 + *face* FACE.

defalcate dī·fǒlkeit †lop off, retrench, deduct XV; commit defalcation XIX. f. pp. stem of medL. *dēfalcāre*, f. *dē* DE- 2 + L. *falc-*, *falx* sickle, scythe; see -ATE³. Cf. F. *défalquer*, Sp. *desfalcar*, It. *diffalcare*. The earlier *defalk* (– F. or medL. inf.) survives in U.S. legal use. So **defalc**A·TION †diminution, reduction, curtailment XV; defection, failure; fraudulent monetary deficiency XVIII. – medL.

defame difei·m †render infamous; attack the good name of. XIV. ME. *diffame*, *defame* – OF. *diffamer*, also *desf-*, *def(f)-*, corr. to Pr. *diffamar*, It. *diffamare* – L. *diffāmāre* spread about as an evil report, f. *dis-* DIF-, DE- 6 + *fāma* FAME. The prefix was replaced on the model of medL. *dēfāmāre* (cf. L. *dēfāmātus* infamous, *dēfāmis* shameful). The first sense prob. belongs strictly to *dēfāmāre*, the second to *diffāmare*. So **defam**A·TION de-, dīfəm- (in corr. senses). XIV (R. Mannyng, Trevisa, Ch.). – (O)F. *diffamation* – late L. *diffāmātiō*. **defamat**ORY -fæ·m-. XVI. – medL.

default difɔ̄·lt in default of, absence, lack (now surviving mainly in phr.); failure to do something XIII (Cursor M.). ME. *defaut(e)* – (i) OF. *défaute*, f. *défaillir*, on the model of *faute* FAULT, *faillir* FAIL; (ii) (O)F. *défaut*, back-formation on *défaute*. Hence **defau·lt** vb. XIV: partly suggested by *défaut*, 3rd pres. sg. ind. of *défaillir*. For the sp. and pronunc. see FAULT.

defeasance difī·zəns (Sc.) discharge (of debt, etc.) XIV; (leg.) condition upon the performance of which an instrument is made void XV; annulment; undoing XVI. – OF. *defesance*, f. *defesant*, prp. of *de(s)faire* (mod. *défaire*) undo, f. *des-*, *dé-* DE- 6+*faire* make; see FACT, -ANCE.

defeat difī·t †undo, ruin, destroy XIV (Ch.); frustrate, nullify XV (Caxton); †disappoint, defraud; discomfit, vanquish XVI (not in Sh. or A.V.). ME. *def(f)ete* – AN. *defeter*, f. *defet*, OF. *deffait*, *desfait*, pp. of *desfaire* (mod. *défaire*) = It. *disfare* :– medL. *disfacere* undo, mar, f. L. *dis-* DE- 6+*facere* make (see FACT). Hence **defea·t** sb. XVI; cf. F. *défaite* = It. *disfatta*. **defea·tISM**. XX. – F. *défaitisme*. **defea·tIST** sb. and adj. XX. – F. *-iste*.

defecate dī·fikeit clear from impurities XVI; remove (fæces) XVIII; void the fæces XIX. f. †*defecate* pp. (XV) – L. *dēfæcātus*, *-āre*, f. *dē* DE- 6+*fæces*, *fæx* dregs; see -ATE[3]. So **defecA·TION**. XVII. – late L.

defect dife·kt, dī·fekt shortcoming, deficiency. XV. – L. *dēfectus*, f. *dēfect-*, pp. stem of *dēficere* leave, desert, fail, f. *dē* DE- 2 +*facere* (see FACT). So **defe·cTION** failing, falling away. XVI. – L. **defe·cTIVE** faulty, wanting. XV. – (O)F. or late L.

defend dife·nd guard from attack; †ward off, prevent, prohibit XIII; vindicate (a cause, person) XV. – (O)F. *défendre* = Pr. *defendre*, Sp. *defender*, It. *difendere* :– L. *dēfendere* ward off, protect, f. *dē* DE- 2+ *-fendere* (only in comps., cf. *offend*), prob. :– IE. **gwhendh-* and rel. to OE. *gūþ* battle, Gr. *phónos* slaughter, Skr. *hánti* strikes, kills. Aphetic FEND. **defe·ndANT** (leg.) person sued)(*plaintiff* XIV; gen. senses are later and obs. – (O)F. *défendant*, sb. use of prp. of *défendre*. **defe·nder** one who wards off an attack XIII; (leg.) defendant XV. – AN. *defendour*; see -ER[2]. **defence, U.S. defense** dife·ns. XIII. ME. *defens* and *defense*, *-ence* – OF. *defens* and (also mod.) *défense* – L. (Rom.) *dēfēnsum*, *dēfēnsa*, sb. uses of n. and fem. pp. of *dēfendere*. **defe·nsIBLE** †defensive; defendable, justifiable. XV. late L. *dēfēnsibilis* (Cassiodorus), f. *dēfēns-*, pp. stem of *dēfendere*; earlier †*defensable* XIII (RGlouc.) – (O)F. *défensable* – late L. *dēfēnsābilis* (Ambrose).

defenestration dīfenistrei·ʃən action of throwing out of a window. XVII. – modL. *dēfenestrātiō(n-)*, f. *dē* DE- 1+*fenestra* window; see -ATION.

defer[1] difɔ̄·ɹ put off, postpone. XIV (Wycl. Bible). ME. *differre*, *deferre* – (O)F. *différer* defer, differ – L. *differre* carry apart, delay, bear in different directions, differ. Often spelt with *diff-* until XVII, but finally differentiated from the ult. identical DIFFER, perh. partly by assoc. with *delay*.

defer[2] difɔ̄·ɹ †submit oneself, submit or refer (a matter) XV; †offer, proffer XVI; submit in opinion *to* XVII. – (O)F. *déférer* – L. *dēferre* carry away, transport, grant, report, refer (a matter), f. *dē* DE- 2+*ferre* BEAR[2]. This word in its later sense is that prob. referred to by Evelyn in 1667 (see O.E.D. *Bizarre*). So **deferENCE** de·fərəns. XVII (Clarendon).– F. *déférence*. Hence **defere·ntIAL**. XIX (Scott, Dickens); after *prudence*, *prudential*, etc.

defiance difai·əns declaration of hostilities XIV; challenge to combat XV; setting at nought XVIII. – (O)F. *défiance* (now only 'distrust'; cf. DIFFIDENCE), f. *défier* DEFY; see -ANCE. Hence **defi·ANT**. XIX.

deficient difi·ʃənt wanting in something. XVI. – L. *dēficient-*, *-ēns*, prp. of *dēficere* undo, take oneself away, leave, fail, f. *dē* DE- 2, 6+*facere* (see FACT). Hence †**defi·cIENCE** XV; **defi·cIENCY** XVII.

deficit de·fisit, dī·fisit amount by which a sum falls short of what is required. XVIII. – F. *déficit* – L. *dēficit* there is wanting, 3rd pers. sg. pres. ind. of *dēficere* (see DEFECT); formerly placed against an item in an account.

defile[1] difai·l make foul or unclean. XIV. Alteration of †*defoul*, †*defoil*, by assocn. with synon. †*befile*, OE. *befȳlan* (f. BE-+ *fȳlan*, f. *fūl* FOUL). The earlier *defoul* (XIII), of which there is an unexpl. var. *defoil* (XIV), was – OF. *defouler*, *defuler* trample down, outrage, violate, deflower, f. *de-* DE- 1+ *fouler* tread, trample (= Pr. *folar*, Sp. *hollar*, It. *follare*) :– Rom. **fullāre* stamp, f. L. *fullō* FULLER. Hence **defi·leMENT**. XVII (Milton).

defile[2] dī·fail, difai·l narrow pass between mountains. XVII. orig. *defilé*, *defilee* – F. *défilé*, sb. use of pp. of *défiler* march by files, f. *dé-* DE- 2+*file* FILE[2]. For the loss of the final syll. cf. ASSIGN[2].

define difai·n determine the limits of; state exactly what (a thing) is. XIV (Ch.). – OF. *définer* = Pr. *definar* – Rom. **dēfīnāre*, for L. *dēfīnīre* (whence OF., Pr. *defenir*, modF. *définir*, Sp. *definir*, It. *definire*), f. *dē* DE- 3+ *fīnīre* FINISH. Early forms in *deff-*, *diff-* are from corr. OF. forms based on L. *diffīnīre* (f. DIS-). So **definite** de·finit having fixed limits. XV (gram. XVIII, after F. *défini*). – L. *dēfīnītus*, pp. of *dēfīnīre*. **defini·TION**. XIV (Wycl. Bible, Ch., Trevisa; before XVI chiefly *diff-*). – (O)F. – L. **definitive** difi·nitiv. XIV (Ch.; rare before XVI). – (O)F. – L.

deflate diflei·t release the air from (an inflated object) XIX; reduce an inflated currency XX. f. DE- 6+*-flate* of INFLATE.

deflect difle·kt turn to one side. XVII. – L. *dēflectere*, f. *dē* DE- 2+*flectere* bend. So **defle·xion, defle·**CTION XVII; see FLEXION.

deflower diflauə·ɹ deprive of virginity, violate. XIV (Wycl. Bible, Gower). – OF. *defflourer*, earlier *desflo(u)rer* (mod. *déflorer*), corr. to Pr. *deflorar*, etc. – Rom. **disflōrāre*, for late L. *dēflōrāre*, f. DE- 6+*flōr-flōs* FLOWER.

deform difɔ̄·ɹm mar the form or beauty of. XV. – OF. *difformer*, *de(s)former* (mod. *difformer*, *déformer*), corr. to Pr. *deformar*, Sp. *desformar*, It. *deformare* – medL. *difformāre*, Rom. **disformāre*, L. *dēformāre*, f. DIS-, DE- 6+*forma* FORM. So **deforma·**TION. XV. – (O)F., L. *dēf-* (medL. *diff-*). **defo·rm**ITY disfigurement, mis-shapenness. XV. – OF. *deformité* (*deff-*, *desf-*) – L. *dēformitās*, f. *dēformis* mis-shapen.

defraud difrɔ̄·d deprive by fraud. XIV (PPl.). – OF. *defrauder* or L. *dēfraudāre*, f. *dē* DE- 3+*fraudāre* cheat, f. *fraud-*, *fraus* FRAUD.

defray difrei· †disburse; discharge (expense). XVI. – (O)F. *défrayer* (†*deff-*, †*desf-*), f. *dé-* DE- 6+†*frai*, †*frait* (usually pl. *frais*, †*fres*) expenses, cost :– medL. *fredum*, *-us* fine for breach of the peace – Frank. **friđu*, cf. OHG. *fridu*, OE. *friþ* peace.

deft deft †gentle, meek XIII; skilful XV; neat, pretty (now dial.) XVI. ME. *defte*, var. of DAFT. The orig. sense of 'fitting, convenient' has passed into that of 'skilful' by transition from an objective to a subjective application; cf. OE. (*ġe*)*hende* near at hand, convenient, in ME. courteous, gentle, nice.

defunct difʌ·ŋkt deceased, dead. XVI. – L. *dēfunctus* discharged (from an office or obligation), deceased, pp. of *dēfungī* discharge, perform, finish (cf. *vītā dēfungī* die), f. *dē* DE- 3+*fungī* perform (see FUNCTION). Cf. (O)F. *défunt*.

defy difai· †renounce allegiance to; (arch.) challenge to a contest; challenge the power of, set at nought. XIV. – (O)F. *défier* = Pr. *desfiar*, It. *diffidare* :– Rom. **disfīdāre*, f. L. *dis-* (see DE- 6)+*fīdus* trustful, rel. to *fidēs* FAITH. Cf. DEFIANCE.

dégagé deigā·ʒei unconstrained. XVII. F., pp. of *dégager* set free, f. *dé-* DE- 6, after *engager* ENGAGE.

degenerate didʒe·nərət that has declined in character or qualities. XV. – L. *dēgenerātus*, pp. of *dēgenerāre* depart from its race or kind, f. *dēgener* debased, ignoble, f. *dē* DE- 2+*gener-*, *genus* KIND[1]. So **dege·nerate** vb. -eit become degenerate. XVI. f. pp. stem of the L. vb.; see -ATE[2], -ATE[3]. **degenera·**TION. XVII. – F.

deglutition dīglūti·ʃən swallowing. XVII. – F. *déglutition* (XVI, Paré) or modL. *dēglūtītiō(n-)*, f. L. *dēglutīre*, f. *dē* DE- 1+*glūtīre* (*gluttīre*) swallow; see GLUTTON and -ITION.

degrade digrei·d reduce to a lower rank. XIV. – (O)F. *dégrader* = Pr., Sp. *degradar*, It. *degradare* :– ecclL. *dégradáre*, f. *dé* DE- 1+*gradus* rank, DEGREE. So **degrad**ATION degrədei·ʃən. XVI. – (O)F. *dégradation* or ecclL. *dēgradātiō*. ¶ The painting term (identical in form) XVIII, meaning 'the gradual lowering of colour or light', is – F. *dégradation* (XVII) – It. *digradazione*, f. *digradare* come down by degrees.

degree digrī· step (now only her. in lit. sense); relative rank XIII; relative condition, relation; academic rank; unit of geometrical measurement XIV; musical interval XVII; unit of temperature XVIII. ME. *degre*, – (O)F. *degré* = Pr. *degra(t)*, Pg. *degrau* :– Rom. **dēgradu-s*, f. L. *dē* DE- 1+*gradus* step, GRADE.

dehiscent dihi·sənt gaping open (spec. bot.). XVII. – L. *dēhiscent-*, *-ēns*, pp. of *dēhiscere*, f. *dē* DE- 2+*hiscere*, inceptive of *hiāre* gape; see HIATUS, -ENT.

dehydrate dīhai·dreit (chem.) deprive of water. XIX. f. DE- 7+Gr. *hudr-*, *húdōr* WATER+-ATE[3].

deictic dai·ktik that proves directly. XVII. – Gr. *deiktikós* showing directly, f. *deiktós*, vbl. adj. of *deiknúnai* show, rel. to L. *dīcere* say (cf. DICTION).

deify dī·ifai make a god of. XIV (R. Rolle). – (O)F. *déifier* – ChrL. *deificāre*, f. *deus* god; see DIVINE, -FY. So **de:ifica·**TION. XIV (Gower).

deign dein think fit, vouchsafe XIII; condescend to give XVI. – (O)F. *degnier*, later *deigner* (mod. *daigner*) = Pr. *denhar*, It. *degnare* :– L. *dignāre*, *dignārī* deem worthy, f. *dignus* worthy (see DIGNITY).

deil Sc. form of DEVIL.

deipnosophist daipnɔ·səfist master of the art of dining. XVII. – Gr. *deipnosophistḗs*, f. *deîpnon* dinner+*sophistḗs* master of his craft (SOPHIST); pl. title of a work by Athenæus, *c.* 230 A.D., in which learned men are represented as dining together and discussing various subjects.

deist dī·ist one who acknowledges the existence of God but rejects revealed religion. XVII. – F. *déiste* (XVI), f. *deus* god (see DIVINE)+*-iste* -IST. ¶ Opposed orig. to *atheist* and synon. with *theist* till *c.* 1700, but finally distinguished from the latter in emphasizing the negative aspect. So **de·**ISM. XVII; cf. F. *déisme*.

deity dī·iti godhood, the Godhead, divine being XIV (PPl., Ch., Trevisa); *the* Supreme Being XV (Lydg.). – (O)F. *déité*, corr. to Pr. *deitat*, Sp. *deidad*, It. *deità* – ChrL. *deitās* (Augustine), rendering Gr. *theótēs* (f. *théos* god), as in Col. ii 9)(*theiótēs* divinity (f. *theîos* divine); see DIVINE, -ITY.

deject didʒe·kt †cast down XV; depress in spirits XVI. f. *dēject-*, pp. stem of L. *deicere*, f. *dē* DE- 1+*jacere* throw (pt. *jēcī*), rel. to Gr. *híēmi* I send, throw (:– **jijēmi*).

déjeuner dei·ʒənei, ||deʒöne luncheon. XVIII. F., sb. use of *déjeuner* break one's fast; see DINE.

del. abbrev. of L. *dēlīneāvit* 'drew', 3rd sg. pt. of *dēlīneāre* DELINEATE.

delaine dĭlei·n light textile fabric. XIX. Short for *muslin delaine* – F. *mousseline de laine* MUSLIN of wool.

delate dĭlei·t inform against. XVI. f. *dēlāt-*, stem of functional pp. of L. *dēferre* DEFER². So **dela·tion**. XVI. – L. ¶ From the same stem are *collate, dilate, oblate, prolate, relate, translate,* with sbs. in *-ation*; *ablative, illative, relative.*

delay dilei· put off till later XIII; impede the progress of XIV. – OF. *delayer*, var. of *deslaier*, presumably f. *des-* DIS-+*laier* leave (of unkn. origin). So **delay·** sb. XIII (Laȝ., later text; RGlouc.). –(O)F. *délai*, f. the vb.; *without delay*, tr. OF. *sans délai.*

del credere del krei·dəri said of the terms of an obligation undertaken by a broker, etc., in becoming responsible for the solvency of the person to whom he sells. XVIII. It.; *del* of the, *credere* belief, trust (:– L. *crēdere*; see CREED).

dele dī·li (typogr.) delete. XVIII. imper. of L. *dēlēre* DELETE; or perh. short for earlier *delea·tur*, 3rd pers. sg. pres. subj. pass. 'let it be deleted'. (The sign used is ₰.)

delectable dile·ktəbl delightful. XIV (Maund.). –(O)F. *délectable* – L. *dēlectābilis*, f. *dēlectāre* DELIGHT; see -ABLE. (Superseded ME. *delitable* XIII – OF. *delitable*, f. *delitier*.) So **delecta·tion**. XIV. –(O)F. – L.

delectus dile·ktəs selection of literary passages. XIX. – L. *dēlectus* choice, f. *dēlect-*, pp. stem of *dēligere* choose out, f. *dē* DE- 2+ *legere* choose (cf. LECTION).

delegate de·ligət person chosen to act for another. XIV. – L. *dēlēgātus*, pp. of *dēlēgāre*, f. *dē* DE- 2+*lēgāre* send on a commission (cf. LEGATE). So **delegate** de·ligeit entrust to another XVI; commission XVII. f. pp. stem of the above vb.; see -ATE³. **delega·tion**. XVII.– L. **de·legacy** delegation XV; body of delegates XVII. f. DELEGATE, after *prelate, prelacy.*

delete dilī·t †destroy, abolish; obliterate. XVII. f. *dēlēt-*, pp. stem of L. *dēlēre* (cf. INDELIBLE). So **dele·tion**. XVI. – L.

deleterious del-, dīlitiə·riəs injurious. XVII. f. medL. *dēlētērius* – Gr. *dēlētḗrios*, f. *dēlētḗr* destroyer, f. *dēleîsthai* injure, destroy; see -IOUS. Preceded by †*deletery* XVI.

delf(t) delf(t) orig. *Delf(t) ware*, kind of glazed earthenware made at *Delf*, now *Delft*, in Holland (so called from the *delf*, i.e. ditch, the name of its chief canal, rel. to DELVE). XVIII.

deliberate dili·bərət well-considered, unhurried. XV. – L. *dēlīberātus*, pp. of *dēlīberāre*, f. *dē* DE- 3+*lībrāre* weigh, f. *lībra* scales (cf. LIBRATION). So **deli·berate** -eit vb. †think over; think carefully. XVI. See -ATE², -ATE³. **delibera·tion**. XIV (Ch.). –(O)F. – L. **deli·berative**. XV. – F. or L.

delicate de·likət †delightful, elegant, dainty; †indolent, †fastidious XIV (Ch., Wycl. Bible); fine, not coarse, rough, or robust XVI; finely sensitive or skilful XVI. –(O)F. *délicat* (rare before XVI) or L. *dēlicātus* (whence also Pr. *delicat*, Sp. *-cado*, It. *-cato*), of unkn. origin, but assoc. in sense-development with L. *dēliciæ* (see next); see -ATE². Hence **de·licacy**. XIV (Ch., Gower); concr. XV.

delicious dili·ʃəs highly pleasing. XIII. – OF. *delicious* (mod. *délicieux*), corr. to Pr. *delicios*, etc. – late L. *dēliciōsus* (Augustine), f. L. *dēlicia*, pl. *-iæ*, f. *dēlicere* allure aside, f. *dē* DE- 2+*lic-*, as in *ēlicere* ELICIT.

delict dili·kt violation of law. XVI. – L. *dēlictum*, sb. use of n. of *dēlictus*, pp. of *dēlinquere* (see DELINQUENT).

delight dilai·t gratification or source of this. XIII. ME. *delit* – OF. *delit* (= Pr. *deleit*, Sp. *deleite*, It. *diletto*), f. stem of *delitier*, etc. :– L. *dēlectāre* allure, charm, frequent. of *dēlicere* (see DELICIOUS). The sp. with *-gh-* on the analogy of native words such as *light* dates from XVI. So **deli·ght** vb. XIII. – OF. *delitier*; the sp. *delite* is retained in some passages of A.V.

delineate dili·nieit trace the outline of. XVI. f. pp. stem of L. *dēlīneāre*, f. *dē* DE- 3+ *līnea* LINE²; see -ATE³.

delinquent dili·ŋkwənt offender against the law. XVII (earlier *delynquaunt*, Caxton, from F.). – L. *dēlinquent-*, *-ēns*, pp. of *dēlinquere* be at fault, offend, f. *dē* DE- 3+ *linquere* leave (cf. LOAN); see -ENT.

deliquesce delikwe·s melt by absorption of moisture. XVIII. – L. *dēliquēscere*, f. *dē* DE- 3+*liquēscere*, f. *liquēre* (see LIQUID).

delirium dili·riəm disorder of the mental faculties. XVI. – L. *dēlīrium*, f. *dēlīrāre* deviate from a straight line, be deranged, f. *dē* DE- 2+*līra* ridge between furrows. See also D.T. Hence **deli·rious**. XVIII.

deliver dili·vəɹ A. set free XIII (AncrR.); disburden XIV; B. give up, give over, surrender XIII (RGlouc.); C. give or send forth, utter XVI. –(O)F. *délivrer* = Pr. *delivrar* :– Gallo-Rom. **dēlīberāre*, f. *dē* DE- 3+*līberāre* LIBERATE. So **deli·verance**. XIII. –(O)F. *délivrance*. **deli·very** handing over, †deliverance XV; being delivered of a child; utterance of words XVI. – AN. *délivrée*, sb. use of fem. pp. of *délivrer*; see -Y³. ¶ For derivs. of L. *dēlīberāre* see DELIBERATE.

dell del deep hollow or valley. OE. *dell* (also in comp. *dellwudu*) = MLG., MDu. *delle* (Du. *del*), MHG. *telle* (G. dial. *telle*; *delle* from LG.) :– Germ. **daljō* (cf. Goth. *ibdalja* slope of a mountain), f. **dal-* (see DALE).

Delphic de·lfik pert. to *Delphi* on the slope of Mt. Parnassus in Greece and the oracle of Apollo there; obscure and ambiguous. XVI. See -IC.

Delphin de·lfin pert. to the edition of Latin classics prepared *in usum Delphini* for the use of the DAUPHIN, viz. the eldest son of Louis XIV of France. XVIII.

delphinium delfi·niəm genus of plants comprising larkspur. XVII. – modL. *delphīnium* – Gr *delphī́nion* larkspur, f. *delphīn-*, *delphin* DOLPHIN; so called from the dolphin-like form of the nectary.

delta de·ltə triangular tract of alluvial land at the mouth of a river, orig. of the Nile. XVI. Name of the fourth letter of the Greek alphabet, Δ, derived from Phœnician *daleth* (◬), applied by Herodotus to the mouth of the Nile, by Strabo to the Indus. So **de·lt**OID resembling the Gr. letter Δ. XVIII. – F. *deltoïde* or modL. *deltoidēs* (Linnæus) – Gr. *deltoeidḗs*.

delude diljū·d cheat into a false opinion. XV. – L. *dēlūdere* play false, mock, f. *dē* DE- 4 + *lūdere* play, f. *lūdus* play, game (cf. LUDICROUS). So **delu·**SION. XV. – late L. **delu·**SIVE. XVII. **delu·**SORY. XV. f. *dēlūs-*, pp. stem of the vb.

deluge de·ljūdʒ great flood. XIV (Ch.). – (O)F. *déluge*, remodelling, after popular formations in *dé-* and *-uge*, of earlier learned *diluvie* = Pr. *diluvi*, Sp., It. *diluvio* – L. *dīluvium*, rel. to *lavere*, *lavāre* wash (cf. ALLUVIAL, ANTEDILUVIAN). Hence **de·luge** vb. XVII.

delve delv dig, lit. and fig. (dial. and literary). OE. *delfan*, pt. *dealf*, *dulfon*, pp. *dolfen* = OFris. *delva*, OS. *bi|delƀan* (Du. *delven*), OHG. *bi|telban* :– WGerm. **delƀ-*, **dalƀ-* **dulƀ-*, which has cogns. in Slavonic. The weak form of the pt. appeared in XIV and of the pp. in XVI, the form *dolven* remaining in full use till then.

demagogue de·məgɔg leader of the people or of a popular faction. XVII. – Gr. *dēmagōgós* (applied at Athens during the Peloponnesian war to the heads of the popular party, the attacks upon whom gave currency to the unfavourable sense of the word), f. *dêmos* people (cf. DEMOCRAT) + *agōgós* leader, f. *ágein* lead (see ACT). Cf. F. *démagogue*. So **demago·g**IC -dʒik, -gik. XIX. **de·magogy.** XVII. – Gr. *demagogiā́*; see -Y[3].

demand dimà·nd authoritative or formal request or claim. XIII. – (O)F. *demande*, f. *demander* (whence **dema·nd** vb. ask for as with authority XV) = Pr., Sp. *demandar*, It. *domandare* ask, Rum. *dimindare* arrange :– L. *dēmandāre* hand over, entrust, f. *dē* DE- 3 + *mandāre* (see MANDATE).

demarcation dīmāɹkei·ʃən marking a boundary, orig. applied in the phr. *line of demarcation* (Sp. *linea de demarcacion*, Pg. *linha de demarcação*) to the division of the New World in XV between the Spaniards and the Portuguese. XVIII. – Sp. *demarcación* (Pg. *demarcação*), f. *demarcar* mark out the bounds of, f. *de-* DE- 3 + *marcar* MARK; see -ATION. Hence by back-formation **de·marc**ATE[3] vb. XIX.

démarche deimā·ɹʃ proceeding. XVII. F., f. *démarcher* march, take steps, f. *dé* DE- 3 + *marcher* MARCH.

deme dīm township of ancient Attica; (biol.) aggregate of cells. XIX. – Gr. *dêmos* territory of a community, people; see DEMOS.

demean[1] dimī·n †carry on, manage XIII; conduct *oneself* XIV. – (O)F. *démener* lead, exercise, practise, (refl.) behave = Pr. *demenar*, It. *dimenare* :– Rom. **dēmināre*, f. L. *dē* DE- 3 + L. *mināre* drive (animals), orig. urge on with threats (L. *minārī* threaten; see MINATORY). Hence, prob. by assoc. with †*havour* (see BEHAVIOUR), **demea·nour** conduct, behaviour. XV.

demean[2] dimī·n lower, humble. XVII. f. DE- 4 + MEAN[1], after *debase*.

demented dime·ntid out of one's mind. XVI. f. *dementātus*, pp. of late L. *dēmentāre*, f. *dēment-*, *-ēns*, f. *dē* DE- 6 + *ment-*, *mēns* MIND; see -ED[1].

démenti deimā·ti statement giving the lie. XVII. F., earlier †*démentie*, f. *démentir*, f. *des-* DE- 6 + *mentir* :– L. *mentīrī* tell lies.

Demerara deməreə·rə epithet of a kind of brown cane sugar. XIX. Name of a part of British Guiana, S. America.

demerit dīme·rit †desert, merit XIV; †sin, offence XV (Lydg.); ill-desert, want of merit XVI. – OF. *de(s)merite* or L. *dēmeritum*, f. pp. stem of *dēmerērī* merit, deserve, f. *dē* DE- 3 + *merērī* MERIT; in Rom. the prefix was taken in a pejorative or negative sense.

demesne dimei·n, dimī·n possession of real estate as one's own; possession, estate. XIV. – AN., OF. *demeine*, later AN. *demesne*, sb. use of adj. belonging to a lord, seigneurial, that is private property, proper :– L. *dominicu-s* pert. to a lord or master (see DOMINICAL); cf. DOMAIN. For the insertion of unetymological *s* cf. MESNE. ¶ In Germ. law, the primary idea in relation to property is possession, not ownership (Roman *dominium*); hence derivs. of L. *dominium* and *proprietas* PROPERTY became assoc. in med. law almost exclusively with possession.

demi- de·mi – F. *demi* :– medL. *dīmediu-s*, for L. *dīmidius* (cf. DEMY), used in comb. to denote things that are half the normal or full size, length, etc., as in her. (XV, Book of St. Albans); in costume, e.g. †*demigown* (XV); in ordnance, e.g. *demi-culverin* (XVI); in music, e.g. *demi-crotchet*, *-quaver* (XVII), *-semiquaver*.

demijohn de·midʒɔn large bulging bottle usu. in a wicker case. XVIII. prob. – F. *dame-jeanne* (XVII, †*dame-jane*), with early assim. to DEMI- and later to the proper name

John; prop. 'Lady Jane'. ¶ The F. word appears to be the source of Sp. *damajuana*, modPr. *damajano*, It. *damigiana*, Arab. *dama-*, *dāmajāna* (whence some have unwarrantably assumed an Arab.-Pers. origin).

demi-monde demimɔ̄·nd class of women of doubtful reputation. XIX. F., 'half-world' (Alexandre Dumas fils, 1855, who used the term for the kind of society midway between the conventional respectable life and the life of licence and vice).

demi-rep demire·p woman of doubtful reputation. XVIII (Fielding, Swift). f. DEMI-+*rep*, short for *reputation* (but the implication is not clear); mentioned by Swift in 'Polite Conversation', 1731–8, among 'some abbreviations exquisitely refined'.

demise dimai·z transfer of an estate XVI; transfer of sovereignty XVII; death (as occasioning this) XVIII. – AN. **demise*, sb. use of fem. pp. of OF. *de(s)mettre* (mod. *démettre*) DISMISS, (refl.) resign, abdicate.

demiurge de·miəːɹdʒ creator of the world (in Platonism). XIX (earlier in L. form). – ecclL. *dēmiūrgus* – Gr. *dēmiourgós* handicraftsman, artisan, etc., f. *dḗmios* public (see DEMOS)+**erg-* WORK.

demnition demni·ʃən Chiefly U.S. euphem. for DAMNATION. XIX (Dickens, Poe).

demobilize dīmou·bilaiz disband (armed forces); also **demo:biliza·tion**. XIX. – F. *démobiliser*, *-isation* (1870); see DE- 7, MOBILIZE. abbrev. **demob** vb. dimɔ·b. XX.

democracy dimɔ·krəsi government by the people. XVI. – (O)F. *démocratie* – late L. *dēmocratia* – Gr. *dēmokratiā*; see DEMOS, -CRACY. So **democrat** de·mŏkræt orig. republican of the French Revolution of 1790. – F. *démocrate*, f. *démocratie*, after *aristocrate*. **democra·tic**. XVII. – (O)F. – medL. – Gr.

demolish dimɔ·liʃ pull or throw down XVI; (joc.) eat up XVIII. – *démoliss-*, lengthened stem of (O)F. *démolir* – L. *dēmōlīrī*, f. *dē* DE-1 +*mōlīrī* construct, f. *mōles* mass; see MOLE³, -ISH². So **demoli·tion** dem-, dīməli·ʃən. XVII. – (O)F. – L.

demon dī·mən (often sp. *dæmon*) inferior divinity, genius, attendant spirit; evil spirit, devil. XV (normally as L. before this date). – medL. *dēmōn*, L. *dæmōn* – Gr. *daimōn* divinity, genius; cf. (O)F. *démon*. In both senses repr. L. *dæmonium*, Gr. dim. *daimónion*. So **demoniac** dimou·niæk (one) possessed by an unclean spirit. XIV (Ch.). – (O)F. *démoniaque* – ChrL. *dæmoniăcus*, f. *dæmonium*. **demoniacal** dīmənai·əkəl. XVII. **demonic** dīmɔ·nik demoniacal XVII (Evelyn); pert. to supernatural power or genius (often sp. *dæmonic*; cf. G. *dämonisch*). XVIII. – late L. *dæmonicus* – Gr. *daimonikós*.

demonetize dīmɔ·nitaiz deprive of standard monetary value. XIX. – F. *démonétiser* (1793), f. *dé-* DE- 7 + L. *monētā* MONEY; see -IZE.

demonstrate de·mənstreit †indicate, exhibit; make evident by proof. XVI. f. pp. stem of L. *dēmonstrāre*, f. *dé* DE- 3+*monstrāre* show; see MONSTER, -ATE³. So **demonstra·tion**. XIV (Ch., Gower). – (O)F. or L. **demo·nstrative** serving as evidence or proof XIV (Ch.); indicating, as in gram. XV. Of manners, effusive XIX. – (O)F. – L.

demoralize dimɔ·rəlaiz corrupt the morals of XVIII (N. Webster); lower the morale of XIX. – F. *démoraliser*, a word of the French Revolution, condemned by La Harpe (Si *Démoraliser* pouvait être français, il signifierait, cesser de parler de morale, 'Langue de la Révolution'); see DE- 7, MORAL, -IZE.

demos dī·mɔs the people or populace. XIX. Gr. *dêmos*, corr. to OIr. *dám*, Ir. *dámh* tribe, family, Gael. *dàimh* relationship.

demote dīmou·t (U.S.) reduce in rank or grade. XIX. f. DE- 7+*-mote*, of PROMOTE.

demotic dīmɔ·tik of the people; spec. of the popular form of ancient Egyptian character. XIX. – Gr. *dēmotikós* popular, f. *dēmótēs* one of the people, f. *dêmos*; see DEMOS and -IC.

demulcent dimʌ·lsənt soothing. XVIII. – L. *dēmulcent-*, *-ēns*, prp. of *dēmulcēre* soothe caressingly, f. *de* DE- 3+*mulcēre* stroke, appease; see -ENT.

demur dimɔ̄·ɹ †linger XIII; †hesitate; put in a demurrer; make difficulties XVII. – OF. *demourer*, *demeur-* (mod. *demeurer*) :– Rom. **dēmorāre*, for L. *dēmorārī*, f. *dē* DE- 3+ *morārī* delay (see MORATORIUM). The present sp. begins in XVI, superseding the normal *demo(u)re*, and appears to be based on *demurrer*. So **demurrage** dimʌ·ridʒ †delay; detention of a vessel beyond the agreed time, payment for this XVII; charge of 1½*d*. per oz. by the Bank of England in exchanging gold or notes for bullion XIX. **demurrer** dimʌ·rəɹ (leg.) pleading which stops an action. XVI. – AN. *demurrer*, sb. use of inf.; see -ER⁵.

demure dimjuə·ɹ †(of the sea) calm XIV; sober, serious XV; †affectedly or unnaturally grave XVII. perh. (with muting of *é* as in ASSIGN², etc.) – AN. *demuré*, OF. *demoré*, pp. of *demorer* (mod. *demeurer*) remain, stay (see prec.), but infl. by OF. *mur*, *meür* grave (mod. *mûr*) :– L. *mātūrus* ripe, MATURE. For the development of meaning cf. *staid*.

demy dĭmai· †(Sc.) half-mark; foundation scholar at Magdalen College, Oxford (L. *semicommunarius* one whose commons were orig. half that of a Fellow) XV; size of paper XVI. ellipt. uses of DEMI-, the sp. with *-y*, †*-ye* being appropriate for the final position when the prefix was written separately.

den¹ den lair of a wild beast OE.; cave XIII; (Sc.) dingle XVI. OE. *denn*, corr. to MLG., MDu. *denne* low ground (WFlem. *den* threshing-floor), OHG. *tenni* (G. *tenne*) floor, threshing-floor :– Germ. **danjam*, **danjō* (cf. medL. *danea*, whence dial. F.

daigne threshing-floor); rel. to DEAN[1]. The basic meaning may be 'open or flat place'.

denarius dinɛə·riəs ancient Roman coin. XVI. L. (ellipt. for *dēnārius nūmmus* coin containing ten asses), f. *dēnī* by tens, distributive of *decem* TEN. Cf. DENIER, DINAR.

dena·tionalize deprive of nationality. XIX (early). – F. *dénationaliser*, a word of the French Revolution; see DE- 7, NATIONAL, -IZE, and cf. *demoralize*.

dendrite de·ndrait tree-like form in stone or mineral. XVIII. – F. *dendrite* – Gr. *dendrī́tēs* pert. to a tree, f. *déndron* tree; see -ITE[2].

dene dīn, **den**[2] den sandy tract by the sea. XIII (fishermen to have *Den & Strond* at Great Yarmouth). The meaning suggests affinity with LG. (whence G.) *düne* and Du. *duin* sand-hill on the coast (see DUNE).

dene-hole dī·nhoul, **dane-hole** dei·nhoul ancient excavation in SE. England and northern France traditionally attributed to the activities of the Danes. XVIII. perh. repr. OE. **Denahol*, f. *Dena*, g. pl. of *Dene* Danes+*hol* HOLE; assoc. by later archæologists with DENE and DEN.

dengue de·ŋgi fever epidemic in E. Africa, etc. XIX. (Earlier also *dangue*.) – W. Indian Sp. *dengue* – Swahili *denga, dinga*, the full name being *ka dinga pepo* lit. kind of cramp plague (evil spirit). The word was identified with Sp. *dengue* fastidiousness, prudery, with mocking reference to the stiffness of the neck and shoulders characteristic of the disease; cf. the synon. W. Indian Negro *dandy* (of the same origin) and *giraffe*.

denier dĭniə·ɹ twelfth of a sou. XV (*denere*); unit of fineness of silk yarn, etc. XIX. – AN. *dener*, (O)F. *denier* = Pr. *dener*, Sp. *dinero*, It. *denaro* :– L. *dēnāriu-s* DENARIUS.

denigrate dī·nigreit, de·n- blacken, lit. and fig. XVI. – pp. stem of L. *dēnigrāre*, f. *dē* DE- 3+*nigrāre*, f. *nigr-*, *niger* black; see -ATE[3]. So **denigra·tion**. XV. Cf. late L. *denigratio* dyeing black.

denim de·nim (formerly) kind of serge, (now) coloured twilled cotton. XVII. orig. *serge de Nim* – F. *serge de Nîmes* 'serge of Nîmes', a manufacturing town in S. France.

denizen de·nizən inhabitant XV; foreigner admitted to residence XVI. Late ME. *deynseyn* – AN. *deinzein*, f. OF. *deinz* within = Pr. *dins, dens* (:– late L. *dē intus* (from within)+*-ein* (:– L. *-āneu-s*). The trisyllabic form (XV) was due to assim. to CITIZEN.

denominate dinɔ·mineit give a name to. XVI. f. pp. stem of L. *dēnōmināre*; see DE- 3, NOMINATE. So **denomina·tion** naming XIV; appellation, designation; (arith.) class of one kind of unit XV; class, sort, sect (of individuals) XVII. – (O)F. or L. **deno·minative** having the function of naming XVII; (gram.) formed from a noun (after Priscian's uses of *denominativus*, tr. Gr. *παρώνυμος*) XVIII. – (O)F. – late L. **deno·minator** (spec. in math.). XVI. – F. *dénominateur* (in math. sense XV) or medL.

denote dinou·t mark out, distinguish by a sign; be the mark of XVI (Sh.); indicate, signify XVII;)(*connote* (1843, J. S. Mill). – (O)F. *dénoter* or L. *dēnotāre*; see DE- 3, NOTE. So (earlier) **denota·tion**. XVI. – F. or L.

denouement deinū·mã, ||denumã final unravelling of the complication of a plot. XVIII (Chesterfield). F., f. *dénouer* (earlier *des-*), f. *des-* DIS- 2+*nouer* :– L. *nodāre* knot, f. *nodus* NODE.

denounce dinau·ns declare to be so-and-so XIII (Cursor M.); give formal information of XIV; declare to be evil XVII; (after modF.) announce formally the termination of XIX. – OF. *denoncier* (mod. *dénoncer*) :– L. *dēnuntiāre* give official intimation, f. *dē* DE- 3+*nuntiāre* make known, report (see ANNOUNCE). Cf. DENUNCIATE.

dense dens thick, crowded. XV (orig. in techn. use, as in modF.); stupid XIX. – F. *dense* or L. *dēnsus*, rel. to synon. Gr. *dásus*, *daulós* (:– **dasulos*) and Alb. *dënt* I make compact. So **de·nsity**. XVII. – F. or L.

dent dent †stroke, blow XIII; hollow made as if by a blow XVI. In the first sense, var. of DINT, in the second f. **dent** vb. XIV, which is prob. aphetic of INDENT.

dental de·ntəl pert. to the teeth. XVI. – medL. *dentālis*, f. L. *dent-*, *dēns* TOOTH; see -AL[1] and cf. F. *dental*. So **de·ntifrice** tooth-paste or -powder. XVI. – F. *dentifrice* – L. *dentifricium* (cf. Gr. *ὀδοντότριμμα*), f. *dent-*, *dēns*+*fricāre* rub (see FRICTION). **dentine** de·ntīn hard tissue of teeth. XIX (1840, R. Owen); see -INE[4]. **de·ntist** dental surgeon. XVIII. – F. *dentiste*, f. *dent* tooth; whence **de·ntistry** 1838. **denti·tion** cutting of the teeth XVII; arrangement of the teeth XIX. – L. *dentītiō(n-)*, f. *dentīre* teethe. So **de·nture** set of (artificial) teeth. XIX. Cf. F. *denture* set of (natural) teeth, *dentier* set of (artificial) teeth.

denude dīnjū·d make naked, lay bare. XV. – L. *dēnūdāre*, f. *dē* DE- 3+*nūdāre* bare, f. *nūdus* NUDE. In Sc. earlier in pp. (XV, Henryson). So **denuda·tion**. XV.

denunciate dinʌ·nʃieit denounce. XVI. f. L. *dēnuntiāt-*, *-āre* DENOUNCE; see -ATE[3]. So **denuncia·tion** †proclamation XV; warning announcement; delation, public condemnation XVI. – (O)F. or L.

deny dinai· say no to. XIII. ME. *denie* – tonic stem-form *deni-* of (O)F. *dénier*, earlier *deneier, denoier* (whence ME. *denay, denoy*) = Pr., Sp. *denegar*, It. *dinegare* :– L. *dēnegā·re* (*dē·negat*), f. *dē* DE- 3+*negāre* (see NEGATION). Hence **deni·al.** XVI; see -AL[2].

deodand dī·ŏdænd chattel which has been the instrument of death forfeited to the Crown for pious uses. XVI. – law F. *deodande* – AL. *deōdanda, -um*, i.e. *Deō danda, -um* that is to be given to God, d. of *deus* god (cf. DEITY), gerundive of *dare* give (cf. DATIVE).

deodar di·ŏdāɹ subspecies of cedar. XIX. – Hindi *dē'odār, dēwdār* :– Skr. *devadāru*, f. *devás* DIVINE + *dāru* wood, timber (see TREE).

deontology dī·ɔntɔ·lədʒi science of duty. XIX (Bentham). f. Gr. *deont-, déon* that which is binding, duty, n. prp. of *deî* it is binding, it behoves (cf. DESMO-) + -LOGY.

depart dipā·ɹt †divide into parts, distribute; †sunder, separate XIII (RGlouc.); go away XIII (AncrR.); leave, quit XIV; die XVI; – (O)F. *départir*, †*despartir*, corr. to Pr. *departir*, Sp., Pg. *de-, desparter*, It. *di-, dispartire* :– Rom. **dē-*, **dispartīre*, for L. *dispertīre* divide; see DE-[2], DIS-[1], and PART. ¶ 'Till death us departe' (i.e. sunder) of the Book of Common Prayer of 1549, was altered in 1662 to 'till death us do part'. So **depa·rt**MENT separately allotted province, division, or part. XVIII. – F. *département*, f. *départir*. (In late ME. – OF. 'departure'). **depart**URE dipā·rtʃəɹ †separation; going away, setting out; deviation. XV. – OF. *departeüre*.

depend dipe·nd be suspended, be in suspense, be resultant or contingent *upon*. XV (Lydg.). – (O)F. *dépendre* – Rom. **dēpendere*, for L. *dēpendēre*; see DE- 1, PENDANT. So **depe·nd**ANT †dependency; dependent person. XVI. – F. *dépendant*, sb. use of prp. of *dépendre*. **depe·nd**ENT pendent XV; contingent XVI; subordinate, subject XVII. orig. *dependant* – (O)F. *dépendant*. Hence **depe·nd**ENCE †dependency XV; dependent condition XVII. – (O)F. *dépendance*. **depe·nd**ENCY dependence XVI; dependent country or province XVII.

dephlogisticated dīflŏdʒi·stikeitid; see PHLOGISTON.

depict dipi·kt represent in colours XVII; portray XVIII. f. *dēpict-*, pp. stem of L. *dēpingere*; cf. pp. *depictyd* (XV, once), †*depict* (XV–XVI) and see DE- 3, PAINT, PICTURE. Superseded †*depaint* (XIV–XIX) and †*depicture* (XVI–XIX).

depilate de·pileit remove hair from. XVI. f. pp. stem of L. *dēpilāre*, f. DE- 3 + *pilāre* deprive of hair, *pilus* hair. So **depil**A·TION. XV. **depilat**ORY dipi·l- adj. and sb. XVII; cf. F. *dépilatoire* (Paré).

deplete diplī·t empty (orig. as by blood-letting). XIX. f. *dēplēt-*, pp. stem of L. *dēplēre*, f. *dē* DE- 6 + *-plēre* FILL. So **deple·**TION. XVII. – late L. *dēplētiō(n-)*, repl. late L. *dēplētūra* blood-letting.

deplore diplɔə·ɹ lament. XVI. – (O)F. *déplorer* or It. *deplorare* – L. *dēplōrāre*, f. *dē* DE- 3 + *plōrāre* wail, bewail. Hence **deplo·r**ABLE. XVII. – F. or late L.

deploy diploi· spread out, trans. and intr. XVIII. – F. *déployer* :– L. *displicāre* unfold, DISPLAY.

deponent dipou·nənt (gram. XV; see below); one who makes a deposition. XVI. – L. *dēpōnent-, -ēns*, prp. of *dēpōnere* lay aside, put down, deposit, (medL.) testify, f. *dē* DE- 1 + *pōnere* place, lay; see -ENT. ¶ Deponent verbs in Latin were orig. reflexive in form and meaning (e.g. *fruor* I enjoy, orig. I delight myself, *prōficiscor* I set out, orig. I put myself forward); but, since in verbs generally the reflexive form had become a passive, these verbs were mistakenly regarded as having 'laid aside' a passive meaning, whereas they had in fact ceased to have a reflexive meaning.

depopulate dīpɔ·pjŭleit †lay waste; deprive of population. XVI. f. pp. stem of L. *dēpopulāre, -ārī* ravage, f. *dē* DE- 3 + *populāre, -ārī* lay waste (f. *populus* PEOPLE), in medL. deprive of inhabitants, by assoc. with Rom. **dispopulāre* (OF. *despeupler*, mod. *dépeupler*, whence *dispeople* XV). So **depopul**A·TION. XV. – L.

deport dipō·ɹt A. †bear with, forbear, refrain XV (Caxton); refl. comport oneself XVI; B. carry away or off XVII. In A – OF. *deporter*, f. *de-* DE- 3 + *porter* carry :– L. *portāre*, rel. to PORT[1] and [2]; in B – F. *déporter* – L. *dēportāre* (see DE- 2). So **depo·rt**MENT †conduct; personal carriage. XVII. – (O)F. *déportement*.

depose dipou·z put down from office, dethrone XIII; lay aside, lay down, remove XIV; testify (to), attest XV. – (O)F. *déposer*, based on L. *dēpōnere* lay aside or down, deposit, entrust, f. *dē* DE- 2 + *pōnere* place; see POSE[1], POSITION. So **deposit** dipɔ·zit something laid up or committed for safe keeping; state of being deposited XVII; place of deposit XVIII. – L. *dēpositum*, sb. use of n. of pp. of *dēpōnere*. ¶ Earlier syns. are †*depose* (XIV, Gower), †*depost* (XIV, Wycl. Bible), †*depositum* (XVI, Rheims N.T.). **depo·sit** vb. place as a pledge or for safe keeping XVII; lay or put down XVIII. – F. †*dépositer* or medL. *dēpositāre*, f. L. *dēpositum*. **depo·sit**ARY one with whom a thing is deposited XVII (Sh.); place of deposit, depository XVIII. – late L. *dēpositārius*; cf. F. *dépositaire*. **depos**ITION dīpəzi·ʃən degradation, dethronement XIV; giving of testimony on oath XV; taking down of Christ from the Cross XVI. – (O)F. *déposition* – L. **depo·sit**ORY[1] keeper of a deposit, depositary XVII; place of deposit XVIII. – medL. *dēpositōrium*. **depot** de·pou, (U.S. dī·pou place for military stores or troops XVIII; depository; (U.S.) railway station XIX. – F. *dépôt*, OF. *depost* – L. *dēpositum* DEPOSIT. Spelt also *depôt, dépôt*, U.S. *depo, deepo*, and formerly pronounced dipou·, U.S. dī·pɔt.

deprave diprei·v corrupt, pervert; †vilify. XIV (PPl., Wycl. Bible). – (O)F. *dépraver* or L. *dēprāvāre*, f. *dē* DE- 3 + *prāvus* crooked perverse, wrong, bad. So **deprav**ITY dipræ·vĭti corruption, esp. (after Jonathan Edwards, 1757) that of human nature due to original sin. XVII. Alteration of PRAVITY after DEPRAVE; in theol. use superseding *pravity* and *depravation* (XVI).

deprecate de·prikeit pray against; plead for the avoidance of. XVII. f. pp. stem of L. *dēprecārī*, f. *dē* DE- 2+*precārī* PRAY; see -ATE[3]. So **depreca·tion** XV. – L. **de·precatory** XVI. – late L.

depreciate diprī·ʃieit lower in value or estimation XV (Hardyng); fall in value or estimation (orig. U.S.) XVIII. f. pp. stem of late L. *dēpretiāre* (medL. *-prec-*), f. *dē* DE- 1 + *pretium* PRICE; see -ATE[3] and cf. F. *déprécier*.

depredation depridei·ʃən making prey or plunder (of a thing). XV (Caxton). – F. *déprédation* – late L. *dēprædātiō(n-)*, f. *dēprædāri*, f. *dē* DE- 3+*prædāri* prey; see -ATION.

depress dipre·s †subjugate XIV; press down XV; bring down in vigour or spirits XV. – OF. *depresser* – late L. *dēpressāre*, frequent. f. *dēpress-*, pp. stem of *dēprimere* press down, f. *dē* DE- 1 + *premere* PRESS. So **depression** dipre·ʃən (astron.) angular distance below the horizon, etc. XIV (Ch.); lowering of condition or powers XV. – (O)F. or L.

deprive diprai·v dispossess, divest, debar. XIV (R. Mannyng). – OF. *depriver* – ecclL. *dēprīvāre*, f. L. *dē* DE- 3 + *prīvāre* deprive (see PRIVATION). So **deprivation** deprivei·ʃən. XV. – ecclL.

de profundis dī proufʌ·ndis Psalm cxxix (cxxx), beginning with these words in the L. version, 'Out of the depths' (have I called upon thee, O Lord), one of the seven penitential psalms used in the office for the dead XV; cry from the depths of misery XIII. L. *dē* out of, and abl. pl. n. of *profundus* (used sb.) deep, PROFOUND.

depth depþ deepness, deep place, deep water. XIV (Wycl. Bible, Ch., Gower). prob. based on ME. *dĕpnes* deepness + -TH[1] (cf. WIDTH); cf. MDu. *diepde*, (also mod.) *-te*, MLG. *dēpede*. ¶ Superseded or supplemented OE. *dīepe, -u, dēopu* and *dēopnes* (see DEEP; OE. *dīepe* corr. to OS. *diupī*, OHG. *tiufī* (G. *tiefe*), ON. *dýpi*, Goth. *diupei* :- CGerm. **deupīn-*).

depute dipjū·t appoint, assign. XV. Partly – (O)F. *députer* – L. *dēputāre* destine, assign, f. *dē* DE- 2+*putāre* consider (see PUTATIVE); partly based on *depute* pp. (XIV), still surviving in Sc. legal use as sb. 'deputy' – (O)F. *député*, the final syll. of which was dropped as in ASSIGN[2], etc. So **deputa·tion** dep- appointment, delegation XIV; body of deputed persons XVIII. – late L. **deputy** de·pjŭti person deputed to act for another. XVI. var. of *depute* sb. (see above) with final syll. of the F. retained; see -Y[5]. Hence **de·putize**. XVIII.

deracinate diræ·sineit pluck up by the roots. XVI (Sh.). f. F. *déraciner* (OF. *des-*), f. *dé-* DE- 6 + *racine* :- late L. *radīcīna*, f. L. *radix* root, RACE[3]; see -ATE[3].

derail direi·l run off or throw off the rails. XIX. – F. *dérailler*, f. *dé-* DE- 2 + *rail* RAIL[2]; in gen. use first in U.S.

derange direi·ndʒ disturb the order or functions of. XVIII. – F. *déranger*, OF. *desrengier*; see DE- 6, RANGE.

Derby dā·ɹbi, (dial., vulgar, and U.S.) də̄·ɹbi name of an English county, OE. *Dēor(a)bȳ*, and title of an earldom named therefrom; hence, name of an annual horse-race founded in 1780 by the twelfth earl of *Derby*; (U.S.) bowler hat. XIX.

derelict de·rilikt forsaken, abandoned; also sb. XVII. – L. *dērelictus*, pp. of *dērelinquere*, f. *dē* DE- 3 + *relinquere* leave (see RELICT). So **dereli·ction** abandonment XVII; reprehensible neglect (of duty, etc.) XVIII. – L.

deride dirai·d laugh to scorn. XVI. – L. *dērīdēre*, f. *dē* DE- 3+*rīdēre* laugh, laugh at (see RISIBLE). So **derision** diri·ʒən. XV. – (O)F. – late L.

derive dirai·v pass. and intr. emanate, take its origin XIV (Ch.); trans. conduct (water) *from* a source *into* a channel XV; †convey, transmit, direct; obtain from a source XVI. – (O)F. *dériver* (corr. to Pr., Sp. *derivar*, It. *derivare*) or L. *dērīvāre*, f. *dē* DE- 2 + *rīvus* brook, stream (cf. RIVAL). So **derivation** derivei·ʃən origination, spec. of a word XV (Bokenham); deviation into a channel; (med.) withdrawal of morbid fluid XV. – F. or L. **derivative** deri·v-. XV (sb. Battlefield Gram., adj. and sb. gram., Palsgr.). – F. – L. (Priscian).

dermat(o)- də̄·ɹmət(ou), də̄ɹmət(ə·) comb. form, varying with the shortened form **dermo-**, of Gr. *dérma -mat-* skin (cf. EPIDERMIS and TEAR[2]), used in many techn. terms.

dern də̄ɹn †concealed, secret OE.; (arch.) dark, drear, dire XV. OE. *derne, dierne* = OFris. *dern*, OS. *derni*, OHG. *tarni* :- WGerm. **darnja*, rel. to OE. *darian* lie hid.

derogate de·rŏgeit †abrogate in part; †detract from, disparage XV; take away a part *from* XV; fall away *from* a standard XVII. f. pp. of L. *dērogāre*, f. *dē* DE- 2 + *rogāre* ask, question, propose (a law). So **deroga·tion**. XV. – (O)F. or L. (only in sense 'partial abrogation of a law'). **derogatory**[2] dirɔ·gətəri. XVI. – late L. Cf. ROGATION.

derrick de·rik †hangman; †gallows XVI; hoisting contrivance XVIII. f. surname of a noted hangman at Tyburn *c.* 1600; Du. *Dierryk*, for *Diederik* = G. *Dietrich*, Goth. *Þiudareiks* (Theodoric) lit. 'people-mighty'.

derring-do deriŋdū· (arch.) feats of daring. XVI (Spenser; the Glosse to The Shepheardes Calender, October, has 'In derring doe, In manhoode and cheualrie'). Taken up from sixteenth-century prints of Lydgate's 'Chronicle of Troy', where *derrynge do* is misprinted for original *dorryng do*, which echoes 'In *dorrynge don* that longeth to a knyght' (in daring to do what appertains to a knight) of Chaucer's 'Troylus & Criseyde' v 837. Lydgate also used the phr. as a fully developed sb. (e.g. 'Chron. Troy' v 136) (1962 *N. & Q.* 369 f.). Its currency in mod. writers is due to Scott's use of *deeds of such derring-do* ('Ivanhoe' xxix).

derringer de·rindʒəɹ (U.S.) small pistol. XIX. f. surname of the inventor.

derry de·ri meaningless word forming part of refrains, as *hegh derie derie* XVI, *hey dery diddle, hey down derry down* XVII, which have been echoed by poets of XIX.

dervish dɔ̄·ɹviʃ Mohammedan ascetic. XVI. – Turk. *derviş* – Pers. *darvēsh, darvīsh* poor, religious mendicant; cf. F., It. *dervis* (the source of early forms in Eng.), Sp. *derviche*, G. *derwisch*.

des- see DIS-.

descant de·skænt (mus.) accompaniment to a plainsong theme XIV (Wyclif); composition in parts; †variation from the normal; varied comment XVI. orig. *deschaunt* – OF. *deschant* (mod. *déchant*) = Pr. *deschans*, Sp. *discante* – medL. *discantus* part-song, refrain, f. L. *dis-* asunder, apart + *cantus* song; see DIS-, CHANT. The present form is due to partial assim. to L.; the retention of the OF. form of the prefix is unusual. So **descant** diskæ·nt make a descant; comment, discourse. XVI. prob. f. the sb.

descend dise·nd come or go down. XIII (Cursor M.). – (O)F. *descendre* = Pr. *deissendre*, Sp. *descender*, It. *descendere* :- L. *dēscendere*, f. *dē* DE- 1 + *scandere* climb (see SCANSION). So **desce·ndANT** issue, offspring. XVI. – (O)F. *descendant*, prp. of *descendre*. **desce·nt** act or fact of descending from an ancestor, transmission by inheritance XIV; downward motion XIV (Ch.; rare before XVI). – (O)F. *descente*, f. *descendre*, after *attente, vente* from *attendre, vendre*.

describe diskrai·b set down in words; delineate. XV. – L. *dēscrībere* write down, copy off, f. *dē* DE- 1 + *scrībere* write (see SCRIPTURE); superseded ME. *descrive* (– OF. *descrivre*, mod. *décrire*). ¶ Formerly confused, through the notion of 'mark down', with DESCRY, as in Milton 'P.L.' IV 567. So **descri·pTION** (Wyclif, Ch.). – (O)F. – L.

descry diskrai· A. †proclaim, declare, †disclose; †cry down, decry XIV; B. catch sight of, discern XIV. – OF. *descrier* cry, publish, DECRY. Sense B appears to have arisen through identification with †*descrie* (– OF. *descrire*), var. of †*descrive* (see prec.), which combined the senses of 'write down, describe' and 'mark down, discern'.

desecrate de·sikreit destroy the sacred nature of. XVII. Formed with DE- 6 as the antithesis of CONSECRATE. So **desecrA·TION.** XVIII. ¶ L. *dēsecrāre* means 'consecrate, dedicate'.

desert[1] dizɔ̄·ɹt worthiness, meritoriousness XIII; action or quality deserving appropriate recompense XIV. – OF. *desert, deserte*, sb. derivs. of *deservir* DESERVE (obs. pp. *desert*, repr. Rom. **dēservitu-s*, for L. *dēservītu-s*).

desert[2] de·zəɹt waste tract of country. XIII (AncrR.). – (O)F. *désert* (= Pr. *desert*, Sp. *desierto*, It. *deserto*, Rum. *deçert*) – ecclL. (Vulgate) *dēsertum*, sb. use of n. of *dēsertus* abandoned, left waste, pp. of *dēserere* sever connexion with, leave, forsake. The L. pp. is the source of (O)F. *désert* adj., whence **de·sert** adj. (XIII, RGlouc.), which is now apprehended as an attrib. use of the sb.

desert[3] dizɔ̄·ɹt forsake, abandon. XV (earliest in Sc.). f. †*desert* pp. or – F. *déserter*, in OF. make desert = Pr. *desertar*, Sp. *desertar*, It. *disertare* (cf. late L. *dēsertāre*), ult. f. L. *dēsertus* DESERT[2]. So **dese·rTION.** XV (Lydg.). – (O)F. – late L.

deserve dizɔ̄·ɹv †become entitled to earn or claim XIII; be worthy to have XIV. – OF. *deservir* (now *desservir*) :- L. *dēservīre* serve zealously or well, f. *dē* DE- 3 + *servīre* SERVE. So **deservedly** dizɔ̄·ɹvidli according to desert. XVI. f. pp. *deserved* + -LY[2]; rendering L. *meritō*, It., Sp. *meritamente*.

deshabille see DISHABILLE.

desiccate de·sikeit, dī·sikeit make quite dry. XVI. f. pp. stem of L. *dēsiccāre*, f. *dē* DE- 3 + *siccāre* make dry, f. *siccus* dry; see -ATE[3]. Stressed *desi·ccate* till XIX. So **desiccA·TION.** XV. – late L.

desiderate dizi·dəreit, dis- feel the want or loss of. XVII. f. pp. stem of L. *dēsīderāre*, f. *dē* DE- 1, 2 + base **sīder-*, as in *consīderāre* CONSIDER; see -ATE[3] and cf. DESIRE. So **desideratum** -ei·təm something wanting and desired. XVII. sb. use of n.sg. of the pp. of the vb. **desi·derATIVE** (gram.) expressing desire. XVI. – late L.

design[1] dizai·n plan, scheme, purpose XVI (Sh.); plan for a work of art XVII. Earliest forms *deseigne, disseigne, designe* – F. †*desseing*, †*des(s)ing* (mod. *dessein* purpose, plan, from which is now differentiated *dessin* drawing, draft), f. †*desseigner* (see next).

design[2] dizai·n A. point out, designate; B. plan, purpose, intend XVI; C. delineate, draw XVII. In form – F. *désigner* indicate, designate, and L. *dēsignāre* mark out, point out, delineate, depict, contrive, DESIGNATE. All the meanings derive ult. from the L. word, but sense B has been affected by DESIGN[1] and F. †*desseigner*, sense C by F. *dessiner*, †*dessigner* (an alteration of *desseigner* – It. *disignare*). So **designate** de·zigneit †indicated XV (once), marked out or selected for office, appointed or nominated. XVII. – L. *dēsignātus*, pp. of *dēsignāre*, f. *dē* DE- 3 + *signāre* mark, SIGN; see -ATE[2]. **de·signate** vb. appoint or nominate for office XVIII; point out, name XIX. f. pp. stem of *dēsignāre*; see -ATE[3]. **designA·TION.** XIV. – (O)F. or L.

desire dizaiə·ɹ wish for. XIII. – (O)F. *désirer* = Pr. *dezirar*, It. †*disiderare* :- L. *dēsīderāre* (see DESIDERATE). So **desi·re** sb. XIV. – (O)F. *désir*, f. the vb. **desi·rOUS.** XIV. – AN. *desirous*, OF. *-eus* (mod. *désireux*) = Pr. *deziros*, It. *desideroso*.

desist dizi·st cease, leave off. xv. – (O)F. *désister* – L. *dēsistere*, f. *dē* DE- 2 + *sistere*, redupl. formation on *stare* STAND.

desk desk rest for a book, writing-paper, etc. XIV (Ch.). Late ME. *deske* – medL. *desca*, prob. based on Pr. *desc*, *desca* basket or It. *desco* table, butcher's block :– L. *discus* quoit, dish, disc (see DISCUS and cf. DAIS, DISH); occas. vars. are *desse* (XVI, Spenser) and *dexe*; *dask*, the common Sc. form XVI–XVIII, is unexplained.

desmo- de·zmou, dezmɔ· comb. form of Gr. *desmós* bond, chain, ligature (rel. to *deîn* bind; cf. DIADEM), used in scientific terms. XIX.

desolate de·sələt left alone; deserted XIV (Ch.); destitute of life, joy, or comfort XV. – L. *dēsōlātus*, pp. of *dēsōlāre* abandon, f. *dē* DE- 3+*sōlus* alone, SOLE; see -ATE². So **desol**ATION desəlei·ʃən utter devastation; dreary sorrow. XIV (Wycl. Bible). – late L. or partly through (O)F.

despair dispɛə·ɹ lose hope. XIV (R. Rolle), f. *despeir-*, tonic form of OF. *desperer* = Pr., OPg. *desperar*, It. *disperare* :– L. *dēspērāre* (see DESPERATE). So **despai·r** sb. XIV. – AN. **despeir*, for OF. *desespeir* (mod. *désespoir*). ¶ Ch. and Gower have *desespeir* sb., Ch. and Lydgate *desespeire* vb.

despatch see DISPATCH.

desperado despərā·dou †one in despair; desperate adventurer. XVII. refash. of the somewhat earlier †*desperate*, sb. use of next (XVI), after Sp. words in -ADO.

desperate de·spərət †despairing, hopeless; reckless from despair XV; to be despaired of, extremely dangerous or serious XV. – L. *dēspērātus* despaired of, pp. of *dēspērāre* despair, f. *dē* DE- 6+*spērāre* hope, f. OL. *spērēs* pl., *spēs* hope; cf. the similar use of the earlier *despaired* (XIV), modelled on OF. *despéré* (now *désespéré*) = It. *disperato*, Sp., Pg. *desperado*; see -ATE². So **desper**A·TION. XIV (Ch.). – OF. – L.

despise dispai·z look down upon in scorn. XIII. f. *despis-*, pres. stem of OF. *despire* :– L. *dēspicere*, f. *dē* DE- 1+*specere* look. (The early vars. in *-ice* show unvoiced s, after OF. *despiss-*, *despisc-*.)

despite dispai·t †scorn; outrage, injury XIII; indignation, vexation, spite XIV. ME. *despit* – OF. *despit* (mod. *dépit*) = Pr. *despiech*, Sp. *despecho*, It. *dispetto* :– L. *dēspectu-s* looking down (upon), f. *dēspect-*, *despicere* (see prec.). Phr. *in despite of* – OF. *en despit de*. Aphetic SPITE. So †**despit**EOUS; see DISPITEOUS.

despoil dispoi·l strip or rob of possessions. XIII. – OF. *despoill(i)er*, *despuillier* (mod. *dépouiller*) = Pr. *despolhar*, Sp. *despojar*, It. *spogliare*, Rum. *despoià* :– L. *dēspoliāre*, f. *dē* DE- 6+*spolia* (see SPOIL).

despond dispɔ·nd lose heart or confidence. XVII. – L. *dēspondēre* give up, resign, abandon (in phr. *animum dēspondēre*, later with obj. dropped, lose heart), f. *dē* DE- 2+*spondēre* promise (cf. SPOUSE). Hence **despo·nd**ENCE, -ENCY, -ENT. XVII.

despot de·spət lord, prince, ruler XVI; absolute ruler, tyrant XVIII (Cowper, Southey, Burke; the vogue of this sense was extended at the time of the French Revolution). – F. *despote*, earlier †*despot* – medL. *despota* – Gr. *despótēs* master, lord, perh. f. **dems-*, rel. to L. *domus* house (cf. DOME), and meaning 'master of the house'. So **despot**IC despɔ·tik. XVII. – F. *despotique* – Gr. *despotikós*. **despot**ISM de·spətizm. XVIII. – F.

desquamation dīskwəmei·ʃən scaling, peeling of skin. XVIII. – F. *désquamation* or modL. *dēsquāmātiō(n-)*, f. *dēsquāmāre* remove the scales from, f. *dē* DE- 6+*squāma* scale; see -ATION.

dessert dizə̄·ɹt course of fruit after dinner. XVII. – F. *dessert* m., *desserte* fem., pp. derivs. of *desservir* remove what has been served at table, f. *des-* DIS- 2+*servir* SERVE. The pronunc. with z, for earlier s from F. *-ss-*, is due to the incidence of the stress on the following syll.

destine de·stin appoint beforehand, as by a supernatural power XIV; set apart, allot XVI. – (O)F. *destiner* – L. *dēstināre* make fast or firm, establish (cf. *dēstina* support, *obstināre* set one's mind on (see OBSTINATE), *præstināre* 'fix the price of beforehand', buy), f. *dē* DE- 3+**stanāre* settle, fix, f. *stare* STAND; cf. Gr. *histánein*, *stanúein* place, OIr. *conosnaim* (:– **con-od-stanāio*) cease, Skr. *sthānam* place, OSl. *stanŭ*, Lith. *stónas* place. Hence **destin**A·TION. XV. – (O)F. or L. The current concrete sense is short for 'place of destination' (XVIII). **destiny** de·stini that which is destined, overruling necessity, fate. XIV. – (O)F. *destinée* = Pr. *destinada*, It. *destinata*, Rom. sb. use of fem. pp. of prec. L. vb.

destitute de·stitjūt †abandoned, forsaken, forlorn XIV (Wycl. Bible); devoid *of* XV; bereft of resources XVIII (this sense prob. arises from a contextual interpretation of *the poore destitute* in Coverdale's tr. of Psalm cii 17, where the meaning is properly 'forlorn'). – L. *dēstitūtus* forsaken, pp. of *dēstituere*, f. *dē* DE- 1, 2 + *statuere* set up, place (see STATUTE).

destrier de·striəɹ (arch.) war-horse. XIII. ME. *destrer* – AN. *destrer*, (O)F. *destrier* = Pr. *destrier* (whence It. †*destriere*) :– Gallo-Rom. **dextrāriu-s* (sc. *equus* horse), f. L. *dext(e)ra* (see DEXTER), the knight's charger being led by the squire with his right hand.

destroy distroi· pull down, demolish, put out of existence, put an end to. XIII (RGlouc., Cursor M.). ME. *destru(e)*, *destrui(e)*, *destrie*, *destroie* – OF. *destruire* (mod. *détruire*) = Pr., Sp. *destruir*, It. *struggere* :– Rom. **dēstrūgere* (formed after pt. *dēstruxī*, pp. *dēstructus*), for L. *destruere*,

f. *dē* DE- 6+*struere* pile up (see STRUCTURE). Hence **destroy·**ER[1]. XIV (Wycl. Bible, Trevisa); short for torpedo-*boat destroyer* 1894. So **destruction** distrʌ·kʃən act of destroying. XIV (R. Rolle). – (O)F. *destruction* = Pr. *destruccio*, etc. – L. *dēstructiō(n-)*, f. *dēstruct-*, *dēstruere*; see above and -TION. **destru·ct**IVE. XV. – (O)F. – late L.

desuetude dīsjū·itjūd, de·-, dī·switjūd †discontinuance, state of disuse. XV. – F. *désuétude* or its source L. *dēsuetūdō*, f. *dēsuēt-*, *dēsuēscere* disuse, become unaccustomed, f. *dē* DE- 6+*suēscere* be wont, prob. f. **swe-* 'self' (cf. SUICIDE), and so lit. 'make one's own'; see -TUDE.

desultory de·səltəri shifting from one place or thing to another XVI; disconnected and irregular XVIII. – L. *dēsultōrius* pert. to a vaulter, superficial, f. *desultor*, f. *dēsult-*, pp. stem of *dēsilīre* leap down, f. *dē* DE- 1+ *salīre* leap; see SALIENT, -ORY.

detach ditæ·tʃ disconnect and separate. XVII (prob. first in mil. use). – F. *détacher*, earlier †*destacher* (whence rare late ME. *distache*, Caxton), corr. to Pr., Sp. *destacar*, It. *distaccare*; f. *des-*, *dis-* DIS- 1+stem of *attacher* ATTACH. So **deta·ch**MENT. XVII. – F.

detail dī·teil, ditei·l *in detail* item by item (after F. *en détail*, opposed to *en gros* in gross); minute account XVII; minute part; (mil.) distribution in detail of the daily orders to the officers concerned, body detached for special duty (after F. *détail du service, distribuer l'ordre en détail*) XVIII. – F. *détail*, f. *détailler* (f. *dé-* DE- 3+*tailler* cut up in pieces), whence **de·tail** vb. deal with in detail XVII; (mil.) XVIII.

detain ditei·n keep under restraint XV; keep waiting XVI. repr. tonic stem of (O)F. *détenir* (AN. *detener*), corr. to Pr., Sp. *detener*, It. *ditenere* :– Rom. **dētenēre*, for L. *dētinēre*, f. *dē* DE- 2+*tenēre* hold; cf. ABSTAIN. So **detai·ner** (leg.) detention. XVII. – AN. *detener*, inf. used sb.; see -ER[4]. **deten**TION dite·nʃən. XV. – F. *détention* or late L. *dētentiō(n-)*, f. *dētent-*, pp. stem of *dētinēre*. **détenu** dei·tənü person detained in custody. XIX. F., pp. of *détenir*.

detect dite·kt †uncover, expose XV; expose the secrecy of XVI. f. *dētect-*, pp. stem of L. *dētegere*, f. *dē* DE- 6 + *tegere* cover (see THATCH); after †*detect* pp. (XIV). So **dete·c**TION. XV. – late L. **dete·ct**IVE. XIX; first in *detective police(man)*; hence ellipt. as sb.

detent dite·nt in clocks and watches, the catch which regulates the striking. XVII (also gen. stop or catch in a machine; in gunsmiths' use *detant*). – F. *détente*, earlier *destente* mechanism in a crossbow by which the string is released, (hence) analogous part in fire-arms, f. *destendre* slacken, f. *des-* DIS- (privative)+*tendre* :– L. *tendere* stretch, TEND. Being assoc. formally with *detent-*, ppl. stem of *detinēre* DETAIN, the word acquired a contradictory meaning (releasing mechanism being often a means of detention). **détente** deitã·t easing of strained relations. XX. F.; see above.

deter ditə̄·ɹ frighten away, discourage *from*. XVI. – L. *dēterrēre*, f. *dē* DE- 2 + *terrēre* frighten (see TERRIBLE). So **deterr**ENT dite·rənt. XIX.

deterge ditə̄·ɹdʒ wipe or clear away (esp. med.). XVII. – F. *déterger* (Paré) or L. *dētergēre*, f. *dē* DE- 2 + *tergēre* wipe. So **dete·rg**ENT also sb. XVII, **dete·rs**IVE cleansing. XVI. – F. *détersif*, f. pp. stem *dēters-* of L. *dētergēre*.

deteriorate ditiə·riəreit make worse XVI; grow worse XVIII. f. pp. stem of late L. *dēteriōrāre*, f. *dēterior* worse, compar. of **dēter-*, f. *dē* down (see DĒ-)+compar. suffix; see -ATE[3].

determine ditə̄·ɹmin bring to an end; come to an end, term, or decision XIV (Wyclif, Ch., Trev.); in former university practice, discuss and resolve a question (cf. below) XVI. – (O)F. *déterminer* = Pr., Sp. *determinar*, etc. – L. *dēterminãre* bound, limit, fix, f. *dē* DE- 3+*termināre* TERMINATE. So **dete·rmin**ANT. XVII; as sb. (math.) tr. modL. *determinans* (Gauss, 1802), whence F. *déterminant* (Cauchy). **determin**A·TION. XIV. (In former university practice, applied to disputations which followed admission to the degree of bachelor of arts and completed the taking of that degree.) – (O)F. – L.

determinism ditə̄·ɹminizm (philos.) doctrine that human action is necessarily determined. XIX (Hamilton, 1846). – F. *déterminisme* (1840) or its source G. *determinismus* (Kant, 1793), which may have been extracted from *prädeterminismus*, if not directly f. *determinieren* – L. *dēterminãre* (see prec.)+*-ismus* -ISM.

detest dite·st †execrate; have abhorrence of. XVI. – L. *dētestāri* denounce, renounce, f. *dē* DE- 4 + *testārī* bear witness, call to witness, f. *testis* witness (see TESTIFY); perh. partly back-formation from **detest**A·TION dī- †execration XV; abhorrence XV. – (O)F. – L.

detinue de·tinju (leg.) detention. XV. – OF. *detenue*, sb. use of fem. pp. of *detenir* DETAIN. Cf. *avenue, issue, retinue.*

detonate dī·tŏneit explode with sudden loud report; also trans. XVIII. f. pp. stem of L. *dētonāre*, f. DE- 3+*tonāre* THUNDER (see -ATE[3]); partly back-formation from **deton**A·TION (XVII) – F. *détonation*, f. *détoner* – L. *dētonāre*. Hence **de·ton**ATOR; XIX.

detour, détour dei·tuəɹ dituə·ɹ, roundabout way. XVIII. – F. *détour* change of direction, f. *détourner* (OF. *destorner*) turn away; see DE- 2, TOUR, TURN.

detract ditræ·kt disparage XV; †take away *from* XVI. f. *dētract-*, pp. stem of L. *dētrahere* draw off, take away, disparage, f. *dē* DE- 2+ *trahere* draw. So **detra·c**TION disparagement XIV; †taking away XVI. – (O)F. – L. See TRACT, TRACTION.

detrain dĭtrei·n unload from or get off a train. XIX. f. DE- 7+TRAIN sb.

detriment de·trimənt loss, damage. XV. – (O)F. *détriment* or L. *dētrīmentum*, f. pt. stem *dētrī-* of *dēterere* wear away, f. *dē* DE- 2 +*terere* rub; see TRITE, -MENT. Hence **detrime·ntAL**[1]. XVII.

detritus ditrai·təs †wearing away by rubbing XVIII; (after F. *détritus*, which superseded the more correct *détritum*) matter produced by such action XIX. – L. *dētrītus*, f. *dētrī-* (see prec.).

detur dī·təɹ annual prize at Harvard University, U.S.A. XVIII. L. 'let there be given', 3rd sg. pres. ind. pass. of *dare* give (cf. DATIVE).

deuce[1] djūs two at dice or cards XV; (at tennis), the point at which each side has scored 40 and the game is *à deux* (It. *a due*) 'at two', i.e. when two successive points must be gained to win the game or set. XVI. – OF. *deus* (mod. *deux*) :– L. *duōs* acc. TWO.

deuce[2] djūs in imprecatory phr. †*a deuce on, the* (†*a*) *deuce take, what the* (†*a*) *deuce*, plague, mischief, (later) the Devil. XVII. – LG. *duus* (in *de duus!*, *wat de duus..!*) = G. *daus* (in *der daus!*, *was der daus..!*, prob. to be identified ult. with prec. as a dicer's exclamation on making the lowest throw, viz. a two. ¶ There is no chronological contact with ME. *deus!* – OF. *deus!* God!

deuterium djūtiə·riəm (chem.) an isotope of hydrogen, symbol D. 1934. modL., f. Gr. *deúteros* (cf. next)+-IUM.

deutero- djū·tərou, djūtərə· before a vowel **deu·ter-** comb. form of Gr. *deúteros* second, also in the sense 'secondary', as in *deu:terocan·onical* XVII (modL. *deuterocanonicus*), *Deu:tero-Isai·ah* later part of the book of Isaiah (ch. xl–lv), writer to whom this is ascribed (XIX).

deuto- djū·tou, djūtə· before a vowel **deut-**, shortened form of DEUTERO- used in chem. to denote the second in a series, as *deuto*·XIDE (1810), and biol. to denote the second or a secondary part, form, or the like.

deutzia djū·tsiə genus of saxifragaceous shrubs. XIX. modL., f. name of J. *Deutz* of Amsterdam; see -IA[1].

Devanagari deivənā·garī Sanskrit alphabet. XVIII (*Dewnagur*, *Devya-nagre*). Skr. (Hindi, Marathi) *dēvanāgarī* (Bengali *devanāgar*), lit. 'divine town script', f. *dēvás* god (cf. DEITY, DIVINE)+*nāgarī* (an earlier name of the alphabet), f. *nāgaran* town; perh. so named from having originated in a certain town.

devastate de·vəsteit lay waste. XVII (rare before XIX; superseded older †*devast* XVI). f. pp. stem of L. *dēvāstāre*, f. DE- 3+*vāstāre* lay waste, f. *vāstus*; see WASTE and -ATE[3]. So **devastA·TION**. XV.

develop dive·ləp unfold, lay open (more fully). XVII. First recorded in dicts. in pp. *developed*; preceded by †*disvelop* (XVI–XVIII). – OF. *desveloper* (in pp. *c.* 1200), mod. *développer* = Pr. *desvolopar*, It. *sviluppare* :– Rom. vb. f. L. *dis-* DIS- 2+**volup-*, **velup-* (as in OF. *voloper* envelop, Pr. *volopar*, It. *viluppo* bundle, truss, *viluppare* wrap up), which has been referred ult. to medL. **faluppa* wisp of straw, chip, of unkn. origin; cf. ENVELOP. So **deve·lopMENT**. XVIII (in Chesterfield in F. form *développement*).

deviate dī·vieit turn aside. XVII. f. pp. stem of late L. *dēviāre*, f. *dē* DE- 2+*via* way; see -ATE[3]. So **deviA·TION**. XVII; – F. – medL.

device divai·s plan, planning; pleasure, fancy XIII; †opinion; design, figure XIV; contrivance XIV. ME. *devis*, later *devise*, from XV *device*; the present form is – OF. *devis* m.; *devise* is – OF. *devise* fem.; the two words, which had an almost identical range of meaning, corr. to Pr. *devis*, *devisa*, It. *diviso*, *divisa* – Rom. derivs. of L. *dīvīs-*, pp. stem of *dīvīdere* DIVIDE. Cf. DEVISE.

devil de·vl the supreme spirit of evil; an evil spirit; malignant being, fiend in human form; printer's apprentice XVII; (highly seasoned) fried or broiled dish XVIII. OE. *dēofol* = OFris. *diovel*, OS. *diubul*, *-al* (Du. *duivel*), OHG. *tiufal* (G. *teufel*), ON. *djǫfull*, Goth. *diabaulus*, *-bulus*. The Goth. forms were directly – Gr. *diábolos* (used in LXX to render Heb. *sātān* SATAN), prop. accuser, slanderer, f. *diabállein* slander, traduce, f. *diá* across+*bállein* throw, cast (cf. BALLISTA). The other Germ. forms were – ChrL. *diabolus*, whence also the Rom. forms, (O)F., Pr. *diable*, Sp. *diablo*, It. *diavolo*, and OSl. *diyavolŭ* (Russ. *d'avol*). One of the earliest Christian adoptions in Germanic. Shortening of the OE. diphthong *ēo* (whence ME. *ē*) in inflected forms, e.g. nom. pl. *dēoflas*, produced the present standard form, but the long vowel is preserved, with suppression of *v*, in ME. *dele*, later *deale* (as in Sh. 'Hamlet'), Sc. *deil* dīl; vocalization of *v* gave ME. *deul*, mod. dial. *dule*. Hence **devil** vb. †play the devil XVI; grill, broil (with hot condiments) XVIII; act as devil to a lawyer or writer XIX. **de·vilish.** XV (Lydg.); see -ISH[1]; cf. MLG., MDu. *duvelsch*, MHG. *tiuvelisch* (G. *teuflisch*). **de·vilRY**. XIV (Barbour); after (O)F. *diablerie*; cf. MDu. *duivel(e)rie*; altered (orig. U.S.) to **de·viltry** XVIII, on the false analogy of *harlotry* or the like. *Devil-may-care* orig. Sc. *deil-ma-care* XVIII, phr. used attrib. in the sense 'wildly reckless', from ellipt. phr. such as 'The devil may care (but I don't, he doesn't, etc.)'.

devious dī·viəs lying out of the way XVI; deviating from the direct way XVII. f. L. *dēvius*, f. *dē* DE- 2+*via* way; see -OUS.

devise[1] divai·z order, appoint XIII; assign by will; plan, plot, contrive XIV. – (O)F.

deviser divide, dispose, dispose of, design, contrive, discourse = Pr., OSp. *devisar*, It. *divisare*, Rom. **dīvīsāre*, f. *dīvīs-*, pp. stem of *dīvīdere* DIVIDE.

devise[2] divai·z testamentary disposition. XVI. – OF. *devise* (see DEVICE) – medL. *dīvīsa*, used for *dīvisiō* DIVISION.

devocalize dīvou·kəlaiz make (a sound) voiceless or non-sonant. XIX (Sweet). f. DE- 7+L. *vōcālis* VOWEL+-IZE.

devoid divoi·d destitute *of*. XV. orig. pp. (contr.) of †*devoid* make void or empty (XIV) – OF. *devoidier*, *-vuidier* (mod. *dévider*), f. *de-* DE- 3+*voider*, *vuider* VOID.

devoir dəvwā·ɹ duty, task XIII; †endeavour XIV; dutiful act of respect XVI. ME. *dever* – AN. *dever*, OF. *deveir* (mod. *devoir*) = Pr. *dever*, Sp. *deber*, It. *devere*, *dovere* :- L. *dēbēre* owe (see DEBIT) used as sb. The ME. pronunc. was dəvē·r, later dĕ·vər, continued in early modEng. *deavour* (cf. ENDEAVOUR); forms of the Parisian F. type (*devoir*) appear in XV and were established later, with approximation to the F. pronunc.

devolve divɔ·lv †roll down XV; pass or cause to pass *to* or fall *upon* another XVI. – L. *dēvolvere*, f. *dē* DE- 1+*volvere* roll (see VOLUME). So **devolu**TION dīvəlʲū·ʃən. XVI. – late L.

Devonian divou·niən pert. to Devon. XVII. f. medL. *Devonia*, f. *Devon* (OE. *Defna|sćīr*; *Defnas* repr. British *Dumnonii* name of the Celtic inhabitants, which was transf. to the Saxon conquerors; cf. W. *Dyfnaint* Devon :- British *Dumnonia*); see -IAN.

devote divou·t appropriate or dedicate as by a vow. XVI. f. *dēvōt-*, pp. stem of L. *dēvovēre*, f. *dē* DE- 3 + *vovēre* VOW. So **devo**·TION. XIII. – (O)F. – L.

devotee devŏtī· person devoted to a cause, esp. religion. XVII (Evelyn). f. prec.+-EE, after *debauchee*, or the like; superseding †*devote*, sb. use of the adj. – F. *dévot* or L. *dēvōtus*, pp. of *dēvovēre*.

devour divauə·ɹ swallow up, consume. XIV. *devour-*, tonic stem of (O)F. *dévorer* (corr. to Pr., Sp. *devorar*, It. *devorare*) – L. *dēvorāre*, f. *dē* DE- 3+*vorāre* swallow (see VORACIOUS).

devout divau·t devoted to divine worship or service. XIII (*devot*, *devout*). – (O)F. *dévot* = Pr. *devot*, Sp. *devoto*, It. *divoto* – L. *dēvōtus*, pp. of *dēvovēre* DEVOTE. The passage of ō to ū (whence present au) in the second syll. had begun before 1300.

dew djū moisture deposited in drops from the atmosphere. OE. *dēaw* = OFris. *dāw*, OS. *dau* (Du. *dauw*), OHG. *tou* (G. *tau*), ON. *dǫgg* (gen. *dǫggvar*) :- CGerm. (not in Goth.) **dawwaz*, *-am* :- IE. **dhawos*, *-om*, the base of which is repr. by Skr. *dhāv* flow, *dhāutís* spring, brook, Gr. *theîn* run, *thoós* swift.

dewan diwā·n (in India) chief minister or officer. XVII. – Hind. – Arab., Pers. *dīwān*, an early sense of which was 'register of accounts', from which it was transf. in India to the officer having charge of the financial department of a state. Cf. DIVAN, DOUANE.

dew-claw djū·klō rudimentary inner toe in dogs. XVI. prob. f. DEW+CLAW, being so called because it touches only the dewy surface of the ground; cf. 'deaw-claw, or water-claw of dogs' (Cotgr.) and next.

dew-lap djū·læp fold of loose skin hanging from the throat. XIV (Trevisa). f. DEW+LAP[1], perh. after ON. **dǫggleppr* (ODa. *doglæp*).

dexter de·kstəɹ (her.) right-hand. XVI. – L. *dexter*, compar. formation expressing the contrast of two sides, f. CIE. base **dex-*, whence Gr. *dexiós* on the right hand (cf. *dexiterós*), together with Indo-Iranian, Balto-Slav., Germ., Celtic, and Albanian cogns.; the primary meaning passes sometimes into 'south', sometimes into 'adroit' and 'valiant'. So **dexter**ITY -e·rĭti manipulative skill, mental adroitness. XVI. – F. – L. **de·xter**OUS, **de·xtr**OUS. f. L. *dexter*.

dextrin de·kstrin (chem.) gummy substance into which starch is converted at high temperatures, having the property of turning the plane of polarization 138·68° to the right, whence its name. – F. *dextrine* (Biot and Persoz, 1833), f. L. *dextrā* on the right hand, abl. fem. of *dexter*; see prec. and -IN.

dextro- de·kstrou used as comb. form of L. *dexter*, *dextr-* right-handed (see DEXTER) or *dextrā* on the right hand, in physical and chemical terms to denote 'turned or turning to the right' with ref. to the property of causing a ray of polarized light to turn to the right; first used by Pasteur.

dey dei commanding officer of the janissaries of Algiers. XVII. – F. *dey* – Turk. *dāī* maternal uncle, friendly title given formerly to older people, esp. among the janissaries.

dhoby dou·bi native Indian washerman. XIX. – Hindi *dhōbī*, f. *dhōb* washing :- Skr. *dhāv* wash (see DEW).

dhooly erron. var. of DOOLIE.

dhoti, dhootie d(h)ou·ti, d(h)ū·ti loincloth worn by Hindus. XVII (*duttee*). Hindi *dhōtī*.

dhow, dow dau native vessel used on the Arabian Sea. XIX. ult. origin unkn.; in Marathi as *ḍāw*, in Arabic as *dāw*. ¶ The sp. with *dh* appears to be an attempt to orientalize the look of the word.

di-[1] di, dai see DIS-.

di-[2] dai, di repr. Gr. *di-*, for *dís* TWICE (see TWO), as in *dígamos* twice married, *dídrakmos* worth two drachmas, *díptukhos* double-folded; see DICOTYLEDON, DIGAMMA, DIGRAPH, DILEMMA, etc. As a living prefix used in chem. in the sense of 'twice, double', with various spec. application, expression the presence of two atoms or molecules, equivalents, etc.

dia- daiə before a vowel **di-** repr. Gr. *dia-*, *di-*, the prep. *dia* (app. alteration of IE. **dis* in two, apart; cf. DIS-) in comps. with the senses 'through', 'thorough(ly)', 'apart', occurring in a few words going back (sometimes through French and Latin) to Gr. originals, as DIALECT, DIATRIBE, and in many mod. scientific and technical formations. **b.** In Gr. medical terms *diá* with a genitive pl. was used to denote the composition of medicaments, as *dià triôn pepereôn phármakon* drug made of three peppers, *dià tessárōn, dià pénte* of four, five ingredients. Many of these were combined into single words by Latin physicians, whence DIAPENTE, DIATESSARON; the formation of some became obscured through apprehending Gr. *-ōn* (*-ων*) as *-on* (*-ον*), which was latinized as *-um*, as in DIACHYLUM. For the similar use in mus. terms see DIAPASON, DIAPENTE.

diabetes daiəbī·tiz disease marked by immoderate discharge of urine containing glucose. XVI. – L. *diabētēs* – Gr. *diabḗtēs*, f. *diabaínein* go through; see DIA- and COME.

diablerie diæ·bləri dealings with the devil, devilry XVIII (Warburton); devil-lore XIX (Scott). – F., f. *diable* DEVIL; see -ERY.

diabolic XIV, **diabolical** XVI daiəbɔ·lik(əl) pert. to the or a devil. – or f. (O)F. *diabolique*, ChrL. *diabolicus*, f. *diabolus* DEVIL; see -IC, -ICAL.

diabolo dià·bəlou the game of devil-on-two-sticks, in which a double cone is made to spin in the air by means of a string attached to two sticks held one in each hand. XX (1907). It. (DEVIL).

diachylon, -um daiæ·kilɔn, əm, **diaculum** daiæ·kjuləm lead-plaster. XIV. – OF. *diaculon, diachilom* – late L. *diachylon*, for L. *diachȳlōn*, repr. Gr. *dià khūlôn* composed of juices; see DIA- b, CHYLE.

diaconal daiæ·kənəl pert. to a deacon. XVII. – ChrL. *diācōnālis*, f. *diāconus* DEACON. So **dia·conate.** XVII. – ChrL. *diāconātus*. Cf. F. *diaconal, diaconat*; see -AL[1], -ATE[1].

diacritic daiəkri·tik serving to distinguish XVII; sb. diacritic sign XIX. – Gr. *diakritikós*, f. *diakrī́nein* distinguish; see DIA-, CRITIC.

diadem dai·ədem royal crown or fillet. – (O)F. *diadème* – L. *diadēma* – Gr. *diádēma* regal fillet of the Persian kings, f. *diadeîn* bind round, f. *diá* DIA-+*deîn* bind.

diæresis daiiə·rĭsis (sign " marking) the separation of a vowel from its neighbour. XVII. – late L. – Gr. *diaíresis*, f. *diaireîn* divide, f. *diá* DIA-+*haireîn* take (cf. HERETIC).

diagnosis daiəgnou·sis determination of the nature of a disease. XVII. –modL. – Gr. *diágnōsis*, f. *diagignṓskein* distinguish, discern, f. *diá* DIA-+*gignṓskein* perceive (see KNOW).

diagonal daiæ·gənəl extending from one angular point of a figure to an opposite one. XVI. **dia·gonally** adv. XV. – L. *diagōnālis*, f. Gr. *diagṓnios*, f. *diá* across, DIA-+*gōníā* angle (cf. KNEE); see -AL[1]. So (O)F.

diagram dai·əgræm illustrative figure. XVII. – L. *diagramma* – Gr. *diágramma* (*-at-*), f. *diagráphein* mark out by lines, f. *diá* DIA-+*gráphein* write; see -GRAM. So **di:agrammatic** -grəmæ·tik. XIX.

dial dai·əl instrument to tell the time of day by the shadow cast by the sun. XV. Obscure deriv. of medL. *diālis*, f. *diēs* day; see -AL[1]. ¶ Outside Eng. only in a single instance in Froissart's Chronicle where it means a daily wheel (*roe jornal*) in a clock.

dialect dai·əlekt particular manner of speech; subordinate variety of a language. XVI. – F. *dialecte* or L. *dialectus* – Gr. *diálektos* discourse, way of speaking, language of a district, f. *dialégesthai* hold discourse, f. *diá* DIA-+*légein* speak (cf. LOGOS). Hence **diale·ctAL**[1] pert. to dialect(s). XIX; *dialectical* was earlier in this sense XVIII. So **diale·ctIC** XVII, -ICAL XVI pert. to logical disputation. **diale·ctic** sb. investigation of truth by discussion XIV (Wycl. Bible); spec. in Kant, etc. XVIII. – (O)F. *dialectique* or L. *dialectica* – Gr. *dialektikḗ* sb. use (sc. *tékhnē* art) of fem. of *dialektikós*; cf. G. *dialektik*. The treatment of L. *dialectica* as n.pl. led to the use of **diale·ctICS**. XVII (Milton). **dialecti·CIAN**. XVII. – F. *dialecticien* (Rabelais).

dialogue dai·əlɔg colloquy, esp. between two persons. XIII. – OF. *dialoge* (mod. *dialogue*) – L. *dialogus* – Gr. *diálogos* conversation, discourse, f. *dialégesthai* converse (see DIALECT). Hence as †vb. express in dialogue; hold a dialogue. XVI (Sh.).

dialysis diæ·lĭsis †statement of disjunctive propositions, asyndeton XVI; (chem.) Graham's name for the separation of the soluble crystalloid substances in a mixture from the colloid XIX. – L. – Gr. *diálusis*, f. *dialúein* part asunder, f. *diá* DIA-+*lúein* set free, LOOSEN.

diamanté diamã·tei material scintillating with powdered crystal, etc. XX. F., pp. formation on *diamant* DIAMOND.

diameter daiæ·mitəɹ transverse line through the centre of a circle, etc., terminated at each end by the circumference. XIV (Ch., Trevisa). – (O)F. *diamètre* – L. *diametrus, -os* – Gr. *diámetros* (sc. *grammḗ* line) diagonal of a parallelogram, diameter of a circle, f. *diá* DIA-+*métron* measure (see METRIC). So **dia·metrAL**[1]. XVI. – (O)F. – late L.; contemp. with **diame·trICAL**. XVI.

diamond dai·əmənd most brilliant and valuable of precious stones. XIII. ME. *diama(u)nt* – (O)F. *diamant* = Pr. *diaman*, Sp., It. *diamante* – medL. *diamant-, diamas*, alteration of L. *adamas* ADAMANT, prob. through a pop. form **adimas* (whence OF. *aimant*, mod. *aimant*, Pr. *aziman* lodestone), and by assocn. with words in DIA-, e.g. Gr. *diaphanḗs* DIAPHANOUS. The differentiation of form in medL. was prob. due to the twofold application of *adamas* to the diamond and the magnet. The disyllabic pronunc. dai·mənd is shown as early as XVII and is recognized by orthoepists of XVIII. For fina l *d* from *t* cf. *card, mound.*

diapason daiəpei·zən (mus.) †octave XIV; harmonious or melodious succession of notes or parts; foundation stop in an organ XVI; scale, range, pitch XVIII. – L. *diapāsōn* – Gr. *diapāsôn*, i.e. *dià pāsôn* (sc. *khordôn*), more fully *hē dià pāsôn khordôn sumphonía* the concord through all the notes, i.e. of the scale; *diá* through (cf. DIA- b) *pāsôn*, g. pl. fem. of *pâs* all, *khordôn*, g. pl. of *khordḗ* CHORD. Cf. (O)F. *diapason*, whence the XVI–XVII stressing *dia·pason* (but Sh., Milton, and Dryden, e.g., have *diapa·son*). By Spenser and imitators anglicized as *diapase*. So **diapente** daiəpe·nti (mus.) interval of a fifth (XIV), XV; †medicine composed of five ingredients XVII. – OF. – late L. – Gr. *dià pénte* through five; see DIA- b.

diaper dai·əpər linen fabric with a small diamond pattern XIV; pattern of this kind XVII; small towel XVI. – OF. *diapre*, earlier *diaspre* = Pr. *diasp(r)e* – medL. *diasprum* – Byzantine Gr. *díaspros*, f. *diá* DIA-+*áspros* white; the orig. meaning of the Gr. word is uncertain. Hence **di·aper** vb., **di·apered** ppl. adj. XIV; cf. (O)F. *diaprer, diapré.*

diaphanous daiæ·fənəs perfectly transparent. XVII. f. medL. *diaphanus* (whence (O)F. *diaphane*, Sp., It. *diafano*, etc.), f. Gr. *diaphanḗs*, f. *diá* DIA-+*phan-, phaínein* show (cf. PHANTASY); see -OUS. So **diaphaneity** -ī·ĭti. XVII (Boyle). – medL. *diaphaneitās*, whence F. *diaphanéité*; earlier †*diapha·nity* (XV) – F. †*diaphanité.*

diaphoretic dai:əfŏre·tik sudorific. XV. – late L. *diaphorēticus* – Gr. *diaphorētikós*, f. *diaphórēsis* perspiration, f. *diaphoreîn* throw off by perspiration, f. *diá* DIA-+*phoreîn* carry, rel. to *phérein* BEAR[2]; see -TIC.

diaphragm dai·əfræm partition dividing the thorax from the abdomen. XVII (earlier in L. form). – late L. *diaphragma* – Gr. *diáphragma*, f. *diá* DIA-+*phrágma* fence, *phrássein* (:– **phrakj-*) fence in, hedge round.

diarchy see DYARCHY.

diarrhœa daiərī·ə· too frequent evacuation of too fluid fæces. XVI (also *diaria, diarie* XV). – late L. *diarrhœa* (Cælius Aurelianus, Isidore) – Gr. *diárrhoia* (Hippocrates), f. *diarrheîn* flow through, f. *diá* DIA-+*rheîn* flow (see STREAM).

diary dai·əri daily record; book to contain this. XVI. – L. *diārium* daily allowance, (later) journal, diary, in form sb. use of n. of *diārius* daily (which, however, is not premediæval), f. *diēs* day (f. a base repr. also by L. *deus* god, Gr. *Zeus*, L. *Jovis*, g. of *Juppiter*, Ir. *dia*, W. *dyw* day); see -ARY. Hence **di·arIST.** XIX.

Diaspora daiæ·spərə the Jews dispersed among the Gentiles. XIX. – Gr. *diasporá*, f. *diaspeírein* disperse, f. *diá* DIA-+*speírein* sow, scatter (cf. SPERM); from Deut. xxviii 25 (LXX) ἔσῃ διασπορὰ ἐν πάσαις βασιλείαις τῆς γῆς.

diastole daiæ·stəli (physiol.) dilatation. XVI. – late L. – Gr. *diastolḗ* separation, expansion, dilatation, f. *diastéllein*, f. *diá* DIA-+*stéllein* place (cf. STOLE[1]).

diatessaron daiəte·sərən †(mus.) interval of a fourth XIV; medicine of four ingredients XV; harmony of the four Gospels XIX. – late L. *diatessarōn*, f. Gr. *dià tessárōn* through, i.e. composed of, four (*diá* DIA-, *tessárōn*, g. of *téssares* FOUR). The last meaning is derived from the title of the earliest work of the kind, Tatian's Euaggélion dià tessárōn 'gospel made up of four' (II).

diatonic daiətɔ·nik (mus.). – (O)F. *diatonique* or its source, late L. *diatonicus* – Gr. *diatonikós* proceeding through, i.e. at the interval of, a tone, f. *diá* DIA-+*tónos* TONE; see -IC.

diatribe dai·ətraib disquisition XVI; severely critical discourse XIX. – F. *diatribe* – L. *diatriba* – Gr. *diatribḗ* employment (of time), study, discourse, f. *diatríbein* consume, waste, while away, f. *diá* DIA-+*tríbein* rub (prob. rel. to L. *terere* rub; cf. TRITE).

dibble di·bl instrument for making holes in the ground. XV (*debylle*). In form a deriv. with -LE of †*dib* vb. (XIV), a syn., and prob. a modified form, of DIP; but the senses of this vb. that are more directly connected with *dibble* are of much later emergence.

dibs dibz pl. children's game played with pebbles or knuckle-bones XVIII (earlier *dibstones*, Locke); money XIX. perh. f. *dib* vb. (see prec.) tap, dip, bob, apprehended as a var. of DAB.

dicast di·kæst member of an ancient Athenian jury. XIX. – Gr. *dikastḗs*, agent-noun f. *dikázein* judge, f. *díkē* judgement (cf. DEICTIC).

dice dais. XIV, earlier *dise, dyse, dees, dēs*, pl. of DIE[2], with the orig. pronunc. of the pl. inflexion as [s] preserved in the spec. coll. use, as in *pence.*

dichotomy daikɔ·təmi division into two parts. XVII. – Gr. *dikhotomíā*, f. *dikhótomos* cut in two, equally divided, f. *dikho-*, comb. form of *díkha* in two, rel. to *dís* (see TWICE)+ **tom-*/*témnein* cut; see -TOMY. So **dicho·to-mIZE.** XVII. **dicho·tomIST.** XVI (Marlowe).

dick[1] dik (sl.) short for DICTIONARY, (hence) fine language, long words. XIX.

dick[2] dik (sl.) short for DEC|LARATION (e.g. *take one's dick*, i.e. one's oath); hence perh. sl. phr. *up to Dick*, up to the proper standard. XIX.

dickens di·kinz euph. substitute for *devil*. XVI (Sh.). prob. a fanciful use of the personal name *Dickens*, f. *Dicken, Dickon*, dim. of *Dick*, alteration of *Rick*, pet-form of *Rickard, Richard*; cf. the use of *Old Harry* and *the Lord Harry, Old Nick*, for the Devil.

dicker di·kəɹ ten, esp. of hides. ME. *dyker* (XII), in latinized forms *dicra* (Domesday Book), *dikra, dicora*, points to an OE. **dicor*, corr. to MLG. *dēker*, MHG. *techer*, (also mod.) *decher* :- WGerm. **decura* – L. *decuria* set of ten (cf. DECURION), which is found as early as III as a measure of hides; the adoption of the term by the Germans is accounted for by the exaction of tributes of skins by the Romans (cf. Tacitus 'Annals' IV 72) and by the frontier trade in skins between the Romans and the northern nations. Hence (perh.) **di·cker** vb. (U.S.) trade by barter, haggle. XIX; a use supposed to be due to the bartering of skins on the N. American frontier.

dicky[1] di·ki he-ass, donkey; †under-petticoat XVIII; driver's or rear seat in a carriage; detached shirt-front; small bird (also *dicky-bird*) XIX. dim. of the proper name *Dick* (cf. DICKENS); see -Y[6].

dicky[2] di·ki (colloq.) shaky, insecure, 'queer'; feeling ill XVIII (Grose, 'It's all Dickey with him'). perh. orig. f. *Dick* in phr. 'I am as queer as Dick's hatband' (Grose); see -Y[1].

dicotyledon dai:kətilī·dən (bot.) flowering plant having two seed-lobes. XVIII. – modL. pl. *dīcotylēdones* (Ray); see DI-, COTYLEDON.

dictaphone di·ktəfoun machine which records and reproduces words received by it. XX (1907). irreg. f. DICTATE + *-phone* of GRAMOPHONE.

dictate diktei·t utter aloud (something to be written down); lay down authoritatively. XVII. f. *dictāt-*, pa. ppl. stem of L. *dictāre* pronounce, prescribe, frequent. f. *dīcere* say (see DICTION). The earlier stressing was *di·ctate*. So **di·ctate** sb. XVI (Hooker). – L. *dictātum*, sb. use of n. pp. of *dictāre*, usu. in pl. *dictāta* rules, precepts. **dicta·TION**. XVII. – late L. **dictA·TOR** ruler with absolute authority. XIV (Trevisa). – L. *dictātor*.

diction di·kʃən †word, phrase XV; choice of phraseology, wording XVII (Dryden). – (O)F. *diction* or L. *dictiō(n-)* saying, mode of expression, (later) word, f. *dict-*, pp. stem of *dīcere* say, rel. to Gr. *deiknúnai* show (cf. DEICTIC), *díkē* justice, Goth. *gateihan* announce, OHG. *zīhan* (G. *zeihen*), OE. *tēon* (:- **teohan*) accuse, ON. *tjá* show, tell; see -TION. ¶ Other derivs. of L. *dīc-* are *abdicate, dedicate, indicate, predicate, vindicate*, with corr. sbs. in *-ation*; *juridical*; *addict, interdict, predict*; *benediction, indiction, jurisdiction, malediction, prediction*; *dictionary*; *dictate, dictum*; *condition*; *index*; *judge*.

dictionary di·kʃənəri book treating the words of a language or an author, their forms and uses. XVI. – medL. *dictiōnārium* (sc. *manuāle* MANUAL) and *dictiōnārius* (sc. *liber* book), f. L. *dictiō* phrase, word; see DICTION, -ARY. ¶ *Dictionarius* was used *c.* 1225 by the Englishman Joannes de Garlandia for a collection of L. words arranged according to subject, and in XIV the Frenchman Peter Berchorius (Pierre Bersuire) wrote a 'Dictionarium morale utriusque testamenti', containing 3,514 words used in the Vulgate, with moral expositions.

dictum di·ktəm saying, utterance. XVI (rare in gen. sense before XVIII). L. 'thing said', sb. use of pp. n. of *dīcere* (see DICTION); repr. earlier (XVI) by †*diton* – F. *dicton*.

didactic didæ·ktik, dai- pert. to a teacher or teaching. XVII. – Gr. *didaktikós*, f. stem *didak-* of *didáskein* teach (cf. DISCIPLE), perh. after F. *didactique*; see -IC.

didapper dai·dæpəɹ dabchick. XV. Reduced form of *dive-dapper* (not recorded so early), extension of *dive-dap* :- OE. **dȳfedoppa*, parallel to *dūfedoppa*.

diddle di·dl (colloq.) cheat, swindle. XIX. prob. back-formation from *diddler* swindler.

didymium didi·miəm (chem.) metallic element. XIX. modL., f. Gr. *dídumos* twin + -IUM; so called from its close association with lanthanium.

die[1] dai cease to live. XII. ME. *deȝen* (Orm *deȝenn*), *deiȝen, deye*, pt. *de(i)ȝede, deide*, of disputed origin: two hypotheses are admissible: (i) that the ME. forms repr. unrecorded OE. **dīeġan*, **dēġan* = OS. *dōian*, OHG. *touwan* (MHG. *töuwen*), ON. *deyja* (in which the orig. strong conjugation is preserved, pt. *dó*, pp. *dáinn*; in the other langs. the vb. is weak) :- Germ. **dawjan* (pt. **dōw*, pp. **dawan-*), f. **daw-*, repr. also in DEAD, DEATH, and Goth. *af|dauiþs* vexed, rel. by gradation to *diwans* mortal, *un|diwanei* immortality; but it is more likely (ii) that the ME. forms were immed. – ON. *deyja* (OSw. *döia*, ODa. *döie*; Sw. *dö*, Da. *döe*). ¶ The tendency of the uncompounded vb. to disappear is illustrated in all the Germ. langs. but Norse; in OE. the words for 'die' were *steorfan, sweltan*, or *wesan dēad*, pt. *wæs dēad* ('be, was dead'). For the development of *die* from ME. *dēȝe*, cf. *dye, eye, high, nigh, thigh*, etc.

die[2] dai pl. **dice** dais cube with sides marked 1, 2, 3, 4, 5, 6, used in games of chance. XIII. ME. *dē, dee*, pl. *dēs, dees* – (O)F. *dé*, pl. *dés* = Pr. *dat*, Sp., It. *dado* :- L. (Rom.) *datum*, sb. use of n. pp. of *dare* give (cf. DATE[1]), spec. play, as in *calculum dare* play a 'man'.

diesis dai·ǐsis (mus.) applied to several intervals smaller than a tone XVI (Morley); (typogr.) double-dagger ‡, which was formerly used to denote a diesis (cf. F. *dièse* sign of a sharp ♯) XVIII. – L. *diesis* – Gr. *díesis*, f. *diïénai* send through, f. *diá* DIA- + *hiénai* send.

dies non dai·īz nɔn day on which no legal business is transacted or which is not reckoned in counting days for legal or other purposes. XIX. Short for legal L. *diēs nōn jūridicus* day not set apart for the administration of justice (cf. JURIDICAL).

diet[1] dai·ət food XIII; customary or prescribed course of food XIV (Ch.). – (O)F. *diète* = Pr., Sp., It. *dieta* – L. *diæta* – Gr. *díaita* course of life. Hence **di·et** vb. XIV; after OF. *dieter*, medL. *diætāre*. **di·et**ARY course of diet. XV. – medL. *diætārium.*

diet[2] dai·ət †day's journey; appointed day or time, meeting, session XV; metal scraped from gold and silver plate assayed day by day at the Mint XVII. – medL. *diēta* day's journey, allowance, work, wages; assoc. with L. *diēs* day, and consequently divorced from prec.

dif- assim. form of DIS- before *f*, as in L. *differre* DIFFER. In Rom. it became *def-*, which in OF. was reduced to *de-*, and this appears in DEFER, DEFY.

differ di·fəɹ have contrary qualities or tendencies XIV (Ch.); be at variance XVI. – (O)F. *différer* (i) put off, DEFER, (ii) be different – L. *differre* (i) bear apart, spread abroad, delay, (ii) tend apart, differ, f. *dis-* DIS- 1 + *ferre* carry, BEAR[2]. The final differentiation of *differ* from DEFER[1] in meaning and pronunc. is due to assoc. with *different.* So **di·ffer**ENT. XIV. – (O)F. *différent* – L. *differēns.* **di·ffer**ENCE. XIV. – (O)F. – L. **differe·nt**IAL. XVII. **differe·nti**ATE[3], -A·TION. XIX. – medL. *differentiāre*; cf. F. *différencier, -entier.*

difficult di·fikəlt not easy, hard XIV; hard to please XVI (from XIX largely replaced by F. *difficile*). Back-formation from *difficulty*, from which a form †*difficul* (XV–XVII) was also derived, and used beside †*difficil* (– F. *difficile*, L. *difficilis*, f. *dis-* DIS- 2 + *facilis* easy, FACILE). **di·fficulty**)(*ease* (Wycl. Bible, Trevisa); something hard to understand XIV (Ch.); reluctance XV. – L. *difficultās*, f. *dis-* DIF- + *facultās* FACULTY; partly through (O)F. *difficulté.*

diffident di·fidənt †distrustful XV; wanting in self-confidence XVIII. – L. *diffīdent-*, *-ēns*, prp. of *diffīdere* mistrust, f. *dis-* DIS- 2 + *fīdere* trust, rel. to *fīdes* FAITH; see -ENT. So **di·ffid**ENCE. XV. – F. or L.

diffraction difræ·kʃən (optics) breaking up of a beam of light. XVII. – F. *diffraction* or modL. *diffractio* (Grimaldi, 1665), f. *diffract-*, pp. stem of *diffringere* break in pieces, f. *dis-* DIF- + *frangere* (see FRACTION).

diffuse difjū·s †confused, indistinct XV;)(*confined* and *condensed* XVIII. – F. *diffus* (fem. *-use*) or L. *diffūsus* extensive, ample, prolix, pp. of *diffundere* pour out or abroad, f. *dis-* DIF- + *fundere* pour. So **diffuse** difjū·z pour or spread abroad. XVI. f. *diffūs-*, pp. stem of *diffundere.* **diffu·**SION †outpouring XIV; spreading abroad XVI; permeation of a fluid by another XVIII. – L.

dig dig make holes in and turn up (the ground) XIII ('Orfeo'); make (a hole) as with a spade; excavate XIV. ME. *digge*, perh. :– OE. **dīcigian*, f. *dīc* DITCH; superseded *delve* and *grave* (OE. *grafan*), orig. conjugated weak (*digged*), as always in Sh., A.V., and Milton; the new *dug* appears XVI (cf. *stuck*, pt. of *stick*). ¶ Chronology and meaning are against deriv. from F. *diguer* furnish with *dikes* (XV), also, spur (a horse), prod, stab.

digamma daigæ·mə Gr. letter ϝ, so called by grammarians of the first century A.D. from its shape, which suggests a combination of two gammas (see DI-, GAMMA) set one above the other. XVII. – L. – Gr. *dígamma.*

digest dai·dʒest methodical or systematic compendium. XIV (orig. of the Digest or Pandects of the Emperor Justinian; later gen.). – L. *dīgesta* 'matters methodically arranged', n. pl. of *dīgestus*, pp. of *dīgerere* divide, distribute, dissolve, digest, f. *dī-* DI-[1] + *gerere* carry (see GERUND). So **digest** di-, daidʒe·st arrange methodically; assimilate (food) in the body XV. f. *dīgest-*, pp. stem of *dīgerere.* **dige·**STION. digesting of food XIV (Ch., Trevisa); etc. – (O)F. – L. ¶ In XVI–XVII *disgest, disgestion* were also current.

dight dait †appoint, ordain; †compose, make OE.; †deal with; † put in order, equip; (arch. or dial.) dress, array, prepare, put to rights XIII. OE. *dihtan* direct, command, appoint, arrange, compose, write, corr. to MLG., MDu. *dichten* compose, institute, contrive (Du. *dichten* invent, compose, versify), OHG. *tichtōn* (G. *dichten*) write, compose verses, ON. *dikta* compose in Latin, invent, contrive – L. *dictāre* appoint, prescribe, DICTATE, in medL. write, compose. ¶ The wide development of this vb. in ME. is repr. in mod. dial. by such specialized applications as 'polish, burnish, smooth', 'winnow', 'wipe'. In the mod. literary lang. used mainly in the contracted pp. *dight*, which was revived by Scott, prob. from Spenser or Milton, after a century of desuetude.

digit di·dʒit any numeral below 10, any of the ten Arabic figures XV; $\frac{1}{12}$ of the diameter of sun or moon XVI; finger, toe; finger's breadth XVII. – L. *digitus* finger, toe, prob. for **dicitus* 'the pointer' and rel. to TOE.

digitalis didʒitei·lis plant of the foxglove family XVII; drug prepared from this XVIII. – modL. (Fuchs, 1542), sb. use (sc. *herba* plant) of L. *digitālis* pert. to the finger, after the G. name of the foxglove, *fingerhut* thimble, lit. 'finger-hat'.

dignify di·gnifai give dignity to. XV. – F. *dignifier* – late L. *dignificāre*; see next and -FY. Frequent in pp. from XIX in sense 'marked by dignity'.

dignity di·gnĭti worth, nobility, honourable estate or office XIII; nobility or gravity of manner XVII (Milton). ME. *dignete*, – OF. *dignete* (mod. *dignité*, with latinized spelling) – L. *dignitās*, f. *dignus* worthy (:– **decnos* fitting, f. *decet* it is fitting or DECENT); see -ITY. Hence **di·gnit**ARY. XVII; after *proprietary*. ¶ From the same base are *condign, dainty, deign, disdain, indignant*.

digraph dai·gràf group of two letters representing one sound. XVIII. f. Gr. *di-* twice, DI-² + *graphḗ* writing (cf. -GRAPHY).

digress daigre·s deviate from a course or from one's subject. XVI (Palsgr.). f. *dīgress-*, pp. stem of L. *dīgredī*, f. *dī-* DI-¹ + *gradī* step, walk, f. *gradus* step (see GRADE). So **digre·s**SION. XIV (Ch.). – (O)F. – L.

dike, dyke daik A. (dial.) ditch XIII; B. embankment XV. – ON. *dík, díki* or MLG. *dīk* dam, MDu. *dijc* ditch, pool, mound, dam (Du. *dijk* dam); see DITCH. In A first recorded from northern and eastern texts, in which it is prob. of Norse origin; in B prob. originating from the Low Countries in connexion with drainage works. So **dike, dyke** vb. XIV (R. Mannyng, PPl., Barbour, Ch.).

dilapidate dilæ·pideit bring (a building) to a state of decay; (arch.) squander. XVI. f. pp. stem of L. *dīlapidāre*, f. *di-* DI-¹ + *lapid-*, *lapis* stone; see LAPIDARY, -ATE³. So **dilapid**A·TION allowing a building to fall into disrepair; (arch.) squandering. XV. – late L. ¶ The application to the deterioration of ecclesiastical property, which is predominant, depends on an etymological interpretation not found in the orig. L. words, which denote wasteful expenditure, squandering, the sense retained in F. *dilapider, -dation*.

dilate dailei·t A. †relate at length XIV (Gower); discourse at large *upon* XVI; B. make wider XV; become wider, expand XVII. – (O)F. *dilater* – L. *dīlātāre* spread out, f. *dī-* DI-¹ + *lātus* wide (cf. LATITUDE). So **dilat**A·TION. XIV (Ch.) – OF. – late L. (cf. Sp. *dilatación*); largely superseded by the shorter **dila·**TION XV, which is improperly formed, as if *dilate* contained the suffix -ATE³; cf. It. *dilazione* and *coercion*.

dilatory di·lətəri tending to cause delay XV; given to delaying XVII. – late L. *dīlātōrius*, f. *dīlātōr* delayer, f. *dīlāt-*, pp. stem of *diferre* DEFER; see -ORY.

dilemma dai-, dile·mə form of argument involving the opponent in the choice of alternatives; choice between two equally unfavourable alternatives. XVI. – L. *dilemma* – Gr. *dílēmma*, f. *di-* DI-² + *lêmma* assumption, premiss (see LEMMA).

dilettante dilitæ·nti amateur of the fine arts; (later) mere amateur. XVIII. It. 'lover (of music or painting)', sb. use of prp. of *dilettare* :– L. *dēlectāre* DELIGHT; see -ANT.

diligent di·lidʒənt constant or persistent in endeavour. XIV. – (O)F. *diligent* – L. *dīligent-, -ēns* assiduous, attentive, adj. use of prp. of *dīligere* esteem highly, love, choose, take delight in, f. *dī-* DI-¹ + *-legere* (as in *neglegere* NEGLECT), prob. rel. to Gr. *alégein* be concerned about, *álgos* pain. So **di·li**GENCE †careful attention; constant endeavour XIV; †dispatch, haste XV. – (O)F. *diligence* – L. *dīligentia*. ¶ As the designation of a public stage-coach *diligence* is a mod. adoption (XVIII) of F. *diligence*, short for *carrosse de diligence* 'coach of speed'; the clipped form *dilly* (XVIII) was formerly used for this, and survives dial. for various kinds of carts, trucks, etc., used in agricultural and industrial operations.

dill dil the plant Anethum graveolens, having carminative properties. OE. *dile* and *dyle*, corr. to OS. *dilli* (Du. *dille*), OHG. *tilli* (G. *dill* from LG.), and MDu. *dulle*, MHG. *tülle*, ON. *dylla*; of unkn. origin.

dillenia dilī·niə genus of E. Indian plants. XVIII. modL., f. name of J. J. *Dillenius*, professor of botany at Oxford 1728–47; see -IA¹.

dilly see DILIGENCE.

dilly-dally di·lidæ:li expressive of vacillation. XVII. redupl., with variation of vowel, of DALLY.

dilute dailjū·t, di- weaken by adding water, etc. XVI. f. *dīlūt-*, pp. stem of L. *dīluere* wash away, dissolve, f. *dī-* DI-¹ + *-luere*, comb. form of *lavāre* wash, LAVE. Hence **dilu·**TION. XVII (Sir T. Browne).

diluvial diljū·viəl pert. to the Flood XVII; (geol.) caused by extraordinary action of water on a large scale XIX. – late L. *dīluviālis*, f. *dīluvium* flood, DELUGE. So **dilu·**VIAN. XVII.

dim dim not clear or bright. OE. *dim(m)* = OFris. *dim*, ON. *dimmr*, rel. to synon. OHG. *timbar* (MHG., mod. dial. *timmer*), OSw. *dimber*, OIr. *dem* black, dark. Hence **dim** vb. XIII; in OE. comps. *ādimmian, fordimmian*, corr. to ON. *dimma* darken.

dime daim †tenth part XIV; $\frac{1}{10}$ of a dollar XVIII. – (O)F. *dime*, †*disme* :– L. *decima* tithe, sb. use (sc. *pars* part) of fem. of *decimus* TENTH.

dimension di-, daime·nʃən measurement, measure. XIV (Trev.). – F. *dimension* – L. *dīmensiō(n-)*, f. *dīmens-*, pp. stem of *dīmetīrī*; see DI-¹ and MEASURE.

dimidiation dimidiei·ʃən halving. XV. – L. *dīmidiātiō(n-)*, f. *dīmidiāt-*, *-āre*, f. *dīmidium* half (cf. DEMY), f. *dī-* DI-¹ + *medius* middle, MID; see -ATION.

diminish dimi·niʃ make smaller, lessen. XV. Resulting from a conflation of †*diminue* XIV (– (O)F. *diminuer* – L. *dīminuere*) and MINISH. In Rom. the prefix has taken the form of DI-¹ (cf. Pr., Sp. *diminuir*, It. *diminuire*); but L. *dīminuere* means 'break up small'. So **diminu·**TION. XIV. – (O)F. *diminution* – L. *dīminūtiō(n)-*, late form of *dēminūtiō*. **dimi·nut**IVE. XIV (as sb. in gram.). – (O)F. *diminutif* – late L. *dī-*, *dēminūtīvus*.

dimissory dimi·səri authorizing dismissal or mission. XIV. – late L. *dīmissōrius* (in *litteræ dimissoriæ*), f. *dīmiss-*, *dīmittere*; see DISMISS.

dimity di·miti stout cotton fabric. XV (*demyt*). – It. *dimito* or medL. *dimitum* – Gr. *dímitos*, f. *dís* DI-[2]+*mítos* thread of the warp; the origin of the final syll. is unkn.

dimorphous daimɔ̄·ɹfəs existing or occurring in two forms. XIX. f. Gr. *dímorphos*, f. *dís* DI-[2]+*morphḗ* form; see -MORPH, -OUS. So **dimo·rphIC** (Darwin).

dimple di·mpl †hollow in the ground XIII; small hollow in the cheek or chin XIV. In place-names (XIII) occurring as *dimpel*, *dympel*, prob. repr. OE. **dympel*, corr. to OHG. *tumphilo* (MHG. *tümpfel*, G. *tümpel*) deep place in water, f. Germ. **dump-*, perh. nasalized form of **dup-* **deup-* DEEP; cf. Eng. dial. *dump* deep hole in pond or river-bed, Norw. *dump* pit, pool, MLG. *dümpelen*, Du. *dompelen* dive, the IE. base of which, **dhumb-*, appears in Lith. *dumbù*, *dùbti* become hollow or deep; see -LE[1].

din din loud noise. OE. *dyne* (:– **duniz*) and *dynn*, corr. to OHG. *tuni*, ON. *dynr* (:– **dunjaz*, *-uz*). So **din** vb. †sing, resound OE.; assail with din, make resound, make a din XVII. OE. *dynian* = OS. *dunian*, MHG. *tünen* roar, rumble, ON. *dynja* come rumbling down, gush, pour :– Germ. **dunjan*. The IE. base **dhun-* is repr. also by Skr. *dhúnis* roaring, Lith. *dundéti* sound.

dinar dīnā·ɹ name of various Oriental coins. XVII. – Arab., Pers. *dīnār* – late Gr. *dēnárion* – L. *dēnārius* (cf. DENIER).

dinder di·ndəɹ denarius or other small coin found on ancient Roman sites, e.g. at Wroxeter. XVIII. var. of *di·nneere*, *de·neere*, DENIER.

dine dain take the principal meal of the day. XIII (RGlouc.). – (O)F. *diner*, earlier *disner* (whence It. *de-*, *disinare*) = Pr. *disnar*, Cat. *dinar* :– Rom. **disjūnāre*, for **disjējūnāre* break one's fast, f. *dis-* DIS- 2+ *jējūnium* fast; see JEJUNE and cf. DÉJEUNER, DINNER.

ding diŋ deal or strike with heavy blows XIII; knock, dash *down*, etc. XIV. prob. of Scand. origin (cf. ON. *dengja* hammer, whet a scythe; (corr. to OE. *dengan* beat, whence dial. *dinge*), OSw. *dängia*, Da. *dænge* beat, bang), corr. to G. *dengeln* whet a scythe, MHG *tengeln*. Conjugated strong in Sc. and north. dial., after *fling*, *sing*.

ding-dong di·ŋdɔ·ŋ redupl. form imit. of the tolling of a bell. XVI.

dinghy, dingey di·ŋgi native Indian rowing-boat; (gen.) small rowing-boat. XIX. – Hindi *ḍiṅgī*, *ḍeṅgī*, dim. of *ḍēṅgā*, *ḍōṅgā* larger kind of boat, sloop, coasting-vessel. The sp. with *gh* is used to indicate pronunc. with g.

dingle di·ŋgl deep hollow, deep narrow cleft; (in literary use, after Milton's 'Comus' 311) dell shaded with trees. XIII (*sea dingle*, in the w. midl. 'Sawles Warde'; not otherwise recorded in literature till Drayton, a Warwickshire man, but occurring in place-names of Lancs and Worcs XIII, and poss. in *Dinglei* of Domesday Book). perh. a dim. form (see -LE[1]); cf. the synon. (dial.) *dimble* (XVI) and DIMPLE; ult. origin unkn.

dingo di·ŋgou wild dog of Australia. XVIII. Native name; cf. *jūnghō* (George's River), *jūgūng* (Turuwul, Botany Bay).

dingy di·nᵈʒi (dial.) dirty; of dark and dull colour or appearance. XVIII. prob. in dial. use long before it is recorded, and perh. to be referred ult. to OE. *dynġe* dung, manured land, f. *dung* DUNG; see -Y[1].

dinky di·ŋki (colloq.) neat, spruce. XIX. f. Sc. and north. *dink* decked out, trim (XVI); of unkn. origin; see -Y[1].

dinner di·nəɹ chief meal of the day. XIII (RGlouc., Cursor M.). ME. *diner* – (O)F. *dîner*, sb. use of *dîner* DINE; see -ER[4].

din(o)- dain(ou) comb. form in modL. terms of Gr. *deinós* terrible (cf. DIRE), denoting certain huge extinct animals, as **dino·rnis** moa (Gr. *órnis* bird) 1843, **di·nosaur** saurian reptile (Gr. *saûros* lizard) 1841, **di·nothere** proboscidean quadruped (Gr. *thēríon* wild beast) 1835.

dint dint †stroke, blow OE.; force of attack or impact XIV (R. Mannyng); (by assoc. with *dent*, *indent*) mark made by a blow, dent XVI. OE. *dynt*, reinforced in ME. by the rel. ON. *dyntr* (*dyttr*), *dynta*. Phr. †*by dint of sword* (XIV–XVIII); *by dint* (earlier *dent* XVI) *of*, by means of XVII. So **dint** vb. XIII (Cursor M., Havelok). – ON. *dynta* (*dytta*).

diocese dai·əsis, -sīs bishop's sphere of jurisdiction. XIV. ME. *diocise* – OF. *diocise* (mod. *diocèse*) = Pr. *diocesa*, *diocezi*, Sp. *diocesis*, It. *diocesi* – late L. *diocēsis*, for L. *diœcēsis* governor's jurisdiction, district, (eccl.) diocese – Gr. *dioíkēsis* administration, government, (Roman) province, (eccl.) diocese, f. *dioikeîn* keep house, administer, f. *di(a)-* thoroughly, through+*oikeîn* inhabit, manage, f. *oîkos* house (cf. WICK[2]). By assim. to L. the F. form became *dioces*, later *diocèse*, and the Eng. forms followed the same course; *diocess* was the prevalent form from XVI, and was retained by some even in XIX (e.g. in The Times). So **diocesAN** daiɔ·sisən pert. to a diocese; sb. bishop. XV. – F. *diocésain* – late L. *diocēsānus*.

diœcious daiī·ʃəs (bot.) having the two sexes in separate individuals. XVIII. f. modL. *Diœcia* (1735) twenty-second class in Linnæus's sexual system of plants – Gr. type **dioikía*, f. **díoikos* having two houses, f. *di-* DI-[2]+*oîkos* house; see -IOUS.

Dionysiac daiŏni·siæk pert. to Dionysus (Bacchus). XIX. – late L. *Dionȳsiacus* – Gr. *Dionūsiakós*, f. *Diónūsos* god of wine; see -AC. In F. *-iaque*. So **Diony·SIAN** (i) in same sense XVII; (ii) pert. to Abbot Dionysius the Little (VI A.D.), who is said to have first dated events from the birth of Christ, of which he fixed the accepted date XVIII. f. L. *Dionȳsius*, adj. of *Dionȳsus*, and the personal name *Dionȳsius*.

diorama daiŏrà·mə see PANORAMA.

dip dip let down into liquid OE.; go down, sink XIV; have a downward inclination XVII. OE. *dyppan* (pt. *dypte*, pp. *dypped*) :- **dupjan*, f. **dup*- **deup*- (see DEEP). Hence **dip** sb. act of dipping XVI; depression; downward inclination XVIII; in full *dip-candle* XIX.

diphtheria difþiə·riə infectious disease affecting chiefly the throat. 1851 (in Dunglison); became current when 'Boulogne sore throat' was epidemic in 1857–8). – modL. – F. *diphthérie* (now *diphtérie*), substituted by Pierre Bretonneau (of Tours, d. 1862) for his earlier *diphthérite* (modL. *diphtherītis*, which was used in Eng.), f. Gr. *diphthérā*, *diphtherís* skin, hide, piece of leather; so named on account of the tough membrane which forms on parts affected by the disease. Hence **diphtheri**·TIC, which is preferred to *diphthe·ric*.

diphthong di·fþoŋ combination of two adjacent vowels or 'vowel-likes' in one syllable XV; used loosely for *digraph* and for the ligatures *æ*, *œ* XVI. In early use often *dipthong* – F. *dipthongue*, †*dypthongue* – L. *diphthongus* (late *dipthongus*) – Gr. *díphthoggos*, f. *dís* DI-² + *phthóggos* voice, sound.

diplo- di·plou comb. form of Gr. *diploûs* twofold, double (see DI-² and FOLD¹), used in techn. terms from XVIII.

diploma diplou·mə official document of state or church; document conferring an honour, privilege, or licence. XVII. – L. *diplōma* – Gr. *díplōma* folded paper, letter of recommendation or conveying a licence or privilege, f. *diploûn* double, fold, f. *diploûs* DOUBLE.

diplomacy diplou·məsi management of international relations by negotiation XVIII; skill in such dealings XIX. – F. *diplomatie*, f. *diplomatique*, after *aristocratie*, *-cratique*. **diplomat**IC diplŏmæ·tik pert. to original official documents; concerned with diplomacy. XVIII. In the former sense – modL. *diplōmaticus* (in Mabillon's 'De re diplomatica', 1681), f. L. *diplōmat*-, DIPLOMA; in the latter sense – F. *diplomatique*, which was so used at the time of the French Revolution (e.g. in *corps diplomatique* body of officials attached to foreign legations). The transition of sense originated from such titles as the 'Codex juris gentium diplomaticus' of G. W. Leibnitz, 1695, and 'Corps universel diplomatique du droit des gens' of Jean Dumont, 1726, in which the word was used in its proper sense as applied to original official documents; but, as the subject-matter of these collections concerned international relations, the word itself was construed as referring directly to these. As sb. **diploma·tic** A. †diplomatist; †diplomacy XVIII; B. (also *-ics*) study of original documents XIX. A. sb. uses of the adj.; B. – F. *diplomatique*, based on modL. *rēs diplōmatica* (Mabillon, 1681). So **diplomat** di·plŏmæt. XIX. – F. *diplomate*, back-formation from *diplomatique*, after *aristocrate*, *-cratique*. **diplo·mat**IST. XIX. f. F. *diplomate* or L. stem *diplōmat*-.

dipsomania dipsoumei·niə morbid craving for strong drink. XIX. modL., f. Gr. *dípsa*, *dípsos* thirst + MANIA. So **dipsoma·ni**AC.

diptera di·ptərə two-winged flies. XIX. modL. – Gr. *díptera* (Aristotle), n. pl. of *dípteros* two-winged (f. *di*- DI-² + *pterón* wing; cf. PTERO-) used sb. (sc. *éntoma* insects). So **di·pter**OUS. XVIII.

diptych di·ptik two-leaved hinged tablet for writing. XVII. – late L. *diptycha* – late Gr. *díptukha* pair of writing-tablets, n. pl. of *díptukhos*, f. *di*- DI-² + *ptukhḗ* fold.

dire daiəɹ dreadful, terrible. XVI. – L. *dīrus*, f. base **dwei*- fear (cf. Gr. *deídein*, *déos* sb. fear, *deinós* terrible (DINO-), *deilós* afraid.

direct di-, daire·kt address (a letter or message), later spec. with the designation written on the outside XIV (Ch.); direct or instruct XV (Lydg.) prob. based immed. on pp. *direct* (Ch.) – L. *dīrectus*, pp. of *dīrigere*, *dē*- straighten, direct, guide, f. *dis*- DI-¹, *dē* DE 3 + *regere* put straight, rule (see REGENT), whence also **dire·ct** adj. straight XIV (Ch.); straightforward, immediate XVI. ¶ The sense-development of the vbs. *direct* and ADDRESS is, in consequence of their origin, closely parallel. So **dire·**CTION action of directing XV; course pursued XVII. – F. or L. **dire·**CTIVE. adj. XV, sb. XVII. – medL. **dire·**CTOR. XV. – AN. *directour* (mod. *directeur*). **dire·ct**ORY adj. serving to direct XV (Lydg.); sb. book of directions XVI; used for F. *Directoire* the executive body in France during part of the Revolution period, consisting of five *directeurs*. XVIII (Washington).

dirge dɜ̄ɹdʒ office of matins for the dead XIII; song of mourning XVI. ME. *dirige* (three syll.), later *dyrge*, *derge*, *dergie* (two syll.), the pl. of which prob. suggested a monosyllabic sg. *dirge*, which appears to be first established in late XVI; the first word of the antiphon to the first psalm in the office: '*Dirige*, Domine, Deus meus, in conspectu tuo viam meam' (cf. Psalm v 8) Direct, O Lord my God, my way in thy sight; imper. of L. *dīrigere* DIRECT.

dirigible di·ridʒĭbl that can be directed or steered. XVI. f. L. *dirigere* DIRECT + -IBLE; as applied in mod. use to aircraft, alteration of *dirigeable* (*c.* 1880) – F. *dirigeable* (1870); see -IBLE, -ABLE.

diriment di·rimənt nullifying. XIX. – L. *diriment*-, *-ēns*, prp. of *dirimere* separate, interrupt, frustrate, f. *dir*- DIS- + *emere* take (cf. EXEMPT); see -ENT.

dirk dǝ̄ɹk dagger. XVI. Earliest in Sc. *durk*, *dowrk*; the present sp. was popularized by Johnson; poss. – Da. *dirk*, *dirik*, Sw. *dyrk*, familiar form of *Diederik* (see DERRICK), used, like G. *dietrich*, LG. *dierker*, for a pick-lock; but the earliest forms and the meaning do not favour this origin.

dirt dǝ̄ɹt (dial.) ordure; unclean matter XIII; (dial.) mud, soil XVII. ME. *drit* – ON. *drit*, corr. to MDu. *drēte* (Du. *dreet*), rel. to the vbs. OE. *ġedrītan* = ON. *drīta*, MDu. *drīten* (Du. *drijten*), with poss. Balto-Sl. cogns. The present metathesized form appears XV.

dis- prefix repr. L. *dis-*, corr. to Germ. **tiz-* (OE. *te-*, *to-*, OFris., OS. *to-*, *te-*, *ti-*, OHG. *za-*, *ze-*, *zi-*) and rel. to Gr. DIA-. It was reduced to *dī-* before some voiced consonants, as in *dīligere* (see DILIGENT), *dīrigere* DIRECT, *dīvīdere* DIVIDE, became *dir-* between vowels in *dirimere* (see DIRIMENT), was assim. before *f*, as in *differre* DIFFER, *difficilis* DIFFICULT, but retained its full form before *p*, *t*, *c*, and *s*.

In Eng. *dis-* appears (i) as repr. *dis-* in words adopted direct from Latin, (ii) as repr. OF. *des-* (mod. *dés-*, *dé-*), organically developed from L. *dis-*, (iii) as repr. late L. *dis-*, Rom. **des-*, substituted for L. *dē-*, (iv) as a living prefix combined with words of no matter what origin.

As an etymol. el. *dis-* occurs (1) with the meanings 'apart', 'asunder', 'separately', as in *discern*, *discuss*, *disperse*, *dispute*, *distend*; hence (2) with privative, negative, or reversive force, as in *disaster*, *displease*, *dissuade*, or with intensive force, as in *disturb*. As a living prefix from XV with such privative or reversive force it (3) forms comp. vbs., as *disestablish* (XVI; of a church, 1838, W. E. Gladstone), *disinter*, *disown*, (4) with sbs. forms vbs. meaning to strip, rid, free or deprive of a quality or character, or reverse a condition, as *dischurch*, *disrobe*, (5) with adjs. forms vbs., as *disable*, (6) with sbs. expresses the reverse or lack of, as *disquiet*, *disrepute*, *disregard*, *disservice*, *disunion*, (7) with adjs. expresses the negative or opposite, as *discourteous*, *disreputable*, and (8) is used with intensive force, as *disannul*. *Dis-* has sometimes replaced earlier *mis-*, as in *dislike*.

disabi·lity incapacity. XVI. DIS- 6. **disable** disei·bl make unable or incapable, incapacitate. XV. DIS- 5. **disabu·se** undeceive. XVII. DIS- 3, 4. **disadva·ntage.** XIV (Wyclif, Trevisa). – (O)F. *désavantage*; DIS- 2. **disaffe·ct** †dislike; (esp. in pp.) alienate the friendship or loyalty of. XVII. DIS- 3. **disaffo·rest** free from the operation of the forest laws. XVI. – AL. *disafforestāre*; DIS- 2. Syns. *de-afforest* (XVII), *deforest* (XVI), *disforest* (XVI). **disagree·** fail or refuse to agree. XV. – (O)F. *désagréer*; DIS- 2. **disallow·** refuse to allow, †approve, accept, acknowledge. XIV (PPl., Gower). – OF. *desalouer*; DIS- 2.

disappear disəpiə·ɹ cease to be visible or present. XV (Lydg.). f. DIS- 3+APPEAR, after F. *disparaître*, the lengthened stem of which, *disparaiss-*, was repr. by †*disparish* XV. ¶ Not in Sh. or A.V. Hence **disappea·rance.** XVIII.

disappoint disəpoi·nt deprive of appointment; frustrate the expectation or fulfilment of. XV. – (O)F. *désappointer*, f. *des-* DIS- 2+ *appointer* APPOINT. Hence **disappoi·ntment.** XVII. ¶ *Disappointed* in Sh. 'Hamlet' I v 77 means 'improperly appointed', 'unprepared'.

disarm disā·ɹm deprive of arms or armament XIV (Ch., fig. tr. L. *exarmare*); reduce to a peace footing XVIII. – (O)F. *désarmer*; see DIS- 2 and ARMS. So **disa·rmament.** XVIII; after F. *désarmement*.

disarray· (arch.) disorder. XIV (in MSS. of Ch., varying with *desray*). – AN. **desarei*, OF. *desaroi*; DIS- 2, ARRAY.

disaster dizā·stəɹ sudden or great calamity. XVI. – F. *désastre* or its source It. *disastro*, f. *dis-* DIS- 2+*astro* (:– L. *astrum*) STAR; lit. 'unfavourable aspect of a star' (cf. *disasters in the sun*, Sh. 'Hamlet' I i 118); cf. Pr., Sp. *desastre*, and Pr. *benastre* good fortune, *malastre* ill fortune, and Eng. *ill-starred* (Sh.). So **disa·strous** †ill-starred, ill-boding XVI; calamitous XVII. – F. *désastreux* – It. *disastroso*; in early use competing with †*disaster* adj., †*disastered* – F. †*désastré* – It. *disastrato*.

disband disbæ·nd break up (as) a band of soldiers. XVI. – F. †*desbander* (mod. *dé-*), f. *des-* DIS- 1+BAND[3], after It. *sbandare*.

disbelie·f want of belief. XVII. DIS- 6. So **disbelie·ve** not to believe. XVII. DIS- 3; superseded *misbelief* (XIII), *-believe* (XIV). **disbu·rden.** XVI. DIS- 4.

disburse disbǝ̄·ɹs pay out. XVI. – OF. *desbourser* (mod. *débourser*, whence †*deburse* XVI), f. *des-* DIS- 2+*bourse* PURSE.

disc, disk disk 'flat' surface of the sun, etc. XVII; discus; circular plate; round and flattened part XVIII. – F. *disque* or its source L. DISCUS.

discard diskā·ɹd reject (a card) from the hand; cast off, abandon, dismiss. XVI. f. DIS- 4+CARD[1], after F. †*descarter*, †*decarter* (whence earlier Eng. †*decard* XVI), which was prob. modelled on It. *scartare* (or Sp. *descartar*).

discern disǝ̄·ɹn, diz- distinguish by the intellect or the vision. XIV. – (O)F. *discerner* – L. *discernere* separate, divide, distinguish, f. *dis-* DIS- 1+*cernere* separate, rel. to Gr. *krínein* (see CRISIS).

discharge distʃā·ɹdʒ disburden, relieve XIV; remove (a charge) XV; acquit oneself of XVI. ME. *descharge* – OF. *descharger* (mod. *décharger*) = Pr., Sp. *descargar*, It. *scaricare*, Rum. *descarca* :– Rom. **discarricāre*; see DIS- 2 and CHARGE. Hence **discha·rge** sb. XV; cf. OF. *descharge* (mod. *dé-*).

disciple disai·pl follower of a doctrine, pupil. OE. *discipul* – L. *discipulus* learner, f. *discere* learn, rel. to *docēre* teach (see DOCTOR); reinforced in ME. by OF. *deciple*; later conformed to the L. sp.

discipline di·siplin chastisement, penitential correction XIII (AncrR.); †instruction, schooling; branch of learning XIV; training in action or conduct XV; system of control over conduct XVI. – OF. *discipline*, †*dece-*, †*des(c)e-* – L. *disciplīna*, f. *discipulus* (see prec.). So **discipli·nARY**. XVI. – medL. *disciplinārius*. **disciplinA·RIAN** XVI.

disclaim disklei·m renounce a claim. XVI. – legal AN. *desclaim-*, tonic stem of *desclamer* (AL. *disclāmāre*), f. *des-* DIS- 2+*clamer* CLAIM. So **disclai·mER**[4] disavowal of a claim. XV. – AN. *disclaimer*, sb. use of inf.

disclose disklou·z uncover, open up to the knowledge of others. XIV (Gower). f. OF. *desclos-*, pres. stem of *desclore* = Pr. *desclaure* :– Gallo-Rom. **disclaudere*; see DIS- 2, CLOSE. Hence **disclo·SURE**. XVI.

discobolus diskɔ·bələs thrower of the discus. XVIII. L. – Gr. *diskobólos*, f. *dískos* DISCUS+**bol-*, var. of base of *bállein* throw (cf. BALLISTA).

disco·lour alter or spoil the colour of. XIV (Wyclif; pp. Gower). – OF. *descolorer* or medL. *discolōrāre*; DIS- 2. So **dis**COLORA·TION. XVII (H. More).

discomfit diskʌ·mfit defeat utterly; thwart, disconcert. XIV. ME. *disconfite*, based on pp. *disconfit* (XIII) – OF. *desconfit*, pp. of *desconfire* (mod. *déconfire*) = Pr. *desconfir*, It. *disconfiggere* :– Rom. **disconficere*, f. DIS- 2+*conficere* put together, frame, complete, finish off, destroy, consume (which in Rom. retained the constructive sense; see CONFECTION). So **disco·mfit**URE. XIV. – OF. *desconfiture* = Pr. *desconfitura*, etc.

disco·MFORT †discouragement, †distress, desolation XIV (Barbour, Ch., Wycl. Bible); being uncomfortable XIX. – OF. *desconfort* (mod. *dé-*). So vb. XIV (RGlouc., R. Mannyng). – OF. *desconforter*. See DIS- 2, 6.

discommon diskɔ·mən †deprive of membership of a community XV; (in universities of Oxford and Cambridge) deprive (a tradesman) of the privilege of dealing with undergraduates; deprive of the right of common or the character of common land. XVI. f. DIS- 4+COMMON. So **disco·mmons** deprive of commons; discommon (a tradesman). XIX. †**disco·mmune** discommon. XVI; after medL. *discommūnicāre*.

disconcert diskənsə̄·ɹt throw into confusion, derange XVII; 'put out' XVIII. – F. †*desconcerter* (mod. *dé-*), f. *des-* DIS- 2+*concerter* CONCERT.

disconsolate diskɔ·nsələt comfortless, cheerless. XIV (Ch.). – medL. *disconsōlātus*, f. L. *dis-* DIS- 2+*consōlātus*, pp. of *consōlārī* CONSOLE.

disconti·nue cause to cease; cease XV. – (O)F. *discontinuer*; DIS- 2. So **disconti·nuance**. XIV (Trevisa). – AN. **disconti·nuous**. XVII (Milton).

discord di·skɔ̄ɹd want of harmony, variance XIII (AncrR., RGlouc.); (mus.) XV (Lydg.). – OF. *descord*, *discord*, f. *des-*, *discorder* – L. *discordāre* be at variance, f. *discord-*, *discors* discordant, f. *dis-* DIS- 2+*cord-*, *cor* HEART. So **disco·rd**ANT. XIV (Ch.). – OF. *des-*, *discordant*.

discount di·skaunt †abatement, deduction; (prob. after It. *sconto*, whence F. *escompte*) deduction made for payment before the due time. XVII. – F. †*descompte* (modern *décompte*), f. *descompter*, whence, if not direct from It. *(di)scontare*, **discou·nt** vb. XVII. See DIS- 2, COUNT[2].

discou·ntenance discourage, disfavour. XVI (Sidney, Spenser). See DIS- 2, 4; partly after F. †*descontenancer*.

discou·rage damp the courage of. XV. – OF. *descourager* (mod. *dé-*); see DIS- 2, 4, COURAGE.

discourse di·skɔ̄(ə)ɹs †reasoning XIV (Ch.); (arch.) conversation, talk; treatment of a subject; †course XVI. ME. *discours* – L. *discursus* running to and fro, (late) intercourse, (med.) argument (whence F. *discours* (XVI), f. *discurs-*, pp. stem of *discurrere* run to and fro, (late) speak at length, f. *dis-* DIS- 1+*currere* run; assim. in form to COURSE. Hence **discou·rse** vb. XVI; partly after F. *discourir*, †*discurre*.

discover diskʌ·vəɹ disclose to knowledge XIII (Cursor M.); reveal, exhibit; †uncover XIV; find out XVI. – OF. *descovrir* (mod. *découvrir*) = Pr., Sp. *descubrir*, It. *discovrire* :– late L. *discooperīre*, f. *dis-* DIS- 2+*cooperīre* COVER. The OF. tonic forms *descuevre*, etc., gave the ME. var. *diskever* (surviving dial.), and the vocalization of *v* between vowels the reduced forms †*discure*, †*diskere*. Hence **disco·very**. XVI; after *recover*, *recovery*; repl. *discovering*.

discre·dit sb. disrepute XVI; distrust XVII; vb. disbelieve; destroy confidence in; bring into discredit XVI; DIS- 6, 3; after It. *discredito*, *-itare*, F. *discrédit*, *-iter*.

discreet diskrī·t showing good judgement XIV; (Sc.) civil, polite XVIII. – (O)F. *discret*, *-ète* = Pr., Sp., It. *discreto* – L. *discrētus* separate, DISCRETE, which in late L. and Rom. took over its new meaning from *discrētiō* DISCRETION.

discrepant di·skrīpənt, diskre·pənt not harmonious or consistent. XV. – L. *discrepant-*, *-āns*, prp. of *discrepāre* be discordant, f. *dis-* DIS- 1+*crepāre* make a noise, creak; see -ANT. So **di·screp**ANCE. XV. **discre·p**ANCY. XVII.

discrete diskrī·t distinct, separate XIV (rare before XVI); discontinuous XVI; (gram., etc.) †adversative, disjunctive XVII. – L. *discrētus*, pp. of *discernere* separate, DISCERN.

Cf. DISCREET. So **discretion** diskre·ʃən discrimination; liberty or power of deciding; sound judgement. XIV (R. Mannyng). – (O)F. – L.

discriminate diskri·mineit make a distinction between, distinguish, differentiate. XVII. f. pp. stem of L. *discrīmināre*, f. *discrīmin-*, *-crīmen* distinction, f. *discernere* DISCERN; see CRIME, -ATE³. So **discrimination**. XVII. – late L.

discursive diskə̄·ɹsiv passing rapidly from one thing to another XVI; ratiocinative XVII. – medL. *discursīvus*, f. *discurs-*; see DISCOURSE, -IVE.

discus di·skəs quoit used in ancient Greek and Roman games. XVII. L. – Gr. *dískos* :– **díkskos*, f. *dikeîn* throw. See DAIS, DESK, DISC, DISH.

discuss diskʌ·s A. †investigate, decide XIV (R. Rolle); examine by argument XV; B. dispel, disperse XIV (Ch.). f. *discuss*, pp. stem of L. *discutere* dash to pieces, disperse, dispel, in Rom. investigate (cf. F. *discuter*, Sp. *discutir*, It. *discutere*), as in late L. *discussio*, *discussor*; f. DIS- 1+*quatere* shake. So **discussion** diskʌ·ʃən. XIV (Rolle). – (O)F. – L.

disdain disdei·n feeling of scorn; †indignation. ME. *desdeyne* (XIV), earlier *dedeyne* (XIII) – OF. *desdeign*, AN. *dedeigne* (mod. *dédain*) = Pr. *desdaing*, Sp. *desdeño*, It. *disdegno*, *sdegno*, deriv. of CRom. **disdignāre*, for L. *dēdignāri* reject as unworthy; see DIS- 2, DEIGN. So **disdai·n** vb. XIV. – OF. *desdeigner* = Pr. *desdegnar*, etc.

disease dizī·z †uneasiness, discomfort; morbid physical condition. XIV. – AN. *des-*, *disease*, OF. *desaise*, f. *des-* DIS- 2, 6+ *aise* EASE.

disembark disėmbā·ɹk put or go ashore. XVI. – F. *désembarquer*, Sp. *desembarcar*, or It. *disimbarcare*; see DIS- 2, EMBARK.

disembogue disėmbou·g †come out of the mouth of a river, etc., into the open sea; (of a river, etc.) discharge itself. XVI (early forms also *disemboque*, *-boke*). – Sp. *desembocar*, f. *des-* DIS- 2+*embocar* run into a creek or strait, f. *en* IN-¹+*boca* mouth :– L. *bucca* (cf. BUCCAL).

disembowel disėmbau·əl remove the bowels from. XVII. Intensive (DIS- 8) of †*embowel* (XVI) eviscerate – OF. *embouler*, alteration of *esbouler*, f. *es-* EX-¹+*bouel* BOWEL. Superseded †*debowel* (XIV), †*disbowel* (XVI).

disfigure disfi·gəɹ mar the figure or form of. XIV (Ch.). – OF. *desfigurer* (mod. *dé-*) = Pr., Sp. *desfigurar*, etc. – CRom. **disfigūrāre*; see DIS-, FIGURE.

disgorge disgō̄·ɹdʒ eject from the throat, vomit forth XV; transf. and fig. XVI. – OF. *desgorger* (mod. *dé-*), f. *des-* DIS- 1, DE- 6+ *gorge* throat, GORGE.

disgrace disgrei·s †disfavour; dishonour, shame, or cause of this. XVI. – F. *disgrâce* – It. *disgrazia*, f. *dis-* DIS- 2+*grazia* GRACE. So **disgra·ce** vb. †disfigure; bring dishonour to. XVI. – F. *disgracier* – It. *disgraziare*.

disgruntled disgrʌ·ntld put out of humour. XVII. f. DIS- 8+*gruntle* grunt, complain (XVI), frequent. of GRUNT+-ED¹.

disguise disgai·z alter the dress of, now only to conceal identity XIV; conceal by a counterfeit appearance XVI. – OF. *desguisier* (mod. *déguiser*) = Pr. *desguisar*, f. Rom. *dis-* DE- DIS-+*guisa* GUISE. Hence **disgui·se** sb. XIV.

disgust disgʌ·st dislike, distaste, (now) strong distaste verging on loathing. XVI. – F. *desgoust* (mod. *dégoût*) or It. *disgusto*, f. *desgouster* (mod. *dégoûter*), *disgustare*, whence **disgu·st** vb. XVII (ppl. adj. *disgu·sting* XVIII, repl. *disgustful* XVII); see DIS- 2, 6 and GUSTO.

dish diʃ broad shallow vessel OE.; applied to certain measures from XV; food served ready for eating XV. OE. *disć* plate, bowl, platter, corr. to OS. *disk* (Du. *disch*) table, OHG. *tisc* plate (G. *tisch* table), ON. *diskr* (perh. – OE.) – L. *discus* quoit, (Vulgate) dish, disc (of a sundial); see DISCUS and cf. DAIS, DESK. Hence **dish** vb. serve up in or as a dish XIV; (sl.) 'do for' (from the notion of food being *done* and *dished* up; cf. '*cook* one's goose', 'settle one's *hash*') XV.

dishabille di·səbīl undress garment or style. XVII. Earliest forms *dishabillie*, *-illee*, *-illié*, *déshabil(l)é*. – F. *déshabillé*, sb. use of pp. of *déshabiller* undress, f. *dés-* DIS- 4 + *habiller* dress (see HABILIMENT). For the muting of final *é* cf. DEFILE², SIGNAL².

dishearten dishā·ɹtn discourage. XVI (Sh.). f. DIS- 3, after *discourage*.

dishevelled diʃe·vld †without head-dress XV; (of the hair) unconfined XVI; fig. disorderly XVII. f. late ME. †*dischevel*, †*dischevelee*, *-y* (Ch.) – OF. *deschevelé*, f. *des-* DIS- 1+*chevel* hair (:– L. *capillu-s*; cf. CAPILLARY); see -ED¹.

dishonest disɔ·nist, diz- †entailing dishonour XIV (Ch.); †unchaste XIV; fraudulent, not straightforward or honest XVII. – OF. *deshoneste* (mod. *déshonnête*); see DIS- 2.

dishonour, U.S. **-or** disɔ·nəɹ, diz- reverse of honour, indignity, disgrace. XIII (Cursor M.). – OF. *deshonor* (mod. *déshonneur*) = Pr., Sp. *deshonor*, It. *disonore* – Rom. **dishonor*, *-ōrem*; see DIS- 2, HONOUR. So as vb. XIV (Wycl. Bible). – OF. *deshonorer* = Pr. *desonorar*, etc., medL. *dishonōrāre*.

disincli·ne(d), **-inclination**. XVII (Clarendon). DIS- 3, 6, 9.

disinhe·rit deprive of an inheritance. XV. f. DIS- 3+INHERIT, superseding †*disherit*, †*deserite* (XIII) – OF. *deseriter* (mod. *déshériter*) = Pr. *deseretar*, etc. – Rom. **desheretare*, f. *des-* DIS- 2+**heretare*, for late L. *hērēditāre* INHERIT.

disinte·r exhume. XVII (Cotgr.). – F. *désenterrer*; see DIS- 2, INTER.

disi·nterested †not interested; impartial, unbiased by personal interest. XVII. repl. †*disinteressed* (XVII, Florio, Donne) – F. *désintéressé*; see DIS- 7, INTEREST.

disjunctive disdʒʌ·ŋktiv disjoining; alternative; adversative; also sb. XV. – L. *disjunctīvus*, f. *disjunct-*, pp. stem of *disjungere*, whence OF. *desjoindre*, *desjoign-* (mod. *déjoindre*), the source of **disjoi·n** XV; see DIS- 1, JOIN, JUNCTION, -IVE.

disk var. of DISC.

dislike dislai·k †displease; not to like. XVI. f. DIS- 2+LIKE[2]; superseded MISLIKE. Hence **disli·ke** sb. †displeasure; distaste, aversion. XVI.

dislocate di·sləkeit put out of place, displace. XVII (Sh.). prob. back-formation from **disloca·tion** (first in medical sense). *c.* 1400. – OF. or medL.; see DIS- 1, LOCATE.

dismal di·zməl †sb. evil days, orig. the unpropitious days, two in each month, of the mediæval calendar XIII; adj. †(of days) unlucky XIV; †(of other things) disastrous; causing dismay or gloom; depressingly dreary XVI. – AN. *dis mal* (XIII) :- medL. *diēs malī* evil days. The (orig. superfluous) addition of *day* to *dismal* led to the apprehension of *dismal* as an adj., which had an extensive sense-development. ¶ occas. Icel. *dismala daga* is doubtless from Eng.

dismantle dismæ·ntl †uncloak; divest, strip. XVII. – F. †*desmanteller* (mod. *démanteler*); see DIS- 2, MANTLE.

dismay dismei· discourage completely. XIII (RGlouc.). – OF. **desmaier*, *demaier* = Pr. *desmaiar* (whence OSp. *desmayar*, It. *smagare*) :- Rom. **dismagāre* deprive of power, f. L. *dis-* DIS- 2+Germ. **mag-* be able, MAY[1] (cf. OF. *esmaier*, whence F. *émoi* excitement, Pr. *esmaiar* disturb, trouble, Pg. *esmagar* crush, overwhelm; ME. *esmay*, *amay* – OF.). Hence **dismay·** sb. XIV.

disme·mber deprive of limbs. XIII (RGlouc.). – OF. *desmembrer* – Rom. **desmembrare*, f. *des-* DIS- 4+L. *membrum* MEMBER.

dismiss dismi·s send away XV; discard, reject XV. First in pp., repr. OF. *desmis* (mod. *démis*) :- medL. *dismissus*, for L. *dīmissus*, pp. of *dīmittere*, f. *dis-* DIS- 1+*mittere* send (see MISSION); preceded by †*dismit* (XIV), and superseded this, together with other forms which were common XVI–XVII, †*dimit*, †*dimiss*, as well as †*demit*. So **dismi·ssion** XVI; after F. †*desmission* (mod. *démission*); largely replaced by **dismi·ssal**[2] XIX.

dismou·nt remove (a thing) from that on which it has been mounted; come down, esp. alight from a horse, etc. XVI. f. DIS- 3+MOUNT, prob. after OF. *desmonter*, etc., medL. *dismontāre*.

disobey· refuse to obey. XIV (Gower). Late ME. *dis-*, *desobeie* – (O)F. *désobéir* = Pr. *desobedir*, etc. – Rom. **desobedīre*, for late L. *inobēdīre*; see DIS- 3, OBEY. So **disobe·dience**, -ENT. XV. – OF.; repl. †*disobeisant* XIV (Ch.) – (O)F. *désobéissant*.

disorder disɔ̄·ɹdəɹ, diz- (arch.) put out of order XV; derange XVI. app. modification after ORDER vb. of earlier †*disordeine* (XIV) – OF. *desordener* (see DIS- 6, ORDAIN). Hence **diso·rder** sb. XVI; after F. *désordre*; whence **diso·rderly**[1]. XVII.

disorganize disɔ̄·ɹgənaiz, diz- destroy the organization or organic connexion of. XVIII (Burke, 1793). – F. *désorganiser* (in common use at the time of the French Revolution), f. *dés-* DIS- 6+*organiser* ORGANIZE.

disparage dispæ·ridʒ †match unequally; bring discredit on XIV; speak of slightingly XVI. – OF. *desparagier*, f. *des-* DIS- 2+*parage* (high) rank, prop. equality of rank = Pr. *paratge* :- Rom. **parāticum*, f. *par* equal; see PEER, -AGE. So **dispa·ragement**. XV. – OF.

disparity dispæ·rĭti inequality, unlikeness. XVI. – F. *disparité* – late L. *disparitās*; see DIS- 2, PARITY.

dispart[1] dispā·ɹt difference between the semidiameter of a gun at the base ring and at the swell of the muzzle; sight-mark allowing for this. XVI. Of doubtful origin; prob. f. next, but there are chronological difficulties.

dispart[2] dispā·ɹt (arch.) part asunder XVI (Spenser); divide, separate XVII. – It. *dispartire* divide, part, or L. *dispartīre* distribute, divide; see DIS- 1, PART; superseded *depart* in the corr. senses.

dispatch, despatch dispæ·tʃ send off post-haste or with expedition; get rid of, dispose of; execute promptly. XVI. prob. at first a term of diplomatic usage; Bishop Tunstall, the earliest known user of the word, was commissioner to Spain 1516–17. – It. *dispacciare* or Sp. *despachar*, f. *dis-*, *des-* DIS- 2 +base of It. *impacciare* hinder, stop, Sp., Pg. *empachar* impede, embarrass; this base is of obscure origin and difficult to relate directly with that of the synon. OF. *empechier* (mod. *empêcher* prevent) IMPEACH, OF. *depéchier* (mod. *dépêcher*), whence Eng. †*depeach* (XV–XVII), which was superseded by *dispatch*. Hence (or – It. *dispaccio*, Sp. *despacho*) **dis-, despa·tch** sb. act of dispatching, message dispatched XVI; superseded †*depeach* (XVI–XVII) – (O)F. *dépêche*. ¶ The sp. with *des-* dates from Johnson's Dictionary, 1755, though J. in his writings used *dispatch*.

dispel dispe·l drive away and scatter. XVII. – L. *dispellere*, f. DIS- 1+*pellere* drive (see PULSE[2]).

dispense dispe·ns A. deal out, distribute, administer XIV; make or put up (medicine) XVI; B. arrange administratively *with*; relax or release administratively XIV (first in Ch., Trev., Wyclif, Gower). – OF. *despenser* (mod. *dépenser* spend) = Pr., Sp. *despensar*, It. *dispensare*) – L. *dispensāre* weigh out, disburse, administer, dispose, (in medL.) deal with a person or a matter according to the requirements of eccl. law (*dispensare cum aliquo, circa aliquem* or *aliquid*, etc.), frequent. of *dispendere*, f. *dis-* DIS- 1+ *pendere* weigh (cf. SPEND). The phr. *dispense with* (medL. *dispensare cum*) has an extensive development: A. †grant (a person) exemption or release; give exemption from (a rule); B. do away with (a requirement), put up with the want of, do without; C. †condone (an irregularity), †deal with indulgently, †manage or do with. So **dispens**A·TION distribution; administration, management (esp. of the divine conduct of the world, repr. N.T. and patristic uses of L. *dispensātiō* and Gr. *οἰκονομία* ECONOMY); act of dispensing with a requirement. XIV. – (O)F. – L. **dispe·ns**ARY place for dispensing medicines XVII; †collection of drugs; †book containing formulæ for making up medicines XVIII. The earlier word was **dispe·nsat**ORY. XVI. – absol. uses of medL. adjs. *dispensārius, dispensātōrius*. **dispe·nser** administrator, steward. XIV. – OF. *despensour* – L. *dispensātor* (which was current in Eng. XIV–early XIX); see -ER[1]. ¶ Hence the surnames *Despenser, Spenser, Spencer*.

dispeople dispī·pl (arch.) depopulate. XV – OF. *despeupler* (mod. *dé-*) = Pr. *despovoar*, etc., Rom. formation on L. *dis-* DIS- 4+*populus* PEOPLE.

disperse dispɔ̄·ɹs cause to separate or scatter XIV; dissipate XVI. – F. *disperser*, f. *dispers* – L. *dispersus*, pp. of *dispergere*, f. *dis-* DIS- 1+*spargere* strew (cf. SPARSE). Hence **dispe·rsal**· XIX; see -AL[2]. **dispe·r**SION. Earliest in spec. meaning of 'Jews dispersed among Gentiles after the Babylonian Captivity', tr. Gr. DIASPORA. XIV (Wycl. Bible, 1 Peter i 2).

dispiteous dispi·tiəs (arch.) pitiless. XIX. Revival of †*despiteous* (XVI), alteration after PITEOUS of †*despitous* (XIV) – OF. *despitos* (mod. *dépiteux*), f. *despit* DESPITE; taken as DIS-7+PITEOUS.

displace displei·s remove from its place. XVI. f. DIS-+PLACE, partly after OF. *desplacer* (mod. *dé-*).

display displei· †unfold; expose to view XIV; exhibit, manifest XVI; show off XVII. – OF. *despleier* (mod. *déployer* DEPLOY), earlier *desplier* = Pr., Sp. *desplegar*, It. *dispiegare* :– L. *displicāre* scatter, (medL.) unfold, unfurl, f. *dis-* DIS- 1, 2+*plicāre* fold (see PLY). Aphetic SPLAY. Hence **display**· sb. XVII.

disPLEA·SE XIV (Ch.), -PLEA·SURE XV – OF. *desplais-, -plaisir*, L. *displicēre*.

disport dispɔ̄·ɹt †divert; refl. enjoy oneself, frolic. XIV (Ch.). – AN. *desporter* (mod. *déporter* DEPORT), f. *des-* DIS- 1+*porter* to carry. So **dispo·rt** sb. (arch.) diversion, pastime. XIV. – OF. *desport*, f. the vb. Aphetic SPORT.

dispose dispou·z put in a suitable place; prepare the mind of, incline (esp. in pp.); make arrangements, ordain events XIV; with *of* †(i) order, control, (ii) put away, get rid of XVI. – (O)F. *disposer*, f. *dis-*+*poser* place, set in order, settle, after L. *dispōnere, -pos-* (see DIS-, POSITION, POSE[1]), tr. Gr. *διατιθέναι*. (L. *dispōnere* is repr. directly by *dispone* XIV, surviving in Sc. law, 'make over, assign'.) Hence **dispo·**SAL[2]. XVII (Milton); superseding earlier †*dispose* (Sh.). So **disposi**TION dispəzi·ʃən arrangement, control, management, bestowal; natural bent, inclination, aptitude. XIV. – (O)F. – L. *dispositiō(n-)*, tr. Gr. *διαθήκη*; not a deriv. of *dispose*, but assoc. with it in form through the adoption of F. *-poser* as the repr. of L. *-pōnere*.

dispraise disprei·z speak in disparagement of. XIII (Cursor M.). – OF. *despreisier* = Pr. *desprezar*, etc. – Rom. **despretiāre*, for L. *dēpretiāre* DEPRECIATE; see DIS- iii. So †**dis**PRI·ZE. XV. – OF. *desprisier*, var. of *despreisier*.

disproof disprū·f refutation, evidence for this. XVI. f. DIS- 6+PROOF, after **dis**PRO·VE XIV (Wyclif). – OF. *desprover*; see DIS- iii.

dispropo·rtion XVI (Eden); also vb. XVI (Sh.). **dis**PROPO·RTIONATE. XVI (Eden); after F. *disproportion, disproportionné*; see DIS- 6, 7.

dispute dispjū·t debate or discourse argumentatively XIII; debate upon XIV; argue against, contest XVI. – (O)F. *disputer* = Pr. *desputar*, etc. – L. *disputāre* estimate, discuss, (Vulgate) contend in words, f. *dis-* DIS- 1 + *putāre* reckon, consider (see PUTATIVE). Hence **dispu·te** sb. XVII. So **disput**A·TION. XIV. – F. – L.; repl. ME. † *disputisoun* (XIII–XV) – OF. *desputeisun*. **disput**ANT di·spjŭtənt. XVII (Dekker).

disquisition diskwizi·ʃən investigation; treatise or discourse in which a subject is investigated. XVII. – (O)F. *disquisition* – L. *disquīsitiō(n-)*, f. *disquīsīt-*, pp. stem of *disquīrere*, f. *dis-* DIS- 1 + *quærere* seek (see QUERY).

disrobe disrou·b divest of garments. XVI. f. DIS- 3 or 4+ROBE vb. or sb., perh. after OF. *desrober*.

disruption disrʌ·pʃən breaking up. XV (Sir T. Browne). – L. *disruptiō(n-)*, f. *disrupt-*, pp. stem of *disrumpere*; see DIS- 1, RUPTURE. So **disru·pt** intr. XVII; trans. XIX. f. the L. pp.

dissect dise·kt cut up. XVII. f. *dissect-*, pp. stem of L. *dissecāre*. So **disse·**CTION. XVII. – medL.; see DIS- 1, SECTION.

disseisin disī·zin (leg.) dispossession of property. XIV. – AN. *disseisine*, OF. *dessaisine*; see DIS- 4, SEISIN. So **dissei·ze**. XIV (R. Mannyng). – AN. *desseisir*.

dissemble dise·mbl †feign XV (Lydg.); †pretend not to see XV; disguise by feigning; intr. conceal one's intentions XVI. Late ME. *dissemile*, *-immil*, alteration of †*dissimule* (XIV) – (O)F. *dissimuler* – L. *dissimulāre* (see DIS- 2, SIMULATE), through *dissimble*, and assocn. with SEMBLANCE. The corr. sb. is DISSIMULA·TION.

disseminate dise·mineit scatter or spread abroad. XVII (Holland). f. pp. stem of L. *dissēmināre*, f. *dis-* DIS- 1 + *sēmin-*, *sēmen* SEED; see -ATE[3]. So **dissemina·tion**. XVII (Sir T. Browne). – L.

dissension dise·nʃən disagreement in opinion. XIII (Cursor M.); freq. sp. *-tion* from XV. – (O)F. *dissension* – L. *dissensiō(n-)*, f. pp. stem of *dissentīre*, whence (partly through F. *dissentir*) **disse·nt** withhold assent or consent XV (Wyntoun); disagree, differ XVI; whence **disse·nt** sb. XVI, **disse·nter**[1] spec. dissentient from prescribed or established religious creed or practice XVII; so **disse·ntient** adj. and sb. XVII. **disse·ntious**. XVI; cf. F. †*dissentieux*, *-cieux*. See DIS- 1, SENTIENT, -SION.

dissepiment dise·piment (bot., zool.) partition. XVIII. – L. *dissæpimentum*, f. *dissæpīre*, f. *dis-* DIS- 1 + *sæpes* hedge; see -MENT.

dissertation disəɹtei·ʃən †discussion; spoken or (usu.) written discourse containing a discussion at length. XVII. – L. *dissertātiō(n-)*, f. *dissertāre* discuss, debate, frequent. of *disserere* treat, examine, discourse, f. *dis-* DIS- 1 + *serere* join, connect, join words in composition (cf. SERIES, SERMON); see -ATION.

dissever dise·vəɹ separate, disjoin XIII; divide into parts XIV. – AN. *des(c)everer*, OF. *desevrer* (modF., techn. *desseuvrer*) = Pr. *desebrar*, It. *sceverare* :– late L. *dissēparāre*; see DIS- 1, SEVER.

dissident di·sidənt at variance XVI; sb. XVIII. – F. *dissident* or L. *dissident-*, *-ēns*, prp. of *dissidēre* disagree, f. *dis-* DIS- 1 + *sedēre* SIT; see -ENT.

dissimilar disi·milar unlike. XVII (Burton). f. DIS- 7 + SIMILAR, after L. *dissimilis*. So **dissimila·tion**. XIX; after *assimilation*. **dissimilitude** dissimilarity. XV. – L.

dissimulate disi·mjŭleit dissemble XV; †pretend not to see XVI. f. pp. stem of L. *dissimulāre*; see DIS- 2, SIMULATE. Earlier †**dissimule** XIV (Ch., Wycl. Bible). – (O)F. –L. So **dissimula·tion**. XIV (Ch., Gower). – (O)F. – L.

dissipate di·sipeit scatter, dispel, disperse XV; squander; distract XVII. f. pp. stem of L. *dissipāre*, f. *dis-* DIS- 1 + **supāre*, **sipāre* throw; see -ATE[3]. So **dissipa·tion**; dissolution XV; †dispersion XVI; squandering XVII; distraction of mind XVIII (Swift), (hence) frivolous diversion, (passing into) dissolute living XVIII. – (O)F. or L.

dissociate disou·ʃieit cut off from association. XVII (Cotgr.). f. pp. stem of L. *dissociāre*, f. *dis-* DIS- 1 + *sociāre* join together, f. *socius* companion; see SOCIAL, -ATE[3]. So **dissocia·tion**. XVII (Cotgr.).

dissoluble diso·ljŭbl that can be dissolved. XVI (More). – OF. *dissoluble* or L. *dissolūbilis*, f. *dissolvere*; see DIS- 1, SOLUBLE. So **dissolute** di·səlʲūt relaxed, lax, remiss XIV (Wycl. Bible); †enfeebled, weak; †unrestrained XV; †disconnected; lax in morals XVI. – L. *dissolūtus* loose, disunited, pp. of *dissolvere* DISSOLVE. **dissolu·tion** separation into parts XIV (Trevisa); †relaxation XV; breaking-up, dispersal XVI; death XVI (More). – (O)F. or L.

dissolve dizo·lv loosen the parts of, spec. †melt, fuse, (now) diffuse in liquid XIV (Wycl. Bible); †release from life, esp. pass. XIV (Ch.); undo (†a knot, bond, union) XIV (Wyclif); intr. XV. – L. *dissolvere*, f. *dis-* DIS- 1 + *solvere* loosen, SOLVE.

dissonant di·sənənt out of harmony, discordant in sound. XV. – (O)F. *dissonant* or L. *dissonant-*, *-āns*, prp. of *dissonāre* disagree in sound, f. *dis-* DIS- 1 + *sonāre* (see SONANT). So **di·ssonance**. XV. – (O)F. or late L.

dissuade diswei·d advise against XV; seek to divert *from* XVI. – L. *dissuādēre*, f. *dis-* DIS- 2 + *suadēre* advise, urge; cf. F. *dissuader*. So **dissua·sion**. XV (Lydg.). – (O)F. or L.

distaff di·stàf stick to hold material to be spun. OE. *distæf*, a peculiarly Eng. word, the Continental word being repr. by MDu. *rocke* (Du. *rok*), whence prob. dial. Eng. *rock* (XIV), OHG. *rokko* (G. *rocken*), ON. *rokkr*; f. the base of MLG. *dise*, *disene* distaff, bunch of flax (LG. *diesse*), rel. to DIZEN; the second el. is STAFF. ¶ Used typically (from XVI) of the female members of a family, spinning being a woman's work or occupation (cf. *distaff women*, Sh., 'Rich. II' III ii 118); e.g. *distaff side*)(*spear side*, *distaff right* (tr. legal L. *jus coli*); cf. F. *tomber en quenouille* (of property, etc.) go to the female side.

distain distei·n stain with colour, dye XIV (Gower); †dim, outshine XIV (Ch.); defile XV (Hoccleve). – OF. *desteign-*, pres. stem of *desteindre*, mod. *déteindre* = Pr. *destenher*, Sp. *desteñir*, It. *stingere* :– Rom. **distingere*; see DIS- 1, TINGE. Aphetic STAIN.

distal di·stəl (anat.) situated away from the centre of the body. 1808 (J. Barclay). irreg. f. next + -AL[1].

distant di·stənt separate XIV (Ch.); far apart; remote XV. – (O)F. *distant* or L. *distant-*, *distāns*, prp. of *distāre*, f. *dis-* DIS- 1 + *stāre* STAND. So **di·stance** †discord, dissension XIII (RGlouc.); extent of space between objects XV; remoteness XVI. – (O)F. – L. *distantia*.

distaste distei·st dislike, aversion. XVI. f. DIS- 6 + TASTE, after OF. *desgoust* (mod. *dégoût*), It. *disgusto* DISGUST.

distemper[1] diste·mpəɹ †disturb or derange the condition of XIV; put out of humour XIV (Ch.); derange the physical or bodily condition of XIV (Wyclif). – late L. *distemperāre* (whence also OF. *destremper*, mod. *détremper*, It. *distemperare*, Sp. *destemplar*), f. L. *dis-* DIS- 2+*temperāre* proportion or mingle duly, TEMPER. Hence, or f. DIS- 6+TEMPER sb. **diste·mper** sb.[1] disturbance of the bodily 'humours' or 'temper', (hence) ill health, disease XVI (spec. of a catarrhal disease of dogs XVIII).

diste·mper[2] †mix with liquid, soak XIV; fig. dilute XVI (Sh.); (f. the sb.) paint in distemper XIX. – OF. *destemprer* or late L. *distemperāre* soak, macerate, f. L. *dis-* DIS- 1, 2+*temperāre* mingle, qualify, TEMPER. Hence (after OF. *destrempe*, mod. *détrempe*) **diste·mper** sb.[2] method of painting on plaster XVII; whiting mixed with size and water used in this XIX.

distend diste·nd †stretch out or apart XIV; swell out from within XVII. – L. *distendere*; see DIS-1, TEND[2]. So **diste·nsION**. XV. – L.; so in F. (XIV).

distich di·stik couple of lines of verse. XVI (Holinshed; earlier in L. form). – L. *distichon* – Gr. *dístikhon*, sb. use (sc. *métron* metre) of n. of *dístikhos* of two rows or verses, f. *di-* DI-[2]+*stíkhos* row, line of verse, rel. to *steíkhein* advance, go, Germ. **steig-* (cf. STIRRUP).

distil(l) disti·l fall in minute drops (Maund.); let fall in minute drops or vapour; vaporize by heat and condense the vapour (Maund., Trev.); also intr. XIV. – (partly through (O)F. *distiller*) L. *distillāre*, for *dēstillāre*, f. *dē* DE- 1+*stillāre*, f. *stilla* drop (cf. Gr. *stílē* drop of water). So **distillA·TION**. XIV (Gower). – L. **disti·llERY** †distillation XVII (Evelyn); place or works for distilling XVIII.

distinct distiŋkt separate, different; clear, plain XIV (in earliest use as implied in the adv.). – L. *distinctus*, pp. of *distinguere* DISTINGUISH; so in (O)F. So **distincTION** disti·ŋkʃən †division, class XIII (AncrR.); discrimination, making a difference XIV (R. Rolle, Wyclif, Trevisa); distinguishing excellence XVII; mark of honour XVIII. – (O)F. – L. **disti·nctIVE**. XV. f. *distinct-*, pp. stem of L. *distinguere*+-IVE.

distingué distæ·ŋgei, ‖distε̃ge having an air of distinction. XIX (Byron). F., pp. of *distinguer* – L. *distinguere* DISTINGUISH.

distinguish disti·ŋwiʃ divide into classes; make, or mark as, different; perceive plainly; make prominent. XVI. irreg. f. (O)F. *distinguer* or L. *distinguere* (adopted earlier as †**distingue** XIV)+-ISH[2]; cf. *extinguish*.

distort distɔ̄·ɹt give a twist to, lit. and fig. XVI (C'tess Pembroke). f. *distort-*, pp. stem of L. *distorquēre*, f. *dis-* DIS- 1+*torquēre* twist. So **disto·rTION**. XVI. – L.; in F. *distorsion*. See TORT.

distract distræ·kt draw away or in different directions. XIV (Wyclif). f. *distract-*, pp. stem of L. *distrahere*, f. *dis-* DIS- 1+*trahere* draw, drag; see TRACT. So **distra·cTION**. XV. – L.; so F. (XIV).

distrain distrei·n (hist.) force to perform an obligation by the seizure of a chattel, etc. XIII; levy a distress XIV; in various casual senses 'press', 'compress', 'oppress', 'strain out' XIV (R. Rolle, Ch., etc.). ME. *destreyne* – OF. *destreign-*, pres. stem of *destreindre* = Pr. *destrenher* :- L. *distringere* (see STRINGENT). Aphetic STRAIN.

distrait distrei· having the attention distracted. XVIII (Chesterfield). F., pp. of *distraire* DISTRACT. ¶ In ME. (Ch.; XIV–XV) 'greatly perplexed' – OF. *destrait*.

distraught distrɔ̄·t mentally distracted XIV (Gower); mentally deranged XV. Alteration of (pp.) adj. *distract* by assim. to *straught*, pp. of STRETCH.

distress distre·s (dial.) strain, stress; strain of adversity; (leg.) act of distraining. XIII (RGlouc., Cursor M.). – OF. *destre(s)ce*, *-esse* (mod. *détresse*) = Pr. *destreissa* :- Gallo-Rom. **districtia* (cf. *angustia* ANGUISH, f. *angustus*), f. pp. stem of L. *distringere* DISTRAIN. So **distre·ss** vb. XIV. – AN. *destresser*, OF. *-ecier*, f. the sb. Aphetic STRESS.

distribute distri·bjūt deal out in portions. XV. f. *distribūt-*, pp. stem of L. *distribuere*, f. *dis-* DIS- 1+*tribuere* grant, assign (cf. TRIBUTE). So **distribu·TION**. XIV. – (O)F. or L.

district di·strikt †territory under the jurisdiction of a feudal lord; portion of territory marked off for a purpose (various spec. uses) XVII; region, quarter XVIII. – F. *district* – medL. *districtus* (power of) exercising justice, territory involved in this, f. *district-*, pp. stem of *distringere* DISTRAIN.

distringas distri·ŋgæs (leg.) writ directing a sheriff to distrain. XV. L., 'thou shalt distrain', 2nd pers. sg. pres. subj. of *distringere* DISTRAIN.

distrust distrʌ·st †intr. be suspicious *of* XV (Lydg.); trans. not to trust XVI. f. DIS- 3+ TRUST, after F. *défier* (cf. DEFY) or L. *diffīdere*.

disturb distɔ̄·ɹb †deprive *of* (AncrR.); agitate (lit. and fig.) XIII. ME. *desto(u)rben* – OF. *desto(u)rber* = Pr. *destorbar* (cf. It. *sturbare*) – L. *disturbāre*, f. *dis-* DIS- 2+ *turbāre* disorder, disturb, f. *turba* tumult, crowd. So **distu·rbANCE**. XIII (RGlouc.). – OF. *desto(u)rbance*.

disuse disjū·z †make (a person) unaccustomed XIV (Barbour); †misuse, abuse XIV (Wyclif); cease to use XV. – OF. *desuser*. Hence **disuse** sb. disjū·s XV. See DIS- 3, 6 and USE.

disyllable, diss- disi·ləbl word or metrical foot of two syllables. XVI (*dissillable*). – F. *dissyllabe*, †*dissill-* – L. *disyllabus* – Gr. *disúllabos*, f. *di-* DI-² +*sullabḗ* SYLLABLE. The sp. with *ss* was regular XVI–XVIII and is still common, the etymol. sp. with *s* being first favoured by scholars in XIX. So **di(s)sylla·b**IC. XVII (Jonson). – F. (XVI), f. L. *disyllabus*.

ditch ditʃ long narrow excavation OE.; (dial.) embankment, dike XVI. OE. *dīć*, corr. to OFris., OS. *dīk* ditch, dike (Du. *dijk*), MHG. *tīch* (G. *teich* pond, pool), ON. *díki* ditch, DIKE; a word of the Baltic coast, of unkn. origin. Hence **ditch** vb. surround with a ditch, dig ditches in XIV; (orig. U.S.) throw into a ditch XIX; not repr. OE. *dīćian* dig, make an embankment.

dither di·ðəɹ quake, quiver. XVII. Var. of (dial.) *didder* (XIV), orig. and still north., of symbolic origin.

dithyramb di·þiræmb Greek choric hymn in honour of Dionysus (Bacchus) XVII; inflated discourse XIX. – L. *dīthyrambus* – Gr. *dīthúrambos*. So **dithyra·mb**IC. XVII.

dittany di·təni labiate plant Origanum Dictamnus. XIV. Late ME. *ditane, diteyne* – OF. *ditan, ditain* :– medL. *dictamu-s*, for L. *dictamnu-s, -um* – Gr. *diktamnon*, reputed to be f. *Diktḗ* the mountain in Crete, a well-known habitat of the plant. The trisyllabic form (*detany*) appears XV; it depends on medL. *ditaneum*, late L. *dictamnium*.

ditto di·tou †of the said month; gen. the aforesaid, the same XVII; duplicate, copy; pl. suit of the same stuff throughout XVIII. – It. *ditto*, Tuscan var. of *detto* said :– L. *dictu-s*, pp. of *dīcere* say (see DICTION); orig., as in It., used to avoid repetition of the name of a month, e.g. 'li 22 di dicembre . . li 26 detto' (the 22 Dec. . . the 26th aforesaid); extended in Eng. commercial usage to 'the same commodity, place, person, or amount'. Cf. F., G., Du. *dito*. abbrev. **do.**

dittography ditɔ·grəfi (palæogr.) unintentional writing of a letter, word, or passage twice. XIX. f. Gr. *dittós* double+-GRAPHY.

ditty di·ti song, lay XIII; †words of a song, theme XVI. ME. *dite(e)* – OF. *dité* composition, treatise :– L. *dictātum*, sb. use of n. pp. of *dictāre* express in language, compose (see DICTATE).

ditty-bag di·tibæg sailor's bag for small necessaries. XIX. So **di·tty-box,** used by American fishermen. Of unkn. origin.

diuretic daijure·tik exciting excretion or discharge of urine. XV. – (O)F. *diurétique* or L. *diūrēticus* – Gr. *diourētikós*, f. *dioureîn* urinate, f. *diá* through+*oûron* URINE.

diurnal daiɔ̄·ɹnəl occupying a day; occurring daily XV; of the day XVII. – late L. *diurnālis*, f. *diurnus*, f. *diēs* day; cf. DIARY, JOURNAL.

diva dī·vă prima donna. XIX. It., 'goddess' :– L. *dīva* female divinity, sb. use of fem. of *dīvus* divine, sb. god, rel. to *deus* (see DEITY).

divagation daivəgei·ʃən deviation, digression. XVI. f. L. *dīvagāt-*, *-ārī*, f. DI-¹, DIS- I +*vagārī* wander; see VAGUE, -ATION.

divan divæ·n, daivæ·n Oriental council of state; court of justice, council chamber XVI; long seat against the wall of a room XVIII; smoking-room with lounges XIX. – F. *divan* or It. *divano* – Turk. *divān* – Arab. *diwān*, *dīwān* – Pers. *dēvān* (now *dīwān*) (orig.) brochure, (hence) collection of poems, muster-roll, register, account-book, office of accounts, custom-house, tribunal, court, council chamber, (cushioned) bench. Cf. DEWAN, DOUANE. ¶ The word has become CEur.

divaricate daivæ·rikeit stretch or spread apart. XVII. f. pp. stem of L. *dīvaricāre*, f. *dis-* DI-¹+*varicāre* stretch (the legs) asunder, f. *varicus* straddling; see VARICOSE, -ATE³. So **di:varic**A·TION. XVI.

dive daiv plunge into or under water; trans. OE.; intr. XIII. OE. *dȳfan* wk. trans. dip, submerge = ON. *dýfa* :– **dūƀjan*, f. Germ. **dūƀ-*; OE. *dūfan* str. intr. did not survive, being replaced by the wk. form (cf. pp. †*bedoven*, = MDu. *be|dūven*), belonging to the Germ. series **dauƀ-* **deuƀ-* **duƀ-*, parallel to **daup-* **deup-* **dup-* DEEP, DIP. Hence **dive** sb. XVII; in the U.S. sense of 'low resort for drinking, etc.' from the sense of the vb. 'dart out of sight'.

diverge daivɔ̄·ɹdʒ proceed on a different course. XVII. – medL. *dīvergere*, f. L. *dis-* DI-¹+*vergere* bend, incline, VERGE. So **dive·rg**ENT, -ENCE. XVII.

divers dai·vəɹz †different, diverse; (arch.) sundry, several, many. XIII. ME. *divers, diverse* – (O)F. *divers*, fem. *diverse* = It., Sp. *diverso* – L. *dīversus* contrary, hostile, separate, different, prop. pp. of *dīvertere* DIVERT. When *divers* became the established form in the second sense the final s became z, as in the pl. of sbs. So **diverse** daivɔ̄·ɹs different; †divers, sundry. XIII (RGlouc.). Identical in origin with prec., in later use differentiated from it in form and pronunc. (cf. *adverse, inverse*), with restriction to the sense of the orig. L. So **dive·rs**ITY. XIV (R. Rolle). – (O)F. – L. **dive·rs**IFY. XV. – OF. *diversifier* – medL. *dīversificāre*.

divert daivɔ̄·ɹt turn aside XV (Lydg.); distract XVI; entertain, amuse XVII. – F. *divertir* = Sp. *divertir*, It. *divertire* – L. *dīvertere* turn out of the way, leave one's husband (cf. DIVORCE), differ (cf. *dēvertere* turn aside), f. *dis-* DI-¹+*vertere* turn (see WORTH²). So **dive·r**SION. XVII. – late L. (medical term, like *diversion* in OF.); the mil. use may be immed. – F. *diversion* or It. *diversione*. **diverticulum** -i·kjŭləm †bypath XVI; (anat.) side-branch of a process XIX. L.; earlier †*diverticle* (XV).

dives dai·vīz (leg.) in *dives costs* costs on the ordinary scale)(*pauper costs* costs on a lower scale imposed on a plaintiff who sued in forma pauperis. XIX. L. 'rich', 'rich man' (occurring in the parable in Luke xvi and gen. taken as the proper name of the rich man in that parable).

divest daive·st strip of covering; dispossess. XVII (Sh.). refash. on L. models in DI- of earlier *devest* (XVI) – OF. *devestir, desvestir* (mod. *dévêtir*) = It. *(di)svestire* – Rom. **disvestīre*; see DIS- 4, VEST.

divide divai·d separate (trans. & intr.) into parts XIV (PPl., Ch., Wyclif); part (an assembly) into separately voting groups XVI. – L. *dīvidere* cleave, apportion, separate, remove, f. *dis-* DI-[1]+ **videre*, f. IE. **widh-*, repr. also by L. *viduus, -a* WIDOW, Skr. *vindhá́te* is empty. Cf. DEVISE[1]. So **dividend** di·vidənd portion of anything divided XV; quantity to be divided XVI. – AN. *dividende* – L. *dīvidendum*, sb. use of n. gerundive of *dīvidere*. **divi·dER**[1]. XVI; pl. dividing compasses XVIII. **divisION** divi·ʒən XIV (Ch., Wyclif, Gower); spec. (math.) XIV; (mus.) execution of a rapid melodic passage, such a passage itself, run (so applied from the splitting of notes up into smaller ones); portion of an army or fleet XVI. – OF. *devisiun* (mod. *division*) – L. **divisor** divai·zəɹ (math.) XV. – F. or L.; see -OR[1].

divine[1] divai·n pert. to God or a god; godlike; heavenly XIV (Ch., Wyclif, Gower); of surpassing excellence XV. ME. *devine, divine* – OF. *devin*, fem. *-ine*, later, by assim. to L., *divin(e)* = Pr. *devin*, Sp., It. *divino* – L. *dīvīnu-s*, f. *dīvus* godlike, god, rel. to *deus* god :– **deiwos*, whence L. *Dies|piter*, voc. *Juppiter* (cf. JOVE and TUESDAY); see -INE. So **divinITY** divi·nĭti. XIV. – (O)F. – L. *dīvīnitās*, in Christian use tr. Gr. θειότης)(θεότης DEITY.

divine[2] divai·n †soothsayer, seer; ecclesiastic, theologian. XIV. ME. *devine* – OF. *devin* (:– L. *dīvīnu-s* soothsayer), later *divin* theologian, after medL. *dīvīnus* doctor of divinity, theologian; sb. use of prec.

divine[3] divai·n make out as by supernatural insight; practise divination. XIV (PPl., Ch., Trevisa). ME. *devine* – (O)F. *deviner*, f. *devin* DIVINE[2], after L. *dīvīnāre* foretell, predict. So **divinA·TION**. XIV (Ch., Wycl. Bible, Trevisa).

divorce divɔ̄·ɹs legal dissolution of marriage. XIV (PPl., Wyclif). – (O)F. *divorce*, corr. to Sp. *divorcio*, It. *divorzio* – L. *dīvortium* separation, divorce, f. *dīvortere*, var. of *dīvertere* DIVERT. So **divo·rce** vb. XIV (Trevisa). – (O)F. *divorcer* – late L. *divortiāre*. Hence **divorcEE·** divorced person. XIX; more freq. in F. form *divorcé(e)*. **divo·rceMENT**. XVI (Tindale, Matt. v 31).

divot di·vət piece of turf. XVI. orig. Sc. *deva(i)t, dewot, diffat, defett, divat, duvat*; of unkn. origin. Now gen. familiar from its use in the laws of golf.

divulge daivʌ·ldʒ, di- †publish abroad XV; reveal (something secret) XVII. – L. *dīvulgāre* make commonly or publicly known, f. *dis-* DI-[1]+*vulgāre* publish, propagate, f. *vulgus* common people (cf. VULGAR). The pronunc. with dʒ, instead of g as in F. *divulguer*, is prob. due to the sp.*-ge*. So **di·vulgATE**[3], -A·TION. XVI. – L.

divvers di·vəɹz †*Div*inity Moderation*s* in the University of Oxford; see -ER[6]. XIX.

divvy di·vi colloq. deriv. of DIV|IDEND + -Y[6]. XIX.

dixie di·ksi iron kettle or pot. XIX. – Hind. *degchi* (repr. by occas. *dechsie*) – Hindi *degachī, -chā*, Panjabi *dekachī, -chā* – Pers. *degcha*, dim. of *deg, dīg* iron pot, kettle.

dizen dai·zn, di·zn †dress (a distaff) with flax XVI; (arch. and dial.) dress up, deck out, BEDIZEN XVII. f. base repr. by the first syll. of DISTAFF; cf. MDu. *disen*, perh. the immed. source. See -EN[5].

dizzy di·zi (dial.) foolish, stupid OE.; giddy XIV. OE. *dysiġ* = OFris. *dusig*, MDu. *dosech, dōsech*, LG. *dusig, dōsig* giddy, OHG. *tusic* foolish, weak, f. WGerm. **dus-*, found also in OE. *dys(e)liċ* foolish, LG. *dusen* be giddy, and with *l*-suffix in LG. *dūsel* giddiness, MDu. *dūselen* (Du. *duizelen*) be giddy or stupid; see -Y[1].

djereed, djinn see JEREED, JINN.

do[1] dū pt. **did**, pp. **done** dʌn trans. A. put, place (cf. DOFF, DON[1], DOUT, DUP); B. perform, execute; C. cause; D. as auxiliary of tense. OE. intr. A. act (in a specified way) OE.; B. fare, get on XIII (Cursor M.); C. (in perf. tenses) make an end XIV (R. Mannyng); D. be (well or ill) XV; E. serve the purpose, suffice XVI (Sh.). OE. *dōn*, pt. *dyde*, pp. *ġedōn*, of which the pt. *dyde* is isolated amongst the Germ. langs., the others having forms corr. to OE. pl. *dǣdon*, Anglian *dēdon* (a type which survived only into ME.), viz. OFris. *dua(n), dede, dēden, dēn*, OS. *dōn, doan, deda, dēdun, gidōn* (Du. *doen, deed, deden, gedaan*), OHG. *tuo(a)n, teta, tātum, getān* (G. *tun, tat, getan*).

In OE. *dōm* is found in late Nhb. beside the usual *dō* in 1st pers. sg. pres. ind.; OE. 2nd and 3rd pers. sg. *dēst, dēþ* (:– **dōist, *dōiþ*) were supplanted in ME. by *dost, doth*, beside which *doest* dū·ist, *doeth* dū·iþ were formed later and became restricted to non-auxiliary uses. OE. prp. *dōnde* was superseded by *doing* (XIV). The OE. pp. *ġedōn*, in which the prefix was constant, became *idon, don*, mod. *done*, with change of vowel as in *dost, doth*, and *does* (which descends from late Nhb. *dōas, dōes*, north. ME. *dōs, dūs*).

This CWGerm. vb., the history of which remains in some points obscure, is based on a widespread IE. **dhō- *dhē- *dhə-*, repr. by Skr. *dádhāmi* put, lay (with pf. *dadhāu*, corr. to OFris., OS. *dede*, OHG. *teta*), Arm. *d|nem*, Gr. *títhēmi* I place (cf. THEME), L. *fa|c|ere* make, do (pt. *fē|cī*, corr. to Gr. aor. *é|thē|ka*), *-dō, -dere* in *addere* ADD, *condere* (see CONDITION), Lith. *déti*, OSl. *dětí* put, lay. Cf. DEED, DOOM, -DOM, and CREED. The meaning 'avail, suffice' is prob. much older than the date of our present evidence, and may derive partly from ON. *gera* make, do (e.g. *þat mun ekki gera* that won't do).

do², **doh** dou (mus.) first note of the scale in solmization. XVIII. – It. *do* (noted as of recent introduction by Lorenzo Penna in 'Li Primi Albori Musicali', 1672), said to be a modification of *du*, altered inversion of UT.

doab dū·əb, dou·əb tract between two confluent rivers. XIX (Wellington, Heber). – Hind. – Pers. *dōāb*, i.e. *do*, TWO, *āb* water.

doat var. of DOTE.

Dobbin dɔ·bin typical name for a draught horse, farm horse. XVI (Sh.). Proper name, var. of *Robbin*, *Robin*, pet form of *Robert*.

dobe, dobie, doby (U.S.) see ADOBE.

docent dou·sənt †adj. teaching XVII; sb. (U.S.) teacher in a college or university (after G.) 1890. – L. *docent-*, *-ēns*, prp. of *docēre* teach; see DOCTOR, -ENT.

Docetic douse·tik, -ī·tik pert. to the Docetæ, sect which held that Christ's body was not human but only appeared to be so. XIX. f. medL. *Docētæ* – Gr. *Dokētaí*, f. *dokeîn* seem, appear; see -IC.

dochmiac dɔ·kmiæk (Gr. pros.) pert. to the *dochmius*, 5-syllabled foot of which the typical form is ∪ – – ∪ –. XVIII. – Gr. *dokhmiakós*, f. synon. *dókhmios* oblique.

docile dou·sail, dɔ·sail teachable XV; tractable XVIII. – L. *docilis*, f. *docēre* teach; see DOCTOR, -ILE, and cf. F. *docile* (XVI).

dock¹ dɔk coarse weedy herb, of genus Rumex. OE. *docce* (also in *sūr|docce*, *wudu|-docce* sorrel), pl. *doccan*, corr. to MDu. *docke|blaederen* (whence G. *dockenblätter*) patience dock, ODa. *å|dokke* (= OE. *ēa|docce* water-dock). ¶ Hence Gael., Ir. *dogha*, OF. (Norm. dial.) *doque*.

dock² dɔk solid fleshy part of a horse's tail; crupper XIV; cut end, stump XVI. perh. identical with OE. *docca* (or *-e*) in *finger-doccan* finger-muscles, and corr. to Fris. *dok* bunch, ball (of twine, etc.), (M)LG. *dokke* bundle of straw, OHG. *tocka* (south G. *docke*) doll; the meanings point to a basic sense 'something round'. Hence **dock** vb. cut short, curtail. XIV (Ch., Wyclif).

dock³ dɔk †bed, hollow (or creek) in which a ship rests, esp. at low water XIV; artificial basin for the reception of ships XV. – MLG., MDu. *docke* (mod. *dok*), of unkn. origin; from Du. and Eng. the word has passed into German (*dock*), Scandinavian (Sw. *docka*, Da. *dokke*), and French (*dock*). Hence **dock** vb. XVI. **do·ck**ER¹ dweller near docks XVIII; dock labourer **XIX**.

dock⁴ dɔk enclosure in a criminal court where the prisoner stands his trial XVI (Warner, B. Jonson). prob. at first a word of rogues' cant and identical with the word repr. by Flem. *dok* cage, fowl-pen, rabbit-hutch, of unkn. origin. From *c.* 1620 to *c.* 1820 current mainly in †*bail-dock* (BAIL); familiarized XIX mainly through the writings of Dickens.

docket dɔ·kit †summary, minute XV; abstract, memorandum, register XVI; endorsement, label XVIII. Of unkn. origin, poss. f. DOCK²+-ET; also sp. *dogget* (XV–XVII); cf. AL. *doggetum* (XV). Hence **do·cket** vb. XVII.

doctor dɔ·ktəɹ teacher; one highly proficient in a branch of learning or holding the highest university degree; spec. doctor of medicine, (hence) medical practitioner. XIV. – OF. *doctour* – L. *doctor*, *doctōrem* teacher, f. *doct-*, pp. stem of *docēre* teach, causative corr. to *discere* learn (:– **di-dc-scō*), referred to an IE. base **dok-* **dek-*, as in Gr. *dokeîn* seem good (cf. DOGMA), *didáskein* learn (cf. DIDACTIC), L. *decet* it is fitting (cf. DECENT), *decus* (cf. DECOROUS), *dexter* right (cf. DEXTEROUS), Skr. *daçasyáti* is gracious, *dákšati*. Hence **do·ctress, do·ctoress** female doctor XV. f. DOCTOR+-ESS¹, after F. †*doctoresse*, late L. *doctrīc-*, *doctrix*, whence Eng. †*doctrice* XV–XVI.

doctrine dɔ·ktrin that which is taught; †instruction, lesson. XIV. (Wycl. Bible, Ch.). – (O)F. *doctrine* – L. *doctrīna* teaching, learning, f. *doctor* (see prec.). So **doctrin**AL¹ dɔktrai·nəl, dɔ·ktrinəl. XV. – late L. *doctrīnālis* (Isidore); earlier as sb. 'text-book' (XV) after OF. *doctrinal*, medL. *doctrināle* (sb. use of n. adj.). **doctrinaire** dɔktrinɛə·ɹ orig. one of a F. political party (soon after 1815) which aimed at an ideal of reconciliation of extremes; (hence) pedantic theorist.

document dɔ·kjŭmənt †instruction; †evidence XV; something written, etc. furnishing evidence XVIII. – (O)F. *document* = Sp., It. *documento* – L. *documentum* lesson, proof, instance, specimen, in medL. written instrument, official paper, f. *docēre* teach; see prec. and -MENT. Hence as vb. †instruct XVII; furnish with documents (as evidence) XVIII; cf. F. *documenter*. Whence **document**A·TION. XVIII.

dod dɔd euph. alteration of GOD, surviving dial. and in (U.S.) *dod burn*, *drat*; *dod-blamed*, *-durned*, *-rotted*, etc.

dodder¹ dɔ·dəɹ parasitic genus of convolvulaceous plants, Cuscuta. XIII. ME. *doder*, corr. to MLG. *dod(d)er*, MHG. *toter* (G. *dotter*). The formal similarity to OS. *dodro* (MDu. *doder*, Du. *door*, *dooier*), OHG. *totoro*, *tutar|ei* (G. *dotter*), rel. further to OE. *dydrin* yolk of egg, has suggested ult. connexion, but proof is wanting.

dodder² dɔ·dəɹ (dial.) tremble, shake XVII; totter, potter XIX. var. of or parallel form to †*dadder* (*dadir* 'frigucio', Catholicon Anglicum). Hence **do·ddery**¹ XX.

doddered dɔ·dəɹd used, after Dryden (1684), of old oaks that have lost the top or branches; expl. erron. by J. as 'overgrown with dodder'; altered form, simulating a pp., of *doddard* (Dryden, 1693), f. *dod* poll, lop (of hair XIII, of trees XV). f. an el. of unkn. origin + *-ard*, as in *pollard*; cf. *doddle oak* (Holland, 1601), and dial. *dodderel* pollard.

dodecagon doude·kəgən (geom.) 12-sided plane figure. XVII. – Gr. *dōdekágōnon*, f. *dṓdeka* 12 (f. *dṓ* TWO + *déka* TEN) + *-gōnos* -angled, *gōníā* angle. So **do:deca**HE·DRON. XVI (Billingsley). – Gr. **do:deca**SY·LLABLE. XVIII.

dodge dɔdʒ palter, haggle, trifle XVI; avoid an encounter with; move to and fro, keep shifting position XVII. Of unkn. origin. sb. XVI.

dodkin see DOIT.

dodo dou·dou extinct bird of Mauritius. XVII ('a strange fowle, which I had at the Iland mauritius, called by ye portingalls a DoDo', 1628, 'the Dodar (a blacke Indian bird)', 1634). – Pg. *doudo* simpleton, fool; applied to the bird because of its clumsy appearance.

doe dou female of the fallow deer OE.; female of hare or rabbit. XVII. OE. *dā*, of unkn. origin; adoption from Celtic has been suggested (cf. Corn. *da*, Ir. *dam* ox, stag), but if a native word it may corr. to Alemanic *de* in place-names, e.g. *De|brunnen, De|wald*; ult. connexion with MDu. *dāme*, OHG. *tāmo, dāmo* (G. *dam-* in *dambock, damhirsch, damwild*), which appear to be – L. *dāma* fallow-deer, presents serious difficulties.

doff dɔf put or take off XIV; (techn.) strip the slivers of wool, etc., from the carding-cylinders XIX. ME. *dof, doffe*, contr. of *do of(fe)*, OE. *dōn of, of dōn* take off, remove; see DO[1], OFF, and cf. DON[1], DOUT, dial. *dup*, for *do up*, i.e. open. ¶ Recorded as a northernism by Ray, by J. as 'obsolete, and scarcely used except by rustics'; restored to literary use by Scott.

dog dɔg quadruped of the genus Canis. Late OE. *docga* (once in a gloss; also g. pl. in place-names, *doggeneford, doggeneberwe*), of unkn. origin; prob. orig. denoting a large or powerful kind, the gen. term being *hund* HOUND, which *dog* finally displaced in this status; it has been adopted in Germ. and Rom. langs., usu. with a limited application, e.g. bulldog, mastiff (at first with the epithet 'English'); e.g. Du. *dog*, †*dogghe*, LG., G. *dogge*, †*dock*, Norw. *dogge*, Sw. *dogg*, F. *dogue*, also *bouledogue*, Sp., Pg., It. *dogo*. ¶ For the formation of the OE. word cf. the animal-names *frocga* FROG, **picga* PIG, **stacga* STAG, **sucga* in *hægsucga* hedge-sparrow, **wicga* beetle in EARWIG. ON. *dugga* useless fellow has been compared. Hence **dog** vb. follow like a dog. XVI. **dogged** dɔ·gid ill-conditioned XIV; †canine XV; pertinacious XVIII; see -ED[2], and cf. *crabbed*, of similar date.

In various comps. *dog-* renders L. or Gr. names, as *dog rose* (XVI, *dogs rose*), medL. *rosa canina*, repr. L. *cynorrodon* (Pliny) – Gr. *kunórodon*, f. *kuno-, kúōn* HOUND + *rhódon* ROSE; *dog's tooth* (XVI), medL. *dens canis*; *dog star* Sirius (XVI), Gr. *kuṓn*, L. *canicula*; *dog days* (XVI), L. *dies caniculares* (see CANICULAR); *dog-tooth* eye-tooth (XIV), pointed ornament (XIX). In *dog-sleep* (XVIII), *dog-watch* (XVII) there is a reference to the light or fitful sleep of a dog.

doge doudʒ chief magistrate of the republics of Venice and Genoa. XVI. – F. *doge* – It. *doge* – Venetian *doze* :– L. *ducem, dux* leader; cf. DUCE, DUKE. So **dogate** dou·geit office of a doge. XVIII. – F. *dogat* – It. (Venetian) *dogato*, f. *doge*; see -ATE[1].

dogger dɔ·gəɹ two-masted fishing vessel. XIV. – MDu. *dogger* trawler, fishing-boat (Du. *dogger* cod-fisher), obscurely rel. to MDu. *dogge* (in *ten dogge varen* go to the cod-fishing; early Du. *dogghe boot* large barque), which appears to be repr. in Icel. *fiski|duggur* pl. used of Eng. fishing-boats visiting Iceland in 1413 (cf. *duggari* one of the crew of a dogger, and Eng. *dogger* occas. so used XVI). Also †*dogger-boat* (XVII – Du.); *Dogger Bank* (Du. *Doggers bank*) name of a great shoal in the North Sea, also called †*Dogger-sands*.

dogg(e)rel dɔ·g(ə)rəl ill-constructed or mean verse. XIV. In earliest use adj. in *rym dogerel* (Ch.), presumably f. DOG (with contemptuous implication as in *dog Latin*, †*dog rime* XVII) + -EREL.

doggo dɔ·gou (sl.) *lie doggo* lie quiet, remain hid. XIX. app. f. DOG + -O, with ref. to the light sleeping of dogs and the difficulty of telling when their eyes are shut whether they are asleep.

dog-gone dɔ·gɔn (U.S. sl.) confound! damn! XIX. app. development of earlier *dog on it* (etc.), of obscure origin, as a euph. substitute for *God damn it*. Cf. Sc. *dagone!* deuce take it!

dogma dɔ·gmə tenet or doctrine laid down. XVII. – L. *dogma* philosophical tenet – Gr. *dógma, dogmat-* opinion, tenet, decree, f. *dokeîn* seem, seem good, think, suppose (cf. DOCTOR). So **dogma·t**IC, -ICAL. XVII. – late L. *dogmaticus* – Gr. *dogmatikós*; so F. *-tique*. **do·gmat**ISM XVII, -IST XVI. – F. **do·gmat**IZE. XVII (A.V., Pref.). – F. or late L.

doily doi·li †woollen stuff for summer wear XVII (*Doily Petticoat*, Dryden); small ornamental napkin or mat XVIII (*Doiley-napkin*, Swift). f. name of *Doiley, Doyley*, who according to Samuel Pegge kept a linen-draper's shop in the Strand, London; see also 'Spectator' No. 283 (1712), 'Philosophical Transactions' XXXIV (1727) 222.

doit doit small Dutch coin. XVI. – MLG. *doyt* = MDu. *duit, deuyt*, perh. to be connected with ON. *þveit* small coin, prop. piece cut off, f. *þvita* cut. **MDu.** dim. *doytkin* was repr. by ME. *doydekin* (XV), later *dodkin*.

doited doi·tid (Sc.) of unsound mind, foolish. XV (Wyntoun). Perh. var. of *doted* (XIV) pp. of DOTE, but *oi* is obscure.

doldrums dɔ·ldrəmz low spirits; becalmed state of a ship, region of calms. XIX. prob. orig. dial. or sl. f. *dol* DULL, perh. after *tantrums*.

dole[1] doul †part, portion OE.; (arch.) lot, share, fate XIII; portion doled out XIV. OE. *dāl* :– **dailaz*; see DEAL[1]. Hence **dole** vb. XV.

dole[2] doul (arch. and dial.) grief, sorrow, lamentation. XIII. ME. *dol*, with variants *doel, deol, del* (obs. before 1500), *dul, duil* (surviving in Sc. *dule*) – OF. *dol, doel, duel*, etc. (mod. *deuil* mourning) :– pop.L. *dolu-s*, f. L. *dolēre* (see DOLOUR). Hence **do·le**FUL[2]. XIII (Laȝ.).

dolerite dɔ·lərait mineral allied to basalt. XIX. – F. *dolérite* (Haüy), f. Gr. *dolerós* deceptive; so named from the difficulty of discriminating its constituents; see -ITE.

dolichocephalic dɔ:likousifæ·lik (ethnol.) long-headed)(*brachycephalic*. XIX. f. Gr. *dolikhós* LONG + *kephalḗ* HEAD + -IC.

doll dɔl †mistress XVI; child's toy-baby XVII; pretty but silly woman XIX. Pet-form of the female name *Dorothy* (e.g. *Doll* Tearsheet in Sh. '2 Henry IV', *Doll* Common in B. Jonson's 'The Alchemist'); *r* becomes *l* as in *Hal, Sal, Moll*, for *Harry, Sarah, Mary*. Hence **dolly** dɔ·li in same senses XVII; also applied to contrivances having a fancied resemblance to a doll XVIII; SEE -Y[6].

dollar dɔ·ləɹ German taler; Spanish peso or piece of eight (i.e. eight reales) XVI; standard unit of coinage in U.S.A., Canada, etc., equivalent to 100 cents XVIII. – early Flem., LG. *daler* (Du. *daalder*) – G. *taler* (formerly also *thaler*), short for *Joachimst(h)aler*, applied to a silver coin made from metal obtained in *Joachimst(h)al* (i.e. 'Joachim's valley') in the Erzgebirge, Germany; thence also It. *tallero*. The forms *doler, dolor* appeared XVI, *dollor, dollar* XVII.

dollop dɔ·ləp †tuft, clump XVI; shapeless lump XIX. perh. of Scand. origin (cf. Norw. dial. *dolp* lump).

Dolly Varden dɔ·li vā·ɹdən name of a character in Dickens's 'Barnaby Rudge', applied to (1) a large hat with one side bent downward and abundantly trimmed with flowers, (2) a print frock with large flower pattern, (3) a Californian trout or char.

dolman dɔ·lmən Turk's long robe open in front XVI (*dolyman*); hussar's uniform jacket worn with sleeves hanging loose; woman's mantle with cape-like appendages XIX. In the first sense – F. *doliman*, in the second – F. *dolman* – G. *dolman* – Magyar *dolmany*; all ult. – Turk. *dōlāmān*.

dolmen dɔ·lmen cromlech. – F. *dolmen* (*dolmin* Latour d'Auvergne 1796, *dolmine* Le Grand d'Aussy 1798), expl. by Legonidec (1821) as Breton *tōl* table, *men* stone; but the Breton form would be **taolvean*, **tōlven*, and the F. word prob. repr. inexactly Cornish *tolmēn* 'hole of stone', applied to enormous blocks of stone found in Cornwall poised on two supporting points so that an aperture is left beneath; cf. *Maen tol*, Cornish place-name in OE. charter of 785.

dolomite dɔ·ləmait (min.) native carbonate of lime and magnesia. XVIII. – F. *dolomite*, also *dolomie*, f. name of Sylvain *Dolomieu*, French geologist (1750–1802); see -ITE.

dolour, U.S. **dolor** dɔ·ləɹ †pain; grief, sorrow XIV. – OF. *dolor, -our* (mod. *douleur*) = Pr., Sp. *dolor*, It. *dolore* :– L. *dolōrem, dolor*, rel. to *dolēre* suffer pain or grief (cf. DOLE[2]). So **do·lor**OUS. XIV. – OF. *doleros* (mod. *douloureux*) – late L. *dolōrōsus*.

dolphin dɔ·lfin cetaceous mammal resembling the porpoise, Delphinus delphis XIII; constellation Delphinus XV (Lydg.); dorado XVII; black bean aphis XVIII. Three types of form have been current: (i) *delfyn, delphin* – L. *delphīnus* – Gr. *delphin-, delphis* (cf. Sp. *delfin*, It. *delfino*); (ii) *dalphyn* – OF. *daulphin* (see DAUPHIN) = Pr. *dalfin* :– Rom. **dalfīnu-s*; (iii) *dolfyn, dolphin*, app. Eng. alterations of (ii). Cf. DELPHIN.

dolt doult dull fellow, blockhead. XVI. prob. earlier in dial. use, and rel. to †*dold* (XV) numb, and *dol(l)*, var. of DULL.

dom[1] dɔm A. Pg. title of dignity; B. title prefixed to the name of Benedictines and Carthusians XVIII. In A, Pg. *dom* = Sp. DON[2] :– L. *dominu-s* master (spec. of a household), f. *domus* house, f. **dem-*, as in Vedic *dám pátis, pátir dán* master of the house, Gr. *despótēs* DESPOT (:– **dems|pot-*). In B, shortening of L. *dominus* DAN.

dom[2] doum cathedral. XIX. G., – L. *domus* (*Deī*) house (of God); cf. DOME.

-dom dəm suffix denoting condition or state, as in *freedom, thraldom, wisdom* state of being free, a thrall, wise, passing to the sense of domain, realm, territory, area, region, in *christendom, dukedom, kingdom*, and the like, and to that of experience, as in *martyrdom*. OE. *-dōm* = OS. *-dōm* (Du. *-dom*), OHG. *-tuom* (G. *-tum*), suffixal use of OE. *dōm* judgement, statute, jurisdiction, DOOM, OHG. *tuom* position, condition, dignity. It has lent itself easily in recent times to occas. and trivial use, as *officialdom, squiredom, theatredom, topsyturvydom*.

domain dŏmei·n estate, lands, dominions XVII; sphere of thought or action XVIII; lordship, in *eminent domain* (tr. modL. *dominium eminens*, Grotius) lordship of the sovereign power over all property XIX. – F. *domaine*, alteration, by assoc. with L. *dominium* (see DOMINION), of OF. *demaine, demeine* DEMESNE. ¶ *Domayne* occurs as a var. reading for *demayne* (i.e. DEMESNE) in Wyntoun's Chronicle II 366, and *domaine landes* is in Skene, 1597.

dome doum (arch.) house, mansion XVI; †cathedral church, DOM²; rounded vault, cupola XVII; vaulted roof, canopy, etc. XVIII. In the first sense – L. *domus* house (see DOMESTIC); in the others – F. *dôme* – It. *domo*, DUOMO house, house of God, cathedral, cupola (as a distinguishing feature of Italian cathedrals) :– L. *domu-s*.

Domesday dū·mzdei the Great Inquisition or Survey of the lands of England made in 1086 by order of William the Conqueror. XII (*domesdei*). ME. form of DOOMSDAY, popular appellation (see 'Dialogus de Scaccario' I xvi) given to the book (*liber de Domesday*) as being the final and inexorable authority on the matters contained in it.

domestic dŏme·stik †pert. to the household; pert. to one's country XVI; of the house, household-; tame XVII; sb. †inmate XVI; household servant XVII. – (O)F. *domestique* – L. *domesticus*, f. *domus* house, rel. to Gr. *dómos*, Skr. *dámas*, OSl. *domŭ*, OIr. *doim* in the house, f. IE. **dom*- **dem*- **dm̥*- (cf. DESPOT, TAME, TIMBER); for the terminal el. of the L. word cf. *rūsticus* RUSTIC, *silvāticus* (see SAVAGE), *viāticus* (see VOYAGE). †*Domestical* is earlier (XV). So **dome·sticate** doum-, dɔm-. XVII. f. pp. stem of medL. *domesticāre*; see -ATE³. **domesti·city**. XVIII; so F. *-icité*.

domicile dɔ·misail dwelling-place XV; place of (permanent) residence XVIII. – (O)F. *domicile* – L. *domicilium*, f. *domus* house (see prec.). Hence **domiciliary** -si·liəri XVIII.

dominant dɔ·minənt ruling, commanding (cf. PREDOMINANT) XV; (mus.) pert. to the fifth note of the scale of any key (also sb.) as dominating it next to the tonic. XIX. – (O)F. *dominant* – L. *dominant-*, *-āns*, prp. of *dominārī* (f. *dominus*), on the pp. stem of which was formed **do·minate**. XVII; see DOM¹, -ANT, -ATE³. **domina·tion** exercise of rule XIV (Ch.); fourth of the nine orders of angels XIV (Trevisa). – (O)F. – L.

domineer dɔminiə·ɹ govern or act imperiously, tyrannize (over). XVI (Sh.). – Du. †*domineren* – F. *dominer* – L. *dominārī*; see prec. and -EER².

dominical dŏmi·nikəl pert. to the Lord or the Lord's Day (Sunday). XV. – (O)F. *dominical* or late L. *dominicālis*, f. *dominicus*, f. *dominus* lord, master; see DOM¹, -ICAL.

Dominican dŏmi·nikən pert. to (a member of) the Order of Friars Preachers (Black Friars). XVII. – medL. *Dominicānus* (whence F. *dominicain*), f. *Dominicus*, L. form of the name of *Domingo* de Guzman (St. Dominic), 1170–1221, founder of an order of preaching friars; see -AN.

dominie dɔ·mini schoolmaster, pedagogue. XVII. sp. of L. *dominē*, orig. term of respectful address to clerics, voc. case of *dominus* master, lord (see DOM¹); cf. †*domine* clergyman (XVII–XVIII), prob. – Du. *dominé*. The present currency is due to the character Dominie Sampson in Scott's 'Guy Mannering'.

dominion dŏmi·njən lordship, sway XV; domains of a feudal lord or sovereign (now, the specific designation of some countries of the British Commonwealth) XIV; (leg.) ownership (L. *dominium*) XVII. – OF. *dominion* – medL. *dominiō(n-)*, f. *dominium* property (cf. CONDOMINIUM), f. *dominus* master, lord (see DOM¹).

domino dɔ·minou A. cloak with a half-mask worn at masquerades, person wearing this XVIII; the mask itself XIX; B. rectangular piece used in the game (*dominoes*) having the under side black and the upper blank or marked with pips XIX. – F. *domino* priest's winter cloak with hood (XVI), hooded masquing garment, name of the game (XVIII); presumably a deriv. of L. *dominus* (see DOM¹). The marked difference of use (A and B) has not been satisfactorily accounted for; the assoc. of the second with the first by reference to the black back of the pieces and the attribution of the game to an abbot *Domino* lack confirmation. From the use of *domino!* at the end of the game it has been generalized as an int. for 'full up!' and as marking the completion of an action.

don¹ dɔn (arch., dial.) put on. XIV (Ch.). In early use also *d'on*, *do'n*; contr. of *do on*; DO¹ (in the sense 'put'). ON adv.; after *c.* 1650 retained in pop. use in north. dial.; revived in literary use by Scott, like DOFF. Walker marks *don* as little used and *doff* as obsolete.

don², Don dɔn Sp. title prefixed to a man's Christian name; Sp. lord or gentleman, Spaniard; distinguished or important man, (dial.) adept; (in English universities) head, fellow, or tutor of a college XVII. Sp. :– L. *dominu-s*. Cf. DAN, DOM¹.

dona, also *donah*, *doner* dou·nə (sl.) woman, girl. XIX. – Sp. *doña* (Pg. *dona*) = It. DONNA :– L. *domina* mistress, lady, f. *domus* house, home (cf. DOMESTIC).

donate dounei·t (chiefly U.S.) make a gift of. XIX. Back-formation from **dona·tion**. XV (Wyntoun). – (O)F. – L., noun of action f. *donāre*, f. *dōnum* gift, f. **dō*- (cf. DATIVE). **do·native**. XV (Lydg.). – L., n. of *dōnātivus*. **do·nor¹**. XV. – AN. *donour*, OF. *doneur* :– L. *dōnātōr(em)*. Hence **donee·**. XVI.

Donatist dou·nətist one of a Christian sect of N. Africa (IV). XV. – late L. *Dōnātista*, f. *Dōnātus* (of uncertain identity); see -IST.

done dʌn pp. of DO¹.

donga dɔ·ŋgə in S. Africa, ravine or gully with steep sides. XIX. Bantu.

dongola dɔ·ŋgŏlə epithet of a race in which a punt or canoe is propelled by paddling by equal numbers of either sex; also of a kind of leather and a red colour. XIX. f. name of a district of the Sudan, N. Africa.

donjon arch. sp. of DUNGEON.

donkey dɔ·ŋki ass. XVIII (Grose). In early use pronounced so as to r.w. *monkey*, whence the proposed derivs. from DUN¹ and from the proper name *Duncan* (cf. *dicky*, *neddy*).

donna dɔ·nə lady; title of courtesy for an It. or (instead of *doña, dona*) a Sp. or Pg. lady. XVII. It. :- L. *domina*, fem. of *dominus* DON². Cf. PRIMA DONNA.

donor see DONATE.

donzella dontse·lla young lady. It., Pr. :- Rom. **dominicella*, dim. of L. *domina* DAME; cf. DAMSEL.

doob dūb dog's-tooth grass, Cynodon Dactylon. XIX. – Hindi *dūb* :- Skr. *dūrvā*.

doodle dū·dl simpleton, noodle XVII; (U.S.) Yankee or Union soldier; larva of tiger-beetle (also **doodle-bug**, which was applied in 1944 to the 'flying bomb'); aimless scrawl on paper XX. In the first sense – LG. *dudel-* in *dudeltopf, -dopp* simple fellow; the connexion of the other senses is doubtful; the last is prob. rel. to dial. vb. *doodle* fritter time away.

doolie dū·li Indian litter or palanquin. XVII (*dowle, doola*). – Hindi *ḍōlī*, dim. of *ḍōlā* swing, cradle, litter :- Skr. *dolā*, f. *dul-* swing.

doom dūm (hist.) statute, ordinance; decision, sentence OE.; trial, judgement XIII; (final) fate XIV. OE. *dōm* = OFris., OS. *dōm* ,OHG. *tuom*, ON. *dómr*, Goth. *dōms* :- CGerm. **dōmaz* lit. that which is set or put, f. **dō-* place, set, DO¹. For the sense-development cf. Gr. *thémis* law (**the-* place), L. *statūtum* STATUTE. Hence **doom** vb. XV.

doom var. of DOUM.

doomsday dū·mzdei Day of Judgement. OE. *dōmes dæġ*, g. of DOOM and DAY; cf. DOMESDAY. So ON. *dómsdagr*, MDu. *doem(e)dach*.

doomster dū·mstəɹ †judge XV; (Sc.) official who formerly recited the judicial sentence XVII (Skene). Alteration of *demester*, DEMPSTER, after DOOM.

door dɔ̄əɹ hinged or sliding barrier for closing an entrance. (i) OE. *duru* (fem. *u*-stem) = OFris. *dure*, OS. *duru*, corr. to other Germ. (orig. pl.) forms with *i*-stem, ODu. *dori* pl. (Du. *deur* fem. sg.), OHG. *turi* pl. (G. *tür* fem. sg.), ON. *dyrr* fem. pl. and n., Goth. *daurōns* fem. wk. pl. (ii) OE. *dor* n., pl. *doru* = OS. *dor*, (O)HG. *tor* gate, Goth. *daur*. The IE. base **dhur-* is repr. also by Skr. *dur, dvār* (orig. dual or pl.), Gr. *thúrā*, L. *foris* (cf. FOREIGN), OIr. *dorus* (:- **dhworest-*), OSl. *dvĭrĭ* gate, *dvorŭ* court, Lith. *dùrys* gate. The ME. descendants of OE. *duru* and *dor* coalesced, *dur* and *dore* existing beside *dure* and *dor*; the form *dore* lasted from XIII to XVII; the sp. *door* (from XVI) implies a ME. *dǭr*, which is confirmed by Sc. *dūr* (in north. Eng. 'Cath. Angl.' *dure, duyr*, 1483); the local pronunc. duəɹ, which reflects this, has been replaced in standard use by dɔ̄əɹ; cf. *floor*. ¶ If one should rime to this word (Restore) he may not match him with (Doore) or (Poore) for neither of both are of like terminant ('Arte of English Poesie', 1589).

dop doup Cape brandy distilled from grape-skins. XIX. – Afrikaans use of Du. *dop* shell, husk.

dope doup (orig. U.S.) lubricating fluid; opium or other narcotic XIX. – Du. *doop* sauce, f. *doopen* dip, mix, adulterate (see DIP), whence **dope** vb.

doppelganger dɔ·plgæːŋgəɹ apparition of a living person, wraith, double. XIX. – G. *doppelgänger* 'double-goer', '-walker' = Du. *dubbelganger*; semi-anglicized by Scott and C. Kingsley as *double-ganger*.

dopper dɔ·pəɹ Dutch Baptist. XVII (B. Jonson). – (with shortening of vowel) Du. *dooper*, f. *doopen* dip, baptize (cf. DOPE).

dor dɔ̄ɹ species of fly or beetle OE.; flying beetle XV. OE. *dora*; cf. MLG. *dorte* drone; prob. imit. of humming noise.

Dora dɔ̄·rə joc. make-up of the initials of *D*efence *o*f the *R*ealm *A*ct (August 1914), forming a common female Christian name.

dorado dŏrā·dou the fish Coryphæna hippuris XVII; the constellation xiphias (swordfish) XIX. – Sp. *dorado* :- L. *dēaurātu-s*, pp. of *dēaurāre* (see DORY¹).

Dorcas dɔ̄·ɹkəs *D. society* church society of ladies for providing clothes for the poor. XIX. Name of a woman disciple 'full of good works', mentioned in Acts ix 36.

doria, dorea dɔ̄·riə kind of striped Indian muslin.

Dorian dɔ̄·riən pert. to Doris, a division of ancient Greece; (mus.) name of one of the ancient Gr. musical modes. XVII. f. L. *Dōrius* – Gr. *Dṓrios*, f. *Dōrís*; see -IAN. So **Dor**IC dɔ·rik Dorian XVI; one of the main dialects of ancient Greek; (hence) rustic; one of the Greek orders of architecture XVII. – L. *Dōricus* – Gr. *Dōrikós*.

Dorking dɔ̄·ɹkiŋ breed of poultry. XIX. Name of a town in Surrey.

dormant dɔ̄·ɹmənt (hist.) fixed, stationary XIV (*table dormant*, Ch.); sleeping; inactive, quiescent XVI. – (O)F. *dormant*, prp. of *dormir* :- L. *dormīre* sleep, rel. to OSl. *drĕmati* (Russ. *dremát'* slumber), and further to Skr. *drā́ti, drā́yati* sleeps, Gr. *édrathon* I slept. So **dormer** dɔ̄·ɹməɹ projecting vertical window in a sloping roof (orig. dormitory window). XVI. – OF. *dormeor*, f. *dormir* sleep + *-eor* -ER². **dormition** dɔ̄ɹmi·ʃən falling asleep. XV (Caxton). – F. – L. **dormit**ORY dɔ̄·ɹmitəri sleeping-chamber. XV. – L. *dormītōrium*, sb. use of n. of *dormītōrius* (Pliny), f. *dormīt-*, pp. stem of *dormīre* sleep; so OF. *dormitoire*. **dorter, -our** dɔ̄·ɹtəɹ (hist.) dormitory (e.g. of a monastery). XIII. – OF. *dortour* (mod. *dortoir*) = Pr. *dormidor* :- L. *dormītōrium*.

dormouse dɔ̄·ɹmaus small hibernating rodent, Myoxus. XV. Of unkn. origin; it has been suggested that it was f. north. dial. *dorm* sleep; cf. the Du. names †*slaepmuys*, †*slaepratte* 'sleep-mouse', '-rat'. Treated as a comp. of *mouse*, with pl. *-mice*, since XVI; but *-mouses* occurs XVI–XVII.

dormy dǭ·ɹmi (in golf) leading by as many holes as there are holes to play. XIX. Of unkn. origin.

dorothy bag dɔ·rəþi bæg lady's open-topped handbag. XX. *Dorothy*, female Christian name, BAG.

dorp dǭɹp †village XVI (Stanyhurst); (S. Africa) small town XX. – Du. *dorp* = OE. *þorp* THORP.

dorsal dǭ·ɹsəl pert. to the back. XV. – (O)F. *dorsal* or late L. *dorsālis*, for L. *dorsuālis*, f. *dorsum* back; see -AL[1]. Cf. DOSSAL. So **dorsi-, dorso-** (see -O-), comb. forms of L. *dorsum*.

dory[1] dǭ·ri the fish Zeus faber (also JOHN DORY). XIV (*darre*). – F. *dorée*, sb. use of fem. pp. of *dorer* gild :– late L. *dēaurāre*, f. *dē* DE- + *aurāre* gild, f. *aurum* gold; so called from its yellowish colour with metallic reflections.

dory[2] dǭ·ri small W. Indian and U.S. boat. XVIII. Of unkn. origin.

dose dous, (Sc.) douz prescribed quantity of medicine. XV. – F. *dose* – late L. *dosis* (which was earlier in Eng. use) – Gr. *dósis* giving, gift, portion of medicine (Galen), f. *didónai* give (cf. DONATION). Hence **dose** vb. XVII; cf. F. *doser*.

doss dɔs (sl.) sb. bed; vb. sleep. XVIII. Earlier *dorse*; f. L. *dorsum* (F. *dos*) back. For the loss of *r* cf. BASS[1], DACE.

dossal dɔ·səl ornamental cloth on or at the back of a chair, an altar, etc. XVII. Also *dossel*, earlier †*dosel*, †*dorsel* – medL. *dossāle*, n. of *dossālis*, for *dorsālis* (see DORSAL); cf. OF. *dossal, -el*. The ME. word was †*dos(s)er* (XIV) – OF. *dossier* (see next).

dossier dɔ·siei ‖ dosje set of documents relating to a matter. XIX. – F. *dossier* bundle of papers in a wrapper having a label on the back (XVII), f. *dos* back (:– L. *dorsum*; cf. DORSAL) + *-ier* (:– L. *-ārium* -ARY).

dost dʌst see DO[1].

dot[1] dɔt (dial.) small lump, clot XVI; minute mark XVII. OE. *dott* (once) head of a boil, perh. in continuous colloq. use (cf. the dim. DOTTLE), but not recorded again till XVI in the gen. sense of 'small knob or lump', when its appearance may be due to Du. *dot* knot, prob. rel. to OHG. *tutto, tutta* nipple (cf. G. dial. *tütte*, MHG. dim. *tüttel* nipple, G. *tüttel* point, dot, jot); for the prob. base **dutt-* cf. OE. *dyttan* (:– **duttjan*), dial. *dit* stop up, plug. Hence **dot** vb. XVIII.

dot[2] dɔt dowry. XIX (Thackeray). – (O)F. *dot* – L. *dōtem*, nom. *dōs*, f. **dō-* give (cf. DONATION). An earlier form was †*dote* (XVI) – F. var. †*dote*.

dote, doat dout A. be silly or weak-minded XIII; B. bestow excessive fondness *upon* XV. ME. *dotie* (perh. OE. **dotian*), corr. to MDu. *doten* be silly (whence OF. *redoter*, mod. *radoter*). In A now usu. *dote*, in B *doat* (from XVI). Hence **do·t**AGE weak-minded senility XIV; cf. F. *radotage*. **do·t**ARD one in his dotage XIV (Ch.); cf. synon. ME. †*dote* (XII), which appears to be the earliest word of this group, and based on MDu. *dote* folly. ME. had also *dotel* fool, dotard (XIV–XV), and vbs. *adote* intr. (XIII–XIV) and *bedote* trans. (XIV–XVI).

doth dʌþ see DO[1].

dott(e)rel dɔ·t(ə)rəl species of plover; dotard. XV. f. DOTE + -REL, the bird was presumably so named from its (alleged) stupidity. ¶ *Dotterel* is applied dial. to a 'doddered', stunted, or decaying tree (XVI), as was also †*dotard* (XVII–XVIII), with which are to be connected dial. *dote* decay, and *doted* decayed (XV); but the relations are obscure.

dottle dɔ·tl †plug XV; plug of tobacco ash in the bottom of a pipe XIX. dim. of DOT[1]; see -LE[1].

dotty dɔ·ti covered with dots; (sl.) of unsteady gait (from phr. *dot and go* or *carry one*, said of one who has a wooden leg, XVIII); of feeble mind, daft XIX. See -Y[1].

douane dua·n custom-house. XVII. – F. – It. *doana, dogana* – Turk, *duwan*, Arab. *diwān* DIVAN.

double dʌ·bl consisting of two. twofold XIII; twice as many XIV. – OF. *doble, duble*, later and mod. *double* = Pr., Sp. *doble*, It. *doppio* :– L. *duplu-s* DUPLE. So **double** vb. XIII. – OF. *dobler, dubler* (mod. *doubler*) :– late L. *duplāre*.

double entendre dū·bl ãtã·dr double meaning, phrase capable of this. XVII (Dryden). F. phr. (rare) 'double understanding'; see DOUBLE, INTEND; anglicized †*double extender* (XVII–XVIII).

doublet dʌ·blit (hist.) close-fitting body garment for men XIV; one of two things exactly alike XVI (philol. one of two words in the same language deriving from the same ultimate word XIX). – (O)F. *doublet*, f. *double*; see prec. and -ET.

doubloon dʌblū·n Sp. gold coin, orig. double of the pistole. XVII. – F. *doublon* or its source Sp. *doblón*, augm. f. *doble* DOUBLE. See -OON.

doubt daut †fear; be in uncertainty XIII (AncrR., Cursor M.). – OF. *doter, duter* (mod. *douter*) = Pr. *dobtar*, Sp. *dudar*, Pg. *duvidar* :– L. *dubitāre* waver, hesitate, rel. to *dubius* DUBIOUS. The latinized sp. with *b* appears XV, following F. †*doubter*. The sense 'fear' was an early and prominent sense, which survives dial.; cf. *redoubtable*. So **doubt** sb. †fear; uncertainty. XIII. – OF. *dote, dute* (mod. *doute*), f. *douter*. Hence **dou·bt**FUL[1]. XIV, which was preceded by †*dou(b)tous* (– OF. *doutous*, mod. *douteux*). **dou·bt**LESS adv. without doubt. XIV.

douce dūs †sweet, pleasant XIV; (Sc.) quiet, sober XVIII. – OF. *dous* (mod. *doux*), fem. *douce* = Pr. *dols*, Cat. *dous*, Pg. *doce*, It. *dolce*, Rum. *dulce* :– L. *dulci-s* sweet, rel. to Gr. *glukús* (cf. GLYCERINE).

douceur dū·sǿɹ †pleasantness; †complimentary speech XVII (Dryden); gratuity, tip XVIII (H. Walpole). – F. *douceur*, earlier †*dousour*, etc. = Pr. *dolzor*, Sp. *dulzor* :– Rom. **dulçōre*, for late L. *dulcōrem*, nom. *dulcor* sweetness, f. *dulcis* sweet; see prec. ¶ An adoption of the OF. word had some currency in ME.

douche dūʃ stream of water applied to the body. XVIII (Smollett). – F. *douche* – It. *doccia* conduit pipe, f. *docciare* pour by drops :– Rom. **ductiāre*, f. *ductus* DUCT.

dough dou mass of flour moistened into a paste. OE. *dāg* = OFris. *deeg*, MLG. *dēch* (Du. *deg*), OHG. *teic* (G. *teig*), ON. *deig*, Goth. *daigs* :– CGerm. **daigaz*, f. **daiʒ-* :– IE. **dhoigh-* **dheigh-* **dhigh-* smear, knead, form of clay (so Goth. *digan*), whence also Skr. *dih* smear, *dēhas* body, Av. *pairi|daēza-* (see PARADISE), Arm. *dēz* heap, L. **fig-* in *fingere* (see FICTION), *figūra* FIGURE, Gr. *teîkhos*, *toîkhos* wall (for **theîkhos*, **thoîkhos*), OSl. *zĭdŭ* clay, Lith. *dýžti* beat soundly, Goth. *digrei* abundance, ON. *digr* stout, big. Cf. LADY.

doughty dau·ti †worthy; valiant, stout. Late OE. *dohtiġ*, new formation prob. after *dohte*, pt. of *dugan* be of use or worthy, replacing *dyhtiġ* (ME. *dühti*), corr. to MLG., MDu. *duchtich* (Du. *duchtig*), MHG. *tühtic* (G. *tüchtig* brave), f. MHG. *tuht* bravery, f. **tug-* of OHG. *tugan* (= OE., OS. *dugan* be worth, competent, strong, ON. *duga*, Goth. **dugan*, in 3rd pres. ind. *daug* is profitable; cf. Lith. *daũg* much, OSl., Russ. *dyúzhiĭ* strong); see -Y[1].

Doukhobors dū·kobǭɹz Russian sect. XIX. Russ. *dukhobórȳ* 'spirit-wrestlers', f. *dukh* spirit+*borót'sya* wrestle.

doum, doom daum, dūm kind of palm. XVIII. – Arab. *daum*, *dūm*.

dour duəɹ, Sc. dūr (Sc. and north.) hard, stern XIV; stubborn, sullen XV. prob. – Gael. *dúr* dull, stupid, obstinate = (M)Ir. *dúr*, which may be – L. *dūrus* hard; but the possibility of an early (Anglian) adoption of the L. word cannot be excluded.

douse[1], dowse daus †strike XVI; strike (sail) XVII; doff; dout XVIII. perh. rel. to similar and partly synon. MDu., LG. *dossen*, Du. *doesen* (Kilian), G. dial. *dusen* beat, strike.

douse[2] daus †plunge in liquid; drench. XVI (Holland). prob. imit. (cf. *souse*), but poss. identical with prec.

douse[3] see DOWSE.

dout daut (dial.) put out, extinguish. XVI. contr. of *do out*; cf. DOFF, DON[2], DUP.

dove dʌv bird of the pigeon family (Columbidæ) XII; appellation of tender affection XIV (Ch.). ME. *duve*, *douve*, *dofe* – ON. *dúfa* = OFris. *dūve*, OS. *dūƀa* (Du. *duif*), OHG. *tūba* (G. *taube*), Goth. *dūbo* :– CGerm. (exc. OE.) **dūƀōn*, presumed to be imit. of the bird's note. See CULVER.

dowager dau·idʒəɹ woman whose husband is dead and enjoys a title or property derived from him. XVI (applied to Mary Tudor, widow of Louis XII, and Catherine of Aragon, styled *Princess Dowager*). – OF. *douag(i)ere*, f. *douage* dower, f. *douer* portion, ENDOW+*-iere* :– L. *-āria* -ARY.

dowd daud †ugly woman XIV (R. Mannyng); shabbily or drably dressed woman XVIII. Of unkn. origin. Hence **dow·dy[1]** sb. XVI; adj. XVII; denoting ugliness until XVIII.

dowel dau·əl headless peg, bolt, etc. XIV. perh. – MLG. *dovel*, corr. to OHG. *tubili* (MHG. *tübel*; G. *döbel*, after LG.), f. Germ. **duƀ-* :– IE. **dhubh-*, whence Gr. *túphos* (:– **thuphos*) wedge. Cf. THOLE.

dower dauəɹ dowry XIV (Ch.); †portion of a deceased husband's estate allowed to a widow XIV. – (O)F. *douaire* – medL. *dōtārium*, f. L. *dōt-*, *dōs* dowry, *dōtāre* endow; cf. -ARY. So **dowry** dauə·ri †dower (R. Mannyng); money that a wife brings her husband XIV. – AN. *dowarie* = (O)F. *douaire*.

dowlas dau·ləs †coarse linen, (now) strong calico. XV. f. name of *Doulas*, *Daoulas*, a town south-east of Brest in Brittany; cf. *lockram*.

down[1] daun †hill OE.; open expanse of high ground, spec. in pl. XIII (RGlouc.); *the Downs* part of the sea within the Goodwin Sands off the east coast of Kent, opposite to the eastern end of the North Downs XV; dune XVI. OE. *dūn* = OFris. *dūne*, OS. *dūna* (Du. *duin*; cf. DUNE), a word of the LG. area, perh. – OCeltic (Gaulish) **dūnom* (cf. place-names *Augusto|dūnum* Autun, *Novio|dūnum*), whence (O)Ir. *dún* fort, W. †*dīn* fort (cf. *dinas* city), cogn. with OE. *tūn* TOWN.

down[2] daun first feathering of young birds. XIV (Ch.). – ON. *dúnn* (also in comb. *æðardún* EIDER-DOWN), whence LG. *dūne*, G. *daune*.

down[3] daun adv. to or in a low or lower position or level. OE. *dūne* in *dūnestīgende* descending (Vespasian Psalter Gloss lxxxvii 5 'descendentibus'), *dūne āstag* descended (Lindisfarne Gospels, Luke iv 31), *dūn* in Peterborough Chronicle (XII) and Ormulum; aphetic of *adūne*, *ofdūne* ADOWN. Hence **down** prep. in a descending direction along. XIV (Cursor M.). **dow·ncast** cast down, ruined; directed downwards. XVII. **dow·nfall[1]** fall from high estate XIII (Cursor M.); descent XV. **downhearted** XVIII (Goldsmith). f. *down* depressed XVII (Jonson). **downright** vertically downwards XIII (Laȝ.); thoroughly, outright XIV; adj. XVI; aphetic of *adounriht*. **dow·nward**. XII: aphetic of †*adownward*, late OE. *adūnweard*.

down[4] daun meaningless word in refrains, as *downe downe downe a downe'a* (Sh.), echoed by later poets; see also DERRY. Hence †**down** sb. refrain of a song. XVII (Cotgr.).

dowse dauz, daus use the divining-rod. XVII (*deusing rod*, Locke, 1691). Of S.W. dial. origin, being proper to Somerset, Devon, and Cornwall; the local pronunc. is deuz, which is shown by Locke, who was born at Wrington, Somerset; the forms *dawze* and *jowse* also occur; the source is unkn.

doxology dɔksɔ·lədʒi formal ascription of praise to God. XVII (Jer. Taylor). – medL. *doxologia* – Gr. *doxologiā*, f. *doxológos* giving glory, f. *dóxa* glory + *-logos* speaking, *légein* speak; see -LOGY.

doxy[1] dɔ·ksi beggar's or vagrant's wench, (gen.) paramour, harlot. XVI. orig. rogues' cant; of unkn. origin.

doxy[2] dɔ·ksi (sl.) opinion. XVIII. Terminal el. of *orthodoxy* and *heterodoxy* used joc. (with ref. to DOXY[1]) as a word. ¶ Cf. 'Orthodox and other dox' (Amory, 1756).

doyen dwa·jɛ̃ senior member of a body (transf. from the position of dean as head of a cathedral chapter). XVII. F.; see DEAN[2].

doyl(e)y see DOILY.

doze douz †stupefy, muddle, perplex; sleep drowsily XVII. prob. much earlier in local use and perh. of Scand. origin, but words of kindred meaning do not corr. exactly in form, e.g. Da. *døse* drowse, mope, *døs* drowsiness, ON. *dúsa* ?doze, *dús*, *dos* lull, calm, Sw. dial. *dusa* slumber. Hence **doze** sb. XVIII.

dozen dʌ·zn set of 12. XIII (Cursor M.). ME. *dozein(e)* – OF. *dozeine*, *-aine* (mod. *douzaine*) = Pr. *dotzena*, Sp. *docena* (It. *dozzina* – F., whence also G. *dutzend*); Rom. deriv. with *-ēna* (as in L. *decēna*, *centēna*, etc. group of 10, 100, etc.) on **do(t)ze* :– **dōdece* :– L. *duodecim* 12, f. *duo* TWO + *decem* (*-im*) TEN.

drab[1] dræb slattern; harlot. XVI. prob. in origin a cant or slang word; perh. from Du. or LG., in which there is a group of similar words meaning 'mud', 'mire', 'dregs', viz. Du. *drab* dregs, LG. *drabbe* thick dirty liquid, mire, *drabbig* muddy (cf. DRABBLE). ¶ Ir. *drabóg* slut, Gael. *drabach* slatternly, are from Eng.

drab[2] dræb †kind of cloth XVI; dull yellowish-brown colour XVII. prob. alteration of †*drap* cloth (of which it was an alternative form XVII–XVIII), due to assim. occurring in such comps. as *drap-de-Berry*, *drab-de-Berry*; *drap* – (O)F. *drap* = Pr. *drap*, in It. *drapo*, Sp. *trapo* rag, – late L. *drappus* perh. of Celtic origin. For the transition of sense in Eng. cf. *drapp-colour* XVII, *drap-coloured*, *Brown Drap* XVIII.

drabble dræ·bl become wet or make wet with muddy water. XIV. – LG. *drabbelen* walk or paddle in water or mire; see DRAB[1] and -LE[2].

drachm dræm †drachma; unit of weight, DRAM. XIV. Late ME. *dragme* – OF. *dragme* or late L. *dragma*, var. of L. *drachma* – Gr. *drakhmḗ* Attic weight and coin, prob. orig. 'handful of coins', f. base **drakh-* of *drássesthai* seize, grasp. Also **drachma** dræ·kmə. XVI. ¶ Cf. *dirhem* (XVIII, Gibbon) – Arab. *dirham* – L. *drachma*.

draconic, Draconic drəkɔ·nik A. pert. to a dragon XVII; B. pert. to Draco (archon at Athens 621 B.C.) or his severe code of laws XVIII. f. L. *drācō(n-)* DRAGON or the proper name *Dracō*, Gr. *Drákōn* + -IC. So **draco·nian, D-.** XIX.

draff dræf dregs, refuse. XIII (Laȝ.). If not orig. a term of beer-manufacture of LG. origin, perh. repr. OE. **dræf* = MLG., (M)Du. *draf*, OHG. **trab*, pl. *trebir* (G. *treber*, *träber* husks, grains), ON. **draf* (Icel. *draf*, Norw. *drav* mash). ¶ Ir., Gael. *drabh* is from Eng.

draft drȧft var. of DRAUGHT, recorded XVI and established since XVIII for certain senses. Hence **draft** vb. XVIII.

drag dræg pull, haul XIV; use a drag to XV. Obscurely developed from OE. *dragan* DRAW, or – cogn. ON. *draga* (Sw. *draga*, Da. *drage*); cf. *swag*, *wag*. Hence or partly – MLG. *dragge* grapnel. **drag** sb. XIV ('harrow', †'float, raft'), XIV ('drag-net'), XVII ('scent, trail'), XVIII ('carriage, coach').

dragée dræ·ʒei sweetmeat used as the vehicle of a drug. XIX. F.; see DREDGE[2].

draggle dræ·gl soil (a garment), etc., by dragging it through wet or mire. XVI (G. Douglas). f. DRAG vb. + -LE[2]. An earlier form was *drakelyn* XV (Promp. Parv.).

dragoman dræ·gəmən interpreter. XVI. – F. †*dragoman* (now *drogman*) – It. *dragomano* – medGr. *dragómanos* – early Arab. *targumān*, now *tarjumān* (see TRUCHMAN), f. *targama*, *tarjama* interpret (see TARGUM). The earlier forms *drog(e)man* (from XIV) and other vars. repr. OF. *drugemen*, Pr. *drogoman*, medL. *dragumannus*. The Eng. word has often been apprehended as a comp. of *man*, and consequently inflected *-men* instead of *-mans*.

dragon dræ·gən huge serpent or reptile (with wings). XIII. – (O)F. *dragon* – L. *dracōnem*, *dracō* (whence also Pr., Sp. *dragon*, It. *dragone*) – Gr. *drákōn*, commonly referred to **drak-* **derk-*, repr. also in Gr. *dérkesthai*, aorist *drakeîn* see clearly, Skr. *darç* see, Av. *darštis* sight, OIr. *derc* eye, OE. *torht* (= OS. *torht*, OHG. *zoraht*) clear, bright.

dragonnade drægənei·d persecution directed by Louis XIV against French protestants in which dragoons were quartered upon the victims. XVIII. – F. *dragonnade*, f. *dragon* DRAGOON; see -ADE.

dragoon drəgū·n †carbine, musket, so called from its 'breathing fire' like a dragon; cavalry soldier, orig. applied to mounted infantry armed with this weapon. XVII. – F. *dragon* DRAGON; see -OON. Hence **dragoo·n** vb. set dragoons upon, force rigorous measures upon. XVII; after F. *dragonner*.

drain drein †strain OE.; draw liquid away in small quantities. XVI. OE. *drēahnian*, *drēhnian*, prob. f. **drēag*- :- Germ. **draug*- (see DRY). The normal repr. of the OE. is drīn, as shown by *drean* (XVI–XVII) and in some dialects; for the present standard pronunc. cf. *great*. Hence **drain** sb. XV. Hence **drai·n**AGE, action of draining, system of drains. XVII.

drake[1] dreik †dragon (cf. *fire-drake*) OE.; (from LG.) kind of cannon; angler's name for species of fly XVII. OE. *draca* = OFris., MLG., MDu. *drake* (Du. *draak*), OHG. *trahho* (G., with MG. initial, *drache*) :- CWGerm. **drako* – L. *dracō* (see DRAGON).

drake[2] dreik male of the duck. XIII (Havelok). To be referred, with G. dial. (LG.) *drake*, *drache*, to WGerm. **drako* (**dreko*), of obscure origin, which forms the second element of OHG. *antrahho*, *antrehho*, for **anutrahho* (G. *enterich*, dial. *endedrach*, *entrach*), the first el. of this compound being OHG. *anut*, *enit*, MHG. *anet*, *ant*, *ente* (G. *ente*) = OE. *ened*, MLG. *anet* (Du. *eend*), ON. *ǫnd*; widespread IE. word for 'duck', repr. by L. *anas*, *anat*-, Gr. *nêssa*, *nâssa*, Lith. *ántis*, OSl. *ąty* duck, and perh. Skr. *ātís* aquatic bird.

dram dræm †drachm, drachma XV; ⅛ fluid ounce, (hence) small draught of cordial or spirituous liquor XVI. – OF. *drame* or medL. *drama*, var. of DRACHMA.

drama drā·mə composition to be acted on a stage. XVII (B. Jonson; in anglicized form †*drame*. XVI). – late L. *drāma* – Gr. *drâma*, -*at*- deed, action, play (esp. tragedy), f. *drân* do, act. So **dramat**IC drəmæ·tik. XVI. – late L. – Gr. **dramatis personæ** dræ·mətis pɔ̄ɹsou·nī (list of) characters in a play. XVIII (Fielding). L. 'persons of a drama'. **dramat**IST dræ·m-. XVII (Cudworth). **dra·mat**IZE. XVIII. Cf. F. *drame*, *dramatique*, -*iste*, -*iser*, all recorded later than the corr. Eng. words. **dra·maturge** -ɔ̄ɹdʒ playwright. XIX. – F. *dramaturge* – Gr. *dramatourgós*, f. *dramato*- + -*ergos* worker (cf. WORK).

drape dreip A. †make into cloth XV; B. cover with drapery. XIX. In A – OF. *draper*, f. *drap* cloth = Pr. *drap* :- late L. *drappus*, poss. of Celtic origin; in B (recorded first from Tennyson) back-formation from DRAPERY, suggested by F. *draper*. So **drap**ER[1] drei·pəɹ dealer in cloth, and now, in other textiles. XIV (PPl.). – AN. *draper*, (O)F. *drapier*, f. *drap*. **dra·p**ERY cloth, textile fabric XIV; business or shop of a draper XV; artistic arrangement of clothing; stuff with which an object is draped XVII. – (O)F. *draperie*.

drastic dræ·stik (of medicines) acting strongly XVII; vigorously effective XIX. – Gr. *drastikós* active, effective, f. *drastós*, ppl. adj. of *drân* do; see DRAMA and -IC. Cf. F. *drastique* (XVIII).

drat dræt mild substitute for 'damn!'. XIX. Aphetic for *od-ra·t* (Fielding), i.e. *Od*, minced form of GOD, and RAT[2].

draught dràft act of drawing XII; that which is drawn or pulled XIII; †move at chess, etc.; pl. game played on a board XIV; †picture, sketch XV; design, plan XVI; (perh. short for †*withdraught*) †cesspool, privy XVI; current of air XVIII. Early ME. *draht*, if not in OE., – ON. **drahtr*, *dráttr*, later reinforced from (M)Du. *dragt* = OHG. *traht* (G. *tracht*), abstr. sb. f. **dragan* DRAW; see -T. Cf. DRAFT.

Dravidian drəvi·diən pert. to the race inhabiting S. India and parts of Ceylon. XIX (R. Caldwell, 'A Grammar of the Dravidian Languages', 1856). f. Skr. *drāviḍa* pert. to *Dravida*, name of a province of S. India; see -IAN.

draw drɔ̄, pt. **drew** drū, pp. **drawn** drɔ̄n general vb. for the expression of various kinds of traction, attraction, extraction, and protraction (infl. in some uses by assoc. with L. *trahere* draw); trace or delineate on a surface XIII; frame, formulate XVI; intr. move, make one's way OE. A CGerm. str. vb.: OE. *dragan*, pt. *drōh*, *drōgon*, pp. *dræ̀gen*, *dragen* = ON. *draga*, *dró*, *drógum*, *dreginn* draw, pull, and (in the sense 'bear, carry', 'wear') OFris. *draga*, OS. *dragan* (Du. *dragen*), OHG. *tragan* (G. *tragen*, *trug*, *getragen*), Goth. (*ga*)*dragan* (only in prp. -*and*). ¶ Not immed. rel. to synon. L. *trahere*.

drawcansir drɔ̄kæ·nsəɹ Name of a fierce swashbuckling character in Villiers's 'The Rehearsal' (1672); burlesque alteration of *Almanzor* of Dryden's 'Conquest of Granada' (1670–2), perh. designed to suggest *draw* and *can* (of liquor).

drawer drɔ̄(ə)ɹ receptacle sliding in and out of a table frame, etc. XVI. f. DRAW + -ER[1], after F. *tiroir* (XIV), f. *tirer* draw (cf. RETIRE).

drawers drɔ̄(ə)ɹz two-legged under-garment suspended from the waist. XVI (given as 'Peddelers Frenche' for *hosen* in Harman's 'Caveat for Cursetors', 1567). f. DRAW + -ER[1] with pl. -*s*.

drawing-room drɔ̄·iŋrūm. XVII. Shortening of *withdrawing-room* (XVI); †*drawing-chamber* is earlier (XVI).

drawl drɔ̄l †crawl or drag along; speak with indolent or affected slowness. XVI. prob. orig. vagrants' cant – EFris., LG., Du. *dralen* delay, linger. ¶ †*Drail*, of similar date, was used in the same senses.

dray drei †sled or cart without wheels XIV; low cart without sides for heavy loads XVI. Late ME. *dreye, draye* (AL. *dreia*), corr. formally (though evidence of continuity is wanting and the meanings are different) to OE. *dræġe* (also *dræġnet*) drag-net, f. base of *dragan* DRAW (cf. MLG. *drage* bier, litter, OHG. *traga*, ON. *draga* trailing load of timber).

dread dred fear greatly. XII. ME. *drēden*, in Ormulum *drædenn, dredenn*, pt. *dredde*; aphetic of OE. *adrǣdan*, late form of *ondrǣdan* = OS. *antdrādan*, OHG. *intrātan*, f. *ond-*, *and-* (as in ANSWER) + a WGerm. base of obscure origin. Hence **dread** sb. XII. **drea·dNOUGHT** thick coat worn in rough weather XIX; specially powerful type of battleship 1906; cf. FEARNOUGHT (XVIII).

dream drīm vision during sleep. XIII (Genesis and Exodus, Cursor M.). ME. *drēm*, identical in form with the ME. repr. of OE. *drēam* joy, jubilation, music, minstrelsy (= OS. *drōm* mirth, noise), but corr. in sense to OFris. *drām*, OS. *drōm* (Du. *droom*), OHG. *troum* (G. *traum*), ON. *draumr*. On the assumption that there has been accommodation of ON. *draumr* to Eng. phonetic conditions, attempts have been made to relate the two meanings to the same original base; on the other hand, the words meaning 'joy' have been connected with Gr. *thrûlos* noise, shouting, those meaning 'dream' with G. *trügen* deceive, ON. *draugr* apparition, through **draugm-*. Hence **dream** vb. XIII (Genesis and Exodus, Cursor M., Havelok). The earliest use was prob. impers. after the impers. use of ON. *dreyma*, e.g. with two accusatives, as in *mik dreymdi draum, draum dreymdi mik* (ME. *a drem dremede me, hem drempte dremes*). ¶ The native OE. words are: *swefn, mǣting* sbs., *swefnian, mǣtan* vbs.

drear driəɹ poet. shortening of DREARY. XVII (Milton, once); partly based on †*drear* sb. dreariness, a back-formation from *dreary* used by Elizabethan archaists (Sackville, Spenser, Bp. Hall).

dreary driə·ri †dire, grievous, †sad, doleful OE.; dismal, gloomy. XVII (Milton). OE. *drēoriġ* bloody, gory, grievous, sorrowful, f. *drēor* gore, flowing blood :- Germ. **dreuzaz*, f. **dreuz-* **drauz-*, whence also OE. *drēosan* drop, fall, OS. *driosan*, Goth. *driusan*, and OS. *drōr*, OHG. *trōr*, ON. *dreyri* gore, blood, MHG. *trūrec* (G. *traurig* sorrowful); see -Y[1]. The comps. **drea·riHEAD** (XIII), **drea·riLY**[2] (OE. *drēoriġlīċe*) were revived by Spenser, who also coined **drea·riMENT**.

dredge[1] dredʒ instrument for dragging the bed of a river, etc. XVI. rel. in some way to early Sc. *dreg* (XV), which may be – MDu. *dregghe* 'harpago', 'verriculum'; but the final cons. of the Eng. word suggests a native origin; no antecedent forms, however, are known to account for this and for the vars. *dradge* (XVI), *dridge* (XVII), *drudge* (XVIII), beside the normal *dredge*. Hence **dredge** vb.[1], **dredgER**[1] XVI (Sc.).

dredge[2] dredʒ A. †sweetmeat containing spice; B. (dial.) mixture of grain. XVI. The forms *dreg(g)e, dradge* are unexpl. alterations of ME. *drag(g)e* (two syll.), *dragie* (XIV–XV) – OF. *dragie*, (also mod.) *dragée*, corr. to Pr., Sp. *dragea*, Sp., Pg. *gragea*, It. *treggea*, which, with medL. *drageia, dragētum, dragāta*, have been referred to L. *tragēmata*, Gr. *tragḗmata* spices, condiments, but the relation is obscure. Sense B is regarded by some as a different word. Hence **dredge** vb.[2] sprinkle with powder XVI (Nashe); whence **dre·dgER**[2] box with perforated lid for sprinkling XVII (Pepys); a var. with *-u-* is found XVII–XIX.

dree drī (dial., arch.) endure, suffer. OE. *drēogan*, pt. *drēah, drugon*, pp. *drogen* perform, endure, f. Germ. **dreug-* **draug-* **drug-*, repr. otherwise by Goth. *driugan* do military service (cf. *ga|drauhts* soldier, *drauhti|witoþ* army) and ON. *drýgja* perpetrate, practise. Revived in literary use by Scott (*dreeing a sair weird*).

dreg dreg (usu. pl.) sediment of liquor; refuse XIV. prob. of Scand. origin (cf. ON. pl. *dreggjar*, MSw. *drägg* 'fæx', Sw. pl. *drägg*), there are poss. cogns. in Balto-Slavic, viz. OPruss. *dragios*, OSl. *droždiję*. The problem of immed. origin is complicated by the occurrence in early modE. of the forms *dragges* and *dredges*. Hence **dre·ggY**[1]. XV (Promp. Parv.); cf. Sw. *dräggig*.

drench drentʃ draught, potion OE.; medicinal dose for an animal XVI. OE. *drenċ* :- Germ. **draŋkiz*, f. **draŋk-*, var. of **driŋk-* DRINK; corr., with variation of declension, to OS. *dranc*, OHG. *tranch* (G. *trank*), ON. *drekka*, Goth. *dragk*. So **drench** make to drink OE. (now spec. in veterinary lang.); †submerge, drown; soak, saturate XIII; wet through XVI. OE. *drenċan* = OFris. *drenza*, OS. *drenkian* (Du. *drenken*), OHG. *trenchen* (G. *tränken*), ON. *drekkja*, Goth. *dragkjan* :- CGerm. **draŋkjan*.

dreng dreŋ (hist.) free tenant (esp. in Northumbria). Late OE. *dreng* ('Battle of Maldon') – ON. *drengr* young man, lad, fellow (Sw. *dräng* man, servant, Da. *dreng* boy, apprentice). Survived till late XIII in literary use, remaining in Sc. for 'low or base fellow' in the regularly developed form *dring*.

dress dres †make or put straight or right; prepare, treat (later, in a specific way) XIV; array, equip, attire XIV; line up (troops) XVIII. – (O)F. *dresser* = Pr. *dressar*, OSp. *derezar*, It. *dirizzare* :- Rom. **dīrectiāre*, f. *dīrectus* DIRECT. Hence **dress** sb. †setting right XVI; personal attire XVII (Sh.).

dresser dre·səɹ sideboard. XV. – OF. *dresseur, dreçor* (mod. *dressoir*; cf. medL. *dīrectōrium*), f. *dresser* prepare; see -ER[2].

dribble dri·bl A. let flow or fall in a trickling stream XVI; B. (football) work the ball forward with repeated touches of the feet XIX. f. *drib* (XVI), modified form of DRIP + -LE[3]. With sense B (perh. a different word) cf. Du. *dribbelen* toddle, trip.

driblet dri·blit small sum or quantity. XVII. f. *drib* vb.; see prec. and -LET; assoc. later with *dribble*.

drift drift driving or driven snow XIII (Cursor M.); driving or being driven XIV; (dial.) drove XV; course, direction; meaning, tenor XVI. orig. – ON. *drift* snowdrift, drifting snow; later – (M)Du. *drift* drove, herd, course, current, impulse, impetuous action = OFris. *drift* in *urdrift* expulsion, MHG., G. *trift* passage of or for cattle, pasturage, drove; f. base of DRIVE; see -T.

drill[1] dril A. bore a hole in XVII; B. train in military evolutions XVI. – MDu. *drillen* bore, turn in a circle, brandish = MLG. *drillen* roll, turn, whence (M)HG. *drillen* turn, round off, bore, drill soldiers. Hence **drill** sb. A. boring instrument; B. military evolutions. XVII. ult. origin unkn.

drill[2] dril W. African baboon. XVII. prob. native name. Now usually MANDRILL.

drill[3] dril small furrow; machine for sowing seed in drills. XVIII. perh. a use of †*drill* small stream, rivulet, of unkn. origin, rel. to †*drill* trickle, drip, which appears to be a var. of THRILL.

drill[4] dril coarse twilled fabric. XVIII. Shortening of *drilling* (XVII), alteration of G. *drillich*, earlier †*drilich* – L. *trilīc-*, *trilix* woven in threefold, f. *tri-* THREE + *līcium* THREAD.

drink driŋk pt. **drank** dræŋk, pp. **drunk** drʌŋk take in liquid by the mouth. OE. *drincan*, pt. *dranc*, *druncon*, pp. *druncen* = OFris. *drinka*, OS. *drinkan* (Du. *drinken*), OHG. *trinchan* (G. *trinken*), ON. *drekka*, Goth. *drigkan* :– CGerm. str. vb. **dreŋkan*, with no ulterior cognates. From XVI *drunk* appears for *drank* in the pt. and is frequent till *c.* 1800; on the other hand, from XVII *drank* was intruded into the pp., prob. to avoid the associations of DRUNK, DRUNKEN. The corr. causative is DRENCH.

drip drip let fall in drops XV (Promp. Parv.); of Scand. origin intr. XVII. – MDa. *drippe* (Da. *dryppe*), f. Germ. **drupp-* (see DROP). In ME. there was a synon. *drepe*, repr. OE. *drēopan* (f. **dreup-*) or more prob. – ON. *drjúpa*. Hence **dri·pp**ING[1]. XV (earlier *drepyng* in concr. sense). ¶ There is no evidence for an OE. **dryppan*.

drive draiv pt. **drove** drouv, pp. **driven** dri·vn force to move before one; move or advance rapidly; carry on vigorously. OE. *drīfan*, pt. *drāf*, *drifon*, pp. *drifen* = OFris. *drīva*, OS. *drīban* (Du. *drijven*), OHG. *trīban* (G. *treiben*, *trieb*, *getrieben*), ON. *drífa*, Goth. *dreiban* :– CGerm. **drīban*, with no certain cogns. outside Germ. The north. repr. *drave* of OE. pt. *drāf* was long in gen. literary use from XVI; *drave* and *drove* are used in Sh. and A.V., only *drove* in Milton's poems. Hence **drive** sb. act of driving XVII; carriage road XIX.

drivel dri·vl dribble, slaver; talk foolishly. XIV (PPl.). ME. *drevele*, *dryuele*, repr. OE. *dreflian*, in prp. glossing medL. *reumaticus* rheumy; a var. †*dravele* points to an OE. var. **dræflian* (cf. DRAFF); see -LE[2].

drizzle dri·zl rain in very fine drops. XVI. perh. earlier in non-literary use (cf. *dwindle*); prob. f. ME. *drēse*, OE. *drēosan* fall = OS. *driosan*, Goth. *driusan* (cf. DREARY); see -LE[3].

drogher drou·gəɹ W. Indian coasting vessel. XVIII. – obs. F. *drogueur* ship that fished and dried herring and mackerel (Jal) – Du. *drooger* dryer, f. *droogen*, f. *droog* DRY.

drogue droug contrivance attached to a harpoon line to check the progress of a whale XVIII; canvas bag towed at a boat's stern to prevent it from broaching to XIX; in aeronautics, canvas cone used as an anchor, etc. XX. Of unkn. origin.

droit droit legal right. XV. – (O)F. *droit* :– Rom. **drectum*, L. *dīrectum*, sb. use of n. of *dīrectus* DIRECT.

droll droul intentionally facetious XVII; unintentionally amusing XVIII. – F. *drôle*, earlier †*drolle*. So **droll** sb. waggish fellow; †farce, puppet-show; †jesting, burlesque. XVII. perh. – MDu. *drolle* little chap. **droll** vb. make fun (of). XVII (Evelyn). – F. †*drôler* play the wag. Hence **dro·ll**ERY †puppet show, comic picture XVI (Sh.); waggery XVII. – F. *drôlerie*.

drome droum short for AERODROME. XX.

-drome droum repr. Gr. *drómos*, as in HIPPODROME, identical with *drómos* running, course, race, rel. to *drameîn*, pf. *dédroma* run, *apodidrā́skein* flee, Skr. *drámati*, Av. part. *dramna-*.

dromedary drʌ·m-, drɔ·midəri light fleet one-humped camel. XIV. – AN. **dromedarie*, OF. *dromedaire* (mod. *dromadaire*), or late L. *dromedārius* (Vulgate), for **dromadārius* (sc. *camēlus* camel), f. *dromad-*, *dromas* dromedary (– Gr. *dromad-*, *dromás* runner; cf. prec.) + *-ārius* -ARY[1].

dromond drɔ·mənd large mediæval ship. XIII. – AN. *dromund*, OF. *dromon(t)*, late L. *dromōn-*, nom. *dromo* – late Gr. *drómōn* large many-oared vessel, f. **drom-* (see -DROME).

drone droun male of the honey-bee. OE. *drān*, *drǣn*; corr. to OS. *drān*, *dreno*, MLG. *drāne*, *drōne* (LG. *drōne*), (with *e*-grade) OHG. *treno* (MHG. *trene*, *tren*, G. dial. *träne*), prob. f. **dran-* **dren-* **drun-* boom (cf. MDu. *drōnen*, *drōnen*, Du. *dreunen*, LG. *drönen*, whence G. *dröhnen*, Icel. *drynja* roar), with which Gr. *an|thrḗnē* wild bee and *ten|thrḗnē*, have been connected. The OE. forms gave normally ME. and mod. dial. *drane*; the form *drone* (XV), which is common to Sc. and Eng., is – (M)LG. *drōne*.

droop drūp hang or sink down. XIII (Cursor M.). ME. *drupe, droupe* – ON. *drúpa* hover, hang the head for sorrow (cf. *drúpr* drooping spirits), f. **drūp-*; see next. Only in Scandinavianized areas till XVI, when it appears to have been adopted into gen. literary use from these areas, where *ū* had remained unchanged.

drop drɔp small quantity of liquid OE. *dropa*, whence ME. *drope* = OS. *dropo*, ON. *dropi* :– Germ. **dropon*; beside OE. **droppa*, whence ME. *droppe* (and the present form) = OHG. *tropfo* (G. *tropfen*) :– Germ. **droppon* (*-pp* :– *-pn-*); f. **drup-*, weak grade of the base of DROOP; cf. DRIP.

dropsy drɔpsi disease marked by accumulation of watery fluid. XIII. Aphetic of *idrop(e)sie* (*þidropsie* becoming *þe dropsie*) – OF. *idropesie* – medL. *(h)ydrōpisia*, for L. *hydrōpisis* – Gr. **hudrṓpisis*, repl. *húdrōps*, dropsy, f. *hudr-, húdōr* WATER.

droshky drɔ·ʃki, **drosky** drɔ·ski Russian low four-wheeled carriage. XIX. – Russ. *drózhki*, pl., dim. of *drógi* waggon, hearse, prop. pl. of *drogá* shaft of a vehicle. So F. *droschki*, G. *droschke*.

dross drɔs scum thrown off from metals in smelting OE.; dreggy matter, refuse. XIV. OE. *drōs* = MDu. *droes(e)* dregs; cf. OE. *drōsna* (g. pl.), MLG. *drōsem*, MDu. *droesen(e)* (Du. *droesem*), OHG. *truosana* (G. *drusen*) dregs, lees.

drought draut dryness. Late OE. *drūgaþ*, f. **drūg-*, base of *drȳġe* DRY; cf. (M)LG. *drogede*, (M)Du. *droogte*, f. *droog* dry. For the Sc. and north. *drouth* (which has been used also by Eng. poets, beside *droughth*), cf. *highth* HEIGHT, and see -T, -TH[1]. Hence **drought**Y[1], **drouth**Y[1] dry; thirsty. XVII.

drove drouv herd or flock of beasts, crowd. OE. *drāf*, f. gradation-var. **ai* of *drīfan* DRIVE; the present form derives from OE. obl. cases with infl. from *drive*. Hence **dro·ver** driver of cattle. XV (*dravere*, Wyntoun); see -ER[1], -IER[1].

drown draun suffer, or subject to, death by water; inundate; overwhelm. XIII (Cursor M.). ME. (orig. north.) *drun(e), droun(e)*, pointing to an OE. **drūnian*, rel. to ON. *drukna* be drowned :– **druŋknan*, f. **druŋk-*, var. of **driŋk-* DRINK. ¶ Superseded *drench*.

drowsy drau·zi inclined to sleep, caused by sleepiness, inactive. XV. prob. based on the stem of OE. *drūsian* be languid or sluggish, f. **drūs-*, var. of base of *drēosan* fall (cf. DREARY). See -Y[1]. Hence, by back-formation, **drowse** be inactive, or heavy or dull with sleep. XVI (Tusser, Sh.). ¶ The long interval of date puts direct continuity with OE. *drūsian* out of the question; the status of early Flem. *droosen* 'dormitare, dormiscere', recorded by Kilian, is dubious.

drub drʌb beat as with a stick; in early use, esp. to bastinado XVII (Herbert's 'Travels', 1634). Ult. repr. Arab. *ḍaraba* dʌrʌba beat, bastinado, *ḍarb* dʌrb beating (in Turk. *durb*, in Pers. *ẓurb*).

drudge drʌdʒ work slavishly. Not certainly recorded before XVI; poss. a continuation with extended meaning of ME. *drugge* (XIII–XIV) drag or pull heavily (but the pronunc. of *gg* in this word is uncertain). So **drudge** sb. servile worker. XV. **dru·dg**ERY. XVI.

drug drʌg medicinal substance. XIV. Late ME. pl. *drogges, drouges* – (O)F. *drogue(s)*, corr. to Pr. *drogua*, Sp., Pg., It. *droga*, of much-disputed origin. ¶ It is not certain that *drug* meaning 'commodity no longer in demand and therefore valueless' (XVII) is the same word in origin; but F. *drogue* is so used, beside *droguet*. Hence **drug** vb. mix with a drug XVII (Sh.); administer drugs to XVIII. So **dru·gg**IST. XVII. – F. *droguiste*. Cf. G. *droge, drogist*, Russ. *drogist*.

drugget drʌ·git kind of woollen stuff formerly used for garments, now for floor-coverings. XVI. – F. *droguet* (whence Sp. *droguete*, etc., G. *droguett*), of unkn. origin.

Druid drū·id one of an order of priests in ancient Britain and Gaul. XVI. – F. *druide* or its source L. pl. *druidæ, druides*, Gr. *druídai* – Gaulish *druides* (= Ir. *draoi*, g. pl. *druadh*, Gael. *draoi, draoidh, druidh*) – OCeltic **derwíjes* (whence W. *derwydd-on*), f. **derwos* (whence W. †*derw* true, Ir. *derb* sure) TRUE, whence the etymol. sense would be '*sooth*sayer'; but another view is that it is based on **dru-* oak, TREE (druidical rites being assoc. with the oak). Hence **drui·di**C(AL). XVII. Also †*dru·idan* (XVI), †*drui·dean* (XVII), **dru·idish** (XVI). ¶ OE. had *drȳ* magician – OIr. *drūi* :– Celtic **dru|wids* knowing certainly.

drum drʌm percussive musical instrument; drummer XVI (*drom, dromme*); tympanum of the ear XVII; drum-shaped object XVIII. Cf. KETTLEDRUM. Shortening of †*drom(b)slade*, †*drombyllsclad* (XVI) drum, drummer, altered – LG. *trommelslag* drum-beat, f. *trommel* (= late MHG. *trum(b)el*, G. *trommel*, f. *trum(b)e*; see TRUMP[1]) + *slag* beat (see SLAY[1]). Hence **drumm**ER[1]. XVI; other forms in occas. use were †*drumslager*, †*drumsler* (Du. *trommel-slager*, etc.), †*drumster*.

drunk drʌŋk inebriated. XIV. Clipped form of DRUNKEN, orig. characteristic of the south; now in standard use only predicative; sb. (sl.) drinking bout; intoxicated person XIX. So **drunk**ARD drʌ·ŋkəɹd one addicted to drinking or who is habitually drunk. XV. prob. – MLG. *drunkert*, f. *drunken*; cf. MDu. *dronker*, Du. *dronkaard*, whence early modF. *dronquart* (pl. *-ars*). **drunken** drʌ·ŋkn (obs. or arch.) intoxicated, drunk OE.; habitually intemperate XVI. OE. *druncen*, pp. of DRINK = OFris. *drunken*, OS. *drunkan* (Du. *dronken*), OHG. *trunchan* (G. *trunken*), ON. *drukkinn*, Goth. **drugkans* (whence *drugkanei* drunkenness), all of which have the same active meaning, for which cf. the pps. G. *vergessen* forgetful, L. *potus* having drunk, *pransus* having dined.

drupe drūp (bot.) stone-fruit. XVIII. – L. *drūpa, druppa* over-ripe olive, specialized in bot. L. (Linnæus) – Gr. *drúppā* olive. Cf. F. *drupe*.

druse drūz crystals lining a rock-cavity. XIX. – F. *druse* – G. *druse* weathered ore = MLG. *drūse, drose*, Du. *droes*.

Druse drūz one of a Mohammedan sect. XVIII. – F. *Druse* – Arab. *Durūz* pl., said to be formed on the designation of Ismail al-darazi (i.e. the tailor), who supported the claim of the Sixth Fatimite Caliph (XI) to be a divine incarnation.

dry drai destitute of moisture. OE. *drȳge* :– **drūgiz*, rel. to (M)LG. *dröge, dreuge*, MDu. *drōghe* (Du. *droog*) :– **draugiz*, f. Germ. **draug-* **dreug-* **drūg-* (not IE.), whence also OE. *drūgian* make or become dry, *drūgaþ* DROUGHT and OHG. *trockan, truckan* (G. *trocken*) dry, OS. *drukno, drokno* adv. Hence **dry** vb. OE. *drȳgan*.

dryad drai·æd wood nymph. XIV (Gower). – (O)F. *dryade* – L. *Dryades*, pl. of *Dryas* – Gr. *Druádes, Druás*, f. *drū-s* TREE; see -AD.

dryasdust drai·əzdʌst name of fictitious person to whom Sir Walter Scott dedicated some of his novels, transf. applied to a student of antiquities, etc., who occupies himself with the driest subjects, or to his works; f. DRY adj. + AS[1] + DUST sb.

duad djū·ĕd group of two. XVII. – Gr. *duás, duad-*, the normal repr. of which is DYAD.

dual djū·əl pert. to two. XVII. (gram. *numerus duālis* dual number, Quintilian, tr. Gr. *duikós*, Dionysius Thrax). – L. *duālis*, f. *duo* TWO; see -AL[1]. Hence **du·al**ISM. XVIII; after F. *dualisme*. So **dual**ITY djuæ·lĭti two-fold condition or character. XIV. – late L.; cf. F. *dualité* (XVI).

duan dū·ən poem; canto. XVIII (Macpherson's 'Ossian'; Burns). Gael. and Ir.

dub dʌb invest with a dignity (spec. that of knighthood) XI; dress, trim XIII; spec. in tanning; smear with grease (cf. DUBBIN) XVII. Late OE. **dubbian*, in phr. *dubbade* (pt.) *tō rīdere*, 'dubbed to knight', knighted, modelled on AN. *aduber a chevalier*. – AN. *duber*, aphetic of *aduber*, OF. *adober* (mod. *adouber*) equip with armour, repair, mend, whence Pr. *adobar* equip, arm, arrange, tame (a hawk), Sp. *adobar* dress, pickle, cook, tan, It. *addobbare* adorn, embellish, fit up, and Icel. *dubba, dybba* (in *dybba til riddara*) dub a knight, arm, dress; of unkn. origin. (AL. *dubbare, dubbator, dubberia* are recorded XIII as techn. terms of leather-dressing; cf. OF. *adouberie* tannery.) Hence **du·bbin, -ing** preparation of grease for softening and waterproofing leather. XVIII; see -ING[1]; for the ending *-in* cf. *tarpaulin*.

dubious djū·biəs doubtful. XVI. – L. *dubiōsus*, f. *dubium* doubt, sb. use of n. of *dubius* doubtful, obscurely f. *duo* TWO, and meaning 'hesitating between two alternatives'; cf. DOUBT. So **dubie**TY djubai·ĭti. XVIII. – late L. *dubietās*.

ducal djū·kəl pert. to a duke or dukedom. XVI. – F. *ducal* (cf. Sp. *ducal*, It. *ducale*), f. *duc* DUKE; see -AL[1].

ducat dʌ·kət Italian coin. XIV ('As fyne as ducat in Venyse', Ch.). – It. *ducato* or its source medL. *ducātūs* DUCHY, whence also (O)F. *ducat*, medGr. *doukáton*. The name was first applied to a silver coin issued in 1140 by Roger II of Sicily (Duke of Apulia) and having the legend R DX AP, i.e. Rogerus Dux Apuliæ, in 1202 to a silver coin of Venice. The first gold ducat was struck at Venice under the doge Giovanni Dandolo; it bore the legend 'Sit tibi, Christe, datus quem tu regis iste *ducatus*', which may have furthered the currency of the name. So **ducat**OO·N. XVII. – F. *ducaton*, It. *ducatone*.

duce dū·tʃei *il Duce*, title assumed by Benito Mussolini as leader of the Fascisti, 1922. It. 'leader' :– L. *ducem*, nom. *dux* (cf. DUKE).

duchess dʌ·tʃis wife of a duke, lady of ducal rank XIV. – (O)F. *duchesse* – medL. *ducissa*, f. L. *duc-, dux*; see DUKE and -ESS[1]. Spelt *dutchess* from XVI to early XIX.

duchy dʌ·tʃi territory of a duke or duchess. XIV. – (i) OF. *duché*, later form of *duchée* fem. :– Rom. **ducitāt-, -tās*, f. *duc-, dux* (see DUKE and -ITY); and (ii) (O)F. *duché* m. = Pr. *ducat*, Sp. *ducado*, It. *ducato* :– medL. *ducātus* (see -ATE[1]).

duck[1] dʌk swimming bird of the genus Anas or family Anatidæ. OE. *duce* or *dūce*, f. base of *dūcan* dive, DUCK[2]. The ME. vars. *duk(ke), dōke* (cf. Sc. *duik*), *douke*, point to orig. variation in the quantity of the stem-vowel. ¶ For the IE. word see DRAKE[2].

duck[2] dʌk plunge into liquid, trans. and intr. XIV (Cursor M.); stoop quickly XVI. ME. *douke, dūke*, repr. OE. **dūcan* = OFris. *dūka*, MLG., MDu. *dūken* (Du. *duiken*), OHG. *tūhhan* (G. *tauchen*), corr. to forms with a short vowel in MHG. *tücken* stoop quickly, G. *ducken* (with LG. initial cons.). The short vowel is evidenced XVI; cf. *suck*.

duck[3] dʌk strong untwilled fabric. XVII; pl. trousers or a suit of this XIX. – (M)Du. *doek* linen, linen cloth (whence Icel. *dúkr*) = OFris., OS. *dōk*, OHG. *tuoh* (G. *tuch*), of unkn. origin.

duct dʌkt †course, direction; †stroke drawn; tube or canal in an animal or vegetable body XVII. – L. *ductus* leading, conduct, command, in medL. aqueduct, f. *duct-*, pp. stem of *dūcere* lead (see TEAM). ¶ Derivs. of L. *dūc-* are: *abduction*, and sbs. in *-tion* corr. to *adduce, deduce, induce, introduce, produce, reduce, seduce, traduce*; *educate*; *duke*; *aqueduct*; *ductile*; cf. TEAM.

ductile dʌ·ktəil malleable; flexible, pliable. XIV. – (O)F. *ductile* – L. *ductilis*, f. *duct-*; see prec. and -ILE.

dud[1] dʌd †coarse cloak XIV (*'birrus*, i. *grossum vestimentum*, a dudde'); pl. (sl.) clothes; (dial.) rags, tatters XVI. Of unkn. origin.

dud[2] dʌd (dial.) delicate, soft, or contemptible person; worthless object XIX; also as adj. XX. perh. transf. use of prec.

dude djūd fastidious or exquisite 'swell'. XIX. orig. Amer. slang; prob. – G. dial. *dude* fool (cf. LG. *dudenkop* 'stupid head').

dudeen dudī·n short clay tobacco-pipe. XIX. – Ir. *dúidín*, dim. of *dúd* pipe; see -EEN[2].

dudgeon dʌ·dʒən feeling of resentful anger. XVI. freq. in phr. *take in dudgeon*; of unkn. origin; identical in form with obs. or arch. *dudgeon* (XV; in AN. *digeon* XIV) kind of wood used for handles of knives, etc., whence *dudgeon dagger* (XVI), which was used attrib. and fig. app. for 'crude, rough'; but transference to the sense 'resentment' would be difficult to account for; a rare, obscure var. †*endugine* (XVII) throws no light.

due djū owing XIII (Cursor M.); proper, suitable XIV; that is to be ascribed *to* XVII. ME. *dew, du(e)* – OF. *deu* (mod. *dû*, fem. *due*) = It. *dovuto*, †*devuto* :– Rom. **dēbūtu-s*, for L. *dēbitu-s* (cf. DEBIT), pp. of *dēbēre* (F. *devoir*) owe :– **dēhabēre* 'have away' (from someone), hold or have what belongs to another; see DE-, HABIT. Also adv. †duly; directly, straight XVI (Sh.). **due** sb. XV (Lydg.). – (O)F. *dû*, sb. use of pp. of *devoir*. Hence **du**LY[2] adv. XIV. Cf. DUTY.

duel djū·əl single combat. XV. – It. *duello* or L. *duellum*, arch. form of *bellum* war, used in medL. for the judicial single combat, whence also F. *duel* (XVI). Hence **du·ell**IST. XVI (Sh.); after It. *duellista* or F. *duelliste*.

duenna djue·nə chief lady-in-waiting; elderly woman acting as family governess XVII; chaperon XVIII. Early forms also *douegna, duegna* – Sp. *dueña* dwe·nja, formerly spelt *duenna* :– L. *domina* lady, mistress (cf. DAME).

duet djue·t (mus.) composition for two performers. XVIII. – G. *duett* or It. *duetto* (in Eng. XVIII–XIX), f. *duo* TWO; the F. term is *duo*, which was anglicized XVI. See -ET.

duff dʌf (dial.) dough; flour-pudding boiled in a bag XIX. north. var. of DOUGH.

duffadar dʌfədā·ɹ (Anglo-Ind.) petty officer of native police. XVIII. – Urdu (– Pers.) *dafa*[c]*dār* subaltern of cavalry.

duffel dʌ·fl coarse woollen cloth with a thick nap XVII (*duffield*, Plot; earlier in N. Amer. use); (U.S.) articles of dress for camping, etc. XIX. f. *Duffel*, name of a town in Brabant.

duffer dʌ·fəɹ (colloq.) incapable or inefficient person; (sl.) counterfeit article; (Australian sl.) unproductive mine. XIX. poss. alteration of Sc. *doofart, dowfart* stupid or dull person, f. *douf* (*dolf* XVI), *dowf* dull, spiritless, app. identical with †*douffe* sb. (Lydg.), perh. – ON. *daufr* DEAF (cf. *daufingi* drone, sluggard).

dufter dʌ·ftəɹ (Anglo-Ind.) bundle of official papers, register. XVIII. – Urdu – Arab., Pers. *daftar* record – Gr. *diphthérā* skin (cf. DIPHTHERIA).

dug dʌg pap, teat. XVI. Of unkn. origin.

dugong dū·gɔŋ large aquatic herbivorous animal. XVIII. ult. – Malay *dūyong*, recorded by Barchewitz (1751) as *dugung*, which was adopted by Buffon (1765) as *dugon* and by Gmelin (1788) as *dugong*.

dug-out dʌ·gaut A. (U.S.) canoe made be hollowing out a tree-trunk; dwelling made by an excavation in the ground XIX; roofed shelter in trench warfare XX. B. superannuated officer in temporary service XX. sb. use of pp. of DIG *out*.

duke djūk sovereign prince, ruler of a duchy XII; †leader, captain, ruler XIII; hereditary title of nobility XIV. ME. *duc, duk* – (O)F. *duc* – L. *ducem*, nom. *dux* leader, rel. to *dūcere* lead (see DUCT).

dulcet dʌ·lsit sweet. XIV. Early form also †*doucet* – (O)F. *doucet* (dim. of *doux*, fem. *douce*), refash. after L. *dulcis*; see -ET.

dulcimer dʌ·lsiməɹ musical string instrument. XV. orig. *doussemer, dowcemere* – OF. *doulcemer, -mele*, corr. to Sp. †*dulcemele*, It. *dolcemelle*, supposed to repr. L. **dulce melos* sweet song (cf. DOUCE, MELIC).

dull dʌl not sharp of wit XIII; not brisk XIV; not clear or bright; tedious XV. – MLG., MDu. *dul*, corr. to OE. *dol* stupid (:– **dulaz*), OS. (Du.) *dol*, OHG. *tol* (G. *toll*); cf. ON. *dulinn* self-conceited. A mutated form, OE. **dyll* (:– **duljaz*), was repr. by early ME. *dill*, which was more frequent. Hence **dull** vb. XIV (Ch.). **du·ll**ARD. XV. prob. – MDu. *dull-, dollaert* = MHG. *tolhart*.

dulse dʌls edible seaweed. XVII. – Ir., Gael. *duileasg* = W. *delysg, dylusg*; various spellings repr. more closely the Celtic forms have been used.

duma dū·mă in Tsarist Russia, elective council, spec. of 1905–17. XX. Russ., 'thought', 'meditation', 'council'; *gosudárstvennaya dúma* State Assembly.

dumb dʌm destitute of speech, mute. OE. *dumb* = OFris., OS. *dumb* (Du. *dom*) stupid, OHG. *tump* stupid, deaf (G. *dumm* stupid), ON. *dumbr*, Goth. *dumbs* mute; of unkn. origin: unaccompanied by speech, as *dumb show* XVI; lacking some quality, etc., normally present XVII; (of a mechanical contrivance) taking the place of a human agent, as *dumb waiter* XVIII. ¶ The orig. sense was prob. 'stupid', 'without understanding', from which the senses 'deaf' and 'dumb' would be developed by specialization in different ways.

dumb-bell dʌ·mbel (i) hist. apparatus like that for swinging a church bell, but without the bell, used for exercise or ringing practice, (ii) pl. pair of instruments held in the hands and swung for exercise. XVIII. f. prec.

dumbfound dʌmfau·nd strike dumb, nonplus. XVII (Urquhart, Otway). prob. f. DUMB+*-found*, of CONFOUND.

dum-dum dʌ·mdʌm soft-nosed bullet. XIX (1897). f. *Dum Dum*, name of a military station and arsenal near Calcutta, India.

dummy dʌ·mi dumb person XVI; imaginary player at whist, etc. XVIII (Swift); dolt XVIII; counterfeit or substituted article XIX. orig. Sc. *dummie*, with var. *dumbie*, f. DUMB+-Y[6].

dump[1] dʌmp fit of melancholy or depression, freq. and now only pl. XVI (Skelton, More); †mournful tune XVI (Udall, Sydney, Sh.). prob. of LG. or Du. origin and a fig. use of MDu. *domp* exhalation, haze, mist, rel. to DAMP.

dump[2] dʌmp †A. throw down or fall with sudden force XIV; B. throw down in a mass (orig. U.S.) XIX. In north. ME. perh. of Scand. origin (cf. Da. *dumpe*, Norw. *dumpa* fall suddenly or with a rush, and Sw. *dimpa*, pt. *damp*, pp. *dumpit*); but an independent imit. origin is possible. Hence as sb. matter dumped, place of dumping. XIX.

dumpling dʌ·mpliŋ pudding more or less globular generally enclosing fruit. XVI. First attributed to the county of Norfolk; much earlier than the simplex *dump*, which is applied to various short thick objects (late XVIII) and is app. f. **du·mpy**[1] adj. short and stout (mid-XVIII); see -LING[1].

dun[1] dʌn dull or dingy brown. OE. *dun(n)* = OS. *dun* 'spadix' date-brown, nut-brown, prob. rel. to OS. *dosan*, OHG. *tusin* (cf. DUSK); prob. not of Celtic origin, but W. *dwn*, (O)Ir., Gael. *donn* may be referred to the same IE. source (**donnos*, **dusnos*).

dun[2] dʌn importunate creditor, agent employed to collect debts. XVII (Earle). abbrev. of †*dunkirk* (XVII, Dekker) privateer, orig. ship from Dunkirk (also †*dunkirker*), transf. dun; f. name of a town on the coast of French Flanders. Hence **dun** vb. XVII (Bacon).

dunce dʌns †disciple of Duns Scotus; †dull pedant; dullard, blockhead XVI. orig. *Duns*, name of John *Duns* Scotus (died 1308), celebrated scholastic theologian, known as the Subtle Doctor, whose works were textbooks, and whose disciples, called Scotists, formed a predominant scholastic sect at the universities until they were attacked by the humanists and reformers; occurring first in contemptuous allusions in Tindale's works in phr. *Duns men*, *Dunces disciples*, whence *duns*, *dunce* was evolved in the above senses.

dunder, also *dander* dʌ·ndəɹ (W. Indies) lees of cane juice. XVIII. f. Sp. *redundar* overflow – L. *redundāre* (see REDUNDANT).

dunderhead dʌ·ndəɹhed blockhead. XVII (Fletcher, who has also †*dunderwhelp*). perh. to be assoc. with dial. *dunner* resounding noise.

Dundreary dʌndriə·ri name of lord *Dundreary*, a character in 'Our American cousin' (1858) by Tom Taylor, an indolent brainless peer, whose long side-whiskers became proverbial.

dune djūn sand-hill on the sea-coast. XVIII. – (O)F. *dune* – MDu. *dūne* (Du. *duin*) = OE. *dūn* DOWN[1].

dung dʌŋ excrement, manure. OE. *dung* = OFris. *dung*, MDu. *dung(e)*, OHG. *tunga* manuring (G. *dung* manure); cf. (with mutated vowel) Sw. *dynga* muck, dung, Da. *dynge* heap, pile, Icel. *dyngja* heap, dung; of unkn. origin. Hence **dung** vb. XIV. (OE. had *dyngian*; cf. OFris. *donga* and *denga*, MHG. *tungen*, G. *düngen*).

dungaree dʌŋgərī· coarse Indian calico. XVII. – Hindi *dungrī*.

dungeon dʌ·ndʒən castle keep (sp. *donjon* by some archaists); strong cell. XIV. –(O)F. *donjon*, also †*danjon*, †*dognon*, †*doignon* = Pr. *domnhon* :- Gallo-Rom. **domniōnem* 'lord's tower' or 'mistress tower' (in medL. *dangio*, *dunjo*, *donjo*, *-jonus*, *domnio*), f. L. *dominus* master, lord (see DOM[1]).

duniwassal dū·niwɔsəl Highland gentleman (of secondary rank). XVI. – Gael. *duine uasal*, i.e. *duine* man (rel. to Gr. *thnētós* mortal :- **dhwn̥tós*, *-thaneîn* die), *uasal* gentle- or noble-born.

dunlin dʌ·nlin red-backed sand-piper. XVI. prob. for **dunling*, f. DUN[1]+-LING[1].

dunnage dʌ·nidʒ light material, brushwood, etc. stowed among a cargo XIV (in AL. form *dennagium*), XV (*donage*), XVII (*dynnage*), XVIII (*dunnage*). Of doubtful origin; the variation in the stem vowel might be accounted for by deriv. from MLG., MDu. *dünne*, *dinne* THIN+-AGE, the notion being 'collection of loose light stuff'.

duo djū·ou (mus.) duet. XVI. (F. *duo*) – It. *duo* – L. *duo* TWO.

duodecimal djuŏde·siməl pert. to 12th parts; based on the number 12. XVIII. f. L. *duodecimus* twelfth, f. *duodecim* twelve, f. *duo* TWO + *decem* TEN; cf. DECIMAL. So **duode·cimo** size of a book in which a page is $\frac{1}{12}$ of a sheet. XVII. modL. (*in*) *duodecimō* 'in a twelfth'; cf. *folio*, *octavo*, *quarto*.

duodenum djuŏdī·nəm (anat.) first portion of the small intestine beginning at the pylorus. XIV. medL. (short for *intestinum duodenum digitorum* 'of twelve digits'; so named from its length), f. *duodēnī*, distributive of *duodecim* twelve (see prec.).

duologue djū·ɔlɔg dramatic piece for two actors. XIX. irreg. f. L. *duo* or Gr. *dúo* TWO, after *monologue*.

duomo dwou·mou Italian cathedral church. XVI (*domo*). It. (see DOME).

dup dʌp (dial.) open. XVI. contr. of *do up*; DO[1] (in sense 'put')+UP adv.; cf DOFF, DON[1].

dupe djūp victim of deception. XVII. – F. *dupe*, earlier †*duppe*, said in a text of XV to be a cant term; joc. application of (dial.) *dupe* hoopoe (of obscure origin), from the bird's stupid appearance. Hence **dupe** vb. XVIII; after F. *duper*.

duple djū·pl twofold. XVI. – L. *duplus*, f. *duo* TWO + **pl-* -FOLD. So **du·plex.** XIX. – L. *duplex*, f. *duo* + *plic-* FOLD².

duplicate djū·plikət adj. consisting of two corresponding parts XV; sb. one of two things exactly alike XVI. – L. *duplicātus*, pp. of *duplicāre*, f. *duplus* DOUBLE; see -ATE². So **du·plicate** vb. -eit XV. **duplica·tion** doubling. XV. – F. or L.

duplicity djupli·sĭti quality of being double-faced. XV (Lydg.). – (O)F. *duplicité* or late L. *duplicitās*, f. *duplic-*, DUPLEX; see -ITY.

durable djuə·rəbl lasting. XIV (Ch.). – (O)F. *durable* (= Sp. *durable*, It. *durabile*) – L. *dūrābilis*, f. *durāre* last, ENDURE; see -ABLE.

duralumin djuræ·ljŭmin aluminium alloy. XX. G., f. *Düren* (in the Rhineland) + *alumin(i)um* ALUMINIUM; invented by A. Wilm (1910); trade-mark of the Dürener Metallwerke A.-G. ¶ The identity of the first syll. of the internationalized form with the stem of L. *dūrus* hard, is accidental.

dura mater djuə·rə mei·təɹ outermost envelope of brain and spinal cord. XV. medL., lit. 'hard mother', tr. Arab. *alumm al-galīḍah* or *al-jāfīyah* 'the hard mother'; so called because it was thought to be the source of every other membrane in the body; cf. PIA MATER. Hence **dur**AL¹. XIX.

durance djuə·rəns †duration, lastingness XV; forced confinement or restraint, now esp. in phr. *durance vile* (Burns), formerly *vile durance* (Burke) and *durance base* (Butler); †stout cloth XVI. – (O)F. *durance*, f. *durer*; see next and -ANCE; in the latter sense infl. by *duress*.

duration dju(ə)rei·ʃən continuance. XIV (Ch.). – OF. *duration* – medL. *dūrātiō(n-)*, f. *dūrāre* harden, endure (whence (O)F. *durer* last, hold out, whence ME. *dure* XIII), f. *dūrus* hard; see -ATION. So **dur**ATIVE djuə·rətiv (gram.) applied to a form which marks action as going on or a state as continuing. XIX. f. pp. of L. *dūrāre*.

durbar də̄·ɹbāɹ court or levee held by a native Indian ruler. XVII. – Urdu – Pers. *darbār* court, f. *dar* door + *-bar* (suffix of place-names).

duress(e) djure·s, djuə·res †hardness, harshness XIV; forcible restraint, imprisonment; constraint XV. – OF. *duresse* :– L. *dūritia*, f. *dūrus* hard; see -ESS².

durian duə·riən prickly fruit of Durio zibethinus. XVI. ult. – Malay *durīan*, f. *dūrī* thorn, prickle. So Du. *doerian*, F. *durion*, It. *durio*.

during djuə·riŋ in or throughout the course of. XIV (Ch.; in Sc. †*durand* XIV–XVI, *-ant* XIV). – (O)F. *durant* = Pr., Cat. *durant*, It., Sp., Pg. *durante* :– Rom. **dūrante*, abl. of L. *dūrāns*, prp. of *dūrāre* last, continue (cf. DURATION and see -ING²). In French *le mariage durant* (e.g.) occurs alongside *durant le mariage* lit. 'the marriage lasting', (hence) in the course of the marriage, being modelled on L. phr. with *durante*, in which either order was possible. Cf. the origin of PENDING and of G. *während* during, prop. prp. of *währen* last (cf. e.g. *in der währenden Arbeit* 'in the lasting work', during the work).

durmast də̄·ɹmāst variety of oak. XVIII. perh. orig. an error for *dunmast*, i.e. DUN¹ (dark-coloured), MAST².

durn see DARN².

durra, dhurra, also *dhourra* du·rə Indian millet. XVIII. – Arab. *ður(r)ah*.

durst see DARE.

dusk dʌsk adj. dark-coloured (OE.); sb. darker stage of twilight XVII; vb. grow dark (OE.). The form *dusk* is difficult to account for (cf., however, for the vowel OE. *ġepuxod*, *ġepuhsod* darkened); it is recorded first from Chaucer and the Wycl. Bible; it was preceded by ME. *dosk* sb., *doskin* vb. (XIII), which are characteristically western forms and repr. OE. *dox* dark, swarthy (:– **duskaz* :– **dhuskos*, whence L. *fuscus* dark, dusky, FUSCOUS; cf. SUBFUSC), and its deriv. *doxian* become dark in colour; these forms are further rel. to OS. *dosan*, OHG. *tusin* darkish (of colour), dull (cf. DUN¹).

dust dʌst solid matter in a minute state of division. OE. *dūst* = OFris. *dūst*, MDu. *donst*, *dūst* (LG. *dust*, Du. *duist* meal-dust, bran), ON. *dust*. The primary notion appears to be 'that which rises in a cloud, as dust, smoke, vapour'; cf. OHG. *tun(i)st* wind, breeze, G. *dunst* vapour. Germ. **dunstu-* points to IE. **dhwns-* **dhwens-*, repr. by Skr. *dhvans* fall to pieces or to dust. Hence **dust** vb. †rise as dust XIII: †reduce to dust XV; soil with dust; free from dust XVI (whence **du·st**ER¹; cf. ON. *dusta*). **du·st**Y¹. OE. *dūstiġ*.

dustoor dʌstuə·ɹ (India) customary commission. XVII. – Urdu – Pers. *dastūr*, f. *dast* hand.

dutch dʌtʃ (vulgar colloq.) wife. XIX. Short for DUCHESS.

Dutch dʌtʃ †German (in the widest sense) XIV (Wyclif); pert. to the people of Holland XVI. – MDu. *dutsch* Dutch, Netherlandish, German (Du. *duitsch* German) = OE. *þēodisċ* Gentile, also sb. a language, OS. *thiudisc* :– Germ. **þeudiskaz* (cf. Goth. *þiudiskō* adv. 'ἐθνικῶς'), f. **þeudā* (OE. *þēod*, etc. people); see -ISH¹. In Germany the adj. was orig. used to render L. *vulgaris* to distinguish 'the vulgar tongue' from Latin, and hence to denote German vernaculars, and consequently the speakers of any of these. This is its earliest use in Eng., but in late XVI it became restricted (exc. in the traditional contrast of 'High Dutch' and 'Low Dutch') to Netherlanders, who were the division of 'Germans' with which the English came into particular contact.

duty djū·ti conduct due towards a superior XIII (RGlouc.); obligation, function; †due charge or fee XIV (Ch.); payment enforced or levied XV (Caxton). – AN. *deweté*, *dueté*, f. *du(e)* DUE; see -TY. Hence **du·te**OUS (Sh.), **du·ti**FUL[1] XVI, **du·ti**ABLE XVIII.

duumvir djuʌ·mvǝɹ one of a pair of co-equal officials. XVI. L., sg. derived from g. pl. *duum virum* of *duo virī* two men (see TWO, VIRILE).

dwarf dwǭɹf creature much below the ordinary size. OE. *dweorg*, *dweorh* = OFris. *dwirg*, MDu. *dwerch* (Du. *dwerg*), OHG. *twerg* (G. *zwerg*), ON. *dvergr* :– CGerm. (exc. Goth.) **dwergaz* :– IE. **dhwergʷhos*, whence also Gr. *sérphos* (:– **ϝérphos*) midge. Hence **dwarf** vb. render dwarfish. XVII. **dwa·rf**ISH[1]. XVI.

dwell dwel †lead astray OE.; †tarry, delay; continue in a place or state XII (Orm); have one's abode XIII; spend time *on* XV. OE. *dwellan*, pt. *dwealde* lead astray, corr. to OS. *bi|dwellian* hinder, MDu. *dwellen* stun, perplex, OHG. *twellen* (MHG. *twellen*) delay, harass, ON. *dvelja* trans. delay, intr. and refl. tarry, stay; f. Germ. **dwel-* **dwal-* **dwul-*, repr. also by OE. *dwelian* lead astray, go astray, OFris. *dwelia* delay, MLG. *dwelen* be stupid, OHG. *gitwelan* be stunned, OE. *dwolian* wander, *dwola* error, heretic, *ġedwolen* perverse. The sense 'abide, stay' was adopted from ON., to which the present existence of the word is mostly due.

dwindle dwi·ndl become smaller and smaller. XVI (Sh.). f. (dial.) *dwine*, OE. *dwīnan* waste away = (M)LG., MDu. *dwīnen*, ON. *dvína*; see -LE[2].

dwt., abbrev. for *pennyweight*, scil. *d* for DENARIUS, *wt.* for *weight*.

dyad dai·æd number two. XVII. – late L. *dyad-*, *dyas* – Gr. *duad-*, *duás*, f. *duo* TWO; see -AD[1]. Cf. DUAD.

dyarchy dai·āɹki government by two rulers. XIX. Usual sp. of *diarchy* by assoc. with *dyad*, f. Gr. *di-* DI-[2]+ *-arkhía*, *arkhé* -ARCHY.

dye dai cause to take, impregnate with, a certain colour, tinge. OE. *dēagian*, of unkn. origin. Not recorded again till late XIV (Ch., Trevisa), though the agent-nouns **dy·**ER[1], **dye·**STER are recorded from XIII; in Anglian areas the ME. words were *lit* (– ON. *lita*), *litster*, from XIII. So **dye** sb. colour produced by dyeing, material used for it. OE. *dēah*, *dēag*, rare ME. *dēh*; the present word is a new formation on the vb. (XVI). The words are peculiarly Eng. The distinction of sp. between this word and *die* became established since the time of Johnson, who has *die* for both, while Addison (e.g.) has *dye* for both. For the phonetic development cf. DIE[1], EYE, LIE[2], TIE.

dyke frequent sp. of DIKE, as in place-names.

dynamic dainæ·mik, di- pert. to force. XIX. – F. *dynamique* (Leibniz, 1692) – Gr. *dunamikós*, f. *dúnamis* strength; see next and -IC. So **dyna·mi**CAL. XIX. **dyna·mi**CS. XVIII.

dynamite dai·-, di·nǝmait high explosive. Coined by Alfred Nobel 1867. f. Gr. *dúnamis* force, rel. to *dúnasthai* (see DYNASTY) + -ITE.

dynamo dai·nǝmou short for *dynamo-machine*, itself short for *dynamo-electric-machine* (1867); for the comb. form see -O-.

dynasty di·nǝsti, dai·- line of kings or princes. XV (Capgrave). – F. *dynastie* or late L. *dynastīa* – Gr. *dunasteiā* power, domination, f. *dunastḗs* (L. *dynastēs*, whence **dy·nast** XVII), f. *dúnasthai* be able or powerful.

dyne dain unit of force in the centimetre-gramme-second (C.G.S.) system. XIX. – F. *dyne*, taken from Gr. *dúnamis* force.

dys- dis- prefix in L. adoptions repr. Gr. *dus-* = Skr. *dus-*, Germ. **tus-* (whence OE. *tō-* (cf. TO-), OHG. *zur-* (G. *zer-*), ON. *tor-*); denoting the reverse of easy, favourable, or fortunate, used in direct derivs. from Gr. and in new (chiefly scientific) formations.

dysentery di·sǝnt(ǝ)ri inflammation of the large intestine. XIV (Wycl. Bible). – OF. *dissenterie* or L. *dysenteria* – Gr. *dusenteriā*, f. *dusénteros*, f. *dus-* DYS- + *éntera* bowels (cf. ENTERIC); see -Y[3].

dyslogistic dislǝdʒi·stik having an unfavourable meaning. XIX. f. DYS- + the basic el. of EU|LOGISTIC.

dyspepsia dispe·psiǝ difficulty of digestion. XVIII. – L. *dyspepsia* (anglicized **dyspe·psy** XVII) – Gr. *duspepsiā*, f. *dúspeptos* difficult of digestion, f. *dus-* DYS- + *peptós* cooked, digested; see PEPTIC, -Y[3].

dyspnœa dispniǝ· (path.) difficulty of breathing. XVII. – L. *dyspnœa* – Gr. *dúspnoia*, f. *dus-* DYS- + *pnoḗ* breathing; rel. to *pneûma* (cf. PNEUMATIC).

dziggetai, dzh- dzi·gǝtai, dʒ- equine quadruped of Central Asia, Equus hemionus. XVIII (Pennant). – Mongolian *dschiggetai*, var. of *tchikketei* (long-)eared, f. *tchikki* ear.

E

e- see EX[1]-.

each ītʃ every one regarded separately. OE. *ǣlċ* = OFris. *ellik*, *elk*, *ek* (WFris. *elk*, *elts*), MLG. *ellik*, MDu. *elic*, *ellic*, (M)LG., (M)Du. *elk*, OHG. *eogilīk* (G. *jeglich*) :– WGerm. phr. **aiwō galīkaz* 'ever alike'; see AYE, LIKE[1], ALIKE. For the disappearance of *l* in similar unstressed position cf. WHICH, SUCH *everich* (EVERY), forms below and

OFris. *ek.* ¶ Other OE. words for 'each' were: *ylć*, whence ME. *ülch, üch, ich, ych*, ILK[1]; *ǣfrić* EVERY; *ġehwilć*, whence ME. *iw(h)ilch, uich*; *ǣġehwilć*, whence ME. *ewilch, euch.*

eager ī·gəɹ †ardent, fierce XIII; keenly desirous or impatient; †pungent, acid (cf. VINEGAR) XIV. – AN. *egre*, (O)F. *aigre* = Pr. *agre*, Sp., It. *agro* :– Rom. **acrum*, for L. *ācrem*, nom. *ācer* pungent, swift, strenuous, f. **ǎk-* be sharp or pointed (cf. ACID, EDGE).

eagle ī·gl large bird of prey ('the king of birds'). XIV (Ch., Wyclif). – AN. *egle*, (O)F. *aigle*, replacing †*aille*, refash. after Pr. *aigla* = Sp. *águila*, Pg. *aguia*, It. *aquila*, Rum. *ăceră* :– L. *aquila*, perh. rel. to *aquilus* dark-brown, and orig. meaning 'dun-coloured bird'. So **eaglet** ī·glit young eagle. XVI. + -ET, after F. *aiglette*, †*eglette*.

eagre ī·gəɹ, (locally) ei·gəɹ tidal bore. The forms are of three types: (i) *higre, hyger, hygre* (XVII–XIX), in AL. *higra* Severn bore (XII, William of Malmesbury); (ii) †*agar* (XVI–XVII), *ager, aiger* (XIX); (iii) *eagre, eager* (XVII–). These perh. ult. repr. OE. *ǣgur, ēgur, ēagor, ēogor* flood, tide; but this can only be if the *g* is a stopped cons., and if such a deriv. as *ēa* river + *gār* spear (cf. BORE[1]) may be assumed, of which, however, there is no confirmation. Forms with *a-, ai-* may be due to Scand. influence (ON. *á* river). ¶ It is difficult to relate ME. *aker, akyr* 'impetus maris', dial. *aiker, acker* ripple.

-ean ī·ən (e.g. in *empyrean, Tacitean*), -iən (e.g. in *cærulean*), and varying (as in *hyperborean, Protean*), suffix formed by adding -AN to *e* or *ē* of L. *-eus, -ēus* (varying with *-æus*), corr. to Gr. *-eos, -eios (-aîos)*; formerly often with parallel forms in *-æan, -eian, -ian*; it has in some words an immed. F. original in *-éen*. There are a few survivals of formations on L. adjs. in *-eus*, viz. *cærulean, hyperborean*; others, such as *gigantean, marmorean, purpurean*, are obs.; their number is larger if one takes in those repr. the comp. L. suffixes *-āceus, -āneus* (see -ACEAN, -ANEAN), which are also the source of -ACEOUS, -ANEOUS. The earliest exx. of the suffix *-ean* date from mid-XVI to early XVII, and the majority are based on proper names, e.g. *Democritean* (*Dēmocritēius*, *Δημοκρίτειος*), *Epicurean* (*Epicūrēus*, *Ἐπικούρειος*), *Euripidean* (*Eurīpidēus*, *Εὐριπίδειος*), *European* (*Eurōpæus*, *Εὐρωπαῖος*), *Herculean* (*Herculeus*), *Prome·thean* (*Promēthēus*, *Προμήθειος*), *Pythagorean* (*Pythagorēus, -īus*, *Πυθαγόρειος*). There are special cases, such as *antipode·an, Tyrole·an*, prob. modelled on *European*; *Aristotelian, Euclidian*, which replaced *Aristotelean, Euclidean*; *Thucydide·an*, prob. after *Æschyle·an, Sophocle·an*, and superseding *Thucydi·dian* (L. *Thūcydidīus*); and *Herodote·an*, prob. after *Thucydide·an*; *Rhadamanthean* has been superseded by *Rhadamanthine*. *Herculean* həɹkjū·liən, həɹkjulī·ən is paralleled by *Heraclean* hiərəklī·ən (L. *Hēraclēus*). See also CÆSAREAN, EMPYREAN, JACOBEAN, PROTEAN.

ea·nling (Sh.) see YEAN.

ear[1] iəɹ organ of hearing. OE. *ēare* = OFris. *āre*, OS., OHG. *ōra* (Du, *oor*, G. *ohr*), ON. *eyra*, Goth. *ausō* :– CGerm. **auzo·n, *au·son*, f. **aus-* :– CIE. **ous-*, whence also Av. *uši* the ears, L. *aurēs, -īs* (cf. *auscultāre* listen, **auzdīre, audīre* hear; see AUSCULTATION, AUDITION), Gr. *ôs, oûs* (:– **oúsos*), g. *ōtós* (:– **ousatós*), OPruss. acc. pl. *ausins*, Lith. *ausìs*, OSl. *ucho*, dual *uši* (Russ. *úkho*), OIr. *au*, mod. *ó*. ¶ One of the CIE. names of parts of the body; cf. *eye, foot, heart, nail, nose*. Hence **ea·r**RING. OE. *ēarhring*.

ear[2] iəɹ spike of corn. OE. *ēar* (Nhb. *æhher*; cf. ACROSPIRE) = OFris. *ār*, OS. *ahar* (Du. *aar*), OHG. *ahir, ehir* n. (G. *ähre* fem.), ON. *ax*, Goth. *ahs* :– CGerm. **aχuz, *aχiz*, rel. to L. *acus, acer-* husk, chaff, f. **ak-* be sharp or pointed, cf. AWN, EDGE.

ear[3] iəɹ (arch., dial.) plough. OE. *erian* = OFris. *era*, OS. *erian*, OHG. *erren*, ON. *erja*, Goth. (CGerm.) *arjan*, f. IE. **ar-*, repr. also by Gr. *aroûn*, L. *arāre*, Lith. *ariù*, OSl. *orją*, OIr. *airim* I plough; (sbs.) Gr. *árotron*, L. *arātrum*, OIr. *arathar*, Arm. *araur* plough.

earing iə·riŋ (naut.) any of a number of small ropes fastening the upper corner of a sail to the yard. XVII (Capt. Smith). perh. f. EAR[1] + -ING[1] or RING.

earl əːɹl warrior; nobleman, prince; JARL OE.; equiv. of *count* XII (in ME. often 'great noble'). OE. *eorl* = OS., OHG. *erl*, ON. *jarl* (runic *erilaR*), of unkn. origin. Hence **ea·rl**DOM. XII.

early əː·ɹli near the beginning of a period. OE. (late Nhb.) *ǣrlīće*, beside *ārlīće*, f. *ǣr* ERE + *-līće* -LY[2], after ON. *árliga*. So **ea·rly** adj. XIII (AncrR.); after ON. *árligr*.

earn əːɹn gain as a reward or wages. OE. *earnian* = MLG. *arnen*, OHG. *arnēn, arnōn* reap :– WGerm. **aznōjan, *aznǣjan*, f. **aznu* (ON. *ǫnn* labour), rel. to OE. *esne* labourer, man, OHG. *esni*, Goth. *asneis* hired labourer, and further to OHG. *aran* (whence MHG. *erne*; G. *ernte* is a new formation) harvest, Goth. *asans* harvest, autumn (whence OPrussian *assanis* autumn).

earnest[1] əː·ɹnist †ardour in battle; seriousness. OE. *eornust, -ost*, with suffix as in OHG. *dionōst* (G. *dienst*) service = MLG. *ernest*, OHG. *ernust* (G. *ernst*), f. **ern-*, repr. also in ON. *ern* brisk, vigorous, Goth. *arniba* safely; of unkn. origin. So **ea·rnest** adj. OE. *eornost(e)* = OFris. *ernst*, MLG. *ernest* (in G. *ernst* adj. has been developed from phr. containing the sb.). **ea·rnest**LY[2]. OE. *eornostlīće*.

earnest² ə·ɹnist money paid as an instalment. XIII. Earliest forms *ernes, eernes*; prob. alteration, with assim. to -NESS, of synon. and contemp. *erles* (Sc. *arles* XVI) – OF. **erles* :– Rom. **arrulas*, dim. (pl.) of L. *arra* pledge, pop. alteration of *arrabō* – Gr. *arrhabōn* – Heb. *ʿērābōn* security f. *ʿerab*; assim. to prec. (*ernest, arnest*) appears XV. ¶ A very rare late ME. *erres* (XV) – OF. *erres* – L. *arras*, is independent.

earth əɹþ *the* ground; *the* world. OE. *eorþe* = OFris. *erthe*, OS. *ertha* (Du. *aarde*), OHG. *erda* (G. *erde*), ON. *jǫrð*, Goth. *airþa* :– CGerm. **erþō*, f. base **er-*, appearing also in OHG. *ero* earth. ON. *jǫrfi* gravel, Gr. *éraze* on the ground, W. *erw* field. Hence **earth** vb. †bury XIV (Barbour); cover *up* with earth XVII; until late XVI only Sc. **earthen** ə·ɹþən. XIII; see -EN³ and cf. OHG. *irdīn*, Goth. *airþeins*; whence **ea·rthen**WARE¹. XVII. **ea·rth**LY¹. OE. *eorþlić*. **ea·rth**QUAKE. XIV; superseding OE. *eorþdyne* (DIN), ME. *erthdin(e)*. **ea·rthy.** XVI; see -Y¹.

earwig iə·ɹwig insect so called because it is supposed to penetrate the ear. OE. *ēarwicga*, f. *ēare* EAR¹+*wicga* earwig, prob. rel. to WIGGLE; cf. synon. ME. *arwygyll* (Promp. Parv.), dial. *arrawiggle*. ¶ For the form of *wicga* cf. DOG, and, for the connexion with *ear*, cf. synon. G. *ohrwurm*, Du. *oorworm*, F. *perce-oreille*, Russ. *ukhovërtka*.

ease īz †opportunity, means; comfort, convenience. XIII (*chapel of ease* XVI). – AN. *ese*, OF. *eise*, (also mod.) *aise* †elbow-room; †favourable occasion, convenience = Pr. *aize* (whence It. †*asio*, AGIO, Pg. *azo* occasion, assistance, aptness) :– Rom. **adjaces* for *adjacēns* (cf. medL. *in aiace* in the neighbourhood), sb. use of prp. of L. *adjacēre* (see ADJACENT). So **ease** vb. relieve, comfort. XIV. orig. – OF. *aisier, aaisier*, f. phr. *a aise* in comfort, at ease (*a* :– L. *ad*); later directly f. the sb.

easel ī·zl standing frame to support a picture. XVII. – Du. *ezel* ASS; cf. uses like *cheval glass, clothes horse*.

easement ī·zmənt relief, convenience; accommodation in or about a house; privilege of using something not one's own XIV; evacuation of bowels XV. – OF. *aisement* (cf. AL. *aisiamentum*), f. *aisier* EASE vb.; see -MENT.

east īst adv. in the direction of the rising sun OE.; sb. (OE. *ēaste* fem.); adj. (in OE. only compar. *ēasterra, ēastra*, superl. *ēast(e)mest*). OE. *ēast-* in comps. (e.g. *ēastende* eastern region, *Ēastangle* East-Anglians, *ēastrīce* the East) = OFris. *āst*, OS., OHG. *ōst* (Du. *oost*, G. *ost*), repr. Germ. **austo-* (with suffix **-nō-* in OE. *ēastan*, OS., OHG. *ōstana*, ON. *austan* from the east); as adv. prob. shortening of **ēaster* = OS., OHG. *ōstar*, ON. *austr* toward the east :– Germ. **austro-*, which is found in the proper names *Ēstranglī* (Bede) East-Anglians, OHG. *Ōstarrīhi* (G. *Österreich*) Austria, Germ.-L. *Austrogotī* (Goth. **Austrogutōs*) Ostrogoths; f. IE. base **aus-*, as in L. *aurōra* (:– **ausōsā*), *auster* (cf. AUSTRAL), Gr. (Æolic) *aúōs* dawn, *aúrion* (:– **ausrion*) to-morrow, Lith. *aušrà*; cf. Skr. *ushā́s* morning, dawn. So †**easter** nearest the east, eastern. XIV–XIX. perh. continuing OE. compar. *ēasterra* (cf. ON. *austarr* more to the east). Hence prob. **ea·ster**LY¹. XVI; cf. Du. *oosterlijk*. **ea·stern** pert. to, lying towards, the east. OE. *ēasterne* = OS., OHG. *ōstroni*, ON. *austrœnn* :– Germ. **austrōnja-*, f. **austro-*. **ea·st**WARD adv. toward the east. OE. *ēastewearde*; hence as adj. XV.

Easter ī·stəɹ festival of the Christian Church commemorating the resurrection of Jesus Christ from the dead. OE. *ēastre*, mainly pl. *ēastron* (g. *ēastrena*, d. *ēastrum*), also *ēastro, -a* = OFris. *āsteron*, MHG. *ōsteren*, OHG. *ōstarūn* (G. *Ostern* pl.); derived by Bede from the name of a goddess whose feast was celebrated at the vernal equinox, *Ēostre*, Nhb. var. of *Ēastre* :– Germ. **Austrōn*, cogn. with Skr. *usrā* dawn (see EAST). Several OE. comps. of the comb. form *Ēaster-* survive: *Ēasterǣfen* Easter Eve, *Ēasterdæġ* Easter Day, *Ēastersunnandæġ* Easter Sunday, *Ēastertīd* Eastertide, *Ēasterwuce* Easter week.

easy ī·zi at ease, free from pain, constraint, or discomfort XII; causing little or no dis comfort or difficulty; not oppressive, severe, or painful XIV. – AN. *aisé*, OF. *aisié* (mod. *aisé*), pp. of *aisier* put at ease (see EASE vb.); the ending has been assim. to -Y¹. Hence *easy-chair* XVIII (Farquhar). **ea·sy** adv. XIV; comb. in *easy-going* XVII; (perh. orig. of horses).

eat īt pt. **ate** et, eit, pp. **eaten** ī·tn con sume for nutriment; destroy by devouring. OE. str. vb. *etan*, pt. *ǣt, æt, ǣton*, pp. *eten*) = OFris. *eta*, OS. *etan* (Du. *eten, aat, gegeten*), OHG. *ezzan* (G. *essen, ass, gegessen*), ON. *eta* (*át, etinn*), Goth. *itan* :– CGerm. **etan*; f. CIE. base **ed-*, whence L. *edere*, Gr. *édein*, Ir., Gael. *ith*, Lith. *édmi*, OSl. *jami*, Skr. *ádmi* I eat, Hittite *etir* they ate. The sp. *ate* of the pt. depends on early ME. *at*, which repr. a short var. of OE. *ǣt*; the pronunc. et is usu. assoc. with the sp. *ate*, but is perh. a shortening of pt. *ēt*. ¶ FRET is a comp. of this vb.

eau F. *eau* :– L. *aqua* water, as in **eau-de-Cologne** ou:dəkəlou·n perfume orig. made at Cologne (Köln), Germany; **eau-de-vie** oudəvī· 'water of life', brandy.

eaves īvz edge of a roof. OE. *efes*, corr. to OFris. *ose*, MLG. *ovese*, Flem. *oose*, MDu. *ovese, ose*, OHG. *obasa, -isa*, MHG. *ob(e)se* (G. dial. *obsen*) eaves, porch, ON. *ups*, Goth. *ubizwa* (in d. sg. *ubiswai*) 'στοά' :– Germ. **obaswa, *obiswa*, prob. f. **ob-* of OVER. The final *s* is treated as the pl. ending and the word takes pl. concord. ¶ ME. *ouese*, s.w. dial. *oaves, ovice, office* point to an OE. **ofes* (beside *ofesć* edge, border, in place-names, parallel to *efesć*). Hence **eavesdropp**ER[1] ī·vzdrɔ:pəɹ one who listens under walls to hear gossip, secret listener. XV. f. ME. *evesdroppes*, prob. – ON. *upsardropi*, corr. to OE. *yfæsdrypæ*, WFris. *oesdrip*, *-drup*, Flem. *oosdrup* eaves; see DRIP, DROP. Hence by back-formation **ea·vesdrop** vb. XVII.

ebb eb reflux of the tide. OE. *ebba* = (M)LG., (M)Du. *ebbe* (Du. *eb*) (whence G., Da. *ebbe*, Sw. *ebb*; also F. dial. *èbe*, if this is not from Eng.) :– WGerm. **abjon*, *-ōn*, f. **ab* (see OF), as if meaning 'a running off or away'. So **ebb** vb. OE. *ebbian* (also in *ā|ebbian*, *be|ebbian* strand a ship) = (M)LG., (M)Du. *ebben* (cf. OS. *ebbiunga*), OHG. *fir|ebbita* subsided, MHG. *eppen* ebb.

Ebenezer ebənī·zəɹ title of some nonconformist meeting-houses, (hence) dissenting chapel. XIX. – Heb. *eben hā 'ezer* 'stone of the help', stone set up as a memorial of help received by Samuel after the victory of Mizpeh (1 Sam. vii 12).

ebonite e·bənait vulcanite. 1861. f. EBONY + -ITE; cf. Du. *eboneit*.

ebony e·bəni hard black wood (esp. of trees of the species Diospyros). XVI (*hebeny*; the solitary ex. of *hebenyf* in Wycl. Bible, Ezek. xxvii 15, appears to be due to misreading Vulg. *ebeninos* (of ebony) as *ebeniuos*). preceded by †*eban* (XV, Lydg.) – OF. *eban* (also *ebaine*, mod. *ébène*) – medL. *ebanus* (whence also Sp., It. *ebano*), var. of L. *ebenus* (also used in ME. and MHG.), *hebenus* – Gr. *ébenos* ebony tree, of Semitic origin (cf. Egyptian *hbnj*, Heb. *hobnīm*); later *ebon* (XVI), latinized (*h*)*eben* (cf. Du. *ebben|boum*, *ebben|hout*, G. *eben|baum*, *eben|holz* ebony tree/wood), which was superseded by forms with *-y*, perh. after *ivory*.

ebriety ībrai·ĭti intoxication. XV. – F. *ébriété* or L. *ēbrietās*, f. *ēbrius* drunk)(*sōbrius* SOBER; see -ITY.

ebullient ibʌ·liənt boiling, effervescent, bubbling over. XVI. – L. *ēbullient-*, *-ēns*, prp. of *ēbullīre*, f. *ē* E- + *bullīre* BOIL[2]; see -ENT. So **ebull**ITION ebʌli·ʃən. XVI (once XIV Lanfranc). – late L.

écarté eikā·ɹtei, ||ekarte card game in which certain cards are thrown out. XIX. F., pp. of *écarter* discard, f. *é-* EX-[1] + *carte* CARD.

ecbatic ekbæ·tik (gram.) denoting result. XIX. – Gr. **ekbatikós*, implied in the adv. *ekbatikôs*, f. *ekbaínein* result, f. *ek* out + *baínein* go; see EX-[2], COME, -IC.

eccentric ėkse·ntrik not concentric XVI (as sb. XV, Lydg.); not central or referable to a centre; irregular, odd XVII; sb. (person) XIX (Scott), after F. (XVIII). – late L. *eccentricus*, f. Gr. *ékkentros*, f. *ek* out, EX-[2] + *kéntron* CENTRE; cf. (O)F. *excentrique*. Hence **eccentri·c**ITY. XVI.

ecclesiastic iklīziæ·stik pert. to the Church XV; sb. clergyman XVII. – F. *ecclésiastique* or ChrL. *ecclēsiasticus* – Gr. *ekklēsiastikós*, f. *ekklēsiastḗs*, in LXX. rendering Heb. *qōheleth* one who addresses a public assembly, in ancient Gr. member of the ecclesia or public assembly of citizens, f. *ekklēsiázein* hold or summon to an assembly, (eccl.) summon to church, f. *ekklēsiā* assembly, (eccl.) church, f. *ekklētós*, pp. adj. of *ekkaleîn*, f. *ek* out, EX-[2] + *kaleîn* call, summon (cf. HALE[2]). So **ecclesia·st**ICAL. XV.

echelon ei·ʃəlɔ̃, -lən military formation in parallel divisions but with no two on the same alignment. XVIII. – F. *échelon*, f. *échelle* ladder :– L. *scāla* SCALE[3]; cf. -OON.

echinus ėkai·nəs (zool.) sea-urchin XIV (Ch.); (archit.) ovolo moulding next below the abacus. XVI. L. – Gr. *ekhînos* hedgehog, sea-urchin, rel. to OE. *iġel* or *īġel* hedgehog, OHG. *igil*, *īgil* (G. *igel*, †*eigel*), ON. *ígull*, OSl. *ježĭ*. Comb. form **echi·no-**. XIX.

echo e·kou repetition of sounds due to reflection of sound-waves. XIV. – (O)F. *écho* or L. *ēchō* – Gr. *ēkhṓ* (cf. *ēkhḗ*, *êkhos* noise), perh. rel. to OE. *swōg* noise, *swōgan*, *swēgan* make a noise. Hence **e·cho** vb. XVI. **echoic** ėkou·ik of the nature of echo, applied by J. A. H. Murray (1880) to words that are held to imitate sounds denoted by them.

éclair ei·klɛəɹ finger-shaped cake of light pastry filled with cream and iced. XIX. F. ('lightning'), f. *éclairer* :– Rom. **exclāriāre*, f. *ex* EX-[1] + *clārus* CLEAR.

éclaircissement eiklɛərsi·smã clearing up, explanation. XVII (Clarendon, Dryden). F., f. *éclairciss-*, *éclaircir* :– Rom. **exclāricīre*, f. *ex* EX-[1] + *clārus* CLEAR; see -MENT.

éclat ei·kla brilliance, lustre, brilliant success. XVII (Evelyn). F., f. *éclater* burst out (OF. *esclater* = Pr. *esclatar*) :– Rom. **esclattare* – Germ. **slaitan*, causative of **slītan* SLIT.

eclectic ėkle·ktik epithet of philosophers not attached to a school XVII; collecting or collected from different sources XIX. – Gr. *eklektikós*, f. *eklektós* selective, f. *eklégein*, f. *ek* out, EX-[2] + *légein* choose = L. *legere*; see LECTION, -IC. Cf. F. *éclectique*.

eclipse ikli·ps interception or obscuration of the light of a heavenly body. XIII (*esclepis*, *clipes*, *clippis*, Cursor M.). – OF. *eclipse*, †*esclipse* (mod. *éclipse*) – L. *eclīpsis* – Gr. *ékleipsis*, f. *ekleípein* be eclipsed, leave its place, fail to appear, be wanting, f. *ek* out, away, EX-[2] + *leípein* LEAVE[2]. Hence **ecli·pse** vb. XIV. – (O)F. *éclipser*.

ecliptic ikli·ptik pert. to an eclipse XIV (Ch.); sb. great circle of the celestial sphere, the apparent orbit of the sun, so called because eclipses happen only when the moon is on or very near this line XIV. – L. *eclīpticus* (in *signa ecliptica*, *linea ecliptica*) – Gr. *ekleiptikós* (also sb. in masc. and n.), f. *ekleípein*; see prec. and -IC. Also **ecli·pt**ICAL. XVI. Cf. F. *écliptique*.

eclogue e·klɔg pastoral dialogue (esp. of Theocritus and Virgil). XV (*ecloog*, Lydg.). – L. *ecloga* short poem – Gr. *eklogḗ* selection, esp. of poems, f. *eklégein* (see ECLECTIC). The common var. *eglog* (XVI–XVIII) reflects (O)F. *églogue*, medL. (Sp., It.) *egloga*, of which the *eg-* is due to assoc. with Gr. *aig-*, *aíx* goat, quasi 'discourse of goatherds'.

ecod var. of *egod*, EGAD. XVIII.

ecology, œcology īkɔ·lədʒi (bot.) study of the relations of plants and animals with their habitat. XIX. – G. *ökologie* (Haeckel), f. Gr. *oîkos* house (used for 'habitat') (cf. WICK[2]); see -LOGY.

economy ikɔ·nəmi management (of a house) XVI; careful management, thrift; administration of a community or establishment XVII; *political economy*, tr. F. *économie politique* XVI. – (O)F. *économie* or L. *œconomia* – Gr. *oikonomíā*, f. *oikonómos* manager of a household, steward, f. *oîkos* house (cf. WICK[1])+-*nómos* managing, *némein* manage (cf. NOMAD); see -Y[3]. So **economic** īkənɔ·mik, ek-, -ICAL adjs. XVI – (O)F. *économique* or – L. *œconomicus* – Gr. *oikonomikós*.

écru ei·krü colour of unbleached linen. XIX. (O)F., f. *é-* (intensive)+*cru* CRUDE.

ecstasy e·kstəsi exalted state of feeling. XIV (Wycl. Bible). Rare before XVI; earlier forms *ex(s)tasie*, *-acy*, the sp. with *ecst-*, accommodated to Gr., appearing XVII; – OF. *extasie* – (with assim. to sbs. in *-sie*, L. *-sia*) late L. *extasis* (Tert.) – Gr. *ékstasis*, f. *eksta-*, stem of *existánai* put out of place (in phr. *existánai phrenôn* drive out of one's wits), f. *ek* out, EX-[2]+*histánai* place (see STAND). So **ecstatic** ėkstæ·tik. XVII. – F. *extatique* (Rabelais) – Gr. *ekstatikós*.

ecto- e·ktou repr. Gr. *ektós* outside (f. *ek* EX-[2] after *entós* = L. *intus* within), used as comb. form in scientific terms such as *e·ctoderm*, *e·ctoplasm*.

ecumenical var. of ŒCUMENICAL.

eczema e·kzimə skin disease. XVIII. – modL. – Gr. *ékzema*, f. *ekzeîn* boil over, (of disease) break out, f. *ek* out, EX-[2]+*zeîn* boil (cf. YEAST).

-ed[1] id (d, t; see below) formative of the pp. of weak verbs, in OE. *-ed*, *-ad*, *-od*, *-ud*, the vowels of which repr. (though not consistently) the thematic vowels characteristic of the class to which the verbs belong, the suffix proper being *-d* :– CGerm. **-ðaz* :– IE. **-tós*, repr. by Skr. *-tás*, Gr. *-tós* (in verbal adjs.), L. *-tus*, Lith. *-tas*. In some OE. verbs, the suffix being added immed. to the base appears as *-d*, after unvoiced cons. as *-t*; e.g. *seald*, pp. of *sellan* SELL, *boht*, pp. of *byćġan* BUY. In ME. the several OE. variants were levelled under *-ed* (*-id*, *-yd*; in western areas *-et*, e.g. *icrunet* crowned; in north. and Sc. *-it*, *-yt*, e.g. *lovit* beloved); and this *-ed* is usu. retained in writing, although the pronunc. is normally reduced to d, or, after unvoiced cons., to t, e.g. *robed* roubd, *hoped* houpt. The pronunc. id occurs regularly in ordinary speech only in the endings *-ded*, *-ted*, but it is often required elsewhere in verse and survives in the public reading of the Bible and the Liturgy. A few pps., as *beloved*, *blessed*, *cursed*, prominent in religious use, have escaped the tendency to contraction when used as adjs.; and *learned* as adj. is pronounced lə̄·ɹnid as dist. from the pp., which is lə̄ɹnd, lə̄ɹnt. From XVI to XVIII commonly (and later in individual usage) *-ed* was replaced by *-t* after a voiceless cons. preceded by another cons. or a short vowel, e.g. *jumpt*, *stept*, *whipt*; this spelling has become universal where a long vowel in the stem has been shortened in the pp., e.g. *crept*, *dealt*, *kept*, *knelt*, *lost*, *meant*, *slept*, *swept*. Where there is a shortened and an unshortened form there is a twofold spelling, as in *leapt* lept, *leaped* līpt.

In certain other classes of verbs there has been gen. contraction in ME. of *-ed* which had begun in inflected forms in OE.: *-ded*, *-ted* became *-d(d)*, *-t(t)*, as in *bled(d)* for OE. *blēded* (see BLEED), *set(t)* for OE. *seted* (see SET[1]); after *l*, *n*, *r*, the ending *-ded* has become *-t*, as in *gilt*, *girt*, *sent*; in some verbs *l*, *m*, *n* at the end of their stem cause the change of *-ed* to *t*, as in *burnt*, *felt*, *smelt*, *spilt*, *unkempt*. Several verbs have parallel forms without contraction, sometimes with difference of use, e.g. *burned* and *burnt*, *leaned* and *leant*, *penned* and *pent*, *roasted* and *roast*, *spoiled* and *spoilt*.

In early ME. *wicke* and *wrecche* were given an adjectival appearance by adding *-ed*, to make *wicked*, *wretched*. Exceptional formations on sbs. are *crabbed*, *dogged*; †*bicched* (cursed) may be similarly based on *bitch*.

In early mod. Eng. certain pps. and other similar forms of foreign origin were extended with *-ed* to assimilate them to native words of similar function; as †*bigot*, *bigoted*; †*devote*, *devoted*; †*elate*, *elated*; *situate*, *situated*; L. and F. pps. were also directly naturalized, as *couped*, *versed*. In scientific use there are variants such as *falcate* and *falcated*, *labiate* and *labiated*, *pinnate* and *pinnated*.

-ed[2] id repr. OE. *-ede* = OS. *-ōdi* :– Germ. **-ōðja-*, and appended to sbs. to form adjs. denoting the possession or the presence of the thing or attribute expressed by the sb., e.g. OE. *hōcede* hooked (f. *hōc*), *hringede* ringed (f. *hring*). This suffix corresponds in function to the *-tus* of L. formations like *caudātus* tailed (f. *cauda* tail), *aurītus* eared (f. *auris* ear); it is now added without restriction to a sb. to form an adj. with the sense 'possessing, provided with, characterized by' (something), as in *booted*, *cultured*, *diseased*, *honeyed* (*honied*), *jaundiced*, *moneyed*, *spurred*, *wooded*, and notably in parasynthetic adjs., as *dark-eyed*, *leather-aproned*, *mealy-mouthed*, *three-pronged*, *weak-kneed*.

In mod. Eng. and to a large extent in ME. there is no formal distinction between **exx.**

of this suffix and ppl. adjs. in -ED[1] derived ult. from sbs. through unrecorded vbs. Even in OE. there is variation between *-ede*, *-ed* (rare), and *-od* (*-ud*), chiefly in parasynthetic comps., as *ānēagede* one-eyed, *blæcfeaxede* black-haired, *langswēorede* long-necked, *rēadstalede* red-stalked, *twihēafdede* two-headed, *twilæpped* having two skirts, *þribeddod* having three beds, *þrifōtud* three-footed. Suffixed parasynthetic adjs. existed beside forms without a *d*-suffix (the latter were extended later with *-ed*, e.g. *heardheort*, *hard-hearted*), e.g. *hwītlocc*, *hwītloccede* white-haired, *twiecge*, *-ecgede* two-edged; other types, with mutation, are repr. by *ānhyrnd* one-horned, *þrihyrne*, *þrihyrnede* three-horned, *fēowerfēte* four-footed, with which cf. ON. *-eygðr* -eyed, *-hyrndr* -horned, which have a ppl. suffix as well as *i*-mutation.

edacious ī-, idei·ʃəs eating, devouring. XIX. f. L. *edāci-*, *edāx*, f. *edere* EAT; see -IOUS.

edaphic idæ·fik (bot.) pert. to the soil. XX. – G. *edaphisch* (Schimper), f. Gr. *édaphos* ground, soil (orig. base, bottom, f. **sed-* SIT); see -IC.

Edda e·də title of two ON. collections (Elder or Poetic E., Younger or Prose E.). XVIII (Gray). ON., of disputed etym.; either f. the name of the great-grandmother in the poem 'Rígsþula' or f. ON. *óðr* poetry. Hence **E·dd**IC, **Edda**IC edei·ik. XIX.

eddish e·diʃ aftergrowth of grass; stubble. XV. Formally identical with OE. *ediscˊ* park, enclosed pasture; the discrepancy of sense is a difficulty, but cf. OE. *ediscˊhenn* quail, perh. 'stubble-hen'; perh. f. *ed-* (see next); cf. OE. *edgrōwung*, ME. *edgrow* aftergrowth.

eddy e·di small whirlpool. XV (Sc. *ydy*). perh. of Scand. origin; the stem-vowel of *ydy* corr. to that of ON. *iða* eddy, whirlpool, which does not, however, account for the terminal *-y*; in any case, prob. f. base of OE. *ed-* again, back = OFris. *et-*, OHG. *et(a)-*, ON. *ið-*, rel. to L. *et* and, Gr. *éti* yet, Gaulish *etic* and, Goth. *iþ* then, but; if of native origin, perh. :- OE. **edwǣǵ*, corr. to MHG. *itwæge* flood, whirlpool (OE. *wǣǵ* wave = OFris. *wēi*, OS., OHG. *wāg*, G. *woge*, ON. *vágr*, Goth. *wēgs*; cf. WAY, WEIGH).

edelweiss ei·dlvais Alpine plant, Filago Leontopodium. XIX. G., f. *edel* noble (cf. ATHELING)+*weiss* WHITE.

Eden ī·dn abode of Adam and Eve (Gen. ii 15) XIV (Wycl. Bible); delightful abode, paradise XVI (Sh.). – L. (Vulg.) *Ēden*, Gr. (LXX) *Ēdén* – Heb. *'ēden*, assoc. with the word meaning 'delight'.

edentate īde·nteit of the order of Edentata, which lack incisor and canine teeth. XIX. – L. *ēdentātus*, f. *ē* E-+*dent-*, *dēns* TOOTH; see -ATE[2]. So **ede·nt**ULOUS toothless. XVIII. f. L. *ēdentulus*.

edge edʒ sharp side of a blade OE.; boundary of a surface XIV. OE. *ecˊǵ* = OFris. *egg*, OS. *eggia* (Du. *egge*), OHG. *ekka* (G. *ecke*), ON. *egg* :- CGerm. (exc. Goth.) **agjō*, f. **ag-* :- IE. **ak-* be sharp or pointed, as in L. *aciēs* edge, sharpness, line of battle, Gr. *akís* point, *akmḗ* ACME, Lith. *akštìs* spit; cf. AWN, EAR[2], and EAGER. Hence **edge** vb. give an edge to XIII; incite XVI (cf. EGG[2]).

edible e·dĭbl fit to be eaten. XVII. – late L. *edibilis*, f. *edere* EAT; see -IBLE.

edict ī·dikt order proclaimed by authority. XV. – L. *ēdictum*, sb. use of pp. n. of *ēdīcere* proclaim, f. *ē* E-+*dīcere* say, tell (cf. DICTION). Superseded earlier adoption (XIII) of (O)F. *édit*.

edification e:difikei·ʃən A. building up of the church, of the soul in holiness, etc. (after Gr. οἰκοδομή in 1 Cor. xiv; cf. Rom. xiv 19) XIV (Wycl. Bible); mental or moral improvement XIV; building XV (now rare or obs.). – L. *ædificātiō(n-)*, f. *ædificāre* EDIFY; see -FICATION. So **edifice** e·difis building. XIV (Ch.). – (O)F. *édifice* – L. *ædificium*, f. *ædis* dwelling, orig. hearth (rel. to Skr. *édhas* kindling wood, Gr. *aíthein* burn, L. *æstus* heat, OE. *ād* funeral pile, fire, OIr. *aed* fire) + *fic-*, wk. form of *facere* make. **edi**FY e·difai build up, lit. and fig. XIV. – (O)F. *édifier* – L. *ædificāre*.

edit e·dit †publish (rare); prepare an edition of XVIII; be the editor of XIX. Formerly occas. *edite*; partly – F. *éditer* publish, edit (itself based on *édition*); partly back-formation from EDITOR. ¶ An earlier ex. of a vb. †*edition* occurs XVIII. So **edi**TION idi·ʃən †publication; †production, creation; one of the forms in which a literary work is produced XVI. – (O)F. *édition* – L. *ēditiō(n-)*, f. *ēdit-*. **editor** e·ditəɹ †publisher XVII (rare); one who prepares an edition XVIII; conductor of a periodical XIX. – L. *ēditor* producer, exhibitor, f. *ēdit-*, pp. stem of *ēdere* put forth, f. *ē*+*dare* put; see E-, EX-[1], DATE[2], -TOR, and cf. F. *éditeur* publisher (XVIII). ¶ Preceded by †*editioner* in the second sense. Hence **edito·r**IAL XVIII; whence F. *éditorial*.

educate e·djŭkeit bring up, provide schooling or tuition for. XV. f. pp. stem of L. *ēducāre*, rel. to *ēdūcere* EDUCE; see -ATE[3]. So **educa·**TION. XVI. – (O)F. or L. Hence **educa·tion**IST XIX, which is earlier than **educa·tional**IST, f. **educa·tion**AL[1] (XVII). **e·ducat**IVE. XIX.

educe idjū·s †lead or draw forth XV; bring out, develop from a latent condition XVII. – L. *ēducere*, f. *ē* E-+*dūcere* lead (cf. DUCT).

edulcorate idʌ·lkŏreit soften. XVII. f. pp. stem of medL. *ēdulcorāre*, f. *ē* E- + *dulcor* sweetness, f. *dulcis* sweet; see DOUCE, -ATE[3].

-ee[1] ī· suffix repr. AN. *-ee, -e,* (O)F. *-é* :- L. *-ātus, -ātum,* endings (m. and n.) of pps. of vbs. in *-āre,* as in *dēputātus* deputy, *mandātum* command (cf. MAUNDY). It occurs earliest (XV) in legal terms of AN. origin, denoting the recipient of a grant or the like, e.g. *feoffee, grantee, lessee, patentee,* on the model of which many others were made, most of which cannot be construed as 'direct' passives, but denote the indirect object of vbs.; in *payee* 'one to whom something is payable' (XVIII), there has been a further departure from the original function. *Legatee* (XVII) is a fresh type, on the model of which *donatee* was formed (contrast *donee*). The common correspondence of agent-nouns in *-or* or *-er,* e.g. *lessor* and *lessee, obligor* and *obligee,* with nouns in *-ee* led to the general application of the suffix, as with *lover* and *lovee* (Richardson), *jester* and *jestee* (Sterne). Many such are nonce-words and remain so; but some, like *addressee* (De Quincey), are permanent. From XVI certain heraldic adjs., such as *nebuly, undy* (earlier *nebule, unde*) have variants with *-ee.* By mid-XVII *-ee* had become the regular repr. of F. *-é* in adopted words; e.g. *congee, debauchee, rappee.* Later exx. are *examinee, illuminee, employee, escapee,* in XX *internee, evacuee.* There are special features in ABSENTEE, COMMITTEE, DEVOTEE, REFUGEE.

-ee[2] ī· suffix used in a few names of garments, primarily with dim. force, as *bootee, coatee, neckatee* (of obscure formation), all of XVIII, and *shirtee* (U.S.); also *goatee* (orig. U.S.), var. *goaty,* perh. a variation on *-ie,* -Y[6], as also in *goalee* goalkeeper, *townee* town-bred person. ¶ In *dungaree, grandee, jamboree, jubilee, marquee, puttee,* in *Pharisee* and *Sadducee,* in *Bengalee, Chinee, Maltee,* and *Portugee,* the source of the el. is different. See -ESE.

eel īl fish of the genus Anguilla. OE. *ǣl* = OFris. *ēl,* OS., OHG. *āl* (Du., G. *aal*), ON. *áll* :- CGerm. (exc. Goth.) **ǣlaz,* of unkn. origin.

een īn see EYE. **e'en** īn see EVEN[1].

-een[1] ī·n terminal el. in names of fabrics, denoting one inferior to or coarser than that denoted by the original word; it repr. F. *-ine,* as in *ratteen* XVII (– F. *ratine*), which was preceded by *shagreen* XVII (irreg. – F. *chagrin*), *camleteen* XVIII (– F. *camelotine*); *velveteen* (XVIII) was modelled on *ratteen, sateen* (XIX) is a modification thereafter of *satin,* and *beaverteen* (XIX) has *-teen* from *velveteen* and *sateen.*

-een[2] ī·n suffix repr. Ir. dim. ending *-in,* as in *boneen* young pig (*banabhin*), *boreen* lane (*botharín*), *buckeen* (XVIII), *caubeen* (*cáibín*), *colleen, dudeen, mavourneen* (XVIII), *spalpeen, squireen.*

e'er ɛəɹ see EVER.

-eer[1] iə·ɹ suffix repr. mostly F. *-ier* :- L. *-ārius* -ARY (in Sp. *-ero,* Pg. *-eiro*; It. *-iere* is from F.), and denoting 'one who is concerned with, handles, or deals with'. Formal conditions vary from word to word, but in several exx. there were earlier vars. in *-er* and *-ier* (which was gen. replaced by *-eer* in XVII); and two words, *charioteer* and *engineer,* go back to ME. antecedents adopted from OF. forms in *-eor* (mod. *-eur*). Of the older words those that date from XVI often begin with *-er,* as *mutiner, pioner, scrutiner,* but there are instances of *-eer* as early as XVI, e.g. *cannoneer, moyleteer* MULETEER. In *pamphleteer, privateer, sonneteer* (all from XVII) a derogatory or contemptuous notion predominates; these provided a model for such words as *crotcheteer, profiteer, racketeer,* and more recently *blackmarketeer,* all of which are formed on words ending in *t.* There are two words denoting inanimate objects, GAZETTEER and MUFFINEER.

Most of the sbs. have deriv. vbs., which are used particularly in the gerund and prp. (*-eering*), and some of them, e.g. *electioneering, mountaineering,* are much commoner than the sbs. to which they belong. In early XIX *foreigneering* appears for 'engaging in foreign matters', modelled on *electioneer*; hence *foreigneer* fɔrəniə·ɹ as a depreciatory var. of *foreigner.*

-eer[2] iə·ɹ repr. Du. *-eeren* – F. inf. ending *-er* :- L. *-āre,* in *commandeer* (XIX), *domineer* (XVI). The obs. *pickeer* (XVII) pillage, skirmish, scout, flirt, wrangle, seems to be – Du. *pickeren* prick, spur (– F. *piquer*), with a strange sense-development; and the form of †*fineer* (later *veneer*) points to Du. *fineeren* refine (gold), veneer (wood).

eerie, eery iə·ri fearful, timid, (now) superstitiously uneasy XIII (Cursor M.); uncanny, weird XVIII. Orig. north. Eng. and Sc. *eri, ery*; derivation from ME. *erȝ, arȝe* cowardly, timid (OE. *earg*) would suit the earliest sense, but the vowel of the stem is not appropriate, and the ending (*-ie,* -Y[1]) would be difficult to account for.

ef- form of *ec-* EX-[1] used before *f.*

efface ėfei·s wipe out, obliterate. XV (Caxton). – (O)F. *effacer,* f. *ex-* EF-+*face* FACE.

effect ife·kt result XIV (Ch.); accomplishment XV; operative influence, impression XVII; pl. goods and chattels XVIII. – OF. *effect* (mod. *effet*) or L. *effectus,* f. *effect-,* pp. stem of *efficere* work out, f. *ex* EF-+*fic-, facere* make, do (cf. FACT). Cf. FECKLESS. Hence **effe·ct** vb. XVI. Also **effe·ctIVE.** XIV (Trevisa). – L. *effectīvus*; cf. (O)F. *effectif.* **effe·ctuAL.** XIV (Ch., Trevisa). – medL. **effe·ctuATE**[3]. XVI. f. medL. *effectuāt-, -āre,* whence F. *effectuer.*

effeminate ife·minət womanish. XIV (Gower). – L. *effēminātus,* pp. of *effēmināre* make feminine, f. *ex* EF-+*fēmina* woman; see FEMININE, -ATE[2]. Hence **effe·minACY.** XVII.

effendi efe·ndi Turkish title of respect. XVII (*aphendi,* Selden). – Turk. *efendī* – Gr. *authéntēs* (pronounced afþe·ndis) lord, master (see AUTHENTIC).

efferent e·fərənt discharging. XIX. – L. *efferent-*, *-ēns*, prp. of *efferre*, f. *ex* EF- + *ferre* BEAR[2]; see -ENT.

effervesce efəɹve·s give off bubbles of gas. XVIII. – L. *effervescere*, f. *ex* + *fervēscere*, inceptive of *fervēre*; see EF-, FERVENT, -ESCE. So **efferve·scENT**, -ENCE. XVII.

effete ėfī·t †that has ceased to bring forth; worn out. XVII. – L. *effētus* that has brought forth young, exhausted as by bearing young, f. *ex* EF- + *fētus* bearing (see FŒTUS).

efficacious efikei·ʃəs producing the desired effect. XVI. f. L. *efficāci-*, *-ax* (whence F. *efficace*), f. *efficere*; see EFFECT and -ACIOUS. So **effica·CITY**. XV. – F. – L. So **efficient** ifi·ʃənt making a thing what it is XIV (*the cause efficient*, Trevisa, tr. L. *causa efficiens*); adequately operative or skilled XVIII. – prp. of L. *efficere*. **effi·ciENCY**. XVI (Hooker). – L.

effigy e·fidʒi portrait, image. Not before XVIII in sg. form, which is based on the L. abl.; earlier in pl. *effigies* and phr. *in effigie* (4 syll.) belong to L. **effigies** efi·dʒiīz, which was in common use XVI–XIX. – L. *effigiēs*, f. *effig-*, stem of *effingere*, f. *ex-* EF- + *fingere* fashion (see FEIGN).

effloresce eflōre·s burst forth as in flower; change to fine powder. XVIII. – L. *efflōrēscere*, f. *ex* EF- + *flōrēscere* (see FLORESCENCE). So **efflore·SCENCE**. XVII. **efflore·SCENT**. XIX.

effluent e·fluənt flowing out XVIII (once XV); sb. XIX. – L. *effluent-*, *-ēns*, prp. of *effluere*, f. *ex* EF- + *fluere* flow (cf. FLUX). So **e·fflu-ENCE**. XVII (once XIV). Cf. (O)F. *effluent*, *-ence*. **effluvium** ėflū·viəm outflow or exhalation of (electric or other) particles; exhalation affecting the sense of smell, (hence, pop.) noxious odour. XVII (Sir T. Browne). L., f. *effluere*, f. *ex* EF- + *fluere* flow (cf. FLUENT). So **efflux** e·flʌks outflow. XVII (Sanderson, H. More, Jer. Taylor). L.; cf. FLUX. **efflu·XION**. XVII (Bacon, Sir T. Browne). – (O)F. or late L.

effort e·fəɹt putting forth of power. XV (Caxton). – (O)F. *effort*, earlier *esforz* nom., f. *esforcier* (mod. *efforcer*) = Pr. *esforzar*, It. *sforzare*, Sp. *esforzar* :– Rom. **exfortiāre*, f. L. *ex* EF- + *fortis* strong (see FORCE).

effrontery ifrʌ·ntəri shameless audacity. XVIII. – F. *effronterie*, f. *effronté* shameless, impudent, OF. *esfronté* = It. *sfrontato* :– Rom. **exfrontātus*, f. **exfrōns*, for late L. *effrōns* barefaced, f. *ex* EF- + *frōns* forehead; see FRONT, -ERY.

effulgent ėfʌ·ldʒent gleaming forth. XVIII. – L. *effulgent-*, *-ēns*, prp. of *effulgēre*; see EF-, FULGENT. So **effu·lgENCE**. XVII (Milton). – late L.

effusion ėfjū·ʒən pouring out or forth, shedding (of blood). XV. – (O)F. *effusion* – L. *effūsiō(n-)*, f. *effūs-*, *effundere*; see EF-, FUSION. So **effu·nd** (now rare). XV; **effu·se**. XVI pour forth. **effu·SIVE**. XVII.

efreet var. of AFREET.

eft eft OE. *efeta* NEWT, surviving dial.

eftsoons eftsū·nz again; (soon) afterwards. OE. *eft sōna* 'afterwards immediately', ME. *eftsōne*, to which advb. -s was added XIV; OE. *eft* (= OFris., OS. *eft*, MLG., MDu. *echt*, ON. *ept*, *eft* :– Germ. **aftiz*, compar. adv. f. **aft-* AFTER) + *sōna* SOON.

egad igæ·d (arch.) euph. excl., veiling *by God*. XVII. Varying with *i gad*, *egod*, *agad*, and *adad*, *adod*; perh. orig. for *A! God!*

egg[1] eg 'ovum'. XIV. – ON. *egg*; superseding ME. *ey* :– cognate OE. *ǣġ* = OS., OHG. (Du., G.) *ei*, Crim.-Gothic *ada* (Goth. **addi-*) :– CGerm. **ajjaz* n., prob. ult. rel. to L. *ōvum*, Gr. *ōión*, OSl. **jaje* (Russ. *yaĭtsó*, dim. *yaíchko*), Ir. *og*, W. *wy* :– **ōwjom*, and further to words for 'bird' in Skr. *vis*, L. *avis* :– **owís*. ¶ Traces of OE. sg. *ǣġ* survived in *aye* (XVI) and of pl. *ǣġru* (= OHG. *eigir*, G. *eier*) in *eyren* (XV).

egg[2] eg incite. First recorded in late Nhb. OE. *ġeeggedon*, pt. pl. of *ġeeggia* – (with *ġe-* Y- prefixed) ON. *eggja*, rel. to *egg* EDGE.

eglantine e·gləntain sweet-briar. XIV. – OF. *églantine* – Pr. *aiglentina*, f. *aiglent* :– Rom. **aculentu-s*, f. (after *spīnulentus* thorny) *acus* needle, *aculeus* prickle, sting, f. **ak-* (see ACRID).

ego e·gou, ī·gou (philos.) *the* conscious or thinking subject; (colloq.) self. XIX. L., the pron. I. So **e·goISM** belief that nothing exists but one's own mind; theory which regards self-interest as the basis of morals XVIII; egotism XIX. – F. *égoïsme* – modL. *egōismus*. **egotISM** e·gotizm practice of talking about oneself; self-conceit, selfishness XVIII (Addison); the *t* may be merely hiatus-filling; but perh. modelled on *despotism*; hence F. *égotisme*. So **e·goIST**, **e·gotIST**. XVIII.

egregious igrī·dʒiəs eminent; gross, flagrant. XVI. f. L. *ēgregius* surpassing, illustrious, f. *ē* out of (EX-[1]) + *greg-*, *grex* flock (cf. CONGREGATE, GREGARIOUS); see -IOUS.

egress ī·gres going out, issuing. XVI. – L. *ēgressus*, f. *ēgress-*, pp. stem of *ēgredī*, f. *ē* EX-[1] + *gradī* step (cf. GRADIENT).

egret ī·gret white heron. XV. – AN. *egrette*, (O)F. *aigrette* – Pr. *aigreta*, f. stem of *aigron*, corr. to (O)F. *héron* HERON; see -ET.

eh ei, dial. ē also spelt *eigh*, Sc. and north. Eng. int. of wonder, doubt, or the like :– north. ME. *ā*, AH = south. ME. *ō* OH. XVI. Cf. ON. *á*. ¶ Two interrog. uses are widespread: (i) appended to an inquiry, 'Is it so?', 'What do you think?' XVIII; (ii) in brusque or rude speech, asking for a repetition of a statement, as an answer to a call, etc., 'What did you say?'. The origin and history of these uses are not clear; they were earlier expressed by *ha?*, e.g. Sh. 'Mer. V.' II v 44, 'Wint.' I ii 270.

eider-down ai·dəɹdaun down from the breast of the **ei·der-duck,** Somateria mollissima. XVIII. – Icel. (ON.) *æðr*, g. *æðar* ai·ðar in *æðarfugl* eider-duck, (Icel.) *æðardún* (see DOWN[3]); from Icel. are also Sw. *ejder (gås), -dun*, Da. *eder(fugl), -duun*, Du. *eider (-eend, -gans), -dons*, G. *eider (-ente, -gans, -vogel), -daunen, -dunen*, whence F. *édredon.*

eidolon aidou·lən unsubstantial image. XIX (Carlyle). Gr. *eídōlon* IDOL.

eight eit 8, viii. OE. *ehta (eahta, ahta)* = OFris. *achta, acht(e)*, OS., OHG. *ahto* (Du., G. *acht*), ON. *átta*, Goth. *ahtau* :– CGerm. **aχtō* :– IE. **oktō*, whence also L. *octō*, Gr. *oktṓ*, (O)Ir. *ocht*, W. *wyth*, Lith. *aštuonì*, Skr. *aštáu*, Av. *ašta*. So **eighteen** eitī·n, ei·tīn OE. *e(a)htatēne*, corr. to OFris. *achtatīne*, OS. *ahtotian* (Du. *achttien*), OHG. *ahtozehan* (G. *achtzehn*), ON. *áttján*; see -TEEN. **eighteen**TH[2] (stress variable). ME. *eȝtetenþe*, repl. OE. *e(a)htotēoþa*; cf. OFris. *achtatīnda, achtendesta, achtiensta*, ON. *áttjándi*. **eigh**TH[2] eitþ, (formerly †*eight*) OE. *e(a)htoþa* = OFris. *achte*, OHG. *ahtodo* (G. *achte*) :– Germ. **aχto·þan*, f. **aχtō*: see -TH[2]; OS. *ahtodo*, Goth. *ahtuda* repr. **a·χtoðan*; OFris. *achtunda*, ON. *áttundi* have forms with *n* on the analogy of SEVENTH. **ei·ghti**ETH[1]. **eighty** ei·ti ME. *eȝteti*, repl. OE. *hunde(a)htatiġ*; cf. OFris. *achtich*; see HUNDRED and -TY[1].

eirenicon aiərī·nikən proposal for peace. XIX (Pusey). – Gr. *eirēnikón*, n. sg. of *eirēnikós*, f. *eirḗnē* peace; see -IC.

eisteddfod eiste·ðvəd congress of Welsh bards. XIX. W., 'session', f. *eistedd* sit, for **eitsedd*, for the second syll. of which see SEAT, SET, SIT.

either ai·ðəɹ, ī·ðəɹ each of the two OE.; one or other of the two XIII; adv. introducing alternatives XIV. OE. *ǣġþer*, contr. form of *ǣġ(e)hwæþer* = OFris. *ēider*, MLG., MDu. *ed(d)er* (as adv.), OHG. *eogihwedar* (MHG. *iegeweder*) :– Germ. phr. **aiwo giχwaþaraz*, i.e. 'ever each of two'; see AY, WHETHER, and cf. EACH.

ejaculate idʒæ·kjŭleit eject (fluid) XVI; utter suddenly XVII. f. pp. stem of *ējaculārī*, f. *ē* E-+*jaculārī* dart, f. *jaculum* dart, javelin, f. *jacere* throw, rel. to Gr. *hiénai* send, throw, utter; see -ATE[3]. So **ejacul**A·TION. XVII.

eject idʒe·kt throw out, expel. XV. f. *eject-*, pp. stem of L. *e(j)icere*, f. *ē* E-+*jacere* (see prec.). **eject** ī·dʒekt sb. (philos.) 1878 (W. K. Clifford). – L. *ējectum*, n. ppl., after *object, subject*. So **eje·c**TION. XV; – L. **eje·ct**MENT. XVI; in legal AN. *ejectement*.

eke[1] īk also OE. *ēc, ēac* = OFris. *āk*, OS. *ōk* (Du. *ook*), OHG. *ouh* (G. *auch*), ON., Goth. *auk*; referred by some to IE. **au* again+**ge*, emphatic particle (cf. Gr. *aû ge* again; and L. *autem* moreover, *aut* or, Skr. *u, utá* and, but, also), by others to EKE[2] (cf. OE. *tō ēacan* in addition, besides).

eke[2] īk (dial.) augment XII; (with *out*) supplement, prolong XVI. OE. **ēacan* (implied in *ēacen*, pp. increased, strong, pregnant; cf. *ēacian* intr. increase) = OFris. *āka*, OS. *ōkian*, ON. *auka*, Goth. *aukan*, rel. to L. *augēre* increase, Gr. *aúkhein*, Lith. *áugu* I grow, f. base **aug-* (cf. Skr. *ṓjas* strength, *ugrás* powerful, and WAX[2]). The OE. sb. *ēaca* increase = OFris. *āka*, ON. *auki*, may have been partly the source of the ME. vb. See also NICKNAME.

-el[1] (ə)l repr. OE. *-el, -ela, -ele* :– Germ. **-ilaz, *-ilon, *-ilōn*, usu. retained as -LE[1], but the old form survives in *hatchel, kernel*.

-el[2] (ə)l repr. OF. *-el* (mod. *-eau*) :– L. *-ellu-s, -ella* (see *libel, novel, satchel, tunnel*).

elaborate ilæ·bərət †produced by labour XVI; highly or minutely finished XVII. – L. *ēlabōrātus*, pp. of *ēlabōrāre*, f. *ē* E-+*labor* LABOUR. So **ela·borate** -eit produce by labour; give finish to. XVII. See -ATE[2] and [3]. So **elabor**A·TION. XV (first in physiol. and chem.). – L. (whence in F.). **ela·bora-t**ORY (arch.) laboratory. XVII (Evelyn).

elæo- ilī·ou comb. form of Gr. *élaion* OIL.

élan ei·lã, ǁelã ardour, impetuosity. XIX. F., f. *élancer* cast or launch forth, f. *é-* EX-[1]+ *lancer* LAUNCH.

eland ī·lənd S. African antelope. XVIII. – S. Afr. use of Du. *eland* elk – G. *elend* (more fully *elentier*) – Lith. *élnis* = OSl. *jelenĭ* stag, rel. to *lani* hind (:– **olnia*), Gr. *ellós* fawn (:– **elnós*), *élaphos* stag (:– **elnbhos*), W. *elain*, pl. *elanedd*, hind, fawn. Animal names on the same base (IE. **oln-, *eln-*) are widespread, appearing also in ELK. F. *élan* (– G.) was repr. in Eng. by *elan* (XVI Hakluyt to XIX) and *ellan* (XVII), G. *elend* by *ellend* (XVII).

elapse ilæ·ps (of time) pass away. XVII. f. *ēlaps-*, pp. stem of L. *ēlābī* slip away; see E- and LAPSE.

elastic ilæ̀·stik †orig. applied to the 'impulsive force' of the atmosphere; spontaneously resuming its normal bulk after contraction, etc. XVII. – modL. *elasticus* (in *virtus elastica*, of the atmosphere, Pecquet's 'Dissertatio Anatomica', 1651) – Gr. *elastikós* propulsive, impulsive, f. **elaϝ-*, stem of *elaúnein* drive. Cf. F. *élastique*. Hence **elasti·c**ITY el-, il-, īlæsti·sĭti. XVII.

elate ilei·t †elevate XVI; (chiefly in pp.) †encourage; puff up XVII. f. *ēlāt-*, stem of pp. of L. *efferre*, f. *ex* EF-+*ferre* BEAR[2]. The L. pp. *ēlātus* was anglicized as *elate* (XVII), but had been adopted earlier, through OF. *elat* proud XIV (Ch.); see -ATE[2] and [3]. So **el**A·TION. XIV (Ch.). – OF. *elacion* and (later) its source L. *ēlātiō*.

elater e·lətəɹ †elasticity XVII; skipjack beetle (Linnæus); (bot.) elastic spiral filament XIX. mod. L. (Pecquet; cf. ELASTIC). – Gr. *elatḗr* driver, f. **elaϝ-*, *elaúnein* drive.

elbow e·lbou bend of the arm. OE. *el(n)-boga* = MDu. *elleboghe* (Du. *elleboog*), OHG. *elinbogo* (G. *ellenbogen*), ON. *ǫlnbogi* :- CGerm. (exc. Goth.) **alinobogon*, f. **alinā* arm (cf. ELL)+**bogon* BOW[1].

eld eld (arch.) age. OE. (Anglian) *eldu*, (WS.) *ieldu* = OFris. *elde*, OS. *eldī*, OHG. *eltī*, ON. *elli* :- CGerm. (exc. Goth.) **alþī*, f. **alþaz* OLD.

elder[1] e·ldəɹ the tree Sambucus nigra. OE. *ellærn*, ME. *eller*, *eldre*, corr. to MLG. *ellern*, *elderne*, *elhorn*, *alhorn*, prob. orig. an adj. formation like (O)HG. *ahorn* maple (corr. to L. *acernus* of maple).

elder[2] e·ldəɹ, **eldest** e·ldist compar. and superl. of OLD. OE. *eldra*, *-e* (*ieldra*, *-e*) = OFris. *alder*, *elder*, OS. *aldira*, OHG. *altiro*, *eltiro* (G. *älter*), ON. *ellri*, Goth. *alþiza* :- CGerm. **alþizon*, f. **alþaz* OLD; see -ER[3]. OE. *eldest* (*ieldest*) = OFris. *eldest*, OHG. *altist* (G. *ältest*), ON. *ellztr*, Goth. *alþista* :- CGerm. **alþistaz*; see -EST. As sb. *elder* was used in OE. and later for 'parent, ancestor', from *c.* 1200 for 'one's senior' or 'superior in age', from XIV (Wycl. Bible) rendering L. *senior* and *senatus*, by Tindale used to tr. N.T. Gr. πρεσβύτερος PRESBYTER (cf. PRIEST); in the Presbyterian and other bodies, title of an office believed to corr. to that of elder in the apostolic church.

eldorado eldŏrā·dou *El Dorado* name of a fictitious place in S. America abounding in gold XVI (Ralegh); fig. source of boundless wealth XIX. Sp., *el* the, *dorado*, pp. of *dorar* gild = F. *dorer* :- Rom. **dēaurāre*, f. *dē* DE-(3)+*aurum* gold.

eldritch e·ldritʃ pert. to elves or fairies; weird, unnatural. XVI (Douglas, Dunbar). Of Sc. origin; poss. from attrib. use of OE. **ælf-*, **elfrīce* 'fairy realm' (see ELF, RICH); early forms were *elri(s)ch*, *-reche*, *-rage*, with occas. *elphrish*; *eldritch* appears to have been established by Burns.

elecampane elikæmpei·n composite plant, Inula Helenium. XIV. ult. – medL. *enula campāna*, i.e. *enula* for L. *inula* (medL. vars. are *elna*, *elena*; cf. OE. *eolone*, *elene* – **iluna* for *inula*) – Gr. *helénion*, and *campana* prob. of the fields (cf. CHAMPAIGN). ¶ The medL. forms *enula*, *elena*, *ala* are repr. by It. *enola*, *-ula*, *(l)ella*, OF. *eaune*, *(i)alne*, F. *aunée*, Sp., Pg. *ala*, MLG., MDu., (O)HG. *alant*.

elect ile·kt picked out, chosen, select XV; (theol.) XVI; chosen for an office (but not yet installed) XVII. – L. *ēlectus*, pp. of *ēligere*, f. *e-* EX-[1]+*legere* choose (cf. LEGION). Preceded by *elite* (Trevisa), *elyte* (Wyntoun) – (O)F. *élit-e* (see ÉLITE). So **ele·ct** vb. choose, esp. by vote. XV. f. corr. pp. stem. **ele·**CTION choosing, choice. XIII (with ref. to representative bodies XVII). – (O)F. *élection* – L. *ēlectiō(n-)*; hence **election**EE·R[1] (first in vbl. sb.) XVIII (Jefferson, Burke). **ele·ct**IVE. XVI (once XV). – (O)F. *électif*, *-ive* – late L. **ele·ct**OR[2], one who has the right to vote XV (prince of the Holy Roman Empire, *Kurfürst*, entitled to elect the Emperor XVI). – (O)F. *électeur*, L. *ēlector*; hence **ele·ctor**AL[1]. XVII (of a German Elector; cf. F. *altesse électorale*). **ele·ctor**ATE[1]. XVII; after F. *électorat*.

electric, -ical ile·ktrik, -ikl pert. to electricity. XVII (Sir T. Browne, Newton). – modL. *ēlectricus* (W. Gilbert, 'De Magnete', 1600), f. L. *ēlectrum* – Gr. *ḗlektron* amber; see -IC, -ICAL. Hence **electric**IAN eliktri·ʃən one skilled in electricity. XVIII (Franklin). **electric**ITY elėktri·sĭti, ĭlek- distinctive property of amber, etc., when excited by friction, of attracting bodies near them, (hence) this state of excitation, and the cause of this phenomenon (formerly regarded as a fluid). XVII (Sir T. Browne). **ele·ctri**FY, **ele·ctri**FICA·TION. XVIII (Franklin).

electro- ile·ktrou, ĭlektrə· comb. form of Gr. *ḗlektron* amber, used in the sense 'electricity', 'electric', as in **electro·**METER (XVIII); *electro-dyna·mic*, *electro·lysis*, *electro-ma·gnet*, *-magne·tical* (Faraday), -PLATE (vb.), *-type*.

electrocution ilektrŏkjū·ʃən execution by electricity. 1890. Alteration, after prec., of †*electricution* (1889), f. *electri|cal exe|cution* (1888); hence by back-formation †*ele·ctricute*, **ele·ctrocute**, which was preceded by **ele·ctr**IZE (1886).

electrode ile·ktroud one of the poles by which electricity is conducted. XIX (Faraday). f. ELECTRIC+Gr. *hodós* way; cf. *anode*, *cathode*.

electron ile·ktrən (phys.) smallest supposed component of matter, carrying a negative charge of electricity. 1891 (applied by G. J. Stoney to the unit of electric charge). f. ELECTRIC+*-on* of *anion*, *cation*, *ion*. Hence **electro·n**IC, -ICS.

electuary ile·ktjuəri medicinal conserve or paste. XIV. – late L. *ēlectuārium*, prob. altered deriv. of synon. Gr. *ekleiktón*, f. *ekleíkhein* LICK up (cf. L. *eclīgma*, Pliny – Gr. *ékleigma*); see EX-[2]. Aphetic †*lectuary*.

eleemosynary e·liimə·sinəri, -mə·z- pert. to (the nature of) alms. XVII. – medL. *eleēmosynārius*, f. ChrL. *eleēmosyna* ALMS; see -ARY.

elegant e·ligənt tastefully ornate, refined and graceful, 'pleasing by minuter beauties' (J.). XVI. – (O)F. *élégant* or L. *ēlegant-*, *-āns*, of the form of a prp. of **ēlegāre*, rel. to *ēligere* select, ELECT. The etymol. sense is 'choosing carefully'; the early sense in L. was 'fastidious, dainty', the later 'choice, tasteful'. So **e·leg**ANCE. XVI. – F. – L.

elegy e·lĭdʒi song of lamentation; poem in elegiac metre. XVI. – F. *élégie* – L. *elegīa* – Gr. *elegeíā* (sb. use of adj., sc. *ōidḗ* ode), f. *élegos* perh. orig. a flute-song, of alien origin; see -Y[3]. So **elegi**AC elidʒai·æk pert. to elegy, written or writing in a metre consisting of alternate hexameters and pentameters. XVI. – F. *élégiaque* – late L. *elegīacus* – Gr. *elegeiakós*, f. *elegeiā*, *elegeîon* (sc. *métron* metre).

element e·limənt one of the four constituents of the universe (earth, water, air, fire) XIII (whence ult. the use in mod. chem. by Davy XIX); constituent portion; pl. rudiments XIV. – (O)F. *élément* – L. *elementum* esp. pl. principles, rudiments, letters of the alphabet, used to tr. Gr. *stoikheîon* step, ground, base, element, etc., f. *stoîkhos* row, rank. Hence **eleme·ntAL**[1]. XV. So **ele-me·ntARY**. XVII (earlier *elementare* XIV, *-air* XVI) – L. *elementārius*, whence F. *élémentaire*.

elemi e·lĭmi stimulant resin. XVI. In full *gum elimi*, modL. *gummi elimi*, prob. of Oriental origin. So F. *élémi*, Sp. *elemi*.

elenchus ile·ŋkəs form of syllogism in refutation. XVII (earlier in anglicized form *elynch* XV, *elench* XVI). L. – Gr. *élegkhos* argument of disproof or refutation.

elephant e·lifənt huge pachydermatous quadruped with a trunk. XIII. ME. *olifaunt*, *-ont*, *-unt*, later (XIV) with assim. to L., *elifant*, etc. – OF. *olifant*, *elefant* (mod. *éléphant*) = Pr. *olifan* – Rom. **olifantu-s* (cf. MDu. *olfant*, Du. *olifant*, W. *oliffant*, Breton *oli-fant*, Cornish *oliphans*, OE. *olfend* camel), alteration of L. *elephantus*, *-phās* (whence OE. *elpend*) – Gr. *elephant-*, *eléphās* ivory, elephant, prob. of alien origin. So **e·le-phantiASIS** -ai·əsis skin disease resembling an elephant's hide. XVI. **elephant-INE**[1] -æ·ntəin. XVII. – L. – Gr.

Eleusinian eljusi·niən pert. to Eleusis in Attica. XVII (*E. mysteries*, Milton). f. L. *Eleusīnius* – Gr. *Eleusínios*, f. *Eleusís*; see -IAN.

elevate e·liveit lift or raise up. XV. f. pp. stem of L. *ēlevāre*, f. *ē* EX-[1] + *levāre* lighten, raise, rel. to *levis* LIGHT[2]. The pp. †*elevate* was earlier. XIV (Ch.); see -ATE[3]. So **eleva·-TION**. XIV (astron., Ch.). – (O)F. or L. **e·levATOR** muscle that raises XVII; machine for raising objects XIX.

eleven ile·vn 11, xi. OE. *endleofon*, *-lufon*, *ellefne*, ME. *endleven(e)*, *elleven(e)* = OFris. *andlova*, *elleva*, *al-*, *elvene*, OS. *elleban*, OHG. *einlif* (Du., G. *elf*), ON. *ellifu*, Goth. *ainlif* :– CGerm. **ainlif-*, f. **ainaz* ONE + **lif-* (appearing also in TWELVE), quasi 'one left (over ten)', plausibly referred to IE. **liq-* LEAVE[2], and connected with *-lika*, the suffix of Lith. numerals 11–19, *vienuó-*, *dvý-*, *try-lika*, etc. Hence **ele·venTH**[2], a new formation (XIV), superseding OE. *endleofeþa*, itself a new formation on *endleofon*, superseding previous *endlyfta*, *ællefta* = OFris. *andlofta*, *ellefta*, OS. *ellifto*, OHG. *einlifto* (Du. *elfde*, G. *elfte*), ON. *ellifti* :– CGerm. (exc. Goth.) **ainlifton*.

elf elf dwarf supernatural being OE.; tricksy or mischievous creature XVI. OE. *elf* (as in g. pl. *dūn|elfa* mountain-nymphs, Castalides), non-WS. var. of **ielf*, late *ylf* (recorded in pl. *ylfe* 'Beowulf' 112, *ylfa ġe-sċeot* disease attributed to evil spirits, dial. *elfshot* XVII, north. *awfshots*) = MDu. *elf* (whence Sw. *elf*, Da. *elv*), beside MHG. *elbe* fem. :– **albiz*, parallel to **albaz*, whence OE. *ælf* (ME. pl. *alven*) = OS., MLG. *alf*, MHG. *alp* (G. *alp* nightmare; *elf* is from Eng.), ON. *álfr* (whence in part Eng. dial. *aulf*, *awf* and †*ouph*, OAF XVII), and **albinnja-*, whence OE. **ielfen*, *elfen*, coll. sg. fem. nymphs, in comps. as *wudu|elfen* Dryads, *sǣ|elfen* Naiads; poss. rel. to Skr. *ṛbhús* name of three semi-divine artificers. Hence **e·lfin** adj. XVI (Spenser), poss. suggested by ME. *elevene*, g. pl. of *elf*, and infl. by *Elphin*, a character of Arthurian romance. **e·lfISH**[1]. XVI. **e·lvISH**[1]. XIV (Ch.).

elicit ėli·sit draw forth or out. XVII. f. *ēlicit-*, pp. stem of L. *ēlicere* draw forth by trickery or magic, f. *ē* E- + *lacere* deceive, rel. to *lax* deceit (cf. DELICIOUS).

elide ilai·d †annihilate; (leg.) annul XVI; omit in pronunciation XVIII. – L. *ēlīdere* crush out, f. *ē* + *lædere* dash (cf. LESION). So **elisION** ili·ʒən suppression of a sound or syllable. XVI. – late L. *ēlīsiō(n-)*, f. *ēlīs-*, pp. stem of *ēlīdere*.

eligible e·lidʒĭbl fit to be chosen. XV. – F. *éligible* – late L. *ēligibilis*, f. *ēligere* choose; see ELECT, -IBLE. Hence **e:ligibi·lITY**. XVII.

eliminate ėli·mineit expel, get rid of. XVI. f. pp. stem of L. *ēlīmināre* thrust out of doors, expel, f. *ē* EX-[1] + *līmin-*, *līmen* threshold; see LIMINAL, -ATE[3]. Hence **eliminA·TION**. XVII.

élite eilī·t *the* pick (*of*). XVIII. F., sb. use of fem. of pp. †*élit*, †*eslit* of *élire*, †*eslire* = Pr. *eslire* :– Rom. **exlegere*, for L. *ēligere* ELECT.

elixir ėli·ksəɹ alchemist's preparation for changing metals to gold or prolonging life. XIV (Ch.). – medL. *elixir* (Roger Bacon) – Arab. *aliksīr*, perh. f. *al* AL-[2] + Gr. *xērion* desiccative powder for wounds, f. *xērós* dry. Cf. F. *élixir*, Sp. *elíxir*, It. *elissire*.

elk elk large animal of the deer kind, Alces malchis. XV (Bk. St. Albans). prob. repr. OE. *elh*, *eolh*, with k for χ as in dial. *dwerk* (OE. *dweorh*) DWARF, *fark* (OE. *fearh*) FARROW, *felk* (OE. *felh*) FELLOE, *selk* (OE. *seolh*) SEAL[1]. OE. had also *ēola* (:– **eolha*), cogn. with OHG. *elaho* (G. *elch*), repr. IE. **elk-*, beside **olkís*, whence Germ. **algiz* (ON. *elgr*, Sw. *älg*) and CSlav. **olsĭ* (Russ. *los'*, OPol. *łoś* elk); cf. L. *alcēs* pl. (Cæsar) and Gr. *álkē* (Pausanias), which are perh. – Germ. See also ELAND.

ell el measure of length (in England 45 inches). OE. *eln* = OFris. *(i)elne*, MDu. *elne*, *elle* (Du. *el*), OHG. *elina* (G. *elle*), ON. *ǫln* (*aln-*) cubit, ell, forearm, Goth. *aleina* (for **alina*) cubit :– CGerm. **alinā* (whence F. *aune*, OSp., It. *alna*, medL. *alena*), orig. 'arm', 'forearm'; cogn. with L. ULNA (:– **olenā*), Gr. *ōlénē*, *ōlḗr*, *ôllon* ELBOW, Arm. *oln* spine, OIr. *u(i)len*, W. *elin*, Skr. *aratnís*, Av. *arəθna-* elbow, and further to Slav. **lak-* (cf. Russ. *lókot'*, elbow, cubit, ell). For *ll* from *ln* cf. *kill*, KILN, MILL.

ellipse ili·ps regular oval figure; (math.) conic section so called, acc. to Apollonius of Perga, because the square on the ordinate is equal to a rectangle whose height is equal to the abscissa and whose base lies along the latus rectum but falls short of it (ἐλλείπει). XVIII; (gram.) ellipsis XIX. – F. *ellipse* – L. *ellīpsis* – Gr. *élleipsis* ELLIPSIS. Hence **elli·p**SOID. XVIII.

ellipsis ili·psis †ellipse XVI; (gram.) omission of words supposed to be essential to the complete form of a sentence XVII. – L. *ellīpsis* (Quintilian) – Gr. *élleipsis* defect, ellipse (conic section), grammatical ellipsis, f. *elleipein* leave out, fall short, fail, f. *en* IN+ *leípein* leave (see LOAN). So **elli·pt**IC XVIII; **elli·pt**ICAL pert. to an ellipse XVII (Hobbes); (gram.) XVIII (Lowth). – Gr. *elleiptikós* (chiefly gram.) defective.

elm elm tree of the genus Ulmus. OE. *elm*, corr. to MLG., OHG. *elm(boum)*, *elmo* (MHG. *elme*, *ilme*, G. dial. *ilm*), and, with vowel variation, ON. *álmr* (Sw., Norw. *alm*), L. *ulmus* (whence OE. *ulm|trēow*, occas. ME., early modEng. *ulm*, MHG., G. *ulme*, †*ulm|boum*, and MDu. *olme*, Du. *olm*, through OF. *olme* = It. *olmo* :- L.), MIr. *lem* (Ir. *leamh*), Gael. *leamhan*, W. *llwyf*; a tree name of WEur. extent.

elocution elǒkjū·ʃən †literary or oratorical style XV (Lydg.); oral utterance or delivery XVII. – L. *ēlocūtiō(n-)*, f. *ēlocūt-*, pp. stem of *ēloquī*; see ELOQUENCE, -TION. Cf. F. *élocution* (XVI).

éloge ei·louʒ encomium XVI; funeral oration. XVIII. – F. – L. *ēlogium* short saying or formula, epitaph, altered – Gr. *elegeîon* ELEGY, initial *e* being replaced by *ē* E- and *-leg-* by the *-log-* of EULOGY. ¶ The L. *elogium* (XVI) and the anglicized *elogy* (XVII) were formerly in use.

Elohist elou·hist any of the authors of those parts of the Hexateuch in which *Elohim* is used as the name of God instead of *Jahveh*. XIX. f. *Elōhīm* (pl., perh. of majesty), one of the Heb. names of God or of the gods, of unkn. origin; see -IST.

eloi(g)n èloi·n (spec. leg.) remove. XVI. – OF. *esloignier* (mod. *éloigner*) :- Rom. **exlongiāre*, for late L. *ēlongāre* (see next).

elongate ī·lɔŋgeit A. †remove XVI (pp. XV); †depart XVII; B. lengthen XVI. f. pp. stem of late L. *ēlongāre* remove, withdraw, prolong, orig. f. *ē* E-+*longē* far off, but later taken as if f. *ē*+*longus* LONG, i.e. 'lengthen out'. So **elong**A·TION. XIV (Ch., in astron. sense). – late L.

elope ilou·p (of woman) run away from husband or home. XVII. – AN. *aloper*, perh. f. ME. **alope(n)*, pp. of **alepe* run away, f. A-[3]+LEAP; cf. MDu. *ontlōpen*, G. *entlaufen* run away. Hence **elo·pe**MENT. XVII; cf. AN. *alopement*.

eloquent e·ləkwənt fervent and powerful in the use of language. XIV (Gower). – (O)F. *éloquent* – L. *ēloquent-*, *-ēns*, prp. of *ēloquī* speak out, f. *ē* EX-+*loquī* speak; see LOCUTION, -ENT. So **e·loqu**ENCE. XIV (Wycl. Bible). – (O)F. – L.

elpasolite elpæ·solait (min.) native fluoride of potassium, aluminium, and sodium. XIX. f. *El Paso* county, Colorado, U.S.A.+-LITE.

else els (with pron.) other; otherwise, if not. OE. *elles* = OFris. *elles*, *-is*, MDu. *els*, OHG. *elles*, *alles*, OSw. *äljes* (Sw. *eljest*), g. sg., corr. to Goth. *aljis*, of CGerm. **aljaz*, cogn. with L. *alius*, Gr. *állos* (cf. ALIEN). Hence **else**WHERE. OE. *elles hwǣr* = MDu. *elswaer*. †**e·lse**WISE otherwise. XVI (Udall, Coverdale).

elucidate èlʲū·sideit make lucid. XVI. f. pp. stem of late L. (Vulg.) *ēlūcidāre*, f. *ē* EX-[1] + *lūcidus* LUCID; see -ATE[3]. **elucid**A·TION. XVI.

elude iljū·d †delude, baffle XVI; slip away from XVII. – L. *ēlūdere*, f. *ē* EX[1]-+*lūdere* play (cf. LUDICROUS). So **elu·**SION †deception XVI; evasion XVII. f. L. *ēlūs-*, *ēlūdere*. **elu·**SIVE. XVIII.

elvan e·lvən in Cornwall, intrusive rock of igneous origin. XVIII. Said to be Corn. *elven* spark, the rock being so hard as to strike fire.

elver e·lvəɹ young eel. XVII. Var. of *eelvare* (XVI), south. form of *eelfare* brood of young eels, f. EEL+FARE, i.e. passage of (young) eels up a river.

Elysium ili·ziəm state or abode of the blessed dead. XVI. L. – Gr. *Elýsion* (sc. *pedíon* plain). Hence **Ely·**SIAN. XVI (*Elisian fieldes*, Spenser; tr. L. *Elysii campi*, Virgil).

elytron e·litrɔn pl. *elytra* (zool.) outer wing-case. XVIII (Goldsmith). – Gr. *élytron* sheath, rel. to *eilúein* envelop, L. *volvere* roll (cf. VOLUTE, REVOLVE).

Elzevir e·lzīviəɹ name (*Elzevier*, *Els-*, latinized *Elzevirius*) of a family of printers (1592–1680) at Amsterdam, The Hague, Leyden, and Utrecht; transf. a book printed by one of them. XVIII.

em em name of the letter M; (typogr.) square of the body of a type, orig. of the type m, used as a unit of measuring the amount of printed matter. XIX; attrib. in *em quad*, *em rule*. Cf. EN.

'em əm orig. unstressed var. of *hem* (OE. *heom*), d. and acc. pl. of the 3rd pers. pron. HE[1]; later felt as a clipped form of THEM. XII (in ME. sometimes tacked on to a vb., as *torndem* turned them).

em-[1] form of EN-[1] before *b*, *p*, *m*; cf. IM-[1].

em-[2] form of EN-[2] before *b*, *p*, *m*.

emaciate èmei·ʃieit make lean. XVII. f. pp. stem of L. *ēmaciāre*, f. *ē* E-+*maciēs* leanness; see MACERATE, MEAGRE, -ATE[3].

emanate e·məneit flow forth, issue. XVIII. f. pp. stem of L. *ēmānāre*, f. *ē* E-[1]+*mānāre* flow. So **emana·tion**. XVI. — late L.

emancipate imæ·nsipeit set free, orig. from the patria potestas. XVII. f. pp. stem of L. *ēmancipāre*, f. *ē* E-[1]+*mancipium*; see MANCIPLE, -ATE[3]. So **emancipa·tion**.

emasculate imà·skjŭleit deprive of virility. XVII. f. pp. stem of L. *ēmasculāre* castrate, f. *ē* E-[1]+*masculus* MALE; see -ATE[3].

embalm ėmbā·m impregnate a dead body with spices. XIII (Cursor M.). ME. *embaume* — (O)F. *embaumer*, f. *en* EM-[1]+*baume* BALM.

embankment ėmbæ·ŋkmənt bank for confining a watercourse XVIII; raised bank for carrying a road XIX. f. *embank* (XVII) enclose with banks, f. EM-[1]+earlier synon. *bank* vb.; see BANK[2], -MENT.

embar ėmbā·ɹ debar; enclose within bars; oppose a barrier to. XV. — (O)F. *embarrer* = It. *imbarrare*, Pr., Sp. *embarrar*; see EM-[1], BAR.

embargo ėmbā·ɹgou prohibitory order on the passage of ships; suspension of commerce, etc. XVI (*inbargo*). — Sp. *embargo*, f. *embargar* arrest, impede :— Rom. **imbarricāre*, f. L. *in* IM-[1], EM-[1]+*barra* BAR.

embark ėmbā·ɹk put on board. XVI. — F. *embarquer*, f. *en* EM-[1]+*barque* BARK[1]; cf. Pr., Sp. *embarcar*, It. *imbarcare*.

embarrass ėmbæ·rəs hamper, perplex. XVII. — F. *embarrasser* (Montaigne) — Sp. *embarazar* — It. *imbarazzare*, f. *imbarrare* EMBAR. So **emba·rras** sb. F., f. the vb.; now only as F.

embassy e·mbəsi function or office of an ambassador; †message of an ambassador XVI; body of persons sent as ambassadors XVII. In early use also *inbase* (rare), *ambassy*. — OF. *ambassée*, *-axée*, *-asée*, corr. to Pr. *ambaissada*, OSp. *ambaxada*, It. *ambasciata*, medL. *ambasc(i)ata* (f. Rom. **ambactiāre*; see AMBASSADOR); see -Y[5]. ¶ Preceded by †*ambass(i)at*, *-(i)ad*, *-axade*, *em-* (XV) — (O)F. *ambassade*, †*-axade* — OSp.; and †*em-*, *ambassage* (XVI, Latimer), perh. based on *ambassade* with ending assim. to *message*.

embattle[1] ėmbæ·tl set in battle array. XIV (Gower). — OF. *embataillier*, f. *en* EM-[1]+*bataille* BATTLE.

embattle[2] ėmbæ·tl furnish with battlements. XIV. f. EM-[1]+OF. *bataillier* (see BATTLEMENT).

embay ėmbei· enclose in or as in a bay. XVI. f. EM-[1]+BAY[1].

embed, (chiefly U.S.) **imbed** ėmbe·d fix firmly in a surrounding mass. XVIII. f. EM-[1], IM-[1]+BED.

embellish ėmbe·liʃ beautify. XIV. f. lengthened stem of (O)F. *embellir*, f. *en*-EM-[1]+*bel* beautiful; see BEAU, -ISH[2]. Hence **embe·llishment**. XVII. — (O)F.

ember e·mbəɹ live coal. OE. *ǣmyrġe*, *ǣmerġe* = MLG. *ēmere*, OHG. *eimuria* pyre (MHG. *eimere*), ON. *eimyrja* (Da. *emmer*, Sw. *mörja*) embers :— Germ. **aimuzjōn*, held to be rel. to OE. *ām* branding-iron, ON. *eimi*, *eimr* steam, vapour, *ím* dust, ashes. ¶ For intrusive *b* cf. *slumber*.

Ember Day e·mbəɹ dei (eccl.) any of the three days (Wednesday, Friday, Saturday of the same week) occurring at the four seasons (ecclL. *quatuor tempora*) in the year at which ordinations take place. Late OE. *ymbrendagas* pl., beside *ymbrenwice* (-week), *ymbrenfæsten* (-fast); the first el. is OE. *ymbren* (sg. and pl.), which may be an alteration of *ymbryne* period, revolution of time, f. *ymb* about, around (rel. to L. *amb-*, Gr. *amphi*; cf. AMPHI-)+*ryne* course (f. **run*- RUN); but the possibility that it is based partly on *quatuor tempora* is suggested by the form of G. *quatember*. ¶ ON. *imbru*-(*dagar*), OSw. *ymber*(*dagar*) are — OE.; OSw. had also *tamperdagar*.

ember-goose e·mbəɹgūs northern diver or loon. XVIII. — Norw. *emmer|gaas*; cf. Icel. *himbrimi*, earlier *himbrin*, and Faeroese *imbrim*.

embezzle ėmbe·zl †make away with XV; †impair; divert wrongfully to one's own use XVI. — AN. *enbesiler*, f. *en* EN-[1]+*besiler* in same sense (whence Eng. *bezzle* †plunder, destroy XV, dial. 'put away' food or drink XVII) = OF. *besillier*, Pr. *besillar* maltreat, ravage, destroy, of unkn. origin; through the var. forms *imbezill*, *imbecill*, assoc. in XVI with L. *imbecillāre* weaken (see IMBECILE).

embitter ėmbi·təɹ make bitter. XVII. f. EM-[1]+BITTER.

emblem e·mblĭm †allegorical picture XV (Lydg.); symbolical representation, figured object with symbolic meaning XVII. — L. *emblēma* inlaid work, raised ornament — Gr. *émblēma* (*-at-*) insertion, f. *emblē-*, *embállein* throw in, insert, f. *en* EN-[2]+*bállein* throw (cf. BALLISTA). Hence **emblema·tic**(AL). XVII; after F. *emblématique* (Rabelais).

embody (formerly **im-**) ėmbɔ·di put into a body XVI; give a body to; incorporate XVII. f. EM-[1]+BODY, after L. *incorporāre* INCORPORATE.

embolism e·mbəlizm intercalation of a day or days in a calendar to correct errors arising from the difference between the civil and the solar year XIV (Trevisa); (path.) plugging of a blood-vessel XIX. — late L. *embolismus* — Gr. *embolismós*, f. *embállein* throw in, f. *en* EM-[2]+*bállein* (see BALLISTA).

embonpoint ãbɔ̃pwɛ̃ plumpness. XVIII. F. (XVI), f. phr. *en bon point* in good condi- -ion (see POINT).

emboss[1] ėmbɔ·s mould in relief XIV (Ch.); cover with protuberances XV. — OF. **embocer*, *imbocer* (XVI), *embosser* (Cotgr.), f. *en* EM-[1]+*boce*, *bosse* BOSS[1].

emboss[2] ėmbɔ·s †(of a hunted animal) take shelter in a wood XIV (Ch.); †drive (a hunted animal) to extremity XVI (Spenser, Sh.); †pass. be exhausted by running, (hence) foam at the mouth XVI (Skelton); (arch.) cover with foam XVI (Elyot). – OF. *embuscher*, var. of *embuschier* AMBUSH.

embouchure ãbuʃǖr mouth of a river or creek. XVIII. F., f. *emboucher* refl. discharge itself by a mouth, f. *en* EM-[1] + *bouche* mouth (cf. BUCCAL); see -URE.

embowel ėmbau·əl early syn. of DISEMBOWEL. XVI. – OF. *emboweler*, alteration (by substitution of *em-* for *es-*) of *esboueler*, f. *es-* EX-[1] + *bouel* BOWEL.

embrace ėmbrei·s clasp in the arms, receive gladly XIV; comprise XVII. – OF. *embracer* (mod. *embrasser*) = Pr. *embrassar*, It. *imbracciare* :- Rom. **imbracchiāre*, f. L. *in* IM-[1] + *bracchium* arm, pl. *bracchia* (see EM-[1], BRACE[2]). Hence **embra·ce** sb. XVI (Sh.); superseding earlier **embra·ce**MENT. XV (Caxton). – OF. *embracement*.

embrangle ėmbræ·ŋgl confuse, perplex. XVII (Butler's 'Hudibras'). f. EM-[1] + OED. *Brangle* v.[1]

embrasure ėmbrei·ʒəɹ opening widening from within. XVIII. – F. *embrasure*, f. *embraser*, varying with *ébraser* bevel off, slope door or window opening from within; of unkn. origin; see -URE.

embrocation embrŏkei·ʃən †fomentation XV; liniment XV. f. medL. *embrocāre*, f. late L. *embroc(h)a* – Gr. *embrokhḗ* lotion, f. *embrékhein* steep, foment, f. *en* EM-[1] + *brékhein* wet (*brokhḗ* rain; cf. Lett. *merga* soft rain) :- **meregh-*; see -ATION.

embroider ėmbroi·dəɹ ornament with needlework. XV. Earlier also *-bro(u)d-*; extension of *embroude* – AN. *enbrouder* (Gower), f. *en-* EM-[1] + *brouder, broisder* (mod. *broder*) = Pr. *broidar* – Germ. **brusdan*; the form *broid-* is partly due to blending with ME. *broiden*, pp. of BRAID. **embroi·d**ERY. XIV (Gower). – AN. *enbrouderie*.

embroil ėmbroi·l bring into confusion or discord. XVII. – F. *embrouiller* — It. *imbrogliare*, Sp. *embrollar*; see EM-[1] and BROIL.

embryo e·mbriou unborn offspring. XVI (varying with *embryon*, *-ion* XVI–XVIII). – late L. *embryo*, *-io*, mistaken form arising from taking *embryon* as a sb. in *-ōn*, *-ōnis*; – Gr. *émbruon* new-born animal, fœtus, f. *en* EM-[2] + *brúein* swell, grow.

embus ėmbʌ·s put on a bus. XX. f. EM-[1] + BUS, after ENTRAIN[2].

emend ime·nd correct XV; remove errors from (a text) XVIII. – L. *ēmendāre*, f. *ē* E- + *menda* fault. So **emend**ATION īmendei·ʃən improvement XVI; correction of a text XVII. – L.

emerald e·mərəld bright green precious stone. XIII. ME. *emeraude* – OF. *e(s)meraude* (mod. *émeraude*) = Pr. *esmerauda*, It. *smeraldo*, Sp. *esmeralda* :- Rom. **smaralda*, *-o*, alteration of L. *smaragdus* – Gr. *smáragdos* SMARAGDUS. The sp. with *-ld* is prob. due to It. or Sp. influence in XVI.

emerge imə̄·ɹdʒ rise out of a liquid XVII; come to light, arise XVI. – L. *ēmergere*, f. *ē* E- + *mergere* dip, MERGE. So **eme·rg**ENCE, **eme·rg**ENCY XVII. – medL. **eme·rg**ENT XV, **eme·r**SION XVII. – late L. (Jerome).

emeritus ime·ritəs honourably discharged from service. XIX. L., pp. of *ēmerērī* earn (one's discharge) by service, f. *ē* E- + *merērī* deserve (see MERIT).

em(e)rod obs. exc. bibl. var. of HÆMORRHOID.

emery e·məri coarse corundum for polishing. XV. – F. *émeri*, *émeril*, var. of †*esmeril* – It. *smeriglio* :- Rom. **smericulum*, f. medGr. *smērí*, Gr. *smúris* polishing powder (see SMEAR).

emetic ime·tik producing vomiting. XVII. – Gr. *emetikós*, f. *émetos* vomiting, f. *emeîn* VOMIT; see -IC.

émeute emœ̄·t popular rising. XIX (Thackeray). F. :- Rom. **exmovita*, sb. use of fem. pp. of **exmovēre* (see EMOTION).

emigrate e·migreit remove from one's country. XVIII. f. pp. stem of L. *ēmigrāre*, f. *ē* E- + *migrāre* MIGRATE. So **emigr**A·TION. XVII. – late L. Cf. F. *émigrer*, *émigration*.

eminent e·minənt conspicuous, signal XV lofty, prominent XVI; exalted, distinguished XVII. f. prp. stem of L. *ēminēre*, poss. rel. to *mōns* MOUNT[1]; see -ENT. So **e·min**ENCE, -ENCY. XVII. – L. Cf. F. *éminent*, *-ence*.

emir ėmiə·ɹ Arab prince or governor; descendant of Mohammed. XVII. – F. *émir* – Sp. *emir* – Arab. *amīr* AMEER.

emissary e·misəri one sent on a mission (often with unfavourable implication). XVII (Jonson, 'The Staple of News', 1625, where it seems to be a novelty). – L. *ēmissārius* scout, spy, f. *ēmiss-*, pp. stem of *ēmittere* EMIT; see -ARY.

emit imi·t send forth, issue. XVII (Bacon, Sir T. Browne). – L. *ēmittere*, f. *ē* E- + *mittere* (see MISSION). So **emi·ss**ION. XVII. – L. (Cf. ADMIT, REMIT, SUBMIT.)

emmenagogue emī·nəgɔg (agent) having the property of exciting the menstrual discharge. XVIII. So **emmenagog**IC -gɔ·dʒik. XVII. f. Gr. *émmēna* menses (f. *en* EM[2] + *mēn-* MONTH) + *agōgós* drawing forth, f. *ágein* lead (cf. AGENT).

emmet e·mit dial. development of OE. *ǣmete* ANT; occurs in Douay Bible, 1609 (in the form *emmote*), and in Johnson's Life of Pope.

emollient imɔ·liənt softening. XVII. f. prp. stem of L. *ēmollīre*, f. *ē* E- + *mollis* soft; see MOLLIFY, -ENT.

emolument imo·ljŭment profit or salary arising from an office, etc. xv. – (O)F. *émolument* or L. *ēmolumentum*, *ēmoli-* gain, orig. prob. 'payment to a miller for the grinding of corn', f. *ēmolere* grind up, f. *ē* E-+*molere* grind; see MILL, -MENT.

emotion imou·ʃən †agitation, tumult XVI; †physical disturbance; disturbance of mind or feeling; affection of the mind, feeling XIX. Rare before second half of XVII; referred to by Evelyn, 1665, as a F. word that might be profitably adopted. – F. *émotion* (*esmocion* XVI), f. *émouvoir* excite, move the feelings of (:– Rom. **exmovēre*; see EX-[1], MOVE), after *mouvoir*, *motion*. Hence **emo·tion**AL[1]. XIX. So **emot**IVE imou·tiv †causing movement XVIII (rare); pert. to or expressing emotion XIX (early). f. pp. stem *ēmōt-* of L. *ēmovēre*. See E-, MOVE.

empanel, im- ėmpæ·nl enrol on a panel. XV. – AN. *empaneller*; see EM-[1], PANEL.

empathy e·mpəþi (psych.) power of understanding things outside ourselves. XX. Rendering, after Gr. *empátheia*, of G. *einfühlung* (Lipps), f. *ein* IN[1]+*fühlung* FEELING; see EM-[2], -PATHY.

emperor e·mpərəɹ sovereign of the undivided Roman Empire, or the Western or Eastern Empire; head of the Holy Roman Empire; title of sovereignty superior to 'king'. XIII. ME. *emperere*, *emperour* – respectively OF. *emperere*, nom. and *emperour*, *-eor*, obl. (mod. *empereur*), semi-pop. – L. *imperā·tor*, *imperātō·rem*, f. *imperāre* command, f. *in* IM-[1]+*parāre* PREPARE, contrive, rel. to *parere* bring forth, produce (cf. PARENT); see -OR[1].

emphasis e·mfəsis intensity of statement XVI; intensity of feeling, etc.; stress or force laid upon anything XVII; prominence XIX. – L. *emphasis* (Quintilian) meaning implied but not directly expressed – Gr. *émphasis* in same sense, orig. (mere) appearance, f. **empha-* in *emphaínein* exhibit, f. *en* EM-[2]+*phaínein* show (see PHASE). So **emph**ATIC ėmfæ·tik strongly expressive. XVIII. – late L. *emphaticus* (cf. F. *emphatique*, Sp., It. *enfatico*) – Gr. *emphatikós*. **emph**A·TICAL †allusive, suggestive; strongly expressed or expressive. XVI.

empire e·mpaiəɹ imperial territory or rule. XIII (RGlouc.). – (O)F. *empire*, earlier *emperie* – L. *imperium*, rel. to *imperātor* EMPEROR.

empiric ėmpi·rik sb. member of the sect of ancient physicians called *Empirici*)(*Dogmatici*); untrained practitioner, quack XVI; adj. XVII (Bacon). – L. *empīricus* sb. (Cicero, Pliny) – Gr. *empeirikós*, f. *empeiriā* experience, f. *émpeiros* skilled, f. *en* EM-[2]+*peîra* trial, experiment (cf. FEAR, PERIL). So **empi·r**ICAL adj. relying or based on experiment. XVI. Cf. (O)F. *empirique*.

emplacement ėmplei·smənt situation; platform for guns. XIX. – F. *emplacement*, f. *en* EM-[1]+*place* PLACE; see -MENT.

employ ėmploi· apply to a purpose XV; use the services of XVI. – (O)F. *employer* = Pr. *implegar* buy, It. *impiegare*, Sp. *emplear*, Pg. *empregar* use, spend :– Rom. *implicāre*, for L. *implicārī* be involved (in) or attached (to), pass. of *implicāre* enfold, involve (see IMPLY). Hence **employ·** sb. XVII. **employ·**ER[1]. XVI (Sh.). **employ·**MENT. XVI (Sh.). **employé** ãplwa·jei employed person. XIX. pp. of *employer* used sb.; anglicized **employ·**EE emploi·ī. XIX (orig. U.S.).

emporium impō·riəm place of commerce, mart. XVI. – L. *emporium* – Gr. *empórion*, f. *émporos* merchant, f. *en* EM-[2]+**por-* (see FARE[1]).

empress e·mpris consort of an emperor. XII (Peterborough Chron.). ME. *emperice*, *emperesse* – OF. *emperesse*, f. *emperere* EMPEROR; see -ESS[1].

empressement ãpre·smã eager cordiality. XVIII (Chesterfield). F., f. *empresser* urge, *s'empresser* be eager, f. *en* EM-[1]+*presser* PRESS.

emprise emprai·z (arch.) enterprise. XIII (Cursor M.). – (O)F. *emprise* = Pr. *empreza*, Sp. *empresa*, It. *impresa* :– Rom. **imprēnsa*, sb. use of pp. fem. of **imprendere* undertake, f. *in* EM-[1], IM-[1] + *pre(he)ndere* take (cf. PREHENSILE).

empty e·m^{p}ti containing nothing, vacant. OE. *ǣmtiġ*, *ǣmet(t)iġ* (also, unoccupied), f. *ǣmetta* leisure :– **āmōtiþa*, perh. f. negative *ā-*+*mōt-* meeting (see MOOT). Hence **e·mpty** vb. XVI (cf. OE. *ġeǣmtiġian*); formerly and still dial. **empt** vb. (OE. *ǣmtian*, f. *ǣmta* leisure).

empyema empaiī·mə (path.) collection of pus. XVII. late L. – Gr. *empúēma*, f. *empueîn* suppurate, f. *en* EM-[2]+*pûon* matter, PUS.

empyrean empai(ə)rī·ən adj. of the highest heaven XVII (Ralegh); sb. (Milton); in ancient cosmology, the sphere of the element of fire, in Christian use the abode of God and the angels. f. medL. *empyreus*, as sb. n. *-eum* (sc. *cælum* heaven) – Gr. *empúrios*, as sb. n. *-ion* (Proclus), f. *en* EM-[2]+*pûr* FIRE; see -EAN. So **empyre·**AL[1] adj. XV (*imperyall*, Caxton).

empyreuma empirū·mə burnt smell. XVII. – Gr. *empúreuma* live coal covered with ashes, f. *empureúein* set on fire, f. *en* EM-[2]+*pûr* FIRE. Hence **empyreum**A·TIC(AL. XVII.

emu ī·mjū †cassowary XVII; †American ostrich (?) XVIII; bird of the Australian genus Dromæus XIX. Earliest forms *emia*, *eme*, later *emeu*, *emew*, orig. – Pg. *ema*. Cf. F. *émeu* (1698), *émou*, Du. *emoe*.

emulate e·mjŭleit strive to equal or rival. XVI. f. pp. of L. *æmulārī*, f. *æmulus* rival, prop. adj. striving, rel. to *imitārī* IMITATE, *imāgō* IMAGE; see -ATE[3]. So **emul**A·TION. XVI. – L. **emul**OUS †imitative (of) XIV; †zealous XVI; emulating, rival XVII. f. L. *æmulus*.

emulsion imʌ·lʃən milky fluid. XVII. – F. *émulsion* or modL. *ēmulsiō(n-)*, f. *ēmuls-*, pp. stem of *ēmulgēre* milk out, f. *ē* E-+*mulgēre* MILK.

emunctory imʌ·ŋᵏtəri cleaning by excretion XVI; cleansing organ or canal XIV. – medL. *ēmunctōrius* (sb. *-ium*), f. *ēmunct-*, pp. stem of L. *ēmungere* wipe or blow the nose, f. *ē* E-+base rel. to MUCUS; see -ORY.

en en (typogr.) unit of measurement in composition (cf. EM)) equivalent to the average width of a letter; attrib. in *en quad, en rule, en score*.

en-[1] en, in (before the sound of k, often passing into ėŋ) prefix repr. (O)F. *en-*, which is the form assumed, as also in Pr., Sp., and Pg., by the L. prefix *in-* (see IN-[1]); before *b* and *p* and occas. before *m* it takes the form EM-[1], but this was not established in Eng. sp. before XVII, *enb-, enp-* being more frequent than *emb-, emp-* in ME., as in OF. and OSp. In OF. and consequently in ME. *en-, em-* often appears as *an-, am-*, which last survives in *ambush*. From an early date IN-[1], IM-[1] have been substituted for *en-, em-*, and vice versa, the former being gen. preferred in XVII; in some words, e.g. *embed, imbed, encase, incase, enclose, inclose*, both are still current, the *i*-forms esp. in U.S.A.; in others, e.g. *imbrue, impair, inquest, im-, in-* have replaced *em-, en-*, where these are historically appropriate; in *ensure* and *insure* the variants have been allocated to different meanings. As a living formative (from XIV) *en-* has been used in senses mainly identical with those of Latin *in-* (IN-[1]): viz. put in, into, or on (something), as *encase, encyst, engarland, enshroud, enthrone, entrain*; bring or come into a certain state, as *enable, encamp, endanger, endear, enslave, enthral, enure*; with emphatic or neutral force, as *enkindle, enlighten, enliven*.

en-[2] en, in repr. Gr. *en-*, the prep. *en* IN used as prefix, as in *enallage, endemic, energy, enthusiasm*; before *b, m, p, ph* it takes the form EM-[2]; before *l* it becomes *el-* (as in ellipse).

-en[1] ən suffix forming (chiefly) dims., as from names of animals; OE. *-en* = OHG. *-īn*, Goth. *-ein* :– Germ. **-īnam*, formally the neuter of **-īnaz* -EN[3], as in *clīewen* CLEW, *ćycen* CHICKEN, *filmen* FILM, *mæġden* MAIDEN, *tiććen*, ME. *ticchen* kid.

-en[2] ən suffix chiefly forming fem. sbs. from mascs., and fem. abstr. and concr. sbs.; OE. *-en* = (O)HG. *-in* :– Germ. **-inī, *injō-*; e.g. OE. *biren* she-bear (f. *bera*), *gyden* goddess (f. *god* GOD), *myneċen* nun (f. *munuc* MONK); VIXEN is the only surviving example of this type (but OE. *fyxen* is found only as adj.); *hæften* custody, *wæċen* watching, vigil; *byrþen* BURDEN, *rǣden* arrangement, rule, condition (see -RED).

-en[3] ən adj. suffix denoting 'pert. to', 'of the nature of', 'made or consisting of'; OE. *-en* = OS. *-in*, OHG. *-īn* (G. *-en*), ON. *-in*. Goth. *-eins* :– CGerm. **-īnaz*, corr. to Gr. *-īnos*, L. *-īnus* -INE[1]. OE. adjs. formed with this suffix have normally mutation of the stem-vowel, as *stǣnen* of stone, f. *stān* stone, *gylden* golden, f. *gold*; these have not survived, but from ME. onwards new adjs. have been extensively formed direct from the sbs., as *earthen, golden, silvern* (*-en* is reduced to *-n* after *r*). Only a few adjs. (as *wheaten, wooden*) are in St. Eng. used with lit. meanings, but in s.w. dial. the application to sbs. denoting material is unlimited, as *glassen, papern*.

-en[4] ən inflexion of the weak declension, ME. reduction of OE. *-an*, as in *oxan* oxen, which was extended to other declensions, esp. in the south and west; permanent exx. of this in Standard Eng. are seen in *children* (pl. of CHILD), *brethren* (pl. of BROTHER), and in dial. *hosen* (see HOSE), *shoon* (see SHOE), *housen, treen*, etc.

-en[5] ən suffix forming verbs based on sbs. and adjs., in OE. *-nian*, ON. *-na*, OHG. *-inōn*, Goth. *-nan*, e.g. OE. *beorhtnian* BRIGHTEN, *fæstnian* FASTEN, *hlosnian* hearken, *lācnian* heal (cf. LEECH), *war(e)nian* WARN, *wilnian* desire, ON. *batna* BATTEN[2], *harðna* HARDEN, OHG. *festinōn* fasten, Goth. *fullnan* be full. The relation *fast* adj. / *fasten* gave a model for such vbs. as *darken, deepen, madden, moisten, widen*; the extension to sbs. began in late ME., e.g. *heighten, lengthen, strengthen*; but several such vbs. appear only very late. Some verbs in *-en* are extensions of earlier forms, e.g. CHASTEN of †*chaste*, HAPPEN (of *hap*), HASTEN of *haste*, HEARTEN of †*heart*, LISTEN of *list*; this took place esp. where a distinctively verbal form seemed desirable.

-en[6] ən suffix forming the regular ending of pps. of strong verbs; OE. *-en* (sometimes with mutation in the stem-syll.), OS., OHG. *-an* (Du., G. *-en*), ON. *-inn, -enn*, Goth. *-ans*, (once) *-ins*, repr. Germ. **-anaz, *-enaz, *-iniz* :– IE. **-ónos, *-énos, *-énis* (OE. and ON. generalized **-en*-forms, and OS., OHG., and Goth. **-on*-forms). Active meanings are shown in *mistaken* (1601), *outspoken* (1808).

enable ėnei·bl †invest with legal status XV; give (legal) power to, supply with means *to do* XVI. f. EN-[1]+ABLE adj.; cf. *able* vb. XIV. (R. Rolle.)

enact ėnæ·kt A. †enter among the acts or public records XV; make into an act, decree XV; B. perform (a play, etc.), act (a part) XVI. f. EN-[1]+ACT sb. and vb., after medL. *inactāre, inactitāre*. Hence **ena·ct**MENT action of enacting, what is enacted. XIX; superseding **ena·**CTION (XVII) and (rare) †**ena·ct** (XV–XVI).

enallage enæ·lədʒi (rhet.) substitution of one grammatical form for another. XVI. late L., – Gr. *enallagē*, f. base of *enallássein*, f. *en* EN-[2]+*allássein* exchange, f. *állos* other (cf. ELSE).

enamel ėnæ·məl glass-like composition laid on a surface. XV. f. **ena·mel** vb. XIV. – AN. *enameler, enamailler*, f. *en* EN-[1]+*amail* – AN. *amail* = OF. *esmail* (mod. *émail*), analogical new formation (for *esmaut*, which is of Pr. origin) on the nom. *esmauz* – Germ. **smalt-* (OHG. *smalz*, G. *schmalz* melted fat), rel. to SMELT[2].

enamour ėnæ·məɹ inspire with ove. XIV (R. Mannyng). – (O)F. *enamourer* (cf. It. *innamorare*, Pr., Sp. *enamorar*), f. *en* EN-[1]+ *amour* love; see AMOUR.

enarthrosis enāɹþrou·sis (anat.) ball-and-socket joint. XVII. modL. – Gr. *enárthrōsis*, f. *énarthros* jointed; see EN-[1], ARTHRITIS, -OSIS.

encænia ėnsī·niə †dedication (of a temple, etc.) XIV; annual commemoration of founders and benefactors at the university of Oxford. XVII (in Caxton anglicized *encenye*). L. – Gr. (*tà*) *egkaínia*, n. pl. 'festival of renewal', f. *en* EN-[2]+*kainós* new. See -IA[2].

encase, incase ėnkei·s enclose (as) in a case. XVII. f. EN-[1], IN-[1]+CASE[2].

encaustic enkō·stik produced by burning in pigments. XVII. – L. *encausticus* (Pliny) – Gr. *egkaustikós*, f. *egkaíein* burn in; see EN-[2], CAUSTIC.

-ence əns suffix – (O)F. *-ence* – L. *-entia*, f. *-ent-* -ENT with abstr. suffix. In popL. *-entia* was superseded by *-antia*, repr. in OF. by *-ance*, e.g. *aparance* (ecclL. *apparentia*) APPEARANCE, *contenance* COUNTENANCE, *oyance* (:– L. *audientia* AUDIENCE), *silance* SILENCE. Later, L. sbs. in *-ntia* were adopted in F. with the L. vowels, e.g. *absence, élégance, présence, tempérance*, and both classes were adopted in ME. with their French forms and meanings; but in early mod. Eng. some sbs. in *-ance* have been altered back to *-ence*, and all sbs. adopted since have followed the L. forms. The result is that mod. spelling shows many variations and discrepancies, e.g. *assist*ance, *consist*ence, *exist*ence, *resist*ance, *subsist*ence; *pertin*ence, *appurten*ance; cf. *ascend*ant, -ent, -ancy, -ency. See also -ENCY. ¶ The pls. of sbs. in *-ence* and *-ency*, sounding alike, tend to be confused, so that (e.g.) *excellences* is freq. miswritten *excellencies*.

enceinte[1] ãsɛ̃·t (esp. fortif.) enclosure. XVIII. F. :– L. *incincta*, pp. fem. of *incingere* gird in; see IN-[1], CINCTURE.

enceinte[2] ãsɛ̃·t pregnant. XVII (in earliest use *enseint, inceint*, after legal AN. *enseint*; later *ensient*; occas. *insented* XVI). F. = Pr. *encencha*, It. *incinta*, Sp. *encinta* :– medL. *incincta* 'ungirded' (Isidore, 'id est sine cinctu'), f. L. *in-* IN-[2]+*cincta*, fem. pp. of *cingere* gird (see CINCTURE).

enchant ėntʃà·nt lay under a spell XIV (Ch., Gower, PPl.); charm XVI (Sh.). – (O)F. *enchanter* :– L. *incantāre*, f. *in* EN-[1]+*cantāre* sing (see CHANT). So **encha·nt**ER[2]. XIII. – OF. *enchanteor, -our* (mod. *-eur*) :– late L. *incantātōrem*; see -ER[1]. **encha·nt**MENT. XIII. – (O)F. **encha·ntress**[1]. XIV (Ch.). – (O)F. *enchanteresse*.

enchase ėntʃei·s adorn with figures in relief XV; set (a jewel) XV; enshrine as a relic XVII. – (O)F. *enchâsser* enshrine, set (gems), encase, f. *en* EN-[1]+*châsse* shrine, casket, CASE[2]. The chronology shows early development of the transf. sense in Eng. (cf. CHASE[2]).

enchiridion en-, eŋkəiri·diən manual. XVI. – late L. – Gr. *egkheirídion*, f. *en* EN-[2]+*kheír* hand (cf. CHIRO-)+*-idion* dim. suffix.

enclave ã·klāv, ãklā·v portion of territory entirely surrounded by alien dominions. XIX (†*enclaved* pa. pple. once XV). F., f. (O)F. *enclaver* = Pr., Cat. *enclavar* : – popL. **inclāvāre*, f. *in* EN-[1] + *clāvis* key, rel. to *claudere* (see CLOSE).

enclitic ėnkli·tik (gram.) 'leaning' its accent on the preceding word. XVII. – late L. *encliticus* (Priscian) – Gr. *egklitikós*, f. *egklínein* lean on, f. *en* EN-[2]+*klínein* LEAN[2]; see -IC.

enclose ėnklou·z shut up or in, surround; insert in a frame, etc. XIV. f. (O)F. *enclos(e)*, pp. of *enclôre* :– popL. **inclaudere*, for L. *inclūdere* INCLUDE. So **en**CLOSURE ėnklou·ʒəɹ. XV. – legal AN., OF. *enclosure*. See also INCLOSE, INCLOSURE.

encomium ėn-, ėŋkou·miəm formal eulogy. XVI. – L. *encōmium* – Gr. *egkṓmion*, sb. use (sc. *épos* speech) of n. of adj., f. *en* EN-[2]+ *kômos* revel (in which a conqueror was led in procession); cf. COMIC. So **enco·miast**. XVII. – Gr. *egkōmiastḗs*, f. *egkōmiázein*; whence also *egkōmiastikós* (in modL. *encōmiasticus*) **encomia·st**IC. XVI.

encore ɔŋkɔ̄ə·ɹ, as sb. ɔ·ŋkɔ̄əɹ once more; repetition of a performance. XVIII. F. (= Pr. *ancara*, OSp. *encara*, It. *ancora*), of disputed origin. Hence as vb. XVIII. ¶ Not so used in French.

encounter ėnkau·ntəɹ meeting in conflict. XIII. – (O)F. *encontre* (cf. Pr. *encontre*, It. *incontro*), f. *encontrer* = Pr., Sp., Pg. *encontrar*, It. *incontrare* :– Rom. **incontrāre*, f. *in* EN-[1]+*contrā* against (cf. COUNTER[6]).

encourage ėnkʌ·ridʒ inspire with courage. XV. – (O)F. *encourager*; see EN-[1], COURAGE.

encrinite e·nkrinait (geol.) fossil crinoid. XIX. f. modL. *encrinus* (Harenberg, 1729) 'stone-lily', f. Gr. *en* EN-[2]+*krínon* lily; see -ITE.

encroach ėnkrou·tʃ †seize wrongfully XIV; trench usurpingly upon XVI. – OF. *encrochier* seize, fasten upon, f. *en* EN-[1]+ *crochier* crook, f. *croc* hook (– ON. *krókr* CROOK).

encumber ėnkʌ·mbəɹ obstruct, hamper. XIV. – (O)F. *encombrer* block up = Pr. *encombrar* (It. *ingombrare*) :– Rom. **incombrāre*; see EN-[1], CUMBER. So **encu·mbr**ANCE. XIV. – OF. *encombrance*.

-ency ənsi suffix – L. *-entia* (see -ENCE and -Y[3]), used in the formation of sbs. denoting qualities or states, from which concr. or semi-concr. senses have been developed in Eng. adoptions, as dist. from the derivs. in -ENCE, which have freq. the sense of action or process in addition to or to the exclusion of that of quality or state. Examples of the difference now gen. established between the suffixes are *recurrence* and *currency*, *emergence* and *emergency*, *excellence* and *excellency*, *confluence* and *fluency*, *dependence* and *dependency*, *permanence* and *permanency*; several forms in *-ency* have become established to the exclusion of parallel forms in *-ence*, as *clemency*, *decency*, *efficiency*, *inconsistency*; *residence* and *presidency* have two types of meaning in full use, whereas *regency* and *transparency* are almost restricted to one.

encyclical ènsi·klikəl intended for universal circulation. XVII (sb. XIX). f. late L. *encyclicus*, f. Gr. *egkúklios* circular, general, f. *en* EN-[2]+*kúklos* circle (CYCLE); see -ICAL.

encyclopædia, U.S. **-pedia** ènsaiklopī·diə †general course of instruction XVI; repertory of information on all branches of knowledge XVII. (Also anglicized, or after F., †*encyclopedie*, *-y*.) – modL. – spurious Gr. *egkuklopaideiā* (in MSS. of Quintilian 'Inst.' I X I, Pliny 'Nat. Hist.' pref.), for *egkúklios paideiā* 'general education', the circle of arts and sciences considered by the Greeks to be essential to a liberal education; see prec. and PEDAGOGUE. Cf. CYCLOPÆDIA.

end end extremity, final limit OE.; †termination, completion XIII; death; event, issue; intended result, purpose XIV; remnant (*candle end*, *odds and ends*) XV. OE. *ende* = OFris. *enda*, *-e*, OS. *endi*, (Du. *einde*), OHG. *enti* (G. *ende*), ON. *endir*, *endi*, Goth. *andeis*, f. CGerm. **andja-* :– IE. **antjó*; cf. Skr. *ántas* end, boundary, death, and OHG. *endi*, ON. *enni* forehead, L. *antiæ* forelock, *ante* before, OIr. *ētan* forehead, *ēt* end, point; Gr. *antí*, *antíos* opposite. ¶ In *East End*, *West End* and *the ends of the earth* there is a historical survival of the sense 'quarter, region' of OE. *ende*. So **end** vb. OE. *endian* = OFris. *endia*, OS. *endiōn* (Du. *einden*), OHG. *entōn* (G. *enden*), ON. *enda*. Hence **e·nd**WAYS, -WISE XVI.

endear èndiə·ɹ †raise the value of XVI; make dear or beloved XVII. f. EN-[1]+DEAR, after F. *enchérir* (f. *en-*+*cher* dear).

endeavour ènde·vəɹ make an effort, strive. XIV. orig. refl.; f. phr. *put oneself in dever* (*devoir*), after F. *se mettre en devoir* do one's utmost; see DEVOIR. Hence **endea·vour** sb. XV.

endemic ènde·mik regularly found among a people or in a country. XVIII (as sb. pl. XVII). – F. *endémique* or modL. *endēmicus*, f. Gr. *éndēmos*, *endḗmios* pert. to a people, native, f. *en* EN-[2]+*dêmos* people; see DEMOS, -IC. Also **ende·mi**AL[1], -ICAL adjs. XVII.

endive e·ndiv the plant Cichorium Intybus. XV. – (O)F. *endive* = Pr., Pg., It. *endivia*, Sp. *endibia* – late L. *endivia* – medGr. *indivi* – L. *intibum*, *intubum* – Gr. *entubon*, of which a dim. *entubion* is extant.

endo- e·ndou, endɔ· comb. form of Gr. *éndon* within, f. *en* IN+**dom-* house (see TOFT), used in many comps. of mod. formation, as *e·ndocarp*, *-derm*, *endo·genous* (Lindley), *endoca·rdiac*; **endo**·gamy marriage (Gr. *gámos*) within a clan or tribe.

endorse èndɔ̄·ɹs write, put one's signature, etc., on the back of XVI; (after **endo·rse**MENT ratification XVII) confirm, countenance XIX. – medL. *indorsāre*, f. L. *in* IN-[1]+*dorsum* back (see DORSAL); superseded earlier †*endoss* (XIV) – (O)F. *endosser* (*dos* :– L. *dorsum*).

endow èndau· enrich, as with property XIV; provide a dower for XVI. – legal AN. *endouer*, f. *en* EN-[1]+(O)F. *douer* :– L. *dōtāre*, f. *dōt-*, *dōs* dowry, rel. to *dare* give (cf. DATE[1]). Hence **endow·**MENT. XV.

endris e·ndris (arch.) recently past. XIV. var., with advb. -S, of *ender* (esp. *this ender night*, XIII, Cursor M.), f. ON. *endr* formerly, *endranær* at some other time, corr. to Goth. *andiz|uh* either (conj.), compar. f. AND.

endue èndjū· The earliest appearance is of *c.* 1400 in the rare sense 'induct'; established in XV in various senses, viz. †(of a hawk) pass food into the stomach, digest; †assume (a form), put on (clothes); invest with property, endow with power, etc. orig. – (O)F. *enduire* (i) = Pr. *enduire*, It. *indurre* :– L. *indūcere* lead in (INDUCE); (ii) a new formation, f. *en* EN-[1]+*duire* :– L. *dūcere* lead; by crossing with L. *induere* put on (a garment), clothe, the word became partly synon. with *endow* and *invest*.

endure èndjuə·ɹ †harden; continue; undergo, bear XIV; tolerate XV. – (O)F. *endurer* = Pr., Sp. *endurar*, It. *indurare* :– L. *indūrāre* harden, f. *in-* EN-[1]+*dūrus* hard. So **endu·r**ANCE. XV. – (O)F.

-ene īn (chem.) terminal el. of the names of certain hydrocarbons (e.g. *benzene*, *naphthalene*, *toluene*), proper to those of the formula C_nH_{2n}, the vowel *e* being used to complete the sequence *a*, *e*, *i*, *o*. Cf. -ANE[2], -INE[5], -ONE.

enema e·nimə injection. XV. – late L. – Gr. *énema*, f. *eniénai* send or put in, inject, f. *en* EN-[2]+*hiénai* send (cf. INJECT).

enemy e·nimi hostile person or community, foe. XIII (Cursor M.). – OF. *enemi* (mod. *ennemi*) = Pr. *enemic*, Sp. *enemigo*, It. *nemico* :– L. *inimīcu-s*, f. *in-* IN-[2]+*amīcus* friend (see AMICABLE); *the Enemy* the Devil (after Luke x 19) XIV (Wycl. Bible), the hostile force XVII (Sh.).

energumen enɔ̄ɹgjū·men possessed person, demoniac. XVIII. – late L. *energūmenus* – Gr. *energoúmenos*, pass. ppl. of *energeîn* work in or upon, f. *en* EN-[2]+*érgon* WORK.

energy e·nəɹdʒi vigour of expression XVI; working, operation; power displayed XVII; vigour or intensity of action XIX (Coleridge); in physics, *actual, kinetic,* or *motive energy* (T. Young), *potential, static,* or *latent energy* (W. Rankine). – F. *énergie* or late L. *energīa* – Gr. *enérgeia* (Aristotle), f. *energḗs* active, effective, f. *en* EN-²+*érgon* WORK; see -Y³. So **energet**IC -e·tik, -ICAL †powerfully operative; full of energy. XVII. – Gr. *energētikós* active, f. *energeîn* operate, effect, f. *en* EN-²+*érgon.* **e·nerg**IZE rouse to or put forth energy. XVIII; cf. F. †*énergiser.*

enervate e·nəɹveit weaken. XVII. f. pp. stem of L. *ēnervāre,* f. *ē* E-+*nervus* sinew, NERVE; stressed *ene·rvate* XVII–XVIII; cf. (O)F. *énerver.* So **enerva·**TION. XV. – late L.

enew ènjū· (arch.) drive (a bird) into the water. XV. – OF. *enewer, eneauer,* f. *en* EN-¹+*eau* (:– L. AQUA) water.

enfeoff ènfe·f invest with a fief. XIV. – AN. *enfeoffer* (AL. *infeoffāre*), OF. *enfeffer,* f. *en* EN-¹+*fief* FIEF. Hence **enfeo·ff**MENT. XV.

Enfield e·nfīld name of a village in Middlesex, near which is a government small-arms factory, applied to rifles, etc. XIX.

enfilade enfilei·d †suite of apartments, the doors of which are placed opposite to each other; fire sweeping a line of works or troops from one end to the other. XVIII. – F. *enfilade,* f. *enfiler* thread on a string, piece from end to end, f. *en* EN-¹+*fil* FILE³; see -ADE.

enforce infɔ̄·ɹs †strengthen physically or morally; †drive by force, use force upon; †refl. and intr. strive XIV; press home, emphasize XV; compel XV. – OF. *enforcier,* (also mod.) *enforcir* :– Rom. **infortiāre,* **infortīre,* f. *in* IN-¹+*fortis* strong (cf. FORT).

enfranchise ènfræ·ntʃaiz, -iz set free; make a person or town municipally 'free' XV; admit to political status XVII. f. *enfranchiss-,* lengthened stem of OF. *enfranchir,* f. *en* EN-¹+*franc, -che* free, FRANK. †*Affranchise* was earlier (XV). The assoc. of the word with FRANCHISE has led to the prevalence of the pronunc. with aiz. Hence **enfra·nchise**MENT -izmənt. XVI (Sh.).

engage èngei·dʒ pledge or secure by a pledge XV; hire for employment XVIII; persuade, win over XVII; attach, charm XVIII; †entangle, involve XVI; employ, occupy XVII; bring or come into conflict XVII. – (O)F. *engager* = Pr. *engatgar,* It. *ingaggiare* :– Rom. **inwadiāre,* f. *in* EN-¹+ **wadium* GAGE, WAGE. So **enga·ge**MENT. XVII. – (O)F.

engender èndʒe·ndəɹ beget, produce. XIV. – (O)F. *engendrer* = Pr. *engenrar,* It. *ingenerare* :– L. *ingenerāre,* f. *in* EN-¹+*generāre* GENDER, GENERATE. So **engendr**URE †generation; descent. XIV. – OF. *engendr(e)ure.* The var. **enge·ndure** (XIV) was used by Lamb and J. R. Lowell.

engine e·ndʒin A. †contrivance, artifice XIII; †ingenuity; †genius XIV; B. machine of war XIII; mechanical contrivance XIV; complex machine (later spec. steam-engine) XVII. – OF. *engin* = Pr. *engenh,* Sp. *ingenio,* It. *ingegno* :– L. *ingenium* natural quality, disposition, or temper, talents, genius, clever device (cf. INGENIOUS). Aphetized GIN². The now old-fashioned or vulgar pronunc. i·ndʒin, which shows a normal development of e+nasal and is evidenced in XV, was stigmatized by Walker as 'very improper' and savouring 'strongly of vulgarity'.

engineer endʒiniə·ɹ designer or constructor of engines or works, orig. of military engines. XIV. – OF. *engigneor, -our* (mod. *ingénieur*) = Pr. *engenhador* :– medL. *ingeniātōrem, -ātor,* f. *ingeniāre,* f. *ingenium* ENGINE. In XVI the forms from OF. were superseded by *en-, inginer,* either after modF. or – It. *ingegnere,* a distinct formation = OF. *engi(g)nier,* Sp. *ingeniero* :– Rom. **ingeniārius*; the ending was later assim. to *-ier,* -EER¹. Hence **enginee·r** vb. intr. XVII; trans. XIX.

England i·ŋglənd OE. *Engla land* (orig.) country of the Angles (see ANGLE), (later) of the Germanic inhabitants of Great Britain; hence OFris. *Angelond,* OS. (Du.) *Engeland,* (O)HG., Icel., etc. *England.* So **Engl**ISH¹ i·ŋgliʃ pert. to England or its inhabitants. OE. *englisć,* occas. *ænglisć* (prop.) pertaining to the Angles, but (in the earliest exx.) pert. to the group of Germanic peoples known coll. as *Angelcynn* (Bede's *gens Anglorum*), lit. 'race of Angles'; also adj. and sb., of their language; hence OFris. *angelsk, anglesk, engelsk, englesk,* OS. (Du.) *engelsch,* MHG. *engel(i)sch,* ON. *Enskr* (mod. *Engilskr,* Sw., Da. *engelsk*). As the name of a language (OE. *englisć,* absol. use of the n. adj.) orig. applied to all the Angle and Saxon dialects spoken in Britain; in its most comprehensive modern use it comprises all the dialects descended from the language of the early Germanic conquerors of Britain. **Englishman** i·ŋgliʃmən OE. *Englisćmon*; whence Du. *Engelschman,* ON. (pl.) *Enskir menn* (Icel. *Englismaðr,* Sw. *Engelsman,* Da. *Engelskmand*). **E·nglish**RY. XVII; in AN. *englescherie,* AL. *englescheria* (XII).

engraft èngrà·ft graft or implant in. XVI. f. EN-¹+GRAFT vb.; repl. †*engraff* (XV–XVIII).

engrail ingrei·l (her.) indent with contiguous curvilinear notches. XIV. (late ME. pp. *engrelede, ingraylit*). – OF. *engresler* (mod. *engrêler*), f. *en* EN-¹+*gresle* (*grêle*) hail; the marks being compared to hailstones.

engrain, ingrain èngrei·n A. †dye with cochineal XIV (PPl.); B. work into the texture or structure of XVII. In sense A – OF. *engrainer* dye, f. phr. *en graine* (whence Eng. *in grain*) where *graine* means cochineal dye; in sense B f. EN-¹+GRAIN. Now mainly in pp. (chiefly *ingrained*) in senses (i) thoroughgoing, incorrigible, (ii) deep-rooted, inveterate.

engrave ėngrei·v carve, †sculpture XVI; represent by lines incised on a metal plate or wood block XVII. f. EN-[1]+GRAVE[2], after F. †*engraver*; pp. *engraven*, *ingraven* was in use XVI–XIX (latterly poet. or arch.).

engross ėngrou·s A. †buy up wholesale XIV; †get together XVI; gain or keep exclusive possession of, occupy exclusively XVII; B. write in large letters, as in legal documents XV (Lydg.). – AN. *engrosser* and AL. *ingrossāre*, in sense A f. phr. *en gros* and *in grossō* in the lump, by wholesale, in sense B f. *en* IN+OF. *grosse*, medL. *grossa* large writing; see GROSS.

enhance ėnhà·ns †raise, exalt XIV; heighten, intensify XV; raise in price XV. – AN. *enhauncer*, prob. alteration of OF. *enhaucer* = It. *innalzare* :– Rom. **inaltiāre*, f. *in* EN-[1]+*altus* high (cf. OLD).

enharmonic enhāɹmɔ·nik (mus.) in which an interval of 2½ tones was divided into 2 quarter tones and a major third. XVII. – late L. *en(h)armonicus* – Gr. *enarmonikós*, f. *en* EN-[2]+*harmoniā* HARMONY; see -IC.

enigma ini·gmə riddle in verse XVI; puzzling problem XVII. – L. *ænigma*, *-mat-* – Gr. *aínigma*, f. base of *ainíssesthai* speak allusively or obscurely, f. *aînos* apologue, fable. So **enigm**ATIC enigmæ·tik. XVII. – F. *énigmatique* or late L. *ænigmaticus*. -A·TICAL XVI.

enjamb(e)ment ėndʒæ·m(b)mənt, ‖ãʒãbmã continuation of sentence beyond second line of couplet. XIX. F., f. *enjamber* stride, f. *en* EN-[1]+*jambe* leg; see JAMB, -MENT.

enjoin ėndʒoi·n A. impose (a penalty, task, etc.) XIII; prohibit by an injunction XVI; B. †join together XIV (Wycl. Bible). f. *enjoi(g)n-*, stem of (O)F. *enjoindre* = Pr. *enjunher*, It. *ingiugnere* :– L. *injungere* join, attach, impose, f. *in* EN-[1]+*jungere* JOIN.

enjoy ėndʒoi· †be joyful XIV; possess or experience with joy XV; refl. (after F. *se (ré)jouir*) XVII. – OF. *enjoier* give joy to, refl. enjoy (cf. It. *ingiojare*), f. *en-* EN-[1]+*joie* JOY, or – OF. *enjoïr* enjoy, rejoice, f. *en-*+*joïr* :– L. *gaudēre*. Hence **enjoy·**MENT. XVI.

enkindle ėnki·ndl cause to blaze up, set on fire. XVI (Udall, Stanyhurst). See EN-[1].

enlarge ėnlā·ɹdʒ make larger or more extensive XIV; †set at large XV; †refl. expand in words; intr. speak at large XVII. – OF. *enlarger*, *-largir*, f. *en-* EN-[1]+*large* LARGE; some of the uses are due to (O)F. *eslargir*, mod. *élargir* set free.

enlighten ėnlai·tn give light to, shed light upon. XIV (rare before XVI). orig. extended form with EN-[1], of †*en-*, †*inlight*, OE. *inlihtan*, f. *in* IN-[1]+*lihtan* LIGHT; later a new formation either f. EN-[1]+LIGHTEN[1] or f. EN-[1]+LIGHT[1]+-EN[5]. Hence **enli·ghten**MENT. XVII (in XIX used as tr. of G. *Aufklärung*).

enlist ėnli·st enrol on the 'list' as a soldier XVII; also fig.; intr. XVIII. f. EN-[1]+LIST[4] sb. or LIST vb. (which is recorded 50 years earlier), perh. after Du. *inlijsten* inscribe on a list or register. Hence **enli·st**MENT. XVIII.

enliven ėnlai·vn †give life to; animate, inspirit; cheer. XVII. Extended form of †*enlive* (XVI), f. EN-[1]+LIFE, after LIVE.[1]

enmity e·nmĭti hatred, hostility. XIII (Cursor M.). – OF. *enemi(s)tié* (mod. *inimitié*) = Pr. *enemistat*, Sp. *enemistad* :– Rom. **inimīcitātem*, f. *inimīcus*; see ENEMY, -ITY.

ennead e·niæd set of nine. XVII. – Gr. *ennead-*, *enneás*, f. *ennéa* NINE. See -AD[1].

ennoble ėnou·bl make noble. XVI (pa. pple. XV). – (O)F. *ennoblir*; see EN-[1], NOBLE.

ennui ɔ·nwi, ‖ã·nwi feeling of lack of interest. XVIII. F. :– L. phr. *in odiō* (see ANNOY). ¶ See quot. from Evelyn s.v. CHICANERY.

enormous inɔ̄·ɹməs †abnormal, monstrous; †irregular, outrageous; of excessive size. XVI. f. L. *ēnormis*, f. *ē* E-+*norma* pattern; see NORM, -OUS. ¶ Nearly contemp. were †*enorm* (after F. *énorme*) and †*enormious* (XV). So **eno·rm**ITY. XV (Caxton). – (O)F. – L.

enough ĭnʌ·f OE. *ġenōg*, *ġenōh* (used in acc. as adv.) = OFris. *enōch*, OS. *ginōg* (Du. *genoeg*), OHG. *ginuog* (G. *genug*), ON *gnógr*, Goth. *ganōhs* :– CGerm. **ganōgaz*, rel. to impers. preterite-present vb. OE. *ġeneah*, OHG. *ginah*, Goth. *ganah* it suffices, f. Germ. **ga-* Y-+**naχ-*, which is repr. also in OE. *beneah* (he) enjoys, requires, Goth. *binah* it is right or needful, and is :– IE. **nak-*, in L. *nancīscī* (pp. *nactus*) obtain, Skr. *naç* reach. The infl. forms of *ġenōg* gave ENOW, which, as repr. OE. nom. and acc. pl. *ġenōge*, was in literary use as the pl. of *enough* at least till XVIII (later with Sc. writers and dial.).

enounce inau·ns enunciate. XIX. – F. *énoncer* – L. *ēnuntiāre* ENUNCIATE, after *announce*, *pronounce*.

enow ĭnau· see ENOUGH.

enrage ėnrei·dʒ †be distracted; †pp. maddened; put in a rage or fury. XVI (pp. *enraged* was used by Trevisa, tr. Barth. *De P.R.*). – (O)F. *enrager*; see EN-[1], RAGE. The trans. use arose in Eng. through the apprehension of pp. *enraged* (F. *enragé*) as a passive.

enrapture ėnræ·ptʃəɹ throw into a rapture, delight intensely. XVIII. f. EN-[1]+RAPTURE, after **enrapt** carried away by ecstasy (XVII Sh.); see RAPT.

enrich ėnri·tʃ make rich. XIV (Wycl. Bible). – (O)F. *enrichir*, f. *en-* EN-[1]+*riche* RICH.

enrol(l) ėnrou·l inscribe on a roll or list, enter among the rolls or records. XIV. – OF. *enroller* (mod. *enrôler*), f. *en* EN-[1]+*rolle* ROLL.

ens enz, pl. *entia* e·nʃiə being, entity. XVI (Sidney, Jonson). L., sb. use of n. of prp. formed from *esse* BE, on the supposed analogy of *absēns* ABSENT, to render Gr. n. *ón* being, prp. of *eînai*. Cf. ESSENCE.

ensample ėnsà·mpl example. XIII. – AN. *ensa(u)mple*, alteration of OF. *assample*, *essemple* EXAMPLE. The mod. arch. use is due to reminiscence of its use in N.T. (e.g. Phil. iii 17, 1 Thess. i 7).

ensconce ėnskɔ·ns †fortify, shelter behind a fortification; establish †secretly or securely. XVI. f. EN-[1]+SCONCE[3]; cf. OF. *esconcer.*

ensemble ãsã·bl all the parts together. XV. F., sb. use of adv. 'together' = It. *insieme*, etc. :- Rom. **insemul*, for L. *insimul* (Statius), f. *in* IN+*simul, semul* at the same time, rel. to *similis* SIMILAR.

ensiform e·nsifɔ̄ɹm sword-shaped. XVI. - modL. *ēnsiformis*, f. *ēnsis* sword (= Skr. *asís*); see -FORM.

ensign e·nsain, (naut., of the flag) e·nsn †battle-cry, watchword; sign, token, badge; banner XIV (naval flag XVIII); ensign-bearer (hence, various military and naval officers) XVI (cf. ANCIENT[2]). - (O)F. *enseigne* = Pr. *ensenha*, Sp. *insignia* :- L. *īnsignia*; see INSIGNIA.

ensilage e·nsilidʒ preservation of green fodder in a pit. XIX (first in U.S.). - F. *ensilage*, f. *ensiler* - Sp. *ensilar*, f. *en* EN-[1]+ *silo*; see SILO, -AGE. So **ensile** ėnsai·l. XIX. - F. *ensiler*.

enslave ėnslei·v make a SLAVE of. XVII (Prynne, Cowley, Howell, Boyle). See EN-[1].

ensue ėnsjū· †follow, in various gen. senses, trans. and intr. XIV; follow in the course of events (now esp. in *next ensuing* with ref. to a date), follow as a result XV. - OF. *ensiw-, ensu-*, stem of *ensivre* (mod. *ensuivre*), corr. to Pr., Cat. *enseguir*, It. *inseguire* :- Rom. **insequere*, for L. *insequī*, f. *in* IN-[1]+ *sequī* follow (cf. PURSUE, SUIT).

ensure ėnʃuə·ɹ †make sure or safe, assure, pledge, guarantee XIV; secure, make certain XVIII. - AN. *enseurer*, alteration of OF. *asseurer* ASSURE. See also the differentiated INSURE.

-ent ənt suffix repr. F. *-ent* (= Sp., It. *-ente*) - L. *-entem*, nom. *-ēns*, ending of prp. of L. vbs. in *-ēre, -ere, -īre*, corr. in sense to -ING[1] (cf. -ANT) and in form belonging to the IE. series **-ont-, *-ent-, *-nt-*, repr. by Skr. *-ant-*, Gr. *-ont-*, Goth. *-and-*, OE. *-end-*. Examples are: *pendent* hanging, *confident* trusting, *salient* leaping; many such ppl. adjs. had become sbs. in Latin or in French; e.g. *adherent, agent, exponent, parent, president, serpent, student*; some are names of inanimate objects or abstractions, as *aperient, coefficient, continent, constituent, current, deterrent, emollient, expedient, orient, solvent, tangent, torrent.* See also -ESCENT, -FACIENT.

entablature ėntæ·blətʃuəɹ (archit.) part of an order above the column XVII; framework of an engine supported by columns XIX. - (partly through F. *entablement*, which was also current in Eng. XVII), It. *intavolatura* boarding, f. *intavolare* board up, f. *in* EN-[1]+ *tavola* TABLE.

entail ėntei·l (leg.) settle (an estate) on a number of persons in succession XIV (Wyclif); †attach as an inseparable appendage XVI; impose (trouble) *upon* XVII; involve as a consequence XIX. f. EN-[1]+ AN. *taile* or *tailé* TAIL[2]. Hence **entai·l** sb. XIV (Wyclif).

entangle ėntæ·ŋgl involve (as) in network, etc. XV. f. EN-[1]+TANGLE; perh. orig. of boats or oars caught in 'tangle' or seaweed.

entelechy ente·liki, **entelechia, -eia** ent:elikai·ə (philos.) realization of a function. XVII. - late L. - Gr. *entelékheia*, f. *en* IN + *télei* d. of *télos* end, perfection + *ékhein* be in a (certain) state; see -Y[3].

Entellus ėnte·ləs East Indian species of monkey, Semnopithecus entellus. XIX. modL., named by Dufresne, 1797, presumably after *Entellus* in Virgil 'Æneid' v 437-72. ¶ Names of other Indian monkeys are of similar origin, *Anchises, Irus, Priamus, Rhesus.*

entente ãtã·t understanding. XIX. F., f. *entendre* INTEND; earliest in *entente cordiale* (*c.* 1840).

enter e·ntəɹ go or come in XIII (Cursor M.); go or come into XIV (R. Rolle); cause to go in, put in or into, insert, introduce XIV (PPl.). - (O)F. *entrer* = Pr. *en-, intrar*, Sp. *entrar*, It. *en-, intrare*, Rum. *întra* :- L. *intrāre*, f. *intrā* within (see INTRA-).

e·nter-, †**entre-** prefix - (O)F. *entre-* :- L. INTER-. All comps. formed with this, exc. *enterprise, entertain*, are either obs. or have been refash. with *inter-*.

enteric ente·rik pert. to the intestines; typhoid. XIX. - Gr. *enterikós*, f. *énteron* intestine, rel. to L. *inter* between, among, *interus* (see INTERIOR, INTERNAL), *intus* within (see INTESTINE); cf. F. *entérique*. So **enteri·**TIS, **entero-**, comb. form of Gr. *énteron*.

enterprise e·ntəɹpraiz work taken in hand, bold undertaking; daring spirit. XV. - (O)F. *entreprise*, sb. use of pp. fem. of *entreprendre* later var. of *emprendre*, whence *emprise* EMPRISE (XIII). (Cf. PREHENSILE.)

entertain entəɹtei·n †keep in a certain state; keep up, maintain; treat; receive, e.g. as a guest XV; †retain in service; engage the attention of XVI; amuse XVII. - (O)F. *entretenir* (infl. *-tient*, †*-teigne*) = Pr. *entretenir*, Sp. *entretener*, It. *intrattenere* :- Rom. **intertenēre*, f. *inter* among, INTER-+*tenēre* hold (cf. TENANT). Hence **entertai·n**MENT. †maintenance, provision XVI; reception (of a guest); meal; amusement XVII; public performance XVIII.

enthral(l) ėnþrɔ̄·l enslave (fig. hold spellbound). XVI. f. EN-[1]+THRALL.

enthrone ėnþrou·n set on a throne. XVII (Sh.). repl. *enthro·nize* (XIV, Gower) - OF. *introniser* - late L. *inthronizāre* - Gr. *enthronizein*, f. *en* EN-[2]+*thrónos* THRONE.

enthusiasm enþjū·ziæzm †prophetic or poetic frenzy; vain confidence in divine inspiration, misguided religious emotion XVII; rapturous or passionate eagerness XVIII. – F. *enthousiasme* or late L. *enthūsiasmus* – Gr. *enthousiasmós* (Plato), f. *enthousiázein* be inspired or possessed by the god, f. *énthous, éntheos* inspired, possessed, f. *en* IN+ *theós* god. So **enthu·siast.** XVII. – F. *enthousiaste* or eccl.L. *enthūsiastēs* designation of a sect – eccl.Gr. *enthousiastés*. **enthusia·stic.** XVII. – Gr. *enthousiastikós* (Plato). Hence **enthu·se** vb. inspire with enthusiasm, become enthusiastic. XIX (orig. U.S. colloq.).

enthymeme e·nþimīm syllogism in which one of the premisses is suppressed. XVI. – L. *enthȳmēma* – Gr. *enthū́mēma*, f. *enthūmeîsthai* consider, reflect, infer, f. *en* EN-[2]+*thūmós* passion, courage, mind, rel. to L. *fūmus* FUME. The current use in logic is due to a misapprehension, found as early as Boethius, of Aristotle's use of the word for 'syllogism drawn from merely probable premisses' as an imperfect syllogism (ἀτελὴς συλλογισμός) and as referring to its form instead of to its matter.

entice èntai·s †incite XIII; allure XIV. – OF. *enticier*, prob. :– Rom. **intītiāre*, f. L. *in* EN-[1]+**tītius*, for L. *tītiō* firebrand, as if 'set on fire, add fuel to' (cf. *inflame*). So **enti·ce**MENT. XIV. – OF. *enticement*, f. *enticier*. ¶ Aphetic TICE.

entire èntaiə·ɹ whole, complete. XIV (Wyclif; in Ch. only the adv. *entirely*); (of animals) not castrated XIX. ME. *enter, entier* – AN. *enter*, (O)F. *entier*, fem. *-ière* = Pr. *entier*, Sp. *entero*, Pg. *inteiro*, It. *intero* :– Rom. **inte·gro*, for L. *i·ntegrum* (nom. *integer*), f. *in-* IN-[2]+**tag-*, base of *tangere* touch (see TANGENT, TACT). The ME. and early modEng. senses 'upright', 'honest', 'sincere' have not survived. So **entire**TY èntaiə·ɹti. XVI. – (O)F. *entièreté*.

entitle èntai·tl give a title to. XIV (Ch.). – AN. *entitler*, OF. *entiteler* (mod. *intituler*) = Pr. *entitolar*, It. *intitolare* – late L. *intitulāre*, f. *in-* IN-[1] (cf. EN-[1])+*titulus* TITLE.

entity e·ntiti being. XVI. – F. *entité* or medL. *entitās*, f. L. *ent-*, ENS; see -ITY.

ento- e·ntou before a vowel **ent-**, comb. form of Gr. *entós* within (= L. *intus*), as in **entozo·on,** parasitic animal living within another. XIX (see ZOO-).

entomo- (before two unstressed sylls.) entəmə·, (before one unstressed syll.) entə·mou, (before a stressed syll.) e:ntəmŏ; **entomology** entəmə·lədʒi science of insects. XVIII. – F. or modL. f. Gr. *éntomon*; see INSECT, -LOGY.

entourage ɔn-, ãturā·ʒ environment; persons in attendance. XIX. F., f. *entourer* surround, f. *entour* surroundings, sb. use of adv. 'round about' = Pr. *entorn*, It. *intorno* :– Rom. **in torno* in the circle (see TURN).

entr'acte ã·trakt interval, or performance of music, etc., between acts of a play. XIX (anglicized XVIII by Chesterfield as *inter-act*). F., f. *entre* between+*acte*; see INTER-, ACT.

entrails e·ntreilz intestines, (formerly) inward parts gen. XIII (Cursor M.). – (O)F. *entrailles* = Pr. *entralhas* – medL. *intrālia* (Reichenau Glossary), alteration of L. *interānea* (whence OF. *entraigne*, Sp. *entrañas*), sb. use of n. pl. of *interāneus* internal, f. *inter* (see INTERIOR). Formerly also sg. as in OF.

entrain[1] èntrei·n draw as an accompaniment or consequence. XVI (now rare). – (O)F. *entraîner*, f. *en* EN-[1] + *traîner* drag (see TRAIN).

entrain[2] entrei·n put on a railway train. XIX. f. EN-[1]+TRAIN sb.

entrance[1] e·ntrəns coming or going in; place of entry. XVI. – OF. *entrance*, f. *entrer* ENTER; see -ANCE. So **e·ntr**ANT sb. and †adj. XVII. – prp. of F. *entrer*.

entrance[2] èntrà·ns put into a trance, carry away as in a trance, overpower esp. with delight. XVI. f. EN-[1]+TRANCE vb.; perh. intended as an intensive formation.

entrap èntræ·p XVI. – OF. *entrap(p)er*, f. *en-* EN-[1]+*trappe* TRAP[1].

entreat èntrī·t †treat XIV; beseech, implore XV. – OF. *entraiter*, f. *en-* EN-[1]+*traiter* TREAT. The sense of 'implore' was carried over from *treat*, which was used intr. and trans. in that sense, which was developed from that of 'deal with'. Hence **entrea·ty** †treatment; earnest request XVI; after TREATY.

entrechat ã·trəʃa caper in dancing in which the feet are struck together rapidly. XVIII. F., alteration (perh. after It. *capriola intrecchiata* intricate caper), earlier †*entrechas, -chasse*, f. *entrechasser* chase in and out, f. *entre* between, INTER-+*chasser* CHASE.

entrée ã·trei entrance, leave of entry XVIII; dish served before the joint. XIX. F.; see ENTRY.

entremets ã·trəmei side dishes. XVIII. F., earlier *entremès*, adopted in ME. XIV, occas. semi-anglicized †*entremetes* (Caxton); f. *entre* between, INTER-+†*mès, mets* MESS.

entrench, in- èntre·nʃ place within a trench XVI; trench (upon) XVII. f. EN-[1], IN-[1]+ TRENCH. Hence **entre·nch**MENT line of trenches, post fortified thereby. XVI (Spenser).

entrepôt ã·trəpou storehouse; mart. XVIII. F. (earlier †*entrepost*, †*-pos*), f. *entreposer* store, f. *entre* among + *poser* place; see INTER-, POSE.

entrepreneur ãtrəprənő̄r director or organizer of (musical) entertainments. XIX. F., f. *entreprendre* undertake (see ENTERPRISE).

entresol ã·trəsɔl storey between ground and first floor. XVIII. F., f. *entre* between, INTER-+*sol* ground.

entropy e·ntrəpi (phys.) quantitative element determining the thermodynamic condition of a substance undergoing a reversible change. 1868. – G. *entropie* (Clusius), f. Gr. *en* EN-[2]+*tropḗ* transformation (see TROPE), after *energy*; see Y[3]. ¶ Clusius, assuming the etymol. meaning of *energy* to be 'work-content' (*Werkinhalt*), devised this term as a corr. designation for 'transformation-content' (*Verwandlungsinhalt*); see 'Poggio Annalen' CXXV 390.

entrust, in- ėntrʌ·st invest with a trust; confide the care of. XVII. f. EN-[1]+TRUST.

entry e·ntri entering, entrance (more esp. leg.) XIII (RGlouc.); passage affording entrance, alley between houses; entering in a book, item entered XV. ME. *entre(e)* – (O)F. *entrée* = Pr. *intrada*, Sp. *entrada*, It. *intrata* :– Rom. **intrāta*, sb. use of fem. pp. of L. *intrāre* ENTER; see -Y[5].

enucleate injū·klieit explain. XVI. f. pp. stem of L. *ēnucleāre* extract the kernel from, make plain, f. *ē* E-+*nucleus* kernel; see NUCLEUS, -ATE[3]. So **enucle**A·TION. XVII. – medL.

enumerate injū·məreit detail as if by counting. XVII. f. pp. stem of L. *ēnumerāre*, f. *ē* E-+*numerus* NUMBER; see -ATE[3]. So **enumer**A·TION. XVI. – F. or L.

enunciate inʌ·nʃieit give expression to XVII; pronounce XVIII. f. pp. stem of L. *ēnuntiāre*, f. *ē* E-+*nuntiāre* ANNOUNCE. So **enunci**A·TION. XVI. – F. or L.

enure injuə·ɹ †inure XV; (leg.) come into operation, be applied *to* XVII. f. EN-[1]+URE.

envelop ėnve·ləp wrap up. XIV (Ch.). ME. *envolupe, -ipe* – OF. *envoluper, -oper* (mod. *envelopper*) = Pr. *envolupar, envelopar*, It. *inviluppare*, f. *in-* EN-[1]+**volup-*, **velup-*, of unkn. origin (cf. OF. *voloper*, Pr. *volopar* envelop, It. *viluppo* tuft, bundle, confusion, intricacy); cf. DEVELOP. So **envelope** e·nvəloup; in the sense of 'cover of a letter' often ã·vəloup, ɔ·nvəloup, after F. XVIII. – F. *enveloppe*, f. the vb.

envious ė·nviəs full of envy. XIII. – AN. *envious*, OF. *envieus* (mod. *-eux*), f. *envie* ENVY, after L. *invidiōsus*; of Pr. *envejos*, Sp. *envidioso*, It. *invidioso*.

environ ėnvaiə·rən surround, encompass. XIV. – OF. *environer* (mod. *-onner*), f. *environ* surroundings, around, f. *en* IN+*viron* circuit, f. *virer* turn, VEER (cf. *entour* s.v. ENTOURAGE). Hence **envi·ron**MENT. XVII (occas. only before XIX). So **environs** e·nvirənz, ėnvaiə·rənz neighbourhood. XVII (Evelyn). F. pl.

envisage ėnvi·zidʒ look straight at; view, contemplate. XIX (Keats). – F. *envisager*, f. *en-* EN-[1]+*visage* face, VISAGE.

envoy[1] e·nvoi conclusion of a poem, etc. XIV (Ch.). – (O)F. *envoi*, f. *envoyer* send, f. phr. *en voie* on the way (so Sp. *enviar*, It. *inviare*); cf. VIÂ. ¶ In ME. and later freq. *lenvoy*, with coalescence of the F. def. art.

envoy[2] e·nvoi minister sent on a diplomatic mission. XVII. Alteration (in late XVII) of F. *envoyé*, sb. use of pp. of *envoyer* (see prec.), which had been adopted earlier unchanged. ¶ For the loss of F. *-é* cf. ASSIGN[2].

envy e·nvi †malice; feeling of mortification and ill will at another's well-being. XIII. – (O)F. *envie* (which early developed the sense 'desire'), corr. to Pr. *enveia*, Sp. *envidia*, Pg. *enveja*, It. *invidia*, semi-pop. – L. *invidia* malice, ill will, f. *invidēre* look maliciously upon, grudge, envy, f. *in* upon, against + *vidēre* see; see EN-[1], VISION. So **e·nvy** vb. XIV (Ch.). – (O)F. *envier*, corr. to Pr. *enveiar*, Sp. *envidiar*, etc. ¶ Older envai· to XVII, still dial., esp. Sc.

enzyme e·nzaim (chem.) catalytic ferment. 1881. – G. *enzym* (Kühne 1876), f. modGr. *énzumos* leavened, f. Gr. *en* IN+*zúmē* leaven (see JUICE).

eo- īou, comb. form of Gr. *ēṓs* (see next).

Eoan īou·ən pert. to the dawn, eastern. XVII (Drayton). f. L. *ēōus* – Gr. *ēôos*, f. *ēṓs* dawn (cf. AURORA, EAST); see -AN.

eocene ī·ŏsīn (geol.) lowest division of the tertiary. XIX (Lyell). f. Gr. *ēṓs* dawn (cf. AURORA)+*kainós* new, recent. So **miocene** mai·o- middle division of the tertiary. f. Gr. *meíōn* less (cf. MINOR). **oligocene** ɔ·ligo- intermediate between eocene and miocene. f. Gr. *olígos* OLIGO-. **pleistocene** plai·sto- (i) newest division of the pliocene, (ii) older division of the post-tertiary. f. Gr. *pleîstos* most (cf. PLUS). **pliocene** plai·o- newest division of the tertiary. f. Gr. *pleíōn* more.

-eous iəs suffix of adjs. the majority of which are formed on L. adjs. in *-eus* (= Gr. *-eos*); these are based on sbs. denoting material things and usu. have the sense 'composed of', as well as that of 'of the nature of, resembling', while the Eng. derivs. have the latter meaning only; exx. are *erroneous, flammeous, gemmeous, igneous, lacteous, ligneous, niveous, puniceous, spadiceous, vitreous*, and (from scholL.) *heterogeneous, homogeneous*. In adoptions of F. adjs. in *-eux* based on sbs. in *-age* the suffix took this form, as in *advantageous, courageous, outrageous, umbrageous*, and in *hideous* and *piteous* (with *dispiteous*) *-eous* has replaced *-ous*; *aqueous* (– F. *aqueux*) and †*atheous* are isolated; in *bounteous, courteous, gorgeous, plenteous*, and *righteous* other endings have been assim. to *-eous*; in *beauteous* and *duteous* the ending has arisen from the addition of -OUS to *-te*, early form of -TY. See also -ACEOUS.

epact ī·pækt number of days by which the solar exceeds the lunar year; number of days in the age of the moon at the new year. XVI (Bk. Com. Prayer, 1552). – (O)F. *épacte* – late L. *epactæ* pl. – Gr. *epaktaí* (sc. *hēmérai* days), fem. pl. of *epaktós*, pp. adj. of *epágein* intercalate, f. *epí* on, EPI-+*ágein* lead, bring (cf. ACT).

eparch e·pāɹk governor of a province; (eccl.) metropolitan. XVII. – Gr. *éparkhos*, f. *epí* EPI- + *arkhós* chief, ruler (cf. -ARCH). So **e·parchy.** XVIII. – Gr. *eparkhiā*; see -Y[3].

epaulet, -ette epəle·t shoulder-piece on a uniform. XVIII. – F. *épaulette*, f. *épaule* shoulder, SPATULA; see -ET, -ETTE.

epenthesis ėpe·nþĭsis (philol.) insertion of a sound between two others. XVII. Late L. (Servius) – Gr. *epénthesis*, f. *epenthe-*, stem of *epentithénai* insert, f. *epí* EPI- + *en* IN + *tithénai* place (see DO[1]). So **epenthe·tic** XIX.

epergne ipə̄·ɹn ornamental centre dish for the dinner table to hold dessert, etc. XVIII (occas. *epargne*). Perh. Eng. use of F. *épargne* saving, economy (f. *épargner* SPARE) derived from phr. *taille* or *gravure d'épargne* metal or etching in which parts are 'spared', i.e. left in relief (cf. *tailler* or *graver en épargne*, and the use of *épargne* for the acid-resisting mixture with which those parts of ornamental work are painted that are to be left plain).

epexegesis epeksidʒī·sis added explanation. XVII. – Gr. *epexḗgēsis*, f. *epexēgeîsthai*; see EPI- and EXEGESIS. Hence **epexege·ti-c(al).** XIX.

ephah ī·fa dry measure (the same as BATH[2]). XVI (*epha*). Heb. *ēiphāh*, believed to be of Egyptian origin (cf. LXX Gr. *oiphí*, Vulgate L. *ēphi*).

ephemeral ėfe·mərəl, ėfī·- existing only for a day or a very short time. XVI. orig. said of a fever; f. (after F. *éphémère*) Gr. *ephḗmeros* (whence fem. and n. in **-a, -on** as sbs. XVI–XVII), f. *epí* EPI- + *hēmérā* day, rel. to * êmar* day; see -AL[1]. So **ephemeris** ėfe·məris, ifī·- table showing the places of heavenly bodies for every day of a period XVI; astronomical almanac XVII. L. – Gr. *ephēmerís* diary, f. *ephḗmeros*.

ephod e·fɔd Jewish priestly vestment. XIV (*ephoth*, Wycl. Bible). – Heb. *ēphōd*, f. *āphad* put on.

ephor e·fɔ̄ɹ Spartan magistrate. XVI (first in L. pl. *ephori*, and anglicized *ephories*). – L. *ephorus* (whence also F. *éphore*) – Gr. *éphoros*, f. *epí* EPI- + **ϝor-*, base of *horân* (see WARE[2]).

epi- e·pi prefix repr. Gr. *epi-*, before an unaspirated vowel *ep-*, before an aspirated vowel *eph-*, a use of the adv.-prep. *epí* on, upon, over, close up in time or space, in addition (to) = Skr. *ápi* moreover, also, at, in :- IE. **epi*, beside **opi* (whence Gr. *ópisthen* from behind, L. *ob* towards, against, in OL. around, near); in many techn. terms, as of anat. and path., e.g. *epididymis, epigastrium, epiglottis, episternum, epithelium*; in chem. and min. used to form terms denoting substances analogous to those denoted by the uncompounded words, as *epichlorohydrin, epidiorite*.

epic e·pik adj. XVI; sb. continuous (poetic) narrative of the doings of heroes XVIII. – L. *epicus* – late Gr. *epikós*, f. *épos*; see EPOS, -IC.

epicedium episī·diəm funeral ode. XVI. L. *epicēdīum*, – Gr. *epikḗdeion*, sb. use of n. of *epikḗdeios*, f. *epí* EPI- + *kêdos* care, spec. funeral observance (see HATE).

epicene e·pisīn (gram.) of common gender. XV. – late L. *epicœnus* – Gr. *epíkoinos*, f. *epí* EPI- + *koinós* common (cf. KOINE).

epicentre e·pisentəɹ point on the earth's surface lying immediately above the focus of an earthquake. XIX. f. EPI- + CENTRE.

epiclesis epiklī·sis (liturg.) invocation of the Holy Ghost in the Eucharist. XIX. – Gr. *epíklēsis*, f. *epikaleîn* call upon; see EPI-, HALE[2].

epicure e·pikjuəɹ †Epicurean; †glutton, sybarite; one who is choice in eating and drinking. XVI. – medL. *epicūrus* one whose chief happiness is in carnal pleasure; appellative use of L. *Epicūrus*, Gr. *Epíkouros* name of an Athenian philosopher, *c.* 300 B.C.

Epicurean e:pikjurī·ən pert. to the philosophy of Epicurus, according to which pleasure is the highest good. XIV. – F. *épicurien*, f. L. *epicūrēus* – Gr. *epikoúreios*, f. *Epíkouros* Epicurus; see prec. and -EAN. Hence **E:picure·an**ISM. XVIII. So **e·picur**ISM (*E-*) philosophy of Epicurus, Epicureanism; †pursuit of pleasure XVI; habits of an epicure XVII; partly f. *Epicūrus*, after F. *épicurisme*; partly f. EPICURE.

epicycle e·pisaikl small circle having its centre on the circumference of a greater, as in the Ptolemaic astronomy. XIV (Ch.). – (O)F. *épicycle* or late L. *epicyclus* – Gr. *epíkuklos*; see EPI-, CYCLE.

epidemic epide·mik of diseases prevalent among a people at a particular time. XVII; sb. XVIII. – F. *épidémique*, f. *épidémie* (hence †*epidemy* XV) – late L. *epidēmia* – Gr. *epidēmíā* prevalence of a disease, f. *epidḗmios*, f. *epí* EPI- + *dêmos* people; see DEMOS, -IC.

epidermis epidə̄·ɹmis (anat.) outer skin. XVII. – late L. (Vegetius) – Gr. *epidermís* (Hippocrates), f. *epí* EPI- + *dérma* skin (cf. TEAR[2]).

epigram e·pigræm short pithy poem XV (Lydg.); †inscription XVI. – F. *épigramme* or L. *epigramma* – Gr. *epígramma*, f. *epí* EPI- + *gráphein* write (cf. GRAMMAR). So **epigraph** e·pigràf inscription XVII; short quotation at the beginning of a work, etc. XIX. – Gr. *epigraphḗ*. Hence **epi·**GRAPHY ėpi·grəfi (science of) inscriptions. XIX.

epigynous ėpi·dʒĭnəs (bot.) placed upon the ovary. XIX. – modL. *epigynus* (Jussieu), f. Gr. *epí* on + *gunḗ* woman (used for 'pistil'); see QUEAN, -OUS.

epilepsy e·pilepsi nervous disease in which the patient falls unconscious ('the falling sickness'). XVI. – F. *épilepsie* or late L. *epilēpsia* – Gr. *epilēpsíā*, f. *epilab-*, stem of *epilambánein* seize upon, attack, f. *epí* EPI- + *lambánein* take hold of, f. IE. **slaph-* seize; see -Y[3]. So **epile·ptic**. XVII. – F. – late L. – Gr. *epilēptikós*. ¶ MedL. vars. *epilentia*, *-enticus*, OF. *epilence*, *-entique*, were repr. by late ME. *epilence*, *epilentik*.

epilogue e·pilɔg conclusion of a literary piece (esp. a play). XV. – (O)F. *épilogue* – L. *epilogus* – Gr. *epílogos*, f. *epí* EPI- + *lógos* speech (cf. -LOGY). So **epilogize** epi·lŏdʒaiz XVII. – Gr. *epilogízesthai*. †**epi·loguize** (Milton).

Epiphany[1] ipi·fəni (feast of) the manifestation of Jesus Christ to the Gentiles. XIII. – (O)F. *épiphanie*, – ecclL. *epiphania* – ecclGr. *epiphánia* n. pl. of **epiphánios*, f. *epiphaínein* manifest, f. *epí* EPI- + *phaínein* show (cf. PHENOMENON); see -Y[3].

epiphany[2] manifestation of a supernatural being. XVII. – Gr. *epipháneia* manifestation, appearance of a divinity, f. *epiphanḗs* manifest, *epiphaínein* (see prec.).

epiphysis ėpi·fisis (anat.) portion of a long bone originating in a separate centre. XVII. modL. – Gr. *epíphusis*, f. *epí* EPI- + *phúsis* growth (cf. PHYSIC). Cf. APOPHYSIS.

epiphyte e·pifait (bot.) vegetable parasite. XIX. f. Gr. *epí* EPI- + *phutón* plant (cf. prec.).

episcopal ipi·skəpəl of a bishop or bishops XV; based on episcopacy XVII. – (O)F. *épiscopal* or ecclL. *episcopālis*, f. *episcopus* BISHOP; see -AL[1]. Hence **episcopalian** -ei·liən. XVIII. **epi·scopally**. XVI; cf. ecclL. *episcopāliter*. So **epi·scopacy** government by bishops. XVII. f. ecclL. *episcopātus*, after *prelacy*. **epi·scopate**[1]. XVII. – ecclL.

episode e·pisoud dialogue between choric songs; incidental narrative XVII; incidental event XVIII. – Gr. *epeisódion*, sb. use of n. of *epeisódios* coming in besides, f. *epí* EPI- + *eísodos* entrance, f. *eis* into + *hodós* way, passage. Cf. F. *épisode* († *episodie*).

epistemology e:pistīmɔ·lədʒi theory of knowledge. XIX. f. *epistemo-*, comb. form of Gr. *epistḗmē* knowledge, f. *epístasthai* know (how to do), f. *epí* EPI- + *stánai* STAND; see -LOGY.

epistle ipi·sl apostolic letter of the N.T. (AncrR.); (gen.) letter. XIV (Ch.). OE. *epistol*, beside *pistol*, ME. *pistle* (XII–XVI; Burns has *pistyl*) – L. *epistola*; ME. *epistle* (XIII) – OF. *epistle* (mod. *épître*) – L. *epistola* – Gr. *epistolḗ*, f. *epistéllein* send, esp. as a message, f. *epí* EPI- + *stéllein* send (cf. STOLE). So **epistolary** ipi·stələri. XV. f. F. *épistolaire* or L. *epistolāris*. **epistoler**[2], **epi·stler** ipi·stləɹ one who reads the epistle at Mass XVI; letter-writer XVII. – F. *épistolier* or medL. *epistolāris*.

epistrophe ipi·strəfi (rhet.) figure of speech in which each sentence or clause ends with the same word. XVII. modL. – Gr. *epistrophḗ*, f. *epistréphein* turn about; see EPI-, STROPHE.

epistyle e·pistail (archit.) architrave. XVII. – F. *épistyle* or L. *epistȳlium* – Gr. *epistúlion*, f. *epí* EPI- + *stûlos* pillar, STYLE[2].

epitaph e·pitàf inscription on a tomb. XIV (Trev.). – (O)F. *épitaphe* – L. *epitaphium* funeral oration – Gr. *epitáphion*, n. of *epitáphios* (in *e. lógos* funeral oration; also as sb.; cf. *epitáphia* n. pl. funeral), f. *epí* EPI- + *táphos* obsequies, tomb.

epithalamium e:piþəlei·miəm nuptial song. XVII (earlier in Gr. form, Spenser, and anglicized *epithalamy*). L. – Gr. *epithalámion*, sb. use of n. of *epithalámios*, f. *epí* EPI- + *thálamos* bridal chamber.

epithet e·piþet adjective, attributive word. XVI. – F. *épithète* or L. *epitheton*, sb. use of n. of Gr. *epíthetos* attributed, pp. adj. of *epitithénai* put on or to, f. *epí* EPI- + *tithénai* place (see DO[1]).

epitome ipi·təmi abridgement, summary. XVI. – L. *epitomē* – Gr. *epitomḗ*, f. *epitémnein* cut into, cut short; see EPI-, TOME. Hence **epi·tomize**. XVI.

epitrite e·pitrait (pros.) foot of one short and three long syllables. XVII. – L. *epitritos* (Gellius) – Gr. *epítritos* in the ratio of 4 to 3, lit. with the addition of one-third, f. *epí* EPI- + *trítos* THIRD.

epoch ī·pɔk point or period of time. XVII (first in L. form *epocha*, and occas. in Gr. form *epoche*, 3 syll.). – modL. *epocha* – Gr. *epokhḗ* stoppage, station, fixed point of time, f. *epékhein* stop, take up a position, f. *epí* EPI- + *ékhein* hold, intr. be in a certain state (cf. SCHEME). Cf. F. *époque*, It. *epoca*, etc. *Epoch-making* XIX (*epoch-forming*, Coleridge) is after G. *epochemachend*.

epode e·poud lyric poem in which a long line is followed by a shorter one XVI; part of a lyric ode following the strophe and the antistrophe XVII (Milton). – F. *épode* or L. *epōdos* – Gr. *epōidós*; see EPI-, ODE.

eponymous ėpɔ·niməs applied to personages from whose names the names of peoples or places are reputed to be derived (e.g. *Brutus*, grandson of Æneas, as mythical founder of *Britain*). XIX (Grote). f. Gr. *epṓnumos* given as a name, f. *epí* EPI- + *ónuma*, var. stem of *ónoma* NAME; see -OUS.

epopee e·popī epic poem or poetry. XVII (Dryden). – F. *épopée* – Gr. *epopoiíā*, f. *épos* word, song (cf. VOICE) + *poieîn* make (cf. POET). So **epos** e·pɔs. XIX. – L. – Gr.

Epsom salt(s) e·psəm sɔ̀lts. XVIII. orig. the salt obtained from *Epsom water*, the water of a mineral spring at *Epsom* in Surrey.

equable e·kwəbl, ī·kwəbl free from fluctuation or variation. XVII. – L. *æquābilis*, f. *æquāre* make level or equal, f. *æquus*; see next and -ABLE. So **equabi·lity**. XVI. – L.

equal ī·kwəl identical in amount, degree, etc. XIV (Ch.); adequate; uniform XVII. – L. *æquālis*, f. *æquus* level, even (cf. *æquor* level surface, sea). Semi-learned (O)F. *égal* (superseding pop. OF. *ewel*, *ivel*) was adopted in Eng. †*egall* (XIV–XVII). So **equal**ITY ikwɔ·lĭti. XIV (Trev.). – OF. – L. Hence **e·qual**IZE. XVI; partly after F. *égaliser*.

equanimity īkwəni·mĭti, ek- †fairness; evenness of temper. XVII.– L. *æquanimitās*, f. *æquanimis*, f. *æquus*; see prec., ANIMUS, -ITY.

equate ikwei·t average XV; make or treat as equal XVII. f. pp. stem of L. *æquāre*, f. *æquus*; see EQUAL and -ATE[3]. So **equa·**TION. equal partition XIV (Ch., Gower, in astrol., Chauliac in med.); (math.) statement of equality, formula affirming the equivalence of two quantities XVI (Dee, Digges, Billingsley). – (O)F. or L.

equator ikwei·təɹ great circle of the celestial sphere (XIV, Ch.); great circle of the earth XVII. – (O)F. *équateur* or medL. *æquātor*, in full *circulus æquator diei et noctis* circle equalizing day and night (cf. EQUINOCTIAL), f. *æquāre* (see prec.).

equerry ikwe·ri, e·kwəri †A. royal or princely stables. B. †officer in charge of these; (now) officer of the royal household in attendance on a prince. XVI. Of mixed origin; the mod. sp. and pronunc. are due to assoc. with L. *equus* horse. The earliest forms are *esquiry*, *escuirie*, *equirrie*, aphetic *quer(r)y*, *quir(r)y* – F. †*escu(i)rie* (mod. *écurie* stable), corr. to Pr. *escura* stable (medL. *scura*, *scuria*) of unkn. origin; sense B seems to be based on OF. *escuyer d'escuyrie* 'SQUIRE of stables', AN. *esquire de qurye*.

equestrian ikwe·striən pert. to horse-riding; of the order of *equites* XVII; mounted on horseback XVIII. f. L. *equestris* (as in *equestris statua*), f. *eques* horseman, knight, f. *equus* horse; see EQUINE, -IAN. Cf. (O)F. *equestre*. So **eque·stri**AL[1]. XVI. Hence **equestrienne** -ie·n horsewoman. XIX; pseudo-F.; fem. of a supposed **équestrien*.

equi- ī·kwi, e·kwi repr. *æqui-*, comb. form of L. *æquus* EQUAL, used in parasynthetic adjs. for 'equal', 'equally', as in *equi*DI·STANT and *equi*LA·TERAL XVI (Billingsley), *equipo·llent* of equal power XV (Hoccleve), *equipo·llence* equality of power (XIV), EQUIVALENT, EQUIVOCAL, all based on F. and L. forms; so, e.g., *equiangular* having all its angles equal XVII, and nonce-formations such as †*equivaliant* (XVI); **e·qui**POISE (XVII) replaced phr. *equal poise*.

equilibrium īkwili·briəm well-balanced condition. XVII (Boyle). – L. *æquilībrium*, f. *æquus* EQUI-+*lībra* balance (see LIBRATION).

equine e·kwain pert. to a horse. XVIII. – L. *equīnus*, f. *equus* horse, rel. to OE. *eoh*, ON. *jór*, Goth. *aihwa-*, OIr. *ech*, Gr. *híppos*, Skr. *açvás*, Pers. *asp*; see -INE[1].

equinox ī·kwĭnɔks, e·k- time and point at which the sun crosses the equator and day and night are equal. XIV (Ch.). – (partly through (O)F. *équinoxe*) L. *æquinoctium*, in medL. *-noxium* (also formerly used in Eng.), f. *æquus* EQUI-+*noct-*, *nox* NIGHT. So **equino·ct**IAL -ʃəl. XIV (Ch.). – (O)F. *équinoxial* – L. *æquinoctiālis*.

equip ikwi·p fit out. XVI. – F. *équiper*, not recorded in this sense before XVI exc. as in AN. *eskipeson* equipment, medL. *eschipāre* man (a vessel); prob. a different word from OF. *eschiper*, *esquiper* put to sea (so OE. *sċipian*), but like it, prob. – ON. *skipa* man (a vessel), fit up, arrange, f. *skip* SHIP. So **equip**AGE ikwi·pidʒ, e·k †equipment, apparatus; †train of attendants XVI; carriage and horses, orig. with attendant servants XVIII. – F. *équipage*. **equi·p**MENT. XVIII. – F. *équipement*.

equitation ekwitei·ʃən riding on horseback. XVI. – F. *équitation* or L. *equitātiō(n-)*, f. *equitāre*, f. *equit-*, *eques* horseman, f. *equus* horse; see EQUINE, -ATION.

equity e·kwĭti fair dealing XIV; (leg.) 'natural justice' XVI (Lambarde). – (O)F. *équité* = Pr. *equitat*, Sp. *equidad*, It. *equità* – L. *æquitās*, f. *æquus*; see EQUI-, -ITY. So **e·quit**ABLE fair, just XVII (Sir T. Browne); valid in equity XVIII. – F. *équitable*, f. *équité*, with the active meaning of the suffix, as in (e.g.) *charitable*.

equivalent ikwi·vələnt of equal value. XV; sb. XVI; – (O)F. *équivalent* – prp. of late L. *æquivalēre*, f. *æquus* EQUI- + *valēre* (see VALUE). So **equi·val**ENCE, -ENCY. XVI. – (O)F. – medL.

equivocal ikwi·vəkəl †nominal only; capable of twofold interpretation XVII; of doubtful genuineness, questionable XVIII. f. late L. *æquivocus* (Mart. Cap.), f. *æquus* EQUAL + *vocāre* call, name (cf. VOCATION); see -AL[1]. So **equi·voc**ALLY. XVI; after late L. *æquivocē*. **equivocation** ikwivŏkei·ʃən †ambiguous use of words XIV (Wycl.); use of words in a double sense in order to mislead XVII (Sh.). – late L. *æquivocātiō(n-)*, f. *æquivocāre* (whence **equi·vocate** XV), f. *æquivocus*. **e·quivoque** -vouk †equivocal XIV (Wycl. Bible); sb. †thing called by the same name as something else XVI; play on words XVII; ambiguity of speech XIX. – (O)F. *équivoque* or late L. *æquivocus*, f. *æquus* EQUAL + *vocāre* call (see VOCATION). ¶ The unique *equivocas* in Usk's 'Testament of Love' (1387) III is perh. L. (*verba*) *æquivoca* equivocal words, with pl. ending -*s*.

er ə̄ repr. an inarticulate sound interpolated by a hesitant speaker. XIX.

-er[1] əɹ suffix denoting one who or a thing which has to do with something and so the regular formative for agent-nouns; OE. *-ere*, earlier *-eri*, late Nhb. *-are*, corr. to OFris. *-ere*, OS. *-ari*, *-iri* (Du. *-er*), OHG. *-āri*, *-ēre* (MHG. *-ære*, G. *-er*), ON. *-ari*, earlier also *-eri*, Goth. *-areis* :– CGerm. **-arjaz*,

-ǣrjaz*, prob. – L. *-ārius* -ARY, of which an accentual var. with *ă* was perh. evolved. In the early Germ. stage, such a deriv. as Goth. ***laisareis* teacher, from **laisō* LORE, became assoc. with *laisjan* teach, and was apprehended as its agent-noun; thus the model was provided for the universal application of the suffix to vb.-stems, as *bæcere* baker, f. *bacan*, *leornere* learner, f. *leornian*, etc. Some Germ. sbs. seem to be directly based on or suggested by L. agent-nouns formed on sbs.: e.g. OE. *bōcere* scribe = OHG. *buochari*, Goth. *bokareis*, f. **bōk-* BOOK, after L. *librārius* copyist, scribe, f. *liber* book; OS. *mulineri*, MDu. *molenāre* (Du. *molenaar*), OHG. *mulināri* (G. *müller*), ON. *mylnari*, after medL. *molīnārius* miller, f. L. *molīna* MILL; direct formations on sbs. occur in OE., e.g. *sangere* singer, f. *sang* SONG, and continued to be made in ME. and later, e.g. *docker* dweller near docks, worker in a dock, *drover* driver of cattle, *hatter* hat-maker (prob. after F. *chapelier*), *slater* layer of slates, *wheeler* wheelwright. OE. *-ere* finally superseded synon. *-a* and *-end* (cf. *hunta* hunter, *ċīepa* trader, *lufiġend* lover) and its ME. repr. *-er(e)*, *-ar(e)* became established as the universal suffix for new creations of agent-nouns. At various dates in ME. and later *-er* was substituted for other suffixes or added superfluously to sbs. of which the endings did not obviously suggest their function; e.g. *astrologer*, *astronomer* superseded †*astrologien*, †*astronomien*; †*alchemister* was formed from *alchemist*; †*cater*, †*fruiter*, †*huckster*, †*poulter*, †*sorcer* (in all of which the *-er* is of alien origin) were extended to *caterer*, *fruiterer*, †*hucksterer*, *poulterer*, *sorcerer*; a native example is †*upholdster*, which became *upholsterer*; prob. on the model of *philosopher*, derivs. of Gr.-L. words in *-graphus*, *-logus* assumed the forms -GRAPHER, -LOGER; an isolated instance is *widower*, in which *-er* provides a masc. counterpart to *widow*. A var. *-ier* is established in the occupational names *clothier*, *collier*, *glazier*, *grazier*, *hosier*, *spurrier*, and dial. in *drovier*, *lovier*, with *-yer* after *w* in *bowyer*, *lawyer*, *sawyer*, †*tawyer*, *whittawyer*; see -IER[1]. ¶ For *sailor*, etc., and such variations as *exciter/excitor* see -OR[1].

Some ordinary agent-nouns are found in titles of periodicals: *adventurer*, *idler*, *rambler*, *tatler*; others in titles of manuals: *reader*, *reciter*, (ready) *reckoner*, *writer*.

Many agent-nouns, esp. those of occupations, as in other Germ. langs. have a wide currency as surnames, as *Baker*, *Hunter*, *Miller*, *Slater*, *Tiler*, *Wheeler*. Similarly in designations of natives or inhabitants, as *Londoner* (cf. Du. *Londenaar*, G. *Londoner*), *Britisher*, *Tynesider*, *New Zealander*, *Icelander*; so *inlander*, *islander*; *northerner*, *southerner*; *cottager*, *villager*; *foreigner* (prob. after *stranger*), *outlander*.

Some personal designations occur esp. as the fixed second el. of comps.; e.g. charcoal-*burner*, new-*comer*, money-*grubber*, lamp-*lighter*, good-*looker*, on*looker*, iron*monger*, self-*seeker*, back*slider*, care*taker*.

Many formations are applied almost exclusively to inanimate objects, particularly to instruments or implements used in specific operations, as *amplifier*, *blotter*, *boiler*, *burner*, *buzzer*, *cracker*, *cutter*, *decanter*, *dredger*, *duster*, *girder*, *growler* (cab), *hopper*, *knocker*, *lighter*, *pointer*, *poker*, *propeller*, *reaper-and-binder*, *rocker*, *roller*, *runner*, *steamer*, *stopper*, *strainer*, *stretcher*, *winder*; (in pl. form mainly) *clippers*, *dividers*, *pincers*, *tweezers* (cf. *scissors*); of diverse origin are *kneeler* pad for kneeling on, *locker* chest that locks up, *liner* steamer of a line, *revolver* 'revolving pistol'; articles of clothing are *blazer*, *boater*, *jumper*, *pinner*, *reefer* 'reefing jacket', *slipper*, *stomacher*, *sweater*; pl. *drawers*, *trousers*; U.S. *diner*, *sleeper* are for 'dining'/'sleeping compartment'; having non-material reference are *appetizer*, *feeler*, *poser*, *reminder*. There are many colloq. and sl. formations in which *-er* expresses 'one', as *backhander*, *blighter*, *deader*, *forty-niner*, *goner*, *last-ditcher*, *napper*, *out-and-outer*, *peasouper*, *penny-a-liner*, *sixfooter*, *sundowner*, *teen-ager*, *ten-tonner*, *three-decker*, *topper*, *whole-hogger*; *lifer* life-sentence; *oner* one who is 'a one'; so *fiver/tenner* £5-/£10-note. Akin to these are derogatory terms like *blighter*, *bounder*, *rotter*, *soaker*, and terms denoting an uncommonly large specimen, a heavy fall or blow, or a big lie (some have the twofold application), as *banger*, *cropper*, *facer*, *header*, *heeler*, *mucker*, *muzzler*, and *smeller* (blow on the nose), *purler*, *stinger*, *stunner* (stunning blow, 'stunning' person or thing), *whopper*. The sp. *-ar* survives in *beggar*, *liar*, *pedlar*. ¶ Other suffixes disguised under the form *-er* are found in *border*, *bracer*, *counter*, *dresser*, *laver*, and others.

-er[2] əɹ repr., in adoptions from French, (i) OF. *-er* :- L. *-āri-s* -AR, or (ii) AN. *-er*, OF. *-ier* :- L. *-āriu-s*, *-āriu-m* -ARY, used sb. Some ME. exx. in *-er* have been refash. with *-ar* after Latin, as (i) ME. *scoler* (– AN. *escoler*, OF. *escolier*) SCHOLAR; so TEMPLAR; (ii) ME. *coler* (– AN. *coler*, OF. *colier*) COLLAR; so CELLAR, POPLAR. Where the L. suffix is the m. *-ārius*, the word has usu. the sense 'person connected with', as *archer*, *banker*, *butcher*, *butler*, *carpenter*, *draper*, *fletcher*, *gaoler*, *gardener*, *grocer*, *mariner*, *officer*, *verger* (so also a few ME. adoptions of OF. sbs. in *-iere*, viz. *chamberer*, *lavender*); where the L. suffix is n. *-ārium*, the sense is 'thing connected with', 'receptacle for', as *antiphoner*, *censer*, *corner*, *danger*, *garner*, *primer*. See also -IER, -OR[2].

-er[3] əɹ suffix of compar. adjs. and advs. A. In adjs., ME. *-er(e)*, *-re* (occas. vars. *-ore*, *-ure*), from OE. *-ra* m., *-re* fem., n., repr. two Germ. suffixes, (i) **-izon-* (OS., OHG. *-iro*, ON. *-ri*, Goth. *-iza*, accompanied by mutation) and (ii) **-ōzon-* (OHG. *-ōro*, ON. *-ari*, Goth. *-ōza*), which were formed on the advb. suffixes **-iz*, **-ōz* (see below). Mutation was retained in a few OE. compars., as *strang* strong, *strengra*, *sćeort* short, *sćyrtra*; traces persist in *better* :– **batizon-* and *elder* :– **alðizon-*; *worse* and *less* contain the suffix **-izon-* in a disguised form. B. In advs., OE. *-or* = OS., OHG. *-ōr*, Goth. *-ōz* :– CGerm. **-ōz*, beside which there was **-iz* (corr. to L. *-is*, as in *magis* more, *nimis* too much, and cogn. with *-ior* of L. compar. adjs.), repr. by ON. *-r* (with mutation) and Goth. *-is* (e.g. *hauhis* higher), and by the mutation in OE. compars. like *leng* longer :– **laŋgiz*, *bet* better :– **batiz*, which were superseded in ME. by regular forms in *-er*. The advs. that take a compar. in *-er* (as distinct from those that take *more*) are mostly those that are identical with their adjs., e.g. *harder, close, tighter*; exceptions are *seldomer, oftener, sooner*; advs. in -LY[2] normally take *more*, but the older use, which admitted forms like *easilier*, survives in poet. usage, as in *keenlier* (Tennyson).

-er[4] əɹ suffix forming iterative and frequent. vbs.; OE. *-(e)rian* = OFris. *-ria*, OS. *-arōn*, MLG., MDu. *-eren*, OHG. *-arōn*, *-irōn* (G. *-ern*), ON. *-ra* :– CGerm. (exc. Gothic) **-rōjan*. There are a few exx. in OE.: *claterian* CLATTER, *fliceriạn* flutter, hover, FLICKER, *floterian* float, *hwǣstrian* whisper, *sćaterian* SCATTER, SHATTER, *stam(e)rian* STAMMER, *sweþrian*, *swiþrian* subside, cease (cf. SWITHER), *wandrian* WANDER; to some there are corr. adjs., as *gliddrian* slip, beside *gliddor*, *slidrian* SLITHER, beside *sliddor*. The number of such words was greatly increased in ME. and later, partly by analogous formations of an echoic or symbolic kind (sometimes from native bases), partly by direct adoption or assimilation of ON. or LG. verbs; e.g. *blunder, bluster, chatter, clamber, fluster, glimmer, glitter, jabber, mutter, patter, pucker, quaver, quiver, shiver, shudder, snigger, stagger, stutter, swagger, titter, totter, waver*.

-er[5] əɹ ending (*-er* :– L. *-āre*) of a number of AN. infins. (= OF. *-er*, *-ir*, *-eir*, or *-re*), used orig. as sbs. in legal language, mostly of XV or XVI: viz. *cesser, demurrer, detainer, disclaimer, misnomer, non-user, remitter, retainer, trover, user, waiver*; *attainder*, †*detainder*, *(sur)rejoinder*, *remainder*; *tender*; the same ending is in *dinner* and *supper*.

-er[6] əɹ suffix (prob. an extended vague application of -ER[1]) used in Eng. public-school and university sl. formations made by adding it to the first syll. or early sylls. of a word, which are themselves sometimes deformed; e.g. *bedder* bedroom, *bedsitter* bed-sitting room, *cupper* cup-tie (match), *Divvers* Divinity Moderations, *ekker* exercise, *footer* football, *fresher* freshman, *Radder* Radcliffe Camera (Oxford), *rugger / soccer* Rugby / Association football, *Toggers* Torpids (boat-races), *Tosher* unattached student (at Oxford); *Adders* Addison's Walk (Magdalen College, Oxford); there have been casual or transitory uses such as *wagger pagger bagger* waste-paper basket.

era iə·rə system of chronology reckoned from a point of time; date from which a period is reckoned XVII; period or epoch XVIII. – late L. *æra*, orig. pl. of *æs*, *æris* copper, in the sense 'counters (for calculation)', used as fem. sg. for 'number used as a basis of reckoning', 'item of an account', 'epoch from which time is reckoned' (Isidore); see ORE. Cf. Sp., It. *era*, F. *ère* (XVI, *la here de Cesar*). First in Spain and southern Gaul prefixed to the number of years elapsed since B.C. 38 (e.g. *æra* DXXXVIII = A.D. 500); the phr. *æra Hispanica* (Spanish era) suggested to Renaissance scholars the phr. *æra Christiana*, *æra Varroniana*, etc.

eradicate iræ·dikeit pull up by the roots. XVI. f. pp. stem of L. *ērādīcāre*, f. *ē* E-, EX-[1] + *rādic-*, *rādix* ROOT; see -ATE[3].

erase irei·z, irei·s scrape or rub out. XVII. f. *ērās-*, pp. stem of L. *ērādere*, f. *ē* E- + *rādere* scrape (see RASOR). **era·**SER[1], as in *ink-eraser*. XIX. Hence **eras**URE irei·ʒəɹ. XVIII. ¶ perh. in early use partly a var. of *arace*, *arase* – OF. *aracier*, var. of *arachier* (mod. *arracher* tear, snatch) = Pr. *arazigar* :– Rom. **adradīcāre*.

Erastian ėræ·stiən. XVII. f. name of Thomas *Erastus* (Liebler), physician of Heidelberg, Germany (1524–83), whose efforts were directed mainly against the use of excommunication, but to whom has been attributed the theory of the supremacy of the State in ecclesiastical affairs; see -IAN.

ere ɛəɹ (arch.) before (of time). OE. *ǣr* = OFris., OS., OHG. *ēr* (Du. *eer*, G. *eher*), Goth. *airis* :– Germ. **airiz*, compar. of **air* (ON. *ár*, Goth. *air*) early, rel. to Gr. *êri* early (adv.), *ēérios* early (adj.), *áriston* (:– **ajeridtom*) breakfast, Av. *ayarə* day; cf. ERST. Hence **ere**LO·NG before the lapse of much time. XVI. **ere**WHI·LE (arch.) some time ago. OE. *ǣrhwīlum*.

erect ire·kt upright. XIV (Ch.; rare before XVI). – L. *ērectus*, pp. of *ērigere* set up, f. *ē* EX-[1] + *regere* direct (cf. REGAL). So **ere·ct** set up or upright XV; raise *into* XVII. f. *ērect-*, pp. stem of *ērigere*. So **ere·c**TION. XV. – F. or L. **ere·ct**OR[1] one who erects XVI; (anat.) muscle causing erection XIX.

-erel see -REL.

eremite e·rimait (arch.) hermit. XIII. – OF. *eremite*, var. of *(h)ermite* HERMIT. So **eremi**·TIC XV, **eremi**·TICAL XVI. – F. *érémitique*, medL. *erēmiticus*.

erethism e·riþizm unusual or morbid excitement. XVIII. – F. *éréthisme* – Gr. *erethismós*, f. *erethízein*, *eréthein* irritate; see -ISM.

erg ɜ̄ɹg (phys.) centimetre-gramme-second unit of work. XIX (1873). – Gr. *érgon* WORK.

ergo ɜ̄·ɹgou therefore. XIV. L., as prep. in consequence of, absol. consequently; rel. to *ergā* opposite, against, towards.

ergot ɜ̄·ɹgət disease of the seed of rye. XVII. – F. *ergot*, OF. *ar(i)got*, *argor* cock's spur, of unkn. origin.

ericaceous erikei·ʃəs (bot.) pert. to the family Ericaceæ (heaths). XIX. modL., f. L. *erīce* – Gr. *eríkē* (earlier *ereíkē*) heath; see -ACEOUS.

eristic eri·stik controversial. XVII. – Gr. *eristikós*, f. *erízein* wrangle, f. *erid-*, *éris* strife; see -IC.

erl-king ɜ̄·ɹlki·ŋ goblin haunting the Black Forest. XVIII (Scott). Partial tr. of G. *erlkönig* 'elder-king' (first in Herder's 'Stimmen der Völker in Liedern', 1778), misunderstanding of Da. *elle(r)konge* (for *elve(r)konge*) king of elves (see ELF, KING).

ermine ɜ̄·ɹmin stoat XII; fur of this, often having the black tails arrayed upon it XIII; (her.) white with black spots XV. – OF. *(h)ermine* (mod. *hermine*) = Pr. *ermini*, Sp. *armiño*, Pg. *arminho*, prob. :– medL. *(mūs) Armenius* 'Armenian mouse', equiv. to L. *mūs Ponticus* (Pliny) 'mouse of Pontus' (Armenia and Pontus were conterminous); cf. medGr. *muōtós* (f. *mûs* mouse) name of an Armenian garment (Julius Pollux, *c.* 180 A.D.). But contact with similar Germ. words is possible, viz. OHG. *harmīn* adj., f. *harmo* stoat, weasel (G. *harme*) = OE. *hearma* glossing L. *megale* (i.e. *mygale*), rel. to Lith. *šzermuõ* weasel; cf. OHG. *harmilī*, MHG. *hermelīn* (G. *hermelin*), which may be either a deriv. of this, or – Rom. **armelīnus*, whence F. *hermeline*, It. *ermellino*, †*armellino*, Sp. *armelina*. obs. or arch. Eng. *ermelin* (Spenser). So **ermines** (her.) fur with white spots on a black ground. XVI. poss. – OF. *hermines*, pl. of *herminet*, dim. of *hermine*.

-ern əɹn suffix in *eastern*, *western*, *northern*, *southern*; OE. *-erne* = OS., OHG. *-rōni*, ON. *-rœnn* :– Germ. **-rōnjaz*, f. **-ro-* (as in **austro-*; see EAST) + **-ōnjaz* = L. *-āneus* -ANEOUS.

erne ɜ̄ɹn (arch.) eagle. OE. *earn* = MLG. *arn*, *arnt* (Du. *arend*), OHG. *arn*, ON. *ǫrn* :– Germ. **arnuz*, rel. to **aron*, whence OHG. *aro* (G. *aar*), ON. *ari*, Goth. *ara*; cf. Gr. *órnis* bird, OSl. *orĭlŭ*, Lith. *erẽlis*, *ẽras*, W. *eryr*, OIr. *irar*, Corn., Bret. *er* eagle.

erode ėrou·d eat or wear away. XVII. – F. *éroder* or L. *ērōdere*, f. *ē* EX-¹ + *rōdere* gnaw (see RODENT). So **ero**SION ėrou·ʒən. XVI. – F. *érosion* – L. *ērōsiō(n-)*, f. *ērōs-*, pp. stem of *ērōdere*.

erotic ėrɔ·tik pert. to the passion of love. XVII. – F. *érotique* – Gr. *erōtikós*, f. *erōt-*, *érōs* sexual love; see -IC. So **erot**ISM e·routizm. XIX; after F. *érotisme*. **ero·tic**ISM. XIX. **eroto**MA·NIA. XIX.

err ɜ̄ɹ go astray; †roam. XIV (R. Mannyng, Rolle, Ch., Wyclif). – (O)F. *errer* = Pr., Sp. *errar*, It. *errare* :– L. *errāre* :– **ersāre*, rel. to Goth. *airzei* error, *airzjan* lead astray, OS., OHG. *irri* astray, angry (G. *irre*), OE. *ierre* gone astray, perverse, angry. ¶ For anger conceived as wandering from a path cf. L. *dēlīrāre* (see DELIRIUM).

errand e·rənd †message; †mission OE.; business on which one is sent XIII; journey taken to convey a message, etc. XVII. OE. *ǣrende* = OFris. *ērende*, OS. *ārundi*, OHG. *ārunti*, *-onti*, *-andi* :– Germ. **ǣrundjam*, obscurely rel. to synon. ON. *eyrindi*, *ørindi*, *erindi* (Sw. *ärende*, Da. *ærinde*) :– Germ. **arundjam*; neither type can be reconciled with the otherwise plausible connexion with OE. *ār*, OS. *ēru*, ON. *árr*, Goth. *airus* messenger.

errant e·rənt A. travelling in quest of adventure, as in *knight errant* XIV; †(leg.) itinerant, in eyre XV; B. †thorough (see ARRANT); C. wandering, straying XV. – (O)F. *errant*, in which two distinct words have coalesced: (i) prp. of OF. *errer*, earlier †*edrer* travel as in quest of adventure (*chevalier errant* knight errant) :– Rom. **iterāre*, for L. *itinerāre* ITINERATE, f. *iter* journey; (ii) prp. of (O)F. *errer* wander, ERR. In C – L. *errant-*, *-āns*, prp. of *errāre*. So **error** e·rəɹ false belief XIII; mistake, wrongdoing XIV; wandering XVI. – OF. *errour*, *errur* (mod. *erreur*) = Pr., Sp. *error*, It. *errore* :– L. *errōrem*, nom. *error* :– **ersor* (see ERR). As with *horror*, *mirror*, *terror*, the sp. continued to vacillate between *-or* and *-our* till *c.* 1800. **erratic** ėræ·tik †wandering, vagrant XIV (Ch., *erratike sterres*, tr. L. *stellæ errantes*, Gr. ἀστέρες πλανῆται planets); (geol.) stray; eccentric or irregular in conduct XIX. – (O)F. *erratique* – L. *errāticus*, f. *errāt-*, pp. stem of *errāre* ERR; see -IC. So **erratum** ėrei·təm error made in writing or printing. XVI. sb. use of n. pp. of *errāre*. ¶ In XVII–XVIII *errata* was used as a sg. with pl. *erratаes*, *errata's*. **erroneous** ėrou·niəs wrong, faulty XIV (Usk); †straying XV. – OF. *erroneus* or f. L. *errōneus* (whence F. *erroné*), f. *errō(n-)* vagabond, f. *errāre*; see -EOUS.

ersatz ɛ̄·ɹzats substitute or imitation. XX. G. 'compensation', 'replacement', f. *ersetzen* replace, f. *er-*, unstressed var. of *ur-* = OFris., OS. *ur-*, *or-*, OE. *or-* + *setzen* SET¹.

Erse ɜ̄ɹs Irish, esp. applied to Irish and Scotch Gaelic. XIV (*ersche*). Early Sc. var. of IRISH.

erst ɜ̄ɹst †earliest, first, (arch.) formerly, before. Also **arst** (XIV–XV). OE. *ǣrest*, superl. corr. to *ǣr* ERE = OS. *ērist* (Du. *eerst*), OHG. *ērist* (G. *erst*) :– WGerm. **airista* (see -EST). Hence **e·rst-**WHILE. XVI (Spenser). after *erewhile*.

erubescent erubeˑsənt blushing. XVIII. – L. *ērubēscent-*, *-ēns*, prp. of *ērubēscere*, f. *ē* EX-¹ + *rubēscere*, f. *rubēre* be RED; see -ESCENT.

eructate irʌ·kteit belch. XVII. f. pp. stem of L. *ēructāre*, f. *ē* E- + *ructāre* belch, rel. to REEK; see -ATE³. So **eruct**A·TION. XV. – L.

erudite e·rʲudait learned. XV. – L. *ērudītus*, pp. of *ērudīre*, f. *ē* EX-¹ + *rudis* RUDE; see -ITE. So **erudi**·TION. XV. – (O)F. or L.

eruption irʌ·pʃən breaking or bursting forth, outbreak. XV. – (O)F. *éruption* or L. *ēruptio(n-)*, f. *ērupt-*, *ērumpere*, f. *ē* EX-[1] + *rumpere* break; see RUPTURE, -TION. So **eru·pt.** XVII. f. L. *ērupt-*; or a back-formation. **eru·pt**IVE. XVII; cf. F. *éruptif*.

-ery əri suffix first occurring (ME. *-erie*, *-erye*) in adoptions from French and subsequently used on the analogy of these in formations on various kinds of base. (O)F. *-erie*, which superseded *-ie* -Y[3] as a living formative, arose from the addition of *-ie* to personal designations in *-(i)er*, *-eur*, to denote quality, condition, action, occupation, or calling; e.g. *archerie* ARCHERY, f. *archer*; *chevalerie* CHIVALRY, f. *chevalier*; *flatterie* FLATTERY, f. *flatteur*. Such comps. came to be apprehended as directly rel. to the ult. base, as *chevalerie* to *cheval* horse; consequently, formations on various kinds of sb. were made, e.g. *diablerie* devilry on *diable* devil, *imagerie* IMAGERY on *image*, *juiverie* JEWRY on *juif* Jew, *loterie* LOTTERY on *lot*; this was extended to adjs., as *effronterie* EFFRONTERY on *effronté*, *sauvagerie* SAVAGERY, and to vbs. as *batterie* BATTERY on *battre*; and the practice was followed in Eng. formations, as *deanery*, *drudgery*, *gunnery*, *slavery*, *thievery*. The suffix enters into many sbs. having a derogatory or contemptuous reference as *buffoonery*, *foolery*, *flummery*, *frippery*, *monkery*, *popery*, *quackery*, *waggery*. The suffix came to be esp. assoc. with -ER[1] and -ER[2], so that all agent-nouns in *-er* have actually or potentially a deriv. in *-ery* denoting condition, occupation, etc., e.g. *bookbindery*, *drapery*, *drysaltery*, *grocery*, *joinery*, *millinery*; hence, by extension, in designations of premises, establishments, environment, fittings, etc., as *bakery*, *crockery*, *deanery*, *machinery*, *nursery*, *orangery*, *ostlery*, *piggery*, *rookery*, *scenery*, *surgery*, *swannery*, *vinery*; the pl. *-eries* is used also beside the sg. in names of wares, as *groceries* (XVII). In some cases it is transferred to the place of manufacture, e.g. *The Potteries* (see POTTERY), on the model of which *The Dukeries* has been applied to an area of Nottinghamshire and Derbyshire containing several ducal seats. The title of the *Fisheries* Exhibition of 1883 led to a colloq. use of *Healtheries* for the later Health Exhibition and of *Colinderies* for the Colonial and Indian Exhibition. See also the reduced var. -RY. ¶ A few F. words in *-erie* have been adopted in recent times, e.g. *causerie*, *lingerie*.

eryngo èri·ŋgou sea holly, Eryngium maritimum; †candied root of this. XVI (Sh.). irreg. – It. or Sp. *eringio* – L. *ēryngium* – Gr. *ērúggion*, dim. of *ḗruggos*.

erysipelas erisi·pələs local febrile disease with red inflammation. XVI (XIV–XV *erisipila*). – L. – Gr. *erusípelas*, perh. f. base of *eruthrós* RED (cf. *erusíbē* red blight) + **pel-* skin, FELL[1].

erythema eriþī·mə inflammation of the skin. XVIII. modL. – Gr. *erúthēma*, f. *eruthaínein* be red, f. *eruthrós* RED.

erythro- èri·þrou comb. form of Gr. *eruthrós* RED, mainly in chem. terms. XIX.

es- prefix occurring in adoptions from OF. with initial *es-* :– L. *ex-* EX-[1]; a few survive with this element unchanged, as *escape*, *escort*; others have been refash. with *ex-*, as *exchange* for *eschange*. ¶ To be distinguished from *es-* produced by the prothesis of *e* to *s* + cons., as in *especial*, *esquire*, *estate*.

escalade eskəlei·d scaling the walls of a fortified place. XVI (Florio). – F. *escalade* – Sp. *escalado* (also used in Eng. XVI–XIX) = It. *scalata*, f. medL. *scalāre* SCALE vb.; see -ADE.

escalator e·skəleitəɹ moving staircase. XX. orig. U.S., f. stem of prec. + -ATOR.

escallop èskæ·ləp, early form of SCALLOP.

escape èskei·p gain one's liberty by flight; get away from. XIV (R. Mannyng, Rolle). The earliest recorded forms are *ascape* and (aphetic) *scape* (– AN., ONF. *ascaper*), with occas. accommodated forms *atscape*, *ofscape*; vars. of this type, *aschape*, *achape* (– OF. *aschaper*), aphetic *schape*, *chape*, were frequent in XIV; the present form is – AN., ONF. *escaper* (mod. *échapper*) = Pr., Sp., Pg. *escapar*, It. *scappare*, Rum. *scăpa* :– CRom. **excappāre*, f. L. *ex* EX-[1] + medL. *cuppa* cloak (see CAP); for the sense-development cf. Gr. ἐκδύειν strip of clothing, get out of, escape. So **esca·pe** sb. (XIII) XIV. in earliest use – OF. *eschap*, f. *eschaper*; later f. the vb. **escap**ADE eskəpei·d escape, runaway flight XVII; flighty piece of conduct XIX (Scott). – F. *escapade* – Pr. or Sp. *escapada*, f. *escapar*. **escap**EE· one who has escaped. XIX. – F. *échappé*, sb. use of pp. **esca·pe**MENT in a clock or watch. XVIII (earlier *scapement*; cf. *scape pinion*, *wheel*). – F. *échappement* (1718), f. *échapper*; the ref. is to the 'escape' of the toothed wheel from its detention by the pallet. In the sense 'escape' XIX (Hood, Froude, George Eliot).

escarpment èskā·ɹpmənt (fortif.) ground cut to form a steep slope; (geol.) abrupt face of a ridge or hill range. XIX. – F. *escarpement*, f. *escarper*; see SCARP, -MENT.

-escent e·sənt suffix repr. F. *-escent* and its source L. *-ēscentem*, nom. *-ēscēns*, prp. ending of vbs. in *-ēscere*, chiefly inceptives f. vbs. of state in *-ēre*, e.g. *liquēscere*, f. *liquēre* be LIQUID; primarily occurring in adjs. – L. prps. (orig. through F.), as *deliquescent*, *effervescent*, *obsolescent*, *putrescent*, the gen. sense being 'beginning to assume a certain state'; later used to form adjs. on sbs., as *alkalescent*, f. *alkali*, and in several words describing the play of light and colour, as *fluorescent*, *iridescent*, *opalescent*, *phosphorescent*. The corr. suffix of the nouns of state is **-escence** e·səns, less freq. **-escency** e·sənsi.

eschalot see SHALLOT.

eschatology eskətɔ·lədʒi theology of 'the four last things' (Death, Judgment, Heaven, Hell). XIX. f. Gr. *éskhatos* last (perh. f. *ex* EX-²)+-OLOGY.

escheat istʃī·t lapsing of an estate to the overlord, estate so lapsed. XIV. – OF. *eschete* :– **excadecta*, sb. use of pp. of Rom. **excadēre* (OF. *escheoir*, mod. *échoir*, Pr. *escazer* fall out, happen, Sp. *escaecer*, Pg. *esquecer* forget, be forgotten), for L. *excidere* fall away, escape, pass away, escape the memory, forget, f. *ex* EX-¹+*cadere* fall (see CASE¹). Hence **eschea·t** vb. XIV. So **eschea·tor**¹. XIV. – AN. *eschetour*. Cf. CHEAT.

eschew istʃū· avoid, shun. XIV. – OF. *eschiver* (mod. *esquiver* – It.) = Pr., Sp. *esquivar* (whence It. *schivare*) :– Rom. **skivāre* – Germ. **skeuχ(w)an* (OHG. *sciuhen*, G. *scheuen*), f. **skeuχ(w)az* SHY¹.

eschscholtzia eʃɔ·ltsiə, (pop.) ėskɔ·ltʃə California poppy. XIX. modL., named 1821 by A. v. Chamisso after J. F. v. *Eschscholtz*; see -IA¹.

escort e·skōɹt armed guard or convoy XVI; accompanying person or persons XVIII. – F. *escorte* – It. *scorta*, sb. use of fem. pp. of *scorgere* guide, conduct :– Rom. **excorrigere*, f. *ex* EX-¹+*corrigere* set in order, CORRECT¹. So **esco·rt** vb. XVIII. – F. *escorter* – It. *scortare*.

escritoire eskritwā·ɹ writing-desk. XVIII. – OF. *escritoire* orig. m. in sense 'study' (mod. *écritoire*) :– L. SCRIPTORIUM. ¶ Also †*escruto(i)re*; the aphetic forms †*scrito(i)re*, †*scrutore*, are earlier (XVII).

escrow ėskrou· (leg.) species of deed. XVI. – AN. *escrowe*, OF. *escroe* :– medL. *scrōda* – Germ. **skrauđ-* SHRED.

esculent e·skjŭlənt suitable for food. XVII. – L. *ēsculentus*, f. *ēsca* food (:– **ēdsqā*), f. **ed-* of *edere* EAT; see -ULENT.

escutcheon ėskʌ·tʃən (her.) shield. XV. – AN., ONF. *escuchon* (OF. *escusson*, mod. *écusson*) :– Rom. **scūtiōnem*, f. *scūtum* shield.

-ese ī·z suffix (always stressed) repr. OF. *-eis* (mod. *-ois*, *-ais*) = Pr., Sp. *es*, Pg. *-es*, It. *-ese* – L. *-ēnsem* (nom. *-ēnsis*), which meant 'belonging to, originating in (a place)', as *hortēnsis*, f. *hortus* garden, *prātēnsis*, f. *prātum* meadow, and in many adjs. of local names, as *Athēniēnsis* Athenian, f. *Athēnæ* Athens. As a living suffix it forms derivs. of names of countries modelled usu. on Rom. prototypes, as *Chinese*, *Japanese*, *Portuguese* (F. *chinois*, *japonais*, *portugais*) and from some names of foreign towns, as *Cantonese*, *Pekinese*, *Milanese*, *Viennese*. Such adjs. are used sb. as names of languages or as designations of peoples; in the latter use formerly with pl. in *-eses*, but now the pl. form is the same as the sg. From words in *-ese* used as pl. illiterate or joc. sg. back-formations have been made, as *Chinee*, *Maltee*, *Portugee*. A frequent mod. application of the suffix is to the diction of authors who are alleged to write a language of their own, as *Carlylese*, *Johnsonese*; modelled on these are *journalese*, *newspaperese*, *guide-bookese*.

esemplastic esemplæ·stik unifying. XIX (Coleridge). irreg. f. Gr. *es* (*eis*) into +*hén*, n. of *heîs* ONE+*plastikós* PLASTIC, after G. *ineinsbildung* unification (Schelling, 1803). ¶ Preceded by the etymol. correct forms *eisenoplasty*, *esenoplastic* in 1810.

Eskimo, (formerly) **Esquimaux** e·skimou member of an American race of Indians inhabiting the Arctic coast. XVIII. – Da. *Eskimo* (Sw. *Eskimå*) – F. *Esquimaux* pl. – N. Amer. Indian word (cf. Abnaki *Eskimantsic*, Ojibway *Ashkimeq*) meaning 'eaters of raw flesh' (cf. Cree *aski* raw, *mow* he eats).

esophagus see ŒSOPHAGUS.

esoteric esoute·rik pert. to the initiated)(*exoteric*. XVII. – Gr. *esōterikós* (Lucian, attributing to Aristotle a classification of his own works into 'esoteric' and 'exoteric'), f. *esōtérō* inner, compar. of *ésō* within, f. *es* (*eis*) into; see IN¹, -THER, -IC.

espalier ėspæ·liəɹ framework for training trees on; fruit-tree so trained. XVII. – F. *espalier* – It. *spalliera* applied to supports for the shoulders, hence to stakes of that height, f. *spalla* shoulder (SPATULA).

esparto espā·ɹtou Spanish grass, Stipa tenacissima. XVIII. – Sp. *esparto* :– L. *spartum* – Gr. *spárton*.

especial ėspe·ʃəl special. XIV (Ch.). – OF. *especial* – L. *speciālis*, f. *speciēs* SPECIES; cf. SPECIAL. Hence **espe·cially**². XVI.

Esperanto espəræ·ntou name of an artificial language invented by L. L. Zamenhof, who brought out 'Langue Internationale, préface et manuel complet' at Warsaw in 1887 under the pen-name of Dr. *Esperanto* (i.e. 'hoping one'); appeared as the name of the language first in 1889.

espionage e·spiənidʒ, espiənā·ʒ, ėspai·ənidʒ spying. XVIII. – F. *espionnage*, f. *espionner*, f. *espion* SPY.

esplanade esplənei·d open level space. XVII. – F. *esplanade* – Sp. *esplanada*, f. *esplanar* :– L. *explānāre* flatten out, level; see EXPLAIN, -ADE.

espousal ėspau·zəl marriage, betrothal. XIV (also in aphetic form *spousal* XIV). – OF. *espusaile*, chiefly *espousailles* fem. pl. (mod. *épousailles*) = Pr. *esposalhas*, OSp. *esposayas* :– L. *spōnsālia*, sb. use of n. pl. of *spōnsālis*, f. *spōnsus* SPOUSE; see -AL². So **espou·se** marry XV; †betroth; adopt, embrace (opinions) XVII. – OF. *espouser* (mod. *épouser*) = Pr. *espozar*, etc. :– L. *spōnsāre*, f. *spōns-*, *spondēre* betroth (see SPONSOR).

esprit esprī· intellect, nous. XVI. F. :– L. *spīritus* SPIRIT.

espy ėspai· †spy upon; descry. XIV. – OF. *espier* (mod. *épier*); see SPY.

-esque e·sk suffix forming adjs., repr. F. *-esque* – It. *-esco* :– Rom. **-iscus* – Germ. **-iskaz* -ISH[1]; in adoptions from It. through F. in the basic sense of 'resembling the style of, partaking of the characteristics of', as in *arabesque, burlesque, Dantesque, grotesque, picaresque, picturesque, romanesque.* It. *-esco* is freely added to names of artists, whence by imitation *Claudesque, Giottesque, Titianesque, Turneresque,* and many nonce-formations on authors' names, as *Browningesque, Kiplingesque, Shawesque.*

Esquimaux see ESKIMO.

esquire èskwaiə·ɹ young man attending on a knight; man ranking immediately below a knight XV; as a title XIV. Early forms *esquyer, -ier* – OF. *esquier* (mod. *écuyer*) = Pr. *escudier* (whence It. *scudiere*, etc.) :– L. *scūtāriu-s* shield-bearer, f. *scūtum* shield (cf. ÉCU). Aphetic SQUIRE is earlier.

ess es pl. *esses* e·siz (as in *Collar of Esses*) the letter S. XVI.

-ess[1] ès suffix forming sbs. denoting female persons and animals – (O)F. *-esse* = Pr. *-esa*, Sp. *-esa, -isa*, Pg. *-eza, -iza, †-essa*, Rum. *-easă* :– CRom. **-essa*, for late L. *-issa* – Gr. *-issa* (:– **-ikjā*; cf. OE. fem. suffix *-iċġe* :– **-igjōn*), as in *basílissa* queen (f. *basileús* king), but esp. in late formations, as *balánissa* bathing-woman, *diakónissa* DEACONESS, on the model of which were formed *abbātissa* ABBESS, and the like. Thence the suffix became generalized for the formation of fem. derivs. of masc. sbs., e.g. F. *comtesse* (f. *comte*), whence Eng. *countess*, and similarly *duchess, hostess, lioness, mistress, princess.* In OF. *-esse* was added to mascs. in *-ere, -eor*, e.g. *enchanteresse* enchantress; so in ME. *-ess* was added to agent-nouns in *-er* and *-ster*, as *†dwelleress, huntress* (Ch.), *seamstress, songstress*, contraction taking place where possible; the older *†governeresse* was reduced to *governess*; similarly we have *adventuress, †conqueress, murderess*; there are several cases of sbs. in *-tor* with fems. in *-tress* (e.g. *actress, benefactress, traitress*), with the result that this ending corr. to F. *-trice*, L. *-trix*. There was gen. extension to other kinds of sb., as *authoress, giantess, goddess, heroess, Jewess, mayoress, poetess, prioress, quakeress, tailoress*, for some of which, however, there are F. models; some have mascs. in *-er, -or*, as *cateress, procuress, sorceress*; *votary* gives *votaress.*

-ess[2] es ME. *-esse* – (O)F. *-esse, †-ece* = Pr. *-ez(z)a*, Sp. *-eza*, It. *-ezza*, Rum. *-eață* :– L. *-itia* (of disputed origin), forming sbs. of quality or condition, as *trīstitia* sadness, f. *trīstis* sad; examples are DURESS, *†humblesse*, LARGESS, *†nobless*, PROWESS, *†richesse* RICHES, all adopted from French, on the analogy of which Spenser formed pseudo-arch. *idlesse.*

essart var. of ASSART.

essay esei· †try, test XV (Caxton); try *to do* XVI; attempt, try to accomplish XVII. Alteration of ASSAY by assim. to F. *essayer* = Pr. *essayar, assajar*, Sp. *ensayar*, It. *(as)saggiare* :– Rom. **exagiāre* weigh, f. late L. *exagium* weighing, balance, f. *exag-*, base of L. *exigere* weigh (cf. EXAMINE). So **essay** e·sei sb. trial, attempt, result of this; form of literary composition. XVI. – (O)F. *essai*, f. *essayer*; whence also It. *saggio*, Sp. *ensayo*, Pg. *ensaio*. Hence **e·ssay**IST. XVII (Chapman, B. Jonson); whence F. *essayiste* (Goncourt), Sp. *ensayista.* ¶ The title of Francis Bacon's 'Essayes | Religious Meditations | Places of perswasion and disswasion', 1597, was adopted from 'Les Essais de Michel seigneur de Montaigne', 1580. Montaigne's application of *essai* varies (cf. 'aux Essais que i'en fay ici' [i.e. de mon iugement]', bk. I, ch. i, and 'Toute cette fricassee que ie barbouille ici n'est qu'vn registre des essais [i.e. experiences] de ma vie', bk. III, ch. xiii; but, presumably because of the content and character of M.'s work, his title was taken by Bacon to mean 'dispersed Meditacions', which is his own description of Seneca's Epistles in the 1607–12 MS. of the 'Essayes'.

esse e·si being, essence. XVI. L. inf. (see BE); used as sb. by the schoolmen. Cf. BENE ESSE.

essence e·səns (theol.) substance XIV; †existence, being XVI; that by which a thing is what it is; chemical (etc.) extract of a substance; perfume XVII. – (O)F. *essence*, corr. to Pr. *essentia*, Sp. *esencia*, It. *essenza* – L. *essentia* (Quintilian, Seneca), f. **essent-*, assumed prp. stem of *esse* be, on the model of Gr. *ousíā*, f. *ont-*, prp. stem of *eînai* be. So **essent**IAL èse·nʃəl. XIV (R. Rolle, Trevisa). – late L. *essentiālis* (Augustine); cf. F. *essentiel*, Pr. *essencial*, etc.

Essene esī·n one of an ascetic and mystical Jewish sect. XVI. – L. pl. *Essēnī* – Gr. *Essēnoí*, presumably of Heb. or Aram. origin.

essoi(g)n esoi·n (leg.) excuse for non-appearance. XIV. – OF. *essoine, essoigne*, f. *essoi(g)ner* :– medL. *exsoniāre*, f. *ex* EX-[1]+ *sonia* lawful excuse – OHG. *sunnia* hindrance = OS. *sunnea* want, lack, ON. *syn* refusal, denial, Goth. *sunja* (recorded only in the sense 'truth'; but cf. *sunjon* vb. excuse), perh. rel. to SIN. So **essoi·n** vb. XV. – OF. *essoignier.*

-est ist suffix forming the superl. of adjs. and advs., repr. two orig. distinct forms: (i) OE. *-ost-, -ust-, -ast-*, corr. to OFris., ON. *-ast-*, OS., OHG., Goth. *-ōst-* :– CGerm. **-ōstaz*; (ii) OE. *-est-, -st-*, with mutation of stem, corr. to OFris., OS., OHG., Goth. *-isto-* :– CGerm. **-istaz.* These two suffixes are comps. of two compar. suffixes, viz. **-ōz-* and **-iz-* (see -ER[3]), with IE. **-to-*, for which there are parallels in Gr. *-isto-*, Skr. *-ishṭha-*. The conditions of the use of *-est* as opp. to that of *most* are similar to those obtaining for -ER[3] and *more*; adjs. in -OUS are a special case, forms like *mervellousest* and *preposterousest* (Butler's 'Hudibras') being mainly occas., and contr. forms like *merveilloust* being regular in XIV–XV and sometimes later.

establish èstæ·bliʃ settle XIV (Ch.); set up and settle XV; install XVI; prove valid XVIII. – *establiss-*, lengthened stem of OF. *establir* (mod. *établir*) = Pr. *establir*, It. *stabilire* – L. *stabilīre*, f. *stabilis* STABLE[2]; see -ISH[2]. Hence **esta·blish**MENT. XV (Caxton). ¶ Aphetic *stablish* is earlier.

estafette estəfe·t mounted courier. XVII. F., – It. *staffetta*, dim. of *staffa* stirrup – Langobardic **staffa* STEP.

estaminet estæ·minei café. XIX (Thackeray). F., – Walloon *staminé* manger, cowhouse, f. *stamō* pole to which a cow is fastened beside the manger in a stall, prob. – G. *stamm* STEM, trunk.

estancia estæ·nsiə, -þia cattle-farm. XVIII. Sp., 'station' = OF. *estance*, It. *stanza* :– medL. *stantia*, f. L. *stant-*, *stāns*, prp. of *stare* STAND. Earlier †*estancion* (XVII), blending of this with Sp. *estacion* STATION.

estate èstei·t (arch.) state, condition, status XIII (AncrR.); outward pomp XIV; class of the body politic XV; interest in property XV; property, possessions XVI; landed property XVIII. Early forms *aestat*, *astat(e)*, *estat* – OF. *estat* (mod. *état*) = Pr. *estat*, Sp. *estado*, It. *stato* – L. *status*, f. *stat-*, pp. stem of *stare* STAND. ¶ Aphetic STATE.

esteem èstī·m A. †value, assess XV (Love); hold in (such-and-such) estimation XVI; B. †judge of XV (Fortescue); account, consider XVI. Earlier forms *estyme*, *esteme*, also *ex-* (as in OF.) – (O)F. *estimer* = Pr., Sp. *estimar*, It. *stimare* – L. *æstimāre* (orig.) fix the price of, estimate, the phonetic repr. of which in F. was †*esmer* (see AIM). The unexpl. ME. development of ĭ to ē, whence mod. ī, is paralleled in *redeem*. So **estee·m** sb. XIV; also aphetic †*steem* (XIV). – (O)F. *estime*. **e·stim**ABLE. XVI. – F. – L. **estimate** e·stimeit †judge, esteem XVI; †value, assess; form an approximate notion of XVII. f. pp. stem of L. *æstimāre*, *-umāre*. Hence, or poss. – L. *æstimātus*, **estimate** sb. e·stimət. XVI. So **estim**A·TION. XIV (Wycl. Bible, Ch.). – (O)F. or L.

ester e·stəɹ (chem.) compound formed by the combination of an acid and an alcohol with elimination of water. XIX. – G. *ester* (Gmelin), arbitrary modification of ETHER, perh. recalling the sound of G. *essigäther*, repr. the group.

estop èstɔ·p stop, esp. in law. XV. – AN., OF. *estop(p)er*, *estouper*; see STUFF. So **estoppel** èstɔ·pəl (leg.) impediment, bar XVI; †obstruction XVII. – OF. *estoup(p)ail*, f. *estouper*; see -AL[2].

estovers èstou·vəɹz (leg.) necessaries allowed by law. XV. pl. of AN. *estover*, sb. use of *estover*, OF. *estoveir*, based on L. *est opus* (cf. ORum. *op este*) it is necessary. Aphetic †*stover* provision of food (XIII).

estrade estrā·d dais. XVII. – F. *estrade* fem., – Sp. *estrado* m. (which was adopted earlier XVI) carpeted part of a room, drawing-room, reception room = Pr. *estrado*, It. *strato* :– L. *strātum* STRATUM.

estrange èstrei·nᵈʒ make strange or a stranger of, alienate. XV. – AN. *estraunger*, OF. *estranger* (mod. *étranger*) = Pr. *estranhar*, Sp. *estrañar*, It. *stranare* :– L. *extrāneāre*, f. *extrāneus* STRANGE.

estray èstrei· stray animal. XVI. – AN. *estray*, f. *estraier*, whence **estray·** vb. XVI. Aphetic STRAY.

estreat èstrī·t (leg.) true copy or note of a document. XIV (first in aphetic form †*strete*). – AN. *estrete*, OF. *estraite*, sb. use of fem. pp. of *estraire* :– L. *extrahere* EXTRACT. Hence **estrea·t** vb. XVI.

estridge[1] e·stridʒ †ostrich XV; ostrich down XIX. – OF. **estruche*, *estruce* (= Pr. *estrus*), var. of *ostruce* OSTRICH.

estridge[2] e·stridʒ goshawk. XIV. ME. *estriche*, ? modification of medL. *asturcus*, *ostric(i)us*, f. late L. *astur*. Cf. OSTRINGER.

estuary e·stjuəri tidal inlet or mouth of a river. XVI. – L. *æstuārium* tidal part of a shore, tidal channel, sb. use (sc. *litus* shore) of n. of **æstuārius* tidal, f. *æstus* swell, surge, tide; see -ARY.

esurient isjuə·riənt hungry. XVII. – L. *ēsurient-*, *-ēns*, prp. of *ēsurīre* be hungry, desiderative vb. f. *ēs-*, pp. stem of *edere* EAT; see -ENT.

-et it suffix forming dims. from sbs., repr. (O)F. *-et* m., *-ette* fem., corr. to Pr. *-et*, *-eta*, Sp. *-ito*, *-ita*, It. *-etto*, *-etta* :– CRom. **-itto*, **-itta*, **-ētto*, *-a*, of unkn. (perh. non-L.) origin; it occurs in many adoptions from French, as *budget*, *bullet*, *crotchet*, *fillet*, *gibbet*, *gullet*, *hatchet*, *mallet*, *pocket*, *pullet*, *sonnet*, *tablet*, *turret*, in most of which there is no longer any consciousness of a dim. force. It became an Eng. formative from XVI, e.g. †*hillet*, *smilet*. The distinction between masc. and fem. suffixes was rarely shown even in ME.; but the sp. *-ete* occas. occurs, e.g. *polete* PULLET; in adoptions of XVI and XVII *-et* often repr. F. *-ette*, e.g. *facet*; cf. *epaulet(te)*. For its use in adjs. see *dulcet*, *russet*, *violet*. The combination in OF. of *-et* with *-el* produced *-elet*, for which see -LET.

etacism ī·təsizm 'Erasmian' pronunciation of Gr. η as ē or ɛ̄. XIX. f. Gr. *êta* name of η + -ISM, with *c* after *labdacism*.

et cetera ètse·t(ə)rə and the rest. late OE. L., *et* and, *cētera* (often *cætera*) the rest, n. pl. of *cēterus* remaining over, perh. f. pronominal stem, or **cae* (= Gr. *kaí*) and + **etero-* other (cf. Umbrian *etru, etram, etraf*).

etch etʃ engrave by 'eating away' the surface with corrosives. XVII. – Du. *etsen* – G. *ätzen* (OHG. *azzen, ezzen*) :- Germ. **atjan*, causative of **etan* EAT.

eternal itə̄·ɹnəl infinite in duration. XIV (*eterneel*, Ch.). – OF. *eternal, -el* (mod. *éternel*) = Pr., Sp. *eternal*, It. *eternale* – late L. *æternālis*, f. *æternus*, for **æviternus*, f. *ævum* age (cf. ÆON); see -AL[1]. So (arch.) **ete·rne.** XIV (Ch.). – OF. *eterne* – L. *æternus*. **ete·rn**ITY. XIV (Ch.). – (O)F. – L.

etesian ėtī·ʒ[i]ən name of certain winds in the Mediterranean area blowing from the NW. for a certain period annually. XVII (Holland). f. L. *etēsius* – Gr. *etḗsios* annual, f. *etes-*, (ϝ)*étos* year; see VETERAN, -IAN.

eth- eþ first part of ETHER used in the formation of names of members of the bicarbon series of hydrocarbons, *ethane, ethene, ethyl* (earlier *ethule*, the form used by Berzelius, inventor of the name); see -ANE[2], -ENE, -YL.

-eth[1] iþ in *twentieth* to *ninetieth*: see -TH[2].

-eth[2] eþ suffix repr. AN. *-et*, OF. *-e(i)t* :- L. *-ātem*, nom. *-ās* (see -Y[4]), as in ME. *bounteþ* BOUNTY, *dainteþ* (XIII) DAINTY, Sc. *purteth* (XVI), later *poortith* POVERTY. ¶ *Pasteth, -yth* in vocabularies of XV appear to be analogical alterations of *pasty*.

Ethanim e·þənim seventh month of the Jewish year (October–November). XVI. Heb. (*yéraḥ hā*) *ēthānīm* month of steady-flowing rivers (*ēthān* ever-flowing).

ether ī·þəɹ clear sky; (phys.) substance permeating space XVII; (chem.) liquid obtained by the action of acid on alcohol XVIII. – (O)F. *éther* or L. *æthēr* – Gr. *aithḗr* upper air, f. base of *aithein* kindle, burn, shine, *aithrā* fine weather, L. *æstās* summer, OIr. *aed* fire. So **ethere**AL[1] iþiə·riəl of the ether; heavenly; airy XVI; impalpable XVII; pert. to ether XVIII. f. L. *æthereus, ætherius* – Gr. *aithérios*. Hence **ethe·real**IZE. XIX.

ethic e·þik adj. pert. to morals XV (now mostly repl. by **e·thical** XVII). – F. *éthique* (Montaigne, 1580) or L. *ēthicus* – Gr. *ēthikós*, f. *êthos*; sb. sg. moral science XIV, after (O)F. *éthique* (XIII), L. *ēthicē*, Gr. (*hē*) *ēthikḗ* (sc. *tékhnē*) XIV; **e·thics** pl. XV; after OF. *étiques*, medL. *ēthica* n. pl. – Gr. *tà ēthiká*. See -IC, -ICAL, -ICS. So **ethos** ī·þɔs characteristic spirit, settled character. XIX. – late L. (Sidon.) – Gr. *êthos* usage, character, personal disposition, f. IE. **swedh-*, f. refl. pron. **swe-* oneself + **dhē-* place, DO[1].

Ethiopian īþiou·piən pert. to Ethiopia; native of Ethiopia, †blackamoor. XIII. f. *Ethiopia, Æthiopia*, f. *Æthiops* Ethiopian, – Gr. *Aithíops*, f. *aíthein* burn, *ṓps* face (see EYE); see -IAN. The earlier form was *Ethiop* (XIV) – L. *Æthiops*. So **Ethiop**IC -ɔ·pik. XVII. – L. – Gr.

ethnic e·þnik †Gentile, pagan XIV; pert. to race XIX. – ecclL. *ethnicus* (whence F. *ethnique*) heathen – Gr. *ethnikós*, f. *éthnos* nation (ecclGr. *tà éthnē* the nations, the Gentiles, rendering Heb. *gōyīm*, pl. of *gōy* nation, esp. non-Israelitish nation). So **ethno·**GRAPHY, **-o·**LOGY XIX; prob. after F. or G.

ethyl e·þil see ETH-.

etiolate ī·tiŏleit blanch. XVIII. f. F. *étioler* (see -ATE[3]), – Norman F. (*s'*)*étieuler* grow into haulm, f. *étieule, éteule* (OF. *esteule*) :- popL. **stupila*, for L. *stipula* straw (cf. STUBBLE). So **e:tiol**A·TION. XVIII.

etiology var. (now U.S.) of ÆTIOLOGY.

etiquette e·tiket, e:tike·t prescribed or conventional code of behaviour. XVIII (Chesterfield, Walpole). – F. *étiquette* (whence It. *etichetta*, Sp. *etiqueta*), the primary sense of which is repr. by TICKET. ¶ OF. *estiquette* means chiefly 'soldier's billet for lodging'; the history of the development in F. from 'label' to 'prescribed routine' is not clear.

etna e·tnə vessel for heating liquid. XIX. f. the name of the volcano *Etna* in Sicily.

-ette e·t suffix, bearing the chief stress in a word, repr. F. *-ette* (OF. *-ete*), and forming dim. sbs., being the fem. corr. to masc. (O)F. *-et* (see -ET). In ME. the F. *-et* and *-ette* were not clearly distinguished, and old adoptions in *-et(t)e* usu. survive with *-et*, e.g. *egret, hatchet, pocket, toilet*. The sp. *-ette* is preserved in adoptions dating from XVII onwards, as *cigarette, coquette, etiquette, gazette, rosette, serviette, statuette, vinaigrette*. In XIX it began to be extended to Eng. sbs., as *leaderette, sermonette, waggonette*, and esp. in names of materials intended as imitations, as *flannelette, leatherette, plushette*.

étui ei·twi small case for small articles. XVII. – F. *étui*, OF. *estui* prison, f. OF. *estuier* shut up, keep, save = Pr. *estojar*, Cat., Pg. *estojar*.

etymology etimɔ·lədʒi origin, formation, and development (of a word), account of this XIV (Trev.); branch of grammar dealing with forms (formerly equiv. to *accidence*) XV. (Earlier form *ethimologie*) – OF. *ethimologie* (mod. *étymologie*) – L. *etymologia* (medL. *ethym-, ethim-*) – Gr. *etumologíā*, f. *etumológos* student of etymology, f. *étumon* literal sense of a word, original form, primary or basic word, sb. use of n. of *étumos* true, whence in L. form **e·tymon** XVI; see -LOGY. So **e:tymolo·**GICAL XVI, **etymo·log**IST XVII, -IZE XVI.

eu- jū prefix repr. Gr. *eu-*, comb. form of Gr. (Epic) *eús* good, brave, used in n. form *eû* as adv. 'well'. Gr. words with *eu-* as first element are predominantly adjs. of the form *eúphōnos* of good sound, well-sounding, EUPHONIOUS. For mod. formations see EUGENIC, etc.; **eurhy·thm**ICS harmony of bodily movement as an object of education. **b.** In bot. applied to forms in which all stages of the life cycle occur.

eucalyptus jūkəli·ptəs myrtaceous genus of plants. XIX. modL. (L'Héritier, 1788), intended to denote 'well-covered' (f. Gr. *eû* EU-+*kaluptós* covered, f. *kalúptein* cover, conceal), the flower before it opens being protected by a cap.

eucharis jū·kəris S. Amer. plant with bell-shaped flowers used for bouquets, etc. XIX. modL. – Gr. *eúkharis* pleasing, f. *eû* EU-+*kháris* grace (cf. next).

Eucharist jū·kərist Sacrament of the Lord's Supper. XIV. – OF. *eucariste* (mod., with latinized ending, *eucharistie*) – ecclL. *eucharistia* – ecclGr. *eukharistíā* giving of thanks, (earlier) gratitude, f. *eukháristos* grateful, f. *eû* EU-+*kharízesthai* show favour, give freely, f. *kharit-*, *kháris* favour, grace (cf. YEARN). So **euchari·st**IC XVII (H. More), -ICAL XVI (T. More).

euchologion jūkolə·giən prayer-book, esp. the ritual of the Gr. Church. XVII (Jer. Taylor). – Gr. *eukhológion*, f. *eukhḗ* prayer+ *-log- légein* say; see -LOGY. Also anglicized †**euchologue,** †**euchology** XVII.

euchre jū·kəɹ card-game originating in U.S.A. XIX (early sp. *euker*, *uker*, *yuker*). Of unkn. origin.

Euclid jū·klid copy of the Elements of Euclid (Gr. *Eukleídēs*), mathematician of Alexandria (*c.* 300 B.C.). XVI. Hence **Eucli·d**IAN XIX, †-EAN XVII; after F. *euclidien*, L. *Euclīdēus*, Gr. *Eukleídeios*.

eudæmonism jūdī·mənizm system of ethics having happiness for its end. XIX (De Quincey). – Gr. *eudaimonismós* (Aristotle), f. *eudaimonízein* call or account happy, f. *eudaímōn* happy, f. *eû* EU-+*daímōn* guardian genius; see DEMON, -ISM. So **eudæ·mon**IST. XIX (Coleridge).

eudiometer jūdiə·mitəɹ instrument for testing the amount of oxygen in air. XVIII (De Magellan). f. Gr. *eúdios* (of weather) clear, f. *eû* EU-+stem of *Diós*, g. of *Zeús* god of the sky and the atmosphere; see -METER.

eugenic jūdʒe·nik concerned with the production of fine offspring; (pl. *-ics*) science of this. 1883 (F. Galton). f. Gr. *eû* EU-+ *gen-* produce (see GENESIS).

eulogy jū·lədʒi discourse in praise of a person. XVI (Spenser) (once †*euloge* XV). – medL. *eulogium*, app. blending of L. *ēlogium* (of obscure origin) inscription on a tomb, etc., and medL. *eulogia* – Gr. *eulogíā* praise, f. phr. *eû légein* speak well of; cf. EU-, -LOGY. Hence **eu·log**IST. XVIII, **eulogi·st**IC. XIX.

eunuch jū·nək castrated male person. XV. – L. *eunūchus* – Gr. *eunoûkhos*, f. *eunḗ* bed+ **okh-* **ekh-* (in *ékhein* keep); the etymol. meaning is therefore 'bedchamber guard'.

euonymus juə·niməs (bot.) genus of shrubs. XVIII. mod. use by Linnæus of L. *euōnymus* (Pliny) – Gr. *euṓnumos* lucky, f. *eû* EU-+**ōnum-*, var. of *ónoma* NAME.

eupatrid jūpæ·trid pl. hereditary aristocracy of ancient Athens. XIX. – L. *eupatridæ*, Gr. *eupatrídai*, f. *eû* EU-+*patḗr* FATHER; see -ID.

eupeptic jūpe·ptik pert. to good digestion. XVII. f. Gr. *eúpeptos* easy of digestion, having a good digestion, f. *eû* EU-+*péptein* digest; see COOK, -IC.

euphemism jū·fimizm (rhet.) figure consisting in the substitution of a favourable for a more accurate but offensive expression. XVII. – Gr. *euphēmismós*, f. *euphēmízein* speak fair, f. *eúphēmos* fair of speech, f. *eû* EU-+*phḗmē* speaking; see FAME, -ISM. Cf. F. *euphémisme* (XVIII). So **euphemi·st**IC. XIX.

euphonium jūfou·niəm (mus.) tenor tuba tuned to B♭. XIX. modL., f. Gr. *eúphōnos*; see next and -IUM.

euphony jū·fəni pleasing quality of sound. XVII (once XV). – F. *euphonie* – late L. *euphōnia* (in Eng. use XVI–XIX) – Gr. *euphōníā*, f. *eúphōnos* well-sounding, f. *eû* EU-+*phōnḗ* sound, voice; see PHONETIC, -Y³. Hence **eupho·n**IOUS. XVIII.

euphorbia jūfɔ̄·ɹbiə the spurge genus. XVII. Alteration (by assim. to -IA¹) of L. *euphorbea* (Pliny), f. *Euphorbus* name of a physician of Juba II, king of Mauritania, who is said to have named the plant after him. So **eupho·rbium** gum resin obtained therefrom. XIV. L.; see -IUM.

euphrasy jū·frəsi the plant eye-bright. XV. – medL. *eufrasia* – Gr. *euphrasíā* cheerfulness, f. *euphraínein* be cheerful, f. *eû* EU-+ *phrḗn* mind; see PHRENOLOGY, -Y³.

euphroe jū·frou (naut.) crow-foot dead-eye. XIX (also *uvrow*, *uphroe*). – Du. *juffrouw* dead-eye, prop. maiden (also *juffer* spar, beam, joint, whence Eng. *ufer* XVIII, †*juffer* XVII), f. *jonk* young+*vrouw* woman (= G. FRAU, ult. based on IE. **pro* before). ¶ The Du. word in its earlier form *jonkvrouw* appears to be repr. in the Sc. nautical term *ȝong frow* (XV–XVI).

euphuism jū·fjuizm precious style of diction characteristic of John Lyly's '*Euphues*, the anatomy of wyt' (1579) and '*Euphues* and his England' (1580). XVI (G. Harvey, 1591). f. Gr. *euphuḗs* well endowed by nature, f. *eû* EU-+*phu-* (BE); see -ISM. Hence **eu·phu**IST. XIX (Scott), **euphui·st**IC. XIX (Carlyle).

Eurasian juərei·ʒⁱən, -ei·ʃⁱən pert. to the continental area comprising Europe and Asia (also *Eurasiatic*); of mixed European and Asiatic (esp. Indian) parentage (formerly called *East Indian* and more recently *Anglo-Indian*). XIX. f. *Eur|ope*+*Asia*, or the comp. *Eurasia*+-AN.

eureka juərī·kə exclamation (Gr. *heúrēka* I have found, pf. of *heurískein* find; cf. HEURISTIC) uttered by Archimedes when he discovered the means of determining by specific gravity the proportion of base metal in Hiero's golden crown (Plutarch's 'Moralia'), hence gen. as an excl. of exultation at a discovery. XVII.

euroclydon juərə·klidən stormy wind mentioned in Acts xxvii 14; also transf. and fig. XVII (A.V.). – N.T.Gr. *euroklúdōn*; the better attested reading is *eurakúlōn*, in Vulg. *euroaquilo* (f. *Eurus* east wind + *Aquilo* north wind), which is reproduced in the Rheims N.T. (1582), R.V. of 1881 reading *Euraquilo*.

European juərəpī·ən pert. to Europe or its countries and inhabitants. XVII (*-ian, -æan, -ean*). – F. *européen*, f. L. *eurōpæus*, f. *Eurōpa* – Gr. *Eurṓpē* (of unkn. origin), first applied to central Greece, later extended to the whole Gr. mainland and then to the land-mass behind it; see -EAN.

eury- juəri L. sp. of comb. form of Gr. *eurús* wide, broad, rel. to Skr. *urús*; used in a few scientific terms, as *eu:rycepha·lic, -gna·thous, -pte·rid, -sto·matous*.

Euskarian jūskɛə·riən Basque, or pert. to the pre-Aryan element in the population of Europe typified by the Basques. XIX. f. *Euskara*, var. of *Eskuara, Uskara*, the Basques' name for their language + -IAN.

eusol jū·səl solution of hypochlorous acid used medicinally. 1915. f. initial letters of *E*dinburgh *U*niversity *Sol*ution, named after the place of its discovery; assoc. with EU-.

Eustachian jūstei·kiən (anat.) epithet of organs or structures discovered by Bartolomeo *Eustachi* (latinized *Eustachius*) of San Severino, Italy (*c.* 1500–74); see -IAN. XVIII.

euthanasia jūþənei·ziə, -ʒ[1]ə gentle and easy death XVII; means of bringing this about XVIII. – Gr. *euthanasíā*, f. *eû* EU- + *thánatos* death, rel. to *thnētós* mortal.

evacuate ivæ·kjueit A. empty out the contents of (esp. the bowels) XVI; †clear of inmates XVII; relinquish occupation of XVIII; B. empty out (contents) XV; remove (inmates or occupants) XVII. f. pp. stem of L. *evacuāre* (Pliny), f. *ē* E- + *vacuus* empty; see VACUUM, -ATE[3]. So **evacua·tion**. XIV. – lateL. **evacuee·**. XX; after F. *évacué*.

evade ivei·d escape (intr. and trans.) XVI; contrive to avoid XVII. – F. *évader* – L. *ēvādere*, f. *ē* E- + *vādere* go (cf. WADE). So **eva·sion**. XV. – (O)F. – L. **eva·sive**. XVIII; cf. F. *ēvasif*.

evaluate ivæ·ljueit work out the value of. XIX. Back-formation, after (O)F. *évaluer*, from **evalua·tion**. XVIII. – (O)F.; see E-, VALUATION.

evanescent evəne·sənt, ī- about to vanish, quickly vanishing. XVIII. – F. *évanescent* – prp. of L. *ēvānēscere*, whence **evane·sce** XIX; see E-, VANISH, -ENT.

evangel ivæ·ndʒəl (arch.) gospel. XIV (earlier aphetic *vangel*, R. Rolle). ME. *evangile* (later assim. to L.) – (O)F. *évangile*, corr. to Pr. *evangeli*, Sp., It. *evangelio* – ecclL. *evangelium* – Gr. *euaggélion* (in eccl. use) good news, (in classical Gr.) reward for bringing good news, pl. sacrifice on receiving good news, f. *euággelos* bringing good news, f. *eû* well, EU- + *aggéllein* announce (cf. ANGEL). The ecclL. form was directly adopted as †*evangelie, -y* (XIV–XVII). So **evange·lic** XV, now more usu. **evange·lical** īvæ̆n-, evæ̆n- pert. to the gospel or gospels; Protestant XVI; as a party designation applied orig. to adherents of the Methodist revival in the Church of England XVIII. – ecclL. *evangelicus* – ecclGr. *euaggelikós*. Cf. G. *evangelisch*, which was extended by Luther to teaching based on the whole of the Bible. **eva·ngelism** preaching of the gospel. XVII (Bacon). **eva·ngelist** writer of one of the four gospels XII; preacher of the gospel XIV (Wycl. Bible, Acts xxi 8, Eph. iv 11, 2 Tim. iv 5). – (O)F. *évangéliste* – ecclL. *ēvangelista* – ecclGr. *euaggelistḗs*. **evangeli·stary** gospel book. XVII. – medL. **eva·ngelize** †intr. XIV, trans. XVII. – ecclL. *ēvangelizāre* – ecclGr. *euaggellizesthai*.

evanish ivæ·niʃ (arch.) vanish out of sight or existence. XV. f. *evaniss-*, extended stem of OF. *evanir*, corr. to It. *svanire* – Rom. **exvanīre*, for L. *ēvānēscere*; see E-, VANISH.

evaporate ivæ·pəreit convert into or become vapour XVI (pa. pple. XIV); reduce to vapour XVII. f. pp. stem of L. *ēvaporāre*; see E-, VAPOUR, -ATE[3]. So **evapora·tion**. XIV (Trevisa). – L.

eve īv (poet.) evening; (eccl.) day before a festival. XIII. In ME. two syll., var. of EVEN[1], orig. southern. ¶ For similar loss of *-n* cf. *clue, game, maid*.

evection ive·kʃən †elevation (rare) XVII; (astron.) inequality in the moon's longitude XVIII. – L. *ēvectiō(n-)*, f. *ēvect-*, *ēvehere* carry forth, elevate; see E-, VEHICLE, -TION.

even[1] ī·vn (poet., dial.) close of the day OE.; eve of a holy day XIV. OE. *ǣfen*, rel. to synon. OFris. *ēvend, io(u)nd*, OS. *āband*, MLG., MDu. *āvont* (Du. *avond*), OHG. *āband* (G. *abend*), perh. repr. respectively pp. and prp. formations on an obscure IE. base **ep-*, in Gr. *epí*, with WGerm. **æƀinj-*, **æƀunj-* :– **ēpinjo-*, **ēpnjo-*, and **æƀanda-* :– **ēponto-*; synon. ON. *aptann* (Sw. *afton*, Da. *aften*) may be another pp. formation on the same base, or (more prob.) a deriv. of the base of AFTER. In contr. form *e'en* arch. and dial. in *All-Hallowe'en, Easter E'en, good e'en*, etc. Cf. EVE, EVENING. Hence **e·vensong, e·ventide**, OE. *ǣfensang, -tīd*.

even[2] ī·vn flat, level (obs. in gen. use; naut. in *an even keel*); uniform, equal, equally balanced OE.; exactly adjusted, precise XIII; of number)(*odd* XIV. OE. *efen* = OFris. *even, iven*, OS. *eƀan* (Du. *even, effen*), OHG. *eban, epan* (G. *eben*), ON. *jafn*, Goth. *ibns* :– CGerm. **eƀnaz*, of unkn. origin. comp. **†even-Christian** fellow-Christian, lit. 'equal Christian'. OE. *efncristen* = OFris. *ivinkerstena*, OHG. *ebanchristani*. So **even** adv. (poet. **e'en** īn) †evenly, equally; (arch.) exactly, fully OE.; in the extreme case XVI. OE. *efne* = OFris. *efne*, OS. *efno* (Du. *even*), OHG. *ebano* (G. *eben*) :– WGerm. **eƀnō*. **even** vb. OE. *efnan* and (*ġe*)*efnian*, f. *efen*.

evening ī·vniŋ †closing of the day OE.; latter part of the day. XV. OE. *ǣfnung*, f. *ǣfnian* grow towards night, f. *ǣfen* EVEN[1]; see -ING[1].

event ive·nt outcome, issue; anything that happens. XVI. – L. *ēventus*, f. *ēvent-*, pp. stem of *ēvenīre* come out, result, happen, f. *ē* E-+*venīre* COME. Hence, or direct from L. *eventu-s*, **eve·ntu**AL[1] †pert. to an event or events; that will take effect in certain contingencies XVII; modelled on *actual*; cf. F. *éventuel* (XVIII). **eve·ntu**ATE[3] have a certain issue, turn out. XVIII. orig. U.S.; prob. after *actuate*.

ever e·vəɹ at all times; at any time; in any case or degree. OE. *ǣfre*, a purely Eng. formation, of unkn. origin (so NEVER). From the meaning the first syll. is prob. the mutation of *ā* ever, AY, as in EITHER; the second el. has been referred to (i) OE. *feorh* life, (ii) OE. *byre* event, occasion (cf. the OE. vars. *ǣbre*, *nǣbre*), the presumed etymol. meanings being resp. 'ever in life' and 'on any occasion'. **e·ver**GREEN XVII adj. (Milton), sb. (Evelyn). **everla·sting** adj. orig. rendering L. *æternus*, *sempiternus* XIV; sb. equiv. to *durance* (XVI–XVII) or *lasting* (XIX). **ever**MO·RE XIII repl. ME. *evermo*, OE. *ǣfre mā*; see MO.

everglade e·vəɹgleid (U.S.) marshy tract under water, (esp. pl.) the vast swampy region of Florida. XIX. Presumably f. EVER (perh. implying 'interminable') + GLADE (with some obscure ref.).

evert ivə̄·ɹt overturn, overthrow XVI; (med.) turn outwards XIX. – L. *ēvertere*, f. *ē* E-+ *vertere* turn (see -WARD). So **eve·r**SION †overthrowing XV; (med.) XVIII. – OF. – L.

every e·v(ə)ri Late OE. *ǣfrić*, *ǣurić*, ME. *efreć*, *æfrech*, *efri(ch)*, *eauer euch*, *euere(l)ch*, *-u(l)ch*, *-i(l)ch*, repr. OE. *ǣfre ǣlć*, **ǣfre ylć*; see EVER, EACH, ILK[2]. Being in origin a comp. of *each*, it differed from it at first only in emphasizing the element of universality in its application; later the words were differentiated, so that *every* regards chiefly the totality, *each* the individuals composing it. Comp. **e·very**BODY XIV (Ch.); **every** ONE XIII (*euerichon*, AncrR.); **e·very**THING XIV (Ch.) (*eauer euch þing* XIII). In **e·verywhere** (XII) two formations have coalesced: (i) *ever*+*iwhere* (OE. *ġehwǣr* anywhere, everywhere), and (ii) *every* (ME. *everilk*)+ *where*.

evict ivi·kt recover (property) XV; expel (a person) by judicial process; †conquer, overcome; †prove XVI. f. *ēvict-*, pp. stem of L. *ēvincere* conquer, obtain by conquering, recover, overcome and expel, eject judicially, prove; see EVINCE. So **evi·c**TION. XVI.

evident e·vidənt visible, obvious, plain. XIV. – (O)F. *évident* or L. *ēvident-*, *-ēns*, f. *ē* EX-[1]+prp. of *vidēre* see (cf. WIT), used in a middle sense ('making itself seen'). So **e·vid**ENCE significant appearance, token XIII; ground for belief XIV; information (given in a legal inquiry) tending to establish fact XVI; clarity XVII (*in evidence* visible, conspicuous, after F. *en évidence* XIX). – (O)F. *évidence* – L. *ēvidentia*, whence (after medL.) **evide·nt**IAL. XVII. **e·vident**LY[2]. XIV (Ch.).

evil ī·vl, ī·vīl)(*good*; bad. OE. *yfel* = OS. *ubil*, OFris., MDu. *evel* (Du. *euvel*), OHG. *ubil* (G. *übel*), Goth. *ubils* :– CGerm. (exc. ON.) **ubilaz*, prob. f. IE. base **up-* (see OVER, UP), the primary sense being 'exceeding due limits'. In OE., as in other early Germ. languages, the most comprehensive adj. expressive of disapproval or disparagement; in mod. colloq. use almost entirely superseded by *bad*, exc. in fixed phr., as *evil eye*; the sb. is more frequent, but is largely confined to the more general senses; in the sense 'disease' (XIII) survives hist. in *the King's evil* scrofula. So **e·vil** adv. OE. *yfle*; survives in literary use in *speak evil* (of), *evil-disposed*, and the like.

evince ivi·ns †overcome; †convince; †prove; make evident. XVII. f. L. *ēvincere* (see EVICT, the older word), f. *ē* E-+*vincere* conquer (see VICTOR).

evirate ī·vireit castrate, emasculate. XVII. f. pp. stem of L. *ēvirāre*, f. *ē* E-+*vir* man; see VIRILE, -ATE[3].

eviscerate ivi·səreit disembowel. XVII. f. pp. stem of L. *ēviscerāre*; see E-, VISCERA, -ATE[3].

evoe ivou·i Bacchanalian cry. XVI (*euohe*) L., prop. disyll. *eu(h)oe* – G. *euoî*.

evoke ivou·k call forth. XVII. – L. *ēvocāre*, f. *ē* E-+*vocāre* call (see VOCATION); poss. after F. *évoquer*. So **evoca·tion** XVII (once, gram., XV). – L. **evoc**ATIVE ivɔ·k-. XVII. – late L.

evolution īvəlʲū·ʃən, ev- unfolding; (mil. and naut.) opening out of a formation, tactical movement; development in detail or from a rudimentary state XVII (spec. in biol. applied first by Charles Bonnet, 1762, to the theory of preformation). – L. *ēvolūtiō(n-)* unrolling of a book, f. *ēvolūt-*, pp. stem of *ēvolvere* (f. *ē* E-+*volvere* roll; see VOLUTE), whence **evo·lve** XVII. Hence by back formation (U.S.) **e·volute** vb. XIX. ¶ F. *évolution* occurs first in mil. sense, 1647, but this use in Eng. is earlier, 1622.

evulsion ivʌ·lʃən forcible extraction. XVII (Chapman). – L. *ēvulsiō(n-)*, f. *ēvuls-*, pp. stem of *ēvellere*, f. *ē* E-+*vellere* pluck (cf. VELLICATION); see -SION.

ewe jū female sheep. OE. *ēowu*, corr. to OFris. *ei*, OS. *ewwi* (MDu. *oie*, Du. *ooi*), LG. *ouw|lamm*, OHG. *ouwi*, *ou* (G. *aue*), ON. *ær* :– CGerm. **awi-* (repr. in Goth. by *awistr* sheepfold = OE. *eowestre*, and Goth. *aweþi* flock = OE. *eowde*) :– IE. **owi-*, repr. also by L. *ovis*, Gr. *ó(ϝ)is*, OIr. *ói*, OSl. *ovica* (Russ. *ovtsá*), Lith. *avìs*, Skr. *ávis* sheep: one of the CIE. animal-names; cf. *cow*.

ewer juəɹ wide-mouthed pitcher. XIV. – AN. **ewere*, ONF. *eviere*, (O)F. *aiguière* :– Rom. **aquāria*, fem. (sc. *olla* pot) of *āquārius* pert. to water, f. *aqua* water; see AQUATIC, -ARY.

ex eks L. *ex* out of (vars. *ec*, *ē*), prep. and prefix (see EX-¹, E-) = Gr. *ex* (vars. *ek*, *eg*; see EX-²), Gaul. *ex-* in *exobnus*, OW. *eh-* in *ehofn* fearless (mod. *eofn*), OIr. *ess-*, with var. *ass-* (Ir. privative prefix *eas-*). Domiciled in Eng. in certain L. phr., as (from XVI) *ex improviso*, *ex opere operato*, *ex professo*, (from XVII) *ex animo*, *ex dono*, *ex hypothesi*; **ex(-)cathedra** kæ·þidrə, kəþe·drə from the CHAIR (i.e. of authority) XIX; **ex(-)libris** ləi·bris 'out of the books' (of somebody), from the LIBRARY (of), (one's) bookplate XIX; **ex(-)officio** ǒfi·ʃiou by virtue of one's OFFICE XVI; **ex(-)parte** pā·ɹti with respect to a PART, (leg.) on one side only XVII. **ex(-)voto** vou·tou (short for *ex voto suscepto* from a vow undertaken) offering made in pursuance of a vow XVIII. **b.** Prefixed to titles of rank after late L. usage in *excōnsul*, nom. evolved from *ex cōnsule* 'from (being) consul', (hence) lately consul; whence gen. with the sense 'former', 'quondam', as in *ex-professor* (so in F., It., etc.), and by further extension prefixed to adjs. (after *ex-consular* XVII) or to sbs. used attrib., as *ex-service*. **c.** In commercial use, with ref. to goods, 'out of', 'landed from' (a ship); similarly *ex warehouse*; 'without', 'exclusive of', as in *ex dividend* (*ex div.*, *x. d.*), *ex interest* (*ex int.*, *ex in.*, *x. i.*).

ex-¹ eks, iks prefix repr. L. *ex-*, the prep. (see prec.) used in combination; its full form remains before a vowel (cf. EXACT, EXONERATE), before *c*, *qu* (cf. EXCURSION, EXQUISITE), *p* (cf. EXPEL, EXPRESS), *s*, as in *exsequī*, *exserere*, *exstare* (but *s* was later dropped; hence the spelling of EXECRATE, EXECUTE, EXERT, EXTANT, EXTIRPATE), and *t* (cf. EXTRACT). *Ex* was reduced (through **egz*) to *ē* before *b*, *d*, *g*, *l*, *m*, *n*, *r*, *i* (*j*), and *u* (cf. EBULLIENT, EDICT, EGRESS, ELECT, EMIT, ENUNCIATE, ERECT, EJECT, EVADE). See E-, ES-. From the orig. sense of going out or forth (cf. EXIT), sometimes with the additional notion of being raised (cf. EXTOL), the prefix acquired that of changing condition (cf. EFFERVESCE) and of completion (cf. EFFECT, EXCRUCIATE, EXHAUST).

ex-² eks, iks prefix repr. Gr. *ex-*, the prep. (see EX) used in combination; before consonants *ek-* EC-.

exacerbate eksæ·səɹbeit increase the bitterness of. XVII. f. pp. stem of L. *exacerbāre*; see EX-¹, ACERB, -ATE³. So **exacerbA·TION.** XVI. – late L.

exact ėgzæ·kt precise, rigorous, accurate (in various applications); †perfect, consummate. XVI. – L. *exactus*, pp. of *exigere* complete, bring to perfection, examine, ascertain, f. *ex* EX-¹+*agere* perform (see ACT). So **exa·ct** vb. demand, esp. by force and with authority. XV. f. *exact-*, pp. stem of L. *exigere* drive out, enforce payment of, require, demand, etc. (as above); cf. EXIGENT. **exa·CTION.** XIV (Wycl. Bible). – L.; so in (O)F. **exa·ctiTUDE** precision of detail, attention to minutiæ; †(as in F.) exactness, perfect correctness. XVIII. – F.

exaggerate ėgzæ·dʒəreit †accumulate, pile up XVI; make (a thing) out greater than it is XVII. f. pp. stem of L. *exaggerāre*, f. *ex* EX-¹ +*aggerāre* heap up, f. *agger* heap, prob. f. *ad* to (AT)+*gerere* carry (see GERENT); see -ATE³. So **exaggerA·TION.** XVI. – L. Cf. F. *exagérer*, *-ération*.

exalt ėgzǒ·lt raise aloft or to a high or higher degree. XV (Lydg.). – L. *exaltāre*, f. *ex* EX-¹+*altus* high (see OLD). **exaltA·TION** lifting up; elevation XIV; elation XV. – (O)F. or late L.; in Eng., as in F., the earliest application is to the feast of the Exaltation of the Holy Cross (14 Sept.).

exam ėgzæ·m short for EXAMINATION. XIX.

examine ėgzæ·min inquire into and test the amount or quality of. XIV. – (O)F. *examiner* – L. *exāmināre* weigh accurately, f. *exāmin-*, *-en* tongue of a balance, weighing, for **exagmen*, f. **exag-*, base of *exigere* examine, weigh (see EXACT). So **examinA·TION.** XIV. – (O)F. – L.

example igzà·mpl object or action to copy or imitate; instance to warn or deter XIV (Wycl. Bible); typical instance XV. – OF. *example* (mod. *exemple*), refash. after L. of *essample* (whence ME. *asample*, arch. *ensample* XIII, aphetic SAMPLE) – L. *exemplum*, f. **exem-*, *eximere* take out (see EXEMPT).

exarch e·ksāɹk governor of a province under the Byzantine emperors; metropolitan in the Eastern Church. XVI. – ecclL. *exarchus* – Gr. *éxarkhos* leader, chief, f. *exárkhein* take the lead, f. *ex* EX-²+*árkhein* rule (cf. ARCH-).

exasperate igzà·spəreit embitter; irritate; †make rugged or harsh. XVI. f. pp. stem of L. *exasperāre*, f. *ex* EX-¹+*asper* rough; see ASPERITY, -ATE³. So **exasperA·TION.** XVI. – L.

excavate e·kskəveit hollow out, dig out. XVI. f. pp. stem of L. *excavāre*, f. *ex-* EX-¹+ *cavāre*, f. *cavus* hollow; see CAVE¹, -ATE³. So **excavA·TION.** XVII. – F. or L.

exceed ėksī·d †pass the limits of; be greater than XIV (Ch.); be superior to XV. – (O)F. *excéder* – L. *excēdere* depart, go beyond, surpass, f. *ex* EX-¹+*cēdere* go. Cf. EXCESS.

excel ėkse·l be superior (to). XV (Lydg.). – L. *excellere* be eminent, (rarely in physical sense) rise, raise, f. *ex* EX-¹+**cellere* rise high, tower (found only in comps.), rel. to *celsus* high, *columna* COLUMN. Cf. F. *exceller* (XVI). So **excellENT** e·ksələnt †exalted, supreme XIV; extremely good XVII (Sh.). – (O)F. – L. **e·xcellENCE, -ENCY** XIV; as a title of honour XIV (Gower).

excelsior ėkse·lsiǭɹ motto of the State of New York, U.S.A. (XVIII) and of the Società degli Alpinisti; used by Longfellow as the refrain of his poem so entitled (1841) and explained by him later as being short for *Scopus meus excelsior est* My goal is higher. L., compar. of *excelsus* high, pp. of *excellere* EXCEL. ¶ The advb. meaning 'higher', 'upwards', commonly attributed to it, is ungrammatical.

except[1] ėkse·pt leave out of account. XV. f. *except-*, pp. stem of L. *excipere*, f. *ex* EX-[1] + *capere* take (see HEAVE); cf. (O)F. *excepter*. So **exce·p**TION action of excepting, case excepted XIV (Ch.); defendant's plea in bar of plaintiff's action XV; objection, demur XVI. – (O)F. – L. Hence **exce·ption**ABLE. XVII (H. More). **exce·ption**AL[1] (after F. *exceptionnel*). XIX. **exce·pt**ING[2] prp. passing into prep., if one excepts, except. XV (Sc. *excepand*).

except[2] ėkse·pt †pp. excepted; prep. if one leaves out of account XIV; †conj. unless XV; otherwise than XVI. – L. *exceptus*, pp. of *excipere* (see prec.). The prep. arose (i) partly from the use of the pp. in concord with a following sb. or pronoun, e.g. *except women*, i.e. women excepted (cf. L. *exceptis vobis duobus* you two excepted, except you two), (ii) partly in imitation of (O)F. *excepté* excepted, and late L. abl. *exceptō*, which was used as a prep. by extension of the classical L. usage with a clause, *exceptō quod* . . except that . . (whence) the conjunctional use of *except*.)

excerpt e·ksǭɹpt extract from a book, etc. XVII. – L. *excerptum*, sb. use of n. pp. of *excerpere*, f. *ex* EX-[1] + *carpere* pluck (cf. HARVEST). So **excerpt** vb. ėksǭ·ɹpt. XVI (pa. pple. once XV). f. *excerpt-*, pp. stem.

excess ėkse·s †extravagant feeling or conduct; overstepping limits of moderation XIV (Ch., Trevisa, Wyclif); fact of exceeding in amount XVI. – (O)F. *excès* – L. *excessus*, f. *excess-*, pp. stem of *excēdere* EXCEED. So **exce·ss**IVE. XIV (Gower). – (O)F. – medL.

exchange ėkstʃei·ndʒ action of exchanging. XIV (Ch.); ME. *eschaunge*, later (by assim. to L.) *exchaunge* – AN. *eschaunge*, OF. *eschange* (F. *échange*), f. *eschanger* (mod. *é-*), whence **excha·nge** vb. XV; see ES-, EX-[1], CHANGE.

exchequer ėkstʃe·kəɹ †chess-board XIII; department of state concerned with the royal revenues, so called orig. with ref. to the table covered with a cloth divided into squares on which the accounts were kept by means of counters XIV (R. Mannyng); court of law theoretically concerned with revenue; office charged with the receipt and custody of public revenue XV (Hoccleve); pecuniary possessions XVII. ME. *escheker* – AN. *escheker*, OF. *eschequier*, earlier *eschaquier* (mod. *échiquier*) = Pr. *escaquier*, Sp. *jaquel*, It. *scaccario* – medL. *scaccārium* chessboard, f. *scaccus* CHECK[1]; see -ER[2]. The form with *ex-* (from XV) is due to assoc. of OF. *es-* with EX-[1], as in *exchange*, *exploit*. Aphetic CHEQUER.

excise[1] ėksai·z †toll, tax XV; duty on commodities (Spenser, with ref. to Holland) XVII (officially adopted 1643 in imitation of Du. practice). – MDu. *excijs* (1406; whence medL. *excisa* 1490), also *accijs* (whence Eng. †*accise* XVII–XVIII, G. *accise*, medL. *accīsia*) – OF. *acceis* :– Rom. **accēnsum*, f. L. *ad* AC- + *cēnsus* tax (see CENSUS).

excise[2] ėksai·z cut out. XVI. f. *excīs-*, pp. stem of L. *excīdere*, f. *ex* EX-[1] + *cædere* cut, with the shape of which may be compared Skr. *khidáti* tear, Gr. *skhizein* split (see SCHISM). So **excis**ION ėksi·ʒən. XV (Caxton). – (O)F. – L.

excite ėksai·t stir up, rouse. XIV (Rolle). – (O)F. *exciter* or L. *excitāre*, frequent. of *exciēre* (pp. *excitus*) call out or forth; see EX-[1], CITE. So **excit**A·TION (partly arch.) encouragement, instigation, stimulation; excitement. XIV (Gower, Maund.). – (O)F. – late L. **exci·te**MENT† instigation, incentive XVII (Sh.); (path.) abnormal activity XVIII; mental stimulation XIX.

exclaim ėksklei·m cry out. XVI. – F. *exclamer* or L. *exclamāre*; see EX-[1], CLAIM. So **exclam**ATION ekskləmei·ʃən. XIV. – (O)F. or L. **exclamat**ORY ėksklæ·m-. XVI.

exclude ėksklū·d shut out or off. XIV. – L. *exclūdere*, f. *ex* EX-[1] + *claudere* shut (see CLOSE). So **exclu·s**ION. XV – L. **exclu·s**IVE. XV. medL. (Cf. F. *exclure*, *exclusion*, *exclusif*.)

excommunicate ekskəmjū·nikeit put out of church communion. XV. f. pp. stem of ecclL. *excommūnicāre*, f. *ex* EX-[1] + *commūnis* COMMON, after *communicāre* COMMUNICATE. Earlier forms were †*excommune* (Caxton), †*excommenge* (XV) – (O)F. *excommunier*, †*escomenger* (:– *excommūnicāre*). So **e:x-communic**A·TION. XV. – late L. ¶ Milton used †*excommunion*.

excoriate ėkskɔ·rieit remove the skin from, flay. XV. f. pp. stem of L. *excoriāre*, f. *ex* EX-[1] + *corium* hide; see -ATE[3]. So **ex-cori**A·TION. XV.

excrement e·kskrimənt †dregs; fæces discharged from the bowels. XVI. – F. *excrément* or L. *excrēmentum*, f. *excrē-*, pp. base of *excernere*, f. *ex* EX-[1] + *cernere* sift (cf. CERTAIN, CRISIS); see -MENT. ¶ Sometimes coalescing with †*excrement* outgrowth (– L. *excrēmentum*, f. *excrēscere*; see next). So **excrementi**·TIOUS. XVI. – modL. **excreta** ėkskrī·tə. XIX. sb. use of n. pl. of *excrētus*, pp. of *excernere*. **excre·**TION. XVII. – F. or L.

excrescence ėkskre·səns outgrowth. XV. – L. *excrēscentia*, f. prp. of *excrēscere* grow out: see EX-[1], INCREASE, -ENCE. So **excre·**SCENT. XVII.

excruciate ėkskrū·ʃieit torture. XVI. f. pp. stem of L. *excruciāre*, f. *ex* EX-[1] + *cruciāre* torment, f. *crux* CROSS; see -ATE[3].

exculpate e·kskʌlpeit free from blame. XVII. f. pp. stem of medL. *exculpāre* (cf. It. *scolpare*), f. *ex* EX-[1]+*culpa* blame; see -ATE[3]. See CULPABLE and cf. INCULPATE.

excursion ėkskɜ̄·ɹʃən †escape; sally, sortie XVI; journey from home XVII. – L. *excursiō(n-)*, f. *excurs-*, pp. stem of *excurrere* run out, issue forth, f. *ex* EX-[1]+*currere*; see COURSE, -ION. Hence **excu·rsion**IST. XIX (Lamb); perh. based on the rare vb. *excursionize*. So **excursus** ėkskɜ̄·ɹsəs separate and detailed discussion of a point in an edition of a classic; also gen. XIX (1802).

excuse ėkskjū·z offer an apology for XIII (AncrR.); obtain exemption or release for; accept as an excuse for or from XIV; serve as an excuse for XVI. ME. *escuse*, *excuse* – OF. *escuser*, (also mod.) *excuser* – L. *excusāre* free from blame, plead in excuse, absolve, dispense with, f. *ex* EX-[1]+*causa* accusation (see CAUSE). So **excu·se** sb. ėkskjū·s. XIV (Ch.). – (O)F. *excuse*, f. *excuser*. The pronunc. with s instead of z in the sb., is due to the analogy of pairs like *use*, *abuse* vbs. and sbs., *advise* and *advice*, where the F. sbs. are masculines ending in *s*.

exeat e·ksiæt †A. stage direction repl. by *exit* XVI; B. permission to go out or leave XVIII. L., 'let him go out', 3rd pers. sg. pres. subj. of *exīre* go out (cf. EXEUNT, EXIT). So in F. (XVII). So **†e·xeant** XV; repl. by EXEUNT.

execrate e·ksikreit express or feel abhorrence of. XVI. f. pp. stem of L. *ex(s)ecrārī* curse, f. *ex* EX-[1]+*sacrāre* devote religiously (either to a deity or to destruction), f. *sacr-*, *sacer* religiously set apart; see SACRED, -ATE[3]. So **execr**A·TION. XIV. – (O)F. or L. **e·xecr**ABLE involving a curse XIV (Wycl. Bible); abominable XV (Caxton). – (O)F. *exécrable* – L. (in act. and pass. senses).

execute e·ksikjūt A. carry into effect, carry out XIV (Ch.); fulfil, discharge XIV (Trevisa); make valid by signing, etc.; carry out the design of, perform XVIII; B. inflict capital punishment on XV (Caxton). – (O)F. *exécuter* (= Pr. *executar*, It. *esecutare*, etc.) – medL. *executāre*, f. *ex(s)ecūt-*, pp. stem of L. *ex(s)equī* follow up, carry out, pursue judicially, punish, f. *ex* EX-[1]+*sequī* follow (cf. SEQUENCE). So **execu·**TION carrying into effect XIV (Ch., Wyclif); infliction of capital punishment XV; enforcement of a judgement; effective action XVI (Sh.). (O)F. – L.; hence **execu·tion**ER[1]. XVI. **executive** ėkse·kjŭtiv. XVII; sb. XVIII (first in Amer. Eng.). f. *execūt-*; cf. (O)F. *exécutif*, revived in late XVIII. **exe·cut**OR[1]. XIII (of an estate). – AN. *execut(o)ur* – L. *execūtor*. Aphetic †*seketur* (XIII), †*sectour* (XIV).

exegesis eksidʒī·sis expository interpretation. XVII. – Gr. *exḗgēsis*, f. *exēgeîsthai* interpret, f. *ex* EX-[2]+*hēgeîsthai* guide (cf. HEGEMONY). So **e·xegete** interpreter. XVIII. – Gr. *exēgētḗs*. **exege·t**IC, -ICAL ·dʒe·tik(l). XVII. – Gr. *exēgētikós*.

exemplar ėgze·mplāɹ, -pləɹ pattern, example XIV (Gower); typical specimen XVII. – (O)F. *exemplaire* – late L. *exemplārium*, f. L. *exemplum* EXAMPLE. The var. *examplar* was widely current from XV (Lydg.). So **exempl**ARY ėgze·mpləri serving as an example. XVI. – late L. *exemplāris*. **exempl**IFY ėgzə·mplifai illustrate by example. XV (Chauliac). – medL. *exemplificāre*, f. L. *exemplum*.

exempt ėgze·mpt †removed, excluded *from* XIV; *exempt from*, not subject to XV. – (O)F. *exempt* – L. *exemptus*, pp. of *eximere* take out, deliver, free, f. *ex* EX-[1]+*emere* take (cf. EMPTION). As sb. formerly used, after F., for an under-officer in the army, and hence (1700) as EXON. So **exe·mpt** vb. XV, **exe·mp**TION. XIV. – (O)F. *exempter*, *exemption* (L. *exemptiō*). ¶ From the same base are *diriment*; *peremptory*, *premium*; *prompt*, *impromptu*; and derivs. of L. *sumere*, viz. *assume*, *consume*, *presume*, *resume*, *subsume*, with corr. sbs.

exenterate ėkse·ntəreit disembowel. XVII (surviving fig. in XIX). f. pp. stem of L. *exenterāre*, f. *ex* EX-[1]+Gr. *énteron* INTESTINE, after Gr. *exenterízein*.

exequatur eksikwei·təɹ (leg.) official authorization. XVIII. L., 'let him perform', 3rd pers. sg. pres. subj. of *exequī* EXECUTE.

exequies e·ksikwiz funeral rites. XIV. – OF. *exequies* = Pr. *ex(s)equias* – L. acc. *exsequiās*, nom. *-iæ* funeral procession or ceremonies, f. *exsequī* follow after, accompany (see EXECUTE).

exercise e·ksəɹsaiz employment, practice XIV; task prescribed for training or testing; religious observance XVI. – (O)F. *exercice* = Pr. *exercici* – L. *exercitium*, f. *exercēre* keep busy or at work (perh. orig. drive forth beasts of tillage), practise, train, administer, disturb, vex, f. *ex* EX-[1]+*arcēre* shut up, keep off, restrain, prevent = Gr. *arkeîn* ward off. Hence **e·xercise** vb. XIV (Ch., Wycl. Bible). Superseded †*exerce* (Ch.) – (O)F. *exercer*, – L. *exercēre*.

exergue ėksɜ̄·ɹg small space on the reverse of a coin, etc., for minor inscriptions. XVII (Evelyn). – F. *exergue* (J. de Bie, 1636), – medL. *exergum*, f. Gr. *ex* outside+*érgon* WORK: prop., something lying outside the (main) work.

exert igzɜ̄·ɹt †discharge, emit; exercise, bring to bear. XVII. f. *exert-*, pp. stem of L. *ex(s)erere* put forth, f. *ex* EX-[1]+*serere* bind, entwine, join (see SERIES). So **exe·r**TION.

exes e·ksiz short for *expenses*. XIX.

exeunt e·ksiʌnt stage direction for certain actors to leave the stage. XV. L., 'they go out', 3rd pers. pl. pres. ind. of *exīre*; see EXIT and cf. EXEANT.

exhale ėgzʰei·l give off as vapour XIV; breathe or blow out XVI. – (O)F. *exhaler* – L. *exhalāre*, f. *ex* EX-[1] + *halāre* breathe. So **exhal**A·TION. XIV (Trevisa, Gower).

exhaust ėgzɔ̄·st draw off or out, drain. XVI. f. *exhaust-*, pp. stem of L. *exhaurīre*, f. *ex* EX-[1] +*haurīre* draw (water), drain. So **exhau·s**TION. XVII.

exhibit ėgzi·bit †offer, furnish, administer XV; submit to view, display XVI. f. *exhibit-*, pp. stem of L. *exhibēre*, f. *ex* EX-[1]+*habēre* hold (cf. HABIT). So **exhibi·**TION †maintenance, allowance XV (surviving in spec. sense of school or college bursary XVII); visible display XIV; public display of objects, etc. XVIII. – (O)F. – late L. (delivery, maintenance).

exhilarate ėgzi·ləreit make cheerful. XVI. f. pp. stem of L. *exhilarāre*, f. *ex* EX-[1]+ *hilaris*; see HILARIOUS, -ATE[3].

exhort ėgzɔ̄·ɹt admonish or encourage earnestly. XIV. – (O)F. *exhorter* or L. *exhortārī*, f. *ex* EX-[1]+*hortārī* encourage (cf. HORTATORY). So **exhorta·**TION. XIV (Wycl. Bible).

exhume ėgzjū·m, ėkshjū·m dig up. XVIII (once XV). – F. *exhumer* – medL. *exhumāre*, f. *ex* EX-[1]+ *humus* ground (cf. HUMBLE). So **exhuma·**TION. XVIII (once XV). – F. – medL. The medL. pp. was adopted earlier in †**exhum**ATE[3] (XVI).

exigent e·gzidʒənt, e·ks- †sb. exigency, extremity XV (Lydg.); adj. urgent XVII (Clarendon); exacting XIX. As sb. – OF. *exigent* sb.; as adj. – L. *exigent-*, *-ēns*, prp. of *exigere* EXACT; see -ENT. So **e·xig**ENCE, -ENCY. XVI. – (O)F. and late L.

exiguous ėgzi·gjuəs, ėks- extremely small. XVII. f. L. *exiguus* scanty in measure or number, f. *exigere* weigh exactly; see EXACT, -UOUS.

exile[1] e·gzail, e·ksail enforced removal or absence from one's country. XIII (Cursor M.). – (O)F. *exil*, latinized refash. of earlier *essil* = Pr. *essilh* – L. *exilium* banishment, f. *exul* exiled person, f. *ex* EX-[1]+ **-ul-*, as in *ambulāre* walk (see AMBLE). So **e·xile**[2] exiled person. XIV. prob. – (O)F. *exilé*, pp. of *exiler*, with muting of the final syll. as in ASSIGN[2], etc., infl. by L. *exul*. **e·xile**[3] vb. make an exile of. XIV. – OF. *exil(i)er* refash. of *essilier* – late L. *exiliāre*, f. *exilium*. ¶ Formerly, and always by Sh. and Milton, str. *exi·le*. **exilic** egzi·lik. XIX.

exility ėgzi·lĭti, ėks- slenderness, tenuity. XV. – L. *exīlitās*, f. *exīlis* thin, lank; see -ITY.

eximious ėgzi·miəs, ėks- excellent, eminent. XVI (Boorde). f. L. *eximius* 'set apart', select, choice, f. *eximere*; see EXEMPT, -IOUS.

exist ėgzi·st have being. XVII (Sh.) ult. – L. *ex(s)istere* emerge, appear, proceed, be visible or manifest, f. *ex* EX-[1]+*sistere* take up a position, redupl. formation on **sta-* STAND; prob. immed. back-formation on **exi·**STENCE †actuality XIV (Ch.), being XV (Lydg.) – (O)F. or late L. **exi·st**ENT XVI. – L. ¶ F. *exister* is later (Descartes, 1637).

exit e·ksit A. (theatr.) direction to a player to leave the stage XVI (repl. *exeat* 'let him or her leave' XV); (hence) departure from the stage XVI (Sh.). B. departure from life, death; egress, outlet, 'he (she) goes out'. XVII. In A 3rd pers. sg. pres. ind. of L. *exīre*, f. *ex* EX-[1]+*īre* go; in B mainly – L. *exitus*, f. pp. stem of *exīre* (cf. ADIT, OBIT, TRANSIT).

exo- e·ksou, eksɔ· prefix repr. Gr. *éxō* outside, f. *ex* EX-[2]+**ō* prep. (= Indo-Iranian *ā*) towards; used in mod. scientific terms)(ENDO-; **exo·gamy** (Gr. *gámos* marriage) custom of a man's taking a wife from outside his clan; **e·xo**GEN (bot.) plant of which the stem grows by deposit on the outside, dicotyledon. – F. *exogène* (De Candolle, 1813), modL. *exogena* (sc. L. *planta* plant), after L. *indigenus* INDIGENOUS.

exodus e·ksədəs departure, spec. of the Israelites out of Egypt (hence, title of the second book of the Pentateuch, which relates this). XVII. – ecclL. *Exodus* – Gr. *éxodos*, f. *ex* EX-[2]+*hodós* way.

exon e·ksɔn officer of the Yeomen of the Guard. XVIII. Later sp. of *exant*, *exaun* officer of cavalry (XVII), var. of EXEMPT intended to repr. F. pronunc. ɛgzã.

exonerate ėgzɔ·nəreit unload, relieve of a burden (spec. the bowels); relieve or free *from* an obligation, reproach, etc. XVI (pa. pple. once XV). f. pp. stem of L. *exonerāre*, f. *ex* EX-[1]+*oner-*, *onus* burden; see ONEROUS, -ATE[3].

exorbitant ėgzɔ̄·ɹbitənt deviating from the right or normal path XV; (grossly) exceeding proper bounds XVII. – prp. of ecclL. *exorbitāre*, f. *ex* EX-[1]+*orbita* ORBIT; see -ANT.

exorcism e·ksɔ̄ɹsizm, -gz- expulsion of an evil spirit by adjuration, etc. XIV. – ecclL. *exorcismus* – ecclGr. *exorkismós*, f. *exorkízein*, f. *ex* EX-[2]+*hórkos* oath; see -ISM. So **e·xor**CIST. XIV (Wycl. Bible). – ecclL. *exorcista* – Gr. *-tḗs*. XIV. **e·xorcise**, -IZE. XV. – F. or ecclL.

exordium ė-gzɔ̄·ɹdiəm, -ks- beginning of a discourse. XVI. – L., f. *exōrdīrī*, f. *ex* EX-[1]+ *ōrdīrī* begin, rel. to *ōrdō* ORDER.

exostosis egzəstou·sis (path.) formation of bone on other bone. XVIII. modL. – Gr. *exóstōsis* (Galen) outgrowth of bone, f. *ex* EX-[2]+*ostéon* bone; see -OSIS.

exoteric eksoute·rik external)(*esoteric*. XVII. – L. *exōtericus* – Gr. *exōterikós*, f. *exōtérō* compar. of *éxō* outside; see EXO-, -IC.

exotic ėksɔ·tik, ėgz- foreign, not indigenous. XVI (Jonson). – L. *exōticus* – Gr. *exōtikós*, f. *éxō*; cf. prec.

expand ėkspæ·nd spread out (trans. and intr.). XV (contr. pp. *expande* XV). – L. *expandere*, f. *ex* EX-[1]+*pandere* spread. So **expanse** ėkspæ·ns wide extent. XVII (Milton, of the firmament of heaven). – modL. *expansum* (n. of *expansus*, pp. of *expandere*), in Eng. context XVII–XVIII, used to render Heb. *rāqī'* (Vulg. *firmamentum*), f. *rāqīa'* spread out. So **expa·n**SION. XVII. – late L.

expatiate ėkspei·ʃieit (arch.) walk about at large XVI; discourse at length XVII. f. L. *ex(s)patiāt-, -ārī*, f. *ex* EX-[1]+*spatiārī* walk, f. *spatium* SPACE; see -ATE[3].

expatriate ėkspei·trieit withdraw from one's native country. XVIII. f. medL. *expatriāt-, -āre*, f. *ex* EX-[1]+*patria* native land (cf. PATRIOT). Hence **expatriA·TION**. XIX.

expect ėkspe·kt †wait, wait for; look for in anticipation. XVI. – L. *ex(s)pectāre*, f. *ex* EX-[1]+*spectāre* look (see SPECTACLE). So **expe·ctANT**. XIV. – L. *expectāns*; **expe·ctANCY**. XVI. **expectA·TION**. XVI. – L.

expectorate ėkspe·ktəreit eject (phlegm) XVII; spit XIX. f. pp. stem of L. *expectorāre*, f. *ex* EX-[1] + *pector-, pectus* breast; see PECTORAL, -ATE[3].

expeditate ikspe·diteit (hist.) cut away from (a dog) three claws or the ball of the forefoot. XVI. f. pp. stem of medL. *expeditāre*, f. *ex* EX-[1]+*ped-, pēs* FOOT, after *excapitāre* behead.

expedite e·kspidait †clear of difficulties; help forward, dispatch. XVII (the pp. *expedite* was used XV, and †*expede* Sc. XVI). f. *expedīt-*, pp. stem of L. *expedīre* extricate (orig. free the feet), make ready, put in order, intr. be serviceable or useful, f. *ex* EX-[1]+*ped-, pēs* FOOT; see -ITE. So **expediENT** ėkspī·diənt conducive to advantage, fit and proper. XIV. f. prp. of the L. vb. **expedI·TION** †prompt action, dispatch; warlike enterprise XV; journey made for a purpose; prompt movement XVI. – (O)F. – L. Hence **expedi·tIOUS**. XV.

expel ėkspe·l drive out or forth. XIV (Ch.). – L. *expellere*, f. *ex* EX-[1]+*pellere* drive, thrust (cf. PULSE[2]). So **expulSION** ėkspʌ·lʃən. XIV. – L. **expu·lsIVE**. XIV (*vertu expulsif*, Ch.).

expend ėkspe·nd pay out, disburse. XV. – L. *expendere*, f. *ex* EX-[1]+*pendere* weigh, pay, rel. to *pendere* hang (see PENDENT); cf. DISPEND, SPEND. Hence **expe·ndituRE**. XVIII; after †*expenditor* officer having charge of expenditure XV–XIX (medL., f. *expenditus*, irreg. pp. of *expendere*, after *venditus* sold). So **expe·nse** spending, money disbursed XIV; pecuniary charge, cost XIV. – AN. *expense*, alteration of OF. *espense* – late L. *expensa*, fem. (sc. *pecunia* money) of pp. of *expendere*. **expe·nsIVE** †lavish; costly. XVII. f. *expens-*, pp. stem of L. *expendere*; assoc. early with *expense*.

experience ėkspiə·riəns †trial; observation of facts; condition or event by which one is affected XIV (Ch., Wycl. Bible, PPl.); knowledge resulting from observation; state of having been occupied in some way XV. – (O)F. *expérience* – L. *experientia*, f. *experīrī* try; see EX-[1], PERIL, -ENCE. Hence vb. XVI. So **experiMENT** ėkspe·rimənt †test, trial; action undertaken to discover or test something. XIV (Wycl. Bible, PPl.). – OF. *experiment* or L. *experīmentum*, f. *experīrī*. Hence vb. †experience, ascertain, test XV (Caxton); make an experiment XVIII. **experime·ntAL**[1]. XV. – (O)F. or medL. **expert** ėkspə̄·ɹt, e·kspə̄ɹt (when not attrib.) trained by experience. XIV (Ch.). – (O)F. *expert*, refash. of †*espert* after L. *expertus*, pp. of *experīrī*. **expert** e·kspəɹt one who is expert, specialist. XIX. – F. *expert*, sb. use of the adj. **expertise** ekspə̄ɹtī·z. XIX. – F.

expiate e·kspieit †bring to an end XVI; avert evil from; do away the guilt of, make amends for XVII. f. pp. stem of L. *expiāre*, f. *ex* EX-[1]+*piāre* seek to appease (by sacrifice), f. *pius* devout, PIOUS; see -ATE[3]. So **expiA·TION**. XV. – L.

expire ėkspaiə·ɹ breathe one's last XV; breathe out XVI. – (O)F. *expirer* – L. *ex(s)pīrāre*, f. *ex* EX-[1]+*spīrāre* breathe (see SPIRIT). So **expirA·TION** coming to an end, †death XVI; breathing out XVII (? XV). – L. Hence **expiRY**[3] ėkspaiə·ri dying, death XVIII (Burns); termination XIX. **expiratORY**[2] ėkspaiə·rətəri pert. to expiration. XIX.

explain ėksplei·n unfold (a matter), give details of XV; †open out, smoothe; assign a meaning to XVII; account for XVIII. – L. *explānāre*, f. *ex* EX-[1]+*plānus* PLAIN. So **explanA·TION** eksplə-. XIV (Wycl. Bible). – L. **explanatORY**[2] ėksplæ·n-. XVII.

expletive ėksplī·tiv serving to fill out; sb. expletive word. XVII (used of a profane oath, etc. XIX). – late L. *explētīvus*, f. *explēre*, f. *ex* EX-[1]+*plēre* fill; see FULL, -IVE.

explicate e·ksplikeit unfold, †lit. and fig. XVI. f. pp. stem of L. *explicāre*, f. *ex* EX-[1]+ *plicāre* fold; see PLY, -ATE[3]. So **explicA·TION**. – F. *explication* (the usual word for 'explanation') or L. So **explicit**[1] ėkspli·sit clearly developed, distinctly expressed. XVII. – F. *explicite* or L. *explicitus*, pp. of *explicāre*. **explicABLE** e·ksplikəbl.

explicit[2] e·ksplisit late L. formula (Jerome) used by scribes to indicate the end of a book or piece, prob. orig. short (on the analogy of INCIPIT) for *explicitus est liber* the book is unfolded or exhibited (see prec.) but regarded as a verb in 3rd pers. sing. ('here ends'), *expliciunt* being used as its pl.

explode ėksplou·d †reject XVI; bring into discredit XVII (now chiefly in pp.); 'go off' or cause to do so with a loud noise XVIII. – L. *explōdere* drive out by clapping, hiss off the stage (cf. APPLAUD, PLAUDIT), f. *ex* EX-[1]+*plaudere* clap the hands. So **explo·SION**. XVII – F or L. **explo·sIVE**. XVII; sb. XIX. Cf. IMPLOSIVE, PLOSIVE. f. *explōs-*, pp. stem.

exploit e·ksploit †progress, success XIV; †attempt to control or capture XV; deed, feat XVI. ME. *esploit, explait, -pleyte, -ployte* – OF. *esplait* achievement, *esploit* m., *esploite* fem. (mod. *exploit*, with latinized prefix) = Pr. *espleit* :– Gallo-Rom. **explictum*, **-ta*, L. *explicitum, -ta* n. and fem. pps. of *explicāre* EXPLICATE; orig. 'something unfolded or put forth'. So **exploi·t** vb. †achieve XIV; †prosper XV; (after modF.) turn to account, make capital out of, esp. in unfavourable sense XIX. ME. *expleite* – OF. *expleiter* accomplish, enjoy (mod. *exploiter*) = Pr. *espleitar* :– Gallo-Rom. **explicitāre*, f. *explicāre*. **exploit**A·TION XIX. – F.

explore ėksplɔ̄ə·ɹ seek to ascertain, examine into XVI; search into (a country, etc.) XVII. – F. *explorer* – L. *explōrāre* search out. So **explor**A·TION. XVI. – F. or L.

exponent ėkspou·nənt interpreting XVI; sb. (math.) index of a power (modL. *numerus exponens*) XVIII; expounder, interpreter XIX. – L. *expōnent-, -ēns*, prp. of *expōnere* EXPOUND. So **expone·nt**IAL (math.) involving the unknown quantity or variable as an exponent. XVIII. – F. *exponentiel* (J. Bernoulli). **expo·n**IBLE (proposition) requiring explanation. XVI. – medL.

export ėkspɔ̄·ɹt †carry away XV; send from one country to another XVII. – L. *exportāre*, f. *ex* EX-[1]+*portāre* carry (cf. PORT[1]). Hence **export** sb. e·kspɔ̄ɹt. XVII. So **export**A·TION. XVII. – L. ¶ F. *export, exporter, exportation* (XVIII) are from Eng.

expose ėkspou·z deprive of shelter; lay open; render liable; disclose XV; exhibit or offer publicly XVII. – (O)F. *exposer*, based on L. *expōnere*; see EXPOUND, POSE[1]. So **exposi**·TION explanation, interpretation XIV (R. Rolle); setting forth in description XIV (Wyclif); (hist.) exposure; displaying to view XVII (after modF, industrial exhibition XIX). – (O)F. or L. **exposit**OR[1] ikspɔ·sitəɹ setter-forth, expounder. XIV (R. Rolle, Trevisa). – (O)F. or late L. **expo·sit**ORY[2]. XVII. – late L. *expositōrius* (Boethius). **expos**URE ėkspou·ʒəɹ action of exposing, being exposed; disclosure to view. XVII (Sh.). Appears first *c.* 1600 along with *composure, disposure*; f. *expose*, after *enclose, enclosure*, which as a pair date from early XVI.

ex post facto eks poust fæ·ktou erron. division of medL. *ex postfacto* (Digest of Justinian) from what is done afterwards, i.e. *ex* from, out of, with abl. of *postfactum*, i.e. *post* after + pp. of *facere* DO[1]. XVII (applied attrib. to an act, etc., operating retrospectively XVIII).

expostulate ėkspɔ·stjŭleit †demand, urge, complain of; make friendly objections. XVI. f. pp. stem of L. *expostulāre*; see EX-[1], POSTULATE. So **expostul**A·TION. XVI. – L.

expound ėkspau·nd set forth in detail; interpret. XIII. ME. *expoune, expounde* – OF. *espondre* (pres. stem *espon-*) = Pr., Sp. *esponer*, It. *esporre*, Rum. *spune* :– L. *expōnere* put out (whence †*expone* XIV), expose, publish, exhibit, explain, f. *ex* EX-[1]+ *pōnere* put, place :– **posinere*, f. **po-* (cf. OSl. *po*, Lith. *pa* with, alongside)+*sinere* place, leave (cf. SITE). Cf. EXPOSE and EXPOSITION (which serves as noun of action to the vbs. *expose* and *expound*). For the formal development cf. COMPOUND.

express ėkspre·s portray, represent XIV (Ch., Wycl. Bible); press out XIV. – OF. *expresser* (= Pr. *espressar*, etc.) – Rom. **expressāre*, f. *ex* EX-[1]+*pressāre* PRESS; repr. in use L. *exprimere* (whence F. *exprimer*). So **expre·ss** adj. explicitly stated XIV (Ch., Gower); specially designed for a purpose XIV (*express train* orig. special train, *c.* 1840; also sb., by ellipsis of *train*). – (O)F. *exprès* (= Pr. *expres*, Sp. *espreso*, etc.) – L. *expressus* distinctly or manifestly presented, pp. of *exprimere*. **expre·ss**ION representation, manifestation XV; pressing out XV. – (O)F. – L. **expre·ss**IVE †tending to expel XIV; full of expression XVII; serving to express XVIII. – F. or medL.

exprobration eksproubrei·ʃən (arch.) reproach. XV. – L. *exprobrātiō(n-)*, f. *exprobrāre*, f. *ex* EX-[1]+*probrum* shameful deed; see OPPROBRIUM, -TION.

expropriate ėksprou·prieit dispossess of property. XVII. f. pp. stem of medL. *expropriāre*, f. *ex* EX-[1]+*proprium* PROPERTY; see -ATE[3]. So **expropri**A·TION. XV (rare before XIX).

expulsion see EXPEL.

expunct ėkspʌ·ŋkt (palæogr.) mark for deletion by a dot above or below. f. pp. stem of L. *expungere* (see next). XVII.

expunge ėkspʌ·ndʒ blot out, efface. XVII. – L. *expungere* mark for deletion by points set above or below, f. *ex* EX-[1]+*pungere* prick; see PUNCTURE, POINT. The Eng. sense is due in part to assoc. with *sponge*.

expurgate e·kspɔ̄ɹgeit amend by the removal of objectionable features. XVII. f. pp. stem of L. *expurgāre*. So **expurg**A·TION. XV (rare before XVII); see EX-[1], -ATE[3], PURGATION. So **e:xpurgato·r**IAL XIX, **expu·rgat**ORY XVII. – modL. *expurgātōrius*, as in *Index Expurgatorius* list of authors and writings forbidden by the Church of Rome to be read unless expurgated.

exquisite e·kskwizit, ėkskwi·zit †ingenious, abstruse, choice XV; †accurate, exact; carefully elaborated; highly cultivated; consummate XVI; intense; keenly sensitive XVII. – L. *exquīsītus*, pp. adj. of *exquīrere* search out, f. *ex* EX-[1]+*quærere* search, seek; see -ITE. Cf. QUERY.

exsert ėksɔ̄·ɹt (biol.) thrust out or forth. XIX. f. *exsert-*, pp. stem of L. *exserere* (see EXERT).

exsiccate e·ksikeit, eksi·keit make dry, dry up. XV. f. pp. stem of L. *exsiccāre*, f. *ex* EX-[1]+*siccāre*, f. *siccus* dry; see -ATE[3].

extant e·kstǣnt, ėkstæ·nt †standing out or forth; (still) existing. XVI. – L. *ex(s)tant-*, *-āns*, prp. of *exstāre* be prominent or visible, exist, f. *ex* EX-¹+*stāre* STAND; see -ANT and cf. F. *extant* (XVII).

extempore ėkste·mpəri without premeditation XVI; adj. XVII; †sb. extempore composition XVI. f. L. phr. *ex tempore* on the spur of the moment, i.e. *ex* out of, *tempore*, abl. of *tempus* time. Also †*extempory* XVII–XVIII. So †**exte·mporAL**¹ XVI, **extempo-rA·NEOUS** XVII. – L. *extemporālis*, late L. *-āneus*. **exte·mporARY** XVII; after *temporary*. Hence **exte·mporIZE**. XVIII.

extend ėkste·nd stretch out XIV (Ch.); enlarge the scope of; stretch forth, hold out XVI. – L. *extendere*, f. *ex* EX-¹+*tendere* stretch, TEND¹. ¶ The leg. sense 'value, assess' (XIV, R. Mannyng) may be an inverse development from *extent* valuation. So **ex-te·nSION** stretching, distension XIV; enlargement XVI; state of being extended, range XVII. – late L. *extensiō(n-)*, *-tent-*; see TENSION. **exte·nsIVE** distended XV; of large extent XVII (Bacon). – F. or late L. **exte·nsOR**¹ (anat.) extending muscle. XVIII. modL. **exte·nt** (hist.) valuation of property XIV (R. Mannyng); (leg.) seizure of lands, etc.; breadth or width of application, etc. XVI (Hooker); length and breadth XVII. – AN. *extente* – medL. *extenta*, sb. use of fem. pp. of *extendere*. **extenuate** ėkste·njueit †make thin, diminish, †disparage the magnitude of; under-rate, seek to lessen the importance of. XVI. f. pp. stem of L. *extenuāre*, f. *ex* EX-¹+*tenuis* THIN. So **extenuA·TION**. XVI. – L. In (O)F. *exténuer*, *-ation*.

exterior ėkstiə·riəɹ outer, situated outside. XVI. – L. *exterior*, compar. formation on *exterus* that is outside (itself a compar.), f. *ex* out = Gr. *ex* EX-¹ and ²; cf. EXTREME; parallel forms are found in W. *eithr* (:– **ektros*) except, *eithaf* (:– **ektəmos*) uttermost, extreme, Ir. *im-eachtar* outside edge.

exterminate ėkstə̄·ɹmineit †expel, banish XVI; destroy utterly XVII. f. pp. stem of L. *extermināre* (in class L. only in first sense; in Vulg. in second sense), f. *ex* EX-¹+*terminus* boundary, TERM; see -ATE³. So **exterminA·TION**. XV. – late L. Cf. (O)F. *exterminer*, *-ation*.

external ėkstə̄·ɹnəl pert. to the outside or exterior. XV. – medL. **externālis*, f. *externus* (whence **extern** XVI), f. *exter(us)* that is outside, f. *ex*; see EX, -AL¹; superseded earlier *extern* in gen. use.

exterritoriality eksteritə̄riæ·liti condition of being considered outside the territory in which one resides. XIX. See EX-¹. In syncopated form **extrality** ėkstræ·lĭti. XX. Also E:XTRA**territoria·lity**. XIX.

extinct ėksti·ŋkt that has burned out XV; that has died out XVI. – L. *ex(s)tinctus*, pp. of *ex(s)tinguere*, f. *ex* EX-¹+*stinguere* quench (see STICK). So **exti·nCTION**. XVI. – L. *extinctiō(n-)*; cf. F. *extinction* (XVI). **extinguish** ėksti·ŋgwiʃ. XVI. irreg. f. L. *ex(s)tinguere*; see -ISH² and cf. *distinguish*.

extirpate e·kstə̄ɹpeit root out. XVI. f. pp. stem of L. *ex(s)tirpāre*, f. *ex* EX-¹+*stirps* stem or stock of a tree; see -ATE³.

extol ėkstou·l, ėkstɔ·l †lift up XV; praise highly, boast of XV. – L. *extollere*, f. *ex* EX-¹+*tollere* raise (cf. TOLERATE).

extort ėkstɔ̄·ɹt obtain by violent or oppressive means. XVI. f. *extort-*, pp. stem of L. *extorquēre*, f. *ex* EX-¹+*torquēre* twist (cf. TORTURE). So **exto·rTION**. XIII (Cursor M.). – late L. *extortiō(n-)*; cf. (O)F. *extorsion* and TORSION. **exto·rtionate.** XVIII (Mrs. Piozzi); superseding †*extortionable* (rare; XVII–XVIII), †*extortionous* (occas.; XVII), †*extortious* (XVI–XVIII), *extortive* (XVII–XIX). **exto·rtionER**¹. XIV.

extra e·kstrə that is beyond the usual XVIII; adv., sb. XIX. prob. short for EXTRAORDINARY, as (earlier) F. *extra* for *extraordinaire*; cf. G. *extra* (XVIII).

extra- e·kstrə L. adv.-prep. *extrā* outside (contr. of *exterā*, abl. fem. of *exterus* EXTERIOR) used to form adjs. on the model of L. *extrāordinārius* EXTRAORDINARY, *extrāmūrānus* extramural (f. *extrā mūrōs* outside the walls), in which an adj. termination is added to a phr. consisting of *extrā* governing an acc.; the analysis of such adjs. is often felt to be *extra*+adj., e.g. *extraordinary* is felt as meaning 'outside of being what is ordinary'. Other early exx. are *e:xtrajudi·cial*, *extramu·ndane* (late L. *extrāmundānus*), *e:xtraparo·chial*, *e:xtraprovi·ncial* (medL. *extrāprovinciālis*), which are all XVII.

extract ėkstræ·kt †pp. derived, descended XV; draw out or forth XVI; take *out of*, copy out XVII. f. *extract-*, pp. stem of L. *extrahere* (whence F. *extraire*, etc.), f. *ex* EX-¹+*trahere* draw (see TRACT). So **extract** e·kstrækt sb. substance extracted XVI; passage excerpted XV (Pecock). – L. *extractum*, sb. use of n. pp. **extra·cTION** lineage, origin XV (Caxton); drawing out XVI. – (O)F. – late L.

extradition ekstrədi·ʃən delivery of a fugitive foreign criminal to the authorities of the government which claims him. XIX (De Quincey). – F. *extradition* (Voltaire), f. L. *ex* EX-¹+*trāditiō* TRADITION. Hence by back-formation **extradite** e·kstrədait (XIX), suggested by F. *extrader* (XVIII).

extrados ekstrei·dɔs (archit.) upper or exterior curve of an arch. XVIII. – F. *extrados*, f. L. *extrā* outside+F. *dos* back :– L. *dorsum* (cf. DOSSAL). Cf. *intrados*.

extraneous ėkstrei·niəs of external origin or position. XVII. f. L. *extrāneus* (see STRANGE); see -EOUS.

extraordinary ekstrəɔ̄·ɹdinəri, ikstrɔ̄·ɹdnri that is out of the usual course XV; exceptional XVI. – L. *extrāōrdinārius*, f. phr. *extrā ōrdinem* out of course, in an unusual manner; see EXTRA-, ORDINARY.

extrapolate ėkstræ·pŏleit find by a calculation based on known terms of a series other terms outside them. XIX (Gladstone, Airy). f. INTERPOLATE by substitution of EXTRA- for *inter-*. So **e:xtrapol**A·TION. XIX.

extravagant ėkstræ·vəgənt epithet of certain papal decrees not contained in particular collections XIV (sb. from XVI); exceeding due bounds XVI. – prp. of medL. *extrāvagārī*, f. *extrā*+*vagārī* wander; see EXTRA-, VAGARY, -ANT. The gen. sense depends on F. *extravagant*, It. *(e)stravagante*. So **extra·vag**ANCE †digression XVII (Milton); unrestrained excess XVII; excessive prodigality XVIII. – F. **extravaga·nza** -gæ·nzə (mus., etc.) extravagant composition. XVIII. – It. *estravaganza* (usu. *strava-*); refash. after EXTRA-.

extravasate ėkstræ·vəseit force (fluid, as blood) out of its proper vessel. XVII. – modL. **extrāvāsāre*, f. *extrā*+*vās* vessel; see EXTRA-, VASE, -ATE[3]. So **extravas**A·TION. XVII; cf. F. *extravaser, -vasation*.

extreme ėkstrī·m last, final (surviving in *extreme unction*) XV; utmost, exceedingly great XV (Fortescue); outermost, farthest XV. – OF. *extreme* (mod. *-ême*) – L. *extrēmus* (superl. corr. to *exterus* EXTERIOR), f. instr. form in *-ē*+superl. suffix **-mo-* (cf. *postrēmus* last, *suprēmus* SUPREME). So **extremi**TY ėkstre·mĭti. XIV. – (O)F. or L.

extricate e·kstrikeit unravel, disentangle. XVII. f. pp. stem of L. *extrīcāre*, f. *ex* EX-[1]+ *trīcæ* perplexities; cf. INTRICATE, and see -ATE[3]. So **extric**A·TION. XVII.

extrinsic ėkstri·nsik †exterior, external XVI; pert. to external aspects or conditions XVII. – late L. *extrinsecus* adj. outer, f. L. *extrinsecus* adv. outwardly (f. *extrā, exter* EXTRA, EXTERIOR+*-im*, as in *interim*)+*secus* alongside of (corr. to Ir. *sech* beside, beyond, OW. *hep* without, Lett. *sec* alongside, Skr. *sácā* with), f. **seqw-* follow (cf. SEQUENCE). The ending was from the first assim. to -IC (cf. INTRINSIC). In (O)F. *extrinsèque*.

extro- e·kstrou alteration of L. *extrā* outside, on the analogy of *intrō-/intrā* inside (cf. *contrō-*); e.g. *extroversion, -vert* XVII.

extrude ėkstrū·d thrust out. XVI. – L. *extrūdere*, f. *ex-* EX-[1]+*trūdere* thrust (cf. THREAT). Hence **extru·**SION. XVI; after *intrusion*.

exuberant ėgzjū·bərənt growing luxuriantly, abundantly fertile; abounding in health and spirits. XV. – F. *exubérant* – L. *exūberant-, -āns*, prp. of *exūberāre*, f. *ex* EX-[1]+*ūberāre* be fruitful, f. *ūber* fertile, rel. to UDDER; see -ANT. So **exu·ber**ANCE. XVII. – F. – L.

exude ėgzjū·d ooze or sweat out. XVI. – L. *ex(s)ūdāre*, f. *ex* EX-[1]+*sūdāre* SWEAT.

exult ėgzʌ·lt †leap up; rejoice exceedingly. XVI. – L. *ex(s)ultāre*, frequent. of *exsilīre*, f. *ex* EX-[1]+*salīre* leap (cf. SALIENT). So **exu·lt**ANT. XVII, **exult**A·TION. XV. – L. Cf. F. *exulter, exultation*.

exuviæ ėgzjū·viī cast skins, shells, etc. XVII. L., clothing stripped off, skins of animals, spoils, f. *exuere* divest oneself, f. *ex* EX-[1]+ **-ou-*, **-eu-* (as in *induere* put on, ENDUE).

eyas ai·əs young hawk taken from the nest. XV (Book of St. Albans). Alteration of †*nias*, †*nyas* – (O)F. *niais* bird taken from the nest, (hence, now) silly person, OIt. *nidiace* :- Rom. **nīd(i)ācem* (*-āx*), f. *nīdus* NEST. For the change of *a nias* to *an yas* cf. ADDER; sp. with *ey-* may be due to assoc. with *ey* EGG[1].

eye ai organ of sight; hole (e.g. of a needle). One of the IE. names of parts of the body (cf. ARM[1]), but wanting in the Celtic group. OE. *ēaġe*, Anglian *ēġe* = OFris. *āge*, OS. *ōga* (Du. *oog*), OHS. *ouga* (G. *auge*), ON. *auga*, Goth. *augo* (Crimean Goth. pl. *oeghene*) :- CGerm. **augon*, rel. ult. to IE. **oq^w-* (but the corr. of Germ. **au* to IE. **o* is inexplicable), on which are based many synon. forms (with various modifications), viz. Skr. (Vedic) *ákshi* eye, number two, (dual) sun and moon, Arm. *akn*, Lith. *akìs*, OSl. (Russ.) *óko*, dual *óči*, Toch. *ak, ek*, Gr. *ósse* (:- **okje*) the two eyes, *ómma* (:- **opma*), *ophthalmós* eye (cf. OPHTHALMIC, OPTIC), *ṓps* face, L. (with dim. suffix) *oculus* (cf. OCULAR), *-ōx* in *atrōx*, ATROCIOUS, *ferōx* FEROCIOUS. The OE. pl. *ēaġan* survives in north. dial. *een* and arch. *eyne* (Spenser); the pl. in *-s* dates from XIV. ¶ For the IE. conditions see esp. Ernout & Meillet s.v. *oculus*. Comps. **eye-**BALL[1]. XVI (Sh.). **eye·bright** plant Euphrasia officinalis, formerly used for weakness of the eyes (f. *bright* in the sense 'brightness', 'light'). XVI. **eye·**BROW. XVI; repl. (dial.) *eyebree* (OE. *ēagbrǣw*). **eye**LASH. XVIII. **eye**LID. XII (*egælid*); cf. OFris. *āchlid, āghlid*. **eye·**SIGHT. XII (*eȝhe sihhþe* Orm). **eye**SORE. XII (*eagesare*). **eye**TOOTH. XVI; perh. after Du. *oogtand*, G. *augenzahn*. **eye·**WI:TNESS. XVI.

eyelet ai·lit small hole worked or perforated in cloth, etc. XIV (Wycl. Bible). Late ME. *oilet, oylette* – OF. *oillet* (mod. *œillet*), dim. of †*oil, œil* :- L. *oculu-s* EYE; see -ET. ¶ The present sp. (*eylet* XVI) and pronunc. are due to assoc. with EYE and -LET.

eyot var. of AIT.

eyre ɛəɪ circuit (*justice in eyre* itinerant judge) XIII; circuit court (sp. *Air* by Scott 'Lay of the Last Minstrel' IV xxxv). – OF. *eire* :- L. *iter* journey. *In eyre* – AN. *en eyre*, as in *justices en eyre* (cf. AN. *justices errauntz*, legal L. *justitiæ itinerantes*).

eyrie, aerie ɛə·ri, aiə·ri nest of a bird of prey. XVI (*airie, ay(e)rie*). – medL. *airea, eyria, aeria, aerea*, prob. f. (O)F. *aire* lair of wild animals, (earlier also) nature, origin, kind (whence ME. *aire*, e.g. *an hauke of noble air*; cf. OF. *un faucon de gentil aire*) = Pr. *agre* family, race, stock :- L. *agrum*, nom. *ager* piece of ground, (hence in Rom.) native country, resting-place, lair (see ACRE and cf. AIR, DEBONAIR). ¶ The sp. *eyerie* was favoured by Spelman in his 'Glossarium', 1664, by assoc. with *ey* EGG[1]; Milton has *Eyries* in 'P.L.' IV 424.

ezod see IZZARD.

F

fa fā (mus.) 4th note in Guido's hexachords XIV; 4th note of an octave XIX. See UT.

Fabian fei·biən pert. to a policy of delay. XIX. – L. *Fabiānus* pert. to a Fabius or the gens Fabia, esp. Quintus *Fabius* Maximus, surnamed Cunctator ('delayer') from his tactics against Hannibal in the Second Punic War. *Fabian Society*, founded 1884 to prosecute a 'Fabian' policy in the furtherance of socialism.

fable fei·bl story, legendary fiction XIII; plot of a play or poem XVII. – (O)F. *fable* – L. *fābula* discourse, story, literary plot, f. *fārī* speak (cf. FAME, FATE). So **fable** vb. tell tales XIV; relate as fiction XVI. – OF. *fabler* – L. *fābulārī*, f. *fābula*.

fabliau fæ·bliou medieval French humorous tale in verse. XIX (Scott). F. (XVI), evolved from OF. (Picard) *fablia(u)x*, pl. of *fablel*, dim. of *fable*; see prec. and -EL².

fabric fæ·brik edifice XV; construction or structure of a building XVII; textile stuff XVIII. – F. *fabrique* (= Pr. *fabriga*, Sp. *fábrica*, It. *fabbrica*) – L. *fabrica*, f. *faber* worker in metal, etc. (cf. FORGE). So **fabri**CATE³ fæ·brikeit construct XV; invent, forge XVIII. f. pp. stem of L. *fabricāre*, f. *fabrica*. **fabric**A·TION XV. – L. *fabricātiōn-em*.

fabulist fæ·bjŭlist composer of fables. XVI. – F. *fabuliste*, f. L. *fābula*; see FABLE, -IST.

fabulous fæ·bjŭləs pert. to, of the nature of, resembling fables. XV. – F. *fabuleux* or L. *fābulōsus*, f. *fābula* FABLE; see -OUS.

faburden see FAUX-BOURDON.

façade fǽsā·d principal front of a building. XVII. – F. *façade*, f. *face*, after It. *facciata*; see next and -ADE.

face feis visage, countenance XIII; hence in many transf. and fig. uses, some of which reflect the primary senses of L. *facies*. – (O)F. *face* = Pr. *fasa*, It. *faccia*, Rum. *faţă* :– Rom. **facia*, alteration of L. *faciēs* (repr. directly by Pr. *fatz*, Sp. *haz*, Pg. *face*) form, appearance, visage, aspect, prob. rel. to *fax* (earlier *facēs*) torch, f. **fac-* appear, shine. Superseded early ME. *onsene*, OE. *ansīen*, *andwlīta*, *-e*. Hence vb. XV. **faci**AL¹ fei·ʃⁱəl †(in *f. sight, vision*) face-to-face XVII; pert. to the face XIX. – medL. *faciālis*; cf. F. *facial* (rare before XIX).

facet fæ·sit one of the sides of a body that has several faces. XVII (*fascet*, Bacon). – F. *facette*, dim. of *face*; see prec. and -ET.

facetiæ fəsī·ʃiī pleasantries. XVII (earlier anglicized †*facecies*; cf. F. *facéties*). L., pl. of *facētia* jest. So **face·t**IOUS. XVI. – F. *facétieux*, f. *facétie* – L. *facētia*, f. *facētus* (whence †**face·te** XVII).

facia var. of FASCIA.

-facient fei·ʃⁱənt terminal el. repr. L. *-facient-*, nom. *-faciēns*, prp. of *facere* DO¹, in *calefacient*, *liquefacient*, *rubefacient*, f. L. *calefacere*, etc.; extended to cases like *calorifacient*, where L. would have the corr. vb. in *-ficāre* and adj. in *-ficus*.

facile fæ·sail easy XV (Caxton); easily led XVI; moving freely XVII. – F. *facile* or L. *facilis*, f. *facere* DO¹; see -ILE. So **facil**ITY fəsi·lĭti. XV. – F. or L. **faci·litate** render easy. XVII. – F. *faciliter* – It. *facilitare*, f. *facile* (– L. *facilis*), after L. *dēbilitāre* DEBILITATE, etc.

facinorous fəsi·nərəs (arch.) criminal, infamous. XVI. – L. *facinorōsus*, f. *facinor-*, *facinus* (bad) deed, f. *facere* DO¹; see -OUS.

facsimile fæksi·mĭli exact copy. XVII. modL. (orig. two words, and formerly so written), f. L. *fac*, imper. of *facere* make, DO¹ + *simile*, n. of *similis* like, SIMILAR.

fact fækt deed (now only in leg. use *after*, *before the fact*, etc.); something that has occurred, what has happened; truth, reality XVI; (pl.) circumstances and incidents of a case XVIII. – L. *factum*, sb. use of n. pp. of *facere* DO¹. Hence (after ACTUAL) **fa·ctual.** XIX (Coleridge). Cf. EFFECTUAL.

faction fæ·kʃən party in a community. XVI. – (O)F. *faction* – L. *factiō(n-)*, f. *facere*; see prec. and -TION, and cf. FASHION, in some senses of which this word was formerly used. So **fa·ct**IOUS. XVI. – F. *factieux* or L. *factiōsus*.

-faction fæ·kʃən repr. L. *-factiō(n-)*, terminal el. of sbs. rel. to vbs. in *-ficere* -FY, e.g. *satisfaction*; extended to cases like *petrifaction*, where the corr. L. vb. would be in *-ficāre*.

factitious fækti·ʃəs †made by art; made up for the occasion. XVII. f. L. *factīcius*, f. *fact-*; see FACT, -ITIOUS.

factitive fæ·ktĭtiv (gram.) expressing the notion of making a thing to be something. XIX. – modL. *factitīvus*, f. L. *fact-*, pp. stem of *facere*; see FACT and -IVE.

factor fæ·ktəɹ agent XV; (math.) any of the quantities which multiplied together produce a given quantity XVII. – F. *facteur* or L. *factor*, f. *fact-*; see FACT, -OR¹.

factory fæ·ktəri A. factorship, agency (Sc.) XVI; B. merchant company's trading station XVI; C. manufactory, works XVII. prob. of mixed origin; in A repr. medL. *factōria* (see FACTOR, -Y³); in B repr. Pg. *feitoria* (= It. *fattoria*, Sp. *factoria*, F. †*factorie* (XV), later *factorerie*); in C, ult. – late L. *factōrium* (recorded in the sense 'oil-press').

factotum fæktou·təm man-of-all-work, †busybody. XVI. – medL. *factōtum*, f. L. *fac*, imper. of *facere* make, DO[1] + *tōtum* the whole (cf. TOTAL); in Eng. context first in appellatives *Johannes Factotum*, *Dominus* or *Magister Factotum* John Do-Everything, Mr. Do-Everything; in XVII occurring without prefixed words, as already earlier in French (†*factoton* XVI) and German (XVI). Cf. the translation-It. *fatutto* fusser.

factum fæ·ktəm statement of a case. XVIII. – F. *factum*, legal use of L. (see FACT).

facula fæ·kjŭlə luminous spot on the sun. XVIII. L., dim. of *fac-*, *fax* torch; cf. FACE, -ULE.

faculty fæ·kəlti ability, capacity; †branch of knowledge (from medL. *facultas*, tr. Gr. *dúnamis* power, as used by Aristotle); department of learning XIV; power; licence XVI. – (O)F. *faculté* – L. *facultās*, f. *facilis* FACILE (cf. early L. *facul* easily); see -TY.

fad fæd crotchety notion or hobby. XIX. Of dial. origin; prob. the second el. of earlier *fidfad* (XVIII), shortening of FIDDLE-FADDLE; deriv. from F. *fadaise* (– Pr. *fadeza*) trifle is improbable.

fade[1] feid lose freshness or brightness. XIV. – OF. *fader*, f. *fade* vapid, dull, faded :– Rom. **fatidu-s*, prob. resulting from a blending of L. *fatuus* silly, insipid, FATUOUS with *vapidus* lifeless, spiritless, VAPID. The common var. †*vade* (XV–XVI) is unaccountable, since no *v-* forms are extant in F.

fade[2] fad insipid. XVIII. F. (see prec.). ¶ The OF. adj. was adopted in ME. in the senses 'pale, wan' and 'faded'.

fæces fī·sīz dregs XV; excrement XVII. L., pl. of *fæx* dregs. Cf. FECULENT.

faerie, faery fei·əri fairyland, var. of FAIRY, perh. based on OF. *faerie*, adopted by Spenser in 'The Faerie Queene' (1590–6) to designate his imaginary world of men and monsters; the special form may have been chosen either to express his peculiar modification of the sense or to exclude unsuitable associations of the usual form *fairy*.

Faeroese, Faroese fɛəroui·z, færoui·z (pert. to) the inhabitants or language of the Faeroe or Faroe Islands (*Faeroes*, *Faroes*), sp. also *Faröe*, †*Feroe* (cf. modL. *Feroa*), situated in the North Sea, between Iceland and the Shetland Islands. XIX. The Scand. names are: Da. *Færørne*, Sw. *Färöarne*, ON. *Færeyjar* 'sheep islands' (f. *fær* sheep, *ey* island). f. above forms + -ESE, after Da., *færøisk*, G. *färöisch*, etc.

fag[1] fæg †something hanging loose; last remnant XV; extreme end XVI (more fully **fag-end** XVII). Of unkn. origin; 'Book of St. Albans' Bj has *the flagg or the fagg federis*.

fag[2] fæg †flag, decline XVI; work hard, toil; tire, weary XVIII; (from the sb.) act as a fag XIX. Of unkn. origin; cf. FLAG[4]. Hence **fag** sb. drudgery, fatigue; in Eng. public schools, junior who performs duties for a senior XVIII (perh. assoc. with *fatigue*).

fag[3] fæg (sl.) cigarette. Abbrev. of *fag-end*. XIX.

faggot fæ·gət bundle of sticks, etc., tied together. XIII. – (O)F. *fagot* – It. *fagotto* (whence also Pr. *fagot*, Sp. *fagoto*), dim. of Rom. **facus*, back-formation on Gr. *phákelos* bundle.

Fahrenheit fæ·rənait, fā·rənhait mercurial thermometer named after its inventor, *Fahrenheit* (1686–1736), Prussian physicist. XVIII.

faience fajã·s porcelain. XVIII. F. *faïence* short for *poterie* or *vaisselle de Faïence*, i.e. pottery or ware of the Italian town Faenza (L. *Faventia*).

fail[1] feil default (now only in *without fail*). XIII. – OF. *fail(l)e*, f. *faillir* (see next).

fail[2] feil be wanting or insufficient; lose power; fall or come short, be in default. XIII. – (O)F. *faillir* be wanting = Pr. *falhir* :– Rom. **fallīre*, for L. *fallere* deceive, and used in the sense 'disappoint expectation, be wanting or defective'. So **failure** fei·ljəɹ default; want of success. XVII. orig. *failer* – AN. (legal) *failer*, for OF. *faillir*, inf. used as sb. (see -ER[5]); altered to *failor*, *-our*, and finally to *failure*, by assim. to the suffixes -OR[2], -URE (cf. *leisure*, *pleasure*).

fain fein (arch.) glad, happy; used advb. gladly, willingly. XII. OE. *fæġ(e)n*, corr. to OS. *fagan*, *-in*, ON. *feginn* :– Germ. **fagin-*, *-an-*, f. CGerm. **faχ-*, repr. by OE. *ġefēon* (:– **gefehan*), pt. *ġefeah*, OHG. *gifehan* rejoice, and OE. *ġefēa*, OHG. *gifeho*, Goth. *faheþs* joy; ult. origin unkn.

fainéant fei·neã idler. XVII. F. (also †*faitnéant*) do-nothing, etymologizing sp. (*fait* does, 3rd sg. of *faire*, *néant* nothing) of OF. *faignant* sluggard, prp. of *faindre* skulk (see FEIGN).

fain(s) fein(z) (sl.) used in formulæ, e.g. *fain(s) I*, *fainit*, deprecating further actions. XIX. var. of *fen*, clipped form of FEND, in the sense 'forbid' or 'ward off'.

faint feint †feigned; †sluggish XIII; †weak, sickly; inclined to swoon XIV; languid, feeble; indistinct XVI. – OF. *faint*, *feint* feigned, sluggish, cowardly, pp. of *faindre feindre* FEIGN. Cf. FEINT. Hence **faint** vb. XIV.

fair[1] fɛəɹ beautiful; pleasing OE.; free from blemish XII; favourable XIII; light-coloured)(*dark* XVI. OE. *fæġer* = OS., OHG. *fagar*, ON. *fagr*, Goth. *fagrs* (only in n. *fagr* fitting; cf. *gafahrjan* prepare) :– CGerm. **fagraz*, prob. f. **fag-* with *r*-suffix as in BITTER; referred by some to IE. **pok-*, repr. by Lith. *púošti* adorn, Lett. *pohsohu* cleanse, sweep.

fair[2] fɛəɹ periodical gathering of buyers and sellers. XIII (D. Sirith). – OF. *feire* (mod. *foire*) = Pr. *feira*, It. *fiera*, Pg. *feira* :– late L. *fēria*, sg. of class. L. *fēriæ* holiday, older *fēsiæ*, rel. to *fēstus* (see FEAST, FERIA, FESTIVE).

fairy fɛə·ri †fairy-land; †fairy-folk; †magic; diminutive supernatural being. XIV. – OF. *faerie, faierie* (mod. *féerie*), f. *fae* FAY[2]; see -ERY. Cf. FAERIE. ¶ The application to a single being is peculiar to Eng. Hence **fai·ry**LAND (Sh.); **fairy-tale** (1750), tr. F. *conte de fées* 'tale of fairies'.

faith feiþ trust; belief; faithfulness; loyalty. XII. ME. *feþ, feiþ* – AN. *fed*, OF. *feid, feit* (pronounced feiþ) FAY[1] = Pr. *fe*, nom. *fes*, Sp., Pg. *fé* (cf. AUTO-DA-FÉ), It. *fede* :– L. *fidem*, nom. *fides* f. **fid-*, var. of **fīd-* in *fīdus* trustworthy, *fīdere* trust, rel. to Gr. *peíthein* (pf. *pépoitha*) persuade, *pístis* faith, *pistós* faithful, Alb. *bē* oath, f. IE. **bhidh-*, **bheidh-*, **bhoidh-* (cf. FEDERAL). Final *-th* may have been supported by *truth*. In theol. uses *faith* renders ecclL. *fides*, which translates Gr. *πίστις* of the N.T. Hence **faith**FUL[1]. XIII (Cursor M.).

fake feik 'do', do for, do up (orig. thieves' sl.). XIX. Later form of †*feak*, †*feague* beat, thrash – G. *fegen* polish, furbish, sweep, (sl.) thrash, scold, rate. Hence as sb.

fakir fakiə·ɹ, fei·kiəɹ, fā·kiəɹ Mahommedan religious mendicant or ascetic. XVII. – (partly through F. *faquir*) Arab. *faqīr* poor, poor man.

Falangist fəlæ·ndʒist adherent of the *Falange* (spec. use of *falange* PHALANX), Sp. Fascist party founded by José Antonio Prima de Rivera in 1933; see -IST.

falbala fæ·lbələ. XVIII; see FURBELOW.

falcate fæ·lkeit (nat. hist.) sickle-shaped. XIX. – L. *falcātus*, f. *falc-*, *falx* sickle; see -ATE[2]. So **fa·lcat**ED[1]. XVIII.

falchion fɔ̄·lʃiən broad curved convex-edged sword. XIV. ME. *fauchoun* – OF. *fauchon* = It. *falcione* :– Rom. **falciō(nem)*, f. L. *falci-*, *falx* sickle. Latinized sp. with *l* appears XVI.

falcon fɔ̄·(l)kən small diurnal bird of prey XIII; light cannon XV (so *falconet* XVI – It. *falconetto*; for such use of a bird-name cf. *musket*). ME. *faucon* – (O)F. *faucon*, obl. case of *fauc* = Pr. *fauc, faucó*, Sp. *halcón*, Pg. *falcão*, It. *falco*, †*falcone* :– late L. *falcō(n-)*, expl. by Festus as f. *falx* scythe, from the bird's sickle-like claws, but perh. – Germ. **falkon*, repr. by OE. personal name *Falca* = OS., OHG. *falco* (Du. *valk*, G. *falke*). The survival of OE. *falcen* (found in place-names, like *heafoc* hawk) is not probable, the earliest endings, *-on, -un*, pointing to AN. origin. So **falcon**ER[2] fɔ̄·(l)kənəɹ. XIV (Ch.). – (O)F. *fauconnier*. ¶ Sp. (*l*) XV after Latin.

falderal fældəræ·l trifle, gewgaw. XIX (earlier XVIII as a meaningless refrain). Obscurely rel. to FAL-LAL.

faldstool fɔ̄·ldstūl movable prayer-desk XVII; armless chair used by prelates, etc. XIX. – medL. *faldistolium* – WG. **faldistōl* = late OE. *fældestōl, fyld(e)stōl* :– Germ. **falþistōlaz*, f. **falþan* FOLD[2] + **stōlaz* STOOL. †*Faldistory* has also been used (XVII–XVIII) – medL. *faldistorium* or Sp., Pg. *faldistorio*, It. *faldistoro*. Cf. FAUTEUIL.

Falernian fəlɜ̄·ɹniən. XVIII. f. L. *Falernus*, name of a territory in Campania, Italy, famed for its wines; see -IAN.

fall[1] fɔ̄l descent XII (Orm); lapse into sin (AncrR.); falling from an erect posture XIII (Cursor M.); downward motion XIV (see WATERFALL), autumn (orig. †*fall of the leaf*); 'falling' article of dress XVI. ME. *fal(l)*, superseding OE. *(ġe)feall* and *fæll, fell, fiell, fyll* (:– **falliz*); partly – ON. *fall* fall, death in battle, sin, downfall (cf. OS., OHG. *fal*); partly a new formation on FALL[3].

fall[2] fɔ̄l trap. OE. *fealle* in *mūsfealle* mouse-trap, surviving in PITFALL, and in Sc. *mouse-faw, ratton-faw*.

fall[3] fɔ̄l pt. **fell,** pp. **fallen** descend, sink; gen.)(*rise*. OE. *feallan, fallan*, pt. *fēoll*, pp. *feallen* = OFris., ON. *falla*, OS., OHG. *fallan* (Du. *vallen*, G. *fallen, fiel, gefallen*) :– CGerm. (exc. Goth.) redupl. str. vb. **fallan*, pt. **fefell-*, rel. to Lith. *pùlti* fall, Arm. *pʻul* downfall. Cf. FELL[4].

fall[4] fɔ̄l (Sc.) cry uttered when a whale is sighted. XVII. Local Sc. pronunc. of WHALE (in Aberdeenshire *wh* is pronounced f).

fallacy fæ·ləsi deception XV (Caxton) (also †*fallas* XIV); logical flaw; delusive notion XVI; delusive nature XVIII. – L. *fallācia*, f. *fallāc-*, *fallāx*, f. *fallere* deceive (cf. FALSE). (†*Fallace* – (O)F. *fallace*, was earlier.) So **fallacious** fəlei·ʃəs. XVI. – (O)F. *fallacieux*. See -ACY, -ACIOUS.

fal-lal fæ·l læ·l piece of finery. XVIII. One of various redupl. formations expressing the notion of something trivial, perh. suggested by FALBALA.

fallible fæ·lĭbl liable to err or be deceived. XV (Hoccleve, Lydg.; Pecock has *fallable*). – medL. *fallibilis*, f. *fallere* deceive; see FALSE, -IBLE.

Fallopian fælou·piən (anat.) applied to parts described by Gabriello *Fallopio* (1523–62), It. anatomist. XVIII; see -IAN.

fallow[1] fæ·lou ploughed or arable land OE.; ground ploughed and harrowed but left uncropped. XVI. OE. *fealh, fealg-* = MLG. *valge* (G. *felge*); used as adj. XIV. Hence **fa·llow** vb. break up (land) as for sowing. OE. *fealgian* = MHG. *valgen, velgen*.

fallow[2] fæ·lou reddish-yellow (now only in *fallow deer*). OE. *falu (fealu)*, obl. *fealwe*, etc. = OS. *falu* (Du. *vaal*), OHG. *falo* (G. *fahl, falb*), ON. *fǫlr* (pl. *fǫlvar*) :– CGerm. (exc. Goth.) **falwaz* :– CIE. **polwos*, f. **pol-* **pel-* **pl-*, as repr. by Skr. *palitás* grey, Gr. *poliós, pelitnós* grey, *pellós* dark-coloured, L. *pallēre* be PALE, *pullus* grey, blackish, (O)Ir., Gael. *liath*, W. *llwyd* (:– **pleitos*) grey, OSl. *plavŭ* (:– **polvŭ*) white. ¶ The Germ. word is the source of F. *fauve*, It. *falbo*.

false fɔ̀ls wrong; untrue, deceitful; spurious. OE. *fals* adj. in *false ġewihta* wrong weights, *falspening* counterfeit penny (cf. ON. *falspeningr*) and sb. (= ON. *fals*) 'fraud, deceit, falsehood' – L. *falsus* adj. and *falsum* sb. n., prop. pp. of *fallere* deceive. In ME. reinforced by or newly – OF. *fals*, *faus*, fem. *false* (mod. *faux*, *fausse*) = Pr. *fals*, Sp., It. *falso* :– L. *falsu-s*, *-a*. Hence **fa·lse**HOOD. XIV (preceded by †*falshede* XIII–XVI). **fa·lsi**FY. XV. – (O)F. or late L. **fa·ls**ITY. XVI. – L. *falsitās*; cf. ME. *fals(e)te* treachery, fraud – OF. *falseté* (mod. *fausseté*).

falsetto fɔlse·tou (mus.) voice of a register above the natural. XVIII. It., dim. of *falso* FALSE.

falter fɔ̀·ltəɹ stumble in step or speech XIV; give way, waver XVI. Of obscure origin; possibly f. ME. *falde* FOLD[2] (which was used esp. of the faltering of the legs and the tongue) + *-ter*, as in TOTTER.

fame feim reputation; †rumour. XIII. – OF. *fame* (now *fâme* in comps. only) – L. *fāma* = Gr. *phḗmē*, (Doric) *phā́mā*, f. **bhā̆-* in L. *fārī*, Gr. *phánai* speak (cf. FABLE, FATE). So **fa·mo**US renowned, celebrated. XIV (Ch.). – AN. *famous*, OF. *fameus* (mod. *-eux*) – L. *famōsus*.

family fæ·mĭli group of relatives, kindred XV; household of parents, children, servants XVI. – L. *familia* household, f. *famulus* servant; see -Y[3]. Earlier Sc. *famyle* (Wyntoun), later *famell* (Douglas) – (O)F. *famille*. So **famili**AR fəmi·ljəɹ. XIV (R. Rolle, Ch.). Early forms *familier*, *famuler* are – (O)F. *familier*, †*famulier*, but forms in *-iar(e)* are also early and reflect the orig. L. *familiāris*. **fami·liar**IZE. XVII. – F. *familiariser* (XVI). **familiar**ITY -æ·rĭti. XIII. – F. – L.

famine fæ·min extreme dearth, extreme hunger. XIV (PPl., Ch., Gower). – (O)F. *famine*, f. *faim* hunger = Pr., Cat. *fam*, It. *fame*, Rum. *foame* :– L. *fame-s* (cf. Sp. *hambre*, Pg. *fome*, Rum. † *foamine* :– Rom. **famini-s*).

famish fæ·miʃ reduce to the extremities of hunger. XIV. Extended form (after vbs. in -ISH[2]) of ME. *fame* (XIV), aphetic – OF. *afamer* (mod. *affamer*) = Pr. *afamar*, It. *affamare* :– Rom. **affamāre*, f. L. *ad* AF- + *famēs* hunger; cf. DISTINGUISH, EXTINGUISH.

fan[1] fæn instrument for winnowing grain OE.; instrument for agitating the air XIV (Ch.). OE. *fann* – L. *vannus*. Hence **fan** vb. OE. *fannian*. **fa·n**LIGHT[2] fan-shaped window over a door. XIX.

fan[2] fæn abbrev. of FANATIC. An early isolated use (*phan*, *fann*) is recorded from late XVII; the present use dates from late XIX and is orig. U.S.

fanatic fənæ·tik †frenzied, as through divine or demonic possession XVI; marked by excessive enthusiasm XVII; sb. †(religious) maniac; unreasoning enthusiast XVII. – F. *fanatique* (Rabelais) or L. *fānāticus* pert. to a temple, inspired by a deity (spec. of priests of Bellona, Cybele, and other goddesses in whose temples they lived), frenzied, f. *fānum* temple, FANE; see -ATIC. Also **fana·t**ICAL. XVI. Hence **fana·tic**ISM. XVII; also †**fa·natism** (XVII–XVIII) – F.

fancy fæ·nsi arbitrary or capricious preference, individual taste XV (†love XVI); imagination (but later dist. from this) XVI; invention XVII. Early forms *fantsy*, *fansey* (Paston Letters), contr. of FANTASY. Hence **fa·ncy** vb. XVI; or partly contr. of *fantasy* vb. (XV) – OF. *fantasier*.

fandangle fæ·ndæŋgl trifling ornament, trinket, tomfoolery. XIX. perh. alteration (after *newfangle*) of FANDANGO, which was occas. used earlier in this sense; cf. dial. *fandangs* trinkets, antics, †*fandangous* (XVIII) nonsensical.

fandango fændæ·ŋgou lively Sp. dance. XVIII. – Sp. *fandango*, perh. of negro origin.

fane fein (poet.) temple. XIV. – L. *fānum*, prob. :– **fasnom* (cf. Oscan *fíisnam*, Umbrian *fesnafe*), and rel. to *fēriæ*, earlier *fēsiæ* (see FERIAL). Often sp. *phane* XV–XVII.

fanfare fæ·nfɛəɹ flourish (of trumpets, etc.). XVII (*famphar*, Montgomerie). – F. *fanfare* of imit. origin.

fang fæŋ †A. capture, catch XI; B. canine tooth, tusk XVI; root of a tooth or prong of this XVII. Late OE. *fang* (repl. native *feng* = ON. *fengr* :– **faŋgiz*) – ON. *fang* capture, grasp, embrace = OFris., OS., OHG. *fang* (Du. *vang* catch, stay, MHG. *vanc*, G. *fang*), f. Germ. **faŋg-*, **faŋχ-*, repr. by OE. *fōn* capture, pt. *fēng*, pp. *fangen* = OFris. *fā*, OS., OHG. *fāhan*, ON. *fá*, Goth. *fāhan*, rel. to L. *pangere* fix (cf. PACT, PEACE); the development of sense B is obscure.

fan-tan fæ·ntæn Chinese gambling game depending on divisions by four. XIX. Chin. *fan t'an* repeated divisions.

fantasia fæntei·ziə musical composition in which form is subordinated to fancy. XVIII. It.; see FANTASY.

fantastic fæntæ·stik †imaginary XIV; †imaginative XV; extravagantly fanciful XVI. – (O)F. *fantastique* – medL. *fantasticus*, late L. *phantasticus* – Gr. *phantastikós*, f. *phantázein* make visible, *phantázesthai* have visions, imagine; cf. next and see -IC. So **fanta·sti**CAL. XV. The sp. with *ph-* was frequent *c.* 1600–1800.

fantasy, phantasy fæ·ntəsi †mental apprehension; †phantom; †delusive imagination; baseless supposition XIV; changeful mood XV; imagination XVI. – OF. *fantasie* (mod. *fantaisie*) = Pr. *fantazia*, etc., It. *fantasia* – L. *phantasia* – Gr. *phantasíā* appearance (later, phantom), mental process, sensuous perception, faculty of imagination, f. *phantázein*; see prec. and -Y[3]. Cf. FANCY.

fantee, fanti fæ·ntī phr. *go fantee* live like a native. XIX (Kipling). Name of a tribe of the Gold Coast, Africa, related to the Ashanti.

fantigue fæntī·g (dial.) state of excitement. XIX. perh. based on FANTASY.

fantoccini fæntotʃī·ni puppet show. XVIII. It., pl. of *fantoccino*, dim. of *fantoccio* puppet, f. *fante* servant, aphetic of *infante* INFANT.

faquir var. of FAKIR.

far fāɹ at or to a great distance. OE. *feor(r)* = OFris. *fēr, fīr,* OS. *fer, ferro* (Du. ver), OHG. *fer, ferro,* ON. *fjarri,* Goth. *fairra* :- Germ. **ferrō,* compar. formation on **fer-* :- IE. **per-,* repr. by Skr. *pára,* Gr. *pérā* further, OIr. *ire* beyond.

farad fæ·ræd (electr.) unit of capacity. 1881. f. name of Michael *Faraday,* English electrician (1791–1867), with assim. to the suffix -AD[1].

farce[1] fāɹs †stuff, cram XIV (Barbour, Ch.); season, 'spice' XIV (Rolle). – OF. *farsir* (mod. *farcir*) = Pr. *farsir* :- L. *farcīre.*

farce[2] fāɹs short dramatic work the sole object of which is to excite laughter. XVI. – F. *farce* (XVI), in OF. stuffing, f. *farcir* :- L. *farcīre* stuff, FARCE[1], in medL. pad out, interlard. The term, in latinized form *farsa, farcia,* was applied in XIII to phrases interpolated in the liturgical *kyrie eleison* (e.g. *kyrie genitor ingenite, vera essentia, eleison*) and to passages in French inserted in the Latin text of the epistle at Mass (cf. medL. *epistola farcita*); hence to impromptu amplifications of the text of religious plays, whence the transition to the present sense was easy. The medL. forms have been anglicized by eccl. antiquaries in the form **farse** for liturgical uses of sb. and vb. Hence **fa·rc**ICAL. XVIII; after *comical, tragical.*

farcy fā·ɹsi disease of horses allied to glanders. XV. Earlier *farcin* – F. *farcin* :- late L. *farcīminum* (Vegetius), beside *farcīmen,* f. *farcīre* FARCE[1]; so named from the purulent eruptions with which the affected animal is 'stuffed'. ¶ For loss of *-n* cf. *booty.*

fardel fā·ɹdl (arch.) bundle, parcel. XIII (Cursor M.). – OF. *fardel* (mod. *fardeau*) burden, load = Pr. *fardel,* It. *fardello* :- dim. of Rom. **fardum* (OIt., Sp. *fardo*; cf. Sp., Pg. *alfarda* notch) – Arab. *fard, farda* notch of an arrow, numbering, camel-load, clothing; see -EL[2].

fare[1] fɛəɹ †journey OE.; passage money XV; passenger XVI; †procedure; †condition; (supply of) food XIII. orig. two words, (i) OE. *fær* str. n. = OHG. *far* transit, landing-place, harbour, ON. *far* :- Germ. **faram*; (ii) OE. *faru* str. fem. = OFris. *fare, fere,* MLG. *vare,* MHG. *var,* ON. *fǫr* :- Germ. **farō,* f. base of next.

fare[2] fɛəɹ †go a journey; get on (well or ill) OE.; †behave, act; happen. XIII. Now only literary. OE. *faran,* pt. *fōr,* pp. *faren* = OFris., ON. *fara,* OS., OHG., Goth. *faran* (Du. *varen,* G. *fahren*) :- CGerm. **faran,* f. **far-* :- IE. **por-* (cf. FORD, EMPORIUM, PORE, PORT[1]). The str. pt. *for* was partly superseded by the pt. *ferd(e)* of synon. *fere* (OE. *fēran*) until the wk. inflexion was regularized to *fared* in XVI. Hence **farewell** str. variable (arch.) int. ('proceed happily'; see WELL[2]), orig. imper. phr. addressed to one setting out, now equiv. to Good-bye!; also as sb. XIV (PPl., Ch., Gower).

farinaceous færinei·ʃ[i]əs of flour or meal. XVII. f. late L. *farīnāceus,* f. *farīna,* f. *far* corn (cf. BARLEY); see -ACEOUS.

farm fāɹm fixed annual payment as rent, etc. XIII (orig. in *to farm, at* or *in farm*); tract of land leased; farm-house XVI. ME. *ferme* – (O)F. *ferme* :- medL. *firma* fixed payment, f. L. *firmāre* fix, settle, confirm, in medL. contract for, f. *firmus* FIRM[1]. Hence **farm** vb. †rent XV; let or lease out XVI. So **fa·rm**ER[2] collector of revenue; bailiff, steward XIV; cultivator of a farm XVI. ME. *fermour* – AN. *fermer,* (O)F. *fermier,* which combined the uses of medL. *firmārius* and *firmātor*; in the more mod. uses apprehended as f. *farm* vb. + -ER[1].

faro fɛə·rou gambling card-game. XVIII. quasi-phonetic sp. of †*Pharaoh,* var. of †*Pharaon,* †*Farro* – F. *pharaon,* title (– late L. *Pharaō(n-),* Gr. *Pharaṓ,* Heb. *Par'ōh* – Egyptian *Per'o* lit. 'great house', i.e. royal house or estate) of the kings of ancient Egypt, which is said to have been applied orig. to the king of hearts in the game.

farouche færū·ʃ shy and repellent. XVIII. F., alteration of OF. *faroche,* beside *forache* (cf. dial. *fourâche,* etc.) = Pr. *ferotge,* It. †*forastico* :- medL. *forasticu-s,* f. L. *foras* out-of-doors (see FOREIGN).

farrago fərei·gou medley. XVII. – L. *farrāgo* orig. mixed fodder for cattle, f. *farr-, far* corn, spelt (cf. BARLEY).

farrier fæ·riəɹ shoeing-smith, veterinary surgeon. XVI. – OF. *ferrier* :- L. *ferrāriu-s,* f. *ferrum* horseshoe, prop. iron (cf. FERREOUS); superseded †*ferrour, ferrer* (XIV–XVIII). Hence **fa·rrier**Y[3] veterinary surgery. XVIII.

farrow[1] fæ·rou †young pig OE.; litter of pigs. XVI. OE. *færh (fearh)* = OS. **farh* (whence dim. MLG. *ferken,* Du. *varken*), OHG. *farah* (whence dim. OHG. *farhilīn,* G. *ferkel*) :- WGerm. **farχaz* :- IE. **porkos,* whence L. *porcus* (see PORK), Gr. *pórkos* pig, Lith. *par̃šas* gelded pig, OSl. *prasę,* OIr. *orc.* Hence **fa·rrow** vb. XIII (pp. *iueruwed*).

farrow[2] fæ·rou (Sc.) not in calf. XV (*ferow*). – Flem. *verwe, varwe,* in *verwekoe, varwekoe,* †*verrekoe* cow that has become barren; of unkn. origin.

farsang fā·ɹsæŋ PARASANG. XVII. Pers.

farsed fāɹst (of speech) embellished XV; (of a liturgical formula) amplified by interpolation XIX. – medL. *farcītus* (as in *epistola farcita* farced epistle), pp. of L. *farcīre* stuff; so F. *épître, hymne farcie.*

fart fāɹt break wind. OE. *_feortan_ (in _feorting_ vbl. sb.), ME. _uerten_ (XIII), corr. to MLG. _verten_, OHG. _ferzan_, MHG. _verzen_, _vurzen_ (G. _farzen_, _furzen_), ON. (with metath.) _freta_ :- CGerm. *_fertan_, *_fartan_, *_furtan_ :- IE. base *_perd-_ *_pord-_ *_pr̥d-_, as repr. by Skr. _pard-_, _pr̥d-_, Av. _pərədən_ (3rd pl.), Alb. _pjerdh_ (1st sg.), Gr. _pérdein_, aor. _épardon_, pf. _péporda_, _pordḗ_ sb., Lith. _pérdžiu_, Russ. _perdét'_.

farther fā·ɹðəɹ to or at a more advanced point or greater distance. XIII; adj. more distant; additional. ME. _ferþer_ (Cursor M.), var. of FURTHER, which came to be used as a compar. of FAR instead of †_farrer_, earlier †_ferrer_, a new formation with -ER[3] on the orig. compar. (OE. _fierr_ :- *_ferriz_). So **fa·rth**EST adj. XIV (_ferþest_), adv. (XVI).

farthing fā·ɹðiŋ fourth of a penny. OE. _fēorþing_, _-ung_, f. _fēorþa_ FOURTH, perh. after ON. _fjórðungr_ quarter; see -ING[3].

farthingale fā·ɹðiŋgeil hooped petticoat. XVI. (Early forms _vard-_, _verd-_, _fard-_) – OF. _verdugale_, _vertugalle_, altered – Sp. _verdugado_, f. _verdugo_ rod, stick, f. _verde_ green (cf. VERT).

fasces fæ·sīz (Rom. antiq.) bundle of rods with an axe in the middle. XVI. L., pl. of _fascis_ bundle, rel. to _fascia_ (see next).

fascia fæ·ʃ[i]ə (archit.) long flat surface or band XVI; (anat.) sheath investing an organ. XVIII. – L. _fascia_ band, fillet, casing of a door, etc., rel. to _fascis_ (see prec.).

fascicle fæ·sikl bundle, cluster XV; part or number of a work XVII. L. _fasciculus_, dim. of _fascis_ (see FASCES). Also **fa·scicule**. XVII; after F.; and in L. form XVIII.

fascinate fæ·sineit cast a spell over, bewitch. XVI. f. pp. stem of L. _fascināre_, f. _fascinum_ spell, witchcraft. So **fascin**A·TION. XVII. – L.

fascine fæsī·n (fortif.) long faggot. – F. _fascine_ – L. _fascīna_, f. _fascis_ bundle.

Fascist fæ·ʃist, fæ·sist orig. member of the _Fascio nazionale di combattimento_ 'national fighting force', formed by Benito Mussolini in March 1919 to combat communism. – It. _fascista_, f. _fascio_ bundle, sheaf, assemblage, association (of forces) = F. _faix_, etc. :- L. _fascis_; see FASCES and -IST. So **Fa·sc**ISM.

fash fæʃ (chiefly Sc.) annoy, trouble. XVI. – early modF. _fascher_ (now _fâcher_) :- Rom. *_fastidicāre_ (cf. Pr. _fastic_ (sb.) disgust, _fastigos_ scornful, _enfastigat_ disgusted), f. L. _fastus_ disdain (cf. FASTIDIOUS).

fashion fæ·ʃən make, shape XIII; mode, manner XIV; established custom, conventional usage XV. ME. _faciun_ (Cursor M.), _fasoun_, _fassoun_ – AN. _fasun_, (O)F. _façon_ = Pr. _faisso_, It. _fazione_ :- L. _factiōn-_, f. _fact-_, _facere_ to make, DO: cf. FACTION. The L. word was used rarely in the sense 'making', chiefly in the sense 'party, sect, faction'; the senses 'manner of action', 'mode', 'custom' are of Rom. development. Hence **fa·shion** vb. XV (Lydg.); after (O)F. _façonner_. **fa·shion**ABLE conforming to the fashion. XVII (Sh.).

fast[1] fàst firm OE.; rapid (evolved from the corr. use of the adv.) XVI; dissipated XVIII. OE. _fæst_ = OFris. _fest_, OS. _fast_ (Du. _vast_), OHG. _festi_ (G. _fest_), ON. _fastr_; prob. orig. :- CGerm. *_fastuz_ (but transf. to other declensions in some langs.), rel. to Arm. _hast_ firm :- *_pazdu_. The base is repr. in Gothic only by _fastan_ keep, guard, observe (a fast) and _fastubni_ observance, fasting; OE. had a mutated _fæstan_ (= ON. _festa_) make fast. So **fast** adv. firmly OE.; closely; quickly; rapidly XIII; dissipatedly XVII (Dryden). OE. _fæste_ = OS. _fasto_ (Du. _vast_), OHG. _fasto_ firmly, closely, quickly (G. _fast_ almost), ON. _fast_ firmly, hard (as of drinking), soundly (as of sleeping) :- Germ. *_fastō_, f. *_fastuz_.

fast[2] fàst abstain from food. OE. _fæstan_ = OFris. _festia_, (M)Du. _vasten_, OHG. _fastēn_ (G. _fasten_), ON. _fasta_, Goth. _fastan_ :- CGerm. *_fastējan_, f. *_fastuz_; see prec. The gen. sense was 'hold fast', hence 'keep, observe' (as in Gothic), of which 'observe abstinence' was a spec. application; cf. the eccl. use of L. _observāre_, _observantia_. So **fast** fàst act or season of fasting. XII. – ON. _fasta_ = OS., OHG. _fasta_; f. Germ. *_fastējan_. The OE. form was _fæsten_, ME. _fasten_ (to XIII). Also **fa·st-day.** XIII; after ON. _fǫstudagr_.

fasten fà·sn †establish, settle OE.; make fast, secure XII; become fixed or attached XIII. OE. _fæstnian_ = OFris. _festna_, OS. _fastnōn_, OHG. _fastinōn_, _fest-_ :- WGerm. *_fastinōjan_, f. *_fastuz_ FAST[1]: see -EN[5].

fasti fæ·stai ancient Roman legal calendar; annals. XVII (B. Jonson). L., pl. of _fāstus_ (_diēs_) lawful (day), i.e. on which courts sat, f. _fās_ right, law (cf. _iūstus_ JUST, f. _iūs_), prob. rel. to _fārī_ speak, and hence prop. 'declaration, sentence'.

fastidious fæsti·diəs †disdainful, scornful XV; easily offended XVII. – L. _fastīdiōsus_, f. _fastidium_ loathing; see -IOUS; cf. F. _fastidieux_. Cf. L. _fastus_, FASH.

fastness fà·stnės quality of being fast; stronghold. OE. _fæstnes_, f. FAST[1]+-NESS; for the concr. use of -NESS cf. _wilderness_ and the parallel use of the abstr. suffix of OF. _ferté_ fortress (= Pr. _fermetat_ :- L. _firmitātem_, _-tās_) and of G. _festung_.

fat[1] fæt well-fed, plump; containing adipose or oily matter, obese; and in various transf. uses; also as sb. fat substance or matter. OE. _fǣt(t)_ = OFris. _fatt_, _fett_, MDu., MLG. _vett_ (Du. _vet_), OHG. _feiʒʒit_ (G. _feist_; _fett_ is – LG.) :- WGerm. *_faitiđa_, pp. formation on *_faitjan_ fatten (OHG. _veiʒʒen_, ON. _feita_), f. Germ. *_faitaz_ adj. fat, repr. by OS. _feit_, OHG. _feiz_, ON. _feitr_ (cf. _feiti_ fatness, _fita_ sb. fat); perh. to be referred to IE. *_poid-_ *_pīd-_, with the basic meaning 'gush forth', as in Gr. _pīdúein_ gush, _pîdax_ spring, OIr. _esc_

(:– *pidska) water, Gael. *uisg* (cf. WHISKY); an extension of *poi- *pī̆ be swollen, gush out, variations of which are seen in several words denoting fatness, e.g. Skr. *pīvā*, Gr. *pîar*, *pī́ōn*, *pīmelḗ*, L. *opīmus*, *pinguis*. So **fat** vb. surviving in arch. *fatted calf*; OE. *fǣttian*. **fa·t**LING[1]. XVI (Tindale). **fa·tt**EN[5]. OE. *(ge)fættnian*. **fa·tt**Y[1]. XIV.

fat[2] obs. form of VAT.

fatal fei·təl †fated; fateful XIV (Ch.); of fate or destiny XV; (in weakened sense) disastrous XVII (Dryden; cf. the trivial use of F.). – (O)F. *fatal* or L. *fātālis*, f. *fātum* FATE; see -AL[1]. So **fatal**ITY fətæ·lĭti. XV – F. or late L. **fa·tal**ISM, -IST. XVII; cf. F. *fatalisme*, *-iste* (XVI), perh. the immed. source, and It. *fatalismo*.

Fata Morgana fā·tə mɔ̄ɹgā·nə mirage seen on the Calabrian coast, once attributed to fairy agency. XIX. It. *fata Morgana* Morgan le Fay (i.e. M. the fairy or witch; see FAY[2]), one of King Arthur's sisters possessing magic powers; *Morgana* (– Arab. *margān* coral – Gr. *margarī́tēs* pearl; cf. MARGUERITE) was used as a female name.

fate feit predetermination of events; predestined lot XIV (Ch.); destiny, spec. fatal end XV; goddess of destiny XV. Not common before XVI; Ch. has three examples, all in 'Troilus & Criseyde' bk. v. Orig. – It. *fato*, later – its source L. *fātum*, sb. use of n. pp. of *farī* speak (cf. FABLE, FAME). The primary sense of the L. word was 'sentence or doom', scil. of the gods; later it was used as the equiv. of Gr. *moîra*, which was orig. 'lot', 'portion', but came to express the impersonal power by which events are determined. The L. pl. *fāta* is repr. by FAY[2]. Hence **fa·te**FUL[1]. XVIII (Pope).

father fā·ðəɹ male parent. CGerm. and IE. term of family relationship like *brother*, etc. OE. *fæder* = OFris. *feder*, OS. *fadar* (Du. *vader*), OHG. *fater* (G. *vater*), ON. *faðir*, Goth. *fadar* (once only, the ordinary word being *atta*) :– CGerm. *fadḗr :– IE. *pətḗr, repr. also by L. *pater*, Gr. *patḗr*, Skr. *pitar-*, Arm. *hayr*, OIr. *athir* (Ir., Gael. *athair*), Toch. *pācar*. ¶ For the change of d to ð cf. *mother*, *gather*, *hither*, *together*, *whether*. Hence **fa·ther**LAND. XVII (esp. tr. Du. *vaderland*, G. *vaterland*).

fathom fæ·ðm †embrace; †cubit; length made by the outstretched arms, 6 feet. OE. *fæþm*, corr. to OFris. *fethem*, OS. *faðmos* pl. two arms outstretched (Du. *vadem*, *vaam* 6 feet), OHG. *fadum* cubit (G. *faden* 6 feet), ON. *faðmr* embrace, bosom :– CGerm. (exc. Goth.) *faþmaz, f. base *faþ- (cf. MHG. *vade*, Goth. *faþa* enclosure) :– IE. *pot- *pet- *pt-, whence also L. *patēre* be open (cf. PATENT), G. *pétalos* spreading, broad (cf. PETAL); formally identical words mean 'thread'. So **fa·thom** vb. †encircle, embrace OE.; take soundings (of), get to the bottom of XVII. OE. *fæþmian*, f. *fæþm*.

fatidic(al) fəti·dik(əl) prophetic. XVII. – L. *fātidicus*, f. *fātum* FATE + *-dicus*, f. weak var. of base of *dīcere* say; see DICTION, -AL[1].

fatigue fətī·g weariness; fatiguing duty or labour XVII (mil. sense XVIII; cf. F. *aller à la fatigue* go on fatigue duty). – F. *fatigue* (corr. to Sp. *fatiga*, It. *fatica*), f. (O)F. *fatiguer* (whence **fatigue** vb. XVII), corr. to Pr., Sp. *fatigar*, It. *faticare* – L. *fatīgāre* exhaust as with riding or working, weary, harass, f. *fatis in *ad fatim*, *affatim* to satiety, abundantly, enough, prop. 'to bursting' (cf. *fatiscāre*, *-ārī* burst open, gape open). See INDEFATIGABLE.

fatuous fæ·tjuəs vacantly foolish XVII; (Sc. law) imbecile, idiotic XVIII. f. L. *fatuus* + -OUS. So **fatu·**ITY. XVII. – F. or L.

faubourg fou·buəɹ(g) suburb. XV. Late ME. *fabo(u)r*, *faubourgh* – F. *faubourg*, †*faulbourg*, †*fauxbourg* (XV), the earlier existence of which is vouched for by medL. *falsus burgus* (XIV) 'false city', i.e. not the city proper. ¶ *Faubourg* superseded OF. *forsborc* (*fors* outside, *borc* city, BOURG) perh. by contact with MHG. *phālburgere*, *fal-* citizens of the PALE (medL. *phalburgenses*).

faucal fɔ̄·kəl pert. to the throat. XIX. f. L. *faucēs* throat (cf. SUFFOCATE); see -AL[1].

faucet fɔ̄·sit (now U.S.) tap for drawing off liquid. XIV. – (O)F. *fausset* – Pr. *falset*, f. *falsar* bore (*fausser* damage, break into).

faugh fɔ̄ excl. of abhorrence. XVI (*fah*, *foh*). imit. of action repelling a disgusting smell.

fault fɔ̇lt †lack, default XIII; defect in character, etc.; error; culpability XIV; (geol.; prob. after F., orig. Walloon, *faille*) break XVIII. ME. *faut(e)* – (O)F. *faute* (= Pr., etc. *falta*) and *faut* :– Rom. *fallita, *fallitum, sb. use of fem. and n. of *fallitus, pp. of L. *fallere* FAIL[2]. (Cf. FALSE.) Hence **fau·lt**Y[1]. XIV; partly after F. *fautif*. The sp. with *l*, following F. †*faulte* (XIV), finally influenced the pronunc.

faun fɔ̄n ancient rural deity. XIV (Ch.; once *fawny*, repr. L. pl.). – (O)F. *faune* or L. *Faunus* god or demigod worshipped by shepherds and farmers and identified with Pan; perh. rel. to *favēre* be FAVOURABLE.

fauna fɔ̄·nə animals of a region or epoch. XVIII. modL. application of the proper name *Fauna* of a rural goddess, sister of Faunus (see prec.); used by Linnæus in the title *Fauna Suecica* (1746), a companion volume to his *Flora Suecica* (1745).

fauteuil fotöj arm-chair XVIII; fou·til seat in a theatre, etc. XX. F. :– OF. *faudestuel*, *faldestoel* – WG. *faldistōl FALDSTOOL.

fautor fɔ̄·tɔ̄ɹ supporter, partisan. XIV (R. Mannyng). ME. *fautour* – (O)F. *fauteur* – L. *fautor*, f. *favēre* FAVOUR; see -TOR.

fauvism fou·vizm style of painting characterized by distortion of the human figure, anarchic design, etc. XX. – F. *fauvisme*, f. *fauve* wild (beast) :– Rom. *falvus – Germ. *falw- FALLOW[2]; see -ISM.

faux-bourdon foubuə·ɹdɔ̃ (mus.) kind of vocal harmony (the application varies). XVIII. F., 'false hum'; the reason for the name is disputed. See FALSE, BOURDON. Anglicized as †*faburdon, -en* (XV) with assim. to BURDEN.

faux pas fou·pa false step, slip. XVII. F.; see FALSE, PACE.

Favonian fəvou·niən gentle, like a west wind. XVII. – L. *favōniānus*, f. *Favōnius* west wind; see -IAN.

favour, U.S. **favor** fei·vəɹ friendly regard; partiality; †attraction, charm XIV; (arch.) appearance, countenance XV (hence *-favoured* -featured, as in *hard-, ill-, well-favoured*); gift as a mark of regard, ceremonial decoration XVI; communication by letter XVII. – OF. *favour, -or* (mod. *faveur*) = Pr., Sp. *favor*, It. *favore* – L. *favor* (*-ōr-*), f. *favēre* regard with goodwill, rel. to *fovēre* cherish (see FOMENT). So **fa·vour** vb. XIV. – OF. *favorer* – medL. *favōrāre*. **fa·vour**ABLE. XIV. – (O)F. – L.

favourite, U.S. **favorite** fei·v(ə)rit one who stands in a person's favour. XVI; adj. XVIII (Addison, Pope). – F. †*favorit* (mod. *favori*, fem. *-ite*) – It. *favorito*, pp. of *favorire*, f. *favore* FAVOUR. In XVII–XVIII used for 'curl or lock hanging upon the temple' (cf. F. *favoris* whiskers). Hence **fa·vourit**ISM. XVIII.

fawn[1] fɔ̄n young fallow deer. XIV (Ch.). ME. *foun*, later *fawn* (XV). – (O)F. *faon*, †*foun*, †*feon* = Pr. *fedon* foal :– Rom. **fētō(n-)*, f. *fētus* offspring, FŒTUS. For sp. and pronunc. cf. LAWN[1].

fawn[2] fɔ̄n (of a dog) show delight XIII; be servile XIV. ME. *vawene* (XIII), *fau(h)ne* (XIV), repr. OE. *fagnian, fahnian*, var. of *fæġnian* rejoice (= OS., OHG. *faganōn*, ON. *fagna*, Goth. *faginōn*), f. *fæġen*, also *fagen* FAIN (the vars. are due to orig. difference of vowel-grade in the suffix, **-in-*, **-an-*); OE. *onfæġnian* is used of the dog Cerberus showing delight *mid his steorte* with his tail.

fay[1] fei faith; surviving in arch. int. *by my fay* (OF. *par ma fei*). XIII. – OF. *fei* (mod. *foi*), earlier *feit, feid* FAITH.

fay[2] fei (arch.) fairy. XIV. – OF. *faie, fae* (mod. *fée*) = Pr., Cat., Pg. *fada*, Sp. *hada*, It. *fata* :– L. *fāta* the Fates (pl. of *fātum* FATE) taken as fem. sg. in Rom.

faze, also *phase* feiz (sl., U.S.) discompose, disturb. XIX. var. of FEEZE.

fealty fiə·lti obligation of fidelity. XIV. ME. *feaute, feute, fealtie* – OF. *feau(l)te, fealte* (mod. *féauté*) = Pr. *fezeltat, feal-* :– L. *fidēlitātem, -tās*, f. *fidēlis* faithful, f. *fidēs* FAITH; see -TY.

fear fiəɹ painful emotion caused by anticipation of evil. XIII. ME. *fēr-e*, repr. OE. *fǣr* sudden calamity, danger, corr. (with variation of decl.) to OS. *vār* ambush, MDu. *vāre* fear (cf. Du. *gevaar* danger), OHG. *fāra* ambush, stratagem, danger, deceit (MHG. *gevære, gevāre* deceit, G. *gefahr* danger), ON. *fár* misfortune, plague :– CGerm. (exc. Goth.) **fǣraz, -am, -ō*. The development of the sense 'alarm, dread' is no doubt mainly due to OE. *fǣran, āfǣran* (see AFEARD) terrify, but the beginnings may perh. be seen in the OE. phr. *būtan fǣre* without (prospect of) risk. Hence **fea·r**FUL[1] causing fear; afraid. XIV. So **fear** vb. frighten OE.; intr. and †refl. feel fear; regard with fear. XIV. OE. *fǣran* (more freq. in comp. *āfǣran*) = OS. *fārōn* lie in wait (MDu. *vaeren* fear), OHG. *fārēn* plot against, lie in wait, endeavour after (MHG. *vāren*, also rarely, fear), ON. *fǽra* taunt, slight. The ult. connexions of the base are unkn.; it is repr. in Goth. only by *ferja* (in acc. pl. *ferjans*) lier-in-wait. Hence **fea·r**NOUGHT (†*fear nothing*) stout woollen cloth. XVIII; cf. DREADNOUGHT.

feasible fī·zibl practicable XV; capable of being dealt with successfully; (with unetymol. development) likely, probable XVII. Early forms are *feseable, fesible*; spellings with *-able* are found as late as XVIII. – (O)F. *faisable*, †*faisible*, f. *fais-*, pres. stem of *faire* (:– L. *facere* DO[1]); see -BLE.

feast fīst religious festival; sumptuous meal or entertainment. XIII. ME. *feste* – OF. *feste* (mod. *fête*) = Pr., Pg., It. *festa*, Sp. *fiesta* :– L. *festa* n. pl. (taken as fem. sg. in Rom.) of *festus* festal, joyous, rel. to *fēria* (see FERIAL), *fānum* FANE. So **feast** vb. XIV. OF. *fester* (mod. *fêter*), f. the sb.

feat[1] fīt deed, esp. a notable one; art, trick XIV (Ch.); surprising trick XVI. ME. *fete*, later *fayte* – OF. *fet*, (also mod.) *fait* = Pr. *fach*, Sp. *hecho*, Pg. *feito*, It. *fatto*, Rum. *fapt* :– L. *factum*, sb. use of n. sg. of *factus* – pp. of *facere* DO[1].

feat[2] fīt †fitting XIV; (arch.) neat XV; apt, dexterous XVI. – OF. *fet* (mod. *fait*) :– L. *factu-s* (see prec.); lit. 'made (for something)'.

feather fe·ðəɹ epidermal appendage of a bird. OE. *feþer* (pl. wings) = OFris. *fethere*, OS. *fethara* (Du. *veer*), OHG. *fedara* (G. *feder*), ON. *fjǫðr* :– CGerm. (exc. Goth.) **feþrō* :– IE. **petrā*, f. **pet-* **pt-*, repr. also by Skr. *pátram* wing, *pátati* fly, Gr. *pterón*, *ptérux* wing, L. *penna* (:– **pet(s)na*) PEN[2], L. *acci|piter* hawk (lit. 'swift-winged'; cf. Gr. *ōku|pétēs*), OIr. *én* (:– **petnos*), OW. *eterim* bird, pl. *atar*, and, further, L. *petere* strive, seek (see PETITION). Hence **fea·ther** vb. furnish with feathers OE.; move like a feather; present a feather edge (of an oar) to the air. XVIII. In OE. *ġefiðrian* (ME. *iuiðeren*); from XIII (in pp.) a new formation on the sb.

feature fī·tʃəɹ †form, shape; †pl. elements constituting bodily form; lineaments of the face XIV; characteristic part XVII. – OF. *feture, faiture* form = Pr. *fachura*, It. *fattura* creation, sorcery, etc., Rum. *făptură* :- L. *factūra* formation, creature, f. *fact-*, pp. stem of *facere* DO[1]; see -URE. Hence **fea·ture** vb. resemble in features; portray the features of. XVIII.

febrifuge fe·brifjūdʒ medicine for reducing fever. XVII. – F. *fébrifuge* – modL. *febrifugus*, f. the same elements as late L. *febrifuga* FEVERFEW.

febrile fe·brail feverish. XVII. – F. *fébrile* or medL. *febrīlis*, f. *febris* FEVER; see -ILE.

February fe·bruəri second month of the year. XIII (repl. OE. *solmōnaþ* 'mud-month'). The earliest recorded forms are *feouereles* and *feouerreres moneð*; the former (which appears to be a purely Eng. var. with dissimilation of *r* . . *r* as in *laurel*) is repr. as late as XVI by *feverell*; the latter is directly – OF. *feverier* (mod. *février*) = Pr. *feurier*, Sp. *febrero*, Pg. *fevereiro*, It. *febbraio*, Rum. *făurar* :- late L. (Rom.) *febrāriu-s*, for L. *februārius*, f. *februa* n. pl. (Sabine *februum* purification) Roman festival of purification held on 15 February. The ME. type *feverer*, Sc. and north. *feveryer*, is repr. as late as XVIII by (partially latinized) *februeer*; the present fully latinized form (*februari*) is found alongside *feverer* in Ch.; *februar* is a characteristically Sc. var.

fecal var. of FÆCAL. **fecial** var. of FETIAL.

feckless fe·klis ineffective, futile; weak, helpless. XVI (James I, Montgomerie; in present use due to Carlyle). f. Sc. *feck*, †*fek* (XV) effect, purport, efficiency, amount, aphetic form of *effeck* (as in *the feck* for *th'effeck*), Sc. var. of EFFECT; see -LESS and cf. Sc. *feckful* (XVI) effective.

feculent fī·kjŭlənt turbid, as with dregs. XV. – F. *féculent* or L. *fēculentus*, f. *fæc-*; see FÆCES and -ULENT.

fecund fī·kʌnd productive, fertile. XIV. – F. *fécond* or L. *fēcundus*, perh. rel. to *fēlix* happy, FŒTUS. So **fecu·nd**ITY. XV. – F. or L.

federal fe·dərəl pert. to the Covenant of Works or of Grace XVII; of states in a political unity XVIII (first with reference to N. America). – modL. **fœderālis*, f. L. *fœder-*, *fœdus* covenant (:- **bhoidhes-*, rel. to *fidēs* FAITH); cf. CONFEDERATE and see -AL[1]. Hence **fe·deral**ISM, -IST. XVIII, -IZE. XIX. So **federa·**TION league for joint action. XVIII (Burke); cf. F. *fédération*.

fee fī estate in land (orig. on feudal tenure); payment for services or privileges. XIV. – AN. *fee* = OF. *feu*, *fiu*, *fieu*, (also mod.) *fief*, pl. *fiez* = Pr. *feu* (whence It. *fio*) :- Rom. **feudum*, medL. *feodum*, *feudum* (IX), also *feaudus*, *feuodium*, which has been derived from Frankish **fehu-ōd* 'cattle-property', i.e. OHG. *fehu* (G. *vieh*) = OE. *fēo*, etc., cogn. with L. *pecu*, *pecus* (cf. PECULIUM, PECUNIARY) and *ōd*, as in ALLODIUM, but the sense is not appropriate. Cf. FIEF.

feeble fī·bl weak. XII. – AN., OF. *feble*, var. of *fieble* (mod. *faible*), later forms of *flieble* = Pr. *feble*, *fible*, *freble* (whence Sp. *feble* weak, deficient in weight), Pg. *febre* short of the legal weight, It. *fievole* weak :- L. *flēbili-s* that is to be wept over, (hence in Rom.) weak, f. *flēre* weep; see -BLE. Hence **fee·b**LY[2]. XIII (*febleliche*).

feed fīd give food to. OE. *fēdan* = OFris. *fēda*, OS. *fōdean* (Du. *voeden*), OHG. *fuoten*, ON. *fœða*, Goth. *fōdjan* :- CGerm. **fōðjan*, f. **fōðon* FOOD. Hence **feed** sb. feeding XVI; (sumptuous or full) meal XIX.

fee-faw-fum fī fɔ̄ fʌm First recorded in Sh. 'King Lear' III iv 188 (1st Folio) as *fie, foh, and fumme*, the excl. of the giant in the nursery tale of Jack the Giant-killer on discovering the presence of Jack; a fuller form is *fe, fi, fo, fum*; used by Dryden (*fee, fa, fum*) as an excl. of murderous intention and for a bloodthirsty person.

feel fīl examine or experience by touch; be conscious (of), perceive, experience. OE. *fēlan* and *ġefēlan* (see Y-) = OFris. *fēla*, OS. *ġifōlian* (Du. *voelen*), OHG. *fuolen* (G. *fühlen*) :- WGerm. **fōljan*, f. **fōl-* :- IE. **pōl-* **pal-* **pl-*, repr. also by OE., OS. *folm*, OHG. *folma* hand, L. *palma* PALM, Gr. *palámē*, W. *llaw*, OIr. *lám* (:- **plāmā*). Hence **feel** sb. XIII. **fee·l**ER[1]. XVII. **fee·l**ING[1]. XII; cf. Du. *voeling*, G. *fühlung*.

feeze, pheeze fīz †drive *away* OE.; (dial., U.S.) frighten, alarm XV; †do for, beat XVI. OE. *fēsian*, of unkn. origin. Cf. FAZE.

feign fein invent or pretend falsely. XIII (Cursor M.). ME. *feigne*, *feine*, *fene* – (O)F. *feign-*, pres. stem of *feindre* = Pr. *fenher*, It. *fingere* (cf. Sp., Pg. *fingir*) :- L. *fingere* form, mould, conceive, contrive; see FICTION, FIGMENT, FIGURE, EFFIGY, DOUGH.

feint[1] feint feigned attack. XVII. – (O)F. *feinte* (= OSp., It. *finta*), sb. use of fem. pp. of *feindre* FEIGN.

feint[2] feint commercial sp. of FAINT, in *feint lines*. XIX.

feis feʃ assembly of chiefs, etc. XVIII; festival of competitions XIX. Ir. *feis*, *fess*.

felicity fili·sĭti happiness. XIV (Ch., Gower). – (O)F. *félicité* (= Sp. *felicidad*, It. *felicità*, etc.) – L. *fēlīcitās*, f. *fēlīc-*, *fēlīx* happy, orig. fertile, rel. to *fēcundus* FECUND, *fētus* FŒTUS; see -ITY. Hence **feli·cit**OUS. XVIII. So **feli·cit**ATE[3] †make happy; congratulate. XVII. f. late L. *fēlīcitāt-*, *-āre*; cf. F. *féliciter*.

feline fī·lain pert. to a cat or cats. XVII. – L. *fēlīnus*, f. *fēlēs* cat; see -INE[1].

fell[1] fel skin, hide. OE. *fel(l)* = OFris., OS. *fel* (Du. *vel*), OHG. *fel* (G. *fell*), ON. *ber|fjall* bear-skin, Goth. *þrūts|fill* 'swelling-skin', leprosy (= OE. *þrūstfell*), *faura|fill* foreskin (cf. also *filleins* leathern) :- CGerm. **fellam* :- IE. **pello-* :- **pelno-*, the base being repr. also by L. *pellis* (:- **pelnis*), Gr. *pélla*, *-pelas* (in *erusípelas* ERYSIPELAS) skin, and FILM.

fell[2] fel hill; wild stretch of land. XIII (Cursor M.). – ON. *fjall* and *fell* hill, mountain, presumably rel. to OS. *felis*, OHG. *felis, felisa* (G. *fels*) rock, and therefore to Skr. *pāṣyam* stone, Gr. *pélla*, (O)Ir. *all* rock (IE. **pels-*).

fell[3] fel (arch.) fierce, cruel, dire. XIII (Cursor M.). – OF. *fel* = Pr. *fel*, It. *fello* wicked :– Rom. **fellō*, the obl. form of which is repr. by FELON.

fell[4] fel strike down. OE. (Anglian) *fellan*, (WS.) *fyllan*, **fiellan* = OFris. *falla, fella*, OS. *fellian* (Du. *vellen*), OHG. *fellen* (G. *fällen*), ON. *fella* :– CGerm. (exc. Goth.) **falljan*, causative of **fallan* FALL[3]. ¶ The identity of this vb. with that in *fell a seam* (XVIII) is uncertain, but the gen. sense 'cause to fall' seems to be applicable.

fellah fe·lă pl. **fellahee·n** Arab peasant. XVIII. – Egyptian Arab. *fellāḥ* husbandman, var. of *fallāḥ*, f. *falaḥa* till the soil.

felloe fe·lou, **felly** fe·li outer rim of a wheel; pl. the sections forming this. OE. *felg*, pl. *felga*, corr. to MLG., MDu. *velge* (Du. *velg*), OHG. *felga* (G. *felge*), of unkn. origin. ¶ For the twofold development cf. BELLOWS, BELLY; there are also north-country vars. *felk, felf, felve*.

fellow fe·lou †partner, associate XI; mate; peer XIII; *good fellow*, agreeable companion; one of a company or corporation XIV; man; in condescending or contemptuous use XV. Late OE. *fēolaga* – ON. *félagi*, f. *fé* (= OE. *feoh* FEE[1]) + **lag-*, base of LAY[1]; primarily, one who lays down money in a joint undertaking (cf. ON. *félag* business partnership). Hence **fe·llow**SHIP XII; after ON. *félagskapr*.

felly var. of FELLOE.

felo de se fī·lou dī sī· one who deliberately puts an end to his life. XVII. Anglo-L. *felo* FELON, *dē sē* of himself.

felon fe·lən adj. (poet.) cruel, wicked; sb. †wicked person; one who has committed felony. XIII. – (O)F. *felon* (OF. nom. *fel*) = Pr. *felon* (*fel*) :– medL. *fellōnem* (It. *fellone* is – Gallo-Rom.), of unkn. origin. So **fe·lony** †villainy, perfidy, crime XIII; (leg.) crime of greater gravity than a misdemeanour XIV. – (O)F. *felonie*; see -Y[3]. Hence **felon**IOUS filou·niəs. XVI.

felt felt stuff of wool (and fur or hair) wrought into a compact substance. OE. *felt*, corr. to OS. *filt* (Du. *vilt*), (O)HG. *filz* :– WGerm. **feltaz*, **feltiz* :– IE. **peldos, -is* (cf. synon. OSl. *plŭstĭ*). See ANVIL, FILTER.

felucca filʌ·kə small Mediterranean vessel. XVII. – It. *feluc(c)a* – Sp. †*faluca* (whence also F. *felouque*), corr. to Pr. *folca* – Arab. *fulk* (now repl. by romanized *falūkah*), perh. – Gr. *ephólkion* sloop.

female fī·meil of the sex which produces offspring (adj. and sb.). XIV (*femele, femal-e, -alle, -aal*). – (O)F. *femelle* = Pr. *femela* :– L. *fēmella*, dim. of *fēmina* woman (see FEMININE). The present form is due to assoc. with *male*, with which it rhymes in Barbour's 'Brus'; *femal* continues till XVII and is the prevailing form in Milton. ¶ The transference of sense in L. (dim.) *femella* young woman (Catullus) to the sense of 'female' took place in popL., in which it came to denote the female of the lower animals (cf. the history of the dim. *masculus* MALE).

feme fem (leg.) wife; *feme covert* married (lit. covered, i.e. protected) woman, *feme sole* unmarried woman. XVI. – AN., OF. *feme* (mod. *femme*) :– L. *fēmina*; see next.

feminine fe·mĭnin female XIV (Ch.); relating to woman; womanly XV; (gram.) in L. *genus femininum*, tr. Gr. θηλυκὸν γένος XIV; (pros.) of rhyme, after F. XVIII (earlier †*female* XVI). – (O)F. *feminin, -ine* or L. *fēminīnus, -īna*, f. *fēmina* woman, prop. 'the suckling one', or 'the sucked one', f. IE. **dhē(i)-* **dhəi-* **dhĭ-*, as in L. *fēlāre* suckle, *fīlius* son (cf. FILIAL), *fēlix* orig. fertile (cf. FELICITY), Gr. *thêsai* suckle, *thḗsato* (aor.) sucked, Skr. *dháyati* sucks, *dhātrī* nurse, OIr. *dēth* (pt.) sucked, (O)Ir. *dínim* I suck, Lett. *dēt*; see -INE[1]. Hence **fe·minin**ISM, and directly from L. *fēmina* **fe·min**ISM; both *c.* 1850; cf. F. *féminisme, -iste* (Dumas fils 1872); **femini·n**ITY. XIV (Ch.), **femi·n**ITY. XV (Lydg.). ¶ Gower has adj. *femeline* once – OF. Other derivs. are **femine**ITY -ī·iti. XIX (Coleridge). f. L. *femineus*. †**feminie** womankind. XIV (Ch.). – OF. *feminie*.

femoral fe·mərəl (anat.) pert. to the femur. XVIII. f. L. *femor-*, *femur* thigh, whence **femur** fī·məɹ. XVIII; see -AL[1].

fence fens †defence XIV; art of fencing XVI; enclosing hedge, wall, etc. XVI; receiver of stolen goods XVII (this sense is from the vb.). ME. *fens*, aphetic of *defens*, DEFENCE. Hence **fence** vb. enclose, screen, protect (lit. and fig.) XV; practise the 'science' of 'defence' with the sword XVI; (sl.) deal in stolen goods XVII. **fe·nc**IBLE capable of making defence XIII (*fensable*); defendable XVI; sb. soldier liable for defensive service at home. Aphetic of †*defensable*, DEFENSIBLE.

fend fend (obs. or arch.) defend XIII; ward off; make an effort XVI, now in *fend for oneself* provide for, look after oneself XVII. Aphetic of DEFEND. Hence **fe·nder** †defender XV; protective device, e.g. cable hung over a ship's side to prevent chafing, fire-guard XVII; see -ER[1].

fenestella feniste·lə small window-like niche. XVIII. L., dim. of *fenestra* window; see -EL[2].

Fenian fī·niən member of a mercenary tribe forming a military force for the support of the king of Eire XIX (Scott); one of a revolutionary organization of Irish in U.S.A. (*c.*1860). f. OIr. *féne* one of the names of the ancient population of Ireland, confused in mod. times with *fiann* body of warriors said to have been the defenders of Ireland in the time of the legendary Irish kings; see -IAN.

fennel fe·nl umbelliferous plant Fæniculum vulgare. OE. *finugl, finule* fem., *fenol, finul* m. – pop. forms, **fēnuclum, -oclum,* of L. *fæniculum,* dim. of *fænum* hay; coincided in ME. with the adoption of OF. *fenoil* (mod. *fenouil*) = Pr. *fenolh,* etc., from the same L. source.

fenugreek fe·njugrīk leguminous plant Trigonella Fœnum Græcum. OE. *fenogrecum,* superseded in ME. by adoption of (O)F. *fenugrec* (= Pr. *fenugrec*) – L. *fēnugræcum,* for *fēnum græcum* 'Greek hay'; the Romans used the dried plant for fodder.

feoff fef (leg.) put in possession of, ENFEOFF. XIII. – AN. *feoffer,* OF. *fieuffer, fieffer,* f. *fief* FIEF. Now repr. by derivs. **feoffEE** fefī·. XV. – AN. *feoffé* (pp.). **feo·ffMENT.** XIV (R. Mannyng). – AN. *feoffement.*

feracious fĭrei·ʃəs prolific. XVII. f. L. *ferāci-, ferāx,* f. *ferre* BEAR[2]; see -ACIOUS. So **feraCITY** fĭræ·sĭti. XV. – L.

feral[1] fiə·rəl deadly; funereal. XVII. – L. *fērālis* pert. to the dead or the lower regions, a term of religious usage, perh. rel. to *fēriæ* (see FERIAL).

feral[2] fiə·rəl wild, savage. XVII. f. L. *ferus* (fem. sb. *fera,* sc. *bestia,* wild animal), rel. to Gr. *thḗr* (Æolic *phḗr*), Lith. *žvėrìs,* OSl. *zvěrĭ,* which repr. the long form **ghwēr-,* OPruss. acc. pl. *swirins*; see -AL[1].

fer-de-lance fɛəɹ də lɑ̃s yellow viper of Martinique. XIX. F., lit. lance-head ('-iron').

feretory fe·rĭtəri portable shrine XIV; chapel for shrines XV. ME. *fertre* – OF. *fiertre* :– L. *feretrum* – Gr. *phéretron* bier, f. *phérein* BEAR[2] with instr. suffix; altered to *fertour* and thence to *feretory* by assim. to words in -TORY.

ferial fiə·riəl, fe·riəl pert. to a weekday XIV; †pert. to a holy day XV. – (O)F. *férial,* or its source medL. *fēriālis,* f. *fēriæ* (cf. FAIR[2]). In ecclL. *fēria* (whence **feria** fiə·riə, in vernacular use from XIX) is used with an ordinal numeral, to designate a particular weekday (e.g. *secunda, tertia,* etc., *fēria* Monday, Tuesday, etc.; so Pg. *segunda, terça,* etc., *feira*), and hence in liturgical use for a weekday as dist. from a Sunday or other feast day. The use appears to have arisen from the naming of the days of the octave of Easter *feria prima, secunda* (etc.), 'first, second' (etc.), 'holy or festival day' (cf. medL. *hebdomada ferialium* 'week of holy days', Easter week); the designation was transferred thence to the days of ordinary weeks, *feria prima* (Sunday) giving way to the proper title of the day and so passing out of use, with the result that *f. secunda, tertia,* etc. (Monday, Tuesday, etc.) survive without any obvious or immediate raison d'être. ¶ From meaning orig. 'festival day', the word has come to mean 'non-festal day'.

ferine fiə·rain (of animals) wild; bestial. XVII. – L. *ferīnus,* f. *fera* wild beast; see FERAL[2], -INE[1].

Feringhee fəri·ŋgī European; Indian-born Portuguese. XVII. – Oriental adoption of FRANK formed with Arab. ethnic suffix (Arab. *faranjī,* Pers. *farangī*).

ferly fɔ̄·ɹli †sudden OE.; (dial., arch.) dreadful, strange, wonderful XIII; sb. marvel, wonder XIII. OE. *fǣrlić,* f. *fǣr* FEAR + *-lić* -LY[1]; cf. MHG. *vǣrlich* (G. *gefährlich*), ON. *fárligr* dangerous.

ferment fɔ̄·ɹmənt leaven; fermentation (lit. and fig.). XV. – (O)F. *ferment* or L. *fermentum,* f. *fervēre* boil (see FERVENT). So **ferment** vb. fəɹme·nt. XIV (Trevisa). – (O)F. *fermenter* – L. *fermentāre*; **fermentA·TION.** XIV (Ch.). – late L.

fern fɔ̄ɹn one of a group of plants (Filices) with feathery fronds. OE. *fearn* = MDu. *væren* (Du. *varen*), OHG. *farn* (G. *farn*) :– WGerm. **farno* :– IE. **porno-,* whence Skr. *parṇám* wing, feather, leaf; rel. further to Lith. *papártis,* Russ. *páporotnik* (O)Ir. *raith* (:– **pratis*). The prim. meaning is doubtless 'feathery leaf'; cf. also Gr. *pterón* feather, *pteris* fern.

ferocious fĭrou·ʃəs fierce. XVII. f. L. *ferōci-, ferōx,* rel. to *ferus* FERAL[2]; for the second el. see EYE. So **feroCITY** -ɔ·sĭti. XVII. – F. or L.

-ferous see -IFEROUS.

ferreous fe·riəs pert. to iron. XVII. f. L. *ferreus,* f. *ferrum* iron; see -EOUS. So **fe·rrIC** XVIII, **fe·rrOUS** XIX (chem.); cf. F. *ferrique, ferreux.* **ferri-** fe·ri, formerly *ferrid-,* comb. form of L. *ferrum* indicating the presence of iron in its ferric state. **fe·rro-** used as comb. form (see -O-) of *ferrum,* (i) min. in names of species containing iron, (ii) chem. designating ferrous compounds.

ferret[1] fe·rit half-tamed variety of the polecat, Putorius furo. XIV. Late ME. *fyrette, forette firette* – OF. *fuiret,* (also mod.) *furet,* by suffix-substitution from OF. *fuiron* (:– Rom. **fūriōnem*), beside *furon* (= Pr. *furon,* Sp. *hurón,* Pg. *furão*) :– late L. *fūrō(n-)* thief, found in the transf. sense in Polemius Silvius and Isidore, f. L. *fūr* thief (cf. FURTIVE). ¶ F. *furet* was adopted in MDu. as *foret, furet* (Du. *fret,* whence G. *frett,* dim. *frettchen*). Hence **fe·rret** vb. XV; cf. F. *fureter.*

ferret[2] fe·rit †floss-silk XVI; stout tape XVII. prob. – It. *fioretti* floss-silk, pl. of *fioretto,* dim. of *fiore* FLOWER.

ferruginous fĭrū·dʒinəs of the nature or colour of iron rust. XVII. f. L. *ferrūgin-, -ūgō* iron rust, dark red, f. *ferrum* iron; see FERREOUS and -OUS.

ferrule fe·rəl band or cap of metal, etc., strengthening the end of a stick or tube. XVII (*ferrel, -il*). Alteration (prob. by assim. to L. *ferrum* iron, and -ULE) of *verrel, -il* (XVII), later form of *vyrelle, -ille, -oll* (XV) – OF. *virelle, virol(e),* mod. *virole* – L. *viriola, -olæ,* f. *viriæ* bracelet. ¶ (The earlier form survives in Sc. as *virl*; AL. has *virella* XIII.)

ferry fe·ri place where boats pass over to transport passengers, etc. XII (in personal names), XIV (Wyclif). The earliest exx. are from north. and eastern areas. – ON. *ferja* ferry-boat, or *ferju-*, as in *ferjukarl*, *-maðr* ferryman, *ferjuskip* ferry-boat = MDu. **vēre* (Du. *veer*), MHG. *vēr(e)* (G. *fähre*) :– Germ. **farjōn*, f. **far-* go (see FARE[1]). So **fe·rry** vb. – ON. *ferja* ferry = OS., OE. *ferian* carry, transport (which survived in ME. *ferie*), OHG. *ferren* (MHG. *vern*), Goth. *farjan* :– CGerm. **farjan*. (Some ME. forms with *v-* suggest Du. influence.)

fertile fǝ̄·ɹtail fruitful. XV. – F. *fertile* – L. *fertilis*, based on pp. formation **fertus* = Gr. *phertós* borne, f. *phérein* BEAR[2]; see -ILE. So **ferti·l**ITY -ti·lĭti. XV. – F. – L. Hence **fe·rtil**IZE. XVII. Cf. F.; earlier †*ferti·lit*ATE[3].

ferule fe·rūl †giant fennel (providing rods) XV; rod used for punishment XVI. – L. *ferula* (also used in Eng.), connected by Isidore with *ferīre* strike.

fervent fǝ̄·ɹvǝnt hot, burning; ardent. XIV. – (O)F. *fervent* – L. *fervent-*, *-ēns*, prp. of *fervēre* boil, glow; see -ENT and cf. FERMENT. So **fe·rv**ID. XVI. – L. *fervidus*. **fe·rv**OUR. XIV. – OF. *fervo(u)r* (mod. *-eur*) – L. *fervor*.

Fescennine fese·nain scurrilous, licentious. XVII (Holland). – L. *Fescennīnus*, f. *Fescennia* town in Etruria on the Tiber, famous for a sort of jeering dialogues in verse (*versus fescennini*); see -INE[1].

fescue fe·skju †straw XIV; small stick for pointing XVI; genus of grasses, Festuca XVIII. Late ME. *festu(e)*, surviving in mod. dial. as *vester* – OF. *festu* (mod. *fétu*) = Pr. *festuc*, It. *festuco* (to which there are corr. fem. forms) :– Rom. **festūcum*, for L. *festūca*. The dissimilative change from *festue* to *fescue* appears XVI.

fesse fes (her.) ordinary consisting of two horizontal lines. XV. – OF. *fesse*, var. of *faisse* :– L. *fascia* band (see FASCIA).

festal fe·stǝl pert. to a feast or festival. XV. – OF. *festal* – late L. *fēstālis*, f. *fēstum* FEAST; see -AL[1]. So **festival** fe·stĭvǝl adj. of a feast-day or festival (now apprehended as the sb. used attrib.) XIV; sb. festal day XVI. – OF. *festival* – medL. *fēstivālis*, f. L. *fēstīvus*, whence **fest**IVE fe·stiv †festal; jovial. XVII; f. *fēstum* FEAST. **festi·v**ITY. XIV. – (O)F. or L.

fester fe·stǝɹ †fistula; ulcer, suppuration. XIII (Cursor M.). – OF. *festre* :– L. *fistula*, with *-re* replacing *-le* as in F. *chapitre* CHAPTER, *épître* EPISTLE. So **fe·ster** vb. generate pus or matter. XIV (PPl.). f. the sb. or OF. *festrir*.

festoon festū·n curved chain of flowers, etc. XVII. – F. *feston* – It. *festone* prop. 'festal ornament', f. *festa* FEAST; see -OON.

fetch fetʃ go in quest of and bring back OE.; cause to come; draw (breath); deal (a blow), make (a stroke) XIV; †arrive at; take (a course) XVI; attract irresistibly XVII (Sh.). Late OE. *feċċ(e)an*, alteration of *fetian* (surviving in dial. *fet*) by combination of t and j (consonantal i) to produce tʃ (as in *ortġeard* ORCHARD); prob. rel. to OE. *fatian*, OFris. *fatia*, OHG. *fazzōn* (G. *fassen*) grasp, perh. orig. 'put in a vessel' (*fat*, VAT).

fête feit, ‖fɛt large entertainment. XVIII. F., mod. form of *feste* FEAST. Hence as vb. XIX after F. *fêter*.

fetial, fecial fī·ʃǝl adj. ambassadorial; sb. herald of war and peace. XVI. – L. *fētiālis* one of a college of priests concerned with the declaration of war and the conclusion of peace, prob. f. **fētis* :– IE. **dhētis* law, f. **dhē-* place, lay down (see DO[1]); see -IAL.

fetish, fetich fe·tiʃ, fī·tiʃ inanimate object worshipped by savages. XVII (*fateish*; earlier in form direct from Pg., *fetisso*). – F. *fétiche* – Pg. *feitiço* charm, sorcery = Sp. *hechizo*, sb. use of the adj. meaning 'made by art' (cf. It. *fattizio*, OF. *faitis*, whence ME. *fetis*, dial. *featish* handsome) :– L. *factītius* FACTITIOUS.

fetlock fe·tlɔk part of a horse's leg behind the pastern-joint, tuft growing there. XIV. ME. *fete-*, *feetlak*, *fitlok*, corr. to MHG. *vizzeloch*, *vizloch*, *-lach* (G. *fissloch*), rel. to G. *fessel* fetlock, deriv. of Germ. **fet-* (:– IE. **ped-*), var. of the base of FOOT.

fetter fe·tǝɹ bond, shackle. OE. *feter*, corr. to OS. pl. *feteros* (Du. *veter* lace), OHG. *fezzera* (early modG. *fesser*), ON. *fjǫturr* :– CGerm. (exc. Goth.) **feterō*, **feteraz*, f. **fet-* :– IE. **ped-* FOOT, as in synon. L. *pedica*, Gr. *pédē*. Hence (or orig. – ON.) **fetter** vb. XIII (Havelok); cf. OFris. *fiteria*, OHG. *fezarōn*, ON. *fjǫtra*.

fettle fe·tl make ready, put in order. XIV. f. (dial.) *fettle*, OE. *fetel* girdle = OHG. *fezzil* (G. *fessel*) chain, band, ON. *fetill* bandage, strap :– Germ. **fatilaz*, f. **fat-* hold (cf. FETCH). Hence **fe·ttle** sb. condition, trim. XVIII.

fetus var. of FŒTUS.

feu fjū (Sc. law) tenure or lease for a fixed return. XV. – OF. *feu*; see FEE. Hence **feu·**AR, †*fear*, *fiar*. XVI.

feud[1] fjūd †active hostility XIII (Cursor M.); state of mutual hostility XV. Of obscure history. Northern ME. *fede*, later mainly Sc. (XIII–XVIII). – OF. *fede*, *feide* – OHG. *fēhida* (G. *fehde*) = OE. *fǣhþ(u)* enmity, OFris. *fāithe*, *fēithe* :– Germ. **faiχiþō*, f. **faiχ-*; see FOE and -TH[1].

¶ In the latter half of XVI the forms *food(e)*, *feood*, *feode*, *fewd* appear in Eng. writings (*deadly* or *mortal feud* corr. to OF. *fede mortel*), in XVI–XVII occas. altered to *foehood*; these forms may repr. attempts to rationalize aberrant vars. of OE. *fǣhþ(u)*, such as *fœþh* (Lambarde 1568).

feud[2] fjūd (hist.) fief. XVII. – medL. *feudum, feodum* (IX), usu. taken to be of Germ. origin, but no evidence can be adduced. So **feu·d**AL[1]. XVII, **feu·dat**ORY. XVI. – medL. *feudālis, feudātōrius* (more freq. *feudātārius*, whence †*feudatary* XVI).

feuille-morte fö̆jmort yellowish brown. XVII. F. 'dead leaf'. ¶ Anglicized *f(i)eulamort, feuill-mort, fuil-de-mort, phyliamort, philemort*, FILEMOT.

feuilleton fö̆jətɔ̃ portion of a page of a newspaper marked off for special matter. XIX. F., f. *feuillet*, dim. of *feuille* leaf, FOIL[1]; cf. -OON.

fever fī·vəɹ disease accompanied by high temperature. OE. *fēfor* m., corr. to MLG. *feber* (whence in mod. Scand.), OHG. *fiebar* m. (G. *fieber*) – L. *febris* fem., of obscure origin, but plausibly referred by some to the base **dheġwh- *dhogwh-* (see FOMENT); reinforced in ME. from AN. *fevre*, (O)F. *fièvre* = Pr., Pg. *febre*, Sp. *fiebre*, It. *febbre* :– L. *febri-s*. Hence **fe·ver**ISH[1]. XIV.

feverfew fī·vəɹ-, fe·vəɹfjū the plant Pyrethrum Parthenium. OE. *feferfuge* – L. *febrifuga, -fugia*, f. L. *febris* FEVER + *fugāre* drive away (*fugere* flee; cf. FUGITIVE); but the mod. form descends from an adoption of AN. **fevrefue, fewerfue* (XIII). The *-fuge* of the OE. form is, however, repr. in *feþerfoy, fedyrfoy* (XIV–XV), forms due to assoc. with *feather* as in the mod. pop. *featherfew*.

few fjū not many. OE. *fēawe, fēawa*, contr. *fēa*, corr. to OFris. *fē*, OS. *fa(o)*, OHG. *fao, fō*, ON. *fár* (whence ME. *fā, fō*), Goth. pl. *fawai*; repr. CGerm. **faw-* :– IE. **pau-*, as in L. *paucus* (cf. PAUCITY), Gr. *paûros* small, L. *paullus* (:– **paurlos*) little, *pauper* POOR.

fey fei (arch., dial.) fated to die, dying. OE. *fǣġe* = OS. *fēgi* (Du. *veeg*), OHG. *feigi* (G. *feige* cowardly), ON. *feigr* :– CGerm. (exc. Goth.) **faigjaz*. After *c.* 1400 chiefly Sc.

fez fez Turkish crimson skull-cap. XIX. – Turk. *fez*, perh. through F.; said to be named after the town *Fez*, capital of Morocco and chief place of its manufacture.

fiacre fiæ·kr, ||fjakr French hackney coach. XVII. Named after the Hôtel de St. *Fiacre*, rue St -Antoine, Paris, where these carriages were stationed.

fiancé m., **fiancée** fem. fiā·sei, ||fjāse betrothed person. XIX. F., pp. of *fiancer* betroth = Pr. *fizansar*, It. *fidanzare* :– Rom. **fidantiāre*, f. **fidantia*, f. L. *fidāre* (see AFFIANCE).

Fian(n) fīn member of the ancient Irish militia; cf. FENIAN. XVIII. Ir.

fiasco fiæ·skou failure, breakdown, orig. in a dramatic or musical performance. XIX. It., in phr. *far fiasco* lit. 'to make a bottle' (see FLASK), which involves an unexplained allusion.

fiat fai·æt authoritative sanction or command. XVII. L. 'let it be done', 3rd sg. pr. subj. of *fierī* (see BE), used as passive of *facere* to do. So **fiant** in the formula *fiant litterae patentes* 'let letters patent be made out'.

fib fib trivial falsehood. XVII. prob. short for *fible-fable* (*fybble-fable* XVI), redupl. formation on FABLE. So vb. XVII.

fibre, U.S. **fiber** fai·bəɹ †lobe of the liver XIV; thread-like body in animal or vegetable tissue; rootlet XVII. – (O)F. *fibre* – L. *fibra*. Hence **fi·br**OUS. XVII; after F. *fibreux*, modL. *fibrōsus*.

fibula fi·bjŭlə clasp, brooch; long bone on the outer side of the leg. XVII. L. *fībula*, perh. f. base of *fīgere, fīvere* FIX.

-fic fik repr. L. *-ficus* making, doing, producing, causing to be (what is denoted by the first element of the comp.), f. weak var. of the stem of *facere* DO[1], forming adjs. (i) from sbs., as *honōrificus* HONORIFIC, *pācificus* PACIFIC, *sacrificus* (cf. SACRIFICIAL); (ii) from adjs., as *beātificus* BEATIFIC, *magnificus* MAGNIFIC; (iii) from vbs., as *horrificus* HORRIFIC, *terrificus* TERRIFIC; (iv) from advs., only in *beneficus* (BENEFICENT), *maleficus* MALEFIC. In medL. and modL. new formations with *-(i)ficus* are numerous, e.g. *prolificus* PROLIFIC, *scientificus* SCIENTIFIC.

-fication fikei·ʃən repr., through F. *-fication*, L. *-ficātiō(n-)*, formative of nouns of action (see -ATION) from vbs. in *-ficāre* -FY. Many L. words with this suffix were adopted in OF. with their corr. vbs. in *-fier*, and from XIV such sbs. have been freely adopted in Eng., e.g. *edification, mortification, purification, sanctification*; and *-fication* is established as the gen. ending for nouns of action related to vbs. in *-fy*, except such as repr. L. vbs. in *-facere* (cf. -FACTION). Formations not based on L. types are exemplified by *beautification* (XVII), *Frenchification, jollification* (XVIII), *transmogrification, uglification*. In scientific lang. there are sbs. in *-fication* having no corr. vb. in regular use, as *dentification, mercurification, nidification*.

fichu fi·ʃū triangular piece of stuff worn on the neck, etc. XIX. F. (*fiʃü*), sb. use of pp. (used perh. in the sense 'put on hurriedly') of *ficher* :– Rom. **fīgicāre*, f. L. *fīgere* FIX.

fickle fi·kl †false, treacherous OE.; changeful, inconstant XIII. OE. *ficol*, rel. to *ġefic* deceit, *befician* deceive (Germ. **fik-*), and further to *fǣcne* deceitful, *fācen* deceit, deceitful (Germ. **faik-*), corr. to OS. *fēkan*, OHG. *feihhan*, ON. *feikn* portent.

fictile fi·ktail moulded by art. XVII. – L. *fictilis*, f. *fict-*, pp. stem of *fingere* fashion; see FEIGN, -ILE.

fiction fi·kʃən something feigned, invention XIV; legal supposition; composition dealing with imaginary events XVI. – (O)F. *fiction*, corr. to Pr. *fiction*, etc. – L. *fictiō(n-)*, f. *fict-*; see prec. and -TION. So **ficti·tious** -i·ʃəs. XVII. f. L. *fictītius*.

fid fid (chiefly naut.) conical pin, square bar; plug of oakum or tobacco. XVII. Of unkn. origin.

-fid fid terminal element repr. L. *-fidus* cleft, divided, f. base of *findere* cleave (see FISSILE), as in *bifid, palmatifid* – (mod)L. *bīfidus, palmātifidus*, etc.

fiddle fi·dl stringed instrument of music played with a bow. OE. *fiþele* = (M)Du. *vedel* (*veel*), OHG. *fidula* (G. *fiedel*), ON. *fiðla* :– CGerm. (exc. Goth.) **fiþula* – Rom. **vītula* (whence F. *viole*, Pr. *viula, viola*, It. VIOLA), f. L. *vītulārī* celebrate a festival, be joyful (cf. *Vītula* goddess of victory and jubilation). Hence **fi·ddle** vb. XIV (PPl.). **fi·ddl**ER[1]. OE. *fiþlere* = ON. *fiðlari*.

fiddle-faddle fi·dlfæ:dl trifling talk or action. XVI. redupl. formation on FIDDLE; cf. G. *fickfack*, and contemptuous formations such as *flim-flam, skimble-skamble*.

fiddley fi·dəli (naut.) iron framework round opening to the stoke-hole. XIX. Of unkn. origin.

fideism fai·diizm mode of thought according to which knowledge depends upon a fundamental act of faith. XIX. f. L. *fides* FAITH + -ISM.

fidelity fi-, faide·lĭti faithfulness. XV. – F. *fidélité* or L. *fidēlitās*; see FEALTY.

fidget fi·dʒit physical uneasiness with spasmodic movements. XVII. prob. f. (dial.) *fidge* (XVI) to move restlessly; the relation with similar synon. forms is undetermined, viz. †*fig* (XVI), (north. dial.) *fitch* (XVII) and *fike* (XIII) – ON. (MSw.) *fíkja*. ¶ A similar series of symbolical formations is (dial.) *fridge* (XVI), †*frig* (XV), †*frike* (OE. *frīcian* dance), all denoting brisk or restless movement. Hence **fi·dget** vb. XVIII.

fiducial faidjū·ʃiəl, fi- (theol.) pert. to trust or reliance. XVII. – late L. *fīdūciālis*, f. *fīdūcia* trust, f. *fīdere* to trust, rel. to *fidēs* FAITH; see -IAL. So **fidu·ci**ARY in trust XVII; (of paper currency) depending on the confidence of the public or on securities (after F. *fiduciaire*) XIX. – L. *fīdūciārius*.

fie fai excl. of disgust or reproach; (now used trivially or joc.). XIII. – (O)F. *fi* :– L. *fī* excl. at perceiving a bad smell; cf. ON. *fý*, which may have contributed to the ME. currency. ¶ Similar ints. are Gr. *phû*, L. *phy, fū, fūfæ*, MHG. *fī, phī* (G. *pfui*), Du. *foei*.

fief fīf feudal estate. XVII. – (O)F. *fief* FEE. Cf. FEOFF.

field fīld open land; piece of land used for pasture or tillage OE.; (prob. after F. *champ*, but cf. OE. *herefeld* 'army field', *wælfeld* 'slaughter field') ground on which a battle is fought XIII (Cursor M.). OE. *feld*, corr. to OFris., OS. *feld* (Du. *veld*; cf. VELD), OHG., G. *feld* (whence Sw. *fält*, Da. *felt*) :– WGerm. **felþu* :– prehistoric **peltus* (adopted in Finnish *pelto* field); ult. rel. to OE. *folde* earth, ground, OS. *folda*, ON. *fold*, the IE. base being **pḷth-*, whence also Gr. *platús* broad, Skr. *pṛthús* broad, *pṛthivī* earth; cf. FLAT[1]. Hence **field** vb. †take the field in fight XVI; act as **fie·ldsman** at cricket, *c.*1820. **field** MARSHAL (in Continental armies) XVII (*marshal of the field* XVI), tr. G. *feldmarschall*, F. *maréchal de camp*); in the British army from XVIII.

fieldfare fī·ldfɛəɹ species of thrush, Turdus pilaris. XIV. Late OE. *feldefare* 'scorellus', ME. *feldefare* (4 syll.), perh. f. *feld* FIELD + stem of FARE[2], but the medial *e* in early forms is not accounted for.

fiend fīnd enemy; the Devil. OE. *fēond* = OFris. *fīand*, OS. *fīond* (Du. *vijand*), OHG. *fīant* (G. *feind*), ON. *fjándi*, Goth. *fijands* :– CGerm. prp. of **fijējan* (OE. *fēogan*, ON. *fía*, Goth. *fijan* hate), rel. to Skr. *pīyati* blames, derides. For origin and sp. cf. FRIEND.

fierce fiəɹs †brave, valiant; †proud; violent and intractable. XIII. – AN. *fers*, OF. *fiers*, nom. of *fer, fier* (mod. *fier* proud) = Pr. *fer*, Sp., It. *fiero* :– L. *feru-s* wild, untamed; see FERAL[2].

fieri facias fai·ərai fēi·ʃiæs (leg.) writ instituting the process for executing a judgement. XV. Law L., 'cause to be made', i.e. *fierī* be made (see FIAT), *facias*, 2nd sing. pres. subj. of *facere* make, DO[1].

fiery faiə·ri of or like fire. XIII. ME. *füri, firy, fyry, fery*, f. FIRE + -Y[1]; cf. OFris. *fiurech* (Du. *vurig*), MHG. *viurec* (G. *feurig*). The present sp. dates from XVI.

fife faif shrill-toned flute-like instrument. XVI (*fiphe, phyfe, fyfe*). – G. *pfeife* PIPE or F. *fifre* – Swiss G. *pfifre* (G. *pfeifer* PIPER).

fifteen, etc., see FIVE.

fig[1] fig (fruit of) fig-tree (Ficus). XIII (AncrR.). – (O)F. *figue* – Pr. *fig(u)a* = Sp. *higa*, Pg. *figa* amulet, It. *fica* pudendum muliebre (cf. Gr. σῦκον) :– Rom. **fīca* (whence OF. *fie*), for L. *fīcus* (whence OF. *fi*, Sp. *higo*, Pg. *figo*, It. *fico*); Rom. and L. forms were adopted in Germ. as (i) OS., OHG. *fīga* (Du. *vijg*, G. *feige*) and (ii) OE. *fīc* (ME. *fike* was prob. – ON. *fíkja*). comp. **fig-**LEAF chiefly with ref. to Gen. iii 7 ('They sowed . . fygge leaves together', Coverdale).

fig[2] fig contemptuous gesture with thumb and fingers. XVI (*figge of Spaine*). – F. *figue* (in phr. *faire la figue* make this gesture; cf. Sp. *hacer la figa*, Pg. *fazer figa*) – It. *fica* (see prec.).

fig[3] dress, equipment. XIX. f. *fig* vb. in phr. *fig out* or *up* to dress or furbish up, orig. said of gingering up horses; var. of †*feague* (XVII), which is perh. – G. *fegen* polish, furbish up, sweep, Du. *vegen* (OS. *fegōn*), f. Germ. **feg-*, rel. to **fag-* of FAIR[1].

fight[1] fait battle, combat. OE. *feohte* wk. fem., *feoht* and *ġefeoht* str. n., corr. to OFris. *fiuht*, OS., OHG. *fehta* (Du. *gevecht*), OHG. *gifeht* (G. *gefecht*); f. base of the verb.

fight[2] fait, pt., pp. *fought* fōt do battle, contend. OE. *feohtan* pt. *feaht*, *fuhton*, pp. *fohten* = OFris. *fiuchta*, OS. *fehtan* (Du. *vechten*), OHG. *fehtan* (G. *fechten*) :- WGerm. **feχtan* (**faχt*, **fuχtum*, **foχtanaz*), formally identical with L. *pectere* comb (cf. PECTINATE), but the connexion of sense is not obvious.

figment fi·gmənt product of fictitious invention. XV (rare before late XVI). – L. *figmentum*, f. **fig-*, base of *fingere* fashion, FEIGN.

figurant m. fi·gjurænt, **figurante** fem. -ãt ballet-dancer; supernumerary on the stage. – F. *figurant*, fem. *-ante*, and It. *figurante*, prps. of *figurer* and *figurare* perform a dancing figure, posture; see next and -ANT.

figure fi·gəɹ A. numerical symbol XIII (*figures of augrim*, AncrR.); B. (bodily) shape or form XIII (Cursor M.); in many senses repr. ult. technical uses of Gr. σχῆμα SCHEME (rhet., gram., logic, math.) from XIV (Ch.); conspicuous appearance distinction, mark XVII. – (O)F. *figure* = Pr., Sp., It. *figura* – L. *figūra*, f. **fig-*; see FEIGN, FIGMENT, -URE. So **fi·gure** vb. XIV. – (O)F. *figurer* – L. *figūrāre*, f. the sb. The L. vb. translated Gr. σχηματίζειν, the pf. part. of which was rendered by L. *figurātus* (whence **figur**ATE[2] XVI), used in the sense of **fi·gur**ATIVE (XIV, Trevisa, – late L. *figūrātīvus*). Cf. *configuration*, *prefigure*, *transfigure*.

figurine fi·gjurīn small carved figure. XIX. – F. *figurine* – It. *figurina*, dim. of *figura* FIGURE; see -INE[1].

figwort fi·gwə̄ɹt name of plants reputed to cure 'the fig' or *ficus*, i.e. piles. XVI. orig. applied to Ficaria, now Ranunculus Ficaria, pilewort; see FIG, WORT.

Fijian fīdʒī·ən pert. to *Fiji* (native name *Viti*) or the archipelago in the Pacific Ocean of which Viti Levu is the principal island; see -AN. XVIII.

filacer, -zer fi·ləsəɹ, -zəɹ former officer of the courts at Westminster, who filed writs. – Law F. *filacer* (-ER[2]), f. AN. *filaz* file of documents – medL. *filacium*, either f. L. *fīlum* thread, FILE[2], or shortening of late L. *chartophylacium* chest for papers – Gr. *khartophulákion*, f. *khártēs* paper, CHART + *phulak-* (*phulássein*) keep, guard.

filament fi·ləmənt tenuous thread-like body. XVI. – F. *filament* or modL. *fīlamentum*, f. late L. *fīlāre*, f. *fīlum* thread, FILE[2].

filbert fi·lbəɹt (nut of) the cultivated hazel. XIV (Gower). Earliest forms *philliberd*, *fylberde*, *filbert* – AN. *philbert*, short for **noix de Philibert* (cf. Norman dial. *noix de filbert*) St. Philibert's nut, so named from its ripening about his day, 22 Aug. (o.s.).

filch filᵗʃ steal. XVI (Awdelay). orig. thieves' slang, of unkn. origin.

file[1] fail metal instrument for abrading surfaces OE.; (sl.) cunning fellow XIX (cf. F. *lime sourde* lit. 'silent file'). OE. *fīl* = OS. *fīla* (Du. *vijl*), OHG. *fīhala*, *fīla* (G. *feile*) :- WGerm. **fīχalā*, which is referred to IE. **pik-* **peik-* cut, repr. also by OSl. *pišati* write, L. *pingere* PAINT, Gr. *pikrós* sharp, bitter. Hence **file** vb.[1] smooth with a file. XIII (AncrR.).

file[2] fail (arch., dial.) defile. OE. *fȳlan* (also with *ā-*, *be-*, *ġe-*) = MLG. *vūlen*, MHG. *viulen* :- WGerm. **fūljan*, f. Germ. **fūlaz* FOUL.

file[3] fail A. string or wire on which papers are strung XVI; collection of papers so preserved or arranged in order XVII. B. (mil.) men constituting the depth of a formation; row of persons, etc., one behind another)(*rank*. XVI. – (O)F. *fil* = Pr. *fil*, Sp. *hilo*, It. *filo* :- L. *fīlum* thread. Hence **file** vb[2]. place on or in a file XV; †place (men) in a file XVI; move in file XVII. Cf. DEFILE[2], ENFILADE.

filemot, philamot fi·līmət. XVII. Alteration of FEUILLE-MORTE; sp. with *ph-* *c.*1650.

filial fi·liəl pert. to a son or daughter. XV. – (O)F. *filial* or ChrL. *fīliālis*, f. L. *fīlius* son, *fīlia* daughter, prob. based on IE. **dhē-* suck, repr. by *fēcundus* FECUND, *fētus* FŒTUS, *fēmina* FEMALE; see -AL[1] and cf. F. *filial*. So **fili**A·TION (theol.) becoming or being a son XV; relationship or descent as of a son XVII. – (O)F. *filiation* – ChrL. *fīliātiō*, f. L. *fīlius*.

filibeg, philibeg, fill- fi·libeg (Sc.) kilt. XVIII. – Gael. *feileadhbeag*, f. *feiladh* fold, plait + *beag* little, as dist. from the large kilt, *feiladhmor*.

filibuster fi·libʌstəɹ †freebooter XVI (*flibutor*, *fleebooter*); piratical adventurer in the W. Indies XVIII; adventurer in Central America and Spanish W. Indies, 1850–60 XIX. The ult. source is Du. *vrijbuiter* FREEBOOTER, of which the earliest Eng. exx. are obvious alterations; the present use begins with the adoption (XVIII) of F. *flibustier* (XVII); this was succeeded (XIX) by the present form – Sp. *filibustero*, which itself is from F. The chronology and mutual relation of the various forms present difficulties.

filic- filis-, filik- stem of L. *filix* fern, as in *fi·lical*, *fili·ciform*, *fi·licoid*. XIX.

filigree fi·ligrī jewel work made with threads and beads. XVII (Evelyn). Alteration of *filigreen*, var. of *filigrane* (XVII–XIX) – F. *filigrane* – It. *filigrana*, f. L. *fīlum* thread (FILE[1]) + *grānum* seed, GRAIN.

filioque filiou·kwi, fai-. XIX. L., 'and [from] the Son', phr. inserted in the Western form of the Nicene Creed to assert the procession of the Holy Ghost from the Son as well as from the Father.

fill[1] fil A. full supply of food OE.; B. quantity that fills XVI. OE. *fyllu* = OHG. *fullī* (G. *fülle*), ON. *fyllr*, Goth. *ufar|fullei* :- CGerm. **fullīn*, f. **fullaz* FULL[1]. In B f. FILL[2], with which this sb. has always been associated.

fill² fil make full OE.; occupy the whole of; execute, fulfil, complete. OE. *fyllan* = OFris. *fullia*, OS. *fullian* (Du. *vullen*), OHG. *fullen* (G. *füllen*), ON. *fylla*, Goth. (CGerm.) *fulljan*; f. **fullaz* FULL¹. Cf. FULFIL.

fill³ fil shaft of cart. XVI (Sh.) dial. var. of THILL.

fillet fi·lit headband; narrow flat band, strip XIV; (cookery) slice of meat or fish XV. ME. *filet* – (O)F. *filet* = Pr. *filet*, Sp. *filete*, It. *filetto* – CRom. dim. of L. *fīlum* thread (FILE³); see -ET.

fillip fi·lip movement made with a finger suddenly released from contact with the thumb XV; (fig.) stimulus XVII. imit. Also as vb. (XVI). Cf. FLIP¹, FLIRT.

fillister fi·listəɹ rabbeting-plane. XIX. perh. based on synon. F. *feuilleret*; for the repr. of F. *feuill-* by *fil-* cf. FILEMOT.

filly fi·li young mare. XV. prob. much older if – ON. *fylja* :– **fuljōn*, parallel to OHG. *fulihha* (MHG. *fülhe*), f. Germ. **ful-* FOAL.

film film †membrane OE; thin pellicle, fine thread XIV. OE. *filmen* membrane, caul, prepuce = OFris. *filmene* skin :– Germ. **filminjam*, f. **felmon* (whence OE. *ǣġ|felma* skin of an egg), f. **fellam* FELL¹. In the senses 'photographic film', 'celluloid roll for cinematographic picture', 'cinema performance' the word has become CEur. Hence **fi·lmy**¹. XVII.

filoselle fi·lŏsel floss silk. XVII. – F. *filoselle*, superseding OF. *filloisel* – It. dial. *filosello*, for **folisello* :– Rom. **follicellus* cocoon (whence OF. *foucel*), for L. *folliculus* FOLLICLE.

filter fi·ltəɹ †felt XIV; piece of felt, etc., for freeing liquids of impure matter XVI; any apparatus for this XVII. – OF. *filtre*, var. of *feltre* (mod. *feutre* felt) = Pr. *feutre*, Sp. *fieltro*, It. *feltro* felt, filter – medL. *filtrum* – WGerm. **filtir* (*-iz*) FELT. Hence vb. XVI. So **fi·ltrATE**³ pass through a filter. XVII. f. pp. stem of modL. *filtrāre*; cf. INFILTRATE.

filth filþ †putrid matter OE.; unclean matter XIII. OE. *fȳlþ* = OS. *fūlitha* (Du. *vuilte*), OHG. *fūlida* :– Germ. **fūlaz* FOUL; see -TH¹. Hence **fi·lthY**¹. XIV.

fimble fi·mbl male plant of hemp, producing a weaker fibre than the female plant (*carl hemp*). XV. Earlier *fem(b)le* – Du. *femel*, LG. *fimel* – F. (*chanvre*) *femelle* 'FEMALE (hemp)', this name being pop. applied to what modern botanists call the male plant.

fimbria fi·mbriə (techn.) fringe. XVIII. Late L. (earlier only pl. *fimbriæ*). Cf. FRINGE. So **fi·mbriate** (her. and nat. hist.) fringed. XIX. – L. *fimbriātus*; see -ATE². **fi·mbriated.** XV (Book of St. Albans).

fin fin propelling and steering organ of fishes. OE. *fin(n)* = MLG. *finne* (whence G. *finne*), MDu. *vinne* (Du. *vin*); a word of the North Sea area, prob. ult. rel. to L. *pinna* feather, wing (cf. PINNACLE) :– **pidnā*, OIr. *ind* end, point :– **pindom*.

final fai·nəl marking an end, putting an end to something; relating to end or purpose. XIV (R. Mannyng, Ch.). – (O)F. *final* or L. *fīnālis*, f. *fīnis* end; see FINE¹, -AL¹. The earliest uses are in *final peace* (tr. medL. *finalis pax* or *concordia*), *final cause* (tr. medL. *finalis causa*, rendering Aristotle's τὸ οὗ ἕνεκα, τὸ τέλος). So **finalITY** fainæ·lĭti. XVI (once; not current till early XIX). – F. – late L. **fi·nalLY**². XIV (Ch); after OF. *final(e)ment*, late L. *fīnāliter*. **fi·nalIZE** put into final form. XX.

finance fi-, fainæ·ns †end; †settlement, payment XIV; †supply, stock; †tax, taxation XV; (pl.) pecuniary resources; management of (public) money XVIII. – (O)F. *finance* †end, †payment, money (cf. AL. *financia* payment XIV), f. *finer* make an end, settle, ransom, bargain for, procure, f. *fin* end, FINE¹. The senses now current are from modF. usage. Hence **fina·ncIAL.** XVIII (Burke). **fina·ncIER.** XVII (Bacon). – F. *financier*.

finch finᵗʃ name of many small passerine birds, esp. of the family Fringillidæ. OE. *finć* = MDu. *vinke* (Du. *vink*), OHG. *fincho* (G. *fink*) :– WGerm. **fiŋkiz*, **fiŋkjon*, perh. of IE. age.

find faind come upon; attain OE.; procure, supply XIII; support, maintain XIV. OE. *findan*, pt. *fand*, *fundon*, pp. *funden* = OFris. *finda*, OS. *findan*, *fīthan* (Du. *vinden*), OHG. *findan* (G. *finden*), ON. *finna*, Goth. *finþan* :– Germ. **finþan*, **fanþ*, **fundum*, **fundonaz* :– IE. base **pent-* (whence OIr. *ētain* I find), perh. identical with the base meaning 'go, journey' (cf. OE. *fēþa*, OHG. *fendo* footsoldier :– **fanþjon*), or a nasalized var. of **pet-* in L. *petere* seek, aim at. The Germ. conjugation should have yielded OE. **fīþan*, **fōþ*; the existing forms are analogical on *bindan* BIND, etc. The form of the pt. *found*, superseding ME. *fōnd*, *foond*, shows assim. to pt. pl. or pp., as in BIND, GRIND, WIND². Hence **find** sb. XIX.

fine¹ fain †end, conclusion XII; final agreement, settlement of a suit; composition paid XIII. – (O)F. *fin* = Pr., Sp. *fin*, Pg. *fim*, It. *fine* :– L. *fīnem*, nom. *-is* end, in medL. sum to be paid on concluding a lawsuit. ¶ For *foot of the fine* see FOOT. So, or – OF. *finer* (see FINANCE), **fine** vb¹. †pay a fine XIII; impose a fine on XVI.

fine² fain consummate in quality XIII (Cursor M.); delicate, subtle; handsome, excellent, admirable XIV; elegant XVI; of the weather XVIII. – (O)F. *fin* = Pr. *fin*, Sp., It. *fino* :– CRom. **fīnus*, f. *fīnīre* FINISH, after such pairs as *grossus*, *grossīre*. The Rom. word was adopted in OHG. *fīn* (G. *fein*), (M)Du. *fijn*, Icel. *fínn*. The later uses, expressing admiring approbation, are of purely Eng. development, and corr. to those of F. *beau*. *Fine arts* (XVIII) tr. F. *beaux arts*. Hence **fine** vb.² refine XIV; make fine, small, etc., XVI.

fine[3] fīn liqueur brandy. XIX. F., short for *fine champagne*, abbrev. of *eau-de-vie* fine *de la* Champagne 'fine brandy of Champagne'.

finesse fine·s †fineness, purity; delicacy, refinement; artfulness, artifice. XV. Many of the earliest exx. of *fynes(se)*, *fines* are spellings of *fineness* (cf. *playnes* for *playnness*, and the like), and it is difficult to determine the date of the adoption of F. *finesse* (= Pr., Sp. *fineza*, It. *finezza*) :- CRom. **fīnitia*, f. **fīnus* FINE[2]; see -ESS[2].

finger fi·ŋgəɹ one of the digits of the hand. OE. *finger* = OFris. *finger*, OS., OHG. *fingar* (Du. *vinger*, G. *finger*), ON. *fingr*, Goth. *figgrs* :- CGerm. **fiŋgraz*, perh. :- IE. **peŋqrós*, f. **peŋqe* FIVE. Cf. FIST[1].

fingering fi·ŋgəriŋ kind of knitting wool. XVII. Earliest forms *fingram*, *fingrum*, *fingrine*; poss. alteration of OF. *fin grain* 'fine grain' (cf. GROGRAM). ¶ Derivation from FINGER seems to be out of the question.

finial fi·niəl †adj. final; sb. (archit.) terminal ornament of an apex or corner. XIV. - AN. **finial* or AL. **finiālis*, f. *fin*, *fīnis* end; see FINE[1], -IAL.

finical fi·nikəl over nice or particular. XVI (Nashe). prob. academic sl. in origin, f. FINE[2]+-ICAL; poss. suggested by MDu. *fijnkens* accurately, neatly, prettily (Kilian). Hence **fi·nick**ING[2] XVII, **fi·nick**Y[1] XIX.

finis fai·nis the L. word placed at the end of a book, etc., XV; conclusion, end XVII. L. (orig. border, frontier). So **finish** fi·niʃ bring to an end, complete XIV; bring to perfection XV. ME. *fenisshe* - OF. *feniss-* (mod. *finiss-*), lengthened stem of *fenir* (altered to *finir*) = Pr. *fenir*, It. *finire* :- L. *fīnīre*, f. *fīnis*; see FINE[1], -ISH[2]. **finite** fai·nait †definite XV; limited XV. - L. *fīnītus*, pp. of *fīnīre*.

Finn fin Germ. name of a people of NE. Europe and Scandinavia calling their country Suomi and speaking a Ural-Altaic language. OE. *Finnas* pl., corr. to G. *Finne*, ON. *Finnr*; recorded as L. *Fennī* (Tacitus 'Germania' xlvi), Gr. *Phínnoi* (Ptolemy). Hence **Fi·nn**IC. XVII. - modL. **Fi·nn**ISH[1]. XVIII; cf. ON. *Finnskr*, G. *finnisch*. **Fi·nno-**, comb. form, as in *Finno-Ugrian*, *-Ugric*, epithet of the westernmost branch of the Ural-Altaic languages.

finnan fi·nən haddock cured with the smoke of green wood, etc. XVIII. Earlier forms *findon*, *findram*, *fintrum*, *findhorn*; name of the river *Findhorn*, confused with *Findon*, a village in Kincardineshire.

fiord, fjord fjɔ̄ɹd long narrow arm of the sea. XVII. - Norw. *fiord* :- ON. *fjǫrðr* :- **ferþuz*; cf. FIRTH, FORD.

fir fɔ̄ɹ coniferous tree (Pinus, Abies, Picea). XIV (Cursor M., Ch., Trevisa). ME. *firr*, *fyrre*, w. midl. *ve(e)r*, *vyrre*; prob. - ON. *fyri-* (in *fyriskógr* fir-wood, etc.) :- Germ. **furχjōn*, f. **furχō*, whence OE. *furh|wudu* fir-wood, OHG. *forha* (G. *föhre*), ON. *fura*, beside OHG. *vereh|eih* (G. †*ferch*), Lombardic *fereha* kind of oak; cf. L. *quercus* (:- **perkus*) oak. ¶ Like BEECH and BIRCH, of Germ. and (partly) IE. extent.

fire faiəɹ principle of combustion; burning material OE.; conflagration XII; heat of fever, passion, etc., XIV; firing of guns XVI (cf. F. *feu*, as in *faire feu* fire a gun). OE. *fȳr* = OFris., OS. *fiur* (Du. *vuur*), OHG. *fiur*, *fūir* (G. *feuer*) :- WGerm. **fūir* (ON. had poet. *fúrr*, *fýrr* m.), corr. to Gr. *pûr*, Umbrian *pir*, Czech *pýř*, Arm. *hūr*, Toch. *por*, *pwār*; cf. Skr. *pāvakás* fire. Hence **fire** vb. OE. *fȳrian* supply with firing; set on fire, lit. and fig. XIII; discharge, explode XVI; burn out (orig. U.S.) XIX.

firkin fɔ̄·ɹkin †cask XIV; quarter of a 'barrel' XV (*ferdekyn*, *ferken*). prob. - MDu. **vierdekijn*, dim. of *vierde* FOURTH; see -KIN.

firlot fə·ɹlət (Sc.) quarter of a boll. XV. Found in AL. *ferthelota* (XIII) prob. - ON. *fjorði hlotr* fourth part (LOT).

firm[1] fɔ̄ɹm fixed, immovable XIV; stable, not yielding XV. ME. *ferm(e)* - (O)F. *ferme* :- L. *firmus*. Conformed XVI to L. sp.

firm[2] fɔ̄ɹm †signature XVI; (style of) a commercial house XVIII. In the earliest use - Sp. *firma*, later - It. *firma*, of the same origin, medL. *firma* (cf. FARM), f. L. *firmāre* strengthen, in late L. confirm by one's signature, f. *firmus* FIRM[1].

firmament fɔ̄·ɹməmĕnt vault of heaven. XIII. - (O)F. *firmament* - L. *firmāmentum*, f. *firmāre* strengthen, f. *firmus* FIRM[1]; see -MENT. The L. word, meaning orig. 'support, foundation', was adopted in the Vulgate, in imitation of LXX Gr. *steréōma* (f. *stereoûn* make firm, f. *stereós* firm) as the rendering of Heb. *rāqīʿa* applied to the vault of the sky, prob. lit. expanse, f. *rāqīaʿ* spread out, beat or tread out, (in Syriac) make firm or solid.

firman fɔ̄·ɹmən edict; licence, permit. XVII. - Pers. *fermān*, OPers. **framānā* command = Skr. *pramāṇam* (right) measure, standard, authority, f. *pra-* PRO-+**mā-* MEASURE.

first fɔ̄ɹst that is before all others. OE. *fyr(e)st* = OFris. *ferost*, *-est*, *ferst*, OS. **furist* (in *furisto* wk. masc. as sb. prince, whence Du. *vorst*), OHG. *furist* (*furisto* prince, whence G. *fürst*), ON. *fyrstr* :- CGerm. **furistaz*, superl. formation on **fur-*, **for-* (see FOR, FORE, -EST, and cf. FORMER, FOREMOST) :- IE. **pr̥*, whence the various formations with superl. suffixes meaning 'first', e.g. Gr. *prôtos* PROTO-, *prṓtistos*, L. *prīmus* PRIME, Skr. *prathamás*. Hence **first**LING[1] first product or offspring. XVI (Coverdale).

firth fɔ̄ɹþ arm of the sea, estuary. XV. orig. Sc. - ON. *fjǫrðr* FIORD.

fiscal fi·skəl pert. to the treasury (spec. in Sc. PROCURATOR *fiscal*); sb. title of certain officials. XVI. - F. *fiscal* or L. *fiscālis*, f. *fiscus* treasury, orig. rush-basket, purse.

fish[1] fiʃ vertebrate water animal with gills. OE. *fisć* = OFris. *fisk*, OS., OHG. *fisc* (Du. *visch*, G. *fisch*), ON. *fiskr*, Goth. *fisks* :– CGerm. **fiskaz* :– **piskos*, rel. to L. *piscis* (cf. PISCINA), Ir. *iasc*, Gael. *iasg* (:– **peiskos*). So **fish** vb. OE. *fisćian*, **fi·sh**ER[1], OE. *fisćere*, also CGerm.; cf. L. *piscārī*, *piscārius*. Hence **fi·sh**Y[1]. XVI. ¶ There is no CIE. word for 'fish'; W. *pysg*, Corn. *pisc* are – L.

fish[2] fiʃ mend (a broken spar, etc.) with a piece of wood (fish or fish-plate). XVII (Capt. Smith). – (O)F. *ficher* fix :– Rom. **fīgicāre*, intensive of L. *figere* FIX. Hence (after F. *fiche*) **fish** sb. (naut.) piece of word used to strengthen another XVII; plate of iron, etc., to protect or strengthen a beam, rail, etc. XIX. Cf. next.

fish[3] fiʃ flat piece of bone, etc., used as a counter in games. XVIII. – F. *fiche*, f. *ficher* (see prec.), assoc. with FISH[1] because of the shape.

fissile fi·sail that may be split. XVII. – L. *fissilis*, f. *fiss-*, pp. stem of *findere* to cleave; see BITE, -ILE. So **fiss**URE fi·ʃəɹ cleft, split. LXIV. – (O)F. *fissure* or L. *fissūra*; **fission** fi·ʃən XIX. – L. *fissiōn-em*.

fist[1] fist clenched hand. OE. *fȳst* = OFris. *fēst*, MLG. *fūst* (Du. *vuist*), OHG. *fūst* (G. *faust*) :– WGerm. **fūsti*, perh. :– **fūχstiz*, for **fuŋχstiz* :– **pn̥qstis* (whence OSl. *pęstĭ* fist), f. zero grade of IE. **peŋqe* FIVE; cf. FINGER. Hence **fi·st**IC XIX, **fi·st**ICAL XVIII. **fi·sticuffs** fighting. XVII; prob. f. *fisty* adj. (XVII)+pl. of CUFF[2].

fist[2] fist breaking wind. First recorded XV, but prob. repr. OE. **fīst* (cf. vbl. sb. *fīsting*), corr., with variety of vowel-grade, to MLG. *vīst*, MDu. *veest*, Du. *vijst*, G. *fist*; cf. also ON. *físa* vb.; Germ. **fisti-* prob. rests on an orig. **fest-* :– IE. **pezd-*, whence L. *pēdere*, Gr. *bdeîn* (:– **bzdeîn*), Lith. *bezdĕti*. ¶ Cf. *wolf's* or *wolves' fist* Fungus Lycoperdon.

fistula fi·stjŭlə long sinuous ulcer. XIV (earlier *fystel*, *fistle* from OF.). L. *fistula* pipe, also in path. sense.

fit[1] (arch. *fytte*) fit division of a poem, canto. OE. *fitt* = OS. **fittia* (preserved in latinized form *vittea* in the preface to 'Heliand'); identified by some with OHG. *fizza* list of cloth (G. *fitze* skein of yarn, †thread with which weavers mark off a day's work) and ON. *fit* hem; but cf. next.

fit[2] fit †dangerous position or experience XIV; paroxysm; sudden state of activity XVI. OE. *fitt* (once) prob. 'conflict', orig. meaning perh. 'juncture', 'meeting', 'match', which might relate or identify this word with prec. Cf. FIT[3], FIT[4]. Hence **fi·t**FUL[1]; usedonce by Sh. ('Macbeth' III ii 23), popularized by Scott.

fit[3] fit well suited, proper XIV; qualified, prepared, ready XVI. perh. pp. of FIT[4], q.v.

fit[4] fit be and make proper or suitable; supply, equip. XVI. In these senses not recorded before late XVI; but a vb. *fitte* marshal forces (XIV) may point to a ME. vb. with the gen. sense 'arrange, adjust, match', which accords in meaning with (rare) ME. *fitte* person's match (XIII). The chronology of the evidence is inadequate for the determination of the relation between this set of words. Hence **fit** sb. XVII. Cf. OUTFIT.

fitch[1], dial. var. of VETCH. XIV (*ficche*, Wycl. Bible); occurs in A.V., Isaiah xxviii 25.

fitchew fi·tʃū polecat and its fur. XIV. – OF. *ficheau*, dial. var. of *fissel* (pl. *fissiaulx*), later *fissau*, dim. of a word appearing in early Du. as *fisse*, *visse*, *vitsche*, whence ult. also synon. **fitch**[2] XVI.

Fitz fits AN. sp. of OF. *fiz* (fits), earlier *filz* (mod. *fils*) :– L. *fīlius* son; survives in surnames in which it is followed by an uninflected genitive, e.g. *Fitzherbert*, *Fitzwilliam*.

five faiv 5, v. repr. inflected *fīfe* (*fīfa*, *fīfum*) of OE. *fīf* = OFris., OS. *fīf* (Du. *vijf*), OHG. *fimf*, *finf* (G. *fünf*), ON. *fimm*, Goth. *fimf* :– CGerm. **fimfi* :– IE. **pempe*, altered by assim. from **peŋqwe*, whence Skr. *pañcha*, Gr. *pénte*, *pémpe*, L. *quīnque* (with assim. of initial *p*), OIr. *cóic*, Gaulish *pempe*, OW. *pimp* (mod. *pump*), Lith. *penkì*, OSl. *pęstĭ* FIST[1]. So **fif**TEEN fiftī·n, fi·ftīn 15, XV. OE. *fīftēne* (*-tīene*) = OFris. *fīftīne*, OS. *fīftein* (Du. *vijftien*), OHG. *fimfzehan* (G. *fünfzehn*), ON. *fimtán*, Goth. *fimftaihun*. Hence **fifteen**TH. Late OE. *fīftēnþa* (XI), ult. superseding OE. *fīftēoþa*, ME. *fiftethe*; northern ME. *fiftend* was – ON. *fimtándi*. **fif**TH[2] fifþ ordinal of five. OE. *fīfta* = OFris. *fīfta*, OS. *fīfto* (Du. *vijfde*), OHG. *fimfto* (G. *fünfte*), ON. *fimti* :– CGerm. (exc. Goth.) **fimfton* :– IE. **peŋqto-* (cf. Gr. *pémptos*, L. *quintus*), f. **peŋqwe* FIVE. The normal *fift* survives dial.; the standard form has *-th* after *fourth* (cf. *sixth*, etc.). **fifty** fi·fti five tens. OE. *fīftiġ* = OFris., OS. *fīftich* (Du. *vijftig*), OHG. *fimfzug* (G. *fünfzig*), ON. *fimmtigr*, Goth. *fimftigjus*; see FIVE, -TY[1]. Hence **fi·fti**ETH[1]. OE. *fīftiġeoþa*, corr. to ON. *fimmtugandi*.

fives faivz game in which a ball is struck with the hand against a wall. XVII. pl. of FIVE. Of uncertain origin, but perh. so called because orig. played by two teams of five persons; cf. 'squaring out the forme of a tennis court .. by this square they (being stript of their dublets) played five to five, with the handball' (Nichols' 'Progresses of Queen Elizabeth').

fix fiks make firm or stable XV; place in a definite position or state XVI. Partly f. pp. †*fix* (XIV, Ch.) – OF. *fix* (mod. *fixe*) or its source L. *fīxus*, pp. of *fīgere* fix, fasten; partly – medL. *fīxāre* (cf. F. *fixer*, Sp. *fijar*, It. *fissare*), f. L. *fīxus*. Cf. AFFIX, PREFIX, SUFFIX, TRANSFIX. Hence **fix** sb. (orig. U.S.). XIX. So **fix**A·TION. XIV (alch., Gower). – medL. **fi·x**ITY. XVII (Boyle). **fi·xt**URE. XVII (Sh. 'Merry Wives' III iii 67, 1st Folio). Alteration, after *mixture*, of †*fixure* (XVII, Drayton). – late L. *fixūra* (Tertullian, Vulg.).

fizgig fi·zgig A. light woman XVI; spinning-top; squib XVII; B. harpoon XVI. The first el. may be †*fise* fart, or FIZZ; the second is GIG[1], which was used early in the senses of 'frivolous person' and 'whipping-top'; for sense B cf. Sp. *fisga* (– G. *fischgabel* fish-hook).

fizz fiz make a hissing sound, as of effervescence. XVII. imit.; cf. next. Hence sb. †disturbance XVIII; effervescing sound; (sl.) champagne XIX.

fizzle fi·zl †break wind silently XVI; (orig. U.S.) come to a lame conclusion, fail XIX. app. f. FIZZ (but this is recorded later)+-LE[3]. Cf. FIST[2].

flabbergast flæ·bəɹgàst confound utterly. XVIII. The pp. is mentioned, along with *bored*, in 1772 ('Annual Register' ii 191) as a new piece of fashionable slang; perh. fanciful formation on FLABBY and AGHAST.

flabby flæ·bi soft and limp XVII (Dryden); nerveless, feeble XVIII. Expressive alteration of synon. *flappy* (XVI), f. FLAP+-Y[1].

flaccid flæ·ksid limp; drooping. XVII. – F. *flaccide* or L. *flaccidus*, f. *flaccus* flabby; see -ID[1].

flag[1] flæg plant of the genus Iris; (formerly) reed, rush. XIV. Related in some way to (i) Du. *flag*, occurring in Bible of 1637, Job viii 11 margin (where A.V. has the same word) and to (ii) Da. *flæg* yellow iris.

flag[2] flæg (E. Anglian) turf, sod XV; flat slab of stone XVII. prob. of Scand. origin; cf. Icel. *flag* spot where a turf has been cut out, ON. *flaga* slab of stone (cf. FLAW[1]). Cf. FLAKE[2], dial. *flaught*.

flag[3] flæg piece of stuff attached to a staff and used as a standard or signal. XVI. perh. orig. an application of †*flag* adj. (see next). ¶ A doubtful ex. of synon. *fagge* (XV) suggests comparison with 'the flagg or the fagg federis' of a hawk's wing (Book of St. Albans, 1486). Adopted in several Germ. langs.

flag[4] flæg †hang down; become limp or feeble. XVI. rel. to †*flag* adj. hanging loose (XVI), of unkn. origin.

flagellant flədʒe·lənt one who scourges himself (as a discipline). XVI. – L. *flagellant-*, *-āns*, prp. of *flagellāre* whip (whence **flagel**LATE[3] flæ̆·dʒĭleit XVII, **flagell**A·TION XV), f. *flagellum*, dim. of *flagrum* scourge; see -ANT.

flageolet flædʒəle·t small wind instrument. XVII (*flajolet*). – F. *flageolet*, dim. of OF. *flag(e)ol*, *flajol* (whence ME. *flagel* XIV) – Pr. *flajol*, of unkn. origin; see -ET.

flagitious flədʒi·ʃəs extremely wicked. XIV (Wycl. Bible). – L. *flagitiōsus*, f. *flāgitium* noisy protest against a person's conduct, scandal, (hence) shameful act, crime, f. *flāgitāre* demand earnestly or vociferously, f. base meaning 'make a noise'; see -IOUS.

flagon flæ·gən large bottle for wine, etc. XV. Late ME. *flakon*, *flagan* – AN. **flagon*, (O)F. *flacon*, earlier **flascon* :– late L. *flascō(n-)* FLASK. For the change of inter-sonant k to g cf. *segrestain* sexton, SUGAR.

flagrant flei·grənt (arch. or obs.) blazing, burning, ardent XV; 'flaming into notice' (J.), glaring, notorious XVIII. – F. *flagrant* or L. *flagrant-*, *āns*, prp. of *flagrāre* burn, blaze, be enflamed, f. **flag-*, repr. a var. of IE. **bhleg-* (cf. FLAME, FULMINATE, PHLEGM, (RE)FULGENT); see -ANT. The second sense derives from the use repr. by F. *en flagrant délit* red-handed, medL. or modL. *(in) flagrante delicto*, late L. *flagrante crimine* (Codex of Justinian), lit. 'the offence raging'.

flail fleil instrument for threshing by hand, OE. **flegil* (repr. once by a late aberrant form *fligel*), in ME. *fleȝȝl* (Orm), *fleil*, *fleyl* = OS. *flegil*, (M)Du. *vlegel*, (O)HG. *flegel* :– WGerm. **flagil-*, prob. – L. *flagellum* scourge, (in Vulgate) flail, whence the Rom. forms OF. *flaiel*, *fleel* (mod. *fléau* scourge), Pr. *flagel*, Sp. *flagelo*, It. *fragello*. Examples of the Eng. word are rare before XV and the later ME. currency was prob. due to adoption from OF. or MDu.

flair flɛəɹ sagacious perceptiveness. XIX. F., f. *flairer* smell :– Rom. **flāgrāre*, for L. *frāgrāre* (see FRAGRANT). ¶ In ME. the OF. word was adopted in the sense 'odour, smell'.

flak flæk anti-aircraft fire (with shift of sense). XX. G., f. initials of *fliegerabwehrkanone* 'aircraft-defence-gun'.

flake fleik one of the small pieces in which snow falls XIV (Ch.); piece of ignited matter thrown off XIV; flat or scaly fragment XV; (arch.) bundle of fibres, lock of hair XVI. immed. source unkn.; the several senses may repr. derivs. of different origin; comparable forms in Scand. langs. are Norw. *flak*, *flāk* patch, flake, *flake* form into flakes, Sw. *is|flak* ice-floe, ON. *flakna* flake off, split. Cf. FLAW[1]. Hence **flake** vb. XV.

flambeau flæ·mbou torch. XVII. – (O)F. *flambeau*, dim. of *flambe*, †*flamble* :– L. *flammula*, dim. of *flamma* FLAME.

flamboyant flæmboi·ənt (orig. archit.) characterized by waved flame-like forms; flamingly coloured. XIX. – F. *flamboyant*, prp. of *flamboyer*, earlier *flambeiier*, f. *flambe*; see prec.

flame fleim ignited vapour; fig. of passion XIV (R. Rolle); visible combustion XV. ME. *flaume*, *flamme*, *flame* – AN. **flaume*, OF. *flame*, (also mod.) *flamme* = Pr. *flama*, Sp. *llama*, Pg. *chamma*, It. *fiamma* :– L. *flamma*, f. base repr. by FLAGRANT. For the origin of the var. †*flambe* (XIV–XVII) see prec. For the pronunc. cf. *angel*, *chamber*, *strange*. So **flame** vb. XIV. – OF. *flamer*, *flammer* (which was superseded by *flamber* XVI).

flamen flei·men †as used by Geoffrey of Monmouth for a supposed grade of priest in heathen Britain XIV (R. Mannyng); priest of a particular deity in ancient Rome XVI. – L. *flāmen*.

flamingo flǽmi·ŋgou bird with long legs and neck and scarlet plumage. XVI. Early forms *flemengo, -ingo* – Pg. *flamengo* – Pr. *flamenc* (whence also Sp. *flamenco*, F. *flamant*), f. *flama* FLAME + Germ. suffix *-iŋg*- -ING[3]; so named because of its bright plumage (cf. the Gr. name *phoinikópteros* lit. 'red-feathered').

flammenwerfer flæ·mənvɛ̄ɹfəɹ flame-throwing weapon. XX. G., f. *flamme* FLAME + agent-noun of *werfen* throw (WARP).

flan flæn disc of metal before stamping; open tart XIX. – F. *flan*; see FLAWN.

flanconade flæŋkŏnei·d thrust in the side at fencing. XVII. – F. *flanconnade*, f. *flanc* FLANK.

flange flænᵈʒ widening part XVII; projecting flat rim XVIII. Partly synon. with †*flanch* (XVIII–XIX); OF. *flanchir* and *flangir* (presumably f. *flanche*, var. of *flanc* FLANK), which are used as syns. of *fléchir* bend, may be the source of the vbs. *flanch* and *flange*, from which the corr. sbs. might be derived; but the chronological evidence does not favour this.

flank flæŋk side of the body of an animal between ribs and hip XII; extreme side of an army XVI. – (O)F. *flanc*, corr. to Sp. *flanco*, It. *fianco* – Frank. **hlanca* side; cf. FLINCH, LINK[1].

flannel flæ·nəl open woollen stuff. XIV. Early forms *flanell*, beside *flan(n)en, flan(n)ing*; the latter are perh. the orig. forms and – W. *gwlanen* woollen article, f. *gwlān* WOOL. ¶ The Eng. word is the source of F. *flanelle*, whence Sp. *flanela, franela*, It. *frannella, frenella*, G. *flanell*, Du. *flanel*. Used ludicrously to designate a Welshman in Sh. 'Merry Wives' v v 172.

flap flæp †blow XIV; fly-flapper XV; loose pendent part XVI. So **flap** vb. strike with something flexible and broad XIV; (of birds) beat the wings XVI. prob. imit., like *clap, slap, rap, tap*; cf. Du. *flap* blow, fly-flapper, lid of a can, *flappen* strike, clap. Hence **fla·p**DOO:DLE (colloq.) nonsense, humbug. XIX. **fla·p**DRA:GON snapdragon. XVI (Sh.). **fla·p**PER[1] one who or a thing which flaps XVI; young partridge XIX (hence sl., young woman XX).

flare flɛəɹ spread out, as hair, etc. XVI; burn with a spreading flame XVII (Milton); in prp. **fla·r**ING[2] showy, gaudy. XVII. Of unkn. origin (perh. Scand.). Hence **flare** sb. XIX. **fla·re-**UP, f. phr. *flare up*. XIX.

flash flæʃ sudden burst of flame or light XVI; sudden rush of water; superficial brilliance; †brilliant or showy person XVII; †(sl.) wig XVII; ornament sewn to the collar of a tunic formerly worn by officers of the 23rd Royal Welch Fusiliers and supposed to be the relic of a queue XIX. f. **flash** vb., the earliest uses of which refer to the rushing or dashing of water (XIV; preceded by an obscure *flaskie* sprinkle XIII), its application to the bursting forth of light or flame being of doubtful occurrence before XVI. Hence **fla·shy**[1] XVI, of which *flash* adj. (XVII) is a partial syn.

flask flàsk †container for wine, clothing XIV; case for gunpowder XVI; (wine) bottle with long narrow neck XVII. In the second sense – F. *flasque*, in the third prob. – It. *fiasco*; the F. form (OF. *flasche, flaske*) repr. medL. *flasca* (Isidore), the It. form medL. *flasco* (cf. Sp. *flasco, frasco*, Pg. *frasco*), acc. *flascōnem* (cf. Pr. *flascon*, It. *fiascone*, F. *flacon* FLAGON); ult. origin dubious; has been referred to L. *vāsculum*, dim. of *vās* VESSEL. ¶ The word appears in Germ. langs. as OE. *flasće, flaxe*, OHG. *flasca* (G. *flasche*), MDu. *flassche* (Du. *vlesch*), whence it has been adopted in various langs., as Lappish *flaskǫ*, Magyar *palaczk*, Pol. *flasza*.

flat[1] flæt level, prostrate XIV; not curved or undulating XV; unqualified; plain; dull; below true pitch XVI; of drink XVII; in many sb. uses from XIV. – ON. *flatr* = OHG. *flaz* :– Germ. **flataz*, of uncertain relationship (connexion with Gr. *platús*, Skr. *pṛthús* broad, L. *planta* PLANT, is plausible in regard to sense, but IE. *t* or *th* does not normally corr. to Germ. *t*; cf. FIELD). Hence **fla·tt**EN[5] vb. XVII; superseded the somewhat earlier **flat** vb.

flat[2] flæt storey of a house; suite of rooms on one floor (Scott). XIX. Alteration by assoc. with prec. of Sc. *flet* inner part of a house (OE. *flet* floor, dwelling = ON. *flet*, etc. :– CGerm. (exc. Gothic) **flatjam*, f. *flataz* FLAT[1]).

flatter flæ·təɹ praise unduly XIII (AncrR.); †fawn; fawn upon. XIV. ME. *flattere*, of unkn. origin; perh. back-formation from **flattery** (XIV) – (O)F. *flatterie*, f. *flatter* vb. flatter (which would normally give *flat* in Eng.), prob. f. Germ. **flat*- FLAT[1], and orig. meaning 'pat, smooth, caress'. ME. syns. based on the cons. skeleton *fl..k* were *flakere, flikere, fleech*; ME. Kentish *ulateri* ('Ayenbite') with initial v suggests a native word, but none is known.

flatulent flæ·tjŭlənt windy. XVI. – F. *flatulent* (Paré) – modL. *flātulentus*, f. L. *flātus* blowing, blast, f. *flāre* BLOW[1]; see -ULENT. So **fla·tul**ENCE XIX, -ENCY XVII.

flaunt flɔ̄nt (intr.) wave gaily or proudly; display (oneself) ostentatiously. XVI. Of unkn. origin; no point of contact can be made with Sw. dial. *flankt* flutteringly, *flanka* flutter, G. dial. *flandern* flutter, waver. ¶ In XVI–XVII the stem entered into several redupl. or jingling collocations, as *flaunt a flaunt* (Gascoigne, Harvey), *flantitanting* (Nashe), *flaunt tant*; also (with A-[1]) *aflaunt*.

flautist flɔ̄·tist player on the flute. XIX. – It. *flautista*, f. *flauto* FLUTE; see -IST.

flavine flei·vain (chem.) yellow dye-stuff. XIX. f. L. *flāvus* yellow + -IN. So **fla·vo**- comb. form.

flavour flei·vəɹ smell, aroma XIV; element in the taste of a substance depending on the sense of smell XVII. – OF. *flaor*, infl. by *savour*; the OF. word, if cogn. with It. †*fiatore*, repr. Rom. **flātor*, blend of L. *flātus* blowing, breath, and *fœtor* stench.

flaw[1] flɔ̄ †flake XIV; fissure, rift; blemish XVII. perh. – ON. *flaga* slab of stone, prob. :– Germ. **flaχ-*, **flag-*, parallel and synon. with **flak-*, whence pp. FLAKE, which *flaw* closely resembles in sense.

flaw[2] flɔ̄ sudden squall, etc. XVI. prob. – MLG. *vlāge*, MDu. *vlāghe* (Du. *vlaag*), the primary sense of which may be 'stroke' (IE. **plak-*; see FLAY).

flawn flɔ̄n custard or cheese-cake, pancake. XIII. – OF. *flaon* (mod. FLAN) :– medL. *fladō(n)-* (cf. It. *fiadone* honeycomb) – Frankish *flado* (Du. *vlade*, *vla* pancake) :– WGerm. **flaþō(n)*, prob. rel. to Gr. *pláthanon* cake-mould, *platús* broad (cf. FLAT[1]).

flax flæks blue-flowered plant, Linum usatissimum, producing textile fibre and linseed. OE. *flæx* (*fleax*) = OFris. *flax*, (M)Du. *vlas*, OHG. *flahs* (G. *flachs*) :– WGerm. **flaχsam*, prob. to be referred to Germ. **flaχ-* **fleχ-* :– IE. **plok-* **plek-* in Gr. *plékein*, L. *plectere*, G. *flechten* plait. Hence **fla·**XEN[3]. XVI.

flay flei strip off the skin of OE.; with skin as obj. XIII. OE. *flēan* (more freq. in comps. *āflēan*, *beflēan*), pt. **flōh*, *flōg*, *-on*, pp. *flæġen*, *flagen* = MDu. *vlae(gh)en* (Du. *vlaen*), ON. *flá* (the source of ME. *flā*, *flō*) :– Germ. **flaχan*, of unkn. origin; str. forms lasted till XV in pt. *flogh*, till XVII in pp. *flain*, *flean*; but wk. forms were current in XVI; for the development cf. *slay*.

flea flī small wingless insect, Pulex. OE. *flēa(h)*, corr. to MLG., MDu. *vlō* (Du. *vloo*), OHG. *flōh* (G. *floh*), ON. *fló*; repr. Germ. base **flauχ-* or perh. **plauχ-* (see FLEE). Hence **flea·**BANE.

fleam flīm lancet. XVI. – OF. *flieme* (mod. *flamme*) = Pr. *flecme* (Sp. *fleme*, Pg. *flame*, It. *fiama* are – F.) :– Rom. **fleutomum* (medL. *fledomum*, *fletoma*), for late L. *phlebotomu-s* – Gr. *phlebotómon*, sb. use of n. of adj. (see PHLEBOTOMY).

fleck flek spot, speck. XVI. The earliest recorded words of the group are **flecked** ppl. adj. dappled XIV and **fleck** vb. XV; the proximate source may be synon. ON. *flekkr* sb., *flekka* vb., or MLG., MDu. *vlecke* (Du. *vlek*) = OHG. *flec*, *fleccho* (G. *fleck*, *flecken*), of unkn. origin.

fledge fledʒ acquire or provide with feathers. XVI. f. †*fledge* adj. (XIV) having feathers (for flight), repr. var. **flećġe* of OE. **flyćġe* recorded only in *unfligge* (x) glossing L. *implumes*; corr. to MDu. *vlugghe* (Du. *vlug*), OHG. *flucchi* (G. *flügge* is from LG.) :– WGerm. **fluggja*, f. **flug-*, weak base of **fleugan* FLY[2]. Hence **fle·dge**LING[1]. XIX; after *nestling*.

flee flī run away (from). OE. *flēon* (pt. *flēah*, *flugon*, pp. *flogen*) = OFris. *flīa*, OS. *fliohan* (MDu. *vlīen*, Du. *vlieden*), OHG. *fliohan* (G. *fliehen*), ON. *flý(j)a* (*fló*, *flugum*) more freq. wk. *flýða*, *flý(i)ðr*; (MSw. *fly*, *flydde*), Goth. *þliuhan* :– CGerm. **þleuχan*, **þlauh*, **þlugum*, **þlogan-*. The str. forms continued till XV; but as early as XIII wk. forms are extant, esp. in texts of northerly provenance, which suggests that they may be of Scand. origin (cf. Sw. pt. *flydde*, Da. *flyede*). *Flee* and *fly* in OE. had identical pt. and pp., and in later usage became interchangeable in sense. In present use, the pt. and pp. of *fly* in the sense 'to run away' are *fled*, the present *flee* (which in north. dial. repr. formally both *flēon* to flee and *flēogan* to fly) having become rhet. or poet.

fleece flīs woolly covering of a sheep, etc. OE. *flēos* = Du. *vlies*, MHG. *vlies* (G. *vlies*) :– WGerm. **fleusaz*, and OE. *flēs* (WS. *flīes*) = MLG. *vlūs*, MDu. *vluus*, MHG. *vlius* (early modG. *fleusz*, *flüsz*) :– WGerm. *flȳs* **fleusiz-*, rel. to MLG., MHG. *vlūs* sheepskin (G. *flaus* woollen coat) :– **flūsaz*; prob. ult. rel. to the base of L. *plūma* feather, PLUME. Hence **fleece** vb. lit. and fig. XVI.

fleer fliəɹ †grin, grimace XIV; laugh mockingly, smile scornfully, gibe XV. prob. of Scand. origin; cf. Norw. and Sw. dial. *flira*, Da. dial. *flire* grin, laugh unbecomingly.

fleet[1] flīt company of ships, naval force. OE. *flēot* (once) ship or ships coll., f. *flēotan* float, swim, FLEET[3].

fleet[2] flīt (dial.) run of water OE.; (hist.) *The Fleet* that flowing into the Thames between Ludgate Hill and *Fleet* Street; (hence) the prison near it XIII. OE. *flēot* (also *flēote* or *-a*), corr. to OFris. *flēt*, (M)Du. *vliet*, MHG. *vliez*, ON. *fljót*, f. Germ. **fleut-* FLEET[3].

fleet[3] flīt †float OE.; (arch.) flow or glide away XII. OE. *flēotan* float, swim = OFris. *fliata*, OS. *fliotan* (Du. *vlieten*), OHG. *fliozan* (G. *fliessen*), ON. *fljóta* float, flow :– CGerm. (exc. Goth.) str. vb. **fleutan*; f. IE. **pleud-* **plud-* (repr. also by Lith. *plústi*, Lett. *pludēt* float, *pludi* flood), extension of **pleu-* **plou-* **plu-* (repr. by Gr. *pleîn* :– **pleϝein* sail, *ploûs* sailing, *ploîon* ship, ON. *fley* (poet.) ship, OSl. *pluti*, Skr. *plávati* swim, sail, L. *pluere* rain; cf. FLY[2]. Surviving mainly in **fleet**ING[2] flī·tiŋ ppl. adj. †floating, swimming OE.; †shifting, inconstant XIII; passing quickly away XVI.

fleet[4] flīt swift. XVI (Skelton). prob. much older if – ON. *fljótr*, **flīotr*, f. Germ. **fleut-* (see prec.).

Flemish fle·miʃ pert. to Flanders or its inhabitants XIV (Ch. has *Flaundryssh*); sb. the form of Dutch spoken in Flanders XVIII. – ON. *Flæmskr* – MDu. *Vlāmisch* (Du. *Vlaamsch*). So assim. to **Fleming** native of Flanders (XIV, Ch.) – ON. *Flæmingi* – MDu. *Vlāming*, f. *Vlām-*, whence *Vlaanderen* Flanders; see -ISH[1], -ING[3].

flense flens cut up the fat of a whale, skin a seal. XIX. – Da. *flense* = Norw. *flinsa*, *flunsa* flay. Also *flench*, *flinch* (Scott).

flesh fleʃ soft substance of an animal body; meat; corporeal form. OE. *flǣsć* = OFris. *flask*, OS. *flēsk* (Du. *vleesch*), OHG. *fleisc* (G. *fleisch*), ON. *flesk* swine's flesh, pork, bacon :– CGerm. (exc. Gothic) **flaiskaz*, *-iz*; an *s*-less form of the base is found in OE. *flǣć* flesh, *flićće* FLITCH, the orig. meaning being 'slice, slit, split' (cf. Lith. *pleikti* slit open a fish). Hence **flesh** vb. reward (a hawk, etc.) with a portion of the quarry; inure to bloodshed, gen. initiate; inflame, incite; plunge into flesh XVI; cf. F. *acharner*. **fle·sh**LY[1] OE. *flǣsćlić*. **fle·sh**POT. XVI (Coverdale). **fle·sh**Y[1]. XIV (Ch.).

fletcher fle·tʃəɹ (hist.) arrow-maker. XIV.– OF. *flech(i)er*, f. *fleche* arrow (whence Pr. *fleca*, Sp. *flecha*, Pg. *frecha*, It. *freccia*), of unkn. origin; see -ER[2]. ¶ Survives as a surname and in the title of a City livery company.

fleur-de-lis flǝ̄ɹdəlī·, ||flördə*li* iris flower; heraldic lily. XIX. The present form superseded the older forms in XIX; late ME. *flour de lys* – OF. *flour de lys*, i.e. *flour* FLOWER, *de* of, *lis* (L. *līlium* LILY); late ME. and early modE. *flower de lice* or *delice* (cf. AN. pl. *fleurs delices* XIII) was assoc. with a fanciful L. *flōs deliciæ* 'flower of delight'; a modified form of this, *flower-de-luce* (XVI, Spenser; in Amer. use since XVII), is unexpl.

fleury, flory flǝ̄·ri, floə·ri (her.) decorated with fleur-de-lis. XV. – OF. *floré*, *flouré* (mod. *fleuré*), f. *fleur* FLOWER; see -Y[5]. So **fleuretté** flǝ̄re·ti. XVI. (O)F., f. *fleurette*, dim. of *fleur*.

flew flū see FLOW, FLY[2].

flews flūz chaps of a hound. XVI (Turbervile). Of unkn. origin.

flex[1] fleks bend. XVI. f. *flex-*, pp. stem of L. *flectere* bend (cf. CIRCUMFLEX, INFLECT, REFLECT). So **fle·x**IBLE. XV (Hoccleve). – (O)F. or L. **flex**ION fle·kʃən bending; inflexion. XVII. – L. *flexiō(n-)*; so F., Sp. **flex·**URE. XVI. – L.

flex[2] fleks flexible insulated electric wire. 1907 (beside *flexible*). Shortening of FLEXIBLE.

flibbertigibbet fli:bəɹtidʒi·bit (dial.) chattering person XV; flighty woman XVI (Latimer); †name of a fiend XVII; character so nicknamed in Scott's 'Kenilworth' (1821); hence, impish urchin. The earliest forms, *flibbergib*, *flebergebet* (also *flepergebet*, Castle Persev.), are perh. imit. of senseless chatter; the expanded form was familiarized by *Flibbertigibbet* in Sh. 'Lear' III iv 20, which is based on *Fliberdigibbet* in Harsnet's 'Popular Impostures' (1603); perh. assoc. with *gibbet*.

flick[1] flik slight blow as with the end or tip of something. XV. imit.; cf. F. *flicflac* cracking of a whip (XVII). Hence **flick** vb. XIX.

flick[2] flik (pl.) cinema show. XX. Short for FLICKER, as in *flicker-palace* cinema.

flicker fli·kəɹ †flutter, hover OE.; †fondle, dally XIII; flutter, vibrate XV; burn fitfully, flash up and die away XVII. OE. *flicorian*, *flycerian* (cf. LG. *flickern*, Du. *flikkeren*), synon. in its earliest use with ME. *flakere*, dial. *flacker*, prob. repr. an OE. **flacorian*, f. *flacor* (of arrows) flying, f. imit. base **flak-*, repr. also in MHG. *vlackern* flicker (G. *flackern*), ON. *flǫkra*, *flǫkta* flutter. Hence **fli·cker** sb. XIX.

flight[1] flait act of flying OE.; collection of beings or things flying together XIII; volley (of missiles) XVI; set of steps (so F. *volée*) XVIII. OE. *flyht*, corr. to OS. *fluht* (M)Du. *vlucht* :– WGerm. **fluχti*, f. weak grade of **fleugan* FLY[2]. Hence **fli·ghty**[1] †swift, rapid XVI; given to flights of fancy, etc.; inconstant XVIII.

flight[2] flait act of fleeing. OE. **flyht* = OFris. *flecht*, OS., OHG. *fluht* (Du. *vlucht*, G. *flucht*), ON. *flótti* :– Germ. **þluχtiz*, f. weak grade of **þleuχan* FLEE.

flimsy fli·mzi slight, frail, trivial. XVII (Dict. of Canting Crew). orig. dial. or sl.; prob. based on **flim-flam** nonsense, humbug, adj. frivolous, vain (XVI), symbolic redupl. formation with vowel variation like *fiddle-faddle*, *whim-wham*. ¶ Connexion with W. *llymsi* bare, empty is not probable, and ON. *flim* lampoon, libel, is remote in sense.

flinch flin[t]ʃ give way, draw back XVI; shrink or wince from pain XVII. – OF. *flenchir*, *flainchir* turn aside – WGerm. **χlaŋkjan*, whence (M)HG. *lenken* bend, turn; rel. to LANK, LINK[1].

flinders fli·ndəɹz (dial.) shivers, splinters. XV. prob. of Scand. origin (cf. Norw. *flindra* thin chip or splinter).

fling fliŋ pt. and pp. *flung* flʌŋ (intr.) move with violence XIII; kick *out*; (trans.) cast, hurl XIV (Barbour). First recorded from the south-eastern texts 'Kyng Alisaunder' and 'Arthour & Merlin'; perh. – ON. unrecorded **flinga*, rel. to *flengja* (Sw. *flänga*, Da. *flænge*) flog, but the sense is remote.

flint flint kind of hard stone. OE. *flint* = MDu. *vlint*, rel. to OHG. (G. dial.) *flins*; perh. rel. to Gr. *plínthos* tile (see PLINTH).

flip[1] flip give a smart blow or jerk to; strike (something) in this way. XVI. prob. contr. of FILLIP; but cf. **flip-flap** (XVI, Skelton), redupl. formation on FLAP, denoting a repeated flapping movement. Hence as sb. XVII (Locke).

flip[2] flip mixture of beer and spirit sweetened and heated with a hot iron. XVII (Congreve). perh. f. prec. vb. with the notion of 'whipping up' into froth.

flippant fli·pənt †nimble, pliant; †voluble, glib XVII; showing unbecoming levity XVIII. f. FLIP[1] + -ANT, perh. in imitation of heraldic adjs., as *couchant*, *rampant*, *trippant*. ¶ *Flip* adj. is used dial. in the first two senses. Hence **fli·pp**ANCY. XVIII.

flirt flɜːt A. †smart stroke; sudden jerk; B. †flighty woman XVI; one who plays at courtship XVIII (Richardson). This, with the corr. vb. of similar date and parallel meanings, seems to be an imit. formation; for the initial sounds cf. *flick*, *flip*, †*flerk*, for the final, *spurt*, *squirt*. Hence **flirta·tion**. XVIII; whence **flirta·tious** XIX.

flit flit remove to another place, trans. and intr. XII (Orm); (naut.) shift (a block, etc.); altered to *fleet* XVIII. – ON. *flytja*, f. **flut-*, weak grade of the base of *fljóta* (see FLEET[3]).

flitch flitʃ side of a hog. OE. *flicce*, corr. to MLG. *vli(c)ke*, ON. *flikki* (whence dial. *flick* from XV) :– Germ. **flikkjam*, f. **flik-*, as in ON. *flik* rag.

flitter fli·təɹ fly or flutter about. XV. f. FLIT + -ER[4]. Cf. G. *flittern* glimmer, OHG. *flitarezzen* flatter. Hence **fli·ttermouse** (dial.) bat. XVI; after Du. *vledermuis* or G. *fledermaus* (OHG. *fledermūs*, f. *fledarōn* flutter). ¶ Syns. of similar form are (dial.) *flickermouse* (XVII, Cotgr., Jonson), *flindermouse* (XV, Caxton), *fluttermouse* (XVIII).

float flout rest on the surface of liquid. Late OE. *flotian* = OS. *flotōn* (MDu. *vlōten*), ON. *flota* :– Germ. **flotōjan*, f. **flot-*, weak grade of base of FLEET[1]. Reinforced in ME. by, if not entirely due to, OF. *floter* (mod. *flotter*) = Sp. *flotar*, It. *fiottare* :– Rom. **flottāre*, prob. – Germ. **flot-*. **floata·tion** see FLOTATION. So **float** sb. floating state OE.; floating object (e.g. cork or quill supporting a baited line); broad, level, shallow vessel. XV. Of mixed origin; OE. *flot* floating = ON. *flot*; OE. *flota* ship, fleet = ON. *floti*; various mod. uses are f. the vb.

flocculent flɔ·kjŭlənt like flocks of wool. XIX. f. L. *floccus* FLOCK[2] + -ULENT.

flock[1] flɔk band or company, esp. of (domestic) animals. OE. *flocc* = MLG. *vlocke*, ON. *flokkr* (in OE. and ON. used only of an assemblage of persons); of unkn. origin. Hence **flock** vb. †trans. and intr. XIII (Laȝ., Cursor M.).

flock[2] flɔk tuft of wool, etc. XIII. – (O)F. *floc* = Pr., Rum. *floc*, Sp. *flueco*, It. *fiocco* :– L. *floccu-s*. The relation to similar synon. Germ. words is undetermined, viz. MDu. *vlocke* (Du. *vlok*), OHG. *floccho* (G. *flocke*), MSw. *flokker*, ON. *flóki* felt, hair, wool; but the MDu. may be partly the source of the Eng. word.

floe flou sheet of floating ice. XIX. prob. – Norw. *flo* layer, level piece :– ON. *fló* layer, stratum. Cf. FLAW[1]. ¶ The earlier word was *flake* (XVI).

flog flɔg beat, thrash. XVII. Recorded as a cant word by Coles 1676. Initial *fl* is characteristic of words imit. of striking or beating, as (dial.) *flack*, *flap*, *flick*, *flirt*; perh. suggested by L. *flagellāre* FLAGELLATE.

flood flʌd flowing in of the tide; body of flowing water; deluge, inundation. OE. *flōd*, corr. to OFris., OS. *flōd* (Du. *vloed*), OHG. *fluot* (G. *flut*), ON. *flóð*, Goth. *flōdus* :– CGerm. **flōðuz*, *-am*, f. **flō-* :– IE. **plō-* (as in Gr. *plṓein* swim, *plōtós* navigable). For the pronunc. cf. *blood*.

floor flɔəɹ level layer of boards, stone, etc. OE. *flōr*, corr. to (M)Du. *vloer*, MHG. *vluor* (G. *flur*), ON. *flór* :– Germ. **flōru-z*; rel. to OIr. *lār*, W. *llawr* :– Celtic **plār-*. Hence **floor** vb. cover with a floor XV; bring to the ground XVII.

floose, fluce flūs small coin of N. Africa, Arabia, India, etc. XVI (*fluss*). – Arab. *fulūs*, pl. of *fals*.

flop flɔp flap heavily, move clumsily; fall, collapse XVII. var. of FLAP, expressive of a duller or heavier sound.

flora flɔ̄ə·rə (*F-*) goddess of flowering plants XVI (Dunbar); plant life of a region, period, etc. XVIII (as a book-title XVII). L., f. *flōr-*, *flōs* FLOWER. So **flo·ral**[1]. XVII. – L. *flōrālis* or directly f. L. *flōr-*.

Florentine flɔ·rəntain inhabitant of (XV), or pert. to Florence, Tuscany XVI. – F. *florentin* or L. *Flōrentīnus*, f. *Flōrentia*; see -INE[1].

florescence flɔ̄re·səns (state or period of) flowering. XVIII. – modL. *flōrescentia*, f. prp. stem of L. *flōrēscere*, inceptive of *flōrēre*; see FLOURISH, -ESCENCE. Cf. *inflorescence*.

floret flɔ̄ə·rit (bot.) small flower. XVII. f. L. *flōr-*, *flōs* FLOWER + -ET.

florid flɔ·rid †flourishing, blooming; (of style) flowery; ruddy. XVII. – F. *floride* or L. *flōridus*, f. *flos*, *flor-* flower; see FLOURISH, -ID[1].

florilegium flɔ̄rilī·dʒiəm methodical collection of (literary) flowers. XVII. modL. (L. *flōs* FLOWER, *legere* gather), tr. Gr. *anthológion* ANTHOLOGY.

florin flɔ·rin gold coin first issued at Florence in 1252 XIV; English gold coin of Edward III's reign XV; two-shilling piece 1849. – (O)F. *florin* – It. *fiorino*, f. *fiore* FLOWER; the coin orig. so named bore the figure of a lily on the obverse and on the reverse the Latin name of the city, *Florentia*, whence the use of OF. and ME. (to early modEng.) *florence* for the coin.

florist flɔ̄·rist, flɔ̄ə·rist cultivator of or dealer in flowers. XVII. f. L. *flōr-*, *flōs* FLOWER + -IST, after F. *fleuriste* or It. *fiorista*.

floruit flɔ·ruit period of 'flourishing'. XIX. L., 3rd sg. pt. indic. of *flōrēre* FLOURISH. ¶ For similar use of such a part of the L. vb. cf. *habitat*, *tenet*, †*tenent*.

flory see FLEURY.

floss flɔs rough silk. XVIII (also *floss-silk*). Early forms also *flosh*, *flox* – F. *floche*, as in *soie floche* floss-silk (hence It. *seta floscia*, Du. *floszijde*), OF. *flosche* down, pile of velvet; of unkn. origin.

flotation, floatation floutei·ʃən floating. XIX. f. FLOAT vb. + -ATION, after F. *flottaison*, as in *ligne de flottaison*. The sp. with *flot-* has been adopted to make the word conform to the foll., and *rotation*.

flotilla flouti·lə small fleet. XVIII. – Sp. *flotilla*, dim. of *flota* = Pr. *flota*, OF. *flote* group, company (mod. *flotte* fleet), rel. to *flot(t)er* FLOAT.

flotsam flɔ·tsəm floating wreckage. XVI. Early forms also *flotsen*, *-son*, *-zam*, *-zan* – AN. *floteson*, f. *floter* FLOAT. For the form cf. JETSAM.

flounce[1] flauns dash or plunge with violent or jerky motion. XVI. Of obscure origin (like *bounce*, *pounce*, *trounce*); connexion with Norw. *flunsa* hurry, Sw. dial. *flunsa* fall with a splash, cannot be asserted.

flounce[2] flauns ornamental appendage to a dress-skirt. XVIII. Alteration, prob. by assim. to FLOUNCE[1], of earlier †*frounce* wrinkle, fold, pleat (Ch., Gower) – (O)F. *fronce*, f. *froncir* wrinkle – Germ. **χruŋkjan* (cf. ON. *hrukka*, MHG. *runke* wrinkle), whence medL. *fruncetura* (Reichenau Glosses). So **flounce** vb. XVIII; cf. †*frounce* vb. wrinkle (XIII), frizz, curl, pleat (XVI).

flounder[1] flau·ndəɹ flat-fish, Pleuronectes Flesus. XIV. – AN. *floundre* (in AL. *flundra* XIII), OF. (mod. Norman dial.) *flondre*, prob. of Scand. origin (cf. OSw. *flundra*, Da. *flynder*, ON. *flyðra* :– **flunþriōn*).

flounder[2] flau·ndəɹ †stumble, plunge or tumble about clumsily. XVI. prob. blending of FOUNDER and BLUNDER, assisted by the frequency of *fl-* in words expressing impetuous, clumsy, or rough movement, e.g. *fling*, *flounce*.

flour flauəɹ 'flower' or finer portion of meal, (now) wheat meal XIII; fine powder resulting from pulverizing XIV. Differentiated sp. of FLOWER (ME. *flour of huete*; cf. F. *fleur de farine* pure wheaten flour); the sp. *flower* continued till early XIX and is the only form recognized by J., though Cruden's Concordance to the Bible (1738) has the distinction.

flourish flʌ·riʃ A. †blossom, flower XIII (Cursor M.); thrive XIV (R. Rolle); be in the prime XIV (Trevisa); B. †adorn, embellish XIII (Cursor M.); C. †display, parade; brandish XIV (Wycl.); brag, swagger XVI. – (O)F. *floriss-*, lengthened stem (see -ISH[2]) of *florir* (mod. *fleurir*) = Pr. *florir*, It. *fiorire* :– Rom. **florīre*, for L. *flōrēre*, f. *flōr-* FLOWER. Hence **flou·rish** sb. A. (dial.) mass of bloom; †vigour, prime XVI; B. embellishment XVII; C. brandishing of a weapon; fanfare XVI.

flout flaut treat mockingly. XVI. perh. – Du. *fluiten* whistle, play the FLUTE, hiss (*uitfluiten*); cf. synon. G. colloq. *pfeifen auf* 'pipe at'.

flow flou move in a current; gush, well forth; be in flood. OE. *flōwan*, pt. *flēow*, pp. *flōwen*, f. Germ. **flō-*, whence also ON. *flóa* flood, MLG. *vlōien*, Du. *vloeien* flow and FLOOD. The sense-development has been infl. by unrelated L. *fluere*, of which it is the usual rendering. The orig. str. conj. *flow*, *flew*, *flown*, began to be superseded by wk. forms in the pt. in early ME.; the pp. persisted till XVIII and survives arch. or as a blunder (esp. in *overflown*, for *overflowed*).

flower flauəɹ A. reproductive organ in plants; blossom; choicest individual XIII (perh. XII, and the earliest use); period of flourishing XIV; state of blooming XVII (*in flower*, †*in flowers*); B. pl. menses; pulverized form of a chemical substance XIV; fungoid growth XVI. ME. *flur*, *flour* – AN. *flur*, OF. *flour*, *flor* (mod. *fleur*) = Pr., Cat. *flor*, It. *fiore*, Rum. *floare* :– L. *flōrem*, nom. *flōs* :– CItalic deriv. with *s* (corr. to OE. *blōstma* BLOSSOM) of IE. **bhlō-* (see BLOW[2], BLADE, BLOOM). In B depending on uses of L. *flōs* and Gr. *ἄνθος*, but the sense 'menses' has been referred by some to L. *fluōrēs*, pl. of FLUOR. Hence **flower** vb. XIII; prob. after OF. *florir*, *flourir* FLOURISH. Hence **flowe·ry**[1]. XIV (Ch.); OE. had *flōrisć*. ¶ Cf. *deflower*, *inflorescence*, and the differentiated FLOUR.

flown floun see FLOW, FLY[2].

fluce see FLOOSE.

flu(e) flū colloq. shortening of INFLUENZA XIX (Southey).

fluctuate flʌ·ktjueit move like a wave, pass to and fro. XVII. f. pp. stem of L. *fluctuāre*, f. *fluctus* current, flood, wave, tempest, f. *fluct-*, pp. stem of *fluere* flow; see -ATE[3]. So **fluctua·tion** vacillation XV; alternate rise and fall XVII. – (O)F. or L.

flue flū chimney, smoke duct in this, etc. XVI (*flew*). Of unkn. origin; the primary meaning is uncertain.

fluent flū·ənt flowing freely or easily (lit. and fig.); ready in speech. XVI. – L. *fluent-*, *-ēns*, prp. of *fluere* flow; see -ENT. ¶ Cf. *fluid*, *flux*, *efflux*; *affluent*, *confluent*, *effluent*, *-ence*; *influence*; *mellifluous*, *superfluous*; *fluctuate*.

fluff flʌf light feathery stuff. XVIII (Grose). prob. of dial. origin and alteration of *flue* †down (XVI), the *f* being symbolic of puffing away some light substance; cf. Flem. *vluwe*, Du. *fluweel*.

fluid flū·id having the property of flowing XV (Chauliac); sb. XVII (Boyle). – (O)F. *fluide* or L. *fluidus*, f. *fluere* flow; see -ID[1]. Hence **flui·dity**. XVII (Florio).

fluke[1] flūk flat fish, esp. flounder OE.; parasitic worm resembling this XVII. OE. *flōc*, corr. to ON. *flóki*, rel. by gradation to MLG., MDu. *flac*, OHG. *flah* (G. *flach*) flat; ult. IE. **plaq-* is further repr. by Gr. *plakoûs*, L. *placenta* flat cake.

fluke[2] flūk triangular plate on either arm of an anchor XVI; triangular extremity of a whale's tail XVIII. perh. transf. use of FLUKE[1], from its shape.

fluke[3] flūk (orig. billards) successful stroke made by chance. XIX. perh. of dial. origin (cf. dial. *fluke* guess, miss in fishing); but poss. a pun on FLUKE[1] with allusion to its syn. FLOUNDER[1].

flummery flʌ·məri (dial.) kind of porridge XVII; transf. mere flattery, humbug XVIII. – W. *llymru*, of unkn. origin; *fl-* (†*thl-*) is used to express the sound of W. *ll-*, as in Shakespeare's *Fluellen* (Llewelyn), and in *Floyd* (Llwyd); cf. †*fluellin* speedwell (– W. *llysiau Llewelyn*).

flummox flʌ·meks (sl.) confound, bewilder. XIX (Dickens). prob. of dial. origin; cf. dial. *flummock* confuse, *flummox* maul, mangle, *flummocky* slovenly, beside *slummock* slattern; imit. or symbolic formations.

flump flʌmp (colloq.) fall or throw *down* heavily. XIX. imit.; cf. *dump, plump, slump*.

flunkey flʌ·ŋki man in livery XVIII; obsequious person XVIII (J. Sinclair, Burns). orig. Sc., brought into Eng. use by Hood and Thackeray; poss. f. *flanker* one who stands at a person's FLANK+-Y[6].

fluo- (chem.) comb. form of FLUORINE. XIX (Davy).

fluor flū·ɔɹ †flux, fluid state; (after Agricola, 1546, tr. G. *flüsse*) one of a class of minerals used as fluxes XVII; mineral of this kind containing fluorine (esp. *fluor-spar*) XVIII. Hence **fluore**·SCENCE, -ESCENT 1852 (Stokes); after *opalescence*. So **flu·orine** non-metallic element of the halogen group. XIX (Davy). – F. *fluorine* (Ampère); see -INE[5].

flurry flʌ·ri sudden gust XVII; sudden agitation or commotion XVIII. f. †*flurr* scatter, ruffle, fly up with a whirr, prob. after *hurry*. Hence **flu·rry** vb. agitate, confuse. XVIII.

flush[1] flʌʃ fly up suddenly. XIII. First in pt. forms *fliste, fluste*, the vocalism of which suggests an OE. **flysćan*, of imit. origin.

flush[2] flʌʃ hand containing cards all of one suit. XVI (Skelton). – OF. *flus, fluz, flux* (whence Flem. *fluys* and Sp. *flux*, It. †*flusso*) – L. *fluxus* FLUX.

flush[3] flʌʃ A. (of liquids) rush out suddenly or copiously XVI; B. emit light or glow suddenly; produce or show heightened colour XVII. orig. identical with FLUSH[1], the notion of sudden movement being common to the two vbs.; the range of meaning is similar to that of FLASH.

flush[4] flʌʃ abundantly full, plentifully supplied XVII (Dekker, Sh.); even, level with XVIII. prob. f. prec.

flushing flʌ·ʃiŋ rough thick woollen cloth. XIX. f. name of *Flushing* (Du. *Vlissingen*), a port in Holland.

fluster flʌ·stəɹ excite, esp. with drink (XV) XVII; intr. for pass. XVII; flurry XVIII. Except for a late isolated and doubtful ME. vbl. sb. *flostyrynge*, first in Sh. 'Othello' II iii 60; of unkn. origin, but resembling in sense Icel. *flaustr* hurry, *flaustra* bustle.

flute flūt cylindrical musical wind-instrument with holes along its length XIV; channel, furrow, groove XVII. The earliest forms are *flowte* (Ch.), *floite* (XIV), in XVI–XVII often *fluit* – OF. *flahute, flëute, flāute* (mod. *flûte*), prob. – Pr. *flāut* (whence also Sp. *flauta*, It. *flauto*), perh. blending of *flaujol, flauja* (cf. FLAGEOLET) with *laut* LUTE. Cf. MHG. *floite* (G. *flöte*), Du. *fluit* – F. So **flute** vb. XIV (Ch.); channel, groove XVI. – (O)F. *flëuter* (mod. *flûter*).

flutter flʌ·təɹ †float to and fro; flap the wings rapidly OE.; quiver, tremble excitedly. XVI. OE. *floterian, -orian* frequent. of Germ. **flut-*; see FLEET[3], -ER[4], and cf. synon. G. *flattern*, †*flotteren*, †*flutteren*.

fluvial flū·viəl pert. to a river. XIV (Trevisa). – L. *fluviālis*, f. *fluvius* river, prop. adj. formation on base of *fluere* flow; see -AL[1]. So **flu·viat**ILE. XVI. – F. – L. *fluviātilis*, f. *fluviātus* moistened, wet, f. *fluvius*.

flux flʌks copious flowing of blood, etc. XIV (Wycl. Bible, PPl.;) (gen.) flowing; continuous succession XVI; incoming tide)(reflux XVII; substance facilitating fusion (earlier †*fluss* – G. *fluss*) XVIII. In early use (XIV–XVII) also †*flix* – (O)F. *flux* or L. *fluxus* (whence also Pr. *flux*, Sp. *fluxo*, It. *flusso*), f. *fluere* flow (cf. FLUENT). So **fluxion** flʌ·kʃən †flow, flowing XVI; (math.) rate of change of a continuously varying quantity XVIII (after Newton). – F. or L.

fly[1] flai winged insect, spec. two-winged insect of the family Muscidæ. OE. *flȳġe, flēoġe* = OS., OHG. *flioga* (Du. *vlieg*, G. *fliege*) :– WGerm. **fleug(j)ōn*, f. **fleugan* (see next); cf. ON. *fluga*.

fly[2] flai move with wings; (now in pres. stem only) flee. OE. *flēogan*, pt. *flēah, flugon*, pp. *flogen* = OFris. *fliāga*, OS. **fliogan* (Du. *vliegen*), OHG. *fliogan* (G. *fliegen*), ON. *fljúga* :– CGerm. (exc. Goth.) **fleugan*, pt. **flaug*, **flugum*, pp. **flugonaz*, f. IE. **pleuk-*, extension of **pleu-*, parallel to **pleud-* FLEET[3]. The normal ME. pt. *flegh* was at first replaced by the type *flough, flow*, which was transferred from the pl. to the sg.; this was finally superseded by *flew*, an unexplained form but perh. due to assoc. with the pt. of FLOW, the pp. of which had become identical with that of *fly*. In comb. applied to things attached by an edge, e.g. *fly-leaf, -sheet, -wheel*. Hence **fly·**ER[1], **fli·er.** XV.

fly[3] flai flight XV; speed-regulating device, compass card, etc. XVI; 'a stage-coach, distinguished by this name, in order to impress the belief of its extraordinary quickness in travelling' (J.) XVIII; light carriage XIX. f. FLY[2].

fly[4] flai (sl.) sharp, wide awake. XIX. prob. f. prec., but the etymol. notion is not clear.

flyboat flai·bout †fast-sailing vessel XVI; swift boat used on canals XIX. orig. – Du. *vlieboot* boat used orig. on the *Vlie*, a channel leading out of the Zuyder Zee; later assoc. with FLY[1]. The word has passed into other Eur. langs., as F. *flibot*, Sp. *flibote*, G. *flieboot*.

foal foul colt or filly. OE. *fola* = OFris. *fola*, OS. *folo*, MDu. *volen*, (also mod.) *veulen*, OHG. *folo* (G. *fohlen* n.), ON. *foli*, Goth. *fula* :– CGerm. **folon*, rel. to synon. L. *pullus*, Gr. *pôlos*, Arm. *ul*. Cf. FILLY.

foam foum aggregation of bubbles formed on the surface of liquid by agitation, fermentation, etc.; frothy saliva. OE. *fām* = (O)HG. *feim* :– WGerm. **faimaz*, *am* :– IE. **poimo-*, rel. to L. *pūmex* PUMICE, OSl. (pl.) *pěny* (Russ. *péna*), Skr. *phénas* foam, corr. to Lith. *spáinė*, L. *spūma* (:– **spoimā*) SPUME. Hence **foam** vb. XIV; superseding OE. *fǣman* (ME. *feme*) = OHG. *feimen* :– WGerm. **faimjan*.

fob[1] fɔb cheat, trick, put *off* deceitfully. XV. Parallel to †*fop* vb. and G. *foppen* quiz, banter. Hence **fob** sb. trick. XVII. ¶ ME. *fobbe* impostor coupled with synon. *faitour* (once in PPl.) is isolated.

fob[2] fɔb small pocket. XVII (Brome). orig. cant term; prob. of G. origin (cf. G. dial. *fuppe* pocket, *fuppen* vb.).

fo'c'sle see FORECASTLE.

focus fou·kəs, pl. *foci* fou·sai, *focus(s)es* fou·kəsiz point towards which lines, rays, etc., converge XVII (Boyle, Hobbes); point at which an object must be situated so that a well-defined image of it may be produced by the lens; centre of activity XVIII. – L. *focus* fireplace, domestic hearth, in pop. lang. repl. *ignis* fire (hence in Rom., e.g. F. *feu*, Sp. *fuego*, It. *fuoco*, Rum. *foc*). So **fo·**CAL[1]. XVIII. – modL. *focālis*.

fodder fɔ·dəɹ (now sl.) food; spec. cattle food. OE. *fōdor* = MLG. *vōder*, (M)Du. *voeder*, OHG. *fuotar* (G. *futter*), ON. *fóðr* :– Germ. **fōðram*, f. **fōð-* (see FOOD, FOSTER).

foe fou adversary in mortal feud or combat, enemy. Early ME. *fā*, *fō*, pl. *fān*, *fōn*, aphetic reduction of *ifā(n)*, *ifō(n)*, OE. *ġefā(n)*, assisted by *fāmon*, *fōman*, late OE. *fāhmon*; OE. *ġefā*, sb. use of *ġefāh* at feud (with) = OHG. *gafēh* (MHG. *gevēch*, *gevē*) :– WGerm. **gafaiχa*, f. **ga-* Y- + **faiχ-* (OE. *fāh* at feud, hostile, OFris. *fāch* liable to punishment), whence also OE. *fǣhþ*, OHG. *(ga)fehida* (see FEUD), and OS. *āfēhian* treat as an enemy; ult. origin unkn. Hence **foe·**MAN. OE.; chiefly poet., revived by Scott.

fœtus fi·təs young in the womb or egg. XIV (Trev.). – L. *fētus* (often miswritten *foetus*) pregnancy, giving birth, young offspring, produce, abstr. sb. parallel to adj. *fētus* pregnant, productive, prob. rel. to *fēcundus* FECUND, *fēmina* woman (see FEMININE).

fog fɔg thick mist. XVI. Identical in form with (dial.) *fog* aftermath grass, long or rank grass (XIV), moss (XV), whence *foggy* boggy, spongy, murky, (of flesh) flabby (XVI), whence perh. (by back-formation) *fog* thick mist (XVI), but the sense-development is not clear, and the evidence is insufficient for a final judgement; possibly ult. of Scand. origin (cf. Norw. *fogg* long-strawed, weak, scattered grass in a moist meadow). ¶ An earlier occurrence of *fog* is implied in *foggage* (privilege of) pasturing cattle on fog, which occurs as AL. *fogagium* c.1200.

fog(e)y fou·gi (colloq.) old-fashioned fellow. XVIII. rel. to sl. *fogram* (XVIII) antiquated, old-fashioned (person), of unkn. origin.

fogger now dial. exc. as in PETTIFOGGER.

foible foi·bl failing, weakness. XVII. – F. *foible*, var. of *faible* FEEBLE.

foil[1] foil tread under foot XIII; overthrow, discomfit; frustrate, ba(u)lk XVI. perh. – AN. **fuler*, var. of (O)F. *fouler* = Pr. *folar*, Sp. *hollar*, It. *follare* :– Rom. **fullāre*, f. L. *fullō* FULLER.

foil[2] foil †leaf; thin sheet of metal XIV; thin leaf of metal placed under a precious stone to increase its brilliance, etc.; a thing that serves by contrast to set off another thing XVI. (i) – OF. *foil* = Pr. *folh*, It. *foglio* :– L. *folium* leaf, perh. rel. to Gr. *phúllon*; (ii) OF. *foille* (mod. *feuille*) = Pr. *folha*, Sp. *hoja*, It. *foglia* :– L. *folia*, pl. of *folium* (n. pl. taken as fem. sg.).

foil[3] foil small-sword with blunt edge and blunted points. XVI. Of unkn. origin.

foin foin thrust with a pointed weapon. XIV. prob. f. OF. *foine*, *foisne* (mod. *fouine*) three-pronged fish-spear :– L. *fuscina* trident.

foison foi·zn (dial.) power, capacity XIII (Cursor M.); (arch.) plenty, abundance XIII. – (O)F. *foison* = Pr. *foizó* :– Rom. **fŭsiōnem*, for L. *fūsiō(nem)* outpouring (see FUSION).

foist foist †palm (a die) so as to be able to introduce it when required; introduce surreptitiously or unwarrantably. XVI. prob. – Du. dial. *vuisten*, f. *vuist* FIST[1]. Cf. JOIST.

fold[1] fould enclosure for domestic animals. OE. *fald*, contr. of *falæd*, *falod*, *-ud*, corr. to OS. *faled*, MLG. *valt*, Du. *vaalt*. Hence **fold** vb. shut up in a fold. OE. *faldian*.

fold[2] fould double or bend over upon itself; lay (the arms) together. OE. *faldan*, *fealdan* pt. *fēold*, pp. *fealden* = MDu. *vouden* (Du. *vouwen*), OHG. *faltan* (G. *falten*), ON. *falda* (pt. *félt*), Goth. *falþan*, pt. *faifalþ* :– CGerm. redupl. str. vb. **falþan*; *t*-extension of IE. **pel-* **pl-* (cf. Gr. *di|paltos*, *di|plásios* twofold, *ha|plóos* simple), with a parallel *k*-extension in L. *plicāre* fold, PLAIT. Hence **fold** sb. XIII (Cursor M.).

-fold fould OE. *-fald* (*-feald*) = OFris., OS. *-fald* (Du. *-voud*), (O)HG. *-falt*, ON. *-faldr*, Goth. *-falþs*, CGerm. terminal el.

rel. to FOLD² and equiv. Gr. *-paltos, -plasios*, and more remotely Gr. *ha|plós* single, *di|plós* double (L. *duplus*); like the Gr. and L. equivs. appended to cardinal numerals and adjs. meaning 'many', orig. with the sense 'folded in two, etc., or many folds', 'plaited in so many strands', becoming chiefly arithmetical multiplicatives. In OE. the adjs. were already used as sbs. and advs. (the advb. notion being expressed also by such phr. as *be fīffealdum, be maniġfealdum*, later †*by fivefold*, †*by manifold*).

foliage fou·liidʒ leaves collectively. XV. Early forms *foillage, fuellage* (assim. later to L. *folium*) – (O)F. *feuillage*, †*foillage*, f. *feuille*; see FOIL², -AGE.

foliation fouliei·ʃən A. being in leaf, arrangement in leaves XVII; B. consecutive numbering of folios XIX. In A f. L. *folium*; see FOIL², -ATION. In B. f. FOLIO.

folic fou·lik (chem.) name of an acid obtained orig. from spinach and abundant in green leaf. XX. irreg. f. L. *folium* FOIL¹+-IC.

folio fou·liou A. leaf of paper, parchment, etc.; page of a ledger, orig. two opposite pages used concurrently; B. *in folio* in the form of a full-sized sheet folded once (hence simply *folio* adj. and sb.). XVI. In A a generalization of the medL. use of the abl. of L. *folium* leaf, FOIL², in references 'at leaf so-and-so' or a latinization of It. *foglio*; in B – It. *in foglio*.

folk fouk (arch.) people, race; (arch.) men, people. OE. *folc* = OFris. *folk*, OS., OHG. *folc* (Du., G. *volk*), ON. *folk* people, army, detachment :- CGerm. (exc. Goth.) **folkam*, the orig. meaning of which is perh. best preserved in ON. Hence **fo·lk-**LORE 1846 (W. J. Thoms). **fo·lk-**SONG XIX. tr. G. *volkslied* (Herder). ¶ From XIV the pl. *folks* has been used, and since XVII is the ordinary form, the sing. being *arch.* or *dial.*

follicle fɔ·likl (anat., etc.) small sac. XVII (Sir T. Browne). – L. *folliculus* little bag, dim. of *follis* bellows, perh. rel. to BALL¹; see -CLE.

follow fɔ·lou go or come after OE.; walk in the footsteps of, copy, imitate. OE. *folgian*, corr. to OFris. *fol(g)ia, fulgia*, OS. *folgon* (Du. *volgen*), OHG. *folgēn* (G. *folgen*), beside OE. *fylgan* (ME. *filȝe*, surviving till XV as *filow, -oe*), ON. *fylgja* accompany, help, lead, follow, pursue; f. CGerm. (exc. Goth.) **fulg-*, of unkn. origin. ¶ OE. *fullgān* (*-gangan*) pt. *fulēode* complete, pursue (a desire), imitate, help = OS. *fullgān* (*-gangan*), OHG. *follegān, -gēn* are distinct in form and orig. in sense.

folly fɔ·li quality or state of being foolish XIII; costly structure considered to have shown folly in the builder XVI. – (O)F. *folie*, f. *fol* foolish, FOOL, corr. to Pr. *fol(h)ia*, It. *follia*; see -Y³. In the second sense derived from a similar use of OF. *folie*, which is preserved in modF. place-names, e.g. *La folie-Beaujon*; the identity with this word is shown (XI) by its being rendered by L. *stultitia*, but there may have been in some instances blending with OF. *fueillee* (mod. *feuillée*) arbour, pleasance, country house (cf. medL. *foleia* and *domus foleyæ* XIII).

fomalhaut fou·məlhɔ̄t (astron.) star in the Southern Fish. XVI. – Arab. *fumᵘ 'lhaut* mouth of the fish.

foment foume·nt bathe with warm lotion; promote the growth of; foster, stimulate. XV. – (O)F. *fomenter* – late L. *fōmentāre*, f. *fōmentum* lotion, poultice, lenitive :- **fovementum*, f. *fovēre* heat, cherish, f. IE. base **dhogʷh-* **dhegʷh-*, repr. also by Skr. *dáhati*, Lith. *degù* burn, Gr. *téphrā* (:- **dhegʷhrā*) ash, ember; cf. DAY.

fond fɔnd (dial.) foolish, silly XIV (R. Rolle); (dial.) foolishly affectionate, doting; †eager, desirous; having a strong liking (for) XVI. ME. *fonned, -yd*, having the form of a pp. of *fon* vb. (recorded later in XIV) be foolish, which is obscurely rel. to †*fon* sb. fool (XIII, Cursor M.). The occurrence in ME. (Wyclif only) and E. Anglian dial. (XVII–XIX) of the sense 'insipid', 'of sickly flavour', has suggested that the vb. *fon* orig. meant 'lose savour'; but this sense is later than that of 'foolish', and its source is of obscure origin; moreover, the chronology of the words as known suggests that ME. *fonned* was directly f. *fon* sb.+-ED² (cf. the etym. of *wicked, wretched*). ¶ Derivation from Scand. as repr. by Sw. *fån(e)*, MDa. *fåne* fool, Icel. *fáni* vain person, swaggerer, though supported by the sense, seems to be ruled out on phonetic and other grounds, unless the shortening of the vowel took place on the addition of *-ed*, and the sb. and vb. *fon* are back-formations.

fondant fɔ·ndənt kind of sweetmeat that melts quickly in the mouth. XIX. F., sb. use of prp. of *fondre* melt; see FOUND², -ANT.

fondle fɔ·ndl †pamper XVII (Dryden); treat with fondness, caress XVIII. Back-formation from †*fondling* (foolish person *c.* 1400, one who is fondly loved or caressed XVII), f. FOND+-LING¹. Cf. *sidle, suckle.*

font¹ fɔnt receptacle for the water used in baptism. Late OE. *font*, var. of *fant* (also in comps. *fantbæþ, -fæt, -hālgung, -hālig, -wæter*, and in ME. *fon(t)stōn, fan(t)stān*) – OIr. *fant, font* – L. *font-, fons* spring, FOUNTAIN, in spec. eccl. use, *fōns* or *fontes baptismi* water(s) of baptism, whence OF. *fonz, fonce* (mod. *fonts*) m. pl., Pr. *font*, It. *fonte*. (OFris. *font, funt*, MDu. *vonte* (Du. *doop|vont*), ON. *funtr* are prob. adoptions of the Eng. word.) ME. shows continuation of the OE. forms as *font, fant, vant*, beside adoption of AN. *funz* (OF. *fonz*) as *funt* (a regular Sc. form), *fount*.

font² var. of FOUNT².

fontanelle fɔntəne·l (anat.) †hollow between muscles XVI; outlet for a discharge XVII; membranous space in the skull of an infant XVIII. – F. *fontanelle* – modL. *fontanella,* latinization of OF. *fontenelle,* dim. of *fontaine* FOUNTAIN; see -EL[2].

food fūd what is taken to support life. Late OE. *fōda* :– *fōðon, a unique formation, the synon. words in other Germ. langs. being f. *fōðjan FEED, viz. ON. *fœði, fœða,* Goth. *fōdeins*; f. Germ. *fōð- *fað- (cf. OHG. *vatēn* pasture, *fatunga* food) :– IE. *păt-, as in Gr. *pateîsthai* eat.

fool[1] fūl A. one deficient in judgement or sense XIII (Laȝ.); professional jester, clown XIV; B. adj. foolish XIII (AncrR.); now only (exc. dial.) as attrib. use of the sb. ME. *fōl* sb. and adj. – OF. *fol* (mod. *fou* mad) = Pr. *fol* (whence Sp. *fol*), It. *folle* :– L. *folli-s* bellows, inflated ball, money-bag, (later fig.) 'windbag', empty-headed person (cf. *follis inflatus* applied by Augustine to a puffed-up person), also used as adj., beside *follus*; perh. rel. to BALL[1], BELLY. Cf. FOLLY. Hence vb. play the fool, make a fool of. XVI (Sh.). **foo·lERY**. XVI (Latimer, Spenser). **foo·lHARDY**. XIII (AncrR.). – OF. *folhardi* 'foolish-bold'. **foo·lsCAP** (*fool's cap*) cap of a professional fool; folio writing- or printing-paper of a kind that orig. bore a watermark representing a fool's cap. XVII.

fool[2] fūl †clotted cream XVI; dish composed of crushed fruit with cream, etc. XVIII. perh. transf. use of prec. suggested by *trifle* (cf. '*Mantiglia,* a kinde of clouted creame called a foole or a trifle', Florio).

foot fut pl. *feet* fīt part of the leg beyond the ankle joint; unit of measurement 12 in.; metrical unit OE.; lowest part XII; what is at the foot or bottom (bottoms, dregs, with pl. *foots*) XV. OE. *fōt,* pl. *fēt* = OFris. *fōt,* OS. *fōt, fuot* (Du. *voet*), OHG. *fuoȥ* (G. *fuss*), ON. *fótr,* Goth. *fōtus*; the CGerm. cons.-stem *fōt- :– IE. *pōd-, which with its vars. *pod- ped- is widespread in the IE. langs. (but not in Celtic), being repr. by Skr. *padám* footstep, *pā́das* foot, Lith. *pėdà* footstep, L. *ped-,* nom. *pēs,* Gr. *pod-,* nom. *poús* foot, *pezōs* (:– *pedjós) on foot, Arm. *otn,* ON. *fet* step, foot as a measure, *feta* make one's way, OE. *fæt* step; see also FETTER, FETLOCK. ¶ The foll. contain the same base: *biped, quadruped, pedal, pedestal, pedestrian*; *impede*; *pawn*; *pioneer*. *Foot of the fine* (legal AN. *pee de la fin*), bottom part of a tripartite indenture recording the particulars of a fine (compromise of a collusive suit for the possession of estate), and remaining with the court, the other two counterparts, which were retained by the parties, being at right angles to it. Hence **foot** vb. dance (now only in arch. *foot it*) XIV; †add *up* XV; walk; strike, etc. with the foot XVI. **foo·tING**[1] (dial.) foothold XIV; (fig. XVI); †walking; dancing; footprint(s) XVI; settled condition XVII (cf. STANDING). **foo·tBALL**[1]. XV. **foo·tFALL**[1]. XVII (Sh.). **foo·tHOLD**. XVII. †**footHOT**. XIII; cf. *hot-foot*. **foo·tMAN** foot-soldier XIII; (dial.) pedestrian XIV; attendant on foot XV. **foo·tPATH**. XVI. **foo·tNOTE**. XIX. **foo·tPACE** walking-pace; raised floor (for an altar). XVI. **foo·tPAD**[2] highwayman who robs on foot. XVII; *pad,* canting use of var. of PATH. **foo·tPATH**. XVI. **foo·tSTALK** petiole, peduncle. XVI (Turner). **foo·tSTEP**. XIV (earlier, once, pl. *fet steppes* XIII). **foo·tSTOOL**. XVI (Palsgr. Coverdale).

footle fū·tl (colloq.) fool about, trifle, potter. XIX (esp. in prp. **foo·tlING**[2] trifling, paltry). perh. alteration, by assoc. with -LE[3], of (dial.) *footer* bungle, idle or potter about, presumably rel. to *footer* contemptible fellow, transf. use of *foutre* (cf. Sh. '2 Henry IV' v iii 103 a footre for the world) – (O)F. *foutre* = Pr. *fotre,* Sp. *hoder,* It. *fottere* :– L. *futuere*; or based on *footy* paltry, worthless (XVIII), var. of *foughty* musty (1600), repr. OE. *fūhtiġ (corr. to OHG. *fūhti,* Du. *vochtig*), f. *fūht* damp = OS., OHG. *fūht* (Du. *vocht,* G. *feucht*).

foozle fū·zl (sl.) waste one's time; bungle. XIX. – G. (Bavarian dial.) *fuseln* work hurriedly and badly; cf. FUSEL.

fop fɔp †fool XV (Promp. Parv.); one who is vain of his appearance, etc. XVII. corr. in form to G. *foppen* hoax. Cf. FOB[1]. Hence **fo·ppERY**. XVI (Bale). **fo·ppISH**[1]. XVII (Sh.).

for fɔ̄ɹ, fɔr, fəɹ prep. †before; representing, instead of; in defence of; with a view to OE.; to obtain, in order *to* XIII; with the object of XIV; in the character of; by reason of, in spite of OE.; in relation to XIV; during XV; conj. (for OE. *for þon þe, for þǣm þe, for þȳ þe* on account of the fact that) because, since XI. OE. *for* = OFris., OS. *for,* Goth. *faur,* prob. reduction of Germ. *fora before (of place and time), repr. by OE. *fore* = OFris., OS., OHG. *fora,* Goth. *faura,* beside OS., OHG. forms with *-i,* viz. *furi* (G. *für*) and ON. *fyrir*; see FORE[2]. Hence **forasmuch** fɔ̄r-, fərəzmʌ·tʃ (arch.) seeing that. XIII (RGlouc.). tr. OF. *por tant que* for so much as; north. *for as mekill,* Sc. also *forasmekle*.

for-[1] fɔ̄ɹ, usu. fəɹ OE. *for-, fær-* = OFris. *for-, fir-,* OS. *for-,* OHG. *fir-, far-* (Du., G. *ver-*), Goth. *fair-, faur-,* corr. to Gr. PERI-, PARA-, L. PER-, POR-, Skr. *pári, purā,* OIr. *ar-, air-*; IE. prefix with variation of form and wide extent of meaning, but esp. implying (1) rejection, exclusion, prohibition, (2) destruction, (3) exhaustion.

for-[2] fɔ̄əɹ var. of FORE-. ¶ Distinct from *for-* in †*forclose,* FORECLOSE, FORFEIT.

forage fɔ·ridʒ food for cattle. XIV. – (O)F. *fourrage,* f. *feurre* = It. *fodero* – Germ. *fōđram FODDER; see -AGE. So **fo·rage** vb. XV. – (O)F. *fourrager,* f. the sb.

foramen forei·men (anat.) opening for the passage of something. XVII. L., f. *forāre* BORE[1].

foray fɔ·rei hostile incursion. XIV (in early use Sc.), prob. f. *foray* vb. (XIV), back-formation from ME. *forayer* forager, raider, var. of *forrier* – OF. *forrier* :– Rom. *fodrārius, f. *fodro FODDER (cf. FORAGE).

forbear[1] fɔ̄ɹbɛə·ɹ †bear, bear with; endure the loss of; abstain from OE. (intr. XIV; spec. leg. refrain from enforcing what is due XVI). OE. *forberan* = OHG. *farberan* restrain, abstain, Goth. *frabairan* endure; f. FOR-[1]+BEAR[2]. Hence **forbea·rANCE**. XVI (orig. leg.).

forbear[2], **forebear** fɔ̄·ɹbɛəɹ arch. or dial. (usu. pl.) ancestor. XV. orig. Sc., f. *for-* FORE- + *bear, beer*, agent-noun of BE.

forbid fəɹbi·d command not to do, etc. OE. *forbēodan* = OFris. *forbiāda*, Du. *verbieden*, OHG. *farbiotan* (G. *verbieten*), Goth. *faurbiudan*; CGerm. (exc. ON., which has *fyrirbjóða*), f. FOR-[1]+BID.

forby fɔ̄ɹbai· prep. †close by XIII (Cursor M.); (Sc.) beside XVI; adv. (dial.) aside, along, past XIV (R. Mannyng); (Sc.) besides XVI. f. FOR adv.+BY; cf. Norw. *forbi*, Sw. *förbi*.

force[1] fɔ̄ɹs strength, power XIII (Cursor M.); body of armed men XIV (Barbour). – (O)F. *force* = Pr. *forsa*, *forza*, Sp. *fuerza*, It. *forza* :– Rom. **fortia*, f. L. *fortis* strong (cf. *comfort*, *effort*, *fort*, *forte*, *fortify*, *fortitude*, *fortress*). So **force** vb. XIII (Cursor M.). – (O)F. *forcer*, f. *force*. **fo·rcIBLE** done by force XV (Hoccleve); †strong; producing a powerful effect XVI. – legal AN., OF., f. *forcer*.

force[2], **foss** fɔ̄ɹs, fɔs (n. dial.) waterfall. In place-names *fors* XI, *foss* XIII; XIV (*forȝ* 'Gawain and the Green Knight' 2173; *force*, var. *fosse* (XV) 'Sir Degrevant' 1655; Camden, anno 1600, gives *The Forses* as a Westmorland name). – ON. *fors*, OWScand. *foss* (Sw. *fors*, Da. *fos*), without cogns. elsewhere in Germ.

force-meat fɔ̄·ɹsmīt meat chopped fine used for stuffing. XVII. f. *force* (XIV), var. of FARCE[1] vb. (cf. Sh. 'Tr. & Cr.' v i 64 *malice forced with wit*)+MEAT.

forceps fɔ̄·ɹseps instrument of the pincers kind, organ shaped like this. XVII. – L. *forceps*, etymologized by Festus as *formucaps* 'because it seizes hot things', f. *formus* hot, WARM+*cap-* of *capere* seize (see HEAVE).

ford fɔ̄ɹd shallow place in a piece of water where one may cross. OE. *ford* = OFris. *forda*, OS. *-ford* in place-names (Du. *voorde*), (O)HG. *furt* :– WGerm. **furdu* (ON. has *fjǫrðr* FIORD :– **ferþuz*) :– IE. **pr̥tús*, repr. also by OW. *rit* (W. *rhyd*) ford, L. *portus* harbour, PORT[1], f. **por-* **per-* **pr̥-* (see FARE and cf. Gr. *Bós|poros* with *Oxena|ford* Oxford; Av. *pərətu-* bridge, ford, *Eu|phrates* 'river with good fords').

fordo fɔ̄ɹdū· pp. **fordone** fɔ̄ɹdʌ·n (arch.) put an end to, destroy, spoil, wreck. OE. *fordōn* = OS. *fardōn* (Du. *verdoen*), OHG. *fartuon* (G. *vertun*); see FOR-[1], DO[1]. In pp. (poet.) exhausted, wearied out XVI (Surrey, Coleridge, M. Arnold).

fore[1] fɔəɹ †earlier XV (Caxton); that is in front XV; sb. in (orig.) Sc. and Anglo-Ir. phr. *to the fore* present, on the spot, surviving; ready, available XVII (Rutherford); conspicuous XIX. Evolved from analysis of comps. of prefix FORE-, e.g. *forehead*, *foreland*, *forepart*.

fore[2] fɔəɹ adv., now only in *fore and aft* from stem to stern, all over the ship. XVII. Not continuous with OE. and ME. *fore*; perh. of LG. origin; cf. Du. *van voren en van achteren*.

fore[3] fɔəɹ int. (in golf) warning cry to people in front of the intended stroke. XIX. prob. aphetic form of BEFORE or AFORE.

fore- fɔəɹ prefix meaning 'before', identical with the adv. *fore* in front, before, OE. *fore* = OFris. *for(e)*, *fara*, OS., OHG. *fora* (Du. *voor*, G. *vor*), Goth. *faura*, perh. :– **forai*, corr. to Gr. *paraí*, a dative formation, the base of which is repr. also in L. *prō*, *præ*, *per* (see PER-, PRE-, PRO-[2]), Gr. *pró*, *pará*, *perí* (see PARA-, PERI-), Skr. *purā́* before.

¶ A few of the foll. comps. had orig. the prefix FOR-[2].

foreARM[1] fɔ̄ərā·ɹm arm beforehand. XVI. **foreARM**[2] fɔ̄ə·rāɹm part of the arm below the elbow. XVIII; cf. Du. *voorarm*, G. *vorderarm*, F. *avant-bras*. **foreCAST** fɔəɹkà·st †contrive beforehand XIV (Wycl. Bible); estimate beforehand XVI. Hence **fo·recast** sb. XV. **foreCASTLE** fou·ksl (whence the sp. *fo'c'sle*) †short raised deck in the bow, orig. a castle-like structure to command the enemy's decks XIV; fore part of a ship XV. **fo·reFA:THER** ancestor. XIII (Cursor M.). – ON. *forfaðir*; superseded OE. *forþfæder*, early ME. *forþfader*; cf. Du. *voorvader* and ChrL. *propator* (Tertullian) – Gr. **fo·reFI:NGER** first or index finger. XV; perh. after Du. *voorvinger*. **fo·reFOOT** one of the front feet. XIV; perh. after Du. *voorvoet* (cf. G. *vorderfuss*). **fo·reFRONT** principal face, foremost part (now dial. exc. fig.). XV (orig. Sc.). (*Foreside* is earlier; cf. Du. *voorzijde*, G. *vorderseite*.) **fo·reGO:ING** preceding. XV. prp. of *forego*. **foreGO·NE** that has gone before. XVI (Sh. in *f. conclusion* 'Oth.' III iii 428). pp. of *forego*, OE. *foregān* go in advance. **fo·reGROUND** part of a view in front and nearest the observer. XVII – Du. *voorgrond*; cf. G. *vordergrund*. **foreHEAD** fɔ·rid part of the face above the eyebrows. OE. *forhēafod* = OFris. *forhāfd* (beside *farahāfd*), MLG. *vorhōved*, Du. *voorhoofd*, G. *vor-*, *vorderhaupt*, *vorkopf*. **foreJU·DGE** judge beforehand. XVI; after F. *préjuger*, L. *præjūdicāre* PREJUDGE. **foreKNOW·LEDGE**. XVI (Coverdale). Cf. **foreKNOW·**. XIV (Ch.). **fo·reLAND** cape, promontory. XIV. Cf. ON. *forlendi* land between hills and sea, Du. *voorland*. **fo·reLOCK**[1] lock of hair growing just above the forehead. OE. *foreloccas* pl. 'antie frontis'; but a new formation in XVI. **fo·reMAN** fɔ̄ə·ɹmən †leader XV; principal juror;

principal of workmen XVI; perh. after ON. *formaðr* captain, leader, or immed. – Du. *voorman* (cf. G. *vormann*). **fo·re**NAME first or Christian name. XVI; after F. *prénom*, L. *prænōmen*, Du. *voornam*, etc. **fo·re**NOON part of the day before noon. XV. **fo·re**PART foremost part. XIV (Sc.). **fo·re**RU:NNER one who goes before to prepare the way (first of John the Baptist) XIII (Cursor M.); one whom another follows XVI (Sh.); tr. L. *præcursor* PRECURSOR. **fo·re**SAIL principal sail set on the foremast. XV; cf. Du. *voorzeil*. **fore**SEE· see beforehand. OE. *forsēon*; but prob. a new formation in ME. after FORESIGHT; perh. orig. tr. L. *prōvidēre* PROVIDE. **fo·re**SHORE. XVIII. **fore-**SHO·RTEN cause to be apparently shortened. XVII (Peacham). prob. – Du. *verkorten*; cf. G. *verkürzen*, and F. *raccourcir*, It. *scorciare*. **fore**SHOW· prefigure, prognosticate; betoken. XVI; not continuous with OE. *foresċēawian* provide, foresee. **fo·re**SIGHT †(divine) providence XIII (Cursor M.); provision for the future XIV; action of foreseeing or looking forward XV; prob. after ON. *forsjá*, *-sjó*, and later felt as etymol. rendering of (O)F. *providence*, L. *prōvidentia*; cf. OHG. *forasiht* (G. *vorsicht*). **fo·re**SKIN. XVI (Coverdale); after G. *vorhaut* (Luther), based on L. *præputium* PREPUCE. **fore**STA·LL †obstruct XIV (Trevisa); buy up (goods) before they reach public markets XIV (PPl.); hinder by anticipation, anticipate in action XVI. Implied earlier in AL. *forstallātio* obstruction, *forstallātor* (XII), AN. *forstallour* forestaller of markets (XIII), f. OE. *for(e)steall* interception, waylaying, ambush. **fo·re**TASTE sb. and vb. XV. **fore**TE·LL predict, prophesy. XIII (Cursor M.); superseding †*foresay*, OE. *foreseċġan* (cf. ON. *fyrirsegja*). **fo·re**THOUGHT †premeditation; previous thought. XIII (Cursor M.); parallel to †*forethink*, OE. *foreþenċan* consider beforehand, and repl. OE. *foreþanc* consideration, forethought, providence. **fo·re**TOP[1] lock of hair at the front XIII; forepart of the crown XIV (Wycl. Bible); top of a foremast XV. **fore**WA·RN warn beforehand. OE. *forewarnian* (trans. and intr.); see **fo·re**WORD preface, introductory remark(s). XIX. tr. G. *vorwort*. (Also pl., as if 'prefatory words'.)

foreclose fɔ̄ɹklou·z exclude, preclude XV; deprive of the equity of redemption, bar (a right of redemption) XVIII. f. *forclos-*, pp. stem of (O)F. *forclore*, f. *for-* + *clore* CLOSE; there has been assoc. with FOR-[1] or with FOR-[2], FORE-. Hence **for**CLO·SURE. XVIII.

foreign fɔ·rĭn †out of doors XIII (rare; *chambre forene* privy, RGlouc.); pert. to another, alien; pert. to another region, not in one's own land XIV; not domestic or native XV. (Not in gen. use before Ch. and Gower.) – OF. *forein*, *forain*, *-e* = Pr. *forá* :– Rom. **forānus* (so in AL., but the more usual forms were *foraneus*, *forinsecus*), f. L. *forās* acc. pl., *forīs* loc. pl. of **fora*, var. of *forēs* DOOR (cf. FOREST). Hence **fo·reign**ER[1] XV; after *stranger*, which it superseded in the sense 'one belonging to another country', for which †*forein* was also used XIV. ¶ For the sp. with *eign* cf. *sovereign*.

forel fɔ·rəl †case, (dial.) book-cover XIII (Cursor M.); parchment dressed to look like vellum XVI (Bk. of Common Prayer, 1549). – OF. *forel* (mod. *fourreau*) sheath, f. *fuerre* – Frank. **fōder*, = OHG. *fōtar* case, cover (G. *futter* lining), Goth. *fōdr* sheath :– Germ. **fōðram*, rel. to Skr. *pấtram* receptacle, f. *pấti* protects.

foremost fɔ̄·ɹməst first in place or order. The present form, dating from XVI, is an alteration, by assocn. with FORE-, of *formost*, itself an alteration, by assocn. with -MOST, of *formest* (XII), f. *forme*, OE. *forma* first (= OFris. *forma*, OS. *formo*), with superl. *-m-* suffix as in L. *prīmus* PRIME) + -EST, *formest* having repl. *fürmest*, *firmest* :– OE. *fyrmest* (= Goth. *frumists*), f. *forma*, the result being a double superl. Cf. FORMER.

forensic fəre·nsik pert. to courts of law. XVII. f. L. *forēnsis*, f. *forum* (cf. *castrēnsis* of a camp); see FORUM, -IC. Earlier **fore·nsi**CAL. XVI.

forest fɔ·rist large tract of land covered with trees. XIII (RGlouc., Cursor M.). – OF. *forest* (mod. *forêt*) – late L. *foresti-s* (*silva*) 'outside wood', royal forest reserved for hunting (Langobardic Laws, Capitularies of Charlemagne), obscurely f. *forīs* out of doors, outside (see FOREIGN); prob. meaning orig. woodland lying outside the park and unfenced; in AL. *foresta*, *forestum* (XI). So **fo·rest**ER[2]. XIII (RGlouc.). – (O)F. *forestier*, f. *forest*; in AL. *forestārius* (XI). ¶ An AN. contr. form is repr. in Eng. by †*foster* XIV–XVII; this survives as a surname, beside *Forster* and *For(r)ester*.

forestall see FORE-.

forfeit fɔ̄·ɹfit †misdeed, misdemeanour XIII (Cursor M.); fine, penalty XV; trivial fine for breach of rule XVII (Sh.). ME. *forfet* – OF. *forfet* crime, (also mod.) *forfait*, f. *for(s)faire* commit crime (medL. *forisfacere*), f. *for(s)-* beyond, outside, sc. what is right (:– L. *forīs* outside; cf. FOREST) + *faire* DO[1]. Hence **fo·rfeit** †sin, transgress XIV; lose the right to XV. **forfeiture** fɔ̄·ɹfitʃəɹ †crime, sin; loss or liability to deprivation. XIV. – (O)F. *forfaiture*, f. *forfait*; see -URE.

for(e)fend fɔ̄ɹfe·nd †forbid; avert XIV (Wycl. Bible); (now U.S.) protect by precautionary measures XVI. f. FOR-[1] (i) + FEND.

for(e)gather fɔ̄ɹgæ·ðəɹ, -gā·ðəɹ (chiefly Sc.) gather together XVI (Douglas); meet *with* XVI. – Du. *vergaderen*, with accommodation to FOR-, GATHER.

forge[1] fɔ̄ɹdʒ smithy XIV (Ch.); furnace for melting metal. – (O)F. *forge* = Pr., Cat. *farga*, *fraga*, Sp. *fraga*, *fragua*, Pg. *fragoa* :– Rom. **faurga* :– L. *fabrica* trade, manufactured object, workshop, forge (see FABRIC). So **forge** vb. shape, fashion (now only in a forge) XIII (Cursor M.); fabricate, make a fraudulent imitation of XIV. – (O)F. *forger* = Pr., Cat. *fargar*, Sp. *fraguar*, *frogar*, Pg. *fragoar* :– L. *fabricāre* FABRICATE. Hence **fo·rg**ER[1]. XIV (Wycl.). **fo·rg**ERY. XVI.

forge[2] fɔ̄ɹdʒ (orig. naut.) make way *ahead*. XVII. Perh. aberrant pronunc. of FORCE vb., similarly used from XVII.

forget fəɹge·t pt. *forgo·t*, pp. *forgo·tten*, arch. and dial. *forgo·t* fail to remember. OE. *forġietan*, pt. *forġeat*, *-ġēaton*, pp. *-ġiten* = OFris. *forjeta*, OS. *fargetan* (Du. *vergeten*), OHG. *firgezzan* (G. *vergessen*); WGerm. vb. f. **fer-* FOR- (i) + **getan* take hold of, GET (q.v. for the phonetic history), the etymol. meaning being 'miss or lose one's hold'. Hence **forge·tful.** XIV (*forȝetful*, Wycl. Bible). Alteration of *forȝetel*, *forgetel*, OE. *forġietel* (= Fris. *forgittel*, Du. *vergetel*) by substitution of -FUL[1] for the final syll. **forge·t-me-not** species of Myosotis. XVI. tr. OF. *ne m'oubliez mie* do-not-forget-me, whence MHG. *vergizmīnniht* (G. *vergissmeinnicht*).

forgett fɔ̄·ɹdʒėt (pl.) side pieces of the finger of a glove. XVII. orig. *forchet* – F. *fourchette*, dim. of *fourche* FORK (see -ET, -ETTE); so called from the shape.

forgive fəɹgi·v pt. *forga·ve*, pp. *forgi·ven* †give, grant; remit, pardon. OE. *forġiefan*; see FOR-[1] (i) and GIVE; corr. to OS. (Du. *vergeven*), OHG. *fargeban* (G. *vergeben*), ON. *fyrirgefa* forgive, Goth. *fragiban* grant; CGerm. tr. of medL. *perdōnāre* PARDON. So **forgi·ve**NESS. OE. *forġief(e)nes*, rarely *-ġiefennes*; cf. Du. *vergiffenis*.

forgo, forego fɔ̄ɹgou· pt. *forewent*, pp. *for(e)gone* †intr. pass away, trans. pass over, neglect; abstain from. OE. *forgān*, pt. *forēode* (ME. *foryode*); see FOR-[1], GO.

fork fɔ̄ɹk pronged instrument for digging OE., for eating XV; divergence into branches, bifurcation XIV. OE. *forca*, *force*, corr. to OFris. *forke*, OS. *furka*, OHG. *furcha* (Du. *vork*, G. *furke*), ON. *forkr*; CGerm. (exc. Goth.) – L. *furca* pitchfork, forked stake, whence (O)F. *fourche*, ONF. *fourque* (which reinforced the word in ME.), Pr., Pg. *forca*, Sp. *horca*, It. *furca*.

forlorn fəɹlɔ̄·ɹn †morally lost, abandoned XII; † ruined, doomed XIV; forsaken, desolate; pitiable, wretched XVI. pp. of ME. *forlēse*, OE. *forlēosan* = OFris. *forliāsa*, OS. *far-*, *forliosan* (Du. *verliezen*), OHG. *firliosan* (G. *verlieren*), Goth. *fraliusan*; CGerm. (exc. ON.), f. **fer-* **fra-* FOR-[1] (i) + **leusan* (see LOSE).

forlorn hope fəɹlɔ̄·ɹn hou·p picked force detailed for an attack, (hence) desperate adventurers, players, etc. XVI; (by misapprehension) hopeless enterprise XVII. – Du. *verloren hoop* 'lost troop', i.e. *verloren*, pp. of *verliezen* (see prec.), *hoop* company (HEAP).

form fɔ̄ɹm A. visible aspect of a thing XIII (RGlouc.); (scholastic philos.) that which makes matter a determinate kind of thing XIV (Ch.). B. character, nature, †degree XIII (class in a school XVI); due observance or procedure XIV (Ch.). C. lair of a hare XIII; long seat without a back XIV (Trevisa); (typogr.) see FORME XV. ME. *forme*, *fourme*, *furme* – (O)F. *forme*, also †*fourme*, †*furme* = Pr., Sp., It. *forma* :– L. *fōrma* mould, shape, beauty (rendering Gr. εἶδος and χαρακτήρ), perh. cogn. with or – Gr. *morphḗ* form, shape (poss. through Etruscan; cf. *catamite*, *person*), but referred by some to *ferīre* strike, as Gr. *túpos* TYPE to *túptein* strike. So **form** vb. give a form to XIII (RGlouc.); be the components of XIV; draw up or dispose in order XVIII. – OF. *fourmer*, (also mod.) *former* – L. *fōrmāre*, f. *fōrma*. **fo·rm**AL[1]. XIV (*cause formal*, Ch.). – L.; cf. (O)F. *formel*. **fo·rmal**ISM. XIX. -IST. XVII; cf. F. *-iste* (XVI). **formal**ITY -æ·lĭti. XVI. – F. **form**A·TION. XV. – (O)F. or L. **fo·rm**ATIVE. XV (Caxton; rare before XVII). – OF.

-form fɔ̄ɹm repr. F. *-forme*, L. *-fōrmis*, f. *fōrma* FORM, termination used to form adjs. meaning (i) 'having the form of', as *ensiform*, *fusiform*, *vermiform*, depending on modL. formations; so *cruciform*, *cuneiform*, *lentiform*, *mammiform*; (ii) 'of (so many) forms', as *multiform*, *triform*, *uniform*, derived from classical L.; so *omniform*.

format fɔ̄·ɹmæt, fɔ̄·ɹma shape and size of a book XIX. – F. (XVIII) – G. *format* (XVII) – L. *fōrmātus* (sc. *liber* book), pp. of *fōrmāre* FORM; so It. *formato*.

forme, form fɔ̄ɹm (typogr.) body of type locked up in a chase for printing. XV (Caxton). spec. use of FORM; so F. *forme*, G. *form*.

former fɔ̄·ɹməɹ earlier in time XII; †first, primeval (as in Ch.'s *the former age*) XIII (Cursor M.); †more forward XIV (Wycl. Bible); first of two)(*latter* XVI. f. ME. *forme* (OE. *forma*; see FOREMOST) + -ER[3]. Hence **fo·rmer**LY[2] †just now; †beforehand XVI (Spenser); in former days XVI (Hakluyt).

formic fɔ̄·ɹmik (chem.) of an acid contained in a fluid emitted by ants. XVIII. f. L. *formīca* ant (cf. Gr. *múrmēx*, PISMIRE); see -IC. Comb. form *form-*, as in *formaldehyde*, **fo·rm**YL (cf. CHLOROFORM).

formidable fɔ̄·ɹmidəbl, fəɹmi·d- giving cause for alarm. XV. – F. *formidable* or L. *formīdābilis*, f. *formīdāre* fear, f. *formīdō* dread, scarecrow (cf. Gr. *morphṓ*); see -ABLE.

formula fɔ̄·ɹmjŭlə set form of words XVII; recipe; rule, etc., expressed by symbols XVIII. – L. *fōrmula*, dim. of *fōrma* FORM; see -ULE. So **fo·rmul**ARY collection or system of formulas. XVI. **fo·rmul**ATE[3]. XIX; after F. *formuler*.

fornication fɔ̄ɹnikei·ʃən sexual intercourse outside marriage. XIII (Cursor M.). – (O)F. *fornication* – late L. *fornicātiō(n-)*, f. *fornicārī* (whence **fo·rnic**ATE[3] XVI), f. *fornic-*, *fornix* arch, vault, vaulted room such as was tenanted by the lower orders and prostitutes, prob. rel. to *fornax*, *furnus* FURNACE; see -ATION. So **fo·rnic**ATOR[1]. XIV (PPl.). – late L.

forrader fɔ·rədəɹ colloq. pronunc. of *forward*ER[3] farther forward, compar. of FORWARD. XIX.

forsake fəɹsei·k pt. *forsook* -su·k, pp. *forsaken* -sei·kn †decline, refuse; give up, renounce. OE. *forsacan*, pt. *forsōc*, pp. *forsacen* = OS. *forsakan* (Du. *verzaken*), OHG. *firsahhan*; WGerm. f. FOR-[1]+*sakan* quarrel, accuse (see SAKE).

forsooth fəɹsū·þ in truth (now only in ironical context). OE. *forsōþ*, i.e. FOR, SOOTH.

forspent fɔ̄ɹspe·nt (arch.) exhausted. XVI (Sackville, Golding). pp. of *forspend*, OE. *forspendan* (cf. OHG. *farspentōn*); see FOR-[1], SPEND.

forswear fɔ̄ɹswɛə·ɹ abjure, repudiate; (intr. and refl.) perjure oneself. OE. *forswerian*; see FOR-[1], SWEAR, and cf. G. *verschwören*, ON. *fyrirsverja*.

forsythia fɔ̄ɹsai·þiə plant of a genus of spring-flowering shrubs. XIX. modL., f. name of William *Forsyth* (1737–1804), Eng. botanist+-IA[1].

fort fɔ̄ɹt fortified place. XV. – (O)F. *fort* or It. *forte*, sb. uses of *fort*, *forte* strong = Pr. *fort*, Sp. *fuerte* :– L. *fortis* (cf. *force*).

fortalice fɔ̄·ɹtelis fortress, (now) small outwork. XV (Wyntoun). – medL. *fortalitia*, *-itium*, f. L. *fortis* strong; see FORT, and cf. Pr., Sp. *fortaleza*, It. *fortalizio*, OF. *fortelesce*, FORTRESS.

forte[1] fɔ̄ɹt strong point or feature. XVII (*fort*). – F. *fort*, sb. use of *fort* (see FORT); the F. fem. form was substituted in Eng. use, as in *locale*, *morale*.

forte[2] fɔ̄·ɹti (mus.) loud. XVIII. It. :– L. *fortis* strong. So **forti·ssimo.** XVIII. It., superl. of *forte*. **fortepiano** (XVIII), original name of the PIANOFORTE.

forth fɔ̄ɹþ forwards (now only in dial. *back and forth*); onwards (surviving in gen. use in *and so forth*); forward, into view; away. OE. *forþ* = OFris., OS. *forth* (Du. *voort*), MHG. *vort* (G. *fort*) :– Germ. **furþa* (cf. Goth. *faurþis* further) :– IE. **pr̥to*, f. base repr. in FORE-. **forthcoming** fɔ̄ɹþkʌ·miŋ about or ready to appear XVI; ready to make advances XIX. f. phr. *come forth*; see -ING[2]. **forth**RIGHT. OE. *forþriht* adj., *-rihte* adv. **forth**WI·TH †at the same time; immediately XIV (Gower); partly short for earlier *forthwithal* (XI), but partly repl. ME. *forth mid* along with, at the same time as, used absol.

fortify fɔ̄·ɹtifəi strengthen against force or attack. XV (Lydg., Pecock, Malory). – (O)F. *fortifier* – late L. *fortificāre*, f. *fortis*; see FORT, -IFY. So **fortifica·tion**. XV. – F. – late L.

fortitude fɔ̄·ɹtitjūd moral strength, courage in endurance. XV. – OF. *fortitude* – L. *fortitūdō*, f. *fortis*; see FORT, -TUDE.

fortnight fɔ̄·ɹtnait period of two weeks in succession. OE. *fēowertīene niht*, ME. *fourten(n)iht* fourteen nights (in which the ancient Germ. reckoning by nights is preserved); cf. SENNIGHT.

fortress fɔ̄·ɹtris military stronghold. XIII. – (O)F. *forteresse* strong place = Pr. *fortareza* :– Rom. **fortaritia* (cf. Gallo-Rom. *vaccaritia* cow-stall, f. *vacca*), f. *fortis* strong (see FORT).

fortuitous fɔ̄ɹtjū·itəs happening by chance. XVII. f. L. *fortuĭtus*, f. *forte* by chance, abl. of *fors* chance :– IE. **bhr̥tis* 'that which is brought', f. base of L. *ferre* BEAR[2]; for the formation cf. *gratuitous*.

fortune fɔ̄·ɹtʃən chance, luck XIII (Cursor M.); (good or bad) luck; position depending on wealth, wealth XVI. – (O)F. *fortune* – L. *fortūna* chance as a divinity, luck, esp. good luck, (pl.) gifts of fortune, (also sg.) riches, orig. sb. use (sc. *dea* goddess) of adj. *fortūnus*, f. *fors* (see prec.). So **fortun**ATE[2] fɔ̄·ɹtʃənət. XIV (Ch., Gower). – L. *fortūnātus*.

forty fɔ̄·ɹti 40, xl. OE. *fēowertiġ* = OFris. *fiuwertich*, OS. *fiwartig* (Du. *veertig*), OHG. *fiorzug* (G. *vierzig*), ON. *fjórir tigir*, Goth. *fidwor tigjus*; see FOUR, -TY[1]. So **fo·rti**ETH[1]. OE. *fēowertiġoþa* = ON. *fertugandi* :– **fiwortigunþon*: see TH[2].

forum fɔ̄·rəm (Rom. antiq.) market-place, spec. in ancient Rome a place of assembly for judicial and other business XV; court, tribunal XVII. – L. *forum*, rel. to *forēs* (outside) DOOR; orig. enclosure surrounding a house. Cf. FOREIGN, FORENSIC.

forward fɔ̄·ɹwəɹd towards the future OE.; towards or to the front, onward. XIV. OE. *forweard*, var. of *forþweard* onwards, continually, f. FORTH+-WARD. Hence **fo·rward** adj. in an advanced state or position; eagerly ready; pert XVI; not continuous with OE. *foreweard* front or first part of. Hence **forward** vb. help forward, advance XVI (Sh.); send forward XVIII. So **fo·rwards.** XIV; cf. OE. *forþweardes* and Du. *voorwaarts*, G. *vorwärts*. See -WARD, -WARDS.

forwea·ry (arch.) tire out XIII; see FOR-[1]. So **forwo·rn** (arch.) worn out XVI; pp. of †*forwear* XIII (Laȝ.), pierce, hollow, with Balto-Sl. cogns.

foss see FORCE[2].

fosse fɔs ditch, trench. XIV (Maund.). – (O)F. *fosse* = Pr., Pg., It. *fossa*, OSp. *fuesa* :– L. *fossa*, f. pp. stem *foss-* of *fodere* dig.

fossick fɔ·sik (Austral. mining) search for gold by digging out crevices, etc.; (sl.) rummage. XIX. Of unkn. origin; cf. dial. *fossick* troublesome person, *fossicking* troublesome, *fossick* make a fuss, bustle about.

fossil fɔ·sil (rock, etc.) dug out of the earth, esp. of remains of the prehistoric past. XVII. – F. *fossile* – L. *fossilis*, f. *foss-*, pp. stem of *fodere* dig; cf. FOSSE and see -ILE.

foster fɔ·stəɹ †nourish, feed OE.; †bring up (a child); promote the growth of XIII; cherish, 'nurse' XIV. OE. *fōstrian* (= ON. *fóstra*), f. *fōster* food, f. **fōð-* FOOD + instr. suffix **-trom*. The stem was used as comb. form in OE. *fōsterbearn*, *-ċild* child as related to those who have reared it as their own, *fōsterbrōþor* / *-sweostor* male / female child reared with another of different parentage, *fōsterfæder* / *-mōdor* one who acts as father / mother to another's child; so *fōsterling* (-LING[1]), foster-child, and corr. forms in ON.; hence *foster-nurse* XVI (Sh.).

fother fɔ·ðəɹ load, cartload OE.; mass, quantity; specific weight or measure XIII. OE. *fōþer* = OS. *fōthar* (Du. *voer*), OHG. *fuodar* (G. *fuder*) :– WGerm. **fōþram*, prob. f. gradation-var. of the base **faþ-* stretch out, as in FATHOM. ¶ G. *fuder* was adopted XVII as *fooder*, *fudder*.

fou fū (Sc.) drunk. XVI. var. of FULL.

foul faul grossly offensive to the senses;)(*clean* OE.;)(*fair* ME. OE. *fūl* = OFris., OS., OHG. *fūl* (Du. *vuil* dirty, G. *faul* rotten, unsound, lazy), ON. *fúll*, Goth. *fūls* stinking :– CGerm. **fūlaz*, f. **fū-* (repr. by ON. *fúinn* rotten, *feyja* let decay :– **faujan*) :– IE. **pū-*, as in L. *pūs* PUS, *pūtēre* stink, rot, *pūtidus* rotten, *putridus* PUTRID, Gr. *púon*, *púos*, *pûar* pus, Lith. *pū́ti* rot (with *l*-cogns. in Lith. *pū́liai* pl. pus, *piaulaĩ* pl. rotten wood), Skr. *pū́yati* stink, *pū́tis* rotten, Arm. *hu* purulent blood.

foulard fūlāɹd, ‖fulār (handkerchief of) silk material. XIX. F., of unkn. origin.

foumart fū·māɹt polecat. XIV. Early forms *folmarde*, *fulmert*, *fullimart*, f. *fūl* FOUL (i.e. stinking) + *mart* (see MARTEN).

found[1] faund set up, establish as on a firm basis. XIII (Cursor M.). – (O)F. *fonder* = Pr. *fondar*, It. *fondare* :– L. *fundāre*, f. *fundus* BOTTOM. So **founda·TION**. XIV (Ch.). – (O)F. – L. Hence **fou·ndER**[1] XIV (R. Mannyng, Trevisa); whence **fou·ndrESS**[1] XV (Lydg.).

found[2] faund melt (esp. metal or glass for casting in a mould). XIV make things thus. – (O)F. *fondre* = Pr. *fondre*, Sp. *fundir*, It. *fondere* :– L. *fundere* pour, melt, pt. *fūdī*, pp. *fūsus* (cf. FUSE[2]), f. IE. **ghud- *gheud-* (in Germ. **gut- *geut-*, repr. by OE. *ġēotan*, OFris. *giāta*, OS. *giotan*, OHG. *giozan*, G. *giessen*, ON. *gjóta*, Goth. *giutan* pour), extension of **ghu- *gheu-*, whence Gr. *khéein*, *kheúein* pour, *khûlos* CHYLE, *khūmós* CHYME, *khū́trā*, *-os* earthen pot, Skr. *juhóti* pour libations, sacrifice, *áhutis* libation; cf. FUTILE. Hence **foundER**[1] XV; perh. after (O)F. *fondeur*, *fonderie*. **fou·ndRY** art of, establishment for, founding metal or glass. XVII.

founder[1] fau·ndəɹ †smash in XIII; †send to the bottom XIV; (of a horse) stumble and fall, go lame XIV (Ch.); fill with water and sink XVI. partly – OF. *fondrer* send to the bottom, submerge, but for the most part aphetic of †*afounder* (XIV), †*enfounder* (XV) – OF. **afondrer*, *esfondrer*, *enfondrer*, mod. *effondrer* (= Pr. *esfondrar*, It. *sfondolare*) :– Rom. **ex-*, *infundorāre*, f. *ex* EX-[1], IN-[1] + **fundor-*, taken as stem of L. *fundus* BOTTOM.

founder[2] fau·ndəɹ finder, spec. in Derbyshire lead-mining XVI; hence, portion of a lead mine given to the first finder of the vein XVII. prob. f. *found*, pp. of FIND + -ER[1].

foundling fau·ndliŋ deserted infant whose parents are not known. XIII. ME. *fundling*, perh. alteration of contemp. and synon. †*funding* (f. *fund-*, pp. stem of FIND + -ING[3]) by substitution of -LING[1]; perh. after (M)Du. *vondeling*, MHG. *vundelinc*.

fount[1] faunt spring, fountain. XVI (Sh., Drayton). prob. back-formation from FOUNTAIN, after *mount*, *mountain*, suggested by F. *fonts* (L. *fons*), which was directly repr. by *font* (XVII; chiefly poet.).

fount[2] faunt (typogr.) set of type of a particular size. XVII (Moxon). Alteration of *font* (which remains an alternative form) †founding, casting (XVI) – F. *fonte*, f. *fondre* FOUND[2], prob. after *vente* sale, *vendre* sell, etc.

fountain fau·ntin (arch.) spring of water XV; artificially formed jet of water XVI. – (O)F. *fontaine* = Pr., Cat., It. *fontana*, Rum. *fîntână* :– late L. *fontāna*, sb. use (sc. *aqua* water) of *fontānus*, f. *font-*, *fons* spring, fountain. Cf. FONT[1].

four fōəɹ 4, iv. OE. *fēower* = OFris. *fiūwer*, *fiōr*, OS. *fiwar*, *fiuwar*, *fiori*, OHG. *fior*, *fier* (Du., G. *vier*), ON. *fjórir*, fem. *-ar*, n. *fjogor*, Goth. *fidwōr*, beside OE. *fyþer-*, *fiþer-*, Frankish *fitter-*, OSw. *fiæþer-*, Goth. *fidur-* (in comps.) :– Germ. **petwor-* :– IE. **qwetwōr-*, whence (with vowel-variation) OW. *petguar* (W. *pedwar*), OIr. *cethir*, L. *quattuor*, Gr. *téssares* (Dor. *tétores*, Æol. *písures*), OSl. *četyri*, Lith. *keturì*, Skr. *catvā́ras*, *catúr-*; orig. inflected, like the words for 2 and 3 and unlike those for 5–10. Cf. QUADRI-. Hence **fourTEEN**. OE. *fēowertīene* = OFris. *fiuwertīne*, OS. *fiertein* (Du. *veertien*), OHG. *fiorzehan* (G. *vierzehn*), ON. *fjórtán*, Goth. *fidwōrtaihun*; whence **fourteenTH**[2], OE. *fēowertēoþa*, ME. *fourtethe*, superseded by *fourtend* (after ON. *fjórtándi*), *-tenþe*, (from XVI) *-teenth*. **fourTH**[2] fōəɹþ OE. *fēo(we)rþa* = OS. *fiorðo* (Du. *vierde*), OHG. *fiordo* (G. *vierte*), ON. *fjórði* :– CGerm. **fi(ð)worþon* :– IE. **qweturto-*, *-twrto*, whence also L. *quartus*, Gr. *τέταρτος*, OSl. *četvrĭtŭ*, Skr. *caturthás*. The ME. types *ferth(e)*, *furth(e)*, *fourt(e)*, were finally superseded by *fourth*. Cf. FORTY.

fowl faul (arch., exc. in *wild-fowl*) bird OE.; domestic cock or hen XVI. OE. *fugol* = OFris. *fugel*, OS. *fugal*, OHG. *fogal* (Du., G. *vogel*), ON. *fugl*, Goth. *fugls* :- CGerm. **foglaz*, **fuglaz*, perh. dissim. form of **fluglaz*, f. **flug-* **fleug-* FLY² (cf. OE. *flugol* fleeing, and Mercian *fluglas heofun* 'volucres cæli', Matt. xiii 32). Hence **fow·l**ER¹. OE. *fug(e)lere*, f. *fug(e)lian* catch wild-fowl.

fox fɔks animal of the genus Vulpis. OE. *fox* = OS. *vuhs* (Du. *vos*), OHG. *fuhs* (G. *fuchs*) :- WGerm. **fuχs*; a corr. CGerm. fem. formation in *-ōn* is repr. by OE. *focge*, MLG. *vohe*, OHG. *foha* (G. dial. *fohe*), ON. *fóa*, Goth. *fauhō*; f. CGerm. **fuχ-* :- **puk-*, assumed base of Skr. *púcchas* tail, Russ., Pol. *pukh* fine woolly hair, down; the name may mean orig. 'the tailed one'. The female is VIXEN. For Eng., LG., and Du. *-o-* for *-u-*, cf. OE. *lox* = OS. *lohs*, MLG., Du. *los* LYNX. ¶ ON. *fox* fraud is – OE. *fox*; cf. OE. *foxung* deception. Hence **fo·x**-GLOVE the plant Digitalis. OE. *foxesglōfa*, f. g. sg. of *fox*; the flower resembles a finger-stall in shape; the Norw. name, *revbjelde* 'fox-bell', shows similar unexpl. assoc. with the animal.

foyer fwa·jei large room in a theatre, etc., for the use of the audience during intervals. XIX. F., hearth, home = Pr. *foguer* :- Gallo-Rom. **focārium*, f. L. *focus* fire (see FOCUS).

fracas fræ·ka, U.S. frei·kəs noisy quarrel. XVIII (Lady Montagu). F., f. *fracasser* – It. *fracassare* make an uproar, of unkn. origin.

fraction fræ·kʃən numerical quantity that is not an integer XIV (Ch.); breaking or its result XV. – (O)F. *fraction* – ChrL. *fractiō(n-)* breaking (as of bread), f. *fract-*, pp. stem of *frangere* BREAK; see -TION. Hence **fra·ction**AL¹. XVII. So **fractious** fræ·kʃəs refractory, (now) cross, peevish. XVIII (Defoe). f. FRACTION (in obs. sense 'discord, dissension'), prob. after *faction* / *factious*. **fract**URE fræ·ktʃəɹ breaking or its result. XV. – (O)F. *fracture* or L. *fractūra*, f. *fract-*. Hence **fra·ctur**ED¹. XVII, whence **fra·cture** vb. XIX.

fragile fræ·dʒail liable to break. XVII (Sh.). – (O)F. *fragile* or L. *fragilis*, f. **frag-*, base of *frangere*. So **fragil**ITY frədʒi·liti. XIV. – (O)F. or L. **frag**MENT fræ·gmənt part broken off. XV. – F. *fragment* or L. *fragmentum*, f. **frag-*. Hence **fra·gment**ARY. XVII (rare before XIX and stigmatized by Johnson, citing Donne, as 'not elegant, nor in use').

fragrant frei·grənt sweet-smelling. XV (Dunbar). – F. *fragrant* or L. *fragrant-*, *-āns*, prp. of *fragrāre* smell sweet; see -ANT. So **fra·gr**ANCE. XVII (Milton; *fra·grancy* XVI).

frail¹ freil rush basket for figs, raisins, etc. XIII. ME. *fraiel* – OF. *fraiel*, of unkn. origin.

frail² freil morally or physically weak (XIII in *frelnes*, Cursor M.); liable to break XIV (Wycl. Bible). ME. *frele*, *freel* – OF. *fraile*, *frele* (mod. *frêle*) :- L. *fragili-s* FRAGILE. So **frai·l**TY. XIV. – OF. *fraileté* – L. *fragilitās*.

fraise freiz (fortif.) palisade XVIII; ruff for the neck XIX. – F. *fraise* transf. use of the word meaning 'mesentery of a calf'.

frambœsia fræmbi·ziə yaws, characterized by raspberry-like excrescences. XIX. modL., f. (O)F. *framboise* raspberry, of disputed origin.

frame freim A. †be profitable; †progress OE.; B. †prepare timber for building XIV; (gen.) shape, construct, contrive XIV. OE. *framian* be of service, make progress, f. *fram* forward (see FROM); cf. ON. *frama* further, advance. The rel. ON. *fremja* (= OE. *fremman*, *fremian*) further, advance, perform, pt. *framði*, pp. *framdr*, prob. infl. the sense-development. Hence **frame** sb. framed work, structure XIV (of heaven and earth, the body XVI); order, plan XVI; whence *fra·mework* XVII (Milton).

franc fræŋk French coin or money of account. XIV (Ch.). – (O)F. *franc*, derived from the legend *Francorum rex* king of the Franks, on gold coins first struck in the reign of Jean le Bon (1350–64).

franchise fræ·ntʃaiz †freedom XIII; legal immunity or privilege XIV; (hist.) district over which a privilege extends XV; (in full *elective f.*) right of voting at a public election XVIII. – (O)F. *franchise*, f. *franc*, fem. *franche* free, FRANK + *-ise*, repr. L. *-itia* -ESS². Cf. ENFRANCHISE.

Franciscan frànsi·skən friar of the order founded by St. Francis of Assisi in 1209. XVI. – F. *franciscain* – modL. *Franciscānus*, f. *Franciscus* Francis; see -AN.

Franco- fræ·ŋkou comb. form of medL. *Francus* FRANK, meaning 'Frankish or French and . . .'; see -O-. XVIII.

francolin fræ·ŋkolin bird of the partridge family. XVII. – F. *francolin* – It. *francolino*, of unkn. origin.

franc-tireur frãtirör one of a corps of light infantry. XIX. F., i.e. *franc* free (see FRANK) + *tireur* shooter, f. *tirer* shoot, of unkn. origin.

frangible fræ·ndʒibl breakable. XV. – OF. *frangible* or medL. *frangibilis*, f. *frangere* BREAK; see -IBLE.

frangipane fræ·ndʒipein perfume obtained from red jasmine XVII; cream for pastry (F. *crème à la frangipane*) XIX. – F. *frangipane*, f. *Frangipani*, name of an Italian marquis who invented a perfume for scenting gloves (cf. F. *gants de frangipane* or *Frangipani*).

frank fræŋk †free XIII; bounteous, generous; †of superior quality (see FRANKINCENSE) XV; ingenuous, candid XVI. – (O)F. *franc* = Pr. *franc*, Sp., It. *franco* :- medL. *francus* free, identical with the ethnic name (see FRANK), which acquired the sense 'free' because in Frankish Gaul full freedom was possessed only by those belonging to or adopted by the dominant people. Hence (from the sense †'free of charge' of the adj.; cf. F. *franc de port* carriage-free) **frank** vb.

superscribe (a letter, etc.) with one's signature to ensure free conveyance, (hence) stamp XVIII; facilitate the passage of XIX.

Frank fræŋk A. of the Germanic nation (or nations) that conquered Gaul and from which the country received the name of France (*Francia*) OE.; B. in the Levant (e.g. Gr. *Φράγκος*), individual of Western nationality XVI. OE. *Franca* = OHG. *Franko*; supposed to be named from their national weapon, OE. *franca* javelin (cf. SAXON).

frankincense fræ·ŋkinsens olibanum. XIV. – OF. *franc encens*; see FRANK (formerly used in the sense 'of superior quality'), INCENSE.

franklin fræ·ŋklin landholder of free but not noble birth. XIII (RGlouc.). ME. *francoleyn, frankeleyn* (3 syll., as in Ch.) – AL. *francālānus*, f. *francālis* (as in *feudum francāle*, synon. with *feudum francum*, OF. *franc fieu*; *francālia* n. pl. territory held without dues; *francāliter* adv. without dues), f. *francus* free, FRANK; see -AL[1], -AN.

frankpledge fræ·ŋkpledʒ system by which each member of a tithing was responsible for every other. XV (*fraunciplegge*). – law L. *franciplegium*, latinization of AN. *fraunc plege*, f. *franc* FRANK + *plege* PLEDGE, mistr. of OE. *friþborh* peace-pledge (*friþ*, f. **frī-* love, as in FRIEND), through the corrupt forms *freoborh, friborh*, in which the first element was identified with *free*.

frantic fræ·ntik †insane XIV; frenzied XVI. Late ME. *frentik, frantik* (forms with *-e-* survived till XVII) – (O)F. *frénétique* – L. *phrenēticus* PHRENETIC. The early change from *-e-* to *-a-* is unaccounted for.

frap fræp A. (dial.) strike XIV; B. (naut.) bind tightly XVI. In A perh. repr. OE. (late Nhb.) *(ġe)fræpġiġa*, which may contain the base of the Rom. word; in B – OF. *fraper* (mod. *frapper*).

frass fræs excrement of larvæ. XIX. – G. *frass* (MHG. *vrāz*), f. *fressen* devour (see FRET[1]).

frate frā·tei friar. XVIII. It. (see FRIAR). ¶ The abbrev. form *fra* is used as a prefix, e.g. *Fra Angelico*.

frater frei·təɹ (hist.) refectory in a religious house. XIII. ME. *freitore, freit(o)ur* – OF. *fraitur*, aphetic of *refreitor* – medL. *refectōrium* REFECTORY. Hence **fra·try**[3]. XIV.

fraternal frətɔ̄·ɹnəl brotherly. XV (Lydg.). – medL. *frāternālis*, f. L. *frāternus*, f. *frāter* BROTHER; cf. (O)F. *fraternel* and see -AL[1]. So **frate·rnity** brotherhood. XIV. – (O)F. – L. **fraternize** fræ·təɹnəiz. XVII. **fra:terniza·tion**. XVIII. – F.

fratricide[1] frei·trisaid, fræ·t- one who kills his (or her) brother. XV. – F. *fratricide* or L. *frātricīda*, f. *frāter*; see prec. and -CIDE[1]. So **fra·tricide**[2]. XVI. – (O)F. *fratricide* or late L. *frātricīdium*; see -CIDE[2].

frau frau German married woman, wife; Mrs. XIX. G. (OHG. *frouwa*) = Du. VROUW. So **fräulein** froi·lain German young lady; Miss. XVII. G. (MHG. *vrouwelīn*), dim. formation.

fraud frɔ̄d deception. XIV (R. Mannyng). – (O)F. *fraude* – L. *fraudem*, nom. *fraus*. So **frau·dulent**. XV (Lydg.). – OF. or L.

fraught frɔ̄t (arch.) laden XIV; stored, supplied XV; attended *with* XVI. pp. of †*fraught* load (a ship) XIV – MDu. *vrachten*, f. *vracht* (whence Eng. *fraught* sb. XIV, now Sc.) = MLG. *vracht* (whence G. *fracht*, Da. *fragt*, etc.), beside *vrecht* FREIGHT, prob. corr. to OHG. *frēht* earnings :– Germ. **fraaiχtiz*, f. **fra-* FOR- + **aiχtiz* acquisition, property (see AUGHT).

fraxinella fræksine·lə cultivated species of dittany. XVII (Evelyn). modL., dim. of L. *fraxinus* ash (cf. BIRCH).

fray[1] frei (arch.) frighten. XIII (Cursor M.). Aphetic of AFFRAY. Hence **fray** sb. (dial.) alarm; disturbance, conflict. XIV.

fray[2] frei †rub XIV (in vbl. sb. *fraying* noise of friction, Barbour); †bruise; †clash, collide XV; spec. (of deer) rub their horns XVI (Turbervile); rub away XVIII (Steele). – F. *frayer*, earlier **freiier* = Pr., Sp., Pg. *fregar*, It. *fregare*, Rum. *freca* :– L. *fricāre* rub, rel. to *friāre* (cf. FRIABLE).

frazzle fræ·zl (U.S.) tear to rags. XIX. First recorded by Forby from East Anglian dial.; perh. a blend of FRAY[2] and dial. *fazzle* tangle. Hence **fra·zzle** sb. pl. frayed ends; phr. *to a frazzle*.

freak frīk sudden change (as of fortune), capricious notion XVI (*fortunes frekes*); capricious prank XVII; product of sportive fancy XVIII; (in full *freak of nature*, L. *lusus naturæ*) monstrous individual of its kind XIX. prob. of dial. origin.

freaked frīkt variegated. XVII (Milton; whence in later poet. use). perh. alteration, by assoc. with *streak*, of *freckt* (Sandys, 1621), based on FRECKLE.

freckle fre·kl brownish spot on the skin. XIV. Early forms are *fracel, frakel*; alteration of (dial.) *freken, fraken* (Ch.) – ON. *freknur* pl. (Sw. *fräkne*, Da. *fregne*). Hence **fre·ckled**[2]. XIV (*yfracled, yfreklet* spotted); in ME. also *frakned, fraknyd*, after ON. *freknóttr*.

free frī not in bondage or subject to control from outside. OE. *frēo* = OFris., OS., OHG. *frī* (Du. *vrij*, G. *frei*), ON. **frīr* (only in comp. *frīdls* :– **frīhals* 'free-necked'; cf. OHG. *frīhals* free man, OE. *frēols*, Goth. *freihals* freedom), Goth. *freis* :– CGerm. **frijaz* :– IE. **prijos*, the stem of which is repr. also by Skr. *priyás* dear (*priyā́* wife, daughter), Av. *fryō*, W. *rhydd* free, OSl. *prijatelji* friend, OE. *frīgu* love, *frēon*, Goth. *frijōn* (see FRIEND), OS. *frī* woman, ON. *Frigg* (cf. FRIDAY). The primary sense is 'dear'; the Germ. and Celtic meaning comes of its having been applied to the members of a household connected by ties of kindred with the head, as opp. to the slaves. The reverse development is seen in L. *līberī* children, orig. the free members of a household. **freebooter** frī·bū:təɹ piratical adventurer. XVI. – Du. *vrijbuiter*, †*-bueter*; cf. FILIBUSTER. **free·**DOM. OE. *frēodōm*; cf. Du. *vrijdom*. **free·ho:ld**ER[1]. XV. tr. AN. *fraunc tenaunt* 'free tenant', one who possesses a **free·hold** estate, AN. *fraunc tenement* 'free holding'. **free** LANCE military adventurer. XIX (Scott); later esp. fig. **free**LY[2]. OE. *frēolīće*. **free·**MAN. OE. *frēoman*; so **free·**WO:MAN. XIV (Wycl. Bible). **free·ma:rtin** hermaphrodite or imperfect female of the ox kind. XVII; of unkn. origin; cf. Ir., Gael. *mart* cow (fattened for the market). **free·**MA:SON †skilled worker in stone (perh. orig. one emancipated from the control of guilds and so free to work where wanted) XIV; member of a fraternity which grew out of the practice of admitting to societies of stonemasons other persons not of that craft (first called *accepted masons*) XVII. **free·**STONE fine-grained sandstone or limestone. XIV. tr. OF. *franche pere*, AL. *lapis liber* (*c.* 1200), the adj. meaning 'of superior quality'. **free·thi:nker** one who refuses to submit his reason to the control of authority. XVIII (once earlier, applied to a sect); cf. Du. *vrijdenker*, F. *libre penseur* (XVII). **free thought.** XVIII (Shaftesbury). **free**WILL unrestrained choice, (theol.) power of directing one's actions without constraint by necessity. XIII; tr. late L. *liberum arbitrium*.

freesia frī·ziə, frī·ʒ[1]ə iridaceous plant from the Cape of Good Hope. XIX. modL. (used by Ecklon for a group of allied plants), f. name of his friend Friedrich H. T. *Freese*, a physician of Kiel, Germany, see -IA[1].

freeze frīz, pt. **froze** frouz, pp. **frozen** frou·zn (impers.) be so cold that ice forms OE.; be converted into ice XIII; convert into ice XV. OE. *frēosan*, pt. *frēas*, pp. *froren* (see FRORE) = MLG., MDu. *vrēsen* (Du. *vriezen*), OHG. *frīosan* (G. *frieren*, with analogical *r* for *s*), ON. *frjósa*, Goth. **friusan* (cf. *frius* frost) :– CGerm. **freusan*, f. **freus- *fraus- *frus-* :– IE. **preus- *prous- *prus-*, repr. by L. *pruīna* hoarfrost, Skr. *pruṣvā́*.

freight freit hire of a transport vessel XV; cargo, lading XVI. – MLG., MDu. *vrecht* (whence also F. *fret*, Sp. *flete*, Pg. *frete*), var. of *vracht* (see FRAUGHT).

French frentʃ pert. to France. Late OE. *frenćisć* :– Germ. **fraŋkiskaz* (whence medL. *Franciscus*, the source of OF. *franceis*, mod. *français*), f. **Fraŋkon* FRANK; see ISH[1]. The contr. form is found in early ME. (*frennsce*, Laȝ.); cf. WELSH, SCOTCH. Some ME. forms with *k*, e.g. *frankis*, *frenkis*, *-isch*, were based on or infl. by ON. *Frankis*(*menn*, etc.). Hence **Fre·nchi·**FY. XVI (Greene, Jonson).

frenzy fre·nzi mental derangement, (passing into) wild agitation of mind. XIV (R. Rolle). ME. *frenesie* – (O)F. *frénésie*, corr. to Pr., It. *frenesia* – medL. *phrenēsia*, for L. *phrenēsis* (whence Pr., Sp., Pg. *frenesi*), f. Gr. *phren-*, *phrḗn* mind; cf. FRANTIC, and see -Y[3].

frequent frī·kwənt †crowded; †commonly practised; †addicted *to* XVI; recurring often, constant, habitual XVII. – (O)F. *fréquent* or L. *frequent-*, *-ēns* crowded, frequent, of unkn. origin (supposed by some to be rel. to *farcīre* stuff, FARCE[1]); see -ENT. So **fre·qu**ENCE. XVI. – (O)F. – L. *frequentia*, whence also **fre·qu**ENCY. XVI. **frequent** frikwe·nt visit, associate with, resort to XV; †practise XV (Caxton). – (O)F. *fréquenter* or L. *frequentāre* (its senses 'crowd', 'celebrate' were also formerly in Eng. use), f. *frequēns*. **freque·nt**ATIVE (gram.) expressing repetition. XV.

fresco fre·skou painting in water-colour on a wall, etc., of which the plaster is not quite dry. XVI. orig. *in fresco*, †*al fresco*, †*a fresco*, repr. It. *affresco*, i.e. *al fresco* 'on the fresh (plaster)'; see FRESH.

fresh freʃ †eager, ardent XII (Orm); brisk, vigorous XIII (Laȝ.); not salty (RGlouc.); new, novel, recent; having the signs of newness, not tainted, sullied, or worn XIV (Rolle); (of wind) XVI. ME. *fresch*, (Orm) *fressh* – OF. *freis*, fem. *fresche* (mod. *frais*, *fraîche*) = Pr. *fresc*, Sp., Pg., It. *fresco* (cf. AL FRESCO, FRESCO) – Rom. **friscu-s* – Germ. **friskaz*, repr. by OE. *fersć* in senses 'not salted, not salt' (continued in rare ME. *ferchse*, *uersse*) = OFris., MDu. *fersc* (Du. *vers*), OHG. *frisc* (G. *frisch*), ON. *ferskr*, perh. rel. to OSl. *prěsinŭ* fresh, Lith. *prė̃skas* unleavened. Hence **fresh**EN[5]. XVII; superseding *fresh* vb. XIV–XVII (later arch.).

freshet fre·ʃit small stream of fresh water XVI; flood XVII. prob. – fem. of OF. *freschet* (as in *fontaine frechette*), f. *frais* FRESH; see -ET.

fret[1] fret †devour OE.; gnaw; also fig. XII; chafe, irritate, vex XIII. OE. *fretan* = MLG., MDu. *vrēten* (Du. *vreten*), OHG. *frezzan* (G. *fressen*), Goth. *fraïtan*; CGerm. (exc. ON.) f. **fra-* FOR-[1] + **etan* EAT. Hence as sb. XV (Lydg.).

fret[2] fret (chiefly in pp. *fretted*) †adorned with interlaced work XIV (R. Rolle); adorned with carved or embossed work XVII (Sh.). prob. – OF. *freter* (in pp. *freté* = AL. *frectatus*, *frictatus*), rel. to *frete* trellis, interlaced work (mod. *frette*), of unkn. origin. So **fret** sb. XIV (Ch.). prob. – OF. *frete*. comp. **fre·t**WORK XVIII.

fret[3] fret (mus.) bar of wood, etc., to regulate the pitch in some stringed instruments. XVI. Of unkn. origin.

Freudian froi·diən pert. to the system of psychoanalysis founded by Sigmund Freud (1856–1939).

friable frai·əbl easily reducible to powder. XVI. – F. *friable* (Rabelais) or L. *friābilis*, f. *friāre* crumble, rel. to *fricāre* (cf. FRICTION, FRAY[2]); see -ABLE.

friar fraiəɹ member of certain religious orders (Franciscans, Augustinians, Dominicans, Carmelites). XIII. ME. *frere* – (O)F. *frère* = Pr. *fraire* brother, friar (whence Sp. *fraile*, †*fraire*), Pg. *freire* :– L. *frātrem*, nom. *frāter* BROTHER (whence It. FRATE). For the phonology cf. *briar*, *entire*, *quire*.

fribble fri·bl †falter; (chiefly dial.) act aimlessly or feebly, fool *away*. XVII (Middleton, Brome, Shirley). Expressive formation (cf. -LE[2]). ¶ Connexion with FRIVOL adj. and vb. is ruled out by chronology.

fricandeau frikãdou· fricassee of veal. XVIII. F. **fricassee** frikəsī· ragout of sliced meat. XVI. – F. *fricassée*, sb. use of fem. pp. of *fricasser* mince and cook in gravy; of unkn. origin.

fricative fri·kətiv (philol.) produced by friction of the breath through a narrow opening of the mouth. XIX. – modL. *fricātivus*, f. L. *fricāre*; see next and -ATIVE.

friction fri·kʃən rubbing (orig. med.). XVI. – F. *friction* (Paré) – L. *frictiō(n-)* (Celsus), f. *fricāre* rub, rel. to *friāre*; see FRIABLE, -TION.

Friday frai·di sixth day of the week. OE. *frīgedæġ* (whence ON. *frjádagr*), corr. to OFris. *frī(g)endei*, MLG., MDu. *vrīdach* (Du. *vrijdag*), OHG. *frīatag* (G. *freitag*); i.e. DAY of *Frīg* = ON. *Frigg* name of the wife of Odin, prop. sb. use of fem. of Germ. **frijaz* noble, FREE; CWGerm. tr. of late L. *Veneris dies* day of the planet Venus (whence F. *vendredi*, It. *venerdì*), based on Gr. Ἀφροδίτης ἡμέρα 'day of Aphrodite'.

friend frend 'one joined to another in mutual benevolence and intimacy' (J.); †lover OE.; (now only pl.; orig. partly after ON. *frǽndi*) relative, kinsman XII. OE. *frēond*, pl. *frīend* = OFris. *friūnd*, OS. *friund* (Du. *vriend*), OHG. *friunt* (G. *freund*), ON. (with change of decl. in the sg.) *frændi*, Goth. *frijonds*; CGerm. prp. formation on **frijōjan* (whence OE. *frēogan*, *frēon*, Goth. *frijōn* love), f. **frijaz* beloved, FREE. For the formation cf. FIEND, which preserves the long vowel, whereas in *friend* there is shortening (usu. held to be due to the comps. *friendly*, *friendship*, in OE. *frēondlić*, *-sćipe*), though it retains the sp. assoc. with the long vowel (which is shown, e.g. in *freend*, *freind*, common in XVI). OE. pl. *frīend*, *frēond* continued in ME. as *frend*; the rare and late *frēondas* became the regular pl. *frendes*, *friends*.

frieze[1] frīz coarse woollen cloth with a nap. XV (*frese*, *frise*). – F. *frise* (whence also G. *fries*) = Sp., Pg. *frisa* – medL. *(*lāna*) *frīsia* FRISIAN wool (so L. *panni frisii* Frisian cloths).

frieze[2] frīz (archit.) member of entablature between architrave and cornice. XVI (*frese*). – F. *frise* – medL. *frisium*, var. of *frigium*, for L. *Phrygium* (sc. *opus*) Phrygian work; cf. L. *phrygiæ vestes*. In It. *fregio*, Sp. *friso*, the relation of which is not clear.

frigate fri·gət (orig.) light swift vessel (later variously applied). XVI. – F. *frégate* – It. *fregata*, †*fragata* (whence Sp. *fragata*), of unkn. origin.

fright frait fear (OE.) sudden or intense fear. OE. *fryhto*, metathetic (Nhb.) var. of *fyrhto* = Goth. *faurhtei* :– Germ. **furχtīn*, f. **furχtaz* afraid, repr. by OE. *forht*, OS. *foroht*, *-aht*, OHG. *foraht*, Goth. *faurhts*; the other WGerm. langs. have a synon. sb. without mutation, viz. OFris. *fruchtia*, OS., OHG. *for(a)hta* (Du., G. *furcht*). No known cogns. outside Germ. So **fright** vb. terrify. OE. (Nhb.) *fryhta*, var. of *fyrhtan* = OFris. *fruchtia*, OS. *forahtian*, OHG. *for(a)htan*, *furihten* (G. *fürchten*), Goth. *faurhtjan*. Cf. AFFRIGHT. Superseded by **fright**EN[5]. XVII (Pepys).

frigid fri·dʒid †cold in 'quality' XV; intensely cold XVII. – L. *frīgidus*, f. *frīgēre* be cold, f. *frīgus* cold = Gr. *rhîgos* :– **srīgos* (with vb. *rhīgeîn*); see -ID[1]. So **frigi·d**ITY. XV. – (O)F. – late L.

frijoles frī·χoles Mexican kidney-bean. XVI (formerly sp. with *s*, *ð*, *z*). Sp. pl. of *frijol*, *frejol*.

frill fril wavy ornamental edging. XVI. contemp. with the corr. vb.; of unkn. origin. The sense 'mesentery of an animal', not recorded till XIX, may have been the original, in which case the development would be similar to that of *chitterling*, F. *fraise*, and G. *gekröse* (i) mesentery, (ii) ruff.

fringe frin^{d}ʒ ornamental border of stuff with dependent threads XIV; edging, border XVII. Late ME. *frenge* – OF. *frenge*, *fringe* (mod. *frange*, whence It. *frangia*, Sp., Pg. *franja*) = Pr. *fremnha*, Rum. *frînghie* cord :– Rom. **frimbia*, metathetic alteration of late L. *fimbria*, earlier only pl. fibres, shreds, fringe. ¶ For the change of e to i before ndʒ cf. *cringe*, *hinge*, *singe*, *swinge*. Hence vb. XV.

fringillaceous frindʒilei·ʃəs of the finch family. XIX. f. L. *fringilla* finch + -ACEOUS.

frippery fri·pəri †old clothes XVI (*freprie*); finery in dress XVII; empty display XVIII. – F. *friperie*, OF. *freperie*, f. *frepe*, *ferpe*, *felpe*, *feupe* rag, old clothes, of unkn. origin; see -ERY.

Frisian, Friesian fri·ziən, fri·ʒiən, frī·- pert. to, an inhabitant of, the language of, Friesland. XVI. f. L. *Frīsiī* (pl.) – the native name OFris. *Frīsa*, *Frēsa*, whence OE. *Frīsa*, *Frēsa*, MDu. *Vriese* (Du. *Vries*), OHG. *Friaso* (G. *Friese*), ON. *Frísir*; see -IAN. Earlier †*Friese* (XV, Caxton) – MDu.

frisk fri·sk move briskly and sportively. XVI. f. *frisk* adj. brisk, lively – OF. *frisque* vigorous, alert, lively, merry, var. of *frische*, *friche*, earlier *frique*, of unkn. origin.

frisket fri·skit (typogr.) frame hinged to the tympan. XVII (Moxon). – F. *frisquette* – modPr. *frisqueto* – Sp. *frasqueta*.

frit frit calcined mixture of sand, etc., to be melted to form glass. XVII. – It. *fritta* (perh. through F. *fritte*), sb. use of fem. pp. of *friggere* FRY[2].

frith[1] friþ wood, wooded country surviving in place-names: *Chapel en le Frith, Frithsden, Pirbright* (*Pirbrigth* XIV, for *Pyrifright* XIII, *Perifrith* XII, OE. *piriġfyrhþe* 'pear-tree wood'); (dial.) sparsely grown land XVI, underwood XVII. OE. (*ġe*)*fyrhþe, fyrhþ* :– Germ. **gafurχþjam*, **furχþi*, perh. f. **furχjōn* FIR.

frith[2] friþ firth. XVI (Holland). var. of FIRTH; perh. infl. by L. *fretum* arm of the sea, formerly its supposed origin.

fritillary friti·ləri plant of the liliaceous genus Fritillaria, esp. F. Meleagris. XVII. – modL. *fritillāria*, f. L. *fritillus* dice-box, presumably applied to the chessboard; so named in ref. to the chequered markings of the corolla. Cf. -ARY.

fritter[1] fri·təɹ portion of batter fried in oil, etc. XIV. – (O)F. *friture* = Pr., Sp. *fritura*, It. *frittura*, Rum. *fripturǎ* :– Rom. **frīctūra*, f. *frict-*, pp. stem of L. *frīgere* FRY[2]; see -URE. The suffix finally became *-er*, through *-our*, *-eur*.

fritter[2] fri·təɹ †break into fragments; do away with piecemeal, waste in trifling. XVII. f. *fritters* fragments (XVII), synon. with earlier (dial.) *flitters* (XVII), expressive alteration of (dial.) *fitters* (XVI), f. †*fitter* break into small fragments, perh. rel. to MHG. *vetze* (G. *fetzen*) rag, scrap; see -ER[4].

Friulian friū·liən pert. to (the language of) Friuli, a district at the head of the Adriatic Sea. f. *Friuli* :– L. *Forojulium*, i.e. *Forum Julii* said to have been founded by Julius Caesar; see -IAN.

frivolous fri·vələs of little importance; lacking in seriousness. XV. f. L. (mainly late) *frīvolus* silly, trifling + -OUS. Hence, by back-formation, colloq. **frivol** vb. (also *frivel, frivvle*). XIX. **frivol**ITY -ɔ·lĭti. XVIII. – F., f. (O)F. *frivole* (whence †*frivol* adj. XV) – L. *frīvolus*.

friz(z) friz curl (the hair) in crisp curls. XVII. Earliest forms *freeze, frize* – F. *friser*, perh. f. *fris-*, stem of *frire* FRY[2]; the vowel appears to have been shortened under the infl. of the earlier FRIZZLE.

frizzle fri·zl frizz (the hair). XVI. First in pp. *frisled*, and earlier than *friz(z)*, of which it might be supposed to be a deriv.; similar Fris. forms such as *frisle* head of hair, *friselen* plait, are doubtfully rel.; perh. – OF. *freselé* plaited.

fro frou prep. (now dial.) from XII (Ormulum); adv. in *to and fro* XIII (*fra and till*, Cursor M.) – ON. *frá* = OE. *fram* FROM.

frock frɔk long eccl. open-sleeved habit; long coat or tunic XIV; skirted outer garment, gown XIV. – (O)F. *froc* = Pr. *froc* (medL. *froccus*), of Germ. origin (cf. OS., OHG. *hroc*; not identical with OHG. *roc*, G. *rock* coat; see ROCHET).

frog[1] frɔg tailless amphibious animal. OE. *frogga*, a pet-form similar to *docga* DOG, **stacga* STAG, *wicga* (see EARWIG); rel. to OE. *forsć, frosć, frox*, ME. *frosh*, dial. *frosk* = MLG., Du. *vorsch*, OHG. *frosc* (G. *frosch*), ON. *froskr* :– Germ. **froskaz*, prob. :– **frudskaz*, f. **frud-* **fraud-* **frūd-*, whence also ME. *frūde, froude* (XII–XV) frog or toad – ON. *frauðr*, OSw. pl. *frødhir* (Da. *frö*), ON. *frauki* (:– **frauðki*); OF. *frois* is from Germ. Hence **froggy** frɔ·gi playful designation of a frog; (sl.; *F-*) contemptuous nickname for a Frenchman, from his eating frogs. XIX; see -Y[6].

frog[2] frɔg pyramidal V-shaped substance in the sole of a horse's hoof. XVII. prob. a transf. use of FROG[1] partly induced by the formal similarity of synon. It. *forchetta* and F. *fourchette*, dim. of *forca, fourche* FORK, whence perh. (dial.) *frush* (cf. 'The French men call it furchette which word our farriers . . do make it a monosyllable, and pronounce it the frush', Topsell, 1607). ¶ Cf. similar uses of words for 'frog', e.g. Gr. *bátrakhos*, Pg. *ranilha*, WFris. *frosk*.

frog[3] frɔg attachment to the waist-belt to carry a sword, etc.; ornamental fastening for a military coat. XVIII (Defoe). Of unkn. origin.

frolic frɔ·lik †joyous; sportive. XVI (*frowlyke*, Bale, 1538). – Du. *vrolijk*, f. (M)Du. *vro* glad, joyous (= OS., OHG. *frao, frō*, G. *froh*, ON. *frár* swift; wanting in Eng.) + *-lijk* -LY[1]. Hence as vb. XVI, whence as sb. XVII; assoc. with -IC.

from frɔm, frəm prep. denoting departure, separation, derivation. OE. *fram, from* = OS., OHG., Goth. *fram*, ON. *frá* FRO; f. *fra-* = PRO- + *-m* suffix (cf. Gr. *prómos* foremost, Umbrian *promom* at first). The primary sense was 'forward'; cf. ON. *fram(m)* = Goth. *framis* (compar.) forward (adv.), OE. *fram, from*, ON. *framr* forward, valiant, OFris. *from* useful (*fromia* make use of); see also FRAME. The sense-development was 'onward', 'on the way', 'away' (from).

frond frɔnd (bot.) leaf-like organ formed by the union of stem and foliage. XVIII. – L. *frond-, frons* leaf, which was applied by Linnæus in a specific sense)(*folium* (FOIL[2]).

front frʌnt (arch.) forehead, face XIII; foremost part XIV. – (O)F. *front* = Pr. *front*, Sp. *frente*, Pg. *fronte*, Rum. *frunte* :– L. *frontem*, nom. *frōns*. **fro·nt**AGE. XVII (rare before XIX). **front**AL frʌ·ntl †ornament for the forehead; movable covering for the front of an altar. XIV. – OF. *frontel* – L. *frontāle* (in pl. *-ālia*), f. *front-*. **front**AL[1] adj. (XVII). **frontier** frɔ·ntiəɹ †front part XIV; boundary of a country XV. Late ME. *frounter(e)* – (O)F. *frontière* = Pr. *fronteira* forehead, Sp. *frontera*, Pg. *fronteira*, It. *frontiera* frontier, AN. *frounter*; Rom. deriv. of L. *frōns*.

Frontignac fronti·njæk muscat wine of *Frontignan*, France. XVII.

frontispiece frʌ·ntispīs principal face of a building XVI; pediment; †front page of a book; illustration facing the title-page XVII. – F. *frontispice* or late L. *frontispicium* examination of the forehead, physiognomy, countenance, façade, f. L. *front-*, *frōns* FRONT+*-spicium*, as in *auspicium* AUSPICE; very early assim. in sp. to *piece*.

frore frɔ̄əɹ (dial.) frozen XIII; (arch.) very cold, frosty XV (Caxton). pp. of FREEZE.

frost frɔ̀st state of freezing, frozen dew or vapour. OE. *frost*, usu. *forst* = OFris. *frost*, *forst*, OS., (O)HG. *frost* (Du. *vorst*), ON. *frost* :- CGerm. (exc. Goth.) **frustaz*, *-am*, f. wk. grade of **freusan* FREEZE+abstr. suffix *-t-*. The form *frost* was doubtless established by ON. influence. Hence **fro·sty**[1]. XIV (Ch.); cf. Du. *vorstig*, OHG. *forstag* (G. *-ig*); OE. had a mutated form *fyrstiġ*.

froth frɔ̀þ aggregation of small bubbles on liquid. XIV (Sir Gawain, Wycl. Bible). – ON. *froða* or *frauð*, f. Germ. **freuþ-* **frauþ-* **fruþ-*, repr. also by the OE. vb. *āfrēoþan* froth. Hence **froth** vb. XIV (Wycl. Bible, Ch.); ON. had a mutated form *freyða*.

frou-frou frū·frū rustling, as of silk. XIX. F., of imit. origin.

frow frau †Dutchwoman XIV; (Dutch or German) wife XVI (superseded by VROUW); cf. FRAU.

froward frou·əɹd perverse, refractory)(*toward*. XIII (Cursor M.). f. FRO+-WARD; superseding the native †*fromward*, OE. *framweard*. ¶ Also as adv. and prep. 'away', 'away from' XII–XVI.

frown fraun knit the brows in displeasure or puzzlement. XIV (Ch.). – OF. *frongnier*, *froignier* (surviving in *re(n)frogner*; corr. to Sp. *enfurruñarse* be surly), f. *froigne* surly look, of Celtic origin (cf. W. *ffroen* nose).

frowzy frau·zi fusty, musty XVII (Otway); dirty and unkempt XVIII. prob. rel. to earlier synon. (dial.) *frowy* XVI (Spenser), †*frowish*, and later *frowsty* (XIX); ult. origin unkn.

fructify frʌ·ktifai bear fruit XIV; make fruitful XVI. – (O)F. *fructifier* – L. *frūctificāre*, f. *frūctus* FRUIT; see -FY. So **fru·ctu**OUS abounding with fruit. XIV (Wycl. Bible). – OF. *fructuous* or L. *frūctuōsus*, f. *frūctus*.

frugal frū·gəl sparing in the use of things XVI; sparingly supplied XVII. – L. *frūgālis*, back-formation from *frūgālior*, *-issimus*, compar. and superl. of *frūgī* indecl. adj. (evolved from phr. *frūgī bonæ* 'to good advantage', serviceable, useful), d. of *frux*, chiefly pl. *frūgēs* produce of the soil (cf. FRUIT); see -AL[1]. So **fruga·l**ITY. XVI. – (O)F. or L.

fruit frūt (esp. pl.) vegetable products gen. XII; edible product of a tree; (arch.) offspring; produce, product XIII. – (O)F. *fruit* = Pr. *fruch*, OSp. *frucho*, It. *frutto* :- L. *frūctu-s* (enjoyment of) the produce of the soil, harvest, fruit, revenue, f. **frūg-*, base of *fruī* enjoy, perh. orig. feed on, *frūgēs* 'fruits' of the earth; the IE. base **bhrūg-* is repr. also by OE. *brūcan* use, enjoy, endure, BROOK[2]. So **fruit** vb. bear fruit. XIV (PPl.). **frui·terer** dealer in fruit XV; extension with -ER[1] of *fruiter* (XV; now chiefly U.S.). – (O)F. *fruitier* (see -ER[2]); later prob. f. *fruit* sb.+-ER[1]. Hence **frui·ter**ESS[1]. XVIII. **frui·tful,** productive of fruit (etc.) XIII. **frui·tless** ineffectual XIV; unproductive XV; unavailing XIX.

fruition frui·ʃən enjoyment, peaceable possession. (XV). – (O)F. *fruition* – late L. *fruitiō(n-)*, f. *fruī* enjoy; see FRUIT, -TION.

frumenty frū·mənti, **furmety** fɔ̄·ɹmīti dish made of hulled wheat boiled in milk. XIV (*frumentee*, *furmente*). – OF. *frumentee*, *fourmentee*, f. *frument*, *fourment* (mod. *froment* wheat) = Pr. *fromen*, OSp. *hormiento*, It. *frumento* :- L. *frūmentum*, perh. f. *fruī*; see FRUIT and -Y[5].

frump frʌmp †sneer, jeer, hoax XVI; (pl., dial.) ill humour, sulks XVII (Dryden); dowdy woman XIX. prob. shortening of (dial.) *frumple* wrinkle (XIV), as vb. – MDu. *verrompelen*, f. *ver-* FOR-+*rompelen* RUMPLE.

frush frʌʃ see FROG[2]. XVII.

frustrate frʌ·streit balk, disappoint. XV. f. *frustrate*, pp. (XV) – L. *frustrātus*, pp. of *frustrāre*, f. *frustrā* in vain, rel. to *fraus* FRAUD; see -ATE[3]. So **frustr**A·TION. XVI. – L.

frustum frʌ·stəm portion of a solid left after the upper part has been cut off by a plane. XVII (Sir T. Browne). L., 'piece cut off', perh. rel. to Gr. *thraustós* breakable.

frutescent frūte·sənt (bot.) becoming shrubby. XVIII. irreg. f. L. *frutex* bush+-ESCENT (for **fruticescent*, L. *fruticescere*). So **fru·tic**OSE shrub-like. XVII. – L. *fruticōsus*, f. *frutic-*, **fru·tex** (bot.) shrub (XVII).

fry[1] frai †offspring; young of fish XIV; young or insignificant creatures XV. Implied in AL. *frium* XIII–XIV. – ON. **frío*, *frjó* seed = Goth. *fraiw* (cf. ON. *frjór* fertile :- **fraiwjaz*), of unkn. origin.

fry[2] frai cook in boiling fat. XIII. – (O)F. *frire* = Pr. *frir*, *fregir*, Sp. *freir*, Pg. *frigir*, It. *friggere*, Rum. *frige* :- L. *frīgere* (cf. Gr. *phrúgein*, Skr. *bhṛjyáti* grill).

fubsy fʌ·bzi fat and squat. XVIII. f. †*fubs* small chubby person (XVII), perh. blending of *fat* and *chub*; see -Y[1], -SY.

fuchsia fjū·ʃə genus of drooping-flowered shrubs. XVIII. modL., named by Charles Plumier (d. 1706), F. botanist, after Leonhard *Fuchs*, G. botanist (XVI); see -IA[1].

fucus fjū·kəs †cosmetic XVI; genus of seaweeds XVIII. – L. *fūcus* rock-lichen, red dye or cosmetic – Gr. *phûkos*, of Semitic origin (cf. Heb. *pūk*). So **fuca·ceous**. XIX.

fuddle fʌ·dl tipple; intoxicate. XVI. Of unkn. origin; rare syns. were †*fuzz*, †*fuzzle*.

fudge[1] fʌdʒ patch up, 'fake', 'cook'. XVII. perh. alteration of earlier *fadge*, occas. *fodge* fit, adjust, and ult. identical with ME. *fage*, dial. *fadge* deceive, beguile, of unkn. origin. Hence **fudge** sb. made-up story, deceit; int. stuff and nonsense! XVIII. ¶ There is no proof of connexion with a certain Captain *Fudge*, nicknamed Lying Fudge (XVII).

fudge[2] fʌdʒ soft sweetmeat made with sugar, milk, chocolate, etc. late XIX (*chocolate fudge*). perh. f. prec.

fuel fju·il material for burning. XIV (Trevisa). – AN. *fuaille, fewaile*, OF. *fouaille* :- Rom. **focālia* (in medL., obligation to furnish or right to demand fuel), f. *focus* fire (see FOCUS).

fug fʌg (sl.) stuffy atmosphere. XIX. perh. a blending of elements of two or more synons., e.g. †*funk* (XVII–XVIII) and †*fogo* offensive smell (early XIX); cf. *fogus* tobacco (XVII), which is perh. a joc. latinization of *fog*, of which, however, *fug* is a Sc. var.

fugacious fjugei·ʃəs fleeting XVII; failing or fading early XVIII. f. L. *fugāci-, fugāx*, f. *fugere* flee; see FUGITIVE, -ACIOUS.

-fuge fjūdʒ terminal el. repr. L. *-fugus*, in the classical period connected directly with *fugere* flee (as in *profugus* fugitive, *refugus* receding), but in later formations (as *febrifugus* FEBRIFUGE, *vermifugus* VERMIFUGE), assoc. with *fugāre* put to flight.

fugitive fju·dʒitiv (one) who takes to flight, †banished XIV (Ch.); sb. XIV (Wycl. Bible). – (O)F. *fugitif, -ive* – L. *fugitīvus, -īva*, f. *fugit-*, pp. stem of *fugere* flee; see BOW[2], -IVE.

fugleman fjū·glmæ̆n model soldier. XIX. – (with simplification of *l . . l*) G. *flügelmann* flank-man, f. *flügel* wing (f. Germ. **flug-* FLY[2]) + *mann* MAN. Hence (by back-formation) **fugle** vb. act as a fugleman or director. XIX (Carlyle).

fugue fjūg (mus.) contrapuntal polyphonic composition. XVI (*fuge*). – F. *fugue* or its source It. *fuga* – L. *fuga* flight, rel. to *fugere* flee (cf. FUGITIVE). Hence **fu·gAL**[1]. XIX.

-ful[1] fəl, fl suffix appended to sbs., forming adjs. like corr. forms in other Germ. langs., orig. with the meaning 'full of', which still survives but has in many instances weakened to 'characterized by', 'fraught with', 'having', 'possessing the qualities or attributes of' what is denoted by the sb. OE. formations are repr. by *careful, harmful, lustful, mindful, rightful, shameful, sinful, sorrowful, wilful, wonderful*; many comps. of OE. origin did not survive, but new ones arose in abundance in ME. and later, as *awful, beautiful, blissful, delightful, dreadful, eventful, fearful, fruitful, gainful, hateful, lawful, manful, masterful, soulful, tearful, thoughtful, woeful, worshipful*; many have both subjective and objective meanings. There are a few OE. formations on adjs.: *deorcful* 'darkful', *slacful* lazy; similar ones of later date are *direful, fierceful*. Based on vb.-stems are *dareful* (Sh.), *mournful, resentful*, the implication being 'apt or inclined to . .'. Special cases are *bashful, forgetful, grateful, thankful*, qq.v.

-ful[2] ful suffix repr. the adj. FULL and forming sbs. denoting a receptacle filled with a substance, and hence the quantity that fills or would fill it. There are a few exx. in OE., the chief of which is HANDFUL (cf. Du. *hondvol*, G. *handvoll*). The suffix soon became of universal application and the number of its comps., permanent or temporary, is limited only by the number of appropriate sbs. OE. *handfull* was treated as a word, not as a syntactical combination, e.g. its d. pl. is *handfullum*. The present pl. is therefore properly *handfuls*, not *handsful* (as some have illogically supposed). Note the unobscured u of this suffix as dist. from -FUL[1]. ¶ The following are of different origin, being direct comps. of the adj. *full*: *bankful(l)* full to the top of the bank, *brimful* full to the brim (which was preceded by synon. OE. *brerdful*), †*topful*.

fulcrum fʌ·lkrəm prop, support, spec. in mech. XVII. – L. *fulcrum* post or foot of a couch, f. base **fulc-* of *fulcīre* support.

fulfil fulfi·l †fill up OE.; †furnish fully; satisfy, carry out XIII. Late OE. *fullfyllan* (once), f. *full* FULL + *fyllan* FILL; a formation peculiar to Eng. ¶ The sense 'carry out, consummate' (a prophecy, promise), 'satisfy' (a desire, prayer) is in origin a Hebraism, lit. tr. Vulgate L. *adimplēre, implēre*, Hellenistic Gr. *plēroûn* fill, used after Heb. *male* fill.

fulgent fʌ·ldʒənt (arch.) glittering. XV. – L. *fulgent-, -ēns*, prp. of *fulgēre* shine; see FLAME and -ENT. Cf. *refulgent*.

fuliginous fjūli·dʒinəs sooty. XVI (applied in old physiol. to certain thick exhalations). – late L. *fūlīginōsus*, f. *fūlīgin-*, nom. *fūlīgō* soot, prob. rel. to *fūmus* smoke, FUME; see -OUS and cf. F. *fuligineux* (*humeur fuligineuse*, Paré), perh. the immed. source.

full ful holding all one or it can; abundant, complete. OE. *full* = OFris. *foll, full*, OS. *ful* (Du. *vol*), OHG. *foll* (G. *voll*), ON. *fullr*, Goth. *fulls* :- CGerm. **fullaz* :- **fulnaz* :- IE. **pl̥nós*, whence also OIr. *lān*, Lith. *pìlnas*, OSl. *plŭnŭ*, Skr. *pūrṇás* – IE. **pol- *pel- *pl-* with the vars. **plē-, *plō-*, are repr. by an extensive series of words expressing fullness or abundance, as OE. *fela*, OHG. *filu* (G. *viel*), Gr. *polús*, Skr. *purús* many, abundant, L. *plēnus* (cf. PLENARY), *-plēre* fill, Arm. *li* full, Gr. *plērēs* full, *plêthos* multitude, *éplēto*, Skr. *áprāt, paprā* he filled.

fuller fu·ləɹ one who cleanses and thickens cloth by treading or beating. OE. *fullere* – L. *fullō*, with native suffix -ER[1]. The L. word (whence also F. *foulon*, It. *follone*) has been connected with a series of words meaning 'white, shining' (Gr. *phálios, phalērós*, Lith. *baltas*, OE. *bǣl* BALEFIRE). *Fuller's earth* (XVI); prob. after Du. *vollers-*

aarde; cf. G. *walkererde* (see WALKER²), F. *terre à foulon*. So **full** ful vb. XIV. prob. back-formation infl. by (O)F. *fouler* or medL. *fullāre*.

fulmar fu·lməɹ sea-bird Fulmarus glacialis. XVII. orig. a word of the Hebrides dial.; perh. f. ON. *fúll* FOUL (with ref. to the bird's offensive smell)+*már* gull, MEW¹.

fulminate fʌ·lmineit thunder forth; orig. a rendering of medL. *fulmināre*, used spec. of formal censure by eccl. authority. XV; also XV in pt. and pp. *fulminat(e)*; see -ATE³. f. pp. stem of L. *fulmināre*, f. *fulmin-*, *-men* lightning, cf. base of *fulgēre* (see FULGENT). So **fulmin**A·TION. XVI. – L.

fulsome fu·lsəm †abundant, plentiful XIII; †well-grown; †satiating, cloying; offensive XIV. f. FULL+-SOME¹; perh., but not necessarily, infl. by ME. *fūl* FOUL.

fulvous fʌ·lvəs reddish-yellow. XVII. f. L. *fulvus*+-OUS; the L. word contains the *w*-suffix characteristic of colour-names.

fumade fjūmei·d smoked pilchard. XVI. – Sp. *fumado*, pp. of *fumar* smoke; see FUME, -ADE. ¶ Corrupted in Cornwall to *fair maid*.

fumble fʌ·mbl speak haltingly; use the hands clumsily. XVI. – LG. *fummeln*, (also Du.) *fommelen*, whence Sw. *fumla*. Cf. *famble* (XV) of faltering utterance (so Sw., *famla*, Da. *famle*).

fume fjūm smoke, vapour (now restricted) XIV; fig., spec. of a fit of petulance XV (Lydg.). – (i) OF. *fum* = Pr., Rum. *fum*, Sp. *humo*, Pg., It. *fumo* :– L. *fūmu-s*; cf. Skr. *dhūmás*, OSl. *dymŭ*; (ii) OF. *fume*, f. *fumer* :– L. *fūmāre* smoke, whence **fume** vb. XIV or directly – L. So **fumigate** fjū·migeit apply smoke or fumes to. XVI. f. pp. stem of L. *fūmigāre*. **fumig**A·TION. XIV (Ch.). – (O)F. or late L. (repl. late L. *fūmigium*).

fumitory fjū·mĭtəri plant of the genus Fumaria. XIV (*fumeterre*, Ch.; *fumyterry*, *fumitorie*, *-arie* XVI). – (O)F. *fumeterre* = Pr. *fumterra* – medL. *fūmus terræ* 'smoke of the earth' (see FUME, TERRA), repr. also by Cat. *fumileterre*, Sp. *filomosterra*, It. *fumosterno*, and in translated form by G. *erdrauch*, Sw. *jordrök*; so named because its growth was supposed to resemble the spread of smoke over the ground: assim. to words in -ARY, -ORY (cf. PELLITORY).

fun fʌn †hoax, practical joke XVII; diversion, sport XVIII (Swift). f. †*fun* vb. hoax (XVII), prob. dial. var. of †*fon* make a fool of (see FOND). Hence **fu·nn**Y¹ comical XVIII; queer, odd XIX. ¶ Giving the definition 'sport, high merriment' Walker says: with great deference to Dr. Johnson, I think *Fun* ought rather to be styled *low merriment*.

funambulist fjunæ·mbjŭlist rope-dancer. XVIII (Evelyn, 1697, had †*funamble*, Bacon, 1605, †*funambulo*, and Sylvester, 1606, †*funambulant*; the L. form was current XVII). f. F. *funambule*, It., Sp. *funambulo*, or their source L. *fūnambulus*, f. *fūnis* rope+*ambulāre* walk; see FUNICULAR, AMBLE, -IST.

function fʌ·ŋkʃən action or activity proper to anything XVI; religious or other public ceremony (after It. *funzione*, Sp. *funcion*, Pg. *função*) XVII; (math.) variable quantity in relation to other variables XVIII (after Leibniz's use of L. *functiō*). – (O)F. *fonction* – L. *functiō(n-)*, f. *funct-*, *fungī* perform (cf. DEFUNCT, PERFUNCTORY); see -TION. Hence **fu·nction** vb. XIX; after F. *fonctionner*. **fu·nction**AL¹. XVII. **fu·nction**ARY¹. XVIII (Burke); after F. *fonctionnaire*, a coinage of the Revolution period, to replace terms of royalist flavour.

fund fʌnd A. †bottom, foundation, basis; B. source of supply; stock of money. XVII. refash. of *fond* after L. *fundus* BOTTOM, piece of land, farm, estate, which is the ult. source of F. *fond* bottom, basis, and *fonds* stock; Eng. *fond* and *fund* were used XVII indifferently in both these senses. Hence **fund** vb. XVIII.

fundament fʌ·ndəmənt foundation; buttocks, anus. XIII. ME. *funde-*, *fondement*, later *fund-*, *fondment* – (O)F. *fondement* :– L. *fundāmentum*, f. *fundāre* FOUND¹ (see -MENT); latinized forms (*fonda-*), antecedent to the present form, appear XIV. So **fundame·ntal**AL¹. XV. – F. *fondamental* (XV) or late L. *fundāmentālis*, whence **fundame·ntal**ISM, -IST *c.* 1920.

funebrial fjunī·briəl funereal, gloomy. XVII. f. L. *fūnebris*, f. *fūnus* FUNERAL; see -IAL.

funeral fjū·nərəl adj. pert. to burial XIV (Ch.); sb. burial ceremonies XVI; burial procession XVIII. The adj. is – OF. *funeral* – late L. *fūnerālis*, f. *fūner-*, nom. *fūnus* obsequies, death, corpse; the sb., of which, after F. use, sg. and pl. were formerly used indifferently, is – OF. *funeraille(s)* – medL. *fūnerālia*; see -AL¹. So **funer**EAL fjuniə·riəl pert. to a funeral, gloomy. XVIII (Pope). f. L. *fūnereus*, f. *fūner-*.

fungible fʌ·ndʒibl (leg.) that can serve for another (thing). XVIII. – medL. *fungibilis*, f. *fungī* perform, enjoy, with meaning as in *fungī vicē* take the place of; see -IBLE.

fungus fʌ·ŋgəs mushroom or the like XVI; spongy excrescence XVII. – L. *fungus*, commonly held to be – Gr. *sphóggos*, *spóggos* SPONGE. So **fu·ng**OUS. XV. – L. *fungōsus*. Cf. F. *fongus*, *fongueux* (XVI, Paré).

funicular fjuni·kjŭləɹ pert. to a hypothetical filament of rarefied matter assumed by Franciscus Linus (1661) XVII; depending on a rope or its tension XIX. f. L. *fūniculus*, dim. of *fūnis* rope+-AR.

funk fʌŋk cowering fear, panic. XVIII (first recorded by Lye as Oxford Univ. sl.). perh. identical with sl. *funk* tobacco smoke (cf. sl. *smoke* fear). So **funk** vb. show fear. XVIII (Horace Walpole, at Eton).

funnel fʌ·nl tube for conducting liquid, etc., into a small opening xv; ventilating shaft xvi. Late ME. *fonel* (prob. orig. a term of the wine trade with the South of France) – Pr. *fonilh*, also *enfonilh* (whence Sp. *fonil*, Pg. *funil*, Breton *founil*, Basque *unila*) :– L. *infundibulum*, (late) *fundibulum*, f. *(in)fundere* pour (in); see FOUND[2].

funny[1] fʌ·ni light boat. xviii (at Cambridge), perh. joc. use of next.

funny[2] see FUN.

fur fɜ̄ɹ (trimming of a garment made from) the hairy coat of certain animals. xiv (Ch., Trevisa). f. **fur** vb. line or trim with fur. xiii; cover, become covered, with a coating (whence a new sb. xix) xvii. – AN. *_furrer_, OF. *forrer* (mod. *fourrer*) line, encase, sheathe (whence Sp., Pg. *forrar*), f. OF. *forre*, *fuerre* – Germ. *_fōðram_ sheath (OE. *fōddor*, OHG. *fuotar*, G. *futter*, ON. *fóðr*, Goth. *fodr*), f. IE. *_pō-_ protect. Hence **furry**[1] fɜ̄·ri. xvii (Milton, Dryden).

furbelow fɜ̄·ɹbəlou pleated border; pl. showy trimming. xviii. Alteration of synon. and contemp. *falbala* – F. *falbala* (xvii), of unkn. origin. ¶ There are similar forms in modPr. and It. dial.

furbish fɜ̄·ɹbiʃ remove rust from, brighten *up*. xiv (Wyclif). – OF. *forbiss-*, lengthened stem (see -ISH[2]) of *forbir* (mod. *fourbir*) = Pr. *forbir*, It. *forbire* – Germ. *_furƀjan_ (OHG. *furben*, MHG. *vürben*).

furcate fɜ̄·ɹkeit forked. xix. – late L. *furcātus*, f. *furca* FORK; see -ATE[2]. So **furca·tion**. xvii (Sir T. Browne).

furious see FURY.

furison fjuə·rizən (now her.) steel used for striking fire from a flint. xvi (*furisine*, Bellenden). – MDu. *vuurijzen*, f. *vuur* FIRE + *ijzen* IRON. In mod. Sc. obscurely altered to *flourice*, *flourish*, *fleurish*, *fleerish*; another obscure var. is *ferris* (xvii).

furl fɜ̄ɹl roll up (a sail, flag, etc.). xvi. – (O)F. *ferler*, earlier *ferlier*, *fermlier*, f. *fer(m)* FIRM + *lier* bind (:– L. *ligāre*; cf. LIGAMENT), the change of *-lier* to *-ler* following the general reduction of inf. *-ier* to *-er*. ¶ By contamination with FARDEL bundle, altered to *fardel*, *furdle* xvi–xvii.

furlong fɜ̄·ɹlɔŋ ⅛ mile. OE. *furlang*, f. *furh* FURROW + *lang* LONG[1]; orig. the length of the furrow in the common field, which was theoretically a 10-acre square.

furlough fɜ̄·ɹlou leave of absence from duty. xvii (*vorloffe*, *fore-loofe*, *furlogh*). – Du. *verlof*, modelled on G. *verlaub*, f. *ver-* FOR-[1] + *_lauƀ-_ LEAVE[1]; Sw. *förlof*, Da. *forlov* are also from Du. The stress on the first syll. seems to show infl. of synon. Du. *oorlof* = G. *urlaub*, abstr. sb. of *erlauben* permit.

furmety see FRUMENTY.

furnace fɜ̄·ɹnis chamber for combustibles to produce intense heat. xiii. – OF. *fornais* m. (= Pr. *fornatz*, Cat. *fornas*, It. *fornace*) and *fornaise* fem. (mod. *fournaise* = Sp. *hornaza*, Pg. *fornaça*) :– L. *fornācem*, *fornāx* and popL. *_fornātia_, f. L. *fornus*, *furnus* oven, rel. to *formus* WARM.

furnish fɜ̄·ɹniʃ †accomplish; supply, provide xv. – OF. *furniss-*, lengthened stem (see -ISH[2]) of *furnir* (mod. *fournir*; whence Pr., Sp., Pg. *fornir*, It. *fornire*) :– CRom. *_fornīre_, alteration of *_formīre_, *_fromīre_ (cf. Pr. *fromir*, *formir*, It. †*frommiare*) – Germ. *_frumjan_ (OS. *frummian*, OHG. *frummen*) promote, accomplish, supply, f. *_frum-_, for the connexions of which see FRAME, FROM, FORMER. So **furniture** fɜ̄·ɹnitʃəɹ †action of furnishing; provision, equipment (with various applications, some obs.); the sense 'movable articles in a room, etc.' is peculiarly Eng. xvi. – F. *fourniture* (OF. *forneture*, AL. *furnitūra*), f. *fournir*.

furore fjurɔ̄·ri enthusiastic admiration. xix (Carlyle). – It. :– L. *furōrem*, nom. *furor*, f. *furere* rage. ¶ L. *furor* was formerly common in Eng. use in this sense (xviii, Swift) as well as in those of 'fury, mania' (xv, *furour*, Caxton, – F. *fureur*), and 'inspired frenzy' (xvi).

furrier fʌ·riəɹ dresser of or dealer in furs. xvi. Alteration, after *clothier*, etc., of ME. *furour* – OF. *forreor* (mod. *fourreur*), f. *forrer* trim with FUR. Hence **fu·rriery**[3]. xviii.

furrow fʌ·rou narrow trench made in the earth. OE. *furh* = OFris. *furch*, MLG., MDu. *vore* (Du. *voor*), OHG. *furuh* (G. *furche*), ON. *for* trench, drain; techn. term of agric. of IE. extent; Germ. base *_furχ-_ :– IE. *_pṛk-_ (L. *porca* ridge between furrows, MIr. *rech*, W. *rhych* furrow, Lith. *pra|paršas* trench, Arm. *herk* fallowland, Skr. *párçānas* cleft). Cf. FURLONG.

further fɜ̄·ɹðəɹ to or at a more advanced point OE.; in addition xii (amplified to *furthermore* xiii); at a greater distance xiv. OE. *furþor*, *-ur*, corr. to OFris. *further*, OS. *furðor* (early modDu. *voorder*), OHG. *furdar*, *-ir*, f. Germ. *_furþ-_ FORTH + compar. suffix (see -ER[3]).

furtive fɜ̄·ɹtiv stealthy. xv (Caxton; rare before xvii). – (O)F. *furtif*, *-ive* or L. *furtīvus*, *-īva*, f. *furt-* in *furtum* theft, *furtim* by stealth, rel. to *fūr* thief = Gr. *phṓr*, f. IE. *_bhŏr-_ *_bher-_ BEAR[2]; see -IVE.

furuncle fjuə·rʌŋkl boil, inflamed tumour. xvii (*froncle* – OF. *froncle* occurs xvi). – L. *fūrunculus* petty thief, knob on a vine ('stealing' the sap), boil, dim. of *fūr* (see prec.).

fury fjuə·ri fierce passion or violence; (*F-*) avenging deity. xiv (Ch.). – (O)F. *furie* = Sp., It. *furia* – L. *furia*, f. *furiōsus*, f. *furere* rage. So **fu·rious**. xiv (Ch.). – OF. *furieus* (mod. *-eux*) – L. *furiōsus*. **furio·sity**. xv (spec. madness, in Sc. law). – OF. or medL.

furze fəːz the shrub Ulex europæus. OE. *fyrs*, of uncertain origin (Gr. *práson*, L. *porrum* leek, corr. formally, but have no connexion of meaning). A pl. form in *-en* which appears XIII survived in S.W. and W. midl. dial.; from the form *furres* taken as pl. a new sg. *fur* was formed XV (Norfolk) and survived in the east midlands. The pronunc. with final z arises from obl. forms, e.g. OE. *fyrsas*, ME. *firses*.

fuscous fʌ·skəs dusky. XVII. f. L. *fuscus* (see DUSK) + -OUS. Cf. SUBFUSC.

fuse[1], **fuze** fjūz cord, casing, etc., fitted with combustible material for igniting explosive. XVII. – It. *fuso* :– L. *fūsu-s* spindle, (hence) spindle-shaped tube orig. used for a bomb, etc.

fuse[2] fjūz melt with intense heat. XVII. f. *fūs-*, pp. stem of L. *fundere* pour, melt, FOUND[2]. So **fu·**SIBLE capable of fusion. XIV (Ch.; readopted XVII). – medL. *fūsibilis*. **fu·**SILE. XIV (Trevisa). – L. *fūsilis*.

fusee fjūzī· †spindle-shaped figure XVI (once); conical pulley XVII; fuse XVIII; match with a large head XIX. – F. *fusée* – popL. **fūsāta* 'spindle-ful', f. L. *fūsus* spindle, FUSE[1].

fusel fjū·zəl *f. oil*, mixture of certain alcohols. XIX. – G. *fusel* bad brandy or other spirits, a LG. word applied also to bad coffee and tobacco; cf. FOOZLE.

fuselage fjū·zilāʒ, -idʒ body of an aeroplane. XX. – F., f. *fuseler* shape like a spindle, f. *fuseau* spindle; see FUSIL[1], -AGE.

fusil[1] fjū·zil (her.) elongated lozenge (orig. representing a spindle covered with tow). XV. – OF. *fusel* (mod. *fuseau*) :– Rom. **fūsellu-s*, dim. of L. *fūsus* spindle; see FUSE[1]. So **fu·silly.** XV (*fesele*). – OF. *fuselé*; see -Y[5] b. **fu·si**FORM. XVIII. – F.

fusil[2] fjūzil †steel for a tinder-box XVI; light musket XVII. – (O)F. *fusil* = It. *fucile*, *focile*, Pr. *fozil* :– popL. **focīle*, f. *focus* (in popL.) fire; see FOCUS. So **fusil**IE·R[2] orig. soldier armed with a fusil. XVII. – F. *fusilier*. **fusill**A·DE discharge of fire-arms. XIX. – F. *fusillade* (1796), f. *fusiller* shoot.

fusion fjū·ʒən melting XVI; union as if by melting. XVIII. – F. *fusion* or L. *fūsiō(n-)*, f. *fūs-*, pp. stem of *fundere* pour; see FOUND[2], -SION. Cf. FOISON.

fuss fʌs excessive commotion, officious activity, needless concern. XVIII (Farquhar, Vanbrugh, Swift). perh. Anglo-Ir., but of unkn. origin. ¶ An attempt to derive it from FORCE (through an assumed local pronunc. fūrs) in the idiomatic phr. *make no force* (XIV–XVI) 'take no account (of)', 'attach no importance (to)', leaves out of account the discrepancy of the date of the currency of this phr. and of the first evidence (1701) for *fuss*, as well as the difference of sense, and the form of the early phr. *keep a fuss* (Swift, 1726).

fustanella fʌstəne·lə white petticoat worn by men as part of the native dress in Greece. XIX, It., f. modGr. *phoústani*, Alb. *fustan*, prob. – It. *fustagno* FUSTIAN.

fustian fʌ·stiən †coarse cloth; thick twilled cotton cloth. XII (*fustane* or *-i*) as adj. fig. bombastic, pretentious XVI. – OF. *fustaigne* (mod. *futaine*), corr. to Pr. *fustani*, Sp. *fustan*, Pg. *fustão*, It. *f(r)ustagno*, repr. medL. (*tēla*) *fustānea*, (*pannus*) *fustāneus*, i.e. cloth of *Fostat*, suburb of Cairo, from which such cloth was exported.

fustic fʌ·stik wood of the sumach, Rhus Cotinus. XV. – F. *fustoc* – Sp. *fustoc* – Arab. *fustuq* – Gr. *pistákē* PISTACHIO. The ending has been assim. to -IC.

fustigate fʌ·stigeit (joc.) cudgel. XVII. f. pp. stem of late L. *fūstigāre*, f. *fūstis* cudgel; see -ATE[3]. So **fustig**A·TION. XVI. – L.

fusty fʌ·sti stale-smelling (of a vessel) XIV (Trevisa), (of bread, etc.) XV (Caxton); also gen. and fig. XVI. – OF. *fusté*, f. *fust* trunk of a tree, barrel = Pr. *fust* stick, barrel, boat, It. *fusto* trunk :– L. *fusti-s* club, stake.

futhork, -ark, fū·þɔ̄ɹk, -ā- Runic alphabet. XIX. Name made up of its first six letters *f*, *u*, *þ*, *ǫ* or *a*, *r*, *k*.

fut fʌt var. of PHUT.

futile fjū·tail ineffectual, useless. XVI. – L. *fūtilis*, better *futtilis*, of which the etymol. meaning is 'that pours out' (hence *futtile*, n. used sb. kind of pitcher; cf. synon. *fūtis*), f. **fud-*, base of *fundere* pour (see FOUND[2]); see -ILE and cf. F. *futile*. So **futil**ITY fjuti·liti. XVII. – F. or L.

futtock fʌ·tək (naut.) one of the middle timbers of the frame of a ship. XIII. ME. (pl.) *votekes*, *futtokes*, *foteken*; of unkn. origin, no evidence is available for deriv. from -OCK.

future fjū·tʃəɹ that is or was to be. XIV (Ch.). – (O)F. *futur-e* – L. *futūru-s*, *-a*, fut. pple. of *esse*, f. **fu-*; see BE. Hence **fu·tur**ISM belief that biblical prophecies are still to be fulfilled XIX; in art use (XX) – F. – It. So **futuri**·TION future occurrence or existence. XVII. – medL. *futūritiō(n-)*, used by St. Bonaventura in discussions of God's foreknowledge; an irreg. formation; cf. F. *futurition* (Fénelon). **futur**ITY fjutʃuə·rìti. XVII (Sh.).

fuze see FUSE[1].

fuzzy fʌ·zi spongy XVII; fluffy XVIII. prob. of Low Du. origin; cf. Du. *voos* spongy, 'rarus & leuis instar fungi' (Kilian), LG. *fussig* spongy (cf. synon. Sc. *fozy* XIX); see -Y[1]. So or hence **fuzz** loose, volatile matter XVII, **fuzz-ball** fungus Lycoperdon Bovista, puff-ball XVI (Gerarde).

Fuzzy-Wuzzy fʌ·ziwʌ:zi soldier's name for a Sudanese warrior, in allusion to his manner of dressing his hair. XIX (Kipling). Jingling formation on prec.

-fy fai suffix forming vbs., the oldest of which were adoptions of F. vbs. in *-fier*, derived from L. vbs. in *-ficāre*, *-ārī* (orig. f. adjs. in *-ficus* -FIC) or modelled on these. The L. vbs. fall into three classes according to the force of the suffix, viz. (i) 'make', 'convert into something', as *ædificāre* EDIFY, *deificāre* DEIFY, *pācificāre* PACIFY, *testificāre* TESTIFY, (ii) 'bring into a certain state', as *certificāre* (late) CERTIFY, *modificāre* MODIFY, *sanctificāre* SANCTIFY (OF. *saintefier*), (iii) with causative sense, as *horrificāre* HORRIFY. In medL. *-ficāre* was substituted for *-facere*, so that F. and Eng. words in *-fier*, *-fy* often corr. to L. vbs. in *-facere*, e.g. *satisfier* SATISFY, *stupéfier* STUPEFY (but in pp. *stupéfait*, beside *stupéfié*). Except in these vbs. and *calefy*, *liquefy*, *putrefy*, *rarefy*, *rubefy*, the suffix normally takes the form -IFY, which has been consequently generalized for new formations (e.g. *codify* c. 1800, *indemnify* XVII) and has been freely used (esp. for trivial and joc. coinages), with the senses: 'make a specified thing', as *speechify*; 'assimilate to the character of something', as *countrify*, *fishify* (chiefly in pp.); 'invest with certain attributes', as *Frenchify*, *happify*. An early ex. is *beautify*, but the analogy on which it is formed is not clear; *crucify* is a special case and *argufy* is unique.

The nouns of action corr. to vbs. in *-ify* end in *-ification*, exc. *petrifaction*, where F. has regularly *pétrification*; those corr. to vbs. in *-efy* end in *-faction*, as *rarefaction*, *stupefaction*.

fylfot fi·lfɔt antiquary's term for the cross cramponnee, swastika, or gammadion, derived from a solitary ex. in British Museum MS. Lansdowne 874, f. 190, the context of which suggests the interpretation 'fill-foot', i.e. a device for filling the foot of a painted window.

G

gab gæb (colloq.) talking, talk. XVIII. var. of dial. *gob* (XVII; *gift of the gob*), prob. a use of north. dial. and sl. *gob* mouth (XVI), which has a var. *gab* (XVIII.) poss. – Gael., Ir. *gob* beak, mouth. ¶ Historically distinct from †*gab* mockery, deceit, idle vaunt, vb. mock, scoff, lie, boast (XIII) – OF. *gab*, *gaber*.

gabble gæ·bl talk volubly XVI (Stanyhurst, Nashe); (of geese) gaggle XVII (Dryden). – MDu. *gabbelen*, of imit. origin. Cf. prec.

gabbro gæ·brou (min.) rock composed of felspar and diallage. XIX. It. (Tuscan) :- L. *glaber*, *-brum* smooth (see GLAD).

gabelle gəbe·l tax, esp. salt-tax. XV. – F. *gabelle* – It. *gabella*, corr. to Sp. *alcabala*, Pg. *alcavala* – Arab. *alqabāla*, i.e. *al* AL-², *qabāla* tribute.

gaberdine gæbəɹdī·n loose upper garment. XVI. Earliest form *gawbardine* – OF. *gauvardine*, *gallevardine* (whence It. *gavardina*), perh. f. MHG. *wallevart* pilgrimage (cf. *pelerine* for the sense); Sp. *gabardina* is closest to the present form, which is used by Sh. ¶ In the form *gabardine* adopted as the name of a dress material XX.

gabion gei·biən (fortif.) wicker basket filled with earth. XVI. – F. *gabion* – It. *gabbione*, augm. of *gabbia* CAGE.

gable gei·bl triangular piece of wall at end of a ridged roof. XIV (*gavel*, *gable*). orig. of twofold origin, – (i) ON. *gafl* and (ii) OF. *gable*, itself prob. – the ON. word; the corr. words in the other Germ. langs. mean 'fork' (OE. *ġeafol*, OHG. *gabala*, G. *gabel*, etc.), the words for 'gable' showing another vowel-grade, e.g. MDu. *ghevel*, OHG. *gibil* (G. *giebel*), Goth. *gibla*; perh. to be referred to IE. **ghebhalā*, whence Gr. *kephalḗ* head.

gaby gei·bi (colloq.) simpleton. XVIII. dial. and sl. in origin; a similar syn. is dial. *gaups*; the suffix is -Y⁶.

gad¹ gæd †metal spike or bar; goad XIII; rod XV. – ON. *gaddr* goad, spike, sting = OHG. *gart*, Goth. *gazds* :- Germ. **gazdaz* (cf. YARD²), rel. to L. *hasta* spear :- **ghastā*. Hence **ga·d-**FLY fly (genus Tabanus or Œstrus) that bites and goads cattle. XVI.

gad² gæd go idly from place to place. XV. prob. back-formation from †*gadling* companion, fellow, low fellow, (later) wanderer, vagabond, OE. *gædeling* (cf. *gæd* fellowship, *ġegada* companion, rel. to GATHER).

gad³ gæd minced pronunc. of GOD in oaths esp. (*by*) *gad!*; cf. BEGAD, EGAD. XVII (*kad* in Sir Hugh Evans's speech in Sh. 'Merry Wives', 1602; *by gads lid*, B. Jonson, 1616). Also †*ged* (XVII–XVIII). Cf. GADZOOKS.

gadget gæ·dʒit (mechanical) contrivance. XIX. orig. a seaman's term; source unkn. but cf. F. *gâchette* catch of a lock, trigger, dim. of *gâche* staple, hook, and dial. F. *gagée* tool; see -ET.

Gadhelic gəde·lik Gaelic (non-Scottish). XVIII (*Gaedhlic*). f. Ir. *Gaedheal*, pl. *Gaedhil*, (OIr. *Góidel*; see GOIDELIC).

gadoid gei·doid pert. to the Gadidæ (codfishes). XIX. f. modL. *gadus* (– Gr. *gádos*) + -OID.

gadroon gədrū·n one of a set of curved lines used in decoration. XVIII. – F. *godron*, prob. rel. to *goder* pucker, crease; see -OON.

gadzooks gædzu·ks (arch.) mild expletive. XVII. perh. for *God's hooks*, i.e. God's nails, scil. of Christ crucified; see GAD³. Also †*gad-*, †*godso(o)kers* (XVII), †*gadswookers*, †*gods sokinges* (XVI).

gaekwar, also **gaikwar, guicower** ga·ekwōɹ native ruler of Baroda, India. XIX. Marathi *gāekwar*, lit. cowherd.

Gael geil Celtic native of the Scottish Highlands. XIX. – Sc. Gaelic *Gaidheal* gai·əl, corr. to Ir. *Gaoidheal*. Hence **Gael**IC gei·lik, gai·əlik, gæ·lik. XVIII; in this dictionary applied to the Celtic language of Scotland. ¶ Dalrymple in his tr. of J. Leslie's History of Scotland, 1596, has *Gathel, Gathelik*.

gaff[1] gæf hook XIII; fishing-spear XVII; steel spur XVIII. – Pr. *gaf*, whence F. *gaffe*, Sp., Pg. *gafa*. comb. **gaff-to·psail**; cf. Norw. *gaff(el)toppseil*, Sw. *gaffeltoppsegel*.

gaff[2] gæf (sl.) secret, in phr. *blow the gaff*. XIX (Vaux). Of unkn. origin.

gaffe gæf (sl.) indiscreet act, faux pas. XIX. – F. *gaffe*, f. *gaffer* – Pr. *gafar* seize, of Germ. origin.

gaffer gæ·fəɹ rustic title for an old or elderly man, 'governor'. XVI. f. contracted form ga·fəðə (resulting from loss of stress) of GODFATHER; cf. GAMMER and synon. F. *compère, commère*, G. *gevatter* gossip.

gag[1] gæg †suffocate, choke XV (Promp. Parv.); stop the mouth of XVI. perh. imit. of the sound made by a choking person, though a poss. Scand. origin may be seen in ON. *gagháls* with the neck thrown back. Hence **gag** sb. XVI.

gag[2] gæg (sl.) impose upon. XVIII (Mme D'Arblay). perh. fig. use of prec. with the notion of thrusting something 'down the throat' of a credulous person. Hence **gag** sb. imposture. XIX. ¶ The connexion of the theatrical *gag* (interpolated expression XIX) is doubtful.

gaga gæ·ga (sl.) daft, half-witted. XX. F., imit. of the enfeebled utterance of extreme old age.

gage[1] geidʒ pledge, security. XIV. – (O)F. *gage* = Pr. *gatge* :– Rom. **gwadjo* – Germ. **waðjam* WED. Cf. WAGE. So **gage** vb. †pledge, pawn; †stake, wager. XVI. – (O)F. *gager* or aphetic of ENGAGE.

gage[2] see GREENGAGE.

gage[3] var. of GAUGE.

gaggle gæ·gl (of geese) cackle. XIV. imit.; cf. MHG. *gāgen, gāgern* cry like a goose; Du. *gaggelen* gabble; ON. *gagl* gosling; and OHG. *gackizōn, gackazzen* (G. *gacksen* cackle). Hence sb. flock (of geese). XV. Cf. -LE[3].

gaiety, gaily see GAY.

gain gein †booty; profit, emolument. XIII. – (O)F. *gain* m., *gaigne* fem. (mod. *gagne*), f. OF. *gaigner* (mod. *gagner*), whence **gain** vb. XIII. – OF. *gaaignier* = Pr. *gazanhar*, Sp. *guadañar* (mow), Pg. *ganhar*, It. *guadagnare* :– Rom. **gwadanjāre* – Germ. **waiþanjan* (OHG. *weidenen* graze, pasture, forage, hunt, fish), f. **waiþō* (OHG. *weida* fodder, pasture, hunting, OE. *wāþ*, ON. *veiðr* hunting); the Rom. words were used in a twofold sense, (i) cultivate land, (ii) win, earn. Hence **gai·n**FUL[1]. XVI.

gainsay geinsei·, pt. *gainsaid* -seid (slightly arch.) deny, contradict. XIII (Cursor M.). f. *gain-*, formerly a common prefix meaning 'against', 'in opposition' (see AGAIN)+SAY[1]; prob. modelled on ON. *gagnmæli* gainsaying; cf. also (O)F. *contredire* CONTRADICT.

gait geit manner of walking. XVI. A particular use of GATE[2], which is otherwise obs. in gen. use; the sp. was established XVIII.

gaiter gei·təɹ outer covering for the ankle or lower leg. XVIII. – F. *guêtre*, †*guietre*, †*guestre* (XV), perh. (in spite of the lateness of date) repr. **wistr-*, metathetic form of Germ. **wirst-* (OHG. **wrist*, G. *rist* ankle) WRIST.

gala gei·lə festive attire XVII; †festivity, gaiety XVIII; festive occasion XIX. – F. *gala* or its source It. *gala* – Sp. *gala* – Arab. *khilʿa* presentation garment.

galacto- gəlæ·ktou comb. form of Gr. *gála*, *galakt-* milk, rel. obscurely to L. *lac* (see LACT-). XVII.

galantine gæ·ləntīn †sauce for fish and fowl XIV (Ch.); jellied meat XVIII. – F. *galantine*, alteration of *galatine* – medL. *galatina*.

galanty gəlæ·nti *galanty show* pantomime of shadows thrown on a screen. XIX. perh. – It. *galanti*, pl. of *galante* GALLANT.

galatea gælətī·ə blue-and-white cotton material (used for children's sailor suits). XIX. f. name of H.M.S. *Galatea*, commanded by the Duke of Edinburgh in 1867.

galaxy gæ·ləksi the Milky Way XIV (Ch.); brilliant assemblage, esp. of women XVII. – (O)F. *galaxie* – medL. *galaxia*, late L. *galaxias* – Gr. *galaxías* (sc. *kúklos* cycle), f. *galakt-*, *gála* MILK; see -Y[3]. ¶ The L. forms were in Eng. use XIV–XVII.

galbanum gæ·lbənəm gum resin from species of Ferula. XIV (Wycl. Bible). – L. – Gr. *khalbánē*, of Sem. origin (cf. Heb. *ḥelbᵉnāh*). Anglicized †*galban(e)* OE.–XVI.

gale[1] geil bog myrtle, Myrica Gale. OE. *gaġel, gaġelle* = MDu. *gaghel*, Du., G. *gagel*; normally repr. by *gaul* (XV–XVII), *gall* (XVI–XIX); the present form is unexpl.; the modL. specific name is from Eng.

gale[2] geil strong wind. XVI. Of unkn. origin; perh. orig. *gale wind*, in which *gale* is an adj.; perh., in spite of the late date, was of Scand. origin, and to be connected with MSw., Norw. *galen* bad (of weather), ON. *galenn* mad, frantic. ¶ It is difficult to connect the similar (O)F. *galerne* westerly wind.

gale[3] geil (Anglo-Ir.) periodical payment of rent XVII; (in the Forest of Dean) freeminer's royalty XVIII. contr. of GAVEL.

galeated gæ·lieitid helmet-shaped; helmeted. XVII. f. L. *galeātus*, f. *galea* helmet +-ED[1]. Also **ga·le**ATE[2]. XVIII.

galeeny gəlī·ni guinea-fowl. XVIII (*galina*). – Sp. *gallina* (*morisca*) '(Moorish) hen' (so in Pg. and It.) – L. *gallīna* (see GALLINACEOUS); the ending assim. to -Y.

Galen gei·lĭn name of a celebrated physician (II A.D.), of Pergamus in Asia Minor; (hence, allusively) physician, doctor. XVI. – L. *Galēnus* (in medL. also *Galiēnus*, whence †*Galien* Ch., Sh.) – Gr. *Galēnós*. Hence **galen**IC(AL) gəle·nik(əl) pert. to Galen, his followers, and his practice, esp. in the use of vegetable medicines XVII; also, pert. to the fourth figure of the syllogism, which was added by him XVIII. **Ga·len**IST 'herb doctor'. XVI (Nashe).

galena gəlī·nə lead ore. XVII. – L. *galena* lead at a certain stage of smelting (Pliny).

galilee gæ·lĭlī porch or chapel at the entrance of a church. XV. – OF. *galilée* – medL. *galilæa*, the proper name (Gr. *Galilaîā*) of a province of Palestine, perh. used in allusion to it as being an outlying portion of the Holy Land; first recorded of Durham cathedral, and taken up thence by antiquarian writers of XIX.

galimatias gælimæ·tiəs, -ei·ʃⁱəs meaningless language. XVII (Urquhart). – F. *galimatias* (Montaigne), of unkn. origin, poss. containing Gr. *-mathía* learning.

galingale gæ·liŋgeil E. Indian aromatic root XIII; also, kind of sedge XVI. – OF. *galingal* – (prob. through Arab. *khalanjān, khaulinjān*, Pers. *khūlanjān*) Chinese *ko liang kiang* 'mild ginger of Ko' (a district of Canton). ¶ Many vars. exist, e.g. medL., medGr., It. *galanga* (F. *galangue*), Du., G. *galgant*; medL. *gallingar*, whence in OE. *gallengar*; Pr., Sp. *garengal*.

gall[1] gōl bile; bitterness. XII (Orm). – ON. *gall* n., corr., with variety of gender, to OE. *ġealla* (surviving in early ME. *ȝalle*), OS. *galla* (Du. *gal*), OHG. *galla* (G. *galle*) :– CGerm. (exc. Gothic) **gallam*, **gallon*, *-ōn*, based on **gholno-*, f. **ghol-* **ghel-*, which is repr. by Gr. *kholḗ, khólos* (see CHOLERIC), L. *fel* bile; cf. YELLOW.

gall[2] gōl swelling, pustule XIV (Ch., *If any wight wol clawe vs on the galle*); bare spot XVI. – MLG., MDu. *galle* (Du. *gal*), corr. to OE. *ġealla* sore on a horse, (M)HG. *galle*, ON *galli* (MSw. *galle*) fault, flaw, perh. identical with prec. GALL[1], the progress of sense being 'bile', 'venom', 'envenomed sore', 'blemish'. (In the Rom. langs. the forms repr. by GALL[3] were used for swelling on a horse's fetlock. Hence **galled** gōld sore from chafing XIV (cf. OE. *ġeallede*); whence **gall** vb. chafe, fret XIV; cf. OF. *galler* scratch, rub.

gall[3] gōl excrescence growing on the oak, etc. XIV. – (O)F. *galle* = It. *gala*, Sp. *galla* L. *galla* (Pliny) oak-apple, gall-nut.

gallant in A and sb., gæ·lənt; in B, gəlæ·nt A. †adj. gorgeous, splendid XV (Lydg.); †fine, stately XVI; chivalrously brave XVI (Sh.); B. attentive to women; amatory XVII (Dryden); sb. (fine) gentleman XIV; lady's man XV. – (O)F. *galant* (whence Sp. *galante*, *galan*, *galano*, It. *galante*), prp. of *galer* make merry, make a show, f. *gale* merrymaking, rejoicing (cf. GALA). Hence **ga·llant**RY. XVII (Sh.). ¶ Has become CEur.

galleon gæ·liən large ship. XVI (*gailȝeown*, Lyndesay). – MDu. *galjoen* – (O)F. *galion*, augm. of *galie* GALLEY or – Sp. *galeon*.

gallery gæ·ləri †covered walk, portico, colonnade XV (Lydg.); long balcony; apartment for the exhibition of works of art XVI (Sh.). – (O)F. *galerie* – It. *galleria* gallery, †church porch – medL. *galeria* (IX), perh. alteration of *galilea* GALILEE by dissim. of *l* . . *l* to *l* . . *r*.

galley gæ·li low flat-built sea-going vessel XIII; large open rowing-boat XVI; ship's kitchen XVIII. – OF. *galie* (mod. *galée*), corr. to Pr. *gale(y)a*, Sp. †*galea*, Pg. *galé*, It. *galea*, †*galia* – medL. *galea* (IX), medGr. *galaîa*, of unkn. origin, but rel. to F. *galère*, Pr., Sp. *galera*, It. *galera*, and medL. *galeida*, MDu., MHG. *galeide*, ON. *galeið*.

galliambic gæliæ·mbik kind of lyric metre, exemplified by Catullus 63. XIX. – L. *galliambus* song of the *Gallī* or priests of Cybele, + -IC; see IAMBIC.

galliard gæ·liəɹd †valiant; (arch.) lively, gay. XIV. – (O)F. *gaillard* = Pr. *galhart* (whence Sp. *gallardo*, It. *gagliardo*), perh. f. Rom. **gallia* strength, power, of Celtic origin (cf. Ir. *gal*, W. *gallu* be able, valour, prowess); see -ARD. As the name of a lively dance (XVI) – F. *gaillarde*, sb. use of fem. adj.

galliass, galleass gæ·liæs (hist.) heavy vessel larger than a galley. XVI. – OF. *gal(l)easse* (mod. *galéace*) – It. *galeaza*, augm. of *galea* GALLEY.

gallic gæ·lik (chem.) name of a crystalline acid occurring in gall-nuts and the tannins. XVIII. – F. *gallique*, f. *galle* GALL[3]; see -IC.

Gallic gæ·lik Gaulish, French. XVII. – L. *Gallicus*, f. *Gallus*, *Gallia* GAUL. So **Ga·llican**. XVI. – F. *gallican*, †(1) French, (2) pert. to the Church of France, or L. *Gallicānus*, f. *Gallicus*. **Ga·llic**ISM. XVII. – F. *gallicisme* (H. Estienne). See -IC, -AN.

galligaskins gæligæ·skinz (arch.) wide hose or breeches XVI; (dial.) leggings XIX. Early forms *gallogascaine*, *galeygascoyne*, *galigascon* (Holinshed, Harrison); preceded by or contemp. with *gally slopes* (Harman), *breeches*, *hose*, and *gaskin* (*gai gallant gaskins*, G. Harvey), *gascoigne hose*; a var. *garragascoyne*, unless a perversion of one of these forms, may point to ult. deriv. from F. †*garguesque*, var. of †*greguesque* – It. *grechesca*, sb. use of fem. of *grechesco*, f. *greco* GREEK (cf. Sp. *gregüescos* wide breeches, and F. *grêgue* – Pr. *grega*); there has been blending with GASCON, but the origin of *galli-* remains unkn.

gallimaufry gælimɔ̄·fri hodge-podge, jumble. XVI. – F. *galimafrée* (OF. *calimafrée*), of unkn. origin.

gallinaceous gælinei·ʃəs pert. to the Gallinæ (domestic poultry, etc.). XVIII. f. L. *gallīnāceus*, f. *gallīna* hen, f. *gallus* cock; see -ACEOUS.

gallinazo gælinā·zou American vulture. XVIII. – Sp. *gallinazo*, augm. of *gallina* hen (see prec.).

gal(l)iot gæ·liət small galley. XIV. – (O)F. *galiote* – It. *galeotta*, dim. of medL. *galea* GALLEY.

gallipot gæ·lipɔt small earthen pot. XV (*gal(e)y pott*). prob. f. GALLEY+POT, as orig. denoting pottery brought in galleys, i.e. from the Mediterranean; cf. Du. *gleipot* (for **galeipot*), *kraakgoed*, *kraakporselein* (orig.) porcelain imported in carracks; also †*galley-halfpenny* (XV) silver coin said to have been introduced in Genoese and other galleys trading to London.

gallium gæ·liəm (chem.) metallic element. XIX. modL. *gallium*, said to be f. L. *gallus* cock, tr. the name of its discoverer, *Lecoq* de Boisbaudran; see -IUM.

gallivant gælivæ·nt, gæ·livænt (colloq.) gad about. XIX. perh. fantastic alteration of *gallant* vb. as used locally; the form suggests blending with LEVANT.

galliwasp gæ·liwɔsp small West Indian lizard. XVIII (Sloane). Of unkn. origin.

ga·llo-, used as comb. form (see -O-) of GALLIC, as in *gallo*NITRATE, *gallo*TANNIC.

Gallo- gæ·lou used as comb. form (see -O-) of L. *Gallus* GAUL.

galloglass gæ·louglàs (hist.) retainer of an Irish chief. XVI. – Ir., Gael. *galló́glach*, f. *gall* foreigner+*óglach* youth, servant, warrior, f. *óg* YOUNG+-*lach*, abstr. suffix. The current form is prob. deduced from pl. *gallogla(gh)s*.

gallon gæ·lən measure of capacity (4 quarts). XIII. – ONF. *galon*, var. of *jalon* :- Rom. **gallone*, f. base of medL. *gallēta* (whence OF. *jaloie* liquid measure), *gallētum* (whence OE. *ġellet* dish, basin, OHG. *gellita*, G. *gelte* pail, bucket), perh. of Celtic origin.

galloon gəlū·n ribbon or braid for trimming. XVII. – F. *galon*, f. *galonner* trim with braid, of unkn. origin; see -OON.

gallop gæ·ləp sb. the most rapid movement of a horse; vb. to perform this. XV. –(O)F. *galop, galoper*, for which see WALLOP.

Galloway gæ·ləwei name of a district in S.W. Scotland, epithet of a breed of horses. XVI (*Galloway Nagges*, Sh.). So **Gallovid**IAN gælovi·diən. XVII (*Gallowedian Nagges*, Lithgow). f. medL. *Gallovidia* – W. *Gallwyddel* = Ir. *Gallgaedheal* 'foreign Gaels'. **Galweg**IAN gælwī·dʒən. XVIII. f. *Gal(lo)way*, after *Nor(ro)way*, *Norwegian*.

gallows gæ·louz apparatus for hanging a person XIII (*galu treo, galwe tree, galwes*); transf. of objects consisting of supports and a cross-piece XVI; 'suspenders' for trousers, braces XVIII (so Du., G. dial. *galgen*). – ON. *gálgi*, also *gálgatré* gallows-tree (whence late Nhb. OE. *galga trē*) = OE. *ġ(e)alga* (*ġalgtrēow*), OFris. *galga*, OS., OHG. *galgo* (Du. *galg*, G. *galgen*), Goth. *galga* :- CGerm. **galgon* (cf. Lith. *žalgà*, Arm. *dzaλk* pole, rod); used in all Germ. langs. for the cross of Christ. Used attrib. or as adj. 'fit to be hanged', villainous, (dial.) mischievous XV; hence (dial.) as adv. (*gallus*) very XIX.

gally gæ·li frighten. XVII. In Sh. 'Lear' III ii 44 in the form *gallow* (still dial.), repr. OE. *āgǣlwan* terrify, of unkn. origin.

galoot gəlū·t (sl.) raw soldier or marine; U.S. (uncouth) fellow. XIX. Of unkn. origin.

galop gæ·ləp lively dance in 2/4 time. XIX. – F. (see GALLOP), also *galope*.

galore gəlɔ̄ə·ɹ in abundance. XVII. – Ir. *go leór* or *lór* (= Gaelic *gu leóir*), i.e. *go* to, *leór* sufficiency; prob. popularized by Scott.

galosh, golosh gəlɔ·ʃ †wooden shoe, patten; (now) over-shoe. XIV. – (O)F. *galoche*, repr. (with abnormal phonetic development) late L. *gallicula* (Jerome), dim. of L. *gallica* (Cicero), sb. use, sc. *solea* shoe, of *gallicus* GALLIC, prob. 'Gaulish sandal'. The present pronunc., superseding the normal gəlɔ·tʃ, is prob. due to the frequent forms *galloshoes*, *goloshoes*, etc. (XVII–XVIII), which are extensions with *shoe*.

galumph gəlʌ·mf bound exultingly. Invented by C. L. Dodgson (Lewis Carroll) in 'Through the Looking-glass', 1871; a 'portmanteau' word combining *gallop* and *triumphant*. Cf. CHORTLE.

galvanism gæ·lvənizm electricity developed by chemical action. XVIII (1797). – F. *galvanisme*, f. the name of Luigi *Galvani*, who first described the phenomenon in 1792; see -ISM. So **galvan**IC -æ·nik XVIII, **ga·lvan**IZE XIX; after F. *galvanique*, *-iser*.

Galwegian see GALLOWAY.

gamash gəmæ·ʃ (arch., dial.) leggings. XVI (Nashe). – F. *gamache* – modPr. *gamacho*, *garamacho* – Sp. *guadamaci* kind of ornamented leather – Arab. *ghadāmasī*, f. *Ghadāmas*, a town in Tripoli where an esteemed kind of leather was made.

gamba gæ·mbə short for VIOLA DA GAMBA. XVI.

gambado[1] gæmbei·dou large boot or gaiter attached to a saddle. XVII. f. It. *gamba* leg (cf. JAMB)+-ADO.

gambado[2] gæmbei·dou bound, spring, caper. XIX (Scott). – Sp. *gambada*, f. *gamba* leg; see prec. and -ADO.

gambeson gæ·mbisən (hist.) padded military tunic. XIII. – OF. *gambeson* (= Pr. *gambaisó*), f. *gambais*, prob. – OFrank. *wamba* belly (see WOMB).

gambier gæ·mbiəɹ astringent extract from the plant Uncaria gambir. XIX. – Malay *gambir* (the decoction is called *getah gambier*; cf. GUTTA PERCHA).

gambit gæ·mbit opening at chess. XVII (*gambett*, 1656). – It. *gambetto* tripping up, f. *gamba* leg (cf. JAMB); first recorded in 1561 by the Spaniard Ruy Lopez in the form *gambito*, whence F. *gambit* (XVIII), which was the form finally established in Eng. (The 1623 Eng. tr. of Greco's work retains the It. form *gambetto*.)

gamble gæ·mbl play games of chance for high stakes. XVIII. prob. continuing †*gamel* (XVI) play games, sport, alteration (with assim. to -LE[3]) of †*gamene*, early form of GAME vb., prob. first through the agent-noun and gerund-prp. form, †*gamner* (XVI) gamester, gambler, †*gamning* (cf. GAMMON[2]).

gamboge gæmbou·dʒ, -bū·dʒ gum-resin, used as a pigment. XVIII. – modL. *gambaugium*, var. of *cambugium*, *cambugia*, *-bogia*, f. *Cambodia*, name of a district in Assam whence the substance is derived.

gambol gæ·mbəl, -boul bound, leap, caper. XVI. Earliest form *gambad(e)* – F. *gambade* – It. *gambata* trip-up, f. *gamba* leg (cf. JAMB); the extant forms show the foll. development, *gambade*, *gambaude*, *gambauld*, *gambold*, *gambol* (XVII). Also as vb. XVI; after F. *gambader*.

gambrel gæ·mbrəl (dial.) stick for stretching XVI; horse's hock XVII (Holland). – ONF. *gamberel*, f. *gambier* forked stick, f. *gambe*, var. of *jambe* leg; see JAMB, -EREL.

gambroon gæmbrū·n twilled cloth for linings. XIX. Presumably f. name of a town on the Persian Gulf.

game[1] geim amusement, diversion OE.; organized amusement or sport XIII (Cursor M.); †sport derived from the chase, (hence) wild animals pursued for sport XIII. OE. *gamen*, *gomen* = OFris. *game*, *gome*, OS., OHG., ON. *gaman*; has been regarded as identical with Goth. *gaman* fellowship (tr. *κοινωνία*, 2 Cor. xiii. 13) (f. Germ. **ga*- Y-+ MAN). For loss of final *n* cf. *clue*, *eve*, *maid*. Hence **game** vb.; a new formation of XIII (AncrR), distinct from OE. *gam(e)nian*, which continued till XVI in *gamening* (cf. GAMMON[2]). **ga·me**SOME[1] XIV. **ga·me**STER XVI.

game[2] geim full of spirit or pluck. XVIII (*die game*, Gay). adj. use of GAME[1] in the sporting sense of 'spirit for fighting, pluck' (cf. *thorough game*, *all game*, *good game*, predicated of one who has these qualities).

game[3] geim (colloq.) lame. XVIII (Grose). Of unkn. origin; cf. synon. dial. *gammy*, perh. – F. *gambi* bent, crooked.

gamete gæmī·t (biol.) each of two cells forming a zygospore. 1886. – modL. *gameta* – Gr. *gametḗ* wife, *gamétēs* husband, f. *gámos* marriage.

gamin gæ·mɛ̃ street Arab. XIX (Thackeray). F., prob. of dial. origin.

gamma[1] gæ·mə third letter of the Gr. alphabet, *Γ*, *γ* XIV (Maund.); the moth Plusius gamma, having gamma-like markings; (math.) of certain functions XIX.

gamma[2] gæ·mə †musical scale, gamut (cf. F. *gamme*, whence Eng. †*gamme*, †*gam* XIV–XVII) XVII.

gammadion gəmei·diən fylfot, swastika (which involves the form of *Γ*). XIX. – late Gr. *gammádion*, f. GAMMA[1].

gammer gæ·məɹ rustic title for an old woman. XVI (*Gammer Gurtons Nedle*). prob. reduction of GODMOTHER (cf. GAFFER), but a sp. *gandmer* (XVI) shows assoc. with GRANDMOTHER.

gammon[1] gæ·mən †ham XV; joint of bacon XVI. – ONF. *gambon* (mod F. *jambon*) ham, f. *gambe* leg (cf. JAMB).

gammon[2] gæ·mən backgammon; term in the game. XVIII. app. survival of *gamen* GAME[1], esp. as repr. in inflected forms such as (pl.) *gamenes* XIII–XVI, and vbl. sb. *gam(e)ning*, *gamner* gamester, gambler (XVI), f. OE. *gamenian* (= ON. *gamna*) sport, game. Hence perh. thieves' sl. *give gammon*, *keep in gammon* keep (a person) in train while robbing him, whence the senses 'talk, chatter' (XVIII), 'humbug, nonsense' (XIX). Also as vb. XVIII.

gammon[3] gæ·mən (naut.) lashing of the bowsprit. XVII. perh. identical with GAMMON[1], the allusion being to the tying up of a gammon or ham (cf. F. *gambe de hune* futtock shroud).

gammy gæ·mi (sl.) bad; (dial.) lame, maimed. XIX. dial. var. of GAME[3].

gamo- gæ·mou comb. form of Gr. *gámos* marriage, as in **gamo**GE·NESIS sexual reproduction (XIX).

gamp gæmp (colloq.) umbrella. XIX. f. name of Mrs. Sarah *Gamp*, monthly nurse in Dickens's 'Martin Chuzzlewit', who carried a large cotton umbrella.

gamut gæ·mət (hist.) lowest note of the medieval musical scale XV; Guido d'Arezzo's 'great scale' comprising the seven hexachords and so all the notes used in medieval music XVI; whole range of notes recognized or playable; (gen.) compass, range XVII. Earliest forms *gammuthe*, *-othe*, *-outh(e)*, contr. of medL. *gamma ut*; see GAMMA[2], UT.

gander gæ·ndəɹ male of the goose. Late OE. *ganra*, *gandra*, corr. to MLG. *ganre* (LG., Du. *gander*); f. the same base as GANNET.

gang gæŋ A. †going, journey XII (Orm); (dial.) way, road XV; B. (dial.) set of articles of one kind XIV; company of workmen, band of persons XVII. – ON. *gangr* m. and *ganga* fem., walking, motion, course (Sw. *gång* walk, pace, 'go', time; Da. *gang* (also) set of knitting-needles) = OE., OS., OHG. (Du., G.) *gang*, Goth. *gaggs*, CGerm. noun of action to **gaŋgan* GO. Hence **ga·ng**STER member of a criminal gang. Late XIX (orig. U.S.).

ganglion gæ·ŋgliən (path.) †tumour in a tendon XVII; (physiol.) complex nerve centre XVIII. – Gr. *gágglion*.

gangrene gæ·ŋgrīn mortification, necrosis. XVI. – F. *gangrène* – L. *gangræna* – Gr. *gággraina* (cf. *góggros* growth on trees). Hence **ga·ngren**OUS. XVII; cf. F. *gangréneux*.

gangue gæŋ matrix of an ore. XIX. – F. *gangue* – G. *gang* vein or lode of metal, techn. use of *gang* course (see GANG).

gangway gæ·ŋwei passage-way, (dial.) thoroughfare. XVII. prob. of continental origin (cf. Da. *gangvej*); see GANG, WAY; not continuous with OE. *gangweġ*.

gannet gæ·nit solan goose. OE. *ganot*, corr. to MLG. *gante*, Du. *gent*, MHG. *ganiz*, *genz*, OHG. *ganazzo*, MHG. *ganze* gander :- Germ. **ganitaz*, **ganoton* (whence L. *ganta*; see GOOSE), f. same base as GANDER.

ganoid gæ·noid having a smooth shiny surface. XIX. – F. *ganoïde*, f. Gr. *gános* brightness; see -OID.

gantlope see GAUNTLET[2].

gantry, gauntry gæ·ntri, gɔ̄·ntri four-footed wooden stand for barrels XIV; platform for a travelling crane, etc. XIX. prob. f. *gawn*, dial. form of GALLON + TREE.

Ganymede gæ·nimīd cup-bearer, (joc.) pot-boy; †CATAMITE. XVI. – L. *Ganymēdēs* – Gr. *Ganumḗdēs* Zeus's cup-bearer.

gaol, jail dʒeil prison. XIII. ME. (i) *gay(h)ole*, *gail(l)e* – ONF. *gaiole*, *gaole*; (ii) *iaiole*, *iaile* – OF. *jaiole*, *jeole* (mod. *geôle*) = It. †*gaiola*, Sp. *gayola* :- Rom. **gaviola*, for **caveola*, dim. of L. *cavea* CAGE. The form *gaol* repr. a pronunc. with g which was current till XVII; the pronunc. repr. by *jail* was equally early (XIII). Comp. **gao·l-**BIRD prisoner in gaol, habitual criminal XVII, with allusion to a caged bird; cf. *gallows-bird*. **gao·l-**DELI:VERY clearing of a gaol of prisoners by bringing them to the assizes XV. So **gaol**ER[2], **jailer, -or**[1] dʒei·ləɹ keeper of a gaol. XIII. ME. *gayholere*, *gailer* and *iailere*, *geilere* – OF. *gaiolere* and *jaioleur*, *jeolier* (mod. *geôlier*).

gap gæp breach in a defence XIV; opening in a mountain range; unfilled space, blank XVI. – ON. *gap* chasm (only in the mythological name *Ginnungagap*; Sw. *gap*, Da. *gab* open mouth, opening), rel. to ON. *gapa* GAPE. Cf. NFris. *gap* (in place-names) cleft, ravine.

gape geip open the mouth wide, stare with open mouth. XIII (contemp. in eastern and western dial.). – ON. *gapa* (Sw. *gapa*, Da. *gabe*) = (M)Du. *gapen*, (M)HG. *gaffen*; in OE. repr. only by *ofergapian* neglect; further relations uncertain. Hence **gape** sb. XVI. ¶ A parallel formation **kap-* is repr. by LG. *kapen*, OHG. *kapfen* keep watch, ME. *bicapen* (beside *bigapen*), *cape* (beside *gape*) in good MSS. of Ch. 'Miller's Tale' 258, 655; 'Troilus' v 1133.

gar gāɹ (dial.) make, cause. XIII (Cursor M.). ME. *gere* – ON. *ger(v)a*, *gǫ(r)va* make, do = OE. *ġierwan* prepare, OS. *garuwian*, *gerwian*, OHG. *garawen* (MHG. *garwen*, *gerwen*, G. *gerben* tan, curry, polish) :- Germ. **garwjan*, f. **garwu-* ready, YARE. The change from *-er-* to *-ar-* prob. took place first in pt. and pp. *gert*. Cf. GEAR.

garage gæ·rāʒ, gæ·ridʒ building for housing automobiles. 1902. – F. *garage*, f. *garer* take care = Pr. *garar* :- Germ. **war-*; see WARE[3], -AGE. Hence as vb.

garb gāɹb †grace, elegance; †style, fashion XVI; fashion of dress, costume XVII. – F. †*garbe* (now *galbe*) – It. *garbo* – Germ. **garwī* (OHG. *garawī* adornment), f. **garw-* (see GAR).

garbage gā·ɹbidʒ offal of an animal XV; refuse, filth XVI. prob. – AN. **garbage*, of unkn. origin.

garble gā·ɹbl †sift, take the pick of XV; make selection from (unfairly or with a bias) XVII. In AL. *garbellāre*, with *garbelāgium* sorting groceries before sale; orig. a term of Mediterranean commerce; – It. *garbellare* sift (corr. to Sp. *garbillar*, F. †*garbeller*) – Arab. *gharbala* sift, select, rel. to *ghirbāl* sieve, perh. – late L. *crībellāre*, f. *crībellum*, dim. of *crībrum* sieve, f. WIE. **krei-* (cf. L. *cernere* sift, DISCERN). ¶ Formerly influenced by *garboil* confuse, disturb (XVI), f. *garboil* sb. confusion, hubbub – OF. *garbouil(le)* – It. *garbuglio*.

garboard gā·ɹbɔ̄əɹd first range of planks or plates laid on the keel. XVII. – Du. †*gaarboord*, perh. f. *garen*, contr. form of *gaderen* GATHER + *boord* BOARD.

garçon gā·rsɔ̃ waiter. XIX. F., obl. case of OF. (mod. dial.) *gars* lad, of disputed origin.

garden gā·ɹdn enclosed cultivated ground. XIV. – ONF. *gardin*, var. of (O)F. *jardin* (whence Sp. *jardin*, It. *giardino*) = Pr. *gardi*, *jardi* :- Rom. **gardīno*, f. **gardo* – Germ. **gardon*; see YARD[1]. Hence **garden** vb. XVI. So **ga·rden**ER[2]. XIII (Cursor M.). – OF. *gardinier*; cf. OHG. *gartinārі* (G. *gärtner*).

gardenia gāɹdī·niə genus of trees and shrubs (Cape jessamine). XVIII. modL., f. name of Alexander *Garden* (d. 1791); see -IA[1].

gare-fowl, gairfowl gɛə·ɹfaul great auk (XVI, *gare*), XVII (*gair-fowl*). – Icel. *geirfugl* (Faroese *gorfuglur*, Sw. *garfogl*), whence Gael. *gearbhul*, F. *gorfou* (penguin).

garfish gā·ɹfiʃ fish having a spear-like snout. XV. app. f. OE. *gār* spear (see GOAD) + FISH[1].

Gargantuan gāɹgæ·ntjuən gigantic, enormous. XVI (Nashe). f. *Gargantua*, name of the large-mouthed voracious giant in Rabelais's work of that name; see -AN.

garget gā·ɹgėt inflammation in cattle, etc. XVI. perh. special use of †*garget* (XIII) throat – OF. *gargate, garguete* – Pr. *gargata* = It. *gargatta*, Sp., Pg. *garganta*, f. **garg-* (see GARGOYLE).

gargle gā·ɹgl wash the mouth and throat with suspended liquid. XVI. – F. *gargouiller* gurgle, †gargle, f. *gargouille* (see next).

gargoyle gā·ɹgoil grotesque spout projecting from a gutter. XV (Lydg.). – OF. *gargouille* throat, with specialized application from the water passing through the mouth of the figure forming the spout; f. base **garg-*, as repr. in L. *gargarizāre* (whence †*gargarize* XVI–XVIII) – Gr. *gargarízein*, of imit. origin.

garial gæ·riæl (also *garr(h)ial, ghuryal*) see GAVIAL.

garibaldi gæribæ·ldi, gæribō·ldi red blouse imitating the red shirt worn by the Italian general Giuseppe *Garibaldi* (1807–82) and his followers. 1862.

garish gɛə·riʃ obstrusively bright; glaring. XVI. Also †*gaurish*, and perh. f. †*gaure* (Ch.) stare, but such a formation with -ISH[1] on a verb is rare.

garland gā·ɹlənd wreath of flowers, etc. XIV; (naut.) band of rope XV. ME. *gerland, garland* – OF. *gerlande, garlande* = Pr., Cat. *gardlanda*, OSp. *guar-*, parallel to Pr. *guirlanda* (whence perh. It. *ghirlanda*, F. *guirlande*), and Sp., Pg. *guirnalda*, Pg. *grinalda*; of unkn. origin.

garlic gā·ɹlik plant of the genus Allium. OE. *gārlēac*, f. *gār* spear (with ref. to the 'cloves' of the plant) + *lēac* LEEK.

garment gā·ɹmənt article of dress. XIV (*garnement, garment*). – (O)F. *garnement* equipment (= OSp. *guarnimiento*, It. *guarnimento*), f. *garnir* GARNISH; see -MENT.

garner gā·ɹnəɹ (rhet.) granary. XII (*gerner*). – AN. *gerner*, OF. *gernier* (mod. *grenier*) :- L. *grānārium* GRANARY; see -ER[2]. Hence vb. (now) store up. XIV.

garnet[1] gā·ɹnit vitreous mineral, a precious kind of which is used as a gem. XIII. ME. *gernet, grenat*, prob. – MDu. *gernate, garnate* – OF. *grenat* – medL. *grānātus* (whence †*granate* XIV–XVIII), perh. transf. use of L. *grānātum* POMEGRANATE, the stone being compared in colour to the pulp of the fruit.

garnet[2] gā·ɹnit (naut.) kind of tackling for hoisting. XV. prob. – Du. *garnaat*, of unkn. origin.

garnish gā·ɹniʃ A. furnish, fit out, embellish XIV (now obs. or rhet., exc. for embellishing a dish of food XVIII); B. (leg.) warn, as with a notice XVI. – (O)F. *garniss-*, lengthened stem (-ISH[2]) of *garnir, guarnir* = Pr. *garnir*, It. *guarnire* – Germ. **warnjan*, prob. rel. to **warnējan*, *-*ōjan* become aware, (hence) guard, defend, provide for (see WARN). Hence **garnish**EE· (leg.). XVII. So **ga·rni**TURE furniture, outfit XVI; ornament XVII, (of a dish) XVIII. – F.

garotte, garrotte gərɔ·t †packing-stick; Sp. method of capital punishment by strangulation XVII (Mabbe); highway robbery by throttling the victim XIX. – Sp. *garrote* orig. cudgel, f. **garr-* (perh. of Celtic origin), whence Pr. *garra* knee-cap, Sp. *garra* claw. So **gar(r)otte** vb. XIX. – F. *garrotter* or Sp. *garrotear*.

garret gæ·rīt †turret, watch-tower XIV; attic room XV. – OF. *garite* (mod. *guérite*), f. *garir* – Germ. **warjan* (cf. next).

garrison gæ·risən †treasure, gift XIII (RGlouc.); †defence XIV; †fortress; defensive force in a fortress XV. – OF. *garison* defence, safety, provision, store, f. *garir* defend, furnish – CGerm. **warjan* defend (whence OE., OS., OHG. *werian*, ON. *verja*, Goth. *warjan*). The later meanings are due to infl. of †*garnison* XIV (Ch.) – (O)F. *garnison*, f. *garnir* fit out, GARNISH. Hence **ga·rrison** vb. furnish with, station as, a garrison XVI; occupy as a garrison XVII.

garron gæ·rən small inferior breed of horse. XVI. – Gael. *gearran*, Ir. *gearrán*.

garrulous gæ·rʲŭləs given to much talking. XVII. f. L. *garrulus*, f. *garrīre* chatter; see -ULOUS. So **garrul**ITY gærū·līti. XVI. – F. †*garrulité* (Calvin) – L.

garter gā·ɹtəɹ band worn above or below the knee. XIV. – OF. *gartier*, var. of *jartier* (also *jartiere*, mod. *jarretière*), f. *garet, jaret* bend of the knee, calf of the leg (whence Sp. *jarrete*, It. *garretto*), prob. of Celtic origin; cf. Breton, W. *gar* leg, ham.

garth gāɹþ yard, garden. XIV. – ON. *garðr* = OE. *ġeard* YARD[1].

gas[1] gæs (hist.) occult principle supposed by van Helmont to be present in all bodies XVII; any completely elastic fluid XVIII. – Du. *gas* (J. B. van Helmont, 1577–1644), based on Gr. *kháos* CHAOS ('halitum illum *Gas* vocavi, non longe a Chao veterum secretum', I have called that spirit *gas*, as being not far removed from the *chaos* of the ancients; the pronunc. of Du. *g* as χ accounts for its being used to repr. Gr. *kh*); perh. suggested by Paracelsus' use of *chaos* for the proper element of spirits such as gnomes. The F. and Sp. form *gaz* was once in Eng. use. Formerly pronounced gās. ¶ Has become CEur. Hence **gas** vb. treat, poison, etc., with gas; (colloq.) talk aimlessly. XIX.

gas[2] gæs (U.S.) colloq. abbrev. of GASOLENE.

gasconade gæskənei·d extravagant boasting. XVIII. – F. *gasconnade*, f. *gasconner* brag, prop. talk like a Gascon, f. *gascon* – L. *Vascō(n-)*, whence also BASQUE; see -ADE.

gash gæʃ long deep cut or cleft. XVI. Later form of †*garsh*, var. of †*garse* (XIII–XVII) – OF. **garse*, f. *garcer, jarcer* scarify (mod. *gercer* chap, crack), Sp. *escarizar*, It. †*(s)carassare* scratch, perh. abnormally repr. late L. *charaxāre* – Gr. *kharássein* (cf. CHARACTER). So **gash** vb. XVI. ¶ For loss of *r* cf. BASS[1], DACE, †*scace* (SCARCE), and perh. next.

gasket gæ·skit (naut.) small rope securing a furled sail. XVII. perh. alteration of †*gassit* (Capt. Smith) – F. *garcette* little girl, thin rope, dim. of *garce*, fem. of *gars* boy (see GARÇON). ¶ For the naut. use of similar words cf. EUPHROE and GRUMMET.

gasolene, -oline gæ·solīn product of the distillation of petroleum, used as fuel for internal-combustion engines. XIX. f. GAS¹+ -OL+-ENE, -INE⁵. Cf. GAS².

gasometer gæsɔ·mitəɹ vessel for holding gas XVII; reservoir for storing illuminating gas XIX. – F. *gazomètre* (Lavoisier, 1789) f. *gaz* GAS¹+-*mètre* – METER.

gasp gàsp catch the breath. XIV (Gower). Early var. *gayspe* – ON. *geispa*, metath. alteration of **geipsa*, f. base of *geip* idle talk, *geipa* talk idly; cf., with weak grade of the base, Sw. dial. *gispa*, Da. *gispe*, OE. *ġipian* yawn (only in prp. *ġipiende*; so OLG. *gipendi* 'patens'), *ġipung* open mouth. Hence **gasp** sb. XVI. ¶ The alt. to *gasp* is expressive.

gasteropod gæ·stərəpɔd mollusc, so called from the ventral position of the locomotive organs. XIX. – F. *gastéropode* (XVIII) – modL. *gasteropoda* n. pl., f. Gr. *gaster-*, *gastḗr* belly +*pod-*, *poús* FOOT. So **gastr**IC gæ·strik pert. to the stomach. XVII. – F. *gastrique* – modL. *gastricus*, f. Gr. *gastr-*, *gastḗr*. **gastro**NOMY gæstrɔ·nəmi art of delicate eating. XIX. – F. *gastronomie* (Joseph Berchoux, 1800).

gate¹ geit opening in a wall capable of being closed by a barrier; barrier itself, esp. framework on hinges. OE. *ġæt*, *ġeat*, pl. *gatu*, corr. to OFris. *gat* hole, opening, OS. *gat* eye of a needle (LG., Du. gap, hole, breach), ON. *gat* opening, passage :– Germ. **gatam* (wanting in HG. and Goth.). Forms with initial *y-*, repr. OE. forms *ġeat*, pl. *ġeatu*, remain in northerly dial. *yett*, *yeat*, and in the surnames *Yates*, *Yeats*; but the standard literary form has been *gate* since XVI.

gate² geit A. (north. dial.) way XIII (Orm); street (surviving in place-names, as *Canongate*) XV; B. †going, journey XIII; manner of going (see GAIT). – ON. *gata* = OHG. *gazza* (G. *gasse* lane), Goth. *gatwō* :– Germ. **gatwōn* (whence Lith. *gàtvė*, Lett. *gatwa*), of unkn. origin (connexion with GET has been assumed by some, as for GATE¹).

gather gæ·ðəɹ bring or come together OE.; infer, conclude (after L. *colligere* collect) XVI. OE. *gaderian* = OFris. *gaderia*, MLG. *gadern*, (M)Du. *gaderen*, MHG. *gatern* :– WGerm. **gadurōjan*, f. **gadurī* TOGETHER. For the change of OE. d to ð cf. FATHER.

gatling gæ·tliŋ machine-gun named after R. J. *Gatling*, first used in the American civil war (1861–5).

gauche gouʃ awkward, clumsy. XVIII (Chesterfield). – F. *gauche* left-handed, f. *gauchir* warp, turn aside – Germ. **walkan* WALK.

Gaucho gau·tʃou, gou·tʃou mixed European and Indian race of the S. American pampas. XIX. Sp., of native origin.

gaud gɔ̄d †trick, sport, jest XIV; (arch.) plaything, toy XV; (pl.) showy things XVII. perh. – AN. deriv. of (O)F. *gaudir* – L. *gaudēre* rejoice.

gaudy¹ gɔ̄·di rejoicing; annual college feast. XVI (*gaudye dayes*). – L. *gaudium* joy, f. *gaudēre* (cf. prec.) or L. *gaudē*, imper. of this vb. Cf. the use in Sp. of L. *gaudeāmus* let us rejoice, *gaudēte* rejoice ye, for 'feast, merrymaking'.

gaudy² gɔ̄·di brilliantly gay, glaringly showy. XVI. prob. the first word of †*gaudy green* (XIV–XVI) yellowish green, prop. green dyed with weld, f. (O)F. *gaude* WELD¹+-Y¹.

gauge, U.S. **gage** geidʒ fixed measure XV; graduated instrument XVII. – ONF. *gauge*, var. of *jauge*, of unkn. origin. For the pronunc. cf. *safe* seif, formerly †*sauf*, *Ralph* reif, formerly †*Rauf*. So **gauge** vb. XV – OF. *gauger* (mod. *jauger*).

gaulin gɔ̄·lin Jamaican egret. XVIII (*gaulding*, Ray). Of unkn. origin.

Gaulish gɔ̄·liʃ pert. to Gaul or the Gauls. XVII. f. *Gaul* Gallia (France and Upper Italy) – F. *Gaule* – Germ. **walχoz* foreigners, pl. of **walχaz* foreign, applied to the Latin and Celtic peoples (cf. WALLACHIAN, WELSH); cf. F. *gaulois* and see -ISH¹.

gault gɔ̄lt (geol.) applied to beds of clay and marl. XVI. Local (E. Anglian) word of unkn. origin, taken up by geologists.

gaunt gɔ̄nt †slim; tall and lean. XV (Promp. Parv.). Of unkn. origin. ¶ There is no evidence of identity with the personal name *de Ga(u)nt*, *le Ga(u)nt* (XIII).

gauntlet¹ gɔ̄·ntlit metal-plated glove of medieval armour. XV. – (O)F. *gantelet*, dim. of *gant* glove (= Pr. *gan*, Cat. *guant*, whence Sp., Pg. *guante*, It. *guanto*) – Germ. **want-*, extant only in ON. *vǫttr* (:– **wantuz*) glove (Sw., Da. *vante*); see -LET.

gauntlet² gɔ̄·ntlit in phr. *run the gauntlet*. XVII. Alteration, by assim. to prec., of †*gantlope* (XVII–XIX) – Sw. *gatlopp*, f. *gata* lane, GATE²+*lopp* course (see LEAP); a term introduced through the Thirty Years War (so G. *gassenlaufen*).

gauze gɔ̄z thin fabric. XVI. – F. *gaze* (Ronsard), prob. f. *Gaza* name of a town in Palestine; cf. Sp. *gasa*, Du. *gaas*, and medL. *gazzatum*. The earliest exx. are Sc. (*gais* XVI, *gadza* XVII). For the pronunc. (shown by the sp. *gawse* in XVII–XVIII) cf. †*bawman* BATMAN, and vɔ̄z, var. pronunc. of VASE.

gavel gæ·vəl (chiefly U.S. and in freemasonry) mallet. XIX. Of unkn. origin.

gavelkind gæ·vəlkaind Kentish form of land-tenure XIII; in Kent and elsewhere, division of a deceased man's property equally among his sons XVI. ME. *gavel(i)kinde*, *-kende*; repr. OE. **gafolġecynd*, f. *gafol* tribute, f. **gaƀ-*, rel. to **geƀ-* GIVE+*ġecynd* KIND¹; presumably orig. tenure by the payment of a fixed service (cf. *socage*). ¶ Various fanciful explanations and forms have been given by antiquaries and lexicographers.

gavial gei·viəl Indian reptile resembling the alligator and the crocodile. XIX. – F. *gavial* – Hind. *ghaṛiyāl* (whence the forms *garial, gharrial*, etc.).

gavotte gəvɔ·t dance resembling the minuet. XVII. – F. *gavotte* – modPr. *gavoto*, f. *Gavot* name in Provence for inhabitants of the Alps.

gawk gō·k (dial.) stupid awkward lout, simpleton (XVII), XIX rel. to *gawk* vb. stare vacantly XVIII, *gawky* adj. XVIII; perh. based on †*gaw* gape, stare XII (*gowenn*, Orm) – ON. *gá* heed; cf. the *k* of *lurk, talk, walk*.

gay gei mirthful, merry XIII; bright-coloured, showy XIV; 'fast', dissipated XVII. – (O)F. *gai*, whence Pr. *gai*, It. *gajo*, of unkn. origin. Also advb. (cf. GEY). So **gaie**TY gei·ĭti. XVII. – (O)F. *gaieté*. Hence **gai**·LY[2]. XIV.

gaze geiz †look with curiosity or wonder, (now) look intently. XIV (Ch.). Of unkn. origin; prob. rel. to the base of ME. *gawe* (cf. ON. *gá* heed), GAWK.

gazebo gəzī·bou turret, look-out. XVIII. perh. joc. f. GAZE, in imitation of L. futures in *-ēbō*.

gazelle gəze·l kind of antelope. XVII. – (O)F. *gazelle*, prob. – Sp. *gacela* – Arab. *ghazāl*.

gazette gəze·t news-sheet. XVII (*gazetta, gazet*). – F. *gazette* or its source It. *gazzetta*, orig. Venetian *gazeta de la novità*, quasi 'a ha'porth of news', so called because sold for a *gazeta*, Venetian coin of small value; see -ETTE. So **gazetteer**[1] gæzĭtiə·ɹ †journalist XVII; geographical dictionary XVIII (from the shortened reference to L. Echard's 'The Gazetteer's; or Newsman's Interpreter: Being A Geographical Index', 1693, used by Echard himself in part II, published in 1704). – F. *gazettier* (XVII) – It. *gazzetiere*.

gear giəɹ equipment; apparatus; stuff. XIII. ME. *gere* – ON. *gervi, gǫrvi*, corr. to OS. *gerwi, garewi*, OHG. *garawī, gar(e)wī* :- Germ. **garwīn-*, f. **garwu-* ready, YARE, whence also **garwjan* GAR.

gecko ge·kou house-lizard. XVIII. – Malay *gēkoq* (the *q* is faint), imit. of the animal's cry.

ged ged (Sc. and north.) pike or luce. XIV. – ON. *gedda*, rel. to *gaddr* GAD; cf. the transf. use of *pike*.

gee dʒī int. word of command to a horse, freq. combined with †*gee, ho*, †*whoa, (h)up*. XVII. Hence as sb. esp. redupl. **gee·-gee** (XIX) child's name for a horse.

geezer gī·zəɹ (sl.) elderly person. XIX. dial. pronunc. of *guiser* masquerader, mummer, f. *guise* †attire fantastically, (dial.) go about in disguise, masquerade, f. GUISE in the sense 'attire'; see -ER[1].

Gehenna gihe·nə place of torture XVI; hell XVII. Earlier anglicized. or – F., *gehenne*.) – ecclL. *gehenna* – Hellenistic Gr. *géenna* (γέεννα τοῦ πυρός hell fire, Matt. v 22, etc.). – late Heb. *gē'hinnōm* place of fiery torment for the dead, fig. use of the place-name *gē' ben Hinnōm* valley of the sons of Hinnom, where, acc. to Jer. xix 5, children were burnt in sacrifice.

geisha gei·ʃə professional dancing and singing girl in Japan. XIX. Jap. *gēisha* 'person of pleasing accomplishments'; taken into Eur. langs. from Eng.

gel dʒel (chem.) semi-solid colloidal solution, classified as hydrogels, alcogels, etc., according to the dispersion medium (water, alcohol, etc.). XIX. First syll. of GELATIN(E) isolated as a word.

gelatine, gelatin dʒe·lətīn, -in basis of jellies. 1800. – F. *gélatine* – It. *gelatina*, f. *gelata* JELLY; see -INE[5]. So **gelatin**OUS dʒĭlæ·tinəs. XVIII. – F. *gélatineux*.

geld[1] geld pp. *gelded, gelt* castrate, emasculate. XIII (Cursor M.). – ON. *gelda*, f. *geldr* barren, whence ME. and dial. *geld* (XIII). So **geld**ING[3] ge·ldiŋ †eunuch; castrated animal. XIV. – ON. *geldingr*, f. *geldr*.

geld[2] geld (hist.) tax paid to the crown by landholders before the Norman Conquest and under the Norman kings. XVII (erron. *gelt*, Holland tr. Camden). – medL. *geldum* (of which a var. *gildum* was adopted by antiquaries as *gild* XVII) – OE. *ġeld, ġield* (see GUILD). Cf. DANEGELD.

gelid dʒe·lid extremely cold. XVII. – L. *gelidus*, f. *gelu* frost, intense cold (cf. COLD); see -ID[1].

gelignite dʒe·lignait variety of gelatin dynamite. XIX. perh. f. GEL(ATIN) + L. *ignis* fire + -ITE.

gem dʒem precious stone. XIV (Ch.).; fig. XIII. – (O)F. *gemme* :- L. *gemma* bud, jewel (cf. COMB); superseded the OE. adoption of the L. word, viz. *ġim(m)*, ME. *ʒimme*. So **ge·mma** (bot.) leaf-bud XVIII. L. **gemma**·TION (bot.) budding. – F., f. L. *gemmāre*.

Gemara gimā·rə later of the two portions of the Talmud. XVII. – Aram. *g^emārā* completion, f. *g^emar* complete.

gemination dʒeminei·ʃən doubling. XVI (Bacon). – L. *gemināti̇ō(n-)*, f. *gemināre* double, whence **ge·mina**TE[3]. XVII (Jonson); f. *geminus*; see GEMINI, -ATION.

gemini early form of JIMINY.

Gemini dʒe·minai the twins Castor and Pollux. XIV. L., pl. of *geminus* double, twin.

gemsbok ge·mzbɔk S. African antelope. XVIII. – Du. *gemsbok* prop. chamois – G. *gemsbock*, f. *gemse* CHAMOIS + *bock* BUCK.

gemshorn ge·mzhɔ̄ɹn (mus.) organ stop. XIX. G., 'chamois horn'; cf. prec.

-gen dʒən repr. Gr. *-genes* (rel. to *génos* KIN), through F. *-gène*, which, by ref. to Gr. *gennân* beget, produce, was used first in *oxygène* OXYGEN, *nitrogène* NITROGEN, by de Morveau and Lavoisier (1787), and later in *endogène* ENDOGEN, *exogène* EXOGEN, by de Candolle (1873), in the sense 'producing', whereas the orig. Gr. formative was used in the senses (i) 'born, produced', as in *eggenḗs* native, and (ii) 'of a (certain or specified) condition', as in *heterogenḗs* HETEROGENEOUS, *homogenḗs* HOMOGENEOUS.

genappe dʒĭnæ·p epithet of a yarn emanating from *Genappe*, town in Belgium. XIX.

gendarme ʒã·dāɹm †mounted armed man XVI; soldier employed in police duties XVIII. – F. *gendarme*, sg. formed on pl. *gens d'armes* 'men of arms', with a new pl. *gendarmes*. Hence **genda·rm**ERY. XVI; after F.

gender dʒe·ndəɹ †kind, sort; (gram.) any of the three 'kinds', masculine, feminine, and neuter, of nouns, adjectives, and pronouns. XIV. – OF. *gendre* (mod. *genre*) = Pr. *genre*, Sp., Pg. *genero*, It. *genere* – Rom. **genero*, f. L. *gener-* GENUS. So (arch.) **ge·nder** vb. – OF. *gendrer* – L. *generāre* GENERATE; cf. ENGENDER.

genealogy dʒīniæ·lədʒi account of one's descent. XIII (Cursor M.). – (O)F. *généalogie* – late L. *geneālogia* – Gr. *geneālogíā*, f. *geneālógos* genealogist, f. *geneá* race, generation; see -LOGY. So **genea**LO·GICAL. XVI; – Gr. **genea·**LOGIST. XVII.

general dʒe·nərəl pert. to the whole, applicable to all XIII; (mil.) of an officer having superior rank and extended command XVI; †sb. (esp. pl.) general idea, principle, etc.; head of a religious order; (mil.) orig. †*general captain*, after F. *capitaine général* XVI. – (O)F. *général* – L. *generālis* (which has been taken into most of the Eur. langs.) pert. to the whole kind, later)(*speciālis* SPECIAL, in dependence on the techn. distinction of *genus* and *species* (repr. the Aristotelian γένος and εἶδος); f. *gener-*, GENUS; see -AL[1]. So **general**ITY -æ·lĭti. XV. – (O)F. – late L. (Earlier †*generalty* XIV, Wyclif; after OF. *generauté*). **ge·neral**IZE. XVIII. – F. *généraliser*. **ge·neral**LY[2]. XIII; after OF. *generalement*, L. *generāliter*, which tr. Gr. γενικῶς. **generali·ssimo** supreme commander. XVII. It., superl. of *generale*.

generate dʒe·nəreit produce (orig. offspring). XVI. f. pp. stem of L. *generāre*, f. *gener-*, GENUS; see -ATE[3]. So **genera·**TION offspring of the same parent(s), etc. XIII (uses mainly dependent on those of *generatio* in the Vulgate); act of generating XIV. – (O)F. – L. **ge·ner**ATIVE. XIV. – late L. (e.g. *virtus generativa*). **ge·ner**ATOR begetter XVII (Sir T. Browne); apparatus for producing power, etc. XVIII. – L.

generic dʒĭne·rik belonging to a genus, general. XVII. – F. *générique* (Descartes, tr. Gr. *genikós*, Aristotle), f. L. *gener-*, GENUS. So **gene·rical.** XV (rare before XVII). See -IC, -ICAL.

generous dʒe·nərəs †nobly born; magnanimous XVI (Sh.); free in giving; ample; of rich quality XVII. – (O)F. *généreux* – L. *generōsus* noble, magnanimous, f. *gener-*, GENUS; see -OUS. So **generos**ITY dʒenəɹɔ·sĭti. XV (rare before XVI). – F. or L.

genesis dʒe·nĭsis first book of the Old Testament OE.; (mode of) origin VII. – L. *genesis* – Gr. *génesis* generation, creation, nativity, horoscope, name of the O.T. book (*ΓΕΝΕΣΙΣ*) in LXX, hence in Vulgate, f. **gen-*, base of *gignesthai* be born or produced (see KIN). Hence **genet**IC dʒĭne·tik pert. to origin. XIX (Carlyle).

genet dʒe·nit civet-cat of S. Europe, W. Asia, and Africa. XV. – OF. *genete* (mod. *-ette*) – Arab. *jarnait*; cf. Sp. *gineta*.

Geneva[1] dʒĭnī·və name of a town in Switzerland assoc. esp. with Calvinistic or extreme puritanical doctrine and practice, often applied to costume, as *G. bands, gown,* †*hat*. Hence **Gene·**VAN. XVI (Abp. Parker).

Geneva[2] dʒĭnī·və spirit otherwise called hollands (flavoured with the juice of juniper berries). XVIII. – Du. *genever*, assim. to prec. in form and pronunc. – OF. *genevre* (mod. *genièvre*) :– **jeniperu-s*, for L. *jūniperus* JUNIPER. Cf. GIN[3].

genial dʒī·niəl (arch.) nuptial XVI; conducive to growth XVII; kindly XVIII. – L. *geniālis* nuptial, productive, joyous, pleasant, f. *genius*; see GENIUS and -AL[1]. ¶ So OF. *genial*; modF. *génial* (marked by genius) is – G. *genial*.

genie dʒī·ni sprite of Arabian demonology. XVIII (Smollett). – F. *génie* GENIUS, used by translators of 'The Arabian Nights' to render the Arab. word (see JINN) which it resembled in sound and in sense; *genii* is used as the pl. in Eng.

genista gĭni·stə (bot.) broom. XVII. L., var. of *genesta* (Virgil, Pliny).

genital dʒe·nitəl pert. to generation; sb. pl. external generative organs. XIV. – (O)F. *génital* or L. *genitālis* (n.sg. and pl. as sb.), f. *genitus*, pp. of *gignere* beget; see KIN, -AL[1].

genitive dʒe·nĭtiv (gram.) pert. to the case which expresses the possessor or source of something. XIV (*genitif*, Trevisa). – (O)F. *génitif*, fem. *-ive*, or L. *genitīvus, -īva* (*gene-*), f. *genit-*, pp. stem of *gignere* beget, produce; see KIN, -IVE. L. *casus genitīvus* (Quintilian, Suetonius) is a rendering of Gr. γενικὴ πτῶσις 'case of production or origin', which was also named κτητική POSSESSIVE, and πατρική, whence L. *casus patricus* (Varro), *patrius* (Aulus Gellius), *paternus* (Priscian).

genius dʒī·niəs tutelary deity or spirit; demon (pl. *genii*; cf. GENIE); characteristic or prevalent disposition or spirit XVI; innate capacity; person as possessing this (pl. *geniuses*) XVII; extraordinary native intellectual power XVIII. – L. *genius* attendant spirit, inclination, appetite, (rarely) intellectual capacity, prob. :– **gṇjos*, corr. to Germ. **kunjam* KIN. (In XVII–XVIII forms repr. F. *génie* and It. *genio* were used in various senses of *genius*.)

Genoa dʒe·nouə name of a city of Italy. XVII. – It. *Genova*, the F. form of which, *Gênes*, is repr. by †*Geane* (XV), JEAN. Hence †**Ge·no**AN. XVII. **Geno**E·SE XVI; after It. *genovese*; the usual adj., of which the foll. syns. have had various periods of currency: †**Genoesi**AN XVII; **Ge·no**VESE XVII (North); †**Ge·noway** XIV (*Janeway*, Maund.; *Jenewey*, Caxton) – OF. *genoueis* – It. *genovese*.

genocide dʒe·nosaid intentional extermination of a race. XX (R. Lemkin, 1945). irreg. f. Gr. *génos* race (KIN) + -CIDE².

-genous dʒĭnəs terminal el. (i) f. L. *-genus* + -OUS, as in *indigenous*; (ii) f. *-gen*, as in (chem.) *hydrogenous*, *nitrogenous*; (iii) f. F. *-gène*, as in (bot.) *endogenous*, *exogenous*.

genre ʒɑ̃r kind, style; painting of subjects of ordinary life. XIX. F., kind (see GENDER).

genro gɛ·nrou elder statesmen of Japan. XX. Jap., 'old men', f. *gen* root, *ro* old.

gens dʒenz pl. *gentes* dʒe·ntīz (Roman antiq.) clan, sept, number of families united by a common name, etc. XIX. L., f. **gen*- produce (cf. GENTILE, KIN).

gent dʒent shortening of GENTLEMAN, in designations (like *esq.* for *esquire*) XVI; hence taken up as an independent word; now vulgar exc. joc. ¶ Cf. the vars. †*gentman*, †*gent'man* of *gentleman* (XVI).

genteel dʒentī·l suited or appropriate to the gentry or persons of quality XVI (B. Jonson); †polished, refined; (vulgar in serious use) stylish, elegant XVII. – F. *gentil*, fem. *-ille*, an earlier adoption of which is repr. by GENTLE. First recorded in the form *gentile*, which was distinguished from GENTILE by retention of the F. pronunc. with final stress, and prob. the nasal sound of the first syll. In Butler's 'Hudibras' II i 747 the form †*gentee* is used, which repr. F. ʒɑ̃ti; cf. JAUNTY.

gentian dʒe·nʃən plant of the genus Gentiana. XIV. – L. *gentiāna* (sc. *herba*), so called, acc. to Pliny, after *Gentius*, a king of Illyria; see -IAN.

gentile dʒe·ntail non-Jewish, †pagan XIV; pert. to a tribe or nation, spec. a gens XVI. – L. *gentīlis* of the same family, stock, or nation, (in eccl. use) heathen, pagan, f. *gent-*, *gēns* race, stock, people, f. **gen*-, base of *gignere* beget (see KIN).

gentility dʒenti·lĭti gentle birth XIV; gentle or genteel state or manner XVI. – (O)F. *gentilité*, f. *gentil*; see next and -ITY.

gentle dʒe·ntl well-born; noble, generous XIII (AncrR., RGlouc., Cursor M.); †domesticated, tame XV; †pliant, soft; mild XVI. – (O)F. *gentil* high-born, noble (in modF. pleasant, kind, agreeable), = Pr., Sp. *gentil*, It. *gentile* :- L. *gentīli-s* belonging to the same gens or stock, (Rom.) belonging to a good family; see also GENTEEL, GENTILE. As sb. (arch.) one of gentle birth XIV (Ch.); larva of the bluebottle, used for bait by anglers XVI (Lyte), spec. use of the sense 'soft'. Hence **ge·ntle**MAN (after OF. *gentils hom*, mod. *gentilhomme*, corr. to It. *gentiluomo*, Sp. *gentilhombre*) XIII (†*gentman* XVI; †*gent'man* XVII, *gemman*, *gem'man* XVI–XIX); whence **ge·ntleman**LY¹ XV (Lydg.). So **ge·ntle**WOMAN XIII.

gentoo dʒentū· penguin of the Falkland Islands. XIX. perh. a use of next.

Gentoo dʒe·ntū Hindu (i.e. pagan, 'gentile', as)(*Moslem*). XVII (Herbert, Dampier). – Pg. *gentio* GENTILE.

gentry dʒe·ntri gentle birth XIV; people of gentle birth XVI. prob. alteration of †*gentrice* (XIII) – OF. *genterise*, var. of *gentelise*, f. *gentil* GENTLE, by assoc. with †*gentle*RY (XIII).

genuflexion, -flection dʒenjufle·kʃən bending the knee. XV. – late L. *genuflexiō(n-)*, f. *genuflectere* (f. *genu* KNEE + *flectere* bend), whence (back-formation) **ge·nuflect** XVII; cf. FLEXION.

genuine dʒe·njuin †natural, native XVI; not spurious or counterfeit XVII. – L. *genuīnus*, f. *genu* KNEE; the orig. ref. was to the recognition of a new-born child by a father placing it on his knees; later assoc. with *genus* race, KIN; see -INE¹.

genus dʒī·nəs (techn.) kind, class. XVI. – L. *genus* birth, race, stock, KIN.

-geny dʒĭni terminal el. = F. *-génie*, modL. *-genia*, based on Gr. adjs. in *-genēs* or the first syll. of GENESIS, meaning 'mode of production', as in *cosmogeny*, *ontogeny*, *physiogeny*, with corr. sbs. in *-genesis* and adjs. in *-genetic*.

geo- dʒī·o(u), dʒiə· repr. *geō-*, comb. form of Gr. *gê* earth, as in many scientific terms of XIX; for older words see below.

geode dʒī·oud concretionary or nodular stone, usu. lined with mineral matter. XVII. – L. *geōdēs* (Pliny) – Gr. *geṓdēs* earthy, f. *gê* earth; cf. F. *géode*.

geodesy dʒiə·dĭsi †land-surveying XVI; (math.) study which determines areas of the earth's surface XIX. – F. *géodésie* or modL. *geōdæsia* – Gr. *geōdaisíā* (*daíein* divide). Hence **geodet**IC -de·tik. XVII.

geography dʒiə·grəfi description of the earth's surface. XVI. – L. *geōgraphia* (partly through F.) – Gr. *geōgraphíā*; see GEO-, -GRAPHY. So **geo**·GRAPHER XVI, **geo**GRA·PHIC XVII, -ICAL XVI.

geology dʒiə·lədʒi †science dealing generally with the earth; science of the earth's crust, strata, etc. XVIII. – modL. *geōlogia*; see GEO-, -LOGY. So **geolo·g**ICAL, **geo·lo**GIST. 1795. ¶ *Geologia* was used in medL. by Richard de Bury for 'science of earthly things'; in modL. in our first sense in a work entitled 'Geologia Norwegica', 1686, and in the title of a work by E. Warren, 1690, and in It. by Fabrizio Sessa, 1687, for the astrological influence of the earth. The present sense, which was made familiar in Eng. by James Hutton's 'Theory of the

Earth', 1795, had appeared in modL. in 'Geologia sive Philosophemata de Genesi ac Structura Globi Terreni', by Dethlevus Cluverus, 1700.

geomancy dʒi·ǒmænsi divination from signs derived from the earth. XIV (PPl., Ch., Maund.). – medL. *geōmantīa*; see GEO-, MANCY. Cf. F. *géomancie* (XV).

geometry dʒiə·mītri science dealing with magnitudes in space. XIV. – (O)F. *géométrie* – L. *geōmetria* – Gr. *geōmetriā*; see GEO-, -METRY. So **geome·tric** XVII, **geome·trical** XVI. – (O)F. *géométrique*, L. *geōmetricus*, Gr. *geōmetrikós*.

George dʒɔ̄ɹdʒ patron saint of England and of the Order of the Garter, an image of whom gives the name to the following things that bear it, viz. (i) jewel forming part of the insignia of the Order XVI (*a joerge of dyamondes*); (ii) †sl., half-crown XVII or guinea (*Yellow George*) XVIII. – L. *Geōrgius* – Gr. *Geṓrgios*.

Georgics dʒɔ̄·ɹdʒiks (pl.) title of Virgil's poetical treatise in four books on husbandry. XVI (G. Douglas). – L. *geōrgica* – Gr. *geōrgiká*, sb. use of n. pl. of *geōrgikós*, f. *geōrgós* husbandman, f. *gê-* (see GEO-) + **erg-* in Gr. *érgon* WORK; see -ICS.

geranium dʒīrei·niəm genus of plants with fruit shaped like a crane's bill XVI; genus Pelargonium XVIII. – L. *geranium* – Gr. *geránion*, f. *géranos* CRANE.

gerent dʒe·rənt (now chiefly in *vicegerent*) ruler. XVI. – L. *gerent-*, *-ēns*, prp. of *gerere*; see GESTATION, -ENT.

gerfalcon dʒɔ̄·ɹfɔ̄(l)kən large kind of falcon. XIV (*ierfakoun*, Wycl. Bible; preceded by an ex. of *gerfauk*). – OF. *gerfaucon*, nom. *gerfaus*, obl. *-fauc*, mod. *gerfaut*) = Pr. *g(u)irfaut*, Cat. *girifalch*, *gerifal*, It. *ger(i)falco* – OFrank. **gērfalco* (G. *ger-*, *gierfalke*) – ON. *geirfálki*, the first el. of which is obscure; see FALCON. ¶ The medL. forms *gyrofalco*, *hierofalco*, have led to unjustifiable attempts to relate the first syll. to L. *gyrāre* GYRATE, and Gr. *hierós* sacred (cf. *falco sacer* SAKER) and *hiérax* hawk.

germ dʒɔ̄ɹm rudimentary form. XVII. – (O)F. *germe* :– L. *germen* sprout, prob. for **genmen* (cf. Skr. *jánman-* birth, origin), f. IE. **gen-* produce, be born (see KIN, -GEN). Preceded by **germen** dʒɔ̄·ɹmen XVII (Sh.), which remains in botanical use.

german dʒɔ̄·ɹmən closely related; now only in *brother-*, *sister-*, *cousin-german*. XIV. – (O)F. *germain* (in OF. also 'brother') = Pr. *german*, and as sbs. Sp. *hermano*, Pg. *irmão* brother :– L. *germānus* genuine, real (as sb. *germānus* brother, *germāna* sister), prob. for **germānus*, f. *germen* GERM; see -AN. Cf. GERMANE.

German dʒɔ̄·ɹmən pert. to Germania or Germany; Germanic. XVI. – L. *Germānus*, perh. of Celtic origin (cf. OIr. *gair* neighbour). The earlier names were *Almain* and *Dutch*. ¶ *German Ocean* (the North Sea) tr. Ptolemy's *Germānikòs Ōkeanós*. So **Germanic** dʒɔ̄ɹmæ·nik. XVII. – L. *Germānicus*; cf. F. *germanique*, G. *germanisch*.

germander dʒɔ̄ɹmæ·ndəɹ plant of the genus Teucrium. XV. – medL. *germandra*, *-drea* (cf. F. *germandrée*, OF. *gemandree*), alteration of *gamandrea* (cf. G. *gamander*), var. of *gamadrea*, for *chamedreos* – late Gr. *khamaidruon*, earlier *khamaidrūs* 'ground-oak', f. *khamaí* on the ground (cf. HUMUS) + *drûs* oak (cf. TREE).

germane dʒɔ̄ɹmei·n closely connected. XIX. var. of GERMAN, due to an echo by Scott (who uses the sp. *germain*) of Sh. 'Hamlet' v ii 165, 1st Folio *more Germaine to the matter*, Qo 1603 *more cosin german*, Qo 1604 *more Ierman*.

germinate dʒɔ̄·ɹmineit sprout, cause to sprout. XVII. f. pp. stem of L. *germināre*, f. *germin-*, *germen*; see GERM, -ATE[3]. So **germina·tion**. XVI. – L.

-gerous see -IGEROUS.

gerrymander dʒe·rimàndəɹ, U.S. ge·ri- (orig. U.S.) manipulate election districts unfairly so as to secure disproportionate representation. 1812 (there are several temporary uses in U.S. about this date). f. name of Elbridge *Gerry*, governor of Massachusetts, who is related to have constructed a district map of the U.S.A. in which the shape of one district suggested to an artist the addition of head, wings, and claws; he exclaimed 'That will do for a salamander!', to which another retorted 'Gerrymander!'

gerund dʒe·rənd verbal noun. XVI (Lilly). – late L. *gerundium*, f. *gerundum*, var. of *gerendum*, gerund of *gerere* carry on (cf. GEST). So **gerundial**[1] gĭrʌ·ndiəl XIX; **gerundive** dʒĭrʌ·ndiv adj. pert. to a gerund XVII; sb. gerund (cf. F. *gérondif*) XV; passive verbal adjective expressing 'to be —ed' XVIII. – late L. *gerundīvus* (sc. *modus* mood).

gesso dʒe·sou plaster of Paris used in painting, etc. XVI. – It. *gesso* :– L. GYPSUM.

gest dʒest (arch.) pl. notable deeds; story, orig. in verse. XIII (Cursor M., Havelok, King Horn). – OF. *geste*, *jeste* – L. *gesta* actions, exploits, sb. use of n. pl. of pp. of *gerere* carry, carry on (cf. GESTATION).

gestalt gəʃta·lt (philos.). XX. G., 'form, aspect', deduced from MHG. *ungestalt* deformity, sb. use of adj. (OHG. *ungistalt*) mis-shapen, f. *un-* UN-[1] + obs. pp. of *stellen* place (see STALL).

gestation dʒestei·ʃən carrying, being carried XVI (Elyot); process of carrying young XVII. – L. *gestātiō(n-)*, f. *gestāre*, frequent. f. *gest-*, pp. stem of *gerere* carry; the presumed base **ges-* has been tentatively connected with ON. *kǫs* heap (cf. L. *agger*) and *kasta* CAST. ¶ From the same base are derived *gest*, *gesticulation*, *gesture*; *congest*, *digest*, *suggest*, with their sbs.; *gerund*; *congeries*; *register*; (*vice-*)*gerent*; *-igerous*.

gesticulate dʒesti·kjŭleit make lively motions with the body. XVII. f. pp. stem of L. *gesticulārī*, f. *gesticulus*, dim. of *gestus* action, GESTURE; see -ATE[3]. So -A·TION. XVII. – L.

gesture dʒe·stʃəɹ †bearing, carriage XV; †attitude, posture; movement of the body XV. – medL. *gestūra*, f. *gest-*, pp. stem of *gerere* (see GERUND).

get get pt. *got*, pp. *got*, U.S. *gotten* gɔt, gɔ·tn obtain, procure; beget; succeed in coming or going *to*, etc. XIII; make oneself, become XVI. – ON. *geta* (pt. *gat*, *gátum*, pp. *getinn*) obtain, beget, guess = OE. **ġietan*, etc. (see below) :– Germ. **getan*, **gat-*, **gētum*, **getanaz*, f. IE. base **ghed-* (**ghod-*) seize, found in L. *præda* (:– **præheda*) booty, PREY, *prædium* estate (cf. PRÆDIAL), and with inserted nasal in L. *prehendere* lay hold of (cf. APPREHEND, etc.), Gr. *khandánein* (aorist *ékhadon*) hold. ¶ Except in Scand., the Germ. vb. appears almost exclusively in comps., e.g. OE. *beġietan*, *forġietan*, *onġietan*, *underġietan* perceive, understand, OFris. *forjeta*, *urjeta* forget, OS. *bigetan*, *fargetan* (Du. *vergeten*), OHG. *gezzan* (in prp. *kezzendi* acquiring), *bi-*, *fergezzan* (G. *vergessen*), Goth. *bigitan*; see further BEGET, FORGET.

The orig. conjugation was repr. in literary use by *get*, *gat*, *getten* as late as XVI; but pp. *gotten* (which survives dial. and U.S.) is found before 1400, by assim. to such schemes as *stele* STEAL, *stal*, *stolen*; the clipped form *got* of the pp., and the pt. *got* (based on the pp.), date from XVI.

geum dʒī·əm avens. XIX. modL. var. of *gæum* (Pliny); as L. for 'avens' by Turner (XVI).

gewgaw gjū·gɔ̄ paltry thing, plaything, trifle. XV (*gwgaw*; later *guygaw*, *guegay*, etc.). Of obscure origin; the phonology of ME. *giuegoue* (AncrR.) is uncertain, and a rare MDu. *ghiveghave* is of doubtful relevance.

gey gei (Sc.) considerable, -ably. XVIII (Ramsay). var. of GAY. Cf. the similar use of *jolly* adv. (XVI).

geyser gei·zəɹ, gai·zəɹ, gī·zəɹ gushing hot spring XVIII; water-heating apparatus XIX. – Icel. *Geysir* proper name of a certain hot spring in Iceland, rel. to *geysa* (ON. *geysa*) gush. Cf. GUST.

ghastly gā·stli †terrible, (now) suggesting the horror of death or carnage XIV; spectre-like, death-like XVI; used advb. XVI. ME. *gastlich*, f. *gaste* terrify (perh. repr. OE. *gǣstan* torment; cf. AGHAST)+*-lich* -LY[1]; the sp. with *gh-* (after GHOST) became current through Spenser.

ghaut gɔ̄t mountain pass XVII; descent to a riverside, landing-place XVIII. – Hindi *ghāṭ* (the development of meaning was in an order the reverse of their appearance in Eng.); applied pl. (*the Ghauts*) by Europeans to two mountain-ranges of India.

ghazal, -el gæ·zĕl species of Oriental lyric poetry. XVIII. – Pers. – Arab. *ghazal*.

ghazi gā·zi champion (against infidels). XVIII. – Arab. *ghāzī*, prp. of *ghazā* fight.

ghee gī clarified butter made from buffalo's milk. XVII. – Hindi *ghī* :– Skr. *ghṛitá-*, pp. of *ghṛi* sprinkle.

gherkin gə̄·ɹkin cucumber for pickling. XVII (*girkin*, Pepys). – early modDu. **(a)gurkkijn* (now *gurkje*, *augurkje*), dim. of *agurk*, *augurk*, *gurk* (whence G. *gurke*, †*gurken*, †*augurken*, Sw. *gurka*, Da. *agurk*); ult. – Slav. word repr. by Slov. *ugorek*, *angurka*, Pol. *ogórek*, Russ. *oguréts*, deriv. with dim. suffix of late Gr. *aggoúrion* (whence Sp. †*angúrria*, It. *anguria*, F. †*angourie*); ult. origin unkn.

ghetto ge·tou Jewish quarter of a town, etc. XVII (Coryat). – It. *ghetto* = Pr. *guet* :– L. *Ægyptus* Egypt. Hence in other Eur. langs., e.g. Russ. *gétto*.

Ghibelline gi·bəlīn, -ain one of the imperialist (anti-papal) party in medieval Italian politics. XVI (G. Harvey). – It. *Ghibellino*, supposed to be – G. *Waiblingen* name of an estate belonging to the Hohenstaufen family, said to have been used as a war-cry by partisans of the Hohenstaufen emperor Conrad III at the battle of Weinsberg, A.D. 1140.

ghost goust soul, spirit OE.; disembodied spirit XIV. OE. *gāst* = OFris. *gāst*, OS. *gēst* (Du. *geest*), (O)HG. *geist* :– WGerm. **gaista* :– **ghoizdos*, which has been connected with Skr. *héḍas* anger, and the presumed base **ghois-* **gheis-* with ON. *geisa* rage, Goth. *usgaisjan*, *usgeisnan* terrify. The sp. with *gh-* is first recorded in Caxton's works and is there prob. due to Flem. *gheest*; it became established late in XVI. See also HOLY GHOST. Hence **gho·st**LY[1]. OE. *gāstlić*.

ghoul gūl spirit preying on corpses. XVIII. – Arab. *ghūl*. In F. *goule*.

Ghurka see GURKHA.

ghyll var. of GILL[3].

giant dʒai·ənt being of superhuman stature. XIII (RGlouc.). ME. *geant* (later infl. by the L. form) – (O)F. *géant*, †*jaiant* = Pr. *jaian*, It. dial. †*zagante*, etc. :– Rom. **gagante*, for L. *gigantem*, nom. *gigās* – Gr. *gigant-*, *gígās*. ¶ The L. form was directly repr. by *ġigant* in OE. and later by *gigant* (XV–XVII).

Giaour dʒauəɹ non-Moslem, Christian. XVI (*Gower*), XVII (*Jaour*, *Giaour*). ult. – Pers. *gaur* infidel (pronounced by the Turks gjaur), var. of *gebr* GUEBRE. So in F. and G.; in It. *giaurro*.

gib gib (name of) a cat. XIV (*Gibbe our cat*). Abbrev. of the name *Gilbert* (cf. *Gibson*).

gibber dʒi·bəɹ chatter incoherently. XVII (Sh.). imit.

gibberish gi·bəriʃ, dʒi·b- unintelligible speech, jargon. XVI. Earlier than *gibber*, but presumably to be connected, the ending being based on names of languages in -ISH[1]. ¶ *Gyberyshe* is found as a field-name in XIV; cf. *gimcrack*.

gibbet dʒi·bit gallows. XIII. – (O)F. *gibet* staff, cudgel, gallows, dim. of *gibe* staff, club, prob. of Germ. origin; see -ET.

gibbon gi·bən long-armed ape, Hylobates. XVIII. – F. *gibbon* (Buffon), f. aboriginal name.

gibbous gi·bəs convex *c.*1400; hump-backed XVII (Sir T. Browne). – late L. *gibbōsus*, f. *gibbus* hump. So **gi·bb**OSE XVII, **gibbos**ITY -ɔ·sĭti *c.* 1400.

gibe, jibe dʒaib speak sneeringly. XVI. perh. – OF. *giber* handle roughly, mod. dial. kick (repr. in modF. by *regimber* buck, rear; cf. JIB), of unkn. origin. Hence **gibe** sb. XVI.

giblets dʒi·blits †appendage XIV; †entrails XV; pl. eatable portions of a bird removed before cooking XVI; odds and ends XVII. – OF. *gibelet* game stew, perh. for **giberet*, f. *gibier* game; cf. Walloon *giblè d'awe* goose giblets, F. *gibelotte* rabbit stew.

gibus dʒai·bəs opera hat. XIX (Thackeray). f. name of inventor.

giddy gi·di †mad, foolish OE.; dizzy; easily distracted, flighty XVI. Peculiar to Eng. OE. *gidiġ*, var. of **gydiġ* :– **guðigaz*, f. **guðam* GOD, the primary sense being 'possessed by a god' (cf. OE. *ylfiġ* insane, f. *ælf* ELF, and Gr. *éntheos* ENTHUSIAST); see -Y[1].

gier-eagle dʒiə·rī:gl vulture. XVII (A.V., Lev. xi 18 *Gier-egle*, Deut. xiv 17 *Geer-eagle*). f. *geire* (XVI) – Du. *gier* vulture (also in *gier-arend* 'vulture-eagle') = OHG. *gīr* (G. *geier*, also in *geieradler*), sb. use of *gīri* greedy.

gift gift giving, thing given. XIII. – ON. *gipt*, corr. to OE. *ġift* payment for a wife, pl. wedding, OFris. *jeft*, OS. *sundar|gift* privilege, MDu. *gift*, *gifte* (Du. *gift* fem. gift, n. usu. *gif* poison), OHG. *gift* fem. gift, poison (G. *gift* fem. gift, n. poison), Goth. *fra|gifts* espousal :– CGerm. **geftiz*, f. **geƀ-*, base of GIVE; see -T. There is no evidence that OE. *ġift* survived, ME. *ȝift*, *yift*, *yeft* being app. itself a new formation on *ȝive*, *ȝeve*, on the model of the ON. word. ¶ Attrib. in *gift horse* (XVII); cf. L. *equi donati dentes non inspiciuntur* (Jerome).

gig[1] gig A. †flighty girl XIII (AncrR.); †whipping-top XV; †fancy, whim XVI (Nashe); (dial.) fun, glee (Mme D'Arblay); (dial.) odd person, fool XVIII; B. (in full *gig-mill*) machine for raising a nap on cloth XVI; light two-wheeled one-horse carriage; light ship's boat XVIII. All these uses may be referred to the gen. notion of light or quick movement, which is also that of the later JIG; but the history of both words is obscure.

gig[2] short for *fishgig*, FIZGIG. XVIII.

gigantic dʒaigæ·ntik †of a giant; having the size of a giant. XVII. f. L. *gigant-*, *gigās* GIANT + -IC. This form finally superseded contemp. or somewhat earlier †*gigantal* (– OF.), *gigantean* (f. L. *giganteus*, Gr. *gigánteios*), †*gigantical*, and †*gigantine* (– obs. F.).

giggle gi·gl laugh in a manner suggestive of foolish levity or uncontrollable amusement. XVI. imit.; cf. Du. *gi(e)chelen*, LG. *giggeln*, MHG. *gickeln*, Russ. *khikhíkat'*.

giglet gi·glit †wanton woman; giddy girl. XIV. perh. f. GIG[1] + -LET.

gigot dʒi·gət (now Sc.) leg of mutton, etc. XVI. – F. *gigot*, dim. of dial. *gigue* (modPr. *gigo*) leg, f. *giguer* hop, jump, of unkn. origin.

Gilbertian gilbə̄·ɹtiən pert. to or characteristic of the humour and absurdity of the characters and situations in the 'Savoy Operas', written by William Schwenck *Gilbert* (1836–1911), with music by Arthur Seymour Sullivan (1842–1900); see -IAN.

Gilbertine gi·lbə̄ɹtain (canon or nun) belonging to a religious order founded by St. Gilbert of Sempringham, *c.* 1140. XVI. – medL. *Gilbertīnus*, f. *Gilbertus*; see -INE[1].

gild[1] gild cover with gold. OE. *gyldan* (in pp. *ġegyld* GILT[1] and comps. *begyldan*, *ofergyldan*) = ON. *gylla* :– Germ. **gulþjan*, f. **gulþam* GOLD.

gild[2] see GUILD.

gill[1] gil organ of respiration in fishes. XIV. – ON. **gil* (whence Sw. *gäl*, †*gel*, Da. *gjælle*) :– **geliz*, rel. to ON. *gjǫlnar* fem. pl. whiskers of the mythical Fenris wold (cf. ODa. *fiske|gæln* fish-gills) :– **gelunaz*, cogn. with Gr. *khelū́nē* lip, jaw, *kheîlos* lip.

gill[2] gil rocky cleft, ravine XI (in place-names), XIV (in literature); narrow stream XVII. – ON. *gil* deep glen, cogn. w. *geil* in same sense. The fanciful sp. *ghyll* was introduced by Wordsworth ('Evening Walk' 54).

gill[3] dʒil ¼ pint. XIV. – OF. *gille*, *gelle*, in medL. *gillo*, *gellus*, late L. *gello*, *gillo* water-pot. ¶ The suggestion that *Gilles* Giles (cf. *jackpot*, *jug*) is the source ignores the *e*-forms.

gill[4] dʒil lass, wench. XV. Short for *Gillian* – F. *Juliane* – L. *Juliāna*, orig. fem. adj. (see -AN) f. *Julius*, Roman gentile name. Cf. JILL.

gillaroo gilərū· Ir. trout. XVIII. – Ir. *giolla ruadh*, i.e. *giolla* fellow (cf. next) + *ruadh* RED.

gillie gi·li attendant on a Highland chief XVII; one who attends on a sportsman XIX. – Gael. *gille* lad, servant = Ir. *giolla* (see prec.).

gillyflower dʒi·liflauəɹ †clove XIV; clove-scented pink, wallflower, etc. XV. ME. *gilofre* (whence dial. *gilliver*), *gerofle*, altered (by assim. to *flower*) to *geraflour* (XV), *gelyflour*, *jillyflower*, *July-flower* (XVI) – OF. *gilofre*, *girofle* (= It. *garofano*) :– medL. *caryophyllum* – Gr. *karuóphullon* clove-tree, f. *káruon* nut + *phúllon* leaf.

gilt[1] gilt gilded. XIV. OE. *ġegyld*; see GILD[1]. *Gilt-edged*, orig. of writing-paper, in commercial use applied to 'paper' (i.e. scrip) of very high value XIX. Hence **gilt** †gilt plate XV; gilding XVI. f. the pp. as used in phr. *of silver and gilt*.

gilt[2] gilt young sow. XIV. – ON. *gyltr* :– **gultjō*, rel. to *gǫltr* :– **galtuz*, whence (dial.) *galt* (XIV); cf. OE. *ġealtborg* swine, OHG. *galza* :– **galtōn*, OE. *gilte* (ME. *yelte*, Devon dial. *ilt*), OHG. *gelza* (G. *gelze*), (M)Du. *gelte* :– **galtjōn*.

gimbals, gymbals dʒi·mbəl (pl.) †joints, links XVI; (naut.) self-adjusting bearings to keep articles horizontal XVIII. var. of GIMMAL.

gimcrack dʒi·mkræk †fanciful notion, dodge; mechanical contrivance; knick-knack; †fop XVII; adj. trivial, trumpery XVIII. ME. *gibecrake* (XIV) perh. small ornament; prob. altered by assoc. with *jim-jam* †trifle, knick-knack (XV); but both elements are obscure. ¶ *Gib(e)crack* is found as a field-name XIII–XVI; cf. *gibberish*.

gimlet gi·mlit boring-tool. XIV. –OF. *guimbelet*, dim. of the Germ. word which appears in Eng. as WIMBLE.

gimmal dʒi·məl finger-ring capable of being divided into two or more rings; (pl.) links in machinery. XVI. Later form (collateral with GIMBALS) of †*gemel*, †*gemew* XIV (pl. twins, Wycl. Bible; hinge; double ring; pl. joints, links). – OF. *gemel*, *gemeau* (mod. *jumeau*) :– L. *gemellus*, dim. of *geminus* twin (see GEMINI); another var. is (dial.) *gimmer* (cf. Sh. '2 Henry VI' I ii 41). Cf. JUMBLE[2].

gimp gimp kind of twist with a cord running through it. XVII. – Du. *gimp* (whence also G. *gimf*, *gimpf*), of unkn. origin.

gin[1] gin (arch.) begin. XII (in ME. pt. *gan* was used as auxiliary, 'did'). Aphetic of *beginne*, *onginne*; see BEGIN.

gin[2] dʒin †ingenuity, craft, trick; (arch.) contrivance, esp. for snaring game. XIII (Orm, Laȝ.). Aphetic – OF. *engin* ENGINE.

gin[3] dʒin ardent spirit distilled from grain and malt. XVIII. abbrev. of GENEVA[2].

gin[4] dʒin female Australian aboriginal. XIX. Native word; cf. N.S. Wales dial. *din*.

ginger dʒi·ndʒəɹ hot spicy root. XIII (Laȝ., AncrR.). ME. *gingivere*, repr. a conflation of OE. *ġinġifer(e)*, *ġinġiber* (which was directly – medL.) with OF. *gingi(m)bre* (mod. *gingembre*) = Pr. *gingevre*, Cat. *(a)gengibre*, Sp. *jenjibre*, Pg. *gengivre*, OIt. *gengiovo*, *zenzavero* (mod. *zenzero*), Rum. *ghimber*– medL. *gingiber*, *zingeber*, L. *zingiber(i)* – Gr. *ziggíberis* – Prakrit *siŋgabēra* – Skr. *çṛŋgavēram*, f. *çṛŋgam* HORN + *vēra-* body; so named from its antler-shaped root. ¶ A widely diffused word, prob. orig. based on an Asian name; the Arab. form with modified final syll., *zanjabīl*, has spread through the Middle East and eastern Europe (e.g. Rum. *zinzifil*, Serb. *dženžefil*); aphetic vars. are repr. by MHG. *ingewer* (G. *ingwer*), Russ. *imbír'*, *inbír'*, Pol. *imbier*. Hence **gi·nger** vb. flavour with ginger; treat (a horse) with ginger, (hence gen.) spirit *up*. XIX.

gingerbread dʒi·ndʒəɹbred A. †preserved ginger XIII; B. cake flavoured with ginger, formerly often coloured and gilded (cf. the phr. *take the gilt off the gingerbread*) XV; adj. tawdry, gimcrack XVIII. Earliest forms *gingebras*, *gyngebre(e)de* – OF. *gingembras*, *-brat* (whence MDu. *gingebraes*, late ON. *gingibráð*) – medL. *gingibrātum*, *-ētum*, f. *gingiber* GINGER + *-ātum* -ATE[1]. The final syll. assumed a form resembling or suggesting *bread*, and for sense B the insertion of *r* in the second syll. completed the semblance of a compound; forms of the type *gingebread* remained in Sc.

gingerly dʒi·ndʒəɹli †elegantly, daintily, mincingly XVI; very cautiously or reluctantly XVII; also adj. perh. f. OF. *gensor*, *genzor*, prop. compar. of *gent* GENT, but used also as a positive, 'pretty, delicate'. See -LY[1], -LY[2].

gingham gi·ŋəm kind of cotton or linen cloth. XVII. – (prob. through Du. *gingang*) Malay *ginggang*, orig. adj. striped. ¶ The word has passed into the mod. Rom. and Germ. langs.

gingili dʒi·ndʒili E. Indian plant (Sesamum indicum) yielding an oil. XVIII. – Hindi, Marathi *jingalī*.

gingival dʒi·ndʒivəl of the gums. XVII. – modL. *gingivālis*, f. L. *gingiva* gum; see -AL[1].

ginglymus gi·ŋ-, dʒi·ŋglimǝs (anat.) joint of which the motion is in only two directions. XVII. modL. – Gr. *gígglumos* hinge. Hence **gi·nglym**OID. XVII.

ginkgo gi·ŋkgou Japanese tree with handsome foliage. XVIII. Jap. – Chinese *yinhing* 'silver apricot'. ¶ Often mis-spelt *gingko*.

ginseng dʒi·nseŋ plant with medicinal root. XVII. – Chinese *jēn shēn* 'man image' (Giles), with allusion to the form of the root.

gipsy, gypsy dʒi·psi member of a nomadic race, called by themselves Romany, of Hindu origin, in XVI supposed to have come from Egypt XVI (Sh.); †rogue; hussy, baggage XVII. Earlier forms †*gipcyan*, †*gipsen*, *-son* (Spenser), aphetic of EGYPTIAN (in the same use). The form *gipsy* may be directly – L. *Ægyptius*; cf. *(by) Mary Gipcy* (Skelton), i.e. Mary of Egypt, Maria Ægyptiaca. Cf. Sp. *gitano* gipsy :– popL. **Ægyptānus*.

giraffe dʒĭrà·f ruminant quadruped of Africa, formerly called *camelopard*. XVII. There are early forms depending on It. *giraffa* and OF. *girafle*, and occas. on Arab., e.g. *ziraph* (cf. OSp. *azorofa*), *iarraff*; the present form (– F. *girafe*, corr. to It. *giraffa*, Sp., Pg. *girafa* – Arab. *zarāfah*) was hardly established before XVIII; in ME. *gerfaunt* and *orafle* occur.

girandole dʒi·rəndoul revolving firework XVII; branched support for candles XVIII. – F. *girandole* – It. *girandola*, f. *girare* – late L. *gyrāre* GYRATE.

girasol dʒi·rəsəl variety of opal having a red glow in bright light. XVI. – F. *girasol* or its source It. *girasole*, f. *girare* (see prec.) + *sole* SUN.

gird[1] gɜːɹd pt., pp. *girt* encircle; invest, endue; fasten (on) as with a belt. OE. *gyrdan* = OS. *gurdian* (Du. *gorden*), OHG. *gurten* (G. *gürten*), ON. *gyrða* :- Germ. **gurðjan*; see GIRTH. Hence **gi·rd**ER[1] main beam supporting joists. XVII (Cotgr. s.v. *solive*).

gird[2] g·ɜ̄ɹd †strike XIII (Laȝ.); †thrust, impel XIII; intr. rush (dial.) XIV; gibe *at* XVI. Of unkn. origin. Cf. GRIDE.

girdle[1] gɜ̄·ɹdl belt worn round the waist. OE. *gyrdel* (earlier *gyrdels*) = MDu. *gurdel* (Du. *gordel*), OHG. *gurtil*, *-ila* (G. *gürtel*), ON. *gyrðill*, f. **gurðjan* GIRD[1]; see -LE[1]. Hence GIRDLE vb. XVI.

girdle[2] gɜ̄·ɹdl (Sc.) iron plate for baking cakes. XV. Metathetic form of GRIDDLE; cf. AL. *girdella* (XII).

girl gɜ̄ɹl †youth or maiden XIII; female child XVI. The ME. vars. *gurle*, *girle*, *gerle* suggest an orig. *ü*, and an OE. **gyrela*, **gyrele* has been proposed, based on **gur-*, repr. prob. in LG. *gör* n. boy, girl; but, as with *boy*, *lad*, and *lass*, certainty is not attainable on the evidence.

giron see GYRON.

girt gɜ̄ɹt surround, gird XVI; take the girth of XVII. f. *girt*, var. (XVI) of GIRTH surviving in techn. uses, infl. by pp. *girt* of GIRD[1].

girth gɜ̄ɹþ band placed round the body of a beast of burden XIV; measurement round a circumference XVII. ME. *gerth* – ON. *gjǫrð* girdle, girth, hoop (:- **gerðu*) = Goth. *gairda* girdle :- Germ. **gerdō*. For other words derived from the vars. **gard-*, **gurd-* see GARTH, GIRD[1], GIRDLE.

gisarme dʒi·zāɹm (hist.) kind of battle-axe or halberd. XIII. – OF. *gisarme*, *guisarme* (whence OSp., Pg. *bisarma*), Pr. *juzarma*, *guisarma* (whence It. †*giusarma*) – OHG. *getīsarn*, f. *getan* (G. *jäten*, †*gäten*) weed + *īsarn* IRON.

gist dʒist (leg.) ground of an action, etc. XVIII; substance or essence of a matter XIX. – OF. *gist* (mod. *gît*), 3rd sg. pres. ind. of *gésir* lie (:- L. *jacēre*), as in law – F. phr. *cest action gist* this action lies; cf. also phr. *gésir en* consist in, depend on.

gith giþ plant of genus Nigella. XIV (Wycl. Bible). (Also †*gitte*, †*git*) – L. *gīt*, *gith*, *gicti*.

gittern gi·tɜɹn (arch.) early form of guitar. XIV. – OF. *guiterne* (perh. through MDu. *giterne*), obscurely rel. to CITHERN and GUITAR.

give giv pt. *gave* geiv, pp. *given* gi·vn hand over OE.; intr. yield XVI. OE. *ġiefan*, *ġefan*, pt. *ġeaf*, *ġēafon*, pp. *ġiefen*, *ġefen* = OFris. *jeva*, OS. *geƀan* (Du. *geven*), OHG. *geban* (G. *geben*), ON. *gefa*, Goth. *giban* :- CGerm. **geƀan*, **gaf*, *gæƀum*, **geƀanaz*, with no certain IE. cogns. OE. *ġ(i)efan* was repr. by ME. *yive*, *yeve*, *yaf*, *yeven*, which prevailed in southern and midland writings till XV; the present form with initial g appears *c*.1200 (in 'Ormulum' beside *ȝifenn*) and is due to Scand., the vowel reflecting OSw. *giva*, ODa. *give*. Cf. the phonetic history of GET.

gizzard gi·zəɹd second stomach of birds. XIV (Ch., tr. L. *jecur*, confused with OF. *guisier*). ME. *giser* (surviving as *gysar* till XVII) – OF. *giser*, *gezier*, *juisier*, also *guisier* (mod. *gésier*) :- Rom. **gicerium*, for L. *gigerium*, only in pl. *-ia*. For the final *d*, which appears XVI, cf. †*garnard*, var. of GARNER, and dial. *scholard*, var. of SCHOLAR. An unexpl. var. *gizzern*, surviving dial., is of about the same age (XIV, Trevisa). The pronunc. with g- (not dʒ-) seems to be due to OF. *guisier*.

glabrous glei·brəs smooth. XVII. f. L. *glaber* hairless, bald (see GLAD) + -OUS.

glacé glæ·sei smooth and highly polished. XIX. F., pp. of *glacer* ice, give a gloss to, f. *glace* ice (see next).

glacial glei·ʃ[i]əl cold, icy; glass-like. XVII. – F. *glacial* or L. *glaciālis* icy, f. *glaciēs* ice, rel. to *gelidus* GELID; see -AL[1].

glacier glæ·siəɹ, glei·ʃəɹ river of ice in a mountain valley. XVIII (*glaciere*). – F. *glacier*, earlier *glacière* (an Alpine word), f. *glace* ice :- Rom. **glacia*, for L. *glaciēs* (see prec.). ¶ Thence also G. *gletscher*, †*gletzer* (XVI).

glacis glæ·si, glei·sis sloping bank, (fortif.) sloping parapet. XVII. – F. *glacis*, f. OF. *glacier* slide, f. *glace* ice (see GLACIAL).

glad glæd †shining, bright; †cheerful, merry; full of joy; rejoicing OE.; suggestive of joy XVII. OE. *glæd* = OS. *glad* (in comp. *gladmōd*), ON. *glaðr* bright, joyous. The orig. sense survives in OHG. *glat* (G. *glatt*) smooth; Germ. **glaðaz* is rel. to OSl. *gladŭkŭ*, L. *glaber* (:- **ghladhro-*) smooth, GLABROUS. Hence **gla·d**SOME[1]. XIV (Ch.). ¶ Words with initial *gl* having 'shining, bright' as the basic sense are: *glade*, *glare*, *glass*, *gleam*, *gleed*, *glim*, *glimmer*, *glimpse*, *glint*, *glister*, *glitter*, *gloaming*, *glow*, *glower*.

gladdon glæ·dən (dial.) iris. OE. *glædene* – **gladina*, f. L. GLADIOLUS.

glade gleid open space in a forest (†spec. for snaring birds) XVI (More); †clear space in the sky XVI. Of unkn. origin; cf. synon. †*glode* (XIV in alliterative verse, and once in XVII); perh. orig. 'bright sunny place' and f. base **glai-* of GLEAM.

gladiator glæ·dieitəɹ in ancient Rome, one who fought with the sword at a public show. XV. – L. *gladiātor*, f. *gladius* sword (presumably of Celtic origin); see -ATOR. Cf. (O)F. *gladiateur*. So **gla:diato·r**IAL XVIII, †**-o·r**IAN XVII; f. L. *gladiātōrius*.

gladiolus glædiou·ləs, glədai·ələs iridaceous plant with sword-shaped leaves. XVI. – L. *gladiolus* (Pliny), dim. of *gladius* sword; repr. in F. by *glaïeul*; anglicized in the form **gla·diol(e)** (XV–XIX).

Gladstone glæ·dstən name of William Ewart *Gladstone* (1808–98), Eng. statesman, used attrib. or ellipt. to designate (i) French wine of which the importation was increased as a result of his reduction of customs duty, (ii) a kind of portmanteau.

Glagolitic glægoli·tik name of the alphabet (of Gr. origin) in which early Sl. translations of the Bible and liturgical texts are written and which is still used by Slavs of the Roman obedience. XIX. – modL. *glagoliticus* (F. *-itique*, G. *-itisch*), f. Serbo-Croatian *glagolica* (*c* = ts), f. *glagól* word (perh. in Sl. dial. letter); see -IC.

glair glɛəɹ white of egg. XIV. – (O)F. *glaire* :– medL. *glarea*, obscure var. of **clarea* (sb. use of fem. of L. adj. *clārus* CLEAR), whence also Pr. *clara*, *glara*, Sp. *clara*, It. *chiara*. Hence **glai·**RY[1] viscid, slimy. XVII.

glaive gleiv †lance, spear XIII; †halbert; (arch.) sword, broadsword XV. – (O)F. *glaive*, †*glavie* †lance, (now) sword = Pr. *glavi*, *glazi*, presumed to be – L. *gladius* sword; but the sense 'lance' (which is also that of MHG., MDu. *glavie*) is not thus accounted for.

glamour glæ·məɹ magic, spell XVIII; magic beauty XIX. orig. Sc., brought into gen. literary use by Scott; alteration of GRAMMAR with the sense of GRAMARYE. For the form with *gl-* cf. medL. *glomeria* (in *magister glomeriæ* title of a former official in the university of Cambridge), prob. – AN. **glomerie*, for *gramarie* GRAMMAR.

glance glàns glide *off* an object struck; †move rapidly XV; make a flash of light; flash a look XVI. The earliest forms *glench*, *glence*, *glanch* suggest an alteration of †*glace* (XIV) glance, glide (– OF. *glacier*; see GLACIS) by crossing with synon. †*glent* (XIII) and *lanch*, LAUNCH[1]. Hence **glance** sb. swift oblique movement; flash, gleam; hurried look. XVI. ¶ Perh. orig. two words.

gland glænd secreting organ of the body. XVII. – F. *glande*, later form of OF. *glandre* (see next).

glander glà·ndəɹ †glandular swelling XV; (pl.) disease of horses XVI. – OF. *glandre* :– L. *glandulæ* pl. throat glands, swollen glands in the neck.

glare glɛəɹ †shine with dazzling light XIII; look fixedly and fiercely XVII. – MLG., MDu. *glaren* gleam, glare, prob. ult. rel. to GLASS.

glass glàs OE. *glæs* = OS. *glas*, *gles*, OHG., G. *glas* :– WGerm. **gla·sam*, of which a var. **glaza·m* is repr. by ON. *gler* glass; prob. rel. to OE. *glǣr*, MLG. *glār* amber, repr. the Germ. word adopted in L. as *glēsum*, *glǣsum* (Tacitus, Pliny).

Glaswegian glàs-, glàzwī·dʒ[1]ən pert. to Glasgow, Scotland. f. modL.

Glauber's salt(s) glɔ̄·bəɹz sɔ̀lt(s) sulphate of sodium. XVIII. named after Johann Rudolf *Glauber* (1604–68), German chemist, by whom it was first artificially made.

glaucoma glɔ̄kou·mə (path.) disease of the eye marked by grey-green haze in the pupil. XVII. L. (Pliny) – Gr. *glaúkōma*, f. *glaukós*; see next and -OMA.

glaucous glɔ̄·kəs dull-green. XVII. f. L. *glaucus* – Gr. *glaukós* bluish-green or grey + -OUS.

glaze gleiz fill with glass XIV; cover with a vitreous substance XV. ME. *glase*, f. obl. form of GLASS. Hence **gla·**ZIER[1]. XIV.

gleam glīm (orig.) brilliant light; (now) subdued or transient light. OE. *glǣm* (:– **glaimiz*), corr. to LG. *glēm*, OHG. *gleimo* glow-worm, and rel. to OS. *glīmo* brightness, OHG. *glīmo* glow-worm, MHG. *glīmen* shine, glow, and further to GLIMMER. Hence **gleam** vb. XIII (w. midl.). In ME. both sb. and vb. occur mainly in alliterative use.

glean glīn gather reaped corn. XIV. – OF. *glener* = Pr. *glenar* :– late L. (Gallo-Roman) *glennare* (VI), prob. f. Gaulish **glenn-* :– Celtic **glendn-* (in OIr. *dighlaim* :– **dē-glendsmn̥*).

glebe glīb soil, earth; field; portion of land attached to a benefice. XIV. – L. *glēba*, *glǣba* clod, land, soil; cf. Pol. *gleba*, Russ. *glýba* clod, and see GLOBE.

glede, gled glīd, gled (arch., dial.) kite, Milvus regalis. OE. *glida*, corr. to MLG. *glede*, ON. *gleða* :– Germ. **gliðon* (**gleðon*), f. **glið-*, weak grade of **glīðan* GLIDE.

glee glī †play, sport; †minstrelsy, music OE. (unaccompanied part-song, of Eng. origin, with one voice to each part XVII); mirth, rejoicing XII. OE. *glēo*, *glīo* = ON. (rare) *glý* :– **gliujam* (not repr. in other Germ. langs.); it was variously treated in OE. as *gliēg-*, *glīg-*, *glīw-*, *glēow-*, nom. *glēo*, the two last giving ME. *glew* and *gle*. Not used by Sh. exc. in the comp. *gleeful* (once, 'Tit. And.' II iii 111), nor by Milton; marked obs. by Phillips (1706); acc. to J., 'not now used except in ludicrous writing, or with some mixture of irony and contempt'.

gleed glīd (arch., dial.) ember. OE. *glēd* = OFris. *glēd*, OS. *glōd-* (Du. *gloed*), OHG. *gluot* (G. *glut*), ON. *glóð* :– Germ. **glōðiz*, f. base of GLOW.

gleek glīk card-game of which three court-cards of the same rank is a special feature. XVI. – OF. *glic*, also *ghelicque* – MDu. *ghelic* (mod. *gelijk*) LIKE[1], perh. the immed. source.

gleet glīt slimy matter, phlegm XIV; morbid discharge XVI. ME. *glet*, Sc. *glit* – (O)F. *glette* slime, filth, (now) litharge, of unkn. origin. The present form was not in common use till XVII; its development is unexpl.

glen glen mountain valley. XV. In early use Sc. *glen*; taken up by Spenser in the forms *glenne*, *glinne*; in gen. Eng. use the form *glen* dates from mid-XVIII. – Gael., Ir. *gleann*, earlier *glenn* = W. *glyn*. ¶ †*Glinnes*, †*glins*, repr. Ir. pl. *gliann*.

Glendoveer glendouvio·ɹ beautiful sprite in Southey's quasi-Hindu mythology. 1810. Alteration of *grandouver* in Sonnerat's 'Voyage aux Indes orientales' (1782–1806), which prob. repr. Skr. *Gandharvas* semi-divine being.

glengarry glengæ·ri Highland cap. XIX. f. name of a town in Inverness, Scotland.

Glenlivet glenli·vĭt variety of Scotch whisky. XIX. f. *Glenlivet* in Banffshire, Scotland, the place of manufacture.

glenoid glī·noid (anat.) pert. to a shallow cavity on certain bones. XVIII. – F. *glénoïde* – Gr. *glēnoeidḗs*, f. *glḗnē* ball or pupil of the eye, (in Galen) shallow joint-socket; see -OID.

glib glib (dial.) smooth and slippery XVI; ready and fluent XVII. rel. to synon. †*glibbery*, corr. formally to Du. *glibberig*, MLG. *glibberich* (LG. *glibbrig*), f. base **glĭb-* (cf. OHG. *gleif* sloping); for expressive *gl-* cf. next.

glide glaid pass easily or smoothly. OE. *glīdan* pt. *glād*, *glidon*, pp. *gliden* = OFris. *glīda*, OS. *glīdan* (Du. *glijden*), OHG. *glītan* (G. *gleiten*) :– WGerm. **glīđan*, of which no cogns. are known (the short base is repr. by OE. *glid(d)er* slippery).

glim glim light, candle, lantern. XVII. orig. in canting lang.; perh. shortening of GLIMMER or GLIMPSE. ¶ Earlier sporadic exx. are of doubtful meaning or status.

glimmer gli·məɹ †shine brightly XIV (Sir Gawain and the Green Knight); shine faintly XV. prob. of Scand. origin (cf. Sw. *glimra*, Da. *glimre*, to which corr. (M)HG., Du. *glimmern*); f. Germ. **glim-* **glaim-*; see GLEAM, -ER[4]. Hence **gli·mmer** sb. XVI. ¶ The present currency of the sb. may be due to Sh.

glimpse glimᵖs †have faint vision XIV (*glimsing*, Ch.); (arch.) shine faintly or intermittently XV; (from the sb.) see momentarily or partially XVIII. deriv. of the base of GLIMMER, perh. repr. an OE. **glimsian* = MHG. *glimsen* :– WGerm. **glimisōjan*. Hence **glimpse** sb. XVI (in Sh. 'Hamlet' I iv 53 *the glimpses of the Moone* the earth by night).

glint glint move quickly, esp. obliquely; shine with flashing light. XIV. Not common till XVIII (Burns), but *glint* sb. is used by Wyatt; alteration of earlier (dial.) *glent* (XIII) in both the above senses and that of 'look askance', prob. of Scand. origin (cf. Sw. dial. *glänta*, *glinta* slip, slide, gleam); cf. GLANCE.

glissade gli·sād sliding movement. XIX. – F. *glissade*, f. *glisser* slip, slide; see -ADE.

glisten gli·sn shine with twinkling light. OE. *glisnian*, f. base of *glisian* (= OFris. *glisa*, MLG. *glisen*), f. Germ. **glis-*, extension of **gli-*, repr. by ON. *gljá* shine, which has been connected with Gr. *khliarós* warm.

glister gli·stəɹ (poet., dial.) glitter. XIV. corr. to and prob. – MLG. *glistern*, (M)Du. *glisteren*, f. Germ. **glis-*; see prec.

glitter gli·təɹ shine with brilliant tremulous light. XIV. – ON. *glitra* = MHG., G. *glitzern*, sparkle, frequent. (see -ER[4]) f. Germ. **glĭt-*, in OS. *glītan*, OHG. *glīʒan* (G. *gleissen*) shine, ON. *glit* brightness, *glita* shine, Goth. *glit|munjan* (of clothes) shine bright; IE. **ghleid-* **ghlid-* appears in Gr. *khlidḗ* luxury.

gloaming glou·miŋ evening twilight. XV (Wyntoun). In the literary language an early-XIX adoption from Sc. writers.

gloat glout †look askance or furtively XVI (Laneham); †cast amorous glances XVII; gaze with intense satisfaction (*over*, *upon*) XVIII. Of unkn. origin; not known to J., who quotes 'Teach . . her deluding Eyes to gloat for You' (Rowe, 'Jane Shore' IV i) with the remark 'This word I conceive to be ignorantly written for *gloar*', i.e. *glore*, *glower*; but it was used by many distinguished writers, being perh. taken up from some dialect in which it may have been adopted from Scand. (cf. ON. *glotta* grin, Sw. dial. *glotta* peep, corr. to (M)HG. *glotzen* stare).

globe gloub spherical body; *the* earth. XVI. – (O)F. *globe* or L. *globus*, rel. to *glēba* GLEBE and referred by some to a base **gel-* roll together, stick, which, with various formatives, is held to be repr. in CLAY, CLEAVE[1], CLEW, CLIMB, CLOT, CLUB, CLUMP, and AGGLUTINATE, (CON)GLOMERATE, GLUE. Hence **glo·b**AL[1]. XX. So **glo·b**OSE. XV (rare before Milton). – L. **glo·b**OUS. XVII. – F. †*globeux* or L. *globōsus*. **globul**AR glɔ·bjŭləɹ. XVII. f. L. *globulus*, dim. of *globus*; freq. used as the adj. of *globe* rather than of *globule*. **glo·b**ULE small spherical body. XVII. – F. *globule* (Pascal) or L. *globulus*.

glomerate glɔ·məreit (bot.) compactly clustered. XVIII. – L. *glomerātus*; cf. CONGLOMERATE, GLOBE.

gloom glūm look sullen; (of the sky, etc.) lower XIV; make dark XVI; look dark XVIII. Late ME. *gloum(b)e*; the earliest evidence is predominantly north.; for the vocalism cf. ROOM (ME. *roum*). Of unkn. origin; Continental forms based on a base **glŭm-* denoting 'muddy', 'turbid', 'foggy' are remote in sense. Hence **gloom** sb. (Sc.) sullen look XVI; darkness, obscurity XVII (Milton; occurs nine times in his poems; prob. back-formation from *gloomy*); melancholy state XVIII. **gloom**Y[1] glū·mi dark, obscure XVI (Sh.); sullen, depressed XVI (Marlowe); depressing, dismal XVIII.

Gloria glɔ̄·riə short for the liturgical *Gloria Patri* (*et Filio et Spiritui Sancto*) Glory be to the Father (and to the Son and to the Holy Ghost), *Gloria in excelsis Deo* Glory to God in the highest, and *Gloria tibi Domine* Glory be to thee, O Lord. XIII.

glory glɔ̄·ri †boastful spirit (see VAINGLORY); resplendent beauty; splendour (in religious lang., of God, heaven, the saints) XIII; exalted praise or honour XIV; halo, nimbus XVII. – OF. (AN.) *glorie* – L. *glōria*. OF. *glore*, (also mod.) *gloire* was repr. by rare ME. *gloire* and gen. Sc. *glor*, *gloir* XIV–XVII. So **glo·ry** vb. exult, †boast. XIV. – L. *gloriārī*, f. *glōria*. **glo·rIFY**. XIV (R. Rolle). – (O)F. – ecclL. **glo·rIOUS**. XIII. – AN. *glori(o)us*, OF. *glorieux* – L. *glōriōsus*; cf. INGLORIOUS, VAINGLORIOUS.

glory-hole glɔ̄·rihoul (sl.) cell to which prisoners are brought on the day of trial; (colloq.) receptacle for a disorderly collection of things; (techn.) small furnace in which goods are re-heated in glass-making. XIX. Of unkn. origin.

gloss[1] glɔs superficial lustre. XVI. Of unkn. origin; words of corr. form are Du. *gloos* glowing, gleaming, Sw. dial. *glossa* gleam, glow, Icel. *glossi* blaze, but no point of contact has been established; *glass* was used as a syn. in XVI, and it is poss. that *gloss* is a modified form of it. Hence **gloss** vb.[1] (infl. by GLOSS[2]) give a specious appearance to, smoothe *over*. XVII. **glo·ssY**[1]. XVI.

gloss[2] glɔs interlinear or marginal explanation; (sophistical) interpretation. XVI. refash. of GLOZE after L. *glōssa*.

glossary glɔ·səri collection of glosses. XIV. – L. *glossārium*, f. *glōssa* GLOSS[2]; see -ARY. Hence **glo·ssarIST**. XVIII (T. Warton).

glosso- glɔ·sou, glɔsɔ· rarely *glotto-*, comb. form of Gr. *glôssa*, *glôtta* tongue, language (cf. GLOSS[2]), as in *glosso*·GRAPHER (Gr. *glōssográphos*), -GRAPHY XVII, **glosso**·LOGY science of language XVIII, *glotto*·LOGY XIX.

glottis glɔ·tis opening at upper part of the trachea and between the vocal chords. XVI. – modL. – Gr. *glōttís*, f. *glôtta*, var. of *glôssa* tongue. Hence **glo·ttAL**[1] applied to percussive sounds made 'when the glottis is suddenly opened or closed on a passage of breath or voice' (Sweet).

glove glʌv covering for the hand. OE. *glōf* corr. to ON. *glófi*, by some taken to be :– Germ. **galōfō*, *-on*, f. **ga-* Y- + base of ON. *lófi* (whence ME., Sc. *loof*), Goth. *lōfa* hand.

glow glou emit (bright) light. OE. *glōwan*, recorded only in prp. *glōwende* and pt. *glēow*, str. vb. corr. to the weak vbs. OS. *glōjan* (Du. *gloeien*), OHG. *gluoen* (G. *glühen*), ON. *glóa*; f. **glō-* (cf. GLEED) :– IE. **ghlō-*, **ghlē-*, whence W. *glo* (:– **ghlōwo-*) coal, Lith. *žlėjà* twilight. Hence **glow·-worm** insect, Lampyris noctiluca, the female of which emits a green light. XIV (Bozon); cf. G. *glühwurm*.

glower glauəɹ (Sc.) stare with wide-open eyes XVI (Dunbar, Lyndesay); scowl XVIII. perh. Sc. var. of synon. (dial.) *glore* (XIV), the earlier sense of which seems to be 'shine, gleam', perh. – LG. *glōren* or Scand. (cf. Icel. *glóra* gleam, stare), rel. to GLOW.

gloxinia glɔksi·niə Amer. tropical plant. XIX. modL., named by L'Héritier after B. P. *Gloxin*, who described the plant in 1785.

gloze glouz flattery, deceit, pretence XIII (RGlouc.); comment, gloss XIV. – (O)F. *glose* – medL. *glōsa*, for L. *glōssa* word needing explanation, the explanation itself – Gr. *glôssa* tongue, language, foreign language, foreign as obscure word. Cf. GLOSS[2]. So **gloze** vb. talk speciously XIII; †gloss, explain; explain away XIV (PPl., Gower). – (O)F. *gloser* gloss, explain. AL. *glossare*.

glucinum glʲusai·nəm (chem.) beryllium. XIX (Davy, 1812); f. **gluci·na**, latinized form of F. *glucine* (Vauquelin, 1798), f. Gr. *glukús* sweet; see -INE[5]. ¶ Gr. υ is abnormally repr. by *u* in these words; contrast GLYCERINE, GLYCO-.

glucose glʲū·kous (chem.) grape-sugar; sugar of the formula $C_6H_{12}O_6$. 1840. – F. *glucose* (1838 in 'Comptes Rendus de l'Académie des Sciences' VII), irreg. – Gr. *gleûkos* must, sweet wine, rel. to *glukús* sweet; see -OSE[2]. Hence **glu·cosIDE**.

glue glū cementing substance. XIV. – (O)F. *glu* = Pr. *glut* :– late L. *glūtem*, *glūs*, for L. *glūten* (cf. GLUTINOUS), rel. to Gr. *gloiá*, *gloiá*, *gliā*, *gloiós* glue, Lett. *glīwe* mucus, Lith. *glitùs* slippery; f. IE. **gloi-* **glei-* **gli-* stick, see CLEAVE[1], etc., and GLOBE. Hence **glue** vb. XIII. – (O)F. *gluer*. **glu·ey**. XIV (Wycl. Bible); see -Y[1].

glum glʌm sullen, looking dejected. XVI. rel. to (dial.) *glum* vb. frown, scowl (XV), var. of †*glom(e)*, †*gloumbe*, GLOOM; for the vocalism cf. *thumb* :– OE. *þūma*.

glume glūm (bot.) husk. XVIII. – L. *glūma* :– **glūbmā*, f. **glūb-* (as in *glūbere* shell) **gleubh-* (see CLEAVE[2]).

glut glʌt feed to repletion, overload with food. XIV. Earliest forms *gloute*, *glotte*, *glotye*, prob. – (O)F. *gloutir* swallow (with causative sense perh. developed in AN.) :– L. *gluttīre* (see GLUTTON).

gluteus glʲutī·əs (anat.) any of the three muscles forming the buttock. XVII. modL., f. Gr. *gloutós* rump, rel. to GLOBE, CLOT, CLUE.

gluten glʲū·tən †albuminous element of animal tissues XVI; sticky or viscid substance XVII; (chem.) nitrogenous part of flour XIX. – F. *gluten* (Paré) – L. *glūten* GLUE. So **glu·tinOUS** gluey. XVI. – (O)F. *glutineux* or L. *glūtinōsus*. **glutinO·SITY**. XIV. – medL.

glutton glʌ·tn A. gormandizer XIII (AncrR.); B. voracious animal, Gulo luscus, wolverene. XVII. – OF. *gluton*, *gloton* (mod. *glouton*) = Pr. *gloton*, It. *ghiottone* :– L. *gluttō(n-)* (whence OF. *glouz*, Pr. *glotz*, It. *ghiotto*), rel. to *gluttīre* swallow, *gluttus* greedy, and further to *gula* throat; cf. Russ. *glot* throat (:– **glŭtŭ*), *glotáti* swallow (:– **glŭtati*). Hence **glu·ttonOUS**. XIV.

glycerin(e) gli·sərīn, -in sweet syrupy liquid obtained from oils. XIX. – F. *glycerin* (Chevreul), f. Gr. *glukerós* sweet, rel. to synon. *glukús* (cf. LIQUORICE), of which the comb. form in gen. use is **glyco-** gləi·ko(u), instead of *glycy-*. Chemically glycerin is an alcohol and its systematic name is *glycerol* (see -OL). Its discoverer, K. W. Scheele (1779), named it *ölsüss* 'oil-sweet'.

glyconic glaikɔ·nik name of a Gr. lyric metre. XVII. – F. *glyconique* – late L. *glyconīus* – Gr. *glukṓneios*, f. *Glúkōn*, name of a Gr. lyric poet; see -IC.

glyph glif (archit.) vertical channel in a frieze. XVIII. – F. *glyphe* – Gr. *gluphḗ* carving, rel. to *glúphein* (see next); cf. TRIGLYPH.

glyptic gli·ptik pert. to carving. XIX. – F. *glyptique* or Gr. *gluptikós*, f. *glúptēs* carver, f. *glúphein* carve, rel. to CLEAVE²; see -IC.

gn- initial cons.-combination common to all Germ. langs. and still retained in most of them with the pronunc. gn, but reduced to n in standard Eng. and in all dials. except in *gnat* and *gnaw* in some Sc. areas.

gnarled nāɹld knobby, knotty. 1623. Once in Sh. ('Measure for Measure' II ii 116, for which the sole authority is the First Folio), and taken up thence by early-XIX writers. var. of **knarled*, **knurled*, f. *knarl*, *knurl*, extensions of *knar* (XIII) rugged rock, knot in wood, *knur*, *knor* (XV) hard excrescence, corr. to MLG., MDu., MHG. *knorre* (Du. *knor*, G. *knorren*) knobby protuberance, rel. to OHG. *chniurig* knobby, rough, MHG. *knūr(e)* knob, knot, rock, blow, buffet, prob. ult. f. Germ. **knus-* strike, knock (OE. *cnossian*, *cnyssan* dash, knock, OHG. *cnussen* press, ON. *knosa* bruise, beat).

gnash næʃ strike the teeth together. XV. Alteration of †*gnacche* (XIV) or †*gnast* (XIII), which had an early var. †*gnaist* – ON. base of echoic origin, repr. by *gnastan*, *gnastran* (also *gnístan*, *gnístran*) gnashing of teeth, *gneista* emit sparks, *gnesta* crash, clatter.

gnat næt small two-winged fly. OE. *gnætt*, corr. to LG. *gnatte*, G. dial. *gnatze*, rel. to MLG. *gnitte*, G. *gnitze*.

gnathic næ·þik, nei·þik pert. to (the alveolus of) the jaws. XIX. f. Gr. *gnáthos* jaw (cf. CHIN)+-IC.

gnathonic neiþɔ·nik parasitical. XVII. – L. *gnathōnicus*, f. *Gnathō(n-)* – Gr. *gnáthōn*, used as proper name of a parasite, f. *gnáthos* jaw; see prec., -IC. So †**gnatho·**NICAL. XVI.

gnaw nɔ̄ pt. *gnawed* nɔ̄d, pp. *gnawed* (from XVIII), *gnawn* nɔ̄n bite persistently. OE. *gnagan*, pt. *gnōg*, pp. *gnagen* = OS. *gnagan*, OHG. *(g)nagan* (G. *nagen*), ON. *gnaga*; parallel forms with initial *k* are in OS., OHG. *knagan* (Du., G. dial. *knagen*), with a corr. Eng. form *knaw* (XV–XVII); distant cogns. are found in Av. *aiwi|γnixta* gnawed, Lett. *gńēga* eating with long teeth; ult. imit.

gneiss nais, gnais (geol.) kind of metamorphic rock. XVIII. – G. *gneiss*, perh. rel. to OHG. *gneisto* (= OE. *gnāst*, etc.) spark, the rock being named from its sheen.

gnomic nou·mik pert. to general maxims. XIX. – Gr. *gnōmikós* (perh. through F. *gnomique*), f. *gnṓmē* opinion, judgement, f. **gnō-*; see KNOW, -IC. So **gno·**MICAL. XVII.

gnomon nou·mɔn indicator, esp. of a sundial; †nose; part of a parallelogram remaining after a similar one is taken from one corner (from the resemblance to a carpenter's square ⏋). XVI. – F. *gnomon* or L. *gnōmōn* – Gr. *gnṓmōn* inspector, indicator, carpenter's square, f. **gnō-*; see KNOW.

gnosis nou·sis higher knowledge of spiritual mysteries. XVIII. – Gr. *gnôsis* investigation, knowledge (cf. 1 Tim. vi 20), f. **gnō-* KNOW.

gnostic nɔ·stik adj. cognitive, intellectual XVII (Stanley); sb. one of a sect of early Christians claiming *gnosis* XVI. – ecclL. *gnōsticus* (sb. pl. Tertullian) – Gr. *gnōstikós* (Plato, Aristotle), f. *gnōstós*, f. **gnō-*; see -IC.

gnu nū, njū S. African quadruped, the wildebeest. XVIII. ult. – Kaffir *nqu*, prob. through Du. *gnoe*; so G. *gnu*.

go gou pt. **went** (see WEND; repl. OE. *ēode* YODE), pp. **gone** gɔ̀n †walk; move along, proceed. OE. *gān*, pres. *gā*, *gǣst*, *gǣþ*, pl. *gāþ*, pp. *ġegān* = OFris. *gān*, *gēn*, pres. 3 sg. *gēt(h)*, *geith*, pp. *gēn*, OS. *-gān*, in *ful|gān* accomplish (Du. *gaan*), OHG. *gān*, pres. *gām*, *gās*, *gāt*, *gāmēs*, *gāt*, *gānt* and *gēn*, pres. *gēm*, *gēs*, etc. (G. *gehen*), Crim-Gothic *geen* (not in the Gothic of Wulfila). As is shown by the OHG. pres. inflexions, orig. a vb. in *-mi*, f. Germ. **gai-*, **gǣ-* :– IE. **ghē(i)-*, prob. repr. in Gr. *kikhēmi* (:– **ghighēmi*) I reach, Skr. *jáhāti* (:– **ghēghēti*) leaves, forsakes, *jíhītē* flees; the relation to GANG is uncertain. The sense 'walk' is preserved in **go·-cart** (XVII) framework on rollers designed to help children to walk. Hence **go-**O·FF (sl.) start; orig. U.S. XIX.

goa gou·ə Tibetan antelope. XIX. – Tibetan *dgoba*.

goad goud pointed rod for driving cattle. OE. *gād* = Lombard *gaida* arrow-head :– Germ. **gaidō*, of which the IE. **ghai-* (as in Gr. *khaîos*, *khaîon* shepherd's staff) is the basis, as also of OE. *gār* spear = OS., OHG. *gēr*, ON. *geirr* :– CGerm. **gaisaz* (in Goth. in proper names, e.g. *Hariogaisus* 'army-spear'). The north. form is repr. by Sc. *gaid* bar of metal (XV–XVII), but in ME. the unrelated *gad* (– ON. *gaddr*) is the commoner word, with the meanings of *goad* and *gaid*.

goal goul terminal point of a race; (in football), posts through which the ball is driven XVI. perh. identical with ME. *gōl* boundary, limit (recorded once in Shoreham's works XIV), which may have survived colloq. in some local game; this indicates a possible OE. **gāl* obstacle, barrier, perh. rel. to OE. *gǣlan* hinder; but the absence of any record of this sb. or its equiv. in other Germ. langs. (ON. *geil* GILL² being too remote in sense) makes this deriv. quite uncertain.

goat gout ruminant of the genus Capra. OE. *gāt* she-goat (the male being called *bucca* BUCK¹ and *gātbucca*), pl. *gēt*, ME. *geet* = OS. *gēt* (Du. *geit*), OHG. *geiȥ* (G. *geiss*), ON. *geit*, pl. *geitr* (whence north. ME. *geet*, *geit*, *get(t)*), Goth. *gaits* :- CGerm. **gaitaz*, rel. to L. *hædus* kid :- IE. **ghaidos*. ¶ The sexes begin to be distinguished by *he-* and *she-* in late XIV. Hence **goat**EE·² (U.S.) beard resembling the tufted beard of a he-goat. XIX. **goatsucker** gou·tsʌ:kəɹ nightjar. XVII. tr. L. *caprimulgus* (f. *capra* goat + *mulgēre* milk), itself tr. Gr. *aigothēlas* (f. *aigo-*, *aíx* goat + *thēlázein* suck).

gob gɔb lump. XIV (Wycl. Bible; also *goubbe, gubbe* XVI). – OF. *gobe, goube* mouthful, lump (mod. *gobbe* food-ball, pill), f. *gober* swallow, gulp, perh. of Celtic origin (cf. Gael. *gob* beak, bill, Ir. *gob* bill, mouth, whence prob. Sc. and north. Eng. *gob* mouth XVI). Cf. GOBBET.

gobang goubæ·ŋ Japanese game. XIX. – Jap. *goban*, said to be – Chinese *k'i pan* chessboard.

gobbet gɔ·bit portion, fragment; lump of food, etc. XIV. – OF. *gobet*, dim. of *gobe* GOB; see -ET.

gobble¹ gɔ·bl swallow hurriedly. XVII (Holland). prob. of dial. origin f. GOB + -LE³.

gobble² gɔ·bl make the characteristic noise of a turkey. XVII. imit., but perh. suggested by prec.

Gobelin gɔ·bəlin, ||goblɛ̃ epithet of tapestry made at *Gobelins*, state factory in Paris, named after its founders. XIX.

goblet gɔ·blit drinking-cup. XIV. – (O)F. *gobelet*, dim. of *gobel*, of unkn. origin; see -ET.

goblin gɔ·blin mischievous and ugly sprite. XIV. prob. – AN. **gobelin* (recorded in F. XV and surviving in Norman dial.), medL. *gobelīnus* (XII, in Ordericus Vitalis as the name of a spirit haunting Évreux, France); prob. appellative use of a proper name, dim. of *Gobel* (now *Gobeau*), which appears to be rel. to *Kobold* (see COBALT). ¶ Connexion with medL. *cobalus* mountain sprite (Agricola), Gr. *kóbālos* rogue, mischievous goblin invoked by rogues, cannot be upheld.

goby gou·bi fish of the genus Gobius. XVIII (Pennant). – L. *gōbius*, var. of *cōbius* – Gr. *kōbiós* some small fish; cf. GUDGEON.

god, God gɔd superhuman being worshipped, deity; the Supreme Being, the Deity. OE. *god* (pl. *godu* n., *godas* m.) = OFris., OS. (Du.) *god* m., OHG. *got* (G. *gott*) m., ON. *god* n., heathen god, *guð* m. and n., God, Goth. *guþ* (pl. *guda* n.). A CGerm. **guð-* points to IE. **ghut-*, pp. formation of uncertain origin, but prob. f. **ghu-*, repr. by Skr. *hū* invoke the gods (cf. *puru|hūtás* 'much invoked', as an epithet of Indra). Hence **go·dd**ESS¹ XIV; **go·d**FATHER, -MOTHER, -DAUGHTER, -SON late OE. *godfæder, -mōdor, -dohtor, -sunu*; cf. GOSSIP; **go·d**CHILD XIII; cf. OE. *godbearn*. **go·d**HEAD XIII. **God's** ACRE churchyard XVII. – G. *Gottesacker* 'God's seed-field', in which the bodies of the dead are 'sown' (cf. Cor. xv 36–44) in hope of the Resurrection. **godsend** gɔ·dsend welcome but unexpected thing. XIX. for †*God's send* (XVII) alteration of ME. *goddes sand* God's message, dispensation, or ordinance (OE. *sand* message, messenger, rel. to SEND). **God**SPEE·D. XV (Henryson). f. phr. *God speed* 'May God prosper' (one). See also GOOD-BYE, GOOD-EVEN. ¶ There are many euphem. perversions of *God* in oaths and asseverations, several of which are inserted here in their alphabetical places; they may be classified as those (i) in which *g* and *d* are retained, as *gad, gawd, ged, gud*; (ii) in which *g* is retained, but the rest of the word is modified, as *gar, gog, golly, gol-, gosh, gaw-, gor-, goy-, gum*; (iii) in which *g* is replaced by *c*, as *cock, cod, cor*, or by *d*, as *dod* (also in *dodrot*); (iv) in which the initial cons. is dropped, as *od, ud*; (v) in which a syll. repr. a prep. is prefixed, as *begad, begar*; *bedad*; *adad, adod, agad, ecod, egad, icod, igad*; (vi) containing the possessive *s*, usu. with other peculiarities, as *ads, ods, uds*; *cocks, cods, cuds*; *gads, gars, gogs, goles, guds*; (vii) in which the possessive is reduced to *s*, as *'sblood, 'sbodikins, 'sdeath, 'slid, swounds* (*zounds*); (viii) in which *God* is reduced to *d*, as *drat* (so *drabbit*). A few of these, as *cock, gog*, are of late-ME. date; of the remainder some half-dozen are recorded from XVI, the rest are of various dates from XVII onwards. The name is also abbreviated, as in *by G—* (also sp. *Gee*), also *G—d*.

godetia godī·ʃⁱə genus of hardy annuals. XIX. f. name of C. H. *Godet*, Swiss botanist; see -IA¹.

godown gou·daun warehouse, store. XVI (*godon*). – Pg. *gudão* – Malay *godong, gadong*, perh. – Telugu *giḍaṅgi* place where goods lie (Tamil *kiḍaṅgu*), f. *kiḍu* lie.

godwit gɔ·dwit marsh-bird resembling the curlew. XVI (Turner, by whom it is used in latinized form *godwitta*, with an obscure syn. *fedoa*). Of unkn. origin; the occas. vars. in *-wipe, -wike* do not suggest a solution. ¶ Casaubon in 1611 rendered the word by L. *Dei ingenium*, i.e. 'God's wit'.

goffer gou·fəɹ, gɔ·-make wavy, crimp. XVIII. – F. *gaufrer* impress with a pattern-tool, f. *gaufre* honeycomb, pastry made on a mould, impressed pattern, AN. *walfre* – MLG. *wāfel*; see WAFFLE, WAFER.

goggle gɔ·gl (dial.) squint, roll the eyes or the head. XIV. prob. frequent. of a base **gog*, expressive of oscillating movement; cf. *jog, joggle*, and see -LE³. So **go·ggle-eyed.** XIV (in Wycl. Bible, Mark ix 47, tr. Vulgate *luscus* squinting). Hence **go·ggle** sb. †squint, stare XVII; (pl.) the eyes; spectacles XVIII.

Goidel goi·dəl Celt of the branch represented by the Irish and the Highlanders of Scotland. XIX. – OIr. *Góidel*; see GAEL. Hence **Goide·lic**.

goitre goi·təɹ morbid swelling of the neck. XVII (*Gouitres of Sauoye*; *the goistre of Piedmont*). – F. *goitre* (dial. *gouitre*), either (i) – Pr. *goitron* (also in OF.) :– Rom. **gutturiōnem*, f. L. *guttur* throat (see GUTTURAL), or (ii) back-formation from F. *goitreux* :– L. **gutturiōsu-s* adj.

goldam, etc. (U.S.) see GOD and cf. GOLLY.

gold gould the most precious metal. OE. *gold* = OFris., OS., OHG. *gold* (Du. *goud*, G. *gold*), ON. *goll*, *gull*, Goth. *gulþ* :– CGerm. **gulþam* :– IE. **ghl̥tom* (whence also OSl. *zlato*, Russ. *zóloto*), f. **ghel-* YELLOW + pp. suffix **-to-* (as in colour-names such as Lith. *geltas* yellow, *báltas* white, Skr. *háritas* yellow). The name *silver* also is common to Germanic and Slavonic. The pronunc. gūld continued till XIX. ¶ Finn. *kulta* was an early adoption from Germ. The flower-name *gold* (OE. *golde*) which survives in MARIGOLD, is presumably a deriv. of this word. Hence **golden** gou·ldn. XIII; superseding †*gilden*, OE. *gylden*; see -EN³. In various collocations immed. tr. L. *aureus*, e.g. *g. age* XV (L. *aurea ætas*), *g. mean* XVI (L. *aurea mediocritas*, Horace), *g. number* XVI (medL. *aureus numerus*), *g. rule* †(math.) the rule of three XVI; the precept of Matt. vii 12 XVII (also *g. law* XVII). **go·ld**FINCH. OE. *goldfinč*; so Du. *goudfink*, G. *goldfink*. **go·ld**SMITH. OE.

golf gɔlf, gɔf ancient ball-game of Scotland. XV (*golf*, *gouff*). Of unkn. origin; there are difficulties of form and use in the way of the commonly given deriv. from (M)Du. *kolf* club, bat. ¶ The pronunc. gɔf is an Eng. attempt to imitate Sc. gɔuf.

golgotha gɔ·lgəþə graveyard. XVII. – Vulgate L. – Gr. *golgothá* – *gogolþā*, Aram. form of Heb. *gulgōleþ* skull; see CALVARY.

goliardic gouliā·ɹdik descriptive of the ribald poetry of a class of clerkly authors (*goliards*), who in XII–XIII were supposed to be named after a certain *Golias*; OF. *goliard* means 'glutton', f. *gole* (mod. *gueule*) :– L. *gula* gluttony. ¶ In ME. occur *gulardous* (R. Mannyng) and *goliardeys* (Ch., PPl.) for *goliard* (used by Caxton), and *gulyardy* for their works (XIV).

golliwog gɔ·liwɔg fanciful invented name for a grotesque doll. XIX (Bertha Upton, of U.S.A.). perh. suggested by *golly*, Negro perversion of *God* (XIX), and *polliwog* (dial. and U.S.) tadpole.

golly gɔ·li (orig. U.S.) substitute for GOD in excls. XIX; cf. *goles* XVIII (Fielding) and U.S. *goldam*, *-darn*, *-dasted* for *goddam*, *-blasted*.

golosh see GALOSH.

goluptious gəlʌ·pʃəs luscious. XIX (John Strang, 1856). perh. perversion of *voluptuous*.

gombeen gɔmbī·n (Anglo-Ir.) usury. XIX. – Ir. *gaimbín*, acc. to Whitley Stokes, repr. a deriv. of OCeltic **km̥bion*, whence medL. *cambium* CHANGE.

gom(b)roon gɔm(b)rū·n Persian pottery. XVII. f. name of a town on the Persian Gulf.

-gon, repr. Gr. *-gōnos* -angled (cf. KNEE), in *heptagon*, *hexagon*, *pentagon*.

gondola gɔ·ndələ light flat-bottomed boat of Venice. XVI. – (Venetian) It. *gondola* (whence F. *gondole*, G. *gondel*, etc.), f. Friulian *gondolà* rock, roll (cf. It. *dondolare* swing, rock). So **gondol**IE·R. XVII. – F. – It.

gonfalon gɔ·nfələn banner, ensign. XVI. – It. *gonfalone* = F. *gonfalon*, later form of *gonfanon* (whence **go·nfanon** XIII) = Pr. *gonfano* – Germ. **gundfano* (= OE. *gūþfana*, ON. *gunnfani*), f. **gund-* :– Germ. **gunþiō* war + *fano* banner (FANON). So **gonfalon**IE·R. XVI. – F. *gonfalonier*, It. *gonfaloniere*.

gong gɔŋ metallic disk producing musical notes when struck. XVII. – Malay *gŏng*, *gŭng*, of imit. origin; whence also Sp. *gongo*, F., G. *gong*. Also **gong-gong.** XVIII; so G.

Gongorism gɔ·ŋgərizm affected diction, akin to euphuism, introduced into Sp. literature by the poet *Góngora* y Argote (1561–1627). XIX. See -ISM.

goniometer gounio·mitəɹ instrument for measuring angles. XVIII. – F. *goniomètre*, f. Gr. *gōníā* angle + *métron* measure; see KNEE, -METER.

gono- gɔ·no(u), before a vowel *gon-*, repr. Gr. *gónos* generation, offspring, semen (see KIN), in scientific terms.

gonoph gɔ·nəf (slang) pickpocket. XIX (Dickens). – Heb. *gannābh* thief.

gonorrhœa gənŏrī·ə inflammatory discharge from urethra or vagina. XVI. – late L. – Gr. *gonórrhoia*, f. *gónos* semen (see KIN) + *rhoía* flux, rel. to *rheîn* flow (see STREAM).

goober gū·bəɹ peanut. XIX. – Angolese *nguba*.

good gud the most general adj. of commendation. OE. *gōd* = OFris., OS. *gōd* (Du. *goed*), OHG. *guot* (G. *gut*), ON. *góðr*, Goth. *gōþs* :– CGerm. **gōðaz*, f. var. of the base **gað-* bring together, unite, as in *gaderian* GATHER, the primary sense being 'fitting, suitable' (cf. OSl. *goditi* be pleasing, *godŭ* suitable time, Russ. *godnyj* suitable). Compared BETTER, BEST; adv. WELL. See also GOODS. Hence **goo·d**LY¹ comely, fair OE.; notable in size XIII (Laȝ.); excellent, proper XIV (Ch.); kindly (in modSc. of fairies) XIV. **goo·d**MAN, as a compd. (i) male head of a house XIV (householder, husband XVI); (ii) †prefixed to designations, names of yeoman, etc., (hence) yeoman, Scottish laird XVI. Similarly (dial.) **goo·d**WIFE XIV; cf. GOODY¹. **goodwill** gudwi·l †virtuous disposition; favourable regard, benevolence OE.; cheerful acquiescence XIII; privilege granted by the seller of a business to the purchaser of trading as his successor XVI. tr. L. *bona voluntas*, F. *bonne volonté*.

good-bye gudbai· farewell. XVI. Early forms *God be wy you, God buy'ye, God b'uy, Godbuy*, contr. of phr. *God be with you* or *ye*, with later substitution of *good* for *God*, after *good day* (XIII), *good night* (XIV, Ch.). So (dial.) **good even** (XV), orig. *God give you good even* (see EVEN[1]), variously reduced to *God dig you den, God ye gooden* (Sh.), *Gud devon, Godden* (Sh.), *Good den*.

goods gudz (pl.) property, possessions XIII (Cursor M.); merchandise, wares XV. Superseded synon. use of sg. *good* (XII); partly after ON. *góðs*, g. sg. of *góð* (n. of *góðr*) used as an indecl. sb. in the sense 'property', partly after L. *bona*, sb. use of n. pl. of *bonus* good; cf. synon. (O)F. *biens* (*c.* 1300).

goody[1] gu·di lowly form of address to a (married) woman. XVI. Hypocoristic f. GOODWIFE; cf. *huzzy*.

goody[2] gu·di sweetmeat. XVIII. Also redupl. *goody-goody* (Swift); f. GOOD, after F. BONBON. See -Y[6].

goody[3] gu·di weakly or sentimentally good. XIX ('Whose goodness, or (if I may be allowed to coin a word, which the times, if not the language, requires) whose *goodiness* . . .', Coleridge). f. GOOD + -Y[6]. Also redupl. **goo·dy-goo·dy** *c.* 1870, earlier *goody-good* (Carlyle).

googly gū·gli (orig. Australian) in cricket, a ball that breaks from the off. XX. Of unkn. origin.

Goorkha see GURKHA.

gooroo, guru gu·rū Hindu spiritual teacher. XVII (Purchas). – Hind. *gurū* teacher, Hindi *guru* priest, sb. use of Skr. *gurús* weighty, grave, dignified (see GRAVE[3]).

goosander gūsæ·ndəɹ the bird Mergus merganser. XVII (*gossander*, Drayton, Ray). prob. f. GOOSE + second el. of *bergander* sheldrake (XVI), which prob. repr. ON. *andar-*, nom. *ǫnd* duck, pl. *andir* (cf. DRAKE[2]).

goose gūs pl. *geese* gīs bird of the genus Anser and allied genera. OE. *gōs*, pl. *gēs* = OFris., MLG. *gōs*, (M)Du., OHG., G. *gans*, ON. *gás* :– CGerm. **gans-* (Sp. *ganso* implies Goth. **gansus*) :– IE. **ghans-*, whence also L. *anser* (:– **hanser*), Gr. *khḗn*, Skr. *haṅsás* m., *haṅsī́* fem., Av. *zāō*, Lith. *žąsìs* goose, OIr. *géis* swan. Cf. L. *ganta* (Pliny) wild goose, of Germ. origin, whence OF. *jante*, Pr. *ganta*, and GANNET. ¶ One of the few bird-names (cf. *crane, drake, sparrow, thrush*) of IE. age; prob. ult. of imit. origin.

gooseberry gu·z-, gū·zbəri edible berry of thorny species of Ribes. XVI. The first el. may be an alteration (by unexpl. assim. to *goose*), of forms such as (dial.) *groser* (XVI) and *gozell* (XVII), repr. remotely (O)F. *groseille*, †*grozelle*, of disputed origin; but immed. deriv. from GOOSE + BERRY is poss.

gopher[1] gou·fəɹ the wood of which Noah's Ark was built. XVII (A.V.). Heb.

gopher[2] gou·fəɹ (orig. U.S.) land tortoise XVIII; pouched rat (Geomys, etc.); ground squirrel XIX. Said to – Canadian F. *gaufre*, a use of the word meaning 'honeycomb', with ref. to burrowing habits; but this is very doubtful (*magofer* occurs earlier in the first sense).

gorblimy gōɹblai·mi (vulgar) for *God blind me*. XIX. See GOD ¶ (ii).

gorcrow gō·ɹkrou (chiefly dial.) carrion crow. XVII (Jonson). f. GORE[1] + CROW[1].

gore[1] gōəɹ †dung, filth OE.; blood shed (and clotted) XVI. OE. *gor* = (M)Du. *goor* mud, filth, OHG. *gor*, ON. *gor* cud, slimy matter, rel. to OIr. *gor*, W. *gôr* matter, pus.

gore[2] gōəɹ triangular piece of land OE.; skirt front, petticoat XIII; triangular piece, spec. of cloth XIV. OE. *gāra* = OFris. *gāra*, MDu. *ghere* (Du. *geer*), OHG. *gēro* (G. *gehre*), ON. *geiri*, rel. to *gār* spear (a spear-head being triangular). Cf. GYRON.

gore[3] gōəɹ †stab XIV; pierce with the horns XVI. Of unkn. origin; early Sc. and north. *gorre* (XV–XVI) seems to rule out a seemingly obvious deriv. from *gore* spear (OE. *gār*).

gorge gōɹdʒ throat XIV; crop of a hawk XV; contents of the stomach (phr. *one's gorge rises*) XVI; neck of a bastion XVII; ravine XVIII. – (O)F. *gorge* throat = Pr. *gorga, gorja*, Sp. *gorga* food of hawks, It. †*gorga* throat :– Rom. **gurga*, for L. *gurges* whirlpool (cf. GURGITATION). Hence **gorge** vb. fill the gorge (of). XIV.

gorgeous gō·ɹdʒəs richly adorned, sumptuously splendid. XV. Early forms *gorgayse, gorges, gorgyas* – OF. *gorgias* fine, stylish, elegant (XV), of unkn. origin; assim. in ending to words in -EOUS.

gorget gō·ɹdʒit throat armour XV; wimple, necklace XVI. – OF. *gorgete*, f. *gorge* throat, GORGE; see -ET.

gorgio gō·ɹdʒiou gipsies' name for one who is not a gipsy. XIX (Borrow). Romany; in G. *gadscho*, in Sp. *gacho*.

gorgon gō·ɹgən terrible- or repulsive-looking person. XVI. Generalized use of the proper name *Gorgon* – L. *Gorgōn-, Gorgō* – Gr. *Gorgṓ*, f. *gorgós* terrible, rel. to (O)Ir. *garg* savage, Gael. *garg* fierce, angry, OSl. (Russ.) *grozá* terror.

gorgonzola gōɹgənzou·lə cheese named from a village near Milan, Italy. XIX.

gorilla gəri·lə largest anthropoid ape. XIX. Adopted by Thomas Savage in 1847 as the specific name of the ape Troglodytes gorilla; from Gr. *gorilla* (only in acc. pl.), occurring as an alleged African name of a wild or hairy man (prop. the female) in an account of Hanno's voyage (V or VI B.C.).

gormandize gō·ɹməndaiz eat gluttonously. XVI. f. †*gormandize* sb. gluttonous feeding (XV) – (O)F. *gourmandise*, f. *gourmand*; see GOURMAND, -IZE.

gorse gɔ̄ɹs prickly shrub, Ulex europæus. OE. *gors, gorst*, which has no immed. Germ. cogns., but points to IE. base ***ghr̥zd-* be prickly or rough, repr. in L. *hordeum* barley (:– **ghr̥zdejum*) and so rel. to Gr. *krīthḗ*, OHG. *gersta* (G. *gerste*) barley :– **gherzdā*.

gorsedd gɔ̄·ɹseð meeting of Welsh bards and druids, esp. as preliminary to the eisteddfod. XVIII. W., 'throne, tribunal', lit. 'high seat'.

gosh gɔʃ Deformation of GOD used in oaths. XVIII (earlier †*gosse* XVI). Cf. LOSH.

goshawk gɔ·shɔ̄k large short-winged hawk. OE. *gōshafoc*, f. *gōs* GOOSE + *hafoc* HAWK; cf. ON. *gáshaukr*.

Goshen gou·ʃən (allus.) place of plenty or of light. XVII. See Gen. xlvi, xlvii, Ex ix 26.

gosling gɔ·zliŋ young goose. XV. orig. *gesling* – ON. *gǽslingr* (Sw., Da. *gàsling*), f. *gás* GOOSE; assim. (XV, Lydg.) to Eng. *goose*; see -LING[1].

gospel gɔ·spəl the 'good tidings' proclaimed by Jesus Christ; any of the four books written by the Evangelists; portion of any of these read at the Eucharist OE.; something 'as true as the gospel' XIII; something 'to swear by' as doctrine to be believed XVII. OE. *gōdspel*, i.e. *gōd* GOOD, *spel* news, tidings (SPELL), rendering of ecclL. *bona annuntiatio, bonus nuntius*, used as literal renderings of ecclL. *evangelium*, Gr. εὐαγγέλιον EVANGEL (cf. Goth. *þiuþspillōn* εὐαγγέλεσθαι, preach the gospel, f. *þiuþ* good, *spillōn* announce; see SPELL). The normal shortening of the *ō* and the apparent appropriateness led to the identification of the first syll. with GOD, which is reflected in all the forms adopted in the Germ. langs. of peoples evangelized from England, viz. OS. *godspell*, OHG. *gotspell*, ON. *guð-, goðspjall*; in ME. *goddspel* occurs in the MSS. of Laȝamon's 'Brut' and *goddspell* in the 'Ormulum'. Hence **go·speller** (which illustrates various uses of -ER[1]), OE. *gōdspellere*, f. *gōdspel* or the corr. vb. *gōdspellian*, †one of the four evangelists (OE.–XVII); †gospel-book, *evangeliarium* XV; one who recites the Gospel at the Eucharist; one who professes the faith of the gospel, esp. fanatically (*hot-gospeller*) XVI.

goss gɔs (sl.) hat. XIX. Short for *gossamer*, trade name of a light silk hat, *c.*1830–50.

gossamer gɔ·səməɹ fine film spun by spiders esp. in autumn. XIV (*gosesomer, gossomer*). ¶The earliest forms suggest deriv. from GOOSE + SUMMER[1], but the allusion is obscure, and is not cleared up by the synon. Continental forms, e.g. G. *altweiber-, mädchen-, Mechtildesommer* (old women's, girl's, Matilda's summer), G. *sommerfäden*, Sw. *sommartråd* (summer threads).

gossip gɔ·sip †sponsor at baptism OE.; †familiar acquaintance XIV; idle talker, tattler XVI; (from the vb.) tittle-tattle, easy talk XIX. Late OE. *godsibb*, corr. to ON. *guðsefi* godfather, *guðsifja* godmother (OSw. *guzsowir* m., *guþsiff, gudzsöff* fem.), comp. of GOD and SIB denoting the spiritual affinity of the baptized and their sponsors. Hence **go·ssip** vb. be or act as gossip XVI (Sh.); talk idly XVII. **go·ssip**RED (hist.) affinity of sponsors XIV; by Scott and others used for 'gossiping, gossip'.

gossoon gɔsū·n (Anglo-Ir.) youth, boy, lackey. XVII. Alteration of †*garsoon* (XVII), earlier †*garsoun* – (O)F. *garçon*; see GARÇON.

got, gotten see GET.

Goth gɔþ name of a Germanic tribe prominent in Europe A.D. III–V, or their language (a member of the East Germanic group). OE. *Gota*, usu. in pl. *Gotan*, was superseded in ME. (XIV, Ch.) by the adoption of late and medL. *Gothī* pl. = Gr. *Góthoi, Gótthoi* pl. – Goth. **Gutōs* or **Gutans* pl. (cf. *Gut þiuda* the Gothic people). So **Go·thic** pert. to the Goths; †Germanic, Teutonic; †medieval, romantic, of the Dark Ages; spec. of the style of architecture characterized particularly by the pointed arch (Evelyn); †barbarous, savage (Dryden); black-letter (type). XVII. – F. *gothique* or late L. *Gothicus*. Cf. SUIOGOTHIC.

gouache gwāʃ water-colour painting with opaque colours. XIX. – F. – It. *guazzo*.

gouge gaudʒ, gūdʒ chisel with concave blade. XV (*goodg*). – (O)F. *gouge* = Pr. *goja*, Sp. *gubia*, Pg. *goiva*, It. *gubbia* :– late L. *gubia, gulbia* (Vegetius, Isidore), perh. of Celtic origin (cf. OIr. *gulba* sting, W. *gylf* beak, Corn. *gilb* borer). Hence **gouge** vb. XVI.

goulash gū·làʃ stew of steak and vegetables XIX; re-deal in contract bridge XX. – Magyar *gulyáshús*, f. *gulyás* herdsman + *hús* meat.

gourd gɔ̄əɹd, guəɹd fruit of cucurbitaceous plants. XIV (R. Mannyng). – AN. *gurde* (William of Wadington), OF. *gourde*, repr. ult. L. *cucurbita* (Columella, Pliny).

gourmand guə·ɹmənd, ‖gurmã †glutton XV; (as F.) judge of good feeding XVIII. – (O)F. *gourmand*, of unkn. origin.

gourmet guə·ɹmei, ‖gurmɛ connoisseur in the delicacies of the table. XIX. – F. *gourmet* (earlier pl. *grommes*) †wine-merchant's assistant, wine-taster, infl. in sense by GOURMAND.

gout gaut disease orig. so named from the notion of the dropping of morbid matter from the blood into the joints. XIII. – OF. *goute* (mod. *goutte*) drop, gout :– L. *gutta* drop, in medL. applied to various diseases marked by 'defluxion of humours'. Hence **gou·ty**[1]. XV (Hoccleve).

govern gʌ·vəɹn rule with authority XIII; direct, regulate, sway XIV; (of grammatical regimen) XVI. – OF. *governer* (mod. *gouverner*) = Pr., Pg. *governar*, Sp. *gobernar*, It. *governare* :– L. *gubernāre* steer, direct, rule – Gr. *kubernân* steer. So **go·vern**ANCE. XIV. – OF. **go·vern**ESS[1] XV (Caxton). Shortening of †*governeress* (XIV, Ch.); see -ESS[1]. **go·vern**MENT. XVI. – (O)F. **go·vern**OR[1].

XIII (Cursor M.). – OF. *governeor* (mod. *gouverneur*) – L. *gubernātor*.

gowan gau·ən (Sc. and north.) chiefly pl., applied to various yellow and white field flowers. XVI. prob. alteration of (dial.) *gollan* (XIV) ranunculus, caltha, chrysanthemum, which is prob. rel. to *gold* in MARIGOLD.

gowk gauk (dial.) cuckoo XIV; fool, half-wit XVII. – ON. *gaukr* = OE. *ġēac*, OFris., OS. *gāk*, OHG. *gouh* (in MHG. fool, G. *gauch*) :– CGerm. (exc. Gothic) **gaukaz*, of imit. origin (cf. OHG. *guckōn* call cuckoo).

gown gaun loose robe. XIV. – OF. *goune*, *gon(n)e* = Pr., OSp. *gona*, It. *gonna* :– late L. *gunna* fur garment (cf. Byz. Gr. *goûna* fur, fur-lined garment). Hence **gow·ns**MAN (earlier †*gownman*) †adult Roman XVI (tr. L. *togātus* 'gowned men'; see TOGA); civilian)(soldier; lawyer, clergyman; university man XVII.

grab[1] græb grasp suddenly or greedily. XVI. prob. – MLG., MDu. *grabben*, to which there is a frequent. formation, Du, LG. *grabbeln* scramble for a thing, whence prob. (dial.) **gra·bble** (XVI) grope, scramble, etc.; f. **grab-*, perh. modification of the base of GRIP[1], GRIPE, GROPE.

grab[2] græb large coasting vessel used in the East. XVII. – Arab. *ghurāb* raven, galley.

grace greis favour XII; prayer of blessing or thanksgiving XIII (till XVI usu. pl., repr. F. *grâces*, L. *grātiæ*); pleasing quality XIV. – (O)F. *grâce* = Pr., Sp. *gracia*, Pg. *graça*, It. *grazia*, semi-pop. – L. *grātia*, f. *grātus* pleasing (see GRATEFUL). So **grac**IOUS grei·ʃəs. XIII (Cursor M.). – OF. *gracious* (mod. *gracieux*), corr. to Pr. *gracios*, etc. – L. *grātiōsus*. Hence **gra·ce**FUL[1] in casual use from XV till late XVI, when the present senses begin. **gra·ce**LESS. XIV (PPl., Ch.).

grackle græ·kl bird of any genus orig. included in Gracula. XVIII. – modL. *grācula*, fem. formed to corr. to L. *grāculus* jackdaw (for the expressive combination of *g* and *r* cf. GARRULOUS).

gradation grədei·ʃən †(rhet.) climax; †gradual progress; series of stages XVI; scale of degrees XVII; ablaut XIX (H. Sweet). – L. *gradātiō(n-)*, f. *gradus* step; see -ATION and cf. F. *gradation*. **grade** greid †angular degree XVI; step, stage, DEGREE XVIII. – L. *gradus* step, or derived F. *grade* (which is partly – It. *grado*). Hence as vb. †in pp. admitted to a degree XVI; arrange in grades XVII. **-grade** greid adj. suffix repr. L. *-gradus* stepping (f. base of *gradus* step, *gradī* step, walk), as in *retrōgradus* RETROGRADE, *tardigradus* TARDIGRADE; hence in modL. formations, as *digitigradus*, *plantigradus*. **gradient** grei·diənt amount of inclination (of a road) to the horizontal, *c.*1830. prob. f. *grade* with ending suggested by *salient*; not connected with the adj. †*gradient* walking (XVII). **gradine** grədī·n set of low steps or seats one above another; shelf at the back of an altar. XIX. – It. *gradino*, dim. of *grado* step, GRADE; cf. F. *gradin* (XVII). **gradual** græ·djuəl, -dʒ- †graded, in steps XVI; proceeding by degrees XVII. – medL. *graduālis*, f. L. *gradus* step, GRADE. (*G. Psalms*, Ps. cxx–cxxxiv, entitled Song of Degrees in A.V., Vulg. *canticum graduum*, tr. Heb. *shīr hamma'alōth*, the meaning of which is disputed.) Also sb. (eccl.) portion of the Eucharistic office between the epistle and the gospel, orig. recited on the steps of the ambo. XVI. – medL. *graduāle*, n. of *graduālis* used sb.; cf. GRAIL[1]. **gradu**ATE græ·djuət, -dʒ- adj. and sb. (one) who has been admitted to a university degree. XV. – medL. *graduātus*, pp. (used sb.) of *graduārī* take a degree, f. *gradus*. **gradus** grei·dəs (pl. *graduses*) short for *Gradus ad Parnassum* (steps to Parnassus), L. title of a dictionary of L. prosody used as an aid to versification. XVIII. ¶ Words formed on the same base (the ultimate relations of which are doubtful) are *aggression*, *congress*, *digress*, *egress*, *ingress*, *progress*, *regress*, *transgress*; *degree*; *ingredient*.

Græcism, Grecism grī·sizm Greek idiom or style. XVI. – F. *grécisme* or medL. *Græcismus*, f. *Græcus* GREEK; see -ISM. So **Græ·ci**ZE, **Gre·ci**ZE. XVII. – L. *Græcizāre*. **Græ·co-, Gre·co-,** mod. comb. form of L. *Græcus*. XVII.

graffito, pl. *-i* græfī·tou drawing or writing scratched on a wall. XIX. – It. *graffito*, f. *graffio* scratching, perh. new formation on *graffiare* scratch, itself f. *graffio* in the sense 'hook' – Germ. **krāppon* (see GRAPE), of which a parallel nasalized var. is repr. by CRAMP.

graft[1] gràft shoot inserted in another stock. XV (Catholicon Anglicum). Alteration, with parasitic *t*, of †*graff* (XIV, Trevisa) – OF. *grafe*, *grefe*, (also mod.) *greffe* – L. *graphium* – Gr. *graphíon*, *grapheîon* stylus, f. *gráphein* write (see GRAPHIC); the transf. of meaning was suggested by the similarity of shape. So **graft** vb. XV. Alteration of †*graff* XIV (PPl., Wycl. Bible), f. the sb.

graft[2] gràft (orig. U.S.) means of making illicit profit; dishonest gains; (political) bribery. XIX. Of unkn. origin; perh. extension of dial. sense 'work' of *graft* (cf. *job*).

grail[1] greil (eccl.) gradual. XIV. ME. *grael* – OF. *grael* :– ecclL. *gradāle*, for *graduāle* GRADUAL.

grail[2] greil platter used by Jesus Christ at the Last Supper, in which Joseph of Arimathea is said to have received his blood at the Crucifixion. XIV. ME. *greal*, *graal* – OF. *graal*, *grael*, *greel*, *greil* :– medL. *gradālis* dish, of unkn. origin. Cf. SANGREAL.

grain[1] grein A. small hard particle XIII; granular texture; †berry, grape; seed, spec. of corn or cereal XIV; smallest Eng. unit of weight XVI (Recorde). B. kermes, which was thought to consist of seeds or berries (phr. *in grain*; cf. INGRAINED); (fast) dye XIV. In A – OF. *grain*, *grein* (mod. *grain*) = Pr. *gran*, Sp., It. *grano*, Pg. *grão* GRAM[1] :– L.

grānum CORN[1]; in B – (O)F. *graine* = Pr., Sp., It. *grana* :– Rom. *grāna fem., orig. pl. of *grānum* n.

grain[2] grein †fork of the body XIII (Cursor M.); (dial.) prong of a fork XV (pl. as sg., also *grainse*; fish-spear with prongs XIX); (dial.) bough XVI. – ON. *grein* division, distinction, branch (Sw. *gren*, Da. *green*), of unkn. origin.

grallatorial grælətɔ̄·riəl (ornith.) wading. XIX. f. modL. *grallātōrius*, f. L. *grallātor* walker on stilts, f. *grallæ* stilts (**grad(s)lā*, f. base of *gradus* step, GRADE); see -ATOR, -IAL.

gralloch græ·ləχ disembowel. XIX. – Gael. *grealach* entrails.

gram[1] græm chick-pea. XVIII. – Pg. †*gram*, *grão* :– L. *grānum* GRAIN[1].

gram[2] var. of GRAMME.

-gram græm repr. Gr. *grámma* something written, letter of the alphabet, rel. to *gráphein* write (cf. GRAPHIC) in (i) words directly derived from Gr., as ANAGRAM, DIAGRAM, EPIGRAM, PROGRAM(ME), or modelled on Gr. types, as CHRONOGRAM, LOGOGRAM, (ii) words compounded with a numeral with *grámma* (or *grammḗ* line), as MONOGRAM, PENTAGRAM. See also TELEGRAM, and, for the denominations of weight in the metric system, GRAMME.

gramarye græ·məri †grammar, learning XIV; occult learning, magic XV (taken up by Scott). – AN. *gramarie* = OF. *gramaire* GRAMMAR; cf. F. *grimoire* book of magic, earlier †*gramoire* (dial. var. of *gramaire*) †Latin grammar. See also GLAMOUR.

gramercy græ·məɹsi (arch.) thanks. XIII. – OF. *grant merci*, i.e. *grant* great, *merci* reward, favour (the etymol. sense being 'May God reward you greatly'); see GRAND, MERCY.

gramineous grəmi·niəs grassy. XVII. f. L. *grāmineus*, f. *grāmin-*, *grāmen* grass (cf. Gr. *grástis* green fodder); see -EOUS.

grammalogue græ·məlɔg in Isaac Pitman's shorthand, word represented by a single simplified sign. XIX. irreg. f. Gr. *grámma* letter (see -GRAM) + *lógos* (LOGOS), taken to mean 'word'.

grammar græ·məɹ †Latin; study of the sounds, forms, and syntax of a language (in earliest use, of Latin). XIV (*gramer-e*). – AN. *gramere*, OF. *gramaire* (mod. *grammaire*) :– **gramadie* – L. *grammatica* – Gr. *grammatikḗ*, sb. use (sc. *tékhnē* art) of fem. of *grammatikós* pertaining to letters (whence, through L. and F., **gramma·tICAL** XVI), f. *grammat-*, *grámma* (see -GRAM). So **grammarIAN** grəmɛə·riən. XIV. – OF. *gramarien* (mod. *grammairien*), f. *gramaire*.

gramme græm XVIII. – F. *gramme* (adopted as the unit of weight in the metric system by a law of 19 frimaire, year viii, i.e. 1799) – Gr. (late L.) *grámma* small weight.

gramophone græ·məfoun instrument for recording and (esp.) reproducing sounds, invented by Emil Berliner of Washington, D.C., 1887. Formed by inverting the first and last sylls. of PHONOGRAM. ¶ Preceded by *graphophone*, 1885, from *phonograph*.

grampus græ·mpəs name for several delphinoid cetaceans. XVI. Earliest forms *graundepose*, *grampoys*, alteration (by assim. to GRAND) of †*gra(s)peys* (XIV). – OF. *grapois*, *graspeis*, also *craspois* :– medL. *craspisci-s*, f. L. *crassus* fat, CRASS, *piscis* FISH.

granadilla grænədi·lə passion-flower. XVIII (earlier in F. form *-ille*; also *grena-*). – Sp. *granadilla*, dim. of *granada* POMEGRANATE.

granary græ·nəri storehouse for grain. XVI. – L. *grānārium* (usu. pl. *-ia*), f. *grānum* GRAIN; see -ARY. Cf. GARNER.

grand grænd great, pre-eminent, main, principal XVI; imposing, sublime XVIII (Addison, Burke). – F. *grand* big, large, tall, lofty, sublime, or its source L. *grandis* full-grown, abundant, grown-up, tall, powerful, lofty, sublime, which in Rom. (Pr. *gran*, Sp., It. *grande*) superseded L. *magnus* in all its uses. (An adoption of AN. *graunt*, OF. *grant*, was current earlier in Eng. XIII–XVI, e.g. in †*grantsire*, later *grandsire*, and in the designation *the graunt* the Great.) The use of F. *grand* to denote the second degree removed in ascent of relationship (in imitation of L. *avunculus magnus* great-uncle, *amita magna* great-aunt, Gr. *megalomḗtēr* grandmother) was adopted, *grandpère*, *grand'mère* being repr. by **gra·ndfa:ther, gra·ndmo:ther** XVI, earlier †*graunt-* XV; it was extended (XVI) to the corr. degree of descent in **gra·ndchild, gra·ndson, gra·nddaugh:ter,** where F. has *petit* little. ¶ Various titles and official designations have been taken over from Rom. langs. in semi-translated form, e.g. *grand duke* (F. *grand duc*, rendering It. *granduca*; cf. G. *grossherzog*), *grand master* (F. *grand maître*), *grand signior* (It. *gran signore*). So also *grand tour* (F. *grand tour* great circuit, sc. of Europe XVII).

grandam græ·ndæm grandmother. XIII. – AN. *graund dame*; see GRAND, DAME (the use of *dame* for 'mother' seems to be AN. only). See also GRANNY.

grandee grændī· Sp. or Pg. nobleman of the highest rank. XVI (*grande*). – Sp., Pg. *grande*, sb. use of *grande* adj. GRAND; the ending was illogically assim. to -EE[1].

grandeur græ·ndjəɹ †height XV; †eminence; transcendent or sublime greatness, lofty dignity. XVII. – (O)F. *grandeur*, f. *grand* great (GRAND). Attempts have been made to anglicize the ending, e.g. *-ure*, *-our* (XVII–XVIII), *-or* (XVIII–XIX).

grandiloquent grændi·ləkwənt of lofty or pompous speech. XVI (Nashe). f. L. *grandiloquus* (whence **grandi·loquous,** G. Harvey), f. *grandis* great, GRAND + *-loquus* speaking, f. *loquī* to speak; see LOCUTION, -ENT.

grandiose græ·ndious producing an effect of grandeur. XIX (Thackeray). – F. *grandiose* – It. *grandioso*, f. *grande* GRAND, after *glorioso*, etc.; see -OSE.

Grandisonian grændisou·niən resembling the ideal of a perfect gentleman as portrayed in the hero of 'The History of Sir Charles Grandison' by Samuel Richardson, 1754; see -IAN. XIX.

grange greindʒ (arch.) granary; farming establishment XIII (Havelok, Cursor M.); outlying farmhouse of an estate XIV (Ch.). – (O)F. *grange* :– medL. *grānica*, sb. use (sc. *villa*) of fem. of **grānicus* pert. to grain, f. *grānum* GRAIN.

grangerize grei·ndʒəraiz illustrate (a book) by the addition of prints, etc. XIX. f. name of Joseph *Granger*, who in 1769 published 'A biographical history of England' with blank leaves for the insertion of portraits, etc.; see -IZE.

granite græ·nit granular crystalline rock. XVII (Evelyn). – It. *granito* (used earlier by Inigo Jones) lit. grained, granular, pp. formation on *grano* GRAIN. (From It. are also F. *granit*, Sp. *granito*, G. *granit*, etc.) Hence **grani·tIC**. XVIII.

granny græ·ni grandmother. XVII (*-ee*, Dryden). f. *grannam* (Sh.), var. of GRANDAM + -Y[6].

grant grànt agree to, allow, concede XIII; bestow formally XIV. – OF. *granter*, *graanter*, *greanter*, alteration of *creanter* guarantee, assure :– Rom. **crēdentāre*, f. *crēdent-*, prp. stem of L. *crēdere* believe, trust (see CREDIT). Hence **grant** sb. XIII.

granule græ·njūl small grain. XVII. – late L. *grānulum*, dim. of *grānum* GRAIN; see -ULE and cf. F. *granule* (XIX). So **gra·nulAR** XVIII; **gra·nulATE**[3], **granulA·TION** XVII; **gra·nulOSE** XIX; **gra·nulOUS** XVI. Cf. F. *granuler*, *granulation* (XVII), *granuleux* (XVI).

grape greip berry of the vine XIII; morbid growth on the pastern of a horse (so F. *grappe*) XVI; more fully *grape-shot* (XVIII) cannon shot consisting of cast-iron balls connected together (cf. G. *traubenkartätschen*) XVII. Earlier in *win|grape* 'wine-cluster', cluster of grapes (XIII), f. *wīn* WINE + *grape* – OF. *grape* (mod. *grappe* bunch of grapes); later in XIII used first in coll. pl., subsequently in sg. (superseding *wīnberie*, OE. *wīnberi(ġ)e* 'wine-berry'). OF. *grape* was prob. a verbal sb. f. *graper* gather (grapes), f. *grape*, *grappe* (= Pr., Sp. *gr̨apa*, It. *grappa*) hook :– Rom. **grap(p)o* – Germ. **krāppon* (OHG. *krāpfo*) hook, rel. to CRAMP. Hence **grape-fruit** (orig. U.S.) shaddock, pomelo. XIX.

graph græf. XIX. orig. (chem.) short for GRAPHIC *formula*, in which lines are used to indicate the connexions of elements; hence in math.

-graph gràf repr. F. *-graphe*, L. *-graphus* – Gr. *-graphos*, which was used (i) in the sense 'written', as *autógraphos* AUTOGRAPH, *kheirógraphos* CHIROGRAPH, (ii) in the sense 'writing', 'describing', as *bibliográphos* writer of books (cf. BIBLIOGRAPHER), *geōgráphos* GEOGRAPHER. Several of the Gr. passive formations have been anglicized, and analogous formations have been made on Gr. models such as *lithograph*, *photograph*, which have been imitated in hybrid formations such as *pictograph* (there are even joc. nonce-words, e.g. *hurrygraph* for 'hurried sketch'). Most of the current words in *-graph* are of the technical order and usu. denote a thing that records or expresses (as if in writing), e.g. *heliograph*, *ideograph*, *phonograph*, *seismograph*, *telegraph*. The Gr. active formations are usu. repr. by forms in **-graphER**[1] grəfəɹ, which furnish agent-nouns for formations in **-graphY**[3] grəfi, as *astronomer* (L. *astronomus*) had been based on *astronomy* (there were, in fact, a few early formations in *-ier*, as *chronographier*, *geographier*). The first words of this type are of early XVI, and by the late XVI *-grapher* had become the regular ending for words ult. devolved from actual or assumed Gr. words in *-gráphos* (but *telegraphist* is the common form, not *telegrapher*). Some words in *-graphy* denote processes or styles of writing or graphic representation, as *brachygraphy*, *calligraphy*, *cryptography*, *orthography*, *photography*, *stenography*, *typography*; but mostly they are names of sciences, as *bibliography*, *geography*, *hydrography*, *lexicography*, *topography*. Hybrid formations like *stratigraphy* are few. The corr. adjs. end in **-graphIC**, **-graphICAL** græ·fik(əl), with advs. in *-gra·phically*.

graphic græ·fik †drawn with pencil or pen (rare); vividly descriptive XVII; pert. to drawing or painting XVIII; characterized by diagrams XIX. – L. *graphicus* – Gr. *graphikós*, f. *graphḗ* drawing, writing (cf. CARVE); so F. *-ique*. So **gra·phICAL** XVII, **gra·phicalLY**[2] XVI.

graphite græ·fait black lead, plumbago. XVIII. – G. *graphit* (Werner, 1789), f. Gr. *gráphein* write (the stuff being used for pencils); see prec. and -ITE.

grapho- græ·fou repr. (sometimes through F.) Gr. *grapho-*, comb. form of *graphḗ* writing.

grapnel græ·pnəl instrument with iron claws, small anchor with three or more flukes. XIV. – AN. **grapenel*, f. synon. OF. *grapon* (mod. *grappin*) – Germ. **krāppon*; see GRAPE, -EL[2].

grapple græ·pl grapnel. XVI. – OF. *grapil* – Pr. *grapil*, f. *grapa* hook (see GRAPE). Hence **gra·pple** vb. XVI.

grasp gràsp †clutch (intr.) XIV; seize with the hand XVI; fig. XVII. Late ME. *graspe*, also *grapse*, perh. :– OE. **grǣpsan* :– Germ. **graipisōn*, parallel to **graipōjan* GROPE; but perh. of LG. origin (cf. LG., EFris. *grapsen*).

grass gràs herbage for fodder OE.; grassy earth XIII; pasture XV; non-cereal gramineous plant XVI. OE. *græs*, *gærs* = OFris. *gres*, *gers*, OS. (Du.), OHG. (G.), ON., Goth. *gras* :– CGerm. **grasam*, f. **gra-* **grō-* (see GREEN, GROW). The metath. form *gærs* is still repr. by dial. *gers*, *girs*. **gra·ss-**

cu:tter native in India employed to cut and bring in hay. XVIII. – Hind. *ghāskaṭ, ghāskaṭā* (Skr. *ghasa* pasture grass), with assim. to *grass* and *cutter*. **grass-green.** OE. *græsgrēne*. **grasshopper** grà·shɔ:pəɹ insect remarkable for leaping and chirping. XV. Extended form of †*grasshop*, OE. *gærshoppa, -e*, Orm *gresshoppe* (f. *gærs* GRASS + *hoppa*, agent-noun of *hoppian* HOP[1]), perh. after OSw. *gräshoppare* or LG. *grashüpper* (G. *grashüpfer*); cf. synon. OS. *feldhoppo* 'field-hopper'. **grass widow** †unmarried woman who has cohabited XVI (More); married woman away from her husband XIX (first in India). The first el. may have alluded orig. to a bed of grass or hay (cf. BASTARD for similar formations). Continental equivalents, with one or both meanings, are MLG. *graswedewe*, Du. *grasweduwe*, Sw. *gräsenka*, Da. *græsenke*; also G. *strohwitwe* 'straw widow'. **gra·ss**Y[1]. XVI (Douglas).

grate[1] greit †grating, grille XIV; †cage, prison XVI; barred frame for holding fuel XVII. – OF. *grate* (Aimé), Sp. *grada* hurdle, corr. to It. *grata* grate, gridiron, hurdle (cf. medL. *grata* lattice), pointing to Rom. **crāta*, **grāta*, for L. *crātis* hurdle.

grate[2] greit †scrape, scarify; rasp small XV; rub harshly *upon* XVI. – OF. *grater* (mod. *gratter*) = Pr., Sp. *gratar*, It. *grattare* :- CRom. **grattāre* – Germ. **krattōn* (OHG. *chrazzōn*, G. *kratzen* scratch). So **gra·ter** grating or rasping instrument. XIV. Partly – OF. *grateor, -our*, partly f. the above vb.; see -ER[1], -ER[2].

grateful grei·tf(ə)l pleasing; thankful XVI. f. †*grate* (XVI) – L. *grātus* (in the same senses), pp. formation corr. to Skr. *gūrtás* welcome, agreeable, thankful, orig. approved, rel. to words of the Indo-Iran. and Baltic groups denoting 'praise' (cf. GRACE, GRATIS); the unusual formation with -FUL[1] may have been suggested by It. *gradevole* pleasing.

gratify græ·tifai †reward, recompense; give pleasure to XVI. – F. *gratifier*, or its source L. *grātificārī* do a favour to, make a present of, f. *grātus*; see GRATEFUL and -FY. So **gratifica·tion**. XVI. – (O)F. or L.

gratin græ·tẽ (cookery) garnishing of grated or rasped material. XIX. – F. *gratin*, f. OF. *grater* GRATE[2].

gratis grei·tis for nothing, freely. XV. – L. *grātīs*, reduction of *grātiīs*, abl. pl. of *grātia* favour, GRACE.

gratitude græ·titjūd †favour, free gift; gratefulness. XVI. – F. *gratitude* or medL. *grātitūdō*, f. *grātus*; see GRATEFUL, -TUDE.

gratuity grətjū·iti †graciousness, favour; gift, present. XVI. – (O)F. *gratuité* or medL. *grātuitās* gift, f. L. *grātus*; see GRATEFUL, -ITY. So **gratu·itous**. XVII. f. L. *grātuitus* freely given, spontaneous; for the formation cf. *fortuitous*.

gratulate græ·tjuleit welcome, greet; CONGRATULATE. XVI. f. L. *grātulāt-, -ārī* (for **grātitulārī*), f. *grātus*; see GRATEFUL, -ATE[3]. So **gratula·tion**. XV. – OF. or L.

gravamen grəvei·men grievance or its presentation XVII; part of an accusation that bears most heavily XIX. – late L. *grāvāmen* physical inconvenience, in medL. grievance, f. L. *gravāre* weigh upon, oppress, f. *gravis* heavy, GRAVE[3].

grave[1] greiv place dug out for a burial. OE. *græf* = OFris. *gref*, OS. *graf*, OHG. *grap* :- WGerm. **graƀa*, parallel to N. and EGerm. **graƀō*, repr. by ON. *grǫf*, Goth. *graba*; f. **graƀ-* GRAVE[2]. The present form descends from OE. obl. forms.

grave[2] greiv (dial.) dig OE.; (dial., orig. from ON.) bury XIII; (arch.) engrave OE. OE. *grafan*, pt. *grōf, grōfon*, pp. *-grafen* dig, engrave, also in *begrafan* bury (cf. OS. *bigraƀan*), OLFrankish *gravan* (Du. *graven*) dig, OHG. *graban* dig, carve (G. *graben* dig; *begraben* bury, *eingraben* ENGRAVE), ON. *grafa* dig, bury, Goth. *graban* dig :- CGerm. **graƀan*, f. **graƀ-* (cf. prec.), **grōƀ-* (see GROOVE); IE. cogns. are OSl. *grebą* I dig, *grobŭ* ditch, Lett. *grebju* I scrape. The strong pt. died out in XV; pp. *graven* survives as a literary arch.; wk. forms appeared in XIV in pt. and pp.

grave[3] greiv weighty, important; serious XVI; plain, sombre XVII; gram.)(*acute* XVII. – (O)F. *grave* or L. *gravi-s* heavy, important, corr. to Skr. *gurús*, Gr. *barús* (cf. BARYTONE), Goth. *kaurus* heavy; cf. BRUTE.

grave[4] greiv †steward of property XII (Orm); in Yorks and Lincs, former administrative official XV. – ON. *greifi* – OLG. *grēve* (cf. GRAVE[6]).

grave[5] greiv clean (a ship's bottom) by burning and tarring; esp. in *graving dock*. XV. The forms †*greve*, †*greave* also occur; since boats were careened on the shore for the operation, prob. f. dial. F. *grave*, var. of *grève* shore – Celtic **gravo-* gravel, pebbles, repr. by Breton *grouan*, GROWAN.

grave[6] greiv foreign title (count); now only as the second member of comps. *landgrave, margrave, palsgrave, rhinegrave*. XVII. – OLG. *grēve*, whence ON. *greifi*; see GRAVE[4].

gravel græ·vl †sand; sand mixed with water-worn stones XIII (Cursor M.); (path.) XV. – (O)F. *gravelle*, dim. of *grave* gravel, coarse sand = Pr., Cat. *grava*; see GRAVE[5], -EL[2]. Hence **gravel-blind,** joc. intensive in Sh. 'Merchant of Venice' II ii 38 of SAND-BLIND; taken up by Sir W. Scott.

graven grei·vn see GRAVE[2].

graveolent grəvi·ələnt smelling strongly. XVII. – L. *graveolent-, -ēns*, f. *grave* advb. n. of *gravis* heavy (GRAVE[3]) + *olēns*, prp. of *olēre* have a smell, rel. to *odor* ODOUR; see -ENT.

graves var. of GREAVES.

gravid græ·vid pregnant. XVI. – L. *gravidus* laden, pregnant, f. *gravis* heavy; see GRAVE[3], -ID[1].

gravitate græ·viteit †exert weight or pressure; be affected by the force of gravity. XVII. f. pp. stem of modL. *gravitāre*, f. L. *gravitās* GRAVITY; see -ATE[3]. So **gravita·tion**. XVII; orig. falling of bodies to the earth or their sinking to their lowest level.

gravity græ·vĭti †influence, authority; seriousness; weighty dignity XVI; physical weight, later only spec. XVII. – (O)F. *gravité* or L. *gravitās*, f. *gravis* GRAVE[3]; see -ITY.

gravure abbrev. of PHOTOGRAVURE. XIX.

gravy grei·vi †dressing for white meats, etc. consisting of broth spiced XIV; fat and juices exuding from flesh during and after cooking XVI. Late ME. *grauey*, *graue*, perh. originating in a misreading of *grane* – OF. *grané* (in printed texts often *gravé*), prob. f. *grain* spice (cf. OF. *grenon* stew); see GRAIN[1], -Y[5].

gray see GREY. Hence **gray·ling**[1] fish of silver-grey colour. XV; whence F. *grelin*.

graze[1] greiz feed on herbage OE.; put to pasture XVI. OE. *grasian*, f. *græs* GRASS; cf. MDu., MHG. *grasen*.

graze[2] greiz touch lightly so as to abrade. XVII (Sh.). The earliest application is to a shot or shaft glancing off a surface; perh. a spec. use of prec., as if 'take off the grass close to the ground'; cf. G. *grasen* browse, pasture, scythe, glance off, Sw. *gräsa* (of a shot) graze, Da. *græsse* pasture, (of a bullet) ricochet. ¶ Distance of date makes it improbable that it is an alteration of ME. *glace* (XIV–XV) glide, glance off.

grazier grei·ziəɹ one who grazes cattle for market. XVI (the earliest recorded use is as tr. medL. *viridarius* VERDERER). f. GRASS + -IER; cf. *glazier*. Formerly assoc. with F. *graissier* fattener.

grease grīs melted fat XIII; fat of a beast of the chase XIV. – AN. *grece*, *gresse*, (O)F. *graisse* = Pr. *graisa*, Sp. *grasa*, It. *grascia* :– Rom. **crassia*, f. L. *crassus* (F., Pr. *gras*, etc., fat); see CRASS. Hence **grease** grīz, grīs. XV. **grea·ser**[1] applied to native Mexicans or Spanish Americans (XIX) from their greasy appearance. **grea·sy**[1] grī·zi, grī·si. XVI.

great greit (dial.) thick, coarse, bulky; large, of considerable size OE.; pregnant XII (Orm); important, eminent XIII (RGlouc.). OE. *grēat* = OFris. *grāt*, OS. *grōt* (Du. *groot*), OHG. *grōʒ* (G. *gross*) :– WGerm. **grautaz*, of unkn. origin, but perh. rel. to GROATS and GROUT[1]. The sense 'large' appears in the OE. period, as also in OHG. and (as the only use) in OS. Thus, *great* became an alternative to *michel* (cf. MICKLE), of which it was later an intensive or affective syn. The forms corr. to OE. *mićel* have been likewise superseded in German and Dutch; with the colloq. substitution of *big* and *large* for *great* cf. the gen. supersession of L. *magnus* in Rom. by *grandis* full-grown, big (see GRAND). The normal ME. compar. *gretter* (:– OE. **grīettra*) was repl. by *greater*, and the analogical *grettest* (XIII–XV) by *greatest*. As in *break*, ei repr. ME. ɛ̄ instead of ī, which was, however, a prevalent pronunc. in XVIII; for a similar infl. of r cf. *broad*. The use of the adj. to designate persons one degree further removed in ascending or descending relationship is after the use of F. *grand*, which reflects that in L. *avunculus magnus* great-uncle, *amita magna* great-aunt. Hence **grea·tly**[2] XII, **grea·tness** late OE. *grētnys*.

greave grīv (usu. pl.) armour for the leg below the knee. XIV. – OF. *greve* calf of the leg, shin, armour (mod. F. dial. *grève*, *graive* upper part of the leg) = Sp. *greba*, of unkn. origin.

greaves, graves grīvz, greivz fibrous refuse of tallow. XVII. orig. a whaler's term – LG. *greven* pl. (whence also Da. *grever*), corr. to OHG. *griubo*, *griobo* (G. *griebe* refuse of lard or tallow), of unkn. origin (OE. *ele|grēofa* may mean 'oil-pot' or 'oil-refuse').

grebe grīb diving bird of genus Podiceps. XVIII (Pennant). – F. *grèbe*, †*griaibe* (Belon), of dial. origin, other vars. being *grèpe*, *gréboz*, *graibioz*.

grece grīs (arch.) steps, stairs XIII (Cursor M.); step, stair XV (in Sh. *grise*, *grize*). – OF. *gres*, *grez*, *greis*, pl. of *gré* (whence ME. *gre(e)* step, degree, surviving in modSc. in the sense 'pre-eminence, mastery') :– L. *gradu-s* step (cf. DEGREE, GRADE).

Grecian grī·ʃən pert. to Greece or the Greeks; sb. †Greek; Greek scholar. XVI. – OF. *grecien* or medL. **græciānus*, f. L. *Græcia* Greece; see -IAN. (*Grekin*, *grecan* had been occas. used earlier.)

greedy grī·di having an inordinate appetite. OE. *grēdiġ*, *grǣdiġ* = OS. *grādag*, OHG. *grātac*, ON. *gráðugr*, Goth. *grēdags* :– CGerm. **grǣðagaz*, *-ugaz*, f. **grǣðuz* hunger, greed (in OE. *grǣdum* d.pl. eagerly, ON. *gráðr*, Goth. *grēdus*), of unkn. origin. Hence **greed** sb., by back-formation. XVII.

greegree grī·grī African charm or fetish. XVII. Of native origin. Cf. F. *grisgris*.

Greek grīk native of Greece OE.; language of Greece XIV (Ch.); cheat, sharper XVI (so F. *grec*); adj. XIV (Ch.); of the Orthodox Eastern Church XVI. OE. *Grēcas* (pl.; and so for the most part till XVI), corr. to MLG. *Grēke*, MDu. *Grieke*, G. *Grieche*, ON. *Grikkir* (pl.), of which the earlier forms are OE. *Crēcas*, OHG. *Chrēch*, Goth. *Krēks* :– Germ. **Krēkaz* – L. *Græcus* (applied by the Romans to the people who called themselves *Hellēnes*; see HELLENE) – Gr. *Graikós* (acc. to Aristotle a prehistoric name of the Hellenes), adj. deriv. of **Graios*, which was used by the Romans in pl. *Graiī* as a poet.

syn. of *Græcī*. So **Gree·k**ISH[1]. OE. *Crēcisċ* (= OHG. *Chrēchisk*); not quite superseded by *Greek* till XVII. Other syns. were †*Grew* (latterly Sc.), ME. *gru* (XIII) – OF. *griu* :– L. *Græcum*; †*Gregeis*, *-ois* XIII–XVI. – OF. *gregois* :– medL. *græciscu-s*. Hence **Gree·k**LING[1] contemptible Greek XVII (Jonson); after L. *Græculus* (Juvenal), dim. of *Græcus*.

green grīn of the colour of growing herbage, verdant OE.; fresh, young, unripe, immature XVII. OE. *grēne* = OFris. *grēne*, OS. *grōni* (Du. *groen*), OHG. *gruoni* (G. *grün*), ON. *grœnn* :– CGerm. (exc. Goth.) **grōnjaz*, f. **grō-*, base of GROW; cf. GRASS. Hence **gree·n**ERY. XVIII (Coleridge). **gree·nga·ge.** XVIII; f. name of Sir William *Gage*, in compliment to whom the plum was so named. **gree·n**HORN perh. orig. ox with green (i.e. young) horns XV; inexperienced person XVII. **gree·ning** †variety of pear; apple which is green when ripe. XVII. prob. – MDu. *groeninc* (Du. *groening*) kind of apple. **gree·n**NESS. OE. **green sickness.** XVI; cf. Du. *bleekzucht*, Gr. *bleichsucht* anaemia.

greet[1] grīt address, salute, esp. with expressions of goodwill OE.; receive with welcome XVII (Sh.). OE. *grētan*, **grœ̄tan* handle, touch, visit, attack, treat, salute = OFris. *grēta* salute, complain, OS. *grōtian* call upon (Du. *groeten* salute), OHG. *gruozzen* address, attack (G. *grüssen* salute) :– WGerm. **grōtjan* cry out, call upon, (hence) provoke to action, assail, address; prob. based on IE. **ghrōd-* **ghrēd-* resound, repr. by Skr. *hrād-*. ¶ Some take this vb. and the next to have a common basis; cf. the double meaning of OFris. *grēta*, and ON. *grǿta* cause to weep, distress.

greet[2] grīt (Sc.) weep. (i) OE. (Anglian) *grētan*, **grǣtan* (prob. str., but once wk. pt. *begrette*) = OS. *grātan* (pt. *griat*, *griot*), MHG. *grazen* (wk.) cry out, rage, storm, ON. *gráta* (pt. *grét*, pp. *grátinn*), Goth. *grētan* (pt. *gaigrōt*) :– CGerm. **grǣtan*, orig. redupl. str. vb. rel. to prec. (ii) OE. *grēotan* (= OS. *griotan*), perh. f. Germ. **ga-* Y- + vb. repr. by synon. OE. *rēotan*.

greffier gre·fiəɹ, ‖grɛfje registrar, clerk, notary. XVI. – F. *greffier* – medL. *graphiārius*, f. *graphium* register, (earlier) stylus – Gr. *grapheîon*, *gráphion* pencil, paint-brush, registry, f. *gráphein* (see GRAPHIC).

gregarious grigɛə·riəs associating in communities. f. L. *gregārius*, f. *greg-*, *grex* flock, herd (cf. OIr. *graig* herd of horses, Gr. *ageírein* assemble, *agorá* (place of) assembly; see -ARIOUS.

Gregorian grigōə·riən pert. to Pope Gregory I (590–604) and the liturgical music ascribed to him; pert. to the calendar as reformed by Pope Gregory XIII (1572–85). XVII. – medL. *grēgoriānus* (whence F. *grégorien*), f. late L. *Grēgorius* – Gr. *Grēgórios*; see -IAN.

gremial grī·miəl pert. to the bosom or lap XVII; (hist.) 'internal', resident (member) XVI; sb. (eccl.) apron for a bishop's lap XIX. – medL. *gremiālis*, *gremiāle*, f. L. *gremium* lap, bosom, perh. rel. to CRAM; see -IAL.

grenade grinei·d pomegranate; small explosive shell. XVI. – F. *grenade* (XVI), alteration of OF. (*pume*) *grenate* POMEGRANATE after Sp. *granada*; so called from its shape. So **grenadier** grenədiə·ɹ †soldier armed with grenades, (now) soldier of a regiment of guards. XVII. – F. *grenadier*; see -IER[2].

grenadine gre·nədīn dress fabric. XIX. – F. *grenadine*, formerly *grenade* silk of a grained texture, f. *grenu* grained, f. *grain* GRAIN + *-u* (:– L. *-ūtus*); see -INE[4].

grey, gray grei colour intermediate between black and white. OE. *grǣġ* = OFris. *grē*, MDu. *grau*, *gra* (Du. *grauw*), OHG. *grāo* (G. *grau*), ON. *grár* :– CGerm. (exc. Gothic) **grǣwaz* :– IE. **ghrēghwos* (the suffix *-wo-* is frequent in colour-adjs., e.g. *yellow*); perh. ult. rel. to L. *rāvus* (:– **ghrāwos*) grey. *Grey Friar*. Franciscan friar. XIV. In sb. use *grey* (XV–XVII) succeeded to BROCK (OE.) and BAUSON (XIV) and was finally superseded by BADGER; perh. a transf. application of the sense 'grey fur'. ¶ Both spellings have analogies in two words in gen. use derived from OE. forms in *-ǣġ* and pronounced with ei, viz. *clay* and *whey*; the practice of printing houses is various and individuals tend to use the vars. with a difference of implication; the *-ey* form is established in *Scots Greys* and *a pair of greys*.

grid grid grating. XIX. Back-formation from GRIDIRON.

griddle gri·dl †gridiron XIII; circular plate for baking cakes on XIV. – OF. *gredil*, *gridil* gridiron (mod. *gril*) :– Rom. **crāticulum*, dim. of *crātis* (cf. CRATE). See GRILL.

gride graid (poet.) pierce. XIV. metath. form of *girde*, GIRD[2], adopted by Spenser from Lydgate and thence used by later writers. The mod. application to a grating or whizzing sound may have been suggested by *grate* and *strident*.

gridiron gri·daiəɹn frame of parallel metal bars used for broiling. XIII. The earliest ex., *gredire*, occurs in the same text (South English Legendary) with *gredile* GRIDDLE, and appears to be an alteration of this by assoc. with *ire* IRON; *e* of the first syll. was raised to *i* in XIV, but the forms *gre(e)diron* persisted till XVII.

grief grīf †hardship, suffering; †displeasure, grievance XIII; †hurt, mischief, injury; mental distress XIV. ME. *gref* – AN. *gref*, OF. *grief* (mod. *grief* grievance, injury, complaint), f. *grever* = Pr. *gravar* cause injury or grief, harass :– Rom. **grevāre*, alteration of L. *gravāre*, f. *gravis* GRAVE[3]. So **grieve**[1] grīv †harass, trouble, hurt; affect with deep sorrow; provoke to anger XIII; feel or show grief XIV. – OF. *grever*. **grie·v**ANCE †injury, distress XIII (Cursor M.); †hurt, disease XIV; ground of complaint XV (Caxton). – OF. *grevance*, f. *grever*.

grieve[2] grīv (hist.) governor of a province, etc., sheriff OE.; (Sc.) farm bailiff XV. OE. (Nhb.) *grǣfa* = WS. *ġerēfa* REEVE[1].

griffe grif claw, (archit., etc.) claw ornament. XIX. – F. *griffe* (anglicized as *griff* by Shelley), f. *griffer* seize as with a claw, f. OF. *grif* claw (of Germ. origin; see GRIP[1]).

griffin[1], **griffon**[1], **gryphon** gri·fin, -ən fabulous animai combining eagle and lion; vulture. XIV. – OF. *grifoun* (mod. *griffon*) = Pr. *griu*, It. *grifone* :– Rom. **grȳphō(nem)*, augm. of late L. *grȳphus*, f. *grȳph-*, *grȳps* – Gr. *grúps*.

griffin[2] gri·fin European newly arrived in India, novice. XVIII. perh. fig. use of prec., but there is no evidence. Also abbrev. *griff* (XIX).

griffon[2] gri·fən breed of dog. XIX. – F. *griffon* (applied to an Eng. dog 1829) GRIFFIN[1].

grig grig †dwarf XIV; short-legged hen XVI; young eel XVII. Of unkn. origin. The phr. *merry grig* extravagantly lively person, synon. and contemp. with *merry Greek* (XVI), was perh. orig. an alteration of the latter (cf. the var. *gay Greek*, and *a grig out of Grece* in the earliest ex. of this word, 'Wars of Alexander', 1753, Dublin MS.).

grill gril gridiron. XVII. – (O)F. *gril*, earlier *graïl*, *greïl*, m. form based on fem. *grille* (see next). So **grill** vb. broil on a gridiron. XVII. – F. *griller*, f. *gril*. Hence a new sb. *grill* broiled meat, etc. XVIII.

grille gril grating, lattice-screen. XVII. – (O)F. *grille*, earlier *graïlle* :– Rom. **grātīcula*, for L. *crātīcula*, dim. of *crātis* (see CRATE, GRATE).

grilse grils (Sc. and north.) young salmon for the year following its first return from the sea. XV. Of obscure origin; the Sc. vars. †*girsil* (XV), †*grissil* (XVI) may be closer to the orig. form (cf. OF. *grisel* grey, GRIZZLE). ¶ Anglo-Ir. synon. *graulse*, *grawls* (XVIII) prob. repr. a Scand. form corr. to Sw. *grålax* 'grey salmon'.

grim grim fierce, cruel OE.; stern or harsh of aspect or demeanour XIV; (of laughter, etc.) unrelenting XVII. OE. *grim* = OFris., OS. (Du.), OHG. *grim* (G. *grimm*), ON. *grimmr* :– CGerm. (exc. Gothic) **grimmaz*, f. **grem-* **gram-* (whence adjs. OE., OS., OHG. *gram*, ON. *gramr* angry, and vbs. OE. *gremian*, OHG. *gremman*, ON. *gremja*, Goth. *gramjan* anger) :– IE. **ghrem-* **ghrom-* (whence Gr. *khremizein* neigh, OSl. *gromŭ*, OPruss. *grumins* thunder). Cf. GRUMBLE.

grimace grimei·s distortion of the countenance. XVII. – F. *grimace*, earlier †*grimache* – Sp. *grimazo* caricature, f. *grima* fright (– Germ. stem of GRIM) with pejorative suffix *-azo* :– L. *-āceum* (cf. -ACEOUS). Hence, or – F. *grimacer*, **grimace** vb. XVIII.

grimalkin grimæ·lkin, -mɔ̄·lkin cat. XVII (*Gray-Malkin* as the name of a fiend, Sh.). f. GREY + MALKIN.

grime graim soil with soot, etc. XV. – MLG., MDu. **grīmen* (cf. Flem. *grijmen*, beside LG. *gremen*). Hence **grime** sb. XVI (Sh.); **gri·my**[1]. XVII.

grimthorpe gri·mþɔ̄ɹp restore (an ancient building) with lavish expenditure rather than skill and taste. XIX. f. name of Sir Edmund Beckett, first Baron *Grimthorpe*, whose restoration of St. Albans Cathedral aroused fierce criticism.

grin grin draw back the lips and show the teeth, in pain or †anger OE., in a smile XV. OE. *grennian*, rel. to OHG. *grennan* mutter (MHG. *grennen* wail, grin) and OHG. *granōn* grunt (MHG. *grannen*), ON. *grenja* howl, OSw. *gränia* roar, gnash the teeth; f. Germ. **gran-*. There is a remarkable similarity in form and sense with a number of Germ. words repr. the gradation-series **grain-*, **grin̥-*, to which GROAN belongs. Hence **grin** sb. XVII.

grind graind reduce to small particles; make a scraping or grating noise OE. (spec. gnash; also trans. XIV); sharpen the edge of XIII; work laboriously (at) XVIII (so *gerund-grinding*). OE. *grindan*, pt. *grond*, *grundon*, pp. *gegrunden*, of which there are no Germ. cogns. An IE. base **ghrendh-* is repr. by L. *frendere* rub away, gnash, Lith. *gréndu* I rub; phr. *grind the face of* (Isa. iii 15) is a Hebraism. Hence **grind** sb. hard task XIX. **gri·nder**[1] tr. L. *molaris* MOLAR. XIV (Trevisa); cf. OE. *grindetōþ*. **gri·ndstone**. XIII.

gringo gri·ŋgou (among Spanish Americans) Anglo-American. XIX. transf. use of Sp. *gringo* gibberish, which some take to be an alteration of *griego* GREEK.

grip[1] grip sb. (i) OE. *gripe* grasp, clutch, corr. to OHG. *grif-* in comb., MHG. *grif* (mod. *griff*) grasp, handle, claw, ON. *grip* grasp, clutch, *gripr* possession, property; (ii) OE. *gripa* handful, sheaf; both f. wk. base of *grīpan* GRIPE. In XV–XVII mainly Sc., prob. through Scand. infl.; mod. techn. uses are mainly f. the vb.; *grip* traveller's hand-bag is short for *gripsack* (both orig. U.S.). So **grip** vb. grasp firmly. OE. (late Nhb.) *grippa*, corr. to MHG. *gripfen*.

grip[2] grip (local) trench, drain. OE. *grypa* (or *-e*) sewer, rel. to *grēop* burrow and MLG. *grüppe*, MDu. *grippe*, *greppe*; f. Germ. **grup-* **greup-* hollow out.

gripe graip †grasp OE.; seize firmly XIII (Orm); †afflict XVI; pinch with pain XVII. OE. *grīpan*, pt. *grāp*, *gripon*, pp. *gripen*) = OFris. *grīpa*, OS. *grīpan* (Du. *grijpen*), OHG. *grīfan* (G. *greifen*), ON. *grípa*, Goth. *greipan*; CGerm. str. vb. (cf. GROPE), with cogn. in Lith. *griebiù*. Weak inflexions were established in XV. Hence **gripe** sb. XIV; in pl. griping pains, colic XVII.

grippe grip influenza. XVIII. – F. *grippe*, f. *gripper* seize – Germ. **gripjan* GRIP[1].

grisaille grizei·l, ‖grizaj painting in grey monochrome. XIX. F., f. *gris* grey (see GRIZZLE[1]) + *-aille* (:– L. *-ālia*).

grisette grize·t French working-class woman. XVIII. F., orig. inferior grey dress fabric, formerly the garb of women of the poorer classes, f. *gris* grey (see prec.)+-ETTE.

griskin gri·skin lean part of pig's loin. XVII. Obscurely f. (dial.) *gris* pig, †occas. pork (– ON. *griss*).

grisly gri·zli causing horror (later in weaker sense). Late OE. *grislić*, f. wk. base of **grīsan* (in *āgrīsan* terrify) = MLG., MDu. *grīsen*; perh. partly aphetic of OE. *angrislić* (cf. *angrisenlīće* terribly); parallel forms are MDu. *grise- grezelijc*, MHG. *grisenlich*, and Du. *grijzelijk*.

grist grist †grinding OE.; corn to be ground XV. OE. *grist* :- Germ. **grinst-*, f. **grindan* GRIND.

gristle gri·sl cartilage. OE. *gristle* = OFris., MLG. *gristel, gerstel*, MHG. *gruschel*, rel. to OE. *grost* gristle; similar synon. forms are OHG. *chrustila* (MHG. *krostel, krustel*); ult. origin unkn.

grit grit sand, gravel, (now) minute stony particles OE.; coarse sandstone XIII; texture of stone XVI; (orig. U.S.) pluck, stamina XIX. OE. *grēot* = OS. *griot*, OHG. *grioȝ* (G. *griess*), ON. *grjót* :- Germ. **greutam* (cf. GROATS, GROUT[1]).

grith griþ (hist.) security, peace. Late OE. *griþ* – ON. *grið* domicile, home, pl. truce, peace, pardon, quarter.

grizzle[1] gri·zl grey. XV (earlier as sb. grey-haired old man XIV, Ch., Gower). – OF. *grisel*, f. *gris* grey (= Pr. *gris*, It. *grigio*; cf. medL. *griseus*) – Germ. **grīsiaz* (OS., MLG. *grīs*, whence MHG. *grīs*, G. *greis* hoary), of unkn. origin. Hence **gri·zzl**ED[1] XV, **gri·zzl**Y[1] XVI. *Grizzly bear* (XVIII), Ursus horribilis.

grizzle[2] gri·zl (dial.) grin XVIII; cry in a fretful or whining fashion XIX. perh. originating in an iron. allusion to 'patient *Grizel*' (Griselda), proverbial type of a meek patient wife.

groan groun utter a loud deep sound of grief or pain. OE. *grānian* :- **grainōjan*, f. Germ. **grain-* **grīn-*, whence also OHG. *grīnan* grin with laughing or weeping (G. *greinen*), MHG. *grinnen* gnash the teeth; cf. MDu. *grinsen* (Du. *grijnsen*) grin. Cf. GRIN.

groat grout small coin. XIV. – MDu. *groot*, MLG. *grōte*, sb. uses of the adj. (= GREAT) in the sense 'thick' (cf. MHG. *grōȝe pfennige* 'thick pennies', and GROSCHEN).

groats grouts hulled grain. Late OE. *grotan* pl., rel. to *grot* fragment, particle (**grut-*), *grēot* GRIT (**greut-*), *grytt* bran, chaff, coarse oatmeal, dial. *grit* (**grutj-*), and *grūt* GROUT[1].

grobian grou·biən (arch.) clownish fellow. XVII (Dekker). – G. *grobian* or its source medL. *Grobiānus* type of boorishness in Germany (XV–XVI), f. G. *grob* coarse, rude, GRUFF; the termination was modelled on names such as *Cyprianus*.

grocer grou·səɹ †dealer in gross; trader in spices, sugar, dried fruits, etc. XV. – AN. *grosser*, OF. *grossier* :- medL. *grossārius*, f. *grossus* GROSS[2]. The Grocers' Company consisted of wholesale dealers in foreign produce, whence the second sense. Hence **gro·**CERY. XV. The sp. with *c* (XV) followed that of †*spicer* (– OF. *espicier*, mod. *épicier* grocer); the extension *greengrocer* 1723.

grog grɔg spirits (orig. rum) and water as served out to the Royal Navy. XVIII. Said to be from 'Old *Grog*', reputed nickname of the Admiral Vernon who gave the order in 1740 for the mixture to be used instead of neat spirit, derived from his wearing a *grogram* cloak. Hence **gro·gg**Y[1] intoxicated XVIII; (of a horse) diseased or weak in the forelegs; shaky, tottering XIX.

grogram grɔ·grəm coarse mixed fabric. XVI (*grow graine, grograyn, grogerane*). – F. *gros grain* 'coarse grain' (see GROSS[2], GRAIN); for the change of final *n* to *m* cf. *buckram, lockram*.

groin groin depression between abdomen and thigh XV; (archit.) intersection of two vaults XVIII. ME. *grynde*, early modE. *gryne*, in late XVI *groin*; perh. transf. use of OE. *grynde* ? orig. depression (recorded only in the sense 'abyss') :- **grundja-*, f. **grundu-* GROUND; cf. the dim. (dial.) *grindle* (XV) narrow ditch or drain. The change of (ī) to (oi) in the pronunc. is paralleled in BOIL[1], HOIST, JOIST.

grommet var. of GRUMMET.

gromwell grɔ·mwəl plant of the genus Lithospermum. XIII. ME. *gromil* – OF. *gromil, grumil* (mod. *grémil*) prob. :- medL. **gruinum milium* 'crane's millet', i.e. n. of late L. *gruīnus*, f. *grūs* CRANE, and *milium* MILLET.

groom grūm, grum A. †boy XIII (AncrR., Havelok); †man XIV; B. †man-servant XIII (RGlouc.; surviving in the spec. sense of horse attendant XVII); officer of the royal household XV; C. BRIDEGROOM XVII (Sh.). ME. *grōm* (with tense *ō*), of unkn. origin; no relation can be established with OF. *grommes* (prob. pl. of *grommet* servant, valet), (M)Du. *grom* fry of fish, offspring, (joc.) children, Icel. *grómr* (XIV in the expansion of 'Snorra Edda'). AN. *gromet*, AL. *grometus* are used in sense B.

groove grūv (dial.) mining shaft, mine XV; channel, hollow XVII. – Du. †*groeve* furrow, ditch (mod. *groef*) = OHG. *gruoba* (G. *grube* pit, ditch), ON. *gróf*, Goth. *grōba*; f. Germ. **grōƀ-*, rel. to **graƀ-* GRAVE[1] and [2].

grope group feel searchingly. OE. *grāpian* = OHG. *greiphōn* :- WGerm. **graipōjan*, f. **graip-* **grīp-* (see GRIP[1], GRIPE).

grosbeak grou·sbīk hawfinch, etc. XVII. – F. *grosbec*, f. *gros* large, GROSS[2]+*bec* BEAK.

groschen grou·ʃən small German coin. XVII. G., (Bohemian) alteration of late MHG. *grosse, gros*, in medL. *denarius grossus* 'thick penny'; see GROSS[2] and cf. GROAT.

gross[1] grous twelve dozen. xv. – F. *grosse*, sb. use (sc. *douzaine* dozen) of fem. of *gros* great; see next and cf. Sp. *gruesa*, Pg., It. *grossa*.

gross[2] grous Late ME. *groos* (XIV, Wyclif) became common first in XV (Lydg., etc.) in senses 'large, bulky' (now obs. or dial.), †'palpable, obvious', †'dense, thick', 'coarse', 'concerned with large masses'. – (O)F. *gros*, fem. *grosse* = Pr. *gros*, Sp. *grueso*, Pg., It. *grosso*, Rum. *gros* :– late L. *grossu-s* (freq. in Vulgate), of similar formation to *bassus* BASE, *crassus* CRASS. Cf. ENGROSS, GROCER.

grot grɔt (poet.) grotto. XVI. – F. *grotte* – It. *grotta* (whence also Sp., Pg. *gruta*) = OF. *crote, croute*, Pr. *crota* :– Rom. **crupta*, **grupta* (L. *crypta*) – Gr. *krúptē* vault, CRYPT. So **grotto** grɔ·tou (rocky) cavern, imitation of this. XVII (earlier *grotta*).

grotesque groute·sk sb. decorative painting or sculpture with fantastic interweaving of forms XVI; adj. pert. to work of such a character, fantastically extravagant XVII; ludicrously incongruous XVIII. Earliest forms *crotescque, -esco, -esko, grot(t)esco, -ko*, from *c.* 1635 *grot(t)esque, -esk*. – F. *crotesque* – (with assim. to OF. *crote* GROT) It. *grottesca*, ellipt. use (for *opera* or *pittura grottesca* grotto-like work or painting) of fem. of *grottesco*, f. *grotta*; finally assim. to F. *grotesque*; see GROTTO, -ESQUE. ¶ The special sense is said to be due to the Rom. application of *grotta* to chambers of old buildings revealed by excavation and containing mural paintings of a certain type.

grouch grautʃ (U.S.) grumble, complain. XX. var. of *grutch* (XIII) – OF. *gruchier*, *grouch(i)er*, of unkn. origin; cf. GRUDGE.

ground graund A. bottom, now only of the sea (cf. AGROUND) OE.; pl. dregs, lees XIV; B. base, foundation, now mainly techn. or fig. (reason, motive XIII) OE.; C. surface of the earth OE.; specific portion of this XIV (pl. enclosed land attached to a building XV). OE *grund* = OFris., OS. *grund* (Du. *grond*), OHG. *grunt* (G. *grund*), Goth. **grundus* (cf. *grundu|waddjus* ground-wall, foundation, *af|grundiþa* abyss) :– Germ. **grunduz*, rel. to ON. *grund* grassy plain, *grunnr* bottom, *grunnr* shallow, *grunn* shoal; no certain cogns. are known, but Lith. *grim̃sti* sink, *gramzdùs* deep-drawing (IE. **ghr̥mt-*) have been compared. Hence **ground** vb. †lay the foundation of XIII; give a basis to XIV (Ch., Wycl., Trevisa); put on the ground or ashore, strand XV (Lydg.).

groundling grau·ndliŋ small fish such as gudgeon and loach XVII; cf. MDu. *grundelinck* (Du. *grondeling*), MHG. *grundelinc* (G. *gründling*) gudgeon; see GROUND, -LING[1]. ¶ The origin of the application to the frequenters of the pit of a theatre (Sh. 'Hamlet' III ii 12) is obscure; a comparison to fishes living at the bottom of the water may have been obvious at the time; the use of *ground* for pit of a theatre (Jonson, 1614) is app. derived from this.

groundsel grau·n^d^səl plant of the genus Senecio. OE. *grundeswyliġe*, earlier *gundæswelġ(i)æ*, which, unless an erron. form for *grund-* in the three closely related glossaries in which it occurs, is presumably f. *gund* pus (cf. REDGUM) + **swulg-* **swelg-* SWALLOW[2], the etymol. meaning being 'pus-absorber', with ref. to its use in poultices to reduce abscesses; on this view, the later OE. form in *grund-* is due to assoc. with GROUND, as if taken to mean 'ground-swallower', with ref. to the rapid growth of the weed.

group grūp assemblage of figures or objects in an artistic design XVII (Dryden); assemblage of persons or things (gen.) forming a unity XVIII. – F. *groupe* – It. *gruppo* (the use of which in Eng. contexts was somewhat earlier) – Germ. ***kruppaz** round mass (see CROP[1]); from It. are also Sp. *grupo*, G. *gruppe*. Hence or – F. **group** vb. XVIII.

grouper grū·pəɹ (also *gruper, garrupa*) any of various fishes of the families Epinephelidæ and Scorpænidæ. XVII (*groper, grooper*). – Pg. *garupa*, prob. native S. Amer. name. For the perversion of form cf. BREAKER[2].

grouse[1] graus gallinaceous bird with feathered feet (Tetrao, Lagopus). XVI (*a brase of grewyses*). The pronunc. points to an orig. ū, which is preserved (perh. locally) in such early forms as *grewes, groose*; poss. orig. pl. of **grue*, to be referred to (i) medL. *grūta*, given as the name of a 'gallus campestris' by Giraldus Cambrensis, or (ii) W. *grugiar*, f. *grug* heath + *iar* hen.

grouse[2] graus grumble. XIX. orig. a soldier's word; its resemblance in form to Norman dial. *groucer*, OF. *groucier*, var. of *grouchier* (see GRUDGE) is remarkable, but immediate connexion with it seems impossible.

grout[1] graut (now obs. or dial.) coarse meal; infusion of malt OE.; coarse porridge XVI; sediment XVII. OE. *grūt*, corr. to MDu. *grūte, gruut* coarse meal, peeled grain, malt, yeast (Du. *gruit* dregs), MHG. *grūʒ* (G. *grauss*) grain, small beer; f. **grūt-*, var. of **graut-* **greut-* **grut-* (see GRIT, GROATS). The later meanings are prob. due to Scand. (cf. ON. *grautr* porridge) and Du. Cf. GRUEL.

grout[2] graut thin mortar. XVII. perh. a use of prec.; but cf. F. dial. *grouter* grout a wall.

grove grouv small wood. OE. *grāf* (:– **graiƀaz, -am*), rel. to *grǣfa* brushwood, thicket (– XVII, Drayton, Holland) :– **graiƀjon*.

grovel grɔ·vl lie prone or prostrate. XVI (Sh.). Back-formation (cf. *suckle*) from **grovelling** grɔ·vəliŋ adj. prone (XVI), attrib. use of the †adv. face downward, in a prone position (XIV), earlier †*grovellings* (XIII), f. *gruf* on the face, on the belly (for phr. *on grufe, ogrufe*) – ON. *á grúfu* (cf. *grufla* go on all fours) + -LING(S)[2].

grow grou, pt. *grew* grū, pp. *grown* groun (orig.) show the development characteristic of living things. OE. *grōwan* (pt. *grēow*, pp. *grōwen*) = OFris. *grōwa*, *grōia*, MDu. *groeyen* (Du. *groeien*), OHG. *gruoan*, ON. *gróa*; CGerm. (exc. Gothic) str. vb. f. **grō-* (see GRASS, GREEN). Hence **grow**TH[1] group action or stage of growing, that which has grown. XVI; there appears to be no historical contact with ON. *gróði*, *gróðr*.

growan grou·ən soft granite in Cornwall. XVIII. Corn. *grow*, W. *gro*; see GRAVE[5].

growl graul make a guttural sound. XVIII. Cf. late ME. *grolle*, *groule*, and *gurle* rumble (said of the belly and thunder), AN. *growler* make the characteristic cry of the crane, OF. *grouller* grumble, scold; but the modern word is prob. an imit. formation independent of any of these.

groyne groin timberwork or masonry run out into the sea. XVI. transf. use of (dial.) *groin* (XIV) snout – (O)F. *groin* (also †cape, promontory) = Pr. *groing*, It. *grugno* :– Rom. **grunnium*, f. L. *grunnīre* grunt.

grub[1] grʌb †dwarfish fellow XIV; insect larva XV; (sl.) food (as grubs are for birds) XVII. Occurs as a surname (*Grubbe*) XIII, prob. orig. as a nickname, and presumably f. next, but the sense-development is not clear.

grub[2] grʌb dig (on the surface) XIII (Cursor M.); labour ploddingly XVIII. perh. to be referred to an OE. **grybban* :– **grubbjan*; cf. OHG. *grubilōn* dig, search closely, MDu. *grobben* scrape together, Du. *grobbelen* root out; f. Germ. **grub-*, rel. to **grab-* GRAVE[1] and [2]. Hence **gru·bb**ER[1]. XIV; survives esp. in *money-grubber* sordid gatherer of wealth (so Du. *grobber*).

Grub Street grʌ·b strīt name of a street near Moorfields, London (now Milton Street), once inhabited by inferior and needy writers, transf. tribe of poor authors and literary hacks. XVII (James Taylor).

grudge grʌdʒ †murmur, grumble; be unwilling to grant. XV. Alteration of †*grutch* (XIII) – OF. *grouchier* (of unkn. origin), perh. infl. by †*aggrege* bear heavily upon (cf. †*aggrogge*, *aggrugge* XV) – OF. *agregier* = Pr. *agreujar* :– **aggreviāre*, f. L. *ad* AG- + Rom. **grevis*, for *gravis* GRAVE[3].

gruel grū·əl †fine meal; liquid food made from oatmeal. XIV. – OF. *gruel* (mod. *gruau*) :– Rom. **grūtellum*, dim. f. Germ. **grūt-* GROUT[1].

gruesome grū·səm inspiring awe or horror. XVI (*growsome*). orig. north. and Sc.; introduced into literature by Scott in the form *grewsome*. f. *grue* XIII (Cursor M.), now Sc. and north., feel horror – Scand. word repr. by OSw. *grua*, ODa. *grue* (= OHG. *in*|*gruēn* shudder, G. *grauen* be awed, shudder, Du. *gruwen* abhor); see -SOME[1].

gruff grʌf (Sc. and techn.) coarse-grained XVI; rough and surly XVII. First in Sc. and prob. orig. in commercial use – Flem. (Du.) *grof* 'crassus, spissus, densus, impolitus, rudis' (Kilian) = MLG. *grof* coarse, OHG. *grob*, *girob* (G. *grob*) :– WGerm. **gaχruƀa*, f. **ga-* Y- + **χruƀ-* **χreuƀ-* (OE. *hrēof* rough, scabby, etc.; cf. Lith. *kraupùs* rough).

grumble grʌ·mbl mutter or murmur (complainingly). XVI (Sidney, Sh.). frequent. f. †*grumme* (XV–XVI) + -LE[3]; cf. (M)Du. *grommen*, MLG. *grommelen* (whence F. *grommeler*, †*gr(o)umeler*), G. *grummeln*; f. imit. Germ. **grum-* (cf. GRIM).

grume grūm clot of blood. XVII. – L. *grūmus* little heap, rel. to OE. *crūma* CRUMB; cf. F. *grumeau* clot. So **gru·mous**. XVII. – modL.

grummet, grommet grʌ·mit (naut.) ring of rope, etc. XV (Cely Pp.) – F. †*grom(m)ette*, *gourmette* chain joining the ends of a bit, f. *gourmer* curb, bridle, of unkn. origin.

grumpy grʌ·mpi surly-tempered. XVIII. prob. of dial. origin; f. *grump*, as in †*humps and grumps* surly or ill-tempered remarks, based on inarticulate noises betokening displeasure; see -Y[1].

Grundy grʌ·ndi surname of an imaginary *Mrs Grundy* who is proverbially referred to as a personification of the tyranny of social opinion; derived from T. Morton's play 'Speed the Plough' (1798), in which Dame Ashfield, constantly fearing the sneers of her neighbour Mrs Grundy, freq. asks 'What will (would) Mrs Grundy say?'

grunt grʌnt make the characteristic sound of a pig. OE. *grunnettan* = OHG. *grunnizōn* (G. *grunzen*), intensive formation on the imit. base **grun-* (OE. *grunian* grunt, OHG. *grun* wailing, MHG. *grunnen*), which has an analogue in L. *grunnīre*, Gr. *grúzein*. The deriv. *gruntle* (dial.) grunt, grumble (XV) is seen in DISGRUNTLED.

Gruyère grū·jɛəɹ, ||grüjēr. cows'-milk cheese. XIX. Name of a town in Switzerland, from which it comes.

gryphon see GRIFFIN[1].

grysbok grai·sbɔk S. African antelope. XVIII. – Afrikaans, f. Du. *grijs* GREY + *bok* BUCK[1].

guacho see GAUCHO.

guaiacum gwai·əkəm tree, wood, and resin of the West Indies. XVI. modL., f. Sp. *guayaco*, *guayacan*, of Haytian origin. Also anglicized **guai·ac** (XVI); cf. F. *gaiac*.

guana see IGUANA.

guanaco gwanā·kou kind of llama. XVII. – Quichua *huanaco*, *-acu*.

guano gwā·nou natural manure found on islands about Peru XVII; artificial (fish-) manure XIX. – Sp. *guano*, S. Amer. Sp. *huano* – Quichua *huanu* dung.

Guarani gwarā·ni (language of) a S. American Indian race inhabiting Paraguay and Uruguay, forming a group with Tupi. XVIII.

guarantee gærəntī· party giving security XVII; act of giving security, security given XVIII (Burke); something providing security XIX. The earliest forms, *garanté, garante*, are perh. – Sp. *garante* = F. *garant* WARRANT; in its later use the word was identified with F. *garantie*, GUARANTY. Hence as vb. be a guarantee for XVIII (Burke); secure (a person or thing) in possession XIX. ¶ As correl. to *guarantor* (XIX), the form is a distinct word, the model being *grantee, grantor*; see -EE[1].

guaranty gæ·rənti security, warranty, undertaking by a guarantor XVI; something that guarantees XVII. – AN. *guarantie*, (O)F. *garantie*, var. of *warantie* WARRANTY.

guard gāɹd †custody; protector, defender XV; body of persons as defenders (with various spec. applications); protection, defence XVI. – (O)F. *garde* (corr. to Pr., Sp., OIt. *guarda*), f. *garder* = Pr., Sp. *guardar*, It. *guardare* :– Rom. **wardāre* – WGerm. **warðo* WARD[1]. So **guard** vb. XVI. f. the sb. or – (O)F. *garder*, †*guarder*. **guardian** gā·ɹdiən protector, defender XV (spec. superior of a Franciscan convent); (leg.) correlative to *ward* XVI. Late ME. *gardein* – AN. *gardein*, OF. *garden*, earlier *gardenc* (mod. *gardien* from XIII, with assim. of suffix to *-ien* -IAN, which was followed in Eng.; cf. Sp. *guardian*, It. *guardiano*). See WARDEN.

guava gwā·və tree of tropical America. XVI (*guayava, -avo*). – Sp. *guayaba, -abo*, of S. Amer. origin.

gubernatorial gjūbəɹneitō·riəl (chiefly U.S.) of a governor or government. XVIII. f. L. *gubernātor* GOVERNOR + -IAL.

gudgeon[1] gʌ·dʒən small freshwater fish XV; bait; gullible person XVI. Late ME. *gogen, gojo(u)n* – (O)F. *goujon* :– L. *gōbiō(n-)*, f. *gōbius* GOBY.

gudgeon[2] gʌ·dʒən pivot of metal, etc. XIV. – (O)F. *goujon* pin, dowel, tenon, dim. of *gouge* GOUGE.

Guebre gī·bəɹ, gei·bəɹ fire-worshipper, Parsee. XVII. – F. *guèbre* – Pers. *gabr*; cf. GIAOUR.

Guelder rose ge·ldəɹrouz snowball-tree, Viburnum Opulus. XVI (*Gelders Rose*, Gerarde). – Du. *geldersche roos* (whence G. *Gelderische rose*, F. *rose de Gueldre*, etc.); f. *Gelderland* or *Gelders*, province of Holland.

Guelph gwelf one of the anti-imperialist party in medieval Italian politics (cf. GHIBELLINE). XVI (*Guelfes*, E. K. in Spenser's 'Shepherds Calendar'). – It. *Guelfo*, medL. *Guelphus* – MHG. *Welf* name of the princely family repr. at the present time by the royal dynasty of Great Britain.

guerdon gə̄·ɹdən (arch.) reward. XIV (Ch.). – OF. *guer(e)don* = Pr. *guierdó*, Sp. *galardon*, It. *guiderdone* :– Rom. (medL.) *widerdōnum* – W. Germ. **widarlōn* (= OHG. *widarlōn*, OE. *wiþerlēan*, f. *wiþer* again + *lēan* payment) with assim. of the second el. to L. *dōnum* gift. So **gue·rdon** vb. XIV (Ch.). – (O)F. *guer(e)doner*, f. the sb.

guerilla gəri·lə irregular war carried on by small bodies; (transf.) one engaged in such warfare. XIX (Wellington, Scott). More freq. sp. of **guerrilla** (so F. *guérilla*) – Sp. *guerrilla*, dim. of *guerra* WAR; introduced into F. and Eng. during the Peninsular War (1808–14).

guernsey gə̄·ɹnzi thick knitted (usu. blue) vest or shirt, worn by seamen. XIX. f. name of one of the Channel Islands; cf. JERSEY.

guess[1] ges †take aim XIII; form an approximate judgement or estimate of XIV. ME. *gesse*, with early var. *agesse* (cf. OSw. *begissa*); perh. orig. naut. and – vars. with *-e-* of MLG., MDu. (Du., Fris.) *gissen*, or OSw. *gissa*, ODa. *gitse*; ult. f. base of GET (cf. ON. *geta* guess) and repr. Germ. types **getisōjan*, **gatisōjan*, **gissjan*, **gessjan*. ¶ The sp. with *gu-* and *gh-* date from XVI; cf. GUEST. So **guess** sb. XIV; cf. MDu. *gisse* (Du. *gis*).

guess[2] ges (with var. *guest*) in **guess-**ROPE XVII (*guestrope*), **guess-**WARP XV (*gyes warpe*), rope for steadying a boat in tow, etc.; perh. orig. based on GUY[1], and assim. later to prec.

guest gest one who is entertained at another's house or table. XIII. – ON. *gestr*; superseding OE. *ġiest, ġest* (whence ME. *ȝest*, occurring beside mixed forms like *güst, gist*) = OS., OHG. (Du., G.) *gast*, Goth. *gasts* :– CGerm. **gastiz* :– IE. **ghostis*, repr. also by L. *hostis* enemy, orig. stranger (whence **hostipot-*, L. *hospit-, hospes* guest, HOST[2]), and OSl. *gostĭ* guest, friend, and prob. (in the weak grade **ghs-*) by Gr. *xénos* (:– **ghsénos*) stranger. ¶ The sp. *gu-*, dating from XVI, marks the stopped g, like the earlier var. with *gh-*; cf. GUESS[1].

guffaw gʌfō· sb. and vb. expressive of loud and boisterous laughter. XVIII. orig. Sc. (Ramsay), of imit. origin; cf. the earlier Sc. synon. *gawf* (XVI).

guicower var. of GAEKWAR.

guide gaid direct the course of. XIV (Ch., Gower). – (O)F. *guider*, alteration of †*guier* (whence ME. †*guy*, early XIV) = Pr. *guizar*, Sp. *guiar*, It. *guidare* :– CRom. **wīdāre* – Germ. **wītan*, f. **wīt-*, gradation-var. of **wit-* (see WIT), repr. by OE., OS. *wītan* blame, OFris. *wīta* guard, keep, Goth. *fra|weitan* avenge, *fair|weitjan* gaze upon (cf. the meanings of other derivs. of this base, OE. *wīse* direction, WISE[1], *wissian* direct, guide, G. *weisen* indicate, direct). So **guide** sb. XIV. – (O)F. *guide* (= It. *guida*), f. the vb.

guidon gai·dən pennant broad next the staff and pointed at the other end. XVI. – F. *guidon* – It. *guidone*, f. *guida* GUIDE.

guild, gild[2] gild confraternity for mutual aid. XIV. The present form is prob. – MLG., MDu. *gilde*, Du. *gild*. (G. *gilde* is from LG.) :– **gelðjōn*, rel. to OE. *ġield, ġild* payment, offering, sacrifice, idol, (also) guild (continued as *ʒild, yeld*), OFris. *geld, ield* money, OS. *geld* payment, sacrifice, reward, OHG. *gelt* payment, tribute (Du., G. *geld* money), ON. *gjald* payment, Goth. *gild* tribute :– CGerm. **gelðam* and ON. *gildi* guild, guild-feast, (also) payment, value :– Germ. **gelðjam*. The base **gelð-* is prob. to be taken in the sense 'pay, offer', so that the sb. would primarily mean an association of persons contributing to a common object.

guilder gi·ldəɹ coin of the Netherlands. XV (*guldren*; later *gildren, gilder*). Alteration (perh. after *kroner*) of Du. *gulden* (which was adopted unaltered in Sc. XVI), prop. adj. of gold, golden (= OE. *gylden*); see -EN[3].

guile gail insidious cunning. XIII. – OF. *guile* = Pr. *guila* (whence Pg. *guilha*), perh. – Scand. **wihl-* WILE. Cf. BEGUILE.

guillemot gi·limɔt sea-bird of the genus Alca. XVII (Ray). – F. *guillemot*, deriv. of *Guillaume* William; cf. the syns. *guillem* (– W. *Gwilym* William) and *willock*. ¶ Other bird names derived from personal names are *dicky, jackdaw, jay, magpie, robin*.

guillotine gilətī·n machine with knife blade for beheading. XVIII (1793). – F. *guillotine* (1790), f. name of Joseph-Ignace *Guillotin*, French doctor who recommended its use.

guilt gilt †offence, crime OE.; †responsibility for something XII; †desert XIII; fact of having committed an offence XIV; state of having wilfully offended XVI. OE. *gylt*, of unkn. origin. Hence **gui·lty**[1]. OE. *gyltig*.

guimp var. of GIMP.

guinea gi·ni name of a portion of the west coast of Africa, first known in Pg. *Guiné*, whence Sp. *Guiné*, F. *Guinée*; applied to things derived thence (or, with vague reference, from some other distant country) as *Guinea fowl* (XVIII), *Guinea hen* (XVI), *Guinea pepper* (XVI) orig. Cayenne pepper, *Guinea pig* (XVII), *Guinea worm* (XVII). The gold coin named *guinea* was first struck in 1663 'in the name and for the use of the Company of Royal Adventurers trading with Africa', being intended for the Guinea trade and made of gold from Guinea.

guipure gipü·r kind of lace and of gimp. XIX. – (O)F. *guipure*, f. *guiper* cover with silk, wool, etc. – Germ. **wīpan* wind round.

guise gaiz style, fashion. XIII (Laʒ.). – (O)F. *guise* = Pr. *guiza*, Sp., It. *guisa* :– Rom. **wīsa* – Germ. **wīsōn* WISE[1]. Cf. DISGUISE.

guitar gitā·ɹ six-stringed instrument of the lute class. XVII (*guittara, guitarra, ghittar, gittar*). orig. – Sp. *guitarra*, later – F. *guitare* (superseding OF. *guiterne* GITTERN) – Sp. itself – Gr. *kithárā*, which was adopted in L. as *ci·thara*, whence Pr. *cedra*, It. *cetera*, and OHG. *cithara* (G. *zither*); see also CITHERN, CITOLE, ZITHER.

gulch gʌlʃ (U.S.) deep ravine. XIX. perh. f. dial. vb. *gulch* swallow, sink in (cf. Norw. *gulka*).

gulden gu·ldən coin of Netherlands and Germany, orig. of gold, later of silver. XVI. – Flem., G. *gulden*, sb. use of adj. of GOLD, golden, = OE. *gylden*, etc. (CGerm. **gulþinaz*).

gules gjūlz (her.) red. XIV. Late ME. *goules, gols, gulles* – OF. *goules, goles* (mod. *gueules*), pl. of *gole, gueule* throat (cf. GULLET), used, like medL. pl. *gulæ*, for pieces of fur used as a neck-ornament and dyed red.

gulf gʌlf kind of bay; chasm, abyss. XIV. – (O)F. *golfe* – It. *golfo* (= Pr. *golfe*, Sp. *golfo*) :– Rom. **colpu-s*, **colphu-s* – Gr. *kólpos*, (late) *kólphos* bosom, fold, gulf :– IE. **qolpos*, **qwolpos* (cf. OE. *hwealf* vault, vaulted, *be|hwielfan* arch over, OHG. *welben* :– **χwalƀjan*, G. *wölben* arch). ¶ For the sense cf. L. *sinus*, G. *busen* bosom, bay.

gull[1] gʌl (dial.) unfledged bird; gosling. XIV. prob. sb. use of †*gull* yellow (– ON. *gulr*). Hence, perh. partly the use of *gull* for 'credulous person, dupe' (late XVI), but cf. the somewhat earlier *gull* vb. dupe, cheat, surviving in **gu·llible**, XIX, which itself may be a transf. use of †*gull* vb. swallow (XVI), rel. to †*gull* sb. throat, gullet (XV) – OF. *gole, goule* (see GULES, GULLET).

gull[2] gʌl long-winged web-footed sea-bird. XV. prob. – W. *gwylan*, Cornish *guilan* = Breton *gwelan, goelann* (whence F. *goéland*), OIr. *foilenn* :– OCeltic **voilenno-*.

gullet gʌ·lit œsophagus XIV (*golet*); water-channel XVI. – OF. **golet, goulet*, dim. of *gole, goule* (mod. *gueule*) :– L. *gula* throat, rel. to OIr. *gelim* I swallow, Skr. *galas* throat, OE. *ċeole*, OS., OHG. *kela* (G. *kehle*) throat; see -ET.

gully gʌ·li †gullet XVI; channel or ravine worn by water XVII; deep gutter XVIII. – F. *goulet* neck of a bottle, outlet, narrow passage of water; see prec.

gulp gʌlp swallow hastily or greedily XV; gasp, choke XVI (*golpe, gulpe*). prob. – MDu. *gulpen* swallow, guzzle, of imit. origin. ¶ (Similar synon. forms of about the same date are †*globbe*, †*glop*, †*gloup*, which are nearer to OSw. *glup* throat, *glupsk* voracious.)

gum[1] gʌm †inside of mouth or throat OE.; firm flesh in which the teeth are fixed. XIV. OE. *gōma*, corr. to OHG. *guomo* (MHG. *guome*) gum, ON. *gómr* roof or floor of the mouth, finger-tip, rel. to OHG. *goumo* (G. *gaumen*); further connexions have been seen in Lith. *gomurỹs* gum, Lett. *gāmurs* windpipe, Gr. *kháos* CHAOS, *khaûnos* yawning, and L. *faux*, pl. *faucēs* throat (IE. **ghĕu-***ghŏu-*).

gum² gʌm viscid secretion from trees. XIV (Ch.). – (O)F. *gomme* = Pr., Sp. *goma*, Pg., It. *gomma* :– Rom. **gumma*, for L. *gummi*, var. of *cummi* – Gr. *kómmi* – Egyptian *kemai*. Hence **gummy**¹. XIV (Trevisa). **gum** vb. †treat with aromatic gums XV; fasten or stiffen with gum XVI; partly after (O)F. *gommer*.

gum³ gʌm. XIX. (sl.) Deformation of GOD, in *by* or *my gum*.

gumbo gʌ·mbou (U.S.) okra plant or pods; soup thickened with the pods; (geol.) local clay or mud. XIX. Of Negro origin; cf. Angola *kingombo* (in Marcgraf, 1648, *quingombo*), f. Bantu prefix *ki*-+*ngombo*.

gum-gum gʌ·mgʌm iron bowl used as a gong. XVII. Presumably Malay; cf. *gong-gong* s.v. GONG.

gumption gʌ·mᵖʃən common sense XVIII (Ramsay); in painting, a vehicle for colour XIX. orig. Sc.; also *rumgumption*, *rumblegumption*; of unkn. origin.

gun gʌn heavy piece of ordnance, cannon XIV; †large engine of war; portable fire-arm XV. ME. *gunne*, *gonne* (1339 instrumenta de latone, vocitata Gonnes; whence AL. *gunna*, *gonna*), prob. repr. pet-form (**Gunna*; in Sw. dial. *Gunne*) of the Scand. female name *Gunnhildr* (f. *gunnr* + *hildr*, both meaning 'war'), which may have been orig. applied to ballistæ or the like; cf. 'una magna balista de cornu quæ vocatur Domina *Gunilda*' (1330–1 in Exchequer Accounts) and '*gonnylde* gnoste', i.e. Gunnild's spark (Political Song temp. Edward II). ¶ For a similar application of a female name cf. *Meg*, the great 15th-century gun in Edinburgh castle. Hence **gunner**¹ gʌ·nəɹ. XIV. (Not f. *gun* vb. XVII.) Whence **gu·nnery**. XVII. Also **gu·npowder** XV, **gu·nshot** XV, **gu·nsmith** XVI, **gu·n-stock**, -**stone** XV.

gunny gʌ·ni coarse material for sacking. XVIII. – Hindi, Marathi *gōnī* :– Skr. *gōṇī* sack.

Gunter gʌ·ntəɹ name of Edmund *Gunter* (1581–1626), Eng. mathematician, after whom several instruments are named, and the source of the U.S. phr. *according to Gunter*, equiv. to Eng. *according to* COCKER.

gunwale, gunnel gʌ·nəl upper edge of a ship's side, formerly serving to support the guns. XV (*gonne walles*). f. GUN+WALE.

gunyah gʌ·nja Australian hut. XIX. – Native name (Port Jackson dial. *gonie*).

gup gʌp (sl., orig. Anglo-Indian) gossip; (hence) vapid talk, blather. XIX. – Hind. *gup*.

gurgitation gə̄ɹdʒitei·ʃən †swallowing XVI (rare); surging up and down, ebullient motion. XIX. – modL. **gurgitātiō(n-)*, f. late L. *gurgitāre* engulf, f. *gurgit-*, *gurges* gulf, abyss. See INGURGITATION, REGURGITATION.

gurgle gə̄·ɹgl †gargle (rare); make the sound of bubbling liquid. XVI. prob. imit., if not directly – similarly formed vbs., e.g. MLG., Du. *gorgelen*, G. *gurgeln*, and It. *gorgogliare*, Pg. *gurgulhar* :– Rom. **gurguliāre*, f. L. *gurguliō* gullet.

Gurkha gə̄·ɹkə, ‖gū·rka (also erron. *Gh-*) one of the ruling Hindu race in Nepal, India. XIX. Native name, f. Skr. *gāus* COW¹+*raksh* guard, protect.

gurnard, gurnet gə̄·ɹnəɹd, gə̄·ɹnit fish of the genus Trigla. XIV. – OF. *gornart*, for **gronart*, f. *gronir*, by-form of *grondir* (= Sp. *gruñir*, It. *grugnire*) :– L. *grundīre*, *grunnīre* GRUNT; see -ARD. ¶ The fish is so named because it makes a grunting sound when caught; cf. the equiv. F. *grondin* (f. *gronder* grumble), G. *knurrfisch*, *knurrhahn* (f. *knurren* grumble), Du. *knorhaan*; also U.S. *grunt*, *grunter* name for fishes of similar habits.

guru var. of GOOROO.

gurry gʌ·ri small native Indian fort. XIX. – Hind. *gaṛhī*, f. *gaṛh* hill fort.

gush gʌʃ flow or rush out violently. XIV. The early evidence points to prob. northern origin, but Scand. forms (ON. *gjósa*, Icel. *gusa*) do not tally; prob. an independent imit. formation (cf. (M)Du. *gutsen*, which, however, may be f. **gut-* pour; see FUSION).

gusset gʌ·sit flexible piece introduced between two adjacent pieces of mail XV; triangular piece let into a garment XVI. – (O)F. *gousset* crescent-shaped piece of armour under the armpit, hollow of the armpit, piece of cloth let in under it and in other parts, (now) waistcoat pocket, formally dim. of *gousse* pod, shell (though this is much later), of unkn. origin.

gust gʌst sudden violent wind. XVI (Sh.). prob. earlier restricted to dial. or naut. use – ON. *gustr*, f. **gus-*, weak grade of the base of ON. *gjósa* gush. Cf. GEYSER.

gustation gʌstei·ʃən tasting, taste. XVI. – L. *gustātiō(n-)*, f. *gustāre*, f. *gustus*; see next and -ATION. So **gu·stative**, **gu·statory**. XVII.

gusto gʌ·stou taste, liking; keen relish; style of a work of art. XVII. – It. *gusto* (= Pr. *gost*, F. *goût*) :– L. *gustu-s* taste, rel. to CHOOSE. A direct adoption from L. in the form *gust* (XV) was current in various senses, (1) taste, (2) liking, (3) flavour, (4) relish; and of F. *goût*, †*goust* (XVI), in the senses (1) liking, relish, (2) æsthetic judgement, (3) flavour (cf. HAUT-GOÛT, HOGO).

gut gʌt (pl.) bowels OE.; (sg.) intestine XIV; narrow passage or channel XVI (Leland). OE. pl. *guttas*, prob. f. base **gut-* of OE. *ġēotan*, Goth. *giutan* pour (see FUSION). Hence **gut** vb. XIV.

gutta percha gʌ·tə pə̄·ɹtʃə inspissated juice of various Malayan trees. XIX. – Malay *getah percha*, i.e. *getah* gum, *percha* tree yielding the juice; assim. to L. *gutta* drop, used in med. and modL. for gum.

gutter gʌ·təɹ †watercourse XIII; shallow trough to carry away water XIV. – AN. *gotere*, OF. *goutiere* (mod. *gouttière*) = Pr., Sp. *gotera* :– Rom. **guttāria* (cf. -ARY), f. L. *gutta* drop (cf. GOUT). Hence **gu·tter** vb. channel XIV; stream XVI; (of a candle) melt rapidly by being channelled on one side XVIII. **gu·tter-snipe** common snipe, also called *mire snipe*; gatherer of refuse, street urchin. XIX. f. *gutter* in dial. sense of 'mud, filth'.

guttle gʌ·tl eat greedily. XVII. f. GUT, after *guzzle*.

guttural gʌ·tərəl pert. to the throat. XVI. – F. *guttural* or medL. *gutturālis*, f. *guttur* throat; see -AL[1].

gutty gʌ·ti gutta-percha ball. XIX. f. *gutta* of GUTTA PERCHA + -Y[6].

guy[1] gai (naut.) rope, chain, etc., used to steady a thing. First in *guy-rope* (*girap* XIV, *gyerope* XV), prob. of LG. origin, as are Du. *gei* brail, *geitouw* clew-garnet, *geiblok* pulley, G. *geitau* clew-line, (pl.) brails (cf. *auf|geien* haul or brail up), F. *gui* main-boom (XVII); cf. GUESS[2].

guy[2] gai effigy of *Guy* Fawkes; grotesque person, 'fright'; (U.S.) man. XIX. Hence **guy** vb. (U.S.) ridicule. XIX.

guzzle gʌ·zl swallow greedily. XVI. poss. – OF. *gosiller*, a deriv. of *gosier* throat, but found only in the senses 'chatter' and 'vomit'.

gwyniad gwi·niæd fish of the salmon kind with white flesh. XVII. – W. *gwyniad*, f. *gwyn* white.

gybe, jibe dʒaib (naut.) swing from one side of the vessel to the other, as a sail; put (a boat) about. XVII. – Du. †*gijben* (mod. *gijpen*, whence G. *geipen*); but initial dʒ is unexplained; cf. JIB[1].

gyle gail fermenting wort; brewing, brew. XIV. – MDu. *ghijl* (Du. *gijl*), rel. to *gijlen* ferment, of unkn. origin.

gymbals var. of GIMBALS.

gymkhana dʒimkā·nə in India, public resort for games; in Europe, athletic sports display. XIX. Alteration, by assim. to *gymnastic*, of Hind. *gendkhāna* 'ball-house', racket court.

gymnasium dʒimnei·ziəm place for athletic exercises. XVI. – L. – Gr. *gumnásion*, f. *gumnázein* train (lit. naked), f. *gumnós* NAKED, NUDE. So **gy·mnast.** XVI. – F. or Gr. *gumnastḗs* trainer of athletes. **gymnastic** -æ·stik adj. and sb. XVI (sb. pl. XVII). – L. *gymnasticus* – Gr. *gumnastikós*.

gymno- dʒi·mnou, dʒimnɔ· comb. form of Gr. *gumnós* naked, in many nat. hist. terms, the earliest of which is *gymnospermous* naked-seeded (XVIII) – modL. (cf. SPERM).

gymnosophist dʒimnɔ·səfist ascetic Hindu philosopher who wore little or no clothing, etc. XVI (earlier once pl. *genosophis* XIV as if based on Gr. **gumnósophos*). – F. *gymnosophiste* (†*gisnocephite*) – L. (pl.) *gymnosophistæ* – Gr. (pl.) *gumnosophistaí*, f. *gumnós* GYMNO- + *sophistḗs* SOPHIST.

gymnotus dʒimnou·təs electric eel. XVIII. modL. (Linnæus), for **gymnonotus*, f. Gr. *gumnós* GYMNO- + *nôton* back, with ref. to the absence of dorsal fins.

gynæceum dʒainīsī·əm (antiq.) women's apartments XVIII; (bot.) female organs (usu. sp. *gynœcium*, by assim. to Gr. *oikíon* house). L. – Gr. *gunaikeîon*, f. *gunaik-*, *gunḗ* woman (see QUEAN).

gynæco-, U.S. **-eco-** gai-, dʒainī·kou, dʒin-, -kɔ·- repr. Gr. *gunaiko-*, comb. form of *gunḗ* woman, female (see QUEAN), as in **gynæco·-**CRACY female rule (XVII, Selden). – F. *gynécocratie* or modL. *gynæcocratia* – Gr. **gynæco·**LOGY. XIX.

gyno- dʒai·nou, dʒi·nou, dʒinɔ· before a vowel **gyn-**, shortened form of GYNÆCO-, used in bot. terms to denote 'pistil', 'ovary', e.g. *Gynandria* (Linnæus) class of plants having stamen and pistil united. So **-gynous** dʒinəs repr. Gr. *-gunos*, used for 'having such-and-such pistils or female organs', e.g. *andro·gynous*, *mono·gynous*.

gyp dʒip (at Cambridge and Durham Univ.) college servant. XVIII (also †*jip*). perh. short for †*gippo* scullion (XVII), transf. use of †*gippo* tunic – (O)F. *jupeau*, dim. of *jup(p)e*.

gypsum dʒi·psəm hydrous calcium sulphate, from which plaster of Paris is made. XVII. – L. (Cato, Pliny; also *-us*) – Gr. *gúpsos*, of Semitic origin (cf. Ass. *gaṣṣu*, Arab. *geçç*, whence Sp. *algez*). The L. word was anglicized as *gips* (XV), *gyps* (XVIII); cf. F. *gypse*, †*gips*. So **gy·ps**EOUS. XVII. f. late L. *gypseus*. ¶ In Rom. langs. pop. forms have the meaning 'plaster', e.g. OF. *gip(se)*, *gif*, *gy*, It. GESSO, Pr. *geis*, Sp. *yeso*, Pg. *gesso*.

gypsy see GIPSY.

gyrate dʒaiərei·t move in a circle or spiral. XIX. f. pp. stem of late L. *gȳrāre*, f. *gȳrus* – Gr. *gûros* ring, circle; see -ATE[3]. So **gyr·a·tion.** XVII. – late L.; cf. F. *giration*. **gyre** dʒaiəɹ revolution, whirl, circle. XVI. – L. *gȳrus*. **gyro-** dʒaiə·rou, dʒaiərɔ· comb. form of Gr. *gûros*.

gyrfalcon var. of GERFALCON.

gyron dʒaiə·rən (her.) ordinary of triangular form. XVI. – (O)F. *giron*, †*geron* gusset, corr. to Sp. *giron*, It. *girone* – OFrank. **gēro* = OHG. *gēro* (see GORE[2]). So **gyro·nny**[5] (her.) divided into gyrons. XIV (*ierownde*; forms with *nn* before XVI).

gyve dʒaiv (arch.) fetter. XIII (*giue*, Laȝ.). Of unkn. origin; a solitary ex. of *gives et manicles* in an AN. text (XIV) may merely reflect the Eng. word; pl. *gyves* (*de draps*) bundles (of cloths) in 'Liber Albus' an. 1419 is difficult to relate because of the meaning; deriv. from OE. *wiþþe* WITH[1] does not account for the long vowel. The traditional pronunc. was with initial g, as is shown by ME. alliterative practice and sp. with *gu-* (XV–XVIII); the present pronunc. with dʒ is due to misinterpretation of *give* when the word had become obs. in oral use. Hence **gyve** vb. XIII (pp. *igwiued*). ¶ Not to be connected with similar and synon. W. *gefyn*, Ir. *geibheann*, Gael. *geimheal*.

H

ha hā excl. denoting surprise, joy, scorn, suspicion, etc. XIII (Cursor M.); †eh? (so ON. *há*) XVI; in hesitating speech XVII (Sh., Jonson). So in many other langs., but not found in OE. in its simple form; for its use to denote laughter see AHA, HA-HA[1] and cf. HE[2], HO.

habeas corpus hei·biæ̆s kō·ɹpəs (leg.) writ requiring a person to be brought before the court. XV. First words of the writ beginning *Habeas corpus ad subjiciendum* (etc.) you shall produce the body [of the person concerned, in court] to undergo [what the court may award]; L. *habeās*, 2nd pers. sg. pres. subj. of *habēre* have, *corpus* body.

haberdasher hæ·bəɹdæʃəɹ dealer in small articles appertaining to dress, formerly of wider application. XIV. prob. – AN. **haberdasser*, **hapertasser* (cf. *haberdasshrie* in an AN. document XV), presumably f. recorded *hapertas* (XV), of unkn. origin and uncertain meaning (Eng. †*haberdash* was used for 'small wares' XV–XVII); see -ER[2]. So **ha·berdash**ERY. XVI.

habergeon hæ·bəɹdʒən sleeveless coat of armour. XIV. – (O)F. *haubergeon*, f. OF. *hauberc* HAUBERK; cf. -OON. Since XVI only hist.; treated in verse (XVII–XVIII) as three or as four syll. with the stress on the second.

habiliment həbi·limənt equipment; †pl. munitions of war; pl. apparel. XV. – OF. *abillement* (later and mod. *habillement*), f. *habiller* render fit, fit out, (hence, by assoc. with *habit*) clothe, dress, f. *habile* ABLE; see -MENT.

habilitate hæbi·liteit (arch. or obs.) qualify. XVII. f. pp. stem of medL. *habilitāre*, f. *habilitās* ABILITY; see -ATE[3]. Survives chiefly in *rehabilitate*.

habit hæ·bit A. apparel, dress XIII; B. mental constitution XIV; settled disposition, custom XVI. ME. (*h*)*abit* – OF. *abit* (later and mod. *habit*) = Pr. (*h*)*abit*, It. *abito* :– L. *habitu-s*, f. *habit-*, pp. stem of *habēre* have, hold, refl. be constituted, be, with cogn. forms in Osco-Umbrian and Celtic. (Cf. Gr. *héxis* state, habit, rel. to *ékhein* have, be conditioned in a certain way.) The range of meaning (in modF. distributed between *habit* dress and *habitude* custom) was fully developed in L. (but the sense 'dress, attire' was not pre-Augustan); cf. *custom*, *costume*. So **habit** A. †dwell (cf. INHABIT) XIV (Ch.); B. dress XVI (Sh.). – (O)F. *habiter* – L. *habitāre*. **habit**A·TION dwelling, abode. XIV. – (O)F. – L. **habitat** hæ·bitæt native locality of an animal or plant. XVIII. – L. 'dwells', 3rd pers. sg. pres. ind. of *habitāre* dwell, inhabit; derived from its use in floras and faunas to introduce the natural place of growth or occurrence of a species (e.g. 'Common Primrose. Habitat in sylvis'). **habitu**AL[1] hæ̆bi·tjuəl †pert. to the inward disposition XVI; pert. to habit, customary XVII. – medL. *habituālis*, f. *habitus* HABIT. So **habi·tu**ATE[3] fix in a habit. XVI. f. late L. *habituāt-*, *-āre*. **habitué** (h)æ̆bi·tjuei habitual visitor. XIX. F., pp. of *habituer* – L. **ha·bi**TUDE constitution, temperament XIV; disposition, habit XVII. – (O)F. – L.

hachish see HASHEESH.

hachure (h)æ·ʃuəɹ (pl.) lines used in hill-shading in physical geography. XIX. – F. *hachure*, f. *hacher* HATCH[3]; see -URE.

hacienda æsie·ndə (in Spain and Sp. colonies) estate with dwelling-house. XVIII. Sp., 'domestic work, landed property' :– L. *facienda*, n. pl. of gerundive of *facere* make, DO[1].

hack[1] hæk cut with heavy blows XII; break up (ground), etc. XVII. OE. (*tō*)*haccian* cut in pieces = OFris. (*tō*)*hakia*, MLG., MDu., (M)HG. *hacken* (Du. *hakken*); CWGerm. deriv. of imit. base **χak-*; cf. synon. OE. *hæććan*, OHG. *hecken*. So **hack** sb. tool for breaking or chopping up XIII; gash, cut, notch XVI. Partly – MLG. *hakke*; partly f. the vb.

hack[2] hæk board for a hawk's meat XVI; rack XVII. By-form of HATCH[1], prob. due to assoc. with its north. dial. var. *heck*.

hack[3] hæk from XVII in various senses of HACKNEY (esp. 'riding-horse' and 'drudge'), of which it is a shortening. Hence vb. make a hack of, etc. XVIII.

hackbut, hagbut hæ·k-, hæ·gbʌt harquebus. XVI. – F. *haquebut*(*e*), alteration of *haquebusche* – MDu. *hakebus*, *hagebus* (Du. *haakbus*), MLG. *hakebusse*, f. *hake*(*n*) HOOK +*bus*(*se*) gun, firearm (cf. BLUNDERBUS), so called from the hook orig. cast on the gun as an attachment.

hackery hæ·kəri native Indian bullock-cart. XVII. – Hindi *chhakṛā* two-wheeled cart.

hackle hæ·kl flax-comb; long feathers on the neck of a domestic cock, etc. XV. By-form of HATCHEL; cf. HECKLE.

hackmatack hæ·kmətæk American larch. XVIII. Amer. Indian (cf. Abnaki *akemantak*).

hackney hæ·kni riding-horse, esp. for hire XIV (in *hakeneyman*, 1308); †common drudge, prostitute XVI; short for *hackney-coach* XVII (Pepys). In AN. *hakenei* (XIV), AL. *hakeneius* (XIII), prob. f. ME. *Hakenei* Hackney in Middlesex, Skeat's view being that horses were raised on the pasture land there and taken to Smithfield market through Mare Street. ¶ Hence (O)F. *haquenée*, Pr. *(f)acanea*, Sp. *hacanea*, It. *(ac)chinea*.

had see HAVE.

haddock hæ·dək fish allied to the cod. XIV. In AL. *haddocus* (XIII); prob. – AN. *hadoc*, var. of OF. *(h)adot*, pl. *hadoz*, *haddos*, of unkn. origin. ¶ For the final cons. cf. HAVOC.

Hades hei·dīz Pluto; the kingdom of Pluto, the lower world; state or abode of the dead. XVI. – Gr. *Háidēs*; in LXX and N.T. Gr. used to render Heb. *sheōl* abode of the dead.

hadji hæ·dʒi pilgrim to the tomb of Mohammed. XVII. – Arab. *ḥājī* pilgrim, f. *ḥajj* pilgrimage. ¶ In CEur. use.

hæmatite, hematite he·mətait, hī·- native sesquioxide of iron. XVII. – L. *hæmatītēs* – Gr. *haimatítēs* (sc. *líthos* stone) 'blood-like stone', f. *haimat-*, *haîma* blood; see -ITE.

hæmat(o)- hī·mət(ou), shortened **hæm(o)-**, comb. forms of Gr. *(h)aîma* blood, as in *hæ:mato-*, *hæmoglo·bin*, *hæmatu·ria*. XIX. **hæmoptysis** -ɔ·ptisis spitting of blood. XVII (Sir T. Browne). modL.; Gr. *ptúein* spit. **hæmorrhage, hemorrhage** he·məridʒ flux of blood. XVII (earlier *emorogie*, *hemoragie*). – F. *hémorr(h)agie*, †*emorogie* – L. *hæmorrhagia* (Pliny) – Gr. *haimorrhagíā*, f. *haimo-* + **rhag-*, base of *rhēgnúnai* break, burst. **hæmorrhoid, hemorrhoid** he·məroid (pl.) piles. XIV. Late ME. *emeroudis*, whence *emerods* (XVI–XVII) – OF. *emeroyde*, later *hémorrhoïdes* (XVI) – L. *hæmorrhoida* – Gr. *haimorrhoís*, acc. *-oída* discharging blood, pl. *-oídes* (sc. *phlébes* veins) bleeding piles, f. *haimórrhoos*, f. *haimo-* + **rhoꜰ-* flow (see STREAM); assim. to L.-Gr. form in XVI.

hafnium hæ·fniəm metallic element discovered in 1923. modL., f. *Hafnia*, L. name of Copenhagen (Køben*havn*), Denmark; see -IUM.

haft hæft handle. OE. *hæft*, *hæfte*, corr. to MLG. *hechte* (Du. *hecht*, *heft*), OHG. *hefti* (G. *heft*), ON. *hepti* :– CGerm. (exc. Gothic) **χaftjam*, f. **χaf-* HEAVE; see -T[1].

hag[1] hæg female evil spirit XIII; repulsive old woman XIV (?). ME. *hegge* (XIII AncrR.), *hagge* (XIV PPl.); rare before XVI. perh. shortening of OE. *hægtesse*, *hegtes* fury, witch = MDu. *haghetisse* (Du. *hecse*), OHG. *hagazissa* (G. *hexe*), of unkn. origin.

hag[2] hæg (Sc. and north.) †gap, chasm XIII (Cursor M.); broken moss-ground (i) piece of soft bog XVII, (ii) spot of firmer ground in a peat bog XIX. – ON. **haggw-*, *hǫgg* gap, breach, orig. cutting blow (whence the Sc. and north. Eng. senses 'cutting, hewing', 'cut wood'), f. **haggwa*, *hǫggva* HEW.

haggard hæ·gəɹd (of a hawk) untamed, wild XVI; †gaunt, lean; wild-looking XVII. – (O)F. *hagard*, perh. f. Germ. **hag-* hedge, bush, HAW[1]; see -ARD. Later infl. in sense by HAG[1] (for which *haggard* occurs XVII–XVIII); cf. dial. *hagged* haggard (XVII).

haggis hæ·gis dish consisting of minced entrails of a sheep, etc., boiled in the maw of the animal; now esp. Scotch. XV (*hagese*, *hagas*). Of unkn. origin; identity of form with †*haggess* magpie has suggested the possibility of its being a transf. use of the source of this, (O)F. *agace*, *agasse* magpie – OHG. *agaz(z)a*; cf. PIE[2].

haggle hæ·gl mangle with cuts XVI; wrangle in bargaining XVII. f. dial. *hag* cut (XIV – ON. **haggw-* *hǫggva* HEW) + -LE[3].

hagio- hæ·giou, hægiɔ· repr. Gr. *hágios* holy, used for 'saint' in **hagio·**GRAPHY, **hagio·**LOGY (XIX) and derivs. **hagio·grapha** books of the O.T. not included in the Law and the Prophets. XVI. late L. – Gr., 'sacred writings'. **hagio**SCOPE hæ·gīoskoup opening in the wall of an aisle, etc., supposed to provide a view of the high altar (also called *squint*). XIX; a modern ecclesiologist's coinage. ¶ The pronunc. with g is irreg.

ha-ha[1] hăhā OE. *ha ha* (see HA); so in many other langs. Cf. AHA.

ha-ha[2] hā·ha sunk fence. XVIII. – F. *haha* (XVII), usu. taken to be so named from the expression of surprise at meeting the obstacle (the F. word is also used for a strikingly ugly woman); redupl. of HA.

haiduk see HEYDUCK.

hail[1] heil frozen vapour falling in pellets. OE. *hæġl* (with var. *hagol*, whence ME. *hawel*), corr. to OFris. *heil*, OS., OHG. (Du., G.) *hagel*, ON. *hagl* :– CGerm. (exc. Gothic) **haȝ(a)laz*, *-am*, rel. to Gr. *kákhlēx* pebble. Hence **hail** vb. XV. (Earlier †*hawele* :– OE. *hagalian* = MHG. *hag(a)len*, ON. *hagla*.)

hail[2] heil excl. of salutation. XII. ellipt. use of †*hail* adj. (ME. phr. *wæs hæil!* 'be whole or healthy', hail!; cf. WASSAIL) – ON. *heill* WHOLE (phr. *kom heill!* welcome! hail!, *far heill!* farewell!). Hence **hail** vb. XII (Orm).

hair hɛəɹ any or all of the filamentous growths on the skin, esp. the head. OE. *hǣr*, *hēr* = OFris. *hēr*, OS., OHG. *hār* (Du., G. *haar*), ON. *hár* :– CGerm. **χǣram* (exc. Gothic), of unkn. origin (there is no CIE. word for hair). The present sp. and pronunc. are abnormal (for **here* or **hear* hiəɹ) and are supposed to be due to assim. to †*haire* hair shirt – (O)F. *haire* – Frankish **hārja* (OHG. *hār(r)a*). Hence **ha·ir-**, **ha·irs-**BREADTH. XVI (earlier *hairbrede* XV). **hai·**RY[1]. XIII (Cursor M.).

hairwood see HAREWOOD.

hake heik cod-like fish, Merlucius vulgaris. XV. perh. for **hakefish*, f. (dial.) *hake* hook (– ON. *haki*; see HOOK); cf. Norw. *hakefisk* applied to fishes having a hooked under-jaw, and OE. *hacod* pike.

hakeem, hakim hakī·m physician. XVII. – Arab. *ḥakīm* wise, learned, philosopher, physician, f. *ḥakama* exercise authority, be wise or learned.

halberd, halbert hæ·lbəɹd, hæ·lbəɹt weapon combining spear and battle-axe. XV. – F. *hallebarde*, †*alabarde* – It. *alabarda* – MHG. *helmbarde* (G. *hellebarde*), f. *helm* handle, HELM[2] + *barde, barte* hatchet (OHG. *barta* = OS. *barda*, ON. *barða*), rel. to *bart* BEARD (cf. ON. *skeggja* halberd, lit. 'the bearded', f. *skegg* beard).

halcyon hæ·lsiən bird fabled to breed on the sea. XIV (*alceon*, Gower). – L. *halcyon, alcyon* – Gr. *alkuṓn* kingfisher (*halkuṓn* by assoc. with *háls* sea and *kúōn* conceiving), rel. to L. *alcēdō*. *Halcyon days* (earlier †*halcyons days*) 14 days during which the kingfisher broods and the sea is calm; L. *alcyonei dies, alcyonides, alcedonia*, Gr. *ἀλκυονίδες ἡμέραι*.

hale[1] heil (dial.) sound, whole XIII (Orm); in robust health XVIII. ME. *hāl*, northern var. of WHOLE, taken into the literary lang. in mod. times.

hale[2] heil draw, pull. XIII. – (O)F. *haler* – OS. *halōn* (= OFris. *halia*, OHG. *halōn, holon*; Du. *halen*, G. *holen* fetch; cf. OE. *ġeholian* acquire), poss. rel. to L. *calāre*, Gr. *kaleîn* call (cf. CALENDS, INTERCALATE).

half hāf being one of two equal parts. OE. *half*, (*healf*) = OFris., OS. (Du.) *half*, (O)HG. *halb*, ON. *hálfr*, Goth. *halbs* :– CGerm. **χalƀaz*. Applied to relatives that are such on one side only, as *half-brother* (XIV, R. Mannyng), *half-sister* (XIII, Laȝ.), prob. – ON. *hálfbróðir, hálfsystur* (pl.); cf. OFris. *halfbrōther*, MLG. *halfsüsken*, Du. *halfbroeder*, MHG. *halpswester*, G. *halbbruder, -schwester*. Comp. **half**PENNY (XIV, R. Mannyng), in OE. *healfpeniġwurþ* (see WORTH), whence †*halpeny, ha'penny* hei·p(ə)ni, †*halp(w)orth, ha'p'orth* hei·pəɹþ. Also sb. †side; one of two equal parts. OE. *half, healf* = OS. *halƀa*, OHG. *halba*, ON. *hálfa* region, part, lineage, Goth. *halba* side, half; ult. connexions doubtful. Cf. BEHALF. So **half** adv. OE. in comb., e.g. *healfcwicu* 'half-alive', half-dead, *healfrēad* reddish, and in correl. use, e.g. *healf man healf assa* half man half ass (onocentaur). Hence **halve** hāv divide into two. XIII; repl. ME. *helfen*, OE. *hielfan* :– **χalƀjan*.

half-pace hā·fpeis raised floor, dais, foot-pace XVI; half-landing XVII. Alteration of *halpace* (XVI), var. of *hau(l)tepase* (XV) – F. *haut pas* 'high step' (see HAUGHTY, PACE).

halibut hæ·libət large flatfish. XV (also *holibut*, from XVII). f. *hāly*, HOLY + BUTT[3]. For the first el. cf. LG. *heilbut, heilige but*, Du. *heilbot*, G. *heilbutt*, ON. *heilagr fiskr* (Icel. *heilagfiski*, Sw. *helgeflundra*, Da. *hellefisk, -flyndre*).

halidom hæ·lidəm (arch.) holy relics. OE. *hāliġdōm* sanctity, holy place or thing = MDu. *heilichdoem*, OHG. *heilagtuom* (cf. ON. *helgidómr*); see HOLY, -DOM. *By my halidom* (XVI) is due to misunderstanding.

halitosis hælitou·sis foulness of breath. XIX. f. L. *halitus* breath, exhalation + -OSIS, used irreg.

hall hōl †spacious roofed place OE.; large public room XI; building for residence of students, business of a guild, etc. XIV; large dining-room in a college, etc., XVI; vestibule, lobby XVII. OE. *hall, heall* = OS., OHG. *halla* (Du. *hall*, G. *halle*), ON. *hǫll* :– CGerm. (exc. Gothic) **χallō*, f. **χal-* **χel-* cover, conceal (cf. HELL).

hallelujah hælilū·jə. XVI (Coverdale). – Heb. *hallelūyāh* praise Jah (i.e. Jehovah), f. imper. pl. of *hallēl* praise. Cf. ALLELUIA.

halliard see HALYARD.

hallo(a) hælou· excl. calling attention and used in greeting. XIX (Dickens). Later form of HOLLO(A). Also (with other vowels in the unstressed syll.) **hello(a)**· XIX, **hillo(a)**· XVIII (*illo* XVII), **hullo(a)**· XIX.

halloo hælū· shout 'halloo' to incite hounds to the chase. XVI. perh. var. of HALLOW[3]. Survives in VIEW-HALLOO. Also *holloo* (XVII–XVIII).

hallow[1] hæ·lou saint. OE. *hālga*, sb. use of definite form of *hāliġ* HOLY; obs. exc. as in ALL-HALLOWS, (Sc.) **Hallow-**E'E·N 31 Oct. (XVIII), (hist.) **Ha·llowmas** All Saints' Day, 1 Nov. (*halwe-, halumesday*, XIV; see MASS[1]).

hallow[2] hæ·lou make or regard as holy, consecrate, bless. OE. *hālgian* = OS. *hēlagōn*, OHG. *heilagōn* (G. *heiligen*), ON. *helga*; CGerm. (exc. Gothic) vb. f. **χailag-* HOLY.

hallow[3] hæ·lou shout so as to incite hounds. XIV. prob. – OF. *halloer*, imit. of shouting (cf. HALLOO).

hallucination həlʲūsinei·ʃən illusory notion. XVII. – L. *hallūcinātiō(n-)*, late form of *ālūcinātiō*, f. *alūcinārī* wander in thought or speech – Gr. *alússein* be distraught or ill at ease, with ending as in *vaticinārī* VATICINATE.

halma hæ·lmə game on a board, characterized by leaping moves. XIX. – Gr. *hálma*, f. *hállesthai* leap, rel. to L. *salīre* (see ASSAIL).

halo hei·lou circle of light round the sun, etc., XVI; nimbus of a saint XVII; fig. XIX. – medL. *halō*, for L. *halōs* (*-ōn-*) – Gr. *hálōs* threshing-floor, disk of the sun, moon, or a shield; cf. F. *halo*, It. *alone*, Sp. *halon*.

haloid hæ·loid like common salt. XIX. f. Gr. *háls* SALT + -OID.

halt[1] hōlt (arch.) lame. OE. *halt*, *healt* = OFris., OS. *halt*, OHG. *halz*, ON. *haltr*, Goth. *halts* :– CGerm. **χaltaz*, of unkn. origin. So **halt** vb. be lame OE.; waver XIV; proceed lamely XV. OE. *healtian*, corr. to OS. *halton*, OHG. *halzēn*, f. the adj.

halt[2] hōlt temporary stoppage on a march or journey. XVII (earlier †*alto* XVI, †*alt* XVII). orig. in phr. *make halt* – G. *halt machen* (whence also F. *faire halte*, It. *far alto*, Sp. *alto hacer*); in the G. phr. *halt* is prob. orig. based on the imper. ('stop', 'stand still') of *halten* HOLD.

halter hō·ltəɹ rope or strap with a noose OE.; rope for hanging XV. OE. *hælfter*, *hælftre*, corr. to OLG. *heliftra* (MLG. *helchter*, MDu. *halfter*, *halter*) :– WGerm. **χalftra-*, **χaliftra*, f. (with instr. suffix) **χalƀ-*; see HELVE.

halyard, halliard hæ·ljəɹd (naut.) tackle for raising and lowering sail, etc. XIV. orig. *halier*, *hallyer*, f. HALE[2]+-IER; altered XVII by assoc. with YARD[2] (cf. LANYARD).

ham[1] hæm hollow or bend of the knee OE.; thigh of a hog used for food XVII. OE. *ham*, *hom* = MLG. *hamme*, OHG. *hamma* (G. dial. *hamm*), rel. to synon. MLG. *hame*, OHG. *hama*, ON. *hǫm*, f. Germ. **χam-* be crooked. Hence **ha·m**STRING one of the tendons at the back of the knee. XVI (Golding); hence as vb. disable (as if) by cutting these XVII (Milton).

ham[2] hæm (now chiefly dial.) plot of pasture or meadow land. OE. *hamm*, *homm* = OFris., MLG., MDu. *hem*; perh. rel. to HEM[1] (cf. EFris., LG. *hamm* piece of enclosed land). ¶ Frequent in place-names, simply or in comb., and not always distinguishable from HAM[3].

ham[3] hæm (antiq.) town, village. XIX. Extracted from place-names having the terminal el. *-ham* (OE. *hām* HOME).

hamadryad hæmədrai·æd wood-nymph. XIV (*ama-*, Ch., Gower). – L. *Hamādryad-*, *-dryas*, Gr. *Hamādruad-*, *-druás*, f. *háma* together (cf. HOMO-)+*drûs* TREE.

hame heim each of the curved pieces forming the collar of a draught-horse. XIV. – MDu. *hame* (Du. *haam*), corr. to MHG. *ham(e)* fishing-rod, of unkn. origin.

Hamitic hæmi·tik pert. to a group of African languages comprising ancient Egyptian, Berber, Galla, etc. XIX. f. *Hamite* descendant of Ham (Hebrew *Kham*), second son of Noah (Gen. vi 10), whose descendants were supposed to have peopled northern Africa; see -ITE, -IC. Cf. *Japhetic*, *Semitic*.

hamlet hæ·mlit small village. XIV. – AN. *hamelet(t)e*, OF. *hamelet* (in AL. *hameletta* XIII), f. *hamel* (mod. *hameau*), dim. f. *ham* (found esp. in place-names of N. France) – MLG. MDu. *ham* HAM[2]; see -LET.

hammam see HUMMUM.

hammer hæ·məɹ beating instrument having a heavy head in which a handle is set transversely. OE. *hamor*, *hamer*, *homer* = OFris. *homer*, OS. *hamur* (Du. *hamer*), OHG. *hamar* (G. *hammer*), ON. *hamarr* hammer, back of an axe, crag; the latter sense of the ON. word and possible connexion with OSl. *kamy*, Russ. *kámen'* stone, suggest that the CGerm. word was orig. applied to a stone weapon.

hammer-cloth hæ·məɹklɔ̄þ cloth covering the seat in a coach. XV (first as the name of an unidentified material). Of unkn. origin.

hammock hæ·mək hanging bed suspended by cords. XVI (*hamaca*, *hammaker*; *hamack*, *-ock* XVII). – Sp. *hamaca* (whence also F. *hamac*), of Carib origin; the ending has been assim. to -OCK. ¶ Du. *hangmat*, G. *hängematte* 'hanging mat', are etymologizing alterations.

hamper[1] hæ·mpəɹ large wicker-work receptacle. XIV. Reduced form of AN. *hanaper* HANAPER.

hamper[2] hæ·mpəɹ obstruct the movement of. XIV. Of obscure formation; the termination appears to be identical with -ER[4].

hamster hæ·mstəɹ rodent Cricetus frumentarius. XVII (Topsell). – G. *hamster* :– OHG. *hamustro* = OS. *hamustra* 'curculio', corn-weevil, rel. to OSl. *chomĕstaru*, the second el. of which is repr. also by Lith. *staras* hamster.

hanaper hæ·nəpəɹ wicker case for documents, (hence) department of the chancery into which fees were paid. XV. – AN. *hanaper*, OF. *hanapier* (AL. *hanaperium* XIII), f. (O)F. *hanap* drinking-vessel, cup – WGerm. **χnapp-* (OE. *hnæp*, OHG. *hnapf*, ON. *hnappr*); see -ER[2]. Cf. HAMPER[1].

hand hænd extremity of the arm comprising palm and fingers OE.; side OE.; source of information, etc. XVI; manual worker XVII (employed person, orig. with reference to skill XVIII); handwriting XIV (spec. *court h.*, *secretary h.*, *Italian h.*). OE. *hand*, *hond* = OFris. *hānd*, *hōnd*, OS. *hand*, pl. *hendi*, OHG. *hant*, pl. *henti* (Du., G. *hand*), ON. *hǫnd*, pl. *hendr*, Goth. *handus*, pl. *handjus*; CGerm., of uncertain origin (there being no CIE. word). Hence **hand** vb. handle (Sh.), furl; lead by the hand; deliver with the hand XVII. Comps.: **ha·nd**BOOK OE. *handbōc*, tr. medL. *manuālis liber*, late L. *manuāle* MANUAL. **ha·nd**CUFF manacle for the hand XVIII (*cuff* is recorded in this sense XVII). **ha·nd**FAST (arch.) betroth XIV (earlier in pp. *hanndfesst*, Orm; – ON. *handfesta*). **ha·nd**FUL[2] OE. **hand**KERCHIEF hæ·ŋkəɹtʃif, also (now dial. or vulgar) **ha·nd**KERCHER square of textile material for wiping the face or covering head and neck. XVI (earlier †*handcoverchief* XV; *pocket h.* XVIII). **ha·nd**MAID XIV (Wycl.

Bible, Trevisa), -MAIDEN XIII female attendant; cf. OE. *handprēost* chaplain, *handþeġen* manservant. **ha·nd**WRI:TING. XVI (Dunbar).

handicap hæ·ndikæp †lottery in which one person challenged an article belonging to another, for which he offered something in exchange, an umpire being chosen to decree the respective values XVII; †*handicap match* match between two horses, in which the umpire decided the extra weight to be carried by the superior horse; so *handicap* (*race*) XVIII; hence gen., and later applied to the extra weight itself, and so to any disability in a contest XIX. Presumably f. phr. *hand i'* (i.e. *in*) *cap*, the two parties and the umpire in the orig. game all depositing forfeit money in a cap or hat. Hence **ha·ndicap** vb. †draw as in a lottery XVII; engage in a handicap; weight race-horses; penalize (a superior competitor) XIX.

handicraft hæ·ndikràft manual skill XV; manual art XVI. Alteration of earlier †*handcraft* (OE. *handcræft*) after next; see CRAFT.

handiwork hæ·ndiwə̄ɹk performance by hand. OE. *handġeweorc*, f. *hand* HAND + *ġeweorc*, coll. formation (see Y-) on *weorc* WORK; analysed in XVI as *handy work* (see HANDY).

handle hæ·ndl part to be grasped by the hand. OE. *handle*, *-la* = MLG. *hantel* (cf. OHG. *hantilla* towel), f. *hand* HAND; see -LE[1]. So **ha·ndle** vb. Late OE. *handlian* feel with the hands, treat of, corr. to OFris. *handelia*, OS. *handlon*, OHG. *hantalōn* (G. *handeln*), ON. *hǫndla* seize, treat; see -LE[3].

handsel, hansel hæ·n[d]səl †omen XII; New Year's gift XIV; earnest money; first use, first-fruits XVI. corr. formally to late OE. *handselen* 'mancipatio', delivery into the hand, and ON. *handsal* giving of the hand, esp. in a promise or bargain (OSw. *handsal*, Sw. *handsöl* money handed over, gratuity, Da. *handsel* earnest money); f. HAND + base of OE. *sellan* give, SELL. Hence as vb. XV. ¶ The characteristic senses of 'omen', 'gift to bring good luck', are not accounted for by those of the OE. and ON. words.

handsome hæ·n[d]səm †easy to handle XV; † handy; † (exc. U.S. dial.) apt, happy; moderately large, considerable; 'beautiful with dignity' (J.); graciously generous XVI. f. HAND + -SOME[1]; parallel formations are G. *handsam*, Du. *handzaam* manageable.

handspike hæ·n[d]spaik wooden bar used as lever. XVII. – Du. †*handspaeke* (now *-spaak*), f. *hand* HAND + MDu. *spāke* pole, rod; assim. to SPIKE[1]. Cf. SPOKE. ¶ Cf. F. *anspect* – Du.

handy hæ·ndi †manual XVI (*handy laboure*); ready to hand; dexterous XVI. In the first sense evolved from HANDIWORK; in the later (for which ME. had *hend*(*e*) :– OE. *ġehende* at hand) a new formation on HAND + -Y[1].

handy-dandy hæ:ndidæ·ndi children's game in which the players guess in which of another's hands an object is. XVI. Rhyming jingle f. HAND, or its infantile dim. *handy*.

hang hæŋ pt. and pp. **hung** hʌŋ, **hanged** hæŋd intr. be attached above without support beneath OE.; trans. attach in this way XIII. The present stem derives from (i) intr. OE. *hangian*, pt. *hangode*, (pp. *hanged* from XIV) = OFris. *hangia*, OS. *hangon*, OHG. *hangēn* (Du., G. *hangen*) :– WGerm. wk. vb. *χaŋgōjan*, *-ǣjan*, (ii) trans. ON. *hanga*, pt. *hékk*, pp. *hanginn* = OE. *hōn* (which continued till XIII), pt. *heng* (till XVI), pp. *hangen* (till XV), OFris. *hūa*, OS. *hāhan*, OHG. *hāhan*, pt. *hiang*, *hieng* (G. *hing*), MLG., MDu. *hān*, MHG. *hāhen*, Goth. *hāhan*, pt. *haihāh* :– CGerm. redupl. vb. *χaŋχan* (further relations in IE. are recognized in L. *cunctārī* delay, Skr. *çáṅkate* hesitate). In north. areas ON. wk. trans. *hengja*, pt. *hengda*, pp. *hengdr* was adopted XII (pt. *henngde*, pp. *henngd*, Orm); the normal change from *heng* to *hing* established the latter as a common north. form, with analogical pt. *hang*, pp. *hung*. Typical ME. midl. inflexions of XIV were: *hangen*, pt. *he*(*e*)*ng*, *hanged*, *ho*(*o*)*ng*, pp. *hanged* (with var. *hong-* for *hang-* throughout); pt. and pp. *hung* were established in literary Eng. in late XVI, with *hanged* largely restricted to the sense 'kill by hanging'. Hence **ha·ng**MAN. XIV (*þe hangeman of tyborne*, PPl.).

hangar hæ·ŋəɹ shed, now spec. for aircraft. XIX (Thackeray). – F. *hangar* (also †*hangard*, †*hanghart*); in medL. *angarium* smith's shed; of unkn. origin.

hanger[1] hæ·ŋəɹ wood on a steep bank. OE. *hangra*, f. *hangian* HANG.

hanger[2] hæ·ŋəɹ one who hangs; pendent or suspending object. XV. f. HANG + -ER[1].

hanger[3] hæ·ŋəɹ short sword. XV. prob. identical with HANGER[2] (the north. dial. var. *hinger* appears to confirm this origin); cf. early modDu. *hangher* rapier, which may be the immed. source.

hangnail (XVII) see AGNAIL.

hank hæŋk loop, coil, skein. XIV (in AL. *hanckus* XIII). – ON. *hanku*, prehistoric form of *hǫnk*, g. *hankar* (cf. *hanki* hasp, clasp; Sw. *hank* string, tie-band, rowel, Da. *hank* handle, ear of a pot). So **hank** vb. loop, noose. XIII. – ON. *hanka* coil.

hanker hæ·ŋkəɹ (dial.) linger, loiter *about*; have a longing *after*, *for*. XVII. f. dial. *hank* (XVI) + -ER[4]; prob. f. *haŋk-*, parallel to *haŋg-* HANG; cf. synon. Du. *hunkeren*, dial. *hankeren*.

hanky hæ·ŋki colloq. for HANDKERCHIEF hæ·ŋkəɹtʃif; see -Y[6].

hanky-panky hæŋkipæ·ŋki jugglery, trickery. XIX. Rhyming jingle based on *hokey pokey*, *hocus pocus*, with possible suggestion of 'sleight of *hand*'.

Hansard ha·nsāɹd colloq. designation of the official record of Parliamentary Debates, which began to be printed in 1805 by T. L. *Hansard*, son of Luke Hansard, who had printed 'Journals of the House of Commons' from 1774.

Hanse hæns merchant guild; entrance fee of such a guild XII; commercial league of German towns XV. First in *hanshus* 'hanse-house', guildhall – MLG. *hanshūs*, and in medL. form *hansa* – OHG. *hansa*, (M)HG. *hanse* (whence MLG. *hanse*, etc.) = OE. *hōs* (instr. only) troop, company, Goth. *hansa* company, crowd :– Germ. **χansō* (whence Finn. *kansa* people, company); of unkn. origin. So **Ha·ns**ARD member of the German Hanse. XIX; **Hanse**ATIC hænsiæ·tik. XVII (Selden). – medL.

hansel see HANDSEL.

hansom hæ·nsəm short for *hansom cab*. XIX. f. name of Joseph Aloysius *Hansom* (1803–82), architect, who registered a Patent Safety Cab in 1834.

hap hæp (arch.) chance, luck; event; †good fortune XIII (Laȝ.); chance, fortuity XIV. – ON. *happ* chance, good luck, rel. to OE. *ġehæp*(*liċ*) fitting, convenient, orderly (cf. OSl. *kobŭ* fate, Czech *koba* consequence). Hence **hap** vb. (arch.) chance, happen. XIV; cf. ODa. *happe*; superseded by **happ**EN[5] hæ·pn. XIV. **hap**LY[2] by chance. XIV (PPl.; in early use varying with *happily*). **happ**Y[1] prosperous XIV (R. Rolle); having a feeling of content XVI. **ha:ppy-go-lu·cky.** XVII.

haplo- hæ·plou, hæplɔ· comb. form of Gr. *haploûs* single, simple, as in *haplo*·GRAPHY *haplo*·LOGY writing/speaking once instead of twice. XIX.

haqueton see ACTON.

hara-kiri hārə-ki·ri suicide by disembowelment. XIX. Jap., f. *hara* belly + *kiri* cut. ¶ Sometimes rendered 'happy dispatch' through a misunderstanding; and often erron. *hari-kari*.

harangue həræ·ŋ vehement address or oration. XV (*arang*; first in Sc.; in Eng. after 1600). – F. *harangue*, earlier †*arenge* – medL. *harenga* (cf. Pr., Sp. *arenga*, It. *arringa* speech), perh. – Germ. **χariχriŋg*- assembly, f. **χarja*- host, crowd (see HARRY) + **χriŋg*- RING.

haras hæ·rəs, ‖ara horse-breeding establishment. XIII (*harace*). – (O)F. *haras*, of unkn. origin.

harass hæ·rəs †tire *out*; trouble, worry. XVII. – F. *harasser*, pejorative deriv. of *harer* set a dog on, f. *hare* cry used for this purpose.

harbinger hā·ɹbindʒəɹ †one who provides lodging, host XII; purveyor of lodging, e.g. for an army XIV; forerunner XVI. ME. *herbergere, -geour* – AN., OF. *herbergere*, obl. case *-geour*, f. *herbergier* provide lodging for, f. *herberge* lodging ∸ OS. (= OHG.) *heriberga* 'shelter for an army', lodging, f. *heri, hari* host, army (see HARRY) + **berg*- protect (see BOROUGH). ¶ The intrusive *n* occurs XV; cf. *celandine*; *messenger, ostringer, passenger, porringer, scavenger, wharfinger*; *nightingale*; *popinjay*.

harbour hā·ɹbəɹ shelter, lodging (arch.) OE.; place of shelter XIII; spec. for ships, port XVI. Late OE. *herebeorg* (perh. – ON.), corr. to OS., OHG. *heriberga* (Du. *herberg*, G. *herberge*), ON. *herbergi*; see prec. Two types evolved in ME., *herberwe, herborouȝ* (surviving in place-names, e.g. Market *Harborough*), and *herber*(*e*), whence the mod. form (with *-ar-* from *-er-*, as in *bark*, etc.). So **ha·rbour** vb. shelter, lodge, entertain; fig. XIV. Late OE. *herebeorgian*, corr. to (M)Du. *herbergen*, OHG. *heribergōn*, ON. *herbergja*. Hence **ha·rbour**AGE. XVI.

hard hāɹd resisting pressure; difficult to endure, severe; intense, violent; sb. beach or jetty for landing XIX. OE. *hard, heard* = OFris. *herd*, OS. (Du.) *hard*, (O)HG. *hart*, ON. *harðr*, Goth. *hardus* :– CGerm. **χarðuz* :– IE. **kratús*, whence Gr. *kratús* strong, powerful (cf. -CRACY). Hence **ha·rd**EN[5] make hard XIII; become hard XV; after ON. *harðna*. Hence **ha·rd**LY[2] †forcibly; †boldly XIII; severely; not easily, (hence) barely, not quite XVI. **ha·rd**SHIP †severity; oppressive condition. XIII (AncrR.). **ha·rd**WARE[1] ironmongery. XVI.

hards, hurds hāɹdz, hɔ̄ɹdz coarser parts of flax or hemp. OE. *heordan* wk. fem. pl., corr. to OFris., OLG. *hēde* (Du. *heede*); of unkn. origin (for the phonology cf. OE. *meord*, OS. *mēd* MEED). Hence **ha·rd**EN[3], **hu·rden** sb. and adj. XV.

hardy hāɹdi courageous, daring XIII; capable of physical endurance XVI. – (O)F. *hardi* (= Pr. *ardit*, It. *ardito*), pp. of *hardir* become bold – Germ. **χarðjan* (cf. OE. *hierdan*, OHG. *herten*, Goth. *gahardjan*, etc.), f. **χarðuz* HARD. Hence **ha·rdi**HOOD. XVII (Milton); preceded by (pseudo-arch.) **ha·rdi**HEAD XVI (Spenser).

hare hɛəɹ rodent of the genus Lepus. OE. *hara* = OFris. *hasa*, MDu. *haese* (Du. *haas*), OHG. *haso* (G. *hase*), ON. *heri* :– CGerm. (exc. Goth.) **χason*, **χazon*; an animal-name of IE. extent, repr. also by W. *ceinach* (based on **kasnī*-), OPruss. *sasins*, Skr. *śaśas* (for **sasas*); prob. sb. use of a colour-adj.; cf. OE. *hasu*, ON. *hǫss* grey, L. *cascus* old, beside OHG. *hasan* grey, L. *cānus* hoary (:– **casnos*). Hence **hare**BELL hɛə·ɹbel wild hyacinth XIV; Campanula rotundifolia XVIII. **hare**BRAIN hɛə·ɹbrein †giddy person; as adj. XVI. **hare-**LIP. XVI (Harman, Sh.). perh. immed. – (with accommodation) Du. *hazenlip*, tr. L. *labium leporinum*; cf. OE. *hærsċeard* 'hare-cleft' (see SHARD), OFris. *hasskerde* (adj.), G. *hasenscharte*, Da. *hareskaar*; F *bec-de-lièvre*.

harem hɛə·rəm women's part of a Mohammedan dwelling-house, or its occupants. XVII. – Arab. *ḥaram* and *ḥarīm* (that which is) prohibited, (hence) sacred place, sanctuary, women's apartments, wives, women, f. *ḥarama* prohibit, make unlawful.

harewood hɛə·ɹwud also *hair, air,* formerly *aire, ayer, ayre* stained sycamore wood. XVII. The first el. is – dial. G. *aehre, ehre,* prob. – Friulian *ayar, ayer, aire* :– Rom. **acre,* for L. *acer* maple.

haricot[1] hæ·rikou kidney bean, French bean. XVII. – F. *haricot* (*febves de h.* XVII), perh. – Aztec *ayacotli.*

haricot[2] hæ·rikou ragout (orig. of mutton). XVIII. – F. *haricot,* earlier *hericoq* (*de mouton*), *hericot,* perh. orig. rel. to OF. *harigoter* cut up, and later assim. to prec.

hari-kari erron. form of HARA-KIRI.

hark hāɹk give ear to XII; listen XIII. ME. *herkien* :– OE. **he(o)rcian* = OFris. *herkia, harkia,* rel. to MLG., MDu., Flem. dial. *horken,* OHG. *hōrechen,* G. *horchen*; cf. HEARKEN. *Hark back* is a hunting phr. arising from the use of 'hark!' as a call to retrace one's course; hence as sb. XVIII.

harlequin hā·ɹlikwin character (associated with Columbine) in It. comedy and Eng. pantomime (clothed in variegated costume, whence the application of the word to animals with variegated coat, plumage, etc.). XVI (*Harlicken, Harlaken,* Nashe, Day). – F. †*harlequin* (mod. *arlequin,* after It. *arlecchino*), later var. of *Herlequin* (also *Hellequin,* as in OF. *maisnie Hellequin,* in medL. *familia Hellequini* or *Herlechini*) leader of the Wild Host or troop of demon horsemen riding by night, also called in medL. *familia Herlethingi* (Walter Map), which has been plausibly referred (as if for **Herlechingi*) to OE. *Herla cyning* king Herla (cf. *De Herla rege* concerning king Herla, in Map's 'De nugis curialium'), whose characteristics have been identified with those of Woden; the circumstances of the transmission of the name from OF. to It., and thence to modF., are not clear. For the It. associations cf. COLUMBINE, PUNCH, ZANY. ¶ *Hurlewaynis kynne* (PPl.) and *H. meyne* (Tale of Beryn), and *Helwayne* (Harsnet, 1603), *Hellwain* (Middleton, *c.* 1605), reflect such phr. as medL. *milites Herlewini* (Peter of Blois).

harlot hā·ɹlət †vagabond, rascal, low fellow XIII (AncrR.); †itinerant jester (R. Rolle); †male servant; †'fellow' XIV (Ch.); prostitute, strumpet XV. ME. *har-, herlot* – OF. *(h)arlot, herlot* young fellow, knave, vagabond = Pr. *arlot* vagabond, beggar, It. *arlotto*; cf. medL. *arlotus, erlotus* glutton, OSp. *arlote, alrote* lazy, OPg. *alrotar* go about begging. Hence **ha·rlot**RY †buffoonery; unchastity XIV; (arch.) harlot XVI.

harm hāɹm hurt, injury. OE. *hearm* = OFris. *herm,* OS., OHG., (G.) *harm,* ON. *harmr* (chiefly) grief, sorrow :– CGerm. (exc. Gothic) **χarmaz,* rel. to OSl. *sramŭ* shame, injury (Russ. *sram* shame, scandal), Pers. *šarm.* So **harm** vb. OE. *hearmian* = OHG. *harmen, hermen.*

harmattan hāɹmæ·tən dry land-wind of Upper Guinea. XVII. f. Fanti or Twi (W. Africa) *haramata.*

harmony hā·ɹməni †melody, music XIV (Ch.); (mus.) combination of notes to make chords; agreement, accord XVI. – (O)F. *harmonie* = Pr., Sp., It. *armonia* – L. *harmonia* – Gr. *harmoniā* joint, agreement, concord, f. **harmo-* of *harmós* joint, *harmózein* fit together. So **harmo·n**IC. XVI. – L. – Gr. *harmonikós.* **harmo·n**IOUS. XVI; cf. (O)F. *harmonieux.* **harmonica** -ɔ·nikə first applied (1762) by B. Franklin to a developed form of musical glasses; fem. sg. or n. pl. (used sb.) of L. *harmonicus.* – (O)F. **harmon**IUM -ou·niəm form of reed organ. – F. *harmonium* (Debain, *c.* 1840), f. L. *harmonia* or Gr. *harmónios* harmonious. **ha·rmon**IZE. XV (Caxton; rare before XVII).

harness hā·ɹnis †baggage, equipment XIII (Cursor M.); trappings of a horse; (arch.) body armour; tackle, gear (now techn.) XIV. ME. *harnais, herneis* – OF. *harneis* military equipment (mod. *harnais*) – ON. **hernest* 'provisions for an army', with assim. of the termination to **-isk-* (cf. OF. *harneschier* equip), f. *herr* army (see HARRY) + *nest* = OE., OHG. *nest* provisions, Goth. *ganists* safety. So **ha·rness** vb. XIV. – OF. (*harnacher*). ¶ The OF. word is the source of Pr., Sp. *arnes,* It. *arnese,* medL. *harnesium,* etc., MHG. *harnasch,* G. *harnisch,* (M)Du. *harnas(ch),* ON. *harn-, herneskja.*

harns hāɹnz (ONc.) brains. XII. Early ME. *hernes* – ON. **herni, hjarni,* corr. to MLG., MDu. *herne* (Du. *hersenen, hersens*), OHG. *hirni* (G. *hirn*) :– Germ. (not OE. or Gothic) **χersni,* rel. to Gr. *krānion* CRANIUM, L. *cerebrum* brain (see CEREBRAL).

harp hāɹp stringed musical instrument. OE. *hearpe* = OS. *harpa* (Du. *harp*), OHG. *harfa* (G. *harfe*), ON. *harpa* :– CGerm. (exc. Gothic) **χarpōn,* whence late L. *harpa* (and the Rom. words derived therefrom). So **harp** vb. OE. *hearpian* = (M)Du. *harpen,* etc., ON. *harpa.*

harpings hā·ɹpiŋz (naut.) wales about the bow of a ship. XVII. Earliest in *cat harpings* (Capt. Smith) ropes or cramps serving to brace in the shrouds of the lower masts; perh. connected with F. *harpe* (cf. next).

harpoon hāɹpū·n barbed spear-like missile. XVII (Purchas). – F. *harpon,* f. *harpe* dog's claw, cramp-iron, clamp – L. *harpē, harpa* – Gr. *hárpē* sickle (cf. L. *sarpere* prune); superseded earlier †*harping*-IRON (XVI), perh. – F. *harpin* boat-hook, f. *harper* grasp, grapple. Hence **harpoon**EE·R[1]. XVII (Purchas).

harpsichord hā·ɹpsikɔ̄ɹd keyboard instrument of music in which the strings were plucked with points. XVII (Cotgr.). – F. †*harpechorde* = It. *arpicordo*, modL. *harpichordium*, f. late L. *harpa* HARP + *chorda* CHORD; the intrusive *s*, found in the earliest instances, is of obscure origin.

harpy hā·ɹpi fabulous monster half woman half bird; also transf. XVI. – (O)F. *harpie* or its source L. *harpȳia*, pl. *-iæ* – Gr. *hárpūiai* 'snatchers', rel. to *harpázein* seize.

harquebus, arquebus (h)ā·ɹkwibəs early portable gun. XVI. – F. (*h*)*arquebuse*, ult. – MLG. *hakebusse* (mod. *haakbus*) or MHG. *hake*(*n*)*bühse* (mod. *hakenbüchse*), which in the F. form †*haquebusche* was adopted in Eng. as *hakbush* XV; f. *hake*(*n*) hook + *bus*(*se*) fire-arm (a hook being orig. cast on the gun). So (**h**)**a:rquebus**IE·R. XVI. – F. (*h*)*arquebusier*; earlier equivs. were *hackbushier*, *hackbutter*, *-buteer*.

harridan hæ·ridən haggard old woman. XVII. Recorded first as a cant word; presumed to be alteration of F. *haridelle* old jade of a horse, of unkn. origin.

harrier[1] hæ·riəɹ hound for hunting the hare XVI; member of a hare-and-hounds team XIX. Early forms *hayrere*, *heirere*, f. *hayre* HARE + -ER[1], after (O)F. *lévrier*, repr. medL. *leporārius* greyhound, sb. use of lateL. adj. f. *lepor-*, *lepus* hare; assim. to next.

harrier[2] hæ·riəɹ one who harries; falcon of the genus Circus. XVI. (In the second sense, early forms *har*(*r*)*oer*, *harrower*.) f. HARROW[1], HARRY + -ER[1].

harrow[1] hæ·rou (arch.) rob, despoil. XIII. ME. *harwe*, *herwe*, var. of *herie* HARRY; in ME. often of the spoiling of Hell by Christ.

harrow[2] hæ·rou toothed timber-frame which is dragged over ploughed land to clean it. XIII (Cursor M.). – ON. **harwjan*, prehistoric form of *herfi*, *hervi* (Sw. *harf*, *härf*, Da. *harv*), rel. obscurely to MLG., MDu. *harke* (Du. *hark*) rake. Hence **ha·rrow** vb. XIII (Cursor M.); fig. lacerate the feelings of XVII (Sh.).

harry hæ·ri make raids OE.; overrun or despoil with an army XIII (Laȝ.); harass XIII (Cursor M.). OE. *hergian*, *herian*, corr. to OFris. *-heria*, OS. *heriōn*, OHG. *herjōn*, ON. *herja* :– CGerm. (exc. Gothic) **χarjōjan*, **χarjōn*, f. **χarjaz* host, army (OE. *here*, MIr. *cuire*, OPruss. *karjis*, Lith. *kãrias* army, and in Gr. *koíranos* 'military commander', lord, king. ¶ Before back vowels (e.g. OE. *hergode* pt., *hergung* vbl. sb.) OE. *g* became ME. *w*, whence the var. HARROW[1]. Conflation with synon. OF. *harier*, *her*(*r*)*ier* is probable.

Harry hæ·ri male Christian name. XIV (Ch.). ME. *Herry* – OF. *Herri*, var. (with assim. of *nr* to *rr*) of *Henri* :– medL. *Henrīcus* – OHG. *Heinrīk* (G. *Heinrich*). *Old Harry* the Devil (XVII); cf. *Old* NICK. *By the Lord Harry* an oath (XVII).

harsh hāɹʃ rough to the touch, taste, or hearing; repugnant to feeling or æsthetic taste. XVI. – MLG. *harsch* (whence G. *harsch*) rough, lit. 'hairy', f. *haer* HAIR; see -ISH[1]. The early form *harrish* implies a MLG. uncontracted form **harisch*; the form *hars* in Pinson's 'Promptorium Parvulorum', if not an error, may repr. LDu. pronunc. ¶ Distinct from the synon. *harsk* XIII (Cursor M.), *hask* (now dial.), which agrees in form (though not in sense) with OSw. *härsk*, Da. *harsk* rancid.

harslet var. of HASLET.

hart hāɹt male of the (red) deer. OE. *heort*, earlier *heorot* = OS. *hirot* (Du. *hert*), OHG. *hir*(*u*)*ȝ* (G. *hirsch*), ON. *hjǫrtr* (:– **herutr*) :– CGerm. (exc. Gothic) **χerutaz*. ¶ An animal-name of wide IE. extent; prob. lit. 'horned beast', and based on IE. **kerw-* (as in L. *cervus* stag, W. *carw* hart, OPruss. *sirwis*, OSl. *srŭna* roe), rel. ult. to HORN.

hartal hā·ɹtəl (in India) day of mourning used as a form of boycott. XX. – Hindi *hartāl*, for *haṭṭāl* 'locking of shops' (Skr. *haṭṭa* shop, *tālaka* lock, bolt).

hartebeest hā·ɹt(ə)bīst S. African antelope. XVIII. Afrikaans (now *hartbees*), f. Du. *hert* HART + *beest* BEAST.

harum-scarum hɛə·rəmskɛə·rəm adv. recklessly XVII; adj. reckless; also sb. XVIII. orig. dial. or slang (*harum starum*, Ray); rhyming jingle perh. f. HARE and SCARE; sometimes taken as *hare 'em*, *scare 'em*.

harvest hā·ɹvist autumn, spec. as the season for gathering the ripened grain OE.; the gathering itself, corn-crop XVI (Tindale). OE. *hærfest* = OFris., (M)Du. *herfst*, OHG. *herbist* (G. *herbst* autumn, in Upper Germany, fruit-harvest), ON. *haust* n. (orig. m.) :– CGerm. (exc. Gothic) **χarƀistaz*, **-ustaz*, f. **χarƀ-* :– IE. **karp-*, as in L. *carpere* pluck, Gr. *karpós* fruit, rel. to OIr. *cirrim* (:– **kirpim*) I chop off, Lith. *kerpù* I shear, Skr. *kṛpāṇas* sword, *-āṇī* scissors. Hence as vb. XIV (Maund.); **harvest-**HOME bringing home the last of the harvest. XVI (Tusser, Sh.).

has see HAVE. **has-been** hæ·zbīn one whose best days are over. XVII (*hesbeene*). orig. Sc.; 3rd sg. pf. ind. of BE.

hash hæʃ cut up (meat) small for cooking; fig. mangle. XVII. – (O)F. *hacher*, f. *hache* HATCHET. Hence **hash** sb. dish of previously cooked meat cut small and heated with gravy. XVII (Pepys); superseded earlier †*hachee*, †*hach*(*e*)*y* – F. *hachis*, f. *hacher* + *-is* (:– Rom. **-āticiu-s*).

hasheesh, -ish (also earlier *hachish*) hæ·ʃīʃ leaves of Indian hemp for smoking or chewing. XVI. – Arab. *ḥashīsh* dry herb, hay, powdered hemp-leaves, intoxicant made therefrom.

haslet hei·slit, **harslet** hā·ɹslit pig's fry, pluck of sheep, etc. XIV. – OF. *hastelet* (mod. *hâtelet, -lette*), dim. of *haste* (*hâte*) spit, roast meat – OLG. *harst* piece of roast meat (cf. Du. *harst* sirloin) = OHG. *harst*; see -LET.

hasp hæsp hinged fastening. OE. *hæpse, hæsp*, corr. to MLG. *haspe, hespe*, OHG. *haspa* (G. *haspe*), ON. *hespa*, rel. further to MLG., Du. *haspel*, OHG. *haspil*. ¶ Most of the Germ. langs. show two meanings, 'fastening, hinge' and 'skein, reel'; whether they belong orig. to the same formation is doubtful.

hassock hæ·sək clump of matted vegetation OE.; cushion for kneeling or resting the feet on, orig. one made from turf or peat XVI. OE. *hassuc*, of unkn. origin; see -OCK. ¶ Not rel. to W. *hesg*; see SEDGE.

hastate hæ·steit spear-shaped. XVIII. – L. *hastātus*, f. *hasta* spear; see YARD[1], -ATE[2].

haste heist swiftness of movement; hurry XIII (Cursor M.); obligation or eagerness to act quickly XIV (Ch.). – OF. *haste* (mod. *hâte*) – WGerm. **χaisti* (OE. *hǣst* violence, fury, ON. *heifst, heipt* hate, revenge, Goth. *haifsts* strife; OE. *hǣste* violent, OFris. *hāste*, OHG. *heisti* powerful); of unkn. origin. (Cf. POST-HASTE.) ¶ The OF. word was adopted in MDu. as *haeste* (Du. *haast*), in MLG. as *hast*, whence G. *hast*. So **haste** vb. XIII (Cursor M). – OF. *haster* (mod. *hâter*), whence also Du. *haasten*, G. *hasten*, Sw. *hasta*, etc.; superseded by **hast**EN[5] hei·sn make haste. XVI. Hence **hasty** hei·sti †speedy; †hurried XIV; precipitate, rash XV. – OF. *hasti, hastif* (mod. *hâtif*), f. *haste*+*-if* -IVE; superseded †*hastif* (cf. *jolly, tardy*).

hat hæt head-covering. OE. *hætt*, corr. to ON. *hǫttr* hood, cowl :– Germ. **χattuz* (cf. ON. *hetta* hood :– **χatjōn*) :– **χadnús*; see HOOD. Hence **ha·tt**ER[1] one who makes and/or sells hats. XIV; after (O)F. *chapelier*, f. †*chapel, chapeau*.

hatch[1] hætʃ half-door, wicket OE.; †movable planking forming a deck, (now) framework covering openings in a deck XIII (implied in AL. *hechia*, 1296); flood-gate XVI. OE. *hæćć, hećć*, corr. to MLG. *heck*, MDu. *hecke* (Du. *hek*); f. Germ. **χak-*, of unkn. origin.

hatch[2] hætʃ bring forth from the egg. XIII. ME. *hacche*, pt. *haȝte*, pp. *yhaht, iheyȝt* and *hacchid, hetchid*, points to an OE. **hæććan*, rel. to MHG. *hecken*, Sw. *häcka*, Da. *hække*, of unkn. origin.

hatch[3] hætʃ inlay XV; engrave lines on XVI. – (O)F. *hacher*, f. *hache* HATCHET.

hatchel hæ·tʃl flax-comb. XVII. Later var. of *hetchel*, ME. *hechele, hechil* (XIII) :– OE. **hæćel*, corr. to (M)LG., (M)Du. *hekel*, (M)HG. *hechel* :– WGerm. **χakila*, f. **χak-* HOOK. Cf. HACKLE, HECKLE.

hatchet hæt·ʃit small or light axe. XIV. – (O)F. *hachette*, dim. of *hache* axe = Pr. *apcha* :– medL. *hapia* – Germ. **χapja* (OHG. *happa, heppa* sickle-shaped knife); see -ET.

hatchment hæ·tʃmənt escutcheon. XVI. Early forms (*h*)*achement, achivment*, shortening of ACHIEVEMENT stressed on the first syll.

hate heit hold in strong dislike. OE. *hatian* = OFris. *hatia*, OS. *haton* (Du. *haten*), OHG. *haȥȥōn, -ēn* (G. *hassen*), ON. *hata*, Goth. *hatan* :– CGerm. **χatōjan*, **-ǣjan*, f. base of **χatis-* (see below). So **hate** sb. XIII; partly – ON. *hatr*, partly f. *hate* vb. under the infl. of **hatred** hei·trid XIII (ME. *haterede*(*n*), f. the vb.-stem+-RED). Both sbs. superseded OE. synon. *hete* (to XIII) = OS. *heti*, OHG. *haȥ* (G. *hass*), ON. *hatr*, Goth. *hatis* :– CGerm. **χatis-* :– IE. **kədes-* (cf. Oscan *cadeis* of enmity, and, with vowel-variation, Av. *sādra-*, Gr. *kêdos* suffering, W. *cawdd* anger, insult, trouble, and with *-t-* suffix, W. *cas*, OIr. *caiss* hatred).

Hattic hæ·tik pert. to the Hatti, conterminous or partly identical with the Hittites. XX. f. Assyrian and Hittite *Khatti*+-IC.

hauberk hō·bəɹk defensive armour for neck and shoulders. XIII. – OF. *hauberc*, also *holberc*, earlier *hausberc* = Pr. *ausberc* (whence It. *osbergo*) :– Frankish **halsberg* (= OHG. *halsberc*, OE. *healsbeorg*, ON. **halsbjǫrg*), f. *hals* neck (cf. COLLAR)+**berg-* protect (cf. HARBOUR).

haugh hāχ, hāf (Sc. and north.) flat land by a river side. ME. *hawch, hawgh*, prob. :– OE. *healh* corner, nook, rel. to *holh* HOLLOW.

haughty hō·ti lofty and disdainful; †eminent, exalted; †high. XVI. Extension with -Y[1] of †*haught*, earlier *haut* (XV) – (O)F. *haut* high :– L. *altus* high (cf. OLD), infl. by Germ. **χauχ-* HIGH. The sp. with *gh* was induced by assim. to words in which the sound denoted by it had become mute, or to *high, height*. ¶ *Haught* was preceded by †*hautain* (XIII) – (O)F. *hautain*.

haul hōl pull, drag; trim (sails) XVI; (of the wind) veer XVIII. Earliest form *hall*; var. of HALE[2]. For the sp. with *au* cf. *crawl*. So **hau·l**IER. XV (*hallier*) – OF. *hallier*, f. *hal*(*l*)*er*.

haulm, halm hōm, hām stems or stalks. OE. *halm* (*healm*) = OS., OHG. (Du., G.) *halm*, ON. *hálmr* :– CGerm. (exc. Gothic) **χalmaz* :– IE. **kolmos*; cf. L. *culmus* haulm, Gr. *kálamos* (whence L. *calamus*) reed, OSl. *slama*, Russ. *solóma* straw; cf. CULM[1].

haunch hōnʃ, hānʃ part of the body between the last ribs and the thigh. XIII (AncrR.). – (O)F. *hanche* = Pr., Sp., It. *anca*, of Germ. origin (cf. LG. *hanke* hind leg of a horse).

haunt hōnt, (old-fashioned) hānt †practise habitually; resort (to) habitually XIII; frequent the company of XV; visit frequently XVI (spec. of ghosts, Sh.). – (O)F. *hanter* – Germ. **χaimatjan* (repr. by OE. *hāmettan* provide with a home, house, ON. *heimta* get home, recover), f. **χaimaz* HOME.

Hausa also *Haussa, H(a)oussa* hau·sə people of northern Nigeria and the Sudan, and their language (much used commercially).

haussmannize hau·smənaiz open out the streets, etc., of (a town). XIX. f. the name of Baron Eugène-Georges *Haussmann*, who when prefect of the Seine (1853–70) remodelled a great part of Paris; see -IZE.

haustellum hōste·ləm (zool.) proboscis of an insect, etc. XIX. modL. dim. of L. *haustrum* machine for drawing water, f. *haust-, haurīre* (see EXHAUST). So **haustorium** -ō·riəm (bot.) sucker of a parasitic plant. XIX. modL., f. late L. *haustor* drainer; see -ORIUM.

hautboy hou·boi wooden wind instrument. XVI. – F. *hautbois*, f. *haut* high+*bois* wood (see BUSH); so named from its high pitch. Superseded by OBOE.

hauteur ou·tə̄ɹ, ‖otǿr loftiness of manner. XVII. F., f. *haut* high+*-eur* -OR².

haut goût see HOGO.

havana həvæ·nə cigar of a kind made in Cuba. XIX. f. name of the capital of Cuba (Sp. *Habana*); cf. F. *havane*.

have hæv, (h)əv pt., pp. **had** hæd, (h)əd the most general vb. denoting possession. OE. *habban*, pt. *hæfde*, pp. *(ġe)hæfd* = OFris. *hebba, hēde, hev(e)d*, OS. *hebbian, habda, habd* (Du. *hebben, hadde, gehad*), OHG. *habēn, habēta, gihabēt* (G. *haben, hatte, gehabt*), ON. *hafa, hafða, haft*, Goth. *haban, habaida, -habaida* (fem.) :– CGerm. **χaƀēn*, **χaƀda*, **gaχaƀdaz*, prob. rel. to **χaƀjan* (IE. **kap-*) HEAVE (connexion with L. *habēre* have, either as cogn. or by adoption therefrom, is doubtful). In OE. all parts of the present had *-bb-* (:– **-ƀj-*), exc. the 2nd and 3rd sg. *hafast, hafaþ* beside *hæfst, hæfþ*, which became in ME. *havest, haveth*, and *hafst, hafþ*, whence (from XIII) *hast* hæst, (h)əst, *hath* hæþ, (h)əþ, while *v* was levelled out into other parts. In weak-stress conditions *v* tended to disappear, whence ME. inf. *han, ha*, Sc. *hae*; loss of *h* resulted in the reduction of the inf. to *n*, the final term being its entire loss, as in Sc. *I wad been* I would have been, *she might been*. ¶ Like *be* and *do*, this verb in all the Germ. langs. came to be used contextually as a fixed element of predication, and esp. as an auxiliary of tense, forming generalized tenses corr. to the L. perfect tenses, e.g. *I have, had, shall have, to have given*, L. *dedī, dederam, dederō, dedisse*.

haven hei·v(ə)n harbour (now rhet. or fig. exc. as in place-names). Late OE. *hæfen, hæfne* (XI) – ON. *hafnar, hǫfn (hafn)* = MLG., MDu. *havene*, Du. *haven* (whence G. *hafen*), rel. to (O)Ir. *cuan* curve, bend, recess, bay = Gael. *cuan* ocean :– **kopno-*.

haversack hæ·vəɹsæk stout canvas bag slung over the shoulder, orig. for a soldier's day rations. XVIII. – F. *havresac* – G. *habersack* orig. bag in which cavalry carried the oats for their horses, f. *haber* oats (OHG. *habaro*; modG. *hafer* is – LG)+*sack* SACK.

Haversian həvə̄·ɹsiən (anat.) pert. to structures in bones discovered by Clopton *Havers*, Eng. anatomist (d. 1702); see -IAN. XIX.

haversine hæ·vəɹsain (math.) half the versed sine. XIX (introduced by J. Inman, 1835). contr. of HALF, VERSED, SINE.

havildar hæ·vildāɹ sepoy non-commissioned officer. XIX. – Hind., Pers. *ḥawāldār* f. *ḥawāla* charge+Pers. *-dār* holding.

havoc hæ·vək in phr. *cry havoc* give the order 'havoc', sound the signal for spoliation; hence *make havoc (of)* plunder, devastate. XV. – AN. *havok* (phr. *crier havok* XIV), alteration of OF. *havo(t)*, of unkn. origin. ¶ For the final cons. cf. HADDOCK.

haw¹ hō fruit of the hawthorn. OE. *haga*, identical in form with *haga* hedge, fence (see HEDGE), connexion with which appears to be shown by the forms of **haw**·THORN, OE. *haga-, haguþorn* = MDu. *hagedorn* (Du. *haagdoorn*), MHG. *hagendorn* (G. *hagedorn*), ON. *hagþorn*; cf. OE. *hæġþorn* 'hedge-thorn'.

haw² hō nictitating membrane in a horse's (dog's, etc.) eye; inflamed state of this. XV.

haw³ hō utterance marking hesitation; also as vb. XVII. Duplicated, as **haw-haw**, which is also used to denote boisterous laughter and affected superiority of utterance. XIX.

hawk¹ hōk bird of prey used in falconry. OE. *hafoc, heafoc*, earlier *hæbuc, habuc* = OFris. *havek*, OS. *haƀuk* (Du. *havik*), OHG. *habuh* (G. *habicht*), ON. *haukr* :– CGerm. (exc. Goth.) **χaƀukaz*, rel. to Pol. *kobuz*, Russ. *kóbets* species of hawk or kite. Hence **hawk** vb. XIV.

hawk² hōk plasterer's hod. XIV. Of unkn. origin. ¶ The use of F. *oiseau* (bird) in this sense suggests identity with prec.

hawk³ hōk clear the throat noisily. XVI (Mulcaster, Stanyhurst, Sh.). prob. imit.

hawker hō·kəɹ itinerant seller. XVI. prob. – LG. (cf. MLG. *hoker*, LG. *höker*, Du. *heuker*); see HUCKSTER. Hence, by back-formation, **hawk⁴** vb. XVI.

hawse hōz (naut.) part of the bows of a ship XIV (Sandahl); space about the stem of a vessel, situation of cables there XVI. Early form *halse* (in AL. *halsa* XIV), prob. – ON. *háls* neck, ship's bow, front sheet of a sail, rope's end (= OE. *heals* neck, prow; cf. COLLAR).

hawser hō·zəɹ (naut.) large rope. XIV. – AN. *haucer, hauceour* (in AL. *haucerus, ausorus, auncerus*), f. OF. *haucier* (mod. *hausser*) hoist = Pr. *alsar*, etc. :– Rom. **altiāre*, f. L. *altus* high (cf. OLD); see -ER².

hawthorn see HAW¹.

hay¹ hei grass cut and dried. OE. *hēġ, hīeġ, hīġ* = OFris. *hā, hē*, OS. *hōi*, OHG. *hewi, houwi* (Du. *hooi*, G. *heu*), ON. *hey* (whence the native word was reinforced), Goth. *hawi* :– CGerm. **χaujam*, f. **χauwan* cut down, HEW.

hay² hei (arch., dial.) hedge. OE. *heġe* :- **χagiz*, f. **χag-*, as in HAW¹, HEDGE. Hence (hist.) **hay·**BOTE. XII (right to take) wood for the repair of fences.

hay³ hei (hist.) winding country dance. XVI (Skelton). Of uncertain origin; perh. – F. (cf. *haye d'allemaigne* XV). Also †*hay de guy* or *guise* XVI (Skelton, Spenser).

haysel hei·səl (E. Anglia) hay season. XVII. f. HAY¹+*sele*, OE. *sǣl* time, season (cf. SILLY).

hayward hei·wəɹd officer having charge of fences and enclosures. XIII (AncrR.). f. ME. *heie, haie*, OE. *heġe*; HAY²+WARD¹.

hazard hæ·zəɹd game at dice XIII; chance, venture XIV; risk, peril; winning opening in a tennis-court, †pocket of a billiard table XVI. – (O)F. *hasard* – Sp. *azar* – Arab. *azzahr, azzār* gaming die. So **ha·zard** vb., **ha·zard**OUS. XVI. – F. *hasarder, hasardeux*.

haze¹ heiz †thick fog; thin mist. XVIII. prob., along with *haze* vb. drizzle (XVII), back-formation from earlier **hazy** hei·zi adj. (orig. naut.) †foggy, (now) misty (XVII), of which the earliest forms *hawsey, heysey, haizy*, beside *hasie, hazy*, together with chronological uncertainty, make the problem of origin difficult.

haze² heiz (dial.) frighten, scare, scold, beat XVII; (naut.) harass with excessive work; (U.S.) subject to brutal horseplay XIX. In the first sense preceded by (dial.) *hazen* (early XVII). OF. *haser* tease, anger, insult, has been compared.

hazel hei·zl small nut-tree, Corylus OE.; reddish-brown colour of the ripe hazel-nut (OE. *hæselhnutu*) XVI (*hasell eyes*, Sh.). OE. *hæsel*, corr. to MDu. *hasel* (Du. *hazelaar* hazel tree, *hazelnoot* hazel nut), OHG. *hasal, -ala* (G. *hasel*), ON. *hasl* (also *hesli*, whence Sc. *heezle*) :- CGerm. (exc. Goth.) **χasalaz* :- IE. **kosolos*, **koselos*, whence also L. *corylus, -ulus* (Rom. forms are based on a var. **colurus*), (O)Ir. *coll*, W. *collen*. Hence **ha·zel-**HEN. XVII. – Du. *haselhoen*, G. *haselhuhn*, so called from the reddish-brown colour; so -GROUSE XVIII.

hazel² hei·zl kind of freestone. XVII. First in *hazel ground*, poss. named from its colour and so a transf. use of prec. But the adj. **ha·zell**Y¹ consisting of a mixture of sand, clay, and earth, is earlier (late XVI).

he¹ hī, hi 3rd sg. m. pers. pron. OE. *he, hē* = OFris. *hi, he*, OS. *hi, he, hie*; f. Germ. demons. stem **χi-*, repr. also in OHG. (Franconian) *er, her, hē* he, d. *himo*, also *hiuru* (:- **hiu jāru*), G. *heuer* this year, OHG. *hiutu* (:- **hiu tagu* this day = OE. *hīodæġ*, OS. *hiudiga*), G. *heute* today, Pr.ON. *hino*, ON. (*h*)*inn* him, *hinig* (:- **hin veg*) 'this way', hither, *hīt* (:- **hīat*) hither, Goth. *himma* to him, *hina* him, *himma daga* today. See also HIM, HIS, HITHER, HENCE, IT. The ult. IE. **ki-* **ko-* is repr. also in L. *cis* on this side, demons. particle *-ce*, OIr. *cē* this, Lith. *šìs*, OSl. *si* this (Russ. *seĭ*), Gr. *e*|*keî* (loc.) there.

he² hī excl. of laughter, usu. repeated *he he, he he he*. OE. *he he*; cf. L. *he, hæ*, G. *hehehe*.

head hed anterior (in man, upper) part of the body, containing the mouth, sense organs, and brain; various transf. uses. OE. *hēafod* = OFris. *hāved, hād*, OS. *hōƀid* (Du. *hoofd*), OHG. *houbit* (G. *haupt*), ON. *haufuð, hǫfuð*, Goth. *haubiþ* :- CGerm. **χauƀuðam, -iðam* the relation of which with L. *caput*, Gr. *kephalḗ* head, Skr. *kapālam* skull, is not clear. Hence **hea·d**LAND strip of land left at the head of furrows OE. (*hēafodland*); promontory XVI. **hea·d**MAN chief. OE. *hēafodmann* (a CGerm. comp.). **hea:d-**QUA·RTERS XVII; cf. G. *hauptquartier*. **hea·ds-**MAN †chief XIV; executioner XVII (Sh.); f. g. of *head*. **hea·d**STRONG violently self-willed. XIV (Trevisa). **hea·d**WAY motion ahead or forward XVIII; for **aheadway* (f. AHEAD). **hea·d**Y¹ headlong (†lit. and fig.) XIV (Wycl. Bible).

-head hed ME.- *hēd*(*e*), repr OE. **-hǣdu*, mutated form corr. to *-hād* -HOOD, and used alongside it from XIII, but surviving in present Eng. only in *godhead* and (arch.) *maidenhead*; orig. attached to adjs., as *boldhede, fairhede*, but extended later to sbs., as *knyhthede, manhede, maydenhede, wommanhede* (all used by Ch.). Pseudo-arch. are *beastlyhead*, DREARIHEAD (Spenser), *lowlihead* (Tennyson).

headborough he·dbʌːrou (hist.) head of a tithing or frankpledge, (later) petty constable. XV (Promp. Parv.). f. HEAD+*borough*, OE. *borh* pledge (see BORROW); repl. *frithborgesheued* (XII) head of the frithborh or frankpledge.

headlong he·dlɔŋ headforemost, precipitately. XV. Alteration, by assoc. with ALONG, of †*headling* (XIII), f. HEAD+-LING² (as in OE. *bæcling* backwards); cf. *sidelong*.

heal hīl make whole, cure. OE. *hǣlan* = OFris. *hēla*, OS. *hēlian* (Du. *heelen*), OHG. *heilan* (G. *heilen*), ON. *heila*, Goth. *hailjan* :- CGerm. **χailjan*, f. **χailaz* WHOLE.

health helþ soundness of body, mind, or spirit OE.; toast drunk to a person's welfare XVI (Sh.). OE. *hǣlþ* = OHG. *heilida* :- WGerm. **χailiþa*, f. Germ. **χailaz* WHOLE; see -TH¹. Hence **hea·lth**FUL¹ salubrious XIV (Trevisa); having good health XVI (superseded in this sense by **hea·lth**Y¹ XVI).

heap hīp collection of things lying one upon another; †great company OE.; (colloq.) a great deal XVII (earlier pl. XVI). OE. *hēap* = OFris. *hāp*, OS. *hōp* (Du. *hoop*; cf. FORLORN HOPE), OHG. *houf* :- WGerm. **χaupaz* (not in Gothic; Icel. *hópr* is from LG.), rel. to MLG. *hūpe*, OHG. *hūfo* (G. *haufen*) :- Germ. **χūpon*; IE. **kūp-* is repr. also by OSl. *kupŭ*, Lith. *kaũpas* heap. Hence as vb. OE. *hēapian* (cf. OHG. *houfōn*).

hear hiəɹ pt., pp. **heard** hɜ̄rd perceive sound (intr. and trans.); listen (to); get to know, be told. OE. Anglian *hēran*, WS. *hīeran* = OFris. *hēra*, *hōra*, OS. *hōrian* (Du. *hooren*), OHG. *hōrren* (G. *hören*), ON. *heyra*, Goth. *hausjan* :- CGerm. **χauzjan*, dubiously connected with Gr. *a|koúein* hear. Hence **hear**SAY hiə·ɹsei report, rumour. XVI. orig. in phr. *by hear say*, tr. OF. *par ouïr dire* (now *ouï-dire*), i.e. *par* by (PER), *ouïr* hear (:- L. *audīre*), *dire* say (:- L. *dīcere*).

hearken, U.S. **harken** hā·ɹkn (arch.) listen (to). OE. *hercnian*, *heorcnian*, f. **he(o)rcian*; see HARK, -EN[5]. The sp. with *ea* is due to assoc. with *hear*.

hearse hɜ̄ɹs catafalque placed over a bier at a funeral XIV (Ch.); †bier, coffin, grave XVII (Sh.); funeral carriage XVII. – (O)F. *herse* harrow, portcullis (so in Eng. in the form *herse*), triangular frame for candles (in AL *hercia* XIII) = It. *erpice* :- medL. *erpica*, Rom. **herpica*, for L. *(h)irpicem*, nom. *(h)irpex* large rake used as a harrow, f. Samnite *(h)irpus* wolf, with ref. to the teeth.

heart hāɹt bodily organ controlling the circulation of the blood, and regarded as the centre of vital functions, the seat of affections, desires, thoughts OE.; dear person; innermost part XIII (so *h. of oak* XVII); vital part; †stomach XVI. OE. *heorte* = OFris. *herte*, OS. *herta* (Du. *hart*), OHG. *herza* (G. *herz*), ON. *hjarta*, Goth. *hairtō* :- CGerm. **χerton* (wk. n., which became wk. fem. in OE. and OFris.). The IE. base **kĕrd-* **krd-* is repr. also by Gr. *kêr* (:- **kērd*), *kardiā*, *kradiā*, L. *cord-*, *cor* (cf. CORDIAL), OSl. *srĭdĭce*, *srŭdĭce* (Russ. *sérdce*), Lith. *širdìs*, OPruss. *seyr*, acc. *sīran*, OIr. *cride*, W. *craidd*, Arm. *sirt*; the synon. Skr. *hṛ́d*, Av. *zərəδaya*, repr. a similar base with a different initial consonant. Hence **hea·rt**EN[5]. XVI; repl. ME. *herte*, OE. *hiertan*.

hearth hāɹþ floor on which a fire is made. OE. *heorþ* = OFris. *herth*, *herd*, OS. *herth* (Du. *haard*), OHG. *hert* (G. *herd*) :- WGerm. **χerþa*, which has been speculatively connected with L. *carbō* coal, CARBON, and *cremāre* burn, CREMATE.

heat hīt quality or condition of being hot. OE. *hǣtu* = OFris. *hēte*, MDu. *hēte*, OHG. *heiȥi* :- WGerm. **χaitin*, f. Germ. **χaitaz* HOT; also OE. *hǣte* (:- **χaitja*); forms from other grades of the base are OS. *hittia* (Du. *hitte*), OHG. *hizza* (G. *hitze*), ON. *hiti*, Goth. *heitō* (fever). So **heat** vb. OE. *hǣtan* = (M)Du. *hēten*, OHG. *heiȥen*, *heizen* (G. *heizen*), ON. *heita* :- Germ. **χaitjan*.

heath[1] hīþ open waste land. OE. *hǣþ*, corr. to OS. *hētha*, MLG., MDu. *hēde*, MHG. *heide* (Du. *heide*, *hei*, G. *heide*), ON. *heiðr*, Goth. *haiþi* :- CGerm. **χaiþiz* :- IE. **kait-*, repr. also by Gaul. *cēto-* in place-names, OW. *coit* (W. *coed*) wood, forest.

heath[2] hīþ plant of the genus Erica. OE. *hǣþ* = OS. *hēth(i)a*, (M)LG., (M)Du. *heide*, OHG. *heida* (G. *heide*) :- WGerm. **χaiþjō*; f. prec.

heathen hī·ð(ə)n not Christian, Jewish, or Mohammedan. OE. *hǣþen* = OFris. *hēthin*, OS. *hēthin* (Du. *heiden*), OHG. *heidan* (G. *heide*), ON. *heiðinn*, in Goth. repr. by *haiþnō* Gentile woman (Mark vii 26, Gr. *Hellēnís*); gen. regarded as a spec. Christian use (perh. originating in Gothic) of Germ. adj. **χaiþanaz*, **χaiþinaz* inhabiting open country, savage, repr. by the ethnic and personal names *Khaideinoí* people of W. Scandinavia (Ptolemy), OE. *(mid) Hǣþnum* ('Widsith' 81), ON. *Heinir* (:- **Heiðnir*), OHG. *Heidanrīh*; f. **χaiþiz* HEATH[1]; see -EN[3]. ¶ Connexion with L. *ethnicī*, Gr. *ethnikoí* ETHNIC, with which the word was often pop. identified, has been suggested but not proved. Hence **hea·then**DOM OE. *hǣþendōm*, **hea·then**ISH[1] OE. *hǣþenisć*; both CGerm. exc. Gothic.

heather he·ðəɹ species of Erica, otherwise called *ling*. XIV. Sc. and north. *hathir*, *haddyr*, *hadder*, *hedder*; the form *hadder* or *hather* (now north. dial.) prevailed in Eng. use from XVI to XVIII, when *heather* is first recorded; of unkn. origin, perh. repr. earlier **hǣddre*; the present literary form appears to be due to assim. to HEATH[1] or [2].

heave hīv (obs. dial. or techn.) lift, raise OE.; cause to rise, throw, cast, haul up XVI; intr. rise XIV. OE. *hebban* (pres. ind. *hebbe*, *hefest*, *hefeþ*, *hebbaþ*), pt. *hōf*, *hafen*, pp. *hæfen* = OFris. *heva*, *hōf*, *heven*, OS. *hebbian*, *hōf*, *haben* (Du. *heffen*, *hief*, *geheven*), OHG. *heffen*, *huob*, *gihaben* (G. *heben*, *hob*, *gehoben*), ON. *hefja*, *hóf*, *hafinn*, Goth. *hafjan*, *hōf*, *hafans* :- CGerm. **χabjan*, **χōf*, **χabana-*, rel. to L. *capere* (pres. ind. *capio*, *capis*, *capit*, *capiunt*) take. The pres. ind. forms in *f* (v) were early levelled out, in some regions by infl. of ON. *hefja*; pt. (with analogical pp.) **hove** survives in some uses, but for the most part weak forms of pt. and pp., already found in late OE. (*hefde*, *hefod*), prevailed.

heave ho hīv hou sailor's call in hauling on a rope. XIX. Preceded by *heave and ho*, †*heue and how(e)* XVI–XVII, and earlier †*heuelow* †*heuylaw* XIII–XV, which was assoc. with *rumbelow*; prob. imper. of HEAVE coupled with HO (the earlier *law* may be LOW[1] adj.).

heaven he·v(ə)n sky, firmament; region of space beyond the sky; habitation of God and his angels, and of beatified spirits; Divine Providence, God OE.; state of bliss XIV (Ch., PPl.). OE. *heofon*, earlier *hefen*, *heben*, in late OE. *heofone*; corr. to OS. *heban*, ON. *himinn* (inflected stem *hifn-* :- **hibn-*), Goth. *himins*; parallel formations with *l*-suffix are OFris. *himul*, OS., OHG. *himil* (Du. *hemel*, G. *himmel*; Sw., Da. *himmel* is from LG.), beside MLG. *hemelte*, OHG. *himilizi* roof, vault (for the sense cf. OE. *hūsheofon*, *heofonhūs* ceiling); the relation of these forms and their ult. origin are disputed.

Heaviside he·visaid name of Oliver *Heaviside* (1850–1925) applied to a *layer* of the atmosphere supposed to aid the transmission of wireless waves.

heavy he·vi having weight. OE. *hefiġ* = OS. *heƀig* (Du. *hevig*), OHG. *hebig*, ON. *hǫfugr*, *hǫfigr* :- CGerm. (exc. Gothic) **χaƀuga-*, **χaƀiga-*, f. **χaƀiz* (OE. *hefe*) weight, f. **χaƀjan* HEAVE; see -Y[1].

hebdomadal hebdɔ·mədəl †lasting seven days XVII; weekly XVIII. – late L. *hebdomadālis*, f. *hebdomad-*, *-as* (whence **he·bdomad** XVI) – Gr. *hebdomás*, f. *heptá* SEVEN. So **hebdo·madARY** (eccl.) religious who takes his or her weekly turn in officiating at divine service. XV. – ecclL. *hebdomadārius*.

Hebe hī·bi daughter of Zeus and Hera, goddess of youth and spring, and cup-bearer of Olympus; transf. waitress. XVII. Personification of Gr. *hḗbē* youthful prime.

hebetate he·biteit make blunt. XVI. f. pp. stem of L. *hebetāre*, f. *hebet-*, *hebes* blunt; see -ATE[3].

Hebrew hī·brū belonging to the Semitic race descended from Abraham, Isaac, and Jacob; Jewish; their language. XIII. ME. *ebreu* – OF. *ebreu*, *ebrieu* (mod. *hébreu*) – medL. *Ebrēus*, for L. *Hebræus* – late Gr. *Hebraîos* – Aram. *ʿebrāyā*, for Heb. *ʿibrī* lit. 'one from the other side' (sc. of the river), f. *ʿēber* the region on the other or opposite side, f. *ʿābar* cross or pass over. So **Hebra**IC hībrei·ik. XIV. – ChrL. *Hebraicus* – late Gr. *Hebraïkós*, f. *Hebra-*, based on the Aram. form. **He·bra**ISM. XVI. – F. or modL. **He·bra**IST XVIII; earlier **Hebri·**CIAN XVI.

Hecate he·kəti Gr. goddess (as identified with Persephone taken to preside over witchcraft). – Gr. *Hekátē*, fem. of *hékatos* far-darting, an epithet of Apollo; formerly also disyllabic (as always, exc. once, in Sh., and in Milton 'Comus' 135 *Hecat*').

hecatomb he·kətoum, -tūm sacrifice of many victims. XVI. – L. *hecatombē* – Gr. *hekatómbē*, f. *hekatón* HUNDRED + *boûs* ox (see COW[1]).

heckle he·kl north. and E. Anglian form of HACKLE. XV. Hence **heckle** vb. dress (flax or hemp) with a heckle XV; examine searchingly; harass (a candidate, speaker) with questions XIX (orig. Sc.).

hectic he·ktik of a wasting fever attended by flushed cheeks XIV; consumptive, wasting, feverish XVII; feverishly active, exciting XX. ME. *etik* – OF. *etique* = Sp., It. *etico* – late L. *hecticus* – Gr. *hektikós* habitual, hectic, consumptive, f. *héxis* habit, state of body or mind, f. *ékhein* intr. (with adv.) be (in such-and-such a state); superseded XVI by the mod. form – F. *hectique* or late L.; cf. EPOCH.

hect(o)- he·kt(ou) F., contr. of Gr. *hekatón* HUNDRED, esp. in terms of the metric system, as *hectare*, *hectolitre*, *hectometre*. XIX.

hector he·ktəɹ play the bully, bully. XVII. f. *Hector* name of 'the prop or stay of Troy', son of Priam and Hecuba, husband of Andromache, sb. use of Gr. adj. *héktōr* holding fast, f. *ékhein* hold. f. the use of the sb. (common in late XVII) for 'swaggering fellow', 'swashbuckler'.

hedge hedʒ row of bushes forming a boundary. OE. *heġġ*, **heċġ* = EFris. *hegge*, MDu. *hegghe* (Du. *heg*), OHG. *hegga*, *hecka* (G. *hecke*) :- WGerm. **χagjō*, rel. to HAW[1], HAY[2]. Hence **he·dge**HOG. XV; so named from frequenting hedgerows and its pig-like snout. **he·dge**ROW. XVI; in OE. *heġġerēwe*.

hedonism hī·dənizm doctrine that pleasure is the highest good. XIX. f. Gr. *hēdonḗ* pleasure (see SWEET) + -ISM. So **he·don**IST.

-hedron he·drən, hī·drən repr. n. sg. (used sb.) of Gr. adjs. ending in *-edros*, f. *hédrā* SEAT, base, in comps. with numerals, as *hexahedron*; corr. adjs. end in *-hedral*, †*-hedrical*.

heed hīd have a care, take notice OE.; care for XIII. OE. *hēdan* = OS. *hōdian* (Du. *hoeden*), OHG. *huoten* (G. *hüten*) :- WGerm. **χōdjan*, f. **χōda* care, keeping (OFris., MLG. *hōde*, OHG. *huota*, G. *hut*). The regular pt. and pp. would have been **hed*; the form *heeded* dates from XVI. Hence **heed** sb. XIII (Cursor M.).

hee-haw hī·hɔ̄ conventional representation of the bray of an ass; loud coarse laugh. XIX. imit. Cf. G. *iah*, †*(h)ika*, †*gigag*, and the vb. *yahen*, †*gigachen*, Du. *giegagen*.

heel[1] hīl hinder part of the foot OE.; also various transf. uses, the earliest of which is 'bottom crust' XIV (PPl.). OE. *hēla*, *hǣla*, corr. to OFris. *hēla*, MDu. *hiele* (Du. *hiel*), ON. *hæll* :- Germ. **χāχil-* :- **χaŋχil-*, f. **χaŋχ-* (whence OE. *hōh* heel, *hōh|sinu* HOUGH, ON. *há|mót* ankle-joint), ult. rel. to Lith. *kìnka*, Lett. *cinksla* hough.

heel[2] hīl incline to one side. XVI. prob. evolved from †*heeld*, †*hield* through apprehending final *d* as a pt.-pp. suffix. OE. *hieldan* = OS. *of|heldian*, MDu. *helden* (Du. *hellen*) :- WGerm. **χalþja*, f. **χalþaz* (OE. *heald* inclined, OFris., OHG. *hald*, ON. *hallr*, with rel. sbs. OFris., MLG. *helde*, OHG. *halda*, ON. *hallr* slope, Goth. *wilja|halþei* inclination of mind).

hefty he·fti weighty, powerful. XIX. Of U.S. and dial. origin; f. (dial.) **heft** weight which is prob. analogically f. *heave*, after *cleft|cleave*, *weft|weave*, etc.; see -Y[1].

hegemony hidʒe·məni, hig- leadership, predominant authority, as of one state of a union, etc. XVI (*aegemonie*; rare before XIX). – Gr. *hēgemoniā*, f. *hēgemṓn* leader, f. *hēgeîsthai* lead, rel. to L. *sāgīre* track, Germ. **sōkjan* SEEK; cf. F. *hégémonie* (XIX) and see -MONY.

hegira, hejira he·dʒirə Mohammedan era. XVI. – medL. *hegira* (whence F. *hégire*, Sp. *hegira*, It. *egira*) – Arab. *hijrah* departure from one's country and friends (spec. *alhijrat* the flight of Mohammed from Mecca to Medina, from which the Mohammedan era is reckoned), f. *hajara* separate, go away.

heifer he·fəɹ young cow (that has not calved). OE. *heahfore, heahfru, -fre*, of unkn. origin. Early forms show threefold development; *heyfer, hayfor*, repr. by the present sp.; *hekfore*, surviving late in dial.; *heffre, -our*, repr. by the present pronunc.

heigh hei excl. of encouragement. XVI (Jonson, Sh.). Later sp. of ME. *he* (XIII), *heh* (XV); cf. OF. *hé*. Also, esp. in Sc. forms *hech, hegh*, expressing displeased surprise, sorrow, etc. So *heigh-ho* (XVI) excl. of weariness or disappointment. See also HEY.

heighday see HEYDAY.

height hait quality of being high; high point. OE. *hēhþu*, (WS. *hīehþu*) = MDu. *hogede, hoochte* (Du. *hoogte*), OHG. *hōhida*, Goth. *hauhiþa* :- CGerm. **χauχiþō*; see HIGH, -TH[1]. Dissimilation of *-hþ* (*-ʒþ*) to *-ht* (*-ʒt*), orig. northern, appears before 1300; cf. *drouth, drought, sleighth, sleight*; *hight* (see -T[2]) was a common sp. XVI–XVII, and dial. *highth*, the form used by Milton, in XVII. The development of ē to ī is evidenced about 1300, whence the present pronunc. (cf. HIGH); the present sp. repr. the older pronunc. with ei. Hence **heigh·**TEN[5]. XVI.

heinous hei·nəs hateful. XIV (Ch.). – OF. *haïneus*, f. *haïne* hatred, f. *haïr* – Germ. **χatjan*, rel. to **χatōjan* HATE; see -OUS.

heir ɛəɹ one who succeeds or is entitled to succeed to an estate. XIII. ME. *eir, eyr* – OF. *eir, heir* (later, *hoir*) = Pr. *her* :- late L. *hērem*, for earlier *hērēdem*, nom. *hērēs*. Hence **hei·**RESS[1]. XVII. **hei·r**LOOM. XV.

hejira see HEGIRA.

hele hīl † hide, keep secret OE.; (local) cover (with earth-tiles). XIII. OE. *hellan, helian* = OS. *hellian*, OHG. *-hellen* :- WGerm. **haljan* f. **χel-* **χal-* **χul-* :- IE. **kel*, repr. in L. *celāre*, Gr. *kalýptein* hide.

helianthus hīliæ·nþəs sunflower genus. XVIII. modL., f. Gr. *hḗlios* SUN + *ánthos* flower (cf. *polyanthus*).

Helicon he·likən mountain in Bœotia, which, sacred to the Muses, is associated along with its fountains with poetical inspiration. XVI (*Eliconys waters*).

helicopter he·likɔptəɹ flying machine sustained by lifting screws. XIX. – F. *hélicoptère*, f. Gr. *heliko-*, HELIX + *pterón* wing (FEATHER).

helio- hī·liou, hīlio· repr. comb. form of Gr. *hḗlios* SUN, as in **he:lio**CE·NTRIC)(*geocentric* XVII; so F. **he·lio**GRAPH various apparatus involving exposure to sun's rays XIX; -GRA·PHIC, relating to **helio·**GRAPHY description of the sun XVIII; use of the sun's light for engraving, etc. XIX; **helio·**METER instrument for measuring the sun's diameter. XVIII. – F. *héliomètre* (Bouguer, 1747). **he·liostat** -stæt apparatus for reflecting the light of the sun. XVIII. – modL. *heliostata*, F. *héliostat* (Gr. *statós* standing, f. **sta-* STAND). **heliotro·p**IC turning in a particular manner under the influence of light. XIX; **-o·trop**ISM.

heliotrope hī·liətroup, he·l- plant of which the flowers turn towards the sun, e.g. formerly, sunflower, marigold, now the genus Heliotropium XVII; green variety of quartz, so called because if thrown into water 'it changeth the raies of the Sun by way of reuerberation into a bloudie colour' (Holland) XVI. – L. *hēliotropium*, medL. also *eliotropus, -tropius*, etc. (formerly used in Eng.), – Gr. *hēliotrópion*, f. *hḗlios* SUN + *-tropos* turning, *trépein* turn (cf. TROPE).

helium hī·liəm (chem.) gaseous element. XIX. f. Gr. *hḗlios* SUN (see -IUM); so named from the discovery of its existence in the solar spectrum by Lockyer in 1868.

helix hī·liks, he·liks spiral object. XVI. – L. *helix* (*helic-*) – Gr. *hélix* (*-ik-*), f. IE. **wel-* roll (cf. VOLUTE, WALLOW). Hence **he·lic**AL[1] spiral. XVII. **he·lic**OID screw-shaped, spiral. XVIII. – modL. – Gr.

hell hel abode of the dead, Hades; place or state of punishment after death. OE. *hel(l)* = OFris. *helle*, OS. *hell(j)a* (Du. *hel*), OHG. *hella* (G. *hölle*), ON. *hel*, Goth. *halja* :- CGerm. **χaljō*, f. **χal-* **χel-* **χul-* cover, conceal (OE. *helian, helan*, mod. dial. *heal, heel*, as in agric., OFris. *hela*, OS., OHG. *helan*, etc.; OE. *hyllan*, Goth. *huljan*, etc.). ¶ The IE. base is repr. also in HALL, HELM[1], HULL[1]; CONCEAL, CELL, CELLAR; CLANDESTINE, COLOUR, OCCULT; SUPERCILIOUS.

hellebore he·libɔ̄əɹ species of plant of the genera Helleborum and Veratrum. XIV (preceded by *eleboryne* XIII). ME. *el(l)ebre, eleure* (Gower has *ele·borum*) – OF. *ellebre, elebore* or medL. *eleborus*, L. *elleborus* – Gr. *(h)elléboros*. Respelt or readopted in the present form in XVI after the prevailing L. and Gr. forms.

Hellene he·līn Greek. XVII. – Gr. *Héllēn*. So **Helle·n**IC. XVII (Milton). **He·llen**ISM. XVII (Holland). **Helleni·**STIC pert. to the modified form of Greek current in Egypt, Syria, etc., after the time of Alexander the Great (IV B.C.).

hello hělou· see HALLO. XIX.

helm[1] helm (arch), helmet. OE. *helm* = OFris., OS., OHG. (Du., G.) *helm*, ON. *hjálmr*, Goth. *hilms* :- CGerm. **χelmaz* :- **kelmos*, f. IE. base **kel-* cover, conceal. From Germ. are OSl. *šlěmŭ*, Lith. *šálmas*, and the Rom. forms (F. *heaume*, etc.). It. *elmo*. For the formation cf. Skr. *śárman-* covering, protection. So **helmet** he·lmit defensive covering for the head. XV (Malory). – OF. *helmet*, dim. of *helme* (mod. *heaume*); see -ET.

helm[2] helm tiller. OE. *helma*, corr. to MLG. *helm* handle, OHG. *helmo, halmo*, ON. *hjalmvǫlr* 'rudder-stick'; of doubtful origin, prob. rel. to HELVE.

helminthology helminþɔ·lədʒi science treating of worms. XIX. f. Gr. *helminth-*, *hélmins* worm, rel. to HELIX; see -LOGY.

helot he·lət serf in ancient Sparta. XVI (*Hylot, Ilot*). – L. *Hēlōtes* pl. – Gr. *Heílōtes*, pl. of *Heílōs*; also *Hīlōtæ* (*Ilōtæ*) – Gr. *Heílōtai*, pl. of *Heilṓtēs*; traditionally derived from *Helos* name of a town in Laconia whose inhabitants were enslaved.

help help that which is furnished to a person for his needs. OE. *help* = OFris. *helpe*, OS. *helpa*, OHG. *helfa*, ON. *hjálp* :– Germ. **χelpō*, f. CGerm. base **χalp-* **χelp-* **χulp-*, whence also **help** vb. OE. *helpan*, pt. *healp*, *hulpon*, pp. *holpen* = OFris. *helpa*, OS. *helpan* (Du. *helpen*), OHG. *helfan* (G. *helfen*), ON. *hjálpa*, Goth. *hilpan*; the IE. base **kelp-* appears also in Lith. *šélpti*, *pa|šalpà* help. The orig. pt. survived till XV in the form †*halp*, which was succeeded by †*holp* (XVI), modelled on the pp. †*holpen*; the weak form *helped* appears XIII, orig. northern. Hence **helpmate** he·lpmeit companion who is a help. XVIII. f. MATE sb., like †*helpfellow* (XVI), doubtless by assoc. with *helpmeet*, which arose from the use of *help-meet for man* (XVII, Dryden), based on *an helpe meet for him* (A.V.) 'a help suitable for him' of Gen. ii. 18, 20.

helter-skelter he:ltəɹske·ltəɹ in disorderly haste. XVI. Rhyming jingle like *harum-scarum*, *hurry-scurry*, perh. based ult. on ME. *skelte* hasten (XIV); cf. the synon. jingles LG. *hulter (de) bulter*, *hulterpulter*, *hullerdebuller*, Du. *holderdebolder*.

helve helv handle of a weapon or tool. OE. *helfe*, WS. *hielfe*, corr. to OS. *helfi* (MDu. *helf*, *helve*), OHG. *halp*; f. WGerm. **χalƀ-* (which appears also in HALTER) :– IE. **kalp-*, as in OPruss. *kalpus* waggon-rail, Lith. *kálpa* cross-piece of a sledge. Cf. HELM[2].

Helvetian helvī·ʃən Swiss. XVI. f. *Helvētia* Switzerland, *Helvētius* pert. to the *Helvētiī* (Gr. *Helouḗtioi*, *Helbḗttioi*) people of Gallia Lugdunensis. So **Helvet**IC -e·tik. XVIII. – L.; see -IAN, -IC.

hem[1] hem edging of cloth or garment OE. (transf. and techn., from XIII); border on a cloth made by doubling in the edge XVII. OE. *hem* (once, Ælfric's Glossary), corr. to OFris. *hemme* enclosed land, presumably rel. to HAM[2]. Hence **hem** vb. edge, border (cloth) XIII; shut *in* XVI. ¶ The forms *hemn* (Wycl. Bible) and *hemny* vb. (XV) are obscure.

hem[2], h'm hem, hm repr. the sound made in clearing the throat, consisting of a guttural or glottal aspiration followed by a nasal murmur with the lips closed. So **hem** vb. XV (in vbl. sb. *hemynge*, Malory).

hemi- hemi repr. Gr. *hēmi-*, comb. el. = L. *sēmi-* SEMI-, Germ. **sāmi-* half (OE. *sām-*, OS., OHG. *sāmi-*); used in many techn. terms in later L., e.g. *hēmicrānia* (see MEGRIM), *hēmicyclium* (whence, through F., **he·micycle** XVII, Jonson), **hemiplegia** -plī·dʒ[i]ə paralysis on one side (XVI, Holland). See also below.

hemiptera hīmi·ptərə (entom.) large order of insects (bugs, lice, plant lice), having wings partly coriaceous partly membranous. XIX. modL., n. pl. of *hēmipterus* (Gr. *pterón* wing, FEATHER).

hemisphere he·misfiəɹ half of a sphere. In the form †*(h)emisperie*, *-sphery* (XIV) – L. *hēmisphærium* – Gr. *hēmisphaírion*, f. *hēmi-* HEMI- + *sphaîra* SPHERE; in the form *hemisphere* (XVI), †*-spere* (XV) – OF. *emisp(h)ere* (mod. *hémisphère*).

hemistich he·mistik (pros.) half-line. XVI. – late L. *hēmistichium* – Gr. *hēmistíkhion*; see HEMI-, STICH.

hemlock he·mlɔk the poisonous plant Conium maculatum. OE. *hymlice*, *hym-*, *hemlic*, of unkn. origin; forms in *hum-*, *hom-* continued till XVI; the alteration of the final syll. to *-lock* (XV) is paralleled in CHARLOCK.

hemorrhoid see HÆMORRHOID.

hemp hemp herbaceous plant Cannabis sativa OE.; fibre of this XIII. OE. *henep*, *hænep* = OS. *hanap* (Du. *hennep*), OHG. *hanaf* (G. *hanf*), ON. *hampr* :– Germ. **χanipiz*, **χanapiz*, rel. to Gr. *kánnabis* (whence L. *cannabis*; cf. CANVAS), Lith. *kanapẽs*, OSl. *konoplja*, Pers. *kanab*.

hen hen female of the domestic fowl OE.; female of other birds XIV. OE. *henn* = OFris., MLG. *henne*, OHG. *henna* (G. *henne*) :– WGerm. **χannja*, f. CGerm. **χanon* cock (OE. *hana*, OFris., OS., OHG. *hano*, Du. *haan*, G. *hahn*, ON. *hani*, Goth. *hano*), rel. to L. *canere* sing, CHANT, Gr. *ēi|kanós* early-crowing, OIr. *canim* I sing. Hence **he·npecked**. XVII.

hence hens from here. XIII. ME. *hennes*, *hens*, f. *henne*, *hen* :– OE. *hio-*, *heonane*, *-one*, *heonan* = OS., OHG. *hinana*, *hinan* (G. *hinnen*), also OE. *hina*, *heona* = MLG., MDu. *hēne* (Du. *heen*), OHG. *hina* (G. *hin*); WGerm. formations on the pronominal base **χi-* HE[1]. Cf. THENCE, WHENCE.

henchman he·n[t]ʃmən squire or page of honour XIV; personal attendant or chief gillie of a Highland chief XVIII; trusty follower, (esp. U.S.) stout political partisan XIX. ME. *hengest-*, *henxst-*, *henx-*, *hensman*, perh. orig. horse attendant (later with elevation of status, as in *groom*, *marshal*), f. OE. *heng(e)st* (= OFris. *hengst*, *hanxt*, MLG. *hengest*, OHG. *hengist*, Du., G. *hengst*, ON. *hestr*) stallion, gelding + MAN. The early history and orig. meaning are obscure, OE. *hengest* being extinct soon after 1200 (except as an el. in proper names containing the name of the reputed founder of Kent), and there being no parallel comp. in the Continental langs. The present currency of the word is due to Scott (who used *hanchman* in 'Waverley' XVI, reproducing the form from E. Burt's Letters, which he edited, but elsewhere has *henchman*, a form well established in XVI and used by Sh.; vars. with *-an-*, *-aun-* were current XV to XVI).

hendeca- he·ndekə, hende·kə comb. form of Gr. *héndeka* eleven, f. *hén*, n. of *heîs* one (cf. SAME)+*déka* TEN; as in **hende·ca**GON (geom.) figure with 11 sides and 11 angles; **he:ndeca**SY·LLABLE. XVIII. f. L. – Gr.

hendiadys hendai·ədis figure of speech in which a single complex idea is expressed by two words connected by a conjunction. XVI. – medL., f. Gr. phr. *hèn dià duoîn* 'one through two' (Servius).

henna he·nə (dye obtained from) Egyptian privet, Lawsonia inermis. XVI. – Arab. *ḥennā'*.

henotheism hênə·þiizm belief in one god as the deity of the individual or tribe. XIX (Max Müller). f. Gr. *heno-*, stem of *heîs* one (cf. SAME)+*theós* god+-ISM.

henry he·nri (electr.) unit of inductance. XIX. f. name of Joseph *Henry* (1797–1878), Amer. physicist.

hepatic hipæ·tik pert. to the liver, liver-coloured. XV. – L. *hēpaticus* – Gr. *hēpatikós*, f. *hēpat-*, *hêpar* liver = L. *jecur*, Skr. *yákṛt*, Lith. *jeknos* pl.; see -IC.

hepta- he·ptə before a vowel **hept-**, comb. form of Gr. *heptá* SEVEN, occurring as the first el. of many Gr. comps., some of which have descended, through L., to mod. langs., many more having been formed in medL. or modL., etc., on Gr. analogies; e.g. **he·pta**CHORD XVIII; **he·pta**GON XVI; **he·ptarchy** XVI (Lambarde; modL. *-archia*, Camden); **he·pta**SYLLABLE XVIII (Gray); **He·ptateuch** -tjūk first seven books of the Bible XVII; Gr. *teûkhos* book.

heptad he·ptæd number or group of seven. XVII. – Gr. *heptad-*, *heptás*, f. *heptá* SEVEN; see -AD[1].

her[1] hɔ̄ɹ, hə genitive of the fem. 3rd pers. pron. OE. *hire* = OFris. *hiri*, MDu. *hare* (Du. *haar*), f. pronominal base **χi-* HE[1]; cf. parallel forms on the base **i-*, viz. OS. *iru*, *iro*, *ira*, *ire*, OHG. *ira*, *iro* (G. *ihr*), Goth. *izōs*. Hence **hers** hɔ̄ɹz absol. pron. XIV. ME. *hires*, *hiris*, *hirs* (see -S), with a parallel (orig. southern) form *hern* (XIV), now dial.

her[2] hɔ̄ɹ, hə orig. dative, later acc. of the fem. 3rd pers. pron. OE. *hire* = OFris. *hiri*, MDu. *hare* (Du. *haar*), f. pronominal base **χi-* HE[1]; cf. the parallel forms on the base **i-*, viz. OS. *iru*, OHG. *iru*, *iro* (G. *ihr*), Goth. *izai*. The use as acc. or direct object began in late Nhb. (X). Hence **her**SE·LF. XII (*hire solf*), in OE. *hire sylfre* (dative).

herald he·rəld officer who delivers proclamations, arranges ceremonial functions, etc.; envoy XIV; forerunner XVI (Sh.); one skilled in heraldry XIX. ME. *heraud*, *herauld* – OF. *herau(l)t* (mod. *héraut*) – Germ. **χariwald-*, f. **χarjaz* army+**wald-* rule, WIELD; cf. *Charioualda* name of a Batavian chief in Tacitus' 'Annals' II xi, OS. *Heriold*, OE. *Hariweald*, ON. *Haraldr* Harold. ¶ It. *araldo*, Sp. *heraldo*, G. *herold* are from OF. Hence **herald**IC hèræ·ldik. XVIII (Warton); **he·rald**RY art of blazoning. XVI.

herb hɔ̄ɹb plant with non-woody stem; medicinal plant. XIII. ME. *erbe*, *herbe* – OF. *erbe* (mod. *herbe*) = Pr. *erba*, Sp. *hierba*, Pg. *herva*, Rum. *iarbă* :– L. *herba* grass, green crops, herb. The sp. with *h* is recorded from the earliest times, but the pronunc. without initial aspirate was regular till early XIX. **herb**A·CEOUS. XVII. f. L. **he·rb**AGE. XIV (Gower). – OF. *erbage* (mod. *herbage*). **he·rb**AL[1] book treating of plants. XVI. – medL. *herbālis* (sc. *liber* book); whence **he·rba**LIST. XVI. **herb**A·RIUM collection of dried plants. XVIII. – late L. *herbārium*, sb. use of n. of adj. repr. by L. *herbārius* botanist, *herbāria* botany (Pliny); see -ARY.

Herculean hɔ̄ɹkjulī·ən, həɹkjū·liən pert. to *Herculēs*, L. alteration of Gr. *Hēraklês*, f. *Hḗrā* wife of Zeus+*kléos* glory, lit. 'having or showing the glory of Hera'. XVI; see -EAN.

herd[1] hɔ̄ɹd company of animals, flock. OE. *heord* = MLG. *herde*, OHG. *herta* (G. *herde*), ON. *hjǫrð*, Goth. *hairda* :– CGerm. **χerðō* :– IE. **kerdhā-*, whence Skr. *çárdhas* troop; cf. OIr. *crod* troop, W. *cordd* tribe, family (:– **kordho-*), OSl. *črěda*.

herd[2] hɔ̄ɹd keeper of a herd. OE. *hirde*, WS. *hierde* = OS. *hirdi*, *herdi*, OHG. *hirti* (G. *hirte*), ON. *hirðir*, Goth. *hairdeis* :– CGerm. **χerðjaz*, f. **χerðō* (see prec.). Hence **herd** vb. intr. XIV; trans. XVI. **he·rds**MAN. XVII. Alteration of *herdman* (OE. *hierdemann*), after *craftsman*.

here hiəɹ in this place. OE. *hēr* = OFris., OS. *hēr*, OHG. *hiar* (Du., G. *hier*), ON. *hér*, Goth. *hēr* (beside OFris., OS. *hīr*); obscurely f. Germ. pronominal base **χi-* this (see HE[1], and cf. HENCE, HITHER). ¶ The form *here* is of early ME. date; cf. THERE.

hereditament herĭdi·təmənt heritable property. XV. – medL. *hērēditāmentum*, f. late L. *hērēditāre*, f. *hērēd-*, *hērēs* HEIR; see -MENT. So **here·dit**ABLE heritable. XV. – obs. F. or medL. **here·dit**ARY descending by inheritance. XVI. – L. *hērēditārius*, f. *hērēditās*. **hered**ITY hire·diti inheritance (rare) XVI; heritable character XVIII; (biol.) XIX. – (O)F. *hérédité*, or L. *hērēditās*, f. *hērēd-*, *hērēs* HEIR.

heresy he·rĭsi unorthodox religious opinion. XIII (AncrR.). ME. *(h)eresie* – OF. *(h)eresie* (mod. *hérésie*) = Sp. *herejia*, It. *eresia* – Rom. **heresia*, for L. *hæresis* – Gr. *haíresis* choice, (hence) course of action or thought, school of thought, philosophical or religious sect, f. *haireîsthai* choose, *haireîn* take. So **heret**IC he·rĭtik one who embraces heresy. XIV (R. Mannyng). – (O)F. *hérétique* – ecclL. *hæreticus* – Gr. *hairetikós* able to choose, f. *haireîsthai*. **here·t**ICAL. XVI (More). – medL.

heriot he·riət (orig.) feudal service consisting of military equipment restored to the lord on the death of a tenant. OE. *heregeatwa*, *-we* (whence medL. *herietum*, *-otum* XII, AN. *heriet*), f. *here* army (cf. HARBINGER) +*ġeatwa* (= ON. *gǫtvar* pl.) trappings.

heritage he·ritidʒ inherited property. XIII (AncrR., RGlouc., Cursor M.). – OF. *(h)eritage* (mod. *hé-*) = Pr. *heretatge*, OSp. *eredage*; f. *(h)eriter*, etc. – ecclL. *hērēditāre*, f. *hērēd-* HEIR. So **he·rit**ABLE. XIV. – (O)F. **he·rit**OR[1]. XV (*-er*). – AN. *heriter* = (O)F. *héritier* :– L. *hērēditārius*; conformed to -OR[1] in XVI (cf. *bachelor*).

hermaphrodite hɜːmæ·frədait being in which parts characteristic of both sexes are combined XV; animal or plant in which male and female organs are present; (naut.) sailing vessel combining characters of two kinds of craft XVIII. – L. *hermaphrodītus* – Gr. *hermaphrόdītos*, orig. proper name of a son of *Hermes* and *Aphrodite*, who grew together with the nymph Salmacis while bathing in her fountain and so combined male and female characters.

hermeneutics hɜːmīnjū·tiks science of interpretation. XVIII (Waterland). – modL. *hermēneutica* – Gr. *hermēneutikḗ*, sb. use (sc. *tékhnē* art) of fem. sg. of adj. (see -IC, -ICS), f. *hermēneutḗs*, agent-noun f. *hermēneúein* interpret, f. *hermēneús* interpreter.

hermetic(al) həɹmėtik(əl) pert. to (the supposed writings of) *Hermes* Trismegistus; (hence) pert. to occult science, esp. alchemy; *h. seal* airtight closure (as used by alchemists). XVII. – modL. *hermēticus*, f. (prob. after *magnēs*, *magnēticus*) *Hermēs Trismegistus* (Gr. Ἑρμῆς τρὶς μέγιστος, late L. *Hermēs termaximus*) 'thrice-greatest Hermes', name given by Neoplatonists, mystics, and alchemists to the Egyptian god Thoth, who was identified with the Grecian Hermes (god of science, etc.) as the author of occult science and esp. alchemy; see -IC, -ICAL. The adv. is earlier in XVII; after modL. *hermēticē*.

hermit hɜ·ːmit religious recluse, esp. of the desert. XIII. ME. *armite*, *(h)ermite*, *(h)eremite* – (O)F. *(h)ermite* (mod. *ermite*) or ChrL. *erēmīta* (medL. *her-*) – Gr. *erēmítēs*, f. *erēmíā* desert, f. *érēmos* solitary, deserted. The initial *h* preserves a medL. variety of sp. Cf. EREMITE. So **he·rmit**AGE. XIII. – (O)F. *(h)ermitage* = Pr. *ermitatge*, etc., medL. *(h)er(ē)mītāgium*; as the name of a French wine (XVII), so called from a ruin on a hill near Valence supposed to have been a hermit's cell.

hernia hɜ·ːniə rupture of abdominal (etc.) wall. XIV (Ch.). – L. *hernia* (medL. also *hirnia*).

hernshaw hɜ·ːnʃɔ̄ see HERONSEW.

hero hiə·rou man of superhuman qualities, demigod XIV (Trevisa; rare before XVI); illustrious warrior XVI; man admired for his great deeds and noble qualities XVII; chief man in a poem, play, etc. XVII (Dryden). In earliest use chiefly pl. *heroes*, with sg. *heroe* (both of 3 syll.) and *heros* – L. *hērōs*, pl. *hērōēs* – Gr. *hḗrōs*, pl. *hḗrōes*. Cf. (O)F. *héros*, †*heroë*, Sp. *heroe*, It. *eroe*. The common *heroe* (XVI–XVIII) was superseded by *hero* (XVII), with pl. *heroes* (2 syll.). So **hero**IC hėrou·ik. XVI. – F. or L. – Gr. *hērōïkós*. **heroi-co·**MIC (J. Warton), -CO·MICAL (Pope), after F. *héroï-comique*, for **hēroïco-comique*. **hero**INE[3] he·rouin. XVII. – F. or L. – Gr. *hērōínē*. **he·ro**ISM. XVIII. – F. *héroïsme*.

heroin he·rouin sedative drug (diacetylmorphin) prepared from morphia. XIX. – G. *heroin*, said to be f. Gr. *hḗrōs* HERO because of the inflated notion of the personality which follows its use; see -IN.

heron he·rən, poet. **hern** hɜːn long-necked long-legged wading bird, Ardea. XIV. ME. *heiroun*, *heroun*, *herne* – OF. *hairon* (mod. *héron*) = Pr. *aigron*, Cat. *agró*, It. *aghirone*, *airone* – Germ. **χaigaron* (whence OHG. *heigaro*; cf. ON. *hegri*), dissimilated form of **χraigron* (cf. OE. *hrāgra*, MLG. *rēger*, MDu. *reiger*, OHG. *reigaro*, G. *reiher* with LG. cons.-change), usu. referred to IE. **qriq-*, whence Gr. *krízein*, aor. *ríxai* utter sharp cries, OSl. *kričati* cry out, etc. Hence **he·ron**RY. XVII. So **heronsew** he·rənsjū (young or little) heron. XIV (Ch.). – OF. *heronceau*, earlier *-cel*, dim. (L. *-cellus*); obs. or dial. vars. are *hernsew* (XV), *heronshew* (XVI).

herpes hɜ·ːpīz (path.) skin disease. XVII. – L. – Gr. *hérpēs* shingles, lit. 'creeping', f. *hérpein* creep (see SERPENT).

herring he·riŋ small N. Atlantic sea-fish, Clupea harengus. OE. *hǣring*, *hēring* = OFris. *hēreng*, MLG. *hērink*, *hārink* (Du. *haring*), OHG. *hāring* (MHG. *hærinc*, G. *häring*, *hering*) :– WGerm. **χēriŋga*, beside which a var. with **χar-* is repr. by medL. *haringus* (whence Pr. *arenc*, F. *hareng*; It. has aberrant *aringa*); poss. orig. 'greyish-white fish', f. HOAR; see -ING[3]. ¶ The long stem-vowel is preserved dial.

Herrnhuter he·rnhūːtər one of the sect of United Brethren or Moravians. XVIII. f. *Herrnhut* 'the Lord's keeping' (HEED), name of their first German settlement.

hertz hɜːts (electr.) frequency of one cycle per second. f. name of H. R. *Hertz* (1857–94), German physicist.

hesitate he·ziteit hold back in doubt. XVII. f. pp. stem of L. *hæsitāre* stick fast, stammer, be undecided, f. *hæs-*, pp. stem of *hærēre* stick, hold fast; see ADHERE and -ATE[3]. So **hesita·**TION. XVII (Bacon). – L.

Hesperian hespiə·riən western. XVI (Surrey), f. L. *hesperius*, Gr. *hespérios*, f. *Hesperia*, Gr. *Hespería* (poet.) land of the west, f. *Hesperus* (used from Ch. onwards), *Hésperos*, as adj. western, as sb. evening star (see VESPER, -IAN).

Hessian he·siən pert. to *Hesse*, a grand duchy of Germany: *H. boot*, top-boot with tassels in front first worn by H. troops XIX; *H. fly*, fly or midge, Cecidomyia destructor, so named because it was erron. supposed to have been carried into America by the H. troops during the War of Independence XVIII; see -IAN.

hest hest (arch.) bidding, BEHEST. XII. ME. *heste*, f. (on the model of abstr. sbs. in *-te*, e.g. *ishefte* creation) *hes*, OE. *hǣs* :– **χaittiz*, f. **χaitan* call (see HIGHT).

hetaira hėtaiə·rə concubine, harlot. XIX. – Gr. *hetaírā*, fem. of *hetaîros* companion, rel. to L. *satelles* SATELLITE. Hence **hetær**ISM hėtiə·rizm open concubinage; tribal communal marriage.

hetero- he·tərо(u), **heter-** comb. form of Gr. *héteros* other, in many techn. comps. (sometimes opp. to *auto-*, *homœo-*, *iso-*, *ortho-*, *syn-*). **he·teroclite,** (gram.) irregularly declined. XVI. – late L. – Gr. *heteróklitos* (*-klitos*, f. *klínein* bend, INCLINE, inflect); **he·terodox**)(*orthodox*. XVII. – Gr. *heteródoxos* (*dóxā* opinion); **he·tero**DYNE. XX; **he:teroge·ne**-OUS -dʒīniəs diverse in kind or nature)(*homogeneous*. XVII; – medL. *heterogeneus*, f. Gr. *heterogenḗs* (*génos* KIND[1]); **heter(o)ou·**SIAN)(*homoousian*, *homoiousian*. XVII.

hetman he·tmən military commander in Poland, etc. XVIII. – Pol. *hetman* (= Czech *hejtman*, Little Russ. *hetman*, Russ. *atamán*) prob. – G. *hauptmann* 'head man', captain, earlier *heubtmann*. Also *ataman* (XIX).

heuristic hjuri·stik serving to find out. XIX. irreg. f. Gr. *heurískein* find (cf. EUREKA), after words in -ISTIC from vbs. in *-ízein* -IZE.

hew hjū pp. **hewn** strike, cut with blows of an axe, etc. OE. *hēawan*, pt. *hēow*, pp. *hēawen* = OFris. *hawa*, *howa*, OS. *hauwan* (Du. *houwen*), OHG. *houwan* (G. *hauen*), ON. *hǫggva* :– CGerm. (exc. Goth.) redupl. str. vb. **χauwan*, pt. **χeχau-*, pp. **χauwan-*; f. IE. **kou-* **kow-*, found also in OSl. *kovą*, *kovati* forge, Lith. *káuju* strike, forge, *kovà* battle.

hexad he·ksæd group of six. XVII. – Gr. *hexad-*, *hexás*, f. *héx* SIX; see -AD[1].

hexa- he·ksə, hėksæ·, hėgzæ·, before vowel **hex-**, comb. form of Gr. *héx* SIX, used like HEPTA-, as in **hexaemeron** heksəī·mərən six days of the Creation. XVI. Late L. – n. of Gr. *hexaḗmeros* (*hēmérā* day); **hexa**GON he·ksəgən, **-agon**AL[1] æ·gənəl. XVI; **-he·dron.** XVI; Gr. *hédrā* seat, base, side of a figure; **hexa**METER hėgzæ·mitəɹ, hėks- (pros.) line of six feet. XVI (Ch. has *exametron*). – L. – Gr. *hexámetros* (see METRE); **he·**XANE[2] paraffin containing six atoms of carbon; **hexapla** he·ksəplə sixfold text (of O.T. or N.T.) in parallel arrangement. XVII; Gr. *hexaplâ*, n. pl. of *hexaploûs* (cf. -FOLD); **hexapod** he·ksəpɔd six-footed animal. XVII (Wilkins, Ray); see FOOT; **he·xastich** group of six lines of verse. XVII (Drayton; earlier *-stichon*). – modL. *hexastichon*; cf. STICHIC; **He·xateuch** -tjūk Pentateuch with Joshua. XIX; cf. HEPTATEUCH.

hey hei excl. to attract attention, express exultation, etc. XIII; used extensively with other words as †*hey go bet* XIV (Ch.); *hey trolly lolly, hey diddle diddle* XVI; *hey-pass* XVI (Marlowe), *hey presto* XVIII (Fielding); *hey-go-mad* XVIII (Sterne). ME. *hei*, *hay*; cf. OF. *hai*, *hay*, Du., G. *hei*, Sw. *hej*. See also HEIGH.

heyday, heigh- hei·dei excl. denoting gaiety, surprise, wonder. XVI (*heyda*, Skelton). The earliest form agrees with LG. *heida*, also *heidi* hurrah! Hence **hey-day** sb. state of exaltation or excitement XVI; prime, bloom XVIII (Smollett, Sterne).

heyduck hei·duk in Hungary and Poland, one of a body of foot-soldiers or retainers. XVII. – Czech, Pol., Serb *hajduk*, in Magyar *hajdú*, pl. *-dúk* – Turk. *haydud* robber, brigand (whence also Bulg. *hajdutin*, mod. Gr. χαϊντούτης).

hey-ho heihou int. perh. of nautical origin and marking the rhythm of heaving or hauling; often used in refrains of songs. XV (*hay hoe, hey how*).

hi hai excl. to attract attention or †to incite. XV (*hy*). ¶ OE. *hiġ lā*, *hyġ lā*, *hī lā hī* means 'alas!', like L. *heu*.

hiatus haiei·təs gap, chasm XVI; interruption of continuity XVII; break between two vowels XVIII. – L. *hiātus* gaping, opening, f. *hiāre* gape (cf. YAWN).

hibernate hai·bəɹneit spend the winter esp. in a state of torpor. XIX (E. Darwin). f. pp. stem of L. *hībernāre*, f. *hīberna* winter quarters, n. pl. of *hībernus* pert. to winter :– **gheimrinos* (cf. Gr. *kheimerinós*), f. *hiems* winter, rel. to Gr. *kheîma* winter, and various forms in Indo-Iranian, Slavonic, Baltic, and Celtic langs. So **hiberna**·TION wintering XVII; (nat. hist.) dormant condition in winter XIX (E. Darwin).

Hibernian haibə̄·ɹniən Irish. XVII. f. L. *Hibernia*, alteration of *Iverna*, *Iuverna*, *Iuberna* – Gr. *Iϝérnē*, *Iérnē* – OCeltic **Iveriu*, acc. **Iverionem* (Ir. *Eriu*, acc. *Eirinn* Erin, later MIr. *Eri*, whence OE. *Īraland* IRELAND); see -IAN.

hibiscus hibi·skəs malvaceous plant. XVIII. L., – Gr. *hibískos*, identified by Dioscorides with *althaíā* ALTHÆA.

hiccough hi·kəp spasm of the respiratory organs accompanied by a resonant gasping noise. XVI. imit.; early forms *hickop*, *hi(c)kup*, which superseded earlier †*hicket*, †*hickock*, of imit. origin; cf. ON. *hixti* sb., *hixta* vb., Du. *hik*, *hikken*, Sw. *hicka*, Da. *hik(ke)*, Russ. *ikát'*, and F. *hoquet*. ¶ The form *hiccough* (XVII) is due to assim. to *cough*, but the pronunc. has not been affected.

hickory hi·kəri N. Amer. tree allied to the walnut. XVII (*-ery*). Shortening of *pohickery* (in Eng. context XVII), the native Virginian form of which is cited as *paw-*, *powcohiccora* for milk or oil extracted from the nuts.

hidalgo hidæ·lgou Spanish gentleman by birth. XVI. Sp., formerly *hijo dalgo*, i.e. *hijo de algo* 'son of something' (*algo* in OSp. and OPg. meant 'possession'), repr. L. *filius* son, *dē* DE, *aliquid* something (cf. ALIQUOT).

hide[1] haid skin. OE. *hȳd* = OFris. *hēd*, OS. *hūd* (Du. *huid*), OHG. *hūt* (G. *haut*), ON. *húð* :– CGerm. (exc. Gothic) **χūðiz* :– IE. **kūtis* (cf. Gr. *kútos*, L. *cutis* CUTICLE). Hence as vb. beat the hide of, thrash, whence (colloq.) **hi·d**ING[1] thrashing. XIX.

hide[2] haid measure of land reckoned as that sufficient to support a free family with dependants. OE. *hīd*, earlier *hīgid*, f. *hīġ-*, *hīw-* (in comb.) = OHG. *hī-*, ON. *hý-*, Goth. *heiwa-*, rel. to L. *cīvis* citizen (see CIVIC), and to a Germ. *n*-stem in OE. *hīwan* (pl.), OFris. *hīuna* members of a household, OHG. *hī(w)un*, ON. *hjún* man and wife; f. IE. **kej-* **ki-* dear, faithful, which with various suffixes is widely represented.

hide[3] haid pt. **hid** pp. **hidden** put or keep out of sight. OE. *hȳdan* = OFris. *hēda*, MDu. *hūden*, LG. *(ver)hüen* :– WGerm. **χūdjan*, prob. based on IE. **keudh-*, repr. also by Gr. *keúthein*, W. *cuddio* hide.

hideous hi·diəs frightful, (hence) frightfully ugly. XIII (Cursor M.). ME. *hidous* – AN. *hidous*, OF. *hidos*, *-eus* (mod. *hideux*), earlier *hisdos*, f. *hide*, *hisde* fear, of unkn. origin. The ending was assim. to -EOUS XVI.

hie hai †strive, exert oneself OE.; (arch.) hasten XII. OE. *hīġian*, of unkn. origin.

hierarchy haiə·rāɹki division of angels comprising three orders XIV (Wyclif, Trevisa); priestly or ecclesiastical rule XVI; body of ecclesiastical rulers XVII (transf. and gen., Milton). ME. *ierarchie*, *gerarchie* (superseded by latinized forms in XVI) – OF. *ierarchie*, *gerarchie* (mod. *hiérarchie* – It. *gerarchia*) – medL. *(h)ierarchia* – Gr. *hierarkhíā*, f. *hierárkhēs* steward of sacred rites, high priest, f. *hierós* sacred, holy + *-arkhēs*, *-arkhos* ruling, ruler; see ARCH-, -Y[3]. So **hie·rarch** ecclesiastical ruler XVI; archangel XVII (Milton). – medL. *hierarcha* – Gr. *hierárkhēs*. **hiera·rch**ICAL. XV. – medL. *-icus* + -AL – Gr.

hieratic haiəræ·tik pert. to a priestly class, (hence) of a style of ancient Egyptian writing. XVII. – L. *hierāticus* – Gr. *hierātikós* priestly, sacerdotal, f. *hierâsthai* be a priest, f. *hiereús* priest, f. *hierós* sacred.

hieroglyphic haiə:rǒgli·fik pertaining to ancient Egyptian writing; sb. character in such picture-writing; symbolic or enigmatic figure. XVI. – F. *hiéroglyphique* or late L. *hieroglyphicus* – Gr. *hieroglyphikós* (n. pl. used as sb. by Plutarch for 'letters, writing'), f. *hierós* sacred + *gluphḗ* carving (cf. CLEAVE[1]). Hence, as back-formation or after F. *hiéroglyphe*, **hie·roglyph** hieroglyphic figure. XVII (*gieroglife*, after It., XVI).

hierophant haiə·rǒfænt expounder of mysteries. XVII. – late L. *hierophanta*, *-ēs* – Gr. *hierophántēs*, f. *hierós* sacred + *-phan-*, base of *phaínein* reveal (cf. PHENOMENON).

higgle hi·gl cavil as to terms. XVII. var. of HAGGLE, expressive of niggling.

higgledy-piggledy hi:gldipi·gldi in huddled confusion. XVI. Rhyming jingle prob. based on PIG with ref. to swine herding together.

high hai having a considerable (or specified) upward extent; exalted. OE. *hēah* (inflexional stem *heaġ-*) = OFris. *hāch*, OS., OHG. *hōh* (Du. *hoog*, G. *hoch*), ON. *hár* (earlier *hǫ́r*), Goth. *hauhs* :– CGerm. **χauχaz* :– IE. **koukos* (cf. Lith. *kaũkas* swelling, boil, *kaukarà* height, hill, and the remoter ON. *haugr* hill, Goth. *hiuhma* heap, Russ. *kúcha* heap, Skr. *kucas* female breast). For the phonology cf. DIE[1], EYE, THIGH; see also HEIGHT. Combs. **hi·gh-**BROW, back-formation from **hi·gh-browed** (orig. U.S.) *c*.1910; **high**CHU·RCHMAN (whence **high church**) succeeded to **high-**FLY·ER XVII; **hi·gh**LAND. OE. *hēahlond* promontory; thereafter (XV) applied spec. to the north and west mountainous district of Scotland; **hi·gh** STREET highway, main road; main street of a town; OE. *hēahstrǣt* often used of the Roman roads; **hi·gh**WAY public road; OE. *hēiweġ*; hence **hi·ghway**MAN. XVII.

high-falutin' haifəlʲū·tin (orig. U.S. sl.) sb. bombastic speech; adj. absurdly pompous. XIX. f. HIGH + obscurely-formed el., which was poss. a whimsical pronunc. of *fluting*, prp. of FLUTE.

high-flown hai·floun †elevated, elated, intoxicated; hyperbolical, bombastic; †extreme in opinion. XVII. orig. f. *high* adv. + old strong pp. of FLOW, from the sense 'in flood', 'swollen'; later assoc. with pp. of FLY[2] (cf. *high-flyer* XVII).

hight hait in literary arch. use now only in pt. 'is called', 'was called', and pp. 'called, named'. The only surviving form of an orig. redupl. CGerm. vb. meaning 'call by name, name, call to do something, bid, command, promise', repr. by OE. *hātan*, pt. *heht*, *hēt*, pp. *hāten* (ME. *hote*, *hiȝt*, *heet*, *hoten*), OFris. *hēta*, OS. *hētan*, OHG. *heizzan* (G. *heissen* call, bid, be called; *es heisst* it is said), ON. *heita*, Goth. *haitan*, pt. *haihait*, pp. *haitans*; f. a base which has been related to L. *ciēre* summon, CITE. This vb. shows the only survival in Eng. of the IE. mediopassive form: OE. *hātte* is called, was called = Goth. *haitada*, the ending of which corr. to Gr. *-tai*. OE. *hātte* did not survive beyond XV; its place had begun to be taken as early as XIII by the active form of the pt. (*heht*, *heȝt*, *hiȝt*, *hight*). The orig. pp. was superseded by forms of the pt. Some active uses remain dial., e.g. Sc. *hecht*, *hicht* promise.

highty-tighty hai:titai·ti var. of HOITY-TOITY. XVII.

hike haik jerk, pull, drag XVIII; move away or off; (latterly) tramp, esp. for pleasure XIX. Of dial. origin.

hilarity hilæ·rĭti cheerfulness XVI; boisterous joy XIX. – F. *hilarité* – L. *hilaritās*, f. *hilaris* = Gr. *hilarós* cheerful, gay; see -ITY. Hence **hilar**IOUS hilɛə·riəs, after *atrocious*, etc.

Hilary hi·ləri name of a saint and doctor of the Church, bishop of Poitiers (died 367), whose feast, falling on 13 January, gives his name to the first of the law and university terms of the calendar year. XVI. – medL. *Hilarius.*

hill hil small mountain. OE. *hyll* = Fris. *hel*, LG. *hull*, MDu. *hille, hil, hul* :– WGerm. (of the LG. area) **χulni* :– **kulnís*, f. IE. base **kl-* **kel-* **kol-*, whence also L. *collis* hill, *celsus* lofty, *culmen* top (see EXCEL, CULMINATE), Gr. *kolōnós, kolṓnē* hill, Lith. *kilnus* high, *kálnas* hill, *kélti* raise; cf. HOLM. Hence **hi·llock**. XIV. **hi·lly**[1]. XIV (Gower).

hillo(a) hilou· var. of HOLLO, with altered quality of the unstr. syll. XVII (Sh.). ¶ Not continuous with obscure ME. *hilla* (XIV).

hilt hilt handle of sword or dagger. OE. *hilt* m. and n. and *hilte* fem., corr. to OS. *hilte, helta*, MLG. *hilte*, MDu. *helte*, OHG. *helza*, ON. *hjalt* :– CGerm. (exc. Gothic) **χeltaz*, **χeltiz*, **χeltjōn*, of unkn. origin (OF. *helt-e, heut-e*, It. *else, elsa* are adoptions from Germ.); phr. *up to the hilt* or †*hilts* (XVI–XVIII) completely. ¶ The pl. *hilts* continues the ME. use of *hiltes*, which goes back to OE. *þā hilt, hiltas*, and *hiltan* (*oð þā hilt* or *hiltan* up to the hilts), coll. pl. *ġehiltu*, ON. *hjǫlt*, the reference of the pl. being to the two cross-pieces of the handle of a sword bounding the middle piece (ON. *meðalkafli*), the lower one being the guard (cf. OE. *hiltlēas sweord* sword without a guard).

him him orig. dative of HE[1], IT; later also as direct object. OE. *him* = OFris. *him*, MDu. *hem(e), him* (Du. *hem*), f. base of HE[1], with inflexion parallel to OS., OHG. *imu, imo* (G. *ihm*), which are f. base **i-* (L. *is* he, *id* it, Goth. *is, ita*, OHG. *er, eȥ*, G. *er, es*). ¶ OE. acc. *hine*, which survives dial. as *en, un*, was superseded by *him* in north. and midl. areas before 1200.

hind[1] haind female of the deer. OE. *hind*, corr. to OS. *hind|calf*, (M)Du. *hinde*, OHG. *hinta* (G. *hinde*), ON. *hind* :– CGerm. (exc. Gothic) **χinþjō* :– IE. **kemti-*, f. **kem-* hornless, repr. by Gr. *kemás* young deer, Skr. *çomas*, Lith. *szmúlas* hornless.

hind[2] haind farm servant; farm bailiff. XVI. Later form of late OE. (north-midl.), ME. *hine* pl. household servants, (hence) sg. servant, esp. farm servant, lad, fellow; presumably developed from OE. *hīna, hīgna*, g. pl. of *hīgan, hīwan* (cf. HIDE[2]), as in *hīna fæder* 'paterfamilias'. For the parasitic *d* cf. ASTOUND, SOUND[2].

hind[3] haind situated at the back, posterior. XIII. This and synon. **hinder**[1] hai·ndəɹ (XIV) appear to be abstracted from OE. *hindeweard* and *hinderweard* backward, back-, *bihindan* BEHIND. The uncompounded OE. *hindan* from behind, *hinder* below (*on hinder* down, behind, backwards), corr. to OHG. *hintana* (G. *hinten*) adv. behind, Goth. *hindana* prep. beyond, and OFris. *hindera*, OS. *hindiro*, MLG. *hinder*, OHG. *hintar* (as adj. *-aro*), G. *hinter*, ON. compar. *hindri*, superl. *hinztr*, Goth. *hindar* prep. beyond, the further relations of which are doubtful. Hence **hi·ndermore**, **hi·ndermost**, and **hi·ndmost**, which all appear in late XIV, having no chronological link with OE. superl. *hindema* (cf. Goth. *hindumists*).

hinder[2] hi·ndəɹ †injure OE.; keep back, delay XIV. OE. *hindrian* = MLG., MDu. *hinderen*, OHG. *hintarōn* (G. *hindern*), ON. *hindra* :– CGerm. (exc. Gothic) **χindarōjan*, f. **χindar*; see prec. Hence **hi·ndrance**. XV.

Hindi hindī (str. variable) Aryan vernacular of N. India. XVIII. – Urdu *hindī*, f. *hind* India; in Pers. *hindwī, hinduvī*, whence formerly in Eng. *Hindevi, Hindawee, Hinduee*, etc. So **Hindu, Hindoo** hindū (str. variable) Aryan of N. India. XVII. – Urdu – Pers. *hindū*, formerly *hindō*, f. *hind* India = Av. *heñdu*, Skr. *sindhu* river, prop. the Indus, (hence) region of the Indus, Sindh. **Hindustani** hindustā·ni formerly *Hindo(o)-, -stanee* language of *Hindustan*, orig. of its Muslim conquerors, being a form of Hindi with admixture of Arabic, Persian, and other elements. XVIII (earlier *Indostan, -stans*). – Urdu – Pers. *hīndūstānī*, f. *hindū*, †*hindō* + *-stān* country + adj. suffix *-ī*.

hine see HIND[2].

hinge hin^{d}ʒ movable joint of a gate or door. XIII (Cursor M.). Of obscure origin; ME. *heng, heeng, hing*, with deriv. (see -LE[1]) *hengle, heengle, hingle*, which survived dial. as hi·ŋgl, he·ŋgl, corr. to MLG., MHG. *hengel* (G. *hängel*), f. the base of HANG; cf. (M)LG. *henge* hinge, Du. *hengel* fishing-rod, handle, *hengsel* hinge, handle. The pronunc. with dʒ (of obscure development) is not evident before XVI. Hence vb. XVII (Sh.).

hinny[1] hi·ni whinny. XV. Earlier *henny* – (O)F. *hennir* :– L. *hinnīre*, to which the word was finally assim.

hinny[2] hi·ni offspring of a she-ass and a stallion. XVII. f. L. *hinnus* – Gr. *ínnos, gínnos*; assim. to prec.

hint hint †opportunity; slight indication or suggestion. XVII (Sh.). Of obscure origin; presumably var. of rare †*hent* grasp, intention, f. *hent* vb., OE. *hentan* seize, of unkn. origin. Hence **hint** vb. XVII.

hinterland hi·ntəɹlænd region behind that lying along a sea or watercourse. XIX. G., f. *hinter* behind (see HIND[3]) + *land* LAND.

hip[1] hip projection of pelvis and top of thigh. OE. *hype* = MDu. *höpe, hüpe* (Du. *heup*), OHG. *huf*, pl. *huffi*, Goth. *hups*, pl. *hupeis* :– Germ. **χupiz*, rel. to HOP[1].

hip[2] hip fruit of the (wild) rose. OE. *hēope, hīope*, corr. to OS. *hiopo* (Du. *joop*), OHG. *hiufo* thornbush, bramble :– WGerm. **χeup-*. ¶ Shortening of the vowel was prob. due to the frequent comps. *hip-bramble* (OE. *hēopbremel*), *hip-tree*.

hip[3] hip †excl. of calling XVIII; as a cheer, in *hip hip hooray* XIX.

hipped hipt morbidly depressed. XVIII. Earlier *hypt, hypp'd*, f. *hyp, hip* (XVIII), short for HYPOCHONDRIA; see -ED². Also **hi·ppISH**¹, *hyppish* (XVIII). Cf. Du. *hiep*, for *hypochonder* hypochondriac.

hippo hi·pou short for HIPPOPOTAMUS. XIX.

hippo- hi·po(u), hipɔ· comb. form of Gr. *híppos* HORSE. **hippoca·mpus** sea-horse. XVI. – L. – Gr. (*kámpos* sea-monster); -CE·NTAUR XVI. – L. – Gr.; **hi·ppogriff** fabulous griffin-like creature. XVII. – F. *hippogriffe* – It. *ippogrifo* (*grifo* :– L. *grȳphus* GRIFFIN¹).

hippocras hi·po(u)kræs wine flavoured with spices. XIV (Ch.). ME. *ypocras* – OF. *ipo-, ypocras*, forms of the name *Hippocrates* (ancient Gr. physician V B.C.) used for medL. *vinum Hippocraticum* 'wine of Hippocrates', the wine being so called because it was strained through 'Hippocrates' bag', a conical bag used as a filter.

Hippocrene hi·po(u)krīn name of a fountain on Helicon, sacred to the Muses, (hence) poetic inspiration. XVII. – L. *Hippocrēnē* – Gr. *Hippokrḗnē*, f. *híppos* horse (cf. EQUINE) + *krḗnē* fountain; so named because fabled to have been produced by a stroke of Pegasus' hoof.

hippodrome hi·pədroum circus (prop.) for horse and chariot races. XVI. – (O)F. *hippodrome* or L. *hippodromus* – Gr. *hippódromos*, f. *híppos* horse + *drómos* race.

hippopotamus hipəpɔ·təməs large quadruped of African rivers. XVI. – L. *hippopotamus* – late Gr. *hippopótamos* (Galen), for earlier *híppos ho potámios* the horse of the river (*potamós* river). ¶ Earlier forms (from XIV) were *ypotam(e), hippotame, ypotamos, -anus* – OF. *ypotame*, medL. *ypotamus*.

hircine hə̄·ɹsain goatish. XVII. – L. *hircīnus*, f. *hircus* he-goat; see -INE¹.

hire haiəɹ payment for the temporary use of a thing; wages, reward. OE. *hȳr* = OFris. *hēre*, OS. *hūria*, MLG., MDu. *hūre* (Du. *huur*) :– WGerm. (of the LG. area) **χūrja*. Hence **hire** vb. OE. *hȳrian* = OFris. *hēra*, MLG., MDu. *hūren* (Du. *huren*). **hi·re-LING**¹. OE. (rare) *hȳrling*; formed afresh in XVI (Coverdale), prob. after Du. *huurling*.

hirsute hə̄·ɹsjūt hairy. XVII. – L. *hirsūtus*, rel. to synon. *hirtus*.

his hiz possessive adj. and pron. OE. *his*, genitive of HE¹ and IT, to which there are parallel forms from the base **i-* (cf. HER) in OS., Goth. *is*, OHG. *is, es* (cf. HIM).

hispid hi·spid bristly, shaggy. XVII. – L. *hispidus*; see -ID¹.

hiss his produce the characteristic sound emitted by geese and snakes. XIV (Wycl. Bible). imit., with an early by-form *hish*. Hence **hiss** sb. XVI.

hist hist excl. enjoining silence. XVII. Aspirated form of †*ist* (XVI), var. of ST (XVI) with the vowel of late ME. WHIST¹.

histo- hi·stou, histɔ· repr. comb. form of Gr. *histós* web, tissue, rel. to *histánai* set up (cf. STAND), as in **histo·LOGY** science of organic tissues. XIX. – F. *histologie*.

history hi·stəri †story, tale; methodical narrative of events, branch of knowledge dealing with these XV; methodical account of natural phenomena XVI. First recorded from Caxton (Gower has one ex. of the F. form *histoire*); – L. *historia* – Gr. *historíā* learning or knowing by inquiry, narrative, history, f. *histōr* knowing, learned, wise man, judge :– **ϝídtōr*, f. **ϝid-* know (see WIT). So **historIAN** histɔ̄·riən. XV (Lydg.). – (O)F. *historien*, f. L. *historia*, after *logicien*, etc. **historIC** histɔ·rik. XVII; **histo·RICAL.** XVI. f. L. *historicus* – Gr. *historikós*.

histrionic histriɔ·nik theatrical, dramatic. XVII. – late L. *histriōnicus*, f. L. *histriō(n-)* actor in stage plays, thought to be of Etruscan origin. See -IC. Also **histrio·nICAL.**

hit hit pt., pp. **hit** light upon XI (pt. *hytte*, AS. Chronicle); strike XIII (Laȝ.). Late OE. (*ġe*)*hittan* – ON. *hitta* light upon, meet with (Sw. *hitta*, Da. *hitte*), of unkn. origin; has taken over the orig. use 'strike' of OE. *slēan* SLAY. Hence **hit** sb. XVI. **hitty-missy** at random. XVI; perh. for **hit I, miss I*; cf. WILLY-NILLY.

hitch hitʃ A. move jerkily XV; B. catch with a hoop, loop, etc. XVII. The earliest records are from E. Anglian areas (Promp. Parv., Skelton); varying with *itch* XVI–XVII; the connexion of A and B is not obvious. Hence as sb. XVII. Also comp. **hi·tch-HIKE.** XX.

hithe, hythe haið haven, landing-place. OE. *hȳþ*, OS. *hūth*, MLG. *-hude* (in place-names); of unkn. origin. ¶ Preserved in the place-names *Hythe, Rotherhithe, Lambeth* (orig. *Lambhithe*), *Chelsea* (OE. *ċealchȳþ*), *Bablockhithe, Hythe* Bridge in Oxford.

hither hi·ðəɹ to this place. OE. *hider*, corr. to ON. *heðra* here, hither, Goth. *hidrē* hither, f. demonstr. base **χi-* (see HE¹, HENCE, HERE) + suffix appearing in L. *citrā* on this side. For the change of d to ð cf. *father, mother, together*.

hive haiv receptacle for a swarm of bees. OE. *hȳf*, f. Germ. **χūf-*, whence also ON. *húfr* ship's hull; cf. L. *cūpa* barrel (see CUPOLA), Gr. *kúpē*, Skr. *kūpas* hole. The present form depends upon OE. obl. forms.

ho hou excl. of surprise, triumph, to attract attention, etc. ('stop!', 'halt!'), and (repeated) of laughter. XIII. Not recorded in OE.; partly – ON. *hó* (whence *hóa* call sheep together) or OF. *ho* halt! Cf. OHO, HEIGH-HO, SOHO, YOHO, and L. *eho* used as a summons, to express surprise, and equiv. to 'eh?'; cf. also HA, HE².

hoar hɔ̄əɹ (arch.) grey-haired, greyish-white. OE. *hār* = OS., OHG. *hēr* old, venerable (G. *hehr* august, stately, sacred), ON. *hárr* hoary, old :– CGerm. (exc. Goth.) **χairaz*, f. base **χai-* (repr. also, with *ð-*

suffix, by OE. *hādor*, OS. *hēdar*, OHG. *heitar*, G. *heiter* bright, ON. *heið* bright sky) :- IE. **koira-* (cf. OSl. *sěrŭ* grey). Survives in **hoa·r**FROST (XIII) and **hoarhound,** HOREHOUND. Hence **hoa·ry**[1] XVI.

hoard hō(ə)ɹd stock, store, treasure. OE. *hord* = OS. *hord, horth* treasure, secret place, OHG. *hort*, ON. *hodd*, Goth. *huzd* :- CGerm. **χuzdam* :- **kuzdhó-*, for **kudhto-*, f. **kudh-* **keudh-* (see HIDE[3]). So **hoard** vb. OE. *hordian* (cf. OHG. *gihurten*, Goth. *huzdjan*). For the sp. cf. *board*.

hoarding hō·(ə)ɹdiŋ temporary fence made of boards. XIX. f. *hoard*, earlier *hord, hourd* (XVIII), which seems to be based ult. on AN. *hourdis, hurdis*, f. OF. *hourd, hort* (– OFrank. **hurð* = OHG. *hurd* HURDLE)+*-is* :- L. *-ītiu-s*; see -ING[1].

hoarhound see HOREHOUND.

hoarse hō(ə)ɹs rough and deep-sounding. XIV. Late ME. *hors-e*, later *hoors, hoarse* (XVI–XVII) – ON. **hārs* (:- **hairsaR*), *háss*; this superseded ME. *ho(o)s*, OE. *hās* (Sc. and north. *ha(a)s, hais*) = OFris. *hās*, MLG. *hēs, hēsch* (Du. *heesch*), OHG. *heis(i)*, (M)HG. *heiser* :- CGerm. (exc. Gothic) **χais(r)az*, **χairsaz*, of unkn. origin.

hoax houks deceive by a fiction; earlier, poke fun at. XVIII. prob. contr. of HOCUS.

hob[1] hɔb rustic, clown XIV; sprite, elf XV. By-form of *Rob* (as in *Kyng Hobbe*, i.e. Robert Bruce, XIV), short for *Robin, Robert* male Christian names (cf. HODGE); now dial. exc. as in **ho·b**GO:BLIN (cf. *Robin Goodfellow*) XVI.

hob[2] hɔb side of a grate, perh. orig. back of a grate formed of a mass of clay XVI (in form *hubbe*); peg or pin as a target XVI. Of unkn. origin; cf. HUB. Hence **ho·b**NAIL nail with a massive head and short tang. XVI.

hobble[1] hɔ·bl †move unsteadily up and down; walk with unsteady rising and falling gait. XIV. prob. of LG. origin (cf. early Du. *hobbelen* toss, rock from side to side, halt, stammer), frequent. of *hobben*.

hobble[2] hɔ·bl fasten together the legs of a horse, etc. XIX. var. of earlier *hopple* (XVI), prob. of LG. origin (cf. early Flem. *hoppelen*), infl. by prec.

hobbledehoy hɔ·bldihoi:, **hobbadehoy** hɔ·bədihoi: clumsy or awkward youth. XVI (*hobledehoye, hobbard de hoy*). Occurs in many forms, the origin of which is uncertain. If the *-l-* forms were the earliest, perh. f. HOBBLE[1] or †*hoball, hobil, hobbel* clown, idiot (XVI); with the *r-* forms and the second part of the word cf. †*hoberd* term of abuse (XV) and *Hoberdidance, Hobbididance* (Sh.) name of a fiend, which are prob. f. by-form of the Christian name *Robert* (cf. HOB[1], HOBBY[1]).

hobby[1] hɔ·bi (arch., dial.) small horse XIV (Barbour); (*h.-horse*) in the morris dance, etc., figure of a horse manipulated by a performer; stick with a horse's head used as a toy XVI; favourite pastime XVII. Earliest forms *hobyn, hoby*, i.e. *Hobin, Hobby* by-forms of the Christian name *Robin* (cf. HOB[1], HODGE). ¶ Hence arch. F. *aubin*, †*hobin*, †*haubby*, whence It. †*ubino*.

hobby[2] hɔ·bi small species of falcon. XV (*hoby*). – OF. *hobé, hobet*, dim. of *hobe* small bird of prey, rel. to F. *hobereau*, OF. *hobel, hober(e)t*: cf. medL. *hobetus, hobelus, oberus*; of unkn. origin.

hobgoblin see HOB[1]. **hobnail** see HOB[2].

hob-nob hɔ·bnɔb drink together XVIII; be on familiar terms XIX. orig. *hob or nob, hob-a-nob, hob and nob*, f. phr. (*drink*) *hob or nob*, etc., drink to one another alternately (cf. 'hob, nob . . giu't or take't', Sh. 'Twelfth Night' III iv 262); continuing earlier *hab-nab, hab or nab* (XVI) get or lose, hit or miss, repr. some part (perh. pres. subj., e.g. *habbe he, nabbe he*) of HAVE and its negative (OE. *habban* and *nabban*).

hobo hou·bou (U.S.) migrant labourer; tramp. XIX (*c.*1890). Of unkn. origin.

hock[1] now only in HOLLYHOCK. OE. *hoc* mallow.

hock[2] hɔk joint of the hind leg XVI; knuckle end of a gammon XVIII. Short for *hockshin* (*hokschyne* XIV), OE. *hōhsinu*; see HOUGH.

hock[3] hɔk German white wine. XVII. Short for †*hockamore* – G. *Hochheimer* (*wein*) wine of *Hochheim* on the Main, Germany.

Hockday hɔ·kdei second Tuesday after Easter Sunday. XII. ME. *hokedei* (3 syll.), of unkn. origin; so **Hock** TUESDAY XIII, **Hock** MONDAY, **Hock**TIDE XV; only hist. after XVII.

hockey hɔ·ki outdoor game of ball played with sticks; stick so used. XIX. Earliest form *hawkey*, of unkn. origin. ¶ In 'hockie stickes or staves', recorded from Galway Statutes of 1527, *hockie* may be for *hooky* hooked; the 'sport' said by Cowper, 5 Nov. 1785, to be called *hockey* at Olney consisted of boys 'dashing each other with mud, and the windows also'. OF. *hoquet* bent stick, shepherd's crook, cannot be connected.

hocus pocus hou·kəs pou·kəs †conjurer, juggler; conjuring formula; jugglery, trickery. XVII (*hocas pocas* 1624, *hokos pokos* 1625). Based ult. on *hax pax max Deus adimax* (XVI), pseudo-L. magical formula coined by vagrant students. Cf. G. *hokus pokus*, as a formula *ox box, ox pox, okos bocos* (XVII). Hence as vb. juggle, hoax. XVII. Also, by shortening, **ho·cus** †sb. juggler; jugglery. XVII; vb. play a trick upon XVII (Head); drug XIX. Cf. HOAX. ¶ Derivation from *Hoc est corpus meum* (This is my body) in the Mass is an unlikely guess.

hod hɔd open receptacle for carrying bricks, etc. XIV; receptacle for holding coal XIX. synon. with, and perh. alteration of, (dial.) *hot* XIII (*hott*, Cursor M.) – (O)F. *hotte* pannier, creel, prob. of Germ. origin.

hodden hɔ·dn (Sc.) coarse woollen cloth. XVIII. Of unkn. origin; *hodden grey*, inversion for the sake of rhyme of *grey hodden* in Ramsay's 'Gentle Shepherd' (1724) V ii (whence in Burns, Scott, etc.), is often written with a hyphen, as if *hodden* qualified *grey* or *hodden-grey* denoted a kind of grey.

Hodge hɔdʒ typical name for an English yokel. XVI. Pet-form of the Christian name *Roger* (ME. *Hogge*; see Ch. 'Cook's Prologue' 12, 21, Gower 'Vox Clamantis' 1791); cf. HOB[1].

hodge-podge see HOTCHPOT.

hodometer, odometer (h)ɔdɔ·mitəɹ instrument for measuring distance travelled by a wheeled vehicle. XVIII. – F. *odomètre*, f. Gr. *hodós* way (cf. PERIOD) + *métron* measure (see -METER).

hoe hou implement for breaking up ground, etc. XIV (in AL. *howa* XIII). ME. *howe* – (O)F. *houe* – OFrank. **hauwa* = OHG. *houwa* (G. *haue*), rel. to *houwan* HEW. The present form, replacing the normal *how*, was established by XVIII; pronounced like *mow* and *throw* acc. to Ray (1674). Hence **hoe** vb. XV (in AL. *howāre* XIII).

hog hɔg swine, esp. castrated swine, barrow-pig OE.; young sheep XIV; coarse or filthy person XV. Late OE. *hogg*, *hocg*, of which derivs. are *hoggaster* XII (cf. late L. *porcaster* young pig), *hogget* XIV, *hoggerel* XVI (AL. *hogerellus* XIII), applied to a boar of a particular age or to a young sheep; perh. of Celtic origin (cf. W. *hwch* pig, sow = Corn. *hogh*). ¶ The orig. application may have emphasized the age or condition of the animal.

hogmanay hɔgmənei· (Sc. and north.) last day of the year. XVII. Corr. in meaning and use to OF. *aguillanneuf* last day of the year, new-year's gift (given and asked for with the cry 'aguillanneuf'), of which the Norman form *hoguinané* may be the immed. source of the Eng. word. ¶ The F. word was meaninglessly analysed as *au-guy-l'an-neuf* (Cotgr.) 'to the mistletoe the new year'.

hogo hou·gou †piquant flavour, relish; †highly seasoned dish; stench. XVII (current till early XIX). Early forms also *hogoe*, *hogoo*; anglicization of F. *haut goût* (XVII, *hautgoust*, *haultgust*, etc.) high flavour (L. *altus* high, *gustus* taste; see OLD, GUSTO).

hogshead hɔ·gzhed large cask for liquids XIV; 52½ imperial gallons XV. f. *hog's*, g. of HOG + HEAD, but the reason for the name is unknown (Kluge compares G. dial. *bullenkop* measure for beer); rendered into L. by *caput porci* ('Liber Albus', an. 1417). ¶ Adopted on the Continent, it appears in altered forms and esp. with assim. of the first el. to 'ox', e.g. MLG. *hukeshovet*, Du. *okshoofd*, G. *oxhoft*, Sw. *oxhuvud*, Da. *oxehoved*.

hoick(s) hoik(s) call to incite hounds. XVII (Topsell). orig. *hoick a* with *boy*, or a hound's name; var. of †*hike*, as in *hike a Bewmont* (XVI, Turbervile); cf. YOICKS.

hoist hoist raise aloft (as by tackle). XVI. Alteration of *hoise* (XVI), perh. through taking the pt. and pp. as the stem-form (cf. *hoist* Sh. 'Hamlet' III iv 207, *hoised* Acts xxvii 40). Earlier forms were *hyse*, *hysse* (XV), Sc. *heis* (XVI), prob. – Du. *hijschen* or LG. *hissen*, *hiesen* (whence also F. *hisser*, It. *issare*, etc., Icel. *hisa*, etc.), but the Eng. forms are earlier than any cited from elsewhere. The word appears early as an int. used in hauling: Eng. *hissa*, *heisau*, Sp. *hiza*, etc. ¶ The change in the stem-vowel of ī to oi is paralleled by *groin*, *joist*.

hoity-toity hoi·titoi·ti sb. riotous behaviour, romping; adj. frolicsome, flighty; int. expressing surprise at flighty conduct. XVII. Rhyming jingle f. †*hoit* indulge in riotous mirth, romp (XVI). Cf. HIGHTY-TIGHTY.

hokey-pokey hou·kipou·ki A. (dial.) hocus pocus; B. cheap sort of ice-cream. XIX. In A alteration of HOCUS POCUS; in B of unkn. origin.

hold[1] hould pt., pp. **held** †guard; keep from getting away, falling, etc.; keep in a certain condition. OE. *haldan* (*healdan*), pt. *hēold*, pp. *h(e)alden* = OFris. *halda*, *helt*, *halden*, OS. *haldan*, *held*, *gihaldan* (Du. *houden*, *hield*, *gehouden*), OHG. *haltan*, *hialt*, *gihaltan* (G. pt. *hielt*), ON. *halda*, *helt*, *haldinn*, Goth. *haldan*, *haihald*, *haldans*; CGerm. orig. redupl. str. vb. with the primitive sense 'watch (cf. BEHOLD), look after', 'pasture (cattle)', as in Gothic, retained in the sense of keeping flocks in OE. *heorde* and *sćēp healdan*, OHG. *hirta haldente*, ON. *halda fé*, *halda geitr*, hence the series 'guard, defend', 'rule', 'possess', 'retain, maintain, sustain'. The word had a wide development of meaning in OE., which was amplified, esp. in combination with advs., by contact with L. *tenere*, F. *tenir*, and their comps. The pp. **holden**, which began to be repl. by the pt. form *held* c.1500, is retained in some formal uses; dial. *hadden*, *hauden*, *hodden* are widespread. Hence, and partly – ON. *hald* hold, fastening, support, custody, **hold** sb. XII. See further, for the senses 'tenure', 'property', COPYHOLD, FREEHOLD, LEASEHOLD; also HOUSEHOLD, STRONGHOLD. **ho·ld**FAST grasp; clamp, staple. XVI; prob. after Du. †*houdvast*, *houvast*.

hold[2] hould cavity in a ship for the stowage of cargo. XVI. Alteration, by assim. to prec., of *hole*, *holl* (XV), prob. – (M)Du. *hol* HOLE.

hole houl hollow place; opening, aperture. OE. *hol*, inflected *hole*, *holes*, etc. = ON. *hol*, orig. n. sg. of *hol* hollow = OFris., OS., (M)Du., OHG. *hol* (G. *hohl*), ON. *holr*, CGerm. (exc. Gothic) **χulaz* (cf. OHG. *hulī*, G. *höhle*, OE. *hylu*, ON. *hola* hollow, hole, *hylr* deep place, pool); ult. f. var. of IE. **kel-* cover, CONCEAL; cf. HELL, HELM[2], HOLLOW. So **hole** vb. make a hole (in). OE. *holian* = OHG. *holōn*, Goth. *-hulōn*.

holiday hɔ·lĭdi religious festival, holy day; day of cessation from work, day of recreation. OE. *hāliġdæġ*, late *hālidæiġ*; also as two words inflected (cf. HOLY DAY).

holla hɔ·lə int. †stop! cease!; shout to excite attention. XVI. – F. *holà*, i.e. *ho* (see HO), *là* there. Cf. HALLO, HOLLO.

holland hɔ·lənd linen fabric orig. named *holland cloth* from *Holland*, a province of the Netherlands, its place of manufacture. XV. – Du. *Holland*, earlier †*Holtlant*, f. *holt* wood (HOLT)+*lant* LAND.

hollands hɔ·ləndz kind of gin. XVIII. Formerly *Hollands genever* and *gin*. – Du. *hollandsch* (pronounced with final s), *hollandsche genever* Dutch gin; see -ISH[1], GIN[2].

hollo hɔ·lou cry out loud. XVI (Boorde). var. of HOLLA; dial. and vulgar *holler*.

hollow hɔ·lou having an empty space inside; concave. XII. ME. *holȝ*, *holu*, inflected *hol(e)we*, attrib. use of OE. *holh* hole, cave, obscurely rel. to *hol* HOLE. The origin of the phr. *beat hollow*, earlier *carry*, *have*, *get it hollow*, used advb. 'thoroughly', is unkn. Hence sb. hollow place XVI (not continuous with the OE. sb.). and **ho·llow** vb. XV.

holly hɔ·li plant of the evergreen genus Ilex. XII (*holi*). Reduced form of OE. *holen*, *holeġn*, ME. *holin*, *-yn*, later *hollen*, Sc. *-in*, rel. to OS., OHG. *hulis* (MHG. *huls*, G. *hulst*), OFrank. **huls*, which is the source of F. *houx*, and further to W. *celyn*, Ir. *cuilenn*, Gael. *cuilionn*.

hollyhock hɔ·lihɔk †marsh mallow, Althæa officinalis XIII; Althæa rosea XVI (W. Turner). f. HOLY+HOCK[1], with ref. to some sacred association; cf. the W. name *hocys bendigaid* 'blessed hock' (in Ir. *ucas*, *(h)ocas*, OIr. *hociamsan*).

holm(e) houm islet, esp. in a river XI; low-lying land by a river XIII. – ON. *holmr* islet in a bay, lake, or river, meadow on the shore, corr. to OE. (poetic) *holm* billow, wave, sea, OS. *holm* hill. It is commonly assumed that the orig. sense was 'hill', which is not recorded in OE., but is found in early ME. (Laȝ.), and that the base is therefore identical with that of HILL.

holm-oak hou·m ouk evergreen oak, Quercus Ilex. XVI. f. *holm* holly (XIV), holm-oak (XVI), alteration of †*holin* HOLLY+OAK.

holo- hɔ·lo(u), before a vowel **hol-**, comb. form of Gr. *hólo-s* whole, entire, in many technical terms.

holocaust hɔ·lŏkōst whole burnt offering XIII ('Genesis and Exodus'); complete sacrifice XV; complete destruction XVII (Milton). – (O)F. *holocauste* – late L. *holocaustum* – Gr. *holókauston*, f. *hólos* whole + *kaustós*, var. of *kautós* burnt, f. *kaíein* burn (cf. CAUSTIC).

holograph hɔ·lŏgràf (letter, etc.) written wholly by the person in whose name it appears. XVII. – F. *holographe* or late L. *holographus* – Gr. *hológraphos*; see HOLO-, -GRAPH.

holster hou·lstəɹ leather case for a pistol. XVII (Butler, 'Hudibras'). corr. to and contemp. with Du. *holster*, but the earlier history of neither word is apparent; the base may be Germ. **χul-* **χel-* CONCEAL.

holt hoult (dial.) wood, copse. OE. *holt* = OFris., OS., ON. *holt*, (M)Du. *hout*, (O)HG. *holz* :– CGerm. (exc. Gothic) **χultam* :– IE. **kḷdos*; cf. OSl. *kladŭ* timber, beam, Gr. *kládos* twig, OIr. *caill*, (mod.) *coill* (:– **kaldēt*), Gael. *coill(e)*, W. *celli*.

holus-bolus hou:ləsbou·ləs all in a lump, all at once. XIX. The earliest evidence is dial.; presumably burlesque latinization of *whole bolus* or repr. assumed Gr. **hólos bôlos* 'whole lump' (see BOLUS).

holy hou·li kept apart for religious use; pert. or conformed to what is divine. OE. *hāliġ*, *-eġ* = OFris. *hēlich*, OS. *hēlag*, *-eg*, OHG. *heilag* (Du., G. *heilig*), ON. *heilagr*, Goth. *hailag* (once only, in n. form) :– CGerm. **χailagaz*, f. **χailaz* WHOLE; the regular equiv. of L. *sanctus*, *sacer*; the primary meaning may have been either 'of good augury' or 'inviolate'. Derivatives and comps. show variety of vowel according to the period of shortening of the OE. stem-vowel *ā*; cf. HALLOW, ALL HALLOWS, HALIDOM, HOLIDAY, HOLLYHOCK, and the proper names *Halliday*, *Halliwell*, *Holliwell*, *Holywell* hɔ·liwel. Hence **holy** DAY hou·li dei: (eccl.) day of special observance as feast or fast. OE. *hāliġ dæġ*; revived in XIX; **Holy** GHOST the Third Person of the Trinity. OE. *se hālga gāst* 'the holy spirit', *hāliġ gāst*, *hāligāst* (often as one word in ME.), tr. ecclL. *sanctus spiritus* (**Holy** SPIRIT XIII); **holy-**STONE hou·listoun piece of sandstone for scouring decks XIX; called *bibles* and *prayer-books* (large and small); cf. Du. *bijbel* (so used) and vb. *psalmzingen* sing psalms, for the operation; said to be so named because the work is done kneeling; **holy** WATER. OE. *hāliġwæter*, ME. *haliwater*; tr. ecclL. *aqua benedicta* 'blessed water'.

hom houm sacred plant of the Persians. XIX. – Pers. *hōm* = Skr. *sōma* SOMA.

homage hɔ·midʒ acknowledgement of allegiance as another's man. XIII. ME. *(h)omage* – OF. *(h)omage* (mod. *hommage*) = Pr. *homenatge*, Sp. *homenage* :– medL. *homināticum*, f. *homin-*, *homō* man (rel. to HUMUS); see -AGE.

home houm house, abode (*long home* grave) OE.; native place XIV; one's own place or country XVI (Sh.). OE. *hām* n. collection of dwellings, village, estate, house, corr. to OFris. *hām*, *hēm*, OS. *hēm* (Du. *heem*), (O)HG. *heim* n., ON. *heimr* m., Goth. *haims* fem. village (a more general sense is seen in Goth. *ana|heims* present, *af|haims* absent); the ult. relations of the Germ. base **χaim-* are disputed. The Germ. acc. of direction without prep. (cf. L. *domum*) survives in the advs. OE. *hām*, (O)HG., ON. *heim*.

¶ The primitive sense 'village' survives in traditional place-names in Eng. *-ham*, G. *-heim*. Hence **home** vb. go home. XVIII; whence (of birds) **ho·mer**[1], **ho·ming**. XIX. **ho·mely**[1] †domestic, familiar; plain, simple XIV; uncomely XVI (Sh.). prob. in part an accommodation of ON. *heimligr*; cf. also OFris. *hēmelīk*, OHG. *heim(e)līch* (G. *heimlich*).

homer hou·məɹ Heb. measure of capacity. XVI. – Heb. *χōmer* 'heap'.

Homeric houme·rik pert. to Homer. XVIII. – L. *Homēricus* – Gr. *Homērikós*; see -IC. So †**Home·rical**. XVI.

homicide[1] hɔ·misəid killer of another human being. XIV. – (O)F. *homicide* – L. *homicīda*, f. shortened stem of *homin-*, *homō* man + *-cīda* -CIDE[1]. So **ho·micide**[2] killing of a human being by another. XIV (Ch.). – (O)F. *homicide* – L. *homicīdium*. Hence **homici·dal**[1]. XVIII (Pope).

homily hɔ·mili religious discourse (to be) addressed to a congregation. XIV (Ch.). Late ME. *omelie* – OF. *omelie* (mod. *homélie*) – ecclL. *homilia* – Gr. *homīliā* intercourse, converse, discourse, (eccl.) sermon, f. *hómīlos* crowd, f. *homoû* together + *ilē* crowd, troop; see -Y[3]. Finally assim. to the L. form in XVI. So **homiletic** -e·tik. XVII. – late L. – Gr. *homīlētikós*, f. *homīlētós*, vbl. adj. of *homīleîn* consort or hold converse with, f. *hómīlos*.

hominy hɔ·mini maize boiled with water or milk. XVII (Capt. Smith). acc. to J. H. Trumbull, from Algonquian *appuminnéonash* parched corn, f. *appwóon* he bakes or roasts + *min*, pl. *minneash* fruit, grain, berry.

homo hou·mo(u) man. XVI ('*Homo* is a common name to all men', Sh.). L., rel. to HUMUS. **homo sapiens** sei·pienz (see SAPIENT), the human species.

homo- hɔ·mo(u), hɔmɔ·, before a vowel **hom-**, comb. form of Gr. *homós* SAME; in many techn. terms)(HETERO-. **homogeneous** -dʒī·niəs of the same kind throughout. XVII. f. scholL. *homogeneus*, f. Gr. *homogene-*, *-genḗs*, f. *gene(s)-*, *génos* KIN; earlier **homoge·neal**[1]. So **homogeneity** -ī·iti. XVII. – scholL. **homologous** hŏmɔ·ləgəs corresponding (spec. math. XVII, biol., chem., etc.) XIX; earlier †**homo·logal**[1] XVI (Dee). **homonym** hɔ·mŏnim the same name to denote different things. XVII. – L. *homōnymum* – Gr. *homṓnumon*, n. of *homṓnumos* (see NAME); cf. medL. *homōnymus* namesake. **homophone** hɔ·mŏfoun applied to words pronounced in the same way but differing in meaning XVII (only in dicts. before XIX). – Gr. *homóphōnos* (*phōnḗ* sound).

homœopathy houmiɔ·pəþi system of medical practice in which 'likes are cured by likes'. XIX (*c.*1830). – modL. *homœopathia*, G. *homöopathie*, f. Gr. *hómoios* like + *-pátheia* -PATHY; cf. ALLOPATHY. So **homœopath** hou·miŏpæþ, **homœopathic** hou:miŏpæ·þik. – G. *homöopath*, *-pathisch*; cf. F. *homéopathe*, *-pathie*, *-pathique*.

homoousian hɔmouau·siən, **homou·sian** (theol.) consubstantial)(*heterousian* and *homoi|ousian*. XVI. – late L. *homoūsiānus*, f. *homoūsius* (Jerome) – Gr. *hom(o)oúsios*, f. *homós* SAME + *ousíā* ESSENCE; see -IAN.)(**homoiousian** hɔmoiau·siən of like substance, believing that the Father and the Son in the Godhead are of like substance. XVIII. – late L. f. Gr. *homoioúsios*, f. *hómoios* like.

homunculus hɔmʌ·ŋkjŭləs diminutive man. XVII. L., dim. of *homō* man; see -CLE.

hone houn whetstone. XIV. spec. use of OE. *hān* stone (often one serving as a landmark) = ON. *hein* :– Germ. **χainō*, prob. to be referred to the same base as Gr. *kônos* CONE, Skr. *çāṇas*, and L. *cōs*, *cōt-* whetstone.

honest ɔ·nist marked by uprightness or probity; †comely, decent XIII (Cursor M.); †honourable, respectable; †chaste XIV. ME. *onest(e)* – OF. *(h)oneste* (mod. *honnête*) = Pr., Sp. *honesto*, It. *onesto* – L. *honestus*, f. **hones-*, *honōs* HONOUR. So **ho·nesty**[3]. XIV (R. Rolle, R. Mannyng, Barbour, Ch.). – OF. *(h)onesté* = Sp. *honestad*, It. *onestà* – L. *honestās*, for **honestitās* (-TY); as a name of the plant Lunaria biennis (XVI, Gerarde) the ref. is to its semi-transparent seed-pods.

honey hʌ·ni sweet fluid collected from flowers by bees OE.; sweetheart XIV; sweetness XVI (Sh.). OE. *huniġ* = OFris. *hunig*, OS. *honeg*, *-ig*, OHG. *honag*, *-ang* (Du., G. *honig*), ON. *hunang* :– CGerm. (exc. Gothic, which has *miliþ* = Gr. *melit-*, *méli*) **χuna(ŋ)-gam*. The sp. with *o* (apart from its use as a graphic var. of *u* next to *n*) points to a widespread ME. form *hōni* (whence Sc. *hinny*, like *brither*, *mither*, from *brōther*, *mōther*). Hence **ho·neycomb**. OE. *huniġcamb*. **ho·neymoon** first month after marriage XVI (J. Heywood); expl. by early writers with ref. to affection of married people changing with the moon. **ho·neysuckle** clover XIII; woodbine, Lonicera XVI. ME. *hunisuccle*, *-soukel*, extension of *hunisuce*, *-souke* (surviving dial.), OE. *huniġsūce*, *-sūge* (f. *sūcan*, *sūgan* SUCK). **honeyed**[1], **honied** hʌ·nid sweetened as with honey. XIV (Ch.).

honk hɔŋk (U.S. and Canada) cry of the wild goose XIX (Thoreau); noise made by a motor-horn XX. imit. Cf. *honc*, earlier *cohonc* (XVIII), N. Amer. Indian name for a wild goose.

honorarium ɔnərɛə·riəm fee for services rendered. XVII (Evelyn). L., gift made on being admitted to a post of honour, sb. use of n. of *honōrārius*, whence **ho·norary**. XVII (Selden). So **honori·fic** conferring honour. XVII. – L. *honōrificus* (Cicero).

honour, U.S. **honor** ɔ·nəɹ renown, reputation XII; high rank or dignity XIII; high respect or esteem; chastity XIV; upright character XVI. ME. *(h)onur, (h)onour, an(o)ur* – AN. *anur, -our,* OF. *(h)onor, (h)onur,* earlier *enor* (mod. *honneur*) = Pr. *enor,* Sp. *honor,* It. *onore* :- L. *honōrem,* nom. *honor,* earlier *honōs* (cf. HONEST). So **ho·nour** vb. XIII. – OF. *onorer, onurer* (F. *honorer*) :- L. *honōrāre,* f. *honōr-.* **ho·nour**ABLE. XV (as an honorific prefix). – (O)F. – L. (Cicero).

honved hɔ·nved Hungarian army in the revolutionary war of 1848–9; (later) militia reserve. XIX. Magyar, f. *hon* home + *ved* defence, corr. to G. *heimwehr.*

hoo hū int. XVII (Sh.) var. of WHOO.

hooch hūtʃ (U.S.) alcoholic liquor, spirits. XX. abbrev. of Alaskan *hoochinoo,* name of tribe that made such liquor.

hood hud soft covering for head and neck. OE. *hōd* = OFris. *hōd,* MDu. *hoet* (Du. *hoed*), OHG. *huot* (G. *hut* hat) :- WGerm. **χōda,* rel. to HAT. Hence **hoo·d**MAN hooded man XVI; blindfolded player in *hoodman-blind,* the older name of *blindman's buff.* **hood**WINK hu·dwiŋk cover the eyes to prevent vision XVI; fig. XVII.

-hood hud OE. *-hād* = OS. *-hēd,*(O)HG. *-heit,* orig. a CGerm. independent sb. meaning 'person', 'sex', 'condition, rank', 'quality', OE. *hād,* OS. *hēd,* OHG. *heit,* ON. *heiðr* (honour, worth), Goth. *haidus* (kind, manner), rel. to ON. *heið* bright sky, Skr. *kētúś* brightness, *kḗtas* form, shape, sign. The transition from independent status to that of suffix is illustrated by the coexistence of OE. *fǣmnan hād* and *fǣmnhād* virginity. This suffix may be added freely to most sbs. denoting a person or a concrete thing to express its condition or state, as OE. *ċildhād* childhood, *prēosthād* priesthood; it lends itself readily to nonce-formations, e.g. *doghood, I-hood, soulhood.* It has been added to a few adjs., e.g. *falsehood, hardihood* (Milton), *likelihood,* †*lustihood,* which superseded formations with the parallel -HEAD. Where comps. in *-head* and *-hood* survive side by side, as in *godhead* and *godhood, maidenhead* and *maidenhood,* there is differentiation of meaning. *Livelihood* is the result of perversion. A few comps. have developed particularized or semi-concrete meanings, as *brotherhood, knighthood, neighbourhood, sisterhood.*

hoodlum hu·dləm (U.S. sl.) street rowdy or loafer. XIX (*c.*1870 in San Francisco). Of unkn. origin.

hoodoo hū·dū (U.S.). XIX (*c.*1880). unexpl. alteration of VOODOO.

hoof hūf pl. *hoofs, hooves* (hūvz) horny growth on the feet of horses, etc. OE. *hōf* = OFris., OS. *hōf* (Du. *hoef*), OHG. *huof* (G. *huf*), ON. *hófr* :- CGerm. **χōfaz* (exc. Gothic), rel. to synon. Skr. *śaphás,* Av. *safa.*

hook huk bent length of metal, etc., for catching hold or hanging. OE. *hōc* = OFris., MLG., MDu. *hōk* (Du. *hoek*) corner, angle, point of land (cf. ON. *hœkja* crutch), rel. to OE. *haca* bolt, OS. *haco* (MDu. *hake,* Du. *haak*), OHG. *hāko* (G. *haken*) hook, ON. *haki* (whence, or from MDu., dial. *hake* XV); Russ. *kógot'* claw, iron hook; cf. HANK. Hence **hook** vb. †bend, curve XIII; attach (as) with a hook XVI.

hookah hu·kə Eastern tobacco-pipe. XVIII. – Urdu – Arab. *ḥuqqah* casket, vase, cup, bottle containing water through which the tobacco-smoke is drawn, in Urdu extended to the whole apparatus.

hooker hu·kəɹ two-masted Dutch vessel XVII; one-masted fishing-smack XIX. – Du. *hoeker,* f. *hoek* HOOK (in earlier *hoekboot*); see -ER[1].

hooligan hū·ligən (young) street rough. *c.* 1898. Said to be f. the name of a rowdy Irish family in London.

hoop[1] hūp circle of metal, etc. XII. Late OE. *hōp* = OFris. *hōp,* MDu. *hoop* (Du. *hoep*) :- Germ. (of the LG. area) **χōpaz,* rel. to ON. *hóp* small land-locked bay.

hoop[2] hūp utter a cry of 'hoop'. XIV (PPl., Ch.). Late ME. *houpe, howpe* – (O)F. *houper,* f. *houp* (imit.). Hence *hooping* (later *whooping*)*-cough.* XVIII. Cf. WHOOP.

hooray hurei·, var. of HURRAH. XIX.

hop[1] hɔp spring on one foot. OE. *hoppian,* corr. to (M)HG. *hopfen,* ON. *hoppa,* f. a base repr. also in OE. *hoppetan,* G. *hopsen,* and prob. cogn. with synon. OSl. *kŭpěti.* Hence **ho·pp**ER[1] creature that hops XIII; part of a grinding-mill having orig. a hopping movement XIV (Ch.).

hop[2] hɔp (ripened cone(s) of) the female hop-plant, Humulus Lupulus. XV (*hoppe*). – MLG., MDu. *hoppe* (Du. *hop*), in OS. *feld|hoppo* = late OHG. *hopfo* (G. *hopfen*). The OE. word was *hymele* = MLG. *homele,* ONorw. *humli* – OSl. *chŭmeli.* ¶ MedL. *huppa, humulus,* Finn. *humala,* and F. *houblon* are from German.

hope[1] houp expectation of something desired. Late OE. *hopa,* also *tōhopa,* corr. to OLG. *tōhopa,* OFris., MLG., MDu. *hope* (Du. *hoop*). Also **hope** vb. Late OE. *hopian* = OFris. *hopia,* (M)Du. *hopen.* Not in OHG.; first in MHG. *hoffe, hoffen*; orig. words belonging to LG. areas, whence they spread to HG. and Scand. (Sw. *hopp, hoppa,* Da. *haab, haabe*); of unkn. origin.

hope[2] houp (Sc. and north. Eng.) piece of enclosed land OE.; small enclosed valley XIV; (from MLG.) inlet, haven XV. Late OE. *hop* = MLG. *hop* (in place-names), MDu. *hop* bay; ult. origin disputed.

hoplite hɔ·plait heavy-armed foot-soldier. XVIII. – F. *hoplite* – Gr. *hoplī́tēs,* f. *hóplon* weapon, pl. *hópla* arms; see -ITE.

hopscotch hɔ·pskɔtʃ children's game of hopping over a pattern of lines. XIX. f. HOP[1] + SCOTCH scored line or mark; earlier †*scotch-hoppers* (XVII), †*hop-scot* (XVIII).

horary hɔ̄·rəri relating to the hours. XVII. – medL. *hōrārius*, f. *hōra* HOUR; see -ARY.

horde hɔ̄ɹd tribe or band of Tartar nomads XVI (*horda, hord*); great troop, gang XVII. – Pol. *horda* (whence F., G., Du. *horde*, Sw. *hord*), corr. to Russ. *ordá*, It., Rum. *orda*; all ult. – Turki *ordī, ordū* camp (see URDU).

horehound, hoarhound hɔ̄ə·ɹhaund the plant Marrubium vulgare, characterized by a white downy pubescence. OE. *hāre hūne*, f. *hār* HOAR + *hūne* 'marrubium', of unkn. origin. For the parasitic *d* cf. ASTOUND, BOUND[2], SOUND[2].

horizon hərai·zən line at which earth and sky appear to meet XIV (Ch., Trevisa, Gower); fig. XVII. Late ME. *orizont(e), orizon* – OF. *orizonte, orizon* (mod. *horizon*) = Sp. *horizonte*, It. *orizonte* – late L. *horīzont-*, nom. *-ōn* – Gr. *horízōn*, sb. use (sc. *kúklos* circle) of prp. of *horízein* bound, limit, define (cf. AORIST) f. *hóros* boundary, limit. In later OF. and Eng. conformed to the L. nom.; in early use stressed on the initial syll. So **horizont**AL[1] hɔrizɔ·ntəl pert. to the horizon XVI; parallel to the plane of the horizon XVII. – F. or modL.

horn hɔ̄ɹn bony excrescence (often curved and pointed) on the head of cattle, etc.; instrument made from or in imitation of this OE.; pointed projection XIII; substance of it XV. OE. *horn* m., corr. to OFris., OS. *horn* m., OHG., ON. *horn* n. (Du., G. *horn*), Goth. *haurn* n. :– CGerm. **χornaz*, **χornam*, rel. to L. *cornū* (whence Celtic *corn*, F. *corne*; see CORN[2]), Skr. *çr̥ṅgam*, and further to Gr. *kéras* (see HART). **horn**BLENDE hɔ̄·ɹnblend (min.). XVIII. – G. **ho·rn**BOOK ABC tablet covered with horn. XVI (Sh.).

hornet hɔ̄·ɹnit insect of the wasp family. The present form appears XV, succeeding to earlier *hernet, harnet*, prob. all – MLG. *hornte*, MDu. *hornte, hornete*, corr. to OE. *hyrnet, hyrnetu*, earlier *hurnitu, hirnitu*, OS. *hornut*, OHG. *hornuz* (G. *hornisse*), which have the appearance of derivs. of HORN (cf. OS. *hornobero* 'horn-bearer', hornet); see -ET.

hornito hɔ̄ɹnī·tou low oven-shaped volcanic mound. XIX. Sp., dim. of *horno* (:– L. *furnus*) oven, FURNACE.

horologe hɔ·rəlɔdʒ timepiece, clock. XIV (Wycl. Bible, Ch.). – OF. *orloge, oriloge* (mod. *horloge*) = Pr. *reloge*, Sp. *reloj*, It. *orologio* :– L. *hōrologium* – Gr. *hōrólogion*, f. *hōrológos*, f. *hṓrā* time, HOUR + *-logos* telling (see -LOGUE). Also **horologium** -lou·dʒiəm, -lɔ·dʒiəm †horologe XVII; (Gr. Ch.) book containing the canonical hours XVIII. L.

horoscope hɔ·rəskoup plan showing the disposition of the heavens at a particular moment. XVI (earlier in L. form). – (O)F. *horoscope* – L. *hōroscopus* – Gr. *hōroskópos* sign in the ascendant at a birth, horoscope, f. *hṓrā* time, HOUR + *skopós* observer (cf. SCOPE).

horrible hɔ·rĭbl exciting horror. XIV. – OF. *(h)orrible* – L. *horribilis*, f. *horrēre* (of hair) stand on end, tremble, shudder; see -IBLE. So **ho·rr**ID[1] bristling, shaggy, rough XVI (Spenser); horrible XVII (Sh.). **ho·rr**OR[2] emotion combining loathing and fear. XIV. – OF. *(h)orrour* (mod. *-eur*) = Pr., Sp. *horror*, It. *orrore* – L. *horrōrem*, nom. *horror*.

horripilation hɔːripilei·ʃən 'goose-flesh'. XVII. – late L. (Vulgate) *horripilātiō(n-)*, f. *horripilāre*, f. *horrēre* (see prec.) + *pilus* hair; see -ATION.

hors d'œuvre (h)ɔ̄ɹdɔ̄·vr dish served as a relish at a meal. XVIII (Pope). F., something out of the ordinary course, prop. 'outside of work'; the els. of the phr. repr. L. *forīs* out of doors, abroad, *dē* of, from, *opera* work. ¶ The usual Eng. pl. *hors d'œuvres* is non-French.

horse hɔ̄ɹs the quadruped Equus caballus OE.; contrivance whose use suggests the service of a horse (cf. CHEVAL-GLASS) XIV (Ch.), XVI. OE. *hors* n. = OFris. *hors, hars, hers*, OS. *hros, hers* (MLG. *ros, ors*, MDu. *ors*, Du. *ros*), OHG. *(h)ros* (MHG. *ros, ors*, G. *ross*) n., ON. *hross* m. :– CGerm. (exc. Gothic) **χorsam*, **χorsaz*, of unkn. origin. The Germ. word was orig. neuter (like *deer, sheep, swine*) and applicable to male and female; OE. nom. sg. and pl. were identical, but pl. *horses* appears in early XIII; the uninflected form survives for 'horse soldiers, cavalry'. In attrib. use often denoting coarseness, roughness, or large size, as *horse chestnut* (XVI; cf. bot. L. *Castanea equina*, G. *rosskastanie*), *laugh* (XVIII), *leech* (XV), *mackerel* (XVII), *mint* (XIII), *play* (XVI), *radish* (XVII). Hence **horse** vb. OE. *horsian*.

¶ The CIE. word is repr. by OE. *eoh* (Runic name), OS. *ehu|skalk*, ON. *jór*, Goth. *aihwa-*, L. *equus*, Gr. *híppos*, OS. *aspa*, Skr. *áçvas*, Lith. *ašvà*, OIr. *ech*, W. *ep* :– **ekwos*.

hortatory hɔ̄·ɹtətəri pertaining to exhortation. – late L. *hortātōrius*, f. *hortāt-*, pp. stem of *hortārī* EXHORT; see -ORY.

horticulture hɔ̄·ɹtikʌltʃəɹ cultivation of gardens. XVII. f. L. *hortus* garden (see YARD[2]), after AGRICULTURE.

hosanna houzæ·nə Jewish liturgical formula, adopted in Christian worship. In OE. and ME. *osanna*, later *hosanna* (Tindale) – late L. *(h)ōsanna* – Gr. *(h)ōsanná* – Heb. *hōshaʿnā*, abbrev. of *hōshīʿāhnnā* save, pray!

hose houz A. article of clothing for the leg OE.; B. flexible pipe for conveying liquid XV. Late OE. *hosa, -e* = OS., OHG., ON. *hosa* (Du. *hoos* stocking, water-hose, G. *hose*) :– CGerm. (exc. Gothic) **χuson, -ōn* (whence Rom. forms, OF. *huese*, OSp. *huesa*, It. *uosa*). Sense B is prob. from Du. Celtic forms are from Eng. Hence **hos**IER[1] hou·ʒ[1]əɹ maker of or dealer in hose. XV.

hospice hɔ·spis house of rest, 'home'. XIX. – (O)F. *hospice* – L. *hospitium* hospitality, lodging, f. *hospit-*, *hospes* HOST[2].

hospital hɔ·spitəl (hist.) hostel, hospice XIII; asylum for the destitute or infirm XV; institution for the care of the sick XVI. – OF. *hospital* (mod. *hôpital*). – medL. *hospitāle*, sb. use of n. of *hospitālis*, f. *hospit-*; see prec. and -AL[1]. Cf. HOSTEL, HÔTEL, SPITAL. So **hospita·l**ITY. XIV. – (O)F. – L. **hosp·it**ABLE affording hospitality. XVI. f. medL. *hospitāre* receive as a guest, f. *hospit-*, HOST[2]. **ho·spitall**ER[2] member of certain charitable religious orders XIV; spiritual officer of a hospital XVI. – OF. *hospitalier* – medL. *hospitālārius*, f. *hospitāle*; see HOSTEL.

hospodar hɔ·spŏdā·ɹ governor in Wallachia and Moldavia. XVII. – Rum. *hospodár* – Little Russ. *hospodár'* = Russ. *gospodár'*, f. *gospód'* lord.

host[1] houst (arch.) army XIII; *h—s of heaven*, *Lord* (*God*) *of h—s* (see SABAOTH) XIV (Wycl. Bible); great company, large number XVII. – OF. (*h*)*ost*, (*h*)*oost* = Pr. *ost*, Sp. *hueste*, It. *oste*, Rum. *oaste* :– L. *hosti-s* stranger, enemy, in medL. army; see GUEST. ¶ The L. *h*, lost in Rom., was restored in OF. and ME. sp., and the aspirate was established in Eng. pronunc.

host[2] houst man who lodges and entertains XIII; (biol.) animal or plant having a parasite XIX (Ray Lankester, tr. G. *wirth*). – OF. (*h*)*oste* (mod. *hôte*) = Pr. *oste*, Sp. *huesped*, It. *ospite*, Rum. *oaspete* :– L. *hospitem*, nom. *hospes* host, prob. f. *hostis* (see prec.). So **host**ESS[1] hou·stis. XIII. – OF. *ostesse* (mod. *hôtesse*). For sp. and pronunc. cf. prec.

host[3] houst †victim, sacrifice; Eucharistic wafer. XIV. – OF. (*h*)*oiste* :– L. *hostia* victim, sacrifice.

hostage hɔ·stidʒ †pledge given for the fulfilment of an undertaking by the handing over of a person; person thus held in pledge. XIII. – (O)F. *ostage*, *hostage* (mod. *otage*) = Pr. *ostatge*, OSp. *hostage*, It. *ostaggio* :– Rom. **obsidāticum*, f. late L. *obsidātus* hostageship, f. *obsid-*, *obses* hostage, f. *ob* OB- + **sed-* SIT; see -AGE. The initial *h* was induced by assim. to the words connected with HOST[2].

hostel hɔ·stəl †place of sojourn, lodging XIII; public place of lodging XIV (Ch.); students' house of residence XVI. – OF. (*h*)*ostel* (mod. *hôtel* HÔTEL) = Pr., Sp. *hostal* :– medL. *hospitāle* HOSPITAL. So **hostel**RY (h)ɔ·slri inn, hostel XIV. (Ch.). – OF. (*h*)*ostelerie* (mod. *hôtellerie*), f. (*h*)*ostelier*; see OSTLER.

hostile hɔ·stail pert. to an enemy, engaged in warfare XVI (Sh.); unfriendly, inimical XVIII. – F. *hostile* or L. *hostīlis*, f. *hostis* enemy; see HOST[1], -ILE. So **hostil**ITY -i·lĭti. XVI (Elyot). – F. or late L.

host(e)ler see OSTLER.

hot hɔt of high temperature, very warm. OE. *hāt* = OFris., OS. *hēt* (Du. *heet*), OHG. *heiȝ* (G. *heiss*), ON. *heitr* :– CGerm. **χaitaz* (exc. Goth., but see HEAT). The typical ME. form was *hǭt*, *hoot*, with compar. *hătter*, *hŏtter* (:– OE. *hăttra*); the *ŏ* of the compar. and superl. *hŏtter*, *hŏttest* appears to have been established in the positive in XVI (as is shown by the sp. *hott*(*e*) and the jingle *Little potte soone whot*). ¶ For *hot-short* see under COLD-SHORT.

hotchkiss hɔ·tʃkis machine-gun and rifle named after the inventor, B. B. *Hotchkiss*. 1880.

hotch-pot hɔ·tʃpɔt mixture, medley XIV (Ch.), spec. in cookery XV; (leg.) collation of properties to secure equality of division XVI. – AN., (O)F. *hochepot*, f. *hocher* shake, prob. of LG. origin + *pot* POT. Altered by rhyming assim. to **ho·tchpotch** XV (*hoche poche*), and further to †*hogpoch* (XV), †*hogepotche* (XVI), †*hodge-potch* (XVI–XVII), **hodge-podge** hɔ·dʒpɔdʒ XVII.

hôtel, hotel houte·l, oute·l large †private or public residence XVII; house for entertainment of strangers and travellers XVIII. – F. *hôtel*, later form of *hostel*; see HOSTEL.

Hottentot hɔ·təntɔt member of a native S. African race. XVII. – Du. Afrikaans *Hottentot*, also †*Ottentot*, †*Hottentoo*, acc. to an early account, imit. word to denote stammering or stuttering, with ref. to the abrupt pronunc. and 'clicks' of the language; early vars. were *Hodmandod*, *Hodmodod*, *Hodmontot* (XVII–XVIII). ¶ Native names for the race were *Khoi-Khoim* 'men of men', *Quae Quae*, *Kwekhena*, *t'Kuhkeub*.

hough hɔk quadruped's hock XIV; leg of beef, etc. XV; hollow behind man's knee-joint XVI (Sc.). ME. *hoȝ*, *houȝ*, prob. f. shortened first el. of OE. *hōhsinu* hamstring, tendon of Achilles (corr. to ON. *hásin*), f. *hōh* heel + *sinu* sinew. Cf. HOCK[2].

hound haund dog (also fig.) OE.; dog kept for the chase XIII; applied contemptuously to a person. OE. *hund* = OFris., OS. *hund* (Du. *hond*), OHG. *hunt* (G. *hund*), ON. *hundr*, Goth. *hunds* :– CGerm. **χundaz* :– **kwntós*, f. IE. **kwn-*, repr. by (O)Ir. *cú* (g. *con*), Gr. *kúōn* (g. *kunós*), Lith. *szuõ* (g. *šuñs*), Arm. *šun*, Skr. *çvās* (g. *çúnas*), Toch. *ku*, and (obscurely) rel. to L. *canis*. ¶ Superseded in gen. sense by *dog*.

hour auəɹ 60 minutes; one of the twelve points on a dial; canonical service of prayer; occasion. XIII. ME. *ure*, *our*(*e*), later *hour*(*e*) – AN. *ure*, OF. *ore*, *eure* (mod. *heure*) = Pr., It. *ora*, Sp. *hora*, Rum. *oară* :– L. *hōra* – Gr. *hṓrā* season, time of day, hour (cf. YEAR); repl. OE. *tīd* TIDE and *stund*. ¶ The latinized sp. with *h-* has not influenced the pronunc., as it has in *herb*, *humble*, *humour*.

houri huə·ri nymph of the Mohammedan paradise. XVIII. – F. *houri* – Pers. *ḥūrī*, f. Arab. *ḥūr*, pl. of *ḥaurā'*; in *ḥūr-al-'ayūn* (females) gazelle-like in the eyes, f. *ḥawira* be black-eyed like the gazelle.

house haus, pl. *houses* hau·ziz building for human habitation, occupation, or worship; household, family OE.; building for a specific activity of a body of people XVI. OE. *hūs* = OFris., OS., OHG. *hūs* (Du. *huis*, G. *haus*), ON. *hús*, Goth. *hūs* (only in *gudhūs* temple) :- CGerm. **χūsam*, of unkn. origin. So **house** hauz put in or receive into a house. OE. *hūsian* = MLG., MDu. *hūsen*, OHG. *hūsōn* (Du. *huizen*, G. *hausen*), ON. *húsa*; f. the sb. Hence **hou·sehold** †contents, etc., of a house XIV (Wycl. Bible); inmates of a house coll. XIV (Maund., Usk); †housekeeping XV (Caxton) – MDu. *huushoud* (cf. HOLD sb.). **housewife** hau·swaif mistress of the household XIII (AncrR.); †HUSSY XVI; HUSSIF XVIII. ME. *hūsewīf*, later *hŭswyfe*, *huswife* (– XVII), f. HOUSE + WIFE. Hence **hou·sewife**RY. XV (*huswyfery*, Promp. Parv.), †-SHIP. XIII (AncrR.).

housel hau·zl (arch.) consecrated host at the Eucharist; holy communion. OE. *hūsl* (whence ON. *húsl*) = Goth. *hunsl* sacrifice, *θυσία*; of unkn. origin.

housings hau·ziŋz cloth covering, esp. for a horse. XIV. f. synon. ME. *house* XIV (in AL. *hu(s)cia* XIII) – OF. *houce* (mod. *housse*) – medL. *hultia* for **hulftia* – Germ. **χulftī* (MDu. *hulfte* pocket for bow and arrow. MHG. *hulft* covering); see -ING[1].

houyhnhnm ʍi·nm combination of letters intended to symbolize a horse's neigh, invented by Swift in 'Gulliver's Travels' (1726) as the name of a race of beings described as horses endowed with reason. Cf. YAHOO.

hovel hɔ·vl, hʌ·vl shed XV; rude dwelling-place XVII. The earliest exx. are from easterly areas; perh. of LG. origin, but no corr. form is known.

hover hɔ·vəɹ, hʌ·vəɹ remain suspended in the air. XIV. frequent. f. synon. ME. *hove* hover, tarry, linger (from XIII), of unkn. origin; see -ER[4].

how[1] hau in what way, by what means. OE. *hū* = OFris. *hū*, *hō*, OS. *(h)wō*, *hwuo* (MLG. *woe*, Du. *hoe*), OHG. *wuo* :- WGerm. **χwō*, adv. formation on **χwa*- WHO, WHAT. ¶ A different synon. formation is repr. by OHG. *(h)wio* (G. *wie*), Goth. *hwaiwa*. Hence **how-beit** haubī·it (arch.) however IT may BE, †conj. although (XIV), formerly with corr. pt. †*how were it* (cf. ALBEIT). **howe**·VER (XIV), **how**SOE·VER (XV), superseded †*how so* (XIII), (dial.) *how*SOME·VER (XIII).

how[2] hau (local) hill, mount, tumulus. – ON. *haugr*, f. Germ. **χauχ*- HIGH.

howdah hau·də seat erected on an elephant's back. XVIII. – Urdu, Pers. *haudah* – Arab. *haudaj* litter carried by camel or elephant.

howitzer hau·itsəɹ short piece of ordnance for high-angle firing. XVI. – Du. *houwitser*; superseding synon. †*howitz* (XVII); both – G. *haubitze*, †*hau(f)enitz*, introduced into German during the Hussite wars – Czech *houfnice* stone-sling, catapult. ¶ The G. word is also the source of F. *obus* †howitzer (now *obusier*), shell, It.*obice*, Sp. *obus*.

howl haul utter a prolonged, loud, doleful cry. XIV (Ch., Gower). corr. to MLG., MDu. *hūlen* (Du. *huilen*), MHG. *hiulen*, *hiuweln*, rel. to OHG. *hūwila* (MHG. *hiuwel*) owl; perh. immed. f. ME. *hūle* (XIII), later *howle* OWL (cf. also L. *ululāre* howl, *ulula* owl, Gr. *hulân* bark).

howlet see OWLET.

hoy[1] hoi cry to excite attention (naut. in hailing or calling aloft). XIV (PPl.). Cf. AHOY.

hoy[2] hoi small sailing-vessel. XV. – MDu. *hoei*, var. of *hoede*, *heude* (mod. *heu*), of unkn. origin.

hoya hoi·ə genus of climbing herbaceous plants. XIX. modL., f. name of Thomas *Hoy*, Eng. gardener + L. fem. suffix -A[1].

hoyden hoi·dn †rude fellow, boor XVI (Nashe); boisterous girl XVII. prob. – (M)Du. *heiden* HEATHEN, gipsy.

hub hʌb nave of a wheel. XVII. prob. identical with HOB[2], of which *hub(be)* is the earliest form, the basic meaning being perh. 'lump, mass'. ¶ Its transf. use (e.g. *hub of the universe*) is mainly due to O. W. Holmes ('Boston State-House is the hub of the solar system', 1858).

hubble-bubble hʌ·blbʌ:bl kind of hookah in which the smoke bubbles through water in a coco-nut shell XVII; bubbling sound XVIII. Rhyming jingle on BUBBLE.

hubbub hʌ·bʌb confused noise, as of shouting XVI (*an yrishe whobub*; *Irish hooboobbes*; *the hobub or the hue and crie*); noisy disturbance XVII. Of Ir. origin; cf. Ir. *abú* used in battle-cries, and Gael. *ub! ubub!* int. of aversion or contempt, *ubh*, *ubh* int. of disgust or amazement. So **hubbuboo** hʌbəbū· XVI (*the Irish hubbabowe*, Spenser).

hubby hʌ·bi colloq. (now vulgar or joc.) for HUSBAND. XVII; see -Y[6].

hubris hjū·bris (academic sl.) wanton insolence. XIX. Gr., with traditional Eng. pronunc.; repr. also by latinized **hybris** hai·bris. XX. So **hubri**·STIC.

huckaback hʌ·kəbæk stout linen fabric with a rough surface. XVII. (Also †*hugaback*, †*hag-a-bag*.) Of unkn. origin.

huckleberry hʌ·klbe:ri (U.S.) low berry-bearing shrub. XVII. prob. alteration of *hurtleberry*, WHORTLEBERRY.

hucklebone hʌ·klboun hip-bone, haunch-bone. XVI. f. *huckle* (XVI), dim. (see -LE[1]) of *huck*; parallel with *huck-bone*, late ME. *hoke-bone* (XV), Sc. *hukebane* (Dunbar), north. dial. *heukbeean*; perh. to be referred ult. to **hūk*-, as repr. in MLG., MDu. *hūken*, *hukken* sit bent, crouch.

huckster hʌ·kstəɹ petty tradesman. xii (*huccstere*, Orm). The earliest repr. of a group based on **huk-*, prob. of LG. origin (but MDu. *hoeker*, *hoekster* hawker, retailer, are not recorded so early), other members being *huckstery* (†*hoxsterye*, †*huckustrye*, also *hokkerie*, etc., PPl.), dial. *huck* vb. (xv), †*hukker* sb. (xiii), *hucker* vb. (xvi); see -STER.

huddle hʌ·dl †conceal; pile or push together in disorderly fashion; crowd together confusedly. xvi. First recorded from G. Harvey and contemp. with †*huddle* adv. confusedly (Coverdale) and prp. *huddling* (Drant; *hudling Horace*, with ref. to L. *satira* hotch-potch); perh. of LG. origin and ult. f. **hūd-* HIDE[3]; see -LE[3].

Hudibrastic hjūdibræ·stik burlesque-heroic like the 'Hudibras' of Samuel Butler (1663–78). xviii. f. *Hudibras* (taken over from Spenser's 'Faerie Queene' ii ii 17), after *fantastic*.

hue hjū †form, aspect; colour. OE. *hēw*, *hēow* form, shape, appearance, colour, beauty = ON. *hý* down on plants (Sw. *hy* skin, complexion), Goth. *hiwi* form, appearance :- Germ. **χiujam*, of unkn. origin.

hue and cry hjūənᵈkrai· outcry calling for the pursuit of a felon. xvi. – legal AN. *hu e cri*, i.e. *hu* outcry (f. *huer* shout, of imit. origin), *e* and, *cri* CRY.

huff hʌf †blow, puff xvi; †bully; (at draughts) remove (an opponent's man) as a penalty (the removal being marked by blowing on the piece; so Sc. *blaw*, G. *blasen*, F. *souffler*). xvii. imit. of the sound of blowing or puffing. Hence **huff** sb. †puff of wind; †gust of anger; fit of petulance. xviii.

hug hʌg clasp tightly. xvi. prob. of Scand. origin; cf. ON. (Norw.) *hugga* comfort, console, rel. to *hugr* thought, feeling, interest, *hugð* interest, affection, *hugsa* think, OE. *hyge* mind, heart, mood, *hogian* think (about), be intent (on), *hogu* solicitude, OFris. *hei*, OS. *hugi*, OHG. *hugu*, OE. *hyċġan* think, etc.

huge hjūdʒ very large or bulky. xiii. ME. *huge*, *hoge*, *howge*, aphetic – OF. *ahuge*, *ahoge*, *ahoege*, of unkn. origin.

hugger-mugger hʌ·gəɹmʌ:gəɹ secrecy xvi; disorder, confusion xvii. Preceded by similar rhyming jingles, *hucker mucker* or *moker* (xvi), and *hoder moder* (xv); prob. based on (dial.) *mucker*, ME. *mokere* hoard, and ME. *hoder* huddle, wrap up; ult. origin unkn.

Huguenot hjū·gənət French Protestant. xvi. – F. *huguenot*, alteration, by assim. to the name of a Geneva burgomaster, Besançon *Hugues*, of †*eiguenot*, pl. †*aignos*, †*huguenaulx* – Du. *eedgenoot* – Swiss G. *eidgenoss* confederate, f. *eid* OATH + *genoss* associate = OE. *ġenēat* companion (CGerm. **ga-* Y- + **naut-* NEAT[1], 'pasturing cattle together').

huh hʌ excl. of suppressed feeling. xvii.

hulk hʌlk A. ship, esp. large ship of burden OE.; body of a dismantled ship (cf. SHEER-*hulk*) xvii (Dryden); B. big unwieldy person xvi (Sh.). Late OE. *hulc*, prob. reinforced in ME. from MLG. *hulk*, *holk(e)*, MDu. *hulc*, *-ke* (Du. *hulk*) = OHG. *holcho* (G. *holk*, *hulk*), whence OF. *hulque*, *hurque*; prob. a Mediterranean word (cf. Gr. *holkás* cargo ship, f. *hélkein* draw, and the derived medL. *hulcus*, *-a*, *-um*).

hull[1] hʌl (dial.) shell of pease and beans. Late OE. *hulu*, f. wk. grade of *helan* cover (cf. HELL, HELM[1]), whence also OE. *hylma*, OHG. *hulla* mantle, head-covering (G. *hülle*) :- **χuljō*, and Du. *huls*, OHG. *hulsa* (G. *hülse* husk, pod) :- **χulisō*.

hull[2] hʌl body or frame of a ship. xv (*hoole*, *hole*, *holle*, Promp. Parv.), perh. sb. use of *hol* HOLLOW, but the transf. from the interior to the exterior of the vessel is a difficulty.

hullaballoo hʌ:ləbəlū· tumultuous noise. xviii (*hollo-ballo*, Smollett). First recorded from northerly sources; occurs with a great variety of forms in the first el., viz. *hollo-*, *halloo-*, *hallo-*, *holli-*, *hulla-*, which corr. to those of the ints. HALLOO, HOLLA, HULLO; the addition of the jingle may have been suggested by *hurlyburly*.

hullo(a) həlou· var. of HALLO, HILLO, HOLLO. xix.

hum hʌm make a low inarticulate murmuring sound. xiv (Ch.). imit.; cf. MHG. (G. dial.) *hummen*, and G. *summen*, *brummen*, Du. *brommen*. Also as int. xvi (Sh.), of very various significance.

human hjū·mən pert. to man. xiv (Trevisa). In earliest use *humain(e)*, *-ayn(e)* – (O)F. *humain*, fem. *-aine* = Sp. *humano*, It. *umano* :- L. *hūmānus*, rel. to *homō* man (cf. HUMBLE); see -AN. The sp. *humane* persisted in gen. use till early xviii, but the form *human* (based directly on L.) occurs in late xvii (Dryden). The variant **humane** hjūmei·n, with differentiated pronunc., became restricted during xviii for the senses (i) characterized by disposition or behaviour befitting a man (formerly spec. †gentle, courteous xv–xvi), and (ii) pert. to studies that tend to humanize or refine (xvii). So **hu·man**ISM †belief in the mere human nature of Christ xix (Coleridge 1812); devotion to human interests or the humanities (*c.* 1830); after **hu·man**IST one devoted to the humanities xvi (earlier †*humanitian*, Holinshed, Jonson) – F. *humaniste* – It. *umanista*. **human**ITY hjumæ·niti humane disposition or conduct xiv (Wycl. Bible, Ch.); human quality or attributes xv (Lydg.; mankind xvi); polite learning, spec. (and from xviii pl.) the ancient Greek and Latin classics, literæ humaniores xv (Caxton; depending on uses of F. *humanité*, It. *umanità*, and ult. L. *hūmānitās* liberal education, as used by Cicero, Aulus Gellius, etc.). – (O)F. – L. Hence **humanit**A·RIAN one who affirms the humanity of Christ xix (Moore); one devoted to humane action or the welfare of the human race *c.* 1830. **hu·man**IZE. xvii (Holland). – F. *humaniser*.

humble hʌ·mbl having a low estimate of oneself XIII; of lowly condition XIV (Ch.). ME. (*h*)*umble* – OF. *umble*, (also mod.) *humble* – L. *humili-s* low, lowly, mean, base, f. *humus* ground, earth, rel. to *homō* man; cf. HUMILIATE, etc. Hence **hu·mble** vb. XIV. ¶ The pronunc. ʌ·mbl, repr. the original, is still used by some old-fashioned speakers.

humble-bee hʌ·mblbī large wild bee, bumble-bee. XV. prob. – MLG. *hummelbē*, *homelbē*, f. *hummel* = (M)Du. *hommel*, OHG. *humbal* (G. *hummel*)+*bē* BEE. Cf. †*humble* rumble, mumble (XIV) and *bumble-bee* (XVI).

humble-pie hʌmblpai· †pie made of the umbles of an animal XVII (rare); phr. *to eat humble-pie* (by assoc. with HUMBLE) to submit to humiliation XIX. f. unexplained var. of UMBLES+PIE[2].

humbug hʌ·mbʌg †hoax, imposture, fraud XVIII; pretence, sham; impostor XIX. Of unkn. origin; its vogue is commented upon in 'The Student', 1751 ('Of the Superlative Advantages arising from the use of the new-invented Science, called the Humbug').

humdrum hʌ·mdrʌm monotonous, commonplace. XVI (once *humtrum*; as sb. in B. Jonson printed in italics as an out-of-the way word); in XVII–XVIII †undecided, shilly-shally. Not common before XVIII; of unkn. origin, but app. based on HUM.

humeral hjū·mərəl pert. to the humerus or the shoulder(s). XVII. – modL. *humerālis*, f. *humerus* (used in anat. for 'upper arm'), with which cf. synon. Goth. *amsans* (acc. pl.), Skr. *ámsas*, Arm. *us*, Gr. *ômos*; see -AL[1].

humetty hjume·ti (her.) said of an ordinary couped so that the extremities do not touch the sides of the shield. XVI. f. †*humet*, †*hawmed* fess or bar so couped – OF. **heaumet*, dim. of *heaume* bar of a rudder+-Y[5].

humid hjū·mid moist. XVI. – F. *humide* or L. *hūmidus*, var. of *ūmidus*, f. *ūmēre* be moist; see HUMOUR and -ID[1]. So **humi·d**ITY. XIV. – (O)F. or L.

humiliate hjumi·lieit †humble XVI; reduce the dignity of XVIII. f. pp. stem of late L. *humiliāre*, f. *humilis* HUMBLE; see -ATE[3]. Earlier †*hu·mile* XV (Caxton) – (O)F. *humilier* – late L. So **humili**A·TION. XIV (Ch.). **humi·l**ITY. XIV. – (O)F. – late L.

hummock hʌ·mək protuberance of earth, etc. XVI. orig. and predominantly in naut. use; of unkn. origin. The orig. vowel of the first syll. is uncertain, the earliest exx. showing *ham-* beside *hom-*, both surviving dial.

hummum, hummam hʌ·mʌm, hʌmā·m Turkish bath or bath-house. XVII (T. Herbert). – Turk. – Arab. *ḥammām* bath, rel. to *ḥummum* coal, fuel, ashes. ¶ A bathing establishment called The Hummums is said to have been set up in 1631 in Covent Garden, London.

humour, U.S. **humor** hjū·məɹ fluid, spec. any of the four chief fluids of the body (blood, phlegm, choler, melancholy) XIV; mental disposition, orig. as determined by the proportion of these XV; mood, temper, inclination XVI; quality of action or speech which excites amusement; faculty of perceiving this XVII. – AN. (*h*)*umour*, OF. (*h*)*umor*, *-ur* (mod. *humeur*) = Pr. *umor*, Sp. *humor*, It. *umore* :– L. (*h*)*ūmōrem*, nom. (*h*)*ūmor*, f. (*h*)*ūm-*, as in HUMID. Hence **hu·mour** comply with the humour of. XVI (Sh.). So **hu·mo(u)r**IST †person subject to 'humours'; humorous or facetious person. XVI. – F. *humoriste*. **hu·mor**OUS †moist, humid; pert. or subject to 'humours' XVI (Sh.); showing humour XVIII (Addison).

hump hʌmp protuberance on the back, etc. XVIII; (sl.) fit of ill humour XIX (perh. from 'humping the back' in sulkiness). Earlier in *humpback*, *-backed* (late XVII), repl. earlier synon. *crump-backed*, and perh. a blending of this with synon. *hunch-backed*; the similar LG. *humpe*, Du. *homp* lump, hunk (whence G. *humpe*) may be related.

humph hʌmf †excl. used as a signal (cf. HEM) XVII (Otway, who uses it also as vb.); excl. of doubt or dissatisfaction XVII (*hmh?*, Jonson).

Humpty-Dumpty hʌ:mᵖtidʌ·mᵖti A. †ale boiled with brandy XVII (by Bentley coupled with the drink *hugmatee*); B. short dumpy person (in the well-known nursery rhyme usu. taken to refer to an egg, which, once broken, cannot be restored). XVIII (Grose). The connexion of the two senses is not clear; f. HUMP and DUMP, but the ending *-ty* is unexpl.

humus hjū·məs (agric.) vegetable mould. XVIII. L., 'mould, ground, soil'.

Hun hʌn member of an Asiatic race of warlike nomads. OE. (pl.) *Hūne*, *Hūnas*, corr. to MHG. *Hūnen*, *Hiunen* (G. *Hunnen*), ON. *Húnar*, also *Hýnar* – late L. *Hunnī*, *Hūnī*, also *Chunnī*, *Chūnī*, medL. also *Hun*(*n*)*ones*, Gr. *Hoûnnoi* – Turki *Hun-yü*. In ME. *Hunuze* (Laȝ.), *Huneys* (R. Mannyng), later *Hun*(*n*)*es*, are of F. origin (OF. pl. *Huns*, 'Chanson de Roland'), partly repr. late L. *Hunniscus*, whence **Hu·nn**ISH[1] (XIX), †*Hunnian*, †*Hunnican* (XVII); cf. MHG. *hiunisch*, G. *hunnisch*, ON. *Húnskr*.

hunch hʌnᵗʃ (dial.) thrust, shove XVI; compress into a hump XVII. So **hunch** sb. †push, thrust XVII; (dial.) lump, hunk XVIII. To be grouped with **hu·nchbacked** humpbacked XVI (whence **hu·nchback** XVIII), which are synon. with †*bunch-backed*, †*hulch-backed* (XVI); of unkn. origin. ¶ OE. *hunćettan* to limp, though formally parallel, does not agree in sense.

hundred hʌ·ndrəd A. ten times ten, 100, C. B. division of a shire, reckoned as 100 hides of land OE. †C. in N. America, political division of a county XVII. Late OE. *hundred* = OFris. *hundred*, OS. *hunderod* (Du. *honderd*), MHG., G. *hundert*, ON. *hundrað* (whence *hundrað*, *-eð* in late Nhb., surviving dial. in *hunderth*): CGerm. (exc.

Gothic), f. *χundam hundred, whence OE., OFris., OS. *hund*, OHG. *hunt*, Goth. (pl. only) *hunda* = L. *centum*, Gr. *he|katón*, Lith. *szimtás*, OIr. *cēt*, OW. *cant*, Skr. *çatám*, Av. *satəm*, Toch. *känt(e)* :- IE. **kmtóm*, poss. for **d(e)kmtóm*, f. **dekm* TEN; the ending is Germ. **raþ* = number (Goth. *raþjō* RATIO). ¶ The pronunc. hʌ·ndəɹd continued in educated use till late XIX. Walker says: 'This word has a solemn and a colloquial pronunciation. In poetry and oratory the first mode [hʌ·ndrəd] is best; on other occasions the last [hʌ·ndəɹd].'

ME. *hundre*, surviving in Sc. *hunder*, is prob. of Scand. origin (cf. Sw. *hundra*). Beside *hund* (which was superseded by *hundred c.*1200), OE. had *hundtēontiġ* = OHG. *zehanzug*, ON. *tíutiger*. ¶ ON. *hundrað* was orig. 120, which use of *hundred* survives in dial. Eng., equiv. to *great* or *long hundred* (XVI); cf. *hundredweight* 112 lb. (XVI).

hung hʌŋ pt. and pp. of HANG.

Hungarian hʌŋgɛə·riən pert. to (native of) Hungary, country of central Europe. XVI. f. *Hungary*, medL. *Hungaria* (F. *Hongrie*), f. *(H)ungarī*, *Ungrī*, *Ugrī* (cf. UGRIAN), medGr. *Oúggroi*, G. *Ungarn*, foreign name of the people called by themselves MAGYAR.

hunger hʌ·ŋgəɹ craving appetite; †famine. OE. *hungor*, *-ur* = OS., OHG. *hungar* (Du. *honger*, G. *hunger*), ON. *hungr* :- Germ. **χuŋgruz* (Gothic has *hūhrus* :- **χuŋχruz*); further relations are doubtful, but Gr. *kágkanos* dry, *kégkein* be hungry, Skr. *kákat* be thirsty, have been compared. So **hu·nger** vb. OE. *hyngran*, *-ian* (= OS. *gihungrian*, Goth. *huggrjan*) was superseded in ME. by *hungeren*, through assim. to the sb.; cf. MLG., MDu. *hungeren* (Du. *hongeren*), OHG. *hungaren* (G. *hungern*). **hun·gr**Y[1]. OE. *hungriġ* = OFris. *hungerig*, OHG. *hung(a)rag* (G. *hungrig*).

hunk hʌŋk (dial., colloq.) large piece cut off. XIX. prob. of LDu. origin (cf. WFlem. *hunke* chunk of bread or meat, of which there are no obvious cogns.).

hunks hʌŋks (arch., dial.) surly old person, miser. XVII (Dekker). Of unkn. origin.

hunt hʌnt go in pursuit of wild animals, trans. and intr. OE. *huntian*, f. wk. grade of base of *hentan* seize (arch. or dial. *hent*), repr. IE. **kend-*, parallel to **kent-* **knt-*, whence OE. *hūþ* booty, OHG. *heri|hundu* spoils of war, Goth. *fra|hinþan* take prisoner, *hunþs* booty, OSw. *hinna* obtain. Hence **hu·nt**ER[1]. OE. *huntere*, evidenced in place-names; superseded OE. *hunta*, which survives in the surname *Hunt*. **hu·ntr**ESS[1]. XIV (Ch.). **hu·nts**MAN. XVI.

hup hʌp call to a horse. XVIII. Cf. Du. *hop!* gee-up.

hurdle hə̄·ɹdl rectangular wattled framework. OE. *hyrdel* :- **χurðilaz*, f. Germ. **χurðiz*, repr. by OS. *hurth*, MLG. *hurt*, *hort*, (M)Du. *horde*, OHG. *hurt* (MHG. *hurt*, pl. *hürte*, *hürde*, G. *hürde*) hurdle, ON. *hurð*, Goth. *haurds* door; based on IE. **krt-* (cf. Gr. *kártallos* basket, L. *crātis* hurdle); see -LE[1]; for the vocalism cf. *bundle*, etc.

hurdy-gurdy hə̄·ɹdigə̄:ɹdi (orig.) rustic instrument having strings producing a drone, with keys to produce the notes of the melody, (later) barrel-organ. XVIII. Rhyming comp. suggested by the sound of the instrument; cf. Sc. and north. *hirdy-girdy* uproar, disorderly noise (XV).

hurl hə̄ɹl †be carried along with violence XIII (Cursor M.); impel or throw with violence XIV. corr. in form and sense to LG. *hurreln* toss, throw, push, dash, but no chronological contact has been established; they are prob. independent imit. formations.

hurly-burly hə̄·ɹlibə̄ɹli commotion, tumult. XVI. Preceded by †*hurling and burling*, a jingling collocation based on †*hurling* (XIV), †*hurl* (XV) strife, commotion, an obs. sense of HURL and its gerund. ¶ Connexion with the similar F. †*hurluburlu* (Rabelais), *hurluberlu*, †*-brelu*, hasty person, and G. *hurliburli* headlong, cannot be demonstrated.

hurrah hurā·, in pop. use **hurray, hooray** hurei· excl. of exultation. XVII. Modification of HUZZA; the connexion, if any, with MHG. *hurrā* (f. imper. of *hurren* hasten, hurry + *ā*) and G. *hurra* (XVIII), LG., Sw., Da. *hurra*, Du. *hoera*, is doubtful; F. *hourra* is from Eng., *houra* from Russ. *urá*. Addison has *whurra*, Goldsmith *hurrea*.

hurricane hʌ·rikən violent wind-storm of the W. Indies. XVI. Earliest forms *furacan(e)*, *-ana*, *-ano*, *haurachana*, *hurricano*, *uracan* – Sp. *huracan* and Pg. *furacão* – Carib *hura-*, *furacan*; from the same source are F. *ouragan*, It. *uracano*, Du. *orkaan*, G., etc. *orkan*. The present form (XVII, T. Herbert) has perh. been influenced by *hurry* in the sense 'disturbance'.

hurry hʌ·ri move (trans. and intr.) with great haste XVI (Sh.); (dial.) agitate XVII. perh. earlier in dial. use, but a n.w. midl. pt. *horyed* (XIV) cannot be certainly identified with this word; otherwise, *whirry* carry along swiftly, is of equal date; similar formations are MHG. *hurren* move quickly, Du. *herrie* agitation. Hence **hu·rry** sb. †commotion, agitation XVI (Holland); excessive haste XVII. In its earliest use synon. with *hurly* (XVI, Sh.). **hu·rry-scu:rry** adv., adj., sb., vb. XVIII (Gray, Richardson, Foote). Jingling extension, perh. infl. by *scud* or *scuttle*.

hurst hə̄ɹst (sandy) eminence; grove, copse. OE. *hyrst*, f. base repr. by OS., OHG. *hurst*, (also mod.) *horst*, which has been referred to the same source as W. *prys* copse, brushwood. ¶ Widespread in proper names, e.g. *Herst*, *Hirst*, *Hurst*; *Ashurst*, *Elmhurst*, *Lyndhurst*; *Amherst*.

hurt hɜ̄ɹt pt., pp. **hurt** †knock, strike; do harm to. XII (*hirrtenn*, Orm). – OF. *hurter* (mod. *heurter*) = Pr. *urtar* (whence It. *urtare*) :– Gallo-Rom. **hūrtare*, perh. of Germ. origin; a very early adoption, as is indicated by the ME. dial. differentiation *hürte, hirte, herte*, OF. *ü* being treated like OE. *y*. So **hurt** sb. †knock, blow; (bodily or material) injury, damage. XIII (Laʒ.). – OF. *hurt*, f. the vb. **hu·rt**ER shoulder of an axle against which the nave strikes. XIII. – (O)F. *hurt(ou)oir*, f. *hurter*.

hurtle hɜ̄·ɹtl (literary or arch.) dash or knock (one thing against another) XIII; come into collision XIV; dash, rush XVI. f. HURT + -LE[3].

hurtleberry hɜ̄·ɹtlberi whortleberry, bilberry. XV. Earlier than synon. *hurt* (XVI) and *whort, whortleberry* (Lyte); of unkn. origin.

husband hʌ·zbənd †master of a household OE.; man joined to a woman in marriage; †tiller of the soil, husbandman XIII; housekeeper, steward XV (*ship's husband* XVIII); †one who manages affairs XVI. Late OE. *hūsbonda* – ON. *húsbóndi* master of a house, husband, f. *hús* HOUSE + *bóndi*, contr. of **bóandi*, **búandi*, sb. use of prp. of *bóa, búa* dwell, have a household = OE., OS., OHG. *būan*, Goth. *bauan* (cf. BOND[2], BOWER[1]). Hence vb. XV; **hu·sband**MAN XIV (R. Mannyng), **hu·sband**RY XIII.

hush hʌʃ repr. an excl. enjoining silence. The earliest recorded word of this form is the vb. 'make or become silent' (XVI), which is followed by adj., int., and sb. in XVII; preceded by †*hust*, int. and adj. XIV (Ch.), (dial.) *husht*; cf. SH, ST, WHISHT. Hence **hushaby** hʌ·ʃəbai word used in lulling a child XVIII; cf. BYE-BYE, LULLABY, ROCKABY. comp. **hu·sh**-MO:NEY money paid for hushing something up. XVIII (Steele, Swift).

husk hʌsk dry outer covering of fruit or seed. XIV (Trevisa). prob. – LG. *hūske* little house, core of fruit, sheath = MDu. *hūskijn* (Du. *huisken*), dim. of *hūs* HOUSE. Hence **hu·sk**Y[1] full of husks, dry as a husk XVI; dry in the throat XVIII; (U.S. and Canada) tough, hefty XIX.

Husky hʌ·ski Eskimo; (*h-*) Eskimo dog. XIX. Supposed to be from ESKIMO.

hussar hʌzā·ɹ one of a body of light horsemen raised in Hungary in XV; hence applied to light cavalry regiments raised elsewhere in Europe XVI. – Magyar *huszar* †freebooter, (later) light horseman – OSerb. *husar, gusar, hursar* – It. *corsaro* CORSAIR.

hussif, huzzif hʌ·zif var. of *huswife*, HOUSEWIFE in the sense 'case of sewing-necessaries'. XVIII.

Hussite hʌ·sait follower of John *Huss*, Bohemian religious reformer (1373–1415). XVI. – modL. *Hussīta* (cf. Du. *Hussiet*); see -ITE.

hussy, huzzy hʌ·zi †housewife XVI; bold, shameless, or †light woman or girl XVII. Reduction of *hŭswif*, HOUSEWIFE; cf. GOODY[1].

husting(s) hʌ·stiŋ(z) sg. (hist.) deliberative assembly XI; court held in Guildhall, London XII (sg.; from XV pl.); †platform in Guildhall on which the members sat XVII; platform from which nomination of candidates for election to parliament was made, (hence) the election itself XVIII. Late OE. *hŭsting* – ON. *húsþing* 'house assembly', one held by a king, etc., with his immediate followers, opp. to the ordinary *þing* (see THING) or general assembly.

hustle hʌ·sl †shake to and fro XVII (Otway); push about roughly XVIII (Smollett). – (M)Du. *husselen, hutselen* shake, e.g. in a cap, frequent. of *hutsen* = MHG. *hutzen* (cf. *hussen* run, *hutschen* push); f. Germ. imit. base **χut-*. The second sense is of Eng. development.

hut hʌt wooden structure for housing troops XVII; mean dwelling of rude construction XVII. – F. *hutte* (whence Sp. *huta*) – (M)HG. *hütte*, OHG. *hutt(e)a* (whence OS. *huttia*):– **χuđjōn*, prob. f. Germ. **χŭđ-* HIDE[3]. ¶ A HG. word which has been adopted elsewhere prob. through military use.

hutch hʌtʃ †chest, coffer XIV (R. Mannyng); box-like pen XVII. – (O)F. *huche*, (dial.) *huge* :– medL. *hūtica* (AL. *hugia* XII), of unkn. origin.

huzza hŭzā· hurrah. XVI (*my youthfulliste hollaes, hussaes, and sahoes*, G. Harvey). Said by writers of XVII–XVIII to have been orig. a sailor's cheer or salute; as such it may be identical with the old hauling-cry †*heisau*, †*hissa* (see HOIST), but G. has *hussa* as a cry of pursuit and exultation. Cf. HURRAH.

hyacinth hai·əsinþ precious stone (cf. JACINTH); plant-name. XVI. – F. *hyacinthe* – L. *hyacinthus* – Gr. *huákinthos* purple or dark-red flower (fabled to have sprung from the blood of Hyacinthus and to bear the initials AI or the int. AIAI), precious stone, a word of pre-Hellenic origin. So **hyaci·nth**INE[2]. XVII. – L. *hyacinthinus* – Gr. *huakínthinos* applied to hair.

Hyades hai·ədīz group of stars near the Pleiades. XVI. – Gr. *huádes* fem. pl., popularly connected with *húein* rain, their heliacal rising being supposed to prognosticate rain, but perh. f. *hûs* SWINE, the L. name being *suculæ* little pigs.

hyaline hai·əlain glass-like, vitreous. XVII. – late L. *hyalinus* – Gr. *huálinos*, f. *húalos* transparent stone, amber, etc., glass (cf. L. *suali|ternicum* reddish amber); see -INE[2]. So **hy·alo-**, comb. form, **hy·al**OID. XIX; F. *hyaloïde*, Gr. *hualoeidḗs*.

hybrid hai·brid sb. and adj. half-breed, mongrel; also fig. XVII (rare before XIX). – L. *hybrida*, *(h)ibrida* offspring of a tame sow and a wild boar, one born of a Roman father and a foreign mother or of a freeman and a slave. Hence **hy·brid**OUS. XVII.

hydatid hai·dətid (path.) watery cyst. XVII (in L. pl. form *hydatides*). – modL. *hydatid-*, *-is* – Gr. *hudatid-*, *-ís*, f. *hudat-*, *húdōr* WATER; see -ID[2].

hydra hai·drə fabulous many-headed snake of Lerna whose heads grew again as fast as they were cut off XVI (earlier in OF. or anglicized forms *ydre, idre, hydre*); genus of freshwater polyps, so named by Linnæus from the fact that cutting it into pieces multiplies its numbers XVIII. – L. *hydra* – Gr. *húdrā* water-serpent (cf. OTTER).

hydrangea haidræ·ndʒ[i]ə genus of shrubs. XVIII. – modL. *hydrangēa* (Linnæus), f. Gr. *hudr-*, *húdōr* WATER + *ággos* vessel; so called with ref. to the cup-like form of the seed-capsule.

hydrant hai·drənt apparatus for drawing water from a main. XIX (orig. U.S.). irreg. f. Gr. *húdr-*, *húdōr* water + -ANT.

hydrate hai·dreit (chem.) compound of water with another compound or an element. *c.* 1800. – F. *hydrate*, f. Gr. *hudr-*, *húdōr* WATER; see -ATE[2]. So **hy·dr**IDE †hydrate; compound of hydrogen with an element or radical XIX.

hydraulic haidrɔ̄·lik pert. to the drawing of water through pipes or operation by water-power. XVII. – L. *hydraulicus* – Gr. *hudraulikós*, f. *hudr-*, *húdōr* WATER + *aulós* pipe; see -IC.

hydro-, before a vowel **hydr-** hai·dr(ou), haidrɔ·, comb. form of Gr. *húdōr* WATER in many terms, mainly techn., of which some came from L. adoptions of Gr. words either direct or through French, but many are of mod. origin (whether through modL. or by immed. derivation); they may be grouped thus: (in gen. terms) **hydro**·GRAPHER, one concerned with **hydro**·GRAPHY description of the waters of the earth's surface XVI (Cunningham), -GRAPHICAL XVI (Dee), **hy·dro**MANCY XIV (Maund.), **hydro**PHO·BIA XVI (Boorde), **hydropon**ICS -pɔ·niks cultivation of plants by means of water without soil (Gr. *pónos* labour) XX; (path.) denoting accumulation of fluid, as **hy·drocele** -sīl tumour of serous fluid XVI, **hydrocephalus** -se·fələs 'water on the brain' XVII (Gr. *hudroképhalon*; *kephalḗ* head); (chem.) denoting combination with water, and (hence) with HYDROGEN (of which it functions as comb. form), as *hydrobro·mic*, *-ca·rbon*, *-chlo·ric*, *-cya·nic*, *-fluo·ric*, *†-sulphu·ric*, **hydro**·XIDE compound of an element or radical with oxygen and hydrogen; (physics) concerned with liquids, as **hy·dro**DYNA·MICS XVIII, -KINE·TIC, -MECHA·NICS XIX, -STA·TICS XVII (Boyle).

hydrogen hai·drədʒən (chem.) gas forming two-thirds in volume of water ('Mr. Lavoisier and others of the French School have most ingeniously endeavoured to shew that water consists of pure air, called by them oxygene, and of inflammable air, called hydrogene', E. Darwin 'Botanic Garden' 1791). – F. *hydrogène* (G. de Morveau, 1787), f. Gr. *hudro-*, *húdōr* WATER; see -GEN.

hydrozoa haidrŏzou·ə (zool.) class of the subprovince Radiaria of the province Radiata in R. Owen's classification. 1843. f. *hydro-*, used as comb. form of HYDRA + pl. of Gr. *zôion* (see ZOO-).

hyena, earlier **hyæna** haiī·nə carnivorous quadruped of a family allied to the dogs. XVI (earlier in OF. or anglicized form *hyene* XIV, in Sh. 'AYL.' IV i 156 *hyen*). – L. *hyæna* – Gr. *húaina*, prop. fem. of *hûs* SWINE, with suffix as in *léaina* lioness, etc.

hygiene haidʒī·n, -dʒiī·n system of principles or rules of health. XIX (earlier, from XVI, in alien forms). – F. *hygiène* (earlier *hygiaine, igieinie* XVI) – modL. *hygieina* – Gr. *hugieinḗ* (sc. *tékhnē* art), sb. use of fem. of *hugieinós* healthful, f. *hugiḗs* healthy :– **sugwijḗs* 'well-living', f. **su-* (Skr. *su-*, Av. *hu-*, OIr. *su-*, *so-*) well + **gwi-* living, QUICK.

hygro- hai·grou, haigrɔ· comb. form of Gr. *hugrós* wet, moist, fluid, as in **hygro**·METER / **hy·gro**SCOPE instruments for measuring / indicating humidity.

hyleg hai·leg (astrol.) ruling planet of a nativity. XVII. – Pers. (Turk.) *hailāj* calculation of a nativity; said by Persian lexicographers to be orig. Gr., meaning 'fountain of life'. Cf. OF. *yleg, ilech*.

hylic hai·lik pert. to matter. XIX. – lateL. *hȳlicus* – Gr. *hūlikós* material, f. *hū́lē* wood, timber, material, matter (whence medL. *hȳlē*, in Eng. use XV–XVIII); see -IC. So **hylo-** hai·lou, hailɔ· comb. form of Gr. *hū́lē*, in techn. terms of nat. hist. (in the sense 'wood, forest') and philos. (in the sense 'matter'). **hylomorph**ISM -mɔ̄·ɹfizm scholastic theory of matter and form XIX; see -MORPH. **hylozo**ISM -zou·izm theory that matter has life XVII; see ZOO-, -ISM.

hymen hai·men (anat.) virginal membrane. XVII. – late L. *hymēn* (Donatus, Servius) – Gr. *humḗn* :– **sjumen-*, f. IE. **sjew-* SEW; cf. F. *hymen* (XVI, Paré). comb. form **hy·meno-,** as in **hymenoptera** haimənɔ·ptərə insects having four membranous wings. XVIII. modL. (Linnæus), n.pl. of *hymenopterus* – Gr. *humenópteros*, f. *humen-*, *-ḗn* + *pterón* wing; see FEATHER, -A[2].

Hymen hai·men Roman god of marriage XVI; †marriage; †wedding hymn XVII. So **hymene**AL[1] -ī·əl, -E·AN XVII. f. L. *hymenæus* – Gr. *huménaios*.

hymn him song of praise to God; spec. metrical composition to be used at a religious service XIII; (gen.) XVI. ME. *imne, ymne* – OF. *ymne* – L. *hymnus* (whence OE. *ymen*) – Gr. *húmnos* song in praise of a god or hero, in LXX rendering various Heb. words meaning a song of praise to God, and hence in N.T. and other Christian writings. The later form was refash. after L.; the loss of final n in pronunc. is shown in XVI (*hymme, imme*). Hence **hymn** vb. XVII (Milton). So

hymnAL[1] hi·mnəl sb. hymn-book. XV. – medL. *hymnāle* (*imnale*). **hymnody** hi·mnədi singing or composing of hymns XVIII; body of hymns XIX. – medL. – Gr. *humnōidíā* (cf. ODE). **hymno**·GRAPHER, **hymno**·LOGY XVII. – Gr.

hyoid hai·oid *h. bone*, horseshoe-shaped bone in the root of the tongue. XIX. – F. *hyoïde* – modL. *hyoīdēs* – Gr. *huoeidḗs*, f. *hû* name of the letter *υ*; see -OID.

hyoscyamus haiosai·əməs genus of solanaceous plants, henbane. XVIII. modL., – Gr. *huoskúamos*, f. *huós*, g. of *hûs* SWINE + *kúamos* bean. Hence **hyoscy·am**INE[5] (chem.) alkaloid obtained from this. XIX.

hypæthral haipī·þrəl open to the sky. XVIII. f. L. *hypæthrus* – Gr. *húpaithros*, f. *hupó* under, HYPO- + *aithḗr* air, ETHER; see -AL[1].

hypallage haipæ·lədʒi (rhet.) figure of speech in which two elements are interchanged. XVI. – late L. *hypallagē* – Gr. *hupallagḗ*, f. *hupó* HYPO- + *allag*-, stem of *allássein* exchange, f. *állos* other (see ALIEN, ALTER).

hyper- hai·pəɹ, haipə̄·ɹ repr. comb. form of Gr. *hupér* prep. and adv. 'over', 'above', 'overmuch', 'above measure', or denoting a condition above or beyond what is denoted by the compounded sb., adj., or vb. (in ancient and medieval music applied to names of modes; chem. now gen. repl. by *per*-). Among the older comps. are: **hype·rbaton** -bətən (rhet.) inversion of logical or natural order. XVI. L. (Quintilian, Pliny) – Gr. *hupérbaton*, n. of *hupérbatos* 'overstepping' (used by Plato and Aristotle of transposition of words); f. *ba- (cf. BASIS). **hype·rbola** -bələ (geom.) conic section having two equal and similar infinite branches, so called because it has an eccentricity greater than unity. XVII. modL. – Gr. *huperbolḗ*, f. *huperbállein* exceed; f. *bállein* throw (cf. BALLISTA). **hype·rbole** -bəli (rhet.) exaggerated statement. XVI (*yperbole*, More). L. (Quintilian) – Gr. (see prec.). So **hyperbol**IC -bɔ·lik. XVI. **hyperbo·l**ICAL. XV. – late L. *hyperbolicus* (Jerome) – Gr. **hyperbor**EAN -bō·riən pert. to the extreme north. XVI (Sylvester). – late L. *hyperboreānus*, f. L. *hyperboreus* – Gr. *huperbóreos*; see BOREAL. **hyp:er**CATALE·CTIC (pros.). XVIII. – late L., repl. L. *hypercatalēctus* – Gr. **hyper**CRI·TICAL extremely or unduly critical. XVII (Camden). f. modL. *hypercriticus* (applied by Camden to the younger Scaliger). **hyperdu·lia** (theol.) superior veneration as paid to the Virgin Mary. XVI (Tindale). medL. **hy·persthene** -sþīn (min.) silicate of iron and magnesium, so called because of its superior hardness. XIX. – F. *hyperstène* (Haüy, 1803); Gr. *sthénos* strength. **hypertrophy** haipə̄·ɹtrəfi (physiol., path.) excessive enlargement. XIX. – medL.; Gr. *-trophíā*, *trophḗ* nourishment; cf. ATROPHY.

hypericum haipe·rikəm genus of plants (St. John's wort). XVI. L. *hyperīcum* – Gr. *hupéreikon*, f. *hupér* HYPER- + *ereíkē* heath.

hyphen hai·f(ə)n sign used to connect two words or parts of a word. XVII. – late L. *hyphen* – late Gr. *huphén* the sign ◡, sb. use of *huphén* together, f. *huph*-, *hupó* under, HYPO- + *hén*, n. of *heîs* one :– *sems, rel. to *homós* SAME. Hence **hy·phen** vb., **hy·phe**NATE[3]. XIX.

hypnotic hipnɔ·tik A. soporific XVII; B. pert. to hypnotism XIX. – F. *hypnotique* (Paré) – late L. *hypnōticus* – Gr. *hupnōtikós* narcotic, f. *hupnoûn* put to sleep, f. *húpnos* sleep; see SWEVEN, -IC. In B, short for *neuro-hypnotic*. Hence **hypnot**ISM hi·pnətizm production of a state resembling deep sleep in which the subject acts only on external suggestion. Short for NEURO-*hypnotism*, coined in 1842 by James Braid, of Manchester, for 'state of nervous sleep', and in 1843 shortened to *hypnotism*, whence he made **hy·pnot**IST, **hy·pnot**IZE.

hypo[1] hi·pou sl. short for HYPOCHONDRIA. XVIII.

hypo[2] hai·pou (photogr.) shortening of *hyposulphite* (of soda). *c.* 1860.

hypo- hai·po(u), hi·po(u), haipɔ·, hipɔ·, before a vowel *hyp*-, repr. Gr. *hup(o)*-, prefix-form of *hupó* under (adv. and prep.) = L. *sub* (see SUB-), in words derived immed. or ult. from Gr. (see below) with meanings 'under', 'beneath', 'below', 'slightly', 'slight' (in ancient music applied to names of modes), and in numerous mod. formations, often)(EPI- OR HYPER-. The earliest pronunc. with hi was superseded by hai, first in stressed positions, and finally in all, exc. in *hypocrisy*, *-crite*, and derivs. **hypocaust** hai·pokōst under-chamber for heating a house or bath. XVII. – L. *hypocaustum* (Pliny) – Gr. *hupókauston*, n. of *hupókaustos* (cf. CAUSTIC). **hypochondria** -kɔ·ndriə A. (anat.) region of the abdomen under the ribs, formerly held to be the seat of melancholy and 'the vapours' XVI; B. morbidity of mind, marked by depression and regarded as due to 'vapours' XVIII (Dryden). – late L.; in A pl. of *hypochondrium* – Gr. *hupokhóndrion* (*khóndros* cartilage); in B taken as fem. in transf. sense. **hy·pocori**·STIC of the nature of a pet-name. XVIII. – Gr. *hupokoristikós*, f. *hupokorízesthai* use endearing terms, f. *kóros*, *kórē* child, boy, girl. **hypocrisy** hipɔ·krĭsi false appearance of goodness. XIII (*ipocrisie*, AncrR.). – OF. *ypocrisie* (mod. *hypo*-) – ecclL. *hypocrisis* – Gr. *hupókrīsis* acting, feigning, f. *hupokrī́nesthai* play a part, pretend (*krī́nein* decide, judge; cf. DISCERN). So **hypocrite** hi·pəkrit. XIII (AncrR.). – (O)F. – ecclL. – Gr. *hupokritḗs* actor, pretender, dissembler. **hypocri·ti**CAL. XVI; Gr. *hupokritikós*; earlier †*-critish* XVI (Tindale, Coverdale). **hypostasis** -ɔ·stəsis †sediment; (theol.) person of Christ, of the Godhead XVI; substance, essence XVII. – ecclL. (Jerome) – Gr. *hupóstasis* (*sta- STAND). **hypotenuse** -ɔ·tənjūs, formerly often †*-thenuse*, side of a right-angled triangle subtending the right angle.

XVI (Digges). – L. *hypotēnūsa* – Gr. *hupoteínousa*, prp. fem. of *hupoteínein* stretch under (cf. TEND), the full expression being ἡ τὴν ὀρθὴν γωνίαν ὑποτείνουσα (sc. γραμμή or πλευρά). **hypothec** haipɔ·þek legal security. XVI. – F. *hypothèque* – late L. *hypothēca* – Gr. *hupothḗkē* deposit, pledge (*thē-* place, DO[1]). So **hypo·thec**ATE[3] mortgage. XVII. f. pp. stem of medL. *hypothēcāre*. **hypothesis** -ɔ·þĭsis †particular case of a general proposition XVI; proposition set as a basis for reasoning; supposition to account for known facts XVII. – late L. – Gr. *hupóthesis* foundation, f. **the-* place, DO[1]. So **hypothe·t**IC XVII, **-the·t**ICAL XVI. – L. – Gr. *hupothetikós*. Cf. F. *hypothétique*.

hypped, hyppish, early variants of HIPPED, HIPPISH. XVIII–XIX.

hypsi- hi·psi repr. Gr. *húpsi* on high, aloft; so **hypso-** hi·pso(u), hipsɔ· repr. Gr. *hupso-* (cf. L. *sus* in *susque dēque* from top to bottom). XIX.

hypsiloid hipsai·loid, hi·ps- U-shaped, or V-shaped. XIX. – Gr. *û psilón* 'slender u' + *-eidḗs* - OID, w. assim. to prec.

hyrax haiə·ræks genus of rabbit-like quadrupeds. XIX. modL. – Gr. *húrax*, prob. rel. to L. *sōrex* shrew-mouse.

hyson hai·sən green tea from China. XVIII. – Chinese *hsi-ch'un* (Cantonese *hei-ch'un*) 'bright spring'. *Young hyson* repr. *yü ch'ien* 'before the rains' (with allusion to the early picking of the leaf).

hyssop hi·səp bushy aromatic shrub; bunch of this used in ceremonial purification. OE. *(h)ysope*, reinforced in ME. by OF. *ysope*, *isope*, later assim. to the source, L. *hyssōpus*, *-um* – Gr. *hússōpos*, *-on*, of Semitic origin (cf. Heb. *ēzōb*).

hysteria histiə·riə functional disturbance of the nervous system, which was thought to be due to disturbance of the uterine functions. XIX. – modL. *hysteria*, f. L. *hystericus* – Gr. *husterikós*, f. *hustérā* womb (see UTERUS); see -IA[1]. So **hyster**IC histe·rik. XVII; modL. *hysterica passio*, tr. Gr. *husterikà páthē*, *husterikḗ pníx*; sb. pl. XVIII. **hyste·r**ICAL. XVII.

hysteron proteron hi·stərən prɔ·tərən figure of speech reversing the proper order of words. XVI. late L. (Servius) – Gr. *hústeron próteron* latter [put as] former; both words have Skr. cogns.

hythe var. of HITHE.

I

I ai nom. pronoun of the 1st person sg. OE. *ić* = OFris., OS. (Du.) *ik*, OHG. *ih* (G. *ich*), ON. *ek(a)*, Goth. *ik* (:– CGerm. **eka* :– **egō*), corr. basically, but with variation of vowel, consonant, and ending, to L. *egŏ*, Rom. **eo* (whence F. *je*, Sp. *yo*, It. *io*, Pg., Rum. *eu*), Gr. *egṓ(n)*, Skr. *ahám*, Av. *azem*, OSl. *(j)azŭ* (Russ. *ja*), Lith. *eo*, Lett., OPruss., Arm. *es*. The reduced form *i* of OE. *ić* appears XII; in stressed position this became ī (whence the mod. ai) and was finally generalized for all positions. The unstressed i remains in north. dial. use, e.g. *wad I* wa·di would I, while in north. use also a new unstressed form a or ə was developed by reduction of ai, əi, and this in turn has been lengthened in stressed positions to ā, ə̄. ME. *ich*, from the unclipped OE. *ić*, survived in southern and western dial. (with vars. *che*, *utch*, *utchy*) and combined with verbs is seen in *chad* I had, *cham* I am, *chill* I will, *chud* I would, etc. ¶ The inflexional system of the pronoun is made up of four distinct bases; see ME, MY (MINE), WE, US, OUR.

-i ai in L. words, i in It. words pl. inflexion of L. masc. sbs. in *-us* and *-er*, and of It. sbs. in *-o* and *-e*, retained in Eng. in learned and techn. use, e.g. *cirri*, *foci*, *radii*; *banditti*, *dilettanti*; *illuminati*, *literati*.

-i- L. stem- or connective vowel as in *omnivorus* OMNIVOROUS, *grānivorus* (f. *grāno-*) GRANIVOROUS, *herbivorous* (*herba-*) HERBIVOROUS; *grāminivorus* GRAMINIVOROUS; *pacificus* (*paci-*) PACIFIC; *uniformis* (*unu-s*) UNIFORM.

-ia[1] iə repr. the termination of L. and Gr. fem. sbs. denoting conditions, qualities, and entities; f. stem- or connective -I- + -A[1]. Exx.: *hydrophobia*, *mania*, *militia*; *dahlia*, *lobelia*; *ammonia*, *morphia*.

-ia[2] iə repr. the termination of L. and Gr. pls. of sbs. in *-ium* or *-e*, and *-ion*, f. stem- or connective -I- + -A[2]. Exx.: *ganglia*, *paraphernalia*, *regalia*; *Mammalia*.

-ial iəl repr. L. *-iālis*, n. *-iāle* (whence F. *-iel*, Sp. *-ial*, It. *-iale*), comp. prefix f. connective or stem-vowel -I- and -AL[1].

iambus aiæ·mbəs (pros.) the foot ⏑ –. XVI. L., – Gr. *íambos* metrical foot, pl. iambic (esp. satirical) verse. Anglicized **iamb** ai·æmb. XIX; cf. F. *ïambe*. So **ia·mb**IC. XVI. – F. *iambique* – late L. *iambicus* – Gr. *iambikós*.

-ian iən, earlier also *-yan*, repr. ult. (sometimes through F. *-ien*), L. *-iānus*, orig. f. *-i-* -I- + *-ānus* -AN, as in CHRISTIAN, ICARIAN, ITALIAN, *Vergiliānus* Virgilian, subsequently by modification of L. forms, as BARBARIAN, EQUESTRIAN, HISTORIAN, PATRICIAN; used in mod. formations on proper names ad libitum, as in *Addisonian*, *Devonian*, *Gladstonian*, *Johnsonian*, *Pickwickian*, *Salopian*, *Wordsworthian*. See also -ARIAN, -ICIAN.

-iana iei·nə see ANA. XVIII (*Shakespeariana*).

iatro- aiæ·trou, comb. form of Gr. *iātrós* physician (*iâsthai* cure), as in *iatroche·mist* XVIII, *ia:tromathema·tical* (Gr. *iātromathēmatikós*) XVII.

ib., ibid., abbrevs. of **ibidem** ibai·dem in the same place, passage, book, etc. XVII. L., f. *ibī* there + *-dem*, as in IDEM, TANDEM.

Iberian aibiə·riən pert. to an ancient people inhabiting parts of the Spanish peninsula, or their language. XVII. f. L. *Ibēria*, f. *Ibēres* – Gr. *I'bēres* Spaniards, also a people of the Caucasus; see -IAN.

ibex ai·beks Alpine wild goat. XVII. – L. *ibex*, prob. Alpine word like *camox* CHAMOIS.

ibis ai·bis bird allied to stork and heron. XIV. – L. – Gr. *îbis*, of Egyptian origin (*heb*).

-ible ĭbl suffix repr. F. *-ible*, L. *-ibilis*, *-ībilis*, f. *-i-*, *-ī-* connective or stem-vowel of vbs. in *-ēre*, *-ere*, *-īre*+*-bilis* -BLE.

-ic ik formerly also *-ick*, *-ik*(*e*), *-ique*, repr. (often through (O)F. *-ique*) L. *-icus*, as in *cīvicus*, *civique* CIVIC, *domesticus* DOMESTIC, *publicus* PUBLIC, or in adoptions from Gr., as in *cōmicus*, *kōmikós* COMIC, *poēticus*, *poiētikós* POETIC. The L. suffix became more widely used in late L. and Rom. in the comp. suffix *-āticus* (see -ATIC, -AGE). In chem., since 1796, depending on the use of F. *-ique* in 'Nomenclature Chimique' (1787), *-ic* has been spec. used to denote acids and other compounds having a higher degree of oxidation than those whose names end in *-ous*, e.g. *sulphuric acid* H_2SO_4)(*sulphurous acid* H_2SO_3.

Derivative abstract sbs. end in **-ic**ITY i·sĭti, as *domesticity*, *publicity*.

Gr. words in *-ikós* were used absol. as sbs. (i) in the m. sg., e.g. *kritikós* CRITIC, *Stōikós* 'man of the porch', STOIC; (ii) in the fem. sg., in names of arts, or systems of thought, knowledge, or action (scil. *tékhnē*, *theōriā*, *philosophiā*), e.g. *hē mousikḗ* MUSIC, *hē ēthikḗ* ETHIC; (iii) in the n. pl., e.g. *tà oikonomiká* things pert. to economy, ECONOMICS, *tà politiká* affairs of state, POLITICS. The distinction between fem. sg. and n. pl. tended to become obliterated, so that *hē taktikḗ* and *tà taktiká*, *hē physikḗ* and *tà physiká* were synonymous. Moreover, in pairs like *physikḗ*, *physiká*, both forms gave L. *physica*, which might be repr. by *physic* or *physics*, according as it was apprehended as fem. sg. or n.pl. Early adoptions in Eng., usu. with *-ique*, *-ike*, after F., were in the sg. form, which has survived in *arithmetic*, *logic*, *magic*, *music*, *rhetoric*. Later, forms in **-ics** (†*-iques*) occur as names of treatises, e.g. *etiques*, i.e. Aristotle's *tà ēthiká*, the Ethics; this form was then applied to the subject-matter of such treatises, as *mathematics*, *physics*, *tactics*, and finally became the accepted form with names of sciences, as *acoustics*, *conics*, *linguistics*, *optics*, or matters of practice, as *athletics*, *gymnastics*, *politics*. More recently the sg. form has been preferred by some, after F. or G. usage, e.g. *dialectic*, *ethic*, *metaphysic*. Names of sciences in *-ics* are now construed as sg., names of practical matters as pl., e.g. 'Mathematics *is* the science of quantity', 'A woman's politics *are* the man she loves'. There are also many sbs. formed from adjs. in *-ic* taken absol., as *cosmetic*, *emetic*, *epic*, *lyric*, *iambic*, *domestic*, *rustic*, *classic*. Words in *-ic* from Gr. or L. are regularly stressed on the penultimate syll. (which normally has a short vowel), as *drama·tic*, *encli·tic*, *fana·tic*, *mecha·nic*, *pole·mic*, *splene·tic*; but in some older adoptions, mainly through French, like *ari·thmetic*, *ca·tholic*, *he·retic*, *lu·natic*, *rhe·toric*, the stress is on the antepenultimate. Pronunciation with a long penultimate is due to recent modelling on classical quantity, as in *cretic*, *exegetic*, *strategic*, and *psychic*, *scenic*; *acetic* is variously pronounced; *nitric* follows *nitre*.

-ical ikl comp. suffix consisting of -IC and -AL[1], repr. (O)F. *-ical*(*e*), late L. *-icālis*, as in *clérical*, *clēricālis*, *grammaticālis*; the number of these was increased in medL., e.g. *chīrurgicālis* SURGICAL, *dominicālis*, *medicālis*, *mūsicālis*, *physicālis*. While F. adjs. in *-ical* are not numerous, Eng. formations are abundant, and are very freq. earlier than corr. words in -IC. A distinction of application is often made where there are parallel forms, e.g. *comic* in 'comic opera', 'the comic muse', *comical* in 'comical attitude', *economic* in 'economic theory', *economical* in 'economical housekeeper', *historic* in 'historic speeches', *historical* in 'English Historical Review', *optic* in 'optic nerve', *optical* in 'optical illusion'. In many cases the main distinction is that one form is more usual than the other, as *artistic*, *authentic*, *epic*, *idiotic*, *linguistic*, *sympathetic*, but *farcical*, *oratorical*, *syntactical*, *theatrical*, *tropical*. Derivative sbs. end in **-ical**ITY ikæ·lĭti, and advs. in **-ically** ikəli, which serves also for adjs. in *-ic*, e.g. *drastic* / *drastically*, *specific* / *specifically*.

Icarian aikɛə·riən pert. to Icarus, son of Dædalus, fabled in Gr. myth. to have flown so high that the wax with which his artificial wings were fastened on melted so that he fell into the sea; (hence) presumptuously ambitious. XVI. f. L. *Icarius* – Gr. *Ikários*, f. *I'karos*; see -IAN.

ice ais frozen moisture. OE. *īs* = OFris., OS., OHG. *īs* (Du. *ijs*, G. *eis*), ON. *íss* :- CGerm. (exc. Gothic) **īsam*, **isaz*, having analogues elsewhere in the Iranian langs. (e.g. Av. *isav-* icy). *Ice cream* (XVIII) is for earlier *iced cream* (XVII). Hence **icy**[1] ai·si; a new formation in XVI, not continuous with OE. *īsiġ*. So **iceberg** ai·sbɜːg †Arctic glacier XVIII; detached portion of this in the sea XVIII. prob. – (M)Du. *ijsberg* (see BARROW[1]), whence also G. *eisberg*, Sw. *isberg*, Da. *isbjerg*.

Icelandic aislæ·ndik pert. to Iceland, large island of the Arctic Ocean between Norway and Greenland; esp. of its language. XVII. sb. the language of Iceland, one of the Germanic group, which retains in its essentials the features of the tongue anciently spoken over the whole Scandinavian region (cf. NORSE). XIX (Southey). f. *Iceland* (ME. *Island*, *Islond* XIII) – ON. *Ísland*, f. *íss* ICE+*land* LAND; see -IC.

ichneumon iknjū·mən N. African weasel-shaped carnivorous quadruped of Egypt, Herpestes ichneumon, which destroys crocodiles' eggs XVI; insect of a family parasitic on the larvæ of others (after Aristotle's use of the name for a spider-hunting wasp) XVII. – L. *ichneumōn* – Gr. *ikhneúmōn* lit. tracker, f. *ikhneúein* track, f. *íkhnos* track, footstep.

ichnography iknɔ·grəfi ground plan. XVI. – F. *ichnographie* or L. *ichnographia* – Gr. *ikhnographíā*, f. *íkhnos* track, trace; see -GRAPHY.

ichor ai·kɔːɹ blood; (Gr. myth.) ethereal fluid flowing in the veins of the gods; (med.) watery discharge. XVII. – Gr. *ikhṓr*.

ichthy(o)- i:kþi(ou), ikþiɔ· repr. comb. form of Gr. *ikhthús* fish, as in **ichthyocolla** -kɔ·lə fish-glue, isinglass. XVII. L. – Gr. (cf. COLLOID); **ichthy**o·LOGY natural history of fishes. XVII (Sir T. Browne); **ichthyosaurus** -sɔ̄·rəs extinct marine animal combining features of fishes and SAURIAN reptiles. XIX (Lyell).

-ician i·ʃən as in *logician, musician, physician, statistician, tactician*, repr. F. *-icien* (e.g. *logicien, †médicien, physicien, rhétoricien*), L. *-iciānus* (whence also Pr. *-iciá*, It. *-iciano*), f. names of sciences in *-ica* -IC(S)+ *-iānus* -IAN. Its use has been extended in U.S., e.g. *beautician* expert in beauty culture (XX), *mortician* undertaker (1895).

icicle ai·sikl pendent formation of ice. XIV (Sir Gawain, PPl.). Late ME. *iisse* (*ysse*) *ikkle, ysekele, iseyokel*, f. ICE+*i(c)kel* (dial. *ickle*), *ȝokyl*, after MSw. *isikil* (= MDa. *isegel*); cf. Norw. *isjøkel, -jokkel*; repl. OE. **īsġiċel* (whence ME. *isechele*), for which *īses ġiċel* 'icicle of ice' is attested; OE. *ġiċel, ġiċela* (ME. *ychele*) :– **jakilaz, -on*, cogn. with ON. *jǫkull* icicle, glacier :– **jakulaz* (cf. ON. *jaki* ice floe). ¶ From ME. *iseyokel* was evolved, by coalescence, dial. *iceshockle*, from which the second el. was detached as *shockle* (XVI), *shoggle* (XVIII).

-icity see -IC.

icon, ikon ai·kɔn †image, picture XVI; (Eastern Ch.) representation in the flat of a sacred personage XIX. – L. *īcōn* (Pliny) – Gr. *eikṓn* likeness, image, similitude, f. **ϝeik-* be like. comb. form **icono-** aikɔ·nŏ, aikənɔ· in the foll.: **ico·noclast** one who favours the destruction of images XVII. – modL. *īconoclastēs* – Gr. *eikonoklástēs* (*klân* break); cf. F. *iconoclaste*; so **iconokla·st**IC XVII. **icono**·GRAPHY †drawing, plan; illustration by means of drawings. XVII. – medL. *īconographia* – G. *eikonographíā*. **icono·stasis** screen bearing icons. – ecclL. – ecclGr. *eikonóstasis* (*stásis* position, station, f. **sta-* STAND); also in Russ. form, *ikonostás*. XIX.

icosahedron aiko(u)səhe·drən, -hī·- solid contained by 20 plane faces. XVI. – Gr. *eikosáedron*, n. of adj. used sb. (sc. *schêma* figure), f. *eíkosi* :– **eϝíkosi* (rel. to L. *vīgintī* twenty) + *hédrā* seat, base (see SIT).

-ics iks see -IC.

icteric ikte·rik pert. to jaundice. XVI. – L. *ictericus* – Gr. *ikterikós*, f. *íkteros* jaundice; see -IC and cf. (O)F. *ictérique*.

ictus i·ktəs metrical stress. XVIII. L. 'blow, stroke', f. *ict-*, pp. stem of *īcere* strike.

id id (biol.) unit of germ-plasm. XIX. G. (Weismann, 1893), the first syll. of *idioplasm* (see IDIO-, PLASM).

id., abbrev. of **idem** ai·dem, i·dem the same name, title, author, as is mentioned above. XVII. L. *īdem* m. (for **isdem*), *idem* n. (for **iddem*), f. *is, id* that one + *-dem*, as in IBIDEM.

-id[1] suffix repr. F. *-ide* – L. *-idus, -ida, -idum*, used to form adjs. chiefly from vbs. with *ē*-stems, as *acidus* ACID, f. *acēre, torridus* TORRID, f. *torrēre*, less freq. from *ĭ*- or cons.-stems, as *fluidus* FLUID, f. *fluere*, and from sbs., as *morbus* MORBID, f. *morbus*.

-id[2] suffix of sbs., repr. F. *-ide* – L. *-idem, -ida*, nom. *-is*, Gr. *-ida*, nom. *-is*, as in *chrysalid, pyramid*; bot. denoting a member of a family, e.g. *irid* of Iridaceæ, *orchid* of Orchidaceæ. In *Æneid, Thebaid*, etc. – L. *Ænēid-, -is, Thēbāid-, -is*, the ending is orig. adj., scil. *mūsa, poēsis* poem.

-id[3] (zool.) in sbs. and adjs. from L. names of families in *-idæ* and of classes in *-ida*, m. and n. pl. respectively of L. – Gr. *-idēs*.

-id[4] early var. of -IDE still retained in U.S.

ide aid fish allied to the carp. XIX (Yarrell). – modL. *idus* (Linnæus) – Sw. *id*. So F. *ide*.

-ide aid formerly also -ID[4], *-yd(e)*, repr. F. *-ide*, †*-yde*, first used in OXIDE – F. *oxyde*, f. *oxygène* OXYGEN, on the analogy of which it is regularly affixed to a shortened form of the name of the element which combines with another element or a radical to form the compound so designated (see also -URET, which it replaced; cf. the synon. *sulphuretted hydrogen* and *hydrogen sulphide*).

idea aidi·ə A. archetype (as in Platonic philosophy), conception, design; †form, figure; mental image, notion. XVI (with special developments in mod. philosophy). – L. *idea* (in Platonic sense) – Gr. *idéā* look, semblance, form, kind, nature, ideal form, model, f. **ϝid-* see (see WIT); analogous in origin and primary meaning to *species* (f. L. *specere* see). Earlier (XV) and still dial. *idee* aidī· – (O)F. *idée*. The comb. form is **ideo-**, as in **ideologue** aidī·əlɔg one who is occupied with (esp. unpractical) ideas XIX. – F. **ide**·AL[1] adj. XVII; sb. XVIII. – F. *idéal* – late L. *ideālis* (Martianus Capella).

idem the same; see ID.

identity aide·ntiti quality of being the same. XVI. – late L. *identitās* (whence also F. *identité*), f. L. *idem* same, prob. after *entitās* ENTITY, but possibly assoc. with *identidem* over and over again, repeatedly, rendering Gr. ταυτότης (Aristotle). Thus *ident(i)-* was established as the comb. form of *idem*; so **ide·ntic**, -ICAL (XVII) – medL. *identicus*, **ide·ntify** (XVII) – medL. *identificāre*.

ideology aidiɔ·lədʒi science of ideas XVIII; ideal or visionary speculation XIX; system of ideas, esp. concerning social and political life XX. – F. *idéologie* (Destutt de Tracy, 1796), f. Gr. *idéā* IDEA + *-logia* -LOGY.

Ides aidz in the ancient Roman Calendar, the 8th day after the Nones. XV. – (O)F. *ides* – L. *īdūs* (pl.), said by Varro to be an Etruscan word.

idio- i·dio(u), idiɔ· repr. Gr. *idio-*, comb. form of *ídios* personal, peculiar, separate.

idiom i·diəm proper language of a people or country, dialect; specific character of a language XVI; expression peculiar to a language XVII. – F. *idiome* or late L. *idiōma* – Gr. *idíōma* property, peculiar phraseology, f. *idioûsthai* make one's own, f. *ídios* own, private. So **idiomA·TIC**. XVIII (Addison).

idiosyncrasy i:diŏsi·nkrəsi peculiarity of constitution or temperament. XVII. – Gr. *idiosugkrāsíā*, *-krāsis*, f. *ídios* IDIO- + *súgkrāsis* commixture, tempering, f. *sún* SYN- + *krāsis* mixture (CRASIS); cf. F. *idiosyncrasie* (XVIII).

idiot i·diət mentally deficient person, natural fool XIII; †ignorant person, clown XIV. – (O)F. *idiot* = It., Sp. *idiota* – L. *idiōta* ignorant person – Gr. *idiṓtēs* private person, plebeian, ignorant, lay(man), f. *ídios* private, peculiar. ¶ Coalescence of *n* of the indef. art. produced (dial.) *nidiot*, *nidget* (XVI). Hence **idiocy** i·diəsi. XVI (*-sy*, Skelton). prob. after *lunatic* / *lunacy*; but cf. Gr. *idiōteíā*; also **i·diotcy**. XIX. **idiotic** idiɔ·tik XVIII, -ICAL XVII; earlier **†i·diotish**[1] XVI–XVIII.

idle ai·dl †empty; worthless, useless; doing nothing, inactive OE.; lazy, indolent XIII. OE. *īdel* = OFris. *īdel*, OS. *īdal* empty, worthless (Du. *ijdel* vain, useless, frivolous, trifling, conceited, *ijl* thin, flimsy, raving), OHG. *ītal* empty, useless (G. *eitel* bare, mere, worthless, vain); WGerm. only (Sw., Da. *idel* are – LG.); ult. origin unkn.; primary meaning prob. 'empty'. Hence **i·dlesse** XVI (Spenser), pseudo-archaism, after *humblesse*, etc., revived by Scott.

Ido ī·dou artificial language based on Esperanto, made public in 1907. The name in the language means 'offspring'.

idol ai·d(ə)l image of a deity XIII; object of devotion; phantom, fiction, false image XVI. ME. *ydel*, *ydol* – OF. *id(e)le*, (also mod.) *idole* – L. *īdōlum* image, form, apparition, (eccl.) idol – Gr. *eídōlon* (same meanings), f. *eîdos* form, shape (cf. IDEA and see WIT). So **idolater** aidɔ·lətəɹ worshipper of idols. XVI. Earlier †*idolatrer*, †*-trour* (XIV Wyclif to XVII Donne), either f. (O)F. *idolâtre* + -ER[1], *-our*, -OR[1], or f. *idolatry*, after *astronomer* / *astronomy*; the present form (XVI) was either a phonetic reduction of *idolatrer* or – F. *idolâtre* – CRom. (medL.) *īdōlatra*, for *īdōlolatra*, *-trēs* – Gr. *eidōlolátrēs* (*latreúein* worship). **ido·latry**[3]. XIII. – (O)F. – CRom. (medL.) *īdōlatrīa*, for ecclL. *īdōlolatrīa* (Tertullian) – Gr. (N.T.) *eidōlolatreíā* (cf. LATRIA). **i·dolize**. XVI (Sylvester); preceded by (arch.) **ido·latrize** XVI (Daniel). **ido·latrous**. XVI. f. †*idolatrer*; superseded †*idola·trical*, †*idolola·trical*.

idyll ai·dil short poem descriptive of a picturesque (rustic) scene or incident. XVII (earlier *idyllium*, *-ion* XVI). – L. *īdyllium* – Gr. *eidúllion*, dim. of *eîdos* form, picture (cf. IDOL, IDEA). Hence **idy·llic**. XIX (earlier *idy·llian* XVIII).

-ie, frequent var. (formerly also †*-ee*) of -Y[6], e.g. *birdie*, *brownie* (XVI, G. Douglas), *dearie* (XVII), *doggie*, *Jeanie*, *Willie*.

-ier[1] iəɹ, with var. *-yer* jəɹ, in agent-nouns based on native words and functioning as -ER[1]. Among the earliest exx. (XIII) are *tiliere*, extension with *-ere* of OE. *tilia* tiller, cultivator, *bowiare* bowyer; these may have served as models for other formations of various and sometimes obscure origin, e.g. *brazier*, *clothier* (preceded by †*clother*), *collier*, *drovier*, *glazier*, *grazier*, *haulier*, *hosier*, *lawyer* (also †*lawer*), *sawyer* (*y* is regular after *w*), *spurrier*.

-ier[2] iə·ɹ repr. F. *-ier* (:– L. *-āriu-s* -ARY), appears first in XVI, as in *bombardier*, *cashier*, *cavalier*, *halberdier*, *harquebusier*; later exx. are *brigadier*, *fusilier*, *grenadier*; in *fina·ncier* the stress is different. For a graphic var. see -EER[1]. ¶ In *farrier* and *furrier* *-ier* repl. *-our* (– OF. *-our*).

-ies iz pl. ending of certain ellipt. words, as *civvies* civilian clothes, *movies* moving pictures, *talkies* talking films, *undies* underclothes.

-iety ai·ĭti suffix repr. F. *-iété* – L. *-ietās* expressing the quality or condition of what is denoted by adjs. in *-ius* -IOUS, as in *anxiety*, *contrariety*, *dubiety*, *(in)ebriety*, *(im)propriety*, *notoriety*, *society*, *variety* (on which was modelled †*rariety* XVI–XVII). A few are based on advs., as *satiety*, *ubiety*.

if conj. introducing a clause of condition or supposition. OE. *ġif*, *ġyf*, corr. (with variation due to stress conditions) to OFris. *jef*, *ef*, *jof*, *of*, OS. *ef*, *of* (Du. *of*), OHG. *ibu*, *oba*, *ube*, also *niba*, *noba*, *nube* if not (G. *ob* whether, if), ON. *ef* if, Goth. *ibai*, *iba* whether, lest, *niba(i)* if not, *jabai* if, although; by some regarded as case-forms of a sb. repr. by OHG. *iba* condition, ON. *ef*, *if*, *efan*, *ifan*, etc., doubt, whence *efa*, *ifa* vb. (but this may be based on the conj.); ult. etym. unkn.

-iferous i·fərəs f. L. *-ifer*, f. stem- or connecting vowel *i* + *-fer* bearing, furnishing, f. base of *ferre* BEAR[2]; orig. in adoptions of L. words in *-fer* or F. words in *-fère*, whence in unlimited use with L. stems, esp. in terms of nat. hist.; see -OUS.

-ify ifai see -FY.

-igerous i·dʒərəs f. L. *-iger*, f. stem- or connecting vowel *i*+base of *gerere* carry (cf. GESTATION); see -OUS.

igloo i·glū Eskimo dome-shaped hut. XIX.

igneous i·gniəs fiery; resulting from the action of fire. XVII. f. L. *igneus*, f. *ignis* fire (rel. to OSl. *ognĭ*, Lith. *ugnìs*, Skr. *agnís*); see -EOUS. **ignite** ignai·t make intensely hot, spec. to the point of combustion or chemical change XVII; trans. set on fire XVIII (Johnson, defining the chemical use); intr. take fire (Todd, 1818, defining the chemical use). f. *ignīt-*, pp. stem of L. *ignīre* set on fire, f. *ignis* fire. So **igni·**TION (chem.) XVII; (pop.) XIX.

ignis fatuus i·gnis fæ·tjuəs will-o'-the-wisp. XVI. modL., 'foolish fire', so named from its erratic flitting from place to place. ¶ Rendered in F. by *feu follet*.

ignoble ignou·bl not noble. XVI. – F. *ignoble* or L. *ignōbilis*, f. *in-* IN-[2]+*gnōbilis* NOBLE. So **ignobi·l**ITY. XV. – L.

ignominy i·gnəmĭni disgrace. XVI. – F. *ignominie* or L. *ignōminia*, f. *in-* IN-[2]+ **gnōmen*, *nōmen* name, reputation; see -Y[3]. So **ignomi·n**IOUS. XVI. ¶ Shortened forms were †*ignomy*, †*ignomious* XVI.

ignoramus ignərei·məs †endorsement made formerly by a grand jury on a bill returned as not a true bill XVI; ignorant person XVII (generalized from the use of *Ignoramus* as a proper name, e.g. of a lawyer in Ruggle's play so entitled, 1615, which was written to ridicule the common lawyer; cf. R. Callis's 'The Case and Arguments against Sir Ignoramus, of Cambridge, in his Readings at Staple's Inn', 1648). L. 'we do not know', in legal use 'we take no notice (of it)', 1st pers. pl. pres. ind. of *ignōrāre* IGNORE.

ignorance i·gnərəns want of knowledge. XIII. – (O)F. *ignorance* – L. *ignōrantia*, f. prp. of *ignōrāre* not to know, misunderstand, disregard, rel. to *ignārus* unaware; see -ANCE. So **i·gnor**ANT. XIV (Ch.). – (O)F. *ignorant*. **ignore** ignɔ̄ə·ɹ †not to know XVII; (of a grand jury) reject (a bill); refuse to take notice of XIX. – (O)F. *ignorer* or L. *ignōrāre*.

iguana igwā·nə large arboreal lizard. XVI – Sp. *iguana*, repr. Carib *iwana* (to which some early forms approximate). Hence, after *mastodon*, **igua·nodon** large fossil lizard.

ihram irā·m Mohammedan pilgrim's dress. XVIII. – Arab. *iḥrām*, f. *ḥarama* forbid (see HAREM).

IHS in ME., late and medL., etc., usually IHS, IHC, ihs, ihc, repr. Gr. ΙΗΣ, IHC, contraction or suspension of ΙΗΣΟΥΣ, IHCOYC JESUS; commonly used as a symbolical or ornamental monogram of the sacred name, and popularly interpreted in various ways.

il-[1] assim. form of L. *in-* IN-[1] before *l*, as in *illuminate*.

il-[2] assim. form of negative *in-* IN-[2] before *l*, as in *illegal*.

-il ĭl former regular var. of -ILE surviving in a few words, viz. *civil*, *fossil*, *utensil*. Cf. APRIL.

-ile ail, (also, esp. formerly) il adj. suffix repr. F. *-il*, chiefly *-ile*, and its sources L. *-ilis*, *-īlis*, which was added to vb.-stems with the senses of capacity or suitability, e.g. *agilis* agile, *fragilis* fragile, and with wider meaning to noun-stems, e.g. *juvenīlis* juvenile, *humilis* humble, *sterilis* sterile.

ilex ai·leks holm-oak, Quercus Ilex. XVI. L., perh. a Mediterranean word.

iliac i·liæk A. (path.) *iliac passion* disease affecting the ileum or third portion of the small intestine. B. (anat.) pert. to the flank. XVI. – late L. *īliacus*, in form a deriv. of *īlia* (i) flanks, (ii) entrails, but the suffix is Gr. and sense A goes with L. *īleus* – Gr. *eileós* colic, prob. rel. to *eílein* roll.

Iliad i·liæ̆d Gr. epic poem (attributed to Homer) concerning the ten years' siege of Ilium (or Troy) by the Greeks. XVI. – L. *Iliad-*, nom. *Ilias* – Gr. *Iliad-*, *Iliás*, sb. use of adj. (sc. *poíēsis* poem) 'pert. to Ilium'. ¶ *Iliad* is used like ÆNEID in sg. and pl.

ilk ilk †same OE.; surviving only in phr. *of that ilk* of the same place or name (e.g. *Guthrie of that ilk* for Guthrie of Guthrie. XVI (erron. *that ilk* that family or set XIX). OE. *ilca* m., *ilce* fem. and n., f. **ĭ-* that, the same (as in Goth. *is* he, OHG. *ir*, also mod. *er*, L. *is* that, *īdem*, *idem* same, Gr. *ín* this one)+**līk-* form (see LIKE and cf. the formation of SUCH, WHICH).

ilka ilkə (now Sc.) each. ME. *ilk a(n)* XII (*illc an*, Orm), i.e. *ilk* :– OE. *ylc* EACH+A[1].

ill il A. (dial.) morally evil XII (Orm); causing harm, pain, or disaster XIII (Bestiary, Genesis and Exodus); of bad quality XIII (Cursor M.); of evil intent XIV (R. Mannyng). B. out of health, sick XV; sb. evil XII (Cursor M.); adv. evilly, badly XII (Orm). – ON. *illr* adj.; *illa* adv., *ilt* n. of adj. as sb.; ult. origin unkn. At first peculiar to areas of Scand. penetration; later much extended regionally in competition with *evil*, but still restricted in standard usage, the adj. being less common than the adv. (which is freely used in composition), and, exc. in predicative use (e.g. *he is ill*), mainly confined to traditional collocations, as *ill health* (ON. *ill heilsa*), *ill temper*, *ill usage*, *ill will* (XIII Cursor M. – ON. *illvili*; later modelled on L. *malevolentia* MALEVOLENCE); *ill-mannered*, *ill-tempered*. Sense B of the adj. appears to have been evolved from ON. impers. use with the neuter as in *mér er illt* I am ill, *varð þeim ilt af* it made them ill. Hence (dial.) **i·lly.** XVI; see -LY[2].

illapse il(l)æ·ps (theol.) falling or sinking into. XVII (Jackson). – L. *illapsus*; see IL-[1], LAPSE.

illative ilei·tiv (gram.) inferential. XVI. – L. *illātīvus*, f. *illātus*, used as pp. of *inferre* INFER; see -IVE. So **illa·**TION inference. XVI. – L.

illegal ilī·gəl. XVII. – (O)F. *illégal* or medL. *illegālis*; see IL-², LEGAL.

illegitimate ilidʒi·tĭmət not born in lawful wedlock XVI; unauthorized XVII. f. late L. *illegitimus* (whence earlier †*illegitime*), after LEGITIMATE; see IL-².

illicit ili·sit not allowed or authorized. XVII. – L.; see IL-², LICIT.

illiterate ili·tərət ignorant of learning or education. XVI. – L.; see IL-², LITERATE.

illth ilþ ill-being)(*wealth*. 1860 (Ruskin). f. ILL + -TH¹.

illuminate ilʲū·mineit light up, give light to XVI; decorate with colour XVIII (superseding †*enlumine* – (O)F. *enluminer*, medL. *inlūmināre*; cf. LIMN) – pp. stem of late L. *illūmināre*, f. *in* IL-¹ + *lūmin, lūmen* LIGHT¹; see LUMINOUS, -ATE³. So **illumin**A·TION spiritual enlightenment XIV (Trevisa); lighting up XVI; embellishment with colour XVII. – (O)F. – late L. **illu·mine** enlighten (first in spiritual sense). XIV (R. Rolle). – (O)F. *illuminer* – L. *illūmināre*.

illuminati ilʲūminei·tai applied to several sects claiming special enlightenment: (i) the Sp. heretics *Alumbrados* XVI; (ii) G. *Illuminaten*, secret society founded by Adam Weishaupt XVIII; (hence gen.) persons claiming special knowledge XIX. L., pl. of *illūminātus*, pp. of *illūmināre* (see prec.), or pl. of It. *illuminato*.

illusion ilʲū·ʒən †deception XIV (R. Rolle); deceptive appearance, etc. XIV (Ch.); perception of an external object involving a false belief XVIII. – (O)F. *illusion* – L. *illūsiō(n-)*, f. *illūdere* mock, jest at (whence rare **illu·de** XV), f. *in-* IL-¹ + *lūdere* play, sport. So **illu·**SORY². XVI. – late L.

illustrate i·ləstreit, (formerly) ilʌ·streit throw light or lustre on; elucidate XVI; exemplify; elucidate with pictures XVII. f. pp. stem of L. *illustrāre*, f. *in* IL-¹ + *lustrāre* illuminate, f. **lukstrom*, rel. to *lūmen* LIGHT¹. Earlier †*illustre* (Caxton). So **illustr**A·TION †illumination XIV; exemplification, example XVI; pictorial elucidation XIX. – (O)F. – L. (Quintilian). **illustr**ATIVE ilʌ·strətiv serving to illustrate. XVII (Sir T. Browne). **illu·str**IOUS distinguished by rank, etc. XVI (Sh.). f. L. *illustris*. Earlier †*illustre* (Dunbar) – F. or L.

im-¹ assim. form of IN-¹ before *p, b, m*.

im-² assim. form of IN-² before *p, b, m*.

image i·midʒ artificial representation of an object, likeness, statue; (optical) counterpart XIII; mental representation XIV (Ch., Gower). – (O)F. *image* = Pr. *image*, Sp. *imagen*, It. *immagine* – L. *imāginem*, nom. *imāgō*, rel. to *imitārī* IMITATE. So **i·mag**ERY. XIV. – OF. *imagerie*, f. *imageur* maker of images. **imagine** imæ·dʒin. XIV (R. Rolle, PPl., Ch., Wyclif, Gower). – (O)F. *imaginer* – L. *imāgināre* form an image of, represent, fashion, (mediopass.) *imāginārī* picture to oneself, fancy. **imagin**A·TION. XIV (R. Rolle, Maund., Trevisa, Ch., Gower). – (O)F. – L. (tr. Gr. φαντασία phantasy). **ima·gin**ABLE. XIV (Ch.). – late L. (Boethius). **ima·gin**ARY. XIV (Wycl. Bible). – L. **ima·gin**ATIVE. XIV (Ch.). – (O)F.

imago imei·gou (entom.) final stage of an insect. XVIII. Mod. use (by Linnæus, 1767) of L. *imāgō* IMAGE.

imam, imaum imā·m priest of a mosque; Mohammedan leader. XVII. – Arab. *imām* leader, f. *amma* precede. Cf. F., Sp. *iman* (used also in Eng.).

imbecile i·mbĭsīl, -il weak XVI; mentally weak, idiotic XIX. Earliest form *imbecille* – F. †*imbécille* (now *-ile*) – L. *imbēcillus, -is*, f. *in-* IM-² + **bēcillum*, var. of *baculum* stick, staff (cf. BACILLUS), the etymol. meaning being 'without support' (*sine baculo*). A notion that the L. form was **imbecilis* (as stated by N. Bailey and Johnson) induced the form in *-ile* and consequently the pronunc. with īl; but J. has *imbe·cile*, as Shelley has. So **imbeci·l**ITY. XVI. – (O)F. – L. Cf. EMBEZZLE. ¶ 'Dr. Johnson, Dr. Ash, Dr. Kenrick, and Entick, accent the word on the second syllable, as in the Latin *imbecilis*; but Mr. Scott and Mr. Sheridan on the last, as in the French *imbecille*. The latter is, in my opinion, the more fashionable, but the former more analogical' (Walker).

imb- U.S. sp. of many words in EMB-.

imbibe imbai·b †A. soak, saturate XIV (Ch.); B. drink in, absorb. XVI. In A – F. *imbiber* soak (not recorded before XVI), in B – its source L. *imbibere*, f. *in* IM¹ + *bibere* drink.

imbricate i·mbrikeit (nat. hist.) covered with scales overlapping like roof tiles. XVII. – pp. of L. *imbricāre*, f. *imbric-, imbrex* roof tile, f. *imber* rain; see -ATE².

imbroglio imbrou·ljou confused heap XVIII; confusion and entanglement XIX. – It. *imbroglio*, f. *imbrogliare* confuse, corr. to F. *embrouiller* EMBROIL; see IM-¹, BROIL¹.

imbrue imbrū· †sully XV; stain *with* blood XVI (More). Early forms *enbrewe, enbrowe* – OF. *embruer, embrouer* bedaub, bedabble, f. *en* IM-¹ + OF. *breu, bro* (cf. mod. *brouet* broth) – Rom. **brodum* (cf. It. *imbrodolare* dirty, bedabble) – Germ. **broð-* BROTH.

imbue imbjū· saturate, impregnate. XVI. In the earliest exx. in pp. f. F. *imbu*, †*imbu(i)t*, or its source L. *imbūtus*, pp. of *imbuere* moisten, stain, imbue.

imburse imbə̄·ɹs XVI. Survives gen. in REIMBURSE.

imide i·maid (chem.) derivative of ammonia in which two atoms of hydrogen are replaced by a diatomic radical. XIX. Arbitrary alteration of AMIDE.

imitate i·miteit make or become like or a copy of. XVI. f. pp. stem of L. *imitārī* copy, rel. to *imāgō* IMAGE and *æmulus* rival, *æmulārī* try to be like, EMULATE; see -ATE³. So **imit**A·TION. XVI. – (O)F. or L. **i·mit**ATIVE. XVI. – late L. **i·mit**ATOR. XVI. – L.

immaculate imæ·kjŭlət spotless. XV. – L. *immaculātus*; see IM-², MACULATE.

immanent i·mənənt indwelling, inherent. XVI (Lyndesay). – prp. of late L. *immanēre* (Augustine), f. *in* IM-¹+*manēre* remain, dwell; see -ENT. So **i·mmanENCE.** XIX (Coleridge), -ENCY. XVII (Pearson).

immarcescible immāɹse·sĭbl unfading. XVI. – late L. *immarcescibilis*, f. *in-* IM-²+*marcēscere, marcēre* fade; see -IBLE.

immaterial imətiə·riəl incorporeal XIV (Trevisa; not freq. before XVI); unimportant XVII (¶ 'This sense has crept into the conversation and writings of barbarians', J.). – late L. (Ambrose, Jerome); see IM-², MATERIAL.

immediate imī·diət having no intermediary; acting or existing without a medium or intervening agency; next adjacent, instant. XVI. – (O)F. *immédiat* or late L. *immediātus*, f. *in-* IM-²+*mediātus* MEDIATE. So **imme·diateLY²**. XV; rendering L. adv. *immediātē*. Hence **imme·diACY** XVII. (Sh.).

immemorial imimō·riəl ancient beyond memory. XVII. – medL. *immemōriālis*; see IM-², MEMORIAL and cf. F. *immémorial*.

immense ime·ns extremely great XV (Caxton); †boundless, infinite XVI. – (O)F. *immense* – L. *immēnsus* immeasurable, f. (after Gr. *ámetros*) *in-* IM-²+*mēnsus*, pp. of *mētīrī* (see MEASURE). So **imme·nsITY.** XV. – (O)F.

immerse imɜ̄·ɹs plunge in liquid. XVII. f. *immers-*, pp. stem of L. *immergere*, f. *in* IM-¹ +*mergere* dip, MERGE. So **imme·rSION.** XVII. – late L.

immigrate i·migreit go and settle in another country. XVII. f. pp. stem of L. *immigrāre*; see IM-¹, MIGRATE. So **i·mmigrANT** XVIII, **immigrA·TION** XVII.

imminent i·minənt impending threateningly, close at hand. XVI. – L. *imminent-, -ēns*, prp. of *imminēre* project, be impending, f. *in-* IM-¹+ **min-* (cf. EMINENT, PROMINENT).

immolate i·mŏleit sacrifice. XVI. f. *immolāt-*, pp. stem of L. *immolāre* (orig.) sprinkle with sacrificial meal (*mola salsa* salted meal), f. *in* IM-¹+*mola* MEAL¹; see -ATE³. So **immolA·TION.** XVI.

immortal imɔ̄·ɹtəl not mortal XIV; lasting, everlasting XVI. – L. *immortālis* (pl. sb. the gods), f. *in-* IM-²+*mortālis* MORTAL; sb. XVII; cf. (O)F. *immortel*. So **immortA·LITY.** XIV. – (O)F. – L. **immortelle** imɔɹte·l everlasting flower. XIX. – F. (for *fleur immortelle*).

immune imjū·n †free, exempt XV; secure from contagion, etc. XIX (*c.*1880 after F. *immune* – L. *immūnis* exempt from a service or charge, f. *in-* IM-²+*mūnis* ready for service (cf. COMMON). So **immu·nITY** exemption from service or liability XIV; non-susceptibility to contagion, etc. (after F. *immunité*) XIX.

immure imjuə·ɹ †wall in; shut within walls XVI; build into a wall XVII. – medL. *immūrāre* (perh. through F. *emmurer*), f. L. *in* IM-¹+*mūrus* wall, early *moiros, moerus* (rel. to *mœnia* fortifications; see MUNITION).

imp imp †young shoot, sapling OE.; scion, offspring, child XIV; 'child' of the Devil, little demon, evil spirit XVI; mischievous child XVII. OE. *impa* or *impe*. So **imp** vb. †graft, engraft OE.; engraft feathers in a bird's wing so as to improve or restore its flight XV; enlarge, eke *out* XVI. OE. *impian*, corr. to OHG. *impfōn* (G. *impfen*), shortened analogues of OHG. *impitōn* (MHG. *impfeten*) – Rom. **impotare*, f. medL. *impotus* graft (Salic Law) – Gr. *émphutos* implanted, engrafted, vbl. adj. of *emphúein* implant, f. *en* IN¹, IN-¹, EM-¹+*phúein* (see BE C). ¶ (O)F. *ente, enter* graft (whence MDu., Du. *ent, ente*) have the same origin. Da. *ympe*, Sw. *ymp, ympa* are from LG.; W. *imp* sb., *impio* vb. are from Eng.

impact i·mpækt striking of one body on another. XVIII. f. *impact-*, pp. stem of L. *impingere* IMPINGE, after CONTACT.

impair impɛə·ɹ make worse or weaker. XIV. ME. *empaire, -peire* – OF. *empeirier* (mod. *empirer*) :– Rom. **impējōrāre* make worse, f. *in-* IM-¹+late L. *pējōrāre* (cf. PEJORATIVE); the prefix was latinized to *im-* XV. The earlier ME. forms were *ampaire, ap(p)aire* – AN. **apairer*, OF. *ampeirier*.

impale impei·l surround with a palisade, fence in XVI (Palsgr.); (her.) combine (coats of arms) palewise; fix upon a stake or point XVII. – F. *empaler* or medL. *impālāre*, f. *in* IM-¹+*pālus* PALE¹.

impanate i·mpəneit embody in bread. XVI. f. pp. stem of medL. *impānāre*, f. L. *in* IM-¹ +*pānis* bread; see -ATE³. So **impanA·TION.**

imparisyllabic impæ:risilæ·bik of Gr. and L. nouns that have not the same number of syllables in all their cases. XVIII. f. L. *impar* unequal, f. *in-* IM-²+*par* equal, PEER¹; see SYLLABIC.

impart impā·ɹt make partaker of XV; make known XVI. – OF. *impartir* – L. *impartīre* (usu. *impertīre*), f. *in* IM-¹+*part-, pars* share, PART.

impasse ẽpa·s, i·mpæs cul-de-sac; insoluble difficulty. XIX (Greville). F. (Voltaire), f. *im-* IM-²+stem of *passer* PASS.

impassible impæ·sĭbl incapable of suffering XIV; incapable of suffering injury XV; incapable of feeling XVI. – (O)F. *impassible* – ecclL. *impassibilis*; see IM-², PASSIBLE. So **impa·ssIVE.** XVII (Milton).

impassion impæ·ʃən inflame with passion. XVI. – It. *impassionare*, f. *in* IM-¹+*passione* PASSION; chiefly in pp. (also †*impassionate*).

impasto impæ·stou laying on of colour thickly. XVIII. It., f. *impastare*, f. *in* IM-¹+ *pasta* PASTE.

impa·tience. XIII (AncrR.). – (O)F. *impatience* – L. (see IM-², PATIENCE). So **impa·TIENT.** XIV (PPl.). – (O)F. – L.

impeach impī·tʃ †impede; accuse, charge XIV (Wyclif); charge with a high misdemeanour; call in question, disparage XVI. ME. *empeche, -esche* – OF. *empecher, -escher* (mod. *empêcher* prevent) = Pr. *empedegar* :– late L. *impedicāre* catch, entangle, f. *in* IM-¹+*pedica* FETTER. Superseded †*appeach* – AN. var. of *empecher*. So **impea·ch**MENT. XIV. – OF. *empe(s)chement*.

impeccable impe·kəbl not liable to sin XVI; faultless XVII. – L. *impeccābilis*, f. *in*- IM-²+*peccāre* sin; see -ABLE.

impecunious impĭkjū·niəs in want of money. XVI (Nashe, Jonson). f. L. *in*- IM-² +*pecunia* money (cf. PECUNIARY).

impede impī·d hinder. XVII (Sh.; †*impedite* is earlier). – L. *impedīre*, f. *in* IM-¹+*ped-, pēs* FOOT. Hence **imped**ANCE impī·dəns (electr.). 1886 (Heaviside). So **impedi**MENT -pe·d- hindrance XIV (Trevisa); †pl. baggage (of an army) XVI. – L. *impedīmentum*, the pl. of which, **impedime·nta**, is used in the second sense (XVI, Holland).

impel impe·l force or constrain *to*. XV (Caxton). – L. *impellere*, f. *in* IM-¹+*pellere* drive (cf. PULSE¹).

impend impe·nd hang threateningly XVI; be imminent XVII; hang *over* XVIII. – L. *impendēre*, f. *in* IM-¹+*pendēre* (see PENDENT).

imperative impe·rətiv (gram.) expressing command; commanding, peremptory XVI; urgent XIX. – late L. *imperātīvus* specially ordered (Macrobius), gram. (Martianus Capella; tr. Gr. προστακτική, sc. ἔγκλισις), f. *imperāt-*, pp. stem of *imperāre* command (cf. EMPEROR); see -IVE.

impe·rfect not perfect. XIV (R. Rolle, Ch.); (gram.) of a tense XVI (Palsgr.); (mus.) XVI (Morley). ME. *inperfit* – (O)F. *imparfait*; see IM-², PERFECT. So **im**PERFE·CTION.

imperial impiə·riəl pert. to an empire or emperor; commanding, majestic, exalted. XIV (Ch., Gower). – (O)F. *impérial* – L. *imperiālis*, f. *imperium* rule, EMPIRE; see -IAL. The sb. uses, 'luggage case for the top of a carriage, the carriage roof itself (XVIII)', 'small beard beneath the lower lip' (1839), are from F. *impériale*. Hence **impe·rial**ISM. XIX, **impe·rial**IST adherent of an empire or emperor XVII (after F. *impérialiste*); advocate of (British) imperialism XIX.

imperil impe·rĭl bring into peril. XVI (*emperill*, Spenser). f. EM-¹ IM-¹+PERIL; prob. after *endanger*.

imperious impiə·riəs †imperial; †sovereign, majestic; overbearing; overmastering. XVI. – L. *imperiōsus*, f. *imperium* command, EMPIRE; see -IOUS and cf. F. *impérieux*.

imperscriptible impəɹskri·ptĭbl for which no written authority can be adduced. XIX. f. L. *in*- IM-²+pp. stem of *perscribere* write out, f. *per* PER- + *scribere* write; see SCRIBE, -IBLE.

impersonal impə̄·ɹsənəl (gram.) used spec. in the 3rd person singular XVI (Whitington); not personal XVII. – late L. *impersōnālis*; see IM-², PERSONAL. Cf. F. *impersonnel*, †*-onal*.

impersonate impə̄·ɹsəneit invest with a personality XVII; assume the person of XVIII. f. L. *in* IM-¹+*persōna* PERSON, after *incorporate*.

impertinent impə̄·ɹtinənt †unrelated XIV (Wyclif); irrelevant XIV (Ch.); inappropriate, not consonant with reason XVI; presumptuously intrusive, insolent XVII. – (O)F. *impertinent* or late L. *impertinens* not pertinent, in medL. inept; see IM-², PERTINENT. Hence (or – F.) **impe·rtin**ENCE. XVII.

impertu·rbable. XV (rare before XVIII). – late L. (Augustine); see IM-², PERTURB, -ABLE.

impe·rvious. XVII. – L.; see IM-², PERVIOUS.

impetigo impĭtai·gou pl. *-igines* i·dʒinīz pustular skin disease. XVI. L., f. *impetere* assail, f. *in* IM-¹+*petere* seek (see PETITION).

impetrate i·mpitreit obtain by entreaty. XVI. f. pp. stem of L. *impetrāre*, f. *in* IM-¹+ *patrāre* bring to an end, f. *patr-, pater* FATHER; see -ATE³ and cf. PERPETRATE. So **impetr**A·TION. XV. – AN. *impetracioun* and L. *-ātiō*.

impetuous impe·tjuəs acting with sudden energy. XIV. – (O)F. *impétueux* – L. *impetuōsus*, f. *impetus* onset, violent impulse, f. *impetere*; see IMPETIGO, -UOUS. **impetus** i·mpitəs. XVII. – L.

impi i·mpi force of Kaffir warriors. XIX, Zulu.

impinge impi·ndʒ †thrust *upon* XVI; strike, dash XVII. – L. *impingere*, f. *in* IM-¹+*pangere* fix, drive in; see PACT and cf. IMPACT.

impious i·mpiəs not pious. XVI. f. L. *impius*; see IM-², PIOUS. So **im**PI·ETY. XIV (R. Rolle). – (O)F. or L.

implacable implæ·kəbl that cannot be appeased. XVI (More). – F. or L.; see IM-², PLACABLE.

implant implā·nt instil. XVI. – F. *implanter* or late L.; see IM-¹, PLANT.

implement¹ i·mplimənt (pl.) equipment, outfit XV; (orig. pl.) apparatus, set of utensils, tools XVI. – medL. *implēmenta* (pl.) noun of instrument corr. to medL. *implēre* employ, spend, extended use (by assoc. with *implicāre* EMPLOY) of L. *implēre* fill up, fulfil, discharge, f. *in* IM-¹+*plēre* FILL.

implement² i·mpliment †essential constituent XVII; (Sc.) fulfilment XVIII. – late L. *implēmentum* filling up, noun of action of L. *implēre* (see prec.). Hence **i·mplement** vb. (orig. Sc.) carry into effect. XIX. So **imple**·TION filling up. XVI. – late L.

implicate i·mplikeit (arch.) intertwine, entangle; involve (as in guilt). XVI. f. pp. stem of L. *implicāre*, f. *in* IM-¹+*plicāre* fold (see PLY); preceded by ppl. adj. *implicate* (see -ATE³). So **implic**A·TION. XV. – L.

implicit impli·sit implied but not plainly expressed XVI; †entangled, entwined XVII. – F. *implicite* (Calvin) or L. *implicitus*, later form of *implicātus*, pp. of *implicāre* (see prec.).

implore implǭə·ɹ beg or pray (for) XVI (Dunbar); beseech (one) XVII (Sh.). – F. *implorer* or L. *implōrāre* invoke with tears, f. *in* IM-¹+*plōrāre* weep.

implosion implou·ʒən bursting inwards; (phonetics) closure of the glottis together with stop contact compressing the enclosed air. XIX. f. IM-¹+-*plosion*, of EXPLOSION. So **implo·**SIVE formed by implosion.

imply implai· †enfold, involve XIV (Ch., Wyclif); involve the truth or existence of; express indirectly XVI. – OF. *emplier* :– L. *implicāre* IMPLICATE. The OF. var. *empleier*, *emploier* is the source of EMPLOY, with which *imply* to some extent overlapped XVI–XVII.

impoli·te. XVII (Drayton). See IM-², POLITE.

import impǭ·ɹt A. carry as its purport, signify, imply XV (Lydg.); be of significance or importance (to) XVI; B. bring in from outside XVI. – L. *importāre*; in A in its med. sense of 'imply, mean' (so F. *importer*, It. *importare*); in B in the orig. sense 'carry in', f. *in* IM-¹+*portāre* bring, carry, rel. to *portus* PORT.¹ Hence **i·mport** A. purport, significance, consequence XVI (Sh.); B. commodity imported XVII. So **impo·rt**ANCE. XVI. – (O)F. *importance* – medL. *importantia* significance, consequence. **impo·rt**ANT. XVI. – F. *important* – medL. *importāns*; cf. It. *importanza*, Sp. -*ancia*, It., Sp. -*ante*.

importunate impǭ·ɹtʃūnət, -tj- persistent in asking. XV. f. L. *importūnus*+-ATE², perh. on the model of *obstinate*. **importune** adj. *c.* 1400. – F. *importun*, -*une* or L. *importūnus* applied to waves and storms)(*opportūnus* OPPORTUNE. **importu·n**ITY. XV. – (O)F. – L. **impo·rtune** vb. XVI. – F. *importuner* or medL. *importūnārī*. The earliest of this group is *importune* adj. with the sense 'burdensome, troublesome', a notion which is common to them all.

impose impou·z †impute XV (Caxton); lay on (in various uses) XVI; exert influence *upon*, as with fraudulent intent or effect XVII. – (O)F. *imposer*, †*emposer*, f. *em-*, *im-* IM-¹+*poser*, to repr. L. *impōnere* place on or into, inflict, set over, lay as a burden, deceive, trick; see POSE¹. Hence **impo·**SING² exacting XVII; impressive XVIII; cf. F. *imposant* (Voltaire, 1732). So **imposition** impəzi·ʃən laying-on of hands XIV (Wycl. Bible); impost XV; exercise imposed as punishment XVIII. – (O)F. or L.

impo·ssible. XIII (Cursor M.). – (O)F. – L.; see IM-². ¶ Recorded earlier than POSSIBLE.

impost¹ i·mpoust tax, duty. XVI (Grafton). – F. †*impost* (now *impôt*) – medL. *impostus*, -*um*, sb. use of *impostus*, *impositus*, pp. of L. *impōnere* IMPOSE.

impost² i·mpoust (archit.) upper course of a pillar XVII (Evelyn); horizontal block supported by upright stones XVIII. – F. *imposte* or its source It. *imposta*, sb. use of fem. pp. of *imporre* :– L. *impōnere* IMPOSE.

impostor impɔ·stəɹ one who imposes on others. XVI. Earlier -*ur(e)*, -*our*, -*er* – F. *imposteur*, corr. to Sp. *impostor*, It. -*ore* – late L. *impostor*, contr. of *impositor* (cf. IMPOST¹), f. pp. stem of L. *impōnere* IMPOSE; see -OR¹. So **impo·st**URE. XVI. – F. – late L.

impost(h)ume impɔ·stjūm (arch.) purulent swelling, abscess. *c.* 1400. – OF. *empostume*, alteration of *apostume*, later form of *aposteme* (whence ME. †*aposteme* XIV) – L. *apostēma* – Gr. *apóstēma* lit. separation (cf. ABSCESS), f. *apostênai*, f. *apó* APO-+*stênai* STAND; finally assim. in prefix and ending to L. IM-¹ and *post(h)umus*.

impotent i·mpətənt physically weak. XIV (Gower). – (O)F. – L.; see IM-², POTENT. **i·mpot**ENCE XV (Hoccleve), -ENCY. XV.

impound impau·nd enclose in a pound XVI; take (an object) into formal custody XVII. f. IN-¹, IM-¹+POUND².

impoverish impɔ·vəriʃ make poor. XV (*emporisshe* Lydg.). f. *empoveriss-*, lengthened stem of OF. *empov(e)rir* (mod. *empauvrir*), f. *em-* (*im-*), IM-¹+*povre* POOR; see -ISH².

imprecation imprikei·ʃən invocation of evil. XVI. – L. *imprecātiō(n-)*, f. *imprecārī* (whence **i·mprecate** XVII), f. *in* IM-¹+*precārī* PRAY; see -ATE³, -ATION. **i·mprecat**ORY². XVI. – medL.

impregnable impre·gnəbl that cannot be overcome. XV. Late ME. *imprenable* – (O)F. *imprenable*, f. *in-* IM-²+*prenable* takeable, f. *pren-*, stem of *prendre* take :– L. *prehendere*; see PREHENSILE, -ABLE. The later forms *impre(i)gnable*, which depend upon OF. vars. (cf. PREGNANT¹), induced the pronunc. with g.

impregnate i·mpregneit make pregnant; imbue, saturate. XVII. f. *impregnate*, pp. (XVI) or – its source late L. *impræg nātus*, f. *in* IM-¹+*prægnāre* be PREGNANT; see -ATE³.

impresario imprisā·riou, -zā·riou organizer of public entertainments. XVIII. It., undertaker, contractor, f. *impresa* undertaking, EMPRISE; see -ARY.

imprescriptible impriskri·ptĭbl that may not be taken away. XVI (Foxe). – F.; see IM-².

impress¹ impre·s stamp, imprint (a mark, etc.), lit. and fig. XIV (Ch.); mark *with* a stamp XVI (Sh.); affect strongly XVIII. (In ME. also *en-*) – OF. *em-*, *impresser*, f. *im-*+*presser* PRESS¹, after L. *imprimere*. Hence **impress** sb. i·mpres stamp, mark. XVI. So **impress**ION impre·ʃən effective action, effect XIV (Ch., Gower); mark produced by pressure XIV (Trevisa); printing XVI; notion impressed on the mind XVII. – (O)F. *impression* – L. *impressiō(n-)* onset, attack, (in Cicero) emphasis, mental impression, f.

impress-, pp. stem of *imprimere*, f. *in* IM-¹+*premere* PRESS. **impre·ssion**ABLE. XIX. – F. *impressionnable*. **impre·ssionist** (of painting). 1881. – F. *impressionniste* (1874), coined in an unfavourable sense with ref. to a picture by Claude Monet entitled *Impression*. **impre·ss**IVE †susceptible XVI (Nashe); making a deep impression XVIII.

impress² impre·s levy, enlist, esp. by force. XVI (Sh.). f. IM-¹+PRESS². Hence **impress** sb. XVII (Sh.).

imprimatur imprimei·təɹ licence to print given by the L. formula *imprimātur* let it be printed, 3rd sg. pres. subj. pass. of *imprimere*; see IMPRINT. XVII.

imprimis imprai·mis in the first place. XV (Paston Lett.). L., assim. form of *in prīmīs* 'among the first things', i.e. *in* IN¹ and *prīmīs*, abl. pl. of *prīmus* first (PRIME).

imprint i·mprint impressed mark or stamp XV (Caxton); publisher's name, etc., on a title-page XVIII. Late ME. *empreynte, -printe* – (O)F. *empreinte*, sb. use of pp. fem. of *empreindre* :– L. *imprimere* impress, f. *in* IM-¹+*premere* PRESS. So **impri·nt** vb. mark by pressure, impress. XIV (Ch.). – OF. *empreinter*; see PRINT.

imprison impri·zn put in prison. XIII (RGlouc.). – OF. *emprisoner* (mod. *-onner*); see IM-¹, PRISON. So **impri·son**MENT. XIV.

impromptu imprɔ·mᵖtju adv. without premeditation; sb. extemporaneous performance. XVII. – F. *impromptu* (Molière) – L. phr. *in promptū* at hand, in readiness (*prōmere*; see PROMPT).

improper imprɔ·pəɹ XVI. – (O)F. or L.; see IM-², PROPER. ¶ Preceded by *improperlich* adv. (Gower), perh. after OF. *impropre-ment* (Oresme).

impropriate improu·prieit annex *to* a person or corporation. XVI. f. pp. stem of medL. *impropriāre* (whence earlier †*improper* XIV–XVIII), f. *in* IM-¹+*proprius* PROPER; see -ATE³.

improve imprū·v (†refl.) make one's profit; turn (an event, etc.) to good account, turn to profit or advantage; now (U.S.) make use of, occupy; enhance, augment XVI; raise to a better quality or condition XVII. Early forms *em-*, *improwe* – AN. *emprower, emprouer* (in AL. *appro(w)are, appruare*), f. OF. *em-* IM-¹+*prou* profit (:– late L. *prōde*, evolved from L. *prōdest* is of advantage), later infl. by PROVE. So **impro·ve**MENT. XV (*emprowement* profitable use, profit).

improvise i·mprəvaiz compose without preparation. XIX (Disraeli). – F. *improviser* or its source, It. *improvvisare*, f. *improvviso* extempore – L. *imprōvīsus* unforeseen, f. *in-* IM-²+*prōvīsus*, pp. of *prōvīdere* PROVIDE. So **improvis**A·TION. XVIII. Both prob. after the earlier adoption of It. *improvisatore* (mod. It. *-provv-*) XVIII (Smollett).

impudent i·mpjŭdənt †immodest XIV (Ch.); unblushingly presumptuous XVI. – L. *impudēns*, f. *in-* IM-²+*pudēns* ashamed, modest, orig. prp. of *pudēre* feel ashamed, shame. So **i·mpud**ENCE. XIV (Ch.).

impugn impjū·n assail. XIV (PPl., Wycl. Bible). – L. *impugnāre*, f. *in* IM-¹+*pugnāre* fight (see PUGNACIOUS).

impulse i·mpʌls act of impelling; stimulation of the mind. XVII. – L. *impulsus*, f. pp. stem of *impellere* IMPEL; cf. PULSE¹. So **impu·ls**IVE impelling to action XVI; actuated by impulse XIX. – (O)F. *impulsif, -ive* (rare before XVIII) or late L. *impulsīvus*.

impunity impjū·nĭti exemption from punishment XVI; security XVIII. – L. *impūnitās*, f. *impūnis* unpunished, f. *in-* IM-²+*pœna* penalty; see PAIN, -ITY.

impure impjuə·ɹ. XVI. – L.; see IM-², PURE. So **impu·ri**TY. XV. – L. Cf. F. *impur, impureté*.

impute impjū·t lay the fault of (a thing) *to* XIV; (theol.) attribute by vicarious substitution XVI. – (O)F. *imputer* – L. *imputāre* bring into the reckoning or charge, f. *in* IM-¹+*putāre* reckon (see PUTATIVE).

in¹ in prep. marking bounds or limits within which. OE. *in* = OFris., OS., OHG. (Du., G.), Goth. *in*, ON. *í*, rel. to L. *in* (older *en*), Gr. *en, enì*, OIr. *i n-, in*, W. *yn*, Lith. *ĩ*, OPruss. *en*, OSl. *vŭ(n-)*, Russ. *v (vo, vn-)* :– IE. **en*, **n̥*. Reduced to *i* before cons. by 1200, and so retained arch. and dial., as in *i' th'* in the, and *i' faith*; cf. HANDICAP. Distinct in origin from **in** adv., which repr. (i) OE. *in(n)*, used with vbs. of motion (cf. INTO) = OFris., OS., Du. *in*, OHG. *īn* (with secondary lengthening), G. *ein*, ON., Goth. *inn*, (ii) OE. *inne*, used with vbs. of position = OFris., OS. *inna*, OHG. *inna, -i, -e*, ON. *inni*, Goth. *inna*, orig. loc. Cf. OE. *hērinne* HEREIN, *þǣrin, -inne* THEREIN. ¶ OE. *innan* adv. and prep. entered into the comp. *wiþinnan* WITHIN.

Arising orig. from syntactical juncture of adv. *in* with a vb. are stable comps. such as *inbred, income, incoming, indwell(ing), ingathering, ingrowing, inlay, inlet, inroad, inset, inturn*, many of the sbs. depending on phrasal units, as *inlet*, f. *let in*. In attrib. or adj. use *in* is or has been variously used, as in *in-land, inshore, inside*, and *in-patient* (sc. in a hospital). Cf. INNER, INMOST.

in² L. *in* (see prec.) with the abl. 'in', with the acc. 'into', 'against', 'towards, for the purpose of', in many phrases frequent in Eng. contexts from XVI onwards, as *in capite* in CHIEF, *in* COMMENDAM, *in extenso, in extremis, in flagrante delicto, in forma pauperis, in medias res, in memoriam, in partibus (infidelium), in pontificalibus, in situ, in statu quo (ante, prius,* or *nunc), in terrorem, in toto, in vacuo*. For designations of sizes of books, e.g. *in-folio*, see the sbs. FOLIO, etc.

in-[1] repr. L. *in-*, the adv. and prep. IN, used in combination mainly with vbs. and their derivs. with the senses 'in, into, within, on, towards, against'; in earlier L. the prefix retained its *n*, but later this was assim. to *l, m, r* (see IL-[1], IM-[1], IR-[1]). In OF. *in-, im-* became *en-, em-* (see EN-[1], EM-[1]) in inherited words, but in learned words *in-, im-* were regularly retained.

in-[2] repr. L. *in-* (whence Sp., It. *in-*), cogn. and synon. with Gr. *a-, an-* A-[4] and CGerm. **un-* UN-[1], as in *fēlix* happy/*infēlix* unhappy, *nocēns* hurtful/*innocēns* innocent; in earlier L. the prefix retained its *n*, but later this was assim. to *l, m, r* (see IL-[2], IM-[2], IR-[2]); before *g* it was reduced to *i-*, as in *ignōrāre* ignore. In a few OF. words this *in-* became *en-*, e.g. L. *inimīcus*, OF. *enemi* enemy, L. *invidia*, OF. *envie* envy; but most F. words containing this prefix are of learned origin and retain *in-* (*il-*, etc.).

-in (chem.) modification of -INE[5] introduced by A. W. von Hofmann for the names of neutral substances such as glycerides, glucosides, bitter principles, proteids, which are thus distinguished from the names of alkaloids and basic substances in *-ine*. Some of such terms were formerly spelt with *-ine* and had passed into popular use before the nomenclature was established, esp. *gelatine* and *margarine*, which are still spelt thus in non-scientific use.

-ina[1] ī·nə L. fem. suffix as in *rēgīna* queen (f. *rēg-, rēx* king), in It. and Sp. and thence in Eng. forming female titles, as CZARINA, and in proper names, as *Clementina*; it is used for some names of musical instruments, as *concertina, flutina, ocarina, seraphina.* Cf. -A[1].

-ina[2] ī·nə n.pl. (sc. *animālia*) of L. *-īnus* -INE[1] used in names of groups of animals, as *Bombycina*, f. generic name *Bombyx*. Cf. -A[2].

inadvertence inədvə̄·ɹtəns lack of attention. XVI. – medL. *inadvertentia*; see IN-[2], ADVERTENCE.

-inæ ai·nī suffix, fem. pl. (sc. *bestiæ* animals) of L. adjs. in *-inus* -INE[1] occurring in names of subfamilies, e.g. *Caninæ* (see CANINE), *Felinæ* (see FELINE).

inamorato inæmorā·tou male lover. XVI. – It. †*inamorato* (now *innam-*), pp. of *inam(m)orare* = OF. *enamourer* ENAMOUR. So **inamora·ta** female lover. XVII.

inane inei·n †empty XVII; empty-headed XIX (Shelley). – L. *inānis* empty, vain. So **inan**ITY inæ·nīti †emptiness; vanity, hollowness XVII; vacuity XVIII. – L.; cf. (O)F.

ina·nimate lifeless. XVI (Foxe). – late L. (see IN-[2]); cf. F. *inanimé*.

inanition inəni·ʃən †emptying of a body XIV; exhausted condition XVIII. – late L. *inānītiō(n-)*, f. *inānīre*, f. *inānis*; see INANE and -ITION; so (O)F.

ina·pt XVIII; so **ina·ptitude** XVII; see IN-[2] and cf. INEPT.

inasmuch inəzmʌ·tʃ in so far *as*, (hence) seeing that, considering that. XIV (Ch., Wyclif; earlier north. *in als mekil*, Cursor M.). tr. OF. *en tant (que)*, repr. L. *in tantum (ut)*, in IN[2], *tantum* so much (n. of *tantus* so great, f. *tam* so). Also INSOMU·CH (XV).

inaugural inɔ̄·gjŭrəl pert. to inauguration. XVII. – F. *inaugural*, f. *inaugurer* inaugurate, after L. *augurālis*; see -AL[1]. So **inau·gu**RATE[3] admit formally to an office XVII; 'begin with good omens' (J.), initiate formally XVIII; initiate the public use of XIX. f. pp. stem of L. *inaugurāre* take omens from the flight of birds, f. *in* IN-[1]+*augurāre* AUGUR. Earlier †*inaugure* (XVI) – (O)F. *inaugurer* or L. **inaugur**A·TION. XVI. – (O)F. or lateL.

inborn (stress variable) † native OE. (newly formed XVII); implanted by nature XVI (G. Douglas). OE. *inboren*, after late L. *innātus* INNATE; cf. Du. *ingeboren*, G. *eingeboren*; see IN-[1], BORN.

Inca i·ŋkə king, or one of the royal family, of Peru before its conquest. XVI. Earlier *Inga*, Sp. alteration of *Inca*, the native form.

incandescent inkænde·sənt glowing with heat. XVIII. – F. *incandescent* – prp. of L. *incandēscere* glow, f. *in*+*candēscere* become white, f. *candidus*; see IN-[1], CANDID, -ENT.

incantation inkæntei·ʃən (use of) formula of words to produce a magical effect. XIV (Gower). – (O)F. *incantation* – late L. *incantātio(n-)*, f. *incantāre* chant, charm, f. *in* IN-[1]+*cantāre* sing, CHANT; cf. ENCHANT and see -ATION.

inca·pable. XVI (Sh.). – F. or late L.; see IN-[2].

incarcerate inkā·ɹsəreit imprison. XVI (preceded by pp. *incarcerate* XV). f. pp. stem of medL. *incarcerāre*, f. *in* IN-[1]+*carcer* prison; see -ATE[3]. So **incarcer**A·TION. XVI. – (O)F. or late L.

incarnadine inkā·ɹnədin, -dain flesh-coloured, crimson, blood-red. XVI (Sylvester). – F. *incarnadin, -ine* – It. *incarnadino*, north. var. of *incarnatino* carnation, flesh-colour, f. *incarnato* INCARNATE; see next and -INE[1]. Hence vb. (Sh. 'Macb.' II ii 62).

incarnate inkā·ɹnət embodied in flesh XIV; flesh-coloured XVI. – ecclL. *incarnātus*, pp. of *incarnārī* be made flesh, f. *in* IN-[1]+*carn-, carō* flesh; see CARNAL, -ATE[2]. The second sense is from F. *incarnat* or modL. So **incarn**A·TION embodiment in flesh XIII (concr. XVIII); †flesh-colour XV. – (O)F. – ecclL.

incendiary inse·ndiəri that sets on fire. XVII (also sb.). – L. *incendiārius*, f. *incendium* burning, fire; see next and -ARY.

incense[1] i·nsens aromatic gum burnt to produce a sweet smell XIII; smoke of this XIV. ME. *ansens, encens* – (O)F. *encens* – ecclL. *incensum*, sb. use of n. of *incensus*, pp. of *incendere* set fire to, f. *in* IN-[1]+**candere* cause to glow (*candēre* glow; see CANDLE). Hence **i·n**CENSE vb. XIV; see CENSE.

incense² inse·ns †set on fire; inflame with wrath. XV. – OF. *incenser*, f. L. *incens-*, pp. stem of *incendere* (see prec.).

incentive inse·ntiv (something) that incites to action. XV. – L. *incentīvus* that sets the tune, that provokes or incites (sb. *-īvum*), f. *incent-*, var. (cf. *incentiō, incentor*) of *incant-*; see INCANTATION, -IVE.

inception inse·pʃən beginning of an undertaking, etc. XV; (at the universities of Oxford and Cambridge) formal entering upon the status of Master or Doctor XVII. – (O)F. *inception* or L. *inceptiō(n-)*, f. *incept-*, pp. stem of *incipere*; see INCIPIENT, -TION. So **ince·pt** vb. (cf. COMMENCE). XIX. **ince·pt-IVE.** XVII.

incessant inse·sənt that does not cease. XVI. – F. *incessant* or late L. *incessant-*, *-āns*, f. IN-² + *cessāns*, prp. of *cessāre* CEASE; see -ANT. So **ince·ssantLY²**. XV; after L. *incessanter*.

incest i·nsest sexual commerce of near kindred. XIII (AncrR.). – L. *incestus*, or *incestum*, sb. use of n. of *incestus* impure, unchaste, f. *in-* IN-² + *castus* CHASTE. So **ince·stUOUS**. XVI. – late L. *incestuōsus*.

inch¹ intʃ twelfth part of a foot. Late OE. *ynće*, corr. to OHG. *unza*, Goth. *unkja* :- **uŋkja* – L. *uncia* twelfth part (see OUNCE¹); cf. MDu. *enke*.

inch² intʃ (Sc.) small island. XV (Wyntoun). – Gael. *innis* iniʃ = (O)Ir. *inis*, W. *ynys*, prob. rel. (obscurely) to L. *insula* ISLE.

inchoate i·nkoueit, i·ŋ- just begun. XVI. – L. *inchoātus*, pp. of *inchoāre*, less correct form of *incohāre* begin; see -ATE². So **incho·ATIVE** spec. gram. of verbs denoting the beginning of an action. XVI. – late L.

incident i·nsidənt liable to befall or occur; attaching itself as a privilege, etc. XV. – F. *incident* or L. *incident-*, *-ēns*, prp. of *incidere* fall upon, happen to, f. *in* IN-¹ + *cadere* fall; see CASE, -ENT. Also sb. accessory event. XV. – (O)F. *incident*, sb. use of adj. Hence **incide·ntAL¹** XVII; after *accidental*. **incide·n-tALLY** XVII; earlier †*incidently* XVI (More).

incinerate insi·nəreit reduce to ashes. XVI. f. pp. stem of medL. *incinerāre*, f. *in* IN-¹ + *ciner-*, *cinis* ashes; see CINERARY, -ATE³. So **incinerA·TION**. XVI. – medL.

incipient insi·piənt beginning. XVII. – L. *incipient-*, *-ēns*, prp. of *incipere* undertake, begin, f. *in* IN-¹ + *capere* take (cf. CAPTURE).

incipit i·nsipit beginning or first words of a literary work. XIX. L., 3rd pers. sg. pres. ind. of *incipere* begin (see prec.); cf. EXPLICIT.

incise insai·z cut into. XVI. – F. *inciser*, f. *incīs-*, pp. stem of L. *incīdere*, f. *in* IN-¹ + *cædere* cut (cf. CÆSURA). So **incisION** insi·ʒən. XV. – (O)F. or late L. **inci·sIVE**. XVI. – medL. So **incisOR¹** insai·zəɹ front (cutting) tooth. XVII (Sir T. Browne). – medL.

incite insai·t urge on. XV. – (O)F. *inciter* – L. *incitāre*, f. *in* IN-¹ + *citāre* set in rapid motion, rouse; see CITE.

incivism see CIVISM.

inclement inkle·mənt †unmerciful; (of weather) not mild XVII (Milton). – F. or L.; see IN-², CLEMENT.

incline inklai·n bend towards a thing, forward or downward. XIII (Cursor M.). ME. *encline* – OF. *encliner*; these Eng. and F. forms survived till XVII, but forms assim. to the L. source *inclināre* finally prevailed; see IN-¹, LEAN². So **inclinA·TION** inklin-. XIV (Ch., Trevisa; Lydg., Caxton; not common till XVI). – (O)F. or L. **inclinO·METER**. XIX.

inclose, inclosure statutory forms of ENCLOSE, ENCLOSURE, in ref. to inclosing land.

include inklʲū·d, iŋ- shut in; comprise. XV. – L. *inclūdere*, f. *in* IN-¹ + *claudere* shut; see CLAUSE. So **inclu·SION**. XVI. – L. **inclu·SIVE** XVI (Sh.); in quasi-adv. use ('from Monday to Saturday inclusive') XVI, based on medL. adv. *inclūsīvē*.

incognito inkɔ·gnitou whose identity is concealed or unavowed. XVII. – It. *incognito* – L. *incognitus* unknown; see IN-², QUAINT. Abbreviated **inco·g.** XVII.

income i·nkʌm, i·ŋ- A. †entrance, arrival XIII (Cursor M.); †fee paid on entering XVI; B. receipts from work, etc., revenue XVII (*income tax* 1799). In ME. use prob. – ON. *innkoma* arrival; later, a new formation on phr. *come in* (cf. OUTCOME); in B preceded by (dial.) *incoming(s)* XVI.

incomme·nsurable (math.) having no common measure. XVI (Billingsley). – late L.; see IN-².

incommode inkəmou·d, iŋ- inconvenience. XVI. – F. *incommoder* or L. *incommodāre*, f. *incommodus* inconvenient; see IN-², COMMODIOUS.

incomprehe·nsible not to be circumscribed; not to be grasped by the understanding XIV (R. Rolle); (hence) that cannot be understood XVII. – L.; so in (O)F.; see IN-².

incomunicado (also erron. *-mm-*) i:nkəmūnikā·dou (U.S.) having no opportunity of communication with others. *c.* 1840. Sp., f. *in-* IN-² + pp. of *comunicar* COMMUNICATE.

inco·ngruous. XVII. – L. *incongruus*; see IN-². So **incongru·ITY**. XVI (Hooker).

inco·ntinence, -ent¹ adj. XIV. – (O)F. or L.; see IN-², CONTINENT.

inco·ntinent² adv. (arch.) without delay, straightway. XV. – OF. *en-*, *incontenant* = Sp., It. *incontinente* – late L. *in continenti*, sc. *tempore* 'in CONTINUOUS time', without an interval. Hence **inco·ntinentLY²**. XV (Caxton).

incorporate inkɔ̄·ɹpəreit, iŋ- put into the body of something XIV; combine or form into one body, adopt into a body XVI. f. pp. stem of late L. *incorporāre*; see IN-¹, CORPORATE. So **incorporA·TION**. XIV. – late L.

incorre·ct. XV. – F. or L. So **incorrigIBLE** inkɔ·rĭdʒĭbl bad beyond correction. XIV (R. Rolle). – (O)F. or L.; see IN-[2], CORRECT.

incrassate inkræ·seit thicken. XVII (Holland). f. pp. stem of late L. *incrassāre*, f. *in* IN-[1]+*crassāre*, f. *crassus* CRASS; see -ATE[3].

increase inkrī·s, iŋkrī·s become or make greater. XIV. ME. *encres* – AN. *encre(s)*-, OF. *encreis(s)*-, stem of *encreistre* :– L. *incrēscere*, f. *in* IN-[1]+*crēscere* grow (see CRESCENT); the prefix was assim. to L. XV. Hence **i·ncrease** sb. XIV (*encre(e)s*, Ch., Wycl. Bible).

increment i·nkrimənt, i·ŋ- increase XV; amount of increase, profit XVII. – L. *incrēmentum*, f. stem of *incrēscere*; see prec., -MENT.

incriminate inkri·mineit charge with a crime. XVIII. f. pp. stem of late L. *incrīmināre* accuse, f. *in* IN-[1]+*crīmen* charge; see CRIME, -ATE[3]. So **incriminA·TION.** XVII.

incrust see ENCRUST. So **incrustA·TION** formation of a crust; hard coating. XVII. – F. or late L.

incubate i·nkjŭbeit, i·ŋ- hatch (eggs). XVIII. f. pp. stem of L. *incubāre*, f. *in* IN-[1]+*cubāre* lie; see CUBICLE, -ATE[3]. So **incubA·TION.** XVII. – L. **i·ncubATOR.** 1857.

incubus i·ŋkjŭbəs, i·n- demon descending upon persons in their sleep XIV (Ch.; earlier *incubi demones*); nightmare XVI; oppressive person or thing XVII. – late L. *incubus*, earlier *incubo*, f. *incubāre*; see prec.

inculcate i·nkʌlkeit, i·ŋ- impress (a thing) upon a person. XVI. f. pp. stem of L. *inculcāre* stamp in with the heel, press in, f. *in* IN-[1]+*calcāre* tread; see CAULK, -ATE[3].

inculpate i·nkʌlpeit, i·ŋ- accuse, blame XVIII; incriminate XIX. f. pp. stem of late L. *inculpāre*; see IN-[1], CULPABLE.

incumbent inkʌ·mbənt falling as a duty or obligation XVI; leaning or resting with its weight XVII. – prp. of L. *incumbere* lie or lean upon, apply oneself to, f. *in* IN-[1]+ **cumbere*, f. nasalized stem corr. to *cubāre* (cf. CUBICLE); see -ENT. The sb. use of 'holder of an ecclesiastical benefice' (XV) is peculiarly Eng., and depends upon an AL. use of *incumbere* for 'possess, occupy'. ¶ From the same base are *concubine, cubicle, incubate, incubus, recumbent, succubus.*

incunabula inkjunæ·bjŭlə earliest stages or first beginnings; books produced in the 'infancy' of printing, i.e. before 1501 A.D. XIX. L. n.pl., swaddling-clothes, cradle, birthplace, infancy, origin, f. *in* IN-[1]+*cūnabula*, f. *cūnæ* cradle, perh. :– **koinā*, rel. to Gr. *koítē* lair, *keîsthai* lie down.

incur inkɔ̄·ɹ, iŋ- †intr. run, fall (*into*); trans. run or fall into, become liable to. XVI. – L. *incurrere*, f. *in* IN-[1]+*currere* run (cf. COURSE); so OF. *encourre*, F. *encourir*. So **incu·rSION** hostile inroad XV; running in or against XVII. – L.

incus i·ŋkəs (anat.) middle one of the three small bones of the ear. XVII. L., 'anvil'.

Ind ind (arch.) India. XIII (*ynde*). – (O)F. *Inde* :– L. INDIA.

indebted inde·tid under obligation. XIII. ME. *an-, endetted* – (with suffix -ED[1]), OF. *endetté*, pp. of *endetter* involve in debt; assim. to L. in prefix and root (medL. *indebitāre*, Pr. *endeptar*, etc.).

indeed indī·d in reality XIV (R. Rolle); as a matter of fact; it is true, truly; (interrog.) Is it so? XVI; as int. of contempt or incredulity XIX. ME. adv. phr. *in dede*, i.e. IN[1] prep., d. of DEED; till *c.* 1600 as two words.

indefatigable indifæ·tigəbl that cannot be wearied. XVI. – F. †*indéfatigable* or L. *indēfatigābilis*; see IN-[2], DE- 3, FATIGUE, -ABLE.

inde·finite (first in gram.). XVI (Palsgrave). – L.; cf. F. *indéfini*; see IN-[2].

indelible inde·lĭbl that cannot be blotted out. XVI (*indeleble*). – F. *indélébile* or L. *indēlēbilis*, f. *in-* IN-[2]+*dēlēbilis*, f. *dēlēre* DELETE; the ending was assim. to -IBLE.

indemnity inde·mnĭti security against contingent injury XV; compensation for loss XVI; legal exemption from liabilities incurred XVII. – (O)F. *indemnité* – late L. *indemnitās*, f. *indemnis* free from loss or hurt, f. *in-* IN-[2]+*damnum*; see DAMAGE, -ITY. So **inde·mnIFY** give indemnity to. XVII.

indent inde·nt make tooth-like incision in, spec. for the purpose of an INDENTURE XIV; make a covenant XV; †contract for XVI; engage (a servant) by contract, orig. in U.S. and Anglo-Indian use XVIII (hence, official requisition for stores as made by an indentured servant XVIII, whence a new sense, make a requisition *for*, draw *upon* XIX); (typogr.) set back from the margin XVII (Moxon). – AN. *endenter*, AL. *indentāre*, f. *in* IN[1]+*dent-*, *dēns* TOOTH. So **indentURE** inde·ntʃəɹ deed between parties with mutual covenants executed in two or more copies, all having their edges correspondingly indented XIV; indentation XVII (Grew). Earliest in MSc. *en-, indenture* – AN. *endenture* (OF. *-eure*), medL. *indentūra* (also *indentātūra*), f. *indentātus*, pp. of *indentāre*. Hence as vb. engage by indenture. XVII.

indepe·ndent not dependent or depending. XVII. f. IN-[1]+DEPENDENT, partly after F. *indépendant*. So **indepe·ndENCE.** XVII. Applied to the Congregational system of church polity *c.* 1640.

index i·ndeks pl. *indexes, indices* i·ndisīz forefinger; pointer; guiding principle; †table of contents; alphabetical list of subjects appended to a book XVI; (math.) XVII; etc. – L. *index*, pl. *indicēs*, forefinger, informer, sign, inscription, f. *in-*+*-dex, -dic-*, as in *jūdex* JUDGE, *vindex* avenger, f. **dik-* point out; cf. INDICATE.

India i·ndiə In OE. *India*, *Indea*, but the present use dates from XVI (prob. immed. after Sp. or Pg.), the ME. form being IND. – L. *India* – Gr. *Indiā*, f. *Indós* the river Indus – Pers. *hind* (OPers. *hiñd'u*) = Av. *heñdu*, Skr. *sindhu* river, spec. the Indus, hence the region of the Indus, Sindh, (by extension, with Greeks and Persians) the country east of this (see HINDUSTAN), also the regions further east (*Further I.*); †applied to America or parts of it after Sp. and Pg. use XVI. Hence **I·ndIAN** adj. and sb. (cf. F. *indien*, medL. *Indiānus*). XV (in early sb. use applied spec. to a mahout); pert. to America and the West Indies XVII (*Indian rubber* XVIII, the earlier form for *India rubber* XIX). †*Indish* was used in XVI; cf. OE. *Indisć*. **Indies** i·ndiz orig. India with the adjacent islands, later called *East Indies*)(*West Indies*, which had come to be applied to lands of the Western Hemisphere which were taken to be part of the Eastern group. XVI. pl. of †*Indie*, *Indy* (XVI–XVII) – L. *India*.

indicate i·ndikeit point out. XVII. f. pp. stem of L. *indicāre* declare, mention, f. *in* IN-[1] + *dicāre* proclaim; cf. INDEX and see -ATE[3]. So **indicA·TION**. XVI (the earliest use is medical, as in F.) – F. – L. **indicatIVE** indi·kətiv. XVI (gram., Palsgrave); suggestive *of* XVII. – (O)F. *indicatif*, *-ive*, – late L. *indicātīvus* (gram.), tr. Gr. ὁριστική (sc. ἔγκλισις).

indict indai·t bring a charge against. XIV. ME. *endite*, later with latinized prefix *indite*, and finally *indict* (XVI). – legal AN. *enditer* (XIII), corr. in form but not in sense to OF. *enditier* declare, dictate, compose, INDITE :– Rom. **indictāre* (in AL. indict XIII), f. *indict-*, pp. stem of L. *indīcere* proclaim, appoint, impose, f. *in* IN-[1] + *dīcere* pronounce, utter (see DICTION). So **indi·ctMENT**. XIV. – AN. *enditement*. The development of the AN., AL., and ME. sense is not accounted for.

indiction indi·kʃən declaration or proclamation, spec. of the Roman emperors fixing the valuation for property tax at the beginning of each fiscal period of 15 years; the period from 1 Sept. 312 instituted by the emperor Constantine by which dates were reckoned, (also) specified year in such a period. XIV (Trevisa). – L. *indictiō(n-)*, f. *indīcere*; see prec. and -TION.

indifferent A. (arch.) impartial, neutral XIV; without interest; neither good nor bad XVI (euphem. not very good XIX); B. †not different; unimportant, immaterial XVI. – F. *indifférent* or L. *indifferēns* making no difference, of no consequence, undiscriminating; see IN-[2], DIFFERENT. Hence **indi·fferENCE**, -ENCY. XVI (More). **indifferentLY**[2]. XIV; after L. *indifferenter*, F. *indifféremment*.

indigenous indi·dʒīnəs produced naturally in a country. XVII. f. L. *indigena* native (adj. and sb.), f. *indi-*, strengthened form of *in* IN[1] + *-gena* (corr. to Gr. *-genḗs*), f. **gen-*, base of *gignere* beget (cf. GENITAL, GENUS).

indigent i·ndidʒənt needy XIV; †wanting, deficient XV. – (O)F. *indigent* – L. *indigent-*, *-ēns*, prp. of *indigēre* lack, f. *indi-* (cf. INDIGENOUS) + *egēre* be in want, need; see -ENT. So **i·ndigENCE**. XIV. – (O)F. or L.

indign indai·n (arch.) unworthy. XV. – (O)F. *indigne* or L. *indignus*, f. *in-* IN-[2] + *dignus* worthy (cf. DEIGN). So **inDI·GNITY** †unworthiness; unworthy treatment. XVI. – F. or L.

indignant indi·gnənt 'inflamed at once with anger and disdain' (J.). XVI (Spenser). – L. *indignant-*, *-āns*, prp. of *indignārī* regard as unworthy, f. *indignus*; see prec., -ANT. So **indignA·TION** †disdain XIV (Ch., Wyclif); anger at what is considered unworthy XIV (Wycl. Bible). – (O)F. or L.

indigo i·ndigou blue powder obtained from plants of the genus Indigofera. XVI. The usual form in XVI–XVII was *indico* – Sp. *indico* – L. *indicum* (Pliny) – Gr. *indikón* (Dioscorides) the blue Indian dye, sb. use of n. of *Indikós* INDIAN; cf. It. *indaco* (XIV). The form *indigo* (XVI), occas. †*endego*, repr. Pg. *indigo*, which passed also into F., Du., G., and Russian. (Cf. MHG. *indich*, early modG. *endigo*, *endich*.)

indire·ct (see IN-[2], DIRECT). XV (Caxton). – (O)F. or medL. Hence **indire·ction,** after *direct* / *direction*. XVI (Sh.).

indiscree·t †without discernment XV; injudicious, unwary XVI (Sh.). – L. *indiscrētus*; cf. F. *indiscret*; so **indiscre·tion**. XIV (R. Rolle). – (O)F. or late L.

indispe·nsable (eccl.) that cannot be allowed or condoned XVI (Cranmer); that cannot be remitted; that cannot be done without XVII. – medL.; see IN-[2], DISPENSABLE.

indisposed indispou·zd †not in order; †unfitted; †ill-disposed XV; out of health XVI; not disposed or inclined XVII. Partly – F. *indisposé* or L. *indispositus* disordered, unprepared; partly directly f. IN-[2] + pp. of DISPOSE. So **indisposI·TION** †unfitness XV; disordered physical state XVI. – F. or f. IN-[2] + DISPOSITION, after prec.

indite indait †dictate; put into words, compose, write. XIV. – OF. *endit(i)er* :– Rom. **indictāre*, f. *in* IN-[1] + *dictāre* declare, DICTATE. Cf. INDICT.

individual indivi·djuəl †indivisible (XV; rare before XVII); existing as a separate entity; pert. to a single person or thing. XVII; sb. XVII. – medL. *indīviduālis*, f. L. *individuus* indivisible, inseparable, f. *in-* IN-[2] + *dīviduus* divisible, f. *dīvidere* DIVIDE; see -AL[1]. Cf. F. *individuel*. So **indivi·dualISM**. XIX; after F. *individualisme*. **i:ndividuA·LITY**. XVII (Selden, Milton).

indivi·sible. XIV (Wyclif; rare before XVI). – late L. *indīvīsibilis*; see IN-[2], DIVISIBLE.

Indo-European iːndoujuərəpī·ən common to India and Europe, spec. applied to the great group of languages spoken over the greater part of Europe and extending into Asia as far as northern India. 1814 (T. Young). Also called *Indo-Germanic*, after G. *indogermanisch* (Klaproth *Asia Polyglotta*, 1823), which repr. the extreme terms of his 'Indisch-Medisch-Sclavisch-Germanisch', used to describe the ethnological chain extending from India to Britain. Others have favoured *Indo-Celtic* as emphasizing Celtic as the most western member of the group. See also ARYAN.

indolent i·ndələnt (path.) painless XVII; averse to exertion XVIII. – late L. *indolent-*, *-ēns* ('dicamus ἀπηλγηκότες indolentes sive indolorios', Jerome in Eph. iv 17–19), f. *in-* IN-[2]+prp. of *dolēre* suffer pain, give pain; see -ENT. So **i·ndol**ENCE. XVI. – F. *indolence* or L. *indolentia* freedom from pain (Cicero, rendering ἀπάθεια). See DOLOUR.

indomitable indɔ·mitəbl †untameable XVII; not to be overcome by difficulties or oppression XIX. – late L. *indomitābilis*, f. *in-* IN-[2]+*domitāre*; see DAUNT, -ABLE.

indoor(s) indɔ̄ə·ɹ(z) inside a house, etc.; adj. pert. to the interior. XVIII. See IN[1], DOOR. For earlier *within-door(s)* XVI.

indri i·ndri babacoote. XIX. misapplication of Malagasy excl. *indry* lo! behold! or *indry izy* there he is!, taken by the F. naturalist Sonnerat for the animal's name.

indubitable indjū·bitəbl not to be doubted. XVIII. – F. *indubitable* or L. *indubitābilis*; see IN-[2], DUBITABLE. Succeeded to †*indubitate* (XV–XVII).

induce indjū·s lead to some action, etc. XIV; †introduce; give rise to, lead to XV; infer XVI. – L. *indūcere*, f. *in* IN-[1]+*dūcere* lead (cf. DUKE); from XIV to XVIII often with *en-* after F. *enduire* (cf. ENDUE). Hence **indu·ce**MENT. XVI (Sh.). So **induct** indʌ·kt (eccl.) introduce formally to a benefice XIV (Wyclif); conduct, introduce XVI (Holland). f. *induct-*, pp. stem of L. *indūcere*. **indu·c**TION (eccl.) XIV (Wyclif); gen. †introduction, initiation XVI; (logic) opp. to *deduction* XV (Capgrave), after Cicero's use of *inductiō*, tr. Gr. ἐπαγωγή (Aristotle); (electr. and magn.) 1812 (Davy). **indu·ct**IVE inducing XVII; (logic) XVII; (electr.) XIX. – late L.

indulge indʌ·ldʒ treat with undeserved favour, gratify by compliance XVII; give free course *to* XVII; take one's pleasure freely *in* XVIII. – L. *indulgēre* (perh. orig.) allow space or time for, (hence) give rein to, prob. rel. to words meaning 'long' (Gr. *dolikhós*, *endelekhḗs* continuous, Skr. *dīrghás*, OSl. *dlŭgŭ* (Russ. *dólgij*)). So **indu·lg**ENCE act of indulging XIV (Wycl. Bible, Ch.); in R.C.Ch. XIV (PPl., Wycl.). – (O)F. – L. **indu·lg**ENT. XVI. – F. or L. **indult** i·ndʌlt special licence or privilege. XVI (first in Sc.). – F. *indult* – late L. *indultum*, sb. use of n. pp. of *indulgēre*.

induna indū·na officer under a chief or king among Zulus, etc. XIX. Zulu, f. nominal prefix *in-*+stem *duna* (cf. *iduna*, pl. *amaduna*) male, sire, lord.

indurate i·ndjureit harden. XVI (Latimer). f. pp. stem of L. *indūrāre*; see ENDURE, -ATE[3]; preceded by pp. †*indurate* XV. So **indur**A·TION. XIV (Ch.). – F. or late L.

indusium indjū·ziəm (anat.) amnion XVIII; (bot.) membranous shield of the sorus of a fern XIX. L., 'tunic', f. *induere* put on, f. *ind-*, strengthened var. of *in* IN[2]+**ew-* (as in *exuere* strip, EXUVIÆ).

industry i·ndəstri †skill, dexterity XV (Caxton); diligence, assiduity; systematic labour, form or kind of this XVI. – (O)F. *industrie* or L. *industria*; see -Y[3]. So **industr**IOUS indʌ·striəs †skilful, ingenious; painstaking, hardworking. XVI. – F. *-ieux* or late L. *-iōsus*. ¶ The L. idiom *dē industriā* 'of set purpose' was formerly repr. by uses of *industrious* for 'intentional, designed' and of the adv. for 'intentionally' (Sh.). **indu·stri**AL[1]. XVI (isolated exx. before XIX). The first ex. is of fruits produced by labour (so obs. F. *industrial*); later partly – F. *industriel*, partly f. INDUSTRY; whence **indu·strial**ISM. XIX (Carlyle).

indwell indwe·l dwell in, inhabit. XIV (Wycl. Bible). f. IN[1]+DWELL, after L. *inhabitāre*.

-ine[1] suffix repr. F. *-in*, fem. *-ine* (= Pr. *-in*, *-ina*, Sp., It., Pg. *-ino*, *-ina*), and its source L. *-īnus*, *-īna* (corr. to Gr. *-înos*, *-ínē*), affixed to nominal and some other stems with the sense 'of or pert. to', 'of the nature of', as *asinīnus*, *canīnus*, *dīvīnus*, *genuīnus*, *masculīnus*, *supīnus*, sometimes in comb. with another suffix, as in *clandestīnus*, *intestīnus*, *vespertīnus*. Formations on proper names, e.g. *Alpīnus*, *Latīnus*, *Saturnīnus*, have provided a pattern for many mod. derivs., as *Algerine*, *Caroline*, *Florentine*, *Johannine*, *Pauline*, *Socotrine*, and in the terminology of nat. hist. *-ine* (pronounced ain) is used freely in adjs. formed on generic names, as *accipitrine*, *passerine*, after *bovine*, *equine*, *murine*; cf. *riverine*. The variation in pronunc. between ain, in, and īn depends on such circumstances as the date of introduction of the word, the channel through which it came, the position of the stress, etc.

-ine[2] suffix forming adjs., repr. F. *-in*, fem. *-ine*, or its source L. *-inus*, *-ina* (corr. to Gr. *-inos*, *-inē*), having in the Rom. langs. and in Eng. the same form and sense as -INE[1]; e.g. *adamantinus*, *corallinus*, *crystallinus*, *hyacinthinus*, *prīstinus*. The pronunc. is now usu. ain, but was formerly in for many words, as *pristine* pri·stin.

-ine[3] suffix of fem. sbs., repr. F. *-ine*, L. *-īna*, Gr. *-ínē*, as in Gr. *hērōínē*, L. *hērōīna*, F. *héroïne* HEROINE (the only survival in Eng.). ¶ In *landgravine* and *margravine*, this form has absorbed G. and Du. *-in* (= -EN[2]). It has been extended in U.S., e.g. *actorine*, *doctorine*.

-ine[4] suffix repr. F. *-ine* (*-in*) or L. *-īna* (*-īnus*), in origin identical with -INE[1], used in abstr. formations on vbs. and agent-nouns, as *doctrīna, medicīna, rapīna, ruīna*, and concr. sbs. on other stems, as *fascīna, ūrīna*. The adjs. in *-īnus, -īna* were used also sb., as in *concubīnus, -īna, consobrīnus* COUSIN, and esp. in personal names, as *Agrippīna, Augustīnus, Constantīnus*. Some are anglicized with *-in*, as *lupin, ruin, Justin.*

In techn. and commercial use this suffix has a vague application and forms names of textile materials, natural and artificial substances, etc., as *brilliantine, dentine, grenadine, nectarine, victorine.*

-ine[5] īn, (restrictedly) ain suffix of chem. terms, in origin a variation of -INE[4], in such names as *gelatine* (now superseded by *gelatin* exc. in pop. use), and those of the four elements *bromine, chlorine, fluorine, iodine*; in later systematic nomenclature restricted (as opp. to -IN) to alkaloids and basic substances, as *caffeine, cocaine, nicotine, strychnine.* Its earlier use in the names of some minerals is now superseded by *-ite.*

inebriate inī·brieit make drunk. XV. f. *inebriate* ppl. adj. (XV) or pp. of L. *inēbriāre*, f. *in-* IN-[1]+*ēbriāre* intoxicate, f. *ēbrius* drunk (cf. EBRIETY); see -ATE[3].

ineffable ine·fəbl that cannot be uttered XV; that must not be uttered XVI. – F. *ineffable* or L. *ineffābilis*, f. *in-* IN-[2]+*effābilis*, f. *effārī* speak out, f. *ex* EF-+*fārī*; cf. FABLE, -ABLE.

ineluctable inilʌ·ktəbl inescapable. XVII. – L., f. *in-*+*ēluctārī* struggle out; see IN-[2], E-, RELUCTANT, -ABLE.

inept ine·pt †(leg.) void XVI; (arch.) unsuited, inappropriate; foolish XVII. – L. *ineptus*, f. *in-* IN-[2]+*aptus* APT.

inequa·lity. XV (Caxton). – OF. or L.; see IN-[2], EQUALITY.

ine·quity unfairness. XVI. f. IN-[2]+EQUITY.

ine·rrant †(of a star) fixed XVII; unerring XIX. – L.; see IN-[2], ERRANT.

inert inə̄·ɹt inactive, inanimate XVII (H. More); sluggish XVIII (Burke). – L. *inert-*, nom. *iners* unskilled, inactive, f. *in-* IN-[2]+ *ars* skill, ART; cf. F. *inerte.* So **inertia** inə̄·ɹʃiə property whereby matter continues in its existing state. XVIII. – L.; see -IA[1].

inescu·tcheon (her.) escutcheon charged on a larger one. XVII (Guillim). f. IN[1]+ ESCUTCHEON.

ine·stimable too great to be estimated XIV (Ch.); priceless XVI. – (O)F. – L.; see IN-[2], ESTIMABLE (which is later).

inevitable ine·vitəbl not avoidable. XV. – L., f. *in-* IN-[2]+*ēvītābilis*, f. *ēvītāre*, f. *ē-* EX-[1]+*vītāre* avoid; see -ABLE.

inexorable ine·ksərəbl not to be moved or prevailed upon. XVI. – F. *inexorable* or L. *inexōrābilis*, f. *in-*+*exorābilis* (equiv. of Gr. ἀπαραίτητος), f. *exōrāre*, f. *ex*+*ōrare* pray; see IN-[2], EX-[1], ORATION, -ABLE.

inexpressible inèkspre·sĭbl unutterable XVII (Donne, Milton); sb. pl. breeches, trousers XVIII (Wolcot, Gibbon); so (in first half of XIX) *ineffables, inexplicables, unmentionables, unutterables* (so F. *inexprimables*).

inexpugnable inèkspʌ·gnəbl that cannot be taken or overthrown. XV (Caxton). – (O)F. *inexpugnable* – L. *inexpugnābilis*, f. *in-* IN-[2] +*expugnābilis*, †*expugnāre*, f. *ex* EX-[1] + *pugnāre* fight; see PUGNACIOUS, -ABLE.

infallible infæ·lĭbl not liable to err. XV (Caxton). – F. or medL. *infallibilis* (Bede); see IN-[2], FALLIBLE. So **infallibi·l**ITY. XVII (A.V., Translators' Preface).

infamous i·nfəməs of ill repute. XIV (Wyclif). – medL. *infamōsus*, for L. *infāmis*; see IN-[2], FAMOUS. So **i·nfam**Y[3]. XV. – (O)F. *infamie*, repl. earlier †*infame* (XIV, Usk) – OF. *infame* – L. *infāmia.*

infant i·nfənt child, (now) young child XIV (Wycl. Bible); (after legal AN.) minor XVI. Late ME. *enfaunt* (with early assim. to L.) – (O)F. *enfant* = Pr. *enfan*, Sp., It. *infante* :– L. *infant-, -fāns*, sb. use of *infāns* unable to speak, f. *in-* IN-[2]+prp. of *fārī* speak; see FABLE, -ANT. So **i·nfan**CY. XV. – L. *infantia.* **infa·nte** XVI/**infa·nta** XVII prince/princess of Spain or Portugal. – Sp., Pg. **i·nfant**ILE. XVII. – F. or L. **i·nfant**INE[1]. XVII. – F. †*infantin*, var. of (O)F. *enfantin.* **infant**RY i·nfantri (coll.) foot-soldiers. XVI. – F. *infanterie* – It. *infanteria*, f. *infante* youth, foot-soldier.

infatuate infæ·tjueit †turn (a thing) to folly; make foolish, possess with foolish passion. XVI. f. pp. stem of L. *infatuāre*, f. *in-* IN-[1]+*fatuus* FATUOUS; see -ATE[3].

infect infe·kt affect with disease; taint, deprave XIV (Ch.); imbue, esp. injuriously XV; †dye, stain XV. f. *infect-*, pp. stem of L. *inficere* dip in, stain, taint, spoil, f. *in-* IN-[1]+ *facere* put, DO[1]. So **infe·c**TION. XIV (Trevisa). – (O)F. or late L.; in Celtic grammar after modL. (Zeuss, 1853). Hence **infe·c**TIOUS. XVI. **infe·ct**IVE. XIV (Trevisa). – medL. (in L. in n.pl. *infectīva* dyes).

infeft infe·ft (Sc. law) var. of ENFEOFF with *t* from pt. and pp. So **infe·ft**MENT. XV.

infer infə̄·ɹ †bring about, induce; †bring in, introduce; draw as a conclusion; imply. XVI. – L. *inferre* bear or bring in, inflict, make (war), cause, in medL. infer, f. *in* IN-[1]+*ferre* BEAR. So **infer**ENCE i·nfərəns. XVI (Hooker, Bacon). – medL. *inferentia* (Abelard), repl. L. *illatiō.*

inferior infiə·riəɹ lower XV (in physical sense now chiefly techn.); of lower or low degree XVI; sb. XVI. – L. *īnferior*, compar. of *īnferus* low, corr. (with superl. *īnfimus*) to Skr. *ádharas, adhamás*; see UNDER, -IOR.

infernal infə̄·ɹnəl pert. to hell XIV (Ch.); hellish, diabolical XV (Lydg.); (colloq.) execrable XVIII. – (O)F. *infernal* – Christian L. *īnfernālis* (Prudentius), f. *īnfernus*, parallel to *īnferus* as *supernus* SUPERNAL to *superus* (*inferni* the shades, *inferna* the lower regions, in Christian use *infernus* hell); see -AL[1].

infest infe·st †attack, assail XV; trouble with hostile attacks, swarm in XVII. – (O)F. *infester* or L. *infestāre*, f. *infestus* hostile, unsafe, perh. lit. 'directed against', f. *in* against (IN[2])+*-festus*, as in *manifestus* MANIFEST.

infidel i·nfidəl non-Christian XV (Malory); professed unbeliever XVI. – F. *infidèle* or L. *infidēlis* unfaithful, (eccl.) unbelieving, f. *in-* IN-[2]+*fidēlis* faithful, f. *fidēs* FAITH. So **infidel**ITY infide·liti. XVI. – (O)F. or L.

infiltrate i·nfiltreit introduce or permeate by filtration. XVIII. f. IN-[1]+FILTRATE, after F. *infiltrer* (Paré). So **infiltra**·TION. XVIII.

infinite i·nfinit (arch.) unlimited in number XIV (Ch.); having no limit or end XV. – L. *infīnītus*; see IN-[2], FINITE. So **infinitesim**AL[1] i:nfinite·siməl reciprocal of an infinite quantity; indefinitely small. XVIII. f. modL. *infīnītēsimus*, f. L. *infīnītus*, after *centēsimus* hundredth. **infinit**IVE infi·nītiv (gram.). XVI (Whitington, Palsgr.). – L. *infīnītīvus*, f. *in-* IN-[2]+*fīnītīvus* definite; in Quintilian and Priscian *infinitus modus* 'unlimited mood', in Diomedes *infinitivus* 'because it has no definite persons or numbers'; tr. Gr. ἀόριστος. **infi·ni**TUDE. XVII (Milton). f. L. *infīnītus*, after *magnitūdō, multitūdō*. **infi·n**ITY. XIV (PPl., Ch.). – (O)F. – L.

infirm infə̄·ɹm †weak, unsound XIV (Ch.); not firm, irresolute XVI; weak through age or illness XVII (Sh.). – L. *infirmus*; see IN-[2], FIRM[1]. So **infi·rm**ARY. XVII (Bacon, Pepys). – medL. *infirmāria* (sc. *domus*), f. L. *infirmus*. In XVIII the common name for a public hospital; hence the traditional name of some provincial hospitals. **infi·rm**ITY. XIV (Barbour, Wycl. Bible). – L.; cf. F. *infirmité*.

infix i·nfiks (philol.) element inserted in the body of a word. XIX. f. pp. stem of L. *infigere*; see IN-[1], FIX.

inflame inflei·m set on fire, lit. and fig. XIV (R. Rolle, Wycl. Bible); make feverish or morbidly hot XVI; aggravate XVII. ME. *inflaume, -flamme* – (O)F. *enflammer* :- L. *inflammāre*, f. *in* IN-[1]+*flamma* FLAME. So **inflamm**ATION infləmei·ʃən. XVI. – L.; so F.

inflate inflei·t blow out as with air. XVI. f. pp. †*inflate* (XV) – L. *inflātus*, pp. of *inflāre*, f. *in* IN-[1]+*flāre* BLOW. So **infla**·TION. XIV (R. Rolle). – L.

inflect infle·kt bend XV; (gram.) vary the termination of XVII; modulate the tone of XIX. – L. *inflectere*, f. *in-* IN-[1]+*flectere* bend (see FLEXION). **inflex**ION, **inflec**TION infle·kʃən bending, curvature XVI; modulation of voice XVI; (gram.) modification of form in declension, etc. XVII. – (O)F. or L.

inflexible infle·ksibl not FLEXIBLE, unbending; rigidly fixed. XIV. – L.; see IN-[2].

inflict infli·kt lay (blows, suffering) upon XVI (Sh.); assail *with* XVI. f. *inflict-*, pp. stem of L. *inflīgere*, f. *in* IN-[1]+*flīgere* (cf. AFFLICT, CONFLICT). So **infli·c**TION. XVI (More). – late L.

inflorescence inflōre·səns arrangement of flowers in a plant. XVI. – modL. *inflōrēscentia* (Linnæus), f. late L. *inflōrēscere* come into flower; see IN-[1], FLORESCENCE.

influence i·nfluəns (astrol.) emanation of ethereal fluid from the heavens affecting mankind XIV (Ch., Trevisa); †infusion of power; †influx XV (Lydg.); insensible action of one *on* another XVI (Sh.); power of ascendancy *over* XVI (Sh.). – (O)F. *influence* or medL. *influentia* (whence also Pr., Sp. *influencia*, It. *influenza*), f. prp. of L. *influere* flow in, f. *in* IN-[1]+*fluere* flow (cf. FLUID); see -ENCE. In the astrol. use medL. *influentia* succeeded to late L. *influxus* (*stellarum* of the stars); in scholL. it acquired the sense 'exertion of power'. Hence **in·fluence** vb. XVII; cf. F. *influencer* (1792). So **influe·nt**IAL. XVI. f. medL. *influentia*.

influenza influe·nzə contagious epidemic febrile disorder. XVIII ('News from Rome of a contagious Distemper raging there, call'd the *Influenza*', 1743). – It. *influenza* INFLUENCE, used spec. for visitation or outbreak of an epidemic (e.g. *influenza di catarro, influenza di febbre scarlattina*), hence absol. epidemic, and esp. 'the epidemic' of 1743.

influx i·nflʌks flowing in; continuous ingression. XVII (Bacon). – F. *influx* or late L. *influxus*, f. *influere* flow in; see IN-[1], FLUX.

inform infə̄·ɹm †give form to XIV (R. Mannyng); give a character to, imbue, inspire XIV (Wyclif); furnish with knowledge XIV (R. Mannyng, R. Rolle); give knowledge of a thing to (a person) XIV (Ch.); †instruct in XIV (R. Rolle). ME. *enfo(u)rme* – OF. *enfo(u)rmer* (mod. *informer*) – L. *informāre* shape, form an idea of, describe, f. *in-* IN-[1]+*forma* FORM. So **info·rm**ANT. XVII. **informa**·TION action of informing XIV (Ch., Trevisa, Gower); (leg.) charge or complaint against a person XV. – (O)F. – L.

infra- i·nfrə prefix repr. L. *infrā* adv. and prep. below, underneath, found occas. in comp. in late and medL., e.g. *infrāforeānus* situated beneath the forum, *infrāmūrānus* lying within the walls, on the model of which are made formations such as *infra-axillary* below the axilla (*infrā axillam*), *inframammary* below the breasts (*infrā mammās*); it is extended to denotation of a condition, as in *infrabestial* below (that of) the beasts; it is attrib. or adverbial in *infraposition*, etc.; **i:nfralapsa·rian** (theol.) pert. to the view that God's election of some was consequent to his prescience of the Fall of Man. XVIII; L. *lapsus* fall, LAPSE. **infra-re·d,** applied to the rays that lie beyond the red end of the spectrum. XIX.

infraction infræ·kʃən violation, infringement. XVII. – L. *infractiō(n-)*, f. *infract-*, *infringere* INFRINGE; cf. FRACTION.

infra dig. infrədi·g. XIX (Scott). abbrev. of L. *infrā dignitātem* beneath (one's) dignity.

infringe infri·ndʒ break into, violate. XVI. – L. *infringere*, f. *in-* IN-¹+*frangere* break (see FRACTION).

infundibulum infʌndi·bjŭləm (anat.) funnel-shaped part in the body. XVIII. L., f. *infundere* INFUSE.

infuse infjū·z pour in XV; instil; steep XVI. f. *infūs-*, pp. stem of L. *infundere*, f. *in* IN-¹+ *fundere* pour (see FUSION). So **infu**·SION XV; concr. XVI. – (O)F. or L.

infusoria infjusɔ̄·riə (zool.) class of protozoa, so called because found in infusions of decaying matter. XVIII. sb. use (sc. *animalcula*) of n.pl. of modL. **infūsōrius*, f. *infūs-*; see prec. and -IA², -ORIOUS.

-ing¹ iŋ suffix forming derivs. orig. of verbs, primarily nouns of action, but subsequently developed in application and meaning in various ways: OE. *-ung* and *-ing* (which superseded the more frequent *-ung* in early ME.) = OFris. *-unge*, *-inge*, *-enge*, OS. *-unga*, MLG., MDu. *-inge*, Du. *-ing*, OHG. *-unga* (G. *-ung*), ON. *-ung*, *-ing* (not known in Gothic and with no cogns. outside Germ.). In OE. the earliest and commonest use of the suffix is in formations from weak verbs, e.g. *ācsung* asking (f. *ācsian* ask), *ćīdung*, *-ing* rebuke (f. *ćīdan* blame, chide), *fēding* (f. *fēdan* feed), *leornung* learning, study (f. *leornian*), *macung* (f. *macian* do, MAKE), *sorgung* (f. *sorgian* grieve). Extension to strong verbs began in OE., e.g. *brecung* breaking, *eting* eating, *hlēapung* leaping, *wrīting*; and before 1200 the suffix was used with verbs of any class, whether native or adopted. Formation on advs. by ellipsis of a verbal notion is typified by *inning*, *offing*, *outing*, (swan-)*upping*, *homing*. Nonce-words are freely formed on words and phrases of many kinds, e.g. *oh-oh-ing*, *hear-hear-ing*, *how-d'ye-doing*, *to-and-fro-ing*.

In OE. itself was developed the notion of a completed action or process or the result of this, (whence) habit, art, e.g. *blētsung*, *-ing* blessing, benediction, *gaderung* collection, assembly, *leornung* learning, study, *tīdung* tidings, *weddung* betrothal, wedding; transference to concrete or material accompaniment or product of a process followed, as in *bedding* bed-clothes, *eardung* dwelling, *innung* contents, revenue, (*ġe*)*mēting* meeting, assembly, convention, *offrung* sacrifice, *sćēawung* spectacle, show; from *trymman* strengthen, confirm, array (TRIM), was formed *trymming* with the series of meanings 'strengthening', 'foundation', 'confirmation', 'edification', 'edifying matter'. Further extensions are: the addition of the suffix to the names of things used or dealt with, or the persons engaged in an action, e.g. *blackberrying*, *fowling*, *gardening*, *hopping* (hop-picking), *nutting*; *buccaneering*, *soldiering*; its use to designate a material thing in which the action or result is embodied, e.g. a *writing* on the wall, the *covering* of a chair, the *landing* of a staircase, a *winding* in a river; the collective designation of material used, e.g. *carpeting*, *edging*, *sheeting*, *trimming*, *trousering*. The existence of a parallel sb. of the same form as the verb (as in *clothes/clothing*, *rail/railing*) has led to the creation of *-ing*-forms without a corresponding verb, as *coping*, *piping*, *scaffolding*, *tubing*. Individualized use, with consequent pluralization, began early and became prominent in later periods, e.g. *a* long *sitting*, three *sittings*; *a* bad *beginning* but *a* happy *ending*; *an outing*, frequent *outings*. In some plurals the concr. use appears almost exclusively, e.g. *earnings*, *filings*, *hangings*, *housings*, *innings*, *leavings*, *trappings*. EVENING and MORNING are special formations.

b. The outstanding development of the verbal sb. in *-ing* is its use as a gerund, so that it may be qualified by adjs. and advs. and may take an object and a predicative noun or adj., e.g. the habit of *rising early*, engaged in *building a house*, you *being strangers* and so much *alike*; (with an object and predicated pp.) after *having* written *a letter*. The germ of such constructions may be seen in such OE. comps. as *āþswerung* swearing of oaths, *feaxfallung* falling-out of hair, *mynsterclǣnsung* purification of a church, *ǣfenrǣding* lection in the evening, *ūtspīwung* expectoration, where the first el. is a sb. in subjective, objective, or adverbial relation, or an adverb, and in such constructions as *oftrǣdliće rǣdinga hāligra bōca* frequent readings of holy books (objective genitive). The attrib. use of the gerund, as in *breeding place*, *counting house*, *dancing lesson*, *feeding ground*, *living room*, *mounting block*, *sinking fund*, *thanksgiving day*, *winning post*, has its antecedent models in the earliest periods; e.g. OE. *cenningstōw* birthplace, *huntingspere* hunting-spear, *wrītingfeþer* pen, ME. *grettinng word* salutation (Orm); the variety of application already in OE. is illustrated by *leornungćild* pupil, *-cniht* disciple, *-mann* student, *-cræft* scholarship, *-hūs* school.

-ing² iŋ suffix of the prp., ME. alteration of OE. *-ende*, later *-inde*, in late Nhb. *-ande* (after ON.) = OFris., OS. *-and* (Du. *-end*), OHG. *-anti*, *-enti*, *-onti* (G. *-end*), ON. *-andi*, Goth. *-ands*, corr. to L. *-ant-* -ANT, *-ent-* -ENT, Gr. *-ont-*, Skr. *-ant-*. The forms *-inde*, *-ende* continued in the Kentish area till XIV, but from the end of XII there was a general tendency to assim. *-inde* to -ING¹, perh. partly through assoc. with AN., (O)F. *-ant*, which is the ending of both prps. and gerunds (*-ant* repr. both L. *-antem*, *-entem* and *-andum*, *-endum*). Several words of ppl. origin or nature are used only or mainly as adjs., e.g. *cunning*, *daring*, *hulking*, *lumping*, *nonjuring*, *strapping*, *swingeing*, *topping*, *unavailing*, *willing*; others (mostly of F. origin) are prepositions, viz. *concerning*, *during*, *excepting*, *notwithstanding*, *pending*, *touching*.

As a morphological feature the prp. enters into the formation of the tenses with the verb *be*, variously known as progressive, continuous, indefinite: e.g. I *am coming*, They *were fighting*; the use is found in the earliest OE.

-ing[3] iŋ suffix forming masc. sbs. based on sbs. or adjs. with the sense 'one belonging to or of the kind of . .', 'possessing the qualities of . .', as a patronymic 'one descended from . .'; OE. *-ing* (corr. to OHG. *-ing*, ON. *-ingr*, *-ungr*) as in: *æþeling* ATHELING, *cyning* KING, *ierming*, *earming* poor wretch, *flӯming* fugitive, *hōring* whoremonger, *lytling* little one; patronymics, as *Æþelwulfing/Wodening* son of Æthelwulf/Woden; gentile names, as *Centingas* men of Kent, *Rēadingas* (Reading), *Gomorringas* people of Gomorra; names of coins, *pending*, *penning* PENNY, *sćilling* SHILLING; fractional parts, *feorþing* FARTHING, *thriding* RIDING (of ON. origin); ME. *efening* equal (Orm) is – ON. *jafningi*. Other words, of various ages from OE. onwards, chiefly names of animals and fruits, are *biffin* (*beefing*), *bunting*, *gelding* (of ON. origin), *golding*, *herring* (OE.), †*hilding*, *jenneting*, *sweeting*, *whiting* (OE.), *wilding*.

inga i·ŋga plant of a (chiefly S. Amer.) genus allied to Mimosa. XVIII (P. Browne). Tupi.

ingeminate indʒe·mineit utter twice, reiterate. XVI. f. pp. stem of L. *ingemināre* redouble, repeat, f. *in* IN-[1]+*gemināre* GEMINATE.

ingenio indʒī·niou (hist.) sugar factory in the W. Indies. XVI (Hakluyt). – Sp. *ingenio* inχē·nio ENGINE (*i. de azúcar* sugar-mill).

ingenious indʒī·niəs †of high intellectual capacity XV; skilful in invention XVI; †used for INGENUOUS XVI. – F. *ingénieux* or L. *ingeniōsus*, f. *ingenium*; see ENGINE, -IOUS.

ingénue ɛ̃ʒenü artless (young) woman. XIX. F., fem. of *ingénu* – L. *ingenuus* (see next).

ingenuous indʒe·njuəs †noble-minded; honourably straightforward XVI; free-born XVII. f. L. *ingenuus* native, inborn, freeborn, noble, frank, f. IN-[1]+**gen-*, base of *gignere* beget; see KIN, -UOUS. So **ingenu**ITY indʒinjū·iti A. †free-born condition; †nobility of character; ingenuousness (now rare); B. †intellectual capacity XVI; skill in contriving XVII. – L. *ingenuitās*; cf. F. *ingénuité*, It. *ingenuità*. The uses of branch B are peculiarly Eng. for *ingeniosity* or **ingeniety*, and depend on the confusion of INGENIOUS and *ingenuous* in XVI–XVII.

ingle i·ŋgl (Sc., etc.) fire, flame, hearth. XVI (Dunbar). perh. – Gael. *aingeal* fire, light.

ingot i·ŋgɔt, -gət †mould in which metal is cast XIV (Ch.); mass of cast metal XV. Origin obscure; form and meaning suggest deriv. from IN[1] and OE. *goten*, pp. of *ġeotan* pour, cast in metal (cf. *inġeotinġ* inpouring, *ingyte* infusion), rel. to L. *fundere* (see FUSION); parallel forms are G. *einguss* infusion, ingot, Sw. *ingöte* neck of a mould for metals, and the vbs. Du. *ingieten*, Sw. *ingjuta*. ¶ Hence F. *lingot* (XV) for *l'ingot*, whence medL. *lingōtus*, Sp. *lingote*, Pg. *linhǫta*.

ingrained ingrei·nd, (before a sb.) i·ngreind. XVI. var. of *engrained*; see ENGRAIN; cf. AL. *ingrānātus* (XIV).

ingratiate ingrei·ʃieit †bring into favour; refl., get oneself into favour. XVII (Bacon). f. L. phr. *in grātiam* into favour (see GRACE) + -ATE[3], after It. †*ingratiare*, *ingraziare*.

ingredient ingrī·diənt something that enters into the formation of a compound or mixture. XV. – prp. of L. *ingredī* enter, f. *in-* IN-[1]+*gradī* step, go: see GRADE, -ENT; cf. F. *ingrédient* (XVI, Paré). Primarily in medical use; the pl. was spelt †*ingredience* XVI–XVII (cf. ACCIDENCE).

ingress i·ngres entrance. XV. – L. *ingressus*, f. pp. stem of *ingredī*; see prec. So **ingres**SION -e·ʃən entrance, invasion. XV (Harding). **ingre·ss**IVE entering in. XVII (gram. inceptive).

inguinal i·ŋgwinəl pert. to the groin. XVII. – L. *inguinālis*, f. *inguin-*, *inguen* (swelling in the) groin = Gr. *adḗn* (:– **ŋgwen-*) gland, ON. *økkr* (:– **eŋkwaz*) tumour; see -AL[1].

ingurgitate ingə̄·ɹdʒiteit swallow greedily. XVI (Levins). f. pp. stem of L. *ingurgitāre*, f. *in* IN-[1]+*gurgit-*, *gurges* whirlpool, gulf. So **ingurgit**A·TION. XVI (Elyot).

inhabit inhæ·bit dwell in, dwell. XIV (Ch., Gower). ME. *en-*, *inhabite* – OF. *enhabiter* or L. *inhabitāre*, f. *in* IN-[1]+*habitāre* (see HABIT).

inhale inhei·l breathe in. XVIII (Pope). – L. *inhālāre*, f. *in-* IN-[1]+*hālāre* (cf. EXHALE). So **inhal**A·TION. XVII. – medL.

inhere inhiə·ɹ exist as an attribute *in* XVI; †remain fixed *in* XVII. – L. *inhærēre*, f. IN-[1]+ *hærēre*; cf. ADHERE. So **inhe·r**ENT. XVI.

inherit inhe·rit †make heir; take or receive as heir. XIV. ME. *en(h)erite* – OF. *enheriter*, f. *en-* IN-[1]+*hériter* :– late L. *hērēditāre*, f. *hērēd-*, *hērēs* HEIR. So **inhe·rit**ANCE. XIV (Gower). – AN. *inheritaunce*. **inhe·rit**OR[1]. XV. **inhe·ri**TRIX. XVI.

inhibit inhi·bit (eccl. law) forbid, interdict XV; restrain XVI. f. *inhibit-*, pp. stem of L. *inhibēre* hold in, hinder, f. *in-* IN-[1]+*habēre* hold (see HABIT). **inhibi**·TION. XIV. – OF. or L.

inhu·man, inhuma·ne. XV (*-ayn*, Caxton). – F. or L.; see IN-[2], HUMAN, HUMANE. **inhuma·n**ITY. XV (Caxton). – F. or L.

inhume inhjū·m bury. XVII. – L. *inhumāre*, f. *in* IN-[1]+*humus* ground (cf. HUMBLE and EXHUME). So **inhum**A·TION. XVII. – F.

inimical ini·mikəl unfriendly, hostile. XVII. – late L. *inimīcālis*, f. *inimīcus*; see ENEMY, -AL[1]. ¶ †*Inimicous* (XVI) and †*inimicitious* (XVII; f. L. *inimīcitia* enmity) were earlier attempts to naturalize the adj.

iniquity ini·kwiti unrighteousness. XIV. – OF. *iniquité* – L. *inīquitās*, f. *inīquus*, f. *in-* IN-[2]+*æquus* just, righteous (see EQUITY).

initial ini·ʃəl pert. to a or the beginning. XVI. – L. *initiālis*, f. *initium* beginning, f. *init-*, pp. stem of *inīre* enter upon, begin, f. *in* IN-[1]+*īre* go, rel. to Skr. *éti* he goes, *imas* we go, Gr. *eîmi* I shall go, *ímen* we go, *íāsi* they go; see -AL[1]. So **initi·**ATE[3]. XVII. **initi**A·TION. XVI (Stubbes). – L. **ini·ti**ATIVE sb. XVIII. – F. **ini·ti**ATORY. XVII.

inject indʒe·kt drive or force in. XVII (Holland). f. *inject-*, pp. stem of L. *inicere* throw in, f. *in* IN-[1]+*jacere* throw (see ADJACENT), rel. to Gr. *hiénai* throw, cast, or send forward. So **inje·**CTION. XVI. – F. or L.

Injun i·ndʒən colloq. and dial. U.S. form of INDIAN. XVII (*Ingin*, *Engiane*, later *Indjon*).

injunction indʒʌ·ŋkʃən authoritative or emphatic admonition. XVI. – late L. *injunctiō(n-)*, f. *injunct-*, *injungere* ENJOIN; see -TION. So **inju·nct**IVE. XVII; cf. F. *injonctif*.

injury i·ndʒəri wrongful action XIV; loss, damage XV; †insult, affront XVI. – AN. *injurie* (mod. *injure* insult) – L. *injūria*, sb. use of fem. of *injūrius* unjust, wrongful, f. *in-* IN-[2]+*jūr-*, *jūs* right; see JURY, -Y[3]. So **injur**IOUS indʒuə·riəs. XV (Henryson). – F. or L.

ink iŋk fluid used in writing and printing XIII; black fluid secreted by cuttle-fish, etc. XVI. ME. *enke*, later *inc(k)*, *inke* – OF. *enque* (mod. *encre*) :- late L. *e·ncautum*, *e·ncaustum* (which with stress *encau·stum* gave Pr. *encaust*, It. *inchiostro*) – Gr. *égkauston* purple ink used by Greek and Roman emperors for their signatures, f. *egkaíein* burn in (see ENCAUSTIC); cf. Jewish F. *anket*, (M)Du. *inkt*. Comp. **i·nk**HORN vessel (orig. a horn) for holding ink XIV; cf. Du. †*inkthoren*; *i. term*, learned or literary word XVI (Bale). Hence **ink** vb. XVI. **ink**Y[1]. XVI.

inkle i·ŋkl linen tape or thread. XVI. Of unkn. origin.

inkling i·ŋkliŋ faint mention or report XIV; hint XVI. f. ME. *inkle* utter in an undertone (XIV), of unkn. origin+-ING[1].

in-law i·nlɔ̄ relative by marriage. XIX. sb. use of phr. denoting connexion by marriage, e.g. *brother-in-law* (*c.* 1300) sister's husband, *father-in-law* (XIV, Ch.) wife's father; after AN. *en ley*, OF. *en loi* (*de mariage*) 'in law (of marriage)'; also used of step-relationship.

inlet i·nlet (prob. after OUTLET) small arm of the sea, creek XVI; f. phr. *let in* (LET[1]) (arch.) admission XVII. ¶ North. ME. *inlate* admission (XIII–XIV) is a distinct word.

inly i·nli (arch.) inwardly; closely, fully. OE. *in(n)līće*, f. *inn* IN[1] (adv.)+-LY[2].

inmate i·nmeit †lodger, subtenant; (fellow) occupier or occupant. XVI. prob. orig. f. INN dwelling (later assoc. with IN[1])+MATE.

inmost i·nmoust, -məst most inward. XIV. Earlier ME. *inmest*, *in(ne)mast* :- OE. *innemest*. f. *in*, *inne* IN[1]; see -MOST.

inn in †dwelling-place OE.; hostelry, hotel; lodging-house for (university or law) students. XIV. OE. *inn* :- **innam* (cf. ON. *inni* :- **innjam*); f. *inne* IN[1].

innards i·nəɹdz (colloq.) see INWARD.

innate inei·t inborn, native. XV. – L. *innātus*, pp. of *innāscī* (see IN-[1], NATIVE).

inner i·nəɹ more within or inward. OE. *inner(r)a*, *in(n)ra* = OFris. *inra*, OHG. *innaro*, *-ero* (G. *innere*), ON. *innri*, *iðri*; compar. f. IN[1] (adv.); see -ER[3]. Hence †**i·nner**MORE adv. XIII; adj. XV. †**i·nner**EST. XIII (Orm). **i·nner**MOST. XV.

innings i·niŋz (cricket, etc.) portion of a game during which a side or player is 'in'. XVIII. f. IN[1] adv.+pl. of -ING[1]; invariable for sg. and pl. in Eng. use; in U.S. a sg. *inning* is current. ¶ No historical connexion with OE. *innung* contents, income, ME. and mod. Eng. *inning* enclosure, (dial.) ingathering.

innocent i·nəsənt free from wrong, sin, or guilt XIV (R. Rolle); not injurious XVII. Also sb. XIV. – (O)F. *innocent* (= It. *innocente*, etc.) or L. *innocent-*, *-ēns*, f. *in-* IN-[2]+*nocēns*, prp. of *nocēre* hurt, injure; see NOXIOUS, -ENT. So **i·nnoc**ENCE. XIV. – (O)F. – L. **innoc**UOUS inɔ·kjuəs harmless. XVI. f. L. *innocuus*, f. *in-*+*nocuus*, f. *nocēre*.

innovate i·nŏveit †renew, †introduce as new; bring in something new. XVI. f. pp. stem of L. *innovāre* renew, alter, f. *in* IN-[1]+*novāre* make new, f. *novus* NEW; see -ATE[3]. So **innov**A·TION. XVI. – L. Cf. RENOVATE.

innuendo injue·ndou †parenthetical explanation or specification; oblique hint or suggestion. XVII. – L., 'by nodding, pointing to, intimating', abl. gerund of *innuere* nod to, signify, f. *in* IN-[1]+*nuere* nod (cf. Gr. *neúein*). ¶ Used in medL. as a formula in legal documents to introduce a precise inference in parenthesis, 'to wit'.

inoculate inɔ·kjŭleit set in (a bud or scion), bud (a plant) XV; implant (a disease); impregnate with the virus of a disease XVIII. f. pp. stem of L. *inoculāre* engraft, implant, f. *in* IN-[1]+*oculus* EYE, bud; see -ATE[3].

inordinate inɔ̄·ɹdinət irregular; immoderate. XIV (Ch., Trevisa). – L. *inordinātus*, f. *in-* IN-[2]+*ordinātus*, pp. of *ordināre* ORDAIN; see -ATE[2].

inosculate inɔ·skjuleit interpenetrate (trans. and intr.). XVII (Grew). f. IN-[1]+L. *ōsculāre* furnish with a mouth or outlet, after Gr. *anastomoûn* (see ANASTOMOSIS).

inquest i·nkwest, i·ŋ- legal inquiry XIII; jury, esp. coroner's jury XIV. ME. *enqueste* – OF. *enqueste* = Pr. *enquesta*, It. *inchiesta* :- Rom. **inquesta*, sb. use of fem. of pp. of **inquǣrere*; see next.

inquire, enquire inkwaiə·ɹ, iŋ- ask about XIII; seek information XIV. ME. *enquere* – OF. *enquerre* (mod. new formation *enquérir*) = Pr. *enquerre*, It. †*inchierere*, *inchiedere* :– Rom. **inquærere*, for L. *inquīrere*, f. *in-* IN-[1] + *quærere* ask (see QUESTION). Both prefix and stem-vowel were conformed to L. in XV, *inquere*, *enquire*, *inquire*. Hence **inquiry**[3] inkwaiə·ri, iŋ- investigation XV; interrogation XVI. Early form *enquery*, f. *enquere*; afterwards assim. to the later form of the vb.

inquisition inkwizi·ʃən, iŋ- inquiry, investigation; judicial inquiry XIV; (R.C.Ch.) ecclesiastical tribunal (the Holy Office) XVI. – (O)F. *inquisition* – L. *inquīsītiō(n-)* (legal) examination, f. *inquīsīt-*, *inquīrere* INQUIRE; see -ITION. So **inquisitive** -i·zitiv. XIV (Ch.). – OF. – late L. **inqui·sitor**. XVI. – OF. – L.

inroad i·nroud hostile incursion, raid. XVI. f. IN[1] + ROAD in the etymol. sense of 'riding'.

insane insei·n not of sound mind. XVI. – L. *insānus*, f. *in-* IN-[2] + *sānus* SANE. So **insa·nity**. XVI. – L.; orig. *insanity of mind*.

inscribe inskrai·b write in or on; (geom.) delineate within a figure XVI; enrol; mark with characters XVII. – L. *inscrībere*, f. *in* IN-[1] + *scrībere* write (see SCRIPTURE). So **inscri·ption**. XIV (concr.). – L.

inscrutable inskrū·təbl that cannot be fathomed by the mind. XV. – late L. *inscrūtābilis* (Hilary, Augustine), f. *in-* IN-[2] + *scrūtārī*; see SCRUTINY, -ABLE.

insect i·nsekt (pop.) small invertebrate animal; (zool.) one of the Insecta. XVII (Holland). – L. *insectum*, pl. *insecta* (Pliny), sb. use of n. of pp. of *insecāre* cut into or up, f. *in* IN-[1] + *secāre* cut (see SECTION); rendering Gr. *éntomon*, pl. *éntoma* (Aristotle), sc. *zôion*, *zôia* animal(s), rel. to *entémnein* cut up or in two (cf. ATOM).

insert insə̄·ɹt set or put in. XVI. f. *insert-*, pp. stem of L. *inserere*, f. *in* IN-[1] + *serere* plant, join, put into (see SOW[2]). So **inse·rtion**. XVI. – late L.

insessores insesō·rīz (ornith.) order of perching birds. XIX. modL., pl. of late L. *insessor*, f. *insess-*, pp. stem of *insidēre*, f. *in* IN-[1] + *sedēre* SIT.

inset i·nset leaf or sheet inserted. XIX. f. pp. *inset*, i.e. set in; see IN[1], SET[1].

inside insai·d sb. inner side or surface XVI; adj. i·nsaid XVII (Sh.); adv. XIX; prep. XVIII. f. IN[1] (attrib.) + SIDE; cf. OUTSIDE.

insidious insi·diəs full of wiles, operating subtly. XVI. – L. *insidiōsus*, f. *insidiæ* ambush, trick, rel. to *insidēre* sit in or upon, be settled, f. *in* IN-[1] + *sedēre* SIT; see -IOUS.

insight i·nsait †mental vision or perception XII (Orm); penetration by the understanding *into* XVI (Sidney). prob. of Scand. and LG. origin; cf. Sw. *insiht*, Da. *insigt*, Du. *inzicht*; G. *einsicht* (XVIII); comp. of IN[1] and SIGHT.

insignia insi·gniə badges, emblems. XVII. L., pl. of *insigne* mark, sign, badge of office, sb. use of n. of *insignis* distinguished (as by a mark), f. *in* IN-[1] + *signum* SIGN (cf. Gr. ἐπίσημος); see -IA[2].

insinuate insi·njueit introduce indirectly or stealthily. XVI. f. pp. stem of L. *insinuāre*, f. *in* IN-[1] + *sinuāre* curve, f. *sinus* curve; see SINUOUS, -ATE[3]. So **insinua·tion**. XVI. – L.

insipid insi·pid tasteless. XVII. – F. *insipide* or late L. *insipidus*, f. *in-* IN-[2] + *sapidus* SAPID. Hence or – F. **insipi·dity**. XVII.

insist insi·st †continue steadfastly *in*; dwell emphatically *on*. XVI. – L. *insistere* stand upon, persist, f. *in* IN-[1] + *sistere* STAND.

insolation insoulei·ʃən exposure to the sun. XVII. – L. *insōlātiō(n-)*, f. *insōlāre*, f. *in* IN-[1] + *sōl* SUN; see -ATION.

insolent i·nsələnt †haughty, arrogant XIV (Ch.); contemptuous of dignity or authority XVII. – L. *insolent-*, *-ēns* unusual, excessive, arrogant, f. *in-* IN-[2] + prp. of *solēre* be accustomed; see -ENT. So **i·nsolence**. XIV (Ch.). – L. Cf. F. *insolent*, *-ence* (XV).

insoluble insɔ·ljŭbl †indissoluble XIV (Wycl. Bible); that cannot be solved XIV (PPl.); that cannot be dissolved in liquid XVIII. – (O)F. or L.; see IN-[2], SOLUBLE.

insomnia insɔ·mniə sleeplessness. XVIII. – L. f. *insomnis* sleepless, f. *in-* IN-[2] + *somnus* sleep + -IA[1]. Anglicized †*insomnie* (XVII). ¶ L. *insomnium* (prop.) dream, tr. Gr. ἐνύπνιον, has been irreg. used for *insomnia*.

insomuch insŏmʌ·tʃ †so much XIV (Wyclif, rare); †inasmuch *as*; to such an extent (*that*) XV. tr. OF. *en tant* (*que*); at first alternative to INASMUCH, but later differentiated.

insouciant insū·siənt, || ɛ̃nsusjɑ̃ unheeding, indifferent. XIX (Scott). F., f. *in-* IN-[2] + *souciant*, prp. of *soucier* care :– L. *sollicitāre* disturb, agitate (see SOLICIT).

inspan inspæ·n (S. Africa) yoke, harness. XIX. – Du. *inspannen*, f. *in* IN[1] + *spannen* stretch, bend, put horses to (see SPAN[2]).

inspect inspe·kt look carefully into or at. XVII. f. *inspect-*, pp. stem of L. *inspicere*, f. *in* IN-[1] + *specere* look (see SPECIES) or – L. frequent. *inspectāre*; cf. F. *inspecter*. So **inspe·ction**. XIV (Gower). – (O)F. – L. **inspe·ctor**[1]. XVII. – L.

inspeximus inspe·ksiməs (leg.) charter in which the grantor avouches to have inspected an earlier charter. XVII. L., 'we have inspected', 1st pers. pl. pt. of *inspīcere* INSPECT; the first word of the document.

inspire inspaiə·ɹ infuse into the mind; impart or suggest by divine agency; †breathe XIV; breathe in XVI. – (O)F. *inspirer* – L. *inspīrāre*, f. *in* IN-[1] + *spīrāre* breathe (see

SPIRIT). So **inspir**A·TION. XIV (R. Mannyng, R. Rolle). – (O)F. – late L.

inspissate inspi·seit, i·nspiseit thicken. XVII (Bacon). f. pp. stem of late L. *inspissāre*, f. *in* IN-[1]+*spissus* thick, dense; see -ATE[3]. So **inspiss**A·TION. XVII (Holland).

install instɔ̄·l invest with or place in an office, orig. by placing in an official stall XVI; (after F.) to place in position XIX. – medL. *installāre*, f. *in* IN-[1]+*stallum* STALL; cf. (O)F. *installer*. So **install**A·TION. XVII. – medL.; so F. Hence **insta·l**MENT[1], U.S. **insta·ll**-installation. XVI.

instalment[2], U.S. **install-** instɔ̄·lmənt †arrangement for payment; agreed part of a sum to be paid XVIII; part supplied at a certain time XIX. Alteration (prob. by assoc. with prec.) of earlier †*estallment*, aphetic †*stallment* (XV) – AN. *estalement* (AL. (*e*)*stallamentum*), f. *estaler* fix (AL. *stallare* pay debts by instalments); see STALL, -MENT.

instance i·nstəns urgency, urgent action (now in phr. *at the instance of*) XIV; †case adduced in objection or disproof; example in support of a general proposition (= medL. *instantia*) XVI; (after Ulpian) process, suit (*court of first i.*, i.e. of primary jurisdiction); hence *in the first i.* as the first step XVII. – (O)F. *instance* eagerness, solicitation, judicial process, new argument rebutting the reply to a previous one – L. *instantia* presence, urgency, pleading or process, in scholL. (prop. *i. contradictionis*) objection, example to the contrary (tr. Gr. *énstasis* objection, f. *enistánai* stand in the way, object), f. *instant-*, *-āns* INSTANT. Hence **i·nstance** vb. †urge XV; cite as an instance XVII.

instant i·nstənt urgent XV; present (of time); of the current month; imminent, immediate XVI. – (O)F. *instant* assiduous, at hand – L. *instant-*, *-āns*, prp. of *instāre* be present or at hand, urge, apply oneself to, f. *in* IN-[1]+*stāre* STAND. As sb. point of time, moment XV; after medL. *instāns* (sc. *tempus*) present moment of time. Hence **i·nstant**LY[2] †urgently; †just now XV; forthwith XVI; after (O)F. *instamment* urgently, L. *instanter* urgently, pressingly. So **instant**A·NEOUS. XVII. f. medL. *instantāneus*, f. *instant-*, after ecclL. *mōmentāneus*.

instate instei·t establish in a position. XVII. f. IN[1]+STATE *sb.* Cf. REINSTATE.

instauration instɔ̄rei·ʃən (arch.) renovation, renewal. XVII. – L. *instaurātiō(n-)*, f. *instaurāre* RESTORE; see IN-[1], -ATION.

instead inste·d in the place or room (*of* another), as deputy or successor XIII; in its stead, as a substitute XVII. orig. written as two words and so regularly till late XVI, when the conjunct form began to appear; phr. *in (the) stead of* (see STEAD), after OF. *en* (now *au*) *lieu de*, which continued L. (*in*) *locō* with gen., 'in the condition or relation (of)'.

instep i·nstep upper part of the foot between toes and ankle. XVI. Earlier forms *instep(pe)*, also *instoppe*, *-stup*, *-stip*; the variation in form prob. points to adoption of a foreign word and away from immed. deriv. from IN[1] and STEP, though the elements are ult. identical with these; for the sense cf. WFris. *ynstap* opening in a shoe for the insertion of the foot ('Dy skoen binne to nau, of to wiid, fen ynstap', the shoes are too narrow, or too wide, in the opening); also LG. *instappen* step in.

instigate i·nstigeit spur or urge on. XVI. f. pp. stem of L. *instīgāre*, f. *in* IN-[1]+*stīgāre* prick, incite, rel. to Gr. *stízein* prick (:- **stigj-*; cf. STIGMA); see -ATE[3]. So **instig**A·TION. XV. – F. or L.

instil insti·l put in by drops; infuse gradually. XVI. – L. *instillāre*, f. *in* IN-[1]+*stillāre*, f. *stilla* drop; cf. DISTIL.

instinct i·nstiŋkt †impulse XV; innate impulse or propensity; intuition XVI (Sh.). – L. *instinctus* instigation, impulse, f. *instinct-*, *instinguere* incite, impel, f. *in* IN-[1]+*stinguere* prick (cf. DISTINCT, EXTINCT); formerly str. *insti·nct*. So **insti·nct** pp. †innate XVI; †impelled, excited XVII (Milton); imbued *with* XVIII. – L. *instinctus* pp. **insti·nct**IVE operating by instinct. XVII. **insti·nctive**LY[2]. XVII (Sh.).

institute i·nstitjūt †purpose; established usage; principle(s) or element(s) of instruction XVI; (after F. *institut* name of the institution created in 1795 to replace the old academies) society to promote an object; building used for this XIX. – L. *institūtum* design, ordinance, precept, sb. use of n. of pp. of *instituere* establish, ordain, arrange, teach, f. *in* IN-[1]+*statuere* set up (see STATUTE). So **i·nstitute** vb. set up, found XV; establish in an office, esp. eccl. XVI. f. pp. stem of *instituere*; preceded by the pp. †*institute* (XIV) and the inf. †*institue*, shortened †*instue* (XIV), – (O)F. *instituer*. **institu**·TION establishment, esp. eccl. in a benefice XIV (Wyclif); established law, etc. XVI; establishment or organization for the promotion of an object XVIII. – (O)F. – L. **institu·tion**AL[1]. XVII.

instruct instrʌ·kt impart knowledge to XV; direct, command XVI; †put in order XVII. f. *instruct-*, pp. stem of L. *instruere* set up, furnish, fit out, teach, f. *in* IN-[1]+*struere* pile up, build (see STRUCTURE); cf. F. *instruire*. So **instru·c**TION imparting of knowledge, teaching; direction, order. XV (Lydg.). – (O)F. – late L. **instru·ct**IVE. XVII. **instru·c**TOR. XV. – F. *-eur*.

instrument i·nstrŭmənt tool, implement XIII (earliest of a musical instrument); something used by an agent; means XIV; legal document XV. – (O)F. *instrument* – L. *instrūmentum*, f. *instruere*; see prec. and -MENT. So **instrume·nt**AL[1] serving as instrument or means XIV (Trevisa); of music composed for instruments XVI; (gram.) of the case denoting 'with' or 'by means of' (after the

Skr. name *karaṇa* means, instrument) XIX. – (O)F. Hence **instrume·ntal**IST player on a musical instrument. XIX (earlier †*instrumentist* XVII; so F. *-iste*). **i:nstrumenta·**TION composition of music for instruments. *c.* 1845. – F. (1824 Stendhal). **i:nstrumenta·l**ITY. XVII (Baxter).

insufflation insʌflei·ʃən breathing upon a person or thing as a means of exorcism XVI; (med.) blowing of air or vapour into the lungs, etc. XIX. – late L. *insufflātio(n-)*, f. *insufflāre*, f. *in* IN-¹+*sufflāre* blow upon, f. *sub* SUF-+*flāre* BLOW¹; see -ATION.

insular i·nsjŭləɹ pert. to an island XVII; characteristic of islanders, as being narrow or prejudiced XVIII. – late L. *īnsulāris*, f. *īnsula* ISLAND; see -AR. So **i·nsul**ATE³ convert into an island XVI; detach, ISOLATE (also electr.) XVIII. **i·nsul**ATOR. *c.*1800.

insulin i·nsjulin specific for diabetes extracted from the *islands* of Langerhans in the pancreas of animals. 1921. f. L. *īnsula* ISLAND; see -IN¹.

insult insʌ·lt glory or triumph *over* XVI; treat with scornful abuse or disrespect XVII. – L. *insultāre*, f. *in* IN-¹+*saltāre*, iterative-intensive f. *salīre* leap, jump (see SALIENT). So **i·nsult** (arch.) attack; affront XVII. – F. *insulte* or – ecclL. *insultus*, f. *in* IN-¹+*saltus* leap. Earlier †**insulta·**TION. XVI. – OF. or L.

insuperable insjū·pərəbl †unconquerable XIV (R. Rolle); unsurmountable XVII (H. More). – OF. or L.; see IN-², SUPERABLE.

insure inʃuə·ɹ. XV. var. of ENSURE, with substitution of IN-¹ for EN-¹, established in the sense of securing payment on death or damage (XVII). So **insu·r**ANCE. XVII; in commercial use repl. ASSURANCE, which is retained in the titles of some long-established companies.

insurgent insə̄·ɹdʒənt one who rises in active revolt. XVIII (Falconer). – F. †*insurgent* (XVIII in connexion with the rising in N. America), – L. *insurgent-*, *-ēns*, prp. of *insurgere* rise up (whence †*insurge* XVI); see IN-¹, SURGE, -ENT. So **insurrec**TION insəre·kʃən rising in arms. XV. – (O)F. – late L. *insurrectiō(n-)*, f. *insurrect-*, *insurgere*.

intact intæ·kt untouched, unblemished. XV. – L. *intăctus*, f. *in-* IN-²+*tāctus*, pp. of *tangere* touch (cf. TANGENT).

intaglio intæ·ljou figure incised or engraved; incised gem. XVII (Evelyn). It., f. *intagliare* engrave, f. *in* IN-¹+*tagliare* cut; cf. ENTAIL.

intake i·nteik taking in or what is taken in, (dial.) place of this. f. phr. *take in*; see TAKE, IN¹. ¶ In north. dial. in the sense of 'inclosure of land' *intack* from XVI, earlier *yntauk* (XIV, 'Selby Cartulary').

integer i·ntidʒəɹ (denoting) a whole quantity. XVI (Digges). – L. *integer* intact, ENTIRE. So **i·ntegr**AL¹ making up a whole, made up of parts which constitute a unity XVI; (math.) XVIII. – late L. *integrālis*, f. *integr-*, *integer*. **i·ntegr**ATE³. XVII; f. pp. stem of L. *integrāre*, f. *integer*. **integra·**TION. XVII. – L. **inte·gr**ITY inte·grĭti. XV. – F. or L.

integument inte·gjŭmənt covering, coating. XVII (Chapman). – L. *integumentum*, f. *integere* cover; see IN-¹, TEGUMENT.

intellect i·ntĭlekt knowing and reasoning faculties of the mind. XIV (Ch., Trevisa). – (O)F. *intellect* or L. *intellectus* perception, discernment, meaning, sense, f. pp. stem of *intellegere*; see below. So **intelle·c**TION understanding. XVII. – L. *intellectiō(n-)*. **intelle·ct**IVE pert. to the understanding. XV. – late L. *intellectīvus*; cf. (O)F. *intellectif*. **intelle·ctu**AL¹ of the intellect; †spiritual, ideal XIV (Trevisa); †intelligent XV; highly gifted with understanding XIX. – L., f. *intellectus* understanding; cf. (O)F. *intellectuel*. **intelle·ctual**ISM. XIX; after G. *intellectualismus*. **intelle·ctual**IST. XVII (Bacon). **i:ntellectua·l**ITY. XVII (Florio). – late L. (Tertullian). **intelligent** inte·lidʒənt quick to understand. XVI (Hawes). – prp. of L. *intelligere*, *-legere* lit. choose among, f. *inter* INTER-+*legere* pick up, gather, choose, read (see LECTION). So **inte·llig**ENCE. XIV (Gower). – (O)F. – L.; hence **intelligenc**ER¹ informer, spy, messenger XVI; as title of a newspaper XVII. **intellige·ntsia, -tzia** the 'intellectuals'. XX. – Russ. *intelligéncija* – Pol. *inteligiencja* – L. *intellegéntia*. **inte·llig**IBLE. XIV (Trevisa, Wycl. Bible).

intemperate inte·mpərət XV (Lydg.). – L. *intemperātus*; see IN-², TEMPERATE. So **inte·mper**ANCE. XV. – (O)F. or L.

intend inte·nd direct the mind or attention XIV (Ch., Gower); design for a purpose XVI (Sh.); various lit. and etymol. senses have been current. ME. *entende*, *in-* – (O)F. *entendre*, †*intendre* (= Pr. *entendre*, Sp. *entender*, It. *intendere*; in the Rom. langs. the sense 'hear' is common) – L. *intendere* extend, direct, intend, promote, f. *in* IN-¹+ *tendere* stretch, TEND¹. So **inte·nd**ANT superintendent, manager (chiefly F. officials). XVII (Evelyn). – F. – L. prp. of *intendere*. **inte·nd**ED¹ purposed, designed; sb. intended spouse XVIII. **inte·nd**MENT †understanding, meaning XIV (Ch., Gower); (leg.) XVI. – (O)F. *entendement*, f. *entendre*. **inte·nse** existing in a very high degree. XIV (*intense cold*, Maund.). – (O)F. *intens(e)* or L. *intensus* stretched, tight, violent, pp. of *intendere*; hence **inte·ns**IFY. XIX (Coleridge). **inte·n**SION tension, intentness, intensity XVII; internal content of a concept XIX (W. Hamilton). **inte·ns**IVE †intense XVI; relating of or pert. to intensity; intensifying XVII (also irreg. *intensative*, *intensitive* XIX);)(*extensive* XIX. **inte·nt**¹ intention XIII (AncrR.); end proposed XIV (R. Rolle; obs. exc. in phr. *to all intents* XVI). ME. *entent*

– OF. *entent* :– L. *intentus*, and *entente* – (O)F. *entente* :– Rom. **intenta*, f. pp. of L. *intendere*. **inte·nt**[2] earnestly attentive or bent *upon*. XVII. – L. *intentus*, pp. of *intendere*. **inte·ntION** †understanding; †meaning, import; purpose XIV; (logic) direction of the mind to an object, conception (medL. tr. of Avicenna) XVI; (theol.) XVII. ME. *entencion* – OF. *entencion* (mod. *intention*) – L. **inte·ntionAL**[1]. XVI. – F. *-ionnel* or medL.

inter[1] intə̄·ɹ bury. XIV (R. Mannyng). ME. *enter(re)* – (O)F. *enterrer* = Pr., Sp. *enterrar*, It. *interrare* – Rom. **interrāre*, f. *in* IN-[1] + *terra* earth (cf. Ir., W. *tír* country), repl. L. *inhumāre* INHUME. The sp. was remodelled on L. Hence **inte·rMENT**. XIV.

inter[2] i·ntəɹ L. prep. 'between', 'among' (cogn. with UNDER), occurring in a few L. phrases current in Eng.: *inter alia* (ei·liə) among other things, *inter nos* (nous) between ourselves, *inter se* (sī) among themselves.

inter- i·ntəɹ, intə̄·ɹ L. prep. (see prec.), repr. in F. by *entre-* (see ENTER-), used as a prefix with the senses: (1) between, in between, in the midst, as in *intercalāre*, *-cēdere*, *-pōnere*, *-venīre*, whence INTERCALARY, INTERCEDE, INTERPOSE, INTERVENE, *interdigitālis* lying between the fingers, INTERREGNUM, *intervallum* INTERVAL; (2) at intervals, as in *intermittere* INTERMIT; (3) with preventive or destructive effect, as in *intercipere* INTERCEPT, *interdīcere* (see INTERDICT), *interficere* kill (f. *facere* DO[1]). The earliest adoptions of such words in Eng. came through F. forms with *entre-* (e.g. *entrechange*, *enterfere*), but in XVI remodelling of these forms on the L. *inter-* began, and at the same time the use of the prefix was widely extended in combination with various radicals, and functioning as adj. or as adv. Meanwhile the prefix had acquired a mutual or reciprocal sense (a trace of which is found in late L. *intermūtātīs manibus* with crossed hands), illustrated by *intercommunion*, *interdependence*, *-ent*, *intermarriage*, *-marry*, *intermingle*, *interplay*, the like of which are numerous. The other large group of comps. in which *inter-* has become a living formative is that in which it governs prepositionally (with the senses 'between', 'among', and 'forming a link between', 'belonging in common to') the sb. implied in the radical part of the comp., on the model of late L. *interamnus* placed between rivers (*amnis* river), *intermūrālis* situated between walls (*mūrus* wall), as in many gen. and techn. words like *interalveolar*, *intercolonial*, *intercollegiate*, *interdenominational*, *interdental*, *international*, *interstellar*, *intervocalic*. The prefix enters freely into combination with sbs. to form attrib. phrases, as in *inter-county* match.

intercalary intə̄·ɹkələri inserted at intervals (in the calendar) XVII; intervening XVIII. – L. *intercalārius*, *-calāris*, f. *intercalāre* (cf. CALENDS. COUNCIL) proclaim the insertion of a day, etc., in the calendar, from pp. stem of which is **inte·rcalATE**[3]. XVII; so **intercalA·TION**. XVI (– F. or L.).

intercede intəɹsī·d †come between XVI; intervene on behalf of another XVII. – (O)F. or L. *intercēdere*, f. *inter* INTER- + *cēdere* go. So **interce·SSION**. XVI (Dunbar, Tindale). – (O)F. or L. **interce·ssOR**[1]. XV. – L.; hence **interce·ssORY**, XVI.

intercept intəɹse·pt seize on the way from one place to another, cut off (a person or thing). XVI. f. *intercept-*, pp. stem of L. *intercipere*, f. *inter* INTER- + *capere* take, seize (see HEAVE). So **interce·pTION**. XVI (Sh.). – F. or L.

intercha·nge exchange mutually. XIV (Ch.). Late ME. *enterchaunge* – OF. *entrechangier*; see INTER-, CHANGE. Hence as sb. XVI. So **intercha·ngeABLE**. XV. – OF.; -ABLY. XIV; after AN. *entrechaungeablement*.

intercommu·nicate have mutual communication. XVI. – AL.; see INTER-, COMMUNICATE. So †**interco·MMON** XV (Lydg.), -COMMU·NE XIV (Ch.). – AN. *entrecomuner*.

intercourse i·ntəɹkōəɹs mutual dealings XV; social or spiritual communication XVI. Earlier *entercourse* – (O)F. *entrecours* – L. *intercursus* (in class. L. only in abl.), f. *intercurrere* run between or among, intervene; see INTER-, COURSE.

interdict i·ntəɹdikt (eccl.) sentence debarring the faithful from church functions and privileges XIII; authoritative prohibition or decree XVII. ME. *entredit* – OF. *entredit* – L. *interdictum* (to which the Eng. word was assim. XVI), sb. use of n. of pp. of *interdīcere* interpose by speech, forbid by decree, f. *inter* INTER- + *dīcere* say (see DICTION). Hence **interdi·ct** vb. XIII; after OF. *entredire* – L. *interdīcere*.

interest i·ntərest, i·ntrėst A. (legal) concern or right *in* XV; advantageous or detrimental relation XVI; matter in which persons are concerned XVII; feeling of one concerned XVIII; B. †injury, damages; money paid for use of money lent XVI. Late ME. alt. of †*interesse*, †*ent(e)resse* (Ch.), partly by addition of parasitic *t*, partly by assoc. with OF. *interest* damage, loss (mod. *intérêt*), app. sb. use of L. *interest* it makes a difference, concerns, matters, 3rd pers. sg. pres. ind. of *interesse* differ, be of importance, f. *inter* INTER- + *esse* BE (the history is, however, obscure). So **i·nterest** vb. invest with a title or share; cause to have or take an interest XVII; affect with a feeling of concern XVIII. Alteration of †*interess* vb. XVI. – F. *intéresser* †damage, concern, f. L. *interesse*; ppl. adj. **i·nterestED**[1] (XVII) was preceded by †**interessed** (XVI) – F. *intéressé*. **i·nterestING**[2]. XVIII. †important (Shaftesbury), apt to excite interest (Sterne); cf. F. *intéressant*.

interfere intəɹfiə·ɹ strike the inside of the fetlock with the hoof of the opposite foot, knock one leg against another XVI; collide, clash, come into opposition, intermeddle *with* XVII; intervene XVIII. – OF. (refl.) *s'entreferir* strike each other, f. *entre-* INTER-+*férir* :– L. *ferīre* strike (cf. OHG. *berjan*, ON. *berja*). Hence **interfe·**RENCE. XVIII. **interfero·**METER. XIX.

interim i·ntərim meanwhile (also *ad interim, per interim*); intervening time, interval of time. XVI. – L. *interim* in the meantime, f. *inter* INTER-+advb. suffix *-im*, orig. ending of acc. sg. of *i-* stems (cf. *partim* partly).

interior intiə·riəɹ situated (more) within. XV (Caxton). – L. *interior* inner, compar. adj. f. *inter* within (see INTER², -IOR).

interjection ejaculation XV; (gram.) XVI (Palsg.). – (O)F. *interjection* – L. *interjectiō(n-)*, f. *interject-*, pp. stem of *intericere* interpose, f. *inter* INTER-+*jacere* throw, cast (cf. ABJECT). So **interje·ct** vb. XVI.

interlace intəɹlei·s. XIV (Ch.). – OF. *entrelacier*; see ENTER-, INTER-, LACE vb.

interlard intəɹlā·ɹd †pass. have alternate layers of fat and lean; diversify by intermixture. XVI. Earlier *enter-* – (O)F. *entrelarder*, f. *entre-* INTER-+*larder* LARD.

interleave intəɹlī·v insert leaves between the leaves of (a book). XVII (Wood). f. INTER-+*leaves*, pl. of LEAF. Hence **i·nter**LEAF. XVIII (Richardson).

interli·ne insert between the lines. XV. – medL. *interlīneāre*; see INTER-, LINE². So **inter**LI·NEAR. XV. – medL. *interlīneāris*.

interlocutor intəɹlɔ·kjŭtəɹ one who takes part in a conversation. XVI (Barclay). – modL., f. L. *interloquī, -locūtiō*; see INTER-, LOCUTION.

interloper i·ntəɹloupəɹ †unauthorized trader XVI; one who thrusts himself into an affair XVII. f. INTER- (as in *intermeddler*)+ *loper* (as in LANDLOPER). Hence **i·nterlope** vb. XVII. ¶ F. *interlope*, †*interlopre* ship trading without authority in countries allotted to a merchant company, and Du., LG. *enterlopen*, are from Eng.

interlude i·ntəɹlʲūd light or humorous dramatic representation, (later XVII–XVIII) comedy, farce XIV; interval in the performance of a play XVII; intervening time or space XVIII. – medL. *interlūdium*, f. *inter* INTER-+*lūdus* play (cf. LUDICROUS).

interme·ddle. ME. *entremedle* (Ch.; Caxton) – AN. *entremedler* = OF. *entremesler*; see INTER-, MEDDLE.

intermediate intəɹmī·diət coming between two things. XVII. – medL. *intermediātus*, f. L. *intermedius*, f. *inter* INTER-+*medius* MID; cf. F. *intermédiat*; see -ATE². So **interme·di**ARY. XVIII; after F. *intermédiaire*.

intermezzo intəɹme·dzou (mus.) piece intervening between two main parts of a composition. XIX. It. – L. *intermedius* (see prec.).

interminable intə̄·ɹminəbl. XIV (Ch.). – (O)F. or late L. ¶ Earlier than *terminable*.

intermit intəɹmi·t leave off, discontinue. XVI. – L. *intermittere*, f. *inter* INTER-+*mittere* let go. So **inter**MI·SSION. XVI. – F. or L.

intern intə̄·ɹn confine within prescribed limits of residence. XIX (*c.* 1865). – F. *interner*, f. *interne* = It. *interno* – L. *internus* inward, internal, f. *inter* INTER² (cf. *externus* EXTERNAL).

internal intə̄·ɹnəl pert. to man's inner nature XVI (Hawes); situated within XVI (Spenser); pert. to the thing or subject itself XVII. – modL. *internālis*, f. *internus*; see prec., -AL¹.

interna·tional existing between nations. XVIII (Bentham). f. INTER-+NATION+-AL¹. So **internationale** -næʃiŏnā·l, ‖ɛ̃tɛrnasjonal revolutionary hymn composed by Eugène Pottier in 1871. F. (sc. *chanson* song).

internecine intəɹnī·sain attended with great slaughter XVII (Butler, 'Hudibras' I i 774 *internecine war*, after L. *internecinum bellum*); (misinterpreted by Johnson in his Dict. as) mutually destructive XVIII. – L. *internecīnus*, f. *interneciō* general slaughter, massacre, extermination, f. *internecāre* slaughter, exterminate, f. *inter* INTER-+*necāre* kill, rel. to *nec-*, *nex* violent death, *nocēre* injure, orig. put to death; see NOXIOUS, -INE¹.

internu·ncio. XVII (Milton). – It. *internunzio*; see INTER-, NUNCIO.

interpellation i:ntəɹpelei·ʃən †pleading, intercession XVI; †interruption XVII; (after modF.) interruption of the order of the day in the French Chamber XIX. – L. *interpellatiō(n-)*, f. *interpellāre* interrupt by speaking, f. *inter* INTER-+-*pellāre* thrust or direct oneself (as in *appellāre* APPEAL).

interplea·der (leg.) suit pleaded between two parties. XVI. – AN. *entrepleder*, sb. use (see -ER⁵) of inf. (see INTER-, PLEAD).

interpolate intə̄·ɹpəleit alter a writing by the insertion of new matter, also gen. XVII; furbish up, alter, falsify, (math.) insert intermediate terms XVIII. f. pp. stem of L. *interpolāre*, f. *inter* INTER-+-*polāre*, rel. to *polīre* POLISH. So **interpol**A·TION. XVII.

interpose intəɹpou·z place between in space or time. XVI. – (O)F. *interposer*, based on L. *interpōnere*; see INTER-, POSE¹. So **interposi**·TION. XV. – (O)F. or L.

interpret intə̄·ɹprit expound the meaning of. XIV (Wyclif). – (O)F. *interpréter* or its source L. *interpretārī* explain, translate, f. *interpret-, -pres* agent, broker, translator, interpreter, f. *inter* INTER-+unkn. element. Hence **inte·rpret**ER¹. XIV. So **interpret**A·TION. XIV. – (O)F. or L.

interregnum intəɹre·gnəm †temporary authority exercised during a vacancy; period intervening between a ruler and his successor. XVI. – L., f. *inter* INTER- + *regnum* REIGN. Earlier †*interreign* (Bellenden), partly – (O)F. *interrègne*.

interrogate inte·rəgeit ask questions of. XV (Caxton). f. pp. stem of L. *interrogāre*, f. *inter* INTER- + *rogāre* ask; see ROGATION, -ATE[3]. So **interroga·tion**. XIV (Ch.). – (O)F. or L. **interrogative** -ɔ·gativ. XVI (Whitington, Palsgr.). – late L. **interro·gatory**. XVI (More; var. *inte·rgatory* XVI–XVII). – late L. (Tertullian).

interrupt intərʌ·pt break in upon. XV (Lydg.). f. *interrupt-*, pp. stem of L. *interrumpere*, f. *inter* INTER- + *rumpere* break (see RUPTURE). So **interru·ption**. XIV (Gower, Caxton). – (O)F. or L.

interse·ct XVII; see INTER-, BISECT; so **interse·ction**. XVI.

intersperse intəɹspɔ̄·ɹs scatter between or among, diversify *with* things at intervals. XVI. f. *interspers-*, pp. stem of L. *interspergere*; see INTER- and DISPERSE.

interstice intɔ̄·ɹstis intervening empty space. XVII (preceded by the L. form). – late L. *interstitium*, f. **interstit-*, pp. stem of *intersistere*, f. *inter* INTER- + *sistere* STAND.

interval i·ntəɹvəl period between two events or actions XIII (Cursor M.); open space between two things XV (Caxton). ult. – L. *intervallum* orig. space between ramparts, f. *inter* INTER- + *vallum* (see WALL), but the earliest forms, *entrewal*, *entervale*, *intervalle*, are – OF. *entreval(e)*, later *-valle* (mod. *intervalle*).

intervene intəɹvī·n †come between XVI; come in in the course of an action, etc. XVII (Bacon). – L. *intervenīre*, f. *inter* INTER- + *venīre* COME. So **interve·ntion**. XV. – F. or L.

interview i·ntəɹvjū meeting of persons face to face. XVI. Earlier form *entervew(e)* – F. †*entreveue*, *-vue*, f. *entrevoir* have a glimpse of, *s'entrevoir* see each other (f. *entre* INTER- + *voir* see), after *vue* VIEW.

intestate inte·steit, -tīt not having made a will. XIV (PPl.). – L. *intestātus*, f. *in-* IN-[2] + *testātus*, pp. of *testārī* bear witness, make a will, f. *testis* witness; see TESTIFY, -ATE[2]. Hence **inte·stacy**. XVIII.

intestine inte·stin internal. XVI (Stewart). – L. *intestīnus*, f. *intus* within (corr. to Gr. *entós*; cf. Gr. *énteron*, as in MESENTERY); sb. (esp. pl.) lower part of the alimentary canal. XVI. – L. *intestīnum*, sb. use of n. of adj. ¶ For the L. formation cf. CLANDESTINE.

intimate i·ntīmət inward, essential, intrinsic; pert. to the inmost thoughts; closely associated (also sb.). XVII. – late L. *intimātus*, pp. of *intimāre*, f. *intimus* inmost, f. *int-* of INTER[2] + superl. suffix (cf. Skr. *ántamas*); see -ATE[2]. Hence **i·ntimacy**. XVII. So **intimate**[3] i·ntimeit make known formally; indicate indirectly. XVI. f. pp. of late L. *intimāre*, f. *intimus*. **intima·tion** formal announcement XV; expression by sign XVI. – (O)F. or late L.

intimidate inti·mideit inspire with fear. XVII. f. pp. stem of medL. *intimidāre*, f. *in-* IN-[1] + *timidus* TIMID; see -ATE[3].

intinction inti·ŋkʃən †dipping, infusion XVI; (eccl.) dipping of the bread in the wine at the Eucharist XIX. – late L. *intinctiō(n-)*, f. *intingere*; see IN-[1], TINCTURE.

intitule intai·tjūl ENTITLE (now leg. in ref. to acts of parliament). XV (Caxton). – (O)F. *intituler* – late L. *intitulāre*.

into i·ntu orig. two words and so written till XVI; OE. *in(n) tō*, i.e. IN[1] adv. expressing motion towards an object, TO prep. marking the place, point, or space entered, reached, or penetrated; in immaterial senses referring to various sorts of introduction, admission, or adaptation.

into·lerable. XV (Lydg.). – F. or L.; see IN-[2].

intone intou·n recite in a singing voice XV (rare before XIX); sing the intonation of a melody XIX. – medL. *intonāre*, f. *in* IN-[1] + *tonus* TONE; in XV–XVI *entone* – OF. *entoner* (mod. *-onner*). So **intona·tion** opening phrase of a plainsong melody XVII: action of intoning, utterance of musical notes; modulation of the voice in speaking XVIII. – medL. *intonātiō(n-)*; so (O)F.

intoxicate intɔ·ksikeit †poison; stupefy with a drug or strong drink. XVI. f. pp. stem of med L. *intoxicāre*, f. *in* IN-[1] + L. *toxicum* poison; see TOXIC, -ATE[3]. So **intoxica·tion**. XV. – F. or medL.

intra- i·ntrə prep., 'on the inside', 'within' (f. *in* IN[2] + *-trā* as in EXTRA-) used occas. in late L. as prefix, as in *intrāmūrānus* lying within the walls; taken up in Eng. techn. language in XIX in similar formations, e.g. *intralo·bular* within the lobe(s).

intra·ctable. XVI. – F. or L.; see IN-[2].

intrados intrei·dɔs (archit.) lower curve of an arch. XVIII. – F. *intrados*, f. L. *intrā* INTRA- + F. *dos* back (cf. DOSSAL).

intransigent intræ·nsidʒənt, -træ·nz- uncompromising. *c.* 1882. – F. *intransigeant* (1875), based on Sp. *los intransigentes* party of the extreme left in the Spanish Cortes, (in 1873–4) extreme republicans; ult. f. *in-* IN-[2] + prp. of L. *transigere* come to an understanding; see TRANSACT, -ENT.

intra·nsitive. XVII. – late L. (Priscian); IN-[2].

intrepid intre·pid fearless, undaunted. XVII (Dryden). – F. *intrépide* or L. *intrepidus*, f. *in-* IN-[2] + *trepidus* agitated, alarmed, f. IE. **trep-* **trop-* **trp-* (cf. Gr. *trapeîn* tread, Skr. *tṛpás*, *tṛpálas* alarmed, hurrying, Lith. *trepséti*, Russ. *tropát'* tread under foot).

intricate i·ntrikīt perplexingly involved. XV (*interkat*, Henryson). – L. *intrīcātus*, pp. of *intrīcāre* entangle, perplex, f. *in* IN-[1] + *trīcæ* trifles, tricks, perplexities, *trīcārī* make difficulties; see -ATE[2].

intrigue intrī·g †intricacy, maze; underhand plotting. XVII. – F. *intrigue*, †*intrique* – It. *intrigo*, *-ico*, f. *intrigare*, *-icare* :– L. *intrīcāre*; see prec. So **intri·gue** vb. XVII. – F. – It. – L.

intrinsic intri·nsik, -zik †inward, inner XV–XVII (later anat. XIX); of its own, proper XVII. – (O)F. *intrinsèque* – late L. *intrinsecus*, f. L. adv. *intrinsecus* inwardly, inwards; from the first the ending was assim. to -IC. So **intri·ns**ICAL, -ICALLY. XVI. ¶ *Intrinsecate* was ridiculed by Marston and used affectedly by Ben Jonson.

intro- i·ntrŏ(u) L. adv. *intrō* to the inside (parallel to INTRA-) used as a prefix in *intrōducere* INTRODUCE, *introitus* INTROIT, *intrōmittere* INTROMIT, acquired extensive currency in Eng. from XVII.

introduce intrədjū·s bring into a society, place, etc. XVI (More); bring into use or action XVII. – L. *intrōdūcere*, f. *intrō* INTRO- + *dūcere* lead, bring (see prec., DUKE). So **introduc**TION -dʌ·kʃən. XIV (Ch.). – (O)F. or L.

introit i·ntroit †entrance; (eccl.) antiphon and psalm recited as the celebrant approaches the altar. XV. – (O)F. *introït* – L. *introitus* entrance, f. *introīre* enter, f. *intrō* INTRO- + *īre* go. Cf. ADIT, EXIT, etc.

intromit intro(u)mi·t interfere. XV. – L. *intrōmittere* introduce, f. *intrō* INTRO- + *mittere* send. So **intro**MI·SSION. XVI. – F. or L.

introspection intro(u)spe·kʃən looking within, as into one's own mind XVII. (Hale, Dryden). Hence **introspe·ct**IVE. XIX (Southey). Cf. INSPECTION and see INTRO-.

introvert introuvə̄·ɹt turn (the mind) upon itself. XVII. – modL. *intrōvertere*, f. *intrō* INTRO- + *vertere* turn (cf. -WARDS). Hence **i·ntrovert** sb. part turned within XIX; (psych.) a wholly self-centred person XX.

intrude intrū·d thrust or force in. XVI. – L. *intrūdere*, f. *in* IN-[1] + *trūdere* thrust (cf. THREAT). So **intru·**SION (leg.) thrusting oneself into an estate or benefice XIV (Usk); uninvited entrance or appearance XVI (Sh.). – (O)F. or medL.

intuition intjui·ʃən †contemplation, view XV (rare before XVII); †regard, reference; (philos.) immediate knowledge or apprehension XVI (Hooker); (gen.) immediate insight XVIII. – Late L. *intuitiō(n-)*; see IN-[1], TUITION. So **intu·it**IVE. XVI (Hooker). – medL. Cf. F. *intuition*, *-itif*.

intussusception i:ntʌssəse·pʃən taking-in of matter from outside XVIII; (path.) introversion of an intestine XIX. – F. or modL., f. L. *intus* within (cf. Gr. *entós*) + *susceptiō(n-)* taking up, f. *suscipere* take up, f. *subs* + *capere* take; see SUS-, HEAVE, -TION.

inundate i·nʌndeit, (formerly) inʌ·ndeit overflow. XVII. f. pp. stem of L. *inundāre*, f. *in* IN-[1] + *undāre* flow, f. *unda*; see WATER, -ATE[3]. So **inund**A·TION. XV. – (O)F. or L.

inure, †**enure** injuə·ɹ accustom, habituate XV (*enewre*, Caxton); †put into operation; (leg.) come into operation XVI. – AN. **eneurer*, f. phr. **en eure* in use or practice, i.e. *en* IN[1], **eure* URE.

inurn inə̄·ɹn put (the ashes of a body) in an urn. XVII (*enurn'd*, Sh.). f. IN-[1] + URN.

invade invei·d make a hostile attack (upon). XV. – L. *invādere*, f. *in* IN-[1] + *vādere* go (see WADE). So **inva·**SION. XVI. – (O)F. or late L.

invagination invædʒinei·ʃən introversion, intussusception. XVII. – modL.; see IN-[1], VAGINA, -ATION.

invalid[1] invæ·lid not valid. XVI. – L. *invalidus*; see IN-[1], VALID. So **inva·lid**ATE[3]. XVI; after F. *invalider*. **in**VALI·DITY. XVI.

invalid[2] i·nvəlīd, -id, (formerly) invəlī·d infirm or disabled from sickness or injury XVII; sb. (spec. disabled soldier or sailor; cf. F. *Hôtel des Invalides*, *Les Invalides* hospital for these in Paris) XVIII. spec. use of prec. with modified pronunc. after F. *invalide*.

inVA·LUABLE of inestimable value XVI; (rare) valueless XVII. See IN-[2].

invar i·nvāɹ alloy of nickel and steel with a negligible coefficient of expansion. Patent name (XX), abbrev. of **in**VA·RIABLE (XVII).

invecked inve·kt (her.) bordered by or consisting of a series of convex lobes (encroaching upon the field). XV (Bk. St. Albans). Anglicized sp. of **invect* – L. *invectus*, pp. of *invehere* carry in (see next); cf. †*inveckit* (Bk. St. Albans) introduced (of one colour *into* another). So **inve·ct**ED[1]. XVII.

inveigh invei· †bring in, introduce XV; give vent to denunciation XVI (More). – L. *invehere* carry in, medio-pass. *invehī* be borne into, attack, assail with words, f. *in* IN-[1] + *vehere* carry (cf. VEHICLE); for the sp. cf. †*conveigh* CONVEY. So **invect**IVE inve·ktiv adj. (arch.) marked by denunciatory or vituperative language XV; sb. speech of this kind XVI. – (O)F. *invectif*, *-ive* adj., *invective* sb. – late L. *invectīvus*, *invectīva* (sc. *ōrātiō*) as sb., f. *invect-*, pp. stem of *invehere*.

inveigle invī·gl, -vei·gl †beguile, deceive XV; gain over by enticement XVI. Earlier *envegle* (*-veugle*) – AN. *envegler* alteration (cf. ENSAMPLE) of (O)F. *aveugler* blind, f. *aveugle* blind, prob. :– Rom. **ab oculīs* 'without eyes'.

invent inve·nt †come upon, find XV; devise, esp. by way of original contrivance XVI. f. *invent-*, pp. stem of L. *invenīre*, f. *in* IN-[1] + *venīre* COME. So **inve·n**TION finding (surviving in *Invention of the Cross* church festival of 3rd May) XV; contrivance (abstr. and concr.) XVI. – L. Cf. F. *inventer* (XVI), *invention* (XIV). **inve·nt**IVE. XV (Lydg.). – OF. **invent**ORY[1] i·nvənt(ə)ri detailed list of articles. XVI. – medL. *inventōrium*, for late L. *inventārium* (whence (O)F. *inventaire*, Sc. †*inventare*, *-aire* XV).

inverness invəɹne·s overcoat with a removable cape. XIX. Name of a town in the Highlands of Scotland (Gael. *Ionar-* or *Inbhirnis* 'mouth of the Ness').

inverse i·nvə̄ɹs, (formerly) invə̄·ɹs inverted (chiefly techn.); also sb. XVII. – L. *inversus*, pp. of *invertere*, f. *in* IN-¹+*vertere* turn (see -WARD). So **inve·r**SION. XVI. **invert** invə̄·ɹt turn in an opposite direction. XVI. – L. *invertere* 'turn in, turn outside in', reverse. Hence **i·nvert** one whose instincts are inverted. XX.

invertebrata invə̄ɹtibrei·tə (sb. pl.) animals having no backbone. XIX (1808). modL. (sc. *animālia* animals), after F. *invertébrés* (Cuvier, 1805), f. *in-* IN-²+*vertèbre*, L. *vertebra* (see VERTEBRATE). Anglicized **inve·rtebrate.** XIX (1826).

invest inve·st A. clothe, spec. with the insignia of office; establish in possession, endow with power; B. enclose with a hostile force XVI; C. put out (money) at interest XVII. – (O)F. *investir* or L. (rare) *investīre* clothe, surround (extended in meaning in medL.), f. *in* IN-¹+*vestis* clothing (see VEST); in C after It. *investire*, the notion being that of giving the capital another 'form'; the use prob. passed from the Levant or Turkey Company to the East India Company. So **inve·stit**URE investing of a person with a dignity, etc. XIV (Trevisa; rare before XVI). – medL. *investitūra*. Hence **inve·st**MENT †clothing XVI (Sh.); investiture XVII (Milton); investing of capital XVII. ¶ *Vestment*, †*vestiment* are of ME. date.

investigate inve·stigeit search into. XVI. f. pp. stem of L. *investīgāre*, f. *in* IN-¹+*vestīgāre* track, trace out; see VESTIGE, -ATE³. So **investig**A·TION. XV. – (O)F. or L.

inveterate inve·tərət established by age or long standing; obstinately embittered. XVI. – L. *inveterātus*, ppl. adj. of *inveterāscere* grow old, f. *in-* IN-¹+*veter-*, *vetus* old; see VETERAN, -ATE². Hence **inve·ter**ACY. XVII.

invidious invi·diəs tending to or entailing odium. XVII. – L. *invidiōsus*, f. *invidia* ill will, ENVY; see -IOUS.

invigilate invi·dʒileit keep watch. XVI. f. pp. stem of L. *invigilāre*, f. *in* IN-¹+*vigilāre* watch, f. *vigil* watchful; see VIGIL, -ATE³.

invigorate invi·gəreit render vigorous. XVII (Sir T. Browne). f. pp. stem of L. **invigōrāre* (cf. F. *envigorer*, etc.), f. *in* IN-¹+*vigor* VIGOUR; see -ATE³.

invincible invi·nsĭbl unconquerable. XV (Lydg.). – (O)F. *invincible* – L. *invincibilis*, f. *in-* IN-²+*vincibilis*, f. *vincere* conquer; see VICTOR, -IBLE.

inviolate invai·ələt not violated, intact. XV (Lydg., Hoccleve). – L. *inviolātus*, f. *in-* IN-²+pp. of *violāre* VIOLATE.

invisible invi·zĭbl. XIV (R. Rolle). – OF. or L.; see IN-², VISIBLE.

invite invai·t ask to come to a place, etc. XVI. – F. *inviter* or L. *invitāre*. So **invita**·TION. XVI. – F. or L. **invitat**ORY² invai·tətəri that invites, spec. to liturgical worship. XIV (R. Rolle); sb. XV.

invoice i·nvois list of items of goods sent to a purchaser. XVI. orig. pl. of †*invoy* (which is, however, recorded only later) – F. †*envoy*, *envoi*; see ENVOY. ¶ For the sp. *-ce* cf. *dice*, *mice*, *pence*, and (in pls. that have become sg.) *bodice*, *truce*. So *once*, *twice*.

invoke invou·k call upon in prayer or attestation. XV (Caxton). – (O)F. *invoquer* – L. *invocāre*, f. *in* IN-¹ + *vocāre* call. So **in**VOCA·TION. XIV. – (O)F. – L.

involucre i·nvŏlʲūkəɹ envelope XVI; (bot.) whorl of bracts XVIII. – F. *involucre* or L. *involū·crum* (also used in Eng. from XVII), f. *involvere* INVOLVE.

inVO·LUNTARY. XVI. – late L.; see IN-².

involve invɔ·lv wrap round, lit. and fig. XIV (Wycl. Bible); implicate in trouble, etc. XIV (Trevisa); implicate in a charge; include XVII. – L. *involvere*, f. *in* IN-¹+*volvere* roll (see VOLUME). So **involute** i·nvəlʲūt rolled or curled up XVII; sb. (math.) XVIII. **involu·**TION involved condition XVII; (arith., alg.) raising of a quantity to any power XVIII, (geom.) system of pairs of points XIX; (physiol.) retrograde change in the body XIX.

inward i·nwəɹd adj. that is within; adv. towards the inside. OE. *innanweard*, *inneweard*, *inweard*, f. *innan*, *inne*, *in(n)* IN¹+ *-weard* -WARD; a CGerm. comp. (cf. MDu. *inne-*, *inwert*, OHG. *inwart* adj., *-wert* adv., ON. *innanverðr* adj.). Also **i·n**WARDS. XIII; cf. MDu. *inwaerts*, MHG. *inwertes*, Icel. *innvortis*, etc.; sb. sg. †entrails OE.; inward part XIV, XIX; pl. internal parts, entrails XIII; vulgarly *innards*.

iodine ai·ədīn, ai·ədain (chem.) non-metallic element which volatilizes into a violet-coloured vapour. 1814 (H. Davy). f. F. *iode* (Gay-Lussac, 1812) – Gr. *iṓdēs* violet-coloured, f. *íon* VIOLET + *-eidēs* -like; see -OID, -INE.⁵ Hence **i·odoform** after CHLOROFORM.

ion ai·ən (chem.) electrically charged particle of an atom or a molecule. XIX (Faraday). – Gr. *ión*, prp. n. of *iénai* go. Cf. ANION, CATION. Hence **i·on**IZE.

-ion iən suffix repr. (O)F. *-ion* – L. *-iō(n-)*, which forms nouns of condition and action from (i) adjs. or sbs., as *commūniō* COMMUNION, f. *communis* COMMON, *dominiō* DOMINION; (ii) verb-stems, as *legiō* LEGION, f. *legere* collect, but chiefly from (iii) pp. or supine stems in *t*, *s*, *x* (see -TION, -SION).

Ionian aiou·niən pert. to (member of) the division of the Hellenes which occupied Attica and established many colonies. XVI. f. L. *Iōnius* – Gr. *Iṓnios*; see -IAN. So **Ion**IC aiɔ·nik (archit.) of an order, (mus.) of an ancient Gr. mode and of the 11th eccl. mode XVI; of a metrical foot, of a dialect of ancient Greek XVII.

ionosphere aiou·nǒsfiəɹ Heaviside layer (an ionized region of the atmosphere). XX. f. ION+-O-+SPHERE.

-ior iəɹ formerly also *-iour* – F. *-ieur*,† *-iour* – L. *-iōrem*, nom. *-ior*, suffix of compar. of adj., as in *anterior, exterior, inferior, interior, junior, posterior, senior, ulterior.* ¶ In *warrior* the ending has another origin.

iota aiou·tə the letter ι, the smallest letter of the Gr. alphabet; (after Matt. v 18, ἰῶτα ἓν ἢ μία κεραία) least particle, atom. XVII. – Gr. *iôta*, of Phœnician origin (cf. Heb. *jōd*). See JOT.

iotacism aiou·təsizm pronunciation of other Greek vowels and diphthongs like *iota*, i.e. as *ī*. XVII. – late L. *iotacismus* – late Gr. *iōtakismós*, f. *iôta* IOTA+*-ismós* -ISM, with hiatus-filling *k*.

I O U aioujū· document bearing these letters constituting acknowledgement of debt. (XVII) XVIII. usu. taken to be a symbolic repr. of *I owe you*.

-ious iəs comp. suffix meaning 'characterized by', 'full of', (i) repr. F. *-ieux*, L. *-iōsus*, f. stem- or connective vowel -I-+*-ōsus* -OUS, or (ii) directly f. a L. suffix consisting of *i* and another suffix (viz. *-ia, -ius, -iō, -iēs, -ium*) +-OUS. See also -ACIOUS, -ITIOUS.

ipecacuanha i:pikækjuæ·nə root of the S. Amer. plant Cephaelis Ipecacuanha, used medicinally. XVII. – Pg. *ipecacuanha* ipikakwānja – Tupi-Guarani *ipe-kaa-guéne* 'low or creeping plant causing vomit' (Cavalcanti). abbrev. colloq. **ipecac** ipikæ·k. XVIII.

ipomœa aipo(u)mī·ə genus of convolvulaceous plants. XVIII. modL. (Linnæus), f. Gr. *ip-*, *îps* worm + *hómoios* like, rel. to *homós* SAME.

ipse dixit i·psi di·ksit personal (dogmatic) assertion. XVI. L. 'he himself said' (it); tr. Gr. αὐτὸς ἔφα, phr. used of Pythagoras by his followers.

ir-[1] assim. var. of IN-[1] before *r*.

ir-[2] assim. var. of IN-[2] before *r*.

irade irā·dei written decree of the Sultan of Turkey. XIX. Turk. – Arab. *irādah* will, desire.

Iranian airei·niən pert. to the Asiatic group of IE. languages comprising Avestic (Zend, Old Bactrian) and Old Persian with their modern representatives. XIX. f. *Irān*, native name of Persia + -IAN.

irascible i-, airæ·sībl easily angered. XVI. – (O)F. *irascible* – late L. *īrāscibilis*, f. *īrāscī* grow angry, f. *īra* IRE; see -IBLE. So **ir**ATE[2] airei·t enraged. XIX. – L. *īrātus*, f. *īra*; ME. had †*irous* in this sense (XIII) – AN. *irous*, OF. *iros* = Pr. *iros*, It. *iroso* :– Rom. **īrōsus*.

ire aiəɹ (poet.) anger. XIII. – (O)F. *ire* = Pr. It. *ira* :– L. *īra*. Hence **i·re**FUL[1]. XIII.

irenicon, eirenicon airī·nikən proposal designed to promote peace. XVII. – Gr. n. of *eirēnikós*, f. *eirḗnē* peace; see -IC.

iridescent iride·sənt displaying colours like those of the rainbow. XVIII (Kirwan). f. L. *īrid-*, IRIS + -ESCENT.

iridium airi·diəm (chem.) white metal of the platinum group. 1803 ('I should incline to call this metal *Iridium*, from the striking variety of colours which it gives, while dissolving in marine acid', Tennant). modL., f. L. *īrid-*, IRIS + -IUM.

iris aiə·ris pl. *i·rides* -īz, *i·rises* species of crystal XIV (Maund.); rainbow XV (Caxton); flat circular coloured membrane in the aqueous humour of the eye; genus of tuberous or bulbous plants XVI. – L. *īris* – Gr. *îris* rainbow, coloured circle, etc., iris (plant), (*I-*) proper name of the female messenger of the gods, whose sign was a rainbow.

Irish aiə·riʃ pert. to Ireland. XIII (Laȝ.). f. OE. *Īras* inhabitants of *Īrland* Ireland (obscurely based on OIr. *Ériu*; see HIBERNIAN) +-ISH[1] (cf. ON. *Í'rskr*).

irk ə̄ɹk †grow weary, be loath XIII (*forhirked* wearied); weary, annoy XV. contemp. with †*irk* adj. weary, loath; of obscure origin. Its first appearance in Scandinavianized areas has suggested deriv. from ON. *yrkja* WORK, Sw. *yrka* claim, demand, insist. Surviving in current Eng. chiefly in **i·rk**SOME[1] †tired, disgusted XV; wearisome, burdensome XVI.

iron ai·əɹn the most abundant and useful metal; chem. symbol Fe. OE. *īren*, perh. for **īrern*, alt. of *īsern* (by assoc. with the var. *īsen*) = OS., OHG. *īsarn* (Du. *ijzen*, G. *eisen*), ON. *ísarn*, Goth. *eisarn* :– CGerm. **īsarnam*, prob. – Celtic **īsarno-* (Gaulish *Ysarno-*, *Iserno-* in place-names, OBret. *hoiarn*, W. *haearn, hayarn*, Ir. *iarann*, Gael. *iarunn*), prob. rel. to L. *æs* (earlier *ais*) bronze, OE. *ār*, Goth. *aiz*, Skr. *áyas*. ME. *ire* survives in s.w. dial. and in the surname *Iremonger*; in north. dial. *iren* was contr. to *irn, yrn*, surviving as *irn, ern, airn*; in Standard Eng. *īren* was syncopated after diphthongization of ī, ai·rən passing to aiə·r(ə)n, thence to ai·ə(ɹ)n. Hence **i·ron**CLAD cased with iron or steel plates, spec. of ships; preceded by *iron-cased, -clothed, -plated, -sided.* XIX. **i·ron**MONGER dealer in ironware. XIV. **iron mould,** orig. -MOLE[1] spot of discoloration caused by iron. XVII (Holland). **i·ron**SIDE nickname of a man of great hardihood XIII (*Edmond yrene syde*, RGlouc.); applied to Oliver Cromwell's troopers 1648.

irony aiə·rəni figure of speech in which the intended meaning is the opposite of that expressed; pretence (as of ignorance; *Socratic irony*) XVI; condition of affairs opposite to that expected (F. *l'ironie du sort* the irony of fate) XVII. – L. *īrōnia* (Cicero) – Gr. *eirōneíā*, f. *eírōn* dissembler; see -Y[3]. So **iron**IC airɔ·nik. XVII. – F. *ironique* or late L. *īrōnicus* (cf. *īrōnicē* adv.) – Gr. *eirōnikós*; preceded by **iro·n**ICAL, -ICALLY. XVI.

irRA·TIONAL XV (Henryson); (math., ult. tr. Euclid's ἄλογος 'without reason') XVI (Recorde). – L.; see IR-[2].

irredentist iride·ntist advocate of the recovery and union to Italy of all Italian-speaking regions. XIX. – It. *irredentista*, f. (*Italia*) *irredenta* unredeemed or unrecovered (Italy); see IR-[2], REDEEM, -IST.

irrefragable ire·frəgəbl incontrovertible, undeniable. XVI. – late L. *irrefrāgābilis*, f. *in*- IR[2]- + L. *refrāgārī* oppose, contest)(*suffrāgārī* (cf. SUFFRAGE); see -ABLE.

irrelevant ire·livənt XVI (Sc.); see IR-[2], RELEVANT. Hence **irre·lev**ANCY. XVI.

irrigate i·rigeit water (land) through channels. XVII. f. pp. of L. *irrigāre*, f. *in* IR-[1] + *rigāre* wet, water; see -ATE[3]. So **irriga**·TION. XVII. – L.

irritate i·riteit †incite; excite to anger, fret XVI; excite to morbid action XVII. f. pp. stem of L. *irrītāre*; see -ATE[3]. Earlier †*irrite* (XV) – (O)F. *irriter*. **i·rrit**ABLE. XVII (H. More). – L. So **irrita**·TION. XVI. – L.

irruption irʌ·pʃən bursting in. XVI. – L. *irruptiō(n-)*, f. *irrupt-*, *irrumpere*, f. *in* IN-[1] + *rumpere* break; see RUPTURE, -TION.

Irvingite ə·ɹviŋait member of the Catholic Apostolic Church, founded on principles promulgated by Edward *Irving* (d. 1834); see -ITE.

is iz see BE.

isabella izəbe·lə greyish yellow, light buff. XVI. In early use always *I. colour*; f. the female name, but the immediate ref. is unkn. Also **isabel** i·zəbel. XIX. – F. *isabelle*.

isagogic aisəgɔ·dʒik introductory. XIX. – L. *īsagōgicus* – Gr. *eisagōgikós*, f. *eisagōgḗ* introduction, f. *eisádgein* introduce, f. *eis* into + *ágein* lead (cf. ACTION); see -IC.

isatin ai·sətin (chem.) crystalline substance, $C_8H_5NO_2$, obtained from indigo. XIX. f. L. *isatis* woad (Pliny) + -IN.

ischiatic iskiæ·tik sciatic. XVII. – medL. *ischiaticus* (after *rheumaticus*), for L. *ischiadicus*, f. *ischiad-*, *iskhiás* pain in the hip, f. Gr. *iskhíon* hip-joint (L. **ischium** i·skiəm XVII, Sir T. Browne); see -IC.

-ise see **-ize**.

-ish[1] iʃ suffix forming adjs.: OE. *-isć* = OFris., OS., OHG. *-isc* (Du., G. *-isch*), ON. *-iskr*, Goth. *-isks* :– CGerm. **-iskaz* = Gr. dim. suffix *-iskos*; in some words reduced to *-sh*, with a var. *-ch*; in Sc. usu. *-is*, with reduced vars. *-s*, *-ce*. In OE., etc., words of old formation (mostly gentile names) have mutation; e.g. *Englisć* ENGLISH, Sc. †*Inglis*, *Scyttisć*, Sc. †*Scottis*, SCOTS (see SCOTTISH, SCOTCH), *Wīelisć* WELSH, Sc. †*Walys*, †*Wallis*, *Denisć*, Sc. †*Dense* (see DANISH), *Frencisć* FRENCH, *Grēcisć*, †*Greekish*; similarly many adjs. of various dates and origins, as *Irish* (XIII), *Flemish*, *Pictish*, *Swedish*. Formations in OE. on common nouns are *ċeorlisć*, *ċierlisć* churlish, *ċildisć* childish, *hǣþenisć* heathenish, *ūtlendisć* foreign; their number was greatly increased in ME., at first with the uncoloured meaning of 'pert. to or of the nature of', but later chiefly on dyslogistic words, as *boorish*, *foolish*, *shrewish*, *thievish*, or with the derogatory force 'having the bad or unpleasant qualities of', as *apish*, *babyish*, *monkish*, *popish*, *selfish*, *womanish*, (with proper names) *Miss Mortineauish* (Tennyson), *Micawberish*, *West-Endish*, (with names of things) *aguish*, *bookish*, *feverish*, (with other parts of speech or phrases) *pettish*, *snappish*, *standoffish*, *ticklish*, *uppish*, *alloverish*.

From XIV onwards *-ish* was added to adjs. with the sense 'approaching the quality of, somewhat, rather', first to adjs. of colour, as *blueish*, *reddish*, *whitish* (Trevisa), *greenish* (Ch.), but later to any (esp. monosyllabic) adjs., often with the intention of being neutral, as *softish*. This use has been extended in XX (prob. after *earlyish*, *latish*) to the qualification of hours of the day or numbers of years to denote 'roundabout', 'or thereabouts', as *four-ish*, *1940-ish*. ¶ Endings of other origin have been assim. to *-ish* in *garish*, *lavish*, *lickerish*, *peevish*, *squeamish*.

-ish[2] iʃ repr. F. *-iss-*, extension of the stem of vbs. in *-ir*, e.g. *abolir* ABOLISH, *périr* PERISH, prp. *abolissant*, *périssant*, 3rd pers. pl. pres. ind. *abolissent*, *périssent*; originating in the *-isc-* of L. inceptive vbs., the use of which in F., Pr., and It. was extended to form a class corr. to L. vbs. in *-īre* and *-ēre*, together with some others that were assim. to these. The earliest forms in Eng. were *-is*, *-ise*, *-iss(e)*, which were superseded by *-ische*, *-ishe*, *-ish*; in Sc. *-is(se)* remained to a later date and appeared in XVI as *-eis(e)*. (In a few words F. *-iss-* is repr. by *-ise* or *-ize*, viz. *advertise*, *aggrandize*, *chastise*, *amortize*; *réjouir*, *réjouiss-* has given *rejoice*.) ¶ Other F. endings have been assim. to this suffix in *admonish*, *astonish*, *diminish*, *distinguish*, *famish*, *lavish*, *minish*, *publish*, *relish*.

isinglass ai·siŋglàs gelatin obtained from air-bladder of sturgeon, etc., fish-glue. XVI (*isomglas*, *ison-*). With assim. to *glass* – early Du. †*huysenblas*, f. †*huysen*, †*huys* sturgeon + †*blas* (mod. *blaas*) bladder (cf. G. *hausenblase*).

Islam i·zlām, -læm, is- Mohammedanism. XIX (Shelley). – Arab. *islām*, f. *aslama* he resigned himself (spec. to God), he became sincerely religious, 4th conjugation of *salama* he became or was safe. Cf. MOSLEM, SALAAM. So **I·slam**ISM XVIII (F. *islamisme*, Voltaire), **I·slam**ITE[1] XVIII (F. *islamite*).

island ai·lənd land completely surrounded by water. OE. (Anglian) *ēġland*, (WS.) *īeġland*, *īġland*, later *īland* = OFris. *eiland*, MDu., MLG. *eilant* (Du. *eiland*), ON. *eyland*; f. OE. *īeġ*, *iġ* island, in comp. water, sea, OFris. *ey* island, OHG. *ouwa* water, stream, watery meadow, island, peninsula (G. *aue*, *au* brook, meadow, pasture), ON. *ey* island :– Germ. **aujō* (repr. in medL. *Austr|avia*, *Scadin|avia*, OE. *Sćedeniġ*, ON. *Skáney*), for **agwjō*, adj. formation on **agwō-* stream, water (whence OE. *ēa*, OFris. *ā*, *ē*, OS., OHG. *aha*, ON. *á*, Goth. *ahwa*), rel. to L. *aqua* water (cf. AQUATIC). The present. sp., dating from XVI, is due to assim. to next.

isle ail (arch. exc. as in place names) island. XIII. ME. *ile*, later *isle* – OF. *ile* (mod. *île*), (latinized) †*isle* = Pr., Sp. *isla*, It. *isola* :– L. *insula*, expl. by the ancients as f. *in salō* 'in the salt sea', but superficial resemblance to Gr. *nêsos*, *nâsos*, and Ir. *inis*, W. *ynys*, may point to gen. adoption from some Mediterranean (non-IE.) source. So **isl**ET ai·lit small island. XVI. – OF. *islette* (mod. *îlette*).

-ism izm repr. F. *-isme*, L. *-ismus* – Gr. *-ismós*, forming nouns of action for vbs. in *-izein* -IZE, e.g. *baptismós* dipping, BAPTISM. (A rel. suffix *-isma*, which expresses rather the finished action, is sometimes the source of *-ism*; see CHARISMA.) A frequent use of *-ismós* was to express the sense of acting like or adopting the habits of a body of people, as *Attikismós* siding with Athenians, Attic fashion or idiom; so *Ioudaïsmós* Judaism, *Khristianismós* practice of Christians, Christianity; on this model was formed medL. *pāgānismus* PAGANISM, whence OF. *paienisme*, *-ime* (cf. PAYNIM). In Eng. *Judaism* is recorded in XV, and from XVI formations with the suffix become numerous. The chief uses are: (1) to form a noun of action naming the process, the completed action, or its result, e.g. *baptism*, *criticism*, *exorcism*, *nepotism*, *ostracism*; (2) with emphasis on conduct, habit, or character, e.g. *barbarism*, *despotism*, *heroism*, *patriotism*, *blackguardism*, *priggism*; (3) forming the name of a system of theory or practice, based on the name of its subject or object, or on the founder's or a promoter's name, e.g. *Arianism*, *Catholicism*, *Epicureanism*, *positivism*, *ritualism*, *Romanism*, *Socinianism*, and (by extension) to designations of doctrines or principles, e.g. *agnosticism*, *altruism*, *bimetallism*, *deism*, *egoism*, *egotism*, *hedonism*, *polytheism*, *romanticism*, *universalism*; (4) forming a term denoting a trait or peculiarity, as of language, e.g. *Americanism*, *Anglicism*, *Gallicism*, *Scotticism*, *colloquialism*, after *archaism*, *barbarism*, *Græcism*, *Hellenism*, *solecism*; for (3) and (4) there is an extensive record of nonce-words. Adjectives of sbs. in *-ism* end in -ISTIC. Hence **ism** izm form of theory or practice of a distinctive character, such as may be designated by a word in *-ism*. XVII ('Jesuitism, Puritanism, Quaquerism, and all Isms from Schism', 1680). The suffix *-ist* has been similarly used as a sb.

iso- ai·so(u), aisɔ·, before a vowel sometimes **is-** ais, comb. form of Gr. *ísos* equal, in many techn. terms, as: **i·sobar** line on a map, etc., connecting places at which the barometric pressure is the same. XIX. Gr. *báros* weight (cf. BAROMETER). **iso·chron**AL[1] XVII, **-chronous** XVIII. f. modL. *isochronus* – Gr. (*khrónos* time) equal in duration. **iso·-**CRACY equality of power. XVII. – Gr. *isokratíā*. **i·sogloss, isome·ric** (chem.) composed of the same elements in the same proportions. XIX. – G. *isomerisch* (Gr. *méros* part). **iso·nomy**[3] equality of laws. XVI (Holland). – It. (modL.) – Gr. *isonomíā* (*nómos* law). **isothe·rm**AL[1] pert. to localities having the same temperature. XIX. f. F. *isotherme* (Gr. *thérmē* heat).

isolated ai·səleitid placed or standing alone. XVIII. f. F. *isolé* – It. *isolato* :– late L. *īnsulātus* made into an island, f. *īnsula* ISLE; see -ATE[2], -ED[1]. Preceded in use by *isolé* (XVIII), which was occas. semi-naturalized as *isolé'd*. Hence **i·solate** vb. (of which *isolated* is now regarded as the pp.) XIX, **isol**A·TION XIX; partly after F. *isoler* (It. *isolare*) and *isolation*.

isosceles aisɔ·sĭlīz (math.) of a triangle, having two sides equal. XVI. – late L. *isoscelēs* – Gr. *isoskelḗs*, f. *ísos* ISO-+*skélos* leg.

isotope ai·sətoup (chem.) element having the same character as another element occupying the same place in the periodic table but differing in atomic weight and certain other properties. 1913 (Soddy). f. ISO-+Gr. *tópos* place (cf. TOPIC). ¶ *Isotopic* was used by Cohen and Miller in a different sense in 1904.

Israel i·zriəl, -eiəl (In OE. in g. pl. *Israela folc*; ME. *israel folk*) – ecclL. (Gr.) *Isrāēl* – Heb. *yisrāēl* 'he that striveth with God', name conferred on the patriarch Jacob (Gen. xxxii 28). So **I·srael**ITE. XIV (Wycl. Bible). – late L. (Vulg.) *Isrāēlīta* – Gr. *Isrāēlī́tēs* – Heb. *yisrāēlī*. **-it**ISH[1]. XVI (Coverdale).

issue i·ʃu, i·sju egress, exit, outflow XIII; offspring, progeny; proceeds; outcome XIV; (leg.) point in question XVI (earlier in *join i.* submit jointly for decision XV); (from the vb.) public giving-out XIX. – (O)F. *issue*, †*eissue* :– Rom. **exūta*, sb. use of fem. of pp. **exūtus*, for L. *exitus*, pp. of *exīre* go out or forth (see EXIT). Hence **issue** vb. XIV. prob. f. (O)F. pp. *issu*, of *issir* (whence ME. *isse*, *ische*) :– L. *exīre*.

-ist ist repr. F. *-iste*, L. *-ista*, *-tēs* – Gr. *-istḗs*, forming agent-nouns from vbs. in *-izein* -IZE, consisting of the agential suffix *-tēs* added to the vb.-stem, as in *baptistḗs* BAPTIST. Several Gr. words were adopted into classical L. (e.g. *citharista* player on the cithara, *grammatista* grammarian, *sophista*, *tympanista* drummer), and many more by Christian writers (e.g. *baptista*, *exorcista*, *psalmista*); later it came into regular use for the designations of observers of particular tenets or rites or the followers of religious leaders (e.g. *Catharista*, *Platonista*, *nōminālista*, *reālista*). In Eng. and the mod. langs. the suffix forms not only agent-nouns having corr. verbs in *-ize*, but analogues of sbs. in *-ism* (e.g. *altruism*, *-ist*), and further, without such reference, names of followers of a leader or a school, of adherents of a party, and of devotees or practisers of a profession or art, e.g. *Bonapartist, botanist, Chartist, copyist, cyclist, diarist, genealogist, nonconformist, philologist, royalist, socialist*; its present wide use is typified by such words as *artist, casuist, florist, Hebraist, humo(u)rist, journalist, materialist, novelist, Second Adventist, semifinalist, tobacconist, ventriloquist*. Cf. -ISM.

-ister istəɹ repr. OF. *-istre*, by-form of *-iste* -IST (perh. after *ministre* minister, etc.), as in *evangelistre*, beside *evangeliste*; so *choristre* (whence ME. †*queristre*, CHORISTER), *sophistre* SOPHISTER.

isthmus i·s(t)məs, i·sþməs narrow neck of land. XVI. – L. *isthmus* – Gr. *isthmós* narrow passage, isthmus, perh. f. **idh-* go (cf. Gr. *íthma* march, *eis|ithmē* entrance).

-istic i·stik repr. F. *-istique*, L. *-isticus* – Gr. *-istikós*, comp. suffix f. *-istḗs* -IST + *-ikós* -IC, as in *sophistikós* SOPHISTIC(AL); but used also where there is a corr. vb. in *-izein* -IZE, and sb. in *-ismós* -ISM but not a sb. in *-istḗs* -IST, as in *kharaktēristikós* CHARACTERISTIC. The use of this suffix was much extended in medL. and mod. langs., and supplies in Eng. the regular adjs. for forms in -IST, as well as for some in -ISM where no deriv. in -IST exists, as *altruistic, Calvinistic, Hellenistic, realistic, socialistic*. Some are used as sbs., e.g. *characteristic, syllogistic(s)*. An alternative secondary form is **-i·st**ICAL, whence the gen. adv. **-i·stical**LY[2]; there is also a parallel **-istic**ATE[3] for related vbs.; e.g. *sophistic, -ical, -ically, -icate(d)*.

it neuter pron. of the 3rd pers. sg.; nom. and acc. of the orig. demonstrative stem **χi-*, whence also HE[1], HIM, HIS, HER. OE. *hit* = OFris. *hit, het*, (M)Du. *het* it, Goth. *hita* this. (The parallel stem **i-* is the base of OS. *it*, OHG. *iʒ*, G. *es* it.) Loss of initial *h* (which is retained dial. for emphasis) took place at first in unstressed positions, but as early as 1200 *it* is found in stressed positions. Reduction to *t* in enclitic position (e.g. *is't* for *is it*) is equally early; in proclitic position (e.g. *'tis*) it is common from XVI. The orig. g. and d. were HIS, HIM; the present g. is ITS. Hence **its**SE·LF. OE. *hit self*; in XVII–XVIII sometimes written *its self*.

itacism i·təsizm pronunciation of Gr. η, ει, οι, υ, υι as ī; substitution of *i* for any of these in MSS. XIX. – modL. *ītacismus*, f. Gr. ἦτα *ī*·ta, with ending as in *rhotacism*.

Italian itæ·ljən pert. to Italy, its people, and its language. XV (of handwriting)(*Gothic* XVI). – It. *italiano* (whence F. *italien*), f. *Italia* Italy; see -IAN. So **Ita·lian**ATE[2] that has become Italian. XVI. – It. *italianato*. **Ita·l**IC pert. to a school of philosophy founded in Magna Græcia XVI; pert. to ancient Italy or its tribes; (*i-*) of printing type introduced by Aldo Manuzio of Venice (see ALDINE) XVII. – L. *Italicus* – Gr. *Italikós*: hence **ita·lic**IZE print in italics XVIII.

Ita·lioT(E) pert. to Gr. colonies or colonists in ancient Italy. XVII. – Gr. *Italiṓtēs*. **I·talo-,** used as comb. form of *Italian*. XVIII.

itch itʃ have or feel irritation of the skin OE.; have a restless desire XIII. OE *ġiććan*, *ġyććan*, corr. to OS. *jukkian*, (M)Du. *jeuken*, OHG. *jucchen* (G. *jucken*), f. Germ. **juk-* (whence also OHG. *jucchido*, MLG. *jeucte*, OE. *ġycþa* itch). So **itch** sb. OE. *ġyćće*. ¶ Initial *ġ* has disappeared as in *if* (OE. *ġif*), *Ipswich* (OE. *Ġipeswić*).

-ite ait suffix corr. to F. *-ite* and Sp., It. *-ito*, G. *-it* – L. *-īta, -ītēs* – Gr. *-ī́tēs*, forming adjs. and sbs. with the sense 'pert. to or connected with', 'member of', as in *hoplī́tēs* heavy-armed (soldier), HOPLITE, *polī́tēs* citizen (see POLITIC). There were many formations in Gr. on proper names, as *Abderī́tēs*, *Stagurī́tēs*; in LXX and N.T. and later Christian use this type was widely extended for the names of sects, heresies, etc., and in late L. and the mod. langs .the suffix has been used without limit for 'follower, devotee, or admirer', as in *Jacobite, Puseyite, Shelleyite, Wycliffite*; these tend to be depreciatory and when used attrib. or as adj. have often the implication 'having the bad qualities of the respective leader or originator'. **b.** In scientific terminology, *-ite* is used after the type of Gr.-L. words in *-ītēs* or *-ītis* in names of fossils and minerals (see AMMONITE, ANTHRACITE, BELEMNITE, HEPATITE, TRILOBITE, on which many terms have been modelled, with an el. expressing a physical character, a locality, or the name of a discoverer, etc.). In chemistry, it is used in the names of certain organic compounds (e.g. glucoses), and in inorganic chem. is the termination of salts of acids denominated by adjs. in *-ous*, e.g. *nitrite/nitrous*. It forms also certain names of explosives, e.g. *cordite, dynamite, lyddite*, and of commercial products such as *ebonite, vulcanite, xylonite*.

item ai·təm adv. likewise, moreover XIV; sb. †maxim, hint; article in an enumeration XVI; detail of news XIX. – L. adv., 'just so', 'in like manner', 'moreover', f. *ita* so (cf. synon. Skr. *iti, ittham*, Av. *iþa*), based on the pronominal stem **i-* (see HE[1], IT), with *-em* as in IDEM. Hence **i·tem** vb. XVII, **i·tem**IZE (esp. U.S.) XIX.

iterate i·təreit do or say again. XVI. f. pp. stem of L. *iterāre* repeat, f. *iterum* again, compar. formation on the pronominal base **i-* (cf. Skr. *ítaras* other); see prec. and ATE[3]. Cf. REITERATE. So **iter**A·TION. XV. – L. **i·ter**ATIVE. XV (Caxton). – F. or late L. (gram. of a vb. denoting repetition).

ithyphallic iþifæ·lik pert. to the phallus carried at the Bacchic festivals; (pros.) composed in the metre of Bacchic hymns. XVII. – late L. *īthyphallicus* – Gr. *īthuphallikós*, f. *īthúphallos*, f. *īthús* straight + *phallós* PHALLUS; see -IC.

-itic i·tik terminal el. of adjs. based on forms in (i) -ITE, (ii) -ITIS.

itinerant əiti·nərənt, iti·n- travelling (spec. of justices in eyre). XVI. – prp. of late L. *itinerārī*, medL. *-āre*, f. L. *itiner-*, *iter* journey, f. **it-* going (cf. *comit-*, *comes* COUNT²), f. IE. **i-* go (L. *īre*, Gr. *iénai*); see TRANSIT, -ANT. So **iti·ner**ARY route of travel; account of a journey XV; guide to travel XVI (Leland). – late L. *itinerārium*; cf. (O)F. *itinéraire*. Cf. AMBIENT, EXIT, INITIAL.

-ition i·ʃən suffix repr. F. *-ition*, L. *-itiō(n-)*, *-ītiō(n-)*, forming nouns of action (see -ION) on verbs with pps. in *-it-* and *-īt-*, as *positiō* POSITION, *audītiō* AUDITION; medL. extension of the application of the suffix is seen in *fūtūritiō* (Bonaventura).

-itious¹ i·ʃəs comp. suffix f. L. *-icius*, *-īcius* + -OUS; these L. endings were commonly written with *t* in medL. manuscripts and this form was perpetuated in ADVENTITIOUS, FACTITIOUS, FICTITIOUS, SUPPOSITITIOUS, etc.; extension of the suffix by analogy is seen in ADSCITITIOUS, EXCREMENTITIOUS, etc.

-itious² i·ʃəs repr. L. *-itiōsus*, *-ītiōsus*, f. *-itiō*, *-ītiō* (of various origins) -ITION + *-ōsus* -OUS, as in AMBITIOUS, SUPERSTITIOUS; similarly NUTRITIOUS, SEDITIOUS.

-itis ai·tis suffix repr. Gr. *-îtis*, prop. forming fems. of adjs. in *-ítēs*, used to qualify *nósos* disease, as *arthrîtis* (disease) of the joints (*árthron*), *pleurîtis* pleurisy (*pleurá* side, rib). On the analogy of these *-itis* came into use in mod. medical L. terminology for names of affections of particular parts, esp. of inflammatory disease, as APPENDICITIS, BRONCHITIS, MENINGITIS, TONSILLITIS. It has been extended in trivial use to the formation of sbs. descriptive of a state of mind or tendency regarded as a disease, e.g. *suffragitis* (Asquith). The deriv. adjs. end in **-itic** i·tik.

-itous itəs comp. suffix f. *-it-* of -ITY + -OUS; corr. to F. *-iteux*, L. *-itōsus*, as L. *calamitōsus*, F. *calamiteux* CALAMITOUS.

its poss. adj. of *it*. XVI ('Musica Transalpina', 1597; in Florio's works 1598, etc.). f. IT + g. -S; superseded *it* (XIV–XVII in literature, later dial.), which was adopted as an unambiguous substitute for HIS (OE. to XVII). Not found in the works of Sh. published in his lifetime, but there are exx. in the First Folio of 1623; in A.V. 1611 there is no ex. of *its*, and only one of *it* (Lev. xxv 5), which disappeared from later editions.

-ity ĭti in ME. *-ite*, *-itie*, repr. (O)F. *-ité*, L. *-itātem*, nom. *-itās*, the form in which *-tās*, *-tātem* -TY usu. appears, the *-i-* being a stem- or connective vowel, as in *suāvitās* suavity, f. *suāvis*, *pūritās* purity, f. *pūrus*, *auctōritās* authority, f. *auctor*; after *i* the suffix became *-etās*, as in *pietās*, *varietās*, f. *pius*, *varius*; it was added to many adj. suffixes, whence the Eng. forms *-acity*, *-ality*, *-anity*, *-arity*, *-bility*, *-idity*, *-ility*, *-ivity*, *-ocity*, *-osity*, *-uity*; its organic repr. in OF. was *-eté* (cf. *safety*, *bounty*, *plenty*, and see -TY). Its trivial use is illustrated by *cuppeity*, after *tableity* (tr. Erasmus's *menseitas*, Gr. τραπεζότης Diogenes Laertius), *womanity* (after *humanity*).

-ium iəm terminal el. of the names of many metallic elements, used first by Davy (1807). CADMIUM was based on †*cadmia*; hence *sodium* on *soda*, etc.

-ive iv in ME. *if(e)*, *-yf(e)* – (O)F. *-if*, fem. *-ive* :– L. *-īvus*, *-īvum*, fem. *-īva*, suffix added mainly to pp. stems, e.g. *actīvus*, *-īva* ACTIVE, *captīvus*, *passīvus*, *nātīvus* inborn, NATIVE, but also to pres. stems, e.g. *cadīvus* falling, f. *cadere*, and to sbs., e.g. *tempestīvus* seasonable, f. *tempestās* TEMPEST. Eng. formations on vb.-stems often assume the appearance of being of the pp. type, as *adoptive*, *selective*; see also -ATIVE. Some L. adjs. were used sb., as *captīvus*, *fugitīvus*; of this usage there is a wide extension in mod. langs. and Eng. (*adjective*, *explosive*, *missive*, *sedative*). In early modEng. the suffix was freq. used with the force of -IBLE, esp. in adjs. of negative meaning, as in *expressive*, *extensive*, *in-* and *unexpressive*, *inflexive*, *insuppressive*. ¶ In *hasty*, *jolly*, *tardy*, the final *f* of the ME. forms *hastyf*, etc., fell away, leaving an ending identical with -Y¹.

ivory ai·vəri hard white substance composing the tusks of elephants, etc. XIII. ME. *ivor*, *yvor(e)*, *yvory* – OF. *yvoire*, AN. **ivorie* (mod. *ivoire*) = Pr. *ivori*, *evori*, *avori*, Cat. *bori*, It. *avorio*, *avolio* – Rom. **eboreum*, f. L. *ebor-*, *ebur* ivory – a form rel. to Egyptian *āb*, *ābu*, Coptic *ebou*, *ebu* elephant, ivory (cf. Heb. *shenhabbīm* ivory, Skr. *íbhas* elephant).

ivy ai·vi climbing evergreen shrub, Hedera Helix. OE. *īfiġ*, obscurely rel. to OHG. *ebah* (mod. G. dial. *efa*, *efai*, *ewich*) and the first el. of MLG. *iflōf*, *iwlōf*, LG., Du. *eilof* (enlarged with the word LEAF), and OHG. *ebahewi*, MHG. *ebehöu*, *ephöu*, G. *efeu* (enlarged with the word HAY¹); of unkn. origin, unless referable to the base of L. IBEX, with the sense 'climber' (cf. Fris., Du. *klimop* ivy, lit. 'climb-up').

iwis, ywis iwi·s (obs. or arch.) certainly, indeed. XII. ME. *ȝewis*, *iwis*, *iwisse* :– OE. *ġewis* = OHG. *giwis* (G. *gewiss*); f. Germ. **ga-*, **gi-* + **wissa-* :– **widto-*, ppl. formation on **wid-* know (see WIT); freq. sp. *i wis*, *I wis*, and misinterpreted as 'I know'.

ixia i·ksiə (bot.) genus of iridaceous plants. XVIII. mod. use of L. *ixia* – Gr. *ixiā́* kind of thistle.

izard i·zārd antelope of the Pyrenees. XVIII. – F. *isard*, Gascon *isart*, perh. of Iberian origin.

-ize, -ise aiz suffix of verbs, repr. F. *-iser* = Sp. *-izar*, It. *-izzare* – late L. *-īzāre* – Gr. *-ízein*, which was used to form both intr. and trans. vbs., as *barbarízein* play the barbarian, side with barbarians (f. *bárbaros* BARBARIAN), *thesaurízein* treasure up (f. *thēsaurós*

TREASURE). Those formed on national, sectarian, or personal names were primarily intr. (cf. ATTICIZE, HELLENIZE); these and others connected with early Christianity were latinized in III or IV (cf. BAPTIZE, EVANGELIZE, CATECHIZE, ANATHEMATIZE, SCANDALIZE, etc.); later medL. formations are typified by CANONIZE, SYLLOGIZE. Many verbs have come into Eng. through French, in which they are spelt with *s*, with the result that *-ise* has been generalized, and is retained, as against *-ize*, in the practice of some printing houses; exx. are *civiliser* CIVILIZE, *humaniser* HUMANIZE. The two orig. uses of the Gr. suffix remain in present usage with specialization in certain fields, viz. 'make or conform to, treat in the way of, what is expressed', 'make that which is denoted by the base of the deriv.', 'act like or in accordance with', 'follow a certain practice', 'treat according to the process of' (an inventor, scientist, etc.), 'charge, impregnate, or influence with, convert into'. The corr. nouns of action end in **-iza·tion**, and agent-nouns in **-izer**[1].

izzard i·zəɹd (arch. or dial.) name of the letter ZED. XVIII. Also *uzzard* (XVII to mod. dial.), †*ezod* (XVI), with other dial. vars. (*izzat, izot, uzzit*).

J

jab dʒæb thrust or poke roughly. XIX. var., orig. Sc., of JOB[1].

jabber dʒæ·bəɹ talk fast and indistinctly. XV (Promp. Parv.). imit.; a contemp. var. (now dial.) is *javer*. Hence as sb. XVIII (Milton has *jabberment*).

jabers dʒei·bəɹz in Ir. phr. *be* (i.e. *by*) *jab(b)ers, Japers (Cripes)*, euphem. deformation of JESUS dʒē·zəs (CHRIST). XIX.

jabiru dʒæ·biru large tropical wading bird. XVIII. Tupi-Guarani.

jabot ʒæ·bou frill on the bosom of a shirt, etc. XIX. – F., 'bird's crop', 'shirt-frill', prob. f. a base **gab-* crop, maw, gullet, to which many Rom. words are referred.

jacamar dʒæ·kəmāɹ bird of the family Galbulidæ. XIX. – F. *jacamar* – Tupi-Guarani *jacamaciri* (Marcgrave, 1648).

jacana dʒæ·kəna bird of the family Parridæ. XVIII. prop. *jaçana* – Pg. *jaçaná* – Tupi-Guarani *jasaná*.

jacaranda dʒækəræ·ndə (ornamental and fragrant wood of) tropical Amer. trees. XVIII. Tupi-Guarani.

jacare dʒæ·kərei S. Amer. alligator. XVIII. Tupi-Guarani.

jacinth dʒæ·sinþ precious stone. XIII. ME. *iacin(c)t* – OF. *iacinte* (mod. *jacinthe*) = Pr. *jiacint*, etc., or medL. *iacintus*, L. *hyacinthus* HYACINTH.

jack[1] dʒæk in numerous transf. applications of the name JACK to implements and machines, or their parts, the male of animals (cf. JACKASS), fishes (esp. pike, orig. young or small pike), etc., from XVI. Hence **jack** vb. (with *up*) hoist with a jack (lifting machine); (sl.) ruin; give up, abandon. XIX.

jack[2] dʒæk A. †jacket; (arch.) leather or iron-plated tunic XIV; B. (leathern) vessel for liquor XVI. – (O)F. *jaque*, of much disputed origin, perh. immed. – Sp., Pg. *jaco* (whence also It. *giaco*), of Arab. origin.

jack[3] dʒæk ship's flag smaller than the ensign. XVII. prob. spec. application of JACK[1] as to an object of a size smaller than the normal. comp. *jack-staff*. XVII.

jack[4] dʒæk (fruit of) an E. Indian tree, Artocarpus integrifolia. XVII (*Iaca*, Purchas; *Jack, Giack*, T. Herbert; *Jawk*, Fryer). – Pg. *jaca* – Malayalam *chakka*.

Jack dʒæk pet-form of the name *John* XIII; figure of a man on a clock XV; †fellow, chap XVI (cf. mod. *every man jack* XIX); sailor XVII (*Jack-Sailor*; cf. *Jack* TAR XVIII); knave of a card suit XVII; (also *j-*) male worker XVII (*jack-of-all-trades*; *cheap-jack, steeple-jack* XIX). ME. *Iacke, Iakke* (disyll.) used from the first as familiar by-form of *John*, perh. through dim. *Jankin*; the resemblance to F. *Jacques* James (:– Rom. **Ja·cobus*, for L. *Jacō·bus* JACOB) is a difficulty. Forms the first el. of various phrasal designations simulating proper names, nicknames, etc., as *Jack-a-Lent, Jack-in-the-box, Jack Straw, Jack-a-dandy, Jack-a-lantern* (= WILL O' THE WISP), *Jack-pudding* (buffoon); also in plant names, esp. of small species.

jackal dʒæ·kōl animal of the dog kind, known as 'the lion's provider'; fig. one who drudges for another. XVII. – (with assim. to JACK) Turk. *chacāl* – Pers. *shagāl, shaghāl*, rel. to Skr. *sṛgāla, çṛgāla*; so F. *chacal*, whence Pg. *chacal*, It. *sciacallo*, G. *schakal*. Formerly str. *jacka·l*.

jackanapes dʒæ·kəneips †ape; pert aping fellow, coxcomb. XVI. First recorded, *c.* 1450, as a nickname (*Jac(k) Napes*) of William de la Pole, first Duke of Suffolk, whose badge was an ape's clog and chain; later, used a quasi-proper name for an ape and a man who performs ape-like tricks; and hence as above. This use of JACK is paralleled in *Jack Straw*, nickname of one of the leaders of the peasants' revolt of 1381; the origin of *Napes* is unkn.; the extended form *jack a napes* suggests assoc. with *Naples* (cf. *fustianapes* for *fustian of Naples*).

jackaroo dʒækərū· Englishman newly arrived in Australia. XIX. f. JACK, with ending from KANGAROO.

jackass dʒæ·kæs he-ass XVIII (Arbuthnot; fig. dolt, blockhead XIX); *laughing j.*, giant kingfisher of Australia, so called from its loud discordant cry XVIII. f. JACK[1] (denoting the male)+ASS.

jackboot dʒæ·kbūt large boot reaching above the knee. XVII. f. JACK[1] (of uncertain application)+BOOT[2].

jackdaw dʒæ·kdɔ̄, (formerly) dʒækdɔ̄· the bird Corvus monedula. XVI (Bale). f. JACK[1] + DAW.

jacket dʒæ·kit outer short upper garment with sleeves. XV. – OF. *ja(c)quet*, dim. of *jaque* JACK[2]; see -ET.

ja·ck-knife large clasp-knife. XVIII (1711). orig. Amer.; presumably based on some application of JACK[1]. A suggested connexion with JOCKTELEG (dial. *jacklag, -leg*) cannot be maintained.

Jacob dʒei·kəb male personal name, being that of the third patriarch in the O.T. (see Gen. xxv, etc.), Heb. *ya'āqōb* 'supplanter', whence Gr. *Iákōbos*, ecclL. *Jacōbus* (see JAMES); in *Jacob's ladder* (i) garden plant *Polemonium cæruleum*, the leaves of which have a ladder-like appearance XVIII, (ii) rope ladder with wooden steps for ascending rigging XIX. ¶ In *Jacob's staff* instrument for taking measurements (XVI); the reference is unknown.

Jacobean dʒækəbī·ən *J. lily*, Sprekelia formosissima (named after St. James the Greater) XVIII; pert. to the age of James I (spec. of a style of architecture); pert. to St. James the Less or his epistle XIX. f. modL. *Jacōbæus*, f. *Jacōbus*; see JACOB, -EAN.

Jacobin[1] dʒæ·kəbin A. Dominican (friar), orig. French member of the order so called from the church of Saint-Jacques (L. *Jacōbus*) in Paris near which they built their first convent XIV; B. member of a French political club established at Paris 1789 near the old convent of the Jacobin friars XVIII (Burke). – (O)F. *Jacobin* – medL. *Jacōbīnus*.

Jacobin[2] dʒæ·kəbin breed of the domestic pigeon with reversed feathers on the back of the neck suggesting a monk's cowl. XVII. – F. *jacobine*, fem. of *Jacobin* (see prec.).

Jacobite[1] dʒæ·kəbait member of a monophysite sect taking its name from *Jacobus* Baradæus, of Edessa (VI). XIV (Maund.). – medL. *Jacōbīta*; see -ITE.

Jacobite[2] dʒæ·kəbait adherent of James II of England after his abdication, or of his family. XVII. f. L. *Jacōbus* JAMES+-ITE.

Jacobus dʒəkou·bəs (hist.) Eng. gold coin of James I's reign issued as the SOVEREIGN. XVII. – ecclL. *Jacōbus* JAMES.

jaconet dʒæ·kŏnet cotton fabric, orig. from India. XVIII. alt. of Urdu *jagannāthī*, f. *Jagannāth(pūrī)* 'Juggernaut-town', in Cuttack, the place of origin.

jactation dʒæktei·ʃən boasting XVI; (path.) tossing of the body to and fro XVII. – L. *jactātiō(n-)*, f. *jactāre* toss about, discuss, boast, frequent. of *jact-*, *jacere* throw (cf. Gr. *hiénai*); see -ATION. So **jactitA·TION** tossing of the body, twitching. XVII. – medL. *jactitatiō(n-)* false declaration tending to someone's detriment, f. *jactitāre*, frequent. of *jactāre*.

jade[1] dʒeid poor or worn-out horse XIV (Ch.); reprehensible woman or girl XVI. Of unkn. origin.

jade[2] dʒeid hard mineral used for implements, etc. XVIII. – F. *jade*; *le jade* was for earlier *l'ejade* – Sp. *ijada* (in *piedra de ijada* 'colic stone') :– Rom. **iliata*, f. L. *ilia* flanks (cf. ILIAC). Cf. synon. NEPHRITE.

jag dʒæg (dial.) stab, prick; slash, pink XIV; make ragged XVI. First in w.midl., varying with *jogge*; not common before XVI; prob. of symbolic formation; cf. RAG, TAG, JOG. Hence **jag** sb. something slashed or ragged. XV. **jaggED[1]** dʒæ·gid. XV (Promp. Parv.).

jäger, jaeger jei·gəɹ German rifleman or sharpshooter, orig. infantryman recruited mainly from foresters XVIII; skua XIX. – G. *jäger* hunter, f. *jagen* (OHG. *jagōn*=OFris. *jagia*) hunt, chase. Cf. YAGER.

jaggery dʒæ·gəri coarse brown sugar. XVI (*gagara, iagra*). – Indo-Pg. *jag(a)ra, jagre* – Canarese *sharkare* – Skr. *śarkarā* SUGAR.

jaghire dʒagiə·ɹ assignment of the king's or government's share of the product of a district to a person as an annuity. XVII. – Urdu – Pers. *jāgīr*, f. *jā* place + *gīr* holding, holder.

jaguar dʒæ·gjuəɹ large animal of the cat kind, Felis onca. XVII. – Tupi-Guarani *jaguara*, said to be prop. generic for carnivorous beast, the spec. name of the jaguar being *jaguareté*.

Jah dʒā in Eng. Bibles repr. Heb. *Yah*, shortening of *Yahwe(h)* JEHOVAH. XVI. So **Jah·VISM** jā·vizm religious system based on the worship of Jahveh; **Jah·VIST** any of the authors of the Hexateuch who use *Jahveh* as the divine name)(ELOHIST XIX.

jail see GAOL.

Jain dʒain non-Brahmin sect of India. XIX. – Hindi *jaina* :– Skr. *jainas* pert. to a saint, f. *jinas* saint, buddha, lit. overcomer, f. *ji* overcome.

jakes dʒeiks (arch.) privy. XVI (*iakes, ia(c)ques, iaxe*). Of unkn. origin; perh. trivial use of the proper name *Jacques* (see JACK) or of the g. of *Jack*, quasi *Jak(k)es*.

jalap dʒæ·ləp, dʒɔ·ləp purgative drug from Exogonium (Ipomœa Purga); the plant itself XVII. – F. *jalap* – Sp. *jalapa*, short for *purga de Jalapa* († *Xalapa*) – Aztec *Xala·pan* 'sand by the water', f. *xalli* sand+ *atl* water + *pan* upon, near.

jalousie ʒæ·luzi blind made with slats sloping upward from without. XIX. – F. *jalousie* JEALOUSY, applied to such a blind or shutter because it allows of seeing without being seen. Prob. – It. *gelosia* in this sense. ¶ Cf. †*jealous glass* translucent glass that cannot be seen through (XVIII).

jam[1] dʒæm press or squeeze tightly, wedge, ram. XVIII. Of symbolic origin; cf. *cham*, CHAMP. Hence **jam** sb., act or result of jamming. XIX.

jam[2] dʒæm conserve of fruit boiled to a pulp. XVIII. perh. identical with prec. sb.

jamb dʒæm side-post of a door, etc. XIV. – (O)F. *jambe* leg, vertical supporting piece = Pr., Cat. *camba*, It. *gamba* :– Rom. **gamba* (**camba*) leg, in late L. hoof, veterinary breeder's term – Gr. (cf. *kampḗ* flexure, joint). ¶ Final b has become mute as in *comb*, *lamb*, *tomb*, *womb*; in *limb* and *thumb* it is not original.

jambo dʒæ·mbou species of Eugenia (rose-apple, etc.). XVI. – vernacular reprs. of Skr. *jambu*, *-ū* rose-apple.

jamboree dʒæmbərī· noisy revel; boy scouts' festival. XIX. Of unkn. origin.

James dʒeimz †*J. Royal*, silver coin of James VI of Scotland XVI; (sl.) sovereign; burglar's jemmy XIX. – OF. *James* = Pr., Cat. *Jaume*, *Jacme*, Sp. *Jaime*, It. *Giacomo* :– Rom. **Ja·comus* for L. *Ja·cobus*, altered form of *Jacō·bus* JACOB. Cf. JEMMY.

jane see JEAN.

jangada dʒæŋgā·də raft of logs or of boats fastened together. XVI. – Pg. *jangada* – Malayalam *changāḍam* – Skr. *saṃghāta* joining together.

jangle dʒæ·ŋgl †chatter, babble XIII (Cursor M.); talk angrily or harshly; also trans. XIV; cause (a bell) to give out a discordant sound XVII (Sh.). – OF. *jangler*, *gengler* = Pr. *janglar*, prob. – Germ. form repr. by (M)Du. *jangelen*.

janissary, janizary dʒæ·nizəri one of the Sultan of Turkey's bodyguard; Turkish soldier; henchman. XVI. Early forms repr. various Rom. forms, the present prevailing sp. reflecting F. *janissaire*; cf. It. *giannizzero*, Sp. *jenizaro*, Pg. *janizaro*, modL. *jeni-*, *janizari*; all ult. – Turk. *yeñitsheri*, f. *yeñi* new, modern + *tsheri* soldiery, militia (– Pers. *charīk* auxiliary forces).

janitor dʒæ·nitɔ̄ɹ door-keeper. XVII. – L. *jānitor*, f. *jānua* door, f. *jānus* arched passage (cf. JANUARY); see -TOR.

Jansenist dʒæ·nsənist adherent of Cornelius *Jansen* (d. 1638), bishop of Ypres, Flanders. XVII; see -IST. Also †*Janse·nian*. XVII.

January dʒæ·njuəri first month of the year. XIV. – L. *Jānuārius*, sb. use (sc. *mensis* month) of adj. of *Jānus*, name of an ancient Italian deity figured with faces looking forwards and backwards; see -ARY. Thence also, or from Rom. **jenuarius*, Pr. *jenovier*, *januer*, Sp. *enero*, †*jenero*, Pg. *janeiro*, It. *gennaio*, *gennaro*. The earliest Eng. forms are *Ieniuer*, *Ieneuer*, *Ianeuer* (XIII) – AN., OF. *Jeneuer*, *Genever* (mod. *janvier*), the type *Janiveer* surviving dial., together with the semi-latinized *Janwar* (Burns).

japan dʒəpæ·n exceptionally hard varnish, which came orig. from Japan. XVII. Like other Eur. forms of the proper name (F., Sp. *Japon*, Pg. *Japão*, It. *Giappone*, Du., G., etc., *Japan*) ult. – Malay *Japang*, *Japung* – Chinese *Jih pun* sunrise, orient (= Jap. *Nippon*), f. *jih* (Jap. *ni*) sun + *pun* (Jap. *pon*, *hon*). Hence vb. XVII. Hence **Japan**E·SE. XVII.

jape dʒeip †A. trick; †B. have carnal knowledge (of); C. jest. XIV (PPl., Ch., Wyclif). Appears to combine the form of OF. *japer* (mod. *japper*) yelp, yap, with the sense of OF. *gaber* mock, deride (cf. GAB). Hence **jape** sb. XIV. ¶ Because of its use in sense B it became gen. obs. during XVI, but was revived with sense C in XIX by Scott and Lamb.

Japhetic dʒəfe·tik pert. to Japheth, one of the sons of Noah (Gen. v 32, etc.), whose descendants were supposed to have peopled Europe and Northern Asia; hence sometimes applied to the Indo-European languages. XIX. f. modL. *Japhetī* descendants of *Japheth*; see -IC. Cf. *Hamitic*, *Semitic*.

japonica dʒəpɔ·nikə gardener's name for certain plants of Japanese origin, of which the specific name is *japonica*; fem. of modL. *Japonicus* JAPANESE.

jar[1] dʒāɹ harsh sound; discord, strife XVI; (from the vb.) act of jarring XIX. So **jar** vb. sound harshly, make a discord (Skelton); cause to vibrate; be at discord or strife. XVI. Early vars. are *gerre*, *ier*, *charre*; prob. imit.

jar[2] dʒāɹ (orig. large) earthen vessel of cylindrical form. XVI. – F. *jarre* = Pr. *jarro*, Sp., Pg. *jarra*, It. *giarra* – Arab. *jarrah*.

jar[3] dʒāɹ in phr. †*at jar*, (*up*)*on the jar*; see AJAR.

jardinière ʒāɹdi·niɛəɹ ornamental vessel for the display of flowers. XIX. F., fem. of *jardinier* GARDENER.

jargon dʒā·ɹgən (arch.) twittering or chattering of birds XIV (Ch.); meaningless talk XIV; debased or hybrid language; speech peculiar to a trade or profession full of gen. unfamiliar terms XVII. Late ME. *iargo(u)n*, *girgoun*, *gargoun* – OF. *jargoun*, *gergon*, *gargon* = Pr. *gergó*, It. *gergo*, *-one*; cf. Sp. *jerga*, *gerigonza*, †*girgonz*, Pg. *giria*, *geringonça*; ult. origin unknown.

jargonelle dʒāɹgəne·l early variety of pear (orig. an inferior gritty kind). XVII. – F. *jargonelle*, dim. of *jargon* JARGOON (cf. -EL[2]).

jargoon dʒāɹgū·n variety of zircon. XVIII. – F. *jargon* – It. *giargone*; prob. to be identified ult. with ZIRCON.

jarl jāɹl chieftain of ancient Scandinavia. XIX. ON. = OE. *eorl* EARL.

jarrah dʒæ·rə mahogany gum-tree of W. Australia. XIX. – native name *djarryl, jerryhl.*

jarvey jā·ɹvi (sl.) coachman. XIX. – *Jarvis* (personal name so used in Grose's 'Dictionary of the Vulgar Tongue', 1796), var. of *Jervis, Gervase* (F. *Gervais*); perh. so applied in allusion to St. Gervase's emblem, a whip or scourge (he having been beaten to death with a leaded scourge).

jasey, jazy dʒei·zi (worsted) wig. XVIII. perh. alteration of JERSEY, so called because made of Jersey yarn.

jasmine dʒæ·smin, **jessamine** dʒe·səmin climbing shrub, Jasminum officinale, with white or yellow flowers. XVI. The two forms (of equal date) repr. F. *jasmin* (= Sp. *jazmin*, Pg. *jasmim*) and †*jessemin* – Arab. *yās(a)mīn* – Pers. *yāsmin, yāsman* (cf. Gr. *iásmē, iasmélaion, iásminon múron* Persian perfume, perh. oil of jasmine). Earlier †*jasme* (XVI).

jasper dʒà·spəɹ precious stone. XIV. – OF. *jaspre*, var. of *jaspe* = Pr. *jaspi*, Sp. *jaspe*, It. *iaspide* – L. *iaspis* (*-id-*) – Gr. *íaspis* (*-id-*), of Oriental origin (cf. Heb. *yashpeh*, Ass. *ashpū*, Arab. *yashb*, Pers. *yashm*).

jaundice dʒɔ̄·ndis, dʒā·ndis disease marked by yellowness of the skin, etc. XIV. – OF. *jaunice* (mod. *-isse*) 'yellowness', f. *jaune* yellow (:– L. *galbinu-s*, f. *galbus*, ult. rel. to YELLOW) + *-ice* :– L. *-ītia.*

jaunt dʒɔ̄nt, dʒānt †ride (a horse) up and down; †trudge about XVI; make a short trip XVII. Also contemp. sb. Of unkn. origin.

jaunty dʒɔ̄·nti †well-bred; †elegant; sprightly. XVII. In early use *jentee, juntee, ja(u)ntee* – F. *gentil* ʒãti (see GENTLE, GENTEEL); assim. later to adjs. in -Y[1].

javelin dʒæ·vəlin light spear thrown with the hand. XVI. – (O)F. *javeline*, alteration of *javelot*, prob. of Celtic origin (OIr. *gabul*, W. *gafl, gaflach*).

jaw dʒɔ̄ one of the bones forming the framework of the mouth, containing the teeth XIV (Ch., Wycl. Bible, Trevisa); (sl.) offensive or tedious talk XVIII (Smollett). Late ME. *iow(e)*, later *iawe*, with occas. vars. *gew, gowe*, beside †*chaw* (XVI–XVII), perh. by blending with CHEW; of unkn. origin.

jawbation see JOBATION.

jay dʒei bird of the genus Garrulus. XIII. – OF. *jay* (mod. *geai*) = Pr. *gai*, Sp. *gayo*, Pg. *gaio* :– late L. *gaius*, beside *gaia* (whence Venetian It. *gazza*); the word has been identified with the L. proper name *Gaius* (cf. the use of other personal names, as *jackdaw, robin*, F. *richard, jacques, colin*, Du. *wouter*).

jazerant, jesserant dʒæ·zərənt, dʒe·s- (hist.) light coat of armour. XIV (*gess-, jesserawnt*). – OF. *jaseran(t), -enc* = Pr. *jazeran*, Pg. *jazerão*, beside Sp. *jacerina*, Pg. *jazerina*, It. *ghiazzerina*; orig. adj. in OF. *osberc (hauberc) jazerant*, Sp. *cota jacerina*, f. Arab. *al|jazīrah* the island (see AL-[2]), pl. *Aljazā'ir* Algiers.

jazz dʒæz kind of ragtime dance, music to which it is danced. 1917. orig. U.S.; *Jas* as a pet-form of *Charles*, name of a Negro musician, has been suggested.

jealous dʒe·ləs suspicious of rivalry XIII; zealous (for) XIV; (dial.) suspicious XVI; suspiciously vigilant XVII. ME. *gelus, ielus* – OF. *gelos* (mod. *jaloux*) = Pr. *gelos*, Sp. *zeloso*, It. *geloso* :– medL. *zēlōsu-s*, f. ChrL. *zēlus* – Gr. *zêlos* ZEAL; see -OUS. ¶ Formerly also scanned as three sylls. So **jea·lousy**[3]. XIII. – OF. *gelosie* (mod. *jalousie*).

jean dʒīn twilled cotton cloth. XVI. orig. *ie(a)ne, ge(a)ne fustian*; attrib. use of *Jene, Gene* – OF. *Janne* (mod. *Gênes*) :– medL. *Janua* Genoa. The F. form with *-s* is repr. by Eng. *geanes, jennes* (XVI), U.S. *jeans.*

jeep dʒīp small utility motor truck. orig. U.S. XX. f. initials *G.P.* dʒī pī 'general purposes', prob. infl. by Eugene the Jeep, name of animal in U.S. comic strip by E. C. Segar.

jeer dʒiəɹ scoff (at) with derision. XVI. Earliest forms are *gy(e)re, geere*; of unkn. origin; *fleer* and *leer* have affinities of form and meaning.

jehad var. of JIHAD.

Jehovah dʒĭhou·və the Lord God. XVI (Tindale, Exod. vi 3, 1530). alt. of the sacred tetragrammaton יהוה JHVH of the Hebrews, the ineffable name of the Almighty, produced by the insertion of the vowel-points repr. the vowels '(ă), ō, ā of *Adonai* as a direction to substitute this for the ineffable name (as is done by Jerome in Exod. vi 3). It is held that the orig. name was *Jahve(h), Yahwe(h).*

Jehu dʒī·hjū (fast) driver. XVII (Dryden). Allusive use of the name of *Jehu*, 'the son of Nimshi, for he driveth furiously' (2 Kings IX 20).

jejune dʒidʒū·n unsatisfying, meagre. XVII. – L. *jējūnus* fasting, barren, unproductive, meagre; cf. DINE.

jelly dʒe·li article of food consisting chiefly of gelatin. XIV. ME. *geli, -y(e)* – (O)F. *gelée* frost, jelly = Pr. *gelada*, Sp. *helada*, It. *gelata* frost :– Rom. *gelāta* (Reichenau Glosses), sb. use of fem. pp. of *gelāre* freeze, f. *gelu* frost (cf. CONGEAL). Hence **je·llied** XVI; (back-formation) **jell** vb. orig. U.S. XIX.

jemadar dʒe·mədāɹ officer below a subahdar, etc. XVIII. – Urdu *jama'dār*, f. Pers. *jama'at* body of men (*jama'* collection) + *dār* holder.

jemima dʒĭmai·mə made-up tie XIX; pl. elastic-sided boots XX. Appellative use of the female name *Jemima*, eldest of the daughters of Job (Job xlii 14).

jemmy dʒe·mi burglar's crowbar. XIX. dim. of JAMES; see -Y[6].

je ne sais quoi ʒənsę̄kwa indescribable something. XVII (Blount, Aubrey). F., 'I know not what'.

jennet dʒe·nit small Spanish horse. XV. – F. *genet* – Sp. *jinete* short-stirruped light horseman – Arab. *Zenāta* Berber tribe famed for horsemanship.

jenneting dʒe·nītiŋ early kind of apple. XVII. f. F. *Jeannet*, pet-form of *Jean* JOHN, as in Norman F. *pomme* (apple) *de Jeannet*; cf. *pere ionette* (PPl., Ch.) and for the ending see -ING[3]. In XVII–XVIII sp. *junetin(g)*, *juneating*.

jenny dʒe·ni pet-form (see -Y[6]) of *Janet* (or *Jane*), used as a prefix to denote a female animal, as *j. ass*, *j. wren* (XVII), and in the names of machines, as *spinning-j.* (XVIII).

jeofail dʒe·feil (leg.) mistake in pleading. XVI. – AN. *jeo fail* I am at fault, i.e. *jeo* (F. *je*) I, *fail*, 1st pers. pres. ind. sg. of *faillir* FAIL.

jeopardy dʒe·pəɹdi †chess problem; †(even) chance; risk of injury or death. XIV (Ch.. Barbour). – OF. *iu* (*ieu*, *giu*) *parti* 'divided play', even game, (hence) uncertain chance, uncertainty (= Cat. *joch partit*, Sp. *juego de partido*, medL. *jocus partītus*, i.e. *jocus* game, JOKE, *partītus*, pp. of *partīrī* divide, PART). For the change of *t* to *d* cf. CARD, DIAMOND, MOUND; forms with *b* for *p* were frequent in XV–XVI, as in LEOPARD; for the sp. *eo* cf. *leopard*, *people*. A shortened form †*jeopard* was current XIV–XVII; cf. **jeo·pard** vb. XIV (disused from *c.* 1650 to *c.* 1820), which was superseded by **jeo·pard**IZE (XVII).

jequirity dʒikwi·rīti woody twining shrub, Indian liquorice. XIX. – F. *jéqwirity* – Tupi-Guarani *jekiriti*.

jerboa dʒə̄ɹbou·ə small rodent, Dipus sagitta, remarkable for its jumping powers. XVII. – medL. *jerbōa* – Arab. *yarbu'*, dial. *jerbō'* flesh of the loins, hence applied to the animal from the highly-developed muscles of its hind legs; in F. *gerbo*, *-boise*, Sp. *gerbo*, *-basia*.

jereed dʒərī·d wooden javelin. XVII. – Arab. *jarīd* midrib of the palm-leaf, rod, lance.

jeremiad dʒerimai·æd lamentation. XVIII. – F. *jérémiade*, f. *Jérémie* – ecclL. *Jeremias* Jeremiah, in allusion to the Lamentations of Jeremiah in O.T.; see -AD[1].

jerfalcon see GERFALCON.

jerk[1] dʒə̄ɹk †stroke with a whip; sharp sudden pull or thrust. XVI. gen. synon. with †*jert* (XVI) and the earlier YERK; all three forms may be phonetically symbolical in origin.

jerk[2] dʒə̄ɹk cure (beef) by cutting it into strips and drying it. XVIII. An earlier form is found in †*jerkin beef* (XVII); repr. Amer. Sp. *charquear*, f. *charqui* – Quichua *echarqui* dried flesh in long strips, and *echarquini* prepare dried meat.

jerkin dʒə̄·ɹkin close-fitting jacket. XVI. Of unkn. origin.

jeroboam dʒerəbou·əm large bowl or wine-bottle. XIX (Scott). So called in allusion to *Jeroboam*, 'a mighty man of valour' (1 Kings xi 28), 'who made Israel to sin' (ibid. xiv 16).

jerry[1] dʒe·ri (sl.) chamber-pot. XIX. Supposed to be short for prec; cf. Y[6].

jerry[2] dʒe·ri (colloq.) unsubstantial(ly), as in *jerry-built*, *-builder*, *-building*. XIX. Said to have arisen in Liverpool; recorded in Lancashire, Yorkshire, and Cheshire glossaries.

jerrymander see GERRYMANDER.

jersey dʒə̄·ɹzi (Jersey) worsted XVI; knitted close-fitting tunic XIX. Name of the largest of the Channel Islands, in which the knitting of worsted articles was a staple industry (cf. *Iarnsey worsted* 1583). Cf. GUERNSEY.

Jerusalem dʒərū·sələm in A.V., O.T. *Ierusalem*, N.T. *Hierusalem*, the latter repr. a Hellenized form with initial aspirate and consequent assim. to *hierós* holy, the former deriving from Gr. ΙΗΡΟΥΣΑΛΗΜ, which prob. approximates to the earlier pronunc. Yerūshālēm of the Heb. name (interpreted as 'possession of peace'). *J.* ARTICHOKE (XVII).

jess dʒes (chiefly pl.) straps for a hawk's legs. XIV (*ges*). – OF. *ges* nom. sg. and acc. pl. (mod. *jet* cast) = Pr. *jet*, Cat. *get*, It. *getto* :– Rom. **jectus*, for L. *jactus* throw, f. *jacere* (cf. EJECT).

jessamine see JASMINE.

Jesse dʒe·si genealogical tree repr. the descent of Jesus Christ from 'the root of Jesse' (Isa. xi 1), the father of David (1 Sam. xvi 12). XV. *J. window*, one containing a J. tree.

jest dʒest †deed, exploit XIII; †idle tale XV; mocking speech; witticism, joke XVI. ME. *geste* – OF. *geste*, *jeste* = Pr. *gesta* history, race :– L. *gesta* doings, exploits, n. pl. of pp. of *gerere* do, perform (cf. GERENT).

Jesuit dʒe·zjuit member of the Society of Jesus, founded by Ignatius of Loyola in 1534. XVI. – F. *Jésuite* or modL. *Jēsuīta*, f. *Jēsūs* + *-īta* -ITE. Hence **Jesui·ti**CAL XVI; after F. *jésuitique*.

Jesus dʒī·səs, **Jesu** dʒī·zju the Founder of Christianity. Not used in OE., in which it was rendered by *Hǣlend* Saviour; in ME. (XII) not usu. written in full, but almost always in the abbreviated forms ihu and ihs, ihus, ihc, ih̄u, etc. (see IHS); repr. ChrL. *Iēsūs*, obl. cases *Iēsū* – Gr. *Iēsoûs*, *Iēsoû* – late Heb. or Aramaic *yēshūa'*, for earlier *y'hōshua'* Joshua, which is explained as 'Jah (or Jahveh) is salvation'. In early mod. Eng. bibles *Iesu* was the distinctive form for the obl. cases; it was frequent in the earlier forms of the Book of Common Prayer, and survives in the Gloria in excelsis Deo and the General Confession at Morning and Evening Prayer. *Jesus'* is often pronounced as if *Jesu's* dʒī·zjūz. Editors of ME. texts have usu. expanded the form ihs as ihesus, but such spellings first appear in print late in xv. In asseverations shortened to *gis(se)*, *iysse*, *Iis* (xvi); in modIr. and U.S. exclamatory use deformed as JABERS, *jebers*, *jeepers*, *jee-whizz*.

jet[1] dʒet hard black form of lignite. xiv (Ch., Trevisa). ME. *geet*, *jeet*, later *jeat*, *jeit* – AN. *geet*, **jeet*, OF. *jaiet*, *jayet* (mod. *jais*) :- L. *gagātēs* – Gr. *gagátēs*, f. *Gágai* town in Lycia, Asia Minor.

jet[2] dʒet †project, protrude, jut xvi; spout forth xvii. – (O)F. *jeter* throw, cast, fling, dart = Pr. *getar*, Sp. *jetar* :- Rom. **jectāre*, for L. *jactāre* (see JACTATION). Hence (partly – F. *jet*) **jet** sb. †projection; †swagger; stream of water, etc., shot out. xvii.

jetsam dʒe·tsəm goods thrown overboard to lighten a vessel and afterwards washed ashore. xvi. Early forms *jetson*, *-sen*, later *-sam* (cf. FLOTSAM), contr. form of JETTISON.

jettison dʒe·tisən action of throwing goods overboard. xv. – AN. *getteson*, OF. *getaison* :- L. *jactātiō(n-)*, f. *jact-*, *jactāre*; see JET[2], -ATION. The contr. form *jetson*, JETSAM having become restricted to the concr. sense, the earlier form was restored in the language of marine insurance to distinguish the action (xviii). Hence **je·ttison** vb. throw overboard (often fig.). xix.

jetty dʒe·ti pier running out into the sea, etc.; †overhanging upper storey. xv. – OF. *jetee*, *getee* projecting part of a building, structure to protect a harbour, sb. use of fem. pp. of *jeter* throw; see JET[2] and cf. JUT.

jeu ʒö play. xviii. F. :- L. *jocu-s* pleasantry, jest, which repl. L. *lūdus* play in Rom.

Jew dʒū person of Hebrew race. xii (*Giw*, *Gyu*, *Iu*, *Iuw*, *Ieu*). – OF. *giu*, earlier *juiu* (mod. *juif*) :- L. *jūdæu-s* – Gr. *ioudaîos*, f. Aram. *y'hūdāi*, Heb. *y'hūdī*, f. *y'hūdāh* Judah, name of a Jewish patriarch and the tribe descended from him. OE. had pl. *Iudeas*, early ME. *Iudeow* (Orm). *Jew's* EAR fungus growing on trees, esp. the elder (on which Judas Iscariot, acc. to legend, hanged himself) xvi; mistr. of medL. *auricula Judæ* Judas's ear. *Jews'* HARP, earlier Jews' TRUMP (xvi), rudimentary musical instrument, the ascription of which to Jews is unexpl. Hence **Jew**ISH[1] dʒū·iʃ. xvi; OE. had *Iudeisć*, early ME. *Iudaysse*, *Iudissk* (Orm). **Jew**RY dʒuə·ri Jews' quarter, ghetto xiii; Jews; †Judea, Palestine xiv. – AN. *juerie*, OF. *juierie* (mod. *juiverie*).

jewel dʒū·əl †costly ornament of gold, silver, or precious stone xiii (fig. 'treasure', 'gem' xiv); precious stone, esp. as an ornament xvi. ME. *iuel*, *iowel*, *gewel* – AN. *juel*, *jeuel*, OF. *joel* (nom. sg. *joiaus*; mod. *joyau*), whence Pr., Sp. *joyel*, It. *gioiello*; of doubtful formation, but ult. based on L. *jocus* jest, in Rom. game, sport. So **jew·ell**ER[2]. xiv. – AN. *jueler*, OF. *juelier* (mod. *joaillier*). **jew·ell**ERY, **jew·el**RY in ME. (xiv) – OF. *juelerie* (mod. *joaillerie*); in mod. use (xviii) a new formation.

Jezebel dʒə·zībəl shameless woman. xvi. Allusive use of the name of the infamous wife of Ahab, king of Israel (1 Kings xvi 31, xix 1, 2, xxi, and 2 Kings ix 30–37).

jib[1] dʒib (naut.) triangular stay-sail xvii (*gibb*); phr. *cut of one's jib* personal appearance (orig. a naut. metaphor) xviii (orig. Amer.). Of unkn. origin; poss. abbrev. of GIBBET, with ref. to the suspension of the sail from the mast-head. So **jib** vb. (naut.) pull a sail round xvii; synon. with Da. *gibbe*, Du. *gijpen*, G. *geipen*, but the initial cons. is against any immed. connexion; cf. GYBE.

jib[2] dʒib projecting arm of a crane. xviii. perh. abbrev. of GIBBET and so identical with prec.

jib[3] dʒib (of a horse, etc.) stop and refuse to go on. xix (*gib*, Jane Austen; *jibb*, Scott). Of unkn. origin; remarkably like OF. *giber* kick, *regiber* (mod. *regimber*), whence ME. (once) *regibben*, but no historical connexion may be supposed.

jibbah dʒibă Egyptian var. of JUBBAH.

jibe see GIBE, GYBE.

jiboya dʒiboi·ə great boa. xvii (*giboya*, Purchas). – Tupi *giboia*.

jiffy dʒi·fi (colloq.) moment, minute. xviii. Of unkn. origin; poss. rel. to *jiffle* fidget (xvii–mod. dial.). Also **jiff.** xviii.

jig dʒig lively springy dance, music for this; †lively ballad, light dramatic performance; (dial., sl.) joke, sport, game. xvi. Of unkn. origin; meaning and chronology do not favour deriv. from OF. *gigue* stringed instrument, fiddle (in senses 'dance' and 'dance tune', prob. from Eng.) = Pr., It. *giga*, of Germ. origin (cf. G. *geige* fiddle). The mod. (xix) applications to various mechanical devices are from **jig** vb. in the sense 'move rapidly or jerkily up and down or to and fro' (xvii), an extension of 'sing or play as a jig' (xvi), which most prob. derives from the sb., not from OF. *giguer* gambol, sport.

jigger[1] dʒi·gəɹ †dancer of a jig xvii; (naut.) small tackle; and in various names of mechanical contrivances similar to those called *jig* xviii. f. prec. + -ER[1].

jigger[2] dʒi·gəɹ. xviii. Later var. of CHIGOE.

jiggered dʒi·gəɹd in (colloq.) *I'm jiggered*, euphem. substitute for a profane or indecent word. xix (Marryat, Dickens).

jiggery-pokery dʒi·gəri pou·kəri (colloq.) underhand or tricky dealing. xix. synon. with and perh. alteration of Sc. and north. dial. *jookery pawkery* (Scott), earlier *juwkry-pawkry* (xvii), jingling formation on (dial.) *jouk* dart, dodge, duck (xvi, G. Douglas), of unkn. origin; see -ERY.

jiggle dʒi·gl move restlessly with slight jerks. xix. Partly f. JIG vb. + -LE[3]; partly modification of JOGGLE, to express smaller movements.

jig-saw dʒi·gsɔ̄ vertically reciprocating saw. XIX (orig. U.S.). f. JIG+SAW.

jihad, jehad dʒĭhā·d religious war of Mohammedans against unbelievers. XIX. Arab.

jill dʒil var. of GILL[4]. XVII.

jilt dʒilt †loose woman XVII (*an old cheating jilt*, Wycherley); 'a woman who gives her lover hopes, and deceives him' (J.) XVII. 'A new canting word' in Blount's 'Glossographia' of 1674, of unkn. origin; hence as vb., the earliest recorded ex. of which (1660) shows a wider sense of 'deceive, cheat'.

jiminy dʒi·mĭni trivial oath. XVII. Earlier *gemini*, prob. of LDu. origin (cf. LG. *jemini*, G., Du. *jemine*, perversion of *Jesu Domine* O Lord Jesus).

jim-jam dʒi·mdʒæm †A. fanciful or trivial article XVI; B. pl. (orig. U.S.) delirium tremens XIX. Fanciful redupl. formation with vowel-alternation, as in *flim-flam*, *whim-wham*, but the basis is unknown.

jimmy dʒi·mi var. of JEMMY.

jingle dʒi·ŋgl give forth a combination of ringing sounds. XIV (*gynglen*, Ch.). imit.; cf. JANGLE, Du. *jengelen*, G. *klingeln* (OHG. *klingilōn*); sp. with *g-* continued till XIX.

jingo dʒi·ŋgou Recorded first (XVII) in conjuror's patter, usu. *hey* or *high jingo*, as a call for the mysterious appearance of something (opp. to *hey presto*), of unkn. origin; then (Motteux's Rabelais, 1694, tr. F. *par Dieu*) in *by jingo!*, a vigorous asseveration. The use of this excl. in the refrain of a music-hall song (1878) by G. W. Hunt, viz. 'We don't want to fight, yet by Jingo! if we do, | We've got the ships, we've got the men, and got the money too' |, gave rise to the slogan of those who supported Lord Beaconsfield in his resistance to the Russian advance on Turkey in 1878 and to the use of *jingo* as a nickname for such supporters, whence it became a gen. term for advocates of a bellicose policy in dealing with foreign powers. Hence **ji·ngo**ISM. 1878.

jink dʒiŋk quick turn so as to elude XVIII (Burns); *high jinks* †frolic at a drinking-party XVII, lively or boisterous sport XIX. So **jink** vb. move with sudden quick motion, make a quick elusive turn. XVIII (Ramsay). orig. Sc., of unkn. origin.

jinn dʒin in Mohammedan demonology, (one of) an order of spirits. XVII (*dgen*). – Arab. *jinn*, pl. of *jinnī* GENIE (also **jinnee** dʒīnī XIX).

jinricksha dʒinri·kʃa light two-wheeled man-drawn vehicle. XIX. – Jap. *jin-riki-sha*, f. *jin* man+*riki* strength, power+*sha* vehicle. Cf. RICKSHAW.

jinx dʒiŋks (U.S.) person or thing that brings bad luck. XX. Of unkn. origin.

jirga(h) dʒiə·ɹga assembly of chiefs of Afghan tribes. XIX. Pushtu.

jitter dʒi·təɹ (U.S.) act in a nervous way. XX. So **ji·tters** sb. pl., **ji·tter**Y[1]. XX.

jiu-jitsu var. of JUJITSU.

job[1] dʒɔb pierce to a slight depth as with a pointed object. XV (Promp. Parv.). Of symbolic origin, expressive of a brief forcible action; cf. BOB[2], STAB (†*stob*), JAB, DAB[1].

job[2] dʒɔb piece of work XVI (*Iobb of werk*); transaction, operation XVII; position of employment XIX (orig. U.S. colloq.). poss. transf. use of †*job* piece, lump (XIV), cart-load (XVI), of unkn. origin.

Job dʒoub patriarch of the O.T. taken as a type of destitution and of patience. XVI.

jobation dʒoubei·ʃən f. †*jobe* rebuke, reprimand (XVII), f. JOB, in allusion to the lengthy reproofs addressed to him by his friends; see -ATION. ¶ The var. *jawba·tion* shows assim. to JAW.

jobbernowl dʒɔ·bəɹnoul stupid head, blockhead. XVI. f. †*jobard* (– F. *jobard*, f. OF. *jobe* stupid, silly)+NOLL.

Jock dʒɔk Sc. var. of JACK; rustic (cf. HODGE). XVI.

jockey dʒɔ·ki pet-form of JOCK; man of the people; lad XVI; †horse-dealer; professional rider in horse-races XVII. f. JOCK+*-ey*, -Y[6]. Hence as vb. ride as a jockey XIX; play the 'jockey' with, outwit, trick XVII.

jocko, jacko dʒɔ·kou, dʒæ·kou chimpanzee. XIX. – F. *jocko* (Buffon, 1766), deduced from *engeco*, prop. *ncheko*, native name in the Gaboon country, W. Africa.

jockteleg dʒɔ·ktəleg (dial.) clasp-knife. XVII. In earliest use Sc., in the form *Jock the leg*, later *jocteleg*; referred by Lord Hailes (*c.*1776) to *Jacques de Liege* (James of Liège), said to have been found inscribed on an old knife as the name of the cutler, but there is no confirmation of this.

jocose dʒŏkou·s characterized by sportive wit. XVII. – L. *jocōsus*, f. *jocus*; see JOKE, -OSE. So **jocul**AR dʒɔ·kjŭləɹ disposed to joking; said or done in jest. XVII. – L. *joculāris*, f. *joculus*, dim. of *jocus*.

jocund dʒɔ·kənd, dʒou·kənd merry, cheerful. XIV (Ch.). – OF. *jocond*, *jocund* = Sp. *jocunde*, It. *giocondo* – L. *jōcundus*, late form of *jūcundus* pleasant, agreeable (:– **juvicundus*), f. *juvāre* help, delight (cf. AID).

jod see YOD. **jodel** see YODEL.

jodhpurs dʒɔ·dpəɹz riding breeches tight from knee to ankle. XIX. f. *Jodhpur*, name of a town in Rajasthan (Rajputana), India.

joey[1] dʒou·i young kangaroo. XIX. Native Australian (Kangaroo Island) *joè*.

joey[2] dʒou·i (sl.) fourpenny piece. XIX. dim. of *Joe*, pet-form of *Joseph*; said to have been named after *Joseph* Hume (d. 1855), who pressed for their coinage; see -Y[6].

jog dʒɔg †stab, prod; give a slight push to, nudge; intr. move as with a jolting pace. XIV. In late ME. in w.midl. texts, varying to some extent with *jag* and †*jug*, all symbolical of stabbing or jerking movement; not common in literature before XVI. Hence **joggLE**² dʒɔ·gl shake to and fro. XVI (G. Douglas).

Johannine dʒouhæ·nain pert. to the apostle and evangelist John. XIX. f. ecclL. *Jōhannēs* JOHN + -INE¹.

johannisberger dʒouhæ·nisbɔ̄ɹgəɹ white wine produced at *Johannisberg* in the Rheingau, Germany. XIX.

John dʒɔn one of the commonest Jewish and Christian names (the name of two saints of the N.T., John Baptist and John Apostle and Evangelist). ME. *Iohan, Ion*, later *Ihon, Iohn, John* (sp. being based partly on abbrevs. of the L. form, *Ihes, Ihōēs, Iohs*, etc.) – late L. (Vulgate) *Iōannēs* (medL. *Iōhannēs*) – N.T. Gr. *Iōánnēs* – Heb. *yōχānān*, for *y'hōχānān*, expl. as 'God (Jah) is gracious'. Cf. OF. *Jehan* (mod. *Jean*), Sp. *Juan*, It. *Giovanni*, G., Du., etc., *Hans*, Russ. *Ivan*, W. *Ieuan, Ifan*, Gael. *Iain*, †*Eòin*, Ir. *Sean* (*Shane*). See also JACK. *John Bull* typical or individual Englishman; from the name of a character repr. the Eng. nation in Arbuthnot's satire 'Law is a Bottomless Pit', 1712. *John* DORY XVIII. Hence **johnnY**⁶, -IE dʒɔ·ni (*J*-) pet-form of *John*; transf. fellow, chap. XVII.

join dʒoin put or bring together XIII (RGlouc.); come or be put together *c*.1300. – *joign*-, pres. stem of (O)F. *joindre* = Pr. *junher*, Sp. *uncir, uñir*, It. *giungere* :– L. *jungere*, f. IE.**jug*- (see YOKE). So **joi·ndER**⁵ joining. XVII (Sh.). – legal AN. *joinder*, sb. use of OF. *joindre*. **joint** dʒoint articulation, as of bones XIII; part so joined XIV; (U.S.) place of resort (orig. of meeting), esp. for illicit purposes XIX. – OF. *joint* and *jointe*, sb. uses of m. and fem. pp. of *joindre*. **joint** adj. joined, combined (now only attrib.) XIV; holding or held in conjunction XV. – (O)F. *joint*, pp. of *joindre*. **jointure** dʒoi·ntʃəɹ †junction, joint XIV (Ch., Wycl. Bible); holding of property jointly, sole estate limited to the wife XV. – (O)F. *jointure* = Pr. *jontura*, Sp. *juntura*, It. *giuntura* :– L. *junctūra* JUNCTURE. ¶ The pronuncs. dʒain, dʒaint (still dial.) are shown by rhyme XVII–XVIII.

joist dʒoist one of the timbers on which the boards of a floor, etc., rest. XIV. ME. *giste, gyste*, early mod. *iust* – OF. *giste* beam supporting a bridge (mod. *gîte*) :– sb. use of L. *jacitum*, n. pp. of *jacēre* lie down (cf. ADJACENT). ¶ The development to *joist* is paralleled by *hoist*.

joke dʒouk something said or done to excite laughter. XVII (*joque*, Eachard). orig. sl.; poss. – L. *jocus* word-play, jest; cf. G. *jucks, jux* joke, spree, and Du. *jok* jest. So **joke** vb. XVII. Hence **jo·kER**¹ jester, merry fellow XVIII; something used in playing a trick; odd card in a pack (orig. U.S.) XIX.

jolly dʒɔ·li (arch.) of gay disposition, lively, festive, jovial; †gallant, brave; †confident; †amorous XIV; splendid, fine; delightful, nice. XVI. ME. *jolif* – OF. *jolif*, (later and mod.) *joli* †gay, †pleasant, pretty = Pr., OCat. *joliu* (whence It. *giulivo*, OSp. *juli*), perh. f. ON. *jól* midwinter festival, feast, YULE, after **festif* FESTIVE. ¶ Final *f* was lost as in *hasty, tardy*.

jolly-boat dʒɔ·libout ship's boat. XVIII. prob. alteration of app. synon. †*jolywat, gellywatte* (XV–XVII), of unkn. origin.

jolt dʒoult move with jerks from one's seat XVI; †butt, nudge XVII. synon. with somewhat earlier †*jot*, but the origin of both words is unkn., as also of the formally corr. first el. of *jolthead* large clumsy head, blockhead (XVI).

jongleur ʒɔ̃·glœ̃r itinerant minstrel in medieval France. XVIII. – F. *jongleur*, alteration of *jougleur* (OF. *jogleor*) :– L. *joculātōrem* jester (see JUGGLER).

jonquil dʒɔ·ŋkwil species of narcissus. XVII. In early use *junquilia* – It. *giunchiglia*; the present form is – modL. *jonquilla* or F. *jonquille* – Sp. *junquillo*, dim. of *junco* :– L. *juncu-s* rush, reed. Formerly pronounced dʒʌ·ŋkwil.

jordan dʒɔ̄·ɹdən †urinal; chamber-pot. XIV. – medL. *jurdanus*, of unkn. origin. ¶ Early forms with *u* do not support the conjecture of deriv. from the river *Jordan*.

Jordan almond fine variety of almond grown esp. at Malaga, Spain. XV. Late ME. *iardyne, jarden*; in medL. *amigdalum jardinum* (*jardanum*); prob. – (O)F. or Sp. *jardin* GARDEN; the present form is found in Gerarde (1597) and shows assim. to *Jordan* (cf. prec.).

jorum dʒɔ̄·rəm large drinking-bowl. XVIII (Fielding). perh. f. name of *Joram*, who 'brought with him vessels of silver, and vessels of gold, and vessels of brass' (2 Sam. viii 10).

joseph dʒou·zif A. in plant-names, name of the spouse of the Virgin Mary. XVI; B. long (riding-)cloak; f. name of the patriarch *Joseph* of the O.T., in allusion to the outer garment which he left behind him (see Gen. xli 48–57).

joss dʒɔs Chinese idol. XVIII. perh. ult. – Pg. †*deos, deus* :– L. *deus* god (cf. DEITY), through Javanese *dejos*; cf. Du. *joosje, josie*.

jostle dʒɔ·sl †meet *with* in an encounter XIV; (trans. and intr.) knock or push (*against*) XVI. f. *just*, JOUST + -LE;³ the formerly prevailing form was *justle*.

jot dʒɔt least part or point. XVI (Tindale). Formerly also *iote, ioate* – L. *iōta* (pronounced jō·ta) – Gr. *iôta* IOTA; cf. Sp., Pg. *jota*, G. *jot*, †*jodt*. Hence (presumably) **jot** dʒɔt vb. set *down* in the briefest form. XVIII (Ramsay). In earliest use Sc., familiarized by Galt and Scott.

joule dʒūl, dʒaul electrical unit, named 1882 after James Prescott *Joule*, English physicist.

jounce dʒauns jolt, bump. XV (Promp. Parv.). Of unkn. origin, like several other vbs. in *-ounce*, viz. *bounce, flounce, pounce, trounce*, all of which are applied to kinds of abrupt or forcible movement.

journal dʒɔ̄·ɹnəl A. †diurnal (service-book) XIV; †itinerary; daily record of transactions; record of events XVI; daily newspaper XVIII. B. part of a shaft or axle that rests on the bearings XIX (1814). – OF. *jurnal, jornal* (mod. *journal*), sb. use of *journal* adj., for earlier *jornel* :– late L. *diurnālis* DIURNAL (cf. AJOURN). Sense B is first recorded from R. Buchanan's 'Shafts of Mills' and 'Millwork', in which *journey* is given as synon.; the use presumably arose in Scottish workshops, but its *raison d'être* is unknown. Hence **jou·rnal**IST. XVII; cf. F. *journaliste* (1704); whence **journalı**·STIC. XIX (Carlyle); **jou·rnal**ISM XIX (1833 in a review of a F. work 'Du journalisme'); after F. (1781). **jou·rnal**IZE enter in a journal XVIII; practise journalism XIX.

journey dʒɔ̄·ɹni †day's travel; spell of travel, esp. by land XIII; (dial.) day's work (hence in *journeyman*, orig. one qualified to work for day wages) XIV; amount produced in a day's work (e.g. at the British Mint) XVI. – OF. *jornee* (mod. *journée* day, day's work or travel) = Pr., Sp. *jornada*, It. *giornata* :– Rom. **diurnāta*, f. L. *diurnum* daily portion, in Rom. langs. day, sb. use of n. of *diurnus* DIURNAL. So **jou·rney** vb. travel. XIV. – AN. *journeyer*.

joust dʒaust, dʒūst combat of two men-at-arms on horseback. XIII. – OF. *juste, jouste*, f. *juster* (mod. *jouter*) bring together, unite, engage on horseback (whence **joust** vb. XIII) = Pr. *jostar* (whence Sp. *justar*, It. *giostrare*) :– Rom. **juxtāre* come together, encounter, f. L. *juxtā* near together, rel. to *jugum* YOKE, *jungere* JOIN.

Jove dʒouv Jupiter. XIV (Ch.). *By Jove* XVI. See next.

jovial dʒou·viəl †under the influence of the planet Jupiter, regarded astrol. as the source of happiness; characterized by mirth. XVI (Spenser, Drayton). – F. *jovial* (XVI) – It. *gioviale*, f. *Giove* Jove, Jupiter :– L. *Jovem, Jovis*, etc., obl. cases of OL. *Jovis* (for which classical L. had the comp. with *pater* father, *Juppiter*, JUPITER, corr. to Skr. *dyaús pitá* 'heaven father'; cf. DEITY, DIVINE); see -IAL. Earlier †*jovy* jovial XV–XVII is – late L. *jovius*; *Jo·vian* (Palsgr.) – F. *jovien*.

jowl[1] dʒoul, dʒaul jaw, jawbone; as in phr. *cheek by jowl*, which repl. *cheek by cheek*. XVI. Later form of *chawle*, reduction of ME. *chauel*, OE. *ćeafl*, corr. to OS. **kaƀal* (in d. pl. *kaflun*), Flem. *kavel* gum, rel. to MHG. *kivel*, Du. *kevel*.

jowl[2] dʒoul, dʒaul dewlap, crop, wattle. XVI. Later form of ME. *cholle* (XIV), OE. *ćeole, -u* = OS., OHG. *kela* (G. *kehle*), throat, gullet, synon. with ME. *choller*, OE. *ćeolur* = OHG. *kelur* (cf. Skr. *gala*).

jowl[3] dʒoul, dʒaul head. (XIV; *jolrap* head-rope.) Later form of *cholle* (XIV), of unkn. origin; of the three sbs. *jowl, j*-forms appear earliest in this.

joy dʒoi pleasurable emotion; state of happiness. XIII. – OF. *joie, joye* (mod. *joie*) = Pr. *joia*, Sp. *joya*, It. *gioia* :– Rom. **gaudia*, fem. for L. *gaudia*, pl. of *gaudium* joy (whence Pr. *joi*), f. *gaudēre*. So **joy** vb. †rejoice XIII (Cursor M.); †ENJOY XIV. – OF. *joïr* (mod. *jouir*) = Pr. *gaudir* :– Rom. **gaudīre*, for L. *gaudēre* rejoice, f. **gawedh*- (cf. synon. Gr. *gētheîn*, f. **gāϝeth*-). So **joy**·ANCE. XVI (Spenser). **joy**·OUS. XIV. – AN. *joyous*, OF. *joios* (mod. *joyeux*).

jubbah dʒʌ·bə, dʒu·bba outer garment of Moslems and Parsees. XVI. – Arab. *jubbah* (whence also F. *jupe* skirt, Pr. *jupa*, Sp. *aljuba*, It. *giubba, giuppa*). Cf. JIBBAH.

jube dʒū·bi rood-loft, choir-screen. XVIII. – F. *jubé* – L. *jubē*, imper. of *jubēre* bid, order, first word of the formula *Jube, domine, benedicere* Sir, bid a blessing, addressed by the deacon to the celebrant before the reading of the Gospel, which, in some places, was done from the rood-loft.

jubilation dʒūbilei·ʃən exultant rejoicing. XIV (Wycl. Bible). – L. *jūbilātiō(n-)*, f. *jūbilāre* (rustic word) call, halloo, (in Chr. writers) shout for joy; see -ATION. Also **ju·bil**ANT. XVII (Milton). ¶ Not orig. rel. to next.

jubilee dʒū·bilī year of emancipation and restoration of the Jews, kept every 50 years (see Lev. xxv); fiftieth anniversary. XIV. – (O)F. *jubilé* (corr. to Sp. *jubileo*, It. *giubileo*). – ChrL. *jūbilæus* (sc. *annus* year) – (with assim. to *jūbilāre*; see prec.) ChrGr. *iōbēlaîos*, f. *iṓbēlos* – Heb. *yōbēl* jubilee, orig. ram, (hence) ram's horn, with which the jubilee year was proclaimed.

JudaIC dʒūdei·ik Jewish XVII; earlier **Juda·**ICAL XV. – L. *Jūdaicus* – Gr. *Ioudaïkós*, f. *Ioudaîos* JEW. So **Juda**ISM dʒū·deiizm Jewish polity. XVI. – ChrL. *Jūdaismus* – Gr. *Ioudaïsmós* (2 Macc. ii 21), f. *Ioudaîos*. So **Ju·da**IZE. XVI. – ChrL. *jūdaizāre* – Gr. *ioudaḯzein* (Gal. ii 14).

judas dʒū·dəs opening through which one can look without being seen. XIX. – F. *judas*, transf. use of the name of the disciple who betrayed Jesus Christ (Matt. xxvi 48).

judge dʒʌdʒ officer appointed to administer the law; arbiter, umpire. XIV. – OF. *juge* = Pr. *jutge*, Sp. *juez*, It. *judice*, Rum. *jude* :– L. *jūdicem*, nom. *jūdex*, f. *jūs* right, law + *-dicus* speaking (see DICTION). So **judge** vb. XIII. – (O)F. *juger* = Pr. *jutjar*, Sp. *juzgar*, It. *giudicare* :– L. *jūdicāre*. **ju·dg(e)**MENT. XIII (RGlouc.). – (O)F. *jugement*, f. *juger*. **judgmat**IC, -ICAL dʒʌdʒmæ·tik judicious. XIX; after *dogmatic*.

judicature dʒū·dikətʃuəɹ action or office of a judge; body of judges. XVI. – medL. *jūdicātūra*, f. pp. stem of *jūdicāre* JUDGE; see -URE.

judicial dʒudi·ʃəl pert. to judgement or a judge XIV; giving judgement XVI. – L. *jūdiciālis*, f. *jūdicium* judgement, f. *jūdic-*, *jūdex* JUDGE; see -IAL. So **judi·**CIOUS exercising good judgement. XVI. – F. *judicieux* = It. *giudizioso*, Sp. *juicioso*.

Judy dʒū·di wife of Punch. XIX. Pet-form of the female name *Judith*.

jug[1] dʒʌg deep vessel with a handle for holding liquid. XVI. prob. a use of the proper name *Jug*, pet-form of *Joan*, *Joanna*, and *Jenny*. sl. prison. XIX.

jug[2] dʒʌg imit. of the notes of the nightingale. XVI (Skelton).

juggernaut dʒʌ·gəɹnɔ̄t (*J-*) title of Krishna, avatar of Vishnu; idol of this carried in an enormous car, under which (it was once said) devotees threw themselves. XVII; also fig. – Hindi *Jagannath* – Skr. *Jagannātha*, f. *jagat-* world + *nāthás* lord, protector.

juggins dʒʌ·ginz (sl.) simpleton. *c.* 1880. perh. a use of the surname *Juggins*, f. *Jug* (see JUG[1]) + suffix as in *Dickens*, *Jenkins*, *Tomkins*; cf. earlier *muggins*.

juggler dʒʌ·gləɹ †jester, buffoon; †magician, wizard; conjurer. XII. ME. *iugelere*, *iugelour*, *iogeler* – OF. *jog-*, *jug-*, *jouglere*, acc. *jogleor*, etc. (cf. JONGLEUR) = It. *giocolatore* :– L. *joculātor*, *-ātōrem* (whence OE. *ġeogelere*), f. *joculārī* jest; also OF. *jogler* = Sp. *juglar*, It. *giocogliere* :– medL. *joculāris* buffoon, sb. use of the adj. (see JOCULAR). So **ju·ggl**ERY. XIII. – OF. *juglerie*. Hence (or – OF. *jugler*) **ju·ggle**. XIV.

Jugoslav, Yugo- jūgouslā·v Southern Slav, pert. to the state of Jugoslavia (proclaimed 30 Oct. 1918). XIX (*Yougo-Slav*, after F.). Austrian German, f. Serb *jugo-*, comb. form of *jug* south + SLAV.

jugular dʒʌ·gjŭləɹ pert. to the neck or throat. XVI. – late L. *jugulāris*, f. L. *jugulum* collar-bone, dim. of *jugum* YOKE; see -AR.

juice dʒūs liquid part of vegetables and fruits. XIII (*iuys*). – (O)F. *jus* – L. *jūs* broth, sauce, vegetable juice (cf. Skr. *yūs*, OSl. *jucha* soup, broth, Gr. *zūmē* leaven), f. **jeu-* mix.

ju-jitsu, -jutsu dʒūdʒi·tsu, -dʒʌ·tsu system of wrestling and physical training. XIX. – Jap. *jūjutsu* (pronounced dʒudʒitsu), f. *jū* (Chinese *jeu* soft, yielding) + *jutsu*, *jutsz* (Chinese *shu*, *shut*) science.

ju-ju dʒū·dʒū W. African fetish. XIX. gen. thought to be – F. *joujou* plaything, redupl. formation on *jouer* play :– L. *jocāre*.

jujube dʒū·dʒūb edible fruit of species of Zizyphus XIV; lozenge of the shape of or flavoured with this XIX. – (O)F. *jujube* or medL. *jujuba*, ult. – L. *zizyphum* – Gr. *zizuphon*. This became in Rom. *zizipus*, *zizupus*, later **zizubo*, **zuzubo*, whence, with change of *z* to *j*, and the use of n.pl. as fem. sg. as in plant-names, *jujuba*.

julep dʒū·lep sweet or syrupy liquor. XIV. – (O)F. *julep*, corr. to Pr. *julep*, Sp. *julepe*, It. *giulebbe*, medL. *julapium* – Arab. *julāb* – Pers. *gulāb* rose-water, f. *gul* rose + *āb* water.

julienne ʒüljɛ·n vegetable soup. XIX. F. (XVIII), for *potage à la julienne*, f. proper name *Jules* or *Julien* (the reason is unkn.).

July dʒulai· seventh month of the year. XIII. – AN. *julie* – L. *Jūlius* (sc. *mensis* month), so named after Caius *Julius* Cæsar, who was born in this month, the orig. name *Quin(c)tilis* being changed to *Julius* after his death and apotheosis. The unexpl. str. *July·* established since Johnson's time. ¶ *July-flower* is a perversion of GILLYFLOWER.

jumble[1] dʒʌ·mbl †intr. move about in disorder; †make a confused or discordant noise; mingle in confusion. XVI. Partly synon. with late ME. †*jumpere*, †*jombre* (Ch., Usk), both app. being formed on a symbolic base with iterative or frequent. suffix. sb. medley, disorder. XVII.

jumble[2] dʒʌ·mbl (now U.S.) sweet cake, formerly made in rings. XVII (*jumbal*). perh. a use of *gimbal*, GIMMAL.

jumbo dʒʌ·mbou big clumsy person, animal, etc. XIX (early). prob. the second element of MUMBO-JUMBO.

jump dʒʌmp move or be moved up and down as with a leap or spring XVI; leap over XVII; (U.S. and Colonial) take summary possession of (a claim) XIX. prob. imit. of the sound of feet coming to the ground; cf. *bump*, *thump*. Words of similar form and meaning are It. dial. *tzumpá*, *dzumbá*, *jumpai*, G. *gumpen*, Da. *gumpe*, Sw. dial. *gumpa*; but these can have no direct contact with the Eng. vb. Hence **jump** sb. XVI.

jumper dʒʌ·mpəɹ loose garment for the torso. XIX. prob. rel. to (obs. or dial). *jump* man's short coat, woman's bodice (XVII), perh. alteration of †*jup* (XVII) – F. *juppe*, var. of *jupe* (see JUBBAH).

junction dʒʌ·ŋkʃən joining. XVIII. – L. *junctiō(n-)*, f. *junct-*, pp. stem of *jungere* JOIN; see YOKE, -TION. Cf. F. *jonction*. So **ju·nc**TURE place of joining XIV (Wycl. Bible); convergence of events XVII. – L. *junctūra* joint (cf. JOINTURE).

June dʒūn sixth month of the year. XIII. – (O)F. *juin* = Pr. *junh*, Sp. *junio*, It. *giugno* :– L. *Jūniu-s* (sc. *mēnsis* month), var. of *Jūnōnius* sacred to the goddess Juno. ME. *juyn* (*ion*) was refash. after L.

jungle dʒʌ·ŋgl (orig.) waste land; (hence) land overgrown with underwood. XVIII. – Hindi, Marathi *jangal* :– Skr. *jangala* dry, dry ground, desert. ¶ Hence G. *dschungel*, F. *jungle*.

junior dʒū·niəɹ younger XVII; of lower standing XVIII; sb. XVI. – L. *jūnior* (:– **juvenior*), compar. of *juvenis* YOUNG.

juniper dʒū·nipəɹ genus of coniferous trees. XIV. – L. *jūniperus*. Cf. GENEVA, GIN[2].

junk[1] dʒʌŋk old rope XV (hence, worthless stuff, rubbish XX); salt meat used on long voyages (compared to pieces of rope) XVIII. Of unkn. origin.

junk[2] dʒʌŋk native sailing vessel, esp. of the China seas. XVII. – F. †*juncque* (mod. *jonque*), Pg. *junco*, or Du. *jonk* – Javanese *djong*, Malay *adjong*.

junker ju·ŋkəɹ young German noble; spec. reactionary member of Prussian aristocracy. XVI (but not common till XIX). G., for earlier *junkher(r)*, f. MHG. *junc* YOUNG + *herre* (mod. *herr*) lord, compar. of *hēr* exalted, eminent.

junket dʒʌ·ŋkit (rush) basket for fish XIV (Wycl. Bible); dish prepared with cream, orig. laid in or on rushes XV; †dainty dish or confection; feast, banquet XVI. – (O)F. *jonquette*, f. *jonc* rush :– L. *juncus*; cf. Pr. *juncada*, medL. *juncata*. In the last two senses preceded by †*junkery* (XV–XVI).

junta dʒʌ·ntə (in Spain and Italy) deliberative or administrative council XVII; body of men combined for a common (political) purpose XVIII. – Sp., Pg. *junta* (whence F. *junte*) = It. *giunta* :– Rom. sb. use of fem. pp. *juncta* of *jungere* JOIN; cf. JOINT. In the latter sense often also **ju·nto** (XVII), with ending assim. to Sp. sbs. in *-o* (cf. -ADO).

Jupiter dʒū·pitəɹ supreme deity of the ancient Romans XIII (in earliest use *Iubiter*); largest of the planets XIII; (alch.) †tin XIV (Ch.); †(her., in blazoning by the names of heavenly bodies) azure XVI. – L.; see JOVIAL. Used in several plant names, esp. tr. L. g. *Jovis*, e.g. *Jupiter's beard*, Barba Jovis.

jurassic dʒuræ·sik (geol.) pert. to oolitic formations of which the Jura mountains chiefly consist. XIX. – F. *jurassique*, f. *Jura*, after *triassique* TRIASSIC.

jurat[1] dʒuə·ræt municipal official or magistrate in the Cinque Ports, the Channel Islands, and some French towns, etc. XV. – L. *jūrātus* (cf. foll.); so F. *jurat*.

jurat[2] dʒuə·ræt (leg.) memorandum of the swearing of an affidavit. XVIII. – L. *jūrātum*, pp. n. of *jūrāre*; see JURY.

juridical dʒuri·dikəl pert. to judicial proceedings. XVI. f. L. *jūridicus*, f. *jūr-*, *jūs* law (with Indo-Iranian cogns.) + *-dicus* saying, f. *dīcere* say (see DICTION). So **jurisconsu·lt** one learned in the law. XVII (Bacon). – L. *jūrisconsultus*, f. *jūris*, g. of *jūs* + *consultus*. **jurisdiction** dʒuərisdi·kʃən exercise of judicial authority. XIII (Cursor M.). Earliest forms *iure-*, *iuridicciou n* – OF. *jure-*, (also mod.) *juridiction*, later conformed to the orig. L. *jūrisdictiō(n-)*; f. *jūris* + *dictiō* declaration; see JURY and DICTION. **juris**PRU·DENCE †skill in law XVII (Coke); system of law XVII; science of law XVIII. – late L. *jūrisprūdentia* (in Cicero *prūdentia jūris*). **jur**IST dʒuə·rist †lawyer XV (Caxton); legal writer XVII (Bacon). – F. *juriste* or medL. *jūrista*, f. *jūr-*, *iūs*. **jur**OR[1] dʒuə·rəɹ member of a jury. XIV (PPl., Wyclif). – AN. *jurour* :– L. *jūrātōrem*. **jury** dʒuə·ri company of men sworn to give a verdict. XIV. Late ME. *iuree* – AN. *juree* (in this sense) – OF. *jurée* oath, juridical inquiry, inquest – (AL. *jūrāta*) sb. use of pp. fem. of L. *jūrāre* swear, f. *jūr-*, *jūs*, an old term of law and religion; cf. JUDGE, JUST; see -Y[5].

jury-mast dʒuə·rimàst, -məst (naut.) temporary mast. XVI. The first el. is perh. identifiable with **iuerie*, recorded as *i(u)were* 'remedium' in Promp. Parv., which may be aphetic deriv. of OF. *ajurie* aid, f. *aju-* pres. stem of *aidier* AID + *-rie* -RY; see MAST[2].

jussive dʒʌ·siv (gram.) expressing command. XIX. f. *juss-*, pp. stem of L. *jubēre* command, prob. f. IE. **jeudh-* set in motion, repr. in Balto-Slavic, Gr., and Indo-Iranian with various sense-developments; see -IVE.

just dʒʌst righteous, fair; well-founded; proper, correct, †exact. XIV. – (O)F. *juste* = Pr. *just*, Sp. *justo*, It. *giusto* – L. *jūstus*, f. *jūs* (cf. JURY). Hence **just** adv. exactly, precisely XIV; precisely (now or then); not more than, barely XVII; not less than, quite XVIII. Cf. F. *juste*.

just see JOUST.

justice dʒʌ·stis exercise of judicial authority XII; judicial officer, judge XII; quality of being just XIV; rightfulness XVI (Sh.). Early ME. *iustise* (Peterborough Chron., Vices and Virtues) – (O)F. *justice* = Pr., Sp. *justicia*, It. *giustizia* – L. *jūstitia* righteousness, equity, f. *jūstus* JUST; see -ICE. So **ju·stic**ER[2] (hist.). XIV (R. Mannyng). – AN. *justicer*, OF. *justicier* – medL. **justiciar** -i·ʃiəɹ (hist. or obs.) XV, **justiciary** -i·ʃiəri XVI. – medL. *justitiārius*; see -AR, -ARY.

justify dʒʌ·stifai †judge, condemn, punish; show to be just; make good, verify XIV; maintain the justice of; make exact, adjust (esp. printing type) XVI. – (O)F. *justifier* – ChrL. *jūstificāre* do justice to, vindicate, f. *justus* JUST: see -FY. So **justifica**·TION. XIV (theol. XVI). – (O)F. or ChrL. **ju·stifi**ABLE. XVI. – F.

jut dʒʌt project, stick *out*. XVI. var. of JET², by assim. to †*jutty* (XV) project, also †*jetty* (XVI), and †*jutty* (XV) pier, JETTY.

jute dʒūt fibre from the bark of Indian trees (genus Corchorus) used for canvas, etc. XVIII. – Bengali *jhōṭo, jhuṭo* :– Skr. *jūṭa*, var. of *jaṭā* braid of hair.

Jute dʒūt member of one of the three Low German tribes which invaded and settled in Britain. XIV (*Iutes*, Trevisa). repr. medL. *Jutæ, Jutī* pl. (Bede), in OE. *Eotas, Iotas* (cf. Icel. *Iótar* people of Jutland in Denmark).

juvenile dʒū·vənail young, youthful XVII (Bacon); sb. young person XVIII. – L. *juvenīlis*, f. *juvenis* YOUNG; see -ILE. †*Juvenal* sb. is earlier. XVI (Sh.). – L. *juvenālis*.

juvenilia -i·liə works produced in one's youth. XVII (Wither, Donne, Dryden). – L. n.pl.

juxtaposition dʒʌ:kstəpəzi·ʃən placing close together. XVII. – F. *juxtaposition*, f. L. *juxtā* (cf. JOUST)+*position*. So **juxtapo·se.** XIX. – F. *juxtaposer*; earlier †*juxtapo·sit*. XVII. See POSE, POSITION.

jynx dʒiŋks wryneck. XVII. – modL. *jynx*, for L. *iynx* – Gr. *íugx*.

K

k- see also C-, KH-.

kaama kā·mə hartebeest. XIX. Said by Burchell to be Hottentot, but current also in Sechuana.

kabaya kəbā·jə light loose tunic. XVI (*cabie, cabaja*). The current form repr. Malay *kabaya* (whence Du. *kabaai*); vars. have occurred repr. F. *cabaye*, Pg. *cabaya, -aia*, all – Arab. *qabāya, qabā'*, Pers. *qabā*.

Kabyle kăbai·l Berber of Algeria or Tunis. XIX. – Arab. *qabā'il*, pl. of *qabīlah* tribe.

kaddish kæ·diʃ portion of the daily ritual of the synagogue. XVII (Purchas). – Aram. *qaddīsh* holy, holy one.

Kaffir kæ·fəɹ, **Kafir** kā·fəɹ infidel; member of a S. African race of the Bantu family. XIX. – Arab. *kāfir*, prp. active of *kafara* deny, be unbelieving; for early forms see CAFFRE.

kailyard see KALE.

kaimakam kaiməkā·m deputy (spec. of the Grand Vizier). XVII. – Turk. *qāimaqām* – Arab. *qa'im maqām* 'one standing in the place of another', i.e. *qā'im* standing, *maqām* place, station.

kainite kai·nait (min.) hydrous chlorosulphate of magnesium and potassium. XIX. – G. *kainit*, f. Gr. *kainós* new+-ITE; named by C. F. Zincken in 1865 with ref. to its recent formation.

kaiser kai·zəɹ emperor. XVI. – G. *kaiser* and Du. *keizer*, †*keiser*, †*keser*, a Germ. adoption of L. CÆSAR through Gr. *kaîsar*, repr. by OE. *cāsere*, OFris. *keisar*, OS. *kēsur, -ar*, ON. *keisari*, Goth. *kaisar*. ME. *caisere* (XII–XV) was – ON.; the mod. use is independent of the ME. currency of the word. The alliterative formula ***king and (or) kaiser*** was common from XIII to XVII, and is recorded dial. in XIX; in literary use it was revived by Scott.

kajawah kadʒā·wa, ka·dʒɔwə camel-litter, pannier. XVII (T. Herbert). Urdu (– Pers.) *kajāwah, kajawah*.

kaka kā·ka N.Z. parrot of the genus Nestor. XVIII. Maori, 'parrot'. So **ka·kapo** N.Z. owl parrot (*po* night), **kakari·ki** green parrakeet ((*r*)*iki* little). XIX.

kakemono kækĭmou·nou wall picture on silk or paper. XIX. Jap., f. *kake-* hang, *mono* thing.

kale, kail keil cabbage XIII (*cale*, Cursor M.); cabbage broth XV (Henryson). north. var. of COLE. Hence **kailyard** cabbage-garden (YARD¹), familiar since 1895 as an epithet of fiction and its authors (*literature of the k., k. school*) describing, with much use of the vernacular, common life in Scotland.

kaleidoscope kəlai·dəskoup optical instrument in which reflections of pieces of coloured glass are made to form varying patterns. 1817 (David Brewster). f. Gr. *kălós* beautiful (cf. CALLI-)+*eîdos* shape (cf. IDEA)+-SCOPE.

kalends see CALENDS.

kali kei·lai prickly saltwort, Salsola Kali XVI; †soda ash XVIII; (*lemon k.*) mixture of tartaric acid and bicarbonate of soda XIX. – Arab. *qalī*; see ALKALI.

kalmia kæ·lmiə genus of Amer. evergreen shrubs. XVIII. modL., f. name of Peter *Kalm*, a pupil of Linnæus; see -IA¹.

kampong kæmpɔ·ŋ Malay village. XIX. See COMPOUND³.

kamptulicon kæmp'jū·likɔn patent floorcloth. 1844. f. Gr. *kamptós* flexible+*oûlos* thick + *-ikón*, n. of *-ikós* -IC.

kana kā·nă Jap. writing, the chief varieties of which are hiragana and katakana. XVIII.

kangaroo kæŋgərū· Australasian marsupial mammal. XVIII. Said by Capt. James Cook (1770) and Joseph Banks (1770) to have been a native Australian name (*kangooroo*), which is supported by some later writers, but denied by others.

kanoon kənū·n species of dulcimer, harp, etc. XIX (Moore). – (Pers. –) Arab. *qānūn*.

kantar kæntā·ɹ measure of weight (100 lb.). XVI (Eden). – Arab. *qinṭār* – medL. *centēnārium*, n. (sc. *pondus* weight) of L. *centēnārius* (f. *centēnī* 100 at a time, f. *centum* HUNDRED), whence modGr. *kentēnári*; cf. QUINTAL.

Kantian kæ·ntiən pert. to Immanuel *Kant* (1724–1804), G. philosopher; see -IAN. XIX (*Kantian*ISM, Beddoes).

kaolin kei·ŏlin fine white porcelain clay. XVIII. – F. *kaolin* – Chinese *kao-*, *kau-ling* name of a mountain (*kao* high, *ling* hill) in N. China, whence the stuff was orig. obtained.

kapok kā·pək fine cotton wool from the seeds of a tree. XVIII (*capoc*). – Malay *kāpoq*, through F. *capoc*, Du. *kapok*, or G. *kapok*.

kaput kapu·t finished, done for. G.; see CAPOT.

Karaite kɛə·reiait member of a Jewish sect which bases its tenets on literal interpretation of the scriptures. XVIII. f. Heb. *q'rāīm* scripturalists, f. *qārā* read; see -ITE.

karma kā·ɹmə fate, destiny (as determined by one's actions in a former state of existence). XIX. Skr. *karma-n* action, effect, fate, f. IE. **qwer-* shape, form.

kaross kərɔ·s skin mantle used by Hottentots, etc. XVIII. Afrikaans *karos*, poss. of Du. origin (*kuras* cuirass has been suggested).

kar(r)oo kərū· barren tract of land in S. Africa. XVIII. Of Hottentot origin, but precise details are unknown.

karyo-, also **caryo-** kæ·riou comb. form of Gr. *káruon* nut, kernel, in biol. terms referring to the nucleus of a cell. XIX.

katabolism kətæ·bəlizm (biol.) destructive metabolism. XIX. f. Gr. *katabolḗ*, f. *katabállein* throw down; see CATA-, BALLISTA, -ISM.

katydid kei·tidid (U.S.) insect of the locust family, producing by stridulation a noise which the name is taken to echo. XVIII.

kava kā·və intoxicating beverage. XIX. SW. Polynesian; also *ava*.

kavass kəvà·s armed police officer. XIX. Turk. – Arab. *qawwās* bow-maker, f. *qaws* bow.

kayak kai·æk sealskin canoe. XVIII. Eskimo.

kayles keilz (dial.) pl. ninepins, skittles. XIV. – (M)Du. *kegel*, †*keyl-* (in *keylbane* skittle-alley) = OHG. *chegil* (G. *kegel*) tapering stick, cone, skittle :– Germ. **kagilaz*, f. **kag-*. Cf. (O)F. *quille* from MDu. or MHG., and W. *ceilys* from Eng.

kazi see CADI.

kea kei·ə parrot of N.Z., Nestor notabilis. XIX. Maori; imit. of the bird's cry.

keck see KEX.

kedge kedʒ warp a ship by winding in a hawser attached to a small anchor. XV. Earliest form *cagge* (XIV), dial. *cadge*; for the variation of *a* with *e* cf. *cag* KEG, *calle* KELL, *cannel* KENNEL[2], *castrel* KESTREL, *catch* KETCH. Hence **ke·dg**ER[1] small anchor or grapnel. XV; **kedge**(-ANCHOR). XVIII.

kedgeree ke·dʒərī Indian dish of rice with condiments; dish made from cold fish, etc., served hot. XVII (*kits-*, *ketch-*, *kichery*). – Hindi *khichṛī* :– Skr. *k'rsara* dish of rice and sesamum.

keech kītʃ lump of congealed fat. XVI (Sh.). Cf. dial. *keech* congeal as fat; of unkn. origin.

keel[1] kīl lowest longitudinal timber (or iron plating) of a ship XIV; (nat. hist.) central ridge XVI (Gerarde). ME. *kele* – ON. *kjǫlr* :– **keluz*. So **kee·l**HAUL, also -HALE. XVII. – Du. *kielhalen*. See KELSON.

keel[2] kīl flat-bottomed vessel, lighter. XIV. ME. *kele* – MLG. *kēl*, MDu. *kiel* ship, boat = OE. *ċēol*, OS. *kiol*, OHG. *chiol* (Du., G. *kiel*) :– CGerm. **keulaz*.

keel[3] kīl (dial.) cool OE.; prevent (a pot) from boiling over XIV. OE. *cēlan* = OFris. *kēla* (Du. *koelen*), OHG. *chuolen* (G. *kühlen*), ON. *kœla* :– Germ. (exc. Gothic) **kōljan*, f. **kōl-* COOL.

keelson see KELSON.

keen[1] kīn †wise; †brave, fierce OE.; having a sharp edge or point; acute, bitter; pungent, biting XIII; ardent, intense XIV; penetrating, acute XVIII. OE. *cēne* = OS. **kōni*, MLG. *kōne* (Du. *koen*), OHG. *chuoni* (G. *kühn*) bold, brave, ON. *kœnn* skilful, expert :– CGerm. (exc. Gothic) **kōnjaz*, which has no certain cogns.

keen[2] kīn (Anglo-Ir.) lament. XIX. – Ir. *caoinim* I wail.

keep kīp, pt., pp. **kept** A. †seize, hold, watch (for); pay regard to, observe OE.; B. take care of, guard XII; preserve, maintain; reserve, withhold, restrain XIV; C. reside, dwell (in) XIV. Late OE. *cēpan*, pt. *cēpte*, of which no cogns. are known. Its sense-development has been infl. by its being used to render L. *servare*, with its comps. *conservare*, *observare*, *præservare*, *reservare*. Its meanings have close affinity with those of *hold*, but the meaning 'support, sustain' of the latter does not belong to *keep*. Hence **keep** sb. A. †care, heed; B. donjon of a castle XIII; C. act of keeping, being kept XVIII; sustenance XIX. (The origin of B is not certain.) **keepsake** kī·pseik thing kept for the SAKE of the giver XVIII (Mme d'Arblay); literary annual containing collections of tales, poems, etc., intended as a gift, common in early XIX.

kef, keif, kief kef, kaif, kīf drowsiness, dreamy intoxication, enjoyment of idleness. XIX. – Arab. *kaif, kef* well-being, enjoyment (in Morocco, etc., Indian hemp).

keffiyeh kefī·jei kerchief. XIX. – Arab. *kaffīyah, kuffīyeh,* perh. – late L. *cofea, cuphia* COIF.

keg keg small barrel. XVII. dial. var. of north. *cag* (XV) – Icel. *kaggi.* ¶ For the change of vowel cf. KEDGE.

kehaya kehajā· Turkish viceroy, etc. XVI (*cahaia*; later vars. are numerous). – Turk. *kiḥayā* – Pers. *katkhudā,* f. *kat* house + *khudā* master.

kell kel. XIV. var. of *calle,* CAUL, of which it has the main senses. ¶ For the change of vowel cf. KEDGE, KEG, KETCH.

kelp kelp large seaweed XIV; calcined ashes of seaweed XVII. Late ME. *cülp(e),* of which *kelp* and rare †*kilpe* appear to be dial. vars.; this variation points to an OE. **cylp.*

kelpie ke·lpi water-sprite of the Scottish Lowlands. XVIII. Of unkn. origin.

kelson, keelson ke·lsən line of timber inside a ship parallel to the keel. XVII. ME. *kelswayn, kelsweyn, kelsyng,* mod. *kelsine,* perh. points to an original **kelswin,* the nearest parallel to which, and the prob. source, is LG. *kielswīn* (whence also G. *kielschwein,* Da. *kølsvin,* Sw. *kölsvin*), f. *kiel* KEEL[1] + (prob.) *swīn* SWINE, used, like *cat, dog, horse,* for a timber. The form *keelson* is due to assim. to KEEL[1].

kempt see UNKEMPT.

ken[1] †make known OE.; (arch., dial.) know XIII. OE. *cennan* (pt. *cende,* pp. *cenned*) = OFris. *kenna, kanna,* OS. *kennian* (Du. *kennen*), OHG. *chennen* (G. *kennen*), ON. *kenna,* Goth. (CGerm.) *kannjan,* f. **kann-* I know, CAN[1]. Properly causative, 'make known', which was the only use in OE. and Gothic, but in Germ. langs. gen. it acquired the sense 'know' at an early period; in Eng. this use may be immed. due to Norse; in Sc. it has displaced *knaw,* KNOW. Hence **ken** sb. †measure of distance at sea; range of vision or perception. XVI.

ken[2] (sl.) house. XVI. Of cant origin.

kennedya kenī·diə genus of leguminous plants. XIX. modL. (Ventenat, 1804), f. name of one *Kennedy,* a Hammersmith gardener.

kennel[1] ke·nəl house for the shelter of a house-dog or hounds. XIV. – AN. **kenil* = OF. *chenil,* It. *canile* :– medL. **canīle,* f. *canis* dog (cf. HOUND). Hence vb. be in, put into, a kennel. XVI.

kennel[2] ke·nəl street gutter. XVI. Later form of *can(n)el* watercourse (XIII), gutter (XIV) – ONF. *canel* = OF. *chanel* CHANNEL[1]. ¶ For the change of vowel cf. KEDGE.

kenosis kènou·sis (theol.) self-renunciation by Jesus Christ of attributes of the divine nature in the Incarnation. *c.* 1870. – Gr. *kénōsis* emptying, f. *kenoûn* (f. *kénos*) empty, with ref. to *heautòn ekénōse* 'he emptied himself' (Phil. ii 7). So **kenotic** kinɔ·tik. XIX. – Gr. *kenōtikós.*

kenspeck ke·nspek dial. (also **-spack**) easily recognizable, conspicuous. XVI. Of Scand. origin, but the immed. source is uncertain; cf. ON. *kennispeki* faculty of recognition, MSw. *kännespaker,* Sw. *känspak,* Norw. *kjennespak* quick at recognizing, f. ON. *kenna* KEN[1] + *spak-, spek-* wise, wisdom. Hence **ke·nspeckle(d)** (Sc. and north.). XVIII; cf. -LE[2].

Kentish ke·ntiʃ OE. *Centisċ,* f. *Cent* – L. *Cantium* (Cæsar), *Kántion* (Diodorus), *Kántion ákron* (Ptolemy), f. OCeltic **kanto-* (i) rim, border, or (ii) white; see -ISH[1].

kentledge ke·ntlèdʒ pig-iron for ballast. XVII. – OF. *quintelage* ballast, with assim. to *kentle* QUINTAL; see -AGE.

kepi kepi French military cap. XIX. F. *képi* – Swiss G. *käppi,* dim. of *kappe* CAP.

ker- (also *ke-, ca-, ka-, co-, che-*) in U.S. vulgar echoic formations designed to imitate the sound of the fall of a heavy body, e.g. *kerslam, -slash, -wallop.* XIX. perh. repr. G. or Du. pp. prefix *ge-* (see Y-).

keratitis kerətai·tis inflammation of the cornea. XIX. f. Gr. *kerat-, kéras* HORN + -ITIS.

kerb kɔ̄ɹb edging of stone for a raised path, etc. XVIII (*kerb-stone*). var. of CURB with quasi-phonetic sp.

kerchief kɔ̄·ɹtʃif (arch.) cloth head-covering. XIII (Cursor M.). ME. *c(o)urchef, kerchif* – AN. *courchef* = (O)F. *couvre-, cuevrechef,* f. *couvrir* COVER + *chief* head (see CHIEF). The form *kerchief,* for **keverchief,* is from the var. *cuevrechef* (cf. ME. *kever* cover, from *cuevr-,* stressed stem of *couvrir*). Hence **handkerchief** hæ·ŋkəɹtʃif. XVI (also **-kercher**). **ne·ckerchief.** XIV (*necke couerchef, neckerchef,* Wycl. Bible).

kerf kɔ̄ɹf cut, spec. of a saw. OE. *cyrf* (ME. *kirf, kerf*) :– Germ. **kurƀiz,* f. **kurƀ-* **kerƀ-* CARVE; cf. ON. *kurfr* chip, *kyrfa* cut, and ME., mod. dial. *carf* (continuing ME. *kerf*).

kermes kɔ̄·ɹmiz, -īz pregnant female of the insect Coccus ilicis, formerly supposed to be a berry; red dye-stuff obtained therefrom; (*k. oak*) evergreen oak on which it lives XVI; (*k. mineral*) red sulphide of antimony XVIII. – F. *kermès* – Arab. (Pers.) *qirmiz* (cf. CRIMSON).

kermis kɔ̄·ɹmis fair, carnival. XVI. – Du. *kermis,* †*-misse,* f. *kerk* CHURCH + *misse* MASS[1]; orig. feast of dedication of a church accompanied by a fair.

kern[1] kɔ̄ɹn light-armed Irish foot-soldier; one of the poorer class among the 'wild Irish'. XIV. – Ir. *ceithern* (ke·hərn, ke·ərn) :– OIr. *ceitern* band of foot-soldiers. Cf. CATERAN.

kern[2] kɜːn part of a metal type extending beyond the body or shank. XVII (Moxon). perh. for **carn* ⁎ F. *carne* corner, salient angle, Norman-Picard var. of OF. *charne* – L. *cardinem, cardō* hinge (cf. CARDINAL).

kernel kɜ·ɹnəl †seed, pip; inner edible part of a nut; (dial.) enlarged gland OE.; nucleus, core XVI. OE. *cyrnel*, dim. of *corn* seed, CORN[1]; other langs. have similar formations without mutation, as MDu. *cornel* coarse meal, MHG. *kornel* a grain; see -EL[1]. The present sp. appears XIV as a var. of north. and midl. *kirnel.*

kerosene ke·rŏsīn product of distillation of petroleum, paraffin oil. XIX (patent of 1854). irreg. f. Gr. *kērós* wax + -ENE.

kerrie ke·ri, **keerie** kiə·ri (now *kierie* in S. Afr.) knobbed stick used by S. African natives. XVIII. – Hottentot or Bushman *kirri*; cf. KNOBKERRY.

kersey kɜ·ɹzi kind of coarse cloth. XIV. prob. f. name of *Kersey* in Suffolk (cf. AL. *panni cersegi* XIII, *carsea* XV, AN. *drap de kersy* XIV); hence F. †*carizé* (whence Sp., It. *carisea*), MDu. *kerzeye* (Du. *karsaai*), etc.

kerseymere kɜ·ɹzimiəɹ twilled woollen cloth. XVIII. alt. of CASSIMERE by assoc. with prec.

kestrel ke·strəl species of small hawk. XV. Earliest form *castrell*, perh. for **casserell* – dial. var. *casserelle* of F. *crécerelle*, †*cresserelle* (dial. *cristel*), f. synon. *crécelle* rattle, kestrel, perh. f. imit. base **krek-* (the bird is supposed to be so called from its cry). ¶ For the vowel cf. KEDGE.

ketch ketʃ two-masted vessel. XVII. Earlier *cache* (XV), perh. f. CATCH. ¶ For the vowel cf. KEDGE.

ketchup ke·tʃəp sauce made from mushrooms, etc. XVIII (earlier *catchup* kæ·tʃəp XVII; *catsup*, Swift). – Chinese (Amoy) *kōechiap, kē-tsiap* brine of fish; cf. Malay *kēchap* (Du. *ketjap*), which is prob. from Chinese.

ketone kī·toun (chem.) any of a class of compounds, the lowest of the series being acetone. XIX. – G. *keton* (Gmelin, 1848), alteration of *aketon* ACETONE.

kettle ke·tl vessel for boiling liquids. XIII. – ON. *ketill* = OE. *ćetel*, WS. *ćietel* (which gave ME. and dial. *chetel*), OS. (Du.) *ketel*, OHG. *kezzil* (G. *kessel*), Goth. **katils* (g.pl. *katilē*) :– CGerm. **katilaz* (whence OPruss. *catils*, Lett. *katlo*, OSl. *kotĭlŭ*, Russ. *kotël*) – L. *catillus*, dim. of *catīnus* deep vessel for serving or cooking food. Hence **ke·ttle-**DRUM drum consisting of a hollow metal hemisphere covered with parchment. XVI.

kex, kecks keks hollow stem of cow-parsnip, etc. XIV (PPl.). The var. *kix, kyx* was regularly current till XVII, and is recorded for mod. dial., together with a derived sg. *keck* (XVII), an extended form *kecksy, kexy* (XVI, *keksyes*, Sh.), also *gix, gicks*, and vars. with *a*, viz. †*casshes* (XVI–XVII), *cax(es)*; metathetic forms are *kesk, kiskey*; perh. of Celtic origin (cf. OCorn. *cegas* hemlock, W. *cegid*, Bret. *kegit* – L. *cicuta* hemlock; also Corn.-Eng. sg. *kager, kaiyer*).

key[1] kī instrument to lock and unlock. OE. *cǣġ* and *cǣġe* = OFris. *kei, kay*; not found elsewhere; of unkn. origin. The pronunc. kī is abnormal; kei (cf. *grey, clay, whey*) prevailed till *c.*1700, but evidence for forms anticipating the present pronunc. (which appears to be of north. origin) is as early as XV.

key[2] older form of QUAY; so **key·**AGE. XV.

Keys kīz pl. of KEY in spec. application to the 24 members forming the elective branch of the legislature of the Isle of Man, more fully *House of Keys*. XV. ¶ The Manx name is *Yn Kiare as Feed* 'The Four-and-Twenty'.

khaki kā·ki dull-brownish yellow; fabric of this colour. XIX (1857; used by the English troops in the Indian Mutiny). – Urdu *khākī* dusty, f. *khāk* (– Pers.) dust.

khalifa kalī·fa. XVIII. repr. Arab. original of CALIPH.

khamsin kæ·msin hot wind in Egypt lasting about 50 days. XVII. – Arab. *khamsīn*, mod. colloq. form of *khamsūn* fifty.

khan[1] kæn, kān title of rulers (later of officials, etc.) in countries of the East. XIV (Maund.). Early forms *caan, can(e), chan(e)* – OF. *chan* or medL. *ca(a)nus, canis* – Turki (hence Arab., Pers.) *khān* lord, prince, altered form of *khāqān*. Cf. CHAM.

khan[2] kæn, kān caravanserai. XIV. – Arab. *khān* inn.

khanjar kæ·ŋdʒāɹ, also **handjar** hæ·ndʒāɹ Eastern dagger. XVII. – Pers. (Arab., Turk., Urdu) *khanjar.*

khedive kėdī·v title of viceroy of Egypt. XIX. – F. *khédive*, ult. – Pers. *khedīv, khidēv* prince, sovereign, var. of *khudaiv* petty god, f. *khudā* God.

khidmutgar, kitmudhgar ki·tmətgāɹ in India, male servant at table. XVIII. – Urdu – Pers. *khidmatgār*, f. Arab. *khidmat* service + *-gār* agent-suffix.

khilat ki·lʌt dress of honour presented by a king, etc. XVII. – Arab. (Urdu, Pers.) *khilʿat*, f. *khalaʿa* reward.

kibble ki·bl large bucket used in mining. XVII. – G. *kübel* (cf. OHG. *miluh-chubilī* milk-pail) = OE. *cyfel* – medL. *cupellus, -a* corn-measure, drinking-vessel, f. *cuppa* CUP.

kibe kaib chilblain. XIV (Trevisa). prob. – W. *cibi* (also *cibwst*).

kibosh kai·bɔʃ in phr. *put the k. on* dispose of finally XIX (Dickens); sb. (app. assoc. with *bosh*) nonsense XIX. Of unkn. origin.

kick kik strike with the foot. XIV (Ch., PPl., Trevisa, Wycl. Bible). Late ME. *kike*, of unkn. origin. Hence **kick** sb. XVI. Other uses in cant or slang, viz. (1) the fashion, (2) sixpence, (3) pl. breeches XVII, are presumably connected, but in what way is unknown. ¶ W. *cicio* vb., Gael. *ceig*, Ir. *cic* sbs. are from English.

kickshaw(s) ki·kʃɔ̄(z) fancy dish in cookery; trifle, gewgaw. XVI. orig. *quelque chose, quelkchose, kickchose, kikeshawes* – F. *quelque chose* kɛkʃōz (formerly an elegant pronunc.) something.

kid[1] kid young of a goat XII (Orm); skin of a kid; (young) child XVI. – ON. *kið* :– **kiðjom*, rel. to OHG. *chizzī, kizzīn* (G. *kitze*) :– **kittīn, *kiðnīn*, f. Germ. **kið-*, of which no cogns. are known. (The *-e* of ME. *kide* is unexpl.) Hence **ki·dd**Y[6] young goat XVI; (sl., colloqu.) little child XIX.

kid[2] small tub. XVIII. perh. var. of KIT[1].

kid[3] (sl.) hoax, humbug. *c.*1810. perh. 'make a kid of', f. KID[1]; *kiddy* has been similarly used. Hence **kid** sb. humbug.

kidnapper ki·dnæ:pəɹ, U.S. *-naper* one who steals children (and others), orig. to provide servants and labourers for the American plantations. XVII. f. KID[1]+*napper*, cant word (XVII) for 'thief' (f. *nap*, var. of NAB+-ER[1]). Hence **ki·dnap** vb. XVII. Formerly stressed *kidna·p, -na·pper.*

kidney ki·dni organ that secretes urine XIV; transf. temperament, nature XVI. Of obscure origin. The existence side by side of ME. sg. *kidnei* and pl. *kidneiren* suggests that the word was a comp. of *ei* egg, pl. *eiren* (OE. *ǣġ*, pl. *ǣġru* EGG[1]), the pl. *kidneires* being partly analogical, partly due to assoc. with ME. and dial. *nere(s)* kidney(s) :– OE. **nēore*, corr. to OHG. *nioro* m. (G. *niere* fem.), ON. *nýra*, rel. to Gr. *nephrós* kidney, scrotum, L. *nefrōnes* loins. On the other hand, if the first el. is (dial.) *kid* pod (:– OE. **cydda* :– **kuddjo-*; see COD[1]), the word may have been OE. **cyd(e)nēora*, the ME. repr. of which was assoc. with *ei, eiren*, the shape of the kidney assisting the comparison.

kief see KEF.

kie-kie kī·kī N.Z. climbing plant. XIX. Maori.

kier kiəɹ vat. XVI (earlier in combs. *boiling-, brewing-, gyle-, gyling-*). – ON. *ker* vessel, tub = OHG. *char*, Goth. *kas*.

kilderkin ki·ldəɹkin cask for liquids, fish, etc.; measure of capacity. XIV. Late ME. *kilderkyn*, alteration of *kyn(d)erkyn* – MDu. *kinderkin*, var. of *kin(n)eken, -kijn*, also *kyntken, -kijn, kindeken* (Du. *kinnetje*), dim. of *kintal, quintal* (G. dial. *kindel*) – medL. *quintāle, -ālus* – Arab. *qinṭar*: see KANTAR.

kill kil †strike, beat XIII; put to death XIV. ME. *cülle, külle, kille, kelle*; these vars. point to an OE. **cyllan* :– Germ. **kuljan*, rel. by gradation to **kwaljan* kill, QUELL. ¶ For the less specific sense cf. EFris. *küllen* vex, strike, beat, OHG. *chollen* vex, kill, martyr, and OE. *slean* SLAY.

killadar ki·lədāɹ in India, governor of a fort or castle. XVIII. – Urdu (Pers.) *qil'adār*, f. Arab. *qal'ah* (pl. *qilā'*) fort+*-dār* holder.

killcrop ki·lkrɔp insatiable brat of popular folk-lore. XVII. – LG. *kīlkrop* = G. *kielkropf* (the second el. being CROP).

kiln kil, kiln furnace for burning or drying. OE. *cylene* :– **cu·lina*, for L. *culī·na* kitchen, cooking-stove (for the shift of stress cf. KITCHEN) :– **cocslīnā*, f. *coquus* COOK. For the var. *kill* and pronunc. kil cf. ELL, MILL.

kilo- ki·lo(u) F. (1795), arbitrarily f. Gr. *khílioi* thousand, in weights and measures, as *ki·logramme* (abbrev. *kilo*), *ki·lometre*, also *kilo·-*; hence in *ki·lo*WATT.

kilt kilt skirt of Highland dress. XVIII. f. north. dial. *kilt* vb. gird or tuck up, of Scand. origin (cf. Sw. dial. *kilta* swathe, Da. *kilte* (*op*) tuck up, OIcel. *kilting, kjalta* skirt, lap).

kimono kimou·nou long Jap. robe with sleeves; in Eur. use, form of dressing-gown. XIX. – Jap.; cf. KAKEMONO.

kin kin family, race; class, kind. OE. *cyn(n)* = OFris. *kin, ken, kon*, OS. *kunni* (Du. *kunne*), OHG. *chunni*, ON. *kyn*, Goth. *kuni* :– CGerm. **kunjam*, f. weak grade of **kin- *kan- *kun-* :– IE. **gen- *gon- *gn-* produce (whence Gr. *génos*, L. *genus* race, kind, sex, GENUS, Gr. *gónos, gégona* I begot, *gígnesthai* become, L. *gignere* beget). The sense 'gender, sex', which was in OE. and early ME., is the only sense in Du. *kunne*, Da. and Sw. *kön*. Cf. AKIN. Hence **ki·ns**FOLK XV, **ki·n**SHIP XIX (Mrs. Browning), **ki·ns**MAN *c.*1200, **ki·ns-**WO:MAN XIV. ¶ For other derivs. of the IE. base, see *agnate, cognate; benign, malign; nation, nature; genus, general; generate; generous; degenerate, regenerate; genius, ingenious; ingenuous, ingénue; indigenous; kind; progeny; -gen, gono-; gentile; genital, genitive, germ, germinate, germane.*

-kin kin suffix forming dims., – MDu. *-kijn, -ken*, MLG. *-kīn* = OHG. *-chīn* (G. *-chen*); of WGerm. extent, but not in OE.; first found (XIII) in personal names, which were adoptions or imitations of dim. or hypocoristic forms current in the Low Countries, e.g. *Watekin* 'little Wat or Walter', *Wilekin* 'little Will'; these have survived in surnames, as *Jenkins* (*Jenkinson*), *Watkin(s), Wilkins, Dickens* (*Dickinson*); formations on common nouns appeared in XIV, but they are not frequent till XVI (*boykin, ladykin, lambkin*); some are plain adoptions from Du. (*catkin, mannikin*); others are of obscure origin (*bumpkin, jerkin*). See also -KINS.

kinchin ki·ntʃin boy, girl, child. XVI (orig. a cant word). – G. *kindchen*, dim. (see -KIN) of *kind* child.

kincob ki·ŋkɔb rich stuff, as damask or gold brocade. XVIII. – Urdu – Pers. *kimkhāb*, f. *kimkhā* damask silk – Chinese *kimsha* smooth satiny stuff, f. *kin* gold; cf. F. *camocan* rich brocade, Russ. *kamká* damask.

kind[1] kaind †birth, descent; nature; manner; race, kin; class, genus, species. OE. *cynd, -e,* earlier *ġecynd, ġecynde* :– **gakundiz, -jam,* f. Germ. **ga-* Y - + **kunjam* KIN + **-diz* :– IE. *-tis* (abstr. suffix). Hence **ki·nd**LY[1] adj. †natural; †lawful OE.; goodnatured. XIV, **ki·nd**LY[2] adv. †naturally OE.; goodnaturedly XIII. OE. *ġecyndelič, -līče.*

kind[2] kaind †natural, native OE.; †wellborn, well-bred; naturally well-disposed XIII; showing benevolence XIV. OE. *ġecynde* :– **gakundjaz,* f. **gakundiz* KIND[1]; the prefix was dropped in early ME.

kindergarten ki·ndəɹgāɹtən school for the instruction of young children according to Fröbel's method. XIX. G., 'children's garden', f. g. pl. of *kind* child+*garten* GARDEN.

kindle[1] ki·ndl set fire to. XII (Orm). f. ON. *kynda*+-LE[3]; suggested by ON. *kindill* candle, torch.

kindle[2] ki·ndl bring forth young. XIII. ME. *kündle, kindle, kendle* perh. :– OE. **(ġe)-cyndlian,* f. *ġecynde,* in ME.; ME. *(i)cünde, kind* birth, KIND[1]; see -LE[3].

kindred ki·ndrid relationship by blood; body of persons so related, kin. XII. ME. *cün-, kinrede(n),* f. KIN+*-rēd(e),* -RED condition. ME. has also *kindreden* (perh. f. KIND[1]), but the present form appears to have arisen from intercalation of *d* between *n* and *r,* as in *thunder.*

kine kain (arch., dial.) cattle. XIII. ME. *cün, kuyn, kyne, ke(e)n,* based on OE. *cȳna,* g. pl. of *cū* COW[1].

kinema, etc., see CINEMA.

kinetic kaine·tik pert. to motion. XIX. – Gr. *kīnētikós,* f. *kīneîn* move; see CITE, -IC.

king kiŋ male sovereign ruler of a state. OE. *cyning,* later *cyng, cing* = OFris. *kin-, kon-, kening,* OS. *kuning* (Du. *koning*), OHG. *chuning* :– Germ. **kuniŋgaz* (not in Gothic; ON. *konungr* has a var. form of the suffix), whence Finnish *kuningas* king, OSl. *kŭnęzĭ* prince, Lith. *kùningas* lord, priest, KNEZ, prob. f. **kunjam* KIN+**-iŋgaz* -ING[3], as if 'scion of the (noble) race' (cf. OE. *dryhten* lord, f. *dryht* army, folk, people, ON. *fylkir* king, f. *folk* people, and Goth. *þiudans* king, f. *þiuda* people, nation). Hence **king**DOM ki·ŋdəm †kingship OE.; realm XIII (Genesis and Exodus, Cursor M.), OE. *cyningdōm*; so OS. *kuningdōm,* G. *königtum,* ON. *konungdómr.* **ki·ng**:FISHER, earlier †*king's-* (XV) small bird with a long beak and brilliant plumage, Alcedo ispida. XVI. So G. *königsfischer,* Da. *kongfiskr.* In comb. applied to large or principal features, as *king-bolt* (XIX), *-post* (XVIII). **king's evil** scrofula, for which the sovereign 'touched'. XIV (Trevisa). tr. medL. *regius morbus*; cf. OF. *le mal le roy,* MDu. *conínces evel.* ¶ Reduced forms in Germ. langs. are repr. by OE. *cyniġ* (cf. *penny*), OS. *kunig,* OHG. *künic,* G. *könig.*

kink kiŋk twist or curl in rope, etc., XVII; mental twist (orig. U.S.) XIX. orig. naut. – (M)LG. *kinke* (Du. *kink*), whence also G. *kink(e),* Sw., Da. *kink,* f. **kiŋk-* bend, var. of **kik-* (as in Icel. *kikna* bend at the knees).

kinkajou ki·ŋkədʒū quadruped of Central and S. America, honey-bear, Circoleptes caudivolvulus. XVIII. – F. *quincajou,* of N. Amer. Indian origin; cf. Algonkin *kwingwaage,* Ojibway *gwingwaage* wolverine.

kino kī·nou substance resembling catechu. XVIII. W. African (Gambia).

-kins kinz dim. suffix, var. of -KIN (from XVI) in certain oath-words, as *bodikins, lakins, maskins, pittikins,* and in words like *babykins, boykins, lambkins.*

kiosk kiɔ·sk open pavilion or summerhouse XVII; light structure for sale of newspapers, etc., XIX. – F. *kiosque* (in It. *kiosco*) – Turk. *kiūshk* pavilion – Pers. *kūshk* palace.

kipper ki·pəɹ A. (?) male salmon in the spawning season OE.; B. salmon, herring, etc., cured by rubbing with salt and drying XVIII. Of obscure history; identical in form with OE. *cypera* (*-e*?), once, in collocation with *leax* salmon = OS. *kupiro,* ME. *kypre, kiper* (XIV), *kepper* (XVI), used app. in sense B; perh. the most plausible conjecture is that of connexion with OE. *copor,* etc., COPPER[1] with allusion to the colour of the male salmon. Hence **kipper** vb. cure (fish) in the above manner. XVIII.

kirk kerk, kǝ̄ɹk (north. and Sc.) church. XII (Orm *kirrke*). – ON. *kirkja* – OE. *ċir(i)ċe* CHURCH.

kirschwasser ki·rʃva:səɹ liqueur made from wild cherries crushed. XIX. G. *kirsch(en)-wasser,* f. *kirsche* CHERRY+*wasser* WATER.

kirtle kǝ̄·ɹtl (obs. or dial.) man's tunic or coat; (arch. or dial.) woman's gown or skirt. OE. *cyrtel* = ON. *kyrtill* tunic :– Germ. **kurtilaz,* f. **kurt-,* usu. taken to be – L. *curtus* short; see CURT, -LE[1].

kismet ki·smet fate. XIX. Turk. *kismet* – Arab. (Pers.) *qismat* portion, lot, fate, f. *qasama* divide.

kiss kis salute or caress with the lips. OE. *cyssan* (pt. *cyste,* pp. *cyssed*) = OFris. *kessa,* OS. *cussian* (Du. *kussen*), OHG. *chussen* (G. *küssen*), ON. *kyssa* :– CGerm. (exc. Gothic, which has *kukjan*; cf. E Fris. *kükken*) **kussjan,* f. **kussaz* a kiss, whence OE. *coss* (to XVI), OFris. *kos,* OS. *cos, kus* (Du. *kus*), OHG. *chus* (G. *kuss*), ON. *koss.* Hence **kiss** sb. XIV, superseding *coss.*

kistvaen ki·stvain tomb constructed of stone slabs. XVIII. – W. *cist faen,* i.e. *cist* (see CHEST) and *faen* (*maen*) stone.

kit[1] kit circular wooden hooped vessel XIV (Barbour); soldier's necessaries packed in a knapsack; outfit; set, lot XVIII. – MDu. *kitte* (Du. *kit* tankard), of unkn. origin.

kit[2] (arch.) small fiddle. XVI. perh. deduced from the first syll. of L. *cithara*, Gr. *kithárā* CITHER.

kit-cat ki·tkæt title of a club of Whig politicians and men of letters. XVIII. Name of *Kit* (i.e. Christopher) *Cat* or *Catling*, keeper of the pie-house in Shire Lane by Temple Bar, London, where the club orig. met.

kitchen ki·tʃin room in which food is cooked. OE. *cyćene* = OS. **kukina* (MLG. *kökene*, MDu. *cokene*, Du. *keuken*), OHG. *chuhhina* (MHG. *küchen*, G. *küche*) :– WGerm. **ko·cina*, for **cocī·na* pop. var. (whence F. *cuisine*, It. *cucina*, etc.) of late L. *coquīna*, f. *coquere* COOK. ¶ One of the Germ. adoptions of L. terms of cookery and gardening, like *cook*, *mint*, *pepper*.

kite kait bird of prey, Milvus, OE.; toy to be flown, consisting of a light frame with a light material stretched across it XVII. OE. *cȳta*; the name, corr. to the base of MHG. *kūze* (G. *kauz*) screech-owl, and other words echoing various cries, may have been given from its shrill plaintive voice.

kith kiþ †knowledge; †native place; †one's friends, fellow-countrymen, neighbours OE.; *kith and kin* country and kinsfolk, (in mod. use) relatives generally XIV. OE. *cȳþ(þ)*, earlier *cȳþþu* = OHG. *chundida* :– Germ. **kunþiþā*, f. **kunþ-* known; see UNCOUTH.

kithe, kythe kaið (Sc. and north.) make known or manifest, display, †confess. OE. *cȳþan* = OFris. *kētha*, OS. *kūðian*, OHG. *kunden*, ON. *kynna*, Goth. *kunþjan*, f. Germ. **kunþ-* (see prec.).

kitmudhgar see KHIDMUTGAR.

kitool, kittul kitū·l jaggery palm, Caryota urens. XIX. – Cingalese *kitūl*.

kitten ki·tn young cat. XIV. Late ME. *kitoun*, *ketoun* – AN. **kitoun*, **ketoun*, var. of OF. *chitoun*, *chetoun* (mod. *chaton*), dim. of *chat* CAT; the ending was assim. to -EN[1]. Hence (dim.) **kit**[3]. XVI.

kittiwake ki·tiweik species of seagull. XVII. imit. of its cry.

kittle ki·tl (orig. Sc. and north. dial.) ticklish, risky, delicate. XVI. f. *kittle* vb. tickle, prob. of ON. origin, corr. to late OE. *kitelung* 'titillatio', noun of action from a vb. repr. by OS. *kitilōn* (Du. *kittelen*), MLG. *ketelen*, OHG. *chizzilōn*, *chuzzilōn* (G. *kitzeln*), ON. *kitla*, f. Germ. **kit-*, **kut-*.

kiwi kī·wi N.Z. bird, apteryx. XIX. Maori.

klepht kleft one of the Greeks who refused to submit to the Turks after the conquest of Greece in XV; brigand XIX. – modGr. *kléphtēs* = Gr. *kléptēs* thief; cf. next.

kleptomania kleptoumei·niə morbid tendency to theft. XIX. f. *klepto-*, comb. form of Gr. *kléptēs* thief, rel. to *kléptein* = L. *clepere*, Goth. *hlifan* steal; see MANIA.

klipspringer kli·pspri:ŋəɹ S. African antelope. XVIII. Afrikaans, f. Du. *klip* rock (see CLIFF)+*springer*, agent-noun (see -ER[1]) of *springen* SPRING.

kloof klūf (in S. Africa) ravine. XVIII. – Du. *kloof* klōf, MDu. *clove* = OHG. *chlobo* (G. *kloben*), etc. :– Germ. **kluƀon* (cf. CLEAVE[1]).

kn- initial cons. combination common to all Germ. langs. (in OE. *cn-*) and still retained by most of them with the pronunc. kn, but reduced in standard Eng. to n, which was finally established XVIII, though current earlier; the orig. pronunc. remains in some Sc. dials., in some others it has become tn.

knack næk trick, dodge XIV (Ch., Wyclif); dexterous faculty; †toy, knick-knack XVI. prob. identical with *knack* sharp blow or sound (XIV); ult. of imit. origin, but perh. immed. – Du., LG. *knak*; cf. *knap* sharp blow (XIV), trick (XVII), of similar imit. origin.

knacker næ·kəɹ A. (dial.) saddler XVI; B. dealer in old horses, horse-slaughterer, etc.; C. (dial. and sl.) old worn-out horse XIX. In A perh. orig. maker of small articles belonging to harness (f. KNACK+-ER[1]); the semantic relation of the senses is obscure.

knapsack næ·psæk stout bag for necessaries carried on the back by soldiers and travellers. XVII. – MLG. *knapsack*, Du. *knapzak*, (whence G. *knappsack*); the first el. is held to be identical with G. *knappen* bite, eat, and the second is SACK[1].

knapweed næ·pwīd species of Centaurea having its petals set on a hard globular head. XV (*knopweed*). f. KNOP+WEED[1]; altered to *knap-* XVI; cf. *strop*, *strap*.

knave neiv †boy; †male servant OE.; base fellow XIII; lowest court card of a suit XVI. OE. *cnafa* = OHG. *knabo* (G. *knabe* boy) :– WGerm. **knaƀon*, rel. obscurely to synon. OE. *cnapa* = OS. *cnapo*, and OHG. *knappo* (G. *knappe* page, squire). Hence **kna·**VERY. XVI. **kna·**VISH[1]. XIV (Ch.).

knead nīd work up (moistened flour) into bread. OE. *cnedan* pt. *cnæd*, *cnǣdon*, pp. *cneden* = OS. *knedan* (in pp. *giknedan*; Du. *kneden*), OHG. *chnetan* (G. *kneten*); WGerm. str. vb. f. **kned-* **knad-*, of which another grade appears in ON. *knoða*. Weak inflexions and analogical pp. *knoden* (cf. *trodden*) appear XIV.

knee nī the joint between the thigh and lower leg. OE. *cnēo(w)* = OFris. *kniu*, *knē*, *knī*, OS. *knio* (Du. *knie*), OHG. *chniu*, *kneo* (G. *knie*), ON. *kné*, Goth. *kniu* :– CGerm. **knewam* :– IE. **gneuom*, f. base **gneu* **geneu* **goneu* (cf. L. *genu*, Gr. *gónu* knee, *gnúx* with bent knee; also **gōn-*, Skr. *jā́nu* knee, Gr. *gōniā́* angle). So **kneel** nīl (pt., pp. *kneeled* nīld, *knelt* nelt) rest on the bent knee(s). OE. *cnēowlian*, corr. to (M)LG. *knēlen*, Du. *knielen*. The form *knelt*, which recalls *felt* and *dealt*, is of recent origin.

knell nel sound of a bell struck or rung. OE. *cnyll*, rel. to *cnyllan* **knell** vb. †bang, knock, ring a bell; the normal midland repr. of these was *knyll(e)* (XIV–XVI), of which there were ME. dial. vars. *knüll(e)*, *knell(e)*; but the present form appears to date from *c.*1500 and may be due to assoc. with *bell*. The base is WGerm. **knell*- **knall*- **knull*-; cf. MHG. *er|knellen* resound, G. *knall*, *knallen*, Du. *knal*, *knallen*, applied to banging or cracking noises.

knez knez (in Slav countries) prince, duke. XVI. – Serb. *knez*, Czech *kněz*, Russ. *knjaz'* :- OSl. *kŭnęzĭ* – Germ. **kuniŋgaz* KING.

knickerbocker ni·kəɹbɔ:kəɹ (pl.) loose-fitting breeches. XIX. f. name of Diedrich *Knickerbocker*, the pretended author of Washington Irving's 'History of New York' (1809). The name is said to have been given to the garment from its resemblance to the knee-breeches of the Dutchman in Cruikshank's illustrations to the History. abbrev. (pl.) **knickers.** *c.*1880.

knick-knack ni·knæk †pretty trick or artifice; light dainty article, trinket XVII. redupl. of KNACK, with alternation of vowel as in *dilly-dally*, *riff-raff*, etc. Hence **kni·ck-kna:ckat**ORY repository of knick-knacks. XVIII; after *conservatory*, etc.

knife naif cutting instrument consisting of a blade fitted in a handle. XI. Late OE. *cnīf* – ON. *knífr* = OFris., MLG. *knīf*, MDu. *cnijf* (Du. *knijf*) :- Germ. **knīƀaz*, of uncertain etym. Hence **knife** vb. XIX.

knight nait †boy, youth OE.; military follower; name of a rank, orig. in military service XI; *knight of the shire c.*1400. OE. *cniht* boy, youth, man of arms, hero = OFris. *knecht*, *kniucht*, OS. *knecht*, OHG. *kneht* (Du., G. *knecht*) :- WGerm. **kneχtaz*, of unkn. origin. The prevailing senses in Continental Germ. are 'servant', 'soldier', in the older periods also 'lad', 'youth'. Hence **knight-**E·RRANT. XIV. **kni·ght**HOOD. XIII (OE. *cnihthād* boyhood). **kni·ght**LY[1]. XIV (OE. *cnihtlić* boyish).

knit nit †tie in or with a knot OE.; draw close together XIV; form a close texture of yarn or thread XVI. OE. *cnyttan* = MLG., MDu. *knutten* (G. dial. *knütten*) :- WGerm. **knuttjan*, f. **knutton* KNOT[1].

knob nɔb small rounded lump or mass XIV (Ch., Trevisa); knoll; small lump of coal, etc. XVII; the head (see NOB) XVIII. – MLG. *knobbe* knot, knob, bud; cf. Flem. *knobbe(n)* lump of bread, etc., Du. *knobbel* bump, knob, knot, and KNOP, NOB, KNUB, NUB.

knobkerry nɔ·bke:ri stick with a knobbed head in S. Africa (where usu. spelt *knopkierie*). XIX. f. KNOB + KERRIE, after Afrikaans *knopkierie*.

knock nɔk strike with a sounding blow. OE. *cnocian* = MHG. *knochen*, ON. *knoka*; f. imit. base (cf. the similar and synon. OE. *cnucian*, MLG. *knaken*, Sw. *knaka*).

knoll[1] noul †summit of a hill; hillock, mound. OE. *cnoll*, corr. to MDu. *knolle* clod, ball (Du. *knol* turnip, tuber), MHG. *knolle* clod (G. *knolle(n)* clod, lump, tuber), ON. *knollr* mountain summit, Norw. *knold* clod, tuber, perh. :- Germ. **knuđlō*, f. base of KNOT[1]; for the formation G. cf. *knödel* seed-bud. ¶ Parallel forms with a different initial are OHG. *hnol* round eminence, *nollo* hill, Du. *nol* hill.

knoll[2] noul toll, ring a knell. XV. f. late ME. *knoll* church bell, tolling, perh. imit. alteration of KNELL.

knop nɔp small round protuberance XIV (Ch.); bud of a flower XIV (Wycl. Bible). prob. – MLG., MDu. *knoppe* (Du. *knop*) = OFris. *knop*, OHG. *chnoph* (G. *knopf* knob, knot, button); the parallel *knap* (XIV) appears to be – ON. *knappr* knob, stud, button; ult. connexions unknown.

knot[1] nɔt intertwining of parts of rope, etc. (fig. something intricate) OE.; hard lump XIII (AncrR.); thickened tissue of a plant (Trevisa); cluster or small group XIV. OE. *cnotta* = Du. *knot*, MLG. *knotte*, MHG. *knotze* knob, knot :- WGerm. **knutton* :- **knudn*-; from other grades are OHG. *chnodo*, *chnoto* (G. *knoten*) :- **knuda·n*, *knu·þan*, ON. *knútr* knot, *knúta* (whence Russ. *knut* KNOUT) :- **knūdn*-, and ON. *knǫttr* (:- **knattuz*) ball. Hence **knot** vb. XVI. **kno·tt**ED[1]. XII (Peterborough Chron.).

knot[2] nɔt red-breasted sandpiper. XVI. Of unkn. origin; later vars. were *knat*, *gnat*. ¶ Camden's conjecture (followed by Drayton, and perpetuated in Linnæus's specific name *Canutus*) that the bird was named after King Canute (*Cnūt*), 'because believed to be a visitant from Denmark', has no foundation.

knout naut, nūt whip, scourge. XVIII. – F. *knout* – Russ. *knut* – Icel. *knútr* (see KNOT[1]).

know nou, pt. **knew** njū, pp. **known** noun perceive, recognize, distinguish XI; be acquainted or familiar with; be aware of or conversant with, apprehend as fact or truth XII. Late OE. (rare) *cnāwan* (in pr. subj. and pp.), earlier *ġecnāwan*, pt. *ġecnēow*, pp. *ġecnāwen*, corr. to OHG. -*cnāen*, -*cnāhen*, ON. pr. ind. *kná*, pl. *knegum*. In the earliest OE. and in OHG. this vb. appears only in comps.; it is absent from LG. and Du. areas and from Gothic; in ON. it had lost the pres. inf. and meant 'can', (as an aux.) 'do', and in OHG. it had lost the orig. str. pt. and pp. An orig. redupl. vb. based on IE. **gn*- **gnē*- **gnō*-, repr. also by CAN[2], KEN[1], and L. *nōscere* (pt. *nōvī*) *cognōscere*, Gr. *gignṓskein*, OSl. *znati*, Skr. *jānā́ti* know, OIr. *gnáth*, Gr. *gnōtós*, Skr. *jñātás* known. ¶ Other derivs. of the IE. base are *cognition*, *incognito*, *noble*, *ignoble*, *notify*, *notion*, *ignorant*, *narrate*.

knowledge nɔ·lidʒ, (arch.) nou·lidʒ †confession; fact of knowing, acquaintance. XIII (Cursor M.). In earliest use north. (*knaulage*), later in gen. use *knowleche*, -*lache*; prob.

f. †**knowledge** vb. acknowledge, recognize (XIII), early ME. *cnaw-*, *cnouleche* :- OE. **cnāwlǣċan* implied in **cnāwlæċung* (a parallel *cnāweläċing* is recorded), f. (*ġe*)*cnāwan* know+*-lǣċan*, f. *lāc* (see -LOCK). Hence **know·ledg(e)ABLE** †(f. the vb.) recognizable XVII; (f. the sb.; orig. dial.) well informed XIX. ¶ For *-dge* cf. PARTRIDGE.

knub nʌb small lump or swelling. XVI (Levins). - MLG. *knubbe*, var. of *knobbe* KNOB.

knuckle nʌ·kl †end of a bone at a joint XIV; spec. bone at a finger-joint XV. Late ME. *knokel* - MLG. *knökel*, corr. to OFris. *knok(e)le*, MDu. *knokel*, *knökel* (Du. *kneukel*), MHG. *knuchel*, *knüchel* (G. *knöchel*), dim. of the base of MLG. *knoke* (Du. *knok*), MHG. *knoche* (G. *knochen*) bone, perh. ult. rel. to KNEE.

knut nʌt, (also) kənʌ·t joc. var. of NUT in sense 'fashionable smart young man', *c.*1910.

koa kou·ə species of acacia of the Sandwich Islands. XIX. Hawaian.

koala kouā·lə Australian arboreal marsupial. XIX. - native names *kūlla*, *kūlā*. The current form *koala* arose perh. as a misreading of *koola*, which was formerly current.

kobold kou·bəld (in G. folk-lore) familiar spirit, goblin, gnome. XIX. - G. *kobold*, MHG. *kobolt* = MDu. *cobout* (Du. *kabouter*), perh. for **kobwalt*, f. *kobe* house, COVE[1]+stem of *walten* rule (see WIELD); cf. OE. *cofgodas*, *-godu* 'house-gods', lares and penates. Cf. COBALT.

kodak kou·dæk photographic camera. XIX. Arbitrary word invented by George Eastman as a trade-mark, patented 1888.

koh-i-noor kouinuə·ɹ famous Indian diamond; also gen. XIX (Thackeray). - Pers. *kōh-i nūr* mountain of light.

kohl koul powder used to darken the eyelids. XVIII. - Arab. *koḥl*; cf. ALCOHOL.

kohl-rabi koulrā·bi cabbage with turnip-like stem. - G. *kohlrabi* - (with assim. to *kohl* COLE) It. *cauli* or *cavoli rape*, pl. of *cavolo rapa* (whence F. *chou-rave*), repr. medL. *caulorapa*; see COLE, RAPE.

koodoo, kudu kū·dū large antelope. XVIII. Xosa-Kaffir (*iqudu*).

kookri see KUKRI. **koola(h)** see KOALA.

kopje, koppie kə·pi small hill in S. Africa. XIX. - Du. *kopje*, Afrikaans *koppie*, dim. of *kop* head = OE. *copp*, (O)HG. *kopf*.

koran kŏrā·n, kōə·rən sacred book of Islam. XVIII (*currawn*). - Arab. *qurān* recitation, f. *qara'a* read; cf. ALCORAN.

Korean, also formerly **Corean** kŏrī·ən pert. to (native of) Korea (Corea), a peninsula in E. Asia. XVIII. f. *Korea*, the Jap. name of which was *Chosen* (*cho sun* 'land of morning calm'); see -AN.

kosher kou·ʃəɹ adj. and sb. of meat prepared according to Jewish law. XIX. - Heb. *kāshēr* right.

kotal kou·təl mountain pass. XIX. Pushto.

kotow, kow-tow koutau·, kautau· Chinese gesture of respect by touching the ground with the forehead. XIX. - Chinese *k'o-t'ou*, f. *k'o* knock+*t'ou* head. Hence vb. act obsequiously. XIX (Disraeli).

kotwal kə·twāl chief officer of police in India. XVI. - (Hindi, Urdu) Pers. *kotwāl*.

koumiss kū·mis fermented liquor made from mare's milk. XVII (*chumis*; earlier in corrupt forms *cosmos*, *cosmus*). - F. *koumis*, G. *kumyss*, Pol. *komis*, *kumys*, Russ. *kumys*, - Tatar *kumiz*.

kourbash, courbash kuə·ɹbæʃ whip of (hippopotamus) hide. XIX. - Arab. *qurbāsh* - Turk. *qirbāch* whip; cf. F. *courbache*.

kraal krāl Central or S. African village; cattle enclosure XVIII. - Afrikaans *kraal* - Pg. *curral*, CORRAL.

kraken krā·kən enormous mythical sea-monster. XVIII. - Norw. *kraken* (*-n* is the suffixed def. art.).

krantz krænts (in S. Africa usu. **krans**) wall of rock. XIX. - Afrikaans, Du. *krans* coronet, chaplet - OHG., (MH)G. *kranz* coronet, circle, encircling ring of mountains, f. a base meaning 'ring'.

Kremlin kre·mlin citadel in a Russian town. XVII. - F. *kremlin* - Russ. *kreml'* citadel, of Tatar origin.

kreutzer kroi·tsəɹ small coin of Germany and Austria, orig. stamped with a cross, XVI (*crocherd*, Boorde). - G. *kreuzer*, f. *kreuz* CROSS, after medL. *denarius crucigerus* 'cross-bearing penny'.

kriegspiel krī·gspīl, ‖krī·kʃpīl game simulating movements in warfare. XIX. G., 'war-game'.

kris(s) see CREESE.

krummhorn kru·mhōɹn obs. wind-instrument; organ reed-stop (see CROMORNE, CREMONA[2]) XVII. G., 'crooked horn'.

krypton kri·ptən (chem.) rare gas discovered by William Ramsay 1898. - Gr. *kruptón*, n. of *kruptós* hidden (see CRYPTIC).

kudos kjū·dəs renown. XVIII (Coleridge). - Gr. *kûdos*.

Ku-Klux-Klan kjūklʌksklæ·n U.S. secret society. XIX. Fanciful invention said to be based on Gr. *kúklos* circle, CYCLE, and CLAN.

kukri, also formerly **kookri** ku·kri curved knife used by Gurkhas. XIX. - Hindi *kukṛī*.

kulak kū·læk well-to-do Russian farmer or trader; peasant proprietor. XIX. - Russ., 'fist', 'close-fisted person'.

kultur kultū·r civilization as conceived by the Germans. XX. G., - L. *cultūra* CULTURE.

kumara, -era ku·mərə (N.Z.) sweet potato, Ipomæa. XVIII. Maori.

kummel ku·məl, prop. *kümmel* küməl German liqueur flavoured with cummin. XIX. - G. *kümmel*, in OHG. *kumil*, var. of *kumīn* - L. (Rom.) *cumīnum* CUMMIN.

kunkur kʌ·ŋkəɹ coarse limestone of India. XIX. – Hindi *kankar* – Prakrit *kakkaram*, Skr. *karkaram*.

kuphar ku·fəɹ circular coracle. XVIII. – Arab. *quffah* circular basket or wicker boat.

kursaal kū·rzāl public building for the use of visitors at a health resort. XIX (Thackeray). G., f. *cur, kur* – L. *cūra* CURE + *saal* hall, room.

kvass kvæs fermented beverage of Russia. XVI (*quass*). Russ. *kvas* (OSl. *kvasŭ* yeast :– **kwātsa-*), cogn. with L. *cāseus* CHEESE (f. **cāso-* :– **kwātso-*).

kyanize kai·ənaiz treat (wood) so as to prevent decay. XIX. f. name of the inventor J. H. *Kyan* (1832) + -IZE.

kyloe kai·lou; also locally *kyley*, etc., repr. old vars. of the Nhb. place-name *Kyloe* (OE. *cȳ-lēah* cow pasture). One of a small long-horned breed of Highland cattle. XIX.

kyrie kiə·riei, -ii, kaiə·ri XVI; short for **kyrie eleison** kiə·riei èlei·isɔn XIV. medL. repr. of Gr. Κύριε ἐλέησον (Kúrie eleḗson) Lord, have mercy, as in the Gr. text of Ps. cxxii(i) 3, Matt. xx 30, 31.

kyrielle kirie·l form of French verse in which couplets end with the same word, which serves as a refrain. XIX. F., f. *kyrie eleison* (see prec.).

kythe see KITHE.

L

la.[1] lā sixth note of the scale. XIV; see UT.

la[2] lā †excl. accompanying a conventional phr. or form of address; later, a mild substitute for *Lord!* or its var. *Lard!* XVI (Sh.). Weakened form of LO; cf. 'They cannot forgeue loe' (T. More), beside 'You doe your selfe wrong indeede—la', and 'La you' (Sh.).

laager lā·gəɹ encampment. XIX. – Afrikaans *lager* (now *laer*) = G. *lager*, Du. *leger*; see LAIR, LEAGUER.

labarum læ·bərəm Roman standard of the late Empire. XVII. – late L. (Prudentius, Tertullian), whence Byz. Gr. *labarón*.

labdanum læ·bdənəm. XVI. med. form of L. *lādanum* (see LADANUM).

labefaction læbifæ·kʃən overthrow, downfall. XVII. f. *labefact-*, pp. stem of L. *labefacere* weaken, f. *labī* fall (see LAPSE)+*facere* make, DO[1]; see -TION.

label lei·bəl †narrow band or strip XIV; narrow strip carrying the seal of a document XVI; slip containing name or description of an object XVII; dripstone XIX. – OF. *label* ribbon, fillet (now *lambeau* rag), prob. – Germ. form rel. to LAP[1], with dim. suffix. Hence vb. XVI (Sh.).

labial lei·biəl pert. to the lips. XVI. – medL. *labiālis*, f. *labia* lips; see LIP, -AL[1]. So **labi**ATE[2] lei·bieit lipped. XVIII. – modL.

labile læ·bail prone to fall. XV. – late L. *lābilis*, f. *lābī* fall, LAPSE; see -ILE.

laboratory læ·bərətəri, ləbɔ·rətəri building set apart for (scientific) research. XVII. – medL. *labōrātōrium*, f. *labōrāt-*, *-āre*; see next and -ORY[1]. Abbrev. **lab** læb. XIX.

labour, U.S. **labor** lei·bəɹ toil, work XIII (Cursor M.); travail of childbirth XVI (Spenser). – OF. *labour, labor* (mod. *labeur* ploughing) – L. *labōrem*, nom. *labor* exertion, trouble, suffering, perh. orig. burden under which one staggers, rel. to *labāre* slip (see LAPSE). So **la·bour** vb. XIV ('till, cultivate'). – (O)F. *labourer* (now chiefly, plough) – Pr. *lavorar* – L. *labōrāre*, f. *labōr-*. **la·bourer.** XIV. – (O)F. *laboureur*; see -ER[1], -ER[2]. **labor**IOUS ləbɔ̄ə·riəs. XIV (Gower; contemp. with †*laborous*, Ch.). – (O)F. *laborieux* – L. *labōriōsus*. Cf. *collaborate, elaborate.* ¶ The Rom. sense of 'ploughing' is developed from L. *boum labores* 'works of oxen', *laborare frumenta ceterosque fructus* cultivate corn and other crops.

laburnum ləbɔ̄·ɹnəm leguminous tree with yellow pendulous flowers. XVI. – L. (Pliny), prob. of foreign origin.

labyrinth læ·bĭrinþ structure made of intercommunicating passages of bewildering complexity. XVI. – F. *labyrinthe* or L. *labyrinthus* – Gr. *labúrinthos*, of non-Hellenic origin. ¶ Several deriv. adjs. have been used: *labyri·nthal* (rare) XVII, †*labyri·nthial* (XVI), *labyri·nthian* (XVI), *labyri·nthic* (XVII), *labyri·nthical* (XVII), *labyri·nthine* (XVII), the last of which remains alone in gen. use.

lac[1] læk dark-red resin, red dye. XVI (*lack(e)*, *lacca*). – (through Du. *lak*, F. *laque*, or Sp., Pg. *laca*, It. *lacca*) Hind. *lākh* :– Prakrit *lakkha* :– Skr. *lākshā*. Cf. LAKE[2], SHELLAC.

lac[2] see LAKH.

lace leis †noose, snare; string or cord for tying XIII; ornamental braid; openwork of cotton, silk, etc. XVI. ME. *las, laas*, (later) *lace* – OF. *laz, las* (mod. *lacs* noose) = Pr. *latz*, Sp. *lazo*, It. *laccio*, Rum. *laţ* :– CRom. **lacium*, for L. *laqueu-s* noose, rel. to *lax* deception, *lacere*, *-licere* entice (cf. DELIGHT). So **lace** vb. XIII. – OF. *lacier* (mod. *lacer*) = Pr. *lasar*, Sp. *lazar*, It. *lacciare* :– CRom. **laciāre*.

lacerate læ·səreit tear the flesh of. XVI. f. pp. stem of L. *lacerāre*, f. *lacer* mangled, torn; see -ATE³.

lacertian ləsə̄·ɹʃiən, -tiən pert. to the lizards. XIX. f. L. *lacerta* LIZARD + -IAN. So **lace·rt**INE¹.

laches læ·tʃiz remissness, neglect XIV (PPl., Gower); (leg.) negligence in the performance of a legal duty XVI. – AN. *laches(se)* = OF. *laschesse* (mod. *lâchesse* cowardice), f. *lasche* (mod. *lâche*) = Pr. *lasc* :– Rom. **lascus*, for L. *laxus* LAX; see -ESS².

lachryma Christi læ·krimə kri·stai strong sweet wine of S. Italy. XVII. L., 'tear of Christ'; in It. *lagrima* (or *-e*) *di Cristo*.

lachrymal læ·kriməl pert. to tears. XVI. – medL. *lachrymālis*, *lacrimālis*, f. *lacrima*, earlier *lacruma* tear, rel. to Gr. *dákru*; see -AL¹. The sp. with *ch* and *y* reflects medL. practice; *y* is retained in Eng. by assoc. with the Gr. word. So **la·chrymat**ORY¹ tear-vase. XVII (Sir T. Browne): after *chrismatory*, etc.

la·chrymOSE tearful. XVII. – L. **la·chrym**OUS. XV (Caxton).

laciniate ləsi·nieit (nat. hist.) jagged, slashed. XVIII. f. L. *lacīnia* tuft, fringe, skirt of a garment + -ATE².

lack læk vb. †be wanting XII; †blame, disparage XIII; be without XIV. So **lack** sb. †defect, fault XII; want, need XIV. The early appearance of these words and the existence of several cogns. suggest the possibility of a CGerm. **lak-* orig. expressing 'deficiency', 'defect', which may have been actually repr. in OE.; cf. OFris. *lek* blame, *lackia*, *leckia*, MLG., MDu. *lak* deficiency, fault, blame (Du. *lak* calumny), *laken* be wanting, blame, ON. *lakr* defective, ODa. *lakke* depreciate; but some uses may be of Scand. or LG. origin.

lackadaisical lækədei·zikəl marked by vapid sentiment. XVIII (Sterne). prop. given to affected or languishing exclamation; f. *lackadaisy* (XVIII), extended form of *lack-a-day* (XVII), aphetic of *alack-a-day*, earlier ALACK *the day* (Sh.) + -ICAL.

lackey, lacquey læ·ki footman, valet. XVI. Formerly also *alakay* (XVI, Sc.) – F. *laquais*, †*alaquais* (whence also It. *lacchè*, Pg. *halaqué*, and G. *lakai*) – Cat. *alacay* (whence also Sp. *(a)lacayo*, Pg. *lacayo*) = Sp., Pg. *alcaide* ALCALDE. Hence as vb. XVI.

laconic ləkɔ·nik (*L-*) Lacedæmonian, Spartan; brief of speech. XVI. – L. *Lacōnicus* – Gr. *Lakōnikós*, f. *Lákōn* member of the Spartan race, renowned for brevity of speech (cf. *βραχυλογία τις Λακωνική*, Plato); see -IC.

lacquer, U.S. **lacker** læ·kəɹ †lac (the dye) XVI; varnish made from a solution of shellac in alcohol XVII. Earlier *la(c)ker* – F. †*lacre* kind of sealing-wax, Sp., Pg. *lacre*, It. †*lacra*; app. unexpl. var. or extension of Sp., Pg. *laca* LAC¹.

lacrosse ləkrɔ·s N. Amer. ball-game played with a racket-like implement called *crosse*. XVIII (*La Crosse*). f. F. (*le jeu de*) *la crosse* '(the game of) the hooked stick'. (O)F. *crosse* prob. – Germ. **krukjō* CRUTCH.

lact- lækt stem of L. *lac*, g. *lactis* milk (cf. Gr. *gála*, g. *gálaktos*; see GALAXY) in derivs.: **lact**A·TION suckling XVII (f. L. *lactāre*), **la·cte**AL¹ XVII (f. L. *lacteus*), **la·ct**EOUS XVII (Sir T. Browne), **lact**E·SCENT XVII milky, secreting a milky juice (f. L. *lactēscere*), **la·ct**IC (chem.) XVIII, whence **la·ct**ATE¹ XVIII, **lacti·**FEROUS XVII (Ray), irreg. comb. form **lacto-** XIX, **la·ct**OSE² XIX.

lacuna ləkjū·nə gap, hiatus. XVII. – L. *lacūna* pool, pond, ditch, cavity, cleft, orig. fem. of an adj. (sc. *aqua*; 'water collected in a hollow'), f. *lacus* LAKE¹.

lacrim-, lacrym- see LACHRIMAL, etc.

lacustrine ləkʌ·strain pert. to a lake. XIX. f. L. *lacus* LAKE¹, after *palūster* marshy (f. *palūs* marsh); see -INE¹.

lad læd †serving-man, varlet XIII (Havelok); youth, young fellow XVI. ME. *ladde*, of unkn. origin; the earliest evidence and even modern currency point to concentration in the east and west midlands and so perh. to Scand. origin (cf. Norw. *aske|ladd* neglected child, (cap.) Boots, *tusse|ladd* duffer, muff). Hence **la·dd**IE. XVI.

ladanum læ·dənəm gum resin derived from Cistus. XVI. – L. *lādanum* – Gr. *lā́danon*, *lḗdanon*, f. *lêdon* mastic.

ladder læ·dəɹ appliance consisting of parallel bars or steps fixed in a close series for ascending and descending. OE. *hlǣd(d)er* = OFris. *hlēdere*, MDu. *lēdere* (Du. *leer*), OHG. *leitara* (G. *leiter*) :– WGerm. **χlaidr-*, f. **χlai-* **χli-* (see LEAN²).

lade leid A. load (a ship, etc.); B. draw (water, etc.), bale. OE. *hladan*, pt. *hlōd*, pp. *ġehladen*, corr. to OFris. *hlada*, OS., OHG. *hladan* (Du., G. *laden*), ON. *hlaða*, Goth. *-hlaþan*; CGerm. str. vb. rel. to OSl. *kladą*, *klasti* lay, place. Cf. LAST². Hence **la·d**ING¹. XV.

la-di-da, lardy-dardy lādidā·(di) affectedly 'swell'. XIX. imit. of 'haw-haw' style of speech.

Ladin ladī·n denoting a group of Romance dialects spoken in the Grisons, the Engadine, and Friuli (Switzerland). – It. *ladino* – L. *Latīnu-s* LATIN.

ladle lei·dl deep long-handled spoon. OE. *hlædel*, f. *hladan* LADE¹; see -LE¹.

lady lei·di †mistress of a household; (arch.) female ruler; (*Our L.*) the Virgin Mary OE.; woman of superior position (hence as a title); wife XIII; woman of refinement XIX. OE. *hlǣfdīġe*, f. *hlāf* LOAF + *-*dīġ-* knead (cf. OE. *dǣġe* kneader of bread, female (farm) servant, dairy-woman, corr. to ON. *deigja* servant-maid, dairy-maid, housekeeper; also DOUGH); like LORD, peculiar to Eng. In ME. there were normal parallel developments *laddi, leddi*, the latter surviving in Sc. *leddy*; the form *lady* descends from ME. *lavedi*. The OE. g. *hlǣfdiġan* (ME. *ladie*) is repr. in *Lady Day* (ME. *ure lefdi day* XIII, i.e. 'Our Lady's day'); so *Lady chapel* XV; also in plant-names, as *lady smock* XVI (contrast *lady's laces, mantle, slipper, thistle*), and *lady-bird*; cf. G. *Marienhuhn*; earlier *lady-cow* (cf. G. *Marienkuh*) and *cow-lady*.

lag[1] læg fail to keep pace, fall behind. XVI. contemp. with **lag** sb.[1] last or hindmost person, and adj. hindmost, falling behind, which may be a perversion of LAST[3] in the series *fog, seg, lag*, which is used dial. in children's games for 'first, second, last'.

lag[2] læg †carry off, steal XVI; (sl.) transport, apprehend XIX. Of. unkn. origin. Hence **lag** sb.[2] (sl.) convict; term of penal servitude. XIX.

lag[3] læg stave of a barrel XVII; lath or strip of material in a covering or casing (whence vb.) XIX. prob. of Scand. origin, cf. Icel. *laggar*, Sw. *lagg* stave (*laggkärl* cask), ON. *lǫgg* rim of a barrel, f. **lag-* LAY[1].

lagan læ·gən goods or wreckage on the sea bottom. XVI. – OF. *lagan* (whence medL. *laganum*), perh. f. ON. *lagn-*, as in *lǫgn*, g. *lagnar* drag-net, f. **lag-* LAY[1].

lager (beer) lā·gəɹbiə·ɹ light kind of beer. XIX. – G. *lagerbier* 'beer for keeping', f. *lager* store (cf. LAAGER, LEAGUER[2]) + *bier* BEER.

lagoon ləgū·n area of brackish water separated from the sea. XVII. – It., Sp. *laguna* (partly through F. *lagune*) :– L. *lacūna* pool (see LACUNA).

laic lei·ik lay. XVI. – late L. *lāicus* LAY[3]. So **la·ic**AL. XVI; **laic**IZE lei·isaiz. XIX.

laidly lē·dli (Sc.) offensive, hideous. XIII (*laithly*, Cursor M.). north. var. of LOATHLY.

lair lɛəɹ †lying down; grave, tomb (Sc. graveyard plot); bed, couch OE.; animal's place of rest XV. OE. *leġer* = OFris. *leger* situation, OS. *legar* bed (Du. *leger* bed, camp, LEAGUER[2]), OHG. *leger* bed, camp (G. *lager*, infl. by *lage* situation; cf. LAGER), Goth. *ligrs*; f. **leg-* (see LIE[1]).

laird lɛəɹd (Sc.) landed proprietor. XV. Sc. form of LORD (north. ME. *laverd*). ¶ For the vocalism cf. BAIRN.

laity lei·ĭti body of lay people. XVI. f. LAY[3] + -ITY; in AN. *laité* (XIV) was used for 'lay property'.

lake[1] leik body of water surrounded by land; †pond, pool XIII; †pit, grave XIV. Early ME. *lac* – (O)F. *lac* – L. *lacu-s* basin, tub, tank, lake, pool, pit, rel. to Gr. *lákkos* hole, ditch, Gael., Ir. *loch* LOCH, LOUGH, OE. *lagu*, ON. *lǫgr* sea, water, OSl. *ląka* marsh. The present form, with long vowel, dating from late XIII, may be due to assim. to OE. *lacu* stream, or to independent adoption of L. *lacus*.

lake[2] leik reddish pigment. XVII. unexpl. var. of LAC[1].

lakh læk hundred thousand (of rupees). XVII. – Hind. *lākh* :– Skr. *laksha* mark, sign, token, 100,000.

Lallan(s) læ·lən; also *Lallans* sb., Scottish dialect. XVIII (Burns). Sc. var. of LOWLAND(S).

lallation lælei·ʃən †childish utterance; pronunciation of r approaching that of l. XVII. – L. **lallātiō(n-)*, f. *lallāre* (Persius) make lulling sounds, such as *lalla*.

lam læm beat soundly. XVI. perh. of Scand. origin (cf. Norw., Da. *lamme* lame, paralyse, based on *lam-* of ON. *lamði* pt., *lamiðr* pp. of *lemja* beat so as to cripple, LAME. Hence synon. (dial.) **lam**BASTE læmbei·st. XVII; preceded by †*lamback* (XVI).

lama lā·mə Buddhist priest of Mongolia and Tibet. XVII. Tibetan *blama* (with silent *b*). So **lamas**ERY lama·səri monastery of lamas. XIX. – F. *lamaserie* (P. E.-R. Huc, *c.*1850), irreg. f. *lama*.

lamantin ləmæ·ntin MANATEE. XVII. – F. *lamantin, -entin*, alteration of Sp. *manaté*, perh. by assoc. with *lamenter* and ref. to the animal's wailing cry.

lamb læm young of the sheep. OE. *lamb* (Nhb. nom. sg. *lemb* :– **lambiz*), pl. *lambru* (Nhb. *lombor, lomboro*) = OFris., OS., OHG. *lamb* (Du. *lam*, G. *lamm*), ON., Goth. *lamb* (in Goth. 'sheep') :– CGerm. **lambaz* (n. of a class corr. to Gr. n. nouns in *-os*, L. in *-us*, as *génos, genus*), adopted in Finn. *lammas*; no certain cogns. are known outside Germ. Hence **lamb** vb. XVII. **la·mb**KIN. XVI (Spenser, Sh.).

lambda læ·mbdə 11th letter of the Gr. alphabet. XIV (Maund.), XVII (Holland). Gr. *lámbda, lábda*. So **la·mbdac**ISM, **la·bda-c**ISM too frequent repetition of l; faulty pronunciation of r resembling l. – late L. *la(m)bdacismus* – Gr. *la(m)bdakismós* (with interpolated *k*). **la·mbd**OID lambda-shaped. XVI. – F. *lambdoïde* – modL. – Gr. *lambdoeidḗs*. -OI·DAL. XVII.

lambent læ·mbənt (of flame) playing lightly upon a surface, shining with soft clear heat. XVII (Cowley). – L. *lambent-, -ēns*, prp. of *lambēre* lick, rel. to LAP[2].

lamboys læ·mboiz (antiq.) skirt in steel of Tudor armour. XIX. Taken up by antiquaries from *lamboys* in Hall's Chronicle of Henry IV, where it may be an error for *Jamboys*, i.e. *jambeaux* (leg-pieces).

lambrequin læ·mbrəkin scarf worn over a helmet XVIII; (U.S.) cornice with a valance, pelmet XIX. – F. *lambrequin* – Du. **lamperkin*, dim. of *lamper* veil; see -KIN.

lame leim crippled or maimed, esp. in the leg. OE. *lama* = OFris. *lam, lom*, OS. *lamo* (Du. *lam*), OHG. *lam* (G. *lahm*), ON. *lami* :- CGerm. (exc. Goth.) **lamon*, orig. weak in the limbs, rel. to OHG. *luomi* dull, slack, gentle, OSl. *lomiti* break. Hence **lame** vb. XIII; first in pp. after ON. *lamiðr*; repl. OE. *lemian* = ON. *lemja* (pt. *lamða*, pp. *lamiðr*).

lamella ləme·lə thin plate. XVII. – L., dim. of LAMINA.

lament ləme·nt demonstrative expression of grief. XVI (Sh.). – L. *lāmentum*; or f. **lament** vb. XVI. – F. *lamenter* or L. *lāmentārī*. So (earlier) **lament**ABLE læ·məntəbl. XV, **lament**A·TION. XIV. – (O)F. or L.

lamia lei·miə fabulous monster with the body of a woman. XVII. L. – Gr. *Lámia* female monster that devoured children, voracious fish.

lamina læ·minə thin plate or scale. XVII. – L. *lāmina, lammina*. Hence **la·min**ATE[2], **-at**ED[1]. XVII.

Lammas læ·məs 1st August, the feast of St. Peter in Chains, observed in A.-S. England by the consecration of bread made from the first ripe corn. OE. *hlāfmæsse*, f. *hlāf* LOAF+*mæsse* festival, MASS[1].

lammergeyer læ·məɹgaiəɹ bearded vulture, Gypætus barbatus. XIX. – G. *lämmergeier*, f. *lämmer*, g. pl. of *lamm* LAMB+*geier* vulture.

lamp læmp vessel containing a substance burnt for the purpose of illumination. XII ('Vices and Virtues'). – (O)F. *lampe* = Pr. *lampe(z)a*, Sp. *lampana*, It. *lampada, -ana* :- late L. *lampada*, f. acc. of *lampas* – Gr. *lampás, lampad-* torch, rel. to *lámpein* shine. comp. **la·mp**BLACK. XVI.

lampas[1] læ·mpəs swelling of the fleshy lining of the mouth in horses. XVI. – (O)F. *lampas*, prob. f. dial. *lãpá* throat, *lãpé* gums, f. nasalized var. of Germ. **lap-* LAP[2].

lampas[2] læ·mpəs A. †glossy crape XIV; B. flowered silk from China XIX. In A prob. – Du. †*lampers* (now *lamfer*); in B – F. *lampas*, †*-asse*, which may be a different word.

lampion læ·mpiən pot of (usu.) coloured glass with oil and wick, used in illuminations. XIX (Thackeray). – F. *lampion* – It. *lampione*, f. F. *lampe* LAMP.

lampoon læmpū·n virulent or scurrilous satire. XVII. – F. *lampon*, said to be f. *lampons* let us drink (used as a refrain), 1st pl. imper. of *lamper* gulp down, booze, nasalized form of *laper* LAP[2]; see -OON. Hence vb. XVII.

lamprey læ·mpri fish having a sucker-like mouth. XII (XIII). – OF. *lampreie* (mod. *lamproie*) = Pr. *lampre(z)a*, Sp. *lamprea*, It. *lampreda* :- medL. *lamprēda* (VIII), whence also OE. *lamprede*, Du. *lampreide*, OHG. *lampreta*, possibly alteration of *lampetra* (V), which is expl. as f. *lambere* lick+*petra* stone (with allusion to the lamprey attaching itself to stones). Cf. LIMPET.

lance làns weapon with a long shaft and an iron or steel head. XIII. – (O)F. *lance* = Pr. *lansa*, Sp. *lanza*, It. *lancia* :- L. *lancea*, of alien origin (Iberian acc. to Varro, from Gr. *lógkhē* acc. to Festus, but prob. Celtic). The F. word was adopted into the Germ. langs. *Lance corporal* (XVIII) was based on LANCEPESADE; *lance sergeant* (XIX) was analogical. So **lance** vb. fling, hurl; (dial.) spring, bound; pierce, make incision in XIV. – (O)F. *lancer*, †*-ier*, f. *lance*; cf. LAUNCH[1]. **la·nc**ER[2] soldier armed with a lance. XVI. – F. *lancier*; cf. late L. *lanceārius*.

lancegay là·nsgei (arch.) kind of lance. XIV (Ch.). – OF. *lancegaye*, perh. alteration, by assoc. with LANCE, of *l'archegaye* ASSEGAI.

lanceolate læ·nsiŏleit shape like a spearhead. XVIII. – late L. *lanceolātus*, f. *lanceola*, dim. of L. *lancea* LANCE; see -ATE[2].

lancepesade lànspĭzā·d (hist.) lance-corporal. XVI. – F. †*lancepessade* (now *anspessade*) 'the meanest officer in a foot company' (Cotgr.) – It. *lancia spezzata* soldier on a forlorn hope, devoted adherent, lit. broken lance, i.e. *lancia* LANCE, *spezzata*, fem. pp. of *spezzare* break :- Rom. **dispettiāre* (DIS-, PIECE); vars. with *-pres-*, *-pris-* (*-z-*) are due to assoc. with Sp., It. *presa* seizure, capture.

lancet là·nsit surgical instrument for making incisions XV; (archit.) applied attrib. to pointed windows XVIII. – (O)F. *lancette*, dim. of *lance*; see LANCE, -ET.

lancinate læ·nsineit pierce. XVII. f. pp. stem of L. *lancināre* tear, rel. to *lacer*; see LACERATE and -ATE[3].

land lænd solid portion of the earth's surface; ground, soil; country, territory, realm, domain; †country (opposed to *town*); ridge in a ploughed field OE.; strip division of a field XIV; (Sc.) building divided into tenements XV. OE. *land* = OFris., OS., ON., Goth. *land*, OHG. *lant* (Du., G. *land*) :- CGerm. **landam*, rel. to OCeltic **landā* (Ir. *land, lann* enclosure, W. *llan* enclosure, church, Cornish *lan* open space, plain, Breton *lann* heath), whence F. *lande* heath, moor, LAUND. The IE. base **londh-* is not evidenced in other langs., but the var. **lendh-* is repr. by OSl. *lędina* heath, desert (Russ. *ljadá, ljadína*), (O)Sw. *linda* fallow land. comp. **la·nd**LA:DY. XVI, after **la·nd**LORD OE. *landhlāford*; **la·nd**MARK[1] OE. *landmearc*. **la·nd**SLIDE U.S. (XIX) equiv. of **la·nd**SLIP XVII. Hence **land** vb. bring to land XIII (K. Horn); come to land XIV (Wycl. Bible); repl. OE. *lendan* :- **landjan*. Whence **la·nd**ING[1] disembarkation XV; platform in a flight of stairs XVIII. ¶ Several foreign comps. have been or are current, as *landamman* (XVIII), *landdrost* (XVIII), *landgrave* (XVI), *landsturm* (XIX), *landtag* (XVI), *landwehr* (XIX).

landau læ·ndɔ̄ four-wheeled carriage. XVIII. Name of a town in Germany where the vehicle was first made. (The G. name is *landauer*, short for *landauer wagen* 'carriage of the people of Landau'.) Hence **landau-**LE·T, **-le·tte**. XVIII.

landloper læ·ndlou:pəɹ (hist.) vagabond. XVI. – MDu. *landlooper*, f. *land* LAND + *loopen* run, LEAP. (Earlier †*landleaper* (XIV), with accommodation to Eng.).

landrail læ·ndreil corn-crake. XVIII. f. LAND + RAIL²; cf. G. *landralle*.

landscape læ·nᵈskeip, læ·nskip picture representing natural inland scenery XVI (*landskip*); view of such scenery XVII (*lantskip*, Milton). – MDu. *lantscap*, (mod.) *landschap* landscape, province (cf. OE. *landsċipe* region, tract, OS. *landskipi*, OHG. *lantscaf*, ON. *landskapr*); see LAND, -SHIP. Adopted from Du. as a painter's term, like *easel*; the form *landskip* repr. the Du. pronunc. la·ndsχəp.

lane lein narrow way or passage. OE. *lane* = OFris. *lana*, *laen*, MDu. *lāne* (Du. *laan*), of unkn. origin.

langrage, -idge læ·ŋgridʒ (hist.) case shot loaded with pieces of iron. XVIII. repl. †*langrel(l)*, *-ill* (XVII Capt. Smith); of unkn. origin.

lang syne læŋsai·n (Sc.) long ago. XVI (Dunbar). Sc. *lang* LONG + *syne*, contr. form of *sithen* SINCE. ¶ Familiar in *auld lang syne* (from Burns).

language læ·ŋgwidʒ body of words as used by a people; form of words, style of expression. XIII. ME. *langage*, later *language* – (O)F. *langage* (AN. also *language*, after *langue* tongue, speech) = Pr. *leng(u)atge* (whence Sp. *lenguaje*, It. *linguaggio*) :– Gallo-Rom. **linguāticum*, f. *lingua* tongue, language; see LINGUISTIC, -AGE.

languish læ·ŋgwiʃ grow weak or faint. XIII (Cursor M.). – (O)F. *languiss-*, lengthened stem of *languir* (= Pr., Sp. *languir*, It. *languire*) :– Rom. **languīre*, for L. *languēre* languish, rel. to *laxus* slack, LAX²; see -ISH². So **la·ngu**ID¹. XVI. – F. or L. **langu**OR² læ·ŋg(w)əɹ †disease, woeful plight, mental distress XIII (Cursor M.); faintness, weariness XVIII. – OF. *languor* (mod. *langueur*) – L. *languor*, *-ōrem*; reinforced later from L.

langur lʌ·ŋgᵘəɹ Indian long-tailed monkey. XIX (Heber). – Hindi *langūr* (Skr. *lāṅgūlin* tailed).

laniard see LANYARD.

laniary læ·niəri (of teeth) adapted for tearing. XIX. – L. *laniārius*, f. *laniāre* tear with the nails, etc.; see -ARY.

laniferous lei-, ləni·fərəs wool-bearing. XVII. f. L. *lānifer*, f. *lāna* WOOL; see -FEROUS. So **lani·**FIC wool-producing. XVII. – L. **lani·**GEROUS wool-bearing. XVII. f. L.

lank læŋk loose, flabby, hollow OE.; straight and flat XVII. OE. *hlanc*, f. Germ. **χlaŋk-*, which appears in (M)HG. *lenken* bend, turn aside, OE. *(h)lanca* hip, loin, OHG. *lancha*; cf. FLANK, FLINCH, LINK¹. Hence **la·nk**Y¹. XVII.

lanner læ·nəɹ species of falcon. XIV. – (O)F. *lanier*, perh. sb. use of *lanier* cowardly (cf. medL. syn. *tardarius*), which was developed from a derogatory application of *lanier* weaver :– L. *lānārius* wool-merchant, f. *lāna* WOOL; see -ER².

lanolin læ·nŏlin fatty matter from sheep's wool. XIX. – G., f. L. *lāna* WOOL + *ol|eum* OIL + -IN.

lansquenet læ·nskənet (hist.) mercenary soldier in Germany; German card-game. XVII. – F. *lansquenet* – G. *landsknecht*, f. g. of *land* LAND + *knecht* in the sense of 'soldier', KNIGHT.

lantern læ·ntəɹn case of glass, etc., containing and protecting a light XIII (Cursor M.); glazed turret-like erection XV. – (O)F. *lanterne* = Pr., Pg., It. *lanterna* :– L. *lanterna*, f. Gr. *lamptḗr* torch, lamp (f. *lámpein* shine; cf. LAMP), after *lucerna* lamp. ¶ The frequent form *lanthorn* is due to assoc. with *horn*, lanterns having been formerly made with horn windows.

lanthanum læ·nþənəm (chem.) rare metallic element. XIX. modL. (Mosander), f. Gr. *lanthánein* escape the notice of; 'it has hitherto lain concealed in oxide of cerium' (1841).

lanuginous lænjū·dʒinəs downy. XVI. f. L. *lānūginōsus*, f. *lānūgō* down, f. *lāna* WOOL, see -OUS.

lanyard læ·njəɹd †whip-lash XV; (naut.) short piece of rope XVII. – (O)F. *lanière*, earlier *lasniere*, f. *lasne*, perh. due to crossing of *laz* LACE and *nasle* – Germ. **nastila-* (G. *nestel* string, lace); adopted earlier as †*lainer* (XIV, Ch.); the final syll. was assoc. with YARD².

Laodicean lei:ŏdisi·ən 'lukewarm, neither cold nor hot', like the church of Laodicea (Rev. iii 15, 16). XVII. f. L. *Lāodicēa*, Gr. *Lāodíkeia*, name of a city in Asia Minor (now Latakia); see -EAN.

lap¹ læp †skirt of a garment; †lobe OE.; †fold of a robe XIII; front part of a skirt and of the body from waist to knees XIII (Laȝ.). OE. *læppa*, corr. to OFris. *lappa*, OS. *lappo*, OHG. *lappa*, with *pp* for *pf* from LG. (G. *lappen*); cf. ON. *leppr* clout, rag, lock of hair; Gr. *lobós* LOBE has been compared. comp. **la·p**DOG. XVII (Evelyn).

lap² læp take up with the tongue. OE. *lapian*, corr. to MLG., MDu. *lapen*, OHG. *laffan*, f. Germ. **lap-*, repr. also by OHG. *gilepphen* swallow, MHG. *leffen*, Icel. *lepja* (:– **lapjan*) lick, OS. *lepil*, MLG. *lepel*, OHG. *leffil* (G. *löffel*) spoon, and rel. to L. *lambere* (see LAMBENT), Gr. *láptein* lick, lap; cf. also LIMPET. OE. *lapian* is repr. directly by ME., dial. *lape*, Sc. *laip*, the present *lap* being prob. due to (O)F. *laper* (of Germ. origin, if not independently imit.).

lap[3] læp wrap, enfold XIII; lay over, so as to cover; project beyond (cf. OVERLAP) XVII. Earlier in †*bilappe*, †*bileppe*, f. *bi-* BE- + *lappe*, **leppe* LAP[1]. Hence **lap** sb. amount by which something overlaps XVIII; act of encircling, turn round a track XIX.

laparo- læ·pərou, læpərɔ· comb. form of Gr. *lapárā* flank, f. *laparós* soft, in medical terms, as *laparo·tomy*. XIX.

lapel ləpe·l part of a coat folded over towards the shoulder. XVIII (Mrs. Piozzi). f. LAP[1] + -EL[1]. Hence **lape·llED**. XVIII (Smollett). ¶ Formation and stress are abnormal.

lapidary læ·pidəri sb. one who cuts stones XIV; adj. suitable for monumental inscriptions XVIII. – L. *lapidārius*, f. *lapid-*, *lapis* stone; see -ARY.

lapilli ləpi·lai fragments of stone from a volcano. XVIII. pl. of It. *lapillo* – L. *lapillus*, dim. of *lapis* stone.

lapis lazuli læ·pis læ·zjŭlai silicate producing ultramarine pigment. XIV (Trevisa). f. L. *lapis* stone + *lazulī*, g. of medL. *lazulum*, varying with *lazur*, *lazurius*, f. Pers. *lāzhward* AZURE.

Lapp læp of the Mongoloid race called by themselves Sabme. XIX. – Sw. *Lapp*, perh. orig. a term of contempt (cf. MHG. *lappe* simpleton), in medL. *Lappo* (*-ōn-*), whence **Lappo·nIAN**. XVII (Topsell). F. *Lapon*.

lappet læ·pit fold, flap XVI; lobe of ear, etc., XVII. f. LAP[1] + -ET.

lapse læps slip of the memory, etc.; fall from rectitude, grace, etc.; termination of a right XVI; gliding, flow XVII (Milton); passing (of time) XVIII. – L. *lapsus*, f. *laps-*, pp. stem of *lăbī* glide, slip, fall, rel. to *labāre* slip, *labor* LABOUR; cf. F. *laps* (*de temps*). So **lapse** vb. fall, pass away XVII; fall in, become void; glide, sink XVIII. Partly – L. *lapsāre* (f. *laps-*), partly f. the sb. ¶ For comps. see COLLAPSE, ELAPSE, RELAPSE.

Laputan ləpjū·tən pert. to Laputa, visionary, chimerical. XIX (Swift's form is *Laputian*). f. *Laputa*, the flying island in 'Gulliver's Travels' III ii (1726); see -AN.

lapwing læ·pwiŋ bird of the plover family, pewit. OE. *hlēapewince*, the first el. of which is formally identical with LEAP[1], and appears in Fris. names of the bird, e.g. *leap*, *ljeap*, *mantsjeleap*, *wyfkeleap*, the second el. contains the base (meaning 'move sideways or from side to side') of OE. *wincian* WINK. Variation of form is shown by ME. *lhapwynche* (Ayenbite of Inwyt), *lappewinke* (Gower), *lapwyng* (Lydg.); the present form is due to assoc. with LAP[3] and WING, 'because he lappes or clappes the wings so often', Minsheu, 1617.

lar lāɹ pl. **lares** lɛə·rīz, **lars** lāɹz household god(s); hearth, home XVI. – L. *lār*, pl. *lārēs*; prob. orig. 'infernal divinities' and hence rel. to *lārua* spectre, ghost (LARVA).

larboard lā·ɹbōɹd, -əɹd side of a ship to the left of a person looking from stern to bows. XIV. orig. *lad(d)borde*, *lathebord*, the second el. of which is BOARD (OE. *bord*, ON. *borði* ship's side), the first is of uncertain origin, but may be from LADE, the orig. sense being 'the side on which deck cargo was taken in'. ¶ The OE. term was *bæcbord* 'the side at the back of the steersman' (the steering-paddle being worked over the right side) = LG., Du. *bakboord* (whence G. *backbord*, F. *bâbord*).

larceny lā·ɹsəni theft. XV (Fortescue). – AN. **larcenie*, f. (O)F. *larcin* :– L. *latrōcinium*, f. *latrō(n-)* brigand, robber, (earlier) mercenary soldier, f. Gr. *látron* pay, *latreús* mercenary, *latreúein* serve (cf. LATRIA).

larch lāɹtʃ coniferous tree, Abies Larix (L. europæa). XVI (introduced by William Turner 1548). – MHG. *larche*, var. of *lerche* (G. *lärche*) :– OHG. **larihha*, **lerihha* – L. *laricem*, nom. *larix*, prob. of alien origin. ¶ The L. form *larix* læ·riks was current XVI–XIX, with var. †*larinx*, †*lari(n)ch*.

lard lāɹd †(fat) bacon or pork; internal fat of swine's abdomen. XV. – (O)F. *lard* bacon = Sp., It. *lardo* :– L. *lār(i)dum*, rel. to Gr. *lārīnós* fat. So **lard** vb. – (O)F. *larder*. **la·rdER**[2] room for storing provisions. XIV. – AN. *larder*, OF. *-ier*, medL. *lardārium*.

lardy-dardy see LA-DI-DA. **lares** see LAR.

large lāɹdʒ †liberal, generous XII; †ample; wide in range or capacity XIII; †broad XIV; great, big XV. – (O)F. *large* (now 'broad, wide') :– L. *larga*, fem. of *largu-s* abundant, bountiful; the fem. early supplanted OF. m. **larc* (= Pr. *larc*, Sp. *largo* long, It. *largo* wide). So **largESS**[2] lā·ɹdʒes †liberality XIII; liberal bestowal of gifts XIV. – (O)F. *largesse* = Pr., Sp. *largueza*, It. *larghezza* :– Rom. **largitia*, f. L. *largus*. **largo** lā·ɹgou (mus.) slow and dignified; movement so marked. XVII. It., 'broad'.

lariat læ·riət rope used for picketing. XIX. – Sp. *la reata* the rope used to tie mules together, f. *reatar* tie up again, f. *re-* RE- + *atar* tie :– L. *aptāre* fit, f. *aptus* APT.

lark[1] lāɹk bird well known for its early morning song. OE. *lāferce*, older *lǣwerce*, *lāuricæ*, corr. to MLG., MDu. *lēwer(i)ke* (Du. *leeuwerik*), OHG. *lērahha* (G. *lerche*), ON. *lævirki* (perh. from Eng.); of unkn. origin. The Sc. var. **laverock** lē·vrək, læ·vərək descends from ME. *laverok*. comp. **la·rkSPUR**. XVI (*larkes spur*, Lyte, Gerarde); so called from the spur-shaped calyx.

lark[2] lāɹk (colloq.) play tricks, frolic. XIX. poss. repr. dial. *lake* play, sport (pronounced lēək) – ON. *leika* = OE. *lācan* play, sport, MHG. *leichen*, Goth. *laikan* dance. Hence **lark** sb. XIX.

larrikin læ·rĭkin street rowdy, hooligan. XIX. Originated in Melbourne, Australia, *c.*1870; perh. f. *Larry*, pet-form of the name *Laurence*, common in Ireland; see -KIN.

larrup læ·rəp (colloq.) thrash. XIX. Of dial. origin; perh. based on *lather* or *leather*.

larum (arch.) læ·rəm. XVI. Aphetic of ALARUM.

larva lā·ɹvə A. †spectre, ghost XVII; B. insect in the grub state XVIII. – L., 'disembodied spirit', 'ghost', 'mask' (cf. LAR); sense B is due to Linnæus, and is an application of the sense 'mask', the notion being that the perfect insect or imago is not recognizable in the larva (Ray, 1691, had spoken of 'the same Insect under a different *Larva* or habit').

larynx læ·riŋks cavity in the throat containing the vocal cords. XVI. – modL. – Gr. *lárugx*; comb. form *lary·ngo-*. Hence **laryngeAL**[1] lǣri·ndʒəl. XVIII. f. modL. *laryngeus*.

lascar læ·skăɹ East Indian sailor. XVII. ult. based on Urdu (– Pers.) *lashkar* army, camp, either as a misuse of this, or through early Pg. *laschar, lasquarin, -im* native (East Indian) soldier, the latter orig. – Urdu adj. *lashkarī* military.

lascivious ləsi·viəs inclined or inciting to lust. XV. – late L. *lascīviōsus*, f. L. *lascīvia* licentiousness, f. *lascīvus* sportive, lustful, wanton, f. adj. **laskos* or vb. **lascāre*, which may be ult. rel. to LUST.

lash[1] læʃ A. make a sudden movement; dash XIV; B. †lavish XVI; C. (from the sb.) flog, scourge XIV. prob. echoic or symbolic, like the contemporary †*lush*; cf. the parallel *dash* / *dush*, *flash* / *flush*, *mash* / *mush*, *smash* / dial. *smush*. Hence **lash** sb. blow, esp. with a whip; flexible part of a whip. XIV. **la·shER**[1]. XVII.

lash[2] †lace XV; (naut.) make fast with a cord XVII. perh. of LG. origin; cf. MDu. *lasche* rag, patch, gusset, Du. *laschen* patch, sew together, scarf (timber).

lashings læ·ʃiŋz (Anglo-Ir.), 'floods', abundance. XIX. f. LASH[1] in sense 'lavish'; see -ING[1].

laspring læ·spriŋ young salmon. XVIII. perh. alteration of **laxpink*, †*lakspynk* (f. LAX[1]+*pink* minnow, young salmon), and interpreted as a contr. of *last spring*.

lass læs girl. XIII (Cursor M.). ME. *lasce, las(se)*; of difficult etym., like *boy, girl, lad*; perh. north. development (cf. *ass* for **ask* ashes, *ass* for *ask* vb., *buss* for *busk* vb.) of **lask* :– ON. **laskwa*, fem. of **laskwar* unmarried, repr. by OSw. *løsk kona* unmarried woman (spec. use of the sense 'unoccupied' or 'having no fixed abode', orig. 'free from ties'; in OIcel. *lǫskr* means only 'weak, good for nothing').

lassitude læ·sitjūd disinclination to exert oneself. XVI. – F. *lassitude* or L. *lassitūdō*, f. *lassus* weary :– **ladtos*, f. **lad-* leave; see LET[1] and -TUDE.

lasso læsū·, læ·sou rope with a noose to catch cattle. XIX. – Sp. *lazo* (in America pronounced la·so) = OF. *laz*, etc., LACE.

last[1] làst †footprint; shoemaker's wooden or iron model of a foot. OE. *lāst* m. footprint, *lǣst* fem. boot, *lǣste* shoemaker's last = MLG. *lēst(e)*, Du. *leest*, OHG. *leist* (G. *leiste-n*) last, ON. *leistr* foot, sock, Goth. *laists* footprint, track; rel. to OS. *lēsa*, OHG. (*wagan*)*leisa* track, rut (G. *geleise, gleise*): all f. CGerm. **lais-* follow a track; cf. Goth. *lais* I know, L. *līra* furrow, *delīrus* (see DELIRIOUS), and LAST[4], LEARN, LORE.

last[2] làst denomination of weight, capacity, or quantity. XIV. OE. *hlæst* load, burden = OFris. *hlest*, (M)LG., (M)Du. *last*, OHG. *hlast* (G. *last*) :– WGerm. **hlatsta-, -sti-*, rel. to **hlatto-* (ON. *hlass* load), f. **hlaþ-* LADE.

last[3] làst following all the others, coming at the end. OE. *latost*, Northumb. *lætest*, corr. to OFris. *letast, lest*, OS. *latst, last, letist* (Du. *laatst, lest*), OHG. *lazzōst, lezzist* (G. *letzt*), ON. *latastr* :– CGerm. **latast-*, **latist-*, superl. of *læt* adj., *late* adv. LATE: see -EST. (*Latest* XVI is a new formation on *late*.) For the reduction of the group *-tst-* cf. BEST.

last[4] làst †follow; †carry out, perform; go on, continue. OE. *lǣstan*, corr. to OFris. *lāsta, lēsta* fulfil, OS. *lēstian* execute, OHG. (G.) *leisten* afford, yield, Goth. *laistjan* follow :– CGerm. **laistjan*, f. **laist-* LAST[1].

latakia lætəkī·ə kind of Turkish tobacco produced near *Latakia*, the ancient Laodicea, seaport of Syria. XIX.

latch lætʃ A. (dial.) loop, noose; B. fastening for door or gate. XIV. In sense A prob. var. of LACE (OF. var. *lache* of *laz*; see next); in sense B prob. f. (dial.) **latch** vb. OE. *læććan* seize, grasp, f. Germ. **lakk-*, prob. :– **lagn-*, rel. to Gr. *lázesthai* (:– **lagj-*), or **laqn-*, rel. to L. *laqueus* noose, LACE.

latchet læ·tʃit (now arch., after Mark i 7) thong, esp. to fasten a shoe. XIV. – OF. *lachet*, var. of *lacet*, f. *laz* LACE; see -ET.

late leit slow, tardy; delayed in time OE.; belonging to an advanced stage XIV; recently dead XV. OE. *læt*, infl. *lætes, lata*, etc. = OFris. *let*, OS. *lat*, OHG. *laz* (G. *lass*), ON. *latr*, Goth. *lats* :– CGerm. **lataz* slow, sluggish, f. **lat-* :– IE. **lad-* (repr. by L. *lassus* weary :– **ladtos*); see LET[1]. Also **late** adv. OE. *late* slowly, at an advanced period = OHG. *laz, lazzo* slowly, lazily. The mod. form *late* repr. infl. forms of OE. *læt*, and OE. adv. *late*. The regular compar. from OE. *lætra* is **latter** læ·təɹ (now restricted, except for phr. like *latter days, latter end*, to uses in contrast with *former*); hence **la·tterLY**[2] XVIII (Richardson); **la·tterMATH** (dial.) AFTERMATH. XVI; **later** lei·təɹ, **la·tEST** (XVI) are new formations, cf. LAST[3].

lateen lætī·n triangular sail. XVIII. – F. *latine*, in *voile latine* 'Latin sail', so called from its use in the Mediterranean; fem. of *latin* LATIN.

latent lei·tənt hidden: opp. to *patent*. XVII. – L. *latent-*, *-ēns*, prp. of *latēre* lie hid; see LETHARGY, -ENT.

lateral pert. to or at the side. XVI. – L. *laterālis*, f. *later-*, *latus* side; see -AL[1]. So F. *latéral*. **lateri-** læ·təri comb. form of L. *later-*, *latus*, having a parallel form **la·tero-** (see -O-). XIX.

laterite læ·tərait (min.) red porous ferruginous rock. XIX. f. L. *later* brick + -ITE[1].

lath lāþ thin narrow strip of wood. OE. *lætt* (corr. to MDu. *latte*, Du. *lat*, G. dial. *latz*) survives in mod. dial. *lat*, but began to be replaced XIV in general use by *laþþe*, which appears to repr. an OE. **læþþ-*, corr. to OHG. *latta* (G. *latte*). Connexion with MHG. *lade* plank (G. *laden* counter, shop) is gen. assumed, but the relation of the Germ. types is obscure; influence from the synon. and prob. cogn. OIr. *slat*, W. *llath* (:- OCeltic **slattā*) is possible. ¶ The Germ. word has been adopted into Rom. langs. (cf. F. *latte*, Sp. *lata*, It. *latta*).

lathe[1] leið administrative district of Kent. XII. irreg. repr. OE. *lǣþ*, corr. to ON. *láð* landed possession, land, rel. to **lǣð-* in Goth. *unlēds* 'unlanded', poor, OE. *unlǣd(e)* wretched.

lathe[2] leið (dial.) barn. XIII (Genesis and Exodus). – ON. *hlaða*, rel. to *hlaða* LADE.

lathe[3] leið supporting structure, stand XV; machine for turning wood, etc. XVII. Varies in its earliest use with †*lare* (Cotgrave s.v. *Tournoir*); the two forms may repr. parallel adoptions of ODa. *lad* (XV) stand, supporting framework, as in *drejelad* turning-lathe, *savelad* saw-bench, *væverlad* loom, perh. a special use of *lad* pile, heap :- ON. *hlað*, rel. to *hlaða* LADE.

lathe[4] leið movable batten of a loom. XVII. cogn. with synon. Sw. *lad*, and so ult. identical with prec.

lather læ·ðəɹ, (formerly) lā·ðəɹ froth made with soap and water. XVI. OE. *lēaðor* washing soda = ON. *lauðr* :- Germ. **lauþram* :- IE. **loutrom*, whence Gr. *loetrón*, *loutrón* bath, OIr. *loathar* 'pelvis', 'canalis', Gaul. *lautra* 'balneo', f. **low-* wash, LAVE + *-tro-* instru. suffix. In its mod. sense f. **lather** vb. cover with lather OE.; become covered with foam XIII. repl. OE. *lēþran*, **līeþran* = ON. *leyðra* :- Germ. **lauþrjan*.

lati- læ·ti comb. form of L. *lātus* broad, as in *lātifolius* broad-leaved, **latifo·li**OUS. XVII.

Latin læ·tin pert. to Latium or the ancient Romans; sb. the Latin language. XIII. – (O)F. *latin* or L. *Latīnus*, f. *Latium* designation of the portion of Italy which included Rome. In OE. the learned form *latin* occurs occas.; the pop. repr. was *lǣden* Latin, language, ME. *leden* speech, utterance (OE. *bōclǣden* 'book language' was spec. Latin). So **La·tin**IST. XVI. – medL. *Latinista*. **Lati·n**ITY. XVII. – L.

latitat læ·titæt (leg.) writ supposing the defendant to lie concealed, etc. XVI. – L., 'he lies hid', 3rd sg. pres. ind. of *latitāre*, frequent. of *latēre* be hid (see LATENT).

latitude læ·titjūd †breadth; angular distance on a meridian, etc. XIV (Ch.); (arch.) extent, scope XVI; freedom from restriction XVII (Bacon). – L. *lātitūdō*, f. *lātus* broad; see -TUDE and cf. (O)F. *latitude*. ¶ The geographical applications of L. *latitudo*, Gr. πλάτος, and *longitudo*, μῆκος, orig. referred to the 'breadth' and 'length' of the oblong map of the known world, whence they came to be used for the distance of any place in the breadthwise and lengthwise direction respectively from the circle which was taken as the origin of measurement. Hence **latitu·di**NAL[1]. XVII (Grew). **la:titudin**A·RIAN. XVII (1662 in 'Brief Account of the new Sect of Latitude-Men' by S. P.).

latria lətrai·ə worship that may be paid only to God)(DULIA. XVI. – Late L. – Gr. *latreíā* service, divine worship, rel. to *latreúein* serve (as with prayer); cf. -LATRY.

latrine lətrī·n privy. XVII. – F. *latrine* – L. *latrīna* bath, privy, contr. of *lavātrīna*, f. *lavāre* wash, LAVE.

-latry lətri repr. Gr. *-latreíā* worship, as in *eidōlolatreíā* IDOLATRY. On this model have been formed (e.g.) *bibliolatry*, *Mariolatry*, and, joc., *babyolatry*, *lordolatry*. The corr. personal designations end in **-later** (Gr. *-latrēs*), the adjs. in **-latr**OUS.

latten læ·tən mixed brass-like metal. XIV. ME. *latoun*, *laton* – OF. *laton*, *leiton* (mod. *laiton*), obscurely rel. to Pr. *lato*, *latun*, Cat. *llautó*, Sp. *(a)laton*, Pg. *latão*, It. dial. *loton*, *lattone*, *lottone*, It. *ottone*, of unkn. origin. ¶ The Rom. word was adopted as Du. *latoen*, ON. *látun*, Russ. *latún'*.

latter see LATE.

lattice læ·tis structure made of laths used as a screen. XIV. – OF. *lattis*, f. *latte* LATH + *-is* :- L. *-ītium*.

latus lei·təs L. *latus* side, as in *latus rectum* (in conic sections). XVIII.

laud lɔ̄d praise; pl. first of the day hours of the Western Church, the psalms of which end with psalms cxlviii–cl (called collectively *laudes*). XIV. – OF. *laude*, pl. *laudes* – L. *laud-ēs*, pl. of *laus* praise. So **laud** vb. praise. XIV. – L. *laudāre*, f. *laud-*. **lau·d**ABLE. XV. – L. (Cicero). **laud**A·TION. XV. – L. **lau·dat**ORY. XVI. – late L.

laudanum lɔ·dənəm preparation of opium. XVI. – modL. *laudanum*, Paracelsus's name for a medicament for which he gives a pretended prescription of costly ingredients but which was early suspected to contain opium, whence the gen. application to opiate preparations; perh. alt. of LADANUM (LABDANUM).

laugh lāf make the characteristic noise expressive of mirth. OE. (Anglian) *hlæhhan* (WS. *hliehhan*), pt. *hlōh*, *hlōgon*, (pp. not recorded) = OFris. *hlakkia*, OS. **hlahhian* (pt. pl. *hlōgun*), OHG. *hlahhan*, pt. *hlōch*, beside *hlahhēn*, pt. *hlahhēta* (Du., G. *lachen*, *lachte*, *gelacht*), ON. *hlǽja*, pt. *hló*, *hlógu*, pp. *hleginn*, Goth. *hlahjan*, pt. *hlōh*; CGerm. str. vb., but later in most of the langs. wholly or partially weak, f. **χlaχ-* **χlōχ-* **χlag-* :- IE. imit. base **klak-* **klōk-* (cf. Gr. *klṓssein* cluck :- **klōkjein*). So **laugh**TER lā·ftəɹ OE. *hleahtor* = OHG. *hlahtar* (whence G. coll. *gelächter*), ON. *hlátr* :- Germ. **χlaχtraz*.

launce lōns sand-eel, Ammodytes. XVII. perh. an application of LANCE.

launch[1] lōnʃ, lānʃ †pierce, lance; hurl, shoot; be set in rapid motion; cause (a vessel) to move from land XIV (fig. XVII); put out from land XVI. – AN. *launcher*, ONF. *lancher*, var. of *lancier* LANCE. Cf. *pinch*.

launch[2] lōnʃ, lānʃ largest boat of a man-of-war XVII; large boat propelled by steam, etc. XIX. – Sp. *lancha* pinnace, perh. of Malay origin; cf. Pg. *lanchara* – Malay *lancharan*, f. *lanchār* quick, nimble.

laund lōnd (arch.) glade, pasture. XIV. – OF. *launde* (mod. *lande*); see LAND, LAWN[2].

laundress lō·ndris, lā·ndris woman who washes and gets up linen, etc. XVI. f. †*launder* (XIV) or the extended form (see -ER[2]) *launderer* (XV) man or woman whose occupation is washing clothes; see -ESS[1]. So **lau·nder** wash and get up (linen). XVI, f. †*launder* sb. **lau·ndry** †washing of clothes; establishment for this. XVI. *Launder* and *laundry* are contr. forms of (i) †*lavender* (XIII) – OF. *lavandier* m., *-ière* fem. = Sp. *lavandero*, *-era*, It. *lavandajo*, *-aja* – Rom. **lavandārius*, f. *lavanda* things to be washed, n. pl. of gerundive of *lavāre* wash, LAVE; (ii) †*lavendry* (XIV) – OF. *lavanderie* (cf. L. *lavandāria* things to be washed); see -RY. For the vocalization of *v* cf. *auger*, *hawk*, *newt*.

laureate lō·riət worthy of the laurel crown, as an eminent poet XIV (Ch.); (in sense of L. *laureus*) of laurel XV; crowned with laurel XVII. – L. *laureātus*, f. *laurea* laurel tree, laurel crown, sb. use of fem. of adj. *laureus*, f. *laurus*; see next and -ATE[2].

laurel lɔ·rəl bay-tree, Laurus nobilis. ME. *lorer* (XIII), *lorel* (XIV) – OF. *lorier* (mod. *laurier*) – Pr. *laurier*, f. *laur* (= OF. *lor*, Cat. *llor*, etc.) :- L. *lauru-s*, prob. of Mediterranean origin. The later form is due to dissimilation of *r* . . *r* to *r* . . *l*; cf. Sp. *laurel*.

laurustinus lɔ̀rəstai·nəs evergreen shrub, Viburnum Tinus. XVII. – modL. *laurus tīnus*, i.e. *laurus* LAUREL, *tīnus* wild laurel.

lava lā·və †stream of molten rock; substance resulting from the cooling of this; fluid matter from a volcano. XVIII. – It. *lava* (Neapolitan dial.) †stream suddenly caused by rain, the lava stream from Vesuvius, f. *lavare* LAVE.

lavabo ləvei·bou, -ā·bou (eccl.) ritual washing of the celebrant's hands. XIX. L., 1st pers. sg. fut. ind. of *lavāre* wash, LAVE; first word of Ps. xxvi 6 '*Lavabo* inter innocentes manus meas' (I will wash my hands in innocency), the recital of which accompanies the ceremony.

lavatory læ·vətəri vessel for washing XIV; lavabo XVI; apartment for washing the hands and face XVII. – late L. *lavātorium*, f. *lavāt-*, pp. stem of *lavāre*; see LAVE, -ORY.

lave leiv (arch.) wash, bathe; pour out. XIII. – (O)F. *laver* = Pr., Sp. *lavar*, It. *lavare* :- L. *lavāre*, corr. obscurely to Gr. *loúein* wash, Arm. *loganam* I bathe. Coalesced in ME. with OE. *lafian* wash by affusion, pour (water), if this vb. survived (= (M)Du. *laven*, OHG. *labōn*, G. *laben* refresh – L. *lavāre*). ¶ ABLUTION, ALLUVION, DELUGE, LATHER, LATRINE, LAVATORY, LOTION, LYE are derivs. of the same base.

laveer ləviə·ɹ (naut.) beat to windward. XVI. – Du. *laveeren*, earlier †*loveren* – F. †*loveer* (mod. *louvoyer*), f. *lof* windward, LUFF; see -EER[2].

lavender læ·vindəɹ fragrant labiate plant, Lavandula vera. XV. – AN. *lavendre*, for **lavendle* – medL. *lavendula*, also *livendula*, *lavindula*, etc. (whence MHG. *lavendel(e)*, G. *lavendel*; cf. It. *lavandula* and *lavanda*, whence F. *lavande*). If the ult. source is L. *lavāre* LAVE, the sense-development is obscure.

laver[1] lei·vəɹ (arch. or rhet.) vessel for washing; baptismal font. XIV. ME. *lavo(u)r* – OF. *laveor*, *laveoir* (mod. *lavoir*) – L. *lavātōrium* LAVATORY[1].

laver[2] lei·vəɹ (edible) seaweed. XVI. – L. *laver* applied by Pliny to a water-plant (whence OE. *laber*).

laverock see LARK[1].

lavish læ·viʃ unrestrainedly liberal or profuse. XV. adj. use of †*lavish* sb., earlier †*lavas* (XV) profusion, prodigality – OF. *lavasse* deluge of rain (cf. OF. *lavis* 'torrent' of words), f. *laver* wash, pour, LAVE; cf. -ISH[1]. Hence **la·vish** vb. XVI.

law[1] lō body or code of rules; an individual rule. Late OE. *lagu* (pl. *laga*), whence ME. *laȝe*, *lawe*, repl. native OE. *ǣ*; – ON. **lagu* (whence OIcel. *lǫg* coll. law), pl. of *lag* layer, stratum, share or partnership, fixed price, set tune :- **lagam*, f. Germ. **lag-* place (see LAY[1], LIE[1]). In various langs. the word for 'law' is derived from bases meaning 'place, set down', e.g. OE. *dōm* DOOM, Gr. *thémis*, L. *statūtum* STATUTE, G. *gesetz* (see SET[1]). See also -IN-LAW. Hence **law·**FUL[1] XIII. **law·**LESS XII; after ON. *lǫgfullr*, *lǫglauss*, **lawyer** lō·jəɹ one versed in the law. XIV (*lawier*, beside *lawer*); see -ER[1], -IER[1].

law² lɔ̄ (north. dial.) hill. XIII (Cursor M.). north. repr. of OE. *hlāw*, var. of *hlǣw*, corr. to OS. *hlēo*, *hlēw-*, OHG. *hleo*, Goth. *hlaiw* :- Germ. **χlaiwaz-*, **χlaiwiz-* :- IE. **kloiwos-*, *-es-*, f. **kloi-* slope (see LEAN²).

law³ lɔ̄ int., orig. asseverative, later excl. of surprise. XVI (Sh.). orig. var. of LA², later coalescing with the excl. *lor'*, = LORD.

lawk(s) lɔ̄k(s) int. Lord! XVIII. var. of *lack!* (XVII), deformation of LORD, perh. suggested by ALACK.

lawn¹ lɔ̄n kind of fine linen. XV. prob. f. *Laon*, name of a town in France, an important place of linen manufacture. ¶ The prevailing early form *laund* shows parasitic *d* as in ASTOUND, BOUND², POUND², SOUND².

lawn² lɔ̄n (arch.) open space between woods XVI; portion of level grass-covered ground kept mown XVIII. Later form of LAUND. ¶ For loss of *d* cf. GROIN.

lawyer see LAW.¹

lax¹ læks salmon. OE. *læx* (WS. *leax*) = LG. *las*, OHG. *lahs* (G. *lachs*), ON. (Sw., Da.) *lax* :- CGerm. (exc. Gothic) **laχs-*, rel. to OPruss. *lasasso*, Lith. *lašišà*, Lett. *lasis*, Russ. *losós'*, Pol. *łosóś*; cf. Toch. *laks* fish. ¶ The OE. word appears to have died out, and the Scand. word, adopted in XIII, continued in local use till XVII; the present currency is due to adoptions from the Continent.

lax² læks (of the bowels) loose XIV; slack, not strict XV. – L. *laxus* loose; see SLACK¹. So **la·xative** relaxing. XIV (Trevisa). – (O)F. or late (medical) L. **la·xity**. XVI. – F. or L.

lay¹ lei pt., pp. **laid** leid cause to lie. OE. *lećġan* pt. *leġde*, pp. *ġeleġd* = OFris. *ledza*, *lega*, *leia*, OS. *leggian* (Du. *leggen*), OHG. *lecken*, *legen* (G. *legen*), ON. *legja*, Goth. (CGerm.) *lagjan*, f. **lag-*, var. of **leg-* LIE¹. The normal repr. of OE. *lećġan*, 1st pers. sg. pres. ind. *lećġe*, pl. *lećġaþ* is seen in ME. *legge* and mod. dial. *ledge* lay (eggs); the standard form *lay* derives from 2nd and 3rd pers. sg. (OE.) *leġest*, *leġeþ*, in which Germ. **g* was orig. followed by **i*, which did not cause gemination of the consonant.

lay² lei short poem of a kind intended to be sung. XIII. – (O)F. *lai*, corr. to Pr. *lais*, of unkn. origin.

lay³ lei not in clerical orders. XIV. – OF. *lai* (now repl. by *laïque*) :- ecclL. *lāicus* – Gr. *lāikós*, f. *lāós* the people. Hence **lay·folk**, **lay·man**. XV.

lay⁴ lei †wager, stake; †layer, stratum; (dial.) impost, tax XVI; line of business, plan of work XVIII (Farquhar, Cibber). f. LAY¹.

layer lei·əɹ A. one who lays XIV; B. thickness of matter spread over a surface; C. shoot or twig pegged down to take root XVII. Several words appeared to have coalesced under one form, all ostensibly f. LAY¹+-ER¹; in sense B the earliest form is *lear*, which may be a var. of LAIR; sense C may be after synon. Du. *af|legger*.

layette leie·t clothes, etc., needed for a new-born child. XIX. F., dim. of OF. *laie* drawer, box – MDu. *laege*; see -ETTE.

lay-fi·gure jointed wooden model of the human figure used by artists. XVIII. f. *lay* as in synon. †**lay**MAN (XVII) – Du. *leeman* for **ledenman*, f. *led* (now *lid*) limb, joint (cf. LIMB).

laystall lei·stɔ̄l †burial-place; place where refuse and dung are laid. XVI. f. LAY¹+ STALL¹.

lazar lei·zəɹ (arch.) poor or diseased person, esp. leper. XIV (*lazre*, *laser*). – (partly through OF. *lasdre*, mod. *ladre*) medL. *lazarus*, appellative use of *Lazarus* name of the beggar in the parable (Luke xvi 20), 'full of sores' – Heb. *El'āzār* (Eleazar) 'God (my) help'; cf. F. *ladre*, Sp. *lázaro*, It. *lazzaro*. So **la·zaret** (XVII) and **lazare·tto** house to receive 'lazars' XVI (slightly earlier *lazar house*); building set apart for quarantine XVII. – F. *lazaret*, It. *lazaretto*.

Lazarist læ·zəɹist one of the Congregation of Priests of the Mission, founded by St. Vincent de Paul (1624) and established in the College of St-Lazare, Paris. XVIII. – F. *Lazariste*, f. *Lazare* Lazarus; see -IST.

lazy lei·zi averse to action or effort. XVI. Early forms *laysie*, *lasie*, *laesy*; perh. of LDu. origin (cf. LG. *lasich* languid, idle). Hence, by back-formation, **laze** vb. XVI.

-le¹ l suffix of sbs., repr. OE. *-el*, as *hlædel* LADLE (varying with *-els* in *brīdel-s* BRIDLE; cf. RIDDLE), *-la*, *-le* (cf. HANDLE), *-ol* (cf. CRADLE, SADDLE), and *-l* (cf. NEEDLE, SETTLE), and corr. to OFris. *-le*, OS., OHG. *-il*, *-al*, *-la* (LG., Du., G. *-el*), ON. *-al*, *-ill*, *-ull*, Goth. *-ils*, and rel. further to IE. *-(*i*)*lo-*, *-(*u*)*lo-*, *(*e*)*lā*, as in L. *cingulus*, *-ula*, *-ulum* girdle, *sella* (:- **sedlā*) saddle, Gr. *hellá* seat, denoting appliances or instruments, like the OE. antecedents of *beetle* (hammer), *bridle*, *cradle*, *girdle*, *hurdle*, *ladle*, *prickle*, *saddle*, *settle*, *shuttle*, *spittle* (small spade), *steeple*, *stickle|back*, *thimble*, beside which there are a few names of animals and plants, as *beetle*, *bramble*, *cockle*, *cuttle|fish*, *thistle* (with which may be grouped *darnel*, *weevil*); cf. *cripple*. The dim. sense exemplified (e.g.) in Skr. *vṛśalás* little or contemptible man, L. *porculus* pigling (cf. Lith. *paršẽlis*, G. *ferkel*), Goth. *Attila* 'Little Father'), was not found in OE. This suffix was not gen. productive, but some adoptions of words containing it were made from ON. and LG., as *axle|tree*, *kettle*, *pickle*, *scuttle*; later formations, such as *bristle*, *cobble*, *noddle*, *nozzle*, and *dottle*, are isolated and obscure; *spittle* (saliva) is a new formation of late-ME. date, the OE. form being *spātl*. In *fowl*, *reel*, *snail*, *stile*, the l has ceased to be syllabic. Cf. -CLE, -CULE, and -EL¹. ¶ In *angle*, *battle*, *bottle*, *candle*, *castle*, *cattle*, *chronicle*, *manciple*, *muzzle*, *participle*, *periwinkle*, *syllable*, *uncle*, etc., the ending is of other origin.

-le[2] l suffix of adjs., repr. OE. *-el, -ol, -ul*, corr. to OFris. *-ol, -el*, OS., OHG. *-al, -il*, Goth. *-ils, -uls*, and rel. further to IE. **ulo-, *-ilo-*, as in L. (esp. with pejorative force) *bibulus, crēdulus, garrulus, pendulus, querulus, tremulus* (cf. Goth. *sakuls* quarrelsome, OHG. *ezzal* greedy, OE. *slāpol* sleepy, *wacol* vigilant), L. *agilis, facilis, similis* similar, *humilis* humble, Gr. *homalós* smooth. Surviving words of OE. date are *fickle, idle, little, mickle, nimble* (with which *evil* may be grouped); *brittle* is of ME. date (XIV, Wycl.).

-le[3] l suffix of verbs with frequent. or dim. force, repr. OE. *-lian*, corr. to OFris. *-lia*, OS., OHG. *-lōn* (Du., G. *-len*), ON. *-la* :- CGerm. **-lōjan*; surviving words of OE. date are *handle, nestle, startle, twinkle, wrestle*. There were many new formations in ME. and modEng., chiefly expressive of repeated action or movement, some being adopted from foreign sources, some being of native echoic or symbolic creation, e.g. *babble, bubble, cackle, chuckle, crackle, dabble, dazzle, drizzle, gabble, giggle, hobble, mumble, niggle, paddle, scribble, shuffle, sparkle, tickle, tootle, topple, wriggle*; redupl. forms are *argle-bargle, fiddle-faddle, tittle-tattle, wiggle-waggle*. Some show shortening of a stem vowel, as *dwindle, prattle, waddle*. *Darkle, sidle, suckle* are back-formations; cf. *grovel*.

lea lī tract of open ground, (hence) grassland. OE. *lēah, lēa*, corr. to OHG. *lōh* 'lucus' (MHG. low brushwood, scrub-land) :- Germ. **lauχ-* :- IE. **louq-*, repr. also by L. *lūcus* grove, Lith. *laũkas* field, Skr. *lokás* open space; the basic meaning was prob. 'clearing', and developed from that of LIGHT[1].

lead[1] led the heaviest of the base metals. OE. *lēad* = OFris. *lād*, MLG. *lōd* (Du. *lood*) lead, MHG. *lōt* (G. *lot*) plummet, solder :- WGerm. **lauda*; ult. rel. to Ir. *luaidhe*, Gael. *luaidh* :- **loudiā*. Hence **lea·dEN**[3] adj. OE.

lead[2] līd take with one, conduct; carry on (now mainly with *life* as obj.); precede, be foremost (in) XIV (first in *lead the dance*). OE. *lǣdan* = OFris. *lēda*, OS. *lēdjan* (Du. *leiden*), OHG. (G.) *leiten*, ON. *leiða* :- CGerm. (exc. Goth.) **laiðjan*, f. **laiðō* LOAD. Hence **lead** sb. XIII (first in northern use; later techn.; 'a low, despicable word' J.). **lea·dER**[1], late OE. *lǣdere*.

leaf[1] līf part of a plant; fold of paper. OE. *lēaf*, corr. to OFris. *lāf*, OS. *lōf* (Du. *loof*), OHG. *loup* (G. *laub*), ON. *lauf*, Goth. *laufs* :- CGerm. **laubaz, -am*, of which there are no certain cognates.

leaf[2] see LEAVE[1].

league[1] līg distance of three miles. XIV. The earliest forms show two types, *leuge* and *leghe*, the first – late L. *leuca, leuga*, late Gr. *leúgē* (of Gaulish origin), the second – the derived Pr. *lega* = (O)F. *lieue*, Sp. *legua*, It. *lega*; the second type has survived. Forms such as †*leuke*, †*leeke*, †*leaque*, reflect late L. *leuca* (Jerome), Gr. *leúkē*.

league[2] līg covenant for mutual assistance. XV. Early forms (*ligg, ligue, leag(u)e, lege*) (i) show deriv. partly from F. *ligue* – It. *liga*, latinized form of *lega*, f. *legare* bind :- L. *ligāre* (cf. LIEN); (ii) partly immed. from It. *lega*. Hence as vb. XVII (Cotgr.). **lea·guer**[1] member of a league. XVI; see -ER[1].

leaguer[2] lī·gəɹ (arch.) military camp; siege. XVI. – Du. *leger* camp, corr. to OE. *leger* LAIR; cf. BELEAGUER.

leak līk hole in a vessel containing or immersed in fluid. XV. So **leak** vb. pass away by a leak XV; allow the passage of fluid through a leak XVI. †**leak** adj. leaky. XVI. prob. all of LG. or Du. origin; cf. MDu. *lek, lēk-* sb. and adj., *lēken* vb. let water through, corr. to OE. *lec* (usu. *hlec*) adj., OHG. *lechen* wk. vb., G. dial. *lech* adj., MHG., G. dial. *lechen* crack, become leaky, ON. *leki* sb., *lekr* adj., *leka* vb.; f. Germ. **lek-*, var. of **lak-* LACK.

leal līl (now Sc.) loyal, faithful, true. XIII (Cursor M.). – AN. *leal*, OF. *leel*, of which the var. *leial* became *loial* LOYAL.

lean[1] līn wanting in flesh. OE. *hlǣne* :- Germ. **χlainjaz*, perh. rel. to Lith. *klýnas* scrap, fragment, Lett. *kleins* feeble.

lean[2] līn recline; incline. ME. *lēnen* :- OE. *hleonian, hlinian*, corr. to OFris. *lena*, OS. *hlinōn* (Du. *leunen*), OHG. *(h)linēn* (G. *lehnen*), f. Germ. **χlĭ-* :- IE. **klĭ-* (cf. Gr. *klîmax* ladder, CLIMAX, L. *clīvus* declivity, Skr. *çri* lean), with *-n-* formative as in Gr. *klīnein* bend, L. *inclīnāre* INCLINE. Cf. LAW[2].

leap[1] līp †run, rush; rise suddenly with both or all four feet to alight in another position. OE. *hlēapan*, pt. *hlēop, hlupon*, pp. *-hlēapen* = OFris. *(h)lāpa*, OS. *-hlōpan* (Du. *loopen*), OHG. *loufan*, earlier *hlauffan* (G. *laufen* run), ON. *hlaupa* (whence Sc. LOUP), Goth. *-hlaupan* :- CGerm. **χlaupan*, without cogns. elsewhere. comp. **lea·p-FROG** game in which one person leaps over another whose crouching position suggests the attitude of a frog. XVI (Sh.). So **leap** sb. OE. **hlīep, hlȳp* (whence ME. *lüpe*) :- **χlaupiz*; cf. OFris. *hlēp*, Du. *loop*, OHG. *hlouf* (G. *lauf*), ON. *hlaup*. **lea·p-YEAR** year having one day (29 February) more than the common year. XIV (Trevisa; prob. much earlier than it is recorded, since ON. *hlaup|ár* is presumably, like other terms of the calendar, modelled on Eng.). The term prob. refers to the fact that in the bissextile year any fixed festival falls on the next weekday but one to that on which it fell in the preceding year; cf. medL. *saltus lunæ* 'leap of the moon', subtraction of a day from the lunar month at the end of a 19-year cycle.

leap[2] līp (dial.) basket. OE. *lēap* = MLG. *lōp*, ON. *laupr*, of unkn. origin.

learn lə̄ɹn pt., pp. **learnt** A. acquire knowledge OE.; B. impart knowledge to, teach (now dial. or vulgar) XIII (Cursor M.). OE. *leornian* = OFris. *lernia, lirnia*, OS. *līnōn* (:- **liznōn*), OHG. *lernēn, lirnēn* (G. *lernen*) :- WGerm. **liznōjan*, **liznējan*, f. **lis-*, weak grade of **lais-* (see LORE[1], LAST[1]). Hence **learn**ED[1] lə̄·ɹnid deeply read, erudite. XVI; in absol. use, after L. *doctus* (pp. of *docēre* teach); succeeding to the sense '(well) instructed', const. *in*, †*of*; preceded by ME., late OE. *lēred*, pp. of *lēran* teach.

lease[1] līs conveyance of property by contract; the contract itself; term for which the contract is made. XV. – AN. *les* = OF. *lais, leis*, f. spec. use of *lesser, laissier* (mod. *laisser*) let, leave (:- L. *laxāre*, f. *laxus* loose, LAX), whence **lease** vb. grant by a lease, let on lease. XVI. Cf. LESSEE.

lease[2] līz (dial.) glean. OE. *lesan* (pt. *læs*) = OFris. *lesa* read, OS., OHG. *lesan* (Du. *lezen*, G. *lesen* gather, read), ON. *lesa*, Goth. (*ga*)*lisan* gather.

leash līʃ thong or line with which dogs are held. XIII. – OF. *lesse*, (also mod.) *laisse*, f. spec. use of *laisser* let (a dog) run on a slack lead; see LEASE[1]. ¶ The development of F. s to Eng. ʃ is paralleled in *crush, cushion, frush* (F. *froisser*).

leasing lī·ziŋ (arch., dial.) lying, falsehood. OE. *lēasung*, f. *lēasian* tell lies, f. *lēas* false, untrue (corr. to OFris. *lās* free, OS., OHG. *lōs*, Du., G. *los*, ON. *lauss*, Goth. *laus* empty, vain; see LOSE, -LESS, LOOSE).

leasow lī·sou, le·zə (dial.) pasture, meadowland. OE. *lǣswe*, obl. form of *lǣs* :- Germ. **lǣswō*, perh. f. base of LET[1], as if 'land let alone' (i.e. untilled). The OE. *lǣs*, obl. *lǣse* have given dial. *lease* pasture, common.

least līst little beyond all others. OE. *lǣst*, contr. of *lǣsest* :- **laisistaz*, f. **laisiz* LESS; see -EST. Hence **lea·st**WAYS, -WISE.

leat līt open watercourse. OE., in *wætergelǣt* water channel; f. base of *lǣtan* LET[1].

leather le·ðəɹ skin prepared for use by tanning; strap, thong OE.; skin XIV. OE. *leþer* (only in comps.) = OFris. *lether*, OS. *leđar* (Du. *leer*), OHG. *ledar* (G. *leder*), ON. *leðr* :- CGerm. (exc. Gothic) **leþram* :- IE. **letrom*, whence also OIr. *lethar*, W. *lledr*, Breton *ler*. Hence **lea·thern,** OE. *leþeren* (see -EN[3]); the earlier OE. form was *liþeren, liþrin* = OS. *litharīn*, OHG. *lidrīn*.

leave[1] līv permission. OE. *lēaf* = OHG. **louba* (MHG. *loube*, G. †*laube*) :- WGerm. **lauƀā*, whence **lauƀjan* permit (OE. *līefan*, etc.). The form *leave* repr. the OE. obl. forms in which the word was esp. frequent (*būtan lēafe* without leave, *be his lēafe* with his permission, *lēafe sellan* give leave); the nom. survives dial. in *leaf*, the form used by sailors and private soldiers. The etymol. meaning is prob. 'pleasure, approval', and the base that of LOVE, LIEF, BELIEVE, FURLOUGH.

leave[2] līv A. have as remainder, cause or allow to remain; B. depart (from). OE. *lǣfan* = OFris. *lēva*, OS. *-lēbian* (in *farlēƀid* left over), OHG. *leiban* (cf. OHG. *bilīban*, G. *bleiben* remain), ON. *leifa*, Goth. *-laibjan* (in *bilaibjan* remain behind) :- CGerm. **laiƀjan* remain, continue, f. **laiƀō* remainder (OE. *lāf* remainder, ON. *leif* heritage, etc., dial. *lave*), of which the vars. **līƀ-* appear in LIFE, LIVE[1]. Referred to an IE. base **loip-* **leip-* **lip-* stick, adhere, repr. by Gr. *līparḗs* persevering, importunate, *lípos* grease, Lith. *lìpti*, OSl. *lĭpěti* adhere, Skr. *lip-, rip-* smear, adhere to.

leaven le·vn substance added to dough to produce fermentation. XIV. ME. *levain* – (O)F. *levain* = Pr. *levam* :- Gallo-Rom. use of L. *levāmen* lit. 'means of raising', only in sense 'alleviation, relief', f. *levāre* lighten, relieve, raise (cf. LEVITY). Hence vb. XV.

lecher le·tʃəɹ grossly unchaste man. XII. – OF. *lichiere* (nom.), *lecheor, -ur* (acc.), f. *lechier* live in debauchery or gluttony (mod. *lécher* lick) = Pr. *lecar*, It. *leccare* – Frank. **likkōn* :- Germ. **likkōjan* LICK. So **le·cher**OUS. XIV (R. Mannyng). – OF. *lecheros*. **le·ch**ERY. XIII. – OF. *lecherie*.

lectern le·ktəɹn reading- or singing-desk in church. XIV. ME. *lettorne, let(t)ron* – OF. *lettrun, leitrun* – medL. *lectrīnum*, f. *lectrum*, f. L. *legere* read (see next), as *mulctrum* milking-pail, f. *mulgēre* milk. The present form goes back to *lectron, lectorn* (XV), which are due to assim. to medL.

lection le·kʃən reading; liturgical lesson. XVI. – L. *lectiō(n-)*, f. *lect-*, pp. stem of *legere* read, orig. gather, choose, rel. to Gr. *légein* collect, say; see -TION. So **lect**URE le·ktʃəɹ †reading XIV; discourse XVI. –(O)F. *lecture* or medL. *lectūra*. Hence **le·cture**SHIP. XVII; orig. office of one appointed to give a series of discourses, e.g. in a church, (later) in a college; repl. (XX) in some universities by the paristic form *le·cturership* (f. **le·ctur**ER[1] XVI). ¶ From the IE. base **leg-* **log-* are derived *collect, elect, select* (with corr. sbs. in *-tion* and *-tor*), *neglect*; *intellect*; *eligible, intelligible, negligible*; *intelligent, negligent*; *prelection, -tor*; *elegant*; *legend*; *legion*; *delight*; *lexicon*; *logic, logos, logistics*; *catalogue, eclogue, epilogue, prologue*; *syllogism*; *logo-, -logue, -logy*.

ledge ledʒ transverse bar or strip XIV; narrow projecting shelf XVI. poss. f. ME. *legge* le·dʒə LAY[1]; cf. MHG. *legge* layer, edge.

ledger le·dʒəɹ A. sb. †book lying permanently in one place XV; principal one of a set of commercial books; horizontal timber, flat slab XVI. B. resident ambassador XVI; adj. †resident, stationary; (mus.) *ledger line* separate short line above or below the stave XVII. Early forms *legger, lidger, ligger*, corr. in sense to Du. *legger, ligger* (f. *leggen* LAY[1], *liggen* LIE[1]) on which the Eng. forms were prob. modelled with phonetic accommodation to ME. *legge* le·dʒə LAY[1], *ligge* li·dʒə LIE[1]; see -ER[1].

lee[1] lī protection, shelter OE.; sheltered side XIV. OE. *hlēo, hlēow-* = OFris. *hli, hly,* OS. *hleo* m., *hlea* fem., ON. *hlé* :- Germ. **χlēw-* (whence **χlēwj-* in ON. *hlý*), not known outside Germ. The naut. sense was mainly from ON. The var. *lew* from OE. *hlēow-* (cf. LUKEWARM) survives locally. Hence **lee**WARD lī·wəɹd, l^jū·əɹd (on) the side turned away from the wind. XVI.

lee[2] lī, usu. coll. pl. **lees** līz sediment, dregs. XIV (Ch., Gower). – OF. *lie* = Pr., Sp., Pg. *lia,* medL. pl. *liæ* (X), – Gaulish **liga* or **ligja* (cf. OIr. *lige*).

leech[1] lītʃ (arch.) physician. OE. *lǣće* = OFris. *letza, leischa,* OS. *lāki,* OHG. *lāhhi,* OSw. *läkir,* Goth. *lēkeis* :- CGerm. **lǣkjaz* :- IE. **lēgios* (cf. Ir. *liaigh*).

leech[2] lītʃ blood-sucking worm, OE. *lǣće,* Kentish *lȳce,* MDu. *lake lieke leke*; orig. a distinct word from prec. but assim. to it.

leech[3] lītʃ (naut.) vertical or sloping side of a sail. XIV *lich(e)* (Sandahl), XV (*leche, lyche,* Sc. *lek*). Obscurely connected with ON. (naut.) *lík* (cf. Sw. *lik,* Da. *lig* bolt rope).

leek līk herb allied to the onion, OE. *lēac,* corr. to MDu. *looc* (Du. *look*), OHG. *louh* (G. *lauch*), ON. *laukr* :- Germ. **laukaz,* **-am* (whence Finnish *laukka,* OSl. *lukŭ*), of which no cogns. are known outside Germ.

leer[1] liəɹ look askance (now only with a sly or malign expression). XVI. Early *leare, le(e)re,* poss. f. *leer* sb. cheek (OE. *hlēor* = OS. *hleor,* etc., ON. *hlýr* pl.), as if 'to look over the cheek'. Hence **leer** sb. XVI (Sh.).

leer[2] liəɹ (dial.) empty. OE. **lǣre* (as in *lǣrnes* emptiness) = OS., OHG. *lāri* (Du. *laar,* G. *leer*) :- WGerm. **lāri,* of unkn. origin.

leet[1] līt court of record held by lords of certain manors. XV (*lete,* Promp. Parv.). – AN. *lete,* AL. *leta* (XI), of unkn. origin. ¶ OE. *lǣþ* administrative district of Kent, which has been proposed as the source, is too remote in sense.

leet[2] līt (mainly Sc.) list of persons eligible or selected for an office. XV (*lite, lytte, lythe*). Of obscure origin, but prob. – AN., OF. *lit(t)e,* var. of *liste* LIST[1].

leetle lī·tl alt. of LITTLE expressive of diminutiveness. XVII.

left left side opposite to the right. XIII. ME. *lüft, lift, left* :- OE. **lyft* (as in *lyftādl* 'left-disease', paralysis), Kentish *left* 'inanis'; the primary sense of 'weak, worthless' is found in EFris. *luf,* Du. dial. *loof,* and the derived sense in MDu., LG. *luchter, lucht, luft,* NFris. *leeft, leefter*; the ult. origin is unknown. ¶ This is one of the words (cf. MERRY) in which a south-eastern (Kentish) form has established itself in gen. English.

leg leg bodily organ of support and locomotion. XIII (Laȝ.). – ON. *leggr* (also in comps. limb, viz. *armleggr, handleggr* arm, *lærleggr, fótleggr* leg; cf. Icel. *uphandleggr* upper arm, *framhandleggr* forearm) :- **lagjaz* (cf. Lombardic *lagi* thigh), of which there are no certain cogns. elsewhere. Superseded SHANK.

legacy le·gəsi †legateship XIV; bequest XV. – OF. *legacie* = Sp. *legacia* – medL. *lēgātia* legateship, f. *lēgātus* LEGATE. In the second and current sense repr. AL. *lēgantia* (XIII), f. *lēgāre* (see LEGATE).

legal lī·gəl pert. to or based upon law. XVI. – (O)F. *légal* or L. *lēgālis,* f. *lēg-, lēx* law (an Italic and Indo-Iran. word); see -AL[1] and cf. LEAL, LOYAL. So **leg**ALITY XV. – F. or medL.

legate le·gət ecclesiastic deputed to represent the Pope XII (Peterborough Chron.); ambassador, delegate XIV. – (O)F. *légat* – L. *lēgātus,* sb. use of pp. of *lēgāre* depute, delegate; see -ATE[1]. So **leg**ATION ligei·ʃən. XV. – (O)F. or L.

legatee legəti· person to whom a legacy is bequeathed. XVII. f. *legate* bequeath (XVI), f. pp. of L. *lēgāre*; see prec., -ATE[3], -EE.

legato legā·tou (mus.) smooth and connected. XIX. It., pp. of *legare* :- L. *ligāre* bind (cf. LIGATURE).

legend le·dʒənd A. story of a saint's life or collection of these XIV; book of liturgical lessons XV; non-historical story; B. inscription, motto XVII. – (O)F. *légende* = Sp. *leyenda,* It. *leggenda* – medL. *legenda,* prop. 'things to be read', n.pl. of gerundive of *legere* read (see LECTION), taken as fem. sg. For the formation cf. PREBEND. So **le·gend**ARY. XVI. – medL. *legendārius* (sb. *-ium*).

legerdemain le·dʒəɹdəmein sleight of hand XV (Lydg.); trickery XVI. – F. *léger de main,* i.e. *léger* (:- Rom. **leviāriu-s,* f. *levis* light), *de* of, *main* hand.

leghorn leghō·ɹn kind of straw plaiting; breed of fowls. XIX. f. place-name *Leghorn* (Italy) – It. †*Legorno,* now *Livorno,* repr. L. *Liburnus.*

legible le·dʒĭbl that can be read, i.e. deciphered. XIV. – late L. *legibilis,* f. *legere* read; see LECTION, -IBLE. **legibi·l**ITY. XVII.

legion lī·dʒən body of infantry in the ancient Roman army; vast host. XIII (Laȝ.). – OF. *legiun, -ion* (mod. *légion*) – L. *legiō(n-),* f. *legere* choose, levy (see LECTION).

legislator le·dʒisleitəɹ one who makes laws. XVII. – L. *lēgis lātor,* i.e. *lēgis* g. of *lēx* law, *lātor* proposer, mover, agent-noun f. *lātus* :- **tlātus,* pp. of *tollere* raise; after phr. *lēgem ferre* propose a law. So **legis**LA·TION. XVII. – late L. *lēgis lātiō.* Hence **le·gisl**ATIVE. XVII. **le·gislat**URE. XVII; after JUDICATURE.

legitimate lidʒi·tĭmət lawfully begotten XV; lawful, regular XVII. – medL. *lēgitimātus,* pp. of *lēgitimāre* declare to be lawful, legitimize, f. L. *lēgitimus,* f. *lēg-, lēx* law. So **legi·timate** -eit vb. XVI. **legitim**A·TION. XV. – medL. See -ATE[2], -ATE[3]. **legi·tim**IST. XIX. – F. (political party). **legi·tim**IZE. XIX. f. L. adj. Cf. LEGAL.

leguminous lėgjū·minəs pert. to pulse; of the pea and bean family (Leguminosæ). XVII. – modL. *legūminōsus*, f. L. *legūmin-*, *-umen* pulse, bean (whence, through F., **legume** le·gjūm beans, peas, etc. XVII; pod of Leguminosæ XVIII); see -OUS.

leisure le·ʒəɹ, lī·ʒəɹ †freedom or opportunity; freedom from occupation, free time. XIV. ME. *leisour*, *-er* – AN. *leisour*, OF *leisir* (mod. *loisir*) = Pr. *lezer* leisure, Cat. *lleer* permission, Pg. *lazer* leisure, opportunity; Rom. sb. use of L. *licēre* be permitted (see LICENCE). Cf. PLEASURE.

leman le·mən (arch.) lover, sweetheart; illicit lover, paramour. XIII. ME. *leofman*, *lefman*, *lemman*, f. *lēof*, *lēf* LIEF+MAN.

lemma le·mə, pl. *lemmata*, *lemmas* (math.) subsidiary proposition XVI; heading, title, theme XVII. – L. – Gr. *lêmma*, pl. *lēmmata* something taken for granted or assumed, theme, argument, title, f. **lab-*, base of *lambánein* take.

lemming le·miŋ small arctic rodent. XVII. – Norw. *lemming*, rel. to Sw. *lemmel*, †*lemb* (pl. *lemmar*), Norw. *lemende*.

lemon[1] le·mən pale-yellow ovate acid fruit, Citrus Limonum. XIV. ME. *lymon* – (O)F. *limon* (now restricted to the lime), corr. to Sp. *limón*, Pg. *limão*, It. *limone*, medL. *limō(n-)*; f. Arab. *līmah*, coll. *līm* fruits of the citron kind (see LIME[2]). So **lemon**A·DE. XVII. – F. *limonade*.

lemon[2] le·mən in *lemon dab*, *lemon sole* certain species of plaice or flounder. XIX. – F. *limande* (XIII; beside *lime*; cf. It. *lima*, *limanda*), of unkn. origin.

lemur lī·məɹ Malagasy nocturnal mammal allied to the monkey. XVIII. – modL. *lemur* (Linnæus), deduced from L. pl. *lemurēs* shades of the departed; so named because of the spectre-like suggestion of the face.

lend lend grant the temporary possession of; grant, bestow. XV. Late ME. *lende*, superseding *lēne(n)* :– OE. *lǣnan*, corr. (with difference of conjugation) to OFris. *lēna*, *lēnia*, Du. *leenen*, OHG. *lēhanōn* (G. *lehnen* enfeoff); f. LOAN. The substitution of *lend-* for *lēn-*, which became established in XV, arose from the fact that the pt. *lende* and pp. *lent* of *lēne*, by assoc. with the conjugation of *bend*, *send*, *wend*, suggested an inf. *lende*.

length leŋ(k)þ quality of being long OE.; long stretch. XVI. OE. *lengþu* (rare, the usual word being *lengu*, *lenge*, which survived till XVII) = Du. *lengte*, ON. *lengd* :– Germ. **laŋgiþō*, f. **laŋgaz* LONG[1]; see -TH[1]. Hence **le·ngthen**[5] XVI; superseding †*length* vb. XIII (Cursor M.). **le·ngthy**[1]. XVII (*c.* 1690, N. Amer.).

lenient lī·niənt softening, relaxing XVII; indisposed to severity XVIII. – L. *lēnient-*, *-ēns*, prp. of *lēnīre* soothe, f. *lēnis* soft, mild; see -ENT. Hence **le·niency**. XVIII (Mme D'Arblay). **lenity** le·nĭti. XVI. – OF. – L.

lenition līni·ʃən (philol.) smoothing or softening of a sound. XIX. f. L. *lēnis*; see prec., -ITION.

leno lī·nou cotton gauze. XIX. prob. – F. *linon* linɔ̃, f. *lin* :– L. *līnum*; see LINEN.

lens lenz piece of glass, etc., with two curved surfaces or one straight and one curved. XVII (Halley). – L. *lens* LENTIL: so called on account of its shape; F. *lentille* is used in the same way.

Lent lent †spring; period from Ash Wednesday to Easter Eve. XIII. Shortened form of ME. *lenten*, OE. *lencten* = MDu. *lentin*, OHG. *lengizin*, *lenzin* :– WGerm. **laŋgitīnaz*, either f. **laŋgita-*, *-ton-* (whence MDu., Du. *lenta*, OHG. *langiz*, *languz*, also *lenzo*, G. *lenz*) with suffix *-īna-*, or f. **laŋgaz* LONG[1]+**tīna-* of Goth. *sinteins* daily, rel. to Skr. *dina*, OSl. *dĭnĭ*, Lith. *dienà* day; the ult. deriv. from LONG[1] is undoubted and may have reference to the lengthening of the day in spring; the eccl. sense of the word is peculiar to Eng. *Lenten* survives in attrib. use and is apprehended as an adj. in -EN[3].

lenticular lenti·kūləɹ lens- or lentil-shaped. XVII. – L. *lenticulāris*, f. *lenticula*; see next and -AR.

lentil le·ntĭl seed of a leguminous plant, Ervum lens, Lens esculenta. XIII. – (O)F. *lentille* :– Rom. **lentīcula*, for L. *lenticula* (whence Sp. *lenteja*, It. *lenticchia*), dim. of *lēns*, *lent-* lentil.

lentisk le·ntisk mastic tree. XV. – L. *lentiscus*, prob. of alien origin.

leonid li·ənid (astron.) one of a group of meteors which appear to radiate from Leo. XIX. f. L. *leōn-* LION+-ID[2].

leonine[1] li·ənain lion-like, pert. to a lion. XIV (Ch.). – (O)F. *léonin*, *-ine* or L. *leōnīnus*, *-īna*, f. *leōn-* LION; see -INE[1]. Identical in form and ult. in origin is **le·onine**[2] in *leonine verse*, Latin verse in which the final word of the line rhymes with that immediately preceding the cæsural pause, from a medieval poet *Leo* or *Leonius*.

leopard le·pəɹd large carnivorous quadruped, Felis panthera. XIII. ME. *leopard*, *leupard*, *lubard*, *lebard* – OF. *leopard*, *leupard*, *lebard* (mod. *léopard*) – late L. *leopardus* – late Gr. *leópardos*, also *leontópardos*, f. *leonto-*, *léōn* LION+*párdos* PARD; so named because supposed to be a hybrid between lion and 'pard'.

leper le·pəɹ leprous person. XIV (Trevisa, Wycl. Bible). prob. arising from attrib. use of †*leper* (XIII) leprosy – (O)F. *lèpre* – late L. *lepra*, cl. *lepræ* (Pliny) – Gr. *léprā*, sb. use of fem. of *leprós* scaly, f. *lépos*, *lepís* scale. The ending *-er* would confirm the tendency to apprehend the word as a personal designation. So **le·prous**. XIII (AncrR.). – OF. *lepro(u)s* – late L. *leprōsus*. Hence **le·prosy**[3]. XVI; repl. †*lepry* (XV).

lepidoptera lepidɔ·ptərə order of insects characterized by scale-covered wings. XVIII. modL. (Linnæus), f. Gr. *lepido-*, *lepis* scale + *pterón* wing (cf. FEATHER); see -A².

leporine le·pərain hare-like. XVII. – L. *leporīnus*, f. *lepor-*, *lepus* hare; see -INE¹.

leprechaun leprəχɔ̄·n in Ir. folk-lore, a pygmy sprite. XVII (*lubrican*), XIX (*lepre(c)haun*). – Ir. *lupracán*, *leipracán*, *lioprachán*, in MIr. *luchrupán*, OIr. *luchorpán*, f. *lu* small + *corp* body (– L. *corpus*; see CORPORAL).

lepto- le·pto(u) comb. form of Gr. *leptós* fine, small, thin, delicate (prop. ppl. adj. of *lépein* scale, peel, rel. to *lepís* shell, scale), in many bot. and zool. terms.

Lesbian le·zbiən pert. to unnatural sexual relations between women; also sb. XIX. L. *Lesbius*, f. *Lesbos* birthplace of Sappho (cf. SAPPHISM) + -IAN.

lese-majesty līzmæ·dʒĭsti treason. XV. – F. *lèse-majesté* – L. *læsa mājestās* hurt or violated majesty, i.e. of the sovereign people; *læsa*, pp. of *lædere* injure (see next), *mājestās* MAJESTY.

lesion lī·ʒən damage, injury. XV. – (O)F. *lésion* – L. *læsiō(n-)*, f. *læs-*, *lædere* injure, hurt; see -SION.

less lės of not so great size or extent; functioning as compar. of *little* (cf. LEAST). OE. *lǣssa* = OFris. *lēssa* :– Germ. **laisizō*, f. **laisiz* (whence OE. *lǣs* = OFris. *lēs* adv.), compar. formation on **laisa-* :– IE. **loiso-* (cf. Gr. *loîsthos* last). Hence **le·ss**EN⁵ vb. XIV, **le·ss**ER³; double compar.

-less lės orig. an adj. rel. to LEASING, LOOSE, LOSE, OE. *lēas* devoid (of), free (from), governing the genitive, e.g. *firena lēas* free from crimes, but more freq. the second el. of adj. compounds, the first el. being a sb., e.g. *wīflēas* without a wife. In some instances the sb. is a noun of action coincident in form with the related vb., and some of the adjs. so formed have the sense 'not to be —ed', 'un—able', e.g. *countless*, *numberless*. On the supposed analogy of these *-less* has been appended (from late XVI) to many verbs, **e.g.** *dauntless*, *fadeless*, *tireless*.

lessee lesī· tenant under a lease. XV. – AN. *lessee*, OF. *lessé*, pp. of *lesser* (mod. *laisser* leave, let); see LEASE¹. So **lesso·r**¹. XV. – AN. *lesso(u)r*.

lesson le·s(ə)n portion of sacred scripture read in divine service; portion of a book to be studied; portion or period of teaching XIII (AncrR.); †lecture XIV. – (O)F. *leçon* :– L. *lectiōnem* LECTION.

lest lest (so) that . . not. OE. *þȳ lǣs þe*, 'whereby less that' (*þȳ* instr. case of the demons. and relative pron., *lǣs* LESS, *þe* relative particle; see THE²), late OE. *þe lǣste*, whence ME. *lest(e)*, by aphesis of the first word of the phr.; cf. for the meaning L. *quōminus* 'whereby less', lest.

let¹ let †leave behind or undone, omit; put out to hire or rent; allow, cause. OE. *lǣtan*, pt. *lēt*, *leort*, pp. *ġelǣten* = OFris. *lēta*, OS. *lātan* (Du. *laten*), OHG. *lāʒan* (G. *lassen*), ON. *láta*, Goth. *lētan* (pt. *lailōt*); CGerm. (orig. reduplicating) vb., f. **lǣt-* (:– **lēd-*), rel. to **lat-* LATE :– **lad-*, repr. by L. *lassus* weary (:– **ladtós*); cf. ALAS, LASSITUDE. The primary sense was prob. 'let go through weariness', as in the Rom. synon. (e.g. F. *laisser*; see LEASE). The strong pp. (still dial. *letten*) began to be superseded by *let* in XIV.

let² lėt (arch.) hinder, prevent. OE. *lettan* = OFris. *letta*, OS. *lettian* (Du. *letten*), OHG. *lezzen*, ON. *letja*, Goth. *latjan* (intr. delay) :– CGerm. **latjan*, f. **lata-* slow, LATE. Hence **let** sb. hindrance. XII.

-let, lėt suffix used since XVI, but not freq. till XVIII, to form diminutives; presumably deduced from *bracelet*, *crosslet*, and the like, which have the appearance of being f. *brace*, *cross*, but which are actually from F. words formed by the addition of *-ette* (-ET) to sbs. ending in *-el* (– L. *-ellum* or *-āle*), or from *tartlet*, which is – F. *tartelette*, dim. of *tarte* TART, through the by-form *tartre*, whence **tarterette*, and by dissimilation *tartelette*.

Armlet, *necklet*, *wristlet*, denoting ornaments for parts of the body, were perh. first suggested by a false analysis of *frontlet*, and furthered by the common *bracelet*.

letch letʃ craving, longing. XVIII. poss. f. by-form of (dial.) *latch* seize, catch hold of (OE. *læććan*), but the transference of meaning is not clear.

lethal lī·þəl deadly, mortal. XVII. – L. *lethālis*, f. *lēthum*, var. of *lētum* death, by assoc. with Gr. *lḗthē* oblivion, used as a proper name in L. (whence **Lethe** lī·þi XVI) for a river in Hades, the water of which, when drunk, produced oblivion of the past; see -AL¹.

lethargy le·þəɹdʒi morbid drowsiness; torpor, apathy. XIV (Ch., Wyclif, Trevisa). Earliest form *litargie* – OF. *litargie* (mod. *léth-*) – late L. *lēthargia* (medL. *litargia*, after medGr. pronunc.) – Gr. *lēthargíā*, f. *lḗthargos* forgetful, f. **lēth-* (cf. prec.), var. of **lath-* in *lanthánein* escape notice, *lanthánesthai* forget, prob. rel. to L. *latēre* be hid (see LATENT). **letharg**IC lėþā·ɹdʒik. XIV (Trevisa; rare before XVI). – L. – Gr.

Lett let member of a people inhabiting Baltic provinces. XIX. – G. *Lette* – native name *Latvi*. Hence **Le·tt**IC (i) Lettish, (ii) in wider use applied to the Baltic langs. **Le·tt**ISH¹ IE. language of the Baltic group; after G. *lettisch*.

letter le·təɹ alphabetic character; epistle; pl. literature, learning. XIII. – (O)F. *lettre* :– L. *littera* (which took over the senses of Gr. *grámma*, pl. *grámmata*; see GRAMMAR) letter of the alphabet, pl. epistle, written document, literature, culture, also *lītera*, var. *leitera* (by false assoc. with *lĭnere* smear), perh. ult. – Gr. *diphthérai* writing tablets. So **letter**ED¹ le·təɹd learned, educated. XIV; after (O)F. *lettré*, L. *litterātus*.

lettuce le·tis plant of the genus Lactuca. XIII. ME. *letus(e)*, obscurely rel. to OF. *laitue* (mod. *laitue*) = It. *lattuga* :- L. *lactūca*, f. *lact-*, *lac* milk, so called with ref. to the milky juice of the plant.

leuco- lʲū·kou before a vowel **leuc-,** comb. form of Gr. *leukós* white (see LIGHT[1]). XVII.

levant lĭvæ·nt decamp, steal away, bolt; esp. of an absconding debtor. XVIII. perh. f. *levant* in sl. phr. *come the l., run or throw a l.*, make a bet with the intention of absconding if it is lost, ult. based on *Levant*, as in the F. phr. *faire voile en Levant*, 'to bee stolne, filched or purloyned away' (Cotgr.). But cf. Sp. *levantarse con algo* seize something.

Levant lĭvæ·nt †the East; eastern part of the Mediterranean. XV. – F. *levant*, sb. use ('point where the sun rises') of prp. of *lever* rise (see LEVY). So **Leva·nt**INE[1]. XVII; after F.

levator livei·tɔ̄ɹ (anat.) muscle that raises. XVII. – late L., agent-noun of L. *levāre* (see LEVY, -ATOR).

levee le·vi, le·vei reception of visitors on rising from bed XVII; assembly held by a sovereign, etc., esp. in the early afternoon XVIII. – F. *levé*, var. of *lever* rising, sb. use of *lever* (inf.) raise, (refl.) rise :- L. *levāre* lift; see LEVY, -EE.

level le·vəl instrument to indicate a line parallel to the horizon XIV; †level condition XV; position marked by a horizontal line XVI; social, etc., plane; level surface XVII. ME. *level, livel* – OF. *livel*, later *nivel* (mod. *niveau*) = Pr. *livel, nivel*, Sp. *nivel*, Pg. *livel, nivel*, It. *nivello* :- Rom. **libellum*, for L. *lībella*, dim. of *lībra* balance, scales (cf. LITRE). Hence adj. XVI, vb. XV.

lever lī·vəɹ bar serving to dislodge a heavy object. XIII. – AN. *lever*, (O)F. *levier*, alteration of OF. *leveor* by substitution of suffix (*-āriu-* for *-ōriu-*), f. *lever* raise (see LEVY); ME. had *levere* and *levour*.

leveret le·vərit young hare. XV. – AN. *leveret*, dim. of *levre*, (O)F. *lièvre* :- L. *leporem*, *lepus* hare (of alien origin); see -ET.

leviathan lĭvai·əþən large aquatic animal in the Bible; †Satan XIV (Wycl. Bible); used by Hobbes for the commonwealth 1651. – L. (Vulg.) *leviathan* – Heb. *livyāthān*.

levigate le·vigeit make smooth. XVII. f. pp. stem of L. *lēvigāre*, f. *lēvis* smooth (cf. Gr. *leîos*)+*-ig-*, var. of base of *agere* do, make; see ACT and -ATE[3]. So **leviga**·TION. XV. – L.

levin le·vin lightning. XIII ('Genesis & Exodus'). ME. *leuen(e)*, first in Scandinavianized areas; prob. of ON. origin, and perh. based on OSw. *liughn|elder* (Sw. *ljung|eld*, Da. *lygn|ild*) lightning flash, f. **leuχ-* (see LIGHT[1]).

levirate lī·vĭreit custom by which a brother of a deceased man marries his widow. XVIII. f. L. *lēuir* brother-in-law (corr. to OE. *tācor*, OSl. *děverĭ*, Homeric Gr. *dāḗr*, Skr. *devár-*) +-ATE[1].

levitate le·viteit rise or cause to rise by reason of lightness. XVII (Marvell). f. L. *levis* light (see LEVITY) after GRAVITATE. So **levita**·TION. XVII (More).

Levite lī·vait descendant of Levi; assistant to a priest XIII (Cursor M.); †deacon XIV (PPl.); †clergyman XVII. – ChrL. *levīta*, *levītēs* – Gr. *leuítēs*, f. *Leuí* – Heb. *Lēvī*. So **levi·t**ICAL. XVI (Coverdale). f. late L. (Vulg.) *levīticus* – Gr. (LXX) *leuītikós*.

levity le·vĭti lightness (physical, mental, or moral). XVI. – L. *levitās*, f. *levis* light, rel. to Gr. *elakhús* short, OSl. *lĭgŭkŭ* light; see -ITY.

levy le·vi action of raising money, an army, etc. XV (*leve(e), levie*). – (O)F. *levée*, sb. use of fem. pp. of *lever* :- L. *levāre* raise, f. *levis* light (see prec. and -Y[5]). Hence **levy** vb. raise (money, taxes, etc.) XIV; raise (an army); make, start (war) XV.

lew lʲū see LEE[1].

lewd ljūd †lay, not clerical OE.; unlearned XIII; †low, vulgar; †ignorant; †ill-conditioned; lascivious, unchaste XIV. OE. *lǣwede*, of unkn. origin; connexion with L. *lāicus* LAY[3] has been suggested.

lewis lʲū·is iron contrivance for raising blocks of stone. XVIII. perh. f. the name *Lewis*. Also called *lewisson, lewising* (XIX).

lewisite lʲū·isait vesicant oily fluid. 1937. f. name of the inventor, W. J. *Lewis* + -ITE.

lexical le·ksikəl pert. to the words of a language; of the nature of a lexicon. XIX. f. Gr. *lexikós* and *lexikón*; see next and -AL[1].

lexicon le·ksikən word-book, dictionary. XVII. – modL. – Gr. *lexikón*, n.sg. (sc. *biblíon* book, BIBLE) of *lexikós* pert. to words, f. *léxis* phrase, word, f. *légein* speak; see LECTION. So **lexico**·GRAPHER, -GRAPHY. XVII.

ley lei var. of LEA, repr. OE. *lēaġe*, etc., obl. forms of OE. *lēah*; now used spec. by agriculturists.

li[1] lī Chinese itinerary measure. XVI.

li[2] lī Chinese weight. XVIII.

liable lai·əbl obliged by law XV; exposed or subject *to* XVI. poss. – AN. **liable*, f. (O)F. *lier* :- L. *ligāre* bind (cf. LIGAMENT, LIEN); but, if this is the origin, the late appearance of the word and its absence from AN. and AL. records are inexplicable. Hence **liabi·l**ITY. XVIII. See -BLE.

liaison liei·zɔ̃ †thickening for sauces XVII; illicit intimacy; (in F. phonetics) consonant-linking XIX; (mil.) co-operation of forces XX. – F. *liaison*, f. *lier* bind (cf. prec.).

liane liā·n tropical climbing and twining plant. XVIII. – F. *liane*, †*liene*, dial. *liorne*, *lierne* clematis (cf. LIERNE), perh. alteration, by crossing with *lier* bind, of dial. F. *viorne*, *vienne* :- L. *viburnum* wayfaring-tree. Also **liana** liā·nə (XIX), which either is a latinization or has arisen from the notion that the word was of Sp. origin.

liar lai·əɹ teller of lies. OE. *lēoġere* (= OHG. *liugari*, ON. *ljúgari*), f. *lēoġan* LIE[2]; see -ER[1]. ¶ For the sp. *-ar* cf. *beggar*, *pedlar*.

lias lai·əs blue limestone rock XVII (*lyas*); (geol.) strata forming the lowest division of the Jurassic XIX. – F. *liais*, OF. *liois* in *marbre liois*, *pierre lioise* some valuable kind of stone or marble, prob. of Germ. origin (cf. OS. *leia*, MHG. *lei(e)* rock, stone).

libation laibei·ʃən pouring out of wine in honour of a god. XIV. – L. *lībātiō(n-)*, f. *lībāre* taste, pour as an offering, rel. to Gr. *leíbein* pour drop by drop, *loíbē* libation, *líba* (acc.) drop; see -ATION.

libel lai·bəl †formal statement or writing XIII; plaintiff's declaration or plea XIV; †published bill or pamphlet XVI; damaging or defamatory statement XVII. – OF. *libel*, (mod.) *libelle* – L. *libellus*, dim. of *liber* book (see LIBRARY). Hence **li·bel** vb. XVI. **li·bel**LOUS. XVII.

liberal li·bərəl pert. to the arts considered 'worthy of a free man'; free in bestowing XIV; †unrestrained XV; free from prejudice XVIII; of political opinion (opp. to *Conservative*, *Tory*) 1801. – (O)F. *libéral* = Sp. *liberal*, It. *liberale* – L. *līberālis*, f. *līber* free :– **louberos*, CItalic **louferos* = Gr. *eleútheros*; see -AL[1]. So **libera·l**ITY. XIV. **li·ber**ATE[3]. XVII. – f. L. *līberāt-*, *-āre*. **libera·**TION. XV. – (O)F. or L.

libertine li·bəɹtin, -ain †freedman XIV (Wycl. Bible; thereafter from XVI); antinomian, free-thinker; licentious man XVI. – L. *lībertīnus*, f. *lībertus* made free, f. *līber* free (see prec.); partly through F. *libertin*.

liberty li·bəɹti freedom XIV (Ch.); leave, permission; privilege, franchise; district of one's privileges XV. – (O)F. *liberté* = Pr. *libertat*, etc. – L. *lībertātem*, *-tās*, f. *līber* free, see LIBERAL, -TY. Hence **liberta·**RIAN. XVIII.

libidinous libi·dinəs lustful. XV. – L. *libīdinōsus*, f. *libīdin-*, *libīdō*, *lubīdō* lust (cf. *libet*, *lubet* it is pleasing); see LIEF, -OUS. **libido** libai·dou, -ī·dou (psych.). XX.

Libra lai·brə (astr.) constellation between Virgo and Scorpio; 7th sign of the zodiac. L., pound weight, balance; the constellation, denoted by ♎, was perh. so named with ref. to the fact that, when the sun enters this part of the ecliptic, the days and nights are equal. Cf. LIRA, LIVRE. ¶ In medL. *libra* was used for 'pound'; hence the abbrevs. *l.*, †*li.*, *lb.* (weight), £ (sterling).

library lai·brəri place to contain books accessible for reading (Ch.); collection of books. XIV. – (O)F. *librairie* (now only 'bookseller's shop') = It., Sp. *libreria*, Pg. *livraria* – CRom. **librārīa* alteration of L. *librāria* bookseller's shop, sb. use (sc. *taberna* shop) of *librārius* pert. to books, f. *libr-*, *liber* book; see -ARY, -Y[3]. So **librar**IAN laibrɛə·riən †scribe XVII; keeper of a library XVIII. f. L. *librārius* + -AN.

libration laibrei·ʃən oscillation, balancing. XVII. – L. *lībrātiō(n-)*, f. *lībrāre* balance, f. *lībra*; see LIBRA, -ATION, and cf. LIVRE, EQUILIBRIUM.

libretto libre·tou text of an opera, etc. XVIII. It., dim. of *libro* book (cf. LIBRARY).

Libyan li·biən pert. to *Libya*, a region of N. Africa, by some applied to the Berber language or the Hamitic group gen. XVII; see -AN.

licence, U.S. **license** lai·səns leave, permission; liberty of action XIV; formal permission from authority; excessive liberty XV; deviation from normal form XVI; licentiousness XVIII. – (O)F. *licence* = Sp. *licencia*, It. *licenza* – L. *licentia*, f. *licent-*, prp. stem of *licēre* be lawful; see LICIT, -ENCE. Hence **li·cense** vb. XV. ¶ The difference of sp. between sb. and vb. is in accordance with the usage exemplified in *practice* sb., *practise* vb., *prophecy* sb., *prophesy* vb., which seems to be based on pairs like *advice* and *advise*, where the difference depends upon a historical phonetic distinction. So **lice·n**TIOUS. XVI. L. (Quintilian).

lich litʃ (dial.) body, corpse. OE. *līċ* = OFris. *līk*, OS. *līc* (Du. *lijk*), OHG. *līh* (G. *leiche*, from MHG. *līche*), ON. *lík*, Goth. *leik* :– CGerm. **līkam* (IE. **līg-* form, repr. in Balto-Sl. by words meaning 'like'). Survives in **li·ch-, ly·ch-**GATE roofed gateway to a churchyard under which the bier is set down at a funeral. XV (*lycheyate*). Cf. LIKE[1], LYKEWAKE.

lichen lai·kən, li·tʃən †liverwort, one of a class of cellular cryptogams XVIII. – L. *līchēn* – Gr. *leikhḗn*. So F. *lichen*, Sp. *liquen*, It. *lichene*.

lichi see LITCHI.

licit li·sit lawful, allowable. XV. – L. *licitus*, pp. of *licēre* be lawful (cf. ILLICIT).

lick lik pass the tongue over. OE. *liccian* = OS. *liccōn*, *leccōn* (Du. *likken*), OHG. *leckōn* (G. *lecken*) :– WGerm. **likkōjan* (whence F. *lécher*, etc.; see LECHER); based ult. on IE. **ligh-* **leigh-* **loigh-*, found in Skr. (Vedic) *reḍhi*, *leḍhi*, Arm. *lizanem*, Gr. *leíkhein*, *likhneúein* lick, *líkhnos* dainty, L. *lingere*, *ligurrīre*, OIr. *ligim*, OSl. *lizati*, Lith. *liẽžti*, Goth. *bi|laigon* lick.

lickerish li·kəriʃ (arch.) dainty; greedy; lecherous. XVI. Alteration by substitution of -ISH[1] of †*lickerous* (XIII) – AN. **likerous*, var. of *lecheros* LECHEROUS (cf. OF. *liquerie*, var. of *lecherie* LECHERY). ¶ Perverted to *liquorish* (XVIII) to express fondness for liquor.

lictor li·ktōɹ officer in ancient Rome. XVI (earlier †*littour* XIV). L., of unkn. origin, but pop. assoc. with *ligāre* bind (cf. LIGAMENT).

lid lid cover of the opening of a vessel OE.; eyelid XIII. OE. *hlid* = OFris. *hlid*, MLG. *lit* (-*d*-), Du. *lid*, OHG. *(h)lit* (now in G. *(augen)lid* eyelid), ON. *hlið* gate, gateway, gap :- Germ. *χlīðam, f. *χlīð- cover, as in OE. *behlīdan*, OS. *bihlīdan* cover, OE. *onhlīdan* OS. *anhlīdan* open (see BE-, UN-[2]), Goth. *hleiþra* tent, hut; IE. **klĭ-* cover, shut, is repr. also in OIr., Balto-Sl., and Gr.

lido lī·dou name of a bathing-place near Venice; transf. public open-air swimming-pool. XX. Venetian It. *lido* :- L. *lītus* shore.

lie[1] lai pt. **lay** lei, pp. **lain** lein be in a prostrate or recumbent position. OE. *liċġan*, pt. *læġ*, pl. *lǣġon*, pp. *leġen* = OFris. *lidz(i)a*, OS. *liggian* (Du. *liggen*), OHG. *liggen*, ON. *liggja* :- CGerm. **ligjan* (OHG. *ligan*, G. *liegen*, Goth. *ligan* are abnormal), f. base **leg- *lag- *lǣg-* :- IE. **legh- *logh- *lēgh-*, repr. also by Gr. *léktron*, *lékhos* bed, *álokhos* bedfellow, *lókhos* lying-in, lying in wait (cf. LOCHIA), ambush, L. *lectus* bed, OSl. *ležati* lie. The form *lie* (repl. normal ME. *liġġe* li·dʒə) resulted from the generalization of the stem of the 2nd and 3rd pers. sg. pres. ind. OE. *liġ(e)st*, *līst*, *liġ(e)þ*, *līþ*; cf. LAY[1]. Hence **lie** sb. XVII.

lie[2] lai pt., pp. **lied** tell an untruth. OE. *lēoġan*, pt. *lēah*, pl. *lugon*, pp. *logen* = OFris. *liāga*, OS. *liogan* (Du. *liegen*, *loog*, *gelogen*), OHG. *liogan* (G. *lügen*, *log*, *gelogen*), ON. *ljúga*, Goth. *liugan*; CGerm. vb. f. **leug- *loug- *lug-* (whence OE. *lyġe* lie); cf. OSl. *lŭža* lie. Hence **lie** sb. untruth. XIII; repl. OE. *lyġe*.

lief līf †adj. beloved, dear. OE. *lēof* = OFris. *liāf*, OS. *liob*, *liof* (Du. *lief*), OHG. *liub*, *liup* (G. *lieb*), ON. *ljúfr*, Goth. *liufs* (*liub-*) :- CGerm. **leuƀaz* :- IE. **leubhos* (whence OSl. *ljubŭ*); see also LEAVE[1], LOVE. As adv. (compared *liever*, *lievest*) dearly, gladly XIII; developed mainly from arch. or dial. phr. *I had as lief*, *I had liever*, i.e. I should hold as dear, dearer, in which *would* was substituted on the analogy of *would rather*.

liege līdʒ entitled to feudal service (as *liege lord*, OF. *lige segnur*) XIII; bound to render this (as *liege man*, OF. *home lige*). - OF. *lige*, *liege* (cf. Pr. *litge*, It. *ligio*, medL. *lēgius*, *līgius*) - medL. *lēticus*, *læticus*, **līticus*, f. *lētus*, *lītus*, prob. - Germ. **lǣþigaz* (cf. G. *ledig* free, unoccupied), **lǣton*, *-az* (cf. Goth. *fra|lēts*, OE. *frēo|lǣta* freedman), f. **lǣt-*, base of LET[1]. ¶ For the survival of the sense 'free' cf. legal *liege poustie* being in health and in possession of one's faculties, OF. *lige poestee*, medL. *līgia potestas*.

lien lī·ən, U.S. līn (leg.) right to retain possession of property. XVI. - F. *lien*, OF. *loien* :- L. *ligāmen* bond, f. *ligāre* (cf. LIGAMENT).

lierne liə̄·ɹn (archit.) short rib in vaulting connecting principal ribs. XIX. - F. (XVI), perh. transf. use of the term for climbing plants (see LIANE).

lieu ljū place, stead. XIII (*liue*). - (O)F. *lieu* :- L. *locu-s* place (cf. LOCUS).

lieutenant lèv-, lèfte·nənt, (U.S.) lute·nənt (arch.) vicegerent XIV; military and naval rank (orig. of one 'holding the place' of a captain) XVI. - (O)F. *lieutenant*, f. *lieu* place + *tenant* holder (see LIEU, TENANT, and cf. LOCUM TENENS), with OF. word-order retained. Forms with *f*, to which the traditional Eng. pronunc. corresponds, appear in XIV, e.g. *leef-*, *leve-*, later *lief-*, *live-*, *liev-*; infl. of LEAVE sb.[1] is possible. Hence **lieu-**TE·NANCY. XV. Also **lieutenant-**GENERAL †vicegerent XV (Caxton); rank next below a general XVI. - F. *lieutenant général*, in which the second word is orig. adj. In **lord-lieutenant** (from XV applied to various officers holding deputed authority from a sovereign) *lieutenant* is adj.

life laif animate existence; course or manner of living. OE. *līf*, corr. to OFris., OS. *līf* life, person (Du. *lijf* body), OHG. *līb* life (G. *leib* body), ON. *líf* life, body :- CGerm. (exc. Gothic) **lībam* (**lībaz*), f. **līb-*, the weak grade of which appears in LIVE[1]. Hence **li·fe**GUARD bodyguard of soldiers. XVII; prob. after Du. †*lijfgarde*, G. *leibgarde* (in which the first el. means 'body'), later assoc. with *life*.

lift lift raise, elevate. XIII (Cursor M.). - ON. *lypta* = MHG., G. *lüften* :- Germ. **luftjan*, f. **luftuz* air, sky (see LOFT). Hence **lift** sb. XVI (Malory).

ligament li·gəmənt short band of animal tissue XIV; ligature XVI. - L. *ligāmentum*, f. *ligāre* bind, tie (cf. ALLY); see -MENT. So **li·ga**TURE. XIV. - late L.

light[1] lait emanation from the sun, etc.; illumination; lighted body. OE. *lēoht*, Anglian *līht* = OFris. *liacht*, OS., OHG. *lioht* (Du., G. *licht*) :- WGerm. **leuχtam* :- **leuktom* (var. **leukotom* is repr. by Goth. *liuhaþ*), f. IE. **leuk- *louk- *lŭk-*, repr. in Gr. *leukós* white, *leússein* see, *lúkhnos* (:- **luksnos*) lamp, L. *lūx*, *lūmen* (:- **leuksmen*) light (cf. LUMINOUS), *lūcēre* (cf. LUCID), *lūna* (:- **leuksnā*) moon (cf. LUNAR), OIr. *luan* moon, *luach* shining, W. *llug* light, ON. *logi* :- **lukón*) flame, OSl. *luča* beam, Skr. *ruc* shine, *rucás* bright. So **light** adj. OE. *lēoht*, *līht* = OFris. *liaht*, OS., OHG. *licht* (Du., G. *licht*). **light** vb. OE. *līhtan* = OS. *liuhtian*, etc., Goth. *liuhtjan*, largely superseded by **light**EN[5]. XIII (Cursor M.). Cf. ALIGHT[2]. comp. **li·ght**HOUSE XVII (Bacon).

light[2] lait of little weight. OE. *lēoht*, *līht* = OFris. *li(u)cht*, OS. *-līht* (Du. *licht*), OHG. *līht(i)* (G. *leicht* easy), ON. *léttr*, Goth. *leihts* :- CGerm. **liŋχtaz*, **-tjaz*, f. **liŋgw-* :- IE. **leñghʷ-*, as in Lith. *leñgvas* light; for the grade **lŋghʷ-* see LUNG. Hence **li·ght**EN[5]. XV.

lightning lai·tniŋ discharge of electricity between groups of clouds. XIV. Special use of *lightening*, vbl. sb. of *lighten* (see LIGHT[1]) with differentiated sp. Superseded ME. *leiting* (XIII), which in turn superseded *leit*, *lait*, OE. *lēġet*, *līġet*, f. base of LIGHT[1].

lights laits lungs (now of slaughtered beasts). XII. ME. *lihte*, pl. of *liht* LIGHT[2] used sb.; cf. the etymol. meaning of LUNG and OIr. *scaman* light, sb. lungs, W. *ysgyfaint* lights, *ysgafn* light, Russ. *lëgkoe* lung, *lëgkiĭ* light.

lign-aloes lainæ·louz aloes, aloes wood XIV (Ch.); aromatic wood of a Mexican tree (Bursera) XIX. – late L. *lignum aloēs* 'wood of the ALOE' (*aloēs*, gen. of *aloē*).

ligneous li·gniəs woody in texture. XVII (Bacon). – L. *ligneus*, f. *lignum* wood (:– **legnom*, f. *legere* COLLECT, fallen branches being collected for burning); see -EOUS.

ligula li·gjŭlə tongue-like strip. XVIII. L., 'strap', 'spoon', var. of *lingula*, f. *lingere* LICK, assoc. with *lingua* TONGUE; cf. -ULE.

like[1] laik having the same character or quality. XII (Orm). ME. *līc*, *līk* – ON. *líkr*, aphetic of *glíkr* = OE. *ġelīć* ALIKE. Hence **li·ken**[5] compare. XIV; cf. MLG. *līkenen*, OHG. *gi|līhinōn*, Sw. *likna*. **li·kewise**. XV.

like[2] laik please, be pleasing OE.; find agreeable, be pleased with XII. OE. *līcian* = OFris. *līkia*, OS. *likōn* (Du. *lijken*), OHG. *līhhēn*, ON. *líka*, Goth. *leikan* :– CGerm. **līkǣjan*, **līkōjan*, f. **līkam* appearance, form (see LICH). **li·k(e)able**. XVIII. **li·king**[1]. – OE. *līcung*.

likely lai·kli probable XIII (Cursor M.); suitable, fit XIV; capable-looking; handsome XV. – ON. *líkligr* (also *glíkligr*), f. *líkr* LIKE[1] + *-ligr* -LY[1]. Also adv. probably. XIV (Wyclif). **li·keness** resemblance, similarity, image, portrait. OE. (*ġe*)*līcnes*.

likin lī·kīn Chinese provincial transit duty. XIX. Chin. LI[2] + *kin* money.

lilac lai·lək shrub Syringa vulgaris. XVII. – F. †*lilac* (now *lilas*) – Sp. *lilac* – Arab. *līlak* – Pers. *līlak*, var. of *nīlak* bluish, f. *nīl* blue, indigo, NIL[1] (cf. Skt. *nīla*, whence Hindi *līl*). The earliest form *lelacke* (Bacon), in mod. dial. *laylock*, may repr. Turk. *leilaq*. So named from the bluish tinge of the flowers of some varieties.

liliaceous liliei·ʃ(i)əs lily-like; (bot.) pert. to the family Liliaceæ. XVIII. – late L. *līliāceus* (Palladius), f. *līlium* LILY; see -ACEOUS.

lillibullero li:libŭliə·rou. XVII (*-burlero*). Refrain perh. orig. burlesquing Irish words.

Lilliputian lilipjū·ʃ(i)ən diminutive. XVIII. f. *Lilliput* name of an imaginary country in Swift's 'Gulliver's Travels' (1726), peopled by pygmies six inches high; see -IAN.

lilt lilt sound (a note), lift up (the voice), sing XIV; sing with a swing XVIII. ME. *lilte* (in †*lilting horn* 'kind of trumpet', Ch.), *lülte*, obscurely rel. to LG., Du. *lul* pipe (Du. *lullepijp* bagpipe; cf. rare Sc. †*liltpipe* XV and Sc. *lill*, *lilt* hole in a wind instrument XVIII). Hence **lilt** sb. (Sc.) song, tune XVIII; swing of a tune or verse XIX.

lily li·li plant of the genus Lilium or family Liliaceæ. OE. *lilie* (weak fem.) – L. *līlium*, perh. – Gr. *leírion*, but the L. and Gr. words may have a common Mediterranean origin. The L. word is almost universally repr. in Germ. and Rom. langs. (cf. FLEUR-DE-LIS).

limb[1] lim part of the body, spec. a member such as the arm, leg, wing; branch (*l. of Satan*, etc., imp, mischievous person; in OE. *dēofles limu* 'devil's limbs'; whence simply *limb* XVII). OE. *lim* n., pl. *limu*, corr. to ON. *limr* m.; prob. rel. to OE. *liþ* limb (= Du. *lid*; see LAY-FIGURE). ¶ The parasitic b prob. arose in obl. forms, as pl. *limes*, was transferred to the nom. sg., and finally disappeared (as in other words in *-mb*).

limb[2] lim A. †limbo of Hell XV; B. edge or boundary of a surface or instrument XVI. – F. *limbe* or its source L. *limbus* (see LIMBO). So **li·mbic** (anat.). XIX. – F. *limbique*.

limbeck li·mbek. XIV. Early forms *lambyke*, *lembike*; aphetic of ALEMBIC.

limber[1] li·mbəɹ shaft; forepart of a gun-carriage. XV. Earliest forms *lymo(u)r*, perh. for **limmer*, **limner* (cf. Sc. *lymnar* XVI), sb. use of medL. *limōnārius* adj., f. *limō(n-)* shaft, of unkn. origin (cf. (O)F. *limon* shaft XII, *limonière* shafts and fore-carriage, medL. *limōnārius* shaft-horse). Hence **li·mber** vb.[1] XIX.

limber[2] li·mbəɹ pl. holes in timbers for the passage of water. XVII. – (O)F. *lumière* lümjēr light, hole (used in the same techn. sense) :– Rom. **lūmināria*, fem. sg. use of pl. of L. *lūmināre* light, lamp, f. *lūmin-*, *lūmen* (see LIGHT[1]).

limber[3] li·mbəɹ flexible, pliant. XVI. perh. from LIMBER[1] in allusion to the to-and-fro motion of shafts or a fore-carriage. Hence **li·mber** (*up*) vb.[2] XVIII.

limbo li·mbou region on the border of Hell XIV; prison, confinement XVI; neglect, oblivion XVII. orig. in phr. *in limbo*, *out of limbo*, repr. medL. *in limbō*, *e limbō*; abl. of L. *limbus* hem, selvage, fringe, in Eng. use from *c*.1400 for *limbo*, from XVII for LIMB[2] B.

lime[1] laim birdlime; mortar, cement; calcium oxide. OE. *līm*, corr. to MDu. *līm* (Du. *lijm*), OHG. *līm* (G. *leim*), ON. *līm*; f. Germ. **līm-*, var. of **laim-* LOAM, ult. rel. to L. *līmus*, which has been referred to **loimos* and **sloimos* SLIME. Hence **lime** vb. XIII.

lime[2] laim fruit of Citrus Medica acida. XVII (Sir T. Herbert). – F. *lime* – modPr. *limo*, Sp. *lima* – Arab. *līmah* (see LEMON[1]).

lime[3] laim linden. XVII (Bacon). unexpl. alteration of *line*, var. of *lind* (see LINDEN).

lime-hound see LYAM.

limen lai·men (psych.) limit below which a stimulus ceases to be perceptible. XIX. L., 'threshold', tr. G. *schwelle* (Herbart, 1824). Cf. SUBLIMINAL.

limerick li·mərik kind of nonsense verse. *c*.1895. Said to be derived from a custom of singing 'Will you come up to Limerick?' at convivial parties at which nonsense verses were extemporized.

liminal li·minəl pert. to the threshold. XIX. f. L. *līmin-*, *līmen* threshold; see -AL[1].

limit li·mit boundary; fixed point. XIV. – L. *līmit-*, *līmes* frontier; cf. F. *limite* (XVI). So **li·mit** vb. XIV. – (O)F. *limiter* or L. *līmitāre*. **limit**A·TION. XIV. – L.

limitrophe li·mitrouf adj., on the frontier XIX; †sb. borderland XVI. – F. *limitrophe* – late L. *limitrophus*, f. *līmit-* LIMIT + Gr. *-trophos* supporting (*tréphein* support, nourish).

limn lim illuminate XV; paint, portray XVI. contr. of †*lumine* (XIV) – OF. *luminer* – L. *lūmināre*, f. *lūmin-*, *lūmen* LIGHT¹. So **lim-ner**¹ li·mnəɹ illuminator XIV; painter XVI. contr. of †*luminer* (XIV), f. *lumine*. ¶ For the vowel cf. *trifle* and for loss of n cf. *autumn*.

limnology limnɔ·lədʒi study of lakes. XIX. f. Gr. *límnē* lake, marsh + -LOGY.

limousine limuzī·n motor-car with closed body. XX. F., f. *Limousin* name of a province of France; orig. caped cloak worn by natives of the province.

limp¹ limp walk lame. XVI. prob. f. †*limp-halt* lame, OE. *lempealt*, *læmpihalt*, f. **lamp-* :– IE. **lomb-* (cf. Skr. *lámbate* hangs down or loose, sinks) + *healt* HALT¹; cf. MHG. *limpfen* limp.

limp² limp wanting in firmness. XVIII. prob. of dial. origin; perh. ult. rel. to prec., the basic sense being 'hanging loose'.

limpet li·mpit mollusc of the genus Patella. ME. *lempet* :– OE. *lempedu* (cf. OHG. *lampfrīda*) – medL. *lamprēda*, *-ida* limpet, LAMPREY.

limpid li·mpid pellucid, clear. XVII. – F. *limpide* or L. *limpidus*, perh. rel. to *limpa*, *lumpa*, later *lympha* LYMPH.

linchpin li·nᵗʃpin pin in an axle-tree to keep the wheel in place. XIV (*lynspin*). ME. *lins* :– OE. *lynis* = WFris. *lins*, OS. *lunisa* (Du. *luns*, *lens*), MHG. *luns*, *lunse* (G. *lünse*); the base is seen also in ME. †*linnail* (XV), †*linpin* (XIV), perh. OE. **lyne* (:– **luni-*), rel. to OHG. *lun*, *luna* (G. dial. *lunn*, *lon*); cf. OHG. *luning* linchpin.

Lincoln green li·ŋkən grīn bright green stuff made at *Lincoln*, county town of Lincolnshire, England, a seat of cloth manufacture (cf. *Lincolnesaye* XIV). XVI.

linden li·ndən lime-tree, Tilia europæa. XVI. In *linden tree* – Du. *lindeboom*, †*lindenboom*, G. *lindenbaum*, f. *linde* (with weak inflexion) + *boom*, *baum* tree (BEAM). The first el. corr. to OE. *lind*, *linde* lime-tree, shield, ON. *lind*, prob. rel. to Gr. *elátē* silver fir (:– **l̥ntā*).

line¹ lain flax; flax thread or cloth. OE. *līn* = OS., OHG. *līn* (Du. *lijn-*, G. *lein-*), ON. *lín*, Goth. *lein* :– CGerm. **līnam* = or – L. *līnum* flax, rel. to Gr. *línon*, Ir. *lín*, Lith. *linaĩ* pl. Now dial. exc. as surviving in LINSEED. Hence **line** vb.¹ apply a layer of material to the inside of (a garment). XIV (Ch.); with ref. to linen being used for the purpose.

line² lain cord, string; string, row, series OE.; thread-like mark, stroke XIII; serial succession XIV; track, course XV. Two words of ult. identical etym. have coalesced: (1) OE. *līne* rope, line, series, rule = MDu. *līne* (Du. *lijn*), OHG. *līna* (G. *leine* cord), ON. *lína*, prob. CGerm. (exc. Gothic) – L. *līnea*; (2) ME. *ligne*, *line* – (O)F. *ligne* = Pr. *linha*, Pg. *linha* :– Rom. **linja*, for L. *līnea*, *līnia*, orig. sb. use (sc. *fībra* fibre) of fem. of *līneus* pert. to flax, f. *līnum*; see prec. Hence **line** vb.² tie with a line, etc. XIV; trace with a line XVI; bring into line (cf. ALIGN) XVII.

line³ lain cover (the bitch). XIV. – (O)F. *ligner*, also *aligner*; identical with LINE vb.², but the sense-development is obscure.

lineage li·niidʒ ancestry, pedigree, ancestors. XIV. – (O)F. *lignage*, †*linage* = Pr. *linhatge*, Sp. *linaje*, It. *lignaggio* :– Rom. **līneāticum*, f. *līnea* LINE²; see -AGE. The sp. *lineage* (XVII) is due to assoc. with *line*; the pronunc. has followed it under the infl. of *lineal*.

lineal li·niəl pert. to a line or lines XIV; in the direct line of descent XV. – (O)F. *linéal* – late L. *līneālis*; see LINE², -AL¹. So **li·ne**AR. XVII. – L. *līneāris*; cf. (O)F. *linéaire*.

lineament li·niəmənt distinctive feature XV; †line, outline XVI. – L. *līneāmentum*, f. *līneāre* make straight, f. *līnea* LINE²; see -MENT. So **line**A·TION. XIV. – L.

linen li·nin adj. made of flax OE.; now, as attrib. use of the sb., made of linen; sb. cloth woven from flax; garments, etc., of this. XIV. OE. *līnen*, *l̆innen* = OFris. (Du.) *linnen*, OS., OHG. *līnin* (G. *leinen*) :– WGerm. **līnīn*, f. **līnam* LINE¹; see -EN³.

liner lai·nəɹ ship or aircraft belonging to a line (LINE²), i.e. a regular succession of vessels plying between certain places. XIX; see -ER¹.

ling¹ liŋ long slender cod-like fish. XIII (Havelok). ME. *leng(e)*, prob. of Du. or LG. origin; cf. Du. *leng*, earlier *lenghe*, *linghe*; rel. to LONG¹ (cf. the synon. Scand. forms, ON. *langa*, Sw. *långa*, Da. *længe*).

ling² liŋ plant of the heather family. XIV. – ON. *lyng*, of unkn. origin.

-ling¹ liŋ suffix, of CGerm. origin, forming sbs., OE., OS., OHG. *-ling*, ON. *-lingr*, Goth. *-liggs*, comp. of **-ila-* -EL¹, -LE¹, and **-iŋga-* -ING³, but treated as a simple suffix. (i) In OE., added to sbs. to form sbs. denoting a person concerned with . ., e.g. *hȳrling* HIRELING; added to adjs. (occas. an adv.) to form sbs. denoting a person having the quality implied, e.g. *dēorling* DARLING, UNDERLING. In ON. the suffix was dim. in force, esp. in names of the young of animals, e.g. *gæslingr* GOSLING, *kiðlingr* young kid. ME. and later formations on the same lines are *fatling*, *grayling*, *nestling*, *sapling*; with unfavourable sense (since *c.* 1600), e.g. *groundling*, *worldling*. Formations on verb-stems are *changeling*, *shaveling*, *starveling*, *suckling* (so *nursling*). Many new dim. formations appear from XVI, e.g. *godling*, *lordling*, *princeling*.

-ling[2] liŋ also *-lings*, *-lins*, adv. suffix, repr. a var. of Germ. **liŋg-* **laŋg-* **luŋg-*, all of which appear in OE., as *bæcling* on or towards the back, *andlang* ALONG[2], *nihtlanges* for a night, *grundlunga, -linga* to the ground; so MLG., MDu. *ling(e)*, Fris. *-lings*, etc. The orig. use to form advs. of direction is continued in ME. *grufelyng* (see GROVELLING), *sideling(s)*; but more numerous are formations in which the suffix denotes condition or situation, as *darkling(s)*, *flatling(s)*.

linger li·ŋgəɹ †dwell XIII; stay behind, tarry, be tardy XVI. north. ME. *lenger*, frequent. (see -ER[4]) of †*leng* linger – ON. *lengja* = OE. *lenġan*, whence ME. *lenge* le·ndʒə = MLG. *lengen*, OHG. *lengen* (G. *längen*) :– Germ. **laŋgjan* prop. make or be long, f. **laŋg-* LONG[1].

lingerie li·nʒəri, ‖lɛ̃ʒri linen (esp. women's) articles collectively. XIX. F., f. *linge* linen :– L. *līneu-s* of linen (f. *līnum* LINE[1]), used sb.; see -ERY.

lingo li·ŋgou foreign language, strange or unintelligible language. XVII. prob. – Pg. *lingoa* :– L. *lingua* TONGUE.

lingot li·ŋgət INGOT. XV. – F.

lingua franca li·ŋgwə fræ·ŋkə orig. mixed jargon based on Italian, used in intercourse with Easterns in the Levant. XVII. It., 'Frankish tongue'; see FRANK, FERINGHEE.

linguist li·ŋgwist one skilled in languages. XVI. f. L. *lingua* TONGUE, LANGUAGE + -IST. Hence **lingui·stic.** XIX (earlier *-ical*). Cf. F. *linguiste, -istique*.

linhay li·nhei shed open in front, often with lean-to roof. XVII (*linny*). Of obscure origin; the first el. may be OE. *hlinian* LEAN[2].

liniment li·nimənt †grease XV; embrocation XVI. – late L. *linimentum*, f. L. *linere* smear, anoint; see -MENT.

link[1] liŋk loop of a chain, etc. XIV (implied in AL. *linkum*). – ON. **hlenkr* (Icel. *hlekkr*, OSw. *lænker*) :– Germ. **χlaŋkjaz*, rel. to OE. *hlenċan* pl. armour, MLG. *lenkhake* pot-hook, MHG. *gelenke* (coll.) flexible parts of the body, *gelenk* joint, link; cf. LANK (basic meaning 'to bend'). Hence **link** vb. XIV.

link[2] liŋk torch. XVI. poss. – medL. *linchinus*, alt. of *lichinus* wick, match, – Gr. *lúkhnos* light, lamp.

links liŋks (pl.) gently undulating sandy ground on the sea-shore (golf-course). OE. *hlincas*, pl. of *hlinc* (whence also dial. *linch* rising ground, ridge), perh. *k*-deriv. of the base of OE. *hlinian* LEAN[2].

linn lin (chiefly Sc.) cascade, pool XVI; precipice XVIII. – Gael. *linne*, Ir. *linn* (earlier *lind*) = W. *llyn*, Corn. *lin*, Breton *lenn*.

Linnæan, Linnean linī·ən. XVIII. f. *Linnæus*, latinized form of the surname of Carl von *Linné*, Sw. naturalist (1707–78); see -AN.

linnet li·nit small song-bird, Linota cannabina. XVI. – OF. (Walloon, Picard) *linette*, earlier *linot* (mod. *linot, linotte*), f. *lin* flax (see LINEN) + Rom. dim. suffix *-ottus*, used in the names of small animals; the bird feeds on the seed of flax and hemp (cf. G. *hänfling*, f. *hanf* hemp, Sw. *hämpling*).

linoleum linou·liəm floor-cloth in which a coating of linseed oil is used. XIX (patented by F. Walton 1860 and 1863). f. L. *līnum* flax, LINE[1] + *-oleum* OIL.

linotype lai·notaip (typogr.) machine for producing lines or bars of words. XIX (patented 1888). For *line o'* (i.e. *of*) *type*.

linseed li·nsīd seed of flax. OE. *līnsǣd*, i.e. LINE[1] + SEED; cf. MHG. *līnsāt*, Du. *lijnsaad*.

linsey li·nzi fabric, (now) of coarse wool on a cotton warp. XV. prob. f. name of *Lindsey* (near Kersey), in Suffolk, where the manufacture is said to have originated (cf. KERSEY). Hence **linsey-wolsey** li:nziwu·lzi. XV; + WOOL, with jingling ending.

linstock li·nstɔk staff to hold a lighted match. XVI. Early *lintstocke* – Du. *lontstok*, f. *lont* match + *stok* stick; assim. to LINT in application to refuse of flax used as tinder.

lint lint flax; dressing for wounds prepared by scraping linen. XIV. ME. *lyn(n)et*, perh. – (O)F. *linette* (known only in the sense 'linseed'), f. *lin* flax, LINE[1] + -ETTE, -ET.

lintel li·ntl upper horizontal of a doorway. XIV. – OF. *lintel* (mod. *linteau*), alteration of **linter*, *lintier* = Pr. *lundar*, Cat. *llindar* :– Rom. **līmitāris*, alt. of *līmināris* pert. to the threshold (used sb.), by crossing of *līmes*, *līmit-* LIMIT with *līmen*, *līmin-* threshold.

lintwhite li·ntʌait linnet. OE. *līnetwiġe*, north. ME. *lynkwhyte*, Sc. *lyntquhyte*, f. *līn* flax, LINE[1] + **twig-* (as in OHG. *zwigōn* pluck; cf. OE. *þisteltwiġe* thistle-finch).

lion lai·ən 'the king of beasts', Panthera leo. ME. *liun, lioun, leoun* – AN. *liun* (F. *lion*) = Pr. *leó*, Sp. *león*, It. *leone*, Rum. *leu* – L. *leō, leōnem* – Gr. *léōn*. (In OE. *lēo*, whence ME. *le* (Orm); cf. OFris. *lawa*, MDu. *leuwe* (Du. *leeuw*), OHG. *lewo* (G. *löwe, leu*), ON. *león, lión*; (partly from Germ.), Lith. *lẽvas*, OSl. *lĭvŭ*; all ult. – L.). So **li·on**ESS[1]. XIII (Cursor M.). – OF. *lionesse*.

lip lip edge of the mouth. OE. *lippa* = OFris. *lippa*, MLG., MDu. *lippe* (whence G. *lippe*), OSw. *lippe, lippa* :– Germ. **lipjon*, rel. to synon. OS. *lepor*, OHG. *leffur, lefs* (G. dial. *lefze*) :– Germ. **lepaz-*, **leps*; f. **lep-* :– IE. **leb-*, rel. to L. *labia, labra* n. pl. lips, Pehlevi *lap* (Pers. *lab*). ¶ F. *lippe* thick lower lip is – LG.

lipo-[1] comb. form of Gr. *lip-*, weak grade of *leípein* leave, be wanting, hence as in *lipogram, lipography*.

lipo-[2], comb. form of Gr. *lípos* fat, in scientific terms.

liquefy li·kwifai reduce to or become a liquid. XVI. – F. *liquéfier* – L. *liquefacere*, pass. *liquefierī*, f. *liquēre*; see LIQUOR, -FY. So **liquefa·**CTION. XV. – F. or late L. **lique**·SCENT. XVIII.

liquid li·kwid adj. neither solid nor gaseous XIV; (of air, sound, light) pure, clear XVI. – L. *liquidus*, f. *liquēre* (cf. LIQUOR). sb. (in phonetics) XVI; liquid substance (formerly *liquor*) XVIII. So **li·quid**ATE[3] †make clear, set out clearly XVI; clear off (a debt) XVIII; set out the liabilities of XIX; (after Russ. *likvidirovat'*) wipe out XX. f. pp. stem of medL. *liquidāre*. The financial senses are due to It. *liquidare*, F. *liquider*. **liquid**A·TION. XVI. **liqu**OR[2] li·kəɹ liquid substance. XIII. ME. *licur, licour* – OF. *licur, licour* (mod. *liqueur*) = Pr., Sp. *licor*, It. *liquore*), – L. *liquōrem, liquor*, rel. to *liquāre* liquefy, filter, *līquī* flow, *liquēre* be fluid, perh. rel. to **liq-, linquere*, LEAVE[1]. F. **liqueur** likɔ̄·ɹ in its specific sense was adopted XVIII.

liquorice, licorice li·kəris rhizome of Glycyrrhiza glabra, preparation from this. XIII. – AN. *lycorys*, OF. *licoresse, -ece* – (with assim. to *licor* LIQUOR) late L. *liquiritia* (whence also It. *liquirizia, legorizia*, MHG. *lakeritze*, G. *lakritze*, Du. *lakkeris*, Sw., Da. *lakrits*) – Gr. *glukúrrhiza*, f. *glukús* sweet (cf. GLYCERINE)+*rhíza* root (cf. RHIZOME). ¶ Rom. langs. have also metathetic forms: OF. *recolisse, regolisse* (mod. *réglisse*), Pr. *regalicia*, Sp. *regaliz(a)*, It. *regolizia*.

lira liə·rə unit of It. currency. XVII. It. – Pr. *liura* = F. *livre*, It. *libbra* :– L. *lībra* pound.

Lisle lail name of a French town, now *Lille* lil, used attrib. as in *L. thread, lace*. XIX.

lisp lisp speak with defective (sibilant) utterance. OE. **wlispian* (only in *āwlyspian*), f. *wlisp, wlips* adj. lisping; cf. MLG. *wlispen, wilspen* (Du. *lispen*), OHG. *lisp* stammering, *lispen* lisp (G. *lispeln*); imit.

lispound li·spaund unit of weight used in the Baltic trade. XVI. – LG., Du. *lispund*, for *livsch pund* 'Livonian pound'.

lissom li·səm lithe and agile. XVIII. Of dial. origin, for **lithsom*, f. LITHE+-SOME[1], with shortening of the first syll.; cf. *lithesome* (XVIII).

list[1] list A. border, edging, strip OE.; B. †boundary; pl. barrier enclosing space for tilting XIV. OE. *līste* = MDu. *lijste* (Du. *lijst*), OHG. *līsta* (G. *leiste*) :– Germ. **līstōn*, which was adopted in Rom. as F. *liste*, It. *lista*. In its application to tilting used to repr. OF. *lisse* (mod. *lice*) = Pr. *lisa*, plausibly referred to Germ. **līstjōn*, f. **līstōn*.

list[2] list †be pleasing OE.; (arch.) desire. XIV. OE. *lystan* = OS. *lustian* (Du. *lusten*), OHG. *lusten* (G. *lüsten*), ON. *lysta* :– CGerm. (exc. Gothic) **lustjan*, f. **lust-* pleasure, LUST. Hence **list** sb. †pleasure, desire XIII; whence **li·st**LESS without zest or spirit XV.

list[3] list (arch.) listen. OE. *hlystan*, f. *hlyst* hearing, corr. to OS., ON. *hlust* :– Germ. **χlustiz* :– IE. **klustis* (cf. Skr. *śruṣṭi* obedience), f. **klus-*, extension of **klu-* hear (see LOUD). So **listen** li·sn OE. *hlysnan*, corr. to MHG. *lüsenen* :– WGerm. **χlusinōjan*; cf. OE. *hlosnian* listen :– **χlusnōjan*.

list[4] list catalogue of names, etc. XVII (Sh.). – F. *liste* (XVI) = Sp., It. *lista* presumably identical with LIST[1], the special application being developed from 'strip' (of paper). Hence **list** vb. XVII.

list[5] list careening or inclination of a ship. XVII. Of unkn. origin. So **list** vb. XVII.

Listerian listiə·riən pert. to the antiseptic methods of surgery promoted by Sir Joseph (later Lord) *Lister*; see -IAN. 1880.

litany li·təni liturgical form of supplication. XIII. ME. *letanie* (later assim. to L.) – OF. *letanie* (mod. *litanie*) = Pr., Sp. *letania*, etc. – ecclL. *litanīa* (whence in OE. *letania*) – Gr. *litaneíā* prayer, entreaty, f. *litanós* suppliant, f. *litḗ* supplication, *litésthai* entreat.

litchi, lichi li·tʃī Chinese fruit. XVI (*lechia, lichea*). Chinese, f. *li-tchi*.

-lite lait final el. in many names of minerals, repr. F. *-lite* (in G. *-lit, -lith*), Gr. *líthos* stone (which is repr. directly by *-lith* in *monolith*, etc., LITHO-).

literal li·tərəl pert. to the or a letter or letters. XIV. – (O)F. *littéral* or late L. *lit(t)erālis*, f. *lit(t)era* LETTER; see -AL[1]. So **li·ter**ARY pert. to letters or literature. XVII. – L. **li·ter**ATE[2] educated, learned XV; literary. XVII. – L. *literātus*; sb. XVI. **li·teratu**RE li·t(ə)rītʃuəɹ polite learning XIV; literary work XVIII. – (partly through F. *littérature*) L. *lit(t)erātūra* (coll.) alphabetic letters, linguistic science, grammar, learning ('grammatice, quam in Latinum transferentes litteraturam vocaverunt', Quintilian). **literatim** -ei·tim letter by letter. XVII. medL., after L. *gradātim* step by step.

litharge li·þāɹdʒ monoxide of lead. XIV. ME. *litarge* – OF. *litarge* (mod. *litharge*) – L. *lithargyrus* – Gr. *lithárguros*, f. *líthos* stone+*árguros* silver, rel. to L. *argentum* silver, ARGENT.

lithe[1] laið †gentle, mild OE.; pliant, supple XV. OE. *līþe* = OS. *līthi*, OHG. *lindi* (G. *lind*) soft, gentle :– WGerm. **linþja-*, f. Germ., IE. **len-*, whence ON. *linr* soft, yielding, OE. *linnan*, OHG., Goth. *-linnan*, ON. *linna* cease (cf. L. *lentus* pliant, slow.)

lithe[2] laið (obs. or arch.) listen. XIII. – ON. *hlýða*, f. *hljóð* listening, sound, rel. to Goth. *hliuma* sense of hearing, OE. *hlēoþor* sense of hearing, music, OHG. *hliudar*, f. **χleu-* hear, LIST[3].

lithia li·þiə (chem.) oxide of lithium. XIX. modL., alteration, after *soda, potassa*, of modL. *lithion* (as if – Gr. *lítheion*, n. of *lítheios* stony, f. *líthos* stone), applied to the fixed alkali to designate its mineral origin. Hence **li·thium** metallic element of the alkaline group. XIX; see -IUM.

litho- liþo(u), liþɔ· comb. form of Gr. *líthos* stone. **litho·**GRAPHY making designs on stone to be printed from. XIX (in fugitive senses XVIII); hence **li·tho**GRAPH, -GRA·PHIC. **litho·**TOMY. XVIII. – late L. – Gr.

lithontriptic liþɔntri·ptik, **lithonthry·ptic** (med.) having the property of breaking up stone. XVII (Sir T. Browne). – F. or modL. *lithontripticus* (corrected later to *-thrypticus*), repr. Gr. (*Φάρμακα τῶν ἐν νεφροῖς*) *λίθων θρυπτικά* (drugs) comminutive of stones (in kidneys); assoc. with *τρίβειν* (rub) suggested 'wearing down'.

Lithuanian liþjuei·niən pert. to Lithuania and its language, a member of the LETTIC group; see -IAN. XVII.

litigation litigei·ʃən †disputation XVI; legal proceedings XVII. – late L. *lītigātiō(n-)*, f. *lītigāt-*, *-āre* (whence **litig**ANT, -ATE[3]), f. *līt-*, *līs* strife, lawsuit (OL. *stlīs*) + *agere* do (see ACT). So **litig**IOUS liti·dʒiəs indulging in litigation. XIV (Wycl. Bible). – (O)F. *litigieux* or L. *lītigiōsus*, f. *lītigium* litigation.

litmus li·tməs blue colouring matter from lichens. XVI. – ONorw. *litmosi*, f. ON. *litr* sb., *lita* vb., whence dial. *lit* dye + *mosi* MOSS.

litotes li·tŏtīz (rhet.) affirmative expressed by the negative of the contrary, as 'a citizen of *no mean* city'. XVII. – late L. – Gr. *lītótēs*, f. *lītós* single, simple, meagre.

litre lī·təɹ unit of capacity in the metric system. XIX. – F. *litre* (1793), suggested by †*litron* old measure of capacity, f. medL. *lītra* – Gr. *lītrā* Sicilian money of account, :– **līþrā*, whence also L. *lībra* LIVRE.

litter li·təɹ †bed XIII (Cursor M.); portable couch XIV; straw, etc., for bedding; number of young brought forth at a birth XV; disorderly accumulation of things lying about XVIII. – AN. *litere*, (O)F. *litière* = Pr. *leitiera*, Sp. *litera*, It. *lettiera* :– medL. *lectāria*, f. *lectus* (F. *lit*) bed; see LIE[1]. Hence **li·tter** vb. furnish (horse, etc.) with litter XIV (Trevisa); bring forth (young) XV (Caxton); strew with litter, scatter disorderly XVIII.

little li·tl not great or big. OE. *lytel* = OS. *luttil* (Du. *luttel*), OHG. *luzzil* (MHG, G. dial. *lützel*) :– WGerm. **lŭttila*, f. **lŭt-*, repr. also by OE. *lyt* adv. little. Compared LESS, LEAST. ¶ Not basically rel. to the synon. and similar EGerm. **lītilaz*, repr. by ON. *lítill*, Goth. *leitils*; but the ON. word affected Eng. regionally, since mod. north. dial. *lātl*, *lāl* repr. ME. *lītel*.

littoral li·tərəl adj. pert. to the shore XVII. sb. region along the shore XIX. – L. *littorālis*, var. of *lītorālis*, f. *lītor-*, *lītus* shore; see -AL[1]. So F. (XVIII).

liturgy li·təɹdʒi service of the Eucharist; form of (Christian) public worship. XVI. – F. *liturgie* or late L. *līturgia* – Gr. *leitourgiā* public service, worship of the gods, f. *leitourgós* public servant, minister, f. **leîtos* public, prob. var. of *lḗïtos* public (cf. **lḗïton* public hall), f. *lēós*, Ionic form of *lāós* people + *-ergos* performing (see WORK); cf. LAY[3]. So **li·tu·rgic**(AL). XVII. – medL. – Gr.

live[1] liv have life, be alive; subsist. OE. (i) *libban*, pres. *libbe*, *liofast*, *liofaþ*, pl. *libbaþ*, pt. *lifde*, (ii) *lifian*, pt. *lifode*, corr. to OFris. *libba*, *liva*, OS. *libbian*, *leƀon*, OHG. *lebēn* (G. *leben*), ON. *lifa* live, remain, Goth. *liban*, pt. *libaida*; f. CGerm. base **lĭƀ-* remain, continue; see LIFE, LEAVE[2].

live[2] laiv living. XVI. Aphetic of ALIVE; repl. older †*lives*, g. of *līf* LIFE.

livelihood lai·vlihud means of living. XVI. Alteration, by assim. to LIVELY and -HOOD, of *livelode* course of life, conduct, maintenance, sustenance, OE. *līflād*, f. *līf* LIFE + *lād* course, way (see LOAD, LODE); cf. OHG. *lībleita* subsistence, provisions.

livelong li·vlɔŋ, lai·vlɔŋ emotional intensive of the adj. *long*. XIV. ME. *lefe longe*, *leve longe*, i.e. LIEF, LONG[1]; cf. G. *die liebe lange nacht* 'the dear long night'. In XVI apprehended as f. LIVE[1] or LIVE[2], and consequently altered in form.

lively lai·vli †living; †vital OE.; vigorous, active XIII; life-like, animated, vivid XIV; gay XVI. OE. *līflić*, f. *līf* LIFE + *-lić* -LY[1]; cf. OHG. *līblīch*, ON. *lífligr*. So **li·ve**LY[2] adv. (OE. *līflīċe*; but newly formed in XIV).

liver li·vəɹ bile-secreting organ. OE. *lifer* = OFris. *livere*, MDu. *lever* (Du. *lever*), OHG. *libara* (G. *leber*), ON. *lifr* :– Germ. **librō*, having no certain cogns. ¶ There is no CIE. name for the liver.

Liverpudlian livəɹpʌ·dliən belonging to (a native of) *Liverpool*, of which the final syll. was joc. altered to *puddle*; see -IAN. XIX.

livery li·vəri dispensing of provisions to retainers XIII (Cursor M.); allowance of provender for horses; suit of clothes for retainers XIV; legal delivery of property XV. – AN. *liveré*, (O)F. *livrée* (whence Sp. *librea*, It. *livrea*), sb. use of fem. pp. of *livrer* DELIVER, dispense :– L. *līberāre*; see -Y[6].

livid li·vid of bluish leaden colour. XVII (Bacon). – F. *livide* or L. *līvidus*, f. *līvēre* be bluish; see -ID[1].

livre līvr old French money of account. XVI. F. :– L. *lībra* pound; cf. LIRA, LITRE.

lixivium liksi·viəm lye. XVII. – late L., sb. use of n. of *lixīvius*, f. *lix* ashes, lye. So **lixi·vi**ATE[3], **li:xivi**A·TION. XVII. – modL.

lizard li·zəɹd reptile of the genus Lacerta. XIV. ME. *lesard(e)* – OF. *lesard*, *-arde* (mod. *léz-*) = Pr. *lazert*, Sp. *lagarto*, It. *lacerta*, repr. L. *lacertus*, *lacerta*, which appears to be identical with *lacertus* muscle; cf. the etym. of MUSCLE. Early forms show variation of vowel (*e*, *i*, *u*) in the first syll.

llama lā·mə S.-Amer. ruminant allied to the camel. XVI. – Sp. *llama* lja·ma, cited as Peruvian in 1535 and 1560.

llano ljā·nou level treeless plain or steppe in the north of S. Amer. XVII. Sp. :- L. *plānum* PLAIN.

Lloyds loidz society of ship brokers and marine underwriters in London; f. name of Edward *Lloyd*, who in 1688 opened a coffee-house, which was a resort of shipping underwriters; so *Lloyd's News* from 1696, *Lloyd's List* from 1726.

lo lou int. repr. (i) ME. *lō* :- OE. *lā*, excl. of surprise, grief, or joy, (with voc.) O!; (ii) ME. *lō*, prob. short for *lōke* :- OE. *lōca*, imper. of *lōcian* LOOK (cf. north. imper. pl. †*los*, and local *loo thee* look you).

loach loutʃ small freshwater fish, Cobitis barbatula. XIV. – (O)F. *loche*, in AL. *lochia* (*c.*1200); of unkn. origin.

load loud †carriage OE.; burden XIII; transf. and fig. XVI (Sh.). OE. *lād* way, journey, conveyance = OHG. *leita* course, leading, procession (G. *leite*), ON. *leið* way, course :- Germ. **laiðō*, whence **laiðjan* LEAD[2]. The development of meaning has been infl. by assoc. with LADE. Cf. LODE. Hence vb. XV.

loadstone, lodestone lou·dstoun magnetic oxide of iron; this used as a magnet. XVI. f. *load*, LODE+STONE; lit. 'way-stone', so named from the use of the magnet in guiding mariners.

loaf[1] louf, pl. *loaves* louvz †bread; portion of bread baked in one mass OE.; moulded conical mass of sugar XIV. OE. *hlāf* = OHG. *leip* (G. *laib*, †*leib*), ON. *hleifr* loaf, Goth. *hlaifs* bread :- CGerm. **χlaiƀaz*. It is uncertain which was the primary sense, 'bread' or 'loaf'. ¶ Adoptions from Germ. are OSl. *chlěbŭ* (Russ. *khleb*), Lith. *kliẽpas*, Finnish *leipä*, etc.

loaf[2] louf (orig. U.S.) spend time idly. XIX. prob. back-formation from contemp. *loafer*, which may be based on G. *landläufer* vagabond, tramp (whence U.S. *landloafer*), f. *land* LAND[1]+*laufen* (dial. *lofen*) run, LEAP[1].

loam loum †clay, earth OE.; clay moistened to form a paste XV; fertile soil mixture XVII. OE. *lām* = (M)Du. *leem*, MLG. *lēm* (whence G. *lehm*), rel. to OHG. *leimo* (G. dial. *leimen*) :- WGerm. **laimaz*, **laimon*, f. **lai-*, **lī̆-* be sticky (see LIME[1]).

loan loun †gift, grant OE.; thing lent, act of lending XIII. – ON. *lán*, corr. to OE. *lǣn* (see LEND), MDu. *lēne* (Du. *leen*), OHG. *lēhan* (G. *lehn*) :- Germ. **laiχwniz*, *-az-* :- IE. **loiqnes-*, *-os-* (cf. Skr. *rēhnas* inheritance, wealth), f. **loiq-* **leiq-* **lĭq-*, repr. also by Gr. *leípein* leave, L. *linquere* (cf. DELINQUENT, RELINQUISH), Goth. *leihwan*, OHG. *līhan* (G. *leihen*), OE. *lēon* lend. Hence vb. XVI (latterly esp. U.S.). comp. **loa·n**WORD word adopted from another language *c.* 1860; after G. *lehnwort* (Ebel, 1856).

loath, loth louþ †hostile; †hateful, loathsome OE.; (f. the vb.) disinclined, unwilling XIV. OE. *lāþ* = OFris. *leed*, OS. *lēð* (Du. *leed*), OHG. *leid* (cf. G. *leid* sorrow, pain, *leider* prop. compar. unfortunately), ON. *leiðr* :- CGerm. (exc. Gothic) **laiþaz*, adopted in Rom. as F. *laid*, Pr. *lait* (whence It. *laido*) ugly. So **loathe** louð be hateful OE.; be averse to, (later) dislike intensely XII. OE. *lāþian* = OS. *lēthon*, ON. *leiða* :- **laiþōjan*. Hence **loa·th**LY[1]. OE. *lāþlić* = OS. *lēðlik*, etc. **loa·th**SOME[1]. XIII.

lob lɔb †pollack XIV; (dial.) bumpkin XVI; pendulous object XVII; lump XIX. prob. of Low Du. origin and repr. adoptions of various dates and sources; cf. EFris. *lob(be)* hanging lump of flesh, MLG., †Du. *lobbe*, *lubbe* hanging lip, Du. *lobbes* bumpkin, gawk. Hence **lob** vb. droop XVI; move or throw heavily XIX (whence *lob* sb. a slow ball).

lobby lɔ·bi †(perh.) monastic cloister XVI; passage or corridor attached to a building XVI (Sh.), spec. in the House of Commons XVII. – medL. *lobium*, *lobia* (see LODGE); prob. orig. in monastic use.

lobe loub roundish projecting part forming a division of an organ. XVI. – late L. *lobus* – Gr. *lobós* lobe of ear or liver, capsule, pod :- **logwós*, rel. to **legw-* in Gr. *lébinthoi* peas, L. *legūmen* pod, *legula* lobe of the ear. So **lo·b**ATE[2] (nat. hist.) lobed. XVIII. – modL. **lob**ULE lɔ·bjūl small lobe. XVII. – modL.

lobelia loubī·liə genus of herbaceous plants. XVIII. modL., f. name of Matthias de *Lobel* (1538–1616), botanist to James I; see -IA[1].

loblolly lɔ·blɔ:li thick gruel XVI; bumpkin XVII. perh. f. dial. *lob* eat or drink up noisily +*lolly* broth, soup. So prob. **lo·bscouse** lɔ·bskaus dish of meat stewed with vegetables and ship's biscuit XVII; in Da. *lapskaus*, Du. *lapskous*.

lobster lɔ·bstəɹ large marine crustacean. OE. *loppestre*, *lopystre*, *lopustre* – L. *locusta* crustacean, LOCUST, with unexpl. *p* for *c*, and *-stre* after agent-nouns in *-stre* -STER (cf. OE. *myltestre* – L. *meretrix*).

local lou·kəl pert. to (a) place. XV (*l. colour* XVIII). – (O)F. *local* – late L. *locālis*, f. *locus* place; see -AL[1]. So **locale** loukā·l locality with special reference; later form of **local** XVIII. – F. *local*, sb. use of the adj. **local**ITY loukæ·lĭti. XVII. – F. or late L. **loc**ATE[3] loukei·t appoint the place of. XVIII. f. L. *locāt-*, *locāre*, f. *locus*. **loca·**TION hiring; placing. XVI. – L. **loc**ATIVE lɔ·k- (gram.). XIX; first used in treating of Skr. grammar.

loch lɔχ (Sc.) lake. XIV (Barbour). – Gaelic *loch*; cf. LOUGH.

lochia lɔ·kiə discharge from uterus after childbirth. XVII. modL. – Gr. *lókhia*, sb. use of n. pl. of *lókhios* pert. to childbirth, f. *lókhos* lying-in (see LIE[1]).

lock[1] lɔk division of a head of hair. OE. *loc*, corr. to OFris., OS. *lok*, MDu. *locke*, Du. *lok*, OHG. *loc*, G. *locke*, ON. *lokkr* :– CGerm. (exc. Gothic) **lokkaz*, **lukkaz* (cf. ON. *lykkja* loop, bend) :– **lugnos*, f. IE. **lug-*, whence Gr. *lúgos* withy, *lugoûn*, *lugízein* bend, Lith. *pa|lugnùs* compliant. Formally coincident and perh. ult. identical with next.

lock[2] lɔk A. contrivance for fastening a door, etc. OE.; mechanism of discharge in fire-arms XVI; B. barrier on a river XIII (?); C. (? f. the vb.) interlocking grip XVI. OE. *loc* = OFris. *lok* lock, OS. *lok* hole, OHG. *loh* (G. *loch*) hole, ON. *lok* lid, end, conclusion (Goth. has *us|luk* opening) :– Germ. **lokam*, **lukam*, f. **luk-* **lūk-* close, enclose, whence CGerm. str. vb. **lūkan*, OE. *lūcan*, pt. *lēac*, pp. *locen*, which was finally repl. by a new deriv. **lock** vb. of the native sb. or an adoption of ON. *loka* (XIII, Cursor M.). The diversity of meaning in the Germ. words suggests that several independent derivs. of the base may have coalesced in form.

lock[3] lɔk as in *lock hospital* (for venereal diseases). XVII (*The Lock*). The 'Lock lazar-house' in Southwark (mentioned 1452) became such a hospital, whence the name was generalized; perh. orig. so called because specially isolated (LOCK[2]).

-lock, suffix surviving only in WEDLOCK, repr. OE. *-lāc*, the second el. of some twelve comps., in which it may be rendered 'actions or proceedings, practice', as *beadolāc*, *feohtlāc*, *heaþolāc* fighting, warfare, *brȳdlāc* nuptials, *rēaflāc* robbery, *wedlāc* pledge-giving, espousals, nuptials; = ON. *-leikr*, identical with *lāc* play, sport, ON. *leikr*, Goth. *laiks* dance, rel. to a vb. repr. by OE. *lācan*, MLG. *lēken*, ON. *leika* (surviving in north. Eng. dial. *laik* play), further connected with various vbs. of the IE. group applied to activities such as playing, leaping, springing, dancing, fighting.

locker lɔ·kəɹ box with a lock. XV. prob. of LDu. origin (cf. Flem. *loker*, Kilian); see LOCK[2], -ER[1], and for the formation cf. *drawer*.

locket lɔ·kit †iron cross-bar of a window XIV; metal plate on a scabbard XVI; †group of jewels in a pattern; †catch or spring to fasten an ornament; small case hung as an ornament from the neck XVII. – OF. *locquet* (mod. *loquet* latch), dim. of (chiefly AN.) *loc* latch, lock f. the Germ. source of LOCK[2].

lockram lɔ·krəm linen fabric. XV. – F. *locrenan*, f. *Locronan*, name of a village in Brittany, the place of manufacture; for the *m* cf. *buckram*.

locomotive lou·kəmoutiv, lou:kəmou·tiv pert. to locomotion; moving by its own powers XVII; of mechanism (e.g. *locomotive engine*, whence *locomotive* sb.) XIX. – modL. *locōmōtīvus*, f. L. *locō*, abl. of *locus* place + *mōtīvus* MOTIVE, after scholastic L. *in locō movērī* = *movērī locāliter* move by change of position in space (cf. Aristotle's ἡ κατὰ τόπον κίνησις). So **loco**MO·TION. XVII. (F. *locomotif*, *-motion* are from Eng.) **lo·co**MOTOR sb. something having locomotive power XIX (Lamb); adj. (after F. *locomoteur*) pert. to locomotion (spec. in anat. and path.).

locum tenens lou·kəm tī·nenz temporary deputy. XVII (earlier Sc. †*locumtenent* XV). medL., 'one holding the place (of another)'; L. *locum*, acc. of *locus* place, and *tenēns*, prp. of *tenēre* hold; cf. LIEUTENANT, TENANT.

locus lou·kəs place, locality (spec. in math.). XVIII. L., 'place'; cf. LIEU.

locust lou·kəst A. destructive insect migrating in swarms XIII; B. fruit of the carob (supposed to have been the food of John the Baptist); carob-tree, etc. XVII. – (O)F. *locuste* – L. *lŏ̄custa* locust, lobster or crayfish, held to be rel. to Gr. *lēkân* leap.

locution lŏkjū·ʃən †utterance; form of expression XV. – (O)F. *locution* or L. *locūtiō(n-)*, f. *locūt-*, pp. stem of *loquī* talk, speak; see -TION.

lode loud †way, journey OE.; watercourse; loadstone XVI; vein of ore (prob. after G. †*leite*) XVII. OE. *lād* LOAD, of which *lode* is a sp.-var. appropriated to the above meanings. **lode**STAR lou·dstāɹ pole star, guiding star. XIV (Ch.); cf. ON. *leiðastjarna*, MHG. *leit(e)sterne*. **lode**STONE see LOADSTONE.

lodge lɔdʒ small house, tent, arbour XIII; small lodging, cottage, etc. XV. ME. *log(g)e* – (O)F. *loge* arbour, summer-house, hut (mod. hut, cottage, box at a theatre, etc.) = Pr. *lotja*, Pg. *loja*, It. *loggia* :– medL. *laubia*, *lobia* LOBBY – Germ. **laubja* (OHG. *louppea*, *louba* sheltered or shady place, booth, hut, MHG. *loube* porch, balcony, hall, G. *laube* arbour, summer-house), prob. f. **lauƀam* LEAF (cf. ME. *lefsel* arbour), but Kluge suggests connexion with ON. *lopt* LOFT.

loess lou·es, lös (geol.) deposit of loam. XIX. G. *löss* f. Swiss G. *lösch* 'loose', f. *lösen* :– **lōsjan*, f. **lōs-* LOOSE.

loft lɔ̀ft †air, sky (see also ALOFT) OE.; upper chamber, attic XIII; gallery, floor, storey XVI. Late OE. *loft* – ON. *lopt* (pronounced loft) air, upper room, balcony, rel. to LIFT. Hence **lo·f**TY[1]. XVI; first recorded in fig. meanings, and even when literal always with rhetorical or emotional implications.

log[1] lɔg bulky mass of wood XIV (Trevisa); (naut.) apparatus for calculating a ship's speed consisting of a thin wooden float attached to a line XVI. prob. earlier; cf. AL. *loggiare* cut into logs XIII; of unkn. origin. In naut. sense (which is held by some to go back to Arab. *lauḥ* tablet) adopted in F. *loch*, †*lok*, Du., G., Da. *log*, Sw. *logg*.

log[2] lɔg (colloq.) short for LOGARITHM.

loganberry lou·gənbe·ri cultivated bramble named after J. H. *Logan*, of U.S.A., by whom it was first grown in 1881.

logaœdic lɔgəī·dik (pros.) composed of dactyls combined with trochees or of anapæsts with iambs. XIX. – late L. *logaœdicus* – Gr. *logaoidikós*, f. *lógos* speech + *aoidḗ* song; see LOGOS, ODE, -IC.

logarithm lɔ·gəriþm (math.) one of a class of functions invented by John Napier of Merchiston (d. 1617) used for abridging calculations. XVII. – modL. *logarithmus* (Napier 1614), f. Gr. *lógos* ratio + *arithmós* number (cf. LOGOS, ARITHMETIC), perh. based on Gr. ἀριθμῶν λόγος *arithmôn lógos* ratio of numbers (Archimedes III B.C.).

logger-head lɔ·gəɹhed †blockhead XVI (Sh.); large head XVI (applied to large-headed animals XVII); instrument with a long handle and bulbous head; *at loggerheads* quarrelling XVII. prob. f. *logger* (recorded only in mod. dialects but prob. earlier) hobble for horses, a deriv. of LOG + HEAD.

loggia lɔ·dʒiə open gallery or arcade. XVII. It.; see LODGE.

logic lɔ·dʒik science that treats of forms of thinking XIV; logical argumentation XVII. – (O)F. *logique* – late L. *logica* – Gr. *logikḗ* (Cicero), for *hē logikḕ tékhnē* the art of reasoning; *logikḗ*, fem. of *logikós*, f. *lógos* reasoning, discourse (see LOGOS). So **lo·gi**CAL. XVI. – medL. **logic**IAN lŏdʒi·ʃən. XIV. – (O)F. *logicien.*

logie lou·gi zinc ornament giving the effect of jewellery. XIX. f. name of the 19th-cent. inventor, David *Logie.*

logistic lŏdʒi·stik pert. to calculation; pl. art of arithmetical calculation. XVII. – late L. *logisticus* – Gr. *logistikós*, f. *logizesthai* reckon, f. *lógos* calculation; see LOGOS, -ISTIC.

logistics lŏdʒi·stiks art of moving and quartering troops and naval units. XIX. – F. *logistique*, f. *loger* quarter, LODGE; see -ISTIC, -ICS.

logo- lɔ·go(u), lɔgɔ· comb. form of Gr. *lógos* mainly in the sense of 'word' (see next). The earliest recorded Eng. words are: **lo·go-griph** kind of enigma involving words (XVI), – F. *logogriphe*, f. Gr. *lógos* + *grîphos* fishing-basket, riddle; **logo·machy** contention about words (XVI) – Gr. *logomakhiā́*. Modern are **logo·**LATRY (Coleridge), **lo·go**TYPE type of several letters cast in one piece. *c.* 1815.

logos lɔ·gɔs 'the Word' of John i 1. XVI. Gr. *lógos* account, ratio, reason, argument, discourse, saying, (rarely) word, rel. to *légein* gather, choose, recount, say (see LECTION).

-logue lɔg, U.S. **-log,** repr. Gr. *-logos*, *-logon* speaking or treating of, chiefly through F., as *analogue, catalogue, dialogue, monologue.* Words with this ending designating persons are now rare or obsolescent (except *ideologue, Sinologue*), derivs. in *-loger*, *-logist*, *-logian* being gen. preferred; cf. †*astrologue*, †*philologue*, †*theologue* and *astrologer, philologist, theologian.* The living formative is **-logist** lədʒist (f. -LOGY + -IST, sometimes after F., e.g. *etymologist*); **-loger** lədʒəɹ survives in *astrologer*, **-logian** lou·dʒiən in *theologian*, which are the earliest formations of their kind.

-logy lədʒi repr. F. *-logie*, medL. *-logia*, Gr. *-logiā́*, which is partly f. *lógos* discourse, speech, partly f. *log-*, var. of *leg-*, *légein* speak; hence derivs. in *-logia* mean either (1) saying or speaking in such-and-such a way, as *brachylogy, eulogy, tautology*, or (2) the science or study with which a person (designated by *-logos* -LOGIST, -LOGER, etc.) is concerned, or that deals with a certain subject. Of the latter class, the first el. is a sb. and in combination ends in *o*, so that the regular form of such words is in *-ology*; exceptions are PETRALOGY and MINERALOGY. Modern formations in *-logy* imply correl. formations in **-lo·gi**CAL, formerly also, now rarely, **-lo·gi**C (F. *-logique*, L. *-logicus*, Gr. *-logikós*) and **-logist** (see prec.).

loin loin part of the body between short ribs and hip-bone. XIV. – OF. *loigne*, eastern var. of *longe* (in modF. loin of veal, = Pr. *lonza*, Sp. *lonja*) :– Rom. **lumbia*, fem. of **lumbeus* LUMBAR, f. *lumbus* loin :– **londhwos*; rel. to OE. *lendenu* pl. loins, OS. *lendin*, OHG. pl. *lentīn* (G. *lende*), ON. *lend*, perh. :– Germ. **landwinjā* (**londhw-*); cf. OSl. *lędvija* (**ləndhw-*), OE. *lundlaga* kidney, ON. *lundir* loins.

loiter loi·təɹ idle, (later) linger indolently. Late ME. *lotere* XIV (PPl.), *loytre* XV (Promp. Parv.), later *leut(e)re* XVI; perh. introduced by vagrants from the Low Countries and – MDu. *loteren* wag about, Du. *leuteren* shake, totter, dawdle (*oi* repr. Du. *ö*), f. base repr. also in MDu. *lutsen* wag about. Cf. G. *lottern.* ¶ The solitary ME. instance of prp. *loltrande* (XI), corrected by some to *loitrande*, may be a deriv. of LOLL.

loll lɔl droop, dangle (intr. and trans.); lean idly XIV; hang out (the tongue) XVII (Sh.). perh. f. a base ult. identical with that of †*lill* (XVI) hang out the tongue; the orig. meaning may have been 'allow to hang loose'.

Lollard lɔ·ləɹd contemptuous name for certain heretics. XIV (implied in *lollardy*, Gower). – MDu. *lollaerd* lit. mumbler, mutterer, f. *lollen* mumble; see -ARD. The Du. name was orig. applied *c.*1300 to the Cellite or Alexian fraternity, also called *lollebroeders*, which was devoted to pious works, and later passed to other bodies, with implication of pretensions to piety and humility. ¶ The by-form †**lo·ller** (Ch., PPl.) was current till XVI; as a personal designation *Lollere* occurs XII.

lollipop lɔ·lipɔp sweetmeat. XVIII. perh. f. dial. *lolly* tongue (cf. LOLL) + POP.

lollop lɔ·ləp lounge, walk with lounging gait XVIII; bob up and down awkwardly XIX. prob. f. LOLL, by assoc. with *trollop.*

Lombard lʌ·mbəɹd one of the Langobardi who conquered Italy in VI and from whom Lombardy took its name; native of Lombardy; money-changer or banker of this nationality XIV (whence *Lombard* Street in London, and Rue des *Lombards* in Paris); †bank, pawnshop XVII. – MDu., MLG. *lombaerd* or F. *lombard* – It. *lombardo*, repr. medL. *Lango-*, *Longobardus* – Germ. **Laŋgobarðaz*, *-on* (OE. pl. *Langbeardas*, *-an*, ON. *Langbarðar*), f. **laŋga-* LONG[1] + ethnic name *Bardi*. See LUMBER[2].

lone loun solitary. XIV. Aphetic of ALONE. Hence **lo·ne**LY[1] XVI, **lo·ne**SOME[1] XVII.

long[1] lɔŋ great from end to end. OE. *lang*, *long* = OFris., OS. *lang*, *long*, OHG. *lang* (Du., G. *lang*), ON. *langr*, Goth. *laggs* :– CGerm. **laŋgaz*. The nature of the relation with L. *longus*, Ir. *long* long, and Gaulish *longo-* (in a proper name) is disputed, and the connexion formerly held between these and synon. Gr. *dolikhós* (cf. DOLICHOCEPHALIC), OSl. *dlŭgŭ*, Skr. *dīrghas*, etc., is now gen. discarded.

long[2] lɔŋ †A. grow long OE.; B. (impers.) arouse desire in OE.; have a yearning desire XIII. OE. *langian* = OS. *langōn* (MDu. *langen* seem long, desire, extend, offer (Du. *langen* offer, present), OHG. *langēn* impers. (G. *langen* reach, extend, suffice), ON. *langa* impers. and pers. desire, long :– CGerm. (exc. Gothic) **laŋgōjan*, **laŋgǣjan*, f. **laŋgaz* LONG[1].

-long lɔŋ suffix forming advs., first appears in *endlong* (XIII), in which it is orig. the adj. LONG, but in analogical formations like *headlong*, *sidelong*, it has, by assoc. with *-ling*, assumed its meaning.

longanimity lɔŋgəni·mĭti long-suffering. XV. – late L. *longanimitās*, f. *longanimis* (f. *longus* long, *animus* mind), after Gr. *makrothumiā*; see -ITY.

longevity lɔndʒe·vĭti long life. XVII. – late L. *longævitās*, f. *longævus* (after Gr. *makraiōn*), f. *longus* long + *ævum* age (cf. AY[1]); see -ITY.

longitude lɔ·ndʒitjūd length (spec. east or west in geog. and astron.; see LATITUDE ¶). XVI (Trevisa, Ch.). – L. *longitūdō*, f. *longus* LONG[1]; see -TUDE and cf. (O)F. *longitude*.

long-shore lɔ·ŋʃɔəɹ frequenting the shore. XIX. Aphetic of *alongshore* (XVIII), i.e. ALONG, SHORE[1]; cf. (*a*)*cross-country*, CROSS[3]. Hence **longshore**MAN.

long-su·fferANCE (arch.) long-suffering sb. (Tindale), adj. (Coverdale). XVI.

loo lū round card game. XVII. Shortening of *lanterloo* (XVII) – F. *lantur*(*e*)*lu*, orig. refrain of a song popular in XVII. Hence **loo** vb. subject to a forfeit at loo. XVII.

looby lū·bi lazy fellow, lout. XIV (*lobye*, PPl.). Of unkn. origin; prob. rel. to LOB.

loofah lū·fă fibrous substance of a plant used as sponge. XIX. Egyptian Arab. *lūfah*.

look luk direct one's sight OE.; have a certain appearance XIII. OE. *lōcian* = OFris. **lōkia* (WFris. *loaitsje*), OS. *lōkon*, MDu. *loeken* :– WGerm. **lōkōjan*, parallel to **logǣjan*, whence OHG. *luogēn* (G. dial. *lugen*) see, look, spy; no further cogns. are known. Hence **look** sb. XII.

loom[1] lūm tool; bucket, tub XIII; weaving machine XV (for earlier *weblome* 'weaving implement' XIV). ME. *lōme*, aphetic of OE. *ġelōma* utensil, implement, f. coll. *ġe*Y- + **lōma*, as in *andlōman* pl. apparatus, furniture.

loom[2] lūm (orig. naut.) move slowly up and down; appear indistinctly. XVI. prob. of LDu. origin; cf. EFris. *lōmen* (whence Sw. dial. *loma*) move slowly, rel. to MHG. *lüemen* be weary, f. *lüeme* slack, soft.

loon[1] lūn (chiefly north. and Sc.) rogue, scamp XV; man of low birth or condition, boor, clown; fellow, boy, lad XVI. orig. north. and Sc. in forms showing ū, which vowel has been preserved in the transference to Southern English.

loon[2] lūn name of various aquatic birds. XVII. prob. alteration of *loom* guillemot, etc. (XVII) – ON. *lómr*.

loony lū·ni (sl.) lunatic. XIX. f. LUN|ATIC, and assoc. with LOON[1]; see -Y[1].

loop lūp A. opening in a wall to look or shoot through XIV (hence *loop-hole* XVI); B. doubling upon itself of a string, etc. XIV; curved piece or part XVII. In sense A identical with AL. *loupa* (XIV) loop-hole, of unkn. origin. The identity of later senses is not certain. In the sense 'outlet, means of escape' *loop-hole* was perh. infl. by Du. *loopgat*, f. *loopen* run + *gat* way, GATE.

loose lūs unbound, unattached XIII; not close XIV; not careful, inexact XVII (Sh.). ME. *lōs* (north. *lous*) – ON. *lauss* = OE. *lēas* lying, untrue, OFris. *lās*, OS., OHG. *lōs*, Goth. *laus* :– CGerm. **lausaz*, f. **laus-* **leus-* **lus-*; see LOSE, LEASING, -LESS. Hence **loose** vb. set free, undo. XIII (*louse*). **loo·**SEN[5]. XIV; cf. ON. *losna* get free.

loosestrife lū·sstraif Lysimachia vulgaris (†L. lutea, Yellow L.), Lythrum Salicaria (†Lysimachia purpurea, Purple L.). XVI (Turner). tr. L. *lysimachia* (– Gr. *lusimákheion*), acc. to a misconception (as old as Pliny) that it is directly f. Gr. *lusi-*, comb. form of *lúein* LOOSE + *mákhē* strife, whereas it is f. *Lusímakhos*, the personal name of its discoverer, an application of the adj. *lusímakhos* loosing (i.e. ending) strife. Hence vb.

loot lūt war booty. XIX. – Hindi *lūṭ*, repr. either Skr. *lōtra*, *lōptra* booty, spoil (f. *lup* = *rup* break), or Skr. *luṇṭ* rob.

lop[1] lɔp cut off branches, etc. of. OE. **loppian*, implied in pp. *lopped* (*æt loppede thorne*, Birch 'Cartularium Saxonicum' iii 240); cf. AL. *loppāre* (XV); perh. f. **lup-*, and rel. to Lith. *lùpti* strip, peel. Hence **lop** sb. smaller branches or twigs. XV.

lop² lɔp hang loosely. XVI. rel. to LOB. Hence **lop-ear(ed).** XVII. **lop-sided.** XIX (earlier *lap-* XVIII).

lope loup (dial.) leap XV; run with long bounding strides XVI. var. of dial. *loup* (XIV) – ON. *hlaupa* LEAP.

lophiodon lofai·ðdɔn (geol.) genus of fossil mammals. XIX. modL., f. Gr. *lóphion*, dim. of *lóphos* crest+*odont-* TOOTH.

loquacious lŏkwei·ʃəs talking much. XVII (Milton). f. L. *loquāci-*, *loquāx*, f. *loquī*; see LOCUTION, -IOUS. So **loquac**ITY lŏkwæ·sĭti XVII. – F. – L.

loquat lou·kwæt fruit of Eriobotrya japonica. XIX. – Chinese *luh kwat* 'rush orange'.

lorch(a) lō·ɹtʃ(ə) fast vessel of Chinese rig. XVII. – Pg. *lorcha*, of unkn. origin.

lord lōɹd master, ruler, †husband OE.; designation of rank XIV; peer of the realm XV. OE. *hlāford*, once *hlāfweard* :– **χlaibward-*, f. **χlaib-* LOAF + **ward-* keeper, WARD¹. The etymol. sense expresses the relation of the head of a household to his dependants who 'eat his bread' (cf. OE. *hlāfǣta* 'bread-eater', servant, and the similar G. *brotherr* 'bread-lord', employer, Sw. *matmoder*, etc., 'meat-mother', mistress). The word is, like LADY, a peculiarly Eng. formation (late OIcel. *lávarðr* is from ME.). It was reduced to one syll. (XIV) by the fall of *v* in *lōverd* and coalescence of the vowels. Hence vb. XIII. **lo·rd**LY¹. OE. *hlāfordlić*. **lo·rd**SHIP. OE. *hlāfordsćipe*.

lore¹ lōəɹ teaching; doctrine; learning. OE. *lār* = OFris. *lāre*, OS., OHG. *lēra* (Du. *leer*, G. *lehre*) :– WGerm. **laizō*, f. **lais-* LEARN.

lore² lōəɹ (nat. hist.) strap-like part. XIX. – L. *lōrum* strap.

lorgnette lōɹnje·t eye-glasses, opera-glass. XIX. F., f. *lorgner* squint, f. *lorgne* squinting. So **lorgnon** lō·ɹnjɔ̃. XIX.

loricate lɔ·rikeit having armour of plates or scales. XIX. – L. *lōrīcātus*, f. *lōrīca* breast-plate, f. *lōrum* strap; see -ATE².

lorikeet lɔrikī·t Malay parrot. XVIII. f. LORY+*-keet*, of PARAKEET.

lorimer, -iner lɔ·riməɹ, -inəɹ (hist.) maker of horses' bits, spurrier, etc. XIII (AncrR.). – OF. *loremier*, *lorenier*, f. *lorain* strap of harness :– Rom. **lōrānum*, f. L. *lōrum* strap, thong; see -ER². ¶ *Lorimer* survives in the title of a London livery company and as a surname.

loriot lɔ·riət golden oriole. XVII. – F. *loriot*, for *l'oriot*, with def. art. incorporated; *oriot* is an unexpl. alteration of *oriol* ORIOLE.

loris lō·ris kind of lemur. XVIII. – F. *loris* (Buffon), said to be – Du. †*loeris* booby, clown.

lorn lōɹn †lost; (arch.) FORLORN. XIII (Cursor M.). contr. form of *loren*, pp. of OE. *lēosan*, ME. *leese* (see LOSE), of which it is the only surviving part.

lorry, lurry lɔ·ri, lʌ·ri long waggon without sides. XIX. Of north-country origin; the sp. *laurie* in the minutes of a meeting of the Liverpool and Manchester Railway of 3 Dec. 1834 suggests that the vehicle was called after an inventor named *Laurie*.

lory lō·ri parrot-like bird of the Far East, etc. XVII. – Malay *lūrī*, dial. var. of *nūrī*, whence *nory*: earlier *lourey*, *lowry*, the present *lory* being due to Buffon's form *lori*.

lose lūz pt., pp. **lost** lɔ̀st orig. intr. †perish, pass. *be lost* be brought to destruction; in late Nhb. OE. appears in trans. senses †(i) destroy, (ii) become unable to find, in the latter meaning finally repl. †*leese* (OE. *lēosan*). OE. *losian*, *losode*, *ġelosod*, f. *los* (see LOSS); corr. to OS. *lōsian*, *-on* (MLG. *lōsen*) become free, ON. *losa* loosen, refl. get loose. The normal repr. of *losian* would be louz, which is found in dial., and is reflected by the sp. *lose*. The pronunc. lūz is presumably due to the infl. of *loose*.

losel lou·zəl (arch.) profligate, scoundrel. XIV. prob. f. *los-*, stem of LOSE; cf. synon. †*lorel* (XIV), f. *loren* LORN, and BROTHEL, f. *broþen*, pp. of *brēoþan* be ruined; see -EL¹.

losh lɔʃ (Sc.) deformation of LORD (cf. GOSH), used in excls. XVIII.

loss lɔ̀s fact of losing or being deprived. XIV (PPl., Ch.). prob. back-formation from *lost*, pp. of LOSE; cf. the synon. contemp. †*lost* (Trevisa, Ch.). Not continuing OE. *los* (only in phr. *tō lose* to destruction), corr. to OHG. *(far)lor*, ON. *los*, f. Germ. **lus-* **laus-* (see LESS, LOOSE), **leus-* (OE. *lēosan*, whence ME. *leese* lose, and LORN; also *forlēosan*, whence FORLORN), extension of IE. **lou-* **leu-* **lu-* (Gr. *lúein* set free, L. *luere*, *solvere* pay, SOLVE).

lot lɔt object used in deciding a matter by appeal to chance; what falls to a person thus OE.; prize in a lottery XVI; plot of land XVII; set of articles XVIII; party or set XVI; large number XIX. OE. *hlot* portion, choice, decision, corr. to OFris. *hlot*, MLG. *lot*, (M)Du. *lot*, ON. *hlutr*, *hluti*; f. **χlut-* (also in OE. *hlȳt* lot), rel. to **χleut-*, in OE. *hlēotan*, OS. *hliotan*, OHG. *liozan*, ON. *hljóta* cast lots, obtain by lot, and to **χlaut-*, in OE. *hlīet* (:– **χlautiz*), OS. *hlōt*, OHG. *(h)lōz* (G. *loos*, *los*), Goth. *hlauts* lot; the primary Germ. sense is unknown. ¶ The Germ. word appears in F. *lot*, It. *lotto* LOTTO, Sp., Pg. *lote*. Cf. ALLOT, LOTTERY.

lotion lou·ʃən liquid preparation for external use XIV; †washing XVI. – (O)F. *lotion* or L. *lōtiō(n-)* washing, f. *lōt-*, *laut-*, pp. stem of *lavāre* LAVE; see -TION.

lottery lɔ·təri scheme for distributing prizes by lot. XVI. prob. – Du. *loterij* (early XVI), whence modL. *loteria*; cf. F. *loterie*, – Du., or It. *lotteria*; see LOT, -ERY.

lotto lɔ·tou, **loto** lou·tou card game on the principle of a lottery. XVIII. – It. *lotto* or its deriv. F. *loto*; see LOT.

lotus lou·təs plant yielding a soporific fruit; water-lily of Asia, etc. XVI. – L. *lōtus* – Gr. *lōtós*, of Semitic origin.

loud laud strongly impressing the sense of hearing. OE. *hlūd* = OFris. *(h)lūd*, OS. *hlūd* (Du. *luid*), OHG. *hlūt* (G. *laut*) :– WGerm. **χluđaz* :– IE. **klūtós*, pp. of **kleu-* **klu-* hear, a base of very wide extent, whence also Gr. *klúein* hear, *klutós* famous, *kléϝos* glory, L. *cluēre* be famed, W. *clywed* heard, OIr. *ro|chluiniur* I hear, OSl. *slava* glory, *slovo* word, Arm. *lu* known, Skr. *śru* hear, *śravas* glory. Cf. LIST[3]. ¶ For the pp. formation cf. *cold, old, sad, uncouth,* and G. *satt, zart.*

lough ləχ in Ireland = Sc. LOCH. XIV. ME. *lowe, loȝe, lou(g)h,* repr. OE. (Nhb.) *luh* pool, strait, gulf – Ir. *loch*; the normal pronunc. of the Eng. word has been superseded by that of Ir. *loch.*

louis lū·i French gold coin. XVII. In full *louis d'or* (of gold); application of the name of many French kings :– *Ludovīcus*, latinization of G. *Ludwig.*

lounge laundʒ move lazily XVI; recline lazily XVII. perh. f. †*lungis* lout, laggard – OF. *longis* :– L. *Longīnus* name of the centurion who pierced the body of our Lord with a spear. Hence sb. XVIII.

loup laup (Sc.) leap. XIV (Barbour). – ON. *hlaupa* LEAP. Also sb. – ON. *hlaup.*

lour lau·əɹ look sullen XIII (King Horn); be dark and threatening XV. Of unkn. origin; similar forms in other langs. are not recorded early enough to be seriously considered as the source, nor are their meanings for the most part appropriate, viz. MHG., MLG. *lūren* (G. *lauern*) lie in wait, early modDu. *loeren* frown, look askance, (now only) lie in wait. ¶ In the second sense coincident in sp. and partly in meaning with LOWER vb. descend.

louse laus parasitic insect, Pediculus, OE. *lūs*, pl. *lȳs* (**lice** lais) = MLG., MDu., OHG. *lūs* (Du. *luis*, G. *laus*), ON. *lús* :– CGerm. (exc. Gothic); cf. W. *lleuen*, pl. *lau.* Hence **lous**Y[1] lau·zi. XIV.

lout laut awkward ill-mannered fellow. XVI. perh. f. †*lout* vb. bend or bow low (OE. *lūtan* = ON. *lúta*).

louver lū·vəɹ dome on a roof XIV; series of sloping boards to admit air and exclude rain XVI. – OF. *lover, -ier* skylight, prob. – Germ. form rel. to those cited s.v. LODGE.

lovage lʌ·vidʒ plant-name. XIV. ME. *lov(e)ache*, alteration (as if *love-ache* 'love parsley'; ME. – (O)F. *ache* parsley :– L. *apium*) of OF. *levesche, luvesche* (mod. *livèche*) :– late L. *levisticum* (sc. *apium*), for earlier *ligusticum*, n. of *ligusticus* Ligurian. ¶ From medL. *lubisticum* (for *levisticum*) were adopted OE. *lufestice*, OHG. *lubestecco*, *-stichal* (G. *liebstöckel*).

love lʌv strong affection or attachment. OE. *lufu* = OFris. *luve*, OHG. *luba* :– **luƀō* (cf. Goth. *brōþrulubō* brotherly love), f. weak grade of WGerm. **leuƀ-* **lauƀ-* **luƀ-*, repr. also by OS. *lubig* loving, OHG. *gilob* precious, and OE., OS., ON. *lof*, OHG. *lob* praise; for the other grades see LIEF, LEAVE[1], BELIEF, BELIEVE. Outside Germ. the base appears in L. *lubet* it is pleasing, *lubīdō* (see LIBIDINOUS), OSl. *ljubŭ* dear, *ljubiti* love, Skr. *lúbhyati* desires. So **love** vb. OE. *lufian* (WGerm.). The sense of 'no score' in games (XVIII) derives from the phr. *for love* without stakes, for nothing (XVII). comps.: †**lo·ve**DAY day of settlement. XIII; tr. medL. *dies amoris.* **lo·ve**LOCK[1]. XVI (Lyly). **lo·ve**LY[1] lʌ·vli †loving, amorous; †lovable; attractive on account of beauty. XIII (Cursor M.). OE. *luflič.* **lo·ve**SOME[1] (arch.) lovable, lovely. OE. *lufsum.*

low[1] lou (north. dial.) flame. XII (Orm). – ON. *logi* = OFris. *loga* :– Germ. **logon*, **lugon* :– **lukón* rel. to MHG., G. *lohe* (also in *lichterloh* in a blaze) :– **luχō* :– **lúkā*, f. **luk-*; see LIGHT[1].

low[2] lou not high or tall. XII. Early ME. *lāh*, inflected *lāȝe* – ON. *lágr* = OFris. *lēge*, *lēch*, MDu. *lage, laech, lege, leech* (Du. *laag*), MHG. *læge* (G. dial. *läg*) flat :– CGerm. (exc. Goth.) **lǣgjaz*, f. **lǣg-*, see LIE[1]. Hence **low** adv. XIII. ME. *lahe, laȝe.* **low·**-LAND less hilly region of a country (spec. Scotland). XVI (*lowland*, Dunbar). Cf. LALLANS. **low·ly** adj. XIV (Ch.); see -LY[1].

low[3] lou characteristic sound made by cattle. OE. *hlōwan*, pt. *hlēow* = OLFrankish *hluoien* (Du. *loeien*), OHG. *hluojen*, ON. *hlóa* (once) roar, redupl. str. vb. f. Germ. **χlō-* :– IE. **klā-*, as in L. *clāmare* shout, Gr. *ki|klēskein* call.

lower lou·əɹ more low, inferior. XII (Orm). ME. *lahre*, compar. of LOW[2] (see -ER[3]). Hence **lower** vb. cause to go down. XVII (Sh.). So superl. **low·**EST. XII (Orm).

loxodromic ləksoudrə·mik pert. to oblique sailing or sailing by the rhumb. XVII. – F. *loxodromique*, f. Gr. *loxós* oblique + *drómos* course; see -IC.

loyal loi·əl faithful to obligations. XVI. – F. *loyal*, OF. *loial, leial* – L. *lēgālis* LEGAL; cf. LEAL. So **loy·al**TY. XIV. – OF. *loialté* (mod. *loyauté*).

lozenge lə·zĭn[d]ʒ rhomb, diamond XIV (Ch.); medicated tablet, orig. diamond-shaped XVI. – OF. *losenge* (mod. *losange*) = Sp. *losanje*, It. *lozanga*; prob. deriv. of the word repr. by Pr. *lausa*, Sp. *losa*, Pg. *lousa* slab, tombstone, and late L. *lausiæ* (*lapides*) stone slabs, slates, of Gaulish or Iberian origin.

L. s. d. elesdī· abbrev. of L. *libræ* pounds (see LIVRE), *solidī* shillings (see SOU), *denariī*, pl. of DENARIUS.

lubber lʌ·bəɹ clumsy fellow, lout XIV; clumsy seaman (cf. *land-lubber*) XVI. ME. *lobre, lobur*, possibly – OF. *lobeor* swindler, parasite, f. *lober* deceive, sponge upon, mock (perh. – MHG. *loben* praise) with assim. in sense to LOB.

lubra lū·bră aboriginal woman of Australia. XIX. – Tasmanian *loubra*, prob. f. *loo, lowa* woman+*proi* big (E. E. Morris).

lubricate lʲū·brikeit make slippery or smooth XVII; treat with oil XVIII. f. pp. stem of L. *lūbricāre*, f. *lūbricus* SLIPPERY, f. IE. **sleub-*; see -ATE³. So **lubri·city** -i·sĭti wantonness XV; slipperiness XVII. – F. – late L.

luce lʲūs pike. XIV (Ch.). – OF. *lus, luis* = Pr. *luz*, Cat. *llus*, It. *luccio* :– late L. *lūcius*.

lucerne lʲusə̄·ɹn plant resembling clover. XVII (often *la lucerne*, with retention of the F. def. art.). – F. *luzerne* – modPr. *luzerno*, transf. use of *luzerno* glow-worm, with ref. to the shiny seeds.

lucid lʲū·sid shining XVI (Spenser); unclouded, clear XVII. – F. *lucide* or It. *lucido* – L. *lūcidus*, f. *lūcēre* shine; see LIGHT¹, -ID¹.

Lucifer lʲū·sifəɹ morning star; Satan. OE. – L. *lūcifer*, f. *lūci-, lūx* LIGHT¹+*-fer* bearing, -FEROUS. As the name of a friction match to produce instantaneous light *Lucifer* succeeded to *Promethean* (both recorded 1831).

luck lʌk fortune good or ill; good fortune. XV. prob. orig. as a gambling term – LG. *luk*, aphetic of *geluk*, in MDu. *ghelucke* (Du. *geluk*) = MHG. *gelücke* (G. *glück* good fortune, happiness), f. *ge-* Y-+a base of unkn. origin; the LG. word was adopted in Icel., OSw. *lukka*, etc. Hence **lu·cky**¹. XV.

lucre lʲū·kəɹ gain, profit (now rare except in *filthy lucre*, Tindale's rendering of *αἰσχρὸν κέρδος* Titus i 11). XIV (Wyclif, Ch.) – F. *lucre* or L. *lucrum* gain, f. IE. **lu- *leu- *lou-*, repr. by Gr. *apolaúein* enjoy, Goth. *laun*, OS., OHG. *lōn* (Du. *loon*, G. *lohn*), OE. *lēan* wages, reward.

lucubration lʲūkjubrei·ʃən (nocturnal) study or its product. XVI. – L. *lūcubrātiō(n-)*, f. *lūcubrāre* work by lamplight, f. *lūc-, lūx* LIGHT¹; see -ATION.

lud lʌd reduced form of LORD, used in excls. and the barrister's address *my Lud*. XVIII.

ludicrous lʲū·dikrəs †sportive, jocular; †frivolous, witty XVII; ridiculous XVIII. f. L. *lūdicrus*, f. *lūdicrum* stage play, f. *lūdere* play (cf. ALLUDE, etc.); see -OUS.

lues lʲū·īz plague. XVII. L.

luff lʌf (naut.) ME. *lof* †perh. a contrivance for altering a ship's course (XIII), often in phr. *wend* or *turn the luff*. – OF. *lof*, prob. of LG. or Du. origin; so also Sp., Pg. *ló*, G. *luv*, Sw. *luf*, Da. *luv*, used of the weather side or part of a ship or sail (in Eng. from XIV): ult. origin and orig. sense obscure. Hence **luff** vb. bring nearer to the wind. XIV (*love*, Gower); perh. immed. – Du. *loeven*.

lug¹ lʌg pull, tug, drag along. XIV. prob. of Scand. origin; Sw. *lugga* pull a person's hair, *lugg* forelock, nap of cloth; perh. rel. to Sc. and north. *lug* (i) flap, lappet XV, (ii) ear XVI, prob. orig. 'something that can be pulled or laid hold of'.

lug² lʌg large marine worm. XVII. perh. of Celtic origin; cf. Anglo-Ir. *lurg*.

luge lʲūʒ sleigh. XX. – F. *luge*, of Swiss (and ult. Gaulish) origin.

luggage lʌ·gidʒ traveller's baggage. XVI (Nashe, Sh.). f. LUG¹+-AGE, after *baggage*; prob. orig. applied joc. to inconveniently heavy baggage.

lugger lʌ·gəɹ vessel with four-cornered sails fore and aft. XVIII. f. *lugsail* (XVII) four-cornered sail hanging obliquely, prob. f. *lug* flap, lappet (XV), ear (XVI), of uncertain origin, but possibly rel. to LUG¹.

lugubrious lʲugjū·briəs doleful, mournful. XVII. f. L. *lūgubris*, f. *lūgēre* mourn (cf. Gr. *leugaléos, lugrós* sorrowful); see -IOUS.

lukewarm lʲū·kwɔ̄ɹm tepid. XIV (Trevisa). f. ME. *luke* (XIII), of which the vars. *leuk, hleuc* suggest deriv. from *lew* (cf. *lew-warm* XV), OE. **hlēow* (in *ġehlēow* warm, *un|hlēow* cold, *hlēowe* warmly) = ON. *hlýr* warm, mild, rel. obscurely to OHG. *lāo* (G. *lau*); cf. LEE¹. See WARM.

lull lʌl soothe to sleep or quiescence. XIV. imit. of the repetition of lu lu or similar sounds (cf. *lully, lulla, lullay* XV) appropriate to singing a child to sleep; cf. Sw. *lulla*, Da. *lulle* hum a lullaby, Du. *lullen*, and further MDu. *lollen* mutter (see LOLLARD) and L. *lallāre* sing to sleep. Hence **lullaby** lʌ·ləbai soothing refrain or song. XVI; cf. BYE-BYE¹, HUSHABY, ROCKABY.

lumbago lʌmbei·gou painful affection of the loins. XVII. – L. *lumbāgo*, f. *lumbus* LOIN, whence medL. *lumbāris*. **lu·mbar**. XVII.

lumber¹ lʌ·mbəɹ move clumsily or heavily. XIV (*lomere*). perh. of symbolic origin.

lumber² lʌ·mbəɹ useless odds and ends XVI; roughly prepared timber XVII. poss. f. LUMBER¹, but later assoc. with *lumber(house)*, *Lumber Street* var. of *lombard* (XVII) pawnshop (considered as a storehouse of odds and ends of property); see LOMBARD.

lumbrical lʌmbrai·kəl pert. to a worm. XVII. –modL.., f. L. *lumbrīcus* worm; see -AL¹.

luminary lʲū·minəri light-giving (celestial) body; source of intellectual, etc., light. XV. – OF. *luminarie* (mod. *-aire*) or late L. *lūminārium*, f. *lūmin-, lūmen* LIGHT¹; see -ARY. So **lu·minous** full of light. XV. – (O)F. *lumineux* or L. *lūminōsus*.

lump¹ lʌmp compact shapeless mass. XIII (Cursor M.). Of unkn. origin; the parallel forms in the Germ. langs. (unless those cited s.v. LUMP² are identical) are not recorded so early; nearest in form and meaning are Da. *lump(e)* lump, Norw., Sw. dial. *lump* block, stump, log; but the presumably orig. sense of 'shapeless piece' is seen also in Du. *lomp*, †*lompe* rag, Du. *lomp*, LG. *lump* coarse, rude (whence G. *lumpen* rag).

lump² lʌmp spiny-finned fish of uncouth appearance, Cyclopterium lumpus. XVI. – MLG. *lumpen*, MDu. *lumpe* (whence modL. *lumpus*), perh. identical with LUMP¹.

lump[3] lʌmp look sulky XVI; (coupled with *like*) be displeased at XIX. Of symbolic sound; cf. *dump, glump, grump, hump, mump*.

lunar lʲū·nəɹ pert. to the moon. XVII. – L. *lūnāris*, f. *lūna* moon; see LIGHT[1], -AR. In *lunar caustic* the meaning is 'of silver', *luna* being used by alchemists for silver. So **lu·n**ARY (now rare). XVI. **luna·**TION time from one full moon to the next. XIV (Maund., Trevisa). – medL. *lūnātiō(n-)*, f. *lūna*.

lunatic lū·nətik orig. affected with the kind of insanity that was supposed to depend on changes of the moon XIII; sb. XIV (PPl., Wyclif). – (O)F. *lunatique* – L. *lūnāticus*, f. *lūna* moon; see prec., -ATIC. Hence **lu·n**ACY. XVI.

lunch lʌnᵗʃ and **luncheon** lʌ·nᵗʃən appear first towards the end of XVI in the sense 'thick piece, hunch, hunk'; perh. – Sp. *lonja* slice, the longer form being prob. an extension on the analogy of *punch* and *puncheon*, *trunch* and *truncheon*. The sense 'slight repast between morning meals' appears XVII, for *luncheon*, and first in the forms *lunchin(g)*; the present use of *lunch* (XIX) is a shortening of this, whence **lunch** vb.

lundyfoot lʌ·ndifut kind of snuff. XIX. Named after *Lundy Foot*, a Dublin tobacconist (XVIII).

lune lʲūn (pl.) fits of frenzy. XVII (Sh.). – L. *lūna* moon (cf. LUNAR, LUNATIC), in medical use 'fit of lunacy', whence also F. *lune*, MHG. *lūne* (G. *laune* whim, caprice).

lunette lʲune·t semicircular object. XVI. – F. *lunette*, dim. of *lune* moon; see prec., -ETTE.

lung lʌŋ respiratory organ in the thorax. OE. *lungen* = OFris. *lungen*, MLG. *lunge*, MDu. *longe* (Du. *long*), OHG. *lungun* (G. *lunge*), corr. to ON. *lunga*; f. Germ. **lung-* :– IE. **l̥ngh-*; see LIGHT[2]. The lungs were so named because of their lightness; cf. LIGHTS.

lunge[1] lʌnᵈʒ sword-thrust. XVIII. Aphetic of *allonge*, *elonge* (XVII), f. vbs. of the same form – F. *allonger* lengthen (in phr. *allonger un coup d'épée* give a sword-thrust), f. *à* AD- + *long* LONG[1]. So **lunge** vb. XVIII. Hence **lu·nge**OUS †(of a fall) heavy; (dial.) rough and violent. XVII.

lunge[2] lʌnᵈʒ †thong XVII; long rope used in training horses XVIII. – F. *longe*, shortening of *allonge* (as in *allonge d'une courroie* piece to lengthen a leather), f. *allonger* (see prec.).

lungi lu·ŋgī loin-cloth. XVII (Sir T. Herbert). – Urdu – Pers. *lungī*, f. synon. *lung*.

lupin lʲū·pin plant of the genus Lupinus. XIV (Trevisa). – L. *lupīnus*, *lupīnum*, prob. rel. to *lupus* WOLF.

lupus lʲū·pəs (path.) ulcerous disease of the skin. XVI. L., 'WOLF'.

lurch[1] lɜ̄ɹtʃ First recorded in *lurch* vb. (XIV) beat at a game in a particular manner; the sb. appears XVI in the senses †game resembling backgammon, final state of the score in a game, †discomfiture, †cheat, swindle, and in phr. †*have in the lurch* have at a disadvantage, *leave in the lurch* leave in unexpected difficulty, which may be in part a modification of *leave in the lash* (of obscure origin). The immed. source appears to be F. †*lourche* (also *l'ourche*) game resembling backgammon, also in phr. *demeurer lourche* be discomfited (orig. in the game), prob. – MHG. *lurz* (mod. dial. *lurtsch* left (hand), wrong, in modG. *lurz werden* fail in a game; cf. MHG *lürzen* deceive (cf. OE. *belyrtan*).

lurch[2] lɜ̄ɹtʃ †be furtively about or in a place XV; get the start of, †be beforehand in securing XVI. perh. var. of LURK, infl. in meaning by LURCH[1]. Hence **lu·rch**ER[1] †forestaller of food; swindler XVI; loiterer; cross-bred dog between sheepdog and greyhound XVII.

lurch[3] lɜ̄ɹtʃ sudden leaning over to one side. (XVIII) XIX. app. orig. in *lee-lurch*, prob. alteration of *lee-larch* (Falconer, 1769), for *lee-latch* (1708) drifting to leeward, f. LEE + †*latch* (XVII) ? leeway, ? lurch, possibly f. F. *lâcher* let go (:– L. *laxāre*, f. *laxus* LAX). Hence **lurch** vb. XIX.

lurdan lɜ̄·ɹdən (obs. or arch.) sluggard, vagabond. XIII (Cursor M.). – OF. *lourdin*, f. *lourd* heavy, OF. *lort* foolish :– L. *lūridu-s* yellow, LURID, which in Rom. assumes many divergent meanings.

lure lʲuəɹ falconer's apparatus to recall a hawk; tempting thing XIV (Ch.); angler's device for alluring fish XVII. – OF. *luere* (mod. *leurre*) = Pr. *loire*, OCat. *lloure* – Germ. **lōþr-* (cf. MHG. *luoder*, G. *luder* bait), prob. rel. to **laþōn* invite (OE. *laþian*, etc.). Hence **lure** vb. XIV (Ch.); cf. F. *leurrer*, OF. *loirrer*. See also ALLURE.

lurid lʲuə·rid wan and sallow, sickly pale XVII; shining with a red glare; yellow-brown XVIII; ominous, 'ghastly' XIX. – L. *lūridus*, f. *lūror* wan or yellowish colour; see -ID[1].

lurk lɜ̄ɹk lie hid or in ambush. XIII (Havelok). perh. f. *lūr-* LOUR + frequent. suffix *-k* as in *talk*.

luscious lʌ·ʃəs sweet and highly pleasant, sweet to excess. XVI. An isolated instance of *lucius* occurs XV, in a MS. which has also *licius*, aphetic of DELICIOUS; but there is no proof of continuity of this with the earliest forms of the present word, *looshious, lousious, lussyous* (XVI), which remain obscure.

lush[1] lʌʃ flaccid, soft XV; succulent and luxuriant. XVII (Sh. 'Tempest' II i 52, and in imitation). poss. var. of *lash* (XV) soft and watery (of plants), by assoc. with prec.

lush[2] lʌʃ liquor, drink. XVIII. perh. joc. application of LUSH[1]. The sl. **lushington** lʌ·ʃiŋtən drunkard (also in phr. e.g. *deal with Lushington* take too much drink) is a joc. use of the surname *Lushington* with punning allusion to this; the 'City of Lushington' was a convivial Society meeting at the Harp Tavern, Russell Street, London, until about 1895.

lust lʌst pleasure, desire, appetite; sexual desire OE.; passionate desire XVII. OE. *lust*, corr. to OFris., OHG. (G.) *lust*, ON. *losti*, Goth. *lustus*, f. CGerm. **lust-* (cf. LIST[2]). Hence **lust** vb. XIII; now only arch., have inordinate desire XVI (Tindale). **lu·st-**FUL[1]. OE. **lu·sty**[1] †joyful; †pleasing XIII; †lustful; powerful, strong XIV; cf. MHG. *lustic*, ON. *lostigr*.

lustre[1] lʌ·stəɹ period of five years. XIV. – L. *lūstrum*, prop. quinquennial purification, perh. :– **loustrom*, f. *lavāre* wash, LAVE. The L. form (XVI) is more usual. So **lustra·tion** expiatory sacrifice, etc., purification. XVII. – L. *lūstrātiō(n)-*, f. *lūstrāre*.

lustre[2] lʌ·stəɹ sheen, gloss; luminosity, brilliance. XVI. – F. *lustre* – It. *lustro*, f. *lustrare* :– L. *lūstrāre* light up :– **lūcstrāre*, f. *lūc-*, *lūx* LIGHT[1]. Hence **lu·strous**. XVII (Sh.).

lustring lʌ·striŋ glossy silk fabric. XVII. – F. *lustrine* or its source It. *lustrino* (said to have been first made at Genoa), f. *lustro* LUSTRE[2]; with assim. to -ING[3].

lute[1] lʲūt stringed musical instrument. XIV. – F. †*lut* (mod. *luth*), earlier *lëut*, prob. – Pr. *laüt* (= Sp. *laud*, Pg. *alaude*) – Arab. *al'ūd* (see AL-[2]). ¶ The Rom. word appears in MHG. *lūte* (G. *laute*), Du. *luit*.

lute[2] lʲūt tenacious clay or cement to stop holes, etc. XIV. – (O)F. *lut* or medL. *lutum*, spec. use of L. *lutum* mud, potter's clay.

luteous lʲū·tiəs of deep-yellow colour. XVII. f. L. *lūteus*, f. *lūtum* yellow weed; see -EOUS.

lutestring lʲū·tstriŋ glossy silk fabric. XVII (Pepys). app. alteration of LUSTRING, which however is evidenced rather later.

luxation lʌksei·ʃən dislocation. XVI. – F. *luxation* (Paré) – late L. *luxātiō(n-)*, f. *luxāre*, f. *luxus* dislocated; see -ATION.

luxury lʌ·kʃəri †lasciviousness XIV; use of and indulgence in choice or costly things XVII; means of such indulgence XVIII. – OF. *luxurie*, var. of *luxure* = Sp. *lujúria*, It. *lussuria* – L. *luxuria*, f. *luxu-s* abundance, sumptuous enjoyment, perh. the noun corr. to *luxus* (see prec.) and meaning orig. 'excess'. In L. and Rom. the word connotes vicious indulgence, the neutral senses of the Eng. word being expressed by *luxus*, F. *luxe* (which has become familiar in Eng. in *train de luxe*, etc.), Sp. *lujo*, It. *lusso*. So **luxuri·ant** lʌgzj-, lʌgʒ-, lʌksjuə·riənt prolific XVI; profusely growing, etc. XVII. – prp. of L. *luxuriāre* grow rank (whence **luxu·riate**[3] XVII, Burton), f. *luxuria*. **luxu·rious** †lascivious, †excessive XIV; self-indulgent XVII. – O(F) – L.

-ly[1] li suffix appended to sbs. and adjs. to form adjs. OE. *-līć*, ME. *-lich*, *-lik*, *-li*, corr. to OFris., OS., OHG. *-līk* (Du. *-lijk*, G. *-lich*), ON. *-ligr*, *-legr*, Goth. *-leiks*. (The vowel was shortened in OE., ON., and G.; the Eng. forms in *-li*, *-ly* are due to ON.). The orig. Germ. adjs. were comps. of **likam* appearance, form, body (cf. LYCHGATE and SUCH, WHICH), e.g. **frijōndlika-* friendly, having the appearance of a friend, **gōðolīka-* goodly, having the appearance or form of what is good, of good appearance. The most general senses in all Germ. langs. are 'having the qualities appropriate to', 'characteristic of', 'befitting'; *-ly* was added to sbs. of alien origin, as *courtly*, *princely*, *scholarly*; formations on designations of things are infrequent, as *earthly*, *heavenly*, *leisurely*, *worldly*. *Deadly*, *likely*, *lively*, *lovely*, *mannerly*, *only*, *stilly* are exceptional in form. A use common to Eng. with other Germ. langs. is to denote periodic occurrence, e.g. *daily*, *yearly*; such adjs. are based on the corr. advs.

When *-ly* is appended to adjs., the derivs. denote a quality allied or approximating to that expressed by the primary, e.g. OE. *lēoflīc* (f. *lēof* LIEF) 'such as may seem dear', beloved, pleasing, *lowly*, *kindly*, *poorly*, *sickly*.

-ly[2] li suffix forming advs. of manner. OE. *-līće*, ME. *-liche*, *-līke*, *-liȝe*, *-li(e)* = OFris. *-līke*, OS., OHG. *-līko* (Du. *-lijk*, G. *-lich*), ON. *-liga*, Goth. *-leikō*: f. -LY[1] with advb. suffix **-ō*. (As in -LY[1] the ME. forms *-li(e)*, *-ly* are due to ON.). In Germ. an adv. with this suffix no doubt orig. implied the existence of a corr. adj. in -LY[1], but in OE. there are some advs. formed immed. on simple adjs., as *bealdlīće* BOLDLY, *swētlīće* SWEETLY; and formations of this type increased greatly in ME. The general sense is 'in a manner characteristic of one who or a thing that is so-and-so' (as defined by the simplex), hence, 'in a so-and-so fashion', 'to a so-and-so degree'. Adverbs referring to moments or periods of time, such as *annually*, *formerly*, *instantly*, *lately*, *latterly*, *quarterly*, *shortly*, *yearly*, were prob. based at first on *early*; *firstly*, *secondly*, etc., were modelled on F. *premièrement*, L. *primo*, etc.; formations on sbs. such as *namely*, *partly* are prob. based on L. *nominatim*, *partim*; *accordingly*, *mostly*, *purposely* are also particular instances; formations on pps., such as *admittedly*, *allegedly*, meaning 'as is admitted, alleged', have become latterly frequent.

Peculiarities of spelling and pronunciation are exemplified by the following: *able*, *ably*, *simple*, *simply*; *idly* (†*idlely*); *whole*, *wholly*; *solely*, *vilely*; *fully* fu·li; *dully* dʌ·l(l)i, *coolly* kū·lli, *foully* fau·lli; *merry*, *merrily*; *dryly*, *drily*; *shyly*, *grayly*; *true*, *truly*; *franticly*, *publicly* (but *heroically*, *poetically*).

lyam lai·əm, **lyme** laim leash for hounds. XIV. – OF. *liem* (mod. *lien*) = Pr. *liams*, Pg. *ligame*, It. *legame* :– L. *ligāmen* LIEN. Hence *lyam-*HOUND bloodhound. XVI.

lycanthropy laikæ·nþrŏpi insanity in which the patient imagines himself a beast (spec. a wolf). XVI. – modL. *lycanthrōpia* – Gr. *lukanthrōpiā*, f. *lukánthrōpos*, f. *lúkos* WOLF + *ánthrōpos* man; see -Y[3].

lyceum laisī·əm the garden in Athens to which Socrates resorted and where Aristotle taught XVI; (after It. *liceo*, F. *lycée*) place of study or instruction XVIII. – L. *Lycēum* – Gr. *Lúkeion* (sc. *gumnásion* GYMNASIUM), n. of *Lúkeios* epithet of Apollo, to whose temple the Lyceum was adjacent.

lychgate see LICH.

lychnis li·knis (bot.) genus of plants (including campion and ragged robin). XVII. – L. – Gr. *lukhnís* some red flower, f. *lúkhnos* lamp (cf. LIGHT[1]).

lycopodium ləikŏpou·diəm (bot.) genus of plants (club-moss). XVIII. modL. – Gr. *lúkos* WOLF + *pod-*, *poús* FOOT; so named from the claw-like shape of the root.

lyddite li·dait kind of high explosive. XIX. f. *Lydd*, name of the town in Kent where it was first tested; see -ITE.

Lydian li·diən pert. to Lydia; spec. of a musical mode. XVI. f. L. *Lȳdius* – Gr. *Lúdios*; see -IAN.

lye lai alkalized water or alkaline solution used for washing. OE. *lēaġ* = MDu. *lōghe* (Du. *loog*), OHG. *louga* (G. *lauge*) lye, ON. *laug* hot bath :- CGerm. (exc. Gothic) **laugō*, f. **lau-* (cf. LATHER) :- IE. **lou-* wash, LAVE.

lykewake lai·kweik (local) watch kept at night over a dead body. XVI. Sc. *likewalk* (G. Douglas), preceded by *lychwake* (XIV Ch., Mirk); perh. – ON. **líkavaka*; see LICH, WAKE[1].

lymph limf (rhet.) water; †sap XVII; colourless alkaline fluid in the body XVIII. – F. *lymphe* or L. *lympha*, prob. hellenized form (by assoc. with Gr. *numphḗ* nymph) of *lumpa*, *limpa* (cf. LIMPID), perh. :- **dumpa* (cf. Oscan *Diumpais* Nymphis). So **lympha·tic** A. †frenzied; B. pert. to lymph. XVII. – L. *lymphāticus* mad, adaption of Gr. *numpholēptós* seized by nymphs (cf. *numphiân* be frenzied); in mod. scientific L. the ending has prob. been assoc. with *spermatic*.

lynch law linᵗʃ lō, earlier †*Lynch's law* (XVIII) infliction of punishment by a self-constituted court. XIX. Named after Captain William *Lynch*, of Pittsylvania, Virginia, U.S.A., who first set up this self-created judicial tribunal. Hence *Judge Lynch*, imaginary authority from whom the sentences imposed were said to proceed. **lynch** vb. condemn and punish (esp. kill) by lynch law.

lynx liŋks feline animal, Lynx, credited with very keen sight. XIV (Rolle). – L. *lynx* – Gr. *lúgx*, rel. to OE. *lox*, OHG. *luhs* (G. *luchs*), OSw. *lō*, Lith. *lúšis*, OPruss. *luysis*, MIr. *lug*; a widespread IE. name, prob. f. **leuk-*, as in Gr. *leússein* see (see LIGHT[1]), the animal being named from its keen sight.

lyre laiəɹ stringed instrument of the harp kind. XIII (*lire*, Laȝ.). – OF. *lire* (mod. *lyre*) – L. *lyra* – Gr. *lúrā*. So **lyric** li·rik. XVI. – F. *lyrique* or L. *lyricus* – Gr. *lurikós*; sb. lyric poem. XVI. **ly·rical**. XVI (Sidney).

M

ma mā see MAMMA[1].

ma'am mæm, məm, m. XVII (*mam*, Dryden), contr. of MADAM. ¶ The old pronunc. mām remains dial., and, repr. by **marm,** in the joc. (orig. U.S.) *school-marm* schoolmistress XIX.

mac mæk person whose name contains the prefix *Mac*. XVII. Ir., Gael. *mac* :- OCeltic **makkos*, rel. to W. *mab*, OW. *map* :- OCeltic **makwos*; a prefix in many Sc. and Ir. names.

macabre məkā·br in *Dance Macabre*, the Dance of Death XV (*daunce of machabree*, Lydg.); (from modF.) gruesome XIX. The form now usual repr. F. *macabre* (XIX), error for OF. *macabré* (*danse macabrée aux Innocens* XV), perh. alt. of OF. *Macabé* Maccabæus (cf. †*Judas Macabré*, medL. *chorea Machabæorum* dance of the Maccabees XV, MDu. *Makkabeusdans* XV); the orig. ref. may have been to a miracle play in which the slaughter of the Maccabees under Antiochus Epiphanes was enacted.

macaco[1] məkei·kou (orig.) S. African (Congo) monkey, (later) monkey of the genus Macacus. XVIII. – Pg. *macaco* – native (Fiot) *makaku* some monkeys, f. *ma* numerical sign + *kaku* monkey. So **macaque** məkā·k. XVII. – F. – Pg.

macaco[2] məkei·kou lemur. XVIII. – F. *mococo* (Buffon); cf. MAKI.

macadam məkæ·dəm applied to a kind of roadway (or the material used for it) invented by John Loudon *McAdam* (1756–1836). Hence **maca·damize**, etc. XIX.

macaroni mækərou·ni Italian wheaten paste in tubes XVI; exquisite, fop XVIII. – It. *maccaroni*, later *maccheroni*, pl. of *macca-*, *maccherone*, f. late Gr. *makaría* barley food (Hesychius). ¶ The sl. application to dandies perh. orig. indicated a preference for foreign food.

macaronic mækərə·nik applied to burlesque verse in which vernacular words are mingled with Latin in a latinized form. XVII. – modL. *macarōnicus* – It. †*macaronico* (*maccheronico*), joc. f. *macaroni* (see prec.). First recorded in 'Carmen macaronicum de

Patavinis' (1490) by Tisi degli Odassi. But the form was popularized by Teofilo Folengo, author of 'Liber Macaronices' (1517), who described his verses as a literary analogue of macaroni ('a gross, rude, and rustic mixture of flour, cheese, and butter').

macaroon mækərū·n small sweet biscuit of ground almonds, etc. XVII. – F. *macaron* – It. *maccarone* MACARONI.

macartney məkā·ɹtni fire-backed pheasant. XIX. f. name of George, Earl *Macartney* (1737–1806), a specimen having been presented to him by the emperor of China.

macassar məkæ·səɹ name of an unguent for the hair made in the early 19th cent. by Rowland & Son and represented to contain ingredients from *Macassar*, name (in the native form *Mangkasara*) of a district in the island of Celebes. XIX (1809). Cf. ANTIMACASSAR.

macaw[1] məkɔ̄· bird of the parrot kind. XVII. – Pg. *macao*, of unkn. origin.

macaw[2] məkɔ̄· palm of the genus Acrocomia. XVII. Carib; cf. Arawak *mocoya, macoya*.

maccoboy mæ·kəboi kind of snuff. XVIII (*macabao, macauba*). f. name of a tobacco called after *Macouba*, district in Martinique.

mace[1] meis heavy club XIII (RGlouc.); sceptre, staff of office XV; old form of billiard cue XVIII. – OF. *masse, mace* (mod. *masse* large hammer, etc.) = Pr. *masa*, Sp. *maza*, It. *mazza* :– Rom. **mattea* club. So **macer**[2] mei·səɹ mace-bearer; (Sc.) official in a court of law. XIV. – OF. *massier*.

mace[2] meis outer covering of the nutmeg. XIV (*macis*). – AL. *macis* (XIII) or (O)F. *macis* (XIV) – L. *macir* red spicy bark from India (Pliny): the form *macis* being apprehended as a pl., a new sg. *mace* was formed from it.

mace[3] meis small gold coin in Malaya. XVI. – Malay *mās*, said to repr. Skr. *māsha* weight of about 17 grains.

macedoine mæ·sidoin, ||masedwan medley of fruits in syrup or jelly. XIX. – F. *macédoine*, presumably a sb. use of OF. adj. – L. *macedonicus* Macedonian.

macerate mæ·səreit soften by steeping; cause to waste away. XVI. f. pp. stem of L. *mācerāre*, f. **māk-*, prob. corr. to **makj-* of Gr. *mássein* knead (cf. MAKE); see -ATE[3]. So **macera·tion**. XV. – F. or L.

machet see MATCHET.

machicolation mætʃikŏlei·ʃən (archit.) opening between corbels supporting a parapet, through which missiles were dropped on the heads of assailants. XVIII. f. *machicolate* (XVIII), f. OF. *machicoler*, AL. *machicollāre*, ult. f. Pr. *machacol* (for **macacol*), f. *macar* beat, crush + *col* neck; see -ATION.

machination mækinei·ʃən plotting, plot. XV. – (O)F. *machination* or L. *māchinātiō(n-)*, f. *māchinārī* contrive, f. *māchina* MACHINE; see -ATION.

machine məʃi·n †structure, fabric XVI; military engine; wheeled vehicle; apparatus for applying mechanical power, etc. XVII. – (O)F. *machine*, corr. to Sp. *maquina*, It. *macchina* – L. *māchina* device, contrivance, engine – *mākhanā́*, Doric form of Gr. *mēkhanḗ*, f. *mē̂khos* contrivance, rel. to Germ. **magan* have power; see MAY[1]. ¶ The F. word has been adopted in all Germ. and Sl. langs. Hence **machi·nery**. XVII; first used of stage appliances.

-machy məki always with connective -o-, repr. Gr. *-makhíā* fighting, in sbs. derived from adjs. in *-makhos* that fights, rel. to *mákhē* battle; e.g. *logomachy* (see LOGO-).

macilent mæ·silənt lean, thin. XVI. – L. *macilentus*, f. *macer* thin, MEAGRE, after *gracilentus* (f. *gracilis*); see -LENT.

mackerel mæ·k(ə)rəl sea-fish, Scomber scomber. XIII (Havelok). – AN. *makerel*, OF. *maquerel* (mod. *maquereau*), first recorded in medL. *macarellus*, from Flanders; of unkn. origin. See -REL.

mac(k)intosh mæ·kintɔʃ applied to a kind of waterproof material invented by Charles *Macintosh* (1766–1843). 1836.

macle mæ·kl twin crystal; dark spot in a mineral. XIX. – F. *macle* – L. *macula* spot, mesh (cf. MAIL[1]). A var. *macule* of the F. word is repr. by **macle, mackle** blur in printing, blurred sheet XVIII, with a corr. vb. blur in printing XVI. – F. *maculer*.

macramé məkrā·mei fringe of knotted cord, etc. XIX. – Turk. *makrama* towel – Arab. *miqramaʰ* striped cloth.

macro- mæ·krou comb. form of Gr. *makrós* long, large, rel. to L. *macer* thin, MEAGRE. The chief and oldest comp. is **ma·crocosm** the universe (XVI) – medL. *macrocosmus*, repr. Gr. **makròs kósmos* 'great world' (see COSMIC); cf. (O)F. *macrocosme*.

macron mæ·krən horizontal mark ¯ placed over a vowel sign to denote length. XIX. – Gr. *makrón*, n. of *makrós* MACRO-.

mactation mæktei·ʃən slaughtering. XVII. – late L. *mactātiō(n-)*, f. pp. of *mactāre* slay; see -ATION.

maculate mæ·kjuleit spotted. XV. – L. *maculātus*, pp. of *maculāre*, f. *macula* spot (cf. MAIL[1]); see -ATE[2]. Now only in contrast with IMMACULATE.

macute məkjū·t (orig.) piece of cloth used as money; money of account (2,000 cowries). XVIII. Native African name (Congolese) *makuta* bundle of palm mats used as currency, f. †*kuta* tie (cf. *kutulula* untie).

mad mæd out of one's mind; foolish, (now) insanely foolish; wildly excited, furious. XIII (*mad, med*). Aphetic of ME. †*amad* (XIII), repr. OE. *ġemǣ̆d(d), ġemǣded*, pp. of **ġemǣdan* render insane, f. *ġemād* insane = OS. *gimēd* foolish, OHG. *gameit, kimeit* foolish, vain, boastful, Goth. *gamaiþs* crippled :- Germ. **gamaiðaz*, f. **ga-* Y-+ **maiða-* :- IE. **moitó-*, pp. formation on **moi-* **mei-* change (cf. L. *mūtāre*); the primary sense appears in Goth. *maidjan* adulterate, *in|maideins* exchange, the corr. ON. *meiða* meaning to cripple. (The simplex **mād* appears in OE. *mādmōd* folly.) Hence **madd**EN[5] mæ·dn. XVIII; superseded **mad** vb. (XIV) in gen. use.

madam mæ·dəm polite title of address used by servants to a mistress (usu. reduced to MA'AM) XIII; †lady of rank, fine lady XVI; kept mistress XVIII; hussy XIX. orig. *ma dame, madame* – OF. *ma dame* (mod. *madame*), i.e. *ma* my, *dame* lady; see DAME and cf. MADONNA. The form **madame** (abbrev. *Mme*) (XVII) is now mainly confined to use with the surname of a French married woman.

madapollam mædəpɔ·ləm kind of cotton cloth. XIX. f. *Madapollam* (:- *Mādhavapalam* – Telugu *Mādhavayya-pālemu*), a suburb of Narsapur, Madras presidency, India.

madder mæ·dəɹ herbaceous climbing plant, Rubia tinctorum, cultivated for a dye-stuff; formerly in wider use. OE. *mædere*, corr. to OHG. *matara*, ON. *maðra* in place-names (Sw. *madra*, Norw. *modra, maure*), obscurely rel. to synon. WFris. *miede*, MLG., MDu. *mēde* (Du. *mede, mee*).

madeira mədiə·rə white wine of Madeira, an island off NW. Africa, once thickly wooded (whence its name). XVI. – Pg. *Madeira*, a use of *madeira* wood, timber = Sp. *madera* :- L. *māteria* MATTER.

mademoiselle mæ:dəmwaze·l title applied to an unmarried Frenchwoman, miss. XVII. F.; *ma* my, *demoiselle* young woman (see DAMSEL).

madid mæ·did moist. XVII. – L. *madidus*, f. *madēre* be wet, rel. to Gr. *madân* be wet, flow; see -ID[1].

madonna mədɔ·nə †my lady, madam XVI; the Virgin Mary, Our Lady, picture or statue of her XVII. – It. *madonna*, i.e. *ma*, old unstressed form of *mia* my (:- L. *mea*), *donna* lady (:- L. *domina*); cf. MADAM.

madrasah, medresseh mədræ·si, -e·si Mohammedan college. XVII. repr. (through Indian, Turkish, or Pers. channels) Arab. *madrasa*[h], f. *darasa* study.

madrepore mæ·dripɔ̄əɹ perforate coral. XVIII. – F. *madrépore* or modL. *madrepora*, – It. *madrepora*, presumably taken by Ferrante Imperato, 'Historia Naturalis' 1599, to be f. *madre* MOTHER (perh. in allusion to the prolific growth of the 'plant')+*poro*, L. *porus* PORE, but the second el. may be L. *pōrus* – Gr. *pôros* calcareous stone, stalactite.

madrigal mæ·drigəl amatory lyrical poem, esp. to be set to music; kind of part song. XVI. – It. *madrigale* (whence F., Sp. *madrigal*) :- medL. *mātricālis* mother-, simple, primitive (*carmen matricale*), f. L. *mātrix* breeding animal, as adj. mother- (cf. medL. *ecclesia matrix* mother church); see MATRIX. ¶ It. *madrigale* was altered later to *madriale*, and *mandriale*, as if 'pastoral song', by assoc. with *mandr(i)a* herd, f. L. – Gr. *mándra* sheepfold.

maelstrom mei·lstrəm whirlpool in the Arctic Ocean off Norway; sb. gen. XVII. – early modDu. *maelstrom* (now *maalstroom*), f. *maalen* grind, whirl round+*stroom* STREAM, whence the Scand. forms, e.g. Sw. *malström*.

Mænad mī·næd Bacchante. XVI. – L. *Mænad-, Mænas* – Gr. *Mainad-, Mainás*, f. *mainesthai* rave (see MANIA).

maffick mæ·fik back-formation from *mafficking*, orig. applied to the uproarious rejoicings in London, etc., on the relief of the siege of *Mafeking* (17 May 1900) in the Boer War of 1899–1902, the place-name being treated as a gerund or prp. in -ING.

mafia mafī·ə violent hostility to law and order; body of people manifesting this. XIX. Sicilian Italian.

mag mæg (colloq.) chatter. XIX. f. MAGPIE, used for 'chatterer' from XVII; cf. *chattermag*.

magazine mægəzī·n, mæ·gəzīn storehouse, spec. for arms; stores, munitions XVI; †storehouse of information XVII; periodical publication, esp. for general readers XVIII ('The Gentleman's Magazine', 1731). – F. *magasin* – It. *magazzino* (Sp. *magacen*) – Arab. *makhāzin*, pl. of *makhzan* storehouse, f. *khazana* store up. ¶ With Arab. article (AL-[2]) prefixed, Sp. has *almacen, almagacen*, Pg. *armazem*.

Magdalen mæ·gdəlin reformed prostitute XVII; home for the reformation of prostitutes XVIII. From *the Magdalen* (XIV, Ch.), after (O)F. *la Madeleine* – ecclL. (*Maria*) *Magdalēna, -lēnē* – Gr. (*María hē*) *Magdalēnḗ* (Mary) of *Magdala*, a town on the Sea of Galilee in Palestine, name of a disciple of Christ 'out of whom went seven devils' (Luke viii 2), identified with the 'sinner' of Luke vii 37, and regarded as a saint by the Church. See MAUDLIN.

mage see MAGUS.

magenta mədʒe·ntə brilliant crimson aniline dye discovered soon after the battle at *Magenta* in N. Italy, where in 1859 the Austrians were defeated by the French and Sardinians. 1860 (*M. red*).

maggot mæ·gət worm, grub XIV (Trevisa); whimsy, crotchet XVII. perh. AN. alteration of ME. *maddo(c)k*, earlier *maðek* (cf. *maked* XV) – ON. *maðkr* (Da. *madike*), a *k*-deriv. (see -OCK and cf. MAWKISH) of the base of OE. *maþa, maþu* = OS. *matho*, OHG. *mado* (Du., G. *made*), Goth. *maþa* :– Germ. **maþon*, **maþō*, of unkn. origin. For the change of k to g cf. *flagon, sugar*.

magic mæ·dʒik art of controlling events by occult means. XIV (Ch.). – OF. *magique* (superseded by *magie*) – late L. *magica* (*magicē* Pliny) – Gr. *magikḗ*, sb. use (sc. *tékhnē* art) of *magikós*, f. *mágos* MAGUS. So **ma·g**IC adj. XIV (Gower), **ma·g**ICAL XVI. (*M. lantern* tr. of modL. *laterna magica* XVII.) **mag**ICIAN mədʒi·ʃən. XIV (*magicien*, Ch.). – (O)F. *magicien*.

magilp see MEGILP.

magisterial mædʒistiə·riəl pert. to a master or magistrate. XVII. – medL. *magisteriālis*, f. late L. *magisterius*, f. L. *magister* MASTER; see -IAL.

magistral mədʒi·strəl †authoritative; devised by a physician for a particular case, †sovereign XVI; (fortif.) principal XIX. – F. *magistral* or L. *magistrālis*; see MASTER, -AL.

magistrate mæ·dʒistrət, -eit officer concerned with the administration of laws XIV; justice of the peace XVII. – L. *magistrātus* magistracy, magistrate, f. *magistr-* MASTER; see -ATE[1] and cf. F. *magistrat*. Hence **ma·gistr**ACY. XVI. **ma·gistrat**URE -trətʃəɹ office of a magistrate. XVII. – F.

magma mæ·gmə †dregs of a semi-liquid substance XV; thin pasty mixture of substances XVII; (geol.) stratum of fluid matter XIX. – L. *magma* – Gr. *mágma* thick unguent, f. base **mag-* of *mássein* knead (cf. MAKE).

magnanimous mægnæ·niməs nobly brave, great-souled. XVI. f. L. *magnanimus*, f. *magnus* great + *animus* mind, after Gr. *megalópsukhos*. So **magnani·m**ITY. XIV. – (O)F. – L. See MAGNITUDE, ANIMAL, -OUS.

magnate mæ·gneit great man. XV (Lydg.; *magnates*, prob. the L. pl., and so until XVIII or XIX). – late L. (Vulg.) pl. *magnātes*, f. *magnus*; see MAGNITUDE and cf. PRIMATE; perh. infl. by F. *magnat* in XVIII.

magnesia mægnī·ʃ[1]ə A. †(alch.) mineral ingredient of the philosopher's stone XIV (Ch.); B. †(spec. *black m.*) manganese XVII; C. (spec. †*white m.*) hydrated magnesium carbonate, used medicinally; (chem.) magnesium oxide, MgO XVIII. – medL. *magnēsia* – Gr. (*hē*) *Magnēsía* (*líthos*) 'the Magnesian stone', (1) loadstone, (2) stone with silvery sheen; the development of sense B is obscure (there may have been simply formal confusion); sense C may depend on modL. *magnēs carneus* 'fleshy magnet', applied to a white powder which adhered to the lips as iron to a magnet. Cf. MAGNET. Hence **magnes**IUM mægnī·ziəm, -ī·siəm, -ī·ʃ[1]əm chemical element, Mg, base of magnesia. XIX (Davy, who applied it first to manganese).

magnet mæ·gnit †magnetic oxide of iron XV (Promp. Parv.); †piece of loadstone; piece of iron or steel having the same attractive properties XVII. – L. *magnēta* (whence OF. *magnete*, perh. in part the source), acc. of *magnēs* – Gr. *mágnēs*, for *ho Mágnēs líthos* (also *ho Magnḗtēs líthos*, *hē líthos Magnêtis*) the Magnesian stone (whence L. *lapis magnēs*, repr. by †*magnes stone* XIV Trevisa to XVII). So **magnet**IC mægne·tik XVII, **-e·t**ICAL XVI. – late L. *magnēticus*; so F. *magnétique*, etc. **ma·gnet**ISM. XVII. – modL. *magnētismus*, **ma·gnet**IZE. XVIII. **magneto-** -ī·tou (see -O-), first in *m.-electric* (1831, Faraday).

magni- mægni comb. form of L. *magnus* great (see MAGNITUDE), as in **magni·loqu**ENT grandiloquent XVII, f. L. *magniloquus* (*loquī* speak; see -ENT).

magnific mægni·fik †renowned; †sumptuous XV (Caxton); (arch.) grand XVI; also **magni·f**ICAL. XVI. – F. *magnifique* or L. *magnificus*; see -FIC. So **magni·fic**ENT great in achievement; †royally munificent; grand, splendid. XVI. – F. *magnificent* or L. *magnificent-*, alt. stem of *magnificus*, after *benevolens* (var. of *-volus*). **magni·fic**ENCE. XIV. – F. or L. **magni·fico** title of magnates of Venice. XVI (G. Harvey). It., sb. use of adj. – L. *magnificus*. **ma·gni**FY A. (arch.) act for the honour of; B. (arch.) augment XIV (Wyclif); C. increase the apparent size of XVII. – (O)F. or L.; sense C is purely Eng.

magnificat mægni·fikæt name of the canticle beginning '*Magnificat* anima mea Dominum' My soul doth magnify the Lord (Luke i 46); 3rd pers. sg. pres. ind. of L. *magnificāre* MAGNIFY.

magnitude mæ·gnitjūd greatness XIV (Trevisa); (relative) size XVI. – L. *magnitūdō*, f. *magnus* great, large, rel. to Gr. *mégas* (cf. MEGA-), Skr. *mahant-* great, Germ. **mikil-* MUCH; see -TUDE.

magnolia mægnou·liə genus of large trees. XVIII. – modL., f. name of Pierre *Magnol* (1638–1715) professor of botany at Montpellier; see -IA[1].

magnum mæ·gnəm bottle containing two quarts. XVIII (Burns). n. sg. of L. *magnus* large (see MAGNITUDE). So **magnum bonum** mæ·gnəm bou·nəm large kind of plum XVIII; kind of potato XIX. n. sg. of L. *bonus* good; 'a large good one'.

magpie mæ·gpai common European bird, Pica caudata, noted for its noisy chatter and pilfering habits. XVII. f. *Mag*, pet-form of *Margaret* + PIE[1]. Earlier (dial.) *maggot-pie* (XVI), f. *Maggot* – (O)F. *Margot*, pet-form of *Marguerite* Margaret.

maguey mæ·gwei, magei· American aloe. XVI. Sp., of Haytian origin.

magus mei·gəs, pl. **magi** mei·dʒai the 'wise men' who came 'from the East' to worship the child Jesus (Matt. ii 1) XIV; member of an ancient Persian priestly caste XVI. – L. *magus* – Gr. *mágos* – OPers. *magus*. Also anglicized **mage** meidʒ wise man, magician. XIV; cf. F. *mage* (XVII). Hence **ma·gIAN**. XVI.

mahal məhā·l private apartments; summer palace XVII; territorial division in India XVIII. – Urdu – Arab. *maḥall*, f. *ḥalla* lodge.

mahaleb mā·həleb kind of cherry. XVI (*macaleb*). – F. *macaleb* (now *mah-*) – Arab. *maḥlab*; later assim. to Arab. in form.

maharajah maharā·dʒə title of some Indian princes. XVII (*mau raja*). – Hind. *mahārājā*, f. *mahā* great (cf. MAGNITUDE) + *rājā* RAJAH. So **mahara·nee.** XIX. – Hindī *mahārānī* (*rānī* queen).

mahatma məhæ·tmə in Esoteric Buddhism, one possessing preternatural powers. XIX. – Skr. *mahātman*, f. *mahā* (see prec.) + *ātmán* soul (cf. OE. *ǣþm*, G. *atem* breath).

mahdi mā·di Mohammedan messiah. XVIII. – Arab. *mahdīy* 'he who is guided right', pp. of *hadā* lead in the right way.

mah-jong mādʒɔ·ŋ game resembling dominoes. XX. Chinese, f. *ma* sparrow, *djung* play.

mahlstick see MAULSTICK.

mahogany məhɔ·gəni wood of a tree of tropical America, Swietenia Mahagoni. XVII (*mohogoney*). Of unkn. origin; adopted as bot. L. by Linnæus (1762) in the form *mahagoni*, whence the various Continental forms.

Mahomet məhɔ·mit. XIV (Wyclif, Ch.). ME. *Mac(h)amete, Mako-* – (O)F. *Mahomet*, †*Mach-*, medL. *Ma(c)hometus* – Arab. *Muḥammad*, now repr. by **Mohammed** mouhæ·mid founder of the religion of Islam. So **Maho·metAN**. XVI. – medL. *Mahometānus*, etc.; so F. **Mahou·nd,** later form (XVI) of †*Mahoun*, †*Mahun* (XIII, Laȝ.). – OF. *Mahun, -um*, shortening of *Mahomet*. Cf. MAUMET.

mahout məhau·t elephant-driver. XVII. – Hindi *mahāut, mahāwat* :– Skr. *mahāmātra* high official, lit. 'great in measure'.

Mahratta, -atti older forms of *Maratha*, MARATHI.

maid meid. XII. Shortening of MAIDEN; in sense 'female servant' XIV (Gower). ¶ For the loss of final *n* cf. *clue, eve, game*.

maidan maidā·n esplanade, parade ground. XVII (Purchas). Pers.

maiden mei·dn girl, young woman; virgin; female servant. OE. *mæġden* n. = OHG. *magatīn* :– Germ. **magadīnam*, dim. (see -EN[1]), f. **magadiz* maid, virgin, which is repr. by OE. *mæġ(e)þ*, OS. *magath*, OHG. *magad* (G. *magd*; whence dim. *mädchen*), Goth. *magaþs*, and is rel. to Germ. **maguz* :– IE. **moghus* boy, young man, whence OE., OS. *magu*, ON. *mǫgr*, Goth. *magus* son, young man, OIr. *mug* slave, Av. *magu* young man. ¶ The application to castles is usu. taken to imply 'virgin', i.e. unviolated, an interpretation not borne out by *Castrum Puellarum* 'maidens' fort', applied to Edinburgh in the Middle Ages. Cf. the equiv. G. *Magdeburg*.

maieutic meijū·tik pert. to the Socratic method of bringing out latent conceptions. XVII. – Gr. *maieutikós* obstetric (used fig. of Socratic methods), f. *maieúesthai* act as midwife, f. *maîa* midwife; see -IC.

maigre meigər involving abstinence from flesh meat. XVII. F.; see MEAGRE.

mail[1] meil ring or plate of armour; armour composed of rings or chain-work XIV; breast feathers of a hawk XV. – (O)F. *maille* mesh = Pr. *malha* (whence It. *maglia*, etc.) :– L. *macula* spot, mesh.

mail[2] meil (now Sc.) payment, tax, tribute. north. repr. of late OE. *māl* – ON. *mál* speech, agreement = OE. *mǣl* speech; prob. contr. form of the word appearing in OE. *mæþel* meeting, discussion, OS., OHG. *mahal* assembly, judgement, treaty, Goth. *maþl* meeting-place (whence medL. *mallum*): in sense the Eng. word corr. rather to ON. *máli* stipulation, stipulated pay. See also BLACKMAIL.

mail[3] meil (now Sc. and U.S.) pack, bag XIII; bag of letters for conveyance by post; person or vehicle conveying this. XVII. ME. *male* – OF. *male* (mod. *malle* bag, trunk) – Germ. (OHG. *mal(a)ha* wallet, bag). Hence vb. (orig. U.S) send by post. XIX.

maim meim mutilating injury. XIV. ME. *maheym* (rare), *maime*, later also *maine*, Sc. †*manyie* – OF. *mayhem, mahaing, main(e)*, f. *mahaignier, mayner* (whence **maim** vb. XIII) = Pr. *maganhar*, It. *magagnare* :– Rom. **mahagnāre*, of unkn. origin. See also MAYHEM.

main[1] mein physical strength (surviving only in *with might and m.*). OE. *mæġen* = OS. *megin*, OHG. *magan, megin*, ON. *magn, meg(i)n*, f. base **mag-* have power; see MAY[1].

main[2] mein (dial.) of great size XIII; strong, mighty (surviving only in sense 'sheer' in phr. *by m. force*); (dial.) great in number or degree XIV; chief in size, extent, or order XV. Partly repr. OE. *mæġen* MAIN[1] in comps., as *mæġenfolc* great company of people, *mæġenstrengo* great strength, *mæġenrǣs* mighty attack, *mæġenbyrþen* heavy load; partly – rel. ON. *megenn, megn* strong, powerful, or *megin* (in combination). There are many special collocations: e.g. *m. chance* XVI, *mainland* XIV (prob. after ON. *meginland*), †*m. sea* XVI (cf. ON. *meginsjór*); *m. drain* XVIII; from these, by ellipsis, arose sb. uses of the *m.*: e.g. (1) prob. from *the m. chance*, a throw in the game of hazard, (hence) the most important part, subject, etc. (now chiefly in phr. *in the m.*) XVI; (2) from *the m. sea*, the high sea XVI; (3) from *m. drain*, chief sewer XVIII. Hence **mai·nLY**[2] †vigorously XIII; †greatly XIV; for the most part XVII (Milton).

main[3] mein (Sc. and north.) †pl. demesne lands XV; home farm XVI. Aphetic of DOMAIN, DEMESNE.

mainour see MANNER[2].

mainpernor mei·npə̄:ɹnəɹ (leg.) surety for a prisoner's appearance. XIV (PPl.). – AN. *mainpernour* (for *-prenour*), f. *mainprendre*, f. *main* hand (:– L. *manu-s*)+*prendre* take, the equiv. of medL. *manūcapere* 'take in the hand', assume responsibility for. So **mai·nprize.** XIV (PPl.). – AN., OF. *mein-*, *mainprise*, f. *mainprendre*; see MANUAL, PRIZE[2].

maintain meintei·n, mən- support the person or cause of XIII (Cursor M.); †practise habitually; carry on, continue; support, provide for XIV. ME. *maintene*, *-teine* repr. tonic stem of (O)F. *maintenir* (AN. *maintener*) = Pr., Sp. *mantener*, It. *mantenere* :– Rom. **manūtenēre*, f. L. *manū*, abl. of *manus* hand +*tenēre* hold. So **maintenANCE** mei·ntĭnəns †demeanour; support of a party or cause (spec. wrongful sustentation of a suit); provision of livelihood XIV. – OF. *maintenance*, f. *maintenir*; cf. Pr. *mantenensa*, etc.

maiolica var. of MAJOLICA.

maison(n)ette meizəne·t small house XIX; part of a house let separately XX. F., dim. of *maison*; see MANSION, -ETTE.

maize meiz Indian corn. XVI (*mais*, *mahiz*, *mayis*, etc.). – F. *maïs*, †*mahiz*, or its source Sp. *maiz*, †*mahiz*, *-is*, †*mayz*, of Carib origin.

majesty mæ·dʒĭsti sovereign power (first of the glory of God) XIII; kingly dignity XVI. –(O)F. *majesté* (earlier *maesté*), corr. to Pr. *maiestat*, etc. – L. *mājestās*, *-tāt-*, f. **mājes-*, var. of **mājōs-* (*mājus*, *mājor*); see MAJOR, -TY. Hence **maje·stIC** XVII, -ICAL XVI.

majolica mədʒɔ·likə fine kind of Italian pottery. XVI. – It. *maiolica*. f. name of the island Majorca, formerly †*Majolica*, where acc. to J. C. Scaliger (1557) the best ware of this kind was made; cf. F. *majolique*, *maïolique*, †*majorique*.

major[1] mei·dʒəɹ officer below the rank of lieutenant-colonel. XVII. – F. *major*, short for *sergent-major* sergeant-major, which orig. designated a much higher rank than at present. Also in *m.-general* (XVII), earlier *sergeant-m.-general* (XVII). – F. *major-général*, where *major* is sb. and *général* adj. (cf. G. *generalmajor*). – L. *mājor*; see next. **major-domo** mei·dʒəɹ dou·mou chief official of a household. XVI. Earliest forms *maior-*, *mayordome* – (partly through F. *majordome*) Sp. *mayordomo*, It. *maggiordomo* – medL. *mājor domūs* (*domūs*, g. of *domus* house) highest official of the royal household under the Merovingians, 'mayor of the palace'. ¶ So *majores domus regiae* at the court of Theodoric (Cassiodorus).

major[2] mei·dʒəɹ greater, first in technical use in logic and math.; constituting the majority. XVI. – L. *mājor* (:– **māgjōs*) compar. of *magnus* great (see MAGNITUDE). Some uses may depend on F. *majeur*, †*maiour*, learned variant of OF. *maour*, acc. of *maire* MAYOR (cf. *Seinte Marie þe maiour*, i.e. Santa Maria Maggiore, XIV). So **majorITY** mədʒɔ·rĭti †superiority; state of being of full age XVI; greater number or part XVII. – F. *majorité* – medL. *mājōritās*. ¶ In the sense 'rank of a major' a distinct word XVIII – F. *majorité*, f. *major* MAJOR[1].

majuscule mədʒʌ·skjūl †capital (letter); (palæogr.) large (also sb.). XIX. – F. *majuscule* – L. *mājusculus* somewhat larger, dim. of *mājor*, n. *mājus*; see MAJOR[2].

make meik pt., pp. **made** meid bring into existence, subject to an operation, cause to be, cause (something to happen). OE. *macian* (early ME. *macan*, *macen*, *makie-n*) = OFris. *makia*, OS. *makōn* (Du. *maken*), OHG. *mahhōn* (G. *machen*) :– WGerm. **makōjan*, f. **mako-* MATCH[1] (MSw. *maka* construct, Sw. *make* move, Da. *mage* manage, arrange, are from LG.); plausibly referred to IE. **mag-* repr. by Gr. *mássein* (aorist pass. *magênai*) knead, *mágeiros* cook, *mageús* baker, OSl. *mazati* anoint, grease. The sense-history is uncertain. OE. *macian* is not very frequent, and is used mainly in factitive and causative meanings, and *hit macian* behave, but in late use the verb, as in early WGerm., corr. in use to L. *facere* do. Hence sb. manner, style, form. XIV. **makER**[1] mei·kəɹ manufacturer, creator XIII (Cursor M.); (arch.) poet (ult. tr. Gr. *poētḗs*) XIV (Usk). See MATCH.[1]

maki mei·ki, mæ·ki lemur. XVIII. – F., repr. Malagasy *maka*.

mal- mæl, formerly often †*male-* (pronounced as one syll.), repr. F. *mal-*, L. *male* badly, ill (cf. MALE-), first in words adopted from F., later generalized, as in *maladministration* XVII, *malconduct* XVIII, *malcontent* XVI, *malodorous* XIX, *malpractice* XVII, *maltreat* XVIII; less freq. repr. OF. adj. *mal*, L. *malus* bad, evil (rel. to IE. **mel-*; cf. Gr. *méleos* vain, useless, unhappy), as in †*maladventure*, †*malease* (cf. MALAISE), †*malengin*, †*maltalent*.

malabathrum mæləbæ·þrəm aromatic leaf (prob. of Cinnamomum), perfumed ointment from this. XVII (Holland). – L. *māla-*, *mālobathrum*, *-on* – Gr. *mālá-*, *mālóbathron* – Skr. *tamālapattra*, f. *tamāla* name of various trees+*pattra* leaf.

malachite mæ·ləkait (geol.) hydrous carbonate of copper occurring as a green mineral. XVI (*melo-*). – OF. *melochite* (now *malachite*) – L. *molochītēs* (Pliny) – Gr. *molokhîtis*, f. *molókhē*, var. of *malákhē* MALLOW.

malaco- mæ·ləkou comb. form of Gr. *malakós* soft, as in *malaco*·LOGY – F. *malocologie* science of molluscs.

malady mæ·lədi ill health, disease. XIII. – (O)F. *maladie*, f. *malade* sick, ill = Pr. *malapte*, *malaute*, Cat. *malalt*, OIt. *malatto* :– Rom. **male habitu-s* 'in bad condition', i.e. L. *male* badly + *habitus* (cf. Massurius Sabinus, *equum nimis strigosum et male habitum*), pp. of *habēre* have, hold; see MAL-, HABIT, -Y[3].

malaga mæ·ləgā white wine exported from *Malaga*, a seaport in the south of Spain. XVII (*Mallego*, *Maligo*).

Malagasy mæləgæ·si pert. to (a native of) Madagascar; sb. its language. XIX (1835). f. *Malegass*, *-gash*, varr. of *Madegass*, *-cass*, after or parallel with F. *malgache*, *madécasse*, adj. f. the name of the island, which is found as *Madagascar* in XVII.

malaguetta mæləgwe·tə capsules of Amomum Meliguetta. XVI. Earlier forms *manguetta*, *manegete*, *mellegette* – F. *maniguette*, †*-guet*, alt. of *malaguette* – Sp. *malagueta*; cf. medL. *melegeta*, poss. dim. of It. *melica* millet; if of Eur. origin, perh. corrupted through some W. Afr. language.

malaise mælei·z bodily discomfort or suffering. XVIII (Chesterfield). – (O)F. *malaise* (adopted in ME. as *males*), f. OF. *mal* bad (L. *malus*) + *aise* EASE.

malander, mallender mæ·lĭndəɹ scabby eruption in horses. XV. – (O)F. *malandre* (= It. *malandre*, etc.) :– L. *malandria* (pl.) pustules on the neck. Also pl. XVII.

malapert mæ·ləpōɹt (arch.) impudent. XV. – OF. *malapert*, f. *mal-* (indicating the opposite) + *apert*, var. of *espert* EXPERT, but apprehended as if f. MAL- improperly + *apert* bold, PERT.

malapropism mæ·ləprɔpizm ludicrous misapplication of language. XIX. f. name of Mrs. *Malaprop*, character in Sheridan's play of 'The Rivals' (1775), remarkable for her misuse of words, f. *malapropos* inopportune(ly) XVII (Dryden) – F. *mal à propos* not to the purpose; see MAL-, APROPOS, -ISM. *Malaprop* was formerly so used, and as adj.

malaria məlɛə·riə fever formerly supposed to be caused by exhalations from marshy places. XVIII (*mal'aria*, H. Walpole). – It. *mal'aria* for *mala aria* 'bad AIR'; cf. MAL-.

male meil pert. to the sex that begets offspring. XIV (Barbour, PPl., Trevisa, Maund., Wycl. Bible). – OF. *male*, earlier *masle* (mod. *mâle*) = (mostly with specialized senses) Pr. *mascle*, Sp. *maslo*, Pg. *macho*, It. *maschio*, Rum. *mascur* :– L. *masculus* (see MASCULINE and cf. MALLARD); in legal use the AN. sp. *masle* continued till XVII.

male-, repr. L. *male-*, comb. form of adv. *male* (see MAL-) in **malediction** mælidi·kʃən cursing, curse. XV. – L. *maledictiō(n-)*; see DICTION and cf. MALISON. **malefactor** mæ·lifæktəɹ evil-doer, criminal. XV. – (partly through OF. *malfaicteur*) L. *malefactor* (*facere* DO[1]). **male**FIC məle·fik productive of evil. XVII. – L. *maleficus*. **male**·FICENT. XVII (Cudworth). **malevol**ENT məle·vələnt disposed to ill will. XVI. – OF. *malivolent* or L. *malevolent-*, *-ēns* (*volēns*, prp. of *velle* WILL). **male·vol**ENCE. XV (Caxton). – OF. or L.

malfeasance mælfī·zəns (leg.) official misconduct. XVII. – AN. *malfaisance*, f. *malfaisour* (adopted in ME. XIV), f. phr. *mal faire* do evil; see MALEFACTOR, -ANCE.

malgré malgre see MAUGRE.

malice mæ·lis †badness XIII (Cursor M.); †harmfulness XIV (Wycl.); mischievous intent XIII (RGlouc.), spec. leg. XVI. – (O)F. *malice* – L. *malitia*, f. *malus* bad; see MAL-. So **malic**IOUS məli·ʃəs. XIII (AncrR.). – OF. *malicius* (mod. *-ieux*) – L. *malitiōsus*.

malign məlai·n evil in nature and effects XIV (Shoreham); (arch.) malevolent XV. – OF. *maligne*, fem. of *malin*, or its source L. *malignus*, f. *malus* evil (cf. MAL-, MALE-, and for the ending BENIGN). **malign** vb. †speak evil, plot XV (Lydg.); †dislike, envy XVI; speak ill of XVII. – OF. *malignier* or late L. *malignāre* contrive maliciously. **malig**NITY məli·gnĭti. XIV (Ch.). – OF. or L. So **malign**ANT məli·gnənt †disposed to rebel XVI (also sb., hist.); of evil effect or disposition XVI. – prp. of L. *malignāre*, f. *malignus* (the use of *ecclesia malignantium* 'congregation of evildoers' in the Vulgate of Psalm xxv[i] 5, used by patristic writers for followers of Antichrist, is the source of *Church Malignant*).

malinger məli·ŋgəɹ feign illness XIX; backformation from **mali·nger**ER[1] (XVIII). app. f. (O)F. *malingre* (as a personal name XIII), perh. f. *mal-* MAL- + *haingre* weak, thin, prob. of Germ. origin (cf. MHG. *hager* thin, lean). Cf. Du. *malenger*, vb. *-eren*.

malison mæ·lisən (arch.) curse. XIII (Cursor M.). – OF. *malison*, *maleison* – L. *maledictiō(n-)* MALEDICTION.

malkin, mawkin mɔ̄·kin †female personal name typical of lower classes XIII; (arch.) slut, drab XVI; (dial.) mop XV; (dial.) scarecrow XVII. dim. of ME. *Malde* Maud, Matilda (OF. *Mahault* – Germ. *Mahthildis* 'strength-battle'); see -KIN.

mall see PALL-MALL.

mallard mæ·ləɹd wild drake or duck. XIV. – OF. *mallart*, (now) *malart*, prob. for **maslart*, f. *masle* MALE; see -ARD. ¶ The ME. vars. *mau(d)lard* agree with this deriv. as much as with that proposed from OHG. proper name *Madelhart* (= OE. *Mæþelheard*), since *madle*, *maule* are AN. and ME. vars. of MALE; cf. AL. *mathlardus*.

malleable mæ·liəbl that may be hammered without breaking. XIV (Ch.). – OF. *malleable* – medL. *malleābilis*, f. L. *malleāre* hammer, f. *malleus*; see MAUL[1], -ABLE.

mallet mæ·lit (wooden) hammer. XV (*mailȝet, mailet*). – (O)F. *maillet*, f. (with *-et* denoting instrument, as in *foret* borer, *jouet* plaything) *mailler* hammer, f. *mail* hammer, MAUL[1].

mallow mæ·lou wild plant, genus Malva. OE. *mealuwe*, *-(e)we* – L. *malva*, rel. to Gr. *malákhē, molókhē*, and prob. of Mediterranean origin. (ME. and dial. vars. are *maul*, pl. *maws*). Cf. MAUVE.

malm mām soft friable rock, light loamy soil. OE. **mealm* (in *mealmstān* friable stone, and *mealmiht* sandy) = ON. *malmr* ore, metal, Goth. *malma* sand, f. **mal-* **mel-* grind (see MEAL[1]); cf. OS., MHG. *melm* dust, from the *e*-var. of the base.

malmaison mælmei·zən variety of carnation. XIX. Short for *souvenirs de Malmaison* 'memories of Malmaison' (the name of the château at which the empress Josephine held her court), orig. the name of a blush rose.

malmsey mā·mzi strong sweet wine. XV (*malmesey*). – MDu., MLG. *malmesie, -eye* (in medL. *malmasia*), f. Gr. place-name *Monemvasia* (*Μονεμβασία*) in the Morea, of which the var. *Malvasia* gave MALVOISIE.

Malpighian mælpi·giən (anat.). XIX. f. name of Marcello *Malpighi* (1628–94), Italian physician; see -IAN.

malt mòlt barley, etc., for brewing. OE. *malt*, (*mealt*) = OS. *malt* (Du. *mout*), (O)HG. *malz*, ON. *malt* :– CGerm. (exc. Gothic) **maltaz* n. (whence Finnish *maltas* and Slovene *mlato*), rel. to Germ. **malta-* or **maltu-* (cf. Skr. *mṛidu*) soft, repr. in OHG. *malt* (G. *malz*) soft, weak, ON. *maltr* rotten; f. base of MELT. Hence **ma·lt**STER. XIV.

maltha mæ·lþə kind of cement XV; bitumen, mineral pitch or tar. XVII. – L. – Gr. *máltha, málthē* mixture of wax and pitch.

Malthusian mælþʲū·ziən pert. to Thomas Robert *Malthus* (1766–1835), who advocated checks on the growth of population; see -IAN.

malvaceous mælvei·ʃʲəs pert. to the mallows. XVII. f. L. *malvāceus* (Pliny), f. *malva* MALLOW; see -ACEOUS.

malversation mælvəɹsei·ʃən corrupt administration. XVI. – F. *malversation*, f. *malverser* – L. *male versārī* (*male* ill, MAL- + *versārī* behave, conduct oneself, f. *vers-*, pp. stem of *vertere* turn (see -WARD, WORTH).

malvoisie mæ·lvoizi (arch.) malmsey. XIV. ME. *malvesin, malvesie* – OF. *malvesie*, from the F. form (cf. It. *Malvasia*) of the place-name *Monemvasia*; see MALMSEY. ¶ The forms in *-in, -yn* suggest an OF. adj. formation; cf. medL. *vinum malvasinum*; the present form is that of modF.

mam mæm (dial.) mother. XVI. prob. repr. a child's earliest instinctive attempts to articulate; cf. MAMMA. ¶ Identical with W. *mam* mother, but this is unlikely to be the immed. source. Hence **mamm**Y[6]. XVI.

mamamouchi mæməmū·tʃi typical pompous-sounding title. XVII (Dryden). The mock-Turkish title conferred by the Sultan on M. Jourdain in Molière's 'Le Bourgeois Gentilhomme' (1670).

mameluke mæ·məlʲūk one of the military body, orig. Caucasian slaves, that seized the throne of Egypt in 1254. XVI. – F. *mameluk* (OF. *mamelus*), It. *mammalucco*, Sp., Pg. *mameluco*, medL. *mameluc, -uchus* – Arab. *mamlūk* slave, sb. use of pp. of *malaka* possess.

mamilla məmi·lə nipple. XVII. L., dim. of *mamma* breast, teat; see next. Hence **ma·mill**ARY. XVII; after L. *māmillāris*.

mamma[1], mama məmā· mother. XVI. repr. redupl. of a syllable instinctively uttered by young children, who are also taught to use it as their word for 'mother', esp. where the ordinary word in the language begins with *m*; of IE. origin, **mammā* being repr. by Gr. *mámmē*, L. *mamma* (mother, teat, breast; see next), OSl., Russ., Lith. *mama*, Ir., W. *mam*. The L. word is repr. in Rom. by F. *maman* XVI, It. *mamma*, Sp. *mama* (*mamá* from F.), Rum. *mumă*. In educated Eng. use pronounced məmā·; dial. and U.S. vars. are mæ·mə, mə·mə. Shortened to **ma** mā (dial. and U.S.) XIX.

mamma[2] mæ·mə (anat.) breast in mammals. XVII. L. (see prec.). Hence **ma·mm**ARY. XVII.

mammal mæ·məl (XIX) animal of the class **mammalia** məmei·liə, who suckle their young XVIII. modL. (Linnæus), n. pl. of L. *mammālis*, f. *mamma*; see prec., -AL[1].

mammee mæmī· large tree of tropical America. XVI. – Sp. *mamei* (whence F. *mamey*), of Haytian origin, whence modL. *mammea* (Linnæus).

mammet see MAUMET.

mammon mæ·mən (personification of) riches. XVI (Tindale, following Luther). Earlier *Mammona* (e.g. in PPl.) as a proper name for 'the devil of covetousness' – late L. (Vulg.) *mam(m)ōna, mam(m)on* – N.T.Gr. *mam(m)ōnâs* (Matt. vi 24, Luke xvi 9, 11, 13) – Aramaic *māmōnā, māmōn* riches, gain.

mammoth mæ·məþ large extinct elephant. XVIII. – Russ. †*mammot* (Ludolf, 1696), now *mámont*, of Ostiak (Siberian) origin. The Eng. form, F. *mammouth*, and G. *mammut* are ult. due to misreading of *ou* for *on* in Tatar *mamont*, said to be f. *mama* 'earth' because the animal was supposed to have burrowed.

mamsell mæmze·l. XIX (Thackeray). – F. *mam'selle* MADEMOISELLE.

man mæn pl. *men* human being; adult male OE.; vassal, manservant XII; (dial.) husband XIII. OE. *man(n), mon(n)*, d.sg. *menn* (:– **menni*), pl. *menn* (:– **manniz*), also *manna, monna*, corr. to OFris. *man, mon*, OS. *man*, OHG. *man* sg. and pl. (Du. *man*, G. *mann*, pl. with numerals *mann*, new formations *mannen, männer*), ON. *maðr*, rarely *mannr* (g. *manns*, pl. *menn*), Goth. *manna*

(g. *mans*, pl. *mans*, *mannans*); the various forms belong to two Germ. stems **mann-*, **mannon-*; a third stem **manno-* is repr. by the tribal names *Alemannī* (see ALEMANIC) and *Marcomannī* 'boundary-people'; a pre-Germ. **manw-*, **mane-* appears in *Mannus* (Tacitus' 'Germania'), a founder of the West Germanic peoples, and links with the base of Skr. *mánu-* man, mankind, *Mánu* progenitor of mankind, *mánusha* man, and OSl. (with *g*-suffix) *mąží*.

The prominent sense in OE. was 'human being', the words distinctive of sex being *wer* and *wīf*, *wǣp(n)man* and *wīfman* WOMAN. In some Germ. langs. this sense is expressed by deriv. (orig. adj.) in *-isk-* -ISH[1] (e.g. OS., OHG. *mennisco*, Du., G. *mensch*), the simple word having at the same time specialized applications of the sense, as in Du. *iemand*, G. *jemand* anybody, Du., G. *niemand* nobody, Du. *men*, G. *man* 'one', people.

The sense 'ship' (as in *Frenchman*) appears in XV; so *merchantman*, *(East) Indiaman*. Among spec. phr. is *man-at-arms* XVI (formerly †*man of arms*, Gower), tr. OF. *homme d'armes* and *à armes*; cf. medL. *homo ad arma* (XIII). The sense of 'piece' used in chess appears uncompounded *c.*1400, and in XV in *chesemen and tabilmenys* (1469), *tabylle man* (1483), after AN. *hum*, medL. *homo*. Hence **man** vb. Late OE. *(ġe)mannian*, with corr. forms in other langs. **ma·n**HOOD, †-HEAD XIII. **ma·nn**ISH[1] †human; masculine XIV (Ch.); pert. to a grown man XVI; characteristic of a male XVIII. repl. OE. *menniscĉ* (of CGerm. origin). **ma·n**SLAUGH:TER XVII (Cursor M.; leg. XV); superseded †*manslaught*, OE. (Anglian) *mannslæht*, the second el. being :- Germ. **slaχtiz*, f. **slaχ-* SLAY.

manacle mæ·nəkl fetter for the hand. XIV. ME. *manicle* – (O)F. *manicle* handcuff, also (as in modF.) gauntlet – L. *manicula* little hand, handle, in medL. gauntlet, dim. of *manus* hand (see MANUAL); assim. later to words in *-acle*. Hence vb. XIV.

manage mæ·nidʒ training of a horse; action and paces of a horse XVI; riding-school XVII. – It. *maneggio* (whence F. *manège*), f. *maneggiare* (= Pr. *manejar*, Sp. *manosear*) :- Rom. **manidiare*, f. *manus* hand (see MANUAL), whence **ma·nage** vb. train (a horse); handle, wield; conduct (an affair), control (a person) XVI; do successfully XVIII. First in the form *manege*, the ending of which was early assim. to -AGE; but in the techn. uses the F. form finally prevailed. In XVII–XVIII the vb. was often identified with F. *ménager* use sparingly (see MÉNAGE). Hence **ma·nage**MENT. XVI.

manakin mæ·nəkin small gaily-coloured passerine bird. XVIII. var. of MANIKIN. ¶ Hence modL. *Manacus* as the generic name.

manatee mænətī· large aquatic cetacean. XVI. – Sp. *manati* – Carib *manattouï*. ¶ Identified with modL. *manātus* having hands, with ref. to the hand-like fins.

manchet mæ·ntʃit (hist.) finest wheaten bread; small loaf of this. XV. perh. f. †*maine* (XV), aphetic of *demaine* in *pain-demaine*+†*cheat* (XV) wheaten bread of second quality; or dim. of AN. **menche* for †*demenche* :- L. *dominica*, fem. of *dominicus* DOMINICAL.

manchineel mæntʃinī·l W. Indian tree Hippomane Mancinella. XVII. – F. *mancenille* – Sp. *manzanilla*, dim. of *manzana* apple, alt. form of OSp. *mazana* (= Pg. *mazãa*) :- L. *matiāna* (sc. *poma*, *mala* apples), n.pl., taken as sg., of *Matiānus*, f. *Matius*, current designation of Gaius *Matius* Calvena, author of a book on cookery, after whom the apple (*malum Matianum*) was prob. named.

manciple mæ·nsipl official who purchases provisions. XIII (AncrR.). – AN., OF. *manciple*, var. of *mancipe* :- L. *mancipium* purchase, slave (orig. one obtained by legal purchase), f. *manus* hand+**cip-*, *capere* take; see MANUAL, CAPTURE.

mancus mæ·ŋkəs (hist.) Anglo-Saxon money of account. OE. *mancus* = OS. *mancus*, OHG. (acc. pl.) *manchussa* – medL. *mancusus*, – Arab. *manqūš*, sb. use (sc. *dīnār* DINAR) of pp. of *naqaša* paint, embroider, engrave, strike (coin).

-mancy repr. (O)F. *-mancie* – late L. *-mantīa* – Gr. *manteíā* divination, f. *manteúesthai* prophesy, f. *mántis* prophet, diviner. Some of the comps. with this ending repr. words recorded in Gr., as *chiromancy*, *necromancy*, others of late L. or medL., as *geomancy*, *hydromancy*; and others have been formed on Gr. models, as *crystallomancy*, *lithomancy*. ¶ Lydgate in 'Assembly of the Gods', *c.*1420, has: Adryomancy, Ornomancy, Pyromancy (l. 869).

mandamus mændei·məs (leg.) royal writ directing the performance of a certain act. XVI. – L. 'we command', 1st pers. pl. pres. ind. of *mandāre* (see MANDATE).

mandarin[1] mæ·ndərin Chinese official (the native name is *kwan*). XVI. – Pg. *mandarim* (after *mandar* command) – Malay *mantrī* – Hindi *mantrī* :- Skr. *mantrin* counsellor, f. *mantra* counsel, f. *man* (see MIND). So F.

mandarin[2] mæ·ndərin small kind of orange. XIX. – F. *mandarine* (sc. *orange*; cf. Sp. *naranja mandarina*), fem. of *mandarin* (see prec.); prob. so named from the yellow of mandarins' costume.

mandate mæ·ndeit, -ĭt command, spec. legal or judicial XVI; commission or contract by which one acts for another XVII. – L. *mandātum*, sb. use of n. pp. of *mandāre* enjoin, commit, f. *manus* hand+**dō* (*dare*) give; see MANUAL, -ATE[1]. So **ma·ndat**ARY XVII, **ma·ndat**ORY XVI. – late L. *mandātārius*, *mandātōrius*.

mandible mæ·ndĭbl jaw, jawbone. XVI. – OF. *mandible*, later *mandibule*, or its source late L. *mandibula*, *-ulum*, f. *mandere* chew.

mandilion mændi·ljən (hist.) loose coat or cassock. XVI. – F. *mandilion* – It. *mandiglione*, augm. of *mandiglia* – F. *mandille*, earlier *mandil* – Sp. *mandil* – Arab. *mandīl* sash, turban cloth, handkerchief – medGr. *mandḗlion* – L. *mantēlium*, *-tēlum* MANTLE.

mandolin mæ·ndəlin instrument of the lute kind. XVIII. – F. *mandoline* – It. *mandolino*, dim. of *mandola*, var. of *mandora*; cf. BANDORE, PANDORE.

mandragora mændræ·gərə plant of S. Europe and the East having emetic and narcotic properties. In OE. in L. form; in ME. anglicized or – (O)F. *mandragore* – medL. *mandragora*, L. *-as* – Gr. *mandragóras*, prob. of pre-Hellenic origin. The L. form has been established since Sh. ('Othello' III iii 330).

mandrake mæ·ndreik mandragora. XIV. ME. also *-ag(g)e*, prob. – MDu. *mandrage*, *mandragre* – medL. MANDRAGORA; alt. to *mandrake* was prob. in allusion to the man-like form of the root of the plant, and assoc. with DRAKE[1] dragon (cf. the var. †*mandragon*) because of the plant's supposed magical properties.

mandrel, -dril mæ·ndrəl A. miner's pick XVI; B. arbor of a lathe XVII; C core of cast or moulded metal XVIII. Of unkn. origin; senses B and C are identical with those of F. *mandrin* (late XVII).

mandrill mæ·ndril largest of the baboons. XVIII. app. f. MAN+DRILL[2].

manducation mændjukei·ʃən eating XVI; chewing XVII. – late L. *mandūcātiō(n)-*, f. L. *mandūcāre*, f. *mandūcō* guzzler, f. *mandere* chew.

mane mein long hair on the back of the neck of certain animals. OE. *manu* = OFris. *mana*, (M)Du. *mane*, OHG. *mana* (G. *mähne*, with irreg. mutation), ON. *mǫn* :– Germ. **manō*. ¶ The orig. meaning of IE. **mon-* appears to have been 'neck'; derivs. with the senses 'neck, nape of the neck, mane' are OIcel. *makki* (Sw., Da. *manke*), OIr. *muin*, *muinel*, *mong*, Skr. *mányā*, and with the sense 'necklace, collar' OE. *mene*, OS. *meni*, OHG. *menni* pl., ON. *men*) :– **mani-*, L. *monīle*, Doric Gr. *mán(n)os*, *mónnos*, Gaulish *maniákēs* (Polybius), OIr. *muince*.

manege mæ·neiʒ see MANAGE.

manes mei·nīz souls of the departed, esp. as beneficent spirits. (XIV) XVII. L. *mānēs* pl., plausibly (but not certainly) referred to *mānis*, *mānus* good, the opposite of which is seen in *im-mānis* cruel.

manganese mæ·ŋgənīz black mineral XVII, later recognized as an oxide of the mineral so named XVIII. – F. *manganèse* – It. *manganese*, unexpl. alt. of medL. *magnēsia* (also *mangnēsia*) MAGNESIA.

mange mein[d]ʒ cutaneous disease of hairy and woolly animals. XIV. ME. *maniewe*, later *mangie*, shortened to *mange* (XVI) – OF. *manjue*, *mangeue* itch, f. *manju-*, pres. ind. sg. stem of *mangier* (mod. *manger*) eat :– L. *mandūcāre* (see MANDUCATION). Hence **ma·ngy**[1]. XVI (Skelton).

mangel-, mangold-wurzel mæ·ŋgəl wɜ̄·ɹzəl variety of beet. XVIII. – G. *mangoldwurzel*, f. *mangold*, †*manegolt* beet+*wurzel* root (cf. WORT). The altered form G. *mangelwurzel*, due to assoc. with *mangel* want, was sometimes tr. 'root of scarcity' (so F. *racine de disette*).

manger mei·ndʒəɹ trough for cattle fodder. XIV (*manyour*, *maniore*). – (O)F. *mangeoire*, f. *mangeure* = Pr. *manjadoira*, Cat. *menjadora*, It. *mangiatoia* :– Rom. **mandūcātōria*, f. *mandūcāt-*; see MANDUCATION.

mangle[1] mæ·ŋgl hack or cut about. XIV. – AN. *mangler*, **mahangler* (cf. medL. *mangulare*), prob. frequent. of *mahaignier* MAIM; see -LE[3].

mangle[2] mæ·ŋgl machine for rolling and pressing laundered clothing, etc. (an old form of which consisted of a stone-filled chest worked with a rack and pinion). XVIII. – Du. *mangel*, short for synon. *mangelstok*, f. *mangelen* mangle+*stok* staff, roller, STOCK; ult. from Gr. *mágganon* (see MANGONEL).

mango mæ·ŋgou fruit of the tropical tree Mangifera indica. XVI (*manga*, *-as*). First – Pg. *manga* (whence modL. *mangas*), later altered to the Du. form *mango* – Malay *maŋgā* – Tamil *mānkāy*, f. *mān* mango-tree +*kāy* fruit.

mangonel mæ·ŋgənel military engine for casting stones. XIII. – OF. *mangonel*, *-elle* (mod. *mangonneau*), corr. to Pr. *manganel*, It. *manganelle*, – medL. *manganellus*, *-gon-*, dim. f. late L. *manganum* – Gr. *mágganon* engine of war, axis of a pulley.

mangosteen mæ·ŋgŏstīn fruit of the E. Indian tree Garcinia Mangostana. XVI. – Malay *manggustan* (now *manggis*).

mangrove mæ·ŋgrouv tree of the genus Rhizophora, esp. R. Mangle. XVII. Early forms *mangrowe*, *mangrave*, later assim. to GROVE; obscurely connected with Pg. *mangue*, Sp. *mangle* (whence F. *mangle*), all recorded XVI, from the Arawaks of Hayti. ¶ Malay *mangi-mangi* may be of Pg. origin.

manhandle mæ·nhændl †wield (a tool) XV; move by force of men alone XIX. f. MAN+HANDLE. The sense 'handle roughly' (XIX) is a distinct development, poss. based on dial. *manangle*, alt. form of MANGLE[1].

mania mei·niə highly excited form of madness XIV (Ch. has *manye*); great enthusiasm, craze XVII. – late L. *mania* – Gr. *maníā*, rel. to *mainesthai* be mad, f. **mn-* **men-*; see MIND, -IA[1]. As a terminal el. it was used in later Gr., e.g. in *gunaikomaníā* mad passion for women, *hippomaníā* passionate love of horses, on the model of which a number of comps. were formed in mod. medical L., e.g. *nymphomania*; later imitations of these are *kleptomania*, *megalomania*. The currency in XVII–XVIII of F. words in *-manie*, e.g. *bibliomanie* mania for books, suggested corr. Eng. formations in *-mania*, some of which were transitory, e.g. *scribbleomania* (Coleridge). The sbs. in *-mania* have corr. adj. forms in *-maniac* (one) affected with the particular mania. So **mani**AC mei·niæk, **mani**ACAL mənai·əkəl. XVII. – late L. *maniacus* – late Gr. *maniakós*.

Manichee mæniki· heretic holding dualistic belief in God and Satan. XIV. – late L. *Manichæus*, f. name of the founder of the sect, *Manes* or *Manichæus*. Also **Manichæ**·AN. XVI.

manicure mæ·nikjuəɹ one who treats 1880, treatment of 1887, the hands and finger-nails. – F. *manicure* (1877), f. L. *manus* hand + *cūra* care; see MANUAL, CURE.

manifest mæ·nifest clearly revealed, obvious. XIV (Ch.). – (O)F. *manifeste* or L. *manifestus*, earlier *manufestus*, f. *manus* hand (see MANUAL) + **festus* struck (cf. *infestus* dangerous), f. base of *dēfendere* DEFEND. So **ma·nifest** vb. XIV (Ch.). – (O)F. *manifester* or L. *manifestāre*. **manifest**A·TION. XV. – late L. **manife·sto** †proof; public declaration. XVII. – It. *manifesto* (f. the vb. *manifestare*), whence also **ma·nifest** sb. †manifestation XVI; †manifesto XVII; list of ship's cargo XVIII.

manifold mæ·nifould numerous and varied. OE. *maniġfeald* = OFris. *manichfald*, OHG. *managfalt* (G. *mannigfalt*), Goth. *managfalþs*, etc.; CGerm. f. MANY + -FOLD. As sb. pl. XIII; see MANYPLIES.

manikin mæ·nikin little man, dwarf XVII (Sh.); artist's lay figure XVIII. – Du. *manneken* (cited by Dee 1570), dim. of *man* MAN; see -KIN. Cf. MANNEQUIN.

manilla[1] məni·lə ring of metal worn by African tribes. XVI. – Sp. *manilla* (= Pg. *manilha*, It. *maniglia*), prob. dim. f. *mano* hand (see MANUAL).

manilla[2] məni·lə short for *Manilla hemp*. XIX; the correct form is *Manila*, name of the capital of the Philippine Islands.

manille məni·l second best trump or honour at quadrille and ombre. XVII (*mallilio*; in Pope *manillio*). The current form is – F. *manille* – Sp. *malilla*, dim. of *mala* used in the same sense, fem. (sc. *carta* card) of *malo* bad.

manioc mæ·niɔk cassava. XVI. Earliest form *manihot*, from F. (but *manioch* is found XVII); repr. Tupi *mandioca*, Guarani *mandio*, which denotes the roots of the plant, the leaves being called *manisoba*, the stalk *maniba*, *maniva*, and the juice *manipuera*.

maniple mæ·nipl (eccl.) vestment worn suspended from the left arm (said to have been orig. a napkin); subdivision of the Roman legion XVI; †handful XVII. – OF. *maniple* (mod. *manipule*) or L. *manipulus* handful, troop of soldiers, f. *manus* hand (see MANUAL) + an unkn. el. ¶ In the eccl. sense the earlier name was *fanon* (XV), and in OE. *handlīn* 'hand-linen'.

manipulation mənipjŭlei·ʃən method of handling chemical apparatus XVIII; manual management or examination XIX. – F. *manipulation* (= Sp. *manipulación*, It. *manipolazione*) – modL. **manipulātiō(n-)*, f. **manipulāre*, f. *manipulus* handful (e.g. of medicinal ingredients); see prec. and -ATION. So **mani·pul**ATE[3] XIX; after F. *manipuler*.

manis mei·nis scaly ant-eater. XVIII. modL. (Linnæus), said to be a spurious sg. of MANES.

manitou mæ·nitū (among Amer. Indians) spirit, fetish. XVII. – Algonkin *manitu*, *manito*, f. *manit* active pple. of a vb. meaning 'surpass' + predic. suffix ('he or it is *manit*').

mankind mænkai·nd human species. XIII (Cursor M.). repl. †*mankin*, OE. *mancynn* (MAN, KIN), by substitution of KIND[1].

manna mæ·nə miraculous food of Exodus xvi OE.; juice from the bark of Fraxinus Ornus (manna ash) XVI. – late L. *manna* – Hellenistic Gr. *mánna* (LXX, NT) – Aramaic *mannā* – Heb. *mān*, corr. to Arab. *mann*, Egyptian *mannu*, the word being prob. anciently current in the Sinaitic wilderness for the exudation of the tree Tamarix gallica. Traditionally derived (cf. Ex. xvi 15) from Aram. *mān hū* what is it? ¶ Current in most European langs. with fig. uses.

mannequin mæ·nĭkin later (F.) form of MANIKIN, in sense 'lay figure', 'dress-maker's model'. XVIII.

manner[1] mæ·nəɹ kind, sort XII; way or mode of action; customary practice; (pl.) moral character; outward bearing XIII; (pl., †sg.) external behaviour XIV (Ch.); method or style XVII. ME. *manere* – AN. *manere*, (O)F. *manière* = Pr. *maneira* (whence Sp. *manera*, It. *maniera*) :– Rom. **manuāria* sb. use of fem. of L. *manuārius* pert. to the hand, in Gallo-Rom. handy, convenient, f. *manus* hand (see MANUAL, -ARY). Hence **ma·nner**ED[2] showing mannerism. XIX; after F. *maniéré*. **ma·nner**ISM. *c.*1800. -IST. XVII (Dryden). **ma·nner**LY[1] and -LY[2]. XIV.

manner[2] mæ·nəɹ in phr. *with the m.* with the stolen thing in one's possession, (hence) in flagrante delicto. XV. orig. *manor*, *maner*, in law-book spelling *mainour* – AN. *mainoure*, *meinoure*, *mainoevere*, OF. *maneuvre* (see next). The etymol. sense would be 'act or fact (of a crime)', but law-F. shows the concrete sense 'thing taken'; the phr. *pris ov mainoure* (taken with 'mainour') was prob. framed to repr. OE. *æt hæbbendre handa ġefangen* taken with the hand holding (the theft).

manœuvre, U.S. **maneuver** mənū·vəɹ, mənjū·vəɹ evolution of naval or military forces. XVIII. – F. *manœuvre* (OF. *manuevre*), f. *manœuvrer* (whence Pr., Pg. *manobrar*, Sp. *maniobrar*, It. *manovrare*, and **manœuvre** vb. XVIII) :– medL. *manuoperāre*, for L. *manū operārī* (*-āre*) work with the hand; see MANUAL, OPERATE.

manometer mənɔ·mitəɹ instrument for measuring the elastic force of fluids. XVIII. – F. *manomètre* (Varignon), f. Gr. *manós* thin, rare; see -METER.

manor mæ·nəɹ †mansion, country residence XIII; †mansion of a lord with the land appertaining XIV; territorial unit, orig. a feudal lordship XVI. ME. *maner(e)* – AN. *maner*, OF. *maneir*, (now) *manoir* dwelling, habitation (latinized *manerium*, *-eria*), sb. use of *maneir* dwell :– L. *manēre* remain, in Rom. dwell; see MANSION. The sp. with *-or* (XVI) is alt. of *mannor*, which succeeded to *manner*, *manoir*. Hence **manor**IAL mənɔ̄·riəl. XVIII; after AL. *manēriālis* (whence †**mane·rial** XVIII).

-mans unexpl. suffix in thieves' cant of XVI–XVII, as *crackmans* hedge, *darkmans* night, *harmans* stocks.

mansard mæ·nsāɹd broken roof. XVIII. – F. *mansarde* (phr. *couvert à la mansarde*, *toit en mansarde*), f. name of the F. architect François *Mansard* (1598–1666).

manse mæns †mansion house XV; (hist.) measure of land sufficient to support a family; ecclesiastical residence XVI. – medL. *mansus*, *mansa*, *mansum* dwelling, house, measure of land, f. *māns-* (see next).

mansion mæ·nʃən †dwelling, abiding; †abiding-place XIV; †manor-house XVI; stately residence XIX. – (O)F. *mansion* – L. *mānsiō(n-)* stay, station, abiding-place, quarters (whence (O)F. *maison* house), f. *māns-*, pp. stem of *manēre* remain, stay, rel. to Gr. *ménein*, *mímnein*, Arm. *mnam* I remain.

mansuetude mæ·nswitjūd (arch.) gentleness. XIV (Ch.). – (O)F., or L. *mānsuētūdō*, f. *mānsuētus* gentle, f. *manus* hand + *suētus* accustomed; see MANUAL, DESUETUDE.

manswear mæ·nswɛəɹ (chiefly Sc.) commit perjury OE.; perjure XIV. OE. *mānswerian*, f. *mān* wickedness (= OFris., OS. *mēn*, OHG. *mein*, surviving in *meineid* perjury, ON. *mein*) :– CGerm. (exc. Gothic) **mainam*, rel. to MEAN[1] + *swerian* SWEAR. So pp. **ma·nsworn** perjured. XIII (Cursor M.).

mantel mæ·ntəl †movable shelter for besiegers; piece of timber supporting the masonry above a fireplace (hence *mantel-piece*, *-shelf*, †*tree*). XV. var. of MANTLE, with senses derived from F. *manteau* (*m. de cheminée*), †*mantel*.

manticore mæ·ntikɔ̄əɹ fabulous monster having a lion's body, a man's head, etc. XIII. – L. *mantichōra* – Gr. *mantikhṓrās*, corrupt reading in Aristotle's 'Historia Animalium' (quoting Ctesias) for *martikhórās* – OPers. word meaning 'man-eater', f. *martīya-* (mod. *mard*) man + χ^v*ar-* (mod. *χurden*) eat.

mantis mæ·ntis insect which holds its fore-legs in a position suggesting hands folded in prayer. XVII. – modL. – Gr. *mántis* prophet, diviner, f. **mn-* (see MANIA).

mantissa mænti·sə †unimportant addition XVII; (math.) decimal part of a logarithm XIX. – L. *mantissa*, *-īsa* makeweight, said to be of Etruscan origin.

mantle mæ·ntl loose sleeveless cloak XIII; applied to various coverings from XIV. ME. *mantel* – OF. *mantel* (mod. *manteau*) = Pr. *mantel*, Sp. *mantillo* :– L. *mantellum*, var. of *mantēlum* (:– **mantergsli-* 'hand-wiper') and rel. to *mantēlium*, *-ēle*, *mantīlium*, *-īle* towel, napkin, table-cloth, with shortened derivs., late L. *mantus*, medL. *mantum* (Isidore), **manta* short cloak, whence Sp., It. *manto* (F. *mante*), Pr. *manta* cloak, Sp. *manta* blanket, tapestry, whence dim. *mantilla* woman's veil; perh. ult. of Celtic origin. Many adoptions of the Rom. forms or their derivs. are or have been current: †**mant** XVII – F. *mante* – Pr. *manta* or Sp. *manto*; **ma·nta** XVII; **ma·nteau** XVII; †**mantee·l** – F. *mantille* – Sp. *mantilla*; MANTEL; **mant(e)let** cape, cloak XIV; movable shelter for men-at-arms XVI; screen for men working a gun XIX. – OF. dim. of *mantel*; **mantelle·tta** XIX – It. dim. of *mantello*; **manti·lla** XVIII – Sp.; **ma·nto** XVII – It. or Sp.; **mantua** mæ·ntjuə loose gown for women XVII; alt. of *manteau* by assoc. with the It. place-name *Mantua*. ¶ Germ. derivs. of L. are OE., OFris. *mentel*, OHG. *mantal* (later *-el*), ON. *mǫttull*. Hence **mantle** wrap in a mantle, cover up XIV; of a hawk spreading its wings XV; become covered *with* a coating XVI; suffuse or be suffused *with* glowing colour XVIII. partly – OF. *manteler*.

Manton mæ·ntən in full *Joe M.*, fowling-piece made by Joseph *Manton* (d. 1835), gunsmith.

manu- mæ·nju repr. abl. sg. of L. *manus* hand (see next) as in MANUFACTURE, MANUSCRIPT; e.g. **manuduc·tion** guidance XVI, **manumi·ssion** XV, after L.

manual mæ·njuəl pert. to the hands; autograph (e.g. in *sign m.* – OF. *seing manuel*). XV. Earliest form *manuel* (later assim. to L.) – (O)F. *manuel* (corr. to Sp. *manual*, It. *manuale*) – L. *manuālis*, f. *manus* hand, rel. to OE. *mund*, OHG. *munt* hand, protection, ON. *mund* hand (cf. Goth. *manwus* ready); see -AL[1]. As sb. small book for handy use (XV) based ult. on late L. *manuāle* (tr. Gr. ἐγχειρίδιον), sb. use of n. of adj.; as a term for the keyboard of an organ (XIX) dist. from *pedal*.

manucode mæ·njukoud bird of paradise. XIX. – F. *manucode* (Buffon), shortening of modL. *manucodiata* (used in Eng. XVI–XVII), – Malay *mānuq dēwāta* 'bird of the gods'.

manufacture mænjufæ·ktʃəɹ †product of manual labour XVI; †manual work; making things by physical labour or mechanical power, thing so made XVII (Bacon). – F. *manufacture* (XVI) – It. *manifattura* (XIV), with refash. after L. *manū factum* made by hand (see MANUAL, FACT, -URE). So **manufa·ctory** XVII; after FACTORY.

manure mənjuə·ɹ †occupy, administer; †till, cultivate XIV; (from the sb.) apply manure to XVI. Earliest forms *maynoyre*, *-oure*, *manour* – AN. *mainoverer*, OF. *man-o(u)vrer* MANŒUVRE; assim. in ending to -URE. Hence **manu·re** sb. dung or compost used for fertilizing XVI; str. *ma·nure* as late as Cowper's 'The Task' (1784); in some dial. (mæ·nəɹ), repr. earlier by *man(n)or*, *-er*, *-ar* (XVI).

manuscript mæ·njŭskript adj. written by hand; sb. writing; codex. XVI. – medL. *manūscrīptus*, i.e. *manū* with the hand, abl. of *manus* and *scrīptus*, pp. of *scrībere* write; see MANUAL, SCRIPTURE, and cf. F. *manuscrit*, It. *manoscritto*, Sp. *manuscrito*.

Manx mæŋks pert. to, people or language of, the Isle of Man. XVI. Earlier *Manks* – (with metathesis) ON. **Manskr* (whence immed. †*Maniske* XVI), f. *Man-* (nom. *Mǫn* :– **Manu* – OIr. *Manu*)+*-skr* -ISH[1].

many me·ni a great number of (with *a*, *an* XIII). OE. *maniġ*, *moniġ*, later *mæniġ*, corr. to OFris. *man(i)ch*, *monich*, *menich*, OS. *manag*, MDu. *menech*, Du. *menig*, OHG. *manag*, *menig* (MHG. *manec*, G. *manch*), OEN. **mangr* (OSw. *mangher*), Goth. *manags* :– CGerm. **managaz*, **manigaz* :– IE. **monogho-* **menogho-*, whence also OSl. *mŭnogŭ* much (Russ. *mnógij*), OIr. *menice* abundant (Ir. *minic*), Gael. *minig* frequent, W. *mynych* often. As sb. in *a* (*great*) *many* (*of*), etc. XVI; orig. modelled on *a few*, but also assoc. with MEINIE. ¶ The old pronunc. mæ·ni survives in **mani**FOLD mæ·nifould (OE. *maniġfeald*); me·ni (from XIII) may be due to the analogy of *ani*/*eni* ANY.

manyplies me·niplaiz (dial.) omasum. XVIII (*monyple*, *manyplus*). f. MANY+pl. of PLY; modelled on synon. *manifold-s* (XIII).

Maori ma·ŏri, mauə·ri (member of) aboriginal race of New Zealand. XIX. – native name, said to mean 'of the usual kind'.

map mæp representation of the earth's surface or of the heavens. XVI. – medL. *mappa*, short for *mappa mundī* 'sheet of the world', i.e. *mappa* (in class. L. table-cloth, NAPKIN), *mundī* g. of *mundus* world. ¶ *Mappa mundi* is repr. by (O)F. *mappemonde* (whence ME. *mappemonde* XIV, Ch.), etc. Hence **map** vb. XVI.

maple mei·pl tree of the genus Acer. In OE. *mapeltrēow*, *mapulder* maple-TREE; cf. OS. *mapulder*, MLG. (with alteration of final element) *mapeldorn*. The simplex is first recorded XIV (Ch.). ¶ A parallel form with orig. *t* instead of *p* is found in OHG. *mazzaltra* (G. *massholder*, *masseller*).

maquis mæ·ki underground patriotic movement in France in the war of 1939–45. F.; 'scrub' – It. *macchia* spot, (hence) thicket appearing as a spot on a mountain side :– L. *macula* (cf. MAIL[1]).

mar māɹ †hinder; †spoil, impair OE.; harm, injure, ruin (now in lighter sense) XIII. OE. *merran* (WS. *mierran*) = OFris. *meria*, OS. *merrian* hinder (Du. *marren* fasten, tie up, loiter), OHG. *marren*, *merren* hinder (MHG. *merren*), ON. *merja* bruise, crush, Goth. (CGerm.) *marzjan* cause to stumble. ¶ The WGerm. **marrjan* was adopted in Rom. and is repr. by OF. *marrir* lead astray, distress (surviving in F. *marri* grieved), Sp. *marrido* grieved, and (with prefix) OF., Pr. *esmarit* strayed, It. *smarrire* bewilder. ¶ Prefixed to sbs. (in object relation) to form comps. meaning 'a person or thing that mars . .'; esp. in the pseudonym 'Martin *Marprelate*' of writers of violent anti-episcopal tracts (1588–9); gen. in *mar-all* (Florio, 1611), *mar-hawk* (Turbervile, 1575), *marplot* (as the name of a character in Mrs. Centlivre's 'Busie Body', 1708).

marabou mæ·rəbū large stork or heron of W. Africa; downy feathers of these birds. XIX. – F. *marabout* – Arab. *murābiṭ*; see next (the stork is said to be *mrabt* holy).

marabout mæ·rəbūt Mohammedan hermit XVII; shrine marking the burial-place of one XIX. In various forms repr. the orig. Arab. or derivs. therefrom; the present form is – F. *marabout* – Pg. *marabuto* – Arab. *murābiṭ* hermit, monk, orig. one who betook himself to a frontier station (*ribāṭ*) to acquire merit against the infidel.

maracock mæ·rəkɔk fruit of Amer. passion-flower. XVII. – Virginian Algonkin.

maranatha mærənæ·þə Aram. phr. (in Gr. form *maranathá*) occurring in 1 Cor. xvi 22, variously interpreted as *māran athā* our Lord has come, or *maranā 'thā* O our Lord, come thou; often erron. regarded as composing with the word preceding it in the text, a formula of imprecation, ANATHEMA *maranatha* (e.g. in the Wycl. Bible 'be he cursid, Maranatha, in the comynge of the Lord'); hence used for a terrible curse.

maraschino mærəskī·nou liqueur made from the marasca cherry. XVIII. It., f. *marasca*, aphetic of *amarasca* (sc. *ciliegia* cherry), f. *amaro* – L. *amārus* bitter.

marasmus məræ·zməs (path.) wasting disease. XVII. modL. – Gr. *marasmós*, f. *maraínein* wither, waste (see AMARANTH).

Marathi mărā·ti pert. to, language of, *Maratha* (a large district of India) :– Skr. *Māhārāshṭra* 'great kingdom'. XVII (*Moratty*).

Marathon mæ·rəþən name of the place at which the Athenians defeated the Persians in 490 B.C., applied to a long-distance foot-race introduced at the revived Olympic Games at Athens (1896) in allusion to the feat of the Gr. runner who brought the news of the battle to Athens.

marauder mərɔ̄·dəɹ one who roves in search of plunder. XVII (*maroder*). – F. *maraudeur*, f. *marauder*, whence, or as back-formation from the agent-noun, **marau·d** vb. XVIII. The F. vb. is f. *maraud* rogue, vagabond, scoundrel (XV), of unkn. origin.

maravedi mærəvei·di Sp. coin. XV. – Sp. *maravedi* – Arab. *Murābiṭīn* (pl. of *murābiṭ* MARABOUT), name of a Moorish dynasty, usu. called *Almoravides* (with prefixed Arab. article AL-²), which reigned at Cordova 1087–1147.

marble mā·ɹbl limestone in a crystalline state. XII (*marbelston*). ME. *marbel, marbre* – OF. *marble*, by dissim. from (O)F. *marbre* = Pr. *marme*, Sp. *mármol*, It. *marmo*, Rum. *marmure* :– L. *marmor* – Gr. *mármaros* shining stone, orig. stone, block of rock, but later assoc. with *marmaírein* shine. ¶ The L. word was adopted early in Germ., as OE. *marma, marm-, marmal-, marmor|stān*, OHG. *marmul* (G. *marmel*), etc.

marc māɹk refuse after grapes are pressed. XVII (*marre*, Holland). – F. *marc*, f. *marcher* tread, MARCH. ¶ An obscure var. *murk, murc, mirk* was current XVII–XIX.

marcasite mā·ɹkəsait (crystallized) iron pyrites. XV. – medL. *marcasīta* (whence also F. *marcassite*, etc.) – Arab. *marqashīṭā* – Pers.; assoc. with -ITE.

marcella māɹse·lə twilled cotton or linen fabric. XIX. f. *Marseilles*, France.

march¹ māɹtʃ third (in the Roman pre-Julian calendar, first) month of the year. XII (*marrch*, Orm). – OF. *march(e)*, north-eastern var. of *marz*, (also mod.) *mars* :– L. *Martiu-s* (sc. *mēnsis* month; lit. month of Mars), whence also Pr. *martz*, Sp., It. *marzo*, and OHG. *marzeo, merzo* (G. *märz*), MDu. *maerte, merte* (Du. *Maart*), etc.

march² māɹtʃ boundary. XIII (RGlouc.). – (O)F. *marche* = Pr., Sp., It. *marca* – Rom. (medL.) *marca* – OFrank. **marka* :– Germ. **markō* MARK¹. So **march** vb. border *upon*. XIV (R. Mannyng). – OF. *marchir*, f. *marche*.

march³ māɹtʃ walk in a military manner. XVI. – (O)F. *marcher* walk, orig. tread, trample (whence mod. techn. felt, full) :– Gallo-Rom. **marcāre*, f. late L. *marcus* hammer. Hence or – F. *marche* (f. *marcher*) **march** sb. XVI. ¶ In the military sense the F. vb. has been adopted in many Eur. langs.

marchioness mā·ɹʃənes wife or widow of a marquis. XVI. – medL. *marchionissa*, f. *marchiō(n-)* prop. captain of the marches, f. *marca* MARCH²; see -ESS¹.

marchpane mā·ɹtʃpein marzipan. XVI. The various forms, *march-, marts-, maza-, -pain(e), -pan(e)*, repr. diverse Continental forms, as F. †*marcepain* (mod. *massepain*), It. *marzapane*, Sp. *mazapan*, G. *marzipan* MARZIPAN (the present current form).

marconigram māɹkou·nigræm wireless telegram. 1902. f. name of Guglielmo *Marconi*, inventor of a system of wireless telegraphy; see -GRAM.

mare¹ mɛəɹ female of the horse, etc. Early ME. *māre* (XII), with stem-vowel from obl. cases of OE. *mearh* horse, finally superseding *mēre* (Ch. has both forms in rhyme), *müre*, OE. **mēre*, **mīere*, *mȳre* :– Germ. (not in Gothic) **marχjōn* (OFris., MLG., MDu. *mer(r)ie*, OHG. *mar(i)ha*, Du. *merrie*, G. *mähre*, ON. *merr*), f. **marχaz* horse (OHG. *marah*, ON. *marr*) :– **markos*, repr. also by Gaulish acc. sg. *márkan* (Pausanias), (O)Ir., Gaelic *marc*, W. *march*. Cf. MARSHAL.

mare² see NIGHTMARE.

maremma məre·mə low marshy land by the sea-shore. XIX. It. :– L. *maritima* (sc. *ōra* shore); see MARITIME.

margarine (strictly) mā·ɹgərīn, (pop.) māɹdʒərī·n legal name (by 50 & 51 Vict. c. 29, an. 1887) for any substitute for butter; repl. OLEO*margarine*, in which *margarine* repr. Chevreul's term for the glyceride of his 'margaric acid', f. F. *margarique* (whence **margar**IC māɹgæ·rik XIX), f. Gr. *márgaron, margarítēs* pearl, with ref. to the pearly lustre of the crystals or scales of the acid.

margaux mā·ɹgou, ‖margo claret made in the commune of *Margaux*, Gironde, France. XVIII (*Margose, -ou*).

margay mā·ɹgei S. Amer. tiger cat. XVIII. – F. *margay* (Buffon), alt. of *margaia* (Claude d'Abbeville 1614) – Tupi *mbaracaïa*.

margin mā·ɹdʒin part just within the boundary of an object. XIV. – L. *margin-, margō*, rel. to MARK¹. Little used in XVII, its place being taken by the altered form **margent** (XVI; earlier *marjant* XV), with which cf. ANCIENT, etc. F. *marge* was adopted in Eng. (now poet.) **marge** māɹdʒ. XV. So **ma·rgin**AL¹. XVI. – medL. **marginalia** māɹdʒinei·liə. XIX (Coleridge). – n. pl. of medL. *marginālis*.

margrave mā·ɹgreiv German title orig. of the governor of a border province. XVI. – MDu. *markgrave* = OHG. *marcgrāvo* (G. *markgraf*); see MARK¹; the second el. is of obscure origin.

marguerite māɹgərī·t daisy. XIX. – F. form (adopted XV–XVII as †*margarete, -ite*) of the female name *Margaret*, ult. – L. *margarīta* – Gr. *margarítēs*, f. *márgaron* pearl, prob. of Oriental origin.

marigold mæ·rigould plant of the genus Calendula. XIV. In early use often pl. *marygoulden, marygoldes*; f. proper name *Mary* (presumably with ref. to the Virgin Mary) + (dial.) *gold*, OE. *golde*, prob. rel. to GOLD. ¶ The marigold is called by names containing 'gold' and 'Mary' in other langs., as Du. *goldbloem*, G. *goldblume*, MLG. *marienblome*, MDu. *marienbloemkijn* 'solsequium'.

marijuana, marihuana mærihwā·nə dried leaves of common hemp, smoked as a narcotic; the plant itself. XIX. Amer.-Sp.

marinade mærinei·d pickle, pickled meat or fish. XVII. – F. *marinade* – Sp. *marinada*, f. *marinar* pickle in brine, f. *marino* MARINE; see -ADE. Hence **marina·de** vb. XVII.

marine məri·n pert. to the sea. XV. – (O)F. *marin*, fem. *marine* = Sp., It. *marino, -ina* :– L. *marīnus*, f. *mare* sea, rel. (with exceptional vocalism) to Goth. *marei*, Ir. *muir*, W., Gaul. *mor* (as in *Aremorici* dwellers near the sea, thence *Armorica*), OSl. *more*; see -INE[1]. So **marinER**[2] mæ·rinəɹ seaman. XIII. – AN. *mariner*, (O)F. *marinier* = Sp. *marinero*, It. *marinaio* :– medL. *marīnārius*, f. L. *marīnus*.

Mariolatry see -LATRY.

marionette mæriəne·t puppet actuated by strings. XVII. – F. *marionnette*, f. *Marion*, dim. of *Marie* MARY; see -ETTE.

marish see MARSH.

marital mæ·ritəl pert. to a husband or to marriage. XVII. – L. *marītālis*, f. *marītus* husband; see MARRY[1], -AL[1].

maritime mæ·ritaim pert. to the sea. XVI. – (partly through F. *maritime*) L. *maritimus*, f. *mari-*, *mare* sea (see MARINE) + *-timus*, as in *fīnitimus* neighbouring, *lēgitimus* LEGITIMATE. Early vars. *maritayne*, *-itan(e)* *-itine* (XVI–XVIII) depend upon F. †*maritain*, †*-aim*, †*-itin*, which show assim. to other suffixes.

marjoram mā·ɹdʒərəm plant of the genus Origanum. XIV (Gower). ME. *majorane*, *mageram* – OF. *majorane* (mod. *marjolaine*, through **marjoraine*) = Pr., Sp., It. *majorana*, Rum. *măgheran* – medL. *majorana* (in Dioscorides *maezurana*, which has been dubiously connected with L. *amāracus*, Gr. *amắrakos*). ¶ The Rom. word has passed into Germ. and other langs.

mark[1] māɹk A. (hist.) boundary (*landmark*); trace, orig. as a sign OE.; B. target XIII (Laȝ.); C. (f. MARK[3]) remark, note XVI. OE. (Anglian) *merc*, (WS.) *mearc* = OFris. *mer(i)ke*, OS. *marka* (Du. *mark*), OHG. *marcha* (G. *mark*), ON. *mǫrk* (recorded only in derived sense 'forest'; Sw., Da. *mark* field, ground), Goth. *marka* :– CGerm. **markō* str. fem., beside which some langs. have reprs. of a n. **markam* sign, landmark, standard, e.g. MDu., MHG., ON. *mark*; rel. to L. *margō* MARGIN, OIr. *mruig* (Ir. *bruig*) boundary, territory, W., etc. *bro* district, Gaulish *brogae* territory (cf. tribal name *Allo|brogēs*), Av. *marəzu* boundary, Pers. *marz* landmark. Hence **ma·rks**MAN XVII (earlier †*markman* XVI); see B above. ¶ The Germ. word and its deriv. vb. were adopted widely in Rom., e.g. OF. *merc*, *marc* m., *marche* fem. MARCH[1], north-eastern and mod. *marque* (which has infl. the native Eng. word), Pr., Sp., It. *marca*.

mark[2] māɹk weight of gold or silver; money of account. OE. *marc*, corr. to OFris. *merk*, MDu. *marc* (Du. *mark*), MHG. *marke*, ON. *mǫrk*; the Germ. forms, which vary in gender, are prob. all – medL. *marcus*, *marca*, whence also F., Pr. *marc*, Sp. *marco*, It. *marco*, *-a*, perh. ult. identical with MARK[1].

mark[3] māɹk A. put a mark upon OE.; B. notice, observe, REMARK XIV. OE. *mearcian* = OFris. *merkia*, OS. *(gi)markon* appoint, observe (Du. *marken*), OHG. *marchōn* plan, ON. *marka* mark, observe :– Germ. **markōjan*, f. **markō* MARK[1]. The Rom. langs. have a corr. vb. from the adopted sb., viz. (O)F. *marquer* (the source of some sense of the Eng. vb.), Pr., Sp. *marcar*, It. *marcare*.

market mā·ɹkit gathering of people for buying and selling XII; public place for this XIII; (opportunity for, rate of) purchase and sale XVI; seat of trade XVII. Early ME. *market* (XII, Peterborough Chron.), recorded earlier in the late OE. comp. *ġēarmarkett* (XI), in which *ġēar* YEAR corr. to the g. of the native term *ġēares ċieping* 'year's market'; both simplex and comp. appear to be – OS. *iārmarket* = OHG. *iārmarchāt*, of which the second el. – L. *mercātus* (in Rom. **marcatus*, whence OF. *marchiet*, mod. *marché*, Pr. *markat-z*), f. *mercārī* buy, f. *merc-*, *merx* MERCHANDISE. Hence vb. (as in *marketable* Sh., *marketing*); cf. G. *markten*.

markhor mā·ɹkōɹ large wild goat. XIX. – Pers. *mārkhōr* lit. 'serpent-eater', f. *mār* serpent + *khōr* -eating.

marl māɹl kind of clayey soil. XIV. – OF. *marle* (still dial.; repl. in modF. by *marne*) :– medL. *margila* (whence also OHG. *mergil*, G. *mergel*), f. (after *argilla* white clay) L. *marga* (whence Sp., OIt., etc. *marga*), said by Pliny to be a Gaulish word (but Bret. *marg* does not corr. phonetically; Bret. *merl* is from F. dial. *merle*, W. *marl* and Ir., Gael. *marla* from Eng.). Hence vb. XIV (Trevisa); so MDu. *marlen*.

marline mā·ɹlin (naut.) small line. XV. Also *marling* – Du. *marlijn*, f. *marren* bind + *lijn* LINE[1], and Du. *marling*, f. *marlen*, frequent. of *marren* + *-ing* -ING[1]; the corr. MLG. *merlink*, *marlink* has passed into other langs., e.g. Sw., Da. *merling*, F. *merlin*. Hence **ma·rlin(g)** SPIKE. XVII (Capt. Smith).

marm mām see MA'AM.

marmalade mā·ɹməleid preserve made by boiling quinces, oranges, etc., to form a consistent mass. XVI. – F. *marmelade* (whence G., Du. *marmelade*, etc.) – Pg. *marmelada* (whence Sp. *marmelada*), f. *marmelo* quince :– L. *melimēlum* – Gr. *melímēlon* kind of apple grafted on a quince, f. *méli* honey (cf. MELLIFLUOUS) + *mêlon* apple; see -ADE.

marmoset māɹməze·t †small monkey, (later) one of the Hapalidæ XIV; †grotesque figure XV (Lydg.); †term of playful reproach XVI. – (O)F. *marmouset* (latinized *marmosetus* XIII) grotesque image, little man or boy, (dial.) ape, of unkn. origin.

marmot mā·ɹmət rodent of the genus Arctomys, inhabiting the Alps and the Pyrenees. XVII (Topsell, citing Scaliger's use of F. *marmot*; *marmotto*, Ray; first naturalized by Goldsmith and Pennant).

– F. *marmotte* (whence Sp., Pg., and It. forms), prob. alt. of Romansh *murmont* :– Rom. **mūrem montis* 'MOUNTAIN MOUSE' (whence OHG. *muremunto*, G. dial. *murmentel*, G. *murmeltier*, etc.).

maroon[1] mərū·n †sweet chestnut of S. Europe XVI; brownish crimson (as of the nutshell); firework (box of pasteboard) XVIII. – F. *marron* – It. *marrone* – medGr. *máraon.*

maroon[2] mərū·n negro of Dutch Guiana and W. Indies XVII; (in full *maroon party*), pleasure party, picnic XVIII. – F. *marron*, †*maron* – Sp. *cimarron* wild, untamed, runaway slave (occas. in Eng. as †*Symeron* XVII), f. *cimarra* furred coat; see -OON. Hence **maroo·n** vb. †pass. and intr. be lost in the wilds XVII; put ashore on a desolate coast XVIII.

marque māɹk †reprisals; *letters of marque*, orig. royal licence authorizing reprisals on a hostile state. XV. – F. *marque* – Pr. *marca*, f. *marcar* seize as a pledge, perh. ult. f. Germ. **mark*- MARK[1], sign.

marquee māɹkī· large tent. XVII (also †*markee*). Spurious sg. form deduced from *marquise* (formerly so used in Eng.) apprehended as pl. and assim. in ending to -EE[2].

marquetry, -terie mā·ɹkĭtri inlaid work. XVI. – F. *marqueterie*, f. *marqueter* variegate, f. *marque* MARK[1]; see -RY.

marquis, marquess mā·ɹkwis ruler (orig.) of a 'march' or frontier district; peer between the ranks of duke and earl XIV; †marchioness XVI–XVII. ME. *marchis*, *markis* – OF. *marchis*, alt. later to *marquis* after the corr. Pr. *marques*, Sp. *marqués*; f. Rom. **marca* MARCH[2]+*-*ese* :– L. -*ēnsem* -ESE; prop. adj., sc. *comēs* COUNT[2]. The sp. with -*ess* (XVI) is used by some holders of the title. ¶ The medL. equiv. was *marchio*; cf. MARCHIONESS. Hence **ma·rquis**ATE[1]. XVI. So **marquise** māɹkī·z kind of pear; †marquee. XVIII. – F., fem. of *marquis.*

marquois mā·ɹkwoiz epithet of a scale used for drawing equidistant parallel lines. XIX (sometimes written *Marquoi's*, *Marquois's*, as if possessive of a proper name). alt. of F. *marquoir* ruler used by tailors, f. *marquer* MARK[3]+-*oir* :– L. -*ōrium* -ORY[1].

marram mæ·rəm bent-grass, Psamma arenaria. XVII. – ON. *marálmr*, f. *marr* sea, MERE[1]+*hálmr* HAULM; chiefly E. Angl.

marrow[1] mæ·rou soft substance in the cavity of bones OE.; central or vital part XV; (*vegetable*) *m.*, fruit of Cucurbita ovifera XIX. OE. *mærh*, *mærg* (WS. *mearh*, *mearg*), corr. to OFris. *merg*, *merch*, OS. *marg* (Du. *merg*), OHG. *mar(a)g* (G. *mark*), ON. *mergr* :– CGerm. (exc. Gothic) **mazgam*, **mazgaz* :– IE. **mozgho*-, which is repr. also in Slav. and Indo-Iranian.

marrow[2] mæ·rou (dial.) companion, mate XV (Promp. Parv.); husband or wife XVI. prob. – ON. *margr* many, fig. friendly, communicative (with special Eng. development).

marry[1] mæ·ri join in or enter into wedlock. XIII (RGlouc., Cursor M.). – (O)F. *marier* = Pr., Sp. *maridar*, It. *maritare*, Rum. *mărita* :– L. *marītāre*, f. *marītus* married, husband (whence (O)F. *mari*, etc.), usu. referred to IE. **mer*- **mor*-, repr. by various words meaning 'young man', 'young woman'. So **marri**AGE mæ·ridʒ wedlock, wedding. XIII (RGlouc., Cursor M.). – (O)F. *mariage* = Sp. *maridaje*, etc., f. the vb.

marry[2] mæ·ri int. XIV (*Marie*). The name of the Virgin MARY used as an oath or ejaculatory invocation; in XVI the oath *by Mary Gipcy*, i.e. by Mary the Egyptian, appears to have suggested the addition of the ints. *gip*, *gup* to *Mary*, and, as these were used in driving horses, *come up* was later substituted for them (*Marry come up* was used in indignation, surprise, or contempt).

Mars māɹz Roman god of war; (astron.); (alch.) iron. XIV (Ch.). – L. *Mārs* (cf. MARTIAL).

Marsala māɹsā·lə species of white wine. XIX. f. name of a town on the west coast of Sicily.

Marseillaise māɹsəlei·z, ‖marsɛjɛ̄z national song of the French Republic, composed 1792. XIX. F., fem. (sc. *chanson* song) of *Marseillais* of Marseilles; so named from having been first sung in Paris by a band of 'fédérés' from Marseilles.

marsh māɹʃ low-lying watery land. OE. *mersć*, *merisć* = MLG. *mersch*, *marsch*, MDu. *mersch(e)* (whence G. *marsch*, Du. *marsk*) :– WGerm. **marisk*-, whence medL. *mariscus*, the source of (O)F. *marais*, †*mareis*, adopted in ME. as *mar(r)eis*, *mar(r)ais* (XIV), altered later to **ma·rish** (XVI), which is found in Spenser, A.V., Milton, Tennyson, and survives dial. Hence **ma·rsh**Y[1]. XIV.

marshal mā·ɹʃəl high officer of state, of the army, †of a court, in charge of ceremonies XIII; †farrier (cf. F. *maréchal-ferrant*) XIV. – OF. *mareschal* (mod. *maréchal*) = Pr. *manescalc-s*, It. *maniscalco*, †*mali*-, †*mari*- (It. *maresciallo*, Sp. *mariscal* are – F.) :– Frankish L. *mariscalcus* (Salic Law) – Germ. **marχaskalkaz* (OHG. *marahscalh*, G. †*marschalk*, later *marschall*), f. **marχaz* horse (see MARE[1])+**skalkaz* (OE. *sćealc*) servant. For the development from the designation of a groom to that of a high officer cf. *constable*. Hence vb. XV. So †**ma·rshal**CY office or rank of marshal XIV (R. Mannyng). – AN. *mareschalcie*, OF. *mareschaucie*; continued in the form **ma·rshalsea** court formerly held before the steward and the knight marshal of the Royal Household, (also) a prison in Southwark under the latter's control; regarded in XVI–XVII as containing the sb. *see*.

marsupial mɑːsjū·piəl of or resembling a pouch XVII; epithet of mammals having a pouch for their young XIX. – modL. *marsūpiālis*, f. L. *marsūpium* pouch – Gr. *marsúpion*, *marsípion*, dim. of *mársipos* purse, bag; see -AL¹.

mart mɑːɹt †market, fair XV; market-place XVI; centre of commerce, emporium XVII. – Du. †*mart*, var. of *markt* MARKET.

martagon mā·ɹtəgən Turk's-cap lily. XV. – F. *martagon* – Turk. *martagān* orig. form of turban adopted by Sultan Muhammed I.

Martello maɹte·lou designation of a so-called tower or small circular fort. XVIII (*Mortella*), XIX (*Martello*). alt., perh. by assoc. with It. *martello* hammer, of the name of Cape *Mortella* in Corsica (It. *mortella* wild myrtle), where there was a tower of this kind which the Eng. fleet captured in 1794.

marten mā·ɹtin fur-bearing animal, †orig. the fur itself. XV. Early forms *martren*, *martro(u)n* – MDu. *martren* – OF. *martrine* marten fur, sb. use (sc. *peau* skin) of *martrin*, f. *martre* (whence ME. *martre* XIII) = It. *martora* – WGerm. **marþr*- (OHG. *mardar*, G. *marder*), ext. form of **marþuz* (OE. *mearþ*, ON. *mǫrðr*), whence (O)F. *marte*, Pr. *mart-z*, Sp. *marta*.

martial mā·ɹʃəl pert. to war or battle XIV (*marcial*, Ch.); pert. to the army, military (*court martial*, *martial law*); warlike XV; of the planet Mars; of iron XVII. – (O)F. *martial* or L. *mārtiālis*, f. *Mārti-*, *Mārs* (for *Māvors*) the Roman god of war, the planet fourth in order of distance from the sun, in medL. iron (after Gr. *A'rēs*); see -IAL. So **Ma·rt**IAN pert. to the planet Mars XIV (*marcien*, Ch.); to the month of March XVII. – OF. *martien* or L. *Mārtiānus* (*Mārtius*).

martin mā·ɹtin bird of the swallow family, Chelidon urbica. XV (Sc. *martoune*). prob. a use of the name *Martin*, a common male Christian name, after St. Martin of Tours. ¶ The proper name is applied in F. to several birds, as *martin-chasseur* hen-harrier, *martin-pêcheur* kingfisher, and the dim. *martinet* to the swift and the martin.

martinet mɑːɹtine·t †system of drill devised by General Martinet XVII; officer who is a stickler for discipline; also gen. XVIII (Moore). f. name of a F. general, drill-master of the reign of Louis XIV.

martingale mā·ɹtiŋgeil A. strap for restraining the movements of a horse's head XVI; B. (naut.) rope for guying down the jib-boom XVIII; C. doubling the stake when losing at cards XIX. – F. *martingale* (Rabelais) in *chausse à la m.* kind of hose fastening at the back, which has been derived from modPr. *martegalo*, fem. of *martegal* inhabitant of *Martigue* in Provence; but connecting links between these forms and with Sp. *almartaga* halter (of Arab. origin), and the relation of senses A, B, C are not known.

Martini¹ mɑːɹtī·ni short for *M.-Henry* (*rifle*), which combines Martini's breech mechanism with Henry's barrel. 1870.

Martini² mɑːɹtī·ni name of a gin-and-vermouth cocktail. XIX. f. name of inventor.

Martinmas mā·ɹtinməs feast of the translation of St. Martin of Tours, 11 Nov. (in Scotland a term-day, in England a time for hiring servants and slaughtering cattle). XIII (RGlouc.). f. *Martin*+MASS¹.

martlet mā·ɹtlit swift; (her.) imaginary bird without feet. XVI. – F. *martelet*, alt. of *martinet*, dim. of *Martin* MARTIN. In the her. sense F. has *merlette* (OF. *merlete*, *meslete*, AN. *mer(e)lot*), dim. of *merle* blackbird (see MERLE), and the orig. intention may have been to represent a 'little blackbird' without feet, later identified with the swift, which has short legs (whence its L. specific name *apus*, Gr. *ápous* footless, in ornithology).

martyr mā·ɹtəɹ (prop.) one who voluntarily undergoes death for the Christian faith. OE. *martir*, corr. to OFris., OS., OHG. *martir* – ecclL. *martyr* – Gr. *mártur*, Æolic and late form of *mártus*, *martur-* witness, (in Christian use) martyr, f. IE. **smer* remember (see MEMORY); reinforced in ME. by OF. *martir*, *martre* (mod. *martyr*); the sp. was finally assim. to the L. form. Hence **ma·rtyr** vb. OE. (*ġe*)*martyrian*, *-martrian*. **ma·rtyr**DOM. OE. So **martyro·**LOGY list of martyrs. XVI. – medL. *martyrologium* – ecclGr. *marturológion* (*lógos* account); in sense 'history of martyrs' a distinct word (see -LOGY). The contr. forms medL. *martilogium*, *-legium*, gave ME. *martiloge*, *-logie*, *-lage* (XIV).

marvel mā·ɹv(ə)l †miracle XIII (Cursor M.); wonderful thing XIV. – (O)F. *merveille*, corr. to Pr. *meravelha*, Sp. *maravilla*, It. *mera-*, *maraviglia* :– CRom. use as fem. sg. of *mirabilia*, n.pl. of L. *mirābilis* wonderful, f. *mirārī* wonder; see MIRACLE, -ABLE. So **marvel** vb. XIII. – (O)F. *merveiller*. **ma·rvell**OUS. XIII. – OF. *merveillos* (mod. *-eux*).

marver mā·ɹvəɹ glass-blower's polished slab of marble or iron. XIX. – F. *marbre* MARBLE; workman's approximation to F. pronunc. marbr.

Mary mɛə·ri mother of Jesus Christ ('the Blessed Virgin Mary'). OE. *Maria*, *Marie*, reinforced in ME. by (O)F. *Marie* – eccl. L. *Maria* – Gr. *Mariā* and *Mariám* – Heb. *Miryām* Miriam (Exod. xv); in asseverations from XIV (cf. MARRY²). ¶ See E. G. Withycombe, 'Dict. Eng. Christian Names'.

marzipan mɑːzipæ·n confectionary made of a paste of pounded almonds, sugar, etc. XIX. – G. *marzipan*, earlier *marcipan*, etymol. alt. (quasi *Marci panis* 'Mark's bread') of *marczapan* – It. *marzapane* MARCHPANE.

mascle mæ·skl †spot; †mesh XIV; (her.) lozenge-shaped charge with lozenge-shaped opening. XV. – AN. *mascle* – AL. *mascula*, alt. of L. *macula* MAIL[1] by assoc. with ME. *mask* (see MESH).

mascot mæ·skət thing supposed to bring good luck. XIX. – F. *mascotte* – modPr. *mascotto*, fem. of *mascot*, dim. of *masco* witch – dial. It. *masca* witch, pl. ghosts of the dead – medL. *masca* witch (Lombardic Laws), of unkn. origin.

masculine mæ·skjŭlin †male (Ch., Trevisa); (gram.) XIV (of rhyme XVI, Sidney); pert. to or characteristic of the male sex XVII. – (O)F. *masculin*, fem. *-ine* – L. *masculīnus*, *-īna*, f. *masculus* MALE; see -INE[1].

mash mæʃ malt mixed with hot water to form wort OE.; warm food of meal for cattle, etc.; pulpy mass. XVI. OE. *māsć* (also in comp. *māxwyrt*) = MLG. *mēsch* (*meschewert*), *māsch*, MHG. *meisch* crushed grapes (G. *maisch*) :– WGerm. **maisk*-, of unkn. origin, but perh. rel. to OE. *miscian* (see MIX). Hence **mash** vb. infuse (malt) XIV; beat into a pulp XVII. ¶ ME. *meshe*, *meysse* (XIII) is independent, pointing to an OE. **mǣsćan* :– **maiskjan*.

masher mæ·ʃəɹ (sl.) fop posing as a lady-killer. Hence **mash** sb.[2] and vb. XIX (acc. to Barrère and Leland in theatrical parlance in U.S.A. *c*.1860).

mashie mæ·ʃi iron golf club with a short head. XIX. poss. – F. *massue* club = Rum. *măciucă* :– Rom. **matteūca*, f. **mattea*, deduced from L. *mateola*.

mask màsk covering to conceal the face. XVI (Berners). – F. *masque* (cf. MASQUE) – It. *maschera* (whence Sp., Pg. *máscara*) = Rum. *măcară* abuse, insult, perh. – Arab. *maskharah* buffoon, f. *sakhira* ridicule. Hence vb. XVI. ¶ With the use of disguises at social gatherings, etc., the word has spread throughout Europe (so medL. *masc(h)a* VII, G., Du., Da. *maske*, Sw. *mask*, Serb. *masca*, Russ. *máska*). An earlier Eng. †*masker* (direct from It.), with var. †*maskeler*, was current in the first half of XVI.

maskinonge mæ·skinəndʒ(i) large pike of the Great Lakes of N. America. XVIII. Recorded in a great variety of forms, due partly to diversities of native dialect, partly to F. pop. etym., which interpreted the word as *masque long* or *allongé* long mask; ult. – Odjibwa *mackinonge*, *micikinonge* (*c* = ʃ), f. *mac*, *mici* great + *kinonge* pike (Cuoq).

maslin[1] mæ·zlin (dial.) brass. OE. *mæstling*, *mæslen* (X), presumably rel. to MHG. *mess(e)* brass (early mod. and dial. G. *mess*, *mesch*, *möss*, *mösch*) and cogns. with suffixes, MDu., MHG. *messinc*, *missinc* (Du., G. *messing*), LG. *mesken* (see -KIN); Icel. *messing*, *mersing* is of LG. origin. Connexion with Czech *mosaz*, Pol. *mosiądz*, has suggested ult. origin in Gr. *Mossúnoikos* pert. to a people living on the shore of the Black Sea; the OE. word antedates the Continental forms and its formation (perh. with -LING[1]) is not certain.

maslin[2] mæ·zlin (dial.) mixed grain. XIV. Many vars. typified by *mestlyon*, *mescellin*, *misselin*, *meslen*, *maslin* – OF. *mesteillon* :– Rom. **mistiliōnem*, f. **mistilium* (whence F. *méteil*), f. L. *mistus*, pp. of *miscēre* MIX; cf. MDu. *mastelūn* (Du. *masteluin*).

masochism mæ·z-, mæ·sŏkizm form of sexual perversion in which a member of one sex takes pleasure in being dominated by one of the other. XIX. f. name of Leopold von Sacher-*Masoch*, Austrian novelist, who described the condition; see -ISM. Hence **masochi·STIC** *a.* XX.

mason mei·sən builder and worker in stone XIII; FREEMASON XV. Earliest forms *machun*, *-oun* – ONF. *machun*; later *mascun*, *masoun* – OF. *masson* (mod. *maçon*) = Pr. *masó*, Pg. *maçâo* :– Rom. **matiōn*- or **maciōn*- (cf. medL. *machio* Isidore VII; *matio* Reichenau Glosses VIII), prob. – Germ. **mattjon* (whence OHG. *mezzo*, *steinmezzo*, G. *steinmetz* stonemason), perh. rel. to MATTOCK. So **ma·sonRY**. XIV (Ch.). – (O)F. *maçonnerie*. **masonIC** mə-, meisɔ·nik esp. pert. to freemasons or freemasonry. XVIII.

mas(s)orah masɔ̄·ra body of tradition relating to the text of the Hebrew Bible. XVII (earlier *masoreth*, Purchas, B. Jonson). repr. Heb. *māsōreth* (Exod. XX 37), where it is interpreted 'bond (of the covenant)', f. *asar* bind, in post-biblical Heb. in the sense 'tradition', as if f. *masur* hand down. So **Mas(s)orete** mæ·sōrīt one who contributed to this. XVI (Golding). – F. *Massoret* and modL. *Massōrēta*; orig. misapplication of *masoreth*, with subseq. assim. of the ending to L. *-ēta*, Gr. *-ētēs*.

masque màsk masked ball; histrionic entertainment consisting of dancing and dumb show XVI; dramatic composition for an entertainment of this kind XVII. var. of MASK, the F. sp. being now restricted to these senses.

masquerade màskərei·d assembly of people wearing masks and diverting themselves with dancing, etc. XVI. First in quasi-Sp. forms *mascarado*, *masquerada* (see -ADO), later superseded by *mascarade*, and (with assim. to MASQUE) *masquerade*; – F. *mascarade* – It. *mascherata* or Sp. *mascarada*, f. *maschera*, *máscara* MASK; see -ADE.

mass[1] mæs, mās Eucharistic service. OE. *mæsse*, *messe*, corr. to OFris., OS. *missa* (Du. *mis*), OHG. *messa*, *missa* (G. *messe*), ON. *messa* – ecclL. *missa* (Rom. **messa*), whence also (O)F. *messe*, Pr., It. *messa*, Sp. *misa*, Pg. *missa*. L. *missa* is a verbal sb. (formed like *collecta* COLLECT[1], *offensa* OFFENCE, *repulsa* REPULSE) from pp. stem *miss*- of *mittere* send, send away (cf. MISSION); it is first recorded from IV (385, St. Ambrose; and 'Peregrinatio

Sylviæ') and in the early centuries is applied to various religious services, but pre-eminently to the Eucharist; the primary meaning is disputed, but many hold that its application to a service results from a transference of meaning in phr. such as *Ite, missa est* Depart, it is the dismissal (i.e. the service is at an end), *Et missæ fiant* And let the dismissals be made (at the end of an office). ¶ The sense 'festival', 'feast day' survives in CANDLEMAS, CHILDERMAS, CHRISTMAS, HALLOWMAS, LAMMAS, MARTINMAS, MICHAELMAS, etc.

mass[2] mæs coherent body of raw material XIV; relatively large body of matter XV; dense aggregation, large amount XVI; solid bulk XVII; (in physics) XVIII. – (O)F. *masse* – L. *massa* – Gr. *mâza* barley-cake, perh. rel. to *mássein* knead, f. **mnq- *menq-* (cf. AMONG, MINGLE). So **mass** vb. XIV. – (O)F. *masser*, f. *masse*.

massacre mæ·səkəɹ indiscriminate killing. XVI. – (O)F. *massacre*, with vars. *maçacre, macecre, macecle*, of unkn. origin. So **massacre** vb. XVI. – (O)F. *massacrer*, f. the sb.

massage mæ·sāʒ curative kneading and rubbing of muscles, etc. XIX. – F. *massage*, f. *masser* apply massage to, used XVIII by French colonists in India, perh. – Pg. *amassar* knead, f. *massa* dough (MASS[2]), but Arab. *mass* handle, *masaḥ* rub, have been suggested; see -AGE. So **masseu·r, -eu·se** XIX.

massicot mæ·sikɔt yellow oxide of lead. XV. Earlier *masticot* – F. *massicot*, †*masticot*, obscurely rel. to It. *marzacotto* unguent, cosmetic, Sp. *mazacote* kali, mortar, prob. based on Arab. *shabbqubtī* Egyptian alum.

massif mæ·sif †block, mass XVI; large mountain mass XIX. – F. *massif*, sb. use of *massif* MASSIVE.

massive mæ·siv forming or consisting of a large mass. XV (Lydg.). – F. *massif*, fem. *-ive*, alt. of OF. *massiz* :– pop. L. **massīceus*, f. *massa* MASS[2]; see -IVE. Finally repl. (arch.) **ma·ssy** XIV (Wycl. Bible, Trevisa), perh. orig. – OF. *massiz*, with later assim. to -Y[1].

massoola mæsū·lə surf-boat used on the Coromandel coast. XVII. Of unkn. origin.

mast[1] màst long pole set up on the keel of a ship. OE. *mæst* = (M)LG., (M)Du., (O)HG. *mast* :– WGerm. **masta* (ON. *mastr*, etc., being – MLG.) :– WIE. **mazdos*, whence poss. L. *mālus* mast, OIr. *matan* club. ¶ The Germ. word was latinized as *mastus* (VIII) and is repr. in Rom. by F. *mât*, Pr. *mast*, with extensions in Pg. *mastro*, Sp. *mastil*.

mast[2] màst fruit of forest-trees, esp. as food for swine. OE. *mæst* = MDu., MLG., OHG. *mast* (in modG. fem.) :– WGerm. **masta* :– **mazdos*, prob. f. base repr. in MEAT.

master mà·stəɹ A. man having control or authority; B. teacher OE. (one who has received an academic degree orig. conveying authority to teach XIV); C. title of rank or compliment XIII; title of presiding officer, etc. XIV. OE. *mægister, magister* (corr. to OFris. *māster* (and OS.) *mēster*, (O)HG. *meister*, ON. *meistari*), a CGerm. adoption from L.; reinforced by OF. *maistre* (mod. *maître*) = Pr. *ma(g)estre-s*, Sp., It. *maestro*, etc. :– L. *magistru-m*, nom. *magister* (OL. *-ester*), usu. referred to *magis* adv. more, as *minister* to *minus* adv. less (but Etruscan forms with *macstr-* are cited, which may be the source). Cf. MISTER[1]. Hence **ma·ster**FUL[1]. XIV. **ma·ster**PIECE XVII; after Du. *meesterstuk* (adopted in Sc. as *meisterstik* XVI) or G. *meisterstück* piece of work qualifying a craftsman. **ma·stery**[3]. ME. *meistrie* (XIII, AncrR.) – OF. *maistrie* (superseded by *maistrise*, mod. *maîtrise*, which was repr. in ME. by *maistris, -ice, -yse*).

mastic mæ·stik gum or resin from Pistachia Lentiscus XIV (Trevisa); the tree XV. – (O)F. *mastic* – late L. *mastichum* (Palladius), *masticha*, varr. of L. *mastichē* (Pliny) – Gr. *mastíkhē*, presumed to be f. *mastikhân* (see next), the substance being used as a chewing-gum in the East.

masticate mæ·stikeit chew. XVII. f. pp. stem of late L. *masticāre* – Gr. *mastikhân* grind the teeth, rel. to *masâsthai* chew, and perh. to synon. L. *mandere*; see -ATE[3]. So **mastica·tion**. XVI. – (O)F. or late L. **ma·sticatory**. XVII. – modL.

mastiff mà·stif dog of a large powerful breed. XIV (R. Mannyng). repr. obscurely OF. *mastin* (mod. *mâtin*) :– Rom. **mānsuētīnus* (Pr. *mastis*, It. *mastino*, etc., are – OF.), f. L. *mānsuētus* tamed, tame, earlier *mānsuēs*, f. *manus* hand (see MANUAL) + base of *suēscere* (pp. *suētus*) accustom, f. *suī* of oneself, *suus* one's own (cf. Goth. *swes* own). The OF. may have become familiar in England in the nom. sg. and obl. pl. form *mastis*, which seems to have been interpreted as **mastifs*.

mastigo- mæ·stigou, -gɔ· comb. form in some scientific words of Gr. *-mástix* scourge, whip, which was used from XVII in the nom. as a second el. of designations of persons and books that deal severely with or are violently critical of a person, institution, etc., as *Homeromastix* (applied to Zoilus), *Histriomastix* (i.e. of the theatre, Prynne 1632), *Satiromastix* (Dekker, used of B. Jonson).

mastodon mæ·stədɔn extinct elephantine mammal having nipple-shaped tubercles on the molars. XIX. – modL., f. Gr. *mastós* breast + *odont-* TOOTH; cf. F. *mastodonte* (Cuvier).

mastoid mæ·stoid (anat., of bones, etc.) nipple-shaped. XVIII. – F. *mastoïde* (Paré) or modL. *mastoīdēs* – Gr. *mastoeidḗs* (ἀποφύσεις μαστοιδεῖς 'mastoid processes', Galen), f. *mastós* (woman's) breast (:–**mədtós*; cf. MAMMA[2], MAST[2]); see -OID.

masturbate mæ·stəɹbeit practise self-abuse. XIX (earlier †*mastuprate* XVII). f. pp. stem of L. *masturbārī*, of unkn. origin, but commonly held to be alt. of **man(ū)-stuprāre* 'defile with the hand'.

mat[1] mæt piece of coarse fabric of plaited fibre OE.; piece of material laid on a surface for protection XV (naut.). OE. *matt, matte, meatte*, corr. to MDu. *matte*, OHG. *matta* (Du. *mat*, G. *matte*); WGerm. – late L. *matta* (whence It. *matta*; parallel late L. *natta* gives F. *natte* map, plait).

mat[2]**, matt** mæt lustreless, dull. XVII. – F. *mat*, identical with *mat* MATE[2]. So **mat** vb. make dull. XVII. – F. *mater*.

matachin mætəʃī·n (antiq.) sword-dancer. XVI. – F. †*matachin* (now *matassin*) – Sp. *matachin*, prob. – Arab. *mutawajjihīn*, active pple. pl. of *tawajjaha* assume a mask, f. *wajh* face.

matador mæ·tədōɹ in Sp. bull-fights, man appointed to kill the bull; principal card. XVII. – Sp. *matador*, f. *matar* kill, f. Pers. *māt* dead (cf. MATE[2]).

match[1] mætʃ A. †mate, fellow OE.; person equal or corresponding XIII; B. †matching of adversaries XIV; contest; matrimonial alliance XVI. OE. *ġemæċċa* :– **gamakjon*, rel. to Germ. **gamakon* (OE. *ġemaca*, dial. *make* match, mate; corr. to OS. *gimaco*, OHG. *gimahho* fellow, equal), sb. use of **gamakaz* (OE. *ġemæć*, OHG. *gimah* well-matched, G. *gemach* easy, comfortable), f. **ga-* Y- + **mak-* fitting; see MAKE. Hence **match** vb. join as a pair or one of a pair in marriage, combat, etc. XIV.

match[2] mætʃ †wick XIV (PPl., Trevisa); piece of inflammable cord, wood, etc., to be ignited XVI (the present domestic article dates from *c*.1830). – OF. *meiche, mesche* (mod. *mèche*), corr. to Pr. *mecca, mecha*, Cat. *metxa*, Sp., Pg. *mecha*, It. *miccia*, which have been referred to L. *myxa* (– Gr. *múxā*) nozzle of lamp (in medL. lamp-wick), with crossing of Rom. **muccare* blow the nose, snuff a wick. ¶ For the Eng. development cf. (dial.) *cratch* cradle from (O)F. *crèche*, *patch* from OF. *peche* PIECE.

match[3] mætʃ that matches, corresponding. XV (*not matche ne lyke to the*, Caxton). Arising from predic. and appositive uses of MATCH[1]; now mainly techn., as in **ma·tch**BOARD (XIX) board having a tongue along one edge and a groove along the other so as to admit of being fitted into others of like form.

matchcoat mæ·tʃkout mantle worn by American Indians. XVII. Earlier *matchco*, prob. – N. Amer. Indian word allied to Odjibwa *matchigode* woman's dress; assim. to COAT.

matchet mæ·tʃit broad heavy knife or cutlass. XVI (*-eto*). – Sp. *machete*, f. *macho* hammer :– late L. *marcus*.

mate[1] meit habitual companion (also in comps.) XIV; (naut.) officer assistant to another XV; one of a wedded pair XVI. – MLG. *mate, gemate* (Flem. *gemaat*, Du. *maat*) = OHG. *gimazzo* :– WGerm. **gamaton*, f. **ga-* Y- (denoting association) + **mat-*, base of MEAT, the lit. sense being 'messmate'.

mate[2] meit at chess, state of the king when he is in check and cannot move out of it; (fig.) total defeat. XIV. ME. *mat* – (O)F. *mat*, in *eschec mat* CHECKMATE. So vb. XIII (AncrR.). – OF. *mater*, f. *mat*.

maté mæ·tei calabash in which leaves of the shrub Ilex paraguayensis are infused, (also) the infusion and the shrub. XVIII. – Sp. *mate* – Quechua *mati*.

material mətiə·riəl consisting of matter XIV (Rolle); pert. to matter)(*formal* XIV (Ch.); of substantial import XVI (More); sb. pl. XVI. ME. *materiel* (rare), *-ial* – (O)F. *matériel*, †*-ial* – late L. *māteriālis* (Tertullian; also sb. *-āle*), f. *māteria* matter; see -AL[1]. ¶ In CEur. use. So **mate·rial**ISM XVIII, -IST XVII (H. More) – modL.; so in F. **mate·rial**IZE. XVIII (Addison).

materia medica mətiə·riə me·dikə remedies used in medicine. XVII. modL., tr. Gr. ὕλη ἰατρική 'healing material'; see MATTER, MEDICAL.

matériel mətei·əriel, ‖materjɛl material equipment or resources. XIX. F., sb. use of adj. *matériel* MATERIAL.

maternal mətə̄·ɹnəl pert. to a mother, motherly. XV (*our english and m. tongue*, Caxton). – (O)F. *maternel* or f. L. *māternus*, f. *māter* MOTHER; see -AL[1]. So **mate·rn**ITY. XVII. – F. – medL.

math mæþ (dial.) mowing, crop mown. OE. *mǣþ*, corr. to MHG. *māt, mād-* (G. *mahd*), f. Germ. **mǣ-* MOW[2]; see -TH[1]. ¶ The normal repr. of the OE. form would be **meath*, but *math* has been generalized from the unstressed form in AFTERMATH, *lattermath*.

mathematic, -ical mæþimæ·tik(əl). XVI. – or f. (O)F. *mathématique* or its source L. *mathēmaticus* – Gr. *mathēmatikós*, f. *mathēmat-, máthēma* something learnt, science, f. **math-* (see MIND), *manthánein* learn; see -IC, -ICAL. As sb. (XIV) ME. *matematik, math-, -ique*, – (O)F. *mathématique* = Sp., It. *matematica* – L. *mathēmatica* (sc. *ars* or *disciplīna*) – Gr. *mathēmatikē* (sc. *tékhnē* or *theōria*), fem. of *mathēmatikós*; now **mathema·t**ICS XVI (Mulcaster); prob. after F. *les mathématiques* (XVI) – L. n. pl. *mathēmatica* (Cicero), Gr. *ta mathēmatiká* (Aristotle). colloq. abbrev. **maths** mæþs XX.

mathesis mǣþi·sis mental discipline. XV. late L. – Gr. *máthēsis* learning, f. **math-*, of *manthánein* learn (cf. prec.). ¶ Formerly str. *ma·thesis* as in Pope 'Dunciad' IV 31.

matico mǣtī·kou (leaves of) the Peruvian shrub Piper angustifolium. XIX. – Sp. *yerba Matico*, i.e. *yerba* HERB, *Matico* dim. of *Mateo* Matthew; said to have been named after a soldier who discovered its styptic properties.

matie mei·ti herring in the best condition for eating. XIX. – Du. *maatjes* (*haring* herring), earlier *maetgens-*, *maeghdekins*, f. *maagd* MAID + *-ken* -KIN.

matins, mattins mæ·tinz canonical hour, prop. a midnight office XIII; Anglican morning prayer; morning song of birds XVI. ME. *matines* – (O)F. *matines* = Pr. *matinas* :- ecclL. *mātūtīnās*, nom. *-īnæ* (prob. sc. *vigiliæ* watches); see MATUTINAL. In medL., masc. sg. and pl. *mātutīnus*, *-īnī* (cf. Sp. *matutino*, *maitines*) were more usual; for the variation of gender cf. *vesperæ*, *vesperī* VESPERS. The sg. *matin* has been used poet. for 'morning', 'morning song', after (O)F. *matin* = Pr. *mati*, It. *mattino* morning :- L. *mātutīnum* (sc. *tempus* time).

matrass mæ·trəs glass distilling vessel. – F. *matras* = Sp. *matraz*, modL. *matracium*, of doubtful origin.

matriarch mei·triāɹk female corr. to patriarch. XVII. f. L. *mātr(i)-*, *māter* mother, after PATRIARCH, which was apprehended as being f. L. *pater* FATHER.

matriculate mətri·kjŭleit insert (a name) in a register, admit into a university, etc. XVI. f. pp. stem of medL. *mātrīculāre*, f. late L. *mātrīcula*, dim. of *mātrīc-* MATRIX; see -ATE[3]. So **matricul**A·TION. XVI. ¶ The words are repr. in the Rom. langs.

matrimony mæ·trĭməni action of marrying, state of being married. XIV. – AN. *matrimonie* = OF. *matremoi(g)ne* (whence ME. *matermoine*, *matrimoi(g)ne*) – L. *matrimōnium*, f. *mātri-*, *māter* MOTHER; see -MONY. So **matrimon**IAL -mou·niəl. XVI. – (O)F. or L.

matrix mei·triks uterus; place or medium of production XVI; enclosing mass; mould XVII. – L. *mātrix* (*-īc-*) pregnant animal, female used for breeding, parent stem, (later) womb, register, roll, f. *mātr-*, *māter* MOTHER, with ending of fem. agent-nouns.

matron mei·trən married woman XIV; married woman having expert knowledge of pregnancy, etc. XV; woman in charge of domestic arrangements XVII. – (O)F. *matrone* = Sp., It. *matrona* – L. *mātrōna*, f. *mātr-*, *māter* MOTHER. ¶ For the suffix cf. COLONY.

matross mətrɔ·s (hist.) soldier next in rank below a gunner. Also *matroze*. XVII. – Du. *matroos* sailor (whence G. *matrose*, Sw., Da. *matros*) – F. pl. of *matelot* sailor.

mattamore mæ·təmōəɹ subterranean chamber. XVII. – F. *matamore* – Arab. *maṭmūra[h]*, f. *ṭamara* store up.

matter mæ·təɹ thing, affair, concern; material of thought, speech, or action; subject or substance of discourse XIII (*subject m.*, tr. L. *subjecta materia*); substance serving as material; (*corrupt m.*) pus XIV; physical or corporeal substance XVII; things written or printed XVII. ME. *materie*, *mat(i)ere* – AN. *materie*, *matere*, (O)F. *matière* – L. *māteria* (also *-iēs*) hard part of a tree, timber, stuff of which a thing is made, cause, occasion, subject of discourse, matter)(mind or form (philos., rendering Gr. ὕλη), orig. substance of which consists the *māter* (MOTHER), i.e. the trunk of a tree regarded as producing shoots. Hence **ma·tter** vb. form or discharge pus; be of importance. XVI.

mattock mæ·tək agricultural tool with metal head having adze-like blade. OE. *mattuc*, of unkn. origin. The ending appears to be the dim. suffix seen in OE. *bealluc* BALLOCK, *bulluc* BULLOCK. ¶ W. *matog*, Gael. *madag* are from Eng.

mattress mæ·trĭs horizontal support for a bed. XIII. ME. *materas* – OF. *materas* (whence G. *matratze*; modF. *matelas* from Pr. *matelas*) cogn. with or – It. *materasso*, parallel with OCat. *almatrach*, Sp., Pg. *almadraque* – Arab. *al-maṭraḥ* (AL-[2]) place where something is thrown, mat, cushion, f. *ṭaraḥa* throw.

mature mətʃuə·ɹ, mətjuə·ɹ fully developed or ripened (lit. and fig.). XV. – L. *mātūrus* timely, early (whence F. *mûr*, etc.), f. **mātu-* (as in next), rel. to *māne* early, in the morning. So **matur**ATE[3] ripen, spec. bring to a head. XVI. f. pp. stem of L. *mātūrāre*, whence **matu·re** vb. XVI (occas. *madure* after OF. *madurer*), **matur**A·TION. XVI. – F. or L. **matu·r**ATIVE causing maturation. *c.*1400. **matu·r**ITY. XIV (Barbour). – L.

matutinal mætjutai·nəl of the (early) morning. XVII. – late L. *mātūtīnālis*, f. L. *mātūtīnus* (whence **ma·tutine** XV), f. *Mātūta* goddess of the dawn, rel. to *māturus* early, MATURE; see -AL[1].

maudlin mɔ̄·dlin †weeping, tearful; weakly sentimental XVII; but the earliest recorded use is as adv. in *maudlin* (†*maudlayne*, †*mawdlen*) drunk XVI. attrib. use of *Maudlin*, ME. *Maudeleyn*, *Maudelen* (XIV) – (O)F. *Madelaine* – ecclL. *Magdalēna* MAGDALEN. The reference to tears comes from pictures in which the Magdalen is shown weeping. ¶ The pronunc. of the saint's name is shown in the statutes of Magdalen College, Oxford, by the sp. *Mawdelayne*.

maugre mɔ̄·gəɹ sb. †ill-will; (arch.) prep. in spite of, notwithstanding (orig. to the displeasure of). XIII. – (O)F. *maugré* (mod. *malgré* prep.) = Pr. *mal grat*, It. *malgrado*, i.e. *mal* bad, evil :- L. *malu-m* (see MAL-), *gré* pleasure (mod. *bon gré mal gré* willy nilly, occas. anglicized †*boon gree mawgree*; cf. *savoir gré* be grateful) :- L. *grātum*, sb. use of n. of *grātu-s* pleasing (cf. GRATEFUL). ¶ F. *malgré* has been used in Eng. since XVII, and It. *malgrado* appears in 1590.

maul, mall mɔ̄l †club XIII; hammer, beetle XIV. ME. *meall*, *mal(e)* – (O)F. *mail* mal[j] = Pr. *malh*, Cat. *mall*, Sp. *maio* threshing-machine, Pg. *malho* flail, It. *maglio*, Rum. *maĭu* :- L. *malleu-s* hammer (cf. OSl. *mlatŭ*, Russ. *mólot* hammer, ON. *mjǫllnir*). Cf.

MALL, MALLET. Hence **maul** vb. †beat down, hammer, batter XIII (*meallin*); damage XVI; handle roughly XVII.

maulstick mɔ̄·lstik light stick used by painters to support the right hand. XVII (*mol-*). – Du. *maalstok*, f. *maalen* paint + *stok* stick; see MOLE[1], STOCK.

maumet mɔ̄·mit, **mammet** mæ·mit †false god, idol XIII (Laȝ.); (arch., dial.) doll, puppet, guy XV; term of abuse XVI. – OF. *mahomet* (cf. Pg. *mafom*) idol, use of the proper name *Mahomet* due to the medieval belief that Mohammed was worshipped as a god. Hence **mau·met**RY (arch.). XIII (Cursor M.).

maund[1] mɔ̄nd (wicker) basket XV; measure of capacity XVI. – (O)F. *mande* – MLG., MDu. *mande* (Du. *mand*) = OE. *mand*, of the survival of which there is no evidence; ult. origin unkn.

maund[2] mɔ̄nd weight current in India, etc. XVII (earlier *mana*; *mao* from Pg.). – Hindi (Pers.) *man*, perh. ult. – Accadian *mana*, whence also Gr. *mnâ*, L. *mina*.

maunder mɔ̄·ndəɹ †grumble XVII; act or talk in a dreamy or inconsequent manner XVIII. perh. a use of †*maunder* (XVII), frequent. of †*maund* (XVI), both being canting words for 'beg', perh. – (O)F. *mendier* :– L. *mendīcāre*; see MENDICANT, -ER[4].

maundy mɔ̄·ndi ceremonial washing of the feet of poor persons on the Thursday next before Easter. XIII. – OF. *mandé* :– med. use of L. *mandātum* command (see MANDATE), first word of the first antiphon sung at the ceremony, viz. '*Mandatum* novum do vobis' (A new commandment give I unto you), taken from the discourse which follows the washing by Christ of the Apostles' feet, John xiii; medL. *mandātum* was used for the ceremony, whence *diēs mandātī* 'day of the maundy' (*Maundy Thursday* XVI). See -Y[5].

Mauser mau·zəɹ in full *M. rifle* military rifle invented by Wilhelm *Mauser* and adopted by the German army in 1871.

mausoleum mɔ̄sŏlī·əm edifice erected as a commemorative burial-place. XVI (Holland; earlier †*Mausole*, James I). – L. *mausōlēum* – Gr. *mausōleîon* the magnificent tomb of *Mausōlus*, king of Caria, erected 353 B.C. at Halicarnassus by his queen Artemisia and accounted one of the seven wonders of the world.

mauve mouv bright but delicate purple dye. XIX. – F. *mauve* mallow, mallow-colour :– L. *malva* MALLOW.

maverick mæ·vərik (U.S.) calf, cow, or steer not having a brand. XIX. f. name of Samuel A. *Maverick*, a Texas cattle-owner who left the calves of his herd unbranded.

mavis mei·vis song-thrush. XIV (Ch.). – (O)F. *mauvis* (whence Sp. *malvís*, It. dial. *marvittse*), obscurely rel. to MBret. *milhuit* (mod. *milfid*) thrush, (O)Corn. *melhuet* lark.

mavourneen məvuə·ɹnīn (Anglo-Ir.) my darling. XVIII. – Ir. *mo mhuirnín* (*mo* my, *muirnín*, dim. of *muirn* affection, love; see -EEN[2]).

maw[1] mɔ̄ stomach. OE. *maga*, corr. to OFris. *maga*, MDu. *maghe* (Du. *maag*), OHG. *mago* (G. *magen*), ON. *magi* :– CGerm. (exc. Gothic) **magon*, *-ōn*.

maw[2] mɔ̄ (dial.) sea-gull. XV. – ON. *már* = OE. *mǣw* MEW[1].

maw[3] mɔ̄ (hist.) card game. XVI. Of unkn. origin.

mawkish mɔ̄·kiʃ †nauseated, without appetite, nauseating XVII; feebly sentimental XVIII. f. *mawk* MAGGOT + -ISH[1].

maxilla mæksi·lə jaw, jawbone. XVII. L. *maxilla*, corr. to *māla* cheek, as *axilla* shoulder-blade to *āla* wing. Hence **maxi·ll**ARY XVII; after L. *maxillāris*.

maxim mæ·ksim †axiom XV; aphoristic proposition; rule of conduct XVI. – F. *maxime* or its source medL. *maxima*, sb. use (for *prōpositio maxima* 'greatest proposition', Boethius) of fem. of *maximus*, superl. of *magnus* great (see MAGNITUDE).

Maxim mæ·ksim *M.(-gun)*, machine-gun invented by Hiram S. *Maxim* (1840–1916).

maximum mæ·ksiməm greatest amount, highest limit. XVIII. – (through F.) modL. *māximum*, sb. use of n. of *māximus* (see MAXIM).

may[1] mei pt. **might** mait †be strong; †be able; be allowed; as an aux. of the subjunctive. A CGerm. vb. belonging by its conjugational form if not by origin to the class of preterite-presents (cf. CAN[2]). OE. *mæġ*, 2nd pers. *meaht*, *miht*, pl. *magon*, pt. *meahte*, *mihte*, corr. to OFris. *mei*, *mugun*, *machte*, OS. *mag*, *maht*, *mugun*, *mahta* (Du. *mag*, *mogen*, *mochte*), OHG. *mag*, *maht*, *magun*, *mahta* (G. *mag*, *mögen*, *mochte*), ON. *má*, *mátt*, *megom*, *mátti*, Goth. *mag*, *magt*, *magum*, *mahta*. The primary sense is 'have power' (cf. the cogn. sbs. MAIN[1], MIGHT), and the IE. base, **mogh-* **mēgh-*, is repr. also by Gr. *mêkhos* contrivance, *mēkhanḗ* MACHINE, OSl. *mogą* I can. It occurs in comps. with vbs. forming advs. meaning 'possibly', 'perhaps', viz. †*may-fall* (XIII), †*maychance* (XVI), *may-hap* (XVI). **may**BE mei·bī. XV (cf. F. *peut-être* perhaps).

may[2] mei blossoms of the hawthorn. XVI. – (O)F. *mai* flowers and branches collected to celebrate 1 May, from the name of the month (see next), dial. hawthorn. So vb. celebrate May-day, chiefly in gerund (*a*)*maying* (XV, Malory), earlier †*amaied* (Gower); cf. MDu. *meyen*, MHG. *meien*, and *meie* may-tree (G. *maibaum*).

May mei fifth month of the year. – (O)F. *mai* = Pr. *mai*, Sp. *mayo*, It. *maggio* :– L. *Maiu-s* (sc. *mēnsis* month) prop. pert. to *Māia*, Italic goddess, daughter of Faunus and wife of Vulcan (later identified with Gr.

T

Maia), perh. for **magiā* and rel. to *magnus* great (see MAGNITUDE); the name has passed into Germ. and Celtic. Hence **May-**DAY 1 May. XV.

maycock mei·kɔk kind of melon. XVI (*macoqwer*). – Algonkin (Powhattan) *mahcawq*.

mayduke mei·djūk kind of sour cherry. XVIII. Conflation of *May cherry* and *duke cherry* (both in Evelyn, 1664).

mayhem mei·hem (leg.) crime of violently inflicting bodily injury. XV. – AN. *ma(i)hem, mahaym* MAIM.

mayonnaise meiənei·z thick sauce as a dressing for salad, etc. XIX (Thackeray). – F. *mayonnaise*, also *magnonaise*, *mahonnaise*, the latter being prob. fem. of *mahonnais* pert. to Port *Mahon*, capital of Minorca, taken by the duc de Richelieu in 1756 (cf. modPr. *faiòu mahonenc* kind of bean).

mayor mɛəɹ chief officer of a municipal corporation. XIII (RGlouc.). ME. *mer, mair* – (O)F. *maire* :- L. *mājor* greater, compar. of *magnus* great (see MAGNITUDE), used sb. in late L. (cf. MAJORDOMO). The sp. *maio(u)r*, common in XVI, prob. reflects the orig. L. form, but as the *i* could be read as a vowel, such forms became coincident with those adopted from F.; the substitution of *y* for *i* was in accordance with the orthographical habits of XVI–XVII. So **mayoral**TY mɛə·rəlti. XIV. – OF. *mairalté*.

mayweed mei·wīd stinking camomile, Anthemis Cotula. XVI. alt. of †*maid-, mayde(n)wede* (XV), for **maithe(n)wede*, f. †*maithe*, †*maithen*, OE. *maġoþe*, *mæġþa* (obl. cases *maġoþan*, *mæġþan*) + WEED.

mazagan mæ·zəgæn variety of broad bean. XVIII. Said to be from *Mazagan* in Morocco, where it grows wild.

mazame məzei·m Amer. species of deer XVIII; Rocky Mountain goat XIX. – F. *mazame* (Buffon) – Mex. *maçame*, pl. of *maçatl* deer, mistaken for sg.

maz(z)ard mæ·zəɹd †mazer; (sl.) head XVII; face, phiz XVIII. alt. of MAZER by assoc. with -ARD.

mazarine mæ·zərīn deep rich blue. XVII. perh. f. name of Cardinal Jules *Mazarin* (1602–61) or the Duchesse de *Mazarin* (died 1699).

maze meiz (dial., arch.) stupefy, daze XIII; bewilder XV (Caxton). synon. *mased*, *amased*, and *bimased* all occur in texts of AncrR., being pps. of parallel formations on *mas-*, which is repr. in OE. by *āmasod* (see AMAZE), of which poss. cogns. are Norw. dial. *mas* exhausting labour, whim, idle chatter, *masa* pass. doze off, and Sw. *mas*, *masa*. Hence **maze** sb. †*the m.*, delusion, deception XIII (RGlouc.); network of winding and intercommunicating paths XIV (Ch.).

mazer mei·zəɹ (hist.) hard (? maple) wood XII; bowl or goblet, orig. of mazer wood XIV. – OF. *masere* (of Germ. origin; in modF. *madré* veined, variegated, like maple-wood), perh. reinforced from MDu. *maeser* maple = OHG. *masar* (G. *maser*) excrescence on a tree, †maple, ON. *mǫsurr* maple, f. **mas-* spot (cf. MEASLES); obs. by 1700, revived by Scott.

mazurka məzə̄·ɹkə lively Polish dance. XIX. – F. *mazurka*, G. *masurka* – Pol. *mazurka* woman of the province of Mazovia. Cf. POLKA.

me[1] mī, mi accusative and dative of the pronoun I. OE. *mē̆* (i) accus., corr. to OFris. *mi*, OS. *mī*, *mē* (Du. *mij*) and further to L. *mē*, Gr. *me*, *emé*, OIr. *mē* (Ir. *mi*), W. *mi*, Skr. *mā*; OE. had also *mec*, corr. to OFris. *mich*, OS. *mik*, OHG. *mih* (G. *mich*), ON., Goth. *mik* :- IE. **mege* (Gr. *emége*), in which a limiting particle **ge* (Gr. *ge* at least) is added (other particles occur in Indo-Iranian and Slavonic); (ii) dative, corr. to OFris. *mi*, *mir*, OS. *mī* (Du. *mij*), (O)HG. *mir*, ON. *mér*, Goth. *mis* :- **mes-*, with suffixed particle of doubtful origin. The base is **me*, on which in all IE. langs. the obl. cases of the pronoun of the 1st person sg. are formed. See MINE[1], MY.

me[2] mī see MI.

mead[1] mīd drink made by fermenting a mixture of honey and water. OE. *medu*, *meodu* = OFris., MLG. (Du.) *mede*, OHG. *metu*, *mitu* (G. *met*), ON. *mjǫðr*, Goth. **midus* (recorded v in Gr. form *médos*):- CGerm. **meduz* :- IE. **medhu-*, whence Gr. *méthu* wine (cf. METHYLATE), OIr. *mid*, W. *medd*, OSl. *medŭ* honey, wine, Lith. *midùs* mead, Skr. *mádhu* honey, sweet drink.

mead[2] mīd (arch.) MEADOW. OE. *mǣd*.

meadow me·dou grass-covered piece of land. XIII. repr. OE. *mǣdwe*, etc., obl. cases of *mǣd* MEAD[2] :- Germ. **mǣdwō* :- **mētwā́* 'mowed land', f. **mē-* MOW[1]; cogn. words of similar meaning but divergent formation are OFris. *mēde*, OLG. *mada* (Du. †*matte*, *mat*), (M)HG. *matte*.

meagre mī·gəɹ lean, thin XIV; poor, scanty XVI. ME. *megre* – AN. *megre*, (O)F. *maigre* (cf. MAIGRE) = Pr. *ma(i)gre*, Sp., It. *magro*, Rum. *macru* :- L. *macrum*, nom. *macer*, rel. to Gr. *makrós* long, *makednós* tall, slender, *mêkos* length; IE. **makró-* (Germ. **magra-*) is repr. by OE. *mæġer*, MLG. (Du.) *mager*, OHG. *magar* (G. *mager*), ON. *magr*.

meal[1] mīl powder of ground grain or pulse. OE. *melu* (*melw-*) = OFris. *mel*, OS. *melo* (Du. *meel*), OHG. *melo* (G. *mehl*), ON. *mjǫl* :- CGerm. (exc. Gothic) **melwam*, f. **mel-* **mal-* **mul-* :- IE. **mel-* **mol-* **ml̥-*, whence OHG., Goth. *malan*, ON. *mala*, L. *molere*, OSl. *mlěti*, Lith. *málti*, OIr. *melim* I grind, W. *malu*, L. *mola* millstone, sacrificial meal, *molīna* MILL, Gr. *múlē*, *múlos* mill, millstone; see also MALM and cf. IMMOLATE, MOLAR.

meal[2] mīl †measure; habitual or customary occasion of taking food OE.; repast XII. OE. *mǣl* mark, sign, measure, fixed time, etc., corr. to OFris. *mēl, māl*, OS. *-māl* sign, measure (Du. *maal* n. meal, m. time), OHG. *māl* time (G. *mal* time, *mahl* meal), ON. *mál* mark, measure, point or portion of time, mealtime, Goth. *mel* time :- CGerm. **mǣlaz, -am*, f. IE. base **mē* MEASURE. The instr. pl. of the OE. word *mǣlum*, in the sense 'measure', 'quantity taken at a time', was used in comb. with sbs., e.g. *dropmǣlum* drop by drop, *limmǣlum* limb by limb (perverted dial. to *limb-small*); these were extended in ME., but the only surviving comp. in gen. use is PIECEMEAL.

mealie mī·li S. Afr. maize. XIX. – Afrikaans *milie* – Pg. *milho* MILLET, perh. through Bantu.

mealy-mouthed mī·limauðd soft-spoken, not outspoken. XVI. var. of contemp. †*meal-mouthed*, f. †*mealmouth* sb. and adj., f. MEAL[1] + MOUTH + -ED[2]; perh. based on a foreign idiom such as G. *Mehl im Maule behalten* (Luther) 'carry meal in the mouth', i.e. lack straightforwardness in speech.

mean[1] mīn have in mind, intend; import. OE. *mǣnan* = OFris. *mēna* signify, OS. *mēnian* intend, make known (Du. *meenen*), (O)HG. *meinen* (now chiefly, have an opinion) :- WGerm. **mainjan*, rel. outside Germ. to OSl. *mĭniti*; f. IE. **men-* (see MIND). Hence **mea·ning**[1] intention, signification. XIV; cf. MDu. *mēninge* (Du. *meening*), OHG. *meinunga* (G. *meinung*).

mean[2] mīn (dial.) common to two or more XII; inferior XIII; undignified, low XIV; ignoble XVII. OE. *mǣne* (rare), ME. *mene*, for OE. *ġemǣne* (ME. *-mene*) = OFris. *gemēne*, OS. *gimēni* (Du. *gemeen*), OHG. *gimeini* (G. *gemein*), Goth. *gamains* :- CGerm. (exc. ON.) **gamainiz*, f. **ga-* Y- + **mainiz* :- **moinis* (repr. in **commoinis*, antecedent form of L. *commūnis* COMMON), f. **moi-* **mei-* change, exchange; see MUTATION, MUTUAL, MUNICIPAL. The development of meaning from 'possessed by all' to 'ordinary', 'not exceptionally good', 'inferior', 'low', was assisted by the coincidence of the native Eng. form with MEAN[3], which was often used disparagingly.

mean[3] mīn †middle; †intermediary; intermediate in time (now only in *mean time, mean while*); intermediate in kind or degree; mediocre, middling. XIV. – AN. *me(e)n*, OF. *meien, moien* (mod. *moyen*) = Pr. *meian*, Sp. *mediano*, It. *mezzano* (cf. MEZZANINE) :- L. *mediānu-s* MEDIAN. Hence **mea·ntime** adv. XVI (Sh.); **mea·nwhile** adv. XV; reduction of advb. phr. *in the m. time* and *m. while* (XIV).

mean[4] mīn (dial.) complain (of), lament. OE. *mǣnan*, rel. to MOAN.

meander miæ·ndəɹ (pl.) windings (of a river, a maze), †intricacies (of affairs) XVI; circuitous course XVII. – (partly through F. *méandre*) L. *mæander* – Gr. *maíandros*, appellative use of the name of a river in Phrygia famous for its notoriously winding course. Hence vb. XVII.

measles mī·zlz infectious disease marked by an eruption. XIV. ME. *maseles* (pl.), prob. – MLG. *masele*, MDu. *masel* pustule, spot on the skin (Du. *mazelen* measles) = OHG. *masala* blood-blister, f. Germ. **mas-* spot, excrescence (cf. MAZER). The change of form from *masel* to *mesel* (whence the present form) appears to be due to assim. to ME. *mesel* leper (– OF. *mesel* :- L. *misellu-s*, f. *miser* wretched, MISERABLE). ¶ Earlier (dial.) *measlings* is prob. of Scand. origin.

measure me·ʒəɹ prescribed or limited extent; action, result, or means of measuring XIII; 'measured' or rhythmic sound or movement XIV. ME. *mesur(e)* – (O)F. *mesure* = Pr., Sp., *mesura*, It. *misura*, Rum. *măsură* :- L. *mēnsūra*, f. *mēns-*, pp. stem of *mētīrī* measure, f. IE. **mēt-* (cf. Skr. *mātram* measure, Gr. *mêtis* prudence, OE. *mǣþ* measure, proportion, power, rank, respect), extension of **mē-* measure (cf. MEAL[2], METRE). So **mea·sure** vb. XIII (Cursor M.). – (O)F. *mesurer* – L. *mēnsūrāre*. **mea·surable** †moderate XIII; that can be measured XVI. – (O)F. *mesurable* – late L. *mēnsūrābilis* MENSURABLE. **mea·surement**. XVIII.

meat mīt food (arch. and dial. exc. as in *meat and drink, flesh meat*) OE.; flesh food XIV. OE. *mete* m. = OFris. *met(e)*, OS. *meti*, ON. *matr*, Goth. *mats* :- CGerm. **matiz* (a parallel **matam* is repr. by OS. *mat*, OHG. *maȝ*), f. **mat-* **met-* measure, METE.

meatus miei·təs passage, spec. in anat. XVII. L., 'passage, course', f. *meāre* go, pass (cf. PERMEATE). comb. form **mea·to-**.

Mecca me·kə name of Mohammed's birthplace, which is a place of Muslim pilgrimage, (hence) sacred spot of resort. XIX. – dial. var. of Arab. *Makkah*. ¶ Dryden (1687) has *Meccan* adj.

mechanic mĭkæ·nik pert. to manual work XIV (Gower), pert. to machines XVII; sb. handicraftsman, artisan XVI; skilled workman, esp. having to do with machinery XVII. – (partly through (O)F. *mécanique*) L. *mēchanicus* – Gr. *mēkhanikós*, f. *mēkhanḗ* MACHINE; see -IC. So **mecha·nical**. XV (first in *art* or *craft m.*, after F. *art mécanique*, L. *ars mēchanica*). **mecha·nics**. XVII. **mechanism** me·kənizm. XVII. **me·chanize**. XVII.

mechlin me·klin name of lace made at *Mechlin* in Belgium (F. *Malines*) XVII (earlier of a black cloth, *meighlyn blac* XV).

mechoacan metʃou·əkæn root of a Mexican species of bindweed. XVI. f. name of a state (now *Michoacán*) of Mexico.

meconic mīkə·nik (chem.) epithet of an acid obtained from opium. XIX (1803). f. Gr. *mḗkōn* poppy+-IC. So **meconIUM** mīkou·niəm †opium XVII; first fæces of a new-born infant (from its dark colour likened to opium juice) XVIII. L. (Pliny) – Gr. *mēkṓneion* (Dioscorides), f. *mḗkōn*.

medal me·dəl †metal disk used as a charm, etc. XVI; coin-shaped piece of metal with an inscription, effigy, etc. XVII. – F. *médaille* – It. *medaglia* = OF. *m(e)aille*, Sp. *medalla* :– Rom. **medallia* :– popL. **metallea* (n. pl.), f. L. *metallum* METAL. So **medallion** mĭdæ·ljən large medal or object resembling this. XVII. – F. *médaillon* – It. *medaglione*, augm. of *medaglia*.

meddle me·dl †mix, mingle; intr. mix or mingle in company or conflict XIV; busy oneself *with* XV. – OF. *medler*, *mesdler*, var. of *mesler* (mod. *mêler*) = Pr. *mesclar*, Sp. *mezclar*, It. *mischiare* :– Rom. **misculāre*, f. L. *miscēre* MIX.

mediæval, medieval mīdiī·vəl, med- pert. to the Middle Ages. XIX. 1827. f. modL. *medium ævum* (Melchior Goldast, 1604) 'middle age'+-AL[1]; see MID, AGE. Cf. F. *médiéval* (1874); preceded by †*middle-aged* (XVIII). So **mediæ·valIST** 1784 (Ruskin; earlier in sense 'one who lived in the Middle Ages'); cf. F. *médiéviste* (1867).

medial mī·diəl †(math.) mean XVI; that is in the middle; ordinary. XVIII. – late L. *mediālis*, f. *medius* MID; see -AL[1] and cf. F. *médial* (XVIII). So **me·dIAN** (first in anat.) *m. vein* XVI; (gen.) middle XVII. – F. *médian* (*veine médiane*) or L. *mediānus*; cf. MEAN[3].

mediastinum mī:diəstai·nəm (anat.) membranous septum between cavities. XVI. modL., sb.n. of medL. *mediastīnus* medial, after L. *mediastīnus* low class of slave. f. *medius* MID.

mediate mī·dieit †halve; effect by intercession XVI; be an intermediary XVII. f. pp. stem of L. *mediāre*, f. *medius* MID; in part prob. back-formation from the much earlier **mediA·TION** XIV (Ch.) – late L. *mediātiō(n-)* (cf. F. *médiation* XV) or **me·diATOR** XIII (Cursor M.) – (O)F. *médiateur*, †*-our* – ChrL. *mediātor*, which was perh. not formed from *mediāre* but directly on *medius* MID, after Gr. *mesítēs* (f. *mésos*) as used in N.T. So **me·diaTRIX** XV, **†-trice** XIV. – late L. (F.).

medical me·dikəl pert. to the healing art. XVII. – F. *médical* (Rabelais) or medL. *medicālis* (Columban), f. L. *medicus* physician, f. base of *medērī*; see REMEDY, -ICAL. So **medicaMENT** mĕdi·kəmənt substance used as a remedy. XIV. – F. *médicament* or L. *medicāmentum*, f. *medicārī* administer remedies to, whence **me·dicATE**[3] XVII, **medicA·TION** XVII. So **medicine** me·d(i)sĭn medicament XIII (AncrR.); art of preserving and restoring health XIV. – OF. *medecine*, *medicine* (mod. *médecine*) = Pr. *mede-*, *medicina*, *metzina*, Sp., It. *medicina* – L. *medicīna* physician's art, physician's laboratory, medicament, f. *medicus*. **medicinAL**[1] mĕdi·sinəl XIV. – (O)F. *médicinal* – L. *medicīnālis*. **me·dico** medical practitioner or student. XVII (Harvey). – It. – L. *medicus*. Also **me·dic** XVII (surviving in U.S.).

medick me·dik plant of the genus Medicago. XV. – L. *mēdica* – Gr. *mēdikḗ*, sc. *póa* ('Median grass').

mediety mĭdəi·ėti †half XV; †(math.) MEAN[3]; (leg.) MOIETY XVII.

mediocre mī·dioukəɹ of middling quality. XVI. – (partly through F. *médiocre*) L. *mediocris* lit. 'of middle height', f. *medius* MID+*ocris* rugged mountain (= Umbrian *ukar* citadel, mountain, Gr. *ókris* point, protuberance, Ir. *ochair*, W. *ochr* edge, Skr. *áśris* corner). So **mediocrITY** -ɔ·krĭti. XVI. – (O)F. – L.

meditate me·diteit consider, study; plan; exercise the mental faculties. XVI. f. pp. stem of L. *meditārī*, frequent. f. IE. **med-* **mēd-* **mod-* measure (see METE, MODE). So **meditA·TION** meditative discourse XIII (AncrR.); action of meditating XIV. – (O)F. – L.

Mediterranean me:ditərei·niən (of water) land-locked XVI; (of land) midland, inland XVII. f. L. *mediterrāneus* inland, in late L. applied to the Mediterranean Sea, *Mare Mediterraneum* (for *Mare Magnum* 'Great Sea'), in which the orig. notion may have been 'in the middle of the earth' rather than 'enclosed by land'; f. *medius* MID+*terra* (corr. to Ir., W. *tir*) land, earth; see -EAN.

medium mī·diəm middle degree or condition; †middle term, mean; intervening substance XVI (whence, pervading or enveloping substance XIX); intermediate agency, means XVII; (in painting) liquid vehicle XIX. – L. *medium* middle, midst, medL. means, sb. use of n. of *medius* MID; cf. F. *médium* (XVI).

medlar me·dləɹ (fruit of) the tree so named, Mespilus germanica. XIV. – OF. *medler*, f. **medle*, for **mesdle*, *mesle* :– L. *mespila*, *-us*, *-um* – Gr. *mespílē*, *méspilon*. ¶ An altered form **nespila* gave OF. *nesple*, mod. *nèfle*, Sp. *nespera*, It. *nespola*; the L. word passed into Germ. as MDu. *mispele*, OHG. *mespila*, *nespila*, Du., G., *mispel*.

medley me·dli †combat, conflict XIV; †combination, mixture XV; (in disparaging sense) XVII. – OF. *medlee*, var. of *meslee* (see **mêlée**) = Pr. *mesclada* :– Rom. **misculāta*, sb. use of fem. pp. of medL. *misculāre* MEDDLE.

medoc mei·dɔk wine produced in *Médoc*, a district of SW. France. XIX.

medulla mĭdʌ·lə marrow, pith. XVII. – L. *medulla*, perh. f. *medius* MID. Hence **medu·lLARY**. XVII; after L. *medullāris*; cf. F. *médullaire* (XVI).

medusa mĭdjū·zə (*M-*) one of the three Gorgons, having snakes for the hair of the head XVI (XIV *Meduse*, Gower); (*m-*) jellyfish, sea-nettle (after Linnæus' use of *Medusa* as a generic name, from the resemblance of some species to a head with snaky curls) XVIII. – L. *Medūsa* – Gr. *Médousa*.

meed mīd †wages, hire OE.; reward, guerdon XIV. OE. *mēd* = OFris. *mēde*, OS. *mēda, mieda*, OHG. *mēta, mieta* (G. *miete*) :– WGerm. **mēda*, rel. to OE. *meord*, Goth. *mizdō* reward (:– Germ. **mizdō, -ōn*); the IE. base **mizdh-* is repr. also by Gr. *misthós*, OSl. *mĭzda*, Skr. *mīḍhám* reward.

meek mīk †gentle, kind; free from pride and self-will XII (Orm); submissive XIV. Early ME. *meoc, mec* – ON. **miúkr, mjúkr* soft, pliant, gentle, rel. to Goth. **mūks* in *mūkamōdei* meekness, and (M)LG. *mūke*, MHG. *mūche* (G. dial. *mauche*) malanders; further cogns. are OIr. *mocht* (:– **mukto-*) gentle, soft, W. *mwytho* soften.

meerkat miə·ɹkæt †monkey XV; S. Afr. name for Cynictis pencillata and Suricata tetradactyla XIX. – Du. *meerkat* = G. *meerkatze* (in OHG. *mericazza*), MLG. *merkatte* lit. 'sea-cat'; perh. orig. alt. of an Oriental name (cf. Hindi *markat*, Skr. *markata* ape) by assim. to words meaning 'sea' and 'cat', with the notion of 'ape from overseas'.

meerschaum miə·ɹʃəm sepiolite found in soft white clay-like masses; tobacco-pipe having a bowl made of this. XVIII. – G. *meerschaum*, f. *meer* MERE[1]+*schaum foam* (SCUM), tr. Pers. *kef-i-daryā* 'foam of sea'.

meet[1] mīt †made to fit XIII (Cursor M.); (rhet.) suitable, fit XIV. Aphetic of earlier ME. *imete* :– OE. (Anglian) **ġemēte*, (WS.) *ġemǣte* = OHG. *gamāẓi* (G. *gemäss*), f. **ga-* Y- +**mǣtō* measure, f. **mǣt-* **met-* measure, METE; the etymol. sense is 'commensurate'. ¶ Words of similar formation on the same base, but of divergent meaning, are OE. *mǣte* insignificant, small, bad, ON. *mætr* valuable, excellent, lawful.

meet[2] mīt pt., pp. **met** come or light upon OE.; come face to face or into contact *with* XIII. OE. *mētan* (Nhb. *mœ̄ta*), also *ġemētan* (see Y-) = OFris. *mēta*, OS. *mōtian* (Du. *moeten*), ON. *mœ̄ta*, Goth. *gamōtjan* :– CGerm. (not in HG.) **ga|mōtjan*, f. **mōtam* meeting, MOOT. Hence **mee·ting**[1] XIII; cf. OE. *ġemēting* 'conventio', 'concilium'.

Meg meg. XVI. Sc. var. of *Mag* (*Magge* XIII; dim. *Maggie*), pet-form of *Margaret*, used for 'hoyden', 'coarse woman', and allusively in various phr.

mega- me·gə, before a vowel **meg-**, comb. form of Gr. *mégas* great (see MAGNITUDE), as in **megali·thic, me·gaphone, megathe·rium** XIX; similarly **megal(o-)** me·gəl(ou), the Gr. stem, as in **me:galoma·nia, me:galosau·rus** (see SAURIAN) XIX.

megilp məgi·lp vehicle for oil colours. XVIII. Some 30 var. spellings are recorded, some of which, with *mac, M[c]*, suggest poss. derivation from a surname; but there is no evidence.

megrim mī·grim severe headache. XIV (Trevisa). Early forms *mygrame, -ane* – (O)F. *migraine* (cf. Sp. *migraña*, It. *magrana*) semi-pop. – late L. *hēmicrānia* – Gr. *hēmikrāniā*, f. *hēmi-* half, HEMI-+*krānion* skull, CRANIUM.

meinie mei·ni (arch.) household, retinue XIII; multitude XIV. – (O)F. *meinée, mesnée* = Pr. *mesnada* (whence Sp. *mesnada, manada*, It. *masnada*) :– Rom. **mansiōnāta*, f. L. *mansiō(n-)* MANSION; see -Y[5].

meiosis maiou·sis (rhet.) †diminishing figure of speech XVI; litotes XVII. – modL. – Gr. *meíōsis*, f. *meioûn* lessen, f. *meíōn* less (see MINOR).

melan(o)- me·lən(ou) comb. form of Gr. *mélās, -an-* black.

melancholy me·lənkəli, -ŋk- †morbid condition of having too much 'black bile'; †ill-temper; sadness and depression. XIV (Ch.). – (O)F. *mélancolie* (= Pr., Sp., It. *melancolia*) – late (medical) L. *melancholia* – Gr. *melagkholiā*, f. *melan-*, *mélās*+*kholḗ* bile; see prec., GALL[1], -Y[3]. So **melancho·lic**. XIV (Ch.). – (O)F. – L. *melancholicus* (Cicero, citing Aristotle) – Gr. **melancho·lious**. XIV (Wyclif, Ch.). – OF. *melancolieus*. Both adjs. were gen. superseded by an adj. use of the sb. (XVI), the termination of which suggests an adj. formation; cf. *dainty*.

Melchite me·lkait orig. Eastern Christian holding the faith as defined by the Councils of Ephesus and Chalcedon. XVII (Purchas). – ecclL. *Melchīta* 'royalist' of the party of the Roman Emperor, f. Syriac *mal'kåyē*, f. *malkå* king; see -ITE.

meld meld (U.S.) declare at pinocle. late XIX. – G. *melden* announce (OHG. *meldōn* = OE. *meldian*, early ME *melde*).

mêlée me·lei irregular or confused fighting. XVII. – F. *mêlée*, earlier *mellée* MEDLEY, whence ME. *mellay* (XIV) hand-to-hand fight, mixed colour.

melic[1] me·lik pert. to poetry intended to be sung. XVII. – L. *melicus* – Gr. *melikós*, f. *mélos*; see MELODY, -IC.

melic[2] me·lik species of grass. XVIII. – modL. *melica* (Linnæus), of unkn. origin.

melilot me·lilət plant of the leguminous genus Melilotus. XV. – (O)F. *mélilot* – L. *melilōtos* – Gr. *melílōtos* sweet kind of clover, f. *méli* honey (cf. MILDEW)+*lōtós* LOTUS.

meliorate XVI; see AMELIORATE.

mell mel (arch., dial.) mingle. XIII. – OF. *meller* (mod. *mêler*), var. of *mesler* MEDDLE.

mellifluous meli·fluəs sweet as if flowing with honey. XV (Caxton). f. OF. *melliflue* (whence rare and late ME. *melliflue*) or its source late L. *mellifluus*, f. L. *mel* honey+ *flu-*; see MILDEW, FLUENT, -OUS.

mellow me·lou soft with ripeness XV; ripe, mature XVI; (of sound, etc.) rich and soft; genial with liquor XVII. perh. from attrib. use of OE. *melu* (*melw-*), ME. *melow* MEAL[1]. ¶ Cf. early ME. *merow*, *meruw*, OE. *mearu* soft, tender (corr. to OHG. *marawi*, *muruwi*, G. *mürbe*), which may have furthered the development.

melodeon mĭlou·diən wind instrument with keyboard; kind of accordion. XIX. alt. of *melodium* (f. MELODY, after *harmonium*), or f. MELODY after *accordion*.

melodrama me·lŏdrāmə (orig.) stage play with appropriate music; (later) sensational play with a happy ending. XIX (Southey). alt. (after *drama*) of earlier *melodrame* – F. *mélodrame*, f. Gr. *mélos* song; see next and DRAMA. Hence **me:lo**DRAMA·TIC.

melody me·lədi sweet music XIII; tune, air XVII; element of musical form)(*harmony* XVIII. – (O)F. *mélodie* – late L. *melōdia* – Gr. *melōidíā* singing, choral song, f. *melōidós* singing songs, musical, f. *mélos* song, rhythmical chant, orig. limb, member (cf. W. *-mal*, Corn. *mal*, pl. *mellow* joint)+*ōid-*; see ODE, -Y[3]. So **melod**IC -ɔ·dik XIX; **melod**IOUS mĭlou·diəs. XIV (Ch.). – OF. (mod. *mélodieux*).

melon me·lən kind of gourd, esp. Citrullus vulgaris. XIV. – (O)F. *melon* = Sp. *melon*, It. *melone* :– late L. *mēlō(n-)*, shortening of *mēlopepō* – Gr. *mēlopépōn*, f. *mêlon* apple+ *pépōn*, sb. use of *pépōn* ripe (cf. PEPTIC).

melt melt liquefy or be liquefied by heat. OE. (1) str. vb. *meltan* (*mealtan*), pt. *mealt* (pl. *multon*), pp. *ġemolten* :– **meltan*, (2) wk. vb. (Anglian) *meltan*, (WS.) *mieltan* = ON. *melta* digest, malt (grain) :– **maltjan* (cf. ON. *maltr* rotten, OHG. *malz* melting, Goth. *gamalteins* dissolution). The base **melt-* **malt-* (see MALT) **mult-* repr. IE. **meld-* **mold-* **mḷd-*, whence Gr. *méldein* melt, L. *mollis* (:– **moldwis*), Skr. *mṛdus* soft; cf. MILD, SMELT[2]. The str. pp. *molten* survives as adj. in literary use.

melton me·ltən epithet of a hunting jacket formerly worn and of a stout cloth. XIX. f. name of *Melton* Mowbray, town in Leicestershire, a famous hunting centre.

member me·mbəɹ organ, limb XIII (R. Glouc.); constituent portion or individual XIV; one elected to a parliament, etc. XV; division of a sentence XVI. – (O)F. *membre* = Sp. *miembro*, It. *membro* :– L. *membrum*, perh. :– **mēmsrom*, with which are compared OIr. *mīr* piece of meat (:– **mēmsro-*), Skr. *māṃsám*, OSl. *męso*, OPruss. *mensā*, Arm. *mis*, Goth. *mimz* meat (:– **mēmso-*), Gr. *mērós* thigh, OSl. *męzdra* membrane (:– **me(m)sro-*, **memsdhro-*).

membrane me·mbrein thin pliable sheet-like tissue. XVI (first in sense 'parchment'). – L. *membrāna* (partly through F.) 'skin covering a part of the body' (prop. sb. use of fem. of adj. in *-ānus* -AN, sc. *cutis* skin), f. *membrum* MEMBER. So **membran**A·CEOUS. XVII. f. late L. **membran**OUS me·mbrənəs. XVI. – F. *membraneux*, f. *membrane*.

memento mime·ntou either of two prayers beginning with *memento* ('remember') in the canon of the Mass XV; reminder, warning XVI; object serving as a memorial XVIII. – L. *mementō*, imper. of *meminisse* remember, redupl. perf. formation ('have brought to mind') on **men-* MIND; F. *mémento* (XVI).

memoir me·mwāɹ, -wɔ̄r †note, memorandum XVI; (pl.) record of events, esp. from a personal or particular source; dissertation on a learned subject XVII. – F. *mémoire* (m.) specialized use of *mémoire* (fem.) MEMORY, arising from the appositional use as in *écrit mémoire*. **me·mor**ABLE worth remembering. XV. – F. or L. **memorandum** meməræ·ndəm 'note to help the memory' (J.). XVI. Derived from the heading of a note of something to be borne in mind, '(It is) to be remembered *that* . . .'; n. sg. of L. *memorandus*, gerundive of *memorāre* bring to mind, f. *memor* (below). **memor**IAL mimɔ̄·riəl preserving a memory XIV (Ch.); sb. commemorative act, record, etc. XV. – (O)F. or L.; cf. IMMEMORIAL. **memo·ria te·chnica** system of mnemonics. XVIII. modL., 'artificial memory' (see TECHNICAL). **memor**IZE me·məraiz cause to be remembered XVI; commit to memory XIX; f. next. **memory** me·məri faculty by which one remembers; recollection, remembrance. XIV. ME. *memorie*, *memoire* – OF. *memorie*, (also mod.) *mémoire* = Sp., It. *memoria* – L. *memoria*, f. *memor* mindful, remembering, redupl. formation on the base **mer-*; see MOURN, -Y[3]. Cf. COMMEMORATE, REMEMBER.

mem-sahib me·msāib (in India) European married lady. XIX. f. *mem*, repr. native pronunc. of MA'AM+SAHIB.

menace me·nəs threat. XIII (Cursor M.). ME. *manas*, *manace* – OF. *manace* (later and mod. *menace*) = Pr. *menasa*, Sp. *(a)menaza*, It. *minaccia* :– L. *mināċia* (only pl. in classL.), f. *mindruc-*, *mindruc*x threatening, f. base of *minārī* threaten, *minæ* overhanging or projecting parts, threats, *eminēre*, *imminēre* (see EMINENT, IMMINENT, PROMINENT), rel. to *mōns* MOUNT. So **me·nace** vb. XIV. – AN. *manasser*, OF. *manacier* (mod. *menacer*) = Pr. *menasar*, etc. :– Rom. **mināciāre*.

ménage meinā·ʒ housekeeping, domestic establishment. XVII. – F. *ménage*, earlier *menaige*, *manaige* :– Rom. **mansiōnāticum*, f. L. *mansiō(n-)* MANSION; see MANAGE.

menagerie mĭnæ·dʒəri collection of wild animals, esp. for exhibition; †aviary. XVIII. – F. *ménagerie* orig. domestic management of cattle, etc., f. *ménage*; see prec. and -ERY.

mend mend (arch.) free from fault or defect XII; †make amends for XIII (surviving in *Least said soonest mended*); restore to wholeness, repair XIV. – AN. *mender*, aphetic of *amender* AMEND (which is later).

mendacious mendei·ʃəs untruthful, lying. XVII. f. L. *mendāci-*, *mendāx* prob. orig. speaking incorrectly or falsely, f. *mendum* defect, fault. So **mendac**ITY -dæ·sīti. XVII.

Mendelian mendī·liən. XX. pert. to the doctrine of heredity of Gregor Johann *Mendel* (1822–84); see -IAN.

mendicant me·ndikənt adj. begging XVI; sb. beggar XV. – pp. of L. *mendīcāre* beg, f. *mendīcus* beggar, f. *mendum* fault, blemish; preceded by †*mendinant*, †*mendivant* (XIV) – OF.; see -ANT.

menhaden menhei·dən fish of the herring family. XVII. – Narragansett Indian *munnawhatteaûg*, prob. rel. to *munnohquohteau* he fertilizes, the fish being used by the Indians for manure.

menhir me·nhiəɹ tall monumental stone. XIX. – Breton *men hir* (*mean* stone, *hir* long) = W. *maen hir*, Corn. *medn hir*; *hir* is cogn. with L. *sērus* late (cf. SINCE).

menial mī·niəl domestic XIV; proper to a domestic servant, servile XVII; sb. XIV. – AN. *menial*, *meignial*, f. *meinie*; see MEINIE, -IAL.

meningitis menindʒai·tis inflammation of the meninges (enveloping brain and spinal cord). XIX. – modL., f. *mēning-*, *mēninx*, Gr. *mênigx*, pl. *mēnigges* mīni·ndʒīz used in Eng. from XVII); see -ITIS.

meno- mī·no(u), comb. form of Gr. *mḗn* MONTH, used in path. terms for 'menses', as in **me·no**PAUSE (Gr. *paûsis*); **menorrhagia** -ræ·dʒiə (Gr. *rhag-*, *rhēgnúnai* break, burst forth); **menorrhœa** -rī·ə (Gr. *-rhoiā́* flow, flux).

menology mīnɔ·lədʒi calendar, esp. of the Orthodox Church. XVII. – modL. *mēnologium* – late Gr. *mēnológion*, f. *mēno-*, *mḗn* MONTH + *lógos* account; see -LOGY.

menses me·nsīz monthly discharge from the womb. XVI. medical use of L. *mēnsēs*, pl. of *mēnsis* MONTH; CATAMENIA.

menshevik me·nʃivik member of the more moderate section of the Russian Socialist party. 1917. – Russ. *Men'shevík* (1903), f. *mén'she* less, compar. of *málуу* little; cf. BOLSHEVIK.

menstruum me·nstruəm uterine secretion XVI; solvent XVII. – L. *mēnstruum*, in class L. only pl. menstrual blood, sb. use of n. of *mēnstruus*, f. *mēnsis* MONTH; cf. prec. The development of the sense 'solvent' in medL. arose from the alchemists' view of the transmutation of base metal into gold by a solvent liquid, which they compared to the development of the sperma in the womb by the agency of the menstrual blood. So **me·nstru**AL[1]. XIV. – L. *mēnstruālis*; cf. F. *menstruel*. **me·nstru**OUS. XVI. – OF. or late L.

mensuration menʃūrei·ʃən measuring. XVI (Digges). – late L. *mēnsūrātiō(n-)*, f. *mēnsūrāre* MEASURE; see -ATION. So in F., etc. So **me·nsur**ABLE measurable, (hence) having assigned limits XVII; (mus.) having fixed rhythm and length of notes XVIII (earlier *mensural* XVII). – F. *mensurable* or late L. *mēnsūrābilis* (also *-ālis*).

-ment mənt suffix forming sbs., repr. (O)F. *-ment* :– L. *-mentum*, which was added to vb.-stems to form sbs. expressing the result or product of an action or the means or instrument of it, e.g. *alimentum* means of nourishment (f. *alere*), *fragmentum* broken piece (f. *frag-*, *frangere*), *ōrnāmentum* that with which a thing is arranged (f. *ōrnāre*), *pavimentum* floor of stones beaten down (f. *pavīre*). In popL. it was extended to the formation of nouns of action (repl. *-tiō* -TION); this was continued in Rom. and is thus widely exemplified in Eng. adoptions from French, e.g. *abridgement*, *commencement*, *government*, *management*, alongside their vbs. *abridge*, etc. This set the fashion for the treatment of *-ment* as if it were native, as in *amazement*, *betterment*, *fulfilment*, *wonderment*; among such formations are many with *be-*, *em-*, *en-*, *im-*, *in-*. A notable range of sense-development is illustrated by *atonement*, *complement*, *compliment*, *embankment*, *escapement*, *government*, *management*, *refreshment*, *settlement*, *statement*. Formations on adjs. are uncommon, as *funniment*, *merriment*, *oddments*; Spenser has *dreriment*, *hardiment*, *iollyment*, *vnruliment*. The corr. adjs. end in **-me·ntal**.

mental[1] me·ntəl pert. to the mind. XV (Hoccleve). – (O)F. *mental* or late L. *mentālis*, f. *ment-* *mēns* MIND; see -AL[1]. Hence **ment**A·LITY. XVII (Baxter).

mental[2] me·ntəl pert. to the chin. XVIII. – F. *mental*, f. L. *mentum* chin; see MOUTH, -AL[1].

menthol me·nþəl crystalline camphor-like substance. XIX. – G. *menthol* (1861), f. *mentha* MINT[2]; see -OL.

mention me·nʃən act of commemorating by speech or writing. XIV. – (O)F. *mention* = Sp. *mencion*, It. *menzione* – L. *mentiō(n-)*, f. base **men-* of *meminisse* remember; cf. COMMENT. So **me·ntion** vb. XVI (Palsgr.). – F. *mentionner* = Sp. *mencionar*, It. *menzionare*, medL. *mentiōnāre*.

mentor me·ntɔ̄ɹ experienced and trusted counsellor. XVIII. – F. *mentor*, appellative use of L. *Mentor* – Gr. *Méntōr*, name of the Ithacan noble whose disguise Athene assumed to act as guide to the young Telemachus in the 'Odyssey'; the name was prob. chosen for its etymol. significance (f. **men-* **mon-* remember, think, counsel; cf. MONITOR). ¶ Its currency in F. and Eng. is derived from its prominence in Fénelon's 'Télémaque' (1699).

menu me·njū bill of fare. XIX. F., sb. use of *menu* small, MINUTE, for *menu de repas* 'list of items of a meal'.

Mephistophelian mĭfistofī·liən. XIX. of the character of *Mephistopheles* mefistɔ·fīlīz (abbrev. *Mephisto* mĭfi·stou) an evil spirit to whom Faust, the hero of the dramas of Marlowe and Goethe (viz. *Doctor Faustus* and *Faust*), sells his soul.

mephitic mifi·tik offensive to the smell, pestilential. XVII. – late L. *mephīticus*, f. L. *mephītis* noxious vapour, (also personified) goddess who averts pestilential exhalations; see -IC.

mercantile mə̄·ɹkəntail pert. to merchandise or commerce. XVII. – F. *mercantile* – It. *mercantile*, f. *mercante* MERCHANT; see -ILE.

Mercator mə̄ɹkei·tə̄ɹ name of Gerardus *Mercator*, latinization of Gerhard *Kremer* (1512–94), Flemish cartographer. XVII (*M.'s projection*).

mercenary mə̄·ɹsĭnəri working merely for monetary reward, hired. XVI (More); sb. XIV (Ch.). – L. *mercēnārius*, earlier *mercennārius*, f. *mercēd-*, *mercēs* reward, wages; see MERCY, -ARY. Cf. (O)F. *mercénaire*.

mercer mə̄·ɹsəɹ dealer in silks and other textiles (surviving as title of a livery company). XIII (AncrR.). – AN. *mercer*, (O)F. *mercier* = Pr. *merc(i)er*, Sp. *mercero*, It. *merciajo* :– Rom. **merciārius*, f. L. *merci-*, *merx* MERCHANDISE; see -ER². So **me·rc**ERY. XIII. – (O)F. *mercerie*.

mercerize mə̄·ɹsəraiz prepare (goods) with chemicals for dyeing. XIX. f. name of John *Mercer*, dyer of Accrington; see -IZE.

merchandise mə̄·ɹtʃəndaiz †exchange of commodities; commodities of commerce. XIII (RGlouc.). ME. *marchaundise*, *mercandise* – (O)F. *marchandise*, dial. †*marcandise*, f. *marchand*+*-ise*, repr. L. *-ītia*. ME. syns. were †*merchandry*, *-dy*. So **merchant** mə̄·ɹtʃənt trader. XIII. ME. *marchand*, *-aunt* – OF. (and mod.) *marchand*, †*march(e)ant* = Pr. *marcadans*, It. *mercatante* :– Rom. **mercātante*, sb. use of prp. of **mercātāre*, f. *mercāt-*, *mercārī*, f. *merc-*, *merx* merchandise, whence also *Mercurius* (see MERCURY). Also as adj. 'relating to trade', in *law m.*, *statute m. c.* 1400; 'serving for transport', as *m. ship* (XIV); 'occupied in commerce', as *m. guild*, *guild m.* (XV), *m. adventurer* (XV); attrib. in *m. tailor* XVI (surviving in *Company of Merchant Taylors*, *Merchant Taylors' School*.

Mercian mə̄·ɹʃiən pert. to, native of, the Anglo-Saxon kingdom of Mercia XVI; the dialect of Old English spoken there XIX. f. medL. *Mercia*, f. OE. *Merċe*, *Mierċe* (pl.) lit. people of 'the march', 'borderers'; see MARCH², -IAN.

mercury mə̄·ɹkjəri (*M-*) Roman divinity identified with the Gr. Hermes (see HERMENEUTIC, HERMETIC), god of eloquence, messenger of the gods, patron of traders, thieves, and roads, guide of departed souls XIV (hence, messenger, go-between, guide XVI); planet nearest the sun (Ch.); quicksilver (Ch.); (after L. *herba mercurialis*) plant-name XIV. – L. *Mercurius*, orig. god of commerce, f. *merc-*, *merx* MERCHANDISE; the application to the planet appears in classL., and like other names of planets, *Mercurius* became in medL. the name of a metal; the application to plants is confined to Eng. So **mercur**IAL mə̄ɹkjuə·riəl XIV (Gower, 'of the planet m.'); volatile XVI. – (O)F. or L.

mercy mə̄·ɹsi forbearance and compassion shown to one who has no claim to kindness. XII. – (O)F. *merci*, now chiefly in sense 'thanks' (see GRAMERCY) and in phr. *à la merci de* in the absolute power of = Pr. *merces*, Sp. *merced*, It. *mercede* :– L. *mercēdem*, nom. *mercēs* pay, reward, wages, fee, recompense, rent, revenue, in ChrL. used for *misericordia* pity, and *gratiæ* thanks. Hence **me·rci**FUL¹. XIII; repl. earlier †*merciable* – OF. **me·rci**LESS. XIV.

mere¹ miəɹ †sea; lake. OE. *mere*, corr., with variations of gender, to OS. *meri* sea (Du. *meer* sea, pool), OHG. *mari*, *meri* (G. *meer*), ON. *marr* sea, Goth. *mari-* in *marisaiws*, *marei* :– CGerm. **mari* :– IE. **mori-* **məri-*, whence OSl. *more* (Russ. *móre*), OIr. *muir* (:– **mori*), W. *mor* (cf. Gaulish *Aremorici* 'dwellers near the sea', whence *Armorica* Brittany), L. *mare* (whence F. *mer*, Pr., Sp. *mar*, It. *mare*).

mere² miəɹ boundary. OE. (*ġe*)*mǣre* = MDu. *mēre*, *meer*, ON. (*landa*)*mæri* landmark :– Germ. **(ga)mairjam*, poss. rel. to L. *mūrus*, earlier *moerus*, *moiros* wall (cf. MURAL).

mere³ miəɹ done without another's help XV; †unmixed, pure; †absolute, entire; that is only what it is said to be XVI. – (in legal use, e.g. *m. motion*) AN. *meer*, OF. *mier* (= Sp., It. *mero*) or its source L. *merus* not mixed, pure. Hence **mere**LY². XVI.

merel me·rəl counter used in the game of *merels*, which is played by two players on a board with pebbles, discs, or pins. XIV (Gower). – OF. *merel* (mod. *méreau*) token coin, counter, also *merelle*, *marelle* board game with counters, f. Rom. **marra* pebbles, shingle (cf. Ladin *mar*, *mara*, pebbles, heap of stone).

meretricious meritri·ʃəs characteristic of a harlot, showily attractive. XVII. f. L. *meretrīcius*, f. *meretrīc-*, *-trix* harlot, f. *merēre* earn money, serve for hire; see -TRIX, -ICIOUS.

merganser mə̄ɹgæ·nsəɹ goosander. XVIII. – modL. *merganser* (Gesner 1555), f. *mergus* diver (water-fowl), f. L. *mergere* dive (see next)+*anser* goose.

merge məːɹdʒ †plunge, immerse XVII; (leg.) extinguish or be extinguished by absorption XVIII. – L. *mergere* dip, plunge; f. IE. **mezg-*, whence also Lith. *masgóti* wash, Skr. *majj-* dive, sink; in legal use through AN. *merger*. Hence **me·rg**ER[5] extinguishment of a right, etc. XVIII; (U.S.) combination of one trading company with another XIX. – sb. use of the AN. vb.

mericarp me·rikāɹp (bot.) portion of a fruit that splits away as a perfect fruit. XIX. – F. *méricarpe*, irreg. f. Gr. *méros* part + *karpós* fruit; see MERO-[1], CARPEL.

meridian mĭri·diən A. †midday XIV; point of sun's or star's highest altitude XV (Lydg.); B. great circle of the earth or a celestial sphere XIV (Ch.); individual locality XVI; adj. XIV (Ch.). – (O)F. *méridien* or L. *merīdiānus* (in sb. uses L. *merīdiānum*, sc. *tempus* time, i.e. noon, medL. *merīdiāna* noon, siesta), f. *merīdiēs*, nom. f. loc. *merīdiē*, by dissim. from **mediei diē* at midday. In sense B ult. for L. *circulus merīdiānus* meridian circle, tr. Gr. *κύκλος μεσημβρινός* (*μεσημβρία* f. *μέσος* MID, *ἡμέρα* day). So **meri·dion**AL[1]. – F. – late L. (after *septentriōnālis*). XIV (Maund.).

meringue məræ·ŋ(g) confection made from pounded sugar. XVIII. – F. *meringue* (1706 in Phillips), of unkn. origin.

merino mərī·nou variety of sheep prized for its fine wool XVIII; stuff made from the wool XIX. – Sp. *merino*, of disputed origin.

merit me·rit fact or condition of deserving XIII (AncrR.); †what is deserved XIII (Cursor M.); something that entitles one to recompense XIV (Wyclif). – (O)F. *mérite* – L. *meritum* price, value, service rendered, sb. use of pp. n. of *merēre*, *-ērī* earn, deserve, rel. to Gr. *meíresthai* obtain as a share, *moîra*, share fate, *méros* part (cf. MERO-[1]). So **me·rit** vb. †reward XV (Caxton); deserve XVI. – F. *mériter*, f. *mérite*. **merito·**RIOUS. XV. f. L. *meritōrius*; earlier †*meritory* (XIV).

merle məːɹl (poet.) blackbird. XV. – (O)F. *merle* = Pr., Sp. *merla*, It. *merla*, *merlo* :– L. *merula*, (late) *merulu-s*. ¶ Distant connexion with synon. Germ. **ams-* (repr. by OE. *ōsle* OUSEL, OHG. *amsala*, G. *amsel*) and W. *mwyalch* is possible.

mermaid mə·ɹmeid fabulous being having the head and trunk of a woman and the tail of a fish. XIV (Ch.). f. MERE[1] + MAID. Also **me·r**MAIDEN. XIV (Ch.). Hence **mer·**MAN. XVII. ¶ Superseded *mer(e)min*, OE. *meremenen*, corr. to OHG. *meremanni*, *meriminna*, Du. *meermin*, ON. *marmennill*.

mero-[1] miə·rou, me·rou before a vowel **mer-**, comb. form of Gr. *méros* part (rel. to *moîra* cf. MERIT), in many techn. terms. XIX.

mero-[2] miə·rou, miərə· comb. form of Gr. *mērós* thigh, rel. to MEMBER. XIX.

-merous mərəs ending of bot. terms denoting (see MERO-[1], -OUS) 'having (a specified number of) parts', as *pentamerous*.

Merovingian merŏvi·ndʒiən pert. to the line of Frankish kings founded by Clovis (*c*.A.D. 500) and to the kingdoms ruled by them. XVII. – F. *mérovingien*, f. medL. *Merovingī* pl., f. L. form (*Meroveus*) of the name of their reputed founder; see -ING[3], -IAN.

merry me·ri †pleasing, agreeable OE. (so orig. in *merry England*, in which it was later apprehended as 'joyous'); full of lively enjoyment XIV (hilarious from drink XVI), (arch., of a saying) amusing XV; (arch.) pleasantly amused XVII (Sh.). OE. *myri(ġ)e* :– Germ. **murgjaz* (cf. MIRTH). Outside Eng. the only cognate corr. in sense is MDu. **merch*, whence *merchte* mirth, *merchtocht* rejoicing, *mergelijc* joyful, *mergen* be merry; but the word may be identical with Germ. **murgjaz* short, repr. by OHG. *murgfāri* of short duration, Goth. *gamaurgjan* shorten, f. IE. **mr̥ghu-*, whence Gr. *brakhús*, Av. *mərəzu-* short; for the sense-development cf. ON. *skemta* amuse, f. *skamt* (SCANT), n. of *skammr* short. The standard form with *e* repr. a predominantly S.E. development; cf. *left*. Hence **me·rri**MENT. XVI. **Merry Andrew** buffoon, clown. XVII (Dryden); of unkn. origin. **me·rry-**MAKE XVI (Spenser), *-ma:king* XVIII; f. phr. *make m.* **me·rry-**THOUGHT furcula between neck and breast of a bird XVII (Dekker); like synon. *wish-bone*, it refers to the custom of two persons pulling the bone so that it breaks between them.

mesalliance meizæ·liãs, ‖mezaljãs marriage with one of inferior social status. XVIII. F.; see MIS-[2], ALLIANCE. The anglicized form **misalli·ance** (used in a gen. sense) is somewhat earlier.

meseems misī·mz (arch.) it seems to me. XIV. f. ME[1] (dative) + 3rd pers. sg. pres. ind. of SEEM.

mesembryanthemum mėse:mbriæ·nþiməm (bot.) genus of plants of which several species open their flowers only about midday. XIX. modL. (Dillenius), for **mesembri-*, f. Gr. *mesēmbriā* noon (f. *mésos* MID, *hēmérā* day) + *ánthemon*, f. *ánthos* flower (cf. ANTHOLOGY).

mesentery me·sĭntəri (anat.) fold of peritonæum. XVI. – medL. *mesenterium* – Gr. *mesentérion*, f. *mésos* MID + *énteron* intestine (cf. ENTERIC).

mesh meʃ open space or interstice of a network. XVI. Early forms also *meish*, *meash*, *mash*, the first two indicating a long vowel; prob. – MDu. *maesche* (Du. *maas*), and *masche*, repr. Germ. **mǣsk-* (whence OHG. *māsca*) and **mask-* (whence OE. *max*. **mæsć* net, *mæscre* mesh, OHG. *masca*, G. *masche*; ON. *mǫskvi*, the source of ME. *mask*).

mesmerism me·zmərizm (production of) a hypnotic state in a person by exercise of another's will-power. *c*.1800. f. name of Friedrich Anton *Mesmer* (1733–1815), Austrian physician + -ISM; so F. *mesmérisme* (1823). Hence **me·smer**IZE. *c*.1830.

mesne mīn (leg.) intermediate, mean. XV. – law F. *mesne*, var. of AN. *meen* MEAN[3]; for the unetymological *s* cf. DEMESNE. So **mesnalty** mī·nəlti condition or estate of a mesne lord. XVI. – law F. *mesnalte*, f. *mesne*, after *comunalte* COMMONALTY.

meso- me·so(u), before a vowel **mes-**, comb. form of Gr. *mésos* middle, MID, used in scientific terms of modern formation (XIX), many of which have correls. in PRO-, PROTO-, META-; those of **mesozoic** -zou·ik (geol.) secondary (1880) are CAINOZOIC tertiary (1838), PALÆOZOIC primary (1838).

mesquite me·skīt leguminous tree of the genus *Prosopis*; species of grass growing in their neighbourhood. XIX. – Mex. Sp.

mess mes A. portion or serving of food, dish of food XIII (Cursor M.); made dish XV; mixed food for an animal XVIII; medley, confused or shapeless mass XIX; B. company of persons eating together XV. – OF. *mes* (in sense A), mod. *mets* (infl. by *metre* place) :- late L. *missu-s* course of food, (earlier) course, round, or heat in sports, f. *miss-*, pp. stem of *mittere* send (out), put forth, cast, (in Rom. use) put, place; cf. *admit, commit, emit*, etc., MISSION. Hence **mess** vb. (dial.) serve up (food) XIV; take one's meals XVIII; make a mess (of) XIX. **me·ss**MATE (sense B) XVIII. **me·ss**Y[1]. XIX.

message me·sidʒ communication sent from one to another. XIII – (O)F. *message* = Pr. *messatge*, Sp. *mensaje*, etc. :- Rom. **missāticum* (in medL. IX), f. *miss-*; see prec. and -AGE. So **messeng**ER[2] me·sindʒəɹ one who carries a message. XIII (AncrR.). ME. *messager* (later *messanger*) – (O)F. *messager*, f. *message*. ¶ For intrusive *n* cf. OSTRINGER, PASSENGER, SCAVENGER, WHARFINGER.

Messiah misai·ə Heb. title applied to a promised deliverer of the Jewish nation, and hence to Jesus of Nazareth. Earlier forms *Messie* XIV (– (O)F. *Messie*), *Messias* XIII – late L. (Vulg.) *Messīās* – Gr. *Messīās* – Aramic *m'shīḥā*, Heb. *māshīªh* anointed (in LXX rendered by *Khristós* CHRIST), f. *māshaḥ* anoint. *Messias* occurs in translations of the Bible down to A.V. (here only in John i 41, iv 25); *Messiah* is an alt. form invented by the translators of the Geneva Bible of 1560, to impart a more Hebraic aspect to the word; it was adopted in A.V. (only in Dan. ix 25, 26). So **Messian**IC mesiæ·nik. XIX. – modL. *Messiānicus*; cf. F. *messianique*, G. *messianisch*.

messieurs me·seɹz, ||mesjö̆. XVII. F., pl. of MONSIEUR.

messuage me·swidʒ orig. portion of land for a dwelling-house, (now) dwelling-house with appurtenances and land assigned thereto. XIV (Ch.). – AN. *mes(s)uage* house, household, AL. *mes(s)uāgium*, supposed to be misreadings of *mesnage, mesnagium* MÉNAGE, but the case is doubtful, the sense development being obscure.

mestizo mistī·zou Sp. or Pg. half-caste; offspring of a Spaniard and an American Indian. XVI. Sp. (= Pg. *mestiço*, Pr. *mestis*, F. *métis*) :- Rom. **mixtīcius*, f. L. *mixtus*, pp. of *miscēre* MIX.

meta mī·tə (Roman antiq.) conical column marking turning-point in a race in the Circus. XVI. L., 'conical object'.

meta- me·tə, mitæ·, before a vowel usu. *met-*, before *h meth-*, repr. Gr. *meta-, met-, meth-*, comb. form of Gr. *metá* with, after (see MID) denoting chiefly sharing, joint action, pursuit, quest, (and esp.) change, corr. to L. TRANS-; used freely (and not always in accordance with Gr. analogy) in scientific terms since *c.*1850, as in anat. and zool. 'behind', 'hinder', 'hindmost' (sometimes correl. with PRO- and MESO-), and in chem. (esp. as distingushing compounds from others in ORTHO- and PARA-).

metabolism mitæ·bəlizm process of chemical change in an organism. XIX. f. Gr. *metabolḗ* change, f. *metabállein*, f. *metá* META- + *bállein* throw; see BALLISTA, -ISM.

metal me·tl any member of the class of substances represented by gold, silver, copper, iron, lead, tin. XIII (RGlouc., Cursor M.). – (O)F. *métal*, †*metail* or its source L. *metallum* mine, quarry, metal – synon. Gr. *métallon*; has become CEur. So **metall**IC mitæ·lik. XVI (Maplet). – F. or L.: earlier **me·tall**INE[1] XV. – F. Hence **me·tall**IZE. XVI. See METTLE.

metamorphosis metəmō·ɹfəsis, me:təmōɹfou·sis. – L. (in pl. as the title of a work by Ovid dealing with changes of shape) – Gr. *metamórphōsis*; see META-, -MORPH, -OSIS. So **metamo·rphose** -fouz. XVI. – F. *métamorphoser*, f. *métamorphose* sb. – L.; also †**metamo·rph**IZE (XVI Sh. to XVIII).

metaphor me·təfəɹ figure of speech involving the transference of a name to something analogous. XVI (Henry VIII). – (O)F. *métaphore* (Jean de Meung) or L. *metaphora* (Quintilian) – Gr. *metaphorá*, f. *metaphérein* TRANSFER; see META-, BEAR[2]. So **metaphor**ICAL -fɔ·rikəl XVI (Latimer), **-pho·ri**CALLY. XVI (Golding); cf. late L. *metaphoricē* adv. (Isidore).

metaphysic metəfi·zik branch of philosophical inquiry which treats of the first principles of things. XIV (Trevisa). – (O)F. *metaphysique* (Oresme) – medL. *metaphysica* fem. sg., for earlier n.pl. (repr. by **metaphy·s**ICS XVI) – medGr. (*tà*) *metaphusikà*, for *tà metà tà phusiká* 'the things (works) after the Physics'; see META-, PHYSIC(s). So **metaphy·s**IC adj. XVI (Tindale), -ICAL XV, -I·CIAN XVI (G. Harvey). ¶ The title of Aristotle's work named *Metaphysics* derives from the fact that the books so designated followed in the received arrangement the treatises on natural science known as *τὰ φυσικά* 'the physics'; although Gr. *metá* does not normally imply 'beyond' or 'transcending' it came to be so interpreted in this word prob. on the model of such a correspondence as *metaphor* and *transfer*.

metatarsus metətā·ɹsəs (anat.) group of bones lying between the tarsus and the toes. XVII. – modL.; see META-, TARSUS.

metathesis mĭtæ·þisis (result of) transposition of sounds or letters in a word. XVII. – late L. – Gr. *metáthesis*, f. *metatithénai* transpose; see META-, THESIS. So **metathet**IC -þe·tik. XIX.

mete mīt (arch.) measure *out*. OE. *metan* = OFris. *meta*, OS. *metan*, OHG. *mezzan* (Du. *meten*, G. *messen*), ON. *meta*, Goth. *mitan* :– CGerm. **metan*; the IE. base **med-* is repr. also by L. *meditārī* MEDITATE, Gr. *médesthai* care for, OIr. *midiur* I treasure, *med* measure, beside **mod-*, of L. *modus* MODE, *modius* bushel, Skr. *mastiš* measure, weight, and MEAT.

metempsychosis mĭtempsikou·sis (formerly often str. on the third syll. after Gr.) transmigration of the soul. XVI. – late L. – Gr. *metempsū́khōsis*, f. *metá* META-+*en* IN +*psūkhḗ* soul (see PSYCHIC).

meteor mī·tiəɹ †atmospheric phenomenon XV; fireball, shooting star XVI (Sh.). – modL. *meteōrum* – Gr. *metéōron*, sb. use of n. of *metéōros* raised up, lofty, f. *metá* META-+ **eōr-*, var. of base of *aeírein* raise. Hence, or partly – medL. *meteōricus*, **meteor**IC mītiɔ·rik †elevated, lofty XVII; †pert. to the atmosphere XVIII; pert. to meteors XIX. Cf. F. *météore*, *météorique*. **me·teor**ITE meteoric stone. XIX (Olmsted); earlier **me·teoro**LITE (*-lithe*, Southey). **meteoro·**LOGY study of atmospheric phenomena. XVII. – F. or modL. – Gr. *meteōrologiā*. **me:teoro**LO·GICAL XVI (Dee); so F. *météorologique* (XVI).

meter[1] mī·təɹ (local) measurer. XIV (Wycl. Bible). f. METE+-ER[1].

meter[2] mī·təɹ apparatus for measuring quantities. XIX. First in *gas m.* (1815); perh. a use of METER[1] suggested by *gasometer* (1790).

-meter mitəɹ terminal el. in names of instruments for scientific measuring, the earliest of which (XVII) were adopted, partly through F., from modL. terms in *-metrum* (intended to repr. Gr. *métron* METRE[1]), e.g. *barometer*, *hygrometer*, *thermometer*, which are not, however, formed according to Gr. analogies. In XVIII and XIX hybrid formations came in, such as *alcoholometer*, *calorimeter*, *galvanometer*, *gasometer*, *lactometer*, *pedometer*, *taximeter*, *voltameter*. Nonce-words of a joc. kind have been frequent, esp. in imitation of Sydney Smith's *foolometer* 'fool-measurer'. The corr. nouns of action end in **-metry** mĭtri (cf. GEOMETRY).

methane me·þein (chem.) light carburetted hydrogen, marsh gas, CH_4. XIX. f. METH|YL +-ANE.

metheglin miþe·glin spiced or medicated mead. XVI. – W. *meddyglyn*, f. *meddyg* medicinal (– L. *medicus* MEDICAL) + *llyn* liquor (= Ir. *linn*, Gael. *linne* pool).

methinks miþi·ŋks (arch.) it seems to me. OE. *mē þyncþ*, ME., early modEng. *me thinketh*, repl. by *methinks* (XVI); see ME and THINK; p.t. **methought** miþɔ̄·t (XIII), repl. OE. *mē þūhte*.

method me·þəd †systematic treatment of a disease; special form of procedure; orderly arrangement. XVI. – F. *méthode* or L. *methodus* – Gr. *méthodos* pursuit of knowledge, mode of investigation, f. *metá* (see MID)+*hodós* way. **method**ICAL miþɔ·dikəl (hist.) belonging to a school of physicians (between 'dogmatists' and 'empirics'); pert. to method XVI; (earlier †*methodic*). – late L. *methodicus* – Gr. **me·thod**IST physician of the methodical school; one who follows a certain method XVI; member of the Holy Club established at Oxford in 1729; member of religious bodies originating in this (cf. WESLEYAN). – modL. *methodista*; hence **me·thod**ISM. ¶ The words have become CEur.

methyl me·þil (chem.) hypothetical radical of wood spirit. 1840. – F. *méthyle* (1840), G. *methyl*, back-formations from F. *méthylène* (1835), G. *methylen* (whence **me·thyl**ENE 1835), f. Gr. *méthu* wine MEAD[1]+*hū́lē* wood. Hence **me·thylated** pp. (see -ATE[3]).

meticulous miti·kjŭləs †timid XVI; over-careful about details XIX. f. L. *metīculōsus* (Plautus), f. *metus* fear, after *perīculōsus* PERILOUS; see -OUS.

métier mei·tjei one's trade, business, or line. XVIII. F. :– Rom. **misterium*, for L. *ministerium* service, MINISTRY, assoc. with *mysterium* MYSTERY.

metonymy mĕtɔ·nĭmi (rhet.) substitution for the name of a thing the name of an attribute of it, etc. XVI. First in late L. form *metōnymia* – Gr. *metōnumiā*, f. *metá* META-+ *ónoma*, Æolic *ónuma* NAME; see -Y[3].

metope me·tóupi (archit.) square space between triglyphs of the Doric frieze. XVI (*methopa*). – L. *metopa* – Gr. *metópē*, f. *metá* between META-+*opaí* holes in a frieze to receive the beam ends.

metre[1], U.S. **meter** mī·təɹ form of poetic rhythm, metrical form, verse. XIV (Rolle, R. Mannyng, Ch.). – (O)F. *mètre*, corr. to Sp., It. *metro*, G. *meter* – L. *metrum* (which was adopted in OE.) – Gr. *métron*. f. IE. **mē̆-* MEASURE+instr. suffix. Also in comps. *dimeter*, *hexameter*, *pentameter*, etc. So **metr**IC[1] me·trik science of metrical form. XVIII; cf. F. *métrique*, G. *metrik*, etc. **me·tr**ICAL pert. to metre XV; relating to measurement XVII. – L. *metricus* – Gr. **me·tr**IST. XVI. – medL. *metrista*.

metre², U.S. **meter** unit of length of the metric system. XVIII. – F. *mètre* – Gr. *métron* (see prec.). So **me·tric²**. XIX.

metro me·trou short for Metropolitan Railway. XX.

metro- me·trou, mĭtro·, comb. form of Gr. *métron* measure (see METRE), as in **me·tronome** instrument for marking time with an inverted pendulum. XIX.

metropolis mĭtro·pəlis (hist.) see of the bishop of a province; chief city. XVI. – late L. *mētropolis* – Gr. *mētrópolis* (Herodotus), f. *mḗtēr* MOTHER + *pólis* city (cf. POLITIC). Cf. (O)F. *métropole*, whence late ME. *metropole* (XIV). So **metropolitAN** metrəpɔ·litən. XVI. – late L. *metropolītānus*, f. Gr. *mētropolī́tēs* citizen of a metropolis, metropolitan bishop. **me:troPOLI·TICAL** XVI. – medL. *metropoliticus*.

mettle me·tl quality of temperament XVI (*Swearing cometh of a hot mettal*, Lyly); (of a horse) vigour, spirit (Sh.); (of persons) XVI. In earliest use (late XVI) *mettal(l)*, *-ell*, vars. of METAL, which began to be established as *mettle* in early XVII to distinguish the fig. uses above defined, which are so far removed from the lit. senses that a graphic differentiation was appropriate.

mew¹ mjū sea-gull. OE. *mǣw*, corr. to OS. *mēu* (MLG., MDu. *mēwe*, Du. *meeuw*; G. *möwe* is from LG) :– Germ. **mai(ʒ)wiz*, rel. to **maiχwaz*, whence OHG. *mēh*, ON. *már* (pl. *mávar*, *máfar*).

mew² mjū cage for hawks while moulting; coop, breeding-cage. XIV. – (O)F. *mue* (corr. to Sp., It. *muda*), f. *muer* moult, shed horns, in OF. also change :– L. *mūtāre* (see MUTATION). So **mew** vb. cast (feathers), esp. of a hawk. XIV. – (O)F. *muer*. A second vb. **mew** put a hawk 'in mew', cage, (transf.) shut *up*, confine XV, is f. the sb. See also MEWS.

mew³ mjū utter the characteristic cry of the cat. XIV. Echoic, varying with †*mewt* (XIV–XVIII), †*mute* (Skelton); cf. MIAOW.

mewl mjūl whimper, whine, mew. XVII (Sh.). Echoic; cf. *miaul*, MIAOW.

mews mjūz royal stables at Charing Cross, London XIV; stabling built round an open space XVII. pl. of (arch. and dial.) *mew* cage, coop (XIV) – (O)F. *mue*, f. *muer* vb. (MEW²).

Mexican me·ksikən pert. to Mexico. XVII. – Earlier Sp. *mexicano* (now *mej-*), f. *Mexico*, f. *Mexitli*, one of the names of the Aztec god of war; see -AN.

mezereon mĭziə·riən shrub Daphne Mezereon. XV (*-ion*). – medL. – Arab. *māzaryūn* (Avicenna).

mezzanine me·zənīn low storey between two higher ones. XVIII. – F. *mezzanine* – It. *mezzanino*, dim. of *mezzano* middle, MEAN³.

mezzotint me·dzoutint †half-tint; method of engraving a metal plate for printing. XVIII. Earlier in It. form **mezzoti·nto** (XVII); f. *mezzo* half (:– L. *mediu-s* MID)+*tinto* TINT.

mho mou (electr.) unit of conductivity. XIX (W. Thomson, later Lord Kelvin). Reversal of OHM.

mi, me mī (mus.) third note of the scale. XVI. See UT.

miaow miau· MEW³. XVII. Echoic; cf. F. *miaou* and *miaul* (XVII) – F. *miauler*.

miasma maiæ·zmə noxious exhalation. XVII. – modL. – Gr. *miasma* defilement, pollution, rel. to *miaínein* pollute (cf. AMIANTHUS). So **mi·asm** XVII; after F. *miasme*.

mica mai·kə †small plate of talc, etc.; mineral consisting essentially of silicate of aluminium occurring in glittering scales or in crystals. XVIII. – L. *mīca* grain, crumb; the modL. use in min. was prob. orig. contextual ('a particle' of . . .), and the development of the specialized meaning was perh. furthered by assoc. with L. *micāre* shine. Hence **micA·CEOUS**. XVIII (Pennant).

Michaelmas mi·klməs feast of St. Michael the archangel, 29 September (a quarter-day). OE. *sancte Micheles mæsse* Saint Michael's mass (see MASS¹), ME. *Mi(ʒh)elmasse* (XIII), *Mykylmes* (XV); *Michael* mai·kl repr. (ult.) Heb. *Mīkhaēl* 'who is like God'.

mickle mi·kl **muckle** mʌ·kl (dial.) great, much. north. and eastern ME. *mikel* (XIII, Ormulum, Bestiary, Cursor M.), later north. *mekil* (whence Sc. *meikle*) – ON. *mikell* = OE. *mićel* MUCH. The var. ME. *mukel* (XIV), later north. *muckle*, arose from assoc. with *muchel*, MUCH. Also adv. XIII, sb. XIV.

micro- mai·krou, before a vowel **micr-**, comb. form of Gr. *mīkrós*, var. of *smīkrós* small, poss. rel to SMALL; used in many scientific terms. **microcosm** mai·kro(u)-kɔzm man viewed as an epitome of the universe. XV (Ludg.). – F. *microcosme* or medL. *mīcro(s)cosmus* – Gr. *mīkròs kósmos* little world. **microMETER** maikrɔ·mitəɹ instrument for measuring very small distances. XVII. – F. *micromètre*. **mi·croPHONE** instrument for intensifying sounds. XVII. **microSCOPE** mai·kroskoup magnifying glass for details. XVII (1656) – modL. *microscopium*.

microbe mai·kroub extremely minute living being, esp. bacterium. XIX. – F. *microbe* (1878, Sédillot), f. Gr. *mikrós* MICRO-+*bíos* life (used for 'living creature'); see BIO-.

micturition miktjuri·ʃən desire to make water, (often simply) making water. XVIII. – L. *micturītiō(n-)*, f. pp. stem. of *micturīre*, desiderative formation on *mict-*, *minct-*, pp. stem of *mingere* make water, formed with nasal infix, like OLith. *minžu* I urinate, on the IE. base **meigh-* repr. by synon. L. *meiere*. Cf. MIXEN.

mid mid (in partitive concord) the middle or midst of. OE. **midd*, only in obl. forms *midde, middes, midne, midre, middum* (cf. AMID), corr. to OFris. *midde*, OS. *middi*, OHG. *mitti*, ON. *miðr*, Goth. *midjis* :– CGerm. **miðja-*, **meðja-* :– CIE. **medhjo-*, whence also L. *medius* (cf. MEDIAL), Gr. *méssos* (:– **methjos*), later *mésos* MESO-, Gaul. *medio-* (as in *Mediolānum*, It. *Milano* Milan), OIr. *mide* middle (sb.), *Mide* Meath, prop. 'middle province', *immedōn* in the middle or interior, OSl. *mežda* limit, *meždu* between, Russ. *mežá* boundary, Skr. *mádhyas*, Av. *maiðyō* in the middle of, Arm. *mēj* middle (sb.); **mi·dday, mi·dnight, mi·dsummer, midwi·nter** occur in OE. both as two words (with *mid* inflected) and as comps.; in the Continental langs. the corr. terms are only comps., exc. ON. *miðr dǫgr, miðr vetr*; **midland** mi·dlənd (XVI), contr. of ME. *middel land* (XIII); **mi·dmost** (XVII) alt. (by assoc. with -MOST) of OE., ME. *midmest*, also OE., OFris. *medemest*; for formation and development cf. FOREMOST; **mi·d**WAY adv. in the middle of the distance XIII. ME. *midwei*, for *o midweie*, OE. *on midweġe*; cf. MDu. *middewech*.

midden mi·dn dunghill, manure heap. XIV. ME. *mydding*, of Scand. origin; identical with Da. *mødding*, earlier *møgdyng(e)*, f. *møg* MUCK+*dynge* heap (cf. DUNG), Norw. dial. *mykjardunge, mitting*.

middle mi·dl so placed as to have the same quantity or number on each side. OE. *middel, midl-* adj. and (by ellipsis) sb. m. = OFris. *middel* adj., OS. *middil-*, in comps. (Du. *middel* adj. and sb.), OHG. *mittil* (G. *mittel* adj. and sb.) :– WGerm. **middila*, f. **middi* :– Germ. **miðja-* MID+*-il* -LE². In OE. and ME. chiefly in superl. *midlest* (now obs. or dial.); in G. the prevailing form is the compar., which is not recorded in Eng.; *middlest* was repl. by **mi·ddle**MOST, north. ME. *midelmast* (XIII). *Middle Ages* (1713), earlier †*Middle Age* (1621), rendering modL. *media ætas* (1518), *medium ævum* (1604).

middling mi·dliŋ †intermediate XV (Haye); of medium size or quality XVI. First in Sc. use, from which it passed into southern use in the reign of James I. prob. f. MID+-LING². Cf. OE. *mydlinga* moderately.

middy mi·di (colloq.) midshipman. XIX (Marryat); see -Y⁶.

midge midʒ small gnat-like insect. OE. *myċġ(e)*, corr. to OS. *muggia* (Du. *mug*), OHG. *mucca* (G. *mücke*), ON. *mý* (Sw. *mygg, mygga*, Da. *myg*) :– Germ. **mugjaz*, **mugjōn*, rel. to L. *musca* fly (cf. MOSQUITO), Gr. *muîa*, Lith. *musẽ*, OSl. (Russ.) *múkha*. Hence **midg**ET mi·dʒit sand-fly (in Canada) *c.*1850; extremely small person *c.*1865.

midrash mi·dræʃ Jewish commentary on the Hebrew scriptures. XVII. – Heb., f. *darash* investigate, search.

midriff mi·drif diaphragm. OE. *midhrif* (= OFris. *midref*), f. **midd* MID+*hrif* belly = OFris. *hrif, href*, OHG. *href*, of obscure origin.

midshipman midʃi·pmən naval rank between cadet and lowest commissioned officer. XVII. Earlier †*midshipsman*, f. †*midships* (see AMIDSHIPS)+MAN. Hence **mi·dship**MITE² XIX.

midst midst middle point or position. XIV. ME. *middest*, alt. of †*middes* (XIV), which was evolved from advb. phr. *in middes, on middes*, which are alterations of *in middan, on middan*, where the prep. governs the dat. of *midde* sb. MIDDLE, or the weak-inflected adj. ¶ For parasitic *t* cf. *amongst, whilst*.

midwife mi·dwaif, (formerly) mi·d(w)if. XIV. prob. f. MID (prep. and adv.) with, together+WIFE in the sense 'woman' (so †*midwoman* XIII), the notion being 'a woman who is *with* the mother at the birth' (cf. the etymol. meaning of *obstetric*). Hence **midwif**ERY mi·d(w)ifri. XV.

mien mīn person's bearing or look. XVI (G. Douglas). Earlier *men, mene, meane, mine*; prob. aphetic of †*demean* sb. (XV; f. the vb.), later assim. to F. *mine* look, aspect.

might¹ mait quality of being able, power, strength. OE. *miht*, for *mieht*, non-WS. *mæht* = OFris. *mecht, macht*, OS., OHG. *maht* (Du., G. *macht*), Goth. *mahts* :– CGerm. **maχtiz* (exc. ON. *máttr* :– **maχtuz*), f. **mag-* be able; see MAY¹, -T¹. Hence **mi·ght**Y¹ OE. *mihtiġ* = OFris. *mahtig*, etc.

might² see MAY¹.

mignonette minjəne·t plant Reseda odorata. XVIII. – F. *mignonnette*, fem. of †*mignonnet*, dim. of *mignon* delicately small, of unkn. origin; see -ETTE.

migraine mi·grein. XVIII (Walpole). – F. (see MEGRIM).

migration məigrei·ʃən moving in flight, etc. from one place to another. XVII. – F. *migration* or L. *migrātiō(n-)*, f. *migrāre*, prob. based on **mei-* change (cf. MUTABLE); see -ATION. So or hence **migr**A·TE³. XVII.

mikado mikā·dou title of emperor of Japan. XVIII. Jap., f. *mi* august+*kado* door. ¶ Cf. *Sublime Porte* 'august gate' as the name of the central office of Ottoman government.

milch milᵗʃ giving milk, in milk. XIII. ME. *mielch, melche, milche*, repr. OE. **mielċe* (cf. *þri|milċe* month of May, in which cows can be milked thrice in the day), :– **melukjaz*, f. **meluk-*, *meolc* MILK. ¶ The form in use in OE. is identical with the sb. = MDu. *melk*, OHG. *melch*, G. *melk*, ON. *mjólkr*.

mild maild †gracious, kind; gentle, not rough OE.; †tame XIII; operating gently XIV; not rough, strong, or severe XV. OE. *milde* = OFris. *milde*, OS. *mildi*, OHG. *milti* (Du., G. *mild*), ON. *mildr*, Goth. *-mildeis*, *-milds* (in *friaþwa|mildeis* loving, *un|mildeis* unkind, *mildiþa* kindness) :- CGerm. **milðjaz*, **milðiz*, f. IE. **meldh-* **mol dh-***m̥ldh-*, whence Gr. *malthakós* (:- **m̥ldhn̥qós*) soft, Skr. *márdh*, *mr̥dh* neglect, despise, OIr. *meldach* pleasing, OSl. *mladŭ* young, tender, L. *mollis* soft (:- **moldwis*); extension of **mel-* **mol-* (cf. MILL[1]).

mildew mi·ldjū †honey-dew OE.; morbid growth on plants, etc. XIV. OE. *mildēaw*, *meledēaw* = OS. *milidou* (Du. *meeldauw*), OHG. *militou* (G., with assim. to *mehl* MEAL[1], *mehltau*), Sw. *mjöldagg*, Da. *meldug*; f. Germ. **meliþ* (Goth. *miliþ*; cf. L. *mel*, Gr. *méli*) honey+**dawwaz* DEW.

mile mail Roman measure of 1,000 paces (*mille passus* or *passuum*) estimated at 1,618 yards; unit of measure derived from this, viz. 1,760 yards in English-speaking countries. OE. *mīl* fem. = MDu. *mīle* (Du. *mijl*), OHG. *mīl(l)a* (G. *meile*), ON. *míla* (prob. from OE.) :- WGerm. **mīlja* – L. *mīlia*, *mīllia*, pl. of *mīle*, *mīlle* thousand. ¶ In Rom. langs. the L. sg. is repr. by F. *mil(le)*, It. *miglio*, the pl. by Pr., Sp. *milla*, Pg. *milha*.

milfoil mi·lfoil yarrow. XIII. – OF. *milfoil* (now *millefeuille*, after *feuille* leaf) :- L. *mīle-*, *mīllefolium*, f. *mīle*, *mīlle* 1000 + *folium* leaf (see FOIL[2]), after Gr. *murióphullon* (*múrios* myriad, *phúllon* leaf); the ref. is to the finely-divided leaves.

miliary mi·liəri resembling millet seed. XVII. – L. *miliārius*, f. *milium* MILLET; see -ARY.

milieu mi·ljö environment. XIX. F., f. *mi* (:- L. *mediu-s* MID)+*lieu* place (:- L. *locu-s*).

militant mi·litənt engaged in warfare XV (*chirche m.*); combative XVII. – F. *militant* or L. *mīlitant-*, *-āns*, prp. of *mīlitāre* serve as a soldier, f. *mīlit-*, *mīles* soldier, perh. of Etruscan origin like *satelles* SATELLITE; see -ANT. So **mi·litar**ISM. XIX. – F. *militarisme*, f. *militaire*. **mi·litar**IST †soldier XVII (Sh.); (now) one dominated by military ideas. **mi·lit**ARY pert. to soldiers or an army. XVI. f. F. *militaire* or L. *mīlitāris*; preceded by †**mi·lit**AR. **mi·lit**ATE[3] †serve as a soldier; †conflict *with*, be evidence *against* XVII. **militia** mili·ʃə †military discipline or service; military force, esp. citizen army. XVI. – L., f. *milit-*; see -IA[1]; cf. F. *milice*.

milk milk fluid secreted by the mammæ of female mammalia. OE. Anglian *milc*, WS. *meol(o)c* = OFris. *melok*, OS. *miluk* (Du. *melk*), OHG. *miluh* (G. *milch*), ON. *mjólk*, Goth. *miluks* :- CGerm. **meluks* fem., f. **melk-* (repr. by the vbs. OE. *melcan*, OHG. *melchan*) :- IE. **melg-* **m̥lg-*, whence OIr. *melg* sb. and the vbs. L. *mulgēre*, Gr. *amélgein*, OSl. *mlěsti*, OIr. *bligim*. Hence vb. OE. *milcian*. comp. **mi·lksop** orig. SOP dipped in milk, (hence) one who is fed on such food, †young infant, (transf.) effeminate fellow XIV (Ch.; as a nickname or surname XIII). Hence **mi·lk**Y[1]; *M. Way* tr. L. *via lactea*; cf. GALAXY. XIV.

mill[1] mil building fitted with apparatus for grinding corn OE.; the apparatus itself XVI; building in which an industry or manufacture is carried on XVI. OE. *mylen* m. and fem. :- **mu·lino*, *-ina*, for late L. *molīnum*, *-īna*, f. and repl. L. *mola* grindstone, mill, rel. to *molere* grind (see MEAL[1]). For the loss of final *n* cf. the common dial. pronunc. kil of *kiln*. comp. **mi·ll**STONE late OE.; cf. Du. *molensteen*, etc. Hence **mill** vb. XVI. ¶ The late L. fem. was adopted in other Germ. langs. and in OSl.; for the native Germ. word for hand-mill see QUERN.

mill[2] mil 1/1000 of a dollar. XVIII. Short for n. of L. *millesimus* MILLESIMAL.

millboard mi·lbɔ̄əɹd stout pasteboard made of coarse matter milled or rolled with high pressure. XVIII. alt. of *milled board*, i.e. board flattened by rolling or beating.

millennium mile·niəm period of 1000 years, spec. that during which Christ will reign on earth (Rev. xx 1–5). XVII. – modL., f. L. *mille* 1000, after *biennium* (see BIENNIAL). So **millenarian** milīnɛə·riən pert. to (sb. one who believes in) the millennium. XVII. f. L. *millenarius*, f. *millēnī*, distributive of *mille*; see -ARIAN; whence also **millen**ARY mi·līnəri. XVI.

millepede mi·lipīd arthropod with many legs. XVII. – L. *millepeda* woodlouse, f. *mille* 1000+*ped-*, *pēs* FOOT.

miller mi·ləɹ one whose trade is grinding corn in a mill, proprietor or tenant of a corn-mill. XIV (PPl., Ch.). Late ME. *mulnere*, *mylnere*, *millere* prob. (with assim. to MILL[1]) – MLG., MDu. *molner*, *mulner* (Du. *molenaar*, *mulder*), in OS. *mulineri*, corr. to OHG. *mulināri* (G. *müller*), ON. *mylnari* – late L. *molīnārius* (CRom., exc. Rum.), f. *molīna* MILL; see -ER[1]. ¶ Superseded OE. *myle(n)-weard* (orig.) custodian of a lord's mill, (later) miller. Three types survive as surnames, *Miller*, *Milner*, *Mil(l)ward*, with var. *Millard*, beside *Mil(l)man*.

millesimal mile·siməl thousandth (part). XVIII. f. L. *millēsimus*, f. *mille* 1000; see -AL[1].

millet mi·lit graminaceous plant, Panicum miliaceum. XIV (Maund.). – (O)F. *millet*, dim. of (dial.) *mil* (whence Eng. †*mill(e)* XVI) = Pr. *melh*, Sp. *mijo*, It. *miglio*, Rum. *meĭŭ* :- L. *milium* (whence OE. *mīl* and late ME. †*mile*), rel. to Gr. *melínē*, Lith. *málnos* pl. (this parallel evidence indicates that the plant was known in primitive IE. times).

milli-, comb. form of L. *mīlle* thousand (see MILE), used esp. in denominations of the metric system to denote the thousandth part of a unit, e.g. *milligramme, millimetre* (XIX).

milliary mi·liəri pert. to a mile or milestone. XVII. – L. *mīl(l)iārius*, f. *mīlle*; see MILE, -ARY.

milliner mi·linəɹ †vendor of fancy ware such as was orig. made at Milan (e.g. *Melane fustian, Myllen bonnettes*); maker-up of articles of female apparel (now esp. hats). XVI (*mylloner, mileyner, milliner*). f. *Milan*, name of the chief city of Lombardy, Italy, famous for textile fabrics and steel-work + -ER[1]. Hence **mi·llin**ERY. XVII.

million mi·ljən a thousand thousands XIV; *the* multitude XVII. – (O)F. *million*, prob. – It. †*millione*, now *milione* (whence also Sp. *millon*, Pg. *milhão*), f. *mille* thousand (see MILE)+augm. suffix *-one*. ¶ The F. word has passed into Germ. and Sl. langs. So **millionaire** miljənɛə·ɹ. XIX. – F. *millionnaire* (XVIII); the F. form and the anglicized *millionary* have also been used.

milt milt A. spleen in mammals OE.; B. (perh. from Du.) soft roe. XV. OE. *milte* and *milt*, corr. to OFris. *milte*, MDu. *milte* (Du. *milt*) spleen, milt of fish, OHG. *milzi* n. (G. *milz* fem.), ON. *milti* :– CGerm. (exc. Gothic) **miltjaz*, **miltjōn*, perh. rel. to **meltan* MELT. ¶ The earlier name for male fish roe was *milk* XIV (so Du. *melk*, G. *milch*, Sw. *mjölke*), the resemblance to which may have assisted the transference of meaning.

mime maim jester, buffoon; farcical drama of the Greeks and Romans. XVII. – L. *mīmus* –Gr. *mîmos* imitator, actor. Cf. F. *mime*, Sp., It. *mimo*. Hence vb. XVII. So **mi·meo**GRAPH mi·miou- stencil device for multiplying manuscript or printed matter. 1889. irreg. f. Gr. *mīméomai* I imitate. **mimesis** maimī·sis imitation. XVI. – Gr., f. *mīmeîsthai*. **mimetic** maime·tik pert. to imitation or mimicry. XVII. – Gr. *mīmētikós*, f. *mīmeîsthai* imitate, f. *mîmos*. **mimi**C mi·mik pert. to a mime or buffoon; imitative; sb. burlesque performer; imitator XVI. – L. *mīmicus* – Gr. *mīmikós*, f. *mîmos*; cf. F. *mimique*, etc. Hence vb., **mi·mic**RY. XVII.

miminy-piminy mi·mini pi·mini overrefined. XIX. Phonetically symbolic; cf. contemp. NIMINY-PIMINY and dial. *mim* (XVII), imit. of pursing the lips.

mimosa mi-, maimou·sə, -ou·zə sensitive plant, Mimosa pudica, and its allies. XVIII. – modL. *mīmōsa* (Colin, 1619), app. f. L. *mīmus* MIME+-*ōsa*, fem. (sc. *herba, planta*) of -*ōsus* -OSE[1], and so named from its imitation of animal sensitiveness.

mina[1] mai·nə unit of weight in the Near East; ancient Greek money. XVI. – L. *mina* – Gr. *mnâ*.

mina[2] mai·nə Indian starling. XVIII. – Hindi *mainā*; vars. with *my-, mai-, -ah, -ar*.

minaret mi·nəret tall slender tower of a mosque. XVII. – F. *minaret* or Sp. *minarete*, It. *minaretto* – Turcized form of Arab. *manārat*, f. *nār* fire (cf. *manār* lighthouse).

minatory mi·nətəri threatening. XVI. – late L. *minātōrius*, f. *mināt-*, pp. stem of *minārī* MENACE; see -ORY[2].

mince mins cut up small XIV; †minimize, disparage; extenuate, moderate; talk, walk, etc., affectedly XVI. – OF. *mincier* :– Rom. **minūtiāre*, f. L. *minūtia* see MINUTIA; dial. vars. with *-ch, -sh* are – OF. dial. *minchier*. Hence sb. minced meat as a dish. XIX. ¶ *Mi·ncemeat, mi·nce-pie·* (both XVII) are for *minced meat, minced pie*.

mind maind memory (surviving in phr. *in m., to m., time out of m.*); thought, purpose, intention; mental faculty. XII. Early ME. *mind(e)*, with dial. vars. *münd(e), mend(e)*, later *meende*; aphetic of *imünd*, etc. :– OE. *ġemynd*, corr. to OHG. *gimunt*, Goth. *gamunds* memory :– Germ. **gamunðiz*, f. **ga-* Y-+**mun-*, weak grade of the series **men-* **man-* **mun-* :– IE. **men-* **mon-* **mn-* revolve in the mind, think. Other Germ. derivs. are: OFris. *minne*, OS. *minnea*, OHG. *minna* (G. *minne*) love; ON. *minni*, Goth. *gaminþi* memory (:– **gamenþjam*); OE. *manian* remind, exhort, advise, *ġe|munan* (present *ġeman*) remember, OS. *far|munan* deny, despise, Goth. *munan* (present *man*) think, believe, *muns* thought, OE. *myne* (:– **muniz*) memory, desire, love. Hence **mind** vb. REMIND; remember, give heed to XIV; (dial.) perceive, notice XV; contemplate XVI; be careful about XVIII. ¶ The IE. base was very prolific; many derivs. are given in the articles AUTOMATON, COMMENT, DEMENTIA, MANIA, MATHESIS, MEMENTO, MEMORY, MENTAL, MENTION, MENTOR, MNEMONIC, MONITION, REMEMBER, REMINISCENT.

mine[1] main poss. adj., of or pert. to ME. OE. *mīn* = OFris., OS., OHG. *mīn* (Du. *mijn*, G. *mein*), ON. *minn*, Goth. *meins* :– CGerm. **mīnaz*, f. IE. locative **meị* of *me* ME + adj. suffix **-no-* (cf. THINE, SWAIN). A case-form of this adj., OE. *mīn*, etc., Goth. *meina* (cf. OSl. *mene*, Lith. *manę* for **menę*, OPers. *manā*), was used as the genitive of I; in Eng. this did not survive the OE. period. In XIII the final *n* of the adj. was already dropped before a cons. in southern and midland Eng.; but it was retained in the north, and survived till XV in Sc. See MY.

mine[2] main dig in the earth for ore, coal, etc. XIII. – (O)F. *miner* = Pr., Sp. *minar*, It. *minare*, perh. orig. Gallo-Rom. deriv. of a Celtic word repr. by Ir., Gaelic *mein* ore, mine, W. *mwyn* ore, †mine. So (or hence) **mine** sb. excavation for mining XIV (R. Mannyng); †mineral, ore XIV (Maund.); so (O)F. *mine* = Pr. *mina, mena* (whence It., Sp. *mina*), medL. *mina*. **mi·n**ER[2] maker of underground mines XIII; excavator for mineral XIV; after OF. *mineor* (mod. *mineur*) = Pr. *minador*. ¶ Has become CEur. esp.

through the use of subterranean methods in warfare (cf. UNDERMINE).

mineral mi·nərəl substance obtained by mining. XV (Lydg.). – OF. *mineral* or medL. *minerāle*, sb. use of n. sg. of *minerālis*, f. *minera* ore – OF. *miniere* mine = Pr. *meniera*, It. *miniera* :– Rom. **minãria* (in AL. XIII), f. **mina*, **mināre* MINE[2]; see -AL[1]. So **mi·neral** adj. XVI. – F. or medL. **mineraLOGY** -æ·lədʒi. science of minerals XVII (Boyle). – modL., of irreg. formation; so **minera·LOGIST.** XVII (Sir T. Browne).

mingle mi·ŋgl mix so as to unite or combine. XIV (*mengel*). f. ME. *meng, ming* mix – ON. *menga* = OE. *mengan*, OFris. *mengja*, (O)HG. *mengen* :– **maŋgjan* (cf. AMONG) + -LE[3], perh. suggested by (M)Du. *mengelen*. Hence **mi·ngle-ma·ngle.** XVI.

miniature mi·nĭtʃəɹ, mi·niətjuəɹ reduced image, small representation XVI; †illumination in manuscripts XVII; portrait on a small scale XVIII; adj. XVIII. – It. *miniatura* – medL. *miniātūra*, f. *miniāre* rubricate, illuminate, f. L. *minium* native cinnabar, red lead, acc. to Propertius of Sp. origin. In the development of the sense 'small portrait' there has prob. been assoc. with the L. stem *min-* (see MINOR); cf. *facies minutæ* (Juvenal XIV 291) of the heads on coins. So **mi·niaturIZE** render minute XX; **mi:niaturizA·TION** XX.

minify mi·nifai diminish in estimated size, etc. XVII. irreg. f. L. *minor* less, *minimus* least (see MINOR, MINIM), after MAGNIFY.

minikin mi·nikin (dial.) playful term for a female XVI; diminutive thing XVIII; adj. dainty, mincing, diminutive XVI. – Du. *minneken*, f. *minne* love (cf. MIND) + *-ken* -KIN.

minim mi·nim A. (mus.) note half the value of a semibreve XV; B. friar of the Ordo Minimorum Eremitarum; C. thing of the least size or importance XVI; single down stroke of the pen XVII. – medL. ellipt. or absol. uses of L. *minimus, -a, -um* least; see MINOR. So **mi·nimIZE.** XIX (Bentham). **mi·nimum** †atom; least amount attainable, etc. XVII; lowest or least value, etc. XVIII. – L., n. of *minimus* used sb. **mi·nimAL**[1] extremely minute XVII.

minion mi·njən †lover, lady-love XVI (Dunbar); favourite (G. Douglas); printing type (cf. F. *mignonne*) XVII. – F. *mignon* (XV), which repl. OF. *mignot*, f. Gaul. **mīno* (cf. OIr. *min* tender, soft) or Gaul. **mino* (cf. OIr. *min* small) + dim. suffix *-ottus*. Cf. MIGNONETTE.

minish mi·niʃ (arch.) lessen, reduce. XIV. – (with assim. to -ISH[2]) OF. *menu(i)sier* = Pr. *menuzar*, It. *minuzzare* :– Rom. **minūtiāre*, f. *minūtus* MINUTE; cf. MINCE, DIMINISH.

minister mi·nistəɹ †servant, subordinate officer XIII; one engaged in the celebration of worship or officially charged with spiritual functions XIV; officer of state XVII. – (O)F. *ministre* – L. *minister* servant, f. **minis-*, var. of *minus* less, adv. of *minor* MINOR, in formation parallel to the correl. *magister* MASTER. So **mi·nister** vb. (arch.) serve, supply, ADMINISTER. XIV. – (O)F. *ministrer* – L. *ministrāre*. **ministerIAL** -tiə·riəl pert. to or characteristic of a minister or ministry. XVI. – F. *ministériel* or late L. *ministeriālis*, f. *ministerium*, but consciously referred to *minister* and *ministry*. **ministrA·TION.** XIV (Rolle). – OF. or L. **mi·nistRY** rendering of service; function of a minister of religion XIV (Wycl. Bible); body of ministers XVI (in politics XVIII). – L. *ministerium* (cf. MISTER[1]).

miniver mi·nivəɹ fur of uncertain identity used for lining and trimming (since *c.*1900 applied to the ceremonial costume of peers). XIII. ME. *meniver, menuver* (the forms with *min-, myn-* date from XV) – AN. *menuver*, (O)F. *menu vair*, i.e. *menu* little (:– L. *minūtus* MINUTE), *vair* variegated fur (:– L. *varius* VARIOUS). *Pured m., m. pure* repr. AN. *meniver puré* powdered miniver, but the pp. has been misinterpreted as 'pure white'.

mink miŋk skin or fur of stoat-like animals of the genus Putorius XV; the animal itself XVII. Early forms *menks, mynkes* (XV–XVI); prob. from the area of the Baltic Sea as the waterway for trading in furs; cf. Sw. *menk, mänk* mink, LG. *mink* otter.

minnesinger mi·nisiŋəɹ German lyric poet of XII–XIV, whose chief theme was love. XIX. G., f. *minne* love (see MIND) + *singer* SINGER.

minnow mi·nou small freshwater fish, Leuciscus phoxinus. XV. Early form *menow*, later *minew* (XVI), perh. orig. repr. OE. **mynwe* (beside recorded OE. *myne* 'capito', 'mena') = OHG. *muniwa* 'capedo' (i.e. L. *capito*), but infl. by ME. *menuse, menise* – OF. *menuise* :– Rom. **minūtia* n.pl. small objects (cf. MINUTIÆ).

minor mai·nəɹ less, smaller; applied first to Franciscan friars (*friars minor*, †*minors*) XIII; from XIV in various techn. uses, the earliest being in logic. – OF. *menour* (:– L. *minōrem*) in *freres menours* (medL. *fratres minores*); in other uses – L. *minor*, which functions as compar. of *parvus* small, and is rel. to *minuere* lessen, Gr. *minúthein*, and *méīōn* less. So **mi·norESS**[1] nun of the second order of St. Francis. XIV. – OF. *menouresse*; a house of the order gave its name to *The Minories* in the City of London. **minorITY** maino·riti. XVI. – F. or medL. ¶ Formations on the same base are COMMINUTE, DIMINISH, DIMINUTION, MINIM, MINISTER, MINUS, MINUSCULE, MINUTE.

minorca minɔ̄·ɹkə black variety of domestic fowl named after *Minorca*, one of the Balearic islands.

Minotaur mi·nŏtɔ̄əɹ fabulous monster confined in the Cretan labyrinth. XIV (Ch., Gower). – OF. *Minotaur* (now *-taure*) – L. *Minotaurus* – Gr. *Minṓtauros*, f. *Mínōs* Minos, king of Crete, whose wife Pasiphae was the mother of the Minotaur + *taûros* bull (cf. STEER[1]).

minster mi·nstəɹ †monastery; church originating in a monastic establishment; large church. OE. *mynster* = OHG. *munistri* (G. *münster*), MDu. *monster*, ON. *mustari* – popL. **monisterium* (whence (O)F. *moutier*, and adoptions in Celtic and Slav.) for ecclL. *monastērium* MONASTERY.

minstrel mi·nstrəl professional entertainer (*menestraus* pl., AncrR.) professional reciter of poetry, esp. with the accompaniment of music (in mod. revived use as F. *ménestrel*). XIII (RGlouc.). ME. *menestral, ministral, -el, men-, minstral, -el* – OF. *menestral, -(e)rel, mini-*, entertainer, handicraftsman, servant – Pr. *menest(ai)ral* officer, attendant, employed person, musician – late L. *ministeriāl-is* official, officer, f. *ministerium* MYSTERY², MÉTIER; see -AL¹. So **mi·nstrelsy** art of a minstrel; body of minstrels XIV; minstrel poetry XIX (Scott). – OF. *menestralsie.*

mint¹ mint †coin OE.; place where money is coined XV. OE. *mynet*, corr. (with variation of gender) to OFris. *menote, munte*, OS. *munita* (Du. *munt*), OHG. *munizza, muniz* (G. *münze*) – WGerm. **munita* (ON, etc. *mynt* is from LG.) – L. *monēta*; see MONEY. Hence **mint** vb. coin XVI; not continuous with OE. *mynetian* = OHG. *munizōn* (G. *münzen*). **mi·nt**AGE. XVI.

mint² mint aromatic labiate plant, Mentha (esp. Mentha viridis). OE. *minte* = OHG. *minza* (G. *minze*) :– WGerm. **minta* – L. *menta, mentha* – Gr. *minthē* (also *minthos*), prob. of Mediterranean origin. ¶ There was also an unexpl. var. WGerm. **muntja*, repr. by MDu. *munte* (Du. *munt*), OHG. *munza* (G. *münze*). ME. *mente* was prob. due to OF. *mente* (now *menthe*) or to MDu. *mente.*

minuet minjue·t, (formerly) mi·njuet stately dance in triple time. XVII. – F., sb. use of adj. *menuet* small, fine, delicate, dim. of *menu* MINUTE², but infl. in form and pronunc. by It. *minuetto* (itself – F.); see -ET.

minus mai·nəs less (a certain quantity); (math.) verbal rendering of the sign –. XV. L. 'less', n. of *minor* (see MINOR) used as adv. The prepositional use (e.g. *four minus three*) appears to have arisen in the commercial arithmetic of the Middle Ages; *minus* is first found in German (XV) as the name of the sign –; It. *meno* is found earlier (XIV) as prep., and Leonardo of Pisa (XIII) uses *plus* and *minus* to denote the excess and deficiency in certain results.

minuscule minʌ·skjūl †(of a letter) small, not capital; (palæogr.))(capital or uncial. XVIII. – F. *minuscule* – L. *minuscula* (sc. *littera* letter), fem. of *minusculus* rather less, dim. of **minwos*, MINOR.

minute¹ mi·nit A. 60th part of an hour or a degree XIV (PPl., Ch.); B. rough draft, memorandum XVI. – (O)F. *minute* (whence also G. *minute*, Du. *minuut*) – late L. sb. use of L. *minūta*, fem. of *minūtus* MINUTE². Sense A rests ult. on medL. *pars minuta prima* 'first minute part', the $\frac{1}{60}$ of a unit in the (Babylonian) system of sexagesimal fractions (cf. SECOND¹ sb.); the system was employed by Ptolemy (A.D. II) to the degrees of the circle, to the 60 sections into which he divided the radius, and to the division of the day; the application to the division of the hour was later. Sense B depends (perh. through F.) on the mediæval use of L. *minūta* (in AL. XIV), which may be for *minuta scriptura* draft in small writing as dist. from the engrossed copy. Hence **minute** mi·nit vb. XVII.

minute² mainjū·t, minjū·t †chopped small XV; †lesser XVI; very small; very precise XVII. – L. *minūtus* (whence F. *menu*; see MENU), pp. of *minuere* lessen, diminish (see MINOR).

minutia, usu. pl. **minutiæ** mai-, minjū·ʃiī very small matters. XVIII. – late L. *minūtia*, pl. *-iæ*, f. *minūtus* MINUTE²; see -Y³.

minx miŋks †pet dog; pert young woman. XVI. Of unkn. origin; deriv. from a form resembling LG. *minske* has been suggested (cf. G. *mensch* wench, hussy; see MAN).

miocene see EOCENE.

miracle mi·rəkl marvellous event to be ascribed to supernatural intervention XII (Peterb. Chron.); wonderful thing; mediæval play based on the life of Christ or the saints XIV. – (O)F. *miracle* (= Pr. *miracle*, Sp. *milagro*, It. *miracolo*) – L. *mīrāculum* object of wonder, f. *mīrārī, -āre* wonder, look at (cf. ADMIRE), f. *mīrus* wonderful, dubiously connected with SMILE. So **miraculous** mĭræ·kjŭləs. XVI. – (O)F. or medL. (*-ōsus*).

mirage mirā·ʒ optical illusion produced by atmospheric conditions involving reflection. XIX. – F. *mirage*, f. *mirer* refl. look at oneself in a mirror – L. *mīrāre*; see prec., -AGE.

mire maiəɹ †swamp, bog; mud. XIV. ME. *müre, myre* – ON. *mýrr* :– **miuzjō* :– **meusjā*, f. Germ. **meus-* **mus-* MOSS.

mirk see MURK.

mirror mi·rəɹ polished surface to reflect images. XIII. ME. *mirour* – OF. *mirour* (mod. *miroir*, from var. *mirēoir*) = Pr. *mirador* mirror, Sp. *mirador* watch-tower, It. *miratore* mirror :– Rom. **mīrātōrium*, f. **mirāt-*, **mirāre* look at, (in pre-classical L.) wonder (L. *mīrārī*; see MIRACLE); from XVI the sp. was modelled on words in -OR².

mirth mɔ̄ɹþ joy, happiness OE.; rejoicing, gaiety XIII; gaiety of mind; diversion, sport XIV. OE. *myr(i)ġþ* (cf. MDu. *merchte*) :– Germ. **murgiþō*, f. **murgjaz* MERRY; see -TH¹.

mirza mə̄·ɹză royal prince; title of honour. XVII. – Pers. *mīrzā*, for *mīrzād*, f. *mīr* prince (– Arab. *amīr* AMEER, EMIR)+*zād* born.

mis-[1] mis OE. *mis-* (ME. *misse-*, *mysse-*, *mys-*, *mes-*) = OFris., OS. *mis-*, OHG. *missa-*, *missi-*, *misse-*, *mes-* (Du. *mis-*, G. *miss-*), ON. *mis-*, Goth. *missa-* (as in *missadeþs* misdeed) :– CGerm. **missa-* (whence **missjan* MISS[1] vb.), meaning predominantly 'amiss', 'wrong(ly)', 'improper(ly)', which is the only sense recognized in new formations, but in OE. there are also exx. of a negative and of a pejorative intensive use. Cf. next.

mis-[2] mis in a few comps. adopted from French, repr. OF. *mes-* (mod. *més-*, *mes-*, *mé-*) = Pr. *me(n)s-*, *menes-*, Sp., Pg. *menos-*, OIt. *menes-*, *minis-*, It. *mis-* :– Rom. **minus-*, a use of L. *minus* (see MINUS) in the senses 'bad(ly)', 'wrong(ly)', 'amiss', 'ill-', and with negative force; at first *mes-*, later assim. to MIS-[1], with which it is broadly synon.

misadventure misədve·ntʃəɹ ill-luck XIII; (leg.) homicide committed accidentally in the course of a lawful act XVI. ME. *misaventure* – OF. *mesaventure*, f. *mesavenir* turn out badly (f. *mes-* MIS-[2]+*avenir* :– L. *advenīre*; cf. ADVENT), after *aventure* ADVENTURE.

misalliance misəlai·əns see MÉSALLIANCE.

misanthrope mi·sənþroup hater of mankind. XVII (earlier in L. or Gr. form XVI). – F. *misanthrope* (Rabelais), modL. *mīsanthrōpus*, Gr. *mīsánthrōpos*, f. *mīs(o)-*, comb. form of base of *mīseîn* hate, *mîsos* hatred+*ánthrōpos* man. So **misanthropy**[3] misæ·nþrəpi. XVII. – F. or modL. – Gr.

misCALL miskɔ̄·l misname XIV; (dial.) revile XV. MIS-[1].

miscarry miskæ·ri †go astray; †come to harm XIV; be prematurely delivered XVI; go wrong, fail XVII (Sh.). – OF. *mescarier*; see MIS-[2], CARRY. Hence **mis**CA·RRIAGE †misconduct; mismanagement; untimely delivery; failure to arrive. XVII.

miscegenation mi:sĭdʒĭnei·ʃən mixture of races. orig. U.S. (said to have been copyrighted in 1863 by D. G. Croly, of New York), irreg. f. L. *miscēre* MIX+GENUS race+-ATION.

miscellaneous misəlei·niəs of mixed character. XVII. f. L. *miscellāneus*, f. *miscellus* mixed, f. *miscēre* MIX; see -ANEOUS. A somewhat earlier adoption was †*miscellane*. So **miscellany** mi·səlǝni, mise·ləni mixture, medley; collection of miscellaneous literary items. XVI. – (with assim. to -Y[3]) F. *miscellanées* fem. pl., or L. *miscellānea* n. pl. (which has been in Eng. use since XVI).

mischance mistʃà·ns ill-luck, calamity. XIII. – OF. *mesch(e)ance* (= Pr. *mescazensa*), f. *mescheoir*; see MIS-[2], CHANCE.

mischief mi·stʃif †misfortune, distress XIII (Cursor M.); harm, injury XIV; cause of harm XVI; conduct causing petty trouble, playful maliciousness XVIII. – OF. *meschief*, *meschef* (mod. *méchef*), f. *meschever* (= Pr. *mescabar*) meet with misfortune (whence **mischie·ve.** XIV), f. *mes-* MIS-[2]+*chever* 'come to a head', happen :– Rom. **capāre*, f. **capum*, L. *caput* head. So **mischievous** mi·stʃĭvəs †unfortunate XIV; harmful XV; disposed to acts of playful malice XVII. – AN. *meschevous*, f. OF. *meschever*. Cf. CHIEF, ACHIEVE.

miscreant mi·skriənt †heretical, infidel XIV; villainous XVI; also sb. with like dates. – OF. *mescreant* (mod. *mécréant*) misbelieving, unbelieving, prp. of *mescroire* (mod. *mécroire*) disbelieve, f. *mes-* MIS-[2]+*croire* :– L. *crēdere*; see CREDIT, -ANT.

misdeed misdī·d evil deed, crime. OE. *misdǣd* = OHG. *missitāt*, Goth. *missadēþs*; see MIS-[1], DEED.

misdemeanour misdĭmī·nəɹ (arch.) misconduct; (leg.) offence less heinous than a felony. XV. MIS-[1]. Hence **misdemea·n**ANT one convicted of a misdemeanour. 1819; repl. †*misdemeanour*, which was in prison use earlier.

misdoubt misdau·t (dial., arch.) have doubts about, be suspicious of. XVI. MIS-[1].

mise mīz, maiz †pl. expenses XV; payment made to secure a liberty XV; (leg.) issue in a writ of right XVI. – OF. *mise* action of setting, expenses, wager, arbitration (whence medL. *misa*, *misia*), f. *mis*, pp. of *mettre* place, set :– L. *mittere* (see MISSION).

miser mai·zəɹ A. †wretch; B. avaricious person. XVI. – L. *miser* wretched, unfortunate. So **miser**ABLE mi·zərəbl A. wretched XVI (Dunbar); B. †miserly XV (Caxton). – (O)F. *misérable* – L. *miserābilis* pitiable, f. *miserārī* be pitiful, f. *miser*. ¶ It., Sp., Pg. *misero* has both senses. Hence **mi·ser**LY[1]. XVI. **miserere** mizəriə·ri fifty-first (fiftieth) psalm, beginning Miserere mei Deus 'Have mercy upon me, O God' XIII; prayer for mercy; †'iliac passion' (strangulated hernia) XVII; misericord (seat) XVIII. imper. sg. of L. *miserērī* have pity, f. *miser*; the last sense is a misuse. **misericord** mize·rikɔ̄ɹd †pity, mercy XIV; dagger for giving the coup de grâce XV; choir seat giving support to one standing XVI. – (O)F. *miséricorde* – L. *misericordia*, f. *misericors* pitiful, f. *miseri-*, stem of *miserērī*+*cord-*, *cor* HEART. **misery**[3] mi·zəri wretchedness of external conditions XIV (Ch.); extreme unhappiness XVI (Coverdale); †miserliness XVI. – AN. **miserie*, for (O)F. *misère*, or – L. *miseria*, f. *miser*.

misfeasance misfī·zəns (leg.) transgression, trespass. XVI (Bacon). – OF. *mesfaisance*, f. prp. of *mesfaire* (mod. *méfaire*), f. *mes-* MIS-[2]+*faire* :– L. *facere* DO[1]; see -ANCE.

misFO·RTUNE bad fortune, ill luck. XV. MIS-[1]; as †vb. XV.

misgive misgi·v A. (of the heart, mind) suggest doubt or foreboding; B. (dial.) fail, miscarry. XVI. f. MIS-¹+GIVE (in A with the ME. sense of 'suggest', in B with meaning as in *give out, give over*).

mishap mishæ·p †ill luck; unlucky accident. XIV (R. Mannyng, Ch.). f. MIS-¹+HAP, prob. after OF. *mescheance* MISCHANCE.

mish-mash mi·ʃmæʃ medley, hodge-podge. XV (*mysse masche*). redupl. of MASH, with variation of vowel.

mishna(h) mi·ʃna collection of *halakhoth* (legal decisions) forming the basis of the Talmud. XVII. – post-biblical Heb. *mishnāʰ* repetition, instruction, f. *shānaʰ* repeat, teach or learn (oral tradition).

miskal mi·skəl Arabian money of account. XVI. ult. – Arab. *misqāl*, local var. of *miþqāl*, f. *þaqala* weigh. The earliest forms *mitigal, mitical* came through Sp. and Pg.

mislike mislai·k (chiefly literary or dial.) not to like OE.; see DISLIKE. Hence **misli·ke** sb. †displeasure XIII; (rare) want of affection, dislike. XVI.

misnomer misnou·məɹ (leg.) mistake in naming XV; use of a wrong name XVII. – AN., sb. use of OF. *mesnom(m)er*, f. *mes-* MIS-²+*nommer* :– L. *nōmināre*; see NOMINATE, -ER⁵.

misogynist mai-, misɔ·dʒinist woman-hater. XVII. f. Gr. *mīsogúnēs*, f. *mīso-*, comb. form of *mīseîn* hate, *mîsos* hatred+*gunḗ* woman (see QUEAN); see -IST.

misprision mispri·ʒən (leg.) wrongful action or omission XV (*m. of treason* or *felony* XVI; often taken to mean 'failure to denounce'); (arch.) misunderstanding, mistake XVI (Sh.). – AN. *mesprisioun* = OF. *mesprison* error, wrong action or speech, f. *mesprendre* (mod. *méprendre*), f. *mes-* MIS-²+*prendre* take (see PRISON).

misprize misprai·z (arch.) despise. XV (Caxton). – OF. *mesprisier* (mod. *mépriser*), f. *mes-* MIS-²+*priser* PRIZE². Hence **mispri·sion** mispri·ʒən contempt. XVI.

misrule misrū·l †disorderly conduct; bad government. XIV (*Lord, Abbot of M.* XV). f. MIS-¹+RULE.

miss¹ mis A. fail to hit or reach OE.; fail to attain XIII; B. discover the absence of XII (Orm.); C. omit XVI. OE. *missan* = OFris. *missa*, (M)LG., (M)Du. *missen*, (O)HG. *missen*, ON. *missa* :– CGerm. (exc. Gothic) **missjan*, f. **misso-* (cf. MIS-¹, AMISS), ppl. formation with *-*to-* on an IE. base **mith-*, repr. by Skr. *mithás*, OSl. *mitě* alternating, cogn. with Skr. *mḗthati* alternates, L. *mūtāre* (see MUTATION), Goth. *maidjan* falsify. So **miss** sb. OE. *miss* loss, corr. to MLG., MHG. *misse* (Du. *mis*), ON. *missa, -ir*.

miss² mis (dial.) kept mistress; title prefixed to the name of an unmarried woman. XVII. Clipped form of MISTRESS; cf. *mass, mess, mus* (from XVI), shortening of *master*, now dial. (*misses and masses* occurs XVIII); cf. MISSIS. Hence **mi·ssy**⁶. XVII.

missal mi·səl mass-book. XIV (*messel*). – medL. *missāle* (whence OF. *messel*, mod. *missel*, the source of some early Eng. instances), use of n. sing. of *missālis* pert. to the Mass, f. *missa* MASS¹; see -AL¹.

missel-thrush mi·səlþrʌʃ thrush (Turdus viscivorus) that feeds on mistletoe berries. XVIII (Goldsmith). Earlier *missel-bird* (XVII, Bacon); f. †*missel* mistletoe, OE. *mistel* = OHG. *mistil* (G. *mistel*), Du. *mistel*, ON. *mistil-*, of unkn. origin.

missile mi·sail adapted for throwing; sb. missile weapon. XVII. – L. *missilis* (n. sg. *missile* as sb.), f. *miss-*; see next and -ILE.

mission mi·ʃən †sending, esp. abroad XVI; sending forth on a service (spec. Mission of the Holy Ghost) or with authority; body of persons sent; commission, errand XVII; establishment of missionaries XVIII; personal duty or vocation XIX; operational sortie XX. – F. *mission* or L. *missiō(n-)*, f. *miss-*, pp. stem of *mittere* let go, send; see -ION. So **mi·ssionARY**. XVII. – modL. *missiōnārius*, whence also F. *missionnaire* (XVII). ¶ For other reprs. of the base see *admit, commit, emit, intermit, omit, permit, submit, transmit*, with corr. nouns of action, etc.; *compromise, demise, promise*; *missile, missive*; MASS¹, MESS¹.

missis, missus mi·siz, -is (illiterate) *the m.*, one's wife; servant's mistress. XIX. Slurred pronunc. of MISTRESS; mi·siz is now the oral equiv. of MRS.

missive mi·siv *letter m.*, (orig. tech.) letter sent by a superior authority XV; †missile XVI; sb. letter (esp. and orig. official), in early use mainly Sc. XVI. – medL. *missīvus* (in *litteræ missivæ*), f. *miss-* (see MISSION)+-*īvus* -IVE. Cf. F. *missive* (XVI) in *lettre missive*; Sp. *letra* and *carta misiva*, etc.

mist mist vapour of water; dimness, obscurity. OE. *mist* = (M)LG., (M)Du. *mist*, Icel. *mistur*, Norw. dial., Sw. *mist* :– Germ. **miχstaz*, f. **mīg-* (cf. Du. *miggelen*, WFris. *miggelje* drizzle) :– IE. **migh-* **meigh-*, as in Gr. *o|míkhlē*, OSl. *mĭgla*, Arm. *mēg*, Av. *maēγa*, Skr. *míh, mēghás* cloud, mist. Hence **mi·sty**¹. OE.

mistake mistei·k †err, transgress XIII (Cursor M.); †take wrongly XIV; misunderstand XV; make a mistake XVI. In earliest use north. – ON. *mistaka* take in error, refl. miscarry (Sw. *misstaga* be mistaken), f. *mis-* MIS-¹+*taka* TAKE. Cf. OF. *mesprendre* (mod. *se méprendre*), which has prob. infl. the meaning. Hence **mista·ke** sb. XVII. **mista·ken** †wrongly supposed XVI; of wrong opinion XVII.

mister¹ mi·stəɹ (obs. exc. arch. and dial.) handicraft, employment; (*this, what*) kind of; office, duty; need, necessity. XIII. – AN. *mester*, OF. *mestier* (mod. MÉTIER) = Pr. *meistier*, Sp. *mestiere* (It. *mestiere*, from F. or Pr.) :– Rom. **misterium*, for L. *ministerium*, see MYSTERY².

mister[2] mi·ster title of courtesy for a man, MR. XVI. Weakened form of MASTER originating from reduced stress in proclitic use; cf. MISTRESS.

mistletoe mi·zltou, mi·sl- parasitic plant Viscum album. OE. *misteltān* (= ON. *mistilteinn*), f. *mistel* mistletoe + *tān* twig (= Du. *teen* withe, OHG. *zein* rod, ON. *teinn* twig, spit, Goth. *tains* twig). The normal development of the OE. word (with obscuration of the final syll.) is repr. by forms such as †*miss-*, †*miscelden*; the current form descends from a var. with strong secondary stress on the final and the same development as in *tān*, late WS. *tā*, TOE.

mistral mi·strāl cold north-west wind of the Mediterranean. XVII. – F. *mistral* – Pr. *mistral* :– L. *magistrālis* MAGISTRAL, sc. *ventus* wind lit. 'master wind'; cf. Sp. *maestral* and *viento maestro*.

mistress mi·stris female correlative of 'master' XIV (Ch., Barbour, Wyclif); feminine title of courtesy; female paramour XV. Late ME. *maistresse* – OF. *maistresse* (mod. *maîtresse*), f. *maistre* MASTER[1] + *-esse* -ESS[1]. Forms in *mis-* (due to light stress) are recorded from XV; cf. MISTER[2]. See also MISS[2], MISSIS.

mi:sundersta·nd XII ('Vices and Virtues'); see MIS-[1]; so **mi:sundersta·nd**ING[1] mistake of meaning XV (Pecock); dissension XVII (Charles I); cf. G. *missverstehen*.

mite[1] mait minute insect; now spec. an acarid, and chiefly the cheese-mite. OE. *mīte* = MLG., MDu. *mīte* (Du. *mijt*), OHG. *mīʒa* gnat :– Germ. **mītōn* (whence F. *mite*), perh. to be referred to **mait-* (OHG. *meiʒan*, ON. *meita*, Goth. *maitan*) cut.

mite[2] mait Flemish coin of very small value; (hence) any small monetary unit; jot, whit XIV; very small object XVI. Recorded first in proverbial phr. 'not worth a mite', and consequently prob. in use long before our records – MLG., MDu. *mīte* (Du. *mijt*) :– Germ. **mītōn*, prob. identical with prec.

mithridatism mi·þrideitizm immunity against the effects of poisons, produced by the administration of gradually increasing doses of the poison itself. XIX. f. *Mithridates*, king of Pontus (d. 63 B.C.), who was said to have made himself immune against poisons by constant use of antidotes. So **mi·thridat**IZE. XIX (Lowell).

mitigate mi·tigeit appease; alleviate, lessen the violence or burden of. XV. f. pp. stem of L. *mītigāre*, f. *mītis* mild, gentle (cf. W. *mwydion* soft parts, Ir. *móith* tender); see -ATE[3]. So **mitig**A·TION. XIV (PPl.) – (O)F. or L.

mitosis maitou·sis division of the nucleus of a cell into minute threads. XIX. – modL., f. Gr. *mítos* thread; see -OSIS.

mitrailleuse mitrajō̆·z machine-gun. XIX (1870 in ref. to the Franco-Prussian war). F., fem. of *mitrailleur*, agent-noun f. *mitrailler*, f. *mitraille* small shot or projectile, in OF. small money, pieces of metal, alt. of *mitaille*, coll. dim. of *mite* MITE[2].

mitral mai·trəl pert. to a mitre XVII; of the left auriculo-ventricular valve of the heart, so called from its shape XVIII. – modL. *mitrālis*, L. *mitra* MITRE; see -AL[1]. So F.

mitre mai·təɹ ceremonial episcopal headdress in the Western Church XIV (Wyclif, Ch.); joint between boards meeting at right angles resembling the outline of a mitre XVII. – (O)F. *mitre* – L. *mitra* – Gr. *mítrā* girdle, belt, headband, turban, perh. of Asiatic origin. ¶ The application to episcopal headdress was suggested by its use in Vulg. and LXX for the Jewish high-priest's turban (Lev. xvi 4, Zech. iii 5).

mitten mi·tn glove-like covering for the hand with a separate division for the thumb only. XIV (Ch.). ME. *mytayne* – (O)F. *mitaine* = Pr. *mitana* (cf. medL. *mitan(n)a*) :– Rom. **medietāna* (sc. *muffula* 'skin-lined glove cut off at the middle', f. L. *medietās* half, MOIETY. Shortened to **mitt.** XVIII.

mittimus mi·timəs (leg.) warrant to the keeper of a prison to hold the person sent. XV. L., 'we send', the first word of the writ; 1st pers. pl. pres. ind. of *mittere* (see MISSION).

mix miks put together in union or combination (XV) XVI; intr. be mixed, associate *with* XVII. As infin. not earlier than the second quarter of XVI; back-formation from pp. *mixed*, var. of †*mixt* (XV in legal use) – (O)F. *mixte* (spec. in AN. law-phr. *accioun mixte* action partly real partly personal) – L. *mixtus*, pp. of *miscēre* mingle, mix, rel. to Gr. *mísgein* (**migsk-*), *mignúnai*, (aorist pass.) *emígēn*, Ir. *meascaim* mix, Lith. *mìšras*, Skr. *miśrás* mixed. ¶ Not repr. OE. *miscian* apportion, which did not survive; with OHG. *misgen*, *miskan* (MHG., MLG., G. *mischen*) this prob. belonged to a WGerm. adoption of L. *miscēre*.

mixen mi·ksən (dial., arch.) dunghill. OE. *mixen* :– **miχsinnja*, f. **miχsa-*, parallel to **miχstuz*, whence OS., OHG, G. *mist*, Goth. *maihstus* dung, f. **mĭg* make water (OE. *micge*, *migga* urine, OE. *mīgan*, LG. *mīgen*, ON. *míga* urinate); for other reprs. of IE. **meigh-* see MICTURITION and cf. OE. *meox*, *miox* dung, OS. *mehs* dunghill.

mixture mi·kstʃəɹ action, fact, or product of mixing. XV. First in techn. use – F. *mixture* (XVI in medicine) or its source L. *mixtūra*, f. *mixt-*, pp. stem of *miscēre*; see MIX and -TURE.

miz(z)en mi·zn (naut.) fore-and-aft sail set on the **mizen mast** (the aftermost mast of a three-masted ship). XV (*mesan*, *-eyn*, *-on*). – F. *misaine* (now, foresail, foremast) – It. *mezzana*, sb. use of fem. of *mezzano* middle; forms with *mi-*, *my-* appear in XVI.

mizzle[1] mi·zl drizzle. XV. orig. north. and eastern; prob. – LG. *miseln* = Du. dial. *miezelen*, WFlem. *mizzelen*, *mijzelen*, frequent. formation (see -LE[3]) on the LG. base found in Du. dial. *mies|regen* drizzle, *miezig*, LG. *misig* drizzling.

mizzle[2] mi·zl (sl.) decamp, be off. XVIII. Of unkn. origin.

mnemonic nīmɔ·nik intended to aid the memory; sb. pl. (after medL. n. pl. XVII) system of rules for this. XVIII. – medL. *mnēmonicus* – Gr. *mnēmonikós*, f. *mnēmon-*, *mnḗmōn* mindful, f. **mnā-* remember (see MIND). So **mnemo·n**ICAL. XVII.

mo mou (dial.; Sc. and north. *mae*) more. OE. *mā* = OFris. *mā(r)*, *mē(r)*, OS., OHG. *mēr* (MDu. *mee*, G. *mehr*), ON. *meir*, Goth. *mais* :– CGerm. **maiz* :– IE. **meis*, with compar. ending *-is* (cf. L. *magis* and see BETTER); cf. MORE, MOST. In OE. used as adv., sb., and adj. ('greater'); the use of *mā* with partitive g. pl., e.g. *mā manna* 'more of men', gave way to simple pl. concord, and the commoner use in later Eng. of adj. and sb. is with pl. reference.

moa mou·ə extinct flightless bird of N.Z. XIX. Maori.

moan moun complaint XIII; (with imit. suggestion) long low inarticulate murmur expressing pain XVII (Milton). ME. *mone*, repr. unrecorded OE. **mān* :– Germ. **main-*, whence **mainjan*, OE. *mǣnan*, ME. *mēne*, which was repl. by **moan** vb. complain (of), lament (for) XVI, from the sb.

moat mout ditch surrounding a town, castle, etc. XIV (PPl.); (dial.) pond, lake XV. ME. *mot(e)*, identical with †*mote* mound, embankment, with transference of sense as in *ditch*, *dike*, *dam*; – OF. *mote*, *motte* clod, hillock, mound, castle hill, castle (mod. *motte* clod, mound), whence MDu. *mote*, medL. *mot(t)a* mound, castle-hill, castle; the survival of apparent cognates in upper Italy, central France, and north Spain suggests a Gaulish origin.

mob[1] mɔb †strumpet; †négligé attire XVII; in full *mob-cap* women's indoor headgear XVIII. var. of *mab* slattern, loose woman (XVI), short for the female name *Mabel*.

mob[2] mɔb disorderly or promiscuous crowd; *the* common mass of people XVII; gang of thieves XIX. Shortening of earlier synon. †*mobile* (XVII), itself for L. *mobile vulgus* the excitable or fickle crowd (Statius, 'Silvæ' II ii 123, Claudian 'Panegyricus de quarto consulatu Honorii' 302); see MOBILE, VULGAR. Hence vb. throng, gather in a mob. XVIII. †**mobi·l**ITY mob. XVII (Dryden); after *nobility*. **mobo·**CRACY rule of the mob. XVIII. ¶ Noted by Swift among the vulgarisms for which he censures Burnet's 'History'; one of a group of shortened forms (as *cit*, *rep*, *pos*, *incog.*) in Addison's 'Spectator' No. 135 (1711).

mobile mou·bail, -·bil movable XV (Caxton); easily moved XIX. – (O)F. *mobile* – L. *mōbilis*, f. **mō-*, *movēre* MOVE; see -ILE. So **mobi·l**ITY. XV (Caxton). – (O)F. – L. **mobil**IZE mou·bilaiz render movable; prepare for active service. XIX. – F. *mobiliser*, f. *mobile*. **mo:biliz**A·TION. XIX. – F. *mobilisation*: earlier in the F. sense of 'conversion into personal property'.

mocassin mɔ·kəsin, mŏkæ·sin leather footgear worn by N.-Amer. Indians. XVII (Capt. Smith). – Powhatan *mo·ckasin*, Ojibwa *ma·kasin*; other dialects have the stress on the second syll., e.g. Narragansett *moku·ssin*, Micmac *mku·ssun*.

mocha, Mocha[1], mou·kə variety of chalcedony. XVII (*mocus*, *moc(h)o*). poss. the same word as next. ¶ G. *mokkastein*, F. *pierre de Mocha*, Sp. *piedra de moca* are prob. from Eng.

Mocha[2] mou·kə applied to fine coffee, orig. that produced in Yemen, in which *Mocha* (the port of shipment) is situated. XVIII. f. name of an Arabian port at the entrance of the Red Sea; cf. F. *moka*.

mock mɔk hold up to ridicule; act or speak in derision XV (*mokke*, *mocque*, *mok*). – OF. *mocquer* (mod. *moquer*, refl. with *de* laugh at) deride, jeer, corr. to Pr. *mocar* :– Rom. **moccāre*, f. **mok-*, repr. by It. dial. *moka* (used in phr. denoting derision), Sp. *mueca* grimace, Pg. *moca* derision. Hence sb. XV, adj. XVI. **mo·ck**ERY. XV (Lydg.). – F. **mo·ck-up** model XX.

mode moud. A. †tune, melody XIV; †mood in grammar and logic XVI; (mus.) form of scale; manner (spec. in philos.) XVII; B. fashion XVII. In A – L. *modus* measure, size, limit of quantity, manner, method, tune, f. IE. **mod-* **med-*; see METE. In B – F. *mode* fem. (with change of gender due to final *e*, retained now for the sense 'fashion', whence Sp., It. *moda*) – L. *modus*; cf. ALAMODE. Hence **mo·d**ISH[1] XVII, **mo·diste** dressmaker. XIX; F. ¶ The word has become CEur.

model mɔ·dl †architect's plans; design, make XVI; representation or figure in three dimensions; exemplar, pattern XVII. – F. †*modelle*, now *modèle* – It. *modello* :– Rom. **modellus*, for L. MODULUS. Hence vb. XVII; after F. *modeler*.

moderate mɔ·dərət avoiding extremes, of medium quantity or quality. XIV (Trevisa). – L. *moderātus* (whence F. *modéré*), pp. of *moderārī*, *moderāre* reduce, abate, control, f. **moder-* :– **modes-* (whence *modestus* MODEST), parallel with **modos*, *modus* MODE. So **moderate** mɔ·dəreit render less violent or intense XV; control, preside over XVI. f. pp. stem of L. *moderāre*, *-ārī*. See -ATE[2] and [3]. So **moder**A·TION XV; pl. in the univ. of Oxford, First Public Examination for B.A., conducted by Moderators. – F. – L. **mo·der**ATOR †ruler XIV (Trevisa); title of various presiding officials XVI. – L.

modern mɔ·dəɹn †now existing; pert. to or characteristic of present or recent times; †ordinary XVI. – (O)F. *moderne* (whence G. *modern*), corr. to Sp., It. *moderno*, or their source late L. *modernus* (VI), f. L. *modo* just now, after L. *hodiernus* of today (f. *hodiē* today). Hence **mo·dern**IST †person of modern times XVI; supporter of modern ways XVIII (Swift); (theol.) XX: after modL. *modernista* (Luther); cf. F. *moderniste* (Rousseau). In recent theol. use from the encyclical Pascendi gregis 'de modernistarum doctrinis' of Pope Pius X (8 Sept. 1907). So **mo·dern**ISM. XVIII (Swift). **mode·rn**ITY mədɔ̄·ɹnĭti. XVII. – medL. **mo·dern**IZE. XVIII. – F.

modest mɔ·dist †well-conducted; having a moderate estimate of oneself; chastely decorous XVI; not excessive XVII; unpretentious XVIII. – (O)F. *modeste* – L. *modestus* keeping due measure, f. **modes-* (see MODERATE)+*-*tos*, ppl. suffix. So **mo·desty**[3]. XVI. – (O)F. or L.

modicum mɔ·dikəm moderate amount. XV (Henryson). – L. *modicum* little way, short time, n. sg. of *modicus* moderate, f. *modus* (due or proper) measure, MODE.

modify mɔ·difai †limit, repress; moderate XIV; (Sc. law) assess award XV; †determine, differentiate XVII; change partially XVIII. – (O)F. *modifier* – L. *modificāre, -ārī*, f. *modus* MODE; see -FY. So **mo:di**FICA·TION. XVI. – (O)F. or L.

modillion moudi·ljən (archit.) projecting bracket in certain orders. XVI. – F. *modillon*, †*modiglion* – It. *modiglione* :– Rom. **mutellione*, f. **mutellus*, for L. *mutulus* MUTULE.

modulate mɔ·djŭleit †make melody XVI; regulate, adjust; attune XVII; pass from one key *to* another XVIII. f. pp. stem of *modulārī* measure, adjust to rhythm, make melody, f. *modulus* (dim. of *modus*) in Eng. use from XVI, and anglicized or – F. **mo·dule.** XVI; see -ATE[3]. So **modul**A·TION. XIV (Trevisa). – L.; so F.; for mus. senses cf. It. *modulare*, *-azione*.

Mœso-Gothic mīsougɔ·þik, -z- pert. to the Mœso-Goths or their language. XIX. – modL. *Mœsogothicus*, f. *Mœsogothī* f. *Mœsī* people of *Mœsia* (corr. to Bulgaria and Serbia)+pl. of *Gothus* GOTH.

mofussil mo(u)fʌ·sil in India, rural localities of a district. XVIII. – Hind. *mufaççil* – Arab. *mufaççal*, pp. of *faççala* divide, separate.

Mogul mou·gʌl, mougʌ·l Mongolian; *The* (*Great* or *Grand*) *M.*, the Emperor of Delhi XVI. – Arab., Pers. *muɣal, -ul*, pronunc. of MONGOL.

mohair mou·hɛəɹ fine camlet made from Angora goat's hair, (later) fabric imitating this. XVI (*mocayare, moochary, mockaire*). ult. – Arab. *mukhayyar* cloth of goat's hair, lit. 'select, choice', pp. of *khayyara* choose; but coming into Eng. through various channels (e.g. F. *moucayar*, It. *moccaiaro*) and later assim. to HAIR.

Mohammedan mouhæ·mĭdən pert. to *Mohammed* (lit. laudable); see MAHOMET, -AN. XVII.

Mohawk mou·hɔ̄k name of a tribe of N.-Amer. Indians of terrifying character XVII; step in skating XIX. Earlier †*Mohock*; Narraganset *Mohowauuck* 'they eat living things' is compared.

mohock mou·hɔk aristocratic street ruffian. XVIII. transf. use of prec.

moidore moi·dɔ̄əɹ Portuguese gold coin. XVIII (*moyodore*). – Pg. *moeda d'ouro* 'coin of gold' (*moeda* MONEY, *ouro* :– L. *aurum* gold).

moiety moi·ĭti half. XV (*moite, moitie*). – OF. *moité*, (also mod.) *moitié* = Pr. *meitat*, Sp. *mitad*, It. *metà* :– L. *medietātem, -tās*, f. *medius* middle, MID; see MEDIETY. The sp. with *-ety* (XVI) is due to latinization.

moil moil (dial., arch.) moisten, soil, bedaub XIV; toil, drudge (as in wet and mire) XVI. – OF. *moillier* wet, moisten, paddle in mud (mod. *mouiller*) :– Rom. **molliāre*, f. L. *mollis* soft (cf. MOLLIFY, EMOLLIENT).

moire mwāɹ, mwɔ̄ɹ, mɔ̄əɹ watered mohair, (later) watered silk. XVII (Pepys). – F. *moire*, later form of *mouaire*, MOHAIR. Also **moiré** mwā·rei, mɔ̄ə·ri watered. XIX. – F. *moiré*, pp. of *moirer* give a watered appearance to.

moist moist †new, fresh; †liquid, watery; slightly wet. XIV (Ch., Gower, Trevisa). – OF. *moiste* (mod. *moite*), perh. :– Rom. **muscidu-s* mouldy, (hence) wet, alt. of L. *mūcidus* (cf. MUCUS) by assoc. with *musteus* new, fresh, f. *mustum* MUST[2]. Hence **moi·st**EN[5] moi·sn; preceded by (dial.) **moist.** XIV (PPl., Wyclif, Trevisa). So **moist**URE. XIV (Ch., Trevisa). alt., by substitution of suffix, of OF. *moi(s)tour* (mod. *moiteur*), f. *moiste*. **moi·st**Y[1] new (of ale) XIV (Ch.); damp; extension of *moist*.

moither moi·ðəɹ worry, perplex XVII; be incoherent or wandering XIX. Of dial. and obscure origin.

mokaddam məkæ·dəm headman. XVII. Hind. – Arab. *muqaddam*, pp. of *qaddama* place in front.

moke mouk (sl., dial.) donkey. XIX. prob. derived from a proper name applied to the ass; cf. 'Mocke hath lost her shoe' (Skelton), where *Mocke* may be the name of a mare or donkey (cf. Skelton's 'mockyshe mare'). ¶ *Mokus* is recorded for Hampshire and Devon. Welsh Gypsy *moχīō* may be from Eng.

molar mou·ləɹ grinding (tooth). XVI. – L. *molāris* of a mill, sb. millstone, grinder tooth, f. *mola* millstone; see MEAL[1], MILL[1], and -AR; cf. F. *molaire* and AN. *dentz moellers*.

molasses məlæ·siz syrup obtained from sugar. XVI (*melasus, molassos, malassos*). – Pg. *melaço* = It. *melazzo* :– late L. *mellāceum* must, n. sg. of **mellāceus* (cf. -ACEOUS), f. *mell-*, *mel* honey (see MILDEW); a fem. form **mellācea* is repr. by Sp. *melaza*, F. *mélasse* (whence It. *melassa*).

mole[1] moul †discoloured spot (cf. IRON-MOULD) OE.; spot or blemish on the human skin (now spec.) XIV. OE. *māl*, corr. to MLG. *mēl*, OHG. *meil*, *meila*, Goth. **mail* (in g. pl. *maile*) :– Germ. **mailam*, **mailōn-*, whence also OE. *mǣlan*, OHG. *meilen* stain.

mole[2] moul small burrowing mammal of the family Talpidæ. XIV (Trevisa). Late ME. *molle, mulle, mole*, prob. – MDu. *mol*, *moll(e)*, (M)LG. *mol*, *mul*, repr. in an early L.-Frankish form *muli* pl. (Reichenau Glosses VII). ¶ Identical in form with OS., OHG. *mol*, (M)HG. *molch* (with suffix as in *habicht* hawk); both words may be in some way rel. to MOULD[1] (cf. MOULDWARP).

mole[3] moul A. (stone) pier or breakwater, (hence) harbour; B. †large mass XVI. – F. *môle* – MGr. *môlos*, *mólos* – L. *mōlēs* shapeless mass, huge bulk (whence sense B), dam, pier. ¶ Gr. *mólos* is also the source of It. *molo* (whence G. *molo*, *mole*), Cat. *moll* (whence Sp. *muelle*, Pg. *molhe*).

molecule mɔ·likjūl, mou·- minute particle of material substance. XVIII. – F. *molécule* (XVII) – modL. *mōlēcula*, dim. of L. *mōlēs* MOLE[3]. Hence **molecul**AR mŏle·kjŭləɹ. XIX; after *corpuscular*.

molest mŏle·st †vex, annoy XIV (Ch.); meddle with injuriously XV. – OF. *molester* or L. *molestāre* trouble, annoy, f. *molestus* troublesome, perh. rel. to *mōlēs* mass, MOLE[3]. So **molest**A·TION. XIV. – (O)F. – medL.

moll mɔl (sl.) prostitute, female paramour. XVII. Appellative use of *Moll*, var. of †*Mall*, pet-form of MARY; cf. MOLLY, MAWKIN. ¶ *Mall* or *Moll Cutpurse* was the familiar nickname of a notorious woman Mary Frith, in the first half of XVII.

mollify mɔ·lifai soften, soothe. XV (Hoccleve, Lydg.). – F. *mollifier* or L. *mollificāre*, f. *mollis* soft, rel. to *molere* grind; see MILL[1], -FY. So **mo·llific**A·TION. XIV (Ch.). – (O)F. – medL.

mollusc mɔ·ləsk one of the Mollusca. XVIII. – F. *mollusque*, f. modL. *mollusca* (XVII), n. pl. of L. *molluscus* soft (used in fem. sg. of a soft nut and in n. sg. of a fungus), f. *mollis* soft (see prec.). ¶ *Mollusca* was applied by Linnæus (1758) to a group of invertebrates forming the second order of the class Vermes.

molly mɔ·li (dial.) lass, wench; (sl.) milksop. XVIII (D'Urfey). f. MOLL + -Y[6]. Hence **mo·lly**-CO·DDLE sb. and vb. XIX.

Moloch mou·lɔk Canaanite idol to whom children were offered as burnt offerings (Lev. xviii 21), represented by Milton as one of the devils; hence transf. XVII. – late L. (Vulgate) *Moloch* – Gr. *Mólokh*, *Molókh* – Heb. *Mōlek*, held to be alt. of *Melek* (king), by substitution after the Captivity of the vowels of *bōsheth* shame.

molten mou·ltn pp. of MELT.

moly mou·li fabulous herb (Odyssey X 305) XVI; liliaceous genus Allium (A. moly, wild garlic) XVII. – L. *mōly* – Gr. *mȏlu*, rel. to Skr. *mūlam* root.

molybdenum mŏli·bdĭnəm (min.) metallic element (symbol Mo). XIX. f. †*molybdena* (XVII), former name of salts of m., use of L. – Gr. *molúbdaina* angler's plummet, f. *mólubdos* lead.

moment mou·mənt very brief portion of time XIV; †small particle XIV; importance, weight XVI; †motive of action XVII (Sh.). – (O)F. *moment* (= Sp., It. *momento*) – L. *mōmentum* (i) movement, moving power, (ii) importance, consequence, (iii) moment of time, particle :– **movimentum*, f. *movēre* MOVE; see -MENT. So **mo·ment**ARY. XVI (Tindale). – L.; in competition during XVI–XVII with derivs. of late L. *mōmentāneus*, viz. †*momentane* XVI after OF. †*momentain*; *momenta·neous* XVII and †*momentany* XVI (after F. *momentané*). Hence **mome·nt**OUS of moment. XVII. **momentum** mo(u)-me·ntəm product of mass of a body by its velocity. XVII. – L.; see prec.

Momus mou·məs L. – Gr. *Mȏmos* god of ridicule (*mȏmos*); transf. captious critic. XVI.

monachal mɔ·nəkəl monastic, monkish. XVI. – (O)F. *monacal* or ecclL. *monachālis*, f. *monachus* MONK; see -AL[1]. So **mo·nach**ISM monasticism. XVI; cf. F. *-isme*.

monad mɔ·næd the number one XVII; ultimate unit of being XVIII; simple organism, element, etc. XIX. – F. *monade* or its source late L. *monad-*, *monas* – Gr. *monás* unit, f. *mónos* alone, MONO-; see -AD[1].

monarch mɔ·nəɹk absolute ruler, (hence gen.) sovereign. XV (Lydg.). – (O)F. *monarque* or late L. *monarcha* – Gr. *monárkhēs*, more freq. *mónarkhos*, f. *mónos* alone (MONO-) + *-arkhos* ruling, *árkhein* rule (cf. ARCH-). So **monarch**AL[1] -ā·ɹk-. XVI, -IAL. XVI; -IC. XVII, -ICAL. XVI; cf. F. *-ique* – Gr. *monarkhikós*. **mo·narch**IST. XVII; cf. F. *-iste*. **mo·narch**Y[3]. XIV (Gower). – (O)F. – late L. – Gr.

monastery mɔ·nəstəri house for religious, esp. monks. XV. – ecclL. *monastērium* – ecclGr. *monastḗrion*, f. *monázein* live alone, f. *mónos* alone, MONO-. In early use also †*monaster* – (O)F. *monastère*. Cf. MINSTER. So **monast**IC mənæ·stik XVI (Sh.); an earlier use (by Pecock XV) of absolute government is erratic. – (O)F. *monastique* or late L. *monasticus* – Gr. *monastikós*, f. *monázein*. **mona·st**ICAL. XV.

monaul mɔnɔ̄·l Impeyan pheasant. XVIII (John Latham). – Hind. *munāl*, *monāl*.

Monday mʌ·ndi second day of the week. OE. *mōnandæġ*, corr. to OFris. *mōne(n)dei*, MLG., MDu. *mān(en)dach* (Du. *maandag*), OHG. *mānatag* (G. *Montag*), ON. *mánadagr*; f. MOON + DAY, tr. late L. *lūnæ diēs* 'day of the moon' (after Gr. *ἡμέρα Σελήνης*), of which the var. *lunis dies* gave OF. *lunsdis* (mod. *lundi*), It. *lunedì* (cf. Pr. *(di)luns*, Sp. *lunes*, Rum. *lunĭ*).

monde mɔ̃d *the* fashionable world. XVIII (Walpole). F., 'world' :- L. *mundu-s* (cf. MUNDANE). Cf. DEMI-MONDE.

monetary mʌ·nĭtəri pert. to coinage or currency (Bentham); pecuniary. XIX. - F. *monétaire* or late L. *monētārius*, f. L. *monēta* MINT[1]; see -ARY.

money mʌ·ni pl. *moneys*, *monies* mʌ·niz coin, cash, esp. in ref. to its purchasing power XIII (S.Eng. Leg.); particular coin or coinage XV. ME. *money(e)*, *-ei(e)*, *mone* - OF. *moneie* (mod. *monnaie* change) = Pr., Sp. *moneda*, Pg. *moeda* (cf. MOIDORE), It. *moneta* :- L. *monēta* mint (in Rome), money, orig. epithet of Juno, in whose temple (also so named) the mint was housed. The pl. *monies* used for sg. has been attributed to Jews since XVI (cf. Sh. 'Mer.V.' I iii 117) and their pronunc. of it rendered by *monish* mʌ·niʃ. So **moneyER**[2] mʌ·niəɹ †money-changer XIII (Cursor M.); †banker, capitalist XVIII; coiner, minter XV (Hoccleve). - OF. *mon(n)ier*, *-oier* (mod. *monnayeur*) :- late L. *monētāriu-s* minter.

mong mʌŋ in ME. XII (Orm) *mang*, *mong*, aphetic of *amang*, AMONG or †*imong*; from XVI (e.g. Sh.) poet. clipping of AMONG, and so written *'mong*. So **mongst** mʌŋst. XVI.

monger mʌ·ŋgəɹ dealer, trader; now used only in conscious analysis of words like *cheesemonger*, *fishmonger*, *ironmonger*, which, with *costermonger*, *scandal-monger*, *whoremonger*, are the commonest exx. OE. *mangere* (= OHG., ON. *mangari*) agent-noun of *mangian* (= OS. *mangōn*, ON. *manga*) :- Germ. **maŋgōjan*, f. L. *mangō* dealer, trader (who furbishes his wares), prob. f. Gr. *magganeúein* trick out; see -ER[1].

Mongol mɔ·ŋgəl pert. to (one of) a yellow-skinned straight-haired Asiatic type of mankind. XVIII. Said to be f. Mongolian *mong* brave. Also, person afflicted with mongolism XX. Hence **MongolIAN** mɔŋgou·liən XVIII. Cf. MOGUL.

mongoose, mungoose mɔ·ŋgūs, mʌ·ŋgūs ichneumon, common in India, Herpestes griseus. XVII. - Marathi *mangūs*. The form *mangoust* (- F. *mangouste* - Sp. *mangosta*) was to some extent current in Eng.

mongrel mʌ·ŋgrəl dog of mixed breed XV; in various transf. uses XVI. Early forms *meng-*, *mang-*, *m(o)ung-*, *mongrel(l)*, the variety of which suggests derivation, with pejorative *-(e)*REL (as in DOGGEREL, SCOUNDREL, WASTREL), from vars. of Germ. **maŋg-* **mong-* mix, MINGLE.

monial mou·niəl (archit.) mullion. XIV (*moinel*). - OF. *moinel* (mod. *meneau*), sb. use of *moi(e)nel* adj. middle, f. *moien* MEAN[3] + *-el* :- L. *-āli-s* -AL[1].

moniliform mɔni·lifɔːɹm necklace-shaped. XIX. - F. *moniliforme* or modL. *monīliformis*, f. *monīle* necklace; see MANE, -FORM.

monish mɔ·niʃ (arch. or obs.) ADMONISH. XIII (Cursor M.). Aphetic - OF. *amonester*.

monism mɔ·nizm doctrine of one (supreme) being; theory which denies the duality of matter and mind. XIX. - modL. *monismus*, f. Gr. *mónos* single; see MONO-, -ISM.

monition mŏni·ʃən warning. XIV. - (O)F. *monition* - L. *monitiō(n-)*, f. *monit-*, pp. stem of *monēre* advise, warn; see MIND, -ITION. So **moniTOR** mɔ·nitəɹ one who warns or advises; senior pupil in a school, etc. XVI; †backboard XVIII; species of lizard supposed to give warning of crocodiles XIX. - L. *monitor*, agent-noun; cf. F. *moniteur*. **mo·nitor** (poet.) to guide XIX; (var. techn. uses) control, regulate XX. f. the sb. **mo·nitORY**[2] warning, admonishing. XV. - L. *monitōrius*.

monk mʌŋk man devoted to the religious life in a community (in a monastery). OE. *munuc* = OFris. *munek*, OS. *munik* (Du. *monnik*), OHG. *munih* (G. *mönch*), ON. *múnkr*; CGerm. (except Gothic) - popL. **monicus*, for late L. *monachus* (cf. **monisterium* MINSTER) - late Gr. *mónakhos*, sb. use of adj. 'single, solitary', f. *mónos* alone (see MONO-); the word belongs, with *nun* and *minster*, to the earliest stratum of ChrL. words adopted in the Germ. langs. Though Gr. *mónakhos* is applied strictly to a solitary or hermit it was early transferred to cœnobites. From pop. L. **monicus* (Rom. **monio*) are derived OF. *monie*, (also mod.) *moine*, Pr. *monge* (whence Sp., Pg. *monge*); the word is CEur. Hence **mo·nkERY**, -ISH[1]. XVI. **mo·nksHOOD** Aconitum Napellus, etc., having hood-shaped flowers. XVI (Lyte, Gerarde). ¶ OE. fem. *mynećenu* nun (see -EN[1]), ME. *minchen*, survives in *Mincing* Lane, London, where there was a nunnery.

monkey mʌ·ŋki mammal of a group closely allied to man. Of unkn. origin; a poss. source has been suggested in a LG. **moneke*, dim. of Rom. **monno*, *-a*, repr. by F. †*monne*, It. *monna*, Sp., Pg. *mono*, *-a*, which has been referred to Turk. *maimun* ape.

mono- mɔ·no(u), -ŏ, mŏnɔ· comb. form of Gr. *mónos* alone, only, single, occurring in numerous words adopted from Gr. (many through late L. or medL.), but in recent times combined with words or stems of any origin, as *monocycle*, *monodrama*, *monomark*, *monoplane*, *monotint*, *monotype*, *monoxide*. The following are of early standing: **mo·noCHORD** one-stringed musical instrument, etc. XV. - (O)F. *monocorde* - late L. *monochordon* - Gr. *monókhordon*, sb. use of n. of *monókhordos* having a single string.

mo·noCHROME painting in different tints of one colour XVII (Evelyn); representation in one colour XIX; the earlier use – medL. *monochrōma*, evolved from Gr. (L.) *monokhrṓmatos* of one colour; later – F. *monochrome* – Gr. *monókhrōmos*. **mono·gamy**Y³ marriage with one person. XVII. – F. – ecclL. – Gr. (*gámos* marriage). **mo·no**GRAM A. †sketch without shading or colour; B. character composed of two or more letters interwoven XVII; in sense A – L. *monogrammus*, attributed by Cicero to Epicurus as descriptive of the gods, by Lucilius used sb. of an unsubstantial or colourless person, a mere shadow (resembling a picture in line only before colour is applied); in sense B – F. *monogramme* – late L. *monogramma*, f. Gr. **monógrammos*. **monograph** mɔ·nŏgràf (nat. hist.) separate treatise on a species, genus, etc.; (more widely) one on a single object or topic. XIX (1821); repl. earlier **mono·**GRAPHY. XVIII (Gilbert White) – modL. *monographia* (XVIII), f. *monographus* (Linnæus) writer of a treatise on a single genus or species; the form in -Y³ was discarded prob. because it suggested an abstract sense (cf. *telegraph* and *telegraphy*). **monolith** mɔ·nŏliþ single block, mass, pillar of stone. XIX. – F. *monolithe* – Gr. *monólithos* (see -LITE). **monologue** mɔ·nŏlɔg dramatic scene or composition in which a single actor speaks. XVII (Dryden). – F. *monologue* (XV), after *dialogue*; cf. late Gr. *monólogos* speaking alone. **mono**MANIA mɔnŏmei·niə madness on a single subject. XIX. – modL. *monomania*, after F. *monomanie*. **monophys**ITE mɔnɔ·fisait one who believes that there is only one nature in the person of Jesus Christ. XVII. – ecclL. *monophysīta* – ecclGr. *monophusī́tēs* (Gr. *phúsis* nature; see PHYSIC). So **mono·thel**ITE. XVI (earlier XV in corrupt forms *monacholite, monalechite*). – medL. *monothelīta* – (with assim. to *-īta*, -ITE) late Gr. *monotheletḗs*, f. *thélein* will. **mo·no**THEISM, -THEIST belief, believer in only one God. XVII (H. More). **mono**TONE mɔ·nətoun having but one tone or note XVIII; sb. utterance on one tone XVII. – modL. *monotonus* – Gr. *monótonos*; so F. **monoton**OUS mənɔ·tənəs XVIII. **mono-tony**Y³ – F. – Gr. *monotoniā*. **mono**TYPE mɔ·nŏtaip inventor's name for a patent type-composing machine. 1895.

monocle mɔ·nəkl single eye-glass. XIX. – F. *monocle*, sb. use of adj. 'one-eyed' – late L. *monoculus*, f. Gr. *mónos* MONO- + *oculus* EYE, after Gr. *monóphthalmos*.

monody mɔ·nədi ode sung by a single voice in Greek tragedy; mournful song, dirge. XVII. – late L. *monōdia* – Gr. *monōidiā*, f. *monōidós* singing alone, f. *mónos* + **ōid-* sing; see MONO-, ODE, -Y³.

monopoly mənɔ·pəli exclusive possession of the trade in some article XVI (More), also fig.; commodity subject to this XIX. – L. *monopōlium* (Suetonius, Pliny) – Gr. *monopṓlion*, *-pōliā*, f. *mónos* MONO- + *pōleîn* sell. Also †**mo·nopole.** XVI – (O)F. *monopole*. So †**mono·pol**ER¹. XVI; after OF. *monopolier*, F. *monopoleur*; repl. by **mono·pol**IST. XVII; cf. It. *monopolista*, G. *monopolist*. **mono·pol**IZE. XVII; cf. F. *monopoliser*.

monsieur məsjö· F. equiv. of MR. XV. F., f. *mon* my, *sieur* lord :– Rom. **seiōre*, for L. *seniōrem*, SENIOR; cf. SIRE, MESSIEURS. Formerly sp. *mounseer* and pronounced maunsiə·ɹ (XVII onwards) and *mossoo* mɔsū· (XIX). So **mon**SEI·GNEUR. XVI, **mon**SI·GNOR, -SIGNO·RE. XVII.

monsoon mɔnsū·n seasonal wind esp. in the Indian Ocean XVI; rainy season (time of the south-west monsoon) XVIII. – early modDu. †*monssoen*, †*monssoyn* (mod. *moesson*, infl. by F. forms) – Pg. *monção*, †*mouçāo* – Arab. *mausim* (whence also Malay *moesim*) fixed season, f. *wasama* mark. ¶ Adopted in Rom. and Germ. langs.

monster mɔ·nstəɹ misshapen creature XIII (Cursor M.); †prodigy; horribly cruel or savage person; huge object XVI. – (O)F. *monstre* – L. *mōnstrum* something marvellous or prodigious, orig. divine portent, f. *monēre* warn (see MONITION, and cf. DEMONSTRATE, REMONSTRATE); for a similar use of *-strum* in a religious term cf. LUSTRUM. So **mo·nstr**OUS. XV – OF. *monstreux* or L. *mōnstrōsus*; earlier †**mo·nstruous.** XIV (Ch.). – (O)F. *monstrueux* – L. *mōnstruōsus* (irreg. formation). **monstros**ITY -ɔ·sĭti. XVI. – late L.

monstrance mɔ·nstrəns (eccl.) vessel in which the Host is exposed. XVI. – medL. *mōnstrantia*, f. prp. stem of L. *mōnstrāre* show, f. *mōnstrum*; see prec. and -ANCE. Cf. G. *monstranz*, F. dial. *monstrance* (for which Standard F. has *ostensoir*. ¶ In late XV and early XVI there was much variety in the form used, e.g. †*moustre*, †*monstyr*, †*mustraunce*? (XV), *monstral*? (Cranmer), †*monstraunt* (Bp. Fisher), †*monstrate* (1524).

montbretia mɔntbrī·ʃ¹ə genus of iridaceous plants. XIX. modL., f. name of A. F. E. Coquebert de *Montbret*, French botanist (1780–1801); see -IA¹.

monte mɔ·nti Spanish card game. XIX. – Sp. *monte* mountain (MOUNT), applied to the stock of cards left after each player has received his share.

month mʌnþ one of the twelve portions into which the year is divided. OE. *mōnaþ* = OFris. *mōnath*, *mōn(a)d*, OS. *mānoth* (Du. *maand*), OHG. *mānōd* (G. *monat*), ON. *mánuðr*, Goth. *mēnōþs* :– CGerm. **mǣnōþ(āz)*, rel. to **mǣnon-* MOON. ¶ The reckoning of time by the revolutions of the moon was CIE.; see MOON for the relation of IE. words for 'moon' and 'month'. Hence **mo·nthly** adj. and adv. XVI; see -LY¹ and ².

monument mɔ·njŭmənt †place of burial (cf. W. *mynwent* graveyard) XIII (Cursor M.); †written document, piece of evidence XV; commemorative object or structure XVI. Early forms also †*mony-*, †*moniment* – (O)F. *monument*, †*moniment* = Sp., It. *monumento* – L. *monumentum*, *monimentum*, f. *monēre* remind; see MONITION, -MENT. Hence **monume·ntAL**[1]. XVII (Sh.); so late L.

-mony məni, repr. (1) L. *-mōnia*, as in *acrimony*, *ceremony*, (2) *-mōnium*, as in *matrimony*, *parsimony*, *patrimony*, *testimony*, and both in *alimony*, *ceremony*; rel. by gradation to *-men* (as in *forāmen* opening), of which *-mentum* -MENT is an extended form.

moo mū. XVI (also *mo*, *mow*). imit. of the characteristic voice of the cow.

mooch, mouch mūtʃ (dial.) play truant XVII; loaf, skulk; steal XIX. Relation to late ME. *mowche* (of doubtful meaning) is uncertain; prob. – OF. *muchier* (Norman dial. *mucher*) hide, skulk, perh. of Gaulish origin.

mood[1] mūd †mind, thought, feeling OE. (to *c.*1400); †pride OE.; †anger XII; frame of mind, disposition. OE. *mōd*, corr. with variety of gender to OFris., OS. *mōd* (Du. *moed*), OHG. *muot* (G. *mut*), ON. *móðr* anger, grief, Goth. *mōþs*, *mōd-* anger, emotion :– CGerm. **mōđaz*, **mōđam*, of which the ult. origin is unkn. Hence **moo·dY**[1] †brave, †proud OE.; †angry XII; subject to fits of ill humour, etc. XVI (Sh.).

mood[2] mūd (logic) class of syllogism; (gram.) form in the conjugation of a verb indicating function; † (mus.) mode. XVI. alt. of MODE by assoc. with MOOD[1].

moolvee mū·lvi Mohammedan doctor of law; learned man. XVII (Purchas). – Urdu *mulvī* – Arab. *maulawiyy* orig. adj. judicial, used sb. in the sense of *maulā* MULLAH, of which it is a derivative.

moon mūn the satellite of the earth OE.; (lunar) month XIV. OE. *mōna* = OFris. *mōna*, OS. *māno* (Du. *maan* fem.), OHG. *māno* (G. *mond*), ON. *máni*, Goth. *mēna* :– CGerm. **mǣnon*, prob. rel. to **mǣnōþ-* MONTH; cogn. words for 'moon' and 'month' based on **mēn(e)s-* are found throughout the IE. langs., e.g. L. *mēnsis* month, Gr. *meís*, *mḗn* month, *mḗnē* moon, Skr. *mā́s* moon, month, Ir. *mí* month, Lith. *mėnesis*, OSl. *měsęcĭ* moon, month; referred ult. to base **mē-*, as in *mētīrī* MEASURE, the moon being the star by which time is measured.

The foll. comps. are of special interest: **moon**CALF †false conception XVI; born fool XVII; perh. after G. *mondkalb* (Luther); cf. G. *mondkind*, MLG. *maanenkind* 'moon-child'. **moon**LIGHT. XIV (Ch.); cf. Du. *maanlicht*, G. *mondlicht*; hence **moonlight**ING[1] operation (esp. illicit) by night *c.*1880. **moon**LIT. XIX (Tennyson). **moon**SHINE moonlight; appearance without substance, empty talk, etc. (orig. *m. in the water*). XV. **moon**STONE. XVII; after L. *selēnitēs* SELENITE. **moon**STRUCK deranged, as if by the influence of the moon (cf. *lunatic*). XVII (Milton); cf. Gr. σεληνόβλητος, -πληκτος. **moon**WORT. XVI (Lyte, Gerarde); after Du. *maankruid*, G. *mondkraut*, late L. *lūnāria*.

moonack mū·næk woodchuck, Arctomys monax. XVII. – Lenape *monachgeu*, f. *monach* dig.

moonshee, munshi mū·nʃi in India, native secretary, teacher of languages. XVIII. – Urdu *munshī* – Arab. *munshī'*, prp. of *ansha'a* compose, causative of *masha'a* grow up.

moonsif mū·nsif native judge in India. XIX. – Urdu *munsif* – Arab. *munçif* just, honest, prp. of *ançafa* be bisected, be impartial, f. *miçf* half.

moor[1] muəɹ, mōəɹ tract of unenclosed waste ground. OE. *mōr* waste land, marsh, mountain, corr. to OS. *mōr* marsh, (M)Du. *moer*, (M)LG. *mōr* (whence G. *moor*, Da. *mor*), OHG. *muor* :– Germ. **mōraz*, **mōram*, perh. rel. to MERE. comp. **moo·r**LAND. OE. *mōrland*.

moor[2] muəɹ, mōəɹ secure a floating boat, etc., to a fixed place. XV. Early mod. *more*, prob. – (M)LG. *mōren*; cf. OE. *mǣrels*, *mārels* mooring-rope, MDu. vbs. *māren*, *mēren* (Du. *meren*), *moeren*.

Moor muəɹ, mōəɹ (in ancient times) native of Mauretania, (later) of north-west Africa (cf. BLACKAMOOR) XIV (Gower, Trevisa, Maund.); Mohammedan, esp. of India XVI. Late ME. *More* – (O)F. *More*, (mod.) *Maure* – L. *Maurus*, medL. *Mōrus* – Gr. *Maûros*. ¶ For **Moo·rISH**[1] (*morys*, XV) cf. MORRIS-DANCE, -PIKE.

Moorpark mōə·ɹpāɹk variety of apricot. XVIII. f. name (*Moor Park*) of Sir William Temple's (1628–99) house.

moorpork see MOPOKE.

moose mūs N.-Amer. animal allied to the elk. Early forms *mus*, *moos* – Narragansett *moos* = Abenaki *mus*, Penobscot *muns*, (according to Trumbull) f. *moosu* he strips or cuts smooth, in allusion to the animal's habit of stripping trees when feeding.

moot mūt assembly of people, esp. for a judicial purpose XII; †argument, discussion XIII; discussion of a hypothetical case in the Inns of Court XVI. Early ME. *mōt*, *imōt* :– OE. *mōt* (in comps. only; later reinforced from ON.), and *ġemōt* :– Germ. **(ga)mōtam*; cf. MDu. *moet*, (also mod.) *gemoet*, MHG. *muoȝe* meeting, attack, ON. *mót*, and MEET[2]; ult. origin unkn. Hence **moot** adj. debatable, arguable XVI; developed from attrib. uses of the sb. (*m. case*, *m. point*).

mop[1] mɔp bundle of yarn, etc., fixed to a stick for use in cleaning. XV. First in naut. use and in the form †*mapp(e)*, which survived till XVIII, the form *mop* appearing XVII (but †*moppe* is recorded for 'rag doll' XV); obscurely rel. to somewhat earlier †*mappel*,

†*mapolt*, *-old* (XV), of which Sc. †*mappat*, †*moppat*, *-et* (XVI) appear to be vars.; ult. connexion with L. *mappa* (see NAPKIN) and dim. *mappula* is poss., but the immed. source remains obscure.

mop[2] mɔp (arch.) grimace, esp. one made by a monkey. Also vb. XVI. Chiefly in phr. *mops and mows*, *mop and mow*; perh. imit. of the pouting of the lips; prob. of LG. origin (cf. Du. *mop* pug-dog, *moppen* be surly, pout).

mope moup (dial.) wander; be listless and dejected. XVI. prob. rel. to †*mope* (XVI), earlier †*mopp(e)* fool (XIV), and †*mop(p)ish* bewildered (XIV), which are perh. of Scand. origin (cf. OSw. *mopa* befool, Sw. dial. *mopa* look discontented, sulk, Da. *maabe* be stupid or unconscious); but cf. prec.

mopoke mou·pouk, **morepork** mɔ̄ə·ɹpɔ̄ɹk name of various Australasian birds. XIX. imit. of the bird's note. ¶ Cf. BOBOLINK.

moquette mɔke·t material used for carpeting. XVIII. – F. *moquette*, said to be alt. of *mocade*, *mockado* (XVI), poss. alt. of It. *mocaiardo* mohair.

mora mɔ̄ə·rə (leg.) delay XVI; (pros.) unit of metrical time XIX. – L. *mora*.

moraine mŏrei·n mountain debris carried down by a glacier. XVIII. – F. *moraine* – Savoyard It. *morêna*, f. southern F. *mor(re)* muzzle, snout :– Rom. **murrum* (cf. MORION).

moral mɔ·rəl pert. to character or conduct. XIV (Rolle, Ch., Trevisa). – L. *mōrālis* (Cicero, tr. Gr. ἠθικός ETHICAL), f. *mōr-*, *mōs* custom, pl. *mōres* manners, character; cf. F., Sp., Pg. *moral*, It. *-ale*; sb. pl. rendering the L. title *Moralia* of certain works XIV; sg. moral lesson XV; pl. moral habits XVII. So **morale** mŏrā·l. F., fem. of *moral* used sb. †morals XVIII; (now, in the sense of F. *moral*) disposition and spirit as of troops XIX. **moral**ITY mɔræ·lĭti. XIV (Ch.). – (O)F. or late L. **mo·ral**IZE interpret morally XV (Hoccleve), -ATION XV (Lydg.). – (O)F. or medL.

morass mɔræ·s wet swampy tract (now only literary exc. in the W. Indies, where it survives with the pronunc. mɔ·rəs). XVII. – Du. *moeras*, †*-asch*, alt. by assim. to *moer* MOOR[1], of MDu. *maras*, *marasch* – (O)F. *marais* MARSH; cf. MLG. *maras*, whence G. *marass*, *morass*, later *morast*.

moratorium mɔrətɔ̄ə·riəm legal authorization to postpone payment. XIX. modL., sb. use of n. sg. of late L. (legal) *morātōrius*, f. pp. stem of *morārī* delay; see MORA, -ORY.

moray mŏrei· tropical species of eel. XVII (Capt. Smith). – Pg. *moreia* = Sp. *morena* – L. *mūræna*, *-ēna* – Gr. *múraina*, rel. to *mûros*, *smûros* eel.

morbid mɔ̄·ɹbid pert. to disease XVII; unwholesome, sickly XIX. – L. *morbidus*, f. *morbus* disease; see -ID[1]. So **morbi**·FIC. XVII. – F. or modL.

morbleu mɔ̄ɹblö· F. oath used chiefly in XVII, euphem. alt. (with assim. to *bleu* blue) of *mortdieu* 'God's death', which was also used, as †*mor du* (Marlowe), †*mortdew*.

mordant mɔ̄·ɹdənt biting. XV (Caxton). – (O)F. *mordant*, prp. of *mordre* bite :– Rom. **mordere*, for L. *mordēre* (see MORSEL).

mordent mɔ̄·ɹdənt (mus.) kind of grace. XIX. – G. *mordent* – It. *mordente*, sb. use of prp. of *mordere* bite (L. *mordēre*); so called in allusion to the force of the 'attack'.

more mɔ̄əɹ A. greater (surviving in (*the*) *m.'s the pity*, *the m. fool you*, etc.). B. existing in greater quantity or degree XIV. C. a greater number of, more numerous XVI. D. additional XIII. OE. *māra*, fem., n. *māre* = OFris. *māra*, OS. *mēro* (MDu. *mēre*, repl. in modDu. by *meerder*), OHG. *mēro* (G. *mehr-*, with compar. suffix *mehrere* several), ON. *meire*, Goth. *maiza* :– CGerm. **maizon*, f. **maiz* MO. In sense B modelled on the use of MO. Hence as sb. late OE., as adv. XII. Hence **moreover** mōrou·vəɹ in phr. *and yet more over* 'and still more beyond' XIV (Ch.); whence, introducing an additional statement, 'besides' (XIV, Wycl. Bible).

-more mɔ̄əɹ use of prec. in advs. denoting place in the compar. degree, many of which have given rise to adjs. of the same form; added chiefly to advs. ending in -ER[3], as *backermore*, *innermore*, *uttermore*; the majority of such words have parallel forms in -MOST. The earliest, *furthermore* (Orm), *farthermore*, and *innermore* (Cursor M.), are based on Scand. forms (ON. *-meir*, OSw. *-mer*), which indicates the immed. source of the use.

moreen mŏrī·n stout stuff for curtains, etc. XVII (*-ine*, Etherege). perh. fancifully f. MOIRE.

morello, -a mŏre·lou, -e·lə dark-coloured bitter cherry. XVII. Of It. form and presumably a use of *morello*, fem. *-a* blackish :– medL. *mo-*, *maurellus*, f. *Maurus* MOOR.

mores mɔ̄ə·rīz (pl.) conventions, customs of social group. XX. – L., pl. of *mōs*, *mōr-* custom (see MORAL).

moresque mōre·sk Moorish. XVII. – F. *moresque* – It. *moresco* (also in Eng. use XVI, beside the Sp. form *morisco*, whence †*morisk*); see MOOR, -ESQUE.

morganatic mɔ̄ɹgənæ·tik applied to a marriage of a man with a woman of inferior station in which wife and children do not share in his rights. XVIII. – F. *morganatique*, G. *morganatisch*, or their source medL. *morganaticus*, evolved from phr. *matrimonium ad morganāticam*, of which the last word is prob. based on Germ. **morgangeba* (G. *morgengabe*) = OE. *morgengifu* (f. *morgen* MORN + **geƀ-* GIVE) gift made by husband to wife on the morning after consummation of the marriage and relieving him of further liability.

morgue[1] mǭɹg, ||morg haughty demeanour. XVI. – F. *morgue*, of unkn. origin.

morgue[2] mǭɹg building in Paris where people found dead are exposed for identification. XIX. Presumed to be identical with prec., the F. word having passed through the intermediate sense of 'place in a prison where prisoners were examined on entry'.

moribund mɔ·ribʌnd about to die. XVIII. – L. *moribundus*, f. *morī* die (see MORTAL). Cf. F. *moribond*, etc.

morion mɔ·riən soldier's helmet without beaver or visor. XVI (in earliest use also *mirrioun, murrion, murren*). – F. *morion* – Sp. *morrion*, f. *morro* :– Rom. **murrum* round object. Cf. MORAINE.

morling mǭ·ɹliŋ wool taken from the skin of a dead sheep. XV. Also †*mortling*, prob. (with substitution of -LING[1] for *-kin*) f. †*mor(t)kin* beast that dies by disease or accident (XV) – AN. *mortekine*, var. of OF. *mortecine* – late L. *morticīna* carrion, n. pl. of L. *morticīnus* (of an animal) that has died (without being slaughtered), f. *mort-, mors* death (see MORTAL); cf. It. *lana morticina* wool of dead animals.

Mormon mǭ·ɹmən member of 'the Church of Jesus Christ of Latter-Day Saints'. Name of the alleged author of 'The Book of Mormon', which Joseph Smith (Manchester, New York, 1830) professed to have translated from the original written on gold plates and miraculously discovered by him.

morn mǭɹn beginning of the day; early part of the day; *the* next morning, *the* next day. (All the senses are CGerm.) OE. *morgen*, inflected *mor(g)n-* = OFris. *morgen, morn*, OS., OHG. *morgan* (Du., G. *morgen*) :– **murganaz*; cf., with variation of suffix, ON. *morgunn, -onn*, inflected *morn-*, also OE. *myrgen-*, ON. *myrginn*, Goth. *maurgins* (:– **murginaz*), and, with different vowel grade of the base, OE. *merġen*, MDu. *margen, mergen*, ON. *merginn* (OSw. *marghan*) :– **marganaz*, **marginaz*. The ult. connexions of the CGerm. base are doubtful. The typical ME. developments of OE. *morġen* were: *morȝen, morwen*; *morun, moren, morn*; *morwe, moru*, MORROW. Hence (after EVENING) **morning** mǭ·ɹniŋ. XIII; ME. also freq. *morwening*.

Morocco mərɔ·kou applied to things originating in the country of north-west Africa so named, esp. to leather of goatskin. XVII. – It. *Marocco*, corr. to Sp. *Marruecos*, F. *Maroc* – Arab. *maγrib-al-aqçā* 'the extreme west'.

moron mǭ·rɔn adult person with the intelligence of a child aged 8 to 12 years. 1910. – n. of Gr. *mōrós* stupid (Skr. *mūrás*).

morose mərou·s of sour unsociable temper. XVI. – L. *mōrōsus* peevish, wayward, fastidious, scrupulous, f. *mōr-, mōs* manner (in the special sense of 'humour', 'fancy'); see MORAL, -OSE[1]. So **moros**ITY mǭrɔ·siti. XVI (now rare). – F. or L.

-morph mǭɹf terminal element repr. Gr. *-morphos*, f. *morphḗ* shape (cf. MORPHO-). The corr. adjs. and abst. nouns end in *-morphic(al), -morphous, -morphism, -morphy*.

morpheme mǭ·ɹfīm (philol.) morphological element. XX. – F. *morphème* (1905), f. Gr. *morphḗ* form, after PHONEME.

morphia mǭ·ɹfiə narcotic principle of opium. XIX. – modL. *morphia*, alt. of *morphium* (named by W. Sertürner after *opium*), f. *Morpheus* (f. Gr. *morphḗ* shape), Ovid's name for the god of dreams, son of the god of sleep. Also **mo·rph**INE[5].

morpho- mǭ·ɹfou, mǭɹfɔ·, comb. form of Gr. *morphḗ* shape, form, as in **morpho·**LOGY branch of biology dealing with living forms, (1830), branch of grammar concerned with the formation and inflexion of words (1869).

morris[1] mɔ·ris dance by persons in fancy costume representing characters esp. from the Robin Hood story. XV. orig. in *mor(e)ys* DANCE; var. of *Moorish* (see MOOR), perh. after Flem. *mooriske dans*, Du. *moorsche dans*; cf. G. *moriskentanz*, F. *danse moresque*. ¶ For the form cf. *morris-pike* (XV), a pike supposed to be of Moorish origin.

morris[2] mɔ·ris (antiq.) game with counters (XVII, Sh.), of which the early name was *merels*, pl. of late ME. *merel* – OF. (later *méreau*), of unkn. origin.

morrow mɔ·rou morning; *the* day after. XIII. ME. *morwe, -ewe, -owe, moru*; see MORN and for the phonology cf. SORROW. Survives in gen. use only in TO-MORROW.

morse[1] mǭɹs fastening of a cope. XV. – OF. *mors* – L. *morsu-s* bite, catch, f. *mors-*, pp. stem of *mordēre* bite.

morse[2] mǭ·ɹs sea-horse or walrus. XVI (*morsse*). Caxton has *mors marine* (XV), corr. to F. *morce marin* (XVI), of which the immed. source is unkn.; ult. – Lappish *moršša*, whence Finnish *morsu*, Russ. *morzh*.

morse[3] mǭɹs system of telegraphy (dots, dashes, and spaces) invented by S. F. B. *Morse* (1791–1872). XIX.

morsel mǭ·ɹs(ə)l bite, mouthful, small piece. XIII. – OF. *morsel* (mod. *morceau*) = It. *morsello*, dim. of *mors, morso* :– L. *morsu-s*; see MORSE[1], -EL[2].

mort[1] mǭɹt (antiq.) note sounded at the death of the deer. XVI. – (O)F. *mort* :– L. *mortem*, nom. *mors* (cf. MORTAL).

mort[2] mǭɹt (dial.) great quantity or number. XVII (Echard). poss. alt. of synon. north. dial. *murth* (– ON. *mergð* multitude, f. *margr* MANY) by assoc. with *mortal* excessive(ly).

mortal mɔ̄·ɹt(ə)l subject to death, human; deadly, fatal XIV; (of sin) XV; of or pert. to death XVI. – OF. *mortal*, latinized var. of OF. (also mod.) *mortel*, whence ME. *mortel*; or directly – L. *mortālis*, f. *mort- mors* death, f. IE. **mor- *mer- *mr̥-* die, as in L. *morī* die, *mortuus* dead, Gr. *brotoí* mortals (see AMBROSIA), *émorten* died (Hesychius), OSl. *mĭrǫ*, Lith. *mìrštu* I die, Skr. *mriyáte* dies, *mr̥tís* death; see -AL[1]. So **mortal**ITY mɔ̄ɹtæ·lĭti. XIV. – (O)F. – L.

mortar[1] mɔ̄·ɹtəɹ A. cup-shaped vessel in which drugs, etc., are pounded with a pestle XIII; B. short piece of ordnance (so named from its squat shape) XVII (orig. *mortar-piece* XVI). ME. partly – AN. *morter*, (O)F. *mortier* = Pr. *mortier*, Sp. *mortero*, It. *mortaio* :– L. *mortārium* (to which the Eng. sp. was finally assim.); partly – LG. (see below). ¶ Not continuous with OE. *mortere*, which corr. to MLG. *mortēr* (Du. *mortier*), OHG. *mortāri* – L.

mortar[2] mɔ̄·ɹtəɹ mixture of lime and sand with water, used for building. XIII. – AN. *morter* = (O)F. *mortier* (see prec.), with transference of meaning from the vessel to the substance produced in it. Cf. MDu., MHG. *morter*, (with dissimilation) *mortel* (Du. *mortel*, G. *mörtel*).

mortgage mɔ̄·ɹgidʒ conveyance of property by a debtor (mortgagor) to a creditor (mortgagee) as security for a money debt. XIV (*morgage*; the sp. *mortgage* was established by legal usage XVI). – OF. *mortgage* 'dead pledge', f. *mort* dead :– popL. var. **mortu-s* of L. *mortuus* (see MORTAL)+*gage* GAGE[1]; AL. *mortuum vadium* (XII). Hence **mo·rtgage** vb. XVI; **mortgag**EE[1] mɔ̄ɹgidʒī·, **mortgag**OR[1] mɔ̄ɹgidʒɔ̄·ɹ. XVI.

mortician mɔ̄ɹti·ʃən (U.S.) undertaker. XIX. f. MORT|UARY+-ICIAN.

mortify mɔ̄·ɹtifai †kill XIV (Ch., Wyclif); bring (the body, etc.) into subjection; (Sc. law) dispose of in mortmain XV; (cookery) make tender by hanging XVI; become gangrenous; humiliate or vex deeply XVII. – (O)F. *mortifier* – ecclL. *mortificāre* kill, (Tertullian) subdue (the flesh), f. *morti-*, *mors* death; see MORTAL, -FY. So **mo:rtifica·**TION subjection of the flesh XIV (Ch.); (Sc. law) disposal in mortmain XV; gangrene, necrosis XVI; humiliation, vexation XVII. – (O)F. – ecclL. (Tertullian).

mortise, -ice mɔ̄·ɹtis hole made in a piece of wood to receive the end of another piece. XIV (Maund.). ME. *mortais*, *-eis* – OF. *mortoise* (mod. *mortaise*) = Sp. *mortaja* – Arab. *murtazz* fixed in, f. *razza*.

mortmain mɔ̄·ɹtmein condition of lands inalienably held by a corporation. XV. – AN., OF. *mortemain* – medL. *mortua manus* (XIII) 'dead hand', i.e. *mortua*, fem. of *mortuus* dead, *manus* hand (cf. MORTAL, MANUAL); the term may be intended as a metaphor for 'impersonal ownership'.

mortuary mɔ̄·ɹtjuəri sb. gift claimed by the parson from the estate of a deceased parishioner XIV (Wyclif); †obsequies XV; dead-house XIX; adj. pert. to burial or death XVI. As sb. orig. – AN. *mortuarie* – medL. *mortuārium*, n. sg. of *mortuārius* (whence the Eng. adj.; cf. F. *mortuaire*), f. *mortuus* dead; see MORTAL, -ARY.

mosaic mŏzei·ik decorative pattern made with small coloured pieces of stone, etc.; also adj. XVI. – F. *mosaïque* – It. †*mosaico*, *musaico* (whence also Sp., Pg. *mosaico*) – medL. *mōsaicus*, *mūsaicus*, obscurely f. late Gr. *mouseîon*, *mousíon* mosaic work (see MUSEUM), whence late L. (*opus*) *mūsēum* and *mūsīvum* (cf. ARCHIVE, OLIVE); so L. *mūsēiārius* worker in mosaic, late Gr. *mousiátōr* id., *mousíōma*, *mousíōsis* mosaic work, *mousioûn* vb. work in mosaic. ¶ OF. had *musec*, *music*, whence rare ME. *musycke* XIV.

Mosaic mŏzei·ik pert. to Moses, the founder and lawgiver of Israel. XVII. – F. *mosaïque* or modL. *Mōsāicus*, f. *Mōsēs*; see -IC.

moselle mŏze·l dry white wine. XVII. – F. name (– G. *Mosel*, in L. *Mosella*) of a river which joins the Rhine at Coblentz and in the neighbourhood of which the wine is produced.

Moslem mɔ·zlĕm, **Muslim** mʌ·z-, mʌ·slim Mohammedan. XVII. – Arab. *muslim*, active pple. of *aslama*; see ISLAM.

mosque mɔsk Mohammedan temple. XIV (*moseach*, *-eak* Maund.), XVI (*muskay*, *mosquee*). The earliest forms are of obscure origin; the present form is a shortening (XVII) of *mosquee*, – F. *mosquée* – It. *moschea* (whence also G. *moschee*) – Arab. *masgid*, local var. of *masjid*, f. *sajada* worship. ¶ There has been much variety of sp., together with adoption of other forms, as from Sp. *mez-*, Pg. *mesquita*, or (direct from Arab.) *masjid*, *mosged*, *muschid*.

mosquito mɔskī·tou kind of gnat (Culex). XVI. – Sp., Pg. *mosquito* (whence F. *moustique*), dim. of *mosca* :– L. *musca* fly (see MIDGE).

moss mɔs A. (dial.) bog, swamp OE.; B. small plant of the class Musci. XIV. OE. *mos* = MLG., MDu. *mos* bog, moss (Du. *mos*), OHG. *mos* (G. *moos*) :– Germ. **musam*, rel. to ON. *mosi* wk. m. bog, moss, and further to OE. *mēos*, OHG. *mios* (G. *mies*) moss (:– Germ. **meus- *meuz-*), ON. *mýrr* MIRE, and outside Germ. to L. *muscus*, OSl. *mŭchŭ* moss :– IE. **mus-*). The application in Eng. to the plant may be due to ON. *mosi*, traces of the formal adoption of which as *mose* are found from XII, appear in place-names, and survive in eastern dial. *mozy* mossy (late ME. *mosy*). Cf. LITMUS.

mossbunker mɔ·sbʌ:ŋkəɹ (U.S.) menhaden. XVII (*marsbancker*), XVIII (*mos-*). – Du. *marsbanker*, of unkn. origin.

most moust greatest OE.; greatest amount of XIV; adv. in the greatest degree OE. The present form repr. partly OE. *māst*, which is recorded only from late Nhb., partly a modification of ME. *mēst*, OE. *mǣst*, by assim. to MO, MORE; *mǭst* is found in XIII in easterly texts (the north. form *māst* survives dial. in *meast*, Sc. *maist*; OE. *māst* = OFris. *māst, maest*, OS. *mēst* (Du. *meest*), (O)HG. *meist*, ON. *mestr*, Goth. *maists* :– CGerm. **maistaz*, f. base of **maiz* MO + *-*ista*- -EST. Hence **mo·st**LY[2] for the most. part. XVI. ¶ The ordinary OE. *mǣst* continued in ME. *mēst*, presumably descended from **māist* (Ch. has *meest* and *moost* in rhyme).

-most moust, məst suffix forming superl. adjs. and advs.; alt. form of OE. *-mest* = Goth. *-umists*, which is a combination of two Germ. (and IE.) superl. suffixes, viz. *-*mo*-, as in OE. *forma* first, L. *prīmus* first (PRIME) and *-*isto*- -EST. The OE. superls. so formed are based mostly on adv.-preps.; see AFTERMOST, FOREMOST, HINDMOST, INMOST, UTMOST (an exception is *midemest* MIDMOST); by analogy, the suffix was added to several adjs. of local or temporal meaning, e.g. *ēastmest* most easterly, *lætmest* latest. It became identified in late OE. and ME. with *mǣst, mēst*, and later with MOST; it was added to compars., as *furthermost, hindermost, outermost, uttermost*, usu. denoting position in place, time, or serial order (an exception is *bettermost*). Cf. -MORE.

mot mou, ‖mo saying. F. 'word' (whence It. MOTTO) :– Gallo-Rom. **mottum*, alt. of L. *muttum* (not) a word or syllable, rel. to (colloq.) *muttire* MUTTER, murmur.

mote[1] mout particle of dust. OE. *mot*, corr. to WFris., Du. *mot* sawdust, dust of turf (in MDu. *steenmot, turfmot*), of unkn. origin. The present form (ME. *moot* XIV) descends from OE. obl. case-forms (*mott*, repr. the uninflected form, survived till XVIII).

mote[2] mout see MUST.

motet moute·t part-song; later spec. harmonized vocal composition, esp. for church use. XIV. – (O)F. *motet*, dim. of *mot* word, saying (see MOTTO); cf. medL. *motetum*, It. *mottetto*, Sp. *motete*; see -ET.

moth mɔþ insect of the genus Tinea or (earlier) its larva OE.; nocturnal lepidopterous insect XVIII ('those butterflies which fly by night, and which the French thence call *papillons nocturnes*, and we vulgarly *moths*', 1753 Chambers's 'Cycl. Supp.'). OE. *moþþe, mohðe*, from the former of which the present form descends, from the latter ME. *moȝðe, mohþe, mouȝthe*, later *mought* and *moath* (XVI); obscurely rel. to synon. MLG., MDu. *motte* (Du. *mot*), (M)HG. *motte*, ON. *motti*.

mother[1] mʌ·ðəɹ A. female parent OE.; term of address to an elderly woman; applied to the B.V.M. XIV; head of community of nuns XVII (Sh.). B. †womb XIV; †hysteria XV. OE. *mōdor* = OFris., OS. *mōdar* (Du. *moeder*), OHG. *muotar* (G. *mutter*), ON. *móðir* :– CGerm. (wanting in Gothic; cf. FATHER) **mōðar*- :– IE. **māte·r*-, whence also L. *māter* (cf. MATERNAL), Gr. (Doric) *mā́tēr*, (Attic, Ionic) *mḗtēr*, OSl. *mati* (*mater*-), OIr. *māthir* (Ir., Gael. *máthair*), Skr. *mātṛ, mātár*-, Tokh. *mācar*. ¶ A Germ. and IE. term of relationship like *father, brother, sister, son*. Important collocations are: *m. country* (XVI), after F. *terre mère*; *m. earth* (XVI), cf. L. *Terra Mater*, taken as a goddess; *m. land* (XVIII); *m. tongue* (XIV, Wyclif), in which *mother* is orig. uninflected g.; *m. wit* (XVI), earlier *moderis*. Hence **mo·ther** vb. be a mother to. XVI. *Mothering Sunday*, Midlent Sunday, so called from the custom of going a-mothering (XVII), i.e. visiting parents, on that day. **mo·ther**LY[1]; OE. *mōdorlić*.

mother[2] mʌ·ðəɹ †dregs, scum XVI (Elyot); (in full *m. of vinegar*) mucilaginous substance produced in vinegar by fermentation XVII (Holland). corr. in form and sense to MDu. *moeder* (mod. *moer*), G. *mutter* MOTHER[1], and in use to F. *mère (de vinaigre)* and Sp., It. *madre*; the orig. notion may have been that the substance was a portion of the 'mother' or original crude substance which remained mixed at first with the refined product. So also in **mo:ther-of-pea·rl** iridescent inner layer of shells (XVI), earlier also †*mother perle*, tr. F. †*mère perle*, corr. to It., Sp. *madreperla*, Du. *paarlmoer*, G. *perlmutter*.

motif moutī·f, mou·tif distinctive constituent feature of an artistic composition. XIX (Mrs. Jameson). F., 'MOTIVE'.

motion mou·ʃən action or process of moving XV (Lydg.); formal proposition XVI. (Several other meanings were formerly current.) – (O)F. *motion* – L. *mōtiō(n-)*, f. *mō*- of *movēre* (*mōtum*) MOVE; see -TION and cf. *commotion, emotion, promotion*. Hence **motion** vb. †propose, move XVI; make a gesture XVIII. **motive** mou·tiv †motion, proposition XIV (PPl.); that which moves a person to act XV (Hoccleve); motif XIX. ME. *motyf, -yve* – (O)F. *motif*, sb. use of adj. – late L. *mōtīvus*, whence **mo·tive** adj. XVI; cf. *locomotive*. So **mo·tiv**ATE[3] supply a motive for or to. XIX (intr. 1863 Lytton); after F. *motiver*.

motley mɔ·tli diversified in colour XIV; sb. †varicoloured fabric XIV (Ch.); particoloured dress of a jester XVI (Sh.). Late ME. *mottelay, -ley*, perh. – AN. **motelé*, f. MOTE[1] (but the formation remains obscure).

motor mou·təɹ agent or force producing motion XVI; machine supplying motive power XIX. – L. *mōtor* (rare, Martial) mover, later in philos. use, f. *mōt-, movēre*; see -OR[1]; prob. partly after F. *moteur*. Hence vb. drive an automobile, whence **mo·tor**IST. XIX. **mo·tor**WAY XX.

mottle mɔ·tl surface variegated with spots; so vb. and ppl. adj. *mottled*. XVII. prob. back-formation from MOTLEY.

motto mɔ·tou orig. word or phrase attached to an emblematic design. XVI. – It. *motto* (see MOT).

motu proprio mou·tjū prɔ·priou papal rescript the terms of which are decided by the pope himself. XIX. L., 'by one's own motion', abl. of *mōtus* motion, *proprius* PROPER.

moufflon mū·flən wild sheep Ovis musimon. XVIII (Goldsmith). – F. *mouflon* (Buffon) – It. *muflone* – Rom. **mufrō(n-)*.

mouillé muje (phonetics) palatalized, fronted. XIX. F., pp. of *mouiller* moisten, make 'liquid' :– Rom. **molliāre*, f. L. *mollis* soft (cf. MOLLIFY).

moujik, muzhik mū·ʒik Russian peasant. XVI (*mousick, musick*). – Russ. *muzhík*.

mould[1], U.S. **mold** mould (dial.) friable earth, surface soil; (poet.) earth of the grave; the earth's surface OE.; garden soil XIV. OE. *molde* = OFris. *molde*, (M)Du. *moude*, OHG. *molta*, ON. *mold*, Goth. *mulda* :– CGerm. **moldō, *muldō*, f. **mul-* (**mel- *mal-*) pulverize, grind (cf. OE. *myl*, MDu. *mul, mol* dust, and MEAL[1]).

mould[2] mould (dial.) top of the head, fontanelle. OE. *molda, -e* = MDu. *moude*, rel. to Skr. *mūrdhán* highest point, head, Gr. *blōthrós* tall, f. IE. *mḷdh-*.

mould[3], U.S. **mold** mould A. native character XIII; (bodily) form XVI; B. pattern or matrix by which a thing is shaped XIV. Presumably metathetic alt. of OF. *modle* (whence modF. *moule*, Sp. *molde*; cf. Pr. *motle*, It. *modano*) – L. MODULUS. Hence **mould** vb. XV.

mould[4], U.S. **mold** mould woolly or furry growth consisting of minute fungi. XV. prob. developed from †*mould*, †*mouled*, pp. of †*moule*, earlier †*muwle* (AncrR.) grow mouldy – ON. **mugla*, rel. to synon. ON. *mygla*. Hence **mou·ld**Y[1]. XIV (Trevisa).

moulder, U.S. molder mou·ldəɹ crumble to dust. XVI. poss. f. MOULD[1] + -ER[4]; but adoption from Scand. is more likely (cf. Norw. dial. *muldra* crumble. **mouldwarp** mou·ldwōɹp (dial.) mole (Talpa). XIV. prob. – MLG. *moldewerp* (whence Da. *muldvarp*) = OHG. *multwurf*, WGerm. comp. of **moldō* MOULD[1] and **warp-* throw, WARP.

moult, U.S. molt moult (of feathers) be shed in the change of plumage XIV (Rolle); shed (feathers) XV. ME. *moute, mowte*, later *molt* (XVI), *moult* (XVII); repr. OE. **mūtian* (as in *mūtung, bimūtian* exchange) = MLG., MDu. *mūten* change, moult, OHG. *mūʒʒōn* (G. *mause(r)n*; cf. Du. *muit* cage for moulting birds); CWGerm. – L. *mūtāre* change (see MUTATION). The intrusion of *l* before *t* (whence the present sp.-pronunc.) resembles that in *assault, fault*. Cf. MEW[2].

mound[1] maund †world XIII; orb intended to represent the globe XVI. – (O)F. *monde* = Sp. *mundo*, It. *mondo* :– L. *mundus* world (see MUNDANE).

mound[2] maund (dial.) hedge, fence; embankment XVI; artificial elevation of earth or stones, tumulus XVIII (Pope). perh. f. the somewhat earlier *mound* vb. enclose with a fence, but the origin of this is unknown.

mount[1] maunt mountain, hill OE.; †earthwork; †mound. XVI. OE. *munt*, reinforced in ME. from (O)F. *mont* = Sp., It. *monte* :– L. *montem, mōns* (cf. EMINENT).

mount[2] maunt go upwards, ascend, rise (Ch., PPl., Gower); cause to ascend, etc., set in position XVI. – OF. *munter*, (also mod.) *monter* = Pr., Sp. *montar*, It. *montare* :– Rom. **montāre*, f. *mont-* MOUNT[1]; for the sense cf. F. *amont* uphill, upstream, and AMOUNT, with which *mount* was synon. XIV–XVIII. Hence **mount** sb. †amount XIV; mounting XV; fitting, setting; ridden animal XIX (for these two senses cf. F. *monture*).

mountain mau·ntĭn hill of notable height. XIII (Laȝ.). – OF. *montaigne* (mod. *-agne*) = Pr., Pg. *montanha*, Sp. *montaña*, It. *montagna* :– Rom. **montānia* or *-ea*, fem. sg. or n. pl. (quasi 'mountainous region') of adj. **montānius, -eus*, f. L. *mont-, mōns* MOUNT[1]; see -AN. Hence **mountain**EE·R[1] XVII (Sh.); superseded †*mountainer*. **mou·ntain**OUS. XV (rare before XVII); partly after F. *montagneux* (= Sp. *montañoso*, etc.).

mountebank mau·ntibæŋk itinerant quack, juggler, etc., appearing on a platform; charlatan. XVI. – It. *montambanco, montimbanco*, for *monta in banco* 'mount (imper.) on bench'; see MOUNT, BANK (cf. rare OF. *montenbancque*).

mourn mōəɹn, muəɹn feel sorrow (for) OE.; lament (a death, someone dead) XIII. OE. *murnan* pt. str. *mearn, murnon*, wk. *murnde*, corr. to OS. *mornon, mornian*, OHG. *mornēn* be anxious, ON. *morna* pine away, Goth. *maurnan* be anxious; prob. to be referred to IE. **(s)mer-*, repr. by Skr. *smárati*, Av. *maraiti* reflect, Gr. *mérimna* care, sorrow, *mérmeros* anxious, L. *memor* mindful (see MEMORY). Hence **mourn**FUL[1]. XVI.

mournival mɔə·ɹnivəl set of four aces or court cards in one hand. XVI (*mornyfle*). – F. *mornifle* in that sense XVI, (now) slap, taunt, the form of which suggests connexion with words meaning 'sniff', as dial. F. *morniflan* sniffing, F. *renifler* snuffle.

mouse maus, pl. **mice** mais small rodent (Mus). OE. *mūs*, pl. *mȳs* = OFris., OS., OHG. *mūs* (Du. *muis*, G. *maus*), ON. *mús*; CGerm. (exc. Gothic) and IE. **mūs-* is repr. also by L. *mūs*, Gr. *mûs*, OSl. *myšĭ*, Skr. *mūṣ-*; f. a base identical with one meaning 'steal, rob'. Cf. MUSCLE. Hence **mouse** vb. mauz. XIII. **mou·ser**[1] mau·zəɹ, -səɹ. OE. *mūsere* mouse-hawk.

mousquetaire muskətĕr one of the soldiers of the French king's household troops. XVIII. See MUSKETEER.

mousse mūs frothy dish. XIX. F., 'moss'.

moustache mŭstā·ʃ hair on the upper lip. XVI. – F. *moustache* – It. *mostaccio* MUSTACHIO.

mouth mauþ cavity in the head used for eating and speaking. OE. *mūþ* = OFris. *mūth*, later *mund*, OS. *mūth*, *mund* (Du. *mond*), (O)HG. *mund*, ON. *munnr*, *muðr*, Goth. *munþs* :– CGerm. **munþaz* (for the loss of *n* in OE., etc., cf. FIVE, OTHER, TOOTH, UNCOUTH) :– IE. **mn̥tos*, corr. to L. *mentum* chin (cf. MENTAL[2]). Hence **mouth** vb. mauð. XIII (Cursor M.).

mouton mū·tən (hist.) F. gold coin bearing the figure of the Lamb of God. XIV (PPl.). – OF. *motoun* sheep (MUTTON).

move mūv change the position of, or one's position; affect, stir, prompt. XIII. – AN. *mover* = OF. *moveir* (mod. *mouvoir*) = Pr., Sp. *mover*, It. *muovere* :– L. *movēre*, pt. *mōvī*, pp. *mōtus* (cf. MOBILE, MOMENT, MOTION, etc.), f. IE. base **mou*- **meu*- **mu*- (with other reprs. in Skr., Gr., and Lith.). Equally common from XIII to XVI was the var. *meve*, *meeve*, earlier *meove*, *moeve*, derived from the OF. forms with radical stress, e.g. 3rd pl. pres. ind. *moevent* (mod. *meuvent*) :– L. *móvent* (contrast *moveir*, *mouvoir* :– L. *movḗre*); cf. PEOPLE, *preve* PROVE. Hence **move** *sb.* (XV), XVII. So **mov(e)**ABLE mū·vəbl. XIV (Ch., Trevisa). – OF. *movable*. **mo·ve**MENT. XIV (not evidenced after Ch., Gower, and Sir G. Haye, till late XVII, when, and later, it appears in various techn. uses). – (O)F. *mouvement* – medL. *movimentum*.

mow[1] mau stack of hay, corn, etc. OE. *mūga*, *mūha*, *mūwa*, corr. to ON. *múgi* swath, (also *múgr*) crowd, and so in comp. *almúge*, *almúgr* (Sw. *allmoge*, Da. *almue*) common people, of unkn. origin.

mow[2] mou cut down (grass, etc.) with scythe or machine. OE. *māwan*, pt. **mēow* (whence ME. and dial. *mew*, superseded gen. by *mowed*), pp. *māwen* (whence *mown*; *mowed* from XVI); CWGerm. vb., in other langs. weak, repr. by OFris. *mēa*, MDu. *maeien* (Du. *maaien*), OHG. *māen* (G. *mähen*), f. **mǣ*- (see MEAD[1]).

mow[3] mau, mou (arch., dial.) grimace. XIV. prob. – OF. *moe*, (also mod.) *moue* †mouth, †lip, pouting; otherwise – MDu. *mouwe*, which may be the source of the OF. word. Hence vb. XV (Lydg.).

Mozarabic mouzæ·rəbik epithet of the ancient ritual of the church in Spain, prob. so called from being used by the Mozarabs after being disused by others. XVIII. f. Sp. *Mozarabe* (in medL. pl. *Mozarabes*) – Arab. *mustaʿrib*, active pp. of desiderative conjugation f. *ʿarab* ARAB; see -IC.

moz(z)etta moze·tə (eccl.) cape with a hood. XVIII. It., dim. of *mozza* (see AMICE).

mpret Albanian title of ruler. – L. *imperātor* EMPEROR.

Mr as a title orig. abbrev. of *Master* XV; †in 16th and 17th cent. used gen. for MASTER, as in *Mr of Arts*, *Mr Gunner*; its present oral equiv. is MISTER[2].

much mʌtʃ †great (surviving in place-names, as *M. Wenlock*); great amount of XIII; adv. greatly; sb. great deal XIV. ME. *muche*, *moche* (with vars. *miche*, *meche*), shortening of *muchel*, *mochel*, repr. late OE. *myćel*, var. of *mićel*; for the development of ü to ʌ cf. *blush*, *crutch*, *cudgel*, *rush*, *such*, *thrush*; the loss of *l* may have been furthered by the relation of *lut* to *lutel* LITTLE, but for the loss of *l* after *ch* cf. *wenchel* WENCH. OE. *mićel* = OS. *mikil*, OHG. *michil*, ON. *mikill* (cf. MICKLE), Goth. *mikils*; CGerm. deriv. of IE. **meg*-, repr. by L. *magnus* (cf. MAGISTRATE, MAGNATE, MAGNITUDE, MAJOR, MASTER), Gr. *mégas* (see MEGA-, MEGALO-), Skr. *mahā*- great (see MAHARAJAH, MAHATMA), *majmán* greatness, Toch. *māka*-, *māk*-; cf. ON. *mjǫk* much, very (:– **meku*-). Hence **mu·ch**LY[2]. XVII (in XIX a new joc. formation). **mu·ch**NESS. XIV (*m. of a muchness* XVIII).

mucilage mjū·silidʒ viscous fluid XIV; gummy secretion XVII; (U.S.) adhesive gum XIX. – (O)F. *mucilage* – late L. *mūcilāgō*, *-āgin-* musty juice, f. *mūcus* MUCUS. Hence **mucilagin**OUS -æ·dʒinəs. XVII.

muck[1] mʌk dung XIII; dirt, filth XIV. prob. of Scand. origin (the earliest ME. exx. are from eastern areas) and – forms rel. to ON. *myki*, *mykr* dung, Da. *møg*, †*mwgh*, *mug*, *mog*, *møk*, Norw. *myk*, f. Germ. **muk*- **meuk*- soft (see MEEK), poss. repr. in rare OE. *hlōs* (pigsty) *moc*.

muck[2] mʌk in *run a muck* (*runs an Indian muck*, Dryden). XVII. Second syll. of AMUCK, wrongly taken to be a sb. preceded by A[1].

muckender mʌ·kĭndəɹ (dial.) handkerchief. XV. prob. – s.w. dial. equiv. of F. *mouchoir*, f. *moucher* clear the nose :– popL. **muccāre*; for the intrusive *n* cf. *colander*.

mucus mjū·kəs viscid or slimy substance. XVII. – L. *mūcus*, also *muccus* mucus of the nose, rel. to synon. Gr. *múxa*, *mússesthai* blow the nose, *muktḗr* nose, nostril (f. **muk*-), also L. *ē|mungere* wipe the nose. So **mu·c**OUS. XVII. – L. *mūcōsus*; cf. F. *muqueux*.

mud mʌd wet and soft earth. XIV. prob. – MLG. *mudde* (LG. *mudde*, *mod*, *mōde*, *mūde*; cf. Du. *modden* dabble in mud), MHG. *mot* (G. dial. *mott*) bog, bog-earth, peat; an extended form of the base is shown in MLG., Du. *modder* mud (whence G. *moder*), MHG. *moter* (G. dial. *motter*). Hence **mu·dd**Y[1]. XVI. **mu·d**LARK grubber or worker in dirty places XVIII; joc. formation after *skylark*.

muddle mʌ·dl †wallow in mud; make muddy, (hence) confuse. XVII. perh. – MDu. *moddelen*, frequent. of *modden*; see MUD, -LE[3].

muezzin mue·zin in Mohammedan countries, public crier who proclaims the hours of prayer. XVI. – dial. var. (with *zz*) of – Arab. *muaððin*, active pple. of *aððana*, frequent. of *aðana* proclaim, f. *uðn* ear.

muff[1] mʌf cylindrical covering for the hands. XVI (B. Jonson). – Du. *mof*, shortening of MDu. *moffel*, *muffel* (corr. to F. *moufle*, It. *mufla*) – medL. *muff(u)la*, of unkn. origin.

muff[2] mʌf awkward person at sport, (gen.) duffer. XIX (Dickens). Of unkn. origin. Cf. WFlem. *moef*, of similar meaning. Hence vb. make a muddle of.

muffin mʌ·fin (dial.) wheat- or oat-cake; flat spongy cake eaten toasted and buttered. XVIII. Of unkn. origin; perh. cf. OF. *moufflet* soft (bread). Hence **muffin**EE·R[1]. XIX.

muffle[1] mʌ·fl wrap up, as in a cloth XV; †blindfold, stifle XVI; deaden the sound of XVIII. perh. aphetic of OF. **amoufler*, *enmoufler*, f. *en-* EN-+*moufle* thick glove (cf. MUFF[1]). Hence **mu·ffl**ER[1] scarf. XVI.

muffle[2] mʌ·fl thick part of upper lip and nose (of beasts). XVII (Holland). – F. *mufle*, of unkn. origin.

mufti mʌ·fti Mohammedan priest or expounder of the law; in Turkey, official head of the state religion. XVI. – Arab. *muftī*, active pple. of *aftā* give a *fetwa* or decision on law. The sense 'plain clothes')('uniform' (XIX) may be a joc. application of this, orig. with allusion to dressing-gown, smoking-cap, and slippers as suggesting the costume of a mufti on the stage.

mug[1] mʌg (dial.) pot, jug XVI; cylindrical drinking-vessel XVII. prob. of Scand. origin (cf. Norw. *mugge*, Sw. *mugg* pitcher with handle, of uncertain connexions).

mug[2] mʌg (sl.) face. XVIII. prob. transf. use of prec., drinking-mugs being freq. made to represent a grotesque face.

mug[3] mʌg (sl.) simpleton, duffer. XIX. perh. transf. use of MUG[2] with ref. to stupid looks. Hence synon. **mu·ggins**, prob. by assoc. with the surname *Muggins*.

muggy mʌ·gi (dial.) moist, damp; (of weather) damp and close. XVIII. f. dial. *mug* sb. mist, drizzle, dull weather (XVIII) or *mug* vb. drizzle (XIV)+-Y[1]; ult. of Scand. origin (cf. ON. *mugga* mist, drizzle, Norw., Sw. dial. *mugg* mould, mildew, prob. rel. to MUCUS).

mugwort mʌ·gwə̄ɹt plant Artemisia vulgaris. OE. *mucgwyrt*, f. base of MIDGE+WORT.

mugwump mʌ·gwʌmp (U.S.) great man, boss; one who holds aloof from party politics. XIX. – Natick (Algonkin) *mugquomp* great chief.

mulatto mjulæ·tou offspring of a European and a Negro. XVI (*mulatow*). – Sp., Pg. *mulato* young mule, (hence) one of mixed race, obscurely f. *mulo* MULE[1]; whence F. *mulâtre* (assim. to *-âtre* -ASTER), It. *mulatto*.

mulberry mʌ·lbəri tree of the genus Morus. XIV. OE. *mōrberie*, **mūrberie* (cf. *mūrbēam* mulberry tree), ME. *murberie* (XIII), corr. to Du. *moerbezie*, OHG. *mōr-*, *mūrberi* (MHG. *mūlber*, G. *maulbeere*); f. **mōr* – L. *mōrum* mulberry, *mōrus* mulberry-tree (perh. of Mediterranean origin)+BERRY; the dissimilation of *r* . . *r* to *l* . . *r*, parallel to that in MHG. and giving the present form, is evidenced XIV (Trevisa).

mulch, mulsh mʌlʃ half-rotten straw. XVII. sb. use of *mulsh* adj. (XV) soft, (dial.) of 'soft' weather, rel. to (dial.) *melsh* mellow, soft, mild (XIV *melch*, *melissche*, Trevisa) :- OE. *mel(i)sć*, *mil(i)sć*, *mylsć*, f. **mel-* **mul-* (see -ISH[1]), whence also MHG. *molwic*, G. *mollig*, *mollecht*, *molsch*, *mulsch* soft, OHG. *molawēn* be soft, cogn. with L. *mollis* tender (cf. MOLLIFY).

mulct mʌlkt inflict a fine on. XV (*multe*). – F. †*multer*, *mulcter* – L. *mulctāre*, prop. *multāre*, f. *mulcta*, *multa* (whence **mulct** sb. XVI), a purely Italic word.

mule mjūl offspring of he-ass and mare (also pop. hinny) XIII (RGlouc.); transf. of various hybrids, e.g. spinning machine consisting of a combination of Arkwright's warping machine and Hargrave's woof machine XVIII. – OF. *mul* m., (also mod.) *mule* fem. = Pr. *mul*, *mula*, Sp., It. *mulo*, *mula* :- L. *mūlu-s* m., *mūla* fem., prob. of Mediterranean origin, the ass not having a CIE. name. ¶ OE. *mūl*, which would have given **mowl*, was prob. inherited from a CGerm. adoption from L.; cf. MLG., OHG. *mūl* (Du. *muil*, G. *maul*, now in comps. *maulesel*, *-pferd*, *-tier*), ON. *múll*. So **mulet**EER[1] mjūlitiə·ɹ mule-driver. XVI. – F. *muletier*, f. *mulet*, f. OF. *mul* (which it superseded); see -ET, -EER[1].

mull[1] mʌl promontory. XIV. In Gael. *maol*; in Icel. *múli*, perh. identical with *múli* snout = OHG. *mūl* (G. *maul*) snout.

mull[2] mʌl make (wine, beer, etc.) into a hot drink with sugar, spices, etc. XVII (*mulled sack*). Of unkn. origin.

mull[3] mʌl (sl.) muddle, mess. XIX. perh. f. (dial.) *mull* pulverize, crumble (XV), f. *mull* dust, ashes (XIV) – (M)Du. *mul*, *mol* (see MULLOCK).

mullah mʌ·lə Mohammedan theologian. XVII. – Pers., Turk., Urdu *mullā* – Arab. *maulā*.

mullein mʌ·lĭn plant of the genus Verbascum (having woolly leaves and yellow flowers). XV. – OF. *moleine* (mod. *molène*) – Gaulish **melēna* (*melinus* 'color nigrus') sb. fem., corr. to Breton *melen*, W. *melyn* yellowish (cf. Gr. *mélās*, *mélaina* black; see MELAN-).

mullet[1] mʌ·lit fish of the genera Mullus and Mugil. xv (*molet*). – OF. *mulet*, dim. f. L. *mullus* red mullet – Gr. *múllos*, rel. to *mélās* black (cf. prec.).

mullet[2] mʌ·lit (her.) five-pointed star. xiv. – AN. *molet*, (O)F. *molette* rowel, dim. of *meule* millstone :– L. *mola* (see MILL[1]). The orig. form was perh. pierced to represent a spur-rowel.

mulligatawny mʌ:ligətɔ̄·ni Indian highly-seasoned soup. xviii. – Tamil *milagutannīr* 'pepper-water' (Yule).

mulligrubs mʌ·ligrʌbz state or fit of depression; (later) colic. xvi (*mulliegrums*, Nashe). Fanciful formation perh. based on *mully* dusty, powdery (xvi), f. (with -Y[1]) *mull* (see MULL[3]) and GRUB; but the early form *mulliegrums* is perh. reminiscent of *grumble*.

mullion mʌ·ljən (archit.) vertical bar dividing the lights of a window. xvi. Metathetic alt. of ME. *munial*, MONIAL, as the contemp. **mu·nnion** is an assim. form (*n* . . *l* to *n* . . *n*).

mullock mʌ·lək (dial.) rubbish, refuse xiv; (Austral.) rock not containing gold xix. f. dial. *mull* (xiv) dust, ashes, rubbish, rel. to OE. *myl* dust, cogn. with (M)Du. *mul*, *mol*, ON. *moli* crumb, *mylja* crush, f. **mul-* (cf. MULL[3], MEAL); see -OCK.

multi- mʌlti comb. form of L. *multus* much, many, esp. in parasynthetic comps. such as *multicaulis* many-stalked; the earliest in Eng. are **multifo·rmity, multi·loquy** (xvi) talkativeness, **multifarious** -fɛə·riəs (xvii) many and various (L. *-fāriam* adv.), and the el. becomes prolific later, esp. in techn. use, e.g. **multila·teral, multino·mial** (after BINOMIAL) xvii; an ex. of the gen. use is **mu:lti**MILLIONAI·RE (1858 O. W. Holmes).

multiple mʌ·ltipl consisting of many elements. xvii. – F. *multiple* – late L. *multiplus*, f. *multus* (see prec.); cf. *duplus* DOUBLE. So **mu·lti·**PLEX. xvi (Recorde, Billingsley). L. (cf. -FOLD). **multipli·c**ITY. xvi. – late L. **mu·ltiply** cause to be much, many, or more; also intr. xiii. – (O)F. *multiplier* – L. *multiplicāre*, f. *multiplic-*, MULTIPLEX. **mu:ltiplic**A·TION. xiv (Ch.). – (O)F. or L. **multi**TUDE mʌ·ltitjūd great number. xiv. – (O)F. – L. **multitu·din**OUS. xvii.

multure mʌ·ltʃəɹ, -tjuəɹ toll of grain carried or flour made. xiii. – OF. *molture*, *moulture* (mod. *mouture*) :– medL. *molitūra*, f. *molit-*, pp. stem of *molere* grind; see MILL[1], -URE.

mum[1] mʌm †inarticulate sound made with closed lips; command to be silent or secret. xiv. imit.; cf. MLG. *mummen*, Du. *mommen*.

mum[2] mʌm (hist.) beer orig. brewed in Brunswick, Germany. xvii. – G. *mumme*, said by Adelung to have been named (1489) after Christian *Mumme*, a brewer of Brunswick, Germany.

mum[3] see MUMMY[2].

mumble mʌ·mbl eat as with toothless gums; speak indistinctly. xiv. ME. *momele*, frequent. formation on MUM[1]; see -LE[3]; cf. LG. *mummelen*, Du. *mommelen*, *mummelen*, G. *mummeln*, Sw. *mumla*, Da. *mumle*, and ME. *mamele* mutter, chatter (corr. formally to OHG. *mammalōn* stammer). Cf. MUMP.

mumbo-jumbo mʌ:mboudʒʌ·mbou grotesque idol said to have been worshipped by African negroes; (transf.) object of unintelligent veneration. xviii. Of unkn. origin.

mumchance mʌ·mtʃàns †dicing game; †masquerade xvi; (dial.) one who acts in dumb show, dummy xvii; adj. silent xvii. – MLG. *mummenschanze*, *-scanze*, *-kanze* game of dice, masked serenade (= MDu. *mommecanse*), f. *mummen* (see MUMMER) + *schanz* – (O)F. *chance* CHANCE.

mummer mʌ·məɹ †mutterer xv; actor (†in dumb show) in a Christmas play xvi. – OF. *momeur*, f. *momer* act in dumb show, rel. to *momon* mask, Sp. *momo* grimace; perh. of Germ. origin (cf. MDu. *momme*, Du. *mom* mask, MLG. *mummen* mask, disguise); see -ER[2]. So **mu·mm**ERY mummer's performance; play-acting. xvi. – OF. *mommerie* (mod. *momerie*); whence Sp. *momeria*, Du. *mommerij*, G. *mummerei*. **mu·mm**ING[1]. xv. ¶ The relative chronology of this group is obscure.

mummy[1] mʌ·mi †medicinal preparation of the substance of mummies, unctuous liquid xiv; †sovereign remedy, etc. xvi; body embalmed for burial xvii. – (O)F. *momie*, †*mumie* (= Sp. *momia*, It. *mommia*) – medL. *mumia* – Arab. *mūmiyā* embalmed body, f. *mūm* wax (used in embalming). Hence **mu·mmi**FY. xvii; after F. *momifier*.

mummy[2] mʌ·mi nursery variety of MAMMY (s.v. MAM). xix. Also **mum.**

mump mʌmp †grimace; (pl.) swelling of the parotid and salivary glands in the neck (with ref. to the appearance produced). xvi. So **mump** vb. mumble, grimace, munch, sulk. xvi. Symbolic repr. of the movement of the lips in muttering and mumbling or chewing. Cf. Icel. *mumpa* take into the mouth, eat greedily, *mumpaskælur* grimace with the mouth, Du. *mompen*, *mompelen* mumble in utterance, G. *mumpfeln*, *-en* mumble in eating.

mumpsimus mʌ·mpsiməs †obstinate adherent to old ways; tradition bigotedly adhered to. xvi. In allusion to the story related in Richard Pace 'De Fructu' (1517) p. 80 of an illiterate English priest, who, when corrected for reading 'quod in ore mumpsimus' (for 'sumpsimus'—what we have taken with our mouths) in the post-communion of the mass, replied 'I will not change my old mumpsimus for your new sumpsimus'.

mun mʌn, mən (dial.) must. xii (Orm). – ON. *muna*, f. the base of MIND; the var. *man* of the pres. sg. gave dial. *maun*.

munch mʌnᵗʃ chew steadily. XIV (Ch.). imit.; cf. *crunch*, *scrunch*.

mundane mʌ·ndein worldly, earthly XV; cosmic XVII. orig. *mondaine* – (O)F. *mondain* – late L. *mundānus* (as sb. in Cicero), f. *mundus* world, (earlier) universe of celestial bodies, spec. use of *mundus* personal adornment, after Gr. *kósmos* (see COSMETIC, COSMOS). Later assim. to L. (see -ANE[1]).

mungo[1] mʌ·ŋgou †mongoose; *m. root*, plant Ophiorhiza Mungo. XVIII. var. of *mungos*, MONGOOSE; acc. to Kæmpfer, 'Amœnitates Exoticæ', 1712, p. 574, the Portuguese called the animal *mungo* and the plant *raje mungo* 'mungo root'.

mungo[2] mʌ·ŋgou superior kind of shoddy (of Yorkshire origin). XIX. perh. a use of Sc. Christian name *Mungo*, in Yorkshire often applied to dogs, with allusion to *mung*, *mong* mixture.

mungoose see MONGOOSE.

municipal mjuni·sipəl †pert. to the internal affairs of a state; pert. to local self-government, esp. of a town. XVI. – L. *mūnicipālis*, f. *mūnicipium* Roman city of which the inhabitants had Roman citizenship, f. *mūnicip-*, *-ceps*, f. *mūnia* civic offices + *capere* take (cf. HEAVE). So **municipa·lITY**. XVIII. – F.

munificent mjuni·fisənt splendidly generous. XVI. f. L. *mūnificent-* (cf. BENEFICENT, MAGNIFICENT), used as stem of *mūnificus*, f. *mūnus* office, duty (cf. MUNICIPAL), gift :– **moinos*, f. **moi-* **mei* **mi-*; see COMMON, IMMUNE, MIGRATE, MUTABLE, and -ENT. So **muni·ficENCE**, †-ENCY. XVI.

muniment mjū·nimənt document preserved as evidence of rights or privileges. XV. – (O)F. *muniment* – L. *mūnīmentum* (in medL.) title-deed, f. *munīre* fortify, secure, earlier *mœnīre*, f. *mœnia* walls, ramparts, rel. to *mūrus*, *mœrus* wall; see MURAL, -MENT.

munition mjuni·ʃən †fortification; AMMUNITION (q.v.). XVI. – (O)F. *munition* – L. *mūnītiō(n-)*, f. *mūnīt-*, *mūnīre*; see prec. and -ITION.

munnion mʌ·njən (see MULLION). XVI.

munshi see MOONSHEE.

muntjak mʌ·ntdʒæk small Asiatic deer. XVIII. – Sunda *minchek*.

mural mjuə·rəl pert. to a wall; (of a crown) embattled. XVI. – (O)F. *mural* (*coronne murail* mural crown) – L. *mūrālis*, f. *mūrus*, earlier *mœrus*, *moiros* wall; see MUNIMENT, -AL[1]. So sb. †wall XV; wall-painting XX.

murder mə̄·ɹdəɹ criminal homicide. OE. *morþor* (ME. *morþre*, *murþre*) = Goth. *maurþr* :– Germ. **murþram*, f. IE. **mrt-* (see MORTAL), repr. also by Germ. **mortam* (whence OE., OS., ON. *morð*, (O)HG. *mord*, Du. *moord*); reinforced in ME. by OF. *murdre* (mod. *meurtre*) – Germ., whence the establishment of the forms with *u* and *d*. So **mu·rder** vb. XIII (*morþren*, *murþren*), prob. f. the sb., there being no clear repr. in ME. of the mutated OE. vb. (*ā-*, *for-*, *of-*) *myrþrian* exc. Orm's *mirrþrenn*. **mu·rderER**. XIII (Cursor M.). partly f. the vb., partly – AN. *murdreour*.

murex mjuə·reks shell-fish yielding a purple dye. XVI. – L. *mūrex*, pl. *mūricēs*, perh. rel. to Gr. *múax* sea-mussel.

muriatic mjuəriæ·tik †pert. to brine; 'marine' (acid), hydrochloric. XVII. – L. *muriāticus*, f. *muria* brine (the acid, 'spirits of salt', being obtained by heating salt with sulphuric acid); see -ATIC.

muricate mjuə·rikeit furnished with sharp points. XVII. – L. *mūricātus*, f. *mūric-*, MŪREX; see -ATE[2].

murk, mirk mə̄ɹk (dial.) darkness. XIII. So adj. dark XIII (Havelok). The ME. evidence points to Scand. origin (ON. *myrkr* sb. and adj. = OS. *mirki* adj.) rather than to OE. *mirce*, though this may have preserved k of an original **kw*, as in *þicce* THICK. Hence **mu·rkY**[1]. XIV (R. Rolle). No cogns. are known outside Germanic.

murmur mə̄·ɹməɹ subdued continuous sound XIV (Maund.); inarticulate complaining XIV (Ch.); softly spoken word(s) XVII. – (O)F. *murmure* or L. *murmur* rumbling noise, murmur, rel. to vb. *murmurāre* (whence (O)F. *murmurer*, Eng. vb. XIV), corr. to Gr. *mormúrein*, Skr. *marmaras* noisy, and with variation OHG. *murmurōn*, *-ulōn* (G. *murmeln*), Du. *murmelen* burble, Lith. *murmė́ti*, *murménti*; redupl. f. imit. base (cf. Du. *morren* murmur, complain).

murphy mə̄·ɹfi (sl.) potato. XIX. f. the common Ir. surname *Murphy*, with allusion to the potato being a staple article of food of the Irish peasant. Cf. synon. *donovan*.

murrain mʌ·rĭn †plague XIV (R. Rolle); infectious disease of cattle XV. – AN. *moryn*, (O)F. *morine*, †*moraine*, f. stem of *mourir*, †*morir* :– Rom. **morīre*, for L. *morī* die (see MORTAL); the F. suffix is that of *ruine* RUIN.

murrey mʌ·ri (arch.) purple-red. – OF. *moré* adj. and sb., *morée* sb. – medL. *morātum*, *-āta*, f. L. *morum* MULBERRY; see -Y[5].

murrhine mʌ·rain (Roman antiq.) pert. to **murra** mʌ·rə fine earth of which precious vases, etc., were made. XVI. – L. *murr(h)inus*, f. *murra*; see -INE[1].

musa mjū·zə plantain or banana tree. XVI. – modL. – Arab. *mauzah*.

muscat mʌ·skæt strong sweet wine (XVI) from the grape so called (XVII). – (O)F. *muscat* – Pr. *muscat*, f. *musc* MUSK; see -ATE[1]. So **muscatel, muskadel** mʌskəte·l, -de·l in the same senses (XIV and XVI). – OF. *muscadel*, *-tel* (cf. It. *-dello*, *-tello*, Sp., Pg. *-tel*); and **muscadine** mʌ·skədain (XVI and XVII) respectively, of doubtful origin.

muscle mʌ·sl contractile fibrous bundle producing movement in an animal body. XVI. – (O)F. *muscle* – L. *mūsculus*, dim. of *mūs* MOUSE, the form and movements of some muscles suggesting those of a mouse (cf. L. *lacertus* lizard, upper arm muscle, F. *souris* mouse, muscle, Gr. *mûs* mouse, fleshy part, OSl. *myšica* arm, Skr. *muṣká-* scrotum, pudendum muliebre); sp. with *-sk(e)l-* survived till XVIII; cf. MUSSEL. So **muscul**AR mʌ·skjŭləɹ. XVII. – modL.; cf. F. *musculaire*. **mu·sculo-,** comb. form of L. *mūsculus*, as in *mu·sculo-arterial* (Coleridge).

muscology mʌskɔ·lədʒi bryology. XIX. – modL. *muscologia*, f. L. *muscus* MOSS; see -LOGY.

muscovado mʌskŏvā·dou unrefined sugar. XVII. – Sp. (*azúcar*) *mascabado*; cf. F. *moscouade*, †*mascovade*.

Muscovy mʌ·skəvi (arch.) Russia. XVI. – F. *Muscovie*, †*Moscovie* – modL. *Moscovia* (see -IA[1]), f. Russ. *Moskvá* Moscow. So **Mu·scov**ITE Russian. XVI. – modL.; so F. *Moscovite*.

muse[1] mjūz be absorbed in thought. XIV (Ayenbite). – (O)F. *muser* †meditate, waste time, trifle = Pr. *musar*, It. *musare* stare vacantly, idle, loiter :– Rom. **musāre*, presumably rel. to medL. *mūsum* (see MUZZLE), but the sense-development is not obvious. Cf. AMUSE.

Muse, muse[2] mjūz goddess inspiring learning and the arts; a poet's inspiring goddess. XIV (Ch.). – (O)F. *muse* or L. *mūsa* – Gr. *moûsa*. Cf. MUSEUM, MUSIC.

museum mjūzī·əm †building devoted to learning and the arts (regarded as 'a home of the Muses'); building for exhibition of objects of art or science (first applied to 'Mr. Ashmole's Museum at Oxford'). XVII. – L. *mūsēum* library, study – Gr. *mouseîon* seat of the Muses, sb. use of n. of *mouseîos*, f. *moûsa* MUSE[1]; the sp. with *æ* was freq. XVII–XVIII. ¶ Of CEur. range.

mush[1] mʌʃ (N.-Amer.) porridge made with meal XVII; (f. the vb.) pulpy mess or substance XIX. prob. symbolic alt. of MASH. So as vb. XVIII. Hence **mu·sh**Y[1] XIX.

mush[2] mʌʃ (sl.) umbrella, short for MUSHROOM. XIX.

musha mʌ·ʃə Ir. excl. of strong feeling. XIX. – Ir. *muise*, var. of *máiseadh*, i.e. *má* if, *is* is, *eadh* it.

mushroom mʌ·ʃrum umbrella-shaped fungus. XV. Late ME. *musseroun*, *musheron*, by assim. *musherom* (XVI) – (O)F. *mousseron* – late L. *mussiriō(n-)* (Anthimus). Hence as vb. XVIII (once, trans.), XIX (intr.).

music mjū·zik art of combining sounds in a certain order for æsthetic effect XIII; sounds in melodic or harmonic combination XIV (Ch.); company of musicians, band XVI; musical score XVII. – (O)F. *musique* – L. *mūsica* – Gr. *mousikḗ*, sb. use (sc. *tékhnē* art) of fem. of *mousikós* pert. to a Muse or the Muses, concerning the arts, poetry, literature, f. *moûsa* MUSE[1]. ¶ Of CEur. range. So **mu·sic**AL[1] pert. to music. XV (Lydg.). – (O)F. – medL. **musi·c**IAN. XIV (*-ien*). – (O)F., f. *musique*.

musk mʌsk odoriferous substance secreted by the musk-deer (Moschus moschiferus). XIV (Trevisa). – late L. *muscus* (Jerome) – Pers. *mushk*, perh. – Skr. *muṣká-* scrotum (the shape of the musk-deer's musk-bag being similar); cf. (O)F. *musc*, etc., Du., G. †*musch*, late Gr. *mósk(h)os*, and medL. *mos(c)hus*, which has been adopted in Germ. langs. ¶ The word has become CEur.

musket mʌ·skit hand-gun for infantry. XVI. – F. *mousquet* (Brantôme), †*-ette* – It. *moschetto*, *-etta* (formerly) bolt from a cross-bow, f. *mosca* fly :– L. *musca*, rel. to Gr. *muîa*, OSl. *mucha* fly, *mŭšica* gnat, and MIDGE. Hence **musket**EER[1] XVI (Marlowe); after F. *mousquetaire*. So **musket**OON short variety of musket with large bore. XVII. – F. *mousqueton* – It. *moschettone*. **mu·sket**RY. XVII. – F. *mousqueterie*.

Muslim mʌ·zlim see MOSLEM.

muslin mʌ·zlin fine cotton fabric. XVII. – F. *mousseline* – It. *mussolina*, *-ino* (whence some early forms), f. *Mussolo* Mosul (Arab. *mauçil*), where muslin was formerly made; cf. -INE[1].

musquash mʌ·skwɔʃ large aquatic rodent, musk-rat. XVII (*mussascus*, *musquassus*, Capt. Smith). – Algonkin (e.g. Abnaki *muskwessu*).

mussel mʌ·sl bivalve mollusc. OE. *muscle*, *muxle*, *musle* (– L.) was superseded by MLG. *mussel*, MDu. *mosscele* (Du. *mossel*) = OHG. *muscula* (G. *muschel*) – Rom. **muscula* (whence OF. *mousle*, F. *moule*), alt. f. L. *musculus*, dim. (see -CLE) of L. *mūs* MOUSE; sp. with *-sk-* survived till XVII, but *-ss-* occurred XV.

Mussulman mʌ·slmən, pl. *-mans* Mohammedan. XVI. – Pers. *musulmān*, prop. adj. f. *muslim* MOSLEM. ¶ With the incorrect pl. *Mussulmen* cf. G. *Muselmänner*.

must[1] mʌst unfermented juice of the grape. OE. *must* = (O)HG. *most* – L. *mustum* (whence also F. *moût*, Sp., It. *mosto*), sb. use of n. of *mustus* new, new-born.

must[2] mʌst †in OE. and ME. *mōste* as pt. of *mōte*, was able or permitted to; as a present (and in certain conditions) a past tense, is obliged or required to. XIII (Cursor M., K. Horn). OE. *mōste*, pt. of *mōt* am permitted or obliged, may, must = OFris. *mōt*, OS. *mōt*, *muot* (Du. *moet*), OHG. *muoz* find room or opportunity, may, must (G. *muss*), Goth. *gamōt* (it) has room, rel. to MLG. *mōte*, OHG. *muoza* (G. *musse*) leisure :– CGerm. (exc. Scand.) **mōtā*, of unkn. origin.

must[3] mʌst mustiness, mould. XVII. Back-formation from MUSTY.

must[4] mʌst (of animals) in a state of dangerous frenzy. XIX. – Urdu *mast* – Pers. *mast* intoxicated.

mustachio mŭstā·tʃiou MOUSTACHE. XVI (*mustaccio, -achio, mastacho*). – Sp. *mostacho* and its source It. *mostaccio* (cf. medL. *mustacia*), based ult. on Gr. *mustak-, mústax* upper lip, moustache, poss. crossing of *mástax* mouth, jaws, and *bústax* moustache.

mustang mʌ·stæŋ wild horse of the American plains. XIX. app. blending of Sp. *mestengo* (now *mesteño*) and *mostrenco*, both applied to wild or masterless cattle, the former being f. *mesta* (:– L. *mixta*, sb. use of fem. pp. of *miscēre* MIX) association of graziers, who appropriated wild cattle that attached themselves to the herds.

mustard mʌ·stəɹd seeds of black and white mustard (species of cruciferous plants of the genus Sinapis, now included in Brassica) powdered and used as a condiment, etc. XIII. – OF. *mo(u)starde* (mod. *moutarde*) = Pr., Cat., Pg., It. *mostarda*, Rum. *mostar*, f. CRom. **mosto*, L. *mustum* MUST[1], whence also Cat. *mostassa*. Sp. *mostaza*; prop. applied to the condiment as orig. prepared by making the ground seeds into a paste with must. ¶ The F. word was adopted into Germ. langs. as MDu. *mostaert* (Du. *-aard*), whence MHG. *mostert* (G. *mostert*).

mustee mʌstī· **mestee** mestī· offspring of a white and a quadroon. XVII. – Sp. *mestizo* mestī·þo; see MESTIZO.

muster mʌ·stəɹ A. †exhibition, display; †pattern, example, sample; B. assembling of soldiers, etc.; assembly, collection. XIV (Wyclif, Ch., Maund.). Late ME. *mostre, moustre* – OF. *moustre* (later in latinized form *monstre*, mod. *montre*) = Sp. *muestra*, Pg., It. *mostra*, repr. CRom. sb. f. **mostrare* :– L. *mōnstrāre* show (cf. MONSTER). So **muster** vb.† show, display XIII (Cursor M.); collect, assemble XV (Lydg.). – OF. *moustrer* (mod. *montrer*).

musty mʌ·sti 'moist and fetid' (J.), smelling of mould. XVI. perh. alt. of MOISTY by assoc. with MUST[1]. A rel. verb and an adj. *must* are contemporary.

mutable mjū·təbl liable to change. XIV (Ch.). – L. *mūtābilis*; see -ABLE. So **mutA·TION** changing XIV (Ch.); (mus.) change from one hexachord to another XVI (Morley); (philol.) change of an initial consonant in Celtic; umlaut XIX. – L. *mūtātiō(n-)*, f. *mūtāt-, mūtāre* change, f. **moit-*, extension of the base **moi-* **mei-*, repr. also in MEAN[2], etc., MUTUAL; cf. (O)F. *mutation*. Hence, by back-formation, **mutA·TE**[3] XIX.

mutch mʌtʃ (dial., esp. Sc.) cap, coif. XV. – MDu. *mutse* (Du. *muts*), corr. to (M)HG. *mütze*, shortened by-forms of MDu. *amutse, almutse* (= MHG. *armuz, almuz*) – medL. *almucia* AMICE.

mutchkin mʌ·tʃkin (Sc.) fourth of old Scots pint (¾ imperial pint). XV. – early mod. Du. *mudseken* (now *mutsje*), dim. of *mudde* (= OS. *muddi*, OHG. *mutti*, G. *mutt*) – L. *modius* bushel; see -KIN.

mute mjūt silent, dumb. XIV (Ch., PPl.). Early forms also *mewet, muwet* (two syll.); – (O)F. *muet*, dim. formation on OF. *mu* = Pr. *mut*, Sp. *mudo*, It. *muto*, Rum. *mut* :– L. *mūtu-s*, f. symbolic syll. **mu*, expressing lack of articulation, as in Gr. *múdos, múndos, mútēs, mukós*, Skr. *mū́kas* dumb, Arm. *munj*, and MUTTER. The form became permanently assim. to L. XVI. Hence vb.

mutilate mjū·tileit deprive of a limb or principal part. XVI. f. pp. stem of L. *mutilāre* cut or lop off, f. *mutilus* maimed; see -ATE[3]. So **mutilA·TION**. XVII. – late L.

mutiny mjū·tĭni open revolt against authority. XVI. f. (after words in -Y[3]) †*mutine* – (O)F. *mutin* rebellious, mutinous, sb. rebel, mutineer, in XVI rebellion, mutiny, f. *muete* (mod. *meute*) = Pr. *mouta* signal, Sp. *muebda* movement, excitement :– Rom. **movita* movement, f. **movit-*, for L. *mōt-* (see MOTION). Hence **mu·tiny** vb. XVI. So **mutinEE·R**[1]. XVII (Sh.), after F. *mutinier*. **mu·tinOUS**. XVI. ¶ Members of the group to which these words belong made their first appearance for the most part (esp. in translations) in the second half of XVI; much variety of formation existed and continued into XVII; the following did not survive: *mutinado* mutineer (cf. Sp. *amotinado*); *mutine* sb. (superseded by *mutiny* and *mutineer*) and adj. (superseded by *mutinous*); *mutine* vb. – F. *mutiner*; *mutiner*; *mutinery* (F. *mutinerie*); *mutinious*; *mutinist*; *mutinize*.

mutter mʌ·təɹ speak almost inaudibly with nearly closed lips. XIV (Ch., Wyclif). Frequentative formation (see -ER[4]) on a base **mut-*, repr. also in MUTE; cf. G. dial. *muttern*, beside synon. ON. *muskra* murmur, Norw. *mustra* whisper, mumble, in Eng. dial. *muster* (XV), L. *mussāre, mussitāre, muttīre*, Gr. *múzein* mutter, moan.

mutton mʌ·tn flesh of sheep XIII; sheep XIV; loose woman XVI. ME. *moto(u)n* – OF. *moton* (mod. *mouton*) = Pr., Cat. *moltó*, OSp. *moton*, It. *montone*, dial. *moltone* :– medL. *multō(n-)*, prob. of Gaul. origin (cf. OIr., Ir. *molt* ram, Gael. *mult* wether, W. *mollt*, Corn. *mols*, Breton *maout* sheep).

mutual mjū·tʃuəl, -tj- felt or done by each to the other XV; respective; pert. to both, common XVI (Sh.). – (O)F. *mutuel* = Sp. *mutual*, f. L. *mūtuus* borrowed, mutual :– **moitwos*, f. **moi-* change, as in *mūtāre*; see MUTABLE, -AL[1].

mutule mjū·tjūl (archit.) projection of stone or wood, modillion. XVI. – F. *mutule* – L. *mutulus*, perh. of Etruscan origin.

muzhik see MOUJIK.

muzzle mʌ·zl A. beast's nose and mouth XV; open end of a gun XVI; B. contrivance confining an animal's mouth XIV (Ch.). Late ME. *mosel* – OF. *musel* (mod. *museau*) = Pr. *muzel* :– Gallo-Rom. **mūsellum*, dim. of medL. *mūsum* (cf. Pr. *mus*, It., OSp. *muso*), of unkn. origin. Hence vb. thrust out the m.; put a m. on. XV.

muzzy mʌ·zi †(of places, etc.) dull, gloomy; stupid, fuddled. XVIII (Mrs. Delany). In early use also *mussy*; words similar in form and meaning are *mossy* †stupid, dull (XVI–XVII), dial. *mosey* mouldy, muggy, hazy, stupid, *mosy* downy (XV), *muzz* study intently, 'mug', fuddle (XVIII), *muzzle* fuddle (XVIII); but their relations and origin are obscure.

my mai (possessive pron.) of or pert. to me. XII. ME. *mī*, reduced form of *mīn* MINE[1], orig. before a cons., as *my son*)(*mine eyes*; cf. THY.

myall[1] mai·əl wild aboriginal of Australia. XIX. Native name in Bigambel (Dumaresque River) *mail* the blacks (*namail* a black).

myall[2] mai·əl Australian acacia. XIX. Native name: in Kamilaroi (Hunter River) *maiāl*.

myceto- maisī·tou comb. form of Gr. *mū́kēs* (*-ēt-*) mushroom.

mylodon mai·lŏdən gigantic extinct sloth. XIX. modL., f. Gr. *múlē*, *múlos* molar, prop. MILL, millstone + *-odōn* TOOTH.

mynheer mainhɛə·ɹ, mənɛə·ɹ Du. equiv. of 'sir', 'Mr'; Dutchman. XVII. – Du. *mijnheer*, f. *mijn* MY + *heer* lord, master (= G. *herr*), repr. compar. of Germ. **χairaz* HOAR (lit.) grey-haired, (hence) honourable, majestic, august (G. *hehr*; cf. L. *senior* SIRE).

myo- mai·ou, maiɔ· comb. form of Gr. *mûs* MUSCLE, as in **myo·**LOGY science of muscles (XVII) – modL.

myopia maiou·piə short-sightedness. XVIII. – modL. – late Gr. *mūōpiā*, f. *mū́ōps*, f. *mū́ein* shut (cf. MYSTERY[1]) + *ṓps* EYE. Hence **myo·pic** -ɔ·pik.

myosotis maiəsou·tĭs plant of the genus so named. XIX. L. – Gr. *muosōtís*, f. *muós*, g. of *mûs* MOUSE + *ōt-*, *oûs* EAR[1]; so called from the soft hairy leaves.

myriad mi·riəd 10,000; countless number. XVI. – late L. *mȳriad-*, *mȳrias* – Gr. *mūriad-*, *mūriás*, f. *mū́rios* countless, innumerable, pl. *mū́rioi* 10,000. Cf. F. *myriade* (XVII); see -AD[1].

myrmidon mə̄·ɹmidən one of a warlike race of Thessaly XIV; †soldier of a bodyguard, faithful follower; unscrupulously faithful attendant XVII. – L. pl. *Myrmidones* – Gr. *Murmidónes*, acc. to legend created orig. from ants (*múrmēkes*).

myrobalan mairɔ·bələn plum-like fruit used now in tanning, etc. XVI. – F. *myrobolan* (= Sp., It. *mirabolano*), or its source L. *myrobalanum* – Gr. *murobálanos*, f. *múron* balsam, unguent + *bálanos* acorn, date, bennut. ¶ Among dyers called *m'rabs*.

myrrh mə̄ɹ gum resin from species of Commiphora. OE. *myrra*, *myrre*, corr. to OS. *myrra* (Du. *mirre*), OHG. *myrra* (G. *myrrhe*), ON. *mirra*; CGerm. (exc. Gothic) = L. *myrrha* (*murrha*, *murra*) – Gr. *múrrā*, of Semitic origin (cf. Arab. *murr*, Aram. *mūrā*); reinforced in ME. from OF. *mirre* (mod. *myrrhe*).

myrtle mə̄·ɹtl †myrtle-berry XIV; plant of the genus Myrtus XVI. – medL. *myrtilla*, *-us* (whence OF. *myrtille*, *-til*, It. *mirtillo*), dim. of L. *myrta*, *-us* – Gr. *múrtos*.

myself maise·lf, mise·lf OE. *mē self* (accus. *selfne*); see ME and SELF; altered to *mi self* (XIII) partly by loss of stress, partly on the analogy of HERSELF, in which *her* was apprehended as genitive; cf. THYSELF, OURSELVES, dial. *hisself*, *theirselves*.

mystagogue mi·stəgɔg one who introduces to religious mysteries. XVI. – F. *mystagogue* or L. *mystagōgus* – Gr. *mustagōgós*, f. *mústēs* initiated person + *agōgós* leading, *ágein* lead (see ACT).

mystery[1] mi·stəri †phr. *in (a) m.*, mystically XIV; religious truth or doctrine; hidden or secret thing XIV; religious rite XVI; (after F. *mystère*) miracle play XVIII. – AN. **misterie* (OF. *mistere*, mod. *mystère*) or immed. – the source L. *mystērium* – Gr. *mustḗrion* secret thing or ceremony, f. **mus-* as in *mústēs* initiated one, *mustikós* MYSTIC. So **mysteri**OUS mistiə·riəs. XVII. – F. *mystérieux*; earlier †*myste·rial* (XVI, Skelton), *-ally* adv. (XV) – late L. (with adv. *mystēriāliter*).

mystery[2] mi·stəri occupation, handicraft, art XIV; trade guild or company XV. – medL. *misterium*, contr. of L. *ministerium* MINISTRY, by assoc. with *mystērium* (see prec.).

mystic mi·stĭk spiritually symbolical XIV; occult, enigmatical; pert. to direct communion with God XVII; sb. exponent of mystic theology; one who practises mystical communion XVII. – (O)F. *mystique* or L. *mysticus* – Gr. *mustikós*, f. *mústēs* initiated one, f. *mū́ein* close (of eyes, lips), *mueîn* initiate. So **my·st**ICAL secret, occult, symbolical XV; pert. to mystics or mysticism XVII. **my·stic**ISM -sizm opinions and practice of mystics. XVIII; so G., F. **mystique** mistī·k. XX. F., sb. use of adj.

mystify mi·stifai bewilder intentionally; involve in mystery or obscurity. XIX (Hazlitt 1814, Southey 1816; 'To bewilder, or in the French phrase, to *mistify* the attentive world', Blackwood's Magazine, 1818, iv 222). – F. *mystifier* (XVIII), irreg. f. *mystère* MYSTERY[1] or *mystique* MYSTIC; see -FY. So **my:stifica·**TION. XIX (1815). – F.; often assoc. with MIST, MISTY, a homonymous deriv.

of which had been used earlier in pp. *mist-*, *mystified* 'beclouded, befogged' (XVIII).

myth miþ, maiþ fictitious narrative usu. involving supernatural things. XIX (*c.*1830). Formerly also *mythe* (cf. F. *mythe*); – modL. *mȳthus*, mai·þəs used in Eng. context (from Coleridge), beside *mythos* (from XVIII) – late L. *mythos* – Gr. *mûthos*. So **mythi**c(AL) mi·þ-. XVII. – late L. *mȳthicus* – Gr. *mūthikós*. **mytho**LOGY miþ-, maiþə·lədʒi †exposition of myths or fables XV (Lydg.); †symbolical story, mythical meaning XVII (Holland); body of myths XVIII (Gibbon). – F. *mythologie* or late L. *mȳthologia* – Gr. *mūthologíā*.

N

nab[1] (OE. *nabban*) see HOB-NOB.

nab[2] næb (colloq.) catch, seize. XVII. Of unkn. origin; parallel to synon. and contemp. *nap* (cant and sl.), which survives in KIDNAPPER.

nabob nei·bɔb Mohammedan official acting as deputy governor in the Mogul empire XVII; rich person, spec. one who has returned from India XVIII (*Mogul Pitt and Nabob Bute*, H. Walpole 1764; Foote *The Nabob* 1773). – Pg. *nababo* or Sp. *nabab* – Urdu *nawwāb*, var. of *nuwwāb* (whence **nawab** XVIII) – honorific pl. of Arab. *nā'ib* deputy, governor, prince (whence **naib** XVII).

nabs næbz (colloq.) *his nabs* himself, †*my nabs* myself. XVIII. Of unkn. origin; cf. synon. NIBS.

nacre nei·kəɹ shell-fish yielding mother-of-pearl XVI; mother-of-pearl XVIII. – (O)F. *nacre*, corr. to Sp. *nácar*, *nácara*, It. *nacchera* (now only 'kettledrum', formerly also 'nacre'), †*naccara*: see NAKER. Hence **na·cr**EOUS, -OUS. XIX.

nadir nei·dəɹ (astron.) †point in the heavens diametrically opposite to another XIV (Ch.); point opposite to the zenith XV; lowest point XVIII. – (O)F. *nadir*, corr. to Sp., It. *nadir* – Arab. *naḍīr* opposite to, over against, opposite point. In the second sense for *naḍīr es-semt* opposite to the ZENITH.

nævus nī·vəs mole on the skin. XIX. L.

naffy næ·fi canteen in charge of N.A.A.F.I. (*N*avy *A*rmy and *A*ir *F*orce *I*nstitutes). f. the initials with terminal el. assim. to -Y[6].

nag[1] næg small riding-horse. XIV. Of unkn. origin; cf. Du. *neg*(*ge*).

nag[2] næg (dial.) gnaw; be persistently worrying or annoying. XIX. Also *gnag*, *knag*; of dial. origin; repr. by *naggy* XVII (*knaggie*) adj.; perh. of Scand. or LG. origin (cf. Norw., Sw. *nagga* gnaw, nibble, irritate, LG. (*g*)*naggen* (XV) irritate, provoke).

Nagari nā·gari. XVIII. = DEVANAGARI.

Nahuatl nā·hwātl name of a group of Central-Mexican langs., f. national name *Nahua*. XIX.

Naiad nai·æd young nymph of the rivers and springs. XVII (Sh.). – L. – Gr. *Nāiad-*, nom. *Nāiás*, rel. to *náein* flow. The pl. *Naiades* (XIV, Gower) repr. F. *Naiades* or L. *Nāiadēs*.

naiant nei·ənt (her.) swimming. XVI. – AN. **naiant* = OF. *noiant*, prp. of *noier*, *noer* swim (mod. *noyer* drown) = It. *nuotare* :– Rom. **notāre*, for L. *natāre* (see NATATION).

naib, naïf see NABOB, NAÏVE.

naik nā·ik, nei·ik Indian title of rank XVI; military officer XVIII. – Urdu *nā'ik* – Hindi *nāyak* chief, officer :– Skr. *nāyaka* leader.

nail neil hard terminal covering of finger and toe; small spike of metal OE.; the applications to (i) measure of weight (now dial.; cf. MDu., MHG. *nagel*) and (ii) measure of length, $\frac{1}{16}$ of a yard, are of uncertain origin. OE. *næġ*(*e*)*l* = OFris. *neil*, OS., OHG. *nagal* (Du., G. *nagel*), ON. *nagl* :– CGerm. **naglaz* (not in Goth., but cf. *nagljan* vb.). IE. base **nogh-* or **noqh-* is repr. also by Lith. *nãgas* nail, claw, *nagà* hoof, OSl. *nogŭtĭ* nail, *noga* foot, Gr. *ónux*, *onukh-*, OPers. *naxun*, Skr. *nakhás*, *nakhám*, rel. further to L. *unguis*, OIr. *ingen*, OW. *eguin*. Hence **nail** vb. OE. *næġlan*; of CGerm. range.

nainsook nei·nsuk cotton fabric of Indian origin. XIX. – Urdu (Hindi) *nainsukh*, f. *nain* eye + *sukh* pleasure.

naissant nei·sənt (her.) issuing from the middle of an ordinary. XVI. – (O)F. *naissant*, prp. of *naître* be born :– Rom. **nascere*, for L. *nāscī*; see NASCENT.

naïve, naive nā·īv, neiv unaffected, artless. XVII (Dorothy Osborne, Dryden). – (O)F. *naïve*, fem. of *naïf* (adopted earlier in Eng. XVI) :– L. *nātīvu-s* NATIVE. So **naïveté** nā·īvtei. XVII (Dryden), anglicized **nai·ve**TY XVIII. Cf. NEIF.

naked nei·kid unclothed; bare (lit. and fig.). OE. *nacod* (early *næcad*) = OFris. *naked*, *-et*, MLG., MDu. *naket* (Du. *naakt*), OHG. *nackut* (G. *nackt*), ON. *nǫkkviðr*, Goth. *naqaþs*, *-ad-* :– CGerm. **naquaðaz*, **-eðaz* :– IE. **nogwodhos*, **-edhos*, ppl. deriv. of **nogw-*, repr. also in L. *nūdus* NUDE, OIr. *nocht* (:– **nogwtos*), Skr. *nagnás*, OSl. *nagŭ* (Russ. *nagój*), Lith. *núogas*.

naker nei·kəɹ (arch.) kettledrum. XIV (not in use later till revived by Scott). – OF. *nacre, nacaire* = It. *nacchera* (cf. medL. *nacara*, medGr. *anákara*) – Arab. *naqqāraḥ* drum. See NACRE.

namby-pamby næ·mbipæ:mbi weakly sentimental, childishly simple. XVIII. joc. redupl. formation (cf. *handy-dandy*) on the name of *Am*brose Philips (d. 1749), author of pastorals, which were ridiculed by H. Carey and Pope (cf. 'So the Nurses get by Heart Namby Pamby's Little Rhimes', Carey; 'Beneath his reign shall . . . Namby Pamby be prefer'd for Wit', Pope 'Dunciad' iii 319, 1733).

name neim particular designation OE.; reputation XIII. OE. *nama, noma* m. = OFris. *nama, noma*, OS. *namo* (Du. *naam*), OHG. *namo* (G. *name*), ON. *nafn, namn* (with retention of *n* and original n. gender), Goth. *namo* n. :– CGerm. **namōn, -on*. An ancient and widespread word (CIE. base **onŏmen-*, **enŏmen-*) repr. by L. *nōmen* (cf. NOMINATE), Gr. *ónoma*, dial. *ónuma, ōnum-* (cf. ANONYMOUS, SYNONYMOUS), OSl. *imę* (Russ. *imja*), Czech *jméno*, OPruss. *emmens*, acc. *emnen*, OIr. *aiṅm*, pl. *anmann*, OW. *anu*, pl. *enuein* (W. *enw*), Arm. *anun*, OPers., Av., Skr. *nāman-*; the long grade appears in the vbs.: OFris. *nōmia*, MLG. *nŏmen*, Du. *noemen*, MHG. *be|nuomen*. So **name** vb. OE. (*ġe*)*namian*, of WGerm. extent; a new formation on the sb. in late ME. repl. ME. *nemne*, OE. *nemnan* :– **namnjan*. **name**LY[2] nei·mli †especially XII; that is to say XV. ME. *name-, nomeliche*, corr. to OFris. *name-, nomelik*, MDu. *namelıke* (Du. *namelijk*), MHG. *nam(e)-, nem(e)līche* (G. *nämlich* especially), ON. *nafnliga* by name; rendering L. *nōminātim* by name, expressly, in detail. **name**SAKE nei·mseik person or thing having the same name as another. XVII. prob. orig. said of persons or things coupled together 'for the *name('s) sake*'.

nankeen næŋkī·n cotton cloth orig. made at *Nankin* or *Nanking*, lit. 'southern capital' (cf. *Pekin* 'northern capital'), chief city of the province of Kiangsu, China. XVIII.

nanny næ·ni children's nurse. Appellative use of pet-form of the female name *Ann(e)*; see -Y[6]. So **na·nny-**GOAT she-goat. XVIII; cf. BILLY-GOAT.

nantz nænts brandy from *Nantes* (the place of manufacture) on the river Loire, France. XVII (*Nants*).

nap[1] næp take a short sleep. OE. *hnappian*, rel. to OHG. (*h*)*naffezan* slumber (MHG. *nafzen*), of unkn. origin. Hence **nap** sb. XIII (Cursor M.).

nap[2] næp surface of cloth raised and cut smooth. XV (*noppe*). – MLG., MDu. *noppe* (whence G., Da. *noppe*), rel. to MLG., MDu. *noppen* trim by shearing the nap. ¶ For the change of vowel cf. *strap*.

nap[3] næp †napoleon (20-franc piece); card-game in which the player who calls five is said to *go nap*, formerly *go the Napoleon*. XIX. Short for *Napoleon*, Christian name of certain emperors of the French, esp. Napoleon I (1769–1821), after whom the coin so named was called.

napalm nei·pām jellied petrol. XX. f. initial sylls. of NA|PHTHA and PALM|ITATE.

nape neip (hollow at) the back of the neck. XIII. ME. *naupe*, of unkn. origin; the similarity of synon. words in Eng. and other langs. does not go beyond the initial *n*; cf. OFris. (*hals*)|*knap*, OHG. (*h*)*nac* (G. *nacken, genick*; see NECK); (O)F. *nuque* (whence It. *nuca*, Sp. *nuca*), of Arab. origin (*nukhā* spinal marrow).

napery nei·pəri household linen. XIV. – OF. *naperie*, f. *nape*; see NAPKIN, -ERY.

naphtha næ·fþə, (vulgarly) næ·pþə inflammable oil from coal. XVI. – L. *naphtha* (Pliny) – Gr. *náphtha*, also *náphthas*, of Oriental origin (cf. Accadian *napṭu*, f. *nafāṭu, nabāṭu* burst into flame); in anglicized form †*napte* (XIV), also †*naphte*, †*napthe* (XVII), partly after F. *naphte* (XVI). Hence **na·phthal**INE[5] (1821, Kidd), with hiatus-filling *l*.

Napier's bones nei·piəɹz bounz slips of bone, etc. used to facilitate multiplication and division according to a method devised by John *Napier* of Merchiston (1550–1617). XVII. So **Napier**IAN neipiə·riən applied to the logarithms invented by him. XIX.

napkin næ·pkin piece of linen for wiping the lips, etc. at table. XV. f. (O)F. *nappe* linen cloth :– L. *mappa* MAP (for the change of *m* to *n* cf. F. *natte* :– L. *matta* MAT, *nèfle* :– L. *mespilus*) + -KIN. ¶ The formation suggests a Du. comp., but none is known.

Napoleon see NAP[3].

napoo nāpū· (orig. soldier's sl.) XX. – F. *il n'y en a plus* there is nothing left.

narcissism nāɹsi·sizm morbid self-love. XX. f. *Narcissus*, in Gr. myth. name of a beautiful youth who fell in love with his own reflection and pined away; see -ISM.

narcissus nāɹsi·səs bulbous plant. XVI. – L. – Gr. *nárkissos*, the termination of which suggests a Mediterranean origin; prob. infl. by *nárkē* numbness (see next), as the plant has narcotic properties.

narcotic nāɹkɔ·tik substance inducing stupor XIV (Ch.); adj. XVII. – (O)F. *narcotique* or medL. *narcōticus*, sb. *-icum* – Gr. *narkōtikós*, sb. *-ikón*, f. *narkoûn* benumb, stupefy, f. *nárkē* numbness, stupor; cf. SNARE and see -OTIC.

nard nāɹd aromatic unguent XIV, derived from the plant so named (cf. SPIKENARD) XVI. – L. *nardus* – Gr. *nárdos*, of Semitic origin (cf. Heb. *nēr'd'*, pl. *n'rādīm*, Arab. *nārdīn*). Cf. OF. *narde* (mod. *nard*).

nare nɛəɹ (arch.) nostril, spec. of a hawk. XIV. – L. *nāris*, pl. *nārēs*, rel. to NOSE.

narghile nā·ɹgili hookah. XIX. – (partly through F. *narghileh, narguilé*) Pers. (Turk.) *nārgīleh*, f. Pers. *nārgīl* coco-nut, of which the receptacle for the tobacco was made.

nark nāɹk (sl.) police spy or informer. XIX. – Romany *nāk* nose (cf. the use of *nose* in the same sense).

narrate næ̆rei·t give an account or history of. XVII (only occas. before *c.*1750; stigmatized as Sc. by Richardson, Johnson, and Beattie; cf. 'the abominable verb "narrate", which must absolutely be proscribed in all good writing', Quarterly Review, 1813, July, 433). f. pp. stem of L. *narrāre* (f. *gnārus* knowing; cf. *ignōrāre* IGNORE), or back-formation from **narr**A·TION (XV). – (O)F. or L. So **narrat**IVE næ·rətiv sb. (in earliest use Sc., spec. in law) XVI; adj. XVII. – F. *narratif, -ive* adj. and †sb. – late L. *narrātīvus.* ¶ In AL. *narrare, narratio,* and *narrator* were used from XII spec. in law with ref. to the statement of a claim or plea.

narrow næ·rou having little breadth OE.; (dial.) parsimonious, 'close'; strict, close XIII; lacking in breadth of view or sympathy XVII. OE. *nearu* (stem *nearw-*) = OS. *naru* (MDu. *nare, naer,* Du. *naar*) :– Germ. **narwaz* (repr. in MHG. *narwe*, G. *narbe*, MLG. *nar(w)e* scar, sb. use of the adj.), of which no certain cogns. are known. So **na·rrow** vb. OE. *nearwian* confine, †oppress, become narrow; but in ME. (XIII) a new formation on the adj.

narthex nā·ɹþeks (archit.) vestibule extendtending across the west end of a church. XVII. – L. *narthēx* – Gr. *nárthēx* giant fennel, stick, casket, and eccl. (as above).

narwhal nā·ɹwəl delphinoid cetacean. XVII. – Du. *narwal* – Da. *narhval* (whence also G. *narwal*, F. *narval*); the second el. is WHALE. The relation to synon. ON. *náhvalr* is obscure; the latter appears to be f. *nár* corpse, and the allusion is supposed to be to the colour of the animal's skin.

nary see NEVER.

nasal nei·zəl pert. to the nose. XVII. – F. *nasal* or medL. *nāsālis*, f. *nāsus* NOSE; see -AL[1]. Also sb. nose-piece of a helmet XV, earlier *nasel* (XIV). – OF. *nasal, -el* – medL. *nāsāle*, sb. use of n. of adj.

nascent næ·sənt being born or produced. XVII. – L. *nāscent-, -ēns*, prp. of *nāscī* be born; see NATAL, -ENT, and cf. NAISSANT.

naseberry nei·zbəri W. Indian tree Sapota Achras. XVII (*nasebury*). – Sp., Pg. *néspera* MEDLAR, with assim. to BERRY.

naso- nei·zou used as comb. form of L. *nāsus* NOSE (for the regular *nasi-*). XIX.

nasturtium nəstɔ̄·ɹʃəm genus of cruciferous plants (watercress, etc.) having a pungent taste XVII; trailing plant of the genus Tropæolum (at first called *Nasturtium indicum* because introduced from Peru) XVIII. – L. *nasturtium* :– **nāstorctiom*; so called 'quod nasum torqueat' because it irritates the nose (Varro); cf. 'nomen accepit a narium tormento' (Pliny); vulgarly corrupted to *nasturtian* (XVIII).

nasty nà·sti filthy, dirty XIV; nauseous XVI; (of weather) foul, dirty XVII; offensive XVIII; ill-natured XIX. Early vars. †*naxty*, †*naxte*, which with †*naskie* (Cotgr., 1611 s.v. *Maulavé*) suggest ult. derivation from an obscure base **nask-* (**nax-*), which appears also in Sw. dial. *naskug, nasket* dirty, nasty; the var. *nesty* (XVI) may indicate blending with a deriv. of Du. *nestig* dirty; see -Y[1].

natal nei·təl pert. to birth or nativity. XIV (Ch.). – L. *nātālis*, f. *nāt-*, pp. stem of *nāscī* be born, f. **gn-* produce; see KIN, -AL[1], and cf. NASCENT, NATION, NATIVE, NATURE, NÉE, ADNATE, COGNATE, INNATE, RENAISSANCE.

natation neitei·ʃən swimming. XVI. – L. *natātiō(n-)*, f. *natāre* swim, frequent. of *nāre*, f. IE. **sna-*, repr. also by Gr. *nḗkhein* swim, Skr. *snāti* bathe, Ir. *snám* swimming, W. *nawf*; see -ATION. So **natato·r**IAL. XIX, **na·tat**ORY[2]. XVIII. – late L. *natātōrius*.

nation nei·ʃən race, people XIII (Cursor M.); *the nations* (i) the heathen, the gentiles XIV, (ii) the peoples of the earth XVII. – (O)F. *nation*, †*nacioun* – L. *nātiō(n-)* breed, stock, race, f. *nāt-*, pp. stem of *nāscī* be born; see NATAL, -TION. So **nation**AL[1] næ·ʃənəl. XVI. **nation**A·LITY. XVII. – F. **na·tional**IZE. XVIII (1800). – F. *nationaliser* (1794). **na·tional**IST. XVIII (early). **native** nei·tiv (hist.) born thrall (cf. NEIF) XV; (astrol.) subject of a horoscope; one born in a particular place XVI; original or usual inhabitant XVII. – medL. *nātīvus*, sb. use of L. *nātīvus* adj. (whence **na·tive** adj. XIV, of one's birth XV), f. *nāt-*, pp. stem of *nāscī*; see NATAL, -IVE; cf. (O)F. *natif, -ive.* So **nativ**ITY nəti·vĭti (festival of) the birth of Jesus Christ, the Virgin Mary, or St. John Baptist XII (*-teð*, Peterborough Chron.); birth XIV. – (O)F. – late L. (Tertullian).

natron nei·trən native sesquicarbonate of soda. XVII. – F. *natron* – Sp. *natron* – Arab. *naṭrūn, niṭrūn* – Gr. *nítron* NITRE.

natter næ·təɹ (colloq.) chatter aimlessly, nag. XIX. Of dial. and imit. origin (often also *gn-, kn-*; cf. LG. *gnatteren*). Also sb. XX.

natterjack næ·təɹdʒæk toad Bufo calamita. XVIII (Pennant). perh. f. prec. (from its loud croak) + JACK (applied dial. to newts and flies).

natty næ·ti neatly smart XVIII; (dial.) deft, clever XIX. orig. dial. or sl.; rel. obscurely to NEAT[2]; the suffix is -Y[1]

nature nei·tʃəɹ essential qualities or innate character *of*; vital powers *of* XIII; inherent power dominating one's action; creative and regulative power in the world XIV; material world XVII. – (O)F. *nature*, corr. to Pr., Sp., It. *natura* – L. *nātūra* (in some uses tr. Gr. *φύσις*), f. pp. stem of *nāscī* (see NATAL). So **natur**AL[1] næ·tʃərəl. XIV. Earlier *naturel* – (O)F. *naturel*, †*natural* – L. *nātūrālis*. (*Natural history* XVI after L. *naturalis historia*, Pliny.) **na·tural**IZE. XVI. – F. *naturaliser*. **na·tural**ISM system of morality having natural basis XVII; extreme form of realism XIX. – F.

naught nɔ̄t nothing. OE. *nāwiht*, *nāwuht*, *nauht* (= OFris. *nawet*, *nauet*, *naut*), f. *nā* NO[3] + *wiht* WIGHT[1]. Cf. NOUGHT. Used predicatively, passing into adj. OE.; superseded by deriv. **naught**Y[1] nɔ̄·ti †poor, needy XIV; †bad, of inferior quality XIV; morally bad (now only in playful use) XVI; (of children) wayward, inclined to disobedience XVII.

naumachia nɔ̄mei·kiə mimic sea-fight. XVI. – L. – Gr. *naumakhíā*, f. *naûs* ship + *mákhē* fight; see NAVY, -IA[1].

naunt see AUNT.

nausea nɔ̄·siə feeling of sickness XVI; strong disgust XVII. – L. *nausea*, *nausia* – Gr. *nausíā*, *nautíā*, seasickness, nausea, f. *naûs* ship (see NAVAL). So **nause**ATE[3] nɔ·sieit reject with nausea; affect with nausea. XVII. f. pp. stem of L. *nauseāre*, f. *nausea*, after Gr. *nausiân*. **nau·se**OUS. XVII; after L. *nauseōsus*.

nautch nɔ̄tʃ East Indian exhibition of professional dancing. XIX. – Urdu (Hindi) *nāch* – Prakrit *nachcha* – Skr. *nṛitja* dancing, f. *nṛit* dance.

nautical nɔ̄·tik(ə)l pert. to seamen or navigation. XVI (*the Nauticall compasse*). f. L. *nauticus* – Gr. *nautikós*, f. *naútēs* sailor, f. *naûs* ship; see NAVAL, -ICAL. Cf. F. *nautique*.

nautilus nɔ̄·tiləs cephalopod which has webbed dorsal arms formerly believed to be used as sails. XVII. – L. – Gr. *nautílos* sailor, nautilus, f. *naútēs* (see prec.).

naval nei·vəl pert. to ships or a navy. XVI. – L. *nāvālis*, f. *nāvis* ship, rel. to Skr. *naús*, acc. *nā́vam*, Gr. *naûs*, g. *neṓs*, for *nēós* (:– **nāϝos*), Ir. *nau*, ON. *nór*; see -AL[1] and cf. (O)F. *naval*.

nave[1] neiv central block of a wheel. OE. *nafu* and *nafa*, corr. to MDu. *nave* (Du. *naaf*), OHG. *naba* (G. *nabe*), ON. *nǫf* :– Germ. **nabō* :– IE. **nobhā*, f. a base repr. also by Lett. *naba* navel, OPruss. *nabis*, Skr. *nā́bhis* nave, navel; cf. NAVEL. ¶ For the primitive origin of names for parts of a cart, cf. *axle*, *linch(pin)*, *waggon*, *wheel*, *yoke*.

nave[2] neiv main body of a church. XVII. – medL. spec. use of L. *nāvis* ship (see NAVAL), whence (O)F. *nef*, Sp., It. *nave* (in both senses). ¶ So G. *schiff*, Du. *schip* ship.

navel nei·vl umbilicus. OE. *nafela* = OFris. *navla*, *naula*, (M)LG., (M)Du. *navel*, OHG. *nabalo* (G. *nabel*), ON. *nafli* :– CGerm. (exc. Goth.) **naƀalon*, based on IE. **nobh-* (cf. NAVE[1]), **onobh-*, repr. also by L. *umbō* boss of shield, *umbilīcus* navel (cf. UMBILICAL), Gr. *omphalós* navel, boss of shield, and, with grade-variation, Skr. *nābhīlam* depression of the navel, and OIr. *imbliu* navel.

navew nei·vju rape, coleseed, Brassica napus. XVI. – OF. **naveu*, earlier *navel*, mod. dial. *naveau* :– L. *nāpus*: see -EL[2].

navicert næ·visɔ̄ɹt certificate of ship's cargo. XX. f. L. *nāvis* ship (see NAVAL) + first syll. of CERTIFICATE.

navicular nəvi·kjŭləɹ (anat.) of bones in the hand and the foot. XVI. – F. *naviculaire* or late L. *nāviculāris*, f. *nāvicula*, dim. of *nāvis* ship; see NAVAL, -AR, and cf. SCAPHOID.

navigable næ·vigəbl admitting of navigation. XVI. – F. *navigable* or L. *nāvigābilis*, f. *nāvigāre* (whence **na·vig**ATE[3] XVI), f. *nāvis* ship (see NAVAL) + *-ig-*, comb. stem of *agere* drive (see ACT). So **naviga**·TION. XVI. – (O)F. or L. **na·vig**ATOR. XVI. – L.

navvy næ·vi labourer employed in excavation and construction of earthworks. XIX. colloq. abbrev. of NAVIGATOR used in this sense (XVIII), prop. one who constructs a 'navigation' or artificial waterway (cf. F. *canal de navigation*).

navy nei·vi †ships, shipping; (arch.) fleet XIV (R. Mannyng); state's ships of war XVI. – OF. *navie* ship, fleet – popL. *nāvia* ship, boat, coll. formation on L. *nāvis* ship; see NAVAL, -Y[3]. ¶ The Rom. langs. show a great variety of derivs. of L. *nāvis*, of which OF. (AN.) *navei*, *navine*, *navire* were repr. in ME. or MSc.

nawab nəwɔ̄·b see NABOB.

nay nei adv. no XII; sb. denial, refusal XIV. ME. *nei*, *nai* (Orm *naȝȝ*) – ON. *nei*, f. *ne* NE + *ei* AY; cf. NO[3]. **nay**WORD nei·wɔ̄ɹd watchword, catchword; byword, proverb. XVI (Sh.); of unkn. origin.

Nazarene næzərī·n (native) of Nazareth in Palestine XIII; follower of Jesus of Nazareth XIV (Acts xxiv 5); one of an early Jewish sect of Christians XVII. – ChrL. *Nazarēnus* – Gr. *Nazarēnós* (Mark i 24), f. *Nazarét*. So **Na·zar**ITE[1] XVI (Coverdale).

Nazarite[2], **Nazir-** næ·zərait Hebrew who had taken a vow of abstinence. XVI (Geneva Bible). f. L. *Nazaræus* (LXX *Naziraîos*), f. Heb. *nāzīr*, f. *nāzar* to separate or consecrate oneself. Earlier forms are direct adoptions of L.; *Nazare*, *Nazarei* (Wycl. Bible), *Nazaree* (Coverdale).

Nazi (nā·tsi, nā·zi) (member) of German National Socialist party XX. repr. pronunc. of *Nati-* in G. *Nationalsozialist*.

nazir nā·ziəɹ title of officials in Mohammedan countries. XVII. – Urdu, Pers. – Arab. *nāẓir* superintendent, inspector, f. *naẓar* sight, vision.

ne nī, ni not (in the mod. period used by Sh., Spenser, Shenstone, Coleridge, and Byron). OE. *ne, ni* (see NAY, NO[1]) = OFris., OS., OHG. *ni, ne,* ON. *né,* Goth. *ni*; corr. to L. *ne-* (as in *nefās* NEFARIOUS, NEUTER, *nullus* NULL, *numquam* never), Lith., OSl. *ne,* Skr. *na,* repr. the short var. of CIE. negative adv. or particle, the long form of which is repr. by L. *nē* that . . not, lest, Gr. *nē-* (as in *nēkēdḗs* free from care, NEPENTHE), Goth. *nē,* Skr. *nā́,* and the weak grade (**n̥*) by IN-[2], UN-[1], the var. *nec-, neg-* by NEGATION, NEGLECT, NEGOTIATE.

neap nīp applied to tides at which high-water level is at its lowest. OE. *nēp* in *nēpflōd*; then not recorded till XV. Of unkn. origin; prob. identical with *nēp* in *forþganges nēp* (OE. 'Exodus' 469) without power of advance, the basic sense being 'wanting, lacking'.

Neapolitan niəpɔ·litən pert. to Naples, Italy. XVI (Sh.). – L. *Neāpolītānus,* f. *Neāpolītēs* (see -ITE), f. (Gr.) *Neāpolis* 'New Town'; see -AN.

near niəɹ adv. (dial.) almost, nearly XII (Orm); to, within, or at a little distance XIII. First in northerly and easterly texts in the form *ner* – ON. *nǽr,* compar. of *ná-* (as in *nábúi, nálægr* neighbouring) NIGH, orig. used with vbs. of motion, e.g. *koma* or *ganga nǽr* come or go nearer (to), whence it was transferred to uses with such vbs. as *standa* (stand) and *vera* (be), corr. to OE. *nēar* (which survived in mod. naut. *no near!* and dial. *never the near,* but was superseded in gen. use by the new formation **nearer** (XVI); it corr. to OFris. *nīar,* OS. *nāhor* (Du. *naar* to, for, after), OHG. *nāhor,* Goth. *nēhwis* :– CGerm. **nēχwiz, *nēχwōz.* Hence **near** prep. close to XIII (Cursor M.); adj. closely placed or related XIV, niggardly XVII. **near**LY[2] niə·ɹli closely XVI; almost XVII; superseded *near* adv. in all exc. the purely physical uses.

neat[1] nīt (arch., dial.) animal of the ox kind; cattle. OE. *nēat* = OFris. *nāt, naet,* OS. *nōt* (Du. *noot*), OHG. *nōʒ* (obs. or dial. *noss, nos*), ON. *naut* (whence north. dial. *nowt* XII) :– CGerm. (exc. Gothic) **nautam,* f. **naut- *neut- *nut-* make use of, enjoy, whence also OE. *nēotan,* OHG. *nioʒan* (G. *geniessen*), ON. *njóta, neyta* (:– **nautjan*), Goth. *niutan* use, enjoy; OE. *nytt* (1) use, (2) useful, OS. *nutti* (Du. *nut*) useful, OHG. *nuz* (G. *nutz, nutzen*) use, Goth. *un|nuts* useless, unprofitable, ON. *nýtr* useful; the IE. base is repr. also by Lett. *-nauda* money, Lith. *naũdyti, pa|nústi* desire, covet.

neat[2] nīt †clean, †clear; free from reductions; trim, smart, elegant, dainty, tidy. XVI. – (O)F. *net* = Pr. *net, ned,* Cat. *net* (whence Sp. *neto,* It. *netto*), Pg. *nedeo,* Rum. *neted* smooth :– L. *nitidu-s* shining, clean, f. *nitēre* shine. Cf. NET[2].

neb neb (dial.) beak, bill; nose; †face OE.; nib; peak, tip. XVI. OE. *nebb* = ON. *nef, nefj-,* rel. to MLG., MDu. *nebbe* (Du. *nebbe, neb*) :– Germ. **nabja-.* Cf. NIB.

nebula ne·bjŭlə film over the eye XVII; cloud-like cluster of stars XVIII. – L. *nebula,* rel. to OE. *nifol* dark, OS. *neƀal* (Du. *nevel*), OHG. *nebul* (G. *nebel*) cloud, ON. *nifl-* (as in *Niflheimr* Hades), *njól* night, OIr. *nél,* W. *niwl,* Gr. *nephélē* cloud, the simple IE. base being repr. by OSl. *nebo* (*nebes-*), Gr. *néphos* cloud, Skr. *nábhas* cloud, mist. So **ne·buly**[5] (her.) wavy like the edges of clouds. XVI. – F. *nébulé,* medL. *nebulātus.* **ne·bul**OUS. XVI. – F. *nébuleux* or L. *nebulōsus.*

necessary ne·sĭsəri inevitably determined XIV (Ch.); not to be done without XIV (Wycl. Bible, Usk); sb. XIV (Rolle). – AN. **necessarie* (OF. *nécessaire*) or L. *necessārius,* f. *necesse* (*esse, habēre*) (be, consider) necessary; see -ARY. Cf. †*necessaire* (XIV, Ch., Gower), Sc. *necessar* (XIV). So **nece·ss**ITY. XIV (Ch., Barbour, Wycl. Bible, Gower, Usk). – (O)F. – L. **nece·ssit**OUS needy. XVII (Cotgr.). – F.

neck nek (back of) that portion of the body lying between head and shoulders OE.; in various transf. uses from XIV. OE. *hnecca,* corr. to OFris. *hnecka, necke,* MDu. *nac, necke* (Du. *nek*), OHG. (*h*)*nac* (G. *nacken* nape), ON. *hnakki* nape :– CGerm. (exc. Gothic) **χnak(j)-,* repr. IE. **knok-,* whence OIr. *cnocc,* OBret. *cnoch* hill, elevation (cf. OHG. *hnack* summit). ¶ In OE. the commoner words for 'neck' were *heals* (ME. and dial. *hals*; cf. HAWSE) and *swēora,* dial. *swire.* Hence **neckerchief** ne·kəɹtʃif. XIV (*necke couerchef, neckerchef*); also (dial.) **ne·ckercher.** XV; see KERCHER and cf. HANDKERCHIEF. So **ne·ckha·ndkerchief.** XVII. **neck**LACE ne·klis ornament of precious stones or metal, etc. worn round the neck. XVI. **ne·ck-**VERSE verse (esp. the beginning of Psalm l[i]) to be recited by one claiming benefit of clergy in order to save his neck.

necro- ne·krou, nėkrɔ·, comb. form of Gr. *nekrós* corpse, rel. to L. *nex* slaughter (cf. INTERNECINE, PERNICIOUS).

necromancy ne·krŏmænsi divination by communication with the dead, 'black magic'. XIII (Cursor M.). Earliest forms in *nigro-, nigra-, negro-* – OF. *nigromancie* (whence in MHG., etc.), corr. to Sp. *nigromancia,* It. *nigro-, negromanzia* – Rom. (medL.) *nigromantia,* alt., by assoc. with *niger, nigr-* black, of late L. *necromantīa* – Gr. *nekromanteiā́,* f. *nekrós*+*manteiā́*; see prec., -MANCY; refash. XVI as in F. after L. and Gr. So **ne·cromanc**ER[2] XIV; after OF. (*-ier*).

necropolis nėkrɔ·pəlis cemetery. XIX. – Gr. *nekrópolis,* f. *nekrós* NECRO- + *pólis* city, -POLIS.

necrosis nėkrou·sis (path.) mortification of tissue. XVII. modL. – Gr. *nékrōsis* state of death, f. *nekroûn* kill, mortify, f. *nekrós*; see NECRO-, -OSIS.

nectar ne·ktəɹ drink of the gods; delicious drink, sweet fluid. XVI. – L. *nectar* – Gr. *néktar*, poss. f. **nek-* death (see NECRO-)+ *-tar*, rel. to Skr. *tarás* triumphing over, *tárati* cross, surmount, overcome, L. *trāns* across; cf. THROUGH. (Cf. the etymol. meaning of AMBROSIA.) So **nectar**EAN -ɛə·riən XVII, -EOUS XVIII, -IAN XVII; after L. *nectareus*, Gr. *nektáreos*, F. *nectaréen*. **nectar**INE[1] ne·ktərin variety of peach. XVII. prob. sb. use of *nectarine* adj.; cf. Du. *nektarperzik*, G. *nektarpfirsich* 'nectar-peach'. **nect**ARY ne·ktəri (bot.) part of a flower that secretes the honey. XVIII. – modL. *nectārium*.

neddy ne·di donkey. XVIII. f. *Ned*, pet form of the Christian name *Edward*+-Y[6]; cf. CUDDY[1], DICKY[1], DONKEY.

née nei distinguishing a married woman's maiden name. F., 'born', fem. pp. of *naître* :– Rom. **nascere*, for L. *nāscī* (see NASCENT).

need nīd †force, constraint; necessity; lack, want; matter requiring action. OE. *nēd*, non-WS. variant of WS. *nīed* (later *nȳd*, whence ME. *nüd*) = OFris. *nēd*, *nāth*, OS. *nōd* (Du. *nood*), OHG. *nōt* (G. *not*), ON. *nauð*, *neyð*, Goth. *nauþs* :– CGerm. **nauðiz*, **nauþiz*, rel. to OPruss. *nautin* need. So **need** vb. be necessary OE.; have need, be in need. OE. *nēodian* (rare), f. *nēod*. Hence **nee·d**FUL[1] †needy XII; requisite, necessary XIV. **nee·d**Y[1] indigent XII; cf. MDu. *nōdich* (Du. *noodig*), OHG. *nōtag*, *-eg* (G. *nötig* necessary), ON. *nauðigr* forced, unwilling. See also NEEDS. ¶ OE. had also *nēad*, without mutation, and a gradation var. *nēod*.

needle nī·dl pointed implement for sewing OE.; magnetized steel of a compass; pillar, obelisk; sharp-pointed mass of rock XIV. OE. *nǣdl* = OFris. *nēdle*, OS. *nādla*, *nāthla*, MLG. *nālde*, OHG. *nādala* (Du. *naald*, G. *nadel*), ON. *nál* (:– **náðl*), Goth. *nēþla* :– CGerm. **nēþlō* :– **nētlā*, f. **nē-* sew, repr. also by MDu. *naeyen* (Du. *naaien*), OHG. *nāian* (G. *nähen*), L. *nēre* spin, Gr. *nêma* thread. Forms with metathesis (ME. *neld*, mod. *neeld*) are common dial. See -LE[1].

needs nīdz of necessity, necessarily. OE. *nēdes*; finally superseding earlier †*need*, OE. *nēde* (*nȳde*, *nīde*), also *nēade*, instrumental case of *nēd*, *nēad* NEED; see -S.

neep nīp (dial.) turnip. OE. *nǣp* – L. *nāpus*, prob. a 'Mediterranean word'. Cf. TURNIP.

neeze nīz (dial.) SNEEZE. XIV. – ON. *hnjósa* = OHG. *niosan*, MLG. *niesen* (G. *niesen*, Du. *niezen*), of imit. origin. ¶ There is one ex. in AV., at 2 Kings iv 35.

nefarious nifɛə·riəs wicked. XVI. f. L. *nefārius* (Cicero), f. *nefās* wrong, wickedness, f. *ne-* NE + *fās* divine permission, command, or law (as opposed to *jūs* human law), assoc. by the ancients with *fārī* speak (see FATE); the formation is parallel to that of *injūrius* INJURIOUS.

negation nigei·ʃən negative statement, denial. XVI. – (O)F. *négation* or L. *negātiō(n-)*, f. *negāre* say no, deny, f. *neg-*, var. of *nec* (cf. NE and NEGLECT, NEGOTIATE); see -ATION. Also **negat**IVE ne·gətiv adj. and sb. XIV. – (O)F. or late L.; hence vb. XVIII.

neglect nigle·kt fail to regard. XVI. f. *neglēct-*, pp. stem of L. *negligere*, *neglegere*, *nec-*, disregard, slight, f. *neg*, var. of *nec* (see NE)+ *legere* choose (see LECTION). Hence sb. XVI; partly after L. *neglēctus*. So **ne·glig**ENCE, -ENT XIV. – (O)F. or L.

negotiate nigou·ʃieit hold conference (*with*) XVI (Sh.); manage; convert into money XVII; (orig. in hunting) succeed in getting over, etc., clear XIX. f. pp. stem of L. *negōtiāri* carry on business, f. *negōtium* business, f. *neg*, var. of *nec*+*ōtium* leisure; see NE, OTIOSE, -ATE[3]. So **negoti**A·TION. XVI. – L.

Negro nī·grou black man, blackamoor. XVI. – Sp., Pg. *negro* :– L. *nigrum*, *niger* black. Also †*nigro* (XVI–XVII), with assim. to L. So **Ne·gr**ESS[1]. XVIII. – F. *négresse*. **negri·llo** and **negri·to.** XIX. – Sp.

negus[1] nī·gəs supreme ruler of Abyssinia. XVI (*neguz*). – Amharic *n'gus* kinged, king.

negus[2] nī·gəs hot spiced drink. XVIII. f. name of the inventor, Colonel Francis *Negus* (died 1732).

neif nīf (hist.) one born in serfdom. XVI. – AN. *neif*, *nief* = OF. *naïf*; see NAÏVE.

neigh nei (of a horse) utter its characteristic cry. OE. *hnǣġan* = MDu. *neyen* (Du. dial. *neijen*), MHG. *nēgen*, of imit. origin; synon. formations are OS. (*to*) *hnechian*; MDu. *nijgen*, *nyen*, MHG. *nyhen*; OE. *hnæggiung* neighing, corr. to ON. *gneggja*, Icel. *hneggja*, Norw. (*k*)*neggja*. Other imit. north. Eng. forms are *neigher* (XVI), *nicher* (XVII), *nicker* (XVIII). Hence **neigh** sb. XVI.

neighbour nei·bəɹ one who lives near. OE. *nēahġebūr*, *nēahhebūr*, f. *nēah* NIGH+*ġebūr* BOOR; corr. to MDu. *nagebuer*, OHG. *nāhgibūr*; cf. OS. *nābūr*, MLG., MDu. *nabur*, MHG. *nāchbūr* (G. *nachbar*); also ON. *nábúi* (Sw., Da. *nabo*), f. *ná-* NEAR+*búa* dwell. Hence **nei·ghbour**HOOD. XV.

neither nai·ðəɹ, nī·ðəɹ A. adv. not either XIII; nor, nor yet XV; B. adj. and sb. not the one or the other XIII. ME. *naiðer*, *neiðer*, alt., after EITHER, of *nauther*, *nouther*, *nather*, *nother*, OE. *nawþer*, *nauþer*, *nāþer*, **nōþer*, contr. of *nāhwæþer* (cf. OFris. *nāhwedder*, *nauder*), f. *nā* NO[1]+*hwæþer* WHETHER.

nemato- ne·mətou comb. form of Gr. *nêma*, *nēmat-* thread (see NEEDLE), used in terms of nat. hist. XIX.

nemertean, -ine nimɜ·ɹtiən, -tain (one) of a class of flat-worms. XIX. f. modL. *Nemertēs* (Cuvier) – Gr. *Nēmertḗs* name of a sea-nymph; see -EAN, -INE[1].

nemesis ne·mĭsis goddess of retribution; retributive justice. XVI. – Gr. *némesis* righteous indignation (also personified), f. *némein* to deal out what is due, rel. to *nómos* custom, law (see NIM).

nenuphar ne·njufāɹ water-lily. XVI. – medL. *nenuphar* (whence also F. *nénufar*, Sp., It. *nenufar*) – Arab. and Pers. *nīnūfar*, *nīlūfar* – Skr. *nīlōtpala* blue lotus, f. *nīl* blue + *utpala* lotus, water-lily.

neo- nī·ou, niə· comb. form of Gr. *néos* NEW, in common use since *c.*1860; there are rare early exx., e.g. *ne:opela·gian* (1647), *neopla·tonism* (*c.*1830). **neologism** niə·lədʒizm innovation in language. XVIII. – F. *néologisme*; also **neo·**LOGY. XVIII. – F.

neophyte nī·ŏfait new convert, novice. XVI. – ecclL. *neophytus* – Gr. N.T. *neóphutos* (1 Tim. iii 6) 'newly planted', f. *néos* NEO- + *phutón* plant (n. of pp. formation on *phúein* cause to be (see BE)). ¶ Not common before XIX. In use somewhat earlier than the Rheims translation in the N.T. (1582), where, in the Preface to the Reader ciij, the question is asked: 'If Proselyte be a received word in the English bibles . . . why may not we be bold to say, Neophyte?' It was rejected by some as an unknown term.

neoteric nīote·rik recent, modern. XVI. – late L. *neotericus* – Gr. *neōterikós*, f. *neṓteros*, compar. of *néos* NEW; see -IC.

nepenthe nipe·nþi drug supposed to banish grief or trouble from the mind XVI (Spenser); plant yielding the drug XVII. Alt., after It. *nepente*, of **nepenthes** nipe·nþīz, also used in Eng. for the drug (XVI) and the pitcher-plant (XVIII) – L. *nēpenthes* (Pliny) – Gr. *nēpenthés* (Odyssey iv 221, qualifying *phármakon* drug), n. of *nēpenthḗs* banishing pain, f. *nē-* NE + *pénthos* grief (see PATHOS).

nephelo- ne·filou comb. form of Gr. *nephélē* cloud (see NEBULA). XIX.

nephew ne·vju, ne·fju brother's or sister's son. XIII. ME. *neveu* – (O)F. *neveu*, also ONF. *nevu*, *nevo* (whence similar ME. forms) = Pr. *nebot*, It. *nepote*, *nipote* :– L. *nepōtem*, *nepōs* grandson, nephew, descendant; CIE. term denoting indirect descent, repr. also by Skr. *nápāt*, OPers. *napā* grandson, Gr. *anepsiós* nephew, OLith. *nepuotis*, *nepotis*, Ir. *nia* (g. *niath*) sister's son, and in Germ. by OE. *nefa* (ME. *neve*), OFris. *neva*, OS. *nevo* (Du. *neef*), OHG. *nevo* (G. *neffe*), ON. *nefi* :– **neƀon*. Cf. NIECE.

nephritic nĕfri·tik affecting the kidneys. XVI. – late L. *nephrīticus* (Celsus) – Gr. *nephrītikós*, f. *nephrītis* (whence, through late L., **nephri·**TIS XVI), f. *nephrós* KIDNEY :– **neghwros*; -IC. So **ne·phro-** comb. form of the Gr. sb. XVII.

ne plus ultra nī plʌs ʌ·ltrə command to go no further; utmost limit. XVII. L. phr., 'not more beyond', said to have been inscribed on the Pillars of Hercules (Calpe, i.e. Gibraltar, and Abyla, mountains on opposite sides of the western entrance to the Mediterranean, fabled to have been parted by the arm of the giant Hercules). Also *non plus ultra* XVII (so in F. from XVII), †*non ultra* XVI.

nepotism ne·pŏtizm favouritism as of a pope, etc. towards nephews XVII. – F. *népotisme* – It. *nepotismo*, f. *nepote* NEPHEW; see -ISM.

Neptunian neptjū·niən (geol.) pert. to the action of water)(*plutonic*, *volcanic*. XVIII. f. L. *Neptūnius*, f. *Neptūnus* god of the sea; see -IAN and cf. F. *neptunien*.

Nereid niə·riid sea-nymph. XVII. – L. *Nēreid-*, nom. *Nēreis* – Gr. *Nēreid-*, *Nērēís*, f. *Nēreús* ancient sea-god, f. base of L. *nāre* swim (see NATATION, -ID, and cf. NAIAD).

neroli niə·rŏli essential oil from the flowers of the bitter orange. XVII. – F. *néroli* – It. *neroli*, said to be from the name of its discoverer, an Italian princess.

nerve nəɹv sinew, tendon XVI; fibrous connexion conveying sensation, etc. between the brain and other parts XVII. – L. *nervus* sinew, bowstring, rel. to Gr. *neûron* (cf. NEURO-) sinew, nerve, and further to L. *nēre* spin (see NEEDLE). Cf. F. *nerf* (whence ME. †*nerf* XIV), It. *nervo*. So **ne·rv**OUS. XIV. – L. *nervōsus*, whence F. *nerveux*, etc. **ne·rv**Y[1]. XVII (Sh.).

nescience ne·ʃiəns lack of knowledge. XVII. – late L. *nescientia*, f. *nescient-*, *-ēns* (whence **ne·sci**ENT XVII), prp. of *nescīre* be ignorant, f. *ne-* + *scīre* know; see NE, SCIENCE.

ness nes headland. OE. *næs(s)*, *nes(s)*, *næsse*, corr. to LG. *nesse*, ON. *nes*, rel. to OE. *næs-*, *nasu*; see NOSE. The generalization of the form *ness*, as opposed to *nass*, is due partly to the prevalence of place-names in *-ness*, partly to ON. *nes*.

-ness suffix expressing state or condition appended to adjs. and pps., in more recent use to prons., advs., and phrs. OE. *-nes(s)*, *-nis(s)* = OFris. *-nesse*, *-nisse*, OS. *-nessi*, *-nissi* (Du. *-nis*), OHG. *-nessi*, *-nissi*, *-nassi* (G. *-niss*), Goth. *-nassus*; f. **n* (of str. pps.) + **-assus*, f. **-atjan* verbal suffix (the vowel-variation *a e i* is unexpl.). A concr. sense is developed in FASTNESS, LIKENESS, WILDERNESS, WITNESS. The use in titles (*highness*, *holiness*) follows that of L. *-tās*. *Forgiveness* is isolated.

nest nest bird's laying- and hatching-place OE.; set of similar objects XVI. OE. *nest* = (M)Du., (O)HG. *nest* :– IE. **nizdo-*, whence also L. *nīdus*, OIr. *net* (mod. *nead*), W. *nyth* nest, Skr. *nīḍá* resting-place; f. **ni* down (cf. NETHER) + **sed-* SIT. Hence **nest** vb. XIII; repl. OE. *nistan* = MDu., (O)HG. *nisten* :– **nestjan*.

nestle ne·sl have a nest OE.; refl. and intr. settle oneself comfortably XVI. OE. *nestlian* = MLG., (M)Du. *nestelen* (cf. OE. *nistl(i)an*, MHG. *nistelen*); see prec. and -LE³. So **nestling** ne·sliŋ young bird in the nest XIV; f. NEST or NESTLE, perh. after MDu. *nestelinc* (mod. *-ling*) = G. *nest-*, *nist(e)ling*.

Nestor ne·stōɹ name of a Homeric hero famous for his age and wisdom, used allus. for a wise old man. XVI (Sh.).

Nestorian nestōə·riən – late L. *Nestōriānus* applied to the heresy according to which Christ is said to have distinct divine and human persons, promoted by *Nestorius*, patriarch of Constantinople 428–*c*.451. XV.

net¹ net 'anything reticulated or decussated, at equal distances, with interstices between the intersections' (J.). OE. *net(t)* = OFris. *net(te)*, OS. *netti*, *net*, (M)Du. *net*, MLG., MDu. *nette*, OHG. *nezzi* (G. *netz*), ON. *net*, Goth. *nati*; the existence of ON. *nót* large net (whence Finn. *nuota*) suggests an IE. base **năd-*, to which some refer L. *nassa* (:- **nadtā*) narrow-necked basket for catching fish. Hence **net** vb. XVI.

net² net †trim, smart, clean, bright XIV; free from deduction XVI. – F. *net*, fem. *nette* NEAT² (whence also Du., Da. *net*, G. *nett*, Sw. *nätt*).

nether ne·ðəɹ lower (now rare exc. in *nether garments*, *n. regions*). OE. *neoþera*, *niþera* = OFris. *nithera*, *nethera*, OS. *nithiri* (Du. *neder* in comps.), MLG. *ned(d)er*, OHG. *nidari*, *-eri*, *-iri* (G. *nieder*), ON. *neðri*; f. CGerm. (exc. Gothic) **niþar* (repr. by OE. *niþer*, etc.) down downwards = Skr. *nitarām*, f. **ni-* down, with compar. suffix.

nettle ne·tl stinging plant (Urtica). OE. *net(e)le*, *netel* = OS. *netila*, MLG. *net(t)ele*, MDu. *netele* (Du. *netel*), OHG. *nezzila* (G. *nessel*), OSw. *netla*, ODa. *næt-*, *nædlæ*, Icel. *netla* :- Germ. **natilōn*, deriv. (see -LE¹) of base of OHG. *nazza*, Icel. *nötu* (*gras*); the reduced grade of the IE. base **nod-* is repr. by Gr. *adíkē* (**n̥d-*) nettle. Hence **nettle** vb. beat or sting with nettles XV; irritate, vex XVI. So Du. *netelen*, G. *nesseln*.

neume njūm (mus., in plainsong) group of notes sung to one syllable XV; sign used in plainsong notation XIX. – (O)F. *neume* – medL. *neuma*, *neupma* – Gr. *pneûma* breath (cf. PNEUMATIC). Also **neu·ma**. XVIII.

neural njuə·rəl pert. to the nerves. XIX. f. Gr. *neûron* NERVE+-AL¹.

neuralgia njuəræ·ldʒə affection of a nerve causing pain. XIX. – modL. *neuralgia*, f. Gr. *neûron* NERVE+*álgos* pain. (In F. *névralgie*.) So **neurasthen**IA¹ -þī·niə, **neuri**·TIS XIX. **neuro-** njuə·rou, njuərɔ· comb. form of Gr. *neûron*, as in **neuro**·LOGY. XVII. – modL. *neurologia* – modGr. *neurología* (cf. F. *névrologie*). **neuro**·TOMY. XVIII. – modL. **neuro·ptera**² order of insects. XVIII; Gr. *pterón* wing (cf. FEATHER).

neuter njū·təɹ neither masculine nor feminine XIV; intransitive; neutral XVI; asexual, sterile XVIII. – (O)F. *neutre* or its source L. *neuter*, f. *ne-* NE+*uter* either of two (cf. NEITHER). So **neu·tr**AL¹ not taking sides; occupying a middle position XVI; (chem.) XVII. – F. †*neutral* or L. *neutrālis* (Quintilian), f. *neutr-*, *neuter*. **neutral**ITY -æ·lĭti. XV. – (O)F. or medL.

névé nei·vei, ‖*neve* granular snow on a glacier; field of frozen snow. XIX. – Swiss F. *névé* glacier :- Rom. **nivātum*, f. L. *niv-*, *nix* SNOW.

never ne·vəɹ at no time. OE. *nǣfre*, f. *ne*+*ǣfre*; see NE, EVER. The contr. form *ner*, *nere* (Laȝ., Cursor M.), with indef. art. *nere a*, *ne'er a*, became (dial.) *narrow a*, *narra*, (esp. U.S.) *nary*. Hence **ne:verthele·ss** notwithstanding XIII (Cursor M.), also †*never the lat(t)er* XIV–XVII; repl. earlier *notheless*, *natheless* OE. *nā þȳ lǣs*, f. *nā*, *nō* NO¹+*thē*, instr. case of THE + LESS; cf. L. *nihilōminus* lit. 'by nothing less'.

new njū not existing before, of recent growth. OE. *nīwe*, *nīowe*, *nēowe* = OFris. *nȳ*, *nī*, OS. *niuwi*, *nigi*, MLG. *nige*, *nie*, MDu. *nieuwe*, *nuwe*, *nie* (Du. *nieuw*), OHG. *niuwi* (G. *neu*), ON. *nýr*, Goth. *niujis* :- CGerm. **neujaz* :- CIE. **newjos*, repr. by Gr. (Ionic) *neîos*, Gaul. *Novio-* (in place-names), OIr. *nūe* (Ir., Gael. *nuadh*, W. *newydd*), OSl. *novŭ*, Lith. *naũjas*, modification of **newos*, repr. by L. *novus* (cf. NOVEL), Gr. *néos*, NEO-, Skr. *návas*.

newel njū·əl pillar forming the centre of a winding stair XIV; post supporting the handrail of a staircase XIX. ME. *nowel* – OF. *nouel*, *noel* knob :- medL. *nōdellus*, dim. of *nōdus* knot (see NODE).

newfangled njū·fæ:ŋgld fond of novelty XV; new-fashioned XVI. alt. (by addition of -ED¹ to impart a more adjectival appearance) of *newefangel* XIV (Ch.), f. *nēwe* adv. of NEW+**fangel*, repr. an OE. **fangol* 'inclined to seize', f. **fang-*; see FANG, -LE². ¶ MDu. *nievingel(heit)* has a different stem-vowel.

news njūz †novelties XIV; tidings XV. pl. of NEW; after OF. *noveles*, pl. of *novele* (mod. *nouvelle*) NOVEL; or after medL. *nova*, pl. of *novum* new thing, sb. use of n. of *novus* NEW. ¶ There is no evidence of contact with synon. Du. *nieuws*, which prob. originated in the phr. *wat nieuws*, *iet(s) nieuws*, in which the form is genitive sg. (cf. OE. *hwæt nīwes*, *aht nīwes*, ME. *what newes*). Hence **new·spa:per**. XVII.

newt njūt small tailed amphibian (Triton). XV. f. *n* of AN (cf. NICKNAME)+*ewt*, var. of *ewet*, EFT. ¶ The change of *f*, *v* to *w* is unusual, but cf. the name *Pewsey*, *Pusey*, from OE. *Pefesiġ*; with the var. *neuft* (B. Jonson) cf. *ewft* (Spenser).

next nekst lying nearest (now only with following sb. or pron. orig. in the dative); nearest in kinship; immediately preceding or succeeding OE.; immediately following in time XII. OE. *nēhst-a*, WS. *nīehst-a* = OFris. *neest-e*, OS. *nā(h)ist-o* (Du. *naast-e*), OHG. *nāhist-o* (G. *nächst-e*), ON. *næstr*, *næsti*; superl. of NIGH (see -EST).

nexus ne·ksəs bond, link XVII; connected group XIX. – L., f. *nex-*, pp. stem of *nectere* bind (cf. CONNECT).

nib nib (dial.) beak, bill XVI; (split) pen-point; (pl.) short handles on the shaft of a scythe XVII; peak, tip XVIII; (pl.) small pieces into which cocoa-beans are crushed XIX. prob. – MDu. *nib* or MLG. *nibbe*, var. of *nebbe* beak, NEB.

nibble ni·bl take little bites (of); fig. carp. XV. prob. of LDu. origin; cf. LG. *nibbeln*, also *gnibbeln*, *knibbeln* gnaw = Du. *knibbelen* gnaw, murmur, squabble, parallel to *knabbelen*, whence †*knabble* (XVI).

niblick ni·blik golf club having a small round heavy head. XIX. Of unkn. origin.

nibs nibz. XIX. See NABS.

niccolite ni·kəlait native arsenide of nickel. XIX. f. modL. *niccolum* NICKEL + -ITE[1].

nice nais †foolish, stupid XIII; †wanton XIV; †coy, shy XV; fastidious, dainty; difficult to manage or decide; minute and subtle; precise, critical; minutely accurate XVI; dainty, appetizing; agreeable, delightful XVIII. – OF. *nice* silly, simple = Pr. *nesci*, Sp. *necio*, It. *nescio* :- L. *nesciu-s* ignorant, f. *ne-* NE + *sci-*, *scīre* know (see SCIENCE). So **nice**TY nai·sĭti. XIV. – OF. *niceté*.

Nicene nai·sīn pert. to (councils of the Church held at) Nicæa (Gr. Níkaia) in Bithynia, esp. of the creed adopted at the first of these (A.D. 325). XV. – late L. *Nīcēnus*, *Nīcænus*.

niche nitʃ recess for a statue, etc. XVII. – (O)F. *niche*, f. *nicher* make a nest, nestle :- Rom. **nīdicare*, f. *nīdus* NEST. ¶ Mainly from F., the word has become CEur.

nick nik notch XV; precise moment XVI. So **nick** vb. make a notch in; hit off; win at the game of hazard; trick, cheat XVI. Of unkn. origin; possibly from Low Du., but no contact of meaning can be made out with the similar Du. *nikken* = G. *nicken* (OHG. *nicchen*) nod, beckon.

Nick nik *Old N.*, the devil. XVII. usu. taken to be abbrev. of the name *Nicholas*, but no reason for such an application is known. ¶ Not connected with NICKER.

nickel ni·kl hard silvery-white lustrous mineral, usu. associated with cobalt. XVIII. Named in 1754 by Axel F. von Cronstedt, Swedish mineralogist; shortening of G. *kupfernickel* 'copper nickel', the mining name of the copper-coloured ore (NICCOLITE) from which the metal was first obtained by Cronstedt in 1751. The second el. of *kupfernickel* appears to be *nickel* dwarf, mischievous demon, the name being given to the ore because it yielded no copper in spite of its appearance (cf. COBALT).

nicker ni·kəɹ water-sprite. OE. *nicor* water-monster = MLG. *necker*, MDu. *nicker*, *necker* (Du. *nikker*), ON. *nykr* :- Germ. **nikwiz*, **nikuz*; cf. OHG. *nihhus* crocodile, *nicchessa* (G. *nix*, *nixe* NIX[2]); based on IE. **nigw-* wash, repr. by Gr. *nízein*, OIr. *nigid*, Skr. *nēnēkti* (p.p.).

nickname ni·kneim name added to or substituted for the proper name, esp. in ridicule. XV. Late ME. *nekename*, f. *n* of AN (cf. NEWT) + †*ekename* (XIV), f. *eke* addition (see EKE[2]) + NAME, after ON. *aukanafn*.

Nicolaitan nikŏlei·itən name of an early Christian sect of obscure character. XVI. – modL. *Nicolaitānus*, f. Gr. *Nicolaítēs* (Rev. ii 6), f. *Nikólaos* Nicholas.

nicotine nikətī·n essential principle of tobacco. XIX. – F. *nicotine*, f. modL. *nicotiāna* (sc. *herba*) tobacco-plant (F. *nicotiane*, whence Eng. †*nicotian* XVI–XVII), f. name of Jacques *Nicot*, French ambassador at Lisbon, by whom tobacco was first introduced into France in 1560; see -INE[5].

nictitate ni·ktiteit blink, wink. XVIII. f. pp. stem of medL. *nictitāre*, frequent. of L. *nictāre* blink, rel. to *cōnīvēre* CONNIVE; see -ATE[3]. So **nictit**A·TION. XVIII.

nid, nide see NYE.

niddering ni·dəriŋ (arch.) base wretch. XVI (*nidering*). erron. form of *nithing*, late OE. *nīðing* – ON. *níðingr* NITHING. The error originated in the 1596 edition of William of Malmesbury's 'De gestis regum Anglorum' p. 68 by the misreading of *niðing* as *nid'ing*, i.e. nidering. The mod. currency of the word is due to Scott. A further corruption is **ni·dder**LING[1]. XVII.

nidification ni:difikei·ʃən nest-building. XVII. – medL. *nīdificātiō(n-)*, f. L. *nīdificāre* (whence **ni·dific**ATE[3] XIX, **ni·di**FY XVII), f. *nīdus* NEST.

nidor nai·dɔ̄ɹ smell from animal substances burned, etc. XVII. – L. *nīdor*; cf. Gr. *knîsa* smell of burnt fat, ON. *hnissa* steam from cooking. So **ni·dor**OUS. XVII (Bacon). – late L.

niece nīs †granddaughter; brother's or sister's daughter. XIII. – (O)F. *nièce* = It. dial. *netsa*, *nezza* :- popL. **neptia*, for L. *neptis*, corr. to Skr. *naptī́s*, Lith. *neptê*, Germ. **niptiz*, whence OE. *nift* (current till XV), OFris., OHG. *nift*, MDu. *nichte* (whence G. *nichte*), Du. *nicht*, ON. *nipt*; a Rom. by-form **nepta* is repr. by Pr. *nepta*, Sp. *nieta*, Pg. *neta*. Cf. NEPHEW.

niello nie·lou black composition for filling in engraved designs, etc. XIX. It. = OF. *neel*, Pr., Sp. *niel* :- L. *nigellu-s*, dim. of *niger* black.

nief nīf, **nieve, neive** nīv (dial.) fist. XIII. ME. *neve* – ON. *hnefi*, *nefi*, which has no known cogns. Current in all north. and Sc. dialects; in Sh. in the form *neafe* (also *newfe*), in B. Jonson in the form *neufe*.

niggard ni·gəɹd sb. stingy person; adj. stingy, miserly. XIV (Ch.). alt., with substitution of suffix -ARD, of earlier †*nigon* (XIV–XVI), f. †*nig* (XIII–XVII); prob. of Scand. origin (cf. Sw. *njugg*, dial. *nugg*, *nygg*, ON. *hnǫggr* (:– **χnauwjaz*), Norw. *nögg*, and NIGGLE), and ult. rel. to OE. *hnēaw* niggardly (:– **χnawaz*), corr. to MDu. *nauwe* (Du. *nauw* narrow, tight), MHG. *nouwe* careful, exact, (*ge*)*nouwe* scarcely (G. *genau* exactly). Hence **ni·ggardly.** XVI; see -LY[1], -LY[2].

nigger ni·gəɹ negro. XVIII. Later form of (dial.) *neeger*, *neger* XVI (– F. *nègre* – Sp. *negro*, whence also Du., G. *neger*), †*niger* XVI–XVIII (– L. *niger*); see NEGRO.

niggle ni·gl do anything in a trifling or ineffective way. XVI (Nashe). prob. of dial. origin in literary use. The modern dial. distribution, mainly northern and eastern, and the correspondence in form and meaning to Norw. *nigla*, point to prob. early adoption from Scand. (cf. NIGGARD).

nigh nai (arch., dial.) near. OE. *nēah*, *nēh*, corr. to OFris. *nei*, *nī*, OS., OHG. *nāh* (Du. *na*, G. *nah*), ON. *ná-* (in comps. like *nábúi* NEIGHBOUR), Goth. *nēhw-* (*nēhw* prep., *nēhwa* adv.); CGerm., of unkn. origin. Fully declined as adj. only in OHG.; in OE. chiefly in advb. use or with obj. dative. The compar. of the adv. is OE. *nēar* NEAR[2], of the adj. *nēarra*, ME. *ner*, *nar*, superl. *nīexst*(*a*) NEXT; the formal relation of these becoming obscured, new forms *nigher*, *nighest* were formed XVI. For the vocalism cf. DIE[1], HIGH.

night nait period of darkness)(*day*. OE. *niht*, for earlier *nieht* with vowel generalized from case-forms in which mutation was regular, the normal (Anglian) nom. being *næht*, *neaht* = OFris., MDu. *nacht*, OS., OHG. *naht* (Du., G. *nacht*), ON. *nátt*, *nótt*, Goth. *nahts*. The CIE. base **nokt-* is repr. also by L. *nox*, *noct-* (cf. NOCTI-, NOCTURN), Gr. *núx*, *nukt-*, OSl. *noštĭ* (Russ. *noch'*), Lith. *naktìs*, OIr. *nocht* (*innocht* tonight), W. *nos* (*peu*|*noeth* every night, *he*|*no* tonight), Skr. *náktā*, *náktis*. ¶ The ancient Germ. reckoning of time by nights is preserved in FORTNIGHT, SENNIGHT; cf. also ON. *mánuðr þritognáttar* 'month of 30 nights', calendar month, W. *wythnos* 'eight nights', week; nec dierum numerum, ut nos, sed noctium computant [sc. Germani], Tacitus, 'Germania' xi; spatia omnis temporis non numero dierum sed noctium finiunt [sc. Galli], Cæsar, 'Bellum Gallicum' vi.

nightingale nai·tiŋgeil bird remarkable for its song, Luscinia. ME. *nihtingale* (XIII), alt. of *nihtegale*, OE. *nihtegala* (*nehte-*, *næhte-*, etc.) = OS. *nahta-*, *nahtigala* (Du. *nachtegaal*), OHG. *nahta-*, *nahtigala* (G. *nachtigall*), ON. *nǽtrgali*; f. Germ. **naχt*(*i*)- NIGHT + **galan* sing (see YELL). ¶ For the intrusive *n* cf. *farthingale*.

nightmare nai·tmɛəɹ female incubus XIII; bad dream with a feeling of suffocation XVI. f. NIGHT + ME. *mare*, OE. *mære* incubus, corr. to MLG. *mar*, MDu. *mare*, *maer*, OHG. *mara* (G. *mahr*), ON. *mara* :– CGerm. (exc. Gothic) **maron*, **marōn* (whence OF. *mare*, surviving in F. *cauchemar* nightmare, f. *caucher* tread upon :– L. *calcāre*). The second el. is rel. to OIr. *Mor*|*rīgain* queen of elves, Pol. *zmora*, Czech *můra* nightmare. Cf. MDu. *nachtmare*, *-mere*, *-merrie*, MHG. *nahtmare* (G. *nachtmahr*, *-mähr*), some of which show assim. to MARE.

nightshade nai·tʃeid plant of genera Solanum and Atropa. OE. *nihtsćada*, corr. to MLG., MDu. *nachtschade*, OHG. *nahtscato* (G. *nachtschatten*); app. f. NIGHT + SHADE, prob. with allusion to the poisonous or narcotic properties of the berries. ME. vars. with *-shode*, *-schede*, and MLG. with *-schede*, are presumably independent alterations due to obscuration of the identity of the second el.

nigri- nai·gri comb. form of L. *niger* (*nigr-*) black, for which the irreg. **nigro-** is more commonly used.

nigrescent naigre·sənt blackish. XVIII. – prp. stem of L. *nigrēscere* grow black, f. *niger* black; see -ESCE, -ENT.

nihil nai·hil nothing, thing of no value; (leg.) return by the sheriff where the party named had no goods on which to levy. XVI. – L. *nihil* (medL. *nichil*), short for *nihilum*, for **nīhīlum*, f. *nī*, var. of *nĕ* NE + *hīlum* small thing, trifle (said to be prop. particle adhering to a seed). Cf. NIL[2].

nihilism nai·(h)ilizm negative doctrines in religion or morals; extreme revolutionary principles involving destruction of existing institutions. XIX. So **ni·hilist** (Sir W. Hamilton). f. NIHIL + -ISM, -IST; in philos. uses after G. *nihilismus* (F. H. Jacobi 1799), *nihilist* (Jean Paul 1804), F. *nihiliste* (1793); extended to the political sense after F. *nihilisme* (– Russ. *nigilízm*), F. *nihiliste* (1793).

nil[1] nil indigo. XVI; see ANIL.

nil[2] nil nothing. XIX. L., contr. of NIHIL.

nilgai see NYLGHAU.

nill nil (arch.) be unwilling, not to will. OE. *nyle* (pres. tense) = OFris. *nil*, *nel*; f. NE + *wile* WILL[2]. Cf. WILLY-NILLY.

nilometer nailɔ·mitəɹ gauge for measuring the height of the river Nile. XVIII. – Gr. *neilométrion*, with assim. to words in -METER.

nim nim (arch.) take OE.; (sl.) steal XVI. OE. *niman*, pt. *nōm, nōmon, nam, nāmon*, pp. *numen* = OFris. *nima*, OS. *niman* (Du. *nemen*), OHG. *neman* (G. *nehmen*), ON. *nema*, Goth. *niman* :– CGerm. str. vb. **neman*, rel. to Gr. *némein* deal out, distribute, possess, occupy; see also NEMESIS, NOMAD, NUMBER. In gen. literary use till XV; rare in XVI; it appears *c.*1600 in canting lang. in the sense 'thieve, pilfer' (cf. Corporal *Nym* in Sh. 'Merry Wives'). ¶ For derivs. see NIMBLE, NUMB.

nimble ni·mbl quick and light in movement or action. ME. *nemel* (XIII), later *nemble, neam(b)le*, app. repr. OE. *nǣmel* quick at seizing, f. **nǣm-* **nem-* take, NIM; superseded by *nymel* (XV), later *nymble*, which may repr. either a phonetic development or an OE. **nimol* (cf. *numol* grasping, biting, *scearpnumol, teartnumol* efficacious); see -LE[2]. ¶ For intrusive *b* cf. THIMBLE.

nimbus ni·mbəs cloud-like splendour investing a god XVII; halo XVIII; rain-cloud XIX. – L. *nimbus* rain, cloud, aureole.

niminy-piminy ni·minipi·mini mincing. XIX. Jingling formation based on NAMBY-PAMBY; cf. MIMINY-PIMINY.

Nimrod ni·mrɔd †tyrant XVII; great hunter XVIII. – Heb. *Nimrōd* valiant, strong; name of 'a mighty one in the earth' and a 'mighty hunter before the Lord' (Gen. x 8, 9).

nincompoop ni·nkəmpūp, -ŋk- simpleton. XVII (*nicom-, nickum-*). The earliest forms suggest deriv. from a proper name, such as *Nicholas* or *Nicodemus* (cf. F. *nicodème* simpleton)+the word repr. by †*poop* cheat, befool (XVI–XVII); cf. †*noddypoop* (XVI); alteration of the first syll. to *nin-* is prob. due to NINNY.

nine nain 9, ix. OE. *nigon* = OFris. *nigun*, OS. *nigun, -on* (Du. *negen*) :– **nigun*, var. of Germ. **niwun* (repr. by OHG. *niun*, G. *neun*, ON. *níu*, Goth. *niun*) :– IE. **(e)newn̥*, repr. by L. *novem* (for **noven*), Gr. *ennéa, eina-, ena-*, OIr. *noi, nóin*, OPruss. *newīnts* ninth, OSl. *devętĭ*, Lith. *devynì* (with *d* . . *n* for *n* . . *n*), Arm. *inn*, Skr., Av. *náva-*, Tokh. *ñu*. So **nine**TEEN. OE. *nigontȳne* = OFris. *niogentena*, OS. *nigentein* (Du. *negentien*), OHG. *niunzehan* (G. *neunzehn*), ON. *nítján*. **nineteen**TH. OE. *nigontēoþa*, etc. **ninth** nainþ. ME. *niȝonþe* (XII), a new formation superseding OE. *nigoþa* = OS. *niguðo*, MLG. *negede*; cf. SEVENTH. **ni·ne**TY[1]. OE. *nigontiġ*. **ninepins**. XVI; see PIN.

ninny ni·ni simpleton. XVI. Appellative use of *Ninny*, pet-form of *Innocent*, with prefixed *n-* (cf. *Ned*, NEDDY) and -Y[6]; cf. '*Innocent*, Innocent, Ninnie (a proper name for a man)' Cotgr. and *Ninny's*, illiterate substitution for *Ninus*' in Sh. 'MND' III i 99, V i 204. In comb. **ninny-hammer**. XVI (Nashe) (cf. *yellow-hammer* as a term of reproach).

niobium naiou·biəm (chem.) metallic element, earlier called *columbium*. XIX. modL., f. *Niobe*, (Gr. myth.) name of the daughter of Tantalus; so named in 1845 by Heinrich Rose, who rediscovered it in the tantalites of Bavaria; see -IUM.

nip[1] pinch XIV (PPl.); snatch, seize smartly XVI; move nimbly XIX. prob. of LDu. origin; cf. †Sc. *gnip* (XIV), †*knip* (XVI). Hence sb. XVI. **ni·pp**ER[1] †thief XVI; costermonger's boy, (hence) youngster XIX.

nip[2] nip †half-pint of ale XVIII; small quantity of spirits XIX. prob. short for †*nipperkin* (XVII) measure of half a pint or less, small quantity of drink, rel. to LDu. *nippen*, whence G. *nippen*, Da. *nippe*.

nipple ni·pl teat. XVI. Early forms also *neble, nible*, perh. dim. of NEB, NIB point; see -LE[1]. ¶ The change from *b* to *p* is unexpl.; unconnected with OE. *nypel* elephant's trunk (Ælfric).

Nippon ni·pɔn see JAPANESE.

nirvana nəɹvā·nə (in Buddhism) extinction of individual existence. XIX. – Skr. *nirvāṇa*, sb. use of n.pp. of *nirvā* be extinguished, f. *nis* out+*vā-* blow (see WIND[1]).

nisi nai·sai (leg.) attached to *decree, order, rule*, to indicate that these are not absolute or final, but are to be taken as valid *unless* some cause is shown, etc. XIX. L. *nisi* unless. So **nisi prius** nai·sai prai·əs writ named from the first two words of the proviso '*nisi prius* justiciarii ad assisas capiendas venerint' *unless* the judges come to take the assize *before* (see Blackstone 'Commentaries', 1768, III 59).

nit nit egg of a louse, etc. OE. *hnitu* = MLG., MDu. *nēte* (Du. *neet*), OHG. *(h)niz* (G. *niss, nisse*) :– WGerm. **χnitō* :– IE. **knidā* (cf. Gr. *konid-, kónis* dust). ¶ Parallel forms are ON. *gnit*, Russ., Pol. *gnída*, OIr. *sned*, Alb. *θενί*.

nithing nai·ðiŋ (arch.) abject wretch, villain; niggard. Late OE. *niþing* – ON. *níðingr*, f. *níð* contumely, libel, insult = OE. *nīþ* enmity, malice, affliction, OFris., OS., OHG. *nīd* (Du. *nijd*, G. *neid* envy), Goth. *neiþ*, CGerm. sb. of which the ult. connexions are unkn.; see -ING[3]. ¶ Cf. NIDDERING.

nitid nit·id shining, glossy. XVII. – L. *nitidus*, f. *nitēre* shine; see -ID[1].

nitre nai·təɹ †sodium carbonate, (now) saltpetre XIV; †supposed nitrous element in air or plants XVII. – (O)F. *nitre* – L. *nitrum* – Gr. *nítron*, of Semitic origin (cf. Heb. *netr* natron, Ass. *nit(i)ru*, Egyptian *ntr*); cf. NATRON. The comb. form is **ni·tro-** nai·trou, naitrɔ·. So **nitr**IC nai·trik applied to an acid produced by the treatment of nitrates with sulphuric acid. XVIII. – F. *nitrique* (1787). **ni·trate** nai·treit XVIII. – F. *nitrate* (1787); see -ATE IC. **ni·tr**OUS pert. to nitre. XVII (the mod. chem. uses date from XVIII). – L. *nitrōsus*; later – F. *nitreux*.

nitrogen nai·trədʒən chief constituent of the atmosphere. XVIII. – F. *nitrogène* (Chaptal, 1790); see NITRO-, -GEN, and cf. OXYGEN. ¶ So named from being a constituent of nitric acid; earlier named *phlogisticated air* or *gas*.

nix[1] niks (sl.) nothing. XVIII. – colloq. G. *nix*, for *nichts*, short for MHG. *nihtesniht* 'nothing of nothing', strengthened form of *niht* nothing :- OHG. *niwiht*, *neowiht*, for **ne eo wiht* 'not ever a thing' (cf. NOUGHT).

nix[2] niks water-sprite. XIX. – G. *nix* m., MHG. *nickes*, OHG. *nihhus*; see NICKER. So **nixie** ni·ksi water-nymph. XIX (Scott) – G. *nixe* fem. :- OHG. *nicchessa*, with assim. of ending to -IE.

nizam nizā·m title of the rulers of Hyderabad 1713–48 XVIII; Turkish regular army XIX. – Urdu, Turk. *nizām* – Arab. *niḍām* order, arrangement, f. *naḍama* arrange, join in order; in the first sense short for *nizām-al-mulk* governor of the empire (*Nizzamuluc* in R. Johnson's 'The Worlde', 1601).

no[1] nou not (in literary use surviving only in *or no* (XV)). OE. *nō*, f. *ne*+*ō*, var. of *ā* ever; cf. NAY. The midl. and south. ME. repr. of OE. *nā* (see NO[3]) coalesced with this and influenced the pronunc. ¶ The phr. *or no* was preceded by *or nōn*, north. *or nān* (XIII), which prob. originated in the ellipsis of a sb.

no[2] nou not any. XIII (*na*, *no*). Clipped form of *nòn*, NONE[1], orig. used (like A[1]) before words beginning with a cons. Comps. **no·**-BODY XIV (R. Mannyng); **no·**HOW XVIII; **no·**WAY(*s*) XIII; NOTHING; **no·**WHERE, **no·**-WHITHER OE.

no[3] nou expressing a negative answer. XIII (AncrR.). midl. and south. ME. form of OE. *nā*, f. NE+*ā* ever (cf. AY). ¶ Earlier practice limited the use of *no* to response to a sentence containing a negative)(*nay*.

no., nº (read as *number*). XVI. abbrev. of L. *numerō* in number, abl. of *numerus* NUMBER; later, perh. after F. *numéro* (– It., Sp. *numero*), standing for 'number' (so-and-so).

Noachian nouei·kiən pert. to Noah (Gen. vi 14, etc.). XVII (Cudworth). So **Noa·-chic**(AL). XVII.

nob[1] nɔb (sl. or colloq.) head. XVII. perh. var. of KNOB.

nob[2] nɔb (colloq.) person of wealth or distinction. XIX. In XVIII Sc. *nab*, *knabb*, the local pronunc. of which may have suggested *nob* to the southerner. Hence **no·bb**Y[1] smart, elegant XIX; in XVIII Sc. *knabby*.

nobble nɔ·bl (sl. or colloq.) tamper with (a racing horse); steal, seize. XIX. prob. var. of (dial.) *knobble*, var. of *knubble* knock, beat, f. KNOB, *knub*+-LE[3].

noble nou·bl illustrious by position, character, or birth; distinguished by splendour or magnificence XIII; of great or lofty character XVI. – (O)F. *noble* = Sp. *noble*, It. *nobile* – L. *nōbilis*, for earlier *gnōbilis* (cf. IGNOBLE), f. **gnō*- KNOW; see -BLE. So **nobi·**LITY. XIV. – (O)F. or L. **noblesse** nou·bles (arch.) nobility. XIII. – (O)F. *noblesse* = Pr. *noblessa*, *-eza*, etc.; see -ESS[2].

nocake nou·keik (U.S.) maize parched and pounded. XVII. Algonkin; cf. Narragansett *nokehick*, Natick *nookhik* maize.

nock nɔk tip of horn on a bow or arrow XIV (Trevisa); (naut.) end of a yard-arm or sail XVI. – MDu. *nocke* (Du. *nock*), whence also G. *nock*.

nocti-, before a vowel **noct-**, comb. form of L. *noct-*, *nox* NIGHT.

noctule nɔ·ktjūl largest species of British bat. XVIII (Pennant). – F. *noctule* (Buffon) – It. *nottola*, *-o*, f. *notte* NIGHT.

nocturn nɔ·ktəɹn division of the office of mattins. XIII. – (O)F. *nocturne* or ecclL. *nocturnus*, *-um*, sb. use of L. *nocturnus* pert. to the night, f. *noct-*, *nox* NIGHT, with *r*-stem as in Gr. *núktōr* by night, *núkteros* nocturnal. So **noctu·rn**AL[1]. XV. – late L. (cf. *diurnus*).

nod nɔd make a quick inclination of the head. XIV (Ch.). perh. of LG. origin; the nearest corr. form is MHG. *notten* (in modG. *notteln*) move about, shake. Hence sb. XVI.

noddy nɔ·di simpleton, noodle; sea-bird, Anous stolidus. XVI. prob. sb. use of †*noddy* adj. foolish, silly (cf. †*noddy peak*, *-poll*, *-poop*), perh. f. NOD+-Y[1]. Cf. synon. †*nodgecock*, *-comb* (XVI).

node noud complication, entanglement XVI; hard tumour; point of intersection XVII. – L. *nōdus* knot, etc., perh. rel. to *nectere* bind (see CONNECT). So **nod**ULE nɔ·djūl. XVI. – L. *nōdulus*; cf. F. *nodule*. **nod**OSE[1] nou·dous knotty. XVIII. – L. **nodos**ITY -ɔ·sĭti. – late L.

noel noue·l Christmas carol. XIX. – F. *noël* NOWEL.

noetic noue·tik pert. to the intellect. XVII. – Gr. *noētikós*, f. *noētós* intellectual, f. *noeîn* think, perceive, f. *noûs*, *nóos* mind.

noggin nɔ·gin mug, cup; small quantity of liquor. XVII. Of unkn. origin. ¶ Gael. *noigean*, Ir. *noigin* are from Eng.

noil noil short pieces and knots of wool combed out of the long staple. XVII. prob. in earlier use and – OF. *noel* :- medL. *nodellu-s*, dim. of L. *nōdus* knot (NODE, NOOSE).

noise noiz loud outcry (survives in *hold one's n.*); †rumour; loud or harsh sound XIII; †agreeable sound XIV; †band of musicians XVI. – (O)F. *noise* outcry, hubbub, disturbance, noisy dispute = Pr. *nausa* noisy confusion, OCat. *noxa* harm, injury, Cat. *nosa* hindrance, OIt. dial. *noxa* dung :- L. *nausea* sea-sickness, NAUSEA. Hence (or – OF. *nois(i)er*) vb. XIV. **noi·s**Y[1]. XVII (Dryden).

noisome noi·səm harmful, injurious XIV (Wycl. Bible); offensive XV. f. †*noy* to trouble, vex, harm, aphetic of ANNOY + -SOME; finally superseding †*noyful*, †*noyous* (XIV).

noli me tangere nou:limitæ·ndʒəri eroding ulcer on the face XIV; species of balsam, Impatiens Noli me tangere XVI; person or thing that must not be meddled with XVII. L., 'touch me not' (cf. Vulgate, John xx 17).

noll nɔl, noul (crown of) the head OE.; †nape of the neck XIV (Wycl. Bible, Trevisa). OE. *hnoll* = MDu. *nolle*, OHG. *hnol* top, summit, crown of the head.

nomad nou·mæd, nɔ·mæd one of a wandering race. XVI. – F. *nomade* – L. *Nomad-*, *Nomas*, pl. *Nomades* pastoral people wandering about with their flocks – Gr. *nomad-*, *nomás* roaming about, esp. for pasture, pl. *Nomádes* pastoral people, f. **nom-* **nem-* (*némein* pasture); see NIM, -AD[1]. So **nomad**IC noumæ·dik. XIX. – Gr. *nomadikós*.

nomenclature nou·mənkleitʃəɹ, nŏme·n-klĭtʃəɹ †name; set of names. XVII. – F. *nomenclature* – L. *nōmenclātūra* (Pliny), f. *nōmenclātor* one who names, f. *nōmen* NAME + *calāre* call; see INTERCALATE, -URE. **nomin**AL[1] nɔ·minəl pert. to a noun XV; †nominalistic (in the medieval sense) XVI; pert. to a name; existing only in name XVII. – F. *nominal* or L. *nōminālis*, f. *nōmen* NAME. Hence **no·minal**ISM XIX, -IST XVII)(*realism*, *-ist*; cf. F. *nominalisme*, *-iste* (1752). **no·minal**LY[2] by name XVII; in name XVIII. **nomin**ATE[3] nɔ·mineit name, esp. officially. XVI. f. pp. stem of L. *nōmināre*, f. *nōmin-*, *nōmen* NAME. **nomin**A·TION. XV. – (O)F. or L. **no·min**ATIVE of the case of the subject of a finite verb. XIV (Trevisa, Wyclif). – (O)F. *nominatif*, *-ive* or L. *nōminātīvus* (sc. *casus* case, Varro), tr. Gr. *onomastikḗ* (sc. *ptôsis* case). **nomin**EE[1] nɔminī· person named or nominated. XVII. f. NOMINATE.

-nomy nəmi, terminal el. of sbs., repr. Gr. *-nomíā* arrangement, management, rel. to *nómos* law, *némein* distribute (see NIM), as in ASTRONOMY, AUTONOMY, ECONOMY, GASTRONOMY, and words formed after these, as *geonomy*, *zoonomy*. The corr. adjs. end in *-no·mic*, *-no·mical*; see -Y[3].

non- nɔn prefix expressing negation, used with sbs., adjs., vbs. (ppl. adjs., gerunds), and advs.; first in the AN. form *noun-* = OF. *non-*, *nom-*, *nun-*, *num-* :– L. *nōn* 'not' used as a prefix. The earliest exx. are *nonpower* (Ch., PPl., Wyclif), *non-residence*, *nonsuit* (Wyclif); similar comps. of a technical kind prevail until XVII, when the application was widened; to the religious and political movements of XVI and XVIII belong *nonconformist*, *nonjuror* (1691), *non-resistance*. The prefix is normally unstressed, but it is stressed in the disyllables *nonage*, *nonsense*, *nonsuit*, as also in *nonchalance*, *nondescript*.

nonage nou·nidʒ period of legal infancy. XIV (PPl.). – AN. *nounage*, OF. *nonage*; see NON-, AGE.

nonagenarian nou:nədʒĭnɛə·riən 90 years old. XIX. f. L. *nōnāgēnārius*, f. *nōnāgēnī*, distributive of *nōnāginta* ninety, f. **novenāginta*, f. *novem* NINE; see -ARIAN. So **nonagesimal**[1] -e·siməl. XVIII. f. L. *nōnāgēsimus* 90th.

nonce nɔns phr. *for the nonce* (orig.) †for the particular purpose, expressly XII (*forr þe naness*, Orm); for the occasion, for the time being XVI. ME. *for þe nanes*, alteration (by misdivision, as in *a newt* for *an ewt*) of *for þen anes*, alt., with advb. -s, of **for þen ane* 'for the one (purpose)', parallel to *to þen ane* (beside *to þen anes*) 'with a view to the one (thing)'; cf. the parallel *ane*, *anes* (see ONCE).

nonchalance nɔ·nʃələns lack of interest or concern. XVII. – (O)F. *nonchalance*, f. *nonchalant* (adopted in Eng. XVIII), f. *non* NON- + prp. of *chaloir* be concerned, first used in (*ne*) *chaut* it is (not) the concern (of), earlier (*ne*) *chieut* :– L. *calet*, 3rd sg. pres. ind. of *calēre* be hot (see LUKEWARM).

nonCONFO·RMIST one who does not conform to the Church of England (or other established church). 1619. So **†nonconfo·rmitan, -fo·rmity** 1618 (Donne).

nondescript nɔ·ndiskript †(nat. hist.) not hitherto described (so contemp. *undescribed*) XVII (Ray); not easily described, neither one thing nor another XIX. f. NON- + *descript* – L. *dēscriptus*, pp. of *dēscrībere* DESCRIBE.

none[1] nʌn no one, nobody; not any. OE. *nān* = OFris. *nēn*, ON. *neinn*; comp. of NE and ONE; cf. OS. *nēn*, (M)Du. *neen*, (O)HG. *nein* no (adv.), and L. *nōn* not :– **nē oinom* 'not ONE (thing)'. As adv. XII; now chiefly in *none the . . .*, *none too . . . .*

noneE·NTITY nɔn- non-existent thing XVI; non-existence; person or thing of no importance XVII. See NON-; cf. †*non-ens* XVII.

nones nounz A. ninth day before the Ides XV; B. the fourth of the day offices of the Church. XVIII. In A – (O)F. *nones* – L. *nōnæ*, acc. *nōnās*, fem. pl. of *nōnus* ninth, f. *novem* NINE; in B f. NONE[2] after *mattins*, *lauds*, *vespers*. Also **none**[2] XIX. – (O)F. *none* (Sp., It. *nona*) – L. *nōna* (sc. *hōra* hour).

nonesuch XVI, now usu. **nonsuch** XVII nʌ·n-sʌtʃ, nɔ·nsʌtʃ unmatched, unrivalled. Extracted from such phr. as 'There is *none such*', but no doubt suggested partly by NONPAREIL; first used in the name of Nonesuch Palace, at Cheam in Surrey, completed 1557.

nonny-nonny nɔ·ninɔ·ni obs. refrain, often used to cover an indelicate allusion (cf. 'these noninos of filthie ribauldry', Drayton). XVI.

non-obstante nɔnɔbstæ·nti (leg.) first two words of a clause in statutes, etc. ('non obstante aliquo statuto in contrarium' any statute to the contrary not standing in the way). XV. medL., *nōn* NOT+*obstante*, abl. of *obstāns*, prp. of L. *obstāre* stand in the way, f. *ob* OB-+*stāre* STAND (cf. OBVIOUS). See NOTWITHSTANDING.

nonpareil nɔnpəre·l having no equal XV (Caxton); unique person or thing XVI (Nashe); size of printing type XVII. – F. *nonpareil*, f. *non-* NON-+*pareil* like :– Rom. **pariculu-s*, dim. of *par* equal (see PAIR).

nonplus nɔ·nplʌs state in which no more can be said or done, esp. in phr. *be at, put to, a nonplus*. XVI. f. L. phr. *nōn plūs* not more, no further (see NON, PLUS); cf. F. †*mettre à nonplus*. Hence as vb. XVI.

non (plus) ultra see NE PLUS ULTRA.

nonsense nɔ·nsens that which is not sense. XVII (B. Jonson). f. NON-+SENSE, after F. *nonsens* (XV). Hence **nonse·ns**ICAL. XVII.

nonsuit nɔ·nsjūt (leg.) cessation or stoppage of a suit. XIV (Wyclif). – AN. *no(u)nsuit*; see NON-, SUIT.

nonyl nɔ·nil (chem.) ninth of the alcohols with formula CnH_{2n+1}. XIX. f. L. *nōnus* NINTH+-YL.

noodle[1] nū·dl simpleton. XVIII. Of unkn. origin.

noodle[2] nū·dl strip of dough as an ingredient of soup. XVIII. – G. *nudel* (of unkn. origin), whence F. *nouilles*.

nook nuk corner, angle. XIII (first in *feower-noked* four-cornered, Laȝamon's 'Brut' 21999; next in Cursor M.). Of unkn. origin. Many of the earliest instances are in texts in which the Scand. element is prominent, but no such Scand. form is known, unless it is repr. by Norw. dial. *nok* hook, bent object. ¶ Gael., Ir. *niuc* is from the Sc. var. *neuk*.

noon nūn †ninth hour of the day reckoned from sunrise, 3 p.m.; †office of nones OE.; †midday meal XII; midday XIII. OE. *nōn*, corr. to OS. *nōn(e)*, (M)Du. *noen*, OHG. *nona*, G. *none*, ON. *nón* – L. *nōna* (sc. *hōra* hour), fem. sg. of *nōnus* ninth (see NINE); cf. NONE[2], NONES. The same shifting of the time denoted, prob. due to the anticipation of the canonical hour or of a meal-time, has taken place also in Du. *noen* and in dial. use of F. *none*. The common phr. *(be)fore noon, after noon* have given rise to the sbs. FORENOON, AFTERNOON. Hence **noo·n**DAY. XV (Coverdale). **noo·n**TIDE. OE. *nōntīd* = MDu. *noentijd*, MHG. *nōn(e)tīt*.

noose nūs loop formed with a running knot. XV (rare before 1600). Late ME. *nōse*, perh. – OF. *nos*, *nous* (= Pr. *nous*, Cat. *nus*, It. *nodo*, Rum. *nod*), nom. sg. and accus. pl. (:– L. *nōdus*, *-ōs*) of *no*, *nou*, later *noud*, mod. *nœud* (:– L. *nōdu-s* NODE). The alternative pronunc. nūz corr. to a disyll. ME. *nō·zə*, which is, however, unaccounted for.

nopal nou·pəl Amer. species of cactus. XVIII. – (F. –) Sp. *nopal* – Mex. *nopalli* cactus.

nor nɔ̄ɹ negative disjunctive particle. XIV. contr. of †*nother* (f. NE), as *or* is of †*other*, †*outher*, and †*wher* of *whether*.

norimon nɔ·rimɔn litter, palanquin. XVII. – Jap. *norimono*, f. *nori* ride+*mono* thing.

norm nɔ̄ɹm model, pattern. XIX (Coleridge). – L. *norma* carpenter's square, pattern, rule, whence also (O)F. *norme* (adopted in Eng. XVII), It. *norma*. So **no·rm**AL[1] rectangular, perpendicular XVII; conforming to a standard XIX (*n. school*, after F. *école normale* 1794) – F. *normal* or (of schools) L. *normālis*, whence also Sp. *normal*, It. *normale*. Hence **no·rmal**CY, **norma·**LITY, **no·rmal**IZE. XIX.

Norman nɔ̄·ɹmən pl. *-mans* native of Normandy XIII (Laȝ.); adj. XVI (*N. English* XVI, *N. French* XVII; (archit.) XVIII). orig. in pl. – (O)F. *Normans*, *-anz*, pl. of *Normant* (mod. *-mand*) – ON. *Norðmaðr*, pl. *-menn*, which was adopted as OE. *Norþmann*, pl. *-menn*, **Norman*, pl. *Normen*, OHG. *Nordman* (Du. *Noorman*, G. *Normanne*); see NORTH, MAN. ¶ The Scand. word is repr. in mod. times (from XVII) by *Northman*.

norn nɔ̄ɹn female fate in Scand. myth. XVIII (Percy). – ON. *norn*, of unkn. origin. Latinized **no·rna** XIX.

Norn nɔ̄ɹn Norwegian. XVII. – ON. *Norrœnn* adj., *Norrœnna* sb. (whence early ME. †*Norren*), for **Norðrœnn*, f. *norðr* NORTH.

Norroy nɔ·roi third King of Arms, whose jurisdiction lies north of the Trent. XV (*-ey*). – AN. **norroi*, f. (O)F. *nord* NORTH + *roi* king (cf. ROYAL).

Norse nɔ̄ɹs (hist.) Norwegian XVI (Hakluyt); sb. and adj. the Norwegian tongue XVII (*Old N.*, the language of Norway and its colonies to the 14th century). – Du. *noorsch*, var. of *noordsch*, f. *noord* NORTH + *-sch* -ISH[1]; cf. OFris. *nor(d)sch*, MLG. *norrisch*, MSw. *norsker*.

north nɔ̄ɹþ pert. to the quarter most remote from the noonday sun. OE. *norþ* = OFris. *north*, *noerd*, OS. *norð* (Du. *noord*), OHG. *nord* (G. *nord*), ON. *norðr*; CGerm. (exc. Gothic), of unkn. origin, the source of (O)F. *nord*, Sp., It. *norte*. So †**no·rth**EN[1]. XII. **no·rther**LY. XVI. **no·rthern** OE.; hence **no·rthern**ER[1]. XIX. †**no·rthern**LY. XVI. **no·rth**ING[1]. XVII (Sturmy). **no·rth**WARD. XII. **no·rth**WARDS. OE.

Northumbrian nɔ̄ɹþʌ·mbriən pert. to Northumbria, that part of England lying north of the Humber. XVII (Drayton). f.

†*Northumber* pl. inhabitants of this, repr. OE. *Norþhymbre*, f. *norþ* north+*Humbre* Humber; see -IAN.

Norwegian nɔːwīˑdʒən pert. to, native of, Norway. XVII. f. medL. *Norvegia* – ON. *Norvegr* (whence late OE. *Norweġ*, mod. *Norway*), f. *norðr* NORTH + *vegr* WAY, (in place-names) region. ¶ Early synonyms were †*Norenish* (Laȝ.), †*Norgan* (Trevisa), †*Norreis* (Laȝ.), NORN, †*Norren* (XII–XIII).

nose nouz organ of smell. OE. *nosu* = OFris. *nose*, MDu. *nōse*, *nuese* (Du. *neus*). Like other names of parts of the body (cf. EAR[1]) of CIE. extent, but the relation of the several forms in obscure; cf. OE. *nasu*, OHG. *nasa* (G. *nase*), ON. *nasar* pl., nom. sg. *nǫs* (perh. secondary), L. *nārēs* pl. nostrils, *nās(s)us* nose, OSl. *nosŭ* (Russ. *nos*), Lith. *nósis*, Vedic (dual) *nāsā*, Skr. *nás* (in some obl. cases); also early ME. *nese* = MLG., MDu. *nese*. Hence vb. perceive by smell XVI; poke *about*, pry XVII. **no·se**GAY. XV (Lydg.); *gay* sb. in the sense 'ornament', 'play thing, toy' (XIV to mod. dial.). **nosey, nos**Y[1] nouˑzi sb. one having a large nose XVIII; adj. evil-smelling; (colloq.) inquisitive XIX.

nosology nɔsɔˑlədʒi classification of diseases. XVIII. – modL. *nosologia*, f. Gr. *nósos* disease; see -LOGY.

nostalgia nɔstæˑldʒ[i]ə home-sickness. XVIII. – modL. *nostalgia*, f. Gr. *nóstos* return home +*álgos* pain; see -IA[1].

nostoc nɔˑstɔk genus of algæ. XVII. Invented by Paracelsus. ¶ 'Nostoch understandeth the nocturnall Pollution of some plethoriall and wanton Star, or rather excrement blown from the nostrills of some rheumatick planet . . in consistence like a gelly' (Charlton, tr. van Helmont's 'Paradoxes', 1650).

Nostradamus nɔstrədeiˑməs seer. XVII (Dryden). Latinization of the name of Michel de *Nostredame* ('Our Lady'), F. physician (1503–66), who published a book of prophecies in rhyme.

nostril nɔˑstrĭl either of the two outer openings of the nose. OE. *nosþyrl*, *nosterl* (= OFris. *nosterl*), f. *nosu* NOSE+*þӯr(e)l* hole :– **þurχil*, f. *þurh* THROUGH. ¶ For the development of *sþ* to *st* cf. LEST, *sćeoldestū* for *sćeoldes þū*.

nostrum nɔˑstrəm medicine or medicament the composition of which is not made public; 'patent' remedy. XVII. L., n. of *noster* our (see US); from the label *nostrum* 'of our own make' formerly attached to such medicines.

not nɔt adv. of negation. XIV (Rolle). Reduced form of *noht*, *noȝt*, NOUGHT. ¶ From XIV to XVI the parallel *nat* (reduction of NAUGHT) was current.

notable nouˑtəbl worthy of note XIV (Rolle); †conspicuous, noticeable XVI; †energetic XVII; – (O)F. *notable* = Sp. *notable*, It. *notabile* – L. *notābilis*, f. *notāre*; see NOTE, -ABLE. The pronunc. nɔˑtəbl is given by XVIII orthoepists, and is retained by later lexicographers as proper to the sense 'capable, managing' (XVIII, later dial.); sb. XV (Caxton). ¶ As sb. pl. (XVI) prominent men of the estates of France liable to be summoned by the King. So **notabil**ITY noutəbiˑlĭti. XIV. – (O)F.

notary nouˑtəri †clerk, secretary; one authorized to draw up deeds. XIV. – L. *notārius* shorthand-writer, clerk, f. *nota* NOTE; see -ARY. The Sc. form was *notar* (XV). – F. *notaire*.

notch nɔtʃ V-shaped indentation. XVI. – AN. *noche* (XIV), perh. f. **nocher* (rel. to *anoccer* add a notch to); cf. L. *inoccare* harrow in (which may have been used transf. for making a score or notch) and rare ME. *oche* vb. ('Morte Arthure'), OF. *oche*, *osche* (mod. *hoche*), f. *o(s)chier* (*hocher*) = Pr. *oscar* nick, notch.

note nout sign denoting a musical sound; musical sound of a certain pitch; †melody, tune; call of a bird XIII; mark, sign, character XIV; abstract, brief record or statement XV; annotation, comment; short letter; distinction; notice, regard XVI; written promise to pay XVII. – (O)F. *note* = Sp., It. *nota* – L. *nota* mark, sign, written character, shorthand sign, note of music, memorandum, critical remark, brand, quality, character. So **note** vb. observe, indicate XIII; mark XV. – (O)F. *noter* – L. *notāre*, f. the sb. **not**Aˑ TION †explanation of a term; †annotation XVI; representation by signs XVIII. – L. or (O)F.

nothing nʌˑþiŋ not any thing. OE. *nān þing*, ME. *nā þing*, later *nǭ þing*; see NO[2], THING, and cf. NOUGHT. Hence **nothing**AˑRIAN. XVIII (first in N. America). **noˑthing**NESS. XVII (Donne).

notice nouˑtis (formal) intimation XV; heed, cognizance XVI; †notion, idea XVII; brief mention in review XIX. – (O)F. *notice* = Sp. *noticia*, It. *notizia* – L. *nōtitia* being known, acquaintance, knowledge, notion, f. *nōtus* known (see KNOW). Hence **noˑtice** vb. †notify XV; mention, refer to XVII; observe, remark XVIII. ¶ Not in gen. use before mid-XVIII; referred to, along with *narrate*, as a Scotticism by Beattie, 1787, and as recently current in America by Franklin in 1789.

notify nouˑtifai †observe; give notice of. XIV (Ch.). – (O)F. *notifier* – L. *nōtificāre*, f. *nōtus* known; see prec. and -FY. So **no:ti**FICATION. XIV (Ch.).

notion nouˑʃən concept, idea. XVI. – L. *nōtiō(n-)* becoming acquainted, examination, conception, idea (Cicero, rendering Gr. ἔννοια, πρόληψις), f. *nōt-*, pp. stem of *(g)nōscere* KNOW; see -TION. So F. (XVII). **noˑtion**AL[1]. XVI. – F. or medL.

noto- nou·tou comb. form of Gr. *nôtos -on* back.

notorious nǒtō·riəs well or generally known; noted *for* some bad quality. XVI. – medL. *nōtōrius* (cf. late L. *nōtōria* notice, news, *nōtōrium* information, indictment), f. *nōtus* known, pp. of *(g)nōscere*; see NOTION, -ORIOUS. Earlier †*notoire* XV – (O)F. *notoire*; †*notory* XIV, *notour* Sc. (surviving in *n. bankrupt*) XV – F. with change of suffix (cf. Du. *notoor*).

notwithstanding nɔtwiðstæ·ndiŋ in *this n.*, *n. this*, etc. in spite of this XIV; adv. nevertheless XV; conj. although XV. f. NOT+prp. of WITHSTAND; after (O)F. *nonobstant*, NON-OBSTANTE, orig. in absol. phr., e.g. *ce nonobstant*, *hōc nōn obstante* this not standing in the way, hence with a clause as regimen (passing into conj.) or without regimen (passing into adv.): F. *nonobstant que*, AN. *nient contrestant que*.

nougat nū·ga sweetmeat made of sugar and almonds. XIX. – F. *nougat* – Pr. *nogat*, f. *noga* nut (:– Rom. **nuca*, for L. *nuce-*, *nux* NUT)+*-at* :– L. *-ātum* -ATE[1].

nought nɔ̄t nothing OE.; adv. (dial.) in no degree; not OE.; †adj. bad, good for nothing XIV. OE. *nōwiht*, f. NE+*ōwiht* OUGHT, var. of *āwiht* AUGHT. Cf. NAUGHT, NOT. ¶ Parallel formations in Germ. are OS. *neo-*, *niowiht*, OHG. *niwiht* (G. *nicht*); OFris. *nāwet*, *nāut*, MDu. *niewet* (Du. *niet*), MHG. *niewet*; OHG. *niwiht* (cf. OE. *ne . . wiht*, Goth. *ni waihts*).

noumenon nau·mənɔn (metaph.) object of purely intellectual intuition. XVIII. – G. *noumenon* (Kant) – Gr. *nooúmenon*, n. of prp. pass. of *noeîn* apprehend, conceive (cf. NOUS).

noun naun (gram.) name of a person or thing. XIV (Trevisa). – AN. *noun* = OF. *nun*, *num* (mod. *nom*) :– L. *nōmen* NAME.

nourish nʌ·riʃ †bring up, nurture; foster (fig.); †suckle, nurse XIII; sustain with proper nutriment XIV. – OF. *noriss-*, lengthened stem (see -ISH[2]) of *norir* (mod. *nourrir*) = Pr. *noirir*, Cat., OSp. *nodrir* :– L. *nutrīre* feed, foster, cherish; see NUTRIMENT. Hence **nou·rish**MENT. XV; repl. earlier †*nouri*TURE XIV (Ch.) – OF. *noureture* (mod. *nourri-*).

nous naus (Gr. philos.) mind, intellect XVII; (colloq.) intelligence, gumption XVIII (sometimes printed in Gr. letters *νοῦς*, as in Byron's 'Don Juan' II cxxx). – Gr. *noûs*, contr. form of *nóos* mind (cf. NOETIC).

Novatian nouvei·ʃən pert. to, member of, a rigorist Christian sect founded by a Roman presbyter *Novatianus* (III). XV (Pecock).

novel nɔ·v(ə)l A. †novelty; †pl. news XV; B. short story of Boccaccio's 'Decameron', etc. XVI; fictitious prose narrative XVII (Milton; 'a kind of abbreviation of a romance', Chesterfield). In A – OF. *novelle* (mod. *nouvelle*) = It. *novella* :– L. *novella*, n. pl. (construed as sing.) of *novellus* (esp. in agricultural use), f. *novus* NEW; in B directly = It. *novella*, orig. fem. (sc. *storia* story) of *novello* new = OF. *novel* (mod. *nouveau*), whence **nov·el** adj. XV. Hence **no·vel**IST †innovator XVI; †newsmonger; writer of novels XVIII; cf. F. *nouvelliste*, It. *novellista*, Sp. *novelista*. **no·vel**TY. XIV. – OF. *novelte* (mod. *nouveauté*).

November nouve·mbəɹ 11th (formerly 9th) month of the year. XIII. – (O)F. *novembre* – L. *November*, also *Novembris* (sc. *mensis* month), f. *novem* NINE; cf. DECEMBER, etc.

novena nouvī·nə nine days' devotion. XIX. – medL. *novēna*, f. *novem* NINE, after L. *novēnārius* of nine days.

novercal nouvə̄·ɹkəl stepmotherly. XVII. – L. *novercālis*, f. *noverca* stepmother, f. *novus* NEW; see -AL[1].

novice nɔ·vis probationer in a religious community XIV; inexperienced person XV. – (O)F. *novice* m. and fem. = Sp. *novicio*, *-icia*, It. *novizio*, *-izia* – L. *novīcius*, *-īcia*, f. *novus* NEW; see -ITIOUS[1]. So **novici**ATE[1] nouvi·ʃiət. XVI. – F. *noviciat* or medL. *novīciātus*.

now nau adv. at the present time; conj. since, seeing that. OE. *nū̆* = OS. *nū̆* (Du. *nu*), OHG. *nū̆* (G. *nun*, with advb. *n* added), ON., Goth. *nū̆*; CIE. adv. of time, repr. also by L. *num*, *nunc*, Gr. *nu*, *nun*, *nûn*, *nūnī*, OIr. *nu-*, *no-* verbal prefix of the present, OSl. *nyně*, Lith. *nù*, *nūnaī*, Skr. *nū*, *nūnám*, Hittite *nu*. Hence **nowaday(s)** nau·ədei(z) at the present time. XIV; + ME. *aday(s)*, resulting from the blending of OE. *on dæġe* and genit. *dæġes*; see -S.

nowel noue·l cry of joy used in celebrating Christmas, retained in carols. XIV. – OF. *nouel*, *noel* (mod. *noël*), obscure var. of *nael*, *neel* = Pr. *nadal*, Sp. *natal*, It. *natale* :– L. *nātālis* (sc. *diēs* day) NATAL.

nowhere nou·ʍɛəɹ in no place. OE. *nāhwǣr*, later *nōhwǣr*, f. *nā* NO[2]+*hwǣr* WHERE. So **no**·WHI:THER. OE. *nā-*, *nōhwider*.

noxious nɔ·kʃəs injurious, harmful. XVII. f. L. *noxius*, f. *noxa* hurt, damage, rel. to *nex* slaughter (cf. INTERNECINE, PERNICIOUS), *nocēre* injure (cf. INNOCENT); see -IOUS.

noyade nwa·jād execution by drowning. XIX. F., f. *noyer* to drown :– L. *necāre* kill without a weapon, (later) drown, f. *nec-*, *nex* slaughter (cf. prec.); see -ADE.

noyau nwa·jou liqueur made from brandy flavoured with kernels. XVIII. F., earlier *noiel* kernel :– Rom. **nucāle*, sb. use of n. of late L. *nucālis*, f. *nuc-*, *nux* NUT.

nozzle nɔ·zl candle-socket; small spout or mouthpiece. XVII. Early forms *nosle*, *nos(s)el*; if f. NOSE+-LE[1], a much earlier existence must be presumed.

nuance nü·ãs shade of feeling, meaning, etc. XVIII (H. Walpole); shade of colour XIX. F. (Cotgr.), f. *nuer* show variations of shades of colour like clouds, f. *nue* cloud :- popL. **nūbe*, L. *nūbēs*; see -ANCE.

nub nʌb †husk of silk XVI; knob, lump XVIII; (U.S.) gist XIX. var. of KNUB.

nubile njū·bail (of women) marriageable. XVII. – L. *nūbilis*, f. *nūbere* take a husband (cf. CONNUBIAL, NUPTIAL, NYMPH); see -ILE.

nucha njū·kə (anat.) †spinal cord; nape of the neck. XIV. medL. – Arab. *nukhāʿ* spinal marrow. (F. *nuque*, †*nuche* were repr. in Eng. by †*nuke*, †*nuche* XVI–XVII.) Hence **nu·ch**AL[1]. XIX.

nucleus njū·kliəs more condensed portion of the head of a comet; central part, kernel. XVIII. – L. *nucleus* nut, kernel, inner part, var. of *nuculeus*, f. *nucula* small nut, dim. (see -ULE) of *nuc-*, *nux* NUT. Hence **nu·cle**AR. XIX.

nude njūd (leg.) not formally attested; †bare, mere XVI; naked, unclothed XVII (rare before XIX, except as sb. *nudes*, *the nude* XVIII, after F. *nu*). – L. *nūdus* :- **now(e)dos*, **nogwedos* NAKED. So **nu·d**ITY. XVII (Cotgr., Evelyn). – (O)F. or late L. **nu·d**IST. XX.

nudge nʌdʒ push gently with the elbow. XVII. Of unkn. origin; perh. in much earlier use and rel. ult. to Norw. dial. *nugga*, *nyggja* push, rub.

nugatory njū·gətəri worthless, useless. XVII. – L. *nūgātōrius*, f. pp. stem of *nūgārī* trifle, f. *nūgæ* jests, trifles; see -ORY[2].

nugget nʌ·git lump, orig. of native gold. XIX. perh. dim. of s.w. dial. *nug* lump, block, unshapen mass, of unkn. origin; see -ET.

nuisance njū·səns injury, harm XV (Hoccleve; now coloured by other senses); injurious or obnoxious thing XV; source of annoyance XIX. – OF. (now arch.) *nuisance* hurt, f. *nuis-*, stem of *nuire* injure :- L. *nocēre* (cf. INNOCENT, NOXIOUS); see -ANCE.

null nʌl not valid (*n. and void*) XVI; insignificant; non-existent XVIII. – (O)F. *nul*, fem. *nulle*, or L. *nūllus*, *-a* no, none, f. *ne* NE+ *ūllus* any, f. *ūnus* ONE. So **nu·ll**IFY make null. XVI. – late L. *nullificāre* despise (Tertullian, tr. Gr. *ἐξουθενεῖν*). **nu:llifica**·TION. 1798 (Jefferson). **nu·ll**ITY. XVI. – F. or medL.

nullah nʌ·lə (in India) river, river-bed, ravine. XVIII. – Hindi *nālā* brook, rivulet, ravine.

numb nʌm deprived of feeling. XV ('nomyn, or take wythe þe palsye, *paraliticus*', Promp. Parv.). Late ME. *nome(n)*, pp. of NIM take, seize. Hence vb. XVII. ¶ For the parasitic *b* cf. THUMB.

number nʌ·mbəɹ sum of individuals or units; full tale or count XIII; multitude, aggregate; aspect or property of things as units; symbol of arithmetical value XIV; (pl.) groups of musical notes, melody; metrical periods, verses XVI. ME. *noumbre*, *nombre*, *numbre* – AN. *numbre*, (O)F. *nombre* = Pr., Cat. *nombre*, It. *novero*, Rum. *număr* :- L. *numeru-s*, perh. rel. to Gr. *némein* distribute (see NIM). The F. word was adopted in Du. *nommer*, G., etc. *nummer*. So **nu·mber** vb. XIII. – (O)F. *nombrer* :- L. *numerāre*.

numbles nʌ·mblz inward parts of an animal as used for food. XIV. – OF. *numbles*, *nombles* pl., corr. to It. dial. *lómbolo*, *nómbolo*, *mombol*, *ombul* :- L. *lumbulu-s*, dim. of *lumbus*; see LOIN and cf. HUMBLE-PIE, UMBLES.

numen njū·men divinity. XVII. – L. *nūmen* divine will, divinity, rel. to *-nuere* nod (only in comps.), Gr. *neúein* nod, incline the head, Skr. *návate* moves. So **nu·min**OUS. XVII. f. L. *nūmin-*, *nūmen*.

numeral njū·mərəl adj. pert. to number; sb. figure denoting a number. XVI. – late L. *numerālis* (Priscian), f. *numerus* NUMBER; see -AL[1]. So **numer**A·TION numbering. XV. – L. **nu·mer**ATOR (arith.). XVI. – F. *numérateur* or late L. **numer**ICAL njume·rikəl. XVII. f. modL. *numericus*. **nu·mer**OUS plentiful, copious, many; measured, rhythmical. XVI. – L. *numerōsus* (in both senses).

numismatic njūmizmæ·tik pert. to coins or coinage. XVIII. – F. *numismatique*, f. L. *numismat-*, *numisma*, var. (infl. by *nummus* coin) of *nomisma* – Gr. *nómisma* current coin, f. *nomízein* have in use, f. *nómos* use, custom, rel. to *némein* hold, possess; see NIM, -ISM, -ATIC.

nummary nʌ·məri pert. to money or coinage. XVII. – L. *nummārius*, f. *nummus* coin; see -ARY.

nummulite nʌ·mjulait (geol.) coin-shaped fossil of a foraminiferous cephalopod. XIX. f. L. *nummulus*, dim. of *nummus* coin; see prec. and -ITE.

numnah nʌ·mnə saddle-cloth. XIX. var. of *numdah* – Urdu *namdā*, f. Pers. *namad* carpet, rug.

numskull nʌ·mskʌl blockhead, dolt (Swift); pate, noddle (Prior). XVIII. f. NUMB+SKULL.

nun nʌn woman vowed to the religious life. OE. *nunne* = OHG. *nunna* (MHG., G. dial. *nunne*), ON. *nunna*, beside ME. *nonne* (partly – OF. *nonne*) = MDu. *nonne* (Du. *non*), G. *nonne* – ecclL. *nonna*, fem. of *nonnus* monk, orig. titles given to elderly persons, whence It. *nonno*, *nonna* grandfather, -mother. **nu·nn**ERY convent for nuns. XIII (Laȝ.). – AN. **nonnerie*.

nunatak nu·nətæk peak or rock in Greenland. XIX. Eskimo.

Nunc dimittis nʌŋk dimi·tis title of canticle beginning in the Vulg. 'Nunc dimittis servum tuum . .', Now lettest thou thy servant depart . . (Song of Simeon, Luke ii 29–32) XVI; transf. permission to depart, departure XVII.

nuncheon nʌ·nʃən (dial.) refreshment orig. taken in the afternoon. XIV. ME. *non(e) shench* (till XVII usu. with final *s*), f. *non* NOON + *shench* draught, cup (OE. *sćenć*, rel. to *sćenćan* :– Germ. **skaŋkjan* give to drink).

nuncio nʌ·nʃiou permanent representative of the Roman See at a foreign court XVI; member of the Polish Diet XVII. – It. †*nuncio*, †*nuntio* (mod. *nunzio*) = Sp., Pg. *nuncio* – L. *nuntius* messenger. Also anglicized (or – F. *nonce*) *nunce* (XVI–XVII).

nuncupative nʌ·ŋkjupeitiv -ətiv (leg.) oral, not written (as a will). XVI. – late L. *nūncupātīvus*, f. pp. of L. *nūncupāre* name, designate, declare, f. **nōmiceps* or *-*capos* 'name-taking', f. *nōmen* NAME + *capere* take (see HEAVE); see -ATIVE.

nunky nʌ·ŋki f. (colloq.) *nuncle*, f. UNCLE with *n*- transferred from *myn* (MY) + -Y[6].

nunnation nʌnei·ʃən addition of final *n* in the declension of Arabic nouns XVIII; addition of inorganic *n* in Middle English forms XIX. – modL. *nunnātiō(n-)*, f. Arab. *nūn* name of the letter *n*; see -ATION.

nuptial nʌ·pʃəl pert. to marriage XV; sb., usu. pl. marriage, wedding. XVI. – F. *nuptial* or L. *nuptiālis*, f. *nuptiæ* wedding, f. *nupt*-, pp. stem of *nubere*; see NUBILE, -IAL.

nurse nɔ̄ɹs person employed to tend children, the sick, etc. XVI. Reduced form of †*norice* †*n(o)urice* (XIII–XVIII) – OF. *nourice* (mod. -*rr*-) :– late L. *nūtrīcia*, sb. use of fem. of L. *nūtrīcius*, f. *nūtrīre* NOURISH. So **nurse** vb. XVI; alt. of †*nurish*, †*norsh* NOURISH, by assim. to the above sb. **nu·rs**ERY †upbringing of children; apartment for nurse and children; ground, etc. for young plants. XVI.

nurture nɔ̄·ɹtʃəɹ †upbringing; †nourishment XIV; fostering care XVII. – OF. *nourture*, contr. of *noureture* (mod. *nourriture*), f. *nourrir* NOURISH, after late L. *nūtrītūra*; see -URE. Hence vb. XV (Lydg.).

nut nʌt fruit consisting of a shell enclosing a kernel. OE. *hnutu* = MLG. *note*, MDu. *note*, *neute* (Du. *noot*, *neut*), OHG. *(h)nuȥ* (G. *nuss*), ON. *hnot* :– Germ. **χnut*-; cf. OIr. *cnū*, W. *cneuen* (pl. *cnau*). A word appearing only in WIE.; cf. L. *nuc*-, *nux*, in which **kn*- is reduced to *n*, but which has an extension in -*k*-, whereas the Germ. langs. have -*t*-.

nutation njūtei·ʃən nodding XVII; oscillation of the earth's axis XVIII. – L. *nūtātiō(n-)*, f. *nūtāt*-, *nūtāre* nod, f. base of -*nuere* nod; see NUMEN, -ATION.

nuthatch nʌ·thætʃ small creeping bird (family Sittidæ). XIV. ME. *notehache*, with later vars. in -*hak*, -*hagge*, which suggest deriv. from NUT and HACK[1], †*hag*, HATCH[2], with allusion to the bird's habit of cracking nuts.

nutmeg nʌ·tmeg hard aromatic seed of Myristica fragrans or officinalis. XIII/XIV. ME. *nute*-, *notemug(g)e*, later *notmyg* (XV), *note*-, *nutmeg* (XVI), partial tr. of AN. **nois mugue*, for OF. *nois mug(u)ede* (also *musguete*; now *noix muscade*) = Pr. *notz muscada*, Sp. *nuez moscada*, It. *noce moscata* :– Rom. **nuce muscāta* 'musk-smelling nut' (L. *nux* NUT, *muscus* MUSK). Cf. AL. *nux mogata*, *mu(s)-gata*; MDu. *note muscate* (Du. *muskaatnoot*), MHG. *muscāt*, etc.

nutriment njū·trimənt food, nourishment. – L. *nūtrīmentum*, f. *nūtrire* nourish, rel. to Skr. *snauti* drips, trickles (said e.g. of a mother's milk): see -MENT. So **nutri·**TION. XVI; so F. **nutri·**TIOUS. XVII. – L. *nūtrītius*, -*īcius*, f. *nūtric*-, *nūtrīx* NURSE. **nu·trit**IVE. XV. – F. – medL.

nux vomica nʌks vɔ·mikə seed of an East Indian tree from which strychnine is obtained. XVI. medL., i.e. *nux* NUT and fem. of *vomicus*, f. L. *vomere* VOMIT.

nuzzer nʌ·zəɹ present from an inferior to a superior. XVIII. Urdu – Arab. *nazr* gift, f. *nazara* he vowed.

nuzzle nʌ·zl †grovel XV; burrow or push with the nose XVI; nestle XVII. perh. orig. back-formation on †*noseling* with the NOSE to the ground (see -LING[2]), but perh. infl. later by Du. *neuzelen* poke with the NOSE, f. *neus*; see -LE[3]. ¶ The identical *nuzzle* †accustom (a dog or hawk) to attack other animals, train, nurse, cherish (XVI), may have the same origin, but the connexion of sense is not obvious.

nyctalopia niktəlou·piə night-blindness. XVII. – late L., f. Gr. *nuktálōps*, f. *nukt*-, *núx* NIGHT + *alaós* blind + *ṓps* EYE.

nye nai (arch.) nest or brood (of pheasants). XV. – OF. *ni* (mod. *nid*) = Pr., Cat. *niu*, Sp., It. *nido* :– L. *nīdu-s* NEST. ¶ *Nide* (XVII) and *nid* (XIX) have also been used.

nylghau ni·lgɔ̄ large Indian antelope. XVIII. – Hind. – Pers. *nīlgāw*, f. *nīl* blue (cf. ANILINE) + *gāw* COW[1]; cf. F. *nilgaut* (XVII); the Hindi form *nīlgāī* is repr. by **ni·lgai.** XIX.

nylon nai·lən proprietary name of a strong plastic material used for yarn, bristles, etc. XX.

nymph nimf (myth.) semi-divine female being XIV (Ch., Gower); young beautiful woman; pupa XVI. – OF. *nimphe* (mod. *nymphe*) – L. *nympha* – Gr. *númphē* bride, nymph, rel. to L. *nūbere* take in marriage (cf. NUBILE). Gr. – L. comb. form **nympho-,** as in *ny·mpholepsy*, *nymphoma·nia* XVIII.

O

o, o' ə (mostly arch. or dial.) reduced form of (i) ON, in ME. varying with *a* (cf. A-[1]) XII; (ii) OF (cf. A-[2]), surviving sparsely in gen. use, e.g. *o'clock, oclock, cat-o'-nine-tails, man-o'-war, will-o'-the-wisp, John o' Groats.*

O ou int. standing before a vocative or introducing a wish or an asseveration. XII. – (O)F. *o* – L. *ō*; cf. Gr. *ô, ṓ*, Goth., OHG. *ō*. ¶ OE. had in this use *lā* LO, *ēa lā*.

-o ou, an addition to a word, or first part of a word, forming a colloq. or sl. expression or a familiar or joc. equiv., as *like billy-o, lie doggo, ammo* (for *ammunition*), *beano* (for *bean-feast*); sometimes, the last syll. of an abbrev. form, as *compo|sition, hippo|potamus, photo|graph*; in *cheer(i)o, right(y)o, -ho*, perh. the int. O, or after *hallo*.

-o- stem- or connective vowel originating in the *-o-* of Gr. comb. forms (often having advb. force), e.g. (from Gr.) *acro-, aero-, cyclo-, geo-, hydro-, logo-, philo-, politico-, pseudo-, xeno-*, and (on L. bases) *oleo-, radio-, serio-*; a special class is that of comp. proper names, as *Anglo-Saxon, Balto-Slavic, Finno-Ugrian, Græco-Latin, Sino-Japanese.* It appears regularly before -CRACY, -GRAPHY, -LOGY, -METER, and so forms stable suffixes with them, e.g. mob*ocracy*, sex*ology*, socio*logy*, fool*ometer*.

oaf ouf half-wit, dolt. XVII (*oph, oaf*). Varying at first with *ouph* (Sh. 1st Folio) and *aufe, aulfe*, the earliest sense of which was 'elf', 'goblin' – ON. *álfr*; see ELF.

oak ouk forest tree bearing the acorn, Quercus. OE. *āc* (pl. *ǣć*) = OFris., MLG. *ēk* (Du. *eik*), OHG. *eih* (G. *eiche*), ON. *eik* :– CGerm. (exc. Gothic) **aiks* (cons.-stem); ulterior connexions unkn. (but L. *æsculus*, Gr. *aigílōps* have been compared); there is no CIE. word for the tree. ¶ OE. *āc* survives in various shapes in place-names, e.g. *A*cton, *Ag*den, *Ea*gle, *Oak*ley, N*oke* (*æt þǣm ācum*), *Knock*holt; Bradd*ock*, Hods*ock*, Matl*ock*; OE. d. sg. *ǣć* in *Each*, Cress*age*, Radn*age*. Hence **oa·k**EN[3]. XIV; cf. OFris., MLG., MDu. *ēken*; OHG. *eichēn* (G. *eichen*).

oakum ou·kəm †tow OE.; fibre obtained by picking old rope XV. OE. *ācumbe, ācum(b)a*, var. of *ǣcumbe, ǣcuma*, corr. to OHG. *āchambi* (MHG. *ākambe, ākamp*), f. *ǣ-, ā-* away, off + **camb-*, stem of *camb* and *cemban* COMB; the etymol. meaning is 'off-combing'.

oar ɔ̄əɹ wooden lever to propel a boat. OE. *ār* = ON. *ár* (Sw. *år*, Da. *aare*) :– Germ. **airō* (whence Finn. *airo*, Lett. *airis*, Lith. *vaĩras*); a word of the North Sea, but perh. ult. rel. to Gr. *eretmós* oar, *erétēs* rower, *eréssein* row, *tri|ḗrēs* TRIREME. Hence **oa·rlock** OE. *ārloc*; see ROWLOCK.

oasis ou·əsis, ouei·sis fertile spot in a desert. XVII (Purchas). – late L. *oasis* – Gr. *óasis* (Herodotus), presumably of Egyptian origin; cf. Coptic *ouahe* (whence Egyptian Arab. *wāh*) dwelling-place, oasis, f. *ouih* dwell. ¶ Traditional Eng. usage favours the pronunc. *oā·sis*; cf. G. and Sp. *oa·sis*, It. *oa·si*.

oast oust kiln for drying malt, hops, lime. OE. *āst* = WFris. *iest*, MLG. *eist* (Du. *eest*) :– Germ. **aistaz*, for **aiþtaz*, f. IE. base **aidh-* (**idh-*, whence Skr. *idhmás* fuel) burn, repr. also by OE. *ād*, OHG. *eit* blazing pile, funeral pyre, L. *ædēs* (earlier *aidis*) hearth, house, *æstus* heat, *æstās* summer, Gr. *aîthos* heat, OIr. *aedh* heat. ¶ In the place-name *Limehouse*, the second el. conceals orig. *ost*.

oat out (pl.) grains of the cereal Avena sativa. OE. *āte*, pl. *ātan*, peculiar to Eng. and of unkn. origin. ¶ Other Germ. langs. have the word **χaƀron* in OS. *haƀoro*, MDu. *hāver(e)*, OHG. *habero* (G. *haber, hafer*; cf. HAVERSACK), ON. *hafri* (whence dial. Eng. *haver*). Hence **oa·t**EN[3]. XV.

oath ouþ solemn appeal to God as a witness OE.; trivial use of sacred names XII. OE. *āþ* = OFris. *ēth, ēd*, OS. *ēth* (Du. *eed*), (O)HG. *eid*, ON. *eiðr*, Goth. *aiþs* :– CGerm. **aiþaz* :– **oitos* (OIr. *ōeth*).

ob- əb, əb comb. form of L. *ob* towards, against, in the way (of), with vars. OC-, OF-, OP-, occas. *o-* (as in OMIT); mostly in words already existing in L.; in mod. scientific L. (hence in Eng. adoptions) in the sense 'inversely', 'in the opposite direction', virtually repr. modL. *obversē* obversely, e.g. *obovate* ovate with the wider end presented.

obbligato əbligā·tou (mus.) a part essential to the effect of a composition)(ad libitum. XVIII. It., sb. use of pp. of *obbligare* OBLIGE.

obdurate ɔ·bdjŭrət hardened or stubborn in resistance. XV. – L. *obdūrātus*, pp. of *obdūrāre*, f. *ob* OB- + *dūrāre* harden; see DURATION, -ATE[2].

obeah ou·biə, **obi** ou·bi charm, fetish; negro witchcraft. XVIII. W. African (cf. Efik *ubio* thing put in the ground to cause sickness or death).

obedient ŏbī·diənt that obeys. XIII (Ancr. R.). – OF. *obédient* – L. *obedient-, -ēns*, prp. of *obēdīre* OBEY; see -ENT. So **obe·di**ENCE. XIII. – (O)F. – L. **obedienti**ARY -e·nʃəri †one subject to obedience XVI; member of a religious body having an office under the superior XVIII. – medL.

obeisance oubei·sens †obedience; respectful salutation XIV (Ch.). – (O)F. *obéissance*, f. *obéissant*, prp. with lengthened stem (see -ISH[2]) of *obéir* OBEY. So **obei·s**ANT. XIII (RGlouc.). – (O)F. *obéissant.*

obelisk ɔ·bəlisk tapering column of stone; any of the signs —, ÷, †. XVI. – L. *obeliscus* small spit, obelisk – Gr. *obelískos*, dim. of *obelós* spit, pointed pillar. So **obelus** ɔ·bīləs (in second sense). XIV. late L. – Gr.

obese oubī·s very fat. XVII. – L. *obēsus* that has eaten himself fat, stout, plump, f. *ob* OB-+*ēsus*, pp. of *edere* EAT. So **obe·sity**. XVII. – F. or L.

obey ŏbei· comply with the bidding of. XIII. ME. *obeie* – (O)F. *obéir*, corr. to Pr. *obezir*, It. *ubbidire* – L. *obēdīre, obœdīre*, f. *ob* OB-+*audīre* hear (see AUDIENCE).

obfuscate ɔ·bfʌskeit darken, obscure. XVI. f. pp. stem of late L. *obfuscāre*, f. *ob* OB-+*fuscāre* darken, *fuscus* dark; see DUSK, -ATE[3]. Earlier †**obfusk** XV (Caxton) – OF. *obfusquer*; later †*offuscate*. XVII; see OF-. So **obfusca·tion**. XVII. – late L. Also †*offuscation*. XVI.

obit ɔ·bit, ou·bit †death, decease; †obsequies; commemoration of the dead XIV. – (O)F. *obit*, corr. to Sp., It. *obito* – L. *obitus* going down, setting, death, f. *obit-*, pp. stem of *obīre* go down, perish, die (for *mortem obīre* meet death), f. *ob* OB-+*īre* go (cf. EXIT).

obiter ɔ·bitəɹ by the way. XVI. L., f. phr. *ob iter*; cf. OB-, ITINERARY.

obituary ŏbi·tjuəri record or announcement of a death. XVIII. – medL. *obituārius*, f. *obitus* OBIT; see -ARY. Also *o. notice*.

object ɔ·bdʒèkt (from classL.) †objection, obstacle XIV (Wyclif); (from medL.) something presented to the sight or observed XIV (Trevisa); (gram.) XVIII. – L. and medL. *objectum* (Duns Scotus), sb. use of the pp. of *obicere* throw towards, place in front of, f. *ob* OB-+*jacere* throw (cf. ABJECT, INTERJECT, SUBJECT, etc.). So **object** vb. əbdʒe·kt bring forward in opposition or as a charge XV; †exhibit, expose XVI. f. *object-*, pp. stem of L. *obicere* or – L. *objectāre* (cf. F. *objecter*, †*objet(t)er*). **obje·ction**. XIV (Wyclif, Trevisa). – OF. or late L.; hence **obje·ctionable** XVIII (Cowper). **obje·ctive** †material)(*formal*; pert. to an object of consciousness XVII; (gram.) XVIII (Lowth); dealing with what is external to the mind (in later use esp. after G. *objectiv*) XIX. – medL. *objectīvus* (Occam; cf. adv. *objectīvē* in Duns Scotus); so F. *objectif* (in adv. *objectivement* XV).

objurgate ɔ·bdʒəɹgeit rebuke severely. XVII. f. pp. stem of L. *objurgāre*, f. *ob* OB-+*jurgāre* quarrel, scold, f. *jurgium* quarrel, strife, f. **jūrig-*, f. *jur-*, *jūs* legal right (cf. JURY)+*agere* do, ACT; see -ATE[3]. So **objurga·tion**, **obju·rgatory**[2]. XVI. – L.

oblate[1] ɔ·bleit person devoted to a religious work. XIX. – F. *oblat* – medL. *oblātus*, sb. use of pp. of *offerre* OFFER; see OBLATION, -ATE[1].

oblate[2] ɔ·bleit (geom.) flattened at the poles. XVIII. – modL. *oblātus*, f. *ob* OB-+*lātus*, as in L. *prōlātus* PROLATE.

oblation ŏblei·ʃən solemn offering. XV. – (O)F. *oblation* or late and ecclL. *oblātiō(n-)*, f. *oblāt-* (*lāt-* :– **tlāt-*, rel. to *tollere*, as in EXTOL) used as pp. stem of *offerre* OFFER; see -ATION.

obley ɔ·blei (hist.) Eucharistic wafer. ME. *uble, ubly, oble, obly* – OF. *ublee, oubleie, oblie* (mod. *oublie*) :– ecclL. *oblāta*, sb. use of fem. pp. of L. *offerre* (see prec.).

oblige əblai·dʒ bind by oath XIII; make indebted, confer a favour on; pass. be bound *to* XVI; constrain XVII. – (O)F. *obliger* – L. *obligāre* bind around or up, bind by oath or other tie, pledge, impede, restrain, f. *ob* OB-+*ligāre* bind; see LIGATURE. The pronunc. oblī·dʒ (corr. to sp. *obleege*, from XVI) survived till early XIX. Hence **obligee**[1], **obligor**[1]. XVI. So **obliga·tion**. XIII. – (O)F. – L. **o·bligatory**. XV. – late L.

oblique əblī·k, (formerly) ŏblai·k having a slanting or sloping direction XV (before XVI only in Trevisa's tr. of Higden's 'Polychronicon' in echoes of the L. text); gram. (L. *casus obliqui, oratio obliqua*) repr. Gr. *πλάγιος*). XVI. – (O)F. *oblique* – L. *oblīquus*, f. *ob* OB-+obscure el. So **obliquity** əbli·kwiti divergence from moral rectitude XV (Hoccleve); oblique direction XVI (Recorde). – (O)F. – L. Hence **obli·quitous** XIX; after *iniquitous* XVI.

obliterate ŏbli·təreit blot out (e.g. a letter). XVI. f. pp. stem of L. *oblit(t)erāre* strike out, erase, f. *ob* OB-+*lit(t)era* LETTER; see -ATE[3].

oblivion əbli·viən forgetfulness XIV (Gower); state of being forgotten XV (Lydg.). – (O)F. *oblivion* – L. *oblīviō(n-)*, f. stem *oblīv-* of *oblīviscī* forget, f. *ob* OB-+**līv-*, of obscure origin. So **obli·vious**. XV; after L. *oblīviōsus*.

oblong ɔ·blɔŋ elongated in one direction, spec. rectangular with adjacent sides unequal. XV. – L. *oblongus* somewhat long, oblong, elliptical, f. *ob* OB-+*longus* LONG.

obloquy ɔ·bləkwi evil speaking against a person or thing. XV. – late L. *obloquium* contradiction, f. *ob* OB-+*loquī* speak; see LOCUTION, -Y[3]. ¶ The early sp. with *-liq-* (XV–XVI) may have been suggested by *oblique*.

obnoxious ŏbnɔ·kʃəs A. †exposed *to* harm; †subject *to* authority XVI; B. (by assoc. with NOXIOUS) †hurtful, injurious; offensive, highly objectionable XVII. – L. *obnoxiōsus* or f. *obnoxius* exposed to harm, subject, liable, f. *ob* OB-+*noxa* hurt, injury; see -IOUS.

oboe ou·bou, (rarely) ou·boi wooden double-reed wind instrument. XVIII. – It. *oboe* (three syll.) – F. *hautbois* HAUTBOY.

obol ɔ·bəl. XVII. Anglicization of **obolus** ɔ·bələs coin of ancient Greece. XVI. L. – Gr. *obolós*, var. of *obelós* OBELISK.

obreption əbre·pʃən obtaining of something by deceit. XVII. – F. *obreption* or L. *obreptiō(n-)*, f. *obrept-*, *obrepere* creep up to, steal upon, f. *ob* OB- + *repere* creep; see REPTILE, -TION.

obscene əbsī·n offensive to the senses, etc.; offensive to decency XVI. – F. *obscène* or L. *obscēnus*, *obscænus* ill-omened, abominable, disgusting, indecent, orig. a term of augury. So **obscen**ITY əbse·nĭti. XVII. (– F.) – L.

obscure əbskjuə·ɹ devoid of light XIV; remote from observation; not manifest to the mind, hard to understand XV. – (O)F. *obscur*, latinized form of earlier *oscur*, *escur* = Pr., Cat. *escur*, OSp. *escuro*, It. *scuro* :– L. *obscūrus*. So **obscu·r**ITY. XV. – (O)F. – L.

obsecration əbsikrei·ʃən earnest entreaty. XIV. – L. *obsecrātiō(n-)*, f. *obsecrāre* entreat, beseech (orig. by the name of the gods), f. *ob* for the sake of + *sacrāre* hold SACRED; see -ATION.

obsequies ɔ·bsĭkwiz funeral rites. XIV (Ch.). Formerly also sg. – AN. *obsequie(s)* = OF. *obseque(s)*, *osseque(s)* (mod. *obsèques*) – medL. *obsequiæ*, prob. alt. of L. *exsequiæ* EXEQUIES, by assoc. with *obsequium*, dutiful service; see next and -Y³.

obsequious əbsī·kwiəs readily compliant XV; servilely compliant XVII. – L. *obsequiōsus*, f. *obsequium*, f. *obsequī* comply with, f. *ob* OB- + *sequī* follow; see SEQUENCE, -IOUS.

observe əbzə̄·ɹv A. attend to in practice, keep to XIV (Gower, Ch.); celebrate, solemnize XVI (Tindale); B. give heed to, watch XIV (Ch.; rare before XVI); C. say by way of remark XVII (Bacon). – (O)F. *observer* – L. *observāre* watch, attend to, guard, f. *ob* OB- + *servāre* watch, keep. So **obse·rv**ANCE. XIII (in sense 'prescribed act or practice'). – (O)F. – L. **obse·rv**ANT applied to Franciscans of the Strict Observance XV; attentive to rule or law; taking notice XVII. **observa·**TION †observance XIV (Wycl. Bible); action of observing XVI. – L. **obse·rvat**ORY¹ building for making observations. XVII (*the new Observatorie in Greenwich Park*, Evelyn). F. *observatoire*, after *conservatory*.

obsess ŏbse·s beset, as a besieging force. XVI (rare in XVIII, revived XIX). f. *obsess-*, pp. stem of L. *obsidēre* sit down before, f. *ob* OB- + *sedēre* SIT. So **obse·ss**ION †siege XVI; being assailed by an evil spirit or a fixed idea XVII. – L.

obsidian əbsi·diən volcanic glass. XVII (*o. stone*). – erron. L. *obsidiānus*, in earliest printed editions of Pliny's 'Natural History', for *obsiānus* (sc. *lapis* stone), so named from its resemblance to a stone found in Ethiopia by one *Obsius*; see -IAN.

obsolete ɔ·bsəlīt fallen into disuse XVI; worn out, effete, effaced; (biol.) indistinct, imperfectly developed XVIII. – L. *obsolētus* grown old, worn out, pp. of **obsolēre* (repr. by inchoative *obsolēscere* grow old, fall into disuse), f. *ob* OB- + *solēre* be accustomed or used. So **obsol**E·SCENT XVIII (J.), -ESCENCE XIX.

obstacle ɔ·bstəkl something that stands in the way. XIV. – (O)F. *obstacle* (earlier *ostacle*) – L. *obstāculum*, f. (with suffix of instrument) *obstāre* stand in the way, f. *ob* OB- + *stāre* STAND; see -CLE.

obstetric ŏbste·trik pert. to a midwife or midwifery. XVIII (Pope). – modL. *obstetricus*, for L. *obstetrīcius*, f. *obstetrīc-*, *-trīx* midwife, lit. 'a woman who is present, i.e. to receive the child', f. *obstāre*; see prec., -TRIX. ¶ Cf. the prob. etymol. sense of *midwife*.

obstinate ɔ·bstinət pertinacious in adhering to one's own course. XIV (R. Rolle). – L. *obstinātus*, pp. of *obstināre* persist, f. *ob* OB- + **stan-* (cf. DESTINE); -ATE². So **o·bstin**ACY. XIV (Gower).

obstreperous əbstre·pərəs clamorous, noisy XVI; unruly, turbulent XVII. f. L. *obstreperus*, f. *obstrepere* shout at, oppose noisily, f. *ob* OB- + *strepere* make a noise.

obstruct əbstrʌ·kt block the way of. XVII. f. *obstruct-*, pp. stem of L. *obstruere* build against, block up, f. *ob* OB- + *struere* pile, build; see STRUCTURE. So **obstru·c**TION. XVI. (– F.) – L.

obtain əbtei·n come into possession of XV (Lydg.); be prevalent XVII. Late ME. *obteine*, *-tene* repr. tonic stem of (O)F. *obtenir* – L. *obtinēre*, f. *ob* OB- + *tenēre* hold (cf. CONTAIN).

obtrude ŏbtrū·d thrust forward. XVI. – L. *obtrūdere* (pp. *obtrūsus*), f. *ob* OB- + *trūdere* thrust (cf. THREAT). So **obtru·s**ION. XVI. **obtru·s**IVE. XVII (Milton).

obtund əbtʌ·nd blunt, deaden. XIV. – L. *obtundere* beat against, blunt, dull, f. *ob* OB- + *tundere* beat (cf. *tudes* hammer), rel. to STUNT. So **obtuse** əbtjū·s A. not sensitive or perceptive; B. greater than a right angle (quasi 'blunted')(*acute*); (bot.) of a leaf, etc., rounded at the extremity. XVI. – L. *obtūsus*, pp. of *obtundere*.

obturate ɔ·btjureit stop up. XVII. f. pp. stem of L. *obturāre*, f. *ob* OB- + *turāre* close up; see -ATE³. So **o·btur**ATOR (anat.) membrane closing the thyroid foramen. XVIII. – medL. (cf. F. *-ateur*, Paré).

obverse ɔ·bvə̄ɹs adj. opposite, (of a figure) narrower at the base or point of attachment than at the apex or top XIX; sb. face of a coin, etc.,)(*reverse* XVII (Sir T. Browne; not common till XIX); counterpart XIX. – L. *obversus*, pp. of *obvertere* turn towards, f. *ob* OB- + *vertere* turn (see VERSE, -WARD).

obviate ɔ·bvieit meet and dispose of. XVI. f. pp. stem of late L. *obviāre* meet in the way, prevent, f. *ob* OB- + *via* way; cf. (O)F. *obvier*; see -ATE³. So **o·bvi**OUS †lying in the way; plainly perceptible. XVII. f. L. *obvius*, f. *obviam* in the way.

oc- ɔk, ək assim. form of OB- before *c*.

ocarina ɔkərī·nə musical instrument having an egg-shaped body with a whistle-like mouthpiece. XIX. – It., dim. of *oca* goose (with ref. to its shape) = Pr. *auca*, OF. *oue* (dial. and mod. *oie*) :– L. *auca* (:– **avica*), f. *avis* bird (cf. AUSPICE)+-*ina* -INE[1].

occasion əkei·ʒən favourable juncture of circumstances; reason, ground, cause XIV (Wycl. Bible, Ch.); juncture calling for action, particular case or time of happening XVI. – (O)F. *occasion* or L. *occasiō(n-)* juncture, opportunity, motive, reason, (later) cause, f. *occās-*, pp. stem of *occidere* go down, set, f. *ob* OB-+*cadere* fall; see CASE[1], -ION. Hence **occa·sion**AL[1] †casual XVI; happening on or limited to a particular occasion XVII; cf. late L. *occāsiōnāliter* as occasion arises, F. *occasionnel* (XVIII). ¶ L. *occāsiō*, through OF. *acheison, achoison*, AN. **ancheisoun* (= Pr. *acaizó*, Pg. *(a)cajão*, It. *(ac)cagione* :– Rom. **accāsiōn-*), was repr. in ME. by *achesoun, anchesoun, encheasoun*, aphetic *chesoun*.

occident ɔ·ksidənt west. XIV (Ch., Gower). – (O)F. *occident* – L. *occident-, -ēns* setting, sunset, west, sb. use of prp. of *occidere* go down, set; see prec., -ENT. So **occide·nt**AL[1] western. XIV (Ch.). – (O)F. or L.

occiput ɔ·ksipʌt back of the head. – L. *occiput, -pit-*, f. *ob* OC-+*caput* HEAD; cf. *sinciput*, comb. form **occi:pito-**. So **occi·pit**AL[1] ɔksi·pitəl. XVI. – F. – medL.

occlude əklū·d shut or stop up. XVI. – L. *occlūdere*, f. *ob* OC-+*claudere* CLOSE. So **occlu**SION əklū·ʃən. XVII; **occlu·s**IVE -siv (phonetics, 'stop'). XIX.

occult əkʌ·lt hidden, secret, recondite XVI; pert. to early sciences held to involve secret and mysterious knowledge XVII. – L. *occultus*, pp. of *occulere*, f. *ob* OC-+**celere*, f. IE. **kel-* CONCEAL. So **occult**A·TION concealment XV; (astron.) of one heavenly body by another XVI. – F. or L., f. *occultāre*, frequent. of *occulere*.

occupy ɔ·kjŭpai †take possession of; have in one's possession; take up, use up; employ, engage XIV (R. Rolle); †lay out, invest XVI. – AN. **occupier*, for (O)F. *occuper* – L. *occupāre* seize, f. *ob-* OC-+*cap-* of *capere* (cf. RECUPERATE). ¶ The rarity of this vb. in XVII and most of XVIII was due to its common sl. use in the sense 'have to do with sexually' (cf. Sh., '2 Henry IV' II iv 161); its occurrence in the Bible of 1611 (ten times) depends on earlier versions. So **o·ccup**ANT. XVI (Bacon). **o·ccupi**ER[1]. XIV; in legal AN. *occupiour*. **occup**A·TION. XIV (Rolle).

occur əkə̄·ɹ †meet *with*; present itself to the mind, in the course of events, etc. XVI. – L. *occurrere* run to meet, present itself, befall, f. *ob* OC-+*currere* run (see CURRENT). So **occu·rr**ENCE əkʌ·rəns that which occurs, event XVII (Sh.; some early exx. may be for *occurrents*); superseded †**occu·r**ENT (XVI). – F. or L.

ocean ou·ʃən †proper name of the great outer sea surrounding the mass of land of the Eastern Hemisphere XIII; any of the main regions into which the water of the globe is geographically divided XIV. ME. *occean(e)* – OF. *occean, -ane* (mod. *océan*) = Sp., It. *oceano* – L. *ōceanus* – Gr. *ōkeanós* orig. the great river (ῥόος Ὠκεανοῖο, Ὠκεανὸς ποταμός, Homer) encompassing the disc of the earth and personified as a god, son of Uranus (heaven) and Gaia (earth). In early use, down to *c.*1650, often *o. sea*, in ME. *sea of (the) o.*, *see occean*, after OF. *mer oceane, oceane mer* (in which *oceane* is fem. adj.), L. *mare oceanum*. So **ocean**IC ouʃiæ·nik. XVII. – medL. *ōceanicus*; so F. *océanique*.

ocelot ɔ·silɔt leopard-like quadruped, Felis pardalis. XVIII (*the Ocelot of Mr. Buffon*, Goldsmith). – F. *ocelot*, Buffon's shortening of Aztec *tlalocelotl*, f. *tlalli* field+*ocelotl* tiger, jaguar, the abbrev. form being transferred from the jaguar to another feline beast.

och ɔχ excl. of surprise, etc., ah! oh! XVI. – Ir., Gael. *och*; cf. OHONE.

ochlocracy əklɔ·krəsi mob-rule. XVI. – F. *ochlocratie* or modL. – Gr. *okhlokratíā*, f. *ókhlos* crowd; see -CRACY.

ochre ou·kəɹ native clayey earth of yellow-to-brown colour. XV. – (O)F. *ocre* – L. *ōchra* (Pliny) – Gr. *ṓkhrā*, f. *ōkhrós* pale yellow, *ôkhros* paleness (cf. Skr. *vy|āghrás* tiger). So **ochre**OUS ou·kriəs. XVIII. f. modL. *ōchreus*. **o·ch(e)r**Y[1] XVI.

-ock ək suffix forming dims.; in OE. *-oc, -uc*, as in *bealloc* BALLOCK, *bulluc* BULLOCK, *cranoc* (dim. of *cran* CRANE), *hassuc* HASSOCK, *meattuc* MATTOCK, *ruddoc* redbreast, (dial.) *ruddock*. The number was extended in ME. and later, as in DUNNOCK, HILLOCK, PADDOCK, PUTTOCK, TUSSOCK; cf. also PARK, POLLACK. Special Sc. formations are *bittock, lassock*, and proper names such as *Bessock, Jamock*.

-ocracy ɔ·kresi, **-ocrat** əkræt see -O- and -CRACY.

o'clock əklɔ·k see O, O'.

ocrea ɔ·kriə (nat. hist.) sheath or investing part. XIX. – L., 'greave', 'legging'.

octa- ɔ·ktə, əktæ· comb. form of Gr. *oktṓ* EIGHT, as in **o·ctagon** (XVII) / **octahe·dron** (XVI, Billingsley) eight-angled / eight-sided figure; see -GON, -HEDRON.

octad ɔ·ktæd group of eight. XIX. – late L. *octad-, octas* – Gr. *oktás*, f. *oktṓ* EIGHT; see -AD[1].

octant ɔ·ktənt eighth part of a circle; (spec. astron.) point 45° (i.e. $\frac{1}{8}$ of 360°) distant from another. XVII. – L. *octant-, -āns* half quadrant (Vitruvius), f. *octō* EIGHT; cf. QUADRANT, SEXTANT.

octave ɔ·ktiv (eccl.) formerly pl. (cf. UTAS), eighth day after a festival, period of eight days beginning with the festival XIV; (pros.) group of eight lines of verse XVI; (mus.) note eight diatonic degrees above a given note (formerly called *eighth*) XVII; interval, or series of notes, between a note and its octave; (fencing) in full *o. parade* XVIII; group of eight XIX. – (O)F. *octave*, superseding semi-pop. *oitieve, utave* (see UTAS) – L. *octāva* (sc. *diēs* day), fem. of *octāvus* eighth, f. *octō* EIGHT. The prosodical sense depends ult. on It. *ottava* (*rima*); the musical sense (medL. *octāva*, sc. *vōx* voice) was in MHG. XIII, in F. XVI. So **octavo** ɔktei·vou size of the page of a book for which the sheets are so folded that each leaf is one-eighth of a full sheet XVII, earlier *in o.* XVI (cf. F. *in-octavo*, Sp. *en octavo*, It. *in ottavo*) 'in an eighth'; abl. of *octāvus*. **octet, -ette** ɔkte·t (mus.) composition for eight instruments or voices; (pros.) group of eight lines. XIX. – It. *ottetto*, or its deriv. G. *oktett*; f. *otto* EIGHT, after *duetto* DUET.

octillion see BILLION.

octo- ɔ·ktou before a vowel *oct-*, comb. form of L. *octō* EIGHT (cf. OCTA-), as in **o:ctogen**A·RIAN (L. *octōgēnārius*) XIX, **octo**SY·LLABLE (late L. *-bus*) XVIII.

October ɔktou·bəɹ tenth (formerly eighth) month of the year. Late OE. *october* – L. *octōber, -bris* (with or without *mensis* month), f. *octō* EIGHT (cf. *December, November, September*); ME. *octobre* – (O)F. *octobre* was superseded by the L. form.

octopus ɔ·ktəpəs cephalopod mollusc having eight 'arms'. XVIII. – modL. *octōpus* – Gr. *oktṓpous* (usu. *oktápous*; cf. L. *octipēs*), f. *octṓ* EIGHT + *poús* FOOT.

octoroon ɔktŏrū·n person having ⅛ negro blood. XIX. f. L. *octō* EIGHT, after QUADROON.

octroi ɔ·ktroi, ‖oktrwa †concession, grant XVII; duty levied on articles on their admission to a town XVIII. F., f. *octroyer* grant (earlier *ot(t)*) = Pr. *autrejar* :– Gallo-Rom. **auctōricāre*, medL. *auctōrizāre* AUTHORIZE.

octuple ɔ·ktjūpl eightfold. XVII. – F. *octuple* or L. *octuplus*, f. *octō* EIGHT + *-plus*, as in *duplus* DOUBLE. So **qua·druple** (late ME.), **qui·ntuple** (XVI), **se·ptuple, se·xtuple** XVII.

ocular ɔ·kjŭləɹ pert. to the eye or eyes. XVI. – F. *oculaire* – late L. *oculāris*, f. L. *oculus* EYE; see -AR. So **o·cul**IST. XVII. – F.

od ɔd (phys.) hypothetical force held by Baron von Reichenbach (1788–1869) to pervade all nature. 1850. Of arbitrary formation. Hence **o·d**IC, **o·dyl** (Gr. *hū́lē* material).

Od, 'od ɔd. XVI (Sh.). Clipped form of GOD used to avoid the overt profanation of the sacred name, as in *Ods-me, Ods my life, Odso, Odsbo·dikins* (XVI–XVIII); var. forms of the genitive were *ads, uds* (XVII). Cf. *od-rot, od-rat* (XVIII), which became DRAT.

odal ou·dəl land held in absolute ownership, as in Scand. countries. XIX. – ON. *óðal* (Norw., Sw. *odal*), corr. to OE. *ǣþel, ēþel, ōþel*, OS. *ōðil*, OHG. *uodal*, f. Germ. **ōþ-* **aþ-*, whence also OE. *æþele* (cf. ATHELING), OHG. *edili* (G. *edel*) noble, OE. *æþelu*, OS. *aðali*, OHG. *adal* (G. *adel*) noble descent, ON. *aðal* native quality, nature. Cf. UDAL.

odalisque ou·dəlisk female slave, concubine. XVII. – F. *odalisque* – Turk. *ōdaliq*, f. *ōdah* chamber in a harem + *-liq* affix expressing function.

odd ɔd that is one in addition to a pair, or remains after a division into pairs; that remains over and above a definite sum or round number XIV; (dial.) single, singular; †unique, distinguished; extraneous, additional XV; not ordinary or normal **XVI.** ME. *odde* – ON. *odda-*, comb. form (in *oddamaðr* third (etc.) man who gives a casting vote, umpire, *oddatala* odd number) of *oddi* point, angle, third or odd number :– **ozdon*, rel. to OE. *ord* point, spot, place, OFris., OS. *ord* point, beginning, origin, OHG. *ort* angle, point, place (G. *ort* place) :– **ozdaz* (with which cf. Gepid personal name *Usdibadus*, and further Lith. *usnìs* thistle, Alb. *ušt* ear of corn) :– **uzdho-* pointed upwards, f. **uz-* up + **dho-* place (see DO[1]). Hence **o·dd**ITY XVIII, **o·dd**MENT XVIII.

odds ɔdz first in phr. *make o. even* (XVI, Dunbar); perh. unequal things, (hence) difference, esp. in favour (Udall), dissension (esp. *at o.*), advantage conceded in wagering (Sh.); presumably subst. pl. of the adj., like NEWS. Also in phr. *odds and ends* (XVIII), prob. of dial. origin, for earlier †*odd ends* (XVI–XVII), in which *end* means 'fragment', as in *candle end(s)*.

ode oud poem of a lyric kind, often in the form of an address and dignified or exalted in style. XVI (Sh.). – F. *ode*, corr. to Sp., It. *oda* – late L. *ōda, ōdē* – Gr. *ōidḗ*, Attic var. of *aoidē* song, lay, f. *aeídein* sing.

-ode oud repr. Gr. *-ṓdēs, -ódes* of the nature of, like, for *-oeidēs* -OID, whence modL. formations in *-ōdium*, e.g. *sarcōdium* SARCODE.

odeum oudī·əm theatre or hall for the performance of music. XVII. – F. *odéum* or L. *ōdēum* – Gr. *ōideîon*, f. *oidḗ* singing (see ODE).

odious ou·diəs hateful. XIV (Wycl., Ch.). – OF. *odious, odieus* (mod. *odieux*) – L. *odiōsus*, f. *odium* (whence **odium** ou·diəm XVII), rel. to *ōdī* I hate.

odometer see HODOMETER.

odonto- oudə·ntou comb. form of Gr. *odṓn, odoús, odont-* TOOTH. XIX.

odour ou·dəɹ scent, smell. XIII. – AN. *odour*, OF. *odor, odur* (mod. *odeur*) – L. *odōrem*, nom. *odor*, rel. to Gr. *odmḗ, osmḗ* smell (cf. OSMIUM), *ózein*, perf. *ódōda* exhale a smell, *dusṓdēs, euṓdēs* ill-, good-smelling, Lith. *úodžiu, úosti* scent out, Arm. *hot* smell, *hototim* I scent, and (with dial. *l*) L. *olēre* smell, stink (cf. REDOLENT), *olfacere* (see OLFACTORY). So **odori·**FEROUS. XV (Lydg.).

f. L. *odōrifer*. **o·dor**OUS. XVI. f. L. *odōrus*; formerly sometimes str. *odo·rous*.

odyssey ɔ·dĭsi long adventurous journey. XIX. transf. use of the name of the Homeric poem (*Odysee* XVII – F. *Odyssée*) describing the ten years' wandering of Odysseus (in L. form, Ulysses). – L. *Odyssēa* – Gr. *Odússeia*, f. *Odusseús*.

œcology see ECOLOGY.

œcumenical, U.S. **ecu-** īkjume·nikəl pert. to the universal church XVI; world-wide XVII. f. late L. *œcumenicus* – Gr. *oikoumenikós*, f. *hē oikouménē* (sc. *gê* earth) the inhabited world, pp. fem. of *oikeîn* inhabit, f. *oîkos* house; see WICK[1], -ICAL, and cf. ECONOMY.

œdema īdī·mə (path.) swelling produced by serous fluid. XVI. modL. – Gr. *oídēma*, *-mat-*, f. *oideîn* swell. Hence **œde·mat**OUS. XVII.

œillade ö·jad amorous glance. XVI (in early use anglicized *oeyliad*, *eliad*, *illiad*; now only as F.). – F. *œillade*, f. *œil* (:– L. *oculu-s* EYE), after It. *occhiata*, f. *occhio* eye; see -ADE.

œno- ī·nou, ĭnɔ· comb. form of Gr. *oînos* WINE.

œsophagus īsɔ·fəgəs gullet. XVI (*ysophagus*). modL. – Gr. *oisophágos*, of which the first el. is unkn. and the second appears to be *-phagos* eating, *phageîn* eat (cf. SARCOPHAGUS), but Aristotle says that the organ gets its name from its length and its narrowness.

œstrus ī·strəs gadfly XVII; frenzy XIX. L. – Gr. *oîstros*, which has been referred to a base repr. also by L. *īra* (:– **eisā*) IRE.

of ɔv, əv prep. expressing removal, separation, derivation, origin, source, spring of action, point of departure in time, cause, agent, instrument, material. OE. *of*, orig. stressless var. of *æf* (surviving only as prefix), corr. to OFris. *af*, *of*, OS. *af*, MLG., MDu. *ave*, *af*, OHG. *aba* adv. and prep., MHG. *abe*, *ab* (Du. *af*, G. dial. *ab*), ON. *af*, Goth. *af* (:– **ab̄*) :– CGerm. adv. and prep. **ab̄(a)* :– IE. **ap*, **apo*, repr. also by L. *ab*, Gr. *apó*, Lith. *apa-*, Skr. *ápa* away from, down from; cf. O, A-[1], OFF. ¶ As a prefix of verbs *of-* was formerly much used to denote removal, destruction, or exhaustion.

of- ɔf, əf assim. form of OB- before *f*.

off ɔ̀f adv. away, so as to be separated, discontinued, etc.; prep. away from, in detachment from. var. of OF from XV, but not finally differentiated from it until after 1600 in the above uses. **off-**HAND ɔ̀fhæ·nd without preparation or premeditation XVII; adj. (also ɔ̀·fhænd) †impromptu; free and easy, unceremonious XVIII.

offal ɔ·fəl (techn., dial.) shavings, chips, scraps XIV (Trevisa); entrails (now with inclusion of head and tail) XV; refuse, garbage XVI. – (M)Du. *afval* extremities of animals cut off, giblets, trotters ('exteriora, trunculi, extremitates membrorum truncatæ, acrocolia anseris', Kilian), shavings, refuse, f. *af* OFF + *vallen* FALL, with assim. to the corr. Eng. elements; cf. G. *abfall* – Du. or LG.

offence, U.S. **offense** əfe·ns (arch.) stumbling, stumbling-block; attack; †harm, damage; act of offending; displeasure; breach of law or decorum. XIV (Ch., Gower, Trevisa, Wycl. Bible). ME. *offens*, *offense* – (O)F. *offens* – L. *offensus* annoyance, and (O)F. *offense* striking against, hurt, wrong, displeasure; both L. forms f. *offens-*, pp. stem of *offendere*, whence or from the deriv. OF. *ofendre* (corr. to Sp. *ofender*, It. *offendere*). **offend** əfe·nd †stumble; †wrong; †attack; wound the feelings of. XIV. See OB-, OF- and DEFENCE, DEFEND. So **offe·ns**IVE pert. to attack; †injurious; repulsive. XVI. – F. *offensif*, *-ive* or medL.; as sb. *the o.* XVIII, after F. *l'offensive*, after It. *l'offensiva*.

offer ɔ·fəɹ present as an act of worship OE.; tender for acceptance or refusal XIV; propose *to do* XV; propound XVI. OE. *offrian* sacrifice, bring an offering = OFris. *off(a)ria*, OS. *offrōn* (Du. *offeren*), ON. *offra*; an early Germ. adoption of L. *offerre* present, offer, bestow (in Christian use, spec. present in sacrifice), f. *ob* OF- + *ferre* bring, BEAR[2]. The OE. word was reinforced from (O)F. *offrir*, which brought in the primary senses. Hence **o·ffer**ING[1] OE. *offrung*. **o·ffer** sb. XV. So **offertory** ɔ·fəɹtəri passage recited at the offering of bread and wine at the Eucharist XIV (Ch.); the offering itself XVI. – ecclL. *offertōrium* place of offering (Isidore), oblation, f. late L. *offert-* (cf. *offertor* offerer III), for *oblāt-* (cf. OBLATION); see -ORY[1] and cf. (O)F. *offertoire*.

office ɔ·fis duty, (obligatory) service; position to which duties are attached; †introit XIII; form of divine service; place for transacting business XIV (Ch.). – (O)F. *office* = Sp. *oficio*, It. *uffizio*, †*officio* – L. *officium*, orig. performance of a task :– **opificium*, f. *opus* work + *-fic-*, *facere* DO[1]. So **offic**ER[2] ɔ·fisəɹ one who holds office XIV; (in army, navy, etc.) XVI. – AN. *officer*, (O)F. *officier* – medL. *officiārius*. **offici**AL[1] əfi·ʃəl sb. XIV. Partly – (O)F. *official*, partly sb. use of adj. (XVI) – L. *officiālis*. **offici**ATE[3] əfi·ʃieit discharge the duties of an office, spec. of a minister at divine service. XVII. f. pp. stem of medL. *officiāre* perform divine service.

officinal əfi·sinəl (of a herb) used in medicine and the arts; (of remedies) sold 'in the shops', made up according to the pharmacopœia. XVIII. – medL. *officīnālis*, f. L. *officīna* workshop, manufactory, laboratory, for *opificīna*, f. *opific-*, *-fex* workman, f. *opus* + *fic-*, *facere* make; see OPUS, -FIC, -AL[1].

officious əfi·ʃəs †eager to please or serve; †dutiful XVI; importunate in offering service; †official XVII; in diplomatic use (after F. *officieux*, It. *uffizioso*) friendly and informal)(*official* XIX. – L. *officiōsus* (or F. *officieux*), f. *officium* OFFICE; see -IOUS.

offing ɔ̀·fiŋ part of the sea visible to an observer on shore or ship; position at a distance off shore. XVII (Capt. Smith; also *offen*, *offin*). perh. f. OFF + -ING[1].

offspring ɔ̀·fspriŋ progeny. OE. *ofspring*, f. *of* OF †'from' + *springan* SPRING. ¶ A formation peculiar to Eng.

oft ɔ̀ft (arch.) many times. OE. *oft* = OFris. *ofta*, OS. *oft(o)*, OHG. *ofto* (G. *oft*), ON. *opt*, *oft*, Goth. *ufta*; CGerm. adv., of obscure origin, perh. pp. formation on a base repr. by ON. *of* great quantity, excess, *of* too, too much. In ME. extended to *oftë* (XII), whence, by further extension (prob. after *selden* SELDOM), **often** ɔ̀·fn. XIV. The comps. *oft-times* (XIV) and *often-times* (XV), repl. †*oft(e)sithe(s)* XIII, repr. OE. *oftsīþum* d. pl., *on oftsīþas* on frequent occasions, but partly also the corr. ON. *optsinnis*, *-sinnum* (for the second el. cf. WIDDERSHINS), with collateral infl. of OF. *sovente(s)fois*.

ogdoad ɔ·gdouæd the number 8, group of eight. XVII. – late L. *ogdoad-*, *-as* – Gr. *ogdoás* (*-ad-*), f. *ógdoos* eighth, *oktṓ* EIGHT; see -AD[1].

ogee ou·dʒī, oudʒī· †ogive XV; S-shaped double curve XVII. prob. reduced form of *ogive*, perh. through the pl. form *ogi(v)es*.

ogham, ogam ɔ·gəm alphabet of the ancient British and Irish. XVII. – OIr. *ogam*, *ogum* (modIr. *ogham*, Gael. *oghum*), traditionally assoc. with the legendary name *Ogma* of the inventor of signs for a secret language (cf. *Ogmios*, name (acc. to Lucian) of a Gaulish deity who presided over language or eloquence).

ogive ou·dʒaiv (archit.) diagonal rib of a vault. XVII. – F. *ogive*, earlier *augive*, *orgive*, of unkn. origin. So **ogi·val** XIX.

ogle ou·gl cast amorous glances (at). XVII. orig. a cant word, prob. of LDu. origin; cf. LG. *oegeln*, frequent. of *oegen* look at, also early modDu. *oogheler*, *oegeler* flatterer, *oogen* cast sheep's eyes at. See -LE[3].

ogre ou·gəɹ man-eating monster of popular story. XVIII (*hogre*). – F. *ogre* (Perrault's 'Contes de Fées', 1697); of unkn. origin; conjectured to have been based on a dial. var. **ogro*, **orgo* of It. *orco* demon, monster = Sp. *huerco*, *(h)uergo* – L. *Orcus* infernal deity. Hence **o·gr**ESS[1].

ogress[2] ou·gres (her.) roundel sable. XVI (Bossewell). perh. alt. of *oglys* 'gonestonys', i.e. gun-stones (Book of St. Albans, 1486), of unkn. origin.

oh ou. XVI. var. of O, formerly used in positions where *O* is now more usual, now chiefly as an excl. of pain, terror, surprise, or disapproval. – F. *oh*, L. *ōh*.

ohm oum unit of electrical resistance. XIX (suggested, along with *ohmad*, at a meeting of the British Association in 1861). f. name of Georg Simon *Ohm*, German physicist (1787–1854).

oho ouhou· excl. expressing surprise, exultation, etc., combining O with HO. XIV.

ohone ohō·n excl. of lament. XV (*ochane*, Henryson). – Gael., Ir. *ochòin*. Cf. OCH.

-oid oid suffix equiv. to *-form*, *-like*, repr. F. *-oïde*, L. *-oīdēs*, from Gr. *-oeidḗs*, f. -O- + *eîdos* form, shape (rel. to IDEA), forming adjs. (predominantly techn.), most of which can be used as sbs., (i) of Gr. formation, as ANTHROPOID, RHOMBOID, (ii) based on non-Gr. words, as OVOID, ALKALOID. So **-oid**AL[1] oi·dəl, **-oide**OUS oi·diəs (modL. *-oïdeus*), forming adjs. on sbs. in *-oid*.

oil oil in early use, liquid expressed from the olive; later, any similar viscid smooth liquid. XII. ME. *oli(e)*, *oile* – AN., ONF. *olie*, OF. *oile* (mod. *huile*) = Pr. *oli*, Sp., It. *olio* – L. *oleum* (olive) oil, for **oleiuom*, **olaiwom* – Gr. *élaiϝon* (cf. *Achīuī* – *Akhaiϝoí* Achaians) OLIVE. The adoption from F. ousted ME. *ele*, OE. *ele*, *œli* = OS. *oli(g)* (Du. *olie*), OHG. *oli* (G. *öl*) – popL. *olium*, L. *oleum*. Hence **oi·l**Y[1]. XVI.

ointment oi·ntmənt preparation of oily matter. XIV. alt., after †*oint* vb. (XIV), of earlier †*oi(g)nement* (XIII) – OF. *oignement* :- popL. **unguimentum*, f. L. *unguentum* UNGUENT; see ANOINT, -MENT.

O.K. oukei·. XIX. orig. U.S.; initials of *Old Kinderhook* (near Albany), name of the birthplace of a Democratic candidate, Martin Van Buren, used first as a slogan and passing into a term of approval, being interpreted as standing for *oll korrect* 'all correct'.

oka, oke ou·kə, ouk Turkish and Egyptian measure of weight. XVII (Purchas). – It. *oca*, F. *oque* – Turk. *ōqah* – Arab. *ūqiyah*, prob. – (through Syriac) Gr. *ougkiā́* – L. *uncia* OUNCE[1].

okapi oukā·pi W. African mammal rel. to the giraffe, first discovered 1900. Mbuba (Congo).

-ol ɔl (chem.) terminal syll. of *alcohol*, used to form names of substances which are alcohols in the wider sense, or compounds analogous to alcohol, e.g. *methol*, *naphthol*, *phenol*. From *phenol* the ending has been transferred to the phenol group.

old ould that has lived long; dating far back into the past; (so many years) of age OE.; as a familiar epithet XVI (Sh.). OE. *ald* (WS. *eald*) = OFris., OS. *ald* (Du. *oud*), (O)HG. *alt* :- WGerm. **alða* (ON. positive supplied by *gamall*; compar. *ellri* ELDER[3], superl. *ellztr* ELDEST; in Goth. *alþeis* old :- **alþijaz*); pp. formation (cf. COLD) on the base of OE. *alan*, ON. *ala* nourish, Goth. *alan* grow up, rel. to OIr. *no|t|ail* who nourishes thee,

L. *alere* nourish, with the parallel formation *altus* high, deep (whence ALTITUDE), *ad|ultus* ADULT. See also ELD. Hence **o·ld**EN[3] ancient. XV (once in Sh.; taken up by Scott).

oleaginous ouliæ·dʒinəs oily, fatty. XVII. – F. *oléagineux*, f. L. *oleāginus* (cf. medL. *oleāgō* oily matter, scraped from the oiled bodies of wrestlers), f. *oleum* OIL; see -OUS.

oleander ouliæ·ndəɹ evergreen shrub Nerium Oleander. XVI (Turner). – medL. *oleander, oliandrum*; cf. (O)F. *oléandre*, Sp. *oleandro, eloendro*, Pg. *(e)loendro*, It. *oleandro*; perh. ult. based on RHODODENDRON, through medL. *laurandrum* (Isidore), *lauri-(d)endrum*, by blending with *laurus* LAUREL (cf. Gr. *ῥοδοδάφνη*, F. *laurier-rose* 'rose-laurel').

olefiant oulī·fiənt, ou·lifaiənt (chem.) *o. gas*, ethylene, so called from its forming an oily liquid with chlorine. XIX. – F. *(gaz) oléfiant* (1795); in form prp. of a vb. **oléfier* make oily, f. L. *oleum* OIL + *-fier* -FY.

oleo- ou·liou used as comb. form of (i) L. *oleum* OIL (XVIII), as in **o·leo**GRAPH picture printed in oil-colours, (ii) *oleic, olein*, as in **o:leo**MA·RGARINE (after F. *oléomargarine*, Berthelot, 1854). XIX.

oleraceous ələrei·ʃəs pert. to pot-herbs. XVII (Sir T. Browne). f. L. *(h)olerāceus*, f. *(h)oler-*, *(h)olus* pot-herb, rel. to *helvus* light bay; see YELLOW, -ACEOUS.

olfactory əlfæ·ktəri pert. to the sense of smell. XVII. – L. **olfactōrius* (repr. by *olfactōria, -ōrium* nosegay), f. *olfactāre*, frequent. of *olfacere* smell (trans.), f. *olēre*; see ODOUR, FACT, -ORY[2]. So **olfacto**·METER. XIX.

olibanum ouli·bənəm aromatic gum-resin. XIV. – medL., ult. repr. Gr. *líbanos* frankincense tree, incense (of Semitic origin; cf. Heb. *lᵉbōriā* incense), perh. through Arab. *al-lubān* (AL-[2]).

oligarchy ɔ·ligāɹki government by the few. XVII. – (O)F. *oligarchie* or medL. *oligarchia* – Gr. *oligarkhiā*, f. *oligárkhēs* (whence **o·lig**ARCH XVII), f. *olígos* few; see -ARCH.

oligocene see EOCENE.

olio ou·liou dish of Sp. and Pg. origin consisting of a medley of meats, vegetables, etc.; hotchpotch, miscellany. XVII. alt. of Sp. *olla* (Pg. *olha*) o·lja :– Rom. **olla*, for L. *ōlla* pot, jar (cf. OLLA PODRIDA); with substitution of *-o* as in -ADO for *-ada*.

olive ɔ·liv (fruit of) the evergreen tree Olea europæa, cultivated for its fruit and oil. XIII. – (O)F. *olive* – L. *olīva* – Gr. *elaiϝā*, rel. to *élaiϝon* OIL. Hence **oliva**·CEOUS. XVIII (Pennant).

oliver ɔ·livəɹ form of tilt-hammer. XIX. perh. f. the personal name *Oliver*.

Oliver ɔ·livəɹ phr. *a Roland for an O.*: see ROLAND.

olla[1] ɔ·lə cooking jar or pot in Spain, etc. XVII. – Sp. *olla* (see OLIO).

olla[2] ɔ·lə palm-leaf. XVII (Purchas). – Pg. *olla* – Malayalam *ōla*.

olla podrida ɔ·lə pɔdrī·də olio. XVI. Sp., 'rotten pot'; *olla* (see OLIO), *podrida* PUTRID. ¶ 'It is called *Podrida*, because it is sod [i.e. boiled] leisurely, til it be rotten (as we say) and ready to fall in pieces' (Mabbe, tr. Aleman's 'Guzmán d'Alfarache', 1622).

-ology ɔ·ledʒi (see -O-, -LOGY); as sb. any of the sciences or departments thereof. *c.*1810.

Olympiad ŏli·mpiæd period of four years from one celebration of the Olympic games (ancient Gr. quadrennial festival) to the next. XVI. – F. *Olympiade* or L. *Olympiad-, -as* – Gr. *Olumpiás*, f. *Olúmpios*, adj. of *O'lumpos* lofty mountain in Thessaly, Greece, home of the gods in Gr. myth.; see -AD[1]. So **Oly·mp**IAN XVI (Sh.), **Oly·mp**IC XVI (Nashe); †-ICAL XV.

-oma ou·mə suffix repr. modL. *-ōma* – Gr. *-ōma*, as in *rhizōma, sárkōma, tríkhōma, phýllōma*, f. vbs. in *-oûsthai*, as *rhizoûsthai* take root, f. *rhiza* ROOT. (i) Used to denote a formation or member of the nature of that denoted by the radical part; now superseded by **-ome** oum, as in *phyllome*, RHIZOME; (ii) Used in names of tumours or other morbid growths, as SARCOMA, *trichoma*.

ombre ɔ·mbəɹ card-game played by three persons with 40 cards. XVII (earlier also *l'hombre, l'ombre*). – Sp. *hombre* (:– L. *hominem*, nom. *homō* man); cf. F. *(h)ombre* chief player at ombre, and the game itself. ¶ 'L'Ombre is a Spanish game at Cards, wherein he who undertakes to play it saith *Jo soy l'Ombre*, i.e. I am the man' (Cotgrave, Wit's Interpreter).

omega ou·migə last letter of the Gr. alphabet (*Ω, ω*); last of a series, end. XVI. – Gr. *ô méga* (cf. MEGA-) 'great o')(*ò mīkrón* 'little o', i.e. long and short 'o'.

omelet(te) ɔ·mlit 'pancake of egges' (Cotgr.). XVII (also *aumelet, am(m)ulet, amlet*). – F. *omelette*, also †*aumelette*, †*amelette*, metath. alt. of †*alumette*, by-form of †*alumelle*, †*alemel(l)e*, which arose from *lemele* blade of a sword or knife, by wrong analysis of *la lemel(l)e* (– L. *lamella*, dim. of *lamina* thin plate of metal); the omelette is presumed to have been named from its thin flat shape.

omen ou·men prophetic sign, augury. XVI. – L. *ōmen, ōmin-*, earlier (acc. to Varro) **osmen*, which was pop. assoc. with *ōs* mouth (cf. ORAL), whence the sense 'word of good or bad augury'. So **omin**OUS ɔ·minəs, ou·minəs. XVI. – L. *ōminōsus*.

omentum oume·ntəm (anat.) caul. XVI. L.

omer ou·məɹ Heb. measure of capacity. 1611 (A.V.).

-ometer ɔ·mitəɹ the el. -METER preceded by -O-, as in *gasometer, olfactometer*.

omit ŏmi·t leave out. XV. – L. *omittere*, f. *ob* OB-+*mittere* send, let go (see MISSION). So **omi·ss**ION. XIV (Wyclif). – (O)F. or late L.

omni- ɔ·mni, ɔmni· comb. form of L. *omnis* all, as in **omni·**POTENT XIV (– (O)F. – L.), **omni**PRE·SENT XVII (– medL.), **omni·-**SCIENCE, **-sci**ENT ɔmni·ʃəns, -ni·siəns, -ənt XVII (– medL.), earlier †**omni·sc**IOUS XVI (f. medL. *omniscius*), **omni·vor**OUS feeding on all kinds of food XVII (f. L. *omnivorus*).

omnibus ɔ·mnibəs (orig. four-wheeled) public passenger vehicle. XIX (1829). – F. *omnibus* (1828), also *voiture omnibus* carriage for all (L. *omnibus*, d. pl. of *omnis* all).

omnium gatherum ɔ·mniəm gæ·ðərəm gathering of all sorts, miscellaneous assemblage. XVI. modL., f. L. *omnium* g. pl. of *omnis* all + mock-L. formation on GATHER, for 'a gathering'. ¶ Earlier †*omnigatherum* (XVI), in XV *omnegadrium* (Hoccleve).

omophagous oumɔ·fəgəs eating raw flesh. XIX. f. Gr. *ōmophágos*, f. *ōmós* raw (= Skr. *āmás*, Ir. *aṁ*, W. *of*); see -PHAGOUS.

omoplate ou·mopleit (anat.) shoulder-blade. XVI. – Gr. *ōmoplátē*, f. *ômos* shoulder (cf. HUMERUS) + *plátē* broad surface, blade (cf. PLANE[1]). Cf. F. *omoplate* XVI.

omphal(o)- ɔ·mfəl(ou) comb. form of Gr. *omphalós* NAVEL. XVII.

omrah ɔ·mrā grandee of a Mohammedan court. XVII (*ombra*, Purchas). – Urdu *umarā* – pl. of Arab. *amīr* AMEER.

on ɔn prep. and adv. expressing the relation of contact with or proximity to a surface (hence with implication of support by it) and motion to or toward a position (later often expressed by *on to*, *o·nto* XVI); in early use covering also some of the uses now expressed by *in* and *at*. (See also UPON.) OE. *on*, orig. unstressed var. of *an* = OFris. *an*, OS., OHG. *ana*, *an* (Du. *aan*, G. *an*), ON. *á*, Goth. *ana* (see ANA-), rel. to Gr. *aná*, *ána* on, upon, Skr. *ā* up, Av. *ana*, OSl. *na*. Hence **o·n**WARD(s) XVI; after *inward(s)*, *upward(s)*.

onager ɔ·nədʒəɹ wild ass. XIV (R. Rolle; afterwards not before Goldsmith's 'Natural History', 1774). – L. *onager* – Gr. *ónagros* for *ónos ágrios*, Skr. *ajríyas* :– IE. **agros* ACRE.

onanism ou·nənizm self-pollution. XVIII. – F. or modL. *onanismus*, f. *Onan* (Gen. xxxviii 9); see -ISM.

once wʌns one time only XII; at any one time, on any occasion XIV. ME. *ānes*, *ōnes*, g. of *ān*, *ōn* ONE (see -s), finally superseding *ēnes*, OE. *ǣnes*, which repl. advb. instr. *ǣne* (ME. *ene*) of *ān* ONE; cf. MDu. *eenes*, MLG. *ēnes*, MHG. *ein(e)s*, G. *einst*. The final *s* retained its voiceless sound and *c.*1500 began to be repl. by *ce*, as in *hence*, *ice*, *mice*, *thrice*, *twice*. The first recorded instance of the *w*-form is a westerly *wonus* (XV); cf. ONE. ¶ See also AT ONCE.

one wʌn first or lowest integral number, I, i. OE. *ān* = OFris. *ān*, *ēn*, OS. *ēn* (Du. *een*), (O)HG. *ein*, ON. *einn*, Goth. *ains* :– CGerm. **ainaz* :– IE. **oinos*, whence also OL. *oinos*, L. *ūnus*, OSl. *inŭ*, OPruss. *ains*, Lith. *v|ienas*, OIr. *óen*, *óin*; in other langs. with other suffixes, as Skr. *ékas* one, Av. *aēva*, Gr. *oîos*, *oîϝos* alone. The orig. OE. vowel is preserved with regular diphthongization (ou) in the comps. ALONE (LONE), ATONE, ONLY; the earliest evidence of development of pronunc. with w is of westerly origin (*won* XV); cf. dial. pronunc. wʌk, wʌts of *oak*, *oats* (OE. *āc*, *ātan*), and ONCE; for a different development see NONE nʌn, NONCE nɔns.

-one oun (chem.) used (i) unsystematically, app. after *ozone*, in *acetone*, *quinone*, (ii) in the nomenclature of Hofmann (1866) for hydrocarbons of the formula C_nH_{2n-4}.

oneiro- o(u)naiə·ro(u) comb. form of Gr. *óneiros* dream, as in **onei·ro**MANCY. XVII.

onerous ɔ·nərəs burdensome XIV; (Sc. law) XVIII. – (O)F. *onéreux*, †*-ous* – L. *onerōsus*, f. *oner-*, ONUS; see -OUS. Cf. EXONERATE.

onion ʌ·njən (bulb of) the plant Allium Cepa. XIV. ME. *unyon*, *oyn(y)on* – AN. *union*, (O)F. *oignon* = Pr. *onhon*, *inhon*, *unhon* :– Gallo-Rom. **unione*, L. *ūnio* (whence OE. *ynne* onion), rustic equiv. of L. *cæpa* (cf. CHIVE).

only ou·nli (dial.) solitary; of which there are no others OE.; single XV. OE. *ānlić*, late var. of *ǣnlić* corr. to MLG. *einlīk*, MDu. *een(e)lijc*. Hence **o·nly** adv. ME. *onliche* (XIII), *-like* (cf. MDu. *eenlīke*, in *al eenlīke*); partly alt. of OE. *ǣnlīće*, after the adj., partly developed from predic. uses of the adj.; see ONE, -LY[1], -LY[2]. ¶ For the pronunc. see ONE; ɔ·nli is widespread in dial. use.

onomasticon ɔnŏmæ·stikɔn vocabulary of proper names. XVIII. – Gr. *onomastikón*, sb. use (sc. *biblíon* book) of n. of *onomastikós* pert. to naming, f. *onomastós* named, *onomázein* vb., f. *ónoma* NAME.

onomatopœia ɔnɔ:mətŏpī·ə, ɔ:nəmætŏpī·ə word-formation based on imitation. XVI. late L. – Gr. *onomatopoiíā* making of words, f. *onomatopoiós*, f. *onomato-*, *ónoma* NAME+ *-poios* -making (see POET). Hence **ono:matopœ**·IC, -POE·TIC. XIX.

onslaught ɔ·nslōt vigorous onset or attack. XVII. Early forms also *anslaight*, *onslat* – early MDu. *aenslag* (mod. *aan-*), f. *aan* ON+*slag* blow, stroke, rel. to *slagen* strike, SLAY[1]; with assim. to †*slaught* (–1600), OE. *slæht* :– **slaχtiz*, f. **slaχan*. ¶ Stated to be Dutch by Phillips 1678; cited by J. only from Butler's 'Hudibras'; said by Todd to be 'not in use'; its present currency is due to Scott.

ontology ɔntɔ·lədʒi study of being. XVIII. – modL. *ontologia* (Jean le Clerc 1692), f. Gr. *onto-*, comb. form of *ón*, g. *óntos* being, n. of *ón*, prp. of *eînai* BE; see -LOGY.

onus ou·nəs burden of responsibility. XVII. – L. 'burden', rel. to Gr. *aniā* grief, dial. *oniā*, Skr. *ánas* wagon.

onymous ɔ·niməs bearing a name (as of the author). XVIII. Extracted from ANONYMOUS.

onyx ou·niks, ɔ·niks variety of quartz much used for cameos. XIII (in form *oniche*; later *onix*; from XVIII *onyx*). – OF. *oniche, onix* – L. acc. *onycha*, nom. *onyx* – Gr. *ónukha, ónux* NAIL, claw, onyx stone. ¶ The Gr. and L. acc. forms, occurring in LXX and Vulgate, were not recognized as such, but were treated as a distinct word in Eng. trs. of the Bible (e.g. Exodus xxx 34) as applied to one of the ingredients of incense in the Mosaic ritual, viz. the operculum of a species of mollusc resembling a finger-nail and emitting a peculiar aroma when burnt.

oo- ou·ŏ, ouə· comb. form of Gr. *ōión* EGG, ovum, in scientific terms: **o·o**LITE (min. and geol.). XVIII. – F. *oölithe*, modL. *oolitēs*; **oo·**LOGY. XIX. – F. *oölogie*, modL. *oologia* (1691); **o·o**SPORE. XIX.

oof ūf (sl.) money. XIX. Shortening of *ooftish*, Yiddish for G. *auf tisch*, i.e. *auf dem tisch* on the table (cf. DISH), said of money laid on the table in gambling (cf. G. *auftischen* vb. serve up).

oomiak ū·miæk large boat made of skins drawn over a frame. XVIII. Eskimo. Cf. KAYAK.

-oon ūn repr. F. *-on* in words with stress on the final syll. adopted XVI–XVIII, e.g. *dragon* DRAGOON, *chalon* SHALLOON, as distinguished from the *-on* of adoptions from AN. (OF.), e.g. *baron, capon, felon*, and of more modern adoptions, e.g. *chignon*; hence repr. gen. F. dim. *-on*, and the corr. It. augm. *-one*, Sp. augm. *-on* – L. *-ōnem*, nom. *-ō*, forming sbs. of the nickname or pejorative type, e.g. *balatrō* jester, *calcitrō* kicker, *nāsō* big-nosed man (cf. *Cicero* 'the fellow with the wart'); exx. of various types of deriv. are *balloon, bassoon, buffoon, cartoon, doubloon, harpoon, lampoon, macaroon, musketoon, octoroon, platoon, pontoon, quadroon*; rarely used as an Eng. formative, as in *spittoon*.

oorali urā·li. XIX. See CURARE.

Oordoo var. of URDU.

ooze[1] ūz †juice, sap OE.; liquor of a tan vat, decoction of bark XVI; (from the vb.) exudation XVIII. OE. *wōs*, corr. to MLG. *wōs(e)* scum, ON. *vás* (MSw. *os, oss, oos*, MDa. *oss, oess, voos*). Cf. next. Hence **ooze** vb. exude, cause to exude XIV (Trevisa); percolate as through pores XVIII. Late ME. *wōse*. Now assoc. with OOZE².

ooze[2] ūz mud, slime. OE. *wāse* = OFris. *wāse*, ON. *veisa* stagnant pool, puddle. ¶ The development of OE. ā after w to ū is paralleled in *two, who, womb*; for the loss of *w* cf. prec. and dial. *ood, ool, ooman* for *wood, wool, woman*.

op- ɔp, əp assim. form of OB- before *p*.

opal ou·pəl iridescent milk-white or bluish stone. XVI. – F. *opale* or L. *opalus* (Pliny), prob. ult. (like late Gr. *opállios*) – Skr. *upalas* precious stone. Hence **opal**E·SCENT.

opaque oupei·k (arch.) dark, dull XV; not transparent XVII. (Formerly often *opake*) – L. *opācus*, partly through F. *opaque*, whence the current sp. So †**opa·**COUS. XVII; **opac**ITY oupæ·sĭti XVII. – F. – L.

ope oup (arch. and dial.) open. XIII. Clipped form of OPEN, with loss of *n* as in pps. *awake, bespoke, broke, wove*. Hence **ope** vb. XV.

opelet ou·plit sea anemone, Anemone sulcata. XIX (1860, Gosse). irreg. f. OPE open + -LET; so called because the tentacles cannot be retracted.

open ou·pn not shut, confined, or covered (with many fig. uses). OE. *open* = OFris. *open*, OS. *opan* (Du. *open*), OHG. *offan* (G. *offen*), ON. *opinn* :- CGerm. (exc. Goth.) **upanaz*, having the form of a strong pp. (see -EN⁶) f. UP, as if meaning 'put or set up' (cf. the sense 'open' of ME. and dial. *up*, G. *auf*). Hence **open** vb. OE. *openian* = OS. *opanon* (Du. *openen*), OHG. *offanōn* (G. *öffnen*).

opera ɔ·pərə musical drama. XVII (Evelyn, Pepys). – It. *opera* (whence also F. *opéra*) = Pr., Cat., Pg. *obra*, Sp. *huebra*, F. *œuvre* :- L. *opera* labour, work produced, fem. coll. corr. to *opus, oper-* work (see OPUS). Hence **operat**IC -æ·tik. XVIII; irreg., after *dramatic*. So (dim.) **opere·tta**. XVIII. – It.

operate ɔ·pəreit †produce an effect (Sh.); effect, produce, bring about XVII; (orig. U.S.) cause or direct the working of XIX. f. *operāt-*, pp. stem of L. *operārī* work, bestow labour upon, f. *oper-*, OPUS; see -ATE³. So **oper**A·TION working, performance XIV (Ch., Gower); surgical act XVI; (mil., math.) XVIII. – (O)F. – L. **o·per**ATIVE XVI; sb. worker, workman XIX. – late L. **o·per**ATOR. XVI. – late L.; cf. F. *opératif, opérateur*.

operculum o(u)pə̄·ɹkjŭləm (zool., etc.) cover, lid. XVIII (Derham). – L., f. *operīre* cover, close, parallel formation to *aperīre* open (cf. APERT); see -CULE.

operose ɔ·pərous laborious (subjectively and objectively). XVII (H. More in *-ly, -ness*). – L. *operōsus*, f. *oper-*, OPUS; see -OSE¹.

ophicleide ɔ·fiklaid musical wind-instrument developed from the ancient 'serpent'. XIX. – F. *ophicléïde* (1811), f. Gr. *óphis* serpent (see next)+*kleid-*, *kleís* key, rel. to L. *clāvis* (see CLEF).

ophidian oufi·diən serpent-like. XIX. f. modL. *Ophidia* order of reptiles, f. Gr. *ophid-*, *óphis* serpent, ult. rel. to *ékhis, ékhidna* viper, Skr. *áhis*; see -IAN. The comb. form of *óphis* (used in scientific terms) is **ophi(o)-**. So **oph**ITE ou·fait. XVII (Evelyn). – L. *ophītēs* (Pliny) – Gr. *ophítēs* (sc. *líthos*) serpentine (stone).

ophthalmia ɔfþæ·lmiə inflammation of the eye. XVI (earlier not naturalized). – late L. (Boethius) – Gr. *ophthalmíā*, f. *ophthalmós* EYE; see -IA[1]. So **ophtha·lmIC**. XVII. – L. – Gr.

opiate ou·pieit containing opium, narcotic XVI; sb. XVII (Jonson, Milton). – medL. *opiātus*; see OPIUM, -ATE[2].

opinion əpi·njən what one thinks, belief XIII (Cursor M.); estimate, estimation XIV. – (O)F. *opinion* – L. *opīniō(n-)*, f. stem of *opīnārī* think, believe (whence **opine** oupai·n XVI), the sb. and vb. being used in philosophical language to repr. Gr. δόξα, δοξάζειν; perh. rel. to *optāre* OPT. So **opi·nionATED** obstinate in belief. XVII. f. †*opinionate* (XVI), prob. repr. medL. **opīniōnātus* (cf. OF. *opinionné*). Former syns. are †**opinatIVE** (XVI) – late L. *opīnātīvus* (cf. F. †*opinatif*, It. †*opinativo*); **opi·nionATIVE**. XVI; a group presumably f. a shortened form of L. *opīniōn-*, repr. also in obs. forms in the Rom. langs. (e.g. F. †*opiniatif*, It. †*opiniato*, †*opiniativo*, Sp. †*opiniatico*), †*opiniate*, *opiniated*, †*opiniative*, all dating from XVI; also †*opinia(s)tre* XVI – F. †*opiniastre* (now *opiniâtre*); see -ASTER.

opistho- oupi·sþou comb. form of Gr. *ópisthen* behind, as in **opi·sthoGRAPH** manuscript written on the back as well as the front. XVII. – Gr. *opisthógraphos*.

opium ou·piəm inspissated juice of a species of poppy. XIV (anglicized †*opie*, Ch.). – L. *opium* (Pliny) – Gr. *ópion*, dim. of *opós* vegetable juice, which has been referred to a base **ăp-* water, repr. in Indo-Iranian and Baltic; cf. (O)F. *opium*.

opodeldoc ɔpoude·ldɔk in the work of Paracelsus (*oppodeltoch*) applied to various medical plasters and believed to have been invented by him. XVII. ¶ For the ending cf. *nostoc*.

opopanax oupɔ·pənæks fœtid gum-resin from the root of Opopanax Chironium. XIV. – L. *opopanax* (Pliny) – Gr. *opopánax* (Dioscorides), f. *opós* juice + *pánax*, n. of *panakḗs* all-healing; see OPIUM, PANACEA.

opossum əpɔ·səm small marsupial, esp. Didelphys virginiana. XVII (*apossoun*, *opassom*, *opassum*). – Virginian Indian *āpassūm* (cf. Ojibway *wābassim*). Cf. POSSUM.

oppidan ɔ·pidən townsman; spec. of a member of Eton College who boards in the town. XVI. – L. *oppidānus*, f. *oppidum* (fortified) town; see -AN.

oppilation ɔpilei·ʃən obstruction. XIV. – late L. *oppīlātiō(n-)*, f. L. *oppīlāre* stop up, f. *ob* OP- + *pīlāre* ram down, stop up (cf. COMPILE, PILLAGE); see -ATION.

opponent əpou·nənt one who maintains a contrary argument XVI; antagonist XVII. – L. *oppōnent-*, *-ēns*, prp. of *oppōnere* (whence †**oppo·ne** oppose XVI) set against, f. *ob* OP- + *pōnere* place (see POSITION).

opportune ɔ·pəɹtjūn adapted to an end or purpose, well timed. XV. – (O)F. *opportun*, fem. *-une* = Sp. *oportuno*, It. *opportuno* – L. *opportūnus* (orig. of wind) driving towards the harbour, (hence) seasonable (cf. *Portunus* protecting god of harbours), f. *ob* OP- + *portus* harbour, PORT[1]. Cf. IMPORTUNE. So **opportu·nITY**. XIV. – (O)F. – L. **o·pportunISM, o·pportunIST**. XIX. – It. *opportunismo*, F. *opportunisme*, etc.; terms first of Italian, and later of French, politics.

oppose əpou·z †confront with objections, pose, appose XIV (Ch., Gower); set against in opposition XVI. – (O)F. *opposer*, based on L. *oppōnere*; see OPPONENT, POSE[1]. The second sense was expressed earlier by †*oppone*. So **opposite** ɔ·pəzit placed over against XIV (Ch.); contrary XVI. – (O)F. *opposite* – L. *oppositus*, pp. of *oppōnere*. **opposI·TION** first in astron. and astrol. XIV (Ch.), and rhet. XV (Lydg.), and otherwise largely techn.; contrary or hostile action XVI (Sh.); (of a party) XVIII. – (O)F. – L.

oppress əpre·s †press hard upon, put down, quell; lie heavy on; keep under wrongfully or tyrannously. XIV. – (O)F. *oppresser* – medL. *oppressāre*, f. *oppress-*, pp. stem of *opprimere*, f. *ob* OP- + *premere* PRESS. So **oppre·ssION**. XIV. – (O)F. – L. **oppre·ssIVE**. XVII. – F. – medL.

opprobrious əprou·briəs conveying injurious reproach. XIV (Trevisa). – late L. *opprobriōsus*, f. *opprobrium* (in Eng. use from XVII; naturalized as †*opprobry* XV) infamy, reproach, f. *ob* OP- + *probrum* shameful deed, disgrace, sb. use of n. of OL. **prober*, **probrus* (*prŏbra* in Aulus Gellius) :- **probheros* put forward (against), f. *pro* PRO-[1] + **bher-* carry, BEAR[2] (cf. L. *prōferre* bring forward, cite, Gr. προφέρειν); see -IOUS.

oppugn əpjū·n †assault, besiege XV; assail in speech or action XVI. – L. *oppugnāre* fight against, f. *ob* OP- + *pugnāre* (see PUGNACIOUS).

opsimathy ɔpsi·məþi learning acquired late in life. XVII. – Gr. *opsimathíā*, f. *opsimathḗs* (whence **o·psimath** -mæþ XIX), f. *opsi-*, *opsé* late + **math-* (cf. MATHESIS); see -Y[3].

opt ɔpt choose, decide. XIX (first used with ref. to the choice by natives of Alsace-Lorraine to be French or German subjects). – F. *opter* – L. *optāre* choose, desire (whence †*optate* XVII), frequent. of **opere* (in OL. *prædopiont* they prefer); see OPINION, and cf. ADOPT, CO-OPT. So **optatIVE** ɔptei·tiv, ɔ·ptətiv (gram.) expressing wish. XVI. – F. *optatif*, *-ive* – late L. *optātīvus* (Priscian), tr. Gr. *euktikḗ égklisis* (ἡ εὐκτική, τὸ εὐκτικόν), f. *eúkhesthai* pray. **opTION** ɔpʃən choice. XVII. – F. or L.; whence **o·ptionAL**[1]. XVIII.

optic ɔ·ptik pert. to sight or the organ of sight. XVI. – (O)F. *optique* or medL. *opticus* (XII) – Gr. *optikós*, f. *optós* seen, visible, f. **op-*; see EYE, -IC. So **o·ptICAL**. XVI. **o·ptICS**. XVI; rendering medL. *optica* – Gr. *tà optiká* (n. pl.).

optimate ɔ·ptimĭt, -eit member of the patrician order in ancient Rome, aristocrat. XVII. – L. *optimāt-*, *-mās*, pl. *-mātēs*, f. *optimus* best, prob. f. *ob* prep. before, in front of+ superl. suffix as in *intimus* INTIMATE, *ultimus* ULTIMATE. So **o·ptimACY**. XVI. – modL. *optimātia*; finally superseded by *aristocracy*.

optime ɔ·ptimi one placed in the second (Senior O.) or third (Junior O.) class in the mathematical tripos at the university of Cambridge. XVIII. adv. of L. *optimus* (see prec.) in phr. *optimē disputāsti* you have disputed very well.

optimism ɔ·ptimizm doctrine of Leibniz ('Théodicée' § 416, 1710), that the present world is the best of all possible worlds XVIII (Warburton 1759, Warton 1782); view that presumes the predominance of good; disposition to hope for or expect the best XIX. – F. *optimisme* (1737 in 'Mémoires de Trévoux', in an account of Leibniz), f. L. *optimum*, sb. use of n. of *optimus* best (see OPTIMATE), applied by him to the world; see -ISM. So **o·ptimIST**. XVIII. **o·ptimum** (that is) best or most favourable. XIX.

opulent ɔ·pjŭlənt abundantly wealthy. XVII. – L. *opulent-*, *-ēns* or *opulentus*, f. **ops*, pl. *opes* resources, wealth (cf. OPUS, COPIOUS); see -ULENT. So **o·pulENCE**. XVI. – L.

opus ou·pəs, ɔ·pəs work, esp. musical composition. XVIII (first in *magnum o.*, *o. magnum* great work). L., rel. to Skr. *ápas*; see also prec. So **opusCULE** opʌ·skjūl – (O)F. – L.; **opu·sculum** a small work XVII.

or[1] ǭɹ (adv., prep., conj.) before; sooner, ere; rather than. XIII (also doubled *or or*; from XV often in *or ever*, *or e'er*, *or ere*). late Nhb. OE. *ār* early, ME. (in Scandinavianized areas) *ār*, later *ǭr* – ON. *ár* = OE. *ǣr* ERE.

or[2] ǭɹ, əɹ particle introducing an alternative. First in 'Ormulum' (*a.* 1200), in which three forms occur: (i) disyll. *oþerr*, (ii) monosyll. *oþþr* before a vowel, which was further reduced to (iii) *orr* before a cons.; the conj. †*other* (XII–XV) seems to have arisen from an alt. of OE. *oþþe* 'or' by assim. of the ending to words expressing an alternative, as *either*, *whether* (cf. the alt. of OHG. *odo*, MHG. *ode*, to *odar*, *oder* by assim. to *weder* neither).

or[3] ǭɹ (her.) the tincture gold or yellow. XVI. – (O)F. *or* :– L. *aurum*.

-or[1] əɹ suffix of agent-nouns repr. ult. (i) L. *-or* chiefly as appended to pp. stems, as in the comp. forms -TOR, -ATOR, *-itor*, and *-(s)sor* (eg. *censor*, *confessor*, *oppressor*, *sponsor*); (ii) L. *-ātōrem*, *-itōrem* (nom. *-ātor*, *-itor*), whence OF. *-ēo(u)r*, later and mod. *-eur* (see -OUR[1]). It has been generalized in legal use for the terms corr. to those in -EE[1]. ¶ In the following *-or* has superseded other endings, e.g. *bachelor*, *chancellor*, *sailor*.

-or[2] əɹ suffix forming (orig.) abstr. sbs., in *error*, *horror*, *languor*, *liquor*, *pallor*, *squalor*, *stupor*, *terror*, *torpor*, *tremor*, repr. ult. L. *-or*, earlier *-ōs* (e.g. *colōs* COLOUR, *honōs* HONOUR), corr. to Skr. *-as*, Gr. *-as*, and rel. for the most part to intr. vbs. in *-ēre*. The earliest forms of the above words were in *-our*, which is the current British spelling in others of the same type (see -OUR[2]). ¶ The ending in the following is of different origins: *manor*, *mirror*, *parlo(u)r*, *razor*, *scissors*, *visor*.

orach(e) ɔ·rətʃ plant of the genus Atriplex. XV (*orage*, *arage*, later *areche*, etc.). – AN. *arasche*, OF. *arache*, *arrace* (mod. *arroche*) = It. *atrepice* :– L. *atriplicem*, *-plex* (or some intermediate form between this and its source) – Gr. *atráphaxus*.

oracle ɔ·rəkl mouthpiece of a deity; divine revelation or message XIV (Ch.); holy of holies in the Jewish temple XV; authoritative or infallible guide XVI. – (O)F. *oracle* – L. *ōrāculum*, f. *ōrāre* speak, plead, pray, ORATE; see -CLE. So **oraculAR** ŏræ·kjŭləɹ. XVII.

oral ō·rəl pert. to the mouth or to speech. XVII. – late L. *ōrālis*, f. L. *ōr-*, *ōs* mouth (cf. OSCULATE), rel. to OE. *ōr* edge, beginning, ON. *óss* river-mouth, Ir. *á*, Skr. *ās-* mouth; cf. F. *oral* (XVIII), and see -AL[1].

orange ɔ·rindʒ (fruit of) an evergreen tree, Citrus Aurantium. XIV (*orenge*). – OF. *orenge* in *pomme d'orenge* (XIV), later and mod. *orange*, corr. to Pr. *auranja*, Cat. *taronja*, Sp. *naranja*, Pg. *laranja*, It. †*narancia* (now *arancia*), *melarancia*, Rum. *năranță*, medGr. *nearantzíon*, of which the point of departure is Spain; ult. – Arab. *nāranj* – Pers. *nārang* (cf. late Skr. *nāranga-*). So **orangeA·DE**. XVIII (– F.), earlier †*orangeado*.

Orange ɔ·rindʒ name of a town (*Arausio* in the ancient province of Gallia Narbonensis) on the Rhône in France, which in 1530 passed to the house of Nassau and so to the ancestors of William III of England ('William of O.', i.e. O.-Nassau), after whom were named (late XVIII) the O. lodges, Orangemen, and O. boys of an ultra-Protestant party in Ireland formally constituted into a secret society in 1795. The coincidence of this name with that of the fruit made the wearing of orange-coloured badges a symbol of attachment to William III and of membership of the O. Society.

orang-outang ŏræ·ŋutæ:ŋ large long-armed man-like ape. XVII. alt. of Malay *ōrang ūtan* jungle dweller, prob. through Du. *orang-utang*, †*oerangoetan* (the native name is recorded in 1631 by Bontius, a Du. East Indian physician); prop. the Malay name for wild races of men misapplied by Europeans. ¶ The word has become CEur.

orator ɔ·rətəɹ †advocate XIV (Ch., Wycl. Bible); †petitioner; (eloquent) public speaker XV; as a university official XVII.

– AN. *oratour* = (O)F. *orateur* – L. *ōrātōrem*, *-ātor* speaker, pleader, f. pp. stem of *ōrāre*, whence (or in part back-formation) **orate** ŏrei·t †plead XVI; deliver a speech XVIII; see -ATE³, -ATOR. So **ora·tion** †petition XIV; formal speech XVI. – L. *ōrātiō(n-)* formal language, discourse, advocate's speech, (eccl.) prayer; cf. ORACLE, ORISON, ADORE.

oratorio ɔrətō·riou (mus.) composition for solo voices and chorus with orchestra, dramatic in character and having a Scriptural theme. XVIII. – It. *oratorio* – ecclL. *ōrātōrium* ORATORY¹; so named from the musical performances held in the church of the *Oratory* of St. Philip Neri in Rome from the latter part of XVI. ¶ 'This evening [8 Nov. 1644] I was invited to heare rare musiq at the Chiesa Nova; the black marble pillars within led us to that most precious Oratory of Philippus Nerius their founder', Evelyn.

oratory¹ ɔ·rətəri place of prayer, esp. a small chapel XIV; title of certain religious congregations in R.C.Ch. (orig. of the O. of St. Philip Neri established in 1564) XVII. – AN. *oratorie* = (O)F. *oratoire* = Pr. *oratori*, Sp., It. *oratorio* – ecclL. *ōrātōrium*, sb. use (sc. *templum* temple) of n. of *ōrātōrius*, f. *ōrāt-*; see prec. and -ORY¹. The OF. var. *oratour*, *-or*, is repr. by ME. *oritore* (XIV), Sc. *orator(e)*, *-our* (XIV–XVI).

oratory² ɔ·rətəri art of the orator, eloquent speaking. XVI (Sh., Sidney). – L. *ōrātōria* (Quintilian), sb. use (sc. *ars* art) of fem. of *ōrātōrius*, f. *ōrātor*; see ORATOR, -ORY². Hence, or directly f. L. *ōrātorius*, **oratorical** -ɔ·rikl XVII, which was preceded by †*oratorial*, †*oratorious*, †*oratory* (all XVI).

orb¹ ɔ̄ɹb †(old astron.) hollow sphere surrounding the earth; †circle, ring; heavenly body XVI; eye-ball, eye XVII; cross-surmounted globe of the regalia XVIII. – L. *orbis* ring, round surface, disc. Hence **orbed²**. XVI (Sh.). So **orbi·cular** circular, spherical. XV. – late L. *orbiculāris*, f. L. *orbiculus*, dim. of *orbis*; see -CULE, -AR.

orb² ɔ̄ɹb (archit.) expl. by many authorities as 'blind window', 'blank panel'. XIV–XVII (in antiquarian use XIX). – AN. *orbe*, AL. *orba*, perh. – sb. use of fem. of L. *orbus* deprived, devoid (of), rel. to ORPHAN; cf. F. *mur orbe* blind wall.

orbit ɔ̄·ɹbit eye-socket XVI; path of a heavenly body XVII. – L. *orbita* wheel-track, course, path (of the moon), in medL. eye-cavity, sb. use of fem. (sc. *via* way) of *orbitus* circular, f. *orb-*, *orbis* ORB¹.

orc ɔ̄ɹk †ferocious (sea-)monster; cetacean of the genus Orca. XVI. – F. *orque* or L. *orca* kind of whale (Pliny) – Gr. *óruga*, acc. of *órux* ORYX.

orchard ɔ̄·ɹtʃəɹd fruit-garden. OE. *ortġeard*, *orċġeard*, *orċe(a)rd* garden, orchard = Goth. *aurtigards* garden (cf. *aurtja* farmer, vine-dresser, and OHG. *ka|orzōn* cultivate); the first element prob. repr. a var. of Germ. **worti-* WORT¹ (cf. MLG. *wortegarde*, MHG. *wurz(e)garte* vegetable garden); the second is YARD¹. The orig. form *ortġeard* was to some extent continued in ME. and later *ortyerd*, but the developed *orcherd* was also re-analysed as *orcheyerd*, *orchyard* (XIV), and with assim. to L. *hortus*, as *hortyard* (XVI).

orchestra ɔ̄·ɹkistrə (formerly str. *orche·stra*) in the ancient Gr. theatre, semicircular area for the chorus XVII; part of a theatre, etc., assigned to musicians; band of musicians itself XVIII. – L. *orchēstra* – Gr. *orkhḗstrā*, f. *orkheîsthai* dance (cf. *orkhēstḗr*, *-tḗs* dancer), middle voice of *orkheîn* put in motion. Hence **orche·stral¹**. XIX.

orchid ɔ̄·ɹkid plant of the orchis family. XIX (Lindley, 1845). f. modL. *Orchideæ* (Linnæus, 1751) or *Orchidaceæ* (Lindley), f. *orchid-*, wrongly assumed stem of L. *orchis* – Gr. *órchis* testicle (with cogns. in Lith., Av., Arm.), applied to the plants from the shape of the tubers in most species.

orchil ɔ̄·ɹtʃil dye prepared from lichens XV; lichen Roccella XVIII. – OF. *orcheil*, *orcele*, *orseil* (mod. *orseille*), perh. to be referred ult. to L. *herba urceolāris* plant for polishing glass pitchers (Pliny), f. *urceolus*, dim. of *urceus* pitcher (cf. URN).

ordain ɔ̄ɹdei·n confer (holy) orders upon; appoint, decree; †arrange, dispose. XIII. ME. *ordeine* – AN. *ordeiner* = OF. *ordener* (pres. *ordeine*), later *-oner* (mod. *-onner*) = Sp. *ordenar*, It. *ordinare* – L. *ōrdināre*, f. *ōrdin-*, *ōrdō* ORDER.

ordeal ɔ̄·ɹdiəl, ɔ̄ɹdī·l ancient mode of trial by subjection to a dangerous physical test OE.; trying experience XVII. OE. *ordāl*, *ordēl* (whence AL. *ordālium*, *ordēla*, *-ēlum*) = OFris. *ordēl*, OS. *urdēli* (Du. *oordeel*), OHG. *urteili* (G. *urteil*) judgement, judicial decision :– Germ. **uzdailjam*, corr. to OE. *ādǣlan*, OS. *adēljan*, OHG. *ar-*, *irteilan* (G. *urteilen*) adjudge as one's share, decide, give judgement :– **uzdailjan* share out, f. **uz-* out + **dailjan* (Goth. *-dailjan*) DEAL. In ME. recorded only in the form *ordal* from Ch. ('Troylus' iii 997), prob. from medL. *ordālium*; thereafter in forms also dependent on medL., *ordale* (Lambarde), *ordele* (Spenser), until XVII, when the present form *ordeal* became current (Verstegan, 'Restitution of Decayed Intelligence', 1605) through etymol. assoc. with DEAL¹. The trisyll. pronunc., recognized by Walker (1775), is due to ignorance of the etymol. sense and assoc. with words in -EAL. ¶ Contains the sole relic in English of the Germ. prefix **uz-*.

order ɔ̄·ɹdəɹ A. rank of angels; grade in the Christian ministry; (gen.) rank, grade; monastic society or fraternity XIII (*o. of chivalry*, etc. XIV); (archit.) system of parts in established proportions XVI; (math.) degree of complexity of form; higher group of animals, etc. XVIII; B. sequence, disposition; method of procedure or action XIV (*in o. to, take o.* XVI); condition of observance of law and usage XV; C. regulation, direction, mandate XVI. ME. *ordre* – (O)F. *ordre*, earlier *ordene* – L. *ōrdinem*, nom. *ōrdō* row, series, course, array, rank (of soldiers), class, degree, captaincy, command, (eccl.) rank in the Church, rel. to *ōrdīrī* begin (cf. EXORDIUM, PRIMORDIAL), *ōrnāre* ADORN. Hence **o·rderLY**[1] arranged in or observant of order XVI; charged with the conveyance or execution of orders XVIII (*o. man, officer, †sergeant*, hence as sb., by ellipsis). **ordinAL**[1] ɔ̄·ɹdinəl †(rare) regular, orderly XIV (Wyclif); of numbers)(*cardinal* XVI; (nat. hist.) pert. to an order XIX. – late L. *ōrdinālis* (Priscian), f. *ōrdin-*, *ōrdō*. So **o·rdinal** sb. book of the order of divine service XIV (Trevisa); form of ordination XVII. – medL. *ōrdināle*, n. sg. of *ōrdinālis* (cf. *manual*). **o·rdinance** A. (arch.) regular arrangement; authoritative direction, spec.)(*law, statute* XIV (R. Mannyng); prescribed usage XIV; B. †provision, supply; spec. military supplies (now *ordnance*) XIV. – OF. *ordenance* (now *ordonnance*) – medL. *ōrdinantia*, f. *ōrdināre* ORDAIN; **o·rdinand** one about to be ordained. XIX. **ordinARY** ɔ̄·ɹdĭnəri A. (eccl. and leg.) one having immediate jurisdiction or authority in juridical matters; B. book of divine service; C. sb. uses of the adj. from XVI. – AN., OF. *ordinarie* (later and mod. *ordinaire*, whence ME. and Sc. *ordinar*) – medL. *ōrdinārius* (sc. *judex* judge, etc.), and in n. sg. *ōrdinārium*. So adj. belonging to the regular order or course; having regular jurisdiction XV; of the usual kind XVI. – L. *ōrdinārius* orderly, usual, f. *ōrdin-*, *ōrdō* ORDER; see -ARY. **ordinA·TION** ordaining. XV. – (O)F. or L., f. *ordināre* ORDAIN. **ordnance** ɔ̄·ɹdnəns establishment for supply of military materials and stores. XVII; contr. of *ordenance*, ORDINANCE. **ordonnance** systematic arrangement. XVII (Evelyn). F., alt. of OF. *ordenance*, after F. *ordonner*.

ordure ɔ̄·ɹdjuəɹ filth, dung. XIV. – (O)F. *ordure*, f. *ord* filthy :– L. *horridu-s* HORRID; see -URE.

ore ɔ̄əɹ native mineral containing a metal which may be extracted from it. OE. *ōra* unwrought metal (corr. to Du. *oer*, LG. *ūr*, of unkn. origin), repr. by *oor(e), oure, ure* from XIV to XVII, which would have survived as **oor* uəɹ, but was superseded by the descendant of OE. *ār* = OS., OHG. *ēr*, ON. *eir*, Goth. *aiz* :– CGerm. **aiz* :– **ajiz*, corr. to L. *æs* crude metal, bronze, money, prob. :– **aj(o)s* (cf. Skr. *áyas* ore, iron).

Oread ɔ̄·riæd mountain nymph. XVI (Spenser). – L. *Orēad-*, *Orēas* – Gr. *Oreiad-*, *Oreiás*, f. *óros* mountain; see -AD[1].

orfray see ORPHREY.

organ ɔ̄·ɹgən in versions of the Bible and allusions thereto, applied to various instruments of music XIII (Cursor M.); musical instrument consisting of pipes supplied with wind and sounded by keys XIV (Ch.); instrument or means of function XV. – OF. *organe*, *orgene* (mod. *orgue*) = Pr. *orgue*, Sp. *órgano*, It. *organo* – L. *organum* instrument, engine, musical instrument, (eccl.) church organ – Gr. *órganon*, f. IE. **worg-* **werg-* WORK; cf. ORGY. So **organIC** ɔ̄ɹgæ·nik †serving as an organ XVI; pert. to organs or an organized body XVIII (chem. XIX). – F. *organique* (anat. XIV) – L. *organicus*. **o·rganISM** †organic structure XVII (Evelyn); organized system or body XVIII. – F. *organisme*. **o·rganIST** player on an organ. XVI. – F. – medL. **o·rganIZE**. XV. – (O)F. – medL.

organdie ɔ̄·ɹgəndi fine translucent muslin. XIX. – F., of unkn. origin.

orgasm ɔ̄·ɹgæzm paroxysm of excitement. XVII. – F. *orgasme* or modL. *orgasmus* – Gr. *orgasmós*, f. *orgân* swell as with moisture, be excited.

orgy ɔ̄·ɹdʒi (pl. *orgies*) secret rites of the worship of Greek and Roman deities, etc. XVI; (sg.) licentious revel XVIII. orig. pl. – F. *orgies* – L. *orgia* – Gr. *órgia* n. pl., f. IE. **worg-* **werg-* WORK; see -Y[3]. So **orgia·stIC**. XVII. – Gr. *orgiastikós*.

-orial ɔ̄·riəl suffix combining L. *-ōrius* -ORY[2] and *-ālis* -AL[1], and usu. identical in sense with *-ory*, e.g. *inquisitorial, territorial, visitatorial*; it is preferred where there is a sb. in *-ory*, e.g. *purgatory / purgatorial*.

oriel ɔ̄·riəl †porch; gallery, balcony, upper storey XIV; windowed recess projecting from a building XV; *o. window* XVIII. ME. *oriole* – OF. *oriol, eurieul* passage, gallery, of unkn. origin; so medL. *oriolum* (XIII) porch, anteroom, upper chamber. ¶ The name of a large house in Oxford (*la* or *le Oriole* XIII), which passed to the provost and scholars of the House of Blessed Mary and gave its name to *Oriel* College.

orient[1] ɔ̄·riənt adj. eastern, (hence, of stones) precious, excellent; sb. *the* East, eastern lands. XIV (Maund., Ch., Gower). – (O)F. *orient* – L. *orient-*, *oriēns* rising, rising sun, east, prp. of *orīrī* rise. Cf. ORIGIN see -ENT. So **orientAL**[1] ɔ̄rie·ntəl. XIV (Ch.). – (O)F. or L.

orient[2] ɔ̄·riənt place so as to face the east XVIII; determine the bearings of; (refl.) ascertain one's bearings XIX. – F. *orienter*, f. *orient*; see prec. So, by extension with -ATE[3], **o·rientate** XIX; prob. after **orientA·TION** situation so as to face east (of a church, east and west), bearing or lie of a thing, determination of bearings XIX, which appears to be directly f. *orient* vb.

orifice ɔ·rĭfis mouth-like opening. XVI. – (O)F. *orifice* – late L. *ōrificium* (Macrobius), f. *ōri-*, *ōs* mouth (see ORAL) + *fic-*, var. of *facere* make, DO[1].

oriflamme ɔ·riflæm sacred banner of St. Denis, of red or orange-coloured silk. XV (also *-flambe*). – (O)F. *oriflambe, -flamme,* in medL. *auriflamma,* f. *aurum* gold (cf. AUREATE)+*flamma* FLAME.

origanum ori·gənəm wild marjoram, etc. XVI. L. – Gr. *orīganon,* perh. f. *óros* mountain+*gános* brightness, joy, pride; preceded by *organ* (OE. to mod. dial.), and *origan* (XV) – (O)F. *origan.*

origin ɔ·ridʒin descent, ancestry XIV; point or place of beginning. XVI. – F. *origine* or L. *orīgin-, orīgō,* f. *orīrī* rise (see ORIENT). So **originAL**[1] əri·dʒinəl pert. to origin (first of *o. sin* XIV, Shoreham); sb. †origin; pattern, exemplar XIV; singular or eccentric person XVII. – (O)F. *original* or L. *orīginālis* (Appuleius). **originA·TION.** XVII. – F. – L. *orīginātiō* derivation of words (Quintilian), f. pp. stem of **orīgināre,* whence **ori·ginATE**[3]. XVII.

oriole ō·rioul name of various yellow-plumaged birds. XVIII. – med. and modL. *oriolus* – OF. *oriol* = Pr. *auriol,* Cat. (Sp.) *oriol* :– L. *aureolu-s,* f. *aureus* golden, f. *aurum* gold.

Orion ŏrai·ən constellation figured as a hunter with belt and sword. XIV. – L. – Gr. *Ōríōn* orig. name in Gr. myth. of a mighty hunter slain by Artemis.

-orious ō·riəs comp. suffix forming adjs. by the addition of -OUS to L. *-ōri-* of *-ōrius* -ORY[2], with which and -ORIAL it is mainly synonymous, but not of like currency.

orison ɔ·rizən (arch.) prayer. ME. *ureisun, oreison, oriso(u)n* – AN. *ur-,* OF. *oreison, orison* (now *oraison*) = Pr. *orazon,* Sp. *oracion,* It. *orazione* :– L. *ōrātiō(n-)* speech, ORATION.

-orium ō·riəm suffix repr. n. sg. of L. *-ōrius,* used in sbs. denoting 'place of . .', 'thing used or requisite for . .', as in *auditorium, crematorium, sanatorium, scriptorium,* and in such techn. terms as *haustorium* sucker, *inductorium* induction coil, *sensorium* seat of sensation. Cf. -ORY[1].

orle ōɹl (her.) band round the shield. XVI. – (O)F. *orle,* also †*ourle* (cf. mod. *ourlet* hem), f. *ourler* hem = Pr., Sp. *orlar,* It. *orlare* :– Rom. **ōrulāre,* f. **ōrula,* dim. of L. *ōra* edge, border, prob. f. *ōr-, ōs* mouth (see ORAL, ORIFICE).

orlop ō·ɹlɔp (orig.) floor or deck with which a ship's hold was covered in; (later) lowest deck. XV (*overloppe*). – (M)Du. *overloop,* f. *overloopen* run over; see OVER-, LEAP.

ormer ō·ɹməɹ sea-ear (edible mollusc). XVII. – Channel Islands F. *ormer* = F. *ormier* :– L. *auris maris* 'ear of the sea' (so called from its resemblance to the ear).

ormolu ō·ɹməlū gold leaf, gilded bronze, gold-coloured alloy. XVIII. – F. *or moulu* 'ground gold', i.e. *or* gold (:– L. *aurum*), *moulu,* pp. of *moudre* :– L. *molere* grind (see MILL).

ornament ō·ɹnămənt †adjunct; accessory equipment (now only of the furnishings of a church); decoration, embellishment. XV. refash. of *ornement* (XIV), after L. *ōrnāmentum,* f. *ōrnāre* ADORN; see -MENT. The earlier forms (XIV) were *ournement, urnement* (XIII) – AN. *urnement,* OF. *o(u)rnement* (mod. *orne-*); these competed also with *aournement* (see ADORNMENT). Hence **o·rnament** vb. XVIII (Pope), whence **o:rnamentA·TION.** XIX; **orname·ntAL**[1]. XVII. So **ornATE**[2] ōɹnei·t highly embellished. XV (Hoccleve). – pp. of *ōrnāre.*

ornithology ōɹniþɔ·lədʒi branch of zoology dealing with birds. XVII (Ray, 1678). – modL. *ornithologia* (Aldrovandus, 1599), f. Gr. *ornīthológos* treating of birds, f. *ornītho-, órnis* bird; see ERNE, -LOGY. ¶ Fuller used it for 'the speech of birds' 1655. So **ornitho·logIST.** 1677 (Plot).

orography ōrɔ·grəfi, **oreography** ōriɔ·grəfi description of mountains. XIX. f. *oro-, oreo-, oreio-,* comb. forms of Gr. *óros* mountain; see -GRAPHY. So **or(e)o·LOGY.** XVIII.

orotund ō·rŏtʌnd marked by fullness and clarity of tone. XVIII. f. L. phr. *ōre rotundō* lit. 'with round mouth', with well-turned speech (Horace 'Ars Poetica' 323), with reduction of *ore ro-* to *oro-.*

orphan ō·ɹfən (one) deprived of parents. XV (Caxton). – late L. (Vulgate) *orphanus* – Gr. *orphanós,* rel. to L. *orbus* bereft, Arm. *orb* orphan. In earlier use (XIV) were †*orphelin,* †*orphenin* – (O)F. *orphelin,* †*orphenin* (cf. Pr. *orfanin*) hypocoristic dim. of *orfene, orfe* = Cat. *orfe,* Sp. *huérfano,* It. *orfano* :– late L.

orphic ō·ɹfik pert. to Orpheus or mysteries associated with him. XVII. – L. *Orphicus* – Gr. *Orphikós,* f. *Orpheús*; see -IC.

orphrey, orfray ō·ɹfri †rich embroidery XIII; ornamental band on a vestment XIV. Falsely inferred sg. from ME. *orphreis* taken as pl. – OF. *orfreis* (mod. *orfroi*) = Pr. *aurfres,* OSp. *aurofres* – medL. *aurifrisium,* alt. of *auriphrygium* gold embroidery, i.e. *aurum Phrygium* 'Phrygian gold' (cf. L. *Phrygia chlamys* embroidered mantle, *phrygiō* embroiderer in gold).

orpiment ō·ɹpimənt yellow arsenic. XIV (Ch.). – (O)F. *orpiment,* corr. to Sp. *oropimiento,* It. *orpimento* – L. *auripigmentum,* f. *aurum* gold+*pigmentum* PIGMENT.

orpin(e) ō·ɹpin succulent herbaceous plant Sedum Telephium, livelong. XIV. – OF. *orpine* yellow arsenic, presumably shortening of *orpiment.*

Orpington ō·ɹpiŋtən breed of poultry. XIX. f. name of *Orpington,* a town in Kent.

orrery ɔ·rəri mechanism for representing the motions of the planets. XVIII. Named after Charles Boyle, Earl of *Orrery,* for whom a copy of the machine invented by George Graham *c.*1700 was made.

orris[1] ɔ·ris (root of) iris. XVI (*oreys, oris, arras*). unexpl. alt. of IRIS.

orris[2] ɔ·ris gold and silver lace pattern. XVIII (*or(r)ice, -ace*). poss. alt. of *orfris* ORPHREY.

ortho- ɔ̄·ɹþou, ɔ̄ɹþɔ·, before a vowel **orth-**, comb. form of Gr. *orthós* (see ARDUOUS) straight, right, correct, in various terms (mostly techn., with specialized applications in chem., cryst., and math.). **orthoepy** ɔ̄ɹþou·ĭpi correct pronunciation. XVII. – Gr. *orthoépeia* (*épos* word). **ortho·**GRAPHY correct spelling. XV. – (O)F. – L. – Gr.

orthodox ɔ̄·ɹþədɔks according with accepted opinion XVI; spec. epithet of the Eastern Church XVIII. – ecclL. *orthodoxus* – Gr. *orthódoxos*, f. *orthós* straight, right (cf. prec.) + *dóxa* opinion, f. base of *dokeîn* seem, rel. to L. *decet* (see DECENT). So **o·rthodox**Y[3]. XVII. – late L. – late Gr.

ortolan ɔ̄·ɹtŏlən species of bunting, Emberiza hortulana. XVII. – F. *ortolan* (Cotgr. 1611) – Pr. *ortolan* gardener – L. *hortulānus*, f. *hortulus* (pl. garden grounds), dim. of *hortus* garden (cf. YARD[1]).

orts ɔ̄ɹts (pl.) fragments of food left over, scraps. XV. – (with pl. suffix) MLG. *ort-e* refuse of food = early modDu. †*ooræte* (cf. Sw. dial. *oräte* refuse fodder, LG. *orten, verorten* leave remains of food or fodder), perh. f. *o(o)r-* out (as in ORDEAL) + *eten* EAT.

-ory[1] əri earlier *-orie* – AN. *-orie* = (O)F. *-oire*, repr. L. *-ōria, -ōrium*, f. and n. of *-ōrius* -ORY[2], used sb. to denote a room or an instrument, as *ambulatory, directory, dormitory, lavatory, oratory, refectory, repository, suppository*, but sometimes with other applications, as in *promontory, territory*; in *priory, rectory* it is formed on a sb. in -OR[1] with -Y[3]. ¶ The groups *glory, history, memory, victory*, and *allegory, category* have a separate history; the ending of the plant names *fumitory, pellitory* is due to alteration.

-ory[2] əri adj. suffix repr. L. *-ōrius*, f. *-ōria*, n. *-ōrium* (partly through F. *-orie*), primarily f. agent-nouns in *-ōr-* -OR[1] + *-ius* -IOUS, as in *amatory, dilatory, initiatory, monitory, satisfactory, supplicatory*; later extended, as in *compulsory, illusory, perfunctory*. Cf. -ORIAL, -ORIOUS.

oryx ɔ·riks species of antelope. XIV. – L. *oryx* – Gr. *órux* stonemason's pickaxe, applied to an antelope or gazelle having pointed horns; perh. rel. to ROUGH; cf. ORC.

Oscan ɔ·skən pert. to (the ITALIC language of) the Osci (e.g. in Campania). f. L. *Oscus* (*Osca lingua*, Varro), adj. of *Oscī*, earlier *Obscī, Opscī, Opicī* (Gr. *Opikoí, O'skoi*); see -AN. **O·sco-**, comb. form, as in *Osco-Umbrian*.

oscillate ɔ·sileit swing backwards and forwards. XVIII. f. pp. stem (see -ATE[3]) of L. *ōscillāre*, f. *ōscillum* little mask of Bacchus hung from the trees, especially in vineyards, so as to be easily moved by the wind (see Virgil 'Georgics' II 387 ff.), dim. of *ōs* face (see ORAL); (or back-formation from) **oscilla·**TION. XVII. – L.

oscitant ɔ·sitənt gaping from drowsiness. XVII. – prp. of L. *oscitāre* gape, acc. to some f. *ōs* mouth + *citāre* put in motion; see ORAL, CITE, -ANT. So **oscita·**TION. XVI. – L.

osculate ɔ·skjuleit kiss; (techn.) bring or come into close contact. XVII. f. pp. stem of L. *ōsculārī* kiss, f. *ōsculum* little or pretty mouth (cf. -CULE), kiss, hypocoristic dim. of *ōs* mouth; see ORAL, -ATE[3]. So **oscula·**TION. XVII. – L.

-ose[1] ous suffix repr. L. *-ōsus*, forming adjs. from sbs. with the meaning 'full of', 'abounding in', e.g. *annōsus* full of years (f. *annus* year), *jocōsus* JOCOSE, *mōrōsus* MOROSE, *verbōsus* VERBOSE. The corr. sbs. end in **-os**ITY ɔ·sĭti, repr. F. *-osité*, L. *-ōsitās*. Cf. -OUS.

-ose[2] ous (chem.) suffix originating in the final syll. of GLUCOSE and used to form names of related carbohydrates, as *cellulose, dextrose, lævose*.

osier ou·ʒiəɹ species of willow, the pliant branches of which are used for basketwork. XIV. – (O)F. *osier*, m. form corr. to fem. (dial.) *osière* :– medL. *ausēria* (VIII), which has been referred to Gaulish **auesā* riverbed (whence Breton *aoz*).

-osis ou·sis terminal el. of many ancient and modL. terms derived from or modelled on Gr. terms in *-ōsis*, which were primarily based on vbs. in *-óein* (*-oûn*) but were later formed directly on sbs. and adjs., e.g. *anchylosis, chlorosis, cyanosis, metamorphosis, sclerosis, thrombosis*; corr. adjs. end in -OTIC.

-osity ɔ·sĭti see -OSE[1], -OUS, and -ITY.

Osmanli oz-, ɔsmæ·nli see OTTOMAN. XIX.

osmium ɔ·zmiəm (chem.) metal of the platinum group, distinguished by a pungent smell. XIX (S. Tennant, 1804). f. Gr. *osmḗ* ODOUR + -IUM.

osmund[1] ɔ·zmənd, ɔ·s- superior quality of iron imported from Baltic regions. XIII. ME. *osemond*, prob. – MLG. *osemunt*, reinforced later from OSw. *osmunder*, ODa. *osmund*; of unkn. origin.

osmund[2] ɔ·zmənd, ɔ·s- flowering fern. XV. – AN. *osmunde*, (O)F. *osmonde*, of unkn. origin.

oso-berry ou·souberi blue-black fruit of western N. Amer. Nuttallia cerasiformis. XIX. f. Sp. *oso* bear :– L. *ursu-s* (cf. ARCTIC) + BERRY.

osprey ɔ·spri sea-eagle, fish-hawk XV; egret plume XIX. – OF. *ospres*, repr. obscurely L. *ossifraga* OSSIFRAGE. ¶ In modF. *orfraie*, †*offraie* (XVI), which is also unexplained.

osseous ɔ·siəs pert. to bone. XVIII. f. L. *osseus*, f. *oss*, *os* bone (:– **ost*-), rel. to Skr. *ásthi*, Gr. *ostéon* OSTEO-; see -EOUS.

ossifrage ɔ·sifreidʒ lammergeyer; osprey. XVII. – sb. uses of L. *ossifragus*, *-fraga* bone-breaking, f. *ossi*-, *os* bone (see prec.) + **frag*-, break (see FRAGMENT). ¶ Identification of Pliny's *ossifraga* with the lammergeyer is held to be supported by this bird's alleged habit of dropping bones from a great height in order to break them. Cf. OSPREY.

ossify ɔ·sifai become or convert into bone. XVIII. – F. *ossifier*, f. L. *ossi*-, *os* bone; see OSSEOUS, -IFY. So **o:ssi**FICA·TION. XVII.

ossuary ɔ·sjuəri charnel-house, bone-urn. XVII (Sir T. Browne). – late L. *ossuārium*, f. *ossu*, var. of *oss*, *os* bone (see OSSEOUS), -ARY.

ostensible ɔste·nsĭbl †that may be shown; †conspicuous; exhibited as actual and genuine. XVIII. – F. *ostensible* – medL. *ostensibilis*, f. *ostens*-, pp. stem of *ostendere*, f. *obs*- OB- + *tendere* stretch; see TENSION, -IBLE. So **oste·ns**ORY[1] monstrance. XIX (earlier in foreign forms *ostensorio*, *-orium*, *-oir*). – medL. *ostensōrium*. **ostent**A·TION display. XV. – (O)F. – L. f. *ostentāre*, frequent. of *ostendere*.

osteo- ɔ·stiou, ɔstiɔ· comb. form of Gr. *ostéon* bone (see OSSEOUS, OSTRACISM), as in **osteo·**LOGY science of bones. XVII. – modL. *osteologia*; **o·steopath, osteo·pathy** (orig. U.S.), *c*.1890, after *homœopath*, *allopath*.

ostiary ɔ·stiəri door-keeper (one of the minor clerical orders). XV. – L. *ōstiārius* (also used in Eng.), f. *ōstium* opening, river mouth, door, f. *ōs* mouth; see ORAL, -ARY.

ostler ɔ·sləɹ (an earlier pronunc. ou·sləɹ survives in the surname *Osler*) stable-man, groom. XV. var. sp. of HOSTLER, restricted since XVI to this sense.

ostmen ou·stmen (pl.) invaders or settlers from Denmark and Norway in Iceland and Ireland. XV. – ON. *Austmenn*, pl. of *Austmaðr*; see EAST, MAN.

ostracism ɔ·strəsizm method of banishment in ancient Greece by voting with potsherds or tiles on which the name of the person proposed to be banished was written. XVI. – F. *ostracisme* or modL. *ostracismus* – Gr. *ostrakismós*, f. *ostrakízein* (whence **o·strac**IZE XVII), f. *óstrakon* shell, tile, potsherd, rel. to *ostakós* crustacean, *ostéon* bone, *óstreon* OYSTER; see OSTEO-, -ISM.

ostreger ɔ·stridʒəɹ, **ostringer** -indʒəɹ (arch.) keeper of goshawks. XIV. – OF. *ostruchier*, *austruchier*, based on *ostour* (mod. *autour*) hawk :– Gallo-Rom. *auceptore*, alt. form (by assoc. with L. *avis* bird) of *acceptore*, for L. *accipiter*, perh. parallel to Gr. *ōkú|pteros* swift-winged. ¶ In XVII also *a(u)stringer*.

ostrei- ɔ·strii (also *ostreo*-) comb. form of L. *ostrea*, *ostreum* OYSTER, as in *o·streicu:lt*URE. XIX.

ostrich ɔ·stritʃ the largest of existing birds, Struthio camelus. XIII. ME. *ostrice*, *-iche*, *-ige* – OF. *ostrice*, *-iche*, *-usce* (mod. *autruche*), corr. to Sp. *avestruz*, Pg. *abestruz* :– Rom. **avistrūthius*, f. L. *avis* bird + late L. *strūthiō* – Gr. *strouthíōn* ostrich, f. *strouthós* sparrow, ostrich. ¶ In class. Gr. called στρουθός, ὁ μέγας στρουθός, and στρουθοκάμηλος.

Ostrogoth ɔ·strougɔþ East Goth. XVII. – late L. pl. *Ostrogothī*, f. Germ. **austro*-, whence OHG., OS. *ōstar*, ON. *austr* eastward (see EAST) + L. *Gothus* GOTH.

-ot ɔt, **-ote** out repr. F. *-ote*, L. *-ōta*, Gr. *-ṓtēs*, expressing nativity in ancient Gr. names, as *Epirot* epaiə·rɔt, Gr. *Epeirṓtēs*, native of Epirus, in mod. names (normally with *-ote*) of inhabitants of certain places in or near Greece, as *Candiote*, *Cypriot(e)*, *Suliote*. ¶ The form *-ot* occurs in the common nouns HELOT, IDIOT, PATRIOT, ZEALOT.

other ʌ·ðəɹ †one of two; *the* remaining (orig. one of two); existing besides OE.; different (as in ANOTHER) XIII. OE. *ōþer* = OFris. *ōther*, OS. *ōðar*, *andar*, OHG. *andar* (Du., G. *ander*), ON. *annarr*, Goth. *anþar* :– CGerm. **anþeraz* :– IE. **ánteros* (compar. formation with **-teros*), whence the orig. sense of alternation (cf. ALTER); parallel to Skr. *ántaras* different, Lith. *añtras*, OPruss. *antars*, based on **an*- as in Skr., Av. *anyas* other. Hence **o·ther-**WISE (OE. *on ōþre wīsan*; cf. ON. *ǫðruvís*).

-otic ɔ·tik repr. ult., through F. *-otique*, L. *-ōticus*, Gr. *-ōtikós*, f. sbs. in *-ōtes* -OT, -OTE, adjs. in *-ōtos*, f. vbs. in *-óein*, *-oûn*, and so rel. to sbs. in -OSIS, e.g. *hypnotic* and *hypnosis*, *sclerotic* and *sclerosis*. Of different formation in Gr. are *demotic*, *erotic*, *exotic*; a mod. analogical formation is *chaotic* on *chaos*.

otiose ou·ʃious of no practical effect XVIII (Paley); (arch.) unemployed XIX. – L. *otiōsus*. f. *otium* leisure (cf. NEGOTIATE); see -OSE. ¶ Earlier were †*otious* XVII (– OF. *ocieus*), *otio·sity* XV (Caxton) – OF.

oto- outou comb. form of Gr. *ōt*-, *oûs* EAR[1]. XIX.

ottava rima ɔtā·va rī·ma (pros.) It. stanza of eight 11-syllable lines rhyming abababcc. XIX. It., 'eighth rhyme' (see OCTAVE, RHYME; cf. TERZA RIMA).

otter ɔ·təɹ aquatic mammal Lutra vulgaris. OE. *otr*, *ot(t)or* = MLG., Du. *otter*, OHG. *ottar* (G. *otter*), ON. *otr* :– CGerm. (not in Goth.) **otraz* :– IE. **udros*, repr. by Skr. *udrás*, Gr. *húdros* water-snake, *húdrā* HYDRA, Lith. *údra*, OSl. *vydra*, f. **ud*- **wed*- **wod*- (see WATER).

otto ɔ·tou unexpl. alt. of *ottar, otter*, vars. of Pers. *attar* ATTAR. XVII.

ottoman ɔ·təmən cushioned seat of the sofa type. XIX. – F. *ottomane* (XVIII), fem. of *ottoman*, adj. of next.

Ottoman ɔ·təmən pert. to the Turkish dynasty founded *c.*1300 by Othman (Osman); Turkish, Turk. XVII (earlier *Othoman, Ottoman*; Byron has *Othman*). – F. *Ottoman*, It. *Ottomano*, medL. *Ottomānus*, medGr. *Othōmānoí*, f. Arab. ʿ*othmānī*, f. ʿ*othmān*; *Osman*, the Turk. pronunc. of *Othman*+Turk. adj. suffix -*li* gives OSMANLI.

oubliette ūblie·t secret dungeon. XIX (Scott). F., f. *oublier* forget = Pr., Cat. *oblidar*, Sp., Pg. *olvidar*, Rum. *uità* :– Rom. **oblītāre*, f. *oblīt-*, ppl. stem of *oblīviscī*; see OBLIVION, -ETTE.

ouch autʃ (arch.) clasp, brooch (in A.V., Ex. xxviii 11, etc.). ME. *ouche*, arising from misdivision of *a nouche* (cf. *adder*) – OF. *nosche, nouche* – OFrank. (= OHG.) *nuskja* buckle, clasp, perh. of Celtic origin.

ought[1] ɔ̄t am bound, was bound, should be bound or obliged. OE. *āhte*, pt. ind. and subj. of *āgan* OWE; (literally) owed as a duty; (through the subj. use) should owe as a duty, passing into ind. use expressing (present or past) obligation, duty, or propriety.

ought[2] ɔ̄t illiterate alt. of NOUGHT in the sense 'cipher', 'zero', arising from misdividing *a nought* as *an ought*. XIX (Dickens).

ouija wī·dʒa, wī·jā (in spiritualism) *o. board*, one lettered with an alphabet for obtaining messages. XX. f. F. *oui* yes+G. *ja* yes.

ounce[1] auns unit of weight ($\frac{1}{12}$ of a pound troy, $\frac{1}{16}$ avoirdupois). XIV (R. Mannyng). ME. *unce* – OF. *unce* (mod. *once*) = Pr. *onsa*, Sp. *onza*, It. *oncia*, †*onza* (see OZ.) :– L. *uncia* twelfth part of a pound or foot (cf. INCH[1]), f. *ūnus* ONE, prob. intended orig. to express a unit.

ounce[2] auns †lynx XIII; mountain panther XVIII (Goldsmith). – AN. **unce*, OF. *once*, beside *lonce* (the *l* of which was taken for the def. art.), corr. to It. *lonza*, repr. Rom. **luncia*, f. *lync-*, *lynx* LYNX (cf. L. *lynceus* lynx-eyed).

our auəɹ pert. to US. A. g. pl. ('of US') of the 1st pers. pron. OE. *ūre* (*ūsser, ūser*) = OFris., OS. *ūser*, OHG. *unsēr*, ON. *vár*, Goth. *unsara*. B. as pron. adj. OE. *ūre* (declined like adjs. in *-e*) = OFris. *ūse*, OS. *unsa* (Du. *onze, ons*), OHG. *unsēr* (G. *unser*), ON. *várr*, Goth. *unsar*. Hence **ours** auəɹz ME. *ūres* (XIII, Cursor M.); repl. †*our* (OE. *ūre* to XVII); *ourn* (Wycl. to mod. dial.); **our**SE·LF XIV, repl. *usself*; with pl. inflexion, *ourse·lven, ourse·lves* XIV.

-our[1] əɹ the older form in many agent-nouns in -OR[1], surviving in SAVIOUR.

-our[2] əɹ surviving spelling in British use (as against U.S. *-or*) in several sbs. in -OR[2], v.z. *ardour, candour, clamour, colour, dolour, favour, fervour, honour, labour, odour, rancour, rigour, rumour, savour, splendour, tumour, valour, vigour*. ¶ The ending in the following has a different origin: *arbour, armour, demeanour, glamour, parlour, succour*; *behaviour* is a special case.

ourali var. of WOURALI.

-ous əs adj. suffix denoting 'characterized by', 'having the quality of', 'full of', 'abounding in', repr. ult. L. *-ōsus, -ōsa, -ōsum* (cf. -OSE[1]); first appearing as *-os, -us* – AN., OF. *-os, -us*, mod. *-eux* (e.g. *coveitos, coveitus* COVETOUS) = Sp., It. *-oso*. The vowel being identified with the repr. of OE. *ū* was, like it, spelt *ou*, the form *-ous* being thus established from *c.*1300, its pronunc. passing from ū through u and a weakened var. of this to the present ə.

The addition of *-ous* to L. stems of many types became the commonest mode of anglicizing L. adjs. ending in *-eus, -ius, -uus, -āci-, -ōci-, -endus, -ulus, -ōrus*, etc., e.g. *aqueous, atrocious, nefarious, stupendous, garrulous*, and of forming adjs. directly from sbs. of all origins; see also -EOUS, -IOUS, -UOUS; rel. sbs. have -OSITY.

In chem. *-ous* indicates a larger proportion of the element denoted by the stem than the termination *-ic*, as *cuprous* oxide, *ferrous* salts, *sulphurous* acid.

ousel, ouzel ū·z(ə)l blackbird. OE. *ōsle* (:– **amsle*) = OHG. *amusla, amsala* (G. *amsel*); see MERLE.

oust aust dispossess XVI; turn out, eject XVII. – AN. *ouster* = OF. *oster* (mod. *ôter*) take away, remove = Pr. *ostar* :– L. *obstāre* oppose, hinder (see OBSTACLE). So **ou·st**ER[5] (leg.) ejection from a possession. XVI. – law F. *ouster*, sb. use of the vb.

out aut adv. of motion or position beyond certain limits; with many transf. and fig. applications. OE. *ūt* = OFris., OS. *ūt* (Du. *uit*), OHG. *ūz* (G. *aus*), ON. *út*, Goth. *ūt*; CGerm. adv. rel. to Skr. prefix *ud-* out (cf. Gr. *hústeros* later :– **udteros*). The comp. prep. *out of* au·təv (lit. forth or proceeding from within; hence, not in or inside) descends from OE. *ūt of* = OS. *ūt af* (see OF). OE. *ūtan(e)*, ME. *uten*, is continued in BUT and WITHOUT. As adj., of restricted use (cf. *outhouse*, OUTSIDE, *out isles, outsize*, and OUT-). As sb. chiefly in techn. uses XVIII. As vb. OE. *ūtian* = OFris. *utia*, OHG. *uzōn*; newly formed XIV (Ch.) and later. **out-and-out** completely XIV; adj. XIX. Hence **out-and-out**ER[1] perfect or extreme one of its kind. XIX. The compar. formed with -ER[3] (*outter, c.*1400) superseded UTTER in certain uses (cf. OUTMOST); hence †*ou·termore* XIV; **ou·ter**MOST XVI, after *innermost, uppermost*.

out- aut repr. OE. *ūt-*, found in some thirty comps. meaning chiefly 'outward(s)', 'outlying', 'foreign', 'exterior, external', much increased in number and extended in application, in ME. and later; e.g. on the model of OE. *ūthealf* outward side are *outside, outskirts, outline*; = 'outside the premises or area', as in *outhouse, outland* (OE. *ūtland*); = 'external', as *out-patient*; on intr. verbal phrases such as *break out, cry out, fit out, lay out, look out* were formed *outbreak, outcry, outfit, outlay, outlook*; on trans. verbal phrases in the sense 'exceed or go beyond a person or thing in something', as *outbid, outdo, outgrow, outlast, outline, outrun*; *out-Herod* (Sh. 'Hamlet' III ii 16) exceed Herod in violence; so e.g. *out-Nero Nero*; *outstrip* (XVI) is based on an obs. vb. meaning 'move swiftly'; similarly with sbs., as *outwit, out-general*; with prepositional sense, as *outdoor* XVIII.

outing au·tiŋ †expedition XIV (Barbour); †expulsion (Promp. Parv.); (orig. dial.) airing, excursion XIX (Clare). Partly f. OUT vb., partly f. the adv.

outlander au·tlændəɹ foreigner XVII; in S. Africa, alien inhabitant XIX. Cf. Du. *uitlander*, G. *ausländer*.

outlaw au·tlɔ̄ one put outside the protection of the law. Late OE. *ūtlaga* – ON. *útlagi*, f. *útlagr* outlawed, banished, f. *út* OUT + **lagu*, *lǫg* LAW. So **ou·tlaw** vb. Late OE. *ūtlagian*. **ou·tlaw**RY. XIV; in AN. *utlagerie, -larie*, AL. *utlagaria, -eria* (f. *utlaga* XI).

outmost au·tmoust, -məst outermost. XIV (Wycl. Bible). alt. of *utmest* (see UTMOST).

outrage au·treidʒ †intemperance, excess, extravagant, violent action; violent injury. XIII. – (O)F. *outrage* = Pr. *oltratge*, Sp. *ultraje*, It. *oltraggio* :– Rom. **ultrāticum*, f. L. *ultrā* beyond; see ULTRA-, -AGE. So **ou·trage** vb. XIV. **outra·geous**. XIV. – OF. *outrageus* (mod. *-eux*).

outré ū·trei, ||utre out-of-the way, eccentric, extravagant. XVIII (Richardson, Fielding). F., pp. of *outrer* †go beyond due limits, f. *outre* :– L. *ultrā* (cf. ULTRA).

outrecuidance ūtrəkwī·dəns (arch.) arrogance, presumption. XV. – (O)F. *outrecuidance*, f. *outrecuider*, f. *outre* beyond (:– L. *ultrā*) + *cuider* think (:– L. *cōgitāre*); see ULTRA-, COGITATE, -ANCE. ¶ Revived by Scott.

outrigger au·tri:gəɹ (naut.) in various senses preceded by, and perh. an alt., by assoc. with RIG, of †*outligger* (XV) 'outlier' (f. OUT + *lig* – ON. *liggja* LIE[1]). ¶ Du. *uitlegger* guard-ship is later in appearance and has not the same meanings.

outright autrait (str. variable) †straight onward, straightway XIII; to the full, completely XIV. f. OUT adv., RIGHT adv.

outSIDE autsaid (str. variable) sb. XVI; adj. XVII; adv. and prep., for *o. of* XVIII; hence **outsi·d**ER[1] (1800, Jane Austen).

outSKIRT au·tskɔ̄ɹt XVI (sg. Spenser; pl. Clarendon). The outer border.

outspan au·tspæn (S. Afr.) unyoke, unharness. XIX. – Du. *uitspannen*, f. *uit* OUT + *spannen* stretch, SPAN[2], put horses to.

outspoken (str. variable) orig. Sc. that is given to speaking out or plainly. XIX. See SPOKEN.

ouzel see OUSEL.

oval ou·v(ə)l egg-shaped. XVI (Dee). – medL. *ōvālis*, f. L. *ōvum* EGG; see -AL[1]. Cf. F. †*oval* (Rabelais). So **ovate**[2] ou·veit. XVIII. – L.

ovary ou·vəri female organ of reproduction. XVII (Sir T. Browne). – modL. *ōvārium* (whence also F. *ovaire* 1690); see -ARY.

ovation ouvei·ʃən (in ancient Rome) lesser triumph XVI; †exultation XVII; enthusiastic applause XIX. – L. *ovātiō(n-)*, f. *ovāre* celebrate a (lesser) triumph, perh. f. Gr. *euoî*, exultant cry at the Bacchanalia; see -ATION.

oven ʌ·vn †furnace; receptacle for food to be cooked by radiating heat. OE. *ofen* = OFris., (M)LG., (M)Du. *oven*, OHG. *ovan* (G. *ofen*), ON. *ofn, ogn*, Goth. **auhns* (acc. sg. *auhn*) :– CGerm. **oχwnaz* :– **ukw(h)nos* (cf. Gr. *ipnós* oven, furnace, Skr. *ukhás* cooking-pot, L. *aulla* (:– **aukslā*) pot, dim. *auxilla*); cf. OE. *ofnet* small vessel.

over ou·vəɹ adv. (also prep. in corr. senses) above (now only in spec. uses); to or on the other side; above a certain quantity OE.; excessively, too XIII; through the whole extent XIV; gone by, done with (XIV) XVII. OE. *ofer* = OFris. *over*, OS. *oƀar* (Du. *over*), OMG. *obar*, OHG. *ubar* prep., *ubiri* adv. (G. *über*, also, from MG., *ober*), ON. *yfir*, Goth. *ufar* :– CGerm. **uƀeri* (LG. and MG. favouring the vowel *o*, the rest *u*) :– IE. **uperi*, compar. formation (cf. Skr. *upári*, Av. *upairi*, Gr. *hupér*, L. *s|uper*; see HYPER-, SUPER-) on **upó* from under towards (see SUB-). **over** adj. ME. *ouere* (XIII) began as a graphic var. of *uuere* (with *o* for *u* before *u*) :– OE. *ufer(r)a, yfer(r)a, -e* (:– **uƀar*, **uƀirōzo-*), which is directly repr. by dial. *uvver*; superseded in gen. use by the advb. form.

over- ouvəɹ repr. OE. *ofer-*, comb. form of prec., of which there are some 300 comps. illustrating several senses and having many of them parallels in other Germ. langs.; the number was increased in ME. and later periods, with modifications and developments of the primary meanings. The chief senses are 'situated above', 'upper', 'in excess', 'extra', 'lying, extending, or moving across', 'passing over a limit or an obstacle', 'beyond in degree or quality', 'covering a surface', 'with dominating or damaging influence or effect'; 'with disturbance of situation', as *overbalance* (XVI), *overcast* (XIII), *overset* (XVI), *overturn* (XIV), OVERWHELM; special uses are those in *overhear* hear without intention (distinct from OE. *oferhīeran* not to listen to); *overlook* look over and beyond and so not to see or notice (distinct from *oversee*, OE. *oferseōn* survey, (later) inspect, superintend); OVERTAKE; *overcoat* (1807 W. Irving) and *overshoe* (*c.*1850) are orig. U.S. and are prob. renderings of the corr. G. or Du. words.

overall ou·vərōl outer covering or garment. XVIII. f. OVER prep.+ALL sb.; partly after F. *surtout* (XVII) SURTOUT.

overplus ou·vəɹplʌs. XIV (Trevisa). Partial tr. of (O)F. *surplus* SURPLUS.

overt ou·vǝ̄ɹt †open, uncovered XIV (Ch.); open to view or knowledge XIV (occas. before XVI). – OF. *overt* (mod. *ouvert*), pp. of *ovrir* (*ouvrir*) open :– L. *aperīre*.

overTA·KE come up with, catch up XIII (AncrR.); come upon suddenly XIV. f. OVER-+TAKE; superseding †*oftake* (Laȝ.), with which cf. OE. *offaran*, *offēran*, *ofrīdan*.

o·verTONE (acoustics, mus.) harmonic. XIX. – G. *oberton* (Helmholtz), for *oberpartialton* 'upper partial tone'.

overture ou·vəɹtʃuəɹ †opening, aperture XIV; opening of negotiations XV; (Sc.) formal motion in an assembly XVI; (mus.) orchestral piece forming the introduction to a work XVII. – OF. *overture* (now *ouverture*) :– L. *apertūra* APERTURE, with infl. from *ouvrir* open.

overweening ouvəɹwī·niŋ presumption, arrogance. XIV (R. Mannyng). f. OVER-, WEEN, -ING[1]; prob. after OUTRECUIDANCE.

overwhelm ouvəɹʍe·lm (dial.) upset. XIV (R. Mannyng); overcome, overpower XVI. f. OVER-+WHELM (which survives otherwise only in poet. and arch. use).

ovi-[1] ou·vi comb. form of L. *ovum* EGG[1], as in *o·vi*DUCT (XVIII).

ovi-[2] ou·vi comb. form of L. *ovis* sheep (see EWE), as in (joc.) *ovicide* sheep-slaughter (Barham).

ovine ou·vain pert. to sheep. XIX. – late L. *ovīnus*, f. *ovis*; see EWE, -INE[1].

ovo- ou·vou used irreg. for OVI-[1]. XIX.

ovoid ou·void egg-shaped. XIX. – F. *ovoïde* (Buffon) – modL. *ōvoīdēs*, f. *ōvum* EGG[1]; see -OID. So **ovoi·d**AL[1]. XVIII.

ovolo ou·vəlou (archit.) convex moulding the section of which is a quarter-circle or ellipse. XVII. – It. *ovolo*, dim. of †*ovo*, *uovo* :– L. *ōvum* EGG[1].

ovule ou·vjūl (bot.) rudimentary seed; (zool.) unfertilized ovum. XIX. – F. *ovule* (Mirbel 1808) – modL. *ōvulum*, dim. of L. *ōvum* (EGG[1]); see -ULE.

ovum ou·vəm egg (female reproductive cell). XVIII. L., EGG[1].

owe ou †A. have, own OE.; B. have to pay XII; C. have as a duty or obligation XII; D. cherish, entertain XIV; have to ascribe or attribute XVI. OE. *āgan*, pres. *āh*, pt. *āhte* = OFris. *āga*, *āch*, *āchte*, OS. *ēgan*, *ēh*, *ēhta*, OHG. *eigan*, *eig*, ON. *eiga*, *á*, *átta*, Goth. *aigan*, *aih*, *aihta*; CGerm. perfect-pres. vb. (cf. CAN[1], DARE, MAY[1]); f. **aig-* :– IE. **oik-* **ik-*, repr. also by Skr. *-iś* possess, own). The orig. conjugation has been repl. by a new one (*owed* XIV) based directly on the inf., and the orig. pt. has become a distinct word (OUGHT[1]) having lost immed. connexion with *owe*. Cf. OWN. In the meaning 'have to pay' *owe* superseded *shall*. A special use of the prp. **ow**ING[2] is in the sense 'attributable to' (XVII), whence the advb. *owing to* because of (XIX, Scott).

owelty ou·əlti (leg.) equality. XVI. – AN. *oweltė*, f. OF. *owel* :– L. *æquālis* EQUAL; see -TY.

owl aul nocturnal bird of prey. OE. *ūle* = OLG. **ūla* (MLG., MDu. *ūle*, Du. *uil*), ON. *ugla* :– **uwwalōn*, parallel with **uwwilōn*, repr. by OHG. *ūwila* (MHG. *iule*, G. *eule*). For the imit. origin cf. L. *ulula*, perh. f. vb. *ululāre* howl; also L. *būbō*, Gr. *búās*, *bûza*. Hence **ow·l**ET. XVI. ¶ Forms with initial *h* are ME. *hule* (XIII), *houlet* (XV); cf. OS. *hūo*, OHG. *hūwo* (G. dial. *uhu*).

own oun pert. to oneself or itself. OE. *āgen* = OFris. *ēgen*, *ēin*, OS. *ēgan*, OHG. *eigan* (Du., G. *eigen*), ON. *eiginn* :– CGerm. (exc. Gothic) **aiganaz*, adj. use of the pp. of OWE, prop. 'possessed', 'owed'. Hence **own** vb. OE. *āgnian* (so OHG. *eiganen*, G. *eignen*, ON. *eigna*) †take possession of; hold as one's own OE. (disused XIV–XVI exc. as repr. in **ow·n**ER[1] (XIV), whence revived XVII by back-formation); acknowledge as one's own, as true or valid, etc. XVII.

ox ɔks pl. **oxen** ɔ·ksn bovine animal, esp. castrated male of the domestic species. OE. *oxa* = OFris. *oxa*, OS., OHG. *ohso* (Du. *os*, G. *ochse*), ON. *uxi*, *oxi*, Goth. *auhsa* :– CGerm. **oχson* :– IE. **uksín-*, repr. also by W. *ych*, pl. *ychyn*, OIr. *oss* stag, Skr. *ukshán* ox, bull, cattle; the ult. relations are unkn. ¶ The only sb. in gen. use that retains the orig. weak pl. (OE. *-an*).

oxalic ɔksæ·lik epithet of a poisonous sour acid existing in the form of salts in wood-sorrel, etc. XVIII. – F. *oxalique* (de Morveau and Lavoisier, 'Nomenclature Chimique', 1787), f. L. *oxalis* (Pliny) – Gr. *oxalís* wood-sorrel (Dioscorides), f. *oxús* sour, acid (cf. OXYGEN); see -IC.

oxide ɔ·ksaid compound of oxygen with another element or with an organic radical. XVIII. – F. *oxide* (de Morveau and Lavoisier, 1787), now *oxyde*, f. *oxygène* OXYGEN + *-ide*, after *acide* ACID. The sp. *oxid* (now U.S.) was suggested by assoc. with *acid*. See prec.

Oxonian ɔksou·niən pert. to Oxford, esp. to its university. XVI. f. *Oxonia*, latinization of OE. *Ox(e)naford*, ME. *Oxen(e)ford*, f. *oxan*, g. pl. of OX+FORD; see -IAN.

oxslip ɔ·kslip flowering herb, hybrid between cowslip and primrose. OE. *oxanslyppe*, f. *oxan*, g. sg. of *oxa* OX+*slyppe* slimy or viscous dropping (see COWSLIP).

oxy- ɔ·ksi repr. *oxu-*, comb. form of Gr. *oxús* sharp, pungent, ACID, used in many scientific terms, in chem. repr. *oxygen*.

oxygen ɔ·ksidʒən (chem.) colourless invisible gas, the most abundant of the elements. XVIII. – F. *oxygène*, intended to mean 'acidifying principle' (acid-producer), f. Gr. *oxús* (see prec.+*-gène* -GEN. The form used as sb. in de Morveau and Lavoisier's 'Nomenclature Chimique', 1787, was *oxigène*; this repl. *oxygène* (1786), short for *principe oxygène* (1785–6), which had succeeded to *principe oxygine* (1777).

oxymoron ɔksimɔ̄·rɔn (rhet.) figure in which contradictory terms are conjoined. XVII. – Gr. *oxúmōron*, n. sg. of *oxúmōros* pointedly foolish, f. *oxús* (see OXY-)+*mōrós* foolish (cf. MORON).

oxytone ɔ·ksitoun (Gr. gram.) having the acute accent on the last syllable. XVIII. – modL. *oxytonus* – Gr. *oxútonos*, f. *oxús* sharp, acute (see OXY-)+*tónos* TONE. So **paro·xytone** pǣr- / **proparo·xytone** proupər- having an acute accent on the penultimate / antepenultimate syllable respectively. XVIII.

oy, oe oi (Sc.) grandchild. XV (*o*). – Gael. *ogha, odha* (ō·ə) = OIr. *au* descendant, Ir. *úa* grandson.

oyer oi·əɹ (leg.) in full *o. and terminer* 'hear and determine', commission to hear and judge indictments. XV. – AN. *oyer* (Britton) = OF. *oïr* (mod. *ouïr*) :- L. *audīre* hear (see AUDIENCE). See -ER[5].

oyez, oyes ouje·s call to command attention, as by a public crier or a court officer. XV (*oyas, oȝes, oyes*). – AN., OF. *oiez, oyez* hear ye!, imper. pl. of *oïr* (see prec.); identified with *O yes* since XV, and often so written.

oyster oi·stəɹ edible bivalve mollusc. XIV. ME. *oistre* – OF. *oistre, uistre* (mod. *huître*) = Pr., Sp. *ostra*, It. †*ostrea* – L. *ostrea* (whence also OE. *ōstre*, (M)Du. *oester*, ON. *ostra*; G. *auster* being from LG.), also *ostreum* from Gr. *óstreon*, rel. to *ostéon* bone (cf. OSTEO-), *óstrakon* (cf. OSTRACIZE).

oz symbol for OUNCE[1]. XVI. – It. *oz*, abbrev. of *onza*, pl. *onze*.

ozokerit(e) ouzou·kərit, -ait, **ozocerit(e)** o(u)zɔ·sərit, -ɔ·kərit, -ait; ouzosiə·rait, -kiə·rait aromatic waxlike fossil resin. XIX. – G. *ozokerit* (Glocker, 1833), f. Gr. *ózein* smell+*kērós* beeswax; see -ITE.

ozone ouzou·n, ou·zoun (chem.) allotropic oxygen, O_3. XIX. – G. *ozon* (C. F. Schönbein, 1840) – Gr. *ózon*, n. prp. of *ózein* smell, rel. to *odmé* ODOUR; thus F. *ozone*; so named from its peculiar smell.

P

pa, pabouch see PAPA, PAPOOSH.

pabulum pæ·bjŭləm food, nutriment. XVII. – L. *pābulum* (:- **pādhlom*), f. base **pā-* of *pāscere*, pt. *pāvī* feed, PASTURE.

paca pæ·kə large rodent of Central and S. America. XVII. – Sp., Pg. *paca* – Tupi *paca* (cf. Guarani *paig*).

pace[1] peis step; rate of progression; †step of a stair, floor raised by a step (surviving in FOOTPACE, HALF-PACE); †mountain pass XIII. ME. *pas, paas* – (O)F. *pas* – L. *passu-s* step, pace, lit. 'stretch (of the leg)', f. *pass-*, pp. stem of *pandere* stretch, extend (cf. EXPAND). Hence **pace** vb. walk with measured pace (along) XVI; set the pace for XIX.

pace[2] pei·si by leave of. XIX. L., abl. of *pāx* PEACE, as in *pāce tuā* by your leave.

pace egg peis eg (north.) Easter egg. XVI. f. north. dial. *pace, pase, paas* (XV), var. of *pask*, PASCH Easter (cf. *ass* for *ask* ash, *buss* for *busk* bush); corrupted to *paste-egg* (XVII). Cf. LG. *paaschey*.

pacha see PASHA.

pachisi pətʃī·si four-handed game played in India, of which ludo is a simplified form. XVIII. – Hindi *pach(ch)īsī*, adj. f. *pach(ch)īs* twenty-five (the highest throw), f. *pach* five.

pachy- pæ·ki comb. form of Gr. *pakhús* thick, as in *pakhúdermos* thick-skinned (*dérma* skin, DERMATO-), on which is based modL. *pachydermata*, whence **pa·chyderm** (after F. *pachyderme*, Cuvier 1797), **pachyde·rmat**OUS XIX.

pacific pəsi·fik making or tending to peace XVI; peaceful XVII (*P. Ocean*, modL. *Mare Pacificum*, so called by Magellan because he found it comparatively free from violent storms). – (O)F. *pacifique* or L. *pācificus*, f. *pāc-*, *pāx* PEACE; see -FIC. Hence **paci·fic**ISM, -IST, usu. in shortened form **pa·cifism, -ist** pæ·sifizm, -ist XX; after F. *pacifisme, -iste*. So **paci**FY pæ·sifai calm, quiet. XV. – (O)F. *pacifier* or L. *pācificāre*. **pacifica**TION. XV. – F. – L.

pack[1] pæk bundle, bale XIII; company, set of people XIV; set of playing-cards XVI; company of animals kept or herding together XVII. – (M)Flem., (M)Du., (M)LG. *pak* (whence ult. also (M)HG. *pack*, Icel. *pakki*, AL. *paccus*, *paka*, F. †*paque*, It. *pacco*, Ir. *paca*); of unkn. origin. So **pack** vb. XIV. – (M)Du., (M)LG. *pakken*; cf. AN. *paker*, *enpaker*, AL. *pakkāre*, *impaccāre*, Icel. *pakka*, etc. Hence **pa·ck**AGE. XVI; earlier †*pakald* (XV), of obscure formation; but AL. *paccāgium* occurs XIII–XIV.

pack[2] pæk †make a plot; †bring into a plot; make up (a jury, etc.) for a wrong purpose; shuffle (cards) fraudulently. XVI. prob. f. †*pact* vb. (f. PACT sb.) by apprehending the final *-t* as an inflexion; cf. †*compack*, occas. var. of *compact*.

packet pæ·kit small pack or package XVI; short for *p.-boat* XVIII. f. PACK[1]+-ET; perh. of AN. formation; F. *pacquet* is from Eng., and Sp. *paquete*, It. *pacchetto* from F. Hence **packet-**BOAT vessel plying between two ports, mail-boat. XVII; orig. boat maintained for the conveyance of 'the packet' of state papers (cf. 'allowance as well for serving the packets by lande as for entertaining a bark to carie over and to returne the packet' 1598–9); hence F. *paquebot*, †*-bouc* (1634), †*paquet-bot* (1718). ¶ Earlier names were †*post-bark*, †*post-boat* (late XVI); cf. 'pacquets postmaster' (1628), 'postmasters frigate' (1637).

paco pā·kou alpaca (the animal) XVII; brown oxide of iron (so called from its colour) XIX. – Sp. *paco* – Quechua *pako* (see ALPACA).

pact pækt covenant, agreement. XV. – (O)F. *pacte*, †*pact* – L. *pactum*, *-us*, sb. uses of pp. of *pacīscī* make a covenant, f. reduced grade of **pāk-*, repr. by *pāx* PEACE.

pad[1] pæd †toad, (dial.) frog. XII. Late OE. or early ME. *pad*, prob. – ON. *padda* = OFris., MDu. *padde* (Du. *pad(de)*, MLG. *padde*, *pedde* (*peddenstōl* toadstool). Cf. PADDOCK[1].

pad[2] pæd (orig. sl., now dial.) path, road XVI; road-horse, nag; highwayman, FOOT-PAD XVII. – LG., Du. *pad* PATH. A word of vagabonds' cant, like others of the class introduced XVI. Hence, or – LG. *padden*, **pad** vb.[1] tread, tramp. XVI. †**pa·dd**ER[1] foot-pad. XVII.

pad[3] pæd †bundle of straw to lie on; soft stuffed saddle XVI; small cushion XVII; hairy foot or paw XVIII; sheets of paper forming a block XIX. prob. of LDu. origin (cf. Flem. †*pad*, *patte*, LG. *pad* sole of the foot). Hence **pad** vb.[2] stuff, fill out. XIX.

pad[4] pæd dull sound of steps on the ground. XVI. Mainly imit., but cf. PAD vb.[1]

paddle[1] pæ·dl spud for cleaning a ploughshare XV; short oar for propelling a canoe, etc.; one of a series of spokes, boards, or floats for propelling a vessel in the water XVII. Of unkn. origin; in the first sense north. dialects have a parallel *pattle* (XIX); the suffix is -LE[1]. Hence **pa·ddle** vb. XVII.

paddle[2] pæ·dl walk or move the feet about in mud or shallow water XVI; toddle XVIII. prob. of LDu. origin; cf. LG. *paddeln* tramp about, frequent. of *padden* PAD vb.[1]; see -LE[3].

paddock[1] pæ·dək frog, toad. XII (in place-name *Padocdailes*). f. PAD[1]+-OCK.

paddock[2] pæ·dək small enclosure of grass land. XVII. alt. of (dial.) *parrock*, OE. *pearroc*, *-uc* PARK. ¶ Cf. *Le (south) par(r)ok* (XIV), later *Paddock Creek* in Essex, *Parrok* (XIV), now *Paddock Wood* in Kent.

paddy[1] pæ·di rice in the straw or in the husk. XVII (*batte* XVI, *batty* XVII). – Malay *pādī*, corr. to Javanese *pārī*, Canarese *bhatta*.

paddy[2] pæ·di Irishman XVIII; fit of temper XIX. Pet-form of Ir. *Padraig* Patrick; see -Y[6].

paddymelon pæ·dimelən small brush kangaroo. XIX. alt. of native name, the first el. of which may be identical with that of Sydney dialect *patagorang* kangaroo.

pad(i)shah pā·diʃā, pā·dʃā title applied to the Shah of Persia, Sultan of Turkey, Great Mogul, etc. XVII. – Pers. *pādshāh*, in poetry *pādishah* :– Pahlavi *pātaχšā(h)* :– OPers. **pātiχšayaθiya*, f. *pati* (= Skr. *pati*) master, lord, ruler + *šāh* king, SHAH.

padlock pæ·dlək portable lock to hang on the object fastened. XV. Of unkn. origin; the simple *pad* appears to be earlier (XIII), perh. identical with PAD[1], the lock being fancifully likened to a toad in shape; see LOCK[1].

padre pā·drei (title of a) minister of religion. XVI. – It., Sp., Pg. *padre* :– L. *patre-m*, *pater* FATHER. ¶ In India taken from Pg.; hence in gen. service use for a chaplain.

paduasoy pæ·djuəsoi silk fabric. XVII. Earliest form *poudesoy* – F. *pou-de-soie*, earlier *pout de soie* (XIV), of unkn. origin; altered to the present form by assoc. with earlier †*Padua say* (XVII), kind of serge (see SAY[2]) from Padua in Italy.

pæan pī·ən song of triumph or exultation. XVI. – L. *pæān* – Gr. *paiā́n* hymn to Apollo invoked by the name *Paiā́n*, Doric var. of Ionic *Paiḗōn*, Attic *Paiṓn*, orig. the Homeric name of the physician of the gods, afterwards Apollo, prop. the Striker, one who heals with magic blows, prp. of *paíein* strike.

pædo-, U.S. **pedo-** pī·dou comb. form of Gr. *paîs*, *paid-* boy, child; as in **pædo-**BA·PTISM infant baptism. XVII. – modL. Cf. PEDAGOGUE.

pæon pī·ən (pros.) metrical foot of four syllables, one long and three short, named, acc. to the position of the long syllable, first, second, third, and fourth pæon. XVII. – L. *pæōn* – Gr. *paiṓn*.

pagan pei·gən heathen. XIV. – L. *pāgānus* rustic, peasant, citizen, civilian; eccl.)(Christian and Jewish, f. *pāgus* (rural) district, the country, orig. landmark fixed in the earth,

f. *pāg- *pəg-, as in *pangere* fix, parallel to *pāk- (see PACT); see -AN. The sense 'heathen' (Tertullian) of *pagānus* derived from that of 'civilian' (Tacitus), the Christians calling themselves enrolled soldiers of Christ (members of his militant church) and regarding non-Christians as not of the army so enrolled. Represented earlier (XIII–XVI) by †*paien*, †*payen* – OF. *paien* (mod. *païen*) = Pr. *paian*, *pagan*, Sp., It. *pagano*; cf. PAYNIM. Hence **pa·gan**ISM. XV.

page[1] peidʒ †boy, lad XIII; †youth in training for knighthood; †male person of low condition; boy (or man) employed as servant or attendant XIV, as in a great household, or (XVIII) a foot-boy or errand-boy at a house, hotel, etc. – (O)F. *page*, perh. – It. *paggio* (cf. Sp. *page*, Pg. *pagem*) – Gr. *paidíon*, dim. of *paid-*, *paîs* boy (cf. PÆDO-).

page[2] peidʒ one side of a leaf of a book, etc. XV. – (O)F. *page* (reduction of *pagene*) – L. *pāgina* vine-trellis, column of writing, page or leaf, f. *pāg- fix (cf. *pāgus* s.v. PAGAN). Earlier †**pagine** (AncrR.) – OF. *pagine*, *-ene*, or direct – L. Hence **page** vb. XVII. So **pagin**ATE[3] pæ·dʒineit. XIX; back-formation from **pagin**A·TION. XIX. – F.

pageant pæ·dʒənt, (now rare) pei·dʒənt †scene acted on a stage XIV; †stage on which scenes were acted, esp. in the open-air performances of the miracle plays XV; †tableau or series of tableaux XVI; brilliant spectacle XIX; since 1907, scenic exhibition of local history. Late ME. *pagyn* (in contemp. AL. *pagina*), of unkn. origin (the uncertainty is complicated by lack of evidence for the chronology of the senses). ¶ With parasitic *d*, *t*, from XIV (cf. *ancient*, *peasant*, *tyrant*). Hence **pa·geant**RY. XVII (Sh.).

pagne pænj cloth, esp. loin-cloth. XVII. – F. *pagne* – Sp. *paño* (in Pg. *panno*, whence Du. *paan*) :– L. *pannu-s* cloth (see PANE).

pagoda pəgou·də idol temple; idol; coin of S. India (from the figure thereon). XVII. – Pg. *pagode*, with substitution of *-a* for *-e*; prob. to be referred ult. to Pers. *butkada* idol temple, f. *but* idol + *kada* habitation, altered by assoc. with Prakrit *bhagodī* divine, holy :– Skr. *bhagavatī* 'god-endowed', divine. Earlier *pagod(e)* late XVI; cf. F. *pagode* (XVII); pronounced *pa·god* and *pago·d*, as in Pope.

pa(h) pā native fort in New Zealand. XIX. Maori *pà*, f. *pà* block up. Earlier †*hippa(h)*, with prefixed def. art. *he*.

Pahlavi pā·ləvi, **Pehlevi** pei·ləvi mode of writing Persian by substituting Semitic equivalents for Persian words. XIX. – Pers. *Pahlavī*, *Pehlevī*, f. *Pahlav* :– *Parthava* Parthia; the system of writing was developed in Parthian times, when the great nobles, the Pahlavāns, ruled.

pail peil vessel of cylindrical or truncated obconical shape made of staves hooped and fitted with a handle. OE. *pæġel* (glossing medL. *gillo* GILL[3]) corr. to (M)Du. *pegel* gauge, scale, mark, LG. *pegel* half a pint, of unkn. origin. ME. forms with final *e* appear to be due to assoc. with OF. *paielle*, *paelle* (mod. *poêle*) pan, bath, liquid measure :– L. *patella* pan; see PATELLA.

paillasse see PALLIASSE.

pain pein (arch.) punishment, penalty (now only in phr.); suffering; †trouble, difficulty XIII; (pl.) trouble taken in doing something XVI (earlier sg. *do one's p.*, etc.). ME. *peine*, *paine* – (O)F. *peine* = Pr., Sp., It. *pena* :– L. *pœna* penalty, punishment, (later) pain, grief – Gr. (Dorian) *poinā́*, (Attic) *poinḗ* expiation, ransom, punishment :– *q^woinā vengeance, price of expiation (cf. OSl. *cěna* price, Av. *kaēnā-* punishment, Skr. *cáyatē* avenge, punish). See PINE[2]. Hence **pai·n**FUL[1] hurtful; †laborious. XIV.

paint peint make (a picture) on a surface in colours XIII (first in *peintunge*, AncrR.); depict in words XV. prob. first in pp. *(i)peint* – (O)F. *peint(e)*, pp. of *peindre* = Pr. *penher*, It. *pingere* :– L. *pingere* embroider, tattoo, paint, embellish, f. nasalized form of **pig-* **peig-* (cf. PICTURE, PIGMENT), repr. also by Skr. *piṅktē* paints, *piñjáras* reddish, and parallel with **peik-* **poik-*, repr. by OE. *fāh*, OHG. *fēh* varicoloured, Goth. *filufaihs*, Gr. *poikílos* (cf. PŒCILO-), Lith. *piešiù*, *piẽšti* paint, write, Skr. *piṃçáti* adorns. Hence **paint** sb. pigment, colour. XVII. So **pai·nt**ER[1]. XIV (R. Rolle). – OF. *peintour*, regimen case of *peintre* = Pr., Sp. *pintor*, It. *pintore* :– CRom. **pinctōrem*, for L. *pictōrem*, *pictor*, f. *pict-*, pp. stem of *pingere*; see -ER[2], -OR[1].

painter[2] pei·ntəɹ rope to secure an anchor, etc. XV. contemp. with †*paint* vb. make fast with a rope, which is prob. a back-formation; of unkn. origin, but cf. OF. *pentoir*, *penteur* strong rope (XV).

pair pɛəɹ set of two; set of parts forming a whole. XIII (e.g. string *of beads* XIV, flight *of stairs* XVI). – (O)F. *paire* = It. *paia* pl. (whence sg. *paio*) :– L. *paria* equal or like things, n. pl. of *pār*, *par-* equal, whence OF. *per* (mod. *pair*) PEER. Formerly often uninflected for the pl. with a numeral; cf. OF. *cinquante paire*, *cent paire*. Hence **pair** vb. XVII. ¶ From L. are also MDu., OHG. *par* (G. *paar*).

Pakistan pākistā·n (at first) Moslem autonomy; (now) Moslem republic in S. Asia. XX. Earlier *Pakstan*, f. initials of *P*unjab, *A*fghan Province, *K*ashmir, *S*ind, and Baluchis*tan*.

paktong pæ·ktɔŋ Chinese nickel silver. XVIII. Cantonese var. of Chinese *peh* (white) *t'ung* (copper).

pal pæl (sl.) comrade, chum. XVII. – Eng. Gypsy *pal* brother, mate = Turk. Gypsy *pral*, *plal* :– Skr. *bhrā́tar-* BROTHER.

palace pæ·lis official residence of a king, pope, bishop XIII; stately mansion XIV; building, often spacious and attractive, for entertainment XIX. ME. *paleis* – OF. *paleis*, (also mod.) *palais*, corr. to Pr. *palatz*, Sp. *palacio*, It. *palazzo* – L. *palātium* orig. name of one of the seven hills of Rome (also called *Mons Palatinus* PALATINE hill), (later) the house of Augustus there situated, the palace of the Cæsars which finally covered the hill.

paladin pæ·lədin one of the Twelve Peers of Charlemagne's court, of whom the Count Palatine was the foremost; (hence) knightly champion or hero. XVI. – F. *paladin* – It. *paladino* – L. *palātīnu-s* pert. to the palace, PALATINE.

palæo-, U.S. **paleo-**, pæ:liou, pælio·- comb. form of Gr. *palaiós* ancient, in many scientific terms often having correlatives in NEO-; among the earliest are **palæo·**GRAPHY – F. *paléographie* – modL. *palæographia* (1708), **pa:læonto·**LOGY XIX; archæol., geol. opp. to MESO-, NEO-, as **pa:læoli·thic, -zo·ic.**

palæstra pəlī·strə wrestling-school. XVI. – L. *palæstra* – Gr. *palaistrā*, f. *palaiein* wrestle. Earlier in form †*palestre* (XV, Lydg.) – (O)F. *palestre*. So **palæ·str**AL[1] (XIV, Ch.).

palafitte pæ·ləfit lake dwelling. XIX. – F. *palafitte* – It. *palafitta* fence of piles, f. *palo* PALE[1] + *fitto* fixed, pp. of *figgere* FIX.

palampore pæ·ləmpɔəɹ chintz bed-cover. XVII. prob. f. *Pālanpur*, name of a town in Guzerat, India, perh. with contamination from Hind., Pers. *palangpōsh* bed-cover.

palankeen, palanquin pælankī·n covered litter used in India and elsewhere. XVI. – Pg. *palanquim* (whence also F., Sp. *palanquin*, It. *palanchino*) – an EIndian word repr. by Pali *pālankī*, Hindi *pālkī* (whence **pa·lkee** XVII) :– Skr. *palyanka*, *paryanka* bed, couch, f. *pari* round about, PERI-. ¶ The final nasal seems to have been a Pg. addition, as in *mandarim* MANDARIN; forms without it, *palanke(e)*, were in use XVII–XVIII.

palate pæ·lət roof of the mouth. XIV (*palet*). – L. *palātum* (used also, by Ennius, for the vault of heaven). (O)F. *palais* was also adopted as *palace*, *pal(a)ys* XV–XVI, a form due to assoc. with L. *palātium* PALACE on account of the roof-like form of the palate (cf. OF. *palais voutis* vaulted palate). Hence **pa·late** vb. taste, relish. XVII (Sh.); **pa·lat**ABLE agreeable to the palate. XVII; **pa·lat**AL[1] pert. to the palate. XIX. – F. *palatal*; earlier †**pala·t**IAL XVIII, and †**palat**IC, **palat**INE (cf. F. *palatin*) XVII. The comb. form of *palate* is **pa·lato-** XVIII.

palatine pæ·lətain (of a count or county) possessing royal privileges XV; sb. lord having sovereign power over a province or dependency of an empire or realm XVI. – F. *palatin(e)* – L. *palātīnus* belonging to the *palātium* PALACE, sb. officer of the Roman imperial palace, chamberlain; hence applied in the Middle Ages to great feudatories exercising royal privileges, such as the rulers of Hungary, the pfalzgraf of the Rhine, the Bishop of Durham, etc. Hence **palatin**ATE[1] pəlæ·tinət territory of a count palatine, county palatine. XVI; cf. F. *palatinat*. Also **palatine** sb. fur tippet worn by women. XVII. – F. *palatine*, so named after the Princess *Palatine*, wife of the Duke of Orleans, brother of Louis XIV.

palaver pəlā·vər parley, conference; profuse or idle talk. XVIII (hence as vb.). – Pg. *palavra* = Sp. *palabra*, Pr. *paraula*, It. *parola*, F. *parole* (cf. PAROLE) :– L. *parabola* PARABLE. ¶ *Palavra* appears to have been used by Pg. traders on the coast of Africa for a parley with the natives, to have been picked up there by English sailors, and to have passed from nautical slang into ordinary colloq. use. Cf. *fetish*.

pale[1] peil pointed stake used in forming a fence; fence of these; limit, boundary XIV; (her.) ordinary consisting of a vertical band XV; territory within determined bounds XVI. – (O)F. *pal*, var. of *pel* (mod. *pieu*) = Pr. *pal*, Sp., It. *palo*, Rum. *par* :– L. *pālu-s* stake (dim. *paxillus*) :– **pakslos* (cf. Gr. *pássalos* peg :– **pakjalos*), f. **pag-*, base of *pangere* fix (see PACT, COMPACT). See PEEL[1,3]. So **pale** vb. enclose with pales. XIV. – (O)F. *paler*, f. *pal*; surviving in **pa·l**ING[1] XV; cf. PALISADE.

pale[2] peil of whitish or ashen colour XIII (Cursor M.); faint, dim XIV. – OF. *pale*, *palle* (mod. *pâle*) – L. *pallidu-s*, whence also Pr. *pale*, Sp. *pálido*, It. *pallido* PALLID. So vb. XIV. – OF. *palir* (mod. *pâlir*), f. *pale*.

paletot pæ·lītou loose outer garment. XIX. – F. *paletot*, formerly †*pal(e)toc*, in ME. †*paltok* (XIV); of unkn. origin. ¶ Also in Sp. *paletoque*, in Breton *paltōk*.

palette pæ·lit artist's tablet to lay and mix his colours on. XVII. – F. *palette*, perh. – It. *paletta* (which has not, however, the artist's sense), dim. of *pala* shovel, blade, plate :– L. *pāla*; see PALLET[2], PEEL[3], -ETTE.

palfrey pō·lfri, pæ·lfri saddle-horse. XII. – OF. *palefrei* (mod. *palefroi*) :– medL. *palefrēdu-s*, for *paraverēdu-s* (v), f. Gr. *pará* beside, extra (see PARA-[1]) + late L. *verēdus* light horse, courier's horse (cf. late Gr. *párippos* led horse); *verēdus* is of Gaulish origin and is a comp. of Celtic **rēdā* (whence L. *ræda* chariot), rel. to RIDE; cf. W. *gorwydd* horse :– **upo|reidos*. ¶ *Paraverēdus* is repr. also in modified forms by Pr. *palafre*, Sp. *palafren*, Pg. *palafrem*, It. *palafreno*; it passed into Germ. and became the ordinary word for a horse, viz. MLG. *pered* (LG. *perd*), MDu. *pert*, *paert* (Du. *paard*), OHG. *pfarifrid*, *pferfrit* (G. *pferd*).

Pali pā·li the language used in the canonical books, etc., of the Buddhists. XVIII. Short for *pālibhāsā*, f. *pāli* line, canon + *bhāsā* language.

palikar pæ·likāɹ member of the band of a Greek or Albanian military chief. XIX (Byron). – modGr. *palikári, pallēkári*, dim. of Gr. *pállax, pállēx* youth (see FOAL).

palimpsest pæ·limpsest †material prepared for writing on and wiping out XVII; parchment, etc., in which the original writing has been erased to make place for a second XIX. – L. *palimpsestus* – Gr. *palímpsestos* (as sb. *-on*, sc. *biblíon* book), f. *pálin* again (cf. POLE[2], WHEEL) + *psestós*, pp. formation on *psên* rub smooth. Cf. F. *palimpseste* (XVI).

palindrome pæ·lindroum word or set of words that reads the same backwards as forwards. XVII. – Gr. *palíndromos* running back again, f. *pálin* again (see prec.) + *drom-, drameîn* run (cf. Skr. *drámati*).

palingenesia pæ:lindʒīnī·siə regeneration. XVII. medL. – Gr. *paliggenesíā*, f. *pálin* (see prec.) + *génesis* GENESIS. Also **palinge·nesy**. XVII. – F. See -IA[1], -Y[3].

palinode pæ·linoud song in which a poet retracts something said before, recantation. XVI. – F. †*palinode* or late L. *palinōdia* – Gr. *palinōidíā*, f. *pálin* (see prec.) + *ōidḗ* song (ODE).

pall[1] pōl A. (arch.) cloth, a cloth, esp. (a) rich cloth OE.; cloth spread on a coffin or hearse XV; B. (arch.) robe, mantle OE.; papal pallium XV; C. 'mantle' of cloud, mist, smoke XV. OE. *pæll* – L. *pallium* Greek mantle, philosopher's cloak, later in various eccl. uses; see PALLIUM.

pall[2] pōl †become dim or faint XIV (Gower); become vapid or stale XV (Lydg.); (fig.) become insipid XVIII; †in various trans. uses XIV (Gower). Aphetic of †*appall*, APPAL.

Palladian pəlei·diən pert. to the school of the It. architect Antonio *Palladio* (1518–80), who imitated ancient Roman architecture. XVIII (Pope, Gibbon). See -IAN.

palladium[1] pəlei·diəm image of Pallas in the citadel of Troy, on which the safety of the city depended XIV (Ch.); safeguard, protection XVI. – L. *palladium* – Gr. *palládion*, f. *Pallad-, Pallás* epithet of the goddess Athene.

palladium[2] pəlei·diəm metal of the platinum group. XIX. – modL.; so named by its discoverer Wollaston from the newly discovered asteroid *Pallas*; see prec. and -IUM.

pallet[1] pæ·lit (straw) mattress. XIV (Ch.). Late ME. *pail(l)et* – AN. *paillete* straw (cf. F. dial. *paillet* bundle of straw), f. *paille* straw :- L. *palea* chaff, straw, which has Balto-Sl. cogns. ¶ For the phonology cf. MALLET.

pallet[2] pæ·lit flat-bladed wooden instrument XVI; flat board; projection which engages with the tooth of a wheel XVIII. – (O)F. *palette*, dim. of *pale* spade, blade (with WF. vocalism, the regular repr. being *pelle*) :- L. *pāla* spade, shovel :- **pakslā*, rel. to *pālus* stake; see PALE[1], PEEL[3], PALETTE.

palliasse, paillasse pæ·liæs straw mattress. XVIII (both forms). – F. *paillasse* – It. *pagliaccio* :- Rom. **paleāceum*, f. L. *palea* (see PALLET[1]); adopted earlier in naturalized form in Sc. *pales, paillyes, pavilyeas* (XVI).

palliate pæ·lieit †cloak, conceal; alleviate (disease, etc.) XVI; disguise the enormity or offensiveness of; †mitigate XVII. f. pp. stem of late L. *palliāre* (*palliātus* cloaked, fig. protected, is earlier), f. PALLIUM; see -ATE[3]. Cf. (O)F. *pallier*. So **pallia·tion**. XVI. – (O)F. – medL. **pa·lliative**. XVI. – (O)F.

pallid pæ·lid wan, pale through death, sickness, etc. XVII. – L. *pallidus*, rel. to *pallēre* be pale; see FALLOW[2] and -ID[1]. So **pa·llor[2]**. XVII. – L.

pallium pæ·liəm large cloak XVI; woollen vestment worn by the pope and conferred by him on archbishops XVII; (zool.) mantle of a mollusc, etc. XIX. – L. *pallium*, rel. to *palla* long wide outer garment of Roman ladies, prob. of Gr. origin, but nothing appropriate is known. ¶ The eccl. vestment, consisting now of a circular band resting on the shoulders with a pendant back and front, is supposed to have developed from a mantle which came to be folded into a band.

pall-mall pælmæ·l, pelme·l †mallet used in the game (also so called) in which a ball was driven through an iron ring XVI; †alley in which this was played, (hence) name of an alley in London XVII, now *Pall Mall*. – F. †*pal(le) mail(le)* – It. *pallamaglio*, f. *palla* ball (collateral var. of *balla* BALL[1]) + *maglio* mallet; see MALL, MALLET.

palm[1] pām tree of the (chiefly tropical) family Palmæ or Palmaceæ; leaf or 'branch' of a palm tree OE.; branch or sprig of a tree substituted for the palm in Palm Sunday processions XIV. OE. *palm, palma, palme* = OS., OHG. *palma* (Du. *palm*, G. *palme*), ON. *pálmr*; CGerm. (exc. Gothic) – L. *palma* PALM[2] (the palm-leaf was likened to the hand with the fingers extended). In ME. the descendant of the OE. words coincided with the repr. of AN. (modF.) *palme*, OF. *paume*. **Palm Sunday** Sunday next before Easter, on which processions are held in which palms are carried. OE. *palmsunnandæġ*, tr. ecclL. *Dominica Palmarum*. Hence **palmy[1]** pā·mi abounding in palms XVII (Milton); flourishing XVII (Sh.).

palm[2] pām part of the hand between the fingers and the wrist; flat part of a deer's horn XIV; measure of length XV. ME. *paume* – (O)F. *paume* = Pr. *pauma*, Sp., It. *palma* :- L. *palma* palm of the hand, part of the trunk of a tree from which branches spring, palm-leaf, palm-tree (see prec.), rel. obscurely to Gr. *palámē* palm of the hand, Ir. *lám* hand, OE. *folm*, OS. *folmōs* pl., OHG. *folma* (cf. FEEL). ME. *paume*, through *paulme* (also OF.), was finally assim. to the L. Hence **palm** vb. XVII.

palma Christi pæ·lmə kristai castor-oil plant. XVI. modL., 'palm of Christ'; so named from the hand-shaped leaves; see PALM², CHRIST.

palmary pæ·lməri of the highest order. XVII. – L. *palmārius* that carries off the palm of victory, f. *palma* PALM¹; see -ARY.

palmate pæ·lmeit shaped like an open hand. XVIII. – L. *palmātus*, f. *palma* PALM²; see -ATE².

palmer pā·məɹ pilgrim from the Holy Land, carrying a palm-branch as a sign XIII; destructive hairy caterpillar, orig. applied to those that migrate or move about in swarms (more fully *p. worm* Joel i 4, Geneva Bible 1560, tr. Heb. *gāzām* prob. locust) XVI. – AN. *palmer, -our*, OF. *palmier* = Sp. *palmero*, etc. :– medL. *palmārius* (XII), f. *palma* PALM¹; see -ER.

palmette pæ·lmet ornament with divisions resembling a palm-leaf. XIX. – F. *palmette*, dim. of *palme* PALM¹; see -ETTE.

palmetto pælme·tou small species of palm. XVI (*palmito*). – Sp. *palmito* dwarf fan-palm, dim. of *palma* PALM¹; later assim. to It. dims. in *-etto*.

palmiped pæ·lmiped having palmate feet. XVII. – L. *palmiped-, -pēs*, f. *palma* PALM²+ *pēs* FOOT.

palmistry pā·mistri divination by inspecting the palm of the hand. XV (*pawmestry*, Lydg.). f. PALM²+*-estry*, of obscure formation, alt. to *-istry* XVI perh. after *sophistry*. Hence by back-formation **pa·lmister**. XV, **pa·lm**IST. XIX; cf. *sophister, sophist*.

palmitic pælmi·tik (chem.) acid contained in palm-oil. XIX. – F., arbitrarily f. *palme* PALM¹; see -IC. Hence **pa·lmit**ATE¹.

palmyra pælmaiə·rə palm, Borassus flabelliformis. XVII. Formerly *palmero, palmeira* – Pg. *palmeira*, Sp. *palmera*, It. *palmero*, f. *palma* PALM¹ (with suffix proper to tree-names); the present sp. suggests assim. to *Palmyra*, name of a city in Syria.

palpable pæ·lpəbl tangible, sensible XIV (Ch.); plainly observable XV (Lydg.); evident, manifest XVII. – late L. *palpābilis*, f. *palpāre* touch soothingly, prob. ult. rel. to FEEL; see -ABLE. So **palp**A·TION handling. XV (Caxton). – F. or L.

palpebral pæ·lpibrəl pert. to the eyelids. XIX. – late L. *palpebrālis*, f. *palpebra* eyelid, rel. to *palpāre*; see prec. and -AL¹.

palpitate pæ·lpiteit beat rapidly and strongly. XVII. f. pp. stem of L. *palpitāre*, frequent. of *palpāre*; see PALPABLE, -ATE³. So **palpit**A·TION. XVII. – L. Cf. F. *palpiter*, *palpitation* (XVI).

palsgrave pɔ̄·lzgreiv count palatine. XVI. – early Du. *paltsgrave* (mod. *paltsgraaf*), f. *palts* palatinate (see PALACE)+†*grave, graaf* count, GRAVE⁶.

palstave pɔ̄·lsteiv form of celt fitting into a split handle. XIX. – Da. *paalstav* :– ON. *pálstafr*, *páll* hoe, spade (– L. *pālus* PALE¹)+*stafr* STAVE.

palsy pɔ̄·lzi paralysis. XIII. ME. *palesi, parlesi* – (O)F. *paralisie* (AN. *parlesie*, Cursor M.) – Rom. **paralisia* (cf. Sp. *perlesia*, It. *paralisia*), for L. *paralysis* – Gr. *parálusis* PARALYSIS. Hence **pa·lsi**ED¹ adj. XVI.

palter pɔ̄·ltəɹ †mumble, babble; †jumble XVI; shuffle in statement or dealing XVII (Sh.). Of the form of a frequent. or iterative in -ER⁴, but the base is unkn.; perh. ult. rel. to next. Cf. †*pelt* haggle, †*pelter* peddling person XVI.

paltry pɔ̄·ltri trashy, worthless. XVI. adj. use (cf. *trumpery*) of (dial.) *paltry* sb. (XVI) rubbish, trash; cf. MLG. *palter-* in *palterlappen* rags, LG. *paltrig* ragged, torn, and prec. Parallel synon. formations are dial. *pelt* (XVI), †*pelting* adj. (XVI, canting term), *peltry* XVI (esp. Sc.); perh. of LG. origin.

paludal pæ·ljudəl, pæljū·dəl pert. to marshes. XIX. f. L. *palūd-, palūs* marsh (cf. synon. Skr. *palvalam*), perh. f. base meaning 'wash, pour'. So **palustr**AL pəlʌ·strəl. XVII. f. L. *palustris*, f. *palūs*. See -AL¹.

paludament pæljū·dəment military or royal cloak. XVII. – L. *paludāmentum*, which, with *paludātus* cloaked, is an ancient ritual term, f. *Paluda* epithet of Minerva; see -MENT.

paly pei·li (her.) divided by vertical lines (palewise). XV. – (O)F. *palé*, f. *pal* PALE¹; see -Y⁵.

pam pæm knave of clubs, as at loo; card game in which this was the highest trump. XVII. abbrev. – F. *pamphile*, which is more nearly repr. by Sc. *pamphie, pawmie*; presumably ult. based on L. proper name *Pamphilus*, Gr. *Pámphilos*.

pampa pæ·mpə, usu. pl. **pa·mpas** vast treeless plain in S. America. XVIII. – Sp. *pampa* – Quechua *pampa* plain.

pamper pæ·mpəɹ †cram with food, feed luxuriously XIV; over-indulge XVI. In ME. also in pp. *forpampred* (Ch.); frequent. (see -ER⁴) of synon. †*pamp* (XIV), dial. *pomp*; prob. of Low Du. origin; cf. G. dial. *pampen, pampfen* cram, gorge, WFlem. *pamperen*, perh. f. nasalized var. of the base of PAP².

pamphlet pæ·mflit small treatise of smaller compass than a 'book' XIV (T. Usk); short treatise or booklet on a matter of current or temporary interest XVI. Late ME. *pamflet, paunflet*, in AL. *panfletus* (Richard de Bury, 1344); generalized use of *Pamphilet, Panflet* (in OF. and MDu. respectively, XIII), vernacular name of the L. amatory poem 'Pamphilus seu de Amore' (XII); for the termination cf. *Catonet* the Distichs of Cato, *Esopet* the Fables of Æsop. ¶ Adopted from Eng. in F. XVIII, whence in G. Hence **pamphlet**EER¹. XVII, earlier †*pamphleter*. XVI.

pan pæn A. broad shallow vessel OE.; †skull (*brain pan*) XIV; B. depression in the ground XVI; C. hard substratum of the soil XVIII. OE. *panne* = OFris., OS. *panna*, (M)LG., MDu. *panne* (Du. *pan*), OHG. *phanna*, *pfanna* (G. *pfanne*) :- CWGerm. **panna* (Scand. forms are prob. from LG.). Initial *p* and HG. *pf* suggest adoption from a foreign source at an early date, and deriv. from L. *patina* (see PATEN) has been proposed. (Lith. and Slav. forms are from Germ.) Hence **pan** vb. wash (gravel, etc.) in a pan, separate the gold; (usu. with *out*) yield gold when so washed; also fig. XIX (*c.*1850). So **pa·n**CAKE XV, prob. after MLG. *pannekōke* (Du. *pannekoek*) = OHG. *pfankuocho* (G. *pfannkuchen*, whence Magyar *pancé*, Rum. *pancovă*); F. *pannequet* is from Eng.

pan- pæn comb. form of Gr. *pas*, n. *pan* all (cf. PANTO-), which was used freely in Gr. with adjs. in the sense 'wholly, completely, of all, by all', and less freq. with sbs. meaning 'all', 'complete' (cf. PANACEA, PANCREAS, PANDECT, PANOPLY, etc.); extensively used in later XIX to express the notion of universality in political or religious activities, as *Pan-African*, *Pan-Anglican* (modL. *Pan-Anglicus* XVII), *Pan-Britannic* (XVIII), *pan-denominational*, *Panslavism*; also in other miscellaneous comps. of a more or less techn. character.

panacea pænəsī·ə universal remedy. XVI. – L. *panacēa* – Gr. *panákeia*, f. *panakḗs* all-healing, f. *pan-* (see prec.) + base of *ákos* remedy; see -A[1].

panache pənā·ʃ plume of feathers XVI; swagger XX. – F. *panache* – It. *pennacchio* :- late L. *pinnāculum*, dim. of *pinna* feather (cf. PINNACLE).

panada pənā·də dish of pulped bread with flavouring. XVI. – Sp. *panada* = Pr. *panada*, It. *panata*, repr. Rom. **panātā*, f. *pānis* bread (cf. PANTRY); see -ADE.

panama pænəmā· name of a town and state in Central America and of the isthmus joining N. and S. America, misapplied to a hat which originated in Jijipapa, Ecuador (hence named *jijipapa* in Latin America). XIX.

pancratium, -ion pænkrēi·ʃ[i]əm, -ən athletic contest combining wrestling and boxing. XVII (Holland). L. – Gr. *pankrátion*, f. *pan-* PAN- + *krátos* strength, mastery.

pancreas pæ·ŋkriæs gland discharging a digestive secretion, sweetbread. XVI. – modL. *pancreas* – Gr. *págkreas*, f. *pan-* PAN- + *kréas* flesh (see RAW). So **pancrea·t**IC. XVII. – modL.

panda pæ·ndə racoon-like animal of the Himalayas. XIX. – Nepali name.

Pandean, -æan pændī·ən pert. to Pan or the pipes reputedly invented by him. XIX. irreg. f. *Pan*, Gr. rural deity + -EAN.

pandect pæ·ndekt compendium of Roman law made by order of the emperor Justinian; complete treatise or digest. XVI. – F. *pandecte* or L. *pandecta*, *-tes* – Gr. *pandéktēs* (pl. *pandéktai* as a title), f. *pan-* PAN- + *dékhesthai* receive (cf. DECENT).

pandemic pænde·mik (of a disease) prevalent over the whole of an area. XVII. f. Gr. *pándēmos*, f. *pan-* PAN- + *dêmos* people (cf. DEMOCRACY); see -IC.

pandemonium pændimou·niəm abode of all devils XVII ('*Pandæmonium*, the high Capital Of Satan and his Peers' Milton 'P.L.' I 756); haunt of great wickedness, (later) place or gathering of lawless violence XVIII. modL., f. Gr. *pan-* PAN- + *daímōn* DEMON; see -IUM. ¶ Hence F. *pandémonium* (*-ion*, Voltaire), It., Sp. *pandemonio*.

pander pæ·ndəɹ go-between in clandestine amours XVI (Lyndesay); one who ministers to base passions or designs XVII. Earliest form *pandar*; appellative use of *Pandare* – It. *Pandaro* (– L. *Pandarus*, Gr. *Pándaros*), name used by Boccaccio and thereafter by Chaucer for the man who procured for Troilus the love of Criseyde (Griseida). The sp. *pander* is due to assoc. with -ER[1]. Hence vb. play the p. *to*. XVII (Sh., Dekker).

pandiculation pæ:ndikjulei·ʃən stretching accompanying yawning. XVII. f. L. *pandiculāt-*, *-ārī*, f. **pandiculus*, *pandus* (with dim. el.) wide apart or open, rel. to *pandere* stretch; see PASS, PACE[1], -ATION.

pandora pændɔə·rə, **pandore** pændɔə·ɹ stringed musical instrument of the cither type. XVI (Morley, Drayton). Also †*pandola*, †*pandure*; – It. †*pandora*, *-iera*, *pandura*, (whence F. *pandore*) – late L. *pandūra* – Gr. *pandoûra*, *-doúrā* three-stringed lute, prob. of Oriental origin. Cf. BANDORE, MANDOLINE.

pandour pæ·nduəɹ (pl.) local force organized in 1741 by Franz Freiherr von der Trenck in Croatia to clear the country of robbers; their rapacity made the word synon. with 'brutal Croatian soldier'. XVIII. – F. *pandour*, G. *pandur* – Serbo-Croatian *pandur* constable, bailiff, summoner, mounted policeman, guardian of the public peace, of fields, etc. (whence Magyar, Rum. *pandur*, Turk. *pandul*), prob. – medL. *banderius* guard of cornfields and vineyards, apparitor (cf. BANNER).

pane pein A. †piece of cloth XIII (Cursor M.); B. section or side (now only in some techn. uses) XIV; C. division of a window XV; panel XVI. ME. *pan*, later *pane* – (O)F. *pan* = Pr. *pan*, Sp. *paño*, It. *panno* :- L. *pannus* cloth, piece of cloth. Sense A survives in COUNTERPANE.

panegyric pænidʒi·rik laudatory discourse. XVII (S. Daniel) – F. *panégyrique* – L. *panēgyricus* public eulogy, sb. use of adj. – Gr. *panēgurikós* pert. to public assembly, f. *panḗguris* general assembly, f. *pan-* PAN- +

-ēguris = *agorá* assembly (cf. CATEGORY). So **panegy·rICAL** adj. XVI (Harvey, Nashe). **panegy·rIST.** XVII (Camden); so F. **pa·negyrIZE.** XVII. – Gr. *panēgurízein.* **panegyrY**[3]. XVI.

panel pæ·n(ə)l piece of cloth placed under the saddle XIII (Cursor M.); saddle consisting of a rough pad XVI; piece of parchment (attached to a writ) on which names of jurors were written, (hence) list of jurymen, jury (cf. EMPANEL) XIV; section of a fence XV; compartment of a door, etc. XVI; thin board used for a painting XVIII; large size of photograph XIX. – OF. *panel* piece of cloth, saddle cushion, piece (mod. *panneau*) = It. *pannello* :– Rom. **pannellu-s*, dim. of *pannus* PANE; see -EL[2].

pang pæŋ brief keen spasm of pain. XVI. In earliest use *pange(s) of deth, panges of child bed*; unexpl. var. of earlier †*pronge* (XV, *prongys of deth, wommanys pronge*), †*prange*; but cf. the OE. variants *pætiġ, prættiġ* PRETTY, *spǣċ, sprǣċ* SPEECH. The forms in *pr-* corr. to MLG. *prange* pinching, early Du. *prang(h)e* oppression, constraint, shackle, Du., LG. *prangen* pinch, Goth. *anapraggan* oppress, ME. *prangled* pressed tightly, Sc. *prang* (varying with *pang*) pack tight, cram.

pangolin pæŋgou·lin scaly ant-eater. XVIII (Goldsmith, after Buffon). – Malay *penggōling* roller, f. *peng-* (denominative element) + *gōling* roll, with ref. to its habit of rolling itself up (cf. 'Javanensibus et aliis populis orientalibus *Panggoeling*, quæ vox *Convolutorem* notat', Seba, 1734).

panic[1] pæ·nik millet. XV. – L. *pānīcum* (whence F. *panic*, It. *panico*, Rum. *părinc*; also OE. *panic*, OHG. *pfenih*, G. *fenich, fench*, etc.), rel. to *pānus* thread wound on a bobbin, swelling, ear of millet – Gr. *pênos* web (*pēníon* bobbin).

panic[2] pæ·nik adj. in *p. fear*, etc. Such as was attributed to the god Pan, a Gr. rural deity, identified by the Romans with Faunus XVII; sb. †contagious emotion so ascribed XVII; sudden and extreme alarm XVIII. – F. *panique*, corr. to Sp., It. *panico*, G. *panisch* – modL. *pānicus* (in *p. terror* tr. πανικὸν δεῖμα, τάραχος πανικός, θόρυβος ὁ καλούμενος πανικός) – Gr. *pānikós* (also n. *-ón* as sb.), f. *Pā̂n* name of a deity part man part goat, whose appearance or unseen presence caused terror and to whom woodland noises were attributed; see -IC. Hence **pa·nickY**[1]. XIX.

panicle pæ·nikl compound (racemose) inflorescence. XVI. – L. *pānicula*, dim. of *pānus*; see PANIC[1], -CLE.

panification pæ:nifikei·ʃən conversion into bread. XVIII. – F. *panification*, f. *panifier* make into bread, f. *pānis* bread (cf. PASTURE); see -FICATION.

panjandrum pændʒæ·ndrəm nonsense word, similating comps. of PAN-, occurring in the farrago of nonsense composed by Samuel Foote in 1755 to test the memory of the retired actor Macklin (see 'Quarterly Review' 1854, xcv 516); hence used as a mock title (orig. 'the Grand Panjandrum') for a pretended great personage.

pannage pæ·nidʒ mast on which swine feed XIV (*pownage*, Ch.); (right of) feeding swine in a forest XV. – OF. *pannage, paan-, pasn-* (mod. *panage*) :– medL. *pāstiōnāticum*, f. *pāstiō(n-)* feeding, pasturing, f. *pāst-*, pp. stem of *pāscere*; see PASTURE, -AGE.

pannier pæ·niəɹ basket, esp. a large one (as carried by a beast of burden, etc.). XIII (Havelok). – (O)F. *panier*, †*pannier* = Pr. *panier*, Sp. *panero* :– L. *pānārium* bread-basket, f. *pānis* bread, prob. rel. to *pāscere* PASTURE.

pannikin pæ·nikin small metal drinking-mug. XIX. f. PAN, after CANNIKIN.

panoply pæ·nəpli complete suit of armour. XVII (used earlier in Gr. or latinized form). – F. or modL. – Gr. *panopliā* full armour of a HOPLITE, f. *pan-* PAN-+*hópla* arms.

panopticon pænɔ·ptikɔn Bentham's name for a circular prison in which warders could at all times observe their prisoners XVIII; show-room XIX. f. Gr. *pan-* PAN-+*optikón*, n. of *optikós* OPTIC (cf. *pánoptos* fully visible). ¶ Earlier (1768) applied to an optical instrument.

panorama pænərà·mə picture of a scene unfolded so as to show the parts in succession XVIII; (fig.) continuous passing scene XIX. Invented by Robert Barker *c.*1789 (who in his patent of 1787 called it 'La nature à coup d'œil', i.e. 'nature at a glance'), f. Gr. *pan-* PAN-+*hórāma* view, f. *horân.*

pansy pæ·nzi common name of Viola tricolor. XV (*pensee*, later *pensy, paunsie*). – (O)F. *pensée* thought, fancifully applied to the plant, f. *penser* think = Pr. *pesar*, Sp. *pensar*, It. *pensare* – L. *pēnsāre* weigh, ponder, consider, in Rom. think (cf. POISE).

pant pænt breathe quickly and hard. XV. – AN. **panter*, based on OF. *pantaisier* be agitated, gasp, pant = Pr. *pantaisar*, Cat. *panteixar*, Pg. *pantegar* jeer, banter :– Rom. **pantasiāre*, for **phantasiāre* be oppressed as with nightmare, gasp with oppression – Gr. *phantasioûn* cause to imagine, make game of, f. *phantasiā* PHANTASY. Hence **pant** sb. XVI. ¶ The syll. *pant-* was taken as a base for the formation of other F. words, as *panteler* pant, *pantoier* gasp, whence *pantoiement* asthma in hawks; perh. first from the sb. and adj. *pantois*, †*pantais* (whence Eng. †*pantais*), in which the second syll. was apprehended as a suffix.

pantaleon pentæ·liən large dulcimer named after the inventor (1705) *Pantaleon* Hebenstreit. XVIII.

pantalet(te)s pæntəle·ts (chiefly U.S.) loose drawers, etc. XIX. f. next + -ETTE.

pantaloon pæntəlū·n Venetian character in Italian comedy represented as a lean and foolish old man XVI; †(pl.) breeches or trousers in fashion after the Restoration XVII (Evelyn, Butler); tight-fitting trousers which superseded knee-breeches XVIII; trousers in general (esp. U.S.) XIX. – F. *pantalon* (XVI) – It. *pantalone* 'a covetous yet amorous old dotard, properly applied in Comedies to a Venetian' (Torriano), alleged to be appellative use of the name of *san Pantal(e)one* patron saint of Venice. Cf. COLUMBINE.

pantechnicon pænte·knikən name of a bazaar of miscellaneous artistic work, intended to be held in a building in Motcomb Street, Belgrave Square, London, which became a large warehouse for furniture; (hence, short for *p. van*) a furniture-removing van. XIX. f. Gr. *pan-* PAN- + *tekhnikón*, n. of *technikós* TECHNICAL.

pantheist pæ·nþiist adherent of the doctrine that God and the universe are identical. XVIII (1705). First used by John Toland (1670–1722), author of 'Christianity not Mysterious', 1696; f. Gr. *pan* all + *theós* god; see PAN-, THEIST. Hence **pa·ntheISM**. XVIII. ¶ F. *panthéisme, -iste* (1712) are from Eng.

pantheon pæ·nþiən, pænþī·ən sacred building in ancient Rome dedicated to all the gods XIV; habitation of all the gods, deities collectively XVI; applied to modern buildings resembling the Pantheon in Rome XVIII. ME. *panteon* – medL. *panteon*; adopted afresh XVI – L. *pantheon* – Gr. *pántheion*, f. *pan-* PAN- + *theîos* divine, *theós* god (see THEISM).

panther pæ·nþəɹ leopard (but in early use with vague reference) XIII; puma, cougar, jaguar XVIII. ME. *panter(e)* – OF. *pantere* (mod. *panthère*) – L. *panthēra* – Gr. *pánthēr*, which was applied to various spotted Felidæ (an Oriental origin has been suspected and Skr. *puṇḍarīkas* tiger has been compared). ¶ The analysis of the Gr. word as *pan-* all + *thḗr* beast gave rise to many fancies and fables.

pantile pæ·ntail (prop.) roofing tile curved to an ogee shape ~. XVII. f. PAN + TILE, prob. after Du. *dakpan* 'roof-pan' (cf. G. *dachpfanne, pfannenziegel* 'pantile').

panto- pæ·ntou, -tŏ before a vowel **pant-**, repr. Gr. *pant(o)-*, comb. form of *pas, pan*, g. *pantós* all (see PAN-).

pantograph pæ·ntŏgràf instrument for the mechanical copying of a design. XVIII. – F. *pantographe* (Bion 1723, who has the erron. form *pento-*), f. Gr. *panto-* + *-gráphos* (see prec. and -GRAPH); cf. 'Pantographice, seu Ars Delineandi res quaslibet per parallelogrammum' by C. Scheiner, 1631. ¶ Various incorrect forms have been used, viz. *pento-, -e-, panta-, panti-*.

pantomime pæ·ntəmaim ancient Roman actor who performed in dumb show XVII (earlier in L. form); dramatic entertainment by gestures to a musical accompaniment; performance of a dramatized tale followed by a transformation scene and clowning XVIII. – F. *pantomime* (XVI) or L. *pantomīmus* – Gr. *pantómīmos* adj. and sb.; see PANTO-, MIME; abbrev. **pa·nto.** So **pantomi·mIC**. XVII. – L.

pantry pæ·ntri room in a house, etc., in which provisions, dining-plate and china, etc., are kept. XIII. – AN. *panetrie*, OF. *paneterie*, f. *panetier* (whence Eng. †*panter* XIII, later †*pant(e)ler* XIV, †*panterer* XV) = Pr. *panetier*, Sp. *panadero*, Pg. *padeiro* baker – Rom. **pānātārius* (in medL. *pāne-, pānitārius*), for *pānārius* (in late L.) bread-seller, f. *pānis* bread (:– **păsnis*, rel. to PASTURE); see -RY.

pants pænts (U.S.) trousers; (in British use) drawers. XIX. Shortening of pl. of PANTALOON.

pap[1] pæp teat, nipple. XII (Orm). ME. *pappe*, prob. immed. from Scand. (cf. Sw. and Norw. dial. *pappe*), ult. f. an imit. base **pap-* expressing blowing out the cheeks and the noise of sucking; cf. L. *papilla*, late L. *papula* nipple, Lith. *pãpas* teat, Lett. *papa* bladder. Cf. next.

pap[2] pæp soft or semi-liquid food for infants. XV. prob. – (M)LG. *pappe*, corr. to MG. *pap* (G. *pappe*), MDu. *pappe*, Du. *pap*, prob. – medL. *pappa* (cf. OF., Sp., Pg. *papa*, It. *pappa*), f. L. *pappāre* eat (whence OF. *paper*, Pr., Sp. *papar*, Rum. *păpa*), ult. derived from baby language (cf. L. *pap(p)a*, used by infants in calling for food; cf. 'cum cibum ac potionem buas ac pappas vocent', Varro).

papa pəpā· father. XVII. – F. *papa* (whence in other Rom. langs.) – late L. *pāpa* – Gr. *páppas, pápas* child's word for father (esp. in voc., as *páppa phíl'* father dear, 'Odyssey' VI 57), shortened *pâ(s)*. At first, like G. *papá* (XVII), in courtly and polite use it remained fashionable till early XIX; subsequently restricted to children's use, but now gen. discarded. Shortened to **pa** pā (dial.) XIX. The var. *pa·ppa* (XVIII) survives in U.S. POPPA, abbrev. **pop.** Cf. POPE.

papacy pei·pəsi office of pope XIV (Gower); papal system XVI. – medL. *pāpātia*, f. *pāpa* POPE; see -ACY. So **pa·PAL**[1]. XIV (Gower). – (O)F. – medL.

papaveraceous pəpeivərei·ʃəs of the poppy family. XIX. f. modL. (bot. family) *Papāverāceæ*, f. *papāver* POPPY; see -ACEOUS.

papaw pəpɔ̄· fruit of the S. Amer. tree Carica Papaya. XVI. Earlier *papaye*, and in foreign forms; – Sp. *papaya*, Pg. *papayo* (whence F. *papaye*) – Carib; the change to *papaw* (XVII) is unexplained.

paper pei·pəɹ substance made of interlaced and compressed fibre for writing, drawing, or printing on, etc.; sheet of this containing a document, etc. XIV; short for *newspaper*; essay, article XVII; set of examination questions XIX. Late ME. *papir* – AN. *papir*, (O)F. *papier* (whence MLG., MHG. *papīr*, G. *papier*, Icel. *pappír*), corr. to Pr. *papier*, Sp. *papel*, It. *papiro* – L. *papȳrus* – Gr. *pápūros* PAPYRUS. Hence **paper** vb. XVI. **paper-hanging.** XVII, **paper-money.** XVII.

papier mâché pæ·piei mæ·ʃei paper pulp shaped by moulding. XVIII. Not of F. origin, though composed of F. words, viz. *papier* PAPER and *mâché*, pp. of *mâcher* chew :– L. *masticāre* MASTICATE. Cf. *équestrienne*, *sacque*.

papilionaceous pəpi:liŏnei·ʃəs like a butterfly. XVII. – modL. *papilionāceus*, f. L. *pāpiliō(n-)* butterfly; see PAVILION, -ACEOUS.

papilla pəpi·lə nipple-like protuberance. XVIII. L., dim. of *papula* (see PAP[1]). So **papi·llARY** pæ·piləri, pəpi·ləri. XVII.

papist pei·pist adherent of the Pope or the papal system, Roman Catholic. XVI. – F. *papiste* or modL. *pāpista*, f. ecclL. *pāpa* POPE; see -IST. Hence **papi·stIC(AL)** pəpi·s-, **pa·pistRY.** XVI. So (by suffix-alt.) **pa·pISH**[1] papistical, popish XVI; (dial.) papist XVII.

papoose pəpū·s. N. Amer. Indian child. XVII. Algonkin (Narragansett *papoos*, Pequot *pouppous*).

papoosh pəpū·ʃ Oriental slipper. XVII. – Pers. *pāpōsh* BABOUCHE; the Turk. *pābutch* is repr. by *pabouch* (XVII).

pappus pæ·pəs (bot.) downy appendage on fruits. XVIII. modL. – Gr. *páppos* (i) grandfather, (ii) down on plants. So **pa·ppOSE**[1]. XVII. – modL.

papyrus pəpaiə·rəs, pl. **-i** ai kind of sedge from which ancient writing material was made XIV (Wycl. Bible); writing material so prepared XVIII. – L. *papȳrus* – Gr. *pápūros* paper-rush, of unkn. (prob. Oriental) origin; cf. PAPER. The comb. form is **papyro-,** as in **papyro·LOGY** (1898), **papyro·LOGIST** (earlier *papyrographer* 1896).

par[1] pāɹ equality of value, equal footing; recognized value of currency, etc. XVII; average amount XVIII. – L. *pār* equal (cf. PAIR, PEER).

par[2] pāɹ in F. expressions, e.g. ME. *par charite* (XIII) out of Christian love, *par compaignie* for company's sake (XIV, Ch., Gower), mod. *par excellence* (XVI) above all others of the kind. – (O)F. *par* (= Pr., Cat. *per*, Rum. *p(r)e*) :– Rom. **pra*, **per ad* (L. *per* PER-, *ad* AD-). See also PARDIE.

para pā·rə small Turkish coin. XVII. – Turk. – Pers. *pārah* piece, portion, coin so called.

para-[1] pæ·rə, pəræ· before a vowel or *h* usu. *par-*, repr. comb. form of Gr. *pará* prep. by the side of, alongside, past, beyond, as in PARABLE, PARADIGM, PARADOX, PARALLEL, PARENTHESIS, PAROCHIAL, PARODY, etc. Also in numerous techn. comps. in which it had cogn. advb. and adj. uses, as 'to one side', 'amiss', 'irregular(ly)', 'wrong(ly)'.

para-[2] pæ·rə repr. F. *para-* – It. *para-*, imper. of *parare* ward off :– L. *parāre* PREPARE; orig. in It. words, e.g. *parapetto* PARAPET, *parasole* PARASOL, but adopted and extended in French, e.g. PARACHUTE, *paracrotte* mudguard, *parapluie* umbrella.

parabasis pəræ·bəsis in ancient Gr. comedy, choric song addressed to the audience. XIX. – Gr. *parábasis*, f. *parabaínein* go aside, step forward; see PARA-[1], COME.

parable pæ·rəbl (arch.) similitude, dark saying, proverb; fictitious narrative or allegory for teaching spiritual truth. XIV. ME. *parabile*, *parable* – (O)F. *parabole* – L. *parabola* comparison, in ChrL. allegory, proverb, discourse, speech – Gr. *parabolḗ* comparison, analogy, proverb, f. *parabállein* put alongside, compare, f. *pará* PARA-[1]+*bállein* cast, throw (cf. BALLISTA). See also PALAVER, PARABOLA, PAROLE.

parabola pəræ·bələ (geom.) plane curve formed by the intersection of a cone by a plane parallel to a side of the cone. XVI (Digges). – modL. – Gr. *parabolḗ* application, spec. in geom. of a given area to a given straight line, f. *parabállein* (see prec.). So **parabolIC** pærəbɔ·lik pert. to parable, metaphorical XVII. – late L. – late Gr.; pert. to a parabola XVIII. **parabo·lICAL** in both senses. XVI. ¶ To the earlier Gr. geometricians, who investigated only sections perpendicular to the surface of the cone, the p. was known as ὀρθογωνίου κώνου τομή = sectio rectanguli coni, the use of παραβολή in this sense (due to Apollonius of Perga, II B.C.) referring to the fact that a rectangle on the abscissa being equal to the square on the ordinate, can be 'applied' to the latus rectum without either excess (as in the hyperbola) or defect (as in the ellipse).

Paracelsian pærəse·lsiən pert. to (follower of) Theophrast Bombast von Hohenheim (1490–1541), Swiss physician, chemist, and natural philosopher, known as *Paracelsus*, a name supposed to be based on PARA-[1] and L. *celsus* high, thus loosely repr. *von Hohenheim* ('high dwelling'). XVI. ¶ To Paracelsus is due the invention of the words *gnome*, *laudanum*, *sylph*.

parachute pæ·rəʃūt umbrella-like apparatus used for descending from a great height. XVIII. – F. *parachute*, f. PARA-[2]+*chute* fall (see CHUTE).

Paraclete pæ·rəklīt title of the Holy Ghost. XV. – (O)F. *paraclet* – ChrL. *paraclētus*, also *-clītus* (Tertullian) – Gr. *paráklētos* advocate, intercessor, f. *parakaleîn* call to one's aid, f. *pará* PARA-[1] + *kaleîn* call (cf. CLAIM). ¶ *Paráklētos* was assoc. by the Gr. Fathers with the Hellenistic sense 'console, comfort' (cf. *paraklḗtōr* comforter).

parade pəreiˑd show, display; mustering of troops for inspection, etc.; place of such assembly; public square or promenade; †parry. XVII. – F. *parade* – Sp. *parada* and It. *parata* (i) display, (ii) parry, (iii) pulling-up of a horse – Rom. **parāta*, sb. use of fem. pp. of L. *parāre* PREPARE, which in Rom. acquired specific applications repr. in the Fr., Sp., and It. words given above; see -ADE. Hence as vb. XVII.

paradigm pæˑrədaim, pæˑrədim pattern, example XV; (gram.) example of the inflexions of a class of words XVI. – late L. *paradīgma* – Gr. *parádeigma* example, f. *paradeiknúnai* show side by side, f. *pará* PARA-[1] + *deiknúnai* show (see TEACH). Cf. F. *paradigme* (XVI).

paradise pæˑrədais garden of Eden; Heaven XII; paradisaical place or state XIII; park, pleasure-ground; (after Luke xxiii 43, etc.) the Intermediate State XVII. ME. *paradis*, also *parais* (XII–XV) – (O)F. *paradis*, also in semi-pop. form *parais* – ChrL. *paradīsus* – Gr. *parádeisos*, first used by Xenophon of the parks of Persian kings and nobles, (hence) garden, orchard, in LXX and N.T. Eden, abode of the blessed – Av. *pairidaēza* enclosure, f. *pairi* around, PERI- + *diz* mould, form (see DOUGH), whence Arm. *pardes*, late Heb. *pardēs*, Pers. (Arab.) *firdaus* garden. Cf. PARVIS. Hence **paradisa**IC -eiˑik. XVIII, **paradisa·**ICAL. XVII; after *Judaic*, *Mosaic*. **paradisi**AC -iˑsiæk, **paradisi**ACAL -aiˑəkl. XVII. – ChrL. *paradīsiacus* – Gr. *paradeisiakós*. ¶ Variants of greater or less currency are *paradisean* XVII, *paradisial* XVIII, *paradisian* XVII, *paradisic* XVIII, *paradisical* XVII.

parados pæˑrədɔs (fortif.) elevation of earth behind a fortified place. XIX. – F. *parados*, f. PARA-[2] + *dos* back :– L. *dorsum* (see DORSAL).

paradox pæˑrədɔks statement or tenet contrary to received opinion; proposition on the face of it (in pop. use, actually) self-contradictory XVI; phenomenon conflicting with preconceived notions XVII. – late L. *paradoxum*, *-doxon*, sb. use of n. of *paradoxus* – Gr. *parádoxos*, f. *pará* PARA-[1] + *dóxā* opinion (cf. DOGMA). Cf. F. *paradoxe* 1580 (Montaigne). Hence **parado·x**ICAL. XVI (in *paradoxically*, Sidney; earlier *paradoxal*, Dee).

paraffin pæˑrəfin orig. colourless or white substance being a mixture of hydrocarbons; spec. a hydrocarbon of the methane series (*p. oil*, kerosene). XIX. – G. *paraffin* (Reichenbach in 'Journal für Chemie und Physik' lix 456, 1830), f. L. *parum* too little, barely (see FEW) + *affīnis* related (see AFFINITY); so named with ref. to its neutral quality and the small affinity it possesses for other bodies.

paragogic pærəgɔˑdʒik (of a letter or syllable) added to a word. XVIII. – modL. *paragōgicus*, f. late L. *paragōgē* – Gr. *paragōgḗ* derivation, addition to the end of a syllable, f. *pará* past, beyond, PARA-[1] + *agōgḗ* leading (cf. ACT). Also **parago·g**ICAL. XVII.

paragon pæˑrəgən pattern of excellence; †match, mate; †comparison; perfect diamond XVI; †double camlet; †black marble XVII; size of printing type XVIII. – F. †*paragon*, now *parangon* (XVI) in the above senses (whence also Sp. *para(n)gón*) – It. *paragone* (XIII) touchstone, comparison – medGr. *parakónē* whetstone, f. Gr. *parakonân* sharpen against, f. *pará* PARA-[1] + *akónē* whetstone, f. **ak-* (see ACID, etc.).

paragraph pæˑrəgràf character ¶ or ⁋ marking a section of a discourse, etc.; passage or section of a book, etc. XVI; short passage or notice in a journal XVII. – (O)F. *paragraphe* or medL. *paragraphus*, *-um* – Gr. *parágraphos* short horizontal stroke written below the beginning of a line in which a break of sense occurs, passage so marked, f. *pará* by the side + *-graphos* written, *gráphein* write; see PARA-[1], GRAPHIC.

parakeet pærəkīˑt small bird of the parrot kind. XVI. Three types are repr.: (i) *parroket*, *-quet*, *perroquet* XVI, (ii) *paraquito*, *-quetto* XVI, (iii) *par(r)akeet* XVII, the last being anglicized forms of the former, which are – (O)F. *paroquet* (mod. *perroquet* parrot), It. *parrocchetto*, *perrochetto*, Sp. *periquito*, the interrelation of which is uncertain. The coexistence of WF. *perrot* (see PARROT), F. *perruche* parakeet (XVII), Guernsey *perrounet* parrot, Sp. *perico* parakeet, suggests that all the forms may be ult. based on a dim. of the name 'Peter' (F. *Pierrot*, Sp. *Perico*).

parallax pæˑrəlæks (astron.) apparent displacement or difference in the apparent position of an object. XVII. – F. *parallaxe* – modL. *parallaxis* – Gr. *parállaxis* change, alternation, mutual inclination of two lines meeting in an angle, f. *parallássein* (*-allakt-*) alter, alternate, f. *pará* PARA-[1] + *allássein* exchange, f. *állos* other (cf. ALTER, ELSE). So **paralla·ct**IC. XVII. – Gr.

parallel pæˑrəlel lying alongside another or one another and always at the same distance apart XVI; precisely similar or corresponding XVII (Sh.). – F. *parallèle* – L. *parallēlus* – Gr. *parállēlos*, f. *pará* alongside + *allḗlous* *-ōn*, etc. pl. one another, redupl. of *állos* other; see PARA- and prec. So **pa:rallelepiped** -eˑpiped figure contained by 6 parallelograms. XVI (in Gr. form, Billingsley). – Gr. *parallēlepípedon*, f. *parállēlos* + *epípedon* plane surface, sb. use of n. of *epípedos* plane, f. *epí* on, EPI- + *pédon* ground. **paralle·logram** 4-sided rectilineal figure with opposite sides parallel. XVI (Billingsley). – F. *parallélogramme* – late L. *parallēlogrammum* – Gr. *parallelógrammon*, sb. use of n. of adj. f. *parállēlos* + *grammḗ* line (cf. -GRAM).

paralogism pəræ·lŏdʒizm false reasoning, fallacy. XVI. – F. *paralogisme* or late L. *paralogismus* – Gr. *paralogismós*, f. *paralogízesthai* reason falsely, f. *parálogos*; see PARA-[1], LOGOS, -ISM.

paralysis pəræ·lĭsis disease involving impairment of motion or feeling. XVI. – L. *paralysis* – Gr. *parálusis*, f. *paralúesthai* be 'loosened' or disabled at the side, pass. of *paralúein*, f. *pará*+*lúein* loosen; see PARA-[1], LOOSE. This form superseded †*paralysie* XIV – (O)F. *paralysie*; see PALSY. So **paralyse,** U.S. **-yze** affect with paralysis. XIX. – F. *paralyser*, f. *paralysie*. **paralyt**IC -li·tik. XIV. – (O)F. – L. – Gr.

paramatta pærəmæ·tə orig. applied to cloth made at *Paramatta* (prop. *Parramatta*) in New South Wales, Australia, where there was formerly a convict establishment in which it was produced; afterwards transf. to a fabric made in England. XIX.

parameter pəræ·mĭtəɹ (math.) third proportional to any given diameter and its conjugate. XVII. – modL. *parameter*, *-metrum* (C. Mydorge, 1631), f. Gr. *pará* beside, subsidiary to + *métron* measure; see PARA-[1], METER.

paramount pæ·rəmaunt (of a feudal lord) superior, supreme. XVI (also †*pera-*). – AN. (Law F.) *paramont*, *peramont* (e.g. *le chef seigneur paramont*), adj. use of adv. *paramont* above (e.g. *son seigneur prochain a luy paramont* his lord next above him), f. (O)F. *par* by+*amont* above; see PAR[2], AMOUNT.

paramour pæ·rəmuəɹ adv. phr. *paramour(s)* by way of (sexual) love, for love's sake, as a lover. XIII. – OF. *par amour(s)* by or through love; see PAR[2], AMOUR. Hence as sb. †(sexual) love; †lover, sweetheart XIII; illicit lover or mistress XIV (Ch.). The sb. use may have arisen partly from a mistaken analysis of the common ME. phr. *to love paramour(s)*. ¶ In early use applied in devotional lang. to God and the Virgin Mary.

paranoia pærənoi·ə (path.) mental derangement marked by delusions, etc. XIX. modL. – Gr. *paránoia*, f. *paránoos* distracted, f. *pará* beside, PARA-[1]+*nóos*, *noûs* mind (cf. NOETIC). Hence **paranoi**·AC adj. and sb.

paranymph pæ·rənimf friend of the bridegroom, groomsman, (also) bridesmaid; †advocate, spokesman. XVI. – late L. *paranymphus*, fem. *-nympha* – Gr. *paránumphos* m. and fem.; see PARA-[1], NYMPH.

parapet pæ·rəpet (fortif.) defence of earth or stone; low wall or barrier XVI; (local) footpath of a street XIX. – F. *parapet* (Rabelais) or its source It. *parapetto* wall breast-high, f. *para-* PARA-[2] + *petto* :– L. *pectu-s* breast (cf. PECTORAL).

paraph pæ·ræf †paragraph XIV; (distinctive) flourish after a signature XVI. – F. *paraphe*, *-afe* – medL. *paraphus*, syncopated form of *paragraphus* PARAGRAPH.

paraphernalia pæːrəfəɹnei·liə articles of personal property which the law allows a married woman to regard as her own XVII; trappings, accessories, appurtenances XVIII. – medL. *paraphernālia*; sb. use (sc. *bona* goods) of n. pl. of *paraphernālis*, f. late L. *parapherna* – Gr. *parápherna* n. pl. articles of property held by a wife besides her dowry, f. *pará* beside, PARA-[1]+*phernḗ* dowry, rel. to *phérein* BEAR[2] (for the formation cf. OE. *bearn* BAIRN); see -AL[1], -IA[2].

paraphrase pæ·rəfreiz expression of the sense of a passage in other words. XVI (also in L. form). – F. *paraphrase* or L. *paraphrasis* – Gr. *paráphrasis*, f. *paraphrázein* tell in other words; see PARA-[1], PHRASE. Hence as vb. XVII.

paraplegia pærəplī·dʒʲə partial paralysis. XVII. modL. – Gr. *paraplēgíā*, f. *paraplḗssein*, f. *pará* PARA-[1]+*plḗssein* strike (**plēgj-*); see -IA[1].

parasang pæ·rəsæŋ Persian measure of length. XVI. – L. *parasanga* – Gr. *parasángēs* – Pers. word now repr. by *farsang*.

parasceve pærəsī·vi eve of the Jewish Sabbath. XVI. – ChrL. *parascēvē* – Gr. *paraskeuḗ* preparation, in N.T. day of preparation for the Sabbath (Mark xv 42, Luke xxiii 54, etc.), in later use, Good Friday, sb. of *paraskeuázein* prepare, f. *pará* PARA-[1] + *skeuázein* make ready, f. *skeûos* instrument, pl. equipment.

paraselene see PARHELION.

parasite pæ·rəsait one who obtains hospitality, etc. by obsequiousness XVI; animal or plant supported by another XVIII. – L. *parasītus* – Gr. *parásītos* one who eats at the table of another, toady, f. *pará* beside, PARA-[1] +*sîtos* food. Cf. F. *parasite* (Rabelais). So **parasi·t**IC -si·tik. XVII. – L. – Gr. **parasi·t**ICAL. XVI.

parasol pærəsɔ·l, pæ·rəsɔl sun-umbrella, sunshade. XVII. – F. *parasol* – It. *parasole*, f. *para-*+*sole* sun; see PARA-[2], SOLAR.

parasynthetic pæːrəsinþe·tik (gram.) based on a syntactical combination or compound, as *hardhearted* from *hard heart*, *get-at-able* from phr. *get at*. XIX. f. late Gr. *parasúnthetos*, f. *pará* beside+*súnthetos*, ppl. formation on *suntithénai* combine, f. *sún* together + *tithénai* put; see PARA-[1], SYN-, THEME.

parataxis pærətæ·ksis (gram.) placing of propositions or clauses side by side without connecting words. XIX. – Gr. *parátaxis*, f. *paratássein* place side by side; see PARA-[1]. So **para**TA·CTIC. XIX.

parboil pā·ɹboil †A. boil thoroughly; B. boil partially XV. – OF. *parboillir* – late L. *perbullīre*; see PER-, BOIL. Sense B is due to assoc. with PART (so in medL. *parbullīre*).

parbuckle pā·ɹbʌkl (naut.) sling or looped rope used for raising and lowering. XVII (Capt. Smith). Early forms *-bunkle, -bunkel,* altered XVIII by assoc. with BUCKLE; of unkn. origin.

parcel pā·ɹsl part, portion, particle, surviving in *part and parcel* XIV (Ch.); separate part, unit, or item XIV; portion of land XV; small party or company XVI (Sh.); quantity of a thing or things put together in a package XVII; quantity of a commodity dealt with XVIII. ME. *parcelle* – (O)F. *parcelle* = Pr. *parcela,* Sp. *partecilla,* It. *particella,* Rum. *părticeà* :– Rom. **particella,* f. L. *particula* PARTICLE. In advb. use 'partly, partially' from XV, e.g. in *parcel-gilt,* becoming obs. XVII, and revived by Scott *c.*1820. Hence **parcel** vb. divide into portions XV; (naut.) cover with canvas strips XVII (Capt. Smith); the latter sense may have a separate origin.

parcener pā·ɹsənəɹ †partner XIII; (leg.) co-heir XVI. – AN. *parcener* = OF. *parçonier* = Pr. *parsonier,* Sp. *parzonero,* Pg. *parceiro,* Rom. **partiōnārius* for **partītiōnārius,* f. L. *partītiō* PARTITION; see -ER², PARTNER.

parch pāɹtʃ dry by exposure to great heat XIV (Trevisa); scorch, shrivel XVI. Also *perch* XIV–XVI, *pearch* XVII, of obscure origin; the assumption that it is a var. of PIERCE (ONF. *perchier*) does not fit the sense, and that it is a specialized use of PERISH is not in accordance with the phonology.

parchment pā·ɹtʃmənt skin of sheep or goat, etc. prepared for writing, etc. XIII (Cursor M.). ME. *parchemin* – (O)F. *parchemin,* earlier *parcamin* :– Rom. **particamīnum,* which resulted from a blending of L. *pergamīna* with *Parthica pellis* 'Parthian skin', leather dyed scarlet (whence OF. *parche* parchment, Pr. *pargue* kind of leather). *Pergamīna* (sc. *charta* paper) writing-material prepared from skins invented at *Pergamum* (now Bergama) is repr. by Pr. *pargami,* Sp. *pergamino,* OIt. *pergamina,* the collateral form *Pergamēna* by Pr. *pergamen.* Assimilation of the ending of the Eng. word to the suffix -MENT appears XV; it is anticipated in medL. *pergamentum* (XI); cf. Du. *perkament, perkement,* (M)HG. *pergament.*

parclose pā·ɹklouz †close, conclusion; partition, screen. XIV. ME. *parclos(e)* – OF. *parclos* m., *parclose* fem., sb. uses of pp. of *parclore,* f. *par-,* L. *per-* thoroughly, PER- 4 + *clore* :– L. *claudere* CLOSE.

pard¹ pāɹd (arch.) panther, leopard. XIII (Cursor M.). OE. *pard*; in ME. – OF. *pard* – L. *pardus* – Gr. *párdos,* of Indo-Iranian origin (cf. Skr. *pṛ́dākus* tiger, panther, Pers. *pārs* panther). See also LEOPARD.

pard² pāɹd (U.S.) mate. XIX. abbrev. of *pardner,* vulgar form (XVIII) of PARTNER.

pardie pāɹdī·, **perdie** pɔ̄ɹdī· (arch. asseveration). XIII. – OF. *par dé* (mod. *pardieu,* colloq. *pardi*) 'by God' :– L. *per Deum*; see PAR², DEITY.

pardon pā·ɹd(ə)n remission of punishment for an offence (spec. papal indulgence) XIII (Cursor M.); excusing of a fault XVI. – OF. *pardun, perdun* (mod. *pardon*) = Pr. *perdo,* Sp. *perdon,* It. *perdono*; f. OF. *pardoner, perduner* (mod. *pardonner*), whence **pa·rdon** vb. XV = Pr., Sp. *perdonar,* It. *perdonare* :– medL. *perdōnāre,* f. L. *per* PER- + *dōnāre* give (see DONATION); cf. FORGIVE. So **pa·rdoner**² (arch.) ecclesiastic licensed to sell pardons. XIV (PPl., Ch.). – AN. *pardoner.*

pare pɛəɹ trim by cutting. XIII (Sir Tristrem). – (O)F. *parer* adorn, arrange, peel (fruit) :– L. *parāre* PREPARE, which in Rom. acquired specialized uses, as in Pr., Sp. *parar* adorn, arrange, It. *parare* ward off (cf. PARADE, PARRY), rel. to *parere* (see PARENT).

paregoric pærigɔ·rik assuaging pain XVII; sb. for *p. elixir* camphorated tincture of opium XIX. – late L. *parēgoricus* – Gr. *parēgorikós* encouraging, soothing (παρηγορικὸν φάρμακον, π. κατάπλασμα, Galen), f. *parēgoreîn* console, soothe, f. *pará* beside + *ēgor-,* var. of *agor-* in *agoreúein* speak in the assembly; see PARA-¹, CATEGORY, -IC.

parenchyma pəre·ŋkimə (anat. and zool.) substance of the liver, etc., (bot.) cellular tissue. XVII. – modL. – Gr. *parégkhuma* (*-mat-*) 'something poured in besides', f. *pará* + *égkhuma* infusion, f. *egkheîn,* f. *en* in + *kheîn* pour; see PARA-¹, EN-², FUSION. The Gr. word was first used by Erasistratus (III B.C.) in the first sense. Hence **parenchy·matous, pare·nchymous.** XVII.

parent pɛə·rənt father or mother; †relative. XV. – (O)F. *parent* (in both senses), corr. to Pr. *paren* related, Sp. *pariente* related, husband (*parienta* wife), It. *parenti* relatives, †parents, Rum. *părinte* father, priest, *părinți* parents :– L. *parentem,* nom. *parēns* father or mother, pl. *parentēs* parents, progenitors, kinsfolk, (prop.) procreators, prp. with athematic stem of *parere* bring forth, rel. to *parāre* PREPARE; see -ENT. So **pa·rentage.** XV (Caxton). – (O)F. **parental**¹ pəre·ntəl. XVII. – L.

parenthesis pəre·nþisis qualifying matter introduced into a passage XVI; device used to mark this, e.g. ( ) [ ] XVIII. – late L. – Gr. *parénthesis,* f. *parentithénai* place in besides; see PARA-¹, EN-², THESIS. So **parenthe·tic(al).** XVII. – medL.

parergon pærɔ̄·ɹgɔn (in painting) something subordinate to the main theme; subordinate piece of work. XVII. – L., extra ornament in art – Gr. *párergon* subordinate or secondary business; see PARA-¹, WORK.

paresis pæ·rĭsis (path.) partial paralysis. XVII. modL. – Gr. *páresis,* f. *pariénai* relax, f. *pará* PARA-¹ + *hiénai* let go.

parget pā·ɹdʒit daub with plaster. XIV (Wycl. Bible, Trevisa). – OF. *pargeter, parjeter* (now dial. fill up joints in masonry), f. *par* through, all over (PAR²) + *jeter* cast

:- medL. *jectare*, for L. *jactāre* throw (see JET[2]); cf. the use of *cast* as in *rough-cast*.

parhelion pāɹhī·liən (astron.) mock sun. XVII. In early use *par(h)elion*, *par(h)elius* – L. *parēlion* – Gr. *parḗlion*, also *-ios*, f. *pará* beside, PARA-[1]+*hḗlios* SUN. So **pa:rasele·ne** mock moon. XVII. modL. (Gr. *selḗnē* moon).

pariah pæ·riə, pɛə·riə, pā·riə member of a low Hindu caste XVII; social outcast XIX. Earlier *parea*, *parrier*, *par(r)iar* – Tamil *paṛaiyar*, pl. of *paṛaiyan* name of the largest of the lower castes in S. India, lit. 'drummer', f. *paṛai* large drum beaten at certain festivals.

parietal pərai·itəl (anat.) pert. to the wall of the body or a bodily organ XVI; (U.S.) pert. to residence within walls of a college XIX. – F. *pariétal* or late L. *parietālis*, f. *pariet-*, *pariēs* wall, partition wall (from Rom. **parētē* are F. *paroi*, It. *parete*, etc.; cf. W. *parwyd*); see -AL[1]. The comb. form is **pari·eto-** XIX.

parish pæ·riʃ district for administrative purposes, orig. township having its own church and priest. XIII. ME. *pa·roche*, *-os(c)he*, *-osse*, *-isshe*, *-esche* – AN., OF. *paroche* and (O)F. *paroisse* – ecclL. *parochia*, alt. (after *parochus* – Gr. *párokhos* public purveyor) of *parœcia* – Gr. *paroikíā* sojourning, f. *pároikos* dwelling near, sojourner, stranger, f. *pará* beside, PARA-[1]+ *oîkos* dwelling, house (see WICK[1]); it is doubtful whether the notion 'neighbour' or 'sojourner' was prevalent in determining the application of *parœcia*, *parochia* (which, moreover, was formerly equivalent to 'diocese' as well as 'parish'). For *-sh* repr. OF. *-ss-* cf. -ISH[2], etc. So **parishioner** pəri·ʃənəɹ inhabitant of a parish XV; superseded earlier †*parishion*, †*parishen* (XIV), alt., after PARISH, of †*paroschian*, *-ien* (XIII), *parochian* – OF. *parochien*, *-ossien* (mod. *paroissien*), f. *paroche*, etc.; -ER[1] was added to suggest more clearly a personal designation.

parisyllabic pæ:risilæ·bik (gram.) having the same number of syllables in the nominative as in the oblique cases. XVII. f. L. *pari-*, *pār* equal, PAR[1]+*syllaba* SYLLABLE+-IC.

park pāɹk enclosed tract of land held by royal grant or prescription for the chase XIII (Laȝ.); (north.) field, paddock XVI; enclosed piece of ground for public recreation; space in a camp occupied by artillery, etc. XVII. – (O)F. *parc* = Pr. *parrec* herd, *pargue* park (whence It. *parco*, Sp., Pg. *parque*) :- medL. *parricus* ('Lex Ripuaria' VIII) – Germ. base repr. by OHG. *pfarrih*, *pferrih* (G. *pferch*) pen, fold, corr. to OE. *pearruc* (see PADDOCK[2]), MLG., MDu. *perc* (Du. *perk*) (Ir., Gael. *pairc*, W. *parc* are from Eng.). Cf. PARQUET. Hence **park** vb. XVI f. the sb.

parkin pā·ɹkin kind of gingerbread. XIX. Of local origin; perh. f. proper name *Parkin*, *Perkin*, dim. of *Per*, Peter.

parky pā·ɹki (colloq.) chilly. XIX. perh. f. PARK+-Y[1], as suggesting the atmospheric conditions of a (London) park.

parlance pā·ɹləns (arch.) speech XVI; mode of speech, idiom XVIII. – OF. *parlance*, f. *parler* :- L. *parabolāre*; see PARLOUR, -ANCE.

parley pā·ɹli speech, talk; (conference for) discussion of terms. XVI. perh. – OF. *parlee*, sb. use of fem. pp. of *parler* speak (see prec.). Hence **parley** vb. XVI. Superseded contemp. †*parle* sb. and vb., of which the vb. was immed. – F. *parler* and the sb. from the vb. So **parleyvoo** pāɹlivū· (joc.) sb. French talk XVIII; Frenchman XIX; vb. talk French XVIII. – F. *Parlez-vous (français)?* Do you speak (French)?

parliament pā·ɹlĭmənt †talk, conference; deliberative assembly XIII; Great Council of the realm XIV. ME. *parlement* – (O)F. *parlement*, f. *parler*; see PARLANCE, -MENT. The present form follows AL. *parliamentum* (XII), which is prob. based on Eng. *parli-*; it appears in XV, when four main forms were current, *parle-*, *-la-*, *-li-*, *-lia-*. Hence **pa:rliament**A·RIAN sb., **parliame·nt**ARY. XVII; cf. F. *parlementaire* adj. (XVII), sb. (XVIII).

parlour, U.S. **parlor** pā·ɹləɹ apartment set aside for conversation in a religious house XIII; smaller room in a mansion, dwelling-house, etc. for private talk, (hence) family sitting-room XIV (Ch.). – AN. *parlur*, OF. *parleor*, *parleur* (mod. *parloir*) = Pr. *parlador*, It. *parlatorio* (cf. medL. *parlātōrium*); f. Rom. **par(au)lāre* (see PARABLE, PAROLE); the ending is assim. to -OUR[2].

parlous pā·ɹləs exposed to danger XIV; dangerously cunning XV. ME. *perlous*, *parlous*, syncopated form of *perelous*, *parelous* PERILOUS.

Parmesan pā·ɹmizən epithet of a cheese made in the province of Parma and elsewhere in N. Italy. – F. *parmesan* – It. *parmigiano*, f. *Parma*.

Parnassian paɹnæ·siən of or belonging to *Parnassus*, poetic XVII; epithet of school of French poetry (*les Parnassiens*) XIX. – L. *Parnassus* – Gr. *Parnassós*, mountain anciently sacred to the Muses. See -IAN.

parochial pərou·kiəl pert. to a parish. XIV. – AN. *parochiel*, OF. *parochial* – ecclL. *parochiālis*, f. *parochia*; see PARISH, -AL[1]. Formerly also †*parochian* XIV. – OF. *parochien* – medL.

parody pæ·rədi imitation of a work so turned as to produce a ridiculous effect. XVI (Jonson). – medL. *parōdia* (Pseudo-Asconius) or Gr. *parōidíā* burlesque poem or song, f. *pará* beside, subsidiary, mock-+ *ōidḗ* song, poem; see PARA-[1], ODE, -Y[3]. **pa·rody** vb. XVIII (Pope), **pa·rod**IST. XVIII; prob. after F. *parodier*, *parodiste*.

parol pæ·rəl oral statement XV; (leg.) pleadings filed in an action XVII; adj. oral XVI – (O)F. *parole*, in Law F. *parol*; see next.

parole pərou·l word of honour XVII; password used by an officer or inspector of the guard XVIII. – (O)F. *parole* word, in the sense 'formal promise, engagement' (as in phr. *parole d'honneur*) :- Rom. **paraula* :- L. *parabola* PARABLE.

paroli pā·rŏli doubling the stake at faro, etc. XVIII. – F. *paroli* – It. *paroli*, f. *pari* like :- L. *pare-m* (see PAIR). Cf. It. *giocare a pari* (Neapolitan *jocà a paro*) play with money added to the original stake.

paronomasia pərənŏmei·ziə playing on words. XVI. – L. – Gr. *paronomasíā*, f. *pará*+ *onomasíā* naming, after *paronomázein* alter slightly in naming, f. *pará*+*ónoma*; see PARA-[1], NAME, -IA[1].

paronymous pərɔ·niməs (of words) radically connected. XVII. f. Gr. *parṓnumos*, f. *pará*+*ónuma*, *ónoma*; see PARA-[1], NAME, -OUS.

parotid pərɔ·tid (anat.) situated beside or near the ear. XVII. – F. *parotide* – L. *parōtid-*, *parōtis* – Gr. *parōtid-*, *parōtís*, f. *pará* PARA-[1] +*ōt-*, *oûs* EAR[1]; see -ID[2].

-parous pərəs, repr. L. *-parus* bearing, producing, rel. to *parere* bring forth (see PARENT), as in *ōviparus* OVIPAROUS, *vīviparus* VIVIPAROUS; hence in numerous later and mod. formations; see -OUS.

paroxysm pæ·rəksizm increase of the acuteness of a disease; violent access, fit. XVII. – F. *paroxysme* – medL. *paroxysmus* irritation, exasperation – Gr. *paroxusmós*, f. *paroxúnein*, f. *pará* in addition, PARA-[1]+ *oxúnein* sharpen, f. *oxús* sharp (cf. OXY-).

paroxytone see OXYTONE.

parpen pā·ɹpən binding stone passing through a wall from side to side. XV (*perpend*, *-poynt*, etc.). – OF. *parpain*, also *per-*, *-pan*, *-pin*, *-poin* (mod. *parpaing*), whence also adj. in *pierre parpaigne*; of much contested origin, but prob. :- Rom. **perpanniu-s*, f. L. *per* through + *pannus* in Rom. use, section of a wall; see PER-, PANEL.

parquet pā·ɹkei flooring consisting of pieces of wood set in a pattern; (U.S.) part of the floor near the orchestra in a theatre. XIX. – (O)F. *parquet* small marked-off space, etc., dim. of *parc* PARK; see -ET.

parr pāɹ young salmon, or coal-fish. XVIII. Of unkn. origin.

parrel, parral pæ·rəl (naut.) band by which the middle of a yard is fastened to a mast. XV. var. of †*parel* (XIV) equipment, apparatus, tackle, aphetic of APPAREL.

parricide[1] pæ·risəid murderer of a father, near relative, or revered person, traitor. XVI. – (O)F. *parricide* or L. *pār(r)icīda*, of uncertain origin, but assoc. by the Romans with *pater* FATHER and *parēns* PARENT; for the second el. see -CIDE[1]. So **pa·rri**CIDE[2] murder of a father, etc. XVI. – F. *parricide* or L. *pār(r)icīdium*; see -CIDE[2].

parrot pæ·rət bird of the genus Psittacus and its congeners. XVI (Skelton). prob. appellative use of F. †*Perrot* (cf. PIERROT), dim. of *Pierre* Peter; *pérot* is given by Littré as a familiar name in modF. for the bird, and *pierrot* for house-sparrow; cf. PARAKEET. ¶ The earlier name was POPINJAY.

parry pæ·ri ward off or turn aside a weapon. XVII. prob. repr. F. *parez* (used as a word of command in fencing), imper. of *parer* – It. *parare* ward off, specialized use of the sense 'prepare' (cf. PARADE).

parse pāɹz, (formerly, and now Sc. and U.S.) pāɹs state the part of speech of. XVI (*pars(e)*, *peirse*, *pearse*, in XVII *parce*, *pearce*). Of doubtful origin; perh. orig. f. ME. *pars* (XIII–XV) parts of speech (– OF. *pars*, pl. of *part* PART), and later infl. by L. *pars*, as in the question *Quæ pars orationis?* What part of speech?; but the forms in *-ea-*, *-ei-* are in any case difficult of explanation.

Parsee, Parsi pāɹsī· descendant of Persians who fled to India to escape Mohammedan persecution. XVII. – Pers. *Pārsī* Persian, f. *Pārs* Persia.

parsimony, parci- pā·ɹsiməni (arch.) care in the use of money XV; stinginess XVI. – L. *parsi-*, *parcimōnia*, *-mōnium*, f. *pars-*, pp. stem of *parcere* refrain, spare; see -MONY and cf. F. *parcimonie*, †*parsi-*. Hence **parsimon**IOUS -ou·niəs. XVI.

parsley pā·ɹsli biennial herb, Petroselinum sativum (Apium Petroselinum). The earliest antecedents of the present form, *percely*, *pers(e)le*, *-ly* (XIV), appear to repr. a blend of (i) OE. *petersilie*, corr. to MDu. *petersilie* (mod. *-selie*), OHG. *petersilia* (G. *petersilie*) – Rom. **petrosilium*, for L. *petroselīnum* – Gr. *petrosélīnon*, f. *pétrā* rock, *pétros* stone +*sélīnon* parsley, with (ii) ME. *percil*, *per(e)sil* (surviving dial. *parsel*) – OF. *peresil* (mod. *persil*), corr. to Pr. *pe(i)resilh*, Sp. *perejil*, Pg. *perrexil*, OIt. *petrosello*, of the same L. – Gr. origin.

parsnip pā·ɹsnip biennial plant, Pastinaca sativa, with pale-yellow root. XIV (Trevisa). The immed. antecedents of the present form, *pars(e)nep* (XVI) are alterations of earlier *pas(se)nep* – (with assim. to ME. *nep*, OE. *nǣp* turnip – L. *nāpus*) OF. *pasnaie* (mod. *panais*) :- L. *pastināca*, whence also (M)Du., (O)HG. *pastinak(e)*. Cf. TURNIP.

parson pā·ɹs(ə)n parish priest XIII; clergyman, minister XVI. ME. *person*, later *parso(u)n* – OF. *persone*, (law F.) *parsone* :- L. *persōna* PERSON, used in the eccl. sense at the Council of Clermont 1096 ('mortuis . . vel mutatis Clericis quos Personas vocant'). The genesis of the application is much disputed, but in England the parson has been long held to be the legal *persona* who could sue and be sued in respect of the parish. So **pa·rson**AGE †benefice XIV (Wyclif); for *p. house* XV. – OF. *personage*.

part pāɹt A. portion of a whole; portion allotted, share XIII; portion of the body XIV;

melody assigned to a voice or instrument XVI; B. region; side XIV. OE., repl. by – (O)F. *part* = Pr. *part*, Sp., It. *parte* :– L. *partem*, *pars* share, part of a whole, side, direction, perh. rel. to *portiō* PORTION, and *parere* produce (see PARENT). Also adv. and adj. in part, partly, partial XVI; cf. AN. *parpaiement* (XIV). So **part** vb. A. divide into parts; B. put or go asunder; C. depart XIII. – (O)F. *partir* = Pr., Sp. *partir*, It. *partire* :– L. (Rom.) *partīre*, *partīrī* divide, distribute, part, f. *parti-*, *pars*.

partaker pāɹtei·kəɹ one who takes a part, participator. XIV. f. PART sb. + *taker*, agent-noun of TAKE, after L. *particeps*; so **parta·king**. XIV (Wycl. Bible), after late L. *participātiō* PARTICIPATION; see -ER[1], -ING[1]. Hence by back-formation **parta·ke** vb. XVI (in XVI–XVII often with pt. and pp. *partaked*, the connexion with *take* being obscured). Cf. G. *teilnehmer*.

parterre pāɹtɛə·ɹ level space in a garden with ornamental flower-beds. XVII. – F. *parterre*, sb. use of phr. *par terre* on or along the ground (L. *par* PAR[1], *terra* earth).

parthenogenesis pā:ɹþĭnoudʒe·nĭsis reproduction without sexual union. XIX (R. Owen). modL., f. Gr. *parthénos* virgin + *génesis* birth, GENESIS.

partial pā·ɹʃ(ə)l A. inclined to favour one party or individual XV (Lydg.); B. pert. to a part XVII (Lydg.). – OF. *parcial* (mod. *partial* in sense A, *partiel* in sense B), corr. to Sp. *parcial*, It. *parziale* – late L. *partiālis*, f. L. *parti-*, *pars* PART; see -AL[1]. So **partia·lity**. XV (*parcialte*, *parcialite*). – (O)F. *parcialté*, *-alité* – medL. **pa·rtially**[2] XV; after late L. *partiāliter* (i) partly, (ii) with partiality, or in sense 'partly' – (O)F. *partiellement*.

partible pā·ɹtibl divisible. XVI. – late L. *partibilis*, f. L. *partīrī* divide, PART; see -IBLE.

participate pāɹti·sipeit take part (in). XVI. f. pp. stem of L. *participāre*, f. *particip-*, *-ceps* taking part, f. *parti-*, *pars* PART + *cip-*, weakened form of *cap-* of *capere* take; see HEAVE, -ATE[3]. So **parti·cipant**. XVI; **participa·tion**. XIV (Ch.). – (O)F. – late L.

participle pā·ɹtisipl (gram.) word that partakes of the nature of a verb and an adjective XIV (Wycl. Bible); †person or thing partaking of two natures XV. – OF. *participle*, by-form of *participe* – L. *participium* (Varro, Quintilian), f. *particeps* (see prec.), after Gr. *metokhḗ* (Dionysius of Halicarnassus), f. *metékhein* partake. ¶ For the parasitic *l* cf. *manciple*, *principle*, *treacle*.

particle pā·ɹtikl small or minute part XIV; (gram.) minor part of speech merely expressing relation XVI. – L. *particula*, dim. of *parti-*, *pars* PART; see -CLE.

particoloured pā·ɹtikʌləɹd partly of one colour and partly of another. XVI. In early use *partie* or *party coloured* beside *particoloured*; amplification of PARTY[2] by combination with *coloured*.

particular pəɹti·kjŭləɹ †partial XIV (Trevisa); pert. to a single individual XIV (Ch.); †private, personal XV; distinguished as an individual XVI; †bestowing marked attention XVII; attentive to details XIX; sb. †part, section; minute part; particular instance; item, detail XVI. ME. *particuler* – OF. *particuler* (mod. *particulier*) – L. *particulāris* (opp. to *universalis*, Apuleius), f. *particula* PARTICLE; see -AR; conformed to L. XVI. So **parti·cularism**. XIX (theol.), after F. *particularisme* (Bossuet) or modL. *particulārismus*; in politics, after G. *partikularismus*. **parti·cularist** XVIII, after F. *particulariste*. **particularity** -æ·rĭti. XVI. – (O)F. *particularité* or late L. *particulāritās* (Cassiodorus, Boethius). **parti·cularize**. XVI. – F. *particulariser*. **parti·cularly**[2] XIV; after late L. *particulāriter* or (O)F. *particulièrement*.

partisan[1] pāɹtizæ·n zealous supporter XVI; guerrilla soldier or chief XVII. – F. *partisan* – It. dial. *partišano*, *partežan*, Tuscan *partigiano*, f. *parte* PART + *-igiano* (Rom. *-*ēse*, L. -*ēnsi-s* + *-*iano*, L. -*iānus* -IAN); cf. COURTESAN, PARMESAN.

partisan[2] pā·ɹtizen long-handled spear, halberd. XVI. – F. †*partizane* (now *pertuisane*, after *pertuiser* bore through, PIERCE) – It. †*partesana*, dial. var. of *partigiana*, sb. use (sc. *arma* arm, weapon) of fem. of *partigiano* (see prec.), so called as being used by some faction.

partition pǎɹti·ʃən action of dividing, orig. of property; (her.) division of a shield XV; division in general XVI. – (O)F. *partition* corr. to Sp. *partición*, It. *partizione* – L. *partītiō(n-)*, f. *partīrī* divide, share, PART; see -ITION. So **pa·rtitive** (gram.) pert. to part of a whole. XVI (Whitington, Palsgr.). – F. *partitif* or medL. *partītīvus*.

partlet[1], **Partlet** pā·ɹtlit (proper name for) a hen. orig. *damoisele Pertelote* (XIV, Ch. 'Nun's Priest's Tale' 50), repr. later by *dame Partlet* (Sh.), occurring as a common noun in early XVII. – OF. *Pertelote*, of unkn. origin.

partlet[2] pā·ɹtlit neckerchief, ruff. XVI. Earlier Sc. and north. †*patelet* (XV, Henryson) – OF. *patelette*, dim. of *patte* paw, band or belt of stuff; see -LET. ¶ The form appears to have been assim. to prec.

partly pā·ɹtli in part. XVI. f. PART + -LY[2], to render L. *partim* (old acc. sg. of *pars* PART) and express the meaning of *in part* (XIV) by means of an adv. corr. to †*wholely*, WHOLLY.

partner pā·ɹtnəɹ partaker, associate XIV; (comm.) XVI; in games XVII; alt. of PARCENER by assoc. with PART.

partners pā·ɹtnəɹz (naut.) framework fitted around a hole or scuttle XIII (*pauteneres* Sandahl). – pl. of OF. *pautonier* servant (= F. *valet*); cf. similar use of *carlings* CARLING[1,2].

partridge pā·ɹtridʒ well-known game-bird, esp. Perdix cinerea. XIII. ME. *partrich*, north. and Sc. *partrick*, also *per-* – OF. *perdriz*, *-triz* (mod. *perdrix*), alt. of *perdiz* – L. *perdicem*, *-ix*, which is CRom. (exc. Rum.), but often in alt. forms, viz. Pr. *perditz*, *perlitz*, Cat. *perdiu*, Sp., Pg. *perdiz*, It. *pernice*, †*perdice*. ¶ The change from final *-che* tʃ to *-dge* dʒ is paralleled in *knowledge*, *sausage*, *smallage*, *Greenwich* gri·nidʒ, *Norwich* nɔ·ridʒ, *Woolwich* wu·lidʒ.

parturient pāɹtjuə·riənt about to bring forth. XVI. – L. *parturient*, *-ēns*, prp. of *parturīre* be in labour, inceptive f. *part-*, pp. stem of *parere* bring forth; see PARENT, -ENT. So **parturi·tion**. XVII. – late L.

party[1] pā·ɹti A. †part, portion; side in a contest, etc.; company or body of persons; person considered in some relation, spec. as litigant, etc. XIII; (now vulgar) individual, person XV; body of adherents XVI; detachment of troops XVII; gathering, assembly XVIII. ME. *parti(e)* – (O)F. *partie* part, share, side in a contest, contract, etc., litigant = Pr., Sp. *partida*, It. *partita* :– Rom. **partīta*, sb. use of fem. pp. of L. *partīrī* PART, whence also Du. *partij*, G. *partei*. Some of the Eng. meanings ('military party', 'political party') are due to later (O)F. *parti*, corr. to Sp. *partido*, It. *partito* :– Rom. **partītum*, n. pp.

party[2] pā·ɹti †particoloured, variegated XIV (Ch., Gower); (her.) of a shield divided into parts of different tinctures XV. – (O)F. *parti* :– L. *partītu-s*, pp. of *partīrī* divide, PART.

parvenu pā·ɹvənju one who from obscurity has (unexpectedly or undeservedly) attained to wealth or position. XIX. F., sb. use of pp. of *parvenir* arrive, reach a position :– L. *pervenīre*, f. *per* PER-[1] + *venīre* COME.

parvis pā·ɹvis court in front of a church, church portico. XIV (Ch.). – (O)F. *parvis*, †*parevis* (beside *pareis*) :– Rom. **paravīsu-s*, for late L. *paradīsus* PARADISE (applied in the Middle Ages to the atrium in front of St. Peter's, Rome).

Pasch pàsk (hist.) Passover; Easter. XII (Peterborough Chron., Orm). ME. *pasch(e)*, *pask(e)*, also pl. *pasches*, *paskes* (esp. Eastertide). – OF. *pasche-s*, *pasque-s* (mod. *Pâques*), corr. to Pr. *pasca(s)*, Sp., It. *pasqua*, Pg. *pascoa* :– Rom. (medL.) *pascua*, alt. (by assim. to *pāscuum* pasture), of ecclL. *pascha* – Gr. *páskhā* – Aram. *paskhā*, rel. to Heb. *pesakh* PASSOVER; from L. are also OFris., OS. *pascha* (Du. *paaschen* pl.), Icel. *páskar* pl.; north. ME. *pask(e)*, whence *pass*, *pace* (in PACE EGG) is due to Scand. So **paschal**[1] pà·skəl. XV. – (O)F. *pascal* – ecclL. *paschālis*.

pasha (formerly also **pacha**) pā·ʃə, pæ·ʃə, pəʃā· Turkish title of officers of high rank. XVII. – Turk. *paşa*, perh. identical with *basha*, f. *bash* head, chief (cf. BASHAW).

pasque-flower pà·skflauəɹ species of anemone. XVI. orig. *passeflower* (Lyte, 1578) – F. *passe-fleur*, f. *passer* PASS sb. + *fleur* FLOWER; altered to *pasque-flower* by Gerarde, 1597, after *pasque*, PASCH, because 'they flower for the most part about Easter'.

pasquil pæ·skwil lampoon published or circulated. XVI. orig. name of the personage on whom anonymous lampoons were fathered, It. *Pasquillo* (whence medL. *Pasquillus*), dim. of *Pasquino*, pop. name of a statue in Rome (disinterred 1501) at which Latin verses (later satirical) were presented.

pass[1] pàs. ME. *pas*, *paas* (XIII), var. of PACE[1] which became restricted to the sense 'passage' (as between mountains, across a river), prob. through contact with F. *pas* (*pas d'une montagne*, *pas d'une rivière*); the sp. was infl. by next.

pass[2] pàs intr. (the most general vb. expressing onward motion); also trans. go by, through, or beyond. XIII (RGlouc., Cursor M.). – (O)F. *passer* = Pr. *passar*, Sp. *pasar*, It. *passare* :– Rom. **passāre* (medL., implied in *passāticum* transport-money), f. *passus* step, PACE. Hence **pa·ssable** that may be passed; that passes muster. XV. – (O)F. *passable*.

pass[3] pàs event, issue XV (Caxton); act of passing; permission to go; lunge, thrust XVI. Partly – F. *passe*, f. *passer*; partly f. PASS[2].

passado pæsā·dou (in fencing) forward thrust. XVI (Sh.). alt. of Sp. *pasada* (cf. Pr. *passada*, It. *passata*, F. *passade*); see -ADO.

passage pæ·sidʒ action of passing; way by which one passes XIII (S. Eng. Leg.); event, act (surviving in *p. of arms*); part of a discourse or musical composition XVI. – (O)F. *passage* = Pr. *passatge* (whence Sp. *pasage*, It. *passaggio*) – Gallo-Rom. **passāticum*, f. **passāre*; see PASS[2], -AGE.

passant pæ·sənt †passing, surpassing XIV; (her.) walking XV. – (O)F. *passant*, prp. of *passer* PASS[2]; see -ANT.

passé pà·sei past one's or its prime. XVIII. – F., pp. of *passer* PASS[2].

passenger pæ·sindʒəɹ †traveller, wayfarer XIV; one who travels in a vessel or vehicle XVI. ME. *passager* – (O)F. *passager*, sb. use of adj. passing, f. *passage* PASSAGE; see -ER[2]. ¶ For the intrusive *n* cf. HARBINGER.

passe-partout pæspāɹtū· master-key XVII; plate of cardboard, etc. cut out to receive a picture XIX. F., f. *passer* PASS[2] + *partout* everywhere (L. *per*, *tōtum*).

passerine pæ·sərain (ornith.) pert. to the Passeres or perchers. XVIII (Pennant). f. L. *passer* sparrow + -INE[1].

passible pæ·sibl capable of suffering. XIV (Rolle). – (O)F. *passible* or ChrL. *passibilis*, f. *pass-*, pp. stem of *patī* suffer; see PATIENT, -IBLE.

passim pæ·sim in many or various places. XIX. L., here and there, everywhere, f. *passus* spread abroad, scattered :– **padtos*, f. **pad-*, base of *pandere* spread out (cf. EXPAND); cf. *paulatim, statim, vicissim.*

passion pæ·ʃən suffering of pain (earliest, of the sufferings of Jesus Christ) XII; †being acted upon; powerful affection of the mind XIV (Ch.); outburst of anger; amorous feeling XVI; sexual impulse; strong predilection XVII. – (O)F. *passion* = Pr., Sp., It. *passione* – ChrL. *passiō* (*n*-) suffering (whence OE. *passiōn*), affection (rendering Gr. *páthos*), f. *pass-*, pp. stem of *patī*; see PATIENT, -ION. So **pa·ssion**ATE[2] prone to anger XV; marked by strong emotion XVI. – medL. *passionātus* (cf. F. *passionné*, etc.). **passion-flower** genus Passiflora. XVII. tr. modL. *flōs passiōnis*; so named from the comparison of the corona to the Crown of Thorns.

passive pæ·siv (gram.) opp. to *active* XIV (Wycl. Bible); suffering action from without XV; (Sc. law) under a liability XVI. – (O)F. *passif, -ive* or L. *passīvus, -īva* (gram. tr. Gr. ὕπτιος), f. *pass-*; see PASSION, -IVE. Hence **passi·**VITY. XVII.

Passover pà·sou:vəɹ Jewish feast, the lamb sacrificed at this, the Paschal Lamb (see Exodus xii 11, 13; 1 Cor. v 7). XVI (Tindale). f. phr. *pass over* pass without touching (PASS[2], OVER prep.), rendering Heb. *pesakh*, f. *pāsakh* pass over (cf. PASCH).

passport pà·spōrt authorization to pass from a port or leave a country. XV. – F. *passeport* (cf. It. *passaporto*), f. *passer* PASS + *port* PORT[1].

past pāst that is gone or has passed away, ago XIV (Cursor M.); (gram.) preterite XVI; sb. *the p.* (F. *le passé*) XVI; *one's p.* XIX. ME. *passed, past*; arising out of the perfect tense of resultant condition of the vb. PASS[2] formed with the vb. 'to be', e.g. *the daies ben* (*i-*) *passed* / (*i*)*past*, corr. to OF. *les jors sont passés.* Hence as prep. beyond in time or place XIII; arising from such construction as 'The day is short and *it is passed* pryme', '*It was passed* 8 of the clokke the space of 2 degrees' (Ch.); whence ellipt. as adv. XIX (e.g. *to go past*).

paste peist flour moistened and kneaded XIV (PPl., Gower); mixture of flour and water used as a glue XVI; applied to various other mixtures XVII. – OF. *paste* (mod. *pâte*) = Pr., Sp., It. *pasta* :– late L. *pasta* small square piece of a medicinal preparation (Marcellus Empiricus, *c.*400) – Gr. *pástē*, pl. *pastá, pastaí* barley porridge, sb. uses of *pastós* sprinkled, f. *pássein* sprinkle. Hence **paste** vb. XVI. **pa·ste**BOARD material made by pasting sheets of paper together XVI; for **pasted board*; cf. the recorded †*pasted paper* (XVI). **past**Y[1] pei·sti. XVII.

pastel[1] pæ·stəl woad. XVI. – F. *pastel* – Pr. *pastel*, dim. of *pasta* PASTE; the leaves of woad are made into a paste for pigment.

pastel[2] pæ·stəl dry paste used for crayon XVII (Evelyn); drawing in this XIX. – F. *pastel*, or its source It. *pastello*; see prec.

pastern pæ·stəɹn †tether or hobble for a horse XIV; part of a horse's foot between fetlock and hoof XVI. ME. *pastron* – OF. *pasturon* (mod. *pâturon*), f. *pasture* (dial. *pâture*) hobble, alt. by change of suffix of **pastoire* (corr. to It. *pastoia* shackle for sheep when being sheared) – medL. *pāstōria, -ōrium*, sb. uses of fem. and n. of L. *pāstōrius* pert. to a shepherd, f. *pāstor* PASTOR.

pasteurize pæ·stəraiz sterilize by the method devised by the F. scientist Louis *Pasteur* (1822–95); see -IZE. XIX.

pasticcio pæsti·tʃiou hotchpotch, potpourri; work of art made up of fragments of an original. XVIII. – It. *pasticcio* pie, pasty, etc. = OF. *pastiz*, Pr. *pastitz* pasty :– Rom. **pastīciu-s*, f. late L. *pasta* PASTE. So **pastiche** pæstī·ʃ. XIX. – F. – It.

pastille pæ·stil roll of aromatic paste; troche, lozenge. XVII. – F. *pastille* – L. *pastillus* little loaf or roll, lozenge, dim. of **pasnis, pānis* loaf; or, dim. of *pasta* PASTE. Sp. *pastilla.*

pastime pà·staim diversion serving to pass the time. XV (Caxton). f. PASS[2] + TIME, rendering F. *passe-temps*, f. *passe*, imper. of *passer* + *temps* time. ¶ The F. word is directly repr. by Sc. †*pastance* XVI.

past-master pà·stmà·stəɹ A. one who has filled the office of master in a guild, etc. XVIII; B. one who is proficient in a subject XIX. In sense A, f. PAST; in B var. of *passed master* (XVI), f. phr. *pass master* graduate as a master in a faculty (cf. †*pass-master* XVI as sb. in this sense).

pastor pà·stəɹ †shepherd; shepherd of souls. XIV (PPl.). – AN., OF. *pastour* (mod. *pasteur*), acc. of *pastre* (mod. *pâtre* shepherd) :– L. *pāstōrem, pāstor* (cf. Pr. *pastre*, Sp. *pastor*, It. *pastore*, Rum. *păstor*), f. **pās-*, extended form of **pā-* in *pāscere* feed, graze; see -TOR. So **pa·stor**AL[1] pert. to shepherds XV; pert. to a spiritual pastor XVI. – L. *pāstōrālis*; cf. (O)F. *pastoral*, etc.; sb. pastoral play or poem XVI. **pa·stor**ATE[1] XVIII.

pastry pei·stri (coll.) articles of food made of flour. XVI. f. PASTE, after OF. *pastaierie*, f. *pastaier* pastrycook; see -RY.

pasture pà·stʃəɹ growing grass for cattle XIII (Cursor M.); †feeding, food XIV. – OF. *pasture* (mod. *pâture*) = Pr., Sp., It. *pastura* :– late L. *pāstūra* (Palladius), f. pp. stem of *pāscere* feed, pasture (cf. PABULUM). So **pa·sture** vb. XIV (Gower). – OF. *pasturer* (mod. *pâturer*). **pa·stur**AGE. XVI. – OF.

pasty pæ·sti, pei·sti meat pie. XIII (Havelok). ME. *paste*(*e*) – OF. *pastée, pasté* (mod. *pâtée, pâté*) :– medL. **pastāta, -tātum*, f. late L. *pasta* PASTE; cf. MDu. *pastei*(*d*)*e* (Du. *pastei*), MHG. *pastēte, -ēde* (G. *pastete*); see -Y[5].

pat pæt A. (dial.) stroke, blow XIV; gentle stroke or tap XIX; B. sound made by patting XVII; C. small mass shaped by patting XVIII. imit., like (dial.) *bat*, of similar date; not evidenced XV–XVI and app. re-formed XVII from **pat** vb. strike XVI, tap or beat lightly XVII. Hence **pat** adv. 'with a fitting stroke', aptly, opportunely; first in phr. *hit pat*.

patagium pætədʒai·əm (anat.) fold of skin. XIX. medL. use of L. *patagium* gold edging of a tunic – Gr. *patageîon*.

Patavinity pætəvi·nĭti characteristics of the dialect of *Patavia* (mod. Padua) in Gallia Cisalpina as seen in the Roman historian Livy. XVII. – L. *patavīnitās*; see -INE[1], -ITY. ¶ Also occas. termed †*Paduanism* (XVI).

patch[1] pætʃ piece of cloth, etc. used to mend a hole, etc. XIV (Wycl. Bible); various transf. uses XVI. Late ME. *pacche*, *patche*, perh. var. of *peche* (AncrR.) – AN. **peche*, OF. *pieche*, dial. var. of *piece* PIECE; for the vocalism cf. CRATCH, MATCH[2]. Hence vb. XV.

patch[2] pætʃ fool, dolt. XVI. Alleged nickname of Cardinal Wolsey's domestic fool; perh. surviving dial. and colloq. as in *cross patch* ill-tempered person.

patchouli pæ·tʃuli, pətʃū·li odoriferous plant (Pogostemon), perfume prepared from it. XIX. – Hind. *pacholī*, referred by some to Tamil *pach*, *pachai-* green, *ilai* leaf.

pate peit head. XIV. Of unkn. origin.

pâté pate pie, PASTY. XVIII. F.; cf. PATTY.

patella pəte·lə (anat.) knee-pan, knee-cap. XVII. – L. *patella*, dim. of *patina*; see next.

paten pæ·tən round shallow dish for the Bread at the Eucharist. XIII (Havelok). ME. *pateyne*, *patyn* – AN. **pateine*, (O)F. *patène* or L. *patina*, *-ena* shallow dish or cooking-pan – Gr. *patánē* plate, dish, rel. to *petannúnai* display, open, *pétalon* PETAL.

patent pei·tənt, pæ·tənt A. in *letters p.*, formerly also *letters p-s*, open letter from an authority recording, enjoining, or conferring something XIV; conferred by these XVI; protected by letters patent, as an invention XVIII; B. (gen.) open, manifest XVI. In A – (O)F. *patent*, *-ente* – L. *patent-*, *patēns*, prp. of *patēre* lie open (see FATHOM); orig. – (O)F. *lettres patentes*, medL. *litteræ patentes*; in B, directly – L. Hence as sb., by ellipsis of *letters* XIV; so AN. *patente*, AL. *patens*.

pater pæ·təɹ A. short for PATERNOSTER (cf. PATTER[1]) XIV; B. (colloq.) pei·təɹ FATHER XVIII. L.

paterfamilias pei:təɹfəmi·liæs male head of a family or household. XV (Lydg.). L., f. *pater* FATHER + arch. g. of *familia* FAMILY.

paternal pətə̄·ɹnəl fatherly; derived from one's father. XVII. – late L. *paternālis*, f. L. *paternus*, f. *pater* FATHER; see -AL[1] and cf. (O)F. *paternel*, etc. So **pate·rn**ITY. XV. – (O)F. or late L.

paternoster pei·təɹ-, pætəɹnɔ·stəɹ the Lord's Prayer OE.; rosary, or a bead of this XIII; form of words used as a charm XIV (Ch.). – L. *pater noster* our Father, the first words of the Lord's Prayer in Latin, whence OF. *pater-*, *patrenostre* (mod. *patenôtre*).

path pàþ way beaten or trodden by the feet; way, course. OE. *pæþ* = OFris. *path*, *pad*, OLG. (Du.) *pad*, OHG. *phad* (G. *pfad*) :- WGerm. **paþa*. Hence **pa·th**WAY. XVI (Tindale). ¶ The cant var. *pad* (XVI), prob. – LG. *pad*, as in *squire* or *gentleman of the pad* (hence *highpad*, and simply *pad*) highwayman, survives in FOOTPAD.

pathetic pəþe·tik pert. to (esp. arousing) the emotions. XVI (earlier *-ical*, G. Harvey). – F. *pathétique* – late L. *pathēticus* – Gr. *pathētikós* sensitive, f. *pathētós* liable to suffer, f. *pathe-* of *páthos*; see next, -IC.

patho- pæ·þou, pəþɔ· repr. comb. form of Gr. *páthos* PATHOS, in modL. formations on Gr. types; **patho·**LOGY study of disease XVII (Cotgr.) – F. or modL.; so **patho-lo·g**ICAL (Boyle), **-o·logist** (Charleton).

pathos pei·þɔs, pæ·þɔs quality in speech, etc. exciting pity or sadness. XVII (Dryden; earlier in Gr. letters and in sense 'pathetic expression'). – Gr. *páthos*, rel. to *páskhein* suffer, *pénthos* grief.

-pathy pəþi terminal el. of ALLOPATHY, HOMŒOPATHY, extended in the sense 'method of cure', e.g. in *electropathy*, *hydropathy*.

patience pei·ʃəns endurance with calmness. XIII (AncrR.; earliest form with *pac-*). – (O)F. *patience*, †*pacience* corr. to It. *pazienza*, etc. – L. *patientia*, f. *patient-*, *-ēns*, prp. of *patī* suffer. So **pa·ti**ENT suffering or enduring without complaint XIV; capable *of* XVII. – (O)F. – L.; as sb. †sufferer (PPl.); one under medical treatment (Ch.).

patina pæ·tinə film produced by alteration of the surface of bronze, marble, etc. XVIII. – It. *patina* (whence F. *patine*) – L. *patina* dish (cf. PATEN).

patois pæ·twa local dialect, spec. of France or French Switzerland; hence gen. XVII (with *jargon*, Sir T. Browne). – (O)F. *patois* 'rough speech', perh. f. OF. *patoier* handle roughly, trample, f. *patte* paw (= Sp., Pg. *pata*), of unkn. origin. Cf. PATROL.

patonce pətɔ·ns (her.) of a cross with the arms expanded ✠. XVI. perh. alt. of **potencé** (XVI) having crutch heads (f. *potent* crutch, var. of *potence* crutch – F. *potence* – L. *potentia* POTENCY.

patriarch pei·triāɹk chief of a family or tribe XII; bishop of certain pre-eminent sees XIII (RGlouc., Havelok); father of an institution XVI; venerable old man XIX. – (O)F. *patriarche* – ecclL. *patriarcha* – Gr. *patriárkhēs* head of a family, f. *patriá* family, clan (f. *patḗr* FATHER) + *-arkhēs* ruler (see -ARCH). So **patriar·ch**AL[1]. XVI. – late L. **patria·rch**ATE[1]. XVII. **pa·tri**ARCHY[3] †patriarchate XVI; patriarchal government XVII. – medL.

patrician pətri·ʃən noble in ancient Rome or the later Roman Empire XV; nobleman, aristocrat XVII. – (O)F. *patricien*, f. L. *patricius*, sb. use of adj. 'of a noble father', f. *patr-*, *pater* FATHER; see -IAN.

patrico pæ·trikou (cant) parson, hedge-priest. XVI. prob. reduced form of earlier *patryng cove*, i.e. *pattering*, ppl. adj. of PATTER[1], COVE[2], quasi 'praying fellow' (cf. †*co* lad, youth XVI–XVII).

patrimony pæ·triməni property inherited from ancestors. XIV (*patrimoyne*). – (O)F. *patrimoine* – L. *patrimōnium*, f. *patri-*, *pater* FATHER + *-mōnium* -MONY; later conformed to L.

patriot pei·triət, pæ·triət †compatriot XVI; (orig., as in F., with commendatory adj.) one whose ruling passion is the love of his country XVII (Jonson). – F. *patriote* – late L. *patriōta* – Gr. *patriṓtēs*, f. *pátrios* of one's fathers, *patrís* fatherland, sb. use of adj. ancestral, f. *patr-*, *patḗr* FATHER; see -OT. ¶ The word fell into disrepute in XVIII, when the present use (for 'good patriot') became frequent in F.; cf. J.'s definition, 'ironically for a factious disturber of the government'. So **patriot**IC -ɔ·tik. XVII. – late L. – Gr. *patriōtikós*. **pa·triot**ISM. XVIII.

Patripassian pætripæ·siən one who holds that the Father suffered with, in, or through the Son. XVI. – ecclL. *patripassiānus* (Isidore), f. *patri-*, *pater* FATHER + *passus* having suffered; see PASSION, -IAN, and cf. F. *patripassien*.

patristic pətri·stik pert. to the Fathers of the Church. XIX. – G. *patristisch*, f. L. *patr-*, *pater* FATHER; see -ISTIC.

patrol pətrou·l going the rounds of a camp, etc.; person or body that does this. XVII. – G. *patrolle*, *-ouille* – F. *patrouille*, f. *patrouiller* (whence ult. **patrol** vb. XVII), alt. of *patouiller* paddle about in mud (cf. OF. *patoier*), f. *patte* paw, foot, with ending from dial. *gadrouille* mud, dirty water. ¶ Of Eur. range, through adoption from F.

patron pei·trən, pæ·trən holder of an advowson; tutelary saint; protector, upholder XIV; (in various uses repr. Rom. ones) †captain or master of a galley, etc. XV. – (O)F. *patron*, corr. to Pr. *padron*, Sp. *patron*, It. *padrone* – L. *patrōnus* protector of clients, advocate, defender; (colloq.) affectionate term of address, f. *patr-*, *pater* FATHER + *-ōnus*, var. of *-ō(n-)*. See also PATTERN. So **patron**AGE pæ·trənidʒ. XV. – (O)F. *patronage*; cf. medL. *patrōnāticum*, *-āgium*. **patron**AL[1] pətrou·nəl, pei·-, pæ·trənəl. XVII. – F. or L. **pa·tron**ESS[1]. XV. **pa·tron**IZE pæt- act towards as a patron. XVI. – †F. or medL.

patronymic pætrəni·mik derived, or forming a derivative, from the name of a father or ancestor. XVII. – late L. *patrōnymicus* (Priscian) – Gr. *patrōnumikós*, f. *patrṓnumos* named from the father, f. *patr-*, *patḗr* FATHER + *ónuma*, *ónoma* NAME; see -IC.

patroon pətrū·n A. †patron (in various senses) XVII; B. U.S. possessor of land and manorial rights granted by the Du. governments of New York and New Jersey to the Du. W. India Company XVIII. In A var. of PATRON after certain Rom. forms; in B – Du. *patroon*. See -OON.

pattamar pæ·təmāɹ †courier XVI; Indian dispatch-boat XVIII. – Pg. *patamar* – Marathi *pattamāri*, f. *patta* tidings + *-māri* carrier.

pattee, patée pæ·tei, pæ·ti (her.) of a cross the arms of which widen out from the centre ✠. XV. – F. *patté(e)*, f. *patte* paw, of unkn. origin; see -Y[5].

patten pæ·t(ə)n wooden shoe, thick-soled shoe. XIV. – (O)F. *patin* (whence Sp. *patin*, It. *pattino*), f. *patte* paw, foot (see prec.) + *-in* (repr. L. *-īnu-s* -INE[1]).

patter[1] pæ·təɹ repeat the paternoster or other prayers, etc. rapidly or glibly XIV; talk rapidly or fluently, esp. in a set formula or in a language not generally understood XV. f. PATER A. Hence **patter** sb. thieves' or beggars' cant, cheap-jack's talk XVIII.

patter[2] pæ·təɹ make a rapid succession of taps or light strokes XVII; run with rapid short steps XIX. frequent. f. PAT vb. + -ER[4].

pattern pæ·təɹn object serving as a model or specimen XIV (Ch.); decorative design XVI. ME. *patron* – (O)F. *patron* PATRON, model, pattern. ¶ The development of sense is from the notion of a patron giving an example to be copied. The change from pæ·trən (still Sc.) to pæ·təɹn is evidenced in XVI; cf. dial. *apern* (apron), *childern*.

patty pæ·ti little pie or pasty. XVIII. alt. of PÂTÉ by assoc. with PASTY.

paucity pō·siti fewness, scantiness. XV. – F. *paucité* or L. *paucitās*, f. *paucus*; see FEW, -ITY.

paulo-post-future pō·lou poust fjūtʃəɹ (gram.) future perfect. XIX. – modL. *paulō post futūrum* (Lascaris, 1494) 'the future by a little after', tr. Gr. ὁ μετ' ὀλίγον μέλλων 'the future after a little'.

paunch[1] pōnᵗʃ belly, stomach. XIV (Barbour, Ch., PPl. Gower). – AN. *pa(u)nche*, ONF. *panche*, var. of OF. *pance* (mod. *panse*) = Pr. *pansa*, Sp. *panza*, It. *pancia*, Rum. *pîntece* :– CRom. **pantice*, L. *pantic-*, *pantex* (esp. pl.) bowels, intestines.

paunch[2] pɔ̄nᵗʃ, pānᵗʃ (naut.) thick mat or wooden shield to prevent chafing. XVII (Capt. Smith). prob. identical with prec. through the use of OF. *pance* for belly armour.

pauper pɔ̄·pəɹ destitute person (in strict legal use, one who was allowed to sue in a court of law *in formâ pauperis* 'in the character of a poor man', i.e. without paying costs). XVI. – L. *pauper* poor (see FEW).

pause pɔ̄z act of ceasing for a (short) time, stop or break in speech, etc. XV (Promp. Parv.; mus. – It. *pausa*). – (O)F. *pause* or L. *pausa* – Gr. *paûsis*, f. *paúein* stop, cease. So **pause** vb. XVI. – F. *pauser* or L. *pausāre*.

pavan pæ·vən stately dance in elaborate costume. XVI. – F. *pavane* – Sp. *pavana*, poss. f. *pavon* :– L. *pāvō(n-)* PEACOCK, with allusion to the ostentatious behaviour of the bird.

pave peiv lay a street, floor, etc. with stones, etc. XIV. – (O)F. *paver*, prob. back-formation from †*pavement* (whence **pa·ve**MENT XIII) = Pr. *pavamen*, etc. (Rum. *pămînt* earth, world) – L. *pavīmentum* beaten or rammed floor, f. *pavīre* beat down, ram. So **paviour** pei·viəɹ. XV. Earlier *pavier*, alt. (see -IER[1]) of *paver* – (O)F. *paveur*; see -OUR[1], -IER[1].

pavilion pəvi·ljən (large peaked) tent XIII; projecting subdivision of a building or façade; building of light construction for pleasure or amusement XVII. – (O)F. *pavillon* tent, canopy :– L. *pāpiliō(n-)* butterfly, tent (as being likened to a butterfly's wings).

pavis pæ·vis large (convex) shield. XIV. Late ME. *paveis* – OF. **paveis*, *pavais* (now *pavois*) – It. *pavese* (whence also Sp. *pavés*) – medL. *pavense* (sc. *scūtum* shield), f. *Pavia* name of a town in Italy where such shields were orig. made. ¶ Revived by Southey and Scott after long desuetude.

pavonine pæ·vonəin pert. to a peacock. XVII. – L. *pāvonīnus*, f. *pavō(n-)* PEACOCK; see -INE[1].

paw pɔ̄ foot of a beast having claws or nails. XIII. ME. *powe*, *pawe* – OF. *powe*, *poue*, *poe* = Pr. *pauta*, Cat. *pota* :– Rom. **pauta* – Germ. **pauta*, repr. by MDu. *pōte* (whence G. *pfote*), Du. *poot*. Hence **paw** vb. XVII.

pawky pɔ̄·ki (Sc.) sly, humorously tricky. XVII. f. *pawk* (XVI, G. Douglas) trick, cunning device, of unkn. origin + -Y[1].

pawl pɔ̄l (naut.) bar to prevent a capstan, etc. from recoiling. XVII (Capt. Smith). poss. – LG., Du. *pal* rel. to adj. *pal* immobile, fixed, of unkn. origin.

pawn[1] pɔ̄n piece of the smallest value in chess. XIV (Ch.). Late ME. *poun* – AN. *poun*, OF. *poon*, *paon*, *peon*, earlier *pehon*, *pedon* pawn = Pr. *pezo*, Sp. *peon* footman, pawn, It. *pedone* footman (fem. *pedona* pawn) :– medL. *pedō(n-)* foot-soldier, f. *ped-*, *pēs* FOOT. Cf. PEON. ¶ The use goes back to Pers. *piyādah*, f. *pai* FOOT.

pawn[2] pɔ̄n pledge, surety XV; state of being pledged XVI. – OF. *pan*, also *pand*, *pant* pledge, security, plunder :– WGerm. **panda* (Icel. *pantr* is from LG.), repr. by OFris. *pand*, OS., MDu. *pant* (Du. *pand*), OHG. *pfant* (G. *pfand*); the Germ. word has been derived by some from OF. *pan* :– L. *pannus* piece of cloth. Hence vb. XVI.

paxwax pæ·kswæks tendon joining spine and occiput. XV (Promp. Parv.; also *pixwex* XVI). alt. of earlier *fax wax*, *fex wex* (XIV), also *fix-fax* (XV), which survived in dial. *fic-fac*, *fig-fag*; presumably f. *fax* (OE. *feax* hair of the head + **weaxe* growth (see WAX[2]). ¶ A further alt. is *taxwax* (*taxywaxy*) XVIII. There are several similar synon. forms in the Germ. langs., but their relationship is obscure: OE. *weald weaxe*, OFris. *walduwaxe*, OHG. *waltowahso*, Upper G. *waldwachs*, with var. MG., LG. *wildwachs*; MLG. *haerwachs*, G. *haarwachs* (for the use of 'hair' for tendon cf. Du. *geel haar* 'yellow hair').

pay[1] pei A. †pacify, please XII; give what is due in discharge of an obligation XIII; render (something due or exacted) XIV. B. (naut.) let out (rope); cause to fall, fall, to leeward XVII. – (O)F. *payer* = Pr., Sp. *pagar*, It. *pagare* :– L. *pācāre* appease, pacify, medL. pay, f. *pāc-*, *pāx* PEACE; the sense 'pay' was developed through that of pacifying a creditor. So **pay** sb. XIII. (O)F. *paie*, f. the vb. Hence **pay·**MENT. XIV. – (O)F. *paiement* = Pr. *pagamen*, etc.

pay[2] pei (naut.) smear with pitch, etc. XVII. – OF. *peier* = Pr., Sp. *pegar* :– L. *picāre*, f. *pic-*, *pix* PITCH.

paynim pei·nim †pagan countries, heathendom XIII; (arch.) pagan, heathen XIV. ME. *painim(e)* – OF. *pai(e)nime* :– ecclL. *pāgānismu-s* heathenism, f. *pāgānus* PAGAN; see -ISM.

pea[1] pī (round seed of) the plant Pisum sativum. XVII. Evolved as if a sg. from PEASE apprehended as a pl. (cf. *as like as two pease*).

pea[2] pī sliding weight of a steelyard, etc. XVIII. Evolved as if a sg. from a supposed pl. *pease*, *pe(i)se*, weight, clock weight, ME. *peis* – OF. *peis* (mod. *poids*) (cf. POISE).

pea[3] pī peak or bill of the fluke of an anchor. XIX. app. naut. pronunc. of PEAK[1].

peace pīs freedom from war, disturbance, or dissension XII (Peterborough Chron.); quiet, stillness, concord XIII (AncrR.). ME. *pais*, *pes* – AN. *pes*, OF. *pais* (mod. *paix*) = Pr. *patz*, Sp. *paz*, It., Rum. *pace* :– L. *pāce-m*, nom. *pāx* peace (cf. PACT, APPEASE). Hence **pea·cemaker.** XV; tr. L. *pācificus* PACIFIC. ¶ For the sp. *-ce* cf. ADVICE.

peaceable pī·səbl disposed to peace, †peaceful. XIV (R. Mannyng, Rolle). ME. *peisible*, *pesible* – OF. *peisible* (mod. *paisible*), with var. †*plaisible*, corr. to Pr. *pazible*, Cat. *pahible*, Sp. *apacible* meek, quiet, pleasant, *aplacible* pleasing, Pg. *aprazivel*, It. *piacevole* agreeable (dial. *pažaivel, plazéul*) :- late L. *placibilis* pleasing, f. *placēre* PLEASE + -*ibilis* -IBLE. ¶ In F. and other Rom. langs. assoc. with and conformed to L. *pāx* PEACE, and in Eng. to adjs. in -ABLE (see -BLE for the active meaning).

peach[1] pītʃ (fruit of) the tree Amygdalus persica. XIV. ME. *peche* – OF. *peche*, earlier *pesche* (mod. *pêche*) = Pr. *persega*, It. *pesca*, Rum. *piersecă* (cf. Sp. *prisco*, Pg. *pecego*) :- medL. *persica* (*pessica*), for L. *persicum* (whence OE. *persoc*, Du. *perzik*, G. *pfirsich*), for *Persicum mālum* 'Persian apple'; see PERSIAN.

peach[2] pītʃ †impeach XV; †inform against; turn informer XVI. Aphetic of *appeach*, ME. *appeche* – AN. **apecher*, for OF. *empecher* IMPEACH.

peacock pī·kɔk male bird of species of Pavo. XIV (PPl., Ch.). ME. *pecok*, f. **pē* (OE. *pēa* :- **pau*) + COCK sb. The ME. var. *pocok*, north. *pacok*, is based on ME. *pō*, *pā* :- OE. *pāwa*; both OE. forms are – L. *pāvō*, whence also MLG. *pāwe* (Du. *pauw*), OHG. *phāwo* (G. *pfau*). ¶ The source of the surnames *Poe, Pay, Pocock, Pe(a)cock*. So **pea·**HEN. XIV. ME. *pehenne*, beside *pohenne*.

pea-jacket pī·dʒæ·kit short stout overcoat. XVIII (first in Amer. sources). prob. (with assim. to JACKET) – Du. *pijjakker*, f. *pij*, MDu. *pīe* (whence †*pee* man's coat of coarse stuff XV–XVII) + *jekker* jacket.

peak[1] pīk pointed extremity; projecting part of the brim of a cap XVI; pointed top of a mountain. XVII. prob. back-formation from *peaked* (*peked* XV), var. of (dial.) *picked* pointed, f. PICK[1] + -ED[2]. In the earliest exx. of the last sense, rendering or repr. Sp., Pg. *pico* and superseding †*pike* (XVI), which is itself from Sp. and Pg., and, like †*pic* (XVII – F. *pic*), applied esp. or orig. to the Peak of Teneriffe. Cf. APEAK.

peak[2] pīk †fall, tumble; †shrink, slink, sneak; look sickly or emaciated (*p. and pine*, Sh. 'Macbeth' I iii 23). Of uncertain status and identity; the following appear to be cogn. in form and meaning: †*peak* dolt (Skelton), †*peak-goose* poor creature (XVI), *peaking* sneaking (Sh.), sickly (XVII), *peakish*, slothful, dispirited, silly (XVI).

Peak pīk hilly district in NW. Derbyshire. OE. *Pēac* in *Pēaclond*, perh. rel. to *Pūca* PUCK, as is suggested by the name Peak's Arse (OE. **Pēaces ærs*, in Domesday Book *Pechesers*) for the Peak Cavern, known also as Devil's Arse at Peak; cf. other place-names, as OE. *Pēacesdel, Pechesdon* (Domesday) Pegsdon, Bedfordshire.

peal[1] pīl †appeal, summons XIV (PPl.); ringing of a bell or bells, esp. as a summons; loud volley of sound XVI; set or ring of bells XVIII. Late ME. *pele*, aphetic of *apele*, APPEAL sb. Hence vb. XVII (Milton).

peal[2] pīl young or small salmon. XVI. First in *salmon pele*, of unkn. origin.

pear pɛəɹ (fruit of) species of Pyrus, esp. P. communis. OE. *pere*, *peru*, corr. to MLG., MDu. *pere* (Du. *peer*) – popL. **pira*, whence (O)F. *poire*, Pr., Sp., It. *pera*, Rum. *pară*), fem. sg. repl. L. *pirum*, of alien and unkn. origin (cf. Gr. *ápion* pear).

pearl pɔ̄ɹl globular or oval gem formed within the shell of a bivalve mollusc XIV; size of printing type between agate and diamond XVII. ME. *perle* – (O)F. *perle* = Pr., Sp., It. *perla* :- Rom. **perla*, prob. for **pernula*, dim. of L. *perna* leg, ham, leg-of-mutton shaped bivalve (cf. It. dial. *perna* pearl, It. *pernocchia* pearl-oyster). ¶ The Rom. word is also the source of OE. *pærl*, OHG. *perala*, *berla* (G. *perle*), MDu. *pārele* (Du. *paarl*). Hence **pearl**ED[2]. XIV (Gower); after F. *perlé*. **pea·r**LY[1]. XV.

pearmain pɛə·ɹmein variety of †pear XV, of apple XVI. Late ME. *par-*, *permayn* – OF. *par-*, *permain* kind of pear (mod. Norman *permaine* kind of apple is from Eng.), prob. – Rom. **Parmānus* (repl. L. *Parmēnsis*) of *Parma*, It. town and province (cf. PARMESAN).

peasant pe·z(ə)nt one who lives in the country and works on the land. XV. – AN. *paisant*, OF. *païsant*, *païsent* (mod. *paysan*), refash. (after -*ant*) of earlier *païsenc*, f. *païs* (mod. *pays*) country (= Pr. *paes*, It. *paese*) :- Rom. **pāgēnsis*, f. *pāgus* country district (cf. PAGAN) + Germ. *-*iŋg*-, denoting origin. Hence **pea·sant**RY. XVI.

pease pīz (arch. or dial.) pea plant or its seed. OE. *pise*, pl. *pisan* – late L. *pisa*, pl. *pisæ*, for earlier *pisum*, pl. *pisa* – Gr. *píson*, pl. *písa*. ME. *pese*, pl. *pesen*, survive as arch. and dial. *pease*, *peason*; see also PEA[1].

peat pīt piece of the vegetable substance of which bogs or mosses consist. XIV. – AL. *peta* (XII), also in *petamora* 'peat-moor', *petaria*, -*er(i)a* peat-bog, perh. f. the Celtic base **pett-*, which is prob. the ult. source of PIECE.

peavey pī·vi lumberer's hook. XIX. f. surname of the inventor.

pebble pe·bl small rounded stone. Late OE. (i) *papel*, *popel* (found only in comb. with *stān* STONE), surviving in dial. *popple* and in the place-names *Popplewick* (Notts), *Poppleford* (Derby), *Poppleton* (Yorks); (ii) *pyppel* in *pyppelrīpig* pebble-stream, surviving in W. midl. *pipple*; a var. of the latter with *b*, **pybbel*, is repr. by s.w. †*puble* (XIII–XIV), midl. †*pibbil* (XIV), later †*pible*, *pibble*, of which *pebble* may be a var. with lowered vowel, unless its ult. origin is to be seen in the dubious OE. local name *pæbbeles hol*.

peccable pe·kəbl liable to sin. XVII. – F. *peccable* – med. L. *peccābilis*, f. *peccāre* sin; see -ABLE. So **peccadillo** pekədi·lou venial or trifling offence. XVI. – Sp. *pecadillo*, dim. of *pecado* (= F. *péché*, etc.) – L. *peccātum*, sb. use of n. pp. of *peccāre*. So **pe·cc**ANT sinning; (med.) morbid XVII; partly after (O)F. *peccant*. **peccavi** pekei·vai. XVI. L., 'I have sinned', 1st sg. pt. of *peccāre*.

peccary pe·kəri Central and S. Amer. quadruped allied to the swine. XVII (*pakeera, pec(c)ary*). – Carib (of Guiana and Venezuela) *pakira*.

peck[1] pek ¼ bushel. XIII. ME. *pek* – AN. *pek* (whence AL. *pecca, peccum* XIII), of unkn. origin, perh. containing the same base as F. *picotin* measure of oats.

peck[2] pek strike or take food with the beak XIV (Ch., Trevisa, Wycl. Bible); strike with pointed tool XVI. prob. – MLG. *pekken* peck with the beak; ult. source unkn.

pecten pe·kten comb-like structure. XVIII. – L. *pecten* (*-in-*) comb, wool-card, pubic hair, rel. to *pectere*, Gr. *pekteîn, pékein* comb, *pékos* fleece, Lith. *pešu* I pull by the hair, OE. *feax*, OHG. *fahs* hair. So **pe·ctin**ATE[2] formed like a comb. XVIII. – L.

pectic pe·ktik (chem.) *p. acid*, gelatinous substance forming a constituent of fruit jellies. XIX. – Gr. *pēktikós*, f. *pēktós* congealed, f. **pēg-* in *pēgnúein* made firm or solid; see -IC. Also **pe·ct**IN, **pe·ct**OSE[2].

pectoral pe·ktərəl pert. to the breast or chest XVI; sb. object worn on the breast XV; medicine for affections of the chest XVII. – (O)F. *pectoral* – L. *pectorālis* (*-āle* breastplate), f. *pector-, pectus* breast, chest.

peculation pekjulei·ʃən wrongful appropriation of property. XVII. f. pp. stem of L. *pecūlārī*, rel. to *pecūlium*; see next and -ATION.

peculiar pĭkjū·liəɹ that is one's own XV; individual, particular XVI; uncommon, odd XVII; sb. parish or church independent of the jurisdiction of the ordinary XVI. – L. *pecūliāris* not held in common with others, f. *pecūlium* property in cattle, private property, f. *pecu* cattle, money (cf. next), rel. to Vedic *páçu*, OE. *feoh* live stock, property, OFris. *fia*, OS., OHG. *fehu* (G. *vieh*), ON. *fé*, Goth. *faihu*; f. IE. base **peku-*. See -AR. Hence **peculiar**ITY -æ·rĭti. XVII.

pecuniary pĭkjū·niəri pert. to money. XVI. – L. *pecūniārius*, f. *pecūnia* money, orig. 'riches in cattle', f. *pecu*; see prec. and -ARY. So **pecu·n**IOUS moneyed (XIV; rare), now repr. by IMPECUNIOUS. – L. *pecūniōsus*.

pedagogue pe·dəgɔg instructor of youth. XIV (Trevisa). – L. *pædagōgus* – Gr. *paidagōgós* slave who took a boy to and from school, f. *paid-, paîs* boy (cf. PAEDO-) + *agōgós* leading, *ágein* lead (see ACT). So **pe·dagog**Y[3] -gɔgi, -gɔdʒi. XVI, **pedago·g**IC. XVII; after F.

pedal[1] pe·dəl lever worked by the foot. XVII. – F. *pédale* – It. *pedale* foot-stalk, tree-trunk (*pedale d'organo* organ pedal) :– L. *pedālis*, f. *ped-, pēs* FOOT; see -AL[1].

pedal[2] pe·dəl lower and thicker part of straw of Italian production. XIX. – It. *pedale*; see prec.

pedant pe·dənt †schoolmaster XVI (Sh.); person who overrates book-learning XVI. – F. *pédant* – It. *pedante*, of obscure origin; the first el. is presumably that of PEDAGOGUE, to which has been added the prp. ending *-ante*, -ANT. In XVI–XVII also †*pedanti(e), -ee*, direct from It. Hence **peda·nt**IC pidæ·ntik. XVII; corr. to F. *pédantesque*, It. *pedantesco*; -ICAL XVI (Sh.). **pe·dant**RY. XVII; after F. *pédanterie* or It. *pedanteria* (used by Sidney).

peddle pe·dl A. follow the occupation of a pedlar XVI; B. busy oneself with trifles XVI. First recorded in *peddling*; in A backformation from *peddler*, PEDLAR; in B prob. var. of PIDDLE by assoc. in form and sense with A.

pedestal pe·distəl base supporting a column, etc. – F. *piédestal* (†*pied d'estal*) – It. *piedestallo*, i.e. *piè* FOOT, *di* of, *stallo* STALL; the first syll. was conformed to L. *ped-, pēs* FOOT.

pedestrian pĭde·striən going on foot; prosaic, uninspired; also sb. XVIII. f. F. *pédestre* or its source L. *pedester, -tr-* going on foot, (after Gr. πεζός) written in prose :– **peditris*, f. **pedit-*, f. *ped-, pēs* FOOT + **-ter-*; see -IAN. Earlier †**pede·str**IAL, †**pede·str**IOUS. XVII.

pediatrician pe:diətri·ʃən one concerned with the health of children. XX. f. Gr. *paid-, paîs* child + *iātrós* physician + -ICIAN. So **pedia·tr**IST.

pedicel pe·disel (bot.) small stalk of a plant. XVII. – modL. *pedicellus*, f. L. *pedīculus* (whence **pe·dic**LE XV), dim. of *ped-, pēs* FOOT.

pedicure pe·dikjuəɹ one whose business is the surgical treatment of the feet (also **pe·dicur**IST); the treatment. XIX. – F. *pédicure*, f. L. *ped-, pēs* FOOT + *curāre* CURE.

pedigree pe·digrī genealogy in tabular form; one's line of ancestors; family descent. XV (*pedegru, -gre, petegreu, -gree*). – AN. **pe de gru* = OF. **pie de grue* crane's foot, i.e. *pie* (mod. *pied* :– L. *pedem, pēs* FOOT), *de* of, *gru* crane (:– L. *grū-s*); so called from the mark /|\ used to denote succession in a genealogical tree; later forms show assim. to *degree*.

pediluvium pedilʲū·viəm foot-bath. XVII. modL., f. L. *ped-, pēs* FOOT + *-luvium* washing, f. *luere* wash (cf. ABLUTION).

pediment pe·dimənt A. triangular gable-like part crowning a façade XVII; B. base, foundation XVIII. Earlier *pedament* (Evelyn), *pedement* (Randle Holme), refash. of *periment* (XVI), expl. as 'corrupt English' for *perimeter* in R. Dallington's 'Hypnerotomachia' 1592, but prob. workman's or rustic's deformation of PYRAMID. Sense B is due to direct assoc. with L. *ped-*, *pēs* FOOT and -MENT, and the present form simulates derivation from these elements.

pedlar pe·dləɹ travelling vendor of small wares. XIV (*pedlere*, PPl.). alt. of †*pedder* (XIII), f. (dial.) *ped* wicker pannier (XIV), of unkn. origin + -ER[1]; for the ending *-ler* cf. (dial.) *tinkler* (XII), beside *tinker*. Hence PEDDLE.

pedology pėdɔ·lədʒi science of soils. XX. – Russ. *pedológiya*, f. Gr. *pédon* ground (cf. Skr. *padám* step, track, place) + -LOGY.

pedometer pėdɔ·mĭtəɹ instrument for recording the number of steps taken. XVIII. – F. *pédomètre* (Bion, 1723), f. *pedo-*, irreg. comb. form (for *pedi-*) of L. *pēs* FOOT; see -OMETER. ¶ F. *podomètre* is earlier, 1712.

pedrail pe·dreil device for facilitating progress of heavy vehicles over rough ground. XX. f. L. *ped-*, *pēs* FOOT + RAIL[2].

pedrero pėdrɛə·rou piece of ordnance for discharging stones. XVI. – Sp. *pedrero* = Pr. *peirier*, It. *petriere*, F. *pierrier* (adopted in Eng. as †*perrier* before 1400) :– L. **petrāriu-s* (cf. medL. *petrāria*), f. *petra* stone (cf. PETRIFY); vars. in *pet(e)r-*, *patar-*, *pater-* have been current since 1600.

peduncle pidʌ·ŋkl (bot.) stalk of flower or fruit. XVIII. – modL. *pedunculus* (Linnæus, 1750), f. L. *ped-*, *pēs* FOOT + *-unculus* -UNCLE.

pee pī (dial., colloq.) make water. XVIII. euphem. or nursery substitute for PISS; cf. F. *faire pipi*.

peek pīk peer, peep. XVI. Early mod. *pe(e)ke* (Skelton), preceded by rare ME. *pike* (Ch.); parallel to *kike*, *keek* (XIV, now Sc. and dial.), which has LG. cogns. Also *peek-bo!* (XVI), superseded by *peep-bo!*

peel[1] pīl †stake, fence of stakes XIV; (prob. short for †*p. house* house defended by a 'peel', XVI) small fortified dwelling or tower on the Scottish Border XVIII (but cf. AL. *pela*, *pelum* tower, castle XIII). – AN. *pel*, OF. *piel* (mod. *pieu*) stake :– L. *pālu-s*, *pālum* PALE[1].

peel[2] pīl A. †plunder, pillage XIII; B. strip outer layer of XV. ME. *peolien*, *pilien*, later *pele*, *pile*, *pill*, repr. OE. **peolian*, **pilian*, recorded only late in *pyleð* peels (intr.) – L. *pilāre*; varies with *pill* in early modEng. and dial. ¶ The differentiation in literary Eng. between *peel* and *pill* may have been assisted by (O)F. *peler* peel, *piller* pillage. Hence **peel** sb. XVI (repl. earlier *pill*) rind, skin; cf. AN. *peel* (XIV).

peel[3] pīl (U.S., dial., and techn.) shovel. XIV (*pele*). – OF. *pele* (mod. *pelle*) = Pr., Sp., It. *pala* :– L. *pāla* :– **pagslā*, f. base of *pangere* fix, plant (cf. PACT). See PALE[1].

peeler pī·ləɹ (hist.) policeman. XIX ('carried off . . by a set of fellows well known in Ireland . . . by the name of Peelers', 1817). orig. nickname for a member of the Irish constabulary founded under the secretaryship (1812–18) of Robert *Peel*; see -ER[1] and cf. BOBBY.

peep[1] pīp (dial.) utter a weak shrill sound. XV (Lydg.). imit.; cf. CHEEP. Hence sb. XV.

peep[2] pīp look through a narrow opening XV; emerge a little into view XVI. For the expressive combination of initial *p* with *ee* cf. PEEK, PEER[2], and dial. *pee*, *pie* (XVII). Hence sb. XVI (of the first appearance of daylight).

peer[1] piəɹ (one's) equal XIII; member of the nobility XIV. – AN., OF. *per*, *peer* (mod. *pair*) = Pr., Sp. *par*, It. *pare* :– L. *pare-m*, *pār* equal; cf. PAIR. Hence **pee·rage** XV, **pee·ress**[1]. XVII.

peer[2] piəɹ look narrowly; peep *out*, show itself XVI. var. of *pire* (XIV) (e.g. Sh. 'Merchant of Venice' I i 19, *piring*), corr. to LG. *pīren*; perh. partly aphetic of APPEAR.

peevish pī·viʃ †silly, foolish XIV (PPl.); †spiteful, malignant XV; †perverse, obstinate; querulous, fretful XVI. Rare before XVI; of unkn. origin, with ending assim. to -ISH[1]. Hence **peeved**[1] pīvd (orig. U.S.) annoyed, vexed. XX. ppl. formation on a supposed verb-stem.

peewit see PEWIT.

peg peg pin or bolt of wood, etc. (cf. *peg-top*) XV; (dial.) tooth; (in stringed instruments) pin with which the tension of the strings is adjusted; step, degree XVI; (orig. Anglo-Indian) measure of drink XIX. First in 'Prompt. Parv.' (*pegge*), prob. of LDu. origin (cf. MDu. *pegge*, Du. dial. *peg* plug, peg, LG. *pigge* peg; also MLG., MDu. *pegel* peg, pin, bolt). Hence **peg** vb. fix with a peg XVI; mark with pegs; *p. out*, die (sl.) XIX.

Pegasus pe·gəsəs winged horse (L. *Pēgasus* – Gr. *Πήγασος*) of Greek and Roman mythology (cf. HIPPOCRENE), by modern writers (first in Boiardo's 'Orlando Innamorato', *c.*1490) repr. as the favourite steed of the Muses and said to carry poets in their 'flights'. XVI. In late ME. (Ch., Lydg.) †*Pegasee* – medL. (*equus*) *Pegasēus*, for L. *Pegaseius* – Gr. *Πηγάσειος*, f. *πηγή* spring.

pejorative pe·dʒərətiv, pī·dʒərətiv, pidʒɔ·rətiv depreciatory in meaning. XIX. – F. *péjoratif*, *-ive*, f. pp. stem of late L. *pējōrāre* make worse, f. *pējor* worse; see -ATIVE.

pekin pīki·n silk stuff. XVIII. – F. *pékin*, f. Chinese place-name (so spelt by Jesuit missionaries) *Pēkīng* 'northern capital')(*Nānkīng* 'southern capital' (see NANKEEN).

pekoe pe·kou, pī·kou superior black tea, so called because the leaves are picked young while the down is on them. XVIII (*peco*, *pack-*

ho). – Chinese (Amoy) *pek-ho*, i.e. *pek*, *pak* (= Mandarin *peh*, *pai*) white, *ho* (= Mandarin *hao*) down, hair.

pelage pe·lidʒ fur, wool, etc. of a quadruped. XIX. – F. *pelage*, f. *poil*, OF. *peil*, *pel* hair (:– L. *pilu-s*), after OF. *pilain* (:– **pilāmen*); see -AGE.

pelagic pėlæ·dʒik pert. to the open sea, oceanic. XVII. – L. *pelagicus*, f. *pelagus* sea – Gr. *pélagos* prop. level surface of the sea; perh. rel. to L. *plānus* PLAIN, PLANE; see -IC.

pelerine pe·lərin mantle, cape. XVIII. – F. *pèlerine* deep collar on a mantle, fem. of *pèlerin* PILGRIM.

pelf pelf †spoil, booty XIV; †property XV; money, 'filthy lucre'; †trash, (now dial.) refuse XVI. – ONF. **pelfe*, recorded as *peuffe* (mod. Norman F. *peufe*), var. of OF. *pelfre*, *peufre* spoil (in AL. *pelfra*, *pelfrum*), rel. to *pelf(r)er* pillage, rob (in AL. *pelf(r)are*), and **pelferie*, *peuferie*, whence Eng. †*pelf* vb. (XIII), †*pelfry* (XV); of unkn. origin; cf. PILFER.

pelican pe·likən large gregarious fish-eating water-fowl OE.; †form of alembic; instrument for extracting teeth XVI. OE. *pellican*, reinforced in ME. by (O)F. *pélican* – late L. *pelicānus* (Jerome) – Gr. *pelekán* (of which there was a parallel form *pelekînos*), prob. f. *pélekus* axe (corr. to Skr. *páraçus*), *pelekân* to hew with an axe, perh. with reference to the appearance or action of the long hooked bill; cf. Gr. *pelekâs* woodpecker.

pelisse pəlī·s fur or furred garment; long mantle worn by women. XVIII. – (O)F. *pelisse* = Pr. *pelisa*, etc. – medL. *pellicia*; see PILCH.

pellagra pelæ·grə disease marked by cracked skin occurring in the Italian rice districts. XIX. – It. *pellagra*, f. *pelle* skin (:– L. *pelli-s* FELL[1]) + *-agra*, after PODAGRA.

pellet pe·lit small ball; ball of stone used as a missile, cannon-shot, (now) small shot. XIV (Gower, PPl, Ch.). Late ME. *pelote*, *pelet* – (O)F. *pelote* = Pr. *pelota* (cf. PELOTA), *pilota*, It. †*pillotta* :– Rom. **pilotta*, dim. of L. *pila* ball, PILL.

pellicle pe·likl thin skin, cuticle, film. XVI. – F. *pellicule* – L. *pellicula*, dim. of *pellis* skin, FELL[1]; see -CLE. Earlier **pe·lli**CULE XIV.

pellitory pe·litəri A. plant Anacyclus Pyrethrum, 'p. of Spain'; B. plant Parietaria officinalis, 'p. of the wall' XVI. In sense A alt. of late ME. *peletre* (XIV) – OF. *peletre*, alt. of *peretre*, corr. to Pr., Sp. *pelitre*, It. *pilatro* – L. PYRETHRUM. In sense B alt. of †*peritorie*, †*paretorie* – AN. *paritarie*, OF. *paritaire* (mod. *pariétaire*) – late L. *parietāria*, sb. use (sc. *herba*) of fem. of *parietārius*, f. *pariet-*, *pariēs* wall. ¶ For the change of ending cf. FUMITORY.

pell-mell pelme·l in mingled confusion, †indiscriminately, in hurried disorder; also adj. and sb. XVI (earlier †*pelly melly* XV). – F. *pêle-mêle*, OF. *pesle mesle*, of which there were early vars. *mesle mesle*, *mesle pesle*, all jingling redupls. on *mesle*, stem of *mesler* (mod. *mêler*) mix, MEDDLE.

pellucid pĭlʲū·sid transmitting light. XVII. – L. *pellūcidus*, f. *pellūcēre*, *perlūcēre* shine through; see PER- (1), LUCID.

pelmet pe·lmėt valance, as to conceal curtain rods. XIX. prob. alt. – F. *palmette* palm-leaf design on a cornice, f. *palme* PALM[1]; see PALMETTE.

peloid pe·loid, pī·loid pert. to muds, peats, etc. XX. f. Gr. *pēlós* clay, mud + -OID. So **pelo-** comb. form of Gr. *pēlós*.

pelota pĭlou·tə Basque game played in a court with a ball. XIX. – Sp. *pelota* ball; see PELLET.

pelt[1] pelt skin with short wool on it XV; raw skin of an animal XVI. Either (1) var. (by a rare kind of syncope) of †*pellet* – OF. *pel(l)ete*, dim. (see -ET) of *pel* (mod. *peau*) :– L. *pelli-s* skin, FELL[1]; or (2) back-formation from PELTRY, perh. after *paste* / *pastry*.

pelt[2] pelt attack with many and repeated blows (now with something thrown) XV; speed along XIX. perh. contr. of PELLET (cf. prec.), as if primarily 'throw stones at'. Cf. colloq. F. *peloter* beat. Hence **pelt** sb. act of pelting; (dial.) outburst of temper XVI; *full p.* at full speed XIX.

peltate pe·lteit shield-shaped. XVIII. – modL. *peltātus*, f. L. *pelta* (bot.) applied to shield-like structures; see -ATE[2]. ¶ L. *peltātus* meant 'armed with a shield'.

peltry pe·ltri undressed skins, fur-skins coll. XV. – AN. *pelterie* (Gower), OF. *peleterie* (mod. *pelleterie* pɛltri), f. *peletier* furrier, f. *pel* (mod. *peau*) :– L. *pellis* FELL[1]; see -RY. ¶ Not exemplified between XVI and XVIII; in mod. use re-adopted through Canadian F.

pelvis pe·lvis (anat.) lowest or hindmost cavity of the trunk in vertebrates. XVII. – L. *pelvis* basin, with cogns. in Skr., Gr., and Sl.; the anat. applications are modern.

pemmican pe·mikən (among N. Amer. Indians) meat prepared by drying, pounding, mixing with fat, etc. XVIII. – Cree *pimecan*, f. *pime* fat, greasy.

pen[1] pen enclosure for domestic animals. Not recorded in literary use before XIV, but presumably repr. OE. *penn*, which is, however, evidenced only in designations of local features of uncertain meaning; implied in OE. *onpennad* 'unpenned', opened, with which has been compared LG. *pennen* bolt, but this is prob. to be connected with PIN. So **pen** vb.[1] enclose, confine. XII; OE. **pennian*, as in *onpennad*; also ME. *bipennen* (XIII).

pen[2] pen instrument, orig. quill, for writing XIII (Cursor M.); (dial.) feather XIV (PPl., Wycl. Bible, Trevisa). ME. *penne* (two syll.) – (O)F. *penne* – L. *penna* feather, pl. pinions, wings, in late L. pen; see FEATHER. Hence **pen** vb.[2] XV. **pe·n**KNIFE. XV; orig. one used for mending quill pens.

penal pī·nəl pert. to punishment. XV. – (O)F. *pénal* or L. *pœnālis*, f. *pœna* PAIN; see -AL[1]. Hence **pe·nal**IZE. XIX. So **penal**TY[2] pe·nəlti punishment imposed. XVI. – legal AN. **penalte* (cf. *severalty, specialty*), for F. *pénalité* – medL. *pœnālitās*.

penance pe·nəns †repentance, penitence; penitential discipline or observance XIII; ordinance for administering this (one of the sacraments) XIV. – OF. *penance* :– L. *pœnitentia* PENITENCE; see -ANCE.

Penates pĭnei·tiz household gods of the Romans. XVI. – L. *Penātēs* pl., f. *penus* provision of food, rel. to *penes* (cf. PENETRATE).

penchant pã·ʃã bent, inclination. XVII (Dryden). – F. *penchant*, sb. use of prp. of *pencher* incline = Pr. *penjar* :– Gallo-Rom. **pendicāre*, f. L. *pendēre* hang (see PENDENT).

pencil pe·nsĭl artist's paint brush XIV (Ch.); writing implement of black lead, chalk, etc.; set of convergent rays XVII; set of straight lines meeting in a point XIX. Late ME. *pensel, -cel* – OF. *pincel* (mod. *pinceau*) = Pr. *pinzel* (whence Sp., Pg. *pincel*) :– Gallo-Rom. **pēnicellum*, for L. *pēnicillum* paint brush, dim. of *pēniculus* brush, dim. of *pēnis* tail, PENIS; see -CULE. Hence **pe·ncil** vb. XVI.

pendant pe·ndənt hanging part XIV; (archit., etc.) truss, spandrel; (naut.) hanging rope, PENNANT; tapering flag, PENNON XV; that by which a thing is suspended XVI; parallel, match XVIII. – (O)F. *pendant*, sb. use of prp. of *pendre* hang; see next.

pendent pe·ndənt hanging, overhanging XV; (gram.) XIX. Late ME. *penda(u)nt* (later latinized) – (O)F. *pendant*, prp. of *pendre* = Pr. *pendre* :– Gallo-Rom. **pendere*, for L. *pendēre* hang, rel. to *pendere* weigh, *pondus* weight; see -ENT. ¶ From the same base are: *appendix, compendium, compensate, depend, dispense, expend, expence, impend, pensile, pension, pensive, perpend, perpendicular, poise, ponder, ponderous, prepense, preponderate, suspend, suspense.*

pendentive pende·ntiv (archit.) each of the spherical triangles formed by the intersection of a hemispherical dome by two pairs of opposite arches. XVIII. – F. *pendentif* (Delorme), f. L. *pendent-, -ēns*; see prec., -IVE.

pending pe·ndiŋ A. awaiting decision XVIII; B. prep. throughout the continuance of XVII. Anglicization of (O)F. *pendant* (see PENDENT) in suspense, not concluded or settled, as in OF. *le plet pendant* the suit being in process, modelled on L. *lite pendente, pendente lite*; for the development of the prep. cf. DURING, NOTWITHSTANDING.

pendulous pe·ndjŭləs hanging down XVII; suspended so as to swing XVIII. f. L. *pendulus* pendent, f. *pendēre*; see PENDENT, -ULOUS.

pendulum pe·ndjŭləm body suspended so as to swing freely, as for regulating movements of a clock's works. XVII (Boyle, 1660). – modL. *pendulum*, sb. use of n. of L. *pendulus* PENDULOUS; after It. *pendolo* (Galileo, 1637); cf. F. *pendule* (1664).

penetralia penitrei·liə innermost parts. XVII. L., pl. of *penetral*, f. stem of *penetrāre*; see next.

penetrate pe·nitreit make a way into. XVI. f., after (O)F. *pénétrer*, pp. stem of L. *penetrāre* place within, enter within, f. *penitus* (cf. *intus* / *intrāre*) inner, inmost, into the inmost recesses, rel. to *penes* within, in the power of. So **pe·netr**ABLE. XV (Lydg.). **penetr**A·TION. XVII (Bacon). – F. – L.

penguin pe·ŋgwin †great auk (of Newfoundland); bird of the southern hemisphere having scaly paddles. XVI. Of unkn. origin; first recorded in both applications in reports published by Hakluyt (1589, 1600); the earliest accounts mention an island of the name; the superficial resemblance to W. *pen gwyn* white head, referred to 1582, has suggested that the name was first applied by Breton fishermen to the northern bird. ¶ F. *pingouin* (1600) is still applied to the great auk, the penguin being *manchot*.

penicillate penisi·leit tufted, pencilled. XIX. f. L. *pēnicillum* PENCIL + -ATE[2]; see next.

penicillin penisi·lin therapeutic drug derived from Penicillium notatum. XX. f. modL. *Penicillium* generic name of moulds, so named from their brush-like sporangia, f. L. *pēnicillum* PENCIL; see -IN.

peninsula pĭni·nsjŭlə piece of land nearly surrounded by water. XVI (Leland). – L. *pæninsula*, f. *pæne* almost (cf. PENITENT) + *insula* ISLAND. Hence **peni·nsul**AR. XVII; after F. *péninsulaire*.

penis pī·nis membrum virile. XVII. – L. *pēnis* tail, usu. male copulatory organ, rel. to Gr. *péos*, Skr. *pásas*.

penitence pe·nitəns †penance XII; contrition leading to amendment XVI (Sh.). – (O)F. *pénitence* – L. *pænitentia*, f. *pænitent-, -ēns*, prp. of *pænitet* (in medL. *pœnitet*) cause want or discontent to, make sorry, perh. rel. to *pæne* scarcely, *pænūria* PENURY; see -ENCE and cf. PENANCE. So **pe·nit**ENT adj. XIV; sb. XV. – (O)F. – L. prp. **penite·nt**IAL. XVI. – late L. *pænitentiālis* (sb. *-āle*). **penite·nti**ARY adj. pert. to penitence XVI; pert. to reformatory treatment of criminals XVIII; sb. official dealing with penitents XV. – medL. *paenitentiārius*.

pennant pe·nənt †pendant; pennon. XVII. Blending in form of PENDANT and PENNON.

Pennant pe·nənt (geol.) name of gritty strata in S. Wales, etc. XVIII. Welsh, f. *pen* head, *nant* valley.

pennon pe·nən long narrow flag or streamer XIV (Barbour, Ch., Trevisa, Gower); (poet.) wing, pinion XVII (Milton). – (O)F. *pennon* = Pr. *peno*, It. *pennone* :– Rom. deriv. of L. *penna* PEN[2]; cf. -OON.

penny pe·ni coin of the value of $\frac{1}{12}$ shilling. OE. *peniġ*, *pæniġ*, pl. *peneġas*, *pæneġas*, earlier *pen(n)ing*, *pending* = OFris. *penning*, *panning*, OS. (Du.) *penning*, OHG. *pfenning*, also *phantinc*, *phenting* (G. *pfennig*), ON. *penningr*, pl. *pengar* money :– Germ. **panniŋgaz*, **pandiŋgaz* (not in Gothic, and the ON. word may be from Eng.), which has been referred to **pand-* PAWN[2] with suffix *-*iŋg*-, as in OHG. *cheisurung* imperial gold coin, SHILLING. OE. pl. *peneġas* gave ME. *peneȝes*, whence *penies*, *pen(n)is*, contr. *pens* XIV, later sp. *pence* (XVI) pens; in comb. with a numeral pəns; *pennies* pe·niz repr. a new formation.

pennyroyal peniroi·əl species of mint, Mentha Pulegium. XVI (*penneryall*, *pene-*, *peny-*). alt. of *puliol(e) reall* (*ryall*) XV – AN. *puliol real*, i.e. OF. *pouliol* (mod. *pouliot*) and *real* ROYAL; *pouliol* corr. to Cat. *poliol*, It. dial. *pelizol*, *poledzol*, etc. :– Rom. **pūlegeōlum*, f. L. *pūle(g)ium*, thyme (whence OF. *pouli*, Pr. *poleg*, Sp. *poleo*, It. *puleggio*, and OHG. *pulei*). The change of *puliol* to *penny* is unexpl.; no intermediate forms are known.

penology pīnɔ·lədʒi scientific study of punishment. XIX. f. L. *pœna* penalty; see PAIN, -OLOGY.

penseroso pensərou·zou melancholy (person). XVIII. From the title of Milton's 'Il Penseroso' (1632) 'the thoughtful man' – It. †*penseroso* (now *pensieroso*), f. †*pensiere* thought – Pr. *pensier*, f. Rom. **pēnsāre* (see PANSY, POISE).

pensile pe·nsail hanging, vaulted. XVII. – L. *pēnsilis*, f. *pēns-*, pp. stem of *pendēre* hang; see PENDENT, -ILE.

pension pe·nʃən fixed or regular payment, spec. out of the revenues of a benefice XIV; payment made by members of a society (as an inn of court) for general expenses XV (hence, consultative assembly of Gray's Inn XVI); annuity for past services XVI; †payment for board and lodging or education; boarding-house (now only as F. pãsjõ) XVII. – (O)F. *pension* – L. *pēnsiō(n-)* payment, rent, f. *pēns-*, pp. stem of *pendere* weigh, pay, rel. to *pendēre*; see PENDENT, -ION. So **pe·nsion**ER[2] one in receipt of a pension; one who makes a stated periodical payment, spec. commoner at Cambridge Univ. XV. – AN. *pensionner*, OF. *pensionnier* – medL. *pensiōnārius* (whence **pe·nsion**ARY XVI).

pensive pe·nsiv plunged in thought. XIV (PPl.). Late ME. *pensyf*, *-yve* – (O)F. *pensif*, *-ive*, f. *penser* think – L. *pēnsāre* weigh, balance, consider, f. *pēns-*; see POISE, -IVE.

pent pent closely confined. XVI. pp. of †*pend* (XV), extended form of PEN vb.[1], due partly to pt. and pp. *penned*; its use has developed, like that of *spent*, independently of the vb.

penta- pe·ntə- repr. Gr. *penta-*, comb. form of *pénte* FIVE, used since late XVII in techn. terms from Gr. elements or on Gr. analogies.

pentacle pe·ntəkl pentagram, pentangle. XVI. – medL. **pentaculum*, f. Gr. *penta-* + *-culum*; see PENTA-, -CLE. Cf. F. †*pentacle* 5-branched candlestick, It. *pentacolo* 5-pointed star.

pentad pe·ntæd number five, group of five XVII; (chem.) XIX. – Gr. *pentad-*, *pentás*, later var. of *pempás*, f. *pémpe*, dial. var. of *pénte* FIVE; see -AD[1].

pentagon pe·ntəgən five-angled figure. XVI (Digges). – F. *pentagone* or late L. *pentagōnum* – Gr. *pentágōnon*, sb. use of n. of *pentágōnos*; see PENTA-, -GON. So **pentagon**AL[1] pentæ·gənəl. XVI (Digges). – F. or medL.

pentagram pe·ntəgræm the figure ☆. XIX. – Gr. *pentágrammon*, sb. use of n. of *pentágrammos* of five lines; see PENTA-, -GRAM. ¶ Called also PENTACLE, *pentalpha* (from its presenting the form of alpha, *A*, in five different positions), PENTANGLE.

pentameter pentæ·mitəɹ (pros.) line of five feet or five stresses. XVI. – L. *pentameter* (whence also F. *pentamètre*) – Gr. *pentámetros*, *-on*, sb. uses of m. and n. of adj. f. *pénte* + *métron*; see PENTA-, METRE.

pentangle pe·ntæŋgl pentagram. XIV (Sir Gawayne). perh. – medL. **pentangulum*, alt. of **pentaculum* PENTACLE after L. *angulus* ANGLE[2].

Pentateuch pe·ntətjūk the first five books of the O.T. XVI (in earliest use pl.). – ecclL. *pentateuchus* – ecclGr. *pentáteukhos*, sb. use of adj., f. *pénte* PENTA- + *teûkhos* implement, vessel, (later) book. Cf. HEPTATEUCH, HEXATEUCH.

Pentecost pe·ntikɔst the Jewish Feast of Weeks; Christian feast observed on the seventh Sunday ('the fiftieth day') after Easter, Whitsunday (cf. Acts ii. 1 for the transf. application). OE. *pentecosten* – acc. of ecclL. *Pentēcostē* – Gr. *Pentēkostḗ*, sb. use (sc. *heortḗ* feast or *hēmérā* day) of fem. ordinal adj. of *pentḗkonta* fifty, f. *pénte* FIVE + *-konta* (cf. L. *quinquā|ginta*); so Goth. *paintekuste*, and d. pl. forms in OS. *te pincoston*, OHG. *zi pfinkustīn* (G. *Pfingsten*); re-adopted in ME. from OF. So **Pentecostal**[1]. XVI. – ecclL.

penthemimer penþimi·məɹ (pros.) catalectic colon of five half-feet. XVII. – late L. – Gr. *penthēmimerḗs*, f. *pénte* FIVE+*hēmimerḗs* halved, f. *hēmi-* HEMI- + *méros* part, MERE[2].

penthouse pe·nthaus, **pentice** pe·ntis subsidiary structure attached to the wall of a main building, esp. one with a sloping roof. XIV. ME. *pentis*, rarely *pendis* – AN. **pentis*, aphetic of OF. *apentis*, *apendis* – med. use of late L. *appendicium* appendage, f. L. *appendere* hang on, attach in a dependent state, f. L. *ad* AP-+*pendere* hang (see PENDENT); refash. (late XIV) by assoc. with HOUSE, as if 'sloping house'.

penultimate pinʌ·ltimət last but one. XVII. f. L. *pænultimus* (f. *pæne* almost + *ultimus* last), after ULTIMATE. Earlier †*penultim* (XVI).

penumbra pinʌ·mbrə (astron.) partly shaded region on the edge of a total shadow. XVII. – modL. (Kepler, 1604), f. L. *pæne* almost + *umbra* shadow; cf. PENINSULA, UMBRAGEOUS.

penury pe·njŭri indigence, want; dearth. XV. – L. *pēnūria*, *pænūria*, perh. rel. to *pæne* almost; see -Y[3].

peon pī·ən (in India) foot-soldier, constable, orderly XVII; (in Sp. America) day-labourer XIX. – Pg. *peão* and Sp. *peon* = OF. *peon* (mod. *pion*) = Pr. *pezó*, It. *pedone* :– medL. *pedō(ne-)* one who goes on foot (in classL. broad-footed man), f. *ped-*, *pēs* FOOT; cf. PAWN[1], -OON, and PIONEER.

peony pī·əni plant or flower of the herbaceous or shrubby genus Pæonia (the root, flowers, and seeds were formerly used in medicine). OE. *peonie* – L. *peōnia*, *pæōnia* – Gr. *paiōniā*, f. *Paiṓn* physician (orig. of the gods); cf. *paiṓnios* medicinal. Between OE. and XV the form *pione* was current – OF. *peone*, *peoine*, *pioine* (now *pivoine*) – L.; this was succeeded by *pionye*, which was finally assim. to L.

people pī·pl nation, race, persons coll., e.g. in relation to a place, person in authority, etc. XIII (Cursor M.); *the* commonalty XIV. ME. *peple*, *poeple*, *people* – AN. *poeple*, *people*, OF. *pople* (also mod. *peuple*) = Pr. *poble*, Sp. *pueblo*, It. *popolo* :– L. *populu-s* (cf. Umbrian *puplum*). For the sp. cf. *jeopardy*, *leopard*. So vb. XV (Caxton). – (O)F. *peupler*.

pep (orig. U.S.) great vigour. XX. abbrev. of PEPPER.

pepper pe·pəɹ pungent aromatic condiment. OE. *piper*, *-or* = OFris. *piper*, OS. *pipari*, *pepar* (Du. *peper*), OHG. *pfeffar* (G. *pfeffer*); W.Germ. (ON. *piparr* being from Eng.) – L. *piper* (whence OF. *peivre*, modF. *poivre*, Pr. *pebre*, etc., It. *pepe*, OSl. *pĭpĭrŭ*) – Gr. *péperi* – Skr. *pippalī́-* berry, peppercorn. In ME. *piper*, *peper*, the latter type prevailing in later Eng.; cf. *lemon*, *level*. Hence vb. XVI; cf. OE. *(ġe)pip(o)rian*. ¶ The spice was known to the Germans at the time of the migrations.

pepsin pe·psin ferment contained in the gastric juice. XIX. – G. *pepsin* (1836), f. Gr. *pépsis* digestion, f. **pep-* COOK, digest; see -IN. So **pept**IC pe·ptik digestive. XVII. – Gr. *peptikós*, f. *peptós* cooked, digestive; cf. DYSPEPTIC. **pept**ONE pe·ptoun (chem.). XIX. – G. *pepton* (C. G. Lehmann, 1849) – Gr. *peptón*, n. of *peptós*.

per pǝ̄ɹ (1) L. prep. 'through', 'by', 'by means of', rel. to PRE- in L. expressions from XV, e.g. *per consequens* consequently, *per se* by or in himself or itself (cf. AMPERSAND); (2) OF. *per* (see PAR[2]), as in phrases repr. by the comp. advs. *peradventure*, *perchance*, *perforce*, *perhaps*; (her.) denoting partition in the direction of an ordinary, e.g. *party per pale*; (3) as an Eng. prep.: by, by means of, e.g. *per bearer*; as indicated or shown by, e.g. *per invoice*, *per margin*, joc. (*as*) *per usual*; (in distributive sense) for each or every, e.g. *so much per head* (cf. L. phr. *per annum* every year, *per capita* 'by the heads', *per centum* PER CENT).

per- pǝ̄ɹ, pəɹ L. prep. *per* (see prec.) used in comp. with vbs., adjs., and their derivs., partly through F., partly directly from L., with the senses: (1) through in space or time, throughout, all over, as in PERAMBULATE, PERVADE; (2) thoroughly, completely, as in PERFECT, PERPETRATE, PERUSE; (3) away, entirely, to destruction, as in PERDITION, PEREMPTORY, PERISH, PERVERT; (4) perfectly, extremely, very, as in PERFERVID. **b.** chem. denoting the (supposed) maximum of some element in a combination: (1) as in *peroxide* compound of oxygen with another element which contains the largest possible proportion of oxygen, (2) as in *perchloride* compound of chlorine with another element or radical containing the maximum proportion of chlorine.

peradventure perədve·ntʃəɹ by chance; PERCHANCE, PERHAPS XIII. phr. *per* or *par auenture* – OF. *per* or *par auenture* (see PAR[2], PER, ADVENTURE); reduced at an early date to †*peraunter*, in late XV assim. to L. spelling; sb. uncertainty, doubt, hazard XVI.

perai pĭrai· voracious freshwater fish of the Orinoco, etc. XVIII (*peri*). – Tupi *piraya* (in Brazil *piranʸa*, whence **piranha** XIX), lit. 'scissors'.

perambulation pəræmbjŭlei·ʃən travelling through a place, tour; spec. for the purpose of recording boundaries XV; bounds XVII. – AN. *perambulation* or medL. *perambulātiō(n-)*, f. L. *perambulāre*, whence **pera·mbulate** XVI, earlier †*peramble*; see PER-, AMBLE, -ATE[3], -ATION. So **pera·mbul**ATOR †traveller, pedestrian; †hodometer XVII; hand carriage for young children XIX.

perceive pəɹsī·v A. apprehend with the mind XIII (Cursor M.); apprehend through the senses XIV; B. †receive, collect XIV. – AN. **perceiver*, OF. **perceivre*, *par-*, var. of *perçoivre* (now repl. by *percevoir*) = Pr. *percebre*, Sp. *percibir*, etc. :– L. *percipere* (i) seize, obtain, collect, (ii) understand, apprehend, f. *per* PER- + *capere* take (see HEAVE). So **percep**TION pəɹse·pʃən A. collection of rents, etc.; †partaking of Holy Communion XV; B. taking cognizance or being aware of objects XVII. In A. – (O)F. *perception*, in B. – L. *perceptiō(n-)* (i) collecting, (ii) perceiving, f. *percept- percipere*. **perce·pt**IBLE †perceptive XVI; cognizable XVII. – OF. or late L. **perce·pt**IVE characterized by perception XVII. **perci·pi**ENT. XVII. – prp. of L. *percipere*.

per cent pəɹse·nt by the hundred, in every hundred. XVI. In earliest exx. *per cento*, *per centum*; often written *per cent.*, as if an abbrev. of *per centum*, which is the form used in Acts of Parliament and legal documents; see PER, CENT; orig. It. business term. Hence **perce·nt**AGE. XVIII (Bentham).

perch[1] pə̄ɹtʃ freshwater fish Perca. XIII. – (O)F. *perche* = Tuscan, Pg. *perca* :– L. *perca* – Gr. *pérkē*, rel. to *pérkos* spotted, dark, *perknós* blackish, bluish, Skr. *pṛ́śnis* spotted, OIr. *erc* striped.

perch[2] pə̄ɹtʃ †pole, stake XIII; fixed bar, esp. for birds to rest upon; linear measure equal to 5½ yards XIV; superficial measure XV. – (O)F. *perche* = Pr. *perga*, It. *pertica* :– L. *pertica*. So **perch** vb. XV. – (O)F. *percher*, f. *perche*.

perchance pəɹtʃà·ns peradventure, perhaps. XIV. orig. phr. – AN. *par chance*, i.e. (O)F. *par* by (PAR[2]), *chance* CHANCE; with later assim. to PER-. So †*percase* XIV – AN. *per cas*, OF. *par cas* (see CASE[1]).

percolate pə̄·ɹkəleit pass or cause to pass through a porous substance. XVII. f. pp. stem of L. *percōlāre*, f. *per* PER- 1 + *cōlāre* strain, f. *cōlum* sieve, strainer; see -ATE[3].

percussion pəɹkʌ·ʃən striking of one body by another. XVI. – (O)F. *percussion* or L. *percussiō(n-)*, f. pp. stem of *percutere* strike or thrust through, f. *per* PER- 1 + *quatere* shake, strike, dash (cf. QUASH).

perdition pəɹdi·ʃən †utter destruction; final spiritual damnation. XIV. – OF. *perdiciun* (mod. *-tion*) or late L. *perditiō(n-)*, f. pp. stem of *perdere* destroy, (hence) lose, f. *per* PER-[3] + *-*dere* (see ADD, -ITION).

perdu pə̄·ɹdjū †*sentinel perdue*, *p. sentinel* post of sentinel, or sentinel himself, in a hazardous position XVI; *be p.* be placed on an outpost, etc. in such a position, (hence) lie in wait XVII, and gen. be concealed (now as F. pɛrd*ü*) XVIII. – (O)F. *perdu* lost, perished, past hope of recovery = It. *perduto* :– Rom. **perdutu-s*, for L. *perditus*, pp. of *perdere*; see prec.

peregrinate pe·rigrineit travel (abroad). XVI (Nashe). f. pp. stem of L. *peregrīnārī* sojourn or travel abroad, f. *peregrīnus* foreign; see next and -ATE[3]. So **peregrina**·TION. XVI (Skelton). – L.

peregrine pe·rigrin applied to a species of falcon, Falco peregrinus, esteemed for hawking XIV (Ch.); foreign, outlandish XVI. In the first use repr. (O)F. *faucon pèlerin* (cf. PILGRIM), medL. *falcō peregrīnus*, so named because the young were not taken like EYAS hawks from the nest, but caught in their passage from the breeding-place; in other uses directly – L. *peregrīnus* foreign, f. *pereger* that is abroad or on a journey, *peregrē* abroad, f. *per* through + *ager* territory, country; see PER- 1, ACRE, -INE[1].

peremptory pe·rəmtəri (leg., orig. Roman) that precludes all debate, question, or delay; decisive, final. XVI. – AN. *peremptorie* = (O)F. *péremptoire* (whence Sc. †*peremptor* XV) – L. *peremptōrius* deadly, mortal, decisive (e.g. *edictum peremptorium*, *peremptoriæ exceptiones*), f. *perempt-*, pp. stem of *perimere* take away entirely, destroy; see PER- 3, EMPTION, -ORY.

perennial pəre·niəl lasting throughout the year or a succession of years. XVII. f. L. *perennis*, f. *per* through + *annus* year; see PER- 1, ANNAL, -IAL. ¶ Earlier †*perennal*.

perfay pə̄ɹfei· (arch. or obs.) in truth. XIII. – OF. *per* or *par fei*; see PAR[2], FAY[1].

perfect pə̄·ɹfikt thoroughly versed or trained; in a complete state XIII (Cursor M.); in a faultless state, accurate XIV; unqualified, unalloyed XVI (Sh.); (arith.) XV; (gram.) of a tense XVI. ME. *parfit* (*-fiȝt*, *-fijt*, *-fight*), *-fite*, later *parfet* XV, (by assim. to L.) *perfect* XV. – OF. *parfit*, *-fite* (mod. *-fait*), corr. to Pr. *perfect*, etc. – L. *perfectu-s*, pp. of *perficere* accomplish, complete, f. *per* PER- 2 + *facere* make, DO[1]. The earliest form survived in mod. dial. *parfit*, and in Sc. *perfit* pərfi·t complete, exact, is distinguished from *pe·rfect* thorough, utter. Hence **perfe·ct** vb. XIV. So **perfe·ct**IBLE. XVII. – medL. **perfe·c**TION †complete state XIII (AncrR.); bringing to completion; condition of being perfect XIV. – (O)F. – L. **perfe·ct**IVE conducing to perfection XVI; (gram. after Slav. usage) expressing completion of an action XIX. – medL.

perFE·RVID. XIX. – modL. *perfervidus* (Buchanan); see PER- 4.

perfidy pə̄·ɹfidi base breach of faith. XVI. – L. *perfidia* (whence F. *perfidie*, Sp., It. *perfidia*), f. *perfidus* treacherous, f. *per* PER- 3 + *fides* FAITH; see -Y[3]. So **perfi·d**IOUS. XVI. – L. *-iōsus*.

perforate pə̄·ɹfəreit make a hole through. XVI. f. pp. stem of L. *perforāre*, f. *per* PER- 1 + *forāre* BORE, pierce; see -ATE[3]. So **perfora**·TION. XV. – (O)F. – medL.

perforce pəɹfɔ̄·ɹs †forcibly XIV; of necessity XVI. – OF. phr. *par force*, with assim. as in PERCHANCE; see PAR[2], PER, FORCE.

perform pəɹfɔ̄·ɹm †complete, finish; †bring about, effect; carry out (an order, etc.) XIV; †construct XV; go through formally XVIII. – AN. *par-*, *perfourmer* (in AL. *performāre*), alt. (after *forme* FORM) of OF. *parfournir* (in medL. *perfurnīre*), f. *par-* PER- 2, 4 + *fournir* FURNISH; cf. Sc. and north. †*perfurnish* (XIV–XVI); the forms *par-*, *perfo(u)rne* were current XIV–XV. Hence **perfo·rm**ANCE. XVI (at first leg.). prob. – AN. **performance*; also †*perform*ATION XVI; so AL. *performātiō*; †*perfor*MENT XVI–XVII, *perform*ING[1] (XIV–XVII).

perfume pə̄·ɹfjūm, (formerly also) pəɹfjū·m odorous vapour, (fragrance of) liquid scent. XVI. In early use also *par-*, but regularly assim. to PER-. – F. *parfum*, f. *par-*, †*perfumer* (whence **perfume** vb. XVI) – It. †*parfumare*, †*per-* (now *pro-*), lit. smoke through; see PER- 1, FUME. Hence **perfu·m**ERY. XVIII. ¶ The perfume industry was prominent in Italy in XVI.

perfunctory pəɹfʌ·ŋktəri done or acting merely by way of duty. XVI. – late L. *perfunctōrius* careless, negligent, f. *perfunct-*, pp. stem of *perfungī* perform, discharge, get rid of, f. *per* PER- + *fungī*; see FUNCTION, -ORY[2].

pergola pə̄·ɹgələ arbour formed with plants trained over a trellis. XVII (Evelyn). – It. *pergola* :– L. *pergula* projecting roof, vine arbour, f. *pergere* come or go forward, f. *per* PER- 1 + **reg-* move in a straight line (see RECTITUDE, RIGHT).

perhaps pəɹhæ·ps maybe, possibly; as may happen. XVI. f. PER 2 + pl. of HAP[1], repl. ME. phr. *by hap(s)* by a single word modelled on *percase*, PERCHANCE. ¶ Instances of *per happous* read in Lydg. are uncertain.

peri piə·ri fairy, orig. malevolent demon, of Persian mythology XVIII; transf. beautiful girl XIX. Anglicized in Richardson's Persian Dictionary, 1777–80, but first popularized in the Eng. translation (1786) of Beckford's 'Histoire du Caliph Vathek' (1782) in pl. form *Peries*, rendering F. *Perises*. – (F. *péri* –) Pers. *perī*, *parī* :– Pehlevi *parīk* evil genius, malevolent elf :– Av. *pairikā* winged.

peri- pe·ri, pəri·, repr. comb. form of Gr. *péri*, *perí* adv. and prep. about, around, roundabout, rel. to L. *per* (see PER, PER-); in older terms often through L. derivs. and new formations (for which see below); in mod. scientific terms (anat. and path.), forming adjs. meaning 'situated or occurring about or around, surrounding or enclosing the part denoted by the second el.', as *peribranchial* around the branchiæ or gills, and forming sbs. denoting a surrounding or enclosing part, in sbs. in -ITIS, which denote inflammation of the region surrounding that denoted by the second el., e.g. *perityphlitis*, of some part adjacent to the CÆCUM.

perianth pe·riænþ (bot.) †calyx, involucre XVIII; outer part of a flower XIX. – F. *périanthe* (Rousseau 1771–7) – modL. *perianthium*, f. Gr. *perí* about, PERI- + *ánthos* flower (cf. ANTHOLOGY), after *pericarpium* PERICARP.

periapt pe·riæpt amulet (worn about the person). XVI. – F. *périapte* – Gr. *periapton*, f. *perí* PERI- + *háptos* fastened, *háptein* fasten.

pericardium perikā·ɹdiəm (anat.) membranous sac enclosing the heart. XVI. – modL. – Gr. *perikárdion* (Galen), f. *perí* PERI- + *kardíā* HEART. Hence **perica·rdi**AC XIX, **perica·rd**IAL XVII, **pe:ricardi·**TIS XVIII.

pericarp pe·rikāɹp (bot.) seed-vessel. XVIII. – F. *péricarpe* or modL. *pericarpium* – Gr. *perikárpion* pod, husk, shell, f. *perí* + *karpós* fruit; PERI-, HARVEST, -IUM.

pericope pĕri·kəpi paragraph. XVII. – late L. *pericopē* – Gr. *perikopḗ* section, f. *perí* PERI- + **kop-* cut; see COMMA.

pericranium perikrei·niəm membrane enveloping the skull. XVI. – modL. *pericranium* – Gr. *perikránion*, sb. use of n. of *perikránios* round the skull; see PERI-, CRANIUM.

peridot pe·ridət †chrysolite XIV; the variety called olivine XVII. In late ME. *peritot* – OF. *peritot* (mod. *-dot*), of which there are several vars.; of unkn. origin.

perigee pe·ridʒī (astron.) point in the orbit of a planet that is nearest to the earth. XVI. In early use varying with forms directly repr. L. and Gr.; – F. *périgée* – modL. *perigēum*, *-æum* – late Gr. *perígeion* (Ptolemy), sb. use of n. of *perígeios* 'close round the earth', f. *perí* PERI- + *géē*, *gaîa*, *gê* earth.

perihelion perihē·liən (astron.) point in the orbit of a heavenly body that is nearest to the sun)(APHELION. XVII. Græcized form of modL. *perihēlium* (Kepler 1596), f. Gr. *perí* PERI- + *hḗlios* SUN.

peril pe·ril risk, danger. XIII (AncrR., Cursor M.). – (O)F. *péril* = Pr. *perilh*, Sp. *peligro*, Pg. *perigo*, It. *pericolo* :– L. *perīc(u)lum* experiment, risk, f. **per-* in *experīrī* try (see EXPERIENCE, PIRATE) + *-culum* -CLE. ¶ Replaced OE. *fǣr*, corr. to G. *gefahr* danger, which may be cogn.; superseded gen. by *danger* except in *at one's p.* Cf. IMPERIL. So **pe·ril**OUS. XIII. – OF. *perillous*, *-eus* (mod. *périlleux*) :– L. *perīculōsu-s*; cf. PARLOUS.

perimeter pəri·mĭtəɹ circumference, periphery. XVI. – F. *périmètre* – L. *perimetros* – Gr. *perímetros*, f. *perí* + *métron*; see PERI-, METER.

period piə·riəd extent of time; end of a course (XIV–XV), XVI; complete sentence, esp. one containing several clauses; full pause at end of this, full stop XVI. In Ch. and Lydg. in the forms *parodie*, *-ye*, also in XV *paryode*, unexpl. alt. of (O)F. *période*, corr. to Sp., It. *periodo* – L. *periodus* cycle, sentence – Gr. *períodos* circuit, revolution, recurrence, course, orbit, rounded sentence, f. *perí* PERI- + *hodós* way, course. So **periodic**(AL) -ɔ·dik(l). XVII. – F. or L. – Gr. *periodikós*. **periodicITY** -i·siti. XIX. – F.

peripatetic pe:ripəte·tik (member) of the school of philosophy founded by Aristotle, who taught in a *perípatos* or walking place in the Lyceum at Athens. XVI. – (O)F. *péripatétique* or L. *peripatēticus* (Cicero, of the philosophy) – Gr. *peripatētikós*, f. *peripateîn* walk up and down, f. *perí* PERI- + *pateîn* tread (cf. *pátos* beaten path); see -IC.

periphery pəri·fəri †layer of air XIV (once, Gower); boundary of a rounded surface XVI (Digges). – late L. *peripheria* – Gr. *periphéreia*, f. *peripherḗs* revolving round, f. *perí* PERI- + *phérein* BEAR[2]; see -Y[3]. Cf. CIRCUMFERENCE. So **peri·pheRAL**[1]. XIX (Barclay). **periphe·ric** (Coleridge), -ICAL. XVII.

periphrasis pəri·frəsis roundabout way of speaking. XVI. – L. *periphrasis* (Quintilian) – Gr. *períphrasis*, f. *periphrázein*, f. *peri*+ *phrázein* declare; see PERI-, PHRASE. So **periphrastic** -fræ·stik. XIX. – Gr. *periphrastikós*; so F. *périphrastique*.

periscope pe·riskoup apparatus for obtaining a view of objects above the ordinary level of vision. XIX (1899). f. Gr. *periskopeîn*, f. *perí* + *skopeîn* look; see PERI-, SCOPE; perh. modelled on **perisco·pic** (1804) enabling one to see for some distance around the axis of vision. ¶ Earlier occas. uses did not survive.

perish pe·riʃ come to a violent or untimely end, cease to exist; pass. be destroyed, lost, injured by exposure, etc. XIII. f. *périss-*, extended stem of (O)F. *périr* = Pr. *perir*, It. *perire*, Sp. *perecer*, Rum. *perì* :– L. *perīre* pass away, come to nothing, lose one's life, f. *per* PER- 3 + *īre* go, *eō* I go, *it* goes, f. **ei-*, **i-*, repr. also by Gr. *eîmi* I shall go, and in Skr., Celtic, and Slav. See -ISH[2]. Hence **pe·rishABLE**. XVII; after F. *périssable*.

perispome pe·rispoum having a circumflex accent on the last syllable. XIX. Shortening of **perispo·menon** – Gr. *perispṓmenon*, n. of prp. pass. of *perispân* draw round, mark with a circumflex, f. *perí* PERI- + *spân* draw.

perissodactyl pəriso(u)dæ·ktil (zool. of ungulates) having an odd number of toes. XIX. – modL. *perissodactylus*, f. Gr. *perissós* uneven, odd + *dáktulos* digit (see DACTYL).

peristaltic peristæ·ltik pert. to the automatic muscular movement in the alimentary canal. XVII. – Gr. *peristaltikós* (Galen) clasping and compressing, f. *peristéllein* wrap up or round, f. *perí* round + *stéllein* place; see PERI-, STOLID, -IC.

peristyle pe·ristail (archit.) colonnade surrounding a building. XVII. – F. *péristyle* – L. *peristȳlum* – Gr. *peristūlon*, sb. use of n. of *perístūlos* having pillars all round; see PERI-, STYLE.

peritoneum pe:ritənī·əm (anat.) serous membrane lining the cavity of the abdomen. XVI. – late L. *peritonæum*, *-ēum* – Gr. *peritónaion*, *-eion*, sb. use of n. of *peritónaios*, f. *perítonos* stretched around, f. *peri* + *-tonos* stretched; see PERI-, TONE.

periwig pe·riwig peruke, wig. XVI. alt., through the stages *perewike*, *-wig*, of *perwike*, *-wick*, vars. of PERUKE (orig. str. *pe·ruke*), in which *-wi-* repr. an attempt to render ü of the F. word.

periwinkle[1] pe·riwiŋkl plant of the genus Vinca. XIV. ME. *pervenke*, *-vinke* – AN. *pervenke*, var. of (O)F. *pervenche* = Sp. *pervenca*, It. *pervinca* :– late L. *pervinca*, earlier *vi(n)ca pervi(n)ca* (Pliny). ¶ Not continuous with OE. *peruince* – L. The mod. form appears XVI as *per(i)wyncle*, prob. by assim. to next.

periwinkle[2] pe·riwiŋkl gastropod mollusc of the genus Littorina. XVI (*purwinkle*, *pere-*, *periwinkle*). Of unkn. origin; OE. *winewinclan* pl., also read as *pinewinclan*, may perh. be repr. by dial. forms in *penny-*; in any case the second el. is the same.

perjure pə̄·ɹdʒəɹ pass. *be p–d* be forsworn or guilty of false swearing XV (now rare), repr. AN., OF. *estre parjuré(z)*; refl. *p. oneself* XVIII, repr. F. *se parjurer* forswear oneself, for which the intr. *perjure* was formerly used XVII–XVIII (so in AN.). – (O)F. *parjurer*, †*per-* – L. *perjūrāre*, refash. of *pe(r)ierāre* break one's oath, f. *per* PER- 3 + *jūrāre* swear (see JUROR). So **pe·rjurY**[3]. XIV. – AN. *perjurie* (modF. *parjure*) – L. *perjūrium*.

perk pə̄ɹk (intr., pass.) carry oneself jauntily, be spruce or smart XIV; (trans.) project or raise in a brisk manner XVI. The earliest instances refer to the action of birds and suggest deriv. from *perk* sb., var. of PERCH[2], or a transf. use of *perk* vb. perch (both now obs. or dial.) – dial. F. **perque*, **perquer*, vars. of *perche*, *percher*. Hence **pe·rkY**[1]. XIX.

perk(s) pə̄ɹk(s) sl. abbrev. of PERQUISITES. 1887. Preceded by Sc. *pirkus* (1824); cf. *parkaseet* (1857).

perlaceous pə̄ɹlei·ʃ[i]əs of the nature of pearl. XVIII. f. modL. *perlāceus*, f. L. *perla* PEARL; see -ACEOUS.

perlustrate pə̄ɹlʌ·streit travel through and survey. XVI. f. pp. stem of L. *perlūstrāre*, f. *per* PER- 1 + *lūstrāre* purify, pass in review, f. *lūstrum* LUSTRE[1]; see -ATE[3].

permafrost pə̄·ɹməfrɔ̀st permanently frozen subsoil. XX. f. PERMA(NENT, FROST.

permanent pə̄·ɹmənənt lasting indefinitely. XV. – (O)F. *permanent* or L. *permanent-*, *-ēns*, prp. of *permanēre* remain to the end; see PER- 1, 2, MANSION. So **pe·rmanENCE**. XV. – (O)F. or medL.

permeable pə̄·ɹmiəbl permitting passage or diffusion through itself. XV. – late L. *permeābilis*, f. *permeāre* (the pp. stem of which gave **pe·rmeate** XVII), f. *per* PER- 1, *meāre* pass, go (cf. CONGEE); see -ABLE.

Permian pə̄·ɹmiən (geol.) pert. to the upper division of palæozoic strata, characteristic of *Perm*, former province of E. Russia. XIX. See -IAN.

permission pəɹmi·ʃən action of allowing, leave. XV. – (O)F. *permission* or L. *permissiō(n-)*, f. pp. stem of *permittere* surrender, allow, f. *per*+*mittere* let go; see PER- 1, 3, MISSION. So **permi·t** vb. XV. – L. *permittere*; hence sb. **pe·rmit** XVIII. **permi·SSIBLE** XV, **permi·SSIVE** XVII (Sh.).

permute pəɹmjū·t †exchange XIV (PPl.); †change, transmute XV; transpose XIX. – L. *permūtāre*, f. *per* PER- 4 + *mūtāre* change. So **perMUTA·TION** †exchange, barter XIV (PPl.); †alteration, transmutation XIV (Ch.); transposition (spec. math.) XVI. – (O)F. or L.

pernicious pəɹni·ʃəs tending to destroy or ruin. XVI. – L. *perniciōsus*, f. *perniciēs* destruction, f. *per* PER- 2+*nec-*, *nex* death, destruction; see INTERNECINE, -IOUS, and cf. (O)F. *pernicieux*.

pernickety pəɹni·kĭti (colloq.) precise about trifles. XIX. orig. Sc., of uncertain origin; such local vars. as *parnickety*, *pernackety* suggest a fanciful alt. of PARTICULAR infl. by Sc. and north. *knick-knack* personal peculiarity (cf. *nick-nacket*, Burns)+-Y[1].

pernoctate pə̄ɹnɔ·kteit pass the night, spec. in prayer, in a certain place to 'keep residence'. XVII. f. pp. stem of L. *pernoctāre*, f. *per* PER- 1+*noct-*, *nox* NIGHT; see -ATE[3]. So **pernoctA·TION**. XVII. – late L. (Ambrose).

peroration perərei·ʃən concluding part of a speech. XV (Capgrave). – F. *péroration* or L. *perōrātiō(n-)*, f. *perōrāre* (whence **pe·roRATE**[3] XVII); see PER- 1, ORATION.

perpend pəɹpe·nd (arch.) ponder. XVI. – L. *perpendere* weigh exactly, consider; see PER- 2, PENDENT.

perpendicular pə̄ɹpəndi·kjŭləɹ situated or having a direction at right angles XIV (Ch.; but not gen. current till XVI); first applied to the third style of English pointed architecture by T. Rickman, 1812–15; sb. XVI. – L. *perpendiculāris*, f. *perpendiculum* plummet, plumb-line, f. *per* PER- 2 + *pendēre* hang; see PENDENT, -CULE, -AR. (Cf. OF. *perpendiculer*, *-ier*, It. *perpendicolare*; F. *perpendiculaire* – L. *perpendiculāris*, *-ārius*.)

perpetrate pə̄·ɹpitreit commit (an evil deed). XVI. f. pp. stem of L. *perpetrāre* perform (in neutral sense), f. *per* PER- 1 + *patrāre* bring about, lit. perform or execute as father, f. *patr-*, *pater* FATHER; see -ATE[3]. So **perpetrA·TION**. XV. – F. or late L.

perpetual pəɹpe·tjuəl lasting or destined to last for ever. XIV (*-el*, Rolle). – (O)F. *perpetuel* – L. *perpetuālis* (Quintilian, who uses it, with *universalis*, to render Gr. καθολικός), f. *perpetuus*, f. *perpet-*, *perpes* continuous, uninterrupted, f. *per* PER-[1]+ *petere* be directed towards (cf. IMPETUS); assim. to L. form XVI; see -AL[1]. So **perpe·tuATE**[3]. XVI. f. pp. stem of L. *perpetuāre*, f. *perpetuus*. **perpetuA·TION**. XIV (Wyclif). – medL. **perpetuITY** pə̄ɹpĭtjū·iti. XV (Hoccleve). – (O)F. – L.

perplex pəɹple·ks trouble with doubt or uncertainty XVI (Sh.); make uncertain or involved through intricacy XVII. Back-formation from *perplexed* (XV), extension of †*perplex* adj. (XIV–XVII) – (O)F. *perplexe* or L. *perplexus* involved, intricate, f. *per* PER- 2 +*plexus*, pp. of *plectere* plait, interweave, involve, f. **plek-*, as in *duplex* twofold, *simplex* SIMPLE, etc.; see PLAIT. So **perple·xITY**. XIV. – (O)F. or late L.

perquisite pə̄·ɹkwizit †property acquired otherwise than by inheritance XV; casual profits or emoluments XVI; gratuity XVIII. – medL. *perquīsītum* acquisition, sb. use of n. of pp. of L. *perquīrere* search diligently for, f. *per* PER- 2+*quærere* seek (see QUERY).

perry pe·ri beverage made from pears. XIV. ME. *pereye*, *perre(e)*, *perrye* – OF. *peré* :– Rom. **pirātum*, f. L. *pirum* PEAR; see -Y[5].

persecute pə̄·ɹsikjūt †pursue, chase; pursue with malignity; †prosecute at law XV (Caxton). – (O)F. *persécuter*, f. L. *persecūt-*, pp. stem of *persequī*, f. *per* PER- 1, 2 + *sequī* follow, SUE. So **persecu·TION**. XIV (Rolle, Barbour, Trevisa, Wyclif). – (O)F. – L.

perseity pə̄ɹsī·iti independent existence. XVII. – medL. *perseitās* (Duns Scotus), f. *per sē* by itself, tr. Aristotle's καθ' αὑτό ('Posterior Analytics' i 4); see -ITY.

persevere pə̄ɹsĭvīə·ɹ continue steadfastly. XIV. – (O)F. *persévérer* – L. *persevērāre* abide by strictly, persist, f. *persevērus* very strict; see PER- (4), SEVERE. Stressed regularly *perse·ver* (and so sp.) till XVII; but the str. *perseve·re* is found sporadically XIV—XVI, is the only form used by Milton, and becomes general in late XVII. So **perseve·rANCE**. XIV. – (O)F. – L.; formerly str. *perse·verance*.

Persian pə̄·ɹʃən pert. to Persia. XIII. Late ME. *persien*, *percien* (Ch., Gower) – OF. *persien* = It. *persiano* – medL. **Persiānus* (repl. L. *Persicus*), f. (after *Asiānus*) *Persia*, f. Gr. *Persís* – OPers. *Pārsa* (mod. *Pārs*, Arab. *Fārs*); assim. to -IAN XVI.

persiflage pə̄·ɹsiflāʒ light banter, raillery. XVIII (Lord Chesterfield). F., f. *persifler* banter, f. *per-* for *par-*+*siffler* whistle :- popL. *sīfilāre*, for L. *sībilāre*; see SIBILANT, -AGE.

persimmon pəɹsi·mən plum-like fruit of the tree Diospyros virginiana. XVII (Capt. Smith). Early forms are *putchamin, pessemmin, posimon* – Algonquian word repr. by Cree *pasiminan*, Lenape *pasimenan*.

persist pəɹsi·st continue firmly *in* a state, etc. XVI; remain in existence XVIII. – L. *persistere*, f. *per* PER- 2 + *sistere* STAND.

person pə̄·ɹsn †character, part played; human being XIII; living body of a human being; individual personality XIV; (theol.) distinction of being in the Godhead XIII; gram. (so L. *persona* in Varro, Gr. *prósōpon* in Dionysius Thrax) XVI. – OF. *persone* (mod. *personne*) = Pr., Sp., It. *persona*, Pg. *pessoa* :- L. *persōna* mask used by a player, one who plays a part, character acted ('dramatis persona'), character or capacity in which one acts person as having legal rights, human being, in Christian use of the Trinity (for Gr. *ὑπόστασις*). perh. f. Etruscan *φersu* mask, and used to render Gr. *prósōpon* face, mask, dramatic part, person (f. *prós* to, towards, *ôps* face). The normally developed var. *parson* (XIV–XVII) has been differentiated with a special meaning; *person* is a reversion to L. form. So **pe·rson**ABLE having a well-formed person. XV. – F. †*personnable*. **pe·rson**AGE †image, effigy; body of a person XV; person of note; person in a drama XVI. – OF. *personage* (mod. *personnage*), corr. to Pr. *personatge*, It. *personaggio*, in medL. *persōnāticum, -āgium*. **pe·rson**AL[1] pert. to a person or individual XIV;)(*real* XV. – OF. *personal, -el* (mod. *personnel*) – L. *persōnālis*. **person**A·LITY. XIV. – (O)F. – late L. **pe·rsonal**TY personal estate. XVI. – law F. *personalté*. **pe·rson**ATE[3] act the part of, IMPERSONATE XVI; represent, typify XVII. f. pp. stem of late L. *persōnāre* (Boethius). **personi**FY pəɹsɔ·nifai. XVIII. – F. *personnifier* (Boileau); hence **perso·ni**FICA·TION. XVIII (Johnson). **personnel** pə̄ɹsene·l body of persons engaged in a service. XIX. – F., sb. use of *personnel* PERSONAL, opposed to *matériel* material equipment, as in *le matériel et le personnel d'une armée*.

perspective pəɹspe·ktiv †optics XIV (Wycl., Trevisa); †optical instrument XIV (Ch.); (after It. *perspectiva*) art of drawing so as to give the effect of solidity and relative size XVI; drawing in perspective XVII. – medL. *perspectīva* (sc. *ars* art), sb. use of fem. of late L. *perspectīvus* (Boethius), f. *perspect-*, pp. stem of *perspicere* look at closely, f. *per*+ *specere* look; see PER- 1, SPECTACLE, -IVE. So **perspe·ctive** adj. †optical XV; pert. to perspective XVII. – late L. So **perspicacious** pə̄ɹspikei·ʃəs of penetrating (mental) vision. XVII. f. L. *perspicāc-, -āx* sharp-sighted, f. *perspicere*; see above and -IOUS. **perspica·**CITY. XVI. – F. or late L. **perspi·c**UOUS †transparent XV; lucid, evident XVI. f. L. *perspicuus*, f. *perspicere*. **perspicu·**ITY. XV. – L.

perspiration pə̄ɹspĭrei·ʃən †breathing through; †evaporation, exhalation; excretion of moisture through the pores XVII. – F. *perspiration* (XVI, Paré), f. *perspirer* – L. *perspirāre* (whence **perspi·re** vb. XVII); see PER- 1, SPIRIT, -ATION.

persuade pəɹswei·d induce to believe or act in a certain way; †induce belief in or practice of, commend, recommend XVI. – L. *persuādēre*, f. *per* PER- 1 or 2 + *suadēre* advise, recommend. So **persua·**SION. XIV. action of persuading XIV (Wycl. Bible, Ch.); religious belief or denomination XVII; (joc.) nationality, sex, sort XIX. – L. *persuāsiō(n-)*; see SUASION and cf. (O)F. *persuader, persuasion*.

pert pə̄ɹt (dial.) expert, intelligent XIII; open, manifest XIV; forward in behaviour XIV (Ch.); (dial.) brisk, lively XVI. Aphetic of †*apert* (in these senses) XIII. – OF. *apert* = Pr. *apert* – L. *apertus* open, pp. of *aperīre* (see APERTURE); partly blended with OF. *aspert, espert* :- L. *expertu-s* expert. ¶ In the first and the last senses often sp. *peart* and perh. apprehended as a distinct word.

pertain pəɹtei·n belong *to*. XIV. Late ME. *partene, -teine* repr. tonic stem of (O)F. *partenir* = Pr. *pertener*, It. *pertenere* – L. *pertinēre* extend, tend or belong (to), f. *per* PER- 1+*tenēre* hold; cf. CONTAIN. So **pe·rtin**ENT relevant, apposite XIV (Wycl.); †appurtenant, suitable XV. – (O)F. *pertinent* or L. *pertinēns*, prp. of *pertinēre*.

pertinacious pə̄ɹtinei·ʃəs persistent in one's opinion or intention. XVII. f. L. *pertināci-*, stem of *pertināx*; see PER- 4, TENACIOUS. Earlier (rare) †*pertinace* – OF. *pertinace*. So **pertina·**CITY. XVI. – F.; earlier †*pertin*ACY XIV (Ch.). – L.

perturb pəɹtə̄·ɹb disturb greatly. XIV (Ch.). – OF. *pertourber* – L. *perturbāre*; see PER- 2, DISTURB. So **perturb**A·TION. XIV (Ch.). – (O)F. – L.

peruke pərū·k †natural head of hair; PERIWIG, WIG XVI. – F. *perruque* (XV, †head of hair) – It. *perrucca, parrucca* (whence also Sp. *peluca*), of unkn. origin.

peruse pərū·z †use up; go through so as to examine, revise, etc. XV; read through XVI. prob. based on AL. **perūsāre, perūsitāre* use up (XIV), f. L. *per* PER- 4+medL. *ūsāre*, L. *ūsitārī* use often, frequent. f. *ūs-* USE. Hence **peru·**SAL[2] XVI (Sh.); earlier †*peruse* sb. XVI.

pervade pəɹvei·d (arch.) pass through; diffuse itself throughout XVII. – L. *pervādere*, f. *per*+*vādere* go; see PER- 1, WADE. So **perva·**SIVE. XVIII. f. pp. stem of *pervādere*.

perverse pəɹvə̄·ɹs turned from the right way, perverted XIV (Ch.); froward, wayward XV (Lydgate). – (O)F. *pervers, -e* – L. *perversus, -a*, pp. of *pervertere* (see below). So **perve·r**SION. XIV. – L. *perversiō(n-)*; cf. F. *perversion*. **perve·rt** †overthrow, subvert; turn aside from a right course or opinion XIV (Ch., Wycl.). – (O)F. *pervertir*, corr. to Pr., Sp. *pervertir*, It. *pervertere*, or their source L. *pervertere* turn round or the wrong way, overturn, ruin, corrupt, f. *per*+ *vertere* turn; see PER- 2, 3, VERSE. **pervert** pə̄·ɹvəɹt perverted or apostate person. XVII. sb. use of †*pervert* adj. (XV–XVI), short for *perverted*, or an analogical formation after *convert* sb.

pervious pə̄·ɹviəs allowing a passage through. XVII. f. L. *pervius*, f. *per* PER-[1]+ *via* WAY. Cf. IMPERVIOUS (XVII).

peseta pesei·tə Spanish silver coin and monetary unit. XIX. Sp., dim. of *pesa* weight :– L. *pēnsa*, pl. of *pēnsum* (see POISE).

pesky pe·ski (U.S. colloq.) plaguy, confounded. XIX. poss. alt. of **pesty*, f. PEST+Y[1].

pessary pe·səri †suppository XIV; instrument to remedy uterine displacement XVIII. – late L. *pessārium*, repl. late L. *pessulum*, f. late L. *pessum, -us* – Gr. *pessós, -ón* draughtboard, oval stone used in a game, medicated plug; see -ARY.

pessimism pe·simizm †the worst condition possible XVIII (Coleridge); tendency to look at the worst aspect of things; (after G. *pessimismus*, Schopenhauer, 1819) doctrine that this world is the worst possible. f. L. *pessimus* worst, rel. to *peior* worse (cf. PEJORATIVE)+-ISM, on the model of *optimism*.

pest pest †pestilence, plague XVI; noxious person or thing XVII. – F. *peste* or L. *pestis* plague, contagious disease. So **pesti·**FEROUS plague-bringing, pernicious. XVI. – L. *pestifer, -ferus*; cf. (O)F. *pestifère*. **pe·stil**ENCE fatal epidemic, spec. bubonic plague. XIV. – (O)F. *pestilence* – L. *pestilentia*, f. *pestilent-, -ēns, -lentus* (whence **pe·stil**ENT XV), f. *pestis*; cf. late L. *pestilis* of the nature of plague, and L. *gracilentus, macilentus*. **pestile·nt**IAL. XIV. – medL. **pe·sti**CIDE[1] pest-killer XX.

pestle pe·sl instrument for pounding in a mortar. XIV (Wycl. Bible). – OF. *pestel* = It. *pestello* – L. *pistillum*, dim. of **pistrum*, f. *pist-*, pp. stem of *pinsare* pound; cf. -EL[2].

pet[1] pet animal domesticated and treated as a favourite; indulged child XVI; darling, favourite XVIII. orig. Sc. and north. dial.; of unkn. origin; formally distinct from †*peat* (XVI) pet (of a woman), (spoilt) girl. ¶ Ir. *peat*, Gael. *peata* are from Sc.

pet[2] pet offence at being slighted. XVI. orig. in phr. †*take the pet*; of unkn. origin. Hence **pe·tt**ISH[1]. XVI.

petal pe·təl each of the divisions of the corolla of a flower. XVIII. – modL. *petalum* (Fabio Colonna, 1649), in medL. metal plate (Isidore) – Gr. *pétalon* lamina, leaf, sb. use of n. of adj. *pétalos* outspread, f. base *pet-*, as in *petánnusthai* unfold.

petard pĭtā·ɹd small engine of war for making a breach XVI (Florio, Sh.); firework XVII. – F. *pétard* (1585), f. *péter* break wind, f. *pet* fart = It. *peto* :– L. *pēditum*, f. *pēdere* break wind; see -ARD.

petasus pe·təsəs (antiq.) low-crowned broad-brimmed hat of the ancient Greeks. XVI (Jonson). – L. – Gr. *pétasos*, f. base **pet-* (see PETAL).

peter pī·təɹ (U.S. mining colloq.) become exhausted, give *out*. XIX (earlier 1812 trans. in sl. use, stop, put an end to). Of unkn. origin.

petiole pe·tioul leaf-stalk. XVIII. – F. *pétiole* – L. *petiolus* little foot, fruit-stalk, specialized by Linnæus ('Petiolus promit folium, et Pedunculus fructificationem', 1751).

petite pətī·t of small stature or dainty figure. XVIII. F., fem. of *petit* PETTY.

petition pĭti·ʃən action of begging or supplicating, orig. in prayer XIV; formally drawn-up request from an inferior to a superior or body in authority XV. – (O)F. *pétition* – L. *petītiō(n-)*, f. pp. stem of *petere* aim at, lay claim to, ask, seek; see -TION. Hence as vb. XVII (Sh.). ¶ To the same base belong APPETITE, COMPETE, IMPETUS, REPEAT.

petrel pe·trəl small sea-bird of the genus Procellaria. XVII. The significance of the early vars. *pitteral, pittrel* is obscure, but as early as 1703 Dampier has the sp. *petrel* and derives the name from that of St. *Peter* in allusion to his 'walking upon the Lake of Gennesareth' (cf. Matt. xiv 30), an expl. supported by Norw. *Soren Peders, Pedersfugl*, G. *Petersvogel*; for the ending cf. *cockerel, dotteral, hoggerel, pickerel*, which may have supplied the analogy. ¶ F. *pétrel* is from Eng.

petrify pe·trifai convert into stone XVI; deprive of movement or feeling XVII. – F. *pétrifier* – L. **petrificāre*, f. *petra* – Gr. *pétrā* rock, stone (also *pétros*, whence *Petrus* 'rock-man', Peter); see -FY. Hence **petrifa·**CTION. XVII (Sir T. Browne); after *stupefy, stupefaction*; superseded **pe·tri**FICA·TION (XVII, Cotgr., Sir T. B.).

petro- pe·trou, petrə· comb. form of Gr. *pétrā* rock or *pétros* stone, as in **petro·**GRAPHY XVII, **petro·logy** XIX (earlier erron. *petra·logy*, Pinkerton).

petrol pe·trəl †petroleum XVI; (after F. *essence de pétrole*) refined petroleum used in internal combustion engines XIX (*c.* 1895). – F. *pétrole* – medL. *petroleum*; see next.

petroleum pĭtrou·liəm mineral oil, occurring in rocks, etc. XVI. – medL. *petroleum* (cf. *petra oleum*, Saxon Leechdom, II 288), f. L. *petra* (see PETRIFY)+*oleum* OIL.

petronel pe·trənel large pistol or carbine. XVI. – F. *petrinal*, var. of *poitrinal*, sb. use of adj. 'pert. to breast or chest', f. *poitrine* :– Rom. **pectorīna*, f. L. *pector-*, *pectus* breast; so called because in firing it the butt end rested against the chest.

petticoat pe·tikout †small coat worn under the doublet XV; (Lydg.); †tunic or chemise XV; skirt dependent from the waist XVI. orig. two words, PETTY and COAT.

pettifogger pe·tifɔgəɹ legal practitioner of inferior status XVI; (gen.) petty practioner XVII. f. PETTY+*fogger*, of unkn. origin (perh. back-formation from this). Hence **pe·ttifogg**ING[1] and [2]. XVI.

pettitoes pe·titouz (orig.) giblets; (later) pig's trotters XVI. In form and sense corr. to F. *petite oie* 'little goose' (L. *auca*), defined by Cotgrave 1611 as 'the giblets of a Goose; also, the bellie, and inwards or intralls, of other edible creatures'; assim. to PETTY and pl. of TOE took place early.

petty pe·ti †small XIV (PPl.); minor, secondary, subordinate XVI. Late ME. *pety*, var. of *petit* (PPl.) – (O)F. *petit* = Pr., Cat. *petit* :– Rom. **pittittu-s*, f. **pit-* (cf. Rum. *pitì* make itself small), repr. in late L. *pitinnus*, *pitulus* very small, and regarded as a symbolic word of child-speech. In some technical phr. *petit* is still retained, e.g. *p. constable*, *p. jury*, *p. larceny*.

petulant pe·tjŭlənt †wanton, lascivious XVI; †pert, saucy XVII; pettishly impatient XVIII. – (O)F. *pétulant* – L. *petulant-*, *-āns*, prp. of **petulāre*, f. *petere* direct oneself to, attack (with formative as in *postulāre*, *ustulāre*); see PETITION, -ANT. So **pe·tul**ANCE XVII, -ANCY XVI.

petunia pĭtjū·niə genus of herbaceous plants closely related to the tobacco plant. XIX. – modL. *petunia* (Jussieu, 1789), f. F. *petun* tobacco (also in Eng. use XVI–XVII) – Guarani *petỹ*; see -IA[1].

pew pjū raised enclosure, stall, or desk in a church, †in a court, etc. XIV (PPl.); pl. fixed benches with backs XVII. Late ME. *pywe*, *puwe* – OF. *puye*, *puie* – L. *podia*, pl. of *podium* elevated place, parapet, balcony (whence OF. *pui* height, mod. *puy*, as in place-names) – Gr. *pódion* base, pedestal, dim. of *pod-*, *poús* FOOT.

pewit, peewit pī·wit, pjū·it lapwing. XIII (*pywet* in place-name), XVI (*puwyt*, *puet*, *-it*). imit. of the bird's call; cf. synon. dial. *pee(s)-weep*, *tewit*, and Flem. *piewitvoghel*, (M)Du. *kievit*, etc., G. *kiebitz*.

pewter pjū·təɹ alloy of tin and lead. XIV. – OF. *peutre*, *peaultre* = Pr. *peltre*, It. *peltro* :– Rom. **peltrum*, of unkn. origin; connexion with SPELTER has been assumed but not established. So **pew·ter**ER[2]. XIV. – AN. *peautrer*, OF. *peautrier* = It. *peltraio*.

pfennig pfe·nix $\frac{1}{100}$ of the German mark. XVI (*phen(n)ing*). G.; see PENNY.

phæton fei·tən four-wheeled open carriage. XVIII. – F. *phaéton* – L. *Phaethōn* – Gr. *Phaéthōn* (myth.) son of Helios (sun) and Clymene, famous for his unlucky driving of the sun-chariot, sb. use of prp. *phaéthōn* shining, rel. to *phaínein* (cf. PHENOMENON), *pháos*, *phôs* light (cf. PHOSPHORUS).

phago- fæ·go(u) repr. Gr. *phago-* eating, *phageîn-* eat, as in *pha·gocyte*. So **-phagous** fəgəs -eating, f. L. *-phagus*, Gr. *-phagos* (cf. SARCOPHAGUS), **-phag**Y[3] fədʒi Gr. *-phagíā*, as in *ichthyophagous*, *-phagy*.

phalanx fæ·ləŋks line of battle, esp. of hoplites in close order XVI; (anat.) joint of a digit XVII; (bot.) bundle of stamens XVIII. – L. *phalanx* (*-ang-*) – Gr. *phálagx* (cf. BALK). So **pha·lange**. – F. – L.

phallus fæ·ləs penis or image of this. XVII. – late L. *phallus* – Gr. *phallós*; see BULL. So **pha·ll**IC. XVIII. – Gr. *phallikós*.

phanerogamous fænərɔ·gəməs (bot.) flowering)(*cryptogamous*. XIX. f. F. *phanérogame* or – modL. *phanerogamus*, f. Gr. *pháneros* visible, evident, rel. to *phaínein* show+*gámos* marriage, sexual union; see PHENOMENON, GAMETE, -OUS.

phantasm fæ·ntæzm illusion XIII; apparition, ghost; imagination, fancy XV; mental image XVI. – (O)F. *fantasme*, †*-esme* – L. *phantasma*; see next. So **phantasmagoria** fæ:ntæzməgɔ̄·riə exhibition of optical illusions; shifting succession of imaginary figures XIX. First recorded 1802, applied to an exhibition in London, prob. – F. *fantasmagorie* (1801), f. *fantasme* with fanciful termination.

phantom fæ·ntəm †illusion, deception XIII (Cursor M.); apparition, spectre XIV; mental illusion, dream image XVI; appearance without substance XVII. ME. *fantome*, *-um*, also *-osme* – OF. *fantosme*, *-ome* (mod. *fantôme*) = Pr. *fantasma*, *-auma*, Sp., It. *fantasma* :– L. *phantasma* – Gr. *phántasma*, f. *phantázein* make visible, f. *phant-*, *phaínein* show (see PHENOMENON). ¶ For the sp. *ph-* cf. PHEASANT.

Pharisee fæ·rĭsī ancient Jewish sect marked by strict observance of the law, (hence) self-righteous person. OE. *fariseus*, early ME. *farisew* (Orm) – late L. *pharīsæus*, *-ēus* – Gr. *pharīsaîos* – Aram. *p'rīshaiyā*, emphatic pl. of *p'rīsh* = Heb. *pārūsh* separated, separatist. The present form is from ME. *f-*, *pharise(e)* – OF. *pharise* – L.

pharmacy fā·ɹməsi administration of medicines XIV; art of preparing drugs XVII; dispensary XIX. – OF. *farmacie* (mod. *pharmacie*) – medL. *pharmacia* – Gr. *pharmakeiā* practice of a *pharmakeús* druggist, f. *phármakon* drug, medicine; see -Y[3]. So **pharmaceut**ICAL -sjū·tikəl. XVII. f. late L. *pharmaceuticus* – Gr. *-keutikós*, f. *pharmakeutḗs*, *pharmakeús* poisoner, druggist, *pharmakeúein* administer drugs. **pharmacopœia** -pi·ə XVII. modL. – Gr. *pharmakopoiiā* (*-poios* -making, -maker).

pharos fɛə·rɔs lighthouse. XVI. Appellative use of L. *Pharos* – Gr. *Pháros* name of an island off Alexandria on which stood a famous tower lighthouse. (Cf. F. *phare.*)

pharynx fæ·riŋks (anat.) cavity behind the nose. XVII. – modL. – Gr. *phárugx* (cf. *pháragx* cleft, chasm). Hence **phary·ng**AL[1], **phary·ngeal** -dʒ[1]əl (modL. *-eus*) XIX.

phase feiz aspect (orig. astron. of a planet). XIX. Partly – F. *phase*, partly new sg. evolved from *phases*, pl. of **phasis** fei·zis, fei·sis (XVII) – modL. *phasis* – Gr. *phásis* appearance, phase, f. **pha-*, as repr. by *phôs*, *pháos* light (cf. PHOSPHORUS).

pheasant fe·zənt long-tailed bright-coloured game-bird, Phasianus. XIII. – AN. *fesaunt*, for (O)F. *faisan* – Pr. *faisan* = Sp. *faisán*, Pg. *faisão*, It. *fagiano* :– L. *phāsiānus* – Gr. *phāsiānós* (sc. *órnis* bird) of Phasis, a river in Colchis, whence the bird is said to have spread westwards. Cf. OHG., MHG. *fasant* (G. *fasan*), Du. *fazant*. ¶ As in *phantom*, there has been etymol. reversion to *ph-*. For parasitic *-t* cf. *tyrant*.

phen- fen, fėn, **pheno-** fe·no(u), fī·no(u), fėnə· repr. Gr. *phaino-*, rel. to *phaínein* shine (cf. PHENOMENON), whence F. †*phène* benzene, *phényle* (see -YL) radical of benzene, *acide phénique* †phenic acid; orig. applied to coal-tar products arising from the manufacture of 'illuminating' gas, later as in *phenacetin*, *pheno-barbitone*.

phenol fī·nəl (chem.) hydroxyl derivative of benzene, carbolic acid. XIX. – F. *phénole*, f. *phène*, *phénique*; see prec. and -OL.

phenomenon finə·mĭnən, pl. **-mena** mĭnə thing or fact perceived or observed XVII (Bacon); immediate object of perception; notable or exceptional fact or occurrence XVIII. Also, in early use, *phaino-*, *phæno-*; – late L. *phænomenon*, pl. *-mena* – Gr. *phainómenon*, *-a*, sb. use of prp. pass. of *phaínein* show, pass. be seen, appear, f. **phan-* (as in *phanerós* visible, clear, *phantasiā* FANTASY), extension of **pha-*; see PHASE, PHOSPHORUS, PHOTO-.

phew fjū vocal gesture of disgust, weariness, etc. XVII. repr. puffing or blowing away with the lips; cf. *pho*, *phoo* (XVII), *foh*, *fah* (XVI), FAUGH.

phial fai·əl vessel (small glass bottle) for holding liquids. XIV. Late ME. *fyole* – (O)F. *fiole* = Pr. *fiola*, It. *fiala* – L. *phiola*, *phiala* saucer, censer – Gr. *phiálē* broad flat vessel.

-phil fil, **-phile** fail repr., through med. and modL. *-philus*, F. *-phile*, Gr. terminal el. *-philos* (which means 'dear to', 'beloved by', as in *Theophilus* dear to God), loving, devoted or favourable to, e.g. modL. *botanophilus* (Linnæus) amateur botanist, BIBLIOPHILE, and many formations like *Anglophil(e)*, for which forms in *phil(o)-* would be etymol. more correct. The corr. adj. suffix is **-phil**OUS filəs, frequent in bot. and zool., with the sense 'having affinity to or preference for', as *ammophilous*, *dendrophilous*, *hygrophilous*; with corr. nouns of state or quality in **-phil**Y[3] fili, **-phil**ISM filizm.

philander[1] filæ·ndəɹ †(passionate) lover. XVII. – Gr. *phílandros*, f. *phílos* loving + *andr-*, *anḗr* man, husband; used as a character-name in poetry and drama. Hence vb. make love, esp. flirtatiously. XVIII.

philander[2] filæ·ndəɹ gen. name for certain marsupials. XVIII (*fil-*). Named after *Philander* de Bruyn, who saw a specimen in 1711.

philanthropy filæ·nþrəpi benevolence towards mankind. XVII. – late L. *philanthrōpia* (formerly also in Eng. use) – Gr. *philanthrōpiā*, f. *philánthrōpos*, f. *phil-* PHILO- + *ánthrōpos* man; see -Y[3]. So **philanthro·p**IC XVIII; after F. **phila·nthrop**IST XVIII.

philately filæ·təli postage-stamp-collecting. XIX (1865). – F. *philatélie* (Herpin, 'Le collectionneur de timbres-poste', 1864), f. Gr. *phil-* PHILO- + *atelḗs* free from tax or charge, *ateleiā* exemption from payment, f. *a-* A-[4] + *télos* payment, charge, tax; see -Y[3]. Gr. *atelḗs* was taken as a passable equivalent of 'free' or 'franco', which was formerly stamped on prepaid letters (before the introduction of the impressed receipt stamp or its successor the adhesive label). Hence **philatel**IC -əte·lik, **phila·tel**IST.

philharmonic fil(h)āɹmɔ·nik devoted to music. XVIII. – F. *philharmonique* – It. *filarmonico*; see PHIL-, HARMONIC.

philibeg see FILIBEG.

philippic fili·pik (pl.) name of the orations of Demosthenes against Philip II, king of Macedon, in defence of Athenian liberty (IV B.C.); hence applied to Cicero's orations against Marc Antony, and gen. to any invective or denunciatory speech. XVI. – L. *philippicus* (in *orationes Philippicæ*) – Gr. *Philippikós* (in Φιλιππικοὶ λόγοι), f. *Phílippos*; see -IC.

Philistine fi·listain one of a people who inhabited the southern sea coast of Palestine and harassed the Israelites; an enemy into whose hands one may fall XVI; †in Germany, one who is not a student at the university; person deficient in liberal culture or of narrow interests XIX. – F. *Philistin* or Vulgate L. *Philistīnus*, also *Palæstīnus*, usually pl. – late Gr. *Philistînoi*, *Palaistînoi* – Heb. *pᵉlishtīm* or *-īīm* (whence Vulgate L. *Philisthiim*, LXX Gr. *Philistieím*), rel. to *pᵉlesheth* Philistia, Palestine. (Earlier Eng. forms of the ethnic name were †*Philistee* (XIV) – Vulgate L. *Philistēus*, and †*Philistian* (XIII) – OF. *philistien* – medL. *Philistiānus*.) The last sense is derived from G. *Philister*, the allusive uses of which were popularized in England by Carlyle, Froude, and Matthew Arnold. This use of G. *Philister* is said to be due to the choice of the passage *Philister über dir, Simson!* the Philistines be upon thee, Samson (Judges xvi) for the text of a sermon preached in 1683 at the funeral of a student killed by townsmen in a riot at Jena. Hence **Phi·listin**ISM. 1831 (Carlyle).

Phillis fi·lis in pastoral poetry, comely rustic maiden, or sweetheart. XVII (Milton). – L. *Phyllis* girl's name in Virgil's and Horace's poetry – Gr. *Phullís* female name (prop. 'foliage'), f. *phúllon* leaf (cf. PHYLLO-); the sp. with *i* instead of *y* may be due to assoc. with Gr. *phílos* dear, beloved (cf. PHILO-).

phillyrea filiri·ə evergreen shrub, native of the Mediterranean. XVII (Evelyn). modL. (Tournefort, Linnæus), for L. *philyrea* – Gr. *philuréā*, app. f. *philúrā* linden tree.

philo- fi·lo(u), filɔ·, before a vowel or *h* **phil-**, repr., often through F. or L., Gr. *phil(o)-*, comb. form of *phílos* meaning 'lover', 'loving' (cf. -PHIL), as in *philósophos* PHILOSOPHER; in many comps. (often nonce-words) from XVII, among which in later use are numerous specimens of the type of Gr. *philéllēn* loving or favourable to the Greeks, **phil**HELLE·NE (Moore, 1825), **phi·lomath** lover of learning XVII (Gr. *philomathḗs*), **phi·loproge·nitiveness** faculty of love of offspring (as a term of phrenology, 1815, Spurzheim), f. pp. stem *prōgenit-* of L. *prōgignere* (cf. PRO-[1], GENITIVE).

philology filɔ·lədʒi †study of literature XVII (Selden); science of language XVIII. – F. *philologie* (XVI; Budé, with reference to 'the lady' of Martianus Capella's 'De nuptiis Philologiæ et Mercurii'; cf. Ch., 'Merchant's Tale' 490) – L. *philologia* (Cicero) – Gr. *philologíā* devotion to dialectic, love of learning and literature, love of language, f. *philólogos* fond of talking, fond of learning, studious of words, whence L. *philologus*; see PHILO-, LOGOS. Hence **philolo·gi**CAL, **philo·logi**ST XVII, **phi·lologue** XVI. modL. *philologicus*, F. *philologue* (Rabelais).

Philomel fi·ləmel, **Philomela** filəmī·lə poetic proper name of the nightingale. XVI (*Philomele*, Spenser). The earlier form was *philomene* (XV–XVI), occas. used as a common noun – medL. *philomena* (XII), alt., presumably by assoc. with *Melpoménē* 'the singing muse', of L. *philomēla* – Gr. *philomḗlē* nightingale.

philosopher filɔ·səfəɹ one versed in philosophy. XIV. – AN. *philo-*, *filosofre*, var. of (O)F. *philosophe* – L. *philosophus* (Cicero) – Gr. *philósophos* 'lover of wisdom', f. *phílos* PHILO- + *soph-* (see SOPHIST); orig. str. *philoso·fre*; *philo·sopher* (OE. had *philosoph*) (assim. to -ER[1]) has prevailed since XVI. So **philoso·phi**C XVII, **philoso·phi**CAL XIV (Ch.) – late L. *philosophicus* (cf. adv. *philosophicē*, corr. to Gr. *philosophikôs*); **philo·sophi**ZE XVI; corr. in use to F. *philosopher*, L. *philosophārī*, Gr. *philosopheîn*. **philo·soph**Y[3] study of things and their causes. XIII (RGlouc.). – OF. *filosofie*, (now) *philosophie*, corr. to Pr. *philosophia*, etc. – L. *philosophia* (Cicero) – Gr. *philosophíā*.

philtre, U.S. **philter** fi·ltəɹ love-potion. XVI. – F. *philtre* – L. *philtrum* – Gr. *phíltron*, f. **phil-*, as in *phílos* dear, *phileîn* love + *-tron*, suffix of instrument or means.

phit fit imit. of certain sounds, e.g. of that made by a bullet. XIX.

phiz fiz face. XVII (*phyz*, *phys*). colloq. shortening of *physnomy*, early var. of PHYSIOGNOMY, of which another var. *physognomy* (XVI–XVII) is repr. by colloq. *physog* fi·zɔg. ¶ Another var., *visnomy*, was current XVI–XVII, survived dial., and was revived by Scott and Lamb.

phleb(o)- fle·b(ou), flébɔ·, comb. form of Gr. *phléps*, *phleb-* vein. **phlebotomy** flébɔ·təmi blood-letting. XIV (earliest form with *fl-*). – OF. *flebothomie* (mod. *phlébotomie* – late L. *phlebotomia* – Gr. *phlebotomíā*, f. *phlebótomos* opening a vein, f. *phlebo-*, *phléps* + **tom-* cut (cf. ATOM). So **phlebo·tomi**ZE. XVI (Nashe). – F. – modL.

phlegm flem mucus, considered as one of the four humours (cold and moist) XIV; as a secretion of membranes XV; coldness or sluggishness supposed to proceed from the predominance of the humour XVI. The present form appears XVI, as the result of assim. to the Gr.-L. original of earlier *fleume*, *fleme*, *fleam(e)* – OF. *fleume* (mod. *flegme*), corr. to Pr. *fleuma*, etc., Sp. *flema*, Pg. *fleima*, *phleu(g)ma* – late L. *phlegma* clammy moisture of the body – Gr. *phlégma* inflammation, morbid humour as the result of heat, f. *phlégein* burn, blaze (cf. PHLOX). **phlegmatic** flegmæ·tik XVI, †**fleu-** (XIV).

phlogiston flɔdʒi·stɔn (old chem.) principle of inflammability. XVIII. – modL. – Gr. *phlogistón*, n. of *phlogistós* burnt up, inflammable, f. *phlogízein* set on fire, f. **phlog-* burn; see next. Hence **dephlogi·sticated** lacking phlogiston (see DE- 6, -ATE[2], -ED[1]) XVIII, as in Priestley's *d. air*, his name for oxygen.

phlox flɔks herbaceous plant of the family Polemoniaceæ. XVIII. – L. *phlox* (Pliny) – Gr. *phlóx* lit. flame, f. **phlog-* **phleg-* :– IE. **bhleg-*, for which see also CONFLAGRATION, FLAGRANT, FLAME, FULMINATE, PHLEGM.

-phobe foub terminal el. – F. *-phobe* – L. *-phobus*, Gr. *-phobos* fearing, f. *phóbos* fear (cf. *phobeîsthai* fear), as in *hydrophobe*, and many comps. with national names, as *Anglophobe*; so **-phobia** fou·biə (– L. *-phobia* – Gr. *-phobíā*) in the sense 'dread', 'horror', as in *hydrophobia*, and *Anglophobia*, etc., some of which are modelled on F. words in *-phobie*.

phœnix, U.S. **phenix** fī·niks mythical bird of gorgeous plumage (mostly red, acc. to Herodotus) living for centuries in the Arabian desert, then burning itself to ashes, from which it emerged with renewed youth. OE., ME. *fenix* – L. *phœnix* and OF. *fenix* (mod. *phénix*), the L. being – Gr. *phoînix* the bird, also date-palm, etc., identical with *phoînix* Phœnician, purple, obscurely connected with *phoinós*, *phoínios* red with blood.

phone[1] foun abbrev. of TELEPHONE. XX.

phone[2] foun (philol.) element of spoken language – Gr. *phōnḗ* sound (see PHONETIC). XIX.

-phone foun terminal el., repr. Gr. *phōnḗ* voice, sound, used in the names of instruments for transmitting, reproducing, or amplifying sound, as *gramophone*, *megaphone*, *microphone*, *radiophone*, *telephone*.

phoneme fou·nīm (philol.) series of variants of a distinctive speech sound. XIX. – F. *phonème* – Gr. *phṓnēma*, f. *phōneîn* speak.

phonetic fŏne·tik pert. to or representing vocal sounds XIX; (sb. pl.) science of speech-sounds XIX (Latham). – modL. *phōnēticus* (G. Zoega, 1797, of notation opp. to *ideographic*) – Gr. *phōnētikós*, f. *phōnētós*, ppl. formation on *phōneîn* speak, f. *phōnḗ* voice, rel. to *phēmí* I speak, *phḗmē*, L. *fāma* FAME; see -IC. Hence **phoneti**·CIAN founĭti·ʃən 1848 (A. J. Ellis).

phoney fou·ni (sl.) deceptive, fraudulent. XX. Of unkn. origin.

phonogram fou·nəgræm character representing a spoken sound 1860 (Pitman); †sound-record made by a phonograph 1884 (see GRAMOPHONE). **phonograph** fou·nəgràf †symbol representing a sound XIX; instrument invented by Thomas A. Edison for automatically recording and reproducing sounds 1877. f. Gr. *phōnḗ* sound + *-graphos* written, *-gráphos* -writing; see prec. and -GRAPH. Cf. F. *phonographé* (Lenoir, 1877). So **phono**·GRAPHY †phonetic spelling XVIII; phonetic shorthand invented by Isaac Pitman in 1837 (named 1840). **phono**·LOGY science of vocal sounds esp. as applied to particular languages. XVIII.

-phore fɔ̄əɹ terminal el. repr. F. *-phore*, modL. *-phorus* – Gr. *-phóros* bearing, bearer, f. **phor-* **pher-* BEAR[2], as in *semaphore*. So **-phor**IC fɔ·rik, **-phor**OUS fərəs.

phosphate fɔ·sfeit (chem.) salt of phosphoric acid. XVIII. – F. *phosphat* (de Morveau, 1787), f. *phosphore* PHOSPHORUS + *-at* -ATE[2].

phosphorus fɔ·sfərəs †morning star; phosphorescent substance; (in early use *Kunkel's p.*) highly inflammable non-metallic element luminous in the dark, accidentally obtained from urine in 1669 by Brandt of Hamburg, who communicated the discovery to Kunkel XVII. – L. *phōsphorus* – Gr. *phōsphóros* light-bringing, sb. (sc. *astḗr* star) morning star, f. *phôs* light + *-phóros* -PHORE. So **phosphor**E·SCE, -E·SCENT. XVIII; cf. F. *phosphorescence*, etc. **phospho·r**IC -fɔ·rik. XVIII. – F. **pho·sphor**OUS. XVIII. **phospho-, phosphor(o)-,** comb. forms of *phosphorus*. Cf. PHÆTON, PHENO-, PHOTO-.

photo- fou·tou, foutə·, before a vowel **phot-,** repr. *phōto-*, comb. form of Gr. *phôs*, *phōt-* light (cf. BEAM), as in **photo·**-METER light-measuring instrument XVIII; later esp. in connexion with photography, as **pho·togravu·re** (F. *gravure* engraving). **pho·to**TYPE plate or block for printing from, produced by a photographic process.

photograph fou·təgràf picture produced by the action of light on a sensitized film. Used for the first time, together with **photogra·phic** and **photo**·GRAPHY, by Sir John Herschel (1792–1871) in a paper read before the Royal Society on 14 March 1839, which was preceded by a use of G. *photographie* in the 'Vossische Zeitung' of 25 February 1839; f. Gr. *phōto-*, *phôs* light + *-graphos* written; see PHOTO-, -GRAPH. ¶ *Photographic* superseded *photogenic* (31 January 1839, Fox Talbot in 'Proceedings of the Royal Society' vol. iv), which is now used for 'offering a good subject for photography'.

phrase freiz style of expression, diction; small group of words in a sentence; pithy expression. XVI. In earliest use also *phrasis*, *-ys* (in Palsgr., 1530, as sg. and pl.), from the pl. of which (*phrases*) a sg. *phrase* appears to have been evolved (cf. PHASE). – L. *phrasis* (Seneca the rhetorician, Quintilian) – Gr. *phrásis* speech, manner of speaking, f. *phrázein* indicate, declare, tell; cf. F. *phrase* (1548), Sp., It. *frase*, Du., G. *phrase*. So **phraseo**LOGY freizio·lədʒi arrangement of words and phrases in speech. XVII. – modL. *phraseologia*, spurious Gr. *phraseologíā*, irreg. formed by M. Neander in the title of his book of locutions collected from Isocrates, 1558 (*ΦΡΑΣΕΟΛΟΓΙΑ ΙΣΟΚΡΑΤΙΚΗ ΕΛΛΗΝΟΛΑΤΙΝΗ* Phraseologia Isocratis Græcolatina), from Gr. *phráseōn*, g. pl. of *phrásis*.

phrenetic frĭne·tik frenzied, FRANTIC. XIV (Ch.; in XVI–XVIII *phrentic*). – (O)F. *frénétique* – L. *phrenēticus* – late Gr. *phrenētikós*, for *phrenītikós*, f. *phrenîtis* delirium, f. *phren-*, *phrḗn* heart, mind; see -ITIS, -IC.

phrenology frĭnɔ·lədʒi study of the cranium as an index of the mental faculties, dependent on the theory of Gall and Spurzheim. 1815. f. Gr. *phreno-*, *phrḗn* mind + -LOGY; designed to cover G. *gehirn- und schädellehre* (1804) encephalology and craniology. Hence **phreno·log**IST, **phrenolo·g**ICAL.

phthalic fþæ·lik abbrev. of NAPHTHALIC. 1857.

phthiriasis þirai·əsis, (f)þairiei·sis condition of the body in which lice multiply. XVI. – L. – Gr. *phthiríāsis*, f. *phtheiriân* be lousy, f. *phtheír* louse; see -ASIS.

phthisic ti·zik pulmonary consumption. XIV. ME. *tisik*, later *ptisike*, *phthisick* – OF. *tisike*, *-ique*, later *ptisique*, *thisique* (repl. by mod. *phtisie*), corr. to Sp., It. *tisica* :– Rom. *(*ph*)*thisica*, sb. use of fem. of L. *phthisicus* – Gr. *phthisikós* consumptive, f. *phthísis*, f. **phthi-*, *phthínein* waste away; see -IC. So **phthisis** tai·sis, ti·sis, (f)þai·sis, (f)þi·sis. XVI. – L. – Gr.

phut fʌt (sl.) *go f.*, be a failure. XIX. f. Hind. *phatna* burst.

phylactery filæ·ktəri small box containing four texts of Scripture worn by Jews as a reminder of the obligation to keep the law. XIV (Wyclif, Trevisa); in various uses from XVII. Early forms *fil-*, *philaterie* – OF. **filaterie*, *-atiere* – Vulgate L. *fyl-*, *phylactērium* – Gr. *phulaktḗrion* safeguard, amulet, f. *phulaktḗr* guard, f. *phulak-*, stem of vb. *phulássein*.

phyllo- fi·lou repr. comb. form of Gr. *phúllon* leaf, perh. rel. to L. *folium*.

phylo- failo(u), failɔ· repr. comb. form of Gr. *phūlḗ*, *phûlon* race (whence modL. **phylum** fai·ləm XIX), as in **phylo·geny** (Gr. *génos* GENUS) racial or tribal history.

physeter faisī·təɹ †large blowing whale XVI; cachalot XVIII. – L. *phȳsēter* – Gr. *phūsētḗr*, f. *phūsân* blow, f. widespread imit. base **phū̆* (cf. PUSTULE).

physic fi·zik healing art, medicine XIII; †natural science XIV; medicinal preparation, medicine XVI. ME. *fisike* – OF. *fisique* medicine (mod. *physique* natural science, now physics) – L. *physica*, *-ē* (Cicero) – Gr. *phusikḗ*, sb. use (sc. *epistḗmē* knowledge) of fem. of *phusikós*, f. *phúsis* nature; see BE, -IC. So **phy·sic** adj. †medical, medicinal XV (*p. garden* XVII); physical, natural XVI. **phy·sical** medical, medicinal XV; natural, material XVI; pert. to physics; bodily, corporeal XVIII. – medL. *physicālis*. **physicist** fi·zisist student of physics. XIX. **physics** fi·ziks natural science XVI; science that treats of matter and energy XVIII; rendering L. n. pl. *physica* – Gr. *tà phusiká* title of Aristotle's physical treatises.

physician fizi·ʃən one who practises the healing art XIII (AncrR.);)(*surgeon* XIV. ME. *fisicien* – OF. *fisicien* (mod. *physicien* physicist), f. *fisique* PHYSIC; see prec., -IAN.

physio- fi·ziou, fiziɔ· repr. *phusio-*, comb. form of Gr. *phúsis* nature (see BE). **physiognomy**[3] fiziɔ·nəmi judging character from bodily lineaments XIV; face, countenance XIV. Late ME. *fisnamye*, *fis-*, *phisonomie*, later *phisnomy* (XV–XVII), *phisognomie* (XVI–XVII), *physiognomy* (XVI) – OF. *phisonomie*, *-anomie* (mod. *physionomie*), corr. to Pr. *phizonomia*, etc. – medL. *phisonomia*, *physionomia* – late Gr. *phusiognōmiā* (recorded once as a miswriting), contr. of Gr. *phusiognōmoníā*, f. *phúsis* nature +*gnōmon-*, *gnṓmōn* interpreter, f. **gnō-* (see KNOW; cf. PHIZ. **physio·graphy**[3] description of natural phenomena XIX; physical geography 1873 (J. Geikie). – F. *physiographie*. So **phy:siogra·phical**. XVIII (Morse). **physio·logy** †natural science, natural philosophy XVI; science of the phenomena of living things XVII. – F. *physiologie* or L. *physiologia* (Cicero) – Gr. *phusiologíā* (Aristotle). So †**physio·loger**[1] XVI; f. late L. *physiologus* – Gr. *phusiológos* one who discourses on nature. **physiolo·gical**. XVII. **physio·logist** †natural philosopher XVII; student of animal or vegetable physiology XVIII.

physique fizī·k bodily structure or build. XIX. – F. *physique* m., sb. use of *physique* PHYSICAL.

physo- fai·sou repr. comb. form of Gr. *phûsa* bellows, bladder, bubble, used in many scientific terms.

-phyte fait terminal el. repr. Gr. *phutón* plant, f. *phúein* (see BE), and denoting a vegetable organism, as in *saprophyte*, *zoophyte*.

phyto- fai·tou, faitɔ· repr. comb. form of Gr. *phutón* (see prec.), used in many bot. terms. **phyto·graphy**, **phyto·logy** description, science of plants. XVII.

pi pai (math.) ratio of the circumference of a circle to the diameter. XIX. English pronunc. of the name of the Gr. letter *Π π* (P p), initial letter of περιφέρεια periphery and περίμετρος perimeter.

piacular paiæ·kjŭləɹ pert. to expiation. XVII. – L. *piāculāris*, f. *piāculum*, f. *piāre* appease, f. *pius* PIOUS; see -CLE, -AR.

pia mater pai·ə mei·təɹ delicate innermost of the three meninges of the brain and spinal cord. XVI. medL. rendering of Arab. *al'umm al raqīqah* the thin or tender mother; cf. DURA MATER.

pianoforte piæ·noufɔ̄ɹt, -fɔ̄·ɹti musical instrument producing tones by means of hammers operated by levers from a keyboard. XVIII (*Piano Forte*, 1767). Like F. *piano-forté* (1774, Voltaire) – It. *pianoforte*, evolved from the descriptive name *gravecembalo col* (or *di*) *piano e forte*, 'harpsichord with soft and loud' (expressing the gradation of tone obtainable, in contrast with the unvarying tone of the harpsichord), used by the inventor Bartolomeo Cristofori of Padua (*c.*1710); *piano e forte* is found 1598 as the name of an instrument of unknown action. Also formerly called †*fortepiano* in It., F., and Eng. (1769). Now usu. abbrev. **piano** piæ·nou. XIX (*c.*1800).

piastre piæ·stəɹ Sp. piece of eight or dollar (*peso duro*); small Turk. coin, the *ghūrūsh* XVII. – F. *piastre* – It. *piastra*, short for *piastra d'argento* 'plate of silver'; *piastra* metal plate, coin, repr. L. *emplastra* (Aulus Gellius), var. of *emplastrum* PLASTER.

piazza piæ·zə, piæ·dzə public square XVI; (erron.) colonnade, covered ambulatory XVII; (U.S.) veranda XVIII. – It. *piazza* = F. *place* PLACE.

pibroch pī·brəχ series of variations for the bagpipe. XVIII. – Gael. *piobaireachd*, f. *piobair* piper (f. *piob* PIPE[1]) + -*achd* suffix of function, etc.

pica pai·kə (typog.) size of printing type. XVI. transf. use of medL. *pica* PIE[3] (but no edition of the 'pie' printed in 'pica' type appears to be known); cf. BREVIER, PRIMER.

picador pikədō·ɹ in bullfighting, mounted man who provokes the bull with a lance. XVIII. Sp., 'pricker', f. *picar* prick = (O)F. *piquer* :– Rom. **piccāre* PICK[2].

picaresque pikəre·sk pert. to rogues, orig. of Sp. literary fiction. XIX. – F. – Sp. *picaresco*, f. *picaro* roguish, knavish, sb. rogue (corr. to It. *piccaro* rascal, beggar); see -ESQUE.

picaroon pikərū·n pirate, pirate ship; rogue. XVII (Capt. Smith). – Sp. *picaron*, augm. of *picaro*; see prec. and -OON.

picayune pikəjū·n (in Louisiana, etc.) Spanish half-real (6¼ cents), (U.S.) 5-cent piece; insignificant object; adj. mean, paltry. XIX. – F. *picaillon* old copper coin of Piedmont, halfpence, cash – modPr. *picaioun*, of unkn. origin.

piccalilli pi·kəlili pickle of chopped vegetables and hot spices. XVIII. prob. fancifully f. PICKLE, with reminiscence of CHILLI.

piccaninny pi·kənini little one, child, esp. child of negro or coloured race. XVII. W. Indian Negro formation on Sp. *pequeño* or Pg. *pequeno* little, small (of unkn. origin); perh. directly based on Pg. dim. *pequenino*.

piccolo pi·kəlou small flute (orig. *p. flute*). XIX. – It. *piccolo* small, f. **pik*- (in It. and Rum.), corr. to synon. **pet*- (in F. and Pr.), and **pek*- (in Sp. and Pg.). See PETTY.

pice pais ¼ anna. XVII. – Hind. *paisā*, perh. f. *pa'ī* PIE[5].

piceous pi·siəs pitchy. XVII. f. L. *piceus*, f. *pic*-, *pix* PITCH[1]; see -EOUS.

pick[1] pik pointed tool for breaking up a surface. XIV (Ayenbite). ME. *pic*, *pykk*, app. collateral form of *pike* pick, pointed object (surviving dial.), OE. *pīc*, rel. to *pīcung* pricking, verbal sb. of **pīcian* or **pīcan* (see next).

pick[2] pik probe with a pointed instrument, etc.; pluck, gather; choose *out*; rob, plunder. XV. Succeeded to *pike* XIV (surviving dial.), prob. through the infl. of F. *piquer* = It. *piccare*, etc., or MLG., MDu. *picken* (Du. *pikken*), whence presumably also Icel. *pikka*, in the senses 'pick', 'peck', 'pierce', 'puncture'.

pick-a-back pi·kəbæk on the shoulders or back like a pack. XVI. Earlier (†*a*) *pick-back*, †*on* or *a pick-pack* (still dial.); it is doubtful whether the orig. form referred to the pitching of a pack on the shoulders or the back on which it is pitched (as, e.g. in G. *huckepack*, -*back*).

pickaxe pi·kæks tool consisting of a curved iron bar with PICK[1]. XV. alt., by assim. of the final syll. to AXE, of ME. *pikois*, -*eis* (surviving in s.w. dial. as *peckis*, *pickis*) – OF. *picois*.

pickerel pi·kərəl young pike. XIV. f. PIKE[1] + -EREL after *cockerel*; in AL. *pikerellus* (XIII).

picket pi·kit A. pointed stake, etc. XVII; B. small detachment of troops (orig. with horses tied to stakes) XVIII. – F. *piquet*, f. *piquer* prick, pierce; see PICK[2], -ET.

pickle pi·kl salt liquor in which food is preserved XIV; article of food so preserved XVII. ME. *pekille*, *pykyl* – MLG., MDu. *pekel* (whence also G. *pökel*), of unkn. origin. Hence vb. XVI.

picnic pi·knik (orig.) social entertainment in which each person contributed a share of the food; (now) outdoor pleasure party with a repast. XVIII (Chesterfield, 1748). – F. *piquenique* (XVII, said by Ménage, 1692, to be of recent introduction); unexplained.

picotee pikətī· variety of carnation. XVIII. – F. *picoté*, pp. of *picoter* mark with pricks or points, f. *picot*, dim. of *pic* point, prick.

picquet pike·t card-game. XVII. – F. *piquet*, †*picquet*, prob. f. *pic* in *faire pic* make sixty, of obscure origin.

picric pi·krik (chem.) *p. acid*. XIX. f. Gr. *pikrós* bitter + -IC. So **pi·cro-**, comb. form of Gr. *pikrós*. XIX.

Pict pikt one of an ancient people of N. Britain. Late ME. (Trevisa) – late L. *Pictī*, identical in form with *pictī* painted or tattooed people (pp. of L. *pingere* PAINT), adopted in OE. as *Pihtas*, var. *Peohtas*, whence ME. *Peght*, Sc. *Pecht*.

picture pi·ktʃəɹ †pictorial representation XV (Lydg.); individual painting or drawing XV (Caxton); visual impression, mental image; graphic description XVI. – L. *pictūra* painting, f. *pict*-, pp. stem of *pingere* PAINT, embroider. Hence vb. XV (Caxton). So **pictur**ESQUE piktʃəre·sk such as would make an effective or striking picture. XVIII (1703 Steele, 1712, 1717 Pope). – (with assim. to prec., to express 'in the style of a picture') F. *pittoresque* – It. *pittoresco* (F. Redi 1664) 'in the style of a painter', f. *pittore* :– L. *pictōrem*, nom. *pictor* painter, f. *pict*- ¶ The earliest evidence available for the F. word is 1720 (*pittoresque*), 1732 (*pittoresquement*), but in 1712 Pope wrote of 'what the French call very *picturesque*'.

piddle pi·dl A. (dial.) trifle XVI; B. (colloq.) urinate XVIII. In A perh. alt. of PEDDLE by assoc. with LG. *piddeln*; in B presumably based on PISS or PEE, after PUDDLE.

pidgin, pigeon pi·dʒin in *P. English*, commercial jargon used esp. in the Far East. XIX (c.1850). Chinese perversion of BUSINESS, used for 'occupation' or 'affair'.

pie[1] pai MAGPIE. XIII (Owl & Nightingale). – (O)F. *pie* = Pr. *piga*, It. *pica* :– L. *pīca* magpie, rel. to *pīcus* green woodpecker, and Skr. *pikás* Indian cuckoo, and referred by some to IE. *(*s*)*pī̆*- be pointed, whence also the Germ. word for woodpecker, (M)Du. *specht*, OHG. *speht* (G. *specht*). ¶ The foll. words, PIE[2], PIE[3], PIE[4], may be all ult. identical with this.

pie[2] pai dish composed of meat, etc., enclosed in paste and baked. XIV. prob. identical with PIE[1] (*pīca* being the medL. equiv.); it has been conjectured that the reason for the application is that the magpie collects miscellaneous objects, and †*chewet* meat or fish pie (perh. identical with F. *chouette* †jackdaw, now owl) and HAGGIS have been compared.

pie[3] pai (liturg.) perpetual almanac and ordinal for the recitation of divine service. XV (Caxton). Rendering of medL. *pīca* (identical with PIE[1]); cf. PICA and PIE[2].

pie[4] pai (typogr.) confused mass of type (spec. *printer's p.*). XVII. perh. tr. F. *pâté* pasty (PIE[2]), as in *caractères tombés en pâté*. ¶ Cf. the synon. G. *zwiebelfische*.

pie[5] pai $\frac{1}{12}$ of an anna. XIX. – Hindi, Marathi *pā'ī* :– Skr. *padī*, *pad* quarter, FOOT (cf. PICE).

piebald pai·bōld of two colours mingled, esp. white and black. XVI. f. PIE[1] + BALD (in the sense 'streaked with white').

piece pīs A. separate or detached portion XIII (w. midl.); (dial.) portion of time or space XIII; quantity (of matter or substance) XIV; B. section of armour, etc. XIV; fire-arm; coin XVI; cask (of liquor) XV; 'man' in a game XVI; C. person XIII (RGlouc.). – ME. *pece*, later *piece* – AN. *pece*, OF. *piece* (mod. *pièce*) = Pr., Cat. *pesa*, Sp. *pieza*, Pg. *peça*, It. *pezza* :– Rom. **pettia* (cf. medL. *petia*, *pecia*, *pet*(*t*)*ium*), prob. of Gaulish origin (cf. W. *peth* quantity, part, Breton *pez* piece :– Brythonic **petti*-, corr. to Goidelic **quett*-, whence OIr. *cuit*, Gael. *cuid* part, share. Cf. PEAT. Hence **piece** vb. XIV. **piece**MEAL[2] piece by piece XIII; repl. OE. *styććemǣlum*.

pied paid particoloured, orig. of black and white like a magpie. XIV. First in *pyed freres*, also called *freres of the pye* and *freres pyes* (Walsingham 'Historia Anglicana' an. 1326) friars wearing a particoloured habit, tr. based on OF. *freres agachies* (F. *agace* magpie); f. PIE[1] + -ED[2].

piepowder pai·pau:dəɹ (hist.) *Court of P.*, *P. Court*, orig. *Court of P-s* summary court formerly held at fairs and markets to administer justice among itinerant dealers, etc. XV. – AN. *piepuldrus* – AL. *pedepulverōsus* dusty-footed, i.e. abl. sg. of L. *pēs* foot, and adj. f. L. *pulver-*, *pulvis* dust (see POWDER).

pier piəɹ one of the supports of the spans of a bridge XII; solid structure extending into the sea, etc., breakwater, jetty XIV; pillar XVII. ME. *per* – AL. *pera* or *pēra*, of unkn. origin. ¶ ONF. *pire* breakwater, boom of a harbour, weir, though corr. in meaning, cannot be formally equated.

pierce piəɹs penetrate with a sharp-pointed instrument. XIII. ME. *perce* (later *pierce* XVI) – (O)F. *percer* = Pr. *pertusar*, It. *pertugiare* :– Rom. **pertūsiāre*, f. L. *pertūsus*, pp. of *pertundere* bore through, f. *per-* PER- + *tundere* thrust (cf. CONTUSION).

Pierian paiiə·riən pert. to Pieria, a region of ancient Macedonia, a seat of the worship of the Muses. XVI. f. L. *Pierius*, f. *Pieria*; see -IAN. (In OE. *Pierisć*.)

pierrot piə·rou French pantomime character; clown with whitened face in fancy costume. XVIII. – F. *pierrot*, appellative use of pet-form of *Pierre* PETER.

pietà pjeita· representation of the Virgin Mary mourning over the body of the dead Christ. XVII. It. :– L. *pietātem* PIETY.

pietism pai·ĭtizm movement for the revival of piety in the Lutheran communion; hence gen. XVII. – G. (modL.) *pietismus*, f. L. *pietās* PIETY; see -ISM. So **pi·et**IST XVII: applied orig. in derision to the followers of P. J. Spener in ref. to the *collegia pietatis* or unions for religious edification formed *c.*1670 at Frankfort, Germany.

piety pai·ĭti †pity XIII; faithfulness to filial (or similar) duties XVI; devotion to religious duties XVII. – OF. *piete* (mod. *piété*) – L. *pietās* dutifulness; f. *pius* PIOUS; see PITY, from which *piety* was not fully differentiated till late XVI.

piezometer paiizɔ·mĭtəɹ instrument for measuring pressure. XIX (1820, J. Perkins). f. Gr. *piézein* press + -(O)METER.

piffle pi·fl trifle (*away*), talk ineffectively. XIX. Of symbolic origin (cf. -LE[3]); so Sc. *piffer*. Hence sb.

pig pig young of swine XIII (AncrR.); swine of any age; oblong piece of metal, ingot (cf. SOW[1]) XVI. ME. *pigge* :– OE. **picga*, **pigga* (of similar formation to *docga* DOG), prob. repr. in OE. *picbrēd* 'swine-food', acorn, and in the proper name *Pigman*

(XII); connexion with synon. LG., early Du. *bigge, big*, MDu. *vigghe*, cannot be made out. Hence **pi·g**TAIL twist of tobacco XVII; plait of hair XVIII.

pigeon[1] pi·dʒĭn †young dove; bird of the family Columbidæ XIV; †young woman, girl; dupe, gull XVI. Late ME. *peion, pyion, pegeon* – OF. *pijon* young bird, esp. young dove (mod. *pigeon*) = Pr. *pijon* (whence Sp. *pichón*, It. *piccione*) :– Rom. **pībiō(n-)*, for late L. *pīpiō(n-)* (whence It. *pippione*), f. imit. base **pīp-*, with corr. verbal forms *pīpiāre, pīpīre, pīpilāre, pīpitāre* (cf. PEEP[1]) and cogns. Skr. *píppaka, pippīkas*, Gr. *pipos, pippízein*.

pigeon[2] see PIDGIN.

pigment pi·gmənt colouring matter. (OE.), XIV. – L. *pigmentum*, f. **pig-*, base of *pingere* PAINT; see -MENT.

pike[1] paik large voracious freshwater fish, Esox lucius. XIV. perh. of OE. date, being prob. repr. in the place-names *Picheburne* (XI), Pickburn in Yorkshire, *Pikemere* (XIII), Pickmere in Cheshire, 'stream/lake where pike were found', and identical with OE. *pīc* point, pick, the fish being so named from its pointed jaw (cf. F. *brochet* pike, f. *broche* spit). OE. *pīc* (also in *hornpīc* pinnacle) corr. to LG. *pīke*, ON. *pík* piked staff, Goth. *peika|bagms* palm tree, of obscure origin, perh. corresp. to L. *fīcus* fig. See also PICKEREL.

pike[2] paik weapon consisting of a long wooden shaft with pointed head. XVI. – (O)F. *pique* = Pr. *piqua*, Sp. *pica*, It. *picca*, CRom. of Germ. origin.

pike[3] paik short for TURNPIKE. XIX (Dickens).

pikelet pai·klit local (w. midl.) name for a kind of crumpet. XVIII. app. short for *barapicklet* (cf. 'our welsh Barrapyclids', Cotgr., s.v. *Popelins*).

pikestaff pai·kstaf A. staff with metal point XIV; B. wooden shaft of a pike XVI. In sense A prob. – ON. *píkstafr*, f. *pík*; see PICK[1] and STAFF; in sense B f. PIKE[2]. ¶ In *as plain as a p.* (XVI) an alt. of *packstaff*, i.e. a staff on which a pedlar supports his pack, with poss. ref. to its smoothness.

pilaster pilæ·stəɹ square or rectangular pillar. XVI. – F. *pilastre* – It. *pilastro*, medL. *pīlastrum*, f. L. *pīla* pillar, PILE[2]; see -ASTER.

pilau, pilaw pilau·, pilɔ̄·, **pilaff** pilā·f Oriental dish of rice. XVII. – Turk. *pilāw, pilāv, -āf* – Pers. *pilāw* (whence Urdu *pilāo, palāo*). Cf. F. *pilau*, It. *pilao*, modGr. *piláphi*, Russ. *piláv*, Rum. *pilaf*.

pilch pilᵗʃ outer garment of skin dressed with the hair or of woollen stuff OE.; saddle pad XVI; baby's wrapper XVII. OE. **pileće*, (late) *pyl(e)će* = OHG. *pelliz* (G. *pelz* fur, furred coat) – medL. *pellicia* cloak, for L. *pellicea*, fem. of *pelliceus*, f. *pellis* skin, FELL[1]; cf. PELISSE, SURPLICE.

pilchard pi·ltʃəɹd small sea-fish, Clupea pilchardus, allied to the herring. XVI (*pilcher, -erd, -ard*). Of unkn. origin; the ending was assim. to -ARD, as in *gurnard*. ¶ Ir. *pilseir* is from English.

pilcrow pi·lkrou paragraph mark ¶. XV. unexpl. alt. of *pylcrafte* (Medulla Gram.), var. of *pargrafte* (Ortus Vocab.), for **pargraf* (cf. AL. *pergraphum*), contr. of *paragraf* PARAGRAPH. Cf. PARAPH.

pile[1] pail †dart, shaft, spike OE.; pointed stake or post, esp. for driving into soft ground for support of a structure XI; (her.) charge of the form Λ XV. OE. *pīl* = MLG., MDu. *pīl* (Du. *pijl*), OHG. *pfīl* (G. *pfeil*) (ON., Sw., Da. forms are – LG.) – L. *pīlum* javelin.

pile[2] pail †pillar, pier; heap of things laid one upon the other XV; heap of combustibles XVI; lofty mass of buildings XVII; series of metal plates in a battery XIX. – (O)F. *pile* heap, pyramid, mass of masonry = Sp., It. *pila* :– L. *pīla* pillar, pier, mole, whence *pīlāre* ram down, heap up, plunder, steal (see COMPILE). Cf. PILLAGE. Hence **pile** vb. heap up. XVI.

pile[3] pail fine soft hair XV; nap of cloth XVI. prob. – AN. *pyle*, var. of *peil* (Liber Albus) kind of cloth, (O)F. *poil* = Pr., Sp., It. *pelo*, Rum. *păr* :– L. *pilus* hair.

pile[4] pail hæmorrhoid. XV. prob. – L. *pila* ball, with ref. to the globular form of an external pile.

pileated pi·lieitid (nat. hist.) having a pileus or cap. XVIII. f. L. *pīleātus*, f. *pīleus, pilleus*; see -ATE[2], -ED[1].

pilfer pi·lfəɹ (obs.) plunder. XIV. Late ME. *pylfre, pelfyr* – AN., OF. *pelfre* (cf. AL. *pelfra*), f. *pelfrer*, whence **pilfer** vb. plunder, (later) steal in small quantities. XVI; see PELF. The form was early affected by assoc. with †*pill* (see PILLAGE).

pilgarlik pilgā·ɹlik bald-headed man; poor creature (U.S. sl., one's poor self). XVII. For earlier *pilled* (i.e. peeled) *garlic* XVI, bald head being likened to a peeled head of garlic.

pilgrim pi·lgrim †wayfarer XII; one who journeys to a sacred place as an act of religious devotion XIII; *P. Fathers* XVIII. ME. *pilegrim* – Pr. *pelegrin* = Cat. *pelegri, peregri*, Sp. *peregrino*, It. *pellegrino*, (O)F. *pèlerin* – L. *peregrīnus* foreign; see PEREGRINE. The Eng. forms, with . . *l* . . *gr* (cf. Icel. *pílagrimr*, MLG. *pilegrim*), suggest derivation through southern France or northern Spain. For final *m* from *n* cf. *buckram, grogram, megrim, vellum*. ¶ So **pi·lgrim**AGE. XIII (*pelrim-, pilegrim-*). – Pr. *pilgrinatge* = (O)F. *pèlerinage*, etc.

pill pil small ball of medicinal substance to be swallowed XV (Caxton); transf. pellet, ball XVI. – MLG., MDu. *pille*, Du. *pil* (whence G. *pille*), presumably – reduced form of L. *pilula* PILULE. Hence **pill** vb. dose with pills XVIII; (sl.) blackball, fail (a candidate).

pillage pi·lidʒ spoliation, plunder. XIV (Gower). – (O)F. *pillage*, f. *piller* plunder (whence *pill* †plunder, pillage, dial. peel XIII, superseding †*pile*, OE. **pilian*, *pylian* XII, in OF. only in *espiller* – Pr. *pilhar*, Cat. *pillar* :– Rom. **pīliāre*, perh. f. L. *pīlum* javelin; see -AGE. Hence vb. XVI (Marlowe, Hakluyt, Nashe).

pillar pi·ləɹ slender or narrow upright supporting a structure. XIII (AncrR.). ME. *piler(e)* – AN. *piler*, (O)F. *pilier* = Pr., Sp. *pilar* :– Rom. **pīlāre*, f. L. *pīla* pillar, pier, PILE[2]; assim. in sp. to words in -AR from XIV.

pillion pi·ljən saddle, esp. a woman's light saddle; also, cushion or pad behind a saddle. XVI (Sc. *pilʒane*, Eng. *pyllyon*). – Gael. *pillean*, *pillin*, Ir. *pillín*, dim. of *pell* (g. sg. and nom. pl. *pill*) couch, pallet, cushion – L. *pellis* skin, FELL[1].

pilliwinks pi·liwiŋks (hist.) sort of thumbscrew. XIV. In Eng. use *pyrwykes*, *pyrewinkes* (XIV–XV), in Sc. use from late XVI *pilli-*, *pinniwinkes*, of which various corrupt vars. occur in later writers; of unkn. origin.

pillory pi·ləri wooden framework erected on a post or pillar and constructed like stocks. XIII. ME. *pillori* – AL. *pillorium* (XII) – (O)F. *pilori*, †*pillori*, †*pellori* (XII), prob. – Pr. *espilori*, of obscure origin (there are many variations of form in OF., Pr., and medL.); poss. (if the forms with single *l* are original) – Rom. **expīlōrium*, f. L. *ex* EX-[1] + *pīla* PILLAR; see -ORY[1]. So vb. XVI; after F. *pilorier*.

pillow pi·lou cushion for support of the head. Late ME. *pilwe* (XIV Chaucer, Gower, Wycl. Bible) :– OE. **pylw-*, obl. stem of *pyle*, later *pylu* (whence ME. *pile*, *pule*, *pele*, dial. *pill*, *peel*), corr. to MLG. *pöle*, MDu. *pēluwe*, *pöluwe* (Du. *peluw*), OHG. *pfuliwī*, *pfulwo* (G. *pfühl*, UG. *pfulwe*, *pfulbe*), repr. WGerm. **pulwī(n)* (II–III) – L. *pulvīnus* cushion, bolster.

pilose pəi·lous hairy. XVIII. – L. *pilōsus*, f. *pilus* hair, PILE[3]; see -OSE[1]. So **pi·lous**. XVII.

pilot pai·lət steersman, esp. for harbour service. XVI. – F. *pilote* – medL. *pilotus* (XV) (whence also Sp., Pg. *piloto*), varying with *pedota*, *pedotta* – MGr. **pēdṓtēs*, f. Gr. *pēdón* oar, pl. rudder, f. **pēd-*, **ped-* FOOT; cf. -OT. (Du. *piloot*, G. *pilot* are also from F.) So vb. XVII; after F. *piloter*.

pilule pi·ljūl pill. XVI. – F. *pilule* – L. *pilula*, dim. of *pila* ball, PILE[4]; see -ULE.

pimento pime·ntou Jamaica pepper or allspice, tree yielding this. XVII. – Sp. *pimiento* – L. *pigmentum* PIGMENT, in medL. spiced drink, (hence) spice, pepper.

pimp pimp pander, procurer. XVII. Of unkn. origin.

pimpernel pi·mpəɹnəl †great burnet, salad burnet; plant Anagallis arvensis. XV. – OF. *pimpernelle* (mod. *pimprenelle*), earlier *piprenelle* (corr. to Sp. *pimpinela*, It. *pimpinella*, medL. *pipinella*) – Rom. **piperīnella*, f. **piperīnus* pepper-like, f. L. *piper* PEPPER, the fruit of burnet resembling peppercorn. ¶ In the Rom. langs. the word has still the first sense; the reason for the transference to the second in Eng. is not known. There is much variation in Germ. derivs., early and modern.

pimple pi·mpl small tumour on the skin. XIV. Nasalized form corr. to late OE. *piplian* (in prp.) break out into pustules; parallel to obs. and dial. var. *pumple* (XVI; cf. F. †*pompette* 'a pumple, or pimple on the nose, or chinne', Cotgr.); similar forms are L. *papula* pustule, Lith. *pãpas* nipple.

pin pin peg OE.; (superseding *preen*, OE. *prēon*) pointed length of stiff wire used as a fastener XIV; (pl.) legs; skittles XVI. Late OE. *pinn*, corr. to MLG. *pin*, (M)LG., (M)Du. *pinne* (Du. *pin*), OHG. *pfinn* (MHG. *pfinne*), Icel. *pinni* – L. *pinna* applied to various objects likened to a wing or feather (cf. PINION, PINNACLE), referred by Quintilian to an adj. **pinnus* pointed, but assoc. in use with *penna* PEN[1], of which it appears as a var. in several senses. Hence **pin** vb. XIV. **pi·n**CU:SHION XVII, earlier †*pinpillow* XVI; **pi·n-**FEA:THER immature feather XVII (earlier *pen-feather*); **pi·n-**MO:NEY allowance made to a woman for dress, etc., typified by the pins used for fastening or adorning garments (cf. 'I give my said daughter Margaret my lease of the parsonadge of Kirkdall Churche . . . to by her pynnes withal' 1542). XVII; **pi·n-**PRICK XIX; in fig. use from 1885 after F. (*politique de*) *coups d'épingle*.

pinafore pi·nəfɔ̄əɹ child's or woman's washable overall. XVIII (*pin-a-fore*, Miss Burney). f. PIN vb. + AFORE, because orig. pinned over the dress in front. Also †*pinbefore* (XIX, Southey). Hence **pi·nn**Y[6]. XIX.

pinaster pai·næstəɹ pine tree, Pinus Pinaster, of south-western Europe. XVI. – L. *pīnaster*, f. *pīnus* PINE[1]; see -ASTER.

pince-nez pɛ̃·snei eyeglasses with clip for the nose. XIX. – F., f. *pincer* PINCH + *nez* NOSE.

pincers pi·nsəɹz tool for grasping or nipping. XIV. ME. pl. *pinsers*, *-ours* – AN. **pincers*, *-ours*, f. OF. *pincier*; see PINCH, -ER[2].

pinch pintʃ compress between the tips of finger and thumb, the teeth, etc.; nip as with cold; stint, restrict XVI. – AN., ONF. **pinchier*, var. of OF. *pincier* (mod. *pincer*) = Sp. *pinchar*, It. *pinzare* :– Rom. **pīnctiāre*, alt. of **punctiāre* (see PUNCHEON) by assoc. with **pīk-* PICK[2].

pinchbeck pi·nᵗʃbek alloy of copper and zinc XVIII; fig. counterfeit, spurious XIX. Named after the inventor, Christopher *Pinchbeck* (died 1732), watch- and toy-maker of Fleet Street, London.

pine[1] pain tree of the coniferous genus Pinus. OE. *pīn* – L. *pīnus*, coalescing in ME. with adoption of (O)F. *pin* (= Pr. *pin*, Sp., It. *pino*, Rum. *pin* :–L.), perh. f. base **pīt-* resin, of Skr. *pītudārus* (lit. 'resin-tree'), Gr. *pítus* pine, and L. *pītuīta* gum (see PITUITARY). Hence **pi·ne-a:pple** A. †pine-cone (cf. Du. *pijnappel*) XIV; B. plant ananas, Ananassa sativa, the collective fruit of which develops from a conical spike.

pine[2] pain †afflict, torment OE.; †cause to languish or waste away XIII; become wasted XV; be consumed with longing XVI. OE. *pīnian*, corr. to MDu., MLG. *pīnen* (Du. *pijnen*), OHG. *pīnōn*, ON. *pína*, rel. to OE. **pīne* (ME. *pine*), OS., OHG. *pīna* (Du. *pijne, pijn*, G. *pein*), ON. *pína*, CGerm. (exc. Gothic) – medL. *pēna*, L. *pœna* (whence also (O)F. *peine* PAIN) PENALTY – Doric Gr. *poinā́* (Attic *poinḗ*) compensation for crime, expiation, punishment.

pinfold pi·nfould pound (later, fold) for cattle, etc. XIV. Late OE. *pundfald*, f. **pund* POUND[2]+*fald* FOLD; hence in ME. and mod. dial. forms *pun(d)-*, *pound-*, *pond-* but from c.1400 assoc. with *pind*, OE. *pyndan* (:– **pnudian*) shut up, dam, and PIN vb. enclose, bar up (XIV).

ping piŋ expressing an abrupt ringing sound. XIX. imit. (cf. PINK[4]). Hence **pi·ng-pong** game like lawn-tennis, played on a table with bats and a celluloid ball. XIX; redupl. after *ding-dong*.

pinguefy pi·ŋgwifai make fat or greasy. XVI. – L. *pinguefacere*, f. *pinguis* fat; see -FY. So **pingu**E·SCENT. XVIII. – prp. of L. *pinguēscere* become fat. **pingu**ID[1] fat, unctuous. XVII. f. L. *pinguis*.

pinguin pi·ŋgwin (fruit of) W. Indian plant Bromelia Pingwin, allied to the pine-apple. XVII. Of unkn. origin.

pinion[1] pi·njən terminal segment of a bird's wing, (gen.) wing. XV. – OF. *pignon* pl. wing-feathers, wings, (now only, gable) :– Rom. **pinniō(n-)*, augm. of L. *pinna* PIN. Cf. PENNON. Hence **pi·nion** vb. cut the pinions of; bind the arms of. XVI.

pinion[2] pi·njən small cog-wheel the teeth of which engage with those of a larger one. XVII. – (O)F. *pignon* (whence Sp. *piñon*), alt. of †*pignol* :– Rom. **pīneolus*, f. L. *pīnea* pine-cone, f. *pīnus* PINE[1].

pink[1] piŋk (small flatbottomed) sailing vessel. XV. – MDu. *pin(c)ke*, small seagoing vessel, fishing-boat (whence also F. *pinque*, Sp. *pinque*, It. *pinco*), of unkn. origin.

pink[2] piŋk species of Dianthus; fig. finest 'flower', embodied excellence *of* XVI (Sh.); adj. of a pale-light-red colour XVIII; hence sb. pink colour, and with spec. application to the scarlet worn by fox-hunters XIX. perh. short for †*pink eye* (see PINK-EYED); cf. synon. F. *œillet*, dim. of *œil* eye.

pink[3] piŋk intr. and tr. prick, pierce XIV; ornament (cloth, etc.) by cutting holes in it, (later) ornament with scalloped edges, etc. XVI. perh. of LDu. origin (cf. LG. *pinken* strike, peck).

pink[4] piŋk imit. of the note of the chaffinch, etc. XIX. Cf. PING.

pink-eyed pi·ŋkaid (dial.) having narrow or half-closed eyes. XVI (Harman). f. *pink eyes* (of which there was a var. *pink nyes*) – early Du. *pinck oogen*, i.e. *pinck* small (cf. Du. *pink* the little finger, etc.), *ooghen*, pl. of *ooghe* EYE; see -ED[2].

pinnace pi·nəs small light sea vessel. XVI. – F. *pinace*, †*pinasse* – It. *pinaccia* or Sp. *pinaza*, which have been referred to Rom. **pīnācea* (sc. *nāvis* ship), f. L. *pīnus* PINE[1], poet. ship; but this does not account for earlier OF. *spinace*, AN. *espynasse*, *spynagtz* pl. (XIV), Eng. †*spinace*, †*spyn(n)es* (XV), AL. *spinacium* (XIV), of which *pinace*, etc. appear to be aphetic derivs.

pinnacle pi·nəkl pointed turret; mountain-peak XIV; highest pitch or point XV. – OF. *pin(n)acle* (mod. *pinacle*) – late L. *pinnāculum*, dim. of L. *pinna* feather, wing, pinnacle; see PIN, -CLE.

pinnate pi·neit resembling a feather. XVIII. – L. *pinnātus* feathered, winged, f. *pinna*; see PIN, -ATE[2]. Also **pi·nnat**ED[1]. XVIII.

pinocle pi·nəkl (U.S.) game of cards resembling bezique. XIX. Of unkn. origin.

pint paint measure of capacity. XIV. – (O)F. *pinte* = Pr., Sp. *pinta* (whence medL. *pinta*), of unkn. origin. Cf. MLG., MDu., MHG. *pinte*.

pintado pintā·dou †chintz; species of petrel; guinea-fowl. XVII. – Pg. (Sp.) *pintado* guinea-fowl, sb. use of pp. ('spotted') of *pintar* :– Rom. **pinctāre*, f. **pinctus*, pp. of L. *pingere* PAINT.

pintle pi·ntl (dial.) penis OE.; pin, bolt XV. OE. *pintel*, dim. f. a base repr. by OFris., LG., Du., G. *pint*; cf. *cuckoo-pint* (XVI), *-pintle* (XV), *priest's pintle* wild arum, and see -LE[1].

pioneer paiəniə·ɹ soldier going in advance of an army to prepare the way XVI; first or original investigator, etc. XVII (Bacon). orig. *pion(n)er* – F. *pionnier*, OF. *paonier*, *peon(n)ier* (corr. to Pr. *pezonier*), f. *paon*, *peon* (see PAWN[1], PEON); orig. str. *pi·oner* (cf. Sh. 'Hamlet' I v 163), the suffix being later assim. to -EER[1].

pious pai·əs faithful to the duties owed to God, parents, etc. XVII (Sh.); practised for the sake of religion or a good object XVII. f. L. *pius*, of Italic range; see -OUS. Cf. F. *pieux* (XVI), perh. the immed. source, and see PIETY.

pip[1] pip disease of birds marked by secretion of thick mucus. XV. – MLG. *pip*, MDu. *pippe* (*pipse*, whence G. *pips*), reduced form corr. to OHG. *pfiffiz* :– WGerm. **pipit* – medL. **pip(p)īta* (whence also (O)F. *pépie*, Pr. *pepida*, Sp. *pepita*, Pg. *pevide*, It. *pipita*), presumably alt. of *pītuīta* (see PITUITARY).

pip[2] pip each of the spots on playing-cards, dice, etc. XVI (Sh.); single blossom of an inflorescence XVIII. Earlier *peepe*, of unkn. origin.

pip[3] pip †pippin (apple) XVI (recorded as a cry of Irish costermongers); seed of fleshy fruits XVIII. Shortening of PIPPIN.

pipe[1] paip musical wind instrument: hollow cylinder or tube OE.; tubular passage or canal XIV; narrow tube used for smoking tobacco XVI. OE. *pīpe* = OFris., MLG., MDu. *pīpe* (Du. *pijp*), OHG. *pfīfa* (G. *pfeife*), ON. *pípa* :– Germ. **pīpa* – CRom. **pīpa*, f. L. *pīpāre* peep, chirp (Varro), of imit. origin (cf. PIGEON); reinforced in ME. by (O)F. *pipe*. So **pipe** vb.[1] OE. *pīpian* play on a pipe. Hence *pi·per*[1]. OE. *pīpere* = G. *pfeiffer*, etc. Also vb.[2] draw through a pipe XVI. ¶ Celtic forms are from Latin or English.

pipe[2] paip large cask for wine, esp. as a measure of capacity (½ tun, 2 hogsheads, or 4 barrels). XIV. – AN. *pipe*, AL. *pipa* XIII; spec. use of PIPE[1] in the tense 'tubular or cylindrical vessel'.

pipe[3] paip account of a sheriff, etc. as sent in and enrolled at the Exchequer; department of the Exchequer concerned with these. XV. – AN. *pipe*, AL. *pipa* (XIII); perh. spec. use of PIPE[1], from the cylindrical shape of a roll (cf. **pipe-roll** XVII) or of a container.

piperaceous pipərei·ʃəs of the nature of pepper. XVII. f. modL. *piperāceus*, f. *piper* PEPPER; see -ACEOUS.

pipette pipe·t narrow pipe or tube. XIX. – F., dim. of *pipe* PIPE[1]; see -ETTE.

pipistrel(le) pi·pistrel small species of bat. XVIII (Pennant). – F. *pipistrelle* – It. *pipistrello*, alt. of *vipistrello*, repr. L. *vespertīliō(n-)* bat, f. *vesper* evening (see VESPER).

pipit pi·pit lark-like bird. XVIII (Pennant). prob. imit. of the bird's short feeble note.

pippin pi·pin (dial.) seed of certain fruits, pip XIII; variety of apple XV. ME. *pepin*, *pipin* – OF. *pepin* (mod. *pepin*, *pépin*), rel. to synon. Sp. *pepita*, It. *pippolo*, *pipporo*, based on obscure **pipp-*.

pipsissewa pipsi·swə Prince's pine, Chimaphila umbellata, XIX. Algonquian (Cree *pipipissekweu*).

piquant pī·kənt †piercing, trenchant XVI; appetizing; exciting keen interest XVII. Early forms *pickant(e)*, *-ande* – F. *piquant*, †*picquant*, prp. of *piquer* prick, sting; see next. Hence **pi·qu**ANCY. XVII (Evelyn).

pique pīk †quarrel or animosity between persons; offence taken. XVI. Earliest forms *pick(e)*, *pike* – F. *pique*, f. *piquer* = Pr., Sp. *picar*, It. *piccare* :– Rom. **piccāre* PICK[2]. Hence vb. XVII.

piqué pī·kei cotton fabric with a raised pattern. XIX. – F. *piqué*, sb. use ('quilted work, quilting') of pp. of *piquer* prick, pierce, back-stitch; see prec.

piragua piræ·gwə, **periagua** periæ·gwə long narrow canoe; two-masted sailing-barge. XVII. – Sp. *piragua* – Carib *piragua* dug-out; alt. by assoc. of the first syll. with *peri-* and *petty* (†*pettiagua*, etc.).

pirate paiə·rət sea-robber XV (Lydg.); marauder XVI; fig. of literary or other plundering XVIII. – L. *pīrāta* – Gr. *peirātḗs*, f. *peirân* attempt, attack, *peîra* attempt, trial :– **perjā*, f. **per-*, as in EXPERIMENT, PERIL. So **pir**ACY paiə·rəsi. XVI. – AL. *pīrātia* – Gr. *peirāteíā*. **pirat**ICAL pairæ·tikl. XVI. f. L. *pīrāticus* – Gr. *peirātikós*. ¶ Of CEur. range.

pirl pɜ̄ɹl, pɛrl (dial.) twist, spin. XV. Of unkn. origin; cf. PURL.

pirogue pirou·g synon. with PIRAGUA. XVII. – F. *pirogue*, prob. – Carib dialect of Cayenne (Galibi).

pirouette pirue·t spinning round on one foot or on the point of the toe. XVIII. – F. *pirouette* orig. kind of dice, of unkn. origin (for the form cf. *girouette* weather-vane).

pis-aller pīzæ·lei last resource. XVII. F., f. *pis* (:– L. *pejus* worse) + *aller* go; based on phr. *au pis aller* 'at the worst procedure'.

piscary pi·skəri right of fishing XV; fishing-ground XVII. – medL. *piscāria* fishing rights, n. pl. used sb. of L. *piscārius*, f. *piscis* FISH; see -ARY. So **piscato·**RIAL XIX, **pi·scat**ORY[2] XVII. f. or – L. *piscātōrius*, f. *piscātor* angler, f. *piscārī* fish, f. *piscis*. **Pisces** pi·sīz twelfth zodiacal constellation and sign of the zodiac. XIV (Ch.), pl. of L. *piscis*. **piscina** pisī·nə, -ai·nə A. fishpond XVI (Hakluyt); B. (eccl.) perforated stone basin for carrying away the ablutions at Mass XVIII. – L. and medL. *piscīna*, f. *piscis*; earlier †*piscine*, in sense A XIII (Cursor M.), in sense B XV (Caxton).

pisé pī·zei clay or earth kneaded and used for building. XVIII. F., sb. use of pp. of *piser* :– L. *pīnsāre* beat, pound, stamp, having cogns. in Indo-Iranian and Balto-Slavonic.

pish piʃ excl. of disgust, etc. XVI (Nashe, Sh.). Hence as vb. XVI (Jonson). Cf. PSHAW.

pismire pi·smaiəɹ ant. XIV (Ch.). ME. *pissemyre*, f. PISS+*mire* ant (prob. of Scand. origin; cf. Da. *myre*, and L. *for|mīca*, Gr. *múrmēx*); so called from the urinous smell of an ant-hill. ¶ Similar names are Fris. *pisimme*, LG. *miegemke*, Norw. *migemaur* (f. **mig-* MICTURITION), Du. †*mierseycke* (*seycke* urine), Finnish *kusiainen* (*kusi* urine).

piss pis urinate. XIII. – (O)F. *pisser* = Pr. *pisar*, It. *pisciare*, Cat. *pixar*, Rum. *pişà* :– Rom. **pissāre*, of echoic origin. ¶ From Rom. (medL.) the word has passed into the Germ. langs. (OFris. *pissia*, (M)LG., (M)Du., G. *pissen*, Da. *pisse*, Sw., Icel. *pissa*) and W. *piso*, *pisio*. Hence sb. XIV (Ch., Wycl. Bible). **pi·ss**ABED dandelion. XVI; after F. *pissenlit*.

pistachio pistā·tʃ[1]ou (fruit of) Pistacia vera or its kernel. XVI (*pistaccio*). Earlier *pistachie*, *pistace* – OF. *pistace*, (also mod.) *-ache*, superseded by Sp. *pistacho* – L. *pistācium* – Gr. *pistákion*, *-ákē* (nut and tree) – Pers. *pistah*.

pistil pi·stil (bot.) female organ of a flower. XVIII. – F. *pistile* (Tournefort, 1694) or L. *pistillum* PESTLE; somewhat earlier the L. form was in use, also after Tournefort.

pistol pi·stəl small firearm. XVI. – F. *pistole* – G. *pistole* (XV in documents relating to the Hussite wars) – Czech *pišt'al*. Cf. the contemp. *howitzer*. The synon. †*pistolet* is rather earlier – F. *pistolet*.

pistole pi·stoul applied to various foreign gold coins. XVI. – F. *pistole*, shortening of *pistolet* (also Eng. XVI).

piston pi·stən disk or short cylinder fitting a tube and used to impart or receive motion from a rod; sliding valve in a cornet. XVIII. – F. *piston* (Pascal) – It. *pistone*, var. of *pestone* pestle, rammer, augm. f. *pest-* in *pestello* PESTLE.

pit pit hole in the ground OE.; hell; hollow in a surface XIII; see also COCKPIT. OE. *pytt* = OFris. *pett*, OS. *putti* (MDu. *putte*, Du. *put*), OHG. *pfuzzi* (G. *pfütze* pool, puddle) :– WGerm. **putti*, *puttja* (ON. *pyttr* is from OE.) – L. *puteus* well, pit, shaft (whence F. *puits*, Pr. *potz*, Sp. *pozo*, It. *pozzo*, Rum. *puţ*, and Ir. *cuithe*, W. *peten*). The south-eastern ME. var. *pett* survives in place-names in Kent and Sussex. Hence **pit** vb. put in a pit; make pits in XV; set (opponents) together in a (cock)pit; match, oppose XVIII. Hence **pi·t**FALL[2]. XIV (Wycl. Bible, Trevisa).

pit-a-pat pi·təpæt with palpitations, with light quick steps. XVI. Earlier *pit pat* (More), also *a-pit-(a-)pat*; imit. of rapidly alternating sounds; cf. PITTER-PATTER.

pitch[1] pitʃ black or dark brown resinous substance. OE. *pić*, corr. to OS. *pik* (Du. *pek*), OHG. *peh* (G. *pech*), ON. *bik*, CGerm. (exc. Gothic) – L. *pic-*, *pix*, which with Gr. *píssa* (:– **pikja*) and Balto-Sl. forms imply a base **pik-*. Hence vb. OE. (*ġe*)*pićian*.

pitch[2] pitʃ †thrust or fix in; fix and erect XIII; set in order or in a fixed place; cast, throw XIV. The ME. conjugation *pic(c)he*, *pihte*, (*i*)*piht* suggests the existence of an OE. **pićć(e)an*, rel. to *pićung* 'stigmata', of unkn. origin; pt. and pp. *pight* were in full use till XVII, but the new form *piched* appears XIV. Hence **pitch** sb. act of pitching; inclination, slope XV; highest point; position taken up XVI.

pitchblende pi·tʃblend (min.) native oxide of uranium. XVIII. – G. *pechblende*, f. *pech* PITCH[1]; see BLENDE.

piteous pi·tiəs †pious; exciting pity XIII; full of pity XIV. ME. *pito(u)s*, *pituo(u)s*, later *pite(o)us* – AN. *pitous*, OF. *pitos*, *piteus* = Pr. *pitos*, *pidos*, Sp. *piadoso*, It. *pietoso* :– Rom. **pietōsu-s*, f. L. *pietās* PIETY, PITY; see -EOUS.

pith piþ medulla of plants; central or vital part OE.; might, mettle XIII; core, marrow XV; gravity XVII (Sh.). OE. *piþa*, corr. to MLG., MDu. *pitte*, *pit* :– **piþ(þ)on*, repr. only in the LG. group, of unkn. origin.

pithecanthrope piþikæ·nþroup ape-man. XIX. – modL. *pithēcanthrōpus* (Haeckel 1868), f. Gr. *píthēkos* ape + *ánthrōpos* man.

pittance pi·təns (hist.) pious donation XIII (AncrR.); small allowance orig. of food XIV (Gower); sparing allowance XVI. ME. *pita(u)nce* – OF. *pi(e)tance*, corr. to Pr. *pitansa*, It. *pietanza* (portion of) food – popL. **pietantia*, f. L. *pietās* PITY; see -ANCE.

pitter-patter pi·təɹpæ:təɹ †pattering repetition XV; PIT-A-PAT XVII.

pituitary pitjū·itəri mucous. XVII. – L. *pītuītārius*, f. *pītuīta* gum, slime, rheum (cf. PINE[1]); see -ARY.

pity pi·ti †clemency, mercy; compassion XIII; †piety XIV. ME. *pite* – OF. *pité* (mod. *pitié*) = Pr. *pietat*, Sp. *piedad*, It. *pietà* :– L. *pietāt-*, *-tās* PIETY. In later L. *pietās*, prop. dutifulness, gratitude, acquired the sense of compassion, kindness; OF. *pite* and *piete* had both senses, but were subsequently differentiated, and this was reflected in the corr. Eng. forms as now used. Hence **pi·ty** vb. XVI (More), perh. after F. **pi·ti**ABLE XV, **pi·ti**FUL[1] XIV, **pi·ti**LESS XV (Hoccleve).

pivot pi·vət short shaft or pin forming a fulcrum XVII; (mil.) XVIII. – (O)F. *pivot*, prob. f. Rom. base repr. by F. dial. *pue* tooth of a comb, harrow, etc., Pr. *pua* (mod. *pivo*), Sp. *pu(y)a* point, of unkn. origin.

pixie, pixy pi·ksi supernatural being akin to a fairy. XVII. The earliest evidence is from Devon and Cornwall, whence and from immediately adjacent counties many uses are recorded, with vars. *pisky*, *pisgy*, *pigsy*; brought into literary use by Coleridge (born in Devon) and Scott (in 'The Pirate', whence it has been ascribed to the Shetlands). The ending, whatever its origin, is assoc. with -IE, -Y[6].

pizzicato pitsikā·tou (mus.) played by plucking the strings. XIX. It., pp. of *pizzicare* pinch, twitch, f. *pizzare*, f. (O)It. *pizza* point, edge.

pizzle pi·zl penis of a bull, etc. XVI (*peezel, pysell*). – LG. *pēsel*, Flem. *pēzel*, dim. of MLG. *pēse*, MDu. *pēze* (Du. *pees* sinew, string, penis), whence also synon. MLG., MDu. *pēserik* (Du. *pezerik*); cf. -EL[1], -LE[1].

placable plæ·kəbl †agreeable XV; capable of being appeased, mild XVI. – OF. *placable* or L. *plācābilis*, f. *plācāre*, pp. stem *plācāt-*, whence **placate** pləkei·t XVII; see PLEASE, -ABLE, -ATE[3].

placard plæ·kaɹd, (formerly) pləkā·ɹd, -ā·ɹt †licence, ordinance, etc., orig. with a thin seal attached to its surface XV; sheet containing a notice on one side of it, to be posted up XVI; †plate of armour, placket, etc. XV. – F. †*placquart, -ard* (mod. *placard*), f. OF. *plaquier* (mod. *plaquer*) lay flat, plaster – MDu. *placken*. ¶ Forms repr. MDu. *plackaert, plackaet* (from F.), viz. *placaet, placcat*, were current XVI–XVIII in the sense 'decree issued in the Netherlands'.

place pleis †space, room; portion of space XIII; space where people dwell; residence; particular spot, passage in a book, etc.; position; situation XIV; office, situation XVI. – (O)F. *place* = Pr. *plasa* (whence Sp. *plaza*), It. *piazza* :– Rom. **plattja* (after **plattus* flat), for L. *platea* broad way, open space – Gr. *plateîa* (sc. *hodós*) broad way, fem. of *platús* broad (cf. FLAT[1] and PLAICE); superseded in gen. use native STEAD and STOW; *take p.*, happen, occur, meant at first 'take effect' (XV). Hence **place** vb. XVI; cf. F. *placer* (XVII).

placebo plæsī·bou (liturg.) vespers for the dead. XIII (AncrR.). First word of the antiphon to the first psalm in the office: '*Placebo* Domino in regione vivorum' (Psalm cxiv 9) I shall please the Lord in the land of the living.

placenta pləse·ntə (anat.) afterbirth XVII (Ray, *p. uterina*); (bot.) part of carpel to which scales are attached XVII (Grew). – L. *placenta* – Gr. *plakóenta* (*-oûnta*), accus. of *plakóeis* (*-oûs*) flat cake, sb. use of adj. f. *plak-*, in *pláx* flat surface.

placer plei·səɹ (U.S.) deposit of sand, etc. XIX. – Amer. Sp. *placer* plasē·r deposit, shoal, rel. to *placel* sandbank, f. *plaza* PLACE.

placet plei·sėt vote of assent. XVI. – L. *placet* it pleases (e.g. *vōbīs* you), 3rd sg. pres. ind. of *placēre* PLEASE.

placid plæ·sid gentle, calm. XVII (Bacon, Milton). – F., or L. *placidus* pleasing, favourable, gentle, f. *placēre* PLEASE; see -ID[1]. Earlier †*placidious*.

placket plæ·kit slit at the top of a skirt. XVII (Sh.). alt. (by assoc. with -ET) of *plackerd* (XVI, Nashe, Greene), PLACARD.

plafond pla·fõ (archit.) ceiling. XVII (*platfond*, Evelyn). – F. †*platfond*, now *plafond*, f. *plat* flat (cf. PLATE)+*fond* bottom (cf. FUND).

plagal plei·gəl (mus.) pert. to an ecclesiastical mode having its sounds comprised between the dominant and its octave. XVI (Morley). – medL. *plagālis*, f. *plaga* plagal mode, f. L. *plagius* – medGr. *plágios* (πλάγιος ἦχος plagal mode), in ancient Gr. oblique, f. *plágos* side; see -AL[1].

plagiarism plei·dʒiərizm wrongful appropriation and publication as one's own. XVII; so **pla·giar**IST XVII, **pla·giar**IZE XVIII. f. **pla·gi**ARY †kidnapper; plagiarist; plagiarism XVII; †adj. plagiarizing XVI. – L. *plagiārius* kidnapper, literary thief (Martial), f. *plagium* man-stealing, kidnapping – Gr. *plágion*. Cf. F. *plagiaire* (XVI).

plagio- plei·dʒiou, before a vowel or *h* **plagi-**, comb. form, repr. Gr. *plágios* oblique, f. *plágos* side (see PLAGAL). XIX.

plague pleig †blow, wound; affliction; malignant epidemic, pestilence. XIV (Wycl. Bible). – L. *plāga* stroke, wound, (Vulg.) pestilence, infection, prob. – Gr. (Doric) *plāgá*, (Attic) *plēgḗ*, f. **plăg-* strike, rel. to L. *plangere* (see PLANGENT). Hence vb. XV (*plaghe* Caxton, after MDu. *plaghen*).

plaice pleis flat-fish Pleuronectes platessa. XIII. – OF. *plaïz, plaïs*, later *plaise, pleisse* (Walloon *playis, pleis*) – late L. *platessa* – unrecorded deriv. of Gr. *platús* broad (cf. FLAT[1]).

plaid plæd, pleid outer garment of Highland costume XVI; stuff of which this is made XVII. – Gael. *plaide* = Ir. *ploid* blanket, of unkn. origin.

plain plein clear, manifest XIII (Cursor M.); †flat, level, even (now PLANE); unembellished; free from duplicity or ambiguity XIV; ordinary, simple XVI. – OF. *plain*, fem. *-e* (surviving in phr. *de plain-pied, plain-chant*, etc.) = Pr. *pla*, Sp. *llano*, Pg. *chão*, It. *piano* (cf. PIANO) :– L. *plānu-s, -a*, f. base **plā-* flat, of obscure connexion. Hence **plai·n**LY[2] XIV (Ch.). So **plain** sb. flat tract of country. XIII (RGlouc.). OF. *plain* (superseded by *plaine* :– L. coll. n. pl.) :– L. *plānum*, sb. use of n. of adj. See also PLANE.

plain-sailing plein sei·liŋ simple or easy course of action. XIX. pop. use (assoc. with the adj. PLAIN) of *plane* (†*plain*) *sailing* (XVII), i.e. navigation by a *plane chart* (XVII), on which the meridians and parallels are represented by equidistant straight lines (a method approximately correct for short distances).

plainsong plei·nsoŋ music composed in the medieval modes and in free rhythm; simple musical theme. XVI. tr. medL. *cantus plānus* (whence F. *plain chant*, It. *canto piano*). So **pla·in-**CHANT. XVIII. – F.; see PLAIN, SONG.

plaint pleint (arch.) lamentation; complaint XIII (AncrR., Havelok); statement of grievance made to a court of law XIV (R. Mannyng). ME. *pleint(e)* – (O)F. *plainte*, sb. use of pp. fem. of *plaindre* and OF. *plaint, pleint* (on which *plainte* was modelled) = Pr. *planh*, Sp. *llanto*, OPg. *chanto*, It. *pianto* :– L. *planctu-s*, f. *plangere* (see COMPLAIN, COMPLAINT, PLANGENT).

plaintiff plei·ntif complainant or prosecutor in a legal suit. XIV. – law-F. *plaintif*, sb. use of (O)F. *plaintif*, fem. *-ive* (f. *plainte* PLAINT), whence **plai·nt**IVE †complaining XIV (Gower); expressive of sorrow XVI.

plaister see PLASTER.

plait plæt, (Sc., U.S.) plēt fold of cloth or similar fabric (now PLEAT) XV; braided band of hair, straw, etc. XVI. – OF. *pleit* fold, manner of folding :– Rom. **plic(i)tum*, sb. use of n. of *plicitus*, pp. of *plicāre* fold (see PLY[1]). Hence vb. XIV.

plan plæn diagram exhibiting the relative position and size of the parts of a thing; project, design. XVIII. (Earlier *plane* XVII) – F. *plan* (XVI) ground-plan, alt. (after *plan* adj. PLANE[4]) of †*plant*, f. *planter*, after It. *pianta* plan of an edifice; see PLANT. ¶ This word and PLANE[3] cover between them the senses of F. *plan*.

planchette plãʃe·t small board used in psychical experiments. XIX. – F. *planchette*, dim. of *planche* PLANK; see -ETTE.

plane[1] plein tree of the genus Platanus. XIV (Wycl. Bible, Trevisa). – (O)F. *plane*, †*plasne* (recorded XV) :– L. *platanu-s* – Gr. *plátanos*, f. stem of *platús* broad (see PLATY-).

plane[2] plein tool for smoothing surfaces. XIV. – (O)F. *plane*, var. (under the infl. of vb. *planer*) of †*plaine* = Cat. *plana* :– late L. *plāna* planing instrument, f. *planāre* PLANE[5].

plane[3] plein plane surface. XVII. – L. *plānum* flat surface, sb. use of n. of *plānus* PLAIN (for which *plane* was introduced to express the geometrical and allied uses; cf. the supersession of F. *plain* by *plan* because of the homophony of *plein* full).

plane[4] plein level, flat. XVII. refash. of PLAIN adj. after F. *plan*, fem. *plane*, which was similarly substituted for *plain*, *plaine* in techn. senses.

plane[5] plein †make level or even; smooth with a plane XIV (also *pleyne, plaine, plain* until XVIII). – (O)F. *planer* = Pr. *planar*, It. *pianare* :– L. *plānāre*, f. *plānus* PLAIN.

planet plæ·nit †(old astron.) heavenly body having an apparent motion among the fixed stars XII (S.Eng. Leg., Cursor M.); (mod. astron.) heavenly body revolving round the sun XVII. – (O)F. *planète* – late L. *planēta*, *planētēs* (only in pl. *planētæ*, for older L. *stellæ errantes*) – Gr. *planḗtēs* wanderer (pl. ἀστέρες πλανῆται wandering stars), f. *planân* lead astray, wander, rel. to *plázein* cause to wander. So **pla·net**ARY. XVII. – late L. *planētārius* (sb. astrologer, Augustine).

plangent plæ·ndʒənt loud-sounding, orig. of waves breaking on the shore. XIX. – L. *plangent-*, *-ēns*, prp. of *plangere* beat (spec. the breast), strike noisily, f. **plag-*, base of Gr. *plázein* (cf. PLANKTON); see COMPLAIN, -ENT.

plani- plæ·ni, pleini· comb. form of L. *plānus* PLAIN, PLANE[4]. **plani·**METRY (XIV, *planemetrie*, Gower; F. *planimétrie*), **pla·ni**SPHERE (XIV, *planisperie*, Gower; medL. *plānisphærium*).

planish plæ·niʃ †level XVI; flatten on an anvil, etc. XVII. f. *planiss-*, lengthened stem of OF. *planir* (now in *aplanir*), f. *plain* PLAIN, PLANE[4]; see -ISH[2].

plank plæŋk long flat piece of smoothed timber. XIII (Sandahl). – ONF. *planke* (mod. dial. *planque*) = (O)F. *planche*, Pr. *planca*, etc. :– late L. *planca* plank, slab, sb. use of fem. of *plancus* flat, flat-footed (used as a cognomen, *Plancus, Plancius, Planciānus*), prob. rel. to Gr. *pláx* flat surface, etc. Hence **plank** vb. cover with planks XV; (orig. U.S.) set down, deposit XIX.

plankton plæ·ŋktən floating or drifting organic life. XIX. – G. *plankton* (V. Hensen, 188.) – Gr. *plagktón*, n. of *plagktós* wandering, drifting, f. base of *plázein* strike, cause to wander, (middle) *plázesthai*.

plant plànt young tree or herb newly planted or intended for planting (OE.), XIV; member of the vegetable kingdom XVI (Turner). OE. *plante*, if it survived, coalesced in ME. with – (O)F. *plante* = Pr. *planta*, Sp. *llanta*, Pg. *chanta*, It. *pianta* :– Rom. use of L. *planta* shoot for planting (whence the OE. word, OHG. *pflanza*, G. *pflanze*, Du. *plant*, ON. *planta*, and Ir. *cland*, W. *plant*), prob. f. *plantāre*, perh. orig. thrust in with the sole of the foot (*planta*; cf. PLANTAIN[1]), whence **plant** vb. OE. *plantian*, reinforced in ME. from (O)F. *planter*; of the same origin. So **plant**A·TION. XV. – F. or L.

plantain[1] plæ·ntin plant of the genus Plantago. XIV (Ch.). – (O)F. *plantain*, †*-ein* = Pr. *plantage*, Sp. *llantén*, Pg. *tanchagem*, Rum. *pătlagină* :– L. *plantāgine-*, nom. *plantāgō*, f. *planta* sole of the foot, so called from its broad prostrate leaves. ¶ The native name is *waybread*.

plantain[2] plæ·ntin tropical plant Musa paradisiaca, allied to the banana; fruit of this. XVI. In early use also *platan* – Sp. *plátano*, *plántano*, identical with the forms meaning 'plane-tree', to which it is prob. that some native words were assimilated (e.g. Galibi *palatana*, Carib *balatana*, Arawak *pratane*).

plantigrade plæ·ntigreid walking on the soles of the feet)(*digitigrade*). XIX. – F.

plantigrade (Geoffroy and Cuvier, 1795) – modL. *plantigradus*, f. *planta* sole + *-gradus* going, walking (cf. GRADE).

plaque plāk ornamental plate or tablet. XIX. – F. *plaque* – Du. *plak* tablet, f. *plakken* stick (cf. PLACARD).

plash plæʃ PLEACH. XV. – OF. *plassier*, *plaissier* :– Rom. **plectiāre*, f. L. *plectere* weave, plait, f. **plek-*, repr. by COMPLEX, etc.

plasma plæ·zmə †form; green variety of quartz XVIII; colourless coagulable liquid of blood XIX; ionized gas XX. – late L. *plasma* mould, image, f. Gr. *plássein* fashion, form (see PLASTIC).

plaster plà·stəɹ A. curative application cohesive to the skin OE.; B. plastic composition to be spread on a surface XIV. OE. *plaster*, corr. to OS. *plāstar*, OHG. *phlastar* (G. *pflaster*), ON. *plástr* – medL. *plastrum*, for L. *emplastrum* (prob. through the infl. of *plasticus* PLASTIC) – Gr. *émplastron* (Galen), f. *emplastós* daubed, plastered, f. *emplássein*, f. *en* EN-[2] + *plássein* (see next); in ME. reinforced in sense B from OF. *plastre* (mod. *plâtre*) = Pr. *plastre*. The once common (now dial.) form *plaister* (XIV–XIX) is based on occas. OF. *plaistre*, of obscure origin. *P. of Paris* (medL. *plastrum parisiense*) was orig. prepared from the gypsums of Montmartre, Paris. ¶ The Celtic forms are from English or French.

plastic plæ·stik characterized by moulding or modelling, causing growth or development XVII (Jonson, Sir T. Browne); capable of being moulded XVIII; of synthetic material XX. As sb., art of modelling figures XVI; plastic substance XX. – F. *plastique* or L. *plasticus* (Vitruvius) – Gr. *plastikós*, f. *plastós*, ppl. adj. f. *plássein*; see PLASMA, -IC.

plastron plæ·strən breast-shield XVI; ornamental front to a bodice; (nat. hist.) ventral part XIX. – F. *plastron* – It. *piastrone*, augm. of *piastra* breastplate (spec. application of the sense 'metal plate', 'lamina') – L. em*plastrum* PLASTER.

plat see PLOT.

platband plæ·tbænd (archit.) flat rectangular moulding XVII; (hort.) narrow bed or strip XVIII. – F. *platebande*, i.e. *plate*, fem. of *plat* (see next) + *bande* BAND[1].

plate pleit flat sheet of (precious) metal, etc. XIII; utensils of metal for the table or house, orig. of silver or gold XIV; shallow vessel for food XV. – OF. *plate* thin sheet of metal = Pr. *plata* metal plate, silver (whence Sp. *plata*, Pg. *prata* silver) – medL. *platta*, sb. use of fem. of *plattus* flat (F. *plat*, etc.), of unkn. origin; cf. MDu. *plāte* (Du. *plaat*), MHG. *plāte* (G. *platte*). In the last sense a separate word – (O)F. *plat* dish = It. *piatto*, sb. use of the corr. masc. adj. Hence vb. cover with metal plates XIV (Ch.).

plateau plæ·tou table-land. XVIII. – F. *plateau*, OF. *platel*, f. *plat*; see prec., -EL[2].

platen plæ·tn †paten XV; flat plate of metal, spec. in a printing-press XVI. – (O)F. *platine*, f. *plat* flat (cf. PLATE) + *-ine* -INE[4].

platform plæ·tfɔ̄ɹm †plane figure or surface; †plan of action, design; †site of a building, etc.; level place for mounting guns XVI; raised level floor of planks, etc. XVIII (spec. raised flooring in a hall from which speeches are delivered, whence, orig. U.S., basis of political or other policy XIX). – F. *plateforme* plan, f. *plate*, fem. of *plat* (see PLATE) + *forme* FORM.

platinum plæ·tinəm rare heavy ductile white metal. XIX (Davy). – modL. alt., in conformity with metal-names in *-um*, of †**platina** (XVIII) – Sp. *platina* platī·na, dim. of *plata* silver (see PLATE).

platitude plæ·titjūd dullness in speech or writing, commonplace remark. XIX. – F. *platitude*, f. *plat* flat (see PLATE), after *certitude*, *exactitude*, etc.; see PLATE, -TUDE.

Platonic plətɔ·nik pert. to Plato, Greek philosopher (c. 429–347 B.C.) XVI; *P. love*, tr. medL. *amor platonicus*, used synon. with *amor socraticus* by Marsilio Ficino (XV), president of Cosmo de' Medici's Accademia Platonica, to denote the kind of interest in young men with which Socrates was credited XVII (Davenant, 'The Platonick Lovers'). – L. *Platōnicus* – Gr. *Platōnikós*, f. *Plátōn*; see -IC. So **Platon**ISM plei·tənizm. XVI. – modL. **Pla·ton**IST XVI. – medL.

platoon plətū·n (mil.) body of infantry. XVII. – F. *peloton* plotõ little ball, group of people, dim. of *pelote* PELLET; see -OON.

platter plæ·təɹ flat dish for food, wooden plate. XIV. – AN. *plater*, f. *plat* dish, sb. use of (O)F. *plat* flat (see PLATE).

platy- plæ·ti comb. form of Gr. *platús* broad (see FLAT[1]), as in **platypus** plæ·tipəs ornithorrhyncus of Australia (XVIII) – Gr. *platúpous* flat-footed (see FOOT).

plaudit plɔ̄·dit act of applause. XVII. Shortening of trisyllabic †*plaudite* (XVI), orig. appeal for applause at the close of a play – L. *plauditē* applaud ye!, 2nd pers. pl. imper. of *plaudere* clap the hands in approval; cf. APPLAUD, EXPLODE.

plausible plɔ̄·zibl †laudable; †acceptable, agreeable; having an appearance of truth or value. XVI. – L. *plausibilis*, f. *plaus-*, pp. stem of *plaudere*; see prec., -IBLE.

play plei exercise oneself, spec. by way of diversion, engage in (a game); perform on (a musical instrument) OE.; move swiftly, briskly, freely; act the character of XIV (Ch., Wyclif). OE. *pleġ(i)an*, *plæġian* = MDu. *pleien* dance, leap for joy, rejoice; doubtfully rel. to OFris. *plega* be wont, OS. *plegan* (Du. *plegen*), OHG. *pflegan* (G. *pflegen*) have charge of, attend to, be in the habit of. So **play** sb. OE. *pleġa*, *plæġa* rapid movement, exercise, sport OE. (cessation of work, being idle XVII); dramatic performance, drama XIV; action, dealing, as in *fair p.*, *foul p.* XVI; *p. of, on*, or *upon words*, after F. *jeu de mots* (Boileau) XVIII. **play·**HOUSE theatre (XVI, Sh.); not continuous with OE. *pleġhūs* 'theatrum'.

plea plī (arch., dial.) action at law, suit XIII; pleading before a court XIV; that which is pleaded XV. ME. *ple*, also *plai, plait, plaid* – AN. *ple, plai*, OF. *plait*, earlier *plaid* agreement, talk, lawsuit, discussion = Pr. *plait*, Sp. *pleito*, It. *piato* – L. *placitum* decision, decree, sb. use of pp. n. of *placēre* PLEASE. Cf. PLEAD.

pleach plītʃ intertwine (branches) to make a fence. XIV. Late ME. *pleche* – OF. **plechier* (mod. dial. *plêcher*), var. of *ple(i)ssier, pla(i)ssier* PLASH.

plead plīd †go to law, argue *with* XIII; address the court as advocate XIV; maintain (a plea), allege formally XV. ME. *plaide, plede* – AN. *pleder*, OF. *plaidier* (mod. *plaider*), f. *plaid* PLEA; cf. medL. *placitāre*, f. *placitum*.

pleasance ple·zəns (arch.) pleasure; pleasantness XIV (Ch.); pleasure ground (cf. F. *plaisance*, †place of delight, and *maison de plaisance* country house) XVI. – (O)F. *plaisance*, f. *plaisant* (whence **plea·**SANT XIV), prp. of †*plaisir* PLEASE.

please plīz A. be agreeable (to), surviving in *if you p.*, where *you* is orig. dative; B. *be pleased* be gratified, (hence) have the desire, choose, be good enough *to* XIV; intr. in the same sense XVI; C. as imper., for †*p. you* 'may it p. you', equiv. to 'be pleased' XVII. ME. *plaise, plese* – OF. *plaisir* (repl. by *plaire*) = Pr. *plazer*, It. *piacere*, Rum. *plăceà* :– L. *placēre* be pleasing, f. base of *placidus* PLACID, *placāre* PLACATE. So **pleasure** ple·ʒəɹ. XIV (Gower; not Ch.). Late ME. *plesir* – OF. *plesir*, (also mod.) *plaisir* :– Rom. sb. use of the inf.; the final syll. was assim. (XV) to -URE; the earlier forms are repr. in dial. *pleezer, plezzer*. Hence (after *comfortable*) **plea·sur**ABLE. XVI.

pleat plīt vb. fold (cloth), gather (drapery) into pleats XIV; sb. fold of cloth or drapery XVI. Early form *plete*, var. of PLAIT. ¶ Both sb. and vb. lapsed in literary use before 1700, but Walker 1791 states that 'There is a corrupt pronunciation of this word [*plait*] as if written *plete*', and this pronunc. prevailed later and re-established the sp. *pleat*.

plebeian plibī·ən pert. to, a member of, the Roman plebs XVI; of low birth or rank XVII. f. L. *plēbēius*, f. *plēb-, plēbs* commonalty of ancient Rome, perh. :– **plēdhw-*, rel. to Gr. *plêthos, plēthús* multitude, f. **plē-* as in L. *plēnus* FULL¹. Cf. (O)F. *plébéien* and see -AN. So **plebiscite** ple·bisit, -ait law enacted by the plebs XVI; direct vote of the whole electorate XIX. – (O)F. *plébiscite* – L. *plēbiscītum*, f. *plēbi-, plēbs*+*scītum* ordinance, sb. use of n. pp. of *sciscere* approve, vote for, rel. to *scīre* know (see SCIENCE); in the second sense familiarized in Eng. through the *plébiscite* which ratified the coup d'état of 1851 in France.

plectrum ple·ktrəm instrument for plucking the strings of the lyre. XVII. – L. *plēctrum* – Gr. *plêktron*, f. *plḗssein* strike, f. **plăk-*, parallel to **plăg-*, repr. by Gr. *plēgḗ*, L. *plāga* PLAGUE, *plangere* strike (cf. PLAINT).

pledge pledʒ bail, surety XIV (Ch.); something handed over as security XV; token of favour or goodwill XVI; solemn promise XIX. Late ME. *plege* – OF. *plege* (mod. *pleige*) :– Frankish L. *plebium* (VI), corr. to *plebīre* (whence OF., Pr. *plevir*) warrant, assure, engage, of unascertained origin, but, in view of the correspondence in meaning with the Germ. base **pleg-* of PLIGHT¹, it is possible that this was crossed with L. *præbēre* furnish, supply (see PREBEND). Hence **pledge** vb. XV; cf. OF. *plegier* (mod. *pleiger*).

pledget ple·dʒit compress of soft material esp. for application to wounds. XVI. Early forms *plaget, pleggat, pleget*, f. synon. **plage*, †*plege* (XVI); corr. to medL. *plāgella* lint plug for a wound, dim. f. L. *plāga* (cf. AL. *plāgiāre, plēgiāre* wound); see PLAGUE, -ET.

plenary plī·nəri complete, full. XVI. – late L. *plēnārius*, f. *plēnus* FULL¹; see -ARY; superseded ME. †*plener*, †*plenar* – AN. *plener*, OF. *plenier* (mod. *plénier*) = Pr. *plen(i)er*, Sp. *llenero* :– late L. *plēnāris*. **plenipotentiary** ple:nipŏte·nʃəri (person) invested with full power. XVII. – medL. *plēnipotentiārius*, f. L. *plēnus* + *potentia* power; see POTENTIAL, -ARY. Cf. contemp. F. *plénipotentiaire*. Shortened colloq. to **plenipo** ple·nipou. XVII (Dryden). **pleni**TUDE ple·nitjūd fullness. XV. – OF. *plenitude* – late L. *plēnitūdō*, f. *plēnus*. **plenteous** ple·ntiəs bearing abundantly, existing in abundance. XIII. ME. *plentivous, -ifous*, later *plentevous, plentuous, plentious, -eous* (cf. BOUNTEOUS) – OF. *plentivous, -evous*, f. *plentif, -ive*, f. *plente*+*-if, -ive* -IVE. **plen**TY ple·nti state of being in abundance. XIII (AncrR.). ME. *plenteth* (surviving as *plentith* XVII), later *plente, -ee, -ie* – OF. *plentet* (= *-eþ*), mod. dial. *plenté* = Pr. *plendat*, Rum. *plinătate* :– L. *plenitāte-, -tās*. Also adj. (XIII; cf. *choice, dainty*). Hence **ple·nti**FUL¹. XV (Malory). **plenum** plī·nəm A. space regarded as filled with matter (opp. to *vacuum*) XVII; B. full assembly XVIII. – L. *plēnum* (Cicero, in sense A), n. of *plēnus*.

pleistocene plai·stosīn see EOCENE.

pleonasm plī·ənæzm (rhet.) redundancy of expression. XVII (earlier in L. form XVI). – late L. *pleonasmus* – Gr. *pleonasmós*, f. *pleonázein* be superfluous, f. *pléon* more, compar. of *polú* much (cf. FULL¹); cf. F. *pléonasme* (1613). So **pleona·stic**(AL). XVII.

plesiosaurus plī:sio(u)sǭ·rəs one of a genus of extinct marine saurian reptiles. modL. (W. D. Conybeare, 1821), f. Gr. *plēsíos* near +*saûros* lizard (see SAURIAN).

plethora ple·þərə, plėþǭə·rə (path.) condition marked by overfullness of blood, etc. XVI; excessive quantity XVII. – late L. *plēthōra* – Gr. *plēthṓrē* fullness, repletion, f. *plḗthein* be FULL. (An irreg. var. *ple·thory*, prob. f. *plethoric*, after *allegoric* / *-ory*, was current from XVII till early XIX.) So **plethor**IC -ɔ·rik. XVII. – F. – late L. – Gr.

pleura pluə·rə (anat.) membrane lining the thorax and enveloping the lungs. XVII. – medL. *pleura* – Gr. *pleurā́* side, rib. So **pleurisy** pluə·rĭsi inflammation of the pleura. XIV. – OF. *pleurisie* (mod. *pleurésie*) – late L. *pleurisis* (Prudentius), in modL. *pleuresis*, for earlier *pleurītis* (Vitruvius) – Gr. *pleurîtis* (Hippocrates), f. *pleurā́*. The adj. is **pleurit**IC -i·tik. XVI. – (O)F. *pleurétique* – L. *pleurīticus* (Pliny) – Gr. *pleurītikós* (Hippocrates). **pleuro-** pluə·rou comb. form of Gr. *pleurā́*.

plexus ple·ksəs (anat.) network of fibres or vessels. XVII. – modL. *plexus*, f. *plex-*, pp. stem of *plectere* interweave, PLAIT.

pliable plai·əbl easily bent or influenced. XV. – F. *pliable*, f. *plier* bend; see PLY[1], -ABLE. So **pli·**ANT. XIV. – (O)F. *pliant*.

pliers plai·əɹz small pincers. XVI. pl. of *plier*, agent-noun f. *ply* bend :– L. *plicāre* FOLD; see PLY[1], -ER[1].

plight[1] plait †danger, risk OE.; (arch.) undertaking, engagement XIII. OE. *pliht* = OFris., (M)Du. *plicht*, OHG. *phliht* (G. *pflicht* duty), f. Germ. **plex-*, whence OE. *pleoh* peril, risk. In the second sense in mod. use prob. deduced from *trothplight*, which was orig. *troth plight* 'plighted troth'. Hence **plight** vb. pledge, engage. XIII (cf. OE. *plihtan* endanger, OHG. *phlihten* engage oneself, MDu. *plichten* guarantee).

plight[2] plait A. †fold, plait XIV (PPl.); B. condition, state XIV. Late ME. *plit*, *plyt* – AN. *plit*, var. of OF. *ploit*, *pleit* fold, PLAIT. In sense B perh. infl. by prec.

plimsoll pli·msəl name of Samuel *Plimsoll*, English politician, to whose agitation the Merchant Shipping Act of 1876 was largely due, in *P.('s) line*, *mark* load-line on the hull of a ship.

plinth plinþ lower square member of the base of a column. XVII. – F. *plinthe* or L. *plinthus* (Vitruvius) – Gr. *plínthos* tile, brick, stone squared for building, prob. of alien origin.

pliocene see **eocene**.

pliosaurus plaio(u)sǭ·rəs extinct marine reptile so called because nearer to the saurian type than the ichthyosaurus. XIX. modL., f. *plio-*, var. of *pleio-*, repr. Gr. *pleíōn* more+*saûros* lizard.

plod plɔd walk heavily; toil laboriously. XVI. Of unkn. origin, but prob. symbolic; connexion with ME. *plodde*, *pludde* (dial. *plud*) puddle, is inappropriate in sense.

plop plɔp imit. of the sound made by a smooth object dropping into water. XIX.

plosive plou·siv (phon.) stop consonant. XX. – F. *plosive*.

plot plɔt A. small piece of ground XI; B. †ground-plan, scheme, outline XVI; plan of a literary work XVII; C. secret plan, conspiracy XVI (Sh.). Properly three words; in A late OE. *plot*, of unkn. origin; in B alteration of *plat* (early XVI, now U.S.), which was orig. a var. of *plot* in sense A, now dial., or (as in *grass plat*, etc.), partly assoc. with late ME. *plat* flat place or space (– (O)F. *plat*, in modF. 'dish'); in C superseding earlier *complot* XVI (– (O)F. *complot* †dense crowd, secret project, of unkn. origin) by assoc. with sense B. Hence **plot** vb. to make a plan of, contrive. XVI (Spenser, Greene).

plough, U.S. **plow** plau implement for cutting furrows in soil. Late OE. *plōh* (pl. *plōges* XII) – ON. *plógr* = OFris. *plōch*, OS. *plōg* (Du. *ploeg*), E.Frank. *phluog*, MHG. *pfluoc* (G. *pflug*) :– Germ. **plōgaz* (whence OSl. *plugŭ*, Lith. *plū́gas*) – north Italic **plōg-*, repr. by Langobardic L. *plōvum* (cf. Lombardic *piò*, Tyrolese *plof*) and Rhætian *plaumorati* (Pliny), and prob. L. *plaustrum*, *plōstrum*, *plōxenum*, *-imum*. The native OE. word was *sulh* (rel. to L. *sulcus* furrow); another Germ. form is ON. *arðr*. Hence vb. XV. **plou·gh**LAND XIII unit of land assessment based on the area tillable by a team of eight oxen in a year. **plou·gh**SHARE XIV, cf. Du. *ploegschaar*, MHG. *phluocschar* (G. *pflugschar*).

plover plʌ·vəɹ name of several grallatorial birds, (pop.) lapwing. XIV. – AN. *plover*, OF. *plovier*, *plouvier* (mod. *pluvier*, alt. after *pluie* rain) = It. *piviere* :– Rom. **ploviārius*, **pluviārius*, f. L. *pluvia* rain (see FLOW[1]). ¶ The name is paralleled in the assoc. with rain by synon. Sp. *pluvial*, G. *regenpfeifer* 'rain-piper', Eng. *rainbird*.

pluck plʌk A. pull off, draw forcibly XIV; B. reject (a candidate) in an examination XVIII. Late OE. *ploccian*, *pluccian*, corr. to MLG. *plucken*, MDu. *plocken* (Flem. *plokken*), ON. *plokka*, *plukka* :– Germ. **plukkōn*, **-ōjan*, a parallel form with mutation **plukkjan* being repr. by OE. **plyććan* (ME. *plicchen*), (M)Du. *plukken*, (M)HG. *pflücken*; prob. all to be referred to Rom. **piluccāre*, whence OF. *peluchier*, ONF. *pelukier*, *plusquier* (mod. Norman and Picard *pluquer* pick, peck), Pr. *pelugar*, Cat. *pellucár*, It. *piluccare* pluck (feathers, grapes), and with EX-[1], OF. *espelucher*, mod. *éplucher* pluck, OIt. *spiluccarsi* lick oneself (of cats), obscurely f. L. *pīlus* hair, PILE[4]; cf. PLUSH. The origin of sense B is obscure; connexion with the Oxford University practice of plucking the proctor's gown at a degree ceremony as a challenge to the granting of a degree is not evidenced. Hence **pluck** sb. act of plucking XV; heart, liver, and lungs of a beast, as being 'plucked' out of the carcass (cf. synon. dial. *gather*) XVII; (orig. pugilistic slang) 'heart', courage, 'guts'; cf. *pluck up heart*, etc. XVIII.

plug plʌg piece of wood, etc. to stop a hole, etc. XVII; cock of water-pipe; tobacco pressed into a cake XVIII. – MLG., MDu. *plugge* (Du. *plug*), of which there are by-forms, MLG. *plügge* (LG. *plüg*), and with different consonant, (M)LG. *plock*, *pluck*, MHG. *pfloc*, *pflocke* (G. *pflock*). (Sw. *plugg*, *pligg*, Da. *plög*, *plök* are from LG., and Ir., Gael. *pluc* from Eng.) Ulterior origin unknown. Hence **plug** vb. XVII; cf. MLG., Du. *pluggen*.

plug-ugly U.S. city ruffian. Of unkn. origin. XIX.

plum plʌm (fruit of) the tree Prunus domestica OE.; dried grape or raisin (as in *p. pudding*) XVII. OE. *plūme*, corr. to MLG. *plūme*, MHG. *pflūme* (G. *pflaume*; in OHG. *pflūmo* plum-tree), ON. *plóma* (perh. – OE.), with by-forms (M)LG., MDu. *prūme* (Du. *pruim*), OHG. *pfrūma* – medL. *prūna* (see PRUNE), orig. pl. of L. *prūnum* plum (cf. *prūnus* plum-tree), parallel to Gr. *proûmnon* plum. The shortening of the vowel, which may have been due to the comp. (OE.) *plūmtrēow* plum-tree (but cf. THUMB), appears XIV in the sp. *plumbe*, but the orig. long vowel remains in north. dial. *plūm*.

plumage plū·midʒ bird's covering of feathers. XV (Caxton). – (O)F. *plumage*, f. *plume* PLUME; see -AGE.

plumb plʌm ball of lead attached to a line. XIII (now familiar chiefly in phr. *out of p.* out of the vertical, and *p.-line* XVI). ME. *plumbe*, prob. – OF. **plombe*, repr. by *plomme* (XIV) sounding-lead :– Rom. **plumba*; later assim. to (O)F. *plomb* = Pr., Cat. *plom* (whence Sp. *plomo*), Pg. *chumbo*, It. *piombo*, Rum. *plumb* :– L. *plumbum* lead, of obscure origin, but prob. from the same source as synon. Gr. *mólubdos*, *mólibos*, *bólimos*, and adopted from a Mediterranean language. Hence **plumb** adj. vertical, adv. vertically. XIV; **plumb** vb. sound with a plummet. XVI; cf. F. *plomber*.

plumbago plʌmbei·gou †yellow and red oxides of lead XVII; black lead, graphite XVIII: genus of plants, leadwort XVIII. – L. *plumbāgō* (i) lead ore, (ii) leadwort, fleawort, f. *plumbum* lead (see PLUMB); used in both senses by Pliny tr. Gr. *molúbdaina* (Dioscorides). Hence **plumbagin**OUS plʌmbæ·dʒinəs. XVIII.

plumber plʌ·məɹ worker in lead. XIV. – OF. *plommier* (mod. *plombier*) :– L. *plumbārius*, f. *plumbum*; see PLUMB, -ER².

plume plūm feather (now spec.). XIV. – (O)F. *plume* = Pr. *pluma*, It. *piuma* :– L. *plūma* (whence rare OE. *plūmfeðer*) small soft feather, down, OHG. *pflūma* (G. *pflaum*, *flaum*, *pflaumfeder*), rel. to OPruss. *plauxdine* feather-bed, Lith. *plùnksna* feather. Hence **plume** vb. furnish with plumes XV; refl. of a bird, to dress its feathers. XVIII.

plummer-block plʌ·məɹblɔk metal box or case for supporting a revolving shaft or journal. XIX (also *plumber-*, *plomer-*). perh. f. a proper name.

plummet plʌ·mit leaden weight attached to a line. XIV (Wycl. Bible). Late ME. *plomet* – OF. *plommet*, *plombet*, dim. of *plomb*; see PLUMB, -ET.

plump¹ plʌmp fall or come down with heavy and abrupt impact XIV; trans. XV; blurt *out* XVI; vote *for* one candidate only XIX. – (M)LG. *plumpen* = (M)Du. *plompen* fall into water (whence G. *plumpen*, Sw. *plumpa*, Da. *plumpe*); of imit. origin. Hence **plump** adv. XVI. In the last sense f. *plump* adv. (e.g. *refuse plump*, †*vote plump*); *plumper* (XVIII) undivided vote.

plump² plʌmp †dull, blockish XV (Caxton); of full and rounded form XVI. Late ME. *plompe* – (M)Du. *plomp*, MLG. *plomp*, *plump* blunt, obtuse, unshapen, blockish (whence G. *plump*), perh. ult. identical with prec. With the second sense cf. MLG. *plumpich* 'corpulentus'.

plumule plū·mjūl (bot.) rudimentary shoot, etc. XVII; (ornith.) down-feather XIX. – F. *plumule* or L. *plūmula* (Columella), dim. of *plūma* PLUME; see -ULE.

plunder plʌ·ndəɹ rob forcibly; appropriate wrongfully, loot. XVII. – (M)HG. *plündern* – (M)LG. *plünderen* pillage, sack, lit. to rob of household effects, f. MHG. *plunder* bedclothes, clothing, household stuff (modG. lumber, trash); cf. MLG., MDu. *plunde*, *plunne* (LG. *plünde*, *plünne*), Du. *plunje* clothes, baggage. First found c. 1630 with ref. to the Thirty Years War, then from 1642 with ref. to the Civil War in England and esp. the action of Prince Rupert's forces. Hence **plu·nder** sb. action of plundering, goods plundered XVII; U.S. (prob. after Du. *plunje*) baggage XIX.

plunge plʌndʒ thrust or cast (*oneself*) *into* liquid; also fig. XIV (Ch., Barbour). – OF. *plungier*, *plongier* (mod. *plonger*) :– Rom. **plumbicāre*, f. L. *plumbum* lead; see PLUMB.

pluperfect plūpə̄·ɹfikt (gram.) pert. to a time earlier than some particular time in the past XVI; more than perfect XIX. – modL. *plūsperfectum*, for L. (*tempus præteritum*) *plūs quam perfectum* '(past tense) more than perfect', tr. Gr. (*χρόνος*) *ὑπερσυντελικός*; cf. F. *plus-que-parfait*.

plural pluə·rəl (gram.) denoting more than one (or two); also sb. XIV (PPl., Trevisa). Late ME. *plurel* – OF. *plurel* (mod. *pluriel*) – L. *plūrālis* (Quintilian) adj. with *numerus, genitivus*, also sb. (sc. *numerus* number), f. *plūr-, plūs* more; see PLUS, -AL[1]. **plu·ral**LY[2] XIV (Wycl.). So **plural**ITY pluræ·liti holding of two or more benefices concurrently by the same person XIV (PPl.); state of being plural XIV (Trevisa); majority XVI (at first Sc., after F. *pluralité*); U.S. excess of votes polled by the leading candidate above those polled by the next XIX. – (O)F. *pluralité* – late L. *plūrālitās*; in the sense 'majority' treated as an immed. deriv. of L. *plūr-, plūs* more. **pluri-** pluəri comb. form of L. *plūr-, plūs* more, *plūrēs* several, used in various techn. terms of XIX. The earliest ex. is *pluripresence*, coined by Johnson)(*omnipresence*.

plus plʌs with the addition of; verbal rendering of the sign + XVII; (electr.) positive(ly) XVIII. – L. *plūs* more, earlier *plous*, perh. for **pleus* (cf. *pleores*, old form of *plūrēs* several), f. **plē̆-*, repr. also by Skr. *prā́yas* most of the time, Av. *frāyah-* more numerous, sb. abundance, *frāyō* more, Gr. *pléōn, plées, pleîstos*, OIr. *līa* (:– **plēis*) more, ON. *fleiri* more, *fleistr* most numerous. Cf. MINUS.

plus-fours plʌsfɔə·ɹz long wide knickerbockers so called because four inches are added to the usual length to produce the overhang. XX. f. PLUS + pl. of FOUR.

plush plʌʃ kind of cloth having a longer nap than velvet. XVI (Nashe). – F. †*pluche*, contr. of *peluche*, f. OF. *peluchier* PLUCK – It. *peluzzo*, dim. of *pelo* (= F. *poil*, Pr. *pel*, Sp. *pelo*) :– L. *pilus* PILE[3].

plutocracy plūtɔ·krəsi rule of wealth or the wealthy. XVII (Urquhart; thereafter not till XIX). – Gr. *ploutokratiā*, f. *ploûtos* wealth, prob. rel. ult. to FULL; see -CRACY. Hence **pluto**CRAT plū·toukræt. XIX.

plutonic plūtɔ·nik (geol.) pert. to the action of internal heat. XVIII (Kirwan). f. Gr. *Ploútōn* (Pluto) god of the infernal regions + -IC; cf. F. *plutonique* (XVI).

pluvial plū·viəl (eccl.) cope. XVII. – medL. *pluviāle* 'rain-cloak', sb. use of n. of L. *pluviālis*, f. *pluvia, pluere* rain, see -AL[1]. **pluvious** characterized by rain, rainy. XV.

ply[1] plai (Sc.) plight, condition XV; fold, layer XVI (in earliest use Sc.); bend, turn, twist XVI (fig. from XVII). – (O)F. *pli*, f. *plier*, †*pleier* (whence **ply** vb. bend, lit. and fig. XIV) :– L. *plicāre*; see FOLD[2] and cf. COMPLEX, EXPLICIT[1], PERPLEX, PLAIT, REPLY.

ply[2] plai apply, employ XIV (Ch., Gower); work away at; solicit earnestly XVI; (naut.) XVI. Aphetic of APPLY.

pneumatic njumæ·tik pert. to wind or air. XVII. – F. *pneumatique* or L. *pneumaticus* (Vitruvius, Pliny) – Gr. *pneumatikós*, f. *pneumat-, pneûma* wind, breath, spirit, f. **pneϝ-* breathe, rel. to OE. *fnēosan* (see SNEEZE); see -IC. So †*pneuma·tical* (somewhat earlier).

pneumonia njumou·niə inflammation of the lungs. XVII. – modL. *pneumonia* – Gr. *pneumoniā*, f. *pneumon-, -ōn* lung, alt., by assoc. with *pneîn, pneûsai* breathe, of *pleúmōn*, rel. to L. *pulmō* lung (cf. PULMONARY).

po pou (colloq.) chamber-pot. XIX. repr. pronunc. of F. *pot* POT.

poach[1] poutʃ cook (an egg) by dropping it without the shell into boiling water. XV (*pocche*, later *potch*; *poach* from XVII). – OF. *pochier* (mod. *pocher*) orig. enclose in a bag, f. *poche* bag, pocket, POKE[1]. The vb. was preceded in Eng. use by *pochee, eyron en poche, eggez pocchez* dishes made from eggs.

poach[2] poutʃ encroach or trespass *on* land, etc., spec. steal game. XVII ('*Pocher le labeur d'autruy*, to poche into, or incroach vpon, another mans imployment, practise, or trade', Cotgr.; 'to poach for power', Dryden, 1682). perh. – (O)F. *pocher* in spec. use of 'pocket'; see prec. and cf. slang use of *bag* vb.

pochard, pockard pou·tʃəɹd, pou·kəɹd, pɔ·- dun-bird, Fuligula or Æthyia ferina. XVI. Of unkn. origin; for the ending cf. *mallard*.

pock pɔk pustule OE.; pl. XIV (see POX). Late OE. *poc, pocc-* = MLG., MDu. *pocke* (Du. *pok*, LG. *pocke*, whence G. *pocke*) :– Germ. **pukno-*, f. **puk-* (repr. also by OE. *pohha, pocca* bag, MHG. *pfoch*).

pocket pɔ·kit bag, sack, as a measure of hops, wool, etc.; small pouch attached to a garment. XV. – AN. *poket(e)*, dim. of *poke* POKE[1], var. of OF. *pochet, pochette* (Norman dial. *pouquet, -ette*). In AL. *poketa, pochettus* POUCH. See -ET. Hence **pocket** vb. XVI; cf. F. *pocheter*. **po·cket ha·ndkerchief.** XVIII (Mme D'Arblay).

pod pɔd seed-vessel of leguminous and cruciferous plants. XVII. prob. back-formation from dial. *podware, podder* (XVI), of unkn. origin, which succeeded to †*codware* (see COD[1], WARE[1]).

podagra pɔ·dəgrə, podæ·grə gout. XV. – L. *podagra* – Gr. *podágrā*, f. *pod-, poús* FOOT + *ágrā* seizure, trap, f. a base meaning 'chase', 'catch'. Earlier †*podagre* (XIII) – OF.

podestà podesta· magistrate in Italian cities. XVI. – It. *podestà*, earlier †*podestate* (whence F. *podestat*, Eng. †*podestat(e)* XVI–XVIII) :– L. *potestātem, potestās* power, authority, magistrate, f. *pot-* (see POTENT).

podge pɔdʒ short fat person. XIX. var. of PUDGE.

podium pou·diəm projecting base XVIII; (zool.) fore or hind foot XIX. L., elevated place, balcony – Gr. *pódion*, dim. of *pod-*, *poús* FOOT.

podo- pɔ·dou, pŏdɔ· comb. form of Gr. *pod-*, *poús* FOOT. XVII.

poem pou·im metrical composition, work in verse. XVI (expressed early by *poesy*). – (O)F. *poème* or L. *poēma* (Plautus) – Gr. *póēma*, early var. of *poíēma* work, fiction, poetical work, f. *poeîn*, *poieîn* make, create, rel. to Skr. *cinṓti*, *cáyati* assemble, heap up, construct, OSl. *činŭ* arrangement, series (base **quoi-*). So **poesy**[3] pou·ĭzi, -ĭsi (arch.) poetry, poem XIV; †POSY XV (Lydg.). – (O)F. *poésie* = Pr., Sp., It. *poesia* – CRom. **poēsia*, for L. *poēsis* – Gr. *póēsis*, *poíēsis* creation, poetry, poem; see -Y[3]. **poet** pou·it writer of poetry. XIII (Cursor M.). – (O)F. *poète* – L. *poēta* (Plautus) – Gr. *poētḗs*, *poiētḗs* maker, author, poet. **po·et-**ASTER. XVI (B. Jonson). – modL. *poētāster* (Erasmus 1521), whence It., Sp. *poetastro*, F. †*poetastre*; after *philosophāster* (Cicero). **poet**IC poue·tik. XVI. – (O)F. *poétique* – L. *poēticus* – Gr. *po(i)ētikós*. **poe·t**ICAL. XIV (Ch.; rare before XVI). **poe·t**ICS treatise on poetry, as that of Aristotle. XVIII. **poetry** pou·ĭtri composition in verse. XIV (Ch., who knew the 'Nova Poetria' of Gaufrei de Vinsauf or Galfridus Anglicus, *c.*1200, in which, as in other early works, *poetria* means the poetic art). – medL. *poētria* (VII), f. L. *poēta*, prob. after L. *geometria* GEOMETRY. ¶ There is no contact with L. *poētria* – Gr. *poētria* poetess.

pogrom pogrɔ·m, pɔ·grəm organized massacre in Russia. XX. – Russ. *pogróm* devastation, destruction, f. *gromit'* destroy.

poignant poi·nənt sharp, pungent. XIV (Ch.). – (O)F. *poignant* :– L. *pungent-*, *-ēns*, prp. of *pungere* prick; cf. POINT and see -ANT.

poilu pwa·lü French private soldier. XX. slang sb. use of F. *poilu* hairy, (sl.) bold, determined, (sb.) stout fellow, fighting man, f. *poil* hair :– L. *pilus* PILE[3].

poinsettia poinse·tiə Mexican species of Euphorbia. XIX. modL., f. name of J. P. *Poinsett*, American minister to Mexico, discoverer of the plant; see -IA[1].

point point A. minute part or particle XIII; small mark, dot; precise position, time, fact, or quality XIV; B. sharp end XIV. In A – (O)F. *point*, in B – (O)F. *pointe*, repr. respectively L. *punctum* (whence also Pr. *punt*, Sp., It. *punto*, Pg. *ponto*), sb. use of n. pp. of *pungere* prick, pierce (cf. PUNGENT), and Rom. (medL.) *puncta* (whence also Pr. *ponta*, Sp., It. *punta*, Pg. *poncha*), corr. use of the fem pp. ¶ The phonetic coalescence in Eng. of *point* with *pointe* combines groups of meaning that are kept apart formally in other langs. (sometimes by distinct words, as in G. *stich* and *spitze*). So **point** vb. XIV. Partly – (O)F. *pointer* (cf. Sp. *puntar*, It. *puntare*, medL. *punctāre*), partly f. the sb.; hence **point**ER[1] in techn. uses from *c.*1500; rod to point with XVII; dog that indicates position of game XVIII. Comps. **point-blank** direct (horizontal) aim or range; also adj. and adv. (XVI, Digges), of unkn. origin, but presumed to involve the sb. *blank* 'white spot in a target'; **point-device** (arch.), orig. *at p. d.*, perfectly, precisely XIV (Ch.); later adj. and adv. without *at*; of unkn. origin, but poss. based on AN. **à point devis* 'arranged to perfection', which may have combined OF. *à point* to perfection, and *à devis* in good order.

pointillism pwæ·ntilizm method of impressionist painters consisting in the use of small dots of colour. XIX. – F. *pointillisme*, f. *pointiller* mark with small points or dots, f. *pointille* – It. *puntiglio*, f. *punto* POINT; see -ISM.

poise poiz †weight XV; balance, equilibrium XVI. – OF. *pois* (mod. *poids*), earlier *peis* = Pr., Cat. *pes*, Sp., Pg., It. *peso* :– CRom. **pēsum*, for L. *pēnsum* weight, sb. use of n. of pp. of *pendere* weigh, rel. to *pendēre* (see PENDENT). So **poise** vb. †weigh XIV; place or hold in equilibrium XVI. f. OF. *poise*, var. of *peise* (whence ME. *peise*, dial. *peise*, *paise*), stem-stressed form of *peser* = Pr. *pezar*, Sp. *pesar*, It. *pesare* :– Rom. **pēsāre*, for L. *pēnsāre*, frequent. of *pendere*.

poison poi·zn †(deadly) potion XIII; substance introduced into an organism that destroys life or injures health XIV (Trevisa). ME. *puison*, *poison* – OF. *puison*, (also mod.) *poison* (in OF. magic potion) = Pr. *pozó*, OSp. *pozon* poison, Pg. *poção* medicine, It. *pozione* drink :– L. *pōtiōn(em)* POTION. So **poison** vb. XIII. – OF. *poisonner* (superseded by *empoisonner*).

poissarde pwa·sărd French market-woman XVIII; French fishwife XIX. – F. *poissarde* low foul-mouthed woman, (assoc. with *poisson* fish) fishwife, fem. of *poissard* pickpocket, rogue, f. *poix* PITCH[1], lit. 'to whom things stick like pitch'; see -ARD.

poitrel poi·trĕl breastplate; stiff stomacher. XV. – OF. *poitral*, earlier *peitral* :– L. *pectorāle* PECTORAL.

poke[1] pouk bag, small sack (now dial. except in 'to buy a pig in a poke'). XIII. – ONF. *poque*, *poke* (cf. AL. *poca*), var. of (O)F. *poche* (cf. POUCH).

poke[2] pouk thrust with the finger or a pointed instrument. XIV (Ch., Wyclif). – (M)LG., (M)Du. *poken* (whence perh. OF. *poquer* thrust out), of unkn. origin. Hence (prob.) **poke** sb. projecting brim of a bonnet. XVIII; so **p.-bonnet**. XIX. **po·k**ER[1] instrument for poking a fire. XVI.

poker[2] pou·kəɹ card-game, a variety of brag. XIX. orig. U.S., of doubtful origin, but cf. G. *poch(spiel)* 'bragging game', f. *pochen* brag, perh. cogn. with POKE[2].

polacre polā·kəɹ, **polacca** polæ·kə three-masted merchant ship of the Mediterranean. XVII (Purchas). – F. *polacre, polaque*, It. *polacra, polacca* = Sp., Pg. *polacra* (whence Du. *polaak*, G. *polack(e), polacker*); identical with the words meaning POLISH, POLE.

poldavy pəldei·vi, **poldavis** pəldei·vis (naut.) coarse canvas. XV. prob. orig. coll. pl. *poldavis*, for **poldavides*, f. *Poldavide* town in Brittany, whence the art of making the stuff was introduced.

polder pou·ldəɹ low-lying land reclaimed from the sea. XVII. repr. in place-names from XI, e.g. *Poldreham* Powderham, *Polre* Poldhurst, *Polr* Polders, of doubtful existence in OE. and prob. – MDu. *polre*, (mod.) *polder* (whence also G. *polder*).

pole[1] poul (orig.) stake; (later) long slender piece of wood used as a support OE.; linear measure of 5½ yards XVI; square measure of 30¼ yards XVII. Late OE. *pāl*, corr. to OFris., (M)LG. *pāl*, MDu. *pael* (Du. *paal*), OHG. *phāl* (G. *pfahl*), ON. *páll*; CGerm. (exc. Gothic) – L. *pālus* stake, prop :– **păkslos*, f. **pāg*- **pāk*- (cf. PACT, etc.).

pole[2] poul each of the two points in the celestial sphere XIV (Ch.); each extremity (north and south) of the earth's axis; each of two opposite points on surface of magnet at which magnetic forces are manifested XVI. – L. *polus* end of an axis – Gr. *pólos* pivot, axis (see WHEEL). Cf. F. *pôle*, in part the source. So **po·lar**. XVI (Recorde). – F. *polaire*, It. *polare*, or modL. *polāris*; whence **polarity** poulæ·rĭti. XVII (Sir T. Browne). **po·larize**. XIX (1811). – F. *polariser* (Malus).

Pole poul †Poland, country of E. Europe XVI; native of this XVII. – G. *Pole*, sg. of *Polen*, in MHG. *Polān*, pl. *-āne* – Polish *Poljane* 'field-dwellers', f. *pole* field. So **Po·lack** (obs. in England; U.S. immigrant from Poland). XVII (earlier †*Polaker*). – F. *Polaque*, G. *Polack* – Pol. *Polak*. Hence **Po·lish**[1] (the language is Western Slavonic). XVIII. Cf. POLACRE.

-pole poul terminal el. repr. (partly through F. *-pole*, L. *-pola*) Gr. *-pṓlēs* seller, dealer, f. *pōleîn* sell, f. a widespread IE. base.

poleaxe pou·læks battle-axe XIV; halbert XVI. ME. *pol(l)ax, -ex* – MDu. *pol(l)aex*, MLG. *pol(l)exe*, f. *pol, polle* POLL[1] + *æx* AXE; later assoc. with POLE[1].

polecat pou·lkæt Putorius fœtidus, of the weasel family. XIV (*polcat*). The first el. is of unkn. origin (OF. *pole, poule* chicken, fowl, has been suggested; see PULLET), the second is CAT.

polemarch pə·limāɹk military commander-in-chief. XVII. – Gr. *polémarkhos*, f. *pólemos* war; see -ARCH.

polemic pŏle·mik disputatious, controversial. XVII. – medL. *polēmicus* – Gr. *polemikós*, f. *pólemos* war; see -IC. Also **pole·mical**. XVII.

polenta pŏle·ntə porridge made from barley, chestnut meal, etc. XVI. – It. *polenta* :– L. *polenta* pearl barley, rel. to POLLEN.

police pəlī·s, (formerly) pə·lis (as still in Scotland and Ireland) †policy; †civil organization XVI; civil administration regulating public order (first with ref. to France, and to Scotland, where Commissioners of Police were established by Queen Anne, 13 December 1714); civil force appointed to maintain public order XVIII (the *New P.* was established for London in 1829). – F. *police* – medL. *polītia* for L. *polītīa*; see POLICY, POLITY. Hence **poli·ceman**[1] XIX (1829), -WOMAN (1853).

policy[1] pə·lĭsi †government, administration XIV (Ch., Gower); prudence in procedure; course of action deemed expedient. XV (Lydg.). – OF. *policie* (in first sense) – L. *polītīa* POLITY. Cf. POLICE.

policy[2] pə·lĭsi in full *p. of assurance* or *insurance* document containing an undertaking to pay certain sums for loss of property. XVI. Earliest form *police* (tr. F. document); – F. *police* – Pr. *polissa, -issia*, Cat. *-ice* = Sp. *póliza*, Pg. *apólice*, It. *polizza* prob. :– medL. *apódissa, -ixa*, alt. of L. *apodīxis* – Gr. *apódeixis* demonstration, proof, f. *apodeiknúnai* (see APODEICTIC).

poliomyelitis pə:liou-, pou:lioumaiəlai·tis (path.) inflammation of the grey matter of the spinal cord. XIX. modL., f. Gr. *poliós* grey + *muelós* marrow; see -ITIS. abbrev. **po·lio**. XX.

poliorcetic pə:liɔ̄ɹse·tik pert. to siegecraft. XIX (De Quincey). – Gr. *poliorkētikós*, f. *poliorkeîn* besiege a city, f. *pólis* city + *orkeîn* besiege. So **po:liorce·tics**. XVI.

-polis pəlis repr. Gr. *pólis* city, as in METROPOLIS, NECROPOLIS; occas. used in the form *-opolis* (see -O-) to form nicknames of towns, e.g. *Cottonopolis* (Manchester), *Porkopolis* (Chicago).

polish pə·liʃ make smooth (and glossy) by friction XIII (Cursor M.); refine XIV. ME. *polis(s* – *poliss-*, lengthened stem of (O)F. *polir* – L. *polīre*, which has been linked as a possible fuller's term with Germ. **felt*- of FELT; see -ISH[2] and POLITE.

Polish see POLE.

polite pəlai·t †polished XV; polished, refined XVI; of refined courteous manners XVII. – L. *polītus*, pp. of *polīre* POLISH.

politic pə·lĭtik †political; characterized by policy, shrewd, judicious XV (Lydg.) sb. pl. science and art of government XVI (Skelton); political affairs or life XVII. – (O)F. *politique* (one of an opportunist party *c.* 1573, temporizer) – L. *polīticus* – Gr. *polītikós* civic, civil, political (used sb. as m. sg., fem. sg., n. pl.), f. *polī́tēs* citizen, f. *pólis* city, state; see -IC. So **political** pŏli·tikəl pert. to the state XVI (T. Wilson); comb. form **poli·tico-** XVIII

(Fielding); **politi·cian** †schemer, intriguer; one versed in politics. xvi. **polity** pɔ·lĭti civil organization, form of government. xvi. – L. *polītia* (Cicero) – Gr. *polīteíā*.

polka pɔ·lkə, pou·lkə lively dance of Bohemian origin, danced at Prague in 1835, in London in 1842. – G., F. *polka* – Czech *pùlka* 'half-step', f. *pùl* half. Cf. MAZURKA.

poll[1] poul A. human head xiii; B. counting by heads (Sh.), (hence) of votes xvii. perh. of LDu. origin (cf. obs. Du., LG. *polle*); but OE. *poll* in place-names, poss. meaning 'hill', may have orig. meant 'head'. Hence **poll** vb. in various senses of independent derivation: cut short, cut off the hair of xiii (pp. *pollid*); cut off the head or top of xvi; count heads, record votes xvii.

poll[2] poul in *poll deed, deed poll*, legal writing polled or cut even at the edge (not indented). xvi. orig. for *pold, polled*, pp. of *poll* vb. (see prec.).

Poll pɔl var. of and contemp. with POLLY xvii (*Pall*), as proper name of a parrot; alt. of *Moll* (xvi); see MOLL.

pollack pɔ·lək sea-fish allied to the cod. xvii. Earlier Sc. *podlok* (xvi), later *podley*; of unkn. origin.

pollard pɔ·ləɹd horned animal that has lost its horns xvi; tree that has been polled or cut back xvii. f. POLL[1]+-ARD. Hence vb. xvii (Evelyn). ¶ Perh. earlier as a name of the hare xiv (*pollart*).

pollen pɔ·lĭn †fine flour xvi; (bot.) powdery substance produced by the anther xviii. – L. *pollen* flour, fine powder, rel. more immed. to POLENTA, *pulvis* POWDER, *puls, pult-* PULSE[2].

pollicitation pɔlisitei·ʃən promising, promise (spec. leg.). xvi. – F. or L. *pollicitātiō*, f. *pollicitārī* bid at auction, f. *pollicērī* promise; see -ATION.

polliwog, polly- pɔ·liwɔg (dial. and U.S.) tadpole. xv. Late ME. *polwygle*, later *porwigle* (xvii), *polwigge* (xvi), *polliwig, polliwog* (xix); f. POLL[1]+WIGGLE and synon. dial. *wig*, alt. by assim. of the vowels of initial and final sylls.

pollute pəlʲū·t render impure. xiv (Wycl. Bible; *pollute* pp. in Ch. and Wyclif). f. *pollūt-*, pp. stem of L. *polluere*, f. **por-* PRO-[1] + base of *lutum* mud. So **pollu·tion**. xiv. – (O)F. *pollution* or late L. *pollūtiō(n-)*.

Polly, polly pɔ·li female name used for a parrot. xvii (*Poolye*, B. Jonson). dim. of POLL; see -Y[6].

polo pou·lou ball game of Oriental origin, first introduced at Calcutta from native Indian practice. xix. – Balti (Indus valley) *polo* ball = Tibetan *pulu*.

polonaise pɔlənei·z female dress orig. suggested by that of Polish women; slow dance of Polish origin. xviii. – F. *polonaise* (sc. *robe* dress, *danse* dance), sb. use of fem. of *polonais* Polish, f. medL. *Polōnia* Poland (cf. POLE).

polonium (chem.) pəlou·niəm radio-active metallic element. xix. – F. (modL.) *polonium*, f. medL. *Polōnia* Poland (see -IUM); so called from the Polish nationality of Mme Curie, who, with her husband, discovered it in pitchblende.

polony pəlou·ni sausage of partly cooked pork. xviii (*pullony sausage*). prob. for *Bolognian sausage* (xvi, Nashe), Bologna, a town in Italy, being noted for a kind of sausage.

poltergeist pɔ·ltəɹgaist noisy mischievous ghost. xix. G., f. *poltern* make a noise, create a disturbance + *geist* GHOST.

poltroon pəltrū·n cowardly or mean-spirited wretch. xvi (Skelton). – F. *poltron*, †*poultron* – It. *poltrone* sluggard, coward (cf. medL. *pultro* xiii St. Francis), perh. f. †*poltro* bed (as if 'lie-abed').

poly- pɔ·li, pŏli· repr. Gr. *polu-*, comb. form of *polús, polú* much, pl. *polloí* many (cf. Skr. *purús*, OIr. *hil*, OHG. *filu*, G. *viel*, OE. *fela*, and FULL); in many techn. terms. **polyanthus** -æ·nþəs cultivated type of primula. xviii. modL. (Gr. *ánthos* flower); **po·lychrome** -kroum work of art, etc. in various colours. xix. – F. – Gr. *polúkhrōmos* (*khrôma* colour); **poly·gamous**. xvii (Purchas), practising **poly·gamy**[3] marriage with several at once (xvi). – F. *polygamie* (Calvin) – ecclGr. *polugamíā* (*gámos* marriage); **polyglot** pɔ·liglɔt (one) who speaks or writes, a work in, several languages. xvii. – F. *polyglotte* – Gr. *polúglōttos* (*glôtta* tongue); **polygon** pɔ·ligən (geom.) many-sided figure. xvi (Digges). – late L. *polygōnum* – Gr. *polúgōnon*, sb. use of n. of adj. *-gōnos*. So **poly·gonal**[1] xviii, †**-gonous** xvii; **polyhedron** -hī·drən, -he·drən many-sided solid. xvi (Billingsley). – Gr. *polúedron* (*hédra* base, side); **po·lymath** person of varied learning. xvii (Burton). – Gr. *polumathḗs* (*manthánein* learn); **polynomial** -nou·miəl (math.) consisting of many terms. xvii. f. modL. *polynomius*, after *binomial*; **polysy·llable** word of many syllables. xvi. f. medL. *polysyllaba* (sc. *vox* word); **po:lysynthe·tic** (cryst.); (philol.) combining several words of a sentence into one. xix. f. Gr. *polusúnthetos*; **polyte·chnic** dealing with various arts. xix – F. *polytechnique* (*École p.* 1795), f. Gr. *polútekhnos*; **polytheism** pɔ·liþiizm belief in many gods. xvii. – F. *polythéisme*, f. Gr. *polútheos*; **polyzoa** pɔlizou·ə (zool.) class of colonial aquatic invertebrates. xix. modL., f. Gr. *zôion* animal; see ZOO-, -A[2].

polygonum pəli·gənəm genus of plants (knotgrass, etc.). xviii. modL. (cf. *-os, -us, -on* Pliny) – Gr. *polúgonon*, f. *pólus* POLY- + *gónu* KNEE.

polyp pɔ·lip †octopus, cuttle-fish, or the like XVI; applied gen. to animals of low organization XVIII. – F. *polype* – L. *polypus*.

polypus pɔ·lipəs †hydra, octopus, etc., polyp; (path.) tumour usu. having ramifications like the tentacles of a polyp. XVI. – L. *polypus* – Doric, Æolic *pṓlupos*, var. of Attic *polúpous* cuttle-fish, f. *polús* POLY-+*poús* FOOT.

pomace pʌ·mĭs mash of crushed apples in cider-making. XVI (*pomes, pomois*). – medL. *pōmācium* cider (f. L. *pōmum* apple), with transference of sense.

pomade pəmā·d scented ointment for the skin and hair (in which apples are said to have been orig. an ingredient). XVI (*pomade*, also *pomado*). – F. *pommade* – It. *pomata* :– medL. **pōmāta*, fem. corr. to n. **pomatum** poumei·təm (f. L. *pōmum*, as prec.), also used in Eng. from XVI; see -ADE.

pomander pɔ·məndəɹ, pŏmæ·ndəɹ ball of aromatic substances carried as a preservative against infection. XV. The orig. form is repr. by *pom(e)amber* (XVI) – AN. **pome ambre*, for OF. *pome d'ambre* – medL. *pōmum ambræ*, *pōmum de ambra* 'apple of AMBER'.

pomegranate pɔ·mgrænət fruit of the tree Punica Granatum, a large roundish many-celled berry with many seeds. XIV. The earliest forms have *poum-* and metathetic *-garnet*, *-garnade*. – OF. *pome grenate*, *p. garnate*, etc., i.e. *pome* (:– Rom. **pōma* for L. *pōmum*) apple, *grenate* (mod. *grenade*) pomegranate = Sp. *granada*, It. *granata* :– Rom. **grānāta* for L. (*mālum*) *grānātum* 'apple having many seeds' (see GRAIN); corr. to medL. *pōmum grānātum*, *pōma grānāta*.

Pomeranian pɔmərei·niən pert. to *Pomerania*, district on the south-east coast of the Baltic Sea. XVIII (*P. puppy*); see -IAN. abbrev. **pom**. XX.

pomi- poumi comb. form of L. *pōmum* fruit, apple, e.g. **pomi·**FEROUS. XVII.

pommel pʌ·ml †round body or prominence; knob terminating the hilt of a sword XIV (R. Mannyng); saddle-bow XV. – OF. *pomel* (mod. *pommeau*) = Pr. *pomel*, It. *pomello* :– Rom. **pōmellum*, dim. of L. *pōmum* fruit, apple. Hence vb. beat as with a pommel. XVI.

pomology poumɔ·lədʒi fruit-culture. XIX. – modL. *pōmologia*, f. L. *pōmum* fruit, apple; see -LOGY, -OLOGY.

pomp pɔmp splendour, magnificence; ostentatious display (surviving in echoes of the liturgical formula in the rite of baptism, *the Devil and all his pomps*, repr. ChrL. *pompa* or *pompæ diaboli*, orig. the processions and shows assoc. with pagan worship). XIV (R. Mannyng, Rolle). – (O)F. *pompe* – L. *pompa* – Gr. *pompḗ* sending, solemn procession, train, parade, display, rel. to *pémpein* send. So **po·mp**OUS. XIV (Ch.). – (O)F. *pompeux* – late L. *pompōsus*.

pompadour pɔ·mpəduəɹ designating dress, furniture, colour, etc. named after the Marquise de *Pompadour*, mistress of Louis XV of France. XVIII.

pom-pom pɔ·mpɔm Maxim automatic quick-firing gun. 1899. imit. of the sound of the discharge.

pompon pɔ·mpɔn ornament on a long pin XVIII; globular chrysanthemum XIX. – F. *pompon*, of unkn. origin.

poncho pɔ·ntʃou S. Amer. cloak. XVIII. – S. Amer. Sp. *poncho* – Araucanian *poncho*.

pond pɔnd small body of still water, orig. of artificial formation. XIII. ME. *ponde*, *poonde*, *pounde*, identical with POUND[2], which survives dial. in this sense; but the vocalism is obscure.

ponder pɔ·ndəɹ †estimate the value of; weigh mentally, meditate upon XIV; intr. XVII (Sh.). – (O)F. *pondérer* consider (mod. *pondérer* balance, moderate) – L. *ponderāre* weigh, reflect upon, f. *ponder-*, *pondus* weight, rel. to *pendere* weigh (see PENDENT, POISE, and cf. PREPONDERATE).

ponderous pɔ·ndərəs physically weighty XIV; laboured in manner XVIII. – L. *ponderōsus*, f. *ponder-*, *pondus*; see prec., -OUS.

pone poun bread of N. Amer. Indians made of maize flour. XVII. – Algonquian, with vars. *apone*, *oppone*, perh. orig. pp. 'baked'.

pongee pɔ·n-, pʌ·ndʒī unbleached Chinese silk. XVIII. – N. Chinese *pun-chī* = Mandarin *pun-kī* 'own loom' or *pun-cheh* 'own weaving', i.e. home-made.

pongo pɔ·ŋgou large anthropoid ape. XVII. – Congolese *mpongo*, *mpongi*, *impungu*.

poniard pɔ·njəɹd dagger. XVI (Sh.). – F. *poignard*, repl. OF. *poignal* (cf. Pr. *coltel ponhal*, Sp. *puñal*, It. *pugnale*) – medL. *pugnālis*, n. *-āle*, f. L. *pugnus* fist, rel. to *pugil* PUGILIST; cf. -ARD.

pontiff pɔ·ntif member of the principal college of priests in ancient Rome; bishop, spec. pope. XVII. – F. *pontife* – L. *pontifex*, *-fic-* (also used in Eng. XVI), f. *ponti-*, *pōns* (see next) + *-fic-*, *facere* make, DO[1]. So **ponti·fi**CAL adj. XV; sb. pl. bishop's vestments XIV; book of episcopal rites XVI. – L. **po:ntificalibus** -kei·libəs, -kā·-, orig. and prop. in phr. (medL.) *in pontificalibus* in pontifical robes (XIV), abl. of n. pl. *pontificālia* used sb. **ponti·fic**ATE[3] officiate as bishop. XIX. f. pp. of medL. *pontificāre*.

pontoon[1] pɔntū·n boat (or other vessel), of which a number are used to support a temporary bridge. XVII (*ponton*). – (O)F. *ponton* :– L. *pontō(n-)* punt, bridge of boats, f. *pont-*, *pōns* bridge, rel. to Indo-Iran. and Balto-Slav. words, with Gr. *pátos*, meaning 'road', 'path', but the relevance of the sense in PONTIFF (if this is 'path-maker') is not clear; see -OON and cf. PUNT[1].

pontoon[2] pɔntū·n (army sl.) alt. of F. *vingt-(et-)un* 'twenty-one' (card game), by assim. to prec. XX.

pony pou·ni small horse. XVII. orig. Sc. *pown(e)y* (cf. '*Pony*, a little Scotch horse', Bailey's Dict. 1730), of uncertain origin; perh. for **poulney* – F. *poulenet*, dim. of *poulain* foal :– late L. *pullāmen*, orig. coll. f. L. *pullus* young animal (cf. FOAL).

pood pūd Russian weight (36 lb.). XVI. – Russ. *pud* – LG. or ON. *pund* POUND[1].

poodle pū·dl breed of pet dog. XIX. – G. *pudel*, taken to be short for *pudelhund*, f. *pudeln* splash in water, the poodle being a water-dog.

poof puf int. (repr. a puff of breath) expressing contempt. XIX. Cf. F. *pouf*.

pooh pu excl. of impatience or disdain XVII (Sh.; *pwh*, *pugh*, later *poh*). Also redupl. XVII (*pough pough*; cf. *pup* XVI and prec.).

Pooh-Bah pūbā· name of a character in W. S. Gilbert's 'The Mikado' (1885) who holds many offices at the same time; joc. made up from the disdainful excls. POOH and BAH.

pool[1] pūl small body of still water. OE. *pōl* = OFris., (M)LG., MDu. *pōl* (Du. *poel*), OHG. *pfuol* (G. *pfuhl*), f. WGerm. **pōl-*, rel. to OE. *pyll* creek (dial. *pill*, of the Severn estuary); further relations uncertain.

pool[2] pūl collective amount of stakes in a card-game, †game at cards XVII; transf. of other games or contests in which the competitors contribute a sum, (hence) common fund, combine XIX. – F. *poule* stake, prop. hen (perh. orig. one set as the target and prize in a game, as in the old *jeu de la poule* 'game of the hen') :– medL. *pulla*, fem. of L. *pullus* young animal, FOAL; cf. Sp. *polla* (whence It. *puglia*) hen (see PULLET), stake at hombre, Walloon *poie*; assoc. with POOL[1] was prob. furthered by the identification of *fish* (in the pool) with F. *fiche* counter, FISH[2]. Hence vb. XIX.

poop pūp stern of a ship. XV (*poupe*, *pouppe* Caxton, *po(p)e*). – OF. *pupe*, *pope* (mod. *poupe*) = Pr., Sp. *popa*, It. *poppa* :– Rom. **puppa*, for L. *puppis* stern.

poor puəɹ having few or no possessions. XIII (Laȝ.). ME. *povere*, *pouere*, *poure*, *pore* – OF. *povre*, (also dial.) *poure* (mod. *pauvre*) = Pr. *paubre*, *paure*, Sp. *pobre*, It. *povero* :– L. *pauper* (Rom. **pauperus*); see FEW and cf. POVERTY. ¶ For similar loss of *v* before *r* cf. CURFEW, KERCHIEF, LORD.

pop pɔp sb., vb., int., and adv., of imit. origin. The earliest uses (XIV), surviving dial., of sb. and vb. have reference to rapping or knocking; not recorded for abrupt explosive sound before XVI (as int. and adv. only XVII); vb. put, pass, move suddenly XVI (Skelton); (sl.) pawn XVIII (Fielding); *pop the question* XVIII; sb. effervescing beverage XIX (Southey). comps. **po·p-**CORN[1] for *popped corn* XIX (U.S.); **po·p-eyed, -eyes** (having) prominent eyes XIX; **po·p-**GUN XVII (Hobbes); **po·pping** CREASE (cricket) XVIII.

pope[1] poup the Head of the R.C. Ch. OE. *pāpa* – ecclL. *pāpa* bishop (Tertullian, Prudentius), from the time of Leo the Great (v) applied spec. to the Bishop of Rome – ecclGr. *pápas*, *papâs* bishop, patriarch, later form of *páppas* father (see PAPA). Cf. F. *pape*, Sp., Pg., It. *papa*; of CEur. range: OS. *pābos*, (M)Du. *paus*, MHG. *bābes(t)*, G. *papst*, ult. – OF. *papes*; cf. OSl. *papežĭ* from HG.). Hence **po·p**ERY the Roman Catholic religion or ecclesiastical system. XVI (Tindale). **po·p**ISH[1]. XVI.

pope[2] poup parish priest of the Orthodox Church in Russia, etc. XVII. – Russ. (OSl.) *popŭ* – WGerm. **papo* (cf. OHG. *pfaffo*) – later Gr. *pápas*; see PAPA, POPE[1].

popinjay pɔ·pindʒei (arch.) parrot XIII; vain or conceited person XVI. ME. *pape(n)iai*, *pope(n)iay*, *-gay* – AN. *papeiaye*, OF. *papegay*, *papingay* (mod. *papegai*) – Sp. *papagayo* (cf. Pr. *papagai*, Pg. *papagaio*; G. *papagei*, Du. *papegaai* are from Rom.) – Arab. *babaghā* (whence also medGr. *papagás*, Pers. *bapghā*): for intrusive *n* cf. MESSENGER; the final syll. is assim. to JAY. ¶ vars. in Eur. langs. are: OF. *papegau* (whence Sc. *papingo* XVI) = Cat. *papagal*, It. *pappagallo*, medL. *pap(p)agallus*, modGr. *papagállos*, MHG. *papegān*, medL. *papagen*, Russ. *popugái*; MLG. *papagoie*, Sw. *papegoja*, Da. *papegøie*.

poplar pɔ·pləɹ tree of the genus Populus. XIV (Wycl. Bible, Trevisa, Ch.). ME. *popler(e)* – AN. *popler*, OF. *poplier* (mod. *peuplier*, with *-ier* characteristic of tree-names), f. *pople* (mod. dial. *peuple*; whence Eng. *popple* XIV, now dial. and U.S.) = Cat. *poll*, Sp. *poblo* :– L. *pōpulus*. ¶ With the form *poplar* (XVI) cf. contemp. *briar*, *cedar*, *medlar*.

poplin pɔ·plin mixed woven fabric. XVIII. – F. †*papeline*, dubiously held to be from It. *papalina*, sb. use of fem. of *papalino* PAPAL, and to be so named because orig. manufactured at Avignon, which was a papal town from 1309 to 1791; see -INE[1]. ¶ F. *popeline* appears to be from English.

poppet pɔ·pit small person or human figure, (hence) pet XIV (Ch.); †puppet XVI; (naut.) short piece of wood XIX. Of obscure origin; based ult. on L. *pūpa*, *puppa* girl, doll; cf. PUPPET, and see -ET.

popple pɔ·pl tumble as water, boil or bubble up. XIV. prob. – (M)Du. *popelen* murmur, babble, quiver, throb, imit. origin. Hence sb. and **po·ppl**Y[1]. XIX.

poppy pɔ·pi plant of the genus Papaver. OE. *popæġ*, *papæġ*, later *popiġ* :– **papāg*, **popāg*, for **pāpau* – medL. **papāuum* (whence OF. *pavou*, mod. *pavot*), alt. of L.

papāver (whence It. *papavero*). ¶ Of wide Eur. extent, with various modifications; but the oldest IE. word for the plant (not Italic or Celtic) is repr. by G. *mohn*, Gr. *mḗkōn*, OSl. *makŭ*.

popsy-wopsy pɔ·psiwɔpsi endearing appellation for a girl. XIX. redupl. formation on dial. *pop* (f. POPPET)+-SY.

populace pɔ·pjŭləs mass of the people. XVI. – F. *populace* – It. *popolaccio*, *-azzo*, f. *popolo* PEOPLE, with pejorative suffix (:- L. *-āceus* -ACEOUS). So **popular** pɔ·pjŭləɹ pert. to the people XV; finding favour with the people XVII. – AN. *populer*, OF. *populeir* (later and mod. *populaire*) or L. *populāris*, f. *populus* PEOPLE. Hence (or – F.) **popularITY** -æ·rĭti XVII, **po·pularIZE** XVIII. **populATE**[3] pɔ·pjŭleit people, inhabit. XVI. f. pp. stem of medL. *populāre*, f. *populus*. **populA·TION** †inhabited place XVI; number of people XVII (Bacon). – late L. *populātiō(n-)* (Sedulius), f. L. *populus*; so in (O)F. **po·pulOUS** full of people. XV. – late L. *populōsus*. ¶ Cl.L. *populari* = ravage, pillage.

porcelain pɔ̄·ɹslĭn fine kind of earthenware. XVI. The earliest forms in *-ana*, *-an* are It. or immed. – It.; superseded by forms – F. *porcelaine*, earlier *pourcelaine* – It. *porcellana* (XIII, Marco Polo) Venus shell, cowrie, polished substance of this, (hence) china ware (from its resemblance to this substance), deriv. in fem. adj. form of *porcella*, dim. of *porca* sow :- L. *porca*, fem. of *porcus* swine (see PORK); the shells are said to have been so named from their resemblance to the vulva of a sow (cf. L. *porcus* 'pudendum', Varro, tr. Gr. *χοῖρος*). Cf. Sp., Pg. *porcelana*, Du. *porselein*, G. *porzellan*, Sw. *porslin*, Da. *porcellæn*.

porch pɔ̄ɹtʃ covered approach to a building XIII; *the P.*, allusively with ref. to the Stoic school XVII. – (O)F. *porche* = Pr. *porge*, It. *portico* PORTICO :- L. *porticus* colonnade, gallery, porch (rendering Gr. *στόα*; cf. STOIC), f. *porta* 'passage', PORT[2].

porcine pɔ̄·ɹsain swine-like. XVII. – F. *porcin*, *-ine* or L. *porcīnus*, f. *porcus* swine; see PORK, -INE[1].

porcupine pɔ̄·ɹkjŭpain rodent of the genus Hystrix bearing defensive spines. XIV. ME. *porc despyne*, later *porke-*, *porcupine* (cf. AL. *porcupina* XV) – OF. *porc espin* (also *porc d'espine*), mod. *porc-épic* – Pr. *porc espi(n)* = Sp. *puerco espin*, etc. :- Rom. **porcospīnus*, f. L. *porcus* pig, PORK+*spīnus* SPINE. Many vars. are found showing kinds of assim.; *porkespick* (XVI–XVII) is after the modF. form; *porpentine* (XVI–XVII) is obscure; the present form shows assim. to L. *porcus*.

pore[1] pɔ̄əɹ minute orifice in a body. XIV (Trevisa). – (O)F. *pore*, corr. to Sp., It. *poro* – L. *porus* – Gr. *póros* passage, pore, f. **por- *per- *pr̥*; see FARE, FORD, PORT. So **po·rOUS**. XIV. – (O)F. *poreux* – medL. *porōsus*. **poro·SITY**. XIV (Trevisa). – medL.

pore[2] pɔ̄əɹ look intently. XIII (King Horn). ME. *pure*, *poure*, *powre*, perh. :- OE. **pūrian*, f. **pūr-*, a mutated form of which (OE. **pȳran*) may be the source of synon. ME. *pire* (XIV). See PEER[2].

porism pɔ̄·rizm, pɔ·rizm geometrical proposition in ancient Gr. mathematics. XIV (Ch., tr. of Boethius; thereafter not before XVII). – late L. *porisma* – Gr. *pórisma* deduction, corollary, problem, f. *porízein* carry, deduce, f. *póros* way, passage; see PORE[1], -ISM. Cf. F. *porisme*.

pork pɔ̄ɹk flesh of the pig used as food XIII; †swine, pig XIV. – (O)F. *porc* = Pr., Pg., It. *porco*, Sp. *puerco*, Rum. *porc* – L. *porcus* swine, hog (see FARROW[1]). Hence **po·rkER**[1] pig raised for food. XVII.

pornographer pɔ̄ɹnɔ·grəfəɹ one who writes of obscene subjects. XIX. f. F. *pornographe* – Gr. *pornográphos*, f. *pórnē* prostitute; see -GRAPHER. So **pornoGRA·PHIC**, **-O·GRAPHY**.

porphyry pɔ̄·ɹfĭri beautiful red or purple stone. XIV. Three types are found: (i) *porfurie*, *-firie* (Ch.) – AN. **porfurie*, **-firie* = OF. *porfire*, mod. *porphyre*, corr. to It. *porfiro*, *-fido*, Sp., Pg. *porfido*, (ii) *purfire*, *porphire*, (iii) *porphyry*; all ult. – medL. *porphyreum*, for L. *porphyrītēs* – Gr. *porphurítes*, f. *pórphuros* PURPLE.

porpoise pɔ̄·ɹpəs small cetaceous mammal, Phocæna communis. XIV. ME. *porpays*, *-poys*, *-pas* – OF. *po(u)rpois*, *-peis*, *-pais* :- Rom. **porcopiscis* (f. *porcus* swine, PORK+*piscis* FISH), for L. *porcus marinus* 'sea hog' (whence Sp. *puerco marino*, It. *porco marino*; cf. G. *meerschwein*, whence F. *marsouin*); forms with the els. reversed are It. †*pesce porco*, Pg. *peixe porco* :- Rom. **pisciporcus*.

porrect pɔre·kt (techn.) stretch out XV; put forward XVIII. f. *porrect-*, pp. stem of L. *porrigere*, f. *por-* = PRO-[1]+*regere* stretch, direct, f. IE. **reg-* (see RIGHT). So **porre·CTION**. XVII. – L.

porridge pɔ·ridʒ †pottage or soup XVI; soft food made with oatmeal XVII. alt. of POTTAGE, intermediate forms being repr. by *podech* (XVI), *podditch*, *-idge*. ¶ Cf. next, and dial. or vulgar *imperence*, *moral*, *geraway*, *geron*, for *impudence*, *model*, *get away*, *get on*.

porringer pɔ·rindʒəɹ bowl for liquid food. XVI. alt., through the var. †*poddinger* (XV), of (dial.) *pottinger*, †*potinger* (XV), †*poteger* – (O)F. *potager*, f. *potage*; see POTAGE, -ER[2]. ¶ For intrusive *n* cf. HARBINGER, etc.; for change of *t* to *r* cf. prec.

port[1] pɔ̄ɹt harbour, haven; town having a harbour. OE. *port* – L. *portus* (see FORD), rel. to *porta* (see next). In ME. prob. a new word – (O)F. *port* = Pr. *port*, Sp. *puerto*, Pg., It. *porto* :- L. *portu-s*.

port[2] pɔ̄ɹt gate, gateway, spec. of a city or walled town XIII (Cursor M.); opening in the side of a ship XIV (Gower). – (O)F. *porte*

= Pr., Pg., It. *porta*, Sp. *puerta*, Rum. *poartă* :– L. *porta* (cf. prec.). Hence **po·rt**HOLE. XVI.

port[3] pɔ̄ɹt (arch.) carriage, bearing XIV (Ch.); †style of living, state XVI. – (O)F. *port*, f. *porter* carry, bear = Pr., Sp. *portar*, It. *portare* :– L. *portāre* (if orig. transport, bring into port), f. *portus* PORT[1]. Hence **po·rt**LY[1] †of dignified bearing, imposing XVI (Skelton); large and corpulent XVI (Sh.).

port[4] pɔ̄ɹt left side of a vessel looking forward. XVII (also in APORT; but no doubt earlier, cf. the vb.). prob. orig. the side turned towards the port (PORT[1]) or place of lading (cf. LARBOARD). Hence vb. put (the helm) to port. XVI.

port[5] pɔ̄ɹt red (also white) wine of Portugal. XVII. Short for †*Oporto wine*, †*Port O Port wine*, later †*Oporto*, †*Porto* (cf. F. *porto*, for *vin de porto*, *vin d'Oporto*), prop. wine from Oporto (Pg. *O Porto* 'the port'; see PORT[1]), the chief port of shipment for Portuguese wines.

portable pɔ̄·ɹtəbl capable of being carried. XIV. – (O)F. *portable* or late L. *portābilis*, f. *portāre* carry; see PORT[3], -ABLE. So **po·rt**AGE transportation, carriage; mariner's venture in cargo. XV. – F. = It. *portaggio* (in medL. *portāgium*, *portāticum*).

portal[1] pɔ̄·ɹtəl stately doorway or gateway. XIV. – OF. *portal* – medL. *portāle*, sb. use of n. of *portālis*, f. *porta* PORT[2]; see -AL[1].

portal[2] pɔ̄·ɹtəl (anat.) pert. to the porta or transverse fissure of the liver; *p. vein*, vena portæ. XIX. – modL. *portālis*, f. L. *porta* PORT[2]; see -AL[1].

portas, portous pɔ̄·ɹtəs (hist.) portable medieval breviary XIV (PPl.); spec. in Sc. law XV. Also *porthous*, *portehors* – OF. *portehors*, f. *porter* carry (see PORT[3]) + *hors* out of doors (:– L. *forīs*, loc. of *forēs* DOOR), corr. to medL. *portiforium*.

portcullis pɔ̄ɹtkʌ·lis grating sliding up and down in grooves at the side of a gateway in a fortress. XIV. ME. *port colice*, *-coles*, *-(e)cules*, *porcules* – OF. *porte coleïce*, i.e. *porte* door (PORT[2]), *col(e)īce*, *coulice* (cf. COULISSE), fem. of *couleïs* gliding, sliding :– Rom. **cōlātīcius*, f. L. *cōlāt-*, *cōlāre* filter.

portend pɔ̄ɹte·nd presage, foreshow. XV. – L. *portendere* (like *ostendere*, a term of augury), f. **por-* = *prŏ-*, PRO-[1] + *tendere* stretch, TEND[1]. So **po·rtent** ominous sign XVI; prodigious thing XVIII. – L. *portentum* strange sign, monster, f. *portendere*. Formerly str. *porte·nt*. **porte·nt**OUS. XVI. – L. *portentōsus*.

porter[1] pɔ̄·ɹtəɹ door-keeper. XIII. – AN. *porter*, (O)F. *portier* = Pr. *portier*, Sp. *portero*, Rum. *portar* – late L. (Vulgate) *portārius*, f. *porta* PORT[1]; see -ER[2].

porter[2] pɔ̄·ɹtəɹ bearer. XIV (Wycl. Bible, PPl.). – OF. *port(e)our* (mod. *porteur*) = Pr., Sp. *portador*, etc. :– medL. *portātōrem*, f. *portāre* carry; see PORT[3], -ER[1], -OR[1].

porter[3] pɔ̄·ɹtəɹ kind of dark-brown beer. XVIII. Earlier *porter* or *porter's ale* (Swift), presumably so named because drunk chiefly by porters and the like. Comp. **po·rter**HOUSE (U.S.) house where porter and other malt liquors are sold; transf. of steaks, etc. supplied there.

portfolio pɔ̄ɹtfou·liou case for keeping papers XVIII; such a case for state documents, (hence) office of a minister of state XIX. Earlier *porto folio*, *portefolio* – It. *portafogli*, f. *porta*, imper. of *portare* carry (see PORT[3]) + *fogli*, pl. of *foglio* leaf, FOIL[1]; alt. by assim. to F. *portefeuille* (XVI).

portico pɔ̄·ɹtikou roofed walk supported on columns. XVII (Jonson). – It. *portico* :– L. *porticus* PORCH.

portière pɔ̄·ɹtiɛəɹ curtain hung over a doorway. XIX (Thackeray). F., f. *porte* door, PORT[2] + *-ière* (:– L. *-āria* -ARY).

portion pɔ̄·ɹʃən part allotted, share XIII (Cursor M.); part of a whole XIV. – OF. *porcion*, (also mod.) *portion* = Pr., Sp. *porcion*, It. *porzione* – L. *portiō(n-)*, attested first in phr. *prō portiōne* portionally, in PROPORTION. So **po·rtion** vb. APPORTION XIV (R. Mannyng); dower XVIII. – OF. *portionner* (medL. *portiōnāre*), f. the sb.

portmanteau pɔ̄ɹtmæ·ntou case for carrying clothing, etc. when travelling. XVI. – F. *portemanteau* official who carries a prince's mantle, valise, clothes-rack, f. *porter* carry (see PORT[3]) + *manteau* MANTLE. Many vars. were formerly current, e.g. *-mantel*, *-mantu*, *-mantua*, *-manty*, *-mantuan*.

portrait pɔ̄·ɹtrĭt delineation of a person (formerly of any object). XVI. – F. *portrait*, sb. use of pp. of OF. *portraire* picture, depict (whence **portray** pɔ̄ɹtrei· XIV), f. *por-* (:– L. *prō* PRO-[1]) + *traire* draw (:– Rom. **tragere*, for L. *trahere*). So **po·rtrait**URE. XIV. – OF. *portraiture*, f. pp. as above.

portreeve pɔ̄·ɹtrīv (now local) chief officer of a town (mayor; later, bailiff). OE. *portġerēfa*, f. *port* town (prob. transf. use of PORT[1]) + *ġerēfa* REEVE[1].

pose[1] pouz A. †suppose or assume XIV (Ch.); lay down (a claim, etc.) XVI; B. place in or assume an attitude XIX. – (O)F. *poser* :– late L. *pausāre* cease, PAUSE (whence also Pr. *pausar* place, rest, Sp. *posar* rest, lodge, lay down, It. *posare* lay down, pose (a model), refl. rest); in Rom. this vb. took over the senses of L. *pōnere*, pt. *posuī*, pp. *positum* place (see POSITION) and became its regular repr. (cf. *appose*, *compose*, *depose*, *dispose*, *expose*, *impose*, *interpose*, *oppose*, *repose*, *suppose*, *transpose*), the application of *pōnere* being specialized in the sense 'lay eggs' (cf. F. *pondre*). So **pose** sb. attitude. XIX (Lady Morgan). – F. *pose*, f. the vb.

pose² pouz †interrogate XVI (Tindale); perplex, nonplus XVI (Donne). Aphetic of APPOSE. Hence **po·ser¹** examiner XVI (Harrison); puzzling problem XVIII (Sheridan).

posh pɔʃ (sl.) tiptop, 'swell'. XX. perh. adj. use of sl. sb. *posh* (i) money, (ii) dandy (XIX), of unkn. origin.

posit pɔ·zit (chiefly in pp.) situate, place; assume, lay down as a basis. XVII. f. *posit-*, pp. stem of L. *pōnere* place. So **posi·tion** pɔzi·ʃən †laying down, affirmation, proposition stated XV; place occupied: (gram.) situation of a vowel in a syllable XVI; posture, attitude XVIII. – (O)F. or L., f. *posit-*, rendering Gr. θέσις THESIS, θέμα THEME. **po·sitive** formally or explicitly stated XIII (Cursor M.); unqualified XV; dealing with fact XVI; affirmative, additive)(*negative* XVII. – (O)F. or L. **po·sitivism** (philos.) 1854. – F. *positivisme* (Comte), for earlier *philosophie positive* (1830). **positron** pɔ·zitrən, f. POSI(TIVE, ELEC)TRON. XX.

posse pɔ·si A. potentiality)(*esse* (often in phr. *in p.* potential(ly) XVI; B. body of men that a sheriff may call to arms, (hence) armed force, strong band XVII. – medL. sb. use of L. *posse* be able (see POTENT¹); in A from scholastic terminology, in B for *posse comitātus* 'force (power) of the COUNTY'.

possess pəze·s †occupy, inhabit; hold as property; put in possession. XV. – OF. *possesser*, f. L. *possess-*, pp. stem of *possīdēre*, f. *potis* (see POTENT) + *sīdere*, rel. to *sedēre* SIT. Earlier †*possede*. XIV–XVII. – (O)F. *posséder*. So **possession** pəze·ʃən XIV (Rolle). – (O)F. or L. **posse·ssive** (gram.) XVI (Palsgr.). – L. *possessīvus* (Quintilian), tr. Gr. *κτητική (πτῶσις* case*)*.

posset pɔ·sit (hist.) drink of hot milk curdled with ale, etc. XV. Of unkn. origin.

possible pɔ·sibl that can or may be. XIV (Rolle). – (O)F. *possible* or L. *possibilis*, f. *posse* be; see POTENT, -IBLE. **possibi·lity.** XIV (Ch.). – (O)F. or late L. ¶ *Impossible* is earlier (XIII).

possum pɔ·səm Aphetic of OPOSSUM; now esp. in colloq. phr. (orig. U.S.) *play p.* pretend to be disabled, with ref. to the opossum's feigning death when attacked. XVII.

post¹ poust stout piece of timber set upright. OE. *post* – L. *postis*, perh. f. *por*- PRO-¹ + base of *stare* STAND; prob. reinforced in ME. from OF. and MLG., MDu. Hence **post** vb.¹ affix to a post. XVII; whence **poster¹** pou·stəɹ bill or placard posted or displayed. XIX (Dickens, 1838); app. on the false analogy of *blotter, poker, roller*.

post² poust †men with horses stationed along a route to carry the king's 'packet' or other letters from stage to stage; †courier, postman; †mail-coach, packet-boat XVI; single dispatch of letters, the mail; short for *post-office*, public department having the conveyance of letters XVII; short for *post-paper*, size of writing-paper, orig. bearing as water-mark a postman's horn XVIII. – F. *poste* – It. *posta* (whence also Sp., Pg. *posta*) – Rom. **posta*, contr. of *posita*, fem. pp. of *pōnere* (see POSITION). Used advb., with post-horses, with haste XVI; e.g. *ride p.*, orig. in phr. *ride in p.* (F. *chevaucher en poste*). Hence or – F. *poster*, **post** vb.² XVI. **po·stage** carriage of letters XVI; charge for this XVII. **po·stal¹**. XIX. – F. Comps. **po·stcard²** 1870 (1 October), after G. *feldpostkarte* (25 June 1870), which was preceded by *postblatt* (1865) and *korrespondenzkarte* (1869). **post-ha·ste** †speed in travelling XVI (Ascham); adv. with all haste XVI (Sh.). From the old direction in the endorsement of letters (*In hast*) *hast post hast*, an exhortation to the post or courier to hasten (i.e. POST sb.², and imper. of the vb. HASTE), later apprehended as *post* sb. used attrib. and *haste* sb. **po·stma:ster¹** one in charge of posts or a post office. XVI; cf. G. *postmeister*, F. *maître des postes*; **post office.** XVII (repl. *letter office*).

post³ poust soldier's station XVI; position taken up by a body of soldiers; position of employment XVII; (naut.) position as full-grade captain XVIII. – F. *poste* (m.) – It. *posto* (whence also Du. *post*, G. *posten*) – Rom. **postu-m*, contr. of popL. *positum*, pp. of *pōnere* (cf. prec.).

post⁴ poust pile of hand-made paper fresh from the mould. XVIII. – G. *posten* parcel, batch, lot – It. *posto* POST³.

post⁵ poust bugle-call warning of the hour for retiring for the night. XIX. prob. short for *call to post* or the like (POST³, first sense).

post⁶ poust L. prep. & adv., earlier *poste*, **posti*, 'after', which has cogns. in Balto-Sl., Indo-Iran., Alb., and Tokh., current in phrases such as *p. bellum* after the war, *p. meridiem* after midday, *post partum* after childbirth. See also POSTERIOR, POSTHUMOUS, PREPOSTEROUS, and next.

post- poust comb. form of POST⁶ as in **postcommu·nion** (liturg.) part of the Eucharistic service following the communion XV (Caxton) – medL.; earlier †*post common* XIV; cf. OF. *pocumenion*; **post-da·te** affix a later date to. XVII (Donne); cf. F. *post-dater*; **po·st-obit** taking effect after a person's death. XVIII; **postpone** pous^t^pou·n, pəs- put off, defer XVI (Dunbar); place after XVII. orig. Sc. – L. *postpōnere*. So **postposi·tion** †(Sc.) postponement; placing after. XVII. **postprandial** -præ·ndiəl occurring after dinner. XIX (Coleridge); L. *prandium*. **postscript** pou·s^t^skript something added after the signature to a letter. XVI. – L. *postscriptum*, sb. use of n. pp. of *postscrībere*.

poste restante pɔstreˈstɑ̃t direction written on a letter which is to remain at the post office till called for; in Eng. use also, department of a post office where such letters are left. XVIII (occas. anglicized †-*tant*). F., '*post* remaining' (see REST).

posterior pɔstiəˈriəɹ latter)(*prior* XVI (More); hinder)(*anterior* XVII; †sb. pl. descendants XVI; (after late L. n. pl. *posteriōra*) hinder parts, buttocks XVII. – L. *posterior*, compar. of *posterus* following, future, f. *post*; see POST[6], -IOR. So **poster**ITY pɔsteˈriti descendants coll. – F. – L.

postern pouˈstəɹn back or side door. XIII. – OF. *posterne* (mod. *poterne*), alt. of *posterle* :– late L. *posterula* (sc. *janua* gate, *via* way), dim. f. *posterus* that is behind (see prec.).

posthumous pɔˈstjuməs born after the father's death; appearing or occurring after death. XVII. f. L. *postumus* last of all, spec. applied as in first sense, used as superl. of *post* after (see POST[6], POST-), later assoc. with *humus* ground, *humāre* bury, whence the sp. with *h*. Earlier †*posthume* (XVI, Sylvester).

postil pɔˈstil marginal note or comment, series of these. XV. – OF. *postille* = Sp. *postila*, It. *postilla* :– medL. *postilla*, conjectured by Du Cange to be L. *post illa* (sc. *verba*) after those words, i.e. of the text, used as a direction to a scribe.

postil(l)ion pŏstiˈljən †forerunner XVI (Sidney); post-boy, swift messenger; one who rides the near horse of a pair XVII. – F. *postillon* – It. *postiglione* post's boy, f. *posta* POST[2] + -*iglione* :– L. -*iliō*(*n*-).

postmaster[2] pouˈstmɑ̀ːstəɹ scholar of Merton College, Oxford. XVI. Of unkn. origin; medL. *portiōnista* one who receives a prescribed 'portion' has been suggested.

postulant pɔˈstjŭlənt petitioner, candidate (spec. for admission to a religious community). XVIII (Chesterfield). – F. *postulant* or L. *postulant*-, -*āns*, prp. of *postulāre* demand; see next.

postulate pɔˈstjŭlət †demand XVI; proposition claimed to be granted, (geom.) problem of self-evident nature XVII. – L. *postulātum* (also used), sb. use of n. pp. of *postulāre*, prob. f. base of *poscere* (see PRAY) with formative as in PETULANT. So vb. pɔˈstjŭleit XVI.

posture pɔˈstʃəɹ, -tj- †position (Bacon); disposition of parts, attitude (Sh.). XVII. – F. *posture* (Montaigne) – It. *postura* :– L. *positūra* position, situation, f. *posit*-, pp. stem of *pōnere* place; see POSITION, -URE. Cf. earlier †*positure* – F. †*positure* or L.

posy pouˈzi A. (arch.) motto, orig. line of verse; B. nosegay. XVI. contr. form of POESY.

pot pɔt round or cylindrical vessel used as a container. Late OE. *pott*, corr. to OFris., (M)LG., (M)Du. *pot* (whence G. *pott*, Icel. *pottr*, etc.) – popL. **pottus* (whence (O)F., Pr. *pot*), perh. alt. of L. *pōtus* drink, in late L. drinking-cup (Venantius Fortunatus), f. *pōt*- (see POTION); prob. reinforced in ME. from OF. ¶ The various Celtic forms are from Eng. or F. The north. word meaning deep hole, pit (XIV) may be identical or may be of Scand. origin; cf. Sw. dial. *putt*, *pott* water-hole, abyss; so prob. **poˈt-**HOLE. XIX. comb. **poˈt-boiˑler** something done merely to gain a livelihood; earlier *pot-boiling* (XVIII); cf. F. *faire bouillir le pot* provide an income; **poˈt**HOOK hook to hang over a fireplace XV; hooked character in writing XVII. **poˈt-huˑnter,** †perh. sycophant, parasite XVI (Nashe, Greene); sportsman who shoots anything he comes across XVIII; (sl.) one who competes in a contest merely for the prize XIX. **pot-**LUCK pɔˈtlʌˈk one's chance of what may be in the pot ready for a meal XVI (Nashe); cf. F. *la fortune du pot*. **poˈt**SHERD (arch.) fragment of earthenware. XIV (-*schoord*, -*scarth*). **pot shot** shot taken at game merely to provide something for the pot, shot aimed directly at something within reach. XIX. **pot-wall**ER[1] pɔˈtwɔːləɹ householder qualified to vote as having a separate fire-place. XVIII. lit. 'pot-boiler'; alt. to **pot-walloper** pɔˈt-wɔːləpəɹ (XVIII) by assim. to WALLOP, now the usual form.

potable pouˈtəbl drinkable. XVI. – F. *potable* or late L. *potābilis*, f. *pōtāre*; see POTION, -ABLE. So **pot**AˈTION. XV. – OF. – L.

potage pɔˈtɑ̃ʒ soup. XVI. – (O)F. *potage* POTTAGE.

potash pɔˈtæʃ (pl.) lixiviated ashes of vegetables evaporated in pots XVII; potassium carbonate (which these contain in crude form); hydroxide or monoxide of potassium XVIII. – Du. *potasschen* (mod. *potasch*); see POT, ASH[2]. So F. *potasse*, whence **potass** pŏtæˈs XVIII. **potassa** pŏtæˈsə modL. form, appropriated to potassium monoxide by Davy, who (1807) coined the name **potassium** pətæˈsiəm, on the model of *magnesia* / *magnesium*, *soda* / *sodium*, to designate the metallic element which is the basis of potash.

potato pəteiˈtou A. (tuber of) Batatas edulis, now dist. as sweet or Spanish potato; B. (tuber of) Solanum tuberosum, widely cultivated for food. XVI. – Sp. *patata* – native name (*batata*) in Hayti for sense A; the transference to sense B was due to the likeness of the two plants in producing esculent tubers.

potent[1] pouˈtənt powerful. XV. – L *potent*-, *potēns*, prp. of **potēre*, *posse* be powerful or able, for *potis esse*; the base **pot*- is repr. also by Skr. *pátis* lord, possessor, husband, Gr. *pósis* spouse, L. *hos|pes*, -*pit*- HOST[1], Lith. *pàt* spouse, Goth. *brūþ|faþs* bridegroom, *hunda|faþs* commander of a century, centurion; see -ENT. So **poˈten**TATE[1]. XIV. – (O)F. *potentat* or L. *potentātus*, f. *potent*-. **potent**IAL pŏteˈnʃəl possible, latent XIV (Trevisa; rare before XVI; in spec. scientific uses XIX); (gram.) of a mood XVI. – OF. *potencial* (now *-tiel*) or late L. *potentiālis* (earlier *potentiāliter* adv.), f. *potentia*, whence **po·t**ENCY XVI, earlier **po·t**ENCE XV (partly – OF. *potence*). **potentilla** poutenti·lə genus of Rosaceæ (Linnæus). XVI. medL., f. L. *potent-*, *-ēns* POTENT + dim. suffix *-illa*; applied early to Garden Valerian, in XVI to Potentilla anserina (silver-weed, goose-grass).

potent[2] pou·tənt (her., of a cross) having the limbs terminating in crutch-heads. XVII (Guillim). attrib. use of †*potent* crutch (XIV, PPl., Ch.), alt. of (O)F. *potence* supporting piece, crutch, gallows (= Sp. *potenza* crutch) – L. *potentia* power, in medL. crutch (XII), f. *potent-*, *potēns*; see prec.

pot(h)een pɔtī·n whisky distilled privately in Ireland. XIX. – Ir. *poitín* (dim. of *pota* POT), in full *uisge poitín* 'little-pot whisky'.

pother pʌ·ðəɹ, pɔ·ðəɹ choking smoke or dusty atmosphere; commotion. XVI. Also *pudder*; the rhymes with *other*, *mother*, and the like point to an orig. stem vowel *ō*, but no source is known; perh. infl. by *bother*.

potion pou·ʃən draught of liquid medicine or poison. XIII. – (O)F. *potion* – L. *pōtiō(n-)* drink, poisonous draught, f. *pōt-*, stem of *pōtāre* drink, *pōtus* having drunk, f. IE. **pō(i)-* **pī̆-*, repr. also by Skr. *pāyin* drinking, Gr. *pé|pōka* I have drunk, *pôma*, *pósis* drink, draught, Skr. *pītás*, *pītíš* drink, and the vbs. Gr. *pī́nein*, OSl. *piti*, Skr. *píbati*, OIr. *ibim*, L. *bibere* (cf. BIBULOUS), for **pibere*; see -TION.

pot-pourri poupu·ri mixture of dried petals kept for perfume XVIII; musical or literary medley XIX. F., 'rotten pot', i.e. *pot* POT, pp. of *pourrir* rot; tr. Sp. OLLA PODRIDA.

pott pɔt var. sp. of POT applied (after F. *papier au pot*) to a certain size of printing-paper, orig. bearing the watermark of a pot.

pottage pɔ·tidʒ dish of vegetables and/or meat boiled to softness XIII; †oatmeal porridge XVII. ME. *potage* – (O)F. *potage* lit. 'what is put in a pot', f. *pot* POT; see -AGE.

potter[1] pɔ·təɹ maker of pots. Late OE. *pottere*; see -ER[1]. Hence or – (O)F. *poterie* **po·tt**ERY potter's factory XV (Caxton), pl. *Potteries* as the name of a district; potter's art, product of this XVIII; cf. AL. *potaria*.

potter[2] pɔ·təɹ (dial.) poke again and again XVI; meddle XVII; (dial.) perplex, bother; trifle, dabble XVIII; move about idly or aimlessly XIX. frequent. of (dial.) *pote*, OE. *potian* thrust, push, PUT[1] (= MLG. *poten*, whence Icel. *pota*, Sw. *påta*); see -ER[4].

pouch pautʃ small bag XIV (Ch.); bag-like cavity in an animal body XV. – ONF. *pouche* (cf. AL. *pocha*, *pucha* XIII), var. of (O)F. *poche* bag, pouch, (now) pocket; cf. POKE[1].

poult poult young of domestic fowl and game-birds. XV. Late ME. *pult*, contr. of *poulet* PULLET. So (arch.) **pou·lter.** XIV. – OF. *pouletier*, f. *poulet*; extended to **pou·lter**ER[1] dealer in poultry XVII, prob. after *poultery*, earlier *pulletrie*, vars. of **poultry** pou·ltri domestic fowls XIV (Ch.); †poultry-farm, -yard, -market (surviving as a street-name in London) XV. – OF. *pouletrie*, f. *pouletier*; cf. AL. *pulletārius*, *poletārius*, *poletria* (XIII); see -ER[1], -RY. ¶ The phonology is as in *boult*, *coulter*, *poultice*, *shoulder*.

poultice pou·ltis soft mass of bread, etc. applied as an emollient, etc. XVI. orig. pl. *pultes*, later taken as sg. – L. *pultes*, pl. of *puls*, *pult-* pottage, pap; see PULSE[2].

pounce[1] pauns claw of a bird of prey, spec. anterior claw of a hawk)(*talon* XV; †stamp or punch, hole pinked in a garment XVI. perh. shortening of PUNCHEON. So **pounce** vb.[1] pink. XIV (Ch.). Hence **pounce** vb[2]. †seize, as a bird of prey XVII; seize *upon* suddenly XVIII; whence **pounce** sb.[2] act of pouncing XIX.

pounce[2] pauns finely powdered sandarac, etc. used to prevent ink from spreading; stamping-powder. XVIII. – (O)F. *ponce* = Sp. *pomez*, Pg. *pomes*, It. *pomice* :– popL. **pōmicem*, for L. *pūmicem*, nom. *pūmex* PUMICE. So **pounce** vb.[3] smooth with pumice or pounce; transfer (a design) with pounce; †powder (esp. the face). XVI. – (O)F. *poncer* polish or erase with pumice, †powder (the face), f. *ponce*.

pound[1] paund measure of weight; English money of account (orig. pound weight of silver). OE. *pund* (pl. *pund*) = OFris., OS. *pund* (MDu. *pont*, Du. *pond*), OHG. *phunt* (G. *pfund*), ON., Goth. *pund* :– CGerm. **pundo* (whence Finnish *punta*) – L. *pondō* (indeclinable) pound weight, orig. instr. abl. of **pondos* (*libra pondō* pound by weight), rel. to **pondes-*, whence L. *ponder-*, *pondus* weight, also to *pendere* weigh, *pendēre* hang; see PENDENT, POISE. ¶ One of the earliest Germ. adoptions from L., prob. contemp. with MINT[1]. The flexionless pl. is often retained with a sum following, and regularly in attrib. use (e.g. *two p. ten*, *five-p. note*).

pound[2] paund enclosure, esp. for cattle; place of confinement. XIV (Wycl.). Earlier only in the comps. ME. *pundbreche* XII breaking open (see BREACH) of a pound, OE. *pundfeald* PINFOLD; of unkn. origin. Hence vb. shut up, confine (cf. IMPOUND). XV.

pound[3] paund break down and crush as with a pestle OE.; strike heavily XVII; move with heavy steps, proceed heavily XIX. Late OE. *pūnian*, ME. *poune* (till XVII), also *ġepūnian*, f. **pūn-* (whence also Du. *puin*, LG. *pün* rubbish), of which no further cogns. are known. ¶ For the final *d*, which appears XVI, cf. ASTOUND, BOUND, COMPOUND[1], *gownd* for GOWN, HIND[1], HOREHOUND, RIBBAND, SOUND[2].

poundage[1] pau·ndidʒ duty of so much per pound sterling. XIV (PPl.). f. POUND[1]+-AGE.

poundage[2] pau·ndidʒ charge for impounded cattle. XVI. f. POUND[2]+-AGE.

pour pōəɹ emit in a stream. XIII. Of unkn. origin. The earlier *pur*, *poure*, *powre*, later *power*, are reflected in mod. dial. pronunc. pauəɹ, which is found in rhymes from Pope to Tennyson and Swinburne, though the two latter show also pōəɹ; the present standard pronunc. is indicated as early as XV by the sp. *pore*, the development of which is unexplained.

pourparler puərpā·ɹlei informal discussion. XVIII. F., sb. use of OF. *po(u)rparler* discuss, f. *po(u)r-* (intensive), PRO-[1]+*parler* speak (see PARLOUR).

pourpoint puə·ɹpoint (hist.) doublet. XV (Lydg.). – OF. *po(u)rpoint*, orig. pp. (as in *gambais p.*) of *pourpoindre* perforate, quilt, f. *pour* (cf. PRO-[1]), substituted for *par* (L. *per*)+*poindre* :– L. *pungere* (see PUNCTURE).

pout paut protrude the lips, in displeasure, XIV. Of unkn. origin; perh. repr. OE. **pūtian*, f. **pūt-* be inflated, which appears to be the base of Sw. dial. *puta* be inflated, Sw., Norw. *puta* pad, Da. *pude* cushion, pillow; cf. prec. Hence **pou·tER**[1] breed of pigeon capable of inflating the crop. XVIII.

poverty pɔ·vəɹti condition of being poor. XII. ME. *poverte* – (i) OF. *poverte* :– L. *paupertās*; this type survived till XVI as *povert*; (ii) OF. *poverté* (mod. *pauvreté*) = Pr. *paubretat*, Sp. *pobredad*, It. *povertà* :– L. *paupertātem*, *-tās*, f. *pauper* POOR; see -TY. ¶ Sc. *poortith* (XVI) repr. OF. *povertet*, with loss of *v* as in POOR and retention of final þ of AN. as in *dainteth*, *plenteth*; see -ETH[2].

powder pau·dəɹ solid matter in minute particles XIII (Cursor M.); gunpowder XIV. – (O)F. *poudre*, earlier *pol(d)re* = Pr. *po(l)dra*, Sp. *polvora*, Rum. *pulbere* :– L. *pulverem*, nom. *pulvis* dust (whence Pr. *pols*, Sp., It. *polvo*, Pg. *po*), rel. to POLLEN; cf. PULVERIZE. So vb. (in earliest use, season, salt). XIII. – (O)F. *poudrer*, or f. the sb.

power pau·əɹ A. dominion, rule, authority XIII; ability XIV; B. body of armed men XIII (RGlouc., Cursor M.); one possessed of authority XIV; deity, divinity XVI; C. (math., etc.) XVI (Billingsley, Digges). ME. *poer*, *pouer* poē·r, puē·r – AN. *poer*, *po(u)air*, OF. *poeir*, later *pooir*, *povoir* (mod. *pouvoir*) = Pr., Sp. *poder*, It. *potere*, sb. use of infs. *poeir*, etc. :– Rom. **potēre*, superseding L. *posse* be able, f. **pot-* (see POTENT); by shift of stress puē·r became pū·ēr, whence pau·əɹ. Hence **pow·erFUL**[1]. XIV.

powwow pau·wau priest or medicine man of N. Amer. Indians; magical rites held by them XVII; conference of Indians, hence gen. congress, palaver XIX. Earlier *powah*, *paw(w)aw*, *powow* – Narragansett (Algonquian) *powah·*, *powwaw·* he dreams, (hence) magician; the two syllables were assimilated early. Hence vb. XVII.

pox pɔks disease marked by pocks, spec. syphilis. XVI. alt. sp. of *pocks*, pl. of POCK; so *chicken-pox*, *cow-pox*, SMALLPOX.

pozz(u)olana pɔts(w)ŏlā·nə volcanic ash. XVIII. It., sb. use of fem. adj. (sc. *terra* earth) pert. to *Pozzuoli* (:– L. *Puteolī* 'little springs', pl. of dim. of *puteus* PIT), town near Naples (Italy) in the neighbourhood of Mount Vesuvius.

practicable præ·ktikəbl that can be carried out, used, etc. XVII (earlier †*practisable* XVI). – F. *praticable*, f. *pratiquer* put into practice, use, f. *pratique*; see below and -ABLE. So **pra·ctICAL** pert. to practice or action (opp. to theory) XVII, which superseded **pra·ctIC** XIV (rare before XVI). – F. †*practique*, var. of *pratique*, or late L. *practicus* – Gr. *praktikós* concerned with action, f. **prak-* (see PRAXIS).

practice præ·ktis scheming, machination; (habitual or continuous) performance; exercise of a profession; (arith.) compendious method of multiplication by aliquot parts (ult. repr. *practica Italica* 'Italian methods', as being first introduced by Italian merchants). XVI. f. *practise*, after ADVICE / *advise*, *device*/*devise*; superseded †**pra·ctIC** (XIV) (Ch., Trevisa). – OF. *practique* (mod. *pratique*) – medL. *practica* – Gr. *praktikḗ*, sb. use of fem. of *praktikós*. **practise** præ·ktis perform (now habitually) XV; implied earlier in **pra·ctisER**[1] XIV (Ch., PPl.). – OF. *pra(c)tiser* or medL. *practizāre* (AL. XIV), alt. of *practicāre*. The change from the earlier str. *practi·se* to *pra·ctise* involved the change of final z to s. So **practitioner** prækti·ʃənəɹ one engaged in the practice of an art, esp. medicine. XVI. Extension with -ER[1] of **practi·CIAN** (XV; chiefly Sc.); cf. dial. *musicianer*, †*physicianer*.

prad præd (sl.) horse. XVIII. – (with metathesis) Du. *paard* – medL. *paraverēdus* PALFREY.

præ- prī see PRE-.

præcipe prī·sipi (leg.) writ requiring something to be done. XV. First of the opening words of the writ, *præcipe quod reddat* enjoin that he render . . ; imper. of *præcipere* (see PRECEPT).

præmunire prīmjunaiə·ri (leg.) in full *p. facias* name of a writ (Stat. 16 Richard II) derived from a formula in the text of it. XV. L. *præmunīre* fortify or protect in front, in medL. (by assoc. with *præmonēre*; see PREMONITION) forewarn, admonish; the words of the writ (1392–3, 16 Richard II) were 'precipimus quod per bonos et legales homines de balliva tua *premunire facias* prefatum propositum quod tunc sit coram nobis' (*that you have* the aforesaid *warned* to appear before us).

prænomen prīnou·mĕn name preceding the nomen, personal name. XVIII. L., f. *præ* PRE-+*nōmen* NAME.

præpostor, pre- prīpɔ·stɔ̄ɹ prefect or monitor at some public schools. XVIII. Syncopated form of *præpositor* PREPOSITOR.

prætor, U.S. **pretor** prī·tɔ̄ɹ magistrate of ancient Rome. XV (Wyntoun). – F. *préteur* or L. *prætor* (*-ōr-*), dubiously analysed as **præitor* 'one who goes before', f. *præ* PRE- + pp. stem of *īre* go + *-or* -OR[1]. So **prætor**IAN prītɔ̄·riən. XV. – L.

pragmatic prægmæ·tik relating to affairs of a state, etc.; †busy, active, officious. XVII (sb. XVI). – late L. *prāgmaticus* (in *pragmatica sanctio*, Codex Justiniani; earlier 'skilled in affairs', Cicero) – Gr. *prāgmatikós*, f. *prāgmat-*, *prâgma* act, deed, affair, f. *prāk-* of *prā́ttein* do. Also (earlier) **pragma·ti**CAL. XVI. So **pra·gmat**ISM (philos.). XIX (W. James 1898); whence in F. and G.; hence **pra·gmat**IST XX (earlier XVII in sense 'pragmatical person').

prairie prɛə·ri great treeless tract of grassland. XVIII. – F. *prairie*, OF. *pra(i)erie* = Sp. *praderia*, It. *prateria* :– Rom.**prātāria*, f. L. *prātum* meadow; see -RY.

praise preiz express the worth of, speak highly of XIII (RGlouc., Cursor M.); (dial.) value, appraise XIV. – OF. *preisier* price, value, prize, praise = Pr. *prezar*, Cat. *prehar*, It. *prezzare* :– late L. *pretiāre*, f. L. *pretium* PRICE; cf. PRIZE[1]. Superseded ME. *herie*, OE. *herian*; in XIV *lose*, *alose* (– OF. *aloser*, f. *los* praise :– L. *laudēs*, pl. of *laus*) were also in use. Hence **praise** sb. XV; superseding ME. *los* and *price*, OE. *herung*; whence **prai·se**WO:RTHY XVI, which replaced †*praiseful* (XIV; Wycl. Bible).

Prakrit prā·krit general name for vernacular dialects developed from Sanskrit. XVIII. – Skr. *prākṛita* original, natural, unrefined, vulgar, vernacular, f. *pra-* before (cf. PRO-[1])+*kṛi* make.

praline prā·līn, prɔ̄·-, prei·- confection made by browning nuts in boiling sugar. XVIII. – F. *praline*, f. name of César de Choiseul, comte de Plessis-*Praslin* (1598–1675), by whom it was invented.

pram[1], praam prām flat-bottomed boat. XVI. – MDu. *prame*, *praem* (Du. *praam*), MLG. *prām(e)* (whence also G. *prahm*, Icel. *prámr*, etc., F. *prame*) = OFris. *prām* – OSl. *pramŭ* (= OHG. *farm* ferry-boat), f. **par-* **per-* **por-*; see FARE.

pram[2] præm short for PERAMBULATOR. XIX.

prance prȧns 'spring and bound in high mettle' (J.). XIV (Ch., Trevisa, Gower). Of unkn. origin; Da. dial. words of similar form and sense suggest a Scand. source, but there are no obvious links.

prang præŋ (Air Force sl.) bomb heavily. XX. Of unkn. origin. Also sb.

prank præŋk †mischievous trick XVI (Skelton), later, mad frolic; also with contemp. †vb. Of unkn. origin; there is no obvious connexion with *prank* deck out, dress up (XVI) or earlier †*prank* sb. and vb., pleat.

prate preit talk idly or aimlessly. XV (Lydg.). – (M)LG., (M)Du. *praten* (whence MHG. *braten*, Icel., Norw., Sw. *prata*, Da. *prate*); prob. of imit. origin; cf. PRATTLE.

pratincole præ·tiŋkoul bird of the genus Glareola, allied to the plover. XVIII (Pennant). – modL. *pratincola* (Kramer 1756), f. L. *prātum* meadow + *incola* inhabitant (cf. COLONY).

pratique præ·tik licence to a ship to hold intercourse with a port after quarantine, etc. XVII (*pratticke*). – (O)F. *pratique* practice, intercourse, corr. to or – It. *pratica* – medL. *practica*, sb. use (sc. *ars* art) of *practicus* PRACTIC.

prattle præ·tl talk childishly or artlessly. XVI. – MLG. *pratelen*, f. *praten* PRATE; see -LE[3]. Hence sb. XVI.

praty prei·ti (also *prawta*, *pritta*, pl. *praes*). XIX. Anglo-Ir. for POTATO, based on Ir. *práta*, *préata*, pl. *prátaidhe*.

prawn prɔ̄n marine crustacean, Palæmon serratus. XV (*prayne*, *prane*). Of unkn. origin.

praxis præ·ksis practice, exercise. XVI. – medL. – Gr. *prâxis* doing, action, f. **prāk-*, base of *prā́ssein* do. Cf. PRAGMATIC.

pray prei ask earnestly, make earnest request or petition. XIII. ME. *preie* – OF. *preier* (mod. *prier*) = Pr., etc. *pregar*, It. *pregare* :– late L. (Rom.) *precāre*, for L. *precārī* entreat, f. **prek-* **pṛk-* (whence *poscere* demand :– **pṛkskere*). So **prayer** prɛəɹ. XIII (Cursor M.). ME. *preiere* – OF. *preiere* (mod. *prière*) = Pr. *pregueira*, Cat. *pregaria* :– Gallo-Rom. **precāria*, sb. use of fem. of L. *precārius* obtained by entreaty (see PRECARIOUS).

pre- prī, pri, pre· (e.g. in *predicate*, *preface*, *premiss*, *preposition*, *presage*, *presence*), prefix repr. F. *pré-* or its source L. *præ-*, later *prē-*, i.e. the adv.-prep. *præ* (of place, rank, time) before, in front, in advance, OL. *prai* = Oscan *prai*, *prae-*, Umbrian *pre*, cogn. with (O)Ir. *ar* before, at, in, Gaul. *are* (as in *Aremorici* that is near the sea, Armorican), OPruss. *prei*, OSl. *pri* near, and rel. to the groups of PER, *prī-* (repr. by PRIME, PRIOR), and *prŏ* (see PRO-[1], PRO-[2]); see also PRETER-.

Many L. comps. of various dates are repr. variously in Eng. (see below), chiefly based on vbs. and corr. sbs., with the meanings 'before', 'previously', 'in advance' (in time or order of succession, action, thought, performance, or execution) in advb. relation to the combined el., as in *preamble*, *precede*, *preclude*, *precursor*, *predestine*, *prefer*, *prefix*, *premature*, *preserve*, *presume*, *pretence*, *pretend*, *prevent*, *previous*, and as in *apprehend, comprehend, predatory, prehensile*; with implication of 'beyond or over all others' as in *precocious, predominate, preeminent, preponderate, prevail*; hence as a living prefix, e.g. in *prejudge* (XII), *prepossess* (XVII); of anterior position, as in (anat.) *precerebellar, -dentate, -hallux*. **b.** In prepositional relation, after modL. *præadamita* (XVII) one who lived before Adam, as in *pre-Alfredian, pre-Cambrian, pre-Hellenic, prehistoric, pre-Raphaelite, pre-Shakespearian.*

preach prītʃ pronounce a public discourse on a sacred subject (AncrR.); proclaim publicly. XIII. ME. *preche* – OF. *prechier* (mod. *prêcher*), earlier *preechier* = Pr. *prezicar*, Sp. *predicar* :– L. *prædīcāre* proclaim, eccl. preach; see PREDICATE. ¶ ChrL. *prædīcāre* was adopted at an early date in the Germ. langs., e.g. OE. *predician*, (OFris. *predikere* preacher), OS. *predikōn*, OHG. *predigōn* (G. *predigen*), ON. *prédika*; so also OIr. *pridchim* I preach. Hence **prea·chMENT**. XIV (R. Mannyng). – OF.; in mod. use a new formation, often with derogatory force.

preamble prīˌæ·mbl preliminary statement. XIV (Ch.). – (O)F. *préambule* – medL. *præambulum*, sb. use of n. sg. of *præambulus* going before, in medL. preliminary, f. *præ* PRE- + stem of *ambulāre* walk; see AMBLE.

prebend pre·bĕnd portion of cathedral revenue granted as stipend to a member of the chapter; land or tithe as source of this XV; †prebendary XVI. – (O)F. *prébende* – late L. *præbenda* pension, pittance, church living, lit. 'things to be supplied', n. pl. of gerundive of L. *præbēre*, f. *præ* forth, PRE- + *habēre* hold, HAVE (cf. *præhibēre*, Plautus). So **pre·bendARY** holder of a prebend. XV. – medL.

precarious prikɛə·riəs (leg.) held by another's favour; dependent on chance XVII; perilous XVIII. f. L. *precārius*, f. *prec-*, *prex* entreaty, prayer; see PRAY, -ARIOUS. Cf. (O)F. *précaire.*

precatory pre·kətəri of the nature of entreaty. XVII. – late L. *precātōrius*, f. pp. stem of *precārī* PRAY; see -ATE[3], -ORY[2].

precaution prikɔ̄·ʃən caution exercised beforehand. XVII. – F. *précaution* – late L. *præcautiō(n-)*, f. L. *præcaut-*, *præcavēre*; see PRE-, CAUTION.

precede prisī·d †surpass, exceed XIV; go before in place or rank XV; go before in time XVI. – (O)F. *précéder* – L. *præcēdere*; see PRE-, CEDE[1]. So **precedENT** pre·sidənt †thing or person that goes before; previous instance or case XV; †adj. preceding XIV (Ch.). Hence **precedENCE** prī·-, -sī·dəns, pre·sidəns. XV.

precentor prise·ntɔɹ leader of the singing of a choir or congregation. XVII. – F. *précenteur* or L. *præcentor*, f. *præcent-*, pp. stem of L. *præcinere*, f. *præ* + *canere* sing; see PRE-, CHANT.

precept prī·sept general command, esp. of divine origin XIV (Wycl. Bible); writ, warrant XV. – L. *præceptum* maxim, order, sb. use of n. pp. of *præcipere* take beforehand, warn, instruct, enjoin, f. *præ* PRE- + *capere* take (see HEAVE). So **prece·ptOR[1]**. XV. – L. Cf. F. *précepte*, †*précept*, *précepteur.*

precession prīse·ʃən (astron.) of the equinoxes. XVI. – late L. *præcessiō(n-)* (Boethius), f. *præcēdere* PRECEDE; modL. *æquinoctiorum præcessio* (Copernicus, *a.* 1530). ¶ Earlier instances XIV–XVI have the sense 'procession'.

précieuse pre·sjōz woman professing refined delicacy of language and taste. XVIII. F., fem. of *précieux* PRECIOUS; popularized by Molière in 'Les Précieuses ridicules', 1659.

precinct prī·siŋkt space enclosed by boundaries; district or province of government. XV. – medL. *præcinctum*, also pl. *præcincta*, sb. uses of n. pp. of L. *præcingere* gird about, encircle, f. *præ* PRE- + *cingere* gird; see CINCTURE.

precious pre·ʃəs of great worth or price XIII (Cursor M.); aiming at choiceness or refinement XIV (Ch.; in mod. use from XVIII, cf. PRÉCIEUSE); egregious, arrant, 'fine' XV. – OF. *precios* (mod. *précieux*), corr. to Pr. *precios*, etc. – L. *pretiōsus*, f. *pretium* PRICE. So **preciosITY** preʃiɔ·sĭti. XIV (Wycl.). – (O)F. – L.

precipice pre·sĭpis †headlong fall XVI (Jonson); vertical steep face of rock, etc. XVII. – F. *précipice* or L. *præcipitium*, f. *præcip-*, *præceps* headlong, steep, or *præcipitāre*, whence **precipitATE[1]** prisi·piteit sb. chem. XVI (modL. *præcipitātum*), adj. prisi·pitĭt headlong, headforemost XVII (L. pp. *præcipitātus*), vb. throw headlong XVI; deposit in solid form from a solution XVII (pp. stem *præcipitāt-*), **precipitA·TION** XVII (– F. or L.); so **preci·pitOUS** precipitate XVII; of the nature of a precipice (superseding earlier †*precipitious* XVII, f. L. *præcipitium*) – F. †*précipiteux* = Sp., It. *precipitoso*, f. L. *præ* before, PRE-, *capit-*, *caput* head (cf. CAPITAL).

précis prei·si concise account or version. XVIII (Chesterfield). – F. *précis*, sb. use of pp. (see next).

precise prisai·s strictly expressed; strict in observance; exact. XVI. – F. *précis*, *-ise* – L. *præcīsus*, *-īsa*, pp. of *præcīdere* cut short, abridge, f. *præ* PRE- + *cædere* cut; cf. CONCISE. So **preci·sely** XV; rendering F. *précisément* (XIV) and L. *præcīsē*. **precisIAN** prisi·ʒən one who is precise, esp. in religious observance, Puritan. XVI. **precisION** prisi·ʒən †cutting short XVII; preciseness XVIII. – F. *précision* or L. *præcīsiō(n-)*; orig. vbl. sb. of action, later abstract sb. corr. to *precise.*

preclude priklū·d shut off. XVII. – L. *præclūdere*, f. *præ* PRE- + *claudere* shut; see CLAUSE, CLOSE.

precocious prikou·ʃəs flowering or fruiting early; prematurely developed. XVII (Sir T. Browne). f. L. *præcoci-*, *-cox*, f. *præcoquere* boil beforehand, ripen fully, f. *præ* PRE- + *coquere* COOK; see -IOUS. So **precos**ITY prikɔ·sĭti. XVII (Howell). – F. or modL.

preconize prī·kənaiz proclaim publicly. XV. – medL. *præcōnīzāre*, f. L. *præcō(n-)* public crier, herald, perh. for **praiwokōn-*, f. *prai* + **wok-*, of *vocāre* call; see PRE-, VOCATION, -IZE.

precursor prikɔ̄·ɹsəɹ forerunner. XVI. – L. *præcursor*, f. *præcurrere*, f. *præ* PRE- + *currere* run; see COURSE, -OR[1].

predatory pre·dətəri pert. or addicted to plundering. XVI. – L. *prædātōrius*, f. *prædātor* plunderer, f. *prædārī* plunder, f. *præda* booty, plunder :– **præheda*, rel. to *præhendere* seize; see PREHENSILE, PREY, -ORY[2].

predecessor prī·disesəɹ former holder of a position. XIV. – (O)F. *prédécesseur* – late L. *prædēcessor*, f. *præ* PRE- + *dēcessor*, f. *dēcēdere* depart; see DECEASE, ANCESTOR.

predestination pridestinei·ʃən God's appointment from eternity of those who shall be saved. XIV. – ecclL. *prædestinātiō(n-)* (Augustine, Boethius), f. *prædestināre* appoint beforehand (in Christian use from III, rendering Gr. προορίζειν in Romans viii 29, 30), f. *præ* PRE- + *destināre* DESTINE. The L. vb. is also the ult. source of **prede·stine** vb. XIV (Wycl) and **prede·stinate** pp. (XIV) and pt. (XV), the latter form being used as present tense from XVI; see -ATE[3]. Cf. (O)F. *prédestination*, *prédestiner* (XII).

predial prī·diəl pert. to land or farms. XVI. – medL. *prædiālis*, f. L. *prædium* farm, estate, f. *præd-*, *præs* surety, bondsman :– **prævid-s*, f. *præ* PRE- + *vad-*, *vās* surety (cf. WED); see AL[1].

predicament pridi·kəmənt category of predication XIV (Wycl.); class, category; situation XVI. – late L. *prædicāmentum* (Augustine, Isidore; tr. Gr. κατηγορία CATEGORY, of Aristotle), f. L. *prædicāre*; see next and -MENT and cf. (O)F. *prédicament*.

predicant pre·dikənt adj. preaching XVII; preacher XVI (now only in Du. form **predikant** predika·nt minister of the Du. Reformed Church, esp. in S. Africa XIX). – L. *prædicant-*, *-āns*, prp. of *prædicāre* PREACH.

predicate pre·dikət (logic and gram.) that which is asserted of the subject. XVI. – late L. *prædicātum* 'quod dicitur de subjecto' (Boethius), tr. Gr. κατηγορεύμενον, n. pp. of *prædicāre* proclaim, declare (cf. PREACH), in medL. predicate, f. *præ* PRE- + *dicāre* make known, rel. to *dīcere* say; see DICTION, -ATE[1]. So **pre·dic**ATE[3] -eit assert, affirm. XVI. f. pp. stem of L. *prædicāre*. **predic**A·TION †preaching XIV; assertion, affirmation XVI. – (O)F. or L. **predic**ATIVE pridi·kətiv (gram.) forming the whole or part of the predicate. XIX.

predict pridi·kt foretell, prophesy. XVII. f. *prædict-*, pp. stem of L. *prædīcere* (whence F. *prédire*, etc.), f. *præ* PRE- + *dīcere* say (see DICTION). (*Predicted* – L. pp. *prædictus* before-mentioned, aforesaid (occurs XVI). So **predi·c**TION. XVI. – L.

predilection prīdile·kʃən mental preference or partiality. XVIII. – F. *prédilection* – **prædīlēctiō(n-)*, f. medL. *prædīligere* prefer, f. *præ* PRE- + *dīligere*; see DILIGENT, -TION.

pre-emption prīe·mᵖʃən purchase before an opportunity is offered to others. XVI. – medL. *præemptiō(n-)*, f. L. *præempt-*, *-emere*, f. *præ* PRE- + *emere* buy. Hence, by back-formation after L. agent-noun *præemptor*, **pre-e·mpt** vb. (chiefly U.S.). XIX.

preen prīn trim (the feathers) with the beak; also transf. XIV (Ch.). Late ME. *preyne*, *prayne*, varying with *proyne* (see PRUNE[2]), of which it may be an alt. by assim. to (dial.) *preen* pin, OE. *prēon*, corr. to MLG. *prēme*, (M)Du. *priem(e)* bodkin, dagger, MHG. *pfrieme* (G. *pfriem*) awl, ON. *prjónn* pin, peg, with ref. to the boring or pricking action of the bird's beak.

prefab prīfæ·b abbrev. of **prefa·bricated** (XX); see PRE-, FABRICATE.

preface pre·fis introduction to a literary work XIV (Ch.); introduction to the canon of the Mass XV (Trevisa). – (O)F. *préface* – medL. *præfātia*, for L. *præfātiō*, f. *præfāt-*, *-fārī*, f. *præ* PRE- + *fārī* speak (see FABLE). Hence vb. XVII. So **pre·fat**ORY[2]. XVII.

prefect prī·fekt governor, chief administrator. XIV. – OF. *prefect* (mod. *préfet*) – L. *præfectus*, sb. use of pp. of *præficere* set over, f. *præ* PRE- + *facere* make, constitute (see FACT). So **pre·fect**URE. XVI. – (O)F. or L.

prefer prifɔ̄·ɹ †advance, promote XIV (Gower, Wycl. Bible); set before others in esteem XIV (Gower); put forward XVI. – (O)F. *préférer* – L. *præferre*, f. *præ* PRE- + *ferre* BEAR[2]. So **prefer**ABLE pre·fərəbl. XVII. – F. *préférable*. **pre·fer**ENCE. XVII. – (O)F. – medL.; hence **prefere·nt**IAL. XIX. **prefe·r**MENT. XV.

prefix prī·fiks verbal element placed before and in combination with another XVII; title prefixed XIX. – modL. *præfīxum*, sb. use of n. of *præfīxus*, pp. of L. *præfīgere* fix in front; see PRE-, FIX. Cf. F. *préfixe* (XVIII). So **prefix** vb. prīfi·ks XV. – (O)F. *préfixer*.

pregnant[1] pre·gnənt (arch.) compelling, cogent. XIV (*'preignant argument*, Ch.; thereafter not till XVI). – F. *preignant* (XVI; perh. earlier in AN.), prp. of *preindre*, earlier *priembre* :– L. *premere* PRESS[1]; see -ANT.

pregnant[2] pre·gnənt with child, with young. XVI. – F. *prégnante* (fem.) or L. *prægnant-*, *-āns*, alt., by assim. to *-āns* -ANT, of *prægnās*, prob. f. *præ* PRE- + base of *(g)nascī* be born (see NASCENT).

prehensile prihe·nsail capable of grasping. XVIII. – F. *préhensile* (Buffon), f. *prehens-*, pp. stem of L. *prehendere*; see APPREHEND, COMPREHEND, PREDATORY, -ILE.

prehistoric prīhistɔ·rik pert. to the period antecedent to historical record. XIX (D. Wilson). – F. *préhistorique*; see PRE-, HISTORIC. Hence **pre**HI·STORY. XIX (Tylor).

prejudge prīdʒʌ·dʒ pass judgement on before trial or inquiry; prejudice. XVI. f. PRE-+JUDGE vb., after F. *préjuger* or L. *præjūdicāre*. So **prejudice** pre·dʒŭdis injury, detriment XIII; †previous or premature judgement XIV; preconceived opinion XVII – (O)F. *préjudice* – L. *præjūdicium*, f. *præ* PRE-+*jūdicium* judgement. **pre·judice** vb. affect injuriously XV; †prejudge XVI; fill with prejudice XVII. – (O)F. *préjudicier*, f. the sb. **prejudic**IAL predʒŭdi·ʃəl injurious XV; †prejudiced XVI. – (O)F. or late L.

prelate pre·lət (eccl.) dignitary of episcopal or similar rank. XIII (Laȝ.). – (O)F. *prélat* = Pr. *prelat*, etc. – L. *prælātus*, (eccl.) sb. use of pp. corr. to *præferre* PREFER; see -ATE[1]. So **pre·l**ACY †office of a prelate; government by prelates. XIV. – AN. *prelacie* – medL. *prælātia*, f. *prælātus*. Hence **prelat**IC(AL) prilæ·t-. XVII.

prelection prīle·kʃən public lecture in a college or university. XVI. – L. *prælectiō(n-)*; see PRE-, LECTION. So **præ**LE·CTOR[1]. XVI. – L.

preliminary prili·minəri introductory to the main business. XVII. – F. *préliminaire* or modL. *prælīmināris*, f. L. *præ* PRE-+ *līmin-*, *līmen* threshold (see LIMINAL).

prelude pre·ljūd introductory action, condition, etc. XVI; (mus.) XVII. – F. *prélude* (Rabelais) or medL. *prælūdium*, f. *prælūdere*. So **pre·lude** vb. (formerly *prelu·de*) serve as prelude to. XVII. – L. *prælūdere* play beforehand, preface, f. *præ* PRE- + *lūdere* play, f. *lūdus* play (cf. LUDICROUS).

premature pri·-, pre·mətʃuəɹ occurring before the time. XVI. – L. *præmātūrus* very or too early, f. *præ* PRE-+*mātūrus* MATURE.

premeditate prime·diteit ponder beforehand. XVI. f. pp. stem of L. *præmeditārī*; see PRE-, MEDITATE. So **premedit**A·TION. XV. – (O)F. or L.

premier pre·miəɹ, prī·miəɹ first in position or rank XV; first in time XVII; sb. prime minister (for *p. minister* XVII – F. *premier ministre* 'first minister') XVIII (first applied to Viscount Charles Townshend 1726). – (O)F. *premier* = Pr. *premier*, Sp. *primero* :– L. *prīmārius* PRIMARY.

premiss, premise pre·mis A. (logic) proposition from which another follows; pl. the two propositions of a syllogism (now distinguished as *major* and *minor premiss*) XIV (Ch., Trevisa). B. (leg., etc.) pl. matters stated previously; subject of a conveyance or bequest; lands and tenements as beforementioned XV; building with its appurtenances XVIII. – (O)F. *prémisse* – medL. *præmissa*, sb. use (sc. *prōpositiō*) of fem. sg. and n. pl. pp. of L. *præmittere* send or set before, f. *præ* PRE-+*mittere* put, send (see MISSION).

premium prī·miəm reward, prize; sum to be paid in an insurance policy, etc. XVII; fee for instruction in a trade, etc.; agio XVIII. – L. *præmium* booty, reward (:– **præimium*), f. *præ* PRE-+*emere* buy, orig. take.

premonition prīməni·ʃən forewarning. XVI (earlier †*premunition*). – F. *premonicion* or late L. *præmonitiō(n-)*, f. L. *præmonēre*, whence **premo·nish** forewarn XVI; after MONISH, ADMONISH; see -ITION. (In medL. *præmonēre* was confused with *præmunīre*; see PRÆMUNIRE.) **premo·nit**ORY[2]. XVII.

prentice pre·ntis. Aphetic of APPRENTICE. XIII (Cursor M.).

preo·ccupy occupy or engage in advance. XVI; after L. *præoccupāre* seize beforehand, F. *préoccuper*. **pre**O:CCUPA·TION. XVI. – F. or L.

prep prep (colloq.) short for *preparation*, *preparatory*. XIX.

prepare pripɛə·ɹ make ready. XV. – F. *préparer* or L. *præparāre*, f. *præ* PRE-+ *parāre* make ready (cf. PARE, PARENT). So **prepar**ATION prepərei·ʃən. XIV (Gower). – (O)F. – L. **preparat**ORY pripæ·rətəri. XV. – late L.

prepense prīpe·ns (in *malice p.*) premeditated. XVIII. For earlier †*prepensed* (XVI), of which the orig. form was †*purpensed* (XV) – AN., OF. *purpensé*, pp. of *purpenser* premeditate, f. *pur-*, *pour-* PRO-[1]+*penser* think (see PENSIVE).

preponderate pripɔ·ndəreit weigh more or heavier. XVII (Cockeram). f. pp. stem of L. *præponderāre*, f. *præ* PRE-+*ponder-*, *pondus* weight; see POISE, -ATE[3]. So **prepo·nder**ANCE XVII (Grew), -ANCY (Sir T. Browne).

preposition prepəzi·ʃən (gram.) part of speech forming adverb-equivalents with nouns and pronouns. XIV (Wycl. Bible, Prologue). – L. *præpositiō(n-)* putting before, (tr. Gr. *πρόθεσις*) preposition, f. *præpōnere*; see PRE-, POSITION. Cf. F. *préposition* (XV).

prepossess prīpəze·s †possess beforehand; cause to be preoccupied; cause to have an opinion beforehand, esp. impress favourably. XVII. f. PRE-+POSSESS, prob. after medL. or modL. *prēpossidēre*. Hence **pre**POSSE·SSION. XVII.

preposterous pripɔ·stərəs inverted in position; contrary to nature or reason. XVI. f. L. *præposterus* 'before-behind', reversed, out of order or season, f. *præ*+ *posterus*; see PRE-, POSTERIOR, -OUS.

prepuce prī·pjūs foreskin. XIV (also †*prepucy* XIV–XV). – L. *præpūtium* (perh. f. *præ* PRE-+an obscure el.), whence F. *prépuce.*

prerogative prirɔ·gətiv prior or peculiar privilege. XIV (Trevisa). – (O)F. *prérogative* or L. *prærogātīva* tribe or century to which it fell by lot to vote first in the comitia, previous choice, prognostic, privilege, sb. use (orig. sc. *tribus* or *centuria*) of *prærogātīvus*, f. *prærogāre* ask first, f. *præ-*+*rogāre* ask; see PRE-, ROGATION, -ATIVE.

presage pre·sidʒ (formerly str. *presa·ge*) prognostic, omen XIV (Gower; not current till XVI); presentiment, foreboding XVI (Sh.). Chiefly – F. *présage*, but in Gower immed. – its source, L. *præsāgium*, f. *præsāgīre* forebode, f. *præ* PRE- + *sāgīre* perceive keenly (cf. SAGACIOUS, SEEK). So **pre·sage** vb. XVI. – F. *présager* or L.

presbyopia prezbiou·piə (path.) failure of eyesight characteristic of old age. XVIII. – modL., f. Gr. *présbus* old man+*ṓps* EYE+ -IA[1].

presbyter pre·zbitəɹ elder in the early Christian church; Christian minister of the second order XVI (Hooker); †presbyterian XVII. – ecclL. *presbyter* (Tertullian) – Gr. *presbúteros* in N.T. 'elder' of the Jewish sanhedrim, 'elder' of the apostolic church, sb. use of compar. (older, elder, senior) of *présbus* old (chiefly sb. old man). Cf. PRIEST. **presby·ter**ATE[1] office of presbyter, body of presbyters. XVII. – ecclL. *presbyterātus*. So **presbyter**IAN -iə·riən pert. to government by presbyters or elders; also sb. XVII. f. ecclL. *presbyterium*. **pre·sbytery** part of a church reserved for the clergy, sanctuary XV; body of presbyters or elders; presbyterianism XVI; (after F. *presbytère*) priest's house XIX. – OF. *presbiterie* – ecclL. *presbyterium* – Gr. *presbutérion*; see -Y[4].

prescience pre·ʃiəns foreknowledge. XIV (Ch., Wycl. Bible). – (O)F. *prescience* – ecclL. *præscientia*, f. *præscient-*, *-ēns* (whence **pre·sci**ENT XVII, Bacon), prp. of *præscīre*, f. *præ* PRE- + *scīre* know (see SCIENCE).

prescribe priskrai·b † hold by prescription XV; lay down as an injunction; order the use of (a medicine, etc.) XVI. – L. *præscrībere*, f. *præ* PRE-+*scrībere* write (see SCRIPT). So **prescri·p**TION (title acquired by) uninterrupted use from time immemorial XIV (Wycl.); limitation of time XV; physician's prescribing of medicine XVI. – (O)F. – L. *præscriptiō(n-)*. **prescri·pt**IVE. XVIII. – late L.

presence pre·zəns fact of being present; †assembly, company XIV; carriage or aspect XVI. – (O)F. *présence* – L. *præsentia*, f. *præsent-*, *-ēns* (whence **pre·sent** adj. through (O)F., XIII Cursor M.), f. *præ* PRE-+-*sēns*, prp. of *sum* I am. So **pre·sent** sb. †presence; thing presented XIII (AncrR.). – OF. *présent* = Pr. *presenz*, Sp., It. *presente* offering, gift; orig.† *in present* in or into the presence (of), hence, as a gift. **present** vb. prize·nt make present XIII; make an offering of XIV. – (O)F. – L. *præsentāre*, f. *præsent-*; see -ENCE, -ENT. **presenta**·TION. XIV (Maund., Wyclif). – (O)F. – late L. **pre·sent**LY[2] †so as to be present XIV (Wyclif); (dial.) at present, now XV (Lydg., Caxton); soon XVI; orig. after medL. *præsentiāliter*.

presentiment prize·ntimənt mental impression of a future event. XVIII. – F. †*presentiment* (mod. *press-*), f. *pré-* PRE- + *sentiment* feeling, SENTIMENT.

preserve prizɔ̄·ɹv keep safe XIV (Barbour); keep alive; keep from physical change XVI; keep (game) for private use XVII. – (O)F. *préserver* – late L. *præservāre*, f. *præ* PRE-+ *servāre* keep, protect, rel. formerly to *servus* SERF). Hence **prese·rve** sb. †preservative; confectionery preparation XVI; wood or water preserved XIX. So **preserva**·TION. XV. – (O)F. – medL. **prese·rv**ATIVE. XIV (Trevisa). – (O)F. or medL.

preside prizai·d occupy the seat of authority. XVII. – F. *présider* – L. *præsidēre*, f. *præ* PRE-+*sedēre* SIT. So **presid**ENT pre·zidənt governor, appointed head. XIV (Ch., Trevisa). – (O)F. *président* – L. *præsident-*, *-ēns*, sb. use of prp. of *præsidēre*. **pre·sid**ENCY. XVI. – Sp., Pg. *presidencia*, It. *presidenza* – medL. *præsidentia*.

presidium prisi·diəm presiding body; standing committee in communistic bodies. XX. Russ. *prezídium* – L. *præsidium*, f. *præsidēre*.

press[1] pres A. crowd, throng XIII; B. instrument used to compress XIV (PPl.); machine for imposing the impression of type on paper, etc.; place for printing XVI; matter printed (*letter-p.*) XVIII. C. large cupboard XIV (Ch.). – (O)F. *presse* (corr. to Pr. *presa*, Sp. *prensa*, It. *pressa*), f. *presser* = It. *pressare* – L. *pressāre*, f. *press-*, pp. stem of *premere* press. So **press** vb. bear down upon or against with force; crowd, push forward XIV; urge XVI. – (O)F. *presser* – L. **press**URE pre·ʃəɹ weight of pain, grief, etc. XIV (Wycl. Bible); action of moral or mental force; action of pressing XVII. – L. *pressūra*, f. *press-*; cf. OF. *pressure*.

press[2] pres force (a man) into the navy or army, impress. XVI. alt., under the infl. of PRESS[1] of †*prest* (XVI), f. †*prest* sb. loan, impost payment in advance, earnest-money paid to a recruit on enlistment XV, enlistment XVI. – OF. *prest* loan, advance pay for soldiers (mod. *prêt*), f. *prester* (*prêter*) afford, lend = Pr., Sp. *prestar*, It. *prestare* :– L. *præstāre* furnish, medL. lend, rel. to *præstō* at hand, within reach. Hence **press** (hist.) impressing of men for service XVI (repl. earlier †*prest*); whence *p.-gang* XVII, *p.-money* XVI (earlier †*prest-money*).

prestige prestī·ʒ †illusion, conjuring trick XVII; brilliance or glamour derived from past success, etc. XIX. – F. *prestige* – L. *præstigium* illusion, more usu. *præstigiæ* fem. pl. juggler's tricks, for **præstrigiæ*, f. *præstringere* bind fast, blind, dazzle (the eyes), f. *præ* PRE- + *stringere* bind, press (see STRICT, STRINGENT).

presto pre·stou (conjurer's word) quickly, at once. XVI. – It. *presto*, adv. use of adj. = OF. *prest* (mod. *prêt*), Pr. *prest*, Sp. *presto* :– Rom. late L. *præstus* ready, quick, for earlier *præstō* at hand. ¶ As a musical direction *presto*, with its superl. *prestissimo*, is an independent adoption (XVII), and short for *tempo presto* quick time.

presume prizjū·m take upon oneself XIV (Barbour, Wycl.); take for granted XIV (PPl., Ch.). – (O)F. *présumer* – L. *præsūmere* anticipate, (later) assume, venture, f. *præ* PRE- + *sūmere* take (cf. ASSUME, etc.). So **presumpt**ION prizʌ·mᵖʃən. XIII (AncrR., Cursor M.). – (O)F. – L. **presu·mpt**IVE. XVI. – F. *présomptif* – late L. **presu·mptu**OUS. XIV. – (O)F. – late L.

pretend prite·nd †(refl.) put oneself forward XIV (Wyclif); profess falsely, feign XV. – F. *prétendre* or – L. *prætendere* stretch forth, put forward, allege, claim, f. *præ* PRE- + *tendere* stretch, TEND². So **pretence**, U.S. **pretense** prite·ns claim XV; purpose, esp. false or alleged XVI. – AN. *pretense* – medL. **prætensa*. **prete·nd**ER¹. XVI. **prete·nsion** assertion of claim. XVII. – medL. *prætensiō(n-)*, also *-tiō(n-)*, f. *prætendere*.

preter-, præter- prī·təɹ prefix repr. L. adv.-prep. *præter* past, by, beyond, more than, besides, compar. formation on *præ* PRE-: e.g. **pretermi·t** leave out, neglect XVI; leave off XIX. – L. (cf. MISSION). **preter**NA·TURAL beyond the range of nature. XVI. – medL. **pre·ter**PLUPE·RFECT pluperfect (†gram., and gen.). XVI. – late L. in *præteritum plusquam perfectum* 'more than perfect past' (Priscian).

preterite, U.S. **-it** pre·tərit past; spec. (gram.) after L. *præteritum tempus* past tense (Quintilian). XIV (Ch.; thereafter not before XVI). – (O)F. *prétérit* or L. *præteritus* gone by, pp. of *præterīre*, f. *præter* PRETER- + *īre* go (cf. *ambit*, *exit*, *transit*).

pretext prī·tekst ostensible reason. XVI (More). – L. *prætextus* outward display, f. *prætext-*, pp. stem of *prætexere* weave in front, border, disguise, f. *præ* PRE- + *texere* weave (see TEXTILE).

pretorian prītɔ̄ə·riən see PRÆTOR.

pretty pri·ti, pru·ti †crafty, wily OE. (only); †clever; ingenious; fine, 'brave' XIV; beautiful in a slight or dainty manner; considerable in quantity XV. OE. *prættig*, corr. to MLG. *prattich* capricious, overbearing, MDu. *(ghe)pertich* brisk, clever, roguish, Du. †*prettig* sportive, humorous; f. WGerm. **pratt-* trick (whence OE. *præt*, surviving in Sc. *prat* perh. through LG. infl., MDu. *parte*, *perte*, Du. *part*, *pret*, ON. *prettr*), of unkn. origin; see -Y¹. ¶ The sense-development is paralleled in some of its features by *canny*, *clever*, *cunning*, *fine*, *nice*.

prevail privei·l †become strong XIV (Trevisa); be superior, gain the ascendant XV; predominate XVII. Late ME. *prevayle* – L. *prævalēre* have greater power (see PRE-), with assim. to AVAIL. So **prevalENT** pre·vələnt †having great power XVI; †predominant; in most extended use XVII. – L. *prævalent-*, *-ēns*, prp. of *prævalēre*.

prevaricate privæ·rikeit †swerve from the right course XVI; act or speak evasively XVII. f. pp. stem of L. *prævāricārī* go crookedly, deviate from the right path, (of an advocate) practise collusion, (Vulg.) transgress, f. *præ* PRE- + *vāricāre* spread the legs apart, straddle, f. *vārus* knock-kneed; see -ATE³. So **prevarica**·TION †deviation from rectitude XIV (Wycl. Bible); †corrupt action XVI; evasive dealing XVII. – L.; so (O)F.

prevenient privī·niənt preceding, spec. theol. of grace. XVII. – L. *prævenient-*, *-ēns*, prp. of *prævenīre*; see next and -ENT.

prevent prive·nt †act in anticipation of XV; anticipate with guidance; forestall by previous measures, hinder. XVI. f. *prævent-*, pp. stem of L. *prævenīre* precede, anticipate, hinder, f. *præ* PRE- + *venīre* COME. So **preve·nt**ION. XVI. – (O)F. or late L. **preve·nt**IVE †anticipatory XVII (Milton); acting as an obstacle XVII; also **preve·nt**ATIVE. XVII.

previous pri·viəs coming or going before XVII; coming too soon (orig. U.S.) XIX. f. L. *prævius*, f. *præ* PRE- + *via* way (cf. DEVIOUS, OBVIOUS, TRIVIAL).

prey prei that which is taken by violence; animal hunted or killed XIII; fig. victim XIV. ME. *praie*, *preie* – OF. *preie* (mod. *proie*) = Pr. *preza*, OSp. *prea*, It. *preda*, Rum. *pradă* :– L. *præda* booty, prob. :– **praiheda*, f. *prai*, *præ* PRE- + **hed-*, base of *præ|hendere*; cf. PREDATORY, PREHENSILE. So **prey** vb. XIII. – OF. *preier*, *preer* :– late L. *prædāre*, for earlier *prædārī*, f. *præda*.

priapism prai·əpizm persistent erection of the penis XVII; licentiousness XVIII. – F. *priapisme* – late L. *priāpismus* – Gr. *priāpismós* (Galen), f. *priāpízein* act Priapus, be lewd, f. *Priāpos* Greek and Roman god of procreation.

price prais A. money, etc. paid for something; †B. value, worth; †C. honour, praise; †D. pre-eminence, superiority; †E. reward, prize XIII. ME. *pris*, later *priis*, *prijs*, and (with final *-e* added to denote length of *i*) *prise*, and finally *price*, with *-ce* as in BODICE, etc. – OF. *pris* (mod. *prix*) = Pr. *pretz*, Sp. *precio*, It. *prezzo*, Rum, *preț* :– L. *pretium* price, value, wages, reward. See PRAISE, PRIZE, which superseded this word in some of its meanings; but *prize* was repl. by **price** vb. assign a price to XV.

prick prik puncture, point, dot OE.; pointed object XIII (Cursor M.); act of pricking XIV. OE. *prica*, also *pricca*, *price* = MLG. *pricke* (LG., Du. *prik*). So **prick** vb. pierce OE.; urge on XIII; mark with dots XIV; raise, erect XVI. OE. *prician* = (M)LG., (M)Du. *prikken*; cf. OE. *āpriċċan* (WGerm. **prikkjan*), whence ME., dial. *pritch*. Words primarily of the LG. area (OS. *prekunga* corr. to OE. sb. *pricung*), the Scand. forms (Icel. *prik*, *prika*, etc.) being adopted thence; of unkn. origin. comp. **p.-song** written vocal music, as being denoted by 'pricks' on paper XVI; earlier *pricked song* XV. ¶ W. *pric* stick, brooch, Ir. *prioca* sting, are from Eng.

pricket pri·kit A. spike on which to stick a candle, candle itself XIV; B. buck in its second year, having straight unbranched horns XV. – AL. *prikettus*, *-um*, dim. f. PRICK; see -ET.

prickle pri·kl †goad OE.; sharp-pointed excrescence of the epidermis. XV. OE. *pricel*, later form of *pricels*, f. base of PRICK (see -LE[1]); corr. to MLG., MDu. *prickel*, *prēkel* (Du. *prikkel*), whence G. *prickel*. Hence **pri·ckly**[1]. XVI.

pride praid high opinion of oneself OE.; consciousness of what is fitting to oneself; (arch.) magnificence, pomp XIII (Laȝ.); *the* prime or flower XV. Late OE. *prȳde*, secondary form (prob. after *prūd* PROUD or ON. *prýði*) of *prȳte*, *prȳtu*, abstr. sb. f. *prūd*, presumably on the model of such pairs as *hlūd* loud/ *hlȳd* sound, noise, *fūl* foul/ *fȳlþ* filth. Hence **pride** vb. †be proud; show *oneself* proud. XIII.

priedieu prīdjö· prayer-desk. XVIII (Walpole). F., f. *prier* PRAY+*Dieu* God, DEITY.

priest prīst clergyman in the second of the holy orders; (sacrificing) minister of religion. OE. *prēost* (with unexpl. *ēo*), corr. to OHG. *priast*, *prēst*, ON. *prestr* (perh. from OE. or OLG.); shortening of the form repr. by OFris. *prēstere*, OS., OHG. *prēster* (MDu., Du., MHG., G. *priester*) – ecclL. *presbyter* PRESBYTER, through pop. **prēster* (whence OF. *prestre*, F. *prêtre*, Sp. *preste*, It. *prete*), repr. in Eng. *Prester John* XIV (– OF. *prestre Jehan*; cf. medL. *presbyter Johannes*, It. *prete Gianni*), title of an alleged Christian priest and king of the East. Hence **prie·st-ESS**[1]. XVII; earlier †*priestress* (XV, XVII) – (O)F. **prie·stHOOD**. OE.

prig prig †tinker XVI; (sl.) thief; †dandy, coxcomb; †as vague pejorative; †precisian, puritan, nonconformist minister XVII; one who affects an offensive propriety XVIII (Smollett, Gray, Johnson). rel. to **prig** vb. steal, haggle XVI; (Sc.) beg XVIII; orig. words of rogues' or thieves' cant (Awdelay, Harman); of unkn. origin. ¶ It is doubtful whether all the applications belong to one and the same word.

prim prim affectedly precise or formal. XVIII. rel. to *prim* sb. and vb., of similar meaning (XVII) and prob. to †*prim* sb. pretty young woman (XVI); perh. all originating in cant or sl. use and ult. – OF. *prin*, fem. *prime* = Pr. *prim* excellent, fine, delicate :- L. *prīmu-s* PRIME[2] (whence also modF. †*prime* fine, delicate).

prima donna prai·mə (prī·mə) dɔ·nə principal female performer in an opera. XVIII. It., 'first lady'; see PRIME[2], DAME.

prima facie prai·mə fei·ʃiī at first sight. XV (Lydg.). L. *prīmā faciē*, i.e. abl. of fem. of *prīmus* first, PRIME[2], and of *faciēs* FACE. ¶ Ch. and Lydg. have *at prime face*.

primage prai·midʒ allowance for the loading of a cargo. XVI. – AL. *prīmāgium*, f. *prīmus* first, PRIME[2]; cf. synon. †*primegilt* (XVI–XVII) – MLG. *primgelt*, and medL. *prīmātor* stevedore; see -AGE.

primal prai·məl primitive XVII (Sh.); principal XIX (Byron, Wordsworth). – medL. *prīmālis*, f. *prīmus* PRIME[2]; see -AL[1].

primary prai·məri earliest, original XV; of the first rank XVI; of the first order or stage XVII; in many techn. uses, as *p. colours*, †*humours*, *planets* XVII. – L. *prīmārius* chief, principal, f. *prīmus* PRIME[2]; see -ARY.

primate prai·mət chief bishop of a province. XIII (Laȝ.). ME. *primat*, later *-ate* – (O)F. *primat* – late L. *prīmat-*, *-ās*, sb. use of L. *prīmās* (Apuleius) of the first rank, chief, f. *prīmus* first, PRIME[2]. So **primatIAL** praimei·ʃəl. XVII. – F. *primatial*, f. medL. *prīmātia* (for earlier *prīmātus*), whence, partly through (O)F. *primatie*, **pri·MACY**. XIV.

primates praimei·tīz, (now anglicized) prai·meits (zool.) highest order of mammalia. XVIII (sg. *primas*, Goldsmith). – modL. use (Linnæus) of pl. of *prīmās*; see prec.

prime[1] praim earliest of the day hours of the Western Church OE.; (arch.) first hour of the day XIII; golden number XIV (R. Mannyng); beginning, earliest time XIV; choicest or finest part, time, etc. XVI. OE. *prīm* – L. *prīma*, sc. *hōra* first (hour), reinforced from (O)F. *prime*, from which or independently from L. the non-eccl. senses were derived; see next. ¶ Cf. TERCE, SEXT, NONE.

prime[2] praim †first in order of time XIV; (arith.) having no integral factors but itself and one XVI (Billingsley); of first rank, importance, or quality XVII (Sh.; *p. minister* PREMIER XVII). – (O)F. *prime* (now only in some phr.) – L. *prīmus* first, f. **prī-*, rel. to *præ* PRE-, *prŏ* PRO-[1], PRO-[2]. Hence **prime** sb. prime number XVI; and in other techn. uses, partly after F. *prime*; cf. prec.

prime[3] praim fill, charge, load. XVI (Douglas). Connected with PRIMAGE, Sc. †*primegilt*, but the basic meaning is not clear.

prime[4] praim cover with a first coat of paint. XVII. perh. f. PRIME[2] after synon. F. *imprimer* (– L. *imprimere* IMPRESS).

primer pri·məɹ, prai·məɹ prayer-book for the laity XIV (PPl.); first reading-book, orig. containing elements of religious instruction XIV (Ch.); size of type (cf. BREVIER) XVI; elementary text-book XIX. – AN. *primer* – medL. *primārius* (sc. *liber* book), *primārium* (sc. *manuale*), sb. uses of m. and n. of L. *primārius* PRIMARY.

primero primεə·rou gambling card-game. XVI. alt. (cf. -ADO) of Sp. *primera* (whence It. *primiera*), fem. of *primero* first :– L. *primārius* PRIMARY. ¶ Associated or identified with †*prima vista* 'first sight' and †*prime* (XVI), which seem to have been applied orig. to a sequence of the best cards.

primeval, -æval praimī·v(ə)l pert. to the first ages of the world. XVII. f. L. *primævus*, f. *prīmus* first, PRIME[2]+*ævum* AGE; see -AL[1].

primitive pri·mĭtiv pert. to early times, original. XIV. – (O)F. *primitif, -ive*, or L. *prīmitīvus* first or earliest of its kind, f. *prīmitus* in the first place, f. *prīmus* PRIME[2]; see -IVE.

primogeniture praimoudʒe·nitʃuəɹ condition of being first-born, right or custom depending upon this. XVII (Bacon). – medL. *prīmōgenitūra*, f. L. *prīmō* adv. of *prīmus* first +*genitūra* birth (after *prīmōgenitus* first-born); see PRIME[2], GENITIVE.

primordial praimɔ̄·ɹdiəl pert. to the beginning. XIV (Trevisa). – late L. *prīmōrdiālis*, f. *prīmōrdium*, sb. use of n. of *prīmōrdius* original, f. *prīmus* PRIME[2]+base of *ōrdīrī* begin; see -IAL.

primrose pri·mrouz plant Primula veris. XV. Late ME. *primerose*, corr. to OF. *primerose* (now, hollyhock), medL. *prima rosa* 'first' or 'earliest rose'; the reason for the name is not known. ¶ Superseded †*primerole* (XIV), dim. formation, perh. more widely used.

primula pri·mjŭlə name of a genus used by Linnæus. XVIII. medL. *prīmula*, fem. (sc. *planta* plant) of dim. (see -ULE) of *prīmus* first, PRIME[2]; orig. in *prīmula vēris* 'little firstling of spring', applied to the cowslip and the field daisy.

primum mobile prai·məm mou·bili supposed outermost sphere added to the Ptolemaic system, carrying with it other spheres in its revolution. XV. medL. 'first moving thing', n. of L. *prīmus* PRIME[2] and *mōbilis* MOBILE; tr. Arab. *al-muḥarrik al-awwal* 'the first mover' (Avicenna).

primus prai·məs presiding bishop in the Scottish Episcopal Church. XIX. – L. *prīmus* PRIME[2].

prince prins sovereign ruler; chief; ruler of a small state XIII (AncrR., RGlouc., Cursor M.); male member of a royal family XIV. – (O)F. *prince*, corr. to Pr. *prince*, Sp., It. *principe* – L. *principem*, nom. *princeps* chief, leader, sovereign, f. *prīmus* PRIME[2]+ *-cip-*, comb. form of stem of *capere* take (see HEAVE).

principal pri·nsĭp(ə)l chief XIII; constituting the primary or original sum XIV; (gram.) XVI; sb. chief, head, superior; original sum XIV; chief actor XVI. – (O)F. *principal* – L. *principālis* first, chief, original, f. *princip-*, *princeps* PRINCE; see -AL[1]. So **principALITY** -æ·lĭti principalship; territory of a prince. XIV. – OF. *principalite* (mod. *principalité* headship of a college); varying in ME. with *principalte* – OF. *principalte* (mod. *principauté* princedom) – late L. *principālitās*. **pri·ncipATE**[1]. XIV. – (O)F. or L.

principia prinsi·piə first principles (of a subject). XVII. pl. of L. *principium* beginning, f. *princip-*, *princeps* chief (cf. PRINCE).

principle pri·nsĭpl †origin, source; fundamental source, quality, truth, etc. XIV (Wyclif, Ch., Trevisa); general law or rule XVI (of nature XIX); (elementary) constituent XVII. – AN. **principle*, var. of (O)F. *principe* – L. *principium* beginning, source, (pl.) foundations, elements, f. *princip-*, *princeps* first in place or time (see PRINCE). ¶ For parasitic *l* cf. *manciple, participle*.

print print impression, impress XIII (Cursor M.); (typographical uses) XV. ME. *prient(e)*, *preint(e)*, *preent(e)*, *prent(e)* (still mod. Sc.), later *print(e)* – OF. *priente, preinte*, sb. use of fem. pp. of *preindre*, older *priembre* = Pr., OSp. *premer*, It. *premere* :– L. *premere* PRESS[1]; cf. (M)LG., (M)Du. *prent*. Hence **print** vb. impress, stamp XIV; (in typographical uses) XVI (earlier *enprynte*, Caxton; see IMPRINT). Hence **pri·ntER**[1]. XVI (*prenter*).

prior[1] prai·əɹ officer of an abbey next below the abbot; head of offshoot of an abbey. XI. Late OE. *prior*, reinforced in ME. by OF. *priur, priour* (mod. *prieur*) – L. *prior* (-*ōr*-), sb. use of *prior* former, elder, superior, compar. (:– **prijos*) f. OL. *pri* (*præ* PRE-) before. So **pri·orESS**[1]. XIII. – OF. *prioresse* = medL. *priōrissa*. **pri·orY**[3]. XIII. – AN. *priorie*, medL. *priōria*.

prior[2] prai·əɹ earlier, anterior; also advb. XVIII. – L. *prior*; see prec. So **priorITY** praiɔ·rĭti. XIV (Usk). – (O)F. – medL.

prism prizm (geom.) solid figure of which the two ends are similar, equal, and parallel rectilinear figures and the sides parallelograms XVI (Billingsley); (optics) transparent body of this form XVII. – medL. *prisma* (Martianus Capella) – Gr. *prîsma, -mat-* (Euclid), lit. thing sawn, f. *prízein* saw vb. (cf. *priôn, príein*). So **prismATIC** -æ·tik. XVIII (Pope). – F. or modL.

prison prizn imprisonment, place of this. XII. – OF. *prisun*, (mod.) *prison* = Pr. *prezó*, Sp. *prision*, It. *prigione* :– L. *prēnsiōnem*, for *præhensiō(n-)*, n. of action f. *præhendere*, f. *præ* PRE-+**hend-*, var. of **hed-* (cf. PREY, GET). So **prisonER**[2] pri·znəɹ. XIII; superseded earlier *prison* so used, as in OF., Sp., It., and medL.

pristine pri·stain pert. to the earliest period. XV. – L. *pristinus*, f. base of *priscus* early, *prīmus* PRIME², with suffix as in *crāstinus* of yesterday, *diūtinus* long-lasting; see -INE¹.

prithee pri·ði (arch.) formula of request. XVI. Earlier *pray the, preythe*, clipped form of *I pray thee.*

private prai·vĭt †applied by Wyclif to the friars; not open to the public XIV (Trevisa); not holding a public position XV. – L. *prīvātus* withdrawn from public life, peculiar to oneself, sb. man in private life, prop. pp. of *prīvāre* bereave, deprive, f. *prīvus* single, individual, private, :– **preiuos* (of CItalic range); see -ATE². Hence **priv**ACY pri·vəsi, prai·vəsi. XV (rare before XVI). **privateer** praivĭtiə·ɹ vessel owned and officered by private persons holding letters of marque, commander of this. XVII; after *volunteer*; earlier called *private man of war.* **privation** praivei·ʃən depriving, being deprived XIV (Rolle, Trevisa). – L. *prīvatiō(n-)*, f. *prīvāre.* **privat**IVE pri·vətiv. XVI (Hooker, Bacon). – F. or L.

privet pri·vit evergreen shrub Ligustrum vulgare. XVI (Elyot, Turner, also *privie*, dial. *privy*). Obscurely rel. to contemp. synon. *primprint* (Turner, Lyte), abbrev. (dial.) *prim, primp*; of unkn. origin.

privilege pri·vĭlidʒ private or particular right. XII. Early ME. *privilegie, privilege* – AN. **privilegie*, (O)F. *privilège* – L. *prīvilēgium* legal provision affecting an individual, prerogative, f. *prīvus* PRIVATE + *lēg-*, *lēx* law (see LEGAL). So vb. – (O)F. *privilégier* – medL. *prīvilēgiāre.* XIV (Ch., Trevisa). So **privy** pri·vi †private; hidden, secret XIII; participating in knowledge (of) XIV; sb. †intimate XIII; private place of easement XIV (Barbour); (leg.) partaker XV. ME. *prive, privey, privy* – (O)F. *privé* (as sb. in OF. familiar friend, private place) :– L. *prīvātu-s* PRIVATE. See -Y⁵. So **pri·**VITY †secret thing; †privacy XIII; (chiefly pl.) private parts XIV; private knowledge XVI. – OF. *priveté, -ité.* ¶ The sense 'place of easement' is found in medL. *priveta, -ata*, OF. *priveit*, MHG. *privēt(e), privāt(e).*

prize¹ praiz †booty XIV (Ch., Gower); ship, etc. captured at sea XVI. – (O)F. *prise* capture (of a ship), booty, captured vessel or cargo = Pr., Sp., It. *presa* :– Rom. **prēsa, *prēnsa*, sb. use of fem. pp. of **prēndere* :– L. *præhendere* seize (see PREY); became identified finally with PRIZE³.

prize² praiz †estimate XV; esteem highly XIV. Late ME. *prise* (earlier Sc. *priss*) – *pris-*, tonic stem of OF. *preisier* PRAISE.

prize³ praiz reward for superiority in a contest. XVI. Differentiated sp. of *pris(e)*, PRICE.

prize⁴ praiz lever up. XVII. f. (dial.) *prize* (XIV) levering instrument – OF. *prise* grasp, seizure, PRIZE¹. See PRY².

pro¹ prou argument or person in favour of a proposal *c.*1400; now only in *pro and con* prouənᵈkɔ·n (reasons) for and against XVI, earlier *pro and* or *et contra* XV (Lydg., Caxton). L. *prō* for, on behalf of, to be grouped with PER, *præ* PRE-, *prī-* as in *prior, prīmus* PRIME²; see PRO-¹, PRO-².

pro² prou short for comps. of PRO-¹, as *professional, proproctor.* XIX.

pro³ prou L. prep. *prō* before, in front of, for, on behalf of, instead of, on account of (see PRO¹), in several phrases domiciled since XV (*pro tempore* temporarily) and esp. XVI (*pro forma* as a matter of form, *pro rata* according to a RATE, proportionally).

pro-¹ prou, prŏ repr. comb. form of L. adv.-prep. *prō* (see PRO¹) having a var. *prōd-* as in *prodigal*, pronounced with ɔ in *procurator, promise, prosecute, prostitute, proverb*; with obscured vowel in *proceed, procure, produce, profane, profound, promote, protect*; as a living prefix chiefly in the senses (1) 'for', 'instead of', 'in place of', as *pro-cathedral*; 'acting as a deputy', in imitation of, as *proconsul*; (2) 'on the side of', 'favouring', as in *pro-Boer, pro-German, pro-war.* For its reflex in F. *pour-, pur-*, see POURPARLER, POURPOINT, PURLIEU, PURLOIN, PURPORT, PURPOSE, PURVEY.

pro-² prou, prɔ repr. comb. form of Gr. *pró* before (of time, position, priority), as in *problem, proboscis, programme, prologue, prophet, prostate, protasis*; in recent scientific terms denoting (1) 'earlier', 'primitive'; **pro·chron**ISM, referring something to a too early date XVII; **propædeutic** proupīdjū·tik pert. to preliminary instruction (Gr. *propaideúein* teach beforehand); (2) 'anterior' (of position), 'front', as **pro**CEPHA·LIC pert. to the fore-part of the head. **prognath**OUS prɔ·gnəþəs having projecting jaws (Gr. *gnáthos* jaw).

proa prou·ə Malay boat. XVI. Early vars. *parao, paroo, prau, prow* – Malay *p(a)rā(h)ū.*

probable prɔ·bəbl †such as to commend itself XIV (Trevisa); †demonstrable XV; having an appearance of truth XVII (Sh.). – (O)F. *probable* – L. *probābilis* provable, credible, f. *probāre*; see PROBE, PROVE, ABLE. So **probabilior**ISM -bi·liŏrizm, -IST XVIII; **probabil**ISM prɔ·bəbĭlizm, -IST XVII; designating tenets based on a greater or less degree of probability.

probang prou·bæŋ (surg.) strip of whalebone with sponge, button, etc. for introducing into the throat. XVII. orig. *provang*, so named by the inventor, W. Rumsey; of unkn. origin (but cf. †*provet* probe – F. *éprouvette*); alt. prob. after PROBE.

probate prou·bət, -beit official proving of a will. XV. – L. *probātum* thing proved, sb. use of n.pp. of *probāre* PROVE; see -ATE¹. So **prob**A·TION testing; proving XV. – (O)F. *probation* or L. *probātiō(n-)*, f. *probāre*; hence **proba·tion**ER². XVII.

probe proub blunt instrument for exploring wounds, etc. XVI. – late L. *proba* proof, medL. examination, f. *probāre*; hence **probe** vb. XVII.

probity prɔ·bĭti, prou·bĭti moral integrity. XVI. – F. *probité* or L. *probitās*, f. *probus* good, honest :– **probhos*, perh. orig. 'growing well' (as crops), f. *prŏ* forward (cf. PRO-¹)+**bhwo*- **bhū* BE (cf. *superbus* SUPERB); see -ITY.

problem prɔ·bləm †difficult question, enigma XIV (Wycl. Bible, Ch.); question proposed for discussion; matter of inquiry; (geom.) proposition in which something is required to be done (Billingsley) XVI. – (O)F. *problème* or L. *problēma* – Gr. *próblēma*, f. *probállein* put forth, f. *pró* PRO-²+ *bállein* throw (cf. BALLISTA, EMBLEM). So **problem**A·TIC XVII, -A·TICAL XVI. – F. or late L. – Gr.

proboscis proubɔ·sis, prŏ- elephant's trunk; elongated (tubular) part of insect's mouth. XVII. – L. *proboscis* (Pliny) – Gr. *proboskís* lit. 'means of providing food', f. *pró* PRO-²+*bóskein* cause to feed.

proceed prŏsī·d go forward, come forth. XIV (Wycl. Bible, Ch., Gower). Late ME. *procede* – (O)F. *procéder* – L. *prōcēdere*, f. *prō* PRO-¹+*cēdere* go; see CEDE. So **proce·d**URE. XVII. – (O)F., f. the vb.

proceleusmatic prou:sėljūsmæ·tik animating; (pros.) consisting of four short syllables. XVIII. – late L. *proceleusmaticus* – Gr. *prokeleusmatikós*, f. *prokéleusma* (-*mat*-), f. *prokeleúein* incite, f. *pro* PRO-²+*keleúein* bid, command; see -ATIC.

process prou·sės fact of going on or being carried on XIV (R. Mannyng, Rolle); proceedings at law XIV; outgrowth XVI; continuous operation XVII. ME. *proces* – (O)F. *procès* – L. *prōcessus*, f. pp. stem of *prōcēdere*; orig. str. *proce·ss*, as still by Milton; but *pro·cess* is as early as Ch. Hence **pro·cess** vb.¹ A. (orig. Sc.) institute a process against XVI; B. treat by a special process XIX. In A – OF. *processer*, f. *procès*; in B f. the sb. So **process**ION prəse·ʃən formal or ceremonial act of going in orderly succession XII; emanation (chiefly theol.) XIV. – (O)F. *procession* – L. *prōcessiō*(*n*-) advance, (later) religious procession, f. *prōcess*-, pp. stem of *prōcēdere*. Hence **proce·ss** vb.² go in procession XIX; for the back-formation cf. *progress* vb.

proclaim prŏklei·m make public announcement of. XIV (Gower). Late ME. *proclame* – L. *prōclāmāre* cry out, f. *prō* PRO-¹+ *clāmāre*; see CLAIM, to the sp. of which this word was assim. So **proclam**A·TION prɔkləm- XV. – (O)F. – L.

proclitic proukli·tik (gram.) of a monosyllable closely linked with the following word and having no accent of its own. XIX. – modL. *procliticus* (Hermann, 1801), f. Gr. *proklínein* lean forward, after late L. *encliticus* ENCLITIC.

proclivity prŏkli·vĭti inclination of mind or character. XVI. – L. *prōclīvitās*, f. *prōclīvis* inclined (whence †**proclive** XVI), f. *prō* PRO-¹+*clīvus* slope (see DECLIVITY).

proconsul proukɔ·nsəl governor of an ancient Roman province XIV (Wycl. Bible); (after F. of the Revolution period) governor of a modern colony, etc. XIX (Scott). – L. *prōconsul*, for *prō consule* (one acting) for the consul; see PRO-¹ (1) and CONSUL. So **proco·nsul**AR. XVII. – L. *prōconsulāris*. Similarly **pro**PRÆ·TOR. XVI. – L., for *prō prætōre*.

procrastinate proukræ·stineit put off to another time. XVI. f. pp. stem of L. *prōcrāstināre*, f. *prō*- PRO-¹+*crāstinus* belonging to tomorrow, f. *crās* tomorrow (for the suffix cf. *pristine*); see -ATE³.

procreate prou·krieit beget, engender. XVI. f. pp. stem of L. *prōcreāre*, f. *prō* PRO-¹+ *creāre* CREATE, after †*procreate* pp. (XV) and (O)F. *procréer*; see -ATE³. So **procre**A·TION. XIV (Ch.). – (O)F. or L.

Procrustean proukrʌ·stiən tending to produce uniformity by violent methods. XIX. f. Gr. *Prokroústēs* name of a fabulous robber of Attica who stretched or amputated his victims to conform them to the length of his bed, f. *prokroúein* beat or hammer out, stretch out, f. *pró* PRO-²+*kroúein* knock, which has Balto-Sl. cogns.; see -EAN.

procto- prɔ·ktou comb. form of Gr. *prōktós* anus, in (mainly) anat. and surg. terms. XIX.

proctor prɔ·ktəɹ †agent, deputy, proxy XIV (Wyclif, Ch.); advocate, attorney XV; university officer representative of the Masters of Arts; representative of clergy in Convocation XVI. Late ME. *proctour*, syncopated form of *procketour*, *procutour*, reduction of *pro·curatour* PROCURATOR. ¶ For the syncope cf. PROXY.

procurator prɔ·kjŭreitəɹ orig. form of PROCTOR, surviving in Sc. *p. fiscal*, public prosecutor of a district. XIII. – OF. *procurateur* or L. *prōcūrātor* manager, agent, deputy, collector in a province, f. *prōcūrāre* PROCURE; see -ATOR, and cf. PROCURER. ¶ For the corr. noun of action see PROXY.

procure prəkjuə·ɹ †contrive; bring about by effort; obtain, win. XIII (RGlouc., Cursor M.). – (O)F. *procurer* – L. *prōcūrāre* take care of, attend to, manage, f. *prō* PRO-¹+ *cūrāre* look after (see CURE). In ME. usu. str. *pro·cure*, whence the weakened forms *pro·cur*, *pro·cre*, *pro·ker*. So **procu·r**ER². XIV (in earliest use, advocate, defender, manager). – AN. *procurour*, OF. *procureur* – L. *prōcūrātōrem*, PROCURATOR.

prod prɔd stab or poke with a pointed instrument, etc. XVI (Coverdale). perh. of purely symbolic origin, but poss. a blending of POKE with dial. *brod* vb. †sprout (XII), goad (XV), rel. to *brod* sb. †sprout (XIII), goad, prick (XIV) – ON. *broddr* = OE. *brord* spike, OHG. *brort* edge :– Germ. **brozdaz*. ¶ There is no obvious connexion with OE. *prod-*, *protbor* boring tool.

prodigal prɔ·digəl extravagant in expenditure. (XV) XVI. – medL. *prōdigālis* (implied in *prōdigāliter*, *prōdigālitās*), f. *prōdigus* lavish, rel. to *prōdigere* drive forward, cast before one, squander, f. *prōd-*, var. of *prō-* PRO-[1]+*agere* drive; see ACT, -AL[1]. So **prodiga·lity**. XIV. – (O)F. – late L. (Boethius).

prodigy prɔ·dĭdʒi †omen, portent XVI; marvel; one of precocious genius XVII. – L. *prōdigium*, f. *prōd-*, var. of *prō* PRO-[1]+an el. variously referred to *aiō* (:– **agjō*) I say, and *agere* (cf. ACT); see -Y[4]. So **prodigious** prədi·dʒəs †ominous, portentous; of the nature of a prodigy. XVI. – L. *prōdigiōsus*; cf. F. *prodigieux* (Rabelais).

prodromus prɔ·drəməs †forerunner; introductory treatise. XVII. – L. *prodromus* – Gr. *pródromos* precursor, sb. use of adj. 'running before', f. *pró* PRO-[2] + *-dromos* running, *drameîn* run.

produce prŏdjū·s bring forward XV; bring into existence; extend in length XVI. – L. *prōdūcere*, f. *prō* PRO-[1]+*dūcere* lead (see DUCT). Hence **produce** sb. prɔ·djūs. XVII. So **product** prɔ·dəkt quantity produced by multiplying XV; thing produced by an operation XVII. – L. *prōductum* (math., Albertus Magnus), sb. use of n.pp. of *prōdūcere*. **production** prədʌ·kʃən. XV. – (O)F. – L. **produ·ctive**. XVII. – F. or late L.

proem prou·ĕm prefatory discourse. XIV (Ch.). Late ME. *proheme* (also *prohemie*) – OF. *pro(h)eme* (mod. *proème*) or L. *prooemium* (medL. *prohēmium*) – Gr. *prooímion* prelude, f. *pró* PRO-[2]+*oímē* song, lay.

profane prŏfei·n secular)(*sacred* XV; ritually impure; characterized by disregard of sacred things XVI. – OF. *prophane* (mod. *profane*) or L. *profānus* (med. *prophānus*) not sacred, uninitiated, impious, lit. 'before, i.e. outside, the temple', f. *prō* PRO-[1]+*fānum* temple, FANE. So **profa·ne** vb. desecrate, violate. XIV (Wycl. Bible). – L. *profānāre*; cf. F. *profaner*. **profana·tion** prɔf-. XVI. – F. or late L. **profanity** prŏfæ·nĭti. XVII (before XIX *profaneness* was more frequent in Eng.)(Sc. and Amer. use). – late L. (Tertullian).

profess prŏfe·ss *be professed* have taken solemn religious vows XIV; trans. declare openly, affirm allegiance to, lay claim to knowledge of, teach as a professor XVI. In earliest use in pp. repl. †*profess* (– (O)F. *profès* = Pr. *profes*, etc. – L. *prōfessus*); later f. *prōfess-*, pp. stem of L. *prōfitērī* declare aloud or publicly, f. *prō* PRO-[1]+*fatērī* CONFESS, rel. to *fābula* FABLE. So **profession** prŏfe·ʃən taking of vows in a religious order XIII (AncrR.); avowal of belief in or obedience to religion; occupation professed XVI. – (O)F. *profession* – L. *prōfessiō(n-)*; hence **profe·ssional**[1]. XVIII. **professor**[1] prəfe·səɹ public teacher of the highest rank in a faculty of learning XIV (Wyclif); one who makes a profession (gen.) XV. – (O)F. *professeur* or L. *professor*. Hence **profe·ssorate**[1]. XIX. So **professorial** prɔfĭsɔ̄ə·riəl. XVIII. f. L. *prōfessōrius*. **professo·riate**[1]. XIX.

proffer prɔ·fəɹ put forward for acceptance. XIII. – AN., OF. *proffrir*, earlier *poroffrir*, *puroffrir*, f. *por* (:– L. *prō* PRO-[1])+*offrir* OFFER. So **pro·ffer** sb. XIV. – AN. *profre* = OF. **poroffre*, f. the vb.

proficient prŏfi·ʃənt †making progress; that has made progress in learning. XVI. – L. *prōficient-*, *-ēns*, prp. of *prōficere* advance, f. *prō* PRO-[1]+*facere* DO[1], make; see -ENT. Hence **profi·ciency**. XVI (Coverdale).

profile prou·fail, -fīl outline, contour, or representation of this. XVII. – It. †*profilo*, now *proffilo* (whence also F. *profil*), f. †*profilare* draw in outline, f. PRO[1]-+*filare* spin, †draw a line – L. *fīlāre*, f. *fīlum* thread; see also PURFLE.

profit prɔ·fit advantage, benefit; revenue, proceeds XIV; gain in a transaction XVII. – (O)F. *profit* = Pr. *profech*, Sp. *provecho*, Pg. *proveito* :– L. *prōfectu-s* progress, profit, f. pp. stem of *prōficere* (see PROFICIENT). So **pro·fit** vb. XIV. – (O)F. *profiter*, f. the sb.; hence **profitee·r**[1]. XIX.

profligate prɔ·fligət †overthrown XVI; abandoned to vice XVI (sb. XVIII). – L. *prōflīgātus* ruined, dissolute, pp. of *prōflīgāre* cast down, ruin, f. *prō* PRO-[1]+base *flīg-* beat (cf. *afflict*, *conflict*, *inflict*); see -ATE[2]. Hence **pro·fligacy**. XVIII.

pro forma see PRO[3].

profound prŏfau·nd showing depth of thought or knowledge XIV; abstruse, recondite; physically deep XV. – AN., OF. *profund*, (also mod.) *profond* earlier *parfund* = Pr. *preon*, Cat. *pregon*, It. *profondo* :– L. *profundu-s*, f. *pro-* PRO-[1] + *fundus* bottom (cf. FOUND[1]). So **profu·ndity**. XV. – OF. or late L.

profuse prŏfjū·s liberal to excess XV; very abundant XVII. – L. *prōfūsus*, adj. use of pp. of *prōfundere* pour forth, f. *prō* PRO-[1]+*fundere* pour; see FUSE. So **profu·sion**. XVI. – F. (Montaigne) or L.

prog[1] prɔg (sl.) victuals, provender. XVII. prob. f. dial. *prog* vb. poke about, as for food, of unkn. origin.

prog[2] prɔg (sl.) proctor at the universities of Oxford and Cambridge (also *proggins*, perh. by assoc. with *juggins*, *muggins*). XIX.

progeny prɔ·dʒĭni offspring. XIII (Cursor M.). – OF. *progenie* – L. *prōgeniēs* descent, family, f. *prō* PRO-¹+ **gen-* (see KIN), after *prōgignere* beget (cf. Skr. *prajā́s*, Av. *frazaintiš* posterity).

prognosis prɔgnou·sis forecast of the course of a case of disease. XVII. – late L. *prognōsis* – Gr. *prógnōsis*, f. *progignṓskein* know beforehand; see PRO-², GNOSIS. So **prognostic** prɔgnɔ·stik previous indication or token XV (Lydg.); symptom XVI. Earlier form *pron-* – OF. *pronostique* (mod. *-ic*) – L. *prognōsticum*, *-con* – Gr. *prognōstikón*, sb. use of n. of adj. f. *progignṓskein*; see -IC. **progno·sticATE**³. XVI. f. pp. stem of medL. *pro(g)nōsticāre*. ¶ An altered form, medL. *prænōsticus*, is repr. by late ME. *prenostik* (Gower, Ch.).

programme, program prou·græm A. †Sc. public notice XVII; B. descriptive notice or plan of intended proceedings XIX. In sense A – late L. *programma* – Gr. *prógramma* public written notice, f. *prográphein* write publicly, f. *pró* PRO-²+*gráphein* write (see CARVE); in sense B – F. *programme*.

progress prou·grės, prɔ·grės onward march; visit of state XV; forward movement XVI. – L. *prōgressus*, f. pp. stem of *prōgredī* go forward, f. *prō* PRO-¹+*gradī* step, walk, go, f. *gradus* step (see GRADE). Hence **progre·ss** vb.; earlier str. *pro·gress*; became obs. in England in XVII, but retained or formed afresh in America, whence it was readopted in England *c.*1800. So **progressION** prŏgre·ʃn. XIV (Ch.). – F. or L. **progre·ssIVE** XVII. – F.

prohibit prouhi·bit forbid. XV. f. *prohibit-*, pp. stem of L. *prōhibēre* hold back, prevent, forbid, f. *prō* in front, PRO-¹+*habēre* hold (cf. *exhibit, inhibit*). So **prohibi·TION**. XIV. – (O)F. or L. **prohi·bitIVE**. XVII. – F.

project prɔ·dʒėkt †design, scheme XIV; †conception, notion XVI; proposal for execution XVII. – L. *prōjectum*, n. of pp. of *prōicere* throw forth, expel. f. *prō* PRO-¹+*jacere* throw. Cf. F. *projet*. So **project** prŏdʒe·kt plan XV; throw forward XVI. f. *prōject-*, pp. stem of L. *prōicere*. Cf. F. *projeter*, earlier †*pourjeter*, which prob. suggested the formation of the Eng. word. **proje·ctILE**. XVII. – modL. *projectilis*. **proje·cTION** action of projecting; earliest in techn. sense of representation of a spherical surface on the flat. XVI (Recorde, Dee). – L.; so (O)F.

prolate prou·leit lengthened in the direction of the polar axis)(*oblate*. XVII. – L. *prōlātus*, used as pp. of *prōferre* bring forward, produce, f. *prō* PRO-¹ + *ferre* BEAR². So **prolA·TION** †utterance; (mus.) relative duration of the minim to the semibreve. XIV (Gower). – L.

prolegomena proulĭgɔ·mĭnə preliminary observations. XVII. pl. of L. *prolegomenon* (also used) – Gr. *prolegómenon*, n. of prp. pass. of *prolégein* say beforehand, f. *pró* PRO-²+ *légein* say (cf. LOGOS).

prolepsis proule·psis, -līp- anticipation, esp. as techn. device in rhet. and gram. XVI. – late L. *prolēpsis* (the pure L. term was *occupatio*) – Gr. *prólēpsis*, f. *prolambánein* anticipate, f. *pró* PRO-² + *lambánein* take. So **prole·pt**IC. XVII. – Gr.

proletarian proulĭtɛə·riən pert. to the lowest class of the people XVII; wage-earning XIX. f. L. *prōlētārius* Roman citizen of the lowest class under the constitution of Servius Tullius, one who served the state not with his property but only with his offspring, (hence) common, low, f. **prōlētus* provided with offspring, f. *prōlēs* offspring, for **prōolēs*, or **proalēs*, f. *prō* PRO-¹+ **ol-* **al-* grow (cf. ADOLESCENT, ALIMENT); see -ARIAN. So **proleta·riATE**¹. XIX. – F. *prolétariat*, f. L. *prōlētārius* (whence F. *prolétaire*, which was current in Eng. in early XIX), and **pro·letARY**. XVII (earlier than *proletarian*).

prolific prŏli·fik producing (much) offspring. XVII. – medL. *prōlificus*, f. L. *prōlēs*; see prec. and -FIC; cf. F. *prolifique*.

prolix prou·liks, prouli·ks lengthy XV (Lydg.); lengthy in discourse XVI. – (O)F. *prolixe* or L. *prōlixus* spreading abroad, extended, lit. 'poured forth', f. *prō* PRO-¹+pp. formation on base of *liquēre* be LIQUID. So **proli·xITY**. XIV (Ch.). – (O)F. – late L.

prolocutor proulɔ·kjutəɹ spokesman of an assembly. XV. – L. *prōlocūtor* pleader, advocate, agent-noun of *prōloquī* speak out; see PRO-¹, LOCUTION. ¶ In medL. *prolocutor* varies with *prælocutor* one who speaks before others; cf. AL. *prolocutor* and *prælocutor parliamenti* Speaker.

prologue prou·lɔg preface to a discourse or drama XIII (Cursor M.); speaker of this XVI. ME. *prolog* – (O)F. *prologue* – L. *prologus* – Gr. *prólogos*, f. *pró* PRO-² + *lógos* speech (cf. LOGOS).

prolong prŏlɔ·ŋ extend in duration XV (†delay, put off, Lydg.); lengthen in space or time XVI. – late L. *prōlongāre*, f. *prō* PRO-¹+*longus* LONG; cf. OF. *prolonguer*, var. of (O)F. *prolonger*, which superseded OF. *por-*, *proloingier* (see PURLOIN). So **prolongA·TION**. XV (Caxton). – (O)F. or late L.

prolusion prouljū·ʒən preliminary attempt, essay, or dissertation. XVII. – L. *prōlūsiō(n-)*, f. pp. stem of *prōlūdere*, f. *prō* PRO-¹+*lūdere* play; see -SION.

promenade prɔmĭnā·d walk taken for exercise or amusement XVI (*purmenade*, *-ado*); place for this XVII. – F. *promenade*, f. *se promener* walk, refl. of *promener* cause to walk, alt. of *pourmener*, f. *pour* (:– L. *prō*) +*mener* lead (:– late L. *mināre* drive, for L. *minārī* threaten); see PRO-¹, MENACE, -ADE. Hence vb. XVI.

Promethean prŏmī·þiən pert. to *Prometheus*, a demigod who stole fire from Olympus and taught men its use. XVI (Sh.). See -EAN. ¶ Applied *c.*1830–60 to a kind of lucifer match.

prominent prɔ·minənt projecting XVI; conspicuous XVIII. – L. *prōminent-, -ēns*, prp. of *prōminēre* jut out, f. *prō* PRO-[1]+base meaning 'jut', repr. also by *mōns* MOUNT[1], *mentum* chin, *minæ* projection of a wall; see -ENT and cf. *eminent, imminent, menace.* So **pro·minENCE.** XVI.

promiscuous prŏmi·skjuəs of mixed or disorderly character. XVII. f. L. *prōmiscuus*, f. *prō* PRO-[1]+*miscēre* MIX; see -UOUS. Hence **promiscu·ITY** prɔm-. XIX.

promise prɔ·mis assurance concerning the future. XIV. – L. *prōmissum*, sb. use of n. pp. of *prōmittere* send or put forth, promise, f. *prō* PRO-[1] + *mittere* send (see MISSION). Hence **pro·mise** vb. XV (Lydg.); after (O)F. *promettre* or L. *prōmittere.* So **pro·missORY.** XVII. – medL. *prōmissōrius.*

promontory prɔ·məntəri point of high land jutting into water. XVI. – medL. *prōmontōrium*, alt. (after *mont-, mōns* MOUNT[1]) of L. *prōmunturium*, gen. considered to be f. *prō* PRO-[1] and a deriv. of *mōns*; cf. -ORY[1].

promote prəmou·t advance in position XIV (Trevisa); further in growth XVI. f. *prōmōt-*, pp. stem of L. *prōmovēre* move forward; see PRO-[1], MOVE. So **proMO·TION.** XV (Caxton). – (O)F. – L.

prompt prɔmpt ready or quick to act. XV. – (O)F. *prompt* or L. *promptus* brought forth, manifest, ready, disposed, pp. of *prōmere* bring forth, f. *prō* PRO-[1]+*emere* take (see EMPTION). So **prompt** vb. incite to action XIV; assist (a speaker) by suggesting what is to be said XV; suggest, inspire XVII. – medL. **promptāre*, f. L. *promptus.* **pro·mptER**[1]. XV (theatr. XVII Sh.).

promulgate prɔ·məlgeit make known publicly. XVI (Palsgr.). f. pp. stem of L. *prōmulgāre* expose to public view, f. *prō* PRO-[1]+base of *mulgēre* MILK, (hence) cause to issue forth, bring to light; see -ATE[3].

prone proun naturally inclined, disposed XIV (Wycl. Bible); bending forward and downward XVI; lying flat XVII. – L. *prōnus*, f. *prō* forward (PRO[3], PRO-[1]), with suffix as in *infernus* INFERNAL, *internus* INTERNAL. So **pronA·TION** (physiol.) putting a fore limb into a prone position. XVII. – F. or medL. (f. late L. *prōnāre*). **pronA·TOR** muscle effecting this. XVIII.

prong prɔŋ forked instrument XV; tine of a fork XVII. In early use also *prang* and varying with (dial.) *sprong* (XV); the form suggests connexion with MLG. *prange* pinching, pinching instrument, horse's barnacle, Du. *prang* pinching, confinement, †shackle, LG., Du. *prangen* press, MHG. *pfrengen* (op-)press, Goth. *ana|praggan* oppress (cf. rare ME. *prangle* press tightly, pinch). Cf. PANG.

pronoun prou·naun (gram.). XVI. f. PRO-[1] instead of+NOUN, after F. *pronom* (XV) and L. *prōnōmen* (Varro, Quintilian) tr. Gr. *antōnumiā* (Aristarchus, Dionysius Thrax), f. *anti* ANTI-+*ónuma, ónoma* NAME. So **pronominAL**[1] prŏnɔ·minəl. XVII. – late L. *prōnōminālis* (Priscian); cf. NOMINAL.

pronounce prŏnau·ns utter formally; speak in a set way. XIV (R. Mannyng, Wyclif, Gower). – OF. *pronuncier* (mod. *prononcer*), for earlier *purnuncier* – L. *prōnuntiāre* proclaim, narrate, f. *prō* PRO-[1] + *nuntiāre* ANNOUNCE. So **pronunciATION** prŏnʌnsiei·ʃən. XV (Lydg.). – (O)F. or L.

pronunciamento prŏnʌ:nsiəme·ntou manifesto. XIX (W. Irving). – Sp. *pronunciamiento*, f. *pronunciar* (– L. *prōnuntiāre* PRONOUNCE)+*-miento* -MENT.

proof prūf that which makes good a statement XIII (AncrR.); action of proving or testing XIV (Wyclif); something produced as a test XVI. Later ME. *prōf* (obl. form *prōve*, pl. *prōves*), superseding earlier *prēf, prēve, preove* – OF. *preve, proeve, prueve* (mod. *preuve*) = Pr. *prova*, Sp. *prueba*, It. *prova* :– late L. *proba*, f. *probāre* PROVE. The substitution of *prōf* for *prēf* was due to assim. to the vb.; the devocalization of *v* to *f* was consequent upon the loss of final *e* (cf. *belief*). Hence **proof** adj. of tested strength XVI (Sh.); prob. from ellipsis of *of* in †*armour of proof* (XV–XVII).

prop prɔp rod, stake, or beam to support a weight. XV (Promp. Parv.). prob. – MDu. *proppe* vine-prop, support, corr. in form to MLG. *proppe* plug, stopper, bung, OHG. *pfropfo* sucker, shoot, graft, but the diversity of sense makes difficulties. Hence or – (M)LG., (M)Du. *proppen*, **prop** vb. XV. ¶ Ir. *propa*, Gael. *prop* are from Eng.

propaganda prɔpəgæ·ndə committee of cardinals charged with the foreign missions of the Church XVIII; systematic scheme for the dissemination of a doctrine or practice XIX. – It. (Sp., Pg.) *propaganda* (whence F. *propagande*), extracted from the modL. title *congregatio de propaganda fide* congregation for propagating the faith; fem. gerundive of L. *prōpāgāre.* **propagate** prɔ·pəgeit multiply specimens of (a plant, etc.); cause to increase or spread. XVI. f. pp. stem of L. *prōpāgāre* (prop.) multiply by means of layers or slips, rel. to *prōpāgō, prōpāgēs* set, layer, offspring, f. *prō* PRO-[1]+**pāg-* fix; see PACT, PAGE[1], -ATE[3]. So **propagA·TION.** XV. – (O)F. or L.

proparoxytone see OXYTONE.

propel prŏpe·l †expel XV; drive forward XVII. – L. *prōpellere*, f. *prō* PRO-[1]+*pellere* drive (see COMPEL). So **propulsION** prŏpʌ·lʃən. XVII (Florio). – medL. *prōpulsiō(n-)*; so F., It.

propensity prŏpe·nsĭti favourable disposition or tendency. XVI. f. *propense* disposed (XVI) – L. *prōpensus* inclining, inclined, pp. of *prōpendēre*, f. *prō* PRO-[1] + *pendēre*; see PENDENT, -ITY.

proper prɔ·pəɹ pert. to oneself or itself or to a person or thing particularly XIII (Cursor M.); strictly pertaining; thorough, complete; excellent, fine XIV; specially adapted XV (cf. the adv.). ME. *propre* – (O)F. *propre*, corr. to Pr., etc. *proprio* – L. *prŏprius* one's own, special, peculiar, prob. f. **prō prīuō* as a PRIVATE or peculiar thing. So **pro·per**LY[2]. XIII (appropriately, fittingly, AncrR.); after (O)F. *proprement*, L. *prŏpriē*. **property** prɔ·pəɹti ownership (esp. private) XIII (Cursor M.); thing or things owned XV (not freq. before XVII); attribute, quality XIV (R. Mannyng); †propriety XIV (Wycl.); portable article for a dramatic performance XV. ME. *proprete* – AN. **proprete*, (O)F. *propriété* – L. *prŏprietās* PROPRIETY.

prophecy prɔ·fisi action or function of a prophet, utterance of a prophet, prediction of events. XIII (AncrR., Cursor M.). – OF. *profecie* (mod. *prophétie*), corr. to Pr., Sp. *profecia*, It. *profesia* – late L. *prophētīa* – Gr. *prophētīā*, f. *prophḗtēs* prophet; see -CY. So **prophesy** prɔ·fisai speak as a prophet. XIV (PPl., Wycl. Bible). – OF. *prophecier*, f. *prophecie*; the differentiation of sp. between vb. and sb. became established after 1700; for the pronunc. of final *-y* cf. vbs. in -FY and *multiply*. **prophet** prɔ·fit inspired revealer of God's will XII; one who predicts XIII (AncrR.). ME. *profete*, *-phete* – (O)F. *prophète* – L. *prophēta*, *-tēs* – Gr. *prophḗtēs* interpreter, spokesman, esp. of the will of a deity, as in LXX and N.T., f. *pró* PRO-[2]+ *-phētēs* speaker, f. *phē-*, *phánai* speak. So **pro·phet**ESS[1]. XIII (Cursor M.). – OF. *prophetesse* – late L. *prophētissa*; **prophet**IC prŏfe·tik. XVI (Sh.), -ICAL. XV. – F. or late L.

prophylactic prɔfilæ·ktik preventive of disease. XVI. – F. *prophylactique* – Gr. *prophulaktikós*, f. *prophulássein* keep guard before; see PRO-[2], PHYLACTERY, -IC.

propinquity prŏpi·ŋkwĭti nearness, proximity. XIV (Ch.; of kinship). – OF. *propinquité* or L. *propinquitās*, f. *propinquus* neighbouring, f. *prope* near (cf. *longinquus*, f. *longe* far off), prob. for **proqe* (cf. *proximus* PROXIMATE); see -ITY.

propitiate prŏpi·ʃieit render propitious. XVII. f. pp. stem of L. *propitiāre*, f. *propitius* favourable, gracious; see -ATE[3]. So **propiti**A·TION. XIV (Wycl. Bible). **propi·tiato**RY[2]. XIII (Cursor M.). – ecclL. **propi·t**IOUS. XV (Bokenham). – OF. *propicieus* or f. L. *propitius*.

propolis prɔ·pŏlis bee-glue, resinous substance with which bees line their hives. XVII. – L. *propolis* (Pliny) – Gr. *própolis* (i) suburb, (ii) bee-glue, f. *pró* PRO-[2]+*pólis* city.

proportion prəpɔ̄·ɹʃən comparative part, share; comparative relation, relative size. XIV. Used by Wyclif, Chaucer, Trevisa, and Gower, but not fully current before XVI; – (O)F. *proportion* or L. *prōportiō(n-)* (Cicero, tr. Gr. ἀναλογία analogy), derived from phr. *prō portiōne* (tr. Gr. ἀνὰ λόγον) proportionally, i.e. *prō* PRO-[1]+abl. of *portiō* PORTION. So vb. make proportionate. XIV. – (O)F. or medL. *prōportiōnāre*. **propo·rtion**ABLE (Ch.). – late L. **propo·rtion**AL[1] (sb., Ch.). – L. **propo·rtion**ATE[2] (Trevisa). – late L.

propose prəpou·z put forward for consideration. XIV. – (O)F. *proposer*, repr. L. *prōpōnere* (see PRO-[1], POSE). Hence **propo·**SAL[2]. XVII. So **proposition** prɔpəzi·ʃən act of propounding or plan propounded XIV (Rolle, Wyclif, Usk); (math.) XVI (Billingsley) – (O)F. or L. (Cicero, tr. Gr. πρόθεσις, πρότασις, πρόβλημα; see PROTHESIS, PROTASIS, PROBLEM), f. pp. stem of *prōpōnere*, whence **propound** prŏpau·nd. XVI, alt. of †*propou·ne*, for earlier **propo·ne** (XIV; chiefly Sc.) – L. *prōpōnere* (for parasitic *d* cf. ASTOUND, COMPOUND, EXPOUND).

propraetor see PROCONSUL.

proprietary prŏprai·ĭtəri grantee of one of certain Amer. colonies; proprietorship XVII; adj. XV. – late L. *proprietārius* (in medL. as sb. holder of property), f. *proprietās* PROPERTY; see -ARY. So **proprietor** prəprai·ətəɹ one who holds something as property. XVII. alt. of prec. by irreg. substitution of suffix -TOR.

propriety prŏprai·ĭti †property XV; fitness, appropriateness XVII; conformity with good usage XVIII. – (O)F. *propriété* – L. *prŏprietās* peculiarity (Cicero; tr. Gr. ἰδιότης), ownership, f. *prŏprius* PROPER; see -ITY.

propulsion see PROPEL.

propylaeum prɔpilī·əm, -pai- entrance to a temple, etc.; introduction. XVIII. L. – Gr. *propúlaion*, sb. use of n. adj. 'before the gate'. f. *pró* PRO-[2]+*púlē* gate.

propylite prɔ·pilait (geol.) volcanic rock so named as opening the Tertiary epoch. XIX. f. Gr. *própulon* gateway, f. *pró* PRO-[2]+*púlē* gate; see -ITE.

prorogue prŏrou·g †extend in time; discontinue the meeting of (a legislative body, etc.) XV. Late ME. *proroge*, later *-rogue* (XVI) – (O)F. *proroger*, †*-guer* – L. *prōrogāre*, f. *prō* PRO-[1]+*rogāre*. So **pro**ROGA·TION prou-, prə- XV. – (O)F. or L.

proscenium prousī·niəm in the ancient theatre, space between background and orchestra XVII; in the mod. theatre, space between curtain and orchestra XIX. – L. *proscēnium* – Gr. *proskḗnion*, f. *pró* PRO-[2]+ *skēnḗ* SCENE.

proscribe pro(u)skrai·b post up the name of (a person) as condemned XVI; denounce, interdict XVII. – L. *prōscrībere* publish in writing, f. *prō* PRO-[1]+*scrībere* write (see SCRIPTURE). So **proscri·p**TION. XIV (Trevisa). – L.

prose prouz form of language not restricted in measure or rhythm XIV; (eccl.) sequence XV (Pecock); matter-of-fact expression XVI; prosy discourse XVII. – (O)F. *prose* – L. *prōsa* (sc. *ōrātiō*, 'straightforward discourse'), sb. use of fem. of *prōsus*, for earlier *prorsus* straightforward, direct, contr. of *prō·versus*, pp. of *prōvertere* turn forwards, f. *prō* PRO-[1] + *vertere* turn (see -WARD). So **prosa**IC prouzei·ik. XVI. – F. or late L. *prōsaicus* (Fortunatus), after *mosaic*. **pro·sy**[1] XIX.

prosecute prɔ·sikjūt follow up, go on with XV; carry on; institute legal proceedings against XVI. f. *prōsecūt-*, pp. stem of L. *prōsequī* pursue, accompany, f. *prō* PRO-[1] + *sequī* follow (see SEQUENCE). So **prosecu·**TION. XVI. – OF. or late L. Cf. PURSUE.

proselyte prɔ·silait convert, spec. to the Jewish religion. XIV. – late (Christian) L. *prosēlytus* – Gr. *prosḗluthos* stranger, sojourner (LXX), convert to Judaism (N.T.), f. 2nd aorist stem (*prosēluth-*) of *prosérkhesthai* come to, approach. Hence **pro·selyt**IZE. XVII (†*proselyte* is somewhat earlier).

prosody prɔ·sədi science of versification. XV. – L. *prosōdia* accent of a syllable (Varro, Quintilian) – Gr. *prosōidíā* song sung to music, tone of a syllable, mark indicating this, f. *prós* to :– **proti* (cf. Skr. *práti* opposite to) + *ōidḗ* song, ODE; see -Y[3]. Cf. F. *prosodie* (XVI).

prosopopœia prɔsŏpŏpī·ə (rhet.) figure by which an imaginary or absent person is represented as acting, (hence) personification. XVI. – L. (Quintilian) – Gr. *prosōpopoiíā* representation in human form, f. *prósōpon* face, person (f. *pròs* to + *ṓps* EYE, face) + *poieîn* make (cf. POET).

prospect prɔ·spekt view afforded by a position XV; spectacle, scene; mental vista XVII (Sh.). – L. *prōspectus* look-out, view, f. *prōspicere*, f. *prō* PRO-[1] + *specere* look (cf. ASPECT). So **prospe·ct** vb. †look forward XVI; explore a region *for* mineral XIX (from the use of the sb. for 'spot giving promise of mineral deposit'). **prospe·ct**IVE. XVI. – obs. F. or late L. **prospe·ctus** prŏspe·ktəs description in advance of a proposed undertaking. XVIII. – L.; prob. after F. use (XVIII).

prosper prɔ·spəɹ be fortunate or successful XV; trans. XVI. – (O)F. *prospérer* or L. *prosperāre*, f. *prosper*, *prosperus* doing well or successfully. So **prosper**ITY prɔspe·rĭti. XIII (AncrR.). – (O)F. – L. **pro·sper**OUS. XV. – F. †*prospereus*, f. L. *prosper*.

prostate prɔ·steit (anat.) gland at junction of neck of the bladder and the urethra. XVII (Sir T. Browne). – F. *prostate* (Paré) – modL. *prostata* – Gr. *prostátēs* one that stands before, guardian, f. *pró* PRO-[2] + *statós* placed, standing, f. **sta-* (see STAND).

prosthesis prɔ·sþĭsis (philol.) addition of a letter or syllable at the beginning of a word. XVI. – late L. *prosthesis* (Charisius, Diomedes) – Gr. *prósthesis*, f. *prostithénai* add, f. *prós* to; see THESIS.

prostitute prɔ·stitjūt †adj. offered or exposed to lust XVI; sb. woman given over to indiscriminate sexual intercourse for hire XVII (Purchas). – L. *prōstitūtus* (fem. *prōstitūta* as sb.), pp. of *prōstituere* expose publicly, offer for sale, prostitute, f. *prō* PRO-[1] + *statuěre* set up, place (see STATUTE). So **pro·stitute** vb. XVI. f. pp. stem of the L. vb. **prostitu·**TION. XVI. – (O)F. or late L.

prostrate prɔ·streit lying with face to the ground. XIV. – L. *prōstrātus*, pp. of *prōsternere* throw in front, cast down, f. *prō* PRO-[1] + *sternere* lay low; see STRATUM, -ATE[2]. So vb. XV. f. the pp. stem; formerly *prostra·te*. **prostra·**TION. XVI. – (O)F. or late L.

protagonist pro(u)tæ·gənist chief personage in a drama XVII; leading person in a contest or cause XIX. – Gr. *prōtagōnistḗs*, f. *prôtos* first, PROTO- + *agōnistḗs* combatant, actor, f. *agōnízesthai* contest, AGONIZE; see -IST.

protasis prɔ·təsis †first part of a play; (gram.) introductory clause of a sentence. XVII. – L. *protasis* (Apuleius, Donatus) – Gr. *prótasis* proposition, problem, etc., f. *proteínein* put forward, tender, f. *pró* PRO-[2] + *teínein* stretch (cf. TEND[2], TENUOUS).

protect prŏte·kt defend from injury. XVI. f. *prōtect-*, pp. stem of L. *prōtegere* cover in front, f. *prō* PRO-[1] + *tegere* cover (see TEGUMENT). So **prote·c**TION. XIV. – (O)F. or late L. **prote·ctor**[1]. XIV. – (O)F. – late L.; hence **prote·ctor**ATE[1]. XVII.

protégé, fem. **-gée** prɔ·tĭʒei one under another's protection. XVIII (Sheridan). F., pp. of *protéger* – L. *prōtegere* PROTECT.

protein prou·tiin, -tīn (chem.) one of a class of organic compounds forming essential constituents of living organisms. XIX. – F. *protéine* (Mulder 1838), G. *proteïn*, f. Gr. *prōteîos* (n. as sb. *-on* chief place), f. *prôtos* first (PROTO-); see -IN. Hence **pro·te**ID[3] prou·tiid. XIX.

pro tem short for *pro tempore* (see PRO[3]).

protest prou·test protestation XIV; formal written declaration XVII; declaration of dissent XVIII. – F. †*protest* (mod. *protêt*), f. *protester* (whence **protest** prŏte·st vb. XV). – L. *prōtestārī* declare formally, f. *prō* PRO-[1] + *testārī* be a witness, assert (see TESTAMENT). So **protest**ANT prɔ·tistənt applied to those who joined in the protest at the Diet of Spires in 1529; (hence) non-Roman-Catholic XVI (1539); (with pronunc. prŏte·stənt) one who protests (gen.) XVII. – L. *prōtestāns*, prp. of *prōtestārī*. **protest**ATION prɔtèstei·ʃən. XIV. – (O)F. – late L.

proteus prou·tiəs, -tjūs (Gr. and Rom. myth.) sea-god fabled to change his shape, transf. and fig. XVI; amœba; genus of amphibians XIX. L. – Gr. *Proteús*. Hence **pro·te**AN changing, varying, XVI.

proto- prou·tou comb. form of Gr. *prôtos* first, obscurely rel. to *pró* PRO-[2]; in many techn. terms; formerly chem. from 1804 (*protoxide*, T. Thomson); **pro·to**MARTYR first martyr, e.g. St. Stephen. XV (Lydg.). – medL. **proto**NO·TARY principal notary, chief clerk. XV (Bokenham). – medL. **protoplasm** prou·tŏplæzm substance constituting the physical basis of life. XIX (1848, Lindley). – G. *prōtoplasma* (H. von Mohl, 1846), f. Gr. *prôtos* first, PROTO-+*plásma* moulded thing (see PLASMA); **proto**TYPE prou·tŏtaip primary type. XVII. – F. or late L. **protozoa** proutŏzou·ə (zool.) division of animals of the most primitive type. XIX (Coleridge). modL. (Goldfuss, 1818), f. Gr. *prōto-* PROTO-+*zôia* animals; see ZOOLOGY, -A[2].

protocol prou·tŏkəl original note or minute of a transaction XVI; original draft or record of a diplomatic document XVII; etiquette of precedence, etc. XIX. orig. *prothocoll* (in earliest use Sc.) – OF. *prothocole* (mod. *protocole*), corr. to Pr. *prothcolle*, Sp. *protocolo*, It. *protocollo* – medL. *prōtocollum* – Gr. *prōtókollon* first leaf of a volume, fly-leaf glued to the case and containing an account of the contents, f. *prôtos* PROTO-+*kólla* glue.

proton prou·tən (phys.) unit of matter associated with a charge of positive electricity. XX. – n. sg. of Gr. *prôtos* first.

protract prŏtræ·kt A. lengthen out; B. draw to scale. XVI. f. *prōtract-*, pp. stem of L. *prōtrahere* prolong, defer, in medL. also in sense B, f. *prō* PRO-[1]+*trahere* draw; cf. PORTRAY. So **protra·ction**. XVI. – F. or late L. **protra·ctor**[1] one who prolongs time, etc.; instrument used in setting off and measuring angles. XVII. – medL.

protrude prŏtrū·d thrust forward; also intr. for refl. or pass. XVII. – L. *prōtrūdere*, f. *prō* PRO-[1] + *trūdere* press, thrust (see THREAT, and cf. ABSTRUSE). So **protru·sion**. XVII (Sir T. Browne). – F. or modL.

protuberant prŏtjū·bərənt bulging beyond the surface. XVII (Sir T. Browne). – prp. of late L. *prōtūberāre*, f. *prō* PRO-[1] + *tūber* bump, swelling; see TUBER, -ANT. So **protu·ber**ANCE. XVII. – modL.

proud praud having a high opinion of oneself OE.; feeling honoured; stately, grand XIII; †valiant XIV; overgrown, tumid XVI. Late OE. *prūd* (also *prūt*) = ON. *prúðr* – OF. *prud*, *prod*, nom. *pruz*, *proz*, *prouz* (mod. *preux*) valiant, gallant = Pr. *proz*, Cat. *prou*, It. *prode* – Rom. **prōdis* (late L. *prōde*, n. in pre-Vulg. *a.* 200), f. L. *prōdesse* be of value, be good, f. *prōd*, var. of *prō* PRO-[1]+*esse* be (cf. ENS). Cf. PRIDE, PRUDE.

prove prūv try, test XII; make good, establish XIII. OE. *prōfian*, succeeded by – OF. *prover* (mod. *prouver*) = Pr. *proar*, Sp. *probar*, It. *probare* :- L. *probāre* test, approve, demonstrate, f. *probus* good (see PROBITY). For the ME. var. *preove*, *preve*, later *prieve*, Sc. *preif*, derived from OF. forms with radical stress (*preuve*, etc.) cf. MOVE. The pp. *proven* prou·vn, prū·vn (orig. Sc. law), belongs to the var. *preve*, and is based on the analogy of †*chese*/*chosen*, *cleave*/*cloven*, *weave*/*woven*.

provenance prɔ·vənəns, -nās place of origin. XIX. F., f. prp. of *provenir* come forth – L. *prōvenīre*, f. *prō* PRO-[1]+*venīre* COME. The form **provenience** prŏvī·niəns, derived immed. from the prp. of the L. vb., is preferred in U.S.A. See -ANCE, -ENCE.

Provençal prŏvā·sæl, prəvənsā·l pert. to Provence, former province in south-east France XVI; the Romance language spoken there XVII. Formerly †*-zal*, †*-cial*; – F. *provençal* – L. *prōvinciālis* PROVINCIAL; the southern part of ancient Gaul, Gallia Narbonensis, which came under Roman rule long before the rest, was familiarly styled (*nostra*) *provincia* the or our province.

provender prɔ·vĭndəɹ †prebend; food, provisions. XIV. – OF. *provendre*, var. of *provende* = It. *profenda* :- Rom. **prōbenda* (whence also OS. *prōvenda*, OHG. *pfruonta*, G. *pfründe*, ON. *prófenda*), alt. of L. *præbenda* PREBEND (cf. PROVOST). ¶ For parasitic *r* cf. PHILOSOPHER.

proverb prɔ·vəːb short pithy saying embodying a general truth. XIV (first in the biblical title, R. Mannyng; in gen. use, Ch., Wycl., Gower). – (O)F. *proverbe* or L. *prōverbium*, f. *prō* PRO-[1]+*verbum* WORD, as if 'a set of words put forth' (cf. the formation of *adagium* ADAGE). So **prove·rb**IAL. XV. – L.

proviant prɔ·viənt provision, commissariat. XVII (introduced by soldiers who served in the Thirty Years War 1618–48). – G. *proviant* (cf. Du. *proviand*) – It. *provianda*, alt. of †*provenda* (see PROVENDER).

provide prəvai·d †(intr.) exercise foresight; furnish for use; fit out. XV. – L. *prōvidēre* foresee, attend to, f. *prō* PRO-[1]+*vidēre* (see VISION); cf. PURVEY. So **provid**ENCE prɔ·vidəns foresight, prevision, timely care XIV (Wycl. Bible, Gower); applied to God XVII. – (O)F. or L. **pro·vid**ENT. XV. – L. (cf. PRUDENT). Hence **provide·nt**IAL. XVII. **provision** prŏvi·ʒən appointment to a see or benefice not yet vacant XIV (Wycl., Trevisa); †foresight, providing in advance; clause providing for a matter; supply of necessaries, etc. XV; supply of food XVII. – (O)F. *provision* – L. *prōvīsiō(n-)*, f. pp. stem of *prōvidēre* PROVIDE; see -ION. Hence **provi·sion**AL[1]. XVII; after F. †*provisionnal* (now *-el*). **proviso** prəvai·zou clause making a condition. XV. – L. *prōvīsō*, abl. sg. n. of pp. of *prōvīdēre* PROVIDE, as used in medL. phr. *prōvīsō quod* (or *ut*) . . it being provided that . . (cf. F. *pourvu que* . .). **provisor** prŏvai·zəɹ holder of a certain grant (now hist. in *Statute of Provisors*); (arch.) one who provides, or purveys XIV. – AN. *provisour* (F. *proviseur*) – L. *prōvīsor*, agent-noun of *prōvīdēre* PROVIDE; see -OR[1].

province prɔ·vins district, region XIV (R. Mannyng); territory outside Italy under Roman rule, hence gen. XIV; department of activity XVII (Bacon). – (O)F. *province* – L. *prōvincia* charge, official duty, administration or region of conquered territory, of unkn. origin. So **provinc**IAL prŏvi·nʃəl. XIV (PPl., Wyclif). – (O)F. – L. Cf. PROVENÇAL. Hence **provi·ncial**ISM. XVIII.

provoke prəvou·k incite, esp. to anger; call forth, evoke. XV. – (O)F. *provoquer* or L. *prōvocāre*, f. *prō* PRO-[1]+*vocāre* call (see VOCATION). So **provoca·**TION, **provoc**ATIVE -vɔ·k-. XV. – (O)F. or (late) L.

provost prɔ·vəst, (in *p. marshal*) prəvou· official set over others (in various spec. uses). Late OE. *profost* (also *prafost*), corr. to MLG., MDu. *provest*, MDu. *proofst* (Du. *proost*), OHG. *probost* (G. *probst, propst*), ONorw. *prófastr*; in ME. reinforced from AN. *provost* (also *prevost*, modF. *prévôt*) – medL. *prōpositus*, used alongside *præpositus*, sb. use of pp. of L. *præpōnere*, f. *præ* PRE-, PRO-[1] + *pōnere* place (see POSITION).

prow prau fore-part of a sailing vessel. XVI. – (O)F. *proue* – Pr. *proa* or It. dial. (Genoese, Sicilian) *prua* = Sp., Pg. *proa*, It. *proda* :– L. *prōra* – Gr. *prôira*, f. base repr. by L. *prō* before, in front of (PRO-[1]). The earlier pronunc. prou continued till early XIX; the present one may be due to assoc. with BOW[3].

prowess prau·is valour, manly courage. XIII (RGlouc.). – OF. *proesce* (mod. *prouesse*) = Pr., Sp. *proeza*, It. *prodezza*; f. OF. *prou* (whence †*prow* adj. worthy, valiant XIV), early *prod*, etc.; see PROUD, -ESS[2].

prowl praul go about in search of something, esp. plunder. XIV (Ch.). Late ME. *prolle*, of unkn. origin. The earlier pronunc. was prōl, proul, Dryden rhyming *controll/prole, proul'd/fold*; the graphic change (XVI) of *prolle* to *proule, prowle* finally induced a change of pronunc.

proximate prɔ·ksimət immediately adjacent XVI; coming next XVII. – L. *proximātus*, pp. of *proximāre* approach, f. *proximus* nearest, superl. of **proqe*, var. of *prope* near (cf. APPROACH, PROPINQUITY); see -ATE[2]. So **proxi·m**ITY nearness. XV. – (O)F. or L.

proxy prɔ·ksi action of a substitute or deputy XV; document authorizing a person to act for another XVI. Earlier forms *procusie, prokecye, proccy*, contr. of †*procracy*, †*pro·curacy* (XIII) – medL. *prōcūrātia*, repl. L. *prōcūrātiō* PROCURATION; see -ACY and cf. PROCTOR.

prude prūd woman who affects excessive modesty or propriety; †also adj. XVIII. – F. *prude* adj. and sb. (Molière), back-formation from *prudefemme*, misunderstood as adj.+sb. but prop. fem. (f. **preu de femme*) corr. to *prud'homme* good man and true, earlier *prodome* (f. **pro de ome* 'fine thing of a man'); cf. PROUD. Hence **pru·d**ISH[1]. XVIII (Pope). So **pru·d**ERY. XVIII (Steele). – F. *pruderie* (Molière).

prudent prū·dənt marked by sound practical judgement. XIV (Wycl. Bible, Ch.). – (O)F. *prudent* or L. *prūdēns* foreseeing, sagacious :– **prōwidēns*, f. *prō* PRO-[1]+prp. of *vidēre* (cf. the new formation *prōvidēns* PROVIDENT). So **pru·d**ENCE. XIV. – (O)F. – L. **prude·nt**IAL. XVII. – medL. or f. L. *prūdentia*.

prune[1] prūn dried fruit of the plum-tree. XIV. – (O)F. *prune* = Pr., OSp. *pruna*, Rum. *prună* :– Rom. **prūna*, fem. sg. for L. n. *prūna*, pl. of *prūnum* – Gr. *proûnon*, later form of *proûmnon* PLUM.

prune[2] prūn trim (feathers) with the beak. XIV. ME. *prune, pruyne*, also *proyne*, Sc. *prunȝe* – pres. stem *poroign-* of OF. *poroindre*, f. *por-* (mod. *pour-*) :– L. *prō-* PRO-[1] +*oindre* :– L. *ungere* anoint (see UNGUENT). Cf. PREEN.

prune[3] prūn lop superfluous growth from. XV (Lydg.). Early forms *prouyne, proine, pruine* – OF. *proignier*, earlier *prooignier* :– Rom. **prōrotundiāre*, f. *prō* PRO-[1]+ **rotundiāre* cut round (whence F. *rogner* clip, prune, †tonsure), f. *rotundus* ROUND.

prunella prune·lə strong (worsted) stuff used for academic gowns. XVII. Of uncertain origin; †*prunello* and *prunella* may be alterations after Sp. or It. of F. *prunelle* (XVIII), derived by some from *prune* plum (PRUNE), as if 'plum-coloured stuff'.

prurient pruə·rjənt itching, having an itching desire XVII; given to lewd thoughts XVIII. – L. *prūrient-, -ēns*, prp. of *prūrīre* itch, long, be wanton; see -ENT. So **prurigo** -ai·gou, **pruritus** -ai·təs itching XVII. L.

Prussian prʌ·ʃən pert. to *Prussia*, a Baltic territory, f. *Prussi* (or *Borussi*), a people belonging to the Balto-Slavic group whose language (*Old P.*) became obsolete in the 17th century; see -IAN. XVII.

prussic prʌ·sik pert. to or derived from *Prussian blue*, which was so called from having been discovered (1704) by Diesbach, a Berlin colour-maker; *p. acid*, hydrocyanic acid, CNH. XVIII. – F. *prussique* (de Morveau, 1787), f. *Prusse* Prussia; see -IC.

pry[1] prai look closely or inquisitively. XIV. Of unkn. origin.

pry[2] prai (dial. and U.S.) prize *up*. XIX. Evolved from PRIZE[4] through apprehending the final cons. as the ending of the 3rd sg. pres. ind.

prytaneum pritənī·əm public hall of a Greek state or city. XVI. – L. *prytanēum* – Gr. *prutaneîon*, f. *prútanis* prince, ruler(at Athens), president, rel. to *protaini* before.

psalm sām sacred song or hymn, spec. one of the collection in the Bible so entitled. OE. *psalm, psealm, s(e)alm* (reinforced in ME. from OF.), corr. to OHG. *(p)salmo* (G. *psalm*), ON. *(p)salmr* – late L. *psalmus* (whence OF. *saume*, F. *psaume*, etc.) – Gr. *psalmós* plucking with the fingers, sounding of the harp, (in LXX and N.T.) song sung to the harp, f. *psállein* pluck, twang, play with the fingers, sing to the harp, perh. rel. to L. *palpāre* (see PALPITATION). So **psalm-IST** sā·mist author of a psalm or psalms. XV. – late L. **psa·lmody**[3]. XIV (Rolle). – late L. *psalmōdia* (Jerome) – Gr. *psalmōidiā*, f. *psalmōidós* psalmist (see ODE). So **psalter** sō·ltəɹ book of psalms OE. *(p)saltere*, corr. to OHG. *(p)salteri*, ON. *(p)saltari* – late L. *psaltērium* – Gr. *psaltḗrion* stringed instrument, (in Christian L. and Gr. writers) the book of Psalms of the O.T., f. *psállein*; ME. *sauter* – AN. *sauter*, OF. *sautier* (mod. *psautier*). **psaltery** sō·ltəri ancient stringed instrument. XIII. ME. *sautre, sautrie* – OF. *sautere, -erie* – L. *psaltērium*; all finally superseded by latinized forms in *ps-*, which have been exclusively used since 1600.

psephology psīfɔ·lədʒi study of the conduct of public elections. XX. f. Gr. *psêphos* pebble, vote (rel. to *psámmos* sandy, L. *sabulum* sand) + -LOGY.

pseudo- (p)sjū·dou before a vowel *pseud-*, repr. comb. el. of Gr. *pseudḗs* false, *pseûdos* falsehood, in comps. adopted (often through L.) from Gr. or modelled on them.

pseudonym (p)sjū·dənim fictitious name. XIX. – F. *pseudonyme* – Gr. *pseudṓnumon*, n. of *pseudṓnumos* (*ónuma, ónoma* NAME), whence **pseudonymous** -ɔ·niməs. XVIII.

pshaw (p)ʃō natural excl. of rejection. XVII. Cf. PISH, †*push* (XVI), TUSH.

psittacosis (p)sitəkou·sis contagious disease of birds, esp. parrots. XIX. modL., irreg. f. L. *psittacus* – Gr. *psittakós* parrot; see -OSIS.

psoriasis (p)sŏrai·əsis (path.) disease of the skin. XIX. – modL. *psōriāsis* – Gr. *psōriāsis*, f. *psōriân* itch, f. *psṓrā* itch, rel. to *psên* scratch, rake, reduce to dust, Skr. *bhas* crush, chew, devour.

psyche (p)sai·ki soul, spirit, mind. XVII. – L. *psȳchē* – Gr. *psūkhḗ* breath, soul, life, rel. to *psū́khein* breathe, blow, cool, *psȳkhrós* cool (whence comb. form **psychro-**). So **psy·chic** XIX, -ICAL XVII (More; rare before XIX); first in senses pert. to soul or mind, from 1878 (*psychical research*) pert. to conditions supposed to be outside the physical domain. – Gr. *psūkhikós* (cf. late L. *psȳchicus* carnal, Tertullian). **psycho-** sai·kou, saikɔ·, comb. form of Gr. *psūkhḗ* used in techn. terms since XVII, but prolifically only since mid-XIX; before a vowel **psych-**, as in **psychiatry** -ai·ətri healing of mental disease (Gr. *hiātrós* healer). **psychology** saikɔ·lədʒi science of the human soul or mind. XVII (only occas. before XIX). – modL. *psȳchologia* (XVI, Melanchthon, Freigius, Goclenius); cf. F., G. *psychologie*. So **psycholo·gical** pert. to psychology; loosely used for 'psychical' XVIII; cf. F. *psychologique*, G. *psychologisch*. In *p. moment* moment at which the mind is prepared to receive what is to happen; through F., a journalistic perversion of G. *das psychologische Moment* through confusion of *der Moment* moment (of time) with *das Moment* operative factor, momentum.

ptarmigan tā·ɹmigən bird of the grouse family, Lagopus alpinus or mutus. XVI. Early forms (in Sc. use) *termigan(t), termagant, tormichan* – Gael. *tarmachan*, of unkn. origin; fancifully sp. *ptarmigan* (after Gr. words with *pt-*, e.g. *pterón* wing) by Sibbald in 'Scotia Illustrata', 1684, and hence by Pennant in his 'Zoology', 1768.

pterido- (p)te·rido(u) repr. comb. form of Gr. *pterís, -id-* fern, rel. to *pterón* (see next).

pterodactyl (p)teroudæ·ktil extinct winged reptile. XIX. – modL. *pterodactylus*, f. Gr. *pterón* wing + *dáktulos* finger; see FEATHER, DACTYL. So **pte·rosaur.** XIX; see SAURUS.

pterygoid (p)te·rigoid wing-like. XVIII. f. Gr. *pterug-, ptérux* wing, fin (cf. prec.) + -OID.

ptisane tizæ·n medicinal decoction, orig. barley-water. XIV. Earlier *tizanne, tysan*, later *ptisane* (XVI) – (O)F. *tisane*, later †*ptisane* – medL. *tisana*, – L. *ptisana* – Gr. *ptisánē* peeled barley, barley-water, f. base of *ptíssein* peel, bray (cf. L. *pinsere* knead; see PESTLE).

Ptolemaic tɔlimei·ik pert. to (the astronomical system of) Ptolemy (L. *-æus*, Gr. *-aîos*) of Alexandria (II A.D.). XVII (earlier **-æ·an**). See -IC.

ptomaine tou·mein, toumei·n gen. name for alkaloid bodies found in putrefying matter. XIX. – F. *ptomaïne* – It. *ptomaina* (Selmi, of Bologna), irreg. f. Gr. *ptôma* (*-at-*) corpse, lit. 'fallen body', f. **p(e)t-* fall (cf. L. *petere* make for; see PETITION). See -INE[5].

puberty pjū·bəɹti condition of having become functionally capable of producing offspring. XIV (Wycl. Bible, Trevisa; not frequent till XVI). – L. *pūbertās* (or the deriv. F. *puberté*), f. *pūber, pūbēs, -is* (*-er-*) adult, *pūbēs* pubic hair; see -TY. So **pubes** pjū·bīz XVI, whence **pu·bic** XIX. **pube·scent** of the age of puberty XVII; downy XVIII. – F. *pubescent* or L. *pūbēscent-, -ēns*, prp. of *pūbēscere* reach the age of puberty. **pube·scence.** XVII.

public pʌ·blik pert. to the people or to a community as a whole XV; sb. *in p.* (tr. F. *en public*, L. *in publicō*) XV; *the* state or commonwealth; *the* community as a whole XVII; short for *p. house* (XVII), i.e. of entertainment

XVIII. – (O)F. *public, -ique* or L. *pūblicus*, based on *pūbes* adult (see prec.) with crossing from *poplicus*, f. *populus* PEOPLE; see -IC. So **pu·blic**AN tax-gatherer XII; keeper of a public house XVIII. – (O)F. *publicain* – L. *pūblicānus* orig. farmer general of the revenues, f. *pūblicum* public revenue, sb. use of n. of *pūblicus*. **pu·blic**IST -isist one learned in international law XVIII; political journalist XIX; publicity agent XX. – F., f. L. (*jūs*) *pūblicum* public law. **public**ITY -i·sĭti being open to public observation XVIII; making things public XX. – F. **pu·bli**CIZE. XX.

publish pʌ·bliʃ make publicly known XIV; issue copies of (a book, etc.) to the public XVI. ME. *puplise, -ische, publishe*, f. stem of OF. *puplier*, (also mod.) *publier* – L. *pūblicāre* make public, f. *pūblicus*; see -ISH². So **public**A·TION. XIV. – (O)F. – L.

puccoon pʌkū·n N. Amer. plant yielding a red pigment. XVII (Capt. Smith). Algonquian.

puce pjūs purplish-brown. XVIII. – (O)F. *puce* flea (*couleur puce* 'flea colour' XVII) :– L. *pūlicem, pūlex*, ult. rel. to FLEA.

Puck pʌk dial. **Pook**? †evil spirit or demon, spec. the Devil OE.; mischievous sprite, called also Robin Goodfellow and Hobgoblin XVI. Late OE. *pūca* (in glosses and place-names) = ON. *púki* mischievous demon; cf. W. *pwca, pwci*, Ir. *púca*; whether Germ. or Celtic origin is prior is uncertain.

pucka see PUKKA.

pucker pʌ·kəɹ contract into wrinkles. XVI. prob. frequent. f. base *pok-* of POKE¹, POCKET, as if 'make pockets', 'form into bag-like gatherings'; see -ER⁴. Cf. F. *faire des poches* bag, pucker. Hence **pu·cker** sb. XVIII.

pud pʌd hand of a child, paw of an animal. XVII. Nursery word of unkn. origin, but poss. var. of PAD. Hence (perh.) **pudsy** pʌ·dzi plump XVIII, poss. alt. to **pudgy** pʌ·dʒi short and thick, whence by back-formation **pudge** short thickset person XIX (cf. PODGE).

pudding pu·diŋ animal's stomach or intestine stuffed with meat, etc. XIII; (dial.) pl. entrails XV; preparation of food with basis of flour boiled, orig. in a bag XVI. ME. *poding, puddyng*, corr. in meaning to (O)F. *boudin*, which it is difficult or impossible to connect formally. ¶ Similar words in Germ. and Celtic langs. are from Eng.

puddle pʌ·dl small dirty pool. XIV (R. Mannyng). ME. *podel*, later *puddel*, dim. of OE. *pudd* ditch, furrow; see -LE¹. Cf. OE. *pydel* (see PIDDLE) and G. dial. *pudel, pfudel*. So **pu·ddle** vb. dabble in mud, etc. XV; make muddy XVI; stir (molten iron) XVIII. Cf. Du. *poedelen*, LG. *pud(d)eln*. ¶ W. *pwdel* is from Eng.

pudendum, pl. **-enda** pjude·ndəm, -də private parts XVII (once XIV). – late L. *pudenda*, sb. use of n. sg. and pl. of *pudendus* gerundive of L. *pudet* it is shameful.

puerile pjuə·rail pert. to a boy or child, esp. in depreciation. XVII. – F. *puéril* or L. *puerīlis*, f. *puer* boy, child (:– **poweros*; cf. Gr. *paîs* child :– **pawis*); see -ILE and cf. PUSILLANIMOUS. So **pueril**ITY pjuəɹi·lĭti. XVI. – F. or L.

puerperal pjuə̄·ɹpərəl pert. to parturition. XVIII. f. L. *puerperus* parturient, f. *puer* child + *-parus* bringing forth; see prec., PARENT, -AL¹.

puff pʌf short emission of air or vapour XIII (AncrR.); swollen or inflated object (light pastry; cf. LG. *puffe, puffebrodt*) XV; (exaggerated) commendation XVII. So vb. expel breath with the lips XIII; inflate XVI. In the earliest exx. *puf* sb., *puffe* vb., pt. *pufte*, the *u* may denote either u or ü, and may repr. OE. **puf* or *pyf(f)* sb., **puffan* or *pyffan* (imper. *pyf*, pt. *pyfte*, prp. *piffende*; also *āpyffan* exhale), corr. to (M)Du. *puffen*, Du. *pof, poffen*, LG. *pof, puf*. The vb. is recorded in 'South English Legendary' (XIII) as *poffe* breathe (r.w. *astoffe* stifle) and in PPl. and Ch. as *poffe, puffe*. Of echoic origin, imit. of the sound of the breath.

puffin pʌ·fin sea-bird of the genus Fratercula. XIV. Late ME. *poffo(u)n, pophyn* (AL. *poffo*), of unkn. origin, perh. Cornish (the earliest reference concerns Scilly in the duchy of Cornwall); prob. assim. later to PUFF on account of the bird's plump or puffed-out appearance.

pug¹ pʌg †term of endearment; †courtesan, harlot; bargeman XVI; †imp; monkey XVII; dwarf breed of dog XVIII; genus of moths XIX. poss. of LDu. origin; cf. WFlem. *Pugge*, substituted for a Christian name, as *Pugge Willems* (De Bo).

pug² pʌg (dial.) pull, tug XVI; in techn. uses expressing stamping or thrusting action XIX. perh. symbolic formation with structure resembling that of *lug, plug, slug, tug*. Cf. WFlem. *pug(ge)* hard prod, kick, knock.

puggaree pʌ·gəri Indian native's light turban XVII; scarf or veil wound round a sun helmet XIX. – Hind. *pagrī*.

pugilist pjū·dʒĭlist boxer. XVIII. f. L. *pugil* (for the ending cf. *vigil*), f. base of *pugnus* fist, *pugnāre* fight, perh. identical with that of *pungere* (pt. *pupugī*) prick (see POINT); cf., however, Gr. *púx* with the fist, *pugmákhos* pugilist, *pugmḗ* fist, boxing; see -IST. **pugn**ACIOUS pʌgnei·ʃəs disposed to fight. XVII. f. L. *pugnāci-, -āx*, f. *pugnāre*, f. *pugnus*. **pugnac**ITY -næ·sĭti. XVII. – L.

puisne pjū·ni younger, junior (now only of judges). XVI. Legal sp. of PUNY.

puissant pjū·isənt, pwi·sənt, pjui·sənt (arch.) powerful. XV. – (O)F. *puissant* = Pr. *poissan* :– Gallo-Rom. **possiantem* (f. L. *posse*), for L. *potentem*, *-ēns* POTENT. So **puiss**ANCE. XV. – (O)F. *puissance* = Pr. *poissansa*, *-ensa*.

puke pjūk vomit. XVI (Sh.; somewhat earlier in *pewkishnesse*, Mulcaster 1581). prob. of imit. origin; cf., for similar expressive elements, LG. (whence G.) *spucken*, Flem. *spukken* spew, spit, and SPEW.

pukka, pucka pʌ·kə of full weight; genuine; reliable, permanent. XVII. – Hindi *pakkā* ripe, mature, cooked, made of brick, firm, strong.

pule pjūl whine, cry plaintively. XVI. prob. of imit. origin; cf. F. *piauler*, dial. *pioular* chirp, whine, and MEWL.

pull pul (dial.) pluck; drag or tug at. Late OE. *pullian*, also *āpullian*, having ostensible similarity in form and sense to LG. *pūlen* shell, strip, pluck, MDu. *polen* 'decorticare' (Kilian), and (M)LG. *pūle*, Du. *peul* husk, shell, the meaning 'pluck, snatch' being prob. the original (cf. PLUCK); the sense 'take a draught of' (XV) is in Du., LG. *pullen*. Hence sb. XIV.

pullet pu·lit young hen of the domestic fowl. XIV (PPl.). – (O)F. *poulet*, fem. *-ette*, dim. of *poule* hen = Pr. *pola*, Sp., It. *polla* :– Rom. **pulla*, fem. of L. *pullus* young animal, chicken (see FOAL); cf. POULTRY.

pulley pu·li grooved wheel for cord to pass over, used for changing direction of power. XIV. ME. *poley* – OF. *polie* (mod. *poulie*) = Pr. *poleja* (whence Sp. *polea*, Pg. *polé*), It. *puleggia* :– Rom. **polidia* (n. pl. used as fem. sg.), pl. of **polidium*, prob. – medGr. **polidion*, dim. of *pólos* POLE[2], also windlass, capstan.

pullicate pu·likət coloured handkerchief orig. made at *Pulicat* on the Madras coast, India. XVIII.

pullman pu·lmən railway carriage constructed as a saloon. XIX. f. name of the designer, George M. *Pullman* (1831–97), of Chicago, U.S.A.

pullulate pʌ·ljūleit sprout XVII; swarm XIX. f. pp. stem of L. *pullulāre* spring forth, grow (whence F. *pulluler* swarm), f. *pullulus*, dim. of *pullus* young of an animal, chick (cf. FOAL); see -ATE[3].

pulmonary pʌ·lmənəri pert. to the lungs. XVIII. – L. *pulmōnārius*, f. *pulmōn-*, *pulmō* lung, rel. obscurely to synon. Gr. *pleúmōn*, OSl. *pljušta* pl., OPruss. *plauti*; see -ARY and cf. F. *pulmonaire*.

pulp pʌlp fleshy part of fruit, etc. XVI; soft formless mass XVII. – L. *pulpa* (whence also F. *poulpe*, It. *polpa*, etc.).

pulpit pu·lpit raised structure from which a sermon is preached. XIV (R. Mannyng). – L. *pulpitum* scaffold, platform, stage, medL. pulpit (whence F. *pupitre*), prob. of alien origin.

pulse[1] pʌls rhythmical dilatation of the arteries. XIV. ME. *pous*, *pouce*, later *puls* – OF. *pous*, later (latinized) *pouls* = Pr. *pous*, Cat. *pols* temple, It. *polso* :– L. *pulsu-s* beating (spec. *vēnārum* of the veins) :– **pelssos* f. base of *pellere* drive, beat. So **pulse** vb. †drive; pulsate. XVI. – L. *pulsāre*, frequent. of *pellere*; **pu·lsa**TE[3]. XVIII; **pulsa·**TION. XVI. – L. Cf. PUSH, REPULSE.

pulse[2] pʌls edible seeds of leguminous plants. XIII. ME. *pols* – OF. *pols* (mod. dial. *poul(s)*, *pou*) :– L. *puls* (*pult-*) thick pottage of meal or pulse (cf. Gr. *póltos* porridge), rel. to POLLEN. Latinized in form from XV.

pulverize pʌ·lvəraiz reduce to powder. XVI. – late L. *pulverizāre* (Vegetius), f. *pulver-*, *pulvis* dust, rel. to POLLEN; cf. F. *pulvériser* (Paré); see POWDER, -IZE. So **pulver**ULENT pʌlve·rʲūlənt powdery, crumbling. XVII. – L.

puma pjū·mə feline quadruped Felis concolor. XVIII. – Sp. *puma* – Quechua *puma*.

pumice pʌ·mis porous kind of lava. XV. Late ME. *pomys* – OF. *pomis* – L. dial. *pōmice-m*, var. of *pūmicem*, nom. *pūmex*; cf. POUNCE[2]. The present sp. shows reversion to the orig. L. form, but the pronunc. has not been infl. OE. *pumić(stān)*, corr. to MLG. *pomes*, MDu. *pums(e)*, OHG. *pumiȝ*, *bumiȝ* (G. *bims|stein*), was not repr. in ME.; the forms *pumysch*, *pomege* (XV), *pumish* (XVI–XVII) were prob. due to assim. of *-is* to -ISH[1], -AGE. (Du. *puimsteen* is based on L. *pūmex*.)

pummel pʌ·ml beat repeatedly, esp. with the fist. XVI. Earlier *pomell*, *poumile*, *pumble*, f. POMMEL, the orig. sense being 'strike with the pommel of a sword (instead of the edge or point)'.

pump[1] pʌmp mechanical device for raising water, etc. XV. In earliest use naut.; corr. to late MDu. *pompe* wood or metal pipe, stone conduit, Du. *pomp* ship's pump, LG. *pump(e)*, whence early modG. *pumpe* (XVI), Sw. *pump*, Da. *pompe*, F. *pompe* (XVI); the evidence is inadequate to decide whether the word was prior in Eng. or LG. The co-existence of synon. Eng. †*plump* (XV–XVII), G. dial. *plumpe*, *plumpfe*, and Cat., Sp., Pg. *bomba*, suggests a series of more or less independent imit. formations. Hence **pump** vb. XVI; cf. Du. *pompen*, etc.

pump[2] pʌmp light close-fitting shoe. XVI. Of unkn. origin; perh. from transf. joc. use of †*pump shoe* (XVI) (part of) the piston of a pump, so applied on account of its fitting close.

pumpernickel pʌ·mpərnikəl German rye bread. XVIII. G., of unkn. origin (earlier lout, booby).

pumpkin pʌ·mᵖkin, (U.S. often pʌ·ŋkin) kind of gourd, Cucurbita Pepo. XVII. alt. (by assim. of the ending to -KIN) of *pumpion*, earlier *pompon* – F. †*pompon* (whence also (M)Du. *pompoen*), nasalized form of †*popon*, var. of **pepon* – L. *pepō(n-)* – Gr. *pépōn* large melon, sb. use of *pépōn* ripe (see COOK), for *síkuos pépōn* kind of melon not eaten till quite ripe (the *sikuos* being eaten unripe).

pun pʌn play on like-sounding words. XVII (Dryden, 1662, Eachard, 1670). prob. one of a group of clipped words which became fashionable in Restoration times (cf. CIT, MOB, NOB, PUNCH²); app. short for †*pundigrion*, which occurs with †*punnet* and *quibble* in 1676 (Roger L'Estrange), 'of which' it is said 'fifteen will not make up one single jest'; it has been conjectured that *pundigrion* may be a fanciful alteration of It. *puntiglio* fine point, PUNCTILIO, †cavil, †quibble. (An earlier term was *clinch*.) Hence vb. XVII (Eachard, 1670). **pu·n**STER. XVII (Congreve); contemp. with *punner*.

punch¹ pʌnᵗʃ †dagger XV (rare); instrument for pricking or piercing XVI, for impressing a design XVII. Shortening of PUNCHEON¹, which it has mostly superseded, if not f. PUNCH⁴; partly synon. with †*pounce*, of obscure origin.

punch² pʌnᵗʃ (capital *P*) hump-backed short grotesque male figure; principal character in the puppet-show of Punch and Judy XVIII; short fat man (also adj.) XVII; one of a breed of thick-set horses (e.g. *Suffolk p.*) XIX. Shortening of PUNCHINELLO.

punch³ pʌnᵗʃ beverage from wine, spirits, mixed with hot water or milk, etc. XVII (1632). Stated by Fryer ('Account of East India', 1698) to be the Marathi and Hindi *pānch* (Skr. *pañchan* FIVE), so named from the five ingredients of the drink; but the mod. pronunc. descends from earlier punʃ, which is not a normal repr. of the *ā* or *a* of the Indian word *pānch*, *panch-* (in comps.). The problem is complicated by the early occurrence of forms which appear to repr. *bowl o' punch*, but which may, however, point to an original of which *punch* is a shortening. ¶ Taken from Eng. into many Eur. langs., as F. *punch*, Du. *punch*, G., Sw., Da. *punsch*, Sp., Pg. *ponche*, Russ. *punsh*.

punch⁴ pʌnᵗʃ (dial.) poke, prod, †stab XIV; pierce with holes; deliver a sharp blow at esp. with the fist XVI. var. of †*pounce* emboss, pink the edge of (XV), prob. of Rom. origin (cf. next).

puncheon¹ pʌ·nᵗʃən pointed tool or †weapon. XIV. Late ME. *pons(y)on*, *ponchon* – OF. *poinson*, *po(i)nchon* (mod. *poinçon*) = Pr. *pounchoun*, Sp. *punzón*, Pg. *punção*, It. *punzone* :– Rom. **punctiōne(m)*, f. Rom. **punctiāre* prick, punch.

puncheon² pʌ·nᵗʃən (mostly Sc.) large cask (esp. one of specific capacity). XV. Identical in form with prec., but if it is the same word the sense-development is obscure.

Punchinello pʌnᵗʃine·lou principal character in an Italian puppet show (see PUNCH²). XVII (Pepys). Current from the outset in two main forms *Policinello* and *Punchinello* (with vars. in *Pon-*, *-elle*). – Neapolitan dial. *Polecenella* (1632, in Silvio Fiorillo's 'La Lucilia costante'), in literary It. *Pulcinella*, perh. based on dim. of *pollecena* young of the turkey-cock (to the hooked beak of which the nose of the mask of Punch bears some resemblance), f. *pulcino* chicken :– Rom. **pullicīnu-s*, f. L. *pullus* (see PULLET). ¶ The forms in *Pun-* appear to have resulted from assim. of *l* to the following *n*.

punctilio pʌŋkti·liou †fine or minute point; minute detail of conduct. XVI (*puntilio*). – It. *puntiglio*, Sp. *puntillo*, dim. of *punto* POINT; with later assim. to L. *punctum*; cf. F. *pointille* – It. So **puncti·li**OUS. XVII. – F. *pointilleux*. **punctual** pʌ·ŋktʃuəl, -tjuəl pert. to a point or dot XIV; †bearing on the point, precise; †minutely observant of rule, etc.; exactly observant of appointed time XVII. – medL. *punctuālis*, f. L. *punctum* POINT; cf. F. *ponctuel* and see -AL¹. So **punctua**·LITY. XVII; cf. medL. *punctuālitās*, F. *ponctualité*. **punctuate** pʌ·ŋktʃueit, -tjueit point out (rare) XVII; put the stops in (a sentence) XIX (formerly *point* XIV). f. pp. stem of medL. *punctuāre* prick, point, etc. (cf. F. *ponctuer*, It. *puntuare*), f. *punctum* POINT; see -ATE³. So **punctua**·TION †pointing of the psalms XVI; insertion of vowel points in Hebrew, etc., of stops in a sentence XVII. – medL. *punctuātiō*; cf. F. *ponctuation*. **puncture** pʌ·ŋktʃəɹ prick, perforation. XIV (rare before XVI). – L. *punctūra*, f. *punct-*, pp. stem of *pungere* prick; see PUNGENT, -URE. Hence vb. XVII.

pundit pʌ·ndit learned Hindu. XVII. – Hindi *paṇḍit* :– Skr. *paṇḍita* learned, skilled, sb. learned man, scholar, rel. to *paṇḍā* understanding, learning; cf. F. *pandit*, †*-ite*, Pg. *pandito*.

pungent pʌ·ndʒənt pricking, sharp, keen. XVI. – L. *pungent-*, *-ēns*, prp. of *pungere* prick, perh. f. base **pug-* of *pugnus* fist, *pugna* fight, *pugil* boxer (cf. PUGILIST, PUGNACIOUS); see -ENT. Superseded †*poinant*, POIGNANT in several senses.

Punic pjū·nik Carthaginian. XV. – L. *Pūnicus*, earlier *Pœnicus*, f. *Pœnus* – Gr. *Phoînix* PHŒNICIAN; see -IC; cf. F. *punique*.

punish pʌ·niʃ cause to suffer for an offence. XIV. ME. *punisse*, *-ische* – (O)F. *puniss-*, extended stem (see -ISH²) of *punir* :– L. *punīre*, earlier *pœnīre*, f. *pœna* PAIN. Hence **pu·nish**MENT. XV. – OF. *punissement*. So **puniti**VE pjū·nitiv. XVII. – F. *punitif*, *-ive* or medL. *pūnītīvus*, f. *punīt-*, pp. stem of *punīre*.

punk[1] pʌŋk (obs. or arch.) strumpet. XVI. Of unkn. origin.

punk[2] pʌŋk (chiefly U.S.) touchwood. XVIII. Of unkn. origin; †*funk* and *spunk* are syns.

punkah pʌ·ŋkə portable fan XVII; fan of cloth stretched on a frame XIX. – Hindi *pankhā* fan :– Skr. *pakshaka* fan, f. *paksha* wing.

punnet pʌ·nit (round) chip basket for fruit or vegetables, serving locally as a measure. XIX. perh. dim. f. *pun*, dial. var. of POUND[1]; see -ET.

punt[1] pʌnt flat-bottomed shallow boat. XV. In earliest use (E. Anglian) *pontebot, punte boot* (BOAT) – MLG. *punte, punto* (LG. *pünte, pünto*) ferry-boat, mud-boat, corr. to late OE. *punt* (which did not survive), MDu. *ponte* (Du. *pont*) ferry-boat, pontoon – L. *pontō* Gaulish transport vessel (Cæsar), PONTOON. Hence vb. XIX.

punt[2] pʌnt at cards, lay a stake against the bank. XVIII. – F. *ponter*, rel. to *ponte* punt in ombre, player against the bank – Sp. *punto* POINT (the Sp. word is used in ombre, quadrille, etc. for the ace of certain suits).

punt[3] pʌnt in Rugby football, kick (the ball) after dropping it from the hands before it reaches the ground. XIX. Appears (with the corr. sb.) in the 'Rules of Football at Rugby School' of 1845; prob. spec. use of dial. *punt* push with force, *bunt* (Warwickshire, in which county Rugby is situated), poss. blending of *bunt* and *put*.

punty, ponty pʌ·nti iron rod used in glass-blowing. XVII. – F. *pontil* – It. *puntello*, dim. of *punto* POINT.

puny pjū·ni †junior, PUISNE; †inexperienced; of inferior size or strength. XVI. – OF. *puisne* (mod. *puîné*), f. *puis* (:– L. *postea* or Rom. **postius*) afterwards + *né* (:– L. *nātu-s*; cf. NATAL) born; the ending has been assim. to -Y[1].

pup pʌp young dog. XVIII. Back-formation f. PUPPY, as if this were a dim. in -Y[6].

pupa pjū·pə chrysalis. XIX. – modL. use by Linnæus (1758) of L. *pūpa* girl, doll; cf. PUPPET.

pupil[1] pjū·pil orphan who is a minor and hence a ward XIV (Wycl. Bible); one under instruction XVI. – (O)F. *pupille* m. and fem. or its source, L. *pūpillus, -illa* orphan, ward, secondary dim. (on *pūpulus, -ula*) of *pūpus* boy, *pūpa* girl.

pupil[2] pjū·pil circular opening in the iris of the eye. XVI. – (O)F. *pupille* or L. *pūpilla* (cf. Sp. *pupila*, It. *pupilla*), secondary dim. of *pūpa* girl, doll, pupil of the eye (see prec.). The application of the L. words to the pupil of the eye is based on, or parallel to, that of Gr. *kórē* maiden, girl, doll, pupil (the allusion being to the tiny images of persons and things that may be seen therein).

puppet pʌ·pit †doll; (human) figure jointed and moving on strings or wires XVI; lathe-head XVII. Earlier in deriv. **pu·ppet**RY (Tindale, 1528); var. of POPPET.

puppy pʌ·pi †lap dog, toy dog XV; young dog XVI (Sh.; also *puppy-dog*); contemptuously of a person XVI. Late ME. *popi(e)*, corr. in form to OF. *popée*, (also mod.) *poupée* doll, lay figure, (contextually) toy, plaything :– Rom. **puppāta*, f. **puppa* (see POPPET, -Y[5]).

purana purā·nə sacred works of Hindu mythology. XVII. – Skr. *purāṇá* pert. to olden times, sb. tale of the past, f. *purā́* formerly (cf. FORE-).

purblind pɜ̄·ɹblaind †quite blind XIII; †blind in one eye XIV; partially blind, short- or dim-sighted XVI. orig. *pur(e) blind*, i.e. *pur(e)*, ME. advb. use of PURE (with assim. to *pour-, pur-*), and BLIND adj. ¶ For the change of sense from 'utterly' to 'partially' cf. PARBOIL.

purchase pɜ̄·ɹtʃəs †contrive, devise (RGlouc.); †procure, acquire XIII (S. Eng. Leg.); buy XIV (PPl.); (naut.) haul in or up (prob. orig. pull in rope with the two hands so as to 'gain' one portion over another) XVI. – AN. *purchacer*, OF. *pourchacier* seek to obtain, procure, f. intensive *pur-, por-, pour-* (:– L. *prō-*, PRO-[1]) + *chacier* (mod. *chasser*) CHASE. So **pu·rchase** sb. XIII (RGlouc.). – AN. *pur-*, OF. *porchas*, f. the vb.

purdah pɜ̄·ɹdă curtain, spec. to screen women from sight XVIII; system of seclusion of Indian women XIX. – Urdu – Pers. *pardah*.

pure pjuəɹ not mixed XIII (RGlouc.); guiltless, innocent XIV (Rolle); chaste XV (Lydg.). – (O)F. *pur*, fem. *pure* = Pr. *pur*, Sp., It. *puro* :– L. *pūru-s*, rel. to Skr. *pavītár-* purifier, *pūtás* purified, (with divergent sense) Ir. *úr*, Gael. *ìr* green, fresh. So **pu·ri**FY, **pu:ri**FICA·TION. XIV. – (O)F. or (late) L. **pu·r**IST one who affects strict purity or correctness. XVIII. – F. *puriste*. **pu·r**ITY. XIII (*purete*, AncrR.). – (O)F. *pureté*, with later assim. to late L.

purée püre soup made from vegetables, etc. pulped and passed through a sieve. XIX. – (O)F. *purée*, f. (with L. suffix *-āta* -ATE[1]) *purer* purify, squeeze (fruits, etc.) to obtain the pulp :– L. *pūrāre*, f. *pūrus* PURE.

purfle pɜ̄·ɹfl adorn with a border. XIV. – OF. *purfiler* = Pr., Sp. *porfilar*, It. *profilare* – Rom. **prōfilāre*, f. *prō* PRO-[1] + *fīlum* (cf. PROFILE).

purge pɜ̄ɹdʒ A. make pure, cleanse, free from guilt XIV (Rolle); B. empty (the bowels) XV. – (O)F. *purger* = Pr., Sp. *purgar*, It. *purgare* :– L. *purgāre* purify, for *pūrigāre*, f. *pūrus* PURE. So **purga·**TION pɜɹg-. XIV. – (O)F. or L. **pu·rg**ATIVE. XV. – O(F.) or late L. **purgat**ORY[1] pɜ̄ɹ·gətəri condition or place of spiritual purging. XIII (AncrR.). – AN. *purgatorie*, (O)F. *purgatoire* – medL. *purgā-*

tōrium (St. Bernard XII), sb. use of n. of late L. *purgātōrius* cleansing, f. pp. stem of *purgāre*. Hence **purgato·rIAL**. XV.

Puritan pjuə·ritən Protestant who aimed at further purification of Reformed doctrine and practice. XVI. f. late L. *pūritās* PURITY + -AN, perh. after F. *puritain* (Ronsard, 1564) or modL. *pūritānus*; prob. modelled on medL. *Cathari*, *Catharistæ* name assumed by the Novatian heretics, f. Gr. *katharós* pure. (†*Catharan* was a contemporary, and †*Catharite* an earlier synon. of *Puritan*.) Hence **puritan**IC, -ICAL -æ·nik(l). XVII. ¶ Early evidence points to its being a self-assumed name, the hostile application being later.

purl¹ pə̄ɹl cord made of twisted gold or silver wire; †pleat, frill XVI; loop on the edge of lace, etc. XVII; inversion of stitches in knitting producing a ribbed appearance XIX (often spelt *pearl*). So vb. XVI. orig. *pyrle*, *pirle*, of unkn. origin. ¶ The last sense of the sb. may be a different word.

purl² pə̄ɹl (of water) whirl with a murmuring sound. XVI. So sb. †small rill XVI; purling motion or sound XVII. prob. imit.; cf. Norw. *purla* bubble up, gush out, Sw. dial. *porla* ripple, gurgle.

purl³ pə̄ɹl revolve, whirl round XVIII; turn head over heels XIX. perh. identical with PURL¹. Hence **pu·rl**ER¹ headlong fall, swingeing blow. XIX.

purlieu pə̄·ɹljū, pə̄·ɹli tract of land on the border of a forest XV; (one's) haunt or bounds; outlying district, esp. of a mean sort XVII. orig. *purlew*, presumably alt. (by assim. to *leu* place, LIEU) of AN. *purale(e)*, *-ley* (str. on the first syll.) perambulation, tract of land between the wider bounds of a forest and those fixed by a perambulation (in AL. *purale*, *porale*, *purlea*), OF. *pouralee*, f. *po(u)raler* traverse, f. *por-*, *pour-* (:- L. *prō* forth) + *aller* go; the colloq. pronunc. is repr. by the form *purley* (XVI; still current XX); cf. *Beaulieu*, pronounced as *Bewley*.

purlin pə̄·ɹlin (archit.) horizontal beam running along the length of a roof. XV. In AL. *perliōn-* (XV), poss. f. L. *per* through, PER- + stem of *ligāre* bind (see LIGATURE; cf. F. *lien* tie in carpentry).

purloin pəɹloi·n † remove, do away with XV; take dishonestly XVI. – AN. *purloigner*, OF. *porloigner*, f. *por-*, *pour-* (:- L. *prō* forth, PRO-¹) + *loign* (mod. *loin*) far (:- L. *longē* far, adv. of *longus* LONG¹).

purple pə̄·ɹpl (orig.) of crimson or other red colour; (later) of a colour obtained by mixing red and blue OE.; sb. XV. OE. (late Nhb.) *purple*, reduced and dissimilated form of *purpuran*, obl. case of *purpure* 'purple' clothing or garment – L. *purpura* (whence also OHG. *purpura*, G. *purpur*, ON. *purpuri*, Goth. *paurpaura*) – Gr. *porphúrā* shellfish that yielded the Tyrian purple dye, dye itself, cloth dyed therewith (cf. PORPHYRY). For dissimilation of *r* . . *r* in this word cf. Pr. *polpra*, OSp. *porpola*, and MARBLE. (Before 1500 the commoner form was *purpur(e)*, partly repr. OE. *purpure*, ME. *purpre*, *purper*, *-ur*, partly – OF. *purpre* (mod. *pourpre*) :- L. *purpura*.)

purport pə̄·ɹpɔ̄ɹt tenor or substance of a document, etc. XV. – AN., OF. *pur-*, *porport* produce, contents, f. *purporter* :- medL. *prōportāre* (in AL. XII), f. L. *prō* PRO-¹ + *portāre* carry, bear (cf. DEPORT, etc.). So **purpo·rt** vb. state, mean. XVI. – OF. *purporter*. Sc. †*proport* is earlier (XIV) – OF. var. *proporter*.

purpose pə̄·ɹpəs object in view XIII (S. Eng. Leg.); intention, aim; matter in hand, now only in phr. *to the p.* XIV; *on p.* by design (XVI, Sh.), earlier (dial.) *a p.* (XVI), *of p.* (XV). – OF. *porpos*, *purpos* (mod. *propos*, after L. *prōpositum*), f. *por-*, *purposer* design, intend (whence **pu·rpose** vb. XIV, Wycl. Bible, Gower, Ch.), f. L. *propōnere* PROPOSE, after *poser* (see POSE¹).

purpresture pəɹpre·stjuəɹ (leg.) illegal enclosure of or encroachment on property. XV. – OF. *pur-*, *porpresture*, alt. of *porpresure*, f. *porprendre* occupy, usurp, enclose, f. *por-* (:- L. *prō* PRO-¹) + *prendre* take (:- L. *præhendere*; see PREY).

purr pə̄ɹ sb. and vb. imit. of the vibratory sound made by a cat; first recorded from Sh. (XVII) in the sb. ¶ Other langs. have various forms containing *r*, as F. *ronron*, G. *schnurren*, Du. *snorren*.

purse pə̄ɹs money-bag of leather, etc. OE. *purs* (with *p* after *pung* purse, *pusa* wallet) – late L. *bursa*, var. of *byrsa* – Gr. *búrsa* leather, bag (cf. BURSAR). OF. *bourse*, Pr., It. *borsa*, Sp., Pg. *bolsa* **purse** vb. pocket XIV (R. Mannyng); wrinkle XVII (Sh.). Hence **purs**ER¹ pə̄·ɹsəɹ †maker of purses; purse-bearer, treasurer, esp. ship's officer who keeps the accounts and provisions, orig. charged only with the commissariat. XV.

purslane, -ain pə̄·ɹslən herb Portulaca oleracea. XIV. Late ME. *purcelan(e)* – OF. *porcelaine*, identical in form with the F. word for PORCELAIN, and prob. assim. to that from L. *porcil(l)āca* (Pliny), more usu. *portulāca* (another name was *porcastrum*, IV).

pursue pəɹsjū· follow with intent to overtake, formerly with hostility. XIII (prosecute at law XVI, esp. Sc.). ME. *pursiwe*, *-sewe* – AN. *pursiwer*, *-suer* = OF. *porsivre* (mod. *poursuivre*) = Pr., Sp. *per-*, *proseguir*, etc. :- Rom. **per-*, **prōsequere*, for L. *prōsequī* PROSECUTE. So **pursu·**ANT consequent and conformable. XVII. **pursu·**ANCE. XVI. **pursuit** pəɹsjū·t †persecution XIV (Wycl., Trev.); †suit, petition XIV (Ch.); act of pursuing XV; following of an occupation XVI. – (O)F. *poursuite* (see SUIT). **pursuiv**ANT pə̄·ɹswivənt junior officer attendant on heralds. XIV (Ch.). – OF. *pursivant*, sb. use of prp. of *pursivre*.

pursy pɜ̄·ɹsi †short-winded XV; (arch.) corpulent XVI. Later form of †*pursive, -if* – AN. *porsif*, alt. of OF. *polsif* (mod. *poussif*), f. *polser* breathe with difficulty, pant :– L. *pulsāre* drive or agitate violently (see PUSH); prob. assoc. with *purse*; for the ending cf. *hasty, jolly, tardy.*

purulent pjuə·rʲulənt of the nature of pus. XVI. – L. *purulent-*, f. *pur-*, PUS; see -ULENT.

purvey pəɹvei· †see to, foresee; provide, supply. XIII (RGlouc.). ME. *porvaie, -veie* – AN. *por-, purveier*, OF. *porveeir* (mod. *pourvoir*) = Pr. *provezer*, Sp. *proveer*, etc. :– L. *prōvidēre* PROVIDE. So **purvey·**OR[1]. XIII (Cursor M.). – AN. *purveur*, OF. *porveour, -eur.*

purview pɜ̄·ɹvju body of a statute, following the preamble XV; scope of a document, etc. XVIII. – AN. *purveu*, OF. *porveu* (mod. *pourvu*), pp. of *porveeir* PURVEY; orig. clause introduced by *purveu est* it is provided, or *purveu que* provided that.

purwanah pəɹwā·nə letter of authority, licence. XVII. – Urdu – Pers. *parwānah.*

pus pʌs matter produced by suppuration. XVI. – L. *pūs*, g. *pūris* (cf. PURULENT, PUTRID, SUPPURATE), having cogns. in Gr., Skr., Arm., Lith., and Germ. (see FOUL).

Puseyite pjū·ziait follower of the Tractarian opinions of the Rev. Edward Bouverie *Pusey* (1800–82); see -ITE. XIX.

push puʃ use force to press or thrust *away*, etc. XIII (pt. *puste*). – AN. **pusser*, (O)F. *pousser*, †*pou(l)ser* (repr. earlier in *repousser* REPULSE) = Pr. *polsar*, Sp. *pujar* :– L. *pulsāre*, frequent. f. *puls-*, pp. stem of *pellere* drive, thrust (cf. COMPEL, etc.). Hence sb. (XVI); cf. F. *pousse* (XV). ¶ For the development of F. *-ss-* cf. BRUSH, -ISH[2], QUASH.

Pushtoo, Pashto pʌ·ʃtū language of the Afghans. XIX.

pusillanimous pjus-, pjūzilæ·niməs faint-hearted, mean-spirited. XVI. f. late L. *pūsillanimis* (rendering Gr. ὀλιγόψυχος), f. *pūsillus* very small, weak (f. *pūsus* boy, *pūsa* girl, rel. to *puer* boy; cf. PUERILE)+*animus* mind; see ANIMATE, -OUS.

puss pus cat, esp. as a call name XVI (also **puss-cat**); hare; applied to a girl or woman XVII. prob. – MLG. *pūs* (also *pūskatte*), Du. *poes*; cf. Ir., Gael. *pus*; of unkn. origin. Hence **puss**Y[6] pu·si. XVIII.

pustule pʌ·stjūl pimple. XIV. – (O)F. *pustule* or L. *pustula* (also *pussula, pusula*) blister, f. imit. base **pu-* **phu-* blow, inflate, repr. with different extensions by Gr. *phûsa* bellows, breath, bubble (cf. PHYSETER), Lith. *pucziù, pūsti* blow, Skr. *pupphusas* lung, *phutkaróti* blow (cf. PHUT). See -ULE.

put[1] put (obs. or dial.) push, thrust, knock, butt (cf. PUTT); transf. in various applications ranging from forcing or urging to placing or setting in a place or position. Fully evidenced from XII onwards; inf. *puten*, pt. *putte*, pp. *put* (later *putted*), repr. OE. **putian* (*u* of uncertain quantity), repr. only in noun of action *putung* instigation; parallel forms are OE. *potian*, ME. *pote, potte*, mod. dial. *pot*, OE. *pȳtan* (*ūt* out), *āpȳtan* put out, ME. *pitte*, pp. *(i)pit*, mod. dial. *pit*; ult. origin unkn. ¶ Similar synon. Scand. dial. forms are of recent date; W. *pwtio*, Gael. *put* are from Eng.

put[2] see PUTT.

putative pjū·tətiv that is such by repute. XV. – (O)F. *putatif* or late L. *putātīvus* (Tertullian), f. pp. stem of L. *putāre* (1) prune, (2) reckon, think (perh. orig. two distinct bases); see -IVE. ¶ The base is repr. also in *amputate, compute, depute, dispute, impute, repute*, and the corr. sbs.

putlock, putlog pʌ·tlɔk, -lɔg short horizontal timber in scaffolding. XVII. perh. f. *put*, pp. of PUT[1]; the form *-lock*, which is much the earlier, is obscure.

putrefaction pjūtrifæ·kʃən rotting, decomposition. XIV. – (O)F. *putréfaction* or late L. *putrefactiō(n-)*, f. L. *putrefacere*, f. *putr-, puter* rotten + *facere* make, DO[1]. So **pu·tre**FY XV. – L. *putrefacere*; cf. F. *putréfier* (XVI). **pu·tr**ID[1] rotten. XVI. – L. *putridus*, f. *putrēre* rot, f. *puter*, rel. to PUS. **putre·**SCENCE XVII, -ESCENT XVIII.

putt, put pʌt (Sc.) †push, shove XVI; throw, hurl (stone or weight) XVIII (spec. in golf of striking the ball). Formally identical with PUT[1], with differentiated pronunc. and pt. and pp. *putted.*

puttee pʌ·ti strip of cloth wound spirally round the leg. XIX. – Hindi *paṭṭī* band, bandage; cf. synon. Skr. *paṭṭa*, f. *paṭ* split, cleave, tear.

putty pʌ·ti jeweller's polishing powder; plasterer's fine cement XVII; glazier's cement for fixing panes XVIII. – F. *potée* potter's glaze, jeweller's putty, loam for moulds, orig. potful (XII), f. *pot*, POT; see -Y[5].

puzzle pʌ·zl embarrass, perplex, bewilder. XVI. – Of late-XVI emergence (*pusle, puzzell*), unless preceded by late ME. pp. *poselet* (r.w. *hoselet* houselled), which, except for chronological difficulties, might be f. POSE[2] (XVI)+-LE[3]; the origin remains unknown. Hence sb. XVII (Bacon).

puzzolana var. of POZZOLANA.

pyæmia, pyemia paiī·miə (path.) blood-poisoning marked by the formation of pus foci. XIX. modL., f. Gr. *púon* PUS+ *haîma* blood (cf. HÆMO-); see -IA[1].

pycno- pi·kno(u), before a vowel **pycn-**, repr. Gr. *pykno-*, comb. form of *puknós* thick, dense, as in **py·cnodont** (Gr. *odont-, odṓn* TOOTH), of the genus *Pycnodus* or family *Pycnodontidæ* of ganoid fishes having obtuse teeth XIX.

pygmy, pigmy pi·gmi member of a race of very small men XIV (Trevisa, Wyclif, Maund.); gen. (also adj.) XVI. In earliest use pl. *pygmeis* – L. *pygmæī*, pl. of *pygmæus* – Gr. *pugmaîos* dwarf(ish), f. *pugmḗ* measure of length from elbow to knuckles, fist (see PUGILIST).

pyjamas, U.S. **pajamas** pidʒā·məz, pədʒā·məz (prop.) loose trousers tied round the waist, (by extension) sleeping suit of these with jacket. XVIII. – Urdu *pāē jāmah*, f. Pers. *pāē, pay* FOOT, *jāmah* clothing.

pylon pai·lən (archit.) gateway XIX; tower, mast, etc. marking a course, supporting a span of wire, etc. XX. – Gr. *pulṓn*, f. *púlē* gate.

pylorus pailō·rəs (anat.) opening from the stomach into the duodenum. XVII. – late L. *pylōrus* (Cælius Aurelianus) – Gr. *pulōrós*, *pulourós* gate-keeper, f. *púlē* gate + *oûros* watcher, warder.

pyo- paiou, before a vowel **py-**, comb. form of Gr. *púon* PUS, as in **pyorrhœa** paiŏrī·ə (path.) discharge of pus. XVIII. modL. (*rhoiā́* flow, flux; cf. RHEO-; RHEUM).

pyramid pi·rəmid monumental (esp. Egyptian) structure with polygonal base and sloping sides meeting in an apex; pile of this shape. XVI (Eden, Dee). orig. used in L. form *pyramis* (*-id-*) – Gr. *puramís*, *-id-* (Herodotus), of alien origin. So **pyramid**AL[1] piræ·midəl. XVI. – medL.

pyre paiəɹ pile of combustible material, funeral pile. XVII (Sir T. Browne). – L. *pyra* – Gr. *purā́*, f. *pur-*, *pûr* FIRE.

pyrethrum pairī·þrəm pellitory of Spain, Anacyclus Pyrethrum XVI; feverfew XIX. L. (Pliny) PELLITORY – Gr. *púrethron* feverfew, perh. f. *puretós* fever (see next).

pyretic pai(ə)re·tik pert. to fever. XIX. – modL. *pyreticus*, f. Gr. *puretós* fever, f. *pûr* FIRE; see -IC.

pyrexia pai(ə)re·ksiə (path.) febrile disease. XVIII. modL., f. Gr. *púrexis*, f. *puréssein* be feverish, f. *pûr*; see prec., -IA[1].

pyrites pĭrai·tīz, pai(ə)- †fire-stone; sulphide of iron. XVI. – L. *pyrītēs* (Pliny) – Gr. *purítēs* sb. use (sc. *líthos* stone) of adj. pert. to fire, f. *pur-*, *pûr* FIRE; see -ITE.

pyro- paiə·ro(u), pai(ə)rə· comb. form of Gr. *pûr* FIRE, in many techn. terms; in Eng. use first in **pyrotechny** pai(ə)·ro(u)tekni †manufacture of gunpowder, firearms, etc.; †technical use of fire XVI; making and use of fireworks XVII. – F. *pyrotechnie* – modL. *pyrotechnia*, (Gr. *tékhnē* art; cf. TECHNICAL). So **pyrote·ch**NIC XVIII, -ICAL. XVII.

pyrrhic pi·rik (pros.) foot of ancient Gr. and L. verse ◡◡. XVII (Jonson). – L. *pyrrhichius* – Gr. *purrhíkhios*, f. *purrhíkhē* war dance; see foll.; -IC.

Pyrrhic[1] pi·rik war-dance of ancient Greeks. XVI. – L. *pyrrhicha* or Gr. *purrhíkhē*, said to be named from the inventor, *Púrrhikhos*.

Pyrrhic[2] pi·rik *P. victory*, one gained at too great cost, like that by Pyrrhus, king of Epirus, over the Romans at Asculum. XIX. f. *Pyrrhus* + -IC.

pyrus paiə·rəs genus of rosaceous trees (pear, apple, etc.). XIX. med. and modL. var. of L. *pirus* PEAR-tree.

Pythagorean paiþægŏrī·ən pert. to Pythagoras, ancient Gr. philosopher (VI B.C.). XVI. Formerly †*Pythago·rian*, *-o·rean* (Cowley, Dryden), in Bailey 1731 *Pythago·rean*, 1736 *Pythagore·an*. f. L. *Pȳthagorēus*, *-īus* – Gr. *Pūthagóreios*, f. *Pūthagóras*; see -EAN.

Pythian pi·þiən pert. to Delphi, its oracle, or priestess of Apollo there. XVII (*P. games*, *P. Apollo*). f. L. *Pȳthius* – Gr. *Pū́thios*, f. *Pū́thōn*; see next and -IAN.

python pai·þən (Gr. myth.) huge serpent slain by Apollo near Delphi XVI; (zool.) genus of large snakes XIX. – L. *Pȳthōn* – Gr. *Pū́thōn*.

pythoness pai·þənės female soothsayer, witch. XIV (Barbour, Ch.). Late ME. *phitones(se)* – OF. *phitonise* (mod. *pythonisse*) – medL. *phītōnissa*, for late L. *pȳthōnissa* (Vulg., 1 Chron. x 13), fem. of *pȳthō* (Deut. xviii 11, etc.)) – late Gr. *pū́thōn* (Acts xvi 16), identical with *pū́thōn* PYTHON; like the F. word finally assim. to the L. form; see -ESS[1].

pyx piks vessel for the reservation of the Host XIV; box at the Royal Mint in which gold and silver coins are deposited to be tested XVI. – L. *pyxis* – late Gr. *puxís* BOX[2]. ¶ The L. form is current as a technical term of anatomy and botany.

Q

qua kwei in the capacity or status of. XVII. L. *quā*, abl. sg. fem. of *quī* WHO, corr. in use to Gr. *ʘ̃*, d. sg. fem. of *ós* who.

quack[1] kwæk (of a duck) utter its characteristic cry. XVII. imit., often repeated; cf. Du. *kwakken*, G. *quacken* croak. ¶ Early vars. are †*quake* XVI (cf. Du. *kwaken*, G. *quaken* croak, quack), †*queke* XIV (cf. Du. *kwekken*), *quackle* XVI (cf. MLG. *quackelen*,

G. *quakeln* prattle). ¶ F. has *coin coin*, G. *gack gack*, *pack pack*, It. *qua qua*, Rum. *mac mac*, Da. *rap rap*.

quack[2] kwæk ignorant pretender to (medical or surgical) knowledge or skill. XVII. Short for **quacksalver** kwæ·ksæːlvəɹ XVI (now rare) – early modDu. *quacksalver* (now *kwakzalver*, whence G. *quacksalber*), of which the second el. is f. *salf*, *zalf* SALVE, and the first is prob. the stem of †*quacken*, *kwakken* prattle. ¶ For the shortening cf. RAKE[3], SAP[4], WAG[2].

quad[1] kwɔd Oxford University abbrev. of QUADRANGLE. XIX.

quad[2] kwɔd abbrev. of (typogr.) QUADRAT (XIX), QUADRUPLET (esp. pl. *quads*) (XIX).

quadragenarian kwɔːdrədʒinɛə·riən (one) forty years old. XIX. f. late L. *quadrāgenārius*, f. *quadrāgēnī*, distrib. of *quadrāgintā*. Also **-a·r**IOUS. XVII. **quadragesimal** kwɔdrədʒe·siməl (of a fast) lasting forty days; of Lent, Lenten. XVII. – late L. *quadrāgēsimālis*, f. **Quadrāgēsima**, name of the first Sunday in Lent and reckoned the fortieth day before Easter, and hence of the whole season, sb. use (sc. *dies* day) of fem. of L. *quadrāgēsimus* fortieth, ordinal of *quadrāgintā* forty, f. *quadrā-*, repr. old n. of *quattuor* FOUR + *-gintā*, corr. to Gr. *-konta*; see -AL[1]. Cf. QUINQUAGESIMA, SEPTUAGESIMA.

quadrangle kwɔ·dræŋgl, kwɔ̆dræ·ŋgl figure having four angles (and four sides) XV; square or rectangular space or court XVI. – (O)F. *quadrangle* or late L. *quadrangulum*, sb. use of n. of *quadrangulus*; see QUADRI-, ANGLE[2]. So **quadra·ngul**AR. XVI – medL. *quadrangulāris* (Boethius), tr. Gr. *tetrágōnos* TETRAGONAL.

quadrant kwɔ·drənt †fourth part, quarter, now only of a quarter-circle; instrument (of the form of a graduated quarter-circle) used for making angular measurements. XIV. – L. *quadrant-*, *-āns* quarter, orig. of the as, f. *quadr-*, for **quatr-*, comb. form of *quattuor* FOUR.

quadrat kwɔ·drət †square XIV; (typogr.) small block of metal used for spacing XVII. – L. *quadrātum* (or the deriv. F. *quadrat*), sb. use of n. of *quadrātus*, pp. of *quadrāre* square (cf. *quadrum* sb., square), f. *quadr-*, var. of *quattuor* FOUR. (*Quadrate* adj. XIV and vb. XVI were formerly current in various senses.) So **quadrat**IC kwɔdræ·tik square; (math.) involving the second and no higher power of an unknown or variable. XVII. – F. *quadratique* or modL. *quadrāticus*, f. *quadrātus*. **qua·drat**URE squaring. XVI. – F. or L.

quadrennial kwɔdre·niəl occurring every four years, lasting for four years. XVII. f. L. *quadr(i)ennium* + -AL[1].

quadri- kwɔ·dri comb. form of L. *quattuor* FOUR, as in **quadri**LA·TERAL XVII, *quadri*LI·TERAL XVIII, **quadripa·rtite** XV (L. *partītus*, pp. of *partīrī* divide).

quadrille[1] k(w)ədri·l card-game played by four persons with forty cards. XVIII. – F. *quadrille* (1725), perh. – Sp. *cuartillo* (f. *cuarto* fourth), with assim. to the original of next.

quadrille[2] k(w)ədri·l any of four groups of horsemen taking part in a tournament, etc.; square dance performed by four couples. XVIII. – F. *quadrille* (1611) – Sp. *cuadrilla*, It. *quadriglia* troop, company, f. *quadra* square (cf. CADRE).

quadrillion kwɔdri·ljən in Great Britain, fourth power of a million; in U.S.A. (as in France), fifth power of a thousand. XVII. – F. *quadrillon*, f. QUADRI- + *m)illion*; cf. BILLION, TRILLION.

quadrivium kwɔdri·viəm see TRIVIUM.

quadroon kwɔdrū·n one who has a quarter of negro blood. XVIII. Earliest forms *quartero(o)n* (through F. *quarteron*) – Sp. *cuarteron*, f. *cuarto* fourth, quarter; later assim. to words in *quadri-*.

quadru- kwɔ·drŭ, kwɔdrū· var. of QUADRI- used before lip-cons., as in **quadru·man**OUS (XVIII) (cf. F. *quadrumane*, Buffon) and next.

quadruped kwɔ·drŭped four-footed animal. XVII (Sir T. Browne). – F. *quadrupède* or L. *quadruped-*, *-pēs*, f. *quadru-* + *pēs*; see prec. and FOOT. So **quadru·ped**AL[1]. XVII. – medL. (Bede), f. L. *quadruped-*. XVI.

quadruple kwɔ·drupl fourfold. XVI. – (O)F *quadruple* – L. *quadruplus*; see QUADRU-, DUPLE. So vb. XIV. – F. or late L. **quadru·plic**ATE[3] adj. and vb. XVII. – L. **quadruplic**A·TION XVI. – late L. **qua·druplet** one of four at a birth. XVIII; after *triplet*; abbrev. QUAD[2].

quære kwiə·ri one may ask, it is a question; question, query. XVI. L. imper. of *quærere* ask, inquire. Now usu. QUERY.

quæstor kwī·stɔ̄ɹ (Rom. antiq.) official having charge of public finances. XIV. – L. *quæstor*, f. **quæs-*, old form of stem of *quærere* (see prec.) + agent-suffix -TOR.

quaff kwȧf drink copiously or deeply. XVI. prob. imit.; in earliest use †*quaft* (More, Coverdale), †*quaught* (Palsgr.); cf. synon. †*quass* (XVI–XVII) – MLG. *quassen* eat or drink immoderately.

quagga kwæ·gə S. African animal allied to the ass and the zebra. XVIII. Said to be orig. Hottentot, but now Xhosa-Kaffir in the form *iqwara* (with guttural r).

quagmire kwæ·g-, kwɔ·gmaiəɹ piece of wet boggy ground. XVI. f. (dial.) *quag* (XVI) + MIRE. The origin of the first el. is obscure; it may orig. denote quaking, as may also the similar els. of synon. and contemp. †*quab-*, †*quack-*, †*quake-*, †*quall-*, †*quave-*, †*quawmire*; perh. the original was *quab-* (cf. *quab(be)*, *quob* in ME. place names XII–XIII) and the source MLG. *quabbe* (Du. *kwabbe*), with later assim. to *quake*, etc.

quail[1] kweil migratory bird allied to the partridge. XIV. – OF. *quaille* (mod. *caille*) = Pr. *calha* (whence OSp. *coalla*, It. *quaglia*) :– medL. *coacula*, prob. of imit. origin like, if not derived from, synon. MLG., MDu. *quackele* (Du. *kwakkel*), OHG. *wahtala*, *qua(h)tala* (G. *wachtel*).

quail[2] kweil fail, give way XV; lose heart, be cowed XVI; also trans. Of unkn. origin. ¶ Not in literary use after *c*.1650 until revived by Scott *c*.1810.

quaint kweint †skilled, clever; †skilfully made, fine, elegant; †proud, fastidious XIII; †strange, unfamiliar XIV; uncommon but attractive XVIII. ME. *cointe*, *queinte* – OF. *cointe*, *queinte* :– L. *cognitu-s* known, pp. of *cognōscere* ascertain, f. *co-* COM- + *gnōscere* KNOW. ¶ The development of the main senses took place in OF.; some of the stages are obscure. For the phonology cf. *acquaint*.

quake kweik shake, tremble. OE. *cwacian*, rel. to *cweććan* (:– **kwakjan*) shake (trans.), in mod. dial. *quetch*, *quatch*; cf. OS. *quekilīk* waving to and fro. ¶ For the symbolic *cw-*, *qu-* cf. QUAVER, QUIVER[2].

Quaker kwei·kəɹ member of the Society of Friends. XVII (1653). f. QUAKE + -ER[1]. 'Shaking and quaking' was attributed to them. Formerly dyslogistic, perh. with ref. to 'Sonne of man, eate thy bread with quaking' (Ezek. xii 18). ¶ Earlier (1647) recorded as being applied to a foreign religious sect of women settled in Southwark.

qualify kwɔ·lifai invest with a quality or condition; modify, moderate. XVI. – F. *qualifier* – med.L. *quālificāre*, f. *quālis* of what kind, f. base of *quī*, *quis* WHO + *-ālis* -AL[1]; see -FY. So **qua:lifica·tion**. XVI – F. or medL. **quality** kwɔ·lĭti †character, disposition; †title, description XIII; attribute, property; nature, kind; rank, position XIV; †profession XVI. ME. *qualite* – (O)F. *qualité* – L. *quālitās* (Cicero, rendering Gr. ποιότης), f. *quālis*. So **qua·litative**. XVII. – late L.

qualm kwām, kwɔ̄m feeling of faintness or sickness XVI; strong scruple of conscience XVII. Of obscure origin; phonetically corr. forms either have inappropriate meanings or cannot be historically connected: OE. *cw(e)alm* pestilence, pain (rel. to QUELL), MLG. *quallem*, G. *qualm* (Du. *kwalm*) thick vapour or smoke.

quandary kwɔ·ndəri, (orig.) kwɔndɛə·ri state of perplexity. XVI (Lily). Also †*quandare* (which is considered to be of L. form by Mulcaster 'First Part of the Elementarie' xvii 111), as if f. L. *quandō* WHEN treated as a verbal form with a corr. infin. *quandare*. Cf. †*backare* back!, †*jocundare* merry mood, †*vagare* VAGARY, all XVI; such formations were perh. modelled on CERTIORARI, of which a common var. was *certiorare*.

quantic kwɔ·ntik (math.) rational, integral homogeneous function of two or more variables. XIX (Cayley). f. L. *quantus* how great (cf. next) + -IC, with ref. to the degree (2nd, 3rd, 4th).

quantity kwɔ·ntĭti size, amount. XIV. – (O)F. *quantité*, corr. to Sp. *c(u)antidad*, It. *quantità* – L. *quantitās* (rendering Gr. ποσότης), f. *quantus* how great, how much, f. base of *quī*, *quis* WHO; see -ITY. So **qua·ntitative**. XVI. – medL. **quantum** kwɔ·ntəm amount required or allotted. XVII. – n. of L. *quantus*.

quaquaversal kweikwəvɔ̄·ɹsəl turning in every direction. XVIII. f. L. *quāquā versus*, i.e. *quāquā* where-, whithersoever, *versus* turned, towards (see -WARD).

quarantine kwɔ·rəntīn A. (leg.) period of forty days during which a widow had the right to remain in her husband's chief mansion house; B. period of isolation of persons and animals suspected of contagious disease. XVII. In sense A – medL. *quarantēna*, *quadrantēna*, f. **quadranta*, for L. *quadrāginta* (see QUADRAGESIMAL); in sense B – It. *quarantina*, f. *quaranta* forty; see -INE[1].

quarenden, quarender kwɔ·rəndən, -dəɹ variety of apple common in Somerset and Devon. XV (*quaryndon*). perh. a use of the place-name *Querendon*, Bucks.

quarrel[1] kwɔ·rəl short square-headed arrow XIII; square or diamond-shaped pane of glass XV. – OF. *quar(r)el* (mod. *carreau*) = Pr. *cairel*, Sp. *cuadrillo*, It. *quadrello* :– Rom. **quadrellu-s*, dim. of late L. *quadrus* square (see QUADRAT).

quarrel[2] kwɔ·rəl †complaint, accusation; ground of complaint XIV; violent contention XVI. ME. *querele* – OF. *querele* (mod. *querelle*) :– L. *querella*, var. of *querēla* complaint, f. *querī* complain (cf. QUERULOUS), with suffix as in *sequēla* SEQUEL. Forms with *quar(r)-* were established by Caxton's time, but *querele* continued till XVII. So **qua·rrel** vb. XIV (isolated in Gower; then not before XVI). In late ME. – OF. *quereler*; afterwards f. the sb. Hence **qua·rrelsome**[1]. XVI (Sh.).

quarry[1] kwɔ·ri parts of a deer placed on the hide and given to the hounds; collection of deer killed XIV; animal hunted or hawked at XV. ME. *quirre*, *querre* – AN. **quire*, **quere*, OF. *cuiree* (mod. *curée*), alt., by crossing with *cuir* leather and *curer* cleanse, spec. disembowel (:– L. *curāre* CURE), of *couree* = Pr. *corada* :– Rom. **corāta* entrails, f. *cor* HEART + *-āta* -EE, -Y[5].

quarry[2] kwɔ·ri open-air excavation from which stone is obtained. XV. – medL. *quarreia*, shortened var. of *quareria* – OF. *quarriere* (mod. *carrière*), f. **carre* = Pr. *caire* :– L. *quadrum* square (sb.) (see QUADRAT); superseded ME. *quarere* (XIV) – AN. **quarere*, OF. *quarriere*. Hence vb. XVIII.

quarry[3] kwɔ·ri alt. of QUARREL[1], prob. after †*quarry* square (XIII–XVII) – OF. *quarré* (mod. *carré*) :– L. *quadrātus* QUADRAT.

quart[1] kwɔ̄ɹt one-fourth of a gallon. XIV. – (O)F. *quarte* = Sp. *cuarta*, It. *quarta* :– L. *quārta*, sb. use of fem. (sc. *pars* part) fourth, ordinal of *quattuor* FOUR.

quart[2] kwɔ̄ɹt position in fencing XVII; sequence of four cards XVIII. – F. *quarte*; cf. CARTE.

quartan kwɔ̄·ɹtən of a fever in which the paroxysms occur every third (acc. to old reckoning, fourth) day. XIII (Cursor M.). ME. *quartain* – (O)F. *quartaine* (sc. *fièvre* fever) :– L. *quārtāna* (sc. *febris*), fem. of *quārtānus*, f. *quārtus*; see prec. and -AN; the present form shows assim. to L.

quarter kwɔ̄·ɹtəɹ one of four parts; measure of 8 bushels XIII; fourth part of a year; region, district XIV; place of residence, pl. soldier's lodgings; assigned position (spec. in *close q-s*); relations with another, terms of treatment XVI; exemption from being immediately put to death XVII. – AN. *quarter*, (O)F. *quartier* :– L. *quartārius* fourth part of a measure, quartern, gill, f. *quārtus* fourth (see QUART). Hence vb. divide into quarters XIV; lodge in quarters XVI (Sh.). **qua·rter**AGE quarterly payment XIV; after OF. or medL. **qua·rter-deck** XVII orig. smaller deck above the half-deck XVII (Capt. Smith). **qua·rter**LY(1) XVI. **qua·rter**LY(2) XVI (her., after AN. *esquartele*), adv. XV. **qua·rter**MASTER officer in navy and army (*q.* in the senses of assigned position and lodging) XV; cf. Du. *kwartiermeester*, etc. **qua·rter**STAFF stout pole used as a weapon. XVI; perh. orig. made from a tree trunk cleft in four.

quartern kwɔ̄·ɹtəɹn quarter, esp. of certain weights and measures XIII. – AN. *quartrun*, OF. *quart(e)ron*, f. *quart* fourth, QUART[1], or *quartier* QUARTER.

quartet(te) kwɔ̄ɹte·t composition for four voices or instruments XVIII (Coleridge); set of four XIX. – F. *quartette* – It. *quartetto* (which was used somewhat earlier in Eng.), f. *quarto* fourth (cf. QUART[1]); see -ET, -ETTE.

quartile kwɔ̄·ɹtil (astr.) pert. to an aspect of two heavenly bodies which are 90° (i.e. ¼ of a circle) distant. XVI. – medL. *quartīlis*, f. *quartus* fourth; see prec. and -ILE.

quarto kwɔ̄·ɹtou size of paper produced by folding a whole sheet twice so as to form four leaves (8 pages) XVI; book made up of such paper XVII. orig. in phr. *in quarto* 'in a fourth' (see QUART[1]); cf. OCTAVO, etc.

quartz kwɔ̄ɹts silica in various forms. XVIII. – (M)HG. *quarz*, *quartz*, var. of *zwerg* DWARF (with East MG. *qu-* for *zw-* and hypocoristic ending as in *Heinz* for *Heinrich*, *Kunz* for *Konrad*); for the application cf. COBALT, NICKEL. ¶ Of CEur. range.

quash kwɔʃ annul, invalidate XIV; bring to nought XVII. – OF. *quasser* (mod. *casser* break) = Pr. *casar*, Sp., Pg. *cansar* weary, tire :– L. *quassāre* shake violently, break to pieces, shatter, freq. of *quatere* (pp. stem *quass-*) shake. Senses connected with those of *shake* and *break* were current XIV–XVII. Cf. CONCUSSION, PERCUSSION. ¶ F. *-ss-* is repr. by *-sh-* as in *brush*, *push*.

quasi kwei·sai as it were XV (Caxton); (a) kind of XVII; seemingly, almost XIX. L., reduced form of *quansei* :– **quānsei*, f. **quām*, acc. sg. fem. (denoting extent) of the base of WHO, WHAT+*sei*, *sī* if.

quassia kwæssi·ə, kwɔ·ʃiə (wood, etc. of) a S. Amer. tree, Quassia amara. XVIII. Named by Linnæus, to whom the virtues of the root were communicated by C. G. Dahlberg, who himself heard of them from a Surinam negro named Graman (i.e. 'grand man') *Quassi* (Ashanti or Fanti *Kwasi*, name given to a child born on a Sunday), the discoverer of the root's properties in 1730.

quaternary kwətɔ̄·ɹnəri sb. set of four things XV; adj. consisting of four things XVII; (geol.) fourth in order (to match *tertiary*) XIX. – L. *quaternārius*, f. *quaternī* four together, f. *quater* four times, f. base of *quattuor* FOUR; see -ARY, cf. TERNARY.

quaternion kwətɔ̄·ɹniən group of four XIV (Wycl. Bible, Acts xii 4); quire of four sheets XVII; (math.) XIX (W. R. Hamilton, 1843). – late L. *quaterniō(n-)*, f. *quaternī* (see prec.).

quatorzain kæ·tɔ̄ɹzein (pros.) poem of 14 lines. XVI. – F. *quatorzaine* set of fourteen, f. *quatorze* fourteen (:– Rom. **quattordecem*, for L. *quattuordecim*)+*-aine* (:– L. *-āna*, fem. of *-ānus* -AN).

quatrain kwɔ·trein (pros.) stanza of four lines. XVI (*quadrain*). – F. *quatrain*, †*quadrain*, f. *quatre* FOUR+*-ain* :– L. *-ānu-* -AN.

quatrefoil kæ·təɹfoil compound leaf or flower of four leaflets. XV. – AN. **quatrefoil*, f. (O)F. *quatre* FOUR + *foil* leaf, FOIL[2]; cf. CINQUEFOIL.

quaver kwei·vəɹ vibrate, tremble XV (Lydg.); trill or shake in singing; also trans. XVI. frequent. (see -ER[4]) of ME. *quave*, *cwauien* (XIII), perh. repr. unrecorded OE. **cwafian*, parallel symbolic formation to *cwacian* QUAKE; ME. *cwakien* and *cwauien* are found in alliterative collocation; cf. the parallel forms under QUAGMIRE. Hence **qua·ver** sb. (mus.) note equal to half a crotchet XVI; shake or trill XVII; tremulous cry, etc. XVIII.

quay kī solid artificial landing-place. XIV. Late ME *key(e)*, later *kay*, and finally *quay* (XVII) by assim. to modF. *quai*; – OF. *kai*, *cay*, north. form corr. to Lyonnese *chai* retaining wall – Gaulish *caio* :– OCeltic **kagio-* (cf. OIr. *cae* enclosed place, house, W. *cae* hedge, OBreton *cai* fence, *caiou* fortifications, mod. *caé* embankment), perh. rel. to Germ. **χag-* HEDGE. ¶ The pronunc. has followed the same lines as in KEY[1]. From F. are also Sp. *cayo* CAY, Du. *kaai*, G., Da. *kai*.

quean kwīn orig. woman; (arch.) from early ME. times, bold impudent woman, jade, hussy; Sc. girl, lass. XV. OE. *cwene* = OS. *cwena* (Du. *kween* barren cow), OHG. *quena*, *quina*, ON. *kvenna*, *kvinna* (g. pl., nom. *kona*), Goth. *qino* woman :- CGerm. **kwenōn* wk. fem., f. IE. base **gwen-*, **gwn-*, repr. by Gr. *gunḗ*, Av. *genā*, OSl. *žena* (Russ. *zhená*), OIr. *ben* woman; cf. QUEEN.

queasy kwī·zi †troublous, unsettled; unsettling the stomach XV; easily upset, inclined to nausea; fastidious, scrupulous XVI. Early forms *coisy*, *quesy*, *quasy*, *queysy* suggest AN., OF. **coisi*, **queisi* or *-ié*, rel. to *coisier* hurt, wound, but there is no evidence.

Quechua ke·tʃuə, **Quichua** ki·tʃuə language of large areas of South America XIX.

queen kwīn wife of a king, woman having sovereign rule. OE. *cwēn* = OS. *quān*, ON. *kvæn* (also *kván*), Goth. *qēns* :- Germ. (exc. HG.) **kwǣniz* str. fem., f. IE. **gwēn-* **gwen-* (see QUEAN). Hence **quee·nLY**. XVI.

queer kwiəɹ odd, strange XVI; out of sorts, drunk XVIII. First recorded from Dunbar and Gavin Douglas; identical in form with and perh. of the same origin as sl. †*queer* bad (XVI, Awdelay, Harman); poss. – G. *quer* cross, oblique, squint, perverse (MHG. *twer*; see THWART). Hence **queer** vb. quiz, puzzle, ridicule XVIII; spoil XIX.

queest kwīst (dial.) ring-dove, wood-pigeon. XV (*quyshte*, *quyste*). perh. syncopated form of CUSHAT.

quell kwel †kill OE.; suppress, extinguish XIV; crush, subdue XVI. OE. *cwellan* = OS. *quellian* (Du. *kwellen*), OHG. *quellen* (G. *quälen*), ON. *kvelja* :- CGerm. (exc. Gothic) **kwaljan*, f. **kwal-* **kwel-*, repr. also by OE. *cwalu* death = ON. *kvǫl* torment, OE. *cwealm* death, torture, plague, OS., OHG. *qualm*, OE. *cwelan* die = OS. *quelan*, OHG. *quelan*; a long vowel appears in OS., OHG. *quāla* (Du. *kwaal*, G. *qual*); the IE. base **gwol-* **gwel-* is repr. by Lith. *gelà*, OSl. *žalĭ* sorrow, OPruss. *golis*, acc. *gallan* death, OIr. *at|balim* I die, Arm. *kełem* I torment.

quench kwentʃ put out, extinguish. XII. ME. *quenchen* :- OE. **cwenċan* (in *ācwenċan*) :- **kwaŋkjan*, causative of OE. **cwincan* (in *ācwincan*) be extinguished = OFris. *quinka* :- **kweŋkan*. Hence **que·nchLESS**. XVI.

quern kwɔ̄ɹn hand-mill. OE. *cweorn(e)* = OFris., OS. *quern* (Du. *kweern*), OHG. *quirn(a)*, ON. *kuern*, Goth. *-quairnus*, f. CGerm. **kwern-* :- IE. **gwern-*, repr. also by Lith. *gìrna*, OSl. *žrŭny*, *žrŭnŭvŭ* (Russ. *zhërnov*), Pol. *żarna*, OIr. *bró* (g. *broon*), W. *breuan*, Skr. *grāvan-*.

querulous kwe·rələs complaining, peevish. XV/XVI. f. L. *querulus* or – late L. *querulōsus*, f. *querī* complain; partly superseding late ME. *querelous* – OF. *querelous* (mod. *querelleux*), f. *querele* QUARREL[2]; see -OUS.

query kwiə·ri anglicization of QUÆRE, with ending assim. to *inquiry*. XVII.

quest kwest (obs. or dial.) inquiry, inquest; search, pursuit XIV; collection of alms XVI. – OF. *queste* (mod. *quête*) = Pr. *questa*, *quista*, Sp. *cuesta*, It. *chiesta* :- Rom. **quæsita* for L. *quæsīta*; sb. use of fem. pp. of *quærere* seek, inquire. Cf. INQUEST. So **quest** vb. go in pursuit of game XIV; search, seek XVII; search for, seek out XVIII. – OF. *quester* (mod. *quêter*) f. the sb.

question kwe·stʃən action of asking; what is asked (about). XIII (Cursor M.). – AN. *questiun*, (O)F. *question* – L. *quæstiō(n)-*, f. *quæst-*, pp. stem of *quærere* see prec.). So **ques·tion** vb. XV. – (O)F. *questionner*. Hence **que·stionABLE**. XVI. **questionnaire** k(w)estjənɛə·ɹ formal list of questions. XIX. F., f. *questionner* + *-aire* -ARY.

questor kwe·stɔ̄ɹ official who delivers papal indulgences. XV. – medL. *questor*, var. of QUÆSTOR.

queue kjū (her.) tail of a beast XVI; long plait of hair XVIII; line of persons, etc. XIX. – F. *queue*, OF. *coe*, *cue* = It. CODA :- L. *cauda* tail.

quibble kwi·bl play on words; equivocating or evasive speech. XVII. f. synon. †*quib* (XVI), prob. f. L. *quibus* (d. and abl. pl. of *quī*, *quæ*, *quod* WHO, WHAT, WHICH) as a word of frequent occurrence in legal documents and so assoc. with verbal niceties or subtle distinctions; see -LE[1]. Hence **qui·bble** vb. †pun; evade the point by a quibble. XVII. ¶ For sl. uses of *quibus* cf. F. *quibus* the wherewithal, cash, Du. *kwibus* fool, coxcomb.

quick kwik (arch.) living, alive OE.; lively, mobile, active; rapid, swift XIII; functionally active XIV. OE. *cwic(u)* = OFris., OS. *quik* (Du. *kwik*), OHG. *quek* (G. *keck*, dial. *kweck* lively, sprightly), ON. *kvikr* :- CGerm. (exc. Gothic) **kwikwaz*, in which the second *k* is of obscure origin, being absent in Goth. **qius* (in pl. *qiwai*) :- **kwiwaz*, f. CIE. base **gwej-* repr. also in L. *vīvus*, Lith. *gývas*, OSl. *živŭ* (Russ. *zhivói*), OIr. *biu*, *beo*, W. *byw*, Skr. *jīvás* living, Gr. *bíos*, *zoé* life (cf. VITAL, VIVID, BIO-, ZOO-). **quick** sb. *the q.*, sensitive flesh in the body. XVI; cf. F. *le vif*. Hence **qui·ckEN**[5] give life to; receive life XIII (Cursor M.); make quick or quicker XVII. In earliest use – ON. *kwikna* (intr.). Comps. **quickLIME** kwi·klaim lime that has been burned but not slaked. XIV; after L. *calx viva* (Vitruvius), F. *chaux vive*. **qui·ckSAND** bed of loose wet sand. XV; f. *quick* in sense of 'mobile' (XIV), corr. to Du. *kwikzand*, G. *quicksand*, Icel. *kviksandr*; OE. had *cweċesand*, f. *cweċċan* shake (rel. to QUAKE); **qui·ckset** live slips set in the ground as for a hedge XV; also adj. XVI; cf. SET sb. and F. *haie vive*. **qui·cksi·lver** mercury. OE. *cwicseolfor* = Du. *kwiksilver*, OHG. *quecsilbar* (G. *quecksilber*), ON. *kviksilfr*; tr. L. *argentum vivum* 'living silver' (Pliny), whence also. F. *vif argent*, It. *argento vivo*.

quickhatch kwi·khætʃ wolverene. XVIII. – Cree (N. Amer. Indian) *okeecoohagees*, *kwekwukao*; from other Algonkian dialects come CARCAJOU, KINKAJOU.

quid[1] kwid sovereign, †guinea. XVII. prob. sl. use of L. *quid* something, perh. with allusion to QUID PRO QUO; cf. F. *quibus* 'the wherewithal'.

quid[2] kwid piece of tobacco, etc. to be chewed. XVIII. dial. var. of CUD (OE. *cwidu*).

quiddity kwi·diti A. essence of a thing XV; B. subtlety, quibble XVI. – medL. *quidditās*, f. *quid* WHAT; see -ITY. Cf. F. *quiddité*.

quidnunc kwi·dnʌŋk inquisitive person, gossip. XVI. f. L. *quid nunc?* WHAT NOW?

quid pro quo kwid prou kwou (in apothecaries' language) one thing in place of another; one thing in return for another, tit for tat. XVI. L. *quid* something, *prō* FOR, instead of, *quō* (abl. of *quid*) something; see WHAT, WHO.

quiescent kwaie·sənt motionless, at rest. XVII. – L. *quiēscent-*, *-ēns*, prp. of *quiēscere* be still, f. *quiēs* quiet; see WHILE, -ENT.

quiet kwai·ət freedom from disturbance or noise. XIV. – AN. *quiete* (as in phr. *en quiete et peas* in quiet and peace), which was orig. OF. *quieté* (adopted in Sc. XV–XVI), f. *quiet* (– L. *quiētus*, pp. of *quiēscere* be QUIESCENT), whence **qui·et** adj. XIV (Wycl. Bible). Cf. COY. Hence **qui·et** vb. XV partly after late L. *quiētāre*; **qui·et**EN[5]. XIX (orig. local). So **qui·et**ISM mysticism characterized by passive contemplation. XVII. **qui·et**UDE. XVI – F. *quiétude* or medL. *quiētūdō*.

quietus kwaiī·təs discharge or acquittance XVI; death XVII (Sh.). Short for *quiētus est* (XV used as sb. in Eng.), medL. formula 'he is QUIT'.

quiff kwif (oiled) lock of hair worn on the forehead. XX. Of unkn. origin; perh. developed from any of various sl. uses.

quill kwil †hollow stem or reed XV (Lydg.); pipe, tube XV; tube or barrel of a feather, esp. as used for writing XVI; spine of the porcupine XVII (Sh.). prob. – (M)LG. *quiele*, of unkn. origin, and obscurely rel. to synon. MHG. *kil* (G. *kiel*).

quillet kwi·lit quibble. XVI. prob. shortening of †*quillity* (XVI), alt. of QUIDDITY (B); cf. *quip* and †*quipy*, †*quiddit* and *quiddity*.

quilt kwilt (orig.) article of bed furniture to lie on, consisting of two pieces of material with padding between; (later) coverlet similarly made, counterpane. XIII. – OF. *coilte*, *cuilte* (mod. *couette*), with var. *coute* (see COUNTERPANE, -POINT), Sp. *colcha* :– L. *culcita* mattress, cushion, rel. to Skr. *kūrcás* bundle, package. Hence **quilt** vb. XVI.

quin kwin abbrev. of QUINTUPLET, chiefly pl. *quins*. XX.

quinary kwai·nəri consisting of fives. XVII. – L. *quīnārius*, f. *quīnī*, distributive of *quinque* FIVE; see -ARY.

quince kwins (fruit of) the tree Pyrus Cydonia. XIV. orig. pl. used coll. of *coyn*, *quoyn* – CF. *cooin* (mod. *coing*), corr. to Pr. *codonh*, Cat. *codony*, It. *cotogno* :– L. *cotōneum* (Pliny), varying with *cydōneum* (apple) of Cydonia (now Canea) in Crete – Gr. *mêlon Kudṓnion*. (From L. *cotōnea*, *cydōnia*, Gr. *kudōniā*, *-éa* are ult. derived OHG. *quitina*, MHG. *quiten*, G. *quitte*, OHG. *chutina*, MHG. *küten*, UG. *kütte(n)*, MDu. *kweede*, Du. *kwee*.) ¶ For similar development of pl. cf. *bodice*, *lettuce*, in which the pronunc. with s is preserved, as also is *pence*.

quincentenary kwinsentī·nəri (pert. to) the 500th anniversary. XIX. irreg. f. L. *quinque* FIVE + CENTENARY. Also **quingentenary** kwindʒentī·nəri. XIX. f. L. *quingentī* 500 after *centenary*.

quincunx kwi·nkʌŋks, -ŋk- arrangement of five objects so placed that four occupy the corners and the fifth the centre. XVII. – L. *quincunx* five-twelfths ($\frac{5}{12}$ of an as was denoted by five dashes arranged as above), f. *quinque* FIVE+*uncia* twelfth, OUNCE[1].

quinine kwinī·n, (U.S.) kwai·nain alkaloid obtained from the bark of cinchona, etc. XIX. f. *quina* (Sp.) bark of cinchona, etc. – Quechua *kina* bark, reduplicated *kinakina*, *kinkina*, whence Sp. *quinquina* (in Eng. use from XVII); see -INE[5].

Quinquagesima kwinkwədʒe·simə †period beginning on the Sunday immediately preceding Lent and ending on Easter Eve XIV; (*Q. Sunday*) the Sunday itself. XVII. medL. sb. use (sc. *dies* day) of fem. of L. *quinquāgēsimus* fiftieth, f. *quinquāginta* fifty; cf. QUADRAGESIMA, etc.

quinque- kwi·nkwi comb. form of L. *quinque* FIVE, as in **qui·nquereme** having five banks of oars (L. *rēmus* oar) XVI.

quinquennial kwinkwe·niəl lasting five years XV (Fortescue); occurring every fifth year XVII. f. L. *quinquennis*, f. *quinque* FIVE+ *annus* year; see BIENNIAL and cf. L. *quinquennālis*.

quinsy kwi·nzi inflammation of the throat. XIV. ME. *quinaci*, *quinesye* – OF. *quinencie* – medL. *quinancia*, f. Gr. *kunágkhē*, f. *kun-*, *kúōn* dog (HOUND)+*ágkhein* throttle. ¶ A frequent var. in ME. is *squina(n)cy* (dial. *squinsy*).

quintain kwi·ntein post set up to be tilted at; exercise of tilting at this. XIV. – OF. *quintaine, -eine* = Pr., It. *quintana*, medL. *quintana, -ena*, usu. taken to be identical with L. *quintāna* market of a camp, f. *quintus* fifth (sc. *manipulus* maniple).

quintal kwi·ntəl 112 lbs. XV. – OF. *quintal* Sp., Pg. *-al*, It. *-ale*, medL. *-āle* – Arab. *qinṭār* KANTAR; cf. KENTLEDGE.

quintessence kwinte·səns substance latent in all things, the extraction of which was one of the objects of alchemy XV (Lydg.); most essential part XVI. – F. *quintessence*, †*quinte essence* – medL. *quinta essentia* FIFTH ESSENCE, the 'æther' of Aristotle ('De Cælo' II 3), the fifth primary body besides the elements of earth, fire, air, and water. Formerly also str. *quintesse·nce*; both stressings are used by Milton. Hence **quintessential** kwintėse·nʃal. XVII.

quintet(te) kwinte·t (mus.) composition for five voices or instruments. XIX. – F. *quintette* – It. *quintetto* (formerly used in Eng. XVIII), f. *quinto* :– L. *quintus* FIFTH; see -ET, -ETTE.

quintillion kwinti·ljən fifth power of a million; U.S. (as in France) cube of a million. XVII. See BILLION.

quintuple kwi·ntjupl fivefold. XVI (Billingsley). – F. *quintuple*, f. L. *quintus* fifth, after *triple*, etc. Hence **qui·ntuplet** pl. set of five. XIX. Cf. QUADRUPLET.

quip kwip Sharp or sarcastic remark. XVI. prob. shortening of †*quippy* (XVI), perh. – L. *quippe* indeed, forsooth (with sarcastic force).

quipu k(w)i·pu knotted device of ancient Peruvians for recording and communicating. XVIII. Quechua.

quire[1] kwaiəɹ †small book, short poem, etc.; set of four sheets of parchment or paper doubled so as to make eight leaves; hence, any gathering of sheets. XV. ME. *quaer*, later *quayer, quair, quere, quire* – OF. *qua(i)er* (mod. *cahier* quire, copy-book) = Pr. *cazern*, It. *quaderno* :– Rom. **quaternum*, f. L. *quaternī* set of four, f. *quater* four times, f. *quattuor* FOUR. ¶ For the development of the pronunc. cf. *quaisy* / *queasy*, *kay* / *key*, and *brere* / *briar*, *frere* / *friar*.

quire[2] see CHOIR.

quirk kwə̄ɹk verbal trick or subtlety XVI; sudden turn or twist XVII. Of unkn. origin.

quirt kwə̄ɹt riding-whip used in Southern U.S. and Sp. America. XIX. – Sp. *cuerda* CORD.

quisling kwi·zliŋ one who collaborates with the enemy. 1940. Surname of Major Vidkun *Quisling*, a Norwegian who collaborated with the Germans when they invaded Norway in World War II.

quit[1] kwit free, clear *of*, XIII. (i) ME. *quīt, quīte* (surviving in QUITE) – OF. *quite* = Pr., Cat. *quiti* (Sp., Pg. *quito*) – L. *quiētus* QUIET; cf. MDu. *quīte, quijt* (Du. *kwijt*), MLG., MHG. *quīt*. Superseded by (ii) later ME. or early mod. *quit(te)* – (O)F. *quitte* – medL. *quittus*, special development of L. *quiētus* (cf. MHG. *quit* (G. *quitt*), ON. *kvittr*).

quit[2] kwit pt., pp. *quitted*, (locally) *quit*. †A. set free, clear, clear off; B. †repay, requite; C. renounce; leave XIV. Late ME. *quitte*, repl. earlier *quite* (XIII), pt. *quitte*, pp. *quit(t)*; – (O)F. *quitter*, earlier *quiter* (cf. medL. *quittāre, quiētāre*), f. *quiētus* QUIET, QUIT[1]. Cf. ACQUIT, REQUITE.

quitch kwitʃ couch grass, Triticum repens. OE. *cwiće* = MLG. *kwēke* (hence G. *kwecke*); supposed to be rel. to *cwic* QUICK with ref. to the vitality of the grass.

quitclaim kwi·tkleim release, acquit; renounce. XIV. – AN. *quiteclamer* declare free, f. *quite* QUIT[1] + *clamer* proclaim (see CLAIM). So sb. †release XV; renunciation XVII. – AN. *quiteclame*, f. the vb.

quite kwait completely, entirely XIV; in the fullest sense, absolutely XVI. adv. use of *quite*, earlier form of QUIT[1] free, clear. (†*Quitely* is found somewhat earlier.)

quitrent kwi·trent rent paid in lieu of services. XV. f. QUIT[1] + RENT[1].

quits kwits †clear, discharged XV; even (*with*) by repayment or retaliation XVII. prob. – colloq. use of medL. *quittus* QUIT[1].

quittance kwi·təns release XIII (AncrR.); release from debt, receipt XIV (R. Mannyng); requital, reprisal XVI (Marlowe). – OF. *quitance* (later *quittance*), f. *quiter* QUIT; see -ANCE.

quiver[1] kwi·vəɹ case for holding arrows. XIII. – AN. **quiver, quiveir*, OF. *quivre, coivre* – WGerm. word repr. by OE. *cocor*, OFris. *koker*, OS. *kokar(i)* (Du. *koker*), OHG. *kohhar(i)* (G. *köcher*); rel. obscurely to medL. *cucurum*, medGr. *koúkouron*, Russ. *kókor* cartridge case (from Du. *koker*).

quiver[2] kwi·vəɹ shake with small rapid movements. XV (Caxton). f. ME. *cwiver* nimble, quick, OE. *cwifer* (in adv. *cwiferlīce*); cf. QUAVER.

qui vive kī vīv phr. *on the qui vive* on the alert. XVIII. F. *Qui vive?* sentinel's challenge to discover to which party the challenged person belongs, lit. 'Long live who?', orig. expecting an answer in the form *Vive le roi, Vive la France*, etc. (cf. VIVAT).

Quixote kwi·ksət enthusiastic visionary. XVII. f. name of Don *Quixote*, now written in Sp. *Quijote* kiχō·te, hero of Miguel de Cervantes' romance. Hence **quixot**IC kwiksɔ·tik. XVIII.

quiz[1] kwiz †eccentric person; one who quizzes XVIII; practical joke, hoax XIX. So **quiz** vb. make fun of, turn to ridicule. XVIII. Of unkn. origin; †*quoz* was a syn. of similar date. Hence **qui·zz**ICAL. XVIII.

quiz² kwiz (dial. and U.S.) question, examine; also sb. examination (spec. oral). XIX. Of unkn. origin.

quod kwɔd prison. XVII. perh. first syll. of QUADRANGLE, but there is no evidence.

quodlibet kwɔ·dlibet question proposed in scholastic disputation; scholastic debate or exercise. XIV. – medL. *quodlibetum*, f. L. *quodlibet* f. *quod* WHAT, *libet* it pleases (see LIBIDINOUS); cf. (O)F. *quolibet*.

quoin koin external angle of a wall or building, corner-stone; wedge, wedge-shaped block. XVI. var. of COIN, formerly current in all senses of this.

quoit koit flat disc thrown as an exercise of strength or skill; pl. sport of throwing quoits at a pin. XV. Earliest form *coyte* (as also in AN. statute of 1388); sp. with *qu-coit* was frequent XV–XIX. XVI–XVIII; of unkn. origin.

quondam kwɔ·ndæm former. XVI. adj. use of L. *quondam* formerly (orig. 'at any given moment'), f. *quom* when (f. **kwo-* WHO)+ generalizing particle *-dam*.

quorum kwɔ̄ə·rəm justice of the peace whose presence was necessary on the bench, later gen. XV; fixed number of persons whose presence is necessary in the transaction of business XVII. g.pl. of L. *quī* WHO; taken from the wording of commissions designating such persons, *quorum vos . . duos* (etc.) *esse volumus* of whom we will that you be . . two (etc.).

quota kwou·tə part or share of a total. XVII. – medL. *quota*, sb. use (sc. *pars* part) of fem. of L. *quotus* of what number, f. *quot* how many (so Skr. *kati*), f. base of *quī*, *quis* WHO; cf. correl. *tot* (see TOTAL). Also **quo·tum**. XVII – medL. *quotum*, *cotum*, n. of *quotus*.

quote kwout †mark with numbers or (marginal) references XIV; cite or refer to; †note XVI; repeat (a passage) *from* a book, etc. XVII. – medL. *quotāre* number, f. *quot* how many, or *quota* QUOTA. Formerly often *cote*, after F. *coter*. So **quotA·TION** †numbering XV; †marginal reference XVI; (typogr.) large quadrat used for filling up blanks (orig. between marginal references); quoting, passage quoted XVII; (comm.) price of stocks, etc. XIX. – medL. *quotātiō(n-)*, f. *quotāre*; cf. F. †*quotation*.

quoth kwouþ (arch.) said. OE. *cwæþ*, pt. of *cweþan* say = OFris. *qwetha*, OS. *queðan*, OHG. *quedan*, ON. *kveða*, Goth. *qiþan* :- CGerm. **kweþan*; early ME. *cwað*, *quaþ*, became *quoth* by rounding of a in contiguity with w in unstressed positions; a common var. XIV–XVI was *quod*. Forms with lack of stress are repr. by former pronuncs. kwəþ, kwɔþ. Hence **quotha** kwou·þə XVI; for *quoth (h)a* said he; fully reduced form is repr. by *catha*, *ketha* (XVI).

quotidian kwouti·diən, kwə- daily, spec. of a fever recurring every day. XIV. ME. *cotidien*, *-ian*, *quot-*, orig. – OF. *cotidien* (mod. *quotidien*), early assim. to L. *quotīdiānus*, earlier *cott-*, *cōtīdianus*, f. *cott-*, *cōtīdiē* (*quot-*) every day, f. base of *quotus* (see QUOTA)+*diēs* day; see -IAN.

quotient kwou·ʃənt result obtained by dividing one quantity by another. XV. – L. *quotiēns* how many times (f. *quot* how many; see QUOTA), taken as a prp. in *-ēns*; cf. F. *quotient* (earlier *quotiens*, which was occas. used in Eng.), It. *quoziente*, Sp. *quociente*.

quo warranto kwou wɔræ·ntou (leg.) writ of Queen's Bench demanding by what warrant a thing is held. XVI. Law L. 'by what warrant'; abl. sg. of *quod* WHAT and *warrantum* WARRANT.

R

rabbet ræ·bit channel or groove made in wood, stone, etc.; rectangular recess. XV. – OF. *rab(b)at*, act of beating down, recess in a wall, f. *rabattre* beat back or down, REBATE; the ending has been assim. to -ET.

rabbi ræ·bai (title of respect given to) a Jewish doctor of the law. XIV (*raby*). – OF. *rab(b)i* (mod. *rabbin*), ecclL. *rabbi* – Heb. *rabbī* my master, f. *rabh* master, with pronominal suffix. So **rabbin** ræ·bin. XVI. – F. *rabbin* or medL. *rabbīnus* (cf. It. *rabbino*, Sp. *rabino*, Du. *rabbijn*, G. *rabbiner*, Russ. *ravvin*) in which the *n* may be due to a Semitic pl. form. Hence **rabbi·NIC(AL)**. XVII.

rabbit ræ·bit burrowing rodent of family Leporidæ (orig. applied to the young, the full-grown animal being called *cony*, which was superseded in gen. use by *rabbit*). XIV (Trevisa). Late ME. *rabet(te)*, perh. – an OF. form repr. by dial. F. *rabotte*, *rabouillet* young rabbit, *rabouillère* rabbit burrow, poss. of LDu. origin (cf. Flem. *robbe*, dim. *robbeke*, Du. †*robett*, Walloon *robète*). ¶ For the use of dims. for this animal cf. L. *cunīculus* CONY, G. *kaninchen*, Du. *kanin(c)ken*.

rabble ræ·bl A. †pack, swarm of animals XIV; disorderly crowd XVI; B. †long string of words XVI, (dial.) rigmarole XVI. Of obscure origin; sense B suggests immed. connexion with (dial.) **rabble** vb. utter in a rapid confused manner (XIV) prob. – MDu. *rabbelen*, LG. *rabbeln*, of imit. origin.

rabid ræ·bid furious, raging XVII; affected with rabies XIX. – L. *rabidus*, f. *rabere* rave, be mad, rel. to Skr. *rábhas* impetuosity, violence; see -ID[1]. So **rabies** rei·biiz canine madness. XVII. – L. *rabiēs*, f. *rabere*.

rac(c)oon rækū·n Amer. nocturnal animal of the genus Procyon. XVII (Capt. John Smith has the forms *rahaugcum, raugroughcum, aroughcun, rarowcun*). – Powhatan (Virginia) dial. of Algonkian. See COON.

race[1] reis †onward movement, rush XIII (Cursor M.); (dial.) running, run XIV; strong current of water (channel for water, e.g. *mill-race* XVI); contest of speed XVI. north. ME., MSc. *rās, raas* – ON. *rás* running, race, rush of water, channel, row, series = OE. *rǣs* running, rush, impetus, attack, MLG. *rās* current; cf. ON. *ras* impetuosity, hurry, *rasa* rush headlong; of unkn. origin. Taken into gen. Eng. use from the north in XVI; hence the pronunc. reis, earlier rēs, orig. rās.

race[2] reis set or class of persons, animals, plants; group of persons, etc. having a common ancestry or character; class of wine or characteristic flavour of this, supposed to be due to the soil XVI; characteristic style of speech or writing XVII. – F. *race* – It. *razza* (XIV, Sacchetti), whence also Sp. *raza*, Pg. *raça*, Du. *ras*, G. *rasse*, Russ. *rása*; of unkn. origin. Hence **rac**IAL rei·ʃ[1]əl. XIX. **rac**Y[1] rei·si (in senses derived from the last two of the sb. above; phr. *racy of the soil*). XVII.

race[3] reis root of ginger. XVI. – OF. *rais, raiz* = Sp. *raiz* :– L. *rādīce- rādīx* root; see RADISH, RADIX.

raceme rəsī·m (bot.) form of inflorescence. XVIII. – L. *racēmus* cluster of grapes. Cf. RAISIN. So **race·mo**SE[1]. XVII.

rachitis rəkai·tis (med.) rickets. XVIII. – modL. – Gr. *rhakhîtis*, f. *rhákhis* spine, ridge; prop. 'inflammation of the spine', but adopted for 'rickets' by the Eng. physician Francis Glisson in his 'De Rachitide sive morbo puerili qui vulgo The Rickets dicitur Tractatus', 1650; see -ITIS.

rack[1] ræk A. †shock, collision XIII; B. mass of driven cloud XIV. prob. of Scand. origin; cf. Norw. and Sw. dial. *rak* (Sw. *vrak*, Da. *vrag*) wreck, wreckage, refuse, f. *reka* drive (cf. ON. *reki* flotsam); but the identity of A and B is not certain.

rack[2] ræk †bar, or framework of bars, esp. used for support or suspension. XIV. ME. *rakke*, occas. *rekke* – Du. *rak*, LG. *rack*, also MDu. *rek* (Du. *rek, rekke*), MLG. *rek(ke)* horizontal bar, shelf, prob. f. *recken* stretch (see RACK[3]).

rack[3] ræk instrument of torture in the form of a frame with a roller at each end. XV. prob. spec. use of RACK[2]. So **rack** vb. stretch the joints of XV (Lydg.), various transf. and fig. uses, stretch, strain, raise (rent) XVI. – MLG., MDu. *racken*, also *recken* = OE. *reććan*, OS. *rekkian*, OHG. *recchan* (G. *recken*), ON. *rekja*, Goth. (CGerm.) **rakjan* stretch, rel. to L. *regere* DIRECT, *porrigere* reach, Gr. *orégein* (cf. RIGHT).

rack[4] ræk horse's gait in which the two feet on each side are lifted simultaneously. XVI (Blundevil). Contemp. with rel. vb.; perh. ult. of Arab. origin (cf. *rekhwet* easy-paced, f. *rekhow* soft, and modGr. (Chios) *rhakhbán* amble). ¶ F. *racquassure* given by Palsgr. for 'rackyng' is otherwise unknown.

rack[5] ræk phr. *to rack (and ruin)* to destruction. XVI. var. of WRACK[1].

rack[6] ræk. Aphetic of ARRACK. XVII.

racket[1] ræ·kit bat of network used in ball games; pl. game played with ball and rackets XVI; (N. Amer.) snow-shoe XVII. – F. *raquette* †palm of the hand, †sole of the foot, racket, battledore, snow-shoe – It. *racchetta*, f. Arab. *rāḥat*, colloq. form of *rāḥa* palm of the hand.

racket[2] ræ·kit disturbance, uproar XVI; social excitement XVIII; trying experience XIX; illicit scheme XX (U.S.). perh. imit. of clattering noise. Hence **ra·cket** vb., **ra·cket**Y[1] XVIII. ¶ Gael. *racaid* is from Eng.

rackrent ræ·krent. XVII (but implied in *rackrented* XVI). f. *rack* in sense 'raise (rent) beyond a normal amount' (XVI 'racke and stretche out the rentes', 1553); see RACK[3], RENT[1].

raddle ræ·dl red ochre. XVI. var. of RUDDLE.

radial rei·diəl pert. to rays or radii. XVI (Dee). – medL. *radiālis*, f. RADIUS; see -AL[1].

radiant rei·diənt shining brightly XV; pert. to radiation XVIII. – L. *radiant-, -āns*, prp. of *radiāre*, f. RADIUS. Hence **ra·di**ANCE XVII (Sh.), -ANCY XVII. So **ra·di**ATE[3] emit rays XVII; spread in all directions from a centre XIX. f. *radiāt-*, pp. stem of *radiāre*. **radia·**TION XVII. – L. **ra·di**ATOR one or that which radiates XIX (in sense 'apparatus for circulating hot water to warm an apartment' orig. U.S.).

radical ræ·dik(ə)l pert. to the moisture inherent in animals and plants XIV (Trevisa); (math., philology, etc.) pert. to a root or radix; inherent, fundamental XVI; going to the root or origin, thorough XVII (*r. reform* XVIII); sb. radical element XVII; advocate of 'radical reform' XIX (at first a term 'in very bad odour' 'The Times' 16 Aug. 1819). – late L. *rādīcālis* (Augustine), f. L. *rādīc-*, RADIX; see -AL[1]. abbrev. **rad** XIX (orig. U.S.). Hence **ra·dical**ISM. XIX.

radicle ræ·dikl (bot.) part of the embryo which develops into the primary root. XVIII. – L. *rādīcula*, dim. of *rādīc-*, RADIX; see -CLE.

radio rei·diou short for *radiotelegraphy* (1904), *-telephony* (1909); see next. ¶ Suggested as the mark of 'wireless' telegrams under the Radio Convention drawn up at Berlin 1906; in foreign langs. the ordinary term for 'wireless' operations.

radio- rei·diou, reidiɔ· used as comb. form of RADIUS (i) anat., as *radio-carpal* pert. to radius and carpus, (ii) pert. to X-rays and other forms of radiation, as *radioactive* (1898), *radio·logy* (1900), *radio·*METER (1875).

radish ræ·diʃ (plant having) fleshy slightly pungent root used as a salad. OE. *rædić* (ME. *redich, radich*) – L. *rādīce-, rādix* root (see RADIX and cf. RACE[3]); late ME. *radish* (XV), alt. of this perh. by blending with F. *radis* (†*radice* XVI) – It. *radice* :– L.

radium rei·diəm (chem.) metallic element emitting rays that penetrate opaque matter, discovered by P. Curie, Mme Curie, and G. Bémont in 1898. modL., f. L. *radius* RAY[1]; see -IUM.

radius rei·diəs †staff of a cross XVI; thicker and shorter bone of the forearm; straight line drawn from the centre of a circle to the circumference XVII; (techn.) rod, bar, ray XVIII. – L. *radius* staff, measuring-rod, spoke, ray, radius of a circle, of the arm, various pointed objects.

radix rei·diks (chiefly techn.) root, basis. XVI. – L. *rādīx* root of a plant; for possible cogns. see ROOT[1].

raff ræf (dial.) abundance, large number XIV; rubbish, trash (see RIFF-RAFF) XV; common run or ruck XVII. perh. of Scand. origin (cf. Sw. *rafs* rubbish, tagrag).

raffia ræ·fiə soft fibre of the leaves of the palm Raphia. XIX. Also *raphia* (rei·fiə), var. of *rofia* roufiə· kind of palm (*rofeer* XVIII), a Malagasy word.

raffle ræ·fl (dial.) game of chance played with three dice XIV (Ch.); (f. the vb.) form of lottery XVIII. – OF. *raffle*, (also mod.) *rafle* (in medL. *raffla*), of which †*raffe*, †*raphe* were syns. in the senses 'throw at dice of all three alike', 'clean sweep'; of unkn. origin. Hence or – F. *rafler* **ra·ffle** vb. XVII.

rafflesia ræflī·ziə, -ʒiə plant of the family Cytinaceæ. XIX. modL., f. name of Sir T. Stamford *Raffles* (1781–1826), British governor of Sumatra, who discovered the plant; see -IA[1].

raft ràft †beam, spar; structure of planks, etc. forming a means of transport over water. XV – ON. *raptr* rafter rel. to OHG. *ravo*, ON. *ráfr, ræ̇fr*, with Balto-Sl. cogns.; cf. next.

rafter rà·ftəɹ beam in a building supporting the roof. OE. *ræfter* = OS. *rehter*, MLG. *rafter, rachter*, rel. to RAFT.

rag[1] ræg small fragment of textile material XIV; remnant, scrap XV; thing (contemptuously) regarded as such XVI. ME. *ragge*, prob. back-formation on **ragg**ED[2] ræ·gid shaggy, rough XIII; of irregular or straggling shape XIV; in rags XIV – ON. *rǫggvaðr* tufted (cf. Norw. *ragget* shaggy); or on **ragg**Y[1] ræ·gi late OE. *racgiġ* 'setosus' (cf. Sw. *raggig* shaggy), f. **racg* – ON. *rǫgg* (**raggw-*) tuft or strip of fur (cf. Norw., Sw. *ragg* rough hair); of unkn. origin.

rag[2] ræg (†piece or mass of) coarse or rough stone XIII (*ragghe*), XIV (*ragston*). Of unkn. origin, but assoc. later with prec.

rag[3] ræg (dial. sl.) scold, rate XVIII; (sl.) annoy, esp. in a rough or noisy fashion XIX. Also in comp. *bally-*, BULLYRAG; of unkn. origin; Da. dial. *rag* opportunity for slander, grudge, has been compared.

ragamuffin ræ·gəmʌfin ill-dressed disreputable-looking man or boy. XVI. Occurs in the form *ragamoffyn* in PPl. C. XXI 283 as the name of a demon, a grandson of Belial; dial. syns. are *ragabash* (XVII), *-brash* (XVIII); perh. based on RAG[1].

rage reidʒ †madness; violent anger, furious passion XIII; violent feeling or desire XIV; fervour, enthusiasm, excitement XVI. – (O)F. *rage* = Pr., Sp. *rabia*, Pg. *raiva*, It. *rabbia* :– Rom. **rabia*, for L. *rabiēs*; see RABIES. So **rage** vb. XIII (Cursor M.). – (O)F. *rager*, f. *rage*.

raglan ræ·glən overcoat without shoulder seams. XIX. f. name of Fitzroy James Henry Somerset, 1st Baron *Raglan*, British commander in the Crimean war.

ragout rægū· meat stewed with vegetables. XVII. – F. *ragoût*, f. *ragoûter* revive the taste of, f. *ra-* (i.e. *re-* RE- 2, 4+*a-*)+*goût* taste (cf. GUSTO).

rag-tag ræ·gtæg rabble, riff-raff. XIX. For older *tag-rag* (XVII), which replaced *tag and rag* (XVI); see TAG[1].

raguly ræ·gjŭli (her.) having short oblique projections. XVII. f. RAG[1] or RAGGY after NEBULY. See -Y[5].

ragweed ræ·gwīd XVII, **ragwort** ræ·gwə̄ɹt XV plant of the species Senecio, esp. S. Jacobæa. XV. f. RAG[1]+WEED[1], WORT[1], the ref. being to the ragged form of the leaves.

raid reid military expedition, orig. on horseback, foray. XV (Wyntoun). Sc. form of ROAD, revived by Scott ('Lay of the Last Minstrel', 1805) and hence generalized, with extension of meaning ('sudden or vigorous onset or attack'). Hence vb. XIX.

rail[1] reil †garment, mantle OE., early ME.; †neckerchief XV; *night-rail* dressing-gown XVI. OE. *hræġ(e)l* = OFris. *(h)reil*, OHG. *(h)regil*, of unkn. origin.

rail[2] reil bar of wood, etc. fixed in a horizontal position XIII; hand-rail of a staircase XV; bar or continuous line of bars laid for wheels to run on (so *railroad, railway*) XVIII. ME. *reyle, raile* – OF. *reille* iron rod = Pr. *relha* lever, crowbar, Sp. *reja* lattice :– L. *rēgula* staff, rod, RULE.

rail[3] reil bird of the genus Rallus or family Rallidæ. XV. – Norman-Picard *raille* (AN. *radle*, OF. *raale*, mod. *râle*) = Pr. *rascla* land-rail, Cat. *rascla* water-rail :– Rom. **rasc(u)la*, perh. of imit. origin.

rail[4] reil utter abusive language. XV. – F. *railler*, †*ragler* – Pr. *ralhar* jest, Sp. *rajar* boast, Pg. *ralhar* scold, It. *ragliare* bray :– Rom. **ragulāre*, f. **ragere* roar, bray, neigh (recorded in a gloss *ragit pullus* the colt neighs), crossing of L. *rugīre* bellow with Rom. **bragere* BRAY. Cf. RALLY[2].

raillery rei·ləri good-humoured ridicule. XVII. – F. *raillerie*, f. *railler* RALLY[2]; a var. †*rallery* (XVII–XVIII) is repr. by the pronunc. ræ·ləri current U.S.A.; see -ERY.

raiment rei·mənt clothes, apparel. XV (Promp. Parv., Malory). Aphetic of *arrayment* (XIV) – AN. *araiement*, OF. *areement*; see ARRAY, -MENT, and cf. (dial.) *ray* †arrange, †dispose, dress (XIV), aphetic of ARRAY.

rain rein condensed vapour of the atmosphere falling in drops. OE. *reġn*, *rēn* = OFris. *rein*, OS., OHG. *regan* (Du., G. *regen*), ON. *regn*, Goth. *rign*; CGerm., but isolated in IE. (the several words for rain are of limited range). So **rain** vb. OE. *reġnian*, also of CGerm. extent; the comps. *rainbow*, *-drop*, *-shower*, *-water*, and **rai·ny**[1] are all of OE. age.

raise reiz set up or upright; build up, construct, produce; remove to a higher position, elevate XII; levy; end (a siege) XIV; to make higher or greater XV. ¶ First recorded from the Ormulum, in which it occurs freely in various senses; ME *reise(n)* – ON. *reisa* = OE. *rǣran* REAR[1].

raisin rei·zn partially dried grape. (XIII.) – (O)F. *raisin* grape = Pr. *razin*, *razim*, Cat. *rahim*, Sp. *racimo* :– Rom. **racīmu-s*, for L. *racēmus* cluster of grapes (see RACEME). The several OF. types were more or less fully repr. in early use (viz. *raizin*, *razin*, *reisin*, *resin*, *roisin* (on the var. *rosin* are based (M)HG. *rosine*, Du. *rozijn*, Da. *rosin*, Sw. *russin*). ¶ Was approximately homophonous with *reason* till late XVIII; the pronunc. rī·zn is defended by Webster in 1828; cf. 'Reason and raisin . . . are pronounced alike in the age of George the Third, by every person who speaks without affectation', H. J. Pye 'Comments on the Commentators of Shakespeare' 1807.

raising-piece wall-plate. XVI (*raysyng or resun pieces*). f. †*rasen*, also *reason* (XVI); OE. *ræsn*, of unkn. origin.

raj rādʒ sovereignty. XVIII.– Hindi *rāj* reign.

raja, rajah rā·dʒă Indian king or prince. XVI (Eden's 'The Decades of the Newe Worlde' 1555). prob. through Pg. *raja* – Hindi *rājā* :– Skr. *rājan*, cogn. with L. *rēg-*, *rēx*, OIr. *rī*, *rīg* king (see RICH).

rake[1] reik implement consisting of a comb-like cross-bar fitted to a long handle. OE. *raca* m., *racu* fem. = MLG., MDu. *rāke* (Du. *raak*), rel. to Goth. *uf|rakjan* stretch out, and by gradation to MLG., MDu. *rēke* (Du. *reek*), OHG. *rehho* (G. *rechen*), ON. *reka*, and OHG. *rehhan*, Goth. *rikan* heap up; Germ. **rak-* **rek-* :– IE. **rog-* **reg-* move in a straight line, stretch, repr. also by RIGHT. So vb. XIII. – ON. *raka* scrape, shave, rake; also f. the sb.

rake[2] reik (naut.) projection of hull at stem and stern beyond the keel line. XVII (Capt. Smith). f. *rake* vb. (XVII, Capt. Smith) have a rake, incline from the perpendicular; prob. rel. to G. *ragen* project (whence Sw. *raka*, Da. *rage*), of unkn. origin. Hence **ra·kISH**[1] having a smart appearance like a fast-sailing ship XIX (W. Irving); partly assoc. with next.

rake[3] reik man of dissipated or loose habits. XVII. Clipped form of *rakel* (XVII; dial.), var. of arch. **rakehell** rei·khel XVI 'suche a feloe as a manne should rake helle for' (Udall, 'Apophthegms of Erasmus' 116b, 1542), f. RAKE[1]+HELL. Cf. QUACK[2], SAP[4], WAG[2]. Hence **ra·kISH**[1]. XVIII.

raki ræ·kī, rakī· aromatic liquor made from grain spirit, etc. XVII. – Turk. *rāqī* (whence modGr. *rhakḗ* brandy spirits).

rallentando rælæntæ·ndou (mus.) direction for reducing the tempo. XIX. It., prp. of *rallentare*, f. *re-* RE- 7+*al-* AD-+*lento* slow.

rally[1] ræ·li reassemble, revive XVI; also intr. XVII. – F. *rallier*, f. *re-* RE-+*allier* ALLY. Hence **ra·lly** sb. XVII.

rally[2] ræ·li treat with good-humoured ridicule. XVII (in early use also *railly*). – F. *railler* RAIL[4]. Cf. RAILLERY.

ram ræm male sheep; battering-ram (after L. *aries*; see ARIES) OE.; weight of a pile-driving machine XV. OE. *ram(m)*, corr. to Fris. *ram*, *room*, (M)LG., (M)Du. *ram*, OHG., MHG. *ram* ram (G. *ramme* rammer), perh. rel. to ON. *ram(m)r* strong. Hence **ram** vb. XIV (cf. MHG. *rammen*), whence **ra·mmER**[1] XV.

ramadan ræmədā·n ninth month (30 days' fast) of the Mohammedan year (supposed orig. to have been a hot month). XVI. – Arab. *ramaḍān* (hence Turk., Pers. *ramazān*), f. *ramaḍa* be hot.

ramble ræ·mbl wander about. XVII. prob. – MDu. *rammelen* (of cats, rabbits, etc.) be excited by sexual desire and wander about, frequent. f. *rammen* copulate with, cover, corr. to OHG. *rammalōn* (G. *rammeln*); ult. f. *ram* RAM; see -LE[3]. Hence **ra·mble** sb. XVII. ¶ The earlier synon. †*romble* (XIV), f. *rome* ROAM, appears to be unconnected.

ramekin, ramequin ræ·məkin cheese with breadcrumbs, etc. baked. XVIII. – F. *ramequin*, of Germ. origin; cf. Flem. †*rameken* toasted bread.

ramify ræ·mifai form branches, branch out. XVI. – (O)F. *ramifier* – medL. *rāmificāre*, f. L. *rāmus* branch; see RADIX and -FY. So **ra:mifica**·TION. XVII. – F.

ramillie ræ·mili wig with long plait and a bow at top and bottom. XVIII. f. *Ramillies* town in Belgium, the scene of the Duke of Marlborough's victory in 1706.

ramoon rəmū·n tops and leaves of West Indian Trophis americana used as fodder. XVIII. – Sp. *ramon*, f. *ramo* branch :– L. *rāmus*; cf. RAMIFY and see -OON.

ramose rămou·s branching. XVII (H. More). – L. *rāmōsus*, f. *rāmus*; see prec., -OSE. So earlier **ram**OUS rei·məs. XVI (Leigh).

ramp[1] ræmp rear or stand on the hind legs (threateningly) XIII (Cursor M.); rage violently XIV (Ch.); (dial.) climb, scramble XVI. – (O)F. *ramper* creep, crawl (a sense rarely repr. in Eng.), climb = It. *rampare*. So **ramp**ANT ræ·mpənt standing with forepaws in the air XIV, spec. in her. XV; violent and unrestrained XVII. – (O)F. *rampant*, prp. of *ramper*.

ramp[2] ræmp inclined plane. XVIII. – F. *rampe*, f. *ramper* RAMP[1].

rampage ræmpei·dʒ behave violently XVIII; push about excitedly XIX. orig. Sc., of unkn. origin; poss. based on RAMP[1].

rampart ræ·mpāɹt mound of earth raised for the defence of a place. XVI. – F. *rempart*, †*rampart*, alt. (by assoc. with *boulevart* BOULEVARD) of †*remper*, †*ramper*, f. *remparer* fortify, f. *re*- RE- 7 + *emparer* take possession of – Pr. *amparar* :– Rom. **anteparāre* put in position before another, f. *ante* ANTE- + *parāre* PREPARE. Adopted earlier in the forms †*rampar*, †*rampere*, †*-ier*, later †*-ire*.

rampion ræ·mpiən species of bell flower, Campanula Rapunculus. XVI. f. some var. of the Rom. forms derived from medL. *rapuncium*, *rapontium* (It. *raperonzo*, F. *raiponce*, Sp. *reponcha*; cf. G. *rapunzel*), presumably f. L. *rāpum* RAPE[2].

rams ræmz (dial.) wild garlic. OE. *hramsa*, *hramse* = MLG. *ramese* (whence G., Da., Sw. *rams*), rel. to Lith. *kermùšė*, Russ. *cheremshá*, OIr. *crem* (Ir., Gael. *creamh*, W. *craf*) wild garlic, Gr. *krómuon* onion. So **ra·msen** OE. *hramsan*, pl. of *hramsa*, *-e*, in later use taken as a sg. with pl. *ramsons*.

ramshackle ræ·mʃækl loose and shaky, rickety. XIX. Later form of **ra·mshackled** XVII, orig. pp. of †*trans(h)ackle* ransack, f. RANSACK + -LE[3].

ranch ràn[t]ʃ hut or house in the country; cattle-breeding establishment. XIX. – Sp. *rancho* (also used in Eng.) mess on board ship, soldiers' quarters, (in S. America) hut for herdsmen, etc.

rancid ræ·nsid having a rank taste or smell. XVII (Sir T. Browne). – L. *rancidus*, f. **rancēre* (in prp. *rancēns*) be putrid; see -ID[1].

rancour, U.S. **rancor** ræ·ŋkəɹ bitter ill-feeling, malignant spitefulness. XIV. – OF. *rancour* (mod. *rancœur*) = Pr. *rancor*, *rencor*, OSp., Pg. *rancor*, Sp. *rencor* :– late L. *rancōrem*, nom. *rancor* rankness, (in Vulg.) bitter grudge, f. **rancēre*; see prec., -OUR[2].

rand rænd (dial.) border, margin OE.; (dial.) strip, long slice XIV; strip of leather used in the sole of a boot or shoe XVI. OE. *rand* brink, bank, shield-boss, shield, corr. to OFris. *rond*, OS. *rand* 'umbo' (Du. *rand* edge, ridge, as in *Witwatersrand*, S. Africa), OHG. *rant* (G. *rand*), ON. *rǫnd* edge, rim of a shield :– CGerm. (exc. Gothic) **randa* (whence Pr. *randa* end, Sp. *randa* lace-edging, It. *randa*), f. **ram*- **rem*-, whence also OHG. *ramft* (G. *ranft* edge, border, crust), OE. *rima* RIM.

randan rændæ·n style of rowing (or boat) in which the middle of three rowers pulls a pair of sculls, the others an oar each. XIX (1828). prob. transf. use of *randem* style of driving in which three horses are harnessed tandem (*randem-tandem* c.1805, jingling formation on TANDEM); but the stress is then difficult to account for.

random ræ·ndəm †impetuosity, great speed or violence (phr. *o* or *in r.*, *with (a) great r.*) XIV; *at (the) r.*, orig. in hawking and the tournament XV; *at r.*, at great speed, (hence) at haphazard, without purpose XVI; †full range of a piece of ordnance, elevation of a gun XVI; adj. XVII (e.g. *random shot*). ME. *rand(o)un* – OF. *randon* (phr. *de* and *a grant r.*, *en un r.*) = Pr. (*a* and *de*) *randon* (whence Sp. *de rondon*, Pg. *de rondão* suddenly, abruptly), rel. to OF. *randir* run impetuously, gallop, f. Germ. **randa* RAND; taken to be orig. a soldier's phr., lit. 'with the shield'. For the dissimilation of *n . . n* to *n . . m* cf. RANSOM.

ranee rā·nī Hindu queen. XVII. – Hindi *rānī* :– Skr. *rājnī*, fem. of *rājan* RAJAH.

range reindʒ A. †rank, file XIII (Cursor M.); row, line, series XVI; B. moving about over an area; area itself XV; extent over which a missile ranges XVI; scope XVII. C. form of fire-grate or cooking apparatus XV. – OF. *range* row, rank, file, f. *ranger* (f. *rang* RANK[1]), whence **range** vb. place in a line, ARRANGE, dispose XIV, take up a position, extend XVI, move over a certain area XVI. Hence **ra·ng**ER[1] (arch.) gamekeeper XV (cf. AL. *rangeator*, *rangiarius* XIV); wanderer XVI; (esp. U.S.) pl. body of mounted troops XVIII.

rank[1] ræŋk row, line; grade of station or dignity. XVI. – OF. *ranc*, var. of *renc* (now *rang*) = Pr. *renc* – Germ. **χreŋgaz* RING[1].

rank[2] ræŋk A. †proud, rebellious OE.; †stout and strong XII; †swift, violent XIII; B. †full-grown OE.; vigorous or luxuriant of growth; coarsely luxuriant XIII; grossly rich or fertile; gross, coarse in manner XIV; of offensively strong smell; absolute, downright XVI. OE. *ranc* proud, stout, valiant, showy in dress = (M)LG. *rank* long and thin, ON. *rakkr* erect, f. Germ. **raŋkaz*; further relations and the primitive sense and later development of meaning are uncertain.

rankle ræ·ŋkl fester (now only fig.) XIV; fret, chafe (as, or as with, a sore) XVI. – OF. *rancler, raoncler* (cf. medL. *ranclāre, ranquillāre*), var. of *draoncler* (mod. dial. *drancler*), f. *rancle, raoncle*, var. of *draoncle* ulcer, festering sore – medL. *dranculus*, for L. *dracunculus*, dim. of *dracō* serpent, DRAGON.

ransack ræ·nsæk †search (a person); search (a place), examine thoroughly XIII; search (a place) with intent to rob, plunder XIV. – ON. *rannsaka* search for stolen goods, f. *rann* house (= OE. *ærn*; cf. BARN) + *-saka*, rel. by gradation to *sœkja* SEEK. The earliest exx. are from northern and eastern texts; used by Ch. and Gower, and in PPl.

ransom ræ·nsəm procuring the release of a prisoner by a payment, sum so paid. XIII (AncrR.). ME. *rans(o)un* – OF. *ransoun, raençon* (mod. *rançon*) = Pr. *rezemson* :– L. *redemptiō(n-)* REDEMPTION. So **ra·nsom** vb. XIII (Cursor M.) – OF. *ransouner* (mod. *rançonner*); for the dissimilation of *n . . n* to *n . . m* cf. RANDOM.

rant rænt †be uproariously merry; declaim in an extravagant manner. XVI (Sh.). – Du. †*ranten* talk foolishly, rave, also †*randen*, whence †*rand* (XVII, B. Jonson). Hence **rant** sb. high-flown declamation; (dial.) boisterous merrymaking. XVII.

ranunculus rənʌ·ŋkjŭləs crowfoot, buttercup. XVI. – L. *rānunculus* little frog, tadpole, medicinal plant (perh. crowfoot), dim. of *rāna* frog, after Gr. *βατράχιον*, dim. of *βάτραχος* frog.

rap[1] ræp strike or knock smartly. XIV. prob. imit.; perh. of Scand. origin: cf. Sw. *rappa* beat, drub, and *clap, flap, slap, tap*. So **rap** sb. XIV; cf. Sw. *rapp*, Da. *rap*.

rap[2] ræp counterfeit coin current in Ireland XVIII (Swift); type of the smallest coin, (hence) least bit XIX. Shortening of Ir. *ropaire*.

rapacious rəpei·ʃəs given to grasping. XVII (Jer. Taylor). f. L. *rapāci-, rapax*, f. *rapere* snatch; see RAPE[3], -IOUS. So **rapa**CITY rəpæ·sĭti XVI (Bacon). – F. or L.

rape[1] reip any of the six administrative districts of the county of Sussex, England. XI (*rap*, Domesday Book; taken up by legal and antiquarian writers from XVI). Identical with OE. *rāp* ROPE (the var. *rope* is found occas. XIV), the reference being to the fencing-off of land with a rope (cf. 'Illam terram suis fidelibus funiculo [with a rope] divisit', Dudo of St. Quentin, in Migne's Patrologia Latina cxli 652); cf. the similarly used cogn. OHG., MHG. *reif*.

rape[2] reip turnip; Brassica producing oil-seed. XIV. – L. *rāpum, rāpa* turnip, obscurely rel. to Gr. *rhápus, rháphus* turnip, *rháphanos, rhaphánē* radish, OSl. *rěpa*, Russ. *répa*, Lith. *rópė*, OHG. *ruoba* turnip.

rape[3] reip take by force XIV; ravish (a woman) XVI. – AN. *raper* – L. *rapere* seize, snatch, take by force (cf. RAPTURE). So **rape** sb. †violent seizure, robbery; carrying away of a person by force XIV; violation of a woman XV. – AN. *ra(a)p, rape* rape of a woman (Britton), f. the vb.

rapid ræ·pid moving with great speed XVII; acting or happening quickly XVIII. – L. *rapidus* lit. carrying along or away, f. *rapere* seize, carry off quickly or violently; see RAPTURE, -ID[1]. So **rapid**ITY rəpi·dĭti. XVII. – F. or L.

rapier rei·piəɹ kind of sword. XVI. prob. – Du. *rapier* or LG. *rappir* (cf. Sc. †*rapper*) – F. *rapière*, orig. *espee rapiere* (1474) 'rapier sword', of unkn. origin.

rapine ræ·pain seizing and taking away by force. XV. – (O)F. *rapine* or L. *rapīna*, f. *rapere* seize; see RAPE[3]. -INE[4].

rapparee ræpərī· Irish pikeman or irregular soldier. XVII. – Ir. *rapaire*, pl. *rapairidhe* (-ī·jə) short pike.

rappee ræpī· coarse snuff, orig. produced by rasping a piece of tobacco. XVIII. – F. (*tabac*) *râpé*, pp. of *râper* RASP.

rapport ræpō·ɹt, ‖ rapōr † report XVI (rare); relationship, connexion XVII. F., f. *rapporter*, f. *re-* RE- 7 + *apporter* bring – L. *apportāre*, f. *ad-* AP- + *portāre* carry (see PORT[3]).

rapprochement raprɔ·ʃmã establishment of harmonious relations. XIX. F., f. *rapprocher*, f. *re-* RE- 7 + *approcher* APPROACH; see -MENT.

rapscallion ræpskæ·liən rascal, vagabond. XVII. Later form of *rascallion* (XVII), f. RASCAL, after †*rampallion* (XVI) ruffian, scoundrel, or later MDu. *rappailie* rabble; cf. for the ending TATTERDEMAL(L)ION.

rapt ræpt taken and carried up *to heaven*, etc. XIV; carried away by force; carried away *in spirit* XV; transported *with* emotion, plunged *in* thought XVI. – L. *raptus*, pp. of *rapere* seize, rel. to Lith. *aprepiu* take by force; cf. RAPE[3], RAPID. So **rapt**URE ræ·ptʃər †carrying off, violent seizure, rape; transport of mind, ecstatic state; rhapsody XVII. – medL. *raptūra* seizure, ecstasy, f. *rapt-*, pp. stem of *rapere*.

rare[1] rɛəɹ †not thick or closely set; few and widely separated; of unusual merit XV; uncommon XVI. – L. *rārus*. Cf. F. *rare* (XVI). So **ra·rė**FY. XIV (Trevisa). – (O)F. *raréfier* or medL. *rārificāre*, extension of L. *rārēfacere*. **rar**ITY rɛə·rĭti. XVI. – F. *rareté*, †*rarité*, or L. *rāritās*. Also †*rari·ety* (XVI), after *variety*.

rare² rɛəɹ underdone. XVII. Later form of *rear*, OE. *hrēr*, of unkn. origin.

rarebit rɛə·ɹbit in *Welsh rarebit* (BIT¹), etymol. alt. of *W. rabbit*. XVIII.

raree-show rɛə·riʃou peep-show. XVII. prob. Savoyard's pronunc. of *rare show*; cf. '*Raree shew men*, poor savoyards who subsist by shewing the magic lanthorn and marmots about London', Grose. The G. name is *raritätenkasten* 'box of rareties'.

rascal rà·skəl †rabble; †young or inferior deer of a herd XIV; †one of the rabble, man of low station XV; low or unprincipled fellow XVI. – OF. *rascaille* (mod. *racaille*), prob. f. ONF. **rasque* = OF. *rasche*, Pr. *rasca* scab, scurf :– Rom. **rāsica*, f. **rāsicāre* (cf. OF. *raschier*, Pr., Sp. *rascar*, Sp., Pg. *rasgar* scratch), f. *rās-*, pp. stem of L. *rādere* scrape, scratch, shave. As adj. XV. Hence **ra·scal**LY¹. XVI (Sh., Jonson).

rase reiz †scratch, slit, slash; scrape XIV; level with the ground, RAZE XVI. – (O)F. *raser* shave close = Pr., Sp. *rasar*, It. *rasare* :– Rom. **rāsāre* (AL. XIII), f. *rās-*; see prec. Cf. ERASE.

rash¹ ræʃ (dial.) active, brisk XIV; hasty or impetuous in action or behaviour XVI. OE. **ræsć* = (M)Du. *rasch*, OHG. *rasc* (G. *rasch*), ON. *rǫskr* doughty, brave :– Germ. **raskuz*, perh. for **raþskuz*, f. **raþ-* RATHE; the existence of the word in OE. may be inferred with probability from the occurrence of *ræsć* storm, *līget|ræsć* lightning, *ræsćan* quiver, flash.

rash² ræʃ superficial eruption of the skin. XVIII. corr. in form to OF. *ra(s)che* skin eruption = It. *raschia* itch, but the late emergence of the word is against direct connexion.

rasher ræ·ʃəɹ slice of bacon or ham (to be) cooked by boiling or frying. XVI (Nashe). Of unkn. origin; the suggestion of a thing 'rashly or hastily roasted' (Minsheu, 1627) is not convincing.

raskolnik ræskɔ·lnik dissenter from the Russian church. XVIII. – Russ. *raskól'nik*, f. *raskól* split, schism.

rasp rɑ̀sp coarse file. XVI. – OF. *raspe* (mod. *râpe*; cf. RAPPEE), f. *rasper* scratch, scrape = Pr., Sp. *raspar*, It. *raspare* :– Rom. **raspāre* (cf. medL. *raspātōrium* rasp) – WGerm. (= OHG.) *raspōn* scrape together, of doubtful origin. So **rasp** vb. scrape as with a rasp XIV; make a grating noise XIX. In ME. – OF. *rasper*; later f. the sb.

raspberry rà·zbəri (fruit of) plant of the genus Rubus. XVII (*ras-*, *resberry*). f. synon. *rasp* (XVI), shortened form of †*raspis* (XVI), †*raspes*, †*respis*, which was used as coll. pl. or as sg. (cf. AL. *raspeium* XIII); it is of unkn. origin, but is identical in form with †*raspis* (XV–XVI) a kind of wine. See BERRY.

rat¹ ræt rodent of some of the larger species of the genus Mus. OE. *ræt*, reinforced in late ME. from (O)F. *rat* = Pr. *rat*, Sp. *rata*, Pg. *rato*, *-a*, It. *ratto* :– Rom. **rattus*, whence (with variations of cons. and vowel) OS. *ratta* (MLG. *rotte*, MDu. *ratte*, Du. *rat*, *rot*), OHG. *ratta* fem., *rato* m. (MHG. *ratte*, *rat*, G. *ratte* fem.), Sw. *råtta*, Da. *rotte*, and OHG. *ratza* (MHG., G. *ratz* m., *ratze* fem.); ult. origin unkn. and historical details uncertain. In ME. *raton* (mod. dial. *ratton*, *ratten*) was the more frequent word. – OF. *raton* (f. *rat* with augm. suffix); vars. with *o*, *rottan*, *-en*, occur from XVI and survive dial.

rat² ræt (mild imprecation) XVII. repr. affected pronunc. of ROT vb. Cf. DRAT.

rata rā·tə large forest tree of New Zealand. XIX. Maori.

ratafia rætəfī·ə cordial flavoured with fruits or their kernels. XVII. – F. *ratafia* (Boileau), prob. of Creole origin and rel. to *tafia* rum.

rataplan rætəplæ·n tattoo, rub-a-dub. XIX. – F. *rataplan*, of imit. origin.

rat-a-tat rætətæ·t sharp rapping sound repeated. XVII. imit. So **rat-ta·t**. XVIII.

ratchet ræ·tʃit set of teeth on the edge of a wheel, etc. in which a cog, etc. may catch. XVII (*rochet*). – F. *rochet* (in OF.) blunt lance-head, (later) bobbin, spool, ratchet (wheel), corr. to or partly – It. *rocchetto* spool, ratchet, dim. f. Rom. **rokk-*; see ROCK³. Later assim. to synon. *ratch* (XVIII) distaff, which may depend upon G. *ratsche*.

rate¹ reit A. †estimated quantity or worth XV; † price XVI; B. quantity in relation to another, value of one thing in respect of that of another XV; fixed relative charge XVI; degree of speed XVII; relative amount of variation XIX; C. †standard, measure XV; class (as of ships) XVII. – OF. *rate* – medL. *rata* (evolved from phr. *pro ratā*, short for *pro ratā parte* or *portiōne* according to an estimated or fixed part, proportionally), fem. of *ratus* (see RATIFY). Hence **rate** vb. †fix the amount of, allot XV; estimate, reckon, assess XVI.

rate² reit chide angrily. XIV (Ch.). Also †*arate* (PPl.), of which *rate* may be an aphetic form; the significance of the occas. vars. †*rehete* (XV), †*rahate* (XVI) is obscure; perh. to be referred to OF. *(a)reter* (of which a var. *aratter* occurs) accuse, blame = Pr. *reptar*, OSp. *rebtar*, *reutar* blame, challenge :– L. *reputāre* REPUTE.

ratel rei·təl S. African carnivore, Mellivora capensis. XVIII. – Afrikaans *ratel*, of unkn. origin.

rath ràþ fortress. XVI. – Ir. *ráth* (now pronounced rā) = Gael. †*ráth*, Gaul. (acc.) *rātin*, *-rātum* in place-names (e.g. *Argentoratum*, Strasbourg).

rathe reið, **rath** ràþ (arch. and dial.) quick, eager OE.; early XIII (in compar.), XV. OE. *hræþ*, var. of *hræd* (ME. and dial. *rad*) = OHG. *(h)rad*, ON. *hraðr*, Goth. **raþs* :- Germ. **χraþaz*, cogn. with Lith. *api|krataĩ* swift, *krečiù*, *krataũ*, MIr. *crothaim* I shake. The form *rathe* is from OE. obl. cases. So **rathe** adv. †quickly, soon OE.; early XIV (now arch. and dial.; comp. *rathe-ripe* XVI). OE. *hraþe*, *hræþe* = MLG. *rade*, OHG. *(h)rado*, Cf. RASH[1].

rather rā·ðəɹ †more quickly, (dial.) earlier, sooner; *the* more readily, *the* more OE.; more properly; somewhat XVI. OE. *hraþor* (= Goth. *raþizo*), compar. of *hræþe* RATHE adv.; see -ER[3]. The pronunc. rei·ðəɹ, which shows normal development of ME. ă in an open syll., is now only dial., as are also pronuncs. with æ, a; cf. *father*, *gather*, *lather*.

ratify ræ·tifai make valid by consent or formal sanction. XIV. – (O)F. *ratifier* – medL. *ratificāre*, f. L. *ratus* fixed, established, pp. of *rērī* reckon, think; see RATE[1], -FY. So **ra:ti**FICA·TION. XV – (O)F. – medL.

ratio rei·ʃiou relation of one quantity to another XVII; †ration XVIII. – L. *ratiō*, f. *rat-*, pp. stem of *rērī* reckon, think; cf. RATION and REASON.

ratiocination ræ:ʃiousinei·ʃən process of reasoning. XVI. – L. *ratiōcinātiō(n-)*, f. *ratiōcinārī* calculate, deliberate, f. *ratiō* REASON; see -ATION. So **ratio·cin**ATE[3], **ratio·cin**ATIVE. XVII; cf. F. *ratiociner*, *-cinatif*.

ration ræ·ʃən, (formerly) rei·ʃən allowance of victuals or provisions. XVIII. In naval and military use – F. *ration* – It. *razione* or Sp. *ración* (cf. medL. *ratio* soldier's ration, in reference to Spain, XIII in Du Cange) – L. *ratiō(n-)* reckoning, computation, sum or number (for other senses see REASON). ¶ Earliest obs. uses in the senses 'reasoning', 'ratio' (XVI–XIX) were immed. from L.

rational ræ·ʃənəl endowed with reason XIV (Trevisa); based on or pert. to reason XVI; (math.) XVI (Billingsley); agreeable to reason, reasonable XVII. – L. *ratiōnālis*, f. *ratiō* REASON; see -AL[1]. Cf. F. †*rational*, mod. *rationnel*). So **rationale** ræʃənei·li reasoned exposition; rational basis. XVII. – modL. *ratiōnāle*, sb. use of n. of *ratiōnālis*. **ra·tional**ISM. XIX; after F. *rationalisme* (1803), G. *rationalismus*. **ra·tional**IST. XVII; after F. *rationaliste* (XVI). **ra·tional**IZE. XIX (Coleridge).

ratlin(e), -ling ræ·tlin, -liŋ (naut.) thin line or rope XV; pl. small lines fastened horizontally on the shrouds XVII. Early forms *ratlin*, *raddelyne*, *radelyng*, of unkn. origin.

rattan rətæ·n species of Calamus, stem of this, switch or stick made therefrom. XVII. var. of earlier *rot(t)ang* – Malay *rōtan*, prob. f. *rāut* pare, trim, strip.

rat-tat(-tat) see RAT-A-TAT.

ratteen rætī·n thick twilled woollen fabric. XVII. – F. *ratine*, of unkn. origin.

rattle ræ·tl give out a rapid succession of short sharp sounds XIV; various transf. uses from XVI. prob. – (M)LG., MDu. *ratelen* = MHG, *razzeln* (G. *rasseln*), of imit. origin. Hence **rattle** sb. rattling sound; instrument for making a rattling noise; plant having a seed-pod that rattles XVI; cf. LG., Du. *rattel*, G. *rassel*. OE. *hrætele*, *hratele* plant-name ('bubonica', 'hierobotanicum') appears to have no historical connexion; but *rattle-bag* child's toy (XVI), which occurs as a surname in *Ratellebagge* ('Rotuli Hundredorum' 1273), may be orig. a comp. of the OE. word (perh. 'rattling seed-pod').

ratty ræ·ti pert. to, infested with, rats; miserable, wretched (like a drowning rat?); irritated. XIX. f. RAT sb. + -Y[1].

raucous rō·kəs hoarse and harsh. XVIII. f. L. *raucus* :- **ravicus*, f. *ravus* hoarse, *ravis* hoarseness; see -OUS. So **rau·**CITY rō·sĭti. XVII – F. or L. *raucitās*.

ravage ræ·vidʒ devastation. XVII. – (O)F. *ravage*, alt., by substitution of -AGE, of *ravine* RAVINE, both being used in the sense 'rush of water'. So **ra·vage** vb. XVII. – F. *ravager*, f. *ravage*.

rave reiv †be mad, (hence) talk wildly. XIV (Ch., Gower). prob. – ONF. *raver*, rel. obscurely to (M)LG. *reven* be senseless, rave, Du. †*ravelen*, *ravotten*.

ravel ræ·vl (dial.) entangle, become entangled XVI; unravel XVII. poss. – Du. *ravelen* tangle, fray out, unweave, corr. obscurely to LG. *reffeln*, *rebbeln*.

ravelin ræ·vəlin (fortif.) outwork of two faces forming a salient angle. XVI. – F. *ravelin* – It. †*ravellino*, (now) *rivellino* = Sp. *rebellin*, Pg. *revelim*, of unkn. origin.

raven[1] rei·vn large black bird with raucous voice, Corbus corax. OE. *hræfn* = OS. *naht|hraƀan* 'nocticorax', MLG., MDu. *rāven* (Du. *raaf*), OHG. *(h)raban*, ON. *hrafn*, beside MDu. *rave*, OHG. *rabo* (G. *rabe*) :- Germ. **χraƀnaz*, **χraƀan*; belongs to a group of imit. words: L. *corvus* raven Gr. *kórax* raven, *korṓnē* crow, Ir. *crú* raven, Skr. *kāravas* crow ('that says *kā*'), Pol. *kruk* raven, Lith. *kraũkia* croaks, Lith. *šárka*, Russ. *soróka* magpie.

raven[2] ræ·vn †take by force, divide as spoil XV; devour voraciously (also intr.). XVI. – (O)F. *raviner* rush, ravage, (now) hollow out, furrow :- Rom. **rapīnāre*, f. L. *rapīna* RAPINE. So **ra·ven**ER[2]. XIV – OF. *ravineor* :- L. *rapīnātōrem*, *-ātor*; **ra·ven**OUS – OF. *ravineux*, f. the vb.

ravin ræ·vin, **raven**[3] ræ·vn (arch.) rapine; voracity; spoil, prey. XIV. – (O)F. *ravine* :- L. *rapīna* RAPINE.

ravine rəvī·n †violence, violent rush (rare) XV; deep narrow gorge, mountain cleft XIX. – (O)F. *ravine* in mod. sense XVII, (formerly) violent rush, impetuosity, fall (of earth), torrent (of water), corr. to Pr. *rabina* impetuosity, ardour :– L. *rapīna* RAPINE, in Rom. (by assoc. with *rapidus* RAPID) impetuous or violent action.

ravish ræ·viʃ seize and carry off (a person), remove from sight XIII (Cursor M.); transport with strong feeling XIV. – *raviss-*, lengthened stem of (O)F. *ravir* = It. *rapire*, Rum. *răpì* :– Rom. **rapīre*, for L. *rapere* seize; see RAPE[3], -ISH[2].

raw rɔ̄ uncooked OE.; in a natural or unwrought state; crude XIV; inexperienced XVI. OE. *hrēaw* = OS. *hrāo* (MDu. *raeu*, *rou*, *ro*, Du. *rauw*), OHG. *(h)rāo*, *rau-*, *rou-*, *rō* (G. *roh*), ON. *hrár* :– CGerm. (exc. Gothic) **χrawaz* :– IE. **krowos*, f. a base repr. also by OIr. *crú*, Lith. *kraũjas*, OSl. *krŭvĭ* blood, Gr. *kréas*, Skt. *kraviś* raw flesh.

ray[1] rei line of light XIV; various techn. senses from XVII. – (O)F. *rai* = Pr. *rai*, Sp. *rayo*, It. *raggio* :– L. *radiu-s*; see RADIUS.

ray[2] rei edible sea-fish allied to the shark (family Raiidæ). XIV. – (O)F. *raie* = Sp. *raya*, It. (prop. Venetian) *razza* :– L. *raia* (Pliny).

raze reiz †scratch, graze; †scrape *out*, erase; sweep away, efface. XVI. var. sp. of RASE.

razor rei·zəɹ instrument for shaving. XIII. ME. *raso(u)r* – OF. *rasor*, *-our* (superseded by *rasoir* :– Rom. **rāsōrium*), f. *raser* RASE; see -OR[1]; the sp. *razor* dates from XVI.

razzia ræ·ziə hostile incursion, raid. XIX. – F. *razzia* – Algerian Arab. *ghāzīah*, var. of Arab. *ghazwah*, *ghazāh* military expedition, f. *ghasw* war.

razzle-dazzle ræ·zldæzl riotous jollity. XIX. Of U.S. origin; jingling formation on DAZZLE.

re[1] rei (mus.) second note of a hexachord or of the octave in solmization. XIV. See GAMUT.

re[2] rī in the matter of, concerning. XVIII (Hearne). abl. of L. *rēs* thing, affair. Also *in re*.

re- (unstressed, mostly) ri, (emph. or with stress, esp. with the sense 'again') rī, (with main or secondary stress, as in *recipe*, *recognize*, *record*, *redolent*, *reference*, *register*, *renovate*, *resolute*, *revolution*) re; repr. L. *re-*, (before a vowel in the classical period) *red-* (e.g. *redimere* REDEEM, *redolēre*, *redundāre* REDOUND) surviving in the doubled cons. of *reddere* RENDER, *religiō* RELIGION, etc.; prefix restricted to the Italic group, having the general sense of 'back' or 'again', occurring in many Eng. words of L. or Rom. origin (cf. F. *re-*, *ré-*, Sp., Pg. *re-*, It. *ri-*), or of Eng. formations freely modelled on these. From the L. was derived an adj. **recos*, repr. in *reciprocus* RECIPROCAL, and an adv. *retrō* backwards, RETRO-. In combination with *a-* the prefix is disguised in *rally*, *rampart*, and *ransom*, and in the non-naturalized *rallentando*, *rapport*, *rapprochement*. The meanings of the L. prefix, which are all repr. in Eng., are: (1) backwards from a point reached or to the starting-point, e.g. *recēdere* RECEDE, *redīre* return, *respicere* look back (see RESPECT), *revocāre* REVOKE; passing sometimes into 'away', e.g. *removēre* REMOVE; (2) back to an earlier state or over to another condition, e.g. *reficere* re-do, remake (see REFECTION), *renovāre* RENOVATE, *repōnere* REPOSE, *restituere* (see RESTITUTION), *resūmere* RESUME; (3) back in a place, from going forward, e.g. *refrēnāre* REFRAIN[1], *remanēre* REMAIN. *retinēre* RETAIN, *residēre* RESIDE, *restāre* REST[2]; (4) again, in return, in repetition or reiteration (the most frequent use in new formations, and sometimes doubled or trebled to express further repetition); (5) in a contrary direction, so that what has been done is annulled or destroyed (= UN-[2]), e.g. *recingere* ungird, *reclūdere* unclose (for later use see RECLUSE), *renuntiāre* RENOUNCE, *reprobare* REPROVE, *resignāre* RESIGN, *revēlāre* unveil, REVEAL; (6) in opposition or conflict, e.g. *rebellis* REBEL, *recrīminārī* RECRIMINATE, *recusāre* refuse (cf. RECUSANT); (7) in response to a stimulus, with intensive force, e.g. *redolēre* (see REDOLENT), *requīrere* REQUIRE, *resolvere* RESOLVE, Rom. **resentīre* RESENT, **resimulāre* RESEMBLE, F. *redouter* (cf. REDOUBTABLE).

Words containing the prefix occur as early as *c*.1200, are prominent in AncrR. and RGlouc., and become more frequent in Ch., PPl., Trev., Wyclif; it became an Eng. prefix in XVI, formations on native words being modelled to some extent on foreign comps., as *recall* on L. *revocāre*, *recast* after F. *refondre*, *renew* on L. *renovāre*. There are double forms with different meanings (with or without hyphen) arising from the coining of new formations from els. identical with those of already existing ones, e.g. *re-cover* (cover again) beside RECOVER. The hyphen in general is used when a *re*-compound is coupled with the simplex, as *bind and rebind*, and when the simplex begins with *e*, as *re-enter*, which in U.S.A. usage is often *re-ënter*.

reach[1] rītʃ stretch *out*, extend (in various lit. and fig. uses). OE. *rǣćan* (pt. *rǣhte*, *rāhte*), also *ġerǣćan* = OFris. *rēka*, *rēts(i)a*, MLG., (M)Du. *reiken*, OHG. (G.) *reichen* :– WGerm. **raikjan*, with which Lith. *raižytis* stretch has been connected. The typical ME. forms of pt. and pp. were *rau(g)hte*, *rau(g)ht* rɔ̄t; the new *reched* appeared *c*.1400, later *reached* XVI. comp. *reach-me-down* ready-made or secondhand (garment); pl. trousers. XIX (Thackeray). f. customer's request, *reach me down* (a garment from a peg or shelf). Hence **reach** sb. continuous stretch, as of a waterway XIII (in place-names); act or extent of reaching XVI.

reach[2] rītʃ †spit, hawk OE.; make efforts to vomit (see RETCH). XVI. OE. *hrǣċan* = ON. *hrǽkja* spit, f. Germ. **χraik-*, repr. also by OE. *hrāca*, ON. *hráki* spittle; of imit. origin (cf. OE. *hroh* phlegm, *hrohian* hawk, clear the throat, dial. *rough*).

react riæ·kt act in turn or in response to a stimulus XVII; move or tend in a reverse direction XIX. f. RE- 5, 7+ACT vb., after F. *réagir* or late L. *reagere*. So **rea·ction** XVII (Florio, rendering It. *reazione*), prob. after F. *réaction* (XVI; in political sense XVIII), whence **rea·ctionary** XIX; partly after F. *réactionnaire* (XVIII in political sense). **reagent** riei·dʒənt (chem.) substance employed to detect the presence of another by the reaction produced XVIII; after *reaction*.

read[1] rīd (now techn.) stomach of an animal. OE. *rēada*, of unkn. origin.

read[2] rīd pt., pp. **read** red †think, suppose, guess; discern the meaning of (chiefly in *read a riddle, a dream*); inspect and interpret aloud or silently (signs representing speech); also intr. OE. *rǣdan* = OFris. *rēda*, OS. *rādan* (Du. *raden* advise, guess), OHG. *rātan* (G. *raten* guess, read (a riddle), advise), ON. *ráða* advise, plan, contrive, rule, explain, read, Goth. *-rēdan* :- CGerm. **rǣðan*, prob. rel. to OIr. *im|rádim* I deliberate, consider, OSl. *raditi* take thought, attend to, Skr. *rādh-* accomplish. Also pp. 'informed by reading', as in *well-read* XVI.

The orig. senses of the Germ. vb. are those of taking or giving counsel, taking charge, controlling (the sense 'advise' has been preserved in Eng. with the form REDE); the sense of considering or explaining something secret or mysterious is common to several langs., but that of interpreting written symbols is peculiar to OE., and ON. (perh. through OE. infl.).

The orig. Germ. conjugation is repr. by OE. (rare) pt. *rēd*, *rēord*, and pp. (*ġe*)*rǣden*, OS. *ried*, *rēd*, and **girādan* (Du. *riet*, *ried*, and *geraden*), OHG. *riat* and *girāten* (G. *riet* and *geraten*), ON. *réð* and *ráðinn*, Goth. *-rairōþ* and **-rēdans* :- CGerm. **rerōð* and **garǣdanaz*; but the usual OE. forms were *rǣdde* and (*ġe*)*rǣd*(*e*)*d*, on the analogy of *lǣdan* LEAD[2], ME. *radde*, *redde* and (*i*)*rad*, (*i*)*red*; since XVII the Eng. inf., pt., and pp. have been identical in spelling. Hence **rea·der**[1]. OE. *rǣdere*; reading-book XVIII. **rea·ding**[1] OE. *rǣding*.

ready re·di in a state of preparation *for* something, prompt, quick. XII–XIII (Ormulum, Laȝ., S.Eng. Leg., Cursor M.). Early ME. *rædi(ȝ)*, *readi*, *redi*, also *ȝeredi*, *ireadi*, extended forms (with -Y[1]) of OE. *rǣde*, usu. *ġerǣde* (ME. *irede*) = OFris. *rēde*, MLG. *rēde*, *gerēde* (Du. *gereed*), OHG. *reiti*, MHG. *gereite*, parallel to OE. *gerād* straight, wise, prudent, -conditioned, MLG. *gerēd*, MHG. *gereit* ready, ON. *reiðr*, *greiðr* ready (whence ME. †*graith*, dial. *gradely*), Goth. *garaiþs* arranged; f. Germ. **raið-* prepare, arrange; connexion with RIDE has been conjectured, the basic meaning 'prepared for a journey' being supposed.

real[1] rī·əl (orig. leg.) pert. to things (as dist. from persons) XV; actually existing or present; that is truly what its name implies XVI. orig. – AN. *real* = (O)F. *réel*; later – its source, late L. *reālis*, f. *rēs* thing, acc. *rem*, corr. to Vedic *rā̆m* riches, *śatá|rā* 'having a hundred riches'; see -AL[1]. So **re·alism** XIX (Coleridge); orig. after G. *realismus* or F. *réalisme*. **re·alist** (philos.) XVII; after F. *réaliste* (XVI). In the sense 'adherent of philosophical realism' earlier †*real* (XVI), after late L. *reālis*. **reality** riæ·lĭti. XVI. – (O)F. or medL. **re·alize, realiza·tion.** XVII (Cotgr.). – F. *réaliser*, *-isation* (XVI). **really**[2] rī·əli. XV; after late L. *reāliter*.

real[2] rī·əl, re·al small Spanish silver coin. XVII. – Sp. *real*, sb. use of *real* ROYAL; in full *real de plata* 'royal coin of silver' (cf. PLATE).

realgar riæ·lgāɹ native disulphide of arsenic. XIV. – medL. *realgar* – Arab. *rehj al-ghār* 'powder of the cave or mine' (*rehj* powder, *al* AL-[2], *ghār* cave). Cf. F. *réalgar*, formerly †*reagal*, †*riagal*, †*realgal*, Sp. *rejalgar*. ¶ In some vars. Arab. *j* is repr. by *s*; cf. OSp. *risalgado*, Pg. *resalgar*, *rosalgar*, It. *risogello*, *risigallo*, medL. *risigallum*, *resegale*, Eng. †*resalgar* (XIV, Ch.), †*rosalger* (XV), †*rosaker* (XVI).

realm relm (now rhet. and techn.) kingdom. XIII (S.Eng. Leg.). ME. *reaume*, later *reame*, *reume*, *realme* (XIV) – OF. *reaume*, *realme* (mod. *royaume*), corr. to Pr. *regeme*, *re(y)alme*, OSp. *rea(l)me*, It. *reame* – L. *regimin-*, REGIMEN; blending with OF. *reiel* ROYAL, etc. produced forms with *-l-*, which finally prevailed in Eng., *realm* being established *c.*1600, *rialm* and *royalme* being earlier prevalent.

ream[1] rīm 20 quires of paper. XIV. – OF. *raime*, *reyme*, *remme* (mod. *rame*), also *riesme*, corr. to Cat. *raima*, Sp., Pg. *resma* – Arab. *risma* bundle of clothes, etc. (whence also It. *risma*, the source of Du. *riem*, G. *ries*, whence Sw., Da. *ris*), f. *rasama* remain fixed, collect into a bundle. ¶ Rag paper was introduced into Spain by the Arabs.

ream[2] (dial.) cream. OE. *rēam* = MLG. *rōm(e)*, (M)Du. *room*, MHG. *milch|roum* (G. *rahm*, dial. *raum*, *rohm*) :- WGerm. **rauma* (ON. *rjómi* is :- gradation-var. **reum-*).

reap rīp cut (grain) for harvest. The present form descends from ME. *repen*, *reopen*, repr. OE. (i) *reopan*, **riopan* (late Nhb. *rioppa*, *rippa*, also *hr-*, with characteristic cons.-doubling), var. of *ripan* (pt. *ripde*, **ripte*), and (ii) **repan* (pt. pl. *rǣpon*); no certain cogns. are known. (OE. pt. pl. *ripon* implies an inf. **rīpan*, pres. *rīpe*, *rīpþ*, repr. by ME. and dial. *ripe*, pt. *rope*. ¶ Various types, some showing admixture, are found in ME., early modE., and mod. dial., viz. inf. *rippe*, *rip*, †*ripe*, pt. *rep*, *rept*, *rope*, pp.†*ropen*, †*repen*, †*rept*, *ripped*, *rope*.)

rear[1] riəɹ set up, lift up, raise (lit. and fig.) OE.; bring up, breed XV; intr. rise on the hind feet XIV. OE. *rǣran* = ON. *reisa*, Goth. *ur|raisjan* awaken :- CGerm. **raizjan*, causative of **reisan* RISE. ¶ Superseded in many senses by the Scand. RAISE.

rear[2] riəɹ hindmost part. XVI. In earliest use military and naval; prob. extracted from phr. *in the rearward* (XV) or simply a shortening of *rearward* or *rearguard*, as the somewhat later VAN[1] is of *vanguard*. ¶ Aphetic deriv. from ARREAR is not supported by the chronology.

rearguard riə·ɹgāɹd †rear portion of an armed force XV (Caxton); portion detached from the main force to protect the rear XVII. – OF. *rereguarde* (cf. F. *arrière-garde*), f. *rer*, *riere* :- L. *retrō* back (see RETRO-)+ *guarde* GUARD. The AN. var. *rerewarde* is repr. by **rea·rward.** XIV; see WARD[1].

rearmouse riə·ɹmaus (dial.) bat (Vespertilio). OE. *hrēremūs*, the first el. of which is of unkn. origin, the second is MOUSE; poss. alt. of synon. *hrēaðemūs*.

reason rī·zn fact or circumstance serving as ground or motive for action; intellectual power, thinking faculty. XIII (AncrR.). Many senses now obs. have been current, as well as phr., which often depend on foreign models. ME. *res(o)un*, *reson*, *reisun* – OF. *reisun*, *res(o)un* (mod. *raison*) = Pr. *razó*, Sp. *razón*, It. *ragione* :- Rom. **ratiōne*, L. *ratiō(n-)* reckoning, account, judgement, understanding, reasoning, method, motive, cause (cf. RATIO, RATION), f. *rat-*, pp. stem of *rērī* think, reckon; see -TION. So **reason** vb. †question, call to account XIV; †hold discourse XV; think connectedly or logically XVI. – OF. *raisoner* (mod. *-onner*), f. *raison*, after medL. *ratiōnāre*. **rea·son**ABLE agreeable to reason XIII (Cursor M.); †endowed with reason; having sound judgement; not exceeding limits assigned by reason XIV. – (O)F. *raison(n)able*, f. *raison*, after L. *ratiōnābilis*. ¶ OF. *re(s)nable* is repr. by *renable* (XIII to mod. dial.) eloquent, fluent.

reasty rī·sti (dial.) rancid. XVI (Tusser). Later form of †*resty* (XIV–XVII) – OF. *resté* left over, pp. of *rester* remain, REST[1]. Other related (dial.) forms are *reesed*, *reezed* (XV), var. of †*rest* (XV); *reest* become rancid (XV); *reasy* adj. (XVII, Cotgr.), RUSTY[2].

Réaumur rei·ǒmjuə, ||reomūr Name of a thermometer invented by René Antoine de *Réaumur* (1683–1757), French physicist. XVIII.

reave rīv pt., pp. **reft** (arch.) commit robbery; despoil; take forcible possession of. OE. *rēafian* = OFris. *rāvia*, *rāva*, OS. *rōƀōn* (Du. *rooven*), OHG. *roubōn* (G. *rauben*), Goth. *bi|raubōn* :- CGerm. **rauƀōjan* (cf. ROB), f. **rauƀ-* (whence also OE. *rēaf* plunder, equipment, clothing = OFris. *rāf*, OS. *rōf*, OHG. *roub*; cf. ON. *reyfi* fleece and ROBE, **reuƀ-* (whence OE. *rēofan* break, tear; cf. BEREAVE, ON. *rjúfa* break, violate); the orig. sense is 'break', as in cogn. L. *rup-*, *rumpere* (see RUPTURE). The prevailing Sc. form is *reive*. Hence **reaver**, Sc. **reiver** rī·vəɹ robber, plunderer (brought into literary use by Scott). OE. *rēafere* = OFris. *rāvere*, MDu. *rōvere* (Du. *roover*), OHG. *roubari* (G. *räuber*).

rebate ribei·t †deduct, subtract; reduce, diminish XV; †dull, blunt XVI. Late ME. *rabat* – (O)F. *rabattre*, f. *re-* RE-+*abattre* ABATE; later alt. by substitution of *re-* for the first syll. Hence **rebate** rī·beit deduction. XVII; cf. F. *rabat*. Formerly †**rebate**MENT. XVI. – OF. *rebatement*.

rebeck rī·bek (hist.) three-stringed fiddle. XVI. – F. *rebec*, †*rabec*, corr. to Pr. *rebec*, Cat. *rabec*, It. †*ribeca*, unexpl. alt. of OF. *ribebe*, *rubebe* (whence ME. *ribibe*, *ru-*, *ribible*), Pr. *rebeb*, It. †*ribeba* – Arab. *rabāb* (dial. *rabēb*) one- or two-stringed fiddle; other perverted forms are OF. *rebelle*, Cat. *rabell*, Sp., Pg. *rabel*, Pg. (with AL-[2]) *arrabil*.

rebel re·b(ə)l adj. that refuses obedience or allegiance XIII; sb. one who does this XIV. In earliest use as predic. adj., later in attrib. position (now felt rather as the sb. used attrib.). – (O)F. *rebelle*. adj. and sb. – L. *rebellis* adj. and sb. (said orig. of the conquered making war afresh), f. *re-* RE- 6+ *bellum* war (cf. BELLICOSE). So **rebel** vb. ribe·l. XIV. – (O)F. *rebeller* – L. *rebellāre*, f. *re-* RE- 6+*bellāre* fight, make war, f. *bellum*. **rebellion** ribe·ljən. XIV. – (O)F. *rébellion* – L. *rebelliō(n-)*. Hence **rebe·lli**OUS. XVI; preceded by †*rebellous* (XV) – F. †*rebelleux*. Cf. REVEL.

rebound ribau·nd bound back. XIV. – OF. *rebonder*, (also mod.) *rebondir*, f. *re-* RE- I+ *bondir* BOUND[4]. Hence or – F. *rebond* sb. XVI.

rebuff ribʌ·f repel bluntly. XVI (Sidney). – F. †*rebuffer* – It. *ribuffare*, *rabbuffare*, f. *ribuffo*, *rabbuffo*, f. *ri-* RE- 6 + *buffo* gust, puff, of imit. origin. So **rebu·ff** sb. XVII (Florio). – F. †*rebuffe* – It. *ribuffo*.

rebuke ribjū·k †break down, force back; chide severely. XIV. – AN., ONF. *rebuker* = OF. *rebuchier*, f. *re-* RE- I+*buschier*, *buchier*, *bukier* beat, strike, prop. cut down wood, f. *busche* (mod. *bûche*) log, prob. of Germ. origin. Hence **rebu·ke** sb. XV.

rebus rī·bəs enigmatic representation of a name, word, etc. by pictures suggesting its syllables. XVII (Camden). – F. *rébus* – L. *rēbus*, abl. pl. of *rēs* thing (see REAL), in the phr. *de rebus quæ geruntur* 'concerning things that are taking place', title given by the clercs de basoche (guild of lawyers' clerks) of Picardy to satirical pieces containing riddles in picture form produced at carnival times.

rebut ribʌ·t †revile, reproach XIII (Cursor M.); †repel, repulse XIV; check XV; (leg.) repel by counter-proof XIX (intr. XVII). – AN. *rebuter*, OF. *reboter*, *-bouter*, f. *re-*, RE- 6+*boter* BUTT[1]. Hence **rebu·tt**AL[2] XIX; so **rebu·tt**ER[5] (leg.) defendant's answer to plaintiff's surrejoinder. XVI.

recalcitrant rikæ·lsitrənt kicking against restraint. XIX. – F. *récalcitrant* – L. *recalcitrant-*, *-āns*, prp. of *recalcitrāre* kick out, (later) be refractory (whence *reca·lcitrate*, *-a·tion* XVII), f. *re-* RE- 6 + **calcitrum* kick, f. *calc-*, *calx* heel; see -ANT.

recall rikɔ̄·l call back; revoke. XVI. f. RE- 1, 2, 3 + CALL, after L. *revocāre* or F. *rappeler*. Hence **reca·ll** sb. XVII.

recant rikæ·nt retract as erroneous. XVI (Lyndesay). – L. *recantāre* recall, revoke (Horace), f. *re-* RE- 5+*cantāre* sing, CHANT, after Gr. *παλινῳδεῖν* (cf. late L. *palinodiam canere* recant, Macrobius). Hence **recan-ta·tion** rī-. XVI. ¶ Terms originating at the Reformation.

recapitulate rīkəpi·tjŭleit go over or repeat again. XVI. f. pp. stem of late L. *recapitulāre*, f. *re-*, RE- 4+*capitulum* section of a writing, CHAPTER; see -ATE[3]; preceded by †*recapitle* (XV, Lydg.) – OF. *recapitler*, var. of *récapituler*. So **re:capitul**A·TION. XIV. – (O)F. or late L.

recast rīkà·st cast (metal) again; refashion. XVIII. f. RE- 4 + CAST, after (O)F. *refondre*.

recede risī·d retire from a place. XV. – L. *recēdere*, f. *re-* RE- 1 + *cēdere* go, CEDE. So **recess** rise·s †retirement, withdrawal XVI; (period of) retirement from occupation; retired, receding, or inner part XVII. – L. *recessus*, f. *recēdere* RECEDE. **rece·ss**ION retirement. XVII. – L. (Vitruvius). **rece·ssion**AL[1] (hymn) sung during the retirement of clergy, etc. after a service. XIX.

receipt risī·t A. recipe. B. reception (of money, etc.); money received XIV (written acknowledgement of this XVII); office for the reception of moneys XV (*r. of the Exchequer*). ME. *receit(e)* – AN. (ONF.) *receite* = OF. *reçoite*, var. (with *-ei-*, *-oi-* from *receivre*, *reçoivre*) of *recete* (mod. *recette*, after It.) = Sp. *receta*, It. *ricetta* – medL. *recepta*, sb. use of fem. pp. of *recipere* RECEIVE. The sp. with *p* appears in OF. *recepte* (XIV), a latinized form of *recete*. ¶ Many uses no longer current depend on early F. uses and on contacts with *receive*.

receive risī·v take to oneself XIII (Cursor M.); accept, take in, admit; be the object of XIV. ME. *receive*, *receve* – OF. *receivre*, var. of *reçoivre* (= Pr. *recebre*, Sp. *recibir*, It. *ricevere*) or later (refash.) *recevoir*, ult. :- L. *recipere*; see RECIPIENT and cf. CONCEIVE, DECEIVE, PERCEIVE. So **recei·**VER[2] XIV – AN. **receivere*, *-our* = OF. *recevere*.

recension rise·nʃən †enumeration, survey XVII; critical revision of a text, text so revised XIX. – L. *recēnsiō(n-)*, f. *recēnsēre* reckon, survey, review, revise, f. *re-* RE- 4+ *cēnsēre*; see CENSOR, -ION.

recent rī·sənt lately done or happened XVI; lately formed or begun XVII. – F. *récent* or L. *recent-*, *recēns*.

receptacle rise·ptəkl containing vessel, place, or space. XV (Lydg.). – (O)F. *réceptacle* or L. *receptāculum*, f. *receptāre*, f. *recept-*, pp. stem of *recipere* RECEIVE.

reception rise·pʃən action of receiving, XIV (Gower, in astron. sense); in gen. sense XV (not freq. til mid-XVII). – (O)F. *réception* or L. *receptiō(n-)*, f. *recipere*; see prec. and -TION. So **rece·pt**IVE. XVI. – medL.

Rechabite re·kəbait one of the Jewish family descended from Jonadab, son of Rechab, who abstained from wine and strong drink and refused to live in houses XIV (Wycl. Bible), hence, total abstainer XVII, dweller in tents XIX. – Vulgate L. *Rechabīta*, used in pl. to render Heb. pl. *Rēkābīm*, f. *Rēkāb* (Jer. XXXV); see -ITE.

réchauffé reiʃou·fei, ‖*reʃofe* warmed-up dish. XIX. F., pp. of *réchauffer* warm up again, f. *re-*+*échauffer*; see RE- 4, CHAFE, -Y[5].

recheat ritʃī·t †assembling of hounds, notes sounded on a horn for this purpose. XV (Malory). f. *recheat* vb. – OF. *racheter*, *rachater* (whence ME. *rechate* XIV) reassemble, rally.

recherché rəʃɔ̄·ɹʃei, ‖rəʃɛrʃe very choice or rare. XVIII. F., pp. of *rechercher* search for carefully, RESEARCH.

recidivist risi·divist one who relapses. XIX. – F. *récidiviste*, f. *récidiver* – medL. *recidīvāre*, f. L. *recidīvus*, f. *recidere* fall back, f. *re-*+*cadere* fall; see RE- 2, CASE, -IVE, -IST. ¶ In much earlier use were †*recidivate* XVI, †*-ation* XV (Lydg.).

recipe re·sĭpi †(imper.) take XIV; sb. formula for a medical prescription XVI, for a dish in cookery XVIII. – L. *recipe*, imper. sg. of *recipere* RECEIVE.

recipient risi·piənt one who or a thing which receives. XVI. – F. *récipient* – It. *recipiente* or L. *recipient-*, *-ēns*, prp. of *recipere* RECEIVE, f. *re-*+*capere*; see RE- 2, HEAVE, -ENT.

reciprocal risi·prəkəl done in return; inversely related XVI; corresponding to each other; (gram.) reflexive XVII. f. L. *reciprocus* moving backwards and forwards, alternating :- **recoprocos*, f. **recos*+**procos*, f. (respectively) RE- and PRO-[1], with **-cos* as in *antīcus* ANTIQUE, *postīcus* (f. *post* after); cf. (O)F. *réciproque*, whence †*reciproque* XVI, common *c.*1570–1620); see -AL[1]. So **reci·procATE**[3]. XVII. f. pp. stem of L. *reciprocāre*, f. *reciprocus*. **reciprocA·TION**. XVI. – F. or L. **recipro·CITY** resiprə·sіti. XVIII. – F. (in medL. 'recurrence', 'reflexive action').

recite risai·t repeat or utter aloud; state or describe in detail. XV (Caxton). – (O)F. *réciter* or L. *recitāre* read out, f. *re-* RE- 7 + *citare* CITE. Hence **reci·TAL**[2]. XVI. So **recitA-TION** resitei·ʃən. XV (Caxton). – (O)F. *récitation* or L. *recitātiō(n-)*. **recitative** resitəti·v adj. and sb. XVII (Evelyn). – It. *recitativo* (also used in Eng. from XVII, Evelyn, Pepys), orig. in *stile recitativo* (cf. 'after the Italian manner (Stylo Recitativo)' B. Jonson 1617), (mus.) manner of declamation combining melody with the rhythms of speech; cf. F. *récitatif* (1690): see -ATIVE and cf. medL. *recitātīvē* in express terms; formerly str. *re·citative* (Johnson), *reci·tative* (Byron, 'Don Juan' IV lxxxvii).

reck rek take care, heed, care, concern oneself. OE. shows two types: (i) **rēċan*, pt. *rōhte* (whence ME. *reche*, *rouhte*, later *rought* till XVII) = OS. *rōkjan*, OHG. *ruohhen*, ON. *rœkja* :– Germ. **rōkjan*; (ii) *reċċan*, the origin of which is obscure, paralleled in *recceléas*, earlier *recci-*, RECKLESS. The present form, which appears as *rek(k)-*, *reck-* in XII and XIII (Ormulum, Havelok, Cursor M.), is due partly to generalization of the *k* of ME. 3rd sg. pr. ind. *rekþ* (OE. *recþ*, which may belong to either **rēcan* or *reċċan*), partly to the infl. of ON. *rœkja*. Forms with a long stem-vowel are indicated by ME. *reke* (XIV), continued in *reak*, *wreak* (XVI–XVII). New pt. and pp. in *-ed* appeared XV.

reckless re·klis careless, negligent. OE. *reċċelēas*, *reċe-*, earlier *reċċileas*, whence ME. *rech-*, *retch(e)less* (to XVII), *reach-* (XVI–XVII), corr. to MLG. *rōkelōs*, (M)Du. *roekeloos*, OHG. *ruahhalōs* (G. *ruchlos*); f. base of RECK + -LESS; forms with *-(c)k-* are extant from Orm's date, by assoc. with the vb. (*rekkenn*).

reckon re·kn A. †recount, relate OE. (once); enumerate, name serially XII (Orm); count, compute XIII; estimate, consider XIV. B. make a calculation, settle accounts with; calculate or design *to* XVI; depend *on* XVII. OE. *ġerecenian* = OFris. *rek(e)nia*, (M)LG., (M)Du. *rekenen*, OHG. *rehhanōn* (G. *rechnen*) :– WGerm. **(ga)rekenōjan*, perh. f. **rekenaz* (OE. *recen*, OFris. *rekon* clear, open) ready, rapid, straightforward.

reclaim riklei·m †call (a hawk) back XIII (Cursor M.); recall, bring back; reduce to obedience XIV (Gower); claim restoration of XVI; bring (land) under cultivation XVIII. – (O)F. *réclamer* – L. *reclāmāre* cry out, exclaim; cf. Pr., Sp. *reclamar*, It. *richiamare*; see RE- 2, CLAIM. So **reclamATION** rekləmei·ʃən. XVI. – F. or L.

recline riklai·n †lay down XV; (of a dial) incline from the vertical XVI; rest in a recumbent position XVII. – OF. *recliner* lean, of a dial (as above), and reinforced from its source L. *reclīnāre* bend back, lay aside, recline, f. *re-* RE- 1 + *-clīnāre* (cf. DECLINE, INCLINE).

recluse riklū·s sb. person shut up from the world for the purpose of religious contemplation XIII (Ancr.R.); person of retired life XVIII; adj. XIV. – (O)F. *reclus*, fem. *recluse*, pp. of *reclure* :– L. *reclūdere* (pp. *reclūsus*) shut up, (earlier) open, f. *re-* RE- 4 + *claudere* CLOSE.

recognition rekəgni·ʃən †(Sc. leg.) resumption of lands by a feudal superior XV; acknowledgement as true or valid XVI; identification of a person or thing XVIII. – L. *recognitio(n-)*, f. *recognit-*, pp. stem of *recognoscere*; see RE- 4, COGNITION. So **recognIZE** re·kəgnaiz †(Sc. leg.) resume possession of XV; †revise, amend; †acknowledge, admit; treat as valid, approve; know again XVI. Early forms *raccunnis* (Sc.), *recognis*, *-nish*, soon assim. to vbs. in *-ise*, -IZE. – OF. *recon(n)iss-*, pres. stem of *reconnaistre* (mod. *reconnaître*) :– L. *recognoscere*. **recognizANCE** rikə·(g)nizəns legal bond or obligation XIV (Ch.); †recognition; †badge XV. – OF. *recon(n)issance* (mod. RECONNAISSANCE); cf. COGNIZANCE.

recoil rikoi·l †beat or drive back XIII (AncrR.); retreat, retire XIV; †go or draw back XV; spring back XVI. – (O)F. *reculer*, corr. to Sp. *recular*, Pg. *recuar*, It. *rinculare* – Rom. **recūlāre*, f. *re-* RE- 1 + *cūlus* posteriors (cf. OIr. *cúl* back, Skr. *kūla-* rearguard); for *oi* repr. F. *ü* cf. FOIL[1]. Hence **recoi·l** sb. XVI, with a rare ME. ex. (XIV); cf. F. *recul* (XVI).

recollect rekəle·kt call back to one's mind XVI. var., with distinctive pronunc., of *recollect* rīkəle·kt †collect; collect again XVI; summon up (one's spirits, courage, etc.) XVII; f. *recollect-*, pp. stem of L. *recolligere*, f. *re-* RE- 1 + *colligere* COLLECT[1]. So **Recollect** re·kəlekt Observantine of the Franciscan order. XVII – medL. *recollectus*, pp. of L. *recolligere*; cf. F. *récollet* (whence **Re·collet** XVII), Sp. *recoleto*, It. *recolletto*. **recolle·cTION** A. (rī-) gathering together again XVI; B. (re-) concentration of thought; recalling to the memory XVII. – F. or medL.

recommend rekəme·nd commend or commit to God (Ch.); †praise, commend XIV (PPl.); mention or introduce with approval; make acceptable XVII. – medL. *recommendāre* (based on F. *recommander*, It. *raccomandare*, etc.), f. *re-* RE- 7 + *commendare* COMMEND. So **re:commendA·TION**. XV. – medL., so F., etc.

recompense re·kəmpens reward, requite. XV. – (O)F. *récompenser* – late L. *recompensāre*, f. *re-* RE- 4, 7 + *compensāre* COMPENSATE. So sb. XV – F. *récompense*, f. the vb.

reconcile re·kənsail bring again into friendly relations or agreement XIV (Wyclif, Trevisa); make compatible XVI. – (O)F. *réconcilier* or L. *reconciliāre*, f. *re-* RE- 2, 7+ *conciliāre* CONCILIATE. So **re:concilia·tion.** XIV (Ch.). – F. or L.

recondite re·kəndait, rikə·ndait †hidden away; removed from ordinary understanding or knowledge. XVII. – L. *reconditus*, pp. of *recondere* put away, hide, f. *re-* RE- 1 + *condere*, put together, compose, hide, f. *com* CON- + base *-dere*, as in *addere* ADD.

reconnaissance, -noiss- rikɔ·nisəns ascertainment of the position and strength of an enemy. XVIII (both forms in Wellington's dispatches). – F. *reconnaissance*, *-oissance*, f. stem of *reconnaître*, later form of *reconnoître* (:- L. *recognoscere* RECOGNIZE), whence **reconnoitre** rekənoi·təɹ make a reconnaissance (of). XVIII (early).

record re·kɔ̄ɹd (leg.) fact of being committed to writing as evidence XIII (Cursor M.); fact of being preserved as knowledge XIV; (leg.) authentic report of proceedings XV; account of a fact in writing, etc. XVI. – (O)F. *record* remembrance, f. *recorder* bring to remembrance = Sp. *recordar*, It. *recordarsi* (cf. OF. *soi recorder* remember) :- L. *recordāre*, usu. *-ārī* (Rom. refl. **sibi recordāre*) think over, be mindful of, f. *re-* RE- + *cord-*, *cor* HEART; whence **record** vb. rikɔ̄·ɹd A. †commit to memory XIV; practise (a song, tune) XV; B. †recall, remember; relate, set down in writing XIV. So **recorder** (1) rikɔ̄·ɹdəɹ magistrate holding a court of quarter-sessions, orig. lawyer appointed by the mayor and aldermen (of London) to keep in mind proceedings of the court, etc. XV. – AN. *recordour*, OF. *recordeur*, f. *recorder*; see -ER[2]. **recorder** (2) rikɔ̄·ɹdəɹ wind instrument of the flute kind. XV (Lydg.). f. *record* vb. in the sense 'practise a tune' + -ER[1].

recount rikau·nt relate, tell in detail. XV. – AN., ONF. *reconter*, f. *re-* RE- 4 + *conter* COUNT. ¶ (O)F. has *raconter*, f. *re-* + *aconter* ACCOUNT.

recoup rikū·p †interrupt XV (rare); (leg.) deduct; recompense for loss or outlay XVII. – OF. *recouper* cut back, retrench, interrupt, re-sell, f. *re-* RE- 1, 2 + *couper* cut, OF. *coper* prop. behead (cf. It. *accoppare* strike down), f. Rom. **cuppa* CUP, transf. head.

recourse rikɔ̄·ɹs †return; †course, movement; resort *to* a person or thing XIV (Ch.); means resorted to XV. – (O)F. *recours* – L. *recursu-s*, f. *recurs-*, *recurrere* run or turn back, resort (see RECUR).

recover rikʌ·vəɹ trans. get or bring back, regain; intr. regain a status. XIV. – AN. *recoverer*, OF. *recovrer* (mod. *recouvrer*), corr. to Pr., Sp. *recobrar*, It. *ricoverare* – L. *recuperāre* RECUPERATE. So **reco·very.** XIV. – AN. *recoverie*, OF. *reco(u)vree*, f. the vb.

recreant re·kriənt confessing oneself vanquished, (hence) cowardly, craven XIV (also sb.); false, apostate XVII (sb. XVI). – OF. *recreant* adj. and sb. use of prp. of *recroire* yield, surrender :- medL. (*sē*) *recrēdere* surrender (oneself), f. *re-* RE- 5 + *crēdere* entrust, believe; see CREED, -ANT, and cf. MISCREANT. ¶ A term of the greatest infamy in the Middle Ages; cf. 'illud verbum odiosum quod recreantus sit', Bracton 'De legibus . . . Angliæ' III II xxxiv § 2.

recreate re·krieit restore to a good or wholesome condition, refresh. XV. f. pp. stem of L. *recreāre*, f. *re-* RE- 2 + *creāre* CREATE. So **recrea·tion** †refreshment, nourishment; refreshment by pleasant occupation. XIV. – (O)F. – L. **re·creative.** XVI; after F. *récréatif*. ¶ Distinct from **re:crea·te** rī- create afresh. XVI.

recrement re·kriment refuse, waste. XVI. – F. *récrément* or L. *recrēmentum*, f. *re-* + *crē-*, pt. and pp. stem of *cernere* separate; see RE- 1, DISCERN, DISCRETION, -MENT, and cf. *excrement*.

recriminate rikri·mineit retort an accusation, accuse in return. XVII. f. pp. stem of med. L. *recrīmināre*, f. *re-* + L. *crīminārī* accuse, f. *crīmin-*, *crīmen*; see RE- 6, CRIME, -ATE[3]. So **recrimina·tion.** XVII. – F. or med. L.

recrudescence rīkrude·səns breaking out afresh. XVIII. f. L. *recrūdēscere*, f. *re-* + *crūdēscere* become raw; see RE- 4, CRUDE, -ESCENCE. So -ENCY XVII, -ENT XVIII.

recruit rikrū·t †reinforcement (abstr. and concr.) of troops; †pl. reinforcements, (hence) one of the men composing these, newly enlisted soldier. XVII. – F. dial. (Hainault) †*recrute* = F. *recrue* (whence somewhat earlier Eng. †*recrew*), sb. use of fem. pp. of *recroître* = Pr. *recreiser*, etc. :- L. *recrēscere*, f. *re-* + *crēscere* grow; see RE- 4, CRESCENT and cf. CREW. So **recrui·t** vb. reinforce; replenish; enlist new soldiers; recover health or vigour XVII; enlist (men) XIX. – F. *recruter*, f. †*recrute*. In ordinary F. use the vb. *recruter* first appeared in gazettes published in Holland and was condemned as barbarous by Racine and others. ¶ The words were adopted in the Germ. langs. (Du. *recruut*, *rekruteeren*, G. *rekrut*, *-ieren*) and in other Rom. langs. (Sp. *recluta*, *-ar*, It. *recluta*, *-are*, Pg. *recruta*, *-ar*).

rectangle re·ktæŋgl right-angled quadri lateral. XVI (Digges). – F. *rectangle* or medL. *rēctangulum*, for earlier *rēctiangulum* (Isidore), sb. use of n. sg. of **rēctiangulus* (after Gr. ὀρθογώνιος), f. L. *rēctus* straight, RIGHT + *angulus* ANGLE[2]. Hence **re·ctangled**[2] XVI (Billingsley), **recta·ngular** XVII; after F.

rectify re·ktifai put right, remedy XIV; refine by chemical process XV; adjust XVI. – (O)F. *rectifier* – medL. *rēctificāre*, f. L. *rēctus* RIGHT; see -FY. So **re:ctifica·tion.** XV – (O)F. or late L.

rectilinear rektili·niəɹ characterized by straight lines. XVII. f. late L. *rēctilīneus*, f. *rēctus* RIGHT+*līnea* LINE[1]; see -AR.

rectitude re·ktitjūd †straightness XV; moral uprightness XVI. – (O)F. *rectitude* or late L. *rēctitūdō*, f. *rēctus* RIGHT; see -TUDE.

recto re·ktou right-hand page of a book when open, front of a leaf. XIX. – L. *rēctō* (sc. *foliō* leaf) on the right side of (a leaf), abl. of *rēctus* RIGHT. Cf. VERSO.

rector re·ktəɹ †ruler, governor XIV (Trevisa); incumbent of a parish whose tithes are not impropriate XIV (PPl.); head of a university, etc. XV. – OF. *rectour* (mod. *recteur*) or L. *rēctor*, *-ōr-*, f. pp. stem of *regere* rule (see REGENT). So **re·ctory**[1] benefice held by a rector XVI; residence XIX. – AN., OF. *rectorie* or medL. *rēctōria*; see -Y[3].

rectum re·ktəm final section of the large intestine, so called from its form in some animals. XVI. – L. *rēctum*, short for *intestīnum rēctum* the straight gut (Celsus), n. of *rēctus* straight (RIGHT).

recueil rəkö·j literary compilation. XV (*recuyell*, Caxton). In XV–XVI in anglicized forms, from XVII in the F. form *recueil*, f. *recueillir* gather together, see RE- 4, CULL.

recumbent rikʌ·mbənt lying down, reclining. XVII. – L. *recumbent-*, *-ēns*, prp. of *recumbere* recline, f. *re-* RE- 1+-*cumbere* (cf. INCUMBENT).

recuperate rikjū·pəreit †recover, regain XVI; restore (esp. in health) XVII; (intr.) recover health, etc. XIX. f. pp. stem of L. *recuperāre*, f. *re-* RE- 2+**cup-* (as in *occupāre* OCCUPY), var. of **cap-* (see HEAVE), with extension as in *tolerāre* TOLERATE. So **recuperA·TION** †recovery XV (Caxton; rare before XVII); restoration of health XIX. – L.

recur rikɔ̄·ɹ go or come back, return (now in abstr. senses) XV; occur again XVII. – L. *recurrere*, f. *re-* RE- 1, 4 + *currere* (see CURRENT). So **recurrENCE** rikʌ·rəns. XVII (Sir T. Browne); **recurrENT** rikʌ·rənt. XVI.

recusant re·kjuzənt Roman Catholic (etc.) who refused to attend services of the Church of England. XVI (Act of Edward VI). – L. *recusant-*, *-āns*, prp. of *recūsāre* refuse, f. *re-* RE- 6+*causa* CAUSE (cf. *accuse*, *excuse*); see -ANT.

red red of the colour of blood, sunset clouds, rubies, glowing coal. A widespread IE. colour-name. OE. *rēad* = OFris. *rād*, OS. *rōd* (Du. *rood*), OHG. *rōt* (G. *rot*), ON. *rauðr*, Goth. *rauþs* :– CGerm. **rauðaz* :– **roudhos*, f. IE. base repr. also by OIr., Gael. *ruadh*, W. *rhudd*, Serb. *rūd*, Lith. *raũdas*, L. *rūfus* RUFOUS (Italic *rōbus*), OE. *rēod*, ON. *rjóðr* red, ruddy, Goth. *gariudi*, Gr. *ereúthein* redden, and L. *ruber* (cf. RUBICUND, RUBRIC), *rubīgō* rust, *russus* (see RUSSET), Gr. *eruthrós*, Skr. *rudhirás* red, *rudhirám* blood, OSl. *rŭděti sja* become red, Lith. *rùdas*; cf. RUDDY, RUST. ¶ The shortening of the stem-vowel is paralleled in *bread*, *dead*, *lead* (metal); the long vowel is retained in the surnames *Read(e)*, *Rede*, *Reid*.

comp. **re·dBREAST**. XV (Lydg., Promp. Parv.); cf. LG. *rōd-*, Du. *roodborstje*; **red deer.** XV (Malory); **red herring.** XV; after (O)F. *hareng saur*; **red lead**[1]. XV; **red-short,** see COLD-SHORT; **redstart** re·dstāɹt singing-bird Ruticilla phœnicurus, having a red tail. XVI; OE. *steort* tail (see START[1]); cf. Du. *roodstartje*, G. *rotsterz* and Eng. *red-tail* (XVI). Hence **re·ddEN**[5] vb. XVII (Cotgr.). **re·ddISH**[1]. XIV (Trevisa).

red- var. of RE-.

-red rid repr. OE. *rǣden* condition, which was freely used as a suffix, as in *brōþorrǣden* brotherhood, *frēondrǣden* friendship, *sibrǣden* relationship. Only a few were retained in ME., but there were some new formations, as *felawrede* fellowship, *gossibrede* GOSSIPRED, *haterede(n)* HATRED, *kinrede(n)* KINDRED. In Sc., by metathesis, the suffix assumed the form *-rend*, *-rand* (*-rent*, *-rant*), as *hatrent*, *manrent* (homage, vassals).

redaction ridæ·kʃən preparation for publication. XIX. – F. *rédaction* – late L. *redactiō(n-)* (Boethius), f. *redact-*, pp. stem of *redigere* drive back, collect, reduce, f. *re-* RED-+*agere* (see AGENT).

redan ridæ·n (fortif.) field-work having two faces forming a salient angle. XVII. – F. *redan*, var. of *redent* notching as of a saw, f. *re-* RE-+*dent* TOOTH.

reddle see RADDLE, RUDDLE.

rede rīd †rule, govern OE.; †guide, guard, appoint XIII; advise, counsel OE.; interpret XVIII. ME. form of READ[2], retained for arch. senses. So **rede** sb. (arch.) counsel; †plan of action; †succour, remedy OE.; tale, story XIV. OE. *rǣd*, corr. to OFris. *rēd*, OS. *rād* (Du. *raad*), OHG. *rāt* (G. *rat*), ON. *ráð* :– CGerm. (exc. Goth.) **rǣðaz*, *-am*, f. base of **rǣðan* READ[2]; cf. READY, RIDDLE.

redeem ridī·m buy back; free (mortgaged property) by payment; free by paying ransom; deliver, spec. from sin XV; make up for, compensate XVI. – F. *rédimer* or L. *redimere*, f. *re-* RE- 2+*emere* buy, orig. take (cf. OSl. *imą*, Lith. *imù* I take, and see EXEMPT, PEREMPTORY, PROMPT). The long vowel of the second syll., paralleled in ESTEEM, is indicated in the earliest forms with *-eme*. (OF. *raembre* :– L. *redimere* is repr. by ME. *raim* XIII–XIV.) Hence **redee·mER**[1]. XV. (Earlier †*redemptor* – OF. or L.) So **redempTION** ride·mᵖʃən action of freeing or delivering; ransom. XIV. – (O)F. *rédemption* – L. *redemptiō(n-)*, f. *redempt-*, pp. stem of *redimere*; cf. RANSOM. **rede·mptorIST** member of the Congregation of the Most Holy Redeemer. XIX – F.

red-gum re·dgʌm papular eruption. XVI. alt., by assim. to GUM[1], of †*redgown(d)*, †*-gown* (XV), later form, infl. by RED, of *radegound* (XIV once, PPl.), f. obscure first el. + (dial.) *gound* pus, esp. from the eyes, OE. *gund* = OHG. *gunt* pus, Goth. *gund* carcinoma, connected by some with Gr. *kanthúlē* swelling.

redintegrate redi·ntigreit restore to completeness or unity. XV. f. pp. stem of L. *redintegrāre*, f. *red-* RE- 2 + *integrāre* INTEGRATE. So **redintegrA·TION**. XV.

redolent re·dŏlənt †sweet-smelling XIV; smelling *of* or *with* XVII (Dryden). – OF. *redolent* or L. *redolent-*, *-ēns*, prp. of *redolēre*, f. *red-* RE- 7 + *olēre* emit a smell, rel. to *odor* ODOUR; see -ENT. So **re·dolENCE**. XV. – OF.

redouble ridʌ·bl double in quantity XV (Caxton); repeat XVI. – F. *redoubler*; see RE- 4, DOUBLE vb.

redoubt ridau·t †small work within a fortification; square or polygonal outwork or field-work. XVII. – F. *redoute*, †*ridotte* – It. †*ridotta*, now *ridotto* (= F. *réduit*, Sp. *reducto*) – medL. *reductus* refuge, retreat, f. pp. stem of *redūcere* draw off, withdraw (see REDUCE). ¶ The intrusive *b* is due to assoc. with next.

redoubtable ridau·təbl to be feared. XIV (Ch.). – (O)F. *redoutable*, f. *redouter* fear, dread (whence *redoubt* vb. XIV), f. *re-* RE- 7 + *douter* DOUBT; see -ABLE.

redound ridau·nd †overflow; †abound; †flow or go back XIV (Wycl. Bible); †resound XIV; turn or contribute to *some advantage* or *disadvantage* XV; attach or accrue *to* XVI. – (O)F. *redonder* = Sp. *redundar*, It. *ridondare* :– L. *redundāre* (see REDUNDANT).

redress ridre·s †set upright again; restore, amend, remedy XIV (Ch., in various applications). – (O)F. *redresser*, †*drecier* = Sp. *redereçar*, It. *ridirizzare* (cf. medL. *redreçare*, *-escere*, *-ssare*, etc.); see RE- 2, 3, DRESS. So **redre·ss** sb. XIV (Ch., Barbour). – AN. *redresse*, *-esce*, f. the vb.

reduce ridjū·s †bring or lead back XIV; bring or restore *to* a condition; bring into subjection, bring down XV; diminish XVI. – L. *redūcere* bring back, restore, replace (whence F. *réduire*, Sp. *reducir*, It. *ridurre*), f. *re-* RE- 2, 3, 4, 5 + *dūcere* lead, bring (see DUCT). So **reducTION** ridʌ·kʃən. XV. – (O)F. or L.

redundant ridʌ·ndənt characterized by superfluity or excess. XVII. – L. *redundant-*, *-āns*, pp. of *redundāre*, f. *red-* RE- 7 + *undāre* (of the sea) be agitated, surge, f. *unda* wave; see WATER, -ANT. So **redu·ndANCE**, **redu·ndANCY**. XVII. – L.

reduplicate ridjū·plikeit make double or twofold XVI; (gram.) XIX. f. pp. stem of late L. *reduplicāre* (pp. in Tertullian), f. *re-* RE- 4 + *duplicāre* DUPLICATE. So **reduplicA·TION** doubling XVI; (gram.) repetition of an element of the radical or base of a word, as in the present and perfect tenses of some IE. langs. XVIII. – late L. *reduplicātiō(n-)* (Martianus Capella, Boethius), tr. Gr. ἀναδίπλωσις; cf. F. *réduplication*.

reed rīd (tall straight stem of) any plant of the genera Phragmites and Arundo. OE. *hrēod* = OFris. *hriad*, OS. *hriod*, OHG. *(h)riot* (Du., G. *riet*) :– WGerm. **χreuđa*, referred to IE. **kru-*, recognized in Tokh.

reef[1] rīf (naut.) horizontal strip of a sail that can be taken in. XIV (*riff*, Gower). – (M)Du. *reef*, *rif* (whence also G. *reff*, *reef*, Sw. *ref*, Da. *rev*) – ON. *rif* (RIB) in same sense; cf. next. Hence **reef** vb. reduce (a sail) by taking in a reef. XVII; cf. Du. *reven*. Hence **ree·fER**[1] reefing-jacket (close-fitting jacket). XIX.

reef[2] rīf ridge of rock at or near the surface of the water XVI; (in gold-mining, orig. Australian) lode of auriferous quartz XIX. Earlier *riff(e)*, in nautical use – MLG. *ref*, *rif*, pl. *rēves*, MDu. *rif*, *ref* (whence also G. *riff*, Sw. *ref*, Da. *rev*) – ON. *rif* (RIB) in same sense; cf. prec.

reek rīk smoke OE.; vapour, steam XIV; exhalation, disagreeable fume XVII. OE. *rēć*, **rieć* = OFris. *reek*, OS. *rōk* (Du. *rook*), OHG. *rouh* (G. *rauch*), ON. *reykr* :– CGerm. (exc. Goth.) **raukiz*, f. **rauk-* **reuk-*. From the second grade is **reek** vb. smoke (trans. and intr.); emit hot vapour OE.; emit unwholesome vapour, stink XVIII. OE. *rēocan* = OFris. *riāka*, (M)Du. *rieken*, OHG. *riohhan* (G. *riechen*), ON. *rjúka*. The normal repr. of the OE. sb. is ME. and dial. *reech*; the *k*-form (which appears first in Cursor M.) is due partly to Scand. infl., partly to assoc. with the native verb. Hence **ree·kY**[1]. XIV; prominently Sc. (*Auld Reekie*, 'Old Smoky', nickname for Edinburgh).

reel rīl winding instrument, orig. for thread or silk OE.; (orig. Sc. f. the vb.) whirling movement, staggering roll; lively dance of Sc. origin XVI. (Gael. *ruidhil*, *ruithil*, *righil* are from Lowland Sc.) OE. *hrēol*, of which no cogns. are known. Hence **reel** vb. (first in northerly texts) wind on a reel; whirl; stagger, sway XIV; dance a reel XVIII.

reeve[1] rīv (chiefly hist.) in Anglo-Saxon times, high official having local jurisdiction; later, variously applied to local officers. OE. *rēfa*, aphetic var. of OE. *ġerēfa*, earlier *ġirǣfa* (late Nhb. contr. form *grǣfa* GRIEVE[2]), f. *ġe-* Y- + **rōf* in *seċġrōf* host of men, *stæfrōf* alphabet = OHG. *ruova*, *ruoba*, ON. *stafróf*. See PORTREEVE, SHERIFF.

reeve[2] rīv pt. and pp. *reeved*, later *rove* (naut.) pass (a rope) through a hole. XVII (Capt. Smith). prob. – Du. *rēven* reef, with shift of meaning.

refection rife·kʃən refreshment, recreation XIV (Rolle); partaking of food, meal, repast XV. – (O)F. *réfection* – L. *refectiō(n-)*, f. pp. stem of *reficere* remake, renew, f. *re-*+ *facere* make; see RE- 2, DO[1], -TION. So **refect**ORY[1] rife·ktəri, re·fiktəri room for taking meals in. XV (Caxton). – late L. *refectōrium* (Gregory); cf. F. *réfectoire.*

refer rifɔ̄·ɹ attribute *to* a source or related thing; have relation or allusion *to* XIV (Ch.); commit *to* an authority, etc. XV. – (O)F. *référer* – L. *referre* carry back, f. *re-* RE- 2+ *ferre* BEAR[2]. **refer**ABLE re·fərəbl. XVII; earlier **referr**IBLE rifɔ̄·rĭbl. XVI. Hence **refer**EE[1] refərī· XVI (leg.); cf. *committee.* **re·fer**ENCE re·fərəns. XVI (G. Harvey, Hooker); cf. *conference, inference*; hence F. *référence.* **refere·ndum** referring a matter to the whole body of voters (as in the Swiss constitution) XIX. gerund or n. gerundive of L. *referre.* **re·fer**ENT (gram.). XIX; – prp. of L. *referre.*

refine rifai·n free from impurity, imperfection, or coarseness. XVI (Stanyhurst, Spenser). f. RE- 7 + FINE vb.[2], partly after F. *raffiner.* Hence **refin·e**MENT XVII, **refi·n**ERY XVIII; after F. *raffinement, raffinerie.*

reflect rifle·kt divert, deflect XV (Lydg.); throw back (beams, etc.), turn one's thoughts *upon* XVII (B. Jonson); cast reproach XVII (Massinger, Clarendon). – OF. *réflecter* or L. *reflectere*, f. *re-* RE-1+ *flectere* bend. So **refle·**CTION, **re**FLE·XION throwing back of light or heat XIV (Ch.); animadversion, imputation; fixing of the thoughts XVII (Clarendon) – (O)F. *réflexion* or late L.

reform rifɔ̄·ɹm A. form again XIV; B. † restore; convert into another and a better form XIV; change for the better XV. – OF. *reformer* (mod. *réformer*) or L. *reformāre* (cf. Sp. *reformar*, It. *riformare*); see RE- 2, 3, FORM vb. In sense A, a new formation since XVI, and now usu. sp. **re-form** and pronounced rī:fɔ̄·ɹm. Hence or – F. *réforme* **refo·rm** sb. XVIII (Butler). So **reform**ADO refɔ̄ɹmā·dou disbanded officer. XVI (B. Jonson). – Sp., sb. use of pp. of *reformar.* **reform**ATION refəɹmei·ʃən improvement, radical change for the better XV (Wyntoun); (hist.) spec., with *R.* XVI; also **re:forma·-tion** rī- new formation. XV. – (O)F. or L. **refo·rmat**ORY adj. XVI (Nashe); sb. institute for the reformation of juvenile offenders XIX.

refract rifræ·kt deflect the course of (light, etc.). XVII. f. *refract-*, pp. stem of L. *refringere*, f. *re-* RE- 1+*frangere* BREAK[1]. So **refra·**CTION † breaking open or up XVI (rare); deflection of rays, etc. XVII. – F. or L.; see FRACTION. **refra·ct**ORY[2] stubborn, unmanageable XVII; resisting the action of heat XVIII. alt. of †*refractary* (XVI, Jonson) – L. *refractārius* (Seneca); cf. F. *réfractaire* (Rabelais). But †*refractorious* is still earlier. ¶ *Refractory* was formerly str. on the first syll.; hence dial. *re·fatory.*

refrain[1] rifrei·n burden of a poem or song (recurring at intervals and so breaking the sequence). XIV (Ch.). – (O)F. *refrain*, †*refrein*, succeeding to earlier *refrait, -eit*, prob. – Pr. *refranh* bird's song, f. *refranhar* – Rom. **refrangere*, for L. *refringere*, f. *re-* RE- 7+*frangere* BREAK.

refrain[2] rifrei·n †restrain; abstain. XIV. – (O)F. *refréner* – L. *refrēnāre* bridle, f. *re-* RE- 3+*frēnum* bridle, rel. to *frendere* grind.

refresh rifre·ʃ impart freshness to, restore to a fresh condition. XIV (Ch., Barbour, Trevisa). – OF. *refreschier, refreschir* (cf. Sp. *refrescar*, It. *rinfrescare*), f. *re-* RE- 2+ *fres*, fem. *fresche* FRESH. Hence **refre·sh**MENT. XIV (Usk).

refrigerate rifri·dʒəreit cause to become cold. XVI (More). f. pp. stem of L. *refrīgerāre*, f. *re-* RE- 2 + *frīgor-, frīgus* cold; see FRIGID, -ATE[3]. So **refriger**A·TION. XV. – L. **refri·ger**ATOR cooler XVII; apparatus for maintaining a cold temperature XIX; earlier **refri·gera**TORY[1] XVII.

reft see REAVE.

refuge re·fjūdʒ shelter from danger or trouble. XIV (Ch.). – (O)F. *refuge*, corr. to Sp., It. *refugio* – L. *refugium*, f. *re-* RE- 1+ *fugere* flee (cf. FUGITIVE). So **refug**EE[1] refjudʒī· one who takes refuge in another country. XVII (*refugie* and *-gee*). – F. *réfugié*, pp. of (*se*) *refugier* take refuge, f. the sb.; the ending was early assim.

refulgent rifʌ·ldʒənt shining with bright light. XVI. – prp. of L. *refulgēre*, f. *re-* RE- 7+*fulgēre* shine; see PHLOX, -ENT.

refund rīfʌ·nd †pour back XIV; pay back, repay XVI. – OF. *refonder* or L. *refundere*, f. *re-* RE- 2+*fundere* pour (see FUSION); in later use based on FUND.

refuse rifjū·z †avoid; decline to accept or *to do* a thing; †renounce XIV; decline to grant XVI. – (O)F. *refuser*, corr. to Pr. *refuzar*, Sp. *rehusar*, It. †*rifusare* – Rom. **refūsāre*, prob. alt. of L. *recūsāre* refuse (see RECUSANT), after *refūtāre* REFUTE. Hence **refu·s**AL[2]. XV. So **refuse** sb. re·fjūs rejected matter. XV (Promp. Parv.). perh. – OF. *refusé*, pp. of *refuser.* ¶ For loss of *é* cf. COSTIVE, SIGNAL[2], TROVE.

refute rifjū·t †refuse XVI (rare); prove in error, disprove XVI. – L. *refūtāre* repel, rebut; see RE- 5, CONFUTE. So **refut**A·TION. XVI. – L.

regal rī·gəl royal, kingly. XIV (Ch.). – OF. *regal* or L. *rēgālis*, f. *rēg-, rēx* king, f. a base common to the Italo-Celtic and Indo-Iranian groups and repr. by Gaulish **rīx* (as in *Dumnorīx, Vercingetorīx*), (O)Ir. *rīg* king, Skr. *sam|rāj-* supreme king, *rājā* RAJA(H), rel. to L. *rēgula* RULE. See -AL[1] and cf. ROYAL. So **regal**ITY rīgæ·lĭti. XV. – OF. or medL.

regale rigei·l entertain or feast in a choice manner. XVII. – F. *régaler* (whence It. *regalare*, etc.), f. *ré-* RE- 7+OF. *gale* pleasure, joy; see GALA, GALLANT.

regalia rigei·liə royal powers or privileges XVI; insignia of royalty XVII. – medL. *rēgālia* royal residence, royal rights, n.pl. of *rēgālis* REGAL; see -IA².

regard rigā·ɹd A. †aspect, look XIV; (arch.) look, glance XV; (hist.) official inspection of a forest XVI; B. †repute, esteem XIV; observation, attention XV; thing to be considered; kindly feeling or wish XVI. – (O)F. *regard*, f. *regarder* (see RE- 1, 7, GUARD vb.), whence **rega·rd** vb. look at, take notice of XV; heed, take into account, consider XVI; concern, have respect or relation to XVII (prp. *regarding*, passing into prep. XVIII). Cf. REWARD. So **rega·rd**ANT (leg.) attached to a manor XV; (her.) looking backwards. – AN., (O)F. *regardant* prp. of the vb.

regatta rigæ·tə boat-race held on the Grand Canal, Venice XVII; hence gen. XVIII. – It. (orig. Venetian) †*regatta*, †*rigatta*, *regata* (whence F. *régate*, Sp. *regata*) 'strife or contention or struggling for the maistrie' (Florio), f. *rigattare* 'to wrangle, sell by retail as hucksters do, to contend, to cope or fight' (ib.), corr. to Sp. *regatear* haggle, sell by retail, contend in sailing.

regelate rī·dʒeleit freeze again. XIX (Tyndall). f. RE- 4+pp. stem of L. *gelāre* freeze (see COLD).

regenerate ridʒe·nəreit cause to be born again or reproduced. XVI. f. pp. stem of L. *regenerāre* (see RE- 4, GENERATE); based on earlier **rege·ner**ATE² adj. re-born, formed anew XV; spiritually re-born XVI. So **regener**A·TION re-creation XIV; spiritual rebirth XV. – (O)F. or L.

regent rī·dʒənt adj. presiding over disputations in a university XIV (Trevisa, *maisters regentes*, tr. L. *magistri regentes*); acting as regent of a country XVI; sb. one who rules, has royal authority, etc. XV. – (O)F. *régent* or L. *regent-*, *-ēns* ruling, ruler, governor, prp. of *regere* rule; see RIGHT, -ENT. So **re·g**ENCY office of a ruler or regent XV; body of persons acting for a sovereign; period during which a regent or regency governs XVIII. – medL. *regentia*.

regicide¹ re·dʒisaid one who kills a king. XVI. f. L. *rēgi-*, stem of *rēx* king (see REGAL) +-CIDE¹, prob. after F. *régicide*. So **re·gi**CIDE² killing of a king. XVII.

régime reiʒī·m †regimen of health; system of government. XVIII. – F. – L. *regimen*, f. *regere* (see REGENT). So **regimen** re·dʒimen regulation of matters pert. to health XIV; rule, government XV; (gram.) government XVI. – L. **regiment** re·dʒ(i)-mənt †rule, government; †control, management; †place under a certain rule XIV (Gower); †regimen of health; body of troops forming a unit XVI. – (O)F. *régiment* – late L. *regimentum* rule, f. *regere*; see REGENT, -MENT. Hence vb. XVII, **regime·n**TAL¹ adj. and sb. pl. XVIII.

region rī·dʒən †kingdom, realm; track of country, division of the world XIV; part or division of the air, a city, the body XVI. – (O)F. *région*, corr. to Sp. *region*, It. *regione* – L. *regiō(n-)* direction, line, boundary, quarter, district, province, f. *regere* direct, guide, rule; see REGENT, -ION. So **re·gion**AL¹ XVII – late L.

register¹ re·dʒistəɹ A. volume in which particulars are systematically entered XIV; B. slider in an organ XVI; plate for regulating the passage of air, heat, or smoke; adjustment of printing type XVII. Late ME. *registre*, *-estre* – (O)F. *registre*, †*regestre* or medL. *registrum*, *-estrum*, alt. of *regestum*, sg. of late L. *regesta* list, register, sb. use of n. pl. of pp. of L. *regerere* transcribe, record, f. *re-* RE- 7+*gerere* carry, carry out, execute (cf. *dīgerere* DIGEST); the senses under B are due to assoc. with F. *régir* guide, manage – L. *regere* (see REGENT). So **re·gister** vb. XIV – (O)F. *régistrer* or medL. *registrāre*, f. *registrum*. **registr**A·TION. XVI. – obs. F. or medL. **re·gistr**RY registration XVI; place of registration; register XVII. Reduced form of *registery* (XV) – medL. *registerium*. **registrar** redʒistrā·ɹ one who keep a register. XVII; superseding in general Eng. use older **re·gistr**ARY (retained in the University of Cambridge) XVI – medL. *registrārius* (f. *registrum*), **re·gister²** (retained in U.S.A. and Madras and 'of the Garter') XVI, ostensibly alt. of †*re·gistrer* XIV (PPl.) – AN. **registrere*= OF. *registreur*, medL. *registrātor* (see -ER²)

regius rī·dʒ¹əs designation of professors appointed by the Crown, instituted by Henry VIII. L., f. *rēg-*, *rēx* king; see REGAL.

reglet re·glit †column of a page XVI; (archit.) narrow band separating mouldings, etc. (Evelyn); (typogr.) narrow strip for making white spaces (Moxon) XVII. – (O)F. *réglet*, also *réglette*, dim. of *règle* RULE¹; see -ET; in archit. sense – It. *regoletto*, f. *regola*.

regnal re·gnəl of a sovereign's reign. XVII. – medL. *regnālis*, f. *rēgnum* REIGN; see -AL¹.

regnant re·gnənt reigning, ruling. XVII. – L. *rēgnant-*, *-āns*, prp. of *rēgnāre* REIGN; cf. F. *régnant* and see -ANT.

regrate rigrei·t (hist.) buy up (commodities) to sell again at a profit. XV. – OF. *regrater*, supposed to be f. *re-* RE- 7 + *grater* (mod. *gratter*) scratch (of Germ. origin). Hence **regra·t**ER¹, -OR¹. XIV (PPl.); in AL. *regratāre* (XIII), *regratārius* (XII).

regress rī·gres return, re-entry. XIV. – L. *regressus*, f. pp. stem of *regredī* go back, f. *re-* RE- 1 + *gradī* step, go, rel. to *gradus*, step, GRADE. So **regre·ss**ION. XVI. – L. **re-gre·ss**IVE. XVII (T. Carew).

regret rigre·t remember with pain or longing XIV; grieve at XVI. – (O)F. *regreter* bewail (the dead) (mod. *regretter*), with var. †*regrater*, whence ME. †*regrate* (XIV–XVII in both senses), corr. to Pr. *regretar*; perh. f. *re-* RE- 7+Germ. **grētan* weep, GREET². So **regre·t** sb. †complaint, lament; sorrow, esp. for something lost. XVI. – (O)F. *regret*, f. the vb.

regular re·gjŭləɹ †subject to a religious rule XIV (Trevisa); conforming to a rule, principle, or standard XVI. Late ME. *reguler* (later with ending assim. to L.) – OF. *reguler* (mod. *régulier*, with change of suffix), corr. to Sp. *regular*, It. *regolare* – L. *rēgulāris* (late in present sense), f. *rēgula* RULE; see -AR. So **re·gular**IZE. XVII (once in a dict.; thereafter not before XIX, after F. *régulariser*). **re·gul**ATE³ control, adjust. XVII. f. pp. stem of late L. *rēgulāre*. Hence **regul**A·TION XVII; rule prescribed XVIII. **re·gul**ATOR. XVII.

regulus re·gjŭləs (astron.) bright star in Leo; †metallic antimony, app. so called from its ready combination with gold; metallic part of a mineral XVI; petty king XVII; golden-crested wren (also called *kinglet*; cf. F. *roitelet*) XIX. L., dim. of *rēg-*, *rēx* king (see REGAL).

regurgitate rigə̄·ɹdʒiteit gush back again XVII; cast out again XVIII. f. pp. stem of medL. *regurgitāre*, f. *re-* RE- 1, 4 + late L. *gurgitāre*. So **regurgit**A·TION. XVII. – medL.

rehabilitate rīhəbi·liteit restore to former status. XVI. f. pp. stem of medL. *rehabilitāre*; see HABILITATE. So **re:habilit**A·TION. XVI. – medL. ¶ In earliest use Sc.

rehearse rihə̄·ɹs recite, relate XIII; practise the performance of XVI. Late ME. *reherce*, *-erse*. – AN. *rehearser*, OF. *reherc(i)er*, perh. f. *re-* RE- 4 + *hercer* harrow (see HEARSE). Hence **rehea·rs**AL² recital XIV (Ch.); practice *of* a play, etc. XVI.

reify rī·ifai convert mentally into a thing. XIX. f. L. *rēs* thing (cf. REAL¹) +- IFY. So **re:ific**A·TION. XIX (Grote).

reign rein (arch.) royal rule, sovereignty, (poet.) sway; †kingdom, realm XIII; period of rule XIV. – OF. *reigne*, (also mod.) *règne*, in OF. always 'kingdom' – L. *rēgnum* (cf. INTERREGNUM), rel. to *rēgula* RULE. So **reign** vb. XIII (R. Glouc., Cursor M.) – OF. *reignier* (mod. *régner*) – L. *rēgnāre*, f. *rēgnum*.

reim rīm (S. Africa) strip of ox-hide. XIX. – Du. *riem* = OE. *rēoma*, etc.

reimburse rīimbə̄·ɹs repay (a sum, a person). XVII. f. RE- 2 + IMBURSE, after F. *rembourser* (repr. immed. by rare Sc. †*ramburse* XVI).

rein¹ rein long narrow strap for guiding a horse. XIII. ME. *rene* – OF. *rene*, *reigne*, *raigne*, *rainne*, etc., earlier *resne*, (AN.) *resne* (mod. *rêne*) = Pr. *renha*, Cat. *regna*, Sp. *rienda*, Pg. *redea*, It. *redine* :– Rom. **retina*, f. L. *retinēre* RETAIN, repl. L. *retināculum* halter, tether. Hence **rein** vb. XIV.

rein² rein reindeer. XVI (*rhen*, *reen*). – Sw., Da. *ren*, †*reen* :– ON. *hreinn* = OE. *hrān*, acc. to some, of Finnish-Lappish origin. From Scand. are also early G. *reen*, *rein(er)*, F. *renne*. **rein**DEER rei·ndiəɹ deer of sub-arctic regions, used for drawing sledges. XIV – ON. *hreindýri* (whence also Sw. *rendjur*, Da. *rensdyr* and adopted in Du. *rendier*, G. *renntier*).

reinette reine·t var. of RENNET².

reinforce rīinfə̄·ɹs strengthen with additional men XVI; also gen. XVII. alt., by analysis into RE- and *inforce*, ENFORCE, of †*renforce* (XVI), often sp. (XVI–XVII) *re'n-*, *r'en-*, *r'in-* – (O)F. *renforcer*, in mil. use prob. – It. *rinforzare*.

reins reinz (arch.) kidneys, loins. XIV (Trevisa, Wycl. Bible, Gower). – (O)F. *reins* :– L. *rēnēs*, pl. of **rēn* kidney (cf. RENAL), whence Sp., It. *rene*. ¶ An instance of *renys* in late OE. Saxon Leechdoms repr. immed. L. *rēnēs*.

reinstate rīinstei·t re-establish in a position XVI; restore to a former state XVIII. See RE- 4.

rei·ntegrate, -a·tion, vars. of REDINTEGRATE, -ATION, after F. or late L. XVI.

reis¹ reis Portuguese money of account. – Pg. *reis* for **reaes*, pl. of *real* = Sp. *real* REAL².

reis², **rais** rais (in Eastern countries) captain of a boat. XVI. – F. *réis*, *rais* (cf. Sp. *arraes*, Pg. *arraes*, *arrais*, with AL-²) – Arab. *rā'is* chief, f. *rā's* head.

reitbuck rī·tbʌk S. African antelope, Cervicapra arundinacea. XVIII (*-bok*). – Afrikaans *rietbok*, f. *riet* REED+*bok* BUCK¹.

reiter rai·təɹ German cavalry soldier. XVI. – G. *reiter* rider, trooper, f. *reiten* RIDE; see -ER¹.

reiterate rīi·təreit. XVI. f. L. *reiterāt-*; see RE- 4, ITERATE. So **reiter**A·TION. XVI. – F. or L.

reiver see REAVER.

reject ridʒe·kt refuse to have, recognize, etc. XV. f. *reject-*, pp. stem of L. *reicere* throw back, discard, f. *re-*, RE- 1 + *jacere* throw; cf. F. †*rejecter*, var. of †*rejetter*, mod. *rejeter* (see JET²). Hence **re·ject** sb. †castaway XVI; thing rejected XIX; f. vb. So **reje·c**TION. XVI. – F. or L.

rejoice ridʒoi·s †enjoy possession of XIV; gladden; †refl. and intr. be joyful XIV (Ch.). ME. *reioshe*, *reioische*, *reioyse*, f. *rejoiss-*, lengthened stem of OF. *re(s)joir* (whence ME. †*reioy*), later *réjouir*, f. *re-* RE- 7+*esjoir* (*éjouir*), f. *es-* EX-¹ + *joir* JOY vb.

rejoin[1] ridʒoi·n reply to a charge or plea XV; say in answer XVII. f. *rejoin-*, stem of (O)F. *rejoindre*; see RE-, JOIN. So *rejoinder* defendant's answer XV; answer to a reply, reply XVI. – AN. **rejoinder*, for (O)F. *rejoindre*, inf. used as sb. (see -ER[5] and cf. *attainder, remainder*).

rejoin[2] rīdʒoi·n join again. XVI. – (O)F. (as prec.) or f. RE- 4+JOIN.

rejuvenate ridʒū·vəneit restore to youth. XIX. irreg. f. RE- 4+L. *juvenis* YOUNG+-ATE[3], after F. *rajeunir* or **rejuven**E·SCENCE renewal of youth (XVII), f. late L. *rejuvenēscere*. **rejuven**E·SCENT (XVIII).

-rel rəl, **-erel** ərəl ME. suffix of diminutive and depreciatory force, repr. OF. *-erel* (mod. *-ereau*), found first in animal names, the earliest of which is *maquerel* (XIII) MACKEREL, followed by DOGGEREL in XIV (Ch.) and in XV by COCKEREL, DOTTEREL, MONGREL, PICKEREL, and later KESTREL, WHIMBREL. Formations of a more general kind are SCOUNDREL, WASTREL.

relapse rilæ·ps fall back into error, illness, etc. XVI. f. *relaps-*, pp. stem of L. *relabī*, f. *re-* RE- 2 + *labī* slip. So sb. XVI; after LAPSE sb. or – F. *relaps*, medL. *relapsus*.

relate rilei·t give an account of XVI; (leg.) refer *back* XVI; bring into connexion or comparison XVII. f. stem of L. *relātus*, functioning as pp. of *referre* REFER, but formally f. the base of *tollere* (cf. EXTOL, SUBLATION); see -ATE[3]. So **rela**·TION narration XIV (Gower); connexion XIV (PPl.); relative XVI. – (O)F. or L. **relat**IVE re·lətiv adj. having relation *to* XVI; sb. (gram.) XIV (Wycl. Bible); (gen.) XV (Lydg.); kinsman XVII. – (O)F. *relatif, -ive* or late L. *relātīvus*.

relax rilæ·ks loosen, †lit. and fig. XV; (Sc.) free from legal restraint XVI; make less strict XVII. – L. *relaxāre*, f. *re-* RE- 7+*laxus* LAX. Cf. RELEASE. So **relaxa**·TION rī-, re- remission of penalty, etc.; release from ordinary occupations XVI; diminution of firmness or strictness XVII. – L.; cf. (O)F. *relaxer, relaxation*.

relay rilei·, rī·lei set of fresh hounds, etc. posted to take up the chase from others XV; set of fresh horses at a stage XVII; relief gang XIX; (stage of) a relay race XX. – OF. *relai* (mod. *relais*), f. *relayer*, f. *re-* RE 3 + *laier*, ult. repr. L. *laxāre* (see LEASE and cf. DELAY), whence or from the sb. **relay** vb. †let go (fresh hounds) XV; provide with relays XVIII.

release rilī·s A. †revoke, cancel XIII; †relieve; remit (now leg.); give up, surrender XIV; B. set free XIV. ME. *relese, -esse* – OF. *relesser, relaiss(i)er* :– L. *relaxāre* RELAX; cf. LEASE. So **relea·se** sb. freeing, deliverance XIV; (leg.) conveyance of an estate XV. – OF. *reles*, f. *relesser*.

relegate re·ligeit send into exile XVI; consign *to* obscurity XVIII; refer for decision XIX. f. pp. stem of L. *relēgāre* send away, refer, f. *re-* RE- I, etc. + *lēgāre* send; see LEGATE, -ATE[3]. Cf. F. *reléguer*.

relent rile·nt †melt, dissolve XIV (Ch.); grow gentle or forgiving XVI. – medL. **relentāre* (cf. L. *relentēscere* slacken), f. *re-* RE- 7+L. *lentāre* bend, medL. soften (so Pg. *relentar*), f. *lentus* flexible, rel. to OE. *līþe* LITHE.

relevant re·livənt pertinent *to*. XVI. In earliest use Sc. and prob. of legal origin; not in gen. Eng. use before 1800. – medL. *relevant-, -āns*, prp. of L. *relevāre* raise up, RELIEVE, in medL. take up, take possession of (a fief), pay a relief for, hold of a landlord. ¶ For the wide development of sense cf. F. *relever* be dependent, It. *rilevare* be of importance or use, *rilevante* important, considerable, Sp. *relevar* exculpate, relieve, exalt, Sp., Pg. *relevante* eminent, excellent, *relevar* be important, suitable, or necessary, exonerate, etc.; and RELIEF[1] A.

reliable rilai·əbl that can be relied upon. XVI (*raliabill*, Sc.). f. RELY + -ABLE. Frequent in gen. use only since *c.*1850, and at first most prominently in Amer. writings; often protested against as a faulty Amer. formation (for *rely-on-able*) but it has analogues in *available, dependable, laughable*. (See Fitzedward Hall 'On English adjectives in *-able*'.) Hence **reli**ABI·LITY. XIX (1816, Coleridge, who uses *reliable* also).

reliance rilai·əns act of relying. XVII (Sh.). f. RELY+-ANCE, after *affiance*. So **reli**·ANT. XIX, chiefly in *self-reliant*.

relic re·lik object remaining as a memorial of a departed saint XIII (souvenir, memento XVII Sh.); pl. remains XIV; surviving trace or memory XVI. ME. *relike* – (O)F. *relique*, orig. pl. – L. *reliquiæ* remains, fem. pl. of *reliquus* remaining, f. *re-* RE- + **liq*ʷ*-*, base of *linquere* leave behind (see RELINQUISH). ¶ OE. had *reliquias* (from L. acc. pl.) and *relicgang* veneration of relics. The sp. *relique* was in use XV–XIX.

relict re·likt †(chiefly Sc.) relic; widow; pl. remains XVI. – L. *relictus*, n. sg. *-um*, n.pl. *-a*, pp. of *relinquere* leave behind, RELINQUISH. In the sense 'widow' (in earliest use Sc.) – OF. *relicte*, late L. *relicta*.

relief[1] rilī·f A. payment made to an overlord on taking possession XIV (R. Mannyng). B. alleviation of distress etc. XIV; release from occupation or duty XVI. – AN. *relef*, (O)F. *relief*, f. *relever* (tonic stem *reliev-*) RELIEVE; for sense A cf. RELEVANT.

relief[2] rilī·f elevation of (parts of) a design from a plane surface. XVII (Evelyn). – F. *relief* – It. *rilievo rilje·vo*, †*rilevo*, f. *rilevare* raise; see next. Earlier †*releve* (B. Jonson), †*relieve* was immed. from the It. forms, which were also in Eng. use before *relief*, as also in *alto relievo, basso relievo, mezzo relievo* high, low, medium relief.

relieve rilī·v assist in trouble or difficulty XIV; ease, mitigate XV; (Sc.) release XVI; (after RELIEF[1]) release from guard or watch XVII; (after RELIEF[2]) bring into relief XVIII. Late ME. *releve* – (O)F. *relever* = Pr., Sp. *relevar*, It. *rilevare* :– L. *relevāre* raise again, succour, alleviate, f. *re-* RE- 7+*levāre* raise, f. *levis* LIGHT[2].

religion rili·dʒən state of life (as of monks) bound by vows and a rule XII; religious order or rule; system of faith in and worship of a divine power XIII; recognition of a divine being to whom worship is due XVI. – (O)F. *religion* = Pr., Sp. *religion*, It. *religione* – L. *religiō(n-)*, obligation (as of an oath), bond between man and the gods, scrupulousness, scruple(s), reverence for the gods; (in late L. from v) religious (monastic) life; by Cicero ('De natura deorum' II xxviii § 72) derived from *relegere* gather together, peruse, but elsewhere connected by him with the idea of obligation (e.g. *religione obstringere*) and more prob. to be derived (as by Servius, Lactantius, and Augustine) from *religāre* bind fast, f. *re-* RE- 7 + *ligāre* bind; see LIGATURE, -ION. So **religi**OUS rili·dʒəs bound by monastic vows; imbued with religion XIII; pert. to religion XVI; sb. as pl. monks, etc. XIII, as sg. XIV. – OF. *religious* (mod. *-ieux*) – L. *religiōsus*. **religio**·SITY. XIV (Wycl. Bible). – L.; in more recent use perh. after F.

relinquish rili·ŋkwiʃ †abandon; desist from XV; resign, surrender XVI. f. *relinquiss-*, lengthened stem of OF. *relinquir* – L. *relinquere*, f. *re-* RE- 7 + *linquere* leave; see LEND, LOAN, -ISH[2].

reliquary re·likwəri vessel to contain relics. XVII. – (O)F. *reliquaire*, f. *relique* RELIC; see -ARY and cf. Sp. *relicario*, It. *reliquiario*, medL. *reliquiārium*, *-iāre*.

relish re·liʃ taste, flavour XVI; appetizing taste; liking, zest XVII. Later form of ME. *reles* taste (XIV), corr. formally to OF. *reles*, var. of *relais* remainder, f. *relaisser* leave behind, RELEASE, but the senses of the Eng. word are not recorded in OF. (taste is regarded as what remains behind after eating). Hence **re·lish** vb. give a relish to; have a taste for XVI; have a certain taste XVII.

reluctant rilʌ·ktənt †struggling, resisting XVII (Milton); unwilling XVIII. – L. *reluctant-*, *-āns*, prp. of *reluctārī* struggle against, f. *re-* RE- 7 + *luctārī* struggle; see -ANT. So earlier **relu·ct**ANCE (1641), -ANCY (1621); other derivs. of the L. vb. are *reluct* vb. (1526), *reluctate* vb. (1643), *reluctation* (1605).

relume riljū·m relight, rekindle XVII (Sh.); illuminate again XVIII. f. RE- 4 + *-lume* of ILLUME, partly after F. *rallumer* or late L. *relūmināre*.

rely rilai· †gather together, assemble, rally (trans. and intr.) XIV (R. Mannyng); †rally *to*, trust, adhere, or be devoted *to* XIV; depend trustfully *on* XVI. – OF. *relier* :– L. *religāre* bind closely, f. *re-* RE- 7+*ligāre* bind; see LIGATURE and cf. ALLY, RALLY. Hence RELIABLE, RELIANCE.

remain rimei·n be left over; continue to exist XIV; stay in a place XV; continue to be XVI. f. *remain-*, *remein-*, tonic stem of OF. *remanoir* = It. *rimanere*, Rum. *rămîneà* :– L. *remanēre*, f. *re-* RE- 7+*manēre* remain (see MANSION); or – OF. *remaindre* = Pr. *remanre* :– Rom. **remanere*, for L. *remanēre*. So **remai·n** sb. remainder, relic, remaining member or part (now chiefly pl.). XV. Earliest instances Sc.; partly – OF. *remain*, f. *remaindre*; partly immed. f. the vb. **remainder** rimei·ndəɹ (leg.) residual interest of an estate XV; what is left over XVI; (math.) XVI (Digges). – AN. *remainder* = OF. *remaindre*; sb. use of inf. (see -ER[5]). Cf. REMNANT.

remand rimā·nd send back XV, spec. (a prisoner) *into custody* XVI. – medL. *remandāre* (in late L. send back word, repeat a command), f. *re-* RE- 2+*mandāre* command, send word (see MANDATE). Hence **rema·nd** sb. XVIII.

remanet re·mənət remainder XVI; (leg.) cause of which the hearing is postponed XVIII. L., 'there or it remains', 3rd sg. pres. ind. of *remanēre* REMAIN.

remark rimā·ɹk †distinguish, point out; take notice of; utter as an observation. XVII. – F. *remarquer*, superseding OF. *remerquier*, *-merchier*, prob. after It. *rimarcare*; see RE- 7, MARK vb. So **rema·rk** sb. †*of* (. .) *remark* worthy of (. .) notice (F. *de* (. .) *remarque*); (an) observation, (a) comment. XVII. – F. *remarque*, f. *remarquer*; cf. It. *rimarco*. **rema·rk**ABLE. XVII. – F. *remarquable*.

remedy re·mĭdi cure for disease; redress, relief XIII; legal redress; small margin within which coins as minted are allowed to vary from the standard XV. – AN. *remedie* = (O)F. *remède*, Sp. *remedio*, It. *remedio* – L. *remedium* medicine, means of relief, in medL. concession, f. *re-* RE- 2, 7+*med-*, stem of *medērī* heal (see MEDICINE). So **remed**IAL rĭmī·diəl. XVII. – late L. *remediālis*. **re·medy** vb. XV. – (O)F. *remédier* (whence also earlier †*remede* XIV) or late L. *remediāre*.

remember rime·mbəɹ retain in or recall to the memory, bear in mind (R. Mannyng); (arch., dial.) remind (Ch.). XIV. – OF. *remembrer* = Pr., Sp. *remembrar* :– late L. *rememorārī* call to mind, f. *re-* RE- 7+*memor* mindful (see MEMORY). So **reme·mbr**ANCE calling to mind, recollection. XIII. – OF. **reme·mbranc**ER[1] official responsible for collection of dues, etc. XV. – AN. *remembrauncer*.

remind rimai·nd †remember, recollect; put in mind *of*. XVII. f. RE-+MIND vb., prob. after †*rememorate* (late L. *rememorārī* REMEMBER), which was current at the time that *remind* first appears. Hence **remi·nd**ER[1]. XVII (H. More; rare before XIX).

reminiscence remini·səns act or fact of remembering. XVI. – late L. *reminiscentia* (Tertullian), f. *reminiscī* remember, f. *re-* RE- 4 + **men-* (see MIND, -ENCE); cf. (O)F. *réminiscence*. So **remini·scENT**. XVIII. Hence by back-formation (usu. joc.) **remini·sce** vb. XIX.

remise rəmī·z coach-house; hired carriage (for *voiture de remise* 'carriage put under cover') XVII; (fencing) second thrust made when the first has missed; (cards) XIX. – F. *remise*, f. *remis*, pp. of *remettre* put back or up, REMIT.

remiss rimi·s †diluted, weak, mild; slack, lax, loose. XV. – L. *remissus*, adj. use of pp. of *remittere* slacken, relax, REMIT.

remit rimi·t A. forgive (sin); abstain from exacting (a penalty) XIV. B. give up, desist from XIV. C. refer for consideration, etc. XIV; put back, XVI; put off XVII; transmit XVII; D. intr. abate XVII. – L. *remittere* send back, slacken, relax, postpone, f. *re-* RE- 1, 2 + *mittere* put, send (see MISSION). Hence **remi·ttANCE** money sent away. XVIII. So **remi·ssION** forgiveness XIII; remitting (*of* debt, etc.) XIV; diminution of force XVII. – (O)F. – L.

remnant re·mnənt (small) part remaining over. XIV. contr. of earlier *remenant* (*c.*1300) – OF. *remenant*, sb. use of prp. of *remenoir*, *-manoir* REMAIN; see -ANT.

remonstrate rimɔ·nstreit, re·mənstreit †demonstrate XVI; †point out (a fault, etc.) *to*; †raise an objection *to*; urge strong reasons *against* XVII. f. pp. stem of medL. *remōnstrāre* demonstrate, f. *re-*+*mōnstrāre* show; see RE- 7, MONSTER, -ATE[3]. So **remo·nstrANCE** †appeal XV (Caxton); †demonstration XVI; formal statement of grievances XVII. – F. †*remonstrance* (mod. *remontrance*) or medL. **remonstrA·TION**. XV (Caxton). – obs. F. or medL.

remora re·mərə sucking-fish, Echeneis remora. XVI: – L. *remora* delay, hindrance, f. *re-* RE- 3+*mora* delay (cf. MORATORIUM); occurs in some texts of Pliny's 'Natural History' XXXII i, where others read *mora*, for the fish called in Gr. ἐχενηΐς 'hold-ship'.

remorse rimɔ̄·ɹs feeling of compunction for wrong done. XIV (in full *r. of conscience* Ch. repr. OF. *remors de conscience*, medL. *remorsus conscientiæ*). – OF. *remors* (mod. *remords*) – medL. *remorsus*, f. *remors-*, pp. stem of L. *remordēre* vex, torment, f. *re-* RE- 7+*mordere* bite (see MORDANT, MORSEL).

remote rimou·t far apart or away. XV (rare before late XVI). – L. *remōtus*, pp. of *removēre* REMOVE.

remount rīmau·nt †set up again XIV (Ch.); replace on horseback XIV; supply with fresh horses XVII. In early use – (O)F. *remonter*; later in part a new formation on RE- 4 and MOUNT[2].

remove rimū·v move from the place occupied. XIV. ME. *remeve*, *remove* – OF. *remeuv-* and *remov-*, stressed and unstressed stems respectively of *removeir* (mod. *remouvoir*) :– L. *removēre*; see RE- 1, MOVE. Hence **remo·VAL**[2]. XVI. **remo·ve** sb. removing, removal XVI; promotion at school from one division or class to another, (hence) title of a class or form XVIII.

remunerate rimjū·nəreit pay for services. XVI. f. pp. stem of L. *remūnerārī* (later *-āre*), f. *re-* RE- 7+*mūnerāre*, *-ārī*, f. *mūner-*, *mūnus* gift, reward (cf. MUNIFICENT); see -ATE[3]. So **remunerA·TION**. XV. – F. or L.

renaissance rīnei·sãs 'revival of learning' in Europe beginning in Italy in the 14th century. XIX (cited as a French term *c.*1840). – F. *renaissance* (in spec. use, short for *r. des arts*, *r. des lettres*), f. *re-* RE- 2, 4+*naissance* birth :– L. *nāscentia*, f. *nāscī* be born (cf. NATION) or f. *naiss-*, pres. stem of *naître* :– Rom. **nascere*; see -ANCE. So **renascENCE** rinæ·səns rebirth, renewal XVIII; substituted for *renaissance* by Matthew Arnold 1869. f. **rena·sCENT** XVIII – L. *renāscent-*, *-ēns*, prp. of *renāscī*. Earlier †**rena·sCENCY** (XVII, Evelyn, Sir T. Browne); cf. It. *rinascenza*.

renal rī·nəl pert. to the kidneys. XVII. – F. *rénal* – late L. *rēnālis*, f. L. *rēnēs* REINS; see -AL[1].

rencounter renkau·ntəɹ meeting of adversaries XVI; chance meeting XVII. – (O)F. *rencontre* (which was in Eng. use XVII–XIX), f. *rencontrer* meet (whence †**rencou·nter** vb. XVI); see RE- 6, ENCOUNTER.

rend rend pt., pp. **rent** tear apart (*asunder*). OE. *rendan* = OFris. *renda*, rel. to MLG. *rende*, and perh. further to Skr. *rándhra-* fissure, slit, split.

render re·ndəɹ A. †repeat, recite XIV; give in return (now as echo of 1 Thess. v 15, 1 Peter iii 9) XV; give *back*; represent, reproduce XVI; B. hand over, give up, surrender XIV; submit (an account, etc.) XV; give, pay XVI; C. bring into a specified state XV; D. melt XIV; give a first coating of plaster XVIII. – (O)F. *rendre*, corr. to Pr. *rendre*, Sp. *rendir*, It. *rendere* :– Rom. **rendere*, alt., after *prendere* (see PRISON), of L. *reddere* give back, give up, recite, represent, imitate, make to be or appear, f. *red-* RE- 1, 3 +*-dere*, as in *addere* ADD, *ēdere* EDIT, etc. ¶ The unusual retention in Eng. of the F. inf. ending is paralleled in TENDER[2]; perh. the AN. infs. *render* and *tender* were taken over without change to avoid collision with REND and TEND, which would have otherwise resulted.

rendezvous rɔ·n-, rã·n-, rã·divū, -deivū place for the assembling of troops; place of meeting. XVI (also *randevou(s)*, etc.). – F. *rendez-vous*, sb. use of *rendez-vous* present or betake yourselves, imper. pl. of *se rendre*, refl. of *rendre* RENDER. Hence as vb. XVII. ¶ Somewhat earlier †*rendy*, repr. F. *rendez*, which was also so used.

rendition rendi·ʃən surrender XVII; (now U.S.) translation, rendering XVII; (U.S.) performance XIX. – F. †*rendition* (cf. Sp. *rendicion*), f. *rendre* RENDER; see -ITION.

renegade re·nigeid apostate XVI; deserter of a cause, etc. XVII. Anglicization of **renegado** renigei·dou (much used XVI–XVIII) – Sp. *renegado* – medL. *renegātus*, sb. use of pp. of *renegāre*; see next and -ADE, -ADO. The medL. word is also the source of It. *rinnegato* (whence F. *renégat*) and †**renegate.** XIV, later RUNAGATE.

renegue rĭnī·g deny, renounce; refuse XVI; revoke at cards XVII. – medL. *renegāre*, f. *re-* RE- 7+L. *negāre* DENY, f. **neg-* not, as in L. *negōtium* (see NEGOTIATE). *Renegāre* was repr. in OF. by *reneier*, whence Eng. †*renay*, †*reny* XIV–XVI.

renew rinjū· make new, restore. XIV (Ch., Wycl. Bible, Trevisa), f. RE- 4+NEW, after earlier ME. †*renovel*, †*renule* (– OF. *renoveler*, *renuveler*), L. *renovāre* RENOVATE. Hence **renew·**AL[2]. XVII.

rennet[1] re·nit curdled milk in a calf's stomach, preparation used in curdling milk for cheese. XV. prob. south-eastern repr. of an OE. **rynet* (f. **run-* RUN) and corr. to (dial.) *runnet* (XV), to which there appears to have been a parallel **rynels* (see -LE[1]), similarly repr. by †*ren(d)lys*, †*renneless*e, †*renels*, dial. *rendles* (cf. Flem. *ren-*, *rin-*, *runsel*, whence G. dial. *ren-*, *runsel*). Cf. also synon. OE. *rynning*, dial. *running* (also *cheese-running* XVI), †*renning* (XV), dial. *earning* (XVII), †*ronnelles* (XVI, rare). The sense is further exemplified in OE. *ġerinnan* (intr.), *ġerennan* (trans.) curdle, *ġerunnen* curdled, OS. *girunnian* (intr.), *girennian* (trans.), G. *gerinnen* (intr.), *rennen* (trans.) curdle. ¶ The ordinary OE. word for rennet was *ċēselyb* prob. 'plant-juice for cheese-making', dial. *cheslip*.

rennet[2] re·nit variety of apple. XVI (*reinet*, *renate*, *runnet*). – F. *reinette*, also *rainette*, prob. f. *raine* tree-frog (:– L. *rāna* frog), the fruit being so named from the spotted markings of some varieties. ¶ The F. form is also used.

renounce rinau·ns give up, abandon. XIV (Wyclif). – (O)F. *renoncer*, corr. to Pr., Sp. *renunciar*, It. *rinunziare* – L. *renuntiāre* announce, proclaim, protest against, f. *re-* RE- 5 + *nuntiāre* bring news, report; cf. *announce*, etc. So **renuncia**·TION. XIV. – (O)F. or L.

renovate re·nəveit renew. XVI (with pp. †*renovate*). f. pp. stem of L. *renovāre*, f. *re-* RE- 2, 4 + *novāre* make new, f. *novus* NEW, NOVEL. So **renova**·TION. XV. – F. or L.

renown rinau·n fact or condition of being widely celebrated. XIV. – AN. *renoun*, *renun*, OF. *renon*, *renom*, f. *renomer* make famous, f. *re-* RE- 7 + *nomer* name (:– L. *nōmināre* NOMINATE). Hence **renow·ned** widely celebrated. XIV (Barbour); after OF. *renomé* (mod. *renommé*), whence ME. †*renomed* (XIII), which this superseded; see -ED[1].

rent[1] rent †source of income XII; †revenue; †tax; payment made by tenant to landlord XIII. – (O)F. *rente* = Pr. *renta*, *renda*, Sp. *renta*, It. *rendita* :– Rom. **rendita*, f. **rendere* RENDER. So **rent** vb. †endow XIV; pay rent for XVI. – (O)F. *renter*, f. *rente*. **re·nt**AL[1] †rent-roll XIV; amount of rent XVII. – AN. *rental* or AL. *rentāle*.

rent[2] rent tear in a piece of stuff. XVI (Coverdale). f. (dial.) *rent* tear, rend (XIV, Ch.), var. of REND based on pt., pp. *rent*.

rentier rã·tiei, ‖rãtje one who derives his income from property or investments. XIX. F., f. *rente* revenue, RENT[1]+-*ier* -ER[2].

rep[1] rep textile fabric with corded surface. XIX. – F. *reps* (which has also been used in Eng.), of unkn. origin.

rep[2] rep (1) school abbrev. of REPETITION XIX; (2) short for *repertory theatre* and *r. company* XX.

repair[1] ripɛə·ɹ betake oneself, resort. XIV. – OF. *repair(i)er* (mod. *repairer*, *repérer*) :– late L. *repatriāre* return to one's country; see REPATRIATE. So **repai·r** sb.[1] (place of) resort. XIV (R. Mannyng). OF. *repaire*, *repeire* (mod. *repaire*, *repère*), f. *repairer*.

repair[2] ripɛə·ɹ † adorn; restore to sound condition. XIV. – (O)F. *réparer* – L. *reparāre*, f. *re-* RE- 2+*parāre* make ready, put in order; see PARE, PREPARE. Hence **repai·r** sb.[2] act of restoring to sound condition, etc. XVI (Sh.). So **repar**ABLE re·p-. XVI. – F. **repar**ATION reparei·ʃən action of repairing XIV; amends XV. – (O)F. – late L.

repand ripæ·nd (nat. hist.) undulating, wavy. XVIII. – L. *repandus* bent backwards, f. *re-* RE- 1+*pandus* bent, *pandere* spread.

repartee repāɹtī· ready reply, quick retort. XVII. – (O)F. *repartie*, sb. use of fem. pp. of *repartir* set out again, reply readily, f. *re-* RE- 4+*partir* PART.

repast ripā·st (quantity of food and drink for) a meal. XIV. – OF. *repast* (mod. *repas*), f. *repaistre*, mod. *repaître* (:– late L. *repascere*), after OF. *past* (:– L. *pastus* fodder, food); see RE- 7, PASTURE.

repatriate rīpæ·trieit, -pei·- restore to his own country. XVII. f. pp. stem of late L. *repatriāre* go back home, in medL. causative, f. *re-* RE- 2+*patria* native land, sb. use (sc. *terra* land) of *patrius*, f. *pater* FATHER; see PATRIOT, -ATE[3]. So **re:patria**·TION. XVI. – medL.

repay ripei· pay back or in return. XVI. – OF. *repaier*; see RE- 2, PAY. So **repay·**MENT. XIV.

repeal ripī·l revoke, rescind. XIV. – AN. *repeler*, for OF. *rapeler* (mod. *rappeler*), f. *re-* RE- 5+*appeler* APPEAL. So **repea·l** sb. XV (Caxton). – AN. *repel*, f. *repeler*.

repeat ripī·t A. say again XIV; say over, recite; say *after* another XVI; B. return to, undergo again XV; do or perform again XVI. Late ME. *repete* – (O)F. *répéter* – L. *repetere*, f. *re-* RE- 4 + *petere* (see PETITION). Hence sb. †repeated word(s), refrain XV; repetition XVI. So **repet**ITION repĭti·ʃən. XVI. – (O)F. or L. **repet**ITIOUS repĭti·ʃəs tiresomely iterative. XVII. **repetit**IVE ripe·titiv. XIX.

repel ripe·l drive, force, or turn back. XV. – L. *repellere*, f. *re-* RE- 1+*pellere* drive (cf. COMPEL, IMPEL). So **repe·ll**ENT. XVII.

repent ripe·nt refl. and intr. feel contrition for XIII (S. Eng. Leg.); be sorry for XIV. – (O)F. *repentir*, f. *re-* RE- 7+OF. *pentir* :– Rom. **pænitīre*, for L. *pænitēre* (see PENITENT). So **repe·nt**ANT XIII; -ANCE XIV; – (O)F. ¶ The native word is RUE[2].

repercussion rīpəɹkʌ·ʃən †repulsion, repulse, recoil; reverberation. XVI. – (O)F. or L.; see RE- 1, 4, PERCUSSION. So **repercu·ss**IVE (med.) repellent. XIV. ¶ Douglas (1501) uses pp. *repercus[si]t* of an echo.

repertory re·pəɹtəri †index, list; storehouse, repository XVI; (after F. *répertoire*) stock of dramatic pieces XIX. – late L. *repertōrium*, f. *repert-*, pp. stem of L. *reperīre* find, f. *re-* RE- 7+**per-*, base of *experīrī* (see EXPERT), *perīculum* PERIL; see -ORY[1].

repine ripai·n feel or show discontent. XVI. f. RE-+PINE[2], after *repent*.

replace riplei·s restore to a former place XVI (Daniel); fill the place of XVIII. f. RE- 2+ PLACE vb., prob. after F. *remplacer* (1549).

replenish riple·niʃ A. (obs. or arch.) fill or stock abundantly XIV (Rolle); B. fill up again XVII (Drayton). f. *repleniss-*, lengthened stem of OF. *replenir*, f. *re-* RE- 4, 7+*plenir* (whence *plenish*, chiefly Sc., XV), f. *plein* :– L. *plēnu-s* FULL; see -ISH[2].

replete riplī·t filled. XIV (Ch., Wycl. Bible). – (O)F. *replet*, fem. *-ète*, or L. *replētus*, pp. of *replēre* fill (see FULL). So **reple·**TION. XIV (Ch., Trevisa). – (O)F. or late L.

replevin riple·vin (writ for) recovery by a person of goods or chattels taken from him. XV. – AN. *replevin*, f. OF. *replevir* recover (whence **reple·vy** XVI), f. *re-* RE- 2+ *plevir* – Germ. **plegjan* PLEDGE.

replica re·plikə reproduction of a work of art. XIX. – It. *replica*, f. *replicare* REPLY.

replication replikei·ʃən reply, rejoinder. XIV (Ch.). – OF. *replicacion* – L. *replicātiō(n-)* folding back, repetition, legal reply, f. pp. stem of *replicāre* unfold, reflect on, reply, f. *re-* RE- 1, 4+*plicāre* fold (see PLY). So **reply** riplai· answer, respond. XIV (Ch.). – OF. *replier* turn back, reply (in this sense repl. by *repliquer*) :– L. *replicāre*. Hence **reply·** sb. XVI.

report ripɔ̄·ɹt rumour XIV (Ch.); account of a matter XV; †musical response, note; resounding noise XVI. – OF. *report*, f. *reporter* :– L. *reportāre* carry back, bear away (spec. an account), f. *re-* RE- 1+*portāre* carry (see FARE). So **repo·rt** vb. relate. XIV (Ch.); etc. – OF. *reporter*. **repo·rt**ER[2] XIV (spec. of legal cases, etc. XVII). – OF. *reporteur*. ¶ The prominent uses corr. to those of OF. *raporter* (mod. *rapporter*), f. *re-*+ *aporter* :– L. *adportāre*.

repose[1] ripou·z †replace XV; place (trust, etc.) *in* XVI. f. RE- 2+POSE[1], after L. *repōnere* replace, restore, store up, lay aside or to rest, r. *re-*+*pōnere* place (see POSITION).

repose[2] ripou·z rest, trans. XV, intr. XVI. – (O)F. *reposer*, earlier *repauser* = Pr. *repausar*, Sp. *reposar*, It. *riposare* :– late L. *repausāre*, f. *re-* RE- 7+*pausāre* PAUSE. So **repo·se** sb. rest. XVI. f. the vb. or – (O)F. *repos* (corr. to Pr. *repaus*, etc.), f. *reposer*.

repository ripɔ·zĭtəri vessel or chamber for storage of things XV (Caxton); storehouse (fig.) XVII; warehouse, mart XVIII. – F. †*repositoire* or L. *repositorium*, f. *reposit-*, pp. stem of *repōnere*; see REPOSE[1], -ORY[1].

repoussé rəpū·sei beaten into relief. XIX. – F., pp. of *repousser*, f. *re-* RE- 7+*pousser* PUSH.

reprehend reprihe·nd reprove, censure. XIV (Rolle). – L. *reprehendere*, f. *re-* RE- 7+ *prehendere* seize (cf. GET). So **reprehe·ns**IBLE. XIV (Wycl. Bible). – late L.; **reprehe·n**SION. XIV (Ch.). – L.; cf. (O)F. *répréhensible*, *répréhension*.

represent reprize·nt †bring into one's presence (Wyclif); bring before the mind (Barbour); display to the eye (Maund.); symbolize (Wyclif) XIV; stand in place of XV (speak for, as in parliament XVII, Cromwell). – (O)F. *représenter* or L. *repræsentāre*, f. *re-* RE- 7+*præsentāre* PRESENT. So **re:present**A·TION †presence, †appearance, likeness XV (Caxton); presentation to the eye, mind, etc. XVI. – (O)F. or L. **represe·nta**TIVE adj. XIV (Usk); sb. XVII (Clarendon). – (O)F. or medL.

repress ripre·s restrain, suppress, reduce. XIV (Ch., Gower). f. *repress-*, pp. stem of L. *reprimere*; see RE- 3, PRESS. So **repre·ss**ION. XIV (Ch.; thereafter not before XVI). – late L., so in F. (XV).

reprieve riprī·v †send back *to* prison; †postpone; delay the punishment of. XVI. First in pp. *reprived*, for earlier *repryed* (*to prison*) – AN., OF. *repris*, pp. of *reprendre*, f. *re-* RE- 1, etc. + *prendre* take (see PRISON). The change of *repry* to *reprive*, and hence to *repre(e)ve*, *reprieve*, is unexplained. Hence **reprie·ve** sb. XVI (Sh.), **reprie·v**AL[2]. XVI (*repriuall*, Sidney).

reprimand re·primànd sharp rebuke. XVII. – F. *réprimande*, †*-ende* – Sp. *reprimenda* – L. *reprimenda*, n.pl. of gerundive of *reprimere* REPRESS. So vb. XVII. – F. *réprimander*, f. the sb.

reprisal riprai·zəl seizing of property in retaliation or by way of indemnity XV; (esp. pl.) act of retaliation in warfare XVIII. – AN. *reprisaille* (XIV) – medL. *repræsāliæ*, *-ālia* (XIII), contr. of *repræ(h)ēnsāliæ*, *-ia* (whence also F. *représaille*, It. *rappresaglia*), f. *repræhēns-*, pp. stem of L. *repræhendere*, f. *re-* RE- 2, 5+*præhendere* take (cf. GET); see -AL².

reproach riprou·tʃ cast up (a thing) *against* a person XV (Caxton); upbraid XVI. – OF. *reprochier* (mod. *reprocher*) = Pr. *repropchar*, Sp. *reprochar*, It. *rimprocciare* :– Rom. **repropiāre* 'bring back near', f. *re-*, RE- 1, 6+*prope* near (see PROXIMATE). So **reproa·ch** sb. XV (Lydg.). – (O)F. *reproche* (corr. to Pr. *repropche*, etc.), f. the vb. (Earlier rare adoptions of these words are †*reproce*, †*repruce* (XIV) – AN. *reproce*, *repruce*, *-er*.)

reprobate re·prŏbeit rejected by God; of abandoned character XVI; also sb. XVI. – late L. *reprobātus*, pp. of *reprobāre* disapprove, f. *re-* RE- 5 + *probāre* approve, PROVE. (The currency is largely due to biblical usage, Vulg. *reprobatus* and A.V. *reprobate* rendering Gr. ἀδόκιμος not approved, not what one ought to be, esp. morally; see e.g. Rom. i. 28, 2 Cor. xiii. 5–7, 2 Tim. iii. 8, Tit. i. 16.) So **re·probate** vb. disapprove of XV; reject, cast off XVI. f. pp. stem of L. *reprobāre*; see -ATE³. **reproba·tion**. XV. – (O)F. or late L.

reproduce rīprədjū·s create anew XVII (Cotgr.); repeat in a copy, etc. XIX. f. RE- 4+PRODUCE vb., after F. *reproduire*. So **reprodu·ction**. XVII (Pearson); after *production*.

reproof riprū·f †shame; †insult (Rolle); censure. XIV. ME. *reprove*, *reprof(e)* – OF. *reprove*, f. *reprover* – late L. *reprobāre*; cf. PROOF, REPROBATE. So **reprove** riprū·v †reject; censure; reprehend. XIV. – OF. *reprover* (mod. *réprouver*).

reptile re·ptail creeping animal XIV (Gower; rare before XVII); mean person XVIII. – (O)F. *reptile* or late L. (Vulg.) *reptile*, n. of late L. *reptilis*, f. *rept-*, pp. stem of *repere* creep, crawl (with Lett. and Lith. cogns.); see -ILE. Also adj. XVII. So **reptilian** repti·liən, f. **repti·lia**² (zool.) XVII.

republic ripʌ·blik †state, common weal; state in which the supreme power resides in the people (Bacon, Clarendon). XVII. – F. *république* – L. *rēspublica*, f. *rēs* affair, thing (see REAL¹) + fem. of *publicus* PUBLIC. Hence **repu·blican** †pert. to the commonwealth; pert. to (sb. advocate of) a republic XVII (earlier †*republical*); partly after F. *républicain* (D'Aubigné XVI); whence **repu·blicanism**. XVII; so F. (XVIII).

repudiate ripjū·dieit put away (a wife); reject XVI; (orig. U.S.) refuse to acknowledge (a debt, etc.) XIX. f. pp. stem of L. *repudiāre*, f. *repudium* divorce, perh. rel. to *ped-*, *pēs* FOOT, as if 'spurn with the foot'; see -ATE³. So **repudia·tion**. XVI. – L. †*Repudy* sb. and vb. show earlier adoption XV.

repugnant ripʌ·gnənt contrary or contradictory *to* XIV (Usk); distasteful *to* XVIII. – F. *répugnant* or L. *repugnant-*, *-āns*, prp. of *repugnāre* (whence **repugn** ripjū·n be contrary, oppose XIV), f. *re-* RE- 6+*pugnāre* fight (cf. PUGNACIOUS, IMPUGN); see -ANT.

repulse ripʌ·ls driving back; refusal, rejection. XVI. – L. *repulsus*, *repulsa*, f. pp. stem of *repellere* REPEL. So vb. XVI; **repu·lsion** †repudiation XV; act of repelling XVI; feeling of being repelled XVIII. – late L.; cf. F. *répulsion*. **repu·lsive**. XVI. – (O)F. *répulsif*, *-ive*, or f. *repulse* vb.

reputation repjutei·ʃən †opinion, estimation (Wycl.); †general estimate (Ch.); high esteem or credit. XIV. – L. *reputātiō(n-)* computation, consideration, f. *reputāre*, f. *re-* RE- 7+*putāre* reckon (see PUTATIVE); see -ATION. Cf. F. *réputation*. So **repute** ripjū·t consider, esteem. XV. – (O)F. *réputer* or L. *reputāre*. Hence **repu·te** †estimate; reputation (in neutral sense) XVI; (in favourable sense) XVII.

request rikwe·st act of asking. XIV. – OF. *requeste* = Pr. Sp. *riquesta*, It. *richiesta* :– Rom. **requæsita*, sb. use of fem. pp. of L. *requærere* REQUIRE. So vb. XVI. f. the sb. or – OF. *requester*, f. *requeste*.

requiem re·kwiəm, rī·- Mass for the departed. XIV (R. Mannyng). – L. *requiem*, acc. of *requiēs* rest, first word of the introit of the Mass, '*Requiem* æternam dona eis, Domine' Rest eternal grant unto them, O Lord; see RE- 7, QUIET.

require rikwaiə·ɹ ask, esp. authoritatively or imperatively. XIV. ME. *requere*, *require* – OF. *requer-*, *requier-*, stem of *requere* (now refash. *requérir*) = Pr. *requerre*, Sp. *requerir*, It. *richiedere* :– Rom. **requærere*, for L. *requīrere*, f. *re-* RE- 7+*quærere* seek, ask. Cf., for assim. of sp. to the L. form, ACQUIRE, INQUIRE. So **requisite** re·kwizit required, necessary XV; sb. XVII. – L. *requisītus*, pp. of *requīrere* search for, pass. be necessary. **requisi·tion**. XVI. – (O)F. or L. Hence vb. XIX (Carlyle); after F. *réquisitionner*. **requite** rikwai·t make return for. XVI. f. RE- 7 + *quite*, var. of QUIT². Hence **requi·tal**². XVI.

reredos riə·ɹdɔs ornamental screen at the back of an altar; (hist.) back of a fireplace. XIV. – AN. **reredos*, aphetic of OF. *areredos*, f. *arere* back (see ARREAR, REAR-)+ *dos* back (cf. DOSS, DOSSAL). Disused after *c.*1550, until revived *c.*1835.

reremouse, rereward see REARMOUSE, REARGUARD.

rescind risi·nd †take away, remove; abrogate, cancel. XVII. – L. *rescindere*, f. *re-* RE- 7+*scindere* cut or tear asunder (see SCISSION, SCISSORS).

rescript rī·skript decretal epistle from the Pope in reply to a question referred; edict, decree. XVI. – L. *rescriptum* imperial decision, sb. use of n. of pp. *rescriptus* of *rescrībere* reply in writing to a petition, etc., f. *re-* RE- 1+*scrībere* write (see SCRIPT).

rescue re·skju deliver from attack, siege, or harm. XIV. ME. *rescowe, reskewe* – *rescou-, reskeu-*, stem of OF. *rescoure, reskeure* (mod. *recourre*) = It. *riscuotere* recover (money) :– Rom. **reexcutere*, f. *re-* RE- 7 + *excutere* shake out, discard, f. *ex* EX-[1] + *quatere* shake (see QUASH). Hence **re·scue** vb. XIV. The contemp. syn. †*rescous* (– OF. *rescousse*, f. *rescourre*) survived in legal sense 'forcible recovery' till XVII.

research risə̄·ɹtʃ intensive searching XVI; investigation directed towards discovery XVII. – OF. *recerche* (now *recherche*). So vb. XVI. – OF. *recercher* = It. *ricercare*. See RE- 7, SEARCH.

reseda risī·də genus of plants including mignonette. XVIII. – L. *resēda*, according to Pliny, f. imper. of *resēdāre* assuage, allay (see SEDATIVE), the formula *resēdā morbīs* 'assuage diseases' having been used as a charm when applying the plant to the reduction of tumours.

resemble rize·mbl be like (Ayenbite); †compare XIV (PPl.). – OF. *resembler* (mod. *ressembler*), f. *re-* RE- 7+*sembler* seem :– L. *similāre*, f. *similis* like (cf. SIMILITUDE). So **rese·mbl**ANCE. XIV (Gower). – AN. *resemblance*.

resent rize·nt orig. †refl. feel pain; show strong feeling; trans. † feel deeply or painfully; feel oneself injured by, show displeasure at. XVII. (Several other uses, now obs., were current XVII–XVIII.) – F. †*resentir*, now *ressentir* (in refl. use XVI; so It. *risentirsi*), f. *re-* RE- 7+*sentir* feel (see SENTIENT). So **rese·nt**MENT. XVII (†*resentiment* somewhat earlier XVI). – F. †*resentiment*, now *ress-*; cf. It. *risentimento*.

reserve rizə̄·ɹv keep for future use; keep or set apart. XIV (pp. *reserved* as adj. XVII). – (O)F. *réserver* – L. *reservāre*, f. *re-* RE- 1+ *servāre* keep, save; cf. CONSERVE, PRESERVE. Hence **rese·rve** sb. A. something reserved; mil., pl. and sg. force(s) kept in r. XVII (whence **rese·rv**IST) after F.; B. self-restraint XVII. So **reserv**ATION rezəɹvei·ʃən. XIV. – (O)F. or late L.

reservoir re·zəɹvwāɹ capacious receptacle for storage, also fig. XVII (Temple, Addison); reserve supply (Cowper). – F. *réservoir*, f. *réserver* RESERVE + *-oir* = ORY[1].

reside rizai·d †take up one's abode XV; dwell permanently XVI; be vested or inherent *in* XVII. prob. orig. back-formation from *resident*, but later infl. immed. by F. *résider* and L. *residēre*. So **re·sid**ENCE act or fact of residing XIV (Ch., Wycl.); place of residence XVI. – (O)F. or medL.; cf. Pr. *residensa*, It. *residenza*, etc. **resid**ENT re·zidənt residing XIV (Wycl. Bible); sb. XV. – (O)F. *résident* or L. *resident, -ēns*, prp. of *residēre* remain behind, rest, f. *re-* RE- 1 + *sedēre* settle, SIT. **reside·nti**ARY one bound to official residence XVI; adj. XVII. – medL.

residue re·zidju that which is left. XIV (PPl., Wycl. Bible). – (O)F. *résidu* – L. *residuum*, sb. use of n. of *residuus* remaining, f. *residēre* remain, RESIDE; see -UOUS. Hence **residu**AL[1] rizi·djuəl. XVI (Billingsley); cf. F. *résiduel*, It. *residuale*. **resi·duum** residue, remains. XVII. L.

resign rizai·n give up, surrender, abandon XIV (Ch., Wyclif); intr. XV. – (O)F. *résigner*, corr. to Sp. *resignar*, It. *rissegnare*. – L. *resignāre* unseal, cancel, give up, f. *re-* RE- 2+ *signāre* SIGN. So **resign**A·TION rezig-. XIV (Trevisa). – (O)F. – medL.

resile rizai·l draw back, shrink, recoil. XVI. – F. †*resilir* or L. *resilīre* leap back, recoil, f. *re-* RE- 1 + *salīre* leap (see SALIENT). So **resili**ENT rizi·liənt returning to the original position. XVII. – L. *resilient-* prp. **resi·li**ENCE. XVII (Bacon).

resin, rosin re·zin, rɔ·zin adhesive substance secreted by plants. XIV. Late ME. *recyn, resyn, rosyn* (Wycl. Bible), *rosine* (Gower). – L. *resīna* (whence Pr. *rezina*, F. *résine* XV, etc.) and medL. *rosīna* (cf. OF. *poix roisine* XIII), prob. collateral adoption, with Gr. *rhētínē*, from some non-IE. source. The medL. *rosīna* is of unkn. origin; other Eng. vars. were †*rosil* (XV), *roset* Sc. (XVI); cf. AL. *rosetum* (XV). So **re·sin**OUS, †**ro·sin**OUS. XVII. – F. *résineux* – L. *resīnōsus*.

resipiscence resipi·səns acknowledgement of error, return to a better opinion. XVI (after long desuetude revived XIX). – F. *résipiscence* or late L. *resipiscentia*, f. *resipiscere* come to oneself again, f. *re-*+*sapere* know; see RE- 4, SAPIENT, -ENCE.

resist rizi·st withstand the action of. XIV (Ch.). – (O)F. *résister* or L. *resistere*, f. *re-* RE- 6 + *sistere* stop, redupl. formation on *stāre* STAND. So **resi·st**ANCE. XV. – F. *résistance*, later form of †*resistence* (whence †**resi·st**ENCE XIV Ch.) – late L.

resolute re·zəlʲūt †determinate, absolute; of fixed resolve. XVI (earlier uses XV were sporadic). – L. *resolūtus*, pp. of *resolvere*. So **resolu**TION rezəlʲū·ʃən †dissolution; resolving into components XIV (Wycl. Bible); decision, determination XVI. – L. noun of action f. L. and CRom. *resolvere* (f. *re-* RE- 7+*solvere* SOLVE), whence **resolve** rizɔ·lv †dissolve (trans. and intr.) XIV (Ch., Trevisa); †soften, slacken XV; separate *into*; answer; solve; determine; †assure XVI; hence sb. XVI (Sh.).

resonance re·zənəns reinforcement of sound. XV (Caxton). – F. †*reson(n)ance* (mod. *résonnance*) – L. *resonantia* echo (Vitruvius), f. prp. stem of *resonāre* RESOUND. So **re·son**ANT. XVI. – (O)F. *résonnant.*

resort rizɔ̄·ɹt †return, revert XIV; betake oneself, repair or proceed *to* XV. –(O)F. *resortir* (mod. *ressortir*), f. *re-* RE- 4+*sortir* go out, of unkn. origin. So sb. that to which one resorts. XIV (Ch.) – (O)F. *ressort*, f. the vb.

resound rizau·nd ring *with* some sound XIV (Ch.); make an echoing sound; (arch.) proclaim, celebrate; (poet.) re-echo XVI. Late ME. *resoune*, f. *re-* RE- 7 + *soune* SOUND³ vb., after OF. *resoner* or L. *resonāre* (cf. RESONANCE).

resource rĭsɔ̄·ɹs means of supplying a want (Cotgr.); possibility of aid; expedient, device (Dryden). XVII. – F. *ressource*, †*-ourse*, sb. use of fem. pp. of OF. (dial.) *resourdre* rise again, recover :– L. *resurgere* (see RESURRECTION).

respect rispe·kt relation, reference XIV (Ch., Trevisa); relationship XV; discriminating regard (Prov. xxiv 23), deferential regard XVI. –(O)F. *respect* (corr. to Sp. *respeto*, It. *rispetto*) or L. *respectus*, f. pp. stem of *respicere* look (back) at, regard, consider, f. *re-* RE- 1+*specere* look (cf. ASPECT). So **respe·ct** vb. regard (also in various obs. senses); refer or relate to (in prp. *respecting* passing into prep. XVIII). XVI. f. *respect-*, pp. stem of L. *respicere*, or its frequent deriv. *respectāre*. In prp. *respecting* passing into prep. XVIII. So **respe·ct**ABLE. XVI; cf. F. *respectable*, etc. **respe·ct**IVE. XVI. F. or medL. Cf. RESPITE.

respire rispaiə·ɹ †(rare) come up to breathe XIV (Usk); breathe again, recover XV; breathe (trans. and intr.) XVI. –(O)F. *respirer* or L. *respīrāre*, f. *re-* RE- 4+*spīrāre* breathe; see SPIRIT and cf. ASPIRE, CONSPIRE. So **respira·tion**. XV (Lydg.). – F. or L. **re·spir**ATOR. XVIII; so F. *respirateur.*

respite re·spit delay or extension of time XIII (S. Eng. Leg.); temporary cessation of labour, etc. XIV. – OF. *respit* (mod. *répit*) = Pr. *respieit* :– L. *respectus* RESPECT. So **re·spite** vb. grant respite to or delay of. XIV (Ch., Gower). – OF. *respitier* :– L. *respectāre.*

resplendent risple·ndənt shining, brilliant. XV. – L. *resplendent-*, *-ēns*, prp. of *resplendēre*, f. *re-* RE- 7 + *splendēre* shine; see SPLENDID, -ENT.

respond rispɔ·nd (liturg.) responsory XIV; response to a versicle XVI. – OF. *respond*, f. *respondre* (mod. *répondre*) = Pr. *respondre*, etc. :– Rom. **respondere*, for L. *respondēre* answer to an engagement, f. *re-* RE- 4 + *spondēre* make a solemn engagement (see SPONSOR). So **respo·nd** vb. answer. XVI. – L. *respondēre*. **respo·nd**ENT one who defends a thesis; (leg.) defendant. XVI.

response rispɔ·ns answer, reply XIV; (liturg.) verse corresponding to a versicle XVII (earlier, responsory XV). ME. *respons* (not continuous with OE. *respons*). – OF. *respons* (mod. *répons*) or *response* (mod. *réponse*) or L. *responsum* (pl. *-a*), f. pp. of *respondēre*. **respo·ns**IBLE †corresponding *to* XVI (B. Jonson); answerable *to* another *for* something; reliable XVII. – F. †*responsible.* **respons**ION rispɔ·nʃən †sum to be paid XV; †response XVI; (Oxford Univ.) first examination for the B.A. degree (in which the candidates 'responderunt in Parviso'). **respo·ns**IVE responding, corresponding. XVI. – F. *responsif*, *-ive*, or late L. **respo·ns**ORY¹ (liturg.) anthem to be recited antiphonally after a lesson. XV. – late L. *responsōrium.*

rest¹ rest A. relief from activity by sleep, intermission of labour, repose of body or mind OE.; repose of death XIV (Wycl. Bible); (mus.) XVI. B. (from the vb). support for a fire-arm XVI; gen. support XVII. OE. *ræst*, *rest* repose, bed, corr. to OFris. *rasta* in *rastelik* restful, OS. *rasta* place of rest, OHG. *rasta* rest, league (G. *rast*), ON. *rǫst*, Goth. *rasta* mile (as a distance after which one rests); on another grade are based MLG. *roste*, *ruste* (whence G. *rüste*), MDu. *ruste*. Further connexions have been seen in OE. *ærn*, *ræn* dwelling (cf. BARN) = Goth. *razn*, and OIr. *ārus* (:– **adrostu-*) dwelling-place. So **rest** vb.¹ take or be at rest; remain OE.; give rest to XIII. OE. *ræstan*, *restan* = OFris. *resta*, OHG. *resten*, *rastōn* (G. *rasten*), and (M)Du. *rusten*. Hence **re·st**FUL¹. XIV. **re·st**LESS. OE. *restlēas*; cf. G. *rastlos*, Du. *rusteloos.*

rest² rest †remainder, remnant; †sum remaining over (XV; reserve fund of a bank XIX); remaining part, number, members XVI; in primero, stakes kept in reserve, freq. in allusive phr. for venture, resolution, stay, residence XVI. –(O)F. *reste*, f. *rester*, whence **rest** vb.² remain so-and-so. corr. to Sp., Pg. *restar*, It. *restare*, *ristare* – L. *restāre*, f. *re-* RE- 1+*stāre* STAND.

rest³ rest in mediæval armour, contrivance fixed to the cuirass to receive the butt-end of a lance. XIV. Aphetic of ARREST sb.; cf. It. *resta*, Pg. *reste*, *riste*, Sp., Pg. *ristre* (hence *enristrar* put the lance in rest).

restaurant re·stərã establishment for the provision of refreshments or meals. XIX. – F. *restaurant*, sb. use (1765; earlier in the sense 'restorative', La Fontaine) of prp. of *restaurer* RESTORE; see -ANT. So **restaurateur** restərătɔ̄ɹ keeper of a restaurant XVIII; †restaurant XIX (somewhat earlier than *restaurant*). – F.

rest-harrow re·sthæ:rou field shrub, Ononis arvensis, with tough roots. XVI. expl. by early writers to mean 'plant that arrests the harrow' (f. aphetic form of ARREST) and so hinders the labourer; cf. OF. *resteboef* 'stop-ox', whence medL. *resta bovis.*

restitution restitjū·ʃən action of giving back XIII (Cursor M.); restoration to a former state XIV (Trevisa, Wycl. Bible); tendency to resume a previous position XVII (Boyle). – (O)F. *restitution* or L. *restitūtio(n-)*, f. *restituere* restore, f. *re-* RE- 4 + *statuere* set up, establish; see STATUTE, -TION.

restive re·stiv †inactive, inert XVI; †obstinate in opinion or action; (of horses) refusing to move or follow a course XVII. Later form (by assim. to -IVE) of †*restif* XV. – OF. *restif* (mod. *rétif*) = Pr. *restiu*, It. *restio* :– Rom. **restīvus* 'inclined to remain stationary', f. *restāre* REST vb.² ¶ With dial. var. *resty* (XVI) cf. HARDY, JOLLY, TESTY.

restore ristɔ̄ə·ɹ give back; build up again; reinstate; renew, re-establish XIII (RGlouc., Cursor M.); bring back *to* an earlier condition XIV (R. Mannyng). – OF. *restorer* (mod. *restaurer*) = It. *ristorare* :– L. *restaurāre* (whence also Sp. *restaurar*, It. *restaurare*); see RE- 2, STORE vb. So **restor**ATION restərei·ʃən action of restoring XVII; (*R*-) re-establishment of the monarchy in England in 1660 XVII. Later form (assim. to the vb.) of *restauration* (XIV) – (O)F. or late L. **resto·rat**IVE adj. and sb. XIV. Var. of †*restaurative* (XIV, Gower, Trevisa) – OF. *restauratif, -ive*.

restrain ristrei·n put a check on, restrict. XIV. ME. *restreyne, restrayne* – OF. *restrei(g)n-, -ai(g)n-*, pres. stem of *restreindre, restraindre* = Pr. *restrenher*, Cat. *restrenyer*, It. *ristringere* :– L. *restringere* bind fast, confine, f. *re-* RE- 2 + *stringere* draw tight (see STRAIN, STRICT). So **restrai·nt.** XV. – (O)F. *restreinte*, f. pp. of *restreindre*. **restrict** ristri·kt confine within limits. XVI (Lyndesay). f. *restrict-*, pp. stem of L. *restringere*. (Stigmatized by Johnson as 'a word scarce English' and included by Beattie in his 'Scotticisms', 1787.) **restri·c**TION. XV (Hoccleve). **restri·ct**IVE. XIV (Maund.). – (O)F. or late L.

result rizʌ·lt arise as a consequence or effect. XV. – medL. (AL.) *resultāre* (whence also F. *résulter*, etc.), fig. use of L. *resultāre* spring back, reverberate, re-echo, f. *re-* RE- 7 + *saltāre* leap (see SALTATION). Hence **resu·lt** sb. (now U.S.) decision, resolution; effect, consequence of action, etc. XVII; cf. Sp., Pg. *resulta*. (†*Resultance*, †*resultancy* were in use somewhat earlier; medL. had *resultātum*, whence F. *résultat*, It. *risultato*.) So **resu·lt**ANT †shining by reflection; resulting XVII; sb. †mathematical result XV; composite effect of forces XIX. prp. of the L. vb.

resume rizjū·m take up, or back, or to oneself again. XV. – (O)F. *résumer* or L. *resūmere* (whence also Sp. *resumir*, It. *risumere*), f. *re-* RE- 2 + *sūmere* take (cf. ASSUME). So **resump**TION rizʌ·mᵖʃən XV. – (O)F. or late L. **résumé** re·zjūmei, rei- summary. XIX. F., sb. use of pp. of *résumer*.

resurge risɔ̄·ɹdʒ rise again. XVI. – L. *resurgere*; see RE- 4, SURGE vb. So **resu·r**GENT. XVIII.

resurrection rezəre·kʃən rising again of Jesus Christ from the dead or of all men at the Last Day. XIII. – (O)F. *résurrection* – late L. *resurrēctiō(n-)*, f. pp. stem of L. *resurgere*; see prec. and -TION; in ChrL. rendering Gr. ἀνάστασις. Hence, by back-formation, **resurre·ct** vb. XVIII.

resuscitate risʌ·siteit restore to life or consciousness. XVI (More). f. pp. stem of L. *resuscitāre*, f. *re-* + *suscitāre* raise, revive, f. *sus-* SUB- + *citāre* put in motion, excite; see RE- 2, SUB-, CITE, -ATE³. Superseded †*resuscite* (XIV–XVI) – (O)F. *ressusciter* or L. So **resuscit**A·TION. XVI. – late L.

ret ret soak (flax, etc.) in water. XV (Promp. Parv.). The E. Anglian forms *reten, retten* corr. to MDu. *reeten*, (also mod.) *reten*; but the north. forms *rayte, rate* point to an ON. **reyta* (repr. by Norw. *røyta*, Sw. *röta*, Da. *röde*), corr. to MLG. *rōten*, MDu. *rooten, roten* (Du. *roten*; dial. also *röten, reuten*), MHG. *rōʒen, rœʒen* (G. *rösten*); rel. to ROT.

retable rī·teibl reredos; shelf or ledge at the back of an altar. XIX. – F. *rétable, retable* – Sp. *retablo* (Pg. *retabolo*) – medL. **retabulum*, for *retrotabulum* (XIII) 'structure at the back of an altar-table' (cf. Pr. *reiretaule*), f. L. *retrō* RETRO-, REAR- + *tabula* TABLE.

retail rī·teil the sale of (commodities) in small quantities XIV; attrib. XVII. – AN. **retaille* (AL. *retallia*, also in phr. *ad retalliam vendere* sell by retail XIV), spec. use of OF. *retaille* piece cut off, shred, f. *retaillier*, f. *re-*, RE- 7 + *taillier* cut (see TAILOR). ¶ This use, which is not in F. or Sp., is prob. of It. origin (cf. medL. *retaiāre, retagliātor*, repr. It. *ritagliare* retail, *ritagliatore* retailer; so It. *ritaglio*, Pg. *retalho, retalhar, retalhiste*). So **retai·l** vb. sell by retail XIV; recount XVI (Sh.). **re·tail**ER¹. XV.

retain ritei·n †restrain XIV (Ch.); keep hold or possession of, keep in one's service; keep in mind XV; keep attached to one XVI. – AN. *retei(g)n-*, repr. tonic stem of OF. *retenir* = Pr., Sp. *retener*, Pg. *reter*, It. *retinere* :– Rom. **retenēre*, for L. *retinēre*, f. *re-* RE- 3 + *tenēre* hold (see TENABLE and cf. CONTAIN, etc.). **retai·n**ER⁵ (authorization of) retaining for oneself XV; fee for retaining a barrister's services XIX. **retai·n**ER¹ maintainer, preserver; dependant on a person of rank. XVI (earlier *-our* = -OR¹). So **rete·n**TION. XIV. – (O)F. or L. **rete·nt**IVE. XIV. – (O)F. or medL.

retaliate ritæ·lieit repay in kind. XVII. f. pp. stem of L. *retaliāre*, f. *re-* RE- + *tālis* of such a kind, f. demons. base **to* (see THAT, THE) + *-ālis* -AL¹ (cf. *quālis* of what kind); see -ATE³. So **retali**A·TION. XVI, **reta·liat**ORY². XIX.

retard ritā·ɹd keep back, delay. XV (Caxton). – (O)F. *retarder* = Sp. *retardar*, It. *retardare* :– L. *retardāre* f. *re-* RE- 3 + *tardus* slow (see TARDY). So **retard**A·TION rī-. XV (Lydg.). – (O)F. or L.

retch retʃ, rītʃ hawk in the throat XVI; make efforts to vomit XIX. var. of REACH².

reticence re·tisəns maintenance of silence. XVII (rare before *c.*1830, being repr. by *reticency*). – L. *reticentia*, f. *reticēre* keep silence, f. *re-* RE- 7 + *tacēre* be silent (see TACIT); cf. F. *reticence*, etc. So **re·tic**ENT. XIX. – L. *reticent-*, *-ēns*.

reticular riti·kjūləɹ resembling or constructed like a net. XVI. – modL. *rēticulāris*, f. L. *rēticulum* RETICULE; see -AR and cf. F. *réticulaire* (XVII). So **reti·cul**ATE². XVII. – L.; so **reti·culat**ED¹. XVIII.

reticule re·tikjūl reticulate structure used in a microscope XVIII; small bag used as a pocket or workbag XIX (*c.*1825; somewhat earlier *ridicule*). – F. *réticule* – L. *rēticulum* network bag, omentum (mod. anat. second stomach of a ruminant XVII), dim. of *rēte* net; see -CULE.

retina re·tinə innermost coating at the back of the eyeball. XIV. – medL. *retina* (whence also F. *rétine*, Sp., It. *retina*), perh. f. L. *rēte* net.

retinue re·tinju †retention in service (Gower); company of persons retained in one's service (Barbour). XIV. – OF. *retenue*, sb. use of fem. pp. of *retenir* RETAIN. ¶ Stressed *reti·nue* XVI–XVIII, as by Spenser, Milton, Bailey's Dict.

retire ritaiə·ɹ draw back, withdraw. XVI. – (O)F. *retirer*, f. *re-* RE- 1 + *tirer* draw; cf. TIER and Sp. *retirar*, It. *retirare*. Hence **reti·r**AL². XVII. **reti·re**MENT. XVI (Sh.; somewhat earlier *re·tire*).

retort¹ ritǭ·ɹt repay, requite; cast back (a charge, etc.) XVI; reply in kind to XVII. f. *retort-*, pp. stem of L. *retorquēre*, f. *re-* RE- 4 + *torquēre* twist (see TORT). Hence **reto·rt** sb. sharp reply. XVI.

retort² ritǭ·ɹt vessel with a long neck used for distillation. XVII. – F. *retorte* (= Sp., It. *retorta*) – medL. *retorta*, sb. use of fem. pp. of L. *retorquēre* (see prec.).

retract¹ ritræ·kt draw back XV; †restrain, withdraw XVI. f. *retract-*, pp. stem of L. *retrahere*, f. *re-* RE- 1 + *trahere* (see TRACT).

retract² ritræ·kt recall, revoke XVI; intr. XVII. – (O)F. *rétracter* or L. *retractāre*, f. *re-* RE- 1 + *tractāre*, frequent. of *trahere*; cf. F. *rétracter*, etc. So **retract**A·TION (pl.) title of a work of St. Augustine containing further treatment and correction of former works XV; recantation XVI; withdrawal from an engagement XVII. – L. *retractātiō*; so F., etc. **retra·c**TION retractation XIV (Ch., rare before XVI). – L. *retractiō*; so F., etc.,

retreat ritrī·t (mil.) signal to retire XIV (Barbour); act of retiring in the face of danger, etc. (Gower); withdrawal into privacy; place of seclusion XV. Late ME. *retret* – OF. *retret*, etc., vars. of *retraite* (whence †*retrait* XV–XVII), sb. uses of m. and fem. pps. of *retraire* :– L. *retrăhere* RETRACT¹. So **retrea·t** vb. retire XV; †retract, revoke XVI. – OF. *retraitier* – L. *retractāre* RETRACT²; assim. to the sb.

retrench ritre·nʃ †cut short, repress; cut down, reduce; also intr. XVII. – F. †*retrencher*, early form of *retrancher*; see RE- 5, TRENCH vb. (†*retranch* is a rare var. XVI–XVII.) So **retre·nch**MENT. XVII. – F. ¶ The use of both words is earlier in fortification (XVI) for inner line of defence.

retribution retribjū·ʃən recompense, requital XIV (PPl., Wycl. Bible); recompense *for* evil XVI. – ChrL. *retribūtiō(n-)*, f. L. *retribuere*, f. *re-* RE- 2 + *tribuere* assign; see TRIBUTE, -TION, and cf. (O)F. *rétribution*. So **retri·but**IVE (in Southey and Shelley str. on the first and third sylls.). XVII (*r. justice* Cudworth; rare before XIX).

retrieve ritrī·v †(of dogs) find again (game that has been lost) XV; recover, regain XVI; bring in (killed or wounded game) XIX. Late ME *retreve* – OF. *retroev-*, *-euv-*, tonic stem of *retrover* (mod. *retrouver*), f. *re-* RE- 4 + *trover* find (cf. TROVE). The usual form in XVI–XVII was *retrive*, with change of vowel as in CONTRIVE; *retrieve* dates from *c.*1650. Hence **retrie·v**ER¹ †dog used to set up game again XV; breed of dog adapted for recovering game XIX.

retro- rī·trou, re·trou prefix repr. L. *retrō-* adv. ('behind') used in combination as in *retrospicere* (cf. RETROSPECT), *retrogradus* (see next), f. *re-* + compar. suffix as in *intrō-* INTRO-; in anat. and path. denoting 'situated behind' the part of the body indicated by the second el., as *retro-ocular*, *-uterine*.

retrograde re·trŏgreid (astron., of planets) moving apparently in a direction contrary to the order of the signs XIV (Ch.); tending or inclined to go backwards XVI. – L. *retrōgradus* (astron.), f. *retrō* + *grad-* step; see RETRO-, GRADE. So **re·trograde** vb. XVI. – L. *retrōgradī*, later *retrōgradāre*. **retrograd**A·TION. XVI. – late L. **retrogre·ss**ION. XVII. – L. **retrōgressiō(n-)*. Cf. F. *rétrograde*, etc., with corr. forms in Sp., Pg., It.

retrospect re·trŏspekt, rī·trou- regard or reference *to* some fact, etc.; survey of the past. XVII. f. *retrōspect-*, pp. stem of L. *retrōspicere* look back, after PROSPECT. So **retrospe·c**TION, **retrospe·c**TIVE. XVII.

retroussé rətrū·sei (of the nose) turned up at the end. XIX. – F., pp. of *retrousser*, f. *re-* RE- 1 + *trousser* TRUSS.

return ritǝ̄·ɹn come or go back, lit. and fig. XIV (Ch.); turn, bring, or send back XV; give back, render XVI (Sh.). – OF. *retorner*, *returner* (mod. *retourner*) = Sp. *retournar*, It. *ritornare* – Rom. **retornāre*; see RE- 1, TURN. So **retu·rn** sb. XIV (Gower). – AN. *retorn*, *return*, f. *retorner*.

reunion rījū·niən coming together again. XVII (Donne). – F. *réunion*, f. *réunir* reunite, after *union*. So **reuni·te.** XVI; cf. AL. *reūnīre*. See RE- 4, UNION, UNITE.

reveal[1] rivī·l disclose in a supernatural manner XIV; divulge by discourse, etc. XV; make visible XVI. – (O)F. *révéler* (= Sp. *revelar*, It. *ri-*, *revelare*) or L. *revēlāre*, f. *re-* RE- 5 + *vēlum* VEIL. So **revelA·TION** revĭl-. XIV (R. Mannyng). – (O)F. or ChrL.

reveal[2] rivī·l side of an opening or recess at right angles to the face of a work. XVII (*revale*, Holme). f. †*revale* lower, bring down – OF. *revaler*, f. *re-* RE- 1 + *avaler* lower, f. *à val* down.

reveille rivæ·li, rive·li morning signal given to soldiers. XVII (*revelley*, *revalley*). – F. *réveillez*, imper. pl. of *réveiller* awaken, f. *re-* RE- 4 + *veiller* :– L. *vigilāre* keep watch (see VIGIL).

revel re·v(ə)l be (riotously) festive. XIV. – OF. *reveler* (refl.) rebel, rejoice noisily :– L. *rēbellāre* REBEL. So **re·vel** sb. XIV. – OF. *revel* (f. the vb.) rebellion, tumult, disturbance, noisy mirth.

revenge rive·ndʒ refl. (XIV, Barbour), pass. (XV) take vengeance; exact retribution for XV. In earliest use Sc. – OF. *revenger*, var. of *revencher* (mod. *revancher*) = Pr. *revenjar* :– late L. *revindicāre*, f. *re-* RE- 7 + L. *vindicāre* VENGE. Hence **reve·nge** sb. XVI; cf. F. †*revenge*, var. of *revenche* (mod. *revanche*).

revenue re·vənju (also str. *reve·nue* XVI to mid-XIX) †yield or profit *of* property; income from possessions XV; (annual) income gen.; department of the civil service dealing with national funds XVII. – (O)F. *revenu*, †*revenue*, m. and fem. pp. of *revenir* :– L. *revenīre* return, f. *re-* RE- 1, 2 + *venīre* COME; cf. AL. *reventus* revenue.

reverberate rivə̄·ɹbəreit †beat or drive back; re-echo; also intr. XVI. f. pp. stem of L. *everberāre*, f. *re-* RE- 1 + *verberāre* strike, beat, f. *verbera* rods, scourge, flogging, with cogns. in Baltic and Sl., and Gr. *rhapís* stick, *rhábdos* stick, rod; cf. F. *réverbérer*, It. *ri(n)verberare*, etc. So **reverberA·TION**. XIV (Ch.; rare before XVI). – (O)F. or late L. **reve·rberatORY** (furnace) so constructed that the flame is forced back upon the substance exposed to it, XVII; cf. F., etc.

revere riviə·ɹ regard with deep respect. XVII. – F. *révérer* or L. *reverērī*, f. *re-* RE- 7 + *verērī* feel awe of, fear (see WARE[2]). So **reverENCE** re·vərəns deep respect XIII (S. Eng. Leg.); gesture indicative of this; condition of being revered; as a title XIV. – (O)F. *révérence* = Sp. *reverencia*, It. *reverenza* – L. *reverentia*. So **reve·rence** vb. XIV. – AN. *reverencer* (Gower); cf. modF. *révérencier*. **re·verend** worthy of reverence (spec. as an epithet of respect) XV; †reverent XVI (formerly in regular use). – (O)F. *révérend* (= Sp., It. *reverendo*, or L. *reverendus*, gerundive of *reverērī*. **re·verENT** †reverend XIV (very freq. XVI–XVII); deeply respectful XV. In first sense – OF. *reverent* or after medL. *reverentissimus* most reverend (of bishops); in second sense – L. *reverent-*, *-ēns* (whence Sp., It. *reverente*). **revere·n-TIAL.** XVI. – F. †*reverencial*, *révérentiel* or medL. **reverentiālis* (adv. *reverentiāliter* reverently).

reverie re·vəri †wild delight, violent or riotous action XIV; †fanciful idea; abstracted musing XVII. In ME. – OF. *reverie* rejoicing, revelry, wildness, rage, f. *rever* revel, act or speak wildly (mod. *rêver* †talk in delirium, dream), of unkn. origin. In XVII–XVIII (often *resverie*) – later F. *resverie*, now *rêverie*; see -ERY.

reverse rivə̄·ɹs opposite, contrary XIV (R. Mannyng, Gower; thereafter not till XVIII); mil. commanding the rear XVIII. – OF. *revers(e)* – L. *reversus*, *-a*, pp. of *revertere*. So sb. A. contrary XIV (Gower, Ch.; thereafter not till XVIII); back of a coin, etc. XVII. B. †back-handed stroke XV; adverse change of fortune XVI. – (O)F. *revers* or †*reverse* – sb. uses of the L. pp. **reve·rse** vb. †bring, send, etc. back; †overthrow; invert, turn the other way. XIV. – OF. *reverser* (now *ren-*) – late L. *reversāre*, f. L. *reversus*. **reve·rSION** (leg.) return of an estate; right of succession. XV. – (O)F. or L. **reve·rSAL**[2]. XV. **reve·rt** †recover consciousness XIII; return, go back XIV. – OF. *revertir* or L. *revertere*, f. *re-* RE- 1, 2 + *vertere* turn (see -WARD).

revetment rive·tmənt (fortif.) retaining wall supporting the face of a rampart. XVIII. – F. *revêtement* (also used in Eng.), f. *revêtir* (whence †*revest* XVII, **revet** XIX) – late L. *revestīre*, f. *re-* + *vestīre* clothe; see RE- 4, VEST, -MENT.

review rivjū· revision; formal inspection XVI; general survey or account XVII. – F. *reveue*, now *revue*, f. *revoir*, f. *re-* RE- 4 + *voir* :– L. *vidēre* see; see VIEW. So or hence vb. †inspect again; revise, survey XVI; etc.; after F. *revoir*, It. *rividere*, etc.

revile rivai·l assail with abuse. XIV (R. Mannyng). – OF. *reviler*, f. *re-* RE- 7 + *vil* VILE; cf. F. *ravilir*, It. *ravvilire*.

revise rivai·z †look *at* or behold again; read over again. XVI. – (O)F. *réviser*, †*reviser* or L. *revīsere*, f. *re-* RE- 4, 7 + *vīsere* VISIT, examine, desiderative and intensive of *vīs-*, *vidēre* see (see WIT). Hence **revi·se** sb. review, revision XVI; revised form of proof-sheet XVII; **revi·SAL**[2]. XVII. So **revisION** rivi·ʒən. XVII. – (O)F. or late L.

revive rivai·v return or restore to consciousness or life. XV. – (O)F. *revivre* (corr. to Pr. *reviure*, etc.) or late L. *revīvere*, f. *re-* RE- 2 + *vīvere* live (see vivid); the causative meaning, which has developed in Eng., corr. to the uses of F. *raviver*, It. *ravivvare*. Hence **revi·val**[2]. XVII; whence **revi·val**ISM, -IST. XIX.

revoke rivou·k †bring back, recall; annul, cancel XIV (Ch., Wyclif); (at cards) fail improperly to follow suit XVI. – (O)F. *révoquer* = Sp. *revocar*, etc. or L. *revocāre*, f. *re-* RE- 1, 2, 3 + *vocāre* call. So **revoca·**TION. XV (Lydg., Wyntoun).

revolt rivou·lt, -ɔ·lt cast off allegiance XVI; affect with disgust XVIII (prp. adj. *revo·lting* XIX). – F. (*se*) *révolter* – It. *rivoltare* (refl. *-arsi*) – Rom. **revolvitāre*, intensive of L. *revolvere* REVOLVE. So **revo·lt** sb. XVI. – F. *révolte* – It. *rivolta*, f. the vb. So **revolution** revəlʲū·ʃən moving of a celestial body in an orbit, time in which this is done XIV (Gower, Ch.); †periodical recurrence XVI; complete change of affairs or reversal of conditions XV; overthrow of established government XVI. – (O)F. *révolution* (corr. to Sp. *revolucion*, It. *rivoluzione*) or late L. *revolūtiō(n-)*, f. pp. stem of *revolvere* REVOLVE; see -TION. Hence **revolu·tion**ARY. XVIII (1774; but in gen. use only after F. *révolutionnaire* 1794). **revolu·tion**IZE. XVIII (1797); after F. *révolutionner* (1795). **revolve** rivɔ·lv †turn or roll back or round XIV (Usk); turn over in the mind, consider XV; cause to travel in an orbit XVII (Milton); intr. of this XVIII. – L. *revolvere*, f. *re-* RE- 1, 7 + *volvere* roll, turn (cf. VOLUBLE). Hence **revo·lv**ER[1] pistol in which a set of loaded barrels or cartridge chambers is revolved. XIX (patented by S. Colt, 1835, American inventor, used by Dickens in 'Martin Chuzzlewit' xxxiii, along with *revolving pistol*).

revulsion rivʌ·lʃən (path.) diminishing a morbid condition in one part by acting on another XVI; drawing away XVII; strong reaction XIX (Scott, Southey). – F. *révulsion* or L. *revulsiō(n-)*, f. *revuls-*, pp. stem of *revellere*, f. *re-* RE- 1 + *vellere* pluck, pull (cf. CONVULSION).

reward riwɔ̄·ɹd †regard; †assign as a recompence; recompense, requite XIV. – AN., ONF. *rewarder* = OF. *reguarder* REGARD. So **rewa·rd** sb. †regard; return, recompence. XIV. – AN., ONF. *reward* = OF. *reguard*, f. the vb.

reynard re·nəɹd proper name of the fox. XIV. – (O)F. *renard*, †*-art*, orig. proper name of the fox (*le goupil*) in the 'Roman de Renart' XIII) – Frank. *Reginhart*, whence MDu. *Reynaert* (*-d*), on which Caxton modelled his form *reynard*. Also ME. *renaud*, later *reynold*, mod. dial. (*mister*) *Reynolds*, showing assim. to ME. *Reinaud* – OF. *Renaud* (cf. OHG. *Reginolt*, G. *Rein(h)old*).

rhabdo- ræ·bdou, ræbdɔ· comb. form of Gr. *rhábdos* rod (see REVERBERATE), as in **rhabdo·**LOGY computation by 'Napier's bones'. XVII – modL. *rhabdologia* (Napier). **rha·bdo**MANCY divination by a rod or wand. XVII (Sir T. Browne) – Gr. *rhabdomanteíā*.

Rhadamanthine rædəmæ·nþain inflexibly severe. XIX (earlier †*-ean* XVII). f. L. *Rhadamanthus*, Gr. *Rhadámanthos* one of the judges in the lower world; see -INE[1].

Rhæto-Romanic rī:touroumæ·nik pert. to the ROMANCE dialects spoken in SE. Switzerland and the Tyrol, sometimes spec. Romansch or Ladin XIX. Also **Rhæ:to-Roma·nce** XIX.

rhapsody ræ·psədi epic poem or part of one suitable for recitation at one time; †miscellany, medley XVI; extravagant effusion XVII. – L. *rhapsōdia*, applied by Cornelius Nepos to a book of Homer – Gr. *rhapsōidíā*, f. *rhapsōidós* rhapsodist, f. *rháptein* stitch + *ōidḗ* song, ODE; see -Y[3]. Hence **rhapsod**IC -ɔ·dik. XVIII, -ICAL, -IST, -IZE. XVII; cf. F. *r(h)apsodie* (XVII), *r(h)apsodiste*, *r(h)apsodier*.

rhatany ræ·təni S. Amer. shrub, Krameria triandra. XIX. – modL. *rhatania* – Pg. *ratanha*, Sp. *ratania* – Quechua *rataña*.

rhea rī·ə three-toed ostrich of S. America. XIX. modL. generic name (Möhring 1752), arbitrary use of the myth. female name L. *Rhea*, Gr. *Rhéā*.

Rhemish rī·miʃ pert. to Rheims (NE. France), formerly †*Rhemes*, or the English R.C. college there, or the N.T. emanating therefrom in 1582 XVI; see -ISH[1].

Rhenish re·niʃ pert. to the Rhine, chief river of Germany XIV; sb. Rhine wine XVI (Sh.). Late ME. *rynis*, *-isch*, *renys* (assim. XVI to L.) – AN. *reneis*, OF. *rinois*, *rainois* – medL. **Rhēnēnsis*, for L. *Rhenānus*, f. *Rhēnus* Rhine; cf. MHG. *rīn(i)sch*, G. *rheinisch*, etc.; see -ISH[1].

rheo- rī·ou, riɔ· comb. form of Gr. *rhéos* STREAM, current, used in scientific terms with the meaning 'electric current', as **rheo·meter, rhe·ostat**. XIX (Wheatstone).

rhesus rī·səs one of the macaques. XIX. modL. specific name, arbitrary use of L. *Rhēsus*, Gr. *Rhêsos*, mythical king of Thrace.

rhetor rī·tɔ̄ɹ professor of rhetoric XIV; (professional) orator XVI. Late ME. *rethor* (later *rhetor*) – late L. *rethor*, var. of L. *rhētor* – Gr. *rhḗtōr*, f. **ϝrā-* (as also in *rhêma* word), f. **wer-* (cf. VERB, WORD). So **rhetor**IC re·tərik art of using language for persuasion. XIV (Ch., Trevisa). Late ME. *ret(h)orique* – OF. *rethorique* (mod. *rhétorique*) – L. *rhētorica* (med.L *reth-*) – Gr. *rhētorikḗ*, sb. use (sc. *tékhnē* art). **rhetoric**AL rītɔ·rikəl. XV. f. L. *rhētŏricus*. **rhetori·**CIAN. XV (Lydg.). – OF.; earlier †*rethorien* XIV (Ch.) – OF. *rethorien*.

rheum[1] rūm watery matter secreted by mucous glands or membranes; mucous discharge, catarrh XIV (Trevisa, PPl.); (poet.) tears XVI (Sh.). Late ME. *reume* – OF. *reume* (mod. *rhume*) = Pr., Sp., It. *reuma* – late L. *rheuma* (Vegetius, Jerome) – Gr. *rheûma* flow, STREAM, bodily humour or defluxion. So **rheum**ATIC -æ·tik consisting of watery discharge XIV; suffering from, characterized by this XVI. – OF. *reumatique* (mod. *rhu-*) – L. – Gr. **rheu·mat**ISM rheumatic disease. XVII. – F. or L. – Gr. **rheu·ma-**TOID. XIX.

rheum[2] rī·əm generic name for the rhubarbs. XVIII. – Gr. *rhêon*. Hence (chem.) **rhe·**IC, **rhe·**IN[1]; after F. *rhéique, rhéine*.

rhinegrave rai·ngreiv count whose domain bordered on the river Rhine. XVI. – MDu. *rijngrave*, G. *rheingraf*; see GRAVE[6].

rhino rai·nou (sl.) money. XVII. In the earliest ex. assoc. with †*rhinocerical* ('The Ready, the Rhino; thou shalt be rhinocerical, my Lad', Shadwell 'Squire of Alsatia' I i), which is recorded also by Grose as a sl. word for 'rich', presumably f. RHINOCEROS in some allusive sense now lost.

rhino- rai·nou, rainɔ· comb. form of Gr. *rhís, rhīnós* nose, pl. nostrils, in scientific terms (XIX).

rhinoceros rainɔ·sərəs pl. *-oses* əsiz large pachyderm with a horn or two horns on its nose. XIII (*ri-, rynoceros*). – L. *rhīnocerōs* (Pliny), pl. *-ōtēs*, in medL. usu. *rīno-* – Gr. *rhīnókerōs*, pl. *-ōtes*, f. *rhīno-, rhīs* nose + *kéras* HORN. Several vars. have been current, as *rhinocerot* (cf. F. *rhinocerot* XVI), pl. *-otes*, pl. *-ceros, -ons* (cf. occas. OF. *rhinocerons*), *-ontes* (after medL.), *-ceroes, -ceri*. Cf. F. *rhinocéros*, Sp., It. *rinoceronte*. So **rhino-cerot**IC -sərɔ·tik. XVIII. – late L.

rhizo- rai·zou, raizɔ· comb. form of Gr. *rhíza* ROOT, in many scientific terms. XIX.

rhizome rai·zoum (bot.) root-like stem. XIX (Lindley). – modL. *rhizōma* – Gr. *rhízōma*, f. *rhizoûsthai* take root, f. *rhíza* ROOT[1].

rhodium[1] rou·diəm rosewood (Convolvulus). XVII. modL. (sc. *lignum* wood), n. of *rhodius* rose-like, f. Gr. *rhódon* ROSE.

rhodium[2] rou·diəm (chem.) white metal of the platinum group. XIX (Wollaston). f. Gr. *rhódon* ROSE + -IUM; so called from the rose colour of a solution of salts containing it.

rhododendron roudŏ-, rɔdŏde·ndrən genus of shrubs akin to azalea. XVII. – L. *rhododendron* oleander (Pliny) – Gr. *rhodódendron*, f. *rhódon* ROSE + *déndron* tree.

rhodomontade see RODOMONTADE.

rhomb rɔm plane figure having the four sides and opposite angles equal. XVI. – F. *rhombe* or L. *rhombus* (whence **rho·mbus** XVI) – Gr. *rhómbos* spinning motion, spinning-top, equilateral parallelogram, lozenge, rel. to *rhémbesthai* roll about, roam. Hence **rho·mb**IC XVII; so **rho·mb**OID adj. XVII, sb. XVI; – F. *rhomboïde* or late L. *rhomboīdēs* – Gr. *rhomboeidḗs* adj., *-és* sb. (sc. *skhêma* figure), -OIDAL. XVII. – modL.

rhopalic roupæ·lik (of lines of verse) in which each word contains one syllable more than the one immediately preceding it. XVII (Sir T. Browne). – late L. *rhopalicus* (Servius), f. Gr. *rhópalon* cudgel thicker towards one end (cf. RHABDO-); see -IC.

rhotacism rou·təsizm excessive use of *r* (Southey); (philol.) conversion of another sound (esp. *s*) into *r*. XIX. – modL. *rhōtacismus* – Gr. **rhōtakismós*, f. *rhōtakízein* make excessive or wrong use of *r*, f. *rhô* letter R; see -ISM, and cf. LAMBDACISM.

rhubarb rū·bāɹb (rootstock of) species of Rheum used in medicine, long imported from China to Europe through Russia and the Levant (*Turkey, Russian, Chinese r.*) XIV; any species cultivated in England or France for their fleshy stalks XVII. Late ME. *rubarbe* – OF. *ru-, reubarbe* (mod. *rhubarbe*) = Pr. *reubarba*, Sp. *riu-*, Pg. *reubarbo* – Rom. **r(h)eubarbum*, shortening of medL. *r(h)eubarbarum*, alt. by assoc. with *rheum* RHEUM[2] (– Gr. *rhêon* rhubarb – Pers. *rēwend*) of *rhabarbarum* foreign 'rha', whence It. *rabarbaro*, G. *rhabarber* (late L. *rhā* – Gr. *rhâ*, said by Ammianus Marcellinus to be called after the ancient name *Rhâ* of the river Volga).

rhumb rʌm, rʌmb (naut.) †line on a chart indicating the course of a ship moving continuously in one direction; point of the compass XVI; angular distance between two successive points XVII. – F. *rumb*, †*rum*, earlier †*ryn* (*de vent* of wind) point of the compass, prob. – Du. *ruim* space, ROOM, altered later by assoc. with L. *rhombus* RHOMB(US); cf. Sp. *rumbo*, Pg. *rumbo, rumo*, It. *rombo*, which may be partly the source of the Eng. word.

rhyme raim. XVII. var. sp. of RIME[2]. So vb. XVII; hence **rhy·mer**[1]. XVII, **rhy·me**STER. XVIII.

rhyncho- ri·ŋkou comb. form of Gr. *rhúgkhos* snout, in scientific terms, as *rhy:nchocepha·lian, rhy·nchophore*. XIX.

rhythm ri·ðm, ri·þm A. †(piece of) rhymed verse XVI; B. metrical movement or flow as determined by the recurrence of features of the same kind XVI; also transf. and gen. XVII. In A graphic var. of RIME[2] (rhyming, e.g., with *time* XVII); in B – L. *rhythmus* or F. *rhythme* – Gr. *rhuthmós*, rel. to *rheîn* flow (IE. **sreu-*; cf. STREAM). So **rhy·thm**IC. XVII, -ICAL. XVI. – F. or L. – Gr.

rial rai·əl applied from XIV to various royal persons and things, esp. (XV–) coins struck in particular reigns (cf. REAL²). – OF. *rial*, var. of *real* REAL¹.

riant rai·ənt smiling, gay. XVI. – F. *riant* – L. *rīdentem*, *-ēns*, prp. of *rīdēre* laugh; see -ANT.

riata riā·tə lariat. XIX. – Sp. *reata*, f. *reatar* to tie again, f. *re-* RE- 4 + *atar* :– L. *aptāre* apply, adjust (cf. ADAPT).

rib rib any of the curved bones articulated to the spine OE.; wife, woman (in allusion to Gen. ii 21) XVI; various transf. and techn. uses from XIV. OE. *rib(b)*, corr. (with variations in gender and declension) to OFris. *ribb*, *rebb*, OS. *ribbi* (Du. *rib(be)*), OHG. *rippi*, *rippa* (G. *rippe*), ON. *rif* :– Germ. **reƀja-*, *-jō*, rel. to OSl. (Russ.) *rebró* (:–**rebhro*) rib, side, and prob. further to OHG. *hirni|reba* brain-pan, cranium, Gr. *orophḗ* roof, *eréphein* roof over.

ribald ri·bəld †retainer of low class XIII; †knave, rascal, licentious person; offensive or scurrilous person XIV; adj. XVI. ME. *ribaud* – OF. *ribaut*, *-ault*, *-auld* (also mod. *ribaud*) = Pr. *ribaut* (whence OSp., OPg., It. *ribaldo*, medL. *ribaldus*), f. OF. *riber* pursue licentious pleasures, f. Germ. base repr. by OHG. *hrība* (MHG. *rībe*) whore, MHG. *rīben* be on heat, copulate. ¶ The Rom. word was adopted in MLG., MDu., MHG., and Icel. So **ri·bald**RY. XIV, †**ribald**Y³. XIII (S. Eng. Leg.). – OF. *ribauderie*, *ribaudie*.

ribband¹ ri·bənd (naut.) any of the long flexible timbers fastened to the ribs of a ship. XVIII. perh. f. RIB+BAND², but poss. identical with next, *ribbon* being so used from the same date.

ribband² see next.

ribbon ri·bn narrow woven band of fine material. XIV (PPl., Ch.). Late ME. *reban*, *riban*, *ryban*, later *ryband* XV, **ri·bband** XVI (freq. till XIX) – OF. *riban* (still dial.), *reuban*, (also mod.) *ruban*, prob. – Germ. comp. of *band* BAND². ¶ The sp. in *-on*, evidenced from XVI, is prob. after *button*, *cotton*; the *d* of *riband* is parasitic, as in *astound*.

ribes rai·bīz pl. currants XVI; (bot.) genus comprising currant and gooseberry XVIII. – medL. *rībēs* – Arab. *rībās* sorrel.

Ribston ri·bstən dessert apple, introduced from Normandy, named after *Ribston* Park, situated between Knaresborough and Wetherby in Yorkshire. XVIII.

rice rais (seeds of) the food plant Oryza sativa. XIII. ME. *rys* – OF. *ris* (mod. *riz*) – It. *riso* (whence also Pr. *ris*) :– Rom. **orīzum*, for L. *orȳza* – Gr. *óruza* (also *óruzon*), of Eastern origin (cf. Skr. *vrīhi*); widespread in the Germ. langs.: MLG., MHG., *rīs* (Du. *rijst*, G. *reis*), MSw. *riis*, Sw., Da. *ris* (Sp., Pg. *arroz* are from Arab. *ar-rozz*, with AL-²).

rich ritʃ †powerful, great; having abundant means OE.; costly, splendid, sumptuous XII; various transf. and fig. uses from XIII. OE. *riċe* = OFris. *rīk(e)*, OS. *rīki*, OHG. *rīchi* (Du. *rijk*, G. *reich*), ON. *ríkr*, Goth. *reiks*, CGerm. – Celtic *rīx* (Ir. *rig*) = L. *rēx* king (cf. RAJAH, ROYAL); reinforced in ME. by (O)F. *riche* orig. powerful = Pr. *ric*, Sp. *rico*, It. *ricco*, of Germ. origin. From the same CGerm. stem are OE. *riċe* = OFris. *rīke*, OS. *rīki*, MLG., MDu. *rīke* (Du. *rijk*), OHG. *rīchi* (G. *reich*), ON. *ríki*, Goth. *reiki* kingdom, realm, royal power, surviving in BISHOPRIC. So **riches** ri·tʃiz abundance of means XIII (Laȝ.). var. (simulating Eng. pls. in *-es*) of †*richesse*, †*richeise* (XII) – OF. *richeise*, *-esce* (mod. *-esse*); f. *riche*+*-eise*, *-esse* -ESS². Cf. ALMS, EAVES.

rick¹ rik stack of hay, etc. OE. *hrēac* = MDu. *rooc*, *roke* (Du. *rook*), ON. *hraukr*, of unkn. origin. The shortening of the vowel, dating from XVI, is paralleled by the widespread dial. var. *ship* of *sheep*.

rick² rik sprain, wrench XVIII; var. of WRICK.

rickets ri·kits disease marked by softening of the bones. XVII ('De Morbo puerili Anglorum, quem patrio idiomate indigenæ vocant The Rickets', D. Whistler, 1645). perh. of local origin, the disease being first observed in Dorset and Somerset; assoc. by medical writers with Gr. *rhakhîtis* RACHITIS, which was adopted as the technical designation. Hence **ri·ckety**¹ affected with r. XVII; shaky, tottering XVIII.

rickshaw ri·kʃɔ̄ also *'rickshaw* (Kipling), *rik(i)sha*, *ricksha*. XIX. Abbreviation of JINRICKSHA.

ricochet ri·kǒʃei, -ʃet (method of firing characterized by) the skipping of a shot along a surface. XVIII. – F. *ricochet*, orig. in phr. *fable* (later *chanson* song) *du ricochet* endless exchange of question and answer, unending argument; the basis of these is unknown. Hence vb. XIX.

rictus ri·ktəs (techn.) throat, orifice, gape. XVIII. L. 'open mouth', f. ppl. stem of *ringī* gape.

rid rid clear (a space); set free *from*, *of* XIII; disencumber *of* XVI. ME. (western) *ruden* (*rudde*, *irud*), north. and eastern *ridde* – ON. *ryðja* (pt. *ruddi*, pp. *ruddr*). Hence **ri·dd**ANCE XVI (Coverdale).

riddle¹ ri·dl puzzling or dark utterance, enigma. OE. *rǣdels*, *rǣdelse* opinion, riddle, corr. to OFris. *riedsel*, OS. *rādisli*, *rādislo* (Du. *raadsel*), OHG. *rādisle* (G. *rätsel*); f. **rǣdan* READ², REDE; see -LE¹. Hence **ri·ddle** vb.¹ speak in riddles; solve a riddle. XVI; whence **ri·ddlemeree** -mirī·, XVIII; fanciful var. of *riddle my rede* or *riddle*. ¶ For the fall of *s* as a supposed pl. ending cf. *burial*, *cherry*, *pea*.

riddle[2] ri·dl coarse-meshed sieve. Late OE. *hriddel*, rel. to synon. *hrīder* and *hrīdrian* sift, of WGerm. extent and based on IE. ***krī̆-** with widespread cogns., as in Gr. *krī́nein* (see CRISIS), L. *crībrum* sieve, *cernere*, *discrīmen* (see DISCERN, DISCRIMINATE), in Germ. ***χrain-** clean, pure (e.g. G. *rein*), etc. Hence **ri·ddle** vb.[2] †sift XIII; pierce with holes XIX.

ride raid pt. **rode** roud, pp. **ridden** ri·dn sit upon and be carried by a horse, etc.; lie at anchor OE.; trans. (of ON. origin) XIII. OE. *rīdan*, pt. *rād*, *ridon*, pp. **riden* = OFris. *rīda*, OS. *-rīdan* (Du. *rijden*), OHG. *rītan* (G. *reiten*), ON. *ríða*, rel. to OIr. *riadaim* I travel, *riad* journey, Gaulish *rēda* chariot (cf. PALFREY). Hence sb. XVIII. **ridER**[1] rai·dəɹ †knight XI; one who rides a horse, etc. XIII; (pl.) additional timbers to strengthen the frame of a ship; additional or supplementary clause XVII; corollary XIX. Late OE. *rīdere*. **ri·ding-COAT**. XVI; adopted in F. as *redingote*.

ridge ridʒ †back, spine; top, crest; coping of a roof; long stretch of high ground; raised strip of arable land OE.; narrow raised part across a surface XVI. OE. *hryċġ* = OFris. *hregg*, OS. *hruggi-* (MDu. *ruc*, Du. *rug*), OHG. *hrucci* (G. *rücken*), ON. *hryggr* (whence ME. and north. dial. *rig* XIII) :- CGerm. (exc. Gothic) **χrugjaz*, having prob. Celtic, Lith., and Skr. cogns. In some transf. senses sparsely recorded in gen. use between OE. and XVI. The ordinary word in OE. for 'back' as a part of the body, whereas *bæc* BACK, which has superseded it in this use, is found mainly in phraseological usage (e.g. *on bæc* ABACK).

ridicule[1] ri·dikjūl †ridiculous thing, nature, character; making fun *of*. XVII. – F. *ridicule* – n. sg. of L. *rīdiculus*, f. *rīdēre* laugh. So **ridicuLOUS** -i·kjŭləs. XVI. f. L. *rīdiculus* or – L. *rīdiculōsus*; cf. F. *ridiculeux*.

ridicule[2] ri·dikjūl – F. illiterate perversion of RETICULE. XIX.

riding rai·diŋ any of the three districts of Yorkshire (East, West, and North). XI. In *Est Treding*, *Estreding*, *Nort Treding* (Domesday Book), *Nort riding*, etc. (XII), alt., by change of *tþ* to *t(t)*, of late OE. **þriding*, **þriðing* (*treding*, *trethine*, *trithing* XI–XIII) – ON. *þriðjungr* third part, f. *þriði* THIRD; see -ING[3]. The pronunc. with ai is a sp.-pronunc. depending on the antiquarian revival of the term in XVI (but Fitzherbert in 1514 has *rydding*).

riem rīm also **reim, rheim** long strip or thong of leather. XIX. – Afrikaans, Du. *riem* = OE. *rēoma* (dial. *rim*), OS. *riomo*, OHG. *riumo* (G. *riemen*), rel. to Gr. *erúein* draw.

rife raif prevalent, widespread; abundant XII; generally current XIV. Once in late OE. *rȳfe*, for **rīfe*; subsequently *rif*, *rijf*, *riue*, in northern, eastern, and w. midl. texts; prob. – ON. *rífr* good, acceptable = WFris. *rjū*, MLG. *rīve*, MDu. *rīve*, *rijf* abundant; cf. ON. *reifa* enrich, *reifr* glad, cheerful.

riff-raff ri·fræf persons of the most disreputable class XV; worthless stuff XVI. f. phr. †*rif and raf* (XIV) one and all, every bit – OF. *rif et raf* (also *ne rif ne raf* nothing at all; '*Il ne luy lairra rif ny raf*, he will strip . . . him of all', Cotgr.), cf. MDu. *rijf ende raf*.

rifle[1] rai·fl despoil; carry off as booty. XIV. – OF. *rifler*, *riffler* graze, scratch, plunder, of unkn. origin.; cf. AL. *rif(f)lātum* spoliation, *rifflerus* robber.

rifle[2] rai·fl spiral groove inside a gun-barrel; (perh. for *rifle* or *rifled gun*) fire-arm having a rifled bore. XVIII. f. *rifle* vb. (XVII) form spiral grooves in – F. *rifler* scratch, scrape, plane, of unkn. origin.

rift rift †rending, splitting XIII (Cursor M.); cleft, fissure XIV (Maund.), orig. north.; of Scand. origin (cf. Norw., Da. *rift* cleft, chink, Icel. *ript* breach of contract); rel. to RIVE.

rig[1] rig fit *out*, esp. with clothes; make ready for sea, supply with tackle XV; provide, fit *up* XVI; fix, adjust XVII. perh. of Scand. origin (cf. Norw. *rigga* bind or wrap up, Sw. dial. *rigga på* harness). Hence **rig** sb. arrangement of masts, sails, etc.; outfit (*rig-out*). XIX; **ri·ggING**[1]. XV; concr. XVI.

rig[2] rig (dial.) banter, ridicule; trick, prank (phr. *run a rig*) XVIII. f. *rig* vb. (XVI) wanton, romp, of unkn. origin.

rigadoon rigədū·n (hist.) lively dance for two persons. XVII. – F. *rigodon*, *rigaudon*, said by Rousseau ('Dictionnaire de Musique') to have been named after its inventor, one *Rigaud*, stated to have been the name of a celebrated dancing-master at Marseilles.

right rait †standard or rule of action; that which is equitably or morally just; just treatment; justifiable claim. OE. *riht* = OFris. *riucht*, OS., OHG. *reht* (Du., G. *recht*), ON. *réttr*; the sb. corr. to **right** adj. †straight; †upright, righteous; just, correct, proper, due; real, true; epithet of the hand that is normally the stronger OE.; (of an angle) of 90° XIV (Ch.); mentally normal XII; correct in opinion, etc. XVI. OE. *riht* = OFris., etc., as in the sb., Goth. *raihts* :- CGerm. ***reχtaz**, pp. formation with IE. ***-to-**; equiv. formations are L. *rēctus* (for *rĕctus*), OIr. *recht* law, W. *rhaith*, Breton *reiz*, Gr. *orektós* upright; f. IE. base ***reg-** denoting movement in a straight line, extension; cf. DIRECT, ERECT, RECTOR, REGENT, REGIMEN, REGION, RULE. So **right** vb. †guide, direct; †set up; set in order, set right, etc. OE. *rihtan*; CGerm. (exc. Gothic) weak vb. **right** adv. OE. *rihte*.

ri·ghtEN[5] set right XIV (rare before XVI). **ri·ght**LY[2]. OE. *rihtlīce.* **righ·t**FUL[1]. OE. *rihtful,* f. the sb.

-right repr. the adj. and the adv. *right,* as in OE. *forþriht(e)* FORTHRIGHT, *upriht(e)* UPRIGHT, after which were formed ME. DOWNRIGHT, OUTRIGHT.

righteous rai·tʃəs upright, virtuous. OE. *rihtwīs,* f. *riht* sb. or adj. + *wīs* manner, state, condition (cf. -WISE and *nīedwīs* necessary, *þearlwīs* severe, and OHG. *rehtwīsig*); ON. *réttvíss* is prob. – OE. Forms in *-wise* were current XIII–XVI, unstr. forms in *-wes, -wos* XV–XVI; the next stage was *-uous* XV–XVI, which gave way to *-eous* (XVI Tindale) by assim. to *beauteous, bounteous, plenteous.* So **ri·ghteous**LY[2]. OE. *rihtwīslīce.* **ri·ghteous**NESS. OE. *rihtwīsnisse.*

rigid ri·dʒid not pliant or yielding; strict XVI; precise in method XVII. – F. *rigide* or L. *rigidus,* f. *rigēre* be stiff; see -ID[1]. So **rig**OUR[2], U.S. **rigor** ri·gəɹ severity, strictness XIV (Ch.), severity, as of climate; severe exactitude; chill with shivering (now usu. *rigor,* the L. form) XVI. sudden chill XVI (in mod. medical use **rigor** rai·gɔ̄ɹ). – (O)F. *rigour,* mod. *rigueur,* corr. to Sp. *rigor,* It. *rigore* – L. *rigōrem, rigor,* f. *rigēre.* **ri·gor**OUS. XIV (Wyclif.; *rigorously* Barbour). – OF. *rigorous* (cf. medL. *rigōrōsus*) – late L. *rigōrōsus.*

rigmarole ri·gmərou̯l rambling or meaningless talk. XVIII. Of dial. origin; alt. of †*ragman roll* list, catalogue (XVI; obs. in literary use *c.*1600), earlier †*roll of ragman. Ragman('s) roll* was used in most of the senses of *rag man* (earlier *rageman,* three syll. as still in Gower 'Confessio Amantis' VIII 2379), which was applied orig. (XIII) to (i) a statute of Edward I and articles of inquisition made under this statute, (ii) a game of chance played with a written roll having strings attached to the items of it, which the players drew; *Rageman* perh. orig. **ragiman* 'ragged man'. It is sometimes treated as a proper name.

rigveda ri·gveida principal sacred books of the Hindus. XVIII. Skr. *ṛigvēda,* f. *ṛic* praise + VEDA knowledge.

rile rail (colloq.) make turbid; disturb in temper, vex. XIX. orig. var. (cf. *jint* for *joint,* etc.) of (dial.) *roil* (XVI), perh. – OF. *ruiler* mix mortar :– late L. *regulāre* REGULATE.

rill ril small stream. XV (but cf. AL. *rilla* XIV). probl. of LDu. origin; cf. LG. *ril(le),* Du., EFris. *ril* (whence G. *rille*); but the ult. source is unknown.

rim rim (raised) edge, margin, verge OE.; outer ring of a wheel XIV. OE. *rima,* esp. in *dæġrima* (ME. *dairime*) break of day, *sǣs rima, sǣrima* (ME. *særime*) sea-shore; *tōþrima* gums, *wudurima* edge of a wood = ON. *rimi* ridge of land, of which no other cogns. are known.

rime[1] raim hoar frost. OE. *hrīm* = (M)Du. *rijm,* ON. *hrím*; rarely evidenced in ME. exc. in †*rime*-FROST (XIII–XVII), corr. to Icel., OSw., *hrímfrost*; from XVI onwards chiefly north., until adopted in gen. literary use in late XVIII.

rime[2] raim †metre XII (Ormulum); consonance of terminal elements in words; (rhyming) verse XIII; word that rhymes XVI. – (O)F. *rime* (:– **ritme*) – medL. *rithmus, rythmus* (used spec. of accentual verse which was usu. rhymed), for L. *rhythmus* RHYTHM. So **rime** vb. XIII. – (O)F. *rimer.* The sp. *rime* (var. *ryme*) prevailed till *c.*1560, when the tendency to respell on classical models led to the use of *rithme, rythme, rhythme* (till *c.*1700); these were succeeded after 1600 by *rhime,* RHYME, and *rime,* which was never discontinued, gained considerable vogue in XVIII and XIX. ¶ F. *rime* was the source of Pr., Sp., It. *rima,* and of forms current throughout the Germ. langs.; so with the vb. *rimer.*

rind[1] raind bark of a tree; crust OE.; peel orsk in XIV. OE. *rind, rinde,* corr., with variation, to OS. *rinda,* MDu. *rinde, rende, runde* (Du. *run*), OHG. *rinta* (G. *rinde*); of unkn. origin.

rind[2] raind iron support of an upper millstone. XIV. prob. – (M)LG. *rīn,* (M)Du. *rijn,* †*rīne,* Flem. *rijne*; the *d* is parasitic.

rinderpest ri·ndəɹpest cattle plague. XIX. G., f. *rinder* cattle, pl. of *rind.*

ring[1] riŋ, circle or circlet of metal, etc.; circular group OE.; various transf. and fig. uses esp. from XIV. OE. *hring* = OFris. *(h)ring,* OS., OHG. *hring* (Du., G. *ring*), ON. *hringr* :– CGerm. (exc. Gothic) **χreŋgaz* (whence Finnish *rengas*). Hence **ring** vb. put a ring or circle around; from XV, with corr. formations in the cogn. langs.; OE. *be-, ymb|hringan* (surround) would have survived as **ringe.* Comps. **ri·ng**DOVE woodpigeon; prob. after LG. or Du. XVI. **ri·ng-**FI:NGER third finger. OE. *hringfinger*; so in other Germ. langs. **ri·nglea·der.** XVI; f. phr. *lead the r.* **ri·ng**LET. XVI. **ri·ng**WORM skin disease marked by circular patches. XV. prob. of foreign origin; cf. Du. *ringworm,* Norw., Da. *ringorm.*

ring[2] riŋ, pt. **rang (rung)** ræŋ, pp. **rung** rʌŋ give out a resonant sound OE.; cause (a bell) to do this XII. OE. *hringan,* corr. to ON. *hringja* (whence Du., G. *ringen*); orig. weak (OE. pt. *hringde,* early ME. *ringde*), but strong forms appear in early XIII (Laȝ.), after *sing.* In earliest OE. a poetical word used of the resounding or clanging of armour; the later application to the ringing of bells was partly due to ON., in which the vb. was so restricted.

rink riŋk †area allotted to a contest XIV (Barbour); stretch of ice for the game of curling XVIII, for skating XIX. Only in Sc. use till XIX; poss. later form of **renk* – OF. *renc* (mod. *rang*) RANK.

rinse rins, (locally) rinz wash *out* with water, etc. XIV. – (O)F. *rincer*, earlier *raincier*, *reincier*, of unkn. origin.

riot raiət †debauched living, dissipation XIII (Ancr R.); †noisy feast, wanton revel; violence, violent disturbance of the peace XIV (Barbour, Gower); (hunting) hound's following the scent of a quarry other than that intended XV (phr. *hunt* or *run riot*; hence fig. use of the latter XVI). – OF. *riote*, *riot* (mod. *riotte*) debate, quarrel = Pr. *riota* (whence OIt. *riotta*), f. OF. *rihoter*, *ruihoter* = Pr. *riotar* quarrel. So **ri·ot** vb. XIV (Ch.). – OF. *riot(t)er*. **ri·ot**OUS (arch.) dissolute, extravagant XIV (Ch.); turbulent XV. – OF. *riotous*, *-eus*.

rip[1] rip tear or pull away vigorously. XV. Of unkn. origin.

rip[2] rip (sl., dial.) worthless thing, old knacker; dissolute person. XVIII. poss. alt. of *rep*, short for *reprobate*.

riparian raipɛə·riən pert. to the banks of a river. XIX. f. L. *rīpārius*, f. *rīpa* bank; see RIVER, -ARIAN.

ripe raip ready for reaping or gathering OE.; in various transf. and fig. uses 'matured, mature' from *c.*1200. OE. *rīpe* = OS. *rīpi* (Du. *rijp*), OHG. *rīfi* (G. *reif*); CWGerm. So **ripe** vb. (arch.) become ripe OE.; make ripe XIV. OE. *rīpian* = OS. *rīpon* (Du. *rijpen*), OHG. *rīfēn* (G. *reifen*); superseded gen. by **ri·p**EN[5] rai·pn. XVI.

riposte ripou·st return thrust in fencing XVIII (*risposte*); effective reply XIX. – F. *riposte*, earlier †*risposte* – Italian *risposta*, sb. use of fem. pp. of *rispondere* RESPOND.

ripple ri·pl (of water) present a surface of small waves. XVII. Hence **ri·pple** sb. U.S. piece of shallow water in a river where rocks cause obstruction; light ruffling of the surface of water XVIII. Of unkn. origin.

Ripuarian ripjuɛə·riən Frank living on the Rhine in the district between the Moselle and the Meuse. XVIII (Gibbon). f. medL. *Ripuārius*; see -IAN. Earlier (rare) **Ri·pu**ARY. XVII.

rise raiz, pt. **rose** rouz, pp. **risen** ri·zn get *up*, go *up*, ascend; rebel; increase XII; come into existence XIII; (dial., techn.) raise XV. OE. *rīsan*, pt. **rās*, pl. **rison*, pp. **risen* (as in *ārās*, etc.) = OFris. *rīsa*, OS., OHG. *rīsan* (Du. *rijzen*, G. *reisen* of the sun), ON. *rísa*, Goth. *ur|reisan* :– CGerm. str. vb., of which no cogns. are known. The simplex *rīsan* is very rare in OE. (as in OS.), the common form being *ārīsan* ARISE; in early ME. the use of *rise* in several senses appears first in the Ormulum, is predominantly north. and may be chiefly due to ON. *rísa*. The proper causative forms are REAR[1] and RAISE. Hence **rise** sb. XV (rare before late XVI).

risible ri·zĭbl inclined to laughter XVI; pert. to laughter; laughable XVIII. – late L. *rīsibilis*. f. *rīs-*, pp. stem of *rīdēre* laugh; see -IBLE and cf. (O)F. *risible*, etc. So **risibi·l**ITY. XVII. – late L. (Boethius).

risk risk chance or peril of destruction or loss. XVII. – F. *risque* – It. *risco*, *rischio*, f. *rischiare*, *risicare* run into danger; of unkn. (much debated) origin. Hence **ri·sk**Y[1]. XIX (J. F. Cooper); later, partly after F. pp. *risqué*.

rissole ri·soul fried ball or cake of meat or fish with bread-crumbs. XVIII. – F. *rissole*, later form of OF. *ruissole*, dial. var. of *roissole*, *roussole* :– Rom. **russeola* (sc. *pasta* paste), sb. use of fem. of late L. *russeolus* reddish, f. *russus* red (see RUSSET). ¶ An early anticipation of this word is *russoles* (pl.) in 'Ayenbite of Inwyt', 1340; and an AN. var. *russ(h)eaulx* (pl.) is repr. by late ME. *rissheus*, *-ewes* (XV).

rite rait formal (esp. religious) procedure or act XIV; general use or practice, esp. in religion XV. – (O)F. *rit*, later *rite* (= Sp., It. *rito*) or L. *rītus* (religious) usage. So **ritu**AL[1] ri·tjuəl pert. to rites XVI; sb. (book containing) prescribed order of the performance of rites XVII. – L. *rituālis*; cf. F. *rituel*, †*-al*, etc.; in sb. use after medL. *rituāle* sb. use of n. sg. **ri·tual**IST one versed in ritual or who advocates its observance. XVII; cf. F. *ritualiste*; hence **ri·tual**ISM. XIX.

rival rai·vəl one who strives to surpass or disputes renown with another. XVI. – L. *rīvālis* one who uses the same stream with another, f. *rīvus* stream (cf. DERIVE); see -AL[1]. Hence vb. XVII, **riva·l**ITY. XVI. – L. (cf. F. *rivalité*, etc.); superseded by **ri·val**RY. XVI.

rive raiv (arch., dial.) tear, rend. XIII (Laȝ., Cursor M.). ME. *rive*, pt. *rōf*, pp. *riven* (pt. and pp. *rived* XVI) – ON. *rífa*, pt. *reif*, *rifu*, pp. *rifinn* = OFris. *rīva*; of unkn. origin.

river ri·vəɹ copious natural stream of water flowing in a natural bed. XIII (R. Glouc.). – AN. *river(e)*, (O)F. *rivière* †river bank, river = Pr. *ribiera* bank, river, Sp. *ribera*, It. *riviera* bank (spec. of the Genoese coast as far as Nice, adopted in Eng. use as **Riviera** riviɛə·rə) :– Rom. **rīpāria*, fem. used sb. (sc. *terra* land) of *rīpārius* RIPARIAN. Hence **ri·ver**INE[1] situated on or pert. to a river; contemp. with **ri·verain** -ein – F. *rive-rain* f. *rivière*. XIX.

rivet ri·vit small nail or bolt. XIV. – OF. *rivet*, f. *river* fix, clinch, of unkn. origin; for the suffix cf. *foret* drill, f. *forer* bore. Hence vb. XIV.

rivière ri·vieəɹ necklace of gems. XIX. F., RIVER.

rivulet ri·vjŭlet small stream. XVI (Harrison) alt. of earlier synon. †*riveret* – F. dim. of *rivière* RIVER, perh. after It. *rivoletto*, dim. of *rivolo*, dim. of *rivo* :– L. *rīvus* stream; see -LET.

rix-dollar ri·ksdɔ:ləɹ (hist.) silver coin and money of account current XVI–XIX in various Eur. countries, XVI. – Du. †*rijksdaler*, f. g. of *rijk* (see RICH)+*daler* DOLLAR.

roach routʃ small freshwater fish, Leuciscus rutilus. XIV. – OF. *roche*, with vars. *roce*, *roque*, of unkn. origin.

road roud A. †riding; †RAID (cf. INROAD) OE.; B. sheltered water where ships may ride XIV; C. line of communication between places (also *roadway*) XVI (Sh.); (gen.) way, course XVI (Sh.). OE. *rād* = O.Fris. *rēd*, MDu. *rēd*, ON. *reið*, rel. to *rīdan* RIDE. Continental words for sense B have divergent forms, e.g. MDu. *rēde*, MLG., G. *reede*. Sense C may be of local origin and generalized from such comps. as OE. *hwēolrād* wheel-track, *strēamrād* course of stream.

roam roum wander, rove. XIII. perh. :– ME. *rāmen* (as in the obscure *rameden* of Laȝ. 7854) with which Gower's rhyming of *rome* with *home* (OE. *hām*) would agree, but the origin remains unknown.

roan[1] roun (of horses, etc.) having a coat in which the prevailing colour is intermingled with another. XVI. – OF. *roan* (mod. *rouan*) = Pr. *rouent*, It., Sp. *roano*, of unkn. origin.

roan[2] roun soft flexible leather used in bookbinding. XIX. Of unkn. origin; identity with †*roan skin* (*royne* XV, *rone* XVI) is not established because of the date.

roar rɔ̄əɹ utter full deep or hoarse prolonged cry OE.; make a loud noise or din XIV (R. Mannyng). OE. *rārian*, corr. to MLG. *rāren*, *rēren*, MDu. *reeren*, OHG. *rēren* (G. *röhren*); WGerm., of imit. origin. Hence sb. XIV (Gower); there is one instance of OE. *ġerār*. ¶ For *roar* (ME. *roore*) confusion, tumult cf. UPROAR.

roast roust cook by exposure to an open fire. XIII (RGlouc.). – OF. *rostir* (mod. *rôtir*), corr. to Pr. *raustir*, Cat. *rostir*, It. *arrostire* – WGerm. **raustjan*, whence Du. *roosten*, OHG. *rōsten* (G. *rösten*), f. *rōst*, *rōsta* gridiron, grill, *rōstpfanna* frying-pan; pp. *roast* (ME. *roste*) survives in *roast beef* XVII (whence F. *rosbif*, earlier †*rot de bif*, Russ. *róstbif*, etc.), *roast meat* XVI.

rob rɔb deprive (one) of by force; plunder, pillage. XIII (AncrR.). – OF. *rob(b)er* = Pr. *raubar*, Sp. *robar*, Pg. *roubar*, It. *rubare*, of Germ. origin; f. base **raub-*, repr. also by REAVE; cf. ROBE. So **ro·bb**ER[2], **ro·bb**ERY. XII. – AN. *rob(b)ere*, *-erie*.

roband rou·bənd (naut.) rope for attaching head of sail to its yard. XIII (Sandahl). ME. *roband*, *-end*, (also *ropbend* XIII, *robyn* XV), – LDu. *raband* (whence Sc. *raband* XVI), f. *ra* (pron. *rå*) sailyard + *band* BAND[1].

robe roub long outer garment. XIII (S. Eng. Leg.). – (O)F. *robe* = Pr. *rauba*, Cat., It. *roba*, (erratically Sp. *ropa*, Pg. *roupa*) :– Rom. **rauba*, of Germ. origin, as ROB, the orig. sense being 'booty', (hence) clothes, regarded as spoil. Hence vb. XIV.

robin rɔ·bin small red-breasted bird, Erithacus rubecula XVI; short for *r. redbreast* XV, both being Sc. in their earliest use. – OF. *Robin*, familiar var. of the masculine name *Robert* (used XV for 'robin'); also *robinet* (XV to mod. dial.). In *round r.* (XVIII) the adj. describes the circular unpunctuated list of names on the document; the reference of the sb. is unkn.

robot rou·bɔt, rɔ·bɔt mechanism doing the work of a man, automaton. XX. – G. *robot*, Czech *robota* compulsory service, rel. to G. *arbeit* work, OE. *earfoþ* difficulty, hardship.

Rob Roy rɔb roi· name (meaning 'Red Robert') of a famous Highland freebooter (1671–1734) given by John Macgregor (1825–92) to a canoe in which he made extensive voyages; (hence) kind of canoe for one person propelled with a double-bladed paddle XIX.

robust roubʌ·st strong and hardy. XVI. – (O)F. *robuste* or L. *rōbustus* oaken, firm and hard, solid, f. *rōbus*, older form of *rōbur* oak, strength :– **reudhos*, f. IE. **reudh-* RED. Hence **robu·st**IOUS; freq. in XVII, becoming rare in XVIII, when Johnson described it as 'now only used in low language, and in a sense of contempt'; revived XIX.

roc rɔk bird of Eastern legend, of enormous size and strength. XVI. In early use in *roche*, *roque*, *ruc*, *ruch* – Sp. †*rocho*, Pg. *roco*, It. †*roche*, Sp., Pg., It. *ruc* – Arab. *rokh*, *rukh(kh)*.

rochet rɔ·tʃit linen vestment of the surplice kind worn by bishops, etc.; (dial.) smock frock. XIV. – (O)F. *rochet*, var. of *roquet* (whence ME. *roket* XIII), corr. to It. *rocc(h)etto*, medL. *rochetum*, etc., dim. f. Germ. base found in OE. *rocc*, OS., (M)Du. *rok*, OHG. *roch* (G. *rock*) coat, ON. *rokkr* (cf. OIr. *rucht* tunic); see -ET.

rock[1] rɔk move from side to side on a pivot. Late OE. *roccian*, prob. f. Germ. **rukk-* move, remove (of which no outside cogns. are known), repr. also by MLG., MDu. *rukken*, *rocken* (Du. *rukken* tug, jerk, snatch), OHG. *rucchan* (G. *rücken* move, push), ON. *rykkja* pull, tug.

rock[2] rɔk solid part of the earth's crust, mass of this. XIV. – OF. *ro(c)que*, var. of (O)F. *roche* (adopted in Eng. XIII and surviving dial.) = Pr., Sp. *roca*, It. *rocca*, *roccia*, medL. *rocca*, *rocha*; of unkn. origin. ¶ Late OE. *stānrocc* 'stone-rock' contains an early adoption of the medL. (Rom.) word. Hence **ro·ck**Y[1]. XV.

rock[3] rɔk (arch., dial.) distaff. XIV. – MLG. *rocken*, MDu. *rocke* (Du. *rok*, *rokken*) or ON. *rokkr* = OHG. *rocco* (G. *rocken*) :– Germ. **rukkon*, of unkn. origin, whence Rom. **rukka*, **rokka* (in Sp. *rueca*, Pg. *roca*, It. *rocca*).

rocket[1] rɔ·kit cruciferous annual, Eruca sativa. XVI. – F. *roquette* (XVI) – It. *rochetta*, var. of *ruchetta* (whence also Sp.

ruqueta), dim. of *ruca* :- L. *ērūca* caterpillar, plant with downy stems.

rocket[2] rɔ·kit cylindrical paper or metal case designed to be projected on ignition of explosive contents. XVII. – (O)F. *roquette* – It. *rocchetto*, dim. of *rocca* ROCK[3]; so called from the cylindrical form. Hence vb. XIX.

rococo rŏkou·kou †old-fashioned; characterized by conventional shell-and-scroll-work, as of the time of Louis XIV and XV of France. XIX. – F. *rococo*, fanciful alt. of *rocaille* pebble- or shell-work, f. *roc* ROCK[2].

rod rɔd straight slender wand XII; stick for measuring with; measure of length and of area XV. Late OE. *rodd*, synon. with Continental forms cited s.v. ROOD, but formally distinct; prob. rel. to ON. *rudda* club (Norw. dial. *rudda*, *rydda* large twig or stick, *rodda* stake).

rodent rou·dənt gnawing, belonging to the Rodentia. XIX. – L. *rōdent-*, *-ēns*, prp. of *rōdere* gnaw (cf. CORRODE, ERODE), rel. to Skr. *rádati* scratch, dig; see -ENT.

rodeo roudei·ou, rou·diou round-up of cattle XIX; exhibition of lassooing, etc. XX. – Sp. *rodeo*, f. *rodear* go round, based on L. *rotāre* ROTATE.

rodomontade rɔdŏmɔntei·d vainglorious or extravagant boast. XVII. – F. *rodomontade* – It. †*rodomontada*, *-ata*, f. F. *rodomont*, It. *-monte* bragger, boaster, appellative use of *Rodomonte* name (lit. 'roll-mountain') of a boastful Saracen leader in Boiardo's 'Orlando Innamorato' and Ariosto's 'Orlando Furioso'. Earlier †*rodomontada*, *-ado* (XVI), with hispaniolized ending; see -ADO. (Also mis-spelt *rhodo-*.)

roe[1] rou small species of deer. OE. *rā*, earlier *rāa*, *rāha* (also *rāhdēor* roe-deer) = OS., OHG. *rēho* (Du. *ree*, G. *reh*), ON. *rá* :- CGerm. (exc. Goth.) **raiχ-* perh. rel. to Lith. and OIr. words meaning 'variegated, spotted'. ¶ OE. had also *rǣġe* hind, corr. to OHG. *rēia*.

roe[2] rou milt or spawn of a fish. XV. Late ME. *row(e)*, *rough*, *roof* :- **roȝe* – MLG., MDu. *roge* = OHG. *rogo* (MHG. *roge*); contemp. forms are dial. *rown* (XV, Promp. Parv.), later *roan* (XVII) – MLG. *rogen* or ON. *hrogn* (Da. *rogn*) = OHG. *rogan* (G. *rogen*), and dial. *rawn* (XV, Catholicon Anglicum), also of Scand. origin (cf. Da. *ravn*), as is likewise F. *rogue*. The relation of the various forms and their ult. origin are obscure.

rogation rougei·ʃən A. (pl.) litanies used on the Monday, Tuesday, and Wednesday before Ascension Day (*R. Days*) XIV; B. (Roman hist.) submission by consuls, etc. of a proposed law to the people XV. – L. *rogātiō(n-)*, in medL. pl. (in sense A) *Rogātiōnēs*, whence Rom. forms, f. *rogāre* ask, orig. stretch towards, rel. to *regere* direct; see RIGHT, -ATION. ¶ From the same base are *abrogate*, *arrogance*, *derogate*, *prorogue*, *surrogate*.

rogue roug one of a class of vagrants XVI (Awdelay, Harman); unprincipled man; mischievous person XVI; (rendering Cingalese *hora*, *sora* :- Skr. *chōra* thief) savage elephant living apart from the herd XIX. orig. one of the numerous canting words that are recorded from mid-XVI; perh. based on †*roger* begging vagabond pretending to be a poor scholar from Oxford or Cambridge (XVI, Copland), prob. f. L. *rogāre* ask, beg (see prec.)+-ER[1]. Hence **ro·gu**ERY. XVI (Sh.). **ro·gu**ISH[1]. XVI.

roil see RILE.

roister roi·stəɹ swaggerer, reveller. XVI. – (O)F. *rustre* ruffian, alt. of *ruste* :- L. *rusticus* RUSTIC; for the repr. of F. ü by Eng. oi cf. †*moil* MULE, †*ois* USE, RECOIL.

Roland rou·lənd legendary nephew of Charlemagne celebrated in the 'Chanson de Roland' and other romances, often with his comrade Oliver; hence phr. (*give*) *a R. for an Oliver*, give as good as one gets, or tit for tat. XVII.

rôle, role roul part or character as in a play. XVII (*rowle*, *roll*). – F. †*roule*, †*rolle*, *rôle* ROLL[1], orig. the 'roll' containing an actor's part.

roll[1] roul piece of parchment, etc. made into cylindrical form XIII (AncrR.); such a piece inscribed with formal records, register XIV (PPl., Ch.); quantity of material, mechanical object in cylindrical form, etc. XVI. – OF. *rolle*, *roulle* (mod. *rôle*; see prec.) = Pr. *role*, *rolle*, *rocle*, *roll*, *roller*, Sp. *rolde* group of persons, It. *rocchio* cylindrical piece of wood or stone :- L. *rotulu-s* (whence also Sp., Pg. *rotulo* list, bill, It. *rotolo*, *ruotolo* roll of parchment, cloth, etc.), var. of *rotula*, dim. of *rota* wheel (ROTA). Hence **ro·ll**-CALL XIX, earlier *ro·ll-ca·lling* list XVIII.

roll[2] roul turn or cause to turn over and over as on an axis or in a socket XIV; coil or cause to coil into a mass; make a reverberating noise XVI. – OF. *rol(l)er*, (also mod.) *rouler*, the source of (M)HG. *rollen* = Pr. *rolar* (whence Sp. *rollar*, Pg. *rolar*, It. *rullare*) :- Rom. **rotulāre* (in AL. XII), f. L. *rotulus* ROLL[1]. Hence **roll** sb.[2] act of rolling. XVII. **roll**ER[1] rou·ləɹ cylindrical object, as of wood, metal, etc. XV.

roller[2] rou·ləɹ crow-like bird with brilliant plumage, Coracius garrulus. XVII. – G. *roller*, f. *rollen* ROLL[2]; known XVII as *Rollar Argentoratensis* and *Strasburg Roller*; so called from its cry (?).

rollick rɔ·lik romp; esp. in prp. *rollicking* boisterously sportive. XIX (Scott). prob. of dial. origin; perh. blending of the vbs. *romp* and *frolic*.

rollock var. of ROWLOCK.

roly-poly rou·li pou·li †worthless fellow XVII (*rowle powle, rowly powly*); name of various games involving the rolling of a ball XVIII; pudding in which a sheet of paste covered with jam, etc. is rolled on itself XIX. Fanciful formation on ROLL; the origin of the first sense is obscure; the second el. may contain POLL[1] (head).

rom rɔm male gipsy. XIX (Borrow). – Romany *rom* man, husband, in various gipsy langs. of the Middle East found as *dom, dōm, dum, lom* – Skr. *ḍoma, ḍomba* minstrel-dancer of low caste. So **Romany** rɔ·məni gipsy, gipsy language. XIX (Vaux, 1812). – Gipsy *Romani*, pl. and fem. of *Romano* adj., f. *Rom.*

Romaic roumei·ik pert. to the vernacular language of modern Greece. XIX. – Gr. *Rōmaikós*, f. *Rṓmē*, used spec. of the Eastern Empire.

Roman rou·mən pert. to (native or inhabitant of) ancient Rome XIII (RGlouc., Cursor M.); pert. to (adherent of) the Roman Catholic Church; (typogr.) based on the characteristic form of the ancient Roman inscriptions XVI. ME. *Romein, -ain* – (O)F. *Romain* – L. *Rōmānus*, f. *Rōma* Rome, capital of Italy; later assim. in sp. to L.; preceded by OE. *Romane, -an* sb. pl.; see -AN. **R. Catholic** (1605), based on the official title of the Roman Church, Ecclesia *Romana Catholica* et Apostolica, 'Roman Catholic and Apostolic Church'.

romance roumæ·ns tale in verse embodying adventure, esp. of mediæval legend XIII (Havelok); fictitious narrative in prose; (after Sp. and F. *romance*) Spanish historical ballad XVII. ME. *roma(u)nz, -a(u)ns* – OF. *romanz, -ans*, fem. *romance* = Pr. *romans* (whence Sp., Pg. *romance*, It. *romanzo*) the vernacular tongue (as dist. from literary Latin), work composed in this :– popL. **rōmānice* 'in the Romanic tongue', adv. of L. *Rōmānicus*, f. *Rōmānus* ROMAN + *-icus* -IC. So **roma·nce** vb. (XIV), XVII. – OF. *romancier*. **roma·nc**ER[2] (XIV), XVII. – OF. *romanceor, -cier.*

Romance roumæ·ns vernacular language of France, later applied to the related tongues. XIV (R. Mannyng). – OF. *romanz*, fem. adj. *-ance* expressed in the vernacular (see prec.), whence medL. *romancium, -ia.*

Romanesque roumənе·sk †(of a language) Romance XVIII; (archit.) pert. to building of Romanized style XIX. – F. *romanesque*, f. *roman* ROMANCE; see -ESQUE.

Romanic roumæ·nik Romance, Romance-speaking. XVIII. – L. *Rōmānicus*, f. *Rōmānus* ROMAN + *-icus* -IC.

Ro·manIST Roman Catholic. XVI (Coverdale). – G. *Romanist* (Luther) or modL. *Romanista* (Luther, 1520). So **Ro·maniz**E render Roman or Roman Catholic. XVII. **Romano-** roumei·nou comb. form (see -O-) of L. *Rōmānus* ROMAN XVII.

Romansh roumæ·nʃ language of Latin origin spoken in the Grisons (East Switzerland). XVII. – native name *Rum-, Roman(t)sch* :– Rom. **Rōmānicē* ROMANCE. Cf. RHÆTO-. See LADIN.

romant roumæ·nt, **romaunt** roumɔ̄·nt (arch.) romance. XVI. – OF. *roma(u)nt*, (later *roman*), deduced (as if an obl. case) from *roma(u)nz* ROMANCE. Hence or – modL. *romanticus* **romant**IC roumæ·ntik of the nature of or suggestive of romances or their imaginative or extravagant qualities. XVII (1650, T. Bayly 'Herba Parietis'). f. *romant*, ROMAUNT (medL. *romantium, -tia*); whence F. *romantique* (1694), G. *romantisch* (1698); renewed from F. and G. in early XIX.

Romany rɔ·məni gipsy; language of the gipsies. XIX. – Romany *Romani* pl. of *Romano*, f. *rom* (see ROM).

romic rou·mik system of phonetic writing 'based on the original Roman values of the letters' (1877, H. Sweet). f. ROMAN + -IC.

Romish rou·miʃ Roman Catholic (chiefly in hostile use). XVI. f. *Rome* (seat of the papal see) + -ISH[1], prob. after Du. *Roomsch*, G. *Römisch*. So †**Ro·m**IST Romanist. XVI.

romp rɔmp frolic boisterously. XVIII. perh. alt. of RAMP with modification of sense. So sb. XVIII.

rondeau rɔ·ndou, rɔ̃do poem with two rhymes throughout and the opening words used twice as a refrain. XVI (rare before late XVII, Dryden). – (O)F. *rondeau*, later form of *rondel* (f. *rond* ROUND), whence **rond**EL[2] rɔ·ndəl. XIV (Gower).

rondo rɔ·ndou (mus.) piece in which a return is continually made to the principal subject. XVIII. – It. *rondo* – F. *rondeau* (see prec.).

Röntgen rə̄·ntjən name of the German scientist Conrad W. *Röntgen*, applied to certain rays. XIX.

rood rūd A. cross, spec. that on which Jesus Christ suffered (*Holy Rood*); crucifix (as on a rood loft or screen); B. (now local) rod, pole, or perch OE.; superficial measure, 40 square poles. XV. In sense A, OE. *rōd* = OFris. *rōd(e)*, OS. *rōda*, OIcel. *róða, -i* (perh. from OE.); in the sense of ROD (only in OE. *seglrōd* sailyard), the Continental forms are OS. *rōda*, MDu. *ro(o)de* (also mod. *roede*), OHG. *ruota* (G. *rute*).

roof rūf (pl. *roofs, rooves*) upper covering of a building; palate of the mouth. OE. *hrōf* = OFris. *hrōf*, (M)LG. *rōf*, MDu. *roof* (Du. *roef* cabin, coffin lid), ON. *hróf* boat shed, of which no certain cogns. are known.

rook[1] ruk black harsh-voiced bird of the crow kind. OE. *hrōc* = (M)LG. *rōk*, MDu. *roec* (Du. *roek*), OHG. *hruoch*, ON. *hrókr* :– Germ. **χrōkaz* (whence F. *freux*), prob. of imit. origin. In the sense 'cheat, swindler, sharper', with corr. vb., a gaming sl. use of late XVI. Hence **roo·kERY**. XVIII.

rook[2] ruk piece at chess also called castle. XIV (R. Mannyng). ME. *rok, roke* – OF. *roc(k), rok*, corr. to Sp., Pg. *roque*, It. *rocco*, and various Germ. forms of the same ult. origin, Arab.-Pers. *rukh*, of uncertain orig. meaning.

room rūm space OE.; †place XIV; chamber in a building XV. OE. *rūm* = OFris., OS., OHG., ON., Goth. *rūm* (Du. *ruim*, G. *raum*, Icel., etc. *rum*), sb. use of CGerm. adj. ***rūmaz* spacious (OE. *rūm*, etc.), f. ***ru-*, which has been connected with L. *rū-s, rū-ris* country. For the vocalism cf. *cooper, droop*, etc. Hence (dial.) **roomTH**[1] rūmþ space. XVI. **roo·mY**[1]. XVII; cf. MLG. *rūmich*, G. *räumig*.

roost rūst perch for fowls. OE. *hrōst* = MDu., Du. *roest* and perh. OS. *hrōst* spars of a roof; of unkn. origin. Hence vb. XVI.

root[1] rūt part of a plant below the earth's surface OE.; source, basis XIV; (math., philol.) XVI. Late OE. *rōt* – ON. *rót* :- Scand. ***wrōt-*, obscurely rel. to L. *rādix* (cf. RADISH), *rāmus* branch, and OE. *wyrt* (see WORT[1]). Hence **root** vb. A. in pp. firmly fixed XIII; B. furnish with roots XIV. C. uproot, eradicate XIV.

root[2] rūt turn over (soil) with the snout. XIV. Later var. of *wroot*, OE. *wrōtan* = (M)LG. *wrōten*, (M)Du. *wroeten*, OHG. *ruozzen*, ON. *róta* (partly the immed. source), rel. to OE. *wrōt*, LG. *wrōte* snout, G. (with instr. suffix) *rüssel* snout, and perh. ult. to L. *rōdere* gnaw (cf. RODENT, ROSTRUM).

rope roup length of strong line or cordage. OE. *rāp* = OFris. *rāp*, (M)LG. *rēp*, (M)Du. *reep*, (O)HG. *reif*, ON. *reip*, Goth. *raip* (in *skaudaraip* shoe-thong) :- CGerm. ***raipaz* (adopted in Finn. as *raippa* rod, twig). ¶ The second el. of STIRRUP.

roquefort rɔ·kfɔ̄ɹ cheese made at *Roquefort*, village in S.W. France. XIX.

roquelaure rɔ·kəlɔ̄əɹ (hist.) man's cloak reaching to the knee. XVIII. – F., f. name of Antoine-Gaston, duc de *Roquelaure* (1656–1738), marshal of France.

roquet rou·ki in croquet, hitting another player's ball with one's own. XIX. presumably arbitrary alt. of CROQUET.

rorqual rɔ̄·ɹkwɔ̄l species of whale. XIX. – F. *rorqual* (Cuvier) – Norw. *røyrkval* :- *reyðarhvalr*, f. *reyðr* (specific name) + *hvalr* WHALE.

rosACEOUS rouzei·ʃəs resembling the roses. XVIII. – L.

rosary rou·zəri base coin current in England in the 13th century XIV (Trevisa); rose-garden XV; set of devotions, spec. that of the B.V.M. ('Our Lady's psalter'), set of beads for its recitation XV. – L. *rosārium* rose-garden, AL. *rosārius* (coin), sc. *nummus* *penny*, sb. uses of n. and m. of adj. f. *rosa* ROSE; see -ARY.

rose rouz plant and flower of the genus Rosa OE.; rose-shaped figure XIV. OE. *rōse*, corr. to MDu. *rōse* (Du. *roos*), OHG. *rōsa* (G. *rose*), ON. *rósa*; CGerm. (exc. Gothic) – L. *rosa* (whence F. *rose*, It., Sp. *rosa*), rel. obscurely to synon. Gr. *rhódon* (cf. RHODODENDRON); reinforced in ME. from (O)F. *rose*. Hence **rosY**[1] rou·zi XIV. (Ch.; rare before XVI); cf. MDu. *rosich*, MHG. *rōsic* (Du., G. *rosig*). So **rosETTE** rouze·t decoration made in the form of a rose. XVIII. – (O)F. *rosette*.

rosemary rou·zməri evergreen shrub, Rosmarinus officinalis. XV. alt., by assoc. with ROSE and MARY, of †*rosmarine* (XIV), either immed. – L. *rōs marīnus*, late L. *rōsmarīnum*, or through (i) OF. *rosmarin* (mod. *romarin*), corr. to Pr. *romari(n)*, It. *rosmarino*, or (ii) MDu. *rosemarine* (Du. *ros(e)marijn*), corr. to MHG. *rosen marin* (G. *rosmarin*), etc. The L. name, which appears also as *marīnus rōs, rōs maris*, and simply *rōs*, means 'sea-dew'.

Rosicrucian rouzikrū·ʃən member of a society reputed to have been founded in 1484 by Christian *Rosenkranz*, the modL. tr. of which, viz. *rosa crucis* or *crux* i.e. 'rose (of the) cross' (cf. *rosy cross* XVII, their alleged emblem), is the basis of the name XVII; see -IAN.

rosin see RESIN.

roster rou·stəɹ, rɔ·stəɹ list or plan exhibiting an order of rotation. XVIII. – Du. *rooster* (i) grating, gridiron, (ii) table, list (from the appearance of a paper ruled with parallel lines), f. *roosten* ROAST; see -ER[1].

rostrum rɔ·strəm (pl. *rostra*) platform for public speakers in ancient Rome, adorned with beaks of captured ships XVI; beak of a galley XVII; platform, stage, pulpit XVIII. – L. *rōstrum* beak, snout, etc. (as above), f. *rōdere* gnaw (see RODENT) + instr. suffix ***-trom.***

rot rɔt undergo decay; trans. XIV (Ch., Wyclif); in imprecations (cf. RAT[2], DRAT) XVI (Sh.). OE. *rotian* = OFris. *rotia*, OS. *rotōn*, MDu. *roten* (also mod. *rotten*, whence G. *ver|rotten*), OHG. *rōzzēn*, rel. to MLG. *rōten*, MHG. *rœzen*; cf. ROTTEN. Hence sb. (but perh. – Scand.) XIII (Cursor M.).

rota rou·tə political club founded in 1659 by J. Harrington, which advocated rotation in the offices of government; rotation, routine; (R.C.Ch.) supreme court for all causes XVII; roster XIX. – L. *rota* wheel, f. widespread IE. base (not repr. in OE.) meaning 'wheel', 'chariot' (cf. G. *rad*). So **ro·tARY** (of motion) circular; operating by rotation. XVIII – medL. *rotārius*. **rotate** routei·t move in a circular track, etc. XIX. f. *rotāt-*, pp. stem of L. *rotāre* turn round, whirl about, revolve. **rotA·TION**. XVI. – L.; so F. *rotation*. Cf. ROTUND, ROUND, ROLL[1], CONTROL.

rote[1] rout (hist.) stringed instrument of the violin class. XIII (Cursor M.). – OF. *rote* = Pr. *rota*; cf. MLG., MDu. *rot(t)e*, OHG. *rot(t)a*; the Rom. and Germ. words are identical with the Celtic word repr. in CROWD[2].

rote[2] rout †custom, habit; regular procedure, routine, esp. in *by rote*. XIV. Of unkn. origin.

rotograph rou·təgràf photographic print of a page, etc. containing a reversed image (proprietary name XIX), f. *roto-*, used as comb. form of L. *rota* wheel + -GRAPH.

rotten rɔ·tn decomposed, putrid XIII; fig. corrupt XIV. – ON. *rotinn*, which has the form of a pp. of the base **raut-* **reut-* **rut-*, repr. by ROT; see -EN[6].

rotund routʌ·nd round, rounded XVIII; sonorous (cf. OROTUND) XIX. – L. *rotundus*, f. *rotāre* ROTATE (cf. *secundus* favourable, f. *sequī* follow). So **rotu·nda,** also †*rotundo*, round-shaped building. XVII (Evelyn). alt. (after L. *rotundus*) of *rotonda* (XVII) – It. *rotonda*, sb. use (sc. *camera*) of fem. of *rotondo* ROUND. **rotu·nd**ITY. XVI. – F. or L.

rouble rū·bl Russian monetary unit. XVI. Earliest forms *rubbel*, *robel*, *ruble*, later *rouble* (after F.). – Russ. *rubl'*, related by some to RUPEE.

roué rū·ei debauchee, rake. XVIII. F., pp. of *rouer* break on the wheel, f. *roue* wheel :– L. *rota* (see ROTA); applied joc. (it is said) by Philip, Duke of Orleans, regent of France (1715–23), to his profligate companions because they were worthy of such punishment.

rouge rūʒ A. *R. Croix* and *R. Dragon*, two pursuivants of the English College of Arms, so called from their badges XV; B. red powder used as a cosmetic XVIII. – (O)F. *rouge* :– L. *rubeu-s* RED. Hence **rouge** vb. XVIII.

rough rʌf not even or smooth OE.; turbulent, violent XIII; harsh, sharp XIV. OE. *rūh* = MLG., MDu. *rūch*, *rū* (Du. *ruig*, *ruw*), OHG. *rūh* (G. *rauh*) :– WGerm. **rūχ(w)az*, rel. to Lith. *rùkti* be wrinkled, *rauka* wrinkle, Skr. *rūkṣás* rough. Hence **rou·gh**EN[5]. XVI. **rou·gh**CAST. XVI. f. *cast* †cover by casting mortar on.

roulette rule·t game of chance played on a table with a revolving centre. XVIII. – F. *roulette*, f. *rouelle*, dim. of *roue* wheel :– L. *rota*; see ROTATION, -ETTE.

Ro(u)manian see **Rumanian**.

round[1] raund A. of the form of a ball XIII (RGlouc.). B. full, complete, plain, straightforward. C. vigorous, severe XIV; plain, straightforward XVI. ME. *rond*, *round* – OF. *rond-*, *round-*, inflexional stem of *ront*, *roont*, earlier *reont* (mod. *rond*) = Pr. *redon*, Sp. *redondo*, It. †*ritondo*, Rum. *rătund* :– Rom. **retundus*, for L. *rotundus* ROTUND. Hence sb. XIV, vb. XIV, adv. XIII; prep., perh. aphetic of AROUND XVII (Sh.).

¶ The F. word has been adopted into most of the Germ. langs.; e.g. MDu. *ront* (Du. *rond*, MHG. *runt* (G. *rund*), (M)Sw. *rund*.

round[2] raund (arch.) whisper. OE. *rūnian*, ME. *rune*, *roune* = OS. *rūnon*, MLG., MDu. *rūnen*, OHG. *rūnēn*, OSw. *runa*; f. OE. *rūn*, ME. *run*, *roun* dark saying, counsel, runic letter, RUNE. For the parasitic *d* cf. BOUND[2], SOUND[2].

roundel rau·ndəl circle, circular object XIII (S. Eng. Leg.); rondeau XIV (Ch.). – OF. *rondel* or *-elle*, f. *rond* ROUND; see -EL[2]; cf. It. *rondello*, *-ella*; adopted freely into Germ. langs., (M)Du. *rondeel*, G., Sw. *rundel*, etc. Cf. RONDEAU, RONDO.

roundelay rau·ndəlei short song with a refrain. XVI. – (O)F. *rondelet* (whence ME. *roundelet*) with ending assim. to VIRELAY or LAY.

roup rūp disease of poultry. XVI (Turberville). Of unkn. origin.

rouse[1] rauz refl. and intr. (of a hawk) shake the feathers XV (Bk. St. Albans); start (game); cause to rise from slumber, etc. XVI. orig. techn. term of hawking and hunting, of unkn. origin. Cf. AROUSE.

rouse[2] rauz (arch.) bumper of liquor, carousal. XVII (Sh.), prob. aphetic of CAROUSE, as in such phr. as *take*, *drink*, *make carouse* being apprehended as *drink*, etc. *a rouse*. But cf. Da. *drikke en rus* get drunk, Du. *roes*, G. *rausch* drunkenness.

rout[1] raut company, troop; disorderly company XIII; †*the r.*, the common herd XIV; riot, uproar XV; fashionable gathering XVIII. ME. *rute*, *route* – AN. *rute* (cf. AL. *ruta*), OF. *route* = Pr. *rota* :– Rom. **rupta*, sb. use (sc. *turba*, *turma* band, crowd) 'broken or fractional company' of fem. of pp. of L. *rumpere* break (see RUPTURE). Cf. next.

rout[2] raut disorderly retreat. XVI. – F. †*route* (in the sense of *déroute*), prob. – It. *rotta* breakage, discomfiture of an army :– Rom. **rupta*, noun of action (for L. *ruptiō*, *ruptūra*) f. *rupt-*, *rumpere* (see prec.). Hence **rout** vb. XVI.

route rūt, (in army use) raut way, course XIII (obs. in ME. in XV; readopted XVI); (mil.) order to march, marching orders XVIII. – OF. *rute*, (also mod.) *route* :– Rom. **rupta*, sb. use (sc. *via* way) of fem. of pp. of *rumpere* (see prec.).

routine rūtī·n regular or unvarying procedure. XVII (*rotine*). – F. *routine*, †*rotine*, f. *route* (see prec.).

rove rouv †A. shoot with arrows *at* a selected mark for finding the range XV; B. wander at random XVI. poss. southernized form of (dial.) *rave* stray (XIV), prob. of Scand. origin (cf. Icel. *ráfa*); sense B prob. due to infl. by ROVER.

rover rou·vəɹ sea-robber, pirate. XIV (Gower). – MLG., MDu. *rōver*, f. *rōven* rob, REAVE.

row[1] rou number of persons or things set in a line. ME. *raw, row* (XIII) points to OE. **rāw* (of doubtful authenticity), var. of *rǣw* (ME. *rew*) :- **rai(g)wa*, prob. obscurely rel. to MDu. *rīe* (Du. *rij*), MHG. *rīhe* (G. *reihe*) :- **reiχwan*, beside OHG. *rīga*, ON. *riga, rega* string :- **rigwa*; cf. Skr. *rēkhā́* stroke, line.

row[2] rou use oars OE.; trans. XIV. OE. *rōwan*, pt. *rēow* (weak inflexions appear XIII) = OFris. **rōia*, MLG. *rōjen* (Du. *roeijen*), MHG. *rüejen* steer (G. *rojen* is – LG.), ON. *róa*, f. Germ. **rō-* steer, belonging to the IE. series **erə- *rē- *rō*, repr. in Gr. *erétēs* rower, *eretmón* oar, *tri|ḗrēs* TRIREME, *triākónt|oros* 30-oared, L. *rēmus* oar, OIr. *ráme* oar, *ro|ráiset* have rowed, Lith. *ìrti* row, *ìrklas*, Skr. *aritā́* rower, *aritras* oar, and RUDDER.

row[3] rau violent commotion, noisy dispute. XVIII. Of sl. or base origin, acc. to Grose 1785 a Cambridge term; the source is unkn. (*towrow* intoxicated is recorded earlier); Todd, 1818, notes it as 'a very low expression'.

rowan rou·ən, Sc. rau·ən mountain ash, Pyrus Aucuparia. XVI (*rountree*). Of Scand. origin; cf. Norw. *rogn* and *raun*, Icel. *reynir*.

rowdy rau·di backwoodsman of a rough type; violent disorderly person. XIX; orig. Amer., but the source is unkn.

rowel rau·əl spur-wheel. XIV. – OF. *roel, roele* (mod. *rouelle* corr. to Pr. *rodella* knee-cap, Sp. *rodilla* knee, It. *rotella* little wheel. :- late L. *rotella*, dim. of *rota* wheel; see ROTATION, -EL[2], and cf. ROULETTE.

rowlock rʌ·lək, ro·l- device forming the fulcrum for the oar in rowing. XVIII. alt., by substitution of ROW[2] for the first syll., of *oarlock*, OE. *ārloc*, f. *ār* OAR + *loc* fastening, LOCK[2].

royal roi·əl pert. to a king or kings. XIV (Ch.). – OF. *roial* (mod. *royal*) :- L. *rēgālis* REGAL. So **roy·al**TY. XIV. (Ch.). – OF. *roialte* (mod. *royauté*); superseded somewhat earlier †*real(te)*, †*trial(te)*. **roy·al**IST. XVII; first in Charles I's reign, perh. modelled on F. *royaliste*.

rub rʌb subject a surface to friction with pressure, trans. and intr. XIV (PPl., Wycl. Bible, Maund.). perh. – LG. *rubben* (whence prob. Sw., Norw., Icel. *rubba*, Da. *rubbe*); ult. origin unkn. Hence **rub** sb. obstacle, produced as if by rubbing a surface (techn., at bowls) XVI; often fig. as in *there's the r.* **rubb**ER[1] rʌ·bəɹ rubbing implement XVI; piece of a substance used for this (short for *India(n) rubber*) XVIII. ¶ The synon. †*rodde*, †*rudde* (XIII–XV) is curiously similar.

rub-a-dub rʌ·bədʌb. XVIII. imit. of drumming sound.

rubber[2] rʌ·bəɹ set of (usu.) three games, as of bowls, whist, etc., the last of which is decisive for victory (†also spec. this game). XVI. The earliest exx. have (*play*) *a rubbers*. Perh. spec. application of RUBBER.

rubbish rʌ·biʃ waste or refuse material. XIV. Late ME. *robous, robys, -ishe, rubbes* – AN. *rubbous*, perh. for **robeus*, pl. of **robel* RUBBLE; assim. to *-ish* and *-idge* (XVIII).

rubble rʌ·bl waste fragments of stone, esp. from demolished buildings XIV; pieces of undressed stone XVI. Late ME *robyl, rubel*, perh. – AN. **robel*, f. OF. *robe* spoils (see ROBE); cf. -EL[1], -LE[1].

rubicund rū·bikənd †inclined to redness XVI (*rubico(u)nd*, Hawes); of ruddy complexion XVII. – F. *rubicond* or L. *rubicundus*, f. *rubēre* be RED.

rubidium rubi·diəm (min.) mineral related to cæsium, lithium, etc. XIX. f. L. *rubidus*, f. *rub-* of *ruber* RED; in allusion to the two red lines in its spectrum; see -IUM.

rubric rū·brik A. †red earth, ruddle XV (Promp. Parv.); B. direction (in red) for the conduct of divine service XIV; heading of a division of a book, etc. XV. Rare before XVII, *rubriche, -ishe* being the usual form XIV–XVI (Ch., Lydg., Caxton). – OF. *rubriche, -ice* (XIII), beside *rubrique*, or its source L. *rŭbrīca* red earth, title of a law, law itself (written with red ochre), sb. use (sc. *terra* earth) of adj. f. *ruber* RED.

ruby rū·bi red precious stone. XIV. – OF. *rubi* (mod. *rubis*), corr. to Pr. *robi*, Sp. *rubi(n)*, Pg. *rubi(m)* – medL. *rubīnu-s*, sb. use (sc. *lapis* stone) of adj. f. base of L. *rubeus, ruber* RED.

ruche rūʃ frill of light material. XIX. – F. *ruche* beehive, and (with allusion to the plaits of a straw hive) frill. – (O)F. *ruche* = Pr. *rusca*, etc. :- medL. *rūsca* bark of tree, of Celtic origin.

ruck[1] rʌk heap, stack, pile XIII (AncrR.); multitude, throng XVI; undistinguished crowd XIX. Of unkn. origin, but perh. Scand. (cf. Norw. synon. *ruka*).

ruck[2] rʌk crease, fold. XVIII (presumably of much earlier occurrence). – ON. *hrukka* (Norw. *hrukka*) :- **hrunka*, rel. to Norw. *rukla, rukka*, MSw. *rynkia* (cf. ME. and dial. *runkle*).

rucksack rʌ·ksæk, ru·k- knapsack. XIX. – G. *rucksack*, f. dial. *rucken* (= *rücken* back, RIDGE) + *sack* SACK[1].

ruction rʌ·kʃən (colloq.) disturbance, disorderly action (esp. pl.). XVIII (rare before XIX). perh. joc. based on L. *ructus* belching

rudder rʌ·dəɹ †steering oar OE.; steering-gear mounted in a boat or ship XIV (R. Mannyng). OE. *roþer* = OFris. *rōther*, MLG. (whence Norw., Da. *ror*), MDu. *rōder* (Du. *roer*), OHG. *ruodar* (G. *ruder*) :- WGerm. **rōþra-* (ON. *róðr* denotes the act of rowing), rel. to ROW[2].

ruddle rʌ·dl red ochre. XVI. f. base of RUDDY; see -LE[1], and cf. contemp. RADDLE, and *reddle* (XVIII).

ruddock rʌ·dək (dial.) redbreast, robin. OE. *rudduc*, rel. to RUDDY; see -OCK.

ruddy rʌ·di red, reddish, orig. of the face. Late OE. *rudiġ*, f. base of *rudu* red colour, redness, rel. to *rēad, rēod*, RED; see -Y[1].

rude rūd in various transf. and fig. senses of 'rough'. XIV (Ch.). – (O)F. *rude* – L. *rudis* unwrought, unformed, uncultivated, uncultured, unpolished, orig. techn. term of handicraft, rel. to *rūdus* rubble. Cf. next and ERUDITE.

rudiment rū·dimənt (pl.) first principles or elements. XVI. – F. *rudiment* or L. *rudīmentum* (Livy, of the early experience of military service), f. *rudis* RUDE, after *elementum* element. Hence **rudime·ntAL**[1]. XVI; now superseded by **rudime·ntARY**. XIX, after F. *rudimentaire*.

rue[1] rū (arch. exc. as surviving in **rue·FUL**[1] XIII) sorrow, regret OE; compassion XIII. OE. *hrēow* = MLG., MDu. *rouwe*, Du. *rouw*, OHG. *(h)riuwa* (G. *reue*), rel. to next.

rue[2] rū affect with contrition or sorrow OE.; affect with pity XII; repent of XII. OE. *hrēowan* (pt. *hrēow*) = OFris. *hriōwa*, OS. *hreuwan* (Du. *rouwen*), OHG. *(h)riuwan* (G. *reuen*); Germ. str. vb. (not in Goth.; cf. ON. *hryggja, hryggva* distress, grieve) of which no cogns. are known. See RUTH.

rue[3] rū shrub of the genus Ruta. (XIV; *ruwe* Wycl. Bible). – (O)F. *rue* = Pr., Sp. *ruda*, It. *ruta*, Rum. *rută* :- L. *rūta* – Gr. *rhūtḗ*, orig. a Peloponnesian word.

ruelle *rüɛl* space between bed and wall; side of bed nearest the wall; bedroom in which a lady of quality received XVII. – (O)F. *ruelle* lane, dim. of *rue* street = Pr., It. *ruga* :- L. *rūga* wrinkle (cf. RUGOSE).

ruff[1] rʌf small freshwater fish of the perch family, Acerina cernua. XV. prob. sb. use of ROUGH; cf. modL. *aspredo* (f. *asper* rough) applied to the fish by John Caius.

ruff[2] rʌf †ruffle on a garment; article of neckwear consisting of linen, etc. starched in folds. XVI. poss. sb. use of *ruff*, ROUGH.

ruff[3] rʌf †former card-game XVI; kind of trump at cards XVII; (from the vb.) act of trumping XIX. – OF. *roffle, rouffle*, earlier *ronfle, romfle*, corr. to It. *ronfa*, poss. alt. of *trionfo* TRUMP[2]. Hence vb. XVI.

ruff[4] rʌf male of the sandpiper, distinguished in the breeding-season by a ruff. XVII. transf. use of RUFF[2].

ruffian rʌ·fiən man of lawless, brutal, or violent behaviour XVI (*ruffian, ruffin*); †pander, bawd XVII. – (O)F. *ruf(f)ian* – It. *ruffiano* (whence also Pr. *rufian, rofian*), supposed to be f. dial. *rofia* scab, scurf, of Germ. origin (OHG. *ruf* scurf).

ruffle[1] rʌ·fl spoil the orderly arrangement of XIII (Cursor M.); (gen.) disorder, disarrange XVI; disturb the mind or temper of XVII. Of unkn. origin. Hence **ru·ffle** sb. disorderly state XVI; ornamental edging to a garment XVIII.

ruffle[2] rʌ·fl (arch.) contend *with*; swagger, hector. XV. Hence **ru·fflER**[1] †one of a class of vagabonds; swaggering fellow. XVI. Of unkn. origin.

rufous rū·fəs reddish. XVIII. f. L. *rūfus*, rel. to *ruber*; see RUBRIC, -OUS.

rug rʌg †rough woollen stuff; piece of thick woollen stuff used as a coverlet XVI; floor mat XIX. prob. of Scand. origin (cf. Norw. dial. *rugga* coverlet, Sw. *rugg* ruffled or coarse hair) and rel. to RAG[1]. So **rugGED**[1] rʌ·gid †shaggy, hirsute XIV; rough, uneven (also fig.) XVI. prob. pp. formation of Scand. origin on the same base; cf. RAGGED.

Rugby rʌ·gbi name of a public school at Rugby in Warwickshire, after which one of the two chief games of football is named. XIX. Hence (sl.) **ru·ggER**[6]. XIX.

rugose rū·gous wrinkled. XVIII. – L. *rūgōsus*, f. *rūga* wrinkle; see -OSE[1].

ruin rū·in (state consequent upon) giving way and falling down XIV (concr. XV); downfall, utter loss XIV. – (O)F. *ruine*, corr. to Sp., It. *ruina* – L. *ruīna*, f. *ruere* fall. So **ru·in** vb. XVI. – (O)F. *ruiner* or medL. *ruīnāre*. **ru·inATE**[3], **ruinA·TION**. XVI. **ru·inOUS**. XIV (Wycl. Bibl.). – (O)F. or L. *ruīnōsus*.

rule rūl principle of procedure, conduct, etc.; code of religious life XIII (AncrR.); standard of estimation, etc.; graduated strip of wood or metal XIV. *rule of thumb* XVII. ME. *riule, reule* – OF. *riule, reule, ruile* :- Rom. **regula*, for L. *rēgula* straight stick, bar, pattern, rel. to *regere* rule (see REGENT), *rēx* (*rēg-*) king. So **rule** vb. govern XIII (AncrR.); mark with lines XV. – OF. *reuler* – late L. *rēgulāre* REGULATE. Hence **ru·lER**[1]. XIV.

rum[1] rʌm spirit distilled from sugar-cane products. XVII. perh. shortening of slightly earlier *rumbullion, rumbustion*, of unkn. origin. ¶ The word has become CEur.

rum[2] rʌm (sl.) queer, odd. XVIII. poss. var. of ROM in collocations like *rum cove*. Also **ru·mmY**[1]. XIX.

Rumanian, Ro(u)manian rūmei·niən pert. to (native of) *Rumania*, a country of S.E. Europe, the natives of which speak a language of the Romanic group having a large element of alien vocabulary; see -IAN. XIX.

rumbelow rʌmbəlou· meaningless combination of syllables used as a refrain chanted by sailors when rowing. XIV. Often coupled with *hevelow, heve* (*and*) *how, hey* (*and*) *how* or *ho*.

rumble rʌ·mbl make a low heavy continuous sound. XIV (Ch.). prob. – MDu. *rommelen, rummelen* (Du. *rommelen*), whence G. *rummeln*, OSw. *rumbla*, etc.; of imit. origin.

ruminate rū·mineit meditate (upon); chew the cud. XVI. f. pp. stem of L. *rūminārī, -āre*, f. *rūmin-, rūmen* throat, gullet, (in mod. scientific use) first stomach of a ruminant; see -ATE[3]. So **ru·min**ANT (animal) that chews the cud. XVII. **rumin**A·TION. XVI (Sh.).

rummage rʌ·midʒ †stowage, orig. in a ship's hold; (dial.) commotion XVI; (from the vb.) overhauling search XVIII. – AN. **rumage* (cf. AL. *rumāgium*, also *runāgium*), aphetic of OF. *arrumage* (mod. *arrimage*), f. †*arrumer*, var. of OF. *arimer, aruner, ariner*, f. *a-* AD-+*run* RUN[2]; see -AGE. *R. sale* is first recorded (XIX) for the sale of unclaimed goods at docks or odds and ends left in a warehouse. Hence **ru·mmage** vb. †stow in the hold, †set (a ship) in order; search (orig. the hold), also intr. XVI.

rummer rʌ·məɹ (arch.) large drinking-glass. XVII. Of LDu. origin; cf. Du. *roemer*, LG. (whence G.) *römer*, f. *roemen*, etc. extol, boast.

rumour rū·məɹ †favourable report XIV (Ch., Trevisa); general report or hearsay XIV (Wycl. Bible). Late ME. *rumur, rumo(u)r* – OF. *rumur, -or* (mod. *-eur*) = Pr. *rumor*, etc. – L.

rump rʌmp hindquarters, buttocks. XV (Promp. Parv.); small or contemptible remainder XVII. prob. of Scand. origin; cf. (M)Da. *rumpe*, (M)Sw. *rumpa*, Icel. *rumpr*; corr. forms in (M)Du., (M)LG., and (O)HG. mean the trunk of the body; the orig. sense may be tree-stump.

rumple rʌ·mpl crease, wrinkle, crumple. XVII. f. *rumple* sb. wrinkle, fold (XVI, Dunbar). – (M)Du. *rompel*, deriv. of MDu. *rompe*, MLG. *rumpe* wrinkle, or – MDu., MLG. *rumpelen, rompelen*, rel. to OE. **rimpan*, in pp. *ġerumpen* contracted, wrinkled, (M)LG., (M)Du. *rimpel* wrinkle, OHG. *rimpfan* (G. *rümpfen*).

rumpus rʌ·mpəs disturbance, row. XVIII (Foote). Of fanciful formation (?).

run[1] rʌn, pt. **ran** ræn, pp. **run** rʌn go along at quicker than walking pace; (gen.) move forward with speed. In finite parts of this vb. the present form with *-u-* is not current before XVI (*runne*), but the var. *ronne* is earlier. The vowel resulted from levelling through from forms in which it was original, viz. pt. pl. *runnen* (OE. **runnon*) and pp. *runne(n), ronnen* (pp. *ġerunnen* coagulated, curdled). OE. *rinnan*, pt. *rann* = OFris. *rinna, renna*, OS., OHG. *rinnan*, (MLG., MDu., G. *rinnen*), ON. *rinna*, Goth. *rinnan*; CGerm. str. vb. of unkn. origin. But the metathesized form of this was commoner in OE., viz. *iernan* (pt. *arn, orn, urnon*, pp. *urnen*), which died out in ME., except for a few survivals in mod. dialects. The common ME. present tense forms *rinne, renne*, were prob. due to ON. *rinna, renna*, with pt. *ran*, pp. *run*, reinforced from the same source. Hence **run** sb. XV (act or spell of running; later in many techn. uses). ¶ Parallel developments are found in BURN[2].

run[2] rʌn (naut.) part of a ship's bottom that rises from the keel and narrows towards either end. XVII. perh. – OF. *run* ship's hold – (M)Du. *ruim* space (ROOM).

runagate rʌ·nəgeit †apostate; (arch.) deserter, runaway; vagabond. XVI. alt. of *ren(n)egate* (see RENEGADE), by assoc. with *renne* RUN and *agate* on the way, away, (f. A-[1]+*gate*, GAIT).

runcible rʌ·nsibl *r. spoon* kind of fork for pickles curved like a spoon and having three broad prongs (one with a sharp edge). XIX. First used by Edward Lear as a nonsense word in *r. cat, r. hat, r. spoon*; supposed to be alt. of *rouncival*, which has been used in many senses of obscure origin, and has been identified with the place-name *Roncesvalles* (*Roncevaux*).

runcinate rʌ·nsineit irregularly saw-toothed. XVIII. – modL. *runcinātus*, f. L. *runcina* joiner's plane (formerly taken also to mean a kind of saw); see -ATE[2].

rundale rʌ·ndeil form of joint occupation of land. XVI. (Sc. *ryndale, rindaill*, later *rendal, rennal*, anglicized *rundale*). f. *rin*, Sc. var. of RUN+*dale*, north. form of DOLE.

rune rūn character of the earliest Germanic alphabet. XVII. Adopted from Danish writers on Northern antiquities, and repr. ON. **rún*, pl. *rúnar, rúnir* secret or hidden lore, runes, magical signs (Sw. *runa*, Da. *rune*) = OE. *rūn* mystery, runic letter, secret consultation, OS., OHG., Goth. *rūna* (cf. ROUND[2]). So **ru·n**IC. XVII (Evelyn). – modL. *rūnicus*. ¶ The words have been adopted into other Eur. langs.; e.g. G., Du. *rune*, F. *rune, runique*; also Finnish *runo* poem, song of the Kalevala, whence *rune* has been so used in Eng., and gen. for 'song, poem, verse' (XIX).

rung rʌŋ stick of rounded form used as a rail, etc. OE.; stave of a ladder XIII. OE. *hrung* = MLG. *runge* (Du. *rong*), OHG. *runga* (G. *runge* from LG.), Goth. *hrugga* ῥάβδος.

runnel rʌ·nl small stream. XVI. Later form (by assim. to RUN) of *rinel*, OE. *rynel, rynele, rinnele*, f. *run-, rin-*, base of RUN[1]; see -EL[1].

runt rʌnt (dial.) old tree-stump XVI (G. Douglas), small breed of cattle XVI; uncouth, ill-conditioned, or dwarfish person; stout variety of domestic pigeon XVII. Of unkn. origin.

rupee rūpī· monetary unit of India. XVII. – Urdu *rūpiyah* :– Skr. *rūpya* wrought silver; cf. ROUBLE.

rupture rʌ·ptʃəɹ breach XV; abdominal hernia XVI; break XVII. – F. *rupture* or L. *ruptūra*, f. pp. stem of *rumpere* break; see REAVE, -URE.

rural ruə·ɹəl pert. to the country)(the town. XV (Lydg.). – (O)F. *rural* or late L.

rūrālis, f. *rūr-*, *rūs* the country :– **rewos* = Av. *ravah-* space, rel. to OSl. *ravĭnŭ* flat, level, and ROOM; see -AL[1].

Ruritania ruəriteiˑniə imaginary kingdom of Central Europe in Anthony Hope's novels (1894, 1898); transf. petty state, esp. as a scene of court romance and intrigue. Hence **-aˑn**IAN. f. L. *rūri-*, *rūs* country + *-tania*, of *Lusitania*, etc.

rusa rūˑsə E. Indian red deer. XIX. modL. – Malay. Cf. BABIROUSSA.

ruse rūz †detour, doubling in the track XV; trick, dodge XVII. – (O)F. *ruse*, f. *ruser* (whence ME. *ruse* repulse in battle, make a detour as a hunted animal) drive back, perh. :– Rom. **ru(r)sāre*, f. L. *rursus* back(wards) :– **reworsos*, f. *re-* RE- 1 + **worsturned* (cf. -WARD, WORTH).

rush[1] rʌʃ plant of the order Juncaceæ. OE. *rysć(e)*, recorded chiefly in place-designations, corr. to MLG., MHG. (Du., G.) *rusch*; the development *u* :– *y* before point-cons. is paralleled in *blush*, *cluster*, etc. OE. *rysć(e)*, with the vars. *resć(e)*, *risć(e)*, **rex(e)*, *rix(e)*, surviving dial. in *resh*, *rish*, *rex*, *rix*, and corr. to MLG., MDu. *risch*, etc., point to a Germ. series **rask-* **resk-* **rusk-*, with poss. further connexions in L. *restis* (:– **rezgtis*) rush, leaf of onion or garlic, rope, cord, Lith. *rẽzgis* basket, *rezgù* plait, Skr. *rájjus* rope.

rush[2] rʌʃ †force out of place, move with force or speed; also intr. XIV (Barbour, Wycl. Bible); the sense-development was prob. infl. by phonetic appropriateness – AN. *russher*, var. of OF. *russer*, *ruser* (see RUSE). ¶ For *-sh* cf. *bushel*, *push*.

rusk rʌsk (piece of) bread re-fired so as to be hard and crisp. XVI. – Sp., Pg. *rosca* twist, coil, twisted roll of bread, of unkn. origin.

Russ rʌs pert. to (native of) Russia. *Rus'*, Russ. name for the Russian lands and people before the sixteenth century. So **Russ**IAN rʌˑʃən. XVI. – medL. *Russiānus* f. *Russia*. (Russ. *Rossiya* prob. – Gr. *Ῥωσία*.)

russet rʌˑsit coarse woollen cloth of reddish-brown or other subfusc colour XIII; adj. reddish-brown XIV (hence sb. russet colour XVI; russet apple XVIII). – AN. *russet*, var. of OF. *rousset*, *rosset*, dim. f. *rous* (mod. *roux*) – Pr. *ros*, It. *rosso* :– L. *russu-s* (:– **rudhsos*) RED; see -ET.

rust rʌst brownish coating formed on iron and steel by oxidation. OE. *rūst* = OS., (O)HG. *rost*, (M)Du. *roest*, based on Germ. **rudh-* **reudh-* **raudh-* RED; cf. synon. ON. *ryð*, OSl. *rŭžda*, Lett. *rūsa* (*rusta* brown colour), L. *rōbīgo*, *rūbīgo*. Hence vb. XIII (AncrR.). **ruˑsty**[1]. OE. *rūstiġ*, with corr. forms in other Germ. langs. ¶ The long quality of the OE. vowel is shown by dial. *roust* (XIV), Sc. *roost*, but shortening may have been very early.

rustic rʌˑstik pert. to the country XV; sb. countryman, peasant XVI. – L. *rūsticus*, f. *rūs* country)(town; cf. F. *rustique* (XIV). So **ruˑstic**AL. XV. – OF. or medL. **ruˑstic**ATE[3] retire to the country XVII; trans. XVIII. f. pp. stem of L. *rūsticārī* live in the country. **rustic**AˑTION. XVII. – L. **rustic**ITY -iˑsiti. XVI. – F. or L.

rustle rʌˑsl give forth a succession of light crisp sounds XIV (Trevisa); (U.S. colloq.) move about vigorously XIX. Of imit. origin; cf. Fris. *russelje*, *risselje*, Flem. †*ruysselen*, *rijsselen*, Du. *ridselen*, *ritselen*.

rusty[2] rʌˑsti reasty, rancid XVI; ill-tempered XIX (Scott). var. of REASTY.

rut[1] rʌt sexual excitement of male deer, etc. XV. – (O)F. *rut*, †*ruit* rutting (time), †bellowing (of stags) = Sp., Pg. *ruido* noise, clamour :– Rom. **rūgitu-s*, for L. *rugītus*, f. *rugīre* roar, f. **ru-*, imit. syll. found elsewhere.

rut[2] rʌt track made in soft ground. XVI. Early forms also *rote*, *roote*, *rupt*; prob. – OF. *rote*, early form of ROUTE; the shortening of the vowel may be due to lack of stress in the comp. †*cartrote*. The form *rit*, which occurs in *cart-ritt* (XVII) and uncompounded in north. dial., is perh. of distinct origin (f. *rit* scratch, incise, in Cumberland dial., cut the first line of a trench or drain with a spade).

ruth rūþ (arch.) pity. XII. Early ME. *reuþe* f. *rewen* RUE[2], prob. after ON. *hryggð*. Survives in gen. literary use in **ruˑth**LESS pitiless. XIV.

ruthenium rūþīˑniəm (chem.) metal of the platinum group, discovered 1828, being first observed in platinum ores in the Ural mountains XIX. f. medL. *Ruthenia* Russia. See -IUM.

-ry ri suffix, reduced form of -ERY used chiefly after an unstressed syll. ending in *d*, *t*, *l*, *n*, or *sh*, and rarely after vocalic els.; exx. of the types are: *heraldry*, *ribaldry*; *casuistry*, *dentistry*, *peasantry*; *chivalry*, *devilry*; *yeomanry*; *Englishry*, *Jewry*; in a few words *-ry* and *-ery* are alternative, *baptist(e)ry*, *jewel(le)ry*.

rybat raiˑbət (Sc.) REVEAL[2]. XVII (*rebatt*), prob. var. of *rabbet*, REBATE.

rye rai the cereal Secale cereale, OE. *ryġe* = ON. *rugr* :– Germ. **rugiz*, an *i*-stem, beside which there is an *n*-stem, **roggan-*, **ruggn-*, repr. by OFris. *rogga*, OS. *roggo* (Du. *rogge*, *rog*), OHG. *rokko* (G. *roggen* is from LG.); from the former type are Finnish *ruis*, Estonian *rukkis*, Lappish *rok*;

from the latter OF. *regon, ragon*, Pr. *raon* maslin; corr. forms in Balto-Sl. are Lith. *rugỹs*, Lett. *rudzis*, OSl. *rŭžĭ* (Russ. *rozh'*), perh. ult. rel. to Gr. (Thracian) *brízā* (:- **wrugjā*). The place of origin and route of transmission are not clear. Hence **rye-grass** A. for earlier *ray-grass* (XVII) species *Lolium* (†*ray* darnel XIV–XVII, of unkn. origin); B. wild rye, Hordeum XVIII.

ryot rai·ət Indian peasant or husbandman. XVII (*riat*, Purchas). – Urdu *ra'īyat, raiyat* – Arab. *ra'īyah* flock, herd, subjects, peasants, f. *ra'ā* pasture, feed.

S

s, -s z repr. OE. g. sg. *-es* of many m. and n. sbs., written universally *'s*, as *boy's, horse's, lady's*, with extension to certain pls., as *men's*; special cases are its use (1) as a euphem. repr. of *God's* (g. of GOD) in oaths, as *'sblood* (XVI), *'sdeath* (XVII), *'slife* (XVII), *'swounds* (XVI; see ZOUNDS); (2) in the terminal el. *-sman*, the extensive use of which, as in *craftsman, helmsman, kinsman, salesman, spokesman, sportsman, tradesman*, is a generalization of the combination found in OE. *stēoresmann* STEERSMAN, *tūnesmann* (occupier of a manor) TOWNSMAN.

b. Identical with the inflexion of the g. sg. is the *-s* surviving in certain advb. forms, viz. *always, eftsoons, needs, nowadays*, (go your) *ways, -wards, -ways*, which are particular instances of the use exemplified by such OE. advs. as *dæġes* by day, *sōþes* in truth, truly, *þances* voluntarily. There were also OE. advs. compounded with *tō* TO and a genitive, as *tōġeġnes* against, *tōmiddes* amidst, by the side of which were synon. *onġeġn* AGAIN, *onmiddan* AMID; hence there arose in ME. mixed forms such as *aȝeines, amiddes*; and *-(e)s* became generalized, as in EFTSOONS, -WARDS, -WAYS. In *once, twice, thrice, hence, thence, whence, since*, the suffix has been otherwise spelt in order to avoid the suggestion of pronunc. with z which is associated with *-ns*, viz. nz. In AGAINST, AMIDST, AMONGST, *anenst* (see ANENT), dial. *onct* (ONCE), there is a parasitic *t*. ¶ In the disjunctive prons. (orig. northern) *hers, ours, theirs, yours* (ME. *hires, heres, ures*, etc.) the *-s* is presumably analogical after *his*, as the *-n* of the parallel dial. *hern, hisn, ourn*, etc. is after *mine, thine*.

Sabæan, Sabean səbī·ən pert. to the ancient people of Yemen in Arabia. XVI (Sidney). f. L. *Sabæus* – Gr. *Sabaîos*, f. *Sába* – Arab. *Saba'* = Heb. *Sh^{e}bā*; see -AN.

Sabaism sei·beiizm star-worship. XVIII. – F. *sabaïsme*, f. Heb. *çābā* host (of heaven), after the presumed etym. of SABIAN; see -ISM.

Sabaoth sæ·beiouþ in phr. *Lord (God) of S.* in Eng. N.T. (Rom. ix 29, Jas. v 4) and **Te Deum**. XIV. – L. *Sabaōth* (Vulg.) – Gr. *Sabaṓth* (LXX and N.T.) – Heb. *ç^{e}bāōth*, pl. of *çābā* army, host.

Sabbatarian sæbətɛə·riən pert. to the observance of the Sabbath (Saturday); sb. observer of the Lord's Day as a Sabbath (7th day of the week). XVII. f. late L. *sabbatārius* (Sidonius), sb. pl. Jews (Martial), f. *sabbatum*; see next, -ARIAN.

Sabbath sæ·bəþ seventh day of the week observed by Jews as a day of rest OE.; the Lord's Day, Sunday XVI; (after F. *sabbat*) midnight meeting of demons and witches XVII. OE. *sabat*, ME. *sabat* (XIII) – L. *sabbatum* and (O)F. *sabbat*, †*sabat* (= Pr. *sabbat* Sabbath, Sp. *sábado*, It. *sabbato* Saturday) – Gr. *sábbaton* – Heb. *shabbāth*, f. *shābath* rest. The sp. with *th* and the consequent pronunc. are due to learned assoc. with the Heb. form. ¶ A pop. L. nasalized form **sambatum* is repr. by F. *samedi* :- **sambatī diēs*, Rum. *sămbătă*, OHG. *sambaȝtag*, G. *samstag*, OSl. *sąbota*. *S. Day* (XIV): cf. OHG. *sambaȝtag* (G. *samstag*), Goth. *sabbato dags*.

sabbatical səbæ·tikəl pert. to the Sabbath; pert. to the seventh year prescribed by Mosaic law to be observed as a Sabbath XVI; hence of an academical year of absence from duty XIX. f. late L. *sabbaticus* – Gr. *sabbatikós*, f. *sábbaton*; see prec., -ICAL.

Sabellian səbe·liən heretic maintaining that the three Persons of the Trinity are merely modes of one divine Person. XV. – ecclL. *Sabelliānus*, f. *Sabellius*, an African heresiarch (III).

Sabian sei·biən adherent of a religious sect of the Arabians XVII; (erron.) star-worshipper XVIII. f. Arab. *çābi'*; see -AN.

Sabine sæ·bain one of a race of ancient Italy. XIV (Trevisa); their language. – L. *Sabīnus*, rel. to *Sabellī* and *Samnium* (see SAMNITE); see -INE[1].

sable[1] sei·bl (fur of) a small carnivore Mustela zibellina. XV. – OF. *sable* (XII) sable fur, also in *martre sable* 'sable-marten' (animal and its fur) – medL. *sabelum* (XII), whence also MLG. *sabel*, Du. *sabel*, Icel. *safal*, *safali*; all ult. of Balto-Sl. origin (cf. Lith. *sàbalas*, Russ. *sóbol'*, with which (O)HG. *zobel* (XI) closely agrees), the word being carried into Germania with the fur trade from Eastern Europe. Cf. ZIBELLINE.

sable[2] sei·bl black colour (spec. in her.); black clothing XIV; adj. XV. – OF. *sable*, whence also Sp., Pg. *sable*, (M)Du. *sabel*; gen. presumed to be identical with prec., but sable fur is brown.

sabot sæ·bou wooden shoe made of a single piece of wood. XVII. – F. *sabot*, of unkn. origin. So **sabot**AGE sæ·bŏtāʒ wilful and organized destruction of machinery, etc. by workers. XX. – F. *sabotage* (1870), f. *saboter* clatter with shoes, execute badly, destroy (tools, etc.), f. *sabot*.

sabre, U.S. **saber** sei·bəɹ cavalry sword with curved blade. XVII (Otway). – F. *sabre*, unexpl. alt. of *sable* – G. *sabel*, local var. of *säbel*, earlier †*schabel* – Pol. *szabla* or Magyar *szblya*. ¶ Introduced into France by German mercenaries. The somewhat earlier Eng. †*sable* was – G. or Du. *sabel*, and Sc. *shab(b)le* – It. *sciab(o)la* or its Pol. or Magyar source.

sabulous sæ·bjŭləs sandy. XVII. – L. *sabulōsus*, f. *sabulum* SAND; see -OUS.

sac sæk bag-like cavity. XVIII. – F. *sac* or L. *saccus* SACK[1] in modL. applications. ¶ See also SACK[4].

saccharine sæ·kərain, -in sugary. XVII. f. medL. *saccharum* SUGAR + -INE[1]. So **sacchar**IN sæ·kərin sweet substance obtained from coal tar XIX; also popularly **-ine** īn. – G. *saccharin* Fahlberg 1879. Hence **sacchari**·METER polariscope for testing sugars. XIX. – F. *saccharimètre*. **saccharo**·METER hydrometer for testing the amount of sugar. XVIII. f. **sa·ccharo-** comb. form of Gr. *sákkharon* SUGAR.

sacerdotal sæsəɹdou·təl pert. to priests or priesthood. XIV. – (O)F. *sacerdotal* or L. *sacerdōtālis*, f. *sacerdōt-*, *-dōs* priest :– **sakrodhōts* 'offering sacrifices', f. **sakro-* SACRED (cf. L. *sacra* sacrifices) + **dhō-* make, DO; see -AL[1].

sachem sei·tʃəm, sæ·tʃəm chief of some Amer. Indian tribes XVII; (U.S.) political chief XIX. – Narragansett *sachem* = Penobscot *sagamo* (see SAGAMORE).

sachet sæ·ʃei small perfumed bag; dry perfume in packet form. XIX (isolated exx. in Caxton). – (O)F. *sachet*, dim. of *sac* SACK[1]; see -ET. ¶ ONF. var. *saquet* is repr. by dial. *sacket* (XV–XIX).

sack[1] sæk large oblong bag open at one end. OE. *sacc* – L. *saccus* bag, sack, sackcloth (whence (O)F., Pr., Rum. *sac*, Sp. *saco*, It. *sacco*), corr. to Gr. *sákkos*, term of commerce for packing-material, of Semitic origin (Heb. *saq* sack, sackcloth, Syriac *saq*, *saqā*, Ass. *šaqqu*). There are corr. forms in MDu. *sak* (Du. *zak*), OHG. *sac(h)*, pl. *secchi* (G. *sack*), ON. *sekkr*, Goth. *sakkus*; the ON. form and OE. *sæċċ* repr. a type **sakkiz*. Comp. **sa·ck**CLOTH coarse textile fabric, esp. as a material for penitential garb. XIV (*sekkclath*); cf. medL. *pannus saccorum*. ¶ A word in gen. Eur. use, from L. or Gr.; cf. Ir., Gael. *sac*, W. *sach*, Russ., Pol., Czech, Serb., Alb. *sak*, Magyar *zsak*. **sack** vb.[1] A. put into a sack XIV; B. dismiss, discharge XIX. In A, partly after medL. *saccāre* or MDu. *sacken*, etc.; in B, f. phr. *give* (a person) *the sack* (XIX), which has analogues in F. *donner son sac à quelqu'un*, (M)Du. *iemand den zak geven*, and in F. vb. *sacquer*.

sack[2] sæk gen. name for a class of white wines from Spain and the Canaries. XVI. orig. (*wyne*) *seck* – F. *vin sec* dry wine (see WINE, SEC); cf. Du. *sek*; also G. *sekt* (†*canarienseckt*) now applied to champagne, formerly †*seck*; perh. orig. applied to dry wines of the sherry class, but later extended to others. ¶ The alt. of *seck* to *sack* is unexplained.

sack[3] sæk plundering. XVI. – F. *sac* (in phr. *mettre à sac* 'put to sack') – It. *sacco* SACK[1] (in phr. *fare il sacco*, *mettere* or *porre a sacco*, *dare il sacco a* pillage, *andare a sacco* be sacked, perh. orig. referring to the filling of bags with plunder, cf. *fare sacco* make a SACK[1] of money). Hence **sack** vb.[2] plunder XVI; cf. medL. *saccāre*, Pr., Sp., Pg. *saquear*, It. *saccheggiare* (whence F. *saccager*).

sack[4] sæk also **sac**, (pseudo-F.) **sacque** loose gown for women XVI; loose-fitting coat XIX. prob. orig. a use of SACK[1], later assoc. with F. *sac* (cf. G. *französischer sack*, Du. *zak*).

sackbut sæ·kbʌt bass trumpet with a slide. XVI. – F. *saquebute*, earlier *-boute*, *-bot(t)e* (XV), recorded earlier in the sense of a hooked lance for pulling a man off his horse, f. *saquer*, var. of OF. *sachier* pull = Sp., Pg. *sacar* (:– Rom. **saccāre*) + *bouter* perh. BUTT[1]. ¶ Used in the Geneva Bible, Dan. iii (and hence in A.V.) to render Aram. *sabb'kā* (repr. in LXX by *sambúkē* and in Vulg. by L. *sambūca*), which, however, denotes a stringed instrument.

sackless sæ·klis (arch., dial.) †undisputed, unchallenged; innocent. Late OE. *saclēas* – ON. *saklauss*, f. *sak-*, *sǫk*; see SAKE[1], -LESS.

sacrament sæ·krəmənt any of certain sacred rites of the Christian Church XII; spec. *the S.*, the Eucharist, Holy Communion XIII; (arch.) sacred or solemn pledge XIV. ME. *sacrement* (also *sa(c)ra-*, by assim. to L.) – (O)F. *sacrement* – L. *sacrāmentum* solemn engagement, caution-money deposited in a suit, military oath, (in ChrL. by recourse to the etymol. meaning) used to render Gr. μυστήριον MYSTERY[1]. f. *sacrāre* hallow, consecrate, f. *sacer* SACRED; see -MENT. So **sacrame·nt**AL[1] XIV

– OF. or late L.; sb. rite analogous to a sacrament XVI. **sacrament**A·RIAN XVI; f. modL. *sacrāmentārius*, applied like Luther's *sacramentirer, sacramenter* to deniers of the Real Presence. So **sacrarium** səkrɛə·riəm sanctuary of a church. XVIII. – eccl. use of L. *sacrārium* place in which sacred objects were kept, f. *sacr-, sacer*. Earlier †*sacrary* (XIV, Wycl. Bible, Trevisa) – OF. *sacrarie, sacraire* or L. **sacred** sei·krid consecrated, dedicated *to* XIV; dedicated to a religious purpose XV; reverenced as holy, secured against violation XVI. orig. pp. (see -ED[1]) of †*sacre* consecrate – (O)F. *sacrer* (= Pr. *sagrar*, It. *sacrare*) – L. *sacrāre* consecrate, dedicate to a divinity, f. *sacr-, sacer* consecrated, holy, rel. to *sancire, sanctus*; see SANCTION, SAINT. **sacrifice** sæ·krifais offering of a slaughtered animal, etc. to a deity; that which is so offered XIII; Jesus Christ's offering of himself XIV; applied to the Eucharist; gen. (so *self-s.*) XVI. – (O)F. *sacrifice* = Pr. *sacrifici*, Sp. *sacrificio*, It. *sagrifizio* – L. *sacrificium*, rel. to *sacrificus*, f. *sacri-, sacer*; see -FIC and cf. the formation of the earlier *sacerdōs*, s.v. SACERDOTAL. Hence vb. XIII; cf. (O)F. *sacrifier*, L. *sacrificāre*. So **sacrific**IAL sækrifi·ʃ(ə)l XVII (Sh.). f. L. *sacrificium*; cf. contemp. †*sacrifical* (XVII) – L. *sacrificālis*, f. *sacrificus*. **sacrilege** sæ·krĭlidʒ violation of a sacred person or thing, prop. theft of a sacred object XIII; profanation XIV. – (O)F. *sacrilège* (= Sp., It. *sacrilegio*) – L. *sacrilegium*, f. *sacrilegus* one who steals sacred things, f. *sacri-, sacer* + *legere* take possession of, after the phr. *sacrum* or *sacra legere* purloin sacred things (see COLLECT, etc.). **sacrileg**IOUS -lĭ·dʒəs, -li·dʒəs XVI. f. L. *sacrilegium*; the pronunc. has been affected by assoc. with *religious*. **sacr**ING[1] sei·kriŋ (hist.) consecration of the Eucharist. XIII. f. †*sacre* consecrate + -ING[1]; hence *sacring-bell* XIV. **sacr**IST sæ·krist one having charge of sacred vessels, etc. XVI. – (O)F. *sacriste*, or medL. *sacrista*, f. *sacr-, sacer*. **sa·crist**AN. XIV. – medL. *sacristānus*; cf. SEXTON. **sa·crist**Y[3] repository in a church for sacred objects. XVII (also †*sextry* XIV–XVII) – F. *sacristie* (earlier *-estie*), It. *sacrestia* or medL. *sacristia*. **sacro-** sei·krou used as comb. form (see -O-) of SACRUM in anat. terms. XIX. **sacrosanct** sæ·krou-, sei·krou-sæŋkt secured by religious sanction. XVII. – L. *sacrōsanctus*, f. *sacrō*, abl. of *sacrum* sacred rite, sb. use of n. of *sacer* + *sanctus*, pp. of *sancīre* (see SANCTION). **sacrum** sei·krəm (anat.) lowest bone of the spine. XVIII. Short for late L. *os sacrum*, tr. Gr. *ἱερὸν ὀστέον* 'sacred bone'.

sad sæd A. †sated, weary OE.; †steadfast, firm; †grave, serious; sorrowful XIV; deplorably disappointing or bad XVII. B. †solid, dense XIII (cf. *sad-iron*, solid flat-iron); dark-coloured (cf. G. *sattblau*, etc.) XVI; (of bread, etc.) that has not 'risen' XVII. OE. *sæd* = OS. *sad* (Du. *zat*), OHG. *sat* (G. *satt*), ON. *saðr*, Goth. *saþs* :– CGerm. **saðaz* :– IE. **sətós*, pp. formation (see -ED[1] and cf. LOUD, OLD) on a base meaning SATISFY and repr. also by Gr. *áatos* (:– **n̥sətós*) insatiate, *hádēn* enough, L. *sat, satis* enough, *satur* sated (cf. SATURATE), OIr. *sathech* satiated, Lith. *sotùs* satisfying. Hence **sadd**EN[5] sæ·dn (dial.) make solid XVI; make sorrowful XVII; repl. †*sad* vb. (XIV) and (dial.) *sade* (OE. *sadian*).

saddle sæ·dl seat for a rider on an animal's back. OE. *sadol, -ul* = MDu. *sadel* (Du. *zadel, zaal*), OHG. *satal, -ul* (G. *sattel*), ON. *sǫðull* :– Germ. (exc. Gothic) **saðulaz*, perh. ult. (but not immed.) to be referred to the *o*-grade of IE. **sed-* SIT, which is repr. in the parallel formations Goth. *sitls* seat (see SETTLE[1]), L. *sella* (:– **sedlā*), Gr. *hellá* seat, OSl. *sedŭlo* saddle, see -LE[1]. Hence vb. OE. *sadolian*.

Sadducee sæ·djusī member of one of the three Jewish sects (the others being Pharisees and Essenes) of the time of Christ. OE. *sad(d)ucēas*, ME. *saduceis, saduce(e)s*, later *Sadduces*, pl.; – late L. *Saddūcæus* – late Gr. *Saddoukaîos*, f. late Heb. *Çaddūqī*, prob. f. personal name *Çaddūq*, in Massoretic vocalization *Çāðōq* Zadok of the Eng. Bible (2 Sam. viii 17, etc.), the high priest of David's time from whom the priesthood of the Captivity and later periods claimed to be descended.

sadism sei·dizm, sā·dizm sexual perversion marked by love of cruelty. XIX. – F. *sadisme*, f. name of the Count (usu. called Marquis) de *Sade* (1740–1814), infamous for his crimes and the character of his writings; see -ISM. Also **sa·d**IST, **sadi**·STIC.

safe[1] seif free from hurt or damage XIII (RGlouc.); free from danger, secure XIV. ME. *sauf, sāf*, orig. inflected *sauve, save* – (O)F. *sauf* (AN. *saf*) = Pr. *salv-s, sal-s*, Sp., It. *salvo* :– L. *salvu-s* uninjured, entire, healthy (cf. SALUTARY, SAVE[1]), corr. in base and suffix to Gr. *hólos* (:– **solϝos*), Skr. *śarvas* whole, all :– IE. **solwos* (cf. OL. *sollus*, W. *holl* whole :– IE. **solnos*; see also SOLEMN, SOLICIT, SOLID). ¶ For the vocalism cf. *chafe, mavis, save, wafer*.

Phrases and comps. *safe and sound* (XIII) reflects F. *sain et sauf*, L. *sanus et salvus, salvus sanus*; *safe conduct* (ME. *sauf condut*, etc. XIII) – (O)F. *sauf conduit*, medL. (Rom.) *salvus conductus*; **sa·fe**GUARD (ME. *sauf garde*, XV; also *saue warde* XIV) – AN. *salve garde*, (O)F. *sauve garde* (AL. *salva gardia* XIV) = Sp., It. *salvaguardia*.

safe[2] seif receptacle for safe keeping. XV (Promp. Parv.). Orig. *save*, f. SAVE[1]; later assim. to prec.

safety sei·fti XIII (Cursor M., 'salvation'), ME. *sauvete* (three sylls. as still in Spenser's *safetie*). – (O)F. *sauveté* = Pr. *saubetat*, Sp. *salvedad* :– medL. *salvitātem, -tās*. See -TY[2].

safflower sæ·flauəɹ (dried petals of) the plant Carthamus tinctorius. XVI (*samfloure*). – Du. *saffloer* or G. *safflor* – OF. *saffleur* – It. †*saffiore*, var. of *asfiore*, *asfrole*, *zaffrole*; infl. by assoc. with *saffron* and *flower*.

saffron sæ·frən (orange-red product of) the plant Crocus sativus XIII; autumn crocus XV. ME. *saffran*, *safron* – (O)F. *safran* (whence also MDu. *saffraen*, Du. *saffraan*, MHG. *saffrān*, G. *safran*), corr. to Pr. *safrá*, It. *zafferano*, (with Arab. article prefixed) Sp. *azafran*, Pg. *açafrão* – Arab. *zaçfarān* (so also in Pers., Turk., Hind.), of unkn. origin. ¶ Of Eur. range.

sag sæg subside XV; hang loose XVI; (naut.) drift XVII. The earliest exx. are from E. Anglian texts; corr. in form to Norw. dial. *sagga* walk slowly and heavily, in sense to MLG. *sacken*, Du. *zakken*, Sw. *sacka*, Norw. dial. *sakka* subside, settle down, Da. *sakke* lag behind, drop astern; perh. ult. of WScand. origin and adopted in LG. and Eng. first in nautical use. Hence **sag** sb. movement to leeward XVI; subsidence XIX.

saga sā·gə mediæval Norse narrative in prose. XVIII. – ON. (Icel.) *saga* SAW[2].

sagacious səgei·ʃəs †of acute perception, esp. of smell; gifted with mental discernment. XVII. f. L. *sagāc-*, *sagāx*, f. **săg-*, repr. also by L. *sāgīre* discern acutely; see SEEK, -IOUS. So **saga**CITY səgæ·sĭti XVI. – F. or L.

sagamore sæ·gəmɔ̄əɹ SACHEM. XVII (Purchas). – Penobscot (Amer. Indian) *sagamo*. See SACHEM.

sage[1] seidʒ plant of the labiate genus Salvia. XIV. ME. *sauge* – (O)F. *sauge* = Pr. *saubja*, Sp., It. *salvia*, Rum. *salbie* :– L. *salvia* 'the healing plant', f. *salvus* SAFE. ¶ For the phonology cf. *chafe*, *gauge*, *safe*, *Ralph* reif.

sage[2] seidʒ wise XIII; sb. man of profound wisdom (in early use chiefly of the seven traditional wise men) XIV. – (O)F. *sage* (whence It. *saggio*), Pr. *satge* :– Gallo-Rom. **sapius* (cf. L. *nesapius* ignorant), f. *sapere* (see SAPIENT).

saggar sæ·gəɹ, **seggar** se·gəɹ in ceramics, protecting case of fire-proof clay. XVIII. perh. a reduction of SAFEGUARD.

Sagittarius sædʒitɛə·riəs zodiacal constellation of the Archer, ninth zone of the zodiac. XIV (Gower). L., f. *sagitta* arrow; see -ARY.

sago sei·gou (starch obtained from the pith of) the palm Metroxylon læve, etc. XVI (*sagu*; later *sagow*, *sagoe*; in XVIII, after Du., *sago*) – (orig. through Pg.) Malay *sāgū*. Cf. F. *sagou* (XVIII), Sp. *sagú*, It. *sogù*, (from Du. or Eng.) G. *sago*.

sagoin səgoi·n small S. Amer. monkey. XVII. – F. *sagouin*, †*sagoin* – Pg. *saguim* – Guarani *sagui*, *çagui*.

sahib sā·ib title used by natives of India in addressing an Englishman or European. XVII. – Urdu use of Arab *ṣāḥib* companion, friend, lord, master.

Sahidic sahi·dik pert. to a dialect of Coptic spoken in Thebes and Upper Egypt. XIX. f. Arab. *ṣa'īd* upper + -IC.

sail seil piece of canvas, etc. fastened to a mast, etc. to catch the wind OE.; similar arrangement attached to the arms of a windmill XV. OE. *seġ(e)l* = OFris. *seil*, OS. *segel* (Du. *zeil*), OHG. *segal*, *-il* (G. *segel*), ON. *segl* :– CGerm. (exc. Goth.) **seglam*, of unkn. origin. So **sail** vb. OE. *seġl(i)an*.

sailor sei·ləɹ one professionally occupied with navigation, mariner. XVI. In earliest use *sayler* (see -ER[1]), later altered by assim. to agent-nouns in -OR[1] (e.g. *tailor*) to distinguish the designation of a regular calling from the unspecialized form.

sainfoin sei·nfoin herb Onobrychis sativa; also lucerne, Medicago sativa. XVII. Early forms *saintfoin*, *St. Foine* – F. †*saintfoin* (mod. *sainfoin*) orig. lucerne – modL. *sanctum fœnum* 'holy hay' (whence *holy hay* XVII, G. *heiligheu*), alt. of *sānum fœnum* 'wholesome hay', which was based on L. *herba medica* 'healing plant', itself erron. alt. of *herba Mēdica*, Gr. *Μηδικὴ πόα* 'Median grass'.

saint seint, (unstr.) sint, s(ə)nt, s(ə)n holy (prefixed to a name, now regarded as the sb. used attrib.); sb. canonized person; one of the elect of God XIV; person of great holiness XVI. OE. *sanct* (to which there are corr. forms in other Germ. langs.), superseded (XII) by *seint(e)*, *sant*, *saint* (before a name with initial cons., *sein*, *sayn*) – OF. *seint*, (also mod.) *saint*, fem. *seinte*, *sainte*, prefixed occas. †*sain* = Pr. *san(c)t*, Sp., Pg., It. *santo* (prefixed before a cons., Pr., Sp., It. *san*, Pg. *são*) :– L. *sanctus* sacred, holy, prop. pp. of *sancīre* (see SANCTION), used sb. in the Vulgate, e.g. Ps. xxix 5. Hence **sai·nt**LY[1]. XVII.

sake[1] seik †strife, contention (in OE. also, legal suit); †guilt OE.; †charge, ground of accusation XII; surviving in phr. *for the sake of* XIII (prob. modelled on ON. *fyrir e-s sakir* or *sǫkum* because of, *fyrir mínum sǫkum* for my behalf, for my part). OE. *sacu* = OFris. *sake*, OS. *saka* (Du. *zaak*), OHG. *sahha* (G. *sache*), ON. *sǫk* :– CGerm. (exc. Goth.) **sakō* affair, thing, cause, legal action, accusation, crime, f. **sak-*, repr. also by OE. *sacan* quarrel, claim at law, accuse, OS. *sakan* accuse, OHG. *sahhan* strive, quarrel, rebuke, OE. *sæċ* (:– **sakjō*), Goth. *sakjō* (:– **sakjōn*) strife (whence Finnish, Lappish *sakko* duty), rel. to **sōk-*, repr. by SEEK. See also FORSAKE, KEEPSAKE, NAMESAKE, RANSACK, SACKLESS.

sake[2] sā·ki fermented liquor made from rice. XVII (*saque*). Jap.

saker sei·kəɹ large lanner falcon, Falco sacer XIV (*sacre*, *sagre*); old form of cannon XVI. – (O)F. *sacre*, corr. to Sp., Pg. *sacro*,

It. *sagro*, medL. *sacer* – Arab. *ṣaqr*; identified with L. *sacer* SACRED, partly through assoc. with Gr. *ἱέραξ* falcon, *ἱερός* sacred. (So MHG. *sacker*, G. *sakerfalk*.) ¶ For the application to a cannon, derived from F. and It., cf. *falconet* (s.v. FALCON), *musket*.

saki sā·ki S. Amer. monkey. XVIII. – F. *saki* (Buffon), irreg. – Tupi *çahy*, corr. to Guarani *çagui* (see SAGOIN), whence Du. *sagwijn*, of which the dim. *sagwijntje* is repr. by **sakawinki** sækəwi·ŋki white-headed saki (XVIII).

salaam səlā·m Oriental salutation, in full (*as*)*salām 'alaikum* peace be unto you, ceremonious obeisance accompanying this XVII. – Arab. *salām* = Heb. *shālōm* peace. Hence vb. XVII.

salacious səlei·ʃəs sexually wanton. XVII. f. L. *salāci-*, *salāx*, f. base of *salīre* leap; see SALIENT, SALTATION, -IOUS.

salad sæ·ləd cold dish of herbs or vegetables. XV. – (O)F. *salade* – Pr. *salada* = OIt. *salata*, Pg. *salada* (cf. It. *insalata*, Sp. *ensalada*) :– Rom. **salāta*, sb. use (sc. *herba*) of pp. fem. of **salāre* (cf. F. *saler*, etc.) salt, f. L. *sāl* SALT. ¶ In gen. Eur. use, e.g. Du. *salade*, G., Da. *salat*, Russ. *salát*.

salamander sæ·ləmàndəɹ lizard-like animal supposed to live in fire XIV; tailed amphibian; poker used red-hot XVII. – (O)F. *salamandre* – L. *salamandra* – Gr. *salamándrā*.

sal-ammoniac sæləmou·niæk ammonium chloride. XIV (*salarmoniak*). – L. *sal ammōniacus*, medL. *sal armōniacum*; see SALT, AMMONIAC.

salary sæ·ləri fixed pay for regular work. XIV (PPl.). – AN. *salarie* = (O)F. *salaire*, Sp., It. *salario* – L. *salārium* orig. money allowed to Roman soldiers for the purchase of salt, (hence) pay, stipend, sb. use (sc. *argentum* money) of *salārius*, f. *sāl* SALT; see -ARY.

sale seil act of selling. Late OE. *sala* – ON. *sala* = OHG. *sala*, f. base of Germ. **saljan* SELL. Hence **sa·l(e)**ABLE. XVI. **sales**MAN sei·lzmən. XVI; see -S.

salempore sæ·ləmpōəɹ blue cotton cloth formerly made at Nellore, India, XVI (*sarampura*, *salampora*) corr. to Du. *salamporij* (XVII), F. *salempouri* (XVIII), prob. f. **Salempur* (*pūr* town) Salem in the province of Madras, India.

salep sæ·ləp nutritive substance made from the tubers of certain orchids. XVIII. – F. *salep*, Sp. *salép*, Pg. *salepo* – Turkish *sālep* – Arab. *sa'leb*, local var. of *tha'leb*, taken to be the shortening of *khasyn 'th-tha'lab* orchis, lit. 'fox's testicles' (cf. *dogstones*). The once common var. **saloop** səlū·p (XVIII) has the derived sense of 'hot drink' consisting of an infusion of salep.

saleratus sælərei·təs (U.S.) impure bicarbonate of potash (soda) used in baking-powders. XIX. – modL. *sāl āërātus* 'AERATED SALT'.

Salian[1] sei·liən XVII. f. L. *Saliī* priests of Mars; referred by the ancients to *salīre* leap; see SALIENT, -IAN.

Salian[2] sei·liən XVII. f. late L. *Saliī* tribe of Franks living near the Zuyder Zee; see -IAN. So **Sal**IC sæ·lik, sei·lik XVI; in *S. law*, tr. *lex Salica*, a Frankish code in which it was provided (LIX § 5) that a woman could have no portion of the inheritance of 'Salic land' (*terra Salica*, the meaning of which is disputed).

salicional səli·ʃənəl (mus.) reedy organ stop. XIX. – G. *salicional*, f. L. *salic-*, *salix* willow, SALLOW[1]. Also **salicet** sæ·liset. XIX. G.; for the ending cf. *dulcet*.

salicyl sæ·lisil (chem.) diatomic radical of **salicy·l**IC *acid*. XIX. – F. *salicyle*, f. L. *salic-*, *salix* SALLOW[1]; see -YL.

salient sei·liənt leaping (first in her.) XVI; jetting forward, pointing outward XVII; prominent XVIII; sb. salient part or angle XIX. – L. *salient-*, *-ēns*, prp. of *salīre* leap; see SALTATION, -ENT; cf. F. *saillant*. *S. point* †the heart as it first appears in an embryo, (hence) first beginning, starting-point (XVII, Sir T. Browne), tr. modL. *punctum saliens* (cf. F. *point saillant*), the source of which is Aristotle's 'Historia Animalium' VI iii *τοῦτο δὲ σημεῖον πηδᾷ καὶ κινεῖται ὥσπερ ἔμψυχον* This point (i.e. the heart appearing as a speck of blood) leaps and moves as if alive.

saline sei·lain, səlai·n pert. to salt XV; sb. salt lake, etc.; saline purge XIX. – medL. *salīnum* (in L. only sb. *sālīnæ* salt works, salt pits, *sālīnum* saltcellar); f. L. *sāl* SALT; see -INE[1].

saliva səlai·və spittle. XVII (anglicized *salyue* c.1400). L. *salīva*. So †**sali·**VAL[1]. XVII. – modL. *salīvālis*. **sali**VARY sæ·livəri. XVIII. – L. *salivārius*. **sa·liv**ATE[3]. XVII. f. pp. stem of L. *salīvāre*. **saliva·**TION production of saliva. XVI. – F. or late L.

salleeman sæ·limæn (hist.) Moorish pirate ship. XVII. f. *Sallee*, name of a Moroccan seaport+MAN, as in *man-of-war*, *merchantman*, *East-Indiaman*.

sallender sæ·lindəɹ earlier *sellender*, (now only pl.) dry scab on a horse's hock. XVI (Fitzherbert). Of unkn. origin, but with a remarkable formal parallel in MALANDER (XV). F. *solandre* is recorded much later (XVII).

sallet sæ·lit, **salade** səlā·d globular head-piece in mediæval armour. XV. – F. *salade*, – Pr. *salada*, It. *celata*, or Sp. *celada* – Rom. **cælāta*, sb. use (sc. *cassis*, *galea* helmet) of fem. pp. of L. *cælāre* engrave, f. *cælum* chisel :– **kaidlom*, f. **kaid-* cut (cf. -CIDE). The form in *-et* arose from reduction of the final syll. due to initial stress.

sallow[1] sæ·lou (dial.) willow. OE. (Angl.) *salh* (repr. directly by dial. *saugh*, †*salfe* XIV) :– Germ. **salχaz* (whence F. *saule*), rel. to

OHG. *salaha* (G. in comp. *sal|weide*) :- **salχōn*, and ON. *selja* (whence north. dial. *seal* XVI, Spenser) :- **salχjōn*, and outside Germ. to L. *salix*, Gr. (Arcadian) *helíkē*, OIr. *sail* (g. *sailech*), W. *helyg*. The forms *sallow* (ME. *salwe*) and (chiefly western and southern) *sally* descend from OE. inflexional *salg-*, *saliġ-*.

sallow[2] sæ·lou of a sickly or brownish yellow. OE. *salo* dusky, dark (cf. *saluwig* dusky, *salwed* darkened) = MDu. *salu*, *saluwe* discoloured, dirty, OHG. *salo*, *salaw-* dark-coloured (G. dial. *sal*), ON. *sǫlr* yellow :- Germ. **salwa-* (whence F. *sale*, It. †*salavo* dirty); cf. Russ. *solóvyj* cream-coloured. For the vocalism, cf. FALLOW[2] yellow.

sally sæ·li sortie from a besieged place XVI; sudden start or outburst XVII; sprightly remark XVIII. – (O)F. *saillie*, sb. use of fem. pp. of *saillir*, refash. (cf. FAIL) of OF. *salir* :- L. *salīre* (see SALTATION). Hence **sa·lly** vb. XVI.

Sally Lunn sæ·li lʌ·n kind of tea-cake. XVIII. Said to be so named after a woman who made and cried them in Bath.

salmagundi sælməgʌ·ndi dish of chopped meat with condiments. XVII. – F. *salmigondis*, †*-gondin* (Rabelais), of unkn. origin.

salmi sæ·lmi ragout of game. XVIII. shortening of F. *salmigondis*; see prec.

salmiac sæ·lmiæk native sal-ammoniac. XVIII. – G. *salmiak*, contr. of L. *sal ammoniacus* SAL-AMMONIAC.

salmon sæ·mən large fish of the genus Salmo, esp. S. salar. XIII (*sa(l)moun*). – AN. *sa(u)moun*, (O)F. *saumon* = Pr. *salmo*, Sp. *salmón*, It. *salmone* :- L. *salmōnem*, *salmō* (Pliny), rel. to *salar* trout or young salmon. ¶ For the repr. of OF. au by æ cf. *savage*, *scabbard*, and the (now vulgar or dial.) pronunc. sæ·sidʒ of *sausage*.

salon sæ·lɔ̃ large reception room. XVIII. – F. *salon*; see next.

saloon səlū·n large apartment for assemblies, etc. XVIII; large cabin or railway carriage; (U.S.) drinking bar XIX. – F. *salon* – It. *salone* (whence also Sp. *salón*, Pg. *salão*), augm. of *sala* (= Pr., Sp. *sala*, OF. *sale*, mod. F. *salle*) – Rom. **sala* hall – Germ. **salaz*, **saliz*, repr. by OE. *sæl*, OHG. *sal* (G. *saal*) and OE. *sele*, OS. *seli*, OHG. *sali*, *seli*, ON. *salr*; see -OON.

saloop see SALEP.

Salopian səlou·piən pert. to Shropshire. XVIII. f. *Salop* sæ·ləp, alternative name of Shropshire, evolved from *Salopesberia* (XI) and *Salopescire* (XI), AN. alt. of ME. forms of OE. *Sćrobbesbyrig* Shrewsbury and *Sćrobbesbyrigscīr* Shropshire; see -IAN.

salpiglossis sælpiglɔ·sis genus of scrophulariaceous plants. XIX. modL., irreg. f. Gr. *sálpigx* trumpet + *glôssa* tongue; so named from its trumpet-shaped corolla.

salsify sæ·lsifi purple goatsbeard, Tragopogon porrifolius. XVIII. – F. *salsifis* (also †*salsefie*, *-fique*, †*sassefrique*) – It. †*salsefica* (mod. *sassefrica*), earlier †*erba salsifica*; of unkn. origin.

salt sɔ̀lt substance (sodium choride) prepared as a condiment OE.; (old chem.) solid non-inflammable substance having a taste XIV; (mod. chem.) compound formed by an acid with a basic radical XVIII. OE. *salt*, *sealt* = OS. *salt* (Du. *zout*), (O)HG. *salz*, ON., Goth. *salt* :- CGerm. **saltam*, sb. use of adj. **saltaz* (see below), extension of IE. (exc. Indo-Iran.) **sal-*, repr. (with variations) by L. *sāl*, *sal-* (whence F. *sel*, Pr., Sp., It. *sale*, Rum. *sare*), Gr. *háls*, OSl. *salĭ* (Russ. *sol'*), Lett. *sâls*, OIr. *salann*, W. *halen*, Toch. *sāle*. So **salt** adj. OE. *s(e)alt* = OFris. *salt*, ON. *saltr*. **salt** vb. OE. *s(e)altan* (pp. *salten*) = MLG. *solten*, Du. *zouten*, OHG. *salzan* (pp. *gisalzan*), ON. *salta*, Goth. *saltan*; cf. L. *sal(l)īre* (*sall-* :- **sald-*; and *salsus* :- **saldtós*). Hence **sa·lty**[1]. XV.

saltation sæltei·ʃən leaping, dancing. XVII. – L. *saltātiō(n-)*, f. *saltāre* dance, frequent. of *salīre* leap, rel. to Gr. *hállesthai*; see -ATION. So **saltato·rial** XVIII, **sa·ltatory**[2] XVII. – L. *saltātōrius*.

saltcellar sɔ̀·ltse:ləɹ small table vessel for holding salt. XV. f. SALT+*saler*, *sel(l)er* – AN. **saler(e)*, OF. *sal(l)iere* (mod. *salière*), also *salier*, corr. to Pr., It. *saliera*; Rom. f. L. *sāl* SALT. The sp. was finally assim. to *cellar*, through *seller*, *sellar*.

saltern sɔ̀·ltəɹn (hist.) salt-works. OE. *sealtærn*, f. *sealt* SALT+*ærn* dwelling, building, house (cf. BARN, RANSACK).

saltigrade sæ·ltigreid (zool.) spider having legs developed for leaping. XIX. – modL. *Saltigradæ* pl., f. L. *saltus* leap +*gradī* step; cf. SALTATION, GRADE.

saltimbanco sæltimbæ·ŋkou mountebank. XVII (Sir T. Browne). – It. *saltimbanco* (whence F. *saltimbanque*), f. *saltare* leap+*in* on+*banco* bench; see SALTATION, BANK[2].

saltire sæ·ltaiəɹ (her.) ordinary in the form of a St. Andrew's cross X. XIV. Early forms *sawturoure*, *sawtire*, later *saltier*, *-ire* – OF. *saut(e)our*, *-ouer*, *sau(l)toir* stirrup cord (perh. forming a deltoid figure when in use), stile with cross-pieces, saltire :- medL. *saltātōrium*, sb. use of n. of *saltātōrius* SALTATORY.

saltpetre sɔ̀·ltpī·təɹ potassium nitrate, nitre. XVI. alt., by assim. to SALT, of †*salpetre* (XIV) – (O)F. *salpètre* – medL. *salpetra*, prob. for **sāl petræ* 'salt of rock', i.e. *sāl* SALT, *petræ*, g. of *petra* (cf. PETRIFY); the substance being so named because it occurs as an incrustation on stones.

salubrious səlʲū·briəs health-giving. XVI. f. L. *salūbris*, f. *salūs* health; see next and -IOUS. So **salu·brity** XV. L.

salutary sæ·ljŭtəri conducive to wellbeing XV (Caxton; earlier †*salutairé*); conducive to health XVII. – (O)F. *salutaire* or L.

salūtāris, f. *salūt-*, *salūs* health, welfare, greeting, salutation, rel. to *salvus* SAFE; see -ARY. So **saluta·tion** greeting in words XIV (Wycl. Bible) – (O)F. *salutation* or L. *salūtātio(n-)*, f. *salūtāre*, whence **salute** səlʲū·t greet XIV (Wycl. Bible; repl. earlier †*salue* – (O)F. *saluer*); (mil. and naval) XVI. **salu·te** sb. XIV; partly – (O)F. *salut* (as sb. to *saluer*), partly f. the Eng. vb.

salvage sæ·lvidʒ payment to persons who have saved a ship or its cargo; action of saving a ship, etc.; property salved XVII. – (O)F. *salvage* – medL. *salvāgium*, f. L. *salvāre* SAVE; see -AGE. Hence, by back-formation, **salve** vb.[2] sælv save from loss at sea or by fire XVIII; **sa·lvor**[1], †*salver* XVII.

salvation sælvei·ʃən saving of the soul XIII (AncrR.); preservation, means of this XIV (Ch.). ME. *sa(u)vacioun*, *salv-* – OF. *sauvacion*, *salv-* (mod. *salvation*) = Pr., Sp. *salvacion*, It. *salvazione* – late L. *salvātiō(n-)*, rendering Gr. σωτηρία, f. *salvāre* SAVE[1]; see -ATION.

salve sāv, sælv healing ointment. OE. *salf*, *sealf(e)* = OS. *salƀa* (Du. *zalf*), OHG. *salba* (G. *salbe*) :– Germ. (not Scand.) **salƀō* :– **solpā*; cf. Skr. *sarpis* clarified butter, *sṛpras* greasy, Gr. *ólpē*, *ólpis* oil-flask, *élpos* oil. So **salve** vb.[1] †anoint OE.; heal, remedy XIII; soothe (irritation, an uneasy conscience) XIX (partly by assoc. with †*salve* clear up, explain – L. *salvāre*). OE. *s(e)alfian* = OFris. *salvia*, OS. *salƀon* (Du. *zalven*), OHG. *salbōn* (G. *salben*), Goth. *salbōn* (whence Goth. *salbons*).

salver sæ·lvəɹ tray for handing things on. XVII. f. F. *salve* tray for presenting objects to the king, or its source Sp. *salva* †foretasting or assaying of food or drink, tray on which assayed food was placed, f. *salvar* SAVE, render safe, assay; the ending *-er* is due to assoc. with *platter*. ¶ *Server* occurs with the same meaning in late XVII and was prob. assoc. with this word through the pronunc. *sarver*.

salvia sæ·lviə genus of Labiatæ, including sage. XIX. modL. (Tournefort, 1700) use of L. *salvia*, SAGE[1].

salvo[1] sæ·lvou saving clause; dishonest mental reservation XVII; expedient for saving one's reputation or soothing one's conscience, etc. XVIII (cf. SALVE vb.[1]). – L. *salvō*, abl. of n. of *salvus* uninjured, intact, SAFE, occurring as the first word of medL. law phr. such as *salvo jure* (abl. of L. *jūs* right) without prejudice to the right of, *salvo servicio forinseco* foreign service excepted (cf. SAVE[2]).

salvo[2] sæ·lvou simultaneous discharge of firearms, esp. as a salute. XVII. repl. earlier (XVI) †*salve* (rarely †*salvee*) and occas. †*salva*, by substitution of *-o* for *-a* (cf. -ADO); ult. – It. *salva* (whence F. *salve*).

sal volatile sæl vəlæ·tili aromatic solution of ammonium carbonate. XVII. – modL. *sāl volātile*; see SALT, VOLATILE.

sam sæm (sl.) oath. XIX. prob. shortening of †*salmon*, †*salomon*, cant term for 'alter or masse' (Harman's 'Caveat', 1567), in phr. †*by the salomon*, †*by salmon* (XVII), presumably a perverted use of L. (Vulg.) *Salomon* Solomon.

Samaritan səmæ·ritən pert. to, native of, Samaria in Palestine XIV; Aramaic dialect spoken in Samaria XVII. – late L. *Samarītānus*, f. Gr. *Samareítēs*, f. *Samareíā*; see -ITE, -AN. (OE. had g.pl. *Samarītāna* and adj. *Samarītānisć*.)

sambo sæ·mbou half-breed, mostly between Negro and Indian. XVIII. – Sp. *zambo* (also in Eng. use XIX), identified with *zambo* bandy-legged; but *Samboses* (pl.) is the name of a W. African tribe in Hawkins's voyage (1564–5) printed by Hakluyt; prob. not the same as *sambo* nickname for a negro (XIX), which may be Foulah *sambo* uncle.

Sam Browne sæm braun officer's belt introduced by General *Sam* J. *Browne* (1824–1901). XX.

sambur sæ·mbəɹ Indian elk. XVII. Hindi.

same seim not different, identical. XII (Orm). – ON. *same* m., *sama* fem., n. = OHG., Goth. *sama* :– Germ. adj. **samaz* (repr. otherwise only by the derived adv., as in OE. *swā same*, OS. *sō sama*, *-o* just as or like, OHG. *sama*, *samo* likewise) :– IE. **somós*, whence also Skr. *samás* level, equal, same, Gr. *homós* (see HOMO-), OIr. *som* same; the vars. **sem-* **sōm-* **səm-* of the base are seen in L. *simul* at the same time, SIMULTANEOUS, *similis* SIMILAR, SANSKRIT, Gr. *heîs* one (:– **sems*), SEEM, and SOME. ¶ Superseded ILK and SELF in gen. use; combined with *self* in *selfsame* (XV, Lydg.) parallel with OHG. *selbsama* in just the same way, Norw., Da. *selvsamme* very same.

samite sæ·mait (hist.) rich silk fabric. XIII. – OF. *samit*, corr. to Pr. *samit*, It. *sciamito*, Sp. *jamete*, ult. – medL. *examitum* – medGr. *hexámiton* (whence also MHG. *samit*, G. *samt* velvet, OSl. *aksamitŭ*), f. Gr. *hexa-* HEXA- + *mítos* thread; the ref. to sixth thread is variously explained.

samlet sæ·mlit young salmon. XVII (Walton). alt. of earlier *samonet* XVI (f. SALMON + -ET) by assoc. with -LET.

Samnite sæ·mnait one of a people of ancient Italy, believed to be an offshoot of the Sabines. XIV (*Sampnites*, Gower). – L. *Samnītēs* (pl.), rel. to *Sabīnus* SABINE; see -ITE.

samovar sæmovā·ɹ Russian tea urn. XIX. – Russ. *samovar*, f. *samo-* self- + stem of *varít'* boil.

Samoyed sæmoi·ed one of a people native to W. Siberia and N. Russ. coastal area XVII; (also *-ede*) breed of dog XIX. – Russ. *samoéd*, prob. f. Lapp. Norw. (Vasmer). ¶ Earlier interpreted as 'self-eater', i.e. 'cannibal', e.g. by Purchas 1613.

sampan sæ·mpæn small Chinese boat. XVII. Chinese *san pan*, f. *san* three, *pan* board.

samphire sæ·mfaiəɹ the plant Crithmum maritimum. XVI (*sampere, sampiere*) – F. (*herbe de*) *Saint Pierre* 'St. Peter's herb'; the later form may be due to assim. to *camphire*, var. of CAMPHOR.

sample sà·mpl †illustrative or confirmatory fact, etc.; †example, warning XIII (Cursor M.); specimen of material or goods XV. Aphetic – AN. *assample*, var. of OF. *essample* EXAMPLE. Hence vb. XVI. Cf. ENSAMPLE.

sampler sà·mpləɹ †example, pattern XIII (Cursor M.); beginner's exercise in embroidery done on canvas XVI. Aphetic – OF. *essamplaire*, var. of *essemplaire* EXEMPLAR.

Samson's post sæ·msənz poust (POST[1]) †kind of mousetrap having a triangular pillar XVI; (naut.) strong pillar or stanchion XVIII. prob. with allusion to Judges xvi 29 ('And Samson took hold of the two middle pillars . . .').

sanatorium sænətɔ̄ə·riəm establishment for the treatment of invalids; room for the sick. XIX. – modL. *sānātōrium*, f. pp. stem of L. *sānāre* heal, f. *sānus* healthy, SANE; see -ATE[3], -ORIUM.

sanbenito sænbĕnī·tou (under the Sp. Inquisition) penitent heretic's garment. XVI. – Sp. *sambenito*, f. *San Benito* St. Benedict; so called ironically from its resemblance in shape to the Benedictine scapular.

sanctify sæ·ŋᵏtifai †consecrate, hallow XIV (Gower); make holy XV. In earliest use *seintifie* – OF. *saintifier*, later influenced by *sanctifier* – ChrL. *sanctificāre* (Tertullian), f. L. *sanctus* holy (SAINT). So **sanctifica·tion**. XVI. – ChrL. *sanctificātiō(n-)*. **sanctimonious** sæŋᵏtimou·niəs †holy, sacred; affecting sanctity. XVII. f. L. *sanctimōnia* sanctity; superseding †**sanctimo·nial** (XVI) – late L.; thence **sa·nctimony** †sanctity XVI; affected holiness XVII. **sanction** sæ·ŋᵏʃən †law, decree XVI; (leg.) penalty exacted to compel obedience; clause of a law prescribing this; motive, etc. involved therein; binding force XVII; influential encouragement XVIII. – F. *sanction* authoritative approval of a law, penalty prescribed in an enactment; (gen.) approval – L. *sanctiō(n-)* act of establishing as inviolable under a penalty, clause decreeing a penalty, f. *sanct-*, pp. stem of *sancīre* render inviolable, decree, ratify, forbid under penalty, f. var. (with nasal infix) of base of *sacer* SACRED; hence vb. XVIII; partly after F. *sanctionner*. **sa·nctity** holiness XIV; sacredness XVII (Sh.); partly (in forms *sauntite, saintite*) – OF. *sain(c)tité* (mod. *sainteté*) = Pr. *sanctetat*, etc.; partly immed. – L. *sanctitās*. **sanctuary** sæ·ŋᵏtjuəri building for religious worship XIV (R. Rolle); part of a church immediately surrounding the altar; sacred place giving immunity from arrest; also fig. XIV (Ch., Wyclif). – AN. *sanctuarie*, (O)F. *sanctuaire*, Pr. *sanctuari*, etc. – L. *sanctuārium*, f. *sanctus*, after SACRARIUM. (OF. forms more commonly had *saint-*, whence Eng. forms in †*saint-*, †*seint-*, *sent-* XIV–XVI.) **sanctum** sæ·ŋᵏtəm holy place of the Jewish tabernacle XVI; short for *sanctum sanctorum* in the second sense XIX. L., n. sg. of *sanctus*. **sanctum sanctorum** sæ·ŋᵏtəm sæŋᵏtɔ̄ə·rəm (also pl. *sancta sanctorum* in sg. sense, as in the Vulgate, Ezek. xliv 13 etc., after the use of LXX) Holy of Holies of the Jewish temple XIV; person's private retreat XVIII. L., n. sg. and n. g. pl. of *sanctus*, tr. (= LXX *τὸ ἅγιον τῶν ἁγίων*) of Heb. *qōdesh haqqodāshīm* holy of holies. **sanctus** sæ·ŋktəs the 'angelic hymn' (see Isa. vi 3), beginning *Sanctus sanctus sanctus* Holy, holy, holy, which concludes the preface to the Eucharistic canon (see also TERSANCTUS). XIV (Wyclif). L. (See SAINT.)

sand sænd material consisting of finely comminuted particles of rocks. OE. *sand* = OFris. *sand, sond*, OS. *sand*, OHG. *sant* (Du. *zand*, G. *sand*), ON. *sandr* :– CGerm. (exc. Gothic) **sandam*, **sandaz* (whence Finn. *santa*) :– **sam(a)dam, -az* (cf. MHG. *sampt*), rel. to Gr. *hámathos* sand, L. *sabulum* (cf. SABULOUS). Hence **sa·ndy**[1]. OE. *sandig*.

sandal[1] sæ·nd(ə)l covering for the sole of the foot XIV (Wycl. Bible); half-shoe for ceremonial wear XV. – L. *sandalium* (pl. *sandalia*, whence as fem. sg. (O)F. *sandale*, Sp. *sandalia*) – Gr. *sandálion*, dim. of *sándalon* (Æolic *sámbalon*) wooden shoe, prob. of Asiatic origin (cf. Pers. *sandal* shoe). ¶ Of CEur. range.

sandal[2] sæ·nd(ə)l scented wood of species of Santalum. XIV. – medL. *sandalum* (with var. *santalum*), whence OF. *sandal*, (also mod.) *santal*, †*sandle*, †*sandre* (whence *sanders* XIV); Sp. *sándalo*, It. *sandalo*, ult. – Skr. *čandanas*, through Pers. *čandal*, Arab. *ṣandal*, late Gr. *sándanon, sántalon*. ¶ Of CEur. range.

sandarac sæ·ndəræk A. realgar XVI; B. resin of a N.W. African tree; †C. bee-bread XVII. – L. *sandaraca* – Gr. *sandarákē, -ákhē*, of Asiatic origin; the connexion between the senses is not clear; cf. F. *sandaraque*, Sp., It. *sandaraca* in A and/or B, Arab. *sandarūs, sandalus* in B, Pers., Urdu *sandaros* in A and B.

sand-blind sæ·ndblaind (arch. and dial.) half-blind, purblind. XV. repr. ult. OE. **samblind*, f. *sam-* half- (as in *samcucu* = OHG *sāmiquec*, half-alive), shortening of WGerm. **sāmi-* (repr. by OS. *sām-*, OHG. *sāmi-*) :– IE. **sēmi-* SEMI- + BLIND; assim. to SAND.

sanders see SANDAL[2].

sandiver sæ·ndivəɹ scum rising through glass in a state of fusion. XIV (*saundyuer*).

corr. of F. *suint de verre* (XVII), i.e. *suint* exudation from wool (formerly †*suin*, **sudin*, f. *suer* sweat :– L. *sūdāre*), *de* of, *verre* glass :– L. *vitrum* (cf. VITREOUS); presumably assim. to SAND.

sandwich sæ·ndwitʃ article of food consisting of two slices of bread with meat, etc. between them. XVIII (Gibbon, 1762). f. name of John Montagu, 4th earl of *Sandwich* (1718–1792), for whom the device was said to have been invented so that he might not leave the gaming-table, at which he spent twenty-four hours without other refreshment.

sane sein sound in mind XVII (*of sane memorie*, repr. law L. *sanæ memoriæ*); †healthy in body. – L. *sānus*. So **san**ITY sæ·nĭti †bodily health XV; mental soundness XVII (Sh.). – L. *sānitās*.

sang-froid sãfrwa· coolness, indifference. XVIII (Chesterfield). F., 'cold blood' (L. *sanguis, frigidus*).

sangreal sæŋgrei·l holy grail. XV. – OF. *saint graal*; see SAINT, GRAIL². ¶ The sp. has been infl. by assoc. with OF. *sang real* royal blood.

sanguinary sæ·ŋgwinəri bloody; bloodthirsty. XVII. – L. *sanguinārius*, f. *sanguin-, sanguis* blood; see -ARY and cf. F. *sanguinaire*, etc. So **sa·nguine** blood-red XIV (Wycl. Bible, Ch., Trevisa); pert. to the physiological complexion in which blood predominates over the other humours XIV (Ch., Gower, Trevisa); disposed to hopefulness XVI. – (O)F. *sanguin*, fem. *-ine* – L. *sanguineus* (whence **sangui·n**EOUS XVI). **sangui·nolent**. XV. – L. See -ULENT.

sanhedrim sæ·nĭdrim highest court and supreme council of the Jews at Jerusalem. XVI. – late Heb. *sanhedrīn* – Gr. *sunédrion* council, f. *sún* together (SYN-)+*hédra* seat (see SIT). ¶ The common incorrect form in *-im* seems to be due to the notion that the orig. *-īn* was the Aram. pl. suffix equiv. to Heb. *-īm*.

sanicle sæ·nikl umbelliferous plant Sanicula europæa. XV. – OF. *sanicle* – medL. *sanicula, -ulum*, perh. f. L. *sānus* healthy (SANE), with ref. to the plant's reputed healing powers.

sanies sei·niiz (med.) thin fœtid pus. XVI. – L. *saniēs*.

sanitary sæ·nitəri pert. to health or to sanitation. XIX. – F. *sanitaire*, f. L. *sānitās* health, f. *sānus* healthy (SANE); see -ARY. Hence (irreg.) **sanit**A·TION. XIX.

sanity see SANE.

sanjak sæ·ndʒæk administrative district of Turkey. XVI. – Turk. *sanjāq* (lit.) banner. So **sa·njak**BEG, -BEY XVI.

sans sænz (arch., chiefly after Sh. 'A.Y.L.' II vii 166) without. XIII. ME. *san, saun, sans, saunz* – OF. *san, sanz* (also mod. *sans*), earlier *sen(s)* = Pr. *sen(e)s*, OSp. *senes, sen* (mod. *sin*), Pg. *sem*, †*sen*, OIt. *sen* :– Rom. **sene*, for L. *sine*, partly infl. by L. *absentiā* (abl.) in the ABSENCE of (whence Pr. *sensa*, It. *senza*). ¶ Before Sh. mainly in phr. direct from OF., e.g. *sans delay, sans fail, sans pity*.

sansculotte sænzkjulɔ·t, ||sãkülɔt in the French Revolution, a republican of the poorer classes in Paris. XVIII (1790). F., f. *sans* without (see prec.) + *culotte* knee-breeches, f. *cul* buttocks :– L. *cūlu-s*; usu. taken to mean lit. 'one who wears trousers (*pantalon*), not knee-breeches'.

sanserif sænse·rif printing type without serifs. XIX. prob. f. SANS+SERIF.

Sanskrit, Sanscrit sæ·nskrit ancient and sacred language of India, the oldest known member of the IE. group. XVII (*Samescretan* Purchas; *Sanscreet*). – Skr. *saṃskṛta* (n. *saṃskṛtam*) put together, well formed, highly wrought, elaborated, perfected, f. *sam* together (rel. to *sama* SAME) + *kṛ* make, do, perform + pp. ending *-to*.

Santa Claus sæ·ntə klɔ̄z imaginary person who brings presents for children on Christmas Eve. XVIII (*St. A Claus*), XIX (*Santiclaus*, Longfellow). orig. U.S. – Du. dial. *Sante Klaas* (Du. *Sint Klaas*) i.e. *sant, sint* SAINT, *Klaas*, abbrev. of *Nicolaas* Nicholas (patron of children).

santon sæ·ntən marabout. XVI. – F. *santon* – Sp. *santon* (= Pg. *santão*), f. *santo* SAINT; cf. -OON.

sap¹ sæp vital juice of plants OE.; sapwood, alburnum XV. OE. *sæp*, corr. to (M)LG., (M)Du. *sap*, OHG. *saf* (G. *saft*, whence Sw., Da. *saft*), prob. repr. Germ. **sapam*, **sappam*, and rel. to ON. *safi* (Sw. *saf*) :– **safon* or **saƀon* :– IE. **sapon-* (cf. L. *sapa* must boiled until it is thick, whence (O)F. *sève*, Pr., Sp. *saba* sap, It. *sapa*). Hence **sa·p**LING¹ young tree XV; young person XVI (Sh.); **sa·p**SKULL simpleton XVIII; cf. SAP⁴.

sap² sæp †undermining a defence; construction of covered trenches to approach a besieged place XVI; trench so constructed XVII. Early forms *zappe, sappe* – It. *zappa* (Piedmontese *sappa*) and the derived F. †*sappe*, †*zappe* (now *sape*) spade, spade-work; cf. Sp. *zapa*, late L. *sappa* (VI), *zappa*. Hence **sap** vb. dig a sap XVI; undermine XVII; weaken insidiously (assoc. with SAP¹, as if 'drain the sap from') XVIII. – F. *saper*, †*sapper* – It. *zappare*; cf. Sp. *sapar*; prob. of Arab. origin.

sap³ sæp (school sl.) studious pupil. XVIII (Chesterfield). perh. f. fig. use of SAP vb.

sap⁴ sæp (colloq.) simpleton XIX (Scott). Short for *sapskull* (XVIII) 'skull of sapwood' (see SAP¹). ¶ Cf. *sappy* foolish (XVII).

sapajou sæ·pədʒū S. Amer. monkey. XVII. – F. *sapajou*, given by d'Abbeville as a Cayenne word.

sapan, sappan sæ·pən dye-wood obtained from the genus Cæsalpina. XVI. – Du. *sapan* – Malay *sapaŋ* (whence also F. *sapan*,

Pg. *sapão*), of S. Indian origin (cf. Tamil *shappangam*, Malayalam *chapaññam*).

saphena səfī·nə name of two veins in the leg. XIV. – medL. *saphena* – Arab. *çāfin*.

sapid sæ·pid savoury, palatable; having a taste. XVII. – L. *sapidus*, f. *sapere*; see next and -ID[1].

sapient sei·piənt (now usu. iron.) wise. XV. – OF. *sapient* or L. *sapient-*, *-ēns*, prp. of *sapere* have a taste, be sensible or wise, rel. to OS. *af|sebbian* perceive, notice, OHG. *int|seffen* notice, taste, OE. *sefa* mind, understanding, OS. *sebo*, ON. *sefi*; see -ENT. So **sa·pi**ENCE. XIV. – OF. – L. *sapientia*. **sapient**IAL sæpie·nʃəl †pert. to wisdom XV; pert. to the 'wisdom' books of the Bible XVI. – F. *sapiential* or ChrL. *sapientiālis*.

sapodilla sæpodi·lə (fruit of) the evergreen tree Achras Sapota. XVII. – Sp. *zapotillo* (whence F. *sapotille*), dim. of *zapote* SAPOTA; the change of *t* to *d* occurs also in Du. *sapodille*, G. *sapodilla*.

saponaceous sæponei·ʃəs soapy. XVIII. f. modL. *sāpōnāceus*, f. L. *sāpōn-* SOAP; see -ACEOUS.

sapor sei·pɔ̄ɹ taste. XV. – L. *sapor*, f. *sapere* have a taste; see SAPIENT and cf. SAVOUR.

sapota səpou·tə (fruit of) the tree Achras Sapota. XVI. In XVI–XVII †*sapote* – Sp., Pg. *zapote* (whence F. *sapote*) – Aztec *tzápotl*; repl. by modL. *sapota*.

Sapphic sæ·fik pert. to Sappho or metres used by her XVI (G. Douglas); also sb. pl. verses in Sapphic metre XVI (Sidney). – F. *saphique*, †*sapphique* – L. *Sapphicus* – Gr. *Sapphikós*, f. *Sapphṓ*, name of the poetess (*c.* 600 B.C.) of Lesbos, Greece; see -IC.

sapphire sæ·faiəɹ blue precious stone. XIII. ME. *saphir*, *safir* – OF. *safir* (mod. *saphir*), corr. to Pr. *safir*, etc. – L. *sapphīrus*, also *sapp(h)ir* – Gr. *sáppheiros* (prob.) lapis lazuli (whence perh. Pers. *saffīr*, Arab. *çafīr*), prob. of Semitic origin (Heb. *sappir*, Jewish Aram. *sampīrīnā* have been further referred to Skr. *çaniprija* 'dear to the planet Saturn', dark-coloured stone (sapphire or emerald).

sapro- sæ·prou, sæprɔ· comb. form of Gr. *saprós* putrid, rel. to *sēpein* rot (see SEPTIC) used in some techn. terms, the earliest of which is **sapro·**PHAGOUS living on decomposing matter XIX; before a vowel *sapr-* as in **sapræmia** -ī·miə septiç poisoning XIX, modL. (Gr. *haîma* blood).

saraband sæ·rəbænd (music for) a slow and stately Spanish dance. XVII (Jonson). – F. *sarabande* – Sp., It. *zarabanda*, of disputed origin.

Saracen sæ·rəsən name of nomadic peoples of the Syro-Arabian desert, (hence) Arab, Moslem; †pagan, infidel. XIII. – OF. *Sar(r)azin*, *-cin* (mod. *Sarrasin*), corr. to Sp. *Saraceno*, It. *Saracino* – late L. *Saracēnus* – late Gr. *Sarakēnós*, perh. f. Arab. *sharqī* eastern, f. *sharq* sunrise, east (cf. SIROCCO). The name was in mediæval times assoc. with Sarah, the wife of Abraham, or with the Hagarens, descendants of Hagar. Cf. SARSEN.

saraf, **sarraf** sarā·f money-changer or banker, in the east. XVI. ult. – Arab. *ṣarrāf*, f. *ṣarafa* exchange, corr. to Heb. *tsāraph* refine, assay (gold, silver); cf. SHROFF.

Saratoga særətou·gə in full *S. trunk* large trunk esp. used by ladies. XIX. prob. f. *S. Springs* name of a summer resort in New York State, U.S.A.

sarbacane sā·ɹbəkein blow-tube for shooting with. XVIII. – F. *sarbacane*. †*-batane* – (with assim. to *canne* CANE) Sp. *zarbatana*, *cerbatana* – Arab. dial. *zarbaṭāna*, for *zab(a)ṭāna*.

sarcasm sā·ɹkæzm cutting expression or remark, sarcastic language. XVI (in L. form) XVII. – F. *sarcasme* (Rabelais) or late L., *sarcasmos* (Charisius) – late Gr. *sarkasmós*, f. *sarkázein* tear flesh, gnash the teeth, speak bitterly, f. *sark-*, *sárx* flesh. So **sarca·st**IC. XVII. – F. *sarcastique*, f. *sarcasme*, after *enthousiasme*, *-astique*.

sarcenet see SARSENET.

sarco- sā·ɹkou comb. form of Gr. *sark-*, *sárx* flesh. **sa·rc**ODE animal protoplasm. XIX. **sarcoma** saɹkou·mə †fleshy excrescence XVII; kind of tumour XIX. – modL. *sarcōma* – Gr. *sárkōma* (Galen), f. *sarkoûn* become fleshy, f. *sark-*, *sárx* flesh; see -OMA.

sarcophagus sāɹkɔ·fəgəs stone reputed by the ancient Greeks to consume corpses and hence used for coffins XVII; stone coffin XVIII. – L. *sarcophagus* – Gr. *sarkophágos*, sb. use of adj. f. *sarko-*, *sárx* flesh + *-phágos* -eating, -PHAGOUS.

sard sāɹd variety of cornelian. XIV (Wycl. Bible). – F. *sarde* or L. *sarda* SARDIUS.

sardelle saɹde·l fish resembling the sardine. XVI. – It. *sardella*, dim. of *sarda* :– L. *sarda* – Gr. *sárdē*. So F.; cf. -EL[2].

sardine[1] sā·ɹdain, -īn precious stone of Rev. iv 3. XIV. – late L. *sardinus* – Gr. *sárdinos*, var. reading for *sárdios* SARDIUS.

sardine[2] sāɹdī·n small fish of the herring family, Clupea pilchardus. XV (*-eyne*). – (O)F. *sardine*, corr. to It. *sardina* – L. *sardīna*; cf. late Gr. *sardḗnē*, *-ī́nē*, *sardînos*, and L. *sarda*, Gr. *sárdā*; prob. connected with the name of the island Sardinia.

sardius sā·ɹdiəs precious stone, sard. XIV (Wycl. Bible). – late L. *sardius* – Gr. *sárdios*, prob. f. *Sardṓ* Sardinia.

sardonic sāɹdɔ·nik (of laughter) marked by bitterness or scorn. XVII (T. Herbert). – F. *sardonique*, alt. of †*sardonien* (whence †**sardo·n**IAN XVI), f. L. *sardonius* – late Gr. *Sardónios* Sardinian, which was substituted for *sardánios* (Homer) as an epithet for scornful laughter from the notion that the word orig. referred to the effects of eating a Sardinian plant (L. *herba Sardonia* or *Sardōa*), which was said to produce facial convulsions resembling horrible laughter; cf. Sp. *sardónico*, It. *sardonico*, and see -IC.

sardonyx sā·ɹdəniks variety of onyx. XIV (*sardonyse*, *-yk*, *-ix*). – L. *sardonyx* – Gr. *sardónux*, presumably f. *sárdios* SARDIUS (f. *Sardis*, capital of Lydia) + *ónux* ONYX.

sargasso sārgæ·sou seaweed found floating in the Gulf Stream and esp. in the S. Sea (bounded by the Azores, the Canaries, and the Cape Verde islands). XVI. – Pg. *sargaço* (whence Sp. *sargazo*, F. *sargasse*), of unkn. origin.

sari, saree sā·rī long wrapping garment of Hindu women. XVIII (*saurry*). – Hindi *sāṛhī*, *sāṛī*.

sark sāɹk (dial.) shirt, chemise. XIII (Cursor M.). ME. (north.) *serk* – ON. *serkr* :– Germ. **sarkiz*, f. base repr. also by OE. *serċe*, *syrċe*, *syr(i)ċ*. Hence **sark** vb. clothe with a sark; (in building) cover (a roọf) with planks XV.

sarmentose sāɹme·ntous (bot.) producing slender prostrate branches or runners. XVIII. – L. *sarmentōsus*, f. *sarmentum* (chiefly pl.) twigs lopped off, brushwood, f. *sarpere* prune, lop, rel. to Gr. *hórpēx* scion, shoot; see -MENT, -OSE[1]. So **sarme·ntous**. XVIII.

sarong sərɔ·ŋ Malay garment wrapped round the waist. XIX. – Malay and Javanese *saroeng* (prop.) sheath, quiver.

sarracenia særəsīn·iə genus of insectivorous plants (side-saddle flower). XVIII. modL., alt. of *Sarracena*; named by Tournefort (1700, after D. *Sarrazin*, of Quebec, who sent him the plant); see -IA[1].

sarsaparilla sā:ɹsəpəri·lə (dried roots of) species of Smilaceæ. XVI. – Sp. *sarzaparrilla* (whence F *salsepareille*, It. *salsapariglia*), f. *zarza* bramble – Arab. *šaraṣ* thorny plant +(prob.) dim. of Sp. *parra* twining plant (attribution to a Dr. *Parillo*, discoverer of the plant's properties, is due to Scaliger).

sarsen sā·ɹsən large boulder. XVII. Earlier in *Saracen's* and *Sarsdon stones*, *Sarsdens*, and supposed to be identical with SARACEN.

sarsenet, sarcenet sā·ɹsənėt soft fine silk material. XV. – AN. *sarzinett*, perh. dim. of *sarzin* SARACEN, suggested by OF. *drap sarrasinois*, medL. *pannus saracenicus* 'Saracen cloth'; see -ET.

sartorial sāɹtōə·riəl pert. to a tailor or tailoring. XIX (Sydney Smith, Carlyle). f. L. *sartor*, f. pp. stem of *sarcīre* patch, botch; see -IAL.

Sarum sɛə·rəm eccl. name of Salisbury. XVI (*the use of S.*). – medL. *Sarum*, evolved from a misinterpretation of *Sarȝ*, mediæval abbrev. of *Sarisburia* Salisbury (OE. *æt Searobyriġ*, later *Særesbyriġ*).

sash[1] sæʃ †turban XVI; scarf worn round the body XVII. orig. *shash* – Arab. *šāš* muslin, turban; alt. by dissimilation of *sh . . sh* to *s . . sh*; cf. next.

sash[2] sæʃ window-frame fitted with glass. First recorded in pl. *shashes* (1681), var. of *chasses*, used as pl. of *chassis* – OF. *chassis* (mod. *châssis*) frame, framework (CHASSIS), f. *chasse* = It. *cassa* :– L. *capsa* box (CASE[2]); for the dissimilation cf. prec.

sasine sei·sin (Sc. law) giving possession of feudal property. XVII. var. of SEISIN, after law-L. *sasina*.

saskatoon sæskətū·n small tree, Amelanchier alnifolia. XIX. – Cree *misāskwatomin*, f. *misāskwat* amelanchier + *min* fruit, berry.

sassaby səsei·bi large S. African antelope. XIX. – Tswana *tsessébe*, *-ábi*.

sassafras sæ·səfræs small tree native to N. America, Sassafras officinale. XVI. – Sp. *sasafrás* or Pg. *sassafraz*, of unkn. origin; so F. (XVI).

Sassenach sæ·sənàχ Gaelic name for 'English'. XVIII (Smollett). – Gael. *Sasunnoch* = Ir. *Sasanach*, f. *Sasan-* (cf. Gael. *Sasunn*, Ir. *Sasana* England) – L. *Saxonēs*, OE. *Seaxe*, *Seaxan* Saxons.

sat pt. and pp. of SIT.

Satan sei·tən, sæ·tən the Devil. OE. *Satan* – late L. *Satān* (Vulgate O.T.) – Gr. *Satā́n* – Heb. *ṣāṭān* adversary, plotter, f. *ṣāṭan* oppose, plot against. From OE. times *Satanas* has also been used – Vulgate L. *Satanās* (whence also F., Sp. *satanas*, OHG., Goth. *Satana*) – Gr. *Satanâs* – Jewish Aram. *ṣāṭānā*, emph. form of *ṣāṭāṇ*. Hence **satan**IC sətæ·nik XVII (Milton), **sata·n**ICAL XVI; cf. F. *satanique*; **Sa·tan**ISM, -IST XVI; so F., and modL. *satanista*. CEur.

satchel sæ·tʃ(ə)l small bag. XIV. – OF. *sachel* :– L. *saccellu-s*, dim. of *saccus* SACK[1]; see -EL[2].

sate seit satisfy to the full. XVII (Sh.). prob. alt. of dial. *sade* (OE. *sadian*, rel. to *sæd* satiated, SAD), by assoc. with SATIATE.

sate seit arch. pt. of SIT.

sateen sətī·n cotton or woollen stuff with satiny surface. XIX. alt. of SATIN, after *velveteen*; see -EEN[1].

satellite sæ·təlait A. attendant on an important person XVI (rare before XVIII; not in J.); B. secondary planet XVII. – (O)F. *satellite* or L. *satellit-*, *satelles*. In sense B the L. word was first applied by Kepler (1611) to the secondary planets revolving round Jupiter.

satiate sei·ʃieit †satisfy XVI; surfeit, glut XVII. f. pp. stem of L. *satiāre*, f. *satis* enough (see SAD), after †*satiate* pp. (XV) – L. *satiātus*; see -ATE[2] and [3]. So **sat**IETY sətai·iti, (formerly) səsai·iti condition of being satiated. XVI (*societie*). – (O)F. *societé* (mod. *satiété*) – L. *satietāt-*, *-tās*, f. *satis*, perh. after *ebrietās*. Cf. INSATIABLE.

satin sæ·tin glossy silk fabric. XIV (Ch.). – (O)F. *satin* – Arab. *zaitūnī*, pert. to the town Tseutung (Tswan-chu-fu) in China (*aṭlas zaitūnī* satin of Zaitun), whence also OF. *zatonin*, *zatony*, Sp. *acetuní*, *setuní*, MIt. *zetani* (It. *setino* after *seta* silk, supposed by some to be the immed. origin of F. *satin*).

satire sæ·taiəɹ poetical (or prose) work in which vices or follies are ridiculed. XVI (Barclay, 'The Shyp of Folys', 1509). – (O)F. *satire* or L. *satira* (whence also Sp. *sátira*, It. *satira*, G. *satire*), later form of *satura* (in earliest use) verse composition treating of a variety of subjects, spec. application of the sense 'medley' (cf. phr. *per saturam* in the lump, indiscriminately); acc. to ancient grammarians this was ellipt. for *lanx satura* 'full dish' (*lanx* dish, *satura*, fem. of *satus* full, rel. to *satis* fully; cf. SAD) dish of various fruits offered to the gods. Formerly assoc. with SATYR and so spelt, from the common notion (found already in some ancient grammarians) that L. *satura* was derived from Gr. *sáturos* satyr, in allusion to the chorus of satyrs which gave its name to the Gr. 'satyric' drama. So **satir**IC(AL) səti·rik(ə)l. XVI. – F. or late L. **satir**IST sæ·tirist. XVI. **sa·tir**IZE. XVII (Jonson). – F. *satiriser*, f. *satire*.

satisfaction sætisfæ·kʃən performance by a penitent of penal and meritorious acts enjoined by his confessor XIII (Cursor M.); payment in full of a debt, etc.; atonement made by Jesus Christ for sin; action of gratifying to the full XIV; release from uncertainty XVI. – (O)F. *satisfaction*, corr. to Pr. *satisfactio*, etc. – L. *satisfactiō(n-)*, f. pp. stem of *satisfacere* (whence, through OF. *satisfier*, **sa·tis**FY XV, Lydg.), f. *satis* enough (cf. ASSET, SAD); see -FACTION, -FY.

satrap sæ·træp governor of a province in ancient Persia. XIV (Wycl. Bible). – (O)F. *satrape* or L. *satrapa*, *satrapēs* – Gr. *satrápēs*, also *exatrápēs*, **exaithrápēs* (implied in *exaithrapeúein* be a satrap) – OPers. *xšaθrapāvan-* 'protector of the country', f. *xšaθra-* country + *pā-* protect. So **sa·trap**Y[3]. XVII (Knolles). – F. or L. – Gr. (*-eíā*).

saturate sæ·tʃəreit, -tj- †satisfy, satiate XVI; cause to combine with the utmost quantity of another substance XVII; soak thoroughly XVIII. f. pp. stem of L. *saturāre*, f. *satur* full, satiated; see SAD, -ATE[3]. So **satur**A·TION. XVI. – late L.; so F. (XVIII).

Saturday sæ·təɹdi seventh day of the week. OE. *Sætern(es)dæġ*, *Sæterdæġ*, corr. to OFris. *saterdei*, MLG. *sater(s)dach*, MDu. *saterdach* (Du. *zaterdag*), tr. of L. *Sāturnī diēs* day of (the planet) Saturn; cf. Ir., Gael. *dia Sathuirn*, W. *dydd Sadwrn*.

Saturn sæ·təɹn Italic god presiding over agriculture OE.; (astron.) one of the primary planets XIV (in OE. *Sæternes steorra*); (alch.) lead XIV (Ch.). – L. *Sāturnus*, poss. of Etruscan origin. So **Saturnalia** -ei·liə festival of Saturn marked by unrestrained revelry XVI (transf. XVIII). L., sb. use of n.pl. of *Sāturnālis*; see -AL[1]. **Saturn**IAN sətə̄·ɹniən ancient Roman metre. XVI. **sa·turn**INE[1] born under Saturn, (hence) of cold and gloomy temperament. XV (Lydg.). – F. *saturnin* – medL. **sāturnīnus*.

satyr sæ·təɹ woodland god or demon, half man half beast, of lustful propensities. XIV (Ch., Trevisa, Gower). – (O)F. *satyre* or L. *satyrus* – Gr. *sáturos*. So **satyr**IC səti·rik epithet of the Gr. drama in which the chorus were habited as satyrs. XVII. – L. – Gr. Cf. SATIRE.

satyrion sæ̆ti·riən kind of orchis. XIV. – L. *satyrion* – Gr. *satúrion*, f. *sátyros* SATYR; named from the plant's supposed aphrodisiac properties.

sauce sɔ̄s liquid preparation taken as a relish with articles of food XIV; piquant addition XVI; (prob. from *saucy*) †impudent person XVI; impudence XIX. – (O)F. *sauce* = Pr., Sp., It. *salsa* :– Rom. **salsa*, sb. use of fem. of L. *salsus* salted, SALT. The etymol. sense is identical with that of *salad*. Hence **sauce** vb. season XV; †belabour, rebuke XVI; address impertinently XIX. **saucy**[1] sɔ̄·si † savoury; insolent towards superiors XVI; (of a ship or boat) †rashly venturous XVI (Sh.); smart XIX.

saucer sɔ̄·səɹ †receptacle for condiments at a meal XIV; shallow circular dish XVII; esp. one to support a cup XVIII. – OF. *saussier*, *saussiere* (mod. only *saucière*) sauce-boat, f. *sauce* SAUCE, prob. after late L. *salsārium*; cf. Sp. *salsera*, It. *salsiera*.

sauerkraut, sourcrout sau·əɹkraut German dish of fermented cabbage. XVII (*sower crawt*). G. (whence F. *choucroute*), f. *sauer* SOUR + *kraut* vegetable, cabbage.

saunter sɔ̄·ntəɹ †muse XV; †wander aimlessly XVII; walk leisurely, stroll XVIII. perh. based on late ME. *sa(w)nterell*, applied contemptuously (together with vbl. sb. *sauntering*) to Jesus Christ in the 'York Plays', with prob. implication of affected sanctity and hence of visionary musing; prob. to be referred (with ME. *sayntrelle*) to *sainterel* (corr. to It. *santarello*), f. *saint* SAINT + *-erel* -REL.

saurian sɔ̄·riən pert. to reptiles of the order Sauria (crocodiles and large extinct lizard-like animals). XV. f. modL. *Sauria* (Brongniart 1799), f. Gr. *saûrā*, *saûros* lizard; see -IAN. So **sau·ro-**, comb. form of Gr. *saûros*, whence modL. *saurus*, repr. in BRONTOSAURUS, ICHTHYOSAURUS, MEGALOSAURUS, PLESIOSAURUS, PLIOSAURUS, PTEROSAUR.

sausage sɔ·sidʒ minced meat enclosed in a thin cylindrical membrane. XV. Late ME. *sausige* – ONF. *saussiche* (var. of OF. *salsice*, mod. *saucisse*) = Sp. *salchicha*, It. *salsiccia*

:- medL. *salsīcia*, n.pl. of *salsīcius* (sc. *farta*, pp. n.pl. of L. *farcīre*, stuff, FARCE[1]), f. *salsus* salted (see SALT, SAUCE). ¶ For the development -idʒ cf. CABBAGE.

sauté sou·tei fried in a pan, being tossed from time to time. XIX. F., pp. of *sauter* leap :- L. *saltāre* (see SALTATION), used trans. in causative sense.

sauterne(s) soutə·ɹn wine of the district of *Sauternes*, near Bordeaux, France. XVIII.

savage sæ·vidʒ that is in a state of nature XIII; of wild or unrestrained behaviour XV (Lydg.); uncivilized XVI; furiously angry XIX; sb. XVI. ME. *sa(u)vage* – (O)F. *sauvage* (AN. also *savage*) = Pr. *salvatge*, Sp. *salvage*, It. *salvaggio* wooded, woodland-, Rum. *sălbatic* :- CRom. **salvāticus*, for L. *silvāticus* woodland-, wild, f. *silva* wood, forest; see SILVAN, -AGE. The var. *salvage* (after OF. *salvage*) was formerly common. XVI–XVII. For æ of the first syll. cf. SALMON. Hence **sa·vag**ERY. XVI (Sh.).

savanna(h) səvæ·nə treeless plain, esp. of tropical America. XVI (*zavanna*, Eden's 'Decades'; hardly naturalized before late XVII). – Sp. *zavana*, *çavana* (pronounced with *s*- in S. Amer. Sp.), said by Oviedo (1535) to be a Carib word.

savant sæ·vã man of learning. XVIII. – F. *savant*, sb. use of orig. prp. of *savoir* know :- Rom. **sapēre*, for L. *sapere* (see SAPIENT).

save[1] seiv make or keep safe XIII; preserve from damnation XIII (AncrR.); reserve, lay aside XIV; avoid or enable to avoid XVII. ME. *sauve*, *salve*, *save* – AN. *sa(u)ver*, OF. *salver*, (also mod.) *sauver* = Pr. *sauvar*, Sp. *salvar*, It. *salvare* :- late L. *salvāre* (theol. rendering Gr. σώζειν) save, f. L. *salvus* SAFE[1].

save[2] seiv (arch.) with the exception of. XIII (Cursor M.). ME. *sauf* and *sauve* – OF. *sauf* (m.) and *sauve* (fem.), orig. varying with the gender of the accompanying sb. (now invariable, *sauf*):- L. *salvō* and *salvā*, abl. sg. of m. or n. and fem. of *salvus* SAFE[1], as used in absolute constr. such as *salvo jure*, *salva innocentia* without violation of right, of innocence, (hence) without injury or prejudice to, with reserve of, *salvo eo ut* . . with the proviso that . ., (passing in Rom. into) excepting, except; so also Sp., It. *salvo*. The later exclusive use of the form *save* is prob. due to the identification of the word with the imper. of SAVE[1]. Cf. SAVING. ¶ Disguised in the first syll. of *sirreverence* XVI, alt. of *sa'* (for *save*) *reverence* with due regard, (hence) human excrement XVI.

saveloy sæ·vəloi kind of sausage. XIX (Dickens). alt. of F. †*cervelat*, (also mod.) *-as* sɛrvəla – It. *cervellata* (corr. to OF. *cervelee*; cf. -ATE f. *cervello* brains :- L. CEREBELLUM.

savey, savvy sæ·vi know. XVIII. Negro and Pigeon Eng., repr. the first word of Sp. *sabe usted* you know (*saber* :- Rom. **sapēre*, for L. *sapere* know; see SAPIENT). Hence sb., practical sense, nous XVIII.

savin(e) sæ·vin shrub Juniperus sabina, XIV. – OF. *savine* (repl. by latinized *sabine*) = Sp. *sabina*, It. *savina* :- L. (*herba*) *Sabīna* 'Sabine plant', fem. of *Sabīnus* SABINE. Widely used in medicine in the Middle Ages; cf. medL. *savīna*, OE. *safēne*, *-īne*, OHG. *sevina*, *sevinboum* (G. *sebenbaum*).

saving sei·viŋ (arch.) except, save. XIV (Ch.). prob. modification of SAVE[2] after TOUCHING.

saviour sei·vjəɹ, U.S. **savior** one who saves, spec. the Redeemer. XIII (Cursor M.). ME. *sauve(o)ur* – OF. *sauvēour* (mod. *sauveur*) = Pr., Sp. *salvador*, etc. :- ChrL. *salvātōrem*, *-ātor* (rendering Gr. σωτήρ, and ult. Heb. *yēshūa'* JESUS), f. *salvāre* SAVE[1]. The change from *-eour* to *-your*, *-iour* is found from XIV.

savory sei·vəri plant of the labiate genus Satureia. XIV. Late ME. *saverey*, perh. repr. (with change of intervocalic ð to v) OE. *sæþerie* – L. *satureia* fem. sg. and n.pl., whence also OE. *saturege*, AN., ME. *satureie*, OF. *sarrie* (whence mod. *sarriette*), Pr. *sadreia*, Sp. *sagerida* and *ajedrea* (– Arab. *akhkhetrīya*, i.e. AL-[2], *khetrīya* – L.), Pg. *saturagem* and *segurelha*, *cigurelha*, Cat. *sajolida*, It. *satureia* and *santoreggia*. ¶ As with many plant-names, the orig. form has undergone obscure alterations; there are several *-v-* forms in local F. and It.

savour, U.S. **savor** səi·vəɹ taste XIII (AncrR.); †smell, aroma XIII (Cursor M.). – OF. *savour* (mod. *saveur*) = Pr., Sp. *sabor*, It. *savore* :- L. *sapōrem*, *sapor* taste, occas. smell, f. *sapere* taste; see SAPIENT, -OUR[2]. So **sa·vour** vb. have a taste XIII (Cursor M.); relish, like XIV (Rolle). – (O)F. *savourer* = Pr. *saborar*, etc. :- late L. *sapōrāre*.

savoury sei·vəri pleasant to the taste XIII; appetizing XIV; fragrant (now chiefly in *unsavoury*) XVI; stimulating to the palate (also sb.) XVII. ME. *savure*, later *savori* – OF. *savouré* sapid, fragrant, f. *savour* (see prec.) + *-é* -ATE[2]; the ending was assim. to -Y[1].

savoy (S-) səvoi· *S. cole*, *cabbage* XVI; *S. biscuit* XVIII. – F. *Savoie*, name of a region of S.E. France.

Savoyard səvoi·əɹd native or inhabitant of Savoy. XVIII. See -ARD.

savvy see SAVEY.

saw[1] sō cutting tool with teeth. OE. **sagu* (in obl. cases *sage*), also *saga* = MLG., MDu. *sage* (Du. *zaag*), OHG. *saga*, ON. *sǫg* :- CGerm. (exc. Goth.) **sagō*, **sagon*, of which the gradation- var. **segō* is repr. by OHG. *sega* (G. *säge*), MDu. *seghe*; rel. to OE. *seax* knife, OFris., OS., OHG. *sahs* :-

*saχsam, f. *sak- *sek- cut (see SECTION). Hence **saw** vb. XIII (pp. *isahet*); orig. with wk. conj., but str. forms appear XV (occas. pt. *suwe*, *sew*, pp. *sawen*, mod. **sawn**).

saw[2] sō †saying OE.; maxim, proverb XIII. OE. *sagu* = OFris. *sege*, MLG., MDu. *sage*, OHG. *saga* (G. *sage*), ON. *saga* SAGA :- CGerm. (exc. Goth.) *sagō, f. base of *sagjan SAY[1]; cf. Lith. *pã|saka* story.

saw[3] see SEE[1].

sawder sō·dəɹ (colloq.) *soft s.* blarney, flattery. XIX. fig. use of *sawder*, var. of SOLDER.

sawney sō·ni (colloq.) nickname for a Scotchman; simpleton. XVII. Sc. local var. of *Sandy* (XV), pet-form of the proper name *Alexander*; see -Y[6]. ¶ The connexion of these two senses and with other uses, such as the sl. use for 'bacon', is doubtful.

sawyer sō·jəɹ one who saws timber. XIV. Late ME. *sawier*, alt. of †*sawer* (f. SAW[1] vb. + -ER[1]) with assim. of the ending to F. *-ier* -ER[2] (cf. *bowyer*, *clothier*, *lawyer*, *paviour*).

Saxe sæks derived from Saxony, as *S. china*. XIX. – F. *Saxe* (also used for *porcelaine de Saxe*, e.g. *un service en saxe*). – G. *Sachsen* Saxony, prop. d.pl. of *Sachse* (see SAXON).

saxhorn sæ·kshōɹn brass musical instrument. XIX. f. name of Charles Joseph *Sax* (1791–1865) + HORN. So **sa·xo**PHONE, invented about 1840 by his son Antoine Joseph, known as Adolphe; see -O-.

saxifrage sæ·ksifreidʒ plant of the genus Saxifraga. XV. – (O)F. *saxifrage* or late L. *saxifraga* (sc. *herba* plant), f. *saxum* rock + *frag-*, base of *frangere* break (see FRAGMENT). ¶ The name 'rock-breaking plant' was prob. given because many species are found growing among stones and in the clefts of rocks.

Saxon sæ·ksən one of a Germanic people, of which one portion, the Anglo-Saxons, occupied S. Britain, while the other, the Old Saxons (modL. *antiqui Saxones*, OE. *Ealdseaxe*) remained in Germany. XIII (RGlouc.). – (O)F. *Saxon* – L. *Saxonem*, nom. *Saxō*, pl. *Saxonēs* = Gr. *Sáxones* – WGerm. *Saxon- (OE. pl. *Seaxan*, *Seaxe*, OHG. pl. *Sahso*, G. *Sachse*), perh. f. *saχsam knife (see SAW[1]), as the name of the characteristic weapon of the people. Cf. FRANK. *Old S.*, language of the Old Saxons, esp. as exemplified in remains of 9th-century poetry ('Heliand', etc.).

saxophone see SAXHORN.

say[1] sei 3 pres. sg. **says** sez, (arch.) **saith** seþ, pt. and pp. **said** sed the verb most widely used to express speaking, with ref. to an object, like L. *dicere*, F. *dire*. OE. *seċġan*, pt. *sæġde*, pp. (*ġe*)*sæġd* = OFris. *sega*, *sedza*, OS. *seggian*, pt. *sagda* (Du. *zeggen*), OHG. *sagēn*, pt. *sagita*, *segita* (G. *sagen*), ON. *segja*, pt. *sagða* :- CGerm. (exc. Gothic) *sagjan and *sagǣjan; the IE. base *soq- *seq- (not extant in Indo-Iran.) is repr. also by OSl. *sočiti*, Lith. *sakýti*, OL. (imper.) *insece*, *inquam* (:- *insquam) I say, Gr. (imper.) *énnepe*, (aorist inf.) *enispeîn*, OW. *hepp* says, OIr. *aithesc* (:- *ati|sqā) answer.

OE. inf. *seċġan*, 1 pres. ind. *seċġe*, pl. *seċġaþ*, etc., are repr. normally by ME. *segge(n)*, etc., *sedgeyng* recitation (R. Mannyng), dial. *zedge* (XVI). These began to be repl. in XII (e.g. inf. *sæʒen*, *sæin*, Peterborough Chronicle) and were finally ousted by forms derived from OE. *sæġ-*, *seġ-*, of 2 and 3 pres. ind. viz. *sæġ(e)st*, *seġ(e)st* sayest, *sæġ(e)þ*, *seġ(e)þ* saith, pt. *sæġde* said, pp. *sæġd*. Hence sb. XVI.

say[2] sei (hist.) serge-like cloth. XIII. – (O)F. *saie* = Pr. *saia* (Sp. *saya*, It. *saja* are from F.) :- L. *saga*, coll. pl. (used as sg.) of *sagum* coarse woollen blanket, military cloak, cloth covering, of Gaulish origin acc. to Polybius.

sayyid sei·jid title of a man tracing his descent from Husain, elder grandson of the Prophet. XVIII (*syed*, *seid*). – Arab. *sayyid* lord, prince; cf. CID.

sbirro sbi·rou, pl. **-i** Italian police officer. XVII. – It. *sbirro*, f. *birro* – medL. *birrus* red, var. of *burrus* – Gr. *purrós*, var. *pursós* fiery-red, f. *pûr* FIRE. ¶ The name refers to the red collar or cape worn by some It. police.

scab skæb A. †skin disease XIII; cutaneous disease in beasts; crust formed over a wound XIV; B. low scurvy fellow XVI; nonunionist XIX. – ON. *skabbr (OSw. *skabber*, Sw. *skabb*, (O)Da. *skab*) = OE. *sċeabb* (see SHABBY). The application to persons may have been due partly to MDu. *schabbe* slut, scold. Hence **sca·bby**[1] XVI perh. after MDu. *schabbich*, *-ig*; repl. *scabbed* (XIII), prob. modelled on OSw. *skabbotter* = late OE. *sċ(e)abbede*, ME. *schabbed*.

scabbard[1] skæ·bəɹd sheath of sword, etc. XIII (RGlouc.). ME. *sca(u)berc*, later *scaberge*, *scaubert*, *scaubard*, aphetic – AN. *escauberc, pl. *escaubers*, *-erz*, *escauberge* (cf. AL. *escauberca*, *scarbagium* XIII), prob. – comp. of OHG. *scala* shell (see SCALE[1]) or *scār*, *scāra* scissors, occas. sword + *berg- protect (as in HAUBERK); alt. of the second syll. to *-bard*, *-bart*, *-berd*, *-bert* is evidenced XIV, but AL. *scauberdum* is as early as XIII. ¶ For æ of the first syll. cf. SALMON, SAVAGE.

scabbard[2] skæ·bəɹd thin board used for splints, veneer, etc. XVII. – MLG. *schalbort*, f. *schale* SCALE[1], SCALE[2] + *bort* BOARD.

scabious skei·biəs plant of the genus Scabiosa (formerly of repute for the cure of skin diseases). XIV. – medL. *scabiōsa* (sc. *herba* plant), of *scabiōsus*, f. L. *scabiēs* roughness, itch, f. *scabere* scratch, scrape; see SHAVE, -IOUS.

scabrous skei·brəs rough with minute points XVII; fig. harsh XVI. – f. L. *scabr-*, *scaber*, f. *scab-* (partly after F. *scabreux*); see prec., -OUS.

scaffold skæ·fəld raised platform or stage XIV; (for the execution of criminals) XVI. ME. *scaffot, scaffald* – AN. **scaffaut*, OF. *(e)schaffaut*, mod. *échafaud*, earlier *escadafaut* = Pr. *escadafalc* :– Rom. **excatafalcum*, f. *ex-* EX-¹ + **catafalcum*; see CATAFALQUE. Hence **sca·ffold**ING¹ XIV. ¶ The word appears in various forms in medL., *scadafale, -faltum, scafaldus*, (AL.) *escafautium, scaffaldum, scafotum* (XIII), *scaffoldum* (XIV); the Rom. word has been adopted in Germ., as Du. *schavot*, G. *schafott*, Da. *skafot*, Sw. *chavott*.

scaglia skā·lja limestone of the Italian Alps. XVIII. It. (see SCALE²). So **scagliola** skāljou·la †scaglia XVI; Italian plaster-work imitating stone XVIII. It. *scagliuola*, dim. of *scaglia*.

scald¹ skōld burn with hot liquor; (dial.) burn. XIII (AncrR.). ME. *scalde, schalde*, aphetic – AN., ONF. *escalder*, OF. *eschalder* (mod. *échauder*) = Pr. *escaudar*, Sp. *escaldar* burn, scorch, scald, make red-hot, It. *scaldare* heat, Rum. *scălda* :– L. *excaldāre* wash in hot water, f. *ex* EX-¹ + L. *cal(i)dus* hot (perh. in the spec. fem. sb. *cal(i)da*, sc. *aqua* water), rel. to *calēre* be warm. Hence **scald** sb. XVII.

scald² skōld (arch., dial.) scabby, scurvy. XVI. Later sp. of *scalled* (XIV), f. (dial.) *scall* (XIII) – ON. *skalli* bald head, f. Germ. **skal-*, whence SCALE¹, SHELL; see -ED².

scald³ see SKALD.

scale¹ skeil †drinking-bowl XIII (Laȝ.); pan of a balance XIV; sg. and pl. weighing instrument XV. – ON. *skál* bowl, pl. weighing-scales = OHG. *scāla* (G. *schale*) :– Germ. **skǣlō*, rel. to **skalō*, whence OE. *sċealu* shell, husk, drinking-cup, weighing scale, OS. *skala* cup (Du. *schaal*), OHG. *scala* shell, husk (G. *schale*); cf. SHALE, SHELL, SKILL. ¶ The normal repr. of ME. *scāle* is *scōle*, which was current XIII–XVII; the characteristic north. form *scale* was established in London speech XVI (Palsgrave, Spenser, Sh.). Hence vb. weigh XVII.

scale² skeil thin horny plate on the skin of animals XIV; lamina of skin, etc. XV; (after F. *écaille*) metal plate worn as an epaulette XIX. Aphetic – OF. *escale* (mod. *écale* husk, chip of stone) – Germ. **skalō* (see SCALE¹), rel. to **skaljō*, whence Rom. (medL.) *scalia* (OF. *escaille*, mod. *écaille* fish-scale, oyster-shell, It. *scaglia* fish-scale, chip of stone). Hence vb. remove scales from. XV. **scal**Y¹ XVI.

scale³ skeil A. †ladder (XV, Lydg.); B. (mus.) series of graduated sounds XVI; C. set of graduations for measuring distances XIV (Ch.; rare before XVI); graduated instrument; D. relative dimension, standard of measurement XVII. – L. *scāla* usu. pl. steps, staircase, (sg., late) ladder (whence OF. *eschiele*, mod. *échelle*, Pr., Sp. *escala*, It. *scala*) :– **scandslā*, f. base of *scandere* climb (cf. SCAN, ASCEND, etc., SCANDAL).

scale⁴ skeil climb, mount. XIV. – OF. *escaler* (cf. ESCALADE) or medL. *scālāre* (whence also Sp. *escalar*, It. *scalare*), f. L. *scāla* SCALE³.

scale-board. XVIII see SCABBARD².

scalene skei·līn (of a triangle) having three unequal sides. XVIII. – late L. *scalēnus* (Ausonius) – Gr. *skalēnós* uneven, unequal, scalene, rel. to *skoliós* oblique, crooked, *skélos* leg, L. *scelus* wickedness, crime, OE. *sceolh* wry, oblique (= MLG. *schēl*, OHG. *scelah*, ON. *skjálgr*), f. a base meaning 'bend'.

scallion skæ·ljən shallot, onion. XIV. – AN. *scal(o)un* = OF. *escalo(i)gne*, Pr. *escalonha*, Sp. *escaloña* :– Rom. **escalōnia*, for L. *Ascalōnia* (sc. *cæpa* onion) shallot, f. *Ascalō* (Gr. *Askálōn*) Ascalon, a port in S. Palestine; (cf. It. *escalogno*, corr. to *Ascalōnium*).

scallop, scollop skæ·ləp, skɔ·ləp kind of shellfish; shell of this, esp. as a pilgrim's badge XIV; formation resembling the edge of a scallop-shell XVII. Aphetic – OF. *escalope*, presumably of Germ. origin (cf. MDu. *schelpe, schulpe* mussel-shell).

scallywag skæ·liwæg (sl.) disreputable fellow. XIX. orig. U.S., of unkn. origin; perh. orig. used for undersized or ill-conditioned cattle.

scalp skælp (dial.) top of the head, skull XIII; integument of this (prob. evolved from †*hairy scalp*, which in the Bible, Ps. lxviii 21, is a literalism from Heb.) XVII. north. ME. *scalp*, prob. of Scand. origin, but the Eng. senses are not found in any Scand. or other Germ. lang.; cf. ON. *skálpr* sheath (Da. dial. *skalp* shell, husk), MLG. *schulpe*, MDu. *schelpe* (Du. *schelp*) shell, the meanings of which suggest deriv. from Germ. **skal-* **skel-* **skul-* SCALE¹, SHELL. Hence vb. remove the scalp of. XVII.

scalpel skæ·lpəl small light knife for surgical operations. XVIII. – F. *scalpel* or L. *scalpellum, -us*, dim. of *scalper, scalprum*, cutting tool, chisel, knife (used in Eng. XVII), f. base of *scalpere* scratch, carve; see -EL².

scammony skæ·məni gum-resin obtained from Convolvulus Scammonia. XV. – OF. *escamonie, scamonee* (mod. *scammonée*) or L. *scammōnea, -ia* (also *-eum, -ium*) – Gr. *skammōniā, -ōnion*. ¶ OE. *scamonie* and rare ME. *scamoine* were casual adoptions.

scamp¹ skæmp idle about mischievously XVI; commit highway robbery XVIII. Implied in †*scampant* XVI (in a burlesque coat of arms, 'a lyther lad scampant, a roge in his ragges'), prob. – MDu. *schampen* slip away, decamp – OF. *escamper, eschamper* = Pr. *escampar*, It. *scampare* :– Rom. **excampāre*, f. *ex* EX-¹ + *campus* field (see CAMP). Hence **scamp** sb. †highway robber or robbery XVIII (cf. †*scamperer* street ruffian,

†*scampsman* highway-man); ne'er-do-well, waster XIX.

scamp[2] skæmp do negligently or hurriedly. XIX. perh. identical with prec., but allied in sense to SKIMP.

scamper skæ·mpəɹ †decamp; run nimbly. XVII. prob. frequent. f. SCAMP[1]+-ER[4].

scan skæn analyse the metre of (XIV) XV; †criticize, test; examine or consider closely; †interpret; †discern XVI; look at searchingly XVIII. – L. *scandere* (pp. *scansus*) climb, (late) 'measure' (verses), with allusion to raising and lowering the foot to mark rhythm; cf. next, and ASCEND, DESCEND. The var. †*scand* was presumably the earlier, though not so shown by the evidence, and was apprehended as pp., from which an inf. *scan* was deduced. So F. *scander* (whence G. *skandiren*, Du. *skandeeren*), Sp. *escandir*, It. *scandere*. So **sca·n**SION. XVII. – L.

scandal skæ·ndəl discredit to religion caused by a religious person; occasion of unbelief, stumbling-block; damage to reputation; grossly discreditable thing; defamatory speech. XVI. – F. *scandale*, corr. to Sp. *escándalo*, It. *scandalo* – ChrL. *scandalum* (Vulg.) cause of offence – Hellenistic Gr. *skándalon* snare for an enemy, cause of moral stumbling, orig. trap (cf. *skandálêthron* spring of a trap), f. IE. **skand-* spring, leap, repr. also by Skr. *skándati*, L. *scandere* (cf. SCAN), MIr. pres. *scendim*, pt. *sescaind*, W. *cy|chwynnu* start. (An independent adoption of OF. *escandle*, *eschandle* is seen in earlier ME. *scandle*, *scha(u)ndle* XIII; cf. SLANDER.) So **sca·ndal**IZE[1] †make public scandal of XV; †be an occasion of stumbling to; slander; disgrace XVI; horrify by impropriety XVII. – (O)F. *scandaliser* or ChrL. *scandalizāre* – ecclGr. *skandalízein*. **sca·ndal**OUS. XVI. – F. or medL.

scandalize[2] skæ·ndəlaiz (naut.) reduce the area of (a sail). XIX. alt. of †*scantelize* shorten (XVII), f. †*scantle* (f. SCANT)+-IZE.

scandaroon skændərū·n †swindler XVII; kind of carrier pigeon (perh. so named because formerly used to take messages from Scanderoon to Aleppo) XIX. f. *Scanderoon* (*Iskanderūn*) name of a seaport in Syria.

Scandinavian skændinei·viən pert. to Scandinavia, which comprises Norway, Sweden, Denmark, and Iceland. XVIII. f. L. *Scandinavia* (Pomponius Mela, Pliny the Elder), erron. for **Scadinavia* – Germ. **Skadinaujā*, repr. by OE. *Scedenīg* ('Beowulf' 1686), ON. *Skáney* (adopted in OE. as *Scōnēg*), name of the southern extremity of Sweden; the terminal el. is **aujō*, OE. *īeg* ISLAND. So **Sca·nd**IAN. XVII. f. the shortened form *Scandia* (Pliny). †**Sca·nd**IC. XVIII.

scansorial skænsɔ̄ə·riəl pert. to climbing, that climbs. XIX. f. L. *scansōrius*, f. *scans-*, pp. stem of *scandere*; see SCAN, -ORIAL.

scant skænt stinted in measure; †parsimonious XIV; limited in extent or amount XVI. – ON. *skamt*, n. of *skammr* short, brief = OHG. *scam*; cf. ON. *skemta* entertain, amuse (lit. make the time short) :- **skammatjan*. Superseded largely by **sca·nty**[1]. XVI. For other exx. of the Scand. n. ending *t* see THWART, WANT.

scantling skæ·ntliŋ measured size; small or scanty amount; †pattern XVI; small piece of wood, etc. XVII. alt., by assoc. with -LING[1], of †*scantlon* gauge (XIII), dimension (XIV), sample (XV), aphetic – OF. *escantillon* (mod. *échantillon* sample), alt. of *eschandillon*, the simplex of which occurs as Pr. *escandel* measure of capacity, parallel to *escandalh* = Cat. *escandall* (whence It. *scandaglio*, Sp. *escandallo*) – medL. **scandalium*, *-ilium*, f. L. *scandere* climb (see SCAN).

scape[1], **'scape** skeip vb. and sb. (obs. or arch.) Aphetic of ESCAPE. XIII. Hence (from the vb.) **scape**GOAT (XVI, Tindale, 1530), intended to render the supposed literal meaning of Heb. *azāzel* (Lev. xvi 8, 10, 26) 'the goote on which the lotte fell to scape' (so Vulg. *caper emissarius*, whence F. *bouc émissaire*); the correct interpretation is prob. 'goat for Azazel' (a demon of the desert). **sca·pe**GRACE 'one who escapes the grace of God' XIX; cf. earlier *want-grace* (XVII).

scape[2] skeip (bot.) long flower-stalk rising from the root. XVII (Holland). – L. *scāpus*, Gr. *skâpos*, rel. to Gr. *skêptron* SCEPTRE.

scape[3] skeip view of scenery. XVIII (G. White). Abstracted from LANDSCAPE.

scaphoid skæ·foid boat-shaped. XVIII. – modL. *scaphoīdēs* – Gr. *skaphoeidḗs*, f. *skáphos* boat; see -OID.

scapular skæ·pjŭləɹ monastic garment covering the shoulders. XV. – late L. *scapulāre*, f. late L. *scapula* shoulder (anat. in Eng. use XVI), earlier pl. *-æ*; see -AR. So **sca·pul**ARY XIII (*scapelori*) – AN. **scapelorie*, var. of OF. *eschapeloyre* (XII) – medL. *scapelōrium*, *scapularium*; assim. to -ARY.

scar[1] skāɹ †rock, crag XIV; precipice XVII; sunken rock XVIII. ME. *skerre*, *scarre*, – ON. *sker* low reef, SKERRY (whence also Gael. *sgeir*); cf. SCAUR.

scar[2] skāɹ trace of a healed wound. XIV (Wycl. Bible). Aphetic – OF. *escharre* (later *escarre*, *eschare*), corr. to Sp., It. *escara* – late L. *eschara* scab (Cælius Aurelianus) – Gr. *eskhárā* hearth, brazier, scab. Hence vb. XVI.

scarab skæ·rəb beetle XVI; gem cut in the form of a beetle XIX. – L. *scarabæus* (earlier in Eng. use XVIII; also anglicized †*scarabee* (XVI, Spenser) – Gr. σκαράβειος, presumably rel. to κάραβος stag beetle.

scaramouch skæ·rəmautʃ stock character of Italian farce, cowardly or foolish boaster constantly cudgelled by Harlequin; rascal, scamp XVII. Early forms *Scaramuzza*, *-moucha*, *-muchio* – It. *Scaramuccia*, joc. use of *scaramuccia* SKIRMISH; hence F. *Scaramouche* (Molière), source of the later and present form. ¶ Popularized in late XVII by the visit to London in 1673 of Tiberio Fiurelli, an impersonator of the part.

scarce skɛəɹs †scanty XIII (RGlouc.); †niggardly; deficient in quantity or number XIV. – AN., ONF. *scars*, aphetic of *escars*, OF. *eschars*, mod. *échars* (of coin) below standard value, (of wind) slight = Pr. *esca(r)s*, Sp. *escaso*, It. *scarso* :– Rom. **excarpsus* plucked out, pp. of **excarpere*, for L. *excerpere* select out, EXCERPT. (Cf. MDu. *schaers*, Du. *schaars* – F.). Hence **sca·rce**LY[2] †scantily, sparingly; only just, not quite. XIII; after (O)F. *écharsement*; **sca·rc**ITY. XIII. – ONF. *escarceté*, OF. *eschar-* (mod. *écharseté*).

scare skɛəɹ terrify. XII (Orm). ME. *skerre*, later *scarre*, *skere* (repr. by dial. *scar*, *skeer*), *skayre*, *skare* (XV), *scare* (XVI) – ON. *skirra* frighten, (also) avoid, prevent, refl. shrink from (cf. Norw. *skjerra*, Sw. dial. *skjarra* scare), f. *skjarr* shy, timid (whence Sc. *scar* XVI, *scaur*); the phonology is obscure. Hence **sca·re**CROW[1] something to frighten away a typical bird from seed. XVI.

scarf[1] skāɹf joint for connecting two timbers into a continuous piece. XIV (Sandahl). orig. naut.; prob. – OF. **escarf* (mod. *écart*), f. **escarver* (mod. *écarver*), perh. f. an ON. base repr. by Sw. *skarf*, Norw. *skarv* piece to lengthen a board or a garment, joint or seam effecting this, Sw. *skarfva*, Norw. *skarva* lengthen in this way); cf. Sp. *escarba*, Pg. *escarva*, LG., Du. *scherf* scarf, Du. vb. *verscherven* (whence G. *verscherben*); all these collateral forms are recorded much later than the Eng. word; the ult. origin remains obscure. Hence vb. XVII (Capt. Smith).

scarf[2] skāɹf broad band of stuff as an article of clothing XVI; (her.) XVII. prob. alt. (by assoc. with prec.) of *scarp*, which is recorded from XVI in the heraldic sense of a diminutive bend sinister. – ONF. *escarpe* = OF. *escherpe* (mod. *écharpe*), whence It. *sciarpa*, Sp. *charpa*, MDu. *scharpe*, Du. *sjerp*, G. *schärpe*; prob. identical with OF. *escarpe*, *escharpe*, *esquarpe*, *escreppe*, pilgrim's scrip suspended from the neck (cf. ON. *skreppa* SCRIP[1]). comp. **sca·rf-**SKIN outer layer of the skin. XVII.

scarify skæ·rifai make incisions or scratches in. XV. – (O)F. *scarifier* – late L. *scarīficāre*, alt. of L. *scarīfāre* – Gr. *skarīphâsthai* scratch an outline, sketch lightly, f. *skárīphos* pencil, stilus; see -IFY. So **sca:ri**FICA·TION. XIV (rare before XVI). – (O)F. or late L.

scarious skɛə·riəs dry and shrivelled. XIX. – F. *scarieux* or modL. *scariōsus* (whence also **sca·ri**OSE[1] XVIII).

scarlatina skāɹləti·nə scarlet fever. XIX. – modL. (Sydenham, 1676) – It. *scarlattina* (Lancelotti, 1537), fem. (sc. *febbre* fever, after medL. *febris scarlatina*) of *scarlattino*, dim. of *scarlatto* SCARLET.

scarlet skā·ɹlit †rich cloth, of various colours, freq. bright-red XIII; bright vivid red colour XV; (adj. XIV, Ch.). Aphetic – OF. *escarlate* fem. (mod. *écarlate*) = Pr. *escarlate* (also *-at* m.), Sp., Pg. *escarlate*, *-ata*, It. *scarlatto*, medL. *(e)scarlata*, *-eta*, *-etum*, whence prob. ON. *skarlat*, *skallat*, MHG. *scharlāt*, also (M)HG. *scharlach* (cf. LAKE[2]), (M)Du. *scharlaken*; the It. form is prob. the source of modGr., Slav., and Turkish forms; ult. origin unkn. (an Oriental source cannot be proved).

scart skāɹt (Sc.) cormorant. XV. MSc. *scarth* – ON. *skarfr*, more closely repr. in Orkney and Shetlands by *scarf* (XVII).

scarus skɛə·rəs parrot-fish. XVII. L., – Gr. *skáros*; supposed by the ancients to chew the cud. Also anglicized as *scar*, †*scare* (XVIII).

scat skæt tax, tribute (now only hist. of countries under Scand. rule) XIV; (in Orkney and Shetland) land-tax XVI. – ON. *skattr* = OE. *sćeat*, OFris. *skett* money, cattle, OS. *skat* (Du. *schat*), OHG. *scaz* (G. *schatz*) treasure, Goth. *skatts* piece of money, money :– CGerm. **skattaz* (whence OSl. *skotŭ* cattle.

scathe skeið (arch., dial.) injury, damage. XIII (Laȝ.). – ON. *skaði* = OE. *sćeaþa* malefactor, (rarely) injury, OFris. *skatha* injury, OS. *skaðo* malefactor, OHG. *skado* (G. *schade*) injury, harm :– Germ. **skaþon*, f. **skaþ-*, whence also Goth. *skaþis* harm, *skaþjan* injure, a var. **skōþ-* being repr. by ON. *skóð* harmful thing, *skœðr* harmful. (The OE. word, with ʃ, is sparsely repr. in ME.) So **scathe** vb. injure XII (Orm); wither, sear XIX. – ON. *skaða* = OE. *sćeaþian*, OFris. *skathia*, OS. *scaðon*, OHG. *skadōn* (Du., G. *schaden*) :– Germ. **skaþōjan*. The sb. survives in gen. literary use in the comp. **sca·the**LESS (XII Orm – ON. *skaðlauss*), the vb. in **scath**ING[2] skei·ðiŋ (poet.) blasting, searing XVIII; fig. as of invective XIX; **unscath**ED[1] ʌnskei·ðd uninjured, orig. Sc. XIV (Sc. Leg. Saints).

scatology skətɔ·lədʒi (path.) diagnosis by the fæces. XIX. f. Gr. *skato-*, *skôr* dung (cf. SCORIA) + -(O)LOGY. So **sca·to**MANCY skæ·t-. XVI.

scatter skæ·təɹ †squander, dissipate; disperse in many directions XIII (*skatere*). prob. var. of SHATTER, with sk- substituted for ʃ- under Scand. influence. ¶ The instance of pt. *scatered* in 'Peterborough Chronicle', an. 1137, is prob. an ex. of *shatter*, since in that text *sc* normally denotes ʃ.

scaup-duck skō·pdʌk duck of the genus Fuligula. XVII (Willughby). f. *scaup* bank providing a bed for shellfish, Sc. var. of *scalp* (XVI) bare piece of rock above water, perh. transf. use of SCALP.

scaur skɔ̄ɹ (Sc.) precipitous bank, cliff. XIX (Scott). var. of SCAR[1].

scavage skæ·vidʒ (hist.) toll formerly levied in London on merchant strangers. XV (Caxton). – AN. *scawage* = ONF. *escauwage*, f. *escauwer* inspect – Flem. *scauwen* = OE. *sċēawian* see (SHOW).

scavenger skæ·vindʒəɹ †officer who took 'scavage' and (later) kept the streets clean; person employed to clean streets XVI. alt. of *scavager* – AN. *scawager*, f. *scawage*; see prec. and -ER[1]; for the *n* cf. *harbinger*, *messenger*, *passenger*, *wharfinger*. Hence by back-formation **sca·venge** vb. XVII.

Scavenger's daughter instrument of torture. XVI (latinized *Scauingeri filia*). alt. of *Skevington*, *Skeffington*, name of the inventor (Leonard S.), Lieutenant of the Tower in Henry VIII's reign.

scazon skei·zən (pros.) choliamb. XVII. – L. *scazōn* – Gr. *skázōn*, sb. use of prp. m. of *skázein* limp, halt.

scenario sinā·riou, ʃeinā·riou outline of the plot of a play. XIX. – It. *scenario* (f. *scena* SCENE), anglicized as †*scenary* XVII.

scend see SEND[2].

scene sīn apparatus for setting forth the action of a play; division of an act of a play; place of an action; †stage performance XVI; †stage of a theatre; view of an action, place, etc.; episode, situation in real life XVII; stormy encounter (so F. *faire une scène*) XVIII. – L. *scēna*, *scæna* stage, scene – Gr. *skēnḗ* tent, booth, stage, scene, rel. to *skiá* shadow (cf. SHIMMER). Cf. F. *scène* (rare before XVII). So **scenery** sī·nəri †dramatic action (Richardson); decoration of a theatre stage (Burke); aggregate of features in a landscape XVIII. alt. of †*scenary* (see SCENARIO) by assim. of the ending to -ERY. **scen**IC sī·nik, se·nik. XVII. – L. *scēnicus* – Gr. *skēnikós*, **sce·n**ICAL XV.

scent sent track (animals) by the smell; †exhale an odour XIV; (from the sb.) perfume XVII. Late ME. *sent(e)* – (O)F. *sentir* feel, perceive, smell = Pr., Sp. *sentir*, It. *sentīre* :– L. *sentīre* feel, perceive. Hence **scent** sb. odour of beast or man as a means of pursuit XIV (Barbour); sense of smell; distinctive odour XV. ¶ The unexpl. sp. *scent* does not appear till XVII.

sceptic, U.S. **skeptic** ske·ptik one who doubts. XVI. – F. *sceptique* (septik) or L. *scepticus*, in sb. pl. *scepticī* followers of the Greek philosopher Pyrrho of Elis (Quintilian) – Gr. *skeptikós*, sb. pl. *skeptikoi* (Aulus Gellius), f. *sképtesthai* look about, consider, observe, f. **skep*-, rel. to **skop*- (as in *skópos*; see SCOPE, -SCOPE) and poss. metathesis of **spek*. So **sce·pt**ICAL. XVII. **sce·ptic**ISM. XVII. – modL. *scepticismus*; cf. F. *scepticisme*. ¶ The sp. with *sk*- and the consequent pronunc. are due to direct recourse to Gr.; it is recorded (along with *sc*-) from XVI, is the only sp. in J.'s Dict., and is the accepted form in U.S.A.

sceptre, U.S. **scepter** se·ptəɹ rod or wand as a symbol of regal or imperial authority. XIII (Cursor M.). ME. *ceptre*, *septre* (with later assim. to L. and Gr.) – OF. *ceptre*, (also mod.) *sceptre*, corr. to Sp. *cetro*, It. *scettro* – L. *scēptrum* – Gr. *skêptron*, f. *skḗptein* prop, *skḗptesthai* prop oneself, lean (on); cf. SHAFT[1].

sch letter-group repr. in its earliest use the sound ʃ, succeeding to OE. *sć*- (see SH); in modern sp. it has this value in *schedule*, *schist*, in a few G. words, e.g. *schnapps*, *schorl*, and (formerly) in Oriental words such as *haschisch*; it repr. s in *schism* (as earlier in *schedule*); it is pronounced sk in words of ult. Gr. origin, as *scheme*, *scholastic*, *school*, and in It. words, e.g. *scherzo*.

schedule ʃe·djūl, (U.S. ske·djul) †ticket, label XIV; †explanatory slip accompanying a document XV; appendix to an act of parliament; classified statement or list XVI. Late ME. *cedule*, *sedule* – (O)F. *cédule*, corr. to Pr. *cedula*, Sp. *cédula*, It. *cedola* – late L. *scedula* small slip of paper, dim. of *sceda*, also *scheda* leaf of papyrus; see -ULE. ¶ In XVI *scedule*, *schedule* reflect the current L. forms, the latter finally prevailing since mid-XVII. The pronunc. se·djūl continued till *c*.1800, but was supplanted by ʃe·djūl. In U.S.A. that with sk (after *scheme*) is current through the authority of Webster.

scheme skīm †figure of rhetoric XVI; †diagram; analytical or tabular statement; plan, design XVII. – L. *schēma* – Gr. *schêma* form, figure, f. **skh*- :– pre-Hellenic **zgh*-, var. of **segh*- (whence Gr. *héxis* habit; cf. HECTIC). The usual medL. rendering of *skhêma* being *figura*, *scheme* was used in XVI–XVII as a syn. of *figure* in several techn. senses. Hence vb. XVIII. So **schem**A·TIC. XVIII. – modL. *schēmaticus*, f. *schēmat*-, *schēma*; cf. G. *schematisch*. **sche·mat**ISM. XVII. – L. – Gr.

scherzando skɔ̄ɹtsæ·ndou (mus.) playfully. XIX. – It. *scherzando*, gerund of *scherzare* play, sport, f. *scherzo* sport, jest, (mus.) lively movement – (M)HG. *scherz*, f. *scherzen*, f. base of *schernen*, f. OHG. *skern* (see SCORN).

schism sizm breach of the unity of the visible Church XIV (Gower); offence of promoting this XV; sect so formed XVI. Late ME. *scisme*, *sisme* – OF. *scisme*, *sisme* (mod. *schisme*), corr. to Pr., It. *scisma*, Sp. *cisma* – ecclL. *schisma* – Gr. *skhísma* rent, cleft, in N.T. division in the Church, f. **skhid*-, base of *skhízein* split, cleave. The sp. was assim. (XVI), as in F., to the L. form. So **schism**A·TIC. XIV (sb., PPl.). – (O)F. – ecclL. – ecclGr.; -ICAL XVI.

schist ʃist (geol.) fissile crystalline rock. XVIII (first in modL. form *schistus*). – F. *schiste* – L. *schistos* (*lapis s.* 'fissile stone', Pliny) – Gr. *skhistós* (*s. líthos* perh. talc), pp. adj. f. **skhid*- (see prec.). Hence **schi·st**OSE[1]. XVIII.

schizo- skai·zou, skaizə·, skidz- comb. form irreg. repr. Gr. *skhizein* split (cf. SCHISM and prec.), used from *c.* 1840 in scientific terms, as *schizodon, schizomycete, schizopod*; **schizophrenia** -frī·niə (path.) 'split mind', condition characterized by cleavage of mental functions, Gr. *phrḗn* mind XX (P. E. Bleuler, of Zurich; modL., after F. *schizophrénie*; see -IA[1]); hence **schizophren**IC -fre·nik adj. and sb. XX.

schnap(p)s ʃnæps spirit resembling Hollands gin. XIX. – G. *schnap(p)s* dram of drink, liquor (esp. gin) – LG., Du. *snaps* gulp, mouthful, f. *snappen* seize, snatch (see SNAP).

schnauzer ʃnau·zəɹ German breed of house dog. XIX. G., f. *schnauze* snout.

schnorkel ʃnō·ɹkəl see SNORKEL.

scholar skɔ·ləɹ pupil in a school; one devoted to learning, learned person XIV; student receiving emolument from a school, etc. XVI. ME. *scoler*, aphetic – OF. *escoler, -ier* (mod. *écolier*) – late L. *scholāris*, f. L. *schola* SCHOOL; see -AR. The L. word was adopted in late OE. *scol(i)ere* pupil, learner, MDu. *scholare, -er*, Du. *scholier*), OHG. *scuolari* (G. *schüler*). Hence **scho·lar**LY[1]. XVII; earlier **scho·lar**LIKE (XVI). **scho·lar**SHIP. XVI.

scholastic skŏlæ·stik pert. to the schoolmen XVI, pert. to education in schools XVII; characteristic of 'the schools', pedantic XVIII; sb. schoolman XVII. – L. *scholasticus* – Gr. *skholastikós* studious, learned, sb. scholar, f. *skholázein* be at leisure, devote one's leisure to learning, f. *skholḗ*; see SCHOOL, -IC, and cf. (O)F. *scolastique*, etc. So **schola·stic**AL. XVI (in all senses earlier). Hence **schola·stic**ISM. XVIII.

scholium skou·liəm, pl. **-ia** iə explanatory note, comment. XVI. – modL. *scholium* – Gr. *skhólion*, f. *skholḗ* learned discussion (see SCHOOL). So **scholiast** skou·liæst commentator. XVI. – late Gr. *skholiastḗs*, f. *skholiázein*, f. *skhólion*; cf. F. *scoliaste* (XVI, Rabelais).

school[1] skūl place or establishment for instruction; body of teachers of a subject in a university (spec. applications vary). OE. *scōl, scolu*, corr. to MLG., MDu. *schōle* (Du. *school*), OHG. *scuola* (G. *schule*), Germ. – medL. *scōla*, for L. *schola* – Gr. *skholḗ* leisure, employment of leisure in disputation, lecture, (later) school; reinforced in ME. by aphetic – OF. *escole* (mod. *école*) = Pr. *escola*, etc. – CRom. *scola*; the adoption of the L. word (which itself superseded *lūdus* prop. game) is CEur.; cf. W. *ysgol*, OIr. *scol* (Ir., Gaẹl. *sgoil*), Russ. *shkola*, etc.; the native name was *lārhūs* 'lore-house'. Hence vb. XVI; cf. G. *schulen*, etc. **schoo·l**MAN (cf. OE. *scōlmann* learner) in mediæval universities, one who treated of logic, metaphysics, and theology. XVI.

school[2] skūl shoal of fish, etc. XIV. – MLG. MDu. *schōle* (Du. *school*) troop, multitude, spec. 'school' of whales = OS. *scola*, OE. *scolu* troop :– WGerm. ***skulo**, perh. orig. division, f. **skul- *skel- *skal-* divide (see SHELL, SKILL).

schooner skū·nəɹ small sea-going fore-and-aft-rigged vessel. XVIII (*skooner, scooner*). Said to be agent-noun (-ER[1]) f. New England vb. **scoon* or **scun* skim along water, for which there is no evidence; adopted in many Eur. langs.

schorl ʃɔ̄ɹl (min.) (black) tourmaline. XVIII. – G. *schörl*, earlier *schrul, schurl, schirl, schir-, schörlich*, of unkn. origin.

schottische ʃɔ·tīʃ, ʃɔtī·ʃ dance resembling the polka introduced into England in 1848. XIX. – G. (*der*) *schottische* (*tanz*) the SCOTTISH dance.

sciagraphy saiæ·grəfi projection of shadows, delineation of light and shade. XVI (*sciographie*). – F. *scia-, sciographie* – L. *scia-, sciographia* – Gr. *skiā-, skiographiā*, f. *skiā-, skiográphos*, f. *skiā́* shadow + *-graphos*; see SHINE[1], -GRAPHY.

sciatic saiæ·tik pert. to or affecting the hip. XVI. – (O)F. *sciatique* – late L. *sciaticus*, alt. of *ischiaticus*, for L. *ischiadicus* (after *-aticus* -ATIC) – Gr. *iskhiadikós* (Hippocrates, Galen, Dioscorides), f. *iskhíon* hip-joint, pl. *iskhía* haunches, hams (cf. medL. *scia* hip). Cf. Pr. *sciatic*, Sp. *ciático*, It. *sciatico*. So **sciatica** saiæ·tikə. XV (*cyetica, sytyca*). – late L. *sciatica* (sc. *passio* morbid affection, illness).

science sai·əns knowledge, esp. of a technical kind. XIV (Rolle). – OF. *science*, corr. to Pr. *sciensa*, Sp. *ciencia*, Pg. *sciencia*, It. *scienza* – L. *scientia*, f. *scient-*, prp. stem of *scīre* know; see -ENCE. The foll. related or deriv. sbs. meaning 'man adept in science' are all ἅπαξ λεγόμενα except the first; †*sciencer* (XVI–XVII), †*scientiate* (XVII), †*sciencist* (XVIII), †*scientman* (XVII); they are repl. by **scient**IST sai·əntist XIX (1840, Whewell). The foll. adjs. were variously current: †*scient* having knowledge or skill (XV Lydg. –XIX) – prp. of L. *scīre* in Rom. largely repl. by *sapere* (cf. SAPIENT); †*sciential* (XV Pecock to XIX) – late L. *scientiālis*; †*scie·ntic*, †*-ical* XVI – F. *scientique*; †*scie·ntious* XVII (only); †*scie·ntive* XVI (only) – OF.; they were finally superseded by **scienti**FIC saiənti·fik (also †**-ical**) XVI (of proof, etc.) demonstrative; concerned with science or the sciences XVI; pert. to science XVIII. – (O)F. *scientifique* or late L. *scientificus*, equiv. to *scientiam faciens* producing knowledge, used primarily in translations of Aristotle's works to render Gr. ἐπιστημονικός (f. ἐπιστήμων possessing knowledge, f. ἐπιστήμη knowledge), and applied first to arguments or proofs, later extended to matters and persons having to do with science. Cf. CONSCIENCE, PRESCIENCE.

scilicet, abbrev. **scil.**, **sc.** sai·liset that is to say, to wit. XIV. L., contr. of *scīre licet* 'it is permitted to know'; *scīre* (see prec.), *licet* 3rd sg. pres. ind. of *licēre* (see LICIT).

scilla si·lə liliaceous plant of the genus Scilla. XIX. – L. *scilla* – Gr. *skílla*. Cf. SQUILL.

scimitar si·mitəɹ short curved one-edged sword. XVI. Introduced in various forms (*cimiterie, cemitere, cymitare, scimitar*) repr. F. *cimeterre, cimiterre*, It. *scimitarra*, †*cimitara*, Sp., Pg. *cimitarra*, Pers. *ṣimṣīr* (whence Gr. *sampsḗrā*).

scincoid ski·ŋkoid resembling a skink. XVIII. – modL. *scincoidēs*, f. L. *scincus* SKINK; see -OID.

scintilla sinti·lə minute particle. XVII (anglicized †*scintill* XVI). – L., spark. So **sci·ntill**ATE[3] sparkle. XVII. f. pp. stem of L. *scintillāre*, f. *scintilla*. **scintilla·**TION. XVII. – L.; so F.

sciolist sai·əlist smatterer. XVII. f. late L. *sciolus*, dim. f. *scius* (cf. CONSCIOUS), f. base of L. *scīre* know; see SCIENCE, -IST.

sciomancy sai·o(u)mænsi divination by the shades of the dead. XVII. – modL. *sciomantīa*, f. Gr. *skio-, skiā́* shadow; see SHINE; -MANCY.

scion sai·ən shoot, slip, graft XIV; heir, descendant XIX. ME. *sioun* – OF. *ciun, cion, sion* (mod. *scion*), perh. alt. of *chion* (as in mod. Picard dial.) – Germ. **kiðon* shoot.

scire facias saiə·ri fei·ʃiæs (leg.) writ requiring the sheriff to summon the party before the court. XV. sb. use of law L. phr. ('you are to do (him) to wit'), the essential formula of the writ.

scirrhous si·rəs pert. to a scirrhus. XVI. – F. *scirrheux* (now *squirreux*) – modL. *scirrhōsus*, f. *scīrrhus* (used in Eng. since XVII) hard tumour (*sciros* in Pliny) – Gr. *skírros, skîros* hard (substance); see -OUS.

scission si·ʃən cutting, division. XV (rare before XVIII). – (O)F. *scission* or late L. *scissiō(n-)*, f. pp. stem of *scindere* cut, cleave, f. IE. **sk(h)id-*, **sk(h)eid-*; cf. Gr. *skhízein* split, separate, and SCHISM, SCHIST, SCHIZO-; see -ION.

scissors si·zəɹz cutting instrument consisting of a pair of pivoted handled blades. XIV (Ch.). Late ME. *sisoures* – (O)F. *cisoires* (now only 'large shears', the sense 'scissors' being appropriated to *ciseaux*, pl. of †*cisel* CHISEL), repr. medL. **cīsōria*, pl. of late L. *cīsōrium*, f. *-cīs-, -cīdere*, var. in comp. of L. *cæs-, cædere* cut (cf. CEMENT, CONCISE). For the ending *-or(s)* see MIRROR. ¶ The sp. with *sc-*, dating from XVI, is due to assoc. with L. *scindere* (see prec. and cf. L. *scissor* carver, in medL. tailor).

sciurine sai·jurain pert. to squirrels. XIX. f. L. *sciūrus* – Gr. *skíouros*, f. *skiā́* shadow + *ourā́* tail; see SHINE, ARSE, -INE[1].

sclaff sklæf (in golf) scrape the ground. XIX. spec. use of Sc. *sclaff* strike with a flat surface, shuffle along, perh. of imit. origin.

sclero- skliə·rou, skliərə· comb. form of Gr. *sklērós* hard (see SKELETON). XIX. So **sclero·**SIS morbid hardening. XIV. medL. *sclērōsis* (usu. *sclīr-*, repr. late Gr. pronunc. of η) – Gr. *sklḗrōsis*, f. *sklēroûn* harden. **sclerotic** -ɔ·tik XVI. – medL.

scoff[1] skɔf contemptuous ridicule XIV; also vb. perh. of Scand. origin; cf. early modDa. *skof, skuf* jest, mockery, *skuffe* jest, mock, also (as now) deceive, disappoint, rel. to OFris. *skof* mockery, OHG. *skoph* poet (cf. SCOP).

scoff[2] skɔf (sl. and dial.) eat voraciously; seize, plunder XIX. orig. var. of synon. (dial.) *scaff* (XVIII), rel. to contemp. *scaff* food; later assoc. with S. African *scoff* food, meal – Afrikaans (Du.) *schoft* (prop.) quarter of a day, (hence) any of the four meals of the day.

scold skould ribald or abusive person (esp. a woman). XIII (the ex. in 'Ormulum' 2192 may mean 'poet, minstrel'). prob. – ON. *skáld* poet, SKALD, in comps. also with dyslogistic implication (e.g. *skáldskapr*, prop. poetry, which has in the Icel. lawbooks the spec. sense of libel in verse), hence (perh. by a spec. Eng. development), libellous, scurrilous, or ribald person. Hence **scold** vb. †quarrel | noisily, (later) be vehement or persistent in reproof or faultfinding (to) XIV (PPl., Trevisa).

scollop see SCALLOP.

scolopendra skɔlŏpe·ndrə †fabulous seafish XVI; centipede, millipede XVII. – L. – Gr. *skolópendra*, prob. of alien origin.

sconce[1] skɔns lantern or screened candlestick carried by a handle XIV; bracket-candlestick XV. Aphetic – OF. *esconse* (i) hiding-place, (ii) lantern or – medL. *sconsa*, aphetic of *absconsa* (sc. *laterna*) dark lantern, sb. use of fem. pp. of L. *abscondere* hide (see ABSCOND).

sconce[2] skɔns (arch. sl.) head. XVI. perh. joc. use of prec.

sconce[3] skɔns (fortif.) small fort or earthwork. XVI. – Du. *schans*, †*schantze* brushwood, screen of brushwood for soldiers, earthwork of gabions – (M)HG. *schanze* (whence also MLG. *schantze*), of unkn. origin; the orig. meaning was perh. 'bundle of twigs'. Cf. ENSCONSE.

sconce[4] skɔns (Univ. sl.) fine in a tankard of ale, etc., e.g. for breach of discipline or convention. XVII. Early exx. have allusions to head-money and being 'taxt by the poul', suggesting that the term arose from a joc. ref. to SCONCE[2]. Hence sb. XVII.

scone skɔn, skoun round cake of wheat or barley meal baked on a griddle, quadrant-shaped section of this. XVI (*scon*, Douglas). orig. Sc., perh. shortening of MLG. *schonbrot*, MDu. *schoonbrot* sχōnbrōt 'fine bread' (see SHEEN).

scoop skūp utensil for baling or ladling XIV; kind of shovel XV. Orig. in nautical and trade use from the Low Countries. – MLG., MDu. *schōpe* (Du. *schoep*) vessel for baling, bucket of a water-wheel = MHG. *schuofe* (G. †*schufe*) :– WGerm. **skōpō(n)*, f. **skōp-* var. of **skap-*, whence **skappjan* draw water (repr. by OS. *skeppian*, Du. *scheppen*, OHG. *scephan*, G. *schöpfen*); cf. SHAPE. Hence **scoop** vb. †ladle or bale out XIV; remove (as) with a scoop XVII. Also in mod. use, orig. U.S., to take up in large quantities; cut out (a rival newspaper editor, etc.) XIX (whence sb. exclusive piece of news).

scoot skūt go suddenly and swiftly. XVIII (naut.). The orig. form is *scout*, which became obs. in early XIX; the present form seems to have been imported later from the U.S.A.; of unkn. origin.

scop skɔp also erron. *scóp*, *scôp* skoup Anglo-Saxon poet or minstrel. XIX (Lytton). Antiquarian revival (with sp.-pronunc.) of OE. *sćop*, *sćeop* (which, if surviving normally, would have become **shop* or **shope*, **shoap*) = OHG. *scof*, rel. to MDu. *schop*, OHG. *scopf* poet, jest, derision, ON. *skop* mocking, railing (cf. SCOFF[1]).

scope skoup object aimed at; room for exercise, free course; range of activity XVI; length of cable at which a ship rides XVII. – It. *scopo* aim, purpose – Gr. *skopós* mark for shooting at, f. **skop-* **skep-*, as in *skopeîn* observe, aim at, examine, *sképtesthai* (cf. SCEPTIC).

-scope skoup terminal el. repr. L. *-scopium* – Gr. *-skópion* (as in *hōroscopium* – *hōroskópion* casting of nativities), f. *skopeîn* (see prec.); extended in medL. use in *microscopium* MICROSCOPE and *tēlescopium* TELESCOPE, on the model of which have been formed terms denoting scientific instruments for enabling the eye or the ear to make observations, e.g. *baroscope*, *gyroscope*, *laryngoscope*, *stethoscope*. The corr. adjs. end in **-sco·pic** skɔpik with advs. in **-sco·pical**LY[2] and nouns of action in **-scopy**[3] skɔpi.

scorbutic skɔ̄ɹbjū·tik pert. to scurvy. XVII. – medL. *scorbūticus*, f. *scorbūtus* scurvy (whence F. *scorbut*, It. *scorbuto*, etc.), perh. for **scorbūcus* – MLG. *schorbūk*, Du. *scheurbuik* (whence G. *scharbock*, Icel. *skyrbjúgr*, etc.), f. MLG., MDu. *schoren* (Du. *scheuren*) break, lacerate + *būk* (*buik*) belly; cf. Du. †*scheurmond* (*mond* mouth) scurvy of the gums, *scheurbeen* (*been* bone) scorbutic affection of the bones.

scorch skɔ̄ɹtʃ heat so as to dry up. XV. rel. obscurely to †*skorkle* (XIV, Ch.), frequent. of **skorke* (cf. *scorrcnenn* in 'Ormulum', which may be – ON. *skorpna* be shrivelled). ¶ With the colloq. use 'cycle or motor at high speed' cf. F. phr. *brûler le pavé* 'burn the road'.

score skɔ̄əɹ A. set of twenty (prob. orig. as marked on a tally) (XI); B. notch, mark, stroke; account of times kept on a tally or board XIV; amount of a bill or reckoning XVI; account, reason XVII; record of points in a game XVIII; C. written or printed piece of concerted music (said to be so named from the practice of connecting the related staves by 'scores' or lines marking off the bars) XVIII. Late OE. **scoru*, pl. *scora*, *-e* – ON. *skor* notch, tally, twenty :– **skurō*, f. **skur-* **sker-* cut, SHEAR. So **score** vb. XIV. partly – ON. *skora*, f. *skor*; partly f. the Eng. sb.

scoria skɔ̄ə·riə slag, clinkers. XVII. – L. *scōria* dross – Gr. *skōriā*, f. *skôr* dung (cf. SCATOLOGY), rel. to OE. *sćearn*, dial. *sharn* dung = OFris. *skern*, ON. *skarn*, etc., pp. formation on Germ. **sker-* **skar-* cut, divide, separate (see SHARE, SHEAR).

scorn skɔ̄ɹn †behave contemptuously XII (Orm); †deride, (now) hold in disdain XIII. Aphetic – OF. *escharnir*, *eschernir* = Pr. *escarnir*, *esquernir*, Sp., Pg. *escarnir*, It. *schernire* :– Rom. **escarnīre*, **eskernīre* – Germ. **skarnjan*, **skernjan*, f. base of OS. *skern*, etc., jest, mockery. So **scorn** sb. XII (Orm). – OF. *escarn*, corr. to Pr. *esquern*, etc., f. the vbs. In sb. and vb. forms with *-a-* and *-o-* are equally early; the origin of the latter is obscure; there are difficulties in the way of referring them to F. †*escorner*, It. *scornare* insult, affront :– Rom. **excornāre*, deprive of horns, dishonour, f. L. *ex* EX-[1] + *cornū* HORN.

scorpion skɔ̄·ɹpiən arachnid whose sting causes intense pain XIII (AncrR.); (after 1 Kings xii 11, 2 Chron. x 11) knotted or armed cord XIV. – (O)F. *scorpion* = Pr., Sp. *escorpion*, It. *scorpione* :– L. *scorpiō(n-)*, extension of *scorpius* – Gr. *skorpíos*.

scorzonera skɔ̄ɹzəniə·rə plant of the genus so named. XVII (earlier †*scorzoner*, Gerarde). – It. *scorzonera* (whence F. *scorsonère*, Sp. *escorzonera*), f. *scorzone* :– Rom. **scurtiōne*, alt. of medL. *curtiō(n-)* poisonous snake, for whose venom the plant may have been an antidote.

scot skɔt payment, contribution; *scot and lot*, taxes levied by a municipal corporation in proportionate shares upon its members XIII. In ME. partly – ON. *skot* (= OE. *sćot* SHOT), partly aphetic – OF. *escot* (mod. *écot*), of Germ. origin; in later use to some extent an antiquarian revival of the OE. form (cf. SCOP). Hence **scot-FREE·** exempt from the payment of scot, fine, etc.; exempt from injury or punishment XVI; there is a parallel *shot-free* (XVI, Sh., Jonson).

Scot skɔt (hist.) one of a Gaelic-speaking people first known in Ireland, and later settled in north Britain (Scotland) OE.; native of Scotland XIV. OE. **Scot*, only in pl. *Scottas* – late L. *Scottus* (*c*.400), whence also OHG. *Scotto* (G. *Schotte*), MDu. *Schotte*, (also mod.) *Schot*. The regular medL. form was *Scōtus*, whence OF. *Escot*, Sp. *Escoto*, It. *Scoto*; a var. *Scŏtus* may be repr. by ON. pl. *Skotar*. Nothing is known of the ult. origin. So **Scotch** skɔtʃ XVI,

Scots XIV (*Scottis*), reduced vars. of **Scottish**[1] XIII (Laȝ.), repl. OE. *Scyttisċ* (cf. (M)Du. *schotsch*, G. *schottisch*, † *schöttisch*, ON. *skotskr*). **Sco·tch**MAN XVI. **Sco·ts**MAN XIV (*Scottis man*, Barbour).

scotch[1] skɔtʃ make an incision in XV (Hoccleve); (from Theobald's emendation of *scorch* in Sh. 'Macbeth' III iv 13) injure or obstruct so as to render harmless for a time XVIII. Of unkn. origin. Hence sb. incision XV; so in HOPSCOTCH.

scotch[2] skɔtʃ block, etc. placed under a circular object to prevent slipping. XVII. occas. *skatch*, which may indicate identity with *scatch* (XVI) stilt – OF. *escache*, whence Du. *schaats* SKATE[2].

Scotist skou·tist follower of the 13th-century theologian Ioannes Duns *Scotus* (the Subtle Doctor); see -IST. XVI.

scoundrel skau·ndrəl unscrupulous or unprincipled person. XVI. Of unkn. origin; deriv. from Sc. and north. *scunner* shrink, flinch, is excluded by the phonology and the Eng. locality of the word, and deriv. from an OF. **esconderel* (f. *escondre* evade :– L. *abscondere* hide, ABSCOND) by its late appearance. See -REL.

scour[1] skauəɹ rid, clear (an area) XIII (Cursor M.); purge XIV (Barbour); cleanse by hard rubbing XIV (Ch.); clear out, get rid of XV (Lydg.); rake with gunshot XVI. prob. introduced by Flemish workmen, and – MLG., MDu. *schūren* (whence G. *scheuern*, (M)Sw. *skura*, Da. *skure*) – OF. *escurer* (mod. *écurer* clean, scour) = Pr., Sp. *escurar*, It. †*sgurare*, †*scurare* :– late L. *excūrāre* (medL. (*e*)*scūrāre*), f. L. *ex* EX-[1] + *cūrāre* take care of, medL. clean, f. *cūra* CURE.

scour[2] skauəɹ move *about* rapidly; pass rapidly over XIV. Of dubious early history and of unkn. origin.

scourer skauə·rəɹ †scout XIV; (arch.) roisterer XVII. Late ME. *scoverour*, aphetic of *descoverour* – OF. *descouvreor*, f. *descouvrir* DISCOVER; afterwards apprehended as agent-noun of SCOUR[2].

scourge skə̄ɹdʒ whip XIII; instrument of divine chastisement XIV; cause of calamity XVI. Aphetic – OF. *escurge*, *escorge*, f. *escorgier* (cf. *escorgiee*, mod. *e*(*s*)*courgée* whip, OIt. *scuriada*, OF. *escourjon* thong of a whip) :– Rom. **excorrigiāre*, f. *ex* EX-[1] + *corrigia* thong, whip, perh. of Gaulish origin. So **scourge** vb. XIII (RGlouc.). – OF. *escorgier*.

scout[1] skaut spy, reconnoitre. XIV. Aphetic – OF. *escouter* (mod. *écouter*) listen, alt. of *ascolter* = Pr. *escoltar*, It. *ascoltare*, etc. :– Rom. **ascultāre*, for L. *auscultāre* (see AUSCULTATION). So **scout** sb. one sent ahead to reconnoitre. XVI. – OF. *escoute*, f. *escouter*; earlier in †*scout-watch* sentinel, spy (XIV), unless this is a comp. of the vb.

scout[2] skaut flat-bottomed boat. XV. – MDu. *schūte* (Du. *schuit*), adopted earlier as *schoute* (XIV), rel. to ON. *skúta* (Da. *skude*) light fast vessel; perh. to be referred to the base of SHOOT in the sense 'move rapidly'.

scout[3] skaut †mock, deride XVII; reject with scorn XVIII. prob. of Scand. origin (cf. ON. *skúta*, *skúti* a taunt, *skútyrði*, *skotyrði* abusive language), prob. f. base of *skjóta* SHOOT. (If so, the word must have been in colloq. use long before it is recorded.) Cf. SHOUT.

scout[4] skaut (at Oxford, hence at Yale and Harvard), male college servant. XVIII. Of unkn. origin; perh. spec. use of SCOUT[1].

scow skau large flat-bottomed square-ended lighter. XVIII. – Du. *schouw*, earlier *schouwe*, *schoude* = LG. *schalde*, rel. to OS. *skaldan* push (a boat) from the shore.

scowl skaul look with louring brows and threatening expression. XIV. First recorded from northerly and eastern areas; prob. of Scand. origin (cf. Da. *skule* cast down one's eyes, give a sidelong look); perh. ult. rel. to late OE. *scūlēgede* squint-eyed (varying with *scȳlēgede*). Hence sb. XVI (Dunbar).

scr- may repr. (1) locally, OE. *scr-*, as in *screed*, the standard development being *shr-*, as in *shred*, *shroud*, (2) ON. *skr-*, as (partly) in *scrape*, (3) OF. *escr-*, as in *screw*, (4) MLG., MDu. *schr-* as in *scrabble*, *scrub* vb., (5) an expressive modification of *cr-*, as in *scrag*[1], *scratch*, *scrunch*.

scrabble skræ·bl make marks at random, scrawl; scratch about XVI; scramble XVII. – MDu. *schrabbelen* frequent. of *schrabben* scratch, scrape; cf. synon. MDu. *schrāven* and SCRAPE.

scrag[1] skræg lean person or animal XVI; lean end of a neck of mutton XVII; neck XIX. perh. alt. of † *crag*(*ge*) XV–XVIII; see SCR- (5). Hence vb. hang by the neck, throttle. XVIII. **scra·ggy**[1] lean. XVII.

scrag[2] skræg (dial.) stump of a tree, rough projection. XVI. Parallel to dial. *scrog* stunted bush, pl. brushwood (XIV), *shrag* rag (XIV), twig (XVI), *shrog* bush, pl. underwood (XV). Implied in ME. **scra·ggy**[1] rough, rugged, ragged. XIII (*scraggi*).

scramble skræ·mbl make one's way by clambering, etc. XVI (Sidney); struggle *with* others for something XVI. Of symbolic form, combining dial. *scamble* and *cramble* (XVI), of allied meaning.

scrannel skræ·nəl (dial.) lean, thin. XVII (Milton 'Lycidas' 124 *s. pipes*, from which subsequent users of the word have inferred the meaning 'harsh, unmelodious'). Obscurely rel. to synon. dial. *scrank* (E. Coles, Dict. 1679), Sc. *scranky* (Ramsay, XVIII), *scranny*; all prob. of ult. Scand. origin and derived from a base repr. by Norw. *skran* shrivelled, *skrank* lean large-boned figure.

scrap[1] skræp pl. remains of food XIV (Trevisa); fragmentary portion XVI. – ON. *skrap* scraps, trifles, f. base of *skrapa* SCRAPE. Hence **scrappy**[1] skræ·pi. XIX.

scrap[2] skræp †villainous plot XVII; struggle, tussle XIX. perh. f. SCRAPE.

scrape skreip remove an outer layer from XIV; rake *together* with effort; draw harshly or noisily over a surface XVI. – ON. *skrapa* or (M)Du. *schrapen* (whence also OF. *escraper*) = OE. *sćrapian* scratch, ME. †*shrape*, rel. to Du., LG. *schrappen* (whence G. *schrappen*), MHG. *schrapfen, schrepfen*; for other prob. cogns. cf. SHARP.

scratch skrætʃ wound the surface of the skin with the nails, etc. XV (Caxton); rub lightly with the finger nails or claws XVI; make linear abrasions on XVII. prob. blending of synon. (dial.) *scrat* (*scratte* XIII) and †*cratch* (*cracche* XIII); the origin of these forms is obscure, but their meaning associates them with the similar MLG., MDu. *kratsen*, OHG. *krazzōn* (G. *kratzen*), OSw. *kratta* scratch; (O)F. *gratter* GRATE[2], OF. *esgrater* (a poss. source of *scrat*), Sp. *gratar*, It. *grattare* are from Germ. Hence sb. result of scratching XVI; mark indicating starting-point XVIII; adj. hastily done, collected, etc. XIX.

Scratch skrætʃ (dial.) usu. *Old S.*, the Devil. XVIII. alt. of (dial.) *scrat*, late ME. *scrate* (XV) hermaphrodite – ON. *skrat(t)i* wizard, goblin, monster, rel. to OHG. *scrato* (G. *schrat*) satyr, sprite.

scrawl skrōl write in a sprawling untidy manner. XVII. perh. transf. use of (dial.) *scrawl* sprawl, crawl (XIV), prob. blending of CRAWL and SPRAWL; cf. SCR- 5. Hence sb. XVII.

scream skrīm utter a shrill piercing cry. XIII. Either aberrant repr. (see SCR-) of late OE. **sćrǣman*, ME. *shreame* (XIII) or – the rel. MDu. **schreemen* (so WFlem.; cf. MDu. *schreem* sb.) = OFris. **skrēma* (WFris. *skrieme* weep).

scree skrī mass of detritus on a mountainside. XVIII. prob. back-formation from *screes*, for **screethes* pl. – ON. *skriða* landslip, rel. to *skríða* slide, glide = OE. *scrīþan*, OS. *skrīðan*, OHG. *skrītan* (G. *schreiten*).

screech skrītʃ XVI. alt. (with expressive lengthening of vowel) of †*scritch* (*scriche* XIII), f. imit. base repr. in OE. *sćriććettan*; cf. (dial.) *screak* (XV), *scrike* (XIV), of Scand. origin (cf. ON. *skrǽkja*, Norw. *scrika*). So *screech-owl* (XVI, Sh.), earlier †*scritch-owl*.

screed skrīd (dial.) fragment severed, torn strip XIV; long roll or list, lengthy discourse XVIII; levelled strip of plaster XIX. prob. var. repr. (see SCR-) of OE. *sćrēade* SHRED.

screen skrīn contrivance to ward off heat, wind, light, etc.; partition in a building XV; (fig.) XVI; sifting apparatus XVI. Aphetic – OFrank. **skrank*, – ONF. *escren*, var. of *escran* (mod. *écran*) = OHG. *skrank*, pl. *skrenk* (G. *schrank* cupboard) bar, barrier, fence (cf. mod. *schranke*). Hence vb. shelter, shield XV; sift XVII.

screever skrī·vəɹ (sl.) pavement artist. XIX. Agent-noun (-ER[1]) of *screeve* (sl.) write, draw pictures on a pavement, perh. – It. *scrivere* :– L. *scrībere* write (see SCRIBE).

screw skrū A. mechanical contrivance of which the operative part is a spiral groove or ridge XV; worm or boring part of a gimlet XVI; (fig.) XVII. B. (from the vb.) act of screwing XVIII; object screwed or twisted up XIX. C. (sl. senses of obscure development) unsound horse; wages, salary XIX. In A – OF. *escroue* fem. (mod. *écrou* m.) either (i) – WGerm. **scrūva*, = MHG. *schrūbe* (G. *schraube*), corr. to MDu. *schrūve* (whence the Scand. forms), or (ii) :– (the source of the Germ. forms) L. *scrōfa* sow (cf. SCROFULA), medL. female screw (for the sense development cf. Sp. *puerca* sow, screw). Hence **screw** vb. XVII (Sh.). **screwed** skrūd (sl.) intoxicated; perh. a joc. variant on *tight*; also (earlier) *screwy*.

scribble skri·bl write carelessly or hastily. XV. – medL. *scrībillāre* (cf. rare L. *conscrībillāre*), dim. formed on L. *scrībere* write (see next); see -LE[3].

scribe skraib doctor of the Jewish law XIV (PPl.); secretary, clerk XIV (Wycl. Bible); copyist, transcriber XVI. – L. *scrība* official or public writer (in Vulg. tr. Gr. *γραμματεύς*, Heb. *sōphēr*), f. *scrībere* trace characters, write, f. IE. base **skreibh*- scratch, incise, repr. also in OIr. and Lith., and by Gr. *skarīphâsthai* scratch (cf. SCRIPT and SHRIVE). For semantic development cf. WRITE. So **scribe** vb. (in carpentry) mark or score (wood, etc.), shape the edge of. XVII. Of obscure development; varying with *scrive*; perh. orig. for *describe*, †*descrive*. ¶ The L. vb. is repr. by many comps. with prefixes, e.g. *ascribe* (*ascription*), *conscribe* (*conscript, conscription*), *describe* (*description*), *transcribe* (*transcript, transcription*).

scrimmage skri·midʒ, **scrummage** skrʌ·midʒ †skirmish XV; noisy contention, confused struggle XVIII (spec. in rugby football XIX; cf. SCRUM). alt. of †*scrimish*, var. of SKIRMISH, with assim. of the ending to -AGE; for the change of iʃ to idʒ cf. dial. *rubbidge* for *rubbish*.

scrimp skrimp scanty. XVIII. In early use Sc.; of unkn. origin; for possible cogns. see SHRIMP and for similar expressive structure cf. SKIMP. So **scrimp** vb. scant, skimp. XVIII.

scrimshaw skri·mʃɔ̄ (sl.) handicrafts practised by sailors on long voyages. XIX. Also *scrimshander, -shandy*; of unkn. origin; perh. f. the surname *Scrimshaw*; cf. for the form *scrimshanker* (soldier's sl.) shirker.

scrip[1] skrip wallet, satchel. XIII (Cursor M.). Aphetic – OF. *escrep(p)e* purse, bag for alms, var. of *escherpe* (mod. *écharpe*) or – ON. *skreppa*, which may itself be – OF.; ult. Germ. ***skerpā** (latinized as *scerpa* equipment).

scrip[2] skrip (dial.) piece of paper with writing on it. XVI (Sh.). perh. alt. of SCRIPT by assoc. with SCRAP.

scrip[3] skrip A. (orig.) receipt for the portion of a loan subscribed, (now) share certificate XVIII; B. trade price of a book 25% below published price XIX. In A short for *sub|scrip|tion (receipt)*; in B for *sub|scrip|tion price*.

script skript piece of writing XIV (examinee's written papers XIX); (kind of) handwriting XIX. In late ME. aphetic – OF. *escript*, for *escrit* (now *écrit*), whence †*scrit(e)* XIII–XV :– L. *scrīptum*, sb. use of n.pp. of *scrībere* write (see SCRIBE). **scrip**TORIUM skriptɔ̄·riəm writing-room. XVIII, (anglicized *scriptory* XV). – medL. **scripture** skri·ptʃəɹ Holy Writ, the Bible XIII (Cursor M.); (arch.) inscription XIV. – L. *scrīptūra*, f. *scrīpt-*, pp. stem of *scrībere*; see SCRIBE, -URE. So **scri·ptur**AL[1]. XVII, – late L. **scriven**ER skri·vənəɹ professional scribe XIV; notary XV. f. ME. *scrivein* (XIII), aphetic – OF. *escrivein* (mod. *écrivain*) = Pr. *escrivá*, etc. :– Rom. **scribano*, f. L. *scrība* SCRIBE, with *-ānus* -AN; see -ER[1].

scritch skritʃ see SCREECH.

scrofula skrɔ·fjŭlə disease characterized by degeneration of the lymphatic glands. XIV. In early use pl. after late L. *scrōfulæ*, dim. f. L. *scrōfa* breeding-sow (supposed to be subject to the disease; cf. synon. Gr. *khoirádes*, pl. of *khoirás* like a hog's back); in sg. form XVIII. Hence **scro·ful**OUS. XVII.

scroll skroul roll of paper or parchment; writing, list, roll; inscribed paper XV; scroll-like ornament XVII. Late ME. *scrowle*, alt., after *rowle*, ROLL, of *scrow* (XIII), aphetic – AN. *escrowe*, OF. *escroe* strip, esp. of parchment – Germ. **skrauđa* SHRED. See ESCROW.

scrotum skrou·təm pouch-like enclosure of the testicles. XVI. – L. *scrōtum*; cf. *scrautum* skin sheath for arrows.

scrouge skrūdʒ, skraudʒ (sl.) crowd out. XVIII (Johnson). alt. of (dial.) *scruze* (XVI, Spenser), perh. blending of SCREW vb. and SQUEEZE.

scrounge skraunᵈʒ (sl.) acquire illicitly. XX. var. of dial. *scrunge* steal.

scrub[1] skrʌb rub hard. XIV. ME. *scrobbe*, beside *shrubbe*, prob. – MLG., MDu. *schrobben, schrubben* (cf. SCR-).

scrub[2] skrʌb low stunted tree XVI (doubtfully XIV); dwarf cattle; mean little fellow XVI. var. of SHRUB; see SCR- 1.

scruff skrʌf nape of the neck. XVIII. orig. alt. of *scuff*, *scuft* (XVIII), of which there is a synon var. *cuff* (XVIII); perh. based ult. on ON. *skoft* (= OHG *scuft*, Goth. *skuft*) hair of the head; cf. (M)HG. *schopf*.

scrum skrʌm XIX. Shortening of *scrummage*, SCRIMMAGE.

scrumptious skrʌ·mᵖʃəs (orig. U.S. colloq.) first rate, 'grand'; (also formerly) fastidious, 'particular' XIX. Of unkn. origin.

scrunch skrʌnᵗʃ (colloq.) XIX. Expressive alt. of CRUNCH; dial. crush, squeeze; see SCR- 5.

scruple skrū·pl A. small unit of weight or measurement; B. thought or doubt troubling the conscience. XVI (occas. †*scrupule*). – F. *scrupule* (corr. to Sp. *escrúpulo*, etc.) or L. *scrūpulus*, *-ulum* in above senses, dim. of *scrūpus* rough or sharp pebble, anxiety (Cicero). **scru·ple** vb. XVII. f. the sb. or – F. **scrupul**OUS skrū·pjŭləs. XV. **scru:pulo·**SITY. XVI – F. or L. ¶ Preceded by †*scriple* (XIV (Wyclif) to XVI.) – L. *scrīpulum*, var. of *scrūpulum*; †*scripulous* (XV–XVII).

scrutator skrūtei·təɹ one who examines closely. XVI. – L. *scrūtātor*, f. *scrūtārī* search, examine, f. *scrūta* trash, rubbish, the orig. application being to the rummaging of rag-pickers or the searching of persons; see -ATOR. So **scrutin**Y[4] skrū·tĭni formal taking of votes XV; close investigation XVII; official examination of votes XVIII. – L. *scrūtinium*. Hence **scrutin**EE·R XVII, earlier †*scrutiner* XVI; see -ER[1], -EER. **scru·tin**IZE. XVII; cf. F. *scrutiner* (XVIII).

scrutoire skrū·twar (arch.) XVII. Aphetic of *escrutoire*, unexpl. var. of ESCRITOIRE.

scry skrai (dial.) descry; act as a crystal-gazer XVI (revived 1894 by Andrew Lang). Aphetic of DESCRY.

scud skʌd move briskly, now esp. of objects driven by the wind. XVI (More). poss. alt. of SCUT, as if to race like a hare.

scudo skū·dou pl. *scudi* silver coin formerly current in Italian states. XVII. It. = OF. *escu* (mod. *écu*), Sp. *escudo* shield, coin bearing a shield :– L. *scūtum* shield.

scuffle skʌ·fl struggle confusedly together. XVI. prob. f. Scand. base (cf. Sw. *skuff*, *skuffa* push) to be referred to Germ. **skuf-* SHOVE.

sculduddery, skul- skʌldʌ·dəri (Sc.) fornication XVIII; obscenity XIX. Of unkn. origin.

sculduggery, skul- skʌldʌ·gəri (U.S.) tricky doings. XIX. Of unkn. origin.

scull skʌl kind of oar. XIV. Of unkn. origin; identity with SKULL is poss. Hence **scull** vb. XVII.

scullery skʌ·ləri (hist.) department of a household concerned with kitchen utensils XV; room attached to a kitchen XVIII. – AN. *squillerie*, for OF. *escuelerie*, f. *escuelier* maker or seller of dishes, f. *escuele* :- Rom. **scūtella* (by assoc. with L. *scūtum* shield), for L. *scutella* salver, waiter, dim. of *scutra* wooden dish or platter; see -ERY.

scullion skʌ·ljən (arch.) servant who performed menial offices in the kitchen. XV (*sculȝon*, Cath. Angl.). Of unkn. origin.

sculpin skʌ·lpin any of several worthless spiny fishes. XVII. perh. alt. of *scorpene* – L. *scorpæna* – Gr. *skórpaina*, presumably f. *skorpíos* SCORPION.

sculpture skʌ·lptʃəɹ art of carving in hard material, products of this. XIV (Gower; rare before XVII; occas. †*sculture* XVI – It. *scultura*). – L. *sculptūra* (whence F. *sculpture*, etc.), f. pp. stem of *sculpere*, var. of *scalpere* (cf. SCALPEL), generalized from the comps. *exsculpere, insculpere*; see -URE. Hence **scu·lpture** vb. (Evelyn; earlier *sculp* †engrave XVI, now chiefly colloq. or joc. XVIII; also **sculpt** XIX), **scu·lpturAL**[1] XIX (Shelley). So **scu·lptOR**[1]. XVII. – L.; cf. F. *sculpteur*.

scum skʌm †foam, froth XIII; film of floating matter on liquid XV; fig. XVI. – MLG., MDu. *schūm* (Du. *schuim*) = OHG. *scūm* (G. *schaum*; cf. MEERSCHAUM), ON. *skúm* :- Germ. **skūman* (whence Pr. *escuma*, OF. *escume*, mod. *écume*, It. *schiuma*), f. **skū-* cover. Hence **scum** vb. †skim XIV (Trevisa); †scour the surface of XV; throw up as scum XVII.

scumble skʌ·mbl spread colour over a picture to soften hard lines, etc. XVIII. poss. f. SCUM vb. + -LE[3].

scuncheon skʌ·nʃən (archit.) bevelled inner edge. XV. Aphetic – OF. *escoinson* (mod. *écoinçon*), f. *es-* EX-[1] + *coin* corner (cf. COIGN) + L. *-siō(n-)* -SION.

scup skʌp (U.S.) fish Pagrus argyrops. XIX. Shortened – Narragansett *mishcup*, f. *mishe* large, *cuppi* scale. Also **scuppaug** skʌ·pɔ̄g XIX; for *mishcuppāuog*, pl. of *mishcup*, Stenotomus versicolor.

scupper[1] skʌ·pəɹ opening in a ship's side on a level with the deck. XV. perh. – AN. aphetic deriv. of OF. *escopir* (mod. *écopir*) :- CRom. **skuppīre* spit, of imit. origin; cf. G. *speigatt* scupper, f. *speien* spit + *gat(t)* hole (GATE[1]).

scupper[2] skʌ·pəɹ (mil. sl.) surprise and massacre; (pass.) be done for. XIX. Of unkn. origin; first recorded at Suakin.

scuppernong skʌ·pəɹnɔŋ variety of muscadine. XIX. name of a river and lake in N. Carolina, U.S.A.

scurf skɔ̄ɹf scales of epidermis characterizing a morbid condition of the skin formerly so called. Late OE. *scurf*, prob. alt. of *sceorf* by the influence of ON. **skurfr*, implicit in *skurfóttr* scurfy, f. base allied to that of OE. *sceorfan* gnaw, *sceorfian* cut into shreds; cf. (M)HG., (M)LG. *schorf* scab, scurf. Hence **scu·rfY**[1]. XVII (isolated ex. XV in Cath. Angl.).

scurrilous skʌ·rīləs coarsely opprobrious or jocular. XVI (Gascoigne). Contemp. with synon. †*scurrile* (Drant), on which it is formed with -OUS; – F. *scurrile* or L. *scurrīlis* (see -ILE), f. *scurra* buffoon. So **scurrilITY** skʌri·lĭti. XVI (Dunbar). – F. or L.

scurry skʌ·ri go rapidly or hurriedly. XIX. Second el. of HURRY-SCURRY used independently. ¶ Chronology seems to preclude connexion with †*scurrier* (XV–XVII) scout.

scurvy skɔ̄·ɹvi characterized by scurf XVI; see -Y[1]. Hence sb., partly ellipt. for †*s. disease* XVI, the spec. application being determined by assoc. with the like-sounding F. *scorbut*, LG. *schorbūk* (see SCORBUTIC).

scut skʌt †hare XV (Promp. Parv.); short erect tail of rabbit, etc. XVI (Palsgr.). rel. to †*scut* adj. short, sb. short garment (Promp. Parv.), †*scut* vb. cut short, dock (Palsgr.); of unkn. origin; connexion with ON. *skutr* (Norw. *skut*) end of a vessel is poss.

scutage skjū·tidʒ (hist.) tax levied on knights' fees, esp. in lieu of military service. XV. – medL. *scūtāgium*, f. L. *scūtum* shield, after OF. *escuage*; see -AGE.

scutate skjū·teit covered with large scales; shield-shaped. XIX. – L. *scūtātus* having a shield, f. SCUTUM; see -ATE[2].

scutch skʌtʃ dress (fibre) by beating. XVIII. – OF. **escoucher*, dial. var. of *escousser* :- Rom. **excussāre*, f. pp. stem *excuss-* of L. *excutere*, f. *ex* EX-[1] + *quatere* shake (cf. QUASH).

scutcheon skʌ·tʃən aphetic var. of AN. *escuchon* ESCUTCHEON. XIV (Ch., Wyclif).

scuttle[1] skʌ·tl †dish, trencher (OE.), XV; (dial.) corn-basket, grain-shovel XIV; wide-mouthed basket XV; bowl-like vessel for coal XIX. Late OE. *scutel* 'catinus' does not seem to have survived; ME. *scutel* is first in northern use – ON. *skutill*, corr. to OS. *skutala* = MLG. *schötele*, MDu. *schotele* (Du. *schotel*), OHG. *scuȥȥila* (G. *schüssel*, whence Lett. *skutelis*); all – L. *scutula* or *scutella*, rel. to *scutra* dish, platter.

scuttle[2] skʌ·tl opening in a ship's deck XV; trap-door XVIII. perh. – F. †*escoutille* (mod. *écoutille*) hatchway – Sp. *escotilla* (the sense 'scuttle' is expressed by the derivs. F. *écoutillon*, Sp. *escotillon*), dim. of *escota* cutting out of cloth, f. *escotar* cut out, f. L. *ex* EX-[1] + Germ. **skaut-* SHEET. Hence **scu·ttle** vb. cut a hole in sides, bottom, or deck of (a ship). XVII.

scuttle[3] skʌ·tl run with quick hurried steps. XV. Parallel with synon. (dial.) *scuddle* XVII, frequent. of SCUD; see -LE[3].

scutum skjū·təm (nat. hist.) shield-shaped part or segment. XIX. techn. use of L. *scūtum* oblong shield.

scye sai tailor's term for the opening in a coat into which a sleeve is inserted. XIX. Sc. and Ulster dial. word of unkn. origin.

Scylla si·lə see CHARYBDIS.

scypho- sai·fou, saifɔ· repr. Gr. *skupho-*, comb. form of *skúphos* large drinking vessel (L. *scyphus*, the comb. form of which is **scyphi-** sai·fi).

scythe saið long-handled long-bladed instrument for mowing. OE. *sīþe*, earlier **sigði* (written *sigdi*) = MLG. *segede*, *sigde* (LG. *seged*, *seid*, *sichte*), ON. *sigðr* :– Germ. **segiþō*, f. **seg-* (:– **sek-* cut; see SECTION), whence also synon. OS. *segisna*, MDu. *seisene* (Du. *zeis*), OHG. *segansa* (G. *sense*). Hence vb. XVI (Sh.). ¶ The sp. with *sc-* (XVII) is prob. due to assoc. with SCISSORS.

Scythian si·ðiən pert. to (one of) a people anciently occupying far-eastern Europe. XVI. f. L. *Scythia* – Gr. *Skuthíā*, f. *Skúthēs* Scythian; -IAN. (The OE. adj. was *Sćiþþisć*.)

'sdeath (see 's) XVII.

se- prefix occurring in derivs. from Latin, repr. *sē* (also *sēd*) prep. and adv. without, apart, as in SECEDE, SECLUDE, SECRET, SECRETE, SEDUCE, SEGREGATE, SEPARATE.

sea sī body of salt water. OE. *sǣ* = OFris. *sē*, OS. *sēo*, *sēu*, d. *sēwa*, OHG. *sēo*, *sē*, d. *sēwe* (Du. *zee*, G. *see*), ON *sǽr*, *sjár*, *sjór*, Goth. *saiws* :– CGerm. **saiwiz*, of unkn. origin (there being no CIE. word). comp. **sea-**COAL (XIII) mineral coal (as dist. from charcoal) is in origin prob. coal derived from the sea (cf. AL. *carbo maris* XIII), not coal brought by sea. (Late OE. *sǣcol* is jet, often got from the sea.)

seal[1] sīl aquatic mammal, spec. Phoca vitulina. OE. *sēol-*, inflexional form of *seolh* (whence Sc. *selch*) = NFris. *selich*, MLG. *sēl*, MDu. *seel*, *zēle*, OHG. *selah*, ON. *selr* :– Germ. **selχaz*, of unkn. origin. The sp. *seal* occurs XV.

seal[2] sīl (piece of wax for impressing) a device used in attesting a document. XIII. – AN. *seal*, OF. *seel* (mod. *sceau*) = Pr. *sael*, Sp. *sello*, It. *suggello*, *sigillo*, Rum. *sugel* :– L. *sigillum* small picture, statuette, seal, dim. of *signum* SIGN. So **seal** vb. – OF. *seeler* (mod. *sceller*), f. *seel*.

seam sīm junction made by sewing; line made by two abutting edges. OE. *sēam* = OFris. *sām*, MDu. *sōm* (Du. *zoom*), OHG. *soum* (G. *saum*), ON. *saumr* – CGerm. (exc. Goth.) **saumaz*, f. **sau-* **su-* SEW. Hence **seam** vb. XVI. **sea·m**STER OE. *sēamestre*, **se·mp**STER XVI sī·mstəɹ, se·mstəɹ. **sea·m-str**ESS[1], **se·mpstr**ESS[1] XVII.

seaman sī·mən one whose occupation is on the sea, sailor, (techn.) sailor below officer rank; OE. *sǣmann*, with Germ. parallels.

séance sei·ãs session of a body of persons, spec. spiritualists' meeting. XIX. F., f. OF. *seoir* :– L. *sedēre* SIT; see -ANCE.

sear[1] siəɹ become withered OE; cause to wither XV (Lydg.); burn, char XVI. OE. *sēarian* = OHG. *sōrēn* :– Germ. **saurōjan*, f. **sauraz* SERE.

sear[2] siəɹ portion of a gun-lock that engages with the notches of the tumbler. XVI. prob. – OF. *serre* grasp, lock, bolt, (now) foot of a bird of prey, f. *serrer* grasp, hold fast. = Pr., Sp. *serrar*, It. *serrare* :– Rom. **serrāre*, for late L. *serāre* bar, bolt, f. *sera* bar for a door.

search sɜ̄ɹtʃ examine thoroughly; look for; also intr. XIV. – AN. *sercher*, OF. *cerchier* (mod. *chercher*) = Pr. *cercar*, It. *cercare* seek, Sp. *cercar* surround :– late L. *circāre* go round, f. L. *circus* CIRCLE. So **search** sb. XVI. – AN. *serche*, OF. *cerche* (†*cherche*), if not f. the vb. XIV.

season sī·z(ə)n (appropriate) time or period XIII (Cursor M.); period of the year (spring, summer, autumn, winter); time of breeding, etc. XIV. ME. *seson*, *-un*, *-oun* – OF. *seson* (mod. *saison*) = Pr. *sazon*, Sp. *sazón*, It. dial. *sason*, *saschun* :– L. *satiō(n-)* sowing, in Rom. time of sowing, seed-time, f. **sə-*, as in L. *satus* sown (cf. SEED, SEMEN, SOW[2]). So **sea·son** vb. render more palatable by the addition of a spice, salt, etc. XIV; bring to maturity XVI. – OF. *saisonner* (repl. by mod. *assaisonner*), f. the sb. Hence **sea·son**ABLE suitable to the time, opportune. XIV (Wyclif, Hoccleve). **sea·son**ABLY. XIV (Usk). **sea·son**AL[1]. XIX. **sea·son**ING[1] †impregnation XVI; savoury addition to a dish (F. *assaisonnement*) XVI. ¶ The sense-development in the vb., as shown in Rom. dialects, is presumed to have been: 'sow', 'cultivate at a favourable time', 'ripen, mature', 'cook well', 'add flavouring to'.

seat sīt †sitting XII (Orm); place or thing to sit on XIII (Laȝ.); place of residence XIII. – ON. *sǽti* = OE. *ġesete*, MDu. *gesaete* (Du. *gezeet*), OHG. *gasāȥi* (G. *gesäss*) :– Germ. **gasǣtjam*, f. **sǣt-* **set-* SIT. Hence vb. XVI.

sebaceous sībei·ʃiəs greasy, oily. XVIII. f. L. *sēbāceus*, f. *sēbum* tallow, rel. to SOAP; see -ACEOUS.

sebesten sibe·stən plum-like fruit of the genus Cordia. XIV. – medL. *sebestēn* – Arab. *sabastān* – Pers. *sapistān*.

sec sek (of wines) dry. XIX. F. :– L. *siccu-s*.

secant sī·kənt in full *s. line*. XVI (Blundevil). – F. *sécant* adj., *sécante* sb. (sc. *ligne*) – modL. use of L. *secant-*, *secāns*, prp. of *secāre* cut; see SECTION, -ANT.

secateurs se·kətɜ̄ɹz pruning clippers. XIX. – pl. of F. *sécateur*, irreg. f. L. *secāre* cut (see SECTION) + *-ateur* -ATOR.

secede sisī·d withdraw *from* an association. XVIII. – L. *sēcēdere*, f. *sē-* SE- + *cēdere* go, CEDE. So **secess**ION sise·ʃən XVII. – F. or L.

seclude siklū·d shut off or away. XV. – L. *sēclūdere*, f. *sē-* SE- + *claudere* shut; see CLAUSE, CLOSE. So **seclu·s**ION. XVII. – medL.

second[1] se·kənd coming next after the first XIII (RGlouc.); next in rank or succession (e.g. *s. lieutenant*) XIV; from XVI in various techn. (mainly ellipt.) uses as sb. – (O)F. *second*, fem. *-onde* = Pr. *segon*, Sp. *segundo*, It. *secondo* – L. *secundus* following, favourable, second, f. base of *sequī* follow (see SEQUENCE). So **se·cond** sb. $\frac{1}{60}$ of a minute. XIV (Ch.). – (O)F. *seconde* – medL. *secunda*, sb. use (sc. *minuta* minute) of fem. of *secundus*, *secunda minuta* 'second minute' being the result of the second operation of sexagesimal division, the first being *prima minuta*. **se·cond**ARY belonging to the second class or order XIV; also sb. XV. – L. *secundārius*; cf. (O)F. *secondaire*, etc.; hence **se·condari**LY[2] XV. ¶ In OE., as in German, there was no proper ordinal for the number two, *ōþer* OTHER being so used; the resulting ambiguity was removed by the adoption of the F. word.

second[2] se·kənd support, back up. XVI (Sidney, Sh., Bacon). – F. *seconder*, corr. to Pr. *segondar*, etc. – L. *secundāre* favour, further, f. *secundus*, see prec.

second[3] sikɔ·nd (mil., etc.) transfer (an officer) temporarily to other duties. XIX. f. F. phr. *en second* in the second rank (said of officers; cf. the use of SECOND *lieutenant*). **seco·nd**MENT. XIX.

seconde səgɔ̃·d (fencing) the second of the eight parries. XVIII. – F. *seconde*, sb. use (sc. *parade*) of fem. of *second* SECOND[1]; the m. was also adopted as †*segoon* (XVIII).

secrecy sī·krəsi secret quality. XVI. repl. †*secretie* (XV), f. *secre* or SECRET + -TY[2] or -Y[3], prob. after *private/privacy*.

secret sī·krit kept from knowledge or observation; sb. secret thing. XIV (PPl., Gower, Trevisa; Ch. has *secre(e)* – OF. *secré*) – (O)F. *secret*, corr. to Pr. *secret*, Sp., It. *secreto* – L. *sēcrētus* (n. *sēcrētum* used sb.), pp. of *sēcernere* (whence *secern* XVII), f. *sē-* SE- + *cernere* separate, distinguish, secrete, (pp. sifted). Cf. CERTAIN, CRIME, CRISIS, CRITIC, DECREE, DISCERN, DISCRIMINATE, EXCREMENT.

secretary se·krĭtəri †confidant XIV (Trevisa); one employed to conduct correspondence, keep records, etc. XV; (after F. *secrétaire d'état*), It. *segretario di stato*, Sp. *secretario de estado*, minister at the head of a department of state XVI. – late L. *sēcrētārius* confidential officer, sb. use of adj. f. *sēcrētus* SECRET (cf. L. *sēcrētārium* n. secret place); see -ARY. So **secretariat** sekrĭtɛə·riət office of secretary. XIX. – F. *secrétariat*; see -ATE[1]. **secretaire** sekrĭtɛə·ɹ writing-bureau. XIX (Scott). – F. *secrétaire* secretary, with transf. meaning prob. suggested by ESCRITOIRE, *secretoire* (XVII–XIX); so It. *segretario*.

secrete[1] sikrī·t produce by secretion. XVIII. f. *sēcrēt-*, pp. stem of L. *sēcernere* separate (see SECRET), partly as a back-formation on **secre·**TION extraction by a gland, etc. of blood, sap, etc. from a substance XVII (Sir T. Browne) – F. *sécrétion* or med. use of L. *sēcrētiō(n-)*. So **secre·**TORY[2]. XVII (Ray).

secrete[2] sikrī·t hide out of sight. XVIII. alt., after L. *sēcrētus* SECRET, of *secret* vb. (XVI), f. the adj.

secrete[3] sikrī·t treat (fur) with nitrate of mercury. XIX. – F. *secréter*, f. *secret* SECRET sb. (in the sense 'secret process'). So **se·cret**AGE. XVIII. – F., f. the vb.

secretive sikrī·tiv addicted to secrecy, indicative of such addiction. XIX. Back-formation from *secretiveness* (also XIX), name in phrenology of a propensity, modelled on F. *secrétivité* (F. J. Gall, 'Introduction au cours de physiologie du cerveau', 1808), f. *secret* SECRET; see -IVE.

sect sekt †class (of persons); †religious order; (now illiterate) sex; religious following; philosophical school XIV; religious denomination XVI; school of opinion XVII (Sh., Jonson). All the earliest uses are found in one or more of the following: Ch., Wyclif, PPl., Trevisa, Gower. – (O)F. *secte* or L. *secta* following (used as cogn. obj. in *sectam sequi* follow a certain course of conduct, follow a person's guidance), party faction, school of philosophy, f. older pp. stem *sect-* (cf. *sectator* follower) of *sequī* follow (see SEQUENCE); cf. Sp. *secta*, It. *setta*. So **sect**ARY se·ktəri member of a (heretical or schismatic) sect, party, or school. XVI. – medL. *sectārius*; cf. F. *sectaire* (XVI). Hence **sect**ARIAN sektɛə·riən adj. and sb. (used in Commonwealth times for Presbyterians and Independents) XVII; whence **secta·rian**ISM XIX (Coleridge); cf. F. *sectarisme*.

section se·kʃən cutting; subdivision of a written or printed work or document; part cut off XVI; drawing of an object as if cut through XVII; sign § XVIII. – F. *section* or L. *sectiō(n-)*, f. *sect-*, pp. stem of *secāre* cut, f. IE. **sek-* (cf. SCYTHE), repr. also in Balto-Sl. and Celtic, and in Germ. by SAW[1]; cf. SEGMENT. ¶ The senses depend ult. on those of Gr. τομή TOME.

sector se·ktəɹ plane figure contained by two radii and the arc of a curve intercepted by them XVI (Billingsley); instrument invented by Thomas Hood for the mechanical solution of mathematical problems (orig. containing a graduated arc) XVI (1589). – late L. techn. use (Boethius) of L. *sector* (agent-n. of *secāre* cut), tr. Gr. τομεύς cutter; see prec. and -OR[1].

secular se·kjŭləɹ A. pert. to the world, worldly XIII (S. Eng. Leg.); not sacred, profane XV; non-religious XVI; B. occurring once in an age XVI; living or lasting for an age or for ages XVII; sb. secular cleric XIII. In A – OF. *seculer* (mod. *séculier*) – L. *sæculāris*, f. *sæculum* generation, age, in ChrL. the World (esp. opp. to the Church); in B immed. – L. *sæculāris*; see -AR. So **secula·**RITY. XVII. – (O)F. or medL.; earlier †*seculerte* XIV prob. – AN.

secundine se·kʌndain, -in after-birth. XIV (Trevisa). – late L. *secundīnæ*, fem. pl. (for which earlier L. had *secundæ*), f. *secundus* following; see SECOND[1], -INE[1].

secure sĭkjuə·ɹ (arch.) feeling no care; safe, certain. XVI. – L. *sēcūrus*, f. *sē-* SE- + *cūra* care (see CURE); cf. SICKER, SURE. Hence **secu·re** vb. make secure XVI; make sure of, get hold of XVIII. So **secu·rITY**. XV. – (O)F. *sécurité* or L. *sēcūritās*.

sedan sidæ·n closed vehicle for one person carried by means of two poles. XVII. poss. based on a dial. var. with *-dd-* of a Rom. deriv. of L. *sella* SADDLE. ¶ 'The streetes (of Naples) are full of gallants on horseback, in coaches and sedans, from hence brought first into England by Sir Sanders Duncomb' (Evelyn 'Diary' 8 Feb. 1645).

sedate sidei·t undisturbed by passion or excitement. XVII. – L. *sēdātus*, pp. of *sēdāre* settle, assuage, calm, f. **sēd-* **sed-*, as in *sedēre* SIT; see -ATE[2]. So **sedA·TION** XVI. – F. or L. **sedatIVE** se·dətiv inducing calm XV. – (O)F. or medL.; sb. XVIII.

sedentary se·dəntəri remaining in one place XVI; pert. to or involving a sitting posture XVII. – F. *sédentaire* or L. *sedentārius*, f. *sedent-*, prp. stem of *sedēre* SIT; see -ENT, -ARY.

sederunt sīdiə·rʌnt (Sc.) sitting of an assembly. XVII. sb. use of L. *sēdērunt* '(there) sat' (viz. the following persons, i.e. at a meeting), 3rd pl. pt. indic. of *sedēre* SIT.

sedge sedʒ coarse grassy rush-like or flag-like plant. OE. *seċġ*, m., n. :– Germ. **sagjaz*, f. **sag-* **seg-* :– IE. **sek-*, repr. by L. *secāre* (see SECTION); cf. EFris. *sige*, LG. *segge*. ¶ For the etymol. notion of 'plant with cutting edge', cf. L. *gladiolus* (f. *gladius* sword), which the OE. word renders in glosses, and OE. *seċġ* fem., sword (:– **sagjō*).

sedilia sidi·liə (n. pl.) series of (three) seats in the sanctuary of a church; rarely sg. **sedile** sidai·li XVIII. – L. *sedīlia*, pl. of *sedīle*, f. *sedēre* SIT; see -ILE, -IA[2].

sediment se·dimənt solid matter falling to the bottom of a liquid. XVI. – F, *sédiment* or L. *sedimentum* settling (cf. late L. *sedimen* sediment), f. *sedēre* SIT, settle; see -MENT.

sedition sidi·ʃən †violent party strife XIV; †revolt, mutiny XVI; behaviour inciting to rebellion XIX. – (O)F. *sédition* or L. *sēditiō(n-)*, f. *sēd-* SE- + *itiō* going, f. *it-*, pp. stem of *īre* go (cf. ITINERARY). So **sedi·tIOUS**[2]. XV. – (O)F. or L.

seduce sidjū·s divert from allegiance or service XV (Caxton); induce (a woman) to surrender her chastity; lead astray XVI. In earliest use *seduise, seduse* – (O)F. *seduis-*, inflexional stem of *séduire*; later assim. to L. *sēdūcere*, f. *sē-* SE- + *dūcere* lead (cf. DUCT). So **seducTION** -dʌ·k- XVI. – F. or L.

sedulous se·djŭləs diligent or persistent in application. XVI. f. L. *sēdulus* eager, zealous, f. *sēdulō* zealously, carefully, for *sē dolō* 'without guile', (hence) with zeal (perh.– Gr. *dólos* ruse); see SE-, -OUS.

sedum sī·dəm (bot.) genus the British species of which are known as stonecrop. XV (*cedum*). L.

see[1] sī, pt. **saw** sō, pp. **seen** sīn perceive with the eyes. OE. *sēon*, pt. *seah*, *sāwon* and *sǣgon*, pp. *(ġe)sewen* = OFris. *sīa*, OS., OHG. *sehan* (Du. *zien*, G. *sehen*), ON. *séa, sía, siá*, Goth. *saihwan*, pt. *sahw*, *sēhwum*, pp. *saihwans* :– CGerm. str. vb. **seχwan* – IE. **seqʷ-*, by some identified with the base of L. *sequī* follow (see SEQUENCE), the etymol. sense being 'follow with the eyes'.

see[2] sī seat, spec. bishop's seat or throne XIII (RGlouc.); episcopal office or authority XIV. – AN. *se, sed*, OF. *sie, sied* :– Rom. **sedem*, alt. (after L. *sedēre*) of *sēdem* (nom. *-es*) seat, f. **sēd-* **sed-* SIT.

seebright sī·brait clary, Salvia sclaria XIX. f. SEE[1] + BRIGHT, after *clear eye*, perverted form of CLARY.

seed sīd that which is or is to be sown; †offspring OE.; †semen XIII. OE. *sǣd*, Anglian *sēd*, corr. to OFris. *sēd*, OS. *sād* (Du. *zaad*), OHG. *sāt* (G. *saat*), ON. *sáð*, Goth. *-sēþs* in *manasēþs* :– CGerm. **sǣðiz*, **sǣðam*, f. **sǣ-* SOW[2]. Hence **seed** vb. XIV (intr., Ch.). **see·dLING**[1]. XVII. **see·dY**[1] full of seed XVI; (sl.) shabby (from the appearance of a plant that has run to seed) XVIII; unwell XIX. Hence **seedlip** sī·dlip basket for seed. OE. *sǣdlēap*; see LEAP[2].

seek sīk pt., pp. **sought** sōt (arch.) try to find or obtain; also intr. OE. *sēċan*, earlier *sœ̄ċan* pt. *sōhte*, pp. *ġesōht* = OFris. *sēka, sēza*, pt. *sōchta*, OS. *sōkian*, pt. *sōhta* (Du. *zoeken*), OHG. *suohhan*, pt. *suohta* (G. *suchen*), ON. *sœkja*, pt. *sótti*, Goth. *sōkjan*, pt. *sōkida*, :– CGerm. **sōkjan*, f. base **sōk-* :– Western IE. **sāg-* **səg-*, repr. also by L. *sāgīre* perceive by scent (cf. PRESAGE), *sāgus* sorcerer, *sāgāx* SAGACIOUS, Gr. *hēgeîsthai* (Doric *hāg-*) lead, OIr. *saigin* I seek, approach. ¶ The normal repr. of OE. *sēċan* survives in n.w. dial. *seech* and in BESEECH. *Seek* is prob. due to generalization of *sēk-* from the forms **sēkst, sēkþ* (2nd and 3rd pres. indic.), furthered by ON. *sœkja*.

seel sīl stitch up the eyes of (a hawk, etc.), also transf. XV. Later form of †*sile* (XIV) – OF. *ciller, siller* or medL. *ciliāre*, f. L. *cilium* eyelid (cf. SUPERCILIOUS).

seem sīm †befit, BESEEM XII (Orm); appear to be XIII. ME. *sēme* – ON. *sœma* honour (MSw. befit), f. *sœmr* fitting, seemly, f. **sōm-*, whence also OE. *sōm* reconciliation, *sēman* (:– **sōmjan*) settle, reconcile, rel. to **sam-* SAME. So **see·mLY**[1]. XIII. ME. *semeliche* – ON. *sœmiligr*, f. *sœmr*.

seep sīp ooze; percolate. XVIII (in recent use through U.S. influence). perh. dial. development of OE. *sipian*, rel. to OFris. *sīpa*, MLG. *sīpen*, MHG. *sīfen*, presumably = OE. *sīpian*, surviving in dial. *sipe*, of unkn. orig.; but the chronological gaps in the evidence make the history of the two vbs. doubtful.

seer[1] siəɹ (tr. Vulg. L. *vidēns*, Gr. *βλέπων*, Heb. *rōēh*) one who sees visions of divine things XIV (Wycl. Bible); one who sees XV; magician, crystal-gazer XVII. f. SEE[1]+-ER[1].

seer[2] siəɹ Indian denomination of weight. XVII. – Hindi *ser*.

seersucker siə·ɹsʌ:kəɹ thin striped crimped fabric. XVIII. E. Indian alt. of Pers. *shīr o shakkar* 'milk and sugar', striped linen garment.

see-saw sī·sō redupl. formation symbolic of alternating movement, based on SAW[1] (as if orig. sung by sawyers), and used in rhythmical jingles, *see saw sacke a downe* (*sacaradown*), *see saw sack a day*, *see saw Margery Daw* XVII; game at which children sitting on each end of a pivoted plank move each other up and down XVIII; plank so used XIX. Hence as vb. XVIII. Cf. Du. *ziegezagen* 'scrape' on a violin.

seethe sīð †boil OE.; soak, steep XVI; be inwardly agitated XVII. OE. *sēoþan*, pt. *sēaþ*, *sudon*, pp. *soden* (SODDEN) = OFris. *siātha*, OS. **sioðan*, in pp. *gesodenemo* 'recocto', OHG. *siodan* (Du. *zieden*, G. *sieden*), ON. *sjóða*, f. Germ. **seuþ*- **sauþ*- **suð*-, the second grade of which is repr. also by ON. *sauðr* sheep ('boiled flesh'), Goth. *sauþs* sacrifice, and OE. *sēaþ* pit, cistern, pond, lake, OFris. *sāth*, MLG. *sōt* (-*d*-) spring, fountain, MHG. *sōt* (-*d*-) cooking, boiling.

segment se·gmənt piece resulting from cutting or division. XVI. – L. *segmentum*, f. *sec*-, stem of *secāre*; see SECTION, INSECT, -MENT.

segregate se·grigeit separate from a body of persons or things. XVI. f. pp. stem of L. *sēgregāre*, f. *sē*- SE-, *greg*-, *grex* flock (cf. EGREGIOUS); based on *segregate* pp. (XV); see -ATE[3]. So **segrega·tion**. XVI. – late L.

seguidilla segidi·lja Spanish dance of ¾ or ⅜ time. XVIII. Sp., f. *seguida* following, sequence, f. *seguir* :– Rom. **sequere*, for L. *sequī* (see SEQUENT).

seid see SAYYID.

seidlitz se·dlits *s. powder* (XIX), named after †*S. salt* and *water* (XVIII), because of its aperient properties; name of a village in Bohemia where there is a spring impregnated with magnesium sulphate and carbonic acid.

seigneur se·njəɹ, ‖sɛŋjœ̄r French feudal lord XVI; in Canada, one of the landed gentry XVIII. – (O)F. *seigneur* :– L. *seniōrem*, SENIOR. The corr. Rom. words are It. SIGNOR, Sp. SEÑOR, Pg. SENHOR. So **seigniory**[3] sei·njəri †lordship XIII (S. Eng. Leg.); feudal lordship XV. Hence **seignio·rial** XIX (earlier **seigneu·rial** XVII).

seine, sean sein large fishing-net. OE. *seġne* = OS., OHG. *segina* :– WGerm. **ságina* – L. *sagēna* (whence OF. *saïne*, mod. *seine*) – Gr. *sagḗnē*; reinforced in ME. from OF.

seisin sī·zin (chiefly leg.) possession. ME. *sesin*(*e*), *seisin*(*e*) – AN. *sesine*, OF. *seisine*, (also mod.) *saisine* (= Pr. *sazina*, OIt. *sagina*), f. *seisir* SEIZE; see -INE[4].

seismic sai·zmik pert. to an earthquake. XIX (Mallet). f. Gr. *seismós* earthquake, f. *seíein* shake; see -IC. So **seismo-**, comb. form of Gr. *seismós*. ¶ The more normal form is repr. by F. *sismique*.

seity sī·iti selfhood. XVIII (Steele). – medL. *sēitās*, f. L. *sē* oneself + -ITY.

seize sīz A. put in (feudal) possession (of); B. take possession or hold of XIII; †C. arrive at XVI; D. (naut.) lash together with cord, etc. XVII (a F. use, the source of which may be Du. *seisen*, derived thence); (of surfaces) unite XIX. – OF. *seisir*, (also mod.) *saisir* = Pr. *sazir* (whence Sp., Pg. *asir*) :– Gallo-Rom., Frankish L. *sacīre* (as in phr. *ad proprium s.*, claim as one's own), Germ. **sakjan*, f. **sak*- process, procedure (see SAKE[1]), which may have been partly conflated with Germ. **satjan* place, settle, SET[1]. Hence **seizure** sī·ʒəɹ. XV.

selachian silei·kiən (pert. to) a shark or allied fishes. XIX. f. modL. *Selachē* (– Gr. *selákhē*, pl. of *sélakhos* shark) or *Selachiī*, after F. *sélacien* (Cuvier); see -IAN.

selah sī·lā Heb. *selāh*, occurring often at the end of a verse in the Psalter and in Habbakuk iii (rendered in LXX by *διάψαλμα*), supposed to be a musical or liturgical direction, perh. indicating a pause.

seldom se·ldəm on few occasions. OE. *seldan* (with late var. *seldum*, due to assim. to *hwīlum* WHILOM), corr. to OFris. *sielden*, MLG., MDu. *selden* (Du. *zelden*), OHG. *seltan* (G. *selten*), ON. *sjaldan*, dative formation on Germ. **selda*-, repr. also in OE. *seldlić*, *sellić* strange, wonderful, *seldsīene* rare, and in Gothic by *sildaleiks* wonderful, *sildaleikjan* be astonished.

select sile·kt specially chosen, picked. XVI. – L. *sēlectus*, pp. of *sēligere* choose out, f. *sē*- apart (SE-) + *legere* collect, choose (see LECTION). So **sele·ct** vb. pick out. XVI. f. pp. stem of the L. vb. **sele·ction**. XVII (Sir T. Browne). – L. Hence **sele·ctive**. XVII.

selenite se·linait sulphate of lime or gypsum (identity of the mineral so named by ancient writers is dubious). XVI. – L. *selēnītēs* (also -*ītis*) – Gr. *selēnítēs* (sc. *líthos*) 'moon(stone)', so called because supposed to wax and wane with the moon, f. *selḗnē* moon, rel. to *sélas* brightness. So **selenium** silī·niəm (chem.) rare non-metallic element. XIX. – modL., f. Gr. *selḗnē*; so named by Berzelius (1818) because of its similarity in properties to *tellurium* (f. L. *tellus* earth), with ref. to the moon's relation to the earth as a satellite.

self self A. (arch.) in apposition with a sb. or pron., e.g. *he self*, superseded by emphatic prons., as *himself*, *ourselves* OE.; B. adj. †*the* same, *the* very OE.; (of a colour) the same throughout XVII; C. sb. (pl. **selves** selvz) individual or particular person XIII; (chiefly philos.) *the* ego XVII. OE. *self* str., *selfa* wk. = OFris. *self, selva*, OS. *self, selbo*, OHG. *selb, selbo* (Du. *zelv, -zelve, -zelfde*, G. *selb-, selbe*), ON. (only str.) *sjálfr*, Goth. (only wk.) *silba* :- CGerm. **selba-*, **selbon-*, of unkn. origin. comps. **se·lf**HOOD XVII; tr. G. *selbheit*; **se·lf**ISH[1] XVII; said to be of Presbyterian coinage. **se·lf**SAME *the* very same XV (Lydg.); cf. OHG. *selbsama* adv., in the very same way, Norw., Da. *selvsamme* adj. ¶ Used extensively in comps. from the OE. period onwards; the 17th century was a period of great productivity in theological and philosophical terms, many of them with parallels in G. *selbst-*.

Seljuk se·ldʒuk epithet of certain Turkish dynasties. XIX. Turk. *Seljūk* name of the reputed ancestor of these. So **Seljuk**IAN seldʒū·kiən. XVII.

sell sel pt., pp. **sold** sould †give up; dispose of for money (orig. in OE. const. with *wiþ* in exchange for). OE. *sellan*, pt. *s(e)alde*, pp. *s(e)ald* = OFris. *sella*, OS. *sellian*, OHG. *sellen*, ON. *selja* give up, sell, Goth. *saljan* offer sacrifice; CGerm. wk. vb., of which cogns. have been recognized in Gr. *heleîn*, OIr. *selaim* take. Cf. SALE.

sellender var. of SALLENDER.

s'elp selp vulgar contr. of *so help* (as in *so help me God*). In ME. *selpe me god* (XIV); cf. MHG. *selftir*, for *so helfe dir* 'so help thee'. Also *s'help, swelp* (XIX).

seltzer se·ltsəɹ effervescent mineral water obtained near Nieder Selters, Prussia; also a similar artificial one. XVIII. alt. of G. *Selterser* (with g. pl. ending), f. *Selters*.

selvage, selvedge se·lvidʒ edge of a piece of woven material finished so as to prevent unravelling. XV. f. SELF+EDGE, after early mod.Du. *selfegghe* (now *zelfegge*), LG. *sülfegge*; cf. synon. Du. *zelfkant* (*kant* border), *zelfeinde* (*einde* end), whence G. *selbende* (now *salband*).

semantic simæ·ntik †relating to signs of the weather XVII (rare); pert. to meaning XIX; sb. pl. science of the meanings of words XX. – F. *sémantique* (rare in form *symentique* XVI; sb. Bréal 'Essai de Sémantique' 1883) – Gr. *sēmantikós* significant, f. *sēmaínein* show, signify, f. *sêma* sign; see -IC. So **semasio**LOGY sīmeisiɔ·lədʒi. XIX. – G. *semasiologie* (1839), f. Gr. *sēmasiā* signification, f. *sēmaínein*. **semato**LOGY sīmatɔ·lədʒi doctrine of signs in relation to knowledge XIX; semasiology XIX.

semaphore se·məfɔ̄əɹ signalling apparatus. XIX. – F. *sémaphore* (1812), irreg. f. Gr. *sêma* sign, signal + *-phoros* -PHORE. So **semapho·r**IC XIX.

semblance se·mbləns †act of appearing XIII (Cursor M.); appearance, likeness XIV (Ch.); outward seeming *of* XVI. – (O)F. *semblance*, f. *sembler* = Pr., Sp. *semblar* (cf. It. *sembrare, semblare*), Rum. *sămăna* :- L. *similāre, simulāre*, see SIMULATE, -ANCE. Superseded earlier †*semblant*.

semée se·mi (her.) covered with many small spots or figures. XVI. – F., pp. fem. of *semer* :- L. *sēmināre* sow, f. *sēmen* SEED.

semeio- sīmai·ou, sīmaiɔ· comb. form of Gr. *sēmeîon* sign, f. *sêma* signal, as in **semeio·**LOGY sign language XVII; branch of medicine concerned with symptoms XIX; so **semeio·**TIC XVII, -ICAL XVI relating to symptoms – Gr. *sēmeiōtikós*.

semen sī·men seed of male animals. (XIV) XVIII. – L. *sēmen*, f. base of *serere* (pt. *sēvī*, pp. *satus*) SOW[2]. Cf. *disseminate*.

semester sīme·stəɹ academic half-year. XIX. – G. – L. *sēmestris* (sc. *cursus* period), f. *sē-*, comb. form of *sex* SIX (as in *sēdecim* sixteen)+*mēnsis* MONTH.

semi- se·mi comb. form repr. L. *sēmi-* (partly through F., It., etc. *semi-*) 'half', (less strictly) 'partly', 'partially', equiv. in meaning to DEMI- and HEMI-, but in much more extensive use. L. *sēmi-* corr. to Gr. *hēmi-*, Skr. *sāmi*, and OS. *sām-*, OHG. *sāmi-*, OE. *sām-* (as in *sambærned* half-burnt, *samcwic* 'half-alive', half-dead, *samsoden* partly cooked, surviving in SAND-BLIND). The L. el. has been in uninterrupted use from the times of Ennius and Plautus, through the post-Augustan, early Christian, mediæval, and modern periods. Typical exx. of techn. usage, besides numerous comps. of a general character with sbs., adjs., and pples., are *sēmicirculus* **se·mi**CIRCLE XVI, late L. *sēmicirculāris* **semi**CI·RCULAR XV, *sēmidiameter* (Boethius) in Eng. use from XVI, ecclL. *sēmichrīstianus* (Jerome), **semi-**A·RIAN, **se:mi-**PELA·GIAN XVII, L. *sēmivocālis* **se·mi**VOWEL XVI; modL. *semimetallum* **se·mi**METAL XVII; (mus). **se·mi**BREVE, -QUAVER XVI, **se·mi**TONE XVII (earlier †*-toyn* XV, †*-tune* XVII), cf. late L. *sēmitonium*; also *demisemiquaver, semidemisemiquaver*; in adjs. and advs. of the type *semi-annual(ly)* recurring every half-year XVIII, *semidiurnal* XVI, *semi-monthly, -weekly*; **semi**CO·LON XVII. See also SESQUI-.

seminar se·mināɹ group of students meeting for systematic instruction. XIX. G. – L. *sēminārium* (see next).

seminary se·minəri †seed-plot XV; place of production, cultivation, or education XVI. – L. *sēminārium*, sb. use of n. of *sēminārius*, f. *sēmin-*, SEMEN; see -ARY. Hence **se·minar**IST one trained in a seminary. XVI.

Semite sī·mait, se·mait Hebrew, Arab, Assyrian, or Aramæan, regarded as a descendant of Shem (Gen. x). XIX. – modL. *Sēmīta*, f. (Vulg.) *Sēm* – Gr. *Sḗm* Shem; see -ITE. So **Semit**IC -i·tik. XIX. – modL.

semolina seməlī·nə hard grains left after bolting of flour. XVIII. alt. of It. *semolino*, dim. of *semola* bran, based on L. *simila* flour (cf. Gr. *semídālis*). Cf. SIMNEL.

sempiternal sempitə·ɹnəl everlasting. XV. – (O)F. *sempiternel* – lateL. *sempiternālis*, f. L. *sempiternus* (whence OF. *sempiterne*, taken into Eng., XIV, by Gower), f. *semper* (f. **sem-* = Gr. *hen-*, *heîs* one) always, for ever + **æviternus* ETERNAL.

sempster, sempstress see SEAMSTER, SEAMSTRESS.

sen sen Jap. copper or bronze coin. XIX.

senarius sīnɛə·riəs (pros.) iambic trimeter. XVI. L. *sēnārius* (sc. *versus* verse, line), sb. use of adj., f. *sēnī* six each, f. *sex* SIX.

senate se·nət supreme governing assembly or council. XIII (Laȝ.). – (O)F. *sénat* (in OF. nom. sg. *senaz*, whence occas. ME. *senas*) = Pr. *senat*, etc. – L. *senātus*, f. *sen-*, *senex* old (man); see SENIOR, -ATE[1]. So **se·nat**OR[1] member of a senate. XIII (Laȝ.). – (O)F. *sénateur* – L. *senātor*, *-ōrem*.

send[1] send pt., pp. **sent** cause or direct to go. OE. *sendan*, pt. *sende*, pp. *ġesended* = OFris. *senda*, *sēnda*, pt. *sante*, OS. *sendian*, pt. *senda*, *sanda*, OHG. *sendan*, *senten*, pt. *sante* (Du. *zenden*, G. *senden*, pt. *sandte*, *sendete*, *gesandt*), ON. *senda* (pt. *senda*, pp. *sendr*), Goth. *sandjan* :– CGerm. **sanðjan*, f. **sanð-* (whence OE. *sand* message, messenger) :– **sanþ-*, causative of **senþ-*, repr. by OE., OS. *sīþ*, OHG. *sind*, *sint*, ON. *sinn*, Goth. *sinþs* journey (cf. WITHERSHINS). comp. **se·nd-**OFF. XIX; orig. U.S.

send[2] send (naut., of a ship) fall with head or stern deep in the trough of the sea. XVII. Often written *'scend*, as if aphetic of DESCEND, which may in fact be the source.

sendal se·ndəl thin rich silk material. XIII (w. midl.). – OF. *cendal*, (also Pr.) *sendal* (whence It. *zendalo*, *zendado*, etc.), obscurely derived from Gr. *sindṓn* SINDON.

senega se·nigə N. Amer. plant Polygala Senega, XVIII. prob. var. of *Seneca* name given by white men to one of the Six Nations of the Iroquois Confederacy living near Lake Seneca, N.Y.

seneschal se·niʃəl official in a great household administering justice, etc. XIV (PPl.) governor XV. – OF. *seneschal* (mod. *sénéchal*) = Pr. *senescal-s*, Sp. *senescal*, It. *siniscalco*, *sescalco* :– medL. *seni-*, *siniscalcus* (Frankish and Alemanic Laws) – Germ. **siniskalkaz*, f. **seni-* old (cf. SENIOR) + **skalkaz* servant (OE. *sċealc*, etc., Goth. *skalks*); cf. MARSHAL.

senhor senjō·ɹ XVIII. Pg. analogue of SEÑOR; fem. **senho·ra,** dim. **senhori·ta**.

senile sī·nail pert. to old age. XVII. – F. *sénile* or L. *senīlis*, f. *sen-* of *senex*; see next and -ILE.

senior sī·niəɹ person superior by reason of age or station XIV (Wyclif); adj. older, elder XV; that ranks higher XVI. – L. *senior*, compar. of *senex* old, rel. to Gr. *hénos* (in *hénē* last day of the moon), Goth. *sineigs* old, *sinista* elder, with other cogns. in Celtic, Baltic, Arm., and Indo-Iran. Cf. SEIGNEUR, SENHOR, SEÑOR, SIGNOR, SIR, SIRE, SENATOR. So **senior**ITY -ɔ·rĭti. XV. – medL.

senna se·nə (leaflets of) a shrub of the genus Cassia. XVI. – modL. *senna*, *sena* – Arab. *sanā*. (Earlier †*sene* XIV – OF. *sené*.)

sennachie se·nəχi in the Scottish Highlands and Ireland, one occupied with the study of traditional lore (Gaelic teller of legendary romances). XVI (*shannaghe*). – Gael. *seanachaidh* (= OIr. *senchaidh*), f. *sean* old (OIr. *sen*; cf. SENIOR).

sennet se·nit set of notes on a trumpet, etc. to announce ceremonial entrances and exits. XVI (Marlowe, Sh.). perh. var. of SIGNET.

sennight se·nait (arch.) week. OE. *seofon nihte* seven nights, ME. *seoueniht(e)*, later *sennyȝt* (XV); see SEVEN, NIGHT, and cf. FORTNIGHT.

sennit var. of SINNET.

señor senjō·ɹ Sp. title of respect for a man. XVII. Sp. :– L. *seniōrem*, SENIOR; fem. **seño·ra** XVI; dim. **señori·ta.**

sensation sensei·ʃən operation of any of the senses, physical feeling XVII; condition of excited feeling XVIII (*make*, *create a s.*, after F. *faire sensation*). – medL. *sensatiō(n-)*, f. L. *sēnsus* SENSE, after late L. *sēnsātus* gifted with sense; see -ATION and cf. (O)F. *sensation*, etc. Hence **sensa·tion**AL[1]. XIX.

sense sens meaning, signification XIV (Wycl. Bible); faculty of perception or sensation; actual perception or feeling XVI. – L. *sēnsus* faculty of feeling, sensibility, mode of feeling, thought, meaning, f. *sēns-*, pp. stem of *sentīre* feel (cf. SENTENCE, SENTIMENT, ASSENT, CONSENT, DISSENT, RESENT); cf. (O)F., Pr. *ses*, Sp. *seso*, It. *senso*. *Common sense*: L. *communis sensus*, tr. Gr. *ἡ κοινὴ αἴσθησις*. Hence **sense** vb. perceive (in several techn. uses). XVI; **se·n**SIBLE perceptible by the senses XIV (Ch.); cognizant, conscious XV (Hoccleve); having good sense XVI. – (O)F. or L. **se·nsit**IVE having sensation. XIV. – (O)F. or medL. **senso·**RIUM seat of sensation in the brain. XVII. – late L. (Boethius). **se·nsu**AL[1] pert. to the senses. XV. – late L.; cf. F. *sensuel*. **se·nsu**OUS pert. to the senses XVII (Milton).

sentence se·ntəns †meaning, sense XIII; †way of thinking; opinion, judgement, or decision pronounced; †apophthegm, maxim XIV; †passage of a writing; grammatically complete expression of a thought XV. – (O)F. *sentence* = Pr. *sentensa*, etc. – L. *sententia* mental feeling, opinion, judgment, (philos.) tr. Gr. *δόξα* and *γνώμη*, f. *sentīre* feel (for the athematic form cf. *parēns* PARENT (*pariō* I bring forth)); see -ENCE. So **sentence** vb. XIV. – (O)F. *sentencier*, **sente·n**TIOUS †full of meaning XV; aphoristic XVI (Hawes, Jonson). – L. *sententiōsus* (Cicero), **senti**ENT se·nʃiənt capable of feeling XVII.

sentiment se·ntimənt †feeling, sensation; mental attitude, opinion; mental feeling, emotion XVII; refined and tender feeling XVIII (Sterne) – (O)F. *sentiment*, refash. of OF. *sentement* (repr. by late ME. *sentement*, Ch.) – medL. *sentīmentum*, f. L. *sentīre* feel (cf. prec.); see -MENT. Hence **sentime·ntal**[1]. XVIII; whence F. *sentimental* (1769), first recorded in tr. of 'A Sentimental Journey through France and Italy' (1768) by Sterne, who is alleged to have used the word in a letter of 1739–40; also G. *sentimental* (1773), *-alisch* (1774); preceded by *sentimented*, 'Prompter', 1735; cf. F. †*sentimenté*.

sentinel se·ntinəl sentry; †duty of a sentry; †military watch-tower XVI; †(in full *private s.*) private soldier XVIII. – F. *sentinelle* (Rabelais) – It. *sentinella*, of unkn. origin; for the fem. gender cf. the originals of *guard, scout, spy, vedette*. Hence vb. XVI (Sh.).

sentry se·ntri †sentinel; armed member of the fighting forces set to keep guard XVII. perh. shortening of †*centrinell*, *-onel* (XVI), vars. of SENTINEL, with assim. to -RY. comp. **se·ntry-go,** †orig. phr. consisting of *sentry* sb. (used vocatively) and imper. of GO; (hence) patrol or duties of a s. XIX.

sepal se·pəl (bot.) division of the calyx. XIX. – modL. *sepalum* (originated and named by N. J. de Necker, 1790, as irreg. modif. of Gr. *sképē* covering + suffix of PETAL). ¶ Necker included petal and sepal under the one term, not recognizing the distinction between corolla and calyx.

separate se·pəreit set apart. XV. f. pp. stem of L. *sēparāre*, f. *sē-* SE- + *parāre* make ready, PREPARE; partly after †*separate* pp. (XV); see -ATE[3]. So **separATION** sepərei·ʃən. XV. – (O)F. – L. **se·paratIST** one who advocates (ecclesiastical) separation. XVII. f. *separate* adj., which was used contemp. as sb. in the same sense.

sepia sī·piə A. cuttlefish XVI; B. rich brown pigment prepared from its inky secretion XIX. – L. *sēpia* – Gr. *sēpiā*. In B prob. (as F. *sépia*) immed. – It. *seppia*.

sepoy sī·poi, sipoi·, **sipahi** sipā·i †(rare) horseman XVII; Indian native soldier under European discipline XVIII. – (prob. through Pg. *sipae*) Urdu – Pers. *sipāhī* horseman, soldier, f. *sipāh* army. Cf. F. *cipaye*, SPAHI.

seps seps very venomous serpent XVI; scincoid lizard XIX. – L. *sēps* – Gr. *sḗps*, cf. base of *sḗpein* rot; cf. next.

sepsis se·psis putrefaction. XIX. – modL – Gr. *sêpsis*, f. *sḗpein* rot, putrefy (cf. *saprós* rotten). So **se·pTIC**. XVII. – L. (Pliny) – Gr. *sēptikós*.

sept sept (Irish) clan. XVI. poss. alt. of *sect* (also so used XVI); cf. AL. *septus* (XVI), and medL. *septa*, repr. OF. *sette* sect, It. *setta*.

September səpte·mbəɹ ninth month of the year, formerly seventh month of the year beginning in March. – L. *September* or (in ME.) F. *septembre*, earlier †*setembre*, f. *septem* SEVEN. (The OE. name was *hærfestmōnaþ* 'harvest month' = OHG. *herbistmānōt*). **septenarius** septinɛə·riəs (pros.) line of 7 feet or stresses. XIX. **septenary** se·ptinəri, septī·nəri. **septennial** septe·niəl see BIENNIAL. **septentrionAL**[1] septe·ntriənəl northern. – L. *septentriōnālis*, f. *septentriōnēs* 'seven plough-oxen', i.e. the seven stars of the Great Bear (f. *septem* SEVEN + pl. of *triō* plough-ox). See -AL[1]. **septet, -ette** septe·t (mus.) composition for seven voices or instruments. XIX. – G. *septet*, f. L. *septem* SEVEN; see -ET, -ETTE. **septi-**[1] se·pti comb. form of L. *septem* SEVEN, e.g. *septifo·lious* seven-leaved (L. *folium* FOIL[1]); **septipa·rtite** (also *septempartite*) divided into 7 parts. XIX. **septillion** septi·ljən see BILLION. **septuagenARIAN** se:ptjuədʒinɛə·riən 70 years old XVIII; also sb. – L. *septuagēnārius*, f. distrib. *septuagēnī*, f. *septuaginta*; see next, -ARIAN. So **septuagenARY** -dʒī·nəri. XVII. **Septuagesima** se:ptjuədʒe·simə third Sunday before Lent XIV (Wyclif); †the seventy days beginning with this (Trevisa); cf. QUINQUAGESIMA, SEXAGESIMA. L. fem. (sc. *diēs* day) of *septuagesimus*, ordinal of *septuagintā* seventy. **Septuagint** se·ptjuədʒint †'the seventy translators of the Old Testament into Greek XVI; the translation traditionally attributed to them (denoted by LXX) XVII. – L. *septuāgintā* 70. **se·ptuple** sevenfold (cf. CENTUPLE) XVII.

septum se·ptəm (anat., bot., zool.) dividing wall or partition. XVIII. – L. *sēptum*, *sæptum*, f. *sēpīre*, *sæpīre* enclose, f. *sēpes*, *sæpes* hedge. So **se·pti-**[2] comb. form, e.g. **se·ptiFORM**.

sepulchre se·pəlkəɹ tomb, burial-place. XII. ME. *sepulcre* – (O)F. *sépulcre* – L. *sepulcrum*, erron. *-chrum*, f. stem of *sepultus*, pp. of *sepelīre* bury. So **sepulchrAL**[1] sipʌ·lkrəl. XVII. – F. or L. **se·pultURE** (arch.) burial. XIII (RGlouc.). – (O)F. *sépulture* – L. *sepultūra*, f. *sepultus*.

sequacious sikwei·ʃəs given to following another (slavishly). XVII. f. L. *sequāci-*, *sequāx*, f. *sequī* follow; see -IOUS. So **sequel** sī·kwəl †train of followers, following XV (Lydg.); what follows as a result XV; ensuing course of affairs, narrative, etc. XVI. – (O)F. *séquelle* or L. *sequēla* (*-ella*), f. *sequī*. **sequela** sikwī·lə pl. **-æ** ī morbid affection resulting from a disease. XVIII. L. **sequENCE** sī·kwəns (liturg.) piece of rhythmical prose or accentual metre following the epistle at Mass XIV (Trevisa); order of succession, run of cards XVI. – late L. *sequentia*, f. *sequent-*, *-ēns* (whence **se·quENT** following XVI), prp. of *sequī*, f. IE. base repr. also by Gr. *hépomai*, Ir. *sechur* I follow. Cf. *consequent, subsequent*, also *obsequies, second, consecutive*.

sequester sikwe·stəɹ set aside, remove XIV (Wyclif); confiscate XVI. – (O)F. *séquestrer* or late L. *sequestrāre*, f. *sequester* depositary of a thing in dispute, lit. 'one standing apart', f. **sequos*, *secus* apart, otherwise, f. IE. **sekʷ*-, repr. also in Indo-Iran., Celtic, and Baltic. So **sequestr**ATE sīkwe·streit. XVI. f. pp. stem of L. *sequestrāre*; **sequestr**A·TION. XIV. – (O)F. or late L.

sequin sī·kwin Italian gold coin XVII; small spangle for the ornamentation of dresses XIX. – F. *sequin* – It. *zecchino*, f. *zecca* (= Sp. *seca*) the mint – Arab. *sekkah* die for coining. Cf. SICCA.

sequoia sikwoi·ə (tree of a) genus of large American conifers (wellingtonia). XIX. – modL. (Endlicher, 1847), from *Sequoiah*, name of a Cherokee Indian, who invented a syllabary for his native language.

serac sĭræ·k tower of ice on a glacier. XIX. Swiss F., orig. name of a compact white cheese, prob. deriv. of L. *serum* whey.

seraglio sĭrā·ljou part of a Mohammedan dwelling-house assigned to women; Turkish palace. XVI. – It. *serraglio* – Turk. – Pers. *serāi* palace. Cf. F. *sérail*, formerly current in Eng. (XVI–XIX).

serai sərai· CARAVANSERAI; Turkish palace. XVII. – Turk. – Pers. *serāi* lodging, residence, palace; cf. prec.

seraph se·rəf one of the seraphim. XVII (Milton). Back-formation from SERAPHIM, *-in*, after *cherub* / *cherubim*, *-in*. So **seraph**IC sĭræ·fik pert. to the seraphim; ecstatic in worship or devotion. XVII. – medL. *seraphicus*; cf. F. *séraphique* (XV), etc. **sera·ph**ICAL. XVI.

seraphim se·rəfim the living creatures with six wings of Isaiah vi, in early Christian interpretation taken to be a class of angels. OE., ME. *seraphin*, later *seraphim* (XVI) – biblical L. *seraphim*, *-in* (= Gr. *seraphím*, *-pheím*) – Heb. *sᵉrāphīm*, pl. of *sārāph*, perh. identical with the word qualifying *nāḥāsh* serpent in Num. xxi, Deut. viii, and Isa. xiv 29, xxx 6 (the 'fiery (flying) serpents' of the Eng. Bible), perh. f. *sāraph* burn (with reference to stinging). From XVI to XVIII the word was freq. taken for a sg., with pl. in *s* (cf. (O)F. *séraphin*).

Serb sə̄ɹb †a Wend of Lusatia; a native, the language, of Serbia. XIX. – Serbian *Srb*. Hence **Se·rb**IAN (formerly *Servian*) XIX.

sere siəɹ (arch.) dry, withered. OE. *sēar* = MLG. *sōr* (LG. *soor*, Du. *zoor*) :– Germ. (of the LG. area, but cf. OHG. *sōrēn* become dry) **sauzaz* :– IE. **sousós*, repr. also by Gr. *aûos*, (Attic) *haûos*, and by Indo-Iran. and Balto-Sl. forms, and rel. to L. *sūdus* dry (:– **suzdos*, **susodos*).

serenade serĭnei·d music performed at night in the open air, esp. by a lover. XVII (Milton has *serenate*, after It.). – F. *sérénade* – It. *serenata* (formerly also, purity, serenity), f. *sereno* SERENE, in the current sense infl. by *sera* evening (:– L. *sēra*, sb. use of fem. of *sērus* late; cf. SOIRÉE); see -ADE. Hence vb. XVII.

serendipity serĭndi·pĭti faculty of making happy discoveries by accident 1754. Coined by Horace Walpole from the title of the fairy-tale 'The Three Princes of Serendip', the heroes of which were always making such discoveries; see -ITY.

serene sĭrī·n (of weather, etc.) clear and calm; honorific epithet of a prince XVI; (of persons) calm, untroubled XVII. In both the early senses first in Sc. (Dunbar) – L. *serēnus* clear, fair, calm (whence F. *serein*, Sp., It. *sereno*). So **seren**ITY sĭre·nĭti first in Sc. (XV) as a title of honour – (O)F. or L.

serf sə̄ɹf †slave XV (Caxton only); person in servitude 'attached to the soil' XVII. – (O)F. *serf* :– L. *servu-s* slave.

serge sə̄ɹdʒ woollen fabric. XIV (Ch.). ME. *sarge*, later *serge* (XVI) – OF. *sarge*, later *serge* (XVI) = Pr. *serga*, *sargua*, Sp. *sarga*, Rum. *sáricǎ* :– Rom. **sārica*, for L. *sērica*, fem. (sc. *lāna* wool) of *sēricus* – Gr. *sērikós* of SILK, orig. pert. to the *Sēres* name of a people anciently inhabiting a part of E. Asia (prob. China). Cf. AL. *sergia* (XIII).

sergeant, serjeant sā·ɹdʒənt †servant XII; † common soldier; †tenant by military service below a knight; officer charged with the arrest of offenders, etc. (now in *s. at arms*); (after law L. *serviens ad lēgem* serjeant-at-law) XIII; officer of the Corporation of London XV; military non-commissioned officer XVI. – OF. *sergent*, *serjant* (mod. *sergent*) = Pr. *serven-s*, Sp. *sirviente*, It. *servente* :– L. *servientem* (see -ANT), prp. of *servīre* SERVE (cf. SERVANT). The two variant forms descend respectively from ME. *sergeaunt*, *seriaunt*; the form with *j* has become appropriated to legal use; *sergeant major* XVI (see MAJOR adj.). Hence **se·rg-, se·rjeant**Y[3] XV; after OF.

sericulture se·rikʌltʃəɹ cultivation of silk. XIX. Shortened – F. *sériciculture*, f. late L. *sēricum* silk, n. of *sēricus*; see SERGE, CULTURE.

series siə·riz, siə·r(i)īz set of things of the same kind (orig. ranged in a line). XVII. – L. *seriēs* row, chain, series, f. *serere* join, connect; cf. F. *série*, Sp., It. *serie*. So **seri**AL[1]. XIX (first of the publication of a literary work). – modL. *seriālis*. **seriatim** siəriei·tim one by one in succession. XVII. medL. (after GRADATIM, LITERATIM); semi-anglicized †*seriatly* (XV); cf. synon. †*seriously* (XIV–XVII) after medL. *seriōsē*.

serif se·rif (typogr.) fine cross-stroke at top or bottom of a letter. XIX. perh. – Du. *schreef* sχrēf dash, line, earlier *schrēve* line, mark, prob. f. Germ. **skreƀ*-, repr. by OHG. *screvōn* scratch in. Cf. SANSERIF.

seringa siri·ŋgə shrub of the genus Philadelphus. XVIII. – F. *seringa* = Pg. *seringa* – L. SYRINGA.

serious siə·riəs of grave or solemn disposition XV; requiring earnest thought XVI. – (O)F. *sérieux* or late L. *sēriōsus*, f. *sērius* (used only of things in classical times), perh. rel. to the Germ. base repr. by OE. *swǣr*, *swār*, OHG. *swār* (G. *schwer*) heavy, with sense-development as in L. *gravis* heavy, GRAVE[3]; see -IOUS. **serio-** siə·riou used as comb. form (see -O-), as in **se·rio-co·mic** (XVIII).

sermon sə̄·ɹmən discourse from a pulpit. XII. ME. *sermun*, *-oun* – AN. *sermun*, (O)F. *sermon* = Pr. *sermo-n*, Sp. *sermon*, It. *sermone* :– L. *sermō(n-)* talk, discourse, referred by the ancients to *serere* join (cf. SERIES), but perh. based on IE. **swer-*, repr. in SWEAR, ANSWER.

sero- siə·rou used as comb. form (see -O-) of SERUM. XIX.

serotine se·rətain late-flowering. XVI. f. L. *sērōtinus*, f. *sērō* adv. of *sērus* late (see SERENADE).

serous siə·rəs pert. to serum. XVI. – F. *séreux* or medL. *serōsus*, f. SERUM.

serpent sə̄·ɹpənt scaly limbless animal that hisses and 'stings' XIV; wind instrument of wood shaped with three U-shaped turns XVIII. – (O)F. *serpent* = Pr. *serpent*, etc. :– L. *serpent-*, *serpēns*, sb. use of prp. of *serpere* creep, cogn. with Gr. *hérpein*, Skr. *sṛp*; see -ENT. So **se·rpent**INE[1]. XIV. – (O)F. – late L.

serpigo sə̄ɹpai·gou creeping skin disease. XIV. – medL., f. *serpere* crawl (cf. prec.). So **serpigin**OUS -i·dʒinəs. XVII. – modL.

serpula sə̄·ɹpjŭlə marine annelid which inhabits a tortuous calcareous tube. XVIII. modL. use of late L. *serpula*, dim. f. L. *serpere* (see SERPENT).

serrate se·reit notched like a saw. XVII – L. *serrātus*, f. *serra* saw; see -ATE[2]. So **se·rrat**ED[1]. XVIII.

serried se·rid in close order. XVII (Milton; in recent currency due to Scott). Either (i) f. (arch.) *serry* press *close together* in the ranks (XVI), prob. f. (O)F. *serré*, pp. of *serrer* (= Pr. *serrar*, Sp. *cerrar*, It. *serrare*) :– Rom. **serrāre* press close, alt. of L. (in comps.) *serāre*, f. *sera* lock, bolt; or (ii) sp. of †*serred* (disyll.), pp. of †*serr* (XVI) – (O)F. *serrer*; see -ED[1].

serum siə·rəm watery animal fluid. XVII. – L. *serum* whey, watery fluid, corr. to Gr. *orós* (**ser-* flow). So F. *sérum* (Paré).

serval sə̄·ɹvəl †lynx; bush cat. XVIII. – modL., F. *serval* (Buffon, 1765) – Pg. (*lobo*) *cerval* 'deer-like wolf' (cf. F. *loup-cervier*), f. *cervo* :– L. *cervu-s* deer; see HART, -AL[1].

servant sə̄·ɹvənt personal or domestic attendant XIII (AncrR.); one under obligation to work for (and obey) another XIV. – OF. *servant* m. and fem. (now only fem. *-ante*), sb. use of prp. of *servir*; see -ANT and cf. SERGEANT. **serve** sə̄ɹv be a servant (to). XIII (AncrR.); many deriv. uses from the same date. – (O)F. *servir* or L. *servīre* (whence also Pr., Sp. *servir*, etc.), f. L. *servus* slave (SERF). So **service**[1] sə·ɹvis condition or work of a servant. XII (*serfise*, *seruise*). – OF. *servise*, (also mod.) *service* = Pr. *servis(i)*, etc., or – L. *servītium* slavery, f. *servus*; in Eng., as in the Rom. langs., providing a noun of action to the vb. **se·rvice**ABLE. XIV (R. Mannyng) – OF. *serviceable*, *-isable*, with suffix in active sense. **serviette** sə̄·ɹvie·t table napkin. XV. In earliest use only Sc. (*seruiot*, *-iat*, later *seruit*), since *c.*1800 re-adopted in gen. Eng. use with F. sp. – (O)F. *serviette* towel, napkin, f. *servir*; see -ETTE and cf. OUBLIETTE. **serv**ILE sə̄·ɹvail pert. to a slave or to laborious or mechanical work XIV (Wycl. Bible; *s. work*, after L. *opus servīle* (Vulg.), tr. Heb. *mᵉléketh ʸăbōdāʰ*); of slavish character XVII. – L. *servīlis*, f. *servus*; cf. (O)F. *servile*. **servi**TOR sə̄·ɹvitəɹ †(man)servant XIV (R. Mannyng); †one who serves in war XVI; former class of exhibitioner at Oxford university XVII. – OF. *servitor* (mod. *serviteur*) – late L. *servītor* (whence also Pr., Sp. *servidor*, It. *servitore*), f. L. *servīre* SERVE. **servi**TUDE sə̄·ɹvitjūd slavery XV; (Sc. leg.) subjection or subservience of property XVI. – (O)F. *servitude* – L. *servitūdō*, f. *servus*. (Earlier †*servitute* – OF. *servitut* or L. *servitūt-*, *-tūs*.) **servo-** sə̄·ɹvou XIX, in **servo-**MO·TOR – F. *servo-moteur* auxiliary motor (see -O-).

Servian sə̄·ɹviən early form of SERBIAN. XVI. f. modL. *Servia*; see -IAN.

service[2] sə·ɹvis the tree Pyrus (Sorbus) domestica. XVI (*sarves*, *servyse*). orig. pl. of †*serve*, OE. *syrfe* :– **surƀjōn* – popL. **sorbea*, f. L. *sorbus* service tree.

Servite sə̄·ɹvait member of the order of the Servants of Mary. XVI. – medL. *Servītæ* pl., f. L. *servus* slave, SERF, in the title of the order, *Servi Beatæ Mariæ*; see -ITE.

sesame se·səmi, (formerly) se·səm, sī·səm E. Indian plant, Sesamum indicum. XV. In early use hardly naturalized and appearing in various forms. – L. *sēsamum*, *sīsamum*, *sēsama*, *-ima* – Gr. *sḗsamon*, *sēsámē* (whence It. *sesamo*, modGr. *sēsámi*), of Oriental origin (cf. Syriac *shūshmā*, Jewish Aram. *shumshᵉmā*, Arab. *simsim*). Since late XVIII the currency of *sesame* is due to translations of 'The Arabian Nights' from F. (*sésame*) and the trisyll. pronunc. to Gr. *sēsámē*.

sesqui- se·skwi prefix expressing superparticular ratio. – L. *sesqui-* :– **sēmisque* a half in addition; see SEMI- and cf. *sestertius* :– **sēmistertius* SESTERCE; in musical terms, e.g. *se:squia·ltera* (denoting the proportion

1½:1) XVI; in other terms, e.g. *se·squipeda·lian* a foot and a half long (after Horace's *sesquipedalia verba*, 'Ars Poetica' 97) XVII; in chem. terms introduced by J. Thomson 1825, denoting a proportion of 3 to 2 between constituents of compounds.

sess var. of CESS (in Ir. use). XVI.

sessile se·sail, se·sil (path.) adhering close to the surface; (nat. hist.) immediately attached to the base XVIII; sedentary XIX. – L. *sessilis*, f. *sess-*, pp. stem of *sedēre* SIT; see -ILE.

session se·ʃən sitting together for conference, spec. judicial sitting XIV (Ch.); continuous series of meetings XVI; act of sitting, occupation of a seat XVII. – (O)F. *session* or L. *sessiō(n-)*, f. *sess-*, *sedēre* SIT; see -ION.

sesterce se·stəɹs ancient Roman coin, orig. equiv. to 2½ asses. XVI. – L. *sestertius* (sc. *nummus* coin) that is two and a half, f. *sēmis* half + *tertius* third; see SEMI-, SESQUI-. So **sestertium** sestə̄·ɹʃiəm 1000 sesterces. XVI. – L., expl. as g.pl. of *sestertius*, with ellipsis of *mille* thousand, taken as n.sg.

sestet(t), -ette seste·t (mus.) composition for six voices or instruments; last six lines of a sonnet. XIX. – It. *sestetto*, f. *sesto* (:– L. *sextu-s*) SIXTH; see -ET and cf. SEXTET.

sestina sestī·nə poem of six six-line stanzas. XIX. – It. *sestina*, f. *sesto* sixth; see prec. So **se·stine.** XVI (Sidney) – F. †*sestine* – It.; cf. SEXTAIN.

set[1] set pt., pp. **set** cause to sit; (hence) the most gen. word for place, put, with many spec. applications lit. and fig. OE.; †subside OE. (late); (of a luminary) go down, sink below the horizon XIII (prob. after ON. refl. *setjask*). OE. *settan*, pt. *sette*, pp. *ġeset(t)*, Anglian *ġeseted* = OFris. *setta*, OS. *settian* (Du. *zetten*), OHG. *sezzan* (G. *setzen*), ON. *setja*, Goth. *satjan* :– CGerm. **satjan*, causative of **setjan* SIT. ¶ Confusion between *set* and *sit* appears XIV.

set[2] set A. setting of a luminary XIV; B. in various applications of the senses 'act of setting', 'manner or position in which a thing is set', 'something that is set' from XV. Mainly f. SET[1]; but sense A may be in part due to ON. *-setr*, *-seta* (as in *sólarsetr*, *-seta* sunset). There is no evidence of survival of OE. *set* place of sunset (cf. OE. *setgang* sunset), pl. camp, stable.

set[3] set number or group of persons XIV; number or collection of things XVI. orig., in sense 'sect' – OF. *sette* :– L. *secta* SECT, but in later developments infl. by SET[1] and apprehended as 'number set together' (cf. SET[2]); the application to things may be partly due to MLG. *gesette* set or suite of things (cf. Da. *sæt* set of china, suit of clothes, G. *satz*).

setaceous sītei·ʃəs like a bristle. XVII. f. modL. *sētāceus*, f. *sēta* bristle; see -ACEOUS.

seton sī·tən thread, etc. drawn through a fold of the skin to maintain an issue XIV; the issue itself XVI. – medL. *sētō(n-)*, app. f. L. *sētā* bristle, in medL. also, silk; cf. (O)F. *séton*, It. *setone*.

settee[1] setī· (hist.) vessel with lateen sails used in the Mediterranean. XVI (*settea*, later *sattee*, *satia*, *settee*). – It. *saettia*, held to be f. *saetta* arrow :– L. *sagitta*.

settee[2] setī· seat to hold two or more persons. XVIII. perh. identical with †*settee* double pinner for the head, the etymol. notion being an object having divisions (cf. 'The soft settee . . . United yet divided, twain at once', Cowper 'The Task' I 75).

setter se·təɹ dog of a breed trained to mark the position of hunted game XVI (cf. *setting dog* XVII); see -ER[1].

setterwort se·təɹwə̄ɹt species of hellebore. XVI. prob. – MLG. *siterwort*, the first el. of which is of unkn. origin; see WORT[1]. Also called †*settergrass* (XIV, *saturgresse*).

settle[1] se·tl †seat OE.; long wooden bench with a high back XVI. OE. *setl*, corr. to MLG., MDu. *setel*, OHG. *sezzal* (G. *sessel*), Goth. *sitls* :– Germ. **setlaz*, **setlam*, rel. to L. *sella* saddle :– **sedlā*, f. **sed-* SIT; see -LE[1].

settle[2] se·tl place in a certain position OE.; come to rest after movement or agitation XIII; sink down XIV; render stable, establish XIV; fix, determine, make an agreement XVI. OE. *setlan* (once) place, implied also in *setlung* sitting-down, setting of the sun, f. *setl* SETTLE[1]. ¶ That the later sense-development was infl. by †*saughtel* reconcile, be reconciled, is improbable, since the latter vb. was obs. before XV.

setwall se·twōl (root of) the East Indian plant Curcuma Zedoaria. XIII. ME. *zedewal*, *zeduale*, *cetewale* – AN. *zedewale*, OF. *citoual* – medL. **zedoāle*, var. of *zedoārium* ZEDOARY.

seven se·vn 7, vii. OE. *seofon*, inflected *seofone*, *-u* = OFris. *sigun*, *soven*, *sogen*, *sav(e)n*, OS. *siƀun*, OHG. *sibun* (Du. *zeven*, G. *sieben*), ON. *sjau*, Goth. *sibun* :– CGerm. **seƀun* :– IE. **septṃ́*, repr. by Skr. *saptá*, Gr. *heptá*, L. *septem*, OSl. *sedmĭ*, Lith. *septynì*, OIr. *secht n-*. So **seven**TEEN. OE. *seofontīene* = OFris. *soventene*, OHG. **sibunzehan* (G. *siebzehn*), ON. *sjautján*. **se·ven**TH[2]. XIV. new formation, directly f. SEVEN + -TH[2], repl. (i) OE. (Anglian) *seofunda*, ME. *sevende* = OFris. *sigunda*, OS. *sivondo*, OHG. *sibunto* (G. *siebente*), ON. *sjaundi* :– Germ. **seƀundo-*, (ii) OE. *seofoþa*, ME. *seveþe*, repl. in ME. by *sevenþe* = OS. *sivoðo* :– Germ. **seƀunþo-*. **se·ven**TY[1]. OE. *(hund)seofontiġ* = OS. *siuntig*, OHG. *sibunzug*, ON. *sjautigr*.

sever se·vəɹ put apart, part, be sundered. XIV. – AN. *severer*, OF. *sevrer* (now, wean) :– Rom. **sēperāre*, for L. *sēparāre* SEPARATE. So **se·ver**AL[1] existing apart; pert. to an individual; also sb. xv. – AN. *several* (whence medL. *severālis*) – medL. *sēparālis*, f. L. *sēpār* separate. **se·ver**ANCE. xv. – AN. *severance*, OF. *sevrance*.

severe sivɪə·ɹ extremely strict xvi; extremely grievous, exacting, or painful xvii. – (O)F. *sévère* or L. *sevērus* (whence also Sp., It. *severo*). So **sever**ITY sive·rīti. xvi. – (O)F. or L.

severy se·vəri (archit.) compartment of a roof or scaffolding. xiv (revived xix). – AN. **civorie*, OF. *civoire* CIBORIUM.

Sèvres seivr, ||sɛvr xix. Name of a town in France, near Paris, designating a costly porcelain.

sew sou pt. **sewed**, pp. **sewn**, **sewed**, soun, soud join together with thread, etc. OE. *siwan*, *siowan* = OFris. *sīa*, OHG. *siuwen*, ON. *sýja*, Goth. *siujan* :– CGerm. **siwjan*, f. IE. **siw-* **sju-*, repr. also by L. *suere*, Gr. *kas|súein*, with Balto-Sl. and Skr. forms (cf. SEAM, SUTRA). For the pronunc. sou cf. *strow*, var. of *strew*; rhymes with *clue*, *new* are found till xvii; cf. Sc. *ʃū*.

sewer[1] sjū·əɹ artificial channel for draining. xv. – AN. *sever(e)*, ONF. *se(u)wiere* channel to carry off overflow from a fishpond (whence medL. *seweria*) :– Rom. **exaquāria* (cf. medL. *exaquātōrium*), f. **exaquāre* (f. L. *ex* EX-[1]+*aqua* water), whence OF. *essever* drain off (cf. *assevour*, *-eur*, *essouere* drain, ditch).

sewer[2] sjū·əɹ (hist.) attendant who arranged a meal and tasted the dishes. xiv. Aphetic – AN. *asseour*, f. (O)F. *asseoir* place a seat for :– L. *assidēre*, f. *ad* AD-+*sedēre* SIT.

sewin sjū·in kind of salmon trout. xvi. Of unkn. origin.

sex seks males or females collectively xiv (Wycl. Bible; rare before xvi); condition in respect of being male or female xvi. – (O)F. *sexe* or L. *sexus* m. (whence also Sp. *sexo*, It. *sesso*), rel. to synon. *secus* n. So **se·xu**AL[1]. xvii. – late L. (Cælius Aurelianus).

sex- seks comb. form of L. *sex* SIX, as in techn. terms, e.g. (zool.) *sexdi·gital*, (chem.) *sexva·lent*; **sexagen**ARIAN se:ksədʒinɛə·riən. xviii, **sexage·n**ARY pert. to 60 xvi, aged 60 xvii; **Sexagesima** seksədʒe·simə xvi (earlier †*-ime* xiv) second Sunday before Lent (cf. SEPTUAGESIMA); **sexage·sim**AL[1] (math.) pert. to or based on 60 xvii; **sex**CENTE·NARY of 600 xviii; of a period of 600 years xix. **sexennial** sekse·niəl see BIENNIAL. **sext** sekst (eccl.) the third of the day hours of the Church, so called because orig. allocated to the sixth hour of the day (midday). xv. – L. *sexta*, sb. use (sc. *hōra* hour) of fem. of *sextus* SIXTH; cf. PRIME.

sextant se·kstənt (astron.) instrument resembling a quadrant having a graduated arc equal to ⅙ of a circle. xvii (Burton). – modL. use (by Tycho Brahe, 1602) of L. *sextant-*, *-āns* sixth part (of an as, etc.), f. *sextus* SIXTH. **sextet(t)**, **-ette** sekste·t. xix. alt. of SESTET after L. *sex* SIX. **sext**ILE se·kstail (astrol.) pert. to the aspect of two heavenly bodies which are 60° or ⅙ of the zodiac distant. xvi. – L. *sextīlis*, f. *sextus* SIXTH. Cf. QUARTILE. **sexti·llion** see BILLION. †**se:xtode·cimo** size of a book in which the leaf is $\frac{1}{16}$ of the sheet, †decimo-sexto; sixteenmo. xvii. **sextuple** se·kstjūpl sixfold. xvii (Bacon); cf. CENTUPLE. **se·xtuplex** sixfold. xvii; cf. DUPLEX, TRIPLEX, etc.

sexton se·kstən sacristan, (later) guardian of a church fabric and churchyard, bell-ringer and grave-digger. xiv. Late ME. *segerstane*, *secristeyn*, *sekesteyn*, *sexteyn*, (from xvi) *sexton* – AN., OF. *segerstein*, *secrestein* – medL. *sacristānus* SACRISTAN.

seyd var. of SAYYID.

sforzando sfɔ̄ɹtsæ·ndou (mus.) direction for emphasis. xix. – It., gerund of *sforzare* use force, vb. f. *s-* EX-[1]+*forzare* :– Rom. **fortiāre* FORCE.

sgraffito sgræfī·tou earlier (xviii) equiv. of GRAFFITO, *s-* repr. L. *ex* EX-[1].

sh ʃ excl. to enjoin silence, also written *'sh* as if an abbrev. of HUSH, of which it is the common int. equiv. xix.

sh digraph repr. the sound ʃ, current since *c.*1200, in the 'Ormulum' (regularly) and 'Trinity College Homilies' (frequently), finally prevailing from Caxton's date and superseding OE. to xiii *sc* (often with graphic *e* before *a*, *o*, *u*), ME. *s* (xii–xiii), *ss* (xii–xiv), *sch* (xii–xiv; till xvii Sc.), *ssh* (xiii–xvi), beside which are the EAnglian ME. var. *x* in *xal*, *xulde* (shall, should), Coverdale's *sz(s)h*, and sporadic *ch* (esp. in *-chipe* -SHIP xiv–xv); cf. -ISH[1], -ISH[2].

shabby ʃæ·bi dingy and faded; contemptibly ungenerous. xvii. Parallel to †*shabbed* (OE. *sċeabbede*), as *scabby* to *scabbed*; f. *shab* scab (OE.), low fellow (xvii), OE. *sċeabb* = ON. **skabbr* SCAB; see -Y[1]. ¶ 'A word that has crept into conversation and low writing; but ought not to be admitted into the language' (J.).

shabrack ʃæ·bræk saddle-cloth. xix. – G. *schabracke*, F. *schabraque*, of East European origin (Russ. *shabrak*, Turk. *čapraq*).

shabunder ʃābʌ·ndəɹ officer at native ports in Indian seas. xvi (*sabandar*). – Pers. *shāhbundar* 'king (SHAH) of the port'; cf. Pg. *xabandar*.

shack ʃæk (N. Amer.) roughly built cabin or shanty. xix. perh. shortened – Mex. *jacal*, Aztec *xacatli* wooden hut, which are more closely repr. by occas. U.S. *shackle*.

shackle ʃæ·kl fetter OE.; transf. uses from xiv. OE. *sċ(e)acul*, corr. to LG. *schäkel* link of a chain, hobble, Du. *schakel*, ON. *skǫkull* wagon-pole, f. Germ. **skak-*, repr. also by OE. *sċeac*, LG. *schake*; see -LE[1]. Hence vb. xv.

shad ʃæd fish of the genus Alosa. Late OE. *sċeadd*, of unkn. origin; cf. W. *ysgadan* pl. (sg. *ysgadanyn*), Ir., Gael. *sgadan* herring.

shaddock ʃæ·dək fruit of Citrus decumana, †pompelmoose. XVII. f. name of Captain *Shaddock* 'Commander of an East-India Ship, who touch'd at that Island [*sc.* Jamaica] in his Passage to England, and left the Seed there' (Sloane, 'A voyage to . . . Jamaica', 1707).

shade ʃeid shadow; protection from glare or heat OE. (concr., as in *lampshade, sunshade* XVII); (after L. *umbra*, Gr. *σκιά*) disembodied spirit (pl. *the shades* Hades); degree of colour XVII; slight degree XVIII. OE. *sċ(e)adu* fem. (obl. cases repr. by SHADOW), and obl. cases *sċeade, sċeadu*, etc. of *sċead* n.

shadow ʃæ·dou comparative darkness; image cast by a body intercepting light; shelter from light and heat. XII. ME. *sceadewe, shadewe*, repr. obl. forms, *sċead(u)we*, of OE. *sċeadu* SHADE, corr. to OS. *scado* (Du. *schaduw*), OHG. *scato* (G. *schatte*, later *schatten*), Goth. *skadus* :- CGerm. (exc. ON.) **skaðwaz*, **skaðwō* :- IE. **skotwós, -wā́* or **skatwós, -wā́*; cf. Gr. *skótos* darkness, Skr. *chādáyati* covers, and OIr. *scāth* shadow, MW. *cisgaud* darkness (W. *sy|sgod, gwa|sgod* shade) :- OCeltic **skāt-*. So **sha·dow** vb. OE. *sċeadwian* (also in *ofer|sċeadwian* overshadow) = OS. *skadowan, skadoian* (Du. *schaduwen*), OHG. *scatewen*, Goth. *-skadwjan*. Hence **sha·dowY**[1]. XIV (Ch.).

shaft[1] ʃàft rod of spear, etc. OE.; long straight part of an object XIV; long bar or rod in a vehicle or machine XVII. OE. *sċæft, sċeaft* = OFris. *sceft*, OS., OHG. *scaft* (Du., G. *schaft*), ON. *skaft* :- CGerm. (exc. Goth.) **skaftaz*, **-am, -iz*, perh. to be referred to IE. **sqăp-*, **sqabh-* support, as in L. *scāpus* shaft, stem, shank, *scamnum* bench, stool, Gr. (Doric) *skâpton* staff, *skēpt|oûkhos* staff-bearer, *skêptein* prop, *skêptron* SCEPTRE.

shaft[2] ʃàft long well-like excavation giving access to a mine XV. – MLG. (whence (M)HG.) *schacht*, prob. spec. application of SHAFT[1], as if the vertical channel were compared to the leg (*schaft*) of a boot.

shag[1] ʃæg rough hair or wool OE.; cloth having a velvet nap XVI; fine-shredded tobacco; in full *s. tobacco*, i.e. a use of the adj. XVIII. Late OE. *sċeacga* (once, in a gloss), rel. to ON. *skegg* beard (:- **skagjam*), OE. *sċeaga* coppice, SHAW, ON. *skagi* promontory (:- **skagon*), *skaga* project, and further to ON. *skógr* wood. Hence **shag** adj. XVI (Sh.), †**shaggED**[2] Late OE. *sċeacgede* (twice, in glosses); superseded by **sha·ggY**[1]. XVI. ¶ Not evidenced before late XVI exc. for the OE. glosses.

shag[2] ʃæg cormorant. XVI. perh. a use of SHAG[1] (sb. or adj.), with ref. to the bird's shaggy crest.

shagreen ʃægrī·n untanned leather. XVII. var. sp. of *chagrin* – F. *chagrin* (whence It. *sagrin*, Du. *sagrijnleer*) – Turk. *sagry* rump, skin of this.

shah ʃā king of Persia. XVI (*shaw, shaugh*). – Pers. *šāh*, shortening of OPers. *χšāyaþiya*. Cf. CHECKMATE.

Shaitan ʃeitā·n Satan, evil spirit XVII; evil-disposed person or animal; dust storm XIX. – Arab. *šaiṭān* – Heb. *sāṭān* SATAN.

shake ʃeik pt. **shook** ʃuk, pp. **shaken** ʃei·kn. †go, move; vibrate, cause to vibrate. OE. *sċ(e)acan*, pt. *sċeōc*, pp. *sċeacen* = OS. *skakan* (pt. *skōk* departed), ON. *skaka*, pt. *skók*, pp. *skekinn* :- Germ. **skakan* (exc. Goth.), with which Skr. *khajati* agitate, churn, has been connected. **shakY**[1] ʃei·ki XVIII.

shako ʃæ·kou military cap. XIX. – F. *schako* – Magyar *csákó*, short for *csákó(s) süveg* peaked cap (*csákos*, f. *csák* peak – G. *zacken* point, spike).

shale ʃeil argillaceous fissile rock. XVIII. prob. – G. *schale* (not used in this sense, but cf. *schalstein* laminated limestone, *schalgebirge* mountain system of thin strata) = OE. *sċ(e)alu* SCALE[1]. So **sha·ly**[1]. XVII.

shall ʃæl, ʃ(ə)l pt. **should** ʃud, ʃəd. CGerm. perfect-present vb., with a new wk. pt. (cf. CAN[2], etc.) orig. meaning †I owe, (hence) †I ought, must, am to, passing thence into a tense-sign of the future and a mark of contingency. OE. *sċeal* (2nd pers. *sċealt* shalt), pl. *sċulon*, pt. *sċeolde* should = OFris. *skel, skil, skilun, skolde*, OS. *skal, skulun, skolda*, OHG. *scal, sculun, scolta* (Du. *zal, zullen, zou*, G. *soll, sollen, sollte*), ON. *skal, skulu, skylda*, Goth. *skal, skulum, skulda*; f. CGerm. (**skel-*) **skal-* **skul-* owe :- IE. **skel-* **skol-* **skḷ-*, repr. also by OE. *ġe|sċola*, OS., OHG. *scolo*, Goth. *skula* debtor, OE. *sċyld*, OFris. *skeld*, OS. *sculd*, OHG. *sculd, sculda* (G. *schuld*) debt, guilt, and, outside Germ., by Baltic forms of similar connotation.

The northern var. *sal* (reduced enclitically to *s*), pt. *suld*, is paralleled by OFris. *sal, sel*, OHG. *sal, sol, sulun*, and this form of the initial sounds has ousted the normal form in G. *soll, sollen, sollte*, and Du. *zal, zou*. The Eng. vb. has no inf. or pples. (the alleged OE. **sċulan*, **sċeolan* are based on insufficient evidence); but elsewhere the inf. is repr. by OHG. *scolan* (G. *sollen*), OS. *sculan*, ON. *skola, skula* (pt. *skylda*), the prp. by OHG. *scolanti* (G. *sollend*), Goth. *skulands*, the pp. by ON. *skyldr* bound by duty, Goth. *skulds* lawful.

shalloon ʃəlū·n woollen fabric. XVII. – (O)F. *chalon* (adopted earlier as †*chalon* blanket, coverlet XIV), f. name of *Châlons-sur-Marne*, France.

shallop ʃæ·ləp sloop; dinghy. XVI. – F. *chaloupe* – Du. *sloep* SLOOP; cf. Sp. *chalupa*, It. *scialuppa*, G. *schaluppe*.

shallot ʃəlɔ·t small onion, Allium Ascalonicum. XVII. Aphetic of †*eschalot* – F. *eschalotte* (now *échalotte*), alt. of OF. *eschaloigne* = Pr. *escalonha*, etc. :– Rom. **iscalonia*, for L. *Ascalōnia* (*cæpa*), (onion) of *Ascalon*, a town in Palestine.

shallow ʃæ·lou not deep. XV. Obscurely rel. to synon. OE. *sćeald*, ME. *schald*; see SHOAL[1].

sham ʃæm sb. †trick, fraud XVII; spurious imitation XVIII; adj. false, counterfeit XVII; vb. †defraud, hoax; †attempt to pass *off*; counterfeit, assume appearance of XVII. Like many words orig. in canting or sl. use, first recorded in late XVII, and of obscure etym.; poss. north. dial. var. of SHAME.

shaman ʃā·mən, ʃæ·mən priest among N. Asiatic tribes. XVII. – G. *schamane*, Russ. *shamán* – Tungusian *samán*; cf. F. *chaman*.

shamble ʃæ·mbl walk with an ungainly gait. XVII (late). f. *shamble* adj. ungainly, shambling (early XVII), perh. orig. in *s. legs*, which may have orig. meant 'legs straddling like those of the trestles of a meat table' (see next); cf. WFris. *skammels* (pl. of *skammel* board on trestles) legs, esp. when badly formed, *skammelje* walk clumsily; cf. G. *schemelbein*, *schemeln*; see -LE[3].

shambles ʃæ·mblz (dial.). meat-market (orig. *flesh s.*) XV; slaughter-house XVI. Colloq. transf. pl. of *shamble* table or stall for the sale of meat (XIV), spec. use of OE. *sć(e)amul* stool, table = OS. *fōt|skamel*, OHG. *fuoʒ|-scamil* footstool (also MDu., MHG. *schamel*, *schemel*, G. *schemel*); CWGerm. – L. *scamellum*, dim. of *scamnum* bench, which has Celtic cognates.

shame ʃeim feeling of disgrace; state of disgrace, circumstance causing this OE.; modest feeling XIV. OE. *sć(e)amu* = OFris. *skame*, *skome*, OS., OHG. *skama* (Du. *schaam-* in comp., G. *scham*), ON. *skǫmm* :– CGerm. **skamō* (not in Goth., but cf. *skaman* vb. below); on the same base are formed OE. *sćand* m. infamous man, *sćand* fem. infamous woman, disgrace, *sćendan* vb. (see SHENT), OHG. *scanda* (G. *schande*) disgrace, *scant* ashamed, Goth. *skanda* disgrace. So vb. OE. *sć(e)amian* intr. and impers., corr. immed. to OS. *skamon*, OHG. *scamōn*, and rel. to OHG. *scamēn*, Goth. *skaman*, and MHG. *schemen* (G. *schämen*), ON. *skemma*. **shamefaced** ʃei·mfeist modest, bashful. XVI. alt. by assim. to FACE, *-faced*, of (arch.) *shamefast*, OE. *sć(e)amfæst*, the second el. being identical with FAST[1], as if 'restrained by shame' (cf. *ǣfæst* 'bound by law', religious, righteous, *þēawfæst* 'bound by virtue', virtuous); but *-fæst* is a common suffix of OE. adjs. equiv. to *-ful*, *-ous*. **sha·me**FUL[1], -LESS. OE. *sć(e)amful*, *-lēas*.

shammy ʃæ·mi XVIII. pronunc. of CHAMOIS. So **shamoy** ʃæ·moi prepare (leather) by working oil into it. XIX.

shampoo ʃæmpū· massage (as now in a Turkish bath) XVIII; wash and rub (the scalp) XIX. – Hind. *chhāmpo*, imper. of *chhāmpnā* (cf. G. *schamponieren*).

shamrock ʃæ·mrɔk plant with trifoliate leaves, now usu. Trifolium minus (lesser yellow trefoil). XVI. – Ir. *seamróg* = Gael. *seamrag*), dim. of *seamar* clover.

shandygaff ʃændigæ·f mixture of beer and ginger-beer or lemonade. XIX. Of unkn. origin.

shanghai ʃæŋhai· (naut. sl., orig. U.S.) render insensible and ship on board a vessel wanting hands (perh. orig. one destined for Shanghai). XIX. f. *Shanghai*, name of a Chinese seaport.

shank ʃæŋk shin-bone, tibia OE.; stem, shaft XVI. OE. *sćeanca*, LG. *schanke*, Flem. *schank* :– WGerm. **skaŋkan*, rel. to MLG. *schenke*, Du. *schenk* leg bone (:– **skaŋkiz*), LG., (M)HG. *schenkel* (:– **skaŋkilaz*); other formations on the series **skiŋk-* **skaŋk-* **skuŋk-* are OS. *scinka* tibia (MLG. *schinke* thigh, ham), OHG. *skinko*, *skinka* (G. *schinken* ham), and OFris. *skunka*, LG. *schunke*; the etymol. meaning is uncertain, but the base corr. formally to that of ON. *skakkr* (:– **skaŋkaz*) wry, distorted, lame, and Gr. *skázein* (:– **sqŋgy*) limp (cf. SCAZON). phr. *Shanks's mare, pony* for 'the legs as a means of transport' is orig. Sc. (XVIII), the pl. of the common noun being joc. turned into a surname. ¶ The primitive sense of LEG (which superseded this word in gen. use) is shown in surnames such as *Cruikshank*, *Longshanks*, *Sheepshanks*.

shanty[1] ʃæ·nti roughly built cabin or hut. XIX. Orig. in N. Amer. use; perh. – Ir. *sean tig* (*toig*) 'old house'.

shanty[2], **chant(e)y** ʃæ·nti sailor's song. XIX. app. corruption of F. *chantez*, imper. of *chanter* sing.

shape ʃeip external or visible form; †sexual organs OE.; guise XVI; form or kind of structure XVII. orig. repr. OE. *ġe|sćeap* creation, creature, form, figure, pudendum, decree, destiny, corr. to OS. *giskapu* pl. creatures, decrees, ON. *skap* condition, pl. fate (*skǫpin* genitals); f. **skap-* base of the vb., of which the sb. came to be later apprehended as a deriv. So **shape** vb. †create; fashion, form. Early ME. new formation on the pp., repl. orig. OE. **sćieppan*, **sćeppan*, pt. *sćōp*, pp. *sćapen*, corr. to OFris. *skeppa*, *skōp*, *eskepen*, OS. **gisceppian*, *-scōp*, **scapan*, Goth. *gaskapjan* *-skōp*, *-skapans*; f. **skap-* create, fashion; first established as a wk. vb. XVI; the OE. pp. survives chiefly in *misshapen*. **sha·pe**LESS. XIII (Cursor M.). **sha·pe**LY[1] †fit, suitable XIV (Ch.); well-shaped XIV (Wycl. Bible).

shard ʃāɹd, **sherd** ʃɜ̄ɹd (dial.) gap; fragment of broken earthenware (cf. POT*sherd*). OE. *sćeard*, corr. to OFris. *skerd* cut, notch, MLG. *skart* crack, chink, MDu. *scarde*, *schart* flaw, fragment (Du. *schaard*), (M)HG. *scharte*, ON. *skarð* notch, gap, sb. uses of the adj. repr. by OE. *sćeard*, OS. *skard*, OHG. *-scart*, ON. *skarðr* :- Germ. **skarðaz* cut, notched, diminished, pp. formation on **skar-* **sker-* SHEAR.

share[1] ʃɛəɹ cutting blade of a plough. OE. *sćær*, *sćear*, corr. to OFris. *sker*, MLG. *schar(e)*, OHG. *scar*, *scaro*, *scare* (G. *schar*); WGerm. deriv. of Germ. **skar-* **sker-* SHEAR. Cf. next. ¶ The present form repr. disyll. obl. forms of the OE. sb., the nom. of which gave ME. *s(c)har*.

share[2] ʃɛəɹ allotted portion XIV; portion of a property owned by a number in common XVI. The earliest exx. are in AN. and AL. documents; repr. spec. development of OE. *sćearu* lit. 'cutting, division', recorded only in senses 'tonsure', 'fork of the body', and in *landsćearu* boundary, *folc-*, *lēodsćearu* division of people, nation, *hearmsćearu* penalty, corr. to OS. *scara* feudal service, troop, also in *harmscara*, MLG. *schare* troop, share, OHG. *scara* troop, share of forced labour (Du. *schaar*, G. *schar* troop, multitude), ON. *skari* :- Germ. deriv. f. **skar-* **sker-* cut, divide, SHEAR. Hence **share** vb. XVI (Spenser, Sh.).

shark ʃāɹk large voracious seafish, Squalus XVI; rapacious or extortionate person XVIII. Said to have been so named by sailors of Capt. John Hawkins's expedition, who brought home a specimen which was exhibited in London in 1569; of unkn. origin. ¶ The available evidence is insufficient to determine connexion with †*shark* parasite, sharper (late XVI) and its syn. †*shirk* XVII–XVIII, or with †*shark* vb. prey *upon* (late XVI), play the parasite or sharper, pilfer.

sharp ʃāɹp having a keen edge or point; keen, acute; severe, harsh; pungent OE.; shrill XIV; (mus.) XVI (Morley); sb. uses date from XIV. OE. *sć(e)arp* = OFris. *skarp*, *skerp*, OS. *skarp* (Du. *scherp*), OHG. *skarf*, *scarpf* (G. *scharf*), ON. *skarpr* :- CGerm. (exc. Goth.) **skarpaz*; cf. OE. *sćearpe* scarification, *sćearpian* scarify, OHG. *scurfen* (G. *schürfen* scratch), and SCRAPE. Hence **sha·rp**EN[5] XV; superseding (dial.) *sharp*, OE. **scierpan*, *sćerpan*; **sha·rp**ER[1], in sense 'cheat', swindler' (XVII); cf. *sharp* vb. swindle (XVII). **sha·rp**LY[2], **sha·rp**NESS. OE.

shatter ʃæ·təɹ (dial.) scatter, disperse XII; break in pieces XV. Origin and relation to SCATTER obscure, there being no evidence for either word before 'Peterborough Chronicle' an. 1137 or between this and *c.*1300. MLG. *schateren* be shattered, resound, laugh uproariously (cf. Du. *schateren*) is prob. an independent imit. formation.

shave ʃeiv scrape, pare away OE.; remove with a razor, use a razor to XIII. OE. *sć(e)afan*, pt. *sćōf*, pp. *sćafen*, *sćeafen* = OS. *scaban*, OHG. *scaban* (Du. *schaven*, G. *schaben*), ON. *skafa*, Goth. *skaban* :- CGerm. **skaƀan*, of doubtful orig.; str. vb. became wk. XIV, with the literary survival str. pp. *shaven*. Hence **sha·ve**LING[1] tonsured ecclesiastic. XVI. **shave**R[1] ʃei·vəɹ one who shaves XV; †plunderer, swindler; (hence colloq.) fellow, chap, wag XVI.

shaw ʃō (dial.) thicket, copse. OE. *sćeaga*, corr. to NFris. *skage* farthest edge of cultivated land, ON. *skagi* promontory, rel. to OE. *sćeacga* (see SHAG[1]). ¶ A common el. in place-names, hence a surname.

shawl ʃōl Oriental oblong article of dress made in Kashmir from the hair of a goat of Tibet XVII; in the West, outer covering for the shoulders (and head) XVIII. Earliest forms *schal*, *scial*, *chal*, *shaul*; ult. – Urdu, etc. – Pers. *shāl*, prob. f. *Shāliāt*, a town in India; adopted in all the main Eur. langs., e.g. Sp. *chal*, It. *scialle*, Rum. *şal*, Du., G. *schal*, Icel. *sjal*, (from Eng.) F. *châle*, †*schale*, G., Da. *shawl*.

shawm ʃōm (hist.) mediæval wind instrument. XIV. ME. *schallemele* (Gower), pl. *chalm(e)yes* (Ch.), *schalmes*, later (sg.) *schalmus*, *shawme* (XVI). – (i) OF. *chalemel* (mod. *chalumeau*) :- Rom. **calamellus*, dim. of L. *calamus* reed – Gr. *kálamos*; (ii) OF. (unexpl.) *chalemie*, whence also MLG., MDu. *schalmeie*, MHG. *schalmīe*, Du., G. *schalmei*; (iii) OF. *chalemeaus*, pl. of *chalemel*.

shay ʃei chaise. XVIII (also *chay*). Back-formation from CHAISE ʃeiz, misapprehended as pl.

she ʃī, ʃi 3rd sg. fem. nom. pers. pron. This form repr. east midl. ME. *scæ* (XII, Peterborough Chronicle), *sȝe*, *sse*, *sche* (XIII), parallel with which there was ME. *scho*, *sho*, north. *sco*, surviving in n.w. dial. *shoo*. These two types appear to descend from divergent developments of OE. fem. demons. pron.-adj. *sio*, *sēo*, acc. *sie* (see THE), resulting from the conversion of the falling diphthongs īo, īe into rising diphthongs jō, jē, viz. sjō, sjē passing into ʃō, ʃē; cf. the development of OE. fem. pers. pron. *hēo*, acc. *hie*, to ME. *ȝho*, *ȝhe* (*oo*, for *hoo*, survives in some northerly dial.). ¶ The necessity for a new form for this pron. arose partly from the coincidence in ME. of OE. *hē* (he) and *hēo* (she) under the form *he*. For the parallel use of the fem. demons. for 'she' cf. OS. and OHG. *siu* (Du. *zij*, G. *sie*) = OE. *sēo*, and OFris. *se*, beside *hiu*, and in ON. the use of the demons. pron. of all genders as a pers. pron.

sheaf ʃīf bundle of reaped corn. OE. *sćēaf* = OS. *skōf* (Du. *schoof*), OHG. *scoub* sheaf, bundle or wisp of straw (G. *schaub*), ON. *skauf* fox's brush :- CGerm. (exc. Goth.) **skauƀaz* (*-am*), f. **skauƀ-* **skeuƀ-* **skuƀ-* (see SHOVE).

shear ʃiəɹ pt. **sheared,**†shore, pp. **sheared, shorn.** cut with a scissor-like instrument. OE. *sćeran*, pt. pl. *sćǣron*, pp. *sćoren* = = OFris. *skera*, OS. *bi|sceran* (Du. *scheren*), OHG. *sceran*, *scar*, *giscoran* (G. *scheren*), ON. *skera*, *skar*, *skorinn* :- CGerm. (exc. Goth.) **skeran*, f. **sker-* **skar-* **skǣr-* **skur-* (cf. SCORE, SHARD, SHARE, SHORE[1]). Hence **shea·rLING**[1] sheep that has been shorn once XIV. **shea·rWA:TER** bird of the genus Puffinus. XVII. **shears** ʃiəɹz pl. (rarely sg.) scissors, now only of a large kind. OE. (i) *sćērero* pl. :- **skǣrizō*, (ii) *sćēara*, pl. of *scēar* fem., corr. to MLG. *schēre*, MDu. *scāre*, *scēre* (Du. *schaer*), OHG. *skār*, pl. *skāri* (whence MHG. *schære*, G. *schere*), ON. *skǽri* n.pl.; f. **skǣr-*. (naut.) pl. (also sp. *sheers*; cf. SHEER-HULK) device on ships for manipulating heavy gear XVII.

sheat-fish ʃī·tfiʃ freshwater fish Silurus glanis. XVI. Earlier *sheath-fish*, prob. f. SHEATH+FISH, after G. *scheid(en)*.

sheath ʃīþ case for a blade. OE. *sćǣþ*, *sćeaþ* = OS. *skēðia* (Du. *scheede*, *schee*), OHG. *sceida* (G. *scheide*), ON. *skeiðir* pl. scabbard :- CGerm. (exc. Goth.) **skaiþiz*, **skaiþjō*, prob. f. **skaiþ-* divide (see SHED[1]), as if orig. 'splitting husk' or 'split stick'; cf. SHIDE and rel. OSw. *skiþa* (Sw. *skida* sheath), ON. *skíða* billet of wood, faggot. Hence **sheathe** ʃīð. XIV.

sheave ʃīv pulley. XIV. repr. OE. **sćife*, rel. to **sćife* (dial. SHIVE) = OFris. *skīve*, OS. *scība*, (M)LG, MDu. *schīve* (Du. *schijf*), OHG. *scība* (G. *scheibe*), f. base meaning variously disc, quoit, wheel, pulley, pane of glass, slice of bread.

shebeen ʃibī·n illicit public house XVIII. Anglo-Ir. *síbín*, *séibín*, f. *séibe* liquid measure, mug + *-in* -EEN[2].

shed[1] ʃed pt., pp. **shed** †separate, divide OE.; (dial.) spill, let fall, pour, send forth as an emanation XII; give forth, diffuse XIV; cast off XVI. OE. *sć(e)ādan*, pt. *sć(e)ād*, *sć(e)ādde*, *sć(e)ādade*, pp. *sć(e)āden*, *ġesćeādad*, corr. directly or with cons.-variation to OFris. *skēda*, *skētha* wk., OS. *skēdan*, *skēthan* (Du. *scheiden*, *scheidde*, *geschieden*), OHG. *sceidan*, *sciad*, *gesceidan* (G. *scheiden*, *schied*, *geschieden*), Goth. *skaidan*, *skaidans* :- CGerm. (exc. ON.) **skaiðan*, **skaiþan* (cf. SHEATH, SHIDE). Beside orig. OE. *sć(e)ādan*, repr. by early ME. *shode*, a var. with falling diphthong *sćēadan* arose, from which the present *shed* descends (with shortening as in *bread*, *dead*). The OE. vb. retained its str. conjugation in WS., but is found only wk. in Nhb.; str. forms persisted to some extent in ME., but wk. forms *schedde*, *sched*, with vars. *schadde*, *schad*, finally prevailed.

shed[2] ʃed †separation OE. (dial.) parting of the hair XIV; ridge of ground dividing valleys (cf. WATERSHED) XVI; spacing between the threads of the warp XVIII. OE. *(ġe)sćēad*, alt. of *(ġe)sćēad* f. base of SHED[1]; cf. OHG. *sceitil* division, G. *scheitel* parting of hair.

shed[3] ʃed slight structure for shelter. XV (*shadde*, Caxton). prob. specialized use of *shad(de)*, *shed(de)* (*ssed(e* Ayenb.), by-forms of SHADE, which itself survives dial. in this sense.

sheen ʃīn (poet.) beautiful, bright, resplendent. OE. *sćēne*, WS. *sćiene* = OFris. *skēne*, OS., OHG. *scōni* (Du. *schoon*, G. *schön*), Goth. *skauns* :- CGerm. (exc. ON.) **skauniz*, **skaunjaz*, f. **skau-* behold (see SHOW). Hence **sheen** sb. brightness. XVII (Sh.); apprehended as abstr. noun of SHINE; whence **shee·nY**[1]. XVII (Milton).

Sheeny ʃī·ni (sl.) Jew. XIX. Of unkn. origin.

sheep ʃīp animal of the genus Ovis. OE. (Anglian) *sćēp*, (WS) *sćǣp*, *sćēap* =OFris. *skēp*, OS. *scāp* (Du. *schaap*), OHG. *scāf* (G. *schaf*) :- WGerm. **skǣpa*, of which no cogns. are known (the ON. word was *fǣr*, the Gothic *lamb*; cf. EWE). In OE. nom. and acc. sg. and pl. became identical through the normal loss of *-u* of the prehistoric pl. **scǣpu*. Hence **shee·pISH**[1]. XII.

sheer[1] ʃiəɹ †bright, shining; (of fabrics) thin, fine; unmixed, unqualified XVI; rising perpendicularly without a break XVIII. prob. alt. of (dial.) *shire* clear, pure, mere, thin, weak, OE. *sćīr* = OFris. *skire*, OS. *skīr(i)*, ON. *skírr*, Goth. *skeirs* :- Germ. **skīraz*, **skīrjaz*, f. **skī-* SHINE. There is no proof of continuity with ME. *schere* (XIII–XIV) free, clear, fine, which was prob. – ON. *skǣrr* (:- **skairjaz*) with change of sk to ʃ; cf. SHEER THURSDAY.

sheer[2] ʃiəɹ (of a ship) turn aside. XVII (Capt. Smith). perh. – (M)LG., (M)HG. *scheren*; identical with SHEAR.

sheer[3] ʃiəɹ (naut.) curve of a ship. XVII. prob. f. SHEAR; cf. synon. F. *tonture* 'shearing' (XVII).

sheer hulk ʃiəɹhʌ·lk hulk of a disused ship fitted with hoisting shears. XVIII. f. *sheers*, SHEARS device for raising masts, etc., the form of which suggests a pair of shears+HULK. ¶ In Dibdin's song 'Tom Bowling', usu. misapprehended as 'mere hulk'.

Sheer Thursday ʃiəɹ þɔ̄·ɹzdi (hist.) Maundy Thursday. XII (*Shereðursdei*). ME. *shere-*, *shire*, corr. to ON. *skǽrr*, *skírr* (cf. SHEER[1]), which were used in the same way and were adopted XII–XIII with sk-.

sheet[1] ʃīt broad piece of linen (etc.) covering OE. (as an article of bedding XIII); piece of paper or parchment for writing or printing on; broad expanse XVI. OE. (Anglian) *sćēte*, (WS.) *sciete* :- **skautjōn*, f. **skaut-* **skeut-* **skut-* (see SHOOT, SHOT), one meaning of which is 'project'. The unmutated stem is repr. by OE. *sćēat* corner, region, lap, bosom, skirt, cloth = OFris. *skāt* skirt, MLG. *schōt*, (M)Du. *schoot* lap, sail-rope, OHG. *scōʒ* (G. *schoss*) skirt, lappet, lap, ON. *skaut* corner, quarter, skirt, bosom, sail-rope, Goth. *skauts* hem of garment, and the forms s.v. SHEET[2].

sheet[2] ʃīt rope attached to lower (leeward) corner of a sail)(*tack.* XIV. repr. OE. *scēata* 'pes veli', but used for *scēatline* (see LINE[2]) = MLG. *schōtlīne* (cf. ON. *skautreip*), prob. after ON. *skaut* or MLG., MDu. *schōte*, both in this sense; phr. *three s—s in the wind*, drunk. (OE. *scēata* corr. to (M)LG. *schōte*, OHG. *scoȝa* skirt, ON. *skauti* kerchief; cf. SHEET[1].)

sheet-anchor ʃī·tæːŋkəɹ largest of ship's anchors. XV (*shute anker*), XVII (*sheet a.*). The earliest forms point to deriv. from †*shoot* sheet of a sail (XV to XVII) – (M)LG. *schōte*, (M)Du. *schoot* (see SHEET[1] and [2]); the connexion in sense is not obvious, but the corr. seems to be confirmed by the substitution of SHEET[2] in XVII.

sheikh ʃeik Arab chief. XVI. ult. – Arab. *šaikh* (prop.) old man, f. *šākha* be or grow old; cf. F. *cheik, scheik*, †*seic*, Sp. *jeque.*

shekel ʃe·k(ə)l Semitic unit of weight, chief silver coin of the Hebrews. XVI (Geneva Bible). – Heb. *šeqel*, f. *šāqal* weigh; repr. earlier in Eng. by †*sicle* (XIII to XVIII) – OF. *sicle* – late L. *siclus* – Gr. *síklos, síglos* – Heb.

shekinah ʃikai·nə manifestation of the Divine Majesty 'between the cherubims' (Exod. XXV 22, etc.). XVII. – late Heb. *šekīnāh*, f. *šākan* rest, dwell.

sheldrake ʃe·ldreik bird of the genus Tadorna. XIV. prob. f. (dial.) *sheld* particoloured, pied, rel. to MDu. *schillede* variegated, f. *schillen* (modDu. *verschillen* differ) diversify+DRAKE[2].

shelf[1] ʃelf horizontal slab of wood, etc. to hold objects XIV (Ch.); ledge or terrace of land XIX (*shelfy* XVIII). – (M)LG. *schelf* shelf, set of shelves, with accommodation to Eng. words in *sh.*, more normally repr. by (dial.) *skelf* (XIV); rel. to OE. *sċylfe* partition, compartment, *sċylf* (also *stānsċylf*) rugged rock, crag, pinnacle; cf. Germ. **skelf-* split. Hence **shelve** vb. †project like a shelf; provide with shelves. XVI.

shelf[2] ʃelf sandbank in the sea or a river. XVI. prob. alt., by assoc. with prec., of synon. †*shelp* (XV), repr. OE. *sċylp* 'scopulus, murex', of unkn. origin.

shell ʃel hard outer covering of an animal, fruit, etc.; scale or scale-like object OE.; hollow or concave object XVI; exterior cover or case (spec. one containing powder and shot) XVII. OE. (Anglian) *sċell*, (WS.) *sċiell* = (M)LG., MDu. *schelle, schille*, Du. *schel, schil* pod, rind, scale, shell, ON. *skel* seashell, Goth. *skalja* tile :– Germ. (not in HG.) **skaljō*, f. **skal-* (cf. SCALE[1] and [2], SHALE). Hence vb. XVI repl. (dial.) *shale* (XIV), *sheel, shel* (XV), which are based on OE. *sċ(e)alu* shell, husk.

shellac ʃelæ·k lac melted into thin plates for use as varnish. XVIII. f. SHELL sb.+LAC[1].

Shelta ʃe·ltə cryptic language of Irish tinkers, gipsies, etc., known also among them as *sheldrū, shelter.* XIX. Of unkn. origin.

shelter ʃe·ltəɹ (structure affording) protection from the elements. XVI. poss. alt. of †*sheltron* phalanx :– OE. *sċieldtruma*, f. *sċield* SHIELD+*truma* troop. Hence vb. XVI (Spenser, Sh.).

shelve ʃelv †tilt XVI; slope gradually XVII. perh. back-formation from *shelvy* having sandbanks (XVI, Sh.), f. SHELF[2]+-Y[1].

shemozzle ʃėmɔ·zl (orig. East End sl.). muddle, quarrel, mêlée. XIX. Also *shlemozzle*; of Yiddish origin, and based on late Heb. *šellō'mazzāl*, i.e. *šel* of *lō'* not *mazzāl* planet, planetary influence, luck.

shent ʃent (arch.) disgraced, ruined. ME. *schent* (XIII) :– OE. *ġesċend*, pp. of *sċendan* put to shame or reproach, ruin, discomfit = OLG. *scendian* (Du. *schenden*), OHG. *scentan* (G. *schänden*) :– WGerm. **skandjan*, f. **skand-* ashamed :– **skamðа-*, pp. formation on **skam-* SHAME.

shepherd ʃe·pəɹd tender of sheep. Late OE. *sċēaphierde*; see SHEEP, HERD[2], and cf. MLG., MDu. *schāphirde*, etc. Hence vb. XVIII, **she·pherd**ESS[1]. XIV.

Sheraton ʃe·rətən name of Thomas *Sheraton* (1751–1806), furniture-maker and designer, applied to his products XIX.

sherbet ʃɔ̄·ɹbət Oriental drink XVII; preparation in powder form for making an effervescing drink XIX. – Turk., Pers. *šerbet* – Arab. *šarāb*, f. *šariba* vb. drink (cf. SHRUB[2], SYRUP).

sherd ʃɔ̄ɹd see SHARD.

sherif, shereef ʃərī·f descendant of Mohammed through his daughter Fatima; sovereign ruler of certain states. XVI. – Arab. *šarīf* noble, glorious, f. *sharafa* be exalted.

sheriff ʃe·rif representative of the royal authority in a shire or county. OE. *sċīrġerēfa*, f. *sċīr* SHIRE+*ġerēfa* REEVE. Several types of form appear in ME. and later periods; the main stress falling orig. on the first etymol. el., considerable modification took place in the second, whence *schir(r)eve, schir(r)ef* (by loss of final *e* and consequent unvoicing of *v*), *shirrif*, Sc. *schirray*; there was also a type *scher(r)eve*, whence *schreve, shrieve* (surviving in SHRIEVALTY), *schrief*, which resulted from the shift of the main stress to the second el.; the present form, *sheriff*, combines the initial stress of the first type with the vowel *e* of the second. The etymol. analytic *shire-reeve* has been used by some antiquaries since XVI. Hence **she·riffalty** XVI; see SHRIEVALTY.

sherry ʃe·ri still white wine of a type orig. made near Xerez (now Jerez), a town in Andalusia, Spain, XVI. alt. of *sherris* (XVI), apprehended as a pl. or derived from *sherris sack* (see SACK[2]), i.e. *Sherries*, repr. old pronunc. of *Xerez.*

sherryvallies ʃe·rivæliz (U.S.) trousers worn (e.g. by teamsters) over others. XVIII. prob. immed. – Pol. *szarawary* (General C. Lee, the first recorded user of the word, having been aide-de-camp to the king of Poland), corr. to Russ. *sharovárȳ*, Gr. *sarábāra* (loose Persian trousers), late and medL. *sarabara*, *saraballa*, etc. – Arab. *šarwāl*, Syriac *šarbâlâ*, prob. – Pers. *šalwār*.

sheva ʃəvā· (in Heb. gram.) sign under a consonant letter to indicate the (supposed) absence of a vowel XVI; (philol.) the vowel ə XIX. – Rabbinic Heb. *šᵉvā*, app. arbitrary alt. of *šaw'* emptiness, vanity. Cf. G. *schwa*.

shew see SHOW.

shewbread ʃou·bred twelve loaves placed every Sabbath 'before the Lord' in the Jewish temple. XVI (Tindale). f. *shew*, var. of SHOW vb. + BREAD, after G. *schaubrot* (Luther), repr. Heb. *léχem pānim* 'bread of presence' (LXX ἄρτοι ἐνώπιοι, NT. ἄρτοι τῆς προθέσεως, Vulg. *panes propositionis*.)

shibboleth ʃi·bəleþ Heb. word used by Jephthah as a test word to distinguish the fleeing Ephraimites, who could not pronounce sh (ʃ), from his own men, the Gileadites (Judges xii 4–6) XIV (Wycl. Bible); (gen.) word used as a test for detecting foreigners; catchword adopted by a party XVII. – Heb. *šibbōleth* stream. Cf. F., G. *schibboleth*.

shicer ʃai·səɹ (sl.) worthless person; (Austral.) unproductive mine. XIX. – G. *scheisser* 'cacator', agent-noun of *scheissen* SHIT. Cf. SHYSTER.

shide ʃaid (dial.) block of wood, board, plank. OE. *sćīd* = OFris. *skīd*, OHG. *scīt* (G. *scheit*), ON. *skíð* (cf. SKI) :– Germ. **skīðam*, f. **skīð-* divide; see SHEATH, SHED[1].

shiel ʃīl (Sc. and north. dial.) shed, shanty, hut. XIII. ME. *shāle*, *shēle*, of unkn. origin. Hence **shie·l**ING[1] piece of pasture for cattle; rough hut. XVI.

shield ʃīld article of defensive armour; (fig.) protection, OE. *sćeld*, *sćield* = OFris. *skeld*, OS., OHG. *scild* (Du., G. *schild*), ON. *skjǫldr*, Goth. *skildus* – CGerm. **skelduz*, prob. orig. 'board' and so f. base **skel-* divide, separate (cf. SCALE[1]). Hence vb. OE. *sćeldan*, *sćildan*.

shift ʃift A. †arrange OE.; B. change XIII; C. alter the position of XIV. OE. *sćiftan* = OFris. *skifta*, MLG. *schiften*, *schichten*, MHG. *schihten* (G. *schichten*), ON. *skipta* divide, separate, change, f. base **skip-* as in ON. *skipa* arrange, assign. Hence **shift** sb. A. expedient, contrivance, evasion; B. †change; (spec.) of clothing; (esp.) woman's chemise XVI; C. change of position, removal XVIII. Hence **shi·ft**Y[1]. XVI.

Shiite ʃai·ait member of the Shiah sect of Mohammedans. XVIII. f. *Shiah* (XVII) – Arab. *šīᶜaʰ* sect, f. *šāᶜa* follow; see -ITE.

shikar ʃikā·ɹ hunting, sport. XVII. – Urdu – Pers. *šikār*.

shillelagh ʃilei·li Irish cudgel. XVIII. f. name of a barony and village in County Wicklow, Ireland, known for its oaks.

shilling ʃi·liŋ money of account equiv. to 12 pence or 1/20 of a pound. OE. *sćilling* = OFris., OS., OHG. *scilling* (MDu., Du. *schelling*, G. *schilling*), ON. *skillingr*, Goth. *skilliggs* :– CGerm. **skillingaz*, of much disputed origin; adopted, in OSl. as *skŭlęzĭ*, OF., Pr., Sp. *escalin*, It. *scellino*, modF. *schelling*.

shilly-shally ʃi·liʃæli phr. *stand* or *go shill I*, *shall I* vacillate, be irresolute XVII; adj. vacillating; sb. vacillation XVIII. f. *shall I*, with variation of vowel, for which cf. DILLY-DALLY, WISHY-WASHY.

shimmer ʃi·məɹ shine with tremulous light. Late OE. *sćymrian*, **sćimerian* = (M)LG., (M)Du. *schēmeren* be shaded or shadowy, glimmer, glitter, G. *schimmern*, iterative (see -ER[4]) f. Germ. **skim-*, extension of **skī-* SHINE[1]; obs. in XVII. Revived by Scott, 'Lay of the Last Minstrel' I xvii (1805); hence sb. (Scott, 1821).

shin ʃin front part of the leg between knee and ankle. OE. *sćinu* = (M)LG., MDu. *schēne* (Du. *scheen*), OHG. *scina*, shin, needle (G. *schiene* thin plate); the basic meaning is prob. 'thin or narrow piece'. OE. *sćia* shin, MHG. *schie* hedge stake.

shindy ʃi·ndi shinty; spree; commotion. XIX. unexpl. alt. of *shinty* (i) game resembling hockey (XVIII), (ii) row, commotion (XIX), later var. of *shinny* (XVII), an earlier name of the game. *Shinny* (XVII) and *shinty* (XVIII) appear to be derived from cries used in the game, *shin ye*, *shin you*, and *shin t'ye* 'shin to you'; other dial. names are *shinnins*, *shinnack*, *shinnup*.

shine[1] ʃain pt., pp. **shone** ʃɔn shed beams of bright light. OE. *sćīnan*, pt. *sćān*, pp. **sćinen* (rare ME. *sinen*) = OFris. *skīna*, OS. *skīnan*, OHG. *scīnan* (Du. *schijnen*, G. *scheinen*), ON. *skína*, Goth. *skeinan* :– CGerm. **skīnan*, f. **skī-* with present-stem formative *-n-* carried through into the pt. and pp. (for cogns. see SHEER[1], SHIMMER). Hence sb. XVI (Skelton); whence (unless f. the vb.) **shi·n**Y[1]. XVI (Spenser, Sh.).

shine[2] ʃain (dial.) convivial party; (colloq.) row, disturbance. XIX. perh. uses of prec. sb., but the senses are notably like those of SHINDY.

shingle[1] ʃi·ŋgl piece of wood used as a house tile. XII. ME. *scincle*, *scingle*, *singel* (whence AL. *cingula* XIV, *shingula* XV), repr., with unexpl. modification, L. *scindula*, later form of *scandula* after Gr. *skhídax*, *skhindalmós*. Hence vb. roof with shingles XVI; (orig. U.S.) cut (the hair) so as to produce the effect of overlapping tiles XIX.

shingle[2] ʃi·ŋgl (beach covered with) small roundish stones. XVI. Of obscure origin and history; forms poss. identifiable with this word appear in place names from Domesday Book onwards, viz. *sincle*, *single*, later with initial *ch*, e.g. *chingel*, esp. in Sc., as *chyngil(l)*, from XV; the relation, if any, with Norw. *singl* coarse sand, small stones, NFris. *singel* gravel, is not determinable.

shingle[3] ʃi·ŋgl subject (puddled iron) to blows and pressure. XVII. – F. *cingler* – G. *zängeln*, f. *zange* TONGS.

shingles ʃi·ŋglz eruptive disease often extending round the middle of the body. XIV (Trevisa). Late ME. *schingles*, *cingules*, *sengles* – medL. use of L. *cingulus*, var. of *cingulum* girdle (f. *cingere* gird; cf. CINCTURE), rendering Gr. *ζώνη* (ZONE), *ζωστήρ* girdle, in this sense.

Shinto ʃi·ntou native religion of Japan. XVIII. – Jap. *shinto* – Chinese *shin tao* way of the gods.

shinty ʃi·nti see SHINDY.

ship ʃip large sea-going vessel. OE. *sćip* = OFris., OS. *skip* (Du. *schip*, *scheep-*, in comb. *scheeps-*), OHG. *skif* (G. *schiff*), ON., Goth *skip* :- CGerm. **skipam*, of unkn. origin; for its adoption in Rom. langs. cf. SKIFF. So **ship** vb. late OE. *sćipian*, corr. to (M)Du. *schēpen*, (M)HG. *schiffen*, ON. *skipa*. Hence **shi·p**MAN (arch.) seaman, sailor, OE. *sćipman*, with Germ. cogns. **shi·p**MENT. XIX. **shi·p**MONEY (hist.) impost for providing ships for the navy. XVII. **shipp**ER[1] ʃi·pəɹ †seaman. late OE. *sćipere*, f. *sćipian*; one who ships goods XVIII. Cf. SKIPPER. **shippound** ʃi·ppaund unit of weight (20 lispounds) used in the Baltic trade. XVI. – MLG. *schippunt*, MDu. *schippond*; see POUND[1]. **ship-shape** ʃi·p-ʃeip trim, orderly. XVIII. orig. †*ship shapen* (XVII) 'arranged in ship fashion', i.e. SHIP sb., and pp. of SHAPE, alt. to *ship shape* and interpreted as 'in the fashion of a ship'. **shi·p**WRECK what is cast up from a wreck XI; destruction or loss of a ship XV. Superseded †*shipbreche* (OE. *sćipbryće*), f. BREACH.

-ship ʃip suffix denoting state or condition: (1) added to adjs. and pps.; of the numerous OE. exx., only HARDSHIP and WORSHIP survive; (2) added to sbs. to denote the state or condition of being what is expressed by the sb., the qualities or character associated with, the power implied by, and spec. the position or dignity designated by the sb., as in OE. *frēondsćipe* FRIENDSHIP, *hlāfordsćipe* LORDSHIP, similarly in *authorship*, *craftsmanship*, *fellowship*, *headship*, *horsemanship*, *kingship*, *stewardship*, *suretyship*, *workmanship*. In *ladyship*, *lordship*, *worship*, like comps. of -NESS, used with poss. adjs. *his*, *her*, *their*, *your* to denote personages bearing the title. In *fellowship*, *scholarship*, *sizarship*, etc. there is transf. application to the emoluments attached to the status. In early mod. Eng. it is added to a sb. to denote a state of life relating to what is denoted by the sb.; *courtship* (Sh.) is the chief instance. TOWNSHIP is the one survival of a group of OE. sbs. with collect. sense.

shire ʃaiəɹ †official charge; †district under a governor, bishop's see, etc.; administrative district later called *county* OE. (hence terminal element in names of counties XII). OE. *sćir* = OHG. *sćira* (in two glosses) care, official charge, poss. :- **skizō* :- **skeisā*, rel. to OItalic **koisā*, repr. by L. *cūra* care, charge, CURE[1].

shirk ʃɜ̄ɹk †practise fraud or trickery; (dial.) slink, sneak away XVII; evade (duty, etc.) XVIII. rel. to †*shirk* sb., perh. – G. *schurke* (cf. SHARK).

shirt ʃɜ̄ɹt undergarment for the trunk. OE. *sćyrte* (once, as an obscure gloss on 'prætexta'), corr. formally to (M)LG. *schört(e)*, *schorte*, MDu. *schorte* (Du. *schort*), G. *schürze* apron, ON. *skyrta* shirt (whence SKIRT), based on Germ. **skurt-* SHORT. Hence **shi·rty**[1] (sl.) out of temper XIX; f. phr. *get* (a person's) *shirt* (*out*), cause him to lose his temper.

shit ʃit void excrement. XVII. Superseding (dial.) *shite*, OE. *sćītan*, pp. *-sćiten* = MLG. *schīten* (Du. *schijten*), OHG. *skīzan* (G. *scheissen*), ON. *skīta*; f. Germ. **skit-* **skīt-* (whence OE. *sćitol* purgative, *sćitte* diarrhœa). Short ĭ was generalized from the pp. **shi·tt**EN[6] XIV (Ch.). prob. based on IE. **skheid-* split, divide (see SCHISM and cf. the etymol. sense of *excrement*). Hence sb. XVI.

shittah ʃi·ta species of acacia. XVII (A.V.). – Heb. *shiṭṭāh* (*ṭṭ* :- *nṭ*; cf. Arab. *sanṭ*, Egyptian *sont* acacia). So **shittim** ʃi·tim acacia wood. XIV (Wycl. Bible). The earliest forms, *sechym*, *cetyne*, *sethim*, are based on Vulg. *setim* – Heb. *shiṭṭīm*, pl. of *shiṭṭāh*.

shive ʃaiv (dial.) slice XIII (AncrR.); thin bung or cork XIX. ME. *schive*, prob. – MLG., MDu. *schīve*, with assim. to Eng. phonetic conditions (see SH-); cf. SHEAVE.

shiver[1] ʃi·vəɹ fragment, chip. XIII (Laȝ.). Early ME. *scifre*, *scivre*, corr. to OHG. *scivaro* splinter (G. *schiefer* slate, for *schieferstein*), f. Germ. **skĭf-* split, whence also SHEAVE, SHIVE. So **shiver** vb. XII (in †*to-shiver*); cf. MDu. *scheveren*, MHG. *schiveren* (G. *schiefern*).

shiver[2] ʃi·vəɹ tremble as with cold or fear. XIII. Early ME. *chivere*, superseded by *shiver* XV, prob. by assoc. with *shake* (cf. *chivere and schake* XIV); perh. orig. referring to chattering of the teeth (cf. *chevere with the chin* XV) and so an alt. by substitution of -ER[4] of ME. *chavele*, *chefle* wag the jaws, chatter, and *chevele*, *chivele* shiver (PPl.), f. OE. *ćeafl* jaw, JOWL.

shoal[1] ʃoul shallow. XVI. alt. of late ME. *schoold*, *schold*, Sc. *schald* (XIV), repr. OE. *sć(e)ald* (only in local names, *æt scealdan* *fleote, on scealdan ford, æt scealdeburnan* Shalfleet, Shalford, Shalbourne) :– **skaldaz*, rel. to SHALLOW. Hence **shoal** sb. shallow place, sandbank XVI; succeeding to late ME. *schald, sholde*, earlier *shelde*.

shoal[2] ʃoul large number of fish, etc., swimming together. late XVI. prob. – MLG., MDu. *schōle* (adopted earlier as SCHOOL[2]), with Eng. sound-substitution (ʃ for Du. sχ).

shock[1] ʃɔk pile of sheaves of grain. ME. XIV, but implied earlier in AL. *socca* (XII), *scoka* (XIII), either repr. OE. **sć(e)oc* or – (M)LG., (M)Du. *schok* shock of corn, group of 60 units (with assim. of sχ to ʃ), in OS. *scok* = MHG. *schoc(h)* heap, also (as in G. *schock*) sixty; of unkn. origin. Hence vb. (in AL. *soccāre* XIV), with agent-noun in OE. g. pl. *sćocere, s(h)oker* (XII–XIII).

shock[2] ʃɔk encounter of armed forces XVI; violent concussion XVII; sudden and disturbing impression on body or mind XVIII. In early use also †*cho(c)k*, †*choque* – F. *choc*, f. (O)F. *choquer* (whence **shock** vb. XVI) = Sp. *chocar*, of unkn. origin. The ppl. adj. **sho·ck**ING[2] (XVIII) appears first in the forms *chocquing, choqueing*, preceded by *choquant* (XVII), the F. prp.

shock[3] ʃɔk thick mass (of hair). XIX. prob. for *shock head*, in which *shock* is adj. (XVII) rough and thick, based on †*shock*, †*shock-dog* poodle (XVII), presumably var. of †*shough* (XVI, Nashe, Sh.), of unkn. origin.

shoddy ʃɔ·di woollen yarn obtained by tearing up refuse rags; cloth made of this, which does not show its origin. XIX. Of dial. but obscure origin. Hence as adj. counterfeit and trashy.

shoe ʃū outer covering for the foot OE.; horseshoe XIV; various transf. senses from XV. OE. *sćō(h)* = OFris. *scōh*, OS. *scōh* (Du. *schoen*), OHG. *scuoh* (G. *schuh*), ON. *skór*, Goth. *skōhs* :– Germ. **skōχaz* or **skōχwaz*, with no known cogns. OE. pl. *sć(e)ōs* is normally repr. by mod. *shoes*; a wk.-inflected pl. appeared XIII and is widespread in dial. *shoon*. Hence **shoe** vb. pt., pp. **shod** ʃɔd OE. *sćōg(e)an* = MLG. *schoi(g)en* (Du. *schoeien*), OHG. *scuohōn* (G. *schuhen*), ON. *skúa*; the doubling of *d* in pt. and pp. (XIV) with consequent shortening of vowel is anticipated in late OE. *unsceōddum fōtum* with unshod feet, and is paralleled in *fled*, pt. and pp. of FLEE.

shoful ʃou·fəl counterfeit money; hansom cab (as an infringement of Hansom's patent) XIX. – Yiddish *schofel* worthless stuff, rubbish, sb. use of adj. 'base, mean', repr. German-Jewish pronunc. of Heb. *šāphāl*.

shog ʃɔg (chiefly dial.) shake, roll (Wyclif); jog along, go steadily on XIV. Late ME. *s(c)hogge*, parallel to contemp. *schokke* move swiftly, MLG., MHG. *schocken* swing, sway; cf. JOG.

shogun ʃou·gun hereditary commander-in-chief of the Japanese army. XVII. – Jap. *shōgun*, for *sei-i-tai shōgun* 'barbarian-subduing great general' (*shōgun* being sound-substitution for Chinese *chiang chiin* 'lead army').

shoo ʃū excl. to drive away birds, etc. XV (*schowe, ssou*, Cath. Angl.). Of instinctive origin; cf. LG. *schu*, (M)HG. *schū*, F. *shou*, It. *scio*. Hence vb.

shoot ʃūt pt., pp. **shot** ʃɔt go swiftly and suddenly; send forth (spec. missiles); wound or kill with a shot. OE. *sćēotan*, pt. *sćēat, sćuton*, pp. *sćoten* (cf. SHOTTEN) = OFris. *skiata*, OS. *skietan*, OHG. *sciozzan* (Du. *schieten*, G. *schiessen*), ON. *skjóta* :– CGerm. (exc. Goth.) str. vb. **skeutan*, f. **skeut-* **skaut-* **skut-*, whence also OE. *sćēat, sćiete* SHEET[1] and [2], *sćot* SHOT, *sćotian* shoot with arrows, *sćyttan* SHUT. Hence sb. (XVI); sloping channel or conduit (cf. SHUTE) XIX. ¶ The phonetic development of *shoot* is as in CHOOSE.

shop ʃɔp building where goods are sold XIII (in AL. *schopa* XI); building set apart for work (XV). Aphetic – AN., OF. *eschoppe* (mod. *échoppe*) lean-to booth, cobbler's stall – MLG. *schoppe*, corr. to OE. *sć(e)oppa* (once, rendering Vulg. 'gazophylacium'), OHG. *scopf* porch, vestibule (G. *schopf* porch, lean-to, cartshed, barn), rel. to OE. *sćypen* (dial. *shippen, -on*) cow-shed, MLG. *schoppen, schuppen* (whence G. *schuppen*) shed.

shore[1] ʃɔ̄əɹ land bordering on a piece of water. XIV. – (with assim. to Eng. phonetics as in foll.) MLG., MDu. *schōre*, perh. f. the base of SHEAR.

shore[2] ʃɔ̄əɹ oblique support for the side of a building. XV. – (with LDu. sχ assim. to ʃ) MLG., MDu. *schōre* (Du. *schoor*) prop, stay. So **shore** vb. prop *up*. XIV. – (M)LG., (M)Du. *schōren*.

shore[3] ʃɔ̄əɹ sewer. XVI. orig. in *common shore*, perh. an application of this phr. (SHORE[1]) in the sense 'no-man's-land at the water-side, where filth was deposited for the tide to wash away'. ¶ Not a var. of SEWER[1] (*common sewer* is later).

short ʃɔ̄ɹt)(*long* OE.; not reaching a certain standard XIV; friable, brittle XV. OE. *sćeort* = OHG. *scurz* :– Germ. **skurtaz* (compar. **skurtizon*, OE. *sćyrtra*); cf. SHIRT, SKIRT. Hence **sho·rt**AGE (orig. U.S.) XIX. **sho·rtco:ming** (censured by De Quincey, 1847, as a Scotticism) XVII; f. phr. *come s.* **sho·rt**EN[5] XVI (More, Palsgr., Coverdale); superseding †*short* vb. (OE. to XVI). **sho·rt**HAND XVII; repl. somewhat earlier †*short-writing*, tr. BRACHYGRAPHY. ¶ For *cold-, hot-, red-short* see COLD-SHORT.

shot ʃɔt act of shooting; that which is shot; payment, share (cf. SCOT) OE. OE. *sć(e)ot*, *ġesć(e)ot* = OFris. *skot*, OS. *sil|scot* 'balista', MLG. *(ge)scot*, OHG. *scoz* and *giscoz* (G.

schoss, geschoss), ON. *skot* :– Germ. **skutaz*, **gaskut*, f. **skut-* **skeut-* SHOOT.

shotten ʃɔ·tn pp. of SHOOT, surviving in (arch.) *s. herring* herring that has spawned (fig. in Sh. '1 Hen. IV' II. iv. 143); see -EN[6].

shoulder ʃou·ldəɹ part of the body at which arm, fore-leg, or wing is attached. OE. *sćuldor* (pl. in *-u*, perh. repr. a dual), corr. to OFris. *skuldere*, MLG. *schuldere* (whence Scand. forms), (M)Du. *schouder*, OHG. *sculter(r)a* (G. *schulter*) :– WGerm. **skuldr-*, of unkn. origin (perh. for **skurdr-*; cf. OHG. *scarti* shoulder-blade); a mutated form is seen in OE. (pl.) *ġesćyldru* = OS. *sculdir*, OHG. *scultirra*. Hence vb. push with the shoulder(s) XIII; support with the shoulder(s) XVI. ¶ For the same conditions cf. COULTER, POULTICE, MOULD, POULTRY.

shout ʃaut loud cry; vb. utter this. XIV. Late ME. *schoute*, poss. repr. a deriv. of **skūt-* **skut-* **skeut-* send forth forcibly, SHOOT; cf. ON. *skúta, skúti* SCOUT[3].

shove ʃʌv pt., pp. **shoved** ʃʌvd thrust, push. OE. *sćūfan*, pt. *sćēaf*, *sćufon*, pp. *sćofen* = OFris. *skūva*, MLG., MDu. *schūven* (Du. *schuiven*), OHG. *sciuban* (G. *schieben*), Goth. *af|skiuban* push away :– CGerm. str. vb. **skeuƀan*, **skauƀ-*, **skuƀ-* (but ON. *skúfa* is wk.). ¶ For the same development of *ū* before *v* cf. DOVE. The str. pt. and pp. began to be repl. by wk. forms in XIV. Cf. SHOVEL.

shovel ʃʌ·vl kind of spade. OE. *sćofl*, corr. to (M)LG. *schuffel*, MDu. *schof(f)el* (Du. *schoffel*) shovel, hoe; with rel. forms showing a long vowel, as in OHG. *scūvala* (G. *schaufel*); f. Germ. **skŭf-* *skŭƀ-* SHOVE; see -EL[1].

show, shew ʃou pt. **showed** ʃoud, pp. **shown** ʃoun †look at, examine OE. – XIV; cause to be seen, point out, exhibit; make known, explain XII (Orm); be seen, appear XIII. OE. *sćēawian* = OFris. *skawia, skowia, schoia*, OS. *skawon* (Du. *schouwen*), OHG. *scouwōn* (G. *schauen*) :– WGerm. wk. vb. **skauwōjan*, f. **skau-* see, look (whence also Goth. *skauns*, etc. beautiful; see SHEEN) :– IE. **sqou-*, repr. in Gr. *thuo|skó(ϝ)os* priest, lit. 'one who attends to sacrifices', a form without initial *s-* being repr. by Skr. *kavís* sage, poet, Gr. *koeîn* observe, L. *cavēre* (see CAVEAT). Hence **show** sb. XIII (Cursor M.); whence **show**Y[1] ʃou·i making a good display, effective XVIII (Addison); superseding †*show*ISH[1] (XVII; freq. in XVIII). ¶ The reversal of meaning from 'see' to 'cause to be seen', found in 'Ormulum', is unexpl., all the continental Germ. langs. retaining the orig. sense. The str. pp. *shown* is attested in 'Ormulum' (*shawenn*); the wk. *showed, shewed* continued till XIX. The sp. *shew, shewn*, repr. orig. a falling diphthong (*sćēaw-*), as against *show*, which repr. a rising diphthong (*sćeāw-*), is now of limited currency.

shower ʃauəɹ fall of rain OE.; copious fall (cf. missiles OE.; of tears, etc. XIV); †conflict, attack, pang XIII. OE. *sćūr* = OFris. *skūr* fit of illness, OS. *skūr*, MDu. *schuur* (Du. *schoer*), OHG. *scūr* (G. *schauer*) :– WGerm. **skūra* m., beside **skūrō* fem. (whence ON. *skúr* shower of rain, of missiles, Goth. *skūra* storm). Hence vb. XVI.

shrapnel ʃræ·pnəl shell that bursts scattering bullets. XIX (*S. shell*, 1806). f. name of General Henry *Shrapnel* (1761–1842), who invented this shell during the Peninsular War.

shred ʃred fragment cut or broken off OE.; fragment of textile material, also fig. XIV. OE. **sćrēad* (pl. *sćrēada*), *sćrēade*, corr. to OFris. *skrēd* hair-cutting, clipping of coin, OS. *skrōd*, MLG. *schrōt, schrāt*, cut off piece (Du. *schroot* – G.), OHG. *scrōt* G. *schrot*); f. WGerm. **skraud-* **skreud-* **skrŭd-* cut; see SHROUD and cf. SCREED. So **shred** vb. †pare, trim OE.; cut into small strips or slices XIV. OE. *sćrēadian* = OFris. **skrēda* (whence *skrēdare* clipper of coin). So vb., pt., pp. **shredded, shred.**

shrew[1] ʃrū mammal of the genus Sorex, formerly held to be venomous. OE. *sćrēawa, sćrǣwa* shrewmouse, rel. to OHG. *scrawaz* dwarf, MHG. *schrawaz, schrat, schröuwel* devil, Icel. *skrǫggr* old man, Norw. *skrogg* wolf, *skrugg* dwarf, Sw. dial. *skrugge* devil, *skragga*. Comp. **shrew**·MOUSE. XVI.

shrew[2] ʃrū †malignant man XIII; person (now, woman) given to railing XIV. perh. transf. use of prec., but poss. spec. application of a word meaning 'ill-disposed being'. **shrew**·ISH[1] †wicked XIV; ill-natured, given to scolding XVI ('I was neuer curst: I haue no gift at all in shrewishnesse' Sh.).

shrewd ʃrūd (dial.) wicked XIV (Mannyng); †hurtful, dangerous, grievous, serious XIV (Trevisa); (arch.) severe, hard XV (Caxton); †cunning, artful, (eulogistically) astute, sagacious XVI. ME. *schrewed(e)*, f. SHREW[2] + -ED[2], as in CRABBED, DOGGED, WICKED, WRETCHED; but some of the senses suggest that the formation is a pp. (-ED[1]) of **shrew**[3] vb. curse (cf. BESHREW), quasi 'cursed'.

shriek ʃrīk utter a loud sharp shrill cry. XVI. Also †*shreak*, †*shreik*; parallel to (dial.) *screak* (XV) – ON. *skrǽkja*; other *shr-* forms are (dial.) *shrike* (XII) and *shritch* (XIII), repr. the base of OE. *sćriććettan*. Cf. SCREECH.

shrievalty ʃrī·vəlti office of a sheriff. XVI. f. *shrieve* (XV–XIX), SHERIFF + *-alty*, repr. OF. *-alté* (mod. *-auté*), as in *mayoralty*.

shrift ʃrift (†penance imposed after) auricular confession. OE. *sćrift*, corr. to OFris. *skrift*, (M)Du. *schrift*, OHG. *scrift* (G. *schrift*), ON. *skript, skrift*; f. SHRIVE; see -T[1]. ¶ The meanings 'penance', 'confession' are confined to Eng. and Scand.

and appear to have arisen from a sense of 'prescribed penalty'; the other langs. have only the senses immed. connected with writing.

shrike ʃraik butcher-bird. XVI (Turner). Of obscure origin; phonetically corr. formations are OE. *sċric* thrush, MLG. *schrīk* corncrake, *sól|skríkja* snow-bunting, Sw. *shrika* jay, rel. to vbs. cited under SHRIEK.

shrill ʃril of high-pitched piercing tone. XIV (Ch.). Contemp. with ME. *shrille* vb.: superseding (dial.) *shille* adj. and vb., OE. **sċiell*, *sċyl*, and **sċiellan*, *sċyllan*; cf. LG. *schrell*, G. *schrill*, rel. to OE. *sċralletan*, Du. *schrallen*, Icel. *skrölta*; f. Germ. **skral-*, **skrel-*.

shrimp ʃrimp crustacean of the genus Crangon; puny person. XIV. Obscurely rel. to MLG. *schrempen* contract, wrinkle, *schrimpen* wrinkle the nose, *schrumpen* wrinkle, fold (whence G. *schrumpfen*), MHG. *schrimpf*, *schrimpfen* contract, ON. *skreppa* slip away, and SCRIMP. Cf. CRIMP.

shrine ʃrain †box, chest; repository for a saint's relics OE.; casket for a dead body, tomb XIV (Ch.), temple, church XVII (Milton). OE. *sċrīn* = OFris. *skrīn*, MLG. *schrīn*, MDu. *schrīne* (Du. *schrijn*), OHG. *scrīni* (G. *schrein*), ON. *skrín*; CGerm. (not in Gothic) – L. *scrīnium* case or chest for books or papers (repr. widely in Rom. and Balto-Slavic).

shrink ʃriŋk pt. **shrank** ʃræŋk, pp. **shrunk** ʃrʌŋk, **shru·nken** †wither, cower, huddle OE.; become reduced in size or extent XIII; retreat, recoil XIV; trans. XIV. OE. *sċrincan*, pt. *sċranc*, *sċruncon*, pp. (*ġe*)-*sċruncen*, corr. to Sw. *skrynka* wrinkle (OSw. *skrunkin*, pp. shrivelled, wrinkled), Norw. *skrekka*, *skrøkka*. *Shrunk*, reduced form of *shrunken* pp., is now differentiated from the latter by being applied to the condition of being contracted by immersion or lowering of temperature.

shrive ʃraiv pt. **†shrove** ʃrouv (cf. SHROVETIDE), pp. **shriven** ʃri·vn hear the confession of OE.; pass. (OE.), refl. and intr. (XIII) make one's confession. OE. *sċrīfan*, pt. *sċrāf*, *sċrifon*, pp. (*ġe*)*sċrifen* assign, devise, impose as a sentence or penance, regard, care for = OFris. *skrīva* write, impose penance, OS. *skrīban*, OHG. *scrīban* write, paint, describe, prescribe (Du. *schrijven*, G. *schreiben* write, spell); WGerm. str. vb. (in ON. wk. and with short *i*, *skrifa*) – L. *scrībere* write (cf. SCRIBE).

shrivel ʃri·vl become, cause to become, contracted and wrinkled. XVI. poss. of ON. *origin* (cf. Sw. dial. *skryvla* wrinkle).

shroff ʃrɔf. XVII. Anglo-Indian alt. of the source of SARAF.

shroud ʃraud A. †garment OE.; winding-sheet; veil, screen XVI; B. †place of shelter XIV; (pl.) crypt, vault XVI; C. (pl.) ship's ropes leading from a mast-head XV. OE. *sċrūd*, corr. to ON. *skrúð* and *skrúði* fittings, gear, ornaments, apparel, furniture, textile fabric, f. Germ. **skrūð-* **skreuð-* cut (see SHRED). Hence **shroud** vb. †clothe; cover, screen XIII; repl. †*shride* :– OE. *sċrȳdan* (**skrūðjan*) = ON. *skrýða*.

Shrovetide ʃrou·vtaid the three days preceding Ash Wednesday. XV. Abnormally f. pt. stem *shrōv-* of SHRIVE+TIDE sb. So *Shrove Tuesday* (XV). ¶ The reference is to the practice of going to confession before Lent.

shrub[1] ʃrʌb woody plant smaller than a tree. OE. *sċrubb* and *sċrybb* (both evidenced once prob. in sense 'shrubbery, underwood'). The basic meaning may be 'rough plant or bush' and the foll. appear to be rel. forms: NFris. *skrobb* broom, brushwood, WFlem. *schrobbe* climbing wild pea or vetch, Norw. *skrubba* dwarf cornel, Da. dial. *skrub* brushwood. Cf. SCRUB[2]. Hence **shru·bb**ERY. XVIII.

shrub[2] ʃrʌb drink prepared from acid fruit, etc. XVIII. – Arab. *šurb*, *šarāb*, f. *šariba* vb. drink; cf. SHERBET, SYRUP.

shrug ʃrʌg shiver, shudder XIV; raise (the shoulders) in disdain, etc. XV. Of unkn. origin; the occas. vars. *shrukke* (XV), *shruck* (XVI) and some affinity of sense suggest comparison with Sw. dial. *skrugge*, *skrukka* crouch, Da. *skrugge*, *skrukke* duck the head, but no point of contact can be made out.

shuba ʃū·ba fur gown or greatcoat. XVI. – Russ. *shúba*.

shuck ʃʌk (dial., U.S.) husk XVII; valueless thing (pl. used as int.) XIX. Of unkn. origin.

shudder ʃʌ·dəɹ tremble convulsively. XIII. ME. *shod(d)er* – MLG. *schōderen*, MDu. *schūderen* (whence G. *schaudern*, Sw. *skudra*), frequent. (see -ER[4]) f. Germ. **skŭd-* shake, repr. in various synon. formations, as OFris. *schedda*, OS. *skuddian*, (M)LG. *schudden*, OHG. *scutten* (G. *schütten*, whence frequent. *schüttern*), *scutisōn*. Hence sb. XVII (Sh.).

shuffle ʃʌ·fl Evidenced in the latter half of XVI in a series of senses expressive of pushing along, putting together, into, or off in a disorderly or evasive manner, and the like. – or cogn. w. LG. *schuffeln*, based on Germ. **skuf-*; see SHOVE, -LE[3].

shun ʃʌn †abhor OE.; avoid, eschew XII. OE. *scunian* (chiefly in *ā-*, *onscunian*); a peculiarly Eng. vb. of unkn. origin.

shunt ʃʌnt †swerve, shy, shrink away XIII; (dial.) shove XVIII; move (a railway train) from one line to another XIX. ME. *schunte*, perh. a deriv. of SHUN.

shut ʃʌt pt., pp. **shut** †fasten (a bolt), (a door, etc.) with a bolt; move (a door, etc.) so as to close an aperture XIII. OE. *sċyttan* (more freq. in the comp. *forsċyttan*) = OFris. *sketta*, (M)LG, (M)Du. *schutten* shut up, obstruct :– WGerm. **skuttjan*, f.

*skut- *skeut- SHOOT. The normal repr. of OE. *sćyttan* is *shit(te)*, the prevailing form down to XVI, except for the south-eastern *shet(te)*, used by Ch. and Gower; the form *shut* was taken into standard Eng. from the west midlands. Hence **shu·tt**ER[1] XVII; short for †*window-shutter* (XVII), repl. earlier †*window-shut* and simple *shut*.

shute ʃūt channel for conveying water to a lower level XVIII; steep channel down which stuff is shot XIX. Partly var. of SHOOT sb., partly var. sp. of CHUTE.

shuttle ʃʌ·tl weaver's instrument for shooting the thread of the weft backwards and forwards. XIV. repr. OE. *sćytel* dart, arrow, corr. to ON. *skutill* harpoon, bolt :- Germ. **scutilaz*, f. **skut-* SHOOT; rel. forms in Scand. langs. have acquired the same sense, viz. Sw., Da. *skyttel*, Da. *skytte*, Norw. *skyt*, *skjøt*; see -LE[1].

shy[1] ʃai †easily frightened OE.; timidly averse to meeting anything XVI; unwilling to commit oneself XVII. OE. *sćēoh* (also in *sćēohmōd* of timid mind) = OHG. **scīoh*, MHG. *schiech* (G. *scheu* is a new formation) :- Germ. **skeuχ(w)az*, whence also OHG. *sciuhen* (G. *scheuen* shun, *scheuchen* scare); rel. by gradation to MDu. *schuwe*, *schu* (Du. *schuw*), Norw. *skygg*, OSw., Da. *sky* :- **sku(g)waz* timid; cf. ESCHEW. ¶ The phonetic development of ʃai from OE. *sćēoh* is parallel to that of THIGH. Hence vb. XVII.

shy[2] ʃai throw (a missile). XVIII. The earliest exx. refer to throwing at cocks with sticks (cf. *cockshy*) and suggest that this vb. was derived from †*shy-cock* (perh. orig.) a cock that refused to fight or to be caught (SHY[1]); but the source remains obscure.

shyster ʃai·stəɹ (U.S. sl.) tricky lawyer, unscrupulous business man, etc. XIX. prob. based on G. *scheisser*, agent-noun of *scheissen* SHIT, with substitution of -STER. Cf. SHICER.

si sī (mus.) seventh note of the scale in solmization. XVIII. – F. *si* – It. *si*, supposed to be made from the initials of *Sancte Iohannes*, for which see UT.

sialagogue sai·ələgɔg medicine that produces saliva. XVIII. – F. *sialagogue* – modL. *sialagōgus*, f. Gr. *síalon* saliva + *agōgós* leading, drawing forth, f. *ágein* lead (see ACT).

siamang sai·əmæŋ large ape with long black hair. XIX. Malay *si(y)āmang*, f. *āmang* black.

Siamese saiəmī·z pert. to, native of, *Siam*. XVII. See -ESE.

sib sib related by blood, now (exc. dial.) spec. of canaries; OE. *sib(b)* = OFris. *sibbe*, MDu. *sib(b)e*, OHG. *sippi*, ON. pl. fem. *sifjar*, Goth. *un|sibjis* (*sibja* relationship), of unkn. origin.

sibilant si·bilənt having a hissing sound. XVII. – L. *sibilant-*, *-āns*, prp. of *sibilāre* hiss, whistle, f. *sibilus* whistling sound, of imit. origin; see -ANT. So **sibil**A·TION. XVII (Bacon). – late L.

Sibyl si·bĭl woman possessing powers of divination. XIII (Cursor M.). – OF. *Sibile* (mod. *Sibylle*) or medL. *Sibilla*, L. *Sibylla*, *Sibulla* – Gr. *Síbulla*, explained in the Doric form *Siobúlla*, by Jerome, as for *Theoboúlē* 'divinely wise'. So **Si·byll**INE[1]. XVI (North). – L.

sic sik L. *sīc* so, thus, used parenthetically to indicate authenticity.

sicca si·kə orig. newly coined rupee. XVII (*secau*, *siccau*). – Hind. *sikka* – Arab. (Pers.) *sikkah* die for coining, impression on money; cf. SEQUIN.

sick sik ill, ailing OE.; out of condition XIV; weary *of* XVI; inclined to vomit, vomiting XVII. OE. *sēoc* = OFris. *siāk*, OS. *siok*, OHG. *sioh* (Du. *ziek*, G. *siech*), ON. *sjúkr*, Goth. *siuks* :- CGerm. **seukaz*, of unkn. origin. There is evidence that *ē* of ME. *sēk* had been raised to *ī* in some areas perh. *c.*1200; the form *sīk(e)*, which rhymes with *līk(e)*, e.g. in Ch. and Gower, and is indicated by the sp. *syke* as late as XVI, was normally shortened in *sickness* (OE. *sēocnes*), whence the form *sick* in the simplex. The raising and shortening of ē were prob. assisted by the forms of OE. *sīclian* be ill, pp. *sĭc(c)lod*, and **sīcol* in bad health, pl. *sīcle*, ME. *sikel*, early modE. *sickle*. Hence **si·ck**EN[5] XII. **si·ck**LY[1] XIV; prob. after ON. *sjúkligr*; whence vb. XVII (Sh.).

sicker si·kəɹ (north. since *c.*1500) safe, secure, sure. OE. *sicor* = OFris., OS. *sikor* (MDu. *seker*, Du. *zeker*), OHG. *sihhur* (G. *sicher*); early WGerm. – late form **sicurus* of L. *sēcūrus* SECURE.

sickle si·kl reaping-hook with toothed edge. OE. *sicol*, *sicel* = MLG., MDu. *sekele*, *sikele* (Du. *zikkel*), OHG. *sichila* (G. *sichel*) – var. **sicila* of (Campanian) L. *secula* (cf. It. *segolo*), f. *secāre* cut (see SECTION).

side ʃaid long surface or part)(top, bottom, or end; place or aspect with reference to a centre; lateral slope, shore, etc. OE.; situation with respect to an opinion XIII. OE. *side* = OFris., OS. *side*, OHG. *sita* (Du. *zijde*, *zij*, G. *seite*), ON. *síða* :- CGerm. (exc. Gothic) **sīðō*, prob. f. **sīðaz* adj. extending lengthways, long, deep, low (OE. *sīd*, MDu. *side*, *zīde*, ON. *síðr*, whence adv. OE. *sīde*, MLG., MDu. *sīde*), and rel. further to OE. *sīþ* late, etc. (see SINCE). Hence **side** vb. XV. **sidelong** sai·dlɔŋ sideways, obliquely; also adj. XVI. alt. of *sideling* (XIV); see -LING[2], -LONG; and cf. MLG., MDu. *sideling(e)*, (Du. *zijdelings*), OSw. *sidholangs*, ODa. *sidelangs*. **sides**MAN sai·dzmən churchwarden's assistant. XVII. alt. of †*sideman* (XVI–XVII), 'a man who stands at the side of a churchwarden'. **si·de**WAYS, †-WISE from one side, laterally, obliquely. XVI. **sid**ING[1] sai·diŋ taking sides XVII; concr. piece of something at the side XVIII. **sidle** sai·dl move obliquely, edge along XVII; back-formation from *sideling, sidelong*, after vbs. in -LE[3].

sideral si·dərəl, sai·dərəl pert. to the stars. XVI. – L. *siderālis*, f. *sider-, sīdus* constellation, star. So **sidereAL**[1] saidiə·riəl. XVII. f. L. *sīdereus*.

siderite si·dərait, sai·dərait †loadstone XVI; various min. uses from XVIII. In early use – F. *sidérite* or L. *siderītēs, -ītis* – Gr. *sidērítēs, -îtis*, f. *sídēros* iron; in later use f. Gr. *sídēros*; see -ITE.

sidero- si·dərou, saidiə·rou comb. f. of Gr. *sídēros* iron, in names of minerals (XVIII), and var. techn. terms.

siege sīdʒ investing of a place with an army. XIII (Cursor M.). ME. *sege* – OF. *sege* (mod. *siège*), f. *assegier* (mod. *assiéger*) BESIEGE. ¶ Distinct from ME. *sege*, later *siege* seat, now only in techn. uses derived from modF. *siège* = Pr. *setge* :– Rom. **sedicum*.

sienna sie·nə (ferruginous earth used as) a reddish-brown pigment. XVIII. Earlier *terra-sienna*, for It. *terra di Sienna* 'earth of Sien(n)a', a town in Tuscany.

sierra sie·rə mountain range in Spain, etc. XVII. – Sp. *sierra* :– L. *serra* saw (cf. SERRATED).

siesta sie·stə afternoon rest taken in hot climates. XVII. – Sp. *siesta* (Pg. *sesta*) :– L. *sexta* (sc. *hōra*) SIXTH hour of the day; cf. SEXT.

sieve siv vessel with a mesh for separating coarser from finer particles. OE. *sife* = MLG., MDu. *seve* (Du. *zeef*), OHG. *sib, sip* (G. *sieb*) :– WGerm. **sibi*, which was applied spec. to the finer kinds as opp. to RIDDLE. The present sp. repr. the ME. *sēve* with orig. ĭ lengthened to ē, but the pronunc. repr. orig. ĭ.

sift sift pass through a sieve. OE. *siftan* = MLG., MDu. *siften, sichten* (Du. *ziften*), whence G. *sichten*; f. **sib-* (see prec.).

sigh sai emit a deep breath expressing weariness, pain, or relief. First in ME. pt. *siȝide, syhid, sighed*, gerund *syȝing, sighing* (XIII), based on the stem of *sihte, siȝte* (pt. †*sight* was in literary use till XVII), wk. pt. of †*siche* :– OE. *sīćan* (orig. str.; cf. pt. *on|sāc*); dial. side-developments are: *sike* (XII), *sick* (XV), evolved from 2nd and 3rd pres. ind. OE. *sīcst, sīcþ*; *sithe* (XIV, now dial.) by a sporadic change of χ to þ, ð; Sc. *sich* siχ (Barbour); *sife, sif*; of unkn. origin. Hence sb. XIV.

sight sait thing seen, spectacle OE.; eyesight, vision; show, display, (hence) lot XIV; device to guide the eye XVI. OE. *sihþ*, more usu. *ġesihþ, ġesiht* (see Y-), corr. to OS. *gisiht*, MLG. *sichte*, MDu. *sicht* (Du. *zicht*), OHG., MHG. *(ge)sicht* (G. *gesicht*; *sicht* XIX – LG.) sight, vision, face, appearance; WGerm. deriv. of **seχ(w)-* SEE[1]; see -T[1]. Hence **si·ghtLY**[1] †visible; pleasing to the sight. XVI; now more freq. in UNSIGHTLY.

sigil sidʒil seal or signet; occult sign. XVII.

sigla si·glə characters used as abbreviations. XVIII. Late L. *sigla*, perh. for *singula*, n.pl. of *singulus* SINGLE; cf. *singulæ litteræ*, so used.

sigma si·gmə name of the Gr. letter Σ, σ, ς (i.e. *s*), uncial C. XVII. So **si·gmOID**. XVII. – Gr. *sigmoeidḗs*.

sign sain gesture to convey a meaning; mark having a meaning, token XIII; division of the zodiac XIV; device for a shop or inn XV. – (O)F. *signe* – L. *signum* mark, token, the organic reprs. of which in Rom. are (O)F. *seing* seal, Pr. *senh*, Sp. *seña*, Pg. *senha* (from the pl.), It. *segno*, Rum. *semn*. So **sign** vb. mark with a sign XIV; affix one's mark or name (to) XV. – (O)F. *signer* – L. *signāre*, f. *signum*. **signal**[1] si·gnəl sign or token (*of*); sign agreed upon XVI (Sh.). – (O)F. *signal*, alteration of earlier *seignal*, corr. to Pr. *senhal*, Sp. *señal*, It. *segnale* :– Rom. (medL.) *signāle*, sb. use of n. of late L. *signālis*, f. *signum* SIGN; see -AL[1]. (As used by Ch. and Gower, an independent early adoption; cf. Gower's use of AN. *signal*.) Hence **si·gnal** vb. XIX. **si·gnalIZE**. XVII. **signal**[2] si·gnəl striking, remarkable. XVII. – F. *signalé*, earlier †*segnalé* – It. *segnalato*, pp. of *segnalare* make illustrious, f. *segnale* (see above). For the loss of final syll. cf. ASSIGN[2], COSTIVE, DEFILE[2]. **si·gnatORY**[2] †used in sealing XVII; (forming) one of those whose signatures are attached XIX. L. *signātōrius*. **signatURE** si·gnətʃəɹ (Sc.) writing presented to the Baron of Exchequer as the ground of a royal grant; person's name as authentication of a document XVI; character. In the first sense repl. Sc. †*signator* – F. *signature* (– It. *segnatura*) or medL. *signātura*, f. pp. stem of L. *signāre*. **signET** si·gnit small seal. XIV (Ch., Gower). – (O)F. *signet* (whence also (M)LG., (M)Du. *signet*) or – medL. *signētum*, dim. of *signe, signum* SIGN. **significANCE** signi·fikəns meaning XV; importance XVIII. – OF. *significance* or L. *significantia*, f. prp. of *significāre*, f. *signum* SIGN; see -ANCE. So **signi·ficANT**. XVI. – L. *significant-, -āns*. **si·gnificA·TION**. XIII (Cursor M.). – (O)F. – L. **si·gnIFY**. XIII. – (O)F. *signifier* – L. *significāre*. **significavit** si:gnifikei·vit (eccl. law) form of writ. XIV (Ch.). 3rd s. pt. ind. of L. *significāre*. Cf. *assign, consign, design, insignia, resign*, etc.

signor, signior sī·njōɹ sir, Mr.; man of distinction or authority. XVI. – It. *signor*, clipped form of *signore* (= SEIGNEUR, SEÑOR, SENHOR) :– L. *seniōrem, senior* SENIOR, SIRE. So **signora** sīnjō·rə title of respect corr. to *madam, Mrs*. XVII.

Sikh sik, sīk member of a military community of the Punjab, established orig. as a religious sect. XVIII. – Hindi *sikh* :– Skr. *sishya* disciple.

silage sailidʒ ensilage. XIX. Alt. f. EN-SILAGE, after SILO.

silence sai·ləns abstinence from speech XIII (AncrR.); absence of sound XIV (Wycl. Bible, Trevisa). – (O)F. *silence*, corr. to Pr. *silenci*, Sp. *silencio*, It. *silenzio* – L. *silentium*, f. *silent-*, *silēns*, prp. of *silēre* be silent; see -ENCE. Similarity of form and meaning are seen in Gr. *sigḗ* silence, *siōpân*, Goth. *ana|silan*, G. *schweigen*. So **si·l**ENT. XVI. – L. prp.

silene sailī·nī genus of caryophyllaceous plants typifying the tribe *Sileneæ*; plant belonging to this; catchfly. XVII. modL. – L. *Sīlēnus* – Gr. *Seilēnós* species of satyr.

Silesia sailī·zjə, -ʃə name of a province in eastern Germany. XVII. Latinized f. G. *Schlesien*.

silhouette silue·t portrait or picture in solid black. XIX. From F. phr. *à la silhouette*, f. name of Étienne de *Silhouette* (1709–67), controller-general in 1759; but divergent reasons are given for the application.

silica si·likə (chem.) dioxide of silicon. *c.*1800. f. L. *silic-*, *silex* flint, after *alumina*, etc. Hence **si·lic**ATE². So **silic**EOUS sili·ʃ¹əs pert. to flint or silica. XVII. f. L. *siliceus*. **sili·c**IUM. XIX (H. Davy, 1808); repl. by **silicon** si·likən. XIX (T. Thomson, 1817).

siliqua si·likwa (bot.) pod of seeds of the mustard family. XVIII. So **si·liqu**OSE¹, **si·liqu**OUS. XVII.

silk silk (fabric made from) the soft lustrous fibre woven by certain moths that feed on mulberry leaves. OE. *sioloc*, *seol(e)c*, for **siluc*, corr. to ON. *silki* pp., and OSl. *šelkŭ* (Russ. *shelk*), Lith. *šilkaĩ*, OPruss. (genitive) *silkas* – L. **sericum*, for *sēricum*, n. of *sēricus*, f. *sēres* – Gr. *Sêres* (see SERGE), oriental people from whom silk was first obtained and passed through Slavonic countries into the Baltic trade. Hence **si·lk**EN³. OE. *soel(o)cen*. **si·lk**WORM. OE. *seolcwyrm*. **si·lk**Y¹. XVII.

sill sil beam forming the foundation of a wall OE.; lower horizontal part of a window opening XV; threshold XVI. OE., *syll*, *sylle* = MLG. *sulle*, *sul*, MDu. *sulle*, rel. to MLG., MDu. *sille*, ON. *svill*, *syll*, and MHG. *swelle*, OHG. *swelli*, *swella* (G. *schwelle* threshold), Goth. *ga|suljan* found, establish, *sulja* sole, and perh. to L. *solea* SOLE¹.

sillabub, syllabub si·ləbʌb dish of milk curdled with wine, etc. XVI. The earliest exx. show *sol-*, *sul-*, *sel-*, *sil-*; together with synon. (dial.) *sillibouk*; of unkn. origin.

silly si·li (dial.) deserving of pity XV; †weakly; †simple, ignorant; feeble-minded, foolish XVI. Later form of *seely* (orig.) happy, blessed :– OE. **sǣliġ* (as in *unsǣliġ* unhappy, *sǣliġliċe*, adv.) and *ġesǣliġ*, corr. to OFris. *sēlich*, OS., OHG. *sālig* (Du. *zalig*, G. *selig*) :– WGerm. **sǣliga*, f. **sǣli* luck, happiness (OE. *sǣl*), sb. f. CGerm. base repr. also by ON. *sǽll* happy, Goth. *sēls* good, and abstr. sb. OE. *sǣlþ*, etc., ON. *sǽld* :– **sǣliþō*.

silo sai·lou pit or underground chamber for storing grain, etc. XIX. – Sp. *silo* (whence also F. *silo*) :– L. *siru-s* – Gr. *sirós* pit to keep corn in. Cf. ENSILAGE.

silphium si·lfiəm Mediterranean plant yielding a gum resin. XVIII. – L. – Gr. *silphion*.

silt silt fine sand, etc., deposited as sediment. XV (Promp. Parv.). The earliest exx. are from E. Anglia; of uncertain origin, but prob. denoting orig. a salty deposit, and so perh. – a Scand. word repr. by Norw., Da. *sylt*, Norw. and Sw. dial. *sylta* salt marsh, sea beach, corr. to OLG. *sulta* (LG. *sulte*, *sülte*; Du. *zult*), OHG *sulza* (G. *sülze*) salt marsh, salt pan, brine, f. Germ. **sult-* **salt-* SALT (cf. OE. *un(ġe)sylt* unsalted, Du. *zilt* salty).

Silurian¹ sailjuə·riən pert. to the ancient British tribe of *Silures* XVIII; (geol.) pert. to a series of palæozoic rocks immediately below the Devonian XIX; see -IAN.

Silurian² sailjuə·riən pert. to the family Siluridæ of fishes. XIX. f. L. *silūrus* – Gr. *sílouros*; see -IAN. Also **Silu·r**OID.

silvan see SYLVAN.

silver si·lvəɹ precious metal ranking next to gold. OE. *siolfor*, *seolfor* = OFris. *sel(o)ver*, OS. *silubar*, *silobar*, OHG. *sil(a)bar*, *silbir* (Du. *zilver*, G. *silber*), ON. *silfr*, Goth. *silubr*, CGerm. **silubr-*, rel. indeterminately to various Balto-Sl. forms, perh. all ult. of Oriental origin.

simian si·miən ape-like. XVII. f. L. *simia*, perh. f. *sīmus* – Gr. *simós* snub-nosed, flat-nosed; see -IAN.

similar si·miləɹ †homogeneous (Bacon); like, alike (Cotgr.) XVII. Earlier *similary* XVI (common in XVII). – F. *similaire* (cf. Sp., Pg. *similar*) or medL. *similāris*, f. L. *similis*, based on IE. **sem-* **som-* (cf. HOMO-, SAME, SIMULTANEOUS); see -AR, -ARY. Hence or – F. **simila·r**ITY. XVII. So **simili**TUDE simi·litjūd. XIV (Ch.). – (O)F. or L.

simmer si·məɹ be at a point short of boiling point. XVII (H. More). Later form of (dial.) †*simper* (XV), perh. of imit. origin; see -ER⁴.

simnel si·mnəl bread made of fine flour. XIII (Havelok). – OF. *simenel* (mod. dial. *simnel*), derived ult. from L. *simila* (whence OHG. *semala*, G. *semmel*), *similāgō*, or Gr. *semídālis* fine flour (cf. SEMOLINA).

simony sai·məni, si·məni traffic in sacred things. XIII (AncrR.). – (O)F. *simonie* – late L. *simōnia*, f. name of *Simon* Magus in allusion to his offer of money to the Apostles Peter and John for the gift of conferring the Holy Ghost (Acts viii 18, 19); see -Y[3]. So **simoniac** si-, saimou·niæk XIV (sb.; adj. XVII). – (O)F. *simoniaque* or medL. *simōniacus*; **simoniac**AL[1] si-, saimŏnai·əkəl. XVI. Several other formations were current XIV–XVI.

simoom simū·m hot suffocating sand-wind. XVIII. – Arab. *samūm*, f. *samm* vb. poison. Cf. F. *simoun*, G. *samum*.

simper si·mpəɹ smile in a self-conscious or affected way. XVI. Similar forms with rel. meanings in Scand. langs., MDu., and G. may be the immed. source or point to a CGerm. imit. origin with the suffix -ER[4]; a close resemblance is seen in *whimper*.

simple si·mpl A. free from duplicity; free from pride XIII; B. of humble condition; ordinary, homely XIII; deficient in knowledge XIV; silly XVII; C. with nothing added XIV; not complex XV. sb. pl. persons of humble status; unlettered people XIV; sg. (gram.) simplex; (arch.) uncompounded substance, herb for use as such XVI. – (O)F. *simple* = Pr., Sp., Pg. *simple* – L. *simplus* (whence It. *scempio*), corr. to Gr. *haplóos*, f. **sm- *sem-* (cf. *semper* always, SEMPITERNAL) **som-* (cf. HOMO-, SAME) + **pl-*, as in *duplus* DOUBLE, *triplus* TRIPLE, etc. (cf. -FOLD). Hence **si·mp**LY[2]. XIII (RGlouc.); with contr. as in *gently*, *nobly*, *singly*. So **simplex** si·mpleks consisting of a single part XVI; sb. (gram.) uncompounded word XIX. L., with second el. as in *duplex*, *multiplex*, *-plic-* (see PLY[1]). **simplic**ITY -i·sĭti. XIV (Ch.). – (O)F. or L., f. *simplic-*, *simplex*. **si·mpli**FY. XVII. – F. – medL. **si:mplific**A·TION. XVII; so F.

simpleton si·mpltən silly person. XVII. f. SIMPLE + -TON, as in many surnames derived from place-names; cf. *idleton* idle fellow (XVIII), †*sillyton* (XVIII), and the use of *-by* (ON. *býr*; cf. BY-LAW), as in *idle(s)by*, *lewdsby*, *rudesby*, *sneaksby*, *sure(s)by*, *wigsby*.

simulacre si·mjuleikəɹ (arch.) image. XIV. – L. *simula·crum* (XVI), which is now esp. used for 'mere image'; f. *simulāre* (see next).

simulate si·mjuleit assume falsely the appearance of. XVII. – pp. stem of L. *simulāre*, f. *similis* SIMILAR; see -ATE[3]. So **simu**LA·TION. XIV. – OF. or L. Cf. DISSEMBLE.

simultaneous siməltei·niəs existing or operating at the same time. XVII. f. L. *simul* at the same time, prob. after *instantaneous* or *momentaneous*; see SAME, -EOUS. ¶ Rare medL. *simultāneus* means 'simulated'; F. *simultané* is recorded only from XVIII.

simurgh si·məɹg monstrous bird of Persian legend. XVIII. – Pers. *sīmurgh*, f. Pahlavi *sīn* (Av. *saēna*, Skr. *cyena*) eagle + *murgh* bird.

sin sin transgression of the divine law. OE. *syn(n)* wrongdoing, offence, (also) enmity (:– **sunjō*), rel. to other Continental forms with dental, as OFris. *sende*, OS. *sundea*, OHG. *sunt(e)a*, *sund(e)a* (G. *sünde*), ON. *synd*; taken to be cogn. with L. *sont-*, *sōns* guilty (see also SOOTH). So **sin** vb. OE. *syngian* (:– **sunnigōjan*), ME. *süngen*, *singen*, *sunigen*, *-ȝen*, was repl. by *sinne*, based on the sb. Cf. ON. *syndgast* refl. vb.

sinapism si·nəpizm mustard plaster. XVII. – F. *sinapisme* or late L. *sināpismus* – Gr. *sināpismós* use of a mustard plaster (*sinā́pisma*), f. *sínāpi* mustard, of Egyptian origin; see -ISM.

since sins adv. †thereupon; from then till now; ago, before now XV; prep. from (a certain time) till now XVI; conj. from the time that; seeing that XV. Late ME. *synnes*, *syns*; either (i) reduced form of †*sithenes* (XIV), f. †*sithen*, OE. *siþþon*, *siþþan*, *sīþ þām* after that (cf. G. *seitdem* since), i.e. *sīþ* after = OS. *sīð*, OHG. *sîd* (G. *seit*), ON. *síðr* less, Goth. *-seiþs* (in *ni þanaseiþs* no longer), prep. compar. adv. meaning 'later', the base of which is rel. to synon. L. *sētius*; or (ii) directly f. (dial.) *sin* (XIV), syncopated form of †*sithen* + -S. For the sp. cf. *hence*, *once*, etc.

sincere sinsiə·ɹ not falsified, adulterated, or feigned. XVI. – L. *sincērus* (whence F. *sincère*, Sp., It. *sincero*). So **since·r**ITY sinse·rĭti. XVI. – L.

sinciput si·nsipʌt (anat.) front part of the skull. XVI. – L. *sinciput*, for **senciput*, f. *sēmi-* half, SEMI- + *caput* HEAD.

sine[1] sain (math.) one of the three trigonometrical functions (cf. *secant*, *tangent*). XVI. – med. use of L. *sinus* bend, bay, fold of toga, bosom (see SINUS), used to translate Arab. *jaib* bosom (cf. JIBBAH) in this sense.

sine[2] sai·ni without. L. (see SUNDER). L. phr. **sine die** sai·ni dai·ī without a day (sc. being specified) XVII; *sine qua non* sai·ni kwei nɔn 'without which (thing *causā*) not', indispensable (thing) XVII; cf. Gr. ὧν οὐκ ἄνευ 'which things not without'.

sinecure sai·nikjuəɹ, si·n- benefice without cure of souls; position with emolument but without duties XVII. – L. (*beneficium*) *sine cūrā*; see SINE[2], CURE.

sinew si·nju tendon OE.; mainstay, chief support (*sinews of war* money, after L. *nervi belli pecunia*, Cicero 'Philippics' v ii 5) XVI. OE. *sin(e)we*, *sionwe*, *seonew-*, obl. forms of *sinu*, *seonu* = OFris. *sini*, *sin(e)*, (M)LG., MDu., MHG. *sene* (Du. *zeen*, G. *sehne*), ON. *sin* :– CGerm. (exc. Gothic) **senawō* (the *w* of the stem appears also in OS. *sinewa* (MDu. *zenuwe*, Du. *zenuw*), OHG. *senawa*.

sing siŋ pt. **sang** sæŋ (formerly also *sung* XVI–early XIX), pp. **sung** sʌŋ, utter with musical inflexions of the voice. OE. *singan*, pt. *sang*, *sungon*, pp. *sungen* = OFris.

siunga, sionga, OS., OHG. *singan* (Du. *zingen*, G. *singen*), ON. *syngva*, Goth. *siggwan* :- CGerm. **seŋgwan*, rel. to Gr. *omphḗ* voice :- **soŋgwā*. comp. **si·ng-song** jingling verse XVII; informal concert XVIII; formed on the model of DING-DONG (XVI).

singe sindʒ burn lightly. OE. *sенćġan* (*sæncġan*), usu. *besenćġan* = OFris. *senga, sendza*, OS. *bisengian* (Du. *zengen*), (M)HG. *sengen* :- WGerm. **saŋgjan*, f. **saŋg-* **seŋg-* **suŋg-*, repr. also by Du. *sengel* spark, MHG. *senge* dryness, *sinc(-g-)* singeing, *sungen*, Icel. *sangr* singed, Norw. *sengla, sengra* smell of burning, OSl. *prě|sąčiti* dry, *sąčilo* oven.

Singhalese see SINHALESE.

single si·ŋgl unaccompanied; unmarried; individual; not double XIV; separate XV; one (*one* or *an*) only XVI. ME. *sengle* – OF. *sengle, single* :- L. *singulu-s* f. *sim-* as in SIMPLE + dim. suffix *-*go*- + *-*lo*-, corr. in formation to Goth. *ainakls* solitary, f. **aina-* ONE + *-*ka*- + *-*la*-. Hence **single** vb. separate, pick out. XVI. **singlet** si·ŋglit unlined undergarment for the trunk. XVIII; f. -ET, after *doublet*.

singleton si·ŋgltən a single card of a suit in the hand. XIX; with -*ton*, as in SIMPLETON, with allusion to the surname *Singleton*. **si·ngLY**[2] adv., with contr. as in *simply*.

singlo si·ŋglou green China tea, orig. obtained from the *Sunglo* hills in the province of Gan-hwuy. XVII.

singular si·ŋgjŭləɹ †alone, solitary; one only; (gram.); †separate, single, personal; †special, particular; not customary, peculiar XVII. ME. *singuler* – OF. *singuler* (mod. *singulier*) – L. *singulāris*, f. *singulī* SINGLE; see -ER[2]. The form in -*er* was not finally displaced by the latinized -*ar* till XVII. So **singula·RITY**. XIV. – (O)F. – late L.

Sinhalese, Sing(h)alese sinhəlī·z, siŋgəlī·z pert. to Ceylon XVIII. f. Skr. *Siṅhalam* Ceylon + -ESE. Also CINGALESE.

sinister si·nistəɹ A. marked by †ill-will, †suspicion, dishonesty XV; unlucky, unfavourable XVI; B. situated on, or directed to, the left side (spec. her.) XV. – (O)F. *sinistre* or L. *sinister* left, f. compar. type in -*is*- on an unidentified base + *-*tro*-, as in *magister* MASTER; str. *sini·ster* till XVIII.

sink siŋk pt. **sank** sæŋk, pp. **sunk** sʌŋk, **sunken** sʌ·ŋkn be submerged; drop to a lower level OE.; trans. (repl. ME. *senchen*, OE. *senćan*) XIII. OE. *sincan*, pt. *sanc, suncon*, pp. *suncen* = OFris. *sinka*, OS., OHG. *sinkan*, MLG., MDu. *sinken* (Du. *zinken*, G. *sinken*), ON. *sǫkkva*, Goth. *sigqan*; CGerm. str. vb., of unkn. origin. The pp. *sunk*, as dist. from *sunken*, now tends to be used of states implying deliberate human agency. Hence **sink** sb. †pit for the receipt of water, conduit XV; basin, etc. of stone, etc. having an escape pipe for water XVI (also fig.).

Sinn Fein ʃin fein Irish movement formed in 1905 by Arthur Griffith. Ir., 'we ourselves'.

sinnet si·nit, **sennit** se·nit (naut.) cordage made by pleating several strands of yarn, etc. XVII. Of unkn. origin.

Sino- sai·nou comb. form of Gr. *Sínai*, L. *Sinæ* the Chinese, in **Sinologue** -lɔg one versed in Chinese civilization, etc. (XIX) modelled on F. or G. comps.

sinter si·ntəɹ incrustation formed by precipitation from mineral waters. XVIII. – G. *sinter* CINDER.

sinuous si·njuəs marked by turns or bends. XVI. – L. *sinuōsus* or F. *sinueux*; see next and -OUS.

sinus sai·nəs (path.) abscess, etc. XVI; (bot., anat.) cavity, depression XVII. – L. *sinus* semicircular fold, bosom, bay.

-sion ʃən, ʒən repr. F. -*sion*, L. -*siō(n-)*, f. *s* of pps. and supines + -*iō(n-)* -ION, as in *adhesion, ascension, delusion, fusion, lesion, pension, suspension, tension, version*.

sip sip imbibe liquid in small quantities XIV (Ch.); trans. XVII. prob. symbolic modification of SUP[1], to express less vigorous action; but cf. LG. *sippen*, which, if early enough, might be the immed. source. Hence sb. XVII.

siphon, syphon sai·fən bent tube for drawing off liquid by atmospheric pressure. XVII. – F. *siphon* or L. *siphō(n-)* – Gr. *sīphōn* pipe, tube. So **siphu·nculus** small canal or tube. XVIII (anglicized *si·phuncle* XIX). L. (Pliny), dim. of *sīphō*; see -UNCLE.

sippet si·pit small piece of bread to be dipped in liquid. XVI. Intended as a dim. of SOP; see -ET and cf. rare †*supet* (XIV) and †*soppet* (XVII).

si quis sai kwis (leg.) notice requesting information. XVI. L. *si* if, *quis* anyone (sc. *invenerit* shall have found, etc.).

sir sɔ̄ɹ, sə title prefixed to the name of a knight or male superior, or used vocatively XIII, later as a gen. term of respect XIV. ME. *sir, ser, sur*, Sc. *scher*, denoting unstressed vars. of SIRE.

sirdar sɔ̄·ɹdāɹ military chief, as in India and Egypt. XVII (Sandys). – Urdu, f. Pers. *sar* head + *dār* possessor.

sire saiəɹ †as a prefixed title or a vocative; †master, sovereign; (arch.) father XIII; male parent of a quadruped XVI. – (O)F. *sire* :- **sieire* :- Rom. **seior*, for L. *senior* SENIOR. Cf. MONSIEUR, SEIGNEUR.

siren saiə·rən (classical myth.) fabulous female monster having an enchanting voice XIV; dangerously attractive person XVI (Sh.); instrument for producing musical tones, invented by Cagniard de la Tour, 1819 (hence, one for making signals). In some early texts (i) *sereyn, -ayn* (Ch.), (ii) *sirene* (Trevisa, Gower) – OF. (i) *sereine, -aine*, (ii) *sirène*, corr. to Sp., It. *sirena*, Pg.

sere(i)a – late L. *Sirēna*, fem. form (cf. -A[1]) of L. *Sirēn* (to which the Eng. word was finally assim.) – Gr. *Seirḗn*, pl. *Seirênes* ('Odyssey' XII 39 ff.).

Sirius si·riəs chief star of the constellation Canis Major, dog-star. XIV (Ch.) – L. *Sīrius* – Gr. *Seírios*.

sirkar sə̄·ɹkār †court, palace of native prince XVII; native agent, etc.; province, state XVIII. – Urdu – Pers. *sarkār*, f. *sar* head + *kār* agent, doer.

sirloin sə̄·ɹloin upper part of a loin of beef. XVI (*surloyn, serlyn*). – OF. **surloigne*, var. of med. and modF. *surlonge*, f. *sur* over, above (see SUR-) + *longe* LOIN. ¶ For the sp. with *sir-* (from XVII) cf. †*sirname* SURNAME, †*sirples* SURPLICE, but its final prevalence may have been due to the fiction that the joint was knighted by an English king.

sirocco sirə·kou oppressively hot and blighting wind blowing from the north coast of Africa. XVII. – F. *sirocco*, earlier †*siroc(h)* – It. *scirocco*, corr. to Pr. *siroc*, Sp. *siroco, jaloque*, Pg. *xaroco, siroco* – Arab. *šarūq*, var. of *šarq* east (wind), f. *šaraqa* (the sun) rose.

sirrah si·rə condescending or contemptuous term of address to men and boys. XVI. Early forms *syrra, sirah*, also *serray, sirry, surry*, later (XIX) **siree** sirī·, prob. repr. late ME. *sīrĕ* SIRE with the last syll. finally assim. to AH.

sir-reverence see SAVE[2].

sirvente sɪrvɑ̃t (pros.) form of poem used by the troubadours. XIX (Scott). – F. *sirvente* – Pr. *sirventes*, the final *s* of which was misapprehended as the pl. ending; of unkn. origin.

sisal si·səl (fibre of) species of Agava, etc. XIX. f. name of a port in Yucatan, Mexico.

siskin si·skin aberdevine. XVI. – MDu. *siseken*, early Flem. *sijsken* (Du. *sijsje*), dim. based on MLG. *sīsek, czitze*, MHG. *zīsec, zīse* (G. *zeisig*), of Sl. origin (cf. Czech *číž*, dim. *čížek*, Russ. *chizh*, dim. *chízhik*); see -KIN.

sister si·stəɹ daughter of the same parent(s) as another person. First in E. Anglian and north. texts (XIII) – ON. *systir*, superseding native forms (*suster, soster*) repr. cogn. OE. *sweoster, swuster, swyster, suster* = OFris. *swester, suster, sister*, OS. *swestar*, MLG., MDu. *suster* (Du. *zuster*), OHG. *swester* (G. *schwester*), Goth. *swistar* :– CGerm. **swestr* :– CIE. **swesr-*, **swesŏr*, repr. in L. *soror* (:– **swesor*) sister, Gr. *éor* daughter, niece, OIr. *siur*, W. *chwaer*, Balto-Sl., Skr., Av., and Arm. Hence **si·ster**HOOD. XIV (Gower); **si·ster**LY[1]. XVI (Levins).

Sistine si·stīn pert. to a pope Sixtus XIX. – It. *Sistino*, f. *Sisto* Sixtus; see -INE[1].

sistrum si·strəm jingling instrument or rattle used by ancient Egyptians. XIV (Trev.). – L. – Gr. *seîstron*, f. *seíein* shake (cf. SEISMIC).

Sisyphean sisifī·ən useless and ineffective like the toil of the legendary Sisyphus in Hades. XVII. – L. *Sisypheius* – Gr. *Sisúpheios*, f. *Sísuphos*; see -EAN.

sit sit pt., pp. **sat** sæt be seated, seat oneself, †be situated OE.; †fit, suit XIII. OE. *sittan*, pt. *sæt, sǣton*, pp. *seten* = OFris. *sitta*, OS. *sittian*, OHG. *sizzan* (Du. *zitten*, G. *sitzen*), ON. *sitja* :– CGerm. (exc. Goth., which has *sitan*) **sitjan*, **setjan*, f. **set-* :– IE. **sed-* **sod-* **sd-*, repr. also by forms s.vv. SEDATIVE, SET, SOOT, NEST.

site sait †place occupied XIV (Ch.); ground on which a building, etc. is set up XV; situation of a place or building XVI. – AN. *site* (XIV) or L. *situs* local position, perh. f. *sit-*, pp. stem of *sinere* leave, allow to remain (cf. SITUATE). Hence vb. XVI.

sith siþ (arch., dial.) since. OE. *siþþa*, ME. *siþþe, siþ(e)*, clipped form of *siþþan* (see SINCE).

sitringee sitri·ndʒī carpet of coloured cotton. XVIII. – Urdu *shatrangi*, f. Pers. *shatranj* chess, with ref. to the orig. chequered pattern.

situate si·tjueit situated. XVI. – late L. *situātus*, f. L. *situs* SITE. Hence **si·tuate** vb., **si·tuated** XVI; see -ATE[2] and [3]. So **situa·**TION. XV. – (O)F. or medL. Cf. medL. *situāre*.

six siks 6, vi. OE. *siex, syx, seox, sex* = OFris. *sex*, OS., OHG. *sehs* (Du. *zes*, G. *sechs*), ON. *sex*, Goth. *saihs* :– CGerm. **seks*, varying in IE. with **sweks*, and repr. by L. *sex*, Gr. *héx*, dial. *ϝéx*, OIr. *sē*, W. *chwech*, etc. So **six**TH[2] sikspþ new formation repl. *sixt(e)*, OE. *siexta* = OFris. *sexta*, OS., OHG. *sensto*, ON. *setti*, Goth. *saihsta*; cf. L. *sextus*, Gr. *héktos*. Cf. SEXT, SEXTANT. **six**TEEN. OE. *siextiene*, etc. **si·x**TY[1], **si·x**TIETH[1], OE. *siextiġ, siextiġoþa*. **sixteen**TH[2], repl. OE. *syxtēoþa*, etc.

size[1] saiz A. (dial.) assize(s); †ordinance for payment of tax, etc. XIII; †fixed standard of food, etc. XIV; B. magnitude XIV. – OF. *sise, size*, aphetic of *assise* ASSIZE, or aphetic var. of Eng. word. So **size** vb.[1] XIV; hence **siz(e)**ABLE sai·zəbl fairly large. XVII. Hence **sizar** səi·zəɹ at the Univ. of Cambridge, an undergraduate receiving a fixed allowance of food, etc. XVI.

size[2] saiz glutinous substance used to produce a ground for gilding, etc., or to mix with colours. XV. perh. identical with SIZE[1], but the history is obscure. Hence vb.[2] XVII.

sizzle si·zl burn with a hissing sound. XVII. imit.; cf. FIZZLE and -LE[3].

sjambok ʃæ·mbək whip made of hide. XIX. – Afrikaans *sam-, tjam-, sjambok* – Malay *samboq, chamboq* – Urdu *chābuk* CHABOUK.

skald skōld poet of ancient Scandinavia. XVIII (Percy). – ON. *skald*, of unkn. origin. Hence **ska·ld**IC. XVIII (Warton).

skat skāt three-handed card game. XIX. – G. *skat* – It. *scarto* (= F. *écart*) cards laid aside, f. *scartare* (see ÉCARTÉ).

skate[1] skeit fish of the genus Raia. XIV. – ON. *skata*.

skate[2] skeit device fixed on the sole of a boot for gliding over ice. XVII. orig. in pl. *scates*, occas. *scatses* – Du. *schaats* (pl. *schaatsen*), in MDu. *schaetse* – ONF. (with unexpl. development of sense) *escace*, OF. *eschasse* (mod. *échasse*) stilt. The final *s* of the Du. word was from the first apprehended as a pl. ending. Hence vb. XVII.

skedaddle skidæ·dl retreat hastily; (gen.) run away, clear out. XIX. First in U.S. mil. sl., unless the earlier Eng. dial. use is taken into account.

skein skein length of thread or yarn put up in a loose knot. XV (Promp. Parv.). Aphetic – OF. *escaigne* (mod. *écagne*) = Pr. *escanha* (cf. medL. *scagna*), of unkn. origin. ¶ Gael. *sgeinnidh*, Ir. *sgainn* are from Eng.

skeleton ske·litən bony frame of an animal. XVI (*sc-*). – modL. *sceleton*, *skeleton* – Gr. *skeletón*, sb. use (sc. *sôma* body) of n. of *skeletós* dried up, f. *skéllein* dry up, rel. to *sklērós* dry (SCLERO-). Cf. F. *squelette*, Sp. *esqueleto*, It. *scheletro*.

skellum ske·ləm rascal. XVII (now only S. African in form *skelm*). – Du. *schelm* sχe·ləm – G. *schelm* (OHG. *skelmo*, *skalmo* rascal, devil, pestilence, carcass).

skene skīn knife or dagger of the Irish kerns and Scottish highlanders. XVI. – Ir. and Sc. Gael. *sgian* (genitive *sceine*, *scine*); cf. W. *ysgien*.

skep skep specific quantity of grain, etc. XI; basket, hamper XIII (Cursor M.); beehive XV. Late OE. *sceppe* (in AL. *sceppa*, *eskeppa* XII) – ON. *skeppa* basket, bushel, rel. to synon. OS. *scepil*, MLG., (M)Du. *schepel*, OHG. *sceffil* (G. *scheffel*); the base of which is repr. also by OS. *skap*, MLG. *scap*, OHG. *scaf* (G. *schaff* tub, vat).

skerry ske·ri rugged insulated sea rock. XVII. Orkney dial., f. ON. *sker* (whence Gael. *sgeir*) SCAR[1].

sketch sketʃ rough drawing; brief account or description. XVII (some exx. still show foreign forms, *schytz*, *schetse*). – Du. *schets* or G. *skizze* – It. *schizzo* (whence also F. *esquisse*, †*esquiche*, Sp. *esquicio*), f. *schizzare* make a sketch :– Rom. **schediāre*, f. L. *schedius* (cf. L. *schedium* extempore poem, late L. *schedia* raft) – Gr. *skhédios* done extempore, f. **skh-*, aorist stem of *ékhein* (cf. SCHEME). Hence vb. XVII (Dryden).

skew skjū †escape XIV; move sideways or obliquely XV; look sideways XVI. Aphetic – ONF. *eskiu(w)er*, *eskuer*, var. of OF. *eschuer* ESCHEW. So **skew** adj. oblique, slanting. XVII. f. the vb. or ASKEW. Also **skew-**WHI·FF. adj. and adv. XVIII.

skewbald skjū·bōld irregularly marked with white and brown or red. XVII. f. synon. †*skued* (XV), of uncertain origin, perh. f. OF. *escu* (mod. *écu*) shield :– L. *scūtum* (cf. L. *scūtulātus* as the colour of a horse, f. dim. of *scūtum*); modelled on PIEBALD.

skewer skjū·əɹ long wooden or metal pin. XVII (Evelyn). var. of dial. *skiver* (XVII), of unkn. origin, but perh. the more original form; cf. ME. *kever*, *kiver*, *cure*, as vars. of *cover*.

ski ʃī, skī snow-shoe. XIX. – Norw. *ski* ʃī (*skji*, *sjii*, *skid*) – ON. *skíð* billet of cleft wood, snow-shoe = OE. *scīd* SHIDE. Cf. F. *ski*, G. *schi*.

skiagram skai·əgræm radiograph. XIX. f. Gr. *skiá* shadow + -GRAM. So **skia·**-GRAPHY XIX; cf. SCIAGRAPHY.

skid skid supporting timber XVII; wooden fender; wheel-locking device XVIII. Of unkn. origin, but in form and sense resembling ON. *skíð* (see SHIDE, SKI). Hence **skid** vb. lock (a wheel) with a skid XVII; (of a wheel) be dragged along by having a skid applied; slip sideways XIX.

skiff skif small sea-going ship XVI; sculling- or racing-boat XVIII. – F. *esquif* (cf. Sp., Pg. *esquife*) – It. *schifo* – Lombardic **skif*, OHG. *schif* SHIP.

skill skil †reason; †what is reasonable XII; †cause, reason; practical knowledge with ability XIII. – ON. *skil* distinction, discernment, knowledge, adjustment, pleading, rel. to *skila* give reason for, expound, decide, *skilja* divide, distinguish, decide, etc., and MLG. *schēle*, (M)Du. *geschil*, *verschil* difference, MLG., MDu. *schillen*, *schēlen* differ, make a difference. Hence **skill**ED[2] skild XVI.

skillet ski·lit saucepan, stew-pan. XV; (*skelet*; in AL. *schiletta* XIV). perh. aphetic – OF. *escuelete* small platter, dim. of *escuele* (mod. *écuelle*) :– popL. *scūtella*, alt. of L. *scutella* SCUTTLE[1]; see -ET.

skilly ski·li thin gruel, soup, etc. XIX. Shortening of *skilligalee* (XIX, Vaux), of unkn. origin.

skim skim clear (a liquid) of surface matter XV; move or act lightly over XVI. Back-formation f. *skimmer* vessel for skimming liquids (XIV), †*skemour*, †*skymour* (later with assim. of ending to -ER[1]) – OF. *escumeure* (mod. *écumoire*), f. *escumer*, f. *escume* SCUM.

skimble-skamble ski·mblskæ:mbl confused, nonsensical. XVI (Sh.).

skimmington ski·miŋtən †shrewish woman; ludicrous procession ridiculing an erring spouse. XVII. poss. – SKIM + -*ton*, after *simpleton*.

skimp skimp scanty. XVII. vb. scrimp XIX. poss. rel. to SCRIMP.

skin skin hide of an animal stripped off XI; derma, epidermis; outer coat or covering XIV. Late OE. *scin(n)* (also *berascin* bear-skin) – ON. *skinn* :– **skinþ-*, rel. to MLG. *schinden* (Du. *schinden*) flay, peel, OHG. *scindan* (G. *schinden*); phr. *The skin of one's teeth* (XVI; Job xix 20, Geneva Bible and A.V.), a literalism from Heb. Hence vb. cover with strip of skin. XV. **skin·NER**[1] one who deals with skins. XIV (Trevisa). Cf. ON. *skinnari* and medL. *peltarius*.

skink skiŋk small lizard. XVI. – F. †*scinc* (now *scinque*) or L. *scincus* – Gr. *skígkos*; cf. SCINCOID.

skip[1] skip leap lightly off the ground XIII (Cursor M.); pass from one thing to another omitting what intervenes XIV. prob. of Scand. origin, but the synon. MSw. *skuppa, skoppa* does not formally agree.

skip[2] skip footman, manservant; spec. college servant at Trinity College, Dublin. XVII. Short for †*skip-kennel* (XVII) lit. gutter-jumper; cf. QUACK[2], WAG[2].

skip[3] skip Shortening of SKIPPER (captain of a team). XIX.

skipper ski·pəɹ master of a small ship. XIV (*Herman, skypper de Dansk*, i.e. Dantzig). – MLG., MDu. *schipper* (whence also OF. *eskipre*, etc.), f. *schip* SHIP; see -ER[1].

skippet ski·pit (hist.) cylindrical wooden box to contain a seal. XIV (Trevisa). Of unkn. origin. Also (dial.) *skibbet*. XIV (Trevisa).

skirl skə̄ɹl cry out shrilly XIV; (of the bagpipes) XVII. prob. of Scand. origin; early forms *scrille, skrille*, corr. to Norw. dial. *skrylla*; ult. imit.

skirmish skə̄·ɹmiʃ irregular engagement between small bodies of fighters. XIV. Late ME. (i) *skarmuch*, aphetic – OF. *escar(a)-muche* – It. *scaramuccia* (whence also Sp. *escaramuza*, Pg. *escarramuça*), of unkn. origin; superseded by (ii) *skarmich, skyrmish*, which were based on OF. *eskermiss-, eskirmiss-* (whence **skirmish** vb. XIV) lengthened stem of *eskermir, eskirmir* (whence ME. *skirme* XIII), also *escremir, escrimir* (modF. *escrimer* fence) = Pr. *escremir*, It. *schermire* – Frankish **skirmjan*, = OHG. *skirmen* (G. *schirmen*) defend. See -ISH[2] and cf. SCRIMMAGE.

skirr skə̄ɹ (poet., arch.) move rapidly XVI; pass rapidly over XVII. synon. with SCOUR[2] but identity with this is not favoured by the forms *skyr, sker*.

skirret[1] ski·rit water-parsnip. XIV. ME. *skirwhit(e)*, perh. f. †*skire* clear, bright (– ON. *skírr* SHEER[1]) + WHITE.

skirret[2] ski·rit instrument for measuring land, aligning trenches, etc. working on a revolving centre-pin. XIX. Of unkn. origin.

skirt skə̄ɹt part of a dress or robe from the waist down XIII (Cursor M.); flap of a saddle, etc. XIV; border, edge XV. – ON. *skyrta* shirt = OE. *sċyrte* SHIRT. ¶ The change of meaning is not accounted for, but the corr. LG. *schört* means 'woman's gown' locally. Hence vb. be on the border of. XVII.

skit skit vain or wanton woman XVI; satirical remark, parody XVIII. So **skit** vb. move lightly and rapidly XVII; make satirical hits XVIII. **ski·ttISH**[1] excessively lively XV; disposed to shy, frolicsome XVI; fickle, coy XVII. perh. all ult. based on ON. **skyt-*, mutation of **skut-* **skeut-* SHOOT; cf. dial. *skite* move rapidly, dart, prob. f. ON. **skȳt-* mutated stem of *skjóta* shoot.

skittle ski·tl (pl.) game of ninepins. XVII. Parallel with *kittle pins* (somewhat later in XVII); cf. †*skayles* (XVI–XVII) and (dial.) KAYLES; of unkn. origin, but the base may be the same as in prec. (cf. Sw., Da. *skyttel* shuttle, marble, gate-bar).

skiver skai·vəɹ thin kind of leather split from a sheepskin. XIX. f. *skive* split – ON. *skifa* (cf. SHIVE).

skivvy ski·vi (sl.) alt. of *slavvy*, SLAVEY. XIX.

skoal skoul health or toast in drinking. XVI (in earliest use Sc. perh. through James VI's visit to Denmark in 1589). – Norw., Da. *skaal*, Sw. *skål*, repr. ON. *skál* bowl. See SCALE[1].

skua skjū·ə predatory gull, Stercorarius. XVII (Ray). – modL. *skua* – Færoese *skúgvur* = ON. *skúfr*, of unkn. origin.

skulk skʌlk move stealthily; conceal oneself. XIII. Of Scand. origin (cf. Norw. *skulka* lurk, lie watching, Sw. *skolka*, Da. *skulke* shirk, play truant).

skull skʌl bony framework of the head, cranium.. XIII (AncrR., S. Eng. Leg.). ME. *scolle, schulle*, of unkn. origin, but remarkably similar to synon. ON. *skoltr* (Norw. *skolt, skult*, Sw. *skult*, dial. *skulle*); repl. OE. *bræġenpanne* brain-pan, *hēafodbolla, -panne* head-bowl, -pan. comp. **skull-**CAP. XVII.

skunk skʌŋk N.Amer. animal of the weasel kind, noted for emitting an offensive smell XVII; contemptible person XIX. – Abenaki (Algonkin) *segankw, segongw*.

sky skai †cloud; *the* vault of heaven, *the* firmament (now the ordinary colloq. word). XIII. – ON. *ský* cloud (:– **skiuja*), rel. to OE. *sċēo*, OS. *skio* (:– **skeuw-*) and (more remotely) OE. *sċuwa*, OHG. *scuwo*, ON. *skuggi* shade, shadow, Goth. *skuggwa* mirror :– **skuwwon*. comp. **sky·**LARK (which soars in the sky while singing) XVII.

Skye skai name of the largest island of the Inner Hebrides used attrib. as in *S. terrier*, a small breed of dog. XIX. Gael. *Sgith* skī.

slab[1] slæb flat, broad, and thick piece. XIII (S. Eng. Leg.). Of unkn. origin.

slab[2] slæb (dial.) marshy place, slush. XVII. So adj. viscid XVII (Sh.). prob. of Scand.

origin (cf. ODa. *slab* mud, Icel., Norw., Sw. *slabb* wet filth). So (dial.) **sla·bb**ER[4] XVI; see SLOBBER, SLAVER.

slack[1] slæk indolent, careless, remiss OE.; loose XIII; dull, inactive XIV. OE. *slæc* = OS., (M)Du. *slak*, OHG. *slach*, ON. *slakr* :- CGerm. (exc. Gothic) **slakaz*, cogn. with L. *laxus* LAX, *languēre* LANGUISH. Hence **slack** vb. XVI. (OE. *slacian* relax efforts; cf. MDu. *slacken*), **sla·ck**EN[5].

slack[2] slæk small or refuse coal. XV (Promp. Parv.). Late ME. and dial. *sleck*, prob. of LDu. origin (cf. LG. *slakk*, Du. *slak*, G. *schlacke* dross).

slade sleid valley, dell; forest glade. OE. *slæd*=OS. *slada*, LG. *slade*, Icel. *slǫðr*, Da., Norw. *slad(e)*. The present form descends from OE. obl. cases.

slag slæg refuse matter from smelting. XVI. – MLG. *slagge*, perh. f. *slagen* strike, SLAY, with ref. to fragments resulting from hammering.

slake sleik A. †relax one's efforts OE.; abate, moderate XIII (Cursor M.); B. †loosen, slacken XII; mitigate, appease, allay XIII; disintegrate (lime) with water XVII. OE. *slacian*, f. *slæc* SLACK[1]; corr. to (M)Du. *slaken* relax, diminish.

slam[1] slæm (at cards) †ruff and honours; winning all the tricks in a game. XVII. perh. shortening of †*slampant*, *-am*, *-aine*, in phr. *give* (one) *the slampant* trick, hoodwink.

slam[2] slæm (dial.) beat XVII; shut with a noise XVIII. prob. of Scand. origin (cf. ON. *slam(b)ra*, Sw. *slämma*, Norw. *slemma*).

slander slà·ndəɹ †be a stumbling-block to XIII (Cursor M.); †disgrace; defame XIV. ME. *sclaundre*, aphetic – AN. *esclaundre*, OF. *esclandre*, alt. of *escandle* SCANDAL. So **slander** vb. XIII (Cursor M.). – OF. *esclandrer*, f. *esclandre*. **sla·nder**OUS †disgraceful, scandalous; characterized by slander or calumny. XV (Hoccleve). – OF. *esclandreux*.

slang slæŋ (orig., but now differentiated from) †cant, jargon XVIII; colloquial language of an undignified kind XIX (Keble, 1818). In its earliest appearance a cant term variously applied ('humbug', 'line of business', 'lay', 'show', 'performance of strolling players', beside the above uses, and as vb. 'defraud'), with gen. implication of irregular or lawless activity variously specialized. The north. dial. sense of 'abusive language' and the colloq. use of the vb. for 'abuse' are notably parallel to Norw. dial. *slengeord* offensive language, (also) new word introduced without special reason, *slengjenamn* nickname, and the phr. *slengje kjæften* 'sling the jaw', utter offensive language; but no immed. connexion can be made out. Hence vb. †exhibit at a fair XVIII; rail, or rail at, abusively (as in *slanging match*) XIX.

slant slànt slope, as of ground XVII; inclination, obliquity XIX. f. earlier adv. XV (*slonte*, later *slant*, *slaunt*), aphetic of ASLANT, and vb. (XVI, *sklaunt*), obscurely rel. to dial. *slent* sb. and vb., which are presumably of Scand. origin. Hence **slantindi·cular** XIX (orig. U.S.); f. *slanting* prp.+PERPEN|DICULAR.

slap slæp smart blow as with the open hand. XVII. – LG. *slapp* (cf. G. *schlappe*), of imit. origin (similar words are *clap*, *flap*, *rap*, *tap*). So vb. and adv. XVII. In comb. with vbs. *slap-bang* XVIII (Grose), *slap-dash* XVII (Dryden).

slash slæʃ cut with a sweeping blow XIV (Wycl. Bible; rare before XVI); cut slits in (a garment); assail severely XVII. perh. aphetic – OF. **esclaschier*, var. of *esclachier* break, obscurely rel. to *esclater*, mod. *éclater* (see SLAT); prob. reinforced by symbolical assoc. with *slit*, *lash*.

slat slæt (dial.) slate XIV; long narrow slip of wood or metal XVIII. Aphetic – OF. *esclat* (mod. *éclat*) splinter, piece broken off, f. *esclater* split, splinter, shatter = Pr. *esclatar*, It. *schiattare*, repr. Rom. **exclatāre*, f. *ex* EX-[1]+imit. base **clat-*.

slate[1] sleit (tablet of) variety of stone that splits readily into plates. XIV (*sclate*, *sklatestane*). – OF. *esclate*, fem. corr. to m. *esclat* SLAT.

slate[2] sleit (sl.) 'knock the hat over someone's eyes'; thrash; assail with abuse. XIX. Of dial. origin, presumably f. prec.

slattern slæ·təɹn untidy and slovenly female. XVII. prob. alt. of synon. dial. *slattering* ('a dirty *slattering* woman', Ray), prp. of *slatter* spill or splash awkwardly, slop, frequent. (see -ER[4]) of *slat* (ME. *sleate*, *sclatte* XIII) dash, perh. of Scand. origin (cf. ON. *sletta* slap).

slaughter slɔ̄·təɹ killing of cattle, etc. for food; killing of a person (cf. *manslaughter*) XIII; carnage, massacre XIV. – ON. **slahtr* (ON. *slátr*, mod. Icel. *slátur* butcher's meat), f. **slaχ-* SLAY[1]; repl. ME. *slaȝt*, repr. OE. **slæht*, **sleaht* (as in *wælsleahta* g. pl.), corr. to OS. *-slahta*, (M)Du. *slacht*, OHG. *slacht* (G. *schlacht* battle), ON. *slátr*, *slátta*. Hence vb., esp. of massacring people and killing cattle XVI.

Slav slāv, slæv member of any of a large group of peoples of Eastern Europe comprising Russians, Bulgarians, Serbs, Poles, Czechs, and Wends. XIV (*Sclave*, Trevisa). In earliest use – medL. *Sclavus*, corr. to medGr. *Sklábos*; so MHG. *Schlaff*, etc.; later, after medL. *Slavus*, F., G. *Slave*; So **Slavon**IAN slǝvou·niǝn XVI, **Slavon**IC -ɔ·nik XVII. f. medL. *S(c)lavōnia*, f. *Slavus*; superseded *Slavon* – F. *Esclavon*. Cf. SLOVAK, SLOVENE.

slave sleiv one who is owned by another person. XIII (S. Eng. Leg.). ME. *sclave*, aphetic – (O)F. *esclave*, prop. fem. of *esclaf* = Pr. *esclau* m., *esclava* fem., Sp. *esclavo*, *-va*, Pg. *escravo*, *-va*, It. *schiavo*, *-va*, Rum. *şchiau*, medL. *sclavus*, *-va*, identical with the ethnic name *Sclavus* SLAV, the Slavonic races having been reduced to a servile state by conquest. Hence **sla·very**. XVI; cf. MDu. *slaverie*, Du. *-erij*, G. *sklaverei*. **slavey** slei·vi, slæ·vi †male servant or attendant; female domestic servant; see -Y[6], **sla·vish**[1]. XVI.

slaver slæ·vəɹ allow saliva to fall. XIV (so also sb.). prob. of symbolic origin like synon. (dial.) *slabber* (XVI), prob. of LDu. origin, and SLOBBER; see -ER[4].

slay[1] slei pt. **slew** slū, pp. **slain** slein (rhet.) †strike; kill. OE. *slēan*, pt. *slōg*, *slōh*, *slōgon*, pp. (*ġe*)*slæġen*, *sleġen*, *slagen* = OFris. *slā*, OS., OHG. *slahan* (Du. *slagen*, G. *schlagen*), ON. *slá*, Goth. *slahan*; the Germ. base **slaχ*- **slag*- **slōg*- strike has no recognizable cogns. The present form of the inf. and pres. stem appeared XIV and is derived from the pp., finally superseding *slea*, *slee* (ME. *slēn*). See SLEDGE[1].

slay[2], **sley** slei instrument for beating up the weft. OE. *sleġe* = OS. *slegi*; f. base of prec.

sleave slīv divide, split (spec. silk into filaments). XVI. OE. *slǣfan* (in comp. *tōslǣfan*), causative f. **slāf*-, rel. to **slīfan* (see SLIVER). Hence **sleave** sb. silk in filaments. XVI; now used only in echoes of Sh. 'Macbeth' II ii 37 Sleepe that knits vp the rauel'd Sleeue of Care.

sled sled sledge, sleigh. XIV (Wycl. Bible). – MLG. *sledde*, corr. to MHG. *slitte* (G. *schlitten*), and rel. to MLG., MDu. *slēde*, Du. *slede*, *slee* (see SLEIGH), OHG. *slito*, *slita*, ON. *sleði*, f. **slid*- **slīd*- SLIDE. Cf. SLEDGE[2].

sledge[1] sledʒ large heavy hammer. OE. *slecġ* = (M)Du. *slegge*, ON. *sleggja* :– **slagj*- f. **slaχ*- strike (see SLAY[2]).

sledge[2] sledʒ carriage mounted on runners. XVII. – MDu. *sleedse* (Du. dial. *sleeds*), rel. to *slēde* SLED.

sleek slīk having a perfectly smooth surface. XVI (Sh.). var. of *slick* (XIV), ME. *slike*, prob. repr. OE. **slice*, rel. to **slician* (as in *niġ|sliced* 'newly polished', glossy) and Icel. *slikja*, Norw. *slikja* be or make smooth. Cf. SLICK.

sleep slīp unconscious state in which the physical powers are suspended. OE. *slēp*, *slǣp* = OFris. *slēp*, OS. *slāp* (Du. *slaap*), OHG. *slāf* (G. *schlaf*), Goth. *slēps* :– CGerm. (exc. ON.; cf. SWEVEN) **slǣpaz*, rel to corr. vb. **slǣpan*, whence OE. *slǣpan*, OS. *slāpan*, etc., and by gradation, to **slap*-, whence LG., Du. *slap* inert, sluggish, G. *schlaff* slack, lax; ult. connexions are doubtful. Hence **slee·per**[1] one who sleeps XIII (AncrR.); stout horizontal timber XVII; apartment for sleeping (orig. U.S.) XIX.

sleet slīt falling snow partially thawed. XIII. repr. OE. **slēte*, **slīete* :– **slautjan*-, rel. to MLG. *slōten* pl. hail, MHG. *slōze*, *slōȥ* (G. *schlosse*) hail(stone) :– Germ. **slautan*-.

sleeve slīv part of a garment to cover the arm. OE. (Anglian) *slēfe*, (WS.) *slīefe*, and *slief*, *slȳf*, corr. to EFris. *slēwe*, NFris. *slēv*, *slīv* sleeve, and ult. rel. to MDu. *sloove*, *sloof* covering.

sleigh slei sledge for transport of passengers or goods. XVIII. orig. N.Amer. – Du. *slee* (see SLED).

sleight slait †craft, cunning XIII; dexterity, adroitness XIV – (surviving gen. in phr. *s. of hand*). ME. *sleȝþ* – ON. *slǽgð* (OSw. *slögdh*, Sw. *slöjd* SLOYD, etc.), f. *slǽgr* SLY. ¶ For the final *-t* cf. HEIGHT.

slender sle·ndəɹ not stout or fleshy XIV; slight XV. Of unkn. origin. ¶ The alleged F. *esclendre* (Palsgr. 1530) and early Flem. *slinder* (Kilian 1599) are of doubtful authenticity; a poss. adj. deriv. of the base of †*slend* vb. slice, split (XIV–XVI), succeeded by (dial.) *slent* (XVII), involves difficulties of meaning and formation.

sleuth slūþ †track, trail XII (Orm); (short for *sleuth-hound* XIV) bloodhound, (hence) detective XIX. – ON. *slóð* track, trail (cf. SLOT[3]).

slew slʲū turn or swing *round* XVIII (*slue*). orig. naut.; of unkn. origin. Hence **slewed** slūd (sl.) intoxicated (XIX).

slice slais †shiver, splinter; applied to various flat utensils XIV; thin, flat, broad piece XV. ME. *s(c)lice*, aphetic – OF. *esclice* (mod. *éclisse*) small piece of wood, etc. f. *esclicier* splinter, shatter (whence **slice** vb. XV) – OFrank. *slītjan* = OHG. *slīȥan* (G. *schleissen*) = OE. *slītan* (see SLIT).

slick slik sleek XIV; smooth-spoken, plausible XVI; adroit, smart XIX; hence adv. (orig. U.S.) XIX. See SLEEK.

slide slaid pt. and pp. **slid** move from place to place smoothly and continuously. OE. *slīdan*, pt. *ā|slād*, *ā|slidon*, pp. *ā|sliden* = LG. *slīden*, MHG. *slīten*, rel. to OE. *slidor* slippery, *slid(e)rian* SLITHER, and the forms s.v. SLED. Hence sb. XVI.

slight slait (dial.) smooth, sleek XIII (Cursor M.); slender, slim; of light texture XIV; small in amount XVI. ME. (orig. north.) *sleght*, *slyȝt* – ON. **slehtr*, *sléttr* level, smooth, soft = OFris. *sliucht*, level, flat, smooth, straight, usual, OS. *sliht*, MLG., MDu. *slecht*, *slicht* simple, defective (Du. *slecht* bad; adv. badly; but *slechts* merely, only, but), OHG. *sleht* level, MHG. *sleht* (G. *schlecht* bad, *schlicht* (after the vb.) smooth, even, plain, simple), Goth. *slaihts* level :– CGerm. **sleχtaz* (whence Pr. *esclet*, It. *schietto*; the base is repr. in OE.

only by *eorþ|slihtes* adv. even with the ground), prob. pp. formation ('levelled'), of obscure origin. So **slight** vb. †smooth, level. XIII (Cursor M.) – ON. **slehta, slétta,* f. *sléttr*; in (obs.) sense 'level to the ground, raze' XVII – Du. *slechten,* LG. *slichten*; in sense 'treat with disdain' XVI (Sh.) f. the adj. in the sense 'of little account'. Hence sb. XVII.

slim slim slender, gracefully thin; slight, poor; (orig. dial.; since 1899 from Afrikaans) cunning, wily. XVII. – LG., Du. *slim,* repr. MLG. *slim(m),* MDu. *slim(p)* slanting, cross, bad = MHG. *slimp (-b)* slanting, oblique, G. *schlimm* grievous, disagreeable, awkward, bad :– Germ. **slimbaz* (cf. OHG. *slimbī* obliquity, inclination), whence Finnish *limppa,* OF. *escleme,* It. *sghembo*; perh. ult. rel. to Lett. *slīps* (:– **slimpas*) oblique, steep.

slime slaim soft sticky mud OE.; viscous fluid XIII. OE. *slīm* = OFris., MLG., MDu., MHG. *slīm* (Du. *slijm,* G. *schleim* phlegm, slime, mucus), ON. *slím* :– CGerm. (exc. Goth.) sb. (whence Finnish *lima*) rel. to Balto-Sl. words meaning 'saliva', 'mucus', and L. *līmus* mud, slime, Gr. *límnē* marsh. Hence **sli·my**[1] XIV (Trevisa, PPl.).

sling[1] sliŋ strap for hurling missiles. XIII (Cursor M.). prob. of LDu. origin (cf. MLG. *slinge,* corr. to OHG. *slinga*), of symbolic origin. See foll.

sling[2] sliŋ device for securing or grasping bulky objects XIV; strap, band, loop for suspension XVIII. The immed. source is doubtful; poss. identical with prec., the senses of LG. *sling-e,* G. *schlinge* noose, snare, arm-sling, to some extent correspond; the Germ. word was adopted in Rom. (OF. *eslingue,* whence Sp. *eslinga*). Hence vb. XVI.

sling[3] sliŋ pt., pp. **slung** slʌŋ throw, cast with or as with a sling. XIII. prob. – ON. *slyngva* str. vb. (pt. *slǫng,* pp. *slunginn*), with corr. wk. vb. *slǫngva*; cf. OHG. *slingan* (G. *schlingen* wind, twist).

sling[4] sliŋ Amer. drink with a basis of spirit; juice of the sugar-cane. XIX. Of unkn. origin.

slink sliŋk pt. pp. **slunk** slʌŋk move stealthily XIV (Ch.); drop (young) prematurely or abortively XVII. repr. OE. *slincan* creep, crawl, corr. to (M)LG. *slinken* subside (whence (O)Sw. *slinka* shake, totter), and (dial.) *slench* (XIV) slink, sneak, repr. OE. **slenćan.*

slip[1] slip semi-liquid mass (cf. the second el. of COWSLIP, OXSLIP) OE.; curdled milk (now U.S.) XV; semi-liquid cementing material XVII. OE. *slipa, slyppe* slime (so *slipig* slimy); cf. Norw. *slip, slipa* slime on fish, and SLOP[2].

slip[2] slip pass lightly, quickly, or quietly XIII (Cursor M.); slide, lose foothold or grasp, err XIV (Rolle); cause to slide, get loose from; let go XVI. prob. – MLG., Du. *slippen* = MHG. *slipfen* (cf. SLIPPERY). Hence **slip** sb. artificial slope XV; leash for a dog; act of slipping or sliding (cf. *landslip* XVII); fault, error XVI; garment readily slipped on XVII.

slip[3] slip small shoot of a plant XV; young person; long and narrow strip XVI. prob. – MLG., MDu. *slippe* (Du. *slip*) cut, slit, strip (but the earliest Eng. sense is not recorded in these langs.).

slipper sli·pəɹ light loose-fitting shoe. XV. cf. (dial.) *slip-shoe* (XVI); presumably f. SLIP[2]; for the use of -ER[1] cf. *drawers.*

slippery sli·pəri giving an insecure foothold or grasp. XVI. First recorded from Coverdale's tr. of the Bible (Ps. xxxv 6), who probably modelled it on Luther's *schlipfferig,* MHG. *slipferig,* f. *slipfern,* extension of *slipfen,* f. Germ. **slip-* as repr. in OE. *slipor* (dial. *slipper*) slippery, morally unstable (cf. SLIP[1]); see -Y[1].

slipshod sli·pʃɔd wearing slippers or very loose shoes XVI; untidy, slovenly XVII. f. SLIP[2] + *shod,* pp. of SHOE vb., after *slip-shoe* (XVI) slipper (cf. OE. *slypesćō* 'soccus').

slipslop sli·pslɔp sloppy mess of food XVII; blundering use of words (with allusion to the mistakes in language made by Mrs. Slipslop in Fielding's 'Joseph Andrews' 1742) XVIII. redupl. f. SLOP[2] with vowel variation.

slit slit pt., pp. **slit** cut into, cut open. XIII. ME. *slitte,* in pp. *islit* (Laȝ.), repr. OE. **slittan,* rel. to *slītan* = OFris. *slīta,* OS. *slītan,* OHG. *slīȥan* (Du. *slijten,* G. *schleissen*), ON. *slíta,* f. CGerm. (exc. Goth.) base having no known cogns. Hence **slit** sb. straight narrow cut. XIII; cf., however, OE. *ġeslit* rending, biting, *slite* tear, rent.

slither sli·ðəɹ glide, slip. XIII. alt. of ME. *slidere* (dial. *slidder*), OE. *sliderian* = MLG. MDu. *slid(d)eren,* G. dial. *schlittern,* frequent. (see -ER[4]) f. weak grade of SLIDE. For the change of *d* to *ð* cf. *hither, together,* etc.

sliver sli·vəɹ slice, splinter. XIV (Ch.). Of obscure formation on the base of (dial.) *slive* (XIV), OE. **slīfan,* occurring in pt. *tō|slāf* split up, but without any known cogns. Hence vb. XVII (Sh.).

slobber slɔ·bəɹ behave (e.g. feed) in a slovenly fashion. XV. Earlier in ME. *bysslober, beslobber* (cf. *slobber* mud, slime XIV), and corr. to Du. *slobberen,* with parallel and gen. synon. contemp. formations in (dial.) *slabber* (XVI) and *slubber* (XVI), Du. *slabberen,* MLG., MDu. *slubberen,* of imit. or symbolic origin. Cf. SLAVER.

sloe slou (fruit of) the blackthorn. OE. *slā(h)* = MLG., MDu. *slē, sleuuwe* (LG. *slē, slī,* Du. *slee*), OHG. *slēha, slēwa* (G. *schlehe*), Sw. *slå(n),* Da., *slaa(en)* :– Germ. **slaiχwōn,* which has been connected with L. *līvēre* be blue (see LIVID), W. *lliw,* Ir. *lī* colour, OSl. (Russ.) *slíva* plum.

slog slɔg A. hit hard; B. plod. XIX. In sense A parallel to synon. dial. *slug*; no further cogns. are found.

slogan slou·gən war-cry, battle-cry XVI (first in Sc. use: *slog(g)orne, sloghorne, slughorne*); party cry or watchword XVIII. – Gael. *sluaghghairm*, f. *sluagh* host (= OIr. *slūag*, W. *llu*)+*gairm* shout, cry.

sloid see SLOYD.

sloop slūp small one-masted vessel, small ship of war. XVII (*slup*) – Du. *sloep*, †*sloepe* (whence F. *chaloupe*, adopted earlier as *shalloop, shalop* XVI); of unkn. origin.

slop[1] slɔp †bag; (dial.) loose tunic or gown XIV; (pl.) wide breeches XV; ready-made garments XVII. OE. *slop*, in *oferslop* surplice, corr. to MDu. *(over)slop*, ON. *(yfir)sloppr*, f. Germ. **slup-*, of which synon. OE. *oferslype*, MHG. *sluf*, ON. *slyppa*, repr. a mutated form, rel. to **slūp-* in OE. *slūpan*, MLG. *slūpan*, OHG. *sliofan* (G. *schliefen*), Goth. *sliupan* glide (cf. L. *lūbricus*; see LUBRICATE).

slop[2] slɔp (dial.) muddy place, slush XIV; liquid food (esp. pl.) XVII; refuse liquid XIX. prob. repr. OE. **sloppe* as in *cūsloppe* COWSLIP, OXSLIP; cf. SLIP[1]. Hence **slo·ppy**[1] slɔ·pi. XVIII.

slop[3] slɔp (sl.) policeman. XIX. Modification of *ecilop*, back-slang for POLICE.

slope[1] sloup †adv. in an oblique direction or position XV. Aphetic of ASLOPE. Hence as †adj. XVI, in comp. †*slope*WISE (XVI), and, by further transference, as vb. intr. take an oblique direction XVI, trans. bring into a slanting position (spec. in military use) XVII, and sb. XVII (partly by analysis of *aslope* as *a slope*, e.g. 'An other ryuere runneth downe a slope' More's 'Utopia') sloping stretch of ground (Cotgr.); inclined direction (Bacon).

slope[2] sloup (sl.) make *off*, decamp. XIX. orig. U.S.; perh. spec. use of prec. vb.

slosh slɔʃ XIX (Southey). var. of SLUSH.

slot[1] slɔt (dial.) bar or bolt for a door, etc. XIII; metal rod, wooden bar XIV. – (M)LG., (M)Du. *slot* = OHG. *sloȥ* (G. *schloss*) door-bolt, lock, castle, f. WGerm. **slut-* (**slūt-*) **sleut-*, whence also OS. *slutil*, OHG. *sluȥȥil* (G. *schlüssel*) key, OFris. *slūta*, MLG., MDu. *slūten* (Du. *sluiten*), OHG. *slioȥan* (G. *schliessen*) close, lock.

slot[2] slɔt (dial.) hollow of the breast bone XIV; elongated narrow depression in wood, etc. XVI. – OF. *esclot* (in first sense), of unkn. origin.

slot[3] slɔt track of an animal XVI (*slott hownd*); deer's foot XIX. – OF. *esclot* horse's hoof-print, prob. – ON. *slóð* track (see SLEUTH).

sloth slouþ inactivity, sluggishness XII; S. Amer. arboreal mammal of sluggish habits XVII. ME. *slauþe, slouhþe*, later †*sloath, sloth* (XVI), f. *slāw, slōw*, SLOW+-TH[1]; repl. OE. *slǣwþ*, ME. *sleuþ(e)*. ¶ For the transf. application to the animal cf. SLUG[1] and F. *paresseuse* slow-moving caterpillar, sb. use of fem. of *paresseux* idle.

slouch slautʃ ungainly fellow XVI; (for *slouch(ed) hat*) hat with flopping brim XVIII; (from the vb.) stooping ungainly carriage XVIII. Hence **slou·ching**[2] prp. adj. XVII, whence **slouch** vb. XVIII. Of unkn. origin; but cf. synon. dial. *slouk* (XVI), *slotch*, and Norw. *slōk*, Icel. *slókr*.

slough[1] slau soft muddy piece of ground. OE. *slōh, slō(g)*, of unkn. origin. ¶ vars. *slow, slew* (XVIII) in U.S. and Canada mean 'marshy or reedy pool (or other water)'.

slough[2] slʌf outer skin shed by a reptile. XIII (Cursor M.). ME. *sloh, sloȝ*, poss. rel. to LG. *sluwe, slu* husk, peel, shell. Hence vb. be shed as skin XVIII; cast off XIX.

Slovak slou·væk, slɔ·vāk, slŏvā·k member of a Slavonic people inhabiting Slovakia in E. Czechoslovakia. XIX. – Slovak, Czech, Russ. *Slovák*.

sloven slʌ·vn †knave, rascal XV; †idle fellow XVI (Skelton); careless or negligent person XVI (Palsgr.). perh. based on Flem. *sloef* dirty, squalid, Du. *slof* negligent.

Slovene slo(u)vī·n member of a Slavonic people inhabiting Slovenia in NW. Yugoslavia; their language. XIX. – G. *Slowene* – Styrian, etc. *Slovenec* (pl. *-enci*), f. OSl. *Slov-* (as also in SLOVAK), held by some to be f. stem of *slovo* word, *sloviti* speak.

slow slou not quick, active, or rapid. OE. *slāw* = OFris. *slēwich*, WFris. *sleau*, OS. *slēu*, (M)Du. *sleeuw, slee*, OHG. *slēo* (G. dial. *schleh*), ON. *slǽr, sljár, sljór* :– CGerm. (exc. Goth.) **slǣwaz* :– IE. **slēwos*, of unkn. origin; cf. SLOTH. Hence **slow** vb. XVI; not continuous with OE. *slāwian* (*forslāwian*). perh. repr. by L. *lævus*, Gr. *laiós* (:– **laiϝós*) left (hand).

slow-worm slou·wəːm small lizard, Anguis fragilis. OE. *slāwyrm* 'regulus', 'stellio'; the first el., which has been assim. to SLOW, is of doubtful origin; it appears, with and without the corr. forms for WORM, in OSw. *slā* (Sw. *orm|slå*), Norw. *orm|slo*.

sloyd, sloid sloid system of manual instruction adopted from Sweden. XIX. – Sw. *slöjd* :– ON. *slǽgð* SLEIGHT.

slubber see SLOBBER.

sludge slʌdʒ mire, ooze XVII; matter mixed with water or slime XVIII. Appears in literature about the same time as the more or less synon. (dial.) *slutch* and SLUSH; but pp. *sluchched* befouled (XIV) is much earlier; prob. all symbolically expressive formations.

slug[1] slʌg sluggard XV; †slow-sailing vessel XVI; slow-moving shell-less land-snail XVIII. Based on a stem *slug-*, repr. also by **slug** vb. be slow or inert (XV) and much earlier by †*sluggy* sluggish (XIII) and †*forslug* neglect through indolence (XIV);

prob. of Scand. origin (cf. Sw. dial. *slogga* be sluggish, Norw. dial. *slugg* large heavy body, *sluggjen* slow, backward). So the synon. adjs. †*slug*, †*slugged* (XV), **slu·gg**ISH[1] (XIV), **slu·gg**ARD XIV (*slogard*), whence †*slu·ggardy* (Ch.), **slu·g**ABED XVI (Sh.). ¶ For the transf. application of *slug* to the snail cf. SLOTH.

slug[2] slʌg irregularly shaped bullet XVII; (typogr.) metal bar, line of type XIX. perh. identical with prec.

slughorn slʌ·ghɔ̄ɹn used for 'trumpet' by Chatterton and Browning through misapprehension of an early form of SLOGAN.

sluice slūs structure for regulating flow of water in a river, etc. XIV (*scluse*). – OF. *escluse* (the source of LG., G., and mod. Scand. forms), modF. *écluse* = Pr. *escluza* (whence Pg. *esclusa*) :– Gallo-Rom. **exclūsa*, sb. use (sc. *aqua* water) of fem. pp. of L. *exclūdere* EXCLUDE. Hence vb. ¶ For the sp. with *ui* (first in XVI) cf. *juice*.

slum slʌm A. †room; B. (orig. *back s.*) dirty or squalid back street, alley, or neighbourhood; C. †gammon, blarney, gipsy jargon; all early XIX. Of cant origin; in gen. use only in sense B. Hence vb. visit slums; **slu·mm**Y[1]. XIX.

slumber slʌ·mbəɹ sleep lightly. XIII (Bestiary). ME. *slūmere*, f. *slūme*, OE. *slūma* or vb. *slūmen* (XIII), north. dial. *sloom*, corr. to MDu., MLG. *slūmen*, MLG. *slummen*, G. †*schlummen*, with parallel formations in MLG., MDu. *slūmeren* (Du. *sluimeren*), MHG. *slummeren*, G. *schlummern*. Hence sb. XIV (Ch.). f. Germ. base repr. also by early ME. *slummi* drowsy (AncrR.). ¶ For the intrusive *b* cf. BRAMBLE, LIMBER.

slump slʌmp fall or sink *into* a bog, etc. XVII; transf. and fig. XIX. Of symbolic origin, like *clump*, *lump*, *plump*. Hence sb. heavy or sudden fall in value. XIX.

slur slɔ̄ɹ A. (dial.) fluid mud XV (*sloor*, *slore*, Promp. Parv.); gliding movement XVI; sliding mechanism XVIII; B. deliberate slight XVII; (mus.) mark indicating a smooth connected passage XIX. Hence vb. A. (dial.) stain, sully; disparage XVII; B. slide XVI; (mus.) XVIII. perh. two or more words have coalesced in sb. and vb.; partly corr. Continental forms are (M)Du. *sloor*, sluttish woman, LG. *slurren* shuffle, (M)LG. *slūren*, MDu. *sloren*, Du. *sleuren*, drag, trail.

slush slʌʃ watery matter resulting from the melting of snow or ice XVII; liquid mud XVIII. contemp. with synon. SLUDGE, *slutch*, with which it forms a series of expressive words paralle to ME. *sloche*, *sliche* (XIV), *sleech* (XVI), and SLOSH, to which the closest foreign parallels are Da. †*slus* sleet, mud, Norw. *slusk* sloppy ground or weather.

slut slʌt dirty slovenly woman XIV (implied in *sluttish*, Ch.); loose woman, hussy XV. Of unkn. origin; contact with Continental words similarly used and having the same cons. framework *sl..t.*, cannot be proved.

sly slai (dial.) skilled, clever XII (Orm); dyslogistic connotations appear very early. ME. *sleh*, *sley*, *sli(ȝ)* – ON. *slœ́gr* clever, cunning, etymol. 'able to strike', f. *slóg-*, pt. stem of *slá* strike (see SLAY[1]); cf. SLEIGHT. For the vocalism cf. DIE[1], etc.

slype slaip covered way from one part of a cathedral, etc. to another. XIX. perh. a use of *slipe* long narrow piece (as of ground XVI–XVII), varying with SLIP, of unkn. origin.

smack[1] smæk taste, flavour OE.; (fig.) trace, tinge, 'touch' XVI. OE. *smæc* = OFris. *smek*, MLG., MDu. *smak* (Du. *smaak*), OHG. *gi|smac* (G. *ge|schmack*). Hence vb. taste XIV, savour *of* XVI; superseding (dial.) *smatch* :– OE. *smæććan* taste = OFris. *smekka*, *smakia*, MLG. *smaken*, MHG. *smecken*, *smacken* (G. *schmecken*).

smack[2] smæk separate the lips with a sharp noise XVI; crack (a whip) XVII; strike sharply with a flat surface XIX. – MLG., MDu. *smacken* (LG., Du. *smakken*); cf. OE. *ġe|smacian* pat, caress, G. *schmatzen* eat or kiss noisily (MHG. *smatzen*, for earlier *smackezen*, f. *smacken*); of imit. origin. So sb. XVI; cf. MDu. *smack*, etc.

smack[3] smæk light single-masted sailing-vessel. XVII. – LG., Du. *smacke*, mod. *smak* (whence also G. *schmacke*, Sw. *smack*, Da. *smakke*, F. *semaque*, Sp. *esmaque*, Pg. *sumaca*, It. *semacca*), of unkn. origin.

small smɔ̄l (dial.) slender, thin; †narrow; of limited size or extent; of fine texture OE.; of low strength or power XII (in AL. *smalemannus* inferior tenant). OE. *smæl* = OFris. *smel*, OS., OHG. *smal* (Du. *smal*, G. *schmal*), ON. *smalr*, Goth. *smals* :– CGerm. **smalaz* (:– IE. **smol-*) in the later Continental langs. mostly 'slender', 'narrow'; the use exemplified in OHG. *smalaȥ nōȥ*, *fihu* (MHG. *smalnōȥ*, *smalvihe*; cf. *smalhirte* shepherd), ON. *smali* small cattle, connects with IE. **mōl-* **mēl-*, repr. by OSl. *malŭ* small, OIr. *mīl* (:– **mēlo-* beast), Gr. *mêlon* sheep. comp. **sma·ll**POX XVI (*small pokkes*; cf. *a pokke small* XV), dist. from *great pox*, the pox proper; cf. F. *petite vérole* (XV).

smallage smɔ̄·lidʒ variety of celery or parsley, esp. Apium graveolens. XIII. ME. *smal ache*, i.e. SMALL, †*ache* – (O)F. *ache* (= Pr. *api*, Sp. *apio*, It. *appio*) :– L. *apium*. ¶ For the change of final tʃ to dʒ cf. *borage*, *partridge*, *spinach*, *Dulwich*, *Greenwich*, *Harwich*, *Norwich*, *Woolwich*.

smalm, smarm smām (dial.) smear, bedaub XIX; plaster *down*; behave fulsomely XX. Hence **sma·lm**Y[1], **sma·rm**Y[1]. Of unkn. origin.

smalt smɔ̄lt glass coloured deep-blue by oxide of cobalt XVI; deep-blue colour XIX. – F. *smalt* (whence also Du. *smalt*, G. *schmalte*), – It. *smalto* = OF. *esmail* (mod. *émail*), nom. *esmauz*, Pr. *esmaut* – Germ. **smalt* (OHG. *smalz*, G. *schmalz*), rel. to SMELT².

smaragd smæ·rægd emerald. XIII. – OF. *smaragde* (usu. *esmaragde*, *-aude* EMERALD) or L. *smaragdus* (also used in Eng. from XIV) – Gr. *smáragdos*, var. of *máragdos* – Prakrit *maragada-* (cf. Skr. *marak(a)tam*) – Semitic **bāraqt* (Heb. *bāreqet*) f. *bāraq* shine.

smart smāɹt be acutely painful OE.; feel sharp pain, suffer severely *for* XII. OE. *smeortan*, pt. **smeart* (only in *fyr|smeortende* fiery, painful, *smeortung* itching) = MDu. *smerten*, (also mod.) *smarten*, OHG. *smerzan* (G. *schmerzen*), based on WGerm. **smert-* **smart-* **smurt-*, perh. rel. to L. *mordēre* bite (cf. MORDANT), Gr. *smerdnós*, *smerdaléos* terrible. So **smart** adj. †biting, stinging XI; causing acute pain XII; brisk, vigorous XII. Late OE. *smeart*. **smart** sb. XII.

smash smæʃ break up or strike at violently. XVIII (Foote; an earlier isolated sl. meaning 'kick downstairs' appears *c*.1700). prob. imit., combining *sm-* of *smack* and *smite* with *-ash* of earlier *bash*, *clash*, *crash*, *dash*, *lash*, *mash*. Hence sb. XVIII.

smatter smæ·təɹ †smirch, defile XIV; †prate, chatter XV; have a superficial knowledge *of* XVI. Of unkn. origin; similar forms, such as Sw. *smattra*, G. *schmettern* sound shrill, smash, etc., do not corr. in sense.

smear smiəɹ †anoint; cover thickly (as) with some greasy matter. OE. *smierwan*, corr. to MLG. *smeren*, OHG. *smirwen* (G. *schmieren*), ON. *smyrva*, *smyrja* :– Germ. **smerwjan*. So **smear** *sb.* †fat, grease, ointment OE.; in later senses f. the vb. OE. *smeoru* = OFris. *smere*, OS., OHG. *smero* (G. *schmer*, Du. *smeer*), ON. *smjǫr*, Goth. *smairþr*; cogn. with Gr. *múron* ointment, *smúris* EMERY.

smectite sme·ktait kind of fuller's earth. XIX. f. Gr. *smēktís*, f. *smḗkhein* rub, cleanse; see -ITE.

smeddum see SMITHAM.

smegma sme·gmə (physiol.) sebaceous secretion. XIX. – L. (Pliny) – Gr. *smêgma*, f. base of *smḗkhein* rub, cleanse.

smell smel pt., pp. **smelled, smelt** A. perceive by the sense of which the nose is the organ; B. have an odour. XII. ME. *smelle*, also *smülle*, *smille*, pointing to OE. **smiellan*, **smyllan*, of which no cogns. are known. Hence sb. XII; superseding *stink* and *stench* in the neutral application of sense B.

smelt¹ smelt small fish, Osmerus sperlanus. OE. *smelt*, *smylt* (in AL. *smeltis*, *-us*, *smyltus* XIV), obscurely rel. to similar Continental names for species of fish; cf. SMOLT.

smelt² smelt fuse (ore) to obtain the metal. XV (implied in *smelter*). – MLG., MDu. *smelten* (whence also Sw. *smälta*, Da. *smelte*) = OHG. *smelzan* (G. *schmelzen*), wk. trans. vb. corr. to str. intr., f. **smelt-*, var. of the base of MELT.

smew smjū saw-billed duck, Mergus albellus. XVII. Obscurely rel. to synon. (dial.) *smee* (XVII), and *smeath* (XVII), Du. *smient*, †*smeente*, LG. *smēnt* widgeon, G. *schmi-*, *schmü-*, *schmeiente* small wild duck (*ente* duck).

smilax smai·læks species of liliaceous plants. XVII. – L. *smīlax* (Pliny) – Gr. *smîlax* bindweed.

smile smail give the face a pleased or amused expression. XIII (Cursor M.). perh. of Scand. origin (cf. Sw. *smila*, Da. *smile*); a parallel form is OHG. **smīlan* (in prp. *smilenter*), MHG. *smielen*; f. (with *l-* suffix) the base repr. by forms cited s.v. SMIRK. Hence sb. XVI; cf. MHG. *smiel*.

smirch smɔ̄ɹtʃ defile, sully. XV. Of unkn. origin. Cf. *besmirch*. XVI (Sh.).

smirk smɔ̄ɹk smile, (later) esp. in a silly manner. OE. *smearcian*, *smercian*, (with *-k* formative) f. **smar-* **smer-* (**smīr-*), repr. by OE. *smerian* laugh at, *bi|smer*, *bi|smerian* scorn, **smǣre* in *gāl|smǣre* given to frivolous laughter, OHG. *smierōn* (G. †*schmieren*) smile, and closely rel. to Skr. *smeras* smiling, more remotely to OSl. *smějǫ sę*, *smijati sę* laugh, Skr. *smáyate* (he) smiles, Gr. *meîdos*, *meidân* laugh. Cf. SMILE.

smite smait pt. **smote** smout, pp. **smitten** smi·tn, (arch. or joc.) **smit** administer a blow to XII; in various applications lit. and fig. now chiefly arch. or joc., superseded in gen. use by *strike* and *hit* except in pp. in fig. uses ('struck', 'impressed', 'infatuated'). OE. *smītan*, pt. *smāt*, *smiton*, pp. *smiten* smear, pollute (also *besmītan* defile) = OFris. *smīta*, OS. *bismītan*, MLG., MDu. *smīten* (Du. *smijten*), OHG. *smīzan* smear, also *bi|smīzan* smear, sully (G. *schmeissen* throw, fling), Goth. *bi|smeitan*, *ga|smeitan* smear :– CGerm. **smītan* (but in Scand. langs. from LG.). ¶ For a similar series of meanings cf. STRIKE.

smith smiþ one who works in iron, etc. OE. *smiþ* = OFris. *smith*, MDu. *smit*, (also mod.) *smid*, OHG. *smid* (G. *schmied*, †*schmid*), ON. *smiðr* :– CGerm. **smiþaz* (in Goth. *aiza|smiþa* coppersmith) orig. prob. craftsman (cf. OE. sense of 'carpenter' and *wīgsmiþ* warrior, ON. *ljóðasmiðr* poet, Icel. *skosmiður* shoemaker, and senses of corr. vbs.); prob. f. IE. **smei-*, repr. by Gr. *smílē* chisel, *sminúē* mattock. So **smith** vb. OE. *smiþian* = OS., OHG. *smithōn*, ON. *smíða*, Goth. *ga|smiþōn*. **smithy** smi·ði smith's workshop, forge. XIII (Cursor M.). – ON. *smiðja*, corr. to OE. *smiþþe* (surviving in early ME. *smiþ(þ)e*), OFris. *smithe*, MLG. *smede* (*smee*), MDu. *smisse* (Du. *smidse*), OHG. *smidda*, *smitta* (G. *schmiede*).

smitham smi·ðəm, **smeddum** sme·dəm fine powder; finest lead ore ground to powder XVII; (Sc.) energy, go XVII. OE. *smed(e)ma* fine flour, meal, of unkn. origin; later assim. to SMITH.

smithereens smiðərī·nz (colloq., dial.) small fragments. XIX. f. (dial.) *smithers* (XIX) + -EEN[2] + pl. *s*. Cf. Ir. *smidirín*.

smock smɔk (dial.) shift, chemise OE.; (short for *s. frock*) loose coarse-linen overall garment XIX. OE. *smoc* = OHG. *smoccho*, ON. *smokkr* (perh. from Eng.); rel. to MHG. *gesmuc* (G. *schmuck* ornament); parallel to forms based on **smūg-*, viz. OE. *smūgan* creep, MHG. *smiegen*, ON. *smjúga* creep into, put on a garment, OE. *æ|smogu* snake's skin, *smygel(s)* burrow. Cf. SMUGGLE.

smoke smouk visible vapour from burning matter. OE. *smoca*, f. wk. grade of the base repr. by MLG. *smōk*, MDu. *smoock* (Du. *smook*), MHG. *smouch* (G. *schmauch*) and OE. *smēoc, smieć, smēć, smić*, (dial.) *smeech, smitch*, and vbs. *smēocan*, (dial. *smeek*), MDu. *smieken*, (M)LG., (M)Du. *smōken*, Flem. *smuik, smuiken* (whence Sc. *smuke*). So vb. OE. *smocian*. Cf. Gr. *smugênai* be consumed with heat, Lith. *smaugti* to be asphyxiated by smoke.

smolt smoult young salmon between a parr and a grilse. XIV (AL. *smoltus* XIV). In earliest use Sc.; of unkn. origin; cf. SMELT[1].

smoot smūt do casual work in a printing house. XVII (Moxon). Of unkn. origin.

smooth smūð having a surface free from irregularities OE.; pleasant, affable XIV; bland, plausible XV. Late OE. *smōþ* (rare, the usual form being *smēþe*, ME. *smethe*, dial. *smeeth*, which was gen. superseded); without certain cogns. Hence **smooth** vb. XV; superseding ME. *smethe* (dial. *smeeth*), OE. *smēþian, smēþan*. **smoo·th**EN[5] XVII.

smother smʌ·ðəɹ (often with *smoke*) dense or stifling smoke. XII. Early ME. *smorðer*, later (with loss of the first *r*) *smoþer*; f. base of OE. *smorian* (dial. *smore*) suffocate, corr. to (M)Du., (M)LG. *smoren* (whence G. *schmoren*), of unkn. origin. Hence vb. (early ME. *smorðren*).

smouch smautʃ (U.S.) pilfer. XIX. perh. alt. of SMOUSE.

smoulder smou·ldəɹ †smother, suffocate XIV; burn and smoke without flame XVI. rel. obscurely to LG. *smöln*, MDu. *smōlen* (Du. *smeulen* smoulder), Flem. *smoel* sultry. ¶ After early XVII discontinued exc. poet. in the prp. *smouldering*, until revived by Scott *c.*1810.

smouse smaus, also †*smouch* Jew. XVIII. – Du. *smous* Jew, usurer, corr. to G. *schmus* talk, patter – Yiddish *schmuoss*, Heb. *šěmūʿōth* tales, news, the reference being to the persuasive talk of Jewish pedlars.

smudge smʌdʒ make a dirty mark or smear on. XV. Hence sb. XVIII. Of unkn. origin, but parallel to synon. *smutch* sb. (XVI), vb. (XVII, Sh.), *smooch* vb. (XVII); cf. the formally corr. pair *sludge* and *slush*, and forms cited s.v. SMUT.

smug smʌg trim, neat, smooth, sleek XVI; marked by self-complacency XIX. Parallel to †*smudge* adj. smart, trim (Nashe), vb. deck out (Nashe, Greene), and corr. in sense to LG. *smuck* pretty (XVII), G. *schmuck* ornament, *schmücken* adorn.

smuggle smʌ·gl convey clandestinely to avoid duty, etc. XVII. Earlier *smuckle*, as in *smuckellor* (1661) – LG. *smukkelen*, with var. *smuggelen* (whence G. and Scand. forms), Du. *smokkelen*, of unkn. origin (reference to the base of OE. vb. *smūgan* creep does not account for the *k*-variant).

smut smʌt blacken, smudge XVI; affect (grain) with smut XVII. So **smut** sb., fungous disease of plants marked by blackness; black or sooty mark; indecent language XVII. Hence **smu·tty**[1] (of grain) XVI; dirty, blackened, obscene XVII. Parallel with obs. synon. formations having the cons.-frame *sm* . . *t* (with var. *sm* . . *d*), as OE. *smitt* smear, *smittian* pollute, *smītan* SMITE, also *besmittian* (ME. *besmit*), *ismotted* pp. (Trevisa), *besmotered* (Ch.) stained, *besmotted, smoterlich* (Ch.), *smotry* (Lydg.) defiled, sullied, *smad* (XV), *smod* stain (XIV), *bismudded, besmuðeled* XIII, and forms cited s.v. SMUDGE; cogn. further with Continental Germ. formations such as LG. *smutt*, MHG. *smotsen, smuz, smutzen* (G. *schmutz, schmutzen*, LG. *smadden*, Du. *smodderen*; cogns. of a type lacking initial *s* are seen in Gr. *múdos* dampness, Lith. *máudyti* bathe, OIr. *muad* cloud.

snack snæk (dial.) bite (esp. of a dog) XV (Hoccleve); share, portion; drop of liquor XVII; morsel of food, light repast, 'bite' XVIII. – MDu. *snac(k)* in the first sense, rel. to *snacken*, var. of *snappen* SNAP (whence Eng. dial. *snack* vb. XIV); MLG. *snacken* chatter (whence G. *schnack* gossip, rumour); perh. orig. imit. of the sound of snapping the jaws together. Cf. SNATCH.

snaffle snæ·fl form of bridle-bit. XVI. prob. of LDu. origin; cf. OFris. *snavel* mouth, (M)LG., (M)Du. *snavel*, corr. to OHG. *snabul* (G. *schnabel*) beak, bill, spout, nose; cf. Lith. *snãpas* beak, bill; see -LE[1].

snag snæg short stump projecting from a tree; sharp projection XVI; (orig. U.S.) trunk or branch in a river, etc. interfering with navigation; hence gen. obstacle XIX. prob. of Scand. origin (cf. ON. *snaghyrndr* sharp-pointed (axe), Norw. dial. *snag, snage* sharp point, spike, Icel. *snagi* peg).

snail sneil gasteropod housed in a shell. OE. *snæġ(e)l, sneġ(e)l* = OS. *snegil*, MLG. *sneil*, OHG. *snegil* (LG. *snagel*), ON.

snigill, f. **snag-*, **sneg-*, rel. to MLG. *snigge*, OHG. *snecko* (G. *schnecke*); cf. -LE[1].

snake sneik reptile of the order Ophidia. OE. *snaca* = MLG. *snake*, ON. *snákr*, *snókr* (Sw. *snok*, Da. *snog*); rel. to OHG. *snahhan* (G. dial. *schnaacken*) crawl, and further to Ir. *snaighim* I crawl.

snap snæp quick or sudden bite XV, catch, effort, sound XVII. So vb. bite quickly or suddenly, seize with sudden action XVI; break clean; make a cracking sound XVII. prob. – (M)LG., (M)Du. *snappen* seize (cf. SNACK vb.), speak hastily; but partly echoic. **snap-** the verb stem has been much used in comb. since XVIII to form terms denoting operations or appliances involving the use of a catch, a snapping movement, or rapid or unexpected action. comp. **sna·p**DRAGON A. antirrhinum XVI (Tusser, Gerarde); B. Christmas game of snatching raisins from burning brandy XVIII (Swift, Steele); in A with fanciful likening of the flower to a dragon's mouth, the lips of which suggest snapping; in B with suggestion of snatching a fiery dragon.

snare snɛəɹ trap consisting of a string with a running noose. Late OE. *sneara* – ON. *snara* = OS. *snari* (Du. *snaar*) string, OHG. *snarahha* snare; rel. to MLG. *snare* harp-string, OHG. *snerhan* bind, knot, ON. *snara* wind, twist. As applied to the strings of gut or rawhide stretched across the lower head of a side-drum prob. – MDu. or MLG. *snare*. Hence **snare** vb. XIV (Wycl. Bible). So synon. **snarl**[1] snāɹl XIV; see -EL[1], -LE[1].

snark snāɹk imaginary animal invented by 'Lewis Carroll' (C. L. Dodgson) in 'The Hunting of the Snark', 1876.

snarl[2] snāɹl make an angry sound with showing of the teeth. XVI. Extension of synon. †*snar* (XVI) – (M)LG. *snarren* = MHG. *snarren* (G. *schnarren*); cf. MHG. *snarche(l)n* (G. *schnarchen*); see -LE[3].

snatch snætʃ make a sudden snap at or seizure of. XIII. Hence **snatch** sb. †catch, hasp; †trap, snare XIV; hasty catch, sudden grab; short period; snack; small amount XVI. Obscurely rel. to SNACK, and north. dial. *sneck* door-latch (XIV); these imply a base **snak-*, repr. by (M)Du. *snakken* gasp, perh. orig. open the jaws suddenly; cf. SNAP.

sneak snīk go stealthily, creep furtively. XVI (Sh.; implied in somewhat earlier *sneakish*). prob. of dial. origin; rel. obscurely to early ME. *snike*, OE. *snican* creep, crawl, ON. *sníkja*.

sneer sniəɹ †snort XVI; smile contemptuously XVII. Hence **sneer** sb. XVIII. perh. of LDu. origin (cf. NFris. *sneer* scornful remark), *sneere* scorn.

sneeze snīz sb. and vb. (make) explosive noise to clear the nostrils. Appears first (XV) in the form *snese* as a substitute in printed texts for an original *fnese* (from OE. *fnēsan*), which had become obs. soon after 1400, being superseded by *nese*, NEEZE for which *snese*, *sneeze* was prob. substituted as more expressive.

snib see SNUB.

snick snik cut, snip XVIII; (in cricket) cut a ball so that it glances off XIX. Deduced from †*snick-a-snee*, †*snickersnee* fight with knives (1705), †*snick or snee*, repl. earlier †*stick or snee* (XVII) – Du. *steken* thrust, STICK, and *snee*, dial. var. of *snijen*, *snijden* cut, repr. CGerm. **snīþan* (OE. *snīþan*, etc., Goth. *sneiþan*).

snider snai·dəɹ breech-loading rifle invented by Jacob *Snider* (died 1860).

sniff snif draw air through the nose audibly. XIV. imit.; cf. next.

snift snift (dial.) sniff. XIV; implied in synon. (dial.) *snifter* (see -ER[1]); perh. – MSw. *snypta*, or MDa. *snyfte*, of imit. origin. *snifting* †*clack*, *pipe*, *valve*, through which air may be expelled.

snigger sni·gəɹ laugh in a half-suppressed manner. XVIII. var. of *snicker* (XVII), of imit. formation (cf. *nicker* neigh); see -ER[4]. Hence sb. (XIX).

snip snip †snap, snatch; cut (up or off). XVI. – LG., Du. *snippen* (cf. G. dial. *schnippen*), of echoic origin (cf. SNAP). Hence (or – LDu. forms) **snip** sb. small piece or amount; cut, incision; (hence) tailor (B. Jonson). XVI.

snipe snaip bird of the genus Gallinago. XIV. prob. of Scand. origin (cf. Icel. *mýri|-snípa*, Norw. *myr-*, *strand|snipa*). The occas. var. †*snippe* (XIV–XVII) corr. to obscurely rel. (M)LG., MDu. *snippe* (Du. *snip*), also *sneppe*, and OHG. *snepfa* (G. *schnepfe*). ¶ The synon. (dial.) *snite*, OE. *snite* (also *wudu|snite*) is of unkn. origin.

snip-snap-snorum snip snæp snō·rəm round card-game. XVIII. – LG. *snipp-snapp-snorum*, of fanciful coinage. ¶ Earlier †*snape snorum* (XVII).

snite snait see SNIPE.

snivel sni·vl run at the nose XIV; be in a tearful state XVII. repr. OE. **snyflan*, implied in late *snyflung* mucus of the nose, f. synon. *snofl*. Cf. LG., Du. *snuffelen* smell out, *snuiven* sniff, Sw. *snövla*, Norw. *snuvla*, Da. *snøvle*, †*snevle*. Hence sb. XV; cf. -LE[3].

snob snɔb (dial.) shoemaker, cobbler; †(Cambridge Univ.) townsman XVIII, †one with no claim to gentility; one who vulgarly admires, etc., one of superior rank, etc. (Thackeray) XIX. Of unkn. origin. Hence **sno·bb**ERY, **sno·bb**ISH[1] (Dickens), **sno·bb**ISM (George Eliot).

snoek snūk (S.Afr.) large edible sea-fish. XIX. Du. (cf. SNOOK).

snood snud hair-band. OE. *snōd* of doubtful origin.

snook snūk kinds of fish, esp. the sea-pike. XVII. – Du. *snoek* = (M)LG. *snōk*, prob. rel. to the base of SNACK. Cf. SNOEK.

snooker snū·kəɹ game combining pool and pyramids. XIX (late). Of unkn. origin. Hence **snoo·ker**ED[1] having one's object-ball covered by another.

snook(s) snūk(s) derisive gesture with thumb to nose (phr. *cock a s.*). XIX (late). Of unkn. origin.

Snooks snuks (colloq.) hypothetical surname of a person not identified or identifiable. Of unkn. origin.

snoop snūp (orig. U.S.) appropriate; go about prying. XIX. – Du. *snoepen* to eat (on the sly).

snooze snūz take a short nap. XVIII. Cant word of unkn. origin, perh. suggested by *snore* and *doze*.

snore snɔ̄əɹ (dial.) snort; make harsh noises in sleep through mouth and nose. XIV. f. imit. base **snor-*, repr. (with expressive additions) by (M)LG., (M)Du. *snorken* (whence dial. *snork* XVI, Tindale), Du. *snorken*, and SNORT; cf. also (M)LG. *snarken*, MHG. *snarchen* (G. *schnarchen*), beside OE. *fnǣran, fnǣrettan* snort.

snorkel snɔ̄·ɹkəl, **schnorkel** ʃnɔ̄·- underwater breathing device, esp. on a submarine. XX. – G. *schnorchel* (in same sense); cf. G. *schnarchen* to snore.

snort snɔ̄ɹt †snore; make an explosive noise by driving the breath through the nostrils. XIV. ult. imit. (cf. prec.); prob. partly alt. of †*fnort* (in some MSS. of Ch.); cf. the history of SNEEZE.

snot snɔt (dial.) snuff of a candle XIV (Wycl. Bible); mucus of the nose XV. prob. – (M)LG., MDu. *snotte*, Du. *snot*, corr. to OE. *ġe|snot*, OFris. *snotta*, MHG. *snuz* (G. dial. *schnutz*), f. Germ. **snūt-* (cf. next). Hence **sno·tty**[1] XVI (Levins); preceded by *sno·ttiness* (Palsgr.).

snout snaut †elephant's trunk; nose, muzzle. XIII. ME. *snūte* – MLG., MDu. *snūt(e)* (Du. *snuit*), whence MSw. *snuta*, Da. *snude*, G. *schnauze*; ult. f. Germ. **snūt-*, whence also late OE. *snȳtan* clear the nose (dial. *snite*) = (M)LG. *snūten*, OHG. *snūzen* (G. *schneuzen* snuff a candle, blow the nose), ON. *snýta* :– **snūtjan* (cf. SNOT).

snow[1] snou frozen vapour of the air falling in flakes. OE. *snāw* = OFris. *snē* (also mod.), OS., OHG. *snēo* (Du. *sneeuw*, G. *schnee*), ON. *snǽr, snjár, snjór*, Goth. *snaiws* :– CGerm. **snaiwaz*, immed. cogn. with Balto-Sl. forms, and Ir. *snigid* it snows, Av. *snaēžaiti*, OIr. *snechta*, parallel to an IE. type without *s-*, repr. by L. *nix, nivis*, Gr. *nípha* (acc.) *niphás, neíphei* it snows, W. *nyf*. Hence **snow** vb. XIII; repl. ME. *snewe*, OE. *snīwan* = MLG. *snīen*, MDu. *snūwen, snīen*, OHG. *snīwan* (G. *schneien*) :– WGerm. **snigwan*; with diff. vowel grade, ON. *snjáva, snjóva*; cf. comps. and derivs. (most of them with Germ. analogues. **sno·w**BALL[1] XIV; cf. AL. *nivenodium*; **sno·w**DROP plant Galanthus nivalis XVII (Boyle); **sno·w**FLAKE XVIII; **sno·w-**SHOE XVII; **sno·w-**WATER XII; **sno·w-**WHITE OE. *snāwhwīt*; **sno·w**Y[1] OE. *snāwig*; analogical str. inflexions, pt. *snew*, pp. *snawn, snown*, remaining dial., date from XIV.

snow[2] snou small sailing-vessel. XVII. – Du. *sna(a)uw* or LG. *snau* (whence also Sw., Da. *snau*, G. *schnaue*, F., etc. *senau*). Of unkn. origin.

snub snʌb rebuke or reprove sharply XIV (Rolle); check, stop (obs. exc. naut.) XVI; (dial.) shorten XVIII. – ON. *snubba* (cf. Norw. and Sw. dial. *snubba*, Da. *snubbe* cut short, make stumpy), rel. to MDa. *snibbe*, MSw. *snybba*, whence (dial.) *snib* rebuke XIII (Cursor M.); ult. origin unkn. Hence adj. short and turned up, in **snub-no·se** and **-no·sed** adj. XVIII (cf. Norw. dial. *snubbnos*); earlier †*snutnose(d)* XVII–XVIII, †*snatnosed* XVI, †*snatted* XIII–XV.

snuff[1] snʌf portion of candle-wick partly consumed XIV (Wycl. Bible). Of unkn. origin (G. synon. *schnuppe* does not corr. phonetically). Hence **snuff** vb. remove the snuff from XV (preceded by *snot* (Wycl. Bible), later dial., extinguish XVII (sl. intr. with *out*, die XIX).

snuff[2] snʌf powdered tobacco for inhaling through the nostrils. XVII. – Du. *snuf*, prob. short for *snuftabak* (so LG. *snuv-*, G. *schnupftabak*), f. MDu. *snuffen* snuffle, whence Eng. *snuff* (XVI) inhale through the nostrils.

snuffle snʌ·fl †sniff *at* in contempt; smell *at*; speak or draw air through the nose. XVI. prob. – LG., Du. *snuffelen* (whence G. *schnüffeln*), f. imit. base **snuf-*, repr. also by SNUFF[2], OE. *snoffa* nausea, *snofl* catarrh; see -LE[3] and cf. SNIVEL.

snug snʌg (of a ship) trim, secure against bad weather XVI; in ease or comfort XVII. First in naut. use and prob. of LDu. origin (cf. LG. *snügger, snögger* slender, smooth, dainty, smart, Du. *snuggher, snoggher* slender, slim, active (mod. *snugger* lively, sprightly), but the meanings are not close. Hence (see -LE[3]) **snuggle** snʌ·gl lie snug or close. XVII.

so sou in such a manner; in that way; to that extent. OE. *swa*, lengthened *swā* (also *swǣ, swē, se*), corr., with variations, to OFris. *sa, so*, OS. *sō*, OHG. *sō, suo* (Du. *zoo*, G. *so*), ON. *svá*, Goth. *swa* (also *swe*), rel. to OL. *suad* so, Oscan *svai, svae* if, *swā* and, Gr. *hōs* (:– **sϝōs*) as, *hóp(p)ōs* (:– **sϝód-pōs*) how. Cf. ALSO, AS, SUCH.

-so sou adv. attached to *wh-* prons. and advs., and *how*, e.g. ME. *hwa so* whoso, *hwer so* whereso (reduced forms of OE. *swā hwā swā, swā hwǣr swā*, etc.), repl. gen. by *-ever* (*whoever, wherever*) and -SOEVER. Cf. -SOME[3].

soak souk steep (trans. and intr.) OE.; permeate thoroughly XIV; percolate XV. OE. *socian*, corr. to WFlem. *soken, zoken*, rel. to OE. *soc* sucking at the breast, f. **suk*-, wk. grade of OE. *sūcan* SUCK. ¶ In OE. perh. only a colloq. word, which could account for its non-appearance in early ME.

soap soup substance composed of certain oils and fats used for cleansing. OE. *sāpe* = (M)LG. *sēpe*, MDu. *seepe* (Du. *zeep*), OHG. *seipha, seifa* (G. *seife*) :- WGerm. **saipō* (ON. *sápa* is prob. from OE.), whence Finnish *saip(p)io, saip(p)ua*, Lappish *saipo*, and L. *sāpō(n-)*, credited to Gaul by Pliny, whence (O)F. *savon*, Pr. *sabó*, Sp. *jabón*, It. *sapone*, Rum. *săpun*. Hence vb. XVI.

soar sɔ̄əɹ fly upwards. XIV (Ch.). Aphetic – (O)F. *essorer* (used refl.) = Pr. *eisaurar* raise into the air, It. (of hawks) *sorare* :- Rom. **exaurāre*, f. L. *ex* EX-[1] + *aura* air in motion (see AURA).

sob sɔb catch the breath convulsively. XII. First evidenced in easterly texts ('Vices and Virtues', 'Havelok', 'Ayenbite of Inwyt') and perh. of LDu. origin (cf. WFris. *sobje*, Du. dial. *sabben* suck).

sober sou·bəɹ temperate in food or drink (R. Mannyng); not drunk or drunken (Wycl. Bible, Trevisa); grave, serious, sedate (PPl., Ch., Gower); subdued in tone XVI (Sh.); restrained in thought, etc. XVII. – (O)F. *sobre* = Sp., It. *sobrio* – L. *sōbrius*)(*ēbrius* (see EBRIETY, INEBRIATE). So **sobr**IETY sobrai·iti. XV. – (O)F. or L.

sobriquet, soubriquet sou·brikei, sū·- nickname. XVII. – F. *sobriquet*, earlier *soubriquet* (XV); identical with *soubriquet* (XIV) tap under the chin, perh. for **souzbequet*, f. *souz* (:- L. *subtus*) under + *bec* BEAK.

socage sɔ·kidʒ (hist.) tenure by service other than knight-service, as by attendance at the court held by the superior in virtue of his right of soke. XIV. – AN. *socage* (AL. *socāgium*), f. *soc*; see SOKE, -AGE.

soccer sɔ·kəɹ see -ER[6].

sociable sou·ʃəbl marked by inclination for companionship. XVI. – F. *sociable* or L. *sociābilis*, f. *sociāre* unite, ASSOCIATE, f. *socius* companion, ally, fellow; see -ABLE. So **sociabi·l**ITY. XV. **soci**AL[1] sou·ʃəl †allied, occurring between allies; marked by mutual intercourse XVI; pert. to human society XVIII (the popularization of this sense was due partly to the title of J. J. Rousseau's 'Le contrat social', 1762) – (O)F. *social* or L. *sociālis* allied, confederate, companionable, sociable, (Ovid) conjugal, f. *socius*; the L. adj. was used by Grotius and Puffendorf in *jus naturale sociale* natural social law. So **so·cial**ISM political doctrine and practice of social organization by which production and administration of all resources are controlled by the community, 1839. – F. *socialisme* (1832); cf. It. *antisocialismo* (Giacomo Giuliana, 1803). **so·cial**IST (1827, R. Owen). **society** sŏsai·iti A. (living in) association XVI (Elyot, More); aggregate of persons living together XVII; B. collection of persons forming a community XVI. – (O)F. *société* = Sp. *sociedad*, It. *società* – L. *societās, -tat-*, f. *socius*; see -ITY, -TY[2]. **societ**A·RIAN pert. to society or its organization XIX (1822, Lamb); cf. F. *sociétaire* (XVIII). **sociology** sousiɔ·lədʒi science dealing with human society. XIX. – F. *sociologie* (Auguste Comte, 1830), irreg. f. (see -O-) L. *socius*. ¶ Grotius used modL. *socialista*, and *socialistus* was applied later to adherents of his.

Socinian sousi·niən (pert. to) a member of a heretical sect denying the divinity of Jesus Christ. XVII. – modL. *Sociniānus*, f. *Socinus*, latinization of *Soz(z)ini*, surname of two It. theologians of XVI.

sock[1] sɔk †light shoe OE.; half-hose XIV; shoe worn by comic actors on the Greek and Roman stage XVI. OE. *socc*, corr. to MLG., MDu. *socke* (Du. *zok*), OHG. *soch* (G. *socke*), ON. *sokkr*; Germ. – L. *soccus* – Gr. *súkkhos, sukkhás*, which may be of Oriental origin, but their connexions are obscure.

sock[2] sɔk (sl.) blow, beating; also vb. XVII. Of unkn. (perh. echoic) origin.

sock[3] sɔk (Eton School sl.) eatables. XIX. Of unkn. origin.

socket sɔ·kit †lance- or spear-head of the form of a ploughshare XIII; cavity to receive an object fitting into it XV – AN. *soket*, dim. of (O)F. *soc* ploughshare (thought to be of Celtic origin) after AL. *vomerulus* (Matthew Paris XIII), dim. of L. *vomer* ploughshare; see -ET.

socle sɔ·kl plain block or plinth serving as a pedestal. XVIII. – F. *socle* – It. *zoccolo* prop. wooden shoe, repr. L. *socculus*, dim. of *soccus* SOCK[1].

sod[1] sɔd piece of grass-grown earth. XV. – (M)LG. *sode*, MDu. *sode* (Du. *zode*) = OFris. *sātha, sāda*, of unkn. origin.

sod[2] sɔd gross term of abuse for a male person; also in milder use. XIX. sl. shortening of SODOMITE.

soda sou·də sodium carbonate. XVI. – medL. *soda* (whence F. *soude*, Sp., It. *soda*), perh. back-formation f. *sodānum* glasswort, based on Arab. *ṣudāᶜ* headache (for which the plant, containing soda, was used as a remedy), f. *sadaᶜ* split. Hence **sodium** sou·diəm (chem.) metal forming the base of soda. XIX (H. Davy 1807).

sodalite sou·dəlait (min.) greenish-blue silicate of aluminium and sodium. XIX. f. SODA + -LITE.

sodality soudæ·liti religious guild for mutual help, etc. XVI. – F. or L., f. *sodālis* member of a brotherhood or corporation; see -ITY.

sodden sɔ·dn †boiled XIII; †dull, stupid, expressionless XVI; saturated with moisture XIX. pp. of SEETHE.

sodomy sɔ·dəmi unnatural sexual intercourse, esp. between males. XIII (RGlouc.). – medL. *sodomia* (whence also (O)F. *sodomie* XIV, Sp. *sodomía*, It. *sodomia*), for ChrL. *peccātum Sodomīticum* (Jerome), *Sodomīta libīdō* (Prudentius) sin, lust of Sodom, f. *Sodoma* (Gr. *Σόδομα*, Heb. *S'dōm*) the city of Sodom in Palestine the wickedness and destruction of which are recorded in Gen. xviii–xix. So **so·domITE** one who commits sodomy XIV; inhabitant of Sodom XV. – (O)F. *sodomite* – late L. *Sodomīta*, Gr. *Sodomī́tēs*; see -ITE.

soever soue·vəɹ poet. **soe'er** soueə·ɹ SO + EVER used with generalizing or emphatic force. XVI. hence as a var. of *-ever*, as in *whosoever*, *whensoever*, *wheresoever*; so (dial.) **some·ver, -some·ver** see -SO, -SOME[3].

sofa sou·fə in the East, dais furnished with cushions and carpets XVII (Purchas); long stuffed couch XVIII. ult. – Arab. *ṣuffaʰ*, through Eur. langs., F. *sofa*, †*sopha*, etc.

soffit sɔ·fit (arch.) under surface or ceiling of an architrave, etc. XVII. Earliest forms *soffita*, *-ito*, later *sof(f)ite*, *soffit* – F. *soffite* or It. *soffito*, *-ita* :– **suffictu-s*, *-icta*, for L. *suffixus* (see SUFFIX).

soft sɔ̀ft A. agreeable OE.; B. gentle, mild XII; C. impressionable, compliant XIII (silly, simple XVII); presenting a yielding surface XIII. Late OE. *sōfte* agreeable, comfortable, luxurious, repl. earlier mutated *sēfte* = OFris. *sēfte*, OS. *sāfti*, OHG. *semfti* (UG. †*senft*) :– WGerm. **samfti*; the un-mutated form, due to influence from the adv. (OE. *sōfte*, etc.), is paralleled in MLG. *sachte*, *safte*, LG. *sacht*, MDu. *sachte*, *safte* (Du. *zacht*), (M)HG. *sanft*; f. WGerm. **samft-*, referred by some to the base **sōm-* of SEEM. Hence **softEN**[5] sɔ̀·fn. XIV (Ch.).

soggy sɔ·gi (dial., U.S.) swampy. XVIII. f. dial. *sog* marsh + -Y[1].

soho souhou· (orig. in hunting) call to direct attention to a hare. XIII. In earliest use varying with *howe*, *he howe*, *here howe*, *howe here*.

soi-disant swadizã self-styled XVIII; pretended XIX. F., *soi* oneself (:– L. *sē*), *disant*, prp. of *dire* say (see DICTION).

soil[1] soil (piece of) ground or earth, land, country; ground as cultivated. XIV. First in several senses from west-midl. texts. – AN. *soil* land, perh. repr. L. *solium* seat (whence F. *seuil* threshold), by assoc. with *solum* (F. *sol*) ground.

soil[2] soil †muddy place; stretch of water as refuge for a hunted animal XV; stain, pollution XVI; filth, ordure (as in *night-soil*) XVII. – OF. **soille*, *souille* (mod. *souille* muddy place, (dial.) *souil* pond, ordure), f. *souiller* SOIL[3].

soil[3] soil A. defile, pollute XIII; sully, tarnish XVI; B. take to water or marshy ground XV. – OF. *soill(i)er*, *suill(i)er* (mod. *souiller*) = Pr. *solhar*, Cat. *sullar* :– Rom. **suculāre*, f. L. *suculus*, *-ula*, dim. of *sūs* SOW[1].

soil[4] soil (dial.) feed (cattle) with green fodder, orig. for purgation. XVII. perh. a use of SOIL[3].

soirée swā·rei evening party. XIX. F., f. *soir* evening :– L. *sērum* late hour, n. of *sērus* late (cf. SINCE).

sojourn sɔ·dʒəɹn, sʌ·dʒəɹn reside, stay. XIII (S.Eng. (Leg). ME. *sorjourni*, *soiourni* – OF. *sorjorner*, *sojorner* (mod. *séjourner*) = Pr. *sojornar*, It. *soggiornare* :– Rom. **subdiurnāre* 'spend the day', f. L. *sub-* SUB- + late L. *diurnum* day (cf. JOURNAL). So **so·journ** sb. XIII. – AN. *su(r)jurn*, OF. *sojor*, etc. (mod. *séjour*), f. the vb.

soke souk right of local jurisdiction; area of this. XIV. – medL. *sōca* – OE. *sōcn* attack, resort, right of prosecution or jurisdiction, administrative district = ON. *sókn* attack, prosecution, concourse, parish, Goth. *sōkns* search, inquiry :– Germ. **sōkniz*, f. **sōk-* (see SEEK). The full form **so·ken** is also used for jurisdictional district (locally, as by Ch., for resort to a particular mill).

sol[1] sɔl sun; (alch.) gold XIV (Ch.); (her.) or XVII. – L. *sōl* SUN.

sol[2] sɔl (mus.) 5th note of Guido's hexachords and hence of the octave. XIV. See GAMUT. Hence **solfa** sɔlfā· set of syllables (do, re, mi, fa, etc.) sung to the notes of the major scale XVI; as vb., repl. †*solf(e)* XIV, surviving in Sc. *sowff* (XVIII) hum or whistle (a tune) softly – (O)F. *solfier*; cf. Sp. *solfear*. So **solfeggio** sɔlfe·dʒiou exercise in which the solfa is employed. XVIII. It., f. *solfeggiare*. **solmization** sɔlmaizei·ʃən solfa-ing. XVIII. – F., f. *solmiser*, f. *sol* SOL[2] + *mi* MI. See -IZE, -ATION.

sola sou·lə L. *sola*, of females, solitary, = SOLE[3]. XVIII. It. (comm.) single bill – L. fem. of *sōlus* SOLE[3]; see -A[1].

solace sɔ·ləs consolation or means of it; †delight, amusement. XIII. – OF. *solas*, *-atz* (mod. dial. *soulas*) = Pr. *solatz*, Sp. *solaz*, It. *solazzo* :– L. *sōlātium*, f. *sōlārī* relieve, console. So **so·lace** vb. XIII. – OF. *solacier* (med. dial. *soulasser*); cf. It. *solazzare*, medL. *sōlātiāre*, etc.

solan sou·lən gannet. XV. In earliest use Sc.; prob. f. ON. *súla* gannet + *and-*, *ǫnd* duck (see DRAKE).

solander sou·lændəɹ box made in the form of a book to contain botanical specimens, etc. XVIII. f. name of D. C. *Solander*, Sw. botanist (1736–82).

solandra soulæ·ndrə genus of tropical Amer. shrubs. XVIII. modL., f. name of D. C. *Solander*; see prec. and -A[1].

solanum soulei·nəm nightshade. XVI. – L. *sōlānum*, f. *sōl* SOL[1]. **solan**A·CEOUS. XIX.

solar sou·ləɹ pert. to the sun. XV. – L. *sōlāris*, f. *sōl* SOL[1]; see -AR and cf. F. *solaire*, etc. So **solarium** soulɛə·riəm sundial; apartment or area exposed to the sun. XIX; cf. SOLLAR and see -IUM.

soldan sɔ·ldən see SULTAN.

solder sɔ·ldəɹ, sou·ldəɹ, sɔ·dəɹ, sɔ̄·dəɹ fusible alloy used for uniting metal surfaces. XIV. Early forms *soudur, soudre, sawdere* (cf. SAWDER), *sod(d)er* – (O)F. *soudure*, f. *souder*, †*solder* (whence †*sold* vb. XIV) = Pr. *soudar*, Sp. *soldar*, OIt. *sodare* :– L. *solidāre* fasten together, f. *solidus* SOLID. Hence vb. XV.

soldier sou·ldʒəɹ one serving in an army for pay. XIII (Cursor M.). Early forms *sawder, -iour, sowdier, -iour, souldeour, so(l)diour* – OF. *soud(i)er, saudier, so(l)dier* (cf. medL. *solidārius*), f. *sou(l)de* (whence †*sold* sb. XIV) pay = Pr. *sol*, Sp. *sueldo*, It., Pg. *soldo* :– L. *solidus* gold coin of imperial times, sb. use (sc. *nummus* coin) of *solidus* SOLID; see -IER[2].

sole[1] soul under-surface of the foot XIV; bottom of a boot or shoe; †foundation; sill XV; lower part, bottom XVII. Late OE. **solu* or **sole* (in miswritten pl. *solen*), corr. to OS., OHG. *sola* (Du. *zool*, G. *sohle*) – popL. **sola* (whence also OF. *suele*, Pr. *sola*, Sp. *suela*, It. *suola*, whence F. *sole*), for L. *solea* sandal, sill (see also next), f. *solum* bottom, pavement, sole of the foot.

sole[2] soul flatfish Solea vulgaris (solea). XIV. – (O)F. *sole* – Pr. *sola* = Sp. *suela* whence It. *soglia*, Pg. *solha* :– Rom. **sola* for L. *solea*, identical with prec., the fish being so named because of its shape.

sole[3] soul single, unmarried (surviving in FEME sole) XIV (Ch.); alone, solitary XV; one and only XV; exclusive XVI. Late ME. *soul(e)* – OF. *soul-e* (mod. *seul-e*) = Pr. *sol*, Sp., It. *solo* :– L. *sōlus* alone, sole. Cf. CONSOLE, DESOLATE.

solecism sɔ·lisizm violation of good grammar or good manners; impropriety. XVI. – F. *solécisme* or L. *solœcismus* – Gr. *soloikismós*, f. *sóloikos* using incorrect syntax, guilty of grammatical impropriety, said by ancient writers (Strabo, etc.) to refer to the corruption of the Attic dialect by Athenian colonists at *Soloi* in Cilicia; see -ISM.

solemn sɔ·ləm accompanied with ceremony; grave, serious. XIV. ME. *solem(p)ne* – OF. *solem(p)ne* (superseded by *solennel*), corr. to Pr., Sp. *solemne*, It. *solenne* – L. *sollemnis, -ennis, -empnis* celebrated ceremonially and at a fixed date, festive, customary, f. *sollus* whole, entire, said by Festus to be an Oscan word; the terminal el. is unexpl. So **solemn**ITY sŏle·mnĭti. XIII (S.Eng. Leg., Cursor M.). – OF. *solem(p)nité* (mod. *solennité*) – L *sollem(p)nitās*. **solemn**IZE sɔ·ləmnaiz. XIV (Wycl.). – OF. *solemniser* – medL. **so:lemniz**A·TION. XV.

solen sou·lən razor-fish. XVII. – L. *sōlēn* – Gr. *sōlḗn* channel, pipe, syringe, shellfish.

solfa, solfeggio see SOL[2].

solfatara sɔlfətā·rə volcanic vent exhaling sulphurous vapour. XVIII. f. name of a sulphurous volcano near Naples, Italy. f. *solfo* SULPHUR.

solferino sɔlfərī·nou bright crimson dye-colour rosaniline. XIX. f. *Solferino*, name of a town in Italy, where a battle was fought in 1859. ¶ Cf. for circumstances of origin MAGENTA, STEENKIRK.

solicit səli·sit A. †disturb, trouble XV; †entreat, petition, incite XVI; B. †manage, attend to (affairs) XV; †urge, plead; sue for; also intr. XVI. – (O)F. *solliciter*, corr. to Pr. *sollicitar*, etc. – L. *sollicitāre* stir, agitate, harass, vex, seduce, entice, (medL.) look after, f. *sollicitus* agitated, f. *sollus* whole, entire (cf. SOLEMN) + *citus* put in motion, pp. of *ciēre* (see CITE). So **solicit**A·TION †management, transaction XV; entreaty XVI. – (O)F. – L. **soli·cit**OR[1] †instigator, †manager, agent, deputy XV (Lydg.); agent in a court of law XVI. – (O)F. *solliciteur* †one who takes charge of business, etc., f. *solliciter*; cf. late L. *sollicitātor*. **soli·cit**OUS troubled, anxious, careful. XVI. f. L. *sollicitus*. **soli·ci**TUDE. XV. – (O)F. – L.

solid sɔ·lid free from empty spaces)(*hollow* XIV (Ch.); of three dimensions XV; of dense consistency; firm and substantial XVI. – (O)F. *solide* (corr. to Sp., It. *solido*), or L. *solidus*, rel. to *salvus* SAFE, *sollus* whole (cf. prec.). Also sb. XV, after F. *solide*, L. *solidum*, sb. use of n. adj. Hence **soli·d**ITY XVI – L.; cf. F. *solidité*. So **solidar**ITY sɔlidæ·rĭti the being fully at one in interests, etc. XIX. – F. *solidarité*, orig. in legal use (XVIII), f. *solidaire* (XVI; whence **so·lid**ARY joint and several XIX), f. *solide*, after L. phr. *in solidum* for the whole, in toto. **solidu·ngu**LATE[2] XIX, **-u·ngul**OUS XVII (Sir T. Browne) soliped; L. *ungula* hoof, f. *unguis* NAIL.

solifidian soulifi·diən (theol.) one who holds that faith alone is sufficient for justification. XVI. – modL. *sōlifidius*, f. L. *sōli-*, comb. form of *sōlus* SOLE[3] + *fides* FAITH; see -IAN.

soliloquy səli·ləkwi talking aloud to oneself. XVII. – late L. *sōliloquium* (Augustine), f. *sōli-*, *sōlus* SOLE[3] + *loquī* speak (see LOCUTION). Hence **soli·loqu**IZE. XVIII.

soliped, -pede sɔ·liped, -pīd animal with uncloven hoof. XVII (Sir T. Browne). – F. *solipède* or modL. *soliped, -pēs*, for L. *solidipēs*, f. *solidus* SOLID + *pēs* FOOT.

solipsism sɔ·lipsizm (philos.) theory that the self is the only object of knowledge. XIX. f. L. *sōlus* SOLE[3] + *ipse* self- + -ISM.

solitary sɔ·litəri alone; marked by solitude. XIV. – L. *sōlitārius*, f. *sōlitās* solitariness, f. *sōlus* SOLE³; see -ITY, -ARY. So **solitaire** sɔ·litɛəɹ recluse; precious stone set by itself; game to be played by one person; loose necktie. XVIII. – (O)F. *solitaire*. **so·litUDE**. XIV (Ch.; not frequent before XVII). – (O)F. or L.

sollar sɔ·ləɹ upper room. XIII (Cursor M.). – AN. *soler*, OF. *solier* = Pr. *solar*, It. *solaio* :– L. *sōlārium* sundial, gallery, terrace, f. *sōl* SOL¹; not continuous with OE. *solor* = OS. *soleri*, OHG. *solări* (Du. *zolder*, G. *söller*), WGerm. adoption of the L. word; see -AR.

solleret sɔ·ləret in the armour of XIV–XV, a shoe of steel plates. XIX. – OF. *sol(l)eret*, dim. of *sol(l)er* (mod. *soulier*) = Pr. *sotlar* :– medL. *subtelāris* (sc. *calceus* shoe), f. late L. *subtel* arch of the sole; see -ET.

solmization see SOL².

solo sou·lou (mus.) part to be sung or played by one performer alone. XVII. – It. *solo* :– L. *solu-s* SOLE³. Hence **so·loIST**. XIX; cf. F. *soliste*.

solstice sɔ·lstis time at which the sun is furthest from the equator and appears to stand still before returning. XIII. – (O)F. *solstice* – L. *sōlstitium*, f. *sōl* SOL¹ + *stit-*, var. of *stat-* (as in STATION).

soluble sɔ·ljŭbl †free from constipation XIV; capable of being melted or dissolved XV; solvable XVIII. – (O)F. *soluble* – late L. *solūbilis*, f. *solvere* loosen, SOLVE; see next, -BLE. So **soluTION** səlʲū·ʃən solving; explanation (Barbour); dissolving (Gower) XIV; breach XVI. – (O)F. – L.

solve sɔlv †loosen, unbind XV; explain, clear up; clear off (a debt) XVI. – L. *solvere* unfasten, free, pay (whence Sp. *solver*, It. *solvere*), for **seluere*, f. **se* SE- + *luere* pay (see LOOSE). So **so·lvENT** able to pay; dissolving (also sb.) XVII. – prp. of L. *solvere*.

somatic soumæ·tik pert. to the body. XVIII. – Gr. *sōmatikós*, f. *sōma(t-)* body; see -IC. So **so·matO-**, comb. form of Gr. *sôma*.

sombre sɔ·mbəɹ marked by gloom XVIII; dark in colour XIX. – (O)F. *sombre*, adj. use of OF. sb. (= Cat., Sp., Pg. *sombra* shade), first in *sombre coup* 'dark blow', bruise, based on Rom. *subombrāre* (cf. Pr. *sozombrar*, *solombrar* shade), f. L. *sub* SUB- 5 + *umbra* shade, shadow (cf. UMBRAGEOUS).

sombrero sɔmbrɛə·rou †Oriental umbrella XVI; broad-brimmed hat XVIII. – Sp. *sombrero* (in full *sombrero de sol*), f. *sombra* shade (see prec.).

some sʌm, (unstr.) səm †a certain; one or other; a certain amount or number of; also as sb. or pron. OE. *sum* = OFris., OS., OHG. *sum*, ON. *sumr*, Goth. *sums* :– CGerm. **sumaz* :– IE. **sm̥mos*, the base of which is repr. also by Gr. *hamôs* somehow, *hamóthen* from some place, *oud|amós* none, Skr. *samás*, Av. *hamō* some, every, Arm. *amēn* every, all. (Cf. SAME.) comps. **so·meBO:DY**, -ONE XIV, **so·meHOW** XVIII, **so·meTHING** OE., **so·meTIME** XIII, -TIMES XVI, **so·meWHAT**, -WHERE XII (Orm). ¶ The word has had greater currency in Eng. than in other Germ. langs., in some of which it is now restricted to dial. use or repr. only in derivs., e.g. Du. *sommige* some, certain, *somtijds*, *somwijlen* sometimes, G. dial. *sum*, *summige*.

-some¹ səm suffix repr. OE. *-sum* = OFris. *-sum*, rel. by gradation to OS., OHG. *-sam* (Du. *-zaam*, G. *-sam*), ON. *-samr*, Goth. **-sams* (in voc. pl. *lustusamans* longed-for), added to sbs., adjs., and vbs., to form adjs. denoting a quality, condition, temperament, etc. of a character expressed or implied by the first el. Of the OE. formations *winsome* remains in literary use, *longsome*, *lovesome* are arch. or dial.; many others are of ME. age, as *cumbersome*, *fulsome*, *gladsome*, *handsome*, *noisome*, *wholesome*; later are *quarrelsome* (Sh.), *tiresome*. In *buxom* and *lissom* the suffix is disguised.

-some² səm repr. OE. *sum* SOME, used after g. pl. of a numeral, as *fiftēna sum* (being) one of (a company of) fifteen, surviving in descriptions of games or contests in which persons of the number designated take part, as *twosome*, *threesome*, *foursome*.

-some³ səm later var. of *-sum*, repr. Scand. rel. adv. *sum*, *som*, surviving in dial. *-somever*, equiv. to -SOEVER, e.g. *whatsomever*.

somersault sʌ·məɹsɔ̀lt leap in which the person turns heels over head. XVI. (Also occas. †*sombersalt*) – OF. *sombresau(l)t*, alt. of *sobresault* (whence Eng. †*sobersault* XVI–XVII), mod. *soubresaut* – Pr. **sobresaut* = Sp. *sobresalto*, f. *sobre* (:– L. *suprā*) above + *saut* (:– L. *saltu-s*) leap; see SUPRA-, SALTATION. Further alt. to *somer-*, *summerset* (XVI). ¶ XVI–XVII sp. also *-saut*. The sp. with *l*, after F. *-sault*, influenced the pronunc. Cf. FAULT.

somnambulism sɔmnæ·mbjulizm walking in one's sleep. XVIII. f. L. *somnus* sleep (cf. INSOMNIA) + *ambulāre* walk (see AMBLE) + ISM. So **somna·mbulIST**, **somnambulA·TION** XVIII.

somni- comb. form of *somnus* sleep, as in **somni·FEROUS** XVII, **somni·FIC** XVIII.

somnolent sɔ·mnələnt inclining to sleep XV; inclined to sleep XVI. – F. *somnolent* (†*somp-*) or L. *somnolentus*, f. *somnus* (see prec.). So **so·mnolENCE**. XIV (Ch.).

son sʌn male child in relation to his parents, 'filius'. OE. *sunu* = OFris., OS., OHG. *sunu* (Du. *zoon*, G. *sohn*), ON. *sunr*, *sonr*, Goth. *sunus* :– CGerm. **sunuz*, rel. more immed. to Balto-Sl. and Indo-Iran. forms (OSl. *synŭ*, Skr. *sūnús*), and remotely to OIr. *suth* (:– **sutu*) offspring, Skr. *sutás* and Gr. *huiús*, *huiós* (:– **suju-s*) son. Cf. BROTHER.

sonant sou·nənt (phon.) uttered with voice. XIX. – L. *sonant-*, *-āns*, prp. of *sonāre* sound; see SOUND[3].

sonata sənā·tə (mus.) †piece of instrumental music)(cantata; now, one for the pianoforte, consisting of three or four movements. XVII. – It. *sonata*, fem. pp. of *sonare* SOUND[2].

song sɔŋ singing; that which is sung. OE. *sang* (*song*) = OFris. *sang, song*, OS. *sang* (Du. *zang*), OHG. *sanc* (G. *sang*), ON. *sǫngr*, Goth. *saggws* :– CGerm. **saŋgwaz*, f. **saŋgw-* **seŋgw-* SING. Hence **so·ngSTER** singer. OE. *sangestre*; whence **so·ngstrESS**[1].

sonorous sənɔ̄·rəs giving out a deep or strong sound. XVII. f. L. *sonōrus*, f. *sonōr-*, *sonor* sound; see SOUND[3], -OUS.

sonnet sɔ·nit (pros.) †short poem; poem of fourteen 10-syllable (five-stress) lines with a particular rhyme-pattern variously arranged. XVI (*sonet*). – F. *sonnet* or its source It. *sonetto*, dim. of *suono* SOUND[3]; see -ET. Hence **sonnetEE·R**[1]. XVII; partly – It. *sonettiere*.

sonsy sɔ·nsi lucky, fortunate XVI; buxom, comely and pleasant XVIII. orig. Sc., Ir. and north. dial.; f. (dial.) *sonse* (XIV) abundance, prosperity – Ir., Gael. *sonas* good fortune, f. *sona* fortunate, happy; see -Y[1].

soon sūn within a short time (†immediately, at once). OE. *sōna* = OFris. *sōn*, OS. *sāno, sān(a)*, OHG. *sān(o)* :– WGerm. **sǣnō* (obs. in nearly all Continental langs.), perh. rel. to Goth. *suns* immediately.

soot sut black carbonaceous deposit from the burning of wood, etc. OE. *sōt* = MLG. *sōt* (G. dial. *sott*), MDu. *soet*, (also mod. dial.) *zoet*, ON. *sót* :– Germ. **sōtam* 'that which settles', with Balto-Sl. and Ir. cogns.; f. IE. **sōd-* **sĕd-* SIT. For the standard pronunc. cf. *book, shook*; for the vulgar sʌt cf. *blood, flood*. Hence **soo·tY**[1]. XIII.

sooth sūþ (arch. as in *in (good) s., s. to say*) truth. OE. *sōþ* = OS. *sōð*, f. corr. adj. OE. *sōþ* = OS. *sōð*, ON. *sannr, saðr* :– Germ. **sanþaz* :– IE. **sontos*, rel. to Goth. **sunjis* true (in fem. *sunja*) :– IE. **sn̥tyós*; with Indo-Iran. cogns. (cf. Skr. *satyás*). So **soo·thfast** truthful, faithful, veracious. Cf. OE. *sōþfæst*; exc. in Sc. legal use not evidenced from XVII until revived by Scott *c.* 1805. **soothsayer** sū·þsei:əɹ †one who speaks the truth; one who claims to foretell the future XIV; *sōþsecġan* tell the truth; cf. OE. *sōþsagu* truth, history; *sayer* agent-noun of SAY.

soothe sūð †prove to be true OE.; †declare to be true; confirm, encourage; †please or flatter by assent; † gloss over XVI; calm, mollify XVII; allay, assuage XVIII. OE. (*ġe*)*sōþian*, f. *sōþ* SOOTH; cf. ON. *sanna* assert, prove.

sop sɔp piece of bread, etc. dipped in liquid OE.; milksop XVII. Late OE. *sopp*, corr. to MLG. *soppe*, OHG. *sopfa* bread and milk, ON. *soppa* (a foreign word), prob. f. wk. grade of the base of OE. *sūpan* SUP (cf. OE. *sopa* draught). So **sop** vb. dip in liquid OE. *soppian* (thereafter not till XVI f. the sb.); drench, soak XVII; become wet XIX. **so·ppING**[2] soaked, soaking wet XIX. **so·ppY**[1] †full of sops XVII; (colloq.) foolishly sentimental XIX.

soph sɔf abbrev. of SOPHISTER (XVII) and SOPHOMORE (XVIII).

sophism sɔ·fizm specious but fallacious argument. XIV. ME. *sophime, -eme* – OF. *sophime* (also mod. *sophisme* after L. and Gr. to which the Eng. form was later assim.) – L. *sophisma* – Gr. *sóphisma* clever device, trick, argument, f. *sophízesthai* devise, f. *sophós* wise, clever; see -ISM. So **so·phIST** XVI. – L. *sophistēs* – Gr. **so·phistER**[1] sophist. XIV (Wycl., PPl., Trevisa). **sophi·stIC.** XVI, -ICAL. XV (Caxton). **sophistiCATE**[3] səfi·stikeit †adulterate XIV (Maund.); corrupt, pervert, falsify, as by debasing admixture XVII. **sophisticA·TION** *c.*1400. – OF. or medL. **so·phistRY** specious or fallacious reasoning. XIV. – OF. *sophistrie* (mod. *-erie*) or medL. *sophistria*.

sophomore sɔ·fŏmɔ̄əɹ at universities (now U.S.) student in his second year. XVII. Earlier *sophumer* (-ER[1]), beside prp. *sophuming*, f. *sophum*, obs. var. of SOPHISM.

sophy sou·fi (hist.) shah. XVI. – Pers. *çafi* surname of the ruling dynasty of Persia from *c.*1500 to *c.*1736, derived from the Arab. epithet *çafi-ud-dīn* ('purity of religion') given to an ancestor of Ismail Safī, founder of the dynasty.

sopite soupai·t put to sleep XVI; put an end to XVII. f. *sōpīt-*, pp. stem of L. *sōpīre* deprive of sense or consciousness, f. *sōpor* deep sleep, f. IE. **sup-* **swep-* (see SWEVEN). So **sopori·FEROUS** soupəri·fərəs, sɔp-producing sleep. XVI. – L. *sopōrifer*. **sopori·FIC.** XVII.

soprano səprā·nou highest singing voice in women and boys. XVIII. – It. *soprano*, f. *sopra* above; see SUPRA-, -AN.

sorb sɔ̄ɹb (fruit of) the service tree XVI; rowan XVIII. – F. *sorbe* or L. *sorbus* service tree, *sorbum* service berry.

Sorb sɔ̄ɹb member of Slavonic race inhabiting Lusatia, E. Saxony. XIX. – G. *Sorbe*, var. of *Serbe* SERB.

sorbet sɔ̄·ɹbit sherbet. XVI. – F. *sorbet* – It. *sorbetto* – Turk. *shorbet* – Arab. *sharbāt* pl. drinks; cf. SHERBET.

sorcerer sɔ̄·ɹsərəɹ practiser of sorcery. XVI (Tindale, Coverdale). Extension, with -ER[1], of late ME. *sorser* – (O)F. *sorcier* :– Rom. **sortiārius*, f. *sort-*, *sors* lot (SORT); see -ER[2]. So **so·rcerESS**[1]. – AN. *sorceresse*; fem. of *sorc(i)er*. **so·rcERY.** XIII (Cursor M.). – OF. *sorcerie*, f. *sorcier*.

sordes sɔ̄·ɹdīz filthy or feculent matter. XVII. – L. *sordēs* pl., rel. to *sordēre* be dirty. So **so·rd**ID[1] foul, dirty (lit. and fig.) XVI; characterized by mean or ignoble motives XVII. – F. *sordide* or L. *sordidus*, f. *sordēre*. See SWART.

sordine sɔ̄·ɹdīn (mus.) muting device. XVI – It. *sordina*, *-ino*, f. *sordo* :– L. *surdus* deaf, mute; see SURD, -INE[1].

sore sɔ̄əɹ †bodily suffering, disease; place where the skin is broken or inflamed; †grief, trouble. OE. *sār* = OFris., OS., OHG. *sēr* (Du. *zeer*, G. †*sehr*), ON. *sár*, Goth. *sair* :– CGerm. **sairam* (*-az*). So **sore** adj. (arch.) painful, grievous; painful, aching, (now) with skin inflamed, etc. OE.; pained, distressed XIII. OE. *sār* = OFris. **sēr*, OS., OHG. *sēr* (Du. *zeer*, G. *sehr*), ON. *sárr* :– Germ. **sairaz* (whence Finn. *sairas* sick, ill). **sore** adv. (arch., dial.) painfully, grievously. OE. *sāre* = OFris. *sēre*, OS., OHG. *sēro* (Du. *zeer*, G. *sehr* greatly, very). **sore**LY[2] OE. *sārlīće*.

sorex sɔ̄·reks shrew-mouse. XVII. L. *sōrex* (*-ic-*), rel. to Gr. *húrax* mouse. So **soric**INE sɔ·risain. XVIII (Pennant). – L. *sōricinus*.

sorghum sɔ̄·ɹgəm Indian millet XVI; Chinese sugar cane; genus of grasses XIX. – modL. *sorghum* – It. *sorgo* (whence F. *sorgho*), perh. :– Rom. **syricum* (cf. medL. *sur(i)cum*) Syrian (sc. *grāmen* grass).

sorites sɔ̄rai·tīz (logic) chain syllogism, in which the conclusion is formed of the first subject and the last predicate. XVI. – L. *sōrītēs* – Gr. *sōreítēs*, f. *sōrós* heap.

sorner sɔ̄·ɹnəɹ (Sc.) sponger. XV. f. *sorn*, f. *sorren* (*sorthyn*, *sorryn* XIII–XIV) service required of vassals in Scotland and Ireland consisting of giving hospitality to the superior or his men – Ir. †*sorthan* free quarters.

sororicide sɔrɔ̄·risaid one who kills his or her sister. XVII. f. *soror* SISTER + -CIDE[1]. So **soro·ric**IDE[2] the killing of one's sister XVIII.

sorrel[1] sɔ·rəl (leaves of) plant of the genus Rumex, having a sour taste. XIV. – OF. *sorele*, *surele* (mod. dial. *surelle*), f. *sur* – Germ. **sūraz* SOUR; see -EL[2].

sorrel[2] sɔ·rəl (horse) of bright chestnut colour. XV. – OF. *sorel* adj., f. *sor* yellowish = Pr. *saur*, *sor*, Sp. *soro*, It. †*sauro* – Frankish **saur* dry; see -EL[2].

sorrow sɔ·rou mental pain or distress. OE. *sorh*, *sorg* = OFris. **sorge*, OS. *sor(a)ga* (Du. *zorg*), OHG. *s(w)orga* (G. *sorge*), ON. *sorg*, Goth. *saurga*; CGerm. sb. of unkn. origin, with corr. vb. OE. *sorgian*, OS. *sorgon*, OHG. *sorgēn* (Du. *zorgen*, G. *sorgen*), beside ON. *syrgja* and Goth. *saurgan*. Hence **so·rrow**FUL[1] OE. *sorhful*; of Germ. range.

sorry sɔ·ri pained at heart OE.; worthless, poor XIII (Gen. & Ex.). OE. *sārig* = OS., OHG. *sērag* (G. dial. *sērich*) :– WGerm. **sairag-*, *-ig-*; f. **sairaz* SORE sb.; see -Y[1]. ¶ ME. *sǫ́ri* XII–XV, *sory* –XVII, was finally assim. to unrelated SORROW.

sort sɔ̄ɹt kind, species XIV (Wyclif, Gower, Ch.); (arch.) manner, way XVI. – (O)F. *sorte* = It. *sorta* :– CRom. **sorta*, alt. of L. *sors*, *sort-* wooden voting tablet, lot, share, fortune, condition, (late) rank (AL. sort, kind). So **sort** vb. †allot; arrange, assort XIV; (arch.) agree or associate *with* XVI. – OF. *sortir* or L. *sortīrī* (f. *sors*); later f. the sb. or aphetic of ASSORT.

sortie sɔ̄·ɹti †knot of ribbon XVII; sally by a besieged garrison XVIII; – F. *sortie* a going out.

sortilege sɔ̄·ɹtilidʒ casting of lots. XIV (Trevisa). – (O)F. *sortilège* (= Sp., It. *sortilegio*) – medL. *sortilegium*, f. *sortilegus* diviner, f. *sort-*, *sors* lot (see SORT) + *legere* choose (see LECTION).

sostenuto sɔstĭnū·tou (mus.) in a sustained manner. XVIII. It., pp. of *sostenere* SUSTAIN.

sot sɔt †fool OE.; habitual drunkard XVI. Late OE. *sott* – medL. *sottus* (*c.*800), of unkn. origin; reinforced from (O)F. *sot*.

sotnia sɔ·tniə squadron of Cossack cavalry. XIX. – Russ. *sótnya* hundred, f. *s(o)t-* (ORuss. *sŭt-*), rel. to Skr. *śatam*, L. *centum* (see HUNDRED).

sotto voce sɔ·tou vou·tʃei in a subdued voice. XVIII. It., i.e. *sotto* under (:– L. *subtus*), *voce* VOICE.

sou su French coin (five centimes). XIX. F., sg. form deduced from *sous*, †*soux*, pl. of OF. *sout* :– *solidus*, sb. use of L. *solidus* SOLID. ¶ Earlier forms are *soulx*, *soul* XVI–XVII, *sous*, *sowse* XVI–XIX.

soubise subī·z †cravat XVIII; kind of onion sauce XIX. f. name of Charles de Rohan *Soubise* (1715–87), F. general and courtier.

soubrette subre·t lady's maid, maid-servant (in a play or opera). XVIII. F. – modPr. *soubreto*, fem. of *soubret* coy, f. *soubra* (Pr. *sobrar* :– L. *superāre* be above; cf. SUPER-).

soubriquet see SOBRIQUET.

souchong sūʃɔ·ŋ fine variety of black tea. XVIII. – Chinese *siao chung* (Cantonese *siu chung*) small sort.

soufflé sū·flei, ‖ *sufle* light dish made by mixing materials with white of egg. XIX. – F. *soufflé*, pp. of *souffler* :– L. *sufflāre*, f. *sub* SUB- 7 + *flāre* BLOW[1].

sough sʌf, sau, Sc. suχ rushing or murmuring of the sea. XIV (Ch.). Late ME. *swo(u)gh*, *swow*, f. *swoghe*, OE. *swōgan* = OS. *swōgan* resound, rel. to OE. *swēgan* sound, Goth. *ga-*, *uf|swōgjan*, *swōgatjan*, *swēgnjan*, sigh (see SWOON). ¶ From XVI chiefly north. dial. until taken up in literary use in XIX.

soul soul †life, animate existence; spiritual or emotional part of man; disembodied spirit of a man OE.; vital principle XIV; essential part *of* XVI. OE. *sāwol, sāw(e)l* = Goth. *saiwala*, corr. to OFris. *sēle*, OS. *sēola* (Du. *ziel*), OHG. *sē(u)la* (G. *seele*), with contr. arising from the fall of *w* at the beginning of a syll. (cf. ON. *sála, sál* – OE.; OSw. *sial, siel* – OS., whence Finn. *sielu*, Lapp. *siello*); CGerm. **saiwalō*, corr. formally to Gr. *aiólos* quick-moving, easily moved (:– **saiwolos*), the soul being primitively conceived as a fleeting or flitting thing.

sound[1] saund †swimming; †sea, water OE.; swimming-bladder of fish XIV; (from Scand.) narrow channel of water XV. OE. *sund* = ON. *sund* swimming, strait (Norw. *sund* swimming, swimming-bladder, strait, ferry, Sw., Da. *sund* strait) :– Germ. **sundam*, f. **sum*- **swem*- SWIM.

sound[2] saund unhurt, uninjured XII (Orm); healthy XIII; based on fact or good grounds XV; solid, ample XVI. Early ME. *sund*, aphetic of *isund*, OE. *ġesund* = OS. *gisund* (Du. *gezond*), OHG. *gisunt* (G. *gesund*) :– WGerm. **gasunđaz* rel. by Kluge to OE. *swīþ* strong, ON. *svinnr* intelligent, prudent, Goth. *swinþs* strong, MHG. *geschwinde* (G. *geschwind* swift) cf. OFris., MLG., MDu. *sunt* (-*d*-), whence Sw., Da. *sund*. Hence **sound** adv. fast *asleep* XIV.

sound[3] saund that which is or may be heard, auditory effect. XIII (Cursor M.). ME. *sun, son, soun* – AN. *sun, soun*, (O)F. *son* = Pr. *son, so*, Sp. *son*, Pg. *som*, It. *suono* :– L. *sonu-s* (whence also OE. *sōn*, ON. *sónn*). So **sound** vb. cause to make a sound XIII; emit a sound XIV. ME. *sune, sone, soune* – AN. *suner*, OF. *soner* (mod. *sonner*) = Pr., Sp. *sonar*, Pg. *soar*, It. *sonare* :– L. *sonāre*, f. *sonus*. ¶ The form with -*d* appears XV, and is established XVI.

sound[4] saund †penetrate XIV; intr. and trans. ascertain the depth of water XV; measure or examine as by sounding XVI. – (O)F. *sonder*, corr. to Sp., Pg. *sondar* use the sounding-lead :– Rom. **subundāre*, f. L. *sub* SUB- + *unda* wave (see WATER). So **sound** sb. †act of sounding XVI; (surg.) instrument for probing XVIII.

sounder sau·ndəɹ herd of wild swine. XIV (Sir Gawain). – OF. *sundre* (also mod. dial. *sonre*), of Germ. origin (cf. OE. *sunor*, corr. to Lombard *sonor|pair* boar, OHG. *swaner*, ON. *sonar|blót, -gǫltr*).

soup sūp liquid food prepared by boiling meat and/or vegetables. XVII. – (O)F. *soupe* (i) sop, (ii) broth poured on slices of bread = Pr., Sp. *sopa*, It. *zuppa* :– late L. *suppa* (Oribasius), f. **suppāre* soak, of Germ. origin; cf. MLG. *soppe*, MHG. *suppe*, and SOP, SUP.

soupçon su·psõ slight trace (of). XVIII. F., repr. OF. *sou(s)peçon* :– late L. *suspectiō(n-)*, for L. *suspiciō* SUSPICION.

sour sauəɹ of tart or acid taste OE.; bitter, extremely distasteful XII; morose, peevish XIII. OE. *sūr* = OS., OHG. *sūr* (Du. *zuur*, G. *sauer*), ON. *súrr* :– CGerm. (exc. Goth.) **sūraz*, having cogns. in the Balto-Slav. langs. Hence **sour** vb. XIV. **sou·r**NESS. OE. *sūrnes*.

source sɔ̄(ə)ɹs A. †rising on the wing; B. fountain-head of a stream; place of origin XIV (Ch.). Late ME. *sours* and *sourse* – OF. *sours, sors* m. and *sourse*, (also mod.) *source* fem., sb. uses of m. and fem. pp. of *sourdre* rise, spring = Pr. *sorzer*, Sp. *surgir*, It. *sorgere* :– L. *surgere* rise, SURGE.

sour-crout sau·əɹkraut. XVII. Anglicization of SAUERKRAUT; cf. F. *choucroute*, †*sorcrote* (XVIII) – Alsatian G. *sūrkrūt*, with assim. to *chou* cabbage.

souse saus steep (meat, etc.) in pickle XIV (Trevisa); plunge in water XV (Malory); drench, soak XVI (Wyatt). f. (dial.) *souse* (XIV) pickled meat – OF. *sous, souz* = Pr. *soulz, sols* – OS. *sultia*, OHG. *sulza* (G. *sülze*) brine, f. Germ. **sult*- **salt*- SALT.

soutache suta·ʃ narrow flat braid. XIX. F. – Magyar *sujtás*.

soutane suta·n cassock. XIX. F. – It. *sottana*, f. *sotto* under :– L. *subtus*.

souter sū·təɹ (Sc. and north.) shoemaker, cobbler. OE. *sūtere*, corr. to OHG. *sūtāri*, ON. *sútari* – L. *sūtor* shoemaker, f. *suere* SEW, stitch; see -TOR, -ER[1].

south sauþ adv. towards the part opposite to the north; adj. OE.; sb. XIII (RGlouc.). OE. *sūþ* = OFris., OS. *sūth* (LG. *sud*), OHG. *sunt* (-*d*-), ON. (with *r*-suffix) *suðr* (:– **sunþr*); MDu. *suut* (Du. *zuid*) and G. *süd* have repl. organically developed forms (**zoud*, **sund*) through the infl. of Fris., LG., or F.; perh. ult. rel. to SUN as being the 'sun-side'. So **souther**LY[1] sʌ·ðəɹli XVI. **southern** sʌ·ðəɹn pert. to the south. OE. *sūþerne* = OFris. *sūthern*, OS. *sūthrōni*, OHG. *sundrōni*, ON. *suðrœnn*; with Sc. var. *southron* sʌ·ðrən XV (Henry, 'Wallace'); in spec. names of plants of OE. date, e.g. **sou·thern**WOOD, Artemisia Abrotanum. OE. Also comp. **south**EAST, -WEST OE., **sou·th**WARD(s) OE.

souvenir sū·vəniəɹ, || suvnīr token of remembrance. XVIII. F. 'memory', 'keepsake', sb. use of *souvenir* :– L. *subvenīre* come to the mind, f. *sub* SUB- + *venīre* COME.

sovereign sɔ·vrin (supreme) ruler XIII; English gold coin of 20 shillings value (first coined 29 Oct. 1490) XVI. ME. *soverein* – OF. *so(u)verain, -ein* (mod. *souverain*) = Sp. *soberano*, It. *sovrano* :– Rom. **superānus*, f. *super* above; see SUPER-. Forms in -*gn*- are found *c.*1400; cf. FOREIGN. Also adj. supreme, paramount. XIV. So **so·ve-**

reignTY[2] XIV. – OF. *so(u)vereinete* (mod. *souveraineté*).

soviet sou·viət, ||savje·t council. XX. – Russ. *sovét.*

sovran sɔ·vrən Milton's sp. of SOVEREIGN, after It. *sovrano* ('Comus' 41, 'PL.' I 246).

sow[1] sau female swine OE.; (so medL. *sus*) structure to cover a besieging force XIII (RGlouc.); (prob. after Du.) oblong mass of metal XVI. OE. *sugu* = OS. *suga*, MLG., MDu. *soge* (Du. *zeug*), rel. to OE. *sū*, OHG. *sū* (G. *sau*), ON. *sýr* (accus. *sú*); f. CIE. base **sŭ-*, the orig. sense of which is unkn., repr. also by L. *sūs* (*suis*) pig, Gr. *hûs* (beside *sûs*), with Alb., Arm., and Toch. parallels, and forms with *k-* suffix, as L. *suculus* young boar, OW. *hucc* (W. *hwch*), OIr. *socc*; and with adj. suffix in SWINE. Hence **sowthi·stle**, ME. *suȝeþistel*, plant of genus Sonchus.

sow[2] sou pt. **sowed** soud, pp. **sown** soun scatter or plant seed so that it may grow. orig. redupl. str. vb., which has become wk. in all the Continental langs. OE. *sāwan*, pt. *sēow*, pp. *ġesāwen*, corr. to OFris. (pp.) *esēn*, OS. *sāian*, pt. *sēu*, *sāida*, OHG. *sāwen*, *sājan*, *sā(h)en*, pt. *sāta* (Du. *zaaien*, G. *säen*), ON. *sá*, pt. *sera*, (late) *sáða*, pp. *sáinn*, Goth. *saian*, pt. *saisō*; CGerm. **sǣjan*, repr. IE. base **sē(j)-*, as in L. pt. *sēvī* (of *serere*), and Balto-Sl., Ir., and in SEED, SEMEN.

soy soi sauce prepared from the soya bean. XVII. – Jap. *soy*, colloq. form of *sho-yu* or *siyau-yu* – Chinese *shi-yu*, *shi-yau*, f. *shi* salted beans used as condiment + *yu* oil. The Jap. form is the source of Malay *soi*, Du. *soja*, *soya*, whence **soya** soi·ə XVII.

spa spā, spɔ̄ (also †*Spau*, †*Spaw*) medicinal spring or well XVII; locality possessing this XVIII. f. name *Spa* of a watering-place in the province of Liège, Belgium, noted for its curative mineral springs.

space speis extent of time or distance. XIII (Cursor M., KAlis.). Aphetic – (O)F. *espace* = Pr. *espaci*, Sp. *espacio*, It. *spazio* – L. *spatium* (in medL. also *spacium*). So vb. place in respect of distance or extent. XVI. – (O)F. *espacer*, or f. the sb. **spac**IOUS spei·ʃəs XIV (Wycl. Bible). – L. *spatiōsus*, or OF. *spacios* (mod. *-ieux*). Cf. SPATIAL.

spade[1] speid tool for digging, etc. ground, turf, etc. OE. *spadu*, *spada*, *-e* = OFris. *spada*, OS. *spado* (Du. *spade*, *spa*), a word of the LG. area (G. *spaten*, OSw. *spadhe*, ODa. *spade*, Icel. *spaði*, etc. are from LG.); rel. to Gr. *spáthē* blade, paddle, shoulder-blade, broadsword (cf. SPATHE).

spade[2] speid (pl.) suit of playing cards with black spade-shaped marks. XVI. – It. *spade*, pl. of *spada* – L. *spatha* – Gr. *spáthē* (see prec.).

spadille spədi·l ace of spades in ombre and quadrille. XVIII. – F. *spadille* – Sp. *espadilla*, dim. of *espada* sword, SPADE[2]. Also †*spadi·llo* (XVII).

spadix spei·diks (bot.) inflorescence consisting of a thick fleshy spike. XVIII. – L. *spădīx* – Gr. *spắdīx* palm-branch.

spae spei (north. and Sc.) prophesy. XIII (Cursor M.). – ON. *spá*, of unkn. origin.

spaghetti spəge·ti Italian variety of alimentary paste. XIX. It., pl. of dim. of *spago* string, of unkn. origin.

spagyric spədʒi·rik alchemical; alchemist. XVI. – modL. *spagiricus*, used and prob. invented by Paracelsus. So **spagyr**IST spæ·dʒirist. XVII. – modL.

spahi spā·hi one of a body of Turkish cavalry XVI; native Algerian horseman XIX. – Turk. (Pers.) *sipāhi*; cf. SEPOY.

spall spɔ̄l chip, splinter. XV (Promp. Parv.). var. of contemp. *spale*, of unkn. origin.

spalpeen spælpī·n labourer, farm-hand XVIII; scamp, rascal XIX. – Ir. *spailpín*, of unkn. origin; see -EEN[2].

spam spæm proprietary name of a variety of tinned meat f. initial and final letters of sp*iced* h*am*. XX.

span[1] spæn distance from tip of thumb to extended tip of little finger (OE.), XIII; small piece or space XIV; short space of time XVI; space between supports of an arch, etc. XVIII. OE. *span(n)* = MLG. *spen(ne)*, (M)Du. *spanne*, OHG. *spanna* (G. *spanne*), ON. *spǫnn* (*spann-*); perh. not continuous with OE., but in ME. prob. – OF. *espan(n)e*, *espan* (mod. *empan*), corr. to It. *spanna*, medL. *spannus*, *-a*, of Germ. origin. Hence vb. †seize XIV; measure with outstretched hand XVI; form an arch over XVII. perh. partly – MLG. *spannen*; not continuous with rel. OE. *spannan*. So **spa·nn**ER[1] orig. †tool for winding up the wheel lock of a firearm XVII, (later) instrument for turning a nut, etc. XVIII. – G. *spanner*, f. *spannen*.

span[2] spæn harness, yoke (e.g. to a vehicle) XVI; (naut.) fix, attach XVIII. – (M)Du. or (M)LG. *spannen* = OE. *spannan*, OHG. *spannan* (G. *spannen*). Cf. INSPAN, OUTSPAN.

spandrel spæ·ndrəl (archit.) space between either shoulder of an arch and the surrounding rectangular framework. XV. perh. f. AN. *spaund(e)re*, poss. f. *espaundre* EXPAND; see -EL[2].

spangle spæ·ŋgl thin piece of glittering metal for ornament XV (Lydg.); small sparkling particle XVI (Spenser). dim. (see -LE[1]) f. synon. †*spange* (XV) – MDu. *spange* (Du. *spang*) = OHG. *spanga* (G. *spange*), or rel. ON. *spǫng*, *spang-* clasp, brooch :– Germ. **spangō* (OE. *spang* is – OS. **spanga*), whence Finn. *panka* buckle, clasp; perh. f. a base meaning 'fasten'.

Spaniard spæ·njəɹd native of Spain, Spanish person. XIV. Late ME. *Spaynard*, aphetic – OF. *Espaignart*, *Espaniard*, f. *Espaigne* (mod. *Espagne*), whence Eng. **Spain** spein (XIII); corr. to Sp. *España*, Pg. *Hespanha*, It. *Spagna* :– late L. *Spānia* (Gr. *Spāniā*) for earlier *Hispānia*, *Ispānia*, whence *Ispania* in OE., but also d. pl. *Spenum*, *Spaneum*; cf. MDu. *Spaengen*, Du. *Spanje*, MHG. *Spanje*, G. *Spanien*, ON. *Spánn*; see -ARD. (An earlier synon. was †*Spaynol* (XIV) – OF. *Espaignol* = Sp. *Español*, It. *Spagnuolo*; cf. SPANIEL.) The early forms in *Spayn-*, *Spain-* were ult. superseded by *Span-* (XV), prob. under the infl. of MDu. *Spaensch* (Du. *Spaansch*); the form *Spaniard* superseded *Spainard* by assoc. therewith. So **Spanis**H[1] spæ·niʃ pert. to Spain XIII (*Spainisce*, Laȝ.); the language of Spain and those parts of America and Asia colonized by the Spaniards from XVI onwards; spec. Castilian, of Central Spain, which is a ROMANCE language allied most nearly to its neighbours Catalan and Portuguese XV (Caxton). ¶ OE. had adj. *Speonisċ*.

spaniel spæ·njəl variety of dog. XIV (*spaynel*, Ch.). Aphetic – OF. *espaigneul* (mod. *épagneul*) :- Rom. **spāniōlūs*, for *Hispāniōlus* Spanish, f. *Hispānia* Spain, see prec.

spank[1] spæŋk smack or slap with the open hand. XVIII. perh. imit. of the sound.

spank[2] spæŋk (dial.) travel with vigour and speed. XIX. Presumably back-formation from **spa·nk**ER[1] †gold coin XVIII; fine large thing XVIII; fast horse XIX; or **spa·nk**ING[2] very large or fine XVII; fast-moving XVIII; of unkn. origin; there is a parallel Sc. *spang* spring, leap, move fast XVI.

spar[1] spāɹ (dial.) rafter of a roof XIII (Cursor M.); (orig. and esp. naut.) pole or length of timber XIV. – ON. *sperra* or aphetic – OF. *esparre* (mod. *épare*, *épar*) or its Germ. source, repr. by MLG., MDu. *sparre* (Du. *spar*), OHG. *sparro* (G. *sparren*), ON. *sparri* (whence also Lith. *spãras*, etc.); cf. MDu. *sperren* (whence ME. *sperre* XII, later *spar*), OHG. *sperren* (G. *sperren*) shut as with a bar. The Germ. base is of unkn. origin.

spar[2] spāɹ †strike out with the feet or a weapon OE.; 'fight with prelusive strokes' (J.) XVIII. OE. *sperran*, *spyrran*, **spierran*, corr. to ON. *sperrask* kick out, of unkn. origin.

spar[3] spāɹ gen. term for certain crystalline minerals (as in *calcspar*, FELDSPAR, *fluorspar*). XVI. – MLG. *spar*, rel. to OE. *spæren* of plaster or mortar, *spærstān* gypsum.

sparable spæ·rəbl small headless wedge-shaped iron nail. XVII. alt. of *sparrow-bill* (XVII), so named from the shape; see SPARROW, BILL[2].

spare spɛəɹ leave unharmed, abstain from destroying, injuring, using OE.; part with, do without, keep in reserve XIII; avoid incurring XIV. OE. *sparian* (also with *ā-*, *ġe-*) = OFris. *sparia*, OS., OHG. *sparōn* (Du., G. *sparen*), ON. *spara* :- CGerm. (exc. Goth.) **sparōjan*. So **spare** adj. XIV. OE. *spær* sparing, frugal = OHG. *spar*, ON. *sparr*.

spark spāɹk A. small particle of fire OE.; vital principle XIV (Wycl. Bible); B. woman of beauty or wit XVI; elegant young man XVII; beau, lover XVIII. OE. *spærca*, *spearca* = (M)LG., MDu. *sparke*, of unkn. origin. ¶ The identity of group B of the senses is doubtful. Hence **spark** vb. XIII (Havelok), **spa·rkle** vb. XII; OE. *spearcian* is of doubtful existence; but cf. MDu., MLG. *sparken*; also (M)Du. *sparkelen* (see -LE[3]).

sparling spā·ɹliŋ (north.) smelt, Osmerus eperlanus. XIV. Aphetic – OF. *esperlinge* (mod. *éperlan*), of Germ. origin (cf. MLG., MDu. *spirlinc*, G. *spierling*).

sparrow spæ·rou small bird of the family Fringillidæ. OE. *spearwa* = OHG. *sparo*, MHG. *sparwe*, ON. *spǫrr*, Goth. *sparwa* :- Germ. **sparwon*, **sparwaz* (in some langs. surviving in comps., e.g. MLG. *sperlink*, G. *sperling*).

sparrowgrass spæ·rougràs XVII. illiterate alt. of †*sparagus* (XVI) – medL., aphetic form of ASPARAGUS, by assim. to SPARROW and GRASS.

sparrowhawk XV. repl. arch. or dial. *sparhawk* f. OE. *spearhafoc*, = ON. *sparrhaukr*, f. stem of *spearwa* SPARROW + *hafoc* HAWK.

sparse spāɹs widely spaced or distributed; orig. Sc. of widely spaced writing XVIII. – L. *sparsus*, pp. of *spargere* scatter, prob. rel. to Gr. *speírein*; cf. F. *épars*, etc.

Spartan spā·ɹtən native of Sparta XV; adj. XVI. – L. *Spartānus*, f. *Sparta* (Gr. *Spartā*, *-ē*); see -AN.

sparus spɛə·rəs sea bream. XVII. – L. – Gr. *spáros*.

spasm spæ·zm sudden or violent muscular contraction. XIV. – (O)F. *spasme* or L. *spasmus*, *spasma* – Gr. *spasmós*, *spásma*, f. *spân* draw, pull, f. IE. **spə-* stretch. So **spasmod**IC -ɔ·dik marked by spasms or twitches XVII, intermittent XIX. – modL. *spasmōdicus*, f. Gr. *spasmṓdēs*, f. *spásma*; see -ODE. **spa·st**IC marked by spasmodic symptoms. XVIII. – L. *spasticus* (Pliny) – Gr. *spastikós*, f. *spân* draw, pull.

spat[1] spæt spawn of shellfish. XVII. – AN. *spat* (XIV), of unkn. origin.

spat[2] spæt short gaiter worn over the instep. XIX. Shortening of *spatterdash* (XVII) long gaiter or legging for protection from splashing, f. SPATTER + DASH[1]; also dial. †*spatterplash*, †*-lash*, *splatter-*, *spattle-dash*(*er*).

spatchcock spæ·tʃkɔk (orig. in Ir. use, later Anglo-Indian) fowl prepared by being summarily split open and grilled. XVIII. Connected by Grose with DISPATCH, but cannot be dissociated from *spitchcock* eel cut into short pieces, dressed, and cooked (XVI), of unkn. origin.

spate speit flood or rising in a river. XV (Wyntoun). orig. north. and Sc., of unkn. origin.

spathe speið (bot.) large sheathing leaf enveloping inflorescence. XVIII. – L. *spatha* (also used in Eng. XVIII) – Gr. *spáthē* (see SPADE[1]).

spatial spei·ʃəl pert. to, occupying, or happening in space. XIX. f. L. *spatium* SPACE + -AL[1].

spatter spæ·təɹ scatter in fragments or drops; splash with drops XVI; also intr. frequent. of imit. base repr. also in LG., Du. *spatten* burst, spout, WFlem. *spatteren*, WFris. *spatterje*; see -ER[4]. Hence *spatter-dash*; see SPAT[2].

spatula spæ·tjŭlə flat elongated implement, XVI. – L. *spatula*, var. of *spathula*, dim. of *spatha* SPATHE. Also **spa·tule.** XV. – (O)F. *spatule* or L.; with alt. of ending †*spature* XIV, whence †*spatter* XVI, also †*spattle* XV. Cf. Du., etc., *spatel.*

spavin spæ·vin hard bony tumour in a horse's leg. XV (Lydg.). Late ME. *spaveyne*, aphetic – OF. *espavin* (cf. medL. *spavenus*, It. *spavenio*) var. of *esparvain* (mod. *éparvin*, dial. *spavagn*, *spavin*) – Germ. **spadwāni*, f. base repr. by EFris. *spadde*, *sparre* + *wan-* (see WANE).

spawn spōn cast spawn XIV–XV; engender XVI. Aphetic – AN. *espaundre* shed roe, var. of OF. *espandre* (mod. *épandre*) shed, spill, pour out :– L. *expandere* EXPAND. Hence **spawn** sb. eggs of fishes, etc. XV.

spay spei remove the ovaries from (a female). XV. Aphetic – AN. *espeier*, OF. *espeer*, f. *espee* (mod. *épée*) sword :– L. *spatha* (see SPADE).

speak spīk pt. **spoke** spouk, pp. **spoken** spou·kn utter words. Late OE. *specan*, pt. *spæc*, *spǣcon*, pp. *ġespecen* (corr. to MDu. *speken*, OHG. *spehhen*); superseding parallel OE. *sprecan*, which did not survive beyond XII = OFris. *spreka*, OS. *sprekan*, OHG. *sprehhan* (Du. *spreken*, G. *sprechen*); WGerm. str. vb., with which cf. ON. *spraki* rumour, *forsprakki* spokesman, ON. *spekjur* fem. pl. talk, parley; W. *ffraeth* eloquent (:– **sphrakto-*) is commonly connected. The conjugation was assim. to *bear* and *break*, pt. *spake* (retained arch. like that of *bare*, *brake*) and pp. *spoken* appearing XIII, pt. *spoke* XVI. Cf. BESPEAK, -SPOKEN, SPOKESMAN. Hence **spea·ker**[1] XIV (of the House of Commons; in 1376–7 Sir Thomas de Hungerford 'avoit les paroles pur les Communes d'Engleterre en cest Parlement').

spear spiəɹ thrusting weapon with a pointed head. OE. *spere* = OFris. *spiri*, *spere*, OS., OHG. *sper* (Du., G. *speer*), ON. (pl.) *spjǫr*, doubtfully rel. to L. *sparus* hunting-spear. Hence vb. XVIII (J.).

spec spek (colloq.) abbrev. of SPECULATION. orig. Amer. XVII.

special spe·ʃ(ə)l exceeding what is usual or common XIII (AncrR., Cursor M.); having a particular purpose XIV. Aphetic – OF. *especial* ESPECIAL or – L. *speciālis*, f. *speciēs*; see -AL[1]; hence **spe·cially**[2] XIII (RGlouc.); after OF. *(e)speciaument*, L. *speciāliter*. **spe·cialist.** XIX. **specia·lity.** XV. – OF. *especialité*. **spec·ialize.** XVII. – F. *spécialiser*. **spe·cialty**[2] XIV. – OF. *(e)specialté*. So **specie** spī·ʃʲī phr. *in s.*, in kind; in the real form XVI; in actual coin XVII; hence sb. coined money XVII; abl. sg. of *speciēs*; cf. the development of EFFIGY.

species spī·ʃʲiz outward form (surviving spec. theol. of the elements in the Eucharist); kind (gen. and spec.) XVI. – L. (sg. and pl.) *speciēs*, f. *spec-* of *specere* look, behold (cf. ASPECT, SPICE, SPY, etc.). **specific** spĭsi·fik XVII (Donne), **speci·fical.** XV having a special determining quality – late L. *specificus*. **specification** spe:sifikei·ʃən. XVII. – medL. **spe·cify.** XIII (Cursor M.). – OF. or medL. *specificāre*. **specimen** spe·simĕn †experiment; †pattern; typical example XVII. – L. *specimen*; so F. **specious** spī·ʃəs †fair to look upon XIV; attractive or plausible but lacking in genuineness XVII. – L. *speciōsus* beautiful, fair-seeming.

speck[1] spek small spot. OE. *specca*, repr. otherwise only in **spe·ckle**[1] XV. – MDu. *spekkel* (Du. *spikkel*). Also vb. XVI; **spe·ckled**[2] XIV, perh. after MDu. *spekelde*, *gespekeld* (Du. *gespikkeld*).

speck[2] spek fat meat, fat of a whale, etc. XVII. – Du. *spek* (MDu. *spec*, MLG. *speck*) or G. *speck* (OHG. *spec*) = OE. *spec*, var. of *spic* = ON. *spik*. So **specksioneer** spekʃəniə·ɹ harpooner on a whaler. XIX. – Du. *speksnijer*, colloq. form of *speksnijder*, f. *spek* + *snijden* cut (= OE. *snīþan*).

specs speks, also *specks*, colloq. abbrev. of *spectacles* (see next). XIX (Hogg).

spectacle spe·ktəkl prepared display, object exhibited XIV (Rolle); device for assisting defective eyesight XIV (sg., Ch.; pl., Lydg.). – (O)F. *spectacle* – L. *spectāculum* public show, spectators in a theatre, f. *spectāre*, frequent. f. *specere* look at (cf. SPECIES). So **specta·tor** onlooker. XVI. – F. or L. **spectre**, U.S. **specter** spe·ktəɹ apparition, phantom. XVII. – F. *spectre* or L. *spectrum*, whence also **spe·ctrum** spectre; coloured band into which a beam of light is decomposed (I. Newton) XVII; comb. form **spectro-**, as in **spe·ctroscope** (after F. or G.). **speculate**[3] spe·kjŭleit †observe, consider XVI; engage in thought XVII; engage in buying and selling for gain XVIII. f. pp. stem of L. *speculārī* spy out, watch, f. *specula*, lookout, watch-tower, f. *specere*. **specula·tion.** XIV (Ch.). **spe·culative.** XIV. – (O)F. or late L. **speculum** spe·kjŭləm surgical instrument for examining XVI; mirror, reflector XVII. – L., f. base of *specere* + *-ulum* (cf. -LE[1]).

speech spitʃ act of speaking. OE. *spēċ*, WS. *spǣċ*, rel. to *specan* SPEAK; repl. earlier *sprǣċ* = OFris. *sprēke, sprētze*, OS. *sprāka* (Du. *spraak*), OHG. *sprāhha* (G. *sprache*), WGerm. sb. f. **sprǣk-* **sprek-* SPEAK. Hence **spee·chify** make a speech or speeches (usu. with derogatory force) XVIII; preceded by **speech** vb. (XVII), used to some extent similarly.

speed spīd †success (surviving in phr. *wish good s.*); quickness. OE. *spēd*, earlier *spœ̄d* = OS. *spōd*, OHG. *spuot*; f. Germ. **spōan* (OE. *spōwan*, OHG. *spuo(e)n* prosper, succeed). Hence **speed** vb. OE. *spēdan*, usu. *ġespēdan* = OS. *spōdian* (Du. *spoeden*), OHG. *spuoten* (G. *spuden, sputen*, from LG.), f. **spōd-*.

speer, speir spiəɹ (Sc. and north.) ask. OE. *spyrian* = OFris. *spera*, OS. **spurian* (cf. the sbs. *spuringa, spuriða*), OHG. *spurren* (G. *spüren*), ON. *spyrja* :- **spurjan*, f. Germ. **spur-* (see SPOOR, SPUR).

spel(l)ican see SPILLIKINS.

spell[1] spel †discourse (cf. GOSPEL) OE.; formula of incantation, first in *night-s.* XIV (Ch.). OE. *spel(l)* = OS., OHG. *spel*, ON. *spjall*, Goth. *spill* recital, tale :- CGerm. **spellam*, rel. to OE. *spellian* = MLG., MDu. *spellen*, OHG. *-spellōn*, ON. *spjalla*, Goth. *spillōn* :- CGerm. **spellam*; of unkn. origin. See GOSPEL. comp. **spe·llbound**[3] enchanted XVIII; hence **spe·llbind** vb., whence (U.S.) **spe·llbi:nder**[1]. XX.

spell[2] spel pt., pp. **spelled,** (usu.) **spelt,** read *out* as if letter by letter XIII (Cursor M.); name or set down the letters of XV (Spellynge, 'sillabicacio', Promp. Parv.); make out, decipher XVI. Aphetic – OF. *espeller, espeler* (mod. *épeler*), *espelir*, for older **espeldre* (whence north. Eng. *spelder* XII), *espeaudre* – Germ. **spellōn* (see prec.).

spell[3] spel relieve (another) at work XVI. Later form of †*spele* take the place of, OE. *spelian*, rel. to *ġespelia, spala* substitute, of unkn. origin. Hence **spell** sb. †relief gang XVI; turn of work taken in relief of another XVII; continuous course of time XVIII.

spellicans var. of SPILLIKINS.

spelt spelt species of grain, Triticum spelta. Rare before XVI; in late OE., ME., and modEng. due to independent adoptions from the Continent of OS. *spelta*, MLG., MDu. *spelte* (Du. *spelt*) = OHG. *spelza, spelta* (G. *spelz*), whence late L. *spelta* (the source of F. *épeautre*, Sp. *espelta*, It. *spelta, spelda*, and Pol. *szpelta*, Czech *špalda*), perh. based on **spel-* split (cf. OE. *speld* splinter).

spelter spe·ltəɹ zinc XVII; zinc alloy XIX. corr. to OF. *espeautre*, MDu. *speauter* (Du., G. *spiauter*), G. *spialter*, and rel. indeterminately to PEWTER.

spence spens (arch.) buttery, pantry XIV (Ch.); (Sc.) parlour XVIII (Burns). Aphetic – OF. *despense* (mod. *dépense*) = Sp. *despensa*, It. *dispensa* :- sb. use of fem. pp. of L. *dispendere* DISPENSE. So †*spencer* steward, butler (surviving as a surname) – AN. *espenser*, for OF. *despenser*.

spencer spe·nsəɹ †kind of wig XVIII; short double-breasted overcoat XVIII; form of life-belt XIX. f. family name *Spencer*; in the several senses respectively after Charles *Spencer*, third earl of Sunderland (1674–1722), George John *Spencer*, second earl *Spencer* (1758–1834), Knight *Spencer* (fl. 1803).

spend spend pt., pp. **spent** give or pay out OE.; use, use up XIII. Partly (i) OE. *spendan* (also in *āspendan, forspendan*, and *spendung*), corr. to MLG., MDu. *spenden*, OHG. *spentōn* (G. *spenden*), ON. *spenna* – L. *expendere* EXPEND; partly (ii) aphetic of *dispend* – OF. *despendre* :- L. *dispendere* distribute, DISPENSE. comp. **spe·ndthrift** XVII; *thrift* being taken in the sense 'substance', 'wealth'; repl. *scattergood*.

sperm spəɹm generative substance of the male. XIV (Ch.). – late L. *sperma* – Gr. *spérma* (*-at-*), f. base of *speírein* sow (cf. SPORADIC), SPORE; comb. form **spe·rmato-** XIX. So **sperma·tic** XVI, **-ical** XV. – late L. – Gr.

spermaceti spəɹməse·ti, -sī·ti fatty substance obtained from the sperm whale or cachalot. XV. – medL. *spermacētī* (so named from an erron. notion of the nature of the substance), f. *sperma* (see prec.) + *cētī*, g. of *cētus* – Gr. *kētos* whale; attrib. in *s. whale* (XVII), shortened to *sperm whale* (XIX); the alt. form *parmacety* was current XVI–XIX.

spew spjū vomit. (i) OE. *spīwan*, pt. *spāw*, *spiwon* = OFris. *spīa*, OS., OHG. *spīwan* (G. *speien*), ON. *spýja*, Goth. *speiwan*; CGerm. str. vb.; (ii) OE. *spēowan, spīowan*, wk. vb.; corr. to L. *spuere*, Gr. *ptúein* (:- **spjūj-*), and Balto-Sl. formations on an IE. base of imit. origin.

sphacelus sfæ·siləs (path.) mortification. XVI. – modL. – Gr. *sphákelos* convulsive movement, painful spasm, gangrene (Hippocrates).

sphagnum sfæ·gnəm (bot.) genus of mosses. XVIII. – modL. – Gr. *sphágnos*.

sphenoid sfī·noid (anat.) irregularly-shaped bone at the base of the skull wedged in between other bones. XVIII. – modL. *sphēnoidēs* – Gr. *sphēnoeidés*, f. *sphḗn* wedge, rel. to SPOON; see -OID.

sphere sfiəɹ globular body or figure; globe conceived as appropriate to a particular planet, hence (one's or its) province or domain XVII. ME. *sper(e)* – OF. *espere*, later (with assim. to Gr. – L.) *sphère* = Sp. *esfera*, It. *sfera* – late L. *sphēra*, earlier *sphæra* – Gr. *sphaîra* ball, globe. So

spheric, spherical sfe·rik(əl) XVI. – late L. *sphē-, sphæricus* – Gr. *sphairikós*. **spheroid** sfiə·roid. XVII.

sphincter sfi·ŋktəɹ (anat.) muscular ring normally closing an orifice. XVI. – late L. *sphincter* – Gr. *sphigktḗr* band, contractile muscle, f. *sphíggein* bind tight (cf. next).

sphinx sfiŋks (Gr. myth.) hybrid monster which propounded a riddle; figure of creature having a human head and breast with a lion's body; inscrutable being XVI; – L. *Sphinx* – Gr. *Sphígx*, g. *Sphiggós* (Bœotian *Phíx*, acc. *Phîka*), presumably f. *sphíggein* (see prec.).

sphragistic sfrədʒi·stik sb. pl. (see -ICS) scientific study of seals or signet rings; adj. pert. to these XIX. – F. *sphragistique* – Gr. *sphrāgistikós*, f. *sphrāgís* seal.

sphygmo- sfi·gmou comb. form of Gr. *sphugmós* pulse, f. **sphug-*, base of *sphúzein* beat, throb. Cf. ASPHYXIA.

spicate spi·keit (bot.) having a spike-like inflorescence. XVII. – L. *spīcātus*, pp. of *spīcāre* furnish with spikes, f. *spīca* SPIKE²; see -ATE².

spice spais aromatic vegetable substance used for its pungency or fragrance. XIII. Aphetic – OF. *espice* (mod. *épice*) :- L. *speciēs* appearance, specific kind, SPECIES, (late) pl. wares, merchandise, after late Gr. use of pl. of *eîdos* form (cf. IDEA) in the senses 'goods', 'groceries', 'spices'. So **spice** vb. season with spice. XIV (PPl.); cf. †**spi·cer²** dealer in spices, druggist. XIII (surviving as a surname) – OF. *espicier* (mod. *épicier* grocer). **spi·cery**. XIII (RGlouc.). **spi·cy¹**. XVI (Turner).

spick and span spikənᵈspæ·n brand new XVII (*speck and span*); trim, spruce XIX. Shortening of (dial.) *spick and span new* (XVI), extension of (dial.) *span-new* (XIII) – ON. *spánnýr* 'new like a freshly shaved chip', f. *spánn* chip (see SPOON¹)+*nýr* NEW; the el. *spick* is prob. due to synon. Du. *spikspelldernieuw, -splinternieuw* 'spike-, splinter-new' (cf. G. *nagelneu* 'nail-new').

spicula spi·kjŭlə (nat. hist.) sharp-pointed feature. XVIII. modL., dim. of L. *spīca* SPIKE². So **spi·culum, spi·cule** (so F.), **spi·culate(d)**. XVIII. See -ULE.

spider spai·dəɹ arachnid of the insectivorous order Araneidæ. OE. *spīþra* (Saxon Leechdoms II 142), ME. *spiþre, spiþer* :- **spinþron*, f. *spinnan* SPIN; cf. synon. OSw. *spinnil*, Sw. *spindel*, Da. *spinder*, OHG. *spinna*, G. *spinne* (lit. female spinner), Du. *spin*, Eng. dial. *spinner* XIII (Bestiary), MDu. *spinnere* (Du. *spinner*).

spiel¹ spīl curling match. XIX. Extracted from BONSPIEL.

spiel² spīl (U.S.) talk, speech. XIX. – G. *spiel* play, rel. to the vb. *spielen* (of WGerm. extent).

spiffing spi·fiŋ (dial., sl.) first-rate, smart. XIX. Of unkn. origin; of prp. form (see -ING²), like *clinking, ripping, topping*, and rel. to *spiff, spiffy*, which connote smartness or spruceness.

spif(f)licate spi·flikeit (dial., sl.) handle roughly, overcome, crush. XVIII. Of fanciful formation.

spignel spi·gnəl (aromatic root of) Meum athamanticum. XVI. perh. contr. of obscure ME. †*spigurnel* (XIV–XV) – medL. *spigurnella*.

spigot spi·gət vent-peg. XIV. Of uncertain origin, but ult. based on L. *spīca* SPIKE², and perh., with change of suffix, – Pr. *espigoun, -gou* = Sp. *espigón*, It. *spigone* rung of a ladder, bar of a chair, bung; cf. Pg. *espicho* spigot :- L. *spīculum*, dim. of *spīcum*, var. of *spīca*, SPIKE².

spike¹ spaik sharp-pointed piece of metal, large nail. XIII. ME. *spyk* (also *spiknail*), of uncertain origin, but corr. to OSw. *spik, spijk* (Sw., Norw. *spik* nail) and perh. shortening of (M)LG., MDu. *spiker* (Du. *spijker*) = MHG. *spîcher* (G. *speicher|nagel*), or of MDu. *spiking* (= OE. *spīcing*, whence ME. *spiking* spike-nail XIII), rel. to SPOKE. Hence **spike** vb. XVII.

spike² spaik A. ear of corn XIV (rare before XVII); inflorescence of sessile flowers on a long axis XVI. B. lavender XVI. – L. *spīca, -us, -um*, rel. to *spīna* SPINE.

spikenard spai·knāɹd aromatic substance from an Eastern plant. XIV. – medL. *spīca nardī* (see SPIKE², NARD), rendering Gr. νάρδου στάχυς, ναρδόσταχυς; or more immed. – OF. *spicanard(e)* or MLG. *spīkenard*, MDu. *spīkenaerde* (Du. *spijknardus*) = MHG. *spīcanarde* (G. *spikenarde* and older variants; cf. mod. shortened forms *narde, spiek*), etc.

spill¹ spil pt., pp. **spilt, spilled** †put to death, destroy, ruin, waste, squander OE.; shed (blood) XII; allow or cause (liquid) to fall or pour XIV (hence intr. XVII). OE. *spillan* = (M)LG., (M)Du. *spillen*, rel. to OE. *spildan* destroy = OS. *spildian*, OHG. *spilden*, ON. *spilla* (:- **spilþjan*), of unkn. origin. Hence **spilth¹** spilþ. XVII (Sh.).

spill² spil splinter or slip of wood, etc. XIII; thin slip of wood, etc. for lighting XIX. *c.*1300 prob. – (M)LG., (M)Du. *spil(l)e* = OHG. *spilla*, MHG. *spille* (G. *spille* spindle, axis, stalk) :- WGerm. **spinla*, f. **spin-* SPIN.

spillikins spi·likinz game with slips of wood, etc. XVIII. f. SPILL²+-KIN.

spin spin pt. **span** spæn, **spun** spʌn, pp. **spun** draw and form into thread OE.; form (a thread) XIII; shoot, gush XIV; revolve XVII. OE. *spinnan*, pt. *spann, spunnon*, pp. *ġespunnen* = (M)Du. *spinnen*, OHG., Goth. *spinnan* (G. *spinnen*), ON. *spinna*; CGerm. str. vb., with cogns.

recognized in Balto-Sl. forms having *sp-* or *p-*.

spinach spi·nidʒ culinary plant Spinacia oleracea. XVI (*spinache* W. Turner, *-age* Palsgr.). prob. – MDu. *spinaetse, spinag(i)e* (Du. *spinazie*) – OF. *espinache, -age* (mod. *épinard*) – Sp. *espinaca* (whence also Cat. *espinach*, It. *spinace*, Rum. *spanac*) – medL. *spinachia, -ium, -acia, -acium* – Arab. *isfināj, isfānāj* (– Pers. *aspanākh*), perh. by assim. to L. *spina* SPINE, with ref. to the prickly seeds of some species; the prob. intermediate channel of adoption, Spain, is illustrated by the names medL. *Hispanicum olus* and F. †*herbe d'Espaigne* (Cotgr.).

spinal spai·nəl pert. to the SPINE. XVI – late L. *spīnālis*; see -AL[1].

spindle spi·ndl slender rod serving to twist and wind thread in spinning OE.; rod serving as an axis XIV. OE. *spinel*, corr. to OFris. *spindel*, OS. *spinnila*, (M)Du. *spindel*, OHG. *spin(n)ila, -ala* (G. *spindel*), f. **spin-* SPIN; see -LE[1]; for intrusive *d* cf. Du. and G. forms. comp. *spindle-side* female line of descent (XIX), used by F. Palgrave and E. A. Freeman as a rendering of OE. *spinlhealf*; cf. G. *spindelseite*, etc., and DISTAFF.

spindrift spi·ndrift continuous driving of spray. XVI. orig. Sc. var. (due to local Sc. pronunc. *speen, spin*, of *spoon*) of *spoondrift* (actually recorded later XVIII), f. SPOON[2]+ DRIFT.

spine spain backbone XIV (rare before XVII); thorn or thorn-like process XV (Lydg.). Aphetic – OF. *espine* (mod. *épine*) = Pr., Sp. *espina*, It. *spina*, or their source L. *spina* thorn, prickle, backbone, prob. rel. to *spīca* SPIKE[2].

spinel spi·nəl, **spinelle** spine·l gem resembling the ruby. XVI. – F. *spinelle* – It. *spinella*, dim. of *spina* SPINE.

spinet spine·t, spi·nit keyed instrument resembling the harpsichord. XVII (Pepys). Aphetic – F. †*espinette* (mod. *épinette*) – It. *spinetta* (whence Sp. *espineta*, modL. *spineta* XVI), prob. (acc. to A. Banchieri, 1608) f. name of the inventor Giovanni *Spinetti* of Venice, whose name Banchieri had seen on a spinet dated 1503.

spinifex spai·nifeks coarse grass of the Australian deserts, having spiny leaves. XIX. – modL. *spīnifex*, f. *spīna* SPINE+*-fex* maker, *facere* make, DO[1].

spinnaker spi·nəkəɹ (naut.) three-cornered sail carried by racing yachts. XIX. Said to be a fanciful formation on *spinks*, mispronunciation of *Sphinx*, name of the first yacht that commonly carried the sail; perh. with reminiscence of SPANKER.

spinney spi·ni copse, esp. for preserving game. XVI. Aphetic – OF. *espinei* (mod. *épinaie*) :– Rom. **spīnēta*, coll. form of L. *spīnētum* (whence It. *spineto*, Rum. *spinet*), f. *spīna* thorn, SPINE[1]. ¶ The use of the word was generalized from particular designations, which are found as early as XIII, and in AN. form (. . *de Spiney*) in XII.

spinster spi·nstəɹ woman (rarely, man) engaged in spinning XIV (PPl.); appended to names of women to denote occupation (e.g. Alicia Moris Spynnestere XIV), later (from XVII) legal designation of one still unmarried. f. SPIN vb.+-STER; perh. after (M)Du. *spinster* (cf. MLG. *spinsterinne*). **spi·nstr**ESS[1] XVII.

spiræa spairi·ə genus of rosaceous plants. XVII (Evelyn). – L. *spiræa* – Gr. *speiraía*, f. *speîra* SPIRE[2].

spiral spaiə·rəl coiled as round a cylinder or cone. XVI (Recorde). – F. *spiral* or medL. *spīrālis* (Albertus Magnus XIII), f. L. *spīra* SPIRE[2]; see -AL[1].

spirant spaiə·rənt (philol. of a consonant) continuant, open. XIX (Whitney). – L. *spīrant-, -āns*, prp. of *spīrāre* breathe; see -ANT. ¶ The L. stem *spīr-* is widely repr. in Eng., with a great diversity of application, as in *aspire, conspire, expire, inspire, perspire, respire* (with *respirator*), *suspire, transpire*, with the large group assoc. with *spirit*; many derivs. depend for sense ult. upon Gr. *pneîn* blow, breathe, *pneûma* breath, spirit.

spire[1] spaiəɹ †stalk, stem OE., (dial.) reeds XIII; shoot, sprout XIV; tapering portion of a steeple XVI (earlier *spere* XV). OE. *spīr* = MLG., MDu. *spier, spīr*, MHG. *spīr* (G. *spier* tip of blade of grass).

spire[2] spaiəɹ coil, spiral. XVI. – F. *spire* It. *spira* – L. *spīra* – Gr. *speîra* coil, winding.

spirit spi·rit A. breath of life; B. vital principle; C. intelligent incorporeal being XIII; immaterial element of a human being; D. vital power XIV; E. †any of four substances so named of the alchemists XIV (Ch.); liquid of the nature of an essence XVII. – AN. *spirit*, aphetic of *espirit*, OF. *esperit*, (also mod.) *esprit* = Pr. *esperit*, Sp. *espíritu*, It. *spirito* – L. *spīritus* breathing, breath, air, life, soul, pride, courage, (in Chr. use) incorporeal being, f. *spīrāre* breathe (cf. *hālitus*, f. *hālāre*); see SPIRANT, and cf. SPRIGHTLY, SPRITE. comb. **spirit-rapping** rapping alleged to be made by disembodied spirits, communication so conveyed, *c.*1850. Hence **spi·rit** vb. (arch.) enliven, inspirit XVI (Sh.); carry *away* mysteriously XVII. **spi·rit**ED[2] full of spirit. XVI (B. Jonson). **spi·rit**ISM, -IST. XIX; preferred by some to *spiritualism, -ist*; cf. F. *spiritisme*, G. *spiritismus*. So **spi·ritu**AL[1] pert. to the spirit XIV (R. Mannyng); ecclesiastical XIV. ME. *spirituel* (later latinized) – (O)F. *spirituel* – L. *spīrituālis*; str. *spiri·tual* XVI–XVIII. **spiritu**A·LITY. XV. – (O)F. or late L. comb. *spiritual-mindedness* XVII, after *spiritually-minded* Tindale, tr. Luther's *geistlich gesinnet*. **spi·ritual**ISM exercise of spiritual faculties, spiritual view XIX (Carlyle, Lytton); *modern s.* (1855). **spi·ritual**TY[1]

†spiritual character; body of ecclesiastics, clergy. XIV. – OF. *spiritualté* – late L. *spīritūalitās*. **spi·rituous** †spirited XVI (B. Jonson); ardent, alcoholic XVII. – F. *spiritueux* or f. L. *spīritu-s*.

spirometer spaiəɹɔ·mitəɹ instrument for measuring breathing-power. XIX. f. L. *spīrāre* breathe; see -OMETER.

spirt spə̄ɹt †short space XVI; slight spell of wind XVIII; brief spell of activity XIX. See SPURT[1].

spit[1] spit pointed rod on which meat is stuck for roasting OE.; sword; small tongue of land XVII. OE. *spitu* = MLG., MDu. *spit, spet* (Du. *spit*), OHG. *spiʒ* (G. *spiess*) :– Germ. **spituz* (whence (O)F. *époi* point of a deer's horn, Sp. *espeto*, It. dial. *spito*), of which a var. **spitj-* is repr. by OHG. *spizza* (G. *spitze*) point.

spit[2] spit pt., pp. **spat** spæt eject saliva (*the very s.*, sl. phr., the exact likeness XIX) OE. late Northumb. (*ġe*)*spittan* = G. dial. *spützen*, f. imit. base **spit-*, of which there are other expressive vars. **spait-*, **spŭt-*, repr. by OE. *spātlian*, *spǣtan* (ME. *spete*, later *spat*), *spǣtlan*, *spǣtl*, *spātl*, *spāld* saliva, MHG. *spiutzen*, ON. *spýta*; see SPITTLE and cf. SPEW.

spit[3] spit spade's depth of earth. XVI. – (M)LG., (M)Du. *spit*, rel. to OE. *spittan* (dial. *spit*) dig with a spade, and hence prob. ult. to SPIT[1].

spital spi·tl (hist.) re-spelling XVII, after the L. original, of †*spittle*, †*spitel*, common vars. (XIII–XVIII) of aphetic form of HOSPITAL; corr. to OHG. *spitāl*, MLG., MHG. *spittel* (G. *spital*, *spittel*).

spitchcock spi·tʃkɔk method of preparing an eel by cutting it up and frying it. XVI. Of unkn. origin; cf. SPATCHCOCK.

spite spait †outrage, insult XIII (Cursor M.); strong ill-will XIV; *in s. of*, in contempt or defiance of, notwithstanding XIV. Aphetic – OF. *despit* DESPITE. So **spite** vb. †regard with contempt XIV; treat maliciously XVI (Sh.). Aphetic – OF. *despiter* – L. *dēspectāre*. Cf. MLG., MDu. *spit*, *spīten* (Du. *spijt*, *spijten*).

spittle spi·tl saliva. XV (Caxton). alt. by assoc. with SPIT[2] of (dial.) *spattle*, OE. *spātl*, *spādl*, *spāld* (ME. *spold*), corr. to OFris., MLG. *spēdel*, f. Germ.**spāt-*, repr. also by OE. *spǣtl*, (†*spettle* XV–XVII), *spǣtan* spit. Hence **spittoon** spitū·n receptacle for spittle. XIX. orig. U.S.

spitz spits Pomeranian dog, having a very pointed muzzle. XIX. – G. *spitz*, also *spitzhund*, spec. use of *spitz* pointed, peaked; see SPIT[1].

splacknuck splæ·knʌk imaginary animal of Brobdingnag in Swift, 'Gulliver's Travels', 1726. Fanciful invention.

splanchnic splæ·ŋknik pert. to the viscera. XVII. – modL. *splanchnicus* – Gr. *splagkhnikós*, f. *splágkhnon*, usu. pl. *-a* inward parts, prob. rel. to *splḗn* SPLEEN; see -IC.

splash splæʃ dash water, etc. upon, also with *water*, etc. as obj., and intr. XVIII. Expressive alt. of *plash*.

splay splei †unfold (a banner) XIV; spread out XV. Aphetic of DISPLAY. Hence sb. (archit.) work deviating from a right angle XVI; adj., as in *splay-foot(ed)* XVI.

spleen splīn gland in the abdomen anciently held to be the seat of (i) melancholy, (ii) mirth XIII; used of various emotions and states of mind XVI (Sh.). Aphetic – OF. *esplen* – L. *splēn* – Gr. *splḗn*, prob. rel. to Gr. *splágkhnon* pluck, L. *liēn*, Skr. *plihán*. comp. **splee·nwort** XVI; after L. *splēnium*, *asplēnon* – Gr. So **splenetic** splīne·tik pert. to the spleen; irritably morose XVI; ill-humoured XVII. – late L. *splēnēticus*, f. *splēn*; so F. Variant synon. forms are: †**splenatic** – medL. *splēnāticus* (so OF. *splénatique*); †**sple·native** XVI–XVII; **splenic** sple·nik. XVII – F. *splénique* (Paré), L. *splēnicus* – Gr.; †**spleni·tic** XVI–XVII; so F.

splendid sple·ndid brilliant, resplendent; magnificent. XVII. – F. *splendide* or L. *splendidus*, f. *splendēre* be bright or shining. From the prp. of the L. vb. are derived †*sple·nd*ANT XVI–XVII, **sple·nd**ENT XV (cf. RESPLENDENT). Various other formations synon. with *splendid*, which finally superseded them, were: †*splendi·d*IOUS XV–XVII, †*sple·ndid*OUS XVII only (B. Jonson); **splend**A·CIOUS XIX fanciful formation after *capacious*, *spacious*. **splendi·**FEROUS XV (now joc., chiefly U.S.) – medL. *splendiferus*, for late L. *splendōrifer*; †*splend*IOUS XVII only. So **sple·nd**OUR[2], U.S. **sple·ndor** great brightness XV; magnificent display, brilliant distinction XVII. – (O)F. *splendeur* or L. *splendor*; hence †**sple·ndor**OUS XVI (Drayton).

splice splais join (ropes) by interweaving the strands XVI; join (two pieces of timber) by overlapping the ends XVII; (sl.) join in marriage XVIII (Smollett). prob. – MDu. *splissen* (whence also Du. dial., G. *splissen*, *spleissen*), but agreeing in vocalism with G. *spleissen* SPLIT; cf. Sw. *splitsa*, Da. *splidse*.

splint splint plate of overlapping metal in mediæval armour XIII; slender or thin slip of wood, etc.; (dial.) splinter XIV; (in farriery) tumour developing into a bony excrescence XVI; laminated coal XVIII. – MLG. *splente*, *splinte*, MDu. *splinte* (Du. *splint*); rel. to next but no cogns. are known.

splinter spli·ntəɹ rough slender piece of wood, etc. XIV (Trevisa). – (M)Du. *splinter*, rel. to prec.

split split break up (a ship) on a rock, etc.; cleave, rend longitudinally. XVI. In earliest use naut. – (M)Du. *splitten*, obscurely rel. to *spletten*, whence earlier Eng. (dial.) *splet* (Palsgr.), *spleet*, and to OFris. *splita*, MLG., MDu. *splīten*, MHG. *splīʒen* (G. *spleissen*); of obscure ult. origin.

splodge splɔdʒ thick clumsy lump or spot. XIX. Expressive alt. of next; cf. WODGE.

splotch splɔtʃ large irregular spot or patch. XVII (Holland). perh. blend of SPOT and †*plotch* (XVI), BLOTCH.

splurge splə̄ɹdʒ (U.S.) ostentatious display. XIX. Of symbolic origin.

splutter splʌ·təɹ (dial.) noise, fuss; violent and confused utterance XVII. loud sputter or splashing XIX. alt. of SPUTTER, by assoc. with *splash*; 'a low word' (J.).

spode spoud china ware manufactured by Josiah *Spode* (1754–1827). XIX.

spoil spoil goods captured from an enemy XIII; (esp. pl.) arms or armour so captured, (also gen.) XVI; refuse material XIX. Aphetic – OF. *espoille* (cf. Sp. *espoja*, It. *spoglia*, *-ie*), f. *espoillier* :– L. *spoliāre*, f. *spolium*, pl. *-ia* skin stripped from an animal, booty. So **spoil** vb. (pt., pp. *spoilt* since XVII). A. strip, despoil XIII; B. damage, ruin XVI; C. deteriorate XVII; *be spoiling for* (orig. U.S.) desire eagerly XIX. – OF. *espoillier*, f. the sb.; or aphetic of DESPOIL.

spoke spouk one of the staves of a wheel OE.; colloq. phr. *put a s. in one's wheel*, (i) attempt to advise or help, (ii) act so as to impede (another) XVII. OE. *spāca* = OFris. *spēke*, *spāke*, OS. *spēca*, OHG. *speihha* (Du. *speek*, G. *speiche*) :– WGerm. **spaikōn*, f. **spaik-* **speik-* SPIKE[1].

-spoken spou·kn as the second el. of a comp. 'speaking in the way denoted by the first el.', e.g. *fair-s.*, *well-s.* (XV), *fine-s.*, *plain-s.* (XVII), based on phr. *speak fair*, etc.; pp. of SPEAK; cf. the similar use of ON. *talaðr*, pp. of *tala* speak.

spokesman spou·ksmən †interpreter; one who speaks on behalf of another XVI; †speaker of an assembly; public speaker XVII. irreg. f. *spoke*, pt. of SPEAK + *-sman* (see -S). ¶ Not connected with rare ME. *spekeman* advocate.

spoliation spouliei·ʃən action of despoiling. XIV. – L. *spoliātiō(n-)*, f. *spoliāre* SPOIL; see -ATION. So F. (XV).

spondee spɔ·ndī (pros.) metrical foot of two long syllables. XIV. – (O)F. *spondée* or L. *spondēus* – Gr. *spondeîos* sb. use (sc. *poús* foot) of adj. f. *spondḗ* libation (see SPONSOR), the spondee being a foot characteristic of melodies accompanying libations. So **spondaic** spɔndei·ik. XVIII. – F. *spondaïque* or late L. *spondaicus*, alt. of *spondīacus* (whence Eng. †*spo·ndiac* XVI) – Gr. *spondeiakós*.

spondulicks spɔndjū·liks (U.S. sl.) money. XIX. Of unkn. origin.

sponge spʌnᵈʒ (piece of) the absorbent skeleton of an aquatic animal with pores in the body wall. OE. *sponge*, corr. to OS. *spunsia* (Du. *spons*) – L. *spongia* (whence OF. *esponge*, mod. *éponge*, It. *spugna*) – Gr. *spoggiā́*, f. *spóggos*, *sphóggos*; reinforced in ME. from OF. Hence vb. XIV; cf. F. *éponger*, †*esponger*, late L. *spongiāre*, Gr. *spoggizein*. So **spo·ngious** spʌ·nᵈʒiəs XIV. – L. *spongiōsus*.

sponsion spɔ·nʃən solemn or formal engagement. XVII. – L. *sponsiō(n-)*, f. pp. stem of *spondēre* promise solemnly, rel. to Gr. *spéndein* pour a libation, promise, *spondḗ* libation, alliance, truce; see -SION. So **spo·nsor**[1] godfather, godmother; one who gives surety. XVII. – L.

sponson spɔ·nsən (naut.) extension beyond the ordinary line or bulk of a vessel. XIX. Formerly also *sponsing*, *sponcing*, of unkn. origin.

spontaneous spɔntei·niəs acting or produced by natural, instinctive, or voluntary impulse. XVII. f. late L. *spontāneus*, f. L. (*suā*) *sponte* of (one's) own accord, abl. of **spōns*, anciently connected with *spondēre* (cf. SPONSION).

spontoon spɔntū·n (hist.) kind of half-pike or halberd. XVIII. – F. †*sponton* (mod. *esponton*) – It. *spuntone*, f. *spuntare* blunt, f. *s-* EX-[1] + *punto* POINT.

spoof spūf (card) game of a hoaxing character; (gen.) hoax, humbug. XIX. Invented by Arthur Roberts (1852–1933), Eng. comedian.

spook spūk (colloq.) spectre, ghost. XIX. – Du. *spook* = (M)LG. *spōk* (whence G. *spuk*), of unkn. origin.

spool spūl bobbin on which thread is wound. XIV. Aphetic – OF. *espole* (mod. *époule*) or – its source, MLG. *spōle* = MDu. *spoele* (Du. *spoel*), OHG. *spuolo*, *-a* (G. *spule*); WGerm., of unkn. origin.

spoom spūm (naut.) run or scud *before* the sea, etc. XVII. alt. of SPOON[2], prob. by assoc. with *boom* (said of a ship making all the way possible).

spoon[1] spūn A. †chip, splinter OE.; B. shallow oval bowl with a long handle XIV. OE. *spōn* = MLG. *spān*, MDu. *spaen*, OHG. *spān* (G. *span* shaving), ON. *spónn*, *spánn*; the Germ. word (adopted in Finn. *panna* shingle) is usu. connected with Gr. *sphḗn* wedge. ¶ The Scand. sense (B) prevailed in this word, as in *dream* and *dwell*. comp. **spoo·nbill**[2] bird of the genus Platalea; after Du. *lepelaar*, f. *lepel* spoon. Hence **spoo·ny**[1] foolish person, silly XVIII; *spoon* was similarly applied contemp. to person making love sentimentally, whence a corr. use of *spoon* vb.

spoon[2] spūn †(naut.) run before the wind or sea, scud. XVI. Of unkn. origin.

spoondrift see SPINDRIFT.

spoonerism spū·nərizm accidental transposition of initial sounds or syllables of words associated in a context, 1900. f. name of the Rev. W. A. *Spooner* (1844–1930), who was said to have been addicted to this; see -ISM.

spoor spuəɹ track, trail. XIX. – Du. *spoor* (in S. African use), repr. MDu. *spo(o)r* =

OE., OHG., ON. *spor* (G. *spur*); rel. to SPUR.

sporadic spŏræ·dik occurring in isolated instances XVII. – medL. *sporadicus* – Gr. *sporadikós*, f. *sporad-*, *sporás* scattered, dispersed, f. base of *sporá* sowing, seed, whence modL. *spora*, used spec. bot., minute reproductive body in flowerless plants, anglicized **spore** spōəɹ. XIX. Cf. F. *sporadique*, etc.; see -IC.

sporran spɔ·rən pouch worn with the kilt of Scottish Highlanders. XIX (Scott). – Gael. *sporan* = Ir. *sparán* purse, MIr. *sboran*, W. *ysbur* – L. *bursa* PURSE.

sport spōɹt pleasant pastime, diversion XV; in full *s. of nature* (tr. L. *lusus naturæ*) XVII; object of diversion XVII (Milton); pl. series of athletic contests XVI. So **sport** vb. †(refl.) amuse oneself XIV; so intr. XV; display XVIII. Aphetic of DISPORT sb. and vb. Hence **spo·rtIVE**. XVI (Sh., Nashe). **spo·rtsMAN**. XVIII (Farquhar) (cf. *spokesman*); earlier †*sporter* (XVII).

spot spɔt moral stain XII; small roundish mark XIII; speck, stain; small piece or particle; small plot or area XIV. perh. – MDu. *spotte*, LG. *spot*, corr. to ON. *spotti* small piece, bit (Norw. *spott* speck, spot, plot of ground), obscurely rel. to OE. *splott* spot, plot of land (cf. *ġesplottod* spotted, and rare ME. *splotti* adj.). (*Spotland*, Lancashire, which appears in XII as *Spotlond*, may be a dissimilated form of **Splotland*.) Hence vb. XV (Hoccleve, Lydg.). **spo·ttED**[2]. XIII, **spo·ttY**[1]. XIV.

spouse spauz wife, husband. XII. Early ME. *spūs(e)* – OF. *spus*, *spous* m., *spuse*, *spouse* fem., aphetic var. of *espous*, *espouse* (mod. *époux*, *épouse*) = Pr. *espos*, *-a*, Sp. *esposo*, *-a*, It. *sposo*, *-a* :– L. *spōnsus* bridegroom, *spōnsa* bride, sb. uses of m. and fem. pp. of *spondēre* betroth (see SPONSOR). So **spou·sAL**[2] †wedlock; ESPOUSAL XIII.

spout spaut pipe for discharge of water, etc. XIV; discharge of water, waterspout XVI. corr. to Flem. *spuyte*, Du. *spuit*, but prob. immed. f. **spout** vb. (XIV) discharge liquid – MDu. *spouten* (Du. *spuiten*), f. imit. base **spūt-*, repr. also in ON. *spýta* spit.

sprag spræg smart, clever. XVI (Sh.). Of unkn. origin; cf. synon. (dial.) *sprack* XVIII; also *sprag* lively young fellow, young salmon or cod XVIII.

sprain sprein wrench (a part of the body) so as to cause pain. XVII. Agrees in form with OF. *espraindre* (see next), but the meaning is distant and the date of emergence is a difficulty. Hence **sprain** sb. XVII.

spraints spreints excrement of the otter. XV. – OF. *espraintes* (mod. *épreintes*), sb. use of fem. pp. of *espraindre* squeeze out, for earlier **espriembre* :– Rom. **expremere*, for L. *exprimere* EXPRESS.

sprat spræt seafish Clupea Sprattus. XVI. Later var. of †*sprot*, OE. *sprot* = MLG., (M)Du. *sprot* (whence G. *sprotte*), of unkn. origin. ¶ For the vocalism cf. STRAP.

sprawl sprōl (dial.) kick convulsively; spread one's limbs awkwardly. OE. *spreawlian*, formed with expressive initial group *spr-* (cf. the foll. words); for the el. *-awl* cf. *crawl*. Obscurely rel. to similar NFris. *spraweli*, Da. *sprelle*, *sprælle* kick or splash about, Sw. dial. *spral(l)a*, Norw. dial. *sprala* struggle.

spray[1] sprei †small twigs, fine brushwood XIII (RGlouc.); slender shoot or twig XIV (Trevisa). Earlier in Devon place-names *Spreyton*, *Sprytown*, in Domesday Book *Espreitone*, *Spreitone* 'farm in brushwood country' and *Sprei* respectively. The ult. origin of OE. **sprǣġ* and synon. *sprǣc* is unkn.

spray[2] sprei water in the form of a fine shower XVII; jet of vapour XIX. orig. *spry*, and so commonly XVII–XVIII; immed. source unkn.; formally corr. to MDu. vb. *spra(e)yen* (whence occas. Eng. †*spray* sprinkle XVI) = MHG. *spræjen*, *spræwen*. Hence vb. XIX.

spread spred pt., pp. **spread** stretch so as to display, send out in various directions XII; overlap *with*; be extended, become diffused XIII. OE. **sprǣdan* (in comps. *ā-*, *ġe-*, *ofer-*, *tōsprǣdan*, and *sprǣdung* diffusion) = OS. *tō|spreidan*, MLG., MDu. *sprēden* (Du. *spreiden*, *spreien*), OHG. *spreitan* (G. *spreiten*) :– WGerm. **spraidjan*, causative of **sprīdan*, repr. by OHG. *sprītan* be extended, with no certain cognates.

spree sprī (colloq.) boisterous frolic. XIX. Of unkn. origin; former vars. *spray*, *sprey*.

sprig[1] sprig small slender nail. XIV. Of unkn. origin.

sprig[2] sprig shoot, twig XV; fig. (cf. *scion*) XVI. Of unkn. origin; LG. has synon. *sprick*.

sprightly sprai·tli animated, brisk. XVI (late). f. *spright* (XVI), var. of SPRITE + -LY[1]. Cf. †*sprightful* (Sh.).

spring[1] spriŋ A. place of rising, as of a stream OE.; B. action or time of rising or beginning XIII; †C. young growth XIII; D. (repl. LENT) first season of the year XVI (earlier †*s. of the year*, †*s. tide* XVI, *s. time* XV, †*springing time* XIV, Trevisa); E. rising of the sea to its extreme height XIV (*s. tide* XVI); F. elastic contrivance XV (fig. impelling agency). OE. *spring* and *spryng* (more freq. in *ǣspring*, *wiellspring* fountain of water, and *ofspring* OFFSPRING, *upspring* rising of the sun, beginning of day etc.), f. **spreŋg-* and **spruŋg* respectively, of the base of next; cf., in sense A, (M)Du., (M)LG., OHG. *spring*; in sense E perh. of LDu. origin.

spring[2] spriŋ pt. **sprang** spræŋ, pp. **sprung** sprʌŋ bound, leap (*up*, etc.); issue *forth*; grow OE.; originate XII; cause (a bird) to rise XVI. OE. *springan* = OFris. *springa*, OS., OHG. *springan* (Du., G. *springen*), ON. *springa* :– CGerm. (exc.

Goth.) *_spreŋgan_, f. base rel. to *_spruŋg-_, repr. in prec. and (O)HG. _sprung_, (M)Du. _sprong_; relation with Gr. _spérkhesthai_ hasten, _sperkhnós_ rapid, has been assumed.

springal(d) spri·ŋgɔ̄l(d) (arch.) youth, stripling. xv (revived in xix by Scott). The oldest forms have _-old_, which gave way to _-ald_, _-al(l)_; presumably f. SPRING[2], but the ending is obscure.

springbok spri·ŋbɔk antelope Antidorcas Euchore. XVIII. Afrikaans, f. Du. _springen_ SPRING[2]+_bok_ goat, antelope (BUCK[1]).

springe sprin^{d}ʒ snare to catch small game, esp. birds. XIII. repr. OE. *_sprenćġ_ :– *_sprangjan_, f. base of SPRING[2].

springhalt spri·ŋhɔ̄lt. XVII. unexpl. alt. of STRINGHALT.

sprinkle spri·ŋkl scatter in drops XIV (Maund.); bedew, bespatter XV; cover with specks of colour XVIII. perh. – (M)Du. _sprenkelen_ (cf. MLG. _sprinkelt_ pp., spotted; so late ME. _sprynkled_); see -LE[3].

sprint sprint †dart, spring XVI; run, etc. fast for a short distance XIX.– ON. *_sprinta_ (Sw. _spritta_); superseding (dial.) _sprent_ (XIV) – ON. *_sprenta_ (Sw. _sprätta_, Da. _sprætte_), prop. the corr. causative wk. vb., but in Eng. chiefly intr.; ult. origin unkn.

sprit sprit pole OE., (naut.) boom or pole crossing a sail diagonally XIV. OE. _sprēot_ = (M)Du., (M)LG. _spriet_, _spret_ (whence G. _spriet_), f. Germ. *_spreut-_ _sprŭt-_; see SPROUT. Cf. BOWSPRIT.

sprite sprait spirit (formerly in various senses, now only) elf, fairy. XIII (Cursor M.). ME. _spryte_, also _spreit_, _sprete_, alt. with lengthened vowel of _sprit_, contr. of SPIRIT. The modified sp. _spright_ XVI (cf. _delight_) was specialized in the senses 'disembodied spirit', 'fairy', 'goblin', and familiarized by Spenser and Sh.; cf. SPRIGHTLY.

sprocket sprɔ·kit triangular piece of timber XVI; projection on the rim of a wheel engaging with the links of a chain XVIII. Of unkn. origin.

sprout spraut shoot forth, spring up. XII. ME. _sprūten_, OE. *_sprūtan_ (in pp. _ā|sproten_), OS. _sprūton_ = MLG. _sprūten_, (M)Du. _spruiten_, MHG. _spriezen_ (G. _spriessen_) :– WGerm. orig. str. vb. *_sprūtan_, f. *_sprŭt-_, as also in OE. _sprȳtan_, _spryttan_, OHG. _spriozan_. Hence or – MLG., MDu. _sprūte_ **sprout** sb. XIII.

spruce sprūs †brisk, lively; trim, neat. XVI. poss. from a particular collocation of _Spruce_ = _Pruce_ Prussia, e.g. _Spruce leather (jerkin)_. Hence vb. XVI.

spruit spruit small watercourse in S. Africa. XIX. Du. (SPROUT).

spry sprai active, brisk. XVIII. The earliest evidence is from S.W. dial. and N. America; of unkn. origin; cf. (dial.) _sprack_ (XVIII), SPRAG (XVI).

spud spʌd †short or poor knife or dagger XV (Promp. Parv.); spade-like implement for digging or weeding XVII; stumpy person or thing XVII; potato XIX. Of unkn. origin.

spume spjūm foam, froth. XIV (Gower). – OF. _(e)spume_ or L. _spūma_, gen. connected with _pūmex_ PUMICE, OE. _fām_ FOAM.

spunk spʌŋk spark; touchwood XVI; fungus growing on trees XVII; (Sc.) lucifer match; spirit, mettle XVIII. Of unkn. origin; cf. PUNK.

spur spɔ̄ɹ device attached to a rider's heel for pricking on his mount. OE. _spora_ _spura_ = OS. _sporo_, OHG. _sporo_ (Du. SPOOR, G. _sporn_, earlier _sporen_), ON. _spori_ :– CGerm. (exc. Gothic) *_spuron_ (whence F. _éperon_, Pr. _esporo_, Sp. _espuera_, Pg. _espora_, It. _sp(e)rone_), based on IE. *_sper-_ strike with the foot (cf. SPURN). Hence vb. XIII (Laȝ.).

spurge spɔ̄ɹdʒ plant of the genus Euphorbia, species of which have been used as purgatives. Aphetic – OF. _espurge_ (mod. _épurge_), f. _espurgier_ :– L. _expurgāre_ (see EX-[1], PURGE).

spurious spjuə·riəs illegitimate XVI; not genuine XVII. f. L. _spurius_ bastard, prop. legal term and perh. of alien origin and allied to _spurcus_ impure.

spurling var. of SPARLING.

spurn spɔ̄ɹn strike with the foot (†intr. and trans.); reject with contempt. OE. _spurnan_, _spornan_, pt. _spearn_, pp. _-spornen_ (more freq. _ætspurnan_), corr. to OS. _spurnan_, OHG. _spornōn_, _spurnan_, ON. *_spurna_, pt. _sparn_; Germ. str. vb. cogn. with L. _spernere_ scorn.

spurr(e)y spʌ·ri plant of the genus Spergula. XVI. – Du. _spurrie_, earlier _sporie_, _speurie_, obscurely based on med. L. _spergula_, whence G. _spergel_, _spörgel_.

spurt[1] spɔ̄ɹt short period, brief unsustained effort. XVI. var. of contemp. SPIRT, of unkn. origin.

spurt[2] spɔ̄ɹt issue in a sudden forcible jet. XVI. var. of contemp. _spirt_, of unkn. origin. Hence sb. XVIII.

sputter spʌ·təɹ spit out in small particles XVI; utter hastily or confusedly XVII. – Du. _sputteren_, of imit. origin; cf. SPLUTTER.

sputum spjū·təm saliva, spittle. XVII. – L. _spūtum_, sb. use of n. pp. of _spuere_ spit; see SPEW.

spy spai one who watches secretly (e.g. an enemy). XIII. Aphetic – OF. _espie_ (= Pr., Cat. _espia_, It. _spia_), f. _espier_ ESPY, whence **spy** vb. act as a spy; catch sight of XIII; – Germ. *_speχ-_, as in MLG. _spēen_, MDu. _spien_ (Du. _spieden_), OHG. _spehōn_ (G. _spähen_), ON. _speja_, _spæja_, repr. IE. *_spek-_ (L. _specere_; see SPECIES), poss. rel. by metathesis with Gr. _skep-_ (see SCEPTIC). ¶ For other derivs. of the base see ASPECT, AUSPICE, CONSPECTUS, CONSPICUOUS, EXPECT, FRONTISPIECE, INSPECT, RESPECT, SPECTRUM, SUSPECT.

squab skwɔb young bird; squat person; sofa, couch, soft cushion. XVII. Of uncertain origin; cf. Sw. dial. *sqvabb* loose fat flesh, *sqvabba* fat woman, *sqvabbig* flabby, and Eng. †*quab* (XVII) squat object (cf. G. *quabbe* soft mass). Also adj. squat. XVII.

squabash skwɔbæ·ʃ crushing blow. XIX (Wilson). f. SQUA|SH+BASH. Also vb.

squabble skwɔ·bl quarrel in a petty manner (Sh.); throw (type) out of line XVII. imit. of noisy confusion; prob. of imit. orig. So sb. Cf. Sw. dial. *sqvabbel.*

squad skwɔd small detail of soldiers. XVII. Aphetic (after next) – F. *escouade*, †*esquade* (XVI), var. of *escadre* – Sp. *escuadra*, It. *squadra*, corr. to F. *écarre* SQUARE.

squadron skwɔ·drən †body of soldiers in square formation; military and naval unit. XVI. – It. *squadrone*, f. *squadra* SQUARE; cf. F. †(*e*)*squadron* (mod. *escadron*), Sp. *escuadron*; cf. -OON.

squails skweilz ninepins. XIX. Of unkn. origin; cf. KAYLES, SKITTLES.

squalid skwɔ·lid repulsively foul. XVI (Spenser). – L. *squālidus*, f. *squālēre* be dry, rough, dirty; see -ID[1]. So **squa·l**OR[2] skwɔ·lər. XVII.

squall skwɔ̄l cry out violently. XVII (Drayton). prob. alt. of SQUEAL by assoc. with BAWL. Hence perh. **squall** sb. sudden and violent gust of wind (and rain). XVIII.

squaloid skwei·loid shark-like. XIX. f. L. *squalus* sea-fish (Varro, Pliny), used in zool. for the shark, rel. to WHALE; see -OID.

squamose skwei·mous, skwəmou·s scaly. XVII. – L. *squāmōsus*, f. *squāma* scale; see -OSE[1]. So **squa·m**OUS. XVI. – F. *squameux* or L.

squander skwɔ·ndər (dial.) scatter, disperse; spend prodigally. XVI (Sh., Nashe). Of unkn. origin.

square skwɛər A. implement for determining a right angle XIII (Cursor M.); B. rectangular figure with four equal sides XIV; rectangular area XVII. Earliest form *squire* (XIII–XVII) chiefly in sense A, later *square* (XV), aphetic – OF. *esquere*, *esquare* (mod. *équerre*) = Pr. *escaire*, Sp. *escuadra*, It. *squadra* :– Rom. **exquadra*, f. **exquadrāre*, f. *ex* EX-[1]+*quadra* square (see QUADRANT). So **square** adj. XIV. – OF. *esquarré*, pp. of *esquarrer* (whence **square** vb. XIV) = Sp. *escuadrar* etc. :– Rom. **exquadrāre.*

squarrose skwæ·rous, skwɔ·rous having scales, etc. standing out at right angles. XVIII. – L. *squarrōsus* scurfy, scabby, prob. for **escharōsus* (with assim. to *squāma* scale), f. Gr. *eskhárā* SCAR; see -OSE[1].

squarson skwā·rsən parish priest who is also squire. XIX (1876 E. A. Freeman; has been attributed to Bishop Wilberforce and others). joc. f. SQU|IRE and P|ARSON.

squash[1] skwɔʃ crush to a flat mess or pulp. XVI. Aphetic – OF. *esquasser* = It. *squassare* :– Rom. **exquassāre*; see EX-[1], QUASH.

squash[2] skwɔʃ kind of gourd. XVII. Short for †(*i*)*squoutersquash* – Narragansett Indian *asquutasquash*, f. *asq* raw, uncooked, the *-ash* being pl. ending, as in SUCCOTASH.

squat skwɔt A. (dial.) crush, flatten XIII; B. refl. and intr. sit in a crouching attitude XV. – OF. *esquatir*, *-ter*, f. *es-* EX-[1]+*quatir* press down, crouch, hide :– Rom. **coactīre*, f. L. *coāctus* (cf. medL. *quactus*), pp. of *cōgere* drive or force together, f. *co-* COM-+ *agere* drive (cf. AGENT). Cf. SWAT[1].

squaw skwɔ̄ N. Amer. Indian woman or wife. XVII. – Narragansett Indian *squaws*, Massachusetts *squa* woman.

squawk skwɔ̄k utter a loud harsh cry. XIX. imit.

squeak skwīk utter a short or slight high-pitched sound XIV (Trevisa; trans. XVI); (sl.) turn informer, 'squeal' XVII (Dryden). imit., combining the initials of SQUEAL and final of SHRIEK; but cf. Sw. *skväka* croak.

squeal skwīl utter a long loud cry XIII (Cursor M.); (sl.) turn informer XIX. imit.; in earliest use northern.

squeamish skwī·miʃ affected with nausea XV; distant, reserved, prudish, fastidious XVI. alt., by substitution of -ISH[1] for -OUS, of ME. *squaymes*, *squeymous*, earlier *scoymus*, *squoymous* (mod. north. dial. *skymous*), aphetic – AN. *escoymos*, of unkn. origin.

squeegee skwīdʒī· implement fitted with rubber for removing moisture from a surface. XIX. Arbitrarily f. *squeege* (XVIII), expressive alt. of SQUEEZE; see -EE[2].

squeeze skwīz press hard, force *out* by pressure. XVI. var. of earlier †*squise*, †*squize* (XVI), intensive of †*queise* (XV), as (dial.) *squench* of *quench*; ult. origin unknown.

squelch skwelᵗʃ crush down (something soft). XVII. imit.; cf. rare *quelch* (XVII).

squeteague skwetī·g (U.S.) weak-fish or sea salmon, Cynoscion regalis. Narragansett Indian.

squib skwib kind of firework; smart hit, lampoon. XVI. prob. imit. of a slight explosion.

squid skwid kind of cuttle fish. XVII (Purchas). Of unkn. origin.

squiffy skwi·fi (sl.) slightly drunk. XIX. Of unkn. origin.

squiggle skwi·gl make wavy or writhing movements. XIX. perh. blend of SQUIRM and WIGGLE, WRIGGLE.

squilgee skwi·ldʒī kind of swab. XIX. perh. blend of SQUELCH and SQUEEGEE.

squill skwil (root of) the sea-onion. XIV. – L. *squilla*, var. of *scilla* – Gr. *skílla.*

squinch skwinᵗʃ (archit.) †stone cut for a scuncheon XV; support constructed across an angle XIX. Shortening of SCUNCHEON.

squint skwint †(looking) obliquely with the eyes differently directed XIV (in *squyntloker*, Trevisa); adj. (as in *s. eye*, *-eyed*), vb. XVI.

Hence sb., strabismus XVII; hagioscope XIX. Aphetic of ASQUINT; cf. late ME. *of skwyn*, analytic var. of *askoyne*.

squire skwaiəɹ young man in attendance on a knight XIII (S. Eng. Leg.); one who attends on a lady XVI (Spenser); country gentleman XVII. Aphetic – OF. *esquier* ESQUIRE. Hence **squi·rearchy** -āɹki class of squires. XVIII; after *hierarchy*. **squire**EE·N[2] petty squire XIX (Maria Edgeworth).

squirm skwǝ̄ɹm writhe like an eel, etc. XVII (Ray, 'South and East Country Words'). Of symbolic origin; prob. assoc. with *worm*.

squirrel skwi·rəl rodent of genus Sciurus, or subfamily Sciurina. XIV (Ch.). Aphetic – AN. *esquirel*, OF. *esquireul*, *escureul* (mod. *écureuil*) = Pr. *escurol*, *esquirol*, Sp. *esquirol* :– Rom. **scūriōlus*, dim. of **scúrius*, for L. *sciūrus* – Gr. *skíouros*, prob. f. *skiā́* SHADE + *ourā́* tail.

squirt skwǝ̄ɹt eject liquid in a thin stream. XIV. Earlier *swirt* and perh. – LG. *swirtjen*, of imit. origin.

squish skwiʃ (dial.) squeeze, squash. XVII. imit. Hence sb. (Univ. sl.) marmalade. XIX.

squit skwit (dial., sl.) insignificant or contemptible person. XIX. prob. rel. to (dial.) *squit* squirt and SQUITTER.

squitch skwitʃ alt. of QUITCH. XVIII.

squitter skwi·təɹ (dial.) squirt, splutter XVI (Nashe); void thin excrement XVII. imit.

st excl. used (i) to impose silence, (ii) drive away or urge on an animal. XIV. So in L., †F., G., Du.; cf. HIST, WHIST[1].

stab stæb use a pointed weapon to wound or kill. XIV (Barbour). The relation to synon. (dial.) *stob* (XVI) is not clear; similar correspondences are seen in *sprat/sprot*, *strap/strop*. Hence sb. XV (Promp. Parv.).

stable[1] stei·bl building for the housing of horses and †cattle. XIII. Aphetic – OF. *estable* m. and fem. stable, pigsty, etc. (mod. *étable* cowhouse), corr. to Pr. *estable*, *-a*, Sp. *establo*, It. *stabbio* sheepfold, Rum. *staul*, *staur* (whence modGr. *staûlos*) :– L. *stabulum*, Rom. **stabula* (pl. used as fem. sg.) stall, enclosure for animals, lit. 'standing-place', f. **st(h)a-*, base of L. *stāre* STAND. Cf. CONSTABLE. Hence, or – OF. *establer* – L. *stabulāre*, **stable** vb. XIV.

stable[2] stei·bl able to remain erect, not liable to fail or vary, steadfast. XIII. – AN. *stable*, OF. *estable* (mod. *stable*), corr. to Pr., Sp. *estable*, Pg. *estavel* :– L. *stabile-m*, *-is*, (with pass. force) firm as a foundation or support, (with active force) standing firm, secure, steadfast, f. **stā*, base of *stāre* STAND; see -BLE. So **stabil**ITY stəbi·lĭti XV (Lydg.). In earliest use also *stablete* – OF. *(e)stableté* – L. *stabilitās*, on which (O)F. *stabilité* and Eng. *stabilitie* were directly modelled. **stabil**IZE stei·-, stæ·bilaiz. XIX. – F. *stabiliser*. **stabl**ISH[2] stæ·bliʃ XIII (Cursor M.). Earlier var. of ESTABLISH, now chiefly used in reminiscences of the Bible and the Prayer Book; in ME. varying with †*stable* (XIII), †*estable* – OF. *establir* (mod. *établir*) – L. *stabilīre*.

staccato stəkā·tou (mus.) with abrupt breaks between successive notes. XVIII. – It. *staccato*, pp. of *staccare*, aphetic of *distaccare* DETACH.

stack stæk pile, heap. XIII (Havelok, Cursor M.); cluster of chimneys XVII (Pepys). – ON. *stakkr* haystack :– Germ. **stakkaz*, prob. in IE. **stognos* (cf. Russ. *stog* haystack). Hence **stack** vb. pile up XIV; (U.S.) pack (cards) fraudulently XIX.

stacte stæ·ktī fragrant spice of the ancients. XIV (Wycl. Bible). L. – Gr. *staktḗ*, sb. use of fem. of *staktós* distilling in drops, f. **stag-*, base of *stázein* flow, drip.

stad stat S. African town or village. XIX. – Du. *stad* = G. *stadt*, rel. to STEAD.

staddle stæ·dl †foundation OE.; young tree left standing; lower part of a rick, etc. XVI; platform on which a rick stands XVIII. OE. *staþol* base, support, tree trunk, fixed position = OFris. *stathul*, OS. *staðal* standing, OHG. *stadal* barn (G. dial. *stadel*), ON. *stǫðull* milking-place :– CGerm. (exc. Goth.) **staþlaz*, f. **sta-* STAND + instr. suffix **-tl-*.

stad(t)holder stæ·thou·ldəɹ †governor of a fortress XVI; in the Netherlands, viceroy of a province, etc. XVII. – Du. *stadhouder* (= G. *statthalter*) tr. LOCUM TENENS, f. *stad* place (STEAD) + *houder*, agent-noun of *houden* HOLD[1].

stadia stei·diə apparatus for measuring distance by optical means. XIX. Of obscure origin; perh. – pl. of STADIUM, which was so used earlier in Eng. So in F. use.

stadium stei·diəm ancient Greek and Roman measure of length XVI; course for foot-racing; stage of a process XVII. – L. *stadium* – Gr. *stádion*, earlier (Argive) *spádion* racecourse, f. *spân* draw (cf. SPAN, L. *spatium* SPACE, SPASM, SPIN), prob. infl. by *stádios* fixed, firm, f. IE. **st(h)a-* STAND.

staff stàf pl. **staves** steivz (now chiefly literary exc. in senses in which STAVE is now the usual sg.), **staffs** stàfs (the only form in C). A. stick, pole, rod OE. (later in many spec. uses); B. †letter OE.; †line of verse XV; †stanza XVI; (mus.) set of horizontal lines for the placing of notes XVII; C. body of officers or persons employed XVIII. OE. *stæf* = OFris. *stef*, OS. *staf* (Du. *staf*), OHG. *stap* (G. *stab*), ON. *stafr* :– CGerm. (exc. Goth.) **stabaz*, of which a var. appears in Goth. **stafs* (d. pl. *stabim*). C is of Continental origin; cf. Du. *staf*, G. *stab* (also *generalstab*, *regimentsstab*; the use being prob. developed from the sense wand of office, 'baton' (cf. 'The Germans Call a Regiment, and all that belongs to it, the Colonel's Staff (den Regiment, oder Colonelstab), for with that the Soldiers are to be ruled' (Astry, tr. Saavedra Faxardo II 249, 1700). Hence vb. provide with a staff of officers, etc. XIX.

staffage stæ·fāʒ accessories of a picture. XIX. – G. *staffage*, pseudo-F. formation on G. *staffieren* fit out, garnish; Cf. OF. *estoffage* furnishing, garnishing, f. *estoffer*, STUFF; see -AGE.

stag stæg male of the (red) deer XII; (north.) young horse XIV; (dial.) full-grown castrated animal XVII; male of birds; (sl.) informer XVIII. OE **stacga*, **stagga*, of similar formation to the OE. animal names *docga* DOG, *frocga* FROG, **picga*, **pigga* PIG, **sucga*, **sugga* (cf. ME. *heġesugge* hedge-sparrow), *wicga* beetle (see EARWIG); perh. orig. 'male animal in its prime' (cf. ON. *staggr*, *staggi* male bird, whence north. dial. *steg* gander, in Icel. also *steggur* tomcat).

stage steidʒ A. storey, floor XIII (Cursor M.); B. †station, position XIII; † C. raised floor, platform XIV (in a theatre XVI); D. division of a journey or process; short for *s. coach* XVII. Aphetic – OF. *estage* dwelling, stay, situation (mod. *étage* storey) = Pr. *estatge* :– Rom. **staticum* standing-place, position, f. L. *stāre* STAND; cf. *-age*. Sense D. perh. arose from a supposed etymol. connexion with STADIUM. So **stagER**[1] stei·dʒəɹ *old s.*, one qualified by long experience. XVI; OF. *estagier* (f. *estage*) inhabitant, resident, is a poss. source.

stagger stæ·gəɹ move involuntarily from side to side; cause to reel or totter. XVI; alt. of (dial.) *stacker* (XIII Cursor M.) – ON. *stakra*, frequent. of *staka* push, stagger. Hence **stagger** sb. spec. pl. as name of a vertiginous disease XVI. Cf. for change of cons. *straggle*, *trigger*.

stagnant stæ·gnənt (of liquid) †that is at rest in a vessel; not running or flowing. XVII. – L. *stagnant-*, *-āns*, prp. of *stagnāre* (hence **sta·gnate** XVII) f. *stagnum* pool; see -ANT, -ATE[3]. Hence **stagnA·TION**. XVII.

staid steid †fixed, permanent; settled in character; of sober or steady demeanour. XVI (*stayed*). adj. use of pp. of STAY vb.

stain stein A. change the colour of, †deprive of colour; sully, blemish; spot or blotch with dirt, etc. XIV; B. impart its colour to, tinge; †ornament with colour XV; colour (fabric, etc.) with pigment XVII, (glass) XVIII. Aphetic of DISTAIN; the development of sense B is obscure. Hence sb. XVI; dye, pigment XVIII.

stair stɛəɹ flight of steps OE.; so in coll. pl. XIV; any one of these XIV. OE. *stǣger* = (M)LG., (M)Du. *steiger* scaffolding, quay :– **staigri*, f. Germ. **staig-* **stig-* climb (cf. STY). ¶ For *staircase* (XVII) see CASE[2].

staithe steið (dial., esp. north.) landing-stage, wharf. XIV (*stath*). – ON. **stapwō*, *stǫð*, rel. to OE. *stæþ* = OS. *stað*, OHG. *stad*, Goth. *staþa* (d. sg.) bank, shore :– CGerm. **staþaz*, **-am*, f. **sta-* STAND; further rel. to OHG. *stado*, MHG. *gestat* (G. *gestade*) shore.

stake[1] steik stout stick or post. OE. *staca*, corr. to OFris., (M)LG., MDu. *stake* (Du. *staak*); sb. of the LDu. area (G. *stake*, *staken*, Sw. *stake*, etc. being – MLG.), f. **stak-* **stek-* (see STICK). Hence **stake** vb. XIV; cf. OE. *stacung* impaling on a stake. ¶ From Germ. are OF. *estaque*, *-ache*, Pr., Sp. *estaca*, It. *stacca*.

stake[2] steik sb. that which is placed at hazard; vb. wager, hazard. XVI (Palsgr.). Of unkn. origin.

stalactite stæ·ləktait, stəlæ·ktait icicle-like deposit of carbonate of lime pendent from a cave-roof. XVII. – modL. *stalactītēs* (Olaus Wormius), f. Gr. *stalaktós* dropping, dripping, f. *stalak-*, base of *stalássein* drip, let drip; see -ITE. So **sta·lagmite** similar deposit rising from the floor of a cave. XVIII. – modL. *stalagmītēs* (Olaus Wormius). f. Gr. *stálagma*, *stalagmós*.

stale[1] steil †wooden upright; long handle, as of a broom. OE. *stalu* (corr. to Flem., Fris. *staal* handle), rel. to *stela* support, stalk (mod. dial. *steal*, *stell*); cf. Gr. *steleá*, *-ón* handle, f. **stel-*.

stale[2] steil †(of liquor) that has stood long enough to clear, (hence) old and strong XIII; that has lost its freshness XVI. prob. – AN., OF. **estale* (mod. *étale*, naut. of stationary water), f. *estaler* come to a stand, STALL[2].

stale[3] steil urinate, esp. of horses. XV. perh. – OF. *estaler* take up a position (see next), in spec. sense.

stalemate stei·lmeit (in chess) position (not properly a mate) in which the player has no allowable move open to him, but is not in check. XVIII. f. synon. †*stale* (XV–XVII), prob. – AN. *estale*, position, f. *estaler* be placed, f. Germ. **stall-*; see STALL[1], MATE[2].

stalk[1] stōk slender stem of plant or flower. XIV. prob. dim. (with *k* suffix), of ME. *stale*, OE. *stalu* side of a ladder, stave (see STALE[1]), rel. to OE. *stela* stalk, support; cf. WFlem. *stalke(n)*, Norw. dial. *stalk*, and parallel NFris. *stelk*, Icel. *stilkur*, OSw., ODa. *stiælke* (Sw. *stjelk*, Da. *stilk*).

stalk[2] stōk †walk stealthily OE.; pursue game by method of stealthy approach XIV (trans. XIX); walk with stiff measured steps XVI ('I stalke, I go softely and make great strides. . . . He stalketh lyke a crane', Palsgr.). Late OE. **stealcian* (repr. in *bistealcian* and vbl. sb. *stealcung*) :– **stalkōjan*, frequent. f. **stal-*, **stel-* STEAL. Hence **sta·lking-horse** horse, or screen simulating one, used in stalking game XVI.

stall[1] stɔ̄l †place, position; division in stable or shed OE.; each of a row of seats in a choir; board in front of a shop for the sale of goods, booth, stand XIV; sheath for the finger, etc. XV (*finger-stall*). OE. *steall* = OFris., (M)Du., OHG. *stal* (G. *stall*), ON. *stallr* pedestal, stall for a horse :- CGerm. (exc. Goth.) **stallaz*, prob. :- **staðlaz*, f. **sta-* STAND, with *-*dhl-* suffix (and corr. to L. *stabulum* STABLE[1]) or with *-*tl-* suffix (and a var. of **staþlaz* STADDLE). In some ME. senses partly – OF. *estal* (mod. *étal*) place, stall in church, etc. = It. *stallo*, of Germ. origin.

stall[2] stɔ̄l A. †have one's abode; B.†install; C. put (an animal) in a stall XIV; †assign, fix; D. come or bring to a stand XV. Of mixed origin; partly (i) – OF. *estaler* stop, sit in choir, f. *estal* (see STALL[1]), (ii) f. STALL[1], and (iii) aphetic of INSTALL. Cf. FORESTALL.

stallion stæ·ljən entire horse. XIV (Wycl. Bible). Late ME. *staloun* – AN. var. (cf. AL. *stalōnus*) of OF. *estalon* (mod. *étalon*) = It. *stallone* – Rom. deriv. (cf. -OON) of Germ. **stall-* STALL[1] (stallions for breeding being kept in the stable); the origin of the form *-ion* (*stalyone* XV) is unkn.; but cf. It. *stallio*.

stalwart stɔ̄·lwəɹt, stæ·l- strongly made; valiant, resolute. XIV (Barbour). Sc. var. of *stalward*, *stalworth*, brought into Eng. use by Scott; OE. *stǣlwierþe* (ME. *stalworþe*, *-worde*, *-warde*), f. *stǣl* place (perh. contr. of **staþl-*, *staþol* STADDLE; cf. occas. ME. *staðelwurðe*)+*weorþ*, *worþ* WORTH[2] adj. ¶ For the final *t* cf. *stewart*, Sc. var. of *steward*.

stamen stei·men †warp, thread; (bot.) male or fertilizing organ of a plant. XVII. – L. *stāmen* warp, thread of warp (pl. *stāmina*; see next) applied by Pliny to the stamens of the lily, corr. to Gr. *stḗmōn* warp, *stêma* some part of a plant (Hesychius), Goth. *stōma*, Skr. *sthāman* station, place :- IE. **st(h)āmon-*, **st(h)āmen-*, f. **st(h)ā-* STAND.

stamina stæ·minə †native elements or rudiments of a thing XVII; †congenital vital capacities; vigour of bodily constitution XVIII; intellectual or moral robustness XIX. – L. *stāmina*, pl. of *stāmen*; see prec. ¶ The senses arise partly from the orig. L. sense 'warp of cloth', partly from the application of L. *stāmina* to the threads spun by the Fates.

stammel stæ·ml (hist.) coarse woollen cloth. XVI (Palsgr.). prob. alt. (with variation of suffix) of †*stamin* (garment of) coarse cloth (XIII) – OF. *estamine* (mod. *étamine*) – fem. of L. adj. *stāmineus*, f. *stāmen* (see prec.).

stammer stæ·məɹ speak with halting articulation OE.; (dial.) stagger XIV. Late OE. *stamerian* = OS. *stamaron*, (M)LG., (M)Du. *stameren* :- WGerm. **stamrōjan*, f. **stamra-* (repr. by OE. *stamor* stammering), f. **stam-*, repr. by OE. *stam(m)*, OHG. *stammēr*, ON. *stamr*, Goth. *stamms* stammering, OHG. *stam(m)ēn*, ON. *stama* stammer, and synon. vbs. with other formatives, (M)LG., (M)Du. *stamelen*, OHG. *stamalōn* (G. *stammeln*), f. WGerm. **stamla-* (OHG. *stamal*) stammering, OE. *stammettan*. Cf. STEM[3], STUMBLE; -ER[4].

stamp stæmp A. †bray, pound XII; B. bring down the foot heavily XIV; C. strike an impression on something XVI. prob. OE. **stampian* = (M)LG., (M)Du. *stampen*, OHG. *stampfōn* pound (G. *stampfen* stamp with the foot, pound, crush), ON. *stappa* :- Germ. **stampōjan*, f. **stampaz*, *-ōn* pestle, mortar (OE. *pil|stampe* pestle, MLG. *stamp*, *stampe*, (O)HG. *stampf*), prob. f. nazalized var. of **stap-* tread, STEP; reinforced or infl. in sense in ME. by (O)F. *estamper* stamp (= Pr., Sp. *estampar*, It. *stampare*), Rom. f. Germ. **stamp-*. Parallel formations are OE. *stempan* pound, bray (*āstempan* stamp with a die, *stempingisern* stamping-iron) = MLG. *stempen*, MHG. *stempfen*. The base has been connected by some with Gr. *stémbein* shake about, handle roughly. Hence or – F. *estampe* **stamp** sb. stamping instrument XV; stamped or impressed mark; kind, character; act of stamping as with the foot XVI.

stampede stæmpī·d (orig. U.S.) sudden rush and flight, orig. of panic-stricken cattle. XIX. – spec. Mex. use of Sp. *estampida* crash, uproar = OF. *estampie*, Pr. *estampida*, It. *stampita*, sb. use of fem. pp. of Rom. **stampīre* – Germ. **stampjan* STAMP.

stance stæns station, position. XVI. – F. *stance* †stay, stanza – It. *stanza* station, stopping-place (see STANZA).

stanch, staunch stānʃ, stɔ̄nʃ stop the flow of; arrest the progress of, allay; †quench, extinguish. XIV. – OF. *estanchier* (mod. *étancher*) = Pr. Sp. *estancar* in similar senses, It. *stancare* weary – CRom. **stancāre*, f. **stancus* (whence OF. *estanc*) dried up, weary, Pr. *estanc* exhausted, weak, Sp. *estanco*, Pg. *estanque* watertight, It. *stanco* exhausted, enfeebled (†*mano stanca* left hand, Rum. *stîng* the left), of unkn. origin. For the rel. adj. see STAUNCH.

stanchion stà·nʃən upright bar or stay. XV. – AN. *stanchon* – OF. *estanchon*, *estanson*, f. *estance* prop, support :- Rom. **stantia* (cf. STANCE, STANZA).

stand stænd pt., pp. **stood** stud A. assume or maintain an erect position on the feet; be upright on a base; be set or placed OE.; B. confront, face XIV; cause to stand, set upright XIX. OE. *standan*, pt. *stōd*, *stōdon*, pp. (*ġe*)*standen* = OFris. *standa*, *stonda*, (pl.) *stōdun*, *stenden*, OS. *standan*, *stōd*, *stōdun*, *-standan* (Du. pt. *stond*), OHG. *stantan*, *stuont*, *stuondum*, *gistantan* (G. pt. *stand*, †*stund*, pp. *gestanden*), ON. *standa*, *stóþ*, *stóþom*, *staþenn*, Goth. *standan*, *stōþ*, *stōþum* (no pp.) :- CGerm. str. vb. **standan*, pt. **stōþ*, pl. **stōðun* (prob. without pp., which has been supplied differently in the several langs.), formed, with suffix **-nd-* (:- IE. **-nt-*) in the pres. stem and **-þ-*, **-ð-* (:- IE. **-t-*) in the perfect stem, on the base **sta-* **stō-* :- IE. **sthə-* **sthā-* stand, cause to stand, [repr. in all branches exc. Arm. and Alb., e.g. L. *stāre*, Gr. *histánai*, OSl. *stati*, Skr. *sthā*, *tisthati*. (In the Germ. langs. exc. Eng., ON., and Gothic, the pres. stem has a shorter form (by infl. of *gān*, *gēn* GO), e.g. OFris., OS. *stān*, OHG. *stān*, *stēn* (Du. *staan*, G. *stehen*), and in some the pp. has similar forms.) The Eng. pp. *standen*, *stand(e)* survived till XVI, when it was superseded by the pt. form *stood*; the wk. formation *standed* (XVI) is rare, but see UNDERSTAND. Hence **stand** sb. †delay OE. (late Nhb.); place of standing, position XIII (Cursor M.); act of standing, stop, halt XVI; appliance to stand on XVII. comp. **sta·ndpoint** (physical or mental) point of view. XIX. f. STAND vb. + POINT sb., after G. *standpunkt* (XVIII), which was modelled on *gesichtspunkt* (XVI), tr. L. *punctum visūs* (cf. F. *point de vue* point of view). **sta·ndstill** cessation of movement. XVIII. f. phr. *stand still* (STILL[1]); cf. G. *stillstand*. ¶ The IE. base is repr. by the foll. and their connexions: *stable, state, station, static, statue, stature, status*; *statute*; *stater*; *stance, stanza*; *circumstance, substance*; *transubstantiation*; *constant, distant, extant, instant*; *destine, predestinate, destiny*; *interstice, solstice*; *assist, consist, desist, exist, insist, persist, resist, subsist*; *superstition*; *constitute, destitute, institute, prostitute, substitute, restitution*; STOOL.

standard stæ·ndəɹd A. military or naval ensign XII; B. (gen.) erect or upright object; stump of tree left standing XIII (in place-names); C. exemplar of measure or weight; level or degree of quality or achievement XV. Aphetic (in AL. *standard(i)um* XII) of AN. *estaundart*, OF. *estendart* (mod. *étendard*), f. *estendre* EXTEND; see -ARD. The group of meanings under B is of mixed origin, but in the majority assoc. with STAND is clear. Hence **sta·ndard**IZE. XIX.

standish stæ·ndiʃ (arch.) stand for writing materials. XV. Of unkn. origin; presumably based on STAND, but the ending is obscure (vars. in *-age*, *-ege*, *-idge* occur XVII–XVIII).

stang stæŋ pole, beam. XIII (Cursor M.). – ON. *stǫng* (corr. to OE. *steng*) = OS., OHG. *stanga* (Du. *stang*, G. *stange*) :- CGerm. (exc. Goth.) **staŋgō*, f. base cogn. with **steŋg-* pierce (see STING). ¶ Surviving esp. in (local) *ride the s.*, be carried astride a pole for the derision of spectators.

stanhope stæ·nəp applied to (i) a light open two-seated vehicle first made for the Hon. and Rev. Fitzroy *Stanhope* (1787–1864), and (ii) a lens and a printing press invented by Charles, third Earl *Stanhope* (1753–1816). XIX.

staniel stæ·niəl kestrel. OE. *stān(e)ġella* 'stone-yeller', f. *stān* STONE + **ġella*, f. *ġellan* YELL (in OE. of the cry of the hawk).

stank stæŋk (local) pond, pool XIII; dam, weir XVII. – OF. *estanc* (mod. *étang*) = Pr. *estanc(s)*, Sp. *estanque* :- Rom. **stancu-*, prob. f. **stancāre* dam up, STANCH.

stannary stæ·nəri *the Stannaries*, the districts comprising the tin mines and smelting works of Cornwall and Devon. XV. – medL. *stannāria* n.pl., f. late L. *stannum* tin, properly *stagnum* alloy of silver and tin (Pliny), whence F. *étain*, Sp. *estaño*, It. *stagno*, perh. of Celtic origin (cf. W. *ystaen*, Bret. *sten*); see -ARY.

stannIC stæ·nik containing tin. XVIII. f. late L. *stannum*; see prec., -IC.

stanza stæ·nzə (self-contained) group of lines of verse. Late XVI (*stanze, stanzo, stanza*) – It. *stanza* standing, stopping-place, dwelling, room, strophe (whence F. *stance*, G. *stanze*) = Pr. *estansa* position, Sp. *estancia* dwelling, room :- Rom. **stantia*, f. L. *stant-*, *stāns*, prp. of *stāre* STAND. Hence **stanza**IC -ei·ik. XIX.

staphyloma stæfilou·mə (path.) protrusion of the cornea. XVI (*-ome*). – modL. – Gr. *staphúlōma*, f. *staphulḗ* bunch of grapes; see -OMA.

staple[1] stei·pl †post, pillar (surviving in place-names) OE.; short U-shaped metal rod or bar XIII (so in AL. *staplus* XII). OE. *stapol*, corr. to OFris. *stapul*, *-el* rung, anvil, crown of a tooth, execution block, MLG., (M)Du. *stapel* pillar, steeple, anvil, emporium, OHG. *staffal* foundation, ON. *stǫpull* pillar, steeple :- CGerm. (exc. Goth.) **stapulaz*; see -LE[1].

staple[2] stei·pl place in which merchants have trading privileges; principal market or commercial centre XV; principal article of commerce or industry XVII; chief object of employment, etc. XIX. – OF. *estaple* emporium, mart (mod. *étape* halting-place) – (M)LG., (M)Du. *stapel* (see prec.). Hence **sta·ple** adj. having the chief place in production or use; orig. qualifying *commodity*. XVII.

staple[3] stei·pl fibre of wool, etc. as determining the quality. XV. perh. f. †*staple* vb. inspect and sort at a staple (see prec.).

star stāɹ luminous celestial body OE., image or figure of one of them XIV. OE. *steorra* = OFris. *stēra*, OS. *sterro* (Du. *ster*, *star*), OHG. *sterro* :- CWGerm. **sterron*, to which a parallel formation is **sternōn*, repr. by OHG. *sterno* (G. *stern*), ON. *stjarna* (whence ME. *sterrne* 'Ormulum'), Goth. *stairnō*; f. IE. **ster-* **stēr-*, repr. by L. *stēlla* (:- **sterlā*), Gr. *astḗr* (*aster-*), *ástron* (cf. ASTRAL), with Indo-Iran., Arm., Toch., and Celtic cogns. *Star Chamber* (XV), orig. †*sterred* (starred) *chamber* (XIV), tr. AL. *camera stellata*, AN. *chambre esteillee* or *des esteilles* (XIV); prob. so called from its decoration. Hence **sta·rry**¹. XIV (Ch.). Late ME. *sterry*. **sta·r-ga:zer**. XVI (Geneva Bible); see GAZE.

starboard stā·ɹbōɹd, -bəɹd right-hand side of a ship)(*larboard*. OE. *stēorbord* (f. *stēor* guidance, steering paddle, rudder (see STEER²)+*bord* BOARD), to which there are corr. continental Germ. forms, whence are F. †*estribord* (mod. *tribord*), Sp. *estribor*, It. *stribordo*. ¶ The etymol. sense refers to the early mode of steering by means of a paddle worked over the right side of the vessel.

starbolins, -bowlines stā·ɹbolinz pl. men of the starboard watch. XVIII. perh. f. prec. +-LING¹; so *larbolins*.

starch stāɹtʃ †stiffen, compose (the features); stiffen (linen, etc.) with starch XV. repr. OE. **sterćan* make rigid (the pp. is found in *sterćedferhþ* of fixed or resolute mind) = OFris. *sterka*, *-ia*, OS. *sterkian*, OHG. *sterken* (Du. *sterken*, G. *stärken*) strengthen :- WGerm. **starkjan*, f. **starkaz* STARK. Hence **starch** sb. substance obtained from flour, used to stiffen fabrics. XV; cf. MDu. *stercke*, MHG. *sterke* (G. *stärke*), G. *stärkmehl*.

stare steəɹ gaze fixedly OE.; (of hair) stand on end XVI. OE. *starian* = MLG. *staren*, OHG. *starēn*, ON. *stara*, f. Germ. **star-* **ster-* be rigid, repr. also by MDu. *star* rigidity of the eyes (Du. *staar* cataract, glaucoma), Du. *staren*, G. *starren* be rigid, OE. *stær(e)blind* quite blind (with cogns. in G., etc.), STARK, STARVE, STERN¹, STEREO-.

stark stāɹk †hard, unyielding; †violent, severe OE.; (arch.) strong, stout XIII; (dial.) rigid, stiff; sheer, absolute XIV; naked XVIII. OE. *stearc* = OFris. *stark*, OS., (O)HG. *stark*, (M)Du. *sterk*, ON. *sterkr*, Goth. **starks* (in proper name *Starcedius*) :- CGerm. **starkaz*, the weak grade of the base being repr. by OHG. *gistorchanēn* grow rigid, Goth. *gastaurknan* dry up, ON. *storkna* curdle, ON. *styrkr* strong, strength; cf. also STARCH, STORK. In *s. blind* (XV) and *s. dead* (XIV) used adv. for 'quite', from the sense 'rigid'; similarly *s. naked* (XVI), for earlier (dial.) *start naked* (XIII) *steort naket*, f. START¹, as if orig. 'naked even to the tail'; synon. forms with other qualifying els. are OE. *stær(e)blind* (see STARE), OFris. *stokknaked*, Du. *spiernakt*, G. *splitternackt* ('stick'-, 'stalk-', 'splinter-naked').

starling stā·ɹliŋ bird of the genus Sturnus. Late OE. *stærlinc*, f. *stær* 'sturnus' (dial. *stare*), corr. to MLG. *star*, OHG. *star* m., *stara* fem. (G. *star*, *stahr*), ON. *stari* :- Germ. **staraz*, **starōn*, rel. to L. *sturnus*; see -LING¹.

starosta stā·rosta head man in a Russian village community. XVI. Russ., Pol. 'elder'.

start¹ stāɹt †tail OE.; (dial.) handle XIV; †point, spur of antler XVI; etc. OE. *steort* = OFris., (M)LG. *stert*, MDu. *staert* (Du. *staart*), (O)HG. *sterz*, ON. *stertr* :- CGerm. (exc. Goth.) **stertaz*, rel. to Gr. *stórthē* point of a spear, *stórthugx* point, boar's tusk, tine of antler, promontory.

start² stāɹt A. †leap, jump (OE.); move with a sudden or violent impulse; issue swiftly XIII; make a sudden involuntary movement; break away XVI; set out for a race XVII; set out on a journey; B. cause to move in such ways XIV. ME. *sterte*, *starte*, *stürte*, repr. OE. **stiertan* or **steortian*, **steartian*, **styrtan* (perh. seen in late Nhb. prp. *sturtende*), f. Germ. **stert-* **start-* **sturt-*, repr. on the Continent by (M)LG. *störten*, (M)Du. *storten*, OHG. *sturzen* (G. *stürzen*) overthrow, pour out, rush, fall headlong, gush out, and MHG. *sterzen*, *starzen* set up or stand stiffly, move briskly.

startle stā·ɹtl †kick, struggle OE. (only); (dial.) rush XIII; †start with surprise, etc.; cause to start (Sh.) XVI. OE. *steartlian*, f. **start-*; see prec. and -LE³.

starve stāɹv †die OE.; die of hunger; cause to die of hunger, cold, etc. XVI. OE. *steorfan*, pt. *stearf*, *sturfon*, pp. *storfen* = OFris. *sterva*, OS. *sterƀan* (Du. *sterven*), OHG. *sterban* (G. *sterben*) :- CWGerm. str. vb., perh. orig. 'be rigid' and thus rel. to ON. *stjarfi* epilepsy, *stjarfr*, *stirfinn* obstinate, *starf* effort, *starfa* toil; outside Germ., cf. OIr. *ussarb* (:- **udsterbhā*) death; extension with -**bh-* of the base **ster-* be rigid (cf. STARE). The orig. str. forms of the pt. became obs. XV, of the pp. XVI. Hence **starva·tion**. First used with ref. to the speech made 6 March 1775 on the Bill for Restraining Trade and Commerce with New England Colonies by Henry Dundas (1742–1811), who said that 'as to the famine which was so pathetically lamented he was afraid it would not be produced by this Act', and consequently received the nickname 'Starvation'.

stasis stei·sis (path.) stoppage of the fluids of the body. XVIII. – modL. – Gr. *stásis*, f. **sta-* STAND.

-stat stæt repr. modL. *-stata*, Gr. *-státēs*, *-statós*, f. **sta-* STAND; first in HELIOSTAT, intended to mean an instrument for causing the sun to appear stationary.

state steit A. condition XIII (Ancr R.); B. †status, (high) rank XIII; 'solemn pomp' (J.); C. estate of the realm XIV; D. commonwealth; body politic, territory belonging thereto XVI; E. (partly from the vb.) statement XVII (spec. mil., report of forces XIX). Partly aphetic of ESTATE, partly direct – L. *status* manner of standing, condition, f. base of *stāre* STAND. Hence vb. †place XVI; set out in due form, declare in words XVI. **sta·tely**¹ befitting or indicating high estate. XIV (Ch.); cf. G. *staatlich*, the sense of 'stately' being expressed by *stattlich* (so Du. *statelijk*). **sta·te**MENT XVIII; repl. *state* sb. E. **stater** stei·təɹ ancient weight and coin. XIV (Wycl. Bible). – late L. *statēr* – Gr. *statḗr*, f. **sta-*, base of *histánai* STAND used in the sense 'weigh'. **sta·tes**MAN (see -S) man concerned with affairs of state. XVI; after F. *homme d'état*; cf. G., Du. *staatsman*. **stat**IC stæ·tik †pert. to weighing or weight XVII; pert. to forces in equilibrium or bodies at rest XVII; pert. to a fixed condition XIX. – modL. *staticus* – Gr. *statikós* pert. to weighing, f. **sta-*; cf. F. *statique*. **sta·t**ICAL. XVI. †**sta·tic** sb. XVI, later altered to **sta·t**ICS XVII. – modL. *statica* – Gr. *statikḗ* (sc. *tékhnē*) science of weighing, fem. of *statikós*. **sta**TION stei·ʃən in spec. or occas. use (e.g. to render the L. word), place assigned or prescribed for some (religious) observance XIV; †act of a play XVI; act of standing (now techn.); standing-place, position; stopping-place (of a conveyance) XVI. – (O)F. *station*, corr. to Sp. *estación*, It. *stazione* – L. *statiō(n-)*, f. **stā-*. Hence or – F. *stationner* **sta·tion** vb. XVIII. **sta·tion**ARY having a fixed station. XV (Lydg.). – L. *statiōnārius*, f. *statiō(n-)*; cf. (O)F. *stationnaire*. **sta·tion**ER[2] †(hist.) bookseller, †publisher XVI; tradesman who sells writing materials (at one time part of the stock-in-trade of a bookseller) XVII. – medL. *statiōnārius* tradesman having a regular 'station' or shop (i.e., not itinerant); cf. Sp. †*estacionario* bookseller, It. †*stazioniere* shopkeeper; whence **sta·tion**ERY articles sold by a stationer, writing materials. XVIII. **stat**IST stei·tist †politician, statesman XVI; statistician XIX. perh. – F. *statiste* or It. *statista* f. *stato* – L. *status*. **stati·st**IC stəti·stik. XVIII. **stati·st**ICAL †political XVII; pert. to **stati·st**ICS, first applied to the political science concerned with the facts of a state or community XVIII; all derived (as F. *statistique*, etc.) immed. – G. *statistisch* adj., *statistik* sb., as used by G. Achenwall (1719-72); whence **statistic**IAN stætisti·ʃən. XIX. **stato-** stæ·tou repr. Gr. *statós* standing. cf. **sta-*, used in scientific terms virtually as comb. form of STATIC and STATICS XIX. **statue** stæ·tju representation in the round of a living being. XIV. – (O)F. *statue* – L. *statua* (whence also Sp. *estátua*, It. *statua*), f. pp. *stat-* of *stare*. (The L. form was in use *c.*1400–XVII.) **sta·tu**ARY maker of statues; art of making them. XVI. – sb. uses of L. *statuārius*, *-āria* (sc. *ars*). **statu**E·SQUE XIX; after *picturesque*. **statu**E·TTE XIX. – F. **stat**URE stæ·tʃəɹ height of a living body. XIII (Cursor M.). – (O)F. *stature* – L. *statūra* (whence also Sp. *estatura*, It. *statura*). **status** stei·təs †height, acme XVII; legal standing XVIII. – L. *status*. **status quo** stei·təs kwou existing state of things. XIX. Based on L. phr. *in statu quo ante*, *prius*, or *nunc* . . . in the STATE in which (things were) before, (or are) now. **statute** stæ·tjūt enactment of a sovereign or legislative authority. – (O)F. *statut* (= Pr. *statuts*, Sp. *estatuto*, It. *statuto*) – late L. *statūtum* decree, decision, law, sb. use of n. pp. of *statuere* set up, establish, decree, f. *status*. **sta·tut**ABLE prescribed or allowed by statute, of statutory quality, etc. XVII. **sta·tut**ORY[2] †enacting; pert. to statutes. XVIII. †*statutary* is earlier (XVII) but rare; cf. med.L. *statūtārius*, *lex statutaria*.

staunch, stanch stɔ̄nʃ, stānʃ watertight; strong, firm XV; (of a sporting dog) reliable XVI; standing firm XVII. – OF. *estanche*, fem. of *estanc*, used as m. XIV (mod. *étanche*); see STANCH.

stauro- stɔ̄·rou comb. form of Gr. *staurós* cross, geol. in terms denoting cruciform formations. XIX.

stave steiv stick or lath of wood XIV (Trev.); verse, stanza XVII; set of lines to carry musical notation XVIII. Back-formation from *staves*, pl. of STAFF. Hence **stave** vb. break up (a cask) into staves XVI; break a hole in (a boat, etc.), make a hole *in*; drive *off* with a staff or stave; keep or ward *off* XVII.

stavesacre stei·vzei:kəɹ plant Delphinium Staphisagria. XIV (*stafisage*, *staphisagre*). – L. *staphisagria* – Gr. *staphìs agríā* 'wild raisin', *staphís* raisin, *agríā*, fem. of *ágrios* wild.

stay[1] stei (naut.) large mast-rope. OE. *stæġ*, corr. to MLG. *stach*, Du. *stag* (whence G. *stag*), ON. *stag* :– Germ. **staga-*, f. **stag-* **staχ-* be firm (cf. STEEL).

stay[2] stei support, prop, lit. and fig. XVI; pl. stiffened underbodice XVII. Partly – OF. *estaye* (mod. *étai*), partly f. **stay** vb. support, sustain (XVI) – OF. *estayer* (mod. *étayer*), of Germ. origin (cf. prec.).

stay[3] stei cease moving, remain; cause to cease, stop, check XV. prob. – pres. stem (AN.) *estai-*, *estei-* of OF. *ester* :– L. *stāre* STAND.

stead sted place, in various applications lit. and fig. (surviving in *in one's s.*, and INSTEAD) OE.; site for a building (surviving in *farmstead*, *homestead*, and place-names) XIII; †framework of a bed (surviving in *bedstead*) XV; advantage, profit (surviving in phr. *stand in good s.*) XIII. OE. *stede*, corr. to OFris. *stede*, *stidi*, OS. *stad*, *stedi* (MLG. *stad*, *stede* place, town), MDu. *stat*, *stede* (Du. *stad* town, *stede*, *stee* place), OHG. *stat* (MHG. *stat*, *stete*, G. *statt* place, adv. prep. instead (of), *stätte* place, site, *stadt* town), ON. *staðr*, Goth. *staþs* place :– CGerm. **stadiz* :– IE. **st(h)ətís*, f. **st(h)ə-* **st(h)ā-* STAND; cf. Skr. *sthíti* standing, position, Gr. *stásis* (see STATIC), L. *statiō* STATION, *statim* adv. immediately. The sense 'advantage' may be due to assoc. with MLG. *stade* opportunity, help = OHG. *stata* condition, opportunity, proper time or place, ON. *staða* position, condition :– Germ. **staðōn*. Hence **steadfast** ste·dfəst fixed in position, etc. OE. *stedefæst* (FAST[1]) =

MLG. *stedevast*, ON. *staðfastr*. So **stead**Y[1] ste·di †fixed, immovable; firm in position or movement; regular in operation or force XVI; not easily perturbed or disturbed XVII. f. STEAD, after MLG., MDu. *stēdig*, *stādig* stable, constant = OHG. *stātīg* (G. *stetig*) :- Germ. **staðigaz*, f. **stað-* (see prec.). Hence **steady** vb. XVI.

steak steik thick slice or strip of meat. XV. – ON, *steik*, rel. to *steikja* roast on a spit, *stikna* be roasted.

steal stīl, pt. **stole** stoul, pp. **stolen** stou·lən take dishonestly OE. (in various uses with immaterial object from XIII); come or go secretly XII (prob. after ON. *stelask* refl.). OE. *stelan*, pt. *stæl*, *stǣlon*, pp. *stolen* = OFris. *stela*, OS., OHG. *stelan* (Du. *stelen*, G. *stehlen*), ON. *stela*, Goth. *stilan*, f. Germ. **stel-* **stæl-* **stul-*, of unkn. origin. The pt. *stal* (in A.V. twice *stale*) began to be superseded by *stole* in XIV, after the pp. Hence **steal**TH[1] stelþ †theft; furtive or underhand action (surviving in *by s.*) XIII. OE. **stǣlþ*, repr. in ME. by *stalþ* and *-stelþ*. Whence **stea·lthy**[1]. XVII (Sh.).

steam stīm vapour, fume OE.; vapour into which water is converted by heat XV. OE. *stēam* = WFris. *steam*, Du. *stoom* :- Germ. **staumaz*. So **steam** vb. OE. *stēman*, *stȳman*.

stearin stī·ərin (chem.) glyceride formed by combination of stearic acid and glycerine. XIX. – F. *stéarine*, f. Gr. *stéar* tallow, suet; see -IN. So **stear**IC sti͵æ·rik derived from or containing stearin. XIX. **steatite** stī·ətait massive variety of talc, soapstone. XVIII. – L. *steatītis*, *-ītēs* (Pliny) – Gr. **steatîtis*, *-ítēs* (sc. *lithos* stone) resembling tallow, f. *steat-*, *stéar*; see -ITE.

steato- stī·ətou used as comb. form of Gr. *stéar* as in **steatopyga** -pai·gə protuberance of the buttocks (Gr. *pūgḗ* rump) as in the females of certain races. XIX. **steat**O·MA encysted fatty tumour. XVI. – L. (Pliny).

steed stīd in OE. stallion; in ME. and early mod. Eng. high-mettled horse, from XVI poet. and rhet. for 'horse'. OE. *stēda* (also *ġestēdhors*), f. base of Germ. **stōðō* STUD[2].

steel stīl artificial variety of iron. OE. (Anglian) **stēle*, earlier *stēli*, *stǣli*, (WS). **stīele*, *stȳle* = OFris. **stēl* (in adj. *stēlen*), OS. *stehli* :- WGerm. **staχljam*, prop. adj. f. Germ. **staχla-*, repr. by MLG. *stāl*, MDu. *stael* (Du. *staal*), OHG. *stahal* (G. *stahl*), prob. f. **staχ-* **stag-* STAY[1]. Hence **stee·ly**[1]. XVI; repl. †*steelen* (OE. *stȳlen*, *stǣlen*); of WGerm. range. comp. **steel**YARD[2] stī·ljāɹd balance consisting of a lever with unequal arms, moving on a fulcrum. XVII.

Steelyard stī·ljāɹd site of the establishment of the Merchants of the Hanse on the north bank of the Thames. XIV. f. STEEL + YARD[1]; mistr. of MLG. *stālhof*, f. *stāl* sample, pattern (erron. identified with prec.) + *hof* courtyard (= G. *hof*).

steenbok stei·nbɔk S. African antelope. XVIII. – Du. *steenbok*, f. *steen* STONE + *bok* BUCK[1]. Cf. STEINBOCK.

steenkerk, steinkirk stī·ŋkə̄ɹk neckcloth with long lace ends. XVII. – F. (*cravate à la*) *Steinkerke*, named from the French victory at Steenkerke, Belgium, 3 Aug. 1692. Cf. *magenta*, *solferino*.

steep[1] stīp †high, towering; †(of eyes) prominent, glaring OE.; precipitous XII. OE. *stēap* = OFris. *stāp* :- WGerm. **staupa*, f. **staup-* **stūp-* (see STOOP[1]). The present sp. points rather to an OE. **stēop*; perh. infl. by STEEPLE; cf., however, *cheek*, *leek*.

steep[2] stīp soak in liquid XIV (Maund.); in various transf. and fig. uses from late XVI. repr. formally OE. **stēpan*, **stiepan* = Sw. *stöpa*, Da. *støbe*, Norw. *støypa* steep (seeds, barley for malting) :- Germ. **staupjan*, f. **staup-* (see STOUP).

steeple stī·pl tall tower OE.; spire XV. OE. *stēpel*, WS. **stiepel*, *stȳpel* :- **staupilaz*, f. **staup-* STEEP[1]; see -LE[1]. Hence **stee·ple-**CHASE (XVIII) orig. race having a church steeple in view as goal (cf. phr. †*hunt the s.*, †*s.-hunting* (XVIII).

steer[1] stiəɹ young (esp. castrated) ox. OE. *stēor* = MLG. *stēr*, OHG. *stior* (Du., G. *stier*), ON. *stjórr*, Goth. *stiur* :- CGerm. **steuraz*, the relation of which with Gr. *taûros*, L. *taurus* bull, is doubtful.

steer[2] stiəɹ guide the course of. OE. *stieran* = OFris. *stiūra*, MLG. *stūren*, (M)Du. *sturen*, *stieren*, OHG. *stiuren* (G. *steuern*), ON. *stýra*, Goth. *stiurjan* settle :- CGerm. **steurjan*, f. **steurō*, whence OE. *stēor* steering, etc. (cf. STARBOARD, STERN[2]). So **steers**MAN stiə·ɹzmən. OE. *stēoresman*, f. g. of *stēor* (see -S), beside *stēorman*; cf. Du. *stuurman*, G. *steuermann*, ON. *stýri-*, *stjórnarmaðr*, whence OF. *esturman*. The base is presumed to be identical with that of Gr. *staurós* post, stake (cf. RESTORE).

steeve[1] stīv compress and stow in a ship's hold. XV. – F. *estiver* or its source Sp. *estivar* :- L. *stīpāre* (cf. CONSTIPATE). See STEVEDORE.

steeve[2] stīv (naut.) incline upwards at an angle. XVII. Of unkn. origin.

stegano- ste·gənou-, -ɔ·- comb. form of Gr. *steganós* covered, as in *steganography* XVI – modL. *steganographia* cryptic writing. So **stego-** ste·gou comb. form of Gr. *stégein* cover, *stégē* covering, *stégos* roof, in scientific terms (XIX). See THATCH.

steinbock stai·nbɔk wild goat of the genus Ibex. XVII. – G. *steinbock*, f. *stein* STONE + *bock* BUCK[1]. Cf. STEENBOK.

steinkerk see STEENKIRK.

stele stīl, stī·lī sculptured upright slab. XIX. – Gr. *stḗlē*. Earlier **stela** stī·lə. XVIII – L. – Gr.

stellar ste·ləɹ pert. to the stars, star-shaped. XVI. – late L. *stellāris*, f. L. *stella* STAR; see -AR. So **ste·llATE**[2] †studded with stars XVI; star-shaped XVII. – L. *stellātus*. **ste·llIFY** place (a person) 'among the stars', deify. XIV (Ch.) – OF. – medL.

stellenbosch ste·lənbɔʃ relegate (one) to an unimportant position where little harm can be done, 1900 (Kipling). f. *Stellenbosch* town and division of Cape Colony, to which officers were sent who had failed in the Kaffir wars.

stellio ste·liou, **ste·llion** lizard with starlike spots. XIV (Wycl. Bible). – L. *stelliō(n-)*, acc. to Pliny f. *stella* STAR.

stem[1] stem main body of the portion of a tree or other plant above ground OE.; stock of a family XVI; upright stroke, etc. XVII; cylindrical or tubular support; (philol.) theme of a word XIX. OE. *stemn*, *stefn* (for corr. forms see STEM[2]) :- Germ. **stamniz*, of which a parallel and synon. formation **stamnaz* is repr. by (M)LG., (M)Du., OHG. *stam* (G. *stamm*), also by OS., ON. *stamn*, recorded only in the naut. sense; f. **sta-* STAND + suffix *-mn* (cf. Gr. *stámnos* earthen jar). Hence vb. †rise erect XVI; remove the stalk from XVIII; (orig. U.S.) derive *from* XX.

stem[2] stem †timber at either end of a vessel OE.; upright at the bow of a vessel XVI. OE. *stemn*, *stefn*, spec. use of STEM[1]; corr., with variation, to OFris. *stevene*, LG., Du. *steven* (whence G. *steven*), and OS. *stamn*, ON. *stamn*, *stafn*. The ON. form was repr. in Eng. by *stam* (XIV–XV) and the LG. in Sc. by *steven* (XVI–XVII); during these periods the native form was rare.

stem[3] stem †intr. stop, delay XIII; trans. stop, check, dam up XV. – ON. *stemma* = (O)HG. *stemmen* :- Germ. **stamjan*, f. **stam-* check (cf. STAMMER).

stem[4] stem head in a certain direction XIV; †ram (a vessel) with the stem XV; make headway against XVI (Sh.).

stemson ste·msən (naut.) timber fitting into the angle formed by stem and kelson. XVIII. f. STEM[2], with *-son*, after KELSON.

stench stentʃ †odour, smell; spec. foul smell. OE. *stenċ* corr. to OS. *stanc*, OHG. *stanch* (Du., G. *stank*); f. **staŋkw-* **steŋkw-* STINK.

stencil ste·nsĭl †ornament with bright colours XIV; (from the sb.) produce with a stencil plate XVIII. Late ME. *stansel*, *stencel* – OF. *estanceler*, *estenceler*, f. *estencele* (mod. *étincelle*) :- Rom. **stincilla*, for L. SCINTILLA (whence Cat., Sp. *centella*) spark. Hence **stencil** sb. perforated plate for producing a pattern by passing a brush over it charged with pigment. XVIII. ¶ The chronology, prob. through lack of early evidence, is doubtful.

Sten gun light machine gun. XX. f. initials of the inventors' surnames, Shepherd and Turpin + *-en*, as in *Bren* gun.

stenography stinɔ·grəfi writing in shorthand. XVII (J. Willis). f. Gr. *stenós* narrow + -GRAPHY.

stentorian stentɔ̄·riən abnormally loud like the voice of Stentor, a Greek warrior in the Trojan war ('Iliad' V 785). XVII. f. *Stentor* + -IAN, after late L. *stentoreus*, Gr. *stentóreios*.

step step pt., pp. **stepped** stept lift the foot and set it down; proceed on foot OE.; fix (a mast, etc.) in its step XVIII. OE. *steppan*, *stæppan*, pt. *stōp*, pp. *-stapen* = OFris. *stapa*, *steppa*, OS. **steppian*, pt. *stōp*, (M)LG., (M)Du. *steppen*, OHG. *stapfōn*, *stepfen* (G. *stapfen*); CWGerm. str. vb., f. **stap-* (whence synon. Continental forms with *-ap-*); wk. forms are found from the end of XIII, and became universal by XVI. So sb. OE. *stepe*, *stæpe* :- **stapiz*; rel. forms in WGerm. descend from **stappaz*, *-on*. No certain cogns. are known.

step- Germ. (exc. Gothic) el. prefixed to terms of relationship to designate a degree of affinity resulting from the remarriage of a widowed parent. OE. *stēop-* (as in *stēopċild* step-child, *stēopfæder* stepfather, *stēopmōder* stepmother, *stēopsunu* stepson), corr. to OFris. *stiāp-*, OS. *stiof-*, (M)Du. *stief-*, MLG. *stēf-*, OHG. *stiof-* (G. *stief*), ON. *stjúp-*; the prim. sense is indicated by its relation to OE. *āstīeped* bereaved, OHG. *stiufen* bereave, and the meaning 'orphan' of OE. *stēopbearn*, *-ċild*. Later formations are *stepbrother*, *-sister* (XV), *stepdame* (XIV).

stephanotis stefənou·tis (bot.) genus of tropical asclepiadaceous plants. XIX. modL. – Gr. *stephanōtís* (fem.) fit for a crown or wreath, f. *stéphanos* crown.

steppe step vast plain in SE. Europe and Siberia. XVII. – Russ. *step'*.

-ster stəɹ suffix repr. OE. *-istræ*, *-istre*, *-estre*, corr. to MLG. *-(e)ster*, (M)Du. *-ster* :- WGerm. **-strjōn*, added to verbal pres. stems and to sbs.; primarily applied to females, but in OE. and LDu. also to males; Survivals from OE. are *seamster* (*sempster*), *songster*, *tapster*, with the surnames *Baxter* (OE. *bæcestre*) and *Webster* (OE. *webbestre*); extraordinary OE. exx. are *miltestre* prostitute (L. *meretrix*) and *wǣpenwīfestre* hermaphrodite ('man-woman-being'), *wītegestre* prophetess; in ME. appear *huckster*, *demestre* (*deemster*, *dempster*), with occas. *bellringestre*, *frutester* (Ch.), and the permanent *brewster*, *maltster*, *spinster*. From XVI *-ster* has been used for comps. having derogatory force, as in *daubster*, *gamester*, *jokester*, *rhymester*, *trickster*, *whipster*; *dabster* and *punster* are neutral; *roadster*, *teamster*, and *tipster* are technical; *gangster* is a modern (U.S.) coinage (1896). A few formations on adjs. date from XVI; as †*lewdster* (Sh.), *youngster* (on which was modelled *oldster*). Feminine formations made with the addition of -ESS[1] are *huckstress*, *sempstress*, *songstress*.

stercoraceous stɜːkəreiˑʃəs pert. to dung. XVIII. f. L. *stercor-*, *stercus* dung + -ACEOUS. So **steˑrcor**ARY. XVII. – L. *stercorārius*. **stercoˑr**EAN, **stercoˑr**EOUS (both rare) XVIII. f. L. *stercoreus*. **steˑrcor**OUS. XVI.

stere stiəɹ cubic metre. XVIII. – F. *stère* – Gr. *stereós* solid.

stereo- steˑriou, stiəˑriou, comb. form of Gr. *stereós* solid (see prec.) in various scientific and technical terms, mostly repr. modL. forms, as in *stereographic(al)*, *-ography* XVII; *stereoˑmetry* XVI (Dee); *steˑreoscope* XIX (Wheatstone, 1838); *steˑreotype* XVIII.

sterile steˑrail, steˑril unproductive, barren. XVI. – (O)F. *stérile* or L. *sterilis*, f. IE. **ster-*, repr. also by Skr. *stariś*, Gr. *steîra* barren cow, Gr. *stériphos*, Goth. *stairō* fem. barren; see STIRK, -ILE. Hence or – (O)F. *stériliser* **steˑril**IZE. XVII. So **steril**ITY stəriˑlĭti. XV (Lydg.) – (O)F. or L.

sterlet stɜˑɹlit small sturgeon. XVI (*sterledey*). – Russ. *stérlyad'*.

sterling stɜˑɹliŋ English silver penny of Norman and later dynasties XIII; (genuine) English money XVI; adj. in *pound s.* etc. (for earlier *pound of s—s* of English money) applied to lawful or standard money XV; of standard or excellent quality XVII. Recorded earlier in OF. *esterlin* (XI or XII), medL. *sterlingus*, *libræ sterilensium* 'pounds of sterlings' (XII); plausibly referred to late OE. **steorling*, f. *steorra* STAR + -LING[1], some of the early Norman pennies bearing a small star.

stern[1] stɜɹn severe, rigorous OE.; expressing displeasure or austerity XIV. OE. **stierne* (implied in *stiernlīce* adv.), late WS. *styrne*:– **sternjaz*, prob. f. **ster-* **star-* be rigid (cf. STARE).

stern[2] stɜɹn hinder part of a ship XIII (King Horn); †steering gear of a ship XIV; tail, buttocks XVI (Turbervile, Jonson). prob. – ON. *stjórn* steering, f. base of *stýra* STEER; but the existence of OFris. *stiārne*, *stiōrne* stern, rudder, may indicate that there was a corr. form in OE.

sternum stɜˑɹnəm (anat.) breast-bone. XVII (earlier †*sternon*). – modL. – Gr. *stérnon* chest, breast, based on IE. **stern-* spread out, repr. e.g. by Gr. *stornúnai* display, L. *sternere* lay low, OHG. *stirna* (G. *stirn*) forehead, OIr. *sernim*, and Skr. and Balto-Sl. forms. comb. form **sterno-**, from XVII.

sternutation stɜɹnjuteiˑʃən (act of) sneezing. XVI. – L. *sternūtātiō(n-)*, f. *sternūtāre*, frequent. of *sternuere* sneeze, rel. to Gr. *ptárnusthai*, Arm. *phřnčel*, and W. *ystrew*, *trew*, OIr. *sreod* sneezing, f. echoic base **pster-*.

stertorous stɜˑɹtərəs pert. to snoring. XIX. f. modL. *stertor* snoring, f. L. *stertere* snore (cf. OIr. *srennim*); see -OUS.

stet stet direction to the printer to restore deleted matter. XIX. 3rd pers. sg. pres. subj. of L. *stāre* STAND; 'let (it) stand'.

stethoscope steˑþəskoup instrument for examining the chest, etc. by auscultation. XIX. – F. *stéthoscope* (Laennec, the inventor, *c.*1819), f. Gr. *stêthos* chest + *skopeîn* look at, observe (see SCOPE).

stetson steˑtsən man's slouch hat with wide brim. XX. Maker's name (*c.*1865).

stevedore stīˑvidōəɹ workman employed in loading and unloading cargoes. XVIII. orig. U.S. – Sp. *estivador*, f. *estivar* stow a cargo = Cat. *estibar*, It. *stivare* (whence F. *estiver*) :– L. *stipāre* press, pack (see STEEVE[1]).

steven steˑvən (dial.) voice. OE. *stefn*, *stemn* corr. to OFris. *stifne*, *stemme*, OS. *stemn(i)a*, *stemma*, OHG. *stimna*, *stimma* (G. *stimme*), Goth. *stibna* :– Germ. (not in ON.) **stemnō*, which has been referred to Gr. *stóma* mouth.

stew[1] stjū A. †stove, heated room; †(arch.) brothel XIV; B. (from STEW[3]) preparation of meat stewed XVIII; (sl.) state of anxiety XIX. ME. *stuwe*, *st(e)we* – OF. *estuve* (mod. *étuve*), corr. to Pr., Cat. *estuba*, rel. to *estuver*, etc., STEW[3].

stew[2] stjū pond or tank for fish. XIV. – OF. *estui* place of confinement, fish-pond (mod. *étui*; cf. TWEEZERS), f. *estoier* put into the sheath or scabbard, shut up, conceal, reserve = Pr. *estoiar*, Pg. *estojar* :– Rom. **studiāre* care for, f. L. *studium* STUDY.

stew[3] stjū bathe in a hot bath XIV; boil slowly in a closed vessel XV (intr. for pass. XVI); confine or be confined closely XVI. – OF. *estuver* (mod. *étuver*), corr. to Pr. *estubar*, It. *stufare* :– Rom. **extūpāre*, **extūfāre* (cf. medL. *stūpa*, *stūfa*), prob. f. EX-[1] + **tūfus* – Gr. *tûphos* smoke, steam (TYPHUS), with poss. infl. from Germ. **stub-* (see STOVE).

steward stjuəɹd officer of a (royal) household OE.; high administrative officer XIV; ship's officer who keeps stores, etc.; (Sc. hist.) magistrate administering crown lands XV; OE. *stiġweard*, *stīweard* (whence Icel. *stívarðr*), f. *stiġ* (prob.) house, hall (cf. *stiġwita* householder, *forestīġe* 'vestibulum, introitum' and STYE) + *weard* WARD[1]. The source of the surname *Stuart* (orig. Sc.); for *-art* cf. STALWART. Hence **stewˑard**RY, usu. **stewˑart**RY (Sc.). XV.

stibium stiˑbiəm black antimony. ME. – L. *stibium* – Gr. *stíbi*, *stímmi* – Egyptian *stm*.

stich stik line, verse. – Gr. *stíkhos* row, line (of objects), line of writing, verse, rel. to *steíkhein* advance, proceed, f. IE. **stigh-* (see STY); cf. DISTICH, HEMISTICH. So **stiˑchic**. XIX. – Gr. *stikhikós*. comb. form **sticho-** as in **stichoˑ**METRY measurement of a manuscript by lines of a certain length. XVIII.

– late Gr. *stikhometriā*. **stichomu·thia** -mjū·þiə,(usu.)**-my·thia** -mi·þiə dialogue in alternate lines of verse. XIX. modL. – Gr. *stikhomūthiā*, f. *mûthos* speech, talk, MYTH.

stick[1] stik rod, staff, or slender piece of wood OE., object in long slender form XV. OE. *sticca* stick, peg, spoon = OFris. *stekk*, MDu. *stecke* (Du. *stek* slip, cutting), OHG. *stecko* (G. *stecken* stick, staff) :– WGerm. **stikkon*, synon. vars. of which with single *-*k*- are repr. by OHG. *stehho*, ON. *stika* stick, yardstick, *kerta|stika* candlestick; f. f. **stik*- **stek*- pierce, prick (see next).

stick[2] stik pt., pp. **stuck** stʌk pierce, thrust; remain fixed OE.; cause to adhere XIII. OE. *stician* = OHG. *stehhan* prick, stab, with parallel forms in (M)LG., (M)Du. *stikken*, OHG. *sticchen*, *sticken* (G. *sticken* embroider); Germ. **stik*- pierce, be sharp (see STICK[1], STITCH) :– IE. **stig*-, **steig*-, repr. by Gr. *stízein* prick (:– **stigj*-), *stigmḗ*, *stígma* STIGMA, L. *in|stīgāre* spur on, INSTIGATE. Hence **sti·ck**Y[1]. XVIII.

stickle sti·kl †act as umpire; †settle (a dispute, etc.); †strive persistently XVI; contend *for* XVII; make difficulties XIX. alt. of †*stightle*, †*stiȝtil* arrange, control (XIII Cursor M.), bestir oneself, strive (XIV), frequent. (see -LE[3]) of †*stight*, OE. *stihtan*, *stihtian* arrange, corr. to ON. *stétta* (:– **stihtan*) support, help (Sw. *stifta*, Da. *stifte*, Icel. *stipta*, are from LG.). Hence **sti·ckl**ER[1] (dial.) moderator, umpire, †active partisan XVI; one who is insistent *for* XVII; synon. †*stiffler*, †*styteler* are earlier (XV).

stickleback sti·klbæk small spiny-finned fish, esp. Gasterosteus aculeatus. XV. f. OE. *sticels* sting, goad, thorn = OHG. *stihhil* goad, ON. *stikill* point of a horn, rel. to *sticol* steep, rough = (O)S. *stekul*, OHG. *stechal* steep, etc., f. **stik*- **stek*- STICK[1] + BACK[1]. ¶ The synon. †*stickling* (XIV) = or – (M)Du. *stekeling* corr. to MHG. *stichelinc* (G. *stichling*); other syns. are *banstickle* (XV), *stanstickle* (XVII); cf. Du. *stekelbaars* 'prickle-perch', G. *stachelfisch*.

stiff stif not flexible, rigid, OE.; (dial.) stalwart; (of wind) strong, steady XIII; steep so as to be difficult XVIII. OE. *stīf*, corr. to MLG., MDu. *stīf*, Du. *stijf* (whence MHG. *stīf*, G. *steif*), ON. *stífr* :– Germ. **stīfaz* :– **stīpos*, rel. to L. *stipāre* (see CONSTIPATE), *stīpes* stake, STIPE, Lith. *stiprùs* strong; cf. STEEVE[1], STIPULATE, STUBBLE. comp. *stiffnecked* XVI (Tindale), after Gr. σκληροτράχηλος, Hebrew *qᵉšēh'ōref* 'hard of neck'. Hence **sti·ff**EN[5]. XVI.

stifle[1] stai·fl joint at the junction of the hind leg and the body in a horse, etc. XIV. Of unkn. origin.

stifle[2] stai·fl cause to choke, suffocate, esp. kill by suffocation. XIV. Of obscure history; in earliest use *stuf(f)le*, varying with †*stuffe*, superseded (XV) by *stiffle* (surviving dial., and recorded XIV as sb. 'asthmatic complaint'), *stifle*; perh. orig. frequent. formation on OF. *estouffer* (mod. *étouffer*) = Pr. *estofar* :– Rom. **extuffāre*, poss. blend of **extūfāre* STEW[3] and **stuppāre* STOP; see -LE[3].

stigma sti·gmə (arch.) mark branded XVI; mark of disgrace, (pl. *stigmata*) mark(s) corresponding to those on the body of the crucified Christ XVIII. – L. *stigma* – Gr. *stígma*, *-mat*- mark made by a pointed instrument, brand, f. **stig*-, as in *stízein* (:– **stigj*-) prick; see STICK[2]. Earlier pl. †*stigmates* (XIV, Trevisa) stigmata of the Passion; cf. F. *stigmate* (XV). So **sti·gmat**IZE †brand XVI; set a brand upon XVII. – F. *stigmatiser* or medL. – Gr. *stigmatízein*, f. *stigmat*-, *stígma*.

stile[1] stail barrier of steps or rails allowing passage through a fence. OE. *stiġel*, corr. to OHG. *stigilla* (MHG. *stiegel*, *stigele*), f. Germ. **stīg*- climb (ref. STIRRUP, STYLE).

stile[2] stail vertical bar of a wooden framework. XVII. prob. – Du. *stijl* pillar, prop, doorpost.

stiletto stile·tou short dagger. XVII. – It. *stiletto*, dim. of *stilo* dagger, STYLUS; see -ET. ¶ By Scott and Browning anglicized as *stylet*, by Meredith as *stilet*.

still[1] stil not moving; (dial.) silent; free from commotion. OE. *stille* = OFris. *stille*, OS., OHG. *stilli* (Du. *stil*, G. *still*) :– WGerm. **stillja*, **stellja*, f. **stel*- be fixed, stand, cf. STALL. S. LIFE (pl. *lifes*) XVII after Du. *stilleven*, also (in XVII) *stilstaand leven*, *stilliggend leven* (whence G. *stilleben*, also in XVIII *stilliegende sachen* 'still-lying objects'), presumably applied orig. to representation not of inanimate objects but of living things in a state of rest. So **still** vb. quiet, calm; very common XVI–XVII, later chiefly poet. OE. *stillan* = OS. (*gi*)*stillian* trans., *stillon* intr., OHG. *stillen* trans., *stillēn* intr., ON. *stilla*. **still** adv. without change of position OE.; †quietly; †without change or cessation, always XIII; until then or now; in or to a further degree XVI; (as sentence adv.) even then, notwithstanding XVII. OE. *stille* = OS., OHG. *stillo* (Du. *stil*, G. *stille*) :– WGerm. **stillō*. **still**Y[1] sti·li †secret XIII; (poet.) quiet XVIII. prob. f. the adv. OE. *stilliċe*, f. *stille* + *-liċe* -LY[2].

still[2] stil apparatus for distillation. XVI. f. †*still* vb. (XIII), aphetic of DISTIL.

stilt stilt (dial.) crutch XIV; †handle of a plough XIV; each of a pair of poles or props with brackets raising a walker's feet above the ground XV; post or pile on which a building is raised XVII. ME. *stilte*, corr. immed. to LG., Flem. *stilte*, Norw. *stilta* :– Germ. **steltjōn*, and rel. to MLG., MDu. *stelte* (Du. *stelt*), OHG. *stelza* (G. *stelze*) :– **steltōn*, Sw. *stylta*, Da. *stylte* :– **stultjōn*, and OFris. *stult*, etc. (see STOUT[1]). Hence **stilt** vb. elevate artificially XVII; the pp. *stilted* in the sense 'artificially or affectedly elevated' is first recorded from Byron (1820), who also used *stiltified*.

Stilton sti·ltən rich cheese made in Leicestershire, so called from having been orig. sold to travellers at a coaching inn in *Stilton*, Huntingdonshire. XVIII.

stimulant sti·mjŭlənt that stimulates; sb. stimulating agent, stimulus XVIII; alcoholic drink XIX. – L. prp. of L. *stimulāre*, f. *stimulus* goad, spur, incentive (in Eng. use from XVII, at first in physiological use), prob. f. **sti-*, repr. also by *stilus* STYLUS and *stinguere* from the pp. stem **sti·mul**ATE³. XVI.

stimy var. of STYMIE.

sting stiŋ pt., pp. **stung** stʌŋ †pierce with a sharp instrument; wound with a sharp-pointed organ. OE. *stingan*, pt. *stang*, *stungon*, pp. *stungen* = ON. *stinga*, pt. *stakk*, *stungu*, pp. *stunginn*, f. **steŋg-* **staŋg-* (whence ON. *stanga* pierce). The vowel of the pp. encroached upon the pt. in XVI. So **sting** sb. act of stinging OE.; stinging organ XIV (Trevisa). OE. *sting*, *styng*.

stingaree stiŋgərī·, sti·ŋgəri. XIX. (U.S. or Austral.) alt. of *sting-ray* (XVII), fish having a sting in the tail; see STING, RAY².

stingo sti·ŋgou strong ale or beer. XVII. f. STING (with ref. to the sharp taste)+-O.

stingy sti·n^{d}ʒi niggardly XVII; (dial.) ill-tempered XVIII, perh. based on a (dial.) var. *stinge* stin^{d}ʒ of STING; see -Y¹.

stink sti·ŋk pt. **stank** stæŋk, pp. **stunk** stʌŋk emit a smell; smell offensively. OE. *stincan* = (M)LG., (M)Du. *stinken*, OHG. *stinchan* (G. *stinken*) :- WGerm. **stiŋkwan*. Cf. STENCH.

stint stint A. (arch. or dial.) cease XII (Ormulum); cause to cease XIII (Cursor M.); B. limit XVI. OE. *styntan* (once), more fully repr. in comps. *āstyntan*, *ætstyntan*, *forstyntan* blunt, dull; corr. to ON. **stynta* (OSw. *stynta*, OIcel. *stytta*) shorten, the source of some Eng. uses :- Germ. **stuntjan*, f. **stunt-* (see STUNT¹). Hence **stint** sb. †cessation, limitation XIII (Cursor M.); amount allotted or fixed XV.

stipe staip (bot.) footstalk. XVIII. – F. *stipe* – L. *stīpes* log, post, tree trunk, in modL. stalk. So **stipes** stai·pīz XVIII. Cf. STIFF.

stipend stai·pend †soldier's pay; salary XV (*stipendy*, *stipende*). – OF. *stipende*, *stipendie* – L. *stīpendium*, for **stipipendium*, f. *stip-*, *stips* money payment, wages, alms+*pendere* weigh, pay (cf. POISE). So **stipe·ndi**ARY stai-, sti- adj. and sb. XVI. – L. *stīpendiārius*; so synon. †*stipe·ndary* XVI–XVII.

stipple sti·pl paint or engrave in dots. XVIII (Goldsmith). – Du. *stippelen*, frequent. of *stippen* prick, speckle, f. *stip* point, see -LE³. So sb. †(pl.) dots used in shading, etc. XVII; method of using such dots XIX.

stipulate sti·pjŭleit make a contract; specify or require as a condition XVII; make a demand for XVIII. f. pp. stem of L. *stipulārī*, acc. to Paulus (*c.*200) f. OL. *stipulus* firm, but connected by some with *stipula* (cf. STUBBLE) from the custom of breaking a straw in confirmation of a promise; see -ATE³. So **stipul**A·TION. XVI. – L.

stir stəɹ move, set in motion, agitate, excite; also intr. OE. *styrian*, corr. to OS. *far|sturian* subvert (MLG. *vorsturen*), MHG. *stürn* stir, poke, MSw. *styr(i)a*, Norw. *styrja* make a disturbance :- Germ. **sturjan*, f. **stur-* (repr. also by ON. *sturla* disturb and prob. by STORM), of which the var. **staur-* is repr. by OFris. *to-*, *ur|stēra*, OHG. *stōren* (G. *stören*); further connexions unknown.

stirk stəɹk young bullock or heifer. OE. *stirc*, *styr(i)c*, Kentish *stiorc* (with doubtful vowel-quantity), perh. f. *stēor* STEER¹+-*oc*, -*uc* -OCK; cf. (with other dim. formations) MLG. *sterke* (whence G. *sterke*, *stärke*), MDu. *sterke* young cow, *stierken* bull calf; but some connect it with Germ. **ster-* of Goth. *stairō* fem. barren (see STERILE).

stirp stəɹp stock of a family. XVI. – L. *stirpis*, *-es*, *stirps* stock, stem (lit. and fig.).

stirrup sti·rəp support for the foot of a rider, orig. a looped rope. OE. *stigrāp* = OS. *stigerēp*, MDu. *steegereep* (WFlem. *steegreep*; the Du. word is *stijgbeugel*), OHG. *stegareif* (G. *stegreif*; the usual word is *steigbügel*), ON. *stigreip*; f. Germ. **stig-* climb (see STILE, STYLE)+**raipaz* ROPE.

stitch stitʃ †prick, puncture OE. only; sharp sudden local pain OE.; (from the vb.) movement of a needle and thread XIII; portion of thread left as a result of this XIV. OE. *stiće* = OFris. *steke*, OS. *stiki* prick, stab. OHG. *stih* (G. *stich*) prick, sting, stitch, Goth. *stiks* point :- CGerm. (not Scand.) **stikiz*, f. **stik-* STICK². Hence **stitch** vb. †stab with pain; fasten with stitches XIII. Hence **stitch**WORT Stellaria holostea, plant reputed to cure the stitch in the side. XIII.

stithy sti·ði anvil. XIII. ME. *steþi*, *stiþi* – ON. *steði* :- **staðjon*, f. Germ. **sta-* STAND. The form is due to assoc. with SMITHY (cf. ME. *stith*, dial. *stith*, for **steþe*, normally – ON. *steði*).

stiver stai·vəɹ small coin of the Low Countries XVI; (colloq.) typical coin of low value XVII. – Du. *stuiver*, in MLG. *stüver* (whence G. *stüber*, Sw. *styfver*, Da. *styver*), prob. based on **stuf-* (cf. STUMP).

stoat stout European ermine, Putorius ermineus, in its brown summer coat (Mustela erminea). XV. Of unkn. origin.

stoccado stəkā·dou thrust with a pointed weapon. XVI. With suffix-substitution – It. *stoccata*, f. *stocco* point of a sword, dagger, of Germ. origin; see STOCK, -ADO.

stock stək A. trunk, stem OE.; B. supporting structure; frame of timber for punishment XIV; C. hollow receptacle XIV; D. massive portion of an instrument XIV (of a gun XVI); E. line of descent (cf. L. *stirps*, G. *stamm*) XIV; F. part of hose (*upper* and *nether*; cf. STOCKING) XV; G. fund, store (as of money) XV; quantity XVII; H. object of contemptuous treatment XVI; I. stiff neck-cloth XVII. OE. *stoc(c)* = OFris. *stokk*, OS., (M)Du. *stok* (G. *stock* stick), ON. *stokkr* trunk, block, log :- CGerm. (exc. Gothic) **stukkaz*, rel. to **stukkjam* piece, repr. by OE. *styćće*, OS., OHG. *stucki* (Du. *stuk*, G. *stück*), ON. *stykki*; of unkn. origin. Used adj. 'kept in stock' XVII. Hence vb. in various senses, that of †'put in the stocks' being the earliest (XIV), 'supply with a stock of' the latest (XVII) in appearance. comp. **sto·ck**-DOVE wild pigeon. XIV; cf. Flem. †*stokduive*; perh. so called from its resting in hollow tree-trunks. **sto·ck**FISH cod, etc. split open and dried. XIII. – (M)Du., (M)LG. *stokvisch* (whence also G. *stockfisch*), variously expl. **stock**GI·LLYFLOWER Matthiola incana. XVI; cf. Flem. *stokviolier*; so called from its woody stem; abbrev. *stock* XVII. **stock**STI·LL motionless. XV; cf. Du., G., and sense H above.

stockade stɔkei·d barrier of stakes or piles. XVII. – F. †*estocade*, alt. of †*estacade* – Sp. *estacada*, f. *estaca* – Rom. – Germ. **stak*- STAKE; see -ADE.

stockinet(te) stɔkine·t knitted textile fabric. XIX. prob. alt., simulating a dim. in -ET, -ETTE, of earlier *stocking-net*.

stocking stɔ·kiŋ close-fitting covering for the leg from foot to knee. XVI. Of obscure formation with -ING[1], repl. †*nether-stock* (NETHER, STOCK), corr. to †*upper stock*, as F. *bas de chausse* (whence *bas* stocking) is parallel to *haut de chausse*.

stodge stɔdʒ fill quite full. XVII. Phonetically symbolic after *stuff* and *podge*. Hence sb. and **sto·dg**Y[1] XIX.

stoep stūp (S. Africa) raised verandah. XIX. – Du. *stoep*, rel. to Germ. **stap*- STEP. In U.S. STOOP[2].

Stoic stou·ik pert. to the school of philosophers founded by Zeno (*c*.300 B.C.); also sb. XVI (in Wycl. Bible *Stoycis* for L. *Stōici*). – L. *stōicus* – Gr. *stōikós*, f. *stoá* the Porch in which Zeno taught at Athens, f. IE. **sthou*- (**sthāu*- **sthū*-) stand, repr. also by STOW, STUD[2]. Also **Sto·ic**AL[1]. XV. (Ch. and Wycl. Bible have forms based on OF. *stoicien*.)

stoker stou·kəɹ one who feeds and tends a furnace. XVII. – Du. *stoker*, f. *stoken* feed (a furnace), MDu., MLG. *stoken* push, poke, f. **stok*-, rel. to **stek*- thrust, prick, STICK; see -ER[1]. Hence by back-formation **stoke** vb. XVII (*stoking-hole*; cf. contemp. *sto·kehole*, tr. Du. *stookgat*, f. *stoken*+*gat* hole).

stole[1] stoul (arch.) long robe; (eccl.) vestment consisting of a narrow strip of stuff worn over and hanging from the shoulders. OE. *stole* fem. *stol* n. – L. *stola* (whence OF. *estole*, mod. *étole*, etc.) – Gr. *stolḗ* equipment, array, clothing, garment, f. **stol*- **stel*- place, array, lead, send (cf. APOSTLE, EPISTLE, SYSTOLE).

stole[2] stoul in *Groom* or *Yeoman of the Stole* officer of the King's Household next below the vice-Chamberlain. XV. var. of STOOL in the sense 'close-stool', surviving traditionally in the designation of the officer, with pronunc. based on sp.; formal assoc. with STOLE[1] has given rise to unwarranted etymol. notions connecting the two words.

stolid stɔ·lid dull and impassive. XVI (rare before XIX; not entered by J. 1755, who has *stolidity*). – F. †*stolide* or L. *stolidus* poss. rel. to *stultus* foolish; see -ID[1]. So **stoli·d**ITY. XVI. – F. †*stolidité* or L.

stolo stou·lou (bot.) prostrate branch that takes root at the tip. XVIII. L. Earlier **stolon** stou·lən XVII – inflexional forms *stolōn*-; cogn. with Gr. *stélekhos* trunk, branch (**sthel*- stand upright).

stoma stou·mə (anat., bot.) small opening. XVII. – modL. use of Gr. *stóma* mouth.

stomach stʌ·mək internal pouch or cavity of the body in which food is digested; abdomen, †chest; appetite *for* XIV; †seat of emotion; †temper, disposition XVI; †courage, pride, anger XVI. ME. *stomak* – OF. *stomaque*, (also mod.) *estomac* = Pr. *estomac*, Sp. *estómago*, It. *stomaco* – L. *stomachus* – Gr. *stómakhos* throat, gullet, mouth of an organ, as of the stomach, (later) stomach, f. *stóma* mouth. So vb. †take offence; †offend, incite XVI; put up with, brook XVII. orig. – F. *s'estomaquer* (refl.) be offended, L. *stomachārī* be resentful, be angry with, f. *stomachus*. **stomach**IC stŏmæ·kik. XVII. – F. or late L. – Gr.

stomacher stʌ·məkəɹ †man's waistcoat XV; part of woman's dress covering the chest XVI. prob. aphetic – OF. *estomachier* (perh. AN., but recorded only once, Palsgr. 1530), f. *estomac* STOMACH+-IER -ER[2]; this would account for the older pronunc. with tʃ, attested by the vars. *stomager* (XV–XVIII) and *stomatcher* (XVIII) and by dicts. from XVIII; but forms with -*k*- are as early as XV.

stone stoun piece of rock or hard mineral substance OE.; measure of weight (14 lb.) XIV (Sir Perc.). OE. *stān* = OFris., OS. *stēn* (Du. *steen*), (O)HG. *stein*, ON. *steinn*, Goth. *stains* :- CGerm. **stainaz*, rel. to OSl. *stēna* wall, Gr. *stíā*, *stîon* pebble. **stone**-BUCK[1] ibex. OE. *stānbucca*; from XVI – G. *steinbock*; cf. STEENBOK, STEINBOCK. **sto·ne-chat,** Pratincola rubicula. XVIII; the clash of pebbles is supposed imit. of the bird's alarm cry. **sto·necrop,** Sedum acre; OE. *stāncrop* (the second el. is not identified); earlier *stone-chatter*, *-smatch*, *-smitch*. **stone's throw** XVI; preceded by †*s. cast* (XIII Cursor M.), *stone's cast* XIV (Trevisa). **stonewall** vb. (f. *stone wall* wall of stone as presenting an obstacle) offer resistance or obstruction XIX. Hence **sto·ny**[1]. OE. *stāniġ*, ult. repl. *stǣniġ*, *stǣnen*, *stāniht*; with similative force, e.g. *stone-blind* XIV, *-deaf*, the earliest being *stone-dead*, *-still* (XIII). Hence vb. XII (pp. *istanedd*, Orm).

stooge stūdʒ (sl.) one who cooperates or deputizes in a subservient fashion. XX. orig. U.S., of unkn. origin.

stook stuk shock of corn. XV. Late ME. *stouk*, corr. to or – MLG. *stūke*, formally = widespread Germ. word (OHG. *stūhha* sleeve, G. *stauche* muff), not agreeing in sense; the present form shows survival of northern vocalism.

stool stūl A. wooden seat for one person OE.; B. base, support, stand XIV; C. seat enclosing a chamber utensil XV; evacuation of the bowels XVI (cf. STOLE[2]); D. (figure of) a bird secured to a stool or perch, serving as a decoy XIX. OE. *stōl* = OFris., OS. *stōl*, OHG. *stuol* (Du. *stoel*, G. *stuhl*), ON. *stóll*, Goth. *stōls* throne :– CGerm. **stōlaz*, f. **stō-* **stā-* STAND + -LE[1], the basic sense being 'stand', 'station'; cf. OSl. *stolŭ* throne seat, Gr. *stḗlē* pillar.

stoop[1] stūp bow or bend down, incline from the vertical; condescend. XVI. OE. *stūpian* = MDu. *stūpen*, ON. *stúpa*, f. Germ. **stūp-*, rel. to **steup-* STEEP[1]. The orig. vowel ū has been retained before the lip-consonant p.

stoop[2] stūp (U.S., Canada) uncovered platform before the entrance of a house. XVIII. – Du. STOEP.

stop stɔp A. fill up, close, plug ; B. bring to a stand or halt XIV; C. come to a stand XVI. OE. **stoppian* in *forstoppian* plug (the ear), corr. to OFris. *stoppia*, G. *verstopfen*, MLG. *stoppen*, OHG. *stopfōn* (G. *stopfen*); see STUFF. Hence **sto·pp**AGE XV. **stopp**ER[1] stɔ·pəɹ. XV; in the sense 'plug, cork' (XVI) repl. *stopple*. XIV.

storax stō·ræks fragrant gum resin. XIV. – L. *storax* – Gr. *stórax*, var. of *stúrax* STYRAX, of alien origin.

store stōəɹ necessaries for future use (now pl.); †live stock XIII (RGlouc., Cursor M.); storage, reserve XIV; sufficient supply, stock laid up XV; animal kept for fattening; warehouse XVII; large shop XVIII. ME. *stor*, aphetic of †*astor* – OF. *estor* (= Pr. *estor*), f. *estorer* (whence **store** vb. XIII; also †*astore*, †*enstore*; cf. AL. *staurāre* XII) :– L. *instaurāre* renew, repair, RESTORE. Hence **sto·r**AGE action and place of storing XVII.

storey, story stō·ri any of the parts one above another of which a building consists XIV; tier of columns XV (cf. CLERESTORY). Aphetic – AL. *(h)istoria*, spec. use of L. *historia* HISTORY, STORY[1]; perh. orig. tier of painted windows (cf. AL. *historia* picture). Hence **storey**ED[2], **storied**[2] stō·rid having storeys. XVII.

storge stō·ɹgī natural affection. XVII. – Gr. *storgḗ*, rel. to *stérgein* love.

storied[1] stō·rid decorated with scenes from history or legend XV (Caxton); recorded in history XVIII (Pope). f. STORY[1] + -ED[1], after medL. *historiātus*, OF. *(h)istorié*.

storied[2] see STOREYED.

stork stōɹk tall white wading bird. OE. *storc* = OS. (Du.) *stork*, OHG. *stor(a)h* (G. *storch*), ON. *storkr* :– CGerm. (exc. Gothic) **sturkaz*, prob. f. **sturk-* **sterk-* (see STARK), the name being supposed to refer to the bird's rigid habit; Balto-Sl. forms are held to be – Germanic.

storm stōɹm violent disturbance of the atmosphere, fig. of affairs OE.; paroxysm, violent access XVI; (from the vb.) assault of troops on a place XVII. OE. *storm* = OS. (Du.) *storm*, (O)HG. *sturm*, ON. *stormr* :– CGerm. (exc. Gothic) **sturmaz*, prob. f. **stur-*, repr. also by STIR. Hence **storm** vb. be tempestuous XV; (of persons) rage (cf. OF. *estormir* make a disturbance) XVI; (after G. *stürmen*, †*störmen*) make an assault (on) XVII. **sto·rmy**[1]. late OE.

Storthing stō·ɹþiŋ Norwegian parliament. XIX. – Norw. *storting*, former *storthing*, f. *stor* great + THING assembly.

story[1] stō·ri †historical relation or anecdote, historical writing XIII (AncrR., Havelok, Cursor M.) XIII; recital of events XIV (Barbour); narrative designed for entertainment, tale XIV; account XVII (Sh.). Aphetic – AN. *estorie* (OF. *estoire*, mod. *histoire*) – L. *historia* (whence OE. *stǣr*, through OIr. *stoir*) HISTORY.

story[2] see STOREY.

stoup stūp (Sc.) pail, bucket XIV; drinking-vessel XV; holy-water vessel against or in a church wall XVIII (substituted by mod. antiquaries for †*stop*, †*stope*). – ON. *staup* = OE. *stēap*, MLG. *stōp*, (M)Du. *stoop*, OHG. *stouf* (G. dial. *stauf*) :– Germ. **staupaz*, *-am*, rel. to OE. *stoppa*, OS. *stoppo* pail :– WGerm. **stoppon*, f. *stup-*. See STEEP[2].

stout[1] staut †proud, fierce, brave; strong in body or build XIV; corpulent XIX. – AN., OF. (NE. dial.) *stout*, for *estout* :– WGerm. **stult-* (OFris. *stult*, MLG. *stolt*, MDu., Du. *stout*, (O)HG. *stolz* proud), perh. rel. to **stelt-* (see STILT).

stout[2] staut 'a cant name for strong beer' (J.) XVII; strong variety of porter XIX. prob. ellipt. for *s. ale* or *s. beer*, the adj. being current XVII–XIX as applied to drink having a good body.

stove stouv †heated chamber or building XV; closed box containing burning fuel XVII; fire grate XVIII. – MLG., MDu. *stove* (Du. *stoof* footwarmer) = OHG, *stuba* (G. *stube* living-room), rel. to OE. *stofa* bathroom, *stuf|bæþ* vapour bath (Scand. forms are prob. of LG. origin), f. **stub-*; connexion with STEW[1], STEW[3] is possible.

stow stou †place XIV; put away to be stored XV; place (cargo) in a ship XVI. Aphetic of BESTOW (based on OE. *stōw* place, surviving in many place-names (= OFris. *stō*) but not continuous with OE. *stōwian* restrain). Naut. sense perh. infl. by Du. *stouwen.* Hence **sto·WAGE.** XIV; cf. AL. *stowagium* (XIV); comp. **sto·WAWAY** person who hides in a ship. XIX; f. phr. *s.* (oneself) *away.*

strabismus strəbi·zməs (med.) squinting. XVII. modL. – Gr. *strabismós*, f. *strabízein* squint, f. *strabós* twisted, squinting (whence L. *strabus*), rel. to *stréphein* (see STREPTO-).

straddle stræ·dl spread the legs wide apart XVI; bestride XIX. frequent. f. **strād *strid* STRIDE alt. of contemp. and synon. *striddle*, back-f. from *striddling(s)* astride (XV), f. **strid-*, wk. var. of STRIDE; see -LE[3].

stradiot stræ·diət cavalry soldier of Greek and Albania. XVI. – It. *stradiotto* (whence F. *estradiot*, formerly in Eng. use) – Gr. *stratiṓtēs* soldier, f. *stratiā́* army.

stradivarius strædivɛə·riəs (colloq. abbrev. **strad**) latinization of the name of Antonio *Stradivari* of Cremona (1649–1737) applied to violins made by him and his relatives.

strafe strāf, streif punish, damage, 'curse'. XX. f. G. phr. *Gott strafe England* God chastise England, current in Germany. Hence sb. fierce assault.

straggle stræ·gl wander scatteringly from the direct course. XIV. perh. alt. of **strackle*, f. (dial.) *strake* move, go, f. **strak-* base of STRETCH; see -LE[3]; for *-gg-* from *-ck-*, *-kk-* cf. *stagger, trigger.*

straight streit not curved or bent XIV; not oblique; honest XVI (obs. in XVII, revived in XIX, from U.S.?); in proper order XIX; adv. XIV (*s. away, s. off* XVII). ME. *streȝt*, *straȝt* (as pp. adj. extended at full length), pp. of *strecche* STRETCH. Hence vb. †(Sc.) stretch XIV; make straight XVI; superseded by **strai·ghtEN**[5] XVII. **straightFO·RWARD** acting in a direct manner. XIX. f. phr. *s. forward* in a direct path onwards. **strai·ghtWAY** †by a direct course XV; immediately XVI (Tindale; also †*-ways* Berners). Cf. L. *rectā viā.*

strain[1] strein †gain, treasure OE.; †generation, offspring XII; †pedigree, ancestry, XIII; race, stock XIV; breed, inherited character XVII. OE. **strēon*, (Nhb. *strion*), aphetic of *ġestrēon* = OS., OHG. *gistriuni*, rel. to OE. (*ġe*)*strēonan*, (*ġe*)*strīenan* gain, get, beget = OHG. (*gi*)*striunen*, f. Germ. **streu-* pile up, rel. to L. *struēs* pile, heap, *struere* build (cf. STRUCTURE). ¶ The normal repr. *streen* (XIV–XVI) of the OE. form has been perverted by assoc. with next.

strain[2] strein A. draw tight, stretch XIII; force the sense or application of; force to extreme effort XV; B. bind or compress tightly (obs. or arch. except in *s. to one's bosom*, etc.); C. press through a filtering medium XIV; D. refl. and intr. exert oneself XIV (in *s. at* make a difficulty of 'swallowing' or accepting XVI, misunderstanding of *s. at a gnat* in Matt. xxiii 24, which means 'strain the liquor if they find a gnat in it'). ME. *strayne, streyne*, aphetic – OF. *estrei(g)n-*, stem of *estreindre* (mod. *étreindre*) = Pr. *estrenher*, Sp. *estreñir*, It. *strignere, stringere*:– L. *stringere* draw tight, bind tightly (see STRINGENT). Hence or – AF. **estreignour* **strai·nER**[1] filter, sieve. XIV.

strain[3] strein section of a piece of music; melody, tune; passage of song or poetry XVI; †stream of impassioned language; tone, style, tenor, drift XVII. rel. obscurely to STRAIN[2] used in the senses 'lift up (the voice) in song', 'utter in song, sing', which are of doubtful origin.

strait streit (arch., dial.) tight, narrow; strict, rigorous; limited in extent XIII; sb. narrow place, (now only) narrow waterway XIV; (now only pl.) straitened circumstances, difficulty, fix XVI; adv. tightly, etc. XII, surviving in gen. use only in *strait-laced* †narrow in scope, mind, etc., excessively rigid (XVI), orig. tightly-laced (*streyght lasyd* XV). ME. *streit*, aphetic – OF. *estreit* tight, close, narrow, sb. narrow place, strait of the sea, distress = Pr. *estreit*, Sp. *estrecho*, It. *stretto* :– L. *strictu-s* STRICT. The var. forms show confusion with *streȝt* STRAIGHT at an early date. Hence **strai·tEN**[5] XVI, superseding †*strait* vb. XIV, and surviving mainly in pp. (*straitened circumstances*, etc. XVIII).

strake streik strip of iron; stripe of colour; ray of light XIV; line of planking in the side of a vessel, breadth of a plank XV. ME. *strake* (in AL. *stracus* 1300), prob. f. **strak-*, base of OE. *streċċan* STRETCH; largely coincident in form and meaning with *streak* from XVI. In the sense 'pit or box for washing ore' (XVIII) prob. orig. applied in pl. to the lining boards.

stramineous strəmi·niəs pert. to straw. XVII. f. L. *strāmineus*, f. *strāmen* straw (f. **strā-*; see STRATUM) + -OUS.

stramonium strəmou·niəm (bot.) solanaceous plant Datura Stramonium. XVII. – modL. *stramonium* (Parkinson 1629), *strammonium* (F. Columna 1592), poss. alt. of Tartar *turman* medicine for horses (whence Russ. *durmán* stramonium).

strand[1] strænd (arch., dial.) land bordering the sea or other water. OE. *strand* = MLG. *strant, -nd-* (whence Du., G. *strand*), ON. *strǫnd*; of unkn. origin. *The Strand*, name of street in London orig. occupying an extent of the shore of the Thames. Hence vb. force on to a shore. XVII; so Du., G. *stranden* (XV), Sw. *stranda*, Da. *strande.*

strand[2] strænd one of the strings twisted together forming a rope or cord. XV (*strond*). Of unkn. origin; connexion with more or less synon. OHG. *streno* (G. *strähne*), MDu. *strēne* (Du. *streen*) is not proved.

strange streindʒ †foreign, alien; belonging to another place; unfamiliar, unknown. XIII. Aphetic – OF. *estrange* (mod. *étrange*) = Pr. *estranh*, Sp. *estraño*, It. *strano*, sb. *stranio*, *strangio*, Rum. *străin* :– L. *extrāneus* EXTRANEOUS; cf. ESTRANGE, earlier †*strange* (Wycl., Gower). So **stranger** strei·ndʒəɹ (arch.) foreigner; guest, visitor; unknown person XIV; new-comer XV. Aphetic – OF. *estrangier* (mod. *étranger*) :– Rom. **extrāneārius*, f. L. *extrāneus*; see prec., -ER[2].

strangle stræ·ŋgl kill by pressing the windpipe, (gen.) choke. XIII. Aphetic – OF. *estrangler* (mod. *étrangler*) = Pr. *estrang(o)lar*, etc. – L. *strangulāre* – Gr. *straggalān*, rel. to *straggálē* halter (see STRING[1]). So **strangulA·TION**. XVI. – L.

strangullion strænggʌ·ljən inflamed state of throat in horses. XV (Caxton). – OF. *(e)stranguillon* (mod. *étranguillon*) – It. *stranguglione* :– Rom. **strangulīō(n-)*, f. L. *strangulāre* STRANGLE.

strangury stræ·ŋgjŭri (path.) slow and painful urination. XIV. – L. *strangūria* – Gr. *straggouríā*, f. *stragg-*, *strágx* drop squeezed out + *oûron* URINE.

strap stræp leather band XVI; strop in naut. use XVII; razor strop XVIII. var. of STROP, with change of vowel before p widespread in dial. use; cf. NAP[2].

strappado stræpā·dou torture in which the victim was hoisted by a rope and dropped with a jerk. XVI. – F. *strapade*, *estrapade* – It. *strappata*, f. *strappare* drag, snatch – OF. *estraper*, var. of *estreper*, *esterper* :– L. *extirpāre* EXTIRPATE; see -ADO.

strapping stræ·piŋ †vigorous, lusty; sturdily built. XVII. Hence **stra·ppER**[1] strapping person. XVII.

Strasbourg stræ·zbɔ̄ɹg, ||ʃtrā·sburχ name of the principal town of Alsace (Elsass), as in *S. linen*, *S. pie*.

strass stræs paste for artificial gems. XIX. – G. *strass*, F. *stras*, f. name of inventor; Joseph *Strasser*.

stratagem stræ·tĭdʒəm artifice to surprise an enemy XV (Caxton); device, trick XVI. – F. *stratagème* = Sp., Pg. *estratagema*, It. *stratagemma* – (with alt. of second syll.) L. *stratēgēma* – Gr. *stratḗgēma*, f. *stratēgeîn* be a general, f. *stratēgós*, commander-in-chief (whence L. *stratēgus* in Eng. use XVII), f. *stratós* army + *-ăg-* lead (see ACT). So **strategIC** -ī·dʒik, -e·dʒik. XIX. – F. *stratégique* – Gr. *stratēgikós*, f. *stratēgós*, *stratēgíā*, whence **strategY**[3] stræ·tĭdʒi. XVII, through F. *stratégie*, Gr. *stratēgíā*.

strath stræþ (Sc.) wide valley or tract of low-lying land. XVI. – Gael. *srath* = Ir. *srath*, *sratha*, W. *ystrad* dale :– **strət-*; cf. Gr. *stratós* encamped army.

stratify stræ·tifai 'range in beds or layers' (J.). XVII. – F. *stratifier* – modL. *strātificāre*, f. L. *strātum*. So **stratificA·TION**. XVII. – modL. **stratigraphic** strætigræ·fik pert. to **strati·GRAPHY** geological study concerned with the strata of the earth's crust. XIX. **stratosphere** strei·tou-, stræ·tousfiəɹ stratum of the atmosphere above the troposphere f. *-sphere* of ATMOSPHERE. XX. **stratum** strei·təm pl. **strata** strei·tə layer (chiefly in spec. uses). XVI. – modL. use of L. *strātum* 'something laid down' (bed-cover, horsecloth, pavement), sb. use of n. pp. of *sternere* lay or throw down, f. IE. **ster-* extend, lay out, for other derivs. of which see CONSTERNATION, PROSTRATE, STRAMINEOUS, STRAW, STREET, STREW, STROMA, SUBSTRATUM. **stratus** strei·təs (meteor.) form of cloud having the appearance of a broad sheet of uniform thickness. XIX. comb. form (see -o-) **strato-** strei·tou, as in *strato-cirrus*, *-cumulus*.

straw[1] strɔ̄ (coll. sg.) stems or stalks of cereals OE.; single stem XII. OE. *strēaw* = OFris. *strē*, OS., OHG. *strō* (Du. *stroo*, G. *stroh*), ON. *strá* (whence ME. *strā*, *strō*) :– CGerm. (exc. Goth.) **strāwam*, rel. to STREW. Cf. L. *strāmen* STREW. comp. **straw-BERRY** strɔ̄·bəri fruit of species of Fragaria. OE. *strēa(w)beriġe*, *strēow-*; the reason for the name is unknown.

straw[2] strɔ̄ (arch.) scatter XII (Orm); cover with something scattered XIII. Differentiated repr. of OE. *streawian* STREW.

stray strei domestic animal that is found wandering. XIII (in AL. XII). – AN. *strey*, aphetic of *astrey* used as sb. So **stray** vb. escape from confinement, wander, roam. XIV. Aphetic – AN., OF. *estraier* (see ASTRAY). Hence (from the sb.) adj. that has escaped from control and goes free. XVII (Topsell).

streak strīk †mark, stroke OE.; thin line of different colour or substance from the rest XVI; stratum of coal or ore XVII; strip of land or water XVIII. OE. *strica* stroke of the pen, mark, line of motion, orbit, corr. in sense and vowel-grade to OFris. *strike*, MLG., MDu. *strēke* (Du. *streek*), (O)HG. *strich*, Goth. *striks*, f. **strik-* (see STRIKE). The normal development of the OE. form is repr. by ME. *strik*; the divergent *strēke* (with *ē* from *ĭ*) was prob. reinforced by MDu. or MLG. *strēke*. Hence **streak** vb. †strike out XV; mark with streaks XVI.

stream strīm course of water, etc.; fig. continuous flow. OE. *strēam* = OFris. *strām*, OS *strōm*, OHG. *stroum* (Du. *stroom*, G. *strom*), ON. *straumr* :– CGerm. (exc. Goth.) **straumaz* :– **sroumos*, f. IE. **srou-* **sreu-* **srŭ-* flow, repr. also by Gr. *rheîn* flow, *rheûma* stream. Hence vb. OIr. *sruaim*, Skr. *srávati* flows. Whence **strea·mER**[1] flag floating in the air. XIII.

street strīt paved road, highway (surviving in names of ancient roads such as Watling Street); road in a town or village. OE. *strǣt* = OFris. *strēte*, OS. *strāta*, OHG.

strāʒ(ʒ)a (Du. *straat*, G. *strasse*); CWGerm. – late L. *strāta* (Eutropius), sb. use (sc. *via* way) of fem. pp. of *sternere* throw or lay down, cf. STRATUM (whence Sp. *estrada*, It. *strada*) an adoption from L. roughly contemp. with MINT[1], POUND, SACK.

Strelets stre·lits, pl. *Streltsy*, (one of) a body of Russian infantry first raised by Ivan the Terrible (1533–84). XVI. – Russ. *streléts* archer, f. *strelyát'* shoot, f. *strelá* arrow. OE. *strǣl*, OS., OHG. *strāla*, G. *strahl* :– Germ. **strēl*.

strength streŋᵏþ quality or condition of being strong. OE. *strengþu* = OHG. *strengida* :– Germ. **straŋgiþō*; see STRONG, -TH[1]. Hence **stre·ngthEN**[5]. XIII; repl. †*strength* XII (pp. *ġestræncþed*, itself repl. OE. *ġestrangod*).

strenuous stre·njuəs vigorous; (now esp.) ardently energetic. XVI (Marston, ridiculed by Jonson). f. L. *strēnuus* brisk, active, valiant, the presumed relation of which with Gr. *strēnḗs* sharp, hard, rough, *strēnos* pride, is not convincing. So **strenu·ITY**. XV. – L. *strēnuitās*.

strepto- stre·ptou comb. form of Gr. *streptós* twisted, pp. adj. of *stréphein* turn, twist (cf. STROPHE), in scientific terms. XIX. **streptoco·ccus** bacteria in which the cocci are arranged in chains. XIX.

stress stres †hardship, affliction; †force, pressure XIV; physical strain; legal distraint XV; overpowering adverse force XVI; emphasis, spec. of utterance XVIII. Aphetic of DISTRESS or, in part, of OF. *estrece, -esse* narrowness, straitness, oppression = Pr. *estreisa* :– Rom. **strictia*, f. L. *strictus* STRAIT, STRICT. So **stress** vb. †constrain, restrain XIV; †distress; overstrain XVI; lay stress on XIX. In earliest use aphetic – OF. *estrecier* = Pr. *estreisar* :– Rom. **strictiāre* (cf. It. *strizzare*), f. L. *strictus*. Later senses are f. the sb.

stretch stretʃ lay at full length; extend OE.; tighten, lengthen, widen by force XIV. OE. *streććan* = OFris. *strekka*, MLG., MDu. *strecken* (Du. *strekken*), OHG. *strecchan* (G. *strecken*) :– WGerm. **strakkjan* (the Scand. forms are – LG.), of doubtful source; cf. STRAIGHT. Hence sb. extension XVI; extent of time or space XVII.

stretto stre·t(t)ou (mus.) in quicker time. XVII. It. :– L. *strictus* STRICT.

strew strū pt. **strewed,** pp. **strewed** (chiefly in active tenses), **strewn** (chiefly in literary use) scatter, sprinkle. OE. *strewian*, *streowian*, corr. to OFris. *strēwa*, OS. *strōian*, OHG. *strewen* (Du. *strooien*, G. *streuen*), ON. *strá*, Goth. **straujan* (in pt. *strawida*); commonly taken to be based on IE. **ster-* as repr. in L. *sternere* (see STRATUM, etc.). Differentiated vars. are STRAW[2] and **strow** strou XIV–XVII (pt., pp. *strowed*, pp. *strown*).

stria strai·ə (archit.) fillet between flutes of columns, etc. XVI; small groove, narrow stripe XVII. – L. *stria* furrow, grooving, perh. :– **strigja*, f. **strig-* (see STRIGIL, STRINGENT). So **stri·ATE**[2], **-atED**[1] XVII. – modL. *striātus*.

stricken stri·kn *s. in years*, †*age*, advanced in age; pp. of STRIKE in the sense 'go' XIV; (arch.) wounded in the chase; struck with a blow XVI; *s. field*, pitched battle XVII (Sc. phr. brought into literary use by Scott, from *strike* in the sense 'fight a battle' (orig. Sc. XIV); afflicted with disease, overwhelmed with grief XVII (cf. 'Yet did we esteem him stricken, smitten of God, and afflicted', Isa. liii 4).

strickle stri·kl rod for levelling contents of a heaped measure OE.; tool for sharpening a scythe XVII. OE. *stricel*, perh. also **stricels* (cf. the forms *stricklace, -les-s* XVII–XIX), with var. *striċel*, repr. by dial. *stritchel*; f. **strik-* STRIKE; cf. Fris. *strikkil*, Flem. *strekel*. Cf. -LE[1].

strict strikt †tight, close; †restricted in space, narrow; (techn.) straight and stiff; in various non-physical senses (for many of which Sh. gives the earliest evidence), close, intricate; rigorous, exact. late XVI. – L. *strictus*, pp. of *stringere* draw tight; see STRIKE.

stricture stri·ktʃəɹ A. (path.) morbid narrowing XIV (rare before XVII); †binding, tight closure; B. †touch, slight trace; incidental comment; (now) adverse criticism XVII. – L. *strictūra*, f. *strict-*, pp. stem of *stringere*, repr. two orig. different words, (A) touch, stroke, fig. blame, rel. to STRIKE, (B) draw tight, rel. to STRANGLE, STRING, STRONG.

stride straid pt. **strode** stroud **strided** †straddle OE.; walk with long steps XII. OE. *strīdan* (once in 3rd sg. pres. ind. *stridit*, *stridæd*; cf. *bestrīdan* BESTRIDE in pt. *bestrād* = (M)LG. *strīden* set the legs wide apart; formally corr. to a set of str. and wk. vbs. meaning 'strive, quarrel', viz. OFris. *strīda*, (M)LG., (M)Du. *strīden*, OHG. *strītan* (G. *streiten, stritt, gestritten*), and OS. *strīdian*, ON. *stríða*, with rel. sbs.; a base expressing strong effort is suggested. Hence sb. XIII; preceded by OE. *stride* and (Nhb.) *strǣde*.

strident strai·dənt making a harsh noise. XVII (Blount 1658; not current before XIX). – L. *strīdent-, -ēns*, prp. of *strīdĕre* creak, f. **streid-*, beside which is *(*s*)*treig-*, repr. by Gr. *trízein* squeak, creak; see -ENT. So **stri·dOR**[2] grating or creaking noise XVII; (path.) harsh vibrating noise XIX. **stri-dulOUS** stri·djŭləs. XVII. f. L. *strīdulus*.

strife straif action of striving together, condition of discord. XIII (AncrR.). Aphetic – OF. *estrif*, rel. to *estriver* STRIVE, of unkn. origin. A synon. form †*strift* (XVII) survived in the traditional phraseology of the Society of Friends; see -T[1].

strigil stri·dʒil instrument for scraping the skin. XVI. – L. *strigilis*, f. **strig-*, base of *stringere* touch lightly (see STRIKE).

strigose strai·gous (nat. hist.) covered with stiff hairs. XVIII. – modL. *strigōsus*, f. L. *striga* furrow, in modL. row of stiff hairs, rel. to STRIA; see -OSE[1].

strike straik pt., pp. **struck** strʌk (see also STRICKEN) A. move, go (now with restriction); B. (obs. or dial.) stroke, smooth OE.; C. lower (a sail, etc.); D. deal a blow XIII; impinge (upon) XIV; E. settle, arrange XVI (partly from phr. *s. hands* XV, partly from L. *fœdus ferire* strike a treaty; F. refuse to work (perh. f. *s. tools*) XVIII. OE. *strīcan*, pt. *strāc*, *stricon*, pp. *stricen* = OFris. *strīka*, MLG. *strīken*, (M)Du. *strijken*, OHG. *strīhhan* (G. *streichen*); WGerm. deriv. of **strīk-* **straik-* :– IE. **strig-* **streig-* **stroig-*; cf. STREAK, STRICKLE, STRIGIL, STROKE. Hence sb. from XIII in various techn. applications.

string[1] striŋ line, cord OE.; number of things strung together XV. OE. *streng* = MLG. *strenge*, MDu. *strenc*, *stranc*, OHG. *stranc*, ON. *strengr* :– CGerm. (exc. Goth.) **straŋgiz* (see STRONG). Hence **string**[2] striŋ pt., pp. **strung** strʌŋ fit (a bow) with its string XVI (isolated ex. of pp. *ystrenged* XIV); make tense XVI; bind (as) with string XVII. f. prec.; the str. conjugation is after *ring*. **string**ED[2] striŋd having a string of strings. First and chiefly in OE. *tȳnstrenged* ten-stringed (Psalm xci 4) and similar combs. **stri·ng**Y[1]. XVII.

stringent stri·ndʒənt †astringent, styptic; †compelling assent XVII; rigorously binding XIX. – L. *stringent-*, prp. stem of *stringere* bind; cf. STRICT and see -ENT. Hence **stri·ng**ENCY. XIX.

stringhalt stri·ŋhōlt disease contracting a horse's hind legs. XVI. Obscurely f. STRING[1]+HALT[1]. Also SPRINGHALT.

strip[1] strip narrow piece (as of textile material). XV. – or cogn. w. (M)LG. *strippe* strap, thong, prob. rel. to STRIPE[2].

strip[2] strip unclothe, denude; doff, tear or peel off. XIII. ME. *stripe*, *strepe*, *strupe*, pointing to an OE. **strȳpan*, **striepan* (as in *bestriepan* plunder, strip), corr. to (M)Du. *stroopen*, OHG., MHG. *stroufen* (G. *streifen*) :– Germ. **straupjan*; shortening of basic vowel began in pt. and pp. before *-pt-* and was thence extended.

strip[3] survives in OUT*strip*.

stripe[1] straip (arch.) stroke with a staff, scourge, etc. XV. Of unkn. origin; Du. *strippen* whip, does not agree in form, and is later.

stripe[2] straip narrow portion of a surface, esp. of different colour or texture XVII (Bacon); narrow strip of cloth, etc., e.g. chevron of soldier's uniform XIX. perh. back-formation on pp. *striped* (XV or XVI) marked with narrow bands, poss. of LDu. origin; cf. MLG., MDu. *strīpe* = MHG. *strīfe*, G. *streifen*.

stripling stri·pliŋ youth passing from boyhood to manhood. XIII. f. STRIP[1]+-LING[1], quasi 'one who is slender as a strip'.

strive straiv pt. **strove** strouv, pp. **striven** stri·vn †be at variance, quarrel, contend or struggle *against*. XIII (AncrR.). ME. *strīven*, aphetic – OF. *estriver*, rel. to *estrif* STRIFE. ¶ *Strive* was taken over into the native conjugation of DRIVE, etc., the only vb. of F. origin to be so treated.

strobilus stroubai·ləs fir-cone XVIII; formation resembling this XIX. – late L. – Gr. *stróbīlos* anything twisted, f. **strob-*, parallel to **strobh-* (cf. STROPHE).

stroke[1] strouk rub softly with the hand or an implement. OE. *strācian* = MLG., MDu. *strēken* (Du. *streeken*), OHG. *streihhōn* (G. *streichen*, which coalesced with *streichen* :– OHG. *strīhhan* strike), f. Germ. **straik-* **strīk-* STRIKE.

stroke[2] strouk act of striking XIII (RGlouc. CursorM.); striking of a clock XV; linear mark XVI; (earlier *s. of God's hands* XVI) seizure by disease XVII. ME. *strōk*, north. *strāk* :– OE. **strāc* :– **straikaz*, f. gradation var. of base of **strīkan* STRIKE.

stroll stroul applied, as a cant word, with *stroller*, in early XVII (Dekker, Jonson), first to itinerant, vagabond, or vagrant persons, later used of aimless or leisurely walking; prob. – G. dial. *strollen*, *strolchen* wander as a vagrant (*strolch* vagabond), of unkn. origin.

stroma strou·mə (anat., etc.) framework of an organ or cell (as of connective tissue). XIX. – modL. use of late L. *strōma* mattress – Gr. *strôma*, f. **strō-* (as in *strōnnúnai* strew, spread), rel. to L. STRATUM.

strombus strɔ·mbəs genus of gasteropods. XVII (Holland). – L. *strombus* spiral shell – Gr. *strómbos*, rel. to *stróbilos* *strobeîn* *streblós* twisted. Angl. as **stromb**. XIX.

strong strɔŋ having great power; powerful, vigorous. OE. *strong*, *strang* (compar. *strenger*, superl. *strengest*) = OS., Fris. *strang*, MDu. *stranc*, ON. *strangr* :– Germ. **straŋgaz*, f. a base of which the mutated form is repr. in OE. (rare) *strenge* severe, MLG., MDu. *strenge* (Du. *streng*), OS. *strang*, OHG. *strengi* (G. *streng*), and for which see further STRING. comp. **stro·ng**-HOLD fortified place. XV. Hence **stro·ng**LY[2] OE. *stronglīċe*. Cf. STRENGTH.

strontia strɔ·nʃ[i]ə monoxide of strontium. XIX (1802). f. **stro·ntian** (XVIII) a former name for strontia and strontium, prop. for native strontium carbonate; from name of a parish in Argyllshire, where are the lead mines in which the mineral was discovered. Hence **stro·ntium** (1808, H. Davy). See -IA[1], -IUM.

strop strɔp (naut.) band of rope, etc. XIV; strip of leather, etc., for sharpening a razor XVIII. – (M)LG., (M)Du. *strop* = OE. *strop* (once in sense 'band, thong', occurs sporadically later, but there is no evidence that the OE. word survived), OHG. *strupf* (cf. MHG., G. *strüpfe* fem.); WGerm. – L. *struppus, stroppus*, presumably – Gr. *stróphos* (cf. next).

strophanthus stroufæ·nþəs (bot.) tropical genus of plants yielding a poisonous drug. XIX. modL., f. Gr. *stróphos* twisted cord (cf. next) + *ánthos* flower.

strophe strou·fi (pros.) series of lines forming a system. XVII. – Gr. *strophḗ* (whence late L. *stropha*) verse unit, lit. 'turning', f. **stroph-* (ANTISTROPHE, CATASTROPHE, as also in *stróphos* cord, string, colic, *stropheús* hinge), **streph-* (as in *stréphein*; cf. STREPTO-). Cf. F. *strophe*, Sp. *estrofa*, It. *strofa, strofe*. Hence **strophIC** strɔ·fik. XIX.

strophiole strɔ·fioul (bot.) excrescence surrounding the hilum of seeds. XIX. – modL. (Gærtner 1788) use of L. *strophiolum*, dim. of *strophium* chaplet – Gr. *stróphion*, f. **stroph-* turn (see prec.).

strow see STREW.

structure strʌ·ktʃəɹ †erection, construction XV; manner of this; edifice, fabric XVII. – (O)F. *structure* or L. *structūra*, f. *struct-*, pp. stem of *struere* build; see STREW, -URE. Hence **stru·cturAL**[1]. XIX.

struggle strʌ·gl contend in close grapple XIV (Ch.); get with difficulty *out of*, etc. XVII. frequent. (see -LE[3]) f. base of obscure origin, prob. symbolic; connexion with ON. *strúgr* ill-will, contention, or with Du. *struikelen*, G. *straucheln* stumble, is dubious.

Struldbrug strʌ·ldbrʌg fanciful name given by Swift in 'Gulliver's Travels' to 'the immortals' in the kingdom of Luggnagg.

strum strʌm play unskilfully on a stringed instrument. XVIII. perh. blend of STRING[1] and THRUM[2].

struma strū·mə (path.) scrofula XVI, scrofulous swelling, goitre XVII, (bot.) swelling at base of petiole XIX. L. *strūma* (*strūmat-*) scrofulous tumour.

strumous strū·məs. XVI. – L. *strūmōsus*, f. prec. + -OUS.

strumpet strʌ·mpit harlot, prostitute. XIV. Of unkn. origin.

strung pp. of STRING[2] †fitted with strings; threaded on a string XVII; in a state of tension XIX.

strut[1] strʌt bar to resist pressure in a framework. XVI. prob. f. next.

strut[2] strʌt †bulge, swell; †protrude stiffly, stand out XIV; †flaunt, swagger; walk upright with stiff step XVI. unexpl. alt. of ME. *stroute*, repr. formally OE. *strūtian* ?be rigid, but a short vowel is seen in (M)HG. *strotzen* and in the Scand. langs.

struthious strū·þiəs pert. to an ostrich. XVIII (Pennant). f. L. *strūthiō* – Gr. *strouthíon*, f. *stroûthos* sparrow, ostrich (cf. THRUSH); see -OUS.

strychnine stri·knīn, -in poisonous vegetable alkaloid. XIX. – F. *strychnine* (Pelletier and Caventou, 1818), f. modL. (Linnæus 1737) use of L. *strychnos* (Pliny) – Gr. *strúkhnos, -on* kind of nightshade; see -INE[5].

stub stʌb stump. OE. *stub(b)* = MLG., MDu. *stubbe*, ON. *stubbr, stubbi* :– Germ. **stubbaz*, **stubbon*; OE. had also *styb* (:– **stubbjaz*), which coalesced with the other form; to pre-Germ. **stŭp-* belong MLG. *stūve*, ON. *stúfr*, Gr. *stúpos* stump, stock, Lett. *stups* fag-end.

stubble stʌ·bl stump(s) of grain-stalks left in the ground. XIII (RGlouc.). – AN. *stuble*, OF. *estuble* (mod. dial. *éteu(b)le*) = Pr. *estobla*, It. *stoppia* :– L. *stupla, stupula*, for earlier *stipula* straw (cf. STIPULATE), rel. to *stipes* (see STIPE).

stubborn stʌ·bəɹn pertinacious in refusing compliance XIV (Ch.); difficult to treat or manage XVI. Late ME. *stibourne*, later *stoburn(e), stuborn*; of unkn. origin (connexion with OE. *stubb, stybb*, **stobb* STUB cannot be proved).

stucco stʌ·kou plaster for covering walls, etc. XVI – It. *stucco* (whence also F. *stuc*, Sp. *estuque, estuco*, G. *stuck*, etc.) – Germ. (prob. Lombardic) word repr. by OHG. *stukki* fragment, piece, (also) crust (see STICK[1]).

stud[1] stʌd A. †post, prop (later as in a building) OE., B. knob, boss, or nail head XV; adjustable button XVI. OE. *studu, stuþu* = MHG. *stud*, ON. *stoð*, rel. to G. *stützen* prop, support. The development of senses is obscure, but there seems to be no doubt of the identity of the word.

stud[2] stʌd establishment for breeding of horses OE.; horses bred by or belonging to one person XVII. OE. *stōd*, corr. to MLG. *stōt*, OHG. *stuot* (G. *stute* mare), ON. *stóð* :– Germ. **stōðam*, **stōðō* (with parallel forms in Balto-Sl.), f. **stō-* STAND. cf. STEED.

studding-sail, stunsail stʌ·nsl sail set on an extension of the yard-arm. XVI (*stoytene sale*). The earliest recorded form has suggested deriv. from MLG., MDu. *stōtinge*, noun of action of *stōten* thrust (Du. *stooten*), cogn. with OS. *stōtan*, OHG. *stōȥan* (G. *stossen*), Goth. *stautan*.

student stjū·dənt one engaged in or addicted to study. XV. – L. *student-, studēns*, prp. of *studēre* be eager or diligent, study; cf. It. *studente*, G., etc. *student*; earlier †*studiant* (XIV), aphetic of †*estudiant* – OF. *estudiant* (mod. *étudiant*) = Pr. *estudian*, etc., sb. use of prp. of *estudier*; a common var. was †*studient* (XIV–XVIII). **studio** stjū·diou sculptor's or painter's workroom

(XIX, *c.*1820). – It. *studio* – L. *studium* STUDY. **studi**OUS stjū·diəs given to study. XIV (Wycl. Bible, Gower). – L. *studiōsus*, f. *studium*.

study stʌ·di †perplexity; serious application of mind, mental effort in learning XIII; room for study, †seat of learning XIV; state of reverie (obs. exc. in *brown s.*). Aphetic – OF. *estudie* (mod. *étude*) = Pr. *estudis*, Sp. *estudio*, It. *studio* – L. *studium* zeal, affection, painstaking application. So **stu·dy** vb. †deliberate, consider XIII (Cursor M.); apply oneself to study XIV. Aphetic – OF. *estudier* (mod. *étudier*) = Pr. *estudiar*, etc., – medL. *studiāre* (f. L. *studium*), for L. *studēre* be zealous, apply oneself, study.

stuff stʌf †equipment, stock; material. XIV. Late ME. *stof(fe)*, *stuff(e)* – OF. *estoffe* (mod. *étoffe*), perh. f. *estoffer* (*étoffer*) vb. = Cat. *estofar*, Sp., Pg. *estofar* – Germ. **stopfōn* (G. *stopfen*) – late L. *stuppāre* plug, STOP up (implied in *stuppator*, caulker), f. *stuppa* tow, oakum, (late L.) cork. So vb. †furnish XIV; line, fill (out) XV. – OF. *estoffer*. Hence **stu·ff**Y[1] †full of substance XVI; (of air) close XIX.

stultify stʌ·ltifai (leg.) prove of unsound mind XVIII; reduce to absurdity XIX. – late L. *stultificāre*, f. L. *stultus* foolish, rel. to *stolidus* STOLID; see -IFY.

stum stʌm unfermented must. XVII. – Du. sb. use of *stom* dumb; cf. F. *vin muet*.

stumble stʌ·mbl trip, make a slip in walking. XIV. – ON. **stumla* (repr. by Norw., Sw. dial. *stumla*, Da. dial. *stumle*), parallel to synon. *stumra* (whence †*stummer* XIV), f. Germ. **stum-* **stam-* (see STAMMER). *stumbling-block* used by Tindale to render Gr. *πρόσκομμα*, by others to render *σκάνδαλον*; phr. *stumble at a block*, i.e. a tree stump (XV).

stump[1] stʌmp part remaining of maimed limb, broken-off end XIV; portion of tree left in the ground after felling; part of a broken tooth left in the gum XV; stub, fag end XVI; short pillar XVII; (in cricket) XVIII. – MLG. *stump*, *stumpe*, (M)Du. *stomp* (whence similar Scand. forms) = OHG., G. *stumpf* sb. uses of corr. adjs.; perh. rel. to STUB and STAMP.

stump[2] stʌmp blunt instrument used for rubbing down hard lines. XVIII. prob. – F. *estompe* – Du. *stomp*, with support from prec.

stun stʌn deprive of consciousness by a blow, etc. XIII (Cursor M.). Aphetic of †*astune*, †*astone* (XIII) – AN. **astoner*, **astuner*, *estuner*, OF. *estoner* (mod. *étonner*) = Pr. *estonar* :– Gallo-Rom. **extonāre*, for L. *attonāre* stun, stupefy, f. *ad* AD- + *tonāre* THUNDER; cf. ASTONISH, ASTOUND. **stu·n-n**ING[2] (colloq.) firstrate, 'topping'. XIX (Dickens, Thackeray).

Stundist ʃtu·ndist, stʌ·ndist member of an Evangelical sect among peasantry of S. Russia, having contacts with German Protestants, *c.*1860. The Russian name of the sect, *Shtunda*, is said to be f. G. *stunde* hour, the name given to their meetings; see -IST.

stunt[1] stʌnt †irritate, provoke XVI; †nonplus; check the growth of (esp. in pp.) XVII. f. *stunt* adj. †foolish (OE.), †short (XV), stubborn (XVI) = MHG. *stunz*, ON. *stuttr* (:– **stuntr*) short :– Germ. **stuntaz*, perh. f. base of STUMP.

stunt[2] stʌnt athletic event or feat, (gen.) enterprise, performance. XIX. orig. U.S. college sl., of unkn. origin.

stupe[1] stjūp piece of steeped tow, etc. for fomenting a wound. XIV. – L. *stuppa* tow – Gr. *stúppē*.

stupe[2] stjūp (colloq., dial.) shortening of STUPID (sb.). XVIII (Bickerstaffe).

stupefy stjū·pifai †stun with amazement XVI (Spenser); make stupid or torpid XVII. – F. *stupéfier* – L. *stupefacere*, f. *stupēre*; see STUPID, -FY. So **stupe**FA·CTION. XVI. – F. – medL.

stupe·ndous. XVII (Pepys). f. L. *stupendus*, gerundive of *stupēre*; earlier †**stupe·nd** (XVII, Burton), †**stupe·ndi**OUS (XVI), the accepted form till XVIII.

stupid stjū·pid wanting in mental perception XVI; †stunned with surprise, grief, etc. XVII (Sh.). – F. *stupide* or L. *stupidus*, f. *stupēre* be stunned or benumbed, f. base **stup-* strike, thrust; see -ID[1]. So **stupi·d**ITY. XVII. – F. or L. **stu·p**OR[2]. XVII.

sturdy stɔ̄·ɹdi †fierce, violent; rough, harsh XIII (RGlouc.); stalwart, strong XIV; sb. stupefying brain disease in cattle XVI. Aphetic – OF. *esturdi*, *estourdi* stunned, dazed, reckless, violent (mod. *étourdi* thoughtless) = It. *stordito*, Pr. *estordit*, stupefied, etc., pp. of *estourdir*, etc. :– Rom. **exturdīre*, f. L. *ex* EX-[1] + *turdus* thrush (taken as a type of drunkenness).

sturgeon stɔ̄·ɹdʒən large fish of genus Acipenser. XIII (Havelok). – AN. *sturgeon*, (O)F. *estourgeon* = Pr. *esturjon*, Sp. *esturion*, It. *storione* :– Rom. **sturiōne* – Germ. **sturjon*, whence OE. *styrġa*, MLG., MDu. *störe* (Du. *steur*), OHG. *sturjo* (G. *stör*), ON. *styrja*, with poss. Balto-Sl. cogns.

stutter stʌ·təɹ speak with checks at and repetitions of certain sounds. XVI. f. late ME. *stutten* (dial. *stut*) + ER[4]; cf. (M)LG. *stötern*, Du. *stotteren*, G. *stottern*. The stem is repr. also in ME. *stotaye* falter, totter, Germ. **stut-* **staut-*, as in MLG. *stöten*, OHG. *stōȥan* (G. *stossen*) strike against.

sty stai inflamed swelling on the edge of an eyelid. XVII. Deduced from dial. *styany* (XV), prop. eye affected with a sty (apprehended as *sty-on-eye*), f. synon. *styan* (:– OE. *stīgend*, lit. 'riser', prp. used sb. of *stīgan* rise, ascend, climb) + EYE. OE.

stiġan corr. to OFris. *stiga*, OS., OHG. *stigan* (Du. *stijgen*, G. *steigen*), ON. *stíga*, Goth. *steigan* :- CGerm. str. vb. **stīgan*, f. **stĭg-* **staig-* :- IE. (not in Latin) **steigh-*, **stoigh-*, *stĭgh-* advance, go, rise, repr. by G. *steíkhein*, *stíkhos* STICH, *stoîkhos* row (cf. STIRRUP).

sty(e) stai enclosed place for swine. XIII. repr. OE. **stī* (as in *stīfearh* 'sty-pig', and prob. some place-names), perh. identical with *stiġ* hall (cf. *stiġweard* STEWARD), corr. to ON. **stí* (only in *svínstí* swine-sty), whence Norw. *sti* flock of sheep or goats, household work esp. concerning the feeding of animals, Da. *svine|sti* :- Germ. **stijam*, of which a parallel formation **stijōn-* is repr. by MLG. *stege*, MDu. *swijnstije*, ON. *stía* pen, fold.

Stygian sti·dʒiən pert. to the river Styx (river of Hell); infernal. XVI. f. L. *Stygius* – Gr. *Stúgios*, f. *Stug-*, *Stúx*, rel. to *stugeîn* hate, *stugnós* hateful, gloomy; see -IAN.

style stail stylus (first in transf. sense in phr. †*turn the s.*, tr. L. *stilum vertere* change the subject); †written work XIII; manner of expression or discourse XIV; proper name or title XIII; manner, fashion XV (of art or architecture XVIII); mode of expressing dates XVI. – (O)F. *style*, †*stile* – L. *stilu-s*. The sp. with *y* is due to the erron. notion that the word repr. Gr. *stûlos* column. Hence **sty·lISH**[1]. XVIII (Jane Austen). **sty·lIST**, **-i·stIC**. XIX. – F. and G.

stylet stai·lėt pointed instrument (e.g. surgical probe) or natural process. XVII. – F. *stylet* – It. *stiletto* (see STILETTO).

stylite stai·lait ascetic living on a pillar. XVII. – eccl. Gr. *stūlī́tēs*, f. *stûlos* pillar; see -ITE.

stylobate stai·lŏbeit (archit.) basement supporting a row of columns. XVII. Earlier **stylobata** stailɔ·bətə. L. – Gr. *stulobátēs*, f. *stûlos* pillar (f. **stŭ-* be erect) + *-batēs*, f. base of *bainein* walk (COME).

stylus stai·ləs writing instrument XVIII; gnomon of a sundial XVIII. – erron. sp. of L. *stilus*; see STYLE.

stymie, stimy stai·mi (in golf) opponent's ball lying in the way of the player's, 1857. Of unkn. origin. Hence vb. (esp. fig.).

styptic sti·ptik having contracting properties. XIV. – L. *stypticus* – Gr. *stuptikós*, f. *stúphein* contract; see -IC.

styrax staiə·ræks. XVI. – L. – Gr.; see STORAX.

suasion swei·ʒən act of urging. XIV (Ch.). – OF. *suasion* or L. *suāsiō(n-)*, f. *suās-*, pp. stem of *suādēre* urge, PERSUADE, f. **swād-*; see next, -ION.

suave sweiv pleasing, agreeable XVI; blandly polite XIX. – F. *suave* or L. *suāvis* SWEET, agreeable. So **suavITY** swæ·vĭti †sweetness XV; pleasurableness XVI; bland urbanity XIX. – (O)F. or L.

sub[1] sʌb L. prep. under, underneath, beneath, at the bottom of (cf. next), corr. to Gr. *hupó*, as *ab* to *apó*, the first word of various L. phrases current from XVII, as *sub judice* 'under a judge', being the subject of judicial inquiry, *sub rosa* 'under the rose', secretly (of unkn. origin), *sub sigillo* under the seal, *sub silentio* in silence, *sub voce* under the word (so-and-so in a list), abbrev. s.v. Cf. SUBPŒNA.

sub[2] sʌb short for SUBORDINATE XVII, SUBALTERN XVIII and various titles, SUBSTITUTE, SUBJECT (U.S.), SUBSCRIPTION, SUBSIST (*money*) XIX.

sub- sʌb, səb prep. *sub* (SUB[1]) under, close to, up to, towards, used in composition with the several meanings given below. The full form is retained before vowels and *b*, *d*, *l*, *n*, *s*, *t*; the *b* is assimilated to *c*, *f*, *g*, *p*, and often to *m* and *r*. A by-form *subs-* was normally reduced to *sus-* in comps. with initial *c*, *p*, *t*. As a living prefix it is capable of being used with words of any origin. Its orig. force is either entirely lost sight of or much obscured in many words, as in *subject*, *suborn*, *subscribe*, *substance*. (Where its form is disguised, as in *succeed*, *suffer*, *suppose*, analysis of the comp. does not readily suggest itself.) The main stress may fall either on the prefix or on the appropriate syll. of the radical el. (for exx. see below); in sense (2), in titles, the stress tends to be level.

It is used with the foll. senses:—(1) under, underneath, below, at the bottom (of), as *subaqueous*, *subterranean*; (2) subordinate, subsidiary, secondary, esp. in titles; subordinately, as *subdeacon*; (3) math. compounded with adjs. expressing a ratio the inverse of that of the radical element, as in *submultiple*, *subtriple*; (4) next below or after, near or close (to), as in *subapostolic*, *subsequent*, *suburb*; (5) incomplete(ly), imperfect(ly), partial(ly), as in *subaci* *subcylindrical*, *subtriangular*; (6) secretly, covertly, as in *suborn*; (7) from below, up, (hence) away, as in *succour*, *suggest*, *suspicion*; (8) in place of another, as in *substitute*; (9) in addition, as in *subjoin*.

suba(h)dar sūbədā·ɹ governor of a province XVII; chief native officer of sepoys XVIII. – Urdu *çūbaʰdār*, f. Arab. *çūbaʰ* province + Pers. *dār* possessor, master.

subaltern sʌ·bltəɹn, sʌbō·ltəɹn of inferior status. XVI. – late L. *subalternus*. Earlier *subalternate* XV; sb., esp. subaltern officer in the army XVII. See SUB- 4, ALTERNATE.

subaudition sʌbōdi·ʃən mentally supplying or 'understanding'. XVIII. – late L. *subauditiō(n-)*, f. *subaudīre* supply mentally, L. f. *sub* + *audire* hear, after Gr. ὑπακούειν; see SUB- 6, AUDITION. So **subauditur** sʌbōdai·təɹ 3rd pers. sg. pres. ind. pass. of the L. vb.

subCO·NSCIOUS. XIX (De Quincey, who used the adv. earlier); see SUB- 5.

subDEA·CON. XIV. – ecclL. *subdiaconus*, also *subdiacon* – ecclGr. *hupodiákonos*; in XIV–XV *su-*, *sodekne* – AN., OF. *su-*, *soudeacne* – ecclL.; see SUB- 2.

subDIVI·DE. – late L. *subdīvidere*. XV. So **sub**DIVI·SION. XVI. – late L.; see SUB- 2.

subdue səbdjū· conquer XIV (Trevisa); bring into subjection XVI. ME. *sodewe*, *sudewe*, later *subdewe* – AN. **soduer*, **su(b)-duer* = OF. *so(u)duire*, *suduire* deceive, seduce = OIt. *soddurre* – L. *subdūcere* withdraw, evacuate, (f. *sub* SUB- 5 + *dūcere* lead, bring (cf. DUKE), with sense derived from †*subdit* subject – L. *subditus*, pp. of *subdere* bring under, subdue, f. *sub* SUB- 1 + *-dere* put (cf. ADD).

suberose sjū·bərous (bot.) cork-like. XIX. – modL. *sūberōsus*, f. *sūber* cork; see -OSE[1]; earlier *suberous* (Evelyn).

subfusc sʌbfʌ·sk of dusky or sombre hue. XVIII. – L. *subfuscus*, var. of *suffuscus*, f. *sub* SUB- 5 + *fuscus* dark (see DUSK).

subjacent sʌbdʒei·sənt underlying. XVII. – L. *subjacent-*, *-ēns*, prp. of *subjacēre*; see SUB- 1, ADJACENT.

subject sʌ·bdʒèkt A. one who is under the dominion of a sovereign, etc. XIV (Rolle, Shoreham); B. (philos.) †substance XIV (Ch., Wycl.); matter operated upon XVI; (gram.) XVII; thinking agent XVIII. ME. *soget*, *suget*, *sugiet*, later *subiect* (XVI) – OF. *suget*, *soget*, *subg(i)et* (mod. *sujet*) = Pr. *suget-z*, Sp. *sugeto*, It. *soggetto* – L. *subjectu-s* m., *subjectum* n. pp. of *subicere*, f. *sub* SUB- 1 + *jacere* throw, cast; so **su·bject** adj. that is under the rule of a power XIV (Mannyng); cf. OBJECT; exposed or liable to XIV (Ch.). – OF. – L. **subject** səbdʒe·kt make subject. XIV (Wycl. Bible, Trevisa). – (O)F. *subjecter* or L. *subjectāre*, frequent. f. *sub(j)icere*, *subject-*. **subje·c**TION. XIV (Rolle). – (O)F. or L. **subje·ct**IVE †pert. to one who is subject XV; pert. to the subject in which attributes inhere XVII; pert. to the thinking subject XVIII. – L.; so F., etc. **su·bject-**MATTER XVI. earlier †*matter subject* XIV tr. late L. *subjecta materia* (Boethius), tr. Gr. ὑποκειμένη ὕλη (Aristotle).

subjoin səbdʒoi·n add at the end or afterwards. XVI. – F. †*subjoindre* – L. *subjungere*, f. *sub* SUB- 9 + *jungere* JOIN.

subjugate sʌ·bdʒŭgeit bring into subjection. XV. f. pp. stem of late L. *subjugāre*, f. *sub* SUB- 2 + L. *jugum* YOKE; see -ATE[3]. So **subjug**A·TION. XVII. – late L.

subjunctive səbdʒʌ·ŋktiv (gram.) †*s. article* (Gr. ἄρθρον ὑποτακτικόν), the relative ὅς ἥ ὅ)('prepositive article' ὁ ἡ τό; †*s. vowel* (L. *vocalis subjunctīva*, F. †*voyelle subjonctive*, Gr. φωνῆεν ὑποτακτικόν) second vowel of a diphthong; designating a mood orig. conceived as proper to subordinate clauses (late L. *modus subjunctīvus*, Gr. ὑποτακτικὴ ἔγκλισις) XVI. – F. *subjonctif* or L. *subjunctīvus*, f. pp. stem of *subjungere* SUBJOIN; see -IVE.

sublapsarian sʌblæpsɛ̂ə·riən (theol.) infralapsarian. XVII. f. modL. *sublapsārius*; see SUB- 4, LAPSE, -ARIAN. Cf. INFRALAPSARIAN, SUPRALAPSARIAN.

sublimate sʌ·blimeit †raise to a high state XVI; act upon so as to produce a refined product XVII. Preceded by pp. *sublimate* (XV), f. pp. stem of L. *sublīmāre*, f. *sublīmis*; see next, -ATE[2,3]. So **sublim**ATE[1] sb. -ət. XVII. **sublime** səblai·m lofty, exalted, in earliest use (XVI) of language or style, later in physical senses. – L. *sublīmis*, *-us*, f. *sub* SUB + an el. variously identified with *līmen* threshold and *līmus* oblique. Cf. F., Sp., Pg. *sublime*. So **subli·me** vb. †sublimate XIV (Ch.); raise to a higher state XVI. – (O)F. *sublimer* or L. *sublīmāre*; **sublim**A·TION. XIV (Gower). **subliminal** səbli·minəl (psych.) applied to states supposed to exist but not strong enough to be recognized. XIX (*c.*1885). f. SUB- 1 + L. *limin-*, *līmen* threshold + -AL[1]; coined to render G. *unter der Schwelle*, sc. *des Bewusstseins* below the threshold of consciousness (Herbart, 1824).

sublunary sʌblʲū·nəri existing or situated beneath the moon. XVI. f. late L. *sublūnāris*, f. *sub* SUB- 1 + *lūna* moon (cf. LUNAR); see -ARY.

submarine sʌ·bmərīn, sʌbmərī·n existing or operating under the surface of the sea. XVII. f. L. SUB + *marinus*; see SUB- 1, MARINE. Cf. F. *sous-marin*. sb. †s. creature XVIII; s. boat XIX.

submerge səbmɔ̄·ɹdʒ cover with water. XVII. – L. *submergere*; see SUB- 1, MERGE. So **subme·r**SION. XVI. – late L.

submit səbmi·t (refl. and intr.) place oneself under control; so trans. XIV (Ch.). – L. *submittere*. So **sub**MI·SSION. XV. – OF. or L. **submi·ss**IVE disposed to submit. XVI (Sidney). – L. **submissīvus*, f. *submiss-*, pp. stem of L. *submittere*. Cf. It. *sommessivo*; also synon. †**submiss** (XVI, Foxe, Lyly).

subordinate səbɔ̄·ɹdinət of inferior grade. XV. – medL. *subordinātus*, pp. of *subordināre* (whence **subo·rdinate** vb. XVI, **subordin**A·TION XVII); see SUB-, ORDAIN, ORDINATION, -ATE[2] and [3].

suborn sʌbɔ̄·ɹn procure by underhand or unlawful means. XVI. – L. *subōrnāre*, f. *sub* SUB- 6 + *ōrnāre* equip (see ORNAMENT). So **suborn**A·TION. XVI. – medL.

subpœna sʌ(ᵇ)pī·nə (leg.) writ issued by a court commanding the appearance of a person. XV. L. *sub pœnā* under a penalty, being the first words of the writ; see SUB, PAIN.

subreption sʌbre·pʃən (eccl. leg.) misrepresentation of the truth. XVII. – L.

subreptiō(n-), f. *subripere*, f. *sub* + *repere* creep (see SUB- 6, REPTILE, -TION).

subscribe səbskrai·b write (one's name) on XV; intr. const. *to* XVI; promise over one's signature to pay XVII. – L. *subscrībere*, L. *sub* SUB- 1 + *scribere* write (see SCRIBE). So **su·bscript** sb. †signature XVIII; adj. written underneath (as in *iota s.*) XIX. – L. *subscriptus*, pp. of *subscribere*. **subscri·p**TION signature at end of a document XV; declaration of assent XVI; contribution to a fund of money XVII. – L.

subsequent sʌ·bsikwənt following in order or in time. XV. – (O)F. *subséquent* or L. *subsequent-*, *-ēns*, prp. of *subsequī*, f. *sub*+ *sequī*; see SUB- 4, SEQUENT.

subservient səbsə·ɹviənt serving as an instrument or means. XVII. – L. *subservient-*, *-ēns*, prp. of *subservīre* (whence **subse·rve** XVII); see SUB- 2, SERVE, -ENT.

subside səbsai·d sink down, die down. XVII. – L. *subsīdere*, f. *sub* SUB- 1 + *sīdere* SETTLE. So **subsid**ENCE sʌ·bsidəns, səbsai·dəns †sediment; sinking or settling to the bottom XVII. – L. *subsīdentia*, f. *subsīdere*.

subsidy sʌ·bsĭdi †help, aid; pecuniary aid granted by parliament, etc. XIV. – AN. *subsidie* = (O)F. *subside* – L. *subsidium* reserve of troops, support, assistance, rel. formally to (rare) *subsidēre*, f. *sub* SUB- 2 + *sedēre* SIT. So **subsidi**ARY səbsi·diəri auxiliary XVI. – L. *subsidiārius*, f. *subsidium*. **su·bsid**IZE. XVIII.

subsist səbsi·st exist as substance or entity XVI; provide for; support oneself *on* XVII. – L. *subsistere* stand still or firm, f. *sub* SUB- + *sistere* STAND. So **subsi·st**ENCE substantial existence XV; provision of support for animal life XVII; *s. money*, money paid on account of wages, etc. XVII; shortened to *subsist money* XIX. – late L.

subsoil sʌ·bsoil substratum of soil just below the surface. XVIII. f. SUB- 1 + SOIL[1].

substance sʌ·bstəns essence XIII (Cursor M.); a being; (philos.) that which underlies phenomena; material, matter; means, wealth XIV. – (O)F. *substance*, corr. to Pr. *sustancia*, Sp. *sustancia*, It. *sostanza* – post-Augustan L. *substantia* being, essence, material property (formally rendering Gr. ὑπόστασις HYPOSTASIS, but used also for οὐσία ESSENCE), f. *substāre*, f. *sub* SUB- + *stāre* STAND. So **substanti**AL[1] səbstæ·nʃəl. XIV. – (O)F. *substantiel* or Chr. L. *substantiālis*, tr. Gr. *hupostatikós* HYPOSTATIC. **substa·ntial**LY[2]. XIV (Trev.); after Chr. L. *substantiāliter*. **substa·nti**ATE[3] give substance to. XVII. f. pp. stem of medL. *substantiāre*, f. *substantia*. **su·bstant**IVE self-existent XV; (gram.) denoting a substance XVI; having substance XIX. – (O)F. *substantif*, *-ive* or late L. *substantīvus*, f. *substantia*; sb. for *noun s.* (late L. *nomen substantivum*) XIV (PPl.); *verb s.* (late L. *verbum substantivum*, Gr. ῥῆμα ὑπαρκτικόν) the verb 'to be' XVI.

substitute sʌ·bstitjūt †appoint as deputy or delegate; put one in place of another. XVI. f. pp. stem of L. *substituere*, f. *sub* SUB- 8 + *statuere* (see STATUTE). So **substitu·**TION. XIV. – late L.

substratum sʌbstrei·təm that which underlies or forms the foundation of a thing. XVII. – modL. sb. use of pp. of L. *substernere*; see SUB- 1, STRATUM.

subsultory sʌbsʌ·ltəri moving by sudden leaps. XVII. f. *subsult-*, pp. stem of L. *subsilīre* f. *sub-* SUB- 7 + *salīre* leap; see SALIENT, -ORY[2]. So **subsu·ltus** convulsive movement. XIX. – modL.

subsume səbsjū·m †bring under, subjoin; state a minor premiss XVI; bring (one idea) *under* another XIX (Coleridge). – medL. *subsūmere*, f. *sub* SUB- 7 + *sūmere* take :– **subs(e)mere* or **sus(e)mere*.

subtend səbte·nd (geom.) extend under, be opposite to. XVI. – L. *subtendere*; see SUB- 1, TEND[2].

subter- sʌ·btəɹ prefix use of L. *subter* adv. and prep. below, underneath, in the sense 'secretly' in **subterfuge** sʌ·btəɹfjūdʒ artifice to evade conviction, censure, etc. XVI. – F. or – late L. *subterfugium*, f. L. *subterfugere* escape secretly (cf. FUGITIVE).

subterranean sʌbtərei·niən living, etc., below the surface of the earth. XVII. f. L. *subterrāneus*, f. *sub* SUB- 1 + *terra* earth (cf. TERRENE); see -AN, -EAN. So **subterra·n**EOUS XVII, which was formerly equally frequent, beside the less common †*subterrene* and *subterre·strial* (XVII).

subtle sʌ·tl of thin or fine consistency; marked by acumen or fine discrimination. XIV. ME. *sutil*, *satil* – OF. *sutil*, *sotil*, *soutil* = Pr. *sutil*, It. *sottile*, Sp. *sutil*, Pg. *subtil* – L. *subtīlis*, prob. orig. a weaver's term, f. **sub tēlā* (passing) under the warp, for **subtēlis*, **subtexlis*, f. **sub texla* (see TEXTURE). So **su·btle**TY[2]. XIV (Rolle). – OF. *su-*, *soutilté* :– L. *subtīlitātem*. Hence **subtly** sʌ·tli. XIV; for the simplification of *ll* cf. *ably*, *simply*, *terribly*. The Latinized var. **subtil(e)**, with corr. pronunc. sʌ·btil (– OF. *subtil*, latinized form of *sutil*), arose in late ME. and remained till modern times along with **su·btilty**, **subti·lity** in arch. or affected use.

subtract səbtræ·kt †withdraw; deduct. XVI. f. *subtract-*, pp. stem of L. *subtrahere* (whence OF. *subtraire*, It. *sottrarre*), f. *sub* SUB- 7 + *trahere* draw (see TRACT). So **subtra·c**TION †withdrawal XIV; taking of one quantity *from* another XV. – late L. *subtractiō(n-)*, in Vulgate tr. Gr. ὑπυστολή, f. L. *subtrahere*. ¶ The parallel forms *substract*, *substraction* (XVI), from late L. *substrahere* (after L. *abstrahere* ABSTRACT), are now illiterate.

subulate sʲū·bjuleit (nat. hist.) awl-shaped. XVIII. – modL. *sūbulātus*, f. L. *sūbula* awl :– **sūdhlā*, cf. L. *suere* SEW.

suburb sʌ·bɜ̄ɹb (esp. pl.) outlying district of a town or city. XIV (Wycl.). – (O)F. *suburbe*, pl. *-es* or L. *suburbium*, pl. *-ia* (medL. also *suburbiō*), f. *sub* SUB- 4 + *urbs* city. So **sub**URBAN səbɜ̄·ɹbən. XVII. – L. *suburbānus*, cf. F. *suburbain*, etc.

suburbIA[2] səbɜ̄·ɹbiə quasi-proper name for suburbs (esp. of London). Late XIX; cf. BELGRAVIA. **suburbica·r**IAN of (six) dioceses around Rome the bishops of which are cardinal bishops. XVII. – late L.; cf. †*urbicarian, urbicary* XVII.

subvention səbve·nʃən †subsidy levied by the state XV; †provision of support XVI; grant of money in aid XIX. – (O)F. *subvention* = Pr. *subventio*, etc. – late L. *subventiō(n-)*, f. *subvenīre* come to the help of, f. *sub* SUB- 7 + *venīre* COME; see -TION. ¶ Readopted from F. in XIX.

subvert səbvɜ̄·ɹt overturn, overthrow. XIV (Wycl. Bible, Ch.). – OF. *subvertir* or L. *subvertere*, f. *sub* SUB- 7 + *vertere* turn (see -WARD, WORTH[3]). So **subve·r**SION. XIV (Wycl. Bible). – (O)F. or late L.

subway sʌ·bwei underground passage or tunnel. XIX (1822; John Williams, of Cornhill, London, patentee of subways, who issued a proposal for *sub-railways* in 1845). f. SUB- 1 + WAY.

succade sʌkei·d fruit preserved in sugar. XV. – AN. *sukade*, ONF. *succade*, also *chuc(c)ade* (see -ADE), of unkn. origin.

succedaneum sʌksidei·niəm substitute. XVII. – modL. use of n. of L. *succēdāneus*, f. *succēdere* come close after; see SUCCEED.

succeed səksi·d come next after another (Barbour, Ch.); follow in the course of events XV (trans. XVI); have a certain issue (now always fortunate) XV; attain a desired end XVI. Late ME. *succede* – (O)F. *succéder* or L. *succēdere* go under or up, come close after, go near, go on well, f. *sub* SUB- 4 + *cēdere* go (see CEDE). So **success** səkse·s †issue, result; †fortune (good or bad); prosperous achievement XVI. – L. *successus* f. pp. stem of *succēdere*. Hence **succe·ss**FUL[1]. XVI (Sh.). **succe·ss**ION. XIV. – (O)F. *succession* or L. *successiō(n-)*, f. *success-*, *succēdere*. **succe·ss**IVE. XV. – medL. **succe·ss**OR[1]. XIII (RGlouc.). – OF. *successour* (mod. *-eur*) – L. *successor, -ōrem*.

succentor səkse·ntɔ̄ɹ †one who takes up the chant after the precentor; precentor's deputy. XVII. – late L. *succentor*; f. *succinere*, f. L. *sub* SUB- 2 + *canere* sing (cf. CHANT); see -OR[1].

succinct səksi·ŋkt †pp. girded, girt XV; adj. brief and concise XVI. – L. *succinctus*, pp. of *succingere*, f. *sub* SUB- 1, 7 + *cingere* gird. So F.

succory sʌ·kəri plant Cichorium Intybus. alt. of *cicoree, sichorie*, early forms of CHICORY, after MLG. *suckerie*, MDu. *sūkerie* (Du. *suikerei*, Flem. †*suykerey*, †*succory*).

succotash sʌ·kŏtæʃ N. Amer. Indian dish of green maize and beans. XVIII. – Narragansett (Algonquian) *msiquatash* (inanimate pl.); cf. SQUASH[2].

succour sʌ·kəɹ help, aid. XIII (AncrR.). ME. *sucurs, soc(o)urs* – OF. *sucurs, socours* (mod. *secours*) = It. *soccorso* :– medL. *succursus*, f. *succurs-*, pp. stem of L. *succurrere*, f. *sub* SUB- 7 + *currere* run (see CURRENT). The final *s* was at an early date (XIII) apprehended as the pl. suffix and a new sg. (*socour*) came into existence, the pl. of which is identical with the old sg. So **su·ccour** vb. XIII. – OF. *socorre* :– L. *succurrere*, and OF. *suc(c)urir* (mod. *secourir*), with change of conjugation.

succubus sʌ·kjŭbəs demon in female form having intercourse with men XVI; strumpet XVII. – medL. *succubus*, m. form with fem. meaning; corr. to late L. *succuba* (used in Eng. from XVI), f. *sub* SUB- 1 + *cub-* lie down (see CUBICLE, INCUBUS, INCUMBENT).

succulent sʌ·kjŭlənt juicy. XVII. – L. *succulentus* (*sūcu-*), f. *succus* (*sūcus*) juice; see -ULENT.

succumb səkʌ·m †bring down, overwhelm XV (Caxton); †(Sc.) fail in a cause XVI; sink under pressure XVII (at first only Sc.). – (O)F. *succomber* or L. *succumbere*, f. *sub* SUB- 1 + *-cumbere* lie (cf. SUCCUBUS). ¶ Noted by J. and by Sinclair (Observations on the Scottish Dialect, 1782) as a peculiarly Sc. word. For the loss of b cf. BOMB.

such sʌtʃ of the kind described or implied. OE. *swilć, swelć, swylć*, ME. *swich, swech, swuch*, mod. dial. *sich*, and *sech*, standard Eng. *such*; for the loss of *w* cf. SO, SOUGH, SWORD, for the loss of *l* cf. WHICH; cogn. Germ. forms are OFris. *sāl(i)k, sēl(i)k, sullik, sulk*, OS. *sulīk*, OHG. *sulīh, solīh* (Du. *zulk*, G. *solch*), ON. *slíkr* (whence ME. *slik-e*), Goth. *swaleiks*; f. **swa*, **swe* so + **līk*- body, form (see LIKE). Hence **su·chlike** (LIKE adj.) of a similar kind XV; cf. dial. *siclike, swilklike*.

suck sʌk draw liquid with the mouth (with the liquid or its source as obj.). OE.; in various fig. uses from XIV. OE. *sūcan*, pt. **sēac, sucon*, pp. *-socen*; str. vb. becoming weak from XIV, corr. to L. *sūgere*, (O)Ir. *súgim*, f. WIE. **sug-*, of which a parallel imit. base **suk-* is repr. by OE. *sūgan*, OS., MLG., MDu. *sūgen* (Du. *zuigen*), OHG. *sūgan* (G. *saugen*), ON. *súga*; cf. SOAK. Hence sb. XII. In phr. *give s.* orig. inf. of the vb. (cf. Du. *te zuigen geven*, G. *zu saugen geben*), but now apprehended as sb. Hence **su·ck**ER[1] young mammal before it is weaned XIV (Wycl. Bible); shoot of a plant XVI; sucking organ, part, etc. XVII.

sucken sʌ·kn Sc. var. of SOKEN. XV.

suckle sʌ·kl give suck to XV. prob. back-formation f. **suckling** sʌ·kliŋ infant at the breast XV, young animal that is suckled XVI, f. SUCK+-LING[1], prob. after MDu. *sūgeling* (Du. *zuigeling*) = MHG. *sōgelinc* (G. *säugling*). ¶ *Suckling* occurs as a surname XIII.

suction sʌ·kʃən sucking. XVII (Bacon). – late L. *sūctiō(n-)*, f. *sūct-*, pp. stem of *sūgere* SUCK; see -TION. So **sucto·rIAL** having organs adapted for sucking. XIX. f. modL. *sūctorius* (npl. *Suctoria*, sc. *animalia*, name of various zoological groups).

sudarium sʲūdɛə·riəm napkin for wiping the face, sweat-cloth. XVII. L. *sūdārium*, f. *sūdor* SWEAT, as used in Vulg., Luke xix 20, John xi 44, Acts xix 12. So †**su·dARY.** XIII (Cursor M.).

sudd sʌd floating vegetation obstructing the White Nile. XIX. – Arab. *sudd*, f. corresp. vb., to obstruct.

sudden sʌd'n coming without warning, unlooked-for, not provided for (with various developments now obs. or arch.). XIII. ME. *soden, sodein, -ain* – AN. *sodein, sudein*, (O)F. *soudain* = Pr. *sob-*, *subtan*, It. *subitano* :– late L. *subitānus*, for L. *subitāneus*, f. *subitus* sudden, pp. of *subire* go stealthily, f. *sub* SUB- 6+*ire* go; cf. EXIT, ITINERARY, PERISH, PRETERITE.

sudorific sʲūdəri·fik promoting sweat. XVII (Bacon). – modL. *sūdōrificus*, f. *sūdor* SWEAT; see -FIC.

suds sʌdz †dregs, filth; †(E. Anglian) flood-water, fen-water; (frothy mass of) soapy water (†barber's lather). XVI. There is no certain evidence for the orig. sense; prob. – MLG., MDu. *sudde*, MDu. *sudse* marsh, bog; early modG. has *seifensod* soap-suds; cf. MHG. *sōt* dish-water, etc. From XVI the phr. *in the suds* was used in various senses mostly obs., viz. in difficulties or disgrace; in the blues; unfinished; being lathered or washed. The base is prob. Germ. **suð-*, wk. grade of SEETHE.

sue sʲū †follow XIII; prosecute (an action), follow up, make a legal claim to (now *sue for*); apply for the grant of (a writ); institute legal proceedings (against) XIV. – AN. *suer, siwer, sure, suir(e)*, f. pres. stem *siu-*, *sieu-*, *seu-* of OF. *sivre* (mod. *suivre*) :– Rom. **sequere* (cf. Pr. *segre, seguir*, Sp. *seguir*, It. *seguire*), for L. *sequī* follow (see SEQUENCE; and cf. ENSUE, PURSUE).

suède sweid undressed kid-skin. XIX. First in *suède gloves*, tr. F. *gants de Suède*, i.e. gloves of Sweden.

suet sʲū·it fat enclosing the kidneys of an ox, etc. XIV. – AN. **suet*, **sewet*, f. *su(e)*, *seu*, OF. *seu, sieu, siu, sif* (mod. *suif*) = Pr. *seu, sef*, Sp. *sebo*, It. *sevo* :– L. *sēbum* tallow, suet, grease.

suffect sʌ·fekt additional consul. XIX. – L. *suffectus*, pp. of *sufficere* substitute; see SUFFICE.

suffer sʌ·fəɹ undergo, endure; tolerate, allow. XIII. ME. *suffre, soffre, soeffre* – AN. *suffrir, soeffrir, -er*, OF. *sof(f)rir* (mod. *souffrir*) = Pr. *su-*, *soffrir*, etc. Sp. *sufrir*, It. *sufferire* :– Rom. **sufferīre*, for L. *sufferre*, f. *suf-* SUB- 7 + *ferre* BEAR[2]. So **su·fferANCE** (arch.) suffering, long-suffering; sanction, permission, toleration (now only in phr. *on s.* and in legal use). XIII. – AN., OF. *suffraunce, soffrance* (mod. *souffrance* suffering) = Pr. *sofrensa*, Sp. *sufrencia*, It. *sofferenza* :– late L. *sufferentia*, f. *sufferre.*

suffete sʌfī·t supreme magistrate in ancient Carthage. XVI. – L. *suffet-*, *suffes*, prop. *sūfes*, of Phœnician origin (cf. Heb. *shōphēt* judge).

suffice səfai·s be enough. XIV. f. OF. *suffis-*, pres. stem of *suffire* :– L. *sufficere*, f. *sub* SUB- + *facere* DO[1]. So **sufficiENT** səfi·ʃənt that suffices or is adequate XIV (Wyclif); †of adequate means or quality XV. – OF. *sufficient* or L. *sufficient-*, *-ēns*, prp. of *sufficere*; superseding earlier †*suffisant* – (O)F. *suffisant*, prp. of *suffire*, of which the corr. sb. was †*suffisance* XIV (Ch., Gower), which was superseded by †*sufficience* XIV (Wyclif) and **suffi·ciENCY** sufficient means or capacity XV. – late L.

suffix sʌ·fiks element attached to the end of a word XVIII; (math.) inferior index XIX. – modL. *suffixum*, sb. use of n. pp. of L. *suffigere*, f. *sub* SUB- 2 + *figere* FIX. So **suffix** vb. subjoin XVII; add as a suffix XVIII. Partly f. L. *suffixus*, partly f. the sb.

suffocate sʌ·fəkeit kill by stopping the breath. XVI. f. pp. stem of L. *suffocāre*, f. *sub* SUB- 1 +*fauces* throat; see -ATE[3].

suffragan sʌ·frəgən bishop considered in relation to his metropolitan, by whom he may be summoned to give his suffrage; subsidiary bishop in the Church of England. – AN., OF. *suffragan*, medL. *suffragāneus*, f. L. *suffragium*; see next and -AN.

suffrage sʌ·fridʒ pl. (intercessory) prayers XIV (Wyclif); vote XVI (More). – L. *suffrāgium*, partly through F. *suffrage* (from XIII); preceded by †*suffragies* prayers (XIII–XVI) – L. *suffrāgia*; of uncertain origin.

suffuse səfjū·z overspread as with fluid, colour, etc. XVI. f. *suffūs-*, pp. stem of L. *suffundere*, f. *sub* SUB-+*fundere* pour. So **sufFU·SION.** XIV (Trev.). – L.

sufi sū·fi one of a Mohammedan sect. XVII. – Arab. *çūfī* 'man of wool', f. *sūf* wool.

sugar ʃu·gəɹ sweet crystalline substance obtained from fruit juices XIII; (old chem.) applied to compounds resembling sugar in form or taste XVII; (mod. chem.) to soluble more or less sweet carbohydrates XIX. ME. *suker* (XIII), *sucre, sugre* (XIV), *suger* (*sugar* from XVI) – OF. *çukre, sukere* (mod. *sucre*) – It. *zucchero*, prob. – medL. *succarum* – Arab. *sukkar* (whence, with AL-[2],

Sp. *azucar*, Pg. *assucar*). The relation of the Arab. form to the type repr. by Gr. *sák-kharon* (cf. SACCHARIN), Pers. *shakar*, Skr. *śarkarā*, and Sl. forms (e.g. Russ. *sakhar*), is not clear. For the change of -k- to -g- cf. FLAGON. So **sugar-ca·ndy** sugar clarified and crystallized. XIV. – OF. *sucre candi* – Arab. *sukkar qandī*, the latter adj. f. *qand* sugar – Pers. *kand* – Skr. *khaṇḍa* sugar in pieces, orig. piece, fragment, f. *khaṇḍ* break. **su·gar-**CANE XVI, -LOAF[1] XV. Hence vb. XV (Lydg.), **su·gar**Y[1] XVI (Spenser).

suggest sədʒe·st cause to be present to the mind. XVI. f. *suggest-*, pp. stem of L. *suggerere*, f. *sub* SUB- 7+*gerere* bear, carry, bring (see GESTATION). So **sugge·s**TION prompting to an action (†in early use, spec. to evil); †false representation or charge XIV; information not upon oath XV. – (O)F. – L. **sugge·st**IVE. (leg.) †resting on information. XVII.

suicide[1] sʲū·isaid one who takes his own life. XVIII. – modL. *suicida*, f. L. *suī* of oneself. So **suicide**[2] taking one's own life. XVII. – mod L. *suicidium*; cf. F. *suicide*, Sp., It. *suicidio*; †*su·icism* was current XVIII. Hence **suici·d**AL[1]. XVIII; earlier † *suicidical*. ¶ All modelled on HOMICIDE.

suint swint grease in the wool of sheep. XVIII. – F. *suint*, earlier †*suing*, f. *suer* sweat.

Suiogothic swīougɔ·þik Swedish; the older Swedish language. XVIII. – modL. *Suiogothicus*, adj. of *Suiones Gothique*, used to denote the *Sviar* Swedens, and *Götar*, older *Gautar*, inhabitants of Gôtland (southern Sweden); see -IC.

suit sʲūt A. (hist.) attendance at court XIII (RGlouc.); B. †pursuit XIV; legal process XV; C. †train, suite XIII (RGlouc.); D. †livery, garb XIII (RGlouc.); E. set, series XV. ME. *siute, siwte, s(e)ute* – AN. *siute*, OF. *sieute, siute* (mod. *suite*) :– Gallo-Rom. **sequita*, sb. use of fem. pp. of **sequere* follow, SUE. The medL. equiv. of *suit* in various senses was *secta* (see SECT, SET[3]). Hence **suit** vb. †sue, pursue XV; provide with apparel; be agreeable or convenient to XVI. Whence **sui·t**ABLE †matching, to match; †agreeing, accordant XVI; fitting, appropriate XVII; after *agreeable*; superseding earlier †*suitlike* (XVI), †*suitly* (XV).

suite swīt A. train of attendants XVII (Dryden); B. succession, series XVIII; C. set of rooms XVIII, of furniture XIX. – F. *suite*; see SUIT. Sense C is of English development.

suitor sʲū·təɹ †frequenter XIII; †adherent XIV; (arch.) petitioner; wooer XVI. – AN. *seutor, suitour, sut(i)er, -or* – L. *secūtor, -ōr-* follower, f. *secūt-*, *sequī* follow, SUE, after *suite* SUIT.

sulcate sʌ·lkeit furrowed. XVIII. – L. *sulcātus*, pp. of *sulcāre* plough, f. *sulcus* (rel. to Gr. *hélkein* draw) groove, furrow, which has been used in Eng. in spec. senses since XVII (Evelyn). So **su·lcated.** XVII; see -ATE[2].

sulk sʌlk indulge in ill-humour. XVIII (Mme d'Arblay). perh. back-formation from somewhat earlier **sulk**Y[1] sʌ·lki adj., used also as sb. for a carriage seated for one person (cf. synon. use of F. *désobligeant* disobliging). *Sulky* was perh. an extension with -Y[1] of an adj. †*sulke* (XVII) hard to dispose of, slow in going off, which may repr. ult. the base **sulk-* of OE. *āsolcen, besolcen* slothful, inactive (*āseolcan* become sluggish, and *besylced* exhausted, *āsolcennys* sloth, tedium).

sullen sʌ·l(ə)n marked by gloomy ill-humour; of gloomy condition or aspect. XVI (Tusser). Later form of †*solein*, †*-eyne* unique, sole, solitary, morose (XIV) – AN. **solein*, **solain*, f. *sol* SOLE[3], after OF. *soltain, soutain* = Pr. *soldan* :– late L. *sōlitāneus*, f. L. *sōlus* SOLE[3].

sully sʌ·li pollute; †intr. for pass. XVI (Sh.). perh. – F. *souiller*; see SOIL[3].

sulphur, U.S. **sulfur** sʌ·lfəɹ greenish-yellow non-metallic element; brimstone. XIV. Late ME. *soufre, solfre, sulph(e)re* – AN. *sulf(e)re*, (O)F. *soufre* = Pr. *solfre*, OSp. *çufre*, Pg. *xofre*, It. *solfo* (with prefixed Arabic *al*, OSp. *açufre*, Sp. *azufre*, Pg. *enxofre*) :– L. *sulfur, -phur, -pur* (pl. *-phura*), perh. rel. to the Germ. word repr. by OE. *swefl*. Comb. form **sulpho-,** before a vowel **sulph-,** now largely superseded by THIO-. XIX. **su·lph**ATE[1]/**su·lph**ITE salt of sulphuric/sulphurous acid. XVIII. – F. *sulphat* / *sulphite*. **su·lph**IDE compound of sulphur with another element. XIX. **sulphur**EOUS sʌlfjuə·riəs pert. to sulphur XVI; †hellish, satanic XVII. (Earlier † *sulphurious* – OF. XV.) **sulphuretted** sʌ·lfjuretid combined chemically with sulphur. XIX. f. *su·lphuret* – modL. *sulphuretum*; see -URET. **sulphur**IC sʌlfjuə·rik *s. acid* H_2SO_4. XVIII, – F., *sulfurique*. **sulphur**OUS sʌ·lfjərəs, (chem.) sʌlfjuə·rəs sulphureous XVI; **su·lphury** sulphurous, -eous. XVI. See Y[1].

sultan sʌ·ltən sovereign of a Mohammedan country XVI; despot, tyrant; sweet-scented annual, Centaurea moschata and C. suaveolens XVII. – F. *sultan* (16th cent.) or medL. *sultānus* – Arab. *sulṭān* power, dominion, ruler, king, f. Aram. *saliṭa* rule, overcome. Cf. the (arch.) doublet **soldan** sɔ·ldən, f. OF. *soldan, soudan*. XIII. So **sultana** sʌltā·nə sultan's wife XVI; mistress, concubine XVIII; purple gallinule; (*s. raisin*) small seedless raisin XIX. – It. *sultana*, fem. of *sultano* sultan. **su·ltan**ATE[1]. XIX.

sultry sʌ·ltri oppressively hot and moist. XVI. f. †*sulter* be sweltering hot (XVI), prob. for **swulter*, rel. to SWELTER; see -Y[1].

sum sʌm quantity *of money*; total amount XIII; summary, epitome (surviving in phr. *sum and substance*, Sh.) XIV; quantity resulting from the addition of quantities XV. ME.

summe, somme – OF. *summe,* (also mod.) *somme* = Pr. *som(m)a,* Sp. *suma,* It. *somma* :– L. *summa* (whence also Du. *som,* G. *summe*), sb. use (sc. *rēs, pars*) main thing, principal part, substance, sum total, of fem. of *summus* :– **supmus,* superl. f. stem of *super, superus* (see SUPERIOR). phr. *sum* TOTAL XIV, tr. medL. *summa tōtālis.* So vb. XIII. – (O)F. *sommer* or late L. *summāre,* f. *summa.* **summa**TION sʌmei·ʃən finding the sum, adding up. XVIII. – modL. *summātiō(n)-,* f. late L. *summāre.*

sumach sjū·mæk, ʃū·mæk preparation of dried leaves of plants of the genus Rhus XIV; plant of this genus XVI. – (O)F. *sumac* = Pr. *sumac, simac,* Sp. *zumaque,* It. *sommaco* or medL. *sumác(h)* – Arab. *summāq.*

summary sʌ·məri comprising the chief points or substance XV; done without delay, (leg.) carried out without certain formalities XVIII (the adv. **su·mmari**LY[2] in corr. sense is XVI; cf. OF. *sommierement,* L. *summātim*). – medL. *summārius* (in classical L. only in n. sb.), f. *summa* SUM; see -ARY. As sb. XVI. – L. *summārium.* Hence **su·mmar**IZE. XIX.

summer[1] sʌ·məɹ second and warmest season of the year. OE. *sumor,* corr. to OFris. *sumur,* OS. *sumar,* MLG. *sommer,* (Du. *zomer*), OHG. *sumar* (G. *sommer*), ON. *sumar* :– CGerm. (exc. Goth.); rel., with different suffixes, to Skr. *sámā* half-year, year, OIr. *sam, samrad,* W. *ham, haf* summer.

summer[2] sʌ·məɹ †packhorse; (archit.) horizontal bearing-beam. XIV. – AN. *sumer, somer,* OF. *somier* (mod. *sommier*) = Pr. *saumier,* It. *somiere* – Rom. **saumārius,* for late L. *sagmārius,* f. *sagma* – Gr. *ságma* packsaddle, f. **sak-* (*sáttein* equip). For the sense-development cf. *horse* and F. *cheval.* Cf. BREASTSUMMER.

summit sʌ·mit topmost part, top. XV (Malory, Caxton). Late ME. – OF. *som(m)ete,* also *somet, sumet* (mod. *sommet*), f. *som, sum* :– L. *summum,* n. sg. of *summus* (see SUM); the sp. with *-it* (from XVII) is due to assim. to †*summity* summit (XIV–XVIII) – (O)F. *sommité* – late L. *summitās* (see -ITY).

summons sʌ·mənz authoritative call, citation. XIII (S. Eng. Leg.). ME. *somouns* – OF. *somonce, sumunse* (mod. *semonce*) = Pr. *somonsa* :– Gallo-Rom. **summonsa,* for L. *summonita,* fem. pp. used sb. of *summonēre.*

summum bonum sʌ·məm bou·nəm chief or supreme good. XVI. L. (Cicero), i.e. *summum* n.sg. of *summus* highest (cf. SUM), *bonum* n.sg. of *bonus* good used sb. (cf. BOON).

sump sʌmp †marsh XV; (dial.) dirty pool; pit for collecting water XVII. – (M)LG., MDu. *sump,* or in mining use, corr. to G. *sumpf,* rel. to SWAMP.

sumpitan sʌ·mpitən blow-gun used by Malays. XVII (T. Herbert). – Malay *sumpītan,* f. *sumpit* blowpipe, prop. narrow.

sumpter sʌ·mᵖtəɹ †driver of a pack-horse XIV; pack-horse XVI. – OF. *som(m)etier,* Pr. *saumatier* :– Rom. **saumatārius,* f. late L. *sagmat-, sagma* – Gr. *ságma* equipment, baggage, packsaddle (see SUMMER[2]).

sumptuary sʌ·mᵖtjuəri pert. to expenditure. XVI. – L. *sumptuārius,* f. *sumptus* expenditure, expense, f. *sumpt-, sūmere* consume, spend; see -ARY and cf. F. *somptuaire,* etc. So **su·mptu**OUS made at great cost XV (Caxton); † spending largely XVI. – (O)F. *somptueux* = Pr. *sumptuos,* Sp. *suntuoso,* etc. – L. *sumptuōsus,* f. *sumptu-s.*

sun sʌn the brightest of the heavenly bodies, the orb of day, OE. *sunne* (fem.) = OFris. *sunne,* OS. *sunna,* OHG. *sunna* (Du. *zon,* G. *sonne*), ON. (poet.) *sunna,* Goth. *sunnō,* beside OE. *sunna* (m.), OHG., OS. *sunno* :– CGerm. **sunnōn, -on*; f. IE. **su-* with *n*-formative, beside **sāu-* with *l*-formative in Homeric Gr. *ēélios* :– **sāwelijos* (Attic *hḗlios*), L. *sōl,* OE. *sōl,* ON. *sól,* Goth. *sauil,* W. *haul.* Hence vb. XVI; **sunn**Y[1]. XIII (Cursor M.). comps. **su·n**BEAM. OE. *sunn(e)bēam.* **su·n**BURN sb. XVII, f. the vb. (XVI) back-formation from *sunburning* (XVI), *sunburnt* (*sunne ybrent* XIV); OE. had sb. *sunbryne.* **su·n**DEW plant of genus Drosera. XVI (Lyte). tr. Du. *son-, sundauw* = G. *sonnentau,* tr. L. *rōs sōlis.* **su·n**DIAL. XVI. **su·ndown** setting of the sun XVII. perh. shortening of †*sunne gate downe* (XV), †*sun go downe* (XVI). **su·n**FLOWER plant whose flowers turn towards the sun; tr. modL. *flōs sōlis* XVI. **su·n**RISE. XV. perh. evolved, through syntactical ambiguity, from a clause such as *before the sun rise* (pres. subjunctive of the vb.); cf. ME. *sonne rist* (XIII). **su·n**SET. OE. (late Nhb.) *sunset*; perh. partly from a clause like *ere the sun set.* **su·n**SHADE parasol. XIX. **su·n**STROKE, for earlier *stroke of the sun,* tr. F. *coup de soleil.* XIX. **su·n-**UP (U.S.) sunrise; after *sun-down* XIX.

sundae sʌ·ndei portion of ice cream served with syrup, etc. XX. orig. U.S.; accepted as alt. of SUNDAY for some obscure reason.

Sunday sʌ·ndi first day of the week. OE. *sunnandæġ* (Nhb. *sunnadæġ*) = OFris. *sunnandei,* OS. *sunnondag,* OHG. *sunnun (-on)-tag* (Du. *zondag,* G. *sonntag*), ON. *sunnudagr*; Germ. tr. of L. *diēs sōlis* = late Gr. *ἡμέρα ἡλίου* 'day of the sun'; surviving as three sylls. till XIV; cf. MONDAY for the formation. ¶ For *S. clothes* cf. F. *s'endimancher* dress in one's S. best (f. *dimanche* Sunday).

sunder sʌ·ndəɹ phr. *in s.,* asunder, apart XIII (Cursor M.). alt. of ASUNDER (OE. *onsundran, -um*) by substitution of IN[1] for ON (*o, a*), partly after ON. *í sundr* (= OHG. *in sunter*). So **su·nder** vb. separate, part. Late OE. *sundrian* (beside *syndrian*), for earlier *āsundrian,* and *ġe-, on-, tōsundrian,* corr. to OHG. *sunt(a)rōn, sund(e)rōn* (G. *sondern*), ON. *sundra*, f. Germ. adv. ('separately') repr. by OE. *sundor*, OFris. *sunder*, OS. *sundar* (MLG. *sunder*; also prep. and conj., Du. *zonder* prep.), OHG. *suntar* (MHG. *sunder* adj., adv., prep., conj., G. *sonder* adv., adj., with var. *sondern* but), ON. *sundr*, Goth. *sundrō*, formed with compar. or oppositive suffix on IE. **su-* repr. also by Skr. *sanitúr* besides, *sanútar* apart from, Gr. *háteros* (Attic *héteros*) one of two, Gr. *áter* without, W. *hanner* half (:- **sṇtero-*), and (without *t*-suffix) L. *sine*, Toch. *sne, snai*, Goth. *inu*, OHG. *āno*, Gr. *áneu* without. So **sundry** sʌ·ndri several, various. OE. *syndriġ* separate, special, private, exceptional, corr. to MLG. *sunder(i)ch*, OHG. *sunt(a)rīc*; see -Y[1]. **sundries** sʌ·ndriz miscellaneous small articles. XIX; cf. *odds*.

sunn sʌn shrub Crotalaria juncea, cultivated for its fibre. XVIII. – Urdu, Hindi *san* – Skr. *çāná* hempen.

Sunni sʌ·ni orthodox Mohammedan, who accepts the *Sunna* (body of tradition) as of equal authority with the Koran. XVII. – Arab. *sunnī* lawful, f. *sunnaʰ* form, way, course, rule.

sunnud sʌ·nʌd deed of grant, charter. XVIII. – Urdu *sunnud* – Arab. *sanad* signature, deed, diploma.

sunnyasee, -asi sʌnjā·si Brahman in the fourth stage of his life. XVII. – Urdu, Hindi *sannyāsī* – Skr. *saṃnyāsin* laying aside, abandoning, ascetic, f. *saṃ* together + *ni* down + *as* throw.

sup[1] sʌp take liquid into the mouth in small quantities. OE. *sūpan*, pt. *sēap* = MLG. *sūpen*, OHG. *sūfan* (Du. *zuipen*, G. *saufen* drink, booze), ON. *súpa* :- CGerm. (exc. Gothic) str. vb.; this vb. continued in ME. *sūpe, sowpe*, pp. *sopen*, giving place to wk. forms with short stem vowel from XIV onwards, which were based partly on OE. (Nhb.) pt. *ġesupede*, pres. ind. pl. *suppas*. Hence sb. XVI.

sup[2] sʌp take supper. XIII. – OF. *super, soper* (mod. *souper*) = Pr. *sopar*, f. Germ. **sup-* (see SOP, SUP[1], and cf. SOUP).

sup- see SUB-.

supari supā·rī areca palm. XVII. Hindi.

supawn səpɔ̄·n (U.S.) maize porridge. XVIII. Natick *saupáun* softened; cf. Du. *sapaen*.

supe sʲūp (sl.) short for next.

super sʲū·pəɹ short for SUPERFICIAL, SUPERFINE, SUPERINTENDENT, SUPERNUMERARY. XIX.

super- sʲūpəɹ prefix repr. L. *super-*, being the adv. and prep. *super* above, on the top of, beyond, besides, rel. to SUB- as Skr. *upári* above, over, moreover, to *úpa* up, hither, to, towards.

The gen. rule for the stressing of *super-* comps. is that the prefix carries a secondary stress, e.g. *su:pera·dd, su:pererога·tion, su:perpho·sphate, su:persubsta·ntial*; but this syll. carries the main stress when a contrast is implied with the radical el., e.g. *su·perman, su·perstructure*; in *supe·rfluous and supe·rlative* the stress is on the second syll. of the prefix.

The chief meanings are: (1) over, above, at the top (of), in advb., prep., or adj. force, as *su·peraltar* (XIV), *-cele·stial* (XVI), *su·perstructure* (XVII); (2) higher in rank, quality, or degree, as *su:peresse·ntial* (XVI), *superm·undane* (XVII), *superse·nsual* (XVII); (3) in or to the highest or a very high degree, (hence) in excess, as *su:perabou·nd, -abu·ndant* (XV, Bokenham, Hoccleve), *su·perfine*; (4) expressing addition, as *supera·dd* (XV), *su·per-tax* (XX). Cf. SUPRA-, SUR-[2].

superable sʲū·pərəbl that can be overcome. XVII. – L. *superābilis*, f. *superāre* overcome, f. *super*; see prec., -ABLE, INSUPERABLE.

superannuated sʲūpəɹæ·njueitid disqualified or impaired by age. XVII. f. medL. *superannuātus*, alt. of *superannātus* (cf. F. *suranné*), f. *super* SUPER- + *annus* year, with assim. to *annuus* ANNUAL; see -ATE[2], -ED[1]. So **su:perannuA·TION**. XVII.

superb sʲupə̄·ɹb of noble or magnificent proportions XVI; grandly furnished XVII. – (O)F. *superbe* or L. *superbus* (whence also It. *superbo*) proud, superior, distinguished, f. *super* above (SUPER-) + **bh-*, as in *probus* (see PROBITY). ¶ Earlier †*superbious*.

supercargo sʲūpəɹkā·ɹgou (naut.) officer who superintends the cargo. XVII. alt., by substitution of SUPER-, of *supra*CARGO (XVII–XIX) – Sp. *sobrecargo*, F. *subrécargue*; cf. modL. *suprācaricārius* (Statutes of Geneva, 1567).

supercilious sʲūpəɹsi·liəs haughtily contemptuous. XVI. – L. *superciliōsus*, f. L. *supercilium* eyebrow, f. *super* SUPER- + *cilium* (lower) eyelid, perh. f. **kel-* hide, CONCEAL.

supererogation sʲū:pərerŏgei·ʃən performance of good works beyond what is required. XVI. – late L. *supererogātiō(n-)*, f. L. *supererogāre*. **su:pererogatORY**[2] -rɔ·gətəri. XVI – scholL. *supererogātōrius*.

superficies sʲūpəɹfi·ʃiīz, -fi·siīz, -fi·ʃīz surface. XVI. – L., f. *super* SUPER- 1 + *faciēs* FACE. Earlier *superfice* (XIV, Ch.) – OF. So **superfi·cial** sʲūpəɹfi·ʃəl †(math.) compounded of two prime factors XIV (Trevisa); pert. to the surface or superficies XV; concerned only with the surface XVI. – late L. *superficiālis*; cf. F. *superficiel*.

superfine sʲū·pəɹfain, sʲūpəɹfai·n †extremely subtle XV; over-refined XVI; extremely fine XVII. – medL. **superfinus* (implied in *superfinitās*), f. L. *super* + medL. *fīnus* FINE[2]. G. *superfin* was applied by Paracelsus to silver of the highest grade. Cf. F. *superfin, surfin*, Sp. It. *sopraffino*.

superfluous sʲupə̄·ɹfluəs that is more than sufficient. XV. f. L. *superfluus*, whence, through F. *superflu*, earlier †*superflue* (XIV), f. *super* SUPER-+*fluere* FLOW; see -OUS. So **superflu·**ITY. XIV (Ch.). – (O)F. – late L.

superhuman sʲūpəɹhjū·mən higher than (that of) man. XVII. – late L. *superhūmānus*; see SUPER-, HUMAN. Cf. F. *surhumain*. ¶ Similar comps. are Gr. ὑπερηνορέων (Homer), ὑπερήνωρ (Hesiod), ὑπεράνθρωπος (Lucan). Cf. SUPERMAN.

superintend sʲū:pərinte·nd have the oversight of. XVII (Bacon). – ecclL. *superintendere*, rendering Gr. *episkopeîn*; see SUPER-, INTEND. So **su:perinte·nd**ENT official having chief charge or oversight; in earliest use applied to Christian ministers in some church polities, as repr. Gr. *epískopos* 'overseer' (see BISHOP). XVI. – ecclL. *superintendent-*, *-ēns*.

superior sʲupiə·riəɹ situated higher XIV (Gower); of higher degree or status XV; *s. to* (†*s. than*) XVI. sb. XV. – OF. *superiour* (mod. *supérieur*), corr. to It. *superiore*, Sp. *superior* – L. *superiōrem*, nom. *-ior*, compar. of *superus* that is above, f. *super*; see SUPER-, -IOR. So **superior**ITY -ɔ·rĭti. XVI. – (O)F. *supériorité* or medL.

superlative sʲupə̄·ɹlətiv (Gram.) XIV (Ch.); surpassing all others XV. – (O)F. *superlatif*, *-ive* = Pr. *superlatiu*, Sp., It. *superlativo* – late L. *superlātīvus*, f. *superlātus* (used as pp. of *superferre*), f. *super* SUPER-+*lāt-* (:– **tlat-*), pp. stem of *tollere* take away (cf. EXTOL); see -IVE.

superman sʲū·pəɹmæn ideal superior type of man. 1903 (G. B. Shaw). tr. of G. *übermensch*, as used in 'Zarathustra' 1883, by F. W. Nietzsche, German philosopher (1844–1900), f. *über* OVER+*mensch* human being (cf. OE. *mennisċ* human). ¶ *Beyondman* (A. Tille, 1896) and *overman* (T. Common, 1901) were earlier renderings, as in F. were *superhomme* (1898) and *surhomme* (Lichtenberger 1901); G. *übermensch* is historically a back-formation from *übermenschlich* (1527, tr. late L. *superhūmānus* SUPERHUMAN).

supernaculum sʲūpəɹnæ·kjŭləm (drink) to the last drop. XVI (*nag-*, Nashe). modL., tr. G. *auf den nagel* (*trinken*) on to the nail. See CAROUSE.

supernal sʲupə̄·ɹnəl existing in the heavens. XV. – OF. *supernal* or medL. *supernālis*, L. *supernus*, f. *super*; see SUPER- and cf. *externus* EXTERNAL.

supernaturAL[1] sʲūpəɹnæ·tʃərəl transcending the natural. XVI. – medL. *supernātūrālis* (Thomas Aquinas), f. L. *super* SUPER 2 + *nātūra* NATURE. So **superna·tural**LY[2]. XV; after medL. *supernātūrāliter*.

supernumerary sʲūpəɹnjū·mərəri beyond the due number. XVII (Bacon). – lateL. *supernumerārius*, f. *super numerum*; see SUPER, NUMBER, -ARY.

superpose sʲūpəɹpou·z place above or upon. XIX. – F. *superposer* (see SUPER- 1, POSE[1]); after L. *superpōnere*. So **su:per**POSI·TION (geom.) XVII; (gen.) XIX. – F. or late L.

superscribe sʲūpəɹskrai·b inscribe on the top or surface of. – L. *superscrībere*, f. SUPER- 1+*scrībere* (see SCRIBE). So **superscri·p**TION. XIV (Wycl. Bible). – late L.

supersede sʲūpəɹsī·d †postpone XV; †desist or refrain from; †render superfluous or void XVI; take the place of something set aside XVII. In early use often *-cede*. – OF. *supercéder*, later *-séder* – L. *supersedēre* (in medL. often *-cēdere*) set above, be superior to, refrain from, omit, f. *super* SUPER- 2+ *sedēre* SIT. **supersedeas** -sī·diæs (leg.) writ commanding the stay of proceedings. XIV (PPl.). L. 'you shall desist', 2nd pers. sg. pres. subj. of *supersedēre*. **superse·s**SION setting aside of a rule, etc. XVIII; substitution of a person in the place of one removed XIX. F. or medL.; an earlier ex. with sense 'desisting' appears in Blount 'Glossographia', 1656, copying Cotgrave.

superstition sʲūpəɹsti·ʃən religious belief or practice founded on fear or ignorance. XV. – (O)F. *superstition* or L. *superstitiō(n-)*, f. *superstāre* stand on or over, f. *super* SUPER- 1 + *stāre* STAND; see -TION. So **supersti·**TIOUS. XIV (Ch.). – (O)F. *superstitieux* or L. *superstitiōsus*.

supersubstantial sʲū:pəɹsəbstæ·nʃəl spiritual (in *s. bread*, i.e. of the Eucharist); transcending all substance. XVI (More). – ecclL. (Vulg.) *supersubstantiālis*, tr. Gr. *epioúsios* Matt. vi 11 in the Lord's Prayer, which is usu. taken to mean '(bread) pert. to the coming day'; see SUPER- 1, 2, SUBSTANTIAL.

supervene sʲūpəɹvī·n occur as something additional. XVII. – L. *supervenīre*, f. *super* SUPER- 4+*venīre* COME. So **superve·n**IENT. XVI. – L. *supervenient-*, *-ēns*, prp. of *supervenīre*.

supervise sʲū·pəɹvaiz †survey XVI (Sh.); have the oversight of XVII. f. *supervīs-*, pp. stem of medL. *supervidēre*, f. L. *super* SUPER- 1 + *vidēre*. So **super**VI·SION. XVII. – medL.

supination sʲūpainei·ʃən action of turning the hand or fore limb so that the back of it is downward or backward. XVII. – L. *supīnātiō(n-)*, f. *supīnāre*, f. *supīnus*; see next, -ATION.

supine sʲū·pain adj. lying on one's back XV; mentally or morally inert XVII. – L. *supīnus*, f. Italic **sup-*, repr. in L. *super* above, *superus* higher, SUPERIOR; see -INE[1]. So sb. form of verbal noun ending in *-tum*, *-tū*, *-sum*, *-sū*. XVI (Lyly). – n.sg. of *supīnus* used sb.; cf. F. *supin*; this usage has not been satisfactorily explained.

supper sʌ·pəɹ last meal of the day. XIII. ME. *supe·r(e)*, *sope·r(e)*, and *su·per*, *so·per*, later *soupper, sopper, supper* – OF. *soper, super* (mod. *souper*), sb. use of *soper* SUP[2]; see -ER[4].

supplant səplà·nt dispossess another, esp. treacherously XIII (implied in *supplanter*, Cursor M., as applied to the Heb. patriarch *Jacob*, whose name has that meaning; see Gen. xxvii); †uproot XVI; †trip up; bring down, bring low XIV. – (O)F. *supplanter* or L. *supplantāre* overthrow, f. *sub* SUB- 7+ *planta* sole of the foot, PLANT.

supple sʌ·pl †soft, yielding XIII (RGlouc.); pliant, flexible XIV (Ch.); compliant XIV. ME. *souple* – (O)F. *souple* :– Rom. **supples*, f. L. *supplex, -plic-* submissive, suppliant, lit. bending under, f. *sub* SUB- 1 + **plic-* bend (see PLIANT).

supplement sʌ·plimənt something added to supply a deficiency XIV (Wycl. Bible, Trevisa); supply, provision, reinforcement XV (Caxton). – L. *supplēmentum*, f. *supplēre* SUPPLY; cf. F. *supplément* (XVI); see -MENT.

suppliant sʌ·pliənt one who supplicates or petitions. XV. – F. *suppliant* (superseding OF. *soupleiant, -oiant*), prp. of *supplier*, †*soupleier* – L. *supplicāre* SUPPLICATE; see -ANT. Also as adj. XVI.

supplicate sʌ·plikeit beg humbly XV; at Oxford University, present a formal petition for a degree XVII. f. pp. stem of L. *supplicāre*, f. *sub* SUB- 7+ †**plic-* bend (see PLIANT); see -ATE[3]. So **su·pplicANT** sb. (Hooker) and adj. (Sh.) suppliant. XVI. – L. prp. of *supplicāre*. **su·pplicat** formal petition. XVII. – L. '(he) supplicates', 3rd sg. pres. ind. of *supplicāre*; used as the first word of a petition. **supplicA·TION**. XIV (Ch., Gower). – (O)F. – L.

supply səplai· †help, succour, complete, supplement; make up for, compensate; fill (another's place) XIV; †fulfil, discharge (office or function) XV; furnish, provide XVI; take the place of, now only as a minister's substitute XVII. Late ME. (in earliest use mainly Sc.) *sup(p)le, sowple*, later *supplie* – OF. *so(u)pleer*, earlier *soup(p)leier, -oier*, later *supplier* (mod. *suppléer*) – L. *supplēre* fill up, make good, complete (whence also Pr., Sp. *suplir*, Pg. *supprir*, It. *supplire*), f. *sub* SUB- 7+*-plēre* fill (*plēnus* FULL). Hence sb. XV (in early use mainly Sc.).

support səpɔ̄·ɹt endure, tolerate (now a gallicism) XIV (Wycl. Bible); strengthen the position of XIV (Gower); furnish sustenance for XV (Lydg.); keep from failing XVI. – (O)F. *supporter* = Pr. *supportar*, etc. – L. *supportāre*, f. *sub* SUB- 7+*portāre* carry (cf. PORT[1]). Hence, or partly – F., sb. XIV (Gower); obs. syns. are †*supportance* (XV), †*supportation* (XIV, Ch.), †*supportment* (XVII), †*supporture* (XVII).

suppose səpou·z †believe, think, guess; assume as a hypothesis XIV; infer hypothetically, incline to think XVII. – (O)F. *sup(p)oser*, f. *sub* SUB- 7+*poser* POSE[1], as a vb. corr. to **supposiTION** sʌpəzi·ʃən †something held to be true as the basis of argument XV; assumption of this hypothetical inference or belief XVI. – (O)F. *supposition* or medL. *suppositiō(n-)*, used as a rendering of Gr. ὑπόθεσις HYPOTHESIS, in older L. recorded only in senses 'placing under' and 'substitution'; cf. POSITION. So **suppositiTIOUS** səpɔziti·ʃəs deceitfully substituted. XVII. f. L. *supposititius, -icius*, f. pp. stem of *suppōnere*. **suppositORY** səpɔ·zitəri plug to be introduced into the rectum. XIV. – medL. *suppositōrium*, n. sg. of adj. f. late L. *supposit-, suppōnere*. Cf. (O)F. *suppositoire* (XIII).

suppress səpre·s put down by force or authority XIV (Wyclif); subdue; keep secret, not to express XVI. f. *suppress-*, pp. stem of L. *supprimere*, f. *sub* SUB- 2+ *premere* PRESS. So **suppre·SSION**. XVI – L. So **suppre·sSIVE**. XVIII (J.).

suppurate sʌ·pjŭreit †cause to form pus XVI; secrete pus XVII. f. pp. stem of L. *suppūrāre*, f. *sub* SUB- 1+*pūs* PUS; see -ATE[3]. So **suppurA·TION**. XVI. – L.

supra- sʲū·prə repr. L. *suprā* adv. and prep., above, beyond, in addition (to), before the time of, in comps. parallel to those of *super-*, but with a different distribution; used in many techn. terms, esp. anat. and zool.)(INFRA- and SUB-. **su:pralapsA·RIAN** pert. to the view that God's election of some was antecedent to the Fall of Man)(*infralapsarian* XVII. **suprali·minal** (psych.) above the threshold of consciousness. XIX; after SUBLIMINAL.

supreme sʲuprī·m A. (poet.) loftiest, topmost; B. highest in authority or rank; of the highest quality or degree. XVI. – L. *suprēmus* (whence also F. *suprême*, Sp., It. *supremo*), f. *suprā*; see prec. and for the formation cf. EXTREME. In sense B first used in titles *s. head* and *s. governor* in the enactments of Henry VIII's and Elizabeth's reigns respectively, dealing with the position of the sovereign as the paramount authority (as against the Bishop of Rome). Hence (after PRIMACY) **supreMACY** sʲupre·məsi. XVI (in earliest use with ref. to the s. head or governor); whence F. *suprématie*, etc.

sur-[1] var. of SUB-.

sur-[2] sə̄ɹ, səɹ – (O)F. *sur-*, earlier *sor-, sour(e)-* :– L. *super*, used in various senses of SUPER-.

sura[1] su·ra fermented juice of species of palm. XVI. – Skr. *surā*.

sura[2] sū·ra section of the Koran. XVII. – Arab. *sūrah*.

surah sʲuə·ra soft twilled silk fabric. XIX. repr. F. pronunc. of SURAT.

sural sʲuə·rəl pert. to the calf of the leg. XVII. – modL. *sūrālis*, f. *sūra*; see -AL[1] and cf. F. *sural*.

surat sʲuræ·t, sʲuə·ræt, su·ræt designating cotton goods orig. made in *Surat*, a town and district in Bombay, India. XVII.

surcease səɹsī·s (arch.) cessation, suspension. XVI. f. *surcease* vb. (arch.) leave off, cease, desist (XV), f. OF. *sursis*, fem. *-sise* (cf. AN. *sursise* omission), pp. of *surseoir* refrain, delay, suspend :- L. *supersedēre* SUPERSEDE; early assim. in sp. to CEASE.

surcharge sɔ̄·ɹtʃāɹdʒ excessive or exorbitant charge. XVII. f. the vb. (XV) – OF. *surcharger*. See SUR-², CHARGE.

surcingle sɔ̄·ɹsiŋgl girth for a horse, etc. XIV. – OF. *so(u)rcengle*, f. *sor-* SUR-²+*cengle* (mod. *sangle*) :- L. *cingula*, f. *cingere* gird.

surcoat sɔ̄·ɹkout outer coat. XIV. – OF. *sur-*, *sourcot*; see SUR-², COAT, and cf. Pr. *sobrecot*, It. *sopracotta*, *sorcotto*, medL. *surcotus*.

surd sɔ̄ɹd (math.) irrational XVI; (phonetics) voiceless XVIII. – L. *surdus* deaf, mute, silent, (of sound) dull, indistinct. ¶ The sense in math. arises from the use of L. *surdus* to render Gr. *ἄλογος* (Euclid, book X, definition 10) speechless, irrational, absurd, through the medium of Arab. *jaðr açamm* lit. 'deaf root'.

sure ʃuəɹ †safe, secure XIV–XVII; trustworthy, steadfast XIV; subjectively certain XIV; objectively certain XV. – OF. *sur-e*, earlier *sëur-e* (mod. *sûr*) = Pr. *segur*, Sp. *seguro*, It. *sicuro* :- L. *sēcūrus* SECURE. So **sure**TY² ʃuə·ɹti †safety, security, certainty; bond entered into for the performance of an undertaking XIV; person undertaking this, bail XV. – OF. *surte*, *sëurte* (mod. *sûreté*) :- L. *sēcūritāt-*, *-tās* SECURITY. **su·rety**SHIP. XVI (Coverdale).

surf sɔ̄ɹf swell of the sea breaking on the shore XVII; mass of foamy water on a shore XVIII. In early use sometimes in phr. *surf of the sea*; continuing in sense and chronology †*suff* (*of the sea*) XVI–XVII, and perh. an alt. of the latter by assoc. with SURGE¹. ¶ Both *suff* and *surf* are first used with ref. to the coast of India.

surface sɔ̄·ɹfis outermost boundary or part of a material body; superficies. XVII. – F. *surface* (XVI), f. *sur* SUR-²+*face* FACE, after L. SUPERFICIES; cf. Sp. *sobrefaz*, †*-haz*, Pg. *sobreface*.

surfeit sɔ̄·ɹfit excess, superfluity (now only as fig. from later sense) XIII (Cursor M.); excessive indulgence esp. in eating or drinking XIV; morbid condition arising from this XVI; nausea, satiety XVII. – OF. *sur-*, *sorfeit*, *-fet* = Pr. *sobrefach* :- Rom. **superfactum*, sb. use of pp. of **superficere* (cf. late L. *superficiens* excessive, OF. *sorfaisant* immoderate), f. *super* SUPER- 3 + *facere* DO, act. Hence **su·rfeit** vb. XIV.

surge¹ sɔ̄ɹdʒ †fountain, source XV (Caxton); rolling swell of the sea XVI; (naut.) slipping back of a rope wound round a capstan XVIII. In the earliest exx. of the first sense tr. OF. *sourgeon* (mod. *surgeon*) and prob. – its base *sourge-*, pres. stem of *sourdre* see next).

surge² sɔ̄ɹdʒ †toss or ride on the waves; †rise, spring; swell or heave, as a large wave XVI; (naut.) slip back, as a rope, etc. XVII. f. OF. *sourge-* (see prec.) or – OF. *sorgir* (mod. *surgir*) – Cat. *sorgir* anchor, *surgir* land, Pr. *sorzer*, It. *sorgere*, OF. *sourdre* :- L. *surgere* rise, beside *surrigere*, f. *sub* SUB- 7+*regere* RULE.

surgeon sɔ̄·ɹdʒən one who heals by manual operation XIV; medical officer in the forces XVI. ME. *surg(i)en*, – AN. *surgien*, also *sirogen*, *cyrogen*, *sur(r)igien*, contr. of OF. *serurgien*, *cir-* (mod. *chirurgien*; cf. CHIRURGEON) = OIt. *cirugiano*, OPg. *celorgião*, *surgião* (mod. Pg. *cirurgião*) – Rom. **chirurgiānu-s*, f. L. *chirurgia* – Gr. *kheirourgíā*, f. *kheirourgós*, f. *kheír* hand+*erg-* WORK. So **su·rg**ERY surgeon's art XIV; medical practitioner's consulting room XIX. – OF. *surgerie*, contr. of *sirurgerie*, f. *sirurgien*. **su·rg**ICAL pert. to surgery or a surgeon. XVIII. alt. of CHIRURGICAL (XVII), after *surgeon*, *surgery*.

suricate sʲuə·rikeit viverrine burrowing carnivore of S. Africa. XVIII. – F. *suricate*, of native S. African origin.

Surinam sʲuərinæ·m S. American country otherwise called Dutch Guiana, in specific names of animals, plants, and products, from XVIII (Goldsmith).

surly sɔ̄·ɹli †lordly, majestic; †masterful, imperious, haughty XVI; churlishly ill-humoured XVII ('As surly as a butchers dog', Ray, 1670). alt. of †*sirly* (XIV–XVII), f. SIR+-LY¹.

surma sɔ̄·ɹma cosmetic powder used by Indian women. XVII. Urdu – Pers. *surma(h)*.

surmaster sɔ̄·ɹmà·stəɹ second master of St. Paul's School, London. XVI. Alt. of orig. *submaster* (= *hypodidascalus* in Erasmus's lett.) – medL. *submagister*, f. *sub-* SUB- 2 + *magister* MASTER.

surmise səɹmai·z †charge *upon*, allege against XV; †devise, suppose XVI; infer conjecturally XVII. f. AN., OF. *surmis(e)*, pp. of *surmettre* – late L. *supermittere* (in medL. accuse), f. *super* SUPER- + *mittere* put. So sb. †allegation XV; conjecture XVI.

surmount səɹmau·nt rise above. XIV (Ch.). – (O)F. *surmonter*; see SUR-², MOUNT².

surmullet sɔ̄·ɹmʌlit red mullet. XVII (Willoughby). – F. *surmulet*, OF. *sor* (mod. *saur*) red, of unkn. orig., + *mulet* MULLET. Cf. SORREL².

surname sɔ̄·ɹneim †name or epithet added to a person's name(s), derived from his birthplace or from some quality or achievement; person's family name)(Christian name XIV. Partial tr. of †*surnoun* (XIV/XV) – AN. *surnoun*, (O)F. *surnom*, f.

sur- SUR-² + *noun* NAME (cf. NOUN), after medL. *super-, suprānōmen* (cf. late L. *supernōmināre*). Hence vb. XVI.

surpass səɹpɑ̀·s go beyond. XVI. – F. *surpasser*, f. *sur-* SUPER- 2 + *passer* PASS.

surplice sə̄·ɹplis long white linen vestment for eccl. use. XIII. – AN. *surplis*, OF. *sourpelis* (mod. *surplis*) = Pr. *sobrepelitz*, etc. – medL. *superpellicium, -eum* (sc. *vestimentum* garment), sb. use of n. of adj. f. *super* SUPER- 1 + *pellicia* fur garment (see PELISSE); so called because orig. put on over furred garments worn in church. The cons. combination *rpl* occasions various deviations from the normal forms.

surplus sə̄·ɹpləs amount remaining in excess. XIV (Ch.). – AN. *surplus*, OF. *so(u)rplus* (mod. *surplus*) = Pr. *sobreplus* – medL. *superplūs*, f. *super* SUPER- 4 + *plūs* more (see FULL). So **su·rplus**AGE (Lydg.). – medL. *surplūsāgium*.

surprise səɹprai·z (mil.) sudden attack or capture XV (phr. *take by s.*); something unexpectedly sudden XVI; feeling caused by this XVII. – (O)F. *surprise* (corr. to Sp., It. *sorpresa*), sb. use of pp. fem. of *surprendre*. So **surpri·se** vb. †overcome *with* desire, etc. XV (Caxton); assail suddenly, take unawares XVI; affect with surprise XVII. prob. first in pp. f. (O)F. *surpris(e)*, pp. of *surprendre* = Pr. *sobreprendre*, etc. :– medL. *superprehendere*, f. L. *super* SUR- + *præhendere* seize (cf. PREHENSILE); the composition of *overtake* is similar. Earlier vars. are †*supprise* sb. (XV), vb. (XIV), and *susprise* vb. (XIV), based on AN. *supris, souspris*.

surrealism sə̄ɹriə·lizm form of art in which interpretation of dream phenomena is attempted. XX. – F. *surréalisme* (A. Breton, 1924); see SUR-², REALISM. So **surre·a**LIST, **surreali·**STIC.

surrebutter sʌribʌ·təɹ (leg.) plaintiff's reply to a defendant's rebutter. XVII. f. SUR-² + REBUTTER, after **sur**REJOI·NDER (XVI), plaintiff's reply to defendant's rejoinder.

surrender səre·ndəɹ (leg.) giving up of an estate or tenancy; giving up of oneself. XV. – AN. *surrender*, OF. inf. *surrendre* used as sb. (see -ER⁵), whence **surre·nder** vb. XV – AN. *surrender*, OF. *surrendre*; see SUR-, RENDER; cf. AL. *superreddere* (XII), *sursumreddere* (XIII).

surreptitious sʌrepti·ʃəs obtained by fraudulent misrepresentation XV; obtained by stealth XVII. f. L. *surreptītius, -icius*, f. *surrept-*, pp. stem of *surripere* seize secretly, (Vulg.) make false suggestions, f. *sub* SUB- 6 + *rapere* seize (cf. RAPTURE); see -ITIOUS.

surrogate sʌ·rəgət deputy, spec. of a judge, bishop. XVII. – L. *surrogātus*, var. of *subrogātus*, pp. of *subrogāre* put in another's place, f. *sub* SUB- 8 + *rogāre* ask, ask for or propose the appointment of (see ROGATION), rel. to *regere* direct (cf. RULE).

surround sərau·nd †A. overflow XV; B. encompass, go round XVII. – AN. *sur(o)under*, OF. *s(o)uronder* overflow, (also) abound, surpass, dominate = Pr. *sobrondar* :– late L. *superundare* overflow (fig.), f. *super* SUPER- + *undāre* rise in waves, f. *unda* wave (see WATER); cf. ABOUND, REDOUND. ¶ Sense B was expressed earlier by *round* (Sh.), of which *surround* was perh. apprehended as an intensive compound.

surtax sə̄·ɹtæks additional tax. XIX. – F. *surtaxe*; see SUR-, TAX.

surtout sə̄·ɹtū, sūɹtū· greatcoat, overcoat. XVII. – F., f. *sur* above (cf. SUR-) + *tout* everything (:– Rom. **tottum*, for L. *tōtum* n. of *tōtus* TOTAL).

surturbrand sə̄·ɹtəɹbrænd (min.) lignite as occurring in Iceland. XVIII. – G. *surturbrand* – Icel. *surtarbrandr*, f. *Surtar*, g. of *Surtr* (rel. to *svartr* SWART), name of a fire-giant + *brandr* BRAND.

surveillance səɹvei·ləns watch kept over a person or thing. XIX. – F., f. *surveiller*, f. *sur-* + *veiller* watch (:– L. *vigilāre*); see SUR-, VIGILANT, -ANCE.

survey səɹvei· oversee, supervise XV; determine the conditions of (a tract of ground); †inspect; take a wide view of XVI. – AN. *surveier, -veir*, OF. *so(u)rveeir* (pres. stem *survey-*) :– medL. *supervidēre*, f. L. *super* + *vidēre* see; cf. SUR-², VISION. Hence **su·rvey** sb. XVI; earlier †**su·r**VIEW. XV. – AN., OF. *surveue*. So **survey·**OR¹. XV. – AN., OF. *sur-, sorve(i)our*.

survive səɹvai·v remain alive, live on XV; outlive XVI. – AN. *survivre*, OF. *sourvivre* (mod. *sur-*) = Pr. *sobreviure*, etc. – L. *supervīvere*, f. *super* + *vīvere* live; see SUPER- 4, VIVID. Hence **survi·**VAL². XVI (Chapman). **survi·**VOR¹. XVI.

susceptible səse·ptibl capable of undergoing or being affected (by) XVII (Bacon); subject to impression XVIII. – late L. *susceptibilis* (Boethius), f. *suscept-*, pp. stem of *suscipere*, f. *sub* SUB- 7 + *capere* take (cf. CAPABLE). So (O)F. An earlier syn. in the first sense was *susce·ptive* (XVI) – late L. *susceptīvus*.

suslik sʌ·slik species of ground squirrel. XVIII. – Russ. *súslik*; cf. F. *souslic, -lik*.

suspect sʌ·spekt, səspe·kt under suspicion; †having suspicion XIV; sb. suspected person XVI; disused in the adj. after c.1700, and in the sb. after c.1600 until revived in XIX after the F. use of the word for 'one suspected of hostility or indifference to the Revolution' (cf. *la loi des suspects* 1793); – (O)F. *suspect* or L. *suspectus*, pp. of *suspicere* look up (to), admire, suspect, f. *sub* SUB- 7 + *specere* look (cf. ESPY); on the pp. stem of this L. vb. was formed **suspe·ct** vb. XV; cf. F. *suspecter*, Sp. *sospechar*, It. *sospettare*, and *inspect, respect*.

suspend səspe·nd A. hold up, put off XIII (S. Eng. Leg.); B. hang (up) XV. – (O)F. *suspendre* or L. *suspendere,* f. *sub* SUB- 7+ *pendēre* hang (see PENDENT). Hence **suspe·nd**ER[1] †one who suspends XVI; (orig. U.S.) that by which something is suspended XIX. So **suspe·nse** condition of being suspended. XV. – AN., OF. *suspens* or *suspense* abeyance, delay, repr. medL. sb. uses of n. and fem. of pp. of L. *suspendere.* XVI. **suspe·n**SION – (O)F. *suspension* or L. (Vitruvius).

suspicion səspi·ʃən action of suspecting. XIV (R. Mannyng). – AN. *suspeciun,* var. of OF. *sospeçon* (mod. *soupçon*) = Pr. *sospeiso,* Pg. *suspeição* :– medL. *suspectiō(n-).* The earliest forms *suspecio(u)n* began to be superseded before 1400 by assim. to OF. *suspicion* or L. *suspiciō.*

suspire səspaiə·ɹ (arch.) sigh (*for*). XV. – L. *suspirāre,* f. *sub* SUB- 7 + *spirāre* breathe (cf. SPIRANT).

sustain səstei·n †support, uphold the course of, keep in being XIII; endure without failing; bear the weight of XIV. ME. *sos-, susteine* – AN. *sustein-,* OF. *so(u)stein-,* tonic stem of *so(u)stenir* (mod. *soutenir*), corr. to Pr., Sp. *sostener,* It. *sostenere* – L. *sustinēre,* f. *sus-* SUB- 7 + *tenēre* hold, keep (cf. TENOR[1], ATTAIN, *sustein-* etc.). So **susten**ANCE sʌ·stinəns means of subsistence XIII (RGlouc., S. Eng. Leg.); act of sustaining XIV (Ch.). – AN. *sustenaunce,* OF. *so(u)stenance* (mod. *soutenance*). **sustent**A·TION. XIV. – (O)F. or L.

susurration. sʲūsʌrei·ʃən whispering. XIV. – late L. *susurrātiō(n)-,* f. L. *susurrāre,* f. *susurrus* whisper (of imit. origin); see -ATION.

sutler sʌ·tləɹ army follower selling provisions to soldiers. XVI. – Du. †*soeteler* (mod. *zoetelaar*), MLG. *suteler, sudeler,* f. †*soetelen* (whence †**suttle** XVII) befoul, perform mean duties, follow a low trade, f. Germ. **suð-* (see SUDS).

suttee sʌ·tī Hindu woman who immolated herself with her husband's dead body XVIII; such immolation XIX. – Hindi, Urdu :– Skr. *satī* faithful wife, f. *sat* good, wise, lit. being, prp. of *as* BE.

suture sʲū·tjuəɹ sewing, stitching; (anat., bot.) junction. XVI. – F. *suture* or L. *sūtūra,* f. *sūt-,* pp. stem of *suere* SEW; see -URE.

suzerain sū·zərein feudal overlord. XIX. – F. *suzerain,* prob. f. *sus* above, up (:– L. *sūsum,* f. *sub* from below, up + *vorsum,* pp.n. of *vertere* turn; cf. -WARD), after *souverain* SOVEREIGN.

svarabhakti svarabha·kti (philol.) development of a glide vowel between two consonants. XIX. Skr. 'sound-separation'.

svelte svelt slim, slender. XIX. F. *svelte* – It. *svelto* :– popL. **exvellitu-s,* pp. of **exvellere,* f. L. *ex* EX-[1] + *vellere* pluck.

swab swɔb mop XVI; absorbent mass of fabric for cleansing XVIII. So vb. (dial.) sway about XV; mop *up* XVIII; **swa·bb**ER[1] member of a crew that swabs decks. XVI. f. Germ. base meaning 'sway about', 'splash in water', as in (M)LG. *swabben* splash, sway, slap, Norw. *svabba* splash, wade, LG. *swabber* (G. *schwabber*) mop, swab, Du. *zwabberen* mop.

swaddle swɔ·dl bind (an infant) in lengths of bandage. XV. f. SWATHE + -LE[3]. The earliest record of the formation is in *swaðelbond* swaddling-clothes XIII; for the phonology cf. FIDDLE. Hence **swa·ddl**ING[1]-*band(s)* XIV, *clothes,* †*clouts* XVI.

swag swæg (dial.) swaying movement XVII; ornamental wreath or festoon XVIII; thief's booty XIX. Sc. vb. (dial.) move or cause to move unsteadily XVI; sink down XVII. Of obscure origin; cf. Norw. *swagga* sway.

swage sweidʒ tool for bending cold metal. XIX. – F. *suage,* earlier *souage,* of unkn. origin. Also **swedge.** XIX.

swagger swæ·gəɹ behave overbearingly as if among inferiors. XVI (Nashe, Sh.). Presumably f. SWAG + -ER[4]. ¶ Chapman (1598) describes it as 'created as it were by a naturall *Prosopopeia,* without etimologie or deriuation'.

Swahili swahī·li (one of) a Bantu people inhabiting Zanzibar and the adjacent coast; their language. XIX. adj. formation on Arab. *sawāḥil,* pl. of *sāḥil* coast.

swain swein †young man attending on a knight; man of low degree XII; †male servant; †man, youth XIII; farm hand, shepherd, rustic; (country) lover XVI. ME. *swein* (Peterborough Chron., Laȝ.) – ON. *sveinn* boy, servant, attendant = OE. *swān* swineherd, MLG. *swēn,* OHG. *swein* (G. dial. *schwein*) :– Germ. **swainaz.* See also BOATSWAIN, COXSWAIN.

swallow[1] swɔ·lou bird of the genus Hirundo. OE. *swealwe* = OS. *swala,* OHG. *swal(a)wa* (Du. *zwaluw,* G. *schwalbe*), ON. *svala* :– CGerm. (exc. Gothic) **swalwōn*; other Germ. types (1) lack *w* in the final syll., (2) have an *m*-suffix, (3) have a dim. *k*-suffix; Russ. *solovej,* Czech *slavík* nightingale are assumed to be cognate.

swallow[2] swɔ·lou take into the stomach through the mouth and gullet; transf. and fig. OE. *swelgan,* pt. *swealh, swulgon,* pp. *swolgen* = OS. *far|swelgan,* OHG. *swel(a)han, swalh, giswolgan* (Du. *swelgen,* G. *schwelgen*), ON. *svelga, svalg, sulgu, solginn* :– CGerm. str. vb. (not in Goth.). f. **swelg-* **swalg-* **swulg-,* repr. also by OE. *ġeswelg* gulf, abyss, OHG. *swelgo* glutton, ON. *svelgr* whirlpool, devourer, *sylgr* draught. ¶ Weak forms of pt. and pp. appeared XIV. The encroachment of the *o* of the pp. and the *a* of the pt. upon the present was from XII and XIII respectively.

swami swā·mi Hindu idol XVIII; Hindu religious teacher XX. – Hindi *svāmī* master, lord, prince (used as a respectful address) :– Skr. *svamin* (also) idol, temple.

swamp swɔmp low-lying wet ground. XVII (Capt. Smith); (local) depression in land XVIII (Ray). Identical in form with (dial.) *swamp* sunk (XIV), the notion of 'depression, subsidence' being perh. the connecting link. Hence vb. (orig. pass.). XVII.

swan swɔn bird of the genus Cygnus. OE. *swan* = OS. *suan*, OHG. **swan*, *swon* (G. *schwan*), ON. *svanr* :– CGerm. (exc. Goth.) **swanaz* str. m., of which vars. **swanon* wk. m. and **swanōn* wk. fem. are repr. by MLG., MDu. *swāne* (Du. *zwaan*), OHG. *swana* (G. dial. *schwane*). perh. appropriated orig. to the 'musical' swan, and so based on IE. **swon-* **swen-*, repr. by Skr. *svanás* noise, *svánati* it sounds, L. *sonere*, *sonāre* SOUND[2], Ir. *sennaim* I make music. comp. **swa·n-upp**ING[1] taking up swans to mark them for ownership. XVI. *upping* f. *up* vb. drive up and catch swans. XVI.

swanimote swɔ·nimout, **swainmote** swei·nmout assembly for superintending the clearance of the king's woods of pigs and cattle. XII. repr. OE. **swānġemōt* 'meeting of swineherds', f. *swān* swineherd + *ġemōt* MOOT; the first syll. was assim. to SWAIN.

swank swæŋk (sl.) behave ostentatiously. XIX. A word of the midland areas, having a wide application as of activity or vigour, taken into gen. sl. use early in XX.

swap, swop swɔp †strike, hit; †move quickly; †strike hands on a bargain XIV; strike (a bargain); exchange *for* XVI. prob. imit. of a smart resounding blow; cf. G. dial. *schwappe* in same sense, *schwappen* make a clapping or splashing noise, and ints. G. *schwapp(s)*, LG. *swaps*. The development of sense from striking to concluding a bargain is paralleled in *strike* and L. *fœdus ferīre* 'strike' a treaty'. Hence **swap, swop** sb. XIV.

sward swɔ̄ɹd †skin of the body, (dial.) rind of pork OE.; upper layer of the earth XV (esp. *greensward* XV; cf. MLG. *grönswarde*). OE. *sweard*, corr. to OFris., MLG., MDu. *swarde* hairy skin, MHG. *swarte* (G. *schwarte* bacon rind, crust), ON. *svǫrðr* skin (of the head), walrus hide, *svard-* in comb., (also) greensward; of unkn. origin. The OE. word, if indeed it survived, was reinforced in ME. by the Scand. and LG. forms.

swarm[1] swɔ̄ɹm body of bees in a compact mass. OE. *swearm* = OS., MLG. *swarm*, OHG. *swar(a)m* (G. *schwarm*), ON. *svarmr* :– CGerm. (exc. Gothic) **swarmaz*, usu. referred to the base of Skr. *svárati* it sounds, L. *susurrus* hum. Hence vb. gather in a swarm or dense crowd. XIV (Ch.). Cf., with mutation, OE. *swirman*, **swierman* = MLG., MDu. *swermen*, MHG. *swärmen* (G. *schwärmen*). But perh. the base is that of SWERVE.

swarm[2] swɔ̄ɹm climb *up* a pole, etc. XVI. Of unkn. origin.

swart swɔ̄ɹt (arch., dial.) of dark colour. OE. *sweart* = OFris., OS. *swart*, OHG. *swarz* (Du. *zwart*, G. *schwarz*), ON. *svartr*, Goth. *swarts* :– CGerm. **swartaz* (a gradation-var. is repr. by ON. *sorta* black colour, *sorte* dark cloud). ¶ A plausible connexion is seen in the base of SORDID.

swarthy swɔ̄·ɹði of dark hue, blackish. XVI. unexpl. alt. of †*swarty*, extension of *swart* with -Y[1] to produce an adjectival appearance.

swash[1] swɔʃ dash violently, make a noise as of clashing swords XVI. imit.; cf. *clash*, *dash*, *crash*, *lash*, *mash*. comp. **swa·sh-**BU:CKLER swaggerer XVI; lit. one who makes a blustering noise by striking his own or his opponent's shield with his sword.

swash[2] swɔʃ (in turning, etc.) inclined obliquely to the axis of the work; (typogr.) having flourished strokes to fill gaps XVII. Cf. †*aswash* crosswise, aslant (XVI). Of unkn. origin.

swastika swæ·stikə, swɔ·- the symbol 卐. XIX. – Skr. *svastika*, f. *svastí* well-being, fortune, luck, f. *sú* good + *astí* being (f. *as* BE).

swat[1] swɔt (dial.) squat XVII; hit smartly XVIII. dial. var. of SQUAT.

swat[2] see SWOT.

swath swɔ̄þ †track, trace OE.; width of grass, etc. cut, measure of grass land; now of grass, etc. reaped XIV. OE. *swæþ* and *swaþu*, corr. to OFris. *swethe*, MLG. *swat*, *swāde* (Du. *zwad*, *zwade*), MHG. *swade* (G. *schwade*). The var. *swathe* sweið is now characteristic of the north.

swathe sweið wrapping of linen, etc. Late OE. **swæþ*, only in d. pl. *swaþum*; rel. to **swathe** vb. late OE. *swaþian*. Cf. SWADDLE.

sway swei †bias; rule, dominion XVI. So vb. move or swing to one side and the other XVI. corr. formally to Du. *zwaaien* swing, wave, walk totteringly, LG. *swājen* move to and fro as with the wind; but preceded by late ME. *sweigh*, *sweye*, applied to sweeping or swinging motion, the vocalism of which corr. to that of ON. *sveigja* bend, (intr.) give way; the history is obscure.

swear swɛəɹ pt. **swore** swɔ̄əɹ, pp. **sworn** swɔ̄ɹn A. take a solemn oath, intr. and trans. B. bind by an oath. C. use profane language XV. OE. *swerian*, pt. *swōr* (rarely *swerede*), pp. *-swaren*, usu. *sworen* = OFris. *swaria*, *swera*, OS. *swerian*, OHG. *swer(i)an*, *swōr*, *gisworan* (Du. *zweren*, G. *schwören*), ON. *sverja* :– CGerm. str. vb. (sporadically wk.) :– Germ. **swarjan* (but Gothic *swaran*) f. **swar-*, repr. also by ON. *svar*, *svara* answer (sb. and vb.), OE. *and|swaru* ANSWER; the ult. origin is disputed. From early times the conjugation has been infl. by *bear*, whence the frequency and persistence of pt. *sware*. comp. **swea·r-**WORD (orig. U.S.). XIX.

sweat swet emit sweat, intr. and trans. work hard. OE. *swǣtan* = MLG., MDu. *swēten* (Du. *zweeten*), OHG. *sweizzan* roast (G. *schweissen* fuse, weld) :- Germ. **swaitjan*, f. **swaitaz*, whence OE. *swāt*, OFris., OS. *swēt* (Du. *zweet*), OHG. *sweiz* (G. *schweiss*), beside **swaiton*, whence ON. *sveiti* sweat; IE. base **swoid-*, whence also L. *sūdor* (:- **swoidōs*), Skr. *svḗdas*; from the grade **swid-* are Gr. *hidrṓs*, W. *chwŷs*, Lett. (pl.) *swiēdri*, Skr. *svídyate*, OHG. *swizzen* (G. *schwitzen*) sweat. **sweat** sb. †life-blood (so OE. *swāt*); hard work XIII; moisture excreted through the pores XIV; colloq. (orig. Sc. and U.S.) state of impatience or anxiety XVIII. Superseded ME. *swote* (OE. *swāt*; see above). **sweat**ER[1] swe·təɹ XVI; vest of wool to protect from cold XIX.

Swede swīd native of Sweden XVII; (for earlier *Swedish turnip* XVII) Brassica campestris, variety Rutabaga XIX. - MLG., MDu. *Swēde* (Du. *Zweed*), prob. - ON. *Svíþjóð* 'people of the Swedes', Sweden, f. *Svíar* Swedes + *þjóð* people.

swedge swedʒ see SWAGE.

sweep swīp pt., pp. **swept** A. remove with or as with a broom or brush; clear (a surface) in this way XIII; B. intr. move with a strong or swift even motion XIV. ME. *swepe*, in earliest use mainly northern, repl. ME. *swōpe* (OE. *swāpan*), either by extension of the vowel *ē* of the pt. (OE. *swēop*), or by development ĭ to ē in OE. **swipian* (pt. *swipode*) scourge, or ON. intr. *svipa*; shortening of vowel in pt. and pp. is shown before 1400. Hence **sweep** sb. in many uses covered by the definitions 'act of sweeping' (from XVI) and 'apparatus for sweeping' (from XV); in the sense 'chimney-sweeper' (XIX) preceded by *chimney-sweep* and †*sweep-chimney* (both XVII). comp. **sweep**STAKE swī·psteik †one who takes the whole of the stakes in a game XV (used as a ship's name till XVII); †total removal XVI; (prize won in) a contest in which the stakes are contributed by the competitors. XVIII.

sweet swīt pleasing to the senses or the mind; dearly loved or prized; kindly, gracious. OE. *swēte* = OFris. *swēte*, OS. *swōti*, OHG. *s(w)uozi* (Du. *zoot*, G. *süss*), ON. *sǿtr* :- Germ. **swōtja-*, **swōti-* (not in Goth., which shows another grade, *suts*), f. **swōt-* :- IE. **swād-* (**swad-*), repr. by Skr. *svādús*, Gr. *hēdús*, *ϝādús* sweet, *hḗdesthai* rejoice, *hēdonḗ* pleasure, *handánein* please (*héadon*, *héada*), L. *suāvis* (:- **swadwis*) SUAVE, *suādēre* advise (prop. make something pleasant to; cf. DISSUADE, PERSUADE). comp. **swee·tbread** pancreas. XVI; perh. OE. *brǣd* flesh = OS. *brādo* ham, calf of leg, etc.; but the reason for the name is unkn. **swee·t**EN[5] make sweet XVI; superseding *sweet* vb. OE. *swētan*. **swee·t**HEART darling XIII; loved one XVI; **swee·t**IE sweetmeat XVIII; sweet one XIX. **swee·t**ING[3] sweetheart XIII; sweet variety of apple XVI. **swee·t**MEAT †sweet cake, etc.; sugarplum, lollipop XV; cf. OE. *swēt-*, *swōtmettas* dainties. **sweet william** species of pink, Dianthus barbatus XVI (Tusser). Hence sb. XIII (Cursor M.); **swee·t**LY[2], -NESS; OE.

swell swel pt. **swelled** sweld pp. **swollen** swou·lən, **swelled** become larger or greater. OE. *swellan*, pt. *sweall*, *swullon*, pp. *-swollen* = OFris. **swella* (in 3rd sg. pres. ind. *swilith*), OS. **swellan* (in 3rd pl. *suellad*), Du. *zwellen*, OHG. *swellan*, *swall*, *s(w)ulum*, *gis(w)ollen* (G. *schwellen*, *schwoll*, †*schwall*, *geschwollen*), ON. *svella*, *sval*, *sullu*, *sollinn* :- Germ. str. vb. **swellan*, to which corr. causative **swalljan* (cf. Goth. *ufswalleins* being puffed up), repr. by MLG., MDu. *swellen*, etc.; no cogns. outside Germ. are known. **swell** sb. †morbid swelling XIII; condition of being swollen, protuberance; heaving of the sea XVII.

swelter swe·ltəɹ be oppressed with heat XV (Lydg.); be oppressive with heat XVI. f. base of (dial.) *swelt* be overcome as with heat (XIV), OE. *sweltan*, pt. *swealt*, *swulton*, pp. *ġeswolten* die, perish = OS. *sweltan*, OHG. *swelzan*, ON. *svelta*, Goth. *swiltan* :- CGerm. str. vb. See -ER[4].

swerve swə̄ɹv turn aside, deviate in movement. XIV. repr. formally OE. *sweorfan*, pt. *swearf*, pp. *sworfen* file, scour.

swift[1] swift moving far in a short time, taking place at high speed. OE. *swift*, f. base of *swīfan* move in a course, sweep (ME. *swive* copulate with) = ON. *svífa*; rel. further to OFris. *swīvia*, OHG. *sweib*, *sweibōn*, *swibōn*, *swebēn*, ON. *sveifla*. Cf. SWIVEL. Hence **swift**[2] (dial.) applied to various swiftly-moving reptiles XVI; bird of the family Cypselidæ XVII. ¶ The sense is peculiar to English.

swift[3] swift (naut.) make fast with ropes drawn taut. XV. prob. rel. to ME. †*swift* (XIV), ? syn. of *swifter* (XVII) rope used for swifting or binding, etc.; presumably of Scand. or LG. origin, and - base repr. by ON. *svipta* reef (sails), *sviftingar* reefing-ropes, Du. *zwichten* take in (sails), *zwichtlings*, *zwichtlijnen* cat-harpings, and ult. allied to SWIFT[1].

swig swig (dial.) drink, liquor (applied dial. to special drinks) XVI; deep draught XVII. Hence **swig** vb. drink eagerly or copiously. Of unkn. origin.

swill swil wash or rinse out OE.; drink greedily or to excess XVI; flow freely XVII. OE. *swillan*, *swilian*, of which no certain cogns. are known. Hence sb. liquid food XVI; copious drinking, liquor XVII.

swim swim pt. **swam** swæm, pp. **swum** swʌm float or progress by moving the limbs on the surface of liquid. OE. *swimman*, pt. *swam(m)*, *swummon*, pp. *swummen* = OS., OHG. *swimman* (Du. *zwemmen*, G. *schwimmen*), ON. *svim(m)a* :- CGerm.

(exc. Goth.) *swemjan, f. *swem- *swam- *swum- (whence OE., ON. *sund* SOUND[1], OFris. *swimma, swommia* swim, Goth. *swumfsl* pool); pt. *swam* superseded normal *swom* by assoc. with *began, drank, sank*. Hence **swim** sb. XVI.

swindle swi·ndl practise fraud. XVIII. back-formation f. **swi·ndl**ER[1] – G. *schwindler* giddy-minded person, extravagant projector, cheat, f. (M)HG. *schwindeln*, OHG. *suintilōn*, frequent. (cf. -LE[3]) of *swintan* (= OE., OS. *swindan*) waste away, languish, lose consciousness, f. **swī-*, repr. also in OE. *swīma*, LG. *swīmel* dizziness.

swine swain animal of the genus Sus, pig. OE. *swīn* = OFris., OS., OHG. *swīn* (Du. *swijn*, G. *schwein*), ON. *svín*, Goth. *swein* :– CGerm. **swīnam*, sb. use of n. of adj. (cf. L. *suīnus*, OSl. *svinŭ* pert. to swine, and see -INE[1]), f. IE. **suw-*, repr. by L. *sūs*, etc. (see SOW[1]). comp. **swi·ne-**HERD[2]; late OE. *swȳnhyrde*. ¶ The orig. use may have been generic or restricted to the young of the animal; for the latter cf. OHG. *geizzīn*, Goth. *gaitein* kid. For parallel uses of the suffix cf. OE. *gǣten* of goats, L. *hædīnus* of kids; OE. *tiċċen* kid, *ċycen* CHICKEN, Du. *veulen* foal; see -EN[1].

swing swiŋ pt., pp. **swung** swʌŋ †A. scourge, flog OE.; †B. move impetuously OE.; C. flourish, brandish (a weapon, etc.) XIV; D. move backwards and forwards XVI. OE. *swingan*, pt. *swang, swungon*, pp. *ġeswungen* = OFris. *swinga, swanga, swenga*, (M)LG. *swingen*, OHG. *swingan* (G. *schwingen* brandish, shake, winnow, swingle, intr. or refl. oscillate, bound, rise); cf. Germ. **sweŋg* **swaŋg* (cf. Goth. *afswaggwidai*, rendering ἐξαπορηθῆναι be in doubt), parallel to **sweŋkan* swink. The vowel of the pp. was finally established in the pt.

Swing swiŋ designating a system of intimidation practised in the south of England in 1830–1, and consisting of threatening letters signed by a fictitious Captain Swing.

swinge swin^{d}ʒ beat, flog, whip. XVI. Later form of ME. *swenge* smite, dash, OE. *swenġan* shake, shatter :– **swaŋgwjan*, as in Goth. *afswaggwidai*. Hence **swinge**ING[2] very forcible or large, immense XVI; cf. *thumping, whopping*. **swinger**ER[1] swi·n^{d}ʒəɹ vigorous or forcible †person or thing. XVI.

swingle swi·ŋgl wooden instrument for beating hemp, etc. XIV. – MDu. *swinghel*, corr. formally to OE. *swingel, swingle* stroke with a rod; see SWING, -LE[1].

swipe swaip drink hastily and copiously; strike *at*. XIX. perh. local var. of SWEEP. Hence sb. heavy blow. XIX.

swipes swaips beer, esp. weak beer. XVIII. perh. f. prec.

swirl swə̄ɹl whirlpool XV (Wyntoun); twist, whirling motion XVIII. orig. Sc., perh. of LDu. origin (cf. Du. *zwirrelen* whirl) and frequent. formation (cf. -LE[3]) on the imit. base seen in MLG. *swirren*, G. *schwirren*, Da. *svirre* whirl.

swish swiʃ make a sound as of an object moving forcibly through air or water. XVIII. imit. So int. and sb.

Swiss swis pert. to, native of, Switzerland. XVI. – F. *Suisse* – MHG. *Swīz* (G. *Schweiz*). So †**Swisser** (XVI–XVII) – MDu. *Switser* or MHG. *S(ch)wycer, S(ch)wītzer* (now *Schweizer*), f. *Swīz(en-)* Switzerland.

switch switʃ slender tapering riding-whip XVI (Sh.); thin flexible shoot XVII; mechanical device for altering direction XVIII; long bunch or coil of hair XIX. In early use also *swits, switz*; prob. – LG. word repr. by Hanoverian dial. *swutsche*, var. of LG. *swukse* long thin stick (cf. *zwuksen* bend up and down, make a swishing noise). comp. **swi·tchback** form of railway used on steep slopes, in which the train or car can be 'switched back' (BACK adv.) or reversed. XIX.

swither swi·ðəɹ hesitate, vacillate. XVI (Douglas). orig. Sc., of unkn. origin.

swivel swi·vl fastening device on which the object fastened turns freely. XIV. f. wk. grade of OE. *swīfan* (see SWIFT)+-EL[1].

swizzle swi·zl intoxicating drink. XIX. Of unkn. origin. Cf. U.S. *switchel*.

swoon swūn fall into a fainting-fit. XIII. perh. back-formation from ME. gerund *swoȝning, swouning, swoning*, f. *iswoȝen, iswowen*, OE. *ġeswogen* overcome, dead, pp. of **swogan*, as in *ā-, oferswogan* suffocate, choke (with weeds), of unkn. origin. So sb., orig. in phr. *i(n) swowne*, etc., alt. of *aswowne*, repr. OE. *āswogen*, pp. of *āswogan*; a var. with parasitic *d*, *swound* sb. (XV) and vb. (XVI), is dialectal.

swoop swūp †sweep along as with trailing garments XVI; †pounce upon XVII; come down suddenly *upon* XVIII. perh. dial. development of ME. *swōpe*, OE. *swāpan* SWEEP.

swoosh swūʃ imit. of the sound made by rushing air or water. XIX. Cf. SWISH.

swop var. of SWAP.

sword sɔ̄ɹd weapon for cutting and thrusting. OE. *sword, sweord, swyrd* = OFris., OS. *swerd*, OHG. *swert* (G. *schwert*), ON. *sverð* :– CGerm. (exc. Goth.) **swerðam*, of doubtful origin. For loss of *w* cf. TWO.

swot, swat swɔt (sl.) vb. and sb. study at school or college. XIX. dial. var. of SWEAT.

-sy si, (after voiced cons.) zi terminal el. of uncertain origin; perh. generalized from *arsy-versy* XVI (f. ARSE + L. *versā*, from VICE VERSA), as in contemp. *topsy-turvy*; in hypocoristic and trivial use, perh. after *Betsy*, pet-form of *Elizabeth*, e.g. *fubsy* fat and squat (XVIII), *pudsy* plump (XVIII), *tricksy* (XVI), *flimsy* (XVIII), *tipsy* (XVI), *tootsy* (XIX), and the group *babsy, ducksy, mopsy, popsy(-wopsy)*.

syagush sjā·gūʃ caracal. XVIII. Urdu, – Pers. *siyāh gūsh* black ear.

sybarite si·bərait person devoted to luxury or pleasure; also adj. XVI. – L. *Sybarita* – Gr. *Subarītēs*, f. *Súbaris*, ancient Greek city of S. Italy, noted for its effeminacy and luxury; see -ITE and cf. F. *sybarite* (XVI).

sycamine si·kəmin, -main black mulberry, Morus nigra. XVI. – L. *sȳcamīnus* – Gr. *sūkáminon*, f. Heb. *shiqmah*, with assim. to *sûkon* fig.

sycamore, sycomore si·kəmɔəɹ species of fig-tree, Ficus Sycomorus XIV; species of maple, Acer Pseudoplatanus XVI. – OF. *sic(h)amor* (mod. *sycomore*) – L. *sȳcomorus* – Gr. *sūkómoros*, f. *sûkon* fig + *móron* mulberry.

syce sais in India, groom, follower on foot of horseman or carriage. XVII. Hind. – Arab. *sāis*, f. *sūs* tend a horse.

sycee saisī· fine uncoined silver in lumps. XVIII. Chinese *sí* (pronounced in Canton *sai, sei*) *sz'* fine silk.

sychnocarpous si:knoukā·ɹpəs (bot.) bearing fruit many times. XIX. f. Gr. *sukhnós* many + *karpós* fruit + -OUS.

sycophant si·kəfənt one of a class of informers in ancient Greece; mean flatterer, toady. XVI. – F. *sycophante* or L. *sȳcophanta* – Gr. *sūkophántēs*, f. *sûkon* fig + **phan-*, base of *phaínein* show (cf. HIEROPHANT, EPIPHANY).

sycosis saikou·sis ulcer or eruption resembling a fig. XVI. – modL. *sycōsis* – Gr. *sūkōsis*, f. *sûkon* fig; see -OSIS.

syenite sai·ənait (min.) crystalline rock allied to granite. XVIII. – F. *syénite*, G. *syenit* – L. *syēnītēs* (sc. *lapis* stone), f. *Syēnē*, Gr. *Suḗnē* town of Upper Egypt, Aswan; see -ITE.

syl- sil assim. from of SYN- before *l*.

syllable si·ləbl vocal sound or sounds uttered with a single effort of articulation. XIV (Ch., Gower, Trevisa). – AN. *sillable*, alt. of OF. *sillabe* (mod. *syllabe*) = Sp. *silaba*, It. *sillaba* – L. *syllaba* (Plautus) – Gr. *sullabḗ*, f. *sullambánein* take, put, or bring together, f. *sun* SYN- + *lambánein* take, f., **lab-*. So **syllab**ARY si·ləbəri set or table of syllables. XVI. – modL. *syllabārium*, n. sg. of late L. *syllabārius*; cf. F. *syllabaire*. **syllab**IC silæ·bik. XVII (†-ICAL XVI). – medL. *syllabicus* – Gr. *sullabikós*; cf. late L. *syllabicē* (adv.). **syllabic**A·TION silæbikei·ʃən. XVII. – medL., f. *syllabicāre* (Priscian). **sylla:bi**FICA·TION formation of or division into syllables. XIX. – medL., f. *syllabificāre*. **syllab**ISM si·ləbizm. XIX; perh. after F. *syllabisme*. **syllab**IZE si·ləbaiz divide into syllables. XVII. – medL. – Gr.

syllabub see SILLABUB.

syllabus si·ləbəs pl. **-bi** bai, **-buses** bəsiz concise statement or table of heads of a discourse, etc. XVII. – modL. *syllabus*, originating in a misprint in early editions (1470) of *syllabos* for *sittýbas*, in Cicero's Letters to Atticus (IV iv), acc. pl. of *sittyba* – Gr. *sittúbā* title-slip or label; *syllabos* was græcized later as συλλάβους, whence a spurious σύλλαβος was deduced and accepted as a deriv. of συλλαμβάνειν put together (cf. SYLLABLE).

syllepsis sile·psis (gram.) figure by which one word or form is made to refer to two or more in the same sentence while strictly applying to only one. XVI. – late L. *syllēpsis* – Gr. *súllēpsis*, f. *sún* SYN- + *lêpsis* taking, f. *lēb- lāb- lab-*, base of *lambánein* take.

syllogism si·lədʒizm argument expressed in the form of two propositions called the premisses and a third called the conclusion. XIV (Trevisa, Gower). Late ME. *silogisme*, occas. *silogime* – OF. *sil(l)ogisme*, earlier *silogime* (mod. *syllogisme*) or L. *syllogismus* (whence also Sp., It. *silogismo*) – Gr. *sullogismós*, f. *sullogízesthai*, intensive of *logízesthai* reckon, compute, conclude, f. *lógos* discourse, consideration, account; see SYN-, LOGOS, -ISM. So **syllogi**·STIC. XVII, -ICAL. XVI. – L. *syllogisticus* (Quintilian) – Gr. *sullogistikós*, f. *sullogízesthai*. **sy·llog**IZE. XV (Lydg.). – OF. *sil(l)ogiser* – late L. *syllogizāre* (Boethius) – Gr. *sullogízesthai*.

sylph silf one of a race of beings supposed to inhabit the air. XVII. – modL. pl. *sylphes* and *sylphi*, G. pl. *sylphen*, of uncertain origin, but perh. based by Paracelsus (Theophrast von Hohenheim) on L. *sylvestris* of the woods and *nympha* nymph. So **sy·lph**ID[1]. XVII. – F. *sylphide*.

sylvan, silvan si·lvən sb. inhabitant of the woods; adj. pert. to a wood or woods, wooded. XVI. – F. *sylvain*, †*silvain*, or L. *silvānus*, *syl-* (only as the name of a god), f. *silva* wood; see -AN. ¶ The sp. with *y* is by assoc. with Gr. *hū́lē* (see HYLIC) wood.

sym- sim assim. form of SYN- before *m*, *b*, *p*.

symbol si·mbəl summary of Christian belief, creed XV (Caxton); something that represents something else XVI (Spenser); written character XVII. – ChrL. *symbolum* (whence F. *symbole*, Sp., It. *simbolo*) – Gr. *súmbolon* mark, token, ticket, watchword, outward sign, covenant, f. *sún* SYN- + **bol-*, as in *bolḗ*, *bólos* a throw (cf. *sum|bállein* put together), rel. to *bállein* throw (cf. BALLISTIC, EMBLEM, PROBLEM). So **symbol**IC(AL) -bɔ·likəl. XVII. – F. *symbolique* or late L. *symbolicus* – Gr. *sumbolikós*. **sy·mbol**IZE †agree, harmonize; have similar qualities (techn. term of early physics said of substances having qualities in common) XVI; be a symbol of XVII.

symmetry si·mĭtri †mutual relation of parts, proportion; due or just proportion.

XVI. – F. †*symmetrie* (mod. *symétrie*) or L. *symmetria* (whence also Sp. *simetria*, It. *simmetria*) – Gr. *summetriā*, f. *súmmetros* commensurable, proportionable, in due measure, symmetrical, f. *sún* SYM-+*métron* measure; see METRE, -Y³. Hence **sym-me·tr**ICAL. XVIII (J.).

sympathy si·mpəþi affinity; agreement; conformity of feelings or temperament. XVI (Sidney, Lyly, Sh., Spenser; earlier in L. form). – L. *sympathīa* (whence F. *sympathie*) – Gr. *sumpátheia*, f. *sumpathḗs* having a fellow-feeling, f. *sún* SYM-+ **path-* base of *páthos* feeling, PATHOS; see -Y³. So **sym**PATHE·TIC. XVII. – modL. – Gr. *sumpathētikós*, f. *sumpatheîn*. **sy·mpath**IZE. be affected like another XVI; have a fellow-feeling XVII. – F. *sympathiser*, f. *sympathie*.

symphony si·mfəni †used vaguely for musical instruments XIII (S. Eng. Leg.); †harmony XV; (mus.) passage for instruments XVII (spec. XVIII). – (O)F. †*sim-*, *symphonie* – L. *symphōnia* instrumental harmony, voices in concert, (Vulg.) musical instrument – Gr. *sumphōniā*, f. *súmphōnos* harmonious, f. *sún* SYM-+*phōnḗ* sound; see PHONETIC, -Y³.

symphysis si·mfisis (anat.) union of two bones. XVI. – modL. *symphysis* – Gr. *súmphusis*, esp. of bones, f. *sún* SYM- + *phúsis* growth (see PHYSIC). *sumphúein* grow together.

symposium simpou·ziəm drinking party, convivial meeting for conversation, etc.; meeting for discussion. XVIII. – L. *symposium* – Gr. *sumpósion*, f. *sumpótēs* fellow-drinker, f. *sún* SYM- + **pot-* (cf. POTION). Earlier (XVI, Sydney) the latinized title of one of Plato's dialogues in which Socrates and others discuss the nature of love. Also **sympo·si**AC convivial; †sb. symposium. XVII. – L. – Gr.

symptom si·mᵖtəm perceptible change in the body indicating disease XVI; (gen.) XVII. Earlier in late L. form *symptōma* – Gr. *súmptōma* chance, accident, mischance, f. *sumpíptein* fall upon, happen to, f. *sún* SYM-+*píptein* fall. So **symptom**A·TIC. XVII, -ATICAL. XVI. – F. or late L. (cf. Gr. συμπτωματικός exposed to chance).

syn- sin latinized form of Gr. *sun-*, comb. form of *sún* prep. together, similarly, alike, in many words of Gr. origin and mod. scientific terms; assim. before *l* to *syl-*, before *b*, *p*, *m* to *sym-*, before simple *s* to *sys-*, before *s*+consonant and *z* to *sy-*.

synæresis siniə·rĭsis contraction of two vowels. XVI. – late L. *synæresis* – Gr. *sunaíresis*, f. *sún* SYN- + *haireîn* take (cf. HERESY).

synagogue si·nəgɔg congregation of Jews for worship XII; building for Jewish worship XIII. ME. *sinagoge* – OF. *sinagoge* (mod. *synagogue*) – late L. *synagōga* – Gr. *sunagōgḗ* meeting, assembly, in LXX. synagogue, f. *sunágein* bring together, assemble, f. *sún* SYN- + *ágein* lead, bring (cf. ACT). The present form, with pronunc. assim. to L., appears regularly from XVI, occas. XIII.

synalœpha sinəlī·fə coalescence of vowels. XVI. – L. *synalœpha* (Quintilian) – Gr. *sunaloiphḗ*, f. *sunaleíphein* smear or melt together, f. *sún* SYN-+*aleíphein* anoint.

synchronic sinkrɔ·nik belonging to the same time. XIX. f. late L. *synchronus* – Gr. *súgkhronos*, f. *sún* SYN-+*khrónos* time (cf. CHRONIC). So **synchro·n**ICAL. XVII. **synchron**ISM si·nkrŏnizm. XVI. – modL. – Gr. **sy·nchron**IZE. XVII. **sy·nchron**OUS coincident in time. XVII. f. late L. *synchronus* – Gr.

syncopation siŋkŏpei·ʃən (gram.) contraction of a word by elision of one or more syllables XVI (Palsgr.); (mus.) beginning a note on a normally unaccented part of the bar and continuing it into the normally accented part XVI (Morley). – medL. *syncopātiō(-n)*, f. late L. *syncopāre*, f. *syncopē*; see next, -ATION.

syncope si·ŋkəpi (path.) failure of the heart's action; grammatical syncopation. XVI. Earlier *syncopis*, incorrect nom. inferred from *syncopin*, var. of L. accus. *syncopen*; also occas. †*syncopa* †*syncop*. – late L. *syncopē* (which superseded it) – Gr. *sugkopḗ*, f. *sún* SYN-+*kop-* strike, cut off.

syncretism si·ŋkritizm union of opposite tenets, etc. XVII; (philol.) merging of cases XX. – modL. *syncrētismus* – Gr. *sugkrētismós*, f. *sugkrētízein*.

synderesis see SYNTERESIS.

syndic si·ndik civil magistrate in some countries of Europe; one deputed to represent a corporation. XVII. – (O)F. *syndic*, †*-ique* delegate, chief magistrate of Geneva, corr. to Pr. *sendegue*, Sp. *sindico*, Pg. *syndico*, It. *sindaco* – late L. *syndicus* delegate of a corporation – Gr. *súndikos* defendant's advocate, f. *sún* SYN-+**dik*, base of *díkē* judgement, *deíknusthai* show; see TEACH, -IC. So **sy·ndical**ISM industrial unionism. XX. – F. *syndicalisme*, f. *syndical*, as in *chambre syndicale* trade union. **sy·ndic**ATE¹ †office of a syndic; body of syndics XVII; combination of financiers or other promoters of enterprise XIX. – F. *syndicat* – medL. *syndicātus*.

syndrome si·ndroum, -drəmi (path.) concurrence of symptoms XVI; †concurrence, concourse XVII. – modL. *syndromē* – Gr. *sundromḗ*, f. *sún* SYN-+**drom-*, *drameîn* run.

syne sain (Sc. and north.) immediately afterwards, thereupon; later; since then XIV; before now, ago XV (esp. in *lang syne* long ago, made familiar by Burns's 'Auld Lang Syne').

synecdoche sine·kdəki (rhet.) figure by which the part is put for the whole or vice versa. – L. *synecdochē* – Gr. *sunekdokhḗ*, f. *sunekdékhesthai*, f. *sún* SYN- + *ekdékhesthai* take up.

synizesis sinizī·sis (gram., pros.) coalescence of two adjacent vowels without forming a recognized diphthong. XIX. – late L. *synizēsis* – Gr. *sunízēsis*, f. *sunizánein* sink down, f. *sún* SYN-+*hizánein*, f. *hízein* sit.

synod si·nəd assembly of clergy. XIV (Trevisa). – late L. *synodus* – Gr. *súnodos* meeting, f. *sún* SYN- + *hodós* way, travel. So **sy·nod**AL[1]. XV. – late L.

synonym si·nənim any of two or more words of the same meaning. XVI. In early use first in pl. in L. form (*-a*) or anglicized (*-es*, *-aes*), later in sg. *-ymum*, *-ymon*, *-ime*, *-yme*. XV. L. *synōnymum* – Gr. *sunṓnumon*, sb. use of n. sg. of *sunṓnumos*, f. *sún* SYN-+ *ónuma* NAME (as in ANONYMOUS). So **synony·mous** sinɔ·niməs. XVII (Donne). **syno·ny·my**[3]. XVII. – late L. – Gr.

synopsis sinɔ·psis tabular arrangement showing general view. XVII. – late L. *synopsis* – Gr. *súnopsis*, f. *sún* SYN- + *ópsis* view. So **syno·p**TIC. XVIII, -ICAL. XVII (Evelyn); see OPTIC.

synovia si-, sainou·viə fluid of the joints in the body. XVII. – modL. *synovia*, *sinovia*, an invention, perh. arbitrary, of Paracelsus (d. 1541), applied by him to the various nutritive fluids in the body. Hence **syno·vi**AL[1]. XVIII. **sinovi**·TIS. XIX.

syntax si·ntæks †orderly arrangement of parts; (gram.) arrangement of words in their appropriate forms and order. XVII. – F. *syntaxe* or late L. *syntaxis* (adopted in Eng. XVI) – Gr. *súntaxis*, f. *suntássein*, f. *sún* SYN- + *tássein* arrange. So **syn**TA·CTIC. XIX, -TA·CTICAL. XVI.

synteresis sintĭrī·sis (theol.) function of conscience serving as a guide to conduct. XVI. medL. – Gr. *suntḗrēsis*, f. *suntēreîn*, f. *sún* SYN-+*tēreîn* watch over, guard. Also †*synderesis*.

synthesis si·nþĭsis proceeding from cause to effect XVII; formation of a compound by combining its elements XVIII. – L. *synthesis* – Gr. *súnthesis*, f. *suntithénai*, f. *sún* SYN-+ *tithénai* (*the-* place, put; see THEME, THESIS). Hence **sy·nthes**IZE. XIX; beside **sy·nthet**IZE. XIX. – Gr. *sunthetízesthai*. So **synthet**IC -e·tik, **-e·t**ICAL. XVII. – F. or modL. (– Gr. *-etikós*).

sypher sai·fəɹ overlap two plank-edges so as to make a flush surface. XIX. var. of CIPHER vb.

syphilis si·filis venereal disease. XVIII. – modL. *Syphilis* title of a poem, in full 'Syphilis sive Morbus Gallicus' (syphilis or the French disease), 1530, by Girolamo Fracastoro, physician, astronomer, and poet, of Verona; the name is used for the disease in the poem itself, which is the story of a shepherd *Syphilus*, represented as the first sufferer (the title *Syphilis* being formed after *Æneis*, *Thebais*, etc.); the term was used systematically by Fracastoro in his 'De Contagione', 1546. *Syphilus* is of unkn. origin. Hence **syphili·**TIC. XVIII. modL. *syphiliticus* (Sauvages); the suffix *-itic*, being the adj. formative of -ITIS, is inappropriate.

syphon, syren see SIPHON, SIREN.

Syriac si·riæk (pert. to) the Semitic language of Syria. XVII. – L. *Syriacus* – Gr. *Suriakós*, f. *Suría*; see -AC. So **Syr**IAN si·riən. XIV. – OF. *sirien* (mod. *syrien*), f. L. *Syrius* – Gr. *Súrios*.

syringa sĭri·ŋgə shrub of the genus Philadelphus. XVII (Evelyn). – modL. *syringa*, f. Gr. *surigg-*, *sûrigx* pipe, SYRINX; first applied (by Lobel 1576) to the mock orange from its stems being used for pipe stems, later (by Linnæus 1735) to the lilac (formerly called *pipe tree*), of which it remains the botanical generic name. Cf. SERINGA.

syringe si·rin[d]ʒ cylindrical instrument consisting essentially of a tube for drawing in and ejecting liquid. XV. – late L. *syringa* (whence OF. *ceringue*, F. *seringue*, etc.) f. L. *syrinx* (see next); orig. *siryng*, *syryng*, which in XVI became assim. to obl. cases of the L. word (hence pl. *syringes* siri·ndʒīz, *syri·nxes*).

syrinx si·riŋks Pan-pipe; narrow rock-cut channels or tunnels XVII; organ of voice in birds XIX. L. – Gr. *sûrigx* pipe, tube, channel, fistula.

Syro- saiə·rou repr. *Suro-*, comb. form of Gr. *Súros*.

syrup si·rəp, U.S. **sirup** thick sweet liquid. – (O)F. *sirop* or medL. *siropus*, *sirupus*, which, with corr. It. *s(c)iroppo*, Sp. *jarope*, derive ult. from Arab. *šarāb* beverage, drink. Cf. SHRUB[2], SHERBET. Hence **sy·rup**Y[1]. XVIII.

systaltic sistæ·ltik pert. to contraction. XVII. – late L. *systalticus* – Gr. *sustaltikós*, f. *sún* SYN-+*staltós*, f. *stal-* *stéllein* place.

system si·stĭm organized or connected group of objects; set or scheme of principles, ideas, etc. XVII. – F. *système* (XVI) or its source late L. *systēma* – Gr. *sústēma* organized whole, f. *sún* SYN-+ **sta-* STAND. So **systemat**IC -æ·tik. XVII. – F. *systématique* (XVI) – late L. **sy·stemat**IZE. XVIII. – F. *systématiser*. **system**IC siste·mik (physiol., path.) XIX. irreg. formation used for differentiation of meaning from *systematic*.

systole si·stəli (physiol.) regular contraction of the heart and arteries. XVI. – late L. *systolē* – Gr. *sustolḗ*, f. *sún* SYN-+ **stol-* **stel-* place, after *sustéllein* contract (cf. STOLE).

systyle si·stail applied to architecture in which the columns are close together. XVIII. – L. *systȳlos* – Gr. *sústūlos*, f. *sún* SYN- + *stûlos* column, pillar.

syzygy si·zidʒi (astron.) †conjunction, (now) conjunction and opposition of two celestial bodies XVII; applied to various unions or combinations XIX. – late L. *sȳzygia* – Gr. *suzugíā* yoke, pair, copulation, conjunction, f. *súzugos* yoked, paired, f. *sún* SYN- + **zug*- YOKE.

T

T tī 20th letter of the Eng. alphabet, in phr. *to a T* (XVII) exactly, to a nicety, perh. for earlier *to a* TITTLE.

-t¹ suffix of abstr. sbs. derived from vbs., repr. IE. *-t-* in -**tis*, -**tus* which is preserved in OE. *-þ* and Germ. *-t*, after guttural, labial, and sibilant cons., e.g. *draught, drift, flight, thirst, thrift*.

-t² phonetic var. of OE. *þ* (as in *health, truth*: see -TH¹), e.g. in *drought, height, sleight, theft*.

-t³ var. of -ED¹, as in *blest, burnt, dreamt, pent, tost*; *blessed, burned, dreamed, penned, tossed*; cf. PAST.

ta tā infantile and joc. colloq. substitute for THANKS. XVIII.

taal tāl *the t.*, the Dutch language of S. Africa, Afrikaans. XIX. – Du. *talu* language, speech, MDu. *tāle* = OE. *taal* TALE.

tab tæb short broad strip, etc. XVII; depending or projecting piece on a dress; label; (U.S.) reckoning, check XIX. prob. of dial. origin; partly synom. with TAG¹.

tabard tæ·bəɹd loose upper garment with short sleeves or none. XIII. – OF. *tabart* = Sp. *tarbardo*, It. *tabarro*; of unkn. origin.

tabaret tæ·bəret fabric of alternate stripes of material. XIX. f. TABBY. Also **tabbarea** tæbərī·ə XIX; **ta·binet** XVIII, based on †*tabine* (XVII).

tabasco təbæ·skou pungent sauce made from capsicum. XVII (*tauasco*). Name of a river and state of Mexico.

tabasheer tæbəʃiə·ɹ siliceous substance forming in the joints of bamboo. XVI. – Pg. or F. form of Urdu (Arab., Pers.) *tabāšīr* chalk, mortar.

tabby tæ·bi silk taffeta, orig. striped XVII; short for *t. cat* (XVII), cat having a striped coat; (colloq.) elderly maiden lady XVIII. – (O)F. *tabis*, †*atabis* (cf. medL. *attābi*) = Sp., It. *tabi* – Arab. *ʻattābiy* name of a quarter of Baghdad in which the stuff was manufactured, named after *ʻAttāb*, great-grandson of Omeyya.

taberdar tæ·bəɹdəɹ name given to certain scholars at the Queen's College, Oxford. XVII. In L. form *taberd(i)us, tabardarius*, f. TABARD + *-ārius* -ARY.

tabernacle tæ·bəɹnækl tent containing the Ark of the Covenant; canopied structure XIII; tent (gen.); dwelling-place, esp. a temporary one XIV; place of worship (not a church) XVII. – (O)F. *tabernacle* or L. *tabernāculum* tent, booth, shed, dim. of *taberna* TAVERN.

tabes tei·bīz slow emaciation. XVII. – L. *tābēs*.

tablature tæ·blətʃuəɹ (mus.) notation, spec. for the lute, flute, etc.; scheme in which the lines of the stave denoted the strings or holes, and signs were placed over them to indicate where these should be stopped. XVI. – F. *tablature* – medL. *tabulātūra*, f. late L. *tabulāre*, f. L. *tabula* TABLE; see -URE.

table tei·bl A. slab, tablet (now mainly techn.) XII; †(pl.) backgammon XIII; †board on which chess, etc. are played; (pl.) leaves of a backgammon board XV (phr. *turn the tables* reverse the situation XVII); B. raised board at which one sits XIII; C. arrangement of numbers, words, etc. XIV (Ch.). – (O)F. *table* = Pr. *taula*, It. *tavola* – L. *tabula* plank, tablet, list, repl. *mensa* in sense B in Gallo-Roman and Italian areas. The L. word was adopted in OE. as *tabule* and *tæfl* (ME. *tavel*) = MLG., MDu. *tāvele*, OHG. *zabal* and *tavala* (Du., G. *tafel*), ON. *tafl*. Hence vb. XV.

tableau tæ·blou picture, graphic description XVII; dramatic grouping of persons, etc. XIX. – F. *tableau*, OF. *tablel*, dim. of *table* (see prec.).

table d'hôte tābldou·t public table or meal at a hotel, etc. XVII (*table de l'hoste, tabl'd host*). F., 'host's table'; see TABLE, HOST².

tablet tæ·blit slab for an inscription or carving XIV; slab or panel for a painting XVI; sheet or leaf or (pl.) a set of them for writing on XVII (Sh.); flat cake, lozenge XVI. – OF. *tablete* (mod. *tablette*), corr. to Pr. *tauleta*, Sp. *tableta*, It. *tavoletta*; Rom. dim. of L. *tabula* TABLE; see -ET.

tabloid tæ·bloid trade-mark term for medicinal tablets patented by Messrs. Burroughs, Wellcome & Co., 14 March 1884; attrib., transf., applied to written or printed matter in condensed form. alt. of TABLET, by substitution of -OID for -ET.

taboo, tabu təbū· consecrated or restricted to a special use; prohibited, inviolable. XVIII (Capt. Cook). orig. – Tongan *ta·bu* (so str. in native use).

tabo(u)r tei·bəɹ hist. (small) drum. XIII (RGlouc.). – OF. *tabour* (mod. *tambour*) – Pr. *tabor, tanbor,* Sp. *tambor,* †*atambor,* It. *tamburo.* Hence **tabr**ET tæ·brit. XIV (*taberett*).

tabouret tæ·bŏret, ||taburɛ low stool, so called from its shape. XVII. – F. *tabouret,* dim. of *tabour*; see prec., -ET.

tabular tæ·bjŭləɹ of the form of a tablet or slab XVII; pert. to a schematic table XVIII. – L. *tabulāris,* f. *tabula* TABLE; see -AR and cf. F. *tabulaire.* Earlier *-ary* (XVI). So **ta·bul**ATE³ arrange in tabular form. XVII. f. pp. stem of late L. *tabulāre,* f. *tabula.*

tacamahac tæ·kəməhæk aromatic resin of Mexico and S. America. XVI. –Sp. †*tacamahaca* (now *tacamaca*) –Aztec *tecomahiyac.*

tacheometer tækiə·mitəɹ instrument for the rapid location of points. XIX. – F. *tachéomètre,* irreg. f. Gr. *takhe-,* stem of *takhús* quick, swift, *tákhos* swiftness; see -METER. Also TACHY·**meter**. XIX.

tachometer tækə·mitəɹ instrument for measuring speed. XIX. f. Gr. *tákhos* speed +METER; cf. prec.

tachy- tæ·ki, tæki· comb. form of Gr. *takhús* swift, as in **tachy**·GRAPHY 'swift writing', shorthand. XVII; **tachy**GRA·PHIC. XVIII.

tacit tæ·sit silent, unspoken, unexpressed. XVII (Bacon). – L. *tacitus,* prop. pp. of *tacēre* be silent (cf. RETICENT), corr. to Goth. *þahan,* and rel. further to OS. *þagian, þagōn,* OHG. *dagēn,* ON. *þagna.* So **ta·citurn** saying little. XVIII (Smollett). – F. *taciturne* or L. *taciturnus,* f. *tacitus,* with ending as in *diurnus, diuturnus, nocturnus.* **tacitu·rn**ITY. XV. – (O)F. or L.

tack¹ tæk A. fastening, as a clasp, sharp-pointed nail, etc. XIV. B. (naut.) rope, wire, etc. to secure sails XV. Parallel to later *tach(e),* the two forms presumably repr. OF. vars. **taque,* (dial.) *tache*; but the relation with the corr. vb. and with *attack, attach, detach* has not been made out. So **tack** vb. A. †attach XIV (Trevisa); fasten loosely or temporarily XV (Promp. Parv.). B. (naut.; from sense B of the sb.) shift the tacks in going about XVI.

tack² tæk †customary payment XIII (Cursor M.); tenure, tenancy XV. prob. – ON. *tak* (beside *taka*) seizure, hold, bail, security, f. *taka* TAKE.

tack³ tæk food-stuff, as in *hard t.*, ship's biscuit. XIX. Of unkn. origin.

tackle tæ·kl apparatus, equipment, gear, rigging. XIII (Genesis and Exodus, Cursor M.), prob. – (M)LG. *takel* (whence also Du. G. *takel,* Sw. *tackel*), f. *taken* = MDu. *tacken* lay hold of; see -LE¹. Hence **ta·ckle** vb. furnish with tackle XIV; harness XVIII; grip, grapple with XIX.

tacky tæ·ki slightly sticky. XVIII. f. TACK¹ (presumably in the gen. sense of holding or fastening together)+-Y¹.

tact tækt A. †sense of touch XVII; B. faculty of mental perception; C. sense of propriety, faculty of doing the right thing at the right time XVIII. – (O)F. *tact* or L. *tactus* touch, f. **tag-,* base of *tangere* touch (see TANGENT). In sense C immed. after F. *tact* (Voltaire, 1769).

tactics tæ·ktiks art of deploying forces in battle. XVII. repr. modL. *tactica* (1616 in title of tr. of Ælian's 'Taktike Theoria') – Gr. *tà taktiká,* n.pl. of *taktikós,* f. *taktós* ordered, arranged, f. base of *tássein* set in order. So **ta·ct**IC adj. XVII, **ta·ct**ICAL XVI. – modL. *tacticus* – Gr. *taktikós.* Hence **tactic**IAN tækti·ʃən. XVIII; after F. *tacticien* (1788).

tactile tæ·ktail pert. to touch. XVII. – L. *tactilis,* f. *tact-,* pp. stem of *tangere* touch; see TANGENT, -ILE. So **ta·ctu**AL¹. XVII. f. L. *tactus* touch.

tadpole tæ·dpoul larva of frog, etc. XV (*taddepol*). f. *tadde* TOAD+*pol* POLL, as if 'a toad that is all head'; the notion of 'head' appears in dial. syns., e.g., as *bullhead, pole-, pollhead.* ¶ In *tadpoles and tapers,* professional politicians, political schemers, from the names of two, Mr. *Tadpole* and Mr. *Taper,* in Disraeli's 'Coningsby' (1844).

tael teil Chinese ounce and standard money of account. XVI. – Pg. *tael,* pl. *taeis* – Malay *tahil, taïl* weight.

tænia, tenia tī·niə band, fillet XVI; tapeworm XVIII. L. – Gr. *tainiā.*

taffeta tæ·fitə silk fabric. XIV. – OF. *taffetas* or medL. *taffata,* ult. – Pers. *tāftah,* sb. use of pp. of *tāftan* shine.

taffrail tæ·freil aftermost part of the poop-rail of a ship. XIX. alt. of *taff(e)rel* †(carved) panel XVII; upper part of the flat portion of a ship's stern XVIII. – Du. *taffereel* panel, picture, for **tafeleel,* dim. of *tafel* TABLE; the final syll. is assim. to RAIL².

Taffy tæ·fi Welshman. XVII. f. attributed pronunc. of *Davy* or *David* (W. *Dafydd*).

tafia tæ·fiə rum-like liquor obtained from molasses. XVIII. Of W. Indian or Malay origin.

tag¹ tæg small pendent piece, orig. on a garment XIV (implied in *tagged*); ornamental pendant; point of metal, etc. at the end of a lace XVI; something appended to a piece of writing, etc., brief quotation XVIII. Of unkn. origin; an early syn. phrase, etc. is †*dag,* which was perh. influenced by TACK. Hence **tag** vb. XVI mark with a tag. †*tag* *and rag* XVI, *tag-rag* XVII rabble, riff-raff, *tag, rag, and bobtail* XVII. Earlier in †*totagge* (XIII) only in fig. sense 'circumstance', presumably derived from the idea of appendage.

tag[2] tæg children's game, otherwise called TIG. XVIII.

tahsildar tʌχsī·ldāɹ chief revenue officer. XVIII. Urdu – Arab., Pers. *taḥsildār*, f. *taḥsil* collection + *dār*, Pers. agent-suffix.

tail[1] teil posterior extremity of an animal OE.; in various transf. senses from XIII. OE. *tæġ(e)l* = MLG. *tagel* twisted whip, rope's end, OHG. *zagal* animal's tail (G. dial. *zagel, zāl*), ON. *tagl* horse's (or cow's) tail, Goth. *tagl* hair of the head, of the camel :– CGerm. **taglaz* :– IE. **doklos*, further connexions of which are doubtful. Hence vb. in many (esp.) specialized senses from XVI.

tail[2] teil (leg.) limitation of a freehold estate or fee to a person. XIV. – (O)F. *taille* cut, division, partition or assessment of a subsidy, tax, f. *taillier* cut, fix the precise form of limit; see TAILOR, TALLY. So **tail** adj. limited by conditions fixed by the donor. XV. – AN. *tailé*, OF. *taillié*, pp. of *taillier*; esp. in *fee-tail* (AN. *fee tailé*); for the fall of final *-é* cf. ASSIGN[2].

tailor tei·ləɹ one whose business is to make clothes. XIII. ME. *taillour, taylo(u)r* – AN. *taillour*, (O)F. *tailleur* cutter, from XVI tailor = Pr. *talaire, talador*, Sp. *tallador* engraver, *tajador* cutter, It. *tagliatore* cutter :– CRom. *tāliātorem, -iātor*, f. *tāliāre* cut = Pr. *talhar*, Sp. *tajar*, It. *tagliare* :– CRom. **tal(l)iāre*, f. L. *tālea* rod, twig, cutting; see -OR[1].

taint teint A. †attaint XIV; B. tint, dye XVI; stain, blemish XVII (Sh.). Partly aphetic of ATTAINT; partly – OF. *teint, taint* :– L. *tinctus* and *teinte* :– medL. *tincta*, sb. uses of pp. of *tingere* TINGE. So vb. †convict XIV; †hit, strike XVI; †tinge, dye XV; affect perniciously XVI.

tais(c)h taiʃ phantom, apparition. XVIII (J.). – Gael. *taibhs* taivʃ, taiʃ = OIr. *taidbse*.

take teik pt. **took** tuk, pp. **taken** tei·kn seize (also in earliest use, touch), capture XII; with various deriv. uses many of which were current by 1200 (Orm). Late OE. *tacan* (chiefly in pt. *tōc*), esp. in phr. modelled on ON. phr., e.g. *tacan tō* – ON. *taka at* begin, *tacan wiþ* – *taka við* receive, *tacan on* – *taka á* touch; also *oftacan* overtake (early XI). – ON. *taka*, pt. *tók* = WFris. *take*, EFris. *tāken*, MDu. *tāken* grasp, seize, catch, rel. by gradation to Goth. *tekan*, pt. *taitok*, pp. *tekans* touch; further connexions uncertain; OE. *oftacan* may point to the native currency of *tacan*. Superseded OE. *niman* (see NIM, NUMB) as the gen. equiv. of L. *capere, sumere*, F. *prendre*, etc. Its conjugation was assim. to that of *shake*, so that *taken* repl. ON. pp. *tekinn*; ME. contr. pp. *(y)tan* is repr. later by *tain(e), tayn(e), ta'en*.

talapoin tæ·ləpoin Buddhist priest or monk. XVI. – Pg. *talapão* – Talaing *tala pōi*.

talar tei·ləɹ garment reaching to the ankles. XVI. – L. *tālāris*, f. *tālus* ankle; see -AR.

talbot tō·lbət kind of hound formerly used for hunting, (her.) figure of this as borne in the arms of the ancient Talbot family. XV. Occurs as the proper name of a dog in Chaucer's Nun's Priest's Tale 562 and *c.*1450 John Talbot, earl of Shrewsbury, is referred to as 'oure goode dogge'; prob. generalized from the family name.

talbotype tō·lbətaip process of photographing on sensitized paper patented by W. H. Fox *Talbot* in 1841, first called *calotype*; see TYPE.

talc tælk species of translucent or shining minerals, e.g. mica. XVI (earlier in L. form XVI). – F. *talc* or medL. *talcum* (in Sp. and It. *talco*) – Arab. *ṭalq* – Pers. *talk*.

tale teil A. †talk, discourse OE.; what is told, story, narrative XI; B. reckoning, number XII. OE. *talu* = OFris. *tale*, OS. *tala* (Du. *taal* speech), OHG. *zala* (G. *zahl* number), ON. *tala* talk, tale, number :– CGerm. (exc. Goth.) **talō* fem., f. **tal-*, as in **taljan* TELL. Sense B was prob. taken from ON. (cf. late Nth. OE. *tal* – ON. *tal* n.).

talegalla tæligæ·lə brush turkey of New Guinea. XIX. modL. (F. *talégalle*) formed by R. P. Lesson (1828) from Malagasy *talèva* and L. *gallus* cock.

talent tæ·lənt A. †inclination, disposition XIII (Cursor M.); B. ancient weight and money of account XIV (Wycl. Bible); C. mental endowment or aptitude XV. – OF. *talent* will, desire = Pr. *talant, talen* = Sp., It. *talento* :– L. *talentum* in Rom. sense of 'inclination of mind' – Gr. *tálanton* balance, weight, sum of money, f. **tal-*, **tla-* bear, endure (cf. THOLE[2]). Sense C is developed from the use of the word in the parable of the talents, Matt. xxv 14–30.

tales tei·līz writ for summoning jurors; list of persons so summoned. XVI. L. *tālēs* pl. of *tālis* such (cf. RETALIATE) in phr. *tales de circumstantibus* such persons from those standing about. L. *tālis* belongs to the group containing *tam* so, *tantus* so great, *tot* so many (cf. the parallel *quālis, quam, quantus, quot*).

talion tæ·liən retaliation. XV (Lydg.). – (O)F. *talion* – L. *tāliō(n-)*, f. *tālis*; see prec., -ION. *lex talionis* principle of exacting compensation, 'eye for eye, tooth for tooth'.

talipot tæ·lipət S. Indian fan-palm. XVII. – Malayalam *tālipat*, Sinhalese *talapata*, Hindi *tālpāt* :– Skr. *tālapattra* leaf of the *tāla* or fan-palm.

talisman tæ·lizmən object endowed with occult powers, used as an amulet or charm.

XVII. – F., Sp. *talisman*, It. *talismano* – medGr. *télesmon*, alt. of late Gr. *télesma* (whence Arab. *ṭilsam*) completion, performance, religious rite, consecrated object, f. *teleîn*, complete, perform (a rite), consecrate, f. *télos* end, result (cf. TELE-).

talk tōk 'speak in conversation' (J.); also trans. XIII. ME. *talkien*, *talken* (first in w. midl. texts), deriv. with *k*-suffix of the base **tal-* of TALE, TELL; cf. *lurk*, *stalk*, *walk*. Hence **ta·lk**ATIVE. XV. **talkee-talkee** tō·kitōki broken English; prattle, chatter. XIX. **ta·lk**IE talking film. XX.

tall tōl †seemly, decent, comely; †doughty, valiant XIV (phr. †*t. of his hands* dexterous, formidable in arms XVI); high of stature, lofty XVI (Palsgr.). repr. OE. *ġe|tæl* swift, prompt (of which sense there are later traces) = OFris. *tel*, OS. *gital*, OHG. *gizal* quick. **ta·ll**BOY tall-stemmed glass XVII; tall chest or bookcase mounted on a high stand XVIII.

tallage tæ·lidʒ tax, levy, orig. one levied by Norman kings. XIII (S. Eng. Leg.). – OF. *taillage*, f. *taillier* cut, shape, determine the form of, limit = Pr. *talhar*, Sp. *tajar*, It. *tagliare* :– Rom. **talliāre*, f. *-tallia* TALLY.

tallith tæ·liþ garment worn by Jews at prayer. XVII. – Rabbinic Heb. *ṭalliþ*, f. *ṭālal* cover.

tallow tæ·lou harder kinds of fat used for candles, soap, etc. XIV. ME. *talȝ*, *taluȝ*, *talow* – MLG. *talg*, *talch* (whence also Du. *talk*, G. *talg*, Icel. *tólg*), of unkn. origin.

tally tæ·li rod of wood marked with notches recording payments XV; reckoning, score XVI; counterpart XVII. – AN. *tallie* = AL. *tallia*, *talia*, for L. *tālea* cutting, rod, stick; the corr. OF. *taille* was adopted earlier in this sense as *tail* (XIV–XVII); cf. TAIL[2]. So **ta·lly** vb. †score, mark down XV; agree, accord XVIII. Cf. medL. *talliāre*.

tally-ho tælihou· huntman's view-halloo. XVIII. Cf. F. *taïaut* (XVII), †*taho*, †*theau* (XVI).

talma tæ·lmə cape, cloak. XIX. f. name of François Joseph *Talma*, F. tragedian 1763–1826. Cf. *roquelaure* (XVIII).

Talmud tæ·lmʌd, -mū·d body of Jewish law (Mishnah) and commentary on this (Gemara). XVI. – late Heb. *talmūd* instruction, f. *lāmad* instruct.

talon tæ·lən claw of a bird of prey, dragon, etc. XIV; spec. Eng. application of the sense †'heel, hinder claw'. – (O)F. *talon* heel = Pr. *talo*, Sp. *talon*, It. *talone* :– Rom. **tālō(n-)*, f. *tālus* ankle-bone.

taluk talu·k district in India as a collectorate. XVIII. – Hind. *taʿalluq*, ult. f. Arab. *ʿalaqa* adhere, be affixed.

talus[1] tei·ləs (fortif.) sloping side of an earthwork XVII; (geol.) sloping mass of detritus XIX. – (O)F. *talus*, of unkn. origin.

talus[2] tei·ləs (anat.) ankle, astragalus. XVIII. L.

tamarind tæ·mărind fruit of the tree Tamarindus indica. XVI. – medL. *tamarindus* (= cf. Sp., It. *tamarindo*) – Arab. *tamr hindī* date of India.

tamarisk tæ·mărisk plant of the genus Tamarix. XV. – late L. *tamariscus*, var. of earlier *tamarix*.

tamasha təmā·ʃə entertainment, public function. XVII (*tomashaw*, *tomasia*, *tamacha*). – Urdu – Arab. (Pers.) *tamāšā* walking about for amusement, entertainment, f. *maša(y)* walk.

tambouki tæmbū·ki *t. grass*, *wood* wild grass and timber of S. Africa. XIX. Afrikaans, f. *Tembu* tribal name + dim. suffix *-kje*.

tambour tæ·mbuəɹ drum XV (Caxton; adopted afresh XVIII); circular frame on which material is stretched; (archit., etc.) XVIII. – F. *tambour*, expressive of *tabour* TABOR. So **tambourine** tæ·mbərī·n †(in uncertain sense) XVI (Spenser; Jonson has *timburine*); musical instrument made of a hoop with parchment stretched over one side and cymbals at the edge XVIII. – F. *tambourin*, dim. of *tambour*. See -INE[4].

tambreet tæmbrī·t duck-billed platypus. XIX. Mallangong (New South Wales).

tame teim domesticated)(wild. OE. *tam* = OFris., (M)LG., (M)Du. *tam*, OHG. *zam* (G. *zahm*), ON. *tamr* :– CGerm. (exc. Goth., but cf. the vb.) **tamaz*, f. IE. **dom-*, repr. also by L. *domāre*, Gr. *damân* tame, subdue. (The form *tame* descends from OE. obl. forms.) Hence **tame** vb. XIV; cf. OHG. *zamōn*; superseding ME. *teme*, OE. *temian* = OFris. *tama*, MLG., (M)Du. *temmen*, OHG. *zemmen* (G. *zähmen*), ON. *temja*, Goth. *gatamjan*.

Tamil, -ul tæ·mil, -əl (language of) a Dravidian race of SE. India. XVIII. – (partly through Du., Pg. *Tamul*) *Tamiḷ*, *Tamiṛ*, native name, in Pali and Prakrit *Damiḷa*, *Daviḷa -iḍa*, Skr. *Dramiḷa*, *-iḍa*, *Draviḍa* DRAVIDIAN.

Tammany tæ·məni name of a Delaware (U.S.A.) chief who flourished about 1683 used to designate the fancifully named 'patron saint' (St. Tammany) of America and hence in the title of a philanthropic society (orig. Sons of St Tammany) and its headquarters (*T. Hall*), and consequently of the political club identified therewith.

tammy[1] tæ·mi fine worsted cloth. XVII. Of unkn. origin.

tammy[2] tæ·mi see next.

Tam o' Shanter tæməʃæ·ntəɹ round Scotch cap. XIX. f. name of the hero of Burns's poem so entitled (1790). Also *Tammy Shanter*, which is abbrev. *tammy* tæ·mi. XIX.

tamp tæmp to stop with clay, etc.; to ram down hard. XIX. Back-formation from TAMPION.

tamper tæ·mpəɹ †work in or temper clay XVI; †scheme, plot; deal improperly, meddle *with* XVII. In all senses the earlier form is *temper*, of which *tamper* was perh. a workman's alteration.

tampion see TOMPION.

tan tæn convert (skin) into leather by steeping in an infusion of astringent bark OE.; make brown by the sun XVI; colloq. (orig. *tan* a person's *hide*) thrash XVII. Late OE. **tannian*, in pp. *ġetanned* and agent-noun *tannere* (see -ER[1]), prob. – medL. *tannāre*, pp. *tannātus*, perh. of Celtic origin; reinforced in ME. from OF. vb. *tan(n)er* = Pr. *tanar*, It. *tannare*, agent-noun *tanere*, *-eor* (cf. medL. *tannātor*). Hence **tan** sb. crushed bark of oak, etc. for tanning XVII; brown or tawny colour XIX. Cf. TAWNY. So **ta·nn**ERY XV; after OF. *tannerie*, medL. *tanneria* (XIII).

tanager tæ·nădʒəɹ passerine bird of the genus Tanagra. XIX. modL. *tanagra* (Linnæus), alt. of Tupi *tangara* (current in Eng. use XVII–XIX).

tandem tæ·ndəm two-wheeled vehicle drawn by two horses harnessed one in front of the other; the horses themselves; also adv. XVIII (Grose, Felton). orig. sl. punning use of L. *tandem* at length (of time) based on phr. *at length* in the sense †'in extended line' (XVIII).

tang[1] tæŋ A. (dial.) serpent's tongue, insect's sting XIV; point or spike, spec. of a metal tool XV; B. penetrating taste XV; slight smack XVI. Of Scand. origin (cf. ON., Da. *tange* point, spit).

tang[2] tæŋ sharp ringing note. XVII. perh. imit. ¶ 'She had a tongue with a tang' (Sh., 'Tempest' II ii 52) may be an early ex., if not a use of TANG[1].

tang[3] tæŋ large coarse seaweed (Fucus). XVIII. Of Scand. origin (Norw., Da. *tang*, Icel. *þáng*); adopted also in Fris., Du., etc.

tanga tæ·ŋgə coin or money of account in India, Persia, and Turkestan. XVI. – Pg. *tanga* – *ṭanka* in various Indian vernaculars :– Skr. *ṭaṅka* weight.

tangent tæ·ndʒənt (geom.) adj. touching at a point XVI; sb. XVI (modL. *tangens*, for *linea tangens* touching line). – L. *tangent-*, *-ēns*, prp. of *tangere* touch. See -ENT. Hence **tangent**IAL tændʒe·nʃəl. XVII.

tangerine tændʒərī·n applied to a small variety of orange obtained from *Tangier* (*Tanger*), seaport of Morocco. XIX. orig. adj. in *T. orange*; see -INE[1].

tangible tæ·ndʒĭbl touchable XVI; discernible by touch XVII; realizable, palpable XVIII. – F. *tangible* or late L. *tangibilis*, f. *tangere* touch; see TANGENT, -IBLE.

tangle[1] tæ·ŋgl †involve (a person) in embarrassment XIV; ENTANGLE XVI. ME. *tangil*, *-el*, var. of *tagil* in Rolle's works; thereafter *tangle* (XVI); of obscure origin. Hence sb. tangled condition. XVII.

tangle[2] tæ·ŋgl gen. term for the larger seaweeds. XVI (earliest Sc.). prob. – Norw. *taangel*, *tongul*, Færoese *tangul*, repr. ON. *þǫngull*.

tango tæ·ŋgou Negro dance adapted to the ballroom. XX. Amer. Sp. (locally, dance and music for this, and instrument of the tambourine kind).

tangram tæ·ngræm Chinese geometrical puzzle. XIX. Of unkn. origin.

tank[1] tæŋk in India, reservoir of water for irrigation, etc.; artificial receptacle for liquids in large quantities. XVII. – Indian vernacular word such as Gujerati *tānkh*, Marathi *ṭānken*, perh. from Skr. *taḍāga* pond, lake. Hence **ta·nk**ER[1], vessel for conveying oil. XX.

tank[2] tæŋk military armoured car of British invention. XX; so named for reasons of secrecy.

tankard tæ·ŋkəɹd †large tub XIV; drinking-vessel (esp. one-handled), XV. Of unkn. origin, but cf. MDu., Du. *tanckaert*.

tanner[1] tæ·nəɹ one who tans hides. OE. *tannere*, f. **tannian* TAN; or – OF. *tanere* :– medL. *tannātor*.

tanner[2] tæ·nəɹ (sl.) sixpence. XIX. Of unkn. origin.

tannin tæ·nin astringent having the property of converting hide into leather. XIX. – F. *tanin* (1798, Proust), f. *tan* TAN + *-in* -IN. So **ta·nn**IC. XIX. – F. *tannique* (1834, Pelouze).

tanrec, tenrec tæ·n-, te·nrek insectivorous mammal allied to the hedgehog. XVIII. F. *tanrec* – Malagasy *tàndraka*, *tràndraka*.

tansy tæ·nzi herbaceous plant, Tanacetum vulgare. XV. – OF. *tanesie* (mod. *tanaisie*) poss. aphetic f. medL. *athanasia* tansy – Gr. *athanasía* immortality; the relation to medL. *tanacētum* is not clear.

tantalize tæ·ntəlaiz torment with disappointment. XVI. f. *Tantalus*, name of a mythical king of Phrygia condemned to stand in Tartarus up to his chin in water which receded as he stooped to drink.

tantalum tæ·ntələm (min.) a rare metal. XIX (discovered in 1802 by Ekeberg). f. *Tantalus* (see prec.), partly with allusion to its non-absorbent quality; the ending follows *aluminum*; see ALUMINIUM.

tantalus tæ·ntələs genus of storks, Tantalus ibis; spirit stand containing decanters locked up but visible. XIX. L. – Gr. *Tántalos*.

tantamount tæ·ntəmaunt that amounts to as much. XVII. f. †*tantamount* sb. equivalent, †*tantamount* vb. amount to as much (both XVII). – AN. *tant amunter* – It. *tanto montare*, i.e. *tanto* as much (:– L. *tantum*, f. *tam* so + -**to-*), *montare* AMOUNT, MOUNT.

tanti tæ·ntai of so much value, worth while; †so much *for*. XVI. – L. *tantī*, g. of n. of *tantus* so much.

tanti·vy tæ·ntivi, tænti·vi †adv. at full gallop; sb. rapid gallop XVII; from *c.*1680, post-Restoration high churchman or Tory, nickname based on a caricature of such clergymen mounted on the Church of England and 'riding tantivy' to Rome. perh. intended to repr. the sound of horses galloping.

tantrum tæ·ntrəm outburst of ill-temper. XVIII (Foote). Of unkn. origin.

Taoism tā·ouizm one of the three religions of China. XIX. f. *Tao tê king* 'book of reason and virtue', in which the system is set forth; see -ISM.

tap[1] tæp device for drawing liquid from a vessel. OE. *tæppa* = MLG., MDu. *tappe* (Du. *tap*), OHG. *zapho*, MHG. *zapfe* (G. *zapfen*), ON. *tappi* :– Germ. **tappon*. Hence **tap** vb. fit with a tap OE.; draw (liquor) with a tap XV. late OE. *tappian* = (M)LG., (M)Du. *tappen*, (M)HG. *zapfen*, f. the cogn. sbs.

tap[2] tæp strike lightly. XIII (*teppe*, AncrR.). Either – (O)F. *taper* or independent imit. formation similar to *flap*, *rap*, *slap*.

tape teip narrow strip of woven fabric. OE. *tæppa* or *tæppe*, repr. obscurely by ME. *tāpe* (Ch.); perh. rel. to OFris. *tapia*, MLG. *teppen* pluck, tear.

taper tei·pəɹ wax candle OE.; long wick coated with wax for use as a spill XIX. OE. *tapor*, *-er*, *-ur* – (with dissimilation of *p* . . *p* to *t* . . *p*) L. *papyrus*, on which the OE. word occurs as a gloss; cf. for the sense Pr. *pabil*, Sp. *pábilo*, Pg. *pavio* wick. Hence **ta·per** adj. becoming continuously narrower in one direction XV; whence **ta·per** vb. XVI.

tapestry tæ·pĭstri decorated textile fabric. XV. alt. of †*tapisery*, †*tapecery* (XV) – (O)F. *tapisserie*, f. *tapissier* tapestry-worker, or *tapisser* cover with carpet, f. *tapis* carpet, OF., Pr. *tapiz* :– Rom. **tappētium*, for late L. *tapētium* – Gr. *tapétion*, dim. of *tápēs*, *-ēt-* tapestry.

tapioca tæpiou·kə prepared flour of the cassava. XVIII (*tipioca*). – Tupi-Guarani *tipioca*, f. *tipi* residue, dregs + *ok*, *og* squeeze out; the present form is due to F., Sp., Pg.

tapir tei·pəɹ swine-like animal of tropical America. XVIII (Goldsmith). – Tupi *tapira*.

tapis tæ·pi phr. *on the t.* (XVII), partial tr. F. *sur le t.* 'on the table-cloth', under discussion; see TAPESTRY.

tappal təpɔ̄·l (Anglo-Ind.) transmission of letters, etc. by relays of runners. XVIII. Of unkn. origin.

tapster tæ·pstəɹ †woman who draws liquor OE.; man who does this XVI(? XV). OE. *tæppestre*, orig. fem. of *tæppere*, agent-noun of *tappian* TAP[1]; see -STER.

tar[1] tāɹ dark thick liquid distilled from wood or coal. OE. *teru*, *teoru*, corr. to MLG. *ter(e)* (LG. *teer*, whence Du., G. *teer*), MDu. *tar*, *ter(re)*, ON. *tjara* :– Germ. **terw-* (cf. OE. *tyrwe*, **tierwe* :– **terwjōn*), gen. held to be f. **trew-* (IE. **drew-*) TREE, the primary application having been to the black oily liquid produced by trees such as pines; cf. Lith. *dervà* pine-wood, tar, Lett. *darva* tar, ON. *tyr|viðr* pine-wood; Finn. *terva* tar is – Germ. Hence **ta·rry**[1]. XVI.

tar[2] tāɹ (colloq.) sailor. XVII (also *Jack Tar* XVIII); short for TARPAULIN.

taradiddle tæ·rədidl petty falsehood. XVIII (Grose).

tarantass tærəntæ·s 4-wheeled Russian travelling carriage. XIX. – Russ. *tarantás*.

tarantella tærənte·lə rapid whirling S. Italian dance. XVIII. – It. *tarantella* (whence F. *tarentelle*), dim. formation on *Taranto* name of a town in Apulia, Italy (the ancient *Tarentum*). The dance was popularly supposed to be a remedy for **tara·ntism** hysterical malady characterized by an impulse to dance (XVII) – modL. *tarantismus* (cf. It. *tarantismo*, F. *tarentisme*), f. *Tarantum*, *Taranto*; the malady itself was pop. attributed to the bite of the tarantula.

tarantula təræ·ntjŭlə large wolf-spider of S. Europe. XVI. – medL. *tarantula* – It. *tarantola* (whence F. *tarentule*), f. *Taranto* (see prec.), where it is commonly found.

taratantara tærətæ·ntərǎ word supposed to be imit. of the sound of a trumpet or bugle. XVI. prob. after L. (Ennius) and It. *taratantara*; cf. medL. *taratantarum* sifting-machine; *taratantara* clapper, rattle.

taraxacum təræ·ksəkəm (drug prepared from) dandelion Leontodon Taraxacum. XVIII. – medL. *taraxacum* – Arab. *ṭar(a)khshaqōq* – Pers. *talkh chakōk* 'bitter herb'.

tarboosh tāɹbū·ʃ Mohammedan fez. XVIII. – Egyptian Arab. *ṭarbūsh*.

tardigrade tā·ɹdigreid slow-paced XVII; (zool.) belonging to the family comprising the sloths XVIII. – F. *tardigrade* or L. *tardigradus* (in n.pl. *Tardigrada* as the name of an order), f. *tardus* slow + *-gradus* stepping, walking; see TARDY, GRADE.

tardy tā·ɹdi slow XV (Caxton); late, behindhand XVII (Milton). Late ME. *tardif*, *-ive* – (O)F *tardif*, *-ive* = Pr. *tardiu*, Sp. *tardío*, It. *tardivo*, Rum. *tărziŭ* :– CRom. **tardīvu-s*, f. *tardus* slow; see -IVE, -Y[1]. Cf. HASTY.

tare[1] tɛəɹ (seed of) vetch; in versions of the Bible (Matt. xiii 25) rendering L. *zīzania*, Gr. *zizánia* injurious weed among corn, darnel, cockle. XIV (Wycl. Bible, later version). Of unkn. origin; MDu. *tarwe*, *terwe* wheat (rel. to Lith. *dirvà* wheat-field) has been compared.

tare[2] tɛəɹ weight of the wrapping, receptacle, or conveyance containing goods. XV. – F. *tare* waste in goods, deficiency, also as in Eng. = Pr., Sp., It. *tara* – medL. *tara* – Arab. *ṭarḥah* what is thrown away, f. *ṭaraḥa* reject.

targe tāɹdʒ (arch.) shield. XIII (RGlouc.). – (O)F. *targe* = Pr. *targua*, It. *targa*, of Germ. origin as repr. by OE. *targa, targe*, ON. *targa* shield, OHG. *zarga*, (M)HG. *zarge* edging, border.

target tā·ɹgit (hist.) light round shield XIV (Maund.); marked with concentric circles to be used as a butt XVIII. dim. of TARGE (see -ET), but of obscure history; the earliest forms in *-get* are ambiguous; they were succeeded by forms in *-gat, -guet*; these follow respectively OF. *target(t)e* and *targuet(t)e* (cf. It. *targhetta*).

targum tā·ɹgəm Aramaic translation or paraphrase of portions of the O.T. XVI. – Chaldee *targūm* interpretation, f. *targēm* interpret; see DRAGOMAN.

tariff tæ·rif †arithmetical table; schedule or system of the rates of customs, item of this XVI; gen. classified list of charges XVIII. – F. *tarif* – It. *tariffa*, Sp. *tarifa* – Turk. *ta'rifa* – Arab. *ta'rīf*, f. *'arafa* notify, make known.

tarlatan tā·ɹlətən kind of thin muslin. XVIII (*tarn-*) – F. *tarlatane*, alt. of *tarnatane*.

tarmac tā·ɹmæk (XX) registered trademark of a kind of *tar* MACADAM (XIX) road material of broken stone with a binder of tar.

tarn tāɹn small mountain lake. XIV. Late ME. *terne, tarne* – ON. **tarnu* (*tjorn, tjǫrn*, Sw. dial. *tjärn, tärn*, Norw. *tjörn*, Da. *tjern*).

tarnation taɹnei·ʃən damnable, -bly. XVIII. var. of *darnation*, euph. var. of DAMNATION; assoc. with *tarnal* (XVIII), aphetic of *eternal*, used as an expression of execration.

tarnish tā·ɹniʃ dim. the lustre of. XVI. – F. *terniss-*, extended stem (see -ISH²) of *ternir* (= It. *ternire* in Florio 1598, but not elsewhere), whence *terne* dim, dull, of unkn. origin; the change of *-er-* to *-ar-* is unparalleled at this date.

taro tā·rou, tæ·rou food plant, Colocasia antiquorum. XVIII (Cook). Native Polynesian name.

tarot tæ·rou one of a set of playing-cards. XVI. – F. *tarot* – It. *tarocco* (pl. *-chi*), of unkn. origin.

tarpaulin tāɹpō·lin (sheet of) tarred canvas XVII (*-ing*, B. Jonson); nickname for a sailor XVII (also †*tarpaulian*); cf. TAR. Of unkn. origin; presumed to be f. TAR + PALL¹ + -ING¹.

tarpon tā·ɹpən jew-fish, Megalops atlanticus. XVII. – Du. *tarpoen*, of unkn. origin.

tarragon tæ·rəgən composite plant Artemisia Dracunculus. XVI. Given first as repr. medL. *tragonia* and *tarchon*, the latter of which goes back to medGr. *tarkhṓn*, which may be an Arab. deformation of Gr. *drákōn*.

tarry tæ·ri (now literary in Great Britain) †delay, retard XIV (R. Mannyng); delay, linger XIV. In earliest use identical in form with ME. *tary* vex, harass, repr. OE. **tærġan, terġan*, and OF. *tarier*, of unkn. origin; but the sense is against identity; for Sc. var. *tarrow* delay, hesitate, cf. *harrow* beside *harry*.

tarsia tā·ɹsiə mosaic inlaid wood. XVII. – It. *tarsia*, of unkn. origin.

tarsus tā·ɹsəs (anat.) posterior parts of the foot. XVII. modL. – Gr. *tarsós* flat of the foot, comb. form **tars(o)-**.

tart¹ tāɹt piece of pastry (now open) with fruit or jam filling. XIV (*Tartes of Turky*). – OF. *tarte* (med.L *tarta* XII), of unkn. origin.

tart² tāɹt sharp to the taste XIV (Ch.; meaning doubtful); sharp or biting in tone XVII. OE. *teart* 'acerrimus', 'asperrimus', *teartlīce* 'acriter', *teartness* 'acerbitas'.

tartan tā·ɹtən (orig. Sc.) woollen cloth woven in stripes crossing at right angles. XVI. perh. – OF. *tertaine*, var. of *tiretaine* cloth half wool, half linen or cotton, of unkn. origin.

tartar tā·ɹtəɹ bitartrate of potash adhering as a crust to the sides of wine casks. XIV (*tartre* Ch., *tartar* Trevisa). – medL. *tartarum* – medGr. *tártaron*, of unkn. origin; cf. modF. *tartre*, Sp., It. *tartaro*. So **tartar**IC tāɹtæ·rik. XVIII. – F. or modL.

Tartar tā·ɹtəɹ native inhabitant of the region of Central Asia extending eastward from the Caspian Sea. XIV (*Tartre*, Ch.). – (O)F. *Tartare* or medL. *Tartarus*; var. **Tatar** tā·tăr XVII; widely current in Europe and the East. So **Tartar**IAN -ɛə·riən. XIV (*-ien*, Maund.). – OF. *tartarien*. **Tartar**IC -æ·rik. XIX.

Tartarus tā·ɹtərəs infernal regions of Gr. and Roman mythology. XVI. L. – Gr. *Tártaros*. So **Tartar**EAN tāɹtɛə·riən, †-EOUS, XVII.

tartrate tā·ɹtreit (chem.) salt of tartaric acid. XVIII. – F. *tartrate*, f. *tartre* TARTAR; see -ATE². So **ta·rtr(o)-** in names of compounds derived from tartaric acid.

Tartuffe tāɹtʌ·f, -tu·f hypocritical pretender to religion, etc. XVII. Gen. use of name of the principal character in Molière's comedy so entitled (1664), taken from It. *Tartufo*, a use of *tartuffo* truffle, as a concealed production.

task tàsk piece of work imposed or undertaken XIII (Cursor M.); †tax, tribute XIV. – ONF. *tasque*, var. of OF. *tasche* (mod. *tâche*) – medL. *tasca*, alt. of *taxa*, f. L. *taxāre* TAX.

tass tæs cup, small goblet. XV (Caxton). – (O)F. *tasse* = Pr. *tassa*, Sp. *taza*, It. *tazza* – Arab. *ṭass, ṭassah* basin – Pers. *tast*.

tassel tæ·sl †clasp, fibula XIII (Cursor M.), pendent ornament consisting of a knob with fringe attached XIV. – OF. *tas(s)el*, of unkn. origin; AL. *tassellus* (XII).

taste teist †examine by touch, try, test; experience or try the flavour of XIII; have a particular flavour XVI. – OF. *taster* (mod. *tâter*) touch, feel, try, taste = Pr., OSp. *tastar*, It. *tastare* :– Rom. **tastāre*, supposed to be blend of L. *tangere* touch (cf. TACT) and *gustāre* taste (cf. GUSTO). So sb. – OF. *tast*, f. the vb. Hence **tasty**[1] pleasant to taste. XVI (in *untasty*).

tat see TIT[3].

ta-ta tæ·tā infantile expression for good-bye. XIX (*tar, tar*, Dickens). Hence sb. tæ·tā in *go ta-ta's* or *for a ta-ta* go for a walk.

Tatar see TARTAR.

tatter tæ·təɹ (chiefly pl.) irregularly torn piece. First recorded in *tatarwagges* (*c.*1400), but implied in earlier *tattered* orig. †clothed in slashed garments (*tatird* Rolle, *tatrid* Wyclif), *tatering* slashing of garments (Wyclif). – ON. **taturr* (Icel. *töturr*, Norw. dial. *totra*), pl. *tǫtrar* rags, rel. to OE. *tættec* rag, and prob. further to OHG. *zæter* rag; cf. deriv. OF. *taterele* ('Aucassin et Nicolete' vi).

tatterdemalian tæ·təɹdĭmei·liən ragged fellow. XVII (Dekker, B. Jonson). f. TATTER or *tattered* (see prec.) + an obscure el.; in early use often *-allian, -allion*.

tatting tæ·tiŋ kind of knotted lace work. XIX. Of unkn. origin; but cf. Sc. *tate* tuft, *tatty* matted (XVI).

tattle tæ·tl †falter, stammer XV (Caxton); talk idly or without reticence XVI. – MFlem. *tatelen*, parallel to the more usual MFlem., MDu., MLG. *tateren*; of imit. origin; see -LE[3]. Cf. TITTLE-TATTLE.

tattoo[1] tætū· signal by beat of drum, etc., for soldiers to return to quarters XVII; military entertainment based on an elaboration of this XVIII. orig. *tap-too, -tow-* – Du. *taptoe* (whence also Sw. *tapto*, Russ. *taptá*), f. *tap* TAP[1] + *toe*, for *doe toe* 'do to', shut; the primary application seems to have been to a signal for the turning off of the taps of barrels of drink at the end of the day; cf. synon. G. *zapfenstreich*, LG. *tappenslag* lit. 'tap-blow'.

tattoo[2] tætū· designs on the skin made by puncturing it and inserting pigments. XVIII (*tattow*). Of Polynesian origin; in Tahiti, Samoa, Tonga *tatau*, in Marquesa *ta-tu*.

tau tɔ̄ name of the Gr. and the Semitic letter T; mark or figure of this shape, St. Anthony's cross. XIII (Cursor M.).

taube tau·bə type of monoplane employed by Germany in the war of 1914–18. G., pigeon; cf. DOVE.

taunt[1] tɔ̄nt †in phr. *taunt pour* (or for) *taunt* tit for tat in reply; †smart rejoinder, witty jibe; scornful reproach or challenge XVI. orig. – F. phr. *tant pour tant* 'so much for so much', like for like (L. *tantum*, n. of *tantus* so great, rel. to *tam* so). Hence **taunt** vb. †answer back; reproach scornfully. XVI.

taunt[2] tɔ̄nt †haughty, (dial.) pert XV; (naut.) tall, of masts and rigging XVI. prob. aphetic of *ataunt* †as much as possible, in full (XIV), with all rigging in use, in full sail (XVII) – (O)F. *autant* as much, f. †*al*, var. of †*el* one more :– Rom. **alid*, for L. *aliud*, n. of *alius* other (cf. ELSE) + *tant* (see prec.); but the development is obscure.

tauromachy tɔ̄rɔ·məki bull-fighting, bull-fight. XIX (Thackeray). – Gr. *tauromakhiā*, f. *taûros* bull + *mákhē* fighting; see -Y[3].

taut tɔ̄t †tense, distended XIV; tightly drawn XVII. For earlier *taught*, alt. (cf. *daughter*) of *tought*, ME. *touht, toȝt*, prob. identical with the common var. *tought* of TOUGH, with the sense influenced by assoc. with *toȝ-*, pp. stem of *tee*, OE. *tēon* draw, pull (see TUG).

tautology tɔ̄tɔ·lədʒi repetition of the same word or phrase or of the same idea in other words. XVI. – late L. *tautologia* – Gr. *tautologiā*, f. *tautológos* repeating what has been said (whence **tauto·logous** XVIII), f. *tautó* the same + *-logos* saying; see -LOGY.

tavern tæv·əɹn house for the sale of drink. XIII. – (O)F. *taverne* = Pr., It. *taverna* :– L. *taberna* (for the suffix cf. CAVERN, CISTERN). So **ta·verner** (arch.) tavern-keeper. XIV – (O)F. *tavernier*; cf. L. *tabernārius*; see -ER[1]. Survives in the surname *Taverner*, beside *Tabberner*.

taw[1] tɔ̄ prepare or dress (raw material), spec. in the conversion of skins into leather. OE. *tawian* rel. to OS. *tōgean*, MLG., MDu. *touwen*, OHG. *zouwen*, ON. (pt.) *tawidō*, Goth. *taujan* :– CGerm. **tawōjan*, **tawjan* do, make, prepare.

taw[2] tɔ̄ large choice or fancy marble. XVIII. Of unkn. origin.

tawdry tɔ̄·dri †short for *t. lace* XVII (Drayton); cheap and pretentious finery; hence adj. of the nature of this XVII. orig. in *Seynt Audries lace, tawdrie lace* (XVI) 'lace' or necktie such as was sold at St Audrey's fair in remembrance of St Audrey, i.e. Etheldrida, or Æþelþryþ (daughter of Anna, king of East Anglia, and patron saint of Ely), who died of a tumour in the throat which she regarded as a just retribution for her youthful fondness for splendid necklaces. ¶ For the metathesis of *t* of *Saint* cf. *Tooley* (Street) from *St Olave's*.

tawny tɔ̄·ni brown with a preponderance of yellow or orange. XIV (PPl.) – AN. *tauné*, OF. *tané* (cf. AL. *taunātus* XIII) dark like tan, f. *tan* TAN. Cf. TENNÉ, -Y[5].

taws(e) tɔ̄z (chiefly Sc.) whip for a spinning top; leather thong used for chastisement. XVI. pl. of *taw* tawed leather, thong, f. TAW[1].

tax tæks determine the amount of (a fine, etc.) XIII; impose a tax on XIV; censure, take to task XVI. – (O)F. *taxer* – L. *taxāre* (whence also OF. *tausser*, Sp. *tasar*, It. *tassare*), perh. Gr. *tássein* (see next). Hence **tax** sb. compulsory contribution. XIV; cf. F. *taxe* (XV), medL. *taxa*. So **taxA·TION**. XIV. – (O)F. – L.

taxi tæ·ksi short (XX) for *taxi-cab*, which is for *taximeter cab* cab fitted with a **taximeter** tæksi·mītəɹ (XIX) automatic contrivance to indicate distance traversed and fare due – F. *taximètre*, f. *taxe* tariff (TAX)+*-mètre* -METER (so It. *tassametro*); slightly earlier *taxameter*, after G. (earlier still, *c.*1875, *taxanom*), with assim. to Gr. *táxis*. Hence vb. travel by t.; (of aircraft) run along the ground before taking off or after alighting XX.

taxidermy tæ·ksidə̄:ɹmi preserving and mounting skins of animals. XIX. f. Gr. *táxis* arrangement (rel to *tássein* order, fix) +*dérma* skin (cf. TEAR[2]); see -Y[3]. Hence **ta·xidermIST**. XIX.

taxonomy tæksɔ·nəmi scientific classification. XIX. – F. *taxonomie* (de Candolle, 1813), irreg. f. Gr. *táxis*; see prec. and -NOMY.

taxwax tæ·kswæks XVIII, **ta·xywa·xy** XIX. See PAXWAX.

tazza tæ·tsa shallow ornamental bowl. XIX. It., see TASS.

T.B. tībī· colloq. abbrev. of *t*ubercle *b*acillus, pop. of tuberculosis.

tcha(h) tʃa repr. an excl. expressing impatience, dissent, etc. XIX (Dickens). Also **tchu(h)**. XIX (Geo. Eliot).

tchick tʃik click made with the tongue against the palate. XIX (Scott). imit. Also **tck** XIX (Kipling).

tea tī (leaves of) a plant, Thea chinensis, Camellia theifera, from which a beverage is made XVII; the beverage itself. Early forms also *tay*, *tey*, repr. the pronunc. tē, tei, still in dial. use, prob. immed. – Du. *tee* – Chinese (Amoy) *t'e*, in Mandarin dial. *ch'a*, whence earlier *cha*, *chaa*, *chia* (XVI). Cf. F. *thé*, Sp. *te*, It. *tè*, G. †*thee*, *tee*.

teach tītʃ pt., pp. **taught** tɔ̄t †show; show by way of information or instruction. OE. *tǣċan* (pt. *tǣhte*, Nhb. *tāhte*):– **taikjan*, rel. to *tācen* TOKEN. The north. type of pt. prevailed; *teached* survived dial. as repr. of ME. *teched* (XIII, Cursor M.).

Teague tīg (former) nickname of an Irishman. XVII. Generalized use of Ir. *Tadhg tēg*, *tīg*, identified with *Thaddeus*, and the var. *Thady*.

teak tīk (wood of) large E. Indian tree, Tectona grandis. XVII (Fryer). – Pg. *teca* – Malayalam *tēkka*.

teal tīl freshwater fowl Querquedula crecca. XIV. rel. to MLG. *tēlink*, MDu. *tēling*, *teiling* (Du. *teling*); ult. origin unkn.

team tīm A. †child-bearing, †offspring, (dial.) family, brood OE.; B. set of draught animals OE.; number of persons in concerted action XVI; †C. (leg.) vouching to warranty OE.; D. (dial., after ON. *taumr*) chain for yoking draught animals XIV. OE. *tēam* = OFris. *tām* bridle, progeny, OS. *tōm*, OHG. *zoum* (G. *zaum*), ON. *taumr* bridle, rein :– CGerm. (exc. Gothic) **taumaz*, prob. for **taugmaz*, f. **tauχ-* draw, rel. to L. *dūcere* (see DUCT). Hence **tea·mSTER**. orig. U.S. XVIII.

teapoy tī·poi three-legged stand. XIX. Hindi, f. *tīn*, in comb. *tir* three+Pers. *pāī* FOOT.

tear[1] tiəɹ drop of fluid shed by the eye. OE. *tēar* (contr. of **teaχor*), ONhb. *tehher*, *tæher* (in MSc. *techyr*) = OFris. *tār*, OHG. *zah(h)ar* (G. *zähre*, orig. pl.), ON. *tár*, Goth. *tagr* :– IE. **dakru-*, repr. also by OL. *dacruma* (L. *lacruma*, *-ima*; cf. LACHRYMOSE), Gr. *dákru*, W. *deigr*, Ir. *dér*.

tear[2] tɛəɹ pt. **tore** tɔ̄əɹ, pp. **torn** tɔ̄ɹn pull asunder by force. OE. *teran*, pt. *tær*, pp. *toren* = OS. *terian*, MLG., (M)Du. *teren*, OHG. *zeran* (G. *zehren*) destroy, consume, Goth. *dis|tairan*; the IE. base **der-* is repr. by Gr. *dérein* flay, Skr. *dṛṇā́ti*.

tease tīz A. separate the fibres of (wool, etc.) OE.; B. irritate by persistent action XVII. OE. *tǣsan* = (M)LG., MDu. *tēzen* (Du. *teezen*), OHG. *zeisan* (G. dial. *zeisen*) :– WGerm. **taisjan* (**taisan*); cf. (dial.) *tose*, *toze* (XIII), repr. OE. **tāsian* :– **taisōjan*. ¶ For the transf. meaning cf. HECKLE.

teasel, teazle tī·zl plant of the genus Dipsacus; the prickly flower heads of which are used for teasing cloth OE., *tǣs(e)l* = OHG. *zeisala* (MHG *zeisel*), f. base of **taisan* TEASE; see -EL[1], -LE[1].

teat tīt nipple of breast or udder. XIII. ME. *tete* – OF. *tete* (later and mod. *tette*) = Pr., Sp. *teta*, It. *tetta*, prob. of Germ. origin (see TIT[1] which it repl. in the standard lang.).

tec tek (sl.) short for DETECTIVE. XIX.

technic te·knik, **te·chnicAL** pert. to art or an art. XVII. – L. *technicus* (Quintilian) – Gr. *tekhnikós*, f. *tékhnē* art, craft, prob. f. IE. **tek-* shape, construct (cf. TECTONIC); see -IC, -ICAL. So **technique** teknī·k manner of artistic execution. XIX (Coleridge). – F., sb. use of adj. – L. *technicus*. **techno·LOGY** scientific study of the arts; technical terminology. XVII. – modL. **technologia* – Gr. *tekhnologíā*. **technolo·gICAL**. XVII. – modL. *technologicus*.

tectonic tektɔ·nik pert. to building or construction. XVII. – lateL. *tectonicus* – Gr. *tektonikós*, f. *tekton-*, *téktōn* carpenter, perh. rel. to L. *texere* (see TEXT).

ted ted (dial.) spread out for drying, scatter. XV. – ON. *teðja*, pt. *tadda*, rel. to *tad* dung, *toddi* small piece (see TOD²), OHG. (G. dial) *zetten* spread.

teddy te·di pet-form (see -Y⁶) of *Edward, Edmund, Theodore*; **te·ddy** BEAR¹, stuffed figure of a bear, with ref. to Theodore Roosevelt, president of U.S.A. 1901–9. **te·ddy** BOY, with ref. to Edward VII of England (1901–10), the style of costume of whose reign is imitated by the boys so named.

Te Deum tī dī·əm opening words of the canticle beginning *Te Deum laudamus* 'Thee God we praise', recited at matins in the Western Church. XIV (Ch.).

tedious tī·diəs, -jəs 'wearisome by continuance' (J.). XV (Lydg.). – OF. *tedieus* or late L. *tædiōsus*, f. L. *tædium* (whence **te·dium** XVII) weariness, disgust, f. *tædēre* be wearisome; see -IOUS.

tee¹ tī letter T or T-shaped object. XV.

tee² tī starting-place at golf. XVIII. Clipped form of earlier †*teaz* (XVII), of unkn. origin.

tee³ tī mark on the ice at curling. XVIII. Of unkn. origin; perh. identical with TEE¹.

tee-hee see TEHEE.

teem tīm †bring forth OE.; be prolific, abound *with* XVI. OE. *tēman* (WS. *tīeman*) :– **taumjan*, f. Germ. **taumaz* TEAM.

teen tīn †injury, hurt OE.; (dial.) spite, malice XII; (arch.) affliction, grief XIII. OE. *tēona* = OFris. *tiona, tiuna*, OS. *tiono*, and OE. *tēon* = ON. *tjón*, Gr. *dúē* misfortune, misery, Skr. *dunóti*.

-teen tīn (str. or unstr. acc. to position) OE. *-*tīene, -tēne, -tȳne* = OFris. *-ten(e), -tīne*, OS. *-tein*, OHG. *-zehan*, Goth. *-taihun* (Du. *-tien*, G. *-zehn*), inflected form of TEN added to cardinals from three to nine. Based on these are the ordinals in **-teen**TH² tīnþ, ME. *-tenþe*, alt. (by assim. to TEN) of *-teþe*, OE. *-teoþa, -teogoþa*, corr. to OFris. *-tinda*, OHG. *-zehanto* (Du. *-tiende*, G. *-zehnte*), ON. *-tándi*. **tee·**PAGE, **-age**R¹. XX.

teeny tī·ni expressive alt. of TINY (cf. *leetle* for *little*). XIX. Also *teeny-weeny*.

teethe tīð cut teeth. XV. f. *teeth*, pl. of TOOTH.

teetotal tītou·təl pert. to total abstinence. XIX. Said to have been first used by one Richard Turner, of Preston, Lancashire, about September 1833, in a speech advocating total abstinence from intoxicating liquors, in preference to abstinence from ardent spirits only. Perh. based on *teetotally* adv., a strengthened form of *totally* (quasi *T-totally*), which is recorded from U.S. in 1832.

teetotum tītou·təm top with four sides lettered to decide the spinner's luck. XVIII. orig. *T totum*, formed by prefixing to L. *tōtum* all, the whole, its initial T, which stood on one of the four sides, the other letters A, D, N, standing for L. *aufer, depone, nihil*. Earlier †*totum* XVII (cf. F. †*totum*, now *toton*).

teg teg sheep (formerly ewe) in its second year. XVI. ME. **tegge*, **tagge* in place-names repr. OE. **tegga*, **tagga*, parallel to OSw. *takka*, Sw. *tacka* ewe. In the formation cf. *earwig*, †*haysugge* hedge-sparrow, *pig, stag*.

tegument te·gjŭment covering, envelope. XV. – L. *tegumentum*, f. *tegere* cover; see THATCH, -MENT, and cf. INTEGUMENT.

tehee tihī· repr. light (derisive) laughter. XIV (Ch.); earlier in gerund †*tihing*.

teichopsia taikɔ·psiə (path.) temporary blindness accompanying ophthalmic headache. XIX. modL., f. Gr. *teîkhos* wall + *ópsis* sight + -IA¹; a frequent symptom is an appearance as of battlements.

teil tīl linden tree. XVI (*teyle*). – OF. *teil*, var. of *til* = Pr. *telh*, It. *tiglio* :– Rom. **tilium*, for L. *tilia* linden tree, F. *teille, tille* linden-bast.

telæsthesia telèsþī·siə perception at a distance. XIX. modL. (Myers, 1882), f. Gr. *têle* TELE- + *aísthēsis* perception (see ÆSTHETIC, -IA¹).

tele- te·li, tile· before a vowel prop. *tel-*, but more often in the full form, repr. Gr. *tēle-*, comb. form of *têle* afar, far off (rel. to *télos* end). comp.: **telegraph** te·ligràf †semaphore, signalling apparatus; apparatus for conveying a message to a distance by electricity XVIII. – F. *télégraphe*, suggested in 1792 by Miot de Mélito instead of the inventor Chappe's own term, *tachygraphe*, and accepted by him. Hence **te·le**GRAM message so sent XIX, **tele·**GRAPHY XVIII, **tele**GRA·PHIC XVIII. **telemeter** tile·mitəɹ instrument for determining the distance of objects XIX. **telepathy** tile·pəþi communication from mind to mind without aid of the senses (Myers, 1882). Gr. *-patheiā* feeling, perception, rel. to *patheîn* suffer, PATHOS. **telephone** te·lifoun apparatus for transmitting sounds to a distant hearer XIX; hence **telephon**IC -fɔ·nik, **telephon**IST tile·fənist; the formation is first exemplified in G. *telephon* (1796); **te·le**PRINTER a type-printing telegraph XX; **tele**SCOPE te·liskoup optical instrument for making distant objects appear nearer and larger. XVII (the It. form was used by Boyle). – It. *telescopio* (Galilei) or modL. *telescopium* (Porta); hence vb. (orig. U.S. XIX) cause to move into another object or collapse like the sliding parts of a telescope. **telescop**IC -skɔ·pik XVIII, †**-sco·p**ICAL XVII. **tele**VI·SION (now usu. te·li-) system of projecting a distant scene or action on a screen by means of photo-electrical and wireless processes XX; **Telex** te·leks system of telegraphy in which printed signals or messages are exchanged by teleprinters connected to the public telecommunication network, f. *tele*printer+*ex*change XX.

telega telei·ga four-wheeled Russian cart. XVI. Russ. *teléga*.

teleo- te·liou, teliɔ· before a vowel **tele-**, repr. *teleo-*, comb. form of Gr. *téleos* (*-eios*) perfect, complete, f. *télos* end, as in **teleo·-**LOGY doctrine of final causes. XVIII. – modL. *teleologia* (Wolf 1728). *b.* Applied in scientific terms to features exhibiting full development.

tell tel pt., pp. **told** tould. A. mention in order, narrate OE.; B. make known, declare; inform; relate OE.; (arch., exc. in *all told, untold wealth, tell one's beads*), mention numerically, count OE.; be of account (e.g. in *telling* ppl. adj.) XVII. OE. *tellan*, pt. *tealde*, pp. *ġeteald* = OFris. *talia, tella*, OS. *tellian*, (M)LG., (M)Du. *tellen*, OHG. *zellen* (*zalta, gizalt*), G. *zählen* reckon, count (cf. *erzählen* recount, relate), ON. *telja* :– CGerm. (exc. Gothic) **taljan*, f. **talō* TALE. Hence **te·ller**[1] one who relates XIII; one who keeps tally XV; one selected to count votes XVII.

tellurium teljuə·riəm (min.) one of the rarer elements. XVIII. modL., named by Klaproth 1798; f. L. *tellūr-, tellūs* earth+ -IUM, in contrast to his own discovery URANIUM.

telpher te·lfəɹ travelling unit in a system of **te·lpher**AGE, transport effected automatically by electricity. XIX (F. Jenkin). contr. form of **telephore*, f. Gr. *têle* TELE-+ *-phoros* bearing (*phérein* BEAR[2]).

telson te·lsən (zool.) last segment of some crustaceans, etc. XIX. – Gr. *télson* limit.

Telugu te·lugū name of a Dravidian people and their language, spoken on the Coromandel coast north of Madras. XVIII. Of unkn. origin; called also *Tenugu*, which native pundits explain as 'mellifluous' and derive from *tēne* honey. The Tamil name is *Vaḍugu* 'the Northern', whence older Pg. *Badages* and older G. *Waruga*.

temerarious teməɹɛ̃ə·riəs unreasonably bold or venturous. XVI. f. L. *temerārius* fortuitous, rash, f. *temere* blindly, rashly, orig. instr. abl. of **temus*, **temer-* darkness rel. to *tenebræ*; see TENEBROUS, -ARIOUS. So **temer**ITY time·rĭti rashness. XV. – L., f. *temere*; cf. F. *témérité*.

temper te·mpəɹ †due mixture of elements XIV (Trevisa); chiefly in various senses of *temperament* and *temperature* from XV; mental balance; frame of mind XVII; (outburst of) ill humour XIX. f. **te·mper** vb. OE. *temprian* (= OS. *temperon*) †mingle, blend; restrain, †regulate OE.; impart due hardness, etc. to (steel) XIV (Ch.). – L. *temperāre* mingle, restrain oneself, perh. orig. combine in due proportion, and rel. to *temper-, tempus* time, due season (but the conditions are obscure). So **tempera** te·mpərə painting in distemper. XIX. – It. in phr. *pingere a tempera*, f. *temperare* – L. **temper**AMENT te·mpərəmənt †due mixture of elements XV (Lydg.); combination of the four cardinal humours XVII, as constituting the natural disposition XIX. – L. *temperāmentum*, f. *temperāre*. **te·mper**ANCE self-restraint, moderation XIV (Rolle), spec. in food and drink XVI. – AN. *temperaunce* – L. *temperantia*. **te·mper**ATE[2] moderate XIV (Trevisa, Wyclif); of the zones lying between the torrid and frigid XVI (cf. Vitruvius' use of the L.). – L. *temperātus*, pp. of *temperāre*. **temperat**URE te·mpərətʃuəɹ †mixture; †temperament XVI; state with regard to heat and cold XVII (Boyle). – F. *température* or L.

tempest te·mpist violent storm. XIII. – OF. *tempeste* (mod. *tempête*) and *tempest* = Pr., It. *tempesta* and Pr. *tempest* :– Rom. **tempesta* and **tempestum*, for L. *tempestās* season, weather, storm, f. *tempus* time, season. So **tempe·st**UOUS. XVI. – late L. *tempestuōsus*; earlier †*tempeste(v)ous, -ious*, after *plente(v)ous*, etc.; see PLENTEOUS.

templar te·mpləɹ A. member of an order of knights orig. occupying a building on or near the site of the Temple of Solomon at Jerusalem XIII; B. barrister of the Inner or the Middle Temple, London XVI. – AN. *templer*, (O)F. *templier* – medL. *templārius* or *templāris*, f. *templum* TEMPLE[1]; see -AR. Established in 1851 as the designation of an organization of total abstainers (the Independent Order of Good Templars), based on the model of an order of freemasons calling themselves Knights Templars, both orig. in U.S.A.

temple[1] te·mpl sacred edifice. OE. *temp(e)l* (– L. *templum*), reinforced in ME. by (O)F. *temple* = Pr. *temple*, Sp. *templo*, It. *tempio* :– L. *templum* space marked out by an augur for taking observations, broad open space, consecrated space, sanctuary, prob. rel. to Gr. *témenos* reserved or sacred enclosure, f. base of *témnein* cut (cf. TMESIS, TOME). Formerly designating headquarters of the Knights Templars (XII) and hence (XIV) the name of two inns of court in London, which stand on the site of buildings once occupied by them.

temple[2] te·mpl flat part of the head between forehead and either ear. XIV (Rolle). – OF. *temple* (mod. *tempe*) = Pr. *templa*, It. *tempia* :– Rom. **tempula*, alt. of L. *tempora*, pl. of *tempus*.

temple[3] te·mpl weaver's stretcher. XV (Cath. Angl.). – F. *temple*, ult. identical with TEMPLE[2].

templet te·mplit plate of timber. XVII (Moxon). prob. f. TEMPLE[3]; see -ET.

tempo te·mpou (mus.) relative speed or rate of movement. XVIII. It. :– L. *tempus* time.

temporal[1] te·mpərəl †temporary; pert. to human life, worldly; secular XIV; (gram., pros.) relating to time or tense XVII. – (O)F. *temporel* or L. *temporālis*, f. *tempor-*, *tempus* time. See -AL[1]. So **tempora·lity** †temporal things XIV; material possessions XV. – late L. *temporālitās*. **te·mporalty**[2] (pl.) temporal things; body of temporal persons or laymen. XIV (Trevisa). **temporary** te·mpərəri lasting for a limited time. XVI. – L. *temporārius*, f. *tempor-*, *tempus*. **temporize** te·mpəraiz adopt a course for the time. XVI. – F. *temporiser* pass one's time, wait one's time – medL. *temporizāre*, f. L. *tempor-*, *tempus*.

temporal[2] te·mpərəl pert. to the temples. XVI. – late L. *temporālis*, f. *tempora*; see TEMPLE[2], -AL[1].

tempt tem^p^t test, try (surviving in *tempt God, fate, fortune, the sea*, etc.); try to attract, entice XIII. – OF. *tempter*, learned form beside *tenter* :– L. *temptāre* handle, feel, try the strength of, test, attempt. So **tempta·tion**. XIII. – OF. – L.

ten ten 10, x. OE. (Anglian) *tēn(e)*, (WS.) *tīen(e)* = OFris. *tiān*, *tēne*, *tīne*, OS. *tehan* (Du. *tien*), OHG. *zehan* (G. *zehn*), ON. *tíu*, Goth. *taihun* :– Germ **teχan*, beside **teχun* :– IE. **dekm̥*, whence also L. *decem* (cf. DECIMAL), Gr. *déka*, OSl. *desętĭ*, Skr. *dáça*, Toch. *śak*. **tenth** tenþ 10th. ME. *tenþe* (XII), alt. by assim. to TEN of *tethe*, OE. *teogoþa* (see TITHE, -TH[2]); cf. Gr. *dékatos*, OSl. *desjătyi*.

tenable te·nəbl, tī· capable of being held. XVI. – (O)F. *tenable*, f. *tenir* hold; see TENANT and -ABLE.

tenace te·nəs at whist, combination of cards controlling the opponent's holding. XVII. – F. *tenace* – Sp. *tenaza* lit. pincers, tongs :– L. *tenācia*, f. *tenāx*.

tenacious tinei·ʃəs holding together, holding fast, persistent. XVI. f. L. *tenāci-*, *tenāx*, f. *tenēre* hold; see next and -IOUS. So **tena·city** -æ·sĭti XVI. – (O)F. or L. *tenācitās*.

tenant te·nənt one who holds land, esp. of a lord; one who holds on lease for a term. XIV. – (O)F. *tenant*, sb. use of prp. of *tenir* hold – (with change of conjugation) L. *tenēre*, rel. to *tendere* stretch, TEND[2], with which it has the pp. (*tentus*) in common. See -ANT. Hence **te·nantry** XIV.

tench ten^t^ʃ freshwater fish, Tinca vulgaris. XIV. – OF. *tenche* (mod. *tanche*) :– late L. *tinca*.

tend[1] tend orig. in various senses of *attend* and *intend* XIV; now only in gen. use, take care of, be in charge of, look after XV. Aphetic of ATTEND and †*entend*, INTEND. Hence or aphetic of ATTENDANCE †**te·ndance**. XVI. Hence **te·nder**[3] †attendant, ministrant XV; boat attending a larger one XVII; car attached to a locomotive XIX; one who has charge of a bar, etc. XIX. Partly f. *attender* (XV), partly immed. f. TEND[1] + -ER[1].

tend[2] tend have a disposition *to* or *towards*. XIV. – (O)F. *tendre* :– L. *tendere* stretch, f. IE. **ten-* **ton-* stretch, extend, for other derivs. of which see TENANT, TENDER[1], TENET, TENOR, TENSE[2], TENT[1], TENUOUS, TETANUS, THIN, TONE.

tendency te·ndənsi fact or quality of tending to something. XVII. – medL. *tendentia* (Bonaventura, Duns Scotus), f. L. *tendent-*, *-ēns*, prp. of *tendere* TEND[2]. Also †**te·ndence** (XVII) – (O)F. *tendance*. See -ENCE, -ENCY. Hence **tende·ntial** -ʃəl, XIX, **tende·ntious** -ʃəs XX, having a (purposed) tendency; cf. F. *tendancieux*, G. *tendenziös*.

tender[1] te·ndəɹ easily broken or injured XIII (AncrR.); having delicacy of feeling XIII (Cursor M.); susceptible to moral or spiritual influences XVI. – (O)F. *tendre* = Pr. *tenre*, *tendre*, Sp. *tierno*, Pg. *tenro*, It. *tenero* :– L. *tener-*, *tener* tender, delicate, f. **ten-* (see TEND[2]).

tender[2] tə·ndəɹ offer for acceptance. XVI. – (O)F. *tendre* :– L. *tendere* stretch, hold forth (cf. TEND[2]). ¶ For the unusual retention of the inf. ending cf. RENDER. Hence sb. formal offer XVI.

tendon te·ndən cord of tissue terminating a muscle XVI. – F. *tendon* or medL. *tendō(n-)*; f. L. *tendere*, tr. Gr. *ténōn* sinew (whence late L. *tenōn*), sb. use of aorist pple. of *teínein* stretch, TEND[2]. Hence **te·ndonous** XVI, superseded by **te·ndinous**, based on modL. *tendin-* (cf. It. *tendine*), which repl. *tendōn-*, on the model of L. words in *-dō*, *-din-*.

tendril te·ndrĭl slender (often spiral) thread-like appendage of a plant. XVI. prob. alt., after F. dim. †*tendrillon*, of †*tendron* young shoot, (pl.) cartilages of the ribs (XIV) – (O)F. *tendron*, earlier *tendrun* tender part or shoot, cartilage = It. *tenerume* shoots :– Rom. **tenerūmen* shoots, f. L. *tener* TENDER[1].

tenebræ te·nibrī Holy Week devotion (matins and lauds) at which candles lighted at the beginning are successively put out. XVII. L (pl.), parallel to Skr. *támaḥ*, g. *támasaḥ*, Lith. *tamsà*, Lett. *timsa* darkness, and referred to **teməsrā* and cogn. with Skr., Baltic, and Celtic forms.

tenement te·nimənt †tenure; holding XIV; dwelling-place XV. – OF. *tenement* (mod. *tènement*) – medL. *tenementum*, f. L. *tenēre* hold (see TENANT) + *-mentum* -MENT.

tenet te·nit doctrine held by a person or party. XVII. – L. *tenet* (he) holds, 3rd pres. sg. of *tenēre* hold (see TEND[2]); superseded earlier †*tenent* (XVI) – L. *tenent* (they) hold, which became obs. during XVIII. ¶ For parallel uses of similar forms cf. *caret*, *habitat*, *incipit*.

tenné te·ni (her.) tawny. XVI. – obs. F. *tenné*, var. of *tanné* TAWNY.

tenner te·nəɹ (colloq.) £10 note. f. TEN + -ER[1].

tennis te·nis ball game played with rackets in a walled court XIV; short for *lawn t.*, earlier *field t.* XIX. Late ME. *tenetz* (Gower), *teneys*, *tenes*, *tenyse*, usu. taken to be – (O)F. *tenez*, imper. of *tenir* hold, take, presumably the server's call to his opponent used as name of the game, which is recorded (XIV) as *tenes*, being intoduced into Italy by French knights early in the year 1325.

tenon te·nən piece fitting into a mortise. XV. – F. *tenon*, f. *tenir* (:– L. *tenēre* hold; cf. TENANT) + *-on* :– L. *-ōn-*.

tenor te·nəɹ A. general sense of a discourse, etc. XIII (Cursor M.); continuous progress XIV (Trevisa); †quality, condition XVI; B. (mus.) voice or part between alto and bass XIV. ME. *tenur*, *-our* – AN. *tenur*, OF. *tenour* (mod. *teneur* course, import), corr. to Sp. *tenor*, It. *tenore* – L. *tenōrem*, *tenor* continuous course, substance, import of a law, etc., f. *tenēre* hold; see TENANT, -OR[2]. Sense B was in OF. *tenor* (mod. *ténor*) – It. *tenore* and medL. *tenor* (to which the Eng. word in all senses has been conformed); the musical sense ('holding or continuous part') is due to the allotting of the melody to that part.

tense[1] tens †time; (gram.) form of a verb indicating time XIV. – OF. *tens* (mod. *temps*) = Pr. *temps*, Sp. *tiempo*, It. *tempo* :– L. *tempus* time (cf. TEMPORAL).

tense[2] tens drawn tight XVII; highly strung XIX. – L. *tensus*, pp. of *tendere* stretch, TEND[2]. So **te·ns**ILE ductile XVII (Bacon); pert. to tension XIX. – medL. **tens**ION te·nʃən condition of being stretched or strained. XVI. – F. *tension* or L. *tensiō(n-)*, f. pp. of *tendere*.

tensOR[1] te·nsɔ̄ɹ (anat.) muscle that tightens some part XVIII; (math.) in quaternions XIX. – modL.

tent[1] tent portable shelter of canvas, etc. XIII (RGlouc.). – (O)F. *tente* :– Rom. **tenta* n.pl. used as fem of **tentum*, for L. *tentōrium* tent, f. *tent-*, pp. stem pf *tendere* stretch, TEND[2], based on the use of phr. *pelles tendere* stretch out skins, in the sense 'pitch tents', 'be encamped'; cf. Pr., It. *tenda*, Sp. *tienda* tent, awning, shop, Rum. *tindă* forecourt, vestibule :– Rom. **tenda*. Hence **tent** vb., **te·nt**ED[1] pp. XVII (Sh.).

tent[2] tent †probe; roll of material for searching a wound XIV. – (O)F. *tente*, f. *tenter* :– L. *temptāre* touch, feel, try, TEMPT.

tent[3] tent deep-red Spanish wine. XVI (*tynt*). – Sp. *tinto* dark-coloured :– L. *tinctus*, pp. of *tingere*, dye, TINGE.

tentacle te·ntəkl sensitive process in animals and plants. XVIII. – modL. *tentāculum* (in earlier use), f. L. *tentāre* var. of *temptāre* feel, try, TEMPT; see -CLE, -CULE.

tentative te·ntətiv of the nature of an experiment. XVI (in *tentatively*, after medL. *tentātīvē*). – medL. *tentātīvus* (also *tentātiva*, fem. sb., whence F. *tentative* attempt), f. pp. stem of L. *tentāre*; see prec. and -ATIVE.

tenter te·ntəɹ wooden frame on which cloth is stretched. XIV. – AN. **tentur* – medL. *tentōrium* (XIII), f. pp. stem *tent-* of L. *tendere* stretch, TEND[2]. The frequent forms of the type *tainter*, *teinter* (XIV–XVII), which are the earliest, suggest assoc. with F. *teindre* dye. comb. *tenterhook* (XV) hook fixed on a tenter, in gen. use now only in fig. phr. *on tenterhooks* (XVI) in a state of painful suspense.

tenth see TEN.

tenuis te·njuis (phon.) unvoiced stop (as p, t, k). XVII. mod use of L. *tenuis* thin, slender, fine, to render Gr. *psīlón*, n. of *psīlós* bare, smooth.

tenuity tənjū·iti thinness, meagreness. XVI. – L. *tenuitās*, f. *tenuis* THIN; see -ITY. Cf. F. *ténuité*. So **tenu**OUS te·njuəs. XVI; superseding earlier *tenuious* f. *tenui-s* + -OUS.

tenure te·njəɹ holding of a tenement, condition under which it is held. XV. – OF. *tenure*, earlier *tenēure* (cf. medL. *tena-*, *tene-*, *tenitūra*), f. *tenir* hold + *-ēure*; see TENANT, -URE.

teocalli tioukæ·li place of worship of the ancient Mexicans. XVII. – Mex. *teocalli*, f. *teotl* god + *calli* house.

tepee tī·pi, tipī· wigwam. XIX. – Sioux, Dakota *tīpī* tent, dwelling.

tephrite te·frait volcanic rock rel. to basalt. XVII. f. Gr. *tephrós* ash-coloured, f. *téphra* ashes; see -ITE and cf. L. *tephrītis*.

tepid te·pid lukewarm. XIV. – L. *tepidus*, f. *tepēre* be warm, rel. to Skr. *tápas* heat, *tápati* burn, OSl. *toplŭ* hot, OIr. *té* hot, W. *tes* heat; see -ID[1].

ter tɔ̄ɹ L. adv. *ter* thrice, used occas. in comp. XVII; spec. in chem. (XIX), now superseded by TRI-.

teraphim te·rəfim idol, image (esp. of household gods) of the Hebrews. XIV (Wycl. Bible). – Vulg. L. *theraphim*, LXX Gr. *theraphín* (Judges xvii 5, Hosea iii 4), etc. – Heb. *tʰeraphīm*, Aram. *-īn*.

teratology terətɔ·lədʒi account of marvels XVII; (biol.) study of abnormalities XIX. f. Gr. *terato-*, *téras* marvel, prodigy + -LOGY.

terce tɔ̄ɹs var. of TIERCE, usual in the name of the canonical hour, XIV (*terse*).

tercel tɔ̄·ɹsl, **tiercel** tiə·ɹsl male hawk. XIV. – OF. *tercel*, also *terçuel* = Pr. *tersol*, Sp. *terzuelo*, It. *terz(u)olo* – Rom. **tertiōlu-s*, f. *tertius* THIRD; perh. so named because it was believed that the third egg of a clutch produced a male bird.

tercet tə̄·ɹset (pros.) set of three lines rhyming together. XVI – F. *tercet* – It. *terzetto*, f. *terzo* (:– L. *tertiu-s* THIRD)+ *-etto* -ET.

terebinth te·rībinþ tree Pistachia Terebinthus, the source of turpentine. XIV. – OF. *t(h)erebinte* (mod. *térébinthe*), corr. to Sp., It. *terebinto*, or their source L. *terebinthus* – Gr. *terébinthos*, earlier *térbinthos, términthos*, of alien origin.

teredo tĭrī·dou boring mollusc, esp. shipworm. XVII. – L. *terēdō* – Gr. *terēdṓn*, f. base **ter-* of *teírein* rub hard, wear away, bore.

terete tərī·t smooth and round (spec. in nat. hist.) XVII. – L. *teret-, teres*.

tergiversation tə̄:ɹdʒivəɹsei·ʃən desertion of a cause, etc.; contradictory behaviour. XVI. – L. *tergiversatiō(n-)*, f. *tergiversārī* (whence **te·rgiversate** XVII) f. *tergum* back +*vers-*, pp. stem of *vertere* turn (see WORTH[3]).

term tə̄ɹm limit in time, period XIII; (pl.) limiting conditions XIV; form in which a matter or subject is expressed, expression XIV – (O)F. *terme* = Pr. *terme*, Sp. *termino*, It. *termine* :– L. *terminu-s*; see below. Hence **te·rm**ER[1] (hist.) one who resorted to London in term XVI. **te·rmin**AL[1] pert. to a boundary XV; situated at or forming the end XIX; sb. terminal element XIX. – L. (or F.). **te·rmin**ATE[3] †determine XVI; bring to an end XVII. f. pp. stem of L. *termināre*, f. *terminus*. **termina·**TION †determination; end XV; (gram.) ending XVI (Palsgr.). – (O)F. or L. **termino·**LOGY system of terms. XIX. – G. *terminologie* or modL. *terminologia*.
terminus tə̄·ɹminəs pl. **-i** ai finishing point XVII; end of a line of railway XIX. – L. *terminus* (an Italic word) limit, boundary, (*T-*) deity presiding over boundaries (orig. rendering Gr. *ὅρος*); in medL. 'term', in extension of the late L. use in rendering mathematical and logical application of Gr. *ὅρος* boundary, limit. Cf. CONTERMINOUS, DETERMINE, EXTERMINATE.

termagant tə̄·ɹməgənt (*T-*) deity attributed to Mohammedans, etc., represented in mystery plays as an overbearing character XIII (Laȝ.); violent domineering person (esp. woman) XVI. Earlier form *tervagaunt*, later *term-* (XIV) – OF. *Tervagan(t)* – It. *Trivigante, -vag-* (Ariosto), expl. as f. L. *tri-* TRI- + *vagant-, -āns*, prp. of *vagārī* wander (cf. VAGUE) and so designating the moon wandering under the names of Selene (Luna), Artemis (Diana), and Persephone (Proserpina), in heaven, earth, and hell respectively.

termite tə̄·ɹmait white ant (genus Termes, family Termitidæ). XVIII. – mod. use (Linnæus) of late L. *termit-, termes* wood-worm, alt. of *tarmes* wood-worm perh. by assim. to *terere* rub.

termor tə̄·rməɹ one who holds property for a term of years. XIV. – AN. *termer*, f. *terme* TERM; see -ER[2].

tern tə̄ɹn sea-bird of the genus Sterna. XVIII (Ray). Of Scand. origin; cf. Da. *terne*, Norw. *terna*, Sw. *tärna* :– ON. *þerna*.

ternary tə̄·ɹnəri threefold, triple. XIV. – L. *ternārius*, f. L. *ternī* three at a time, three by three, f. *ter* thrice; see THREE, -ARY. So **te·rn**ATE[2]. XVIII. – modL. *ternātus*.

terp tə̄ɹp type of artificial mound found in Friesland. XIX. – Fris. *terp* (pl. *terpen*) :– OFris. *therp*, var. of *thorp* village, THORP.

terpene tə̄·ɹpīn (chem.) hydrocarbon of the formula $C_{10}H_{16}$. XIX. f. *terp-* in *terpentine*, obs. form of TURPENTINE+-ENE.

Terpsichorean tə̄ɹpsikərī·ən pert. to dancing. XIX. f. Gr. *terpsikhórē* muse of dancing and of the dramatic chorus, f. *térpein* delight+*khorós* dance, CHORUS; see -EAN.

terra te·rə L., It. 'earth', as in **t. cotta** kɔ·tə unglazed pottery. XVIII. It. 'baked earth' (*cotta* :– L. *cocta*, fem. pp. of *coquere* COOK); **t. firma** fə̄·ɹmə †mainland; dry land. XVII. L., 'firm land' (fem. of *firmus* FIRM); **t. incognita** inkɔ·gnitə unexplored territory. XVII (Capt. Smith). L., 'unknown land'. **terræ filius** te·rī fi·liəs person of obscure parentage XVI; (Univ. of Oxford) formerly orator privileged to make humorous comments at a public act XVII. L. 'son of the earth', therefore, of unknown origin.

terrace te·ris †gallery, balcony; raised level walk. XVI. – OF. *terrace*, (also mod.) *-asse* †rubble, platform = It. *terraccia, -azza* bad soil, *-azzo*, Sp. *terraza*, Pg. *terraço* :– Rom. **terrāceu-s, -ācea*, f. L. *terra* earth (cf. Ir., W. *tir* country); see -ACEOUS.

terrain te·rein, tract of country as fit for something. XVIII. F. – pop. L. **terrānum*, var. of L. *terrēnum* TERRENE.

terramare terəmā·ɹ, -mɛə·ɹ ammoniacal earth found in the valley of the Po, Italy. XIX. – F. *terramare* – It. dial. *terramara*, for *terra marna*, i.e. *terra* earth + *marna* MARL.

terrapin te·rəpin American turtle. XVII. – Abenaki *turepé*, Lenape *turupe* little turtle, with ending *in* of obscure origin.

terraqueous terei·kwiəs composed of, living in, land and water, chiefly in *t. globe*. XVII. f. medL. *terraqueus*, *terra* earth + *aqua* water, after AQUEOUS; hence F. *terraqué-e* (Voltaire); so Sp. *(el globo) terrácueo*, It. *terracqueo*.

terrene terī·n earthly. XIV. – AN. *terrene* – L. *terrēnus*, f. *terra* earth; for the ending cf. *serene*.

terreplein tɛə·ɹplein, || tɛrəplɛ̃ (fortif.) sloping bank behind a wall or rampart XVI; level base for a battery XVII. – F. *terre-plein* – It. *terrapieno*, f. *terrapienare* 'fill with earth', f. *terra* (:– L. *terra* earth)+ *pieno* (:– L. *plēnus*) FULL.

terrestrial tère·striəl earthly, mundane xv; pert. to the earth xvi. f. L. *terrestris*, f. *terra* earth (rel. to Ir., W. *tir* country); for the formation cf. L. *campestris, silvestris*; see -IAL. ¶ Earlier †*terrestre* (esp. in *paradis t.* – OF.). xiv.

terret te·rit circular ring. xv. Late ME. *tyret*, var. of *toret* – OF. *toret, touret*, dim. of *tour* TOUR, TOWER; see -ET.

terrible te·rĭbl exciting terror xv (Lydg.); very violent, severe, or bad, excessive. xvi. – (O)F. *terrible* – L. *terribilis*, f. *terrēre* frighten; see -BLE.

terrier[1] te·riəɹ register of landed property. xv. – OF. *terrier*, sb. use of adj. (cf. F. *registre terrier*) :– medL. *terrārius* (as in *liber terrārius*), f. L. *terra* land.

terrier[2] te·riəɹ small breed of dog. So called from its pursuing the quarry into its earth. xv (Promp. Parv.). – early modF. (*chien*) *terrier* – medL. *terrārius*, f. L. *terra* earth; cf. prec.

terrific təri·fik causing terror. xvii (Milton). – L. *terrificus*, f. *terrēre*, frighten, rel. to *tremere*; see TREMOR, -FIC. So **te·rri**FY. xvi. – L. *terrificāre*; cf. F. *terrifier* (xviii).

terrine see TUREEN.

territory te·rĭtəri land belonging to †a town, a ruler or state. xv. – L. *territōrium*, f. *terra* land, after *dormitōrium, prætōrium*. So **territo·r**IAL. xviii. – late L.

terror te·rəɹ intense fear. xiv. First in Sc. (*terrour*) – OF. *terrour* (mod. *terreur*) :– L. *terrōrem*, nom. *terror* (-OR[2]). So **te·rror**ISM, -IST. xviii. – F. *terrorisme, -iste*.

terry te·ri loop raised in pile-weaving left uncut. xviii. Of unkn. origin.

tersanctus tɜ̄ɹsæ·ŋktəs (liturg.) SANCTUS. xix. Cf. TRISAGION.

terse tɜ̄ɹs †smoothed, polished, neat; †polite, refined xvii; neatly concise xviii. – L. *tersus*, pp. of *tergēre* wipe (cf. DETERGENT).

tertian tɜ̄·ɹʃən (of a fever) of which the paroxysms occur every third (i.e. every alternate) day; also sb. xiv (Ch., Trevisa, PPl.). – L. *tertiānus*, f. *tertius* THIRD; see -IAN. So **terti**ARY tɜ̄·ɹʃəri pert. to (a member of) the third series, order, etc. xvi. – L. *tertiārius*, f. *tertius*. **tertium quid** tɜ̄·ɹʃiəm kwid 'third something'; (old chem.) third substance distinct from its two components. xviii. late L., tr. Gr. τρίτόν τι (Plato); n. of *tertius* THIRD, *quid*, n. of *quis* somebody.

terza rima tɛ·rtsa rī·ma It. form of verse rhyming a b a, b c b, c d c, of the 'Divina Commedia' of Dante. It., fem. of *terzo* THIRD, *rima* RHYME.

tessellated te·sĭleitid formed with a mosaic pattern. xvii. f. L. *tessellātus* (or the derived It. *tessellato*), f. *tessella*, dim. of *tessera*; see next, -ATE[2], -ED[1].

tessera te·sərə small quadrilateral tablet, esp. as used in mosaic; (hist.) square tablet on which watchword, etc., was written; hence (gen.) symbol, token. xvii. – L. *tessera* – Gr. *téssera*, n. of *tésseres*, Ionic var. of *téssares* FOUR.

test test A. cupel used in treating gold and silver alloys or ore xiv (Ch.; rare before xvi); B. 'means of trial' (J.) xvi. – OF. *test* pot (mod. *têt* cupel), :– L. *testū, testum*, by-form of *testa* tile (Rom. head), in B mainly f. the vb. Hence **test** vb., first in pp. (xvii, Sh.); 'to test' is stigmatized by Southey as an Americanism.

testaceous testei·ʃ[i]əs (zool.) having a shell; shell-like. xvii. f. L. *testāceus*, f. *testa* tile, earthern pot, potsherd, shell; see -ACEOUS.

testament te·stəmənt will disposing of property and appointing an executor xiv (R. Mannyng); †covenant between God and man; each of the two divisions of the Holy Scripture or Bible xiii (Cursor M.) (*Old* and *New Testaments*, L. *vetus* and *novum testamentum*, Gr. παλαιὰ and καινὴ διαθήκη.) – L. *testāmentum*, f. *testārī* bear witness, make a will, f. *testis* witness; see MENT. So **testame·nt**ARY. xv. – L.

testamur testei·məɹ (in Univ. use) examiners' certificate that a candidate has satisfied them. xix. L. 'we testify', 1st pers. pl. pres. indic. of *testārī* bear witness, f. *testis*.

testator testei·təɹ one who makes or has made a will. xv. – AN. *testatour* – L. *testātor*, f. *testārī*.

tester[1] te·stəɹ canopy over a bed. xiv (Wyclif). – medL. *testerium, testrum, testura* f. Rom. **testa* head (L. *testa* tile); cf. OF. *testiere*, F. *têtière*, It. *testiera*, Sp. *testera*, having various applications with ref. to the head.

tester[2] te·stəɹ (hist.) obscure alt. of TESTON; later, sixpence.

testicle te·stikl semen-secreting glandular organ of male mammals. xv (*-icules*). – L. *testiculus*, dim. of *testis* witness (the organ being evidence of virility). So **testi·cul**AR. xvii.

testify te·stifai bear witness to. xiv (PPl.). – L. *testificāre, -ārī*, f. *testis* witness; see -FY.

testiMONY te·stiməni evidence; spec. in Scriptural lang., of the Mosaic law, etc., repr. Vulg. *testimonium*, LXX τὸ μαρτύριον, Heb. *hēdūth*, as in Ex. xxx 6, Num. i 50, ix 15, xvii 4. **testimoni**AL[1] -mou·niəl adj. & sb. – (O)F. or late L. xv.

testis te·stis (anat.) testicle. xvii. L., 'witness'.

teston, testoon te·stən, testū·n (hist.) It. coin bearing the head of a duke; shilling of Henry VII, etc., being the first Eng. coins to bear a portrait. xiv. – F. †*teston*, It. †*testone*, f. *teste, testa* head :– L. *testa* tile (in Rom. head); see -OON.

testudo testjū·dou screen resembling a tortoise's shell for the protection of armed forces. XVII. L. *testūdo*, f. *testa* pot, shell (see TEST), *testu* pot-lid.

testy te·sti †headstrong, impetuous XIV (Ch.); prone to be easily irritated XVI. Late ME. *testif* – AN. *testif*, f. OF. *teste* (mod. *tête*) head :– L. *testa* shell, earthen vessel, tile, (Rom.) head; see -IVE. Cf. HASTY, JOLLY, TARDY.

tetanus te·tənəs spasm and rigidity of the muscles. XVI (in late ME. anglicized *tetane*). – L. – Gr. *tétanos*, f. base of *teínein* stretch (cf. TONE).

tetchy te·tʃi easily irritated. XVI (Sh.). prob. f. *tecche*, var. of *tache* spot, blemish, fault – OF. *teche*, (also mod.) *tache*, perh. of Germ. origin; see -Y[1].

tête-à-tête tei·tatei·t private conversation between two. XVII. F., 'head to head' (see TESTY).

tether te·ðəɹ rope, etc. to tie up a beast. XIV (first in north. texts). – ON. *tjóðr*, corr. to WFris. *tyader*, *tieder*, MLG., MDu. *tūder*, *tudder* (Du. *tuier*), OHG. *zeotar* fore-pole, repr. Germ. ***teuđr-**, ***tūdr-**; f. ***teu-** fasten. Hence **tether** vb. XV.

tetra- te·trə, tètræ· before a vowel *tetr-*, – Gr. *tetra-*, comb. form of *téttares*, *téttara* FOUR, as in **te·tra**CHORD XVII, spec. chem. signifying four atoms or groups XIX.

tetrad te·træd group of four. XVII. – Gr. *tetrad-*, *tetrás*, f. *téttares*; see prec. and -AD[1].

te·traGON four-angle figure. XVII; **tetragon**AL[1] -æ·gənəl. XVI; **tetragra·mmaton** Heb. word written JHVH JEHOVAH. XIV. Gr., f. *grámma*, *-at-* letter. **tetra**HE·DRON four-sided figure. XVI (Billingsley). **tetra**LOGY tetræ·lədʒi series of four related dramas. XVII. – Gr. *tetralogíā*. **tetra**METER -æ·mitəɹ (pros.) element of four measures. XVII. – late L. *tetrametrus* – Gr. *tetrámetros*. **te·trastich** strophe of four lines. XVI. – L. *tetrastichon* – Gr. *tetrástikhon* (cf. DISTICH). **tetra**SY·LLABLE. XVI. – Gr. *tetrasúllabos*.

tetrarch te·trāɹk, tī·trāɹk ruler of one of four divisions of a country, subordinate ruler. XIV (Wycl. Bible). – late L. *tetrarcha*, cl. L. *-ēs* – Gr. *tetrárkhēs*, f. *tetra-* (see above) + *-arkhēs* ruling. So **te·trarch**Y[3] XV.

tetter te·təɹ pustular eruption of the skin. OE. *teter*, cogn. with Skr. *dadru* skin disease, f. *dṛ* to crack; cf. Lith. *dedervinẽ* tetter; repr. in OHG. *zittaroh* and G. *zitteroch* (dial.), *zittermal*, *zitterflechte* tetter, ringworm; cf. late L. *derbita* (whence F. *dartre*, etc.), W. *darwden*.

tettix te·tiks cicada. XVIII. modL. – Gr. *téttix*.

Teuton tjū·tən member of a people of unknown race reckoned among the peoples of Germania (see GERMAN). XVIII. – L. *Teutonī*, *Teutones* (pl.), f. IE. base meaning 'people', 'country', 'land'. So **Teuton**IC tjutɔ·nik pert. to this people, later identified with *Germanic*. XVII (*T. Knights*, *T. Order*, military order of German knights). – F. *teutonique* – L. *Teutonicus*. comb. form **Teut(o)-** XIX.

text tekst wording of a passage; very words and sentences; short passage used as a motto, subject of discourse, etc. XIV (PPl.); theme XVII (Sh). ME. *text(e)*, *tixt(e)* – ONF. *tixte*, (also modF.) *texte* – L. *textus* tissue, style of literary work (Quintilian), in medL. the Gospel, written character, f. pp. of *texere* weave. So **textile** te·kstail adj. and sb. woven (fabric). XVII. – F. *textile* or L. *textilis*.

textuAL[1] te·kstjuəl †well-read in texts XIV Ch.); pert. to the or a text, esp. of the Scriptures XIV. – (O)F. *textuel*. **tex**TURE te·kstʃəɹ, -tjuəɹ †weaving XV; character of a textile fabric, also fig. XVII. – L. *textūra*, f. *text-*, pp. of *texere*. Cf. CONTEXT, PRETEXT.

th consonantal digraph usu. repr. the unvoiced and voiced open consonants denoted phonetically by þ (runic thorn) or θ (Greek theta) and ð (crossed d), occurring mainly in words of OE. and ON. origin, e.g. *cloth*, *clothes*, *throat*, *though*, *thwart*, *thy*, and in words of Gr. origin, usu. through L., as *authentic*, *orthography*, *throne*; traces of AN. phonology are seen in *faith*, Sc. *poortith* POVERTY (see -ETH[2]); Oriental aspirated varieties of t are repr. in *thakur*, *thug*.

-th[1] þ suffix denoting action or process, formed on vb.-stems (1) in words such as *bath*, *birth*, *death*, *math*, of prim. Germ. age, (2) in others of later emergence, as *growth*, *spilth*, *tilth*; (3) in OE. words of quality or condition, in *-þu*, *-þo* (:– Germ. *-iþō*) based on adjs., as *breadth*, *filth*, *health*, *length*, *mirth*, *strength*, *truth*; of ME. date are *dearth*, *depth*, *sloth*, *wealth*, of later date are *width*, *illth* (Ruskin). See further -T[1], -T[2].

-th[2] þ suffix of ordinal numbers from *fourth* upwards, repr. OE. *-þa*, *-þe*, or *-oþa*, *-oþe*; in *fifta*, *sixta*, *ellefta*, *twelfta* phonetically modified; in the sp. of *eighth* *th* is a simplification; with the tens (*twenty*, etc.) the ending is *-eth* (OE. *-oþa*, *-oþe*). OE. formations in *-oþa* were regularly repl. in ME. or late OE. by new forms in *-nþe*, based on the cardinals, as *seofoþa* by *seuenþe*, *teoþa* (from *teogoþa*) by *tenþe*; cf. *elevenþe* repl. OE. *endlyfta*.

thakur tʰā·kur lord, noble. XVIII. – Hindi *ṭhákur*:– Skr. *ṭhákkura* deity.

thalamus þæ·ləməs (anat.) part of the brain at which a nerve originates; receptacle of a flower. XVIII. – L. *thalamus* – Gr. *thálamos* inner chamber, rel. to *thólos* vault.

thalassic þəlæ·sik pert. to the sea or inland seas. XIX. – F. *thalassique* (Brongniart 1829), f. Gr. *thálassa*; see -IC.

thaler tā·ləɹ German silver coin. XVIII. – G. *t(h)aler* DOLLAR.

thallium þæ·liəm (chem.) metallic element, so named from the green line distinguishing its spectrum. XIX. – modL. *thallium* (Crookes 1861), f. L. *thallus* (used spec. in bot.), Gr. *thallós* green shoot; see -IUM.

Thames temz the river on which London is situated. OE. *Temes(e)* – L. *Tamēsis*, *Tamēsa*, medL. *T(h)amisa* – British *Tamesā*; phr. *set the T. on fire*, work wonders (XVIII).

than ðən, (quoted alone) ðæn conjunctive particle used after comparatives and *other* (with its comps.) and *else*. OE. *þanne*, *þonne*, *þænne*, orig. identical with the temporal adv. THEN, from which it was not finally differentiated in form until *c.*1700. For the development of the conjunctive use in WGerm. cf. OS. *than*, (M)Du. *dan*, OHG. *thanne*, *danne*, *denne* (G. *denn* for, *dann* then), while Du. *dan* has both meanings).

thanatism þæ·nətizm belief in the destruction of the soul at death. XIX. f. Gr. *thánatos* death + -ISM.

thane þein †(military) servant or attendant; (hist.) in AS. times, one who held lands by military service OE.; (Sc. hist.) man holding lands of the King XV. OE. *þeġ(e)n* = OS. *thegan* man, OHG. *degan* boy, servant, warrior, hero (G. *degen* warrior), ON. *þegn* freeman, liegeman :– CGerm. (exc. Goth.) **þegnaz* :– IE. **teknós* pp. formation on base **teq-*, **toq-* (cf. Gr. *téknon*, Skr. *táknam-* child), repr. also by Gr. *tíktein* (:– **titk-*) bring forth, *tékos* child, *tókos* birth, *tokeús* parent. The sp. *thane* is derived from Sc. usage of XV–XVI as a var. of *thayn* through Holinshed and Sh. (as in 'Macbeth'). See THEGN.

thank þæŋk †thought; †kindly thought, favour, gratitude; expression of gratitude (now only pl. *thanks*, OE. *þancas*; cf. L. *grates*, *gratiæ*). OE. *þanc* = OFris. *thank*, *thonk*, OS. *thank*, MDu., OHG. *danc* (Du., G. *dank*), Goth. *þagks* :– Germ. **þaŋkaz* (but ON. *þǫkk* :– **þaŋku* fem.), f. **þaŋk-*, **þeŋk-* (see THINK). So **thank** vb. OE. *þancian* = OS. *thankon*, OHG. *dankōn* (Du., G. *danken*). comps. *tha·nko:ffering* XVI (Tindale, Great Bible), *tha·nksgi:ving* XVI (Tindale, Coverdlae). Hence **tha·nk**FUL[1] showing gratitude; †deserving gratitude. OE. *þancfull*. **tha·nk**LESS ungrateful; that brings no thanks. XVI. phr. **thank you** þæ·ŋkju XV for *I thank you*; cf. G. *danke*.

that[1] ðæt demons. pron. orig. n. of THE. OE. *þæt*, corr. to OFris. *thet*, OS. *that*, (M)Du. *dat*, OHG. *daz* (G. *das*), ON. *þat*, Goth. *þata* (with suffix). :– IE. **tad*, repr. also by Skr. *tát*, Gr. *tó*, L. *topper* quickly (for **todper*, with *-per* as in *semper*, etc.), in *is|tud*, n. of *iste*, OSl. *to*. As adj. XII (Orm), with pl. THOSE; as adv. XV.

that[2] ðət relative pron. equiv. to *who* and *which*, in OE. a generalized use of the n. of THE (cf. THAT[1]), repl. OE. and ME. indeclinable *þe*.

that[3] (usu. instr.) ðət as a relative or conjunctive particle in uses developed from those of THAT[1] and THAT[2]; the development is CGerm., with differentiation of sp. (*dass*) in modG., and affix in Goth. *þatei*; for the evolution cf. Gr. ὅτι, from the n. of relative pron. ὅστις, L. *quod*, n. of *quī* WHO.

thatch þætʃ roof (a building), esp. with straw. XIV (Trevisa). repr. OE. *þeććan*, pt. *þeahte*, *þehte* = OFris. *thekka*, OS. *thekkian*, OHG. *decchan* (Du. *dekken*, G. *decken*), ON. *þekja* :– CGerm. (exc. Goth.) **þakjan*, f. **þakam* (OE. *þæć* = MDu. *dac*, Du. *dak*, OHG., G. *dach* roof, ON. *þak* roof, thatch), f. **þak-* :– IE. **tog-* **teg-* cover, repr. also by L. *tegere* (cf. INTEGUMENT, TILE). Hence **thatch** sb. XIV (Trevisa). The normal repr. of OE. *þeććan* is (dial.) *thetch*; the present form is due to assim. to *thack* sb. (OE. *þæc*, ON. *þak*).

thaumaturge þɔ̄·mətɔ̄ɹdʒ wonder-worker. XVIII. Earlier *-urg* – medL. *thaumaturgus* – Gr. *thaumatourgós*, f. *thaumat-*, *thaûma* wonder + *-ergos* working (see WORK); later assim. to F. *thaumaturge*.

thaw þɔ̄ reduce to a liquid state OE.; intr. XIV. OE. *þawian* = MLG. *dōien*, Du. *dooien*, OHG. *douwen* (cf. G. *verdauen* digest) :– WGerm. **þawōjan* (cf. ON. *þeyja* :– **þaujan*), of unkn. origin. Hence **thaw** sb. XV.

the[1] ðə, (before a vowel) ði, (emph.) ðī demons. adj. (definite article). Late OE. (Nhb. and N. Mercian) *ðĕ*, ME. *þe*, at first nom. m., but ult. superseding all cases of OE. m. *sĕ*, fem. *sēo*, *sīo*, n. *þæt*, corr. to OFris. *thi*, *thiu*, *thet*, OS. *se*, *thē*, *thie*, *thiu*, *that* (Du. *de*, *dat*), OHG. *der*, *diu*, *daz* (G. *der*, *die*, *das*), ON. *sá*, *sú*, *þat*, Goth. *sa*, *sō*, *þata* (with suffix). The orig. CGerm. **sa*, **sō*, **þat* = Gr. *ho*, *hē* (dial. *há*), *tó* (:–**tod*), Skr. *sa*, *sá*, *tat*; cf. L. *ip|se* same, self, Ir., Gael., Gaulish *so* this, L. *is|tud*; except in ON. and Gothic the orig. nom. m. and fem. were superseded by forms in *þ-* from the same stem as the neuter *þæt* and the oblique cases.

Survivals of the OE. d. inflexions are seen in place-names containing relics of ME. *atten* and *atter* (see AT), e.g. *Noke* (OE. *æt þǣm āce* or *ācum* at the oak or oaks), the river-name *Ray*, *Rea* (OE. *æt þǣre ēa* at the watercourse); the final *t* of OE. *þæt* THAT[1] survives in dial. *tone*, *tother* (OE. *þæt ān* the one, *þæt ōþer* the other). Cf. also NONCE for a relic of *þǣm*.

the[2] ðə (preceding an adj. or adv. in the compar. or superl. degree, e.g. *the more fools they*, *the more the merrier*, *the less said*, *the sooner mended*) by that amount; by how much . . . by so much. repr. OE. *þē*, varying with *þȳ*, *þon*, instr. of THE[1], THAT[1] (e.g. *þȳ māra* the greater, *þȳ mā* the more); cf. LEST.

the-, var. of THEO- before a vowel, as in **thea·ndr**IC, **theanthro·p**IC pert. to God and man, divine and human, **the**ARCHY þī·əɹki rule of God, – or f. ecclGr. *theandrikós* (f. *théandros* god-man; *anḗr* man), *theánthrōpos* god-man, *thearkhíā*. All XVII.

Theatine þiə·tain member of a congregation founded by St. Cajetan with John Peter Carafia (then archbishop of *Chieti*). XVI. – mod. L. *Theatīnus*, f. *Teate*, ancient name of *Chieti* in Italy; see -INE[1].

theatre þiə·təɹ in antiquity, open-air structure for plays and spectacles XIV (Ch.); playhouse XVI. – OF. *t(h)eatre* (mod. *théâtre*) or L. *theātrum* – Gr. *théātron* 'place for viewing', f. *theâsthai* behold. From *c.*1550 to *c.*1700 the prevailing sp. was *theater*, now retained in U.S.A. So **theatr**ICAL þiæ·trikəl XVI; sb. pl. XVII. – late L. *theātricus* – Gr. *theātrikós*.

Thebaid þī·beiid poem relating to Bœotian Thebes. XVIII. – L. *Thēbaid-*, *-ais* – Gr. *Thēbaid-*, *-aís*. So **The·b**AN. XIV (Ch.). pert. to, native of, Thebes.

theca þī·kə receptacle, cell, case. XVII. – L. *thēca* – Gr. *thḗkē* case, cover, f. IE. **dhē-* place (see DO[1]), comb. form *théco-* XIX.

thee ðī, ði acc. and d. of 2nd personal pron. sg. OE. (i) accusative *þec*, *þeh*, later *þē* = OFris. *thi*, OS. *thic*, *thī*, OHG. *dih* (G. *dich*), ON. *þik*, Goth. *þuk* :- CGerm. **þeke* :- **tege*, f. **te* (repr. by L. *tē*, Gr. *sé*, Doric *té*); (ii) dative *þē* = OFris., OS. *thī*, (O)HG. *dir*, ON. *þér*, Goth. *þus* :- CGerm. **þez* :- **tes*. The vowel was orig. short, but was lengthened under stress. The acc. and d. have been undistinguishable in form since IX (exc. in late Nhb. X). Hence **thee** vb. XVII. Cf. THOU.

theft þeft action of a thief; (arch.) thing stolen. OE. (WS.) *þīefþ*, later *þȳfþ*, *þȳft*, non-WS. *þēofþ*, *þēoft* = OFris. *thiūfthe*, *thiūfte*, ON. *þýfð*, *þýft* :- Germ. **þiūƀiþō*, f. *þeuƀaz* THIEF + **-iþō* -T[2].

thegn þein form favoured by some mod. historians (e.g. Stubbs, Freeman) to repr. OE. *þegn* as designating a tenant by military service or a man of knightly rank. See THANE.

their ðɛəɹ of them. XII (*þeȝȝre* Ormulum). – ON. *þeir(r)a*, g. pl. of *sá*, *sú*, *þat* THE, THAT, used also as g. pl. of the 3rd personal pron. Cf. THEM, THEY. Hence **theirs** ðɛəɹz XIII (Cursor M.); see -S.

theism þī·izm belief in one God, esp. as creator and supreme ruler.)(DEISM. XVII (Cudworth). f. Gr. *theós* god. So **the·**IST XVII, **thei·st**IC XVIII, **-i·st**ICAL XVII. Cf. F. *théisme*, *théiste* (Voltaire).

them ðem, ðəm d. and acc. of THEY. ME. *þeim* (*þeȝȝm*, Orm). – ON. *þeim* (= OE. *þǣm*) d. pl. of *sá*, *sú*, *þat* (see THEIR).

theme þīm subject of a discourse XIII (Cursor M.); exercise, essay; inflexional base or stem XVI. ME. *teme* – OF. **teme* (*tesme*) – L. *thēma* (to which it was soon conformed in sp.) – Gr. *théma* proposition, f. **the-* base of *tithénai* place (see DO[1]). So **them**ATIC þīmæ·tik. XVIII. – Gr. *thematikós*.

then ðen at that time, in that case, that being the case (cf. *now then*). ME. *þenne*, *þanne*, *þann* (XII), OE. *þænne*, *þanne*, *þonne* = OFris. *thenne*, *thanne*, *than*, OS. *thanna*, *than*, OHG. *danne*, *denne* (Du. *dan*, G. *dann*), f. demons. base **þa-* (see THAT, THE).

thence ðens from there. XIII. ME. *þannes*, *þennes*, *þens*, f. *þanne*, *þenne* thence, OE. *þanone*, *þanon* = OFris. *thana*, OS., OHG. *danana*, *danān* (Du. *dan*, G. *dannen*) :- WGerm. **þanana*, for which Gothic had *þaþrō*.

theo- þī·ou, þiə· comb. form of Gr. *theós* god (cf. THEISM). See THE-.

theodicy þiə·disi vindication of the divine attributes. XVIII. – F. *théodicée*, title of a work by Leibniz (1710), f. Gr. *theós* God + *díkē* justice; the ending is assim. to -Y[3].

theodolite þiə·dəlait portable surveying instrument for measuring (orig. horizontal) angles. XVII. Earlier (1571) in modL. form *theodelitus* (Leonard or Thomas Digges, its probable inventor); of unkn. origin.

theogony þiə·gəni generation or genealogy of the gods. XVII. – Gr. *theogoníā*, f. *theós* god + **gon-* **gen-*; see GENESIS, -Y[3].

theology þiə·lədʒi 'the science of things divine' (Hooker). XIV (PPl., Ch.). – (O)F. *théologie* – L. *theologia* – Gr. *theologíā*, f. *theológos* one who treats of the gods, f. *theós* god; see -LOGY. By Gower used for metaphysics, after Abelard. So **theolog**IAN þiəlou·dʒiən one versed in theology. XV (Caxton). – (O)F. *théologien*, f. *théologie* or L. *theologia*; synon. formatives that have been current are **theo·log**ER[1] XVI, **theo-logi·**CIAN XVI, **theo·log**IST XVII, **the·ologue** XV (earliest in Sc.) – L. *theologus* – Gr. *theológos*. **theolog**IC þiələ·dʒik XV; **-lo·gi**CAL XVI (first of the virtues of faith, hope, and charity, after medL. 'virtutes theologicæ', Albertus Magnus) scriptural; earlier **theo·logal** (XV, Caxton) – (O)F.

theorbo þiɔ̄·ɹbou kind of lute. XVII. – It. *tiorba* (of unkn. origin), with alteration of ending as in some words in -ADO; cf. F. *téorbe*, *théorbe*. The sp. with *th-* is presumably due to assoc. with THEO-.

theorem þiə·rəm general proposition demonstrable by argument. XVI (Recorde, Billingsley; Hooker). – F. *théorème* (Rabelais) or late L. *theōrēma* – Gr. *theṓrēma* speculation, theory, (in Euclid) proposition to be proved)(problem, f. *theōreîn* be a spectator, look at, f. *theōrós* (see THEORY). So **theoret**IC(AL) þiəre·tik(l) †speculative, contemplative; pert. to theory. XVII. – late L. *theōrēticus* (Ambrose) – Gr. *theōrētikós*, f. *theōrētós*, f. *theōreîn*. Hence **theoreti·**CIAN. XIX.

theory þiə·ri mental conception, scheme of thought. XVI (Hooker). – late L. *theōria* (Jerome) – Gr. *theōriā* contemplation, speculation, sight, f. *theōrós* spectator, f. *thea-* base of *théā* sight, contemplation, *theâsthai* look upon, contemplate (cf. THEATRE). Hence **theo·rIST**. XVI. ¶ *Theory* was preceded by *theorique* (Gower) – OF. **the·orIZE** form theories. XVII. – medL. *theōrizāre*.

theosophy þiɔ·səfi system of philosophical speculation basing the knowledge of nature on that of the divine nature. XVII. – medL. *theosophia* – late Gr. *theosophiā*, f. *theósophos* f. *theós* god+*sophós* wise; see -Y[3]. Hence **theo·sophIST**, earlier **theo·sophER**[1], **-so·phIC(AL)** XVII.

therapeutic þerəpjū·tik (pl., formerly sg.) art of healing XVI; adj. healing, curative XVII. – F. *thérapeutique* or late L. *therapeutica* – Gr. *therapeutikḗ*, sb. (sc. *tékhnē* art) of *therapeutikós*, f. *therapeutḗs* minister, f. *therapeúein* administer to, treat medically, f. *therap-*, *théraps* attendant, minister: see -IC. So **the·rapy**[3] medical treatment. XIX – modL. *therapīa* – Gr. *therapeiā*; often as second el. of a compound, e.g. *psychotherapy*.

there ðeər, ðəɹ A. in, at, or to that place. B. used to indicate existence or occurrence. OE. *þǣr*, *þēr* = OFris. *thēr*, OS. *thār*, OHG. *dār* (Du. *daar*, G. *da*); cogn. with ON., Goth. *þar*; f. demons. base **þa-* (see THE, THAT) + adv. suffix *-r*, as in *here*, *where*; as with *these* and *ere* a final *e* was developed in early ME., whence the present sp. The comps. *thereabout*, *-after*, *-at*, *-in*, *-of*, *-on*, *-out*, *-to*, *-with* are of OE. date.

theriac þiə·riæk (arch.) antidote. XVI. – L. *thēriaca*, *-cē* – Gr. *thēriakḗ*; see TREACLE.

therio- þiə·riou, before a vowel **theri-**, repr. Gr. *thērion* (cf. *-therium*, as in *megatherium*), dim. of *thḗr* wild beast (cf. FERAL[2]).

thermal þə̄·ɹməl pert. to hot springs. XVIII. – F. *thermal* (Buffon), f. Gr. *thérmē* heat, *thermós* hot; see -AL[1].

thermite þə̄·ɹmait mixture of finely divided aluminium and oxide of iron, etc. producing on combustion very great heat. XIX. – G. *thermit*, f. Gr. *thérmē*; see next, -ITE.

thermo- þə̄·ɹmou repr. comb. form of Gr. *thérmē* heat, *thermós* hot, in many scientific terms.

thermometer þəɹmɔ·mitəɹ instrument for measuring temperature. XVII. – F. *thermomètre* or modL. *thermometer*, f. Gr. *thérmē*, *thermós*+*métron*; see prec. and -METER. ¶ Cf. Of Thermometry or the Weather-glass (1669 Worlidge 'System of Agriculture' 257 margin).

thero- þiə·rou repr. Gr. *thēro-*, comb. form of *thḗr* wild beast (cf. FERAL[2]).

Thersitical þəɹsi·tikəl abusive, scurrilous. XVII. f. Gr. *Thersítēs*, name of an ill-tongued Greek at the siege of Troy, rel. to *thársos* (Lesbian *thérsos*) courage (cf. DARE); see -ICAL.

thesaurus þisɔ̄·rəs treasury, spec. of knowledge. XIX. – L. *thēsaurus* TREASURE (Plautus) – Gr. *thēsaurós*.

these ðīz pl. of THIS. Early ME. *þēse* (XIII), normally developed from *þise* (Orm), f. *þis* THIS+pl. suffix *-e*; superseded *þās*, *þōs*, THOSE, which became the pl. of THAT[1]. ¶ The influence of early forms such as *þēs*, *þǣs*, *þēos*, is doubtful.

thesis þī·sis, þe·sis, pl. **theses** -īz A. proposition, theme XVI; (theme of) a dissertation XVII. B. (pros.))(ARSIS unaccented or unstressed element XIV (Trev.); accented or stressed element XIX; – late L. *thesis* (in prosodical sense, Martianus Capella) – Gr. *thésis* placing, setting, corr. to L. *con|diti|ōn-* CONDITION, Skr. *-dhitis*, rel. by gradation to **dhētis* DEED.

Thespian[1] þe·spiən pert. to *Thespiæ* or *Thespia*, town on the slope of mount HELICON; poetic. XVII (Chapman, Jonson, Drayton); see -IAN. So **ThespiAD**[1] muse. XVII (Chapman). – L. *Thespiades* pl.

Thespian[2] þe·spiən pert. to *Thespis*, traditional father of Gr. tragedy, tragic, dramatic. XVII; sb. tragedian XIX; see -IAN.

theurgy þī·əɹdʒi magic of the Egyptian Platonists XVI; divine agency in human affairs XIX. – late L. *theūrgia* – Gr. *theourgiā*, f. *theós* god+*-ergos* working; see THEO-, WORK, -Y[3].

thew þjū †custom, habit OE.; †(good) quality, virtue XIII; (pl.) bodily powers, physical endowments XVI. OE. *þēaw* usage, conduct = OS. *thau*, OHG. *thau*, *dau* discipline, of unkn. origin. ¶ The current application to sinews or tendons depends largely on Scott's association of Shakespearian instances of the sense 'strength, vigour' with bodily features. For earlier sense-development cf. L. *mōs* custom, pl. *mōrēs* morals.

they ðei pl. of HE[1], SHE, IT, pron. of the 3rd person. XII. ME. *þei* (*þeȝȝ*, Orm) – ON. *þeir* (= OE. *þā*), pl. of demons. *sá*, *sú*, *þat*; repl. OE. *hī*, *hīe*, pl. of *hē*, *hēo*, *hit*.

Thibetan see TIBETAN.

thick þik of (comparatively) large measure through; dense. OE. *þicce* = OS. *thikki*, OHG. *dicchi* (Du. *dik*, G. *dick*), ON. *þykkr* :– CGerm. (exc. Goth.) **þeku-*, *þekwia-*, of unkn. origin. Hence **thi·ckEN**[5]. XV. **thi·ckNESS**. OE.

thicket þi·kit dense growth of shrubs, etc. OE. *þiccet*, f. *þicce* THICK.

thief þīf one who steals. OE. *þīof*, *þēof* = OFris. *thiāf*, OS. *thiof*, OHG. *diob* (Du. *dief*, G. *dieb*), ON. *þjófr*, Goth. *þiufs*; CGerm. word of which no further cogns. are known. Cf. THEFT.

thigh þai upper part of the leg. OE. (Anglian) *þēh*, (WS.) *þēoh*, *þīoh* = OFris. *thiāch*, ODu. *thio* (Du. *dij*), OHG. *dioh*, ON. *þjó* :- CGerm. (exc. Goth.) **þeuχam*, f. IE. **teuk-* **tauk-* **tuk-*, whence Lith. *táukas*, OSl. *tukŭ* fat, Lith. *tùkti* be fat, OIr. *tōn* posteriors (:- **tukná*), Av. *tavsa-* leg. OE. *þēh* is repr. immed. by mod. north. *thee*; *thigh* descends from ME. *þīh* (XII), with ē̜ raised to ī, as in *die*, *high*, *nigh*, *shy*. Cf. THOUSAND, THUMB.

thill þil shaft. XIV. Formally coincident with OE. *þille* board, planking (rel. to synon. *þel*, *þelu*; cf. DEAL[2]); but the sense is so distant that, without further evidence, it is unsafe to connect them. The var. *fill* appears in Sh. in *fill-horse*.

thimble þi·mbl †finger-stall OE. (only); bell-shaped finger-cap used in sewing XV (Hoccleve). OE. *þȳmel*, f. *þūma* THUMB; see -LE[1].

thin þin having little thickness, density, or depth. OE. *þynne* = OFris. *thenne*, OS. *thunni*, OHG. *dunni* (Du. *dun*, G. *dünn*), ON. *þunnr* :- CGerm. (exc. Goth.) **þunnuz* (:- **þunw-*), based on IE. **tn-*, zero-grade of **ten-* **ton-* (see TEND[2]).

thine ðain of or pert. to THEE. OE. *þīn* = OFris., OS. *thīn*, OHG. *dīn* (Du. *dijn*, G. *dein*), ON. *þínn*, Goth. *þeins* :- CGerm. **þīnaz* :- IE. **t(w)einos*, f. **tū̆* THOU; cf. MINE and synon. Toch. *tañę*.

thing þiŋ A. †(deliberative or judicial) assembly; †legal process or charge OE. (only); affair, business; deed, act OE.; that which is said XIII; B. that which exists, being OE. (inanimate object XVII); OE. *þing* = OFris., OS. *thing*, OHG. *ding*, *dinc*, assembly for deliberation and/or business, ON. *þing* :- Germ. **þingam*. Hence, with meaningless additions, †*thingum* (XVII), *thingumbob* (XVIII Smollett, Miss Burney), *thingummy* þi·ŋəmi XVIII (Mme D'Arblay), *thingamajig*, *thingumabob*.

Thing þiŋ in Scand. countries, public meeting, legislative council, court of law. XIX. - Scand. *þing*; see prec. and cf. ALTHING, STORTHING.

think þiŋk pt., pp. **thought** þɔ̄t conceive in the mind, consider, exercise the mind; believe. OE. *þenċan*, pt. *þōhte*, pp. *ġeþōht* = OFris. *thanka*, *thenka*, *thenza*, OS. *thenkian*, *thāhta*, OHG. *denken*, *dāchta* (G. *denken*, *dachte*), ON. *þekkja*, *þátta*, Goth. *þagkjan*, *þāhta*; factitive formation on OE. *þyncan* (see METHINKS), perh. orig. meaning 'cause to appear to oneself'. The closeness in form of ME. *þenche*, *þinche*, pt. *þohte*, *þouhte* (from OE. *þenċan*, *þōhte*) and ME. *þünche*, *þinche*, *þenche*, pt. *þuhte*, *þouhte* (from OE. *þynċan*, pt. *þūhte*) and the virtual identity in meaning of *i thinke* and *me thinketh*, *as him thouhte* and *as he thouhte*, led to the forms METHINKS, METHOUGHT; for the *k*-form cf. SEEK.

thio- þai·ou before a vowel *thi-*, repr. comb. form of Gr. *theîon* sulphur; also *thion-*. XIX.

third þɔ̄ɹd ordinal of the numeral three. Sb. third part XIV; musical interval XVI. OE. (late Nhb.) *þird(d)a*, *-e*, var. of *þridda* (whence ME. and Sc. till XVIII *thrid*) = OFris. *thredda*, OS. *thriddio*, OHG. *dritto* (Du. *derde*, G. *dritte*), ON. *þriði*, Goth. *þridja* :- CGerm. **þriðjaz* :- IE. **tritjós* (cf. Skr. *tṛtíyas*, Gr. *trítos*, Lesbian *tértos*, L. *tertius*, OSl. *tretij*, W. *trydydd*), f. stem of THREE. Hence **thi·rd**LY[2]. XVI. **third-**RATE. XVII. **thirteen** (str. various) 13, xiii. OE. *þrēotīene* = OS. *thriutein*, OHG. *drīzehan* (Du. *dertien*, G. *dreizehn*), ON. *þrettán*; the OE. form was repr. by *threteen* as late as XVII, the standard methathetic form appearing XV (*þirttene*). **thirteen**TH[2] (str. various) 13th. OE. *þrēo-*, *þrīetēoþa*, ME. *þritteþe*, *þreottenþe* (XII) (*þrittende* from ON. *þrettándi*), *þrittenþe* (XIV), *þirttenth* (XV), *thirteenth* (XVI); so OFris. *threttinda*, OHG. *drittozehanto*, etc. **thir**TY[2] þɔ̄·ɹti 30, XXX. OE. *þrītiġ* = OS. *thrītig*, OHG. *drîzzug* (Du. *dertig*, G. *dreissig*), ON. *þrírtegr*, Goth. (acc.) *þrins tiguns*. **thi·rtieth** 30th. OE. *þrītigoþa*, *þritteogoþa*, ME. *thrittethe*, remodelled in the present form on the cardinal with metathesis. **thirtytwomo** þɔ̄ɹtitū·mou reading of the symbol 32mo, xxxiimo, designating a book with 32 pages to the sheet, cf. *sixteenmo*, *twelvemo*.

thirlage þɔ̄·ɹlidʒ see THRALL.

thirst þɔ̄ɹst uneasy sensation due to want of drink. OE. *þurst* = OS. *thurst* (Du. *dorst*), (O)HG. *durst* :- WGerm. **þurstu* (cf. ON. *þorsti*, Goth. *þaurstei*); f. **þurs-* :- IE. **trs-* **tors-*, repr. also by L. *torrēre* dry, parch (cf. TORRID), Skr. *tṛ́ṣyati* thirst, OIr. *tart*. So **thirst** vb. suffer thirst OE.; impers. XII (Orm). OE. *þyrstan* (till late ME. also impers.) = OS. *thurstian*, OHG. *durstan* (Du. *dorsten*, G. *dürsten*), ON. *þyrsta*.

this ðis, pl. THESE. demons. pron. and adj. indicating a person or thing present or near. The form *this* in generalized use dates from *c.*1200 (Orm); it is identical with the OE. n. nom. and acc. and the stem of most of the inflected forms. OE. *þes* m., *þēos* fem., *þis* n., corr. to OFris. *this*, *thius*, *thit*, OS. **these*, *thius*, *thit*, OHG. *dese*, *deser*, *desiu*, *diz*, ON. *þessi*, *þetta*; WGerm. and ON. formation on **þa-* (see THE, THAT) and deictic **-se*, **-si* (poss. = OHG. *sē*, Goth. *sai* behold!). The earlier formation is seen in ON. (runic) *sási*, *súsi*, *þatsi*, acc. sg. *þansi*, *þási*, *þatsi*, d. *þaimsi*, n.pl. *þausi* (cf. with deictic IE. $k^{u}e$ = L. *-ce* in *hic*, *hujusce*, etc. this, Goth. *-(u)h* in *sah*, *soh*, *þatuh* this). The *þ-* forms were ult. extended throughout the paradigm, and, whereas orig. the first alone was inflected (e.g. OHG. n. nom. *dese*, g. sg. *desse*, pl. *dese*), the second el. came to be inflected also (e.g. OHG. g. sg. *desses*

= OE. *þisses*); finally the first el. ceased to be inflected. As adv. equiv. to *thus* in various uses (XIV; now esp. in *this much, this far*, and the like), perh. from OE. instr. *þȳs, þīs*, or acc. sg. n. *þis*. Hence **thi·**SWISE. XIII (Cursor M.).

thistle þi·sl prickly plant of the genus Carduus and closely allied genera. OE. *þistel* (some mod. dials. authenticate *ī*, e.g. Somerset dai·sl) = OS. *thistil*, OHG. *distil, distila* (LG. *diestel, dîstel*, Du. *distel*, G. *distel*, also *diestel*), ON. *þistill* :- Germ. **þistilaz, -ilō*, of unkn. origin.

thither ðiðəɹ to that place. OE. *þider*, alt. by assim. to *hider* HITHER, of earlier *þæder*, corr. to ON. *þaðra* there, thither, f. demons. base **þa-* of THAT, THE+suffix denoting 'towards' (IE. **trā(d)*, as in L. *intrā* within, *extrā* outside, Skr. *tátra* there, then). ¶ For the change of d to ð cf. FATHER.

thitsi þi·tsi black varnish tree. XIX. - Burmese *thitsi* (written *sachchē*), f. *thit* tree, wood+*asī* (in comb. *-si*) gum.

thlaspi þlæ·spi genus of cruciferous plants. XVI. - modL. - Gr. *thláspi, -is*.

thole[1] þoul peg, pin, spec. in the gunwale of a boat. OE. *þol(l)* = OFris. *tholl*, MLG., MDu. *dolle* (Du. *dol*), ON. *þollr* fir tree, tree, peg, referred to Germ. **þul-*, IE. **tul-* (cf. Gr. *túlos* peg), extension of **tu-* swell parallel to **tum-* (see THUMB, TUMOUR). The vars. *thoule, thowle*, corr. to the present oarsman's pronunc. þaul, appear XVII; they are prob. due to assoc. with DOWEL. The want of evidence between the OE. period and XV (Promp. Parv.) prob. indicates loss of the OE. word and its supersession by the ON.

thole[2] þoul (arch., dial.) suffer. OE. *þolian* = OFris. *tholia*, OS. *tholon, tholian*, OHG. *dolōn, dolēn*, ON. *þola*, Goth. *þulan*; CGerm. f. **þul-* repr. weak grade of IE. **tol-* **tel-* **tḷ-* raise, remove, of CIE. extent (exc. Balto-Sl.), as in Gr. *tlênai* endure, bear, *tálanton* balance, TALENT, L. *tollere* raise, *tulī* (pt.) bore.

Thomas tɔ·məs common male Christian name. - late L. *Thōmās*, Gr. *Thōmâs*, of Aram. origin ('twin'); name of 'the doubting Apostle' (see John xx 25). Cf. TOM, TOMMY.

Thomist tou·mist follower of *Thomas* Aquinas (c. 1225–74) the Angelic Doctor XVI. - medL. *Thōmista*, f. L. *Thōmās*; see prec., -IST. Cf. F. *thomiste* (Pascal). Hence **Tho·m**ISM. XVIII.

thong þɔŋ narrow strip of hide or leather. OE. *þwang, þwong*, which became *þong* (XIII) by absorption of *w* in *o* = OFris. *thwang*, MLG. *dwank* constraint, OHG. *dwang* rein (MHG. *dwanc, twanc*, G. *zwang*), f. Germ. **þwaŋg-*, whence also late Nhb. pl. *ðuuencgu*, Anglian *þwænga*, corr. to ON. *þvengr* :- **þwaŋgiz*, rel. further to OE. *ġeþwinglod* bound up, OFris. *thwinga*, OS. *thwingan*, OHG. *thwingan, dw-*, ON. *þvinga* force, constrain.

thorax þō·ræks (anat.) part of the body between the neck and the abdomen. XVI. - L. *thōrāx* - Gr. *thṓrāx* (*-āko-*) breastplate, breast, chest. So **thorac**IC -æ·sik. XVII. - medL. - Gr.

thorium þō·riəm (chem.) dark-grey metallic element. XIX. - modL. *thorium* (Berzelius, 1828–9), f. *Thor* Norse god+-IUM.

thorn þɔːɹn A. sharp-pointed process on a plant; thorn-bearing plant (cf. HAWTHORN); B. runic character þ. OE. *þorn* = OS. *thorn* (Du. *doorn*), (O)HG. *dorn*, ON. *þorn*, Goth. *þaurnus* :- CGerm. *þurnuz* :- IE. **tṛnus*, f. **tṛn- tern-*, as repr. also by OIr. *tráinín* small stalk of grass, OSl. *trŭnŭ* thorn, Skr. *tṛ́ṇam* grass-stalk, Gr. *térnax* cactus prickle. Hence **tho·rn**Y[1]. OE. *þorniġ* (Ælfric, Wulfstan).

thorough þʌ·ɹə obs. or arch. as adv. and prep. in senses of *through*; in gen. use as adj. Application of the adv.: fully executed, affecting every part XIII; disyllabic development, *þuruh*, of OE. *þurh* THROUGH, paralleled in OS. *thuru(h)*, OHG. *duruh*, as also in *borough, furrow, marrow, sorrow*. comp. **tho·rough**BASS[3] (mus.) bass part extending through a composition. XVII; **tho·rough-bred** XVIII; **tho·rough**FARE XV (earlier *thurghfare*, Ch.); cf. G. *durchfahrt*; **tho·roughgoing** XIX (Scott, who has also *thoroughgaun*).

thorp þɔːɹp (arch., hist.) hamlet, village. OE. *þrop*, occas. (prob. from ON.) *þorp* = OFris. *thorp, therp* (cf. TERP), OS. *thorp* (Du. *dorp*), OHG. (G.) *dorf* village, ON. *þorp* hamlet, farmstead, Goth. *þaurp* field, land, estate :- CGerm. **þurpam*, of uncertain origin, but connected by some with W. *tref* town, OBret. *treb* dwelling, Gaulish tribal name *Atrebates* 'occupiers'.

those ðouz, pl. of THAT[1]. OE. *þās*, ME. (southern) *þōs*, pl. of THIS; from XIV, first in northern and later in midland and southern speech, pl. of demons. pron. and adj. *that*; repl. *thō* (OE. *þā*, pl. of *se, sēo, þæt* THE), which remained in literary use till XVI, and survives in Sc. and north. dial. as *thae*.

thou ðau pron. denoting the person (or thing) addressed. OE. *þŭ* = OFris., OS. *thŭ* (LG. *du*), OHG. *dŭ* (G. *dŭ*), ON. *þú*, Goth. *þu* :- CGerm. repr. of IE. **tŭ*, whence also L., OIr., Av. *tū*, Gr. (Doric) *tú*, Attic *sú* (after acc. *sé*, d. *soí*), OSl. *ty*, Lith. *tù*, W. *ti*, Skr. *tvám* (after *ahám* I), Toch. *tu*; see also THEE, THINE, THY. Hence **thou** vb. XV; cf. THEE vb.; so Icel. *þúa*, medL. *tuāre, tuisāre*, ME. *thowtyn* (Promp. Parv.), G. *dutzen*, F. *tutoyer*; It. *tuizzare*. ¶ Eng. has generalized the long str. form, G. the short unstr. form.

though ðou, (Sc. and north. Eng.) þō adv. for all that; conj. notwithstanding that. XII. ME. *þŏh* (in Orm *þohh*), **þōh*, prehistoric form of ON. *þó* (OEN. *þau*), earlier **þauh* = OE. *þēah* (whence ME. *þeh*, *þeih*, *þeigh*, and *þah*, *þauh*, *þauȝ*, which were obs. before 1500), OFris. *thăch*, OS. *thoh* (Du. *doch*), OHG. *doh* (G. *doch*), Goth. *þauh* or, yet; CGerm. advb. formation on pron. base **þa-* THE, THAT+(in Goth. *-uh*) the particle repr. by L. *-que*, Gr. *té*, Skr. *ca* and.

thought þōt action or act of thinking; †anxiety, solicitude XIII; very small amount XVI. repr. OE. *þōht* and the more freq. *ġeþōht* = OS. *githāht* (Du. *gedachte*), OHG. *gidāht* :- Germ. **ʒaþaŋχt-*, f. **þaŋkjan* THINK; cf. synon. ON. *þótti*, *þóttr*, Goth. *þūhtus*, f. **þuŋχt-*.

thousand þau·zənd 1000, M. OE. *þūsend* = OFris. *thūsend*, OS. *thūsundig*, OHG. *thū-*, *dusunt* (Du. *duizend*, G. *tausend*), ON. *þúsund*, Goth. *þūsundi* :- CGerm. **þusundi*, cogn. with Balto-Sl. **tūssntjā* (repr. by Lith. *túkstantis*, OSl. *tysęšta*, Russ. *týsyacha*), the first el. of which has been identified with the base of L. *tumēre* swell, Skr. *tuvi* much, the second el. with *hundred* (cf. ON. *þúshundrað* 1000), the etymol. meaning being 'many hundreds'. ¶ There is no CIE. word as with the earlier numbers.

thrall þrōl villein, serf, slave, OE. *þræl* (first in late Nhb.) – ON. *þræll*, perh. :- **þraχilaz*, f. Germ. **þraχ-* **þreχ-* run; cf. Goth. *þragjan* run, OHG. *dregil*, *drigil* servant, (prop.) runner. Hence **thrall** vb. (arch.) bring into bondage, ENTHRALL. XIII (Laȝ.). **thra·l**DOM (XII). ¶ The Sc. var. *threll* (XIV) became *thril(l)*, which by metathesis became *thirl*, whence, from the two forms, were derived †*thrillage* (XIV–XV) and *thirlage* (XVI).

thranite þrei·nait rower in one of the tiers of a trireme. XIX. – Gr. *thrānítēs*, f. *thrânos* bench (cf. *thrónos* seat, THRONE); see -ITE.

thrash þræʃ A. thresh (corn, etc.) XVI (Sh.); B. chastise by beating XVII; C. (naut.) beat (one's way); D. lash out, plunge XIX. metathetic alt. of an early form repr. by OE. *þærsćan*, parallel with *þersćan* THRESH, which is now the prevalent form in sense A.

thrasonical þrəsɔ·nikəl given to boasting. XVI. f. L. *thrasō(n-)* – Gr. *Thrásōn* name of the braggart soldier in Terence's 'Eunuchus', f. *thrasús* bold, resolute, rel. to *thársos*, Lesbian *thérsos* (cf. THERSITICAL); see DARE, -ICAL.

thread þred cord composed of spun fibres of flax, etc. OE.; length of yarn forming a constituent of such fabric XII; transf. and fig. XIV. OE. *þrǣd* = OS. *thrād*, OHG. *drāt* (Du. *draad*, G. *draht*), ON. *þráðr* :- Germ. **þrǣðuz*, f. **þrǣ-* twist (see THROW). Hence **thread** vb. XIV. **threa·d**BARE leaving bare the thread of warp and woof. XIV (PPl., Ch.); fig. XV (Hoccleve).

threat þr·et †throng, troop; †oppression, affliction OE.; denunciation of evil to come (? OE.), XI. OE. *þrēat* m., cogn. with ON. *þraut* fem. struggle, labour, f. Germ. **þraut-* **þreut-* **þrut-* base of OE. *þrēatian* (see below), *þrēotan* trouble, Du. *ver|drieten*, weary, OHG. *ir|driozan* (MHG. *ver|driezen*, G. *ver|driessen* annoy) vex, Goth. *us|þriutan* trouble; prob. cogn. with L. *trūdere* thrust (cf. ABSTRUSE, OBTRUDE). So vb. (arch. or dial.) OE. *þrēatian*, superseded by **threa·-t**EN[5] (OE. *þrēatnian*) †press, urge, from XIII utter threats against, from XVII (Sh.) be ominous (of).

three þrī 3, iii. OE. *þrī*, *þrīe* m., *þrīo*, *þrēo* f., n. = OFris. *thrē*, *thriā*, *thriū*, OS. *thria*, *threa*, *thriu*, OHG. *drī*, *drīo*, *driu* (Du. *drie*, G. *drei*), ON. *þrír*, *þriár*, *þriú*, Goth. **þreis*, *þrija* :- CGerm. **þrijiz* :- IE. **trejes*, whence also L. *trēs*, *tria*, Gr. *treîs*, *tría*, Skr. *tráyas*, etc. Cf. THIRD, THIRTEEN, THIRTY, THRICE, TRI-, TRIO. **three-halfpence** þrīhei·pəns (*-halpenys* XV), **-halfpenny** -hei·peni, **halfpennyworth**, **-ha'porth** hei·pəɹþ (*-halpworthe* XV). **three**PENCE þre·pəns, þri·pəns, þrʌ·pəns XVI, **three·**PENNY -pəni. XV; **threepe·nnyworth, -penn'orth** -pe·nəɹþ (†*-penneard* XVII).

threnody þre·nŏdi lament for the dead, dirge. XVII. – Gr. *thrēnōidiā*, f. *thrênos* whence late L. *thrēnus* (also medL. *thrēna*), Eng. *threne* (XV)+*ōidḗ* ODE; see -Y[3].

thresh þreʃ separate the grain from (corn) by beating, etc. ME. *threshe-n* (XII), continuing metathetic alt. of OE. *þersćan*, pt. *þærsć*, *þursćon*, pp. *þorsćen* = MLG., MDu. *derschen* (LG., Du. *dorschen*), OHG. *dreskan* (G. *dreschen*), ON. *þreskja*, Goth. *þriskan*, f. CGerm. **þersk-* :- IE. **tersk-*, repr. in Balto-Sl. by words denoting 'crackle', 'crash', 'rattle'. ¶ The Germ. word is the source of a widespread Rom. vb. with senses 'trample', 'dance' (OF. *treschier*, Sp. *triscar*, It. *trescare*). Hence **thre·sh**ER[1] person or machine that threshes XIV; shark so named from the upper division of its tail with which it lashes an enemy XVII. Cf. THRASH.

threshold þre·ʃould sill of a doorway, entrance to a building. OE. *þersćold*, *þerxold*, *þresćold*, *þrexold*, *-wold* = ON. *þreskǫldr*, *-kjǫldr* (Norw., Sw. *tröskel*, Da. *dør|tærskel*); cf. OHG. *driscūfli* (G. dial. *drischaufel*); the first el. is OE. *þersćan* THRASH, in the primitive sense of 'tread, trample', the second el. is not identifiable. ¶ The great variety of forms in Eng. is equalled or exceeded in rel. langs.

thrice þrais three times. XII. ME. *þriȝes*, *þries*, f. (with *-es -s*) *þrie* :- OE. *þrīga*, var. of *þrīwa* = OFris. *thria*, OS. *thriuuo*, *thrīo* (peculiar to the Saxon-Frisian group). f. **þri-* THREE + advb. *-a*, with cons. glide intervening; cf. TWICE. ¶ Spelt with *-ce* to express final voiceless s, as *dice*, *mice*, *once*, *twice*.

thrift þrift †thriving condition XIII; †prosperity, success; †gains, savings XIV;

industry; economical management; plant Armeria maritima XVI. – ON. *þrift*, f. *þrífask* THRIVE; see -T[1]. Hence **thri·fty**[1] thriving; †worshipful, respectable XIV; careful of expenditure XVI.

thrill þril A. †pierce (lit. and fig.) XIII (Cursor M.); B. affect, be affected, with a wave of emotion XVI (Sh.); C. †hurl (a piercing weapon) XVII; D. quiver XVIII. Metathetic var. of (dial.) *thirl*, OE. *þȳrlian*, f. *þȳr(e)l* perforation, hole, aperture (see NOSTRIL) :– **þyrhil*, **þurhil*, f. *þurh* THROUGH + -EL[1]; cf. the adjs. OE. *þȳrel*, OHG. *dur(i)hhil* perforated. The rise of the last senses C and D is not clearly accounted for. Hence sb. XVII.

thrips þrips minute insect infecting plants. XVIII. – L. (Pliny) – Gr. *thríps*, pl. *thrîpes* wood-worm.

thrive þraiv pt. **throve** þrouv, pp. **thriven** þri·vn; also pt., pp. **thrived** þraivd (XIV) † grow, increase XIII (Orm); prosper XIII (Cursor M.). ME. *þrīve*, pt. *þrāf*, later *þrōf*, pp. *þriven* (XIV). – ON. *þrífask*, pt. *þreifsk*, refl. of *þrífa* lay hold of suddenly, grasp (cf. the similar use of *takask*, refl. *taka* seize, TAKE).

throat þrout front part of the neck, passage through it to lungs or stomach. OE. *þrote*, *þrotu* = OHG. *drozza* (MHG. *drozze*, whence G. *drossel*; see THROTTLE), f. Germ. **þrut-* **þrūt-* (repr. also by ON. *þroti* swelling, OE. *þrūtian*, ON. *þrútna* swell, *þrútinn* swollen), to which there is a parallel synon. Germ. **strut-* repr. by OS. *strota* (Du. *strot*) throat, OFris. *strotbolla*, beside OE. *þrotbolla*, OFris. *throtbolla* Adam's apple, and MHG. *strozze*, whence It. *strozza* throat, *strozzare* strangle). If the basic meaning is 'thrust out, project, swell', the application to the throat was prob. in ref. to the appearance of the front of it. Hence **throa·ty**[1]. XVII.

throb þrɔb (of the heart) beat strongly XIV (*þrobbant* prp., PPl., obs. *frob* XVI); (gen.) pulsate XIX. Presumably of imit. origin. Hence sb. XVI (Spenser, Lyly).

throe þrou †spasm, paroxysm XII; agony of death XIII; violent convulsion or struggle XVII. ME. *þrowe*, north. *þrawe* (Sc. *thraw*), sp. *throe* (XVII) perh. by assoc. with *woe*; poss. repr. obscurely OE. *þrēa*, *þrawu* threat, calamity, with influence from *þrōwian* suffer.

thrombosis þrɔmbou·sis (path.) coagulation of the blood. XVIII. – modL. – Gr. *thrómbōsis* curdling, f. *thromboûsthai* become curdled or clotted, f. *thrómbos*, lump, clot, whence modL. **thro·mbus** (used in Eng. from XVII); see -OSIS.

throne þroun seat of state, of a deity XIII; third (from Col. i 16) order of angels XIV. ME. *trone* (XIII–XVI), (assim. early to the L. form) *throne* – OF. *trone* (mod. *trône*) – L. *thronus* – Gr. *thrónos* elevated seat. Hence **throne** vb. (arch.) ENTHRONE XIV; be enthroned XVII (Sh.).

throng þrɔŋ A. crowd XIII (Cursor M.); B. crowding, crowded condition XIV. In sense A – ON. *þrǫng*, corr. to OE. *ġeþrang*, MLG., MHG. *gedrang* (G. *drang* crowd, pressure); cf. OHG. *drangōd*, *githrengi*, MLG., MHG. *gedrenge* (G. *gedränge*); in sense B f. **throng** vb. †press, crush; push one's way XIV; form a crowd, crowd round, press upon XVI; fill *with* a crowd XVII. The vb. is prob. orig. f. (dial.) *throng* adj. pressed close together (XIV) – ON. *þrǫngr* narrow, close, crowded, rel. to OE. *þringan* press, crowd, throng = OS. *thringan*, OHG. *dringan* (Du., G. *dringen*), ON. *þryngva*, also to Goth. *þreihan*; the Germ. base **þriŋg(w)*- **þriŋχ(w)*- is rel. to a widespread IE. base with reprs. seen in Av., Lith., and Celtic.

throstle þrɔ·sl thrush, mavis. OE. *þrostle* = OS. *throsla*, OHG. *drōscala* (G. *drossel*), f. Germ. **þrau(d)st-*, *-sk-*, based on IE. formations repr. by L. *turdus*, Celtic and Balto-Sl. names of the bird. See THRUSH[1].

throttle þrɔ·tl compress the throat of, so as to suffocate. XIV. Late ME. *throtel*, *-il*, perh. f. THROAT + -LE[3]. ¶ Not f. much later (dial.) *throttle* throat (XVI), which has the form of dim. of THROAT, like synon. G. *drossel* (f. MHG. *drozze*, OHG. *drozza*), whence †*drosseln*, *erdrosseln* strangle.

through þrū prep. from end to end or from side to side of; by the agency or means of; adv. from end to end. OE. *þurh* = OFris. *thruch*, OS. *thurh*, *thuru*, (M)Du. *door*, OHG. *duruh*, *-ih*, *dur* (G. *durch*, dial. *dur*) :– WGerm. **þurχ*, of which a var. **þerh* is repr. by OE. (late Nhb.) *þerch*, *þærch*, Goth. *þairh* through, OHG. *derh* perforated; cf. further OE. *þȳrel* hole (see NOSTRIL); the basic **tr-* is seen in OIr. *tre*, *tri*, L. *trāns* across. The metathetic forms (*þruh*, etc.) appear *c.*1300 and became universal in XV. Cf. THOROUGH, THRILL. comp. **through**OU·T adv. right through, OE. *þurhūt*, prep. XI; cf. modG. *durchaus*.

throw þrou pt. **threw** þrū, pp. **thrown** þroun twist (now only dial. or in techn. sense of preparing and twisting raw silk into thread XV); from XIII in various uses of *cast*. OE. *þrāwan*, pt. *þrēow*, pp. *þrāwen* = OS. *thrāian*, OHG. *drāen*, *drājen*, *drāwen* (Du. *draaien*, G. *drehen*); WGerm. str. vb. (Da. and Sw. forms are – LG.), based on IE. **ter-*, repr. by L. *terere* rub (see TRITE), Gr. *teírein* wear out, *trêma* hole, Lith. *trinù* I rub, OIr. *tarathar* borer. Hence sb. XVI. ¶ Superseded OE. *weorpan* (see WARP) as the gen. vb. for throwing, sharing various senses with *cast*, which is of Scand. origin.

thrum[1] þrʌm end of a warp-thread left unwoven, short piece of waste thread. XIV. repr. OE. *þrum* in (*under*)*tungeþrum* ligament of the tongue = MDu. *drom*, *drum* (mod. Du. has *dreum* thrum), OHG., MHG. *drum* end-piece, remnant (G. *trumm* end-piece, *trümmer* remnants, ruins), f. Germ. **þrum-* **þram-* (whence ON. *þrǫmr* :- **þramuz*); the IE. base **tr̥m-* is repr. also by L. *terminus, termō*, Gr. *térma* end, TERM.

thrum[2] þrʌm play on a stringed instrument XVI; strum upon XVII; recite in sing-song fashion; drum (*on*) XVIII. Of imit. origin. ¶ 'Anon to our gitterne, thrumpledum, thrumpledum thrum' (Udall 'Royster Doyster' II i, *c*.1550).

thrush[1] þrʌʃ bird of the genus Turdus. OE. *þrysće* (:- **þruskjōn*), rel. to synon. OE. *þrǣsće*, **þrēasće* = OHG. *drōsca* (:- **þrauskōn*); cf. THROSTLE.

thrush[2] þrʌʃ A. disease (esp. of infants) marked by white specks in the mouth XVII (Pepys); B. in the horse, inflammation of the frog of the hoof XVIII. Of unkn. origin; but in sense A cf. Sw., ODa. *tørsk*, Da. *troske*; in sense B FRUSH.

thrust þrʌst use the force of impact (upon). XII. Early ME. *þrüste* (in w.midl. *tothruste* pt. XII), e.midl. *þriste* (Havelok), *þreste* – ON. *þrýsta* (:- **þrūstjan*), which has been referred to IE. **trŭd-*, whence L. *trūdere* (cf. ABSTRUSE, EXTRUDE, INTRUDE, PROTRUDE). Hence **thrust** sb. XVI.

thud þʌd †(Sc.) come with a blast or gust XVI (Douglas); produce a dull heavy sound XVIII. prob. identical with OE. *þyddan*, ME. *thüdde* thrust, push (:- **þudjan*), rel. to OE. *þoddettan* push, beat (:- **þudatjan*) and *þoden*, ME. *þode*, early mod. *thode* (Bunyan) violent wind. Hence **thud** sb. blast, gust XVI (Douglas); heavy blow XVIII; dull heavy sound XIX. In earliest use Sc. and north. dial.; not in gen. Eng. use before XIX, when it became familiar (*c*.1850), prob. through writers whose works show local colouring, e.g. Emily Brontë, George Eliot.

thug þʌg (*Thug*) professional robber and murderer in India, (hence) cut-throat, ruffian. XIX. – Hindi, Marathi *ṭhag* cheat, swindler. So **thuggee·** system practised by the thugs. XIX. – Hindi *ṭhagī*.

thuja þjū·dʒə now the more usual form of THUYA. XVIII. modL. (Linnæus).

Thule þjū·li name of an island supposed by Polybius to be the northernmost region in the world. OE., ME. *Tyle, Tile* (Alfred, Ch., Trevisa), mod. *Thule* (XVI) – L. *Thūlē, Thȳlē* – Gr. *Thoúlē, Thū́lē*, of unkn. origin.

thumb þʌm short innermost digit of the hand. OE. *þūma* = OFris., OS. *thūma*, MLG., MDu. *dūme* (Du. *duim*), OHG. *dūmo* (G. *daumen*) :- WGerm. **þūmon* (ON. has *þumalfingr*; cf. THIMBLE); repr. IE. **tum-*, one of several extensions of **tu-* swell, as seen also e.g. in THOLE[1], THOUSAND, TUMOUR, TUMULT, TUMULUS. The parasitic *b* found in pl. *þumbes* (XII), sg. *þoumbe* (XIII), had no permanent effect on the pronunc. Hence vb. XVI.

Thummim þʌ·mim Heb. *thummīm* perfection, var. of *tummīm*, pl. of *tōm* completeness. XVI. See URIM.

thump þʌmp strike or beat heavily. XVI. So as sb. XVI. imit.; similar forms are EFris. *dump* knock, Icel., Sw. dial. *dumpa* vb. thump.

thunder þʌ·ndəɹ loud noise accompanying lightning. OE. *þunor* = OFris. *thuner*, OS. *thunar*, OHG. *donar* (Du. *donder*, G. *donner*), ON. *þórr* :- CGerm. (exc. Gothic) f. IE. **tn-* **ton-*, as in L. *tonāre* thunder. So vb. OE. *þunrian* = Du. *donderen*, G. *donnern*. ¶ In *thunderbolt* (XV), *thunderstroke* (XVI) the reference is to the supposed destructive power of thunder as the accompaniment of lightning.

thurible þjuə·ribl censer. XV (*turrible, thoryble*, Promp. Parv.). – (O)F. *thurible* or L. *t(h)ūribulum*, f. *t(h)ūr-*, *t(h)ūs* incense – Gr. *thúos* sacrifice, offering, incense. So **thu·rifer** one who carries a thurible. XIX. – ecclL. (cf. -FEROUS); earlier **thuri·bul**ER[2] (XVI) – OF. *thuribulier* – medL. *thūribulārius*.

Thursday þə̄·ɹzdi fourth day of the week. OE. *þur(e)sdæġ*, for *þunresdæġ*, f. g. of *þunor* THUNDER; partly assoc. with ON. *þórsdagr*; corr. to (M)Du. *donderdag*, OHG. *donarestac* (G. *donnerstag*), rendering late L. *Jovis dies* Jupiter's day (whence F. *jeudi*, It. *giovedì*).

thus ðʌs in this manner, like this, to this extent. OE. *þus* = OS. *thus*, (M)Du. *dus*, of unkn. origin. Hence **thu·s**NESS in (joc.) *this thusness* ('A. Ward'). **thu·s**WISE (arch.). XIV. ¶ A similar formation is (M)Du. *zus*, (M)LG *züs*, OHG., MHG. *sus*.

thuya þū·jə one of a genus of conifers. XVIII. irreg. repr. of Gr. *thúia*, var. of *thúā*, name of the source of THYINE wood. See THUJA.

thwack þwæk beat or strike as with a stick. XVI. imit.; cf. (dial.) *thack*, OE. *þaccian*, ME. *thakke*. Hence sb. XVI.

thwart[1] þwɔ̄ɹt (arch.) adv. and prep. athwart XIV; adj. obstinate, perverse XIII. Early ME. *þwert* (Orm *þwerrt*), first in comp. adv. *þwert out* thoroughly, and prep. *þwert over* across, adj. perverse – ON. *þvert*, orig. n. of *þverr* transverse, cross = OE. *þwe(o)rh* crooked, cross, perverse, OHG. *dwerh, twerch*, G. *zwerch* (in comp. *überzwerch* across, *zwerchfell* diaphragm), Goth. *þwairhs* cross, angry :- CGerm. **þwerχwaz*, f. IE. **twerk-* **twork-*, as in L. *torquēre* twist; cf. ATHWART.

thwart[2] þwɔ̄ɹt rower's bench. XVIII. Appears 1736 in Bailey's folio dict. as a var. of *thought*, which is evidenced from XIV (Sandahl) as a var. of earlier n. dial. *thoft*, OE. *þofte* = MDu. *dofte, dochte* (Du. *doft*), OHG. *dofta* (G. *ducht, duft* is from LG.), ON. *þopta* :- Germ. **tuftō*, taken to be f. a base meaning 'squat'. The absence of evidence for *thoft* between 1513 (Douglas) and mod. Sc. (Jamieson) and north. dial. and the replacement of *thought* by *thwart* (presumably under the influence of THWART[1]) render the history obscure.

thy ðai clipped form of THINE (ME. *þi* XII).

Thyestean þaiestī·ən; -e·stiən pert. to *Thyestes*, in ancient Gr. legend brother of Atreus, who at a banquet made him eat of the flesh of his two sons; see -EAN. XVII (Milton).

thyine þai·in epithet of a tree mentioned in Rev. xviii 12. XIV (Wycl. Bible, *tyyn*). – L. *thȳinus* – Gr. *thúïnos*, f. *thúā* THUYA; see -INE[1].

thylacine þai·ləsain native Tasmanian 'wolf', a carnivorous marsupial. XIX. – F. *thylacine*, modL. *thylacīnus*, f. Gr. *thū́lakos* pouch; see -INE[1].

thyme taim fragrant aromatic herb of the genus Thymus. XIV (Trevisa). – (O)F. *thym* – L. *thymum* – Gr. *thúmon* (also *-os*). f. *thū́ein* burn sacrifice, f. base **dhu-* cause to smoke.

thyro- þaiə·rou used as comb. of next. XIX (in modL. XVII).

thyroid þaiə·roid (anat.) *t. cartilage* Adam's apple; *t. gland, t. body* one of the 'ductless glands'. XVIII. – F. †*thyroide* (Paré) or modL. *thyroidēs* (Blancard) – Gr. *thuroidḗs*, erron. for *thureoeidḗs* (χόνδρος θυρεοειδής thyroid cartilage, Galen), f. *thureós* stone put against a door, oblong shield (as door-shaped), f. *thúrā* DOOR; see -OID.

thyrsus þə̄·ɹsəs pl. *thyrsi* þə̄·ɹsai (Gr. and Roman antiq.) staff or spear tipped with a pine-cone ornament; (bot.) form of inflorescence. XVIII. – L. – Gr. *thúrsos* stalk of a plant.

thyself ðaise·lf emph. and refl. vars. of THOU and THEE. ME. *þi sülf, þi self* (XIII), repl. *þē self* (OE. to XIV), i.e. THEE and SELF; cf. MYSELF.

tiara tiā·rə conical cap of ancient Persians XVI; pope's triple crown XVII; lady's ornamental headband XVIII. – L. *tiāra* – Gr. *tiā́ra, tiā́rās*, partly through It. *tiara*; in all senses preceded by anglicized *tiar(e)*, partly due to (O)F. *tiare*.

Tibetan, Thibetan tibe·tən, tibī·tən, ti·betən of or pert. to *Tibet*, a country of central Asia, or its language. XIX. The current Eur. name of the country (called by the Tibetans *Bod*, pronounced as Bhöd, Bhöt) repr. *Tö-bhöt*, i.e. 'High Bod', native name of the plateau bordering Mongolia, China, and Kashmir, by which Eur. travellers approached Tibet; see -AN.

tibia ti·biə larger of the two bones of the lower leg. XVIII. – L. *tībia* shin-bone, flute. So **ti·bi**AL[1]. XVI. – L.

tical tikā·l, ti·kəl former Siamese silver coin. XVII. – Pg. *tical*, repr. native *ṭaṅkā*.

tice tais (dial.) Aphetic of †*attice, -ise*, ENTICE, but earlier than these forms and prob. immed. – OF. *atisier*. Hence sb. yorker (in cricket).

tick[1] tik kind of mite. OE. **ticca* or **tīca* (recorded once as *ticia* VIII), ME. *tyke, teke*, later *ticke* (XVI), corr., with variation of vowel and cons., to MLG., MDu. *tēke* (Du. *teek*), OHG. *zēcho* (G. *zecke*), f. WGerm. **tīk-* **tikk-*; the ME. forms may be partly due to MLG. or MDu.; Arm. *tiz* bug, and Ir. *dega* stag-beetle are compared.

tick[2] tik (dial.) touch or tap lightly, esp. toy, dally XIII (*ticki*, AncrR.); make short quick beats XVIII; mark with a dash, etc. XIX. prob. imit. So **tick** sb. slight touch XV (*tek*; in the game of tick or tig XVII Drayton); quick dry sound XVII; small dot or dash XIX. The parallel LG. *tikk* touch, moment, instant, Du. *tik* pat, touch, *tikken* pat, tick, MHG. *zic* slight touch or pressure, spot, crafty conduct, OHG. *zekōn* pluck (MHG. *zicken* push), Norw. *tikke* touch lightly (from LG.), may point to a WGerm. base, or the various forms may be independent expressive formations.

tick[3] tik case or cover of a mattress or pillow, (hence) material of this. XV (*tikke, tēke, tȳke*). corr. to and prob. immed. – MLG., MDu. *tēke* and MDu. *tīke* (Du. *tijk*), rel. to OHG. *ziahha, ziecha* (G. *zieche* bed-tick, pillow-case); WGerm. – L. *thēca* – Gr. *thḗkē* case, f. IE. **dhē-* place (see DO[1]).

tick[4] tik in phr. (*go, run, play*) *on tick* on credit, on trust XVII; short for TICKET (used in similar phr. *go on the ticket*, etc., from *c.*1600).

ticket ti·kit (short) written notice, label; †voucher, warrant, promise to pay (phr. *on the t.*; cf. TICK[4]) XVI; slip bearing evidence of the holder's title to something XVII; (U.S.) list of candidates for election XVIII; *the t.*, the correct thing XIX. Aphetic – F. †*étiquet* (cf. ETIQUETTE), OF. *estiquet(te)*, f. *estiquier, estequier* fix, stick, var. of *estichier, estechier* – MDu. *steken*; see -ET. Hence vb. XVII.

tickle ti·kl †be thrilled (R. Mannyng); excite agreeably XIV (Ch.); touch, stroke, or poke so as to excite XV. prob. frequent. of TICK[2]; see -LE[3]. For synon. words with similar cons. structure, cf. OE. *tinclian, citelian*, (dial.) *kittle*, OHG. *kizzilōn* (G. *kitzeln*, dial. *zicklen*), ON. *kitla*, L. *titillāre* TITILLATE. Hence **ti·ck**LISH[1]. XVI; superseding (dial.) *tickle* (XVI) in senses 'delicate', 'precarious'.

ticktack ti·ktæ·k expressive of duplicated or alternating ticking sound. XVI. Cf. Du. *tiktak*, G. *ticktack*, F. *tic-tac*. So **ti·ck-ti·ck**. XVIII, **ti·ck-to·ck** (of the ticking of a clock). XIX.

ticky ti·ki (S. Africa) threepenny piece. XIX. perh. native alt. of a Eur. word, e.g. TICKET, or Du. *stukje* little piece.

tidal tai·dəl pert. to the tide or tides. XIX. f. TIDE[1] B+-AL[1]. ¶ Of techn. origin and currency.

tiddlywink ti·dliwiŋk A. (sl.) beershop; B. (pl.) game played with (1) dominoes, (2) counters. XIX. Of unkn. origin; with A cf. sl. *tiddly* a drink, drunk.

tide[1] taid A. †portion of time, season, age; †hour; (arch.) point of time, due time; definite time of day or of the year (surviving in *eventide, noontide, springtide*); church anniversary or festival (arch. except as in *Eastertide, Shrovetide, Whitsuntide*) OE.; B. swelling of the sea or its alternate rising and falling XIV. OE. *tīd* = OS. *tīd* (Du. *tijd*), OHG. *zīt* (G. *zeit*), ON. *tīð* :- CGerm. (exc. Goth.) **tīdiz*, f. **tī-* (cf. TIME) :- IE. **dī* **dā(i)*- divide, cut up, repr. by Gr. *daíesthai* divide, distribute, *daís, daitē* portion, meal, *daímōn* DEMON, Skr. *dáyatē* share, *dā́ti, dyā́ti* cut, harvest, share, Arm. *ti* age, years, time, Gr. *dêmos* DEME. In B prob. after MLG. *(ge)tīde, tīe*, MDu. *ghetīde* (Du. *tij, getij*), a special development of the sense 'fixed time'. So **tide** (arch.) happen, befall. OE. *tīdan*, earlier *ġetīdan*, f. the sb. ¶ Often sp. *'tide*, as if for BETIDE.

tide[2] taid flow or carry along like the tide XVI; get *over*, surmount XVII. f. TIDE[1] B.

tidings tai·diŋz (pl.; formerly also sg.) piece of news. Late OE. *tīdung*, prob., with assim. to -ING[1], anglicization of ON. *tíðendi, -indi* events, news, f. *tíðr* adj. happening, occurring + nominal suffix; various types of form exist in ME., showing different stages of adaptation and blending of ON. and native features; the ON. forms are directly repr. by *tiþennde* (Orm), *tiðind* (Laȝ.). Cf. G. *zeitung* newspaper.

tidy tai·di in good condition, of good appearance XIII; timely, seasonable (presumably the orig. sense); excellent, worthy XIV; of neat habits or appearance XVIII; pretty good, pretty big XIX; sb. object for keeping persons or things neat XIX. ME. *tīdi*, f. *tīd* time, TIDE[1] + -Y[1]. Cf. OHG. *zītig* (G. *zeitig*), Du. *tijdig* timely.

tie tai that with which anything is fastened OE.; fig. bond, connexion XVI; equality between competitors XVII. OE. *tēah (tēag-), tēg* = ON. *taug* rope :- Germ. **taugō*, f. **tauχ-* (cf. TEAM, TOW[2]). So **tie** vb. make fast. OE. *tīġan*, late form of WS. **tieġan*, Anglian **tēġan* (ME. *teȝen*) :- Germ. **taugian* (cf. ON. *teygja* draw).

tier tiəɹ row, rank of seats, shelves, etc. XVI (*tier, tire*); - (O)F. *tire* sequence, rank, order, f. *tirer* draw, draw out = Pr., Sp. *tirar*, It. *tirare* :- Rom. **tīrāre*, of unkn. origin.

tierce tiəɹs †third part XV; third hour of the day (9 a.m.); canonical office said at this hour (TERCE) XIV; wine measure or cask XVI; third of the parries in fencing; sequence of three playing cards XVII; (mus.) note two octaves and a major third above a fundamental note XVII; (her.) division of a shield into three equal parts XIX. - (O)F. *tierce, terce* :- L. *tertia*, sb. use of fem. of *tertius* THIRD.

tiff tif †slight fit of temper; slight quarrel. XVIII. prob. of dial. origin, but no source is known.

tiffany ti·fəni kind of thin transparent silk. XVII (Holland, Cotgr.). perh. punning use (quasi transparency) of *tiffany* - OF. *tifanie* :- ecclL. *theophania* - Gr. *theopháneia, -phánia* EPIPHANY. f. *theós* god + *phan-* appear; cf. dial. sense 'fine sieve'.

tiffin ti·fin in India, etc., a light midday meal. XVIII. For *tiffing*, gerund of (sl. or dial.) *tiff* drink, sip (XVIII; cf. '*Tiffing*, eating, or drinking out of meal time', Grose, 1785), var. of synon. *tift* (XVIII), rel. to *tiff* liquor (XVII), sip or drink (XVIII).

tig tig touch, pat; touch in the game of tick or tig. XIX. Hence **tig** sb. touch, pat XVIII; game in which players are chased and touched when caught XIX. var. of TICK[2].

tiger tai·gəɹ large feline quadruped Felis tigris. XIII. ME. *tygre* - (O)F. *tigre* = Pr., etc. *tigre* - L. *tigri-s* (whence OE. pl. *tigras, -es*) - Gr. *tígris*. Cf. G., Sw., Da. *tiger*, Du. *tijger*. Hence **tigr**ESS[1] tai·grės. XVII; after F. *tigresse*.

tight tait †dense XIV; of close construction so as to exclude air, etc. (cf. *air-tight, water-tight*); firmly fixed; taut; (dial.) capable, vigorous XVI; (dial.) neat, trim XVII; close-fitting XVIII; (sl.) close-fisted; drunk XIX. prob. alt. of *thight* (surviving dial. in *thite, theat*, impervious, dense, close), perh. orig. in †*tonnet(h)ight* (XIV) designating tonnage; - ON. **þehtr, þéttr* watertight, of close texture = OE. *þiht* firm, solid (as in comps. *magaþiht, meteþiht*), MLG., MDu. *dicht* (whence G. *dicht* dense, close) :- **þiŋχtaz*, f. **þiŋχ-* grow, repr. by OE. *(ġe)þēon*, OE. *githīhan*, OHG. *gidīhan* (G. *gedeihen* grow, thrive), Goth. *(ga)þeihan*. As sb. pl. for *tight breeches, trousers* XIX (Marryat, Dickens). Hence **ti·ght**EN[5]. XVIII.

til til plant Sesamum indicum. XIX. Hindi *til* :- Skr. *tilá*.

Tilbury ti·lbəri †A. Sixpenny piece said to have been the fare from Gravesend to Tilbury Fort XVIII; B. light two-wheeled carriage named from the inventor XIX.

tilde ti·ldɛ sign ~ placed over *n* in Spanish to indicate the palatalized sound. XIX. - Sp. *tilde*, corr. to F. *titre*, It. *titolo* - L. *titulu-s* TITLE, TITTLE.

tile tail thin slab of burnt clay for roofing, paving, etc. OE. *tiġele* (*tiġule*), corr. to OS. *tiegla* (Du. *tegel*), OHG. *ziagal*, *-ala* (G. *ziegel*), ON. *tigl* – L. *tēgula*, f. IE. **tĕg-* cover; see THATCH.

till[1] til labour upon, cultivate. OE. *tilian* strive after, attempt, obtain, treat, cure, (late) cultivate = OFris. *tilia* get, cultivate, OS. *tilian*, *tilon* obtain (Du. *telen* produce, beget, raise, cultivate), OHG. *zilōn*, *zilēn* (G. *zielen* aim, strive), Goth. *gatilon* :– Germ. **tilōjan*, **tilējan*, f. **tilam* aim, goal (see TILL[2]). Hence **ti·llAGE**. XV.

till[2] til prep. (Sc. and north.) to OE.; up to the time of XIV; conj. to the time that XII. OE. (Nhb.) *til*, prep. with d. = OFris. *til* (with d.), ON. *til* (with g.); prob. from advb. use of Germ. sb. **tilam*, repr. by OE. *till* fixed point, station, MLG. *til*, *tel* aim, point of time, OHG. *zil* (G. *ziel* end, limit, goal), ON. *aldr|tili* 'end of life', death, Goth. *til* opportunity; hence prop. 'with the limit or goal of' (the place or time specified); for further relations see TILL[1]. In ME. (and later) use due to adoption of the ON. word.

till[3] til †small box, etc. contained within a larger one XV; box or drawer for holding cash in a shop XVII. Of unkn. origin. ¶F. *tille*, which corr. in form but is not recorded before XVIII, is derived by some from the Eng. word; if, however, its source is ON. *þilja* plank, DEAL, it must be much earlier and could possibly be the source of the Eng. word.

tiller ti·ləɹ beam or stock of a crossbow XV; bar or beam attached to the rudder-head XVII. Late ME. *tiler*, *telor* – AN. *telier* weaver's beam :– medL. *tēlārium*, f. L. *tēla* web (see TOIL[2]).

tilt[1] tilt †throw down or over; †fall over XIV; move unsteadily up and down; cause to lean or slant XVI. Late ME. *tilte*, *tylte* may repr. OE. **tyltan*, later form of **tieltan* :– **taltjan*, f. **taltaz* (OE. *tealt* unsteady, whence *tealtian* totter); but perh. of Scand. origin (cf. Norw. *tylten* unsteady, Sw. *tulta* totter). Hence **tilt** sb. inclination. XVI.

tilt[2] tilt covering of coarse cloth, esp. awning over a cart or boat XV; in Labrador, etc. fisherman's or woodcutter's hut XIX. var. of *tild*, *teld* (= (OH)G. *zelt*), perh. influenced by TENT.

tilt[3] tilt barrier separating combatants in an exercise in which the participants ride against each other with lances; the combat itself XVI. Of unkn. origin.

tilth tilþ tillage, husbandry; †harvest OE.; tilled land XIV. Late OE. *tilþ*, *tilþe*, f. *tilian* TILL[1]; see -TH[1].

timar timā·ɹ in Turkey, fief held by military service. XVII. – Turk. – Pers. *tīmār* attendance, watching.

timbal ti·mbəl (arch.) kettledrum. XVII. – F. *timbale*, alteration after *cymbale* cymbal of †*tamballe* – (with assim. to *tambour* drum) Sp. *atabal* – Arab. *aṭṭabl* drum (*aṭ-* is AL-[2]). See ATABAL.

timbale tɛ̃bal membrane resembling a drumhead in certain insects; dish of meat, etc. cooked in a crust, so called from its shape. XIX. F. (see prec.).

timber ti·mbəɹ †building, edifice; †building material, (later) wood for building; growing trees OE.; wooden object, spec. beam XIV. OE. *timber* = OFris. *timber*, OS. *timbar*, OHG. *zimbar* (G. *zimmer* room), ON. *timbr* :– CGerm. **timram* (cf. Goth. *timrjan* build, *timrja* builder) :– IE. **demrom*, f. **dĕm-* **dŏm-* **dm̥-* build see DESPOT, DOME, TOFT.

timbre tæ·mbəɹ, ti·mbəɹ, tɛ̃br quality of a musical or vocal sound. XIX. (O)F. *timbre* (orig.) timbrel, bell struck with a hammer, table-bell, (whence) sound or sonorous quality as of a bell :– Rom. **timbano*, – medGr. *tímbanon*, Gr. *túmpanon* TYMPANUM.

timbrel ti·mbrəl tambourine-like instrument of percussion. XVI (*timberal*, Dunbar). perh. dim. of synon. †*timbre* (XIII) – OF. *timbre*; see prec. and -EL[2].

time taim limited stretch of continued existence; period or point in the course of this OE.; indefinite continuous duration XIV. OE. *tīma* = ON. *tími* time, good time, prosperity :– Germ. **tīmon*, f. **tī-* stretch, extend + *-mon-*. The notion is also expressed in OE. and the other Germ. langs. (not Gothic) by another deriv. of the same base, viz. TIDE, which was superseded by *time* in the strictly temporal senses. Hence **time** vb. †befall XIII; fix, note, etc. the time of XIV. **timely** tai·mli well-timed, †early. XII; modelled on *timely* adv., OE. *tīmlīċe* (cf. ON. *tímaliga*); see -LY[1], -LY[2]. **time**OUS tai·məs (chiefly Sc.) timely. XV. **ti·mepiece**. XVIII; the sense of PIECE is 'specimen of handicraft, production', as in *mantelpiece*, *masterpiece*.

timenoguy tai·mənŏgai· (naut.) rope fastened at one end to the fore-rigging and at the other to the anchor-stock. XVIII. prob. ult. based on (O)F. *timon* wagon-pole, tiller (:– L. *tēmō(n-)* beam, pole, rel. to OE. *þīxl* pole, shaft, OS. *thīsla*, OHG. *dīhsala*, G. *deichsel*, ON. *þísl* :– Germ. **þeŋχslō*) and GUY[1].

timid ti·mid easily frightened. XVI (Sc.). – F. *timide* or L. *timidus*, f. *timēre* fear; see -ID[1].

timocracy taimɔ·krəsi polity with a property qualification for its ruling class XVI; polity in which love of honour is the dominant motive with the rulers XVII. – (O)F. *timocratie* – medL. *tīmocratia* – Gr. *tīmokratíā*, f. *tīmḗ* honour, value + *-kratíā* -CRACY.

timorous ti·mərəs feeling fear. xv. – (O)F. *temoros, -eus* (mod. *timoreux*) – medL. *timorōsus*, f. L. *timor* fear, f. *timēre*; see TIMID, -OUS.

tin tin white highly malleable metal. OE. *tin* = OFris., (M)LG., (M)Du. *tin*, OHG. *zin* (G. *zinn*), ON. *tin* :– CGerm. (exc. Gothic) **tinam*, of unkn. origin, perh. a pre-IE. word of western Europe.

tinamou ti·nəmū XVIII. – F. *tinamou* – Galibi *tinamu*.

tincal ti·ŋkəl, **tincar** ti·ŋkəɹ crude borax. XVII. Malay *tingkal* – Skr. *ṭankaṇa*, and Urdu *tankār, tincār*.

tincture ti·ŋktʃəɹ †dye, pigment XIV; hue, colour (spec. in her.) XV; †imparted quality, tinge; †(Alch.) supposed spiritual principle XVI; †essential principle of a substance; solution of a medicinal principle XVII. – L. *tinctūra* dyeing, f. *tinct-*, pp. stem of *tingere* dye, TINGE; see -URE.

tindal ti·ndəl native petty officer of lascars; foreman of a gang. XVII. – Hind. *taṇḍel* – Malayalam *taṇḍal*, Telugu *taṇḍelu*.

tinder ti·ndəɹ dry material that readily takes fire from a spark. OE. *tynder, tyndre*, corr. (with variation in suffix and gender) to (M)LG. *tunder* (Du. *tonder*), OHG. *zuntara* (G. *zunder*), ON. *tundr*, f. Germ. **tund-* (whence also OHG. *zunten* kindle, Goth. *tundnan* be kindled), **tend-* (whence MHG. *zinden* burn, glow), **tand-*, whence OE. causative *-tendan*, dial. *tind* kindle, ignite, Goth. *tandjan* (:– **tandjan*), OHG. *zantaro* glowing coal, ON. *tandri* fire, spark.

tine tain sharp projecting point, spec. of an antler. OE. *tind* = MLG. *tind*, OHG. *zint*, ON. *tindr*, rel. to synon. MLG. *tinne*, OHG. *zinna*. ¶ For the loss of final *d* cf. GROIN, LAWN², WOODBINE.

tinea ti·niə ringworm. XVII. – L. *tinea* gnawing worm, moth, worm in the body.

ting tiŋ sound (a small bell, etc.) XV; emit a high singing note XVI. imit. Also *ting-tang*.

tinge tinᵈʒ impart a slight change of colour to XV. – L. *tingere* dip in liquid, moisten. Cf. Gr. *téngein* moisten, wet.

tingle ti·ŋgl be affected with a ringing or thrilling sensation. XIV (Wycl. Bible, Trevisa). perh. modification of TINKLE by assoc. with RING².

tinker ti·ŋkəɹ mender of pots, kettles, etc. XIII; (dial.) gipsy, itinerant trader, etc. XVI. perh. repr. OE. **tinecere*, f. **tinecian* work in tin, f. *tin(n)* TIN, with *k*-formative as in *smearcian* SMIRK; but the appearance of synon. (north.) *tinkler* at an earlier date (XII) is then difficult to account for.

tinkle ti·ŋkl (of the ears) ring, tingle XIV (Wycl. Bible); give forth short sharp ringing sounds XIV.

tinnitus tinai·təs (path.) ringing or singing in the ears. XIX. – L. *tinnītus*, f. *tinnīre* ring, tinkle, of imit. origin.

tinsel ti·nsəl †attrib. embellished with gold or silver thread; sb. fabric so embellished; thin plates, strips, etc. of shining metal used for ornament XVI; fig. showy but valueless stuff XVII. First in *tinsell(e) saten*, prob. repr. AN. **satin estincelé* (cf. *tinselt saten*. XVI), with loss of final *-é* as in COSTIVE; hence, by ellipsis, used sb. (O)F. *estincelé* (in which the *s* had become mute in XIV), f. *estincele* (mod. *étincelle* spark), repr. popL. **stincilla*, f. L. SCINTILLA.

tint tint (slight or delicate) hue. XVIII (Pope). Alt. (perh. by assim. to It. *tinto*) of †*tinct* (XVII Sh.). – L. *tinctus* dyeing, f. pp. stem of *tingere* dye, TINGE. Hence as vb. XVIII. A painter's word.

tintinnabulum tintinæ·bjŭləm small tinkling bell. XVI. – L., f. *tintinnāre* (whence F. *tinter*), beside L. *tintinnīre*, redupl. f. *tinnīre* (see TINNITUS). Hence **ti:ntinnabul**A·TION. XIX (Poe).

tiny tai·ni very small. XVI (late). In the earliest exx. always preceded by *little*; extension with -Y¹ of monosyllabic synon. †*tine* (XIV), of unkn. origin.

-tion ʃən ME. *-cio(u)n*, repr. (O)F. *-tion*, earlier *-cion, -ciun*, repr. L. *-tiō(n-)*, comp. suffix f. *-t-* of a pp. stem + *-iō(n-)* -ION; orig. expressing the state or condition of being what the pp. imports, e.g. *complētiō* COMPLETION, the condition of being *complētus* COMPLETE, thence transferred to the action or process involved, and so (like -ING¹) acquiring a concr. or quasi-concr. notion, as in *dictiō* DICTION, *nātiō* birth, brood, NATION, *ōrātiō* mode of speaking, speech, ORATION. So **-tious** ʃəs repr. L. *-tiōsus*, forming adjs. rel. to sbs. in *-tion*, as *ambition/ambitious, nutrition/nutritious*.

tip¹ tip fine or slender extremity XV; vb. (first in pp.) furnish with a tip XIV (*tipped with horn, t. with 'blak,'* Ch.) prob. earlier in colloq. use, the base being repr. in early XIV by †*tipping* pendant. – ON. *typpi* sb., *typpa* vb., *typptr* tipped, topped, edged, *typpingr* edging, f. Germ. **tupp-* TOP¹; prob. reinforced by – (M)LG., (M)Du. *tip* apex, extremity = MHG. *zipf*, of which there is a deriv. (M)LG., (M)Du. *tippel*, Du. *tepel*, MHG., G. *zipfel*.

tip² tip tap or touch lightly. XIII. First in fig. use in AncrR. (*uort þe nede tippe*, AN. version *desque le besoing le touche* until necessity touch him) and thereafter not till XVI; (hence prob.) orig. in rogues' cant, give, hand, pass XVII; give a gratuity to XVIII. perh. orig. identical with TIP¹, as if 'touch the point of', or 'touch as with a point'; cf. LG., Du. *tippen*. Hence **tip** sb. gratuity XVIII; friendly hint (prob. f. phr. *tip the wink* give a private warning (XVII)) XIX. Hence **ti·p**STER. XIX.

tip[3] tip (dial.) overturn, be overturned XIV; incline, tilt; empty out by tilting XVII. orig. *tīpe*, in literary use till XVII and still dial., the distribution suggesting Scand. origin. If the orig. conjugation was *tīpe, tĭpte, tĭpt* (cf. *kēpe, kĕpte, kĕpt*), the pt. and pp. prob. affected the inf.; contact with TIP[2] prob. furthered the change.

tipcat ti·pkæt game in which a 'cat' (short piece of wood tapered at both ends XVII) is struck with a stick. f. TIP[2]+CAT XIX.

tippet ti·pit (hist.) long narrow piece of cloth as part of a dress XIV; garment covering the shoulders XV; (eccl.) clergyman's scarf XVI. Of unkn. origin; prob. – AN. deriv. of TIP[1] (see -ET).

tippler ti·plə1 †retailer of drink, tapster XIV; (from the vb.) habitual drinker XVI. Of unkn. origin; similar forms of cognate meaning are Norw. dial. *tipla* drip slowly, *tippa* drink in small quantities, but connexion with these cannot be established. Hence, presumably by back-formation, **tipple** vb. †retail drink XV; drink habitually XVI.

tipstaff ti·pstàf †staff with a tip carried by some officials; such an official, bailiff, etc. XVI. Alt. of *tipt* (*tipped*) *staff*; see TIP[1].

tipsy ti·psi slightly drunk. XVI. f. TIP[3]+-SY.

tiptoe ti·ptou (pl.) the tips of the toes. XIV (*on his tiptoon*, Ch.); phr. *on t.* XV; adv. XVI (Sh.). f. TIP[1]+TOE.

tiptop ti·ptɔ·p sb. highest point; adj. very highest. XVIII. redupl. of TOP[1], prob. with assoc. of TIP[1].

tirade tairei·d volley of words; section of verse on a single theme. XIX. – F. *tirade* – It. *tirata* volley, f. *tirare* = Pr., Sp. *tirar* :– CRom. **tīrāre* draw, of unkn. origin; see -ADE.

tire[1] taiə1 †fail, give out; become exhausted; exhaust, weary. OE. *tēorian*, freq. in comps. *ātēorian, ġetēorian*, of unkn. origin. There is no evidence for this word between late OE. and XIV, when and in XV (also in comp. *fortyred*) it is predominantly north.; the development of vowel (*tēre* to *tīre*) is paralleled in *briar, friar, quire*. Hence **ti·re**SOME[1]. XVI (Dunbar).

tire[2] taiə1 †get ready, equip; †attire XIV; dress (the hair or head) XVI. Aphetic of ATTIRE. Hence (arch.) *tiring house* XVI, *-room* XVII, dressing-room of a theatre.

tire[3] see TYRE[1].

tirl tɔ̄1l (dial.) turn, twirl; (in ballad poetry, and as revived by Scott) *t. at the pin* rattle the latch of a door. XVI. Metathetic form of *trill* (XIV, Ch.) twirl, spin, prob. of Scand. origin (cf. Sw. *trilla*, Da. *trille*).

tiro, tyro taiə·rou beginner, novice. XVII. In earliest use pl. *tyrones* (with occas. sg. †*tyron*) – L. *tīrō*, pl. *tīrōnēs*, in medL. also *tȳrō, -ōnēs*, young soldier, recruit, beginner.

Tironian tairou·niən *T. notes* system of shorthand said to have been introduced by *Tiro*, the freedman of Cicero. XIX. – L. *Tīrōniānus*, in *notæ Tīrōniānæ*; see -IAN.

tissue ti·ʃu (arch.) rich cloth, esp. interwoven with gold or silver; †band of rich stuff XIV (Ch.); woven fabric XVI; (fig.) fabric, network XVIII; animal or vegetable substance XIX. – OF. *tissu*, sb. use of pp. of *tistre* :– L. *texere* weave; see TEXTURE.

tit[1] tit (dial. and vulgar) TEAT. OE. *tit*, corr. to (M)LG. *titte*, Du. *tit*, (M)HG. *zitze* (from Germ. comes the Rom. form in It. *zizza*, Pr., Sp. *teta*, F. *tette*). Also (dial.) **titty**[6] ti·ti. XVIII.

tit[2] tit (dial.) small horse, (later) nag; (dial.) girl, young woman XVI; short for *titmouse* XVIII. Occurs much earlier in comps. TITMOUSE (XIV) and *titling* †small kind of stockfish (XIV), (dial.) hedge-sparrow, titlark, titmouse (XVI), prob. of Scand. origin (cf. Icel. *titlingr* sparrow, Norw. dial. *titling*, small size of dried stockfish).

tit[3] in phr. *tit for tat*, blow in return for another, retaliation (cf. synon. †*tip for tap*). XVI. var. of *tat*.

Titan tai·tən the sun-god XV (Lydg.); (pl.) family of giants, born of Uranus and Gæa, (sg.) ancestor of these XVII (Milton); (gen.) giant XIX (Scott). – L. *Tītan, -ān-*, elder brother of Kronos – Gr. *Tītā́n*, pl. *Tītânes*; so F., Sp., G. *Titan*, etc. Hence **Titan**IAN taitei·niən, **Titan**IC taitæ·nik. XVII; after L. and Gr.

titanium taitei·niəm (chem.) metallic element in group IV of the periodic system. XVIII. Named by Klaproth 1795; f. Gr. *Tītā́n* TITAN, after *uranium*, also named by him; see -IUM.

titbit ti·tbi·t delicate or toothsome morsel XVII; interesting item XVIII. Earliest form *tyd bit*, i.e. *tid*, dial. word equiv. to *nice*, and glossed in XVII by 'wanton', and in XVIII by 'nice, delicate' (Bailey) and 'tender, soft, nice' (J.) and poss. repr. by obscure stages OE. *tīdre, tiddre* weak, frail, infirm = OFris. *teddre*; the second el. is BIT[2].

tithe taið adj. (arch.) tenth OE.; sb. tenth part of annual produce paid to the Church XII; tenth part XVI. OE. *tēoþa*, contr. of *teogoþa*, ME. *tiȝ(e)þe, tīþe*; see TENTH. Hence **tithe** vb. OE. *tēoþian, teogoþian* grant a tithe of. So **ti·thing**[1] church tithe; company orig. of ten householders in the system of frankpledge. OE. Anglian *tīġeþing*; WS. *tēoþung*.

Titian ti·ʃiən picture by *Titian*, anglicization of *Tiziano* Vecellio, Venetian painter (died 1576), who favoured a 'red' colour for the hair. XIX.

titillate ti·tileit tickle. XVII. f. pp. stem of L. *tītillāre*, prob. rel. to *titta* TEAT. So **titill**A·TION (pleasurable) excitation. XV; tickling XVII. – (O)F. or L. ¶ Variants in *titul-* have been current, as in medL. and OF.

titivate ti·tiveit make smart, touch up. XIX. Earlier *tid(d)ivate*, perh. f. TIDY after *cultivate*.

title tai·tl †inscription or legend; ground of right or claim XIII (Cursor M.); descriptive appellation; (eccl.) certificate of presentation to a benefice, etc. XIV; legal right to possession XV. – OF. *title* (mod. *titre*) = Pr. *tiltre*, Sp. *tilde*, It. *titolo* – L. *titulus* placard, inscription, title. Cf. TILDE, TITTLE, TITULAR.

titmouse ti·tmaus small bird of the genus Parus. XIV. ME. *titmōse*, f. TIT[2]+*mōse*, OE. *māse* = MLG., MDu. *mēse* (Du. *mees*), OHG. *meisa* (G. *meise*) :– WGerm. *maisōn* (ON. has a deriv. form *meisingr*). In XVI, when *mose* had been long obs. as an independent word and had become stressless in *titmose*, assoc. with MOUSE produced *titmouse*, with pl. *titmice*.

titrate ti·treit (chem.) ascertain the amount of a constituent in, by volumetric analysis. XIX. f. F. *titrer*, f. *titre* TITLE, qualification, fineness of gold or silver, (chem.) proportioning of the fixed quantity of a reagent used in analysis; see -ATE[3].

titter ti·təɹ laugh in a suppressed manner. XVII. imit.

tittle ti·tl point or dot over or under a letter XIV (Wycl. Bible); smallest part or amount XV; *to a t.* (cf. G. *bis aufs tüttelchen*) with minute exactness XVII; cf. T. Late ME. *titel*, *-il* – L. *titulus* TITLE, in medieval sense of 'little stroke', 'accent'.

tittle-tattle ti·tltæ:tl idle talk or chatter. XVI (Skelton). redupl. formation on TATTLE or combination of this with (dial.) *tittle* (XIV). Cf. LG. *titel-tateln*, and *prittle-prattle* XVI.

tittymeg ti·timeg whitefish (Coregonus) of N. Amer. lakes. XVIII. Algonquin (Ojibway *atikameg*, Menominee *attaikummeeg*, Chippeway *adikumaig*).

titubate ti·tjubeit stagger, totter. XVI. f. pp. stem of L. *titubāre*, expressive redupl. formation; see -ATE[3].

titular ti·tjŭləɹ pert. to, serving as, or existing only in title. XVIII. – F. *titulaire* or modL. *titulāris*, f. *titulus* TITLE; see -AR.

tizzy ti·zi (sl.) sixpenny piece. XIX. Of unkn. origin.

tmesis tmī·sis (gram.) separation of the elements of a word by interposing another. XVI. – Gr. *tmêsis* cutting, f. **tm-* **tem-* **tom-* cut (see TOME).

T.N.T. tīentī· initial of the els. of *trinitrotoluene*, *-toluol*.

to tu, tə, (str.) tū prep. expressing motion or direction towards an object, addition, or the notion of the dative; with inf. meaning 'for the purpose or with the object of' (doing something), e.g. *tō dōnne*, *to wyrćenne* (later *wyrćanne*), hence serving without meaning as a sign of the inf.; adv. (with full stress) surviving as in *to and fro*, *shut to*, and the like, and in TOO. OE. *tō* adv. and prep. (mainly with dat.) = OFris., OS. *tō* (Du. *toe* adv.), OHG. *zō*, *zuo*, (G. *zu*) :– WGerm. **tō* (essentially adv.), alongside OE. (ME.) *te* = OFris., OS. *te*, *ti* (Du. *te*), OHG. *ze*, *zi*, *za* :– WGerm. **ta* prep. (ON. has *til* TILL[1]; Gothic *du*), perh. a proclitic form of **tō*. The IE. base **dŏ*, *dĕ* is repr. also by L. *en|do in|du* (poet.) in, *in|di-* within (cf. INDIGENOUS), *dō|nec* until, Gr. *oîkon|de* homewards, Balto-Sl. *da*, *do* to, till. See also TODAY, TOMORROW, TO-NIGHT, and cf. dial. *to-year*, this year, OE. *nū tō ġēare*.

toad toud tailless amphibian of the genus Bufo. OE. *tāda*, *tādde* (in g. sg. in place-names), shortening of *tādiġe*, *tādie*, early ME. also *tadde* (XII); cf. TADPOLE; of unkn. origin and unusual formation. comp. **toa·d**STOOL mushroom (XV *tode stole*), earlier *tad(e) stole* (XIV).

toady tou·di servile parasite. XIX. Based on *toad-eater* tou·dī:təɹ charlatan's attendant who ate toads (held to be poisonous) XVII, fawning flatterer, humble friend or dependant XVIII; see -Y[6]. Hence vb. XIX.

toast[1] toust parch XIV (Trevisa); brown (bread, etc.) by exposure to heat XIV. – OF. *toster* roast, grill, corr. to Sp. *tostar*, It. *tostare* :– Rom. **tostāre*, f. *tost-*, pp. stem of L. *torrēre* parch (cf. TORRENT, TORRID). Hence sb. toasted bread. XV.

toast[2] toust orig. favourite lady whose health is drunk to. XVII. Said to have been so named as being supposed to flavour the bumper like a spiced toast (TOAST[1]) in drink.

tobacco təbæ·kou (leaves of) species of Nicotiana, forming a substance used for smoking in a pipe, for chewing, as snuff, etc. XVI. alt. of earlier *tabac(c)o* (1577) – Sp., Pg. *tabaco*, acc. to Oviedo (1535) Carib name applied to the pipe in which the herb was smoked, but this is disputed, Las Casas (1552) stating that it denoted a roll of the leaves smoked like a cigar. Cf. F. *tabac*, Du., G., Russ. *tabak*, Da., Sw. *tobak*; the relation to the name of the island *Tobago* is doubtful. Hence **tobacconIST** təbæ·kənist †tobacco-smoker XVI (Jonson); seller of tobacco XVII. The inserted *n* is euphonic.

Tobin tou·bin *T. bronze*, alloy invented by J. A. *Tobin*, of the U.S. navy. XIX.

toboggan təbɔ·gən light sledge or similar vehicle used for transport over snow. XIX. With many vars. *c.*1830–1870 – Canadian F. *tabaganne* – Algonquian word of which closely similar vars. are Micmac *tobākun*, Abnaki *udābāgan*.

toby tou·bi (thieves' sl.) the highway; (transf.) highway robbery. XIX. Supposed to be alt. of Shelta *tobar* road.

Toby tou·bi familiar form of the name *Tobias* used as the name of (1) a jug or mug in the form of a stout old man with a three-cornered hat, (2) a trained dog in the Punch-and-Judy show. XIX (Dickens).

toccata təkā·tə (mus.) piece for keyboard instruments intended to exhibit touch and technique. XVIII. It., sb. use of fem. pp. of *toccare* TOUCH.

Toc H tɔk eitʃ signaller's name for *T+H*, denoting *Talbot H.*, name of a society of comradeship from the war of 1914–18 formed in memory of Gilbert *Talbot*.

Tocharian, Tokh- tokā·riən, -ɛə·riən (pert. to) an extinct Indo-European language of which remains have been discovered in Turkestan. XX. – F. *tocharien*, f. Gr. *Tokhároi* (Strabo) nomad Chinese tribes identified with the Yuechi. So **Tocha·rish**, after G. *tocharisch*; see -IAN, -ISH[1].

tocher tɔ·χər (Sc. and n. dial.) dowry. XV (*toquhyr*). – Ir., OGaelic *tochar* (modGael. *tochradh*) assigned portion, f. (OIr.) *tochuirim* I put to, assign, f. *cuirim* I put.

toco, toko tou·kou (sl.) chastisement. XIX. – Hind. *thōkō*, imper. of *thoknā* censure, blame.

tocsin tɔ·ksin alarm signal given by a bell. XVI (*tocksaine*). – F. *tocsin*, OF. *touquesain*, *toquassen* – Pr. *tocasenh*, f. *tocar* strike TOUCH+*senh* bell (SIGN).

tod[1] tɔd (dial.) fox. XII. north. word of unkn. origin.

tod[2] tɔd weight used for wool XV; bushy mass (esp. of ivy) XVI. prob. of LDu. origin (cf. LG. *todde* bundle, pack); cf. ON. *toddi* bit, piece, OHG. *zot(t)a*, *zata*, MHG. *zotte* *tuft of wool*. See TED.

today tədei· on this very day OE.; in these days XIII (Cursor M.); sb. this day XVI; this present time XIX. OE. *tōdæġ*, f. *tō* TO+ *dæġ* DAY. Cf. TO-NIGHT.

toddle tɔ·dl †toy *with*; walk with short unsteady steps. XVI. Of unkn. origin.

toddy tɔ·di sap obtained from species of palm XVII; beverage made with whisky and hot water and sugar XVIII. Earlier also *tarrie*, *terry*. – Hind. *tāṛī*, f. *tāṛ* palm tree :– Skr. *tāla* palmyra.

to-do tədū· activity, business, bustle, fuss. XVII. Evolved from such phr. as *with much* or *more to do*, in which *much* and *more* were orig. sbs. but were later apprehended as adjs. with *to-do* as a sb. on the model of ADO.

toe tou each of the digits of the foot. OE. *tā* (OMerc. *tāhæ*), pl. *tān* (ME. *tō*, pl. *to(o)n*, *to(o)s*)= MLG. *tē*, (M)Du. *tee*, OHG. *zēha* (G. *zeh*, *zehe*), ON. *tá* (pl. *tǽr*) :– CGerm. (exc. Goth.) **taiχ(w)ōn*, of unkn. origin. Hence vb.

toff tɔf (sl.) stylish or smart person. XIX. The occas. var. *toft* may point to an alt. of TUFT as applied to noblemen and gentlemen-commoners at the university of Oxford.

toffee tɔ·fi sweetmeat made from sugar or treacle. XIX. alt. of earlier north. *taffy*; vars. *tuffy*, *toughy* show assoc. with TOUGH; of unkn. origin.

toft tɔft site of a house. Late OE. *toft* – ON. *topt*, beside *tomt* :– **tumft-*, with which cf. Gr. *dápedon* (:– **dm̥pedom*) level surface, building site.

tog tɔg (sl.) †outer coat XVIII; (pl.) clothes XIX. prob. shortening of cant *tog(e)mans* cloak, loose coat (XVI–XVII), f. F. *toge* or L. *toga* (see next) + *-man(s)*, as in *darkman(s)* night, etc.

toga tou·gə (antiq.) outer garment of a Roman citizen. XVI. – L., rel. to *tegere* cover (cf. DETECT, PROTECT). Hence **toga**ED[2] tou·gəd XIX; earlier †*toged* (Sh.). Based on L. *togātus*, whence **to·gate** XIX, **to·gated** XVII.

together təge·ðəɹ into one company OE.; in one company or body XIII, ME. *togedere* (east midl. in earliest use *togeddre*, Orm, *to gider*, *-iddre* XIII), repl. *togadere*, OE. *tōgædere* = OFris. *togadera*, *-ere*, MDu. *tegadere* (Du. *-er*); LDu. formation on **tō* TO+**gad-*, as in OE. *gæd* fellowship, *ġegada* associate, Du. *gade*, MDu. *ghegade*, comrade, GATHER. Cf. ALTOGETHER. ¶ For ð from d cf. *father*.

toggle tɔ·gl (orig., naut.) device, e.g. a pin, to hold a thing in place. XVIII. Of unkn. origin.

tohu-bohu tou·hjūbou·hjū utter confusion, chaos. XIX. – F. *tohu-bohu* (Voltaire) – Heb. *thōhū wabhōhū* emptiness and desolation (Gen. i 2), earlier repr. by †*tohu and bohu*, †*tohuvabohu*.

toil[1] toil †verbal dispute, strife, turmoil XIII; (from the vb.) severe labour XVI. – AN. *toil* = OF. *tooil*, *touil*, *tueil* bloody mêlée, trouble, confusion, f. *tooillier* (see below). So **toil** vb. †contend in a lawsuit, dispute; labour arduously XIV. – AN. *toiler* dispute, wrangle = OF. *tooillier* (mod. *touiller* mix, stir up) :– L. *tudiculāre* stir about, f. *tudicula* machine for bruising olives, f. **tud-*, base of *tundere* beat, crush (cf. CONTUSION, OBTUSE).

toil[2] toil (sg. and pl.) net(s) set to enclose game. XVI. – OF. *toile*, *teile* (mod. *toile* cloth, linen, web) = Pr., Sp. *tela* :– L. *tēla* :– **texlā*, f. **tex-* weave (see TEXTILE), which some have related to Gr. *téktōn* (cf. ARCHITECT) and *tékhnē* (cf. TECHNICAL).

toilet toi·lĭt †cloth wrapper XVI; cloth cover for a dressing table, furniture of this, the table itself; dressing XVII; (lady's) dress XIX. – F. *toilette*, dim. of *toile* TOIL[2]; see -ET. ¶ An OF. var. *tellette*, *teilete*, is repr. by *tillet* (XV).

toise toiz French lineal measure of 6 (French) feet. XVI. – (O)F. *toise, teise* = It. *tesa* :– Rom. **tesa*, for *tensa*, sb. use (sc. *bracchia* arms) of n.pp. (taken as fem.) of L. *tendere* stretch, TEND[2].

tokay tokei· rich sweet wine made near *Tokay* (Tokaj) in Hungary. XVIII (Swift). – F. *vin de Tokay*, G. *Tokayerwein*, tr. Magyar *tokajibor* (*bor* wine).

token tou·kn sign, symbol, signal OE.; stamped piece of metal XVI; quantity of press work XVII (Moxon). OE. *tāc(e)n* = OFris. *tēk(e)n*, OS. *tēcan*, OHG. *zeihhan* (Du. *teeken*, G. *zeichen*), ON. *teikn* :– Germ. **taiknam* (not in Goth., which has *taikns* :– **taikniz*), rel. to **taikjan* show, TEACH. So **token** vb. OE. *tācnian* = MLG. *tēkenen*, OHG. *zeihhanen, -ōn* (G. *zeichnen*), Goth. *taiknjan*; cf. BETOKEN.

toko see TOCO.

tolbooth tou·l-, tɔ·lbūð, -būþ †customhouse XIV; town hall, guildhall; town prison (orig. cells under the town hall) XV. f. TOLL[1]+BOOTH stall or shed of a tax-collector. Cf. G. *zollbude*, Da. *toldbod*.

tolderol tɔ·ldərɔ·l jovial refrain of a song. XVIII. Cf. FALDERAL.

toledo tŏlī·dou (arch.) *T.* (*blade, sword*), one made at Toledo in Spain, long famous for finely tempered swordblades. XVI (Jonson).

tolerable tɔ·lərəbl bearable, endurable XV; †allowable; passable, moderate XVI. – (O)F. *tolérable* – L. *tolerābilis*, f. *tolerāre* bear, endure; see -ABLE. So **to·ler**ANCE †endurance XV; disposition to be indulgent. XVIII. – (O)F. *tolérance* – L. *tolerantia*. **to·ler**ANT disposed to tolerate. XVIII. – F. *tolérant*, prp. of *tolérer*. **to·ler**ATE[3] †endure; allow to exist XVI. – pp. stem of L. *tolerāre*. **toler**A·TION †endurance; †permission; forbearance XVI; allowance of the exercise of religion XVII. – F. – L. The use of *tolerance, -ant, -ate, -ation* acquired a special vogue from XVII with the rise of the idea of religious toleration and the passing of the Act of Toleration 1689. The base is that of L. *tollere* raise (cf. EXTOL) having cogns. in pp. *lātus* (for **tlātus*) carried, Gr. *étlān, étlēn* I bore.

toll[1] toul payment for a privilege OE.; charge for a right of passage XV. OE. *toll* = OHG. *zol* (G. *zoll*), ON. *tollr* m., with by-forms OE. *toln* (†*tolne* XI–XV), OFris. *tol(e)ne*, OS. *tolna* fem. – medL. *tolōneum*, alt. of late L. *telōneum* – Gr. *telṓnion* toll-house, f. *telṓnēs* collector of taxes, f. *télos* toll, tax.

toll[2] toul (of a bell or the ringer) give forth a sound from a bell repeated at regular intervals. XV. perh. spec. use of *toll* pull, usu. fig. entice, OE. **tollian*, rel. to *for|tyllan* seduce.

tolu tou·lju, touljū· epithet of a balsam obtained from the *tolu tree*, Myrospermum toluiferum. XVII. Name of a town in Colombia, S. America. Hence **toluol** tou·ljuəl (chem.) earlier term for **to·lu**ENE, obtained by Deville 1841 from tolu balsam. (Cf. T.N.T.)

Tom tɔm familiar abbrev. of THOMAS, used (i) as the name of certain large bells (XVII), and long guns (XIX, *Long Tom*); (ii) in designations originating in quasi-proper names as **tom-**FOOL †half-witted man (XVI); buffoon (XVII); stupid person (XVIII), hence **tomfoo·**LERY (XIX); **tom-**NO·DDY puffin (XVIII), foolish person (XIX); (iii) as the colloq. designation of a male cat, originating in 'The Life and Adventures of a Cat' (1760) in which the hero, a male cat, is called *Tom the Cat*; superseding earlier *Gib* (Gilbert); hence dim. **Tomm**Y[6] tɔ·mi spec. short for *Tommy Atkins* familiar form of *Thomas Atkins*, name of a typical private soldier in the British army arising out of its use in specimen forms of description in official regulations from 1815. Also **tom**BOY tɔ·mboi †bold boy or woman; wild romping girl XVI; **tom**TIT tɔ·mti·t TITMOUSE (XVIII, Steele, Addison); applied to a diminutive object: hence in *Tom Thumb* (XVI) dwarf or pygmy of popular story and in allusive uses.

tomahawk tɔ·məhōk N. Amer. Indian's axe. XVII. – Renape *tämähāk* (in Capt. J. Smith *tomahack*), shortening of *tämähākan* cutting instrument, f. *tämähāken* he uses for cutting, f. *tämäham* he cuts.

toman tomā·n 10,000; Persian coin worth 10,000 dinars. XVI. – Pers. *tūmān, tumān, tuman*.

tomato təmā·tou fruit of Solanum Lycopersicum or Lycopersicum esculentum. XVII. Earlier *tomate* – F. *tomate* or Sp., Pg. *tomate* – Mex. *tomatl*; *tomato, tomata*, and *tomatum* were pseudo-Sp. and L. modifications (XVIII).

tomb tūm place of burial, sepulchral monument. XIII. ME. *toumbe, tumbe* – AN. *tumbe*, (O)F. *tombe* = Sp. *tumba*, It. *tomba* :– late L. *tumba* (Prudentius) – Gr. *túmbos* mound, tomb.

tombac tɔ·mbæk E. Indian alloy of copper and zinc. XVII. – F. *tombac*, with early vars. from Sp. *tumbaga*, Pg. *tambaca* – Malay *tambāga* copper.

tombola tɔ·mbŏlə kind of lottery resembling lotto. XIX. – F. *tombola* or It. *tombola*, f. *tombolare* turn a somersault, tumble.

tomboy see TOM.

tome toum †volume of a literary work; (large or heavy) book XVI. – F. *tome* – L. *tomus* – Gr. *tómos* slice, piece, roll of papyrus, volume (cf. -TOMY).

-tome[1] toum terminal el. (= F. *-tome*), repr. Gr. *-tómon*, n. of *-tómos* -cutting, forming names of surgical instruments used in separations expressed by the corr. words in -TOMY, as *lithotome*.

-tome[2] (toum) terminal el. repr. Gr. *tomḗ*. Cutting, section, segment, as *myotome*.

tomentose toume·ntous closely covered with down. XVII. – modL. *tōmentōsus*, f. L. *tōmentum* stuffing for cushions; see -OSE[1].

Tommy tɔ·mi familiar form of TOM; see -Y[6]. Soldier's name for brown bread, workman's name for food XVIII; simpleton, tom-noddy XIX. See also under TOM.

tomorrow təmɔ·rou adv. for or on the day after today XIII; sb. the day after this day, the morrow XIV. ME. *to mor(e)we*, earlier *to morwen* (mod. dial. *to morn*), OE. *to morġenne*, i.e. d. of *morġen* MORN, MORROW.

tompion tɔ·mpiən watch made by Thomas *Tompion* (1639–1713), known as the father of English watchmaking. XVIII (Pope, Swift).

tom-tom tɔ·mtɔm native E. Indian drum. XVII. – Hind. *tam tam* (so F.); cf. Sinhalese *tamaṭṭama*, Malay *tong tong*.

-tomy təmi terminal el. repr. Gr. *-tomíā*, often through L. *-tomia*, F. *-tomie*, forming abstract sbs. from adjs. in *-tómos* cutting, f. **tom-* **tem-* **tm̥-* cut (cf. TOME, TMESIS).

ton[1] tʌn unit used in measuring the carrying capacity of a ship, orig. space occupied by a tun of wine XIV; measure of capacity for solid commodities; 20 cwt. XV. Identical in origin with TUN, of which it is a differentiated var. established in these senses since late XVII. Cf. TONNAGE.

ton[2] tɔ̃ the vogue, the mode. XVIII. – F. *ton* :– L. *tonu-s* TONE.

-ton tən terminal el. of many town names, repr. unstressed development of OE. *tūn* TOWN, and consequently in many surnames, e.g. *Longton*, *Somerton*, whence extended to form designations of persons and things, as *simpleton*, *singleton*.

tondo tɔ·ndou circular painting. XIX. – It. *tondo* round, circle, aphetic of *rotondo* ROUND.

tone toun musical sound or note (with various applications) XIV; larger interval between notes in the diatonic scale (cf. SEMITONE); pitch, modulation of voice, etc.; degree of tension; style of thought, etc. prevailing state of conduct, etc. XVII; any of the nine plainsong tones; word or syllable accent; quality of colour XIX. repr. various adoptions of (O)F. *ton* (= Pr., Sp. *ton*, Pg. *tom*, It. *tuono*) or its source L. *tonus* tension, sound, tone – Gr. *tónos* (f. **ton-* **ten-* **tn-*; cf. TEND[2]) with the same senses, the application to musical notes being perh. partly due to assoc. with base of L. *tonāre* THUNDER. So **tonAL**[1] tou·nəl pert. to tone or tones. XVIII. – medL. *tonālis*; in mod. use after F. **tonA·LITY**. XIX.

tonga[1] tɔ·ŋgə two-wheeled vehicle used in India. XIX. – Hindi *tāngā*.

tonga[2] tɔ·ŋgə drug extracted from a Fijian plant. XIX. Said to be an arbitrary invention.

tongs tɔŋz two-limbed gripping implement. OE. *tang* and *tange* (pl. *tangan*), corr. to OFris. *tange*, OS. *tanga*, OHG. *zanga* (Du. *tang*, G. *zange*), ON. *tǫng* (:– **tanguz*) :– CGerm. (not in Goth.) **tang-* :– IE. **dank-* bite, repr. also by Gr. *dákos* biting animal, *dáknein* bite, Skr. *dáçati* bites, *dámça-* biting. Cf. OHG. *zangar*, MLG., MDu. *tang(h)er* biting, ON. *tangi* point of land. Cf. TANG[1].

tongue tʌŋ muscular organ in the mouth used in tasting and speaking; speech, language OE.; tongue-like object XIV. OE. *tunge* = OFris. *tunge*, OS. *tunga*, OHG. *zunga* (Du. *tong*, G. *zunge*), ON. *tunga*, Goth. *tuggō* :– CGerm. **tuŋgōn*, rel. to L. *lingua* – **dingua*.

tonic tɔ·nik pert. to tension XVII; increasing or restoring the tone of the body; (mus.) pert. to the keynote XVIII (*tonic solfa*, introduced by John Curwen 1852); pert. to tone in speech XIX; sb. tonic medicine XVIII; keynote XIX. – F. *tonique* or modL. *tonicus* – Gr. *tonikós*, f. *tónos* TONE.

to-night tənai·t on the night following this day OE.; on this present night XIII (Cursor M.); †(dial.) last night XIII (Laȝ.); sb. this night, the night following this day XIII (Cursor M.). Cf. TODAY. OE. *tōniht*, f. *tō* TO + *niht* NIGHT. Cf. dial. *to-year* this year; in OE. *nū tō ġēare*.

tonite tou·nait high explosive, cotton powder. XIX. f. L. *tonāre* THUNDER; see -ITE.

tonka tɔ·ŋkə *t. bean*, seed of Dipterix odorata. XVIII. – Negro name in Guiana.

tonnage tʌ·nidʒ duty levied on wine imported in tuns XV; †charge for the hire of a ship at so much per ton of her burden XVI; charge per ton of freight; shipping in relation to carrying capacity XVII; carrying capacity of a ship expressed in tons of 100 cubic feet XVIII. – OF. *tonnage*, AL. *tonnagium* (XIII), f. *tonne* TUN; later assoc. directly with TON[1]; see -AGE.

tonneau tɔ·nou rear body of a motor car. XX. – F., spec. application of *tonneau* cask (OF. *tonnel*), dim. of *tonne* TUN.

tonsil tɔ·nsĭl (usu. pl.) gland at either side of the back of the mouth. XVII (Holland). – F. *tonsilles* (Paré) or L. *tonsillæ* pl.

tonsorial tɔnsɔ̄·riəl pert. to a barber. XIX. f. L. *tonsōrius*, f. *tonsor* barber, f. *tons-*; see next and -IAL.

tonsure tɔ·nʃəɪ shaving of the head. XIV (Trevisa). – (O)F. *tonsure* or L. *tonsūra*, f. pp. of *tondēre* (*tons-*) shear, clip, f. **tond-* **tend-* (cf. Gr. *téndein* gnaw), f. **tem-* cut (Gr. *témnein*) **tom-* (cf. TOME, -TOMY): see -URE.

tontine tɔntī·n a financial system. XVIII. – F. *tontine*, f. name of Lorenzo *Tonti*, Neapolitan banker who initiated the scheme in France *c.*1653.

too tū in addition, besides, moreover; †exceedingly; in excess, excessively. str. form of TO adv., so sp. since XVI.

tool tūl 'any instrument of manual operation' (J.). OE. *tōl* = ON. *tól* (n. pl.) :– Germ. **tōwlam*, f. **tōw-* **taw-*, whence OE. *tawian* prepare, OS. *tōgean* make, MLG., MDu. *touwen* (Du. *touwen* curry), OHG. *zouwen*, ON. (Runic) *tawido* made, Goth. *taujan* make; see -EL[1], TAW[1].

toot tūt sound a horn. XVI. prob. – (M)LG. *tūten*, unless a parallel imit. formation. Hence **too·tle**. XIX; see -LE[3].

tooth tūþ pl. **teeth** tīþ OE. *tōþ*, pl. *tēþ* = OFris. *tōth*, pl. *tēth*, OS. (Du.) *tand*, OHG. *zan*, pl. *zeni* (G. *zahn*, *zähne*), also *zand*, pl. *zendi*, ON. *tǫnn*, pl. *tenn* :– Germ. **tanþuz*, beside Goth. *tunþus*; CIE. **dont-* **dent-* **dn̥t-* is repr. by Skr. *dán*, acc. *dántam*, Gr. *odṓn*, *odónt-*, Æolic *édont-*, L. *dēns*, *dent-*, OIr. *dét*, W. *dant*, Lith. *dantìs*; prp. formation on **ed-* EAT, the literal meaning being therefore 'the eater or chewer'. Cf. TUSK.

tootsy tu·tsi (colloq.) child's or woman's small foot. XIX (Thackeray). Playful alt. of FOOT + -SY.

top[1] tɔp (dial.) tuft (of hair; etc.), crest; highest point or part OE.; upper part or covering (platform at head of mast XV (†*top-castle* XIV–XVI), uppermost part of a high boot XVII); first or foremost part XV. Late OE. *topp* = OFris. *topp* tuft, (M)Du. *top* crest, summit, tip, (O)HG. *zopf* plait, tress, ON. *toppr* top, tuft :– CGerm. (exc. Gothic) **toppaz*, whence OF. *top*, *toup*, (whence F. *toupet*, cf. TOUPEE), the source of Sp., Pg. *tope*, Pg. *topo*. Hence **top** vb. deprive of the top XIV; put a top on; overtop XVI. **to·pper**[1] exceptionally good person or thing XVIII; top-hat, tall hat XIX. comp. **topga·llant** top at head of topmast (XV), so called as having a superior position and making a brave show; also attrib. in *t. sail*, *yard*. **top saw·yer** sawyer who works the upper handle of a pit saw; also fig. XIX.

top[2] tɔp circular toy having a point on which it is made to spin. Late OE. *top* (once); further evidence is not freq. until after 1400; the origin is unkn.; words similar in form and meaning in G. and F., but their relations are obscure; perh. the word is to be identified with prec.

topaz tou·pæz precious stone. XIII. ME. *topace* – OF. *topace*, (also mod.) *topaze* = Pr. *topazi*, Sp. *topacio*, It. *topazio* – L. *topazus*, *-azius*, *-ion* – Gr. *tópazos*, *-azion*.

tope[1] toup small species of shark. XVII (Ray). Of unkn. origin; perh. Cornish.

tope[2] toup clump or plantation of trees. XVII. – Telugu *tōpu*, Tamil *tōppu*.

tope[3] toup dome or tumulus to contain relics, etc. XIX. – Hind. (Panjabi) *tōp* :– Prakrit, Pali *thūpo* :– Skr. *stūpa*.

tope[4] toup drink (heavily). XVII. perh. alt. of synon. †*top* XVI (of unkn. origin) by assoc. with †*tope* (XVII) int. used as a pledging formula in drinking – F. *tôpe*.

topee, topi topī· Indian name for the European hat, esp. sun helmet· XIX. – Hindi *ṭopī* hat.

tophus tou·fəs soft porous stone, esp. deposited by calcareous springs XVI; (path.) gouty deposit XVII. – L. *tōphus*, var. of *tōfus*; cf. TUFA, TUFF.

topiary tou·piəri pert. to the trimming of shrubs into ornamental or fantastic shapes. XVI. – F. *topiaire* (Rabelais, 1548) – L. *topiārius*, f. *topia* (sc. *opera* work) fancy or landscape gardening – Gr. *tópia*, pl. of *tópion*, dim. of *tópos* place (see TOPIC); see -ARY. Hence sb., clipping of trees into artificial shapes. XX.

topic tɔ·pik †adj. pert. to or of the nature of a COMMONPLACE; sb. (pl.) name of Aristotle's treatise τὰ τοπικά (lit. matters concerning commonplaces) XVI; †consideration, argument, head XVII; subject of a discourse, matter, theme XVIII. – Gr. *topikós*, f. *tópos* place; through L. *topica* (n. pl.) as the title of Aristotle's treatise; see -IC. So **to·pical** local; †pert. to general maxims XVI; pert. to subjects or current affairs XIX.

topo- tɔ·pou, tɔpɔ· comb. form of Gr. *tópos* place, locality. **topo·graphy** description of the features of a locality. XV. – late L. *topographia* – Gr. *topographiā*. So **topo·grapher**[1] XVII (Florio), **-gra·phic** XVII, **-gra·phical** XVI; cf. F. *topographe*, etc.; **topo·nymy**[3], place-names of a region XIX.

topple tɔ·pl (dial.) tumble about; fall through being top-heavy. XVI. f. TOP vb. + -LE[3].

topsy-turvy tɔpsitə·ɹvi with the top (or the higher) where the bottom (or the lower) should be. XVI (Roy, Palsgr.). Earliest records have *topsy tervy* or *tyrvy*; but the somewhat later forms *topset*, *topside*, may point to the origin in pp. *set* or sb. *side*, but there is nothing certain known concerning either el.; for the second el. connexion with †*tirve* (turn) has been suggested, and an OE. **tierfan* (= OHG. *zerben*, MHG. *zirben* turn over) assumed as the base of OE. *tearflian* roll over, wallow; for the suffix see -Y[1].

toque touk small cap or bonnet. XVI. – F. *toque*, corr. obscurely to It. *tocca*, *tocco*, Sp. *toca*, Pg. *touca*, of unkn. origin.

tor tɔɹ high rock, pile of rocks (esp. in local names). OE. *torr*, of British origin (cf. OW. *twrr* bulge, belly, Gael. *tòrr* bulging hill).

-tor L. terminal el. f. *-t-* of pps. + -OR¹, as in *actor, inventor*. Cf. -ATOR.

Torah tōə·rə Mosaic law, Pentateuch. XVI. – Heb. *tōrāh* direction, instruction, doctrine, law, f. *yārāh* throw, (in Hiphil) show, direct, instruct.

torch tōɹtʃ light to be carried in the hand consisting of inflammable material. XIII (S. Eng. Leg.). – (O)F. *torche* = Pr. *torca*, Cat. *torca* wisp of straw, Sp. *tuerca* screw, Pg. *tocha* torch :– Rom. **torca*, for L. *torqua* (Varro), var. of *torquēs* necklace, wreath, f. *torquēre* twist (cf. TORMENT, etc.); the primary meaning is taken to have been 'something twisted, as tow'.

toreador təriədōə·ɹ bull-fighter. XVII. – Sp. *toreador*, f. *torear* fight (bulls) in the ring, f. *toro* bull :– L. *taurus* bull. ¶ *Torero* is the word now in Sp. use.

toreutic torū·tik pert. to working in metal or ivory. XIX. – Gr. *toreutikós*, f. *toreúein* work in relief; see -IC.

torii tō·riī decorative gateway of a Shinto temple. XIX. Jap., of disputed origin.

torment tō·ɹment †torture with the rack, etc. (S. Eng. Leg); state of severe suffering; †violent storm XIII. OF. *torment*, (and mod.) *tourment* = Pr. *tormen*, Sp., It. *tormento* :– L. *tormentum* (:– **torquementum*) engine for throwing missiles, cord, cable, instrument of torture, f. *torquēre* twist. So **torment** tōɹme·nt XIII. – (O)F. *tourmenter*, f. *torment* sb.; cf. late L. *tormentāre*. **torme·ntor¹**. XIII. – OF. *tormentēor*.

tormentil tō·ɹməntil herb Potentilla Tormentilla (T. repens). XV. – (O)F. *tormentille* – medL. *tormentilla*, of unkn. origin.

tornado tōɹnei·dou †violent thunderstorm of the tropical Atlantic XVI; rotatory storm of Africa, etc. XVII. Earliest form *ternado*, later *turnado, tournado, tornado*; perh. orig. altered – Sp. *tronada* thunderstorm (f. *tronar*), later assim. to *tornar* TURN; see -ADO.

torpedo tōɹpī·dou flat fish of the genus Torpedo which emits electric discharges XVI; case charged with gunpowder to explode under water, self-propelled submarine missile XIX. L. *torpēdō*, f. *torpēre* be stiff or numb (cf. next).

torpid tō·ɹpid benumbed, lacking animation or vigour. XVII. – L. *torpidus*, f. *torpēre* be sluggish; see -ID¹. So **to·rpor²**. XVII. – L.

torque tō·ɹk necklace, twisted band. XIX. – F. *torque* – L. *torquēs*, f. *torquēre*.

torrefy tɔ·rifai roast. XVII. – F. *torréfier* – L. *torrefacere*, f. *torrēre*; see next, -FY.

torrent tɔ·rənt swift stream of water. XVII (Sh.). – F. *torrent* – It. *torrente* – L. *torrente-m, torrēns*, sb. use of prp. (scorching, (of streams) boiling, roaring, rushing) of *torrēre* scorch; see THIRST and -ENT. Hence **torrentIAL** tɔre·nʃəl. XIX; after F. *torrentiel*. So **to·rrID¹** scorched, scorching hot. XVI; *t. zone* (medL. *torrida zona*), region between the tropics. – F. *torride* or L. *torridus*.

Torricellian toriᵗʃe·liən, -se·liən applied to experiments and apparatus used in determining atmospheric pressure. XVII. *Torricelli*, It. physicist (1608–47), see -AN.

torsion tō·ɹʃən †griping XV; twisting, twist XVI. – (O)F. *torsion* – late L. *torsiō(n-)*, by-form of *tortiō*, f. *tort-*, *torquēre* (cf. TORT).

torso tō·ɹsou trunk of the human body. XVIII. – It. *torso* stalk, stump, core, trunk of a statue (whence also F. *torse*) :– L. *thyrsu-s*; see THYRSUS.

tort tōɹt †injury, wrong XIV (rare before XVI); (leg.) breach of a duty XVI. – OF. *tort* = Pr. *tort*, Sp. *tuerto*, It. *torto* :– medL. *tortum* (IX), sb. use of n. of L. *tortus*, pp. of *torquēre* twist, wring. ¶ Cf. the relation of *wring* and *wrong*.

torticollis tōɹtikɔ·lis (path.) wry-neck. XIX. – modL., f. L. *tortus* + *collum* neck; see prec. and COLLAR.

tortilla tōɹtī·ljə in Mexico, thin round cake of maize flour (XVII, Dampier). – Sp. *tortilla*, dim. of *torta* round cake = (O)F. *tourte*, Pr., Sp., It. *torta*, Rum. *turtă* :– late L. (Vulgate) *tōrta*.

tortoise tō·ɹtəs reptile of the order Chelonia. XV. The earliest exx. show a variety of forms reflecting medL. *tortūca*, (O)F. *tortue*, and (occas.) Sp. *tortuga*; the present form (of obscure origin) appears in XVI.

tortuous tō·ɹtjuəs full of twists or turns. XV (Lydg.). – OF. *tortuous* (mod. *tortueux*) – L. *tortuōsus*, f. *tortus* twisting, f. *tort-*, *torquēre*; see TORT, -UOUS.

torture tō·ɹtʃəɹ (infliction of) excruciating pain. XVI. – (O)F. *torture* or late L. *tortūra* twisting, writhing, torment, f. *tort-*; see prec., -URE. Hence vb. XVI (Sh.).

torus tō·rəs pl. **tori** -ai (archit.) large convex moulding XVI. – L. *torus* swelling, bolster, round moulding. Hence **torula** tɔ·rʲūlə. XIX. modL. dim. (cf. -ULE). Cf. F. *torule* (m.).

torve tōəɹv grim, fierce-looking. XVII. – L. *torvus*. So **to·rvID¹**, **to·rvOUS**. XVII.

Tory tōə·ri (hist.) from *c*.1645 one of the dispossessed Irish who became outlaws, rapparee; in 1679–80 applied to anti-exclusioners; from 1689, member of one of the two great political parties of Great Britain. Presumably – Ir. **tóraighe* tō·rije pursuer, implied in *tóraigheachd* pursuit, f. *tóir* pursue.

tosh tɔʃ (sl.) trash, rubbish, nonsense. XIX (late). Of unkn. origin.

toss tɔ̀s pt., pp. *tossed, tost* tɔ̀st throw or pitch about; in earliest use freq. of the sea;

hence in various applications, in mod. use with special ref. to throwing *up* or *into the air*. XVI. Of unkn. origin; perh. Scand., but Norw., Sw. dial. *tossa* strew, spread, corr. in form only; W. *tosio* is from Eng.

tot[1] tɔt (colloq.) very small child XVIII; small drinking vessel; dram of drink XIX. Of dial. origin.

tot[2] tɔt (colloq.) sum *up*. XVIII. f. *tot*, abbrev. of TOTAL. ¶ *Tot* was formerly used (XVI–XVIII) to mark an item, indicated by *tot* or *T*, as having been levied or received; this is L. *tot* so much; hence as vb., cf. AL. *totāre*, AN. *totter* mark with a *t*.

total tou·təl pert. to or comprising the whole. XIV. – (O)F. *total* = Sp. *total*, It. *totale* – scholastic L. *tōtālis*, f. *tōtum* the whole, sb. use of n. of *tōtus* entire, whole. So **total**ITY toutæ·lĭti. XVI. – scholastic L. *tōtālitās*; cf. (O)F. *totalité*. **to·tal**LY[2]. XVI; after scholastic L. *tōtāliter*; cf. (O)F. *totalement*. **to·taliz**ATOR apparatus for registering the total of operations, spec. the number of tickets sold to betters on a horse race. XIX. f. *to·tal*IZE (XIX, Coleridge).

totem tou·təm among Amer. Indians, hereditary badge of a tribe or group. XVIII. Of Algonquian origin. Various other forms have been cited, viz. *totam*, *toodaim*, *ododam*; the initial *t* is expl. by some as the final letter of a preceding poss. pron. (cf. Ojibway *ototeman* his relatives), the basic form being *ote* or *otem* (*aoutem* in Lescarbot's 'Histoire de la Nouvelle France', 1609), and the basic meaning 'mark' or 'family, tribe'.

tother tʌ·ðəɹ (dial.) *the t.* the other. XIII. ME. *þe toþer*, for *þet oþer*, orig. n. of OE. *se ōþer* the other, the second; see THE, THAT, OTHER.

totter tɔ·təɹ †swing XII; rock to and fro on its base XIV; move with unsteady steps XVII. ME. *toter* swing – MDu. *touteren* swing (so dial. *totter* sb. XIV, Du. *touter* sb.) :– OS. **taltrōn* = OE. *tealtrian* totter, stagger, whence dial. *tolter* adj. XV, *tolter* vb. XVI.

toucan tū·kæn, tukā·n bird of the genus Rhamphastos, with enormous beak and brilliant colouring. XVI. – Tupi *tucana*, Guarani *tucā*, *tucã*, whence also F. *toucan* (XVI), Sp. *tucan*, Pg., It. *tucano*, G. *tukan*.

touch tʌtʃ put a part of the body upon (with many transf. and fig. applications). XIII. ME. *toche*, *tuche*, *touche* – OF. *tochier*, *tuchier* (mod. *toucher*) = Pr., Sp., Pg. *tocar*, It. *toccare* strike (a bell, etc.), touch, Rum. *tocà* announce with a clapper, knock :– CRom. **toccāre* make a sound like *toc* (cf. Pr. *toc*, It. *tocco* stroke of a bell), of imit. origin. Much used in comps., spec. with ref. to ready ignition (prob. from OF. *toucher* set fire), as in †*touch-powder* (XV) priming-powder (whence *touch-hole* XVI), ***tou·chwood*** wood used as tinder (XVI); also ***tou·chstone*** stone to test gold and silver alloys (XVI), based on OF. *touchepierre* (now *pierre de touche*; cf. Sp. *piedra de toque*). Hence **touch**Y[1] tʌ·tʃi easily moved to take offence, †easily ignited, risky XVII perh. partly an alt. of TETCHY.

touching prep. concerning, relating to XIV – (O)F. *touchant*, prp. of *touch(i)er*; the F. form was current in Eng. XIV–XV.

tough tʌf of strongly cohesive substance OE.; severe, violent XIII; capable of great endurance XIV; difficult to solve XVII. OE. *tōh*, OHG. *zāh*, MLG. *tā* :– **taŋχuz*, f. base repr. also (with *-ja* suffix) by MLG. *tei*, Du. *taai*, OHG. *zāhi* (G. *zäh*).

toupee tū·pi (artificial) lock of hair. XVIII. – F. *toupet* tuft of hair esp. over the forehead, f. OF. *toup*, *top*; see TOP[1], -ET. Superseded by **toupet** tū·pei. XVIII.

tour tuəɹ *one's* turn, spell of duty XIV; †circular movement XV; travelling round, circuitous journey XVII. – (O)F. *tour*, earlier *tor* = Pr. *tor*, *tors* :– L. *tornus* – Gr. *tórnos* lathe (cf. TURN). Hence vb. make a tour (of). XVIII. **tou·r**IST. XVIII, **tou·r**ISM XIX; cf. F. *tourisme*, *-iste*.

tourmaline tuə·ɹməlin brittle pyro-electric mineral orig. from Ceylon. XVIII. – F. *tourmaline* 1771, G. *turmalin* 1707, Du. *toermalijn* 1778, Sp., It. *turmalina*, ult. f. Sinhalese *toramalli* cornelian.

tournament tuə·ɹ-, tɔ̄·ɹnəmənt medieval tilting match. XIII. ME. *turne-*, *tornement* – AN. vars. of OF. *tur-*, *torneiement*, f. *torneier*; see next, -MENT.

tourney tuə·ɹni, tɔ̄·ɹni tournament. XIII. – OF *tornei* (mod. *tournoi*), f. *torneier* (whence ME. vb.) = Pr. *torneiar*, Sp. *tornear*, It. *torneggiare* :– Rom. **tornidiāre*, f. L. *tornus* TURN.

tourniquet tuə·ɹnikei (surg.) instrument involving a screw for checking flow of blood through an artery. XVII. – F. *tourniquet* (XVI), taken to be alt. of OF. *tournicle*, var. of *tounicle*, *tunicle* coat of mail, TUNICLE, by assoc. with *tourner* TURN.

tousle tau·zl pull about roughly, dishevel. XV. frequent. f. (dial.) *touse*, ME. *tuse*, *touse* in *to|tuse* (XIII), *be|touse* (XIV), repr. OE. **tūsian* = LG. *tūsen* pull or shake about, OHG. *zir|zūsōn*, *er|zūsen* tear to pieces, clear of undergrowth, G. *zausen*, rel. to L. *dūmus*, earlier *dusmus* bushes, brambles, Ir. *doss* bush; see -LE[3]. Cf. also *towser* large dog as used in bear- and bullbaiting XVII.

tout taut †peep, peer XIV; (sl.) watch, spy on XVII; solicit custom or votes importunately XVIII. ME. *tūte* :– OE. **tūtian*, f. **tūt-* project, stick out, repr. by OE. *tȳtan* (once) peep out, become visible, MLG. *tūte* horn, funnel (LG. *tūte*, *tūt* spout), MDu. *tūte* nipple (Du. *tuit* spout, nozzle), ON. *túta* teat-like prominence. Hence **tout** sb. †thieves' scout XVIII; touter for custom, etc. XIX.

tow[1] tou fibre of flax, etc. XIV (PPl., Chaucer). – MLG. *touw* :– OS. *tou* = ON. *tó* wool, tow, rel. to **tow-* in OE. *towcræft* spinning, *towhūs* spinning-house, *towlic* pert. to weaving, *towtōl* spinning implement, and Du. *touwen* spin- **taw-* (see TOOL).

tow[2] tou †drag OE.; draw (a vessel) on the water by a rope XIV (but cf. *towage*). OE. *togian* = OFris. *togia*, MLG. *togen*, OHG. *zogōn*, ON. *toga* :– CGerm. (exc. Goth.) **togōjan*, f. **tog-* (**tug-*), cf. TEAM, TIGHT. For the pronunc. cf. BOW. So **tow·**AGE charge for towing a vessel XVI; action of towing XVII. orig. – AN. *towage*, AL. *towagium* (XIII in both senses), f. ME. *towe*, *toȝe* tow.

toward tou·(w)əɹd adj. †coming, future, impending OE.; †promising, disposed to learn, docile)(FROWARD XIII; favourable, propitious)(UNTOWARD XIX. OE. *tōweard* = OS. *tōward*, *-werd*, OHG. *zuowart*, *-wert* 'directed forwards', f. Germ. **tō* TO+ **warð-* -WARD. Hence **toward** təwō·ɹd, toəɹd, tōɹd in the direction of, prep. OE. *tōweard*, n. of the adj. orig. construed with g. later with d.; only Eng. **to**WARDS in same sense. OE. *tōweardes*. ¶ The pronunc. of the preps. with the stress on the second syll. is now the commoner; it appears to be referred to as a vulgarism in Chesterfield's Letters 27 Sept., 1749. 'The vulgar man goes *to wards* and not *towards* such a place.' See also Walker's Pronouncing Dictionary.

towel tau·əl cloth for wiping something dry. XIII. ME. *towaile*, *towelle*, *touel* – OF. *toail(l)e* (mod. *touaille*) = Pr. *toalha* (whence Sp. *toalla*, It. *tovaglia*) :– Germ. **þwaχljō* (OHG. *dwahila*, G. dial. *zwehle* napkin), f. **þwaχan* wash (OE. *þwēan*, OS. *thwahan*, OHG. *dwahan*, ON. *þvá*, Goth. *þwahan*); cf. OE. *þwæhl*, *þwēal*, OHG. *dwahal* bath, ON. *þváll* soap, Goth. *þwahl* bath; see -EL[1], -LE[1].

tower tau·əɹ tall strong structure. XII. ME. *tūr*, later *tour*, *towr* – AN., OF. *tur*, *tor* (later and mod. *tour* = Pr. *tor*, Sp., It. *torre* :– L. *turrem*, nom. *-is*, corr. to Oscan (acc.) *tiurri*) – Gr. *túrris*, *túrsis*, *túrsos*. Hence vb. rise to a great height; soar like a hawk. XVI.

town taun †enclosure, garden, yard; (now Sc.) building(s) on a piece of enclosed land, farmstead; (dial.) cluster of buildings or houses OE.; inhabited place having an independent administration XII (without article XIII); inhabitants of a town XIV (opp. to university XVII); (U.S.) division for local or state government XIX. OE. *tūn* = OFris., OS. *tūn*, OHG. *zūn* (Du. *tuin* garden, G. *zaun*) fence, hedge, ON. *tún* :– CGerm. (exc. Goth.) **tūnaz*, **tūnam*, rel. to Celtic **dūn-* in the place names (e.g. *Augustodunum* Autun), OIr. *dūn*, W. *din* fort, castle, camp, fortified place. In senses later than OE. times it is the equiv. of L. *villa* orig. farm, country house, and its deriv. F. *ville*. comps. and derivs. **town-**CLERK. XIV. **townee** taunī· one of the townspeople XIX; earlier U.S. **towny**. **town-**SHIP. OE. *tūnsċipe*. **tow·ns**MAN. OE. *tūnesman* †villager, villain; man of a town XV.

toxic tɔ·ksik poisonous XVII; due to poisoning XIX. – medL. *toxicus*, f. L. *toxicum* poison – Gr. *toxikón* (*phármakon*) (poison) by smearing arrows, n. of *toxikós*, f. *tóxa* pl. (bow and) arrows, f. *tóxon* bow; see -IC. Hence **to·x**IN poison produced by a microbe. XIX.

toxophilite tɔksɔ·filait devotee of archery. XVIII. f. *Toxophilus*, title of a book (1545) by Roger Ascham, intended to mean 'lover of the bow', f. Gr. *tóxon* bow+*-philos* -PHIL; see -ITE. Hence **toxo·phil**Y[3] (addiction to) archery. XIX.

toy toi A. †amorous play XIV; †sportive or fantastic action, antic, trick XV; B. trifling object; thing to play with XVI. Of unkn. origin; there are serious gaps in the early evidence; MDu. *toi* (Du. *tooi*) attire, finery, agrees in form but not in sense.

trace[1] treis †path, course XIII (Cursor M.); †series of footprints, track XIV; vestige, mark XVII. – (O)F. *trace* = Pr. *trasa*, Sp. *traza*, Pg. *traça*, It. *traccia*, f. corr. vbs. OF. *tracier* (mod. *tracer*), Pr. *trasar*, Sp. *trazar*, Pg. *traçar*, It. *tracciare* :– Rom. **tractiāre*, f. L. *tractus* TRACT[3]; so **trace** vb. A. proceed in a line or track; B. make marks on a plan, etc. XIV. – OF. Hence **tra·**CERY †place for tracing XV; intersecting rib-work in a Gothic window XVII.

trace[2] treis pair of ropes, etc. attached to the collar of a draught animal XIV; each of these XV. ME. *trais*, first as coll. pl. later as sg. – OF. *trais*, pl. of *trait* draught, harness-strap = Pr. *trach* convulsion, Sp. *trecho* space, distance of time, It. *tratto* :– L. *tractu-s* draught, f. pp. stem of *trahere* draw (cf. TRACT[3], TRAIT).

trachea trəkī·ə (anat.) tube extending from the larynx to the bronchi. XVI (early in *trache arteria* or *arterie* XV, and later in anglicized forms such as *arter trache*, and *trachiartere*). – medL. *trāchēa*, for late L. *trāchīa* (Macrobius) – Gr. *trākheîa* (sc. *arteriā* artery), fem. of *trākhús* rough.

trachyte træ·kait, trei·kait species of gritty volcanic rock. XIX. – F. *trachyte* (Haüy), f. Gr. *trākhús* rough or *trākhútēs* roughness.

track træk mark left by the passage of something XV (Malory); line of travel or motion XVI; path laid down XIX. – (O)F. *trac*, perh. – LDu. (MDu., LG.) *tre(c)k* drawing, draught, pull (cf. TREK), but the phonology is difficult. Hence or – F. *traquer* **track** vb. XVI.

tract[1] trækt tractate, (later) short pamphlet. XV, poss. shortening of L. *tractātus* TRACTATE. Hence **tract**A·RIAN writer of tracts, spec. of contributors to the 'Tracts for the Times' 1833–41 published at Oxford.

tract[2] trækt (liturg.) item replacing the Alleluia in the Mass from Septuagesima to Easter Eve. XIV (Trevisa) – medL. *tractus*, spec. use of L. *tractus* (see next), but of uncertain development.

tract[3] trækt act of drawing or something drawn in various uses identical with those of TRACE[1] and TRACK (rare before XVI), now chiefly 'stretch or extent of territory' (so in L. from the notion of area contained by lines drawn). – L. *tractus*, f. pp. stem of *trahere* draw.

tractable træ·ktəbl easy to manage. XVI. – L. *tractābilis*, f. *tractāre* TREAT; see -ABLE. ¶ The earlier word was *treatable* (XIV) – (O)F.

tractate træ·kteit treatise. XV (Caxton). – L. *tractātus*, f. *tractāre* TREAT; see -ATE[1].

traction træ·kʃən drawing, draught XVII; drawing of vehicles or loads along a road (hence *t. engine*) XIX. – F. *traction* or medL. *tractiō(n-)*, f. pp. stem of *trahere* draw; see TRACT, -ION. So **tra·ctor**[1] (med.) device to be drawn or rubbed over the skin XVII; instrument for pulling XIX; traction engine XX.

trade treid †course, way, track XIV; regular practice of a business or profession; buying and selling in this XVI. – MLG. *trade* track (OS. *trada* = OHG. *trata*), f. **trad-* **tred-* TREAD: attrib. *t. wind* orig. any wind that blows in a constant direction (XVII), f. phr. † *blow trade* blow in a regular or habitual course.

tradition trədi·ʃən that which is handed down as belief or practice in a community XIV; delivery, transmission XVI. – (O)F. *tradicion*, (also mod.) *-tion*, or L. *trāditiō(n-)*, f. *trādere* hand over, deliver, f. *trāns* TRANS- + *dāre* give; see -ITION. Hence **tradi·tional**[1]. XVII. F. *traditionnel*, medL. *traditiōnālis*.

traduce trədjū·s †transport; †translate; †transmit; propagate; speak evil of (falsely). XVI. – L. *trādūcere*, f. *trāns* TRANS- + *dūcere* lead (see DUCT).

traffic træ·fik transportation of goods for purposes of trade XVI; passing to and fro of people, etc. XIX. Early records have the forms *traffigo, -ico, trafficque* – F. *traf(f)ique* (mod. *trafic*), corr. to Pr. *trafec*, Sp. *tráfico*, †*tráfago*, Pg. *tráfego*, It. *traffico* (usu. taken to be the source of the F.); of unkn. origin (the first syll. may repr. L. *trāns*).

tragacanth træ·gəkænþ medicinal mucilaginous substance obtained from Astragalus. XVI. – F. *tragacante* or L. *tragacantha* – Gr. *tragákantha* goat's-thorn, f. *trágos* he-goat + *ákantha* thorn.

tragedy træ·dʒidi dramatic piece (†earlier, tale) having a disastrous ending XIV (Ch., Lydg.); calamitous event XVI. – (O)F. *tragédie* – L. *tragœdia* – Gr. *tragōidíā*, usu. taken to be f. *trágos* goat + *ōidḗ* ODE (but the history is disputed). So **tragedian** trədʒī·diən tragic poet XIV (Ch.); tragic actor XVI. – OF. *tragediane*, F. *tragédien*. Earlier †*tragician* XV (Lydg.). **tragic** træ·dʒik pert. to or resembling tragedy. XVI. – F. *tragique* (Rabelais) – L. *tragicus* – Gr. *tragikós*, f. *trágos*, but assoc. with *tragōidíā*. **tra·gical**. XV (Caxton). **tra:gico·medy** composition combining tragic and comic elements. XVI (Sidney). – F. *tragicomédie* or It. *tragicommedia* – late L. *tragicōmœdia*, for *tragicocōmœdia* (Plautus).

tragelaph træ·gəlæf capriform antelope or the like. XVII. – L. *tragelaphus* – Gr. *tragélaphos*, f. *trágos* goat + *élaphos* deer.

tragopan træ·gŏpæn pheasant of the genus Ceriornis (Tragopan); having fleshy horns. XIX. – L. – Gr. *tragópān*, f. *trágos* goat + *Pán* Pan.

trail treil intr. hang down and drag along XIV (R. Mannyng); trans. drag or draw along XIV. prob. of mixed origin – OF. *traillier* or MLG., MFlem. *treilen* haul (a boat), which point to CRom. or popL. **tragulāre* (to which OE. *trægelian* 'carpere' conforms), f. L. *trāgula* drag-net, etc. Cf. TRAWL.

train trein tarrying, delay XIV (R. Mannyng); thing that drags or trails XV (first of the trailing part of a garment); sequence or series XV; number of carriages, etc. coupled together XIX. – (O)F. *train* m., *traine* fem. (both XII), f. OF. (orig.) *trahiner*, *traîner* (mod. *traîner*) = Pr. *traginar*, Sp. *trajinar*, It. *trainare* :– Rom. **tragināre*, f. **tragere*, f. L. *trahere* draw; the OF. vb. is the orig. source of **train** vb. †draw, allure, etc. XV; instruct and discipline XVI.

train-oil trei·noil oil obtained by boiling from whale blubber, etc. XVI. repl. earlier *train*, *trane* (XV) – (M)LG. *trān*, MDu. *traen* (Du. *traan*) = G. *tran*, rel. to *träne* tear, drop (cf. TEAR[1]).

traipse *see* TRAPES.

trait trei, treit †stroke XVI; feature, characteristic XVIII. – F. *trait* = Pr. *trait* :– L. *tractu-s* drawing, draught, TRACT[1].

traitor trei·təɹ one who betrays or is false. XIII. – OF. *traitour*, *-ur* = Pr., Sp. *traidor*, It. *traditore* :– L. *trāditōrem*, nom. *trāditor* (whence (O)F. *traitre*), agent-noun f. *trādere* deliver, betray, f. *trāns* TRANS- + *-dere*, *dāre*, give; see -TOR.

trajectory træ·dʒiktəri, -e·ktəri path of a body moving by force. XVII. – medL. *trājectōrius*, f. *trājec-*, pp. stem of *trāicere*, f. *trāns* + *jacere* throw; see TRANS-, INJECT, -ORY[1].

tralatitious trælətі·ʃəs A. metaphorical XVII; B. traditional XVIII. f. L. *trālātīcius*, var. of *trānslātīcius* preserved by transmission, customary, usual (Cicero), metaphorical (Varro), f. *trānslāt-*, pp. stem of *transferre* TRANSFER; see -ITIOUS[1].

tram[1] træm A. †contrivance, lit. and fig. XIV; B. loosely twisted silk thread used for weft XVII. In A – (O)F. *trame* woof, cunning device, machination :– L. *trāma* woof; in B a new adoption from modF.

tram[2] træm (Sc.) shaft of a barrow or cart XVI (Dunbar); (coalmining, north.) frame or skeleton truck for carrying coal-baskets, perh. orig. carried by hand, later drawn as a sledge or on wheels XVI; (short for *tram-line*) line or track of wood, stone, or iron; (short for *tramroad*, *-way*) road laid with such lines; (short for *tram-car*) passenger car running on tram-lines XIX. (in AL. *trama* XIV) – MLG., MDu. *trame* balk, beam, rung of a ladder, of unkn. origin; the sense-development is obscure and is not paralleled in LG. or Du.

trammel træ·ml fishing-net having three layers of netting XIV; hobble for a horse XVI; thing that hinders free action XVII. – (O)F. *tramail*, mod. *trémail* (whence Sp. *trasmallo*, Pg. *trasmalho*, It. *tramaglio*) – medL. *tramaculum*, var. of *tremaculum*, *tri-* (Salic Law), perh. f. L. *tri-* three, TRI- + *macula* mesh (cf. MAIL[1]). Hence **trammel** vb. in several techn. uses XVI; (fig.) hinder the action of XVIII.

tramontane trəmɔ·ntein lying beyond the mountain (spec. the Alps) from Italy. XVI (Nashe). – It. *tramontana* north wind, pole star, *tramontani* dwellers beyond the mountains – L. *trānsmontānus*, f. TRANS- + *mont-*, *mōns* MOUNT[1].

tramp træmp stamp, tread heavily XIV (Wycl. Bible); walk steadily XVI. prob. of LDu. origin and based on Germ. stem **tramp*; cf. MLG. *trampen*.

trample træ·mpl †tramp, stamp XIV (Wycl. Bible); tread *upon* XVI. f. TRAMP + -LE[3]. Cf. (M)HG., LG. *trampeln*.

trance tràns †extreme dread or doubt XIV; suspension of consciousness, hypnotic state (Ch.). – OF. *transe* (mod. *trance*), f. *transir* depart, be benumbed – L. *trānsīre* (see TRANSIT).

tranquil træ·ŋkwil undisturbed, serenely quiet. XVII (Sh.). – F. *tranquille* or L. *tranquillus*.

trans- tràns, trànz comb. form of L. prep. *trāns* across, beyond, over, corr. to Umbrian *tra(ha)f*, *tra(ha)* with cogns. in Skr., Celtic, and Germ. (see THROUGH). In several L. vbs. and their derivs. the prefix was reduced to *trā* before a cons., e.g. *trādere* (see TRADITION), *trāicere* (see TRAJECTORY); *ss* resulting from composition with an initial *s* is simplified, as in *transcribe*.

transact trànzæ·kt, -sæ·kt †do business, treat XVI; carry through, manage XVII. f. *transact-*, pp. stem of L. *transigere* drive through, accomplish, f. *trāns* TRANS- + *agere* drive, do. So **transa·ction** †adjustment of a dispute XV; action of transacting, matter transacted XVII. – late L.; cf. (O)F. *transaction*; see ACT, ACTION.

transcend trànse·nd pass (a limit) or the limits of XIV (Rolle); rise above, surpass XV (Lydg.); †go beyond, climb over XVI. – OF. *transcendre* or L. *tran(s)scendere* climb over, surmount, f. *trāns* TRANS- + *scandere* climb (cf. SCANSION). So **transce·nd**ENCE XVII (Sh.), -ENCY XVII. – late L. *transcendentia*. **transce·nd**ENT XVI; **transcende·nt**AL[1] XVIII (in current use due mainly to Kantian philosophy).

transcribe trànskrai·b make a copy of XVI; transliterate XVII. – L. *transcrībere*; TRANS-, SCRIBE, SCRIPTURE. So **tra·nscript** written copy. XIII. ME. *transcrit* – (O)F. *transcrit*; later (XV) assim. to L. *transcriptum*, sb. use of n. pp. of *transcrībere*. **transcri·p**TION. XVI. – F. or late L.

transect trànse·kt cut across. XVII. f. TRANS- + *sect-*, pp. stem of L. *secāre* cut (cf. SECTION).

transept trà·nsept transverse part of a cruciform church, either arm of this. XVI (Leland, who freq. uses the L. form also). – modL. *transeptum* 'cross division'; see TRANS-, SEPTUM; hence F. (XIX).

transfer trànsfə̄·ɹ convey from place to place XIV (Wycl. Bible); make over by legal process XVI; convey (a design) from one surface to another XIX. – L. *transferre* (or F. *transférer*), f. *trāns* TRANS- + *ferre* BEAR[2]; the basis of the L. vb. is Gr. *μεταφέρειν* (cf. METAPHOR). Agent-nouns *transferer*, *transferor*, *transferrer*. Hence **tra·nsfer** sb. XVII. So **tra·nsfer**ENCE. XVII.

transfigure trànsfi·gəɹ change in appearance. XIII (Cursor M.). – (O)F. *transfigurer* or L. *trānsfigūrāre*, f. *trāns* TRANS- + *figūra* FIGURE. So **transfigura·**TION. XIV (first in ref. to the change in the appearance of Jesus Christ as narrated in Matt. xvii, Mark ix 2, 3). – (O)F. or L.

transfix trànsfi·ks impale upon a sharp point. XVI (Spenser). f. *trānsfix-*, pp. stem of L. *trānsfigere*, cf. F. *transfixer*, see TRANS-, FIX.

transform trànsfɔ̄·ɹm change the form of. XIV (Rolle). – (O)F. *transformer* or L. *trānsformāre*; see TRANS-, FORM. So **transforma·**TION. XV. – (O)F. or late L.

transfuse trànsfjū·z pour from one place to another. XV. – L. *trānsfūs-*, pp. stem of *trānsfundere*; see TRANS-, FUSE[2].

transgress trànsgre·s, -nz- go beyond the bounds prescribed by law, etc. XVI (Tindale) – *trānsgress-*, pp. stem of L. *trānsgredī*; see TRANS-, DIGRESS. So **transgre·ss**ION. XV (Lydg.). – (O)F. – L.

tran(s)ship. XVIII. f. TRANS- + SHIP vb.

transient trà·nziənt, -ns-, -nʃ-, -nʒ- passing by or away. XVII. – L. *transiēns* (obl. *transeunt-*, repr. in some uses by **transeunt**), prp. of *transīre* pass over, f. *trāns* TRANS- + *īre* go; cf. AMBIENT. **transit** trà·nsit, -nz- passage from one point to another. XV (astron. XVII). – L. *transitus*; cf. ADIT. **transi·**TION trànsi·ʃən, -i·ʒən, -nz- passage from one condition or action to another. XVI. – (O)F. or L. **transit**IVE trà·nzītiv, -ns- (gram.) taking a direct object; passing into another condition. XVI. – late L. *transitīvus* (Priscian); **transit**ORY² trà·nzitəri, -ns- not lasting or continuing. XIV (Ch.). – AN. *transitorie*, (O)F. *transitoire* – ChrL. *transitōrius*, f. L. *transit-*; see TRANSIT.

transire trànsaiə·ri, -nz- warrant permitting the passage of merchandise. XVI. L., f. *trāns* TRANS- + *īre* go.

translate trànslei·t A. remove from one place to another; B. turn from one language into another. XIII (Cursor M.), prob. first in pp. *translate* – L. *translātus*, functioning as pp. of *transferre* TRANSFER; but perh. reinforced by OF. *translater*, medL. *translātāre*. **transl**A·TION, **transla·**TOR¹. XIV. – OF. or L.

transliterate trànsli·təreit replace (letters of one language) by those of another for the same sounds. XIX (Max Müller). f. TRANS- + L. *littera* LETTER + -ATE³. So **tra:nsliter**A·TION. XIX. ¶ Preceded by a nonce-use of *translettering* (1802).

translucent trànsliū·sənt †shining through XVI; transparent XVII. – L. *translūcent-*, *-ēns*, prp. of *translūcēre*; see TRANS-, LUCID.

transmarine trànsmərī·n, -z- that is beyond the sea. XVI. – L. *transmarīnus*; see TRANS-, MARINE.

transmigration trànsmaigrei·ʃən, trænz- †removal of the Jews into captivity at Babylon XIII; passage from one place to another XIV; passage of the soul at death into another body, metempsychosis XVI. – late L. *trānsmigrātiō(n-)* change of country (in Vulgate, 1 Esdras vi 16, the Babylonian Captivity), f. *trānsmigrāre*, whence **transmigrate** (stress variable) XVII (pp. XV); see TRANS-, MIGRATE, -ATION.

transmit trànsmi·t, -nz- send across a space XIV; pass on by communication; cause to pass through a medium XVII. – L. *transmittere*; cf. F. *transmettre* (XVI), OF. *trametre*. So **transmi·ss**ION. XVI. – L. *transmissiō(n-)*; see TRANS-, MISSION.

transmogrify trànsmɔ·grifai, -nz- (colloq.) transform, esp. into a strange shape. XVII. Of obscure origin; in the New Canting Dict. 1725 it is suggested that the preferable form is *transmigrafy*; poss., therefore, it is based on *transmigrate* used for 'transform, transmute' (*transmigration* was similarly used earlier in XVII); see -IFY.

transmutation trànsmjūtei·ʃən, trænz- †change of condition XIV (Wycl.); conversion into something else XIV (Trevisa); (alch.) XV; (biol.) XVII (Bacon). – (O)F. *transmutation* or late L. *transmūtātiō(n-)*, f. L. *transmūtāre*, whence **transmu·te** vb. XV, replacing †*transmue*, *-mew* (– (O)F. *transmuer*); see TRANS-, MUTATION.

transom træ·nsəm cross-beam, esp. spanning an opening. XIV. Early forms *traversayn*, *transyn*, *-ing* (Sandahl XIII–XV) – (O)F. *traversin* in same sense, f. *traverse* TRAVERSE. For *-syn*/ *-son* cf. *kelsine* KELSON.

transparent trànspɛə·rənt, -pæ·rənt that can be seen through XV; (fig.) XVI (Sh.). – (O)F. *transparent* – medL. *trānspārēns*, *-ent-*, f. L. *trāns* TRANS- + *pārēre* APPEAR. So **transpa·r**ENCY. XVI.

transpire trànspaiə·ɹ emit as vapour XVI; pass out as vapour XVII; escape from secrecy to notice (J.), leak out XVIII; (hence, by misapprehension, first U.S.) happen XIX. – F. *transpirer* or medL. *trānspirāre*, f. L. *trāns* TRANS- + *spirāre* breathe (cf. SPIRIT).

transplant trànsplà·nt remove from one place to another. XV. – late L. *trānsplantāre*; see TRANS-, PLANT, and cf. F. *transplanter*.

transpontine trànspɔ·ntain that is across the bridge, spec. any of the London bridges, i.e. south of the Thames, and so pert. to the drama of Surrey-side theatres in XIX. f. TRANS- + L. *pont-*, *pōns* bridge (cf. PONTOON) + -INE¹.

transport trànspɔ̄·ɹt convey from place to place XIV (Ch.; fig.); carry away with emotion XVI. – OF. *transporter* or L. *trānsportāre*, f. *trāns* TRANS- + *portāre* carry (cf. PORT³). Hence or – (O)F. *transport* (cf. medL. *transportus* transferment) conveyance from one place to another or means of this XV; state of being 'carried out of oneself' XVII. Hence **transport**A·TION conveyance XVI (penal removal XVII).

transpose trànspou·z †change into something else XIV (Wyclif, Gower); change the position or order of XVI. – (O)F. *transposer*, f. *trans-* TRANS- + *poser* POSE. So **trans**POSI·TION. XVI. – F. or late L.

transubstantiation trànsəbstænʃiei·ʃən change of substance XIV (Trevisa; spec. of the Eucharistic bread and wine XVI, Tindale). – medL. *tran(s)substantiātiō(n-)* (XI), f. *tran(s)substantiāre*, whence **transubsta·ntiate** XVI (as pp. earlier XV). Cf. (O)F. *transubstantier*, *-tiation*, and see -ATE³, -ATION. Hence **co:nsubstantia·tion** (XVI, Hooker; after modL.) controversialist's term to designate the Lutheran doctrine of the Eucharistic presence in, with, and under the substantially unaltered bread and wine; see CON-.

transume trànsjū·m make an official copy of. XV. – late L. *tran(s)sūmere*.

transumpt trànsʌ·mpt copy, transcript. XV. – medL. *tran(s)sumptum*, sb. use of n. pp. of *tran(s)sūmere*.

Transvaal trȧns-, trȧnzvā·l state of the Union of South Africa, separated from the Orange Free State by the river Vaal. f. TRANS- + *Vaal*, tributary of the Orange River.

transverse trȧnsvə̄·ɹs, -nz- lying across. XVII (Burton). – L. *trānsversus*, pp. of *trānsvertere* turn across; see TRANS-, VERSE. So **transve·rsAL**[1]. XV – medL.

trap[1] træp contrivance for catching animals OE.; movable covering as of an opening in a floor XIV; means of confining and releasing objects XVI; (perh. for *rattle trap*) small carriage on springs XIX. OE. *træppe* (in *coltetræppe* Christ's thorn), *treppe*, corr. in form and sense to MDu. *trappe*, Flem. *trape*, medL. *trappa*, OF. *trape* (mod. *trappe*), Pr., Pg. *trapa*, Sp. *trampa*, but the mutual relations are obscure. So **trap** vb. OE. *be|treppan*. **tra·pPER**[1]. XVIII.

trap[2] træp (min.) igneous rock. XVIII. – Sw. *trapp* (Bergman 1766), so named from the stair-like appearance, f. *trappa* stair.

trapes, traipse (colloq., dial.) walk in slovenly or aimless fashion. XVI. Of unkn. origin. Hence sb. sloven, draggletail. XVII.

trapeze trəpī·z gymnastic apparatus consisting of a crossbar supported by two ropes. XIX. – F. *trapèze* – late L. *trapezium* (see next).

trapezium trəpī·ziəm (geom.) in the Euclidean sense, irregular quadrilateral XVI; in the restricted sense used by Proclus, quadrilateral having only one pair of opposite sides parallel XVII. – late L. *trapezium* – Gr. *trapézion*, f. *trápeza* table, for **tetra-peza*, f. IE. **quetr* FOUR + **pedja* (f. *ped-* FOOT). So **trapezOID** træ·pizoid, trəpī·zoid quadrilateral no two sides of which are parallel. XVIII; – modL. *trapezoidēs* – late Gr. *trapezoeidḗs*.

trapping træ·piŋ (chiefly pl.) covering spread over harness. XIV (Trevisa); (in wider use) external ornaments XVI. f. base of synon. †*trappo(u)r* (XIII) – AN. **trapour* (cf. AL. *trappātūra*), var. of OF. *drapure*, f. *drap* cloth (cf. DRAPER); with substitution of -ING[1].

Trappist træ·pist monk of a Cistercian community established in 1664 by De Rancé, abbot of La *Trappe*, Normandy. XIX. – F. *Trappiste*, f. *La Trappe*; see -IST.

traps træps (colloq.) personal effects, belongings. XIX. Of uncertain origin; perh. contr. of TRAPPINGS.

trash træʃ broken twigs, etc.; worthless stuff. XVI. Of unkn. orig.

traumatic trōmæ·tik caused by a wound. XVII. – late L. *traumaticus* – Gr. *traumatikós*, f. *traumat-*, *traûma* wound (**trau·ma** XVIII), rel. to *titrṓskein* wound; see -IC.

travail træ·veil (arch.) labour, toil; labour of childbirth. XIII. – (O)F. *travail* painful effort, trouble, work = Pr. *trebalh*, Sp. *trabajo*, Pg. *trabalho*, It. *travaglio*, f. (O)F. *travailler* (whence obs. or arch. vb. XIII) = Pr. *trebalhar* work (whence It. *travagliare*), Sp. *trabajar*, Pg. *trabalhar* :– Rom. **trepāliāre*, f. medL. *trepālium* instrument of torture, presumably f. L. *trēs*, *tria* THREE + *pālus* stake (so called from its shape). The etymol. meaning of the vb. was 'put to torture', whence, through the refl. use ('put oneself to pain') the sense 'toil, labour', which survives in F., whereas the Eng. vb. ult. became restricted to the sense 'journey', with the sp. **travel** træ·vl (Sc. *travel* XIV), an application not evolved in F. Hence **tra·vellER**[1] (Sc. *traualoure* XIV). *traveller's joy*, kind of clematis which adorns the wayside XVI (Gerard); **travelogue, -log** træ·vələg talk or lecture about travel. XX. irreg. + *-logue* of *monologue*, *dialogue*.

traverse træ·vəɹs run, move, or pass across or through; act against or in opposition to. XIV. – (O)F. *traverser* = Pr. *traversar*, Sp. *travesar*, It. *traversare* :– late L. *trāversāre*, *trānsversāre*, f. *trānsversus*, pp. of *trānsvertere*, f. *trāns* TRANS- + *vertere* turn; see WORTH[3], -WARD(S). So **tra·verse** sb. something that crosses (lit. and fig.). XIV. – OF. *travers* and *traverse* = Pr. *travers*, *traversa*, Sp. *traviesa*, Pg. *travessa*, It. *traverso*, *traversa*, partly f. corr. vbs., partly repr. sb. uses of n. and f. pps.; cf. medL. *tra(ns)versa*. ¶ From XV to mod. dial. forms without *r* in the second syll., due to lack of stress, were current; cf. Sp. and Pg. *r*-less forms.

travertin(e) træ·vəɹtin, -tīn concretionary limestone deposited from water containing lime. XVIII. – It. *travertino*, for earlier †*tivertino* :– L. *tīburtinus* (sc. *lapis* stone), adj. of *Tībur* (now *Tivoli*) in ancient Latium; see -INE[1].

travesty træ·vĭsti grotesque or ludicrous imitation. XVII (Butler, 1674). freq. in XVII in *Virgil travesti(e)*, adoption of the title of Scarron's 'Le Virgile travesty en vers burlesques' (1648); earlier (1656) †*travested*, for *travestied* – F. *travesti*, It. *travestito*, pps. of *travestir*, *-ire*, f. L. *tra-* TRANS- + *vestīre* clothe (see VEST, -ED[1]).

trawl trōl fish with a drag-net XVII; use a seine-net to catch fish XIX. prob. – MDu. *traghelen* drag, rel. to *traghel* drag-net, perh. – L. *trāgula* drag-net, obscurely f. *trahere* draw. See TRAIL. Hence **trawl** sb. XVIII, short for *trawl-net* (XVII). **traw·lER**[1] one who fishes with a trawl-net XVI; vessel using trawl-nets XIX. ¶ A reading *trawelle* (1481–90) is doubtful. If genuine, it would give priority to the sb.

tray trei shallow open vessel, now a flat board with raised rim. OE. **trēġ*, **trīeġ*, recorded only late as *trīġ* = OSw. *trø* corn-measure :– Germ. **traujam*, f. **trau-*, **treu-* wood (see TREE).

treachery tre·tʃəri action of a traitor. XIII (AncrR., Cursor M.). – (O)F. *trecherie*, (also mod.) *tricherie*, f. *tricher* cheat = Pr. *tricar*, OIt. *treccare*; see TRICK, -ERY. So **trea·cherous**. XIV. – OF. *trecherous*, f. *trechour* traitor.

treacle trī·kl †salve regarded as an antidote to venomous bites, etc. XIV; †in names of plants of reputed medicinal value XV; †sovereign remedy XVI; uncrystallized syrup produced in refining sugar XVII. ME. *triacle* – OF. *triacle* = Pr. *triacla*, Sp., It. *triaca*, Pg. *triaga* :– L. *thēriaca* – Gr. *thēriakḗ*, sb. use (sc. *antidotos*) of fem. of adj. f. *thēríon* wild beast, venomous animal, dim. of *thḗr* (cf. FERAL[2]). For the parasitic *l* cf. PARTICIPLE, PRINCIPLE, SYLLABLE. The application to the syrup of sugar arose presumably from this being used as a vehicle for medicine.

tread tred pt. **trod** trɔd, (arch.) *trode* troud, pp. **trodden** trɔ·dn, *trod* step or walk upon; intr. with *on*, *upon* OE.; thresh by trampling XIV. OE. *tredan*, pt. *træd*, *trǣdon*, pp. *treden* = OFris. *treda*, OS. *tredan*, OHG. *tretan* (Du. *treden*, G. *treten*) :– CWGerm. **treðan*, of which the wk. grade **truð-* is repr. by ON. *troða*, *trað*, *tráðum*, *troðinn*, Goth. *trudan*; no cogns. are known outside Germ. The conjugation was infl. by assoc. with that of *break* (OE. *brecan*, pp. *brocen*), with that of the ON. vb., and of OE. (wk.) *treddian*. Hence **tread** sb. XIII (AncrR.); cf. TRADE. comp. **trea·d-**MILL. XIX. **trea·d**WHEEL instruments operated by the treading of men or animals to give motion to machinery. XVI.

treadle tre·dl †step, stair OE.; lever worked with the foot XV. OE. *tredul*, f. *tredan*; see prec. and -LE[1].

treason trī·zən betrayal of trust XIII; violation by a subject of his allegiance XIV. ME. *treison*, *tresoun* – AN. *treisoun*, *tres(o)un*, OF. *traison* (mod. *trahison*) = Pr. *traizon*, Sp. *traición* :– L. *trāditiō(n-)*, f. *trādere* deliver up, BETRAY, f. *trāns* TRANS- + *-dere* give. Hence **trea·son**ABLE perfidious XIV (Barbour; chiefly Sc. till XVII).

treasure tre·ʒəɹ wealth, riches; valued thing. XII (Peterborough Chron.). ME. *tresor* = (O)F. *trésor* = Cat. *tresor*, OSp., OIt. dial. *tresoro* :– Rom. **tresaurus*, unexpl. alt. of L. *thēsaurus* (see THESAURUS), which is repr. by Pr. *tezaur*, Sp., It. *tesoro*, Pg. *thesouro*. Hence **trea·sure** vb. XIV (Wycl. Bible, tr. L. Vulg. *thēsaurizāre*; rare before XVII). For the sp. *-ure* (XV) cf. *leisure*, *measure*, *pleasure*. So **trea·sur**ER[2]. XIII. – AN. *tresorer*, (O)F. (mod.) *trésorier*, f. *trésor*, after late L. *thēsaurārius*. **treasure trove** tre·ʒəɹ trouv treasure found hidden of unknown ownership. XVI (also *trovey*). – AN. *tresor trové* (in AL. *thesaurus inventus* XII), i.e. *tresor* TREASURE, *trové*, pp. of *trover* (mod. F. *trouver*) find. The ending *-é* has become mute as in ASSIGN[2], etc. (see -Y[5]); earlier repr. by tr. †*treasure found(en)* XV.

So **trea·sury**. XIII. – OF. *tresorie*, for *tresorerie*, f. *tresor*, after medL. *thēsaur(ār)ia*; see -Y[3].

treat trīt deal *with* XIII (RGlouc.); also trans. from XIV. ME. *trete* – AN. *treter*, OF. *tretier*, *traitier* (mod. *traiter*) = Pr. *traitar*, Sp. *trechar* prepare fish, It. *trattare* :– L. *tractāre* drag, handle, manage, investigate, discuss, negotiate, f. pp. stem of *trahere* draw (cf. TRACT, TRACTATE, TRACTION). So **treat** sb. †agreement, treaty XIV; entertainment XVII. So **treatise** trī·tiz book or writing in which a subject is treated. XIV. – AN. *tretis*, OF. **traitiz*, f. *traitier*. **trea·t**MENT action or manner of treating. XVI; cf. (O)F. *traitement*.

treaty trī·ti †literary treatment, discussion XIV (Wycl. Bible); discussion of terms XIV (Ch.); covenant, contract XV. ME. *trete(e)* – AN. *treté*, (O)F. *traité* :– L. *tractatu-s* TRACTATE. See -Y[5].

treble tre·bl threefold, triple XIV; sb. quantity 3 times as great as another XV; (mus.) highest or upper part in a harmonized composition, soprano XIV. – OF. *treble* – L. *triplus* TRIPLE. The development of the musical use is obscure. It has been held that *triplus* may have been loosely used for 'third', thus denoting the part added above the *altus* and *bassus* ('high' and 'low'), or the descant and the canto fermo.

trecento treˌtʃe·ntou short for *mil trecento* 1300: see CINQUECENTO.

tree trī perennial plant having a woody stem and of considerable height and size; piece of wood (as in *axle t.*, *cross t.*, *swingle t.*, *saddle t.*, *boot t.*, and *treenail*) OE.; pedigree XIII. OE. *trēo(w)* = OFris. *trē*, OS. *trio*, *treo* (MDu. *-tere*), ON. *tré*, Goth. *triu* :– Germ. **trewam* (not in OHG. and now obs. in Du. and LG.), f. zero-grade of IE. **deru-* **doru-*, repr. by Skr. *dā́ru*, *dru-* tree, Gr. *dóru*, pl. *doûra* wood, spear, *drûs* tree, oak, Lith. *dervà* pinewood, OIr. *daur*, W. *derwen* oak. Hence **tree**NAIL, **tre**NAIL trī·neil, tre·nəl cylindrical pin of hard wood used in fastening timbers together. XIII.

trefa, trifa trei·fə, trai·fə flesh meat not slaughtered according to Jewish law. XIX. – Heb. *ṭrēphāh* flesh of an animal torn, as by a wild beast, f. *ṭāraf* tear, rend.

trefoil tre·foil, trī·foil plant of genus Trifolium, having triple leaves. XIV. Late ME. *treyfoyle*, *trifolie* – AN. *trifoil* – L. *trifolium* (whence OF. *trefeuil*, Pr. *trefuelh*, It. *trifoglio*), f. *tri-* TRI- + *folium* leaf, FOIL.

trek trek (S. Africa) make a journey by ox wagon, (hence) travel. Also sb. XIX. – Afrikaans, (M)Du. *trekken* draw, pull, travel = OFris. *trekka*, (M)LG. *trekken*.

trellis tre·lis grating used as a support or screen. XIV. Late ME. *trelis* – OF. *trelis*, *-ice* :– Rom. **trilīcius*, *-ia*, f. L. *trilīc-*, *-līx*, f. *tri-*, TRI- + *līcium* thread of a warp.

tremble tre·mbl shake with fear, etc. XIV (R. Mannyng). – (O)F. *trembler* = Pr. *tremblar*, Sp. *temblar*, It. *tremolare* :– Rom. **tremulāre* rel. to L. *tremulus* TREMULOUS.

tremendous trime·ndəs terrific, dreadful XVII; immense XIX. f. L. *tremendus*, gerundive of *tremere* tremble, tremble at, rel. to TREMOR; see -OUS.

tremolando tremŏlæ·ndou (mus.) with tremulous effect. XIX. It. prp. of *tremolare* TREMBLE. So **tre·molo**. XIX.

tremor tre·məɹ †terror XIV (Ch.); involuntary shaking of the body; tremulous movement, as of the earth XVII. – OF. *tremour* and (later) L. *tremor*, rel. to *tremere*, Gr. *trémein* tremble, *trómos* trembling, Lith. *trìmti*, Lett. *tremt*, f. **trem*-, to which there is a parallel **tres*- in Sl. and Indo-Iranian. So **tre·m**ULOUS. XVII. f. L. *tremulus*.

trenail var. of *treenail*; see TREE.

trench trenᵗʃ †track cut through a forest XIV; long narrow excavation XV. – OF. *trenche* cutting, cut, ditch, slice, f. *trenchier* (mod. *trancher*) cut (whence **trench** vb. XV) = Pr. *trencar*, Sp. *trincar* :– Rom. **trincāre* – L. *truncare* (see TRUNCATED). Cf. ENTRENCHMENT.

trenchant tre·nᵗʃənt cutting (lit. and fig.). XIV. – OF. *trenchant* (mod. *tranchant*), prp. of *trancher*; see prec., -ANT.

trencher tre·nᵗʃəɹ †cutting instrument; board on which food was served XIV (hence *t.-man* feeder, eater XVI); (also *t.-cap*) academic cap thought to resemble a square platter XVIII. – AN. *trenchour*, OF. *trencheoir*, f. *trenchier* TRENCH. See -ER², -OR¹.

trend trend †revolve, roll OE.; take a specified direction XVI. OE. *trendan* (in comps. *for|trendan* close by rolling up a stone, *sin|trendan* in prp. round in form), f. Germ. **trend*- **trand*- **trund*-, repr. also by OE. *trinda* round lump, ball, *ātrendlian* roll away, and forms cited s.v. TRUNDLE, *syn|trændel* round, *trændende* steep, OE. *trandel*, *trindel*, *tryndel* round object (in place-names). Hence sb. the way something turns away, general direction. XVIII.

trental tre·ntəl set of thirty requiem masses. XIV. – OF. *trentel* and medL. *trentālis*, f. popL. **trenta*, for L. *trīginta* thirty, f. *trēs* TRI- + **gint*- ten.

Trentine tre·ntain Tridentine. XVII. f. *Trent* (see TRIDENTINE) + -INE¹.

trepan tripæ·n (surg.) saw for cutting out pieces of bone. XIV. – medL. *trepanum* – Gr. *trúpanon* borer, f. *trupân* pierce, bore, *trúpē* hole. So vb. and **trepan**A·TION. XIV. – (O)F. *trépaner*, *trépanation*; cf. G. *trepanieren*.

trepidation trepidei·ʃən tremulous agitation, flurry; vibration, tremor. XVII. – L. *trepidātiō(n-)*, f. *trepidāre*, f. *trepidus*; see INTREPID, -ATION.

trespass tre·spəs transgression XIII (S.Eng. Leg.); actionable wrong or offence XIV. – OF. *trespas* (mod. *trépas*), f. vb. *trespasser* (mod. *trépasser* pass away, die), whence ME. *trespasse* XIV = Pr., Sp. *traspasar*, It. *trapassare* – medL. *transpassāre* (see TRANS-, PASS²).

tress tres plait or long lock of hair. XIII (S. Eng. Leg.). – (O)F. *tresse*, †*tresce* = Pr. *tressa*, It. *treccia*, beside (O)F. *tresser*, †*trecier* = It. *trecciare*, of unkn. origin.

-tress tris comp. suffix formed by the addition of -ESS¹ to sbs. in *-ter*, *-tor*, as *actor* | *actress*, *hunter* | *huntress*.

tressure tre·sjuəɹ, tre·ʃəɹ †headdress XIV; (her.) diminutive orle XV; (numism.) circular enclosure XVIII. Earlier *tressour* – OF. *tressour* :– L. **triciātōrium*; later *tressure* – OF. *tress(e)ure*. See TRESS, -URE.

trestle tre·sl support consisting of a bar with diverging legs. XIV. – OF. *trestel* (mod. *tréteau*) :– Rom. **transtellum*, dim. of L. *transtrum* beam; see -EL².

tret tret allowance of 4 lb. in 104 lb., after deduction of tare. XV. poss. – AN., OF. *tret*, var. of *trait* draught (cf. TRAIT), but the sense-development is obscure.

trews trūz close-fitting garment for buttocks and thighs. XVI (Sc.). – Ir. *trius*, Gael. *triubhas* (sg.); cf. TROUSERS.

trey trei three at cards, etc. XIV (Ch.). – OF. *trei*, *treis* (mod. *trois*) = Prov. *trei-s*, Sp. *tres*, It. *tre* :– L. *trēs* THREE.

tri- trai (occas.) tri repr. L. and Gr. *tri-* (partly through F.), comb. form of L. *trēs*, Gr. *treîs* THREE, *trís* thrice, used in many technical terms with the senses 'three', 'three times', 'triple', 'triply'. Adoptions and adaptations and new formations are made in conditions similar to those of comps. of BI-, the main difference being that there is a larger proportion of Gr. originals in *tri-*.

triad trai·æd set of three. XVI. – F. *triade* or late L. *triad-*, *trias* – Gr. *triad-*, *triás*, f. *tri-* THREE; see -AD¹.

trial¹ trai·əl act of trying, fact of being tried. XVI. – AF. *trial*, also *triel* (latinized *triallum*, perh. the immed. source), f. *trier* TRY; see -AL².

trial² trai·əl (gram.) of a form used to express three (cf. TRINAL). XIX. f. TRI- (after **dual**) + -AL¹.

trialogue trai·ələg colloquy between three persons. XVI (More). – medL. *trialogus* formed by the substitution of TRI- for *di-* of L. *dialogus* DIALOGUE, on the erron. supposition that this is DI-².

triangle trai·æŋgl a three-sided figure. XIV (Trevisa). – (O)F. *triangle* or L. *triangulum*, sb. use of n. of *triangulus* three-cornered, f. *tri-* TRI- + *angulus* ANGLE. So **tria·ngul**AR. XVI. – late L.

triarchy trai·ɑ̄ɹki government by three rulers jointly; group of three districts each under its own ruler. XVII. f. TRI- + Gr. *-arkhiā* government, -ARCHY, or – Gr. *tri-arkhiā* triumvirate. Cf. TETRARCH, -ARCHY.

trias trai·əs three, triad XVII; (geol. after G. *trias* 1834) series of strata between the Jurassic and Permian, so called because divisible into three groups XIX. – late L. *trias* – Gr. *triás* TRIAD. Hence **triass**IC traiæ·sik. XIX; after G. *triassisch*.

tribe traib community of persons claiming a common ancestor, spec. each of the 12 divisions of Israel (XIII) XIV (Wycl., Gower); one of the political divisions of the ancient Roman people; race of people; class or set of persons XVI; group in the classification of animals, etc. XVII. First in pl. †*tribuz* (XIII), †*tribus* (XIV) – (O)F. *tribus* pl. of *tribu* or L. *tribūs*, pl. of *tribus*, whence immed. *tribe* (XIV, Wycl.); the L. word has been supposed to be based on **tri-* THREE. Hence **tri·b**AL[1] XVII. **tribes**MAN trai·bzmən. XVIII (Southey); f. *tribe's*.

triblet tri·blit cylindrical rod for forging nuts, etc. XVII (Cotgr.). – F. *triboulet*, of unkn. origin.

tribrach tri·bræk (pros.) foot of 3 short syllables. XVI. – L. *tribrachys* – Gr. *tri-brakhus*, f. *tri-* TRI- + *brakhús* short (cf. MERRY).

tribulation tribjulei·ʃən great affliction or misery. XIII (AncrR.). – (O)F. *tribulation* – ecclL. *trībulātiō(n-)*, f. L. *trībulāre* press, (esp. pass. in Christian use) oppress, afflict, f. *trībulum* threshing-sledge, f. **trī-*, var. of **ter(e)-* rub (see ATTRITION, CONTRITION, DETRITUS, THROW, and TRITE).

tribune[1] tri·bjūn, trai·- officer in the administration of ancient Rome. XIV. – L. *tribūnus*, prob. orig. sb. use of adj. (sc. *magistratus*) 'magistrate of a tribe', f. *tribus* TRIBE. So **tribun**AL tri-, treibjū·nəl dais, raised throne, judgement seat; court of justice XVI; place of judgement, judicial authority XVII. – (O)F. *tribunal* or L. *tri-būnal, -āle*.

tribune[2] tri-, trai·bjūn saloon in the Galleria degli Uffizi in Florence, Italy XVII (Evelyn); apse of a basilica; dais, rostrum, bishop's throne XVIII. – F. *tribune* – It. *tri-buna* – medL. *tribūna*, for L. *tribūnal*.

tribute tri·bjūt tax paid to a superior XIV; transf. and fig. XVI. – L. *tribūtum*, sb. use of n. of *tribūtus*, pp. of *tribuere* assign, allot, grant, prop. to divide among the tribes, f. *tribus* TRIBE. Cf. F. *tribut* (XV). So **tri·bu-t**ARY paying tribute XIV (Wycl. Bible); paid in tribute XVI (Sh.); subsidiary, auxiliary XVII (*rivers*, Sh.). – L. *tribūtārius*, f. *tri-būtum, -us*; sb. one who pays tribute (XIV) XV; tributary stream XIX (W. Irving).

trice trais phr. †*at a t., in a t.* in an instant, instantly, XV. f. *trice* vb. pull, haul – MDu. *trīsen* (Du. *trijsen* hoist) = MLG. *trīssen* (whence G. *triezen*, Da. *trisse* hoist), rel. to MDu. *trīse*, etc. windlass, pulley, of unkn. origin.

-trice tris suffix of fem. agent-nouns, F. repr. of -TRIX, formerly freq., as in *directrice, mediatrice, victrice*.

triceps trai·seps having three heads or (of a muscle) points of origin. XVI. – L. *triceps*, f. *tri-* TRI- + *-ceps*, adj. comb. form corr. to *caput* HEAD (cf. BICEPS).

trichi tri·tʃi short for *Trichinopoli* (cigar), name of a district and city in Madras, India. XIX.

trichinosis trikinou·sis disease due to trichinæ (parasitic worms) in the alimentary canal. XIX. f. modL. *trichina*, f. Gr. *trīkhinos* of hair, f. *trikh-, thríx* hair. See -INE[2], -OSIS.

tricho- tri·kou-, trai·kou, before a vowel **trich-**, repr. comb. form *trikho-* of Gr. *thríx* hair.

trichotomy tri-, traikɔ·təmi threefold division. XVII. f. Gr. *tríkha* in three, triply, after DICHOTOMY.

trick trik A. crafty or mean device XV (Hoccleve); dexterous artifice XVI; B. (bad or unpleasant) habit XVI; C. (her.) sketch of a coat of arms XVI; D. cards played and won in a round XVI. – OF. *trique*, dial. var. of *triche*, f. *trichier* (mod. *tricher*) = Pr. *tricar*, It. *triccare* deceive, cheat. Hence (presumably) **trick** vb. A. cheat; B. attire, deck; C. sketch, draw in outline XVI; in B perh. assoc. with F. †*s'estriquer* 'to tricke, decke, or trimme up himselfe' (Cotgr.), in C with Du. *trekken* 'delineare' (Kilian), 'to delineate, to make a draught' (Hexham). **tri·ck**ERY. XVIII. **trick**SY tri·ksi smart, spruce XVI (Latimer); playful, whimsical XVI (Sh.); ticklish XIX. **tri·ck**Y[1] deceitful XVIII; difficult to handle XIX.

trickle tri·kl flow in successive drops. Forms with variation of vowel and cons. have been current since XIV, intended to be imit. of the sound of falling drops, viz. *trygle, trikle, trekel, trigle, trinkle, tringle*; see -LE[3]. Hence sb. XVI.

triclinium traikli·niəm couch on three sides of a dining table. XVII. – L. *triclīnium* – Gr. *triklī́nion*, dim. of *triklīnos* dining room with three couches, f. *tri-* TRI- + *klī́nē* (see CLINIC).

tricolour, -color trai·kʌləɹ three-coloured, esp. of the red, white, and blue French national flag. XVIII (Scott). – F. *tricolore* – late L. *tricolor (-ōr-)*, f. *tri-* TRI- + *color* COLOUR.

tricorne trai·kɔ̄ɹn three-horned (creature, hat). XVIII. – F. *tricorne* or L. *tricornis*, f. *tri-* TRI- + *cornū* HORN.

tricot tri·kou knitting. XIX. – F. *tricot*, f. *tricoter*, of unkn. origin.

trictrac tri·ktræk form of backgammon. XVII. – F. *tric-trac*, imit. of the clicking noises made by pieces in the game.

tricycle trai·sikl three-wheeled velocipede. XIX. f. TRI-+CYCLE; hence in F. ¶ Earlier (1827) in F. a three-wheeled coach.

trident trai·dənt three-pronged instrument. XVI (Nashe). – L. *tridēns, -dent-*, f. *tri-* TRI-+*dēns* TOOTH.

Tridentine traide·ntain pert. to the city of Trent in Tyrol and the Council of the Roman Catholic Church held there 1545–63. XVI. – medL. *Tridentīnus*, f. *Tridentum* Trent; see -INE[1].

triennial traie·niəl lasting three years; recurring every three years. XVII. f. late L. *triennis* of three years, *triennium* period of three years, f. *tri-* TRI-+*annus* year; see ANNUAL, -AL[1]. Cf. BIENNIAL.

trifid trai·fid divided into three. XVIII. – L. *trifidus*, f. *tri-* TRI-+*fid-*, base of *findere* split (cf. FISSION).

trifle trai·fl †false or idle tale XIII (AncrR.); matter of little value XIII (S. Eng. Leg.); trinket, knick-knack XIV; slight piece, small sum; light confection XVI. ME. *truf(f)le* – OF. *truf(f)le* by-form of *truf(f)e* deceit, gibe, corr. to It. *truffa*, Sp., Pg., *trufa*; of unkn. origin. Hence vb. XIV; earlier in †*bitrufle* cheat, delude. ¶ The form *trifle*, dating from XIV, is ambiguous for the orig. pronunc. of *i*.

triforium traifɔ̄·riəm (archit.) gallery in the wall over the arches at the sides of nave and choir, first found in Gervase of Canterbury (*c*.1185) in ref. to Canterbury Cathedral, taken up by antiquaries. XVIII. Of unkn. origin.

trigger tri·gəɹ movable catch or lever. XVII. Earliest form *tricker* (which was usual till *c*.1750 and is in widespread dial. use) – Du. *trekker*, f. *trekken* pull; see TREK, -ER[1].

triglyph trai·glif (archit.) in the Doric order, block with three vertical grooves. XVI. – L. *triglyphus* – Gr. *trígluphos*, f. *tri-* TRI-+*gluphḗ* carving (cf. CLEAVE).

trigonometry trigənɔ·mitri branch of mathematics dealing with the measurements of triangles. XVII. – modL. *trigōnometria*, f. Gr. *trígōnon* triangle; see TRI-, -GON, -METRY.

trilby tri·lbi man's soft felt hat; (pl.) bare feet. XIX. Name of the heroine of a novel entitled 'Trilby', by George du Maurier, as applied to articles used in the dramatized version of the novel, and to the heroine's use of bare feet.

trill tril tremulous utterance of a note XVII (Lovelace); vibration of tongue, etc. in pronouncing a consonant XIX. – It. *trillo*, †*triglio*; so vb. XVII (Pepys). – It. *trillare*.

trillion tri·ljən third power of a million (in France and U.S.A., a thousand billions). XVII (Locke). – F. *trillion* (N. Chuquet) or It. *trilione*, formed like BILLION on *million* with substitution of TRI-.

trilobite trai·ləbait (palæont.) member of a group of extinct arthropodous animals having a three-lobed body. XIX. – modL. *trilobītes*, f. Gr.; see TRI-, LOBE, -ITE.

trilogy tri·lədʒi group of three related literary works. XIX. – Gr. *trilogiā*, f. *tri-* TRI-+*lógos* discourse; see -Y[3], -LOGY.

trim trim well equipped, esp. neatly made. XVI. Earliest in the adv. *trimly* (Dunbar); rel. to vb. *trim*, of approximately even date, which became widely applied in the first half of XVI, but is of obscure origin, since, though formally it could repr. OE. *trymian, trymman* strengthen, confirm (f. *trum* firm, strong), there is no connecting evidence of unequivocal character between the OE. period and 1500. Hence **trim** sb. (XVI, Sh.) trim condition (often of a ship), proper array or equipment; **tri·mmER**[1] one who trims XVI, spec. in statecraft, between opposing parties (XVII), chiefly in unfavourable sense but formerly taken to be one who 'keeps even the ship of state'.

trimeter tri·mitəɹ (pros.) verse of three measures. XVI. – L. *trimetrus* – Gr. *trímetros*, f. *tri-* TRI- + *métron* measure, METRE[1].

trin trin (pl.) three young born at one time, (sg.) one of these. XIX. app. alt. of TWIN by assim. to TRI-.

trine train triple XIV (Ch.); (astrol.) pert. to the aspect of two heavenly bodies that are a third part of the zodiac distant from each other; fig. benign XV. – OF. *trin*, fem. *trine* :– L. *trīnus* threefold, f. *trēs, tria* THREE, + multiplicative suffix. So **trinAL**[1] trai·nəl. XVI (Spenser); (gram.) expressing three XIX. – medL. *trīnālis* (Adamnan), f. L. *trīnus*.

trinitro- trainai·trou (chem.) formative denoting that three nitro-groups (NO_2) have replaced three hydrogen atoms in the substance designated by the second el. Cf. T.N.T.

trinity tri·niti (*T-*) being of God in three Persons; God three in one XIII; (*t-*) set of three. – (O)F. *trinité*, corr. to Pr., Sp. *trinidad*, It. *trinità* :– L. *trīnitāt-, -tās* (in Christian use (Tert.), based on Gr. *triás* TRIAD) triad, trio, f. *trīnus* TRINE; see -ITY. So **trinitA·RIAN**. XVI. The earliest uses are †(1) holding unorthodox opinions about the Trinity, (2) belonging to the order of the Holy Trinity XVII; since XVIII the sense 'relating to the Trinity, holding the doctrine of the Trinity' has been established. f. modL. *trīnitārius* (XVI); cf. F. *trinitaire* (Calvin).

trinket tri·ŋkit †small article belonging to an outfit; small ornament or decoration. XVI. Of unkn. origin.

trinomial trainou·miəl (math., etc.) consisting of three terms. XVIII. f. TRI-+ *-nomial* of BINOMIAL.

trio trī·ou composition for three voices or instruments. XVIII. – It. *trio* (partly through F.), f. L. *trēs*, n. *tria* THREE, after *duo*.

triolet trī·-, trai·əlet (pros.) stanza of 8 lines in which the 1st line is repeated as the 4th and 7th and the 2nd as the 8th. XVII. – F. *triolet*, f. *trio* (see prec.) and -LET.

trip trip A. tread or step lightly XIV (Ch.); B. cause to stumble by striking the foot (feet) from under the body; make a false step XV; C. (naut.) †tack XVII; raise (an anchor) clear from the bottom (cf. ATRIP) XVIII. – OF. *treper*, *trip(p)er* = Pr. *trepar* – MDu. *trippen* skip, hop, rel. to OE. *treppan* tread, trample. Hence **trip** sb. A. 'stroke or catch by which the wrestler supplants his antagonist' (J.) XV (Lydg.); B. light movement with the feet XVI; short journey XVII. **tri·ppER**[1] one who trips XIV; excursionist XIX.

tripartite traipā·ɹtait divided into or involving three parts. XIV (Lydg.). – L. *tripartītus*, f. *tri-* TRI- + pp. of *partīrī* divide, PART.

tripe traip stomach of an ox, etc. used for food. XIII. – (O)F. *tripe* = Pr. *tripa*, It. *trippa*, of unkn. origin.

triphthong tri·fþɔŋ combination of three vowels in one syllable. XVI. – F. *triphtongue*, f. *tri-* TRI-, after DIPHTHONG.

triple tri·pl threefold; treble XVI; sb. XV. – (O)F. *triple* or L. *triplus* – Gr. *triploûs*, f. *tri-* TRI-+*pl-* (see FOLD[2]), for L. *triplex*. Hence **tripLET** tri·plit set of three, as of lines of verse XVII, notes of music XIX; after DOUBLET. **tri·plex** (anglicized XVII Sh.). So **triplicate** tri·plikət threefold, triple XV; sb. XVIII. – L. *triplicātus*, pp. of *triplicāre*, f. *triplic-*, *-plex*. **triplicITY** tripli·sĭti threefold condition; division into three groups of the signs of the Zodiac XIV (Trevisa). – late L. *triplicitās*, f. *triplic-*, *-plex*.

tripod trai·pɔd three-legged vessel or support (spec. stool). XVII (Holland, Chapman). – L. *tripod-* (nom. *-pūs*) – Gr. *trípous*, *-pod-*, f. *tri-* TRI-+*poús* FOOT.

tripos trai·pɔs †tripod XVI; at Cambridge Univ., formerly, bachelor of arts appointed to dispute humorously at Commencement (so called from the tripod on which he sat), (hence) set of verses written for this, (later) list of candidates qualified for honours in mathematics printed on the back of the paper containing the verses, (subsequently) final honours examination for the bachelor's degree, first in mathematics, later in other subjects XVII (Pepys). Unexpl. alt. of L. *tripūs* – Gr. *trípous* TRIPOD.

triptych tri·ptik tablet or card folded in three XVIII; picture or carving hinged in three divisions XIX. f. TRI-, after DIPTYCH; cf. F. *triptyque*.

triquetrous traikwe·trəs three-cornered. XVII (Sir T. Browne). f. L. *triquetrus*; see TRI-, -OUS, WHET.

trireme trai·rīm ancient galley with three banks of oars. XVII (Holland). – (O)F. *trirème* or L. *trirēmis*, f. *tri-* TRI-+*rēmus* oar.

trisagion trisæ·giən (liturg.) Eucharistic hymn beginning with a threefold invocation of God ('Holy, Holy, Holy') XVII. – Gr. *trisávgion*, n. of *triságios*, f. *trís* thrice (see THREE) + *hágios* holy. Cf. TERSANCTUS, SANCTUS.

trisect traise·kt divide into three parts. XVII. f. TRI-+*sect-*, pp. stem of L. *secāre* cut, after BISECT.

triste trist dismal, gloomy. XVIII. F. – L. *tristis*. Anglicized *trist* (now obs.) from XV.

tritagonist traitæ·gənist, tri- third actor in a Gr. tragedy. XIX. – Gr. *tritagōnistḗs*, f. *trítos* THIRD+*agōnistḗs* actor, f. *agōnízesthai* (see AGONIZE).

trite trait worn out by use. XVI. – L. *trītus*, pp. of *terere* rub; cf. TRIBULATION, THROW.

trithing trai·ðiŋ (hist.) see RIDING.

Triton trai·tən (Gr. and Rom. myth.) sea-god, son of Poseidon and Amphitrite XVI; (zool.) genus of marine gasteropods XVIII.

triturate tri·tjureit pulverize. XVII. f. pp. stem of late L. *trītūrāre* thresh corn, f. L. *trītūra* rubbing, threshing, f. *trīt-*, pp. stem of *terere*; see TRITE, -URE, -ATE[3].

triumph trai·əmf (Roman hist.) solemn entry of a victorious general into Rome XIV (Ch., Trevisa); victorious achievement XIV. – OF. *triumphe* (mod. *triomphe*) – L. *triumphus*, earlier *triumpus*, prob. – Gr. *thríambos* hymn to Bacchus (Dionysus). So **tri·umph** vb. XVI. **triu·mphAL**[1], **triu·mphANT** XV. – (O)F. or L. Cf. TRUMP[2].

triumvir traiʌ·mvə̄r (Rom. hist.) one of a board of three coordinate magistrates. XVI. – L. *triumvir*, sg. deduced from pl. *triumvirī* (also *trēsvirī*, III *virī*), back-formation from *trium virōrum*, g. pl. of *trēs virī* three men. So **triu·mvirATE**[1] -vĭrət. XVI. – L. *trium virātus*.

triune trai·jūn (of the Godhead) three in one. XVII. f. TRI- + L. *ūnus* ONE. So **triU·NITY**. ¶ Earlier †*trinune*, †*-union*, †*-unity* (cf. TRINE).

trivet tri·vit stand or support for a pot, etc., orig. three-footed. XV. Late ME. *trevet*, repr. OE. *trefet* (recorded once in doubtful application) – L. *triped-*, *tripēs*, f. *tri-* TRI-+ *pēs* FOOT, after Gr. *trípous* TRIPOD.

trivial tri·viəl pert. to the trivium of mediæval learning XV; †such as may be met with anywhere XVI (Nashe); of small account XVI (Sh.); (nat. hist.) specific; popular XVIII. – L. *triviālis*, f. next; see -AL[1].

trivium tri·viəm in the Middle Ages, the lower division of the seven liberal arts (grammar, rhetoric, logic), the upper four (QUADRIVIUM) being arithmetic, geometry, astronomy, and music. XIX. – medL. use of L. *trivium*, place where three roads meet f. *tri-* TRI- + *via* way.

-trix triks suffix of L. fem. agent-nouns corr. to mascs. in -TOR, as *adjūtrix, imperātrīx, venātrīx*, fems. of *adjūtor* helper, *imperātor* commander, *venātor* hunter; such sbs. were adopted from XV from L. of various periods, as *administratrix, executrix, mediatrix, testatrix*; (geom.) applied (sc. *linea* line) to certain straight lines or curves, as *directrix, tractrix*. Cf. -TRICE.

troche troutʃ flat round tablet or lozenge. XVI. Early in pl. *trochies, trotches* (whence sg. *troch-e*), alt. of *trocis, -isce, -iske* (*c*.1400 to XVIII) – F. *trochisque* – late L. *trochiscus* – Gr. *trokhískos* small wheel or globe, pill, lozenge, dim. of *trokhós* wheel; rel. to *trékhein* run.

trochee trou·ki (pros.) foot consisting of a long followed by a short syllable (–⏑). XVI. – L. *trochæus* – Gr. *trokhaîos* (sc. *poús*) running, tripping (foot), f. *trókhos* running, course, rel. to *trékhein* run, with poss. Sl., Celtic, and Germ. cogns. **trochaic** troukei·ik. XVI. – L. *trochaicus* – Gr. *trokhaikós*. Cf. F. *trochée, trochaïque*.

trochilus trɔ·kiləs small Egyptian bird said to have picked crocodile's teeth. XVI. L., – Gr. *trokhílos*, f. var. stem of *trékhein* run.

trocho- trɔ·kou comb. form of Gr. *trokhós* wheel, disc (see prec.).

troglodyte trɔ·glŏdait cave-dweller (chiefly prehistoric). XVI. – L. *trōglodyta* – Gr. *trōglodútēs*, corrupt form of *trōgodútēs* (V B.C.) after *trōglē* hole.

troika troi·ka Russ. vehicle drawn by three horses abreast. XIX. Russ., f. *tróe* THREE.

Trojan trou·dʒən pert. to, native of, ancient Troy; roisterer, good fellow; brave fellow. XVII. repl. earlier *Troian* (XIV, Ch.), *Troyan* (XV) – L. *Trōiānus*, f. *Trōia* Troy; see -AN. ¶ OE. had *Troiānisć*.

troll[1] troul †A. move about or to and fro XIV (PPl.); B. roll, bowl XV; C. sing in full round voice XVI; D. angle with a running line XVII. Of doubtful identity in all senses; F. *trôler* (†*troller*) wander casually, and (M)HG. *trollen* stroll, toddle, have been compared.

troll[2] troul Scand. myth., one of a supernatural race of giants, dwarfs, or imps. XIX. (preceded by a Sc. ex. of XVII). – ON., Sw. *troll* (Da. *trold*); of unkn. origin.

trolley trɔ·li low truck or cart. XIX. Of dial. origin; cf. local *troll*, †*trole* (XVII), presumably f. TROLL[1], and the similar *lorry, rolly, rully*.

trollop trɔ·ləp sluttish or loose woman. XVII (Wither). Of unkn. origin; for form and sense cf. TRULL.

trombone trɔmbou·n large loud-toned wind instrument of music, with a sliding arrangement for extending the tube. XVIII. – F. *trombone* (earlier †*trombon*) or its source It. *trombone*, augm. of *tromba* TRUMP[1]; cf. -OON.

tromometer troumɔ·mitəɹ instrument for measuring earth-tremors. XIX. f. Gr. *trómos* trembling (rel. to *trémein*; see TREMOR) + -METER.

tronk trɔŋk (S. Africa) prison. XVII (*trunke*), Afrikaans – Pg. *tronco* TRUNK.

troop trūp body of soldiers, (pl.) armed forces; number of persons collected together XVI; signal on a drum for assembling troops XVII. (Early also *troupe, trowpe*) – F. *troupe* (whence It. *truppa*), poss. back-formation from *troupeau* flock, herd (= Pr. *tropel*), dim. f. medL. *troppus* (sc. *de jumentis*) herd of mares, prob. of Germ. origin. Hence vb. gather in a troop XVI; *t. the colour* beat the drum for the reception of the colour at the mounting of the guard XVII; **troo·per**[1] cavalry soldier (first in Scotland of the Covenanting Army 1640).

tropæolum tropī·ələm S. Amer. genus of herbs. XVIII. modL. (Linnæus 1737), f. L. *tropæum* TROPHY; so called from the resemblance of the leaf to a shield and of the flower to a helmet.

trope troup (rhet.) use of a word or phrase in a sense not proper to it, figure of speech XVI (Tindale); (Liturg.) phrase introduced into the text for musical embellishment XIX. – L. *tropus* figure of speech – Gr. *trópos* turn, rel. to *trépein* turn (cf. OL. *trepit* turns). So **tro·per** book of tropes. OE. *tropere* – medL. *troperium*, var. of *tropārium*; cf. OF. *trop(i)er*.

trophic trɔ·fik pert. to nutrition. XIX. – Gr. *trophikós*, f. *trophḗ* nourishment.

tropho- trɔ·fou comb. form of Gr. *trophḗ*, rel. to *tréphein* nourish, used in scientific terms. XIX.

trophy trou·fi erection serving as a memorial of victory in war; prize, booty; monument, memorial XVI. – F. *trophée* – L. *trophæum*, earlier *tropæum* – Gr. *trópaion*, sb. use of n. of *tropaîos*, f. *tropḗ* turning, putting to flight, defeat, rel. to *trépein* turn (cf. TROPE).

tropic trɔ·pik †each of the two solstitial points XIV (Ch.); each of the two circles of the celestial sphere touching the ecliptic at the solstitial points; either boundary of the torrid zone XVI; pl. region between these XIX; adj. tropical XVI. – late L. *tropicus* (whence also F. *tropique*, etc.) – Gr. *tropikós* (1) pert. to the 'turning' of the sun at the solstice, (2) figurative, sb. (sc. *kúklos* circle), f. *tropḗ* turning; see TROPE, -IC. So **tro·pical** pert.

to a tropic XVI (of the torrid zone XVII); metaphorical XVI. So **tropicopolitan** trɔ·pikoupɔ·litən (nat. hist.) belonging to the tropics. XIX (1878, P. L. Sclater); after *cosmopolitan*.

trot[1] trɔt gait of a quadruped between walking and running. XIII (Cursor M.). – (O)F. *trot*, f. *troter* (mod. *trotter*), whence **trot** vb. XIV (PPl., Ch.); Rom. **trottāre* (Pr., Sp. *trotar*, It. *trottare*), of Germ. orig.; cf. OHG. *trottōn* (G. *trotten*), intensive f. base of *tretan* step, walk, TREAD. Hence **tro·tter**[1] trotting horse XIV; (pl.) feet of a quadruped, esp. used for food (? XIV), XVI; cf. OF. *trotier*, medL. *trotārius*.

trot[2] trɔt old woman, hag. XIV. ME. *trat(t)e*, early mod. *trot* (XVI), obscurely rel. to AN. *trote* (Gower), of unkn. origin.

troth trouþ, trɔþ (arch.) good faith, loyalty; plighted word; †truth XVI. Later form of ME. *trouth(e)*, *trowth(e)*, var. with stress-shifting and assim. to TROW of *treowþ* TRUTH. Cf. BETROTH.

troubadour trū·bəduəɹ Provençal lyric poet. XVIII. – F. *troubadour* – Pr. *trobador* = OF. *troveor*, nom. *trovere* TROUVÈRE, f. Pr. *trobar*, OF. *trover* (mod. *trouver*) compose, (later) invent, find (whence Sp. *trovar*, It. *trovare*), of much disputed origin.

trouble trʌ·bl mental distress XIII; public disturbance XIV; pains, exertion; *in* or *into tr.* liable to punishment, etc. XVII. – OF. *truble*, *turble*, *tourble* (mod. *trouble*), f. *tourbler*, etc. (mod. *troubler* = Pr. *treb(o)lar*, Rum. *tulbura*), whence **trouble** vb. XIII. :– Rom. **turbulāre*, f. **turbulus* (whence (O)F. *trouble* disturbed, turbid), for L. *turbidus* TURBID. Hence **trou·blesome** †full of trouble; giving trouble. XVI. So **trou·blous**. XV. – OF. *troubleus*.

trough trɔ̄f oblong open vessel, esp. to contain liquid; *t. of the sea* hollow on the surface between waves XVII. OE. *trog* = OFris., OS. *trog*, OHG. *troc* (Du., G. *trog*), ON. *trog* :– CGerm. (exc. Gothic) **trugaz* :– IE. **drukós*, f. **dru-* wood, TREE.

trounce trauns † afflict, harass; thrash, belabour XVI; censure severely XVIII. Of unkn. origin; connexion with OF. *troncer*, *troncher* cut, cut off a piece from, retrench, cannot be made out.

troupe trūp company of players, dancers, etc. XIX. – F. (TROOP).

trousers trau·zəɹz †trews; loose-fitting garment for the loins and legs XVII. Extension, after DRAWERS, of (arch.) *trouse* (XVI) – Ir., Gael. *triubhas* TREWS; attrib. usu. in sg. form, e.g. *trouser leg*.

trousseau tru·sou bride's outfit of clothes, etc. XIX. F., dim. of *trousse* TRUSS.

trout traut freshwater fish Salmo fario. Late OE. *truht* – late L. *tructa* (also CRom. exc. Rum.).

trouvère trūvɛə·ɹ one of a school of epic poets of N. France. XIX (Southey has *trouveur* 1795). F., and OF. *trovere*, obl. *troveor* = Pr. *trobador* TROUBADOUR.

trove short for TREASURE TROVE.

trover trou·vəɹ (leg.) act of finding and keeping possession of a property. XVI. – AN. sb. use of OF. *trover* (mod. *trouver* find; cf. TROUBADOUR); see -ER[5].

trow trou, trau (arch., esp. in *I trow*) believe, suppose. Of mixed origin; (1) OE. *trēowian*, *trēowan*, f. *trēow* truce, with secondary stressing of the diphthong; (2) OE. *trūwian*; cf. TRUCE, TRUE, TRUST.

trowel trau·əl tool consisting of a plate of metal or wood with a short handle. XIV. ME *truel*, *trowel* – OF. *truele* (mod. *truelle*) – medL. *truella*, alt. of L. *trulla* ladle, scoop, f. *trua* skimmer, spoon.

troy troi system of weights used for precious stones and metals. XIV. orig. in phr. *marc. de troye*, *pound of troye*; said to be taken from a weight used at the fair of *Troyes* (Aube, France), with which cf. the Sc. form †*trois*, †*troyis*.

truant trū·ənt †sturdy beggar, idle rogue XIII (S. Eng. Leg.); pupil absent from school without leave XV; adj. XVI. – OF. *truant* (mod. *truand*) = Pr. *truan* (whence Sp. *truhan*, Pg. *truão*) :– Gallo-Rom. **trūgant-*, prob. of Celtic origin (cf. W. *truan*, Gael. *truaghan* wretched).

truce trūs suspension of hostilities. XIII. ME. *trew(e)s*, *trues* (repl. OE. pl. *trēowa*, used as sg.), pl. of *tru(w)e*, OE. *trēow*, corr. to OFris. *trouwe*, *triūwe*, *triōwe*, OS. *treuwa*, OHG. *triuwa* (Du. *trouw*, G. *treue*), Goth. *triggva* covenant; the same base (**treww-*) is recognized in Gr. *droós* firm, OIr. *derb*, W. *drūd* strong; cf. TROW, TRUE, TRUST.

truchman trʌ·tʃmən interpreter. XV. Late ME. *tourcheman* (Caxton) – medL. *turchemannus* (whence also F. *trucheman*, Sp. *truchimán*, It. *turcimanno*) – Arab. *turjamān*; cf. DRAGOMAN, TARGUM.

trucial trū·ʃ[i]əl pert. to a truce regulating the relations of Arab sheiks to each other and to the British Government, 1876. f. TRUCE + -IAL, prob. after *fiducial*.

truck[1] give in exchange XIII (AncrR.); barter away XVII; pay otherwise than in money XIX. ME. *trukie*, later *trukke* – AN. **truquer*, OF. **troquer* (reflected in medL. *trocāre*) = Pr. *trucar*, Sp. *trocar*, of unkn. origin. Hence sb. (cf. AN. *truke* XIV) barter XVI; dealings, traffic XVII; payment in kind, goods supplied instead of wages. XVIII.

truck[2] trʌk small solid wooden wheel or block XVII; wheeled vehicle for heavy weights XVIII. poss. shortening of next.

truckle trʌ·kl pulley, sheave; small roller or wheel under a bed, etc. XV; (short for *t.-bed* XV) low bed running on castors, usu. pushed under a high bed when not in use XVII. Late ME. *trocle, trokel, trookyll* – AN. *trocle* – L. *trochlea* – Gr. *trokhiliā, -eiā* sheaf of a pulley. Hence vb. †occupy a truckle-bed XV; yield obsequiously *to* XVII.

truculent trʌ·kjŭlənt, trū-· marked by a hostile, merciless temper or behaviour. XVI. – L. *truculentus*, f. *truc-, trux* fierce, savage; see -ULENT.

trudge trʌdʒ †be off, depart; walk laboriously XVI. Early forms also †*tredge*, (dial.) *tridge*; of unkn. origin.

trudgen trʌ·dʒən hand-over-hand stroke in swimming familiarized by one John *Trudgen* about 1865.

true trū steadfast; trustworthy OE.; consistent with fact XIII; real, genuine XIV. OE. *ġe|trīewe, trēowe*, later *trȳwe* (ME. *trewe, truwe, tru*) = OFris. *triūwe, trouwe*, OS. *triuwi*, OHG. *gi|triuwi* (Du. *getrouw*, G. *treu*), ON. *tryggr*, Goth. *triggws*, f. the CGerm. sb. repr. by TRUCE. The sp. *true* dates from XV.

truffle trʌ·fl underground (edible) fungus. XVI. prob. – Du. *truffel*, †*truffele* – F. *truffle* (now *truffe*), perh. to be referred ult. to popL. **tūfera*, for L. *tūbera*, pl. of *tūber* TUBER.

truism trū·izm self-evident truth. XVIII (Swift). f. TRUE + -ISM.

trull trʌl (arch.) drab, trollop; †girl, wench. XVI. one of a group of nearly synon. sbs. having initial *tr*, as TROLLOP, TROT², †*trug* (XVI); cf. It. †*trucca*, G. *trulle, trolle*.

truLY² trū·li adv. of TRUE, OE. *trēowlīċe*.

trump¹ trʌmp (arch.) trumpet. XIII (RGlouc.) ME. *trompe* – (O)F. *trompe* = Pr. *tromba, trompa*, Sp. *trompa*, It. *tromba* – OHG. *trumpa, trumba*, ON. *trumba*, prob. of imit. origin. So **trump** vb. XIII (Cursor M.). – (O)F. *tromper*.

trump² trʌmp card of a suit that ranks above all others XVI (Latimer); first-rate fellow XIX. alt. of TRIUMPH, also used by Latimer in this sense and for an obs. card-game; cf. the pun in Sh., 'Ant. and Cleop.' IV xii [xiv] 20. 'She . . . has pack'd cards with Cæsar and false played my glory Unto an enemy's triumph'. Hence **trump** vb. put a trump on (a trick); †get in the way XVI; †bring *up* or forward; get *up* unscrupulously XVII.

trumpery trʌ·mpəri †fraud, trickery XV; trash, rubbish XVI; adj. paltry, trashy XVI. – (O)F. *tromperie*, f. *tromper* deceive, of unkn. origin; see -ERY.

trumpet trʌ·mpit musical wind instrument of narrow bore. XIII. – (O)F. *trompette*, dim. of *trompe* TRUMP¹; see -ET. Hence or – (O)F. *trompeter* **tru·mpet** vb. XVI (Palsgr., Coverdale), **tru·mpetER¹** XV.

truncated trʌ·ŋkeitid having a part cut off. XV (her.). – f. L. *truncātus* (whence prob. *truncāre*), f. *truncus* TRUNK; see -ATE², -ED¹. So **truncA·TION**. XVI. – late L.

truncheon trʌ·nʃən †piece broken off; †fragment or shaft of a spear XIII; short thick staff; staff as symbol of authority XVI. – OF. *tronchon* (mod. *tronçon*), repr. Rom. **trunciō(n-)*, f. L. *truncus* TRUNK.

trundle trʌ·ndl small wheel, roller, or revolving disc. XVI. So vb. roll, bowl XVI. Earlier in *trundle-tail* curly-tailed dog (XV) and *trundle-bed* truckle-bed (XVI). The late and casual appearance of this form as compared with *trendle* (OE. *trendel* circular or spherical object) and *trindle* (early ME. *trindel* wheel), with which it makes a group related by vowel-gradation, involves difficulty in connecting it with OE. words containing *u* or its mutation *y*, as in *trundulnis* 'circuitus', *sintrundel, -tryndel* round, *tryndeled* 'circumtectum', *healftryndel* hemisphere; for the basic forms cf. TREND; see -LE¹.

trunk trʌŋk A. main stem of a tree XV (Caxton); B. human or animal body XV; C. chest, box XV (Promp. Parv.); D. (assoc. partly with TRUMP¹) †pipe, tube; elephant's proboscis XVI (Eden); † pl. trunk-hose XVI. Late ME. *tron(c)k* – (O)F. *tronc*, = Pr. *tronc*, Sp., It. *tronco* :– L. *truncus*. comp. **trunk-HOSE** (hist.) full bag-like breeches. XVII.

trunnion trʌ·njən each of a pair of gudgeons on a cannon XVII; each of a pair of similar supports XVIII. – (O)F. *trognon*, of unkn. origin.

truss trʌs bundle, pack XIII (AncrR.); (naut.) tackle or fitting for a yard XIII; (surg.) supporting appliance XVI. – OF. *trusse, torse* (mod. *trousse*) = Pr. *trossa*, Sp. *troxa*, perh. f. correl. obs. OF. *trusser* (mod. *trousser*), whence ME. *trusse* (XIII), Pr. *trossar*; Sp. *troxar*, of unkn. origin.

trust trʌst confidence XIII (AncrR.); reliability, fidelity XV; thing or person committed to one XVII; (short for *t. company*) body of traders controlling a business XIX. So vb. have confidence (in) XIII. Of obscure history, the primary difficulty being the absence of OE. evidence; early ME. forms of sb., adj., and vb. are of five types: *trust(e)*, beside *trūst(e), trist(e), trest(e)*, which corr. to a possible OE. **tryst*, **trystan*, and *trost(e)* which is presumably – ON. *traust* help, support, confidence, *traustr* firm, strong, confident, with deriv. vb. *treysta* (whence ME. *traiste*); parallel forms are MLG., MDu. *trost* (Du. *troost*), (O)HG. *trōst* consolation, Goth. *trausti* covenant, the formation being ult. that of an abstr. noun on the base **tru-* of TRUE, TROW. Hence **tru·stY¹**. XIII (AncrR.). **trustEE¹**· XVII.

truth trūþ quality of being true, †faith, loyalty OE.; something that is true XIV (PPl.). OE. *trīewþ, trēowþ* corr. to OHG. *triuwida*, ON. (pl.) *trygðir* plighted faith; f. TRUE; see -TH[1] and cf. TROTH. Hence **tru·th**FUL[1] (of statements, etc.) XVI; (of persons) XVIII; (of ideas, artistic or literary presentation, etc.) XIX.

try trai A. examine and determine, esp. judicially XIII (Cursor M.); †B. separate; C. test; attempt XIV; D. (naut.) lie to XVI. – OF. *trier* sift, pick out = Pr., Cat. *triar*, a Gallo-Rom. vb. of unkn. (perh. Gaulish) origin. Sense D. has been explained as 'to attempt by a judicious balance of canvas to keep a ship's bow to the sea' (hence **try·**SAIL trai·seil, -səl XVIII).

trypanosoma tri:pənousou·mə genus of protozoa, species of which are parasitic in the blood. XIX. modL., f. Gr. *trúpanon* borer+*sôma* body.

trypsin tri·psin chief digestive ferment of the pancreatic juice. XIX. perh. for **tripsin*, f. Gr. *trîpsis* rubbing, f. *tríbein* rub; so named because first obtained by rubbing down the pancreas with glycerin; see -IN.

tryst trist, traist (chiefly Sc. before XIX) mutual appointment to meet. XIV (Barbour). spec. use of †*trist*, at first prob. extension of the sense 'appointed station in hunting', var. of †*tristre* – OF. *triste, tristre* (cf. AL. *trista, tristra* XII, perh. – ME. *trist*): see TRUST.

tsar tsāɹ var. of CZAR. XVII.

tsetse tse·tsi dipterous insect Glossina morsitans. XIX. Tswana (language of Bechuanaland).

tuatara tūətā·rə large lizard having a dorsal row of spines. XIX. Maori, f. *tua* on the back+*tara* spine.

tub tʌb open wooden vessel of staves and hoops XIV (Ch.); (orig. *bathing tub*) XVI; heavily-built boat; (joc.) pulpit (hence †*tubman*, †*tubpreacher*, *tub-thumper* preacher in a tub) XVII. prob. of LDu. origin (cf. MLG., MDu. *tubbe*, also MFlem., Du. *tobbe*); of unkn. origin.

tuba tjū·bə brass wind instrument of bass pitch. XIX. It. – L. *tuba* war trumpet.

tube tjūb hollow (cylindrical) body long in proportion to its diameter. XVII. – F. *tube* or L. *tubus*, rel. to *tuba* (see prec.).

tuber tjū·bəɹ thickened portion of the underground stem of a plant. XVII. – L. *tūber* hump, swelling. So **tuber**CLE tjū·bəɹkl small rounded projection XVI; (path.) swelling or nodule XVII. – L. *tūberculum*, dim. of *tūber*. **tube·rcul**AR, **tube·rc**ULOUS XVIII. – modL. **tuberculo·**SIS disease characterized by the formation of tubercles (tubercle-bacilli). XIX.

tuberose[1] tjū·bərous, (erron.) tjū·brouz liliaceous plant Polianthes tuberosa, having a tuberous root. XVII (Evelyn). – L. fem. of *tūberōsus* (see next).

tuberOSE[2] tjū·bərous tuberous. XVIII. So **tubero·**SITY. XVI. **tu·ber**OUS of the form or nature of a tuber. XVII. – F. *tubéreux*, or L. *tūberōsus*.

tubi- tjūbi comb. form of L. *tubus* TUBE. So (erron.) **tubo-**. XIX.

tubule tjū·bjūl small tubular structure. XVII. – L. *tubulus*, dim. of *tubus* TUBE. So **tu·bul**AR. XVII.

tuck[1] tʌk fold or pleat of drapery XIV; gathering of ends XVII; hearty meal XIX (hence *tuck-shop* pastry-cook's shop); f. **tuck** vb. pull or gather up; put up or away XIV; consume (food) XVIII (also intr. *tuck in* XIX). – MLG., MDu. *tucken* (= OHG. *zucchen*, G. *zucken* twitch, snatch), f. base of Germ. **teuχ-* (cf. TUG).

tuck[2] tʌk rapier. XVI. Early forms *toke, tocke, touke*, prob. – F. dial. *étoc*, OF., Pr. *estoc* = It. *stocco*, of Germ. origin (cf. G. *stock* stick).

tuckahoe tʌ·kəhou (U.S.) N. Amer. name for the edible roots of various plants. XVII (Capt. Smith). Algonquian.

tucker tʌ·kəɹ piece of lace, etc. worn at the neck (cf. BIB). XVII. f. TUCK[1], -ER[1].

tucket tʌ·kit flourish on a trumpet. XVI (Sh.). f. †*tuck* beat the drum, sound on a trumpet. XIV. – ONF. *toquer* = Pr., Sp. *tocar*, It. *toccare* TOUCH; see -ET.

-tude tjūd suffix repr. F. *-tude*, L. *-tūdō, -tūdin-*, forming abstr. nouns on adjs., as *altitude, aptitude, fortitude, gratitude, latitude, longitude, multitude, solitude*, derived from L. either directly or through F.; *attitude, decrepitude*, and *platitude* show special features.

Tudor tjū·dəɹ Welsh surname *Tewdwr* as that of the line of English sovereigns from Henry VII to Elizabeth I, descended from Owen Tudor, who married the widow of Henry V. XVIII.

Tuesday tjū·zdi third day of the week. OE. *Tīwesdæg* = OFris. *tīesdei*, OHG. *zīestag* (G. dial. *zīstig*), ON. *týsdagr, týrsdagr*; f. g. of *Tīw* (= OHG. *Zīo*, ON. *Týr*, name of a Teutonic deity identified with Mars :– Germ. **Tīwaz*, cogn. with L. *deus*; see DIVINE[1])+*dæġ* DAY; tr. L. *dies Martis* day of Mars (whence F. *mardi*, It. *martedì*).

tufa tjū·fə (geol.) porous stone. XVIII. † It. *tufa*, local var. of *tufo* – late L. *tōfus, tōphus*. So **tuff** tʌf. XVI. – F. *tuffe, tufe, tuf* – It. *tufo*; cf. G. *tuffstein*. See TOPHUS.

tuffet tʌ·fit tuft or tussock. XVI. prob. alt. of next by substitution of -ET.

tuft tʌft bunch as of hairs XIV (Ch.); clump XVI; tassel on a cap, e.g. as worn by a titled undergraduate XVII. Earlier *toft*, presumably – OF. *tofe, toffe* (mod. *touffe*), of unkn. origin; for the parasitic *t* cf. *draft, graft*, vulgar *paragraft*.

tug tʌg pull forcibly. XIII (AncrR.). Earliest form *togge*, f. weak grade of Germ. **teuχ*- (repr. by OE. *tēon*, OHG. *ziohan*, G. *ziehen*) draw, pull :- IE. **deuk*- (repr. by L. *dūcere* lead; cf. DUCT, DUKE). Hence sb. (chiefly pl.) chains, traces, studs, to maintain attachment, connexion, etc. XIII; act of pulling, or struggling XVI (*tug of war*, N. Lee 1677); (dial.) timber waggon XVIII; small powerful vessel for towing XIX.

tuism tjū·izm use of the pronoun of the second person. XIX (Coleridge). f. L. *tū* THOU + -ISM, after *egoism*.

tuition tjui·ʃən †guardianship, tutelage XV; instruction of a pupil XVI. – (O)F. *tuition* – L. *tuitiō(n-)* protection (Cicero), f. *tuērī* look after; see -ITION. Cf. TUTOR.

tulip tjū·lip bulbous plant of the liliaceous genus Tulipa. XVII (earlier in forms *tulip(p)a*, *-ipan(t)* XVI) – modL. *tulipa*, F. †*tulipan*, *tulipe* (cf. Sp. *tulipan*, Pg. *tulipa*, It. *tulipano*, Du. *tulp*, G. *tulpe*, Sw. *tulpan*, Da. *tulipan*, Russ. *tyul'pán*) – Turk. *tul(i)band* (now *tülbend*) – Pers. *dulband* TURBAN. First mentioned in W. Europe by Busbecq (*c.*1554), in Eng. by Lyte (1578) and Gerarde (1597); the expanded flower was thought to resemble a turban.

tulle tjūl, tul, ||tül fine silk bobbin-net. XIX. F., named from Tulle, in Corrèze, France, where it was first made.

tumble tʌ·mbl †dance with posturing; fall helplessly XIII; cause to fall XIV. ME. *tumbel*, Sc. *tummyll* – MLG. *tummelen* = OHG. *tumalōn* (G. *tummeln*), frequent. (see -LE[3]) f. base of OHG. *tūmōn* (MHG. *tūmen*), *tūmalōn* (MHG. *tūmeln*, G. *taumeln*); cf. OE. *tumbian* dance, MHG. *tumben*, ON. *tumba* tumble; the same base is the source of OF. *tumer*, *tumber* (now *tomber* fall), Sp. *tumbar*, and It. *tomare* and *tombolare*. Hence **tu·mbl**ER[1] †acrobat XIV (Rolle); lurcher XVI; variety of domestic pigeon XVII (so called from their action); footless goblet (made so as not to stand upright) XVII (later, barrel-shaped glass with solid bottom).

tumbrel, -il tʌ·mbrəl instrument of punishment identified with the cucking-stool XIV; tip-cart, dung-cart XV. – OF. *tomb-*, *tumberel* (mod. *tombereau*), in AL. *tumb(e)rellus, -um*, f. *tomber* fall, see TUMBLE, -EL[2].

tumid tjū·mid swollen. XVI. – L. *tumidus*, f. *tumēre* swell; see -ID. So **tumour**, U.S. **tumor** tjū·məɹ †act of swelling, swollen condition; swollen part (now spec.) XVI. – L. *tumor, -ōr-*, f. *tumēre*; see -OUR[2], -OR[2]. Cf. TUMULT, TUMULUS.

tummy tʌ·mi alt. (partly euph.) of STOMACH; see -Y[6].

tump tʌmp (local) mound, hillock. XVI (Nashe). Of unkn. origin.

tum-tum tʌ·mtʌm XIX. imit. of strumming. Also *tum-ti-tum*, *tum-tiddy-tum*.

tumult tjū·mʌlt commotion of a multitude XV (Lydg.); (gen.) disturbance XVI. – (O)F. *tumulte* or L. *tumultus* (cf. Skr. *tumula* tumult, noisy). So **tumu·ltu**ARY. XVI. – L. *tumultuārius* (of troops) raised hastily. **tumu·ltu**OUS. XVI. – (O)F. or L.

tumulus tjū·mjuləs, pl. **-li** lai sepulchral mound. XVII. – L. *tumulus*, rel. to *tumēre* swell. For the formation cf. CUMULUS.

tun tʌn large cask OE.; †tub, vat, etc. XIII; measure of wine, etc. equiv. to 4 hogsheads XV. OE. *tunne*, corr. to OFris., MLG., MDu. *tunne*, *tonne* (Du. *ton*), OHG. *tunna* (G. *tonne*), late ON. *tunna* – medL. *tunna* (whence F. *tonne*, etc., cf. TUNNEL), prob. of Gaulish origin. Hence **tu·n**DISH (local) funnel. XIV. Cf. TON[1].

tundra tʌ·ndrə vast level treeless region of Russia. XIX. – Lappish.

tune tjūn † sound, tone; air, melody XIV (Trevisa); proper intonation or pitch XV. Late ME. *tune*, *tewne*, unexpl. var. of TONE. Cf. *entune* vb. (Ch.).

tungsten tʌ·ŋstən (min.) †calcium tungstate; heavy steel-grey metal. XVIII. – Sw. *tungsten*, f. *tung* heavy + *sten* STONE.

tunic tjū·nik body garment or coat of various kinds; (nat. hist.) sheath, integument. XVII. – F. *tunique* or L. *tunica*. So **tu·nicle** †small tunic XIV; dalmatic XV. – OF. *tunicle* (alt. of *tunique*) or L. *tunicula*, dim. of *tunica*; see -CLE.

tunnel tʌ·nl †tubular net for catching birds XV; †shaft, flue XVI; subterranean passage XVIII. – OF. *tonel* (mod. *tonneau* tun, cask), f. *tonne* TUN; see -EL[2].

tunny tʌ·ni large edible sea-fish of the genus Orcynus. XVI. (Also early *ton(n)y*.) – (O)F. *thon* – Pr. *ton* = It. *tonno* :- L. *thunnu-s* – Gr. *thúnnos*; the ending *-y* is unexpl.

tup tʌp male sheep, ram. XIV. Chiefly north. and Sc.; in earliest use *tope*, *toupe*; of unkn. origin.

tupelo tū·pelou N. Amer. tree of the genus Nyssa. XVIII. Creek Indian; *ito* tree, *opilwa* swamp.

Tupi tū·pi (language of) a tribe and stock of S. Amer. Indians of Brazil. XIX. Tupi, 'comrade'. ¶ The *lingo geral*, i.e. 'general language', the commercial language used by Portuguese and Amazon Indians, is a debased form of this.

tu quoque tjū kwou·kwi L. phr., 'thou also', used in retorting a charge. XVII.

Turanian tjurei·niən pert. to, member of, a people using an Ural-Altaic language. XVIII. f. Pers. *Turān*, applied)(*Irān* by Firdusi (*c.*1000) to the region beyond the Oxus; see -IAN.

turban tə̄·ɹbən Eastern headdress of Muslim origin. XVI. Three main types are repr. by *tolibant*, *tulipan*, *turban(t)* – F.

†*tolliban*, †*tulban*, †*turbant* (mod. *turban*), It. †*tolipano*, *-ante*, Sp., Pg., It. *turbante* – Turk. *tülbend* – Pers. *dulband*. Cf. TULIP.

turbary tə̄·ɹbəri turf-land XIV; right to cut turf XVI. – AN. *turberie*, OF. *tourberie* (medL. *turbāria*), f. *tourbe* TURF; see -ARY.

turbid t·ə̄ɹbid thick with suspended matter; also fig. XVII (Bacon). – L. *turbidus*, f. *turba* disturbance, crowd, beside *turbō* whirlwind, reel, whirl, spinning-top, perh. – Gr. *túrbē* confusion, disorder; see -ID[1].

tu·rbinAL[1] tə̄·ɹbinəl XVI, **tu·rbin**ATE[2], **-at**ED[1] top-shaped. XVII. f. L. *turbin-*, *turben*, var. of *turbō* (see prec.).

turbine tə̄·ɹbain rotary motor driven by water, air, or steam. XIX. – F. *turbine* (1824), stem of *turbō* (see prec.). comb. form **turbo-** tə̄·ɹbou. XIX.

turbit tə̄·ɹbit small variety of domestic pigeon. XVII. prob. f. L. *turbō* top, from its shape. Hence **turbit**EE·N[2]. XIX.

turbot tə̄·ɹbət large flat fish Rhombus maximus. XIII (Havelok). – OF. *turbot* – OSw. *törnbut* (= early mod. Eng. *thornbut*), f. *törn* THORN + *but* BUTT[3].

turbulent tə̄·ɹbjŭlənt disorderly, unruly. XVI (Coverdale). – L. *turbulentus*, f. *turbāre* disturb, agitate, *turba*; see TURBID, -ULENT.

Turco tə̄·ɹkou Chilean bird Hylactes megapodius; Zouave soldier. XIX. – Sp., Pg., It. *Turco* TURK.

Turcoman tə̄·ɹkomæ̆n member of a branch of the Turkish race east of the Caspian Sea. XVI. – Pers. *turkumān* (partly through medL. *turcomannus*, F. *turcoman*), f. *turk* TURK + *māndan* resemble.

turd tə̄ɹd (piece of) excrement. OE. *tord* = MDu. *tort*, *torde* (also in comps. OE. *tordwifel*, †Du. *tortwevel*, ON. *tordýfill* 'turd-weavil', dung-beetle) :– Germ. **turdam* :– IE. **dr̥tom*, pp. formation on **dr-* **der-* TEAR[2]; a mutated form is seen in OE. *tyrdel* (see -EL[1], -LE[1]), early mod. Eng. *tirdle*, *terdle*, dial. *treddle*, *truddle* pellet of dung.

tureen tjurī·n deep table vessel with a lid. XVIII. Earlier forms *terrene*, *-ine* – F. *terrine* large circular flat-bottomed earthenware dish, sb. use of fem. of OF. *terrin* earthen :– Rom. **terrinus*, f. L. *terra* earth; see TERRESTRIAL, -INE[1].

turf tə̄ɹf sod of grass; greensward OE.; slab of peat XIII (Havelok). OE. *turf*, corr., with variation of gender and declension, to OFris., OS. (Du.) *turf* (LG. *torf*, whence G. *torf*), OHG. *zurba*, *zurf*, ON. *torf*, *torfa*; CGerm. sb. (not in Gothic), f. **turb-* (whence medL. *turba*, OF. *tourbe*; cf. TURBARY) :– IE. **drbh-*, the base of Skr. *darbhá* tuft of grass.

turgid tə̄·ɹdʒid swollen, distended XVII; of inflated style XVIII. – L. *turgidus*, f. *turgēre* swell; see -ID[1]. So †**tu·rg**ENT. XV, **turge**·SCENCE. XVII, -E·SCENT. XVIII.

Turk tə̄ɹk member of a numerous and extensive family of the human race of Central Asia and speaking languages belonging to a branch (the Turkic) of the Ural-Altaic group; native of Turkey (Seljuk or Osmanli) XIV. transf. XVI. Of unkn. origin. Hence **Tu·rk**IC. XIX. **Turk**ISH[1] tə̄·ɹkiʃ pert. to Turkey or the Turks. XVI. repl. †*Turkes* (XIV), *Turkeys* – OF. *turqueis* (mod. *turquois*) = Pr. *turques*, It. *turchese*, medL. *Turcensis*.

turkey tə̄·ɹki †guinea-fowl; large gallinaceous bird of American origin (genus Meleagris) XVI. The name of the country (the land of the Turks), first applied to the African bird prob. because it was orig. brought from New Guinea by the Portuguese through Turkish dominions, and later applied to the American bird, to which it became restricted, and to which *Meleagris*, the name by which the guinea-fowl was known to the Greeks and Romans, was attached by Linnæus in his classification.

Turkey tə̄·ɹki land of the Turks (T. in Europe and T. in Asia). XIV (Ch.). – F. *Turquie*, medL. *Turchia*, *Turquia*, f. *Turc*, *Turcus*; cf. -Y[3].

Turki tu·rki Turkish native, †horse. XVIII. – Pers. *turkī*, adj. formation.

turmeric tə̄·ɹmərik (powder made from) the root-stock of the East Indian plant, used in curry powder, etc.; curcuma. XVI. Early forms also *tarmaret*, *tormarith*, which appear to be – F. *terre mérite*, modL. *terra merita* (XVI), perh. alt. of some native form; the ending shows assim. to -IC.

turmoil tə̄·ɹmoil †agitate, distress; †live or move in agitation; (dial.) toil, drudge. XVI. The senses corr. to the transf. senses of MOIL, and, like these, are first recorded in pass. and refl. use. Hence **tu·rmoil** sb. agitation, commotion. XVI; of unkn. origin.

turn tə̄ɹn vb. of extensive sense-development the basic notions of which are rotation and deviation from a course, one of its earliest senses with reference to the operation of a lathe still remaining in use. ME. forms repr. early OE. *tyrnan* (viz. *türne*, *terne*, *tyrne*) were superseded by *turne*, *terne*, derived from OE. *turnian*, giving the present form, and prob. reinforced from OF. *turner*, *torner* (mod. *tourner*) = Pr., Sp., Pg. *tornar*, It. *tornare* :– L. *tornāre*, f. *tornus* lathe – Gr. *tórnos* lathe, circular movement (whence vb. *torneúein*), taken to be cogn. with L. *terere* rub (cf. TRITE, *teres* polished, smooth). Comp. **tu·rn**COAT. XVI. **tu·rn**KEY one who has charge of keys. XVII. **tu·rn-**OUT action or manner of turning out. XVII. **tu·rn-**OVER person or thing that is turned over or transferred XVII; tart of which one half of the paste is turned over the other XVIII; amount of business done, etc. XIX. **tu·rn**PIKE spiked barrier XV; barrier for collection of toll XVII (*t. road* XVIII). **tu·rn**SCREW screwdriver. XIX; cf. F. *tournevis*. **tu·rn**SPIT dog or person kept to turn a roasting spit. XVI; cf. F. *tourne-broche*, whence †*turnbroach* (XV). **tu·rn**STILE revolving gateway regulating passage. XVII; earlier †*turningstile* (Cotgr.). **tu·rn-**TABLE revolving platform or disc. XIX. **tu·rn-**UP part of a garment that is turned up XVII; card turned up XIX. Hence **tu·rn**ER² one who fashions objects of wood, etc. on a lathe. XIV. – OF. *tornere*, *-eor* – late L. *tornātor*, *-ātōrem*. **turning-**POINT point marked by change of procedure. XIX (1841, Keble), prob. modelled on G. *wendepunkt*.

turnip tə̄·ɹnip (root of) Brassica Rapa, var. depressa. XVI. Early forms *turnepe* (XVI–XVII), *-nep* (XVI–XIX); the first el. is indeterminable; the second is *neep*, OE. *nǣp* – L. *nāpus* turnip, prob. of Mediterranean origin.

turnsole tə̄·ɹnsoul violet blue or purple colouring matter XIV; plant yielding this, the flowers of which face the sun XVI. – (O)F. *tournesole* – Sp. *tornasol*, It. *tornasole*, f. L. *tornāre* TURN + *sōl* sun.

turpentine tə̄·ɹpəntain orig. resin of the terebinth tree, (now) any oleoresin from a conifer. XIV. Forms *ter(e)bentine*, *turbentyne*, *terpentine* – OF. *ter(e)bentine* – L. *ter(e)benthina* (sc. *rēsīna* resin), f. *terebinthus* TEREBINTH; see -INE¹.

turpeth tə̄·ɹpeþ cathartic drug obtained from Ipomæa Turpethum. XIV. earlier *turbit(h)* – medL. *turbit(h)um*, *turpetum* – Pers., Arab. *turbiḍ*, *-beḍ*, whence also F. *turbith*, † *-bit*, Sp., Pg. *turbit*.

turpitude tə̄·ɹpitjūd shameful character. XV (Caxton). – F. *turpitude* or L. *turpitūdō*, f. *turpis* base, disgraceful; see -TUDE.

turps tə̄ɹps oil of turpentine. XIX. f. first syll. of TURPENTINE + pl. ending *-s* used coll.; prob. workman's colloq.

turquoise tə̄·ɹkoiz precious stone, of sky-blue to apple-green colour, found in Persia. XIV (Trevisa). Late ME. *turkeis*, later *turkes*, *turques* (XV), *turkoise*, *turquoise* (XVI) – OF. *turqueise*, later *-oise* = Pr., Sp. *turqueza*, It. *turchese*, for *pierre turqueise*, etc. 'Turkish stone', so called from being first known in Turkestan or conveyed through Turkish dominions.

turret tʌ·rit small tower. XIV (*turet*, *touret*). – OF. *torete*, *tourete*, dim. of *tur*, *tor*, *tour* TOWER; see -ET.

turtle¹ tə̄·ɹtl dove of the genus Turtur. OE. *turtla* m., *turtle* fem. = OHG. *turtulo* m., *-ula* fem., also *turtulatūba* (G. *turteltaube*) = MLG. *torteldūve*, MSw. *turturdufva* (so **tu·rtle**DOVE. XIII); in OE. and ME. also *turtur*, in ME. *turture* partly – OF. *turtre* (mod. *tourtre*) or ON. *turturi*; all – L. *turtur*, of imit. origin (for change of *r* to *l* cf. PURPLE). Cf. Sumerian *turturhu*, Heb. *tūr*.

turtle² tə̄·ɹtl marine tortoise. XVII. perh. alt. of F. *tortue* TORTOISE, but the existence of a var. *turckle* (Purchas) may point to a native (Bermudan) name. phr. *turn t.* (orig. †*the t.*) capsize (XIX), with allusion to turning turtles over so as to incapacitate and capture them.

Tuscan tʌ·skən Etruscan; pert. to Tuscany, region of Italy. XVI. – F. *tuscan*, It. *toscano* – L. *Tuscānus*, f. *Tuscī*, pl. *of Tuscus*, called also *Etruscī*; see -AN.

tush tʌʃ (arch.) excl. of impatience or contempt. XV. Cf. rare †*twish* (XVI), PISH. Hence **tu·sh**ERY, coined by R. L. Stevenson for pseudo-arch. romantic literature. XIX.

tusk tʌsk long-pointed tooth. ME. (XIII) metathetic alt. of OE. *tux* (var. of *tusc*, whence ME. *tush*, surviving dial. and as applied to Indian elephants) = OFris. *tusk*, *tosk*; not certainly known outside the Anglo-Frisian area. If the vowel of the OE. word is long, of which there is no evidence, it may repr. **tunþsk-*, f. **tunþus* TOOTH.

tussive tʌ·siv pert. to a cough. XIX. f. L. *tussis* cough + -IVE.

tussle tʌ·sl †pull or push roughly XV (Henryson); struggle vigorously XVII. perh. f. (dial.) *touse* (whence TOUSLE) = Fris. *tūsen*, MLG. *tōsen*, OHG. *er|zūsen*, *zir|zūsōn* (G. *zausen*); see -LE³.

tussock tʌ·sək tuft of hair XVI; tuft or matted growth of grass, etc. XVII. contemp. with synon. (dial.) *tusk* (of unkn. origin), of which it is prob. an alt. form with assim. to -OCK.

tussore tʌ·sɔəɹ coarse brown silk. XVII (*tessar*, *-ur*). – Urdu – Hindi *ta·sar* (:– Skr. *tasara*) shuttle, assim. to *salempore*, etc.

tut tʌt natural excl. of impatience, etc. XVI (Skelton). The front or palatal click, denoted otherwise by *tchick*, *tck*. ¶ Sc. *toot*, *toots* expresses mild expostulation.

tutelage tjū·təlėdʒ guardianship as of a ward. XVII. f. L. *tūtēla* keeping, f. pp. stem of *tuērī* watch, look after; see -AGE. So **tu·tel**ARY. XVII. – L. *tūtēlārius*; cf. F. *tutélaire*.

tutenag tjū·tĭnæg alloy of copper, zinc, and nickel. XVII (also *too-*, *-aga*, *-agal*). – Marathi *tuttināg*, said to be f. Skr. *tuttha* copper sulphate + *nāga* tin, lead; cf. Pg. *tutenaga*, F. *toutenague*.

tutiorist tjū·ʃiərist one who in cases of conscience favours the course of greater moral safety. XIX. f. L. *tūtior* safer, compar. of *tūtus* safe, pp. of *tuērī*; see next and -IST.

tutor tjū·təɹ †guardian XIV (PPl., Wycl. Bible, Trevisa); one employed as an instructor, esp. of youth XIV (Trevisa); supervisor of an undergraduate XVII. – ME. *tutour* – AN., OF. *tutour* (mod. *tuteur*), or L. *tūtor*, agent-noun (see -TOR) f. *tuērī* look at or after, protect. Cf. TUITION.

tutsan tʌ·tsən name of various plants to which healing properties are attributed. XV. – AN. †*tutsaine*, F. *toute-saine*, f. *toute*, fem. of *tout* all, + *saine*, fem. of *sain* wholesome (see SANE).

tutti tu·ti (mus.) direction that all performers are to take part. XVIII. It., pl. of *tutto* :– L. *tōtus* (see TOTAL).

tutty tʌ·ti crude oxide of zinc. XIV (*tutie*). – OF. *tutie* = Sp., Pg. *tutia* – medL. *tutia* – Arab. *tūtiyā* (prob. of alien origin).

tu whit tu whoo tuʍi·t tuʍū· imit. of the call of an owl. XVI (Sh.). Cf. †*twyt* (Lyly).

tuxedo tʌksī·dou dinner-jacket. XIX. f. name of a fashionable country club at *Tuxedo* Park, near New York.

tuyere twī·jɛəɹ nozzle conveying blast. XVIII. – F. *tuyère*, f. *tuyau* pipe, prob. based ult. on an imit. **tūt*.

twaddle twɔ·dl senseless or trifling talk. XVIII. Also *twiddle-twaddle* (XVIII). alt. of *twattle* (XVII) and †*twittle-twattle* (XVI); the corr. vb. (dial. *twattle*) is earlier (XVI) and varied formerly with †*twittle*, itself alt. of *tittle* (see TITTLE-TATTLE); *w* of the altered forms is unexpl.

twain twein (arch.) two. OE. *tweġen*, corr. to OFris., OS. *twēne*, OHG. *zwēne* (G. arch. *zween*), nom. and acc. m. of the numeral of which fem. and n. are repr. by TWO. In ME. *twein(e)* became a secondary form of *two*, used following its sb.; its use in the marriage service of the Book of Common Prayer and in the A.V. of the Bible, and its convenience as a rhyme-word, have contributed to its retention in arch. lang. (phr. *in t.*, into two parts, asunder XIV).

twang twæŋ sound produced by plucking string of bow, harp, etc. XVI; vocal sound modified by passage through the nose; individual or local pronunciation XVII. imit., the *tw-* expressing the sound of plucking, the *-ang* resonance.

twankay twæ·ŋkei variety of green tea. XIX. – Chin. *Tong* (or *Taung*)*ké* or *-kei*, dial. var. of *Tunki* or *Tunchi* name of two streams and a town in China.

twayblade twei·bleid orchidaceous plant of genus Listera (in U.S. Liparis), having two broad leaves springing from stem or root. XVI (Lyte, Gerarde). tr. medL. *bifolium*; f. *tway*, clipped form of TWAIN + BLADE.

tweak twīk pull with a twist or jerk. XVII (Holland, Sh.). prob. alt. of (dial.) *twick*, OE. *twiccian* = OHG. *zwicchan*, rel. to TWITCH.

tweed twīd twilled woollen cloth. XIX. Trade name originating in an accidental misreading (by James Locke, a London merchant, as is alleged by some) of *tweel* or *tweeled*, Sc. forms of TWILL, TWILLED, assisted by assoc. with the river *Tweed*.

tweedle twī·dl make a succession of sounds on a fiddle, etc. XVII. imit. of the sounds, combined playfully in *tweedledum and tweedledee* to indicate two rival musicians (XVIII).

tween twīn aphetic of †*atween* or BETWEEN XIV. Hence **twee·NY**[6] between-maid (one assisting two others) XIX.

tweet twīt imit. of the twittering of a small bird. XIX.

tweezers twī·zərz small pincers or nippers. XVII. alt., by assoc. with *nippers*, *pincers*, *pliers*, or *scissors*, of †*tweezes*, pl. of †*tweeze* case of small instruments, aphetic of †*etweeze*, repr. pl. of ÉTUI.

twelve twelv 12, xii. OE. *twelf*, inflected *twelfe* = OFris. *twelef*, *twelf*, *tolef*, OS. *twelif*, *twilif*, OHG. *zwelif* (MDu. *twalef*, Du. *twaalf*, G. *zwölf*), ON. *tólf*, Goth. *twalif* (*-lib*); CGerm. prob. f. **twa-* TWO + **lif-* as in ELEVEN. Hence **twe·lvemo** 12mo, XIImo, duodecimo. XIX. So **twelfTH**[2] twelfþ 12th. OE. *twelfta* = OFris. *twil(i)fta*, MDu. *twalefde*, OHG. *zwelifto* (Du. *twaalfde*, G. *zwölfte*), ON. *tólfti*, f. *twelf*, etc.; the new formation with *-the* substituted for *-te* appeared XIV and became general from XVI, though *twelft*, *twelt* survives dial. *T. day*, Epiphany, 12th day after Christmas Day. *T. Night*, night of this as time of merrymaking (whence *t. cake*, XVIII).

twenty twe·nti 20, xx. OE. *twentiġ* = OFris. *twintich*, OS. *twēntig*, OHG. *zweinzug* (G., orig. dial., *zwanzig*); the first el. is obscure; cf. ON. *tuttugu*, Goth. *twai tigjus*; see -TY[1]. Hence **twe·ntiETH** 20th. OE. *twentiġoþa*; cf., with other suffixes, late ME. *twentiest* (so O.Fris. *twintigosta*, MHG. *zweinzigeste*, G. *zwanzigste*); Icel. *tuttugasti*, beside ON. *tuttugti*, *tugtugti*, *twítugti*, north. ME. *twentiand* (after ON. *tuttugandi*).

twi- twai prefix meaning 'two', 'twice', 'double', 'doubly', OE. *twi-*, *twy-* (= OFris. *twi-*, OHG. *zwi-*, ON. *tví-*; rel. to TWO). Of the 45 or so OE. comps. none survived exc. (arch.) *twifold*, (dial.) *twibill* two-edged **axe**, mattock, *twi-* being gen. repl. by *two-*, as *twofold* (ME. *twafald* XII, OE. *twifeald*), *two-headed* (OE. *twihēafdode*).

twice twais on two occasions XII; two times as much (as) XIV. Early ME. *twiġes* (Peterborough Chronicle, an. 1120), f. *twiġe*, earlier *twiġ(e)a* = OFris. *twīa*, OS. *tuuīo* (f. **twi-* TWO) + *-es*, -S. Cf. THRICE.

twiddle twi·dl †trifle XVI; turn about esp. with the fingers XVII. prob. intended to combine the notions of *twirl* and *fiddle*.

twig[1] twig minor shoot of a tree or shrub. OE. (late Nhb.) *twigge*, obscurely rel. to *twiġ*, *twī*, corr. to ODa. *tvige* (Da. dial. *tvege*) fork (cf. Skr. *dvikā́* consisting of two) and (with long vowel) MLG. *twīch* (*-g-*), Du. *twijg*, OHG. *zwīg* (G. *zweig*); all based on Germ. **twi-* (:– IE. **dwi-*); cf. TWAIN, TWIN, TWINE, TWO.

twig[2] twig (sl.) look at, perceive XVIII; understand XIX. Of unkn. origin, perh. an application of *twig* pull XVIII (cf. *twick*, TWEAK).

twilight twai·lait (period of) half light. XV (†*twilighting* occurs late XIV). f. TWI- + LIGHT[1]; cf. Du. †*tweelicht*, LG. *twelecht* (whence G. *zwielicht*).

twill twil woven fabric having parallel ridges. XIV. orig. north. and Sc. reduction of †*twilly*, ME. †*twyle*, OE. *twili* = OHG. *zwilīh* (G. *zwillich*), whence MLG., Du. *zwilk*, semi-tr. of L. *bilīc-* (*bilīx*) two-threaded, f. *bi-* BI- + base of *līcium* thrum, thread. ¶ The Sc. form is *tweel*; see TWEED.

twin twin twofold, double OE.; in *t. brother*, etc. XVI (Sh.); forming a pair XVI; sb. pl. two born at a birth. Late OE. *twinn*, earlier *ġetwinn* adj. and sb., corr. to ON. *tvinnr*, *tvennr* twofold, double :- Germ. **twisnaz*; cf. OE. *ġetwisan*, OS. *gitwisan*, MLG. *twesen*, LG. *twēschen* (pl. *-s*) twins, OHG. *zwiniling* (G. *zwilling*) twin, *zwinal* twin-born; IE. **dwisno-* is repr. also by Lith. *dvynù* twins; f. **dwi-* TWI- (for formative *n* cf. L. *bīnī* two each).

twine twain thread of two or more strands. OE. *twīn*, *twiġin* linen = Du. *twijn* twine, twist, f. Germ. **twi-* TWI-, with *n*-formative as in OFris. *twīne*, Goth. *tweihnai* two each, ON. *tvinni* twisted thread; cf. TWIN. Hence vb. XIII (Laȝ.).

twinge twindʒ (dial.) pinch, squeeze OE.; (arch.) cause sharp pain to XVII. OE. *twenġan* = MLG. *twengen*, OHG. *zwengen*, f. Germ. **twaŋg-*, repr. by MHG. *zwange* tongs, *zwangen* pinch, OHG. *zwangōn*. Hence sb. †pinch XVI; sharp wringing pain XVII.

twink twiŋk †wink, blink XIV; (arch.) twinkle XVII. corr. to MHG. *zwinken* (cf. G. *zwinkern* blink, wink, twinkle).

twinkle twi·ŋkl emit tremulous radiance OE.; wink XIII (obs. exc. in arch. *twinkling of an eye* XIV R. Mannyng). OE. *twinclian*, f. base of TWINK; see -LE[3].

twirl twɜːl spin rapidly XVI; twiddle (the thumbs) XVIII. prob. alt. by assoc. with *whirl*, of †*tirl* (XVI), metathetic var. of TRILL.

twist twist †A. divided object or part (band of a hinge, twig, junction of two parts in the body) XIV; B. cord of threads intertwined XVI (of tobacco XVIII); C. act of twisting, turning on an axis, or spinning XVI. Of complicated history; partly dependent on OE. *twist*, in comps. denoting a hinged or branched object, viz. *candeltwist* snuffers, *mæst twist* mast rope, stay, *yltwist* bird-trap, and in place-names prob. denoting 'fork'; presumably f. the base **twis-*, identical with that of TWIN, TWINE. So **twist**, vb. †divide into branches; wring, wrench XIV; combine, unite (threads) XV. Of mixed origin; partly f. the sb. ¶ The sense 'discussion' and 'disagree', 'quarrel' of LDu. *twist*, *twisten*, MHG., G. *zwist* is not found in Eng.

twit twit find fault with, taunt. XVI. In earliest use *twite*, *twight*, aphetic of †*atwite*, OE. *ætwītan* reproach with, f. *æt-* from, away (denoting opposition) + *wītan* (dial. *wite*) corr. to OFris. *wīta*, OS. *wītan*, OHG. *wīȝan*, ON. *víta* punish, Goth. *-weitan* (*fraweitan* avenge), rel. to OE. *wīte* = OFris. *wīte*, OS. *wīti*, OHG. *wīȝȝi*, ON. *víti* punishment, based on a var. of **wit-* know (see WIT), the development of sense being parallel to that of L. *animadvertere* 'observe, consider, censure, punish'.

twitch twitʃ pull or jerk sharply. First in *to|twiċċhe* (XII–XIV) pull apart, corr. to LG. *twikken*, OHG. *gizwickan*, (M)HG. *zwicken*, f. Germ. **twik-*, repr. also by OE. *twiċċian* (dial. *twick*) pluck.

twite twait species of linnet. XVI. imit. of the bird's call.

twitter twi·təɹ utter light tremulous notes, as a bird. XIV (Ch., Trevisa). imit. with -ER[4]; cf. OHG. *zwizzirōn*, MHG. *zwizzern* (G. *zwitschern*) and, with a different initial, Du. *kwetteren*, Sw. *qvittra*, etc.

twixt, 'twixt twikst (arch.) aphetic of †*atwixt*, BETWIXT. XIII (Cursor M.).

twizzle twi·zl (dial., colloq.) twirl, twiddle. XIX. alt. of TWIDDLE or dial. *twistle* (XVIII), f. TWIST; see -LE[3].

two tū 2, ii. OE. *twā* fem., *twā*, *tū* n. = OFris. *twā*, OS. *twā*, *twō*, n. *twē*, OHG. *zwā*, *zwō*, n. *zwei* (Du. *twee*, G. *zwei*), ON. *tveir* m., *tvær* fem., *tvau* n., Goth. *twai* m., *twōs* fem., *twa* n., cogn. with Skr. *dwau* m., *dwe* fem. and n., Gr. *dúo* (*dō* in *dṓdeka* twelve), L. *duo* m. and n., *duæ* fem. (popL. **duī* m., **dua* n.), Lith. *dù*, OSl. *dŭva* m., *dŭvě* fem. and n. (Russ. *dva* m. and n., *dve* fem.), OIr. *dau*, *dō*, W. *dau*; IE. **d(u)wo(u)* with various modifications (see also TWAIN, TWI-). comps. **two**·FOLD consisting of two combined. XII. ME. *twafald*, repl. *twifald*, OE. *twyfeald*. **two**PENCE tʌ·pəns. XVI (*tuppens*). **two**PENNY tʌ·pəni adj. XVI (Sc. *tuapenny*).

-ty[1] ti final syll. of the tens. OE. *-tiġ* = OFris. *-tich*, OS. *-tig*, OHG. *-zug* (Du. *-tig*, G. *-zig*); ON. *tigr* and Goth. *tigus* are separate words, not suffixes (e.g. *tveir tigir*, *twai tigjus* twenty). Cf. Skr. *daśát-*, Gr. *dekás*, *-ad-* (IE. **dekmt-*) DECADE. ¶ Cardinal numbers in *-ty* were orig. construed as sbs. with g. pl., e.g. *twentiġ wintra* 20 years.

-ty[2] ti suffix denoting state or condition; early ME. *-teð*, *-te* (XII), *-tee*, later *-tie*, *-tye* – (O)F. *-té* (AN. *-tet*, *-ted*, *-teth*) = Pr. *-tat*, *-dat*, Sp. *-dad*, Pg. *-dade*, It. *-tà*, Rum. *-tae* :- L. *-tātem*, nom. *-tās*; see also -IETY, -ITY. In OF. such types as *bonitātem* became disyllabic, viz. *bontet* BOUNTY, so that *-tet* (mod. *-té*) became the regular form of the suffix. Special cases are *difficulty*, *faculty*, *honesty, majesty, penalty, personality, property, shrievalty, sovereignty, subtlety*; AN. *-teth* is repr. as late as XVI in *plenteth* PLENTY, and in Sc. *boundith, dainteth, poortith* (POVERTY).

tycoon taikū·n foreigners' title for the Shogun of Japan XIX; (fig., sl.) business magnate XX. – Jap. *taikun*, f. Chin. *ta* great + *kiun* prince.

tyke taik dog, esp. cur, mongrel; ill-conditioned fellow XIV; in full *Yorkshire t.* Yorkshireman XVII. – ON. *tík* bitch (Norw. *tik* bitch, vixen); cf. MLG. *tike* bitch; Germ. **tigōn*, corr. to Gr. dial. *díza* goat (:– **digjá*).

tymp timp mouth of the hearth of a blast furnace. XVII, app. shortening of next.

tympan ti·mpən †tympanum OE.; (typogr.) in a printing press, frame for equalizing pressure XVI. OE. *timpana* and ME. *timpan* (in renderings of biblical passages) – L. *tympanum* (see next) reinforced by (O)F. *tympan* = Sp., It. *timpano*.

tympanites timpanai·tīz (path.) distension of the abdomen by gas. XIV. late L. – Gr. *tumpanítēs* (Galen), f. *túmpanon* TYMPANUM.

tympanum ti·mpənəm drum, tambourine, etc.; ear-drum XVII. L. – Gr. *túmpanon* drum, f. nasalized var. of base of *túptein* strike.

tynwald ti·nwəld, tai·n- annual convention in the Isle of Man. XV. – ON. **þingwall-*, stem of *þingvǫllr*, f. *þing* assembly, THING + *vǫllr* field, level ground. ¶ Of the same origin are the place-names *Tinwald* (Dumfriesshire), *Dingwall* (Ross-shire), *Tingwall* (Shetland).

type taip emblem XV (Henryson); mark, stamp XVI; characteristic or representative form XVII; block carrying a letter or figure used in printing XVIII. – F. *type* or L. *typus* – Gr. *túpos* blow, impression, image, figure, f. base of *túptein* strike, beat. comp. **typewrit**ER[1] tai·prai:tər superseded *type-writing machine*, of equal date XIX. Hence **type** vb. use, make a copy of with, a typewriter. **typ**IC ti·pik typical. XVII (Donne). – F. *typique* – late L. *typicus* – Gr. *tupikós*, f. *túpos*. **ty·p**ICAL of the nature of a type. XVII. – medL. *typicālis* (Thomas Aquinas), f. *typicus*. **ty·pi**FY. XVII (Wither, Sir T. Browne). **ty·p**IST tai·pist †compositor; one who uses a typewriter. XIX. **typo**GRAPHY taipɔ·grəfi printing. XVII (Evelyn). – F. *typographie* (XVI) or modL. *typographia* (Bernard of Verona 1493), f. Gr. *túpos* TYPE. **typo**GRA·PHICAL. XVI. – modL. **typo·**GRAPHER printer. XVII (Sir T. Browne). F. *typographe* or modL. *typographus*.

-type taip repr. F. *-type*, L. *-typus*, Gr. *-túpos*. f. *túptein* (see prec.), as in *antitype, archetype, electrotype, prototype, stereotype*.

typhlitis tiflai·tis (path.) inflammation of the cæcum. XIX. – modL., f. Gr. *tuphlón* cæcum, n. of *tuphlós* blind, used sb.; see -ITIS.

typhoon taifū·n cyclonic storm in the China seas. XVI. – Chinese *tai fung*, dial. vars. of *ta* big, *fêng* wind; cf. G. *taifun, teifun*, F. *typhon*. Earlier †*tuffoon* (XVII), identified in form with †*touffon* (XVI), †*tuffon* (XVII) violent storm in India – Pg. *tufão* – Hind. (– Arab.) *ṭūfān* hurricane, tornado, beside which there was a contemp. †*typhon* (XVI) – L. *tȳphōn* – Gr. *tūphôn*, rel. to *tū́phein* (see TYPHUS).

typhus tai·fəs infectious fever. XVIII. – modL. *tȳphus* (De Sauvages) – Gr. *tûphos* smoke, vapour, stupor, f. *túphein* smoke. Hence **typhoid** tai·foid resembling typhus; applied spec. to a fever marked by intestinal inflammation and formerly supposed to be a variety of typhus. XVIII. f. TYPHUS + -OID; cf. F. *typhoïde*.

tyranno- tairæ·nou comb. form of Gr. *túrannos* TYRANT, as in *tyrannosaurus*.

tyrant taiə·rənt absolute ruler; despotic ruler XIII (RGlouc., Cursor M.). ME. *tira(u)nd, tirant*, pl. *tiraunz*, also *tyran* – OF. *tyrant, tiran* (mod. *tyran*) = Pr. *tiran*, Sp. *tirano*, It. *tiranno* – L. *tyrannus* – Gr. *túrannos*. (OF. *tyrant* is analogical after forms in -ANT.) So **tyrann**IC ti-, tairæ·nik. XV (Caxton). – (O)F. **tyra·nn**ICAL. XVI; preceded by †*tirannysh* (Gower). **tyrann**OUS ti·rənəs. XV. **ty·rann**Y[3] ti·rəni. XIV. – (O)F. *tyrannie* – late L. *tyrannia* – Gr. *turanniā*. **ty·rann**IZE. XV. – (O)F. *tyranniser*.

tyre[1], tire taiər †curved plating for the rim of a wheel XV; rim of metal forming a continuous hoop XVIII, later, endless cushion of rubber for the same purpose XIX. perh. a use of TIRE[2] (aphetic of ATTIRE). ¶ The sp. with *y* is now used in Great Britain.

tyre[2] taiər (in India) curdled milk. XVII (Purchas). – Tamil *tayir*.

Tyrian ti·riən pert. to Tyre, ancient Phœnician city on the Mediterranean, spec. of a purple or crimson dye obtained from molluscs. XVI. f. L. *Tyrius*, f. *Tyrus* Tyre; see -IAN.

tyro see TIRO.

tzar see TSAR, CZAR.

tzigane tsigā·n Hungarian gipsy. XIX. – F. *tzigane* (with *tz* of G. origin) – Magyar *czigány*.

U

ubication jūbikei·ʃən location. xvii. – medL. *ubicātiō(n-)* (cf. Sp. *ubicación*, Pg. *ubicação*), f. *ubicāre* (cf. Sp. *ubicarse* be in a determinate place), f. L. *ubĭ* where = Umbrian *pufe*, Oscan *puf* :– *quubī (cf. L. *alicubī* elsewhere, *necubī* nowhere), f. base of *quī* WHO, with loc. ending; see -ATION. So **ub**IETY jubai·iti condition in respect of place – medL. *ubietās*. **ubiqu**ITY- jubi·kwiti quality of being everywhere at one and the same time. xvi. – modL. *ubīquitās* (cf. F. *ubiquité*, Sp. *ubicuidad*), f. L. *ubīque* everywhere, f. *ubī* + generalizing *-que*. Hence **ubi·quit**OUS. xix, which was preceded by **ubiqu**A·RIAN. xviii. So **ubiquit**A·RIAN. xvii, **ubi·quit**ARY. xvi, f. or – modL. *ubīquitārius* (cf. F. *ubiquitaire*, Sp. *ubiquitario*).

U-boat jū·bout German submarine. xx. – G. *U-boot*, for *unterseeboot* 'under-sea boat'.

udal jū·dəl of lands held by an old pre-feudal form of freehold tenure. xvi (*outhell, uthall, udall*). Orkney and Shetland form of ON. *óðal*, Norw. *odal, odel*, ODAL.

udder ʌ·dəɹ mammary glands in cattle, etc. OE. *ūder* = OFris., OS. *ūder*, MLG., MDu. *ūder* (Du. *uier, uijer*), OHG. *ūter* (G. *euter*) :– WGerm. *ūðr-; cf. OFris. *iāder*, OS. *ieder*, MLG. *jeder, jüdder*, ON. (with unexpl. cons.-change) *júgr, júr* :– *euðer; IE. *ūdhr- is repr. by L. *ūber* teat, udder, as adj. fertile, copious, Gr. *oûthar*, Skr. *ū́dhar*. ¶ The OE. long vowel has been shortened as in *adder, fodder*.

udometer jūdɔ·mitəɹ rain-gauge. – F. *udomètre*, irreg. f. L. *ūdus* damp; see -METER.

ugh ʌ, u repr. of a cough xviii; int. of disgust xix.

ugly ʌ·gli †frightful, horrible, terrible; morally offensive xiii; physically offensive, repulsive to the eye xiv; causing offence or disquiet; hazardous, dangerous; cross, ill-tempered xvii. Appears first in northern and eastern texts; – ON. *uggligr* to be feared, f. *ugga* fear (whence dial. *ug* cause to fear, abhor xiii); see -LY[1]. So **u·g**SOME[1] horrible. xiv; chiefly north. dial. and Sc.; its literary currency in mod. times is prob. due to Scott.

Ugrian (j)ū·griən pert. to a Ural-Altaic people called *Ugry* by early Russ. writers; see -IAN. xix. comb. form **U·gro-** as in *Ugro-Finnish*.

uhlan ū·læn cavalryman, lancer in Continental armies. xviii. – F. *uhlan*, G. *u(h)lan* – Pol. *ułan, hułan* (also in Czech, Russ., etc.) – Turk. *oğlan* youth, servant (cf. *oğul* child).

uitlander ei·tləndəɹ in S. Africa, foreigner, alien. xix. Afrikaans, f. Du. *uit* OUT + *land* LAND; see -ER[1].

ukase jukei·s decree, orig. of Russian emperor. xviii. – Russ. *ukáz*, f. *ukazát'* show, order, decree.

Ukrainian jukrei·niən, jukrai·niən pert. to the *Ukraine*, country of the U.S.S.R. xix. f. Pol., Russ. *Ukraina* lit. border, frontier, marches, f. *u-* at, beside + *kraj* edge, brink; see -IAN.

ukulele jūkilei·li Hawaiian guitar. xix. native name.

-ular jŭləɹ repr. L. *-ulāris* (sometimes through F. *-ulaire*), f. *-ulus, -ula, -ulum* -ULE + *-āris* -AR, as in L. *populāris* POPULAR, *rēgulāris* REGULAR, *sæculāris* SECULAR. Some adjs. function as if connected directly to the bases of derivs. in *-ule*, as *granular, valvular*, apprehended as f. *grain, valve*.

ulcer ʌ·lsəɹ open sore. xiv. – (O)F. *ulcère* or – L. *ulcer-*, nom. *ulcus*, rel. to Gr. *hélkos* wound, sore, Skr. *árças* piles. So **u·lcer**ATE[3]. xv, **ulcer**A·TION. xiv; **u·lcer**OUS. xvi – L. *ulcerāt-, -āre, -ātiō(n-), -ōsus*.

-ule jūl suffix repr. F. *-ule* – L. *-ulus, -ula, -ulum*, as in *capsula* CAPSULE, *globulus* GLOBULE, *grānulum* GRANULE. Some words in *-ule* that were temporarily current, e.g. †*scrupule*, gave way finally to earlier forms in -LE[1]; others, e.g. †*formule*, to the orig. L. form. The corr. adjs. end in -ULAR, -ULOSE, -ULOUS.

ulema ū·ləmə body of Muslim doctors in the law under the authority of the Sheik-ul-Islam xvii; one of these xix. – Arab. (Turk., Pers.) *ʿulemā*, pl. of *ʿālim* learned, f. *ʿalama* know. So F. *ouléma, uléma*, Sp. *ulema*, etc.

-ulent jŭlənt repr. L. *-ulentus*, used to form adjs. usu. with the sense of 'abounding in, full of', as *corpulentus* CORPULENT, *fraudulentus* FRAUDULENT, *opulentus* OPULENT, *pūrulentus* PURULENT, *truculentus* TRUCULENT. Variants with *o* and *i* are repr. by *violentus* VIOLENT, *pestilentus* PESTILENT, *somnolentus* SOMNOLENT.

ullage ʌ·lidʒ amount by which a cask or bottle falls short of being full. xv (*oylage, ulage*). – AN. *ulliage* (cf. AL. *oillagium, eolagium, ullagium, oculagium*) = OF. *ouillage, œillage*, Pr. *ulhage, oulhage*, f. OF. (also mod.) *ouiller, eullier, œiller* (cf. AL. *oillare*) = Pr. *ulhar, oulhar* fill up (a barrel) :– Gallo-Rom. *oculāre, f. L. *oculus* EYE, used in the sense of bung-hole; see -AGE.

ullagone ʌləgɔ·n cry of lamentation. xix. – Ir. *olagón, ologón, olagán*, of imit. origin.

ulmic ʌ·lmik (chem.) derived from the bark of the elm. XIX. – F. *ulmique*, f. L. *ulmus* ELM; see -IC.

ulna ʌ·lnə (anat.) larger inner bone of the fore-arm. XVI. – L. *ulna* ELL. So **u·ln**AR. XVIII. – modL. *ulnāris*.

-ulose jŭlous adj. suffix repr. L. *-ulōsus*, compounded of *-ulus* -ULE and *-ōsus* -OSE[1] and f. sbs. in *-ulus*, *-ula*, *-ulum*. Some Eng. formations are based on existing L. adjs., as *calculose*; others are analogical, as *granulose*. Forms in *-ulose* from the same bases as others in *-ulous* are usu. either older forms now repl. by the commoner *-ulous* or later forms differentiated for specific uses.

-ulous jŭləs adj. suffix repr. L. *-ulōsus* -ULOSE and *-ulus*; to the former belong *crapulous*, *fabulous*, *meticulous*, *populous*, *scrupulous*, to the latter *bibulous*, *credulous*, *garrulous*, *sedulous*. In a few instances L. adjs. of both types exist, as *querulus*, *querulōsus* QUERULOUS, *rīdiculus*, *rīdiculōsus* RIDICULOUS.

ulster ʌ·lstəɹ king-of-arms for Ireland XVI; long loose overcoat of rough cloth introduced by J. G. McGee & Co. of Belfast, capital of Ulster 1867 and thence called *U. overcoat*. Name of the most northerly province of Ireland, the earlier form of which was *Ulvester* (AN. *Ulvestria*, AL. *Ulvestera*, *-tira*) – ON. *Ulfastir*, also *Ulaztir*, *Ulaðstir*, f. Ir. *Ulaidh* men of Ulster; the el. *-ster*, which appears also in *Leinster*, *Munster* (Ir. *Laighean*, *Mumha*), is perh. to be referred to (O)Ir. *tír* land = L. *terra* (see TERRESTRIAL). *Ulton*IAN, the adj. of *Ulster*, is f. medL. *Ultonia* Ulster, f. *Ult-*, stem of OIr. *Ulaid* Ulster, whence also Anglo-Ir. †*Ultagh* Ulsterman (XVII).

ulterior ʌltiə·riəɹ beyond what is immediate or present XVII; locally more remote XVIII. – L. *ulterior* further, more distant, compar. of **ulter* (cf. ULTRA and the rel. of *inferior* with *infra*); cf. F. *ultérieur*, etc. So **ultim**ATE[1] ʌ·ltimət (of an end, stage, etc.) last, final. XVII – medL. *ultimātus*, pp. of late L. *ultimāre* come to an end (Tertullian), f. L. *ultimus*, superl. of **ulter*; see -ATE[2]. **ultimatum** ʌltimei·təm final terms; final point, extreme limit. XVIII. – modL., sb. use of n. of *ultimātus*; in the second sense *ultimate* was used earlier; the L. form is in gen. use in Continental langs. **ultimo** ʌ·ltimou †on the last day XVI; of the last month XVII. abl. (sc. *diē* day or *mense* month) of *ultimus*.

ultra ʌ·ltrə extreme royalist or partisan of any sort. XIX. orig. used by Lady (Sydney) Morgan (1817) after F. *ultra*, short for *ultra-royaliste* (cf. next).

ultra- ʌ·ltrə prefix repr. L. *ultrā* beyond, rel. to *ulterior*, etc. (see above), occurring in L. *ultrāmundānus* that is beyond the world or universe (cf. MUNDANE), medL. *ultrāmarīnus*, *-montānus* ULTRAMARINE, -MONTANE; in mod. use (from early XIX) a living prefix denoting (1) prepositionally, surpassing the limits of (the specified concept), as *ultra-human*, *ultra-fidian* (Coleridge) going beyond mere faith; (2) adverbially, marked by an extreme degree of the quality denoted by the adj. qualified (this sense prob. originating by imitation of F. *ultra-révolutionnaire*, *ultra-royaliste*; (3) spec. in *ultra-violet* applied to the rays beyond the violet end of the visible spectrum; so †*ultra-red* (XIX, now INFRA-*red*); (4) denoting instruments recording very minute measurements, as *ultramicroscope*.

ultraism ʌ·ltrəizm extreme opinion. XIX. f. ULTRA + -ISM. So **u·ltra**IST. Cf. G. *ultraismus*.

ultramarine ʌltrəmərī·n A, applied to a blue pigment obtained orig. from lapis lazuli XVI; B, situated beyond the sea XVII. In B – It. †*oltramarino* (mod. *oltre-*) in *azzurro oltramarino* 'azure from overseas' (cf. Sp., Pg. *azul ultramarino*), the substance being of foreign origin; later assim. to medL. *ultrāmarīnus* (see ULTRA-, MARINE).

ultramontane ʌltrəmɔ·ntein (one) representing the R.C. church beyond (i.e. north of) the Alps and so not favouring extreme views of papal authority XVI (Bacon); (orig. from the French point of view) pert. to the R.C. Church beyond (i.e. south of) the Alps, (and hence) the Italian party favouring such views XVIII. – medL. *ultrāmontānus* (whence also F. *ultramontain*, It. *oltremontano*, etc.); see ULTRA-, MOUNT[1], -ANE[1].

ultroneous ʌltrou·niəs voluntary. XVII. f. L. *ultrōneus*, f. L. *ultrō* at a distance, moreover, into the bargain, of one's own accord, f. base of *uls* beyond, *ulter* (see ULTERIOR); for the ending cf. *spontāneus* SPONTANEOUS, *idōneus*.

ululate ʌ·ljŭleit, jū·ljŭleit howl. XVII. f. pp. stem of L. *ululāre* (whence F. *ululer*, etc.), of imit. origin; see -ATE[3]. So **ulul**A·TION. XVI. – obs. F. or late L.

um əm, m int. expressing hesitation or doubt. XVII.

umbel ʌ·mbəl (bot.) inflorescence in which the flowers are borne upon nearly equal pedicels springing from a common centre. XVI (Gerarde). – F. †*umbelle* (mod. *ombelle*) or L. *umbella* sunshade, dim. of *umbra* shadow; see UMBRA. So **umbellifer** ʌmbe·lifəɹ. XVIII, **umbelli**·FEROUS. XVII – F. †*um-*, *ombellifère*, modL. *umbellifer*.

umber[1] ʌ·mbəɹ grayling. XV. – OF. *umbre*, (also mod.) *ombre*, orig. *ombre de mer* and *de rivière* :– L. *umbra* UMBRA.

umber[2] ʌ·mbəɹ kind of brown earth used as a pigment. XVI. – F. *ombre* or It. *ombra* (also *terre d'ombre*, *terra di ombra* 'shadow earth'), either identical with the words derived from L. *umbra* (cf. prec.) or from

L. *Umbra*, fem. of *Umber* belonging to the ancient province of *Umbria*, Italy (cf. *Umbrica creta* 'Umbrian chalk', Pliny).

umbilical ʌ·mbilaik(ə)l, ʌmbi·lik(ə)l pert. to the navel. XVI. – medL. *umbilīcālis*, f. L. *umbilīcus*, f. base of UMBO + *-l-* deriv. + suffix *-*īko*-; see -AL[1].

umbles ʌ·mblz. XV. var. of NUMBLES; in attrib. use *umble-pie* (XVII, Pepys); cf. HUMBLE-PIE.

umbo ʌ·mbou boss of a shield; round or conical projection. XVIII. – L. *umbō*; NAVEL.

umbra ʌ·mbrə phantom, ghost XVI; uninvited guest accompanying an invited one; (astron.) shadow (cf. PENUMBRA) XVII. – L. *umbra* shadow, shade, phantom, etc.; cf. UMBER[1] and [2].

umbrage ʌ·mbridʒ †shade, shadow XV (Lydg.); shade of trees, (hence) foliage XVI; †shadowy appearance, semblance; †suspicion, inkling, pretext; displeasure, resentment XVII. – OF. *umbrage*, (also mod.) *ombrage* = Pr. *ombratge*, It. *ombraggio* :– Rom. **umbrāticum*, sb. use of n. of L. *umbrāticus* pert. to retirement or seclusion, f. *umbra* (see prec.). The last sense is first used in phr. *give u. to*, modelled on F. *donner ombrage à* make jealous or suspicious. Hence **umbrage**OUS ʌmbrei·dʒəs shady XVI; suspicious, jealous XVII. – (O)F. *ombrageux*.

umbratile ʌ·mbrətail umbrageous XVI; shadowy, unsubstantial XVII. – L. *umbrātilis* keeping in the shade, secluded, f. *umbra* (cf. prec.); see -ILE and cf. F. *ombratile*, etc.

umbre ʌ·mbəɹ African bird Scopus umbretta. XVIII (Pennant). – F. *ombre* or L. *umbra* shade, after modL. *umbretta*, whence **umbre·tte**. XIX.

umbrella ʌmbre·lə circular sunshade or portable protection against bad weather. XVII (also *-ello*). – It. *ombrella*, *ombrello* (whence F. *ombrelle*), dim. of *ombra* :– L. *umbra* (shadow, shade), after *umbella* UMBEL. ¶ late L. *umbrella* occurs in glosses.

Umbrian ʌ·mbriən pert. to *Umbria*, ancient province of Italy, or the Italic dialect spoken there. XVII (Holland).

umlaut u·mlaut (philol.) change in the sound of a vowel due to partial assimilation to an adjacent sound. XIX. G. (Klopstock 1774; familiarized through Jacob Grimm's 'Grammatik' 1819, I. 9); f. *um-* about + *laut* sound (see LOUD). Cf. ABLAUT.

umph mf usu. HUMPH. XVI (*umff*), XVII–XVIII (*umh*), XVIII (*umph*).

umpire ʌ·mpaiəɹ one who decides between disputants or arbitrators. XV (Lydg.). Late ME. *owmpere*, *umpere*, arising from misdivision of *a noumpere*, as *an oumpere* (cf. *anoonpier* . . . the seyd *nounpier* 'Paston Letters', an. 1424, and ADDER, APRON, AUGER); †*noumpere* (XIV–XV) – OF. *no(u)mper*, f. *no(u)n-* NON- + *per* PEER, i.e. a third man called in to decide between two. Hence as vb. XVI. ¶ For the development of ē to ī (whence aiə) before r cf. BRIER[1], FRIAR, QUIRE[1], TIRE[1].

umpty ʌ·mpti signaller's sl. for 'dash' used in reading morse code messages; by assoc. with numerals in -TY[1] used for an indefinite fairly large number; whence **umptee·n**, after numerals in -TEEN. XX.

umquhile ʌ·mʌʍail †sometimes XII (Peterborough Chron.); (arch.) formerly, sometime XIV; adj. former, late XV. Sc. form of *umwhile*, repr. ult. OE. *ymb(e) hwīle*, i.e. *ymb(e)* around, about, (of time) after, with cogns. in all Germ. langs. exc. Gothic, and rel. to AMPHI-, and acc., dat. of *hwīl* time, WHILE.

un[1] ən, n dial. survival of OE. *hine*, accus. of HE. XVII (*'hun*, B. Jonson).

un[2], **'un** ən, n dial. and vulgar form of ONE; reduction of ōn, but often sp. with an apostrophe as if for *wun*.

un-[1] ʌn OE. *un-* = OFris. *un-*, *on-*, *oen-*, (M)Du. *on-*, OS. (LG.), (O)HG., Goth. *un-*, ON. *ú-*, *ó-*, corr. to OIr. *in-*, *an-*, L. *in-* IN-[2], Gr. *an-*, *a-* A-[4], AN-[2], Arm. *an-*, Skr. *an-*, *a-* :– IE. **n̥-*, gradation-var. of *ne* not (see NE). This prefix, expressing negation or contradiction, is capable of being compounded with adjs., advs., pples.

It has been most frequently used with pples. and adjs., but there has been restriction with short simple adjs. (e.g. *unblithe*, *unbold*, *unbroad*, *unfast*, *unglad*, *unslack*, *unstrong*), there being usu. available simple forms with opposite positive meanings; but *unclean*, *uneven*, *unmild*, *untrue*, *unwise*, etc. are of OE. date (some of them of Germ. extent), while *unable*, *undue*, *uneasy*, *unjust*, *unlike*, *unsafe* (Hooker, Sh.) are notable exx. of comps. with adjs. of alien origin. On the other hand derivs. from adjs. in *-able*, *-al*, *-ant*, *-ar*, *-ary*, *-ent*, *-ful*, *-ible*, *-ic(al)*, *-ish*, *-ive*, *-ous*, *-y* are very numerous; *uncomeatable* (XVII, Congreve) and *ungetatable* (XIX) are notably elaborate formations, with an extreme case in Ben Jonson's *un-in-one-breath-utterable*. Formations with pples. appear freely from OE. times onwards. There are several comps. in common use of which the simplex is now obs. or rare, or not current in the relevant senses, as *unbounded*, *undaunted*, *unfailing*, *unfeeling*, *ungainly*, *unmeaning*, *unprincipled*, *unruly*, *unsightly*, *unspeakable*, *untiring*, *untrodden*, *unwieldy*. Adjectives of certain types have not usu. been susceptible of the combination, as *big*, *great*, *huge*, *vast*, *fat*, *fond*, *large*, *long*, *near*, *stupid*, *ugly*, *wrong*; Keats's *untremendous* is a fanciful coinage. Participles with pendent particles are freely used, e.g. *uncalled-for*, *unreferred-to*, *unthought-of*.

There are many parallel formations with IN-[2], esp. in the earlier periods, e.g. ***inactive***, *inconstant, immeasurable, insatiable,* beside *unactive, unconstant, unmeasurable, unsatiable*; *moral*, and its distinguishable negatives, *immoral, unmoral, amoral*, make an exceptional series.

A pejorative sense ('bad', 'evil') of the prefix was exemplified in OE., e.g. *un(ġe)weder* bad or stormy weather (cf. G. *unwetter, ungewitter*), *untīd* wrong time (cf. UNTIMELY), *unwyrd* misfortune; it continued into ME. with limited currency, and survived in Sc. dial. in a formation on an alien word, viz. *unbeest* wild beast, monster (XIII–XIX), with which cf. G. *untier*.

The stress is normally on the basic syll. exc. in attrib. use, e.g. *u·nearned income, u·ntold riches*, or contrasted use, e.g. *even and u·neven patches*.

un-[2] ʌn prefix expressing reversal or deprivation. OE. *un-, on-, an-* = OFris. *und-, un(t)-, and-, on(t)-*, OS. *ant-* (Du. *ont-*), OHG. *ant-, int-* (G. *ent-*), orig. identical with *and-* in OE. *andswaru* ANSWER, *andlong* ALONG[2]. Most of the OE. formations have a simple vb. as their base, as *unbindan* unbind, *undōn* UNDO, *unġeocian* unyoke, and denote reversal of the action; the few denoting removal or deposition were increased later, as *unfasten, unfix, unhorse* (a rider), *unlace, unnail, unsettle, unstitch*, as also those denoting freedom or release, as *unbosom, uncage, unearth, unhorse* (a carriage), *unhouse, unsheathe, unsphere*; from late XVI comps. denoting deprivation of a quality or status appear, as *unchurch, unking, unman*.

The redundant use of the prefix is rare, the chief ex. being *unloose* (cf. OE. *unliesan*, ME. *unlese*), with dial. *unbare, unrip* (XVI), *unstrip*, etc.

Both *un-*[1] and *un-*[2] may be repr. in such a pp. form as *unsaddled*, which may mean 'not saddled or having a saddle' or 'removed from or deprived of a saddle'.

una ju·nə catboat. Name of the first boat of the kind brought from America to England in 1853.

unable ʌnei·bl not able XIV (Wyclif, Gower); physically incapable XVI (in later use Sc.). f. UN-[1]+ABLE, after (O)F. *inhabile* or L. *inhabilis*.

unaneled ʌnənī·ld not having received extreme unction. XVII (Sh. 'Hamlet' I v 77). f. UN-[1] + pp. of †*anele* (XIV), f. *an-* + †*ele* anoint (f. OE. *ele* OIL), after OF. *enuiler* (mod. *enhuiler*), whence ME. *anoil, enoil*; see -ED[1].

unanimous junæ·niməs of one mind or opinion. XVII. f. L. *ūnanimus*, (late) *ūnanimis* (whence †*unanime* freq. 1600–50), f. *ūnus* ONE + *animus* mind; see ANIMATE, -OUS). So **unani·mity** XV. – (O)F. or L.

una·nswerable †discrepant; not admitting of an answer; not responsible *for*. XVII. So **una·nswerab**LY[2] XVI. **una·rm** XIV, **una·rmed** XIII; see UN-[1], UN-[2]; partly after (O)F. *désarmer* DISARM. **unawares** ʌnəwɛə·ɹz without being aware; without warning. XVI (Coverdale). alt. of *unwares* (XII), var. of *unware* (XII), adv. f. OE. *unwær* = ON. *úvarr*; see UN-[1], AWARE, -S. So **unawa·re** adv. XVI (Sh.); adj. XVIII (Swift).

unbeknown ʌnbinou·n in adv. phr. *u. to* without the knowledge of. XVII. Hence, with *-st* (f. -s with parasitic *t*), **unbeknow·nst** (dial. or vulgar). XIX; earlier †*unknow·nst*.

unbend ʌnbe·nd relax XIII; straighten XVII; free oneself from restraint XVIII. f. UN-[1]+BEND vb. **unbe·nding** unyielding, inflexible XVII; remaining erect XVIII. f. UN-[1] + prp. of BEND (-ING[2]). **unbloody** ʌnblʌ·di OE. (rare) *unblōdiġ*; spec. *u. sacrifice* of the Eucharist. XVI. **unbosom** ʌnbu·zəm disclose. XVI (Sh.). UN-[2]; cf. Du. *ontboezemen*. **unbou·nd** OE. *unbunden*; UN-[1]; cf. (M)Du. *ongebonden*, etc. **unbou·nded** XVI (Florio). UN-[1]. **unbri·dled** XIV (Ch.). UN-[1]. **unbroken** ʌnbrou·kn XIII (Cursor M.). UN-[1]; cf. (M)Du. *ongebroken*, (M)HG. *ungebrochen*. **unbu·rden** XVI. UN-[2].

uncanny ʌnkæ·ni †A. malicious XVI; B. (dial.) careless, unreliable XVII; C. not safe to deal with XVIII; D. of a mysterious or weird nature XIX. orig. Sc. and north.; f. UN-[1]+CANNY; sense D is of Eng. development.

unchancy ʌntʃà·nsi (chiefly Sc.) ill-fated XVI; dangerous, unsafe XVIII (Burns). UN-[1]. **unchurch** ʌntʃɔ̄·ɹtʃ exclude from membership of a church. XVII. UN-[2].

uncial ʌ·nʃiəl A. pert. to an inch or an ounce XVII; B. (palæog.) after late L. *unciales litteræ* (Jerome, Prologue to 'Job'), having the large rounded forms characteristic of early Gr. and L. manuscripts XVIII. – L. *unciālis*, f. *uncia* INCH[1], OUNCE[1]; see -AL[1]. ¶ For sense B cf. F. *oncial* (1587); the orig. application is obscure; in Jerome's 'uncialibus, ut vulgo dicunt, litteris' (the emendations *initialibus* and *uncinalibus* have been proposed).

unciform ʌ·nsifɔ̄ɹm hook-shaped. XVIII. – modL. *unciformis*, f. *uncus* hook (cf. Gr. *ógkos* and ANGLE[2]); see -FORM. So **uncin**ATE[2] ʌ·nsineit hooked. XVIII. – L. *uncinātus*, f. *uncīnus*, f. *uncus* (see -INE[1]).

uncle ʌ·ŋkl father's or mother's brother, aunt's husband XIII; *one's u.* pawnbroker (cf. Du. *oom Jan* 'uncle John') XVIII. – AN. *uncle*, (O)F. *oncle* = Pr. *oncle*, *avoncle*, Rum. *unchiu* :– late L. *aunculu-s* uncle, for earlier *avunculus* maternal uncle (*patruus* being paternal uncle), dim. (see next) of **awon-*, var. of the base of L. *avus* grandfather (:– **awos*), *ava, avia* grandmother, which is repr. also by OPruss. *awis*, OSl. *uj*, Lith. *avýnas*, Arm. *hav*, W. *ewythr*, Bret. *eonter* uncle (:– **awentēr*), ON. *ái* great-grandfather, *afi* grandfather.

¶ Superseded ME. *eme* (whence the surname *Eames*), OE. *ēam* = OFris. *ēm*, MLG., MDu. *ōm* (Du. *oom*), OHG. *ōheim* :- Germ. **awuŋχaimaz*, the first el. of which contains the same base.

-uncle ʌŋkl suffix repr. OF. *-uncle*, and its source, L. *-unculus*, *-uncula*, a comp. form with *-ulus*, *-ula*, -ULE, on *-unc-* (as in *homunciō* little man); see CARBUNCLE, PEDUNCLE. Also *-uncule* in *homuncule*; cf. RANUNCULUS.

unco ʌ·ŋkŏ adj. strange, unusual XV (*uncow*); remarkable, great XVIII; adv. extremely (esp. in *the unco guid* 'the rigidly righteous', Burns) XVIII. north. and Sc. clipped form of UNCOUTH; cf. UNKID.

uncomeatable ʌnkʌmæ·təbl inaccessible. XVII (*-ible*, Congreve). Cf. UNGETATABLE. ¶ 'A low, corrupt word' (J.). **unconscionable** ʌnkɔ·nʃənəbl not conscientious; not reasonable, unreasonably great, etc. XVI. UN-[1]. **unco·nscious**. XVIII. UN-[1]. **uncouple** ʌnkʌ·pl release (dogs) from the leash XIV; disconnect XVI. f. UN-[2]+COUPLE, after (O)F. *découpler*; cf. (M)Du. *ont-koppelen*.

uncouth ʌnkū·þ †unknown; †unfamiliar; (dial.) unusual OE.; †unfrequented; uncomely, awkward XVI. OE. *uncūþ* = MDu. *oncont* (Du. *onkond*), OHG. *unkund*, ON. *úkunnr*, Goth. *unkunþs*; CGerm. f. UN-[1]+ pp. of **kunnan* know (see CAN[2]). Cf. UNCO, UNKID.

uncover ʌnkʌ·vəɹ lay open. XIII (Cursor M.). UN-[2]; cf. (O)F. *découvrir* DISCOVER.

unction ʌ·ŋkʃən A. anointing as a rite or symbol XIV (Trevisa); B. (after 1 John ii 20 and 'spiritalis unctio' of the hymn 'Veni, Creator Spiritus') spiritual influence XIV (Wycl. Bible); spiritual feeling XVII; C. lubrication, ointment XVI. – L. *unctiō(n-)*, f. *unct-*, pp. stem of *ung(u)ere*; see UNGUENT, -TION. (Cf. (O)F. *onction*, Sp. *unción*, It. *unzione*.) So **unc**TUOUS ʌ·ŋktjuəs greasy, oily XIV (Trevisa); fat, rich XV. – medL. *unctuōsus*, f. L. *unctus* unction.

undaunted ʌndɔ̄·ntid †untamed XV; †(Sc.) unrestrained XVI; not discouraged XVI.

undee, undy ʌ·ndi (her.) wavy. XIV (*ounde*), XVI (*unde*). – OF. *undé* (mod. *ondé*), f. *unde*, *onde* wave; see UNDULATION, -Y[5]. ¶ *Undated*, f. medL. *undātus*, was also used XV–XVI.

under ʌ·ndəɹ adv. and prep.)(*above*, *over*. OE. *under* = OFris. *under*, OS. *undar* (Du. *onder*), OHG. *untar* (G. *unter*), ON. *undir*, Goth. *undar* :- CGerm. **unðer-* :- IE. **n̥dhero-*, compar. formation (cf. Skr. *ádharas* adj. lower, *adhás* below, Av. *aðarō*, L. *inferus* lower, Skr. *adhamás*, L. *infimus* lowest). Hence *u·nder*MOST. XVI.

under- ʌ·ndəɹ prefix[1], repr. OE. *under-*, comb. form of UNDER adv. and prep. = OS. *undar-*, etc. (see prec.) denoting lower or inferior position or locality, status or rank; defect, or insufficiency; sometimes rendering (O)F. *sous-*, L. *sub-*, *subter-*, *subtus-*; in numerous OE. applications, which, however, often cease to be commonly repr. until XVI or later.

under- ʌ·ndəɹ prefix[2] originating in the coalescence of UNDER prep. with a following sb., the resulting comp. forming an adj. or adv., e.g. *underfoot* (XII), UNDERGROUND (XVI), UNDERHAND, *undersea* (XVII).

undergo ʌndəɹgou· pt. **-we·nt,** pp. **-go·ne** †undermine OE.; †pass under; endure, submit to XIII; experience XVI (Sh., Milton). Late OE. *undergān* (with Germ. cogns.); cf. L. *subīre* (F. *subir*).

undergraduate ʌndəɹgræ·djuət student in statu pupillari at a university. XVII (Laud); shortened to **undergra·d** (XIX). Hence irreg. **u:ndergradu**E·TTE (XX).

underground (with varying str.) adv. XVI; adj. XVII. UNDER-[2].

underhand ʌndəɹhæ·nd adv., as attrib. adj. ʌ·ndəɹhænd, secret(ly), covert(ly). XVI. f. UNDER+HAND; cf. OF. adv. phr. *à* or *par sous main*, Du. *onderhandsch* adj., Da. *underhaanden* adv. ¶ *Under hand* occurs in OE. and ME. in several senses unconnected with the modern use.

underhung ʌ·ndəɹhʌŋ having the lower jaw projecting beyond the upper. XVII. f. UNDER+*hung*, pp. of HANG.

underlay· place beneath, support. OE. *underleċġan* = (M)Du. *onderleggen*, etc.; see UNDER-[1], LAY[1].

underlie· †be subject to; submit to OE.; subtend XVI; form a basis to XIX. OE. *underliċġan* = (M)Du. *onderliggen*, etc. See UNDER-[1], LIE[1].

underling ʌ·ndəɹliŋ subordinate. XII. f. UNDER (in the sense 'in a state of subjection') + -LING[1].

undermine ʌndəɹmai·n mine beneath XIV; overthrow by underhand means XV. f. UNDER+MINE[2], prob. after MDu. *ondermineren* (cf. Du. *ondermijnen*).

undern ʌ·ndəɹn †third hour of the day OE.; †midday (OE.), XIII; (dial.) afternoon or evening XV; (dial.) light meal taken in the afternoon XVII. OE. *undern* = OFris. *undern*, *-en*, OS. *undorn*, *-ern*, OHG. *untorn*, *-arn* (Du. dial. *onder*, G. dial. *untern*, *undern*, *unnern*), ON. *undorn*, *-arn*, Goth. *undaurn-* in *undaurni|mats* ἄριστον; CGerm. formation meaning 'morning' or 'midday', prob. f. UNDER in the sense of 'between' (for the formation cf. L. *inter|nus* INTERNAL). OE. *ǣr undern* before midday, in the morning, ME. *erunder*, survived dial. as *earnder*, *eender*, *yeender* forenoon, and OE. *ofer undern* after midday, in the afternoon, as *orndorn*, *ournder*.

underneath ʌndəɹnī·þ prep. beneath, below; adv. down below. OE. *underneoþan*, f. UNDER+*neoþan* (see BENEATH); cf. ODa. *underneden.*

understand ʌndəɹstæ·nd grasp or know the meaning (or the fact) of OE.; recognize as present or implied XVI. OE. *understandan* = OFris. *understonda*, OIcel. (as a foreign word) *undirstanda*; cf. MLG. *understān* understand, step under, MDu. *onderstaen* (Du. *-staan*), MHG. *understān, -stēn* (G. *unterstehen*), and with another prefix, OE. *forstandan*, OS. *farstandan*, OHG. *firstantan*, MHG. *verstān, -stēn* (G. *verstehen*), MDu. *verstaen* (Du. *-staan*). Hence **understa·nd**ING[1] intellect, intelligence. XI. late OE. (tr. L. *intelligentia*; cf. MSw. *undirstandning*, Icel. *undirstaðning*); (pl.; joc. sl. or colloq.) footwear; legs, feet XIX. ¶ In XV–XVI three forms of the pp. were current, *understanden, understand(e), understanded*, the last of which occurs in no. XXV of the Thirty-nine Articles of Religion (1563) and is echoed in mod. writing ('understanded of the people'); pp. *understood* appears after 1550. For a similar use of a comp. of the vb. 'stand' cf. Gr. *epistánai* understand, know.

understrapper ʌ·ndəɹstræpəɹ underling, subordinate. XVIII. f. UNDER-[1]+(prob.) *strapper* in dial. sense of 'labourer' or 'one who grooms a horse' (cf. STRAP).

undertake ʌndəɹtei·k †entrap XII (Orm); †accept, receive; take in hand, take in charge XIII; †commit oneself XIV; become surety *for* XVI. f. UNDER-[1]+TAKE; cf. OSw. *undertake*; superseded OE. *underfōn*, ME. *underfo, -fong* (see FANG), and *underniman* (see NIM), ME. *undernime*, which survived till XV. Hence **u·ndertak**ER[1] †helper; one who undertakes a task XIV; contractor, now only for *funeral-undertaker* XVII. **underta·k**ING[1] †enterprise; pledge, promise. XIV.

u·ndertone low or subdued tone; undercurrent of feeling, etc. XIX. f. UNDER-[1]+TONE.

underwrite ʌndəɹrai·t write underneath XIV (in pp.); †subscribe (a document) XVI; spec. (a policy of insurance) XVII (hence **u·nderwri·ter**). f. UNDER-[1]; tr. L. *subscrībere* SUBSCRIBE (cf. rare OE. *underwritan*; Du. *onderschrijven*, G. *unterschreiben*).

undies ʌ·ndiz (colloq.) pl. women's undergarments. XX. f. *under-* in UNDERCLOTHES, UNDERWEAR, etc., with pl. of -Y[6] as in *frillies* (XIX). Cf. *unders* XVIII (Fielding).

undine ʌ·ndīn water-nymph. XIX (also *ondine*). – modL. *undina*, also *undena* (Paracelsus 'De Nymphis, etc.', Works 1658 II 391), f. *unda* wave; see WATER; -INE[1]; whence also F. *ondine*, G. *undine*. ¶ Familiarized by F. H. K. de la Motte Fouqué's romance 'Undine' (1811).

undo ʌndū· A. unfasten; B. annul, make of no effect; bring to nought, destroy, ruin OE.; † C. expound XIII. OE. *undōn* = OFris. *un(d)dua*, (M)Du. *ontdoen*, OHG. *intuon*; see UN-[2], DO[1]. The absence of evidence in XVIII for sense A suggests that it came into present literary use through Scott, from whom the earliest exx. are recorded in XIX. Hence **undone** ʌndʌ·n ruined, destroyed XIV; chiefly predic., but current XVII–XVIII in attrib. use.

undoubted ʌndau·tid XV; UN-[1], pp. of DOUBT. Hence **undou·bted**LY[2]. XV.

u·ndress[1], **undre·ss** partial or informal dress. XVII. UN-[1]+DRESS sb. So **undre·ssed** not dressed, trimmed, clothed XV.

undre·ss[2] divest of clothes. XVI (Sh.). UN-[2].

undue ʌndjū·, ʌ·ndjū not owing; improper, unseasonable XIV (Trevisa); excessive XVII. f. UN-[1]+DUE, after (O)F. *indû*, L. *indēbitus*. So **undu·ly**. XIV; after (O)F. *indûment*, †*non deuement* (both XIV).

undulate ʌ·ndjŭleit move in or as in waves. XVII. f. pp. stem of L. *undulāre* (whence F. *onduler*, Sp. *undular*, It. *ondulare*); cf. L. *undulātus* waved, f. late L. *undula*, dim. of *unda* wave; see WATER, -ULE, -ATE[3]. So **undula·tion** XVII (Sir T. Browne, Evelyn). **u·ndulat**ORY[2]. XVIII; cf. F. *ondulatoire*, etc.

undy see UNDEE.

undying ʌndai·iŋ immortal. XIII (*vndeiand*, Cursor M.), UN-[1], prp. of DIE[1].

unearth ʌnə̄·ɹþ exhume XV; expel (an animal) from its earth XVII; (fig.) bring to light XIX. f. UN-[2] + EARTH sb., partly after (O)F. *déterrer*. **uneasy** ʌnī·zi marked by discomfort. XIII (S. Eng. Leg.). UN-[1]. **uneath** ʌnī·þ (arch.) with difficulty; hardly, scarcely. OE. *unēaþe*, f. *un-* UN-[1] + *ēaþe* easily (corr. to OS. *ōðo*, OHG. *ōdo*, ON. *auð-*). **unemployment** ʌnèmploi·mənt. XIX; superseded contemp. *unemploy*. **unending** ʌne·ndiŋ interminable, everlasting. XVII. f. UN-[1]+prp. of END vb. **une·qual**. XVI; earlier †*unegall*. **uneven** ʌnī·vn. OE. *unefen*; CGerm. (exc. Gothic); see UN-[1], EVEN[2]. **unfai·ling**. XIV. UN-[1]. **unfa·sten**. XIII (AncrR.). UN-[2]. **unfeeling** ʌnfī·liŋ. OE. *unfēlende*; UN-[1], prp. of FEEL vb. **unfi·t** XVI. UN-[1]. **unfi·tting**. XVI. UN-[1]; superseded earlier and common †*unsitting* XIV (Ch., Gower). **unfi·x** XVI (Sh.). -UN[2]. **unfold** ʌnfou·ld open the folds of; disclose. OE. *unfealdan*; see UN-[2], FOLD[2], and cf. (M)Du. *ontvouden*, G. *entfalten*. **unfreque·nted**. XVI (Sh.). UN-[1]. **unfrock** ʌnfrɔ·k degrade (cleric). XVII (Milton), f. UN-[2]+FROCK, partly after F. *défroquer* (XV). **ungainly** ʌngei·nli clumsy, awkward. XVII (Cotgr.). f. UN-[1]+(dial.) *gainly*, after *ungain* (dial.) not straight; inconvenient (XV) – ON. *úgegn*, f. *ú-* UN-[1]+*gegn* (cf. AGAIN); see -LY[1].

ungetatable ʌngetæ·təbl unapproachable. XIX. Cf. UNCOMEATABLE.

ungodly ʌngɔ·dli irreligious, wicked. XVI (Tindale). UN-[1]; cf. Du. *ongoddelijk*, G. *ungöttlich*.

unguent ʌ·ŋguənt ointment, salve. XV. – L. *unguentum*, f. *unguere* anoint, rel. to Skr. *anákti* anoints, *aktás* anointed, OPruss. *anktan*, OIr. *imb*, W. *ymenyn*, Bret. *amann*, OHG. *ancho* butter.

ungulate ʌ·ŋgjŭleit hoof-shaped, hoofed. XIX. – late L. *ungulātus*, f. *ungula* claw, hoof, f. *unguis* NAIL; see -ULE, -ATE[2].

unhand ʌnhæ·nd take the hand(s) off. XVII (Sh.). f. UN-[2]+HAND sb.

unhandy ʌnhæ·ndi not easy to handle; lacking in dexterity. XVII. UN-[1].

unhappy ʌnhæ·pi †causing misfortune XIII (Cursor M.); unfortunate, ill-fated, (later) wretched in mind, marked by misfortune XIV. f. †*unhap* misfortune, mishap (XIII, AncrR.) – ON. *úhapp*, f. *ú-* UN-[1]+ *happ* HAP sb.; see -Y[1].

unhi·nge. XVII. UN-[2]. **unho·rse.** XIV (Gower). UN-[2]. **unhou·se.** XIV. UN-[2]; cf. MDu., MLG. *onthusen*.

uni- jū·ni repr. L. *ūni-*, comb. form of L. *ūnus* ONE, a single, repr. by only a few words before or during the classical period, freely used in XIX in techn. terms, to some extent modelled on its Gr. homologue MONO-.

Uniat, -ate jū·niæ̆t (pert. to) a member of an Orthodox Eastern church in communion with the R.C.Ch. XIX. – Russ. *unijat*, f. *unija* – L. *ūniō* UNION.

unicameral[1] -kæ·mərəl consisting of one CHAMBER. XIX. UNI-+CAMERA+-AL[1].

unicorn jū·nikɔ̄ɹn fabulous one-horned equine beast XIII; carriage drawn by three horses arranged one and two XVIII. – (O)F. *unicorne* – L. *unicornis* one-horned, (Vulg.) unicorn, f. *ūnus* ONE+*cornū* HORN, rendering Gr. *monókerōs* (f. *mónos* only, *kéras* HORN).

uniform jū·nifɔ̄ɹm of one or the same form XVI (Palsgr.); sb. (after F.) distinctive uniform dress XVIII. – (O)F. *uniforme* (= Sp., Pg., It. *uniforme*) or L. *ūniformis*, f. *ūnus* UNI-+*forma* FORM. So **unifo·rm**ITY. XV (of importance in English history because of the three acts of uniformity of 1549, 1559, and 1662, concerning conformity in respect of religious practice). – (O)F. or late L.; hence **u:niformit**A·RIAN one who believes that geological phenomena take place continuously and with uniformity. XIX (Whewell).

unify jū·nifai make one. XVI. – (O)F. *unifier* or late L. *ūnificāre*; see UNI-, -FY. So **u:nific**A·TION. XIX.

unilateral jūnilæ·tərəl pert. to one side only. XIX. f. UNI-+LATERAL; cf. F.

union jū·niən, jū·njən act or fact of uniting or being united XV; body of units joined together XVII; textile fabric composed of two or more materials XIX; short for various combs., as *U. flag*, *U. jack* XVIII, *u. house* poor-house or workhouse of a union of parishes under the Poor Laws XIX. – (O)F. *union* or ecclL. *ūniō(n-)* the number one, unity, f. *ūnus* ONE; see -ION. *U. flag*, national flag introduced to symbolize the union of the crowns of England and Scotland XVII; *u. jack*, orig. small union flag flown as a jack (see JACK[3]) XVII. Hence **u·nion**ISM. XIX, **u·nion**IST one who favours the formation or maintenance of a union XVIII; in British politics, relating to the maintenance of parliamentary union between Great Britain and Ireland XIX.

unique junī·k of which there is only one; unparalleled. XVII (also †*unic*, †*unick*). – F. *unique*, †*unic* m. L. *ūnicus* one and only, alone of its kind (whence also Sp., It. *unico*), f. *ūnus* ONE; see -IC. ¶ Reintroduced at the end of XVIII; 'an affected and useless term of modern times' (Todd 1818).

unison jū·nisən, -zən (mus.) identity of pitch XVI; exact agreement. XVII. – (O)F. *unison* (mod. *unisson*) or late L. *ūnisonus* of the same sound, f. *ūnus* ONE+*sonus* SOUND[3]. (For *vnysoune* in York Mystery Plays XXV 262 read *vrysoune* ORISON.) So **unison**OUS yuni·sənəs). XVIII.

unit jū·nit (math.) indivisible whole regarded as the base of number XVI; single individual XVII; quantity serving as a standard of measurement XVIII. f. L. *ūnus* ONE, prob. after *digit*. Introduced by John Dee (1570): 'Note the worde, Vnit, to expresse the Greke Monas, and not Vnitie: as we haue all, commonly, till now, vsed' (Preface to Billingsley's Euclid *iij margin).

unitarian jūnitɛə·riən one who affirms the unipersonality of the Godhead. XVII. f. modL. *ūnitārius* (XVI), f. L. *ūnitās* UNITY; see -ARIAN and cf. TRINITARIAN.

unite junai·t trans. make one XV; intr. form one (*with*) XVII (Sh., Milton). f. *ūnīt-*, pp. stem of L. *ūnīre* join together, f. *ūnus* ONE. (The earlier †*une* and contemp. †*uny* had considerable currency; perh. after OF. *unier*, (O)F. *unir*.) So **un**ITY jū·nĭti fact or condition of being one XIII (Cursor M.); †UNIT XV; the number one XVI; in dramatic composition XVII (Dryden). – (O)F. *unité* (cf. Sp. *unidad*, It. *unità*) – L. *ūnitās* (Varro, after Gr. ἑνότης).

universal jūnivə̄·ɹsəl comprehending the whole XIV (Ch.); pert. to the universe XIV (Gower); of the Church Catholic, forming a whole XV; widely learned or accomplished; (logic) pert. to the whole of a class or genus; also sb. XVI. – OF. *universal* (mod. *-el*) or L. *ūniversālis*, f. *ūniversus*; see next and -AL[1]. So **universa·l**ITY. XIV (once by Ch., thereafter not evidenced till XVI) – (O)F. or late L. (Boethius). **unive·rsally.** XIV (Trevisa); cf. late L. *ūniversāliter*. **unive·rsal**ISM. XIX, -IST. XVII.

universe jū·nivɔ̄ːs A. †*in u.* (L. *in universum*) universally XIV (Ch.); B. the whole of created things XVI; the world XVII. – (O)F. *univers* (cf. Sp., It. *universo*) or L. *ūniversum* the whole world (Cicero, tr. Gr. τὸ ὅλον 'the whole', Plato, Aristotle), sb. use of n. of *ūniversus* all taken together, lit. 'turned into one', f. *ūnus* UNI- + *versus*, pp. of *vertere* turn (see VERSE, -WARD).

university jūnivɔ̄·ɹsĭti whole body of teachers and scholars engaged in the higher branches of learning in a certain place. XIV. – (O)F. *université* – L. *universitās* the whole, the whole number (of), the universe, (in later juridical lang.) society, guild, corporation (whence the med. academic use *universitas magistrorum et scholarium*), f. *ūniversus*; see UNIVERSE, -ITY.

unkempt ʌnke·mᵖt having dishevelled hair XV (Lydg.); †(of language) inelegant, rude XVI (Spenser; prob. after It. *incontos*, L. *incomptus* unadorned). var. of *unkem(be)d*, (cf. MHG. *ungekembet*, ON. *úkembdr*) f. UN-¹ + pp. of *kemb*, OE. *cemban* comb = OS. *kembian*, OHG. *kemben*, *chempen* (G. *kämmen*), ON. *kemba* :- Germ. **kambjan*, f. **kambaz* COMB.

unkid ʌ·ŋkid (dial.) unknown, unfamiliar XIII (Cursor M.); awkward, troublesome XVII; lonely; dismal, uncanny XVIII. ME. *unkid(d)*, f. UN-¹ + *kid(d)*, pp. of (dial.) *kithe*, OE. *cȳþan* make known :- **kunþjan*, f. **kunþ-*, pp. stem of **kunnan* (see CAN²); cf. UNCO, UNCOUTH.

unless ʌnle·s (*not*) on a less condition *than* XIV (Maund.); except it be that, if . . . not XV (first with *than* or *that*, later without XVI); prep. except, but XVI. Late ME. phr. *o(n) lesse*, also *in lesse* (followed by *than*), modelled on (O)F. *à moins que* = Sp. *a menos que*, It *a meno che*, repr. Rom. **ad minus quam* 'at less than'; when the phr. had coalesced into one word (*onless*), lack of stress on the first syll. together with the negative implication of the word led to assim. to UN-¹. ¶ Formerly sometimes used for *lest* (XVI), confused with it, and sp. †*unlest* (XVI).

unle·ttered. XIV (Rolle). UN-¹; cf. ILLITERATE. **unlicked** ʌnli·kt not licked into shape. XVI (Sh.). UN-¹.

unlike ʌ·nlai·k, ʌ·nlaik, ʌnlai·k not like, different XII (Orm); (dial.) unlikely XIV. The early distribution of the word in northern and eastern areas suggests orig. accommodation of ON. *úlíkr*, *úglíkr* = OE. *unġelīć* (ME. *uniliche*), OFris., MLG. *unlik* (Du. *onlijk*), OHG. *ungilih* (G. *ungleich*); CGerm. exc. Gothic; see UN-¹, LIKE¹. So **unLI·KELY¹**. XIV (Barbour); cf. ON. *úlíkligr* improbable.

unloose ʌnlū·s relax; release XIV (PPl.); unfasten XVI (Tindale). f. UN-², LOOSE; cf. OE. *onliesan*, ME. *unlese*. **unlucky** ʌnlʌ·ki UN-¹. XVI (Palsgr.). **unmake** ʌnmei·k UN-². XV (Lydg.). **unman** ʌnmæ·n deprive of manly qualities. XVI (Marston). UN-²; cf. (M)Du. *ontmannen*, etc., (M)HG. *entmannen*. **unma·sk.** XVI (Sidney, Sh.). UN-.² Cf. Du. *ont-*, G. *entmasken*; perh. partly after F. *démasquer* (1564).

unmentionable ʌnme·nʃənəbl not to be mentioned XIX (Carlyle); sb. pl. trousers XIX (1830; orig. U.S. euph.). f. UN-¹ + *mention*ABLE. ¶ Synonyms are *inexpressibles* (1790), *ineffables* (1823), *inexplicables* (1836–7, Dickens), *unutterables* (1843), *unwhisperables* (1837).

unmi·tigated. XVI (Sh.). UN-¹. **unmi·xed.** XVI. UN-¹. **unmu·zzle.** UN-², **unmu·zzled.** UN-¹. XVI (Sh.). **unnai·l.** XV (Malory). UN-². **unna·tural.** XV. UN-¹. **unne·rved.** XVII (Sh.). UN-². **unpai·d.** XIV (Barbour, Trevisa). UN-¹. **unpa·ralleled.** XVI (Drayton). UN-¹.

unready ʌnre·di not ready or prepared XIII (Cursor M.); not prompt XVI. f. UN-¹ + READY. ¶ From XVI (Stow) used as a form of †*unredy* (XIV, Trevisa), f. *unrede* (see -Y¹), OE. *unrǣd* (with Germ. cogns.) lack of counsel or wisdom (see REDE), traditional epithet from XIII of king Ethelred II, originating in the jingling collocation *Æthelred Unred* 'Noble Counsel, Evil Counsel'.

unreal ʌnrī·əl. XVII (Sh.). UN-¹; **unrea·lity.** XVIII. **unreason** ʌnrī·zən †injustice XIV (Cursor M.); †*Abbot of U.*, (Sc.) XV–XVI mock personage in revellings; inability to act reasonably XIX. UN-¹. **unrea·sonable.** XIV (Rolle). UN-¹.

unreliable ʌnrilai·əbl not to be relied on. XIX (De Quincey, who attributes the word to Coleridge, is himself credited with the suggestion of *unrelyuponable*). See RELIABLE.

unruly ʌnrū·li undisciplined, disorderly. XIV. f. UN-¹ + †*ruly* orderly (XIV), f. RULE + -Y¹; modelled on OF. *rieulé/desrieulé*.

unsaid ʌnse·d OE. *unsǣd*, with Germ. cogns. (exc. Gothic). UN-¹. **unsay** (OE., once). XV. UN-². **unseat** ʌnsī·t. XVI (Spenser). UN-². **unsee·mly.** XIII. UN-¹; cf. ON. *úsœmiligr*. **unsee·n.** XII. UN-¹. **unse·ttle.** XVI. UN-². **unsex** ʌnse·ks. XVII (Sh.). UN-². **unshi·p.** XV. UN-²; cf. Du. *ontschepen*, G. *entschiffen*. **unsi·ghtly.** XV. UN-¹; cf. MDu. *onzicht(e)lijk*, etc.

unspeakable ʌnspī·kəbl A. that cannot be expressed in words XIV. B. indescribably bad XIX (*u. Turk*, Carlyle). f. UN-¹ + SPEAK + -ABLE, after L. *ineffābilis* INEFFABLE; cf. F. *indicible* (XV).

unsteady ʌnste·di. XVI; cf. OFris., MDu. *unstedich*, MHG. *unstætec* (G. *unstätig*).

unstrung ʌnstrʌ·ŋ having the string(s) relaxed XVI (Florio); unnerved. XVII. UN-¹, UN-².

unsung ʌnsʌ·ŋ not sung XV; not celebrated in song XVII (Milton); UN-¹.

unsymme·trical. XVIII (J.). UN-¹. **unsyste-ma·tic(al).** XVIII (Burke). UN-¹.

untidy ʌntai·di †untimely, unseemly XIII; not in good order XIV. f. UN-¹ with parallels in the Germ. langs.

untie ʌntai· OE. *untīġan*; UN-².

until ʌnti·l, ʌ·ntil syn. of TILL², adv. and conj. XIII. First in northern and eastern texts (Havelok, Cursor M., R. Mannyng), f. ON. **und*, retained in *unz*, *undz*, for **und es* 'till that', and corr. to OE., OFris., OS. *und* (combined with **te* in OS. *unti*, *unt*, OHG. *unzi*, *unz*, Goth. *unte*)+TILL², the meaning being thus duplicated.

untimeous ʌntai·məs (chiefly Sc.) untimely. XV. alt., by assim. to adjs. in -OUS (cf. WONDROUS) of †*untimes* (XIII, Cursor M.), adj. genitive of †*untime* OE. *untima* bad season, calamity = ON. *útími* misfortune, affliction; see UN-¹, TIME.

untiring ʌntaiə·riŋ not growing weary. XIX. f. UN-¹+prp. of TIRE¹ (intr.).

unto ʌ·ntu, ʌntū· to (in all uses exc. as marking an inf.); (arch.) until XIII. First in northern and eastern texts; f. (Scand.) *un-* of UNTIL+(native) TO. ¶ OS. *untō* is unconnected.

untold ʌntou·ld, ʌ·ntould †not reckoned OE.; immense, vast XIV; not recounted XIV (Ch.). OE. *unteald*; cf. (M)Du. *ongeteld*, etc.

untouchable ʌntʌ·tʃəbl that cannot or may not be touched. XVI (sb. non-caste Hindu XX). UN-¹.

untoward ʌntou·(w)əɹd, ʌntəwɔ̄·ɹd †disinclined; intractable; †awkward, ungainly; unlucky XVI; unpropitious XVII. f. UN-¹+TOWARD adj. Earlier (XV) in *untowardly* adj. and *untowardness*.

untrodden ʌntrɔ·dn not trodden on, untraversed. (XIV), XVI. UN-¹.

untrue ʌntrū· unfaithful OE.; false; wrong XIV. OE. *untrēowe*, with CGerm. cogns.

untruth ʌntrū·þ †unfaithfulness OE.; falsehood XV. UN-¹; cf. ON. *útrygð*. Hence **untru·th**FUL¹.

untutored ʌntjū·təɹd. XVI (Sh.). UN-¹.

unused ʌnjū·zd. XIII (RGlouc.). UN-¹.

unusual ʌnjū·ʒuəl, -zjuəl. XVI. UN-¹.

unutterable ʌnʌ·təɹəbl above or beyond description. XVI. Cf. F. *indicible*, UNMENTIONABLE.

unwashed ʌnwɔ·ʃt. XIV (applied by Sh. to an artisan). UN-¹. Earlier †*unwa·shen* (OE. *unwæscen*).

unwell ʌnwe·l not in good health. XV. Before late XVIII mostly north., Sc., Anglo-Ir.; said to have been generalized through Lord Chesterfield's use. UN¹-.

unwe·pt. XVI (Sh.). UN¹-.

unwieldy ʌnwī·ldi †impotent, feeble XIV (Ch.); awkward in movement; difficult to handle XVI. f. UN-¹+*wieldy* (obs. exc. as back-formation from this word), extended form with -Y¹ of †*wield*, OE. *wielde*, *ġewielde* vigorous, active :- *(*ga-*)*walðja-*, f. **walð-*, base of WIELD; superseding earlier †*unwelde*, †*unweldly* (XIII).

unwilling. OE. *unwillende*; newly formed in XVI; UN-¹.

unwi·se. OE. *unwīs*; of CGerm. range; UN-¹.

unwitting ʌnwi·tiŋ not knowing or aware, OE. *unwitende*, of CGerm. range; rare after 1600 till XIX (Southey). Hence **unwi·tting**LY². XIV (Barbour, Wycl. Bible.

unwo·rthy worthless; not worthy, undeserving XIII; unmerited; not befitting (one) XIV. UN-¹; cf. MDu. *onwerdich*, ON. *úverðugr*.

-uous juəs suffix repr. L. *-uōsus* or deriv. OF. *-uous* (mod. *-ueux*), f. *u*-stems + *-ōsus* -OSE¹, -OUS, as in †*monstruous*, *sinuous*, *sumptuous*; or f. L. *u*-stems+-OUS, as in *arduous*, *conspicuous*, *exiguous*, *incongruous*, *promiscuous*, *strenuous*, *superfluous*. So **-u·**ITY, **-uo·**SITY. ¶ In XV–XVI *rightwis* RIGHTEOUS became *rightuous*.

up ʌp to or at an elevated position. repr. two OE. words (i) *up*, *upp* (said primarily of motion) = OFris. *up*, *op*, OS. *up* (Du. *op*), ON. *upp*, (ii) *uppe* (said primarily of position) = OFris., OS. *uppa*, ON. *uppi*; rel. to OHG. *ūf* (G. *auf*). The use of *up* adv. to express complete consumption was prob. adopted from Scand. (e.g. ON. *drekka upp*, drink up). See also UPON. By ellipsis of preps., such as *against*, *along*, etc., a new prep. was developed to form collocations like *upstairs*. XVI.

up- ʌp prefix repr. OE. *up-*, *upp-*, corr. to OFris. *op-*, *up-*, (M)Du. *op-*, OS., (M)LG. *up-*, OHG. *ūf-* (G. *auf-*), ON. *upp-*. In OE. there were some thirty comps. showing considerable variety of formation (a prominent sense was 'of the heavens'), the chief survival being UPLAND. There were several comps. with pa. pples., fewer with prps. Many formations of ME. and later date in all groups were of temporary vogue, and there were many fresh coinages in either old or new senses; *upgrow* (XV), *upgrowth* (XIX), and *uplift* sb. (XIX), *uplift* vb. (XIV) show typical divergence of date.

up-a-daisy ʌ·pədeizi encouraging excl. on lifting a child from the ground. XVIII (*-dazy*, Swift); also dial. *upaday*; cf. *lackadaisy*, beside (*a*)*lackaday*. Cf. UPSIDAISY.

upanishad upæ·niʃəd division of Vedic literature dealing with the Deity, creation, and existence. XIX. Skr., f. *upa* near to+*ni-shad* sit, lie down.

upas jū·pəs Javanese tree. Antiaris toxicaria. XIX. – Malay *ūpas* poison, in *pōhun* or *pūhun ūpas* poison-tree. Fabled to have existed in Java, having poisonous properties such that it destroyed life for many miles around, XVIII ('London Magazine', in an article purporting to be translated from one written by Foersch, a Dutch surgeon at Samarang; hence in Erasmus Darwin's 'The loves of the plants', 1789.)

upbraid ʌpbrei·d †adduce as a fault OE.; find fault with, carp at; censure, reprove soundly XIII. Late OE. *upbrēdan* (Wulfstan), perh. after ON. **uppbregða* (cf. MSw. *upbrygdha*), f. *upp* UP+*bregða* = OE. *breġdan* BRAID. ¶ The foll. forms, with variation of prefix, have been in use: *abraid, em-, imbraid, umbraid* XIV–XVI; cf. Da. *bebreide*.

upbringing ʌ·pbriŋiŋ rearing and training. XVI. Gerund of †*upbring* (XIII), with Germ. cogns.

upheaval ʌphī·vəl (geol.) raising by volcanic action. XIX (Lyell); hence freq. fig. f. *upheave* (XIII; spec. in geol. XIX), f. UP-+HEAVE; see -AL².

uphill ʌ·phil (str. variable) ascent XVI; adj. †high, elevated; going upwards, arduous XVII; adv. XVII. f. UP prep.+HILL.

uphold ʌphou·ld support, sustain. XIII (AncrR., Cursor M.). Of CGerm. extent exc. Goth.; f. UP-+HOLD¹; cf. OE. *upheald* supporter, maintenance.

upholsterer ʌphou·lstərəɹ one who makes and repairs furniture in which woven fabrics are used. XVII. Extended form with -ER¹ of †*upholster* (XV) dealer in or repairer of small or secondhand articles, f. UPHOLD+-STER, a parallel formation to earlier synon. *upholder* (XIV), which remained current locally. Hence **upho·lster** vb. XIX, **upho·lst**ERY. XVII.

uphroe jū·frou; see EUPHROE.

upkeep ʌ·pkīp maintenance in good condition XIX, f. phr. *keep up* maintain (XVI).

upland ʌ·plənd (arch.) land lying away from the sea; high ground XVI; also adj., repl. earlier *uplandish* (XIV; cf. OE. *uplendisċ* rustic). f. UP, used adj., raised, elevated+LAND sb. ¶ For the first sense cf. ON. *Upplǫnd* eastern inland counties of Norway, Sw. *Uppland* district in central Sweden, MDa. *Opland* Sweden, Norw. *uppland*, Da. *opland* inland country.

upmost ʌ·pmoust, -məst uppermost, highest. XVI (Geneva Bible). f. UP+-MOST.

upon əpɔ·n on. XII (Orm). First in eastern and northern texts; f. UP+ON, after ON. *upp á* (OSw. *up a, uppa*, Sw. *på*, Norw., Da. *paa*); distinct from OE. *uppan*, ME. *uppon, uppe(n), up* prep. on, upon.

upper ʌ·pəɹ higher, top. XIV (not common before XV). f. UP+-ER³; opp. to NETHER and rendering L. *superior* SUPERIOR; cf. MDu. *upper* (Du. *opper*), LG. *upper*. Hence sb., XIX. **u·pper**MOST. XV (preceded by †*upperest* and *uppermore*).

uppish ʌ·piʃ from XVII in various sl. uses implying elevation or elation, f. UP+-ISH¹.

upright ʌ·prait (stress var.) erect, perpendicular OE.; †lying on the back OE. (late); of unbending rectitude XVI; sb. †vertical face XVI; architectural elevation; upright part or member XVII. OE. *upriht*, corr. to OFris. *upriucht*, (M)Du. *oprecht*, OHG. *ūfreht* (G. *aufrecht*), ON. *uppréttr*; CGerm. (exc. Gothic); see UP-, RIGHT.

uproar ʌ·prɔəɹ A. †insurrection, tumult; B. outcry, noise of tumult XVI. Used first by Tindale (1526) and Coverdale (1535) in their translations of passages where Luther's Bible has *aufruhr*. – Du. *oproer* (in Du. Bible of 1531, 2 Kings xi 14 margin), in MDu. *uproer*, MLG. *uprōr*, f. *op* UP-+*roer*, *rōr* = OS. *hrōra*, OHG. *ruora* (G. *ruhr*) motion (cf. OE. *hrēran*, ON. *hrœra* move); in B influenced by ROAR. Hence **uproa·ri**OUS. XIX.

upse-, upsidaisy, vars. of UP-A-DAISY. XIX.

upset ʌpse·t †A. set up, raise, erect XIV (in pp. R. Mannyng, Gower); (Sc.) make good XVI. B. overthrow, overturn XIX; throw into disorder XIX. f. UP+SET¹. For A senses cf. (M)Du. *opzetten*, MHG. *ūfsetzen* (G. *aufsetzen*); in B superseding *overset*.

upshot ʌ·pʃɔt †final shot in an archery match, fig. parting shot; †mark aimed at; †end, conclusion XVI; *in the u.* at last XVI, (hence) result, issue (Sh.) f. UP-+SHOT.

upside down ʌ·psai(d)dau·n so that the upper surface or part is underneath. XVI. Alt. of (dial.) *upsidown* (XV), var. of †*upsedown*, †*up sadown*, for earlier †*up so down* (XIV), orig. meaning 'so as to be upset or overturned'. The form of this phr. is difficult to account for, there being no appropriate use of *so*; but †*up so doun* may itself be a perversion of †*up to doun* (RGlouc. Chronicle 6831), with var. †*up adoun*, which may be modelled on (O)F. *de haut en bas* 'from high to low'. The present form, and †*up set* (or †*upset*) *down*, are due to attempts to express intelligibly the meaning 'with the upper side (set) down'.

upsides ʌpsai·dz even or quits *with*. XVIII. orig. Sc.; f. UP, SIDE sb., -S. Cf. MSw. *upsidhes*.

upstairs ʌpstɛə·ɹz so as to ascend a flight of STAIRS; see UP. XVI (Sh.).

upstart ʌ·pstāɹt (one) newly or suddenly risen in position. XVI. equiv. to contemp. †*start-up*, f. *start*, pp. of START²+adv. UP; cf. *upstart* vb., (now rare) start up (XIV).

uptake ʌ·pteik (Sc.) capacity for understanding. XIX (Scott). f. *uptake* vb. XVIII (Sc.) understand, f. UP+TAKE.

upward ʌ·pwəɹd to or towards a high or higher position. OE. *upweard*, corr. to MLG. *upwart*, MDu. *opwaert* (Du. *opwaart*), MHG. *ūfwert*; see UP, -WARD. So

u·pWARDS. OE. *upweardes*, corr. to OS. *upwardas* (Du. *opwaarts*), MHG. *ūfwertes* (G. *aufwärts*).

ur ə̄ var. of ER. XIX (O. W. Holmes).

ur- ūr primitive, original, earliest. G. prefix as in *ursprache* primitive language.

uræmia juərī·miə (path.) presence in the blood of urinary constituents. XIX. modL., f. Gr. *oûron* URINE + *haîma* blood (cf. HÆMO-).

uræus juərī·əs representation of the sacred asp or serpent on the headdress of ancient Egyptian deities and kings. XIX. modL. – Gr. *ouraîos* (Horapollo) – Egyptian. perh. infl. by Gr. *ourá* tail.

Ural juə·rəl name of a mountain chain forming the north-eastern boundary of Europe with Asia XVIII; *U.-Altaic* pert. to the region including the Urals and the ALTAIC mountains, its inhabitants or their speech; Turanian, Finno-Tartar; also with comb. from *Uralo-* jurei·lou in *Uralo-Altaic*, *-Finnic* XIX. Also **Ural**IAN jurei·liən. XVIII; cf. F. *ouralien*.

uranism juə·rənizm homosexuality. XIX. – G. *uranismus*, f. Gr. *ouránios* heavenly, taken to mean 'spiritual', f. *ouranós* heaven (cf. URANUS); see -ISM.

uranium jurei·niəm (chem.) metallic element. XVIII. modL. (Klaproth, 1789), f. URANUS + -IUM; cf. TELLURIUM (Klaproth 1798).

urano- juə·rənou, juərənɔ· comb. form of Gr. *ouranós* sky, heaven(s), roof of the mouth; e.g. **urano·**GRAPHY (XVII), **urano·**METRY (XVIII); *u·ranoplasty* plastic surgery of the hard palate (XIX).

Uranus juə·rənəs planet situated between Saturn and Neptune. XIX. So named (in conformity with names of major planets called after classical deities) by Bode (1747–1826) – L. *Ūranus* – Gr. *Ouranós* husband of Gæa (Earth) and father of Cronos (Saturn); superseded the name 'the Georgian (sidus)', *Georgium sidus*, which was given to it in honour of George III by Sir William Herschel, who discovered it in 1781.

urban ə̄·ɹbən pert. to a town or city. XVII (rare before XIX; cf. next). – L. *urbānus*, f. *urb-*, *urbs* city; see -AN and cf. next and SUBURBAN.

urbane əɹbei·n †urban XVI; having the manners or culture characteristic of town life; civil, polite XVII. – (O)F. *urbain*, *-aine* or L. *urbānus*, *-āna*; see prec. and -ANE[1]. So **urban**ITY əɹbæ·niti refined civility; †polished wit; city or town life. XVI. – (O)F. or L. ¶ For the difference of form, stress, and meaning between *urban* and *urbane*, cf. *human*, *humane*.

urceolate ə̄·ɹsiŏleit pitcher-shaped. XVIII. – modL. *urceolātus*, f. L. *urceolus*, dim. of *urceus* pitcher; see URN, -ATE[2].

urchin ə̄·ɹtʃin hedgehog XIII; (dial.) deformed person; mischievous youngster; little fellow, brat XVI. ME. *urchon*, beside *yrichon* (XIII), *hirchon*, *irchoun* – ONF. *herichon*, **ir(e)chon*, **urchon*, vars. of OF. *heriçon* (mod. *hérisson*, dial. *hérichon*, *irechon*, *hurchon*) = Pr. *erisó* :– Rom. **hēriciōnem*, f. L. *hērīcius*, late form of *ērīcius* hedgehog (whence Pr. *eritz*, Sp. *erizo*, Pg. *ouriço*, It. *riccio*, Rum. *ariciu*), f. *(h)ēr* = Gr. *khḗr*. ¶ Initial *h* has been mobile and the form of the final syll. has varied greatly, *-in*, †*yn* dating from XV.

Urdu uə·ɹdū variety of Hindustani, the standard language of Mussulmans. XVIII. – Hind. *urdū*, of Pers. origin, for *zabān i urdū* language of the camp; Pers. *urdū* camp. – Turkī *ordu* (see HORDE).

ure juəɹ use, esp. in phr. *bring*, *come*, *put in ure*. XV. – AN. **eure* = OF. *evre*, *euvre*, *uevre* (mod. *œuvre*) :– L. *opera*, pl. of *opus* work, used as fem. sg. (see OPERA). Cf. INURE, MANURE.

-ure jəɹ, juəɹ (combined with *s* and *t* giving ʒəɹ and tʃəɹ), suffix repr. (O)F. *-ure* – L. *-ūra* (whence also Sp., Pg., It. *ura*, Rum. *-ură*), denoting primarily action or process or the result of this, (hence) office or rank, collective body or organization; usu. affixed to pps., but in L. *figūra* FIGURE being exceptionally attached to a present vb.-stem. The earliest adoptions, mainly through F., were *figure*, *nature*, *scripture*, *stature* (XIII), *censure*, *culture*, *jointure*, *literature*, *pressure*, *tonsure* (XIV). Later formations, as *composure*, *exposure*, were based on stems of L. origin, a few are of Rom. origin, e.g. *verdure*, *denture*, or formed on an Eng. stem, e.g. *wafture* (XVII). Various other F. endings have been assim. to this in Eng. adoptions, as in *leisure*, *manure*, *pleasure*, *tenure*, *treasure*. Cf. also *armour*.

urea juə·riə carbamide, a constituent of urine. XIX. modL. – F. *urée*, f. Gr. *oûron* URINE or *oureîn* urinate. The comb. form is *ureo-*.

ure-ox juə·rɔks aurochs. XVII. – G. *urochs*, var. of *auerochs*; see URUS, OX.

-uret jŭret (chem.) suffix added to a stem or truncated word, now gen. replaced by -IDE. – modL. *-urētum* (also *-orētum*), proposed in 1787 by French chemists, who in F. forms preferred the ending *-ure* (De Morveau, 1787); first used *c.*1790, after F. words in *-ure*, in *hydruret*, *phosphuret*, *sulphuret*, it was extended to other terms, such as *carburet* (cf. CARBURETTOR), *nitruret*, *ioduret*, and later still further; it survives in *carburetted* (whence *-ettor*) and *sulphuretted*.

ureter jurī·təɹ (anat.) urinary duct. XVI. – F. *uretère* or modL. *ūrētēr* – Gr. *ourētḗr*, f. *oureîn* make water, f. *oûron* URINE. So **urethra** jurī·þrə tube which discharges urine from the bladder. XVII. – late L. *ūrēthra* – Gr. *ourḗthrā*, f. *oureîn*.

urge ɜːdʒ demand or entreat insistently; press or drive forward. XVI. – L. *urgēre* press, drive, compel, perh. f. IE. **wereg-*, whence also OE. *wrecan* WREAK. So **u·rgENT**. XV. – (O)F. *urgent* – prp. of L. *urgēre*. Hence **u·rgENCY**. XVI.

-uria juə·riə final el. in L. form repr. Gr. *-ouríā*, f. *oûron* (see URINE, -IA[1]) in terms of path. denoting morbid conditions of the urine, e.g. *albuminuria, hæmaturia*.

uric juə·rik pert. to urine. XVIII. – F. *urique*, f. Gr. *oûron* URINE; see -IC.

-urient juə·riənt suffix – L. *-ūrient-*, *-ūriēns*, prp. ending of L. desiderative vbs. in *-ūrīre*, as ESURIENT, PARTURIENT.

Urim juə·rim objects worn in or on the Jewish high-priest's breastplate. XVI (Matthew's Bible, 1537). – Heb. *ūrīm*; usu. in the collocation *Urim and Thummim* (both words are of doubtful origin), for which Coverdale has 'light and perfectnesse', following Luther's 'licht und recht', corr. to LXX δήλωσις καὶ ἀλήθεια (Vulg. 'doctrina et veritas' or 'perfectio').

urinal juə·rinəl †glass vessel to hold urine for inspection XIII (Laȝ.); †vessel for chemical solution XIV (Ch.); chamber-pot XV; place provided for passing urine XIX. – (O)F. *urinal* = Pr. *urinal*, etc. – late L. *ūrīnal*, sb. use of n. of late *ūrīnālis* urinary, f. *ūrīna*; see -AL[1].

urine juə·rin fluid discharged from the bladder. XIV. – (O)F. *urine* = Pr. *urina*, etc. – L. *ūrīna* (adopted in the chief Eur. langs.), perh. distantly rel. to Gr. *oûron*. So **uri·nARY**. XVI. – medL. **ūrīnārius*. **u·rinATE**[3] make water. XVI. f. pp. stem of medL. *ūrīnāre* (in classical L. dive).

urn ɜːn vessel in which to preserve the ashes of the dead XIV (Ch.); vessel for holding voting-tablets or the like XVI; oviform pot or pitcher XVII (*tea urn* XVIII). – L. *urna* (whence also F. *urne*, Sp., It. *urna*) :– **urcnā*, rel. to *urceus* pitcher (cf. L. *orca* butt, tun, Gr. *úrkhē* jar); prob. all of alien origin.

urning ɜ·ɹniŋ male homosexual. – G. *urning*, f. (*Venus*) *Urania*, taken to mean 'heavenly love' and applied by Ulrich to homosexuality as being 'spiritual' (Kluge); cf. URANISM.

uro-[1] juə·rou, jurɔ· comb. form of Gr. *oûron* URINE, as in *uro·logy*, *u:ropoie·tic* (XVIII), *uro·scopy* (XVII), and various chemical terms.

uro-[2] juə·rou, comb. form of Gr. *ourā́* tail, as in *urodele*.

ursine ɜ·ɹsain pert. to or like a bear. XVI. – L. *ursīnus*, f. *ursus* bear; see ARCTIC, -INE[1].

urticate ɜ·ɹtikeit sting like a nettle. XIX. f. pp. stem of medL. *urticāre*, f. L. *urtīca* nettle (whence modL. *urticāria* nettle-rash, in Eng. use from XVIII); see -ATE[3]. So **urticA·TION** stinging. XVII. – medL.

urubu urubū· black vulture of America. XVII. Tupi.

urucu urukū· anatta. XVII (Purchas). Tupi. ¶ Adopted through F. as *roucou* XVII.

urucuri urukū·ri Brazilian palm-tree. XIX. Tupi.

urus juə·rəs AUROCHS. XVII. – L. *ūrus* (Gr. *oûros*). – Germ. **ūrus* (OE., OHG. *ūr*, ON. *úrr*). ¶ In anglicized form †*ure* (cf. F. †*ure*) current XVI–XVII.

us ʌs, əs objective of WE. OE. *ūs* = OFris., OS. *ūs*, (M)Du. *ons*, (O)HG. *uns*, ON. *oss*, Goth. *uns* :– CGerm. **uns* :– IE. **ns*, reduced grade of **nes* (Skr. *nas*). ¶ The present form repr. a generalization of the unstr. var. *ŭs*, the orig. long form being repr. in ME. by *ous*, *ows* ūs.

usage jū·zidʒ, jū·sidʒ habitual use, custom, or conduct. XIII (Cursor M.). – (O)F. *usage* = Pr. *uzatge* (whence Sp. *usaje*, It. *usaggio*) :– L. *ūsus* USE; see -AGE. So **u·SANCE** †usage XIV; period allowed for the payment of a bill of exchange XVII. – OF. *usance* = Pr. *uzansa*, Sp., It. *usanza* :– Rom. **ūsantia*, f. **ūsāre*. **USER**[5] jū·zəɹ (leg.) continual use or enjoyment. XIX; evolved from †*abuser*, *non-user* (XVII).

use jūs act or manner of using, fact of being used. XIII. ME. *us* – (O)F. *us* (surviving in *les us et coutumes*) = Pr. *us*, Sp., It. *uso* :– L. *ūsus* use, usage, f. *ūs-*, pp. stem of *ūtī* use (earlier *oetī*, for **oitī*). Hence **u·seFUL**[1], **u·seLESS**. XVI (Sh.). So **use** jūz observe (a custom, rite, etc.), follow as a custom XIII; engage in, employ, deal with; habituate, accustom XIV (*be used to* XV); intr. be accustomed now only in pt. XIV. – (O)F. *user* †employ (now *user de*), consume, wear out = Pr. *uzar*, Sp. *usar*, It. *usare* :– Rom. **ūsāre*, f. L. pp. stem *ūs-*.

usher ʌ·ʃəɹ officer having charge of the door of a hall, etc. XIV (Ch.); officer whose ceremonial duty it is to precede a person of rank; (fig.) precursor; assistant master in a school XVI. – AN. *usser* = OF. *ussier*, *uissier* (mod. *huissier*) :– medL. *ūstiārius* (VI), for L. *ōstiārius* door-keeper, f. *ōstium* door, f. *ōs* mouth (see ORAL), -ER[2]. Hence vb. XVI. ¶ For *-sh-* from OF. *-ss-* cf. CUSHION, -ISH[2], PUSH.

Usnea ʌ·sniə genus of lichens. XVI. – medL. *usnea* – Arab., Pers. *ushnah* moss.

usquebaugh ʌ·skwibɔ̄ WHISKY[1]. XVI. – Ir. and Sc. Gael. *uisge beatha* 'water of life' (cf. AQUA VITÆ, F. *eau de vie* brandy), i.e. *uisge* WATER, *beatha* life (see VITAL). ¶ The usual form is *-baugh*, repr. Ir. Gael. pronunc., the vars. in *-bae* (†*iskie bae*, †*usquabah*, *whisky bae*) the Sc. Gael.

ustilago ʌstilei·gou smut on grain. XVI. – mod. use of late L. *ustilāgō* f. *ust-*, pp. stem of *ūrere* burn.

usual jū·ʒuəl, jū·zjuəl that is in ordinary or common use. XIV. – OF. *usual*, (also mod.) *usuel*, or late L. *ūsuālis* (whence Pr. *uzual*, etc.), f. *ūsus* USE; see -AL[1]. Hence **u·sual**LY[2]. XV.

usucapion jūzjukei·piən (leg.) acquisition of ownership by long use. XVII. – F. *usucapion* or L. *ūsūcapiō(n-)*, f. *ūsūcapere*, f. *ūsū*, abl. of *ūsus* USE + *capere* take, seize (see CAPTURE). So **usuca·p**TION. XVII. – OF. or medL.

usufruct jū·zjufrʌkt right of temporary possession or use. XVII. – medL. *ūsūfrūctus* (cf. late L. *ūsūfrūctuārius*), for L. *ūsusfrūctus*, more fully *ūsus et frūctus*, *ūsus frūctusque* use and enjoyment; see USE, FRUIT. Earlier †*usufruit* XV – (O)F. *usufruit*.

usurp juzə̄·ɹp appropriate wrongfully to oneself. XIV. – (O)F. *usurper* – L. *ūsūrpāre* seize for use, prob. for **ūsūripāre*, f. *ūsū*, abl. of *ūsus* USE + *rapere* seize (see RAPE[3]). So **usurp**A·TION. XIV. – (O)F. or L.

usury jū·ʒəri, jū·zjŭri lending money at interest XIV; (arch.) interest on money lent XV. – AN. **usurie* = (O)F. *usure* or medL. *ūsūria*, f. L. *ūsūra*, f. *ūsus* USE; see -Y[3]. Hence **usur**IOUS juʒuə·riəs, -zj-. XVII. So **u·surer**[2]. XIII – AN. *usurer*, OF. *usureor*, (also mod.) *usurier*, f. *usure* (= Pr. *uzura*, Sp., It. *usura*) :– L. *ūsūra*, f. *ūsus*.

ut ʌt, ut (mus.) first note of Guido Aretino's hexachords, and of the octave in modern solmization (see DO[2]). – (O)F. *ut*; the lowest of the series *ut*, *re*, *mi*, *fa*, *sol*, *la*, *si*, said to be taken from the office hymn for St. John Baptist's day: *Ut* queant laxis *re*sonare fibris / *Mi*ra gestorum *fa*muli tuorum / *Sol*ve polluti *la*bii reatum, / *S*ancte *I*ohannes. See GAMUT.

utas jū·təs (hist.) octave of a church festival. XIV (Trevisa). Reduced form of *utaves*, varying with *eotas*, *eoytaves*. – OF. *outaves*, *oectaves*, var. of *oitieves* :– L. *octāvās* (*dies*), accus. pl. of *octāva* (*diēs*) eighth day.

utensil jute·nsĭl †(coll. sg.) domestic vessels or implements XIV; domestic implement, etc. XV; sacred vessel; in full *chamber u.* XVII. – OF. *utensile* (mod. *ustensile*) – medL. *ūtēnsile*, sb. use of n. of L. *ūtēnsilis* fit for use, useful (n.pl. *ūtēnsilia* implements, materials), f. *ūtī* USE. Earlier str. *u·tensil*, as by Sh., Milton, J., and till *c.*1800; but the present str. is recorded by Bailey in 1730. L. *ūtēnsilia* was anglicized as †*utensilies* XV–XVII.

uterus jū·tərəs (anat.) womb. XVII. – L. *uterus* belly, womb, obscurely rel. to Skr. *udáram*, Gr. *hóderos*, OPruss. *weders* belly. So **u·ter**INE[1] having the same mother XV; pert. to the uterus XVII. – late L. *uterīnus*.

utility juti·lĭti usefulness XIV (Ch.); useful thing or feature XV. – (O)F. *utilité* – L. *ūtilitās*, f. *ūtilis* useful, f. *ūtī* USE; see -ILE, -ITY. Hence **utilit**A·RIAN. XVIII (Bentham, 1781). So **uti**LIZE jū·tilaiz make useful, convert to use. XIX. – F. *utiliser* (1792) – It. *utilizzare*, f. *utile* :– L. *ūtilis*. **u·tiliz**A·TION. XIX. – F. (1812).

utmost ʌ·tməst, -moust outermost OE.; of the highest degree XIV; †latest, last XV; also sb. †furthest part OE.; extreme degree or limit XV. OE. *ūtmest*, var. of *ūtemest*, f. *ūt*, *ūte* + *-mest*; see OUT adv., -MOST. Cf. OUTMOST, UTTERMOST.

utopia jutou·piə name of Sir Thomas More's imaginary republic XVI; place or condition of ideally perfect government XVII. – modL. *ūtopia* 'no-place', f. Gr. *ou* not + *tópos* place; see TOPIC, -IA[1]. **Uto·p**IAN. XVI. – modL. *Ūtopiānus* (More, 1516).

utraquist jū·trəkwist (theol.) one who upholds communion in both kinds. XIX. – modL. *u·trāquistā*, f. L. *utrāque*, in phr. *sub utrāque specie* under both kinds; see -IST.

utricle jū·trikl small sac or bladder. XVIII. – F. *utricle* or L. *ūtriculus*, dim. of *ūter* leather bottle; see -CLE.

utter[1] ʌ·təɹ outward, outer OE.; extreme, total XV. OE. *ūter(r)a*, *ūttra*, compar. formation (see -ER[3]) on *ūt* OUT, corr. to OFris. *utt(e)ra*, *ūtera*, MDu. *ūtere* (Du. *uiter-*), OHG. *ūʒaro* (G. *äusser*); for shortening of *ū* cf. *udder*. Hence **u·tter**LY[2] †plainly, straight out XIII; absolutely, completely XIV (Ch.); cf. MLG., MDu. *ūterlike* (Du. *uiterlijk*), MHG. *ūʒerliche* (G. *äusserlich*). **u·tter**MOST outermost; utmost. XIV.

utter[2] ʌ·təɹ give out audibly, speak, pronounce; †reveal; †put on the market, sell; give currency to (coin, etc.). XIV. – MDu. *ūteren* (Du. *uiteren*) drive away, speak, show, make known, OFris. *ūtia*, *ūtria*, MLG. *ūtern* turn out, sell, speak, demonstrate, with assim. to UTTER[1]; prob. introduced partly as a term of commerce. Hence **u·tter**ANCE[1] †disposal by sale; speaking, speech. XV.

utterance[2] ʌ·tərəns extremity of force, esp. in phr. (now arch.) *to the u.* to the utmost limit. XIII. – (with assim. to UTTER[1]) (O)F. *outrance*, †*oultrance*, f. *ou(l)trer* go beyond bounds (cf. OUTRAGE, OUTRÉ) = Pr. *oltrar*, It. *oltrare* :– Rom. **ultrāre*, f. L. *ultrā* beyond; see ULTRA, -ANCE.

utu ū·tu (N.Z.) recompense, satisfaction. XIX. Maori.

uva jū·və grape, raisin XVII (Evelyn); *uva ursi* bearberry XVIII; leaves of this or infusion of them XIX. – L. *ūva* grape, cluster of grapes, etc., uvula.

uvea jū·viə (anat.) †posterior coloured surface of the eye XVI; middle coat or vascular tunic of the eye XVIII. – medL. *ūvea*, f. L. *ūva* (see prec.).

uvula jū·vjŭlə fleshy prolongation hanging from the pendent margin of the soft palate. XIV. – late L. *ūvula* (whence (O)F. *uvule*, etc.), dim. of L. *ūva* grape; see UVA, -ULE.

uxorious ʌksɔ̄·riəs excessively devoted to one's wife. XVI. f. L. *uxōrius*, f. *uxor* wife; see -IOUS.

V

vacant vei·kənt not held or occupied XIII; devoid of contents XIV; free from occupation XVI; expressionless, inane XVIII. In early use – (O)F. *vacant*; not freq. before late XVI, the word appears to have been taken in afresh from L. *vacant-*, *-āns*, prp. of *vacāre* be empty or unoccupied, with arch. var. *vocāre*; see VOID, -ANT. So **va·**CANCY. XVI.

vaca·TE[3] make void or vacant XVII; withdraw from XVIII. f. pp. stem of L. *vacāre*. **vaca·**TION release from occupation XIV (Ch.); period of formal suspension of activity XV. – (O)F. or L.; abbrev. **vac** væk XVIII.

vaccine væ·ksin, -īn in *v. disease* cowpox, *v. matter* or *virus vaccine*, *v. inoculation* vaccination. XVIII (1799). – L. *vaccinus*, as used in modL. *variolæ vaccinæ* cowpox (E. Jenner, 1798), *virus vaccinus* virus of cowpox used in vaccination; f. *vacca* cow; see -INE[1]. Also sb. vaccine matter. XIX. – F. *vaccine*. Hence **vaccina·**TION inoculation with vaccine against smallpox, 1800.

vaccinium væksi·niəm genus of plants bearing edible berries (spec. bilberry). XVIII. – L.; perh. rel. to *hudkinthos* HYACINTH.

vacillate væ·sileit swing or sway unsteadily XVI; waver XVII. f. pp. stem of L. *vacillāre* sway, totter, after (O)F. *vaciller*; see -ATE[3]. So **vacilla·**TION. XV. L.; cf. F. *vacillation* (XVI).

vacuity vəkjū·iti emptiness; empty space; vacancy of mind. XVI. – (O)F. *vacuité* or L. *vacuitās*, f. *vacuus* (whence **va·**CUOUS XVII), f. *vacāre* be VACANT. So **vacuum** væ·kjuəm emptiness, empty space XVI. sb. use of n. sg. of *vacuus*; used in modL. to repr. Aristotle's τὸ κενόν 'the empty', defined as τόπος ἐστερημένος σώματος 'place bereft of body' (Physics IV i).

vade-mecum veidimī·kəm handy book of reference. XVII. – F. (XVI) – modL. *vademecum*, sb. use of L. *vāde mēcum* go with me, i.e. imper. of *vādere* go (cf. EVADE, INVADE) and *mēcum*, i.e. *mē* ME, *cum* with (cf. COM-, CON-). Cf. G. *vademekum* (XVI).

vadose vei·dous (geog.) pert. to water lying above the permanent water level. – L. *vadōsus* shallow, f. *vadum* ford; see -OSE[1].

vagabond væ·gəbɔnd wandering without settled habitation XV (Lydg.); sb. itinerant beggar XV; idle good-for-nothing XVII. – (O)F. *vagabond* or L. *vagābundus*, f. *vagāri* wander, f. *vagus* wandering, VAGUE (cf. *errābundus* wandering to and fro, *moribundus* MORIBUND). ¶ Superseded somewhat earlier †*vacabond* (Lydg.) – (O)F. *vacabond*, alt. of *vagabond* after *vaquer*, L. *vacāre* (see VACANT).

vagary vəgɛə·ri †roaming, ramble; †wandering in speech; †frolic, prank XVI; capricious or eccentric act XVII; fantastic notion XVIII. – L. *vagārī* wander (see prec.). ¶ Forms with initial *f* (*fagary*, *fegary*, *figary*) appear XVII and survive in dial.

vagina vədʒai·nə canal connecting vulva with uterus XVII; sheath, theca XVIII. – L. *vāgīna* sheath, scabbard (joc. in Plautus, 'Pseudolus' 1181, of the female vagina).

vagrant vei·grənt (person) wandering from place to place and maintaining himself by begging, etc. XV. Late ME. *vagaraunt* – AN. *vagarant*, *vagaraunt(e)* (XIV–XV in Godefroy), app. f. L. *vagārī*+*-ant* -ANT. AN. vars. were *wakerant*, *wacrant*, *walcrant*.

vague veig not definite or precise. XVI. – F. *vague* – L. *vagus* wandering, inconstant, uncertain (whence also Pr. *vage*, Sp., It. *vago*).

vail[1] veil †benefit, profit XV (Lydg.); (arch.) casual profit or emolument XV; pl. gratuities, perquisites XVI. f. †*vail* vb. avail, profit XIII – OF. *vail-*, tonic stem of *valoir* be of value – L. *valēre* be strong, powerful, of value (cf. AVAIL, VALE[2], VALID, VALOUR).

vail[2] veil (arch.) lower XIV; doff XV. Aphetic of †*avail*, †*avale* descend, lower – (O)F. *avaler* lower, swallow = Pr. *avallar*, It. *avvallare* :- Rom. **advallāre*, f. L. *ad vallem* to the VALLEY, i.e. down. Cf. AMOUNT.

vain vein worthless, futile XIII (Cursor M.); †senseless, silly XIV; having an inordinate opinion of oneself XVII. – (O)F. *vain*, fem. *vaine* :- L. *vānus*, *-a* empty, without substance (whence Pr. *va*, Sp., It. *vano*), rel. to *vacuus* VACANT, *vastus* WASTE. The phr. *in vain* reflects (O)F. *en vain* = Pr. *en van*, Sp. *en vano*, It. *in vano* :- pop. L. **in vānum* (sb. use of n.); cf. L. *in vānum cēdere* come to naught. So **vain**GLO·RY idle boasting, empty pride (Cursor M.), after (O)F. *vaine gloire*, L. *vāna glōria* (Livy); **vain**GLO·RIOUS. XV; after OF. *vaneglorieus*, medL. *vānaglōriōsus* (*vāniglōrius*); so Sp., It. *vanaglorioso*. Cf. VANITY.

vair vɛər fur from the squirrel with grey back and white belly XIII (Cursor M.); (her.) fur having spaces tinctured alternately XVI. – (O)F. *vair* = Pr. *vair*, It. *vaio* :- L. *variu-s* particoloured; see VARIOUS and cf. MINIVER.

vaivode see VOIVODE.

vakeel, vakil vəkī·l agent, representative; envoy, ambassador XVII; native attorney in Hindu law-courts XIX. – Urdu *vakīl*, *wakīl*. Cf. WAKEEL.

valance væ·ləns drapery attached lengthwise and hanging down. XV. perh. – AN. **valance*, f. *valer* lower, aphetic of (O)F. *avaler*; see VAIL[2], -ANCE. But the occurrence of pl. forms such as *valandes* (XVI), *-ents* (XVII) may indicate deriv. from the pl. of the prp. used sb. (cf. ACCIDENCE).

vale[1] veil valley. XIII (Cursor M.). ME. *vale, vaal, vaile* – (O)F. *val* = Pr. *val*, Sp., It. *valle*, Rum. *vale* :– L. *vallē-s, valli-s*; cf. VALLEY.

vale[2] vei·li farewell. XVI. – L. *valē*, imper. of *valēre* be strong or well; cf. VALID.

valediction vælidi·kʃən farewell taking, farewell utterance. XVII. – L. **valedictiō(n-)*, f. *valedīcere*, i.e. *valē dīcere* say farewell; see prec. and DICTION. So **valedi·ct**ORY[2]. XVI.

valenciennes vælənsie·n, valã·sjɛn kind of lace named from *Valenciennes*, a town of northern France celebrated for lace-manufacture. XVIII.

valency vei·lənsi (chem.) capacity of an atom to combine with other atoms. XIX. – late L. *valentia* power, competence, f. *valēre* be powerful (cf. VALE[2]); see -ENCY.

valentine væ·ləntain person chosen or drawn by lot on St. Valentine's day as one's sweetheart for the coming year XV; folded paper with the name of a person to be drawn as a valentine XVI; missive love-token sent on 14 February XIX. f. (O)F. *Valentin* – L. *Valentinus* name of two Italian saints whose festival falls on 14 February.

valerian vəliə·riən herbaceous plant of the genus Valeriana. XIV (Ch.). – (O)F. *valériane* – medL. *valeriana* (whence also (M)HG. *baldrian*).

valet væ·lit, væ·lei gentleman's manservant. XVI. – (O)F. *valet*, also †*vaslet*, †*varlet* (see VARLET) = Pr. *vaslet*, Cat. *vaylet* (It. *valletto* is from F., Pg. *varlete* from Pr.) :– Rom. **vassellittus*, dim. of **vassus* (see VASSAL).

valetudinary vælitjū·dinəri not in robust health, constantly concerned with one's ailments XVI; sb. XVIII. – L. *valētūdinārius*, in ill health, f. *valētūdin-, -tūdō* state of health, f. *valēre* be strong or well; see VALE[2], -TUDE, -ARY. Hence **valetudin**A·RIAN adj. and sb. XVIII. Cf. F. *valétudinaire* (XIV).

Valhalla vælhæ·lə in Scand. myth., hall assigned to those who die in battle. XVIII ('The *Valkyriur* . . . conducted them to *Valhalla*', Gray 1768). – modL. *Valhalla* – ON. *Valhall-, -hǫll*, f. *valr* those slain in battle (= OE. *wæl*, OS., OHG. *wal*), perhaps rel. to L. *vulnus* wound) + *hǫll* HALL. See VALKYRIE.

vali vălī· civil governor in Turkey. XVIII. – Turk. *valī* – Arab. *walī* WALI; cf. VILAYET.

valiant væ·liənt †stalwart; courageous, bold. XIV, ME. *vailaunt, valiaunt* – AN. *valiaunt*, OF. *vail(l)ant* (mod. *vaillant*) :– Rom. **valiente*, for *valent-, -ēns*, prp. of L. *valēre* be strong; see VALE[2], -ANT.

valid væ·lid adequate in law XVI; well founded and applicable XVII. – F. *valide* or L. *validus* strong, powerful, effective, f. *valēre*; see VALE[2], -ID[1]. So **valid**ITY vəli·dĭti. XVI. – F. or late L.

valise vælī·z, -s travelling case, portmanteau. XVII (B. Jonson). – F. *valise* – It. *valigia* (cf. Sp. *balija*); in medL. *valesia, -ium, -isia*; of unkn. origin.

valkyrie væ·lkiri in Scand. mythology, war-maiden who hovers over battle-fields and conducts fallen warriors to Valhalla. XVIII (Bishop Percy). – ON. *Valkyrja* 'chooser of the slain', f. *valr* those slain in battle (cf. VALHALLA) + **kur-* :– **kuz-*, reduced grade of **keuz-* CHOOSE. Cf. OE. *wælcyriġe* 'Bellona', 'Erinys', 'Gorgo', witch, sorceress. G. *Walküre* is – the ON. word.

valley væ·li hollow lying between hills. XIII (RGlouc.). – AN. *valey*, OF. *valée* (mod. *vallée*) = Pr. *vallada*, It. *vallata* :– Rom. **vallāta*, f. L. *vallis, -ēs*; see -Y[6].

vallota vælou·tə genus of amaryllidaceous plants. XIX. modL., f. name of Antoine *Vallot*, French botanist (1594–1671).

vallum væ·ləm rampart of earth, etc. XVII (Holland). L., coll. f. *vallus* stake, palisade; cf. INTERVAL.

valonia vælou·niə acorns of certain species of oak. XVIII. – It. *vallonia* (whence F. *vallonée*) – modGr. *balánia, belánia*, pl. of *baláni, beláni* (Gr. *bálanos*) acorn = L. *glāns* GLAND.

valour væ·ləɹ A. †value, worth XIV; B. (after *valorous*) courage in conflict, prowess XVI. – OF. *valour* (mod. *valeur* value) = Pr. *valor* worth, strength, succour, Sp. *valor*, It. *valore* :– late L. *valōr-, valor*, f. *valēre* be strong, powerful, worth; see VALE[2], -OUR[2]. So **va·lor**OUS valiant, courageous. XV (Caxton). – OF. *valerous* (mod. *valeureux*) or medL. *valōrōsus*.

valse vōls waltz. XVIII. – F. *valse* – G. *walzer* WALTZ.

value væ·lju adequate equivalent; material or monetary worth; †worth, worthiness; relative status or estimate XIV; amount represented by a symbol XVI. – OF. *value*, fem. pp. formation from *valoir* be worth :– L. *valēre* be strong, healthy, effective, be worth; see VALE[2]; cf. Sp. *valua*, It. *valuta*. Hence vb. estimate the value of XV; consider of value XVI; whence **va·lu**ABLE. XVI, **valu**A·TION. XVI (cf. OF., Sp. *valuacion*). (From XV to early XVII †*valure* was a frequent variant, alt. form of *valuur, valur*, after -URE.)

valve vælv either of the leaves of a folding door XIV (Trevisa); one of the halves of a hinged shell; (anat.) membranous fold;

device resembling a flap, lid, etc. XVII. – L. *valva* leaf of a door, (chiefly pl.) folding doors, prob. rel. to *volvere* roll (see INVOLVE, REVOLVE, VOLUTE). Cf. F. *valve*, Pg. *valva*. So **va·lvul**AR. XVIII. – modL. *valvulāris*, f. *valvula*, dim. of L. *valva*.

vambrace væ·mbreis defensive armour for the arm. XIV. ME. *vaun(t)bras* – AN. *vauntbras*, aphetic of OF. *avantbras*, f. *avant* before (:– Rom. **ab ante*) + *bras* arm (:– L. *bracchium* – Gr. *brakhíōn*, f. *brakhús* short); cf. ADVANCE, AVAUNT, BRACE[1].

vamose vəmou·s, **vamoose** vəmū·s (orig. U.S.) to make off, decamp. XIX. – Sp. *vamos* let us go :– L. *vādāmus* 1st pers. pl. pres. subj. of *vādere* go (cf. EVADE, INVADE, PERVADE).

vamp[1] væmp part of hose covering the foot and ankle XIII; part of a boot or shoe covering the front of the foot XVII. – AN. **vaumpé*, aphetic of OF. *avantpié* (mod. *avantpied*), f. *avant* before (see prec.) + *pie(d)* :– L. *pede-m*, *pēs* FOOT. Hence **vamp** vb. provide with a vamp, patch XVI; produce as by patching XVII; extemporize (an accompaniment, etc.) XVIII. ¶ For the fall of AN. *-é* cf. ASSIGN[2], COSTIVE, etc.; the full form was repr. by †*vamp(e)y* XV–XVII.

vamp[2] væmp (sl.) woman who employs her sexual attraction unscrupulously. XX. Shortening of next.

vampire væ·mpaiəɹ preternatural malignant being, supposed to suck blood; person who preys upon others; (after Buffon) kind of bat supposed to suck blood. XVIII. – F. *vampire* or G. *vampir* – Magyar *vampir* – identical form in Sl. langs., in which there are vars. such as Bulg. *vapir*, Russ *upýr'*, Pol. *upiór*; the ult. origin may be Turk. *uber* witch.

vamplate væ·mpleit plate on a lance serving as a guard for the hand. XIV. – AN. *vauntplate*, f. *vaunt-*, aphetic of (O)F. *avant-* before (see VAMP[1]) + *plate* PLATE.

van[1] væn winnowing basket or shovel XV; shovel used in testing ore, etc.; (poet.) wing XVII; sail of a windmill XIX. Southern and western var. of FAN[1] prob. reinforced by (O)F. *van* or L. *vannus*. ¶ For initial *v* repl. *f* cf. †*vade*, †*vardingale*, VANE, VAT, VENEER, VENT[2], VIAL, VIXEN.

van[2] væn. XVII. Short for VANGUARD.

van[3] væn covered vehicle for conveying goods. XIX. Shortening of CARAVAN.

vanadium vənei·diəm chemical element. XIX. – modL. *vanadium* (Sefström, 1830), f. ON. *Vanadís* name of the Scand. goddess Freyja; see -IUM.

Vandal væ·ndəl member of a Germanic tribe which invaded Western Europe in the fourth and fifth centuries A.D., and in 455 sacked Rome XVI; destroyer of beautiful or venerable things XVII. – L. *Vandalus*, pl. *Vandalī* (Pliny), also *-aliī*, *-iliī* (Tacitus), *-ulī* – Germ. **Wandal-*, *-il-*, *-ul-* (repr. by OE. *Wendlas* pl., OHG. *Wentil-* in personal names, G. *Wandale*, ON. *Vendill*); cf. F. *Vandale*, etc. Hence **va·ndal**ISM. XVIII; after F. *vandalisme* (Henri Grégoire *c.*1793).

Vandyke vændai·k portrait by Vandyke; lace or linen collar in the style of those depicted in his portraits XVIII; deep-cut point on a garment, etc. XIX. Name of Sir Anthony *Vandyke* (anglicized form of *Van Dyck*), Flemish painter 1599–1641. Hence as vb. provide with deep-cut points or zigzag ornament. XVIII.

vane vein plate of metal rotating on a spindle to show the direction of the wind XV; sail of a windmill; sight of a surveying instrument XVI; web of a feather XVIII. Southern and western var. of †*fane* (1) flag, banner, (2) weather-cock, OE. *fana* = OFris. *fana, fona*, OS., OHG. *fano* (G. *fahne*), Goth. *fana* cloth :– Germ. **fanon* :– pre-Germ. **ponon-*, rel. to L. *pannus* piece of cloth, OSl. *o|pona* curtain, *ponjava* piece of cloth, curtain. Cf. VAN[1].

vang væŋ (naut.) rope for steadying the gaffs of a sail. XVIII. – Du. *vang* in *vanglijn* painter.

vanguard væ·ngāɹd foremost division of an army. XV. Earlier *vandgard*, var. of †*vantgard*, aphetic of †*avantgard* (XV) – (O)F. *avant-garde*, †*avangarde*, f. *avant* before (:– Rom. **ab ante*) + *garde* GUARD. Earlier forms were †*vantward* (XIII), †*avantward* (XIV), †*vanward* (XV), *vaward* (XIV), the latter being familiar in echoes of Sh. '2 Hen. IV' I ii 200.

vanilla vəni·lə (pod of) climbing orchid, Vanilla planifolia XVII; aromatic substance obtained therefrom XVIII. – Sp. *vainilla*, dim. of *vaina* sheath :– L. *vāgina* VAGINA. In early use in various (esp. perverted) forms, e.g. *vaynilla*, *vanello*, *-il(l)io*; *-illo*; finally assim. to F. *vanille*. Cf. It. *vainiglia*, Pg. *bainilha*.

vanish væ·niʃ disappear rapidly. XIV (R. Mannyng). Aphetic – *e(s)vaniss-*, lengthened stem (see -ISH[2]) of OF. *e(s)vanir* = It. *svanire*, Pg. *esvahir* (cf. Pr. *esvanezir*) :– Rom. **exvānīre*, for L. *ēvānēscere*, f. *ē-* EX-[1] + *vānus* empty, VAIN.

vanity væ·nĭti vain or worthless thing XIII; quality of being vain XIV. – (O)F. *vanité* = Sp. *vanidad*, It. *vanità* :– L. *vānitātem*, *-tās*, f. *vānus* VAIN; see -ITY.

Van John væn dʒɔ·n sl. perversion of VINGT-UN. XIX.

vanquish væ·ŋkwiʃ overcome, defeat. XIV. Early forms *vencus* (Sc. *vincus*), *venquis*, *venquisshe*, the *ven-* forms being superseded by *van-* in XVI, by assoc. with late OF. *vain-*, and the ending assim. to -ISH[2] in XV; f. pp. *vencus* and pt. *venquis* of OF. *veintre*, *vaintre* (mod. *vaincre*) :– L. *vincere* conquer (cf. VICTOR).

vantage vàntėdʒ †advantage, profit XIII (Cursor M.); position of superiority XV; †additional amount XVI; (in lawn tennis) XIX. – AN. *vantage*, aphetic of OF. *avantage* ADVANTAGE.

vant-brace var. of VAMBRACE. XIV.

vapid væ·pid flat, insipid (of beverages) XVII; (of talk, etc.) XVIII. – L. *vapidus*, rel. to *vappa* flat or sour wine, and perh. further to *vapor* VAPOUR; see -ID[1].

vapour vei·pəɹ steam, steamy exhalation XIV (Ch., Wyclif); (pl.) exhalations arising in the human body XV; (arch.) morbid condition resulting from these XVII. – (O)F. *vapeur*, †-*our* (= Sp. *vapor*, It. *vapore*) or L. *vapōre-m, vapor* steam, heat; see prec. and -OUR[2]. So **va·por**OUS. XVI. f. late L. *vapōrus* or – late L. *vapōrōsus*; cf. F. *vaporeux*.

Varangian vəræ·ndʒiən one of the Scand. rovers who in IX–X overran parts of Russia and reached Constantinople. XVIII (Gibbon). f. medL. *Varangus* – medGr. *Bárangos* – (through Slav. langs.) ON. *Vǽringi* (pl. *Vǽringjar*), prob. f. *vár* (pl. *várar*) plighted faith; see -IAN.

varec(h) væ·rek seaweed XVII; carbonate of soda obtained from it XIX. – F. *varec(h)*, OF. *warec, vrec* – ON. **wrek* WRECK.

variable vɛə·riəbl liable to vary. XIV (Ch., Trevisa). – (O)F. *variable* – L. *variābilis*, f. *variāre*; see VARY, -ABLE. Hence **va·riabi·l**ITY. XVIII. So **vari**ANCE vɛə·riəns variation, difference XIV; discrepancy; dissension XV (*at v.* XVI). – OF. *variance* – L. *variantia*, f. *variāre*. **va·ri**ANT †inconstant, not uniform (Ch.); diverse, differing (*from*) XIV; sb. XIX. – (O)F. *variant*. **vari**A·TION †difference, divergence XIV (Ch.); fact or instance of varying XVI. – (O)F. or L.

varicose væ·rikous (of a vein) affected with a varix. XVIII. – L. *varicōsus*, f. *varic-, varix* dilated vein (in Eng. use from XIV, comb. form *varico-* in *varicocele* (XVIII), f. Gr. *kḗlē* tumour); see -OSE[1].

variegate vɛə·riėgeit make varied XVII. f. pp. stem of L. *variēgāre* (Apuleius), f. L. *varius* VARIOUS; see -ATE[3]. So **variega**·TION. XVII.

variola vərai·ələ (med.) smallpox. XVIII. – late L. *variola* pustule, pock, f. L. *varius* speckled, variegated, VARIOUS.

variorum vɛəriō·rəm edition of a work containing the observations of various commentators. XVIII. g. pl. m. of L. *varius* VARIOUS in phr. *editio cum notis variorum* 'edition with the notes of various' (editors).

various vɛə·riəs †variable, changeable XVI; varied, variegated; (with pl.) differing from one another XVII (Milton). f. L. *varius*; see -IOUS. So **vari**ETY vərai·ĭti. XVI. – (O)F. or L.

varlet vā·ɹlit attendant, e.g. on a knight XV; knave, rascal XVI. – OF. *varlet*, var. of *vaslet, vadlet* VALET.

varmint vā·ɹmint (dial.) vermin XVI; troublesome or mischievous creature XVIII. var. of *varmin* VERMIN, with parasitic *t* as in *peasant, tyrant*.

varnish vā·ɹniʃ solution of resinous matter used for providing a hard shiny coat XIV; fig. XVI. ME. *vernisch* – (O)F. *vernis* (whence also Du. *vernis*, G. *firnis*) = Pr. *vernitz* Sp. *barniz*, It. *vernice* :– medL. *veronice-m, veronix* (VIII) fragrant resin, sandarac, or – medGr. *bereníkē*, prob. appellative use of the town-name (Berenice, in Cyrenaica). So **va·rnish** vb. XIV. – OF. *verniss(i)er, -ic(i)er* = It. *verniciare* (cf. Pr. *envernizar*, Sp. *barnizar*), f. the sb. (F. *vernir, -iss-* XVI is a new formation on the sb.).

varsity vā·ɹsĭti XIX (earlier †*versity* XVII). colloq. clipped form of UNIVERSITY; cf. *varsal* (XVII), early †*versal* (XVI, Sh.), for *universal*.

varsovienne vāɹsouvie·n dance resembling Polish national dances. XIX. F., fem. of *varsovien*, f. *Varsovie* Warsaw.

varvel vā·ɹvəl metal ring attached to a hawk's jess. XVI. Earlier †*vervel* – (O)F. *vervelle*, †*varvelle*, syncopated form of *vertevelle* :– Rom. **vertibella*, beside **vertibellum* (whence F. *verveux*, It. *bertovello* hoop-net), dim. of late L. *vertibulum* joint, f. *vertere* turn (cf. VERTEBRA) with suffix of instrument as in L. *infundibulum* funnel. (Cf. dial. *vardle* XVI, *vartiwell* XVIII eye of a hinge, hinge.)

vary vɛə·ri undergo change, cause to change. XIV (Ch., Wyclif, Trevisa). – (O)F. *varier* or L. *variāre* (whence also Sp. *variar*, It. *variare*), f. *varius* VARIOUS. Hence **varied** vɛə·rid diverse XVI (Sh.); variegated XVIII; see -ED[1] and cf. F. *varié*, L. *variātus* (Apuleius); twice in Sh., but not gen. current before XVIII (Prior, Pope).

vascular væ·skjŭləɹ pert. to tubular vessels. XVII. – modL. *vāsculāris*, f. L. *vāsculum*, dim. of *vās* vessel; see next and -AR.

vase vāz, (formerly) vōz, (earlier, now U.S.) veis, veiz ornamental vessel of circular section. XVII. F. *vase* – L. *vās*, earlier also *vāsum, vāsus* vessel, dish, implement, utensil, pl. military baggage. Rhymes used by Swift, Byron, Emerson, Whittier, and Lowell show the pronunc. veis. (In XVII the L. pl. *vāsa* was used as pl. and s. in Eng. contexts.) A comb. form **vaso-** vei·sou is used in physiol. and path. terms relating to vascular parts XIX.

vaseline væ·səlīn, væ·z- proprietary name, registered as a trade mark in 1872 by the Chesebrough Manufacturing Company, for an ointment or lubricant obtained from petroleum. XIX. irreg. f. G. *wasser* va·sər WATER + Gr. *él|aion* OIL + -INE[5].

vassal væ·səl tenant in fee XIV; transf. and fig. XV. – (O)F. *vassal* = Pr. *vasal* (whence Sp. *vasallo*, It. *vassallo*) :– medL. *vassallus* man-servant, retainer, of Celtic origin; the simplex *vassus* (see VAVASOUR) corr. to OGaulish *-vassus* in personal names, e.g. *Dagovassus*, OBret. *uuas* (Bret. *goaz*), W. *gwas*, Ir. *foss* servant. So **va·ssal**AGE. XIV – OF. *vassalage* (mod. *vasselage*) = Pr. *vassalatge*.

vast vàst of immense size or amount. XVI. – L. *vastus* waste, uncultivated, immense (whence also F. *vaste*, Sp., It. *vasto*), pp. formation on a base **wās-*, repr. also by L. *vānus* (:– **wăsnos*) VAIN, *vascus* empty, Ir. *fás* empty, and WGerm. **wōst-* (OE. *wēste*, OS. *wōsti*, OHG. *wuosti*, Du. *woest*, G. *wüst*). Hence **va·sty**[1]. XVI (Sh.).

vat væt cask or tun for liquid. XIII. Southern and western var. of *fat*, OE. *fæt* = OFris. *fet*, OS. *fat* (Du. *vat*), OHG. *faʒ* (G. *fass*), ON. *fat* :– CGerm. (exc. Gothic) **fatam* vessel, cask, rel. to OFris. *fatia*, MLG. *vaten*, OHG. *faʒʒōn* (G. *fassen* hold, contain, seize), f. **fat-*, whence also OE. *fetel*, etc. (see FETTLE); IE. **pŏd-* is repr. also by Lith. *púdas* pot, Lett. *puods*, OPruss. dim. *podalis*. For initial *v* cf. VAN[1].

Vatican væ·tikən palace of the Pope on the Vatican Hill in Rome. XVI. – F. *Vatican* or L. *Vāticānus* (sc. *collis* hill, *mōns* mountain); see -AN.

vaticinate vəti·sineit predict. XVII. f. pp. stem of L. *vāticinārī*, f. *vātēs* seer, prophet, poet, rel. to Ir. *fáith* poet, W. *gwawd* song of praise, and Germ. **wōð-* (whence OE. *wōd* mad, *wōþ* song, OHG. *wuot* rage, ON. *óðr* possessed, inspired, *óðr* poetry, Goth. *wōd-*, **wōþs* possessed). So **vaticin**A·TION væt·-. XVII (Holland). – L.

vaudeville vou·dəvil light popular song XVIII; light stage performance interspersed with songs XIX. – F. *vaudeville* †typical song or play, theatrical piece interspersed with rhymes, alt. of *vaudevire* (XV), f. *Vau de Vire* 'valley of Vire', name of a region of Calvados, Normandy, the songs of which had a vogue in XV.

Vaudois vou·dwa. XVI. F. :– medL. *Waldensis* WALDENSIAN.

vault[1] vòlt arched roof or ceiling XIV; burial chamber XVI. ME. *voute*, *vaute* – OF. *voute*, *vaute* (mod. *voûte*) = Pr. *volta*, *vouta*, Pg., It. *volta* :– Rom. **volta*, **volvita*, pp. fem. (for *volūta*) of L. *volvere* turn (cf. VOLUTE). So **vault** vb. – OF. *vouter* (mod. *voûter*). The sp. with *l* appeared XV (after later OF. usage), and permanently influenced the pronunc. as in FAULT. Hence **vau·lt**AGE. XVI (Sh.).

vault[2] vòlt †leap on to (a horse) XVI; leap with the support of the hand XVII. – OF. *volter*, *voulter* turn (a horse), gambol, leap = Cat. *voltar* upset, Pg. *voltar* roll, It. *voltare* :– Rom. **voltāre*, **volūtare* or **volvitāre*, frequent. f. L. *volvere* roll (see VOLUTE); assim. to prec.

vaunt vōnt (arch.) boast; prob. orig. refl. XIV – AN. *vaunter*, (O)F. *vanter* = Pr. *vantar* :– late L. *vānitāre*, later *vantare*, f. *vānus* VAIN; partly aphetic of earlier †*avaunt* (– OF. *avanter*).

vaunt-courier vō·nt-, vā·ntkuriəɹ one of an advance guard; forerunner (now in echoes of Sh. 'Lear' III ii 5). XVI. Also *van-courier*; aphetic of *avant-courier* – F. *avant-courrier*; cf. COURIER.

vavasour væ·vəsuəɹ feudal tenant immediately below a baron. XIII. ME. *vauasour*, *-er*, later also *valvasour* (XVI–) – OF. *vavas(s)our* (mod. *vavasseur*) – medL. *vavassor*, supposed, but without conclusive evidence, to derive from medL. *vassus vassōrum* 'VASSAL of vassals'. Cf. Pr. *va(l)vasor*, It. *valvassore*, *barbassoro*.

vaward see VANGUARD.

veal vīl flesh of a calf XIV (Ch.); (dial.) calf XV. – AN. *vel*, *veel* = OF. nom. *veiaus*, obl. *veel* (mod. *veau*), Pr. *vedel*, Cat. *vedell*, It. *vitello* :– L. *vitellu-s*, dim. of *vitulus* calf, perh. orig. 'yearling' (cf. Gr. *ϝételon* yearling, f. *ϝétos* year; the base is repr. also by Skr. *vatsás* calf, OE. *weþer* WETHER, Goth. *wiþrus* lamb).

vector ve·ktōɹ †(astron.) for *radius v.* variable line drawn to a curve from a fixed point XVIII; (math.) quantity having direction as well as magnitude XIX (W. R. Hamilton, 1843). – L. *vector* carrier, traveller, rider, agent-noun f. *vect-*, pp. stem of *vehere* carry; see WAY, -TOR.

Veda vei·də any of the four ancient sacred books of the Hindus. XVIII. – Skr. *vēda* knowledge, sacred knowledge, sacred book, f. **wid-* know (see WIT[2]). Hence **Ved**IC vei·dik, vī·dik pert. to the Vedas; sb. the language of these, an early form of Sanskrit. XIX. – F. *védique* or G. *vedisch*.

vedette vide·t mounted sentry in advance of outposts. XVII. – F. *vedette* scout, sentinel – It. *vedetta*, alt. (after *vedere* see) of south It. *veletta*, f. Sp. *vela* watch, f. *velar* watch (= F. *veiller*, etc.) :– L. *vigilāre*; see VIGILANT, -ETTE.

veer[1] viəɹ †run *out* (a line) XV; allow to drift further off XVI; pay out (a cable) XVII. – (M)Du. *vieren* let out, slacken (whence also G. *vieren*, *fieren*, Sw. *fira*, Da. *fire*) = OHG. *fieren*, *fiaren* give direction to.

veer[2] viəɹ change course or direction (spec. clockwise) of wind. XVI. – (O)F. *virer* = Pr., Sp. *virar*, It. *virare* :– Rom. **vīrāre*, perh. alt. of L. *gȳrāre* GYRATE, by assoc. with a verb beginning with *v*, e.g. *vertere* turn or *vibrāre* shake.

vega[1] vei·gə fertile plain in Spain and Spanish America. XVII. – Sp. (Cat.) *vega* = Pg. *veiga*.

vega[2] vī·gə (astron.) α Lyræ. XVII. – Sp. (medL.) *vega* – Arab. *wāqi'* falling, in *al nasr al wāqi'* 'the falling vulture', constellation Lyra.

vegetable ve·dʒitəbl †having the life characteristic of a plant XIV; pert. to plants XVI; sb. plant XVI; plant cultivated for food XVIII. – (O)F. *végétable* or late L. *vegetābilis* animating, vivifying, f. L. *vegetāre* animate, enliven, f. *vegetus* active, f. *vegēre* be active; see WAKE[3], -ABLE. So **ve·getAL**[1]. XV. – medL. **vegetālis* (whence F. *végétal*, etc.). **vegeta·RIAN**. XIX (the Vegetarian Society was formed at Ramsgate in 1847). irreg. f. *vegetable*. **ve·getATE**[3] grow or develop after the manner of a vegetable XVII; live the life of a vegetable, i.e. a dull monotonous existence XVIII. f. pp. stem of L. *vegetāre*. **vegetA·TION** growth as of plants XVI; concr. XVII. – L. (whence F. *végétation*, etc.). **ve·getATIVE** pert. to growth. XIV (Trevisa). – (O)F. *végétatif, -ive* or medL. *vegetātivus*; a reduced form *ve·getive* was common XVI–XVII. **vegete** vidʒī·t healthy. XVII. – L. *vegetus*.

vehement vī·imənt intense, severe; very forcible. XV. – (O)F. *véhément* or L. *vehement-, -ēns* impetuous, violent, perh. for **vēmēns* 'deprived of mind' (cf. *vēcors* cowardly), altered by assoc. with *vehere* carry (see WAY). So **ve·hemENCE**. XVI. – F. – L.

vehicle vī·ikl, vī·hikl medium of application or transmission (first in medical use); means of conveyance or transport. XVII. – F. *véhicule* (XVI, Paré) or L. *vehiculum* (also current XVII–XVIII), f. *vehere* carry; see WAY, WEIGH, -CLE. So **vehiculAR** vihi·kjŭləɹ. XVII. – late L.

vehmgericht vei·mgərixt, ||fē·m- (hist.) secret tribunal active in Westphalia from XII to XVI. XIX (Scott). – G. *vehmgericht* (now *fe(h)mgericht*), f. *vehm* (of unkn. origin) + *gericht* court, tribunal (OHG. *girihti*), rel. to *recht* RIGHT.

veil veil article of attire covering head or face; piece of cloth used as a hanging XIII; fig. XIV. – AN. *veile* and *veil* = OF. *voile* and *voil* (mod. *voile* m. veil, fem. sail) :– L. *vēla* pl. sails and *vēlum* sg. sail, curtain, veil. L. *vēlum* veil is referred by some to **weslom* (f. **wes-* as in *vestis* VEST[1]), and so distinguished from *vēlum* sail :– **wegslom*, f. **weg-* of *vehere* carry (see WAY); others assume the same origin, viz. **wegzlom*, f. **weg-* weave (OIr. *figim* I weave, W. *gwen* weave; cf. WAX[1]). Hence **veil** vb. XIV (Wycl. Bible) f. the sb. after OF. †*veiler*, F. *voiler* or L. *vēlāre*.

vein vein A. tubular vessel in which blood is conveyed through the animal body XIII (of a leaf XVI); B. †small channel through which water flows XIII; line of deposit of mineral or earthy matter XIV; C. strain of some quality; natural tendency; characteristic style; personal disposition; humour, mood XVI. – (O)F. *veine* = Pr., Sp., It. *vena* :– L. *vēna* (cf. VENOUS). Like Gr. φλέψ L. *vena* was used of mineral deposits, watercourses, and the veins of leaves; it was further applied to the innate or inward part or nature of a thing, natural disposition, (poetic) genius. F. *veine* is used absol. for *veine poétique* (phr. *se sentir en veine* be inspired); cf. *in the vein* in a suitable mood (Sh.). Hence **vei·nY**[1]. XVI.

velar vī·ləɹ A. (archit.) resembling a sail XVIII; B. pert. to the velum XIX. – L. *vēlāris* (whence also F. *vélaire*, etc.), f. *vēlum* curtain; see VELUM, -AR.

veld, formerly **veldt** felt, (erron.) **velt** unenclosed country in S. Africa. XIX. Afrikaans *veld*, earlier *veldt* FIELD.

veld(t) shoe felt ʃū S. African light shoe of untanned hide. XIX. – Afrikaans *veldschoen* (now *velskoen*), ult. by assim. to VELD of earlier *velschoen*, f. *vel* skin, FELL[1] + *schoen* SHOE.

velitation velitei·ʃən skirmish. XVII. – L. *vēlitātiō(n-)*, f. *vēlitāre*, f. *vēlitēs*, pl. of *vēles* light-armed soldier, perh. rel. to *vēlox*; see VELOCITY, -ATION.

velleity velī·iti low degree of volition. XVII. – medL. *velleitās* (whence also F. *velléité*, etc.), f. L. *velle* to wish, WILL[2]; see -ITY.

vellum ve·ləm fine parchment prepared from calf-skin. XV (*velim*). – (O)F. *vélin*, f. *veel* VEAL + *-in* -INE[1]; for the change of *n* to *m* cf. *pilgrim*, *venom*.

velocipede vilɔ·sipīd (hist.) 'a wheel carriage to ride cock-horse upon, sitting astride and pushing it along with the toes, a rudder-wheel in hand' (Keats); invented by Baron Drais and patented in England 1818; early form of pedal bicycle XIX (*c*.1850). – F. *vélocipède*, f. L. *vēlox* (see next) + *ped-*, *pēs* FOOT.

velocity vilɔ·siti swiftness of motion XVI; rapidity of operation XVII. – (O)F. *vélocité* or L. *vēlōcitās*, f. *vēlox* swift, rapid, f. **vegslo-*, f. base of *vegēre*; see VEGETABLE, -ITY.

velour vəluə·ɹ hatter's plush pad XVIII; fabric with velvety pile XIX. – F. *velours* (whence †*velure* velvet XVI), alt. of OF. *velous* = Pr. *velos* prop. adj. (sc. *drap* cloth) :– L. *villōsus* hairy, downy, f. *villus* tuft of hair, pl. down, prob. rel. to *vellus* fleece, f. *vellere* pluck.

velum vī·ləm (anat.) soft palate XVIII; (zool., bot.) membranous structure XIX. modL., in full *v. palati*, *v. pendulum* veil of the palate, pendulous veil; see VEIL.

velvet ve·lvit fabric of silk having a dense smooth pile XIV; soft downy skin of a deer's horn XV. ME. orig. three syll. (cf. the vars. *velowet*, *velewet*) – OF. *veluotte*, f. *velu* velvety = Pr. *velut*, Sp. *velludo*, It. *velluto* (for **villuto*) velvety, velvet – medL. *villūtus*, f. L. *villus* down (cf. VELOUR); *veluet* passed through the stage *velwet* (XV–XVI) on its way to *velvet*. Hence **velvetEE·N** XVIII.

venal vī·nəl exposed for sale; capable of being bought over XVII; mercenary XVIII. – L. *vēnālis*, f. *vēnum* that is for sale (also *vēnō*, later *vēnui*), obl. cases of **vēnus* (cf. *vēnīre* be sold, lit. 'go for sale', *vendere* sell, VEND), rel. to Gr. *ônos* purchase price, *ōnḗ* purchase, *ōneîsthai* buy, Skr. *vasnás* price, *vasnám* wages, Arm. *gin* price, *gnem* I buy :– **wesno-* **wosno-*; see -AL¹.

venatic vīnæ·tik pert. to hunting. XVII. – L. *vēnāticus*, f. pp. stem of *vēnārī* hunt; see VENERY¹, -ATIC.

vend vend sell; give utterance to. XVII. – (O)F. *vendre* or L. *vēndere*, f. *vēnum* (see VENAL) + *-dere*, var. of *dare* give (cf. ADD). So **ve·nder, ve·ndor** (the second is the more technical sp.). XVI. – AN. *vendor, -dour* (modF. *vendeur*); see -ER¹, -OR; hence **vend**EE·. XVI. **ve·nd**IBLE saleable. XIV (Wycl. Bible). – L.

vendace ve·ndĭs small freshwater fish Coregonus vandesius. XVIII. – OF. *vendese, -oise* (mod. *vandoise*) – Gaulish **vindēsia*, f. **vindos* white (cf. OIr. *find*, W. *gwynn* white).

vendetta vende·tə blood-feud. XIX. – It. *vendetta* :– L. *vindicta* vengeance; see VINDICTIVE.

vendue vendjū· (U.S. and W. Indies) public sale, auction. XVII. – Du. *vendu*, †*vendue* – (O)F. (now dial.) *vendue* sale, f. *vendre* VEND.

veneer vĭniə·ɹ cover with a thin coating of finer wood. XVII. Recorded first in the gerund *faneering*, later *fineering* (common in XVIII), *veneering* (from early XVIII) – G. *furni(e)rung, fourni(e)rung*, vbl. sb. of *furniren* – (O)F. *fournir* FURNISH. So **venee·r** sb. XVIII. The loss of *r* in the (unstr.) first syll. is seen also in Da. *finer*, Sw. *faner*, Russ. *fanera*.

venerable ve·nəɹəbl worthy of being revered. XV. – (O)F. *vénérable* or L. *venerābilis* (whence also Sp. *venerable*, etc.), f. *venerārī*; see -ABLE. So **ve·ner**ATE³. XVII. f. pp. stem of L. *venerārī*, f. *vener-*, *venus*; see VENERY². **venera**·TION. XV – (O)F. or L.

venereal vĭniə·riəl pert. to sexual desire or intercourse XV; (of disease) communicated by sexual intercourse XVII. f. L. *venereus*, f. *vener-*, *venus* love; see VENERY². Several parallel forms have been current, with varying range of meanings, based on L. *venereus* or *venerius*: †**vene·r**EAN, †**vene·r**EOUS, †**vene·r**IAL. XVI; † **vene·r**IAN. XV; †**venerien.** XIV (Ch., Gower) – (O)F. *vénérien*; †**vener·**IOUS. XVI; also †**v·ener**OUS. XVI; cf. F. †*vénéreux*.

venery¹ ve·nəɹi sport of hunting; †animals hunted. XIV. – (O)F. *vénerie*, f. *vener* = Rum. *vînà* :– Rom. **vēnāre*, for L. *vēnārī* hunt; see -ERY, and cf. VENISON.

venery² ve·nəri indulgence of sexual desire. XV. – medL. *veneria*, f. L. *vener-*, *venus* love (personified as a goddess by the ancient Romans); see WISH, -ERY.

venesection venise·kʃən phlebotomy. XVII. – medL. *vēnæ sectiō* 'cutting of a vein'; see VEIN, SECTION.

Venetian vĭnī·ʃən pert. to Venice, a city in NE. Italy. XV (Lydg.). Late ME. *Venicien* – OF. *Venicien* (mod. *Vénitien*); later assim. to medL. *venetiānus*, f. L. *Venetia* (It. *Venezia*). *Venetian blind, red* XVIII.

vengeance ve·ndʒəns act of avenging oneself or another. XIII (Cursor M.). – (O)F. *vengeance*, f. *venger* (whence arch. **venge** XIII) = Pr. *venjar*, Sp. *vengar*, It. *vendicare* :– L. *vindicāre* VINDICATE; see -ANCE. So **ve·nge**FUL¹. XVI (Spenser). f. *venge*, after *revengeful*; cf. *avengeful* (XVI).

venial vī·niəl (theol., of sin) not mortal XIII (Cursor M.); that may be excused XVI. – OF. *venial* (mod. *véniel*) – late L. *veniālis*, f. *venia* forgiveness, indulgence, f. base of *venus*; see VENERY², -IAL.

venire XVII, short for **venire facias** vĭnaiə·ri fei·ʃiæs writ requiring a sheriff to summon a jury. XV. L. *venire* COME, *faciās* you are to cause, 2nd pers. sg. pres. subj. of *facere* DO¹, make.

venison ven·zən, (U.S.) ven·izən, (Sc.) ve·nisn flesh of an animal killed in the chase XIII; (arch.) beast of the chase XIV. ME. *veneso(u)n, venisoun* – OF. *veneso(u)n, -ison* (mod. *venaison*) = Pr. *venaizó* :– L. *vēnātiō(n-)* hunting, hunt, game, f. *vēnārī*; see VENERY¹, -ATION.

venite vĭnai·ti invitatory psalm at matins. XIII. – L. *venite*, imper. pl. of *venīre* COME; first word of Psalm xc[i]v, beginning 'Venite, exultemus Domino' O come, let us sing unto the Lord.

venom ve·nəm poison, lit. and fig. XIII. – ME. *venim* – OF. *venim*, (also mod.) *vénin* :– Rom. **venīmen*, alt. (after L. words in *-īmen*) of L. *venēnum* potion, drug, poison (whence Pr. *veré*, Cat. *verí*, It. *veleno*, Rum. *venin*), perh. :– **wenesnom* love potion, f. *venus* love (see VENERY²). So **ve·nom** vb. XIV; now rare, cf. *envenom*. **ve·nom**OUS XIII; poisonous XIV. – (O)F. *venimeux*, f. *venim*, after late L. *venēnōsus*.

venose vī·nous veined. XVII. – L. *vēnōsus*, f. *vēna* VEIN; see -OSE¹. So **ve·n**OUS. XVII (Bacon); pert. to a vein or veins XVII; contained in the veins)(*arterial* XVIII.

vent¹ vent †provide with an outlet for gas, etc. XIV (Wycl. Bible, Trevisa); †discharge (fluid); give free course to, utter XVI; intr. †(of animals) scent, (of others, etc.) rise to the surface to breathe XVI. prob. aphetic of †*avent* (XIV) – OF. *aventer*, var. of *esventer* (mod. *éventer*) create wind, expose to the air, divulge, scent = Pr., Cat. *esventar*, It. *sventare*, Rum. *zvînta* :– Rom. **exventāre*, f. L. *ex* EX-¹ + *ventum* WIND¹. Hence (partly after F. †*esvent, évent*) **vent** sb. A. †discharge, utterance; issue, outlet XVI; means of outlet, opportunity of escape XVII; B. anus; aperture, outlet XVI; way out XVII.

vent[2] vent opening or slit in a garment. XV. var. of (dial.) *fent* (XV) – (O)F. *fente* slit :– Rom. **findita* (repl. L. *fissa*), sb. use of fem. pp. of L. *findere* cleave, split (see FISSURE). ¶ For the *v* cf. *vade* FADE[1], VAN[1].

vent[3] vent disposal by sale. XVI. – (O)F. *vente* = Pr., Pg. *venda*, Sp. *venta*, It. *vendita* :– Rom. **vēndita*, fem. pp. formation on L. *vēndere* VEND.

ventage ve·ntidʒ (arch.) finger-hole in a wind instrument. XVII (Sh. 'Hamlet' III ii 373). f. VENT[1] + -AGE.

ventail ve·nteil †neck-piece of armour; lower part of the front of a helmet. XIV. – OF. *vantail* or *vantaille* (= Pr. *ventalha*, It. *ventaglia*), f. *vent* WIND[1]. See -AL[2].

venter ve·ntəɹ A. any of two or more wives who have borne children to the same man XVI; B. belly, abdomen XVII. In A – law-F. *venter*, for (O)F. *ventre* :– L. *venter* belly; in B. immed. – L. Two comb. forms are used in medical terms, **ventri-** and **ventro-** (see -O-). XIX.

ventiduct ve·ntidʌkt passage serving to introduce cool or fresh air. XVII. f. L. *ventus* WIND[1] + *ductus* DUCT.

ventil ve·ntil valve controlling wind supply in an organ. XIX. – G. *ventil* – It. *ventile* – medL. *ventile* sluice.

ventilate ve·ntileit †blow away XV (once); investigate freely, sift by discussion XVI; give free utterance to; †winnow; †increase (flame), set (air) in motion; blow upon XVII; supply with fresh air XVIII. f. pp. stem of L. *ventilāre* brandish, fan, winnow, agitate, in late L. discuss, air a subject (whence also F. *ventiler*, etc.), f. *ventus* WIND[1]; see -ATE[3]. So **ventilA·TION** †motion in the air XV; †fanning, blowing XVI; free course of the air; aeration; admission of fresh air; free discussion XVII. – (O)F. or L. (exposure to the air, Pliny; in AL. discussion). **ve·ntilATOR** apparatus or opening for removing vitiated air and introducing a fresh supply. XVIII (S. Hales, 1743); hence F. *ventilateur*, etc.

ventosity ventɔ·siti flatulence XIV (Trevisa); bombast. XVI. – (O)F. *ventosité* or late L. *ventōsitās*, f. L. *ventōsus*, f. *ventus* WIND[1]; see -OSITY.

ventricle ve·ntrikl (anat.) any of the cavities of the heart, brain, etc. XIV ('Lanfranc's Cirurgie'). – L. *ventriculus*, dim. of VENTER; see -CLE.

ventriloquY[3] ventri·ləkwi speaking so that the sound appears to come from somewhere other than the speaker. XVI. – modL. *ventriloquium*, f. *ventri-*, VENTER + *loqui* speak, after Gr. ἐγγαστρίμυθος 'speaking in the belly' is superseded largely by **ventri·loquISM**. XVIII, f. **ventri·loquIST**. XVII, which superseded †**ventriloquus** (XVII–XVIII) – late L. (Tertullian).

venture ve·ntʃəɹ; -tjəɹ chance XV (chiefly, after 1500, in phr. *at a v.* at random, by chance); chancy or speculative enterprise XVI. Aphetic of *aventure* ADVENTURE, partly through apprehending *a-* as the indef. article (esp. in phr. *at aventure*). So **venture** vb. (in various applications, trans., refl., and intr.; chiefly from XVI) XV (Lydg.; often *venter* XV–XVII). Aphetic of *aventure* ADVENTURE vb. Hence **ve·nturER**[1]. XVI; also short for *merchant adventurer* (XV), *m. venturer* (XVI). **ve·nturOUS**. XVI, **ve·ntureSOME**[1]. XVII.

venue ve·nju A. †assault, attack XIV; thrust, esp. in fencing; fencing bout XVI (earlier in naturalized form *veny*; cf. dial. *vally* value). B. †arrival XIV (rare); (leg.) place where an action is laid or to which a jury is summoned XVI; place of meeting, locality XIX. – (O)F. *venue*, sb. use of pp. fem. of *venir* :– L. *venīre* COME.

Venus vī·nəs A. ancient Roman goddess of beauty and love OE.; beautiful woman; †venery XVI. B. (astron.) second planet in distance from the sun XIII; †(alch.) copper XIV, (her.) green XVI; (member of) genus of bivalve molluscs XVIII. See VENERY[2].

venville ve·nvil form of tenure in parishes adjoining the forest of Dartmoor, giving certain privileges in the use of the forest. XIV. Earliest forms *wengefeild*, *vennefeild*, *vyndefeld*, in which the second el. was replaced by VILL, and the first el. is of unknown origin.

veracious vĭrei·ʃəs observant of the truth XVII; conforming to the truth XVIII. f. L. *vērāci-*, *verāx*, f. *vērus* true; see VERY, -IOUS. So **veracity** vĭræ·sĭti. XVII. – F. or medL.

verandah, (U.S.) **-da** vəræ·ndə open portico along the side of a house. XVIII. – Hindi *varandā* (cf. Bengali *bārāndā*) – Pg. *varanda*, †Sp. *baranda* railing, balustrade, balcony, of unkn. origin. F. *véranda* is from Eng.

veratrine ve·rətrain poisonous alkaloid obtained from species of Veratrum. XIX. – F. *vératrine*, f. L. *vērātrum* hellebore; see -INE[5].

verb vəɹb (gram.) part of speech serving to predicate. XIV (Wycl. Bible, Prologue). – O(F). *verbe* or L. *verbum* WORD. So **ve·rbAL**[1] dealing with words XV (Caxton); consisting of words, oral; pert. to a verb XVI; concerned with words only XVII. – (O)F. *verbal* or late L. *verbālis*. **verbatim** vəɹbei·tim word by word. XV. medL.; cf. LITERATIM. **verbiAGE** vǝ·ɹbiidʒ excessive accumulation of words XVIII; wording XIX. – F. *verbiage*, f. †*verbeier* chatter, f. *verbe* + *-eier* :– Rom. *-*idiāre* – Gr. *-ízein*. Cf. Pg. *verbiagem*. **verbo·SE**[1] wordy, prolix. XVII – L. *verbōsus*. **verbo·SITY**. XVI. – L.

verbascum vəɹbæ·skəm mullein. XVI. L. (Pliny), whence Sp., Pg., It. *verbasco.*

verbena vəɹbī·nə (Roman antiq.) L., usu. pl., certain leaves or twigs used in sacred rites; vervain. XVI.

verb(um) sat. sap. vɜ̄·ɹb(əm) sæt sæp Shortening abbrev. of L. *verbum satis sapienti* a word to the wise (is) enough.

verdant vɜ̄·ɹdənt green (of vegetation). late XVI. Of obscure origin; perh. – OF. *verdeant*, prp. of *verdoier* (mod. *-oyer*) = It. *verdeggiare* (*-iante*) :– L. **viridiāre*, f. *viridis* green, VERT[1]; with reduction to two syll. after prps. in -ANT and assoc. with VERDURE.

verd antique vɜ̄ɹd ǟntī·k variety of green serpentine marble. XVIII. – F. †*verd antique* (now *vert a.*); also in It. form **ve·rde anti·co.** XVIII; see VERT[1], ANTIQUE.

verderer vɜ̄·ɹdərəɹ royal forester. XVI. – AN. *verderer*, extended form of *verder* = (O)F. *verdier* :– Rom. **viridāriu-s*, f. L. *viridis* green, VERT[1]; see -ER[2].

verdict vɜ̄·ɹdikt decision of a jury. XIII. ME. *verdict* – AN. *verdit* = OF. *veir-, voirdit*, f. *veir, voir* :– L. *vērum* true + *dit* :– L. *dictum* saying, speech, sb. use of n. pp. of *dicere* say; see VERY, DICTION. The sp. with *ct* became current XVI; the ME. form, with loss of *t*, survives in dial. *vardy*.

verdigris vɜ̄·ɹdigris green rust of copper. XIV. ME. *verdegres, vertegres* – OF. *vertegrez*, earlier *vert de Grece* (mod. *vert-de-gris*) 'green of Greece' (see VERT[1]), latinized *viride grecum*. The reason for the name is unkn.; cf. synon. G. *grünspan* (MHG. *grüenespān*, more usu. *spāngrüen*) 'Spanish green', medL. *viride Hispanicum*. The formation was at an early date obscured and various corruptions ensued.

verditer vɜ̄·ɹditəɹ pigment made by adding chalk to a solution of nitrate of copper. XVI. – OF. *verd de terre* (mod. *vert d. t.*) 'green of earth'; see VERT[1], TERRA.

verdure vɜ̄·ɹdʒəɹ, -djəɹ fresh green colour; green herbage XIV; †rich tapestry ornamented with vegetation; †freshness; †taste, savour, odour XVI. – (O)F. *verdure* (cf. Pr., Sp., Pg., It. *verdura*), f. †*verd* green; see VERT[1], -URE. From XV to XVII freq. by-forms were †*verder*, †*verdour* – OF. *verdour*; cf. Pr., Sp., Pg. *verdor*, It. *verdore* and see -OR[2].

verge[1] vɜ̄ɹdʒ penis (now only after modF.) XIV; rod or wand of office XV; *within the v.* (tr. AN. *dedeinz la verge*, in AL. *infra virgam*) within the area subject to the Lord High Steward (with ref. to his rod of office); extreme edge, margin, bank, border XV; space within a boundary, scope XVII (Dryden, 'and verge enough for more', imitated by Gray, and echoed later). – (O)F. *verge* = Pr., Sp., It. *verga*, Rum. *vargă* :– L. *virga* rod. Hence **verge** vb. †border, edge XVII; border (*up*)*on*, esp. fig. XVIII.

verge[2] vɜ̄ɹdʒ †descend towards the horizon; move in a certain direction, incline, tend. XVII. – L. *vergere* bend, incline; cf. CONVERGE, DIVERGE.

verger vɜ̄·ɹdʒəɹ official bearing a rod before a church or university dignitary. XV. – AN. **verger* (cf. late L. *virgārius*), f. *verge* VERGE[1]; see -ER[2].

verify ve·rifai prove to be true XIV; ascertain the correctness of XVI. – (O)F. *vérifier* – medL. *vērificāre*, f. *vērus* true; see VERY, -FY. So **ve:rif**ICA·TION. XIV. – (O)F. or medL.

verily ve·rĭli in truth XIII (Cursor M.); in versions of the Bible, rendering Vulg. L. *amēn*, Gr. *amḗn* AMEN XIV. ME. *verraily, verreli, verrili*, f. VERY + -LY[2], after OF. *verrai(e)ment* (mod. *vraiment*), and AN. *veirement* = OF. *voirement* (:– Rom. **vērāmente*), whence †*verement*, †*verament*, †*veriment* (all XIV).

verisimilar verisi·mĭləɹ having the semblance of truth. XVII. f. L. *vērisimilis, vērī similis* 'like the truth', i.e. g. sg. of *vērus* true, *similis* like. So **ve:risimi·li**TUDE. XVII. – L. See VERY, SIMILAR, SIMILITUDE.

verity ve·rĭti truth XIV; true statement or opinion XVI. ME. *verite* – (O)F. *verité*, repl. OF. *verté* = Pr. *verdat*, Sp. *verdad*, Pg. *verdade*, It. *verità* :– L. *vēritātem*, nom. *-tās*, f. *vērus* true; see VERY, -ITY. So **ve·rit**ABLE †true; genuine, real XV (Caxton); (after modF.) that is really so XIX. – (O)F. *véritable*; out of use by *c.*1650, said by Webster 1828 to be 'little used', re-adopted *c.*1830.

verjuice vɜ̄·ɹdʒūs acid juice of unripe fruit. XIV. – OF. *vertjus*, (also mod.) *verjus*, i.e. *vert jus* 'green juice'; see VERT[1], JUICE.

vermeil vɜ̄·ɹmil (arch.) vermilion; adj. XV; sb. XVI (Spenser); (from modF.) silver gilt, gilt bronze XIX. – (O)F. *vermeil* = Pr. *vermelh*, Sp. *bermejo*, Pg. *vermèlho* :– L. *vermiculu-s* little worm, grub, used in Vulg. Ex. xxxv 25 for *coccum* scarlet (see COCHINEAL), dim. of *vermis* WORM. See VERMILION.

vermi-, comb. form of L. *vermis* WORM, as in **ve·rmi**CIDE[1]. XIX, **ve·rmi**FUGE adj. XVII, sb. XVIII, **vermi·**PAROUS. XVII, **vermi·**VOROUS. XVIII, some of which have L. or F. antecedents.

vermicelli vɜ̄ɹmise·li, -tʃe·li wheaten paste, of Italian origin, prepared in long slender hard threads. XVII. – It. *vermicelli*, pl. of *vermicello*, dim. of *verme* :– L. *vermis* WORM.

vermicular vəɹmi·kjŭləɹ †peristaltic XVII; pert. to a worm or worms, vermiform XVIII. – medL. *vermiculāris*, f. L. *vermiculus* (whence **vermicle.** XVII, **vermicule.** XVIII), dim. of *vermis* WORM, after F. *vermiculaire*; see -CULE, -AR. So **vermicul**A·TION being infested with worms; tortuous boring, as of a worm. XVII. – L. (Pliny), f. *vermiculāri* be worm-eaten.

vermilion vəɹmi·ljən cinnabar or red mercuric sulphide XIII; colour of this, bright red XIV. ME. *vermelyon* – OF. *vermeillon* (corr. to Pr. *vermelhó*, Sp. *bermellón*, *-millón*, It. *vermiglione*), f. *vermeil* VERMEIL.

vermin vɜ̄·ɹmin animals of a noxious or offensive kind. XIII. – OF. *vermin*, (also mod.) *vermine* :– Rom. **verminum*, *-ina*, f. L. *vermin-*, *vermis* WORM; see -INE[1]. So **ve·rmin**OUS. XVII. – F. or L.

vermouth, -muth vɜ̄·ɹmūt, -mūþ alcoholic cordial of white wine flavoured with wormwood, etc. XIX. – F. *vermout* – G. *wermut* (see WORMWOOD), with assim. to the early G. sp. *wermuth*.

vernacular vəɹnæ·kjŭləɹ pert. to the native language. XVII. f. L. *vernāculus* domestic, native, indigenous (applied by Varro to native Roman words), f. *verna* home-born slave; see -AR. Also sb. XVIII.

vernal vɜ̄·ɹnəl pert. to the spring. XVI. – L. *vernālis*, f. *vernus* of the spring, f. *vēr* spring; see -AL[1]. So **verna·**TION (bot.) arrangement of leaves or fronds in the bud. XVIII. – modL. (Linnæus), f. *vernāre* bloom, f. *vernus*.

vernicle vɜ̄·ɹnikl cloth with which, according to legend, a woman wiped the face of Jesus Christ on the way to Calvary and on which his features were impressed; representation of this. XIV (PPl., Ch.). – OF. *vernicle*, alt. of *vernique*, (also mod.) *véronique* – medL. *veronica*, which has been supposed to be a perversion of **vēra icōn* 'true image' (see VERY, ICON) and was subsequently taken as the name of the woman herself. For the parasitic *l* cf. *barnacle*, *chronicle*. An equally old var. is *vernacle*, of obscure origin; cf. medL. *vernaculum*. An earlier (rare) syn. is †*veroni* XIII (Cursor M.) – AN. **veronie*. *Veronica* (XVII, Evelyn) has also been current.

vernier vɜ̄·ɹniəɹ movable scale for taking minute measurements. XVIII. – F. *vernier*, f. name of Paul *Vernier* (1580–1637), French mathematician, who described it in 'Quadrant nouveau de mathématiques', 1631.

veronal ve·rənəl diethyl-malonyl-urea, used as a hypnotic. XX. – G. *veronal* (Emil Fischer), f. *Verona*, name of an It. town; said to be so named because the German inventor was on his way to the town at the time the choice of name was discussed; see -AL[1].

veronica vĭrɔ·nikə plant of a scrophulariaceous genus. XVI. Obscure use of the name *Veronica* (see VERNICLE).

verrucose verū·kous full of warty excrescences. XVII. – L. *verrūcōsus*, f. *verrūca*, ult. rel. to WART; see -OSE[1].

versatile vɜ̄·ɹsətail changeable, inconstant. XVII (Bacon). – F. *versatile* or L. *versātilis*, f. *versāt-*, pp. stem of *versāre*, frequent. of *vertere* turn; VERSE, -ILE.

verse vɜ̄ɹs metrical line; versicle OE.; section of a psalm or canticle XII (now merged into: one of the small sections into which a chapter of the Bible is divided XVI); metrical composition XIII (Cursor M.); group of metrical lines, stanza (a sense of Eng. development) XIV. OE. *fers*, corr. to OFris. *fers*, MLG., OHG. (Du., G.), ON. *vers* – L. *versus* turn of the plough, furrow, line, row, line of writing, verse, f. *vers-*, pp. stem of *vertere* turn (see -WARD, WORTH[3]); reinforced or repl. in ME. by adoption of (O)F. *vers* (= Pr. *vers*, Sp., Pg., It. *verso*), from the same L. source. ¶ The division of chapters of the Bible into 'verses', introduced in the folio edition of Stephanus' Gr. N.T. in 1551, was adopted by Whittingham in his Eng. N.T. of 1557 and in the Geneva Bible of 1560.

versed[1] vɜ̄ɹst (math.) in *v. sine* (XVI). tr. modL. *sinus versus*, i.e. L. *sinus* SINE[1], *versus* turned, pp. of *vertere* turn (cf. VERSE, VERSION); the L. phr. tr. Arab. rendering of Prakrit *utkrama-jīvā* 'inverse-order sine' (*jīvā*, by-form of Skr. *jyā*, Vedic *jiā* bowstring).

versed[2] vɜ̄ɹst experienced or skilled in. XVII. – F. *versé* or its source L. *versātus*, pp. of *versāri* stay, be situated, be occupied or engaged, pass. of *versāre*, frequent. of *vertere* turn; see VERSION, -ED[1]. ¶ In XVIII–XIX the sense was borne also by *versant* – L. *versāns* prp. (cf. CONVERSANT).

versicle vɜ̄·ɹsikl (liturg.) short sentence or phrase recited antiphonally with a response XIV; little verse XV. – (O)F. *versicule* or L. *versiculus*, dim. of *versus* VERSE; see -CLE.

versicoloured vɜ̄·ɹsikʌləɹd of changing colour. XVIII. f. L. *versicolor*, f. *versus*, pp. of *vertere* turn (see -WARD, WORTH[3]) + *color* COLOUR; see -ED[2]. Earlier occas. adoptions were †*verse-coloured*, †*versicolo(u)r* (XVII).

versify vɜ̄·ɹsifai write in verse. XIV (PPl., Ch.). – (O)F. *versifier* – L. *versificāre* (Lucilius); see VERSE, -IFY. So **versifica·**TION. XVII. – L. (Quintilian). **versifi**ER[1] vɜ̄·ɹsifaiəɹ XIV (Rolle, Trevisa); syns. (XVII) with various implications are *versemaker*, *-man*, *-monger*, *verser*. – AN. *versifiur*, OF. *-fiour*, *-fieur*. See -FY, -ER[2].

version vɜ̄·ɹʃən rendering from one language into another XVI; particular form of a statement, document, etc. XVIII. (O)F. *version* – medL. *versiō(n-)* (whence also Sp. *versión*, It. *versione*), f. *vers-*, pp. stem of *vertere* turn; see VERSE, -SION.

verso vɜ̄·ɹsou back of the leaf of a book (denoted by v., v°, ^{v}), being the side presented to the eye when the leaf has been turned over. XIX. – L. *versō* (sc. *foliō*) '(the leaf) being turned', abl. sing. of pp. of *vertere* turn (see VERSION).

verst vɜ̄ɹst Russ. measure of length ($\frac{2}{3}$ of an Eng. mile). XVI. – Russ. *versta*, partly through G. *werst* and F. *verste*.

versus vɜ̄·ɹsəs (leg.) against. XV. – medL. (XIII) use of L. *versus* towards, in the sense of *adversus* against; cf. ADVERSE.

vert[1] vɜ̄ɹt green vegetation in a wood XV; (her.) green XVI. – (O)F. *vert* = Pr. *vert*, Sp., It. *verde* :– L. *virid-*, *viridis* green, rel. to *virēre* be green (see -ID[1]).

vert[2], **'vert** vɜ̄ɹt colloq. shortening of CONVERT sb., PERVERT sb., designed to repr. either or both. XIX.

vertebra, pl. **-æ** vɜ̄·ɹtibrə, -ī joint of the spinal column. XVII. – L. *vertebra*, f. *vertere* turn (see VERSION); for the formation cf. *palpebræ* eyelids; prop. pivot of bone; cf. Plato, Timæus, 74a ἐξ αὐτοῦ (of bone) σφονδύλους (vertebræ) πλάσας ὑπέτεινεν οἷον στρόφιγγας (like pivots). So **ve·rtebr**ATE[2]. XIX. – L. (Pliny); cf. INVERTEBRATE.

vertex vɜ̄·ɹteks (geom.) point opposite the base XVI (Dee); zenith; top, summit XVII. – L. *vertex, vertic-* whirl, vortex, crown of the head, highest point, f. *vertere* turn (see VERSION). So **ve·rtic**AL[1] pert. to the zenith XVI; perpendicular, at right angles to the axis, etc. XVIII. – F. or late L.

vertigo vɜ̄·ɹtigou, (formerly) vəɹtai·gou, -īgou swimming in the head. XVI. – L. *vertīgō*, stem *vertīgin-*, whence *vertīginōsus* **vertigin**OUS vəɹti·dʒinəs. XVII.

vervain vɜ̄·ɹvein herbaceous plant Verbena officinalis. XIV (Gower). – (O)F. *verveine* – L. *verbēna* VERBENA.

verve vɜ̄ɹv †special vein or bent in writing XVII (Dryden); spirit, dash, go XIX. – (O)F. *verve* †form of expression, †empty chatter, †whim, vigour – L. *verba*, pl. of *verbum* WORD.

very ve·ri adj. true XIII; exact, precise, actual; sheer XIV; mere XVI; adv. †truly, really XIV; highly, extremely XV. ME. *verray* – OF. *ver(r)ai* (mod. *vrai*) = Pr. *verai* :– Rom. **vērāius*, obscurely f. L. *vērus* true :– IE. **wēros*, whence also OS., OHG. *wār* (Du. *waar*, G. *wahr*), OIr. *fír*, W. *gwir*. The termination was assim. to -Y[1]. See also VERILY.

Very *light*. XX. f. name of the inventor, S. W. *Very*.

vesica vī·sikə †copper vessel used in distilling XVII; *v. piscis* 'fish bladder', painted oval figure used as an aureole XIX. – L. *vēsīca, vessīca, vensīca* bladder, blister; cf. Skr. *vastís* belly, bladder, (O)HG. *wanst* belly. So **vesic**AL ve·sikəl pert. to the urinary bladder. XVIII. – late L. **ve·sic**ATE[3] blister. XVII. f. pp. stem of late L. *vēsīcāre*. So **vesic**A·TION blistering. XVI. **ve·sic**LE small sac or cyst XVI; small elevation of the cuticle containing fluid XVIII. – F. *vésicule* or L. *vēsīcula*. **ve·sico-,** used as comb. form (see -O-) of L. *vēsīca*.

vesper ve·spəɹ A. evening star, Hesperus XIV (Gower); evening XVII (Sh.); B. pl. †public disputations held on the eve of the commencement of a bachelor of arts XVI; pl. sixth of the canonical hours, evensong XVII. A. – L. *vesper* evening star, evening = Gr. *hésperos* (see HESPERIAN); B. – OF. *vespres* (mod. *vêpres*) = Pr. *vespras*, Sp. *vísperas* – ecclL. *vesperās*, acc. pl. of L. *vespera* evening, eventide (= Gr. *hespérā*); modelled on *mātūtīnās* MATINS.

vessel ve·səl †(coll. sg.) domestic utensils; article designed to serve as a receptacle; in and after biblical use (as in Acts ix 15, Rom. ix 22, 2 Tim. ii 21, 1 Peter iii 7, rendering L. *vas*, Gr. σκεῦος), human body or person; boat or ship XIII (Cursor M.). – (i) AN. *vessel* = OF. *vaissel* (mod. *vaisseau* vessel, vase, ship) = Pr. *vaisel*, Sp. *vasillo*, It. *vascello* :– late L. *vascellum* small vase, dim. of *vās* vessel (see VASE); (ii) AN. *vessele* = (O)F. *vaisselle* pots and pans, plate :– Rom. **vascella*, pl. of L. *vascellum* used as coll. sg. fem.

vest[1] vest (hist.) loose outer garment; †vestment; sleeveless garment worn by men beneath the coat (retained in tailors' use for 'waistcoat'), introduced by Charles II XVII; undergarment for the upper part of the body worn next to the skin XIX. – F. *veste* – It. *veste* garment :– L. *vestis* clothing, attire, garment. f. **wes-* (see WEAR[1]). So **ve·sti**ARY pert. to dress. XVII. – L. *vestiārius*. **vestiar**IAN vestiɛə·riən concerned with (the use of) vestments XIX. **ve·stm**ENT garment, article of clothing XIII (Cursor M.); spec. in eccl. use XIV. ME. *vestiment, vestement* (3 syll.) – OF. *vestiment, vestement* (mod. *vêtement*) = Pr. *vestiment(a)*, Sp. *vestimenta*, It. *vestimento* – L. *vestīmentum*, cf. *vestīre* clothe, f. *vestis*. **ve·str**Y[3] room in a church in which clerics robe, and vestments, etc., are kept XIV; assembly of parishioners XVI. – AN. **vest(e)rie*, alt. of (O)F. *vestiaire*, †*vestiarie* (whence earlier Eng. *vestiary* XIII), by assoc. with *-erie* -ERY. **ve·st**URE (article of) apparel XIV (Ch.); (leg.) what grows upon the land, except trees XV. – OF. *vesture* (mod. *vêture*) – medL. *vestūra*, for late L. *vestītūra*, f. L. *vestīre*.

vest[2] vest A. settle (a person) in the possession of something or (a thing) in the possession of some one, invest XV. B. clothe XVI. In both uses first in pp. *vested* (-ED[1]) – OF. *vestu*, pp. of *vestir* (mod. *vêtir*) clothe, †invest (e.g. *vestir et ensaisiner, vestu et mis en possession*) = Sp. *vestir*, It. *vestire* :– L. *vestīre* clothe, spec. with the imperial purple (Ammianus), in medL. put in possession, as by investing a person with the insignia of an office, f. *vestis* VEST[1]. Cf. INVEST, which is later.

Vesta ve·stə (Roman myth.) female deity, goddess of the household XIV; one of the minor planets; kind of wax or wood match XIX. L., corr. to Gr. *Hestíā*, personification of *hestíā* hearth, house, household. So **Ves·t**AL[1], *v. virgin* one of the priestesses having charge of the sacred fire in the temple of Vesta in ancient Rome XV; pert. to, chaste as, a priestess of Vesta; sb. vestal virgin, chaste woman XVI. – L. *vestālis.*

vestibule ve·stibjūl entrance hall or court XVII; (anat., zool.) XVIII. – F. *vestibule* (perh. – It. *vestibulo*) or L. *vestibulum.*

vestige ve·stidʒ trace of something lost or gone XVII; slight trace XVIII. – F. *vestige* – L. *vestigium* sole of the foot, footprint, trace. rel. to *vestigāre* track (cf. INVESTIGATE).

Vesuvian visū·viən pert. to Vesuvius, a volcano on the Bay of Naples, Italy XVII; sb. (so named by Werner 1795) mineral compound found in Vesuvian lavas XVIII. f. *Vesuvius*; see -IAN.

vet vet colloq. shortening of VETERINARY *surgeon* or of its equiv. *veterinarian* sb. Hence as vb. subject to (professional) examination XIX.

vetch vetʃ (fruit of) plants of the genus Vicia XIV (Ch., Wycl. Bible, Trevisa). Late ME. *fecche, ficche* (mod. dial. *fitch*) and *vecche* (also *vache, fatch* XVI, mod. dial. *vatch*) – AN., ONF. *veche* = OF. *vece* (mod. *vesce*), Pr. *vesa*, Cat. *vessa*, It. *veccia* :– L. *vicia*. (Forms with *a* are spec. west-country.) Hence **ve·tch**LING[1] plant of the genus Lathyrus. XVI.

veteran ve·tərən experienced soldier XVI; adj. XVII. – F. *vétéran* or L. *veterānus* (whence also Sp., It. *veterano*), *veter-, vetus* old, rel. to OSl. *vetŭchŭ*, Lith. *vẽtušas* old, and perh. further to Gr. *ϝétos* year, Skr. *vatsás* calf; year, and the words cited s.v. WETHER; see -AN.

veterinary ve·tərīnəri pert. to the treatment of cattle and domestic animals. XVIII. – L. *veterinārius*, f. *veterinus* pert. to cattle (*veterinæ* fem. pl., *veterina* n. pl. cattle), perh. f. *veter-, vetus* (see prec.), as if the orig. ref. was to animals past work; see -INE[1], -ARY. So **ve:terin**A·RIAN. XVII (Sir T. Browne). Cf. F. *vétérinaire* (XVI).

veto vī·tou prohibition designed to prevent a proposed act XVII; after F. *véto* (1790) act of a competent person or body of preventing legislation XVIII (A. Young, 1792). – L. *vetō* I forbid (1st pers. sg. pres. ind. of *vetere*), used by the Roman tribunes of the people in opposing measures of the senate, etc. Hence vb. XVIII.

vex veks trouble, afflict, annoy. XV. – (O)F. *vexer* – L. *vexāre* (whence also Sp. *vejar*, Pg. *vexar*, It. *vessare*) shake, agitate, disturb, f. ppl. stem (cf. CONVEX) of *vehere* carry (see WAY). So **vexa·**TION. XV. – (O)F. – L.; whence **vexa·**TIOUS. XVI.

vexillum veksi·ləm banner; (bot.) large external petal of a papilionaceous flower. XVIII. L., military ensign, f. base of *vehere* carry (cf. VEHICLE).

via[1] vai·ə (astron.) *Via Lactea* the Milky Way XVII; *via media* mī·diə intermediate course XIX. L. 'way', 'road'; see WAY.

via[2], **viâ** vai·ə by way of. XVIII. L. *viā*, abl. of *via* VIA[1].

viable[1] vai·əbl capable of living or existing. XIX. – F. *viable*, f. *vie* life (:– L. *vīta*); see -ABLE. So **viabi·li**TY[1]. XIX. – F.

viable[2] vai·əbl traversable. XIX. – L. (VIA[1]) + -ABLE. So **viabi·li**TY[2]. XIX. – F.

viaduct vai·ədʌkt elevated structure carrying a roadway. XIX. f. L. *via* VIA[1], after *aqueduct*; cf. F. *viaduc.*

vial vai·əl vessel of moderate size for liquids. XIV (Ch., Wycl. Bible Rev. XV 7, XVI 1). ME. *viole*, alt. of *fiole* PHIAL. For the *v* cf. VENT[2].

viand vai·ənd article or kind of food, orig. and esp. pl. XIV (Maund.). – (O)F. *viande* †food, (now) meat = Pr., Sp. *vianda* :– Rom. **vi(v)anda* fem. sb. alt. of L. *vivenda* (cf. F. *offrande* offering and L. *offerenda*), gerundive of *vīvere* live (cf. VIVID) taken in sense of 'servant à la vie'.

viaticum vaiæ·tikəm Holy Communion as administered to the dying; necessaries for a journey. XVI. – L. *viāticum* travelling money, provisions for a journey, sb. use of n. of *viāticus*, f. *via* VIA[1]; see -ATIC and cf. VOYAGE.

vibrant vai·brənt †agitated, energetic XVI; vibrating XVII. – prp. of L. *vibrāre*, move rapidly to and fro, brandish, shake, be agitated, f. IE. **wib- *weib-*, repr. also by WHIP, WIPE; see -ANT. **vibra·**TE[3] swing to and fro. XVII. f. pp. stem of L. *vibrāre*. So **vibra·**TION. XVII – L. **vi·brat**ORY[2]. XVIII; cf. F. *vibratoire*, Sp., Pg. *vibratorio.*

vibrio vi·briou (zool.) bacterioid organism having a vibratory motion. XIX. modL., f. L. *vibrāre* VIBRATE after F. *vibrion.*

viburnum vaibə̄·ɹnəm shrub of the genus so named, e.g. guelder rose, laurustinus. XVIII. L., 'wayfaring-tree', Viburnum Lantana.

vicar vi·kəɹ representative of God on earth XIII (Cursor M.); the Pope as Vicar of Christ; person acting in a parish for the parson or rector, (later) incumbent of a parish of which the tithe is impropriated or appropriated; bishop's deputy XIV. – AN. *vikere, vicare*, (O)F. *vicaire* (now) assistant curate, deputy – L. *vicārius* substitute, deputy (whence also Sp., It. *vicario* and Eng. †*vicary* XIV–XVII, surviving as a surname), f. **vicis* change, alteration, time, turn; see VICE[4], -AR. Hence **vic·ar**AGE. XV; after *parsonage*. **vicari**ATE[1] vikɛə·rieit. XVII. – medL. **vicar**IOUS vikɛə·riəs, vai- taking the place of another. XVII. f. L. *vicārius.*

vice[1] vais corruption of morals, wicked practice XIII (RGlouc., Cursor M.); fault, defect XIV. – (O)F. *vice* – L. *vitium* physical or other defect, fault, vice, whence also Pr. *vetz*, OSp. *vezo* custom, use, It. *vezzo* usage, amusement, pl. endearments. So **vic**IOUS vi·ʃəs depraved, immoral XIV; (of a horse) inclined to be savage XVIII. – (O)F. *vicieux* – L. *vitiōsus*. Cf. VITIATE.

vice[2] vais †winding staircase XIV; †screw XV; tool with two jaws opening and closing by means of a screw XV/XVI – (O)F. *vis* = Pr. *vit, vitz*, Sp. *vid* vine, It. *vite* vine, screw :– L. *vitis* vine, vine stem, prop. tendril, plant with tendrils, rel. to *viēre* twine, *vimen* osier (see WITHE).

vice[3] vais orig. sb. use of the prefix VICE- in the sense 'deputy'; in more recent use, the second el. is usu. implied or expressed in the context.

vice[4] vai·si in place of. XVIII. L., abl. of **vix*, extant only in obl. forms *vicis, vicem, vice, vicēs, vicibus*, for the prob. connexion of which see WEEK. Cf. next and VICAR, VICISSITUDE.

vice- vais repr. L. *vice* in place of (see prec.), which, prop. construed with a genitive, was prefixed immed. to a nominative in late L., e.g. *vice-quæstor* (cf. *prōquæstor*), and so used widely in medL., e.g. *vicecancellarius, -comes, -dominus, -gerens, thesaurarius*, whence OF. *vi(s)chancellier, vi(s)conte* VISCOUNT, *vi(s)dame* VIDAME, *vicegerent, -regent, -treasurer* (XVI). The oldest Eng. exx., of which *vice-chancellor* (XV) is the earliest, show the prefix in the OF. forms *vis-, vi-*, which were later replaced by the L. form, except in *viscount*.

vicennial vaise·niəl (Sc. law) extending to 20 years. XVIII. f. late L. *vicennium*, f. *vicies* 20 times.

viceroy vai·sroi governor of a country by authority of the supreme ruler. XVI. – F. *viceroy*, †*visroy* (mod. *viceroi*), f. *vice-* VICE- + *roi* king :– L. *rēgem, rēx*. So **vice**ROYALTY (str. variable). XVIII. – F. *viceroyauté*.

vicesimal vaise·siməl. XVII. – L. *vīcēsimus* twentieth, f. *vīcēnī* twenty each + -AL[1]. See VIGESIMAL.

vice versa vai·si vɜ̄·ɹsə contrariwise, conversely. XVII. L. 'the position being reversed'; *vice*, abl. of **vix* (see VICE[4]), and abl. sg. fem. of *versus*, pp. of *vertere* (see VERSE).

vicinage vi·sinidʒ neighbourhood. XIV. – OF. *visenage* (mod. *voisinage*) – Rom. **vicīnāticum*, f. L. *vicinus*; see -AGE. So **vici·n**ITY. XVI. – L. *vicinitās*, f. *vicinus* neighbouring, neighbour, prop. of the same quarter or village, f. *vīcus* cluster of dwellings, street, quarter of a town, village, corr. to Goth. *weiks* and rel. to Gr. (ϝ)*oîkos*, Skr. *vēśás* house.

vicious vi·ʃəs A. pert. to vice XIV (R. Rolle); addicted to vice XIV (Ch.); (of horses, etc.) inclined to be savage XVIII (cf. F. *cheval vicieux* Diderot, *beste vicieuse* Amyot); B. (leg.) made void XIV; impaired by fault or defect XVI; *v. circle*, after F. *cercle vicieux* (Descartes), modL. *circulus vitiosus* XVIII. – OF. *vicious* (mod. *vicieux*) – L. *vitiōsus*, f. *vitium* VICE[1]; see -IOUS.

vicissitude vaisi·sitjūd, visi·s- mutation, mutability XVI; change in human affairs XVII. – (O)F. *vicissitude* or L. *vicissitūdō*, f. *vicissim* by turns, f. *vic-* turn; see VICE[4], -TUDE.

victim vi·ktim living creature offered in sacrifice XV; one who suffers death or severe treatment XVII. – L. *victima* (whence also F. *victime*, Sp. *victima*, It. *vittima*), perh. rel. to Goth. *weihan*, etc. to consecrate. The Rhemish (followed by the Douay) translators of the Bible were the first to use the word freely; the general currency dates only from late XVII. Hence **vi·ctim**IZE. XIX; F. has *victimer*.

victor vi·ktəɹ one who overcomes. XIV (Rolle). – AN. *victo(u)r* or L. *victor*, f. *vict-*, pp. stem of *vincere* conquer, f. nasalized var. of **wik-*; see WIGHT[2], -OR[1].

Victoria viktɔ̄·riə. XIX. Name of the Queen of Great Britain (1837–1901) given to various objects: a gigantic water-lily (Victoria regia), a luscious red plum, a light four-wheeled carriage (said to have been first so named by the French). Hence **Victo·r**IAN. 1851 (the year in which Victoria in Australia was so named); **vi·ctor**INE[4] lady's fur tippet. XIX.

victory vi·ktəri state or fact of having conquered XIV; Roman goddess of victory XVI. – AN. *victorie* = (O)F. *victoire* = Sp. *victoria*, It. *vittoria* – L. *victōria*, f. *victor*; see VICTOR and -Y[3]. So **victor**IOUS viktɔ̄·riəs. XIV – AN. *victorious* = (O)F. *victorieux* – L.

victual vi·tl (coll. sg. and pl.) provisions for food, articles of food. XIV. ME. *vitaile(s)* – OF. *vitaille*, later (and mod.) *victuaille* = Pr. *vit(o)alha*, Sp. *vitualla*, It. *vettovaglia* :– late L. *vīctūālia* n.pl. of *victūālis*, f. L. *victus* livelihood, f. base of *vivere* live; see VIVID, -AL[1]. The normal development to *vit(t)el* (XV–XVI) is repr. by the present pronunc., while the sp., first infl. by F. *victuaille*, was finally assim. entirely to L. So **victual** vb. XIV. – OF. *vitaillier, vi(c)tuaillier*. **victuall**ER[2] vi·tləɹ. XIV (PPl., Wycl.). – OF. *vitaill(i)er, -our*.

vicuna vikjū·nə, vikū·njə S. Amer. animal, Auchenia vicunna XVII; vicuna cloth XIX. – Sp. *vicuña* (Pg. *vicunha*) – Quechua. ¶ The F. form *vigogne*, var. †*vigone*, and a latinized form of this, *vigonia*, have been used.

vidame vī·dæm in France, one who held lands from a bishop as his representative. XVI. – F. *vidame*, OF. *visdame* – medL. *vicedominus*, f. *vice-* VICE- + *dominus* lord (cf. DAN, DOM[1], DON[2]).

vide vai·di see, refer to. XVI. L. *vidē*, imper. sg. of *vidēre* (see WIT[2]). abbrev. v., †*vid.*

videlicet vaidī·liset, vi- that is to say, namely. XV. L. *vidēlicet*, f. *vidē*, stem of *vidēre*+*licet* it is permissible; see WIT[2], LICENCE. Abbrev. †*vid.*, †*videl.*, †*vidz(t).*, VIZ.

vidimus vai·dimǝs (leg.) copy of a document bearing an attestation that it is authentic. XV. L. *vīdimus* we have seen, 1st pers. pl. perf. of *vidēre* see (see VISION). So in (O)F.

vidonia vidou·niǝ dry white wine of the Canary Islands. XVIII. Of unkn. origin.

vidual vi·djuǝl pert. to a widow. XVI. – late L. *viduālis*, f. *vidua* WIDOW; see -AL[1]. So **vidu·**ITY widowhood. XV. – (O)F. or L.

vie vai make a challenge XV; enter into rivalry *with* XVII. prob. aphetic of late ME. *avie, envie* – OF. *envier* outbid = Sp., Pg. *envidar*, It. *invitare* :– L. *invītāre* INVITE, in Rom. challenge, make a bid; but the early chronology is uncertain, the reading *vie* in Ch. 'Dethe of Blaunche' 173 being prob. incorrect.

vielle vjel hurdy-gurdy. XVIII. – F. *vielle*, OF. *viele*; see VIOL.

view vjū A. †formal inspection XV; exercise of the faculty of sight; sight, look, vision XVI. B. mental vision XV; conception, opinion XVI; survey; aim, intention XVII. – AN. *vewe, vieue*, OF. *veue* (mod. *vue*), ppl. sb. from *veoir* (mod. *voir*) to see, f. L. *vidēre* see; see WIT[2]. Hence (or aphetic of †*aview* – F. *avuer*, †*aveuer*, f. *à* AD-+*vue*) **view** vb. XVI.

vigesimal vai-, vidʒe·simǝl pert. to 20. XVII. f. L. *vigēsimus*, var. of *vīcēsimus* VICESIMAL.

vigia vi·dʒiǝ (naut.) warning on a sea chart of hidden danger. XIX. – Pg. *vigia* look-out, f. *vigiar* :– L. *vigilāre* watch (see next).

vigil vi·dʒil eve of a church festival XIII; watch XVII. – (O)F. *vigile*. – L. *vigilia* watch, watchfulness, f. *vigil* awake, alert, rel. to *vigēre* be vigorous or lively; see WAKE[1]. So **vi·gil**ANT wakeful and watchful. XV. – L. *vigilant-, -āns* (whence also F. *vigilant*), prp. of *vigilāre* keep awake, f. *vigil.*

vigneron vinjǝrɔ̃ wine-grower. XV. (O)F. *vigneron*, f. *vigne* VINE, with intercalated r.

vignette vine·t ornamental design on a blank space in a book XVIII; photograph of head (and shoulders) XIX. – (O)F. *vignette* (whence also Sp. *viñeta*, It. †*vignetta*), dim. of *vigne* VINE; see -ETTE. ¶ The F. word was adopted earlier as †*vinet* orig. trailing ornament in imitation of leaves, tendrils, etc. (XV).

vigour, U.S. **vigor** vi·gǝɹ active strength or force XIV; legal force XV; energetic action XVII. – OF. *vigour* (mod. *vigueur*) = Pr., Sp. *vigor*, It. *vigore* – L. *vigōrem*, *vigor* liveliness, activity, f. *vigēre* be lively, flourish; see WAKE[3], WAX[2], EKE[2], and -OUR[2]. So **vi·gor**OUS. XIV (not in gen. use before XVII). – OF. *vigorous* (mod. *vigoureux*) – medL. *vigōrōsus*. Cf. INVIGORATE.

viking vai·kiŋ, vi·kiŋ Scandinavian searover. XIX. First appears in Icel. form *vikingr* (G. Chalmers, 1807) or var. of this, *vikinger, -ir*, later *viking* (Longfellow), also *wiking* (E. A. Freeman). – ON. (Icel.) *víkingr* (X), commonly held to be f. *vík* creek, inlet + *-ingr* -ING[3], as if 'frequenter of inlets of the sea'; but the existence of the word in Anglo-Frisian (in OE. as early as VIII in *wīcingsċeaþa* 'piraticus', in OFris. *wītsing, wīsing*) suggests that it originated in that linguistic area, in which case it was prob. f. OE. *wīc*, OFris. *wīk* (see WICK[2]) in the sense of 'camp', the formation of temporary encampments being a prominent feature of viking raids.

vilayet vilā·jet province ruled by a vali. XIX. Turk, f. *wālī* VALI. Cf. BLIGHTY.

vile vail of low or base quality or character. XIII. – (O)F. *vil* m., fem. *vile* = Pr., Sp. *vil*, It. *vile* :– L. *vīli-s* of low value or price, cheap, common, mean, base. So **vili**FY vi·lifai †debase in value XV (freq. in XVII); depreciate in language XVI. – late L. *vilificāre* (Jerome). **vilipend** vi·lipend treat contemptuously XV; represent as contemptible XVI. – (O)F. *vilipender* or L. *vilipendere*, f. *vīlis* + *pendere* consider (cf. PERPEND).

vill vil (leg. and hist.) territorial division under the feudal system, corr. to township or civil parish XVI (Bacon); (poet.) village XVII. – AN. *vill* = OF. *vile, ville* farm, country house, village, collection of villages round a city (mod. *ville* town) – L. *villa*; see next.

villa vi·lǝ country residence, orig. one with farm buildings, etc. XVII; residence in the suburbs of a town or in a residential district (XVIII; Johnson; 'suburban villas' Cowper). Partly – L. *villa* country house, farm (whence (O)F. *ville*, Pr., Sp., It. *villa*) :– **wīcslā*, f. **wīcus* WICK[2]. Partly – It. *villa*. So **vill**AGE vi·lidʒ – (O)F. *village* = Pr. *villatge* (whence Sp. *villaje*, It. *villaggio*) :– coll. deriv. of L. *vīlla*.

villain vi·lǝn base fellow, (later) depraved scoundrel, (hist.; often sp. VILLEIN by mod. historians) feudal serf, peasant cultivator in subjection to a lord XIV. ME. *vilein, vilain* – OF. *vilein, vilain* (mod. *vilain*; also adj. ugly, vile, low) = Pr. *vilá*, Sp., It. *villano*, Pg. *villão* :– Rom. **villānu-s* (medL., whence *villan* XVI–XIX), f. L. *vīlla*; see prec., -AN. So **vi·llain**OUS. XIV; superseded †*villain* adj. and †*villains* (– OF. *vilains*,

-eins :- Rom. nom. **villānus*). **villainy** vi·ləni. XIII. – (O)F. *vilenie*; the present sp. was not established before XIX, when it finally displaced *villany*, earlier *vilany*, ME. *vileinie*.

villanelle viləne·l †rustic song or tune XVI (Sidney); pastoral or lyric poem in stanza form with two rhymes throughout XIX. – F. *villanelle* – It. *villanella*, fem. of *villanello* rural, rustic, f. *villano* peasant, VILLAIN.

villatic vilæ·tik pert. to a (Roman) villa, rustic. XVII ('tame v. Fowl', Milton). – L. *villāticus*, f. *vīlla* VILLA, after *silvāticus* SAVAGE.

villegiatura viledʒətjuə·rə residence in the country. XVIII (Walpole, Smollett). It., f. *villeggiare* to stay in the country, f. *villa* country house, VILLA.

villein vi·lein (hist.) see VILLAIN. So **villeinAGE** vi·lənidʒ tenure of land by bond-service. XIV. – AN., OF. *vilenage*, medL. *villenagium*.

villous vi·ləs covered with numerous thick-set stout hairlike projections. XIV – L. *villōsus* (whence also **villo·SE**[1] XVIII), f. *villus* tuft of hair, pl. hair, down; see -OUS and cf. F. *villeux*.

vim vim (orig. U.S.) force, energy, 'go'. XIX. usu. supposed to be – L. *vim*, acc. of *vīs* strength, energy, corr. to Gr. *ϝīs*, *ϝīn*; but it is poss. a symbolic formation.

vimineous vimi·niəs made of or producing flexible twigs. XVII. f. L. *vīmineus*, f. *vīmin-*, *vīmen* osier; see WITHE and -EOUS.

vinaceous vainei·ʃəs wine-coloured. XVII. f. L. *vīnāceus*, f. *vīnum* WINE; see -ACEOUS.

vinaigrette vineigre·t A. small two-wheeled carriage formerly used in France (said to be so called from resembling the carts which carried an itinerant vinegar-seller's barrels) XVII; B. smelling-bottle XIX. F., f. *vinaigre* VINEGAR; see -ETTE. ¶ Sense B is not F.

Vincentian vinse·nʃ'ən pert. to St. Vincent of Lérins (d. *c.*450 A.D.); see -IAN. XIX.

vincible vi·nsĭbl that may be overcome (spec. in theol. *v. ignorance*). XVI. – L. *vincibilis*, f. *vincere* overcome; see VICTOR, -IBLE. Cf. INVINCIBLE.

vinculum vi·ŋkjŭləm bond, tie XVII (Cudworth); (math.) straight line drawn over two or more terms XVIII. L., f. *vincīre* bind; cf. -ULE.

vindicate vi·ndikeit †set free XVI; †avenge; clear from censure, justify; defend the claims of XVII. f. pp. stem of L. *vindicāre* (also *vendicāre*) claim, set free, punish, avenge, f. *vindic-*, *vindex* claimant, protector, deliverer, avenger; see -ATE[3]. (†*Vendicate* was current *c.*1530–1620.) So **vindicA·TION** †avenging. XV (Caxton); defence against censure, etc. XVII. – OF. or L. **vindi·ctIVE** revengeful. XVII. f. L. *vindicta* vengeance, f. *vindic-* (cf. *senecta* old age); preceded by *vindicative* (XVI) – (O)F. or medL.

vine vain grape-bearing plant. XIII. – OF. *vine* (also mod.) *vigne* = Pr., Pg. *vinha*, Sp. *viña*, It. *vigna*, Rum. *vie* :- L. *vīnea* vineyard, vine, sb. use of fem. of *vīneus* pert. to wine, f. *vīnum* WINE.

vinegar vi·nigəɹ liquid formed by the acetous fermentation of wine. XIII (Cursor M.). ME. *vinegre*, later *vineger* (XV–XVII), *vinegar* (from XVI) – OF. *vyn egre* (mod. *vinaigre*), corr. to Pr., Sp., Pg. *vinagre*, It. *vinagro*, repr. Rom. **vīnum acrum* (for L. *acre*) 'sour wine'; see WINE, EAGER. The sp. with *-ar* was perh. adopted to suggest pronunc. with g, although the difficulty does not seem to have been felt with EAGER.

vineyard vi·njəɹd plantation of vines. XIV (R. Rolle). f. VINE+YARD[1]; superseding ME. *winyard*, OE. *wīnġeard* = OS. *wīngardo* (Du. *wijngaard*), OHG. *wīngart*, ON. *víngarðr*, Goth. *weinagards* (CGerm. comp. of WINE and YARD[1]).

vingt-et-un vɛ̃teœ̃, **vingt-un** vɛ̃tœ̃ round game of cards in which the object is to make the number 21. XVIII. F. 'twenty (and) one'; *vingt* :- L. *vīgintī* (cf. Gr. dial. *ϝíkati*, Attic *eíkosi*), *un* :- L. *ūnu-s* ONE. Cf. VAN JOHN, PONTOON[2].

vinous vai·nəs pert. to wine. XVII. – L. *vīnōsus*, f. *vīnum* WINE; see -OUS and cf. F. *vineux*. So **vino·SITY**. XVII (Sir T. Browne). – late L.

vintage vi·ntidʒ crop of a vineyard XV (since XVIII spec. with ref. to the age or year of a wine); grape harvest XVI. alt., by assoc. with †*vinter*, VINTNER, and assim. of the ending to -AGE, of late ME. *vyndage* (Wycl. Bible), *vendage* (PPl.) – (O)F. *vendange* = Pr. *vendemia*, Sp. *vendimia*, It. *vendemmia* :- L. *vindēmia*, f. *vīnum* WINE+*dēmere* take away, f. *dē* DE-+*emere* buy.

vintner vi·ntnəɹ wine merchant. XV (*vyntenere*, Lydg.). – AL. *vintenārius* (XIII), var. of *vini-*, *vin(e)tārius* – AN. *viniter*, *vineter* (whence ME. †*vinter*, which *vintner* superseded), OF. *vinetier* = Pr. *vinatier*, Sp. *vinatero*, It. *vinattiere* – medL. *vīnātārius*, *-ētārius*, f. L. *vinētum* vineyard, f. *vīnum* WINE; see -ER[2].

viol vai·əl stringed musical instrument played with a bow. XV. Earlier forms *vyell* (Caxton), *viall*. – OF. *viel(l)e* (mod. *vielle* viol, hurdy-gurdy), alt. of *viole* – Pr. *viola*, *viula* (whence also Sp., It. *viola*), prob. rel. to FIDDLE; the present form (– F. *viole*) dates from XVI. So **viol da gamba**. XVIII (earlier *gambo* (XVI–XVII) – It. *viola da gamba* 'leg-viol', i.e. the instrument when played being placed between the legs.

viola[1] vai·ələ †violet XV (Lydg., Henryson); single-coloured pansy XIX. – L. *viola*, violet, rel. to Gr. *ϝíon*. So **violA·CEOUS**. XVII. f. L. *violāceus* violet-coloured.

viola[2] vaiou·lə alto or tenor violin. XVIII. – Sp., It. *viola*, prob. – Pr. *viola*; see VIOL.

violate vai·əleit infringe, transgress; ravish, rape; desecrate, profane XV; disturb violently XVII. f. pp. stem of L. *violāre*, f. *vīs* force, acc. *vim* (cf. VIM), corr. to Gr. *ϝίς*, acc. *ϝῖν*; see -ATE³. So **viola·tion**. XV. – (O)F. or L. **vi·olence** exercise of force. XIII. – (O)F. *violence* – L. *violentia*, f. *violent-*, *-ēns*, beside *violentus*, whence (O)F. *violent*, the source of Eng. **vi·olent**. XIV.

violet vai·əlĭt A. plant of the genus Viola; B. dress of purplish-blue, the colour itself XIV. – (O)F. *violette*, †*-ete* in both senses and (O)F. *violet* in the second sense, dims. of *viole* – L. *viola* VIOLA¹. ¶ A disyllabic pronunc., noted by *vi'let*, now vulgar, is evidenced from XVII (Dryden).

violin vaiəli·n four-stringed musical instrument played with a bow, fiddle. XVI (Spenser). – It. *violino*, f. *viola* VIOLA². Hence **vi·olinist**. XVII; so It. *violinista*, F. *violiniste*.

violoncello vai:ələntʃe·lou bass violin. XVIII. – It., dim. of *violone* double-bass viol; abbrev. 'CELLO.

viper vai·pəɹ adder. XVI (Tindale). – (O)F. *vipère* or L. *vīpera* serpent :– **vivipera*, f. *vīvus* alive (cf. VIVID)+*parere* bring forth (cf. PARENT). *nourish a v. in one's bosom* is after L. 'in sinu viperam habere' (Cicero), 'viperam nutricare sub ala' (Petronius). **vi·perine¹**. XVI. – L. *vīperīnus*. Hence **vi·perous**. XVI.

virago virei·gou †name given by Adam to Eve, after the use in Vulg. Gen. ii 23 ('Hæc vocabitur virago, quoniam de viro sumpta est') OE.; man-like or heroic woman, female warrior (as in L.) XIV (Trevisa); bold or violent woman XIV (Ch.). – L. *virāgō*, obscurely f. *vir* man (see VIRILE).

virelay vi·rəlei short-lined poem on two rhymes. XIV (Ch.). – (O)F. *virelai*, alt. of †*vireli* (perh. orig. a refrain) after *lai* LAY².

virement viə·ɹmənt, ||virmã application of resources intended for one end to the purposes of another. XX. – F. *virement* (as in *virement de fonds*), f. *virer* turn (cf. VEER²)+ *-ment* -MENT.

vireo vi·riou small American bird. XIX. L. (Pliny) perh. greenfinch.

virescent vire·sənt greenish. XIX. f. L. *virescent-*, *-ēns*, prp. of *virescere* become green, f. *virēre* be green (cf. VERT¹); see -ENT, -ESCENT.

virgate vǝ̄·ɹgeit early land-measure. XVII. – medL. *virgāta* (Domesday Bk.), f. L. *virga* rod, VERGE¹; a rendering of OE. *ġierdland*; see -ATE¹.

Virgilian, Ver- vəɹdʒi·liən pert. to the Roman poet Publius *Vergilius* Maro (70–19 B.C.). XVI (Douglas). – L. *Vergiliānus*; see -IAN. The sp. with *-ir-* is found in Eng. use as early as the OE. translation of Boethius ('*Firgilies* freond and lareow'); cf. F., Sp., Pg., It. usage (all with *-ir-*).

virgin vǝ̄·ɹdʒin unmarried or chaste woman or girl XIII (first in eccl. use, of one venerated by the Church); adj. XVI (of a fortress, etc. that has never been taken XVIII). – AN., OF. *virgine*, *-ene* (mod. *vierge*), corr. to Pr., Cat. *verge*, Sp. *virgen*, Pg. *virgem* – L. *virginem* (whence also It. *vergine*, Rum. *vargurǎ*), acc. of *virgō*. So **vir·ginal¹**. XV. – (O)F. or L. As sb. (sg. and pl.) applied to a keyed musical instrument (XVI) perh. so called because it was intended for young ladies of Parthenia, i.e. maiden's songs, title of the first music published for it in England. **virgi·nity**. XIII (Cursor M.). – (O)F. *virginité* – L. *virginitās*. *Virgin wax* (orig.) unused beeswax, (later) white wax XIV. tr. medL. *cera virginea*; cf. F. *cire vierge*.

Virginia vəɹdʒi·niə part of N. America in which the first English settlement was made in 1607; applied to a variety of tobacco grown there (XVII) and to various plants and animals. f. L. *virgin-*, *virgō* VIRGIN, in honour of Queen Elizabeth I of England, 'the *Virgin* Queen'; see -IA¹. Hence **Virgi·nian** sb. XVI.

Virgo vǝ̄·ɹgou constellation lying between Leo and Libra; sixth sign of the zodiac. XIV (Gower, Ch.). L., 'virgin'.

virgouleuse vǝ̄ɹgulǝ̄·z juicy winter pear. XVII. F., fem. (sc. *poire* pear) of *virgouleux*, adj. of *Virgoulée*, repr. pop. pronunc. of *Villegoureix* village of Limousin, France, where the fruit originated. ¶ Apprehension of the final cons. as the pl. sign has produced U.S. *vergaloo*, *-l(i)eu* (XIX), which is applied to the white doyenne or Warwickshire bergamot.

virgule vǝ̄·ɹgjūl sloping or vertical line used in mediæval MSS. as a mark of punctuation. XIX. – F. *virgule* comma – L. *virgula*, dim. of *virga* rod, VERGE¹.

virid vi·rid green. XVI (Fairfax). – L. *viridis*, f. *virēre* be green; see -ID¹. So **viri·dity**. XV (Lydg.).

virile vi·rail, vaiᵊ·rail pert. to or characteristic of a man. XV (Caxton). – (O)F. *viril* or L. *virilis*, f. *vir* man = OE. *wer* (cf. WERGELD), OFris., OS., OHG. *wer*, OIr. *fer*, W. *gŵr* :– IE. **wiros*, beside **wīros*, whence Lith. *výras*, Skr. *vīrás*; see -ILE. So **virility** viri·lĭti. XVI. – (O)F.

virtu, vertu vəɹtū·, vǝ̄·ɹtū taste for works of art. XVIII (Richardson; *object*, etc. *of virtu* curio, antique, Goldsmith). – It. *virtù* (see VIRTUE) used in this sense. ¶ The form *vertu* follows F. sp. without justification, as the It. sense has never been current in F.

virtue vǝ̄·ɹtʃu, -tju †power, influence; efficacy, conformity to moral principles; excellence XIII; (arch.) high merit or accomplishment; †valour XIV. – (O)F. *vertu* = Pr. *vertut*, OIt. *vertù* (see VIRTU), Rum. *vǎrtute* strength :– L. *virtūtem*, nom. *virtūs* valour, worth, merit, moral perfection, f. *vir* man (cf. *juventus* youth, *senectus* old age), corr. to OE. *wer* (cf. WERGELD). So **vi·rtu**AL[1] †effective XIV; that is so in essence or effect XVII. – medL. *virtuālis*; cf. F. *virtuel*, It. *virtuale*, etc. **vi·rtual**LY[2]. XV; cf. medL. *virtuāliter*. **virtuoso** vəɹtjuou·sou one having special knowledge (and skill) in an art. XVII. – It. – late L. *virtuōsus*, whence, through (O)F. *vertueux*, **vi·rtu**OUS †valiant XIII; righteous XIV.

virus vaiə·rəs venom XVI; (path.) poison of a disease XVIII. – L. *vīrus*, rel. to OIr. *fí* poison, Gr. *ἰός* venom, rust, Skr. *viṣám*, Av. *viša-*. So **virulent** vi·rjŭlənt. XIV. – L. *vīrulentus* poisonous.

vis vis XVII. L. *vīs* (acc. *vim*, pl. *vīrēs*) strength, quantity, number, pl. forces, corr. to Gr. *ϝίς*, acc. *ϝîn*. Cf. VIM.

visa vī·zə certificate of examination on a passport. XIX. – F. *visa* – mod. use of L. *vīsa* 'things seen', n.pl. of pp. of *vidēre* see (cf. VISION), put on a document to testify that it has been verified. Superseding **visé** vī·zei f. *viséd* (early XIX), anglicization of F. *visé*, pp. of *viser* look attentively at, scrutinize :– Rom. **vīsāre*, f. L. *vīs-*, pp. stem of *vidēre*.

visage vi·zidʒ face. XIII (Cursor M.). – (O)F. *visage*, f. OF. *vis* (cf. next) = Pr. *vis*, OSp., It. *viso* :– L. *vīsus* sight, appearance, in Rom. face, f. pp. base of *vidēre*; see VISION, -AGE.

vis-à-vis vīzavī· either of two persons facing each other; carriage for two sitting face-to-face. XVIII. (O)F., 'face to face'; OF. *vis* face (see prec.), *à* to (:– L. *ad*), *vis*.

viscacha viskæ·tʃə S. Amer. rodent (Lagidium, Lagostomus). XVII. – Sp. *viscacha* (also *biscacha*) – Quechua *(h)uiscacha*.

viscera vi·sərə internal organs of the body. XVII. L., pl. of *vīscus*; see VISCUS.

viscid vi·sid glutinous, sticky. XVII. – late L. *viscidus*, f. L. *viscum* mistletoe, birdlime; see -ID[1]. So **viscous** vi·skəs. XIV – AN. *viscous* (Gower) or late L. *viscōsus*, f. *viscum*. **visco·**SITY. XV. – (O)F. or medL.

viscount vai·kaunt (hist.) deputy of a count or earl, (high) sheriff XIV (Trevisa); member of the fourth order of the British peerage XV. AN. *viscounte* (OF. *visconte*, *viconte*, mod. *vicomte*) = Sp. *visconde*, It. *visconte* – medL. *vicecomitem*, *-comes* (see VICE-, COUNT[2]). ¶ The sp. preserves the orig. OF. form *vis-*, and the pronunc. derives from its clipped form *vi-*.

viscus vi·skəs soft internal organ of the body. XVIII. L.; cf. VISCERA.

visé see VISA.

visible vi·zĭbl that can be seen. XIV (Rolle). – (O)F. *visible* or L. *vīsibilis*, f. *vīs-*, pp. stem of *vidēre*; see VISION, -IBLE. So **visibi·l**ITY. XVI. – F. or late L. (Tertullian).

Visigoth vi·zigəþ one of that branch of the Goths which established a kingdom in Spain. XVII. – late L. *Visigothus* (usu. pl. *-gothī*; so Gr. *Ouisígotthoi*), the first el. of which may mean 'west')(OSTROGOTH 'East Goth'.

vision vi·ʒən something that appears to be seen otherwise than by ordinary sight XIII; seeing something not present to the eye XIV; bodily sight XV. – (O)F. *vision* – L. *vīsiō(n-)* sight, thing seen, f. *vīs-*, pp. stem of *vidēre* see; see WIT[2], -ION. Hence **vi·sion**ARY adj. XVII; sb. XVIII; perh. made current by the title of J. Desmarets's comedy 'Les visionnaires' (1638).

visit vi·zit (of God) come to, in order to comfort or benefit; go to persons in sickness, etc. to comfort them; †make trial of XIII; deal severely with, assail, afflict; punish, requite XIV; go to see in a friendly way XIV (attend as a physician XVI); go to in order to inspect, for worship, etc. XIV. The earlier uses are based on those of L. *visitare* in the Vulgate. – (O)F. *visiter* (= Sp. *visitar*, It. *visitare*) – L. *vīsitāre* go to see, frequent. of *vīsāre* view, see to, visit, f. *vīs-*, pp. stem of *vidēre* see (see prec.). So sb. XVII. – F. *visite*, f. *visiter*; or immed. f. the vb. **vi·sit**ANT. XVI. – F. or L. **visita·**TION. XIV. – (O)F. – late L. (Tertullian, Vulgate). **visitato·**RIAL. XVII. **visit**OR (formerly also **visiter**) vi·zitəɹ. XIV. – AN. *visitour*, (O)F. *visiteur*, f. *visiter*; the sense 'one who pays a friendly visit or stays on a visit' (XVII, Sh.) was earlier (XVI) borne by *visitant*.

visne vī·ni (leg.) neighbourhood, vicinage XV; jury summoned from the neighbourhood in which the cause of an action lies XVII. – AN., OF. *visné* = Pr. *vezinat* :– Rom. **vīcīnātus*, f. L. *vīcīnus* neighbour; see VICINITY, -ATE[1].

visnomy XVI (now arch. or dial.) = PHYSIOGNOMY (var. senses).

vison vai·sən American mink. XVIII. – F. *vison* (Buffon), of unkn. origin.

visor, vizor vai·zəɹ part of a helmet covering the face; mask (see VIZARD). XIV. ME. *viser* – AN. *viser* = (O)F. *visière*, f. OF. *vis* face; see VISAGE, WIT[2], -OR[2]. ¶ The form *-or* (XVI) of the termination is a modification of the earlier var. *-our* (XV–XVII) and its permanence is prob. due to a desire to avoid identity with -ER[1].

vista vi·stə view, prospect; opening in a wood, etc. affording a view; fig. XVII. – It. *vista*. ¶ The earliest form is †*visto*, which exhibits the tendency to substitute *-o* for *-a* in adoptions of Rom. words; cf. -ADO.

visual vi·ʒuəl, vi·zjuəl proceeding from the eye XV (Lydg.); pert. to sight or vision XVII; pert. to the object of sight XVIII. – late L. *vīsuālis*, f. *vīsu-s* sight; cf. F. *visuel*, etc.; see VISION, -AL[1]. Hence **vi·sual**IZE form a mental picture of. XIX (Coleridge).

vital vai·təl pert. to life XIV (Ch.; *v. spark* Pope); sustaining or essential to life XV (†*v. spirit(s)*; †*v. air* oxygen XVIII); endowed with life; life-giving XVI; essential or indispensable to the existence of something XVII. – (O)F. *vital* = Sp. *vital*, It. *vitale* – L. *vītālis*, f. *vīta* life :– **vivita*, f. *vivus* living; see VIVID and -AL[1]; sb. pl. **vitals** XVII. – L. *vītālia* n.pl. used sb. So **vita·lITY** vital force, principle of life XVI; active force, vigour XIX. - L. **vi·talIZE.** XVII.

vitamin vi·təmin, vai·təmin any of a group of certain essential food elements. XX. Earlier *vitamine* -main; – G. *vitamine* (Casimir Funk, 1913), f. L. *vīta* life (cf. prec.) + *amine* AMINE. ¶ So named because it was first believed that an amino-acid was present, the sp. being later modified in order to avoid the suggestion.

vitellus vite·ləs (biol.) yolk of egg. XVIII. L.

vitiate vi·ʃieit render faulty or corrupt XVI; render of no effect XVII. f. pp. stem of L. *vitiāre* (after †*vitiate* pp. XV), f. *vitium* VICE[1]; see -ATE[2], -ATE[3]. So **vitiA·TION.** XVII. – L.

vitreous vi·triəs of or resembling glass. XVII. f. L. *vitreus* of glass, glassy, clear, transparent, f. *vitrum* glass; see -EOUS. So **vi·triFY.** XVI. – F. *vitrifier* or medL. **vitrificāre*.

vitriol vi·triəl sulphate of iron, copper, etc. XIV (Ch.); *oil of v.* concentrated sulphuric acid XVI. – (O)F. *vitriol* or medL. *vitriolum* (Albertus Magnus, XIII), f. L. *vitrum* glass; so named on account of the glassy appearance of vitriol salts. Cf. It. *vet-, vitri(u)olo*, Sp. *vitriolo*. So **vitriolIC** -ɔ·lik. XVII; cf. F. *vitriolique*.

Vitruvian vitrū·viən pert. to Marcus *Vitruvius* Pollio, Roman writer on architecture. XVIII. See -IAN.

vitta vi·tə L. 'band', 'fillet', 'chaplet'; used in various deriv. techn. senses from XVII.

vituline vi·tjŭlain pert. to a calf. XVII. – L. *vitulīnus*, f. *vitulus* calf, prob. rel. to WETHER; see -INE[1], VEAL.

vituperate vaitjū·pəreit blame in strong language. XVI. f. pp. stem of L. *vituperāre*, f. *vitu-*, for *viti-*, stem of *vitium* VICE[1] (for the formation cf. *recuperāre* RECUPERATE); see -ATE[3]. So **vituperA·TION.** XV. – OF. or L., not common before XIX; there is a gap in both words between mid-XVII and early XIX (Scott).

Vitus vai·təs name of a Christian martyr of Rome under Diocletian, associated with convulsive ailments (*St. Vitus's dance*, chorea XVII).

viva[1] vī·və cry of 'long live . . .!', cheer, hurrah. XVII (Evelyn). It., 3rd sg. pres. sub. of *vivere* :– L. *vīvere* live (see VIVID). So **vivat** vai·væt. XVII (Cowley). – F. or L. (3rd sg. pres. subj. of *vivere*).

viva[2] vai·və (colloq.) short for **viva voce** vai·və vou·si oral examination, 'with living voice', abl. of fem. of L. *vīvus* (see VIVID) + *vōx* VOICE (cf. late Gr. ζώῃ φωνῇ).

vivacious vai-, vivei·ʃəs full of liveliness or animation. XVII. f. L. *vivāci-*, *vivāx* conscious or tenacious of life, lively, vigorous, f. *vīvus* alive, *vīvere* live; see VIVID, -ACIOUS. So **vivacITY** -æ·sĭti. XV. – (O)F. – L.

vivarium vai-, vivɛə·riəm enclosed place for keeping live animals, esp. fish. XVI (Holland). L. 'warren, fishpond', sb. use of *vīvārius*, f. *vīvus*; see prec. and -ARY.

vivid vi·vid full of life, lively. XVII. – L. *vīvidus*, f. *vīvere* be living, *vīvus* alive, lively, corr. to Skr. *jī́vati*, *jīvás*, rel. to Gr. *bíos* life (cf. BIO-), *zên* (cf. ZOO-), and QUICK; see -ID[1].

viviparous vaivi·pəres, vi- bringing forth young in a live state. XVII. f. L. *vīviparus*, f. *vīvus* (see prec.) + *-parus* bring forth (cf. PARENT); see -OUS.

vivisection vivise·kʃən dissection of a living animal body. XVIII. f. *vīvi-*, comb. form of L. *vīvus* alive (cf. prec.) + SECTION, after *dissection*.

vixen vi·ksn she-fox. XV. Late ME. *fixene fox* 'vixen of the fox'; not recorded in OE., which had *fyxe* and adj. *fyxen*, but there is a parallel sb. in late OHG. *fuhsin*, MHG. *vühsinne* (G. *füchsin*); see FOX, -EN[2]. ¶ For initial *v*, not recorded before late XVI, cf. VAN[1], VANE; the *f*-form continued till early XVIII.

viz = VIDELICET. XVI. repr. medL. *viȝ*, in which *ȝ* is the normal symbol for the termination *-et*.

vizard vi·zəɹd mask. XVI. alt. of *visar* (XV–XVI), *vizar* (XVI–XVII), vars. of VISOR; for a similar substitution of -ARD see MAZ(Z)ARD.

vizier vi·ziəɹ in Mohammedan countries, high official, viceroy, etc. XVI. Early forms *vezir*, *vizir* – F. *visir*, *vizir* or Sp. *visir* – Turk. *vezīr* – Arab. *wazīr*, *wezīr* porter.

vizierate vizī·əreit dignity of a vizier. XVII. – Arab. *wizārat*, *-et* with assim. to prec. and -ATE[1].

vizor see VISOR.

Vlach vlæk Wallachian, Rumanian. XIX. – Bulg., Serb *Vlach* = OSl. *Vlachŭ* Rumanian, Italian, Czech, *Vlach* Italian, Russ. *Voloch*, etc. – Germ. (OHG.) *Walh* (cf. OE. *wealh*) foreigner, whence also medGr. *Blákhos*. Cf. WALLACHIAN.

vocable vou·kəbl word. XVI. – F. *vocable* or L. *vocābulum*, f. *vocāre* call; see VOCATION, -BLE. Reintroduced XVIII by Sc. writers; mentioned as a Scotticism by Beattie 1787. So **vocabulARY** vŏkæ·bjŭləri list of words with their meanings attached XVI; range of words in a written language, etc. XVIII. – medL. *vocābulārius*, *-ārium*; see -ARY; cf. GLOSSARY.

vocal vou·kəl pert. to or uttered or formed by the voice. XIV (rare before XVI). – L. *vōcālis* uttering voice, f. *vōc-*, *vōx* VOICE; see -AL[1]. Hence **vo·cal**ISM exercise of the voice; (philol.) system of vowels. XIX. **vo·cal**IST †speaker XVII (rare); vocal musician XIX.

vocation vo(u)kei·ʃən calling to a state of life, function, etc. XV (Lydg.). – (O)F. *vocation* or L. *vocātiō(n-)*, f. *vocāre* call. So **vocat**IVE vɔ·kətiv (gram.). XV. – (O)F. *vocatif* or L. *vocātivus* (Aulus Gellius, Charisius, Priscian).

vociferate vousi·fəreit cry out loud. XVII. f. pp. stem of L. *vōciferārī*, f. *vōci-*, *vōx* VOICE+*fer-*, stem of *ferre* BEAR[2]; see -ATE[3]. So **vocifer**A·TION. XIV|XV. – (O)F. or L. **voci·fer**OUS. XVII (Chapman); see -IFEROUS.

vodka vɔ·dkə ardent spirit orig. distilled in Russia. XIX. – Russ. *vódka*, dim. of *vodá* WATER.

voe vou (Orkney and Shetland dial.) bay, inlet. XVII. Norw. *vaag*, ON., Icel. *vágr* = OE. *wǣg* wave, rel. to WEIGH.

vogue voug †*the v.* foremost place in estimation, greatest currency XVI; popular esteem; course of success; prevailing fashion XVII. – F. *vogue* – It. *voga* rowing, fashion, f. *vogare* row, be going well = Pr., Pg. *vogar*, Sp. *bogar*, presumably of Germ. origin and f. the base repr. by (M)HG. *wogen* wave, float, be borne by the waves, rel. to WAY.

voice vois sound(s) produced by the organs of utterance, in man freq. representing thought or opinion XIII; expressed will or choice, vote XIV; vocal capacity, as for singing XVII. – AN. *voiz*, *voice*, OF. *vois*, *voiz* (also mod. *voix*) = Pr. *votz*, Sp. *voz*, It. *voce*, Rum. *boace* :- L. *vōcem*, *vōx* (cf. VOCAL). Hence **voice** vb. speak of, state XV; give utterance to XVII; endow with voice. XVIII.

void void not occupied, empty XIII; ineffective, useless XIV; having no legal force XV. sb. empty space XVII. – OF. *voide*, dial. var. of *vuide* (mod. *vide*) fem., superseding *vuit* m. = Pr. *vueid*, Cat. *buit*, It. *vuoto* :- Rom. **vocitu-s* pp. formation on **voc-*, repr. also in L. *vocivus*, with parallel **vac-* of *vacāre* (see VACANT).

voivode voi·voud, **vaivode** vei·voud local ruler in south-eastern Europe. XVI. – earlier Magyar *vajvoda* (now *vajda*) and Bulg., Serb. *vojvoda*, Cz. *vojevoda*. Also *waywode* XVII.

Volapük, -puk vɔ·ləpük, -puk artificial language invented in 1879 by a German priest, Johann M. Schleyer. f. *vol*, alt. of Eng. *world*+connecting vowel *a*+*pük*, alt. of *speech*.

volatile vɔ·lətail evaporating rapidly; lively. XVII. – (O)F. *volatil* or L. *volātilis*, f. pp. stem of *volāre* fly. See -ILE.

volcano vɔlkei·nou mountain or hill having an opening called a crater through which lava, etc. is expelled. XVII. – It. *volcano*, †*vulcano* (whence also F., Sp. *volcan*), Pg. *vulcão* – L. *Volcānu-s*, *Vulcānu-s* Roman god of fire. So **volcan**IC vɔlkæ·nik. XVIII. – F. *volcanique*, f. *volcan*.

vole[1] voul winning of all the tricks in certain card games. XVII (Dryden). – F. *vole*, f. *voler* :- L. *volāre* fly.

vole[2] voul mouse-like animal (short-tailed field mouse, water-rat, etc.). XIX. orig. *vole-mouse* – Norw. **vollmus* (cf. Icel. *vollarmús*), f. *voll* field (ON. *vǫllr*; cf. WOLD)+*mus* MOUSE.

volitant vɔ·litənt flitting. XIX. – prp. of L. *volitāre*, frequent. of *volāre* fly; see VOLE[1], -ANT.

volition vo(u)li·ʃən willing, resolving. XVII. – F. *volition* or medL. *volitiō(n-)*, f. *volō* I wish, WILL[2]; see -ITION.

volley vɔ·li simultaneous discharge of firearms or flight of missiles; utterance of many words, etc.; phr. *at the v.* (after F. *à la volée*) of a ball in its flight before it touches the ground, etc., (fig.) without consideration, at random XVI; return stroke at a ball before it has touched the ground XIX. – (O)F. *volée* = Pr., Sp. *volada*, It. *volata* :- Rom. **volāta* flight, sb. use of pp. fem. of L. *volāre* fly; see VOLE[1], -Y[3]. Hence **vo·lley** vb. XVI.

volplane vɔ·lplein aeronautical glide. XX. For F. *vol plané*, i.e. *vol* flight (f. *voler* fly; cf. VOLE[1]), *plané*, pp. of *planer*.

Volscian vɔ·lʃ[1]ən one of an ancient people inhabiting E. Latium. XVI (*Volscan*). f. L. *Volsci*, pl. of *Volscus* (whence late ME. *Vulce*, later *Volsce*)+-IAN.

volt voult unit of electromotive force. XIX. Named after Alessandro *Volta* (1745–1827), Italian physician and chemist, whence also **volta**IC vɔltei·ik. XIX (H. Davy).

volt(e) vɔlt †*volta*, *lavolta*, a kind of dance XVI; sudden movement to avoid a thrust in fencing XVII. – F. *volte* – It. *volta*, sb. use of fem. pp. of *volgere* to turn :- L. *volvere* (see VOLUME).

volte-face vɔlt(ə)fæ·s right-about, complete change of attitude. XIX (Scott). – F. *volte-face* – It. *voltafaccia* 'turn-face', f. *voltare* :- Rom. **volvitāre*, frequent. of *volvere* roll (see VOLUME)+*faccia* FACE.

voluble vɔ·ljŭbl †variable; †rotatory; rapid and fluent (of speech). XVI. – F. *voluble* or L. *volūbilis*, f. *volū-*, as in VOLUME, VOLUTE; see -BLE. So **volubi·l**ITY. XVI. – F. or L.

volume vɔ·ljŭm (hist.) roll of parchment, etc. forming a book; tome XIV (Wycl., Trevisa, Ch.); size, bulk †(of a book) XVI, (of other things) XVII; (poet.) coil, convolution XVII. Late ME. *volym*, *volum*, *volume* – OF. *volum*, (also mod.) *volume* = Sp. *volumen*, It. *volume* – L. *volūmen* roll of writing, book, fold, wreath, eddy, f. *volū-*, var. of base **wolw-* of *volvere* roll = Gr. *eilúein* (cf. *eilūma* envelope, covering), f. IE. **wel- *wol-* turn (see HELIX, WALLOW). ¶ Forms such as *volym*, *volum*, repr. vo·lim, vo·ləm, remained till XVI and XVIII respectively; the present form (XV) F. *volume*, L. *volūmen* shows assim. to F. and L. Cf. *lettuce*, *minute*, *custom* (*costume*). So **volumin**OUS vəljū·minəs. XVII. – late L. *volūminōsus*; cf. F. *volumineux*.

voluntary vɔ·ləntəri depending on free choice. XIV (Usk; the adv. is used by Ch.); sb. piece of music selected by an organist to be played e.g. while a congregation departs XVIII. – (partly after (O)F. *volontaire*, †*voluntaire*) L. *voluntārius*, f. *voluntās* will, for **voluntitās*, f. prp. form of the same type as *eunt-* going (f. *volō* I WILL) + *-tās* -TY²; see -ARY. So **voluntEE·R** one who voluntarily offers his services, orig. mil. XVII. – F. *volontaire* – L. *voluntārius* (pl., sc. *milites* soldiers); the suffix was assim. to -IER² and (later) -EER. Hence **voluntee·ring** (XVII, Dryden), whence by back-formation **voluntee·r** vb. XVIII (J.).

voluptuous vəlʌ·ptʃuəs, -tjuəs pert. to sensual pleasure. XIV (Ch.). – (O)F. *voluptueux* or L. *voluptuōsus*, f. *voluptās* pleasure, f. *volup* agreeably, f. **wol- *wel-* WILL² (cf. Gr. *elpís* hope); see -UOUS. So **volu·ptu**ARY. XVII. – L. *voluptuārius*, later form of *voluptārius*, f. *voluptās*. **voluptu**O·SITY. XIV (Gower).

volute vɔ·ljūt spiral conformation. XVII. – F. *volute* or L. *volūta*, pp. of *volvere* roll (see WALLOW). Earlier †**volu·ta**. XVI–XVIII.

volva vɔ·lvə (bot.) membrane covering fungi. XVIII. L., f. *volvere* roll, wrap.

vomer vou·məɹ (anat., etc.) applied to various bones. XVIII. L. 'ploughshare'.

vomit vɔ·mit matter ejected from the stomach through the mouth. XIV (Trevisa, Ch., Wycl. Bible). – OF. *vomite* or L. *vomitus*, f. *vomere* vomit (whence F. *vomir*), rel. to Skr. *vámiti*, Gr. *emeîn* (see EMETIC). So **vo·mit** vb. spew. XIV. f. *vomit-*, pp. stem of L. *vomere* or – L. frequent. *vomitāre*. **vomi**·TION. XVII. – F. †*vomition* or L.

voodoo vū·dū use of or belief in sorcery, etc. current among W. Indies and U.S. Negroes and creoles. XIX. – Dahomey *vodu*. Somewhat earlier in F. form *vaudoux*.

voortrekker vōɹtre·kəɹ Boer pioneer in S. Africa. XIX. Du., f. *voor-* FORE- + *trekken* TREK.

voracious vərei·ʃəs greedy for food. XVII. f. L. *vorāci-*, *vorāx*, f. *vorāre* DEVOUR; see -IOUS. So **vora**CITY vəræ·siti. XVI. – (O)F. or L.

-vorous vərəs terminal el. forming adjs., f. L. *-vorus* devouring, eating (see DEVOUR, -OUS), as in *carnivorous*, *herbivorous*, *omnivorous*.

vortex vō·ɹteks supposed rotation of the cosmic matter XVII; violent eddy; (fig.) XVIII. – L. *vortex* eddy, whirlpool, whirlwind, var. of *vertex* VERTEX.

vorticism vō·ɹtisizm principles of a school of painting originating in 1913 among some members of 'the London Group'. f. L. *vortic-*, VORTEX, taken in the sense of the artist's conception of relations in the universe; see -ISM.

votary vou·təri one bound by vow to a religious life or devoted to a pursuit, etc. XVI. f. *vōt-*, pp. stem of L. *vovēre* vow + -ARY. Hence **vo·tar**ESS¹. XVI. So **vo·tar**IST. XVII (Sh.).

vote vout indication of opinion by appointed means. XV (in earliest use Sc.; less specific obs. senses occur XVI–XVIII). – L. *vōtum* vow, wish (whence also Sp., Pg., It. *voto*), sb. use of n. pp. (**vovetom*) of *vovēre* vow, desire; hence F. *vote*. So **vote** vb. give a vote (for); †vow, †devote. XVI (before 1600 exclusively Sc.). f. *vōt-*, pp. stem of L. *vovēre*. Cf. OF. *voter* (in mod. use from Eng.), Sp., Pg. *votar*, It. *votare*. So **vo·t**IVE. XVI. – L. *vōtīvus*, whence also Sp., Pg., It. *votivo*, F. *votif*, *-ive*.

vouch vautʃ cite as witness XIV; guarantee the truth of XVI; be surety or witness *for* XVII. – OF. *vocher*, *voucher* summon, invoke, claim, obscurely repr. L. *vocāre* call (see VOCATION). So **vou·ch**ER⁵ summoning of a person into court to prove a title XVI; piece of evidence, esp. written XVII (Sh.). – AN. sb. use of OF. inf. *voucher*. **vouch**SAFE vautʃsei·f confer, bestow, esp. in condescension; show a gracious willingness XIV. orig. as two words, f. VOUCH warrant + SAFE, adj. in predic. use, e.g. *He vouchede hyt saufe on us*; in early use with great variety of form in the first el., the identity and meaning of which became obscured.

voussoir vū·swāɹ (archit.) one of the stones forming part of an arch or a vault. XVIII. f. modF. (OF. *vousoir*, *-our* adopted in ME. XIV–XV) :– popL. *volsōrium*, f. **vols-*, pp. stem of *volvere* roll (see VOLUME).

vow¹ vau solemn promise, esp. of a religious nature. XIII (S. Eng. Leg., RGlouc.). – AN. *vou*, *vu(u)*, OF. *vo*, *vou* (mod. *vœu*) :– L. *vōtum* VOTE. So vb. make a vow. XIII (Cursor M.). – (O)F. *vouer*, f. *vou*.

vow² vau affirm, asseverate. XIV. Aphetic of AVOW.

vowel vau·əl sound produced by vibration of the vocal cords without audible friction. XIV. – OF. *vouel*, var. of *voiel* (superseded by later OF. *voielle*, mod. *voyelle*) :– L. *vōcālem* (*sonum*) or *vōcāle* (*signum*) 'VOCAL sound or sign' (the L. sb. *vōcālis* is fem., sc. *littera* letter).

vox vɔks in *v. angelica*, *v. humana* ('angelic, human VOICE'), organ stops imitative of vocal sounds. XVIII. L. *vōx* (*vōc-*), f. base widely repr. in IE.

voyage voi·idʒ journey (spec. by water). XIII. ME. *ve(i)age, vaiage, viage* – AN. *voiage*, OF. *ve(i)age, vayage* (mod. *voyage*) = Pr. *viatge* (whence Sp. *viaje*, Pg. *viagem*, It. *viaggio*) :– L. *viāticum* money or provisions for a journey, in late L. journey (see VIATICUM). So **voy·age** vb., **voy·ager** XV (Caxton) = (O)F.

vraic vreik seaweed found in the Channel Islands. XVII. – F. dial. *vraic*, var. of *vrec*, *vrac* – MLG., Du. *wrak* WRACK²; cf. VAREC.

vraisemblance vrɛsãblãs verisimilitude. XIX (Scott). F., f. *vrai*; see VERY, SEMBLANCE.

vril vril mysterious force assumed to have been discovered in Lytton's 'The Coming Race', 1871. Arbitrary invention.

vrouw, vrow vrau Dutch woman or matron. XVII. Du. *vrouw* (OS. *frūa* = OHG. *frouwa*, G. *frau*).

vulcanite vʌ·lkənait † pyroxene; preparation of indiarubber and sulphur hardened by heat. XIX. f. *Vulcan* (L. *Vulcānus*), name of the ancient Roman god of fire+-ITE.

vulcanize vʌ·lkənaiz treat (indiarubber) with sulphur to render it more durable. XIX. Named by Brockedon, friend of the English chemist Hancock, who invented it, f. *Vulcan* (see prec.)+-IZE.

vulgar vʌ·lgəɹ that is in common or ordinary use XIV (Ch., Lydg.; rare before XVI); ordinary, common, commonplace XVI; lacking in refinement XVII; sb. †*the* vernacular XV (Lydg.); †(chiefly pl.) common or vulgar person; *the v.* the common people; †(pl.) sentences, etc. in English to be translated into Latin XVI; †Vulgate edition XVII. – L. *vulgāris*, f. *vulgus*, *volgus* the common people; see -AR. The sb. uses depend on those of medL. (*vulgāre* vulgar tongue, vernacular, *vulgārēs* common people) and (O)F. (*le vulgaire* the common herd), etc. So **vu·lgar**ISM †ordinary expression XVII (rare); vulgar expression, quality, etc. XVIII; **vulgarity** -gæ·rĭti †common people XVI; †common use, quality, etc. XVII; vulgar character XVIII. – late L.; cf. F. *vulgarité* (1800). **vu·lgar**IZE †be vulgar XVII; make vulgar XVIII. – modL. *vulgārizare* (whence also F. *vulgariser*, It. *volgarizzare*). **vulgate** vʌ·lgət in common use as a version of the Bible, spec. the Latin of St. Jerome completed in about 405 A.D. XVII (Douay Bible, 1609); sb. the V. Bible XVIII; received text of the Bible; ordinary reading in a text XIX. – late L. *vulgāta* (sc. *ēditiō* edition, *lectiō* reading), *vulgātus* (sc. *textus* text), fem. and m. pp. of L. *vulgāre* make public or common, f. *vulgus*; see -ATE². **vulgus** vʌ·lgəs school task consisting of a set of Latin or Greek verses. XIX. alt. of †*vulgars* (XVI), tr. modL. *vulgāria*, sb. use of n. pl. of L. *vulgāris*, used as the title of Latin–English phrase-books by J. Anwykyll (1483), W. Horman (1519), and R. Whitington (1520); the ending was perh. assim. to GRADUS.

vulnerable vʌ·lnərəbl that may be wounded XVII (Sh.); open to attack XVII (of a place XVIII). – late L. *vulnerābilis* wounding, f. *vulnerāre* wound, f. *vulner-*, *vulnus* wound; L. *invulnerābilis* was earlier and was used with the more usual pass. sense of the suffix *-ābilis* -ABLE. So **vu·lner**ARY used for healing wounds XVI; also sb. XVII. – L. *vulnerārius* (Pliny).

vulpine vʌ·lpain fox-like. XVII. – L. *vulpīnus*, f. *vulpēs*, *volpēs* fox; see -INE¹.

vulture vʌ·ltʃəɹ large bird of prey of the order Raptores. XIV (Ch., Wycl. Bible, Trevisa). – AN. *vultur*, OF. *voltour* (mod. *vautour*), corr. to Pr. *voltor*, It. *avoltojo*, Rum. *vultúr* :– L. *vulturius*, f. *vultur*, *voltur*. Some early forms show dependence rather on OF. *voutre* :– L. *vultur*; a normal development is seen in *vulter* (XVI–XVII); the present pronunc. continues ME. *vulture* and has prob. been established by assoc. with *-ture* as in *creature*. So **vu·ltur**INE¹. XVII. – L.

vulva vʌ·lvə (anat.) external organ of generation in the female. XVI. – L. *vulva*, *volva* womb, matrix.

W

Waac wæk member of the *W*omen's *A*rmy *A*uxiliary *C*orps 1917.

wabble see WOBBLE.

wacke wæ·kə (geol.) sandstone-like rock. XIX. – G. *wacke* (MHG. *wacke* large stone, OHG. *wacko* pebble) miner's word adopted by the geologist Werner.

wad wɔd †wadding; (dial.) bundle of hay, etc. XVI; tightly-rolled bundle XVIII. In form and early meaning corr. to AL. *wadda* wadding (XIV); obscurely rel. to Du. *watten* (whence G. *watte*), F. *ouate*, It. *ovatta* padding, cotton-wool, Sp. *bata* dressing-gown, which has been referred to Arab. *bāṭin* padded clothes. Hence **wad** vb. put a wad in (a gun, etc.) XVI; lay up in bundles XVII; **wa·dd**ING¹ material for wads. XVII, esp. cotton-wool. Cf. Sw. *vadd* (from Eng.), Da. *vat* (from Du. or G.), Russ. *váta*, G. *wattieren*, *-ierung*, Sw. *waddera*, *-ering*, Da. *vattere*, *-ering* pad, padding.

waddle wɔ·dl walk with swaying motion. XVII (Sh.). perh. frequent. of WADE; see -LE[3]. Late ME. *wadill*, meaning app. 'fall heavily' is difficult to connect with the mod. use.

wade weid †go OE.; walk through water or any liquid XIII (OE. in *oferwadan* wade over). OE. *wadan*, pt. *wōd* = OFris. *wada*, MDu., MLG. *waden* (Du. *waden* wk.), OHG. *watan* (G. *waten* wk.), ON. *vaða* :- CGerm. (exc. Goth.) **waðan* go, go through; f. IE. **wădh-*, repr. by L. *vādere* go, *vadāre* wade through, *vadum* ford (cf. OE. *wæd*, ON. *vað* ford).

wadi, -y wā·di ravine or gully turned into a watercourse. XIX. – Arab. *wādī*.

wadmal wɔ·dməl woollen fabric. XIV. – ON. *vaðmál*, prob. for **váðmál*, f. *váð* cloth, WEED[2]+*mál* measure (see MEAL[2]).

wadset wɔ·dset (chiefly Sc.) pawn, mortgage. XIV. f. *wad*, Sc. var. of WED sb.+SET[1]; prob. developed from OE. phr. **tō wedde settan* put to pledge (*tō wedde lećgan* and *sellan* are recorded; cf. OE. *wedd settan* deposit a pledge). Hence sb. XV.

wafer wei·fəɹ very light thin crisp cake XIV (PPl., Ch.); thin disc of unleavened bread used at the Eucharist XVI; disc used for sealing, etc. XVII. – AN. *wafre*, var. of ONF. *waufre*, (O)F. *gaufre* (see GOFFER) – MLG. *wāfel* WAFFLE.

waffle wɔ·fl (U.S.) batter-cake. XIX. – Du. *wafel*, early *waefel* = MLG. *wāfel* (see WAFER); as F. *gaufre* has also the sense 'honeycomb', it is inferred that the Germ. word had orig. this meaning and is rel. to OHG. *wabo, -a* (G. *wabe*) honeycomb (cf. WEAVE[1]).

waft wɔft †convoy; convey safely by water XVI; †pass or propel through the air XVII; carry through the air or through space XVIII (Pope). Back-formation from †*wafter* armed vessel used as a convoy (XV *wa(u)ghter*) – LG., Du. *wachter* guard, f. *wachten* guard (see WAIT). Hence **waft**URE wɔ·ftjuəɹ waving; first as Rowe's emendation in his edition of 1709 of *wafter* in earlier editions of Sh. 'Julius Cæsar' II i 246.

wag[1] wæg trans. †stir, move XIII; sway from side to side XIV; intr. †brandish, wave XIII; move to and fro XIV. ME. *waggen*, iterative formation on OE. *wagian* totter, sway), ME. *waȝe, waw(e)* = MLG., MDu. *wagen*, OHG. *wagōn*, ON. *vaga* (cf. *vagga* cradle). So **waggle** wæ·gl. XV; see -LE[3] and cf. (M)LG., Du. *waggelen* stagger, totter (whence (M)HG. *wackeln*), which may be the immed. source. Cf. WIGGLE.

wag[2] wæg mischievous boy, youth, chap; habitual joker XVI. prob. shortening of †*waghalter* (of which †*wagstring* and †*wagwith* were vars.) one who is likely to swing in the hangman's noose, gallows-bird XVI (see WAG[1], HALTER). ¶ For similar abbreviations see QUACK[2]. Hence **wa·gg**ERY. XVI (Lyly), **wa·gg**ISH[1]. XVI (Sh.).

waggon, wagon wæ·gən strong four-wheeled vehicle for transport; †carriage, car, chariot XVI; covered vehicle for conveyance by road; truck, van running on a mining roadway or (later) railway line XVII. Early forms *wagan, wag(h)en* – Du. *wagen*, †*waghen* WAIN. (Hence F. *wagon* railway carriage.) So **wa·g(g)on**ER[1]. XVI. – Du. *wagenaar*, †*waghenaer*. Hence **wag(g)on**E·TTE four-wheeled (open) carriage. XIX.

wagtail wæ·gteil small bird of the genus Motacilla. XVI. f. WAG[1]+TAIL[1], with ref. to the continual characteristic wagging of its tail; cf. earlier †*wagstert*, †*-start* (START[1]) XV, and MLG. *wagestert*, Du. *kwikstaart* 'quick-tail', Sw. *vippstjert*, Da. *vipstjært*, F. *hochequeue* 'shake-tail'.

waif weif piece of property found ownerless XIV (PPl.); person without home or friends, unowned child XVIII (Cowper). – AN. *waif*, *weif* (AL. *wavium, weyvum*), var. of ONF. *gaif*, fem. *gaive* (cf. early modF. †*wayves, choses gayves* or *guesves*), prob. of Scand. origin (cf. ON. *veif* something wavering or flapping, rel. to *veifa* wave). Often in phr. *waifs and strays*, or †*straifs*, cf. ME. *weyues and streyues*.

wail weil express pain by prolonged piteous cries. XIV. – ON. **weila* (cf. *veilan* wailing), f. *vei* int. = OE. *wā* WOE; the recorded ON. vb. is *væ̆la* (whence *væ̆l*, *væ̆lan*), f. *væ̆* int. Hence **wail** sb. XIV.

wain wein large open vehicle for heavy loads; astron. used of the Great Bear (see CHARLES'S WAIN). OE. *wæġ(e)n*, *wǣn* waggon = OFris. *wein*, OLow Frankish *reidi|wagan*, (M)LG., Du. *wagen*, OHG. *wagan* (G. *wagen*), ON. *vagn* cart, barrow :- CGerm. (exc. Goth.) **wagnaz* or **wegnaz* :- IE. **woghnos* or **weghnos* (whence OIr. *fén* waggon), f. **wogh-* **wegh-* carry (cf. WAY, WEIGH), whence Gr. *ókhos* (:-**woghos*) chariot, OSl. *vozŭ* (Russ. *voz* cartload), Skr. *vahanam* chariot, ship.

wainscot wei·nskət superior oak boarding imported from the Continent XIV; panelling of wood XVI. – MLG. *wagenschot*, presumably, f. *wagen* WAGGON+*schot* (?) boarding planking (cf. *bokenschot* superior beechwood); the first el. of this comp. (which was taken over into Fris., Flem., and Du.) is of doubtful identity; it has been referred by some to OFris. *wāch* = OE. *wāg*, OS. *wēg* wall.

waist weist middle section of the body XIV; middle part of a ship XV; narrowest or slenderest part XVII. Late ME. *wast, waast*, later *waste, waist* (which was rare till adopted in Johnson's Dict. 1755). Believed to repr. OE. **wæst*, for **weahst* (cf. early ME. *wacste* greatness), corr. to ON. **wahstur* (Icel. *vöxstr*, g. *vaxtar*), Goth. *wahstus* growth, size, f. Germ. **waχs-* grow, WAX[2]. comp. **wai·st**COAT wei·s[t]kout, we·skət. XVI.

wait weit A. †watch as an enemy or spy XII; †await; remain, stay XIV; defer action XVII; B. serve at table XVI. – ONF. *waitier*, var. of OF. *guaitier* (mod. *guetter* watch for) = Pr. *guaitar*, It. *guatare* – Germ. **waχtan* (OHG. *wahtēn*, MHG. *wahten*, f. **wak-* WAKE[1]). So **wait** sb. †watch; †watchman; as in phr. *lie in wait*, etc. XV; pl. town musicians XIII (singers and musicians performing in the streets at Christmastide XVIII). Partly – ONF. **wait, wet*, f. the vb. *waitier*; partly f. the Eng. vb.

wait-a-bit wei·təbit applied to certain S. Afr. shrubs with joc. ref. to their hooked and clinging thorns. XVIII. tr. Afrikaans *wacht-een-beetje* (now *wag-'n-bietjie*).

waiter wei·təɹ †watcher, watchman XIV; †attendant, servitor XV; man who waits on guests XVII; (for *waiting salver*, in which *waiting* is gerund used attrib.) small tray XVIII. f. WAIT + -ER[1]. Hence **waitRESS**[1] †handmaid XVI (rare); woman or girl who waits at table XIX.

waive weiv †outlaw XIII; relinquish, abandon XIV, (esp. a right) XV; refrain from enforcing (a rule), or from persisting in or entering upon (an action) XVII. – AN. *weyver* (whence AL. *waiviare*) = var. of OF. *gaiver, guesver* make a 'waif' of, abandon, f. *gaif* WAIF. So **wai·VER**[5] (leg.) dispensing with a requirement. XVII. – AN. (Law F.) *weyver* (Britton XIII), sb. use of inf.

wake[1] weik watching, watch, vigil OE. (spec. beside a dead body; hence, observances incidental to this XV); vigil of a church festival, esp. as an occasion of merrymaking XIII. OE. **wacu* (only in *nihtwacu* night-watch), corr. to MLG., MDu. *wake* (Du. *waak*), OHG. *wahha* (G. *wache*) watch, watching, wakefulness, ON. *vaka* watch, vigil, eve; rel. to WAKE[3]. In the last sense prob. – ON. *vaka* (cf. *Jónsvaka* St. John's Eve, 23rd June, Midsummer festivities).

wake[2] weik track left on the water's surface by a moving vessel. XVI. prob. – MLG. *wake* – ON. **vaku* (*vǫk*), *vaka* hole or opening in ice, perh. orig. one made for itself by a vessel (whence also Du. *wak*, and G. *wake* hole or channel in ice); the sense 'vessel's track' is rare and local outside Eng.; perh. ult. f. Germ. **wakw-* moist, damp, rel. to Gr. *hugrós*, L. *ūvidus* (:– **ugwidos*) moist.

wake[3] weik A. remain awake OE.; become awake; B. rouse from sleep XIII. (i) OE. str. vb. **wacan* (repr. by *onwacan, āwacan* AWAKE) only in pt. *wōc*, corr. to ON. **vaka* (repr. by pp. *vakinn* awake); (ii) OE. wk. vb. *wacian* = OFris. *wakia*, OS. *wakōn*, OHG. *wahhēn, -ōn* (G. *wachen*), ON. *vaka*, Goth. *wakan* :– CGerm. **wakǣjan*, **wakōjan*, f. **wak-* (see also WATCH) :– IE. **wog-* **weg-* be lively or active (see VEGETABLE, VIGOUR, VIGIL), vars. of which in form and meaning are seen in Goth. *wōkains* wakeful, *wokrs*, OE. *wōcor*, ON. *okr* growth, increase, usury, and OE. *ēac* (see EKE). Sense B, which is expressed in OE. by *weććan* (:– **wakjan*), depends partly on ON. *vaka* (intr. and trans.). Hence **wa·keFUL**[1]. XVI (Coverdale).

wakeel wəkī·l var. of VAKEEL.

waken wei·kn become awake; rouse from sleep. XII. – ON. *vakna* wake up = OE. *wæcnan*, also *wæcnian* (recorded only in the sense 'rise, spring, be derived'), Goth. *ga|waknan* (prp. only), f. CGerm. **wak-*; see -EN[5].

wake-robin wei·krɔːbin Arum maculatum, lords-and-ladies, cuckoo-pint (U.S. various other plants). XVI (Palsgr., Gerarde). Of unkn. origin.

wakon wei·kən MANITOU. XVIII. – Dakota *wakaŋ*, sb. use of adj. 'spiritual, sacred, consecrated'. ¶ J. F. Cooper 'The Prairie' xxviii has the form *wahcondah*.

Wal(l)ach wɔ·lək = VLACH. XVIII.

Waldensian wɔlde·nsiən pert. to the *Waldenses* adherents of a religious sect which originated through the preaching of Peter *Waldo* of Lyons, France, *c.*1170. XVII. See -IAN.

wale weil weal on the flesh OE.; horizontal timber round the top of the sides of a boat XIV; raised line in a fabric XVI; ridge of a horse's collar XVIII. Late OE. *walu* ridge of land, etc., weal = LG. *wāle* weal, ON. *vala* knuckle, rel to WEAL[2]. Cf. CHANNEL[2], GUNWALE.

Waler wei·ləɹ horse imported from Australia, esp. New South Wales. XIX. f. *Wales* + -ER[1].

wali wā·li var. of VALI. XIX.

walk[1] wōk intr. †roll, toss; †move about, journey, go OE.; travel on foot, (trans.) traverse on foot XIII; lead at a walk XV. OE. *wealcan*, pt. *wēolc*, pp. *ġewealcen*, corr. to (M)LG., (M)Du. *walken* full, work (felt), cudgel, OHG. **walchen*, in pps. *gewalchen, forwalchen* felted, matted, MHG. *walken*, pt. *wielc*, pp. *walken* knead, roll (paste), full, cudgel, drub, ON. *valka* drag about, torment, refl. wallow; f. Germ. **walk-*, of unkn. origin. Hence sb. XIV (Ch.). See foll.

walk[2] wōk full (cloth). XV. – (M)LG., (M)Du. (see prec.); perh. partly from the agent-noun **walkER**[1] wō·kəɹ (surviving dial. till XIX and as a surname) in OE. *wealcere*, (M)LG., (M)Du. *walker*, OHG. *walkāri* (G. *walker*); ult. identical with WALK[1].

Walker wō·kəɹ excl. expressing incredulity. XIX. More fully *Hookey W.*; of unkn. origin.

walkyrie wɔ·lkiri var. of VALKYRIE.

wall wōl rampart; defensive structure enclosing a town, etc.; lateral or vertical division of a building. OE. *wall* (WS. *weall*), corr. to OFris., OS., (M)LG., (M)Du. *wal* (MHG., G. *wall* is from MLG.) – L. *vallum* rampart, orig. palisading, f. *vallus* stake. Hence **wall** vb. XIII (OE. had *ġeweallod* walled). Comp. **wa·llflower** gilliflower, Cheiranthus, which grows wild on old walls, in quarries, etc. XVI (Lyte, Gerarde). tr. Du. *muurbloem*, G. *mauerblume*.

wallaby wɔ·ləbi small species of kangaroo. XIX. – native Australian *wolabā*.

Wallachian, Walachian wəlei·kiən pert. to Wal(l)achia, area of SE. Europe whose inhabitants speak a Romance language (Walachs or Vlachs). XVII. f. medL. *Wal(l)achia*, f. Sl. forms repr. Germ. **Walh-* (cf. WELSH); see -IAN.

wallah wɔ·lə in words of native Indian languages adopted by European residents, e.g. *howdah-w.* elephant accustomed to carrying a howdah, PUNKAH-*w.*, hence, by extension, in *competition-w.* XVIII. – Hindi *-wālā*, terminal el. expressing relation forming adjs. and sbs., apprehended by Europeans as a sb. meaning 'man', 'fellow'.

wallet wɔ·lĭt bag for provisions for a journey, pilgrim's scrip, pedlar's pack XIV (Ch. *wale·t* and *wa·let*); (orig. U.S.) pocket-book to hold papers XIX. prob. – AN. **walet*, the base of which may have been Germ. **wall-* roll (see WELL[1] and [2]) with which some connect OE. *weallian* = MLG. *wallen*, OHG. *wallōn* (G. *wallen*) go on pilgrimage :- WGerm. **wallōjan*; see -ET.

wall-eyed wō·laid having eyes of an excessively light colour or showing divergence of some kind. XIV (*wawil|eȝed*, *waugle eghed*). – ON. *vagleygr*, f. **vagl* (surviving in Icel. *vagl* film over the eye, Sw. *vagel* sty in the eye)+*-eygr* -eyed, f. *auga* EYE; see -ED[2]. Hence by back-formation **wall eye**. XVI.

wall-knot wō·lnɔt, **wale-knot** wei·lnɔt knot made on the end of a rope by unlaying and intertwining the strands. XVIII. rel. obscurely to Norw., Sw. *valknut*, Da. *valknude* double knot, secure knot, in Norw. also, gammadion, swastika, G. *waldknoten* (with assim. to *wald* wood, forest), in hunting parlance, double knot.

Walloon wəlū·n one of a people of Gaulish origin and speaking a dialect of French inhabiting south-eastern Belgium XVI; their language XVII. – F. *wallon* – medL. *Wallō(n-)*, f. Germ. **walχaz* foreign. Cf. VLACH, WALLACHIAN, WELSH, -OON.

wallop wɔ·ləp †gallop XIV; †bubbling motion; violent noisy movement XVI; beat of the heart, resounding blow XVIII. So **wallop** vb. †gallop XIV; boil, bubble XVI; make violent noisy movements XVIII; beat soundly XIX. – ONF. *walop*, var. of (O)F. *galop*, and its source *waloper*, *galoper* (whence MHG. *walop* and *walopiren*) GALLOP. The imit. suggestiveness of the words has furthered in Eng. the development of a variety of colloq. uses (perh. of joc. origin), esp. since *gallop* prevailed (XVI) in the more dignified uses.

wallow wɔ·lou roll about or from side to side. OE.; be plunged *in* degraded living XIII. OE. *walwian* (WS. *wealwian*) :- WGerm. **walwōjan*, rel. to *wielwan* trans. roll = Goth. *af-*, *at-*, *faur|walwjan* (cf. *walwisōn* intr. roll); f. Germ. **walw-* **welw-* :- IE. **wolw-* **welw-*, whence Gr. *elustheís* rolled, wrapped, *élutron* wrapper, case, L. *volvere* roll (cf. VOLUME).

Wallsend wō·lzend designating orig. coal from a now exhausted local seam, (later) coal of a certain quality and size. XIX (Dickens). Name of a town in Northumberland, so named from its situation at the end of the Roman wall.

wallwort wō·lwəɹt dwarf elder, Sambucus Ebulus. OE. *wealhwyrt*, f. *wealh* foreign+*wyrt* WORT[1].

walnut wō·(l)nʌt nut of Juglans regia. Late OE. *walh-hnutu* (once), corr. to MLG. *wallnut* (whence (M)HG. *walnuss*), MDu. *walnote* (Du. *walnoot*), ON. *walhnot* :- Germ. formation, prob. orig. of the LDu. area, on **walχaz* foreign and **χnut-* NUT. Cf. MHG. *wälhisch nuȥ* (G. dial. *wälsche nuss*), Flem. *walsche not* (Kilian), a LG. equiv. of which was adopted in ME. as †*walsh note* (XIV); cf. OF. *noix gauge* (mod. dial. *gaug*, *gok* walnut), repr. Rom. **nux gallica* 'French nut'. ¶ The reprs. of simple L. *nux* in Rom. langs. mean 'walnut'.

walrus wɔ̄·lrəs sea-horse, morse. XVII. prob. – Du. *walrus*, *-ros* (whence also G. *walross*, Sw. *hvalross*, Da. *hvalros*), alt., after *walvisch* 'whale-fish', by inversion of the els. of such forms as OE. *horschwæl*, ON. *hrosshvalr* ('horse-whale'), but the mutual relations are obscure.

waltz wōls, wōlts dance performed to music in triple time; also vb. XVIII. – G. *walzer* the dance, f. *walzen* roll, revolve, dance the waltz, f. Germ. **walt-*, extension of **wal-* roll (see WELTER). Cf. VALSE and Du. *wals*.

wampee wɔmpī· (fruit of) an Asiatic tree, Clausena Wampi. XIX. – Chinese *hwang pi* 'yellow skin'.

wampum wɔ·mpəm beads threaded on strings used by N. Amer. Indians as currency, etc. XVII. Shortening of somewhat earlier *wampumpeag* (which was falsely analysed as *wampum*+*peag*), a word of the Algonquian langs., f. *wap* white (cf. WAPITI)+*umpe* string+pl. suffix *-ag*.

wan wɔn †dusky, dark; livid, leaden-hued OE.; pallid, unusually pale XIII (Cursor M.). OE. *wan(n)*, of unkn. origin and having no certain cogns., poss. rel. to WANE.

wand wɔnd (dial.) straight, slender stick XII (Orm); slender stem, sapling XIII (Cursor M.); rod or staff of office; magic rod XV. – ON. **wandur* (*vǫndr*) = Goth. *wandus* :– **wanduz* (not in WGerm.), prob. f. **wand-* **wend-* turn, WEND, the basic notion being that of flexibility (supported by dial. uses as above). Comp. **wa·nds**MAN verger. XIX; see -S.

wander wɔ·ndəɹ move aimlessly about OE.; deviate without purpose *from* XV. OE. *wandrian* = OFris. *wondria*, MLG., MDu. *wanderen* (whence (M)HG. *wandern*, Sw. *wandra*, Da. *vandre*) :– WGerm. **wandrōjan*, f. **wand-* **wend-* WEND; see -ER[4].

wanderoo wɔndərū· prop. langur monkey of Ceylon, usu. misapplied, after Buffon, to the lion-tailed macaque of Malabar. XVII. – Sinhalese *wanderu* monkey, rel. to Hindi *bandar* :– Skr. *vā̆nara* monkey, perh. orig. 'forest-dweller', f. *vanar-* forest.

wane wein grow less, decrease, spec. of the periodical decrease of the visible illuminated portion of the moon. OE. *wanian* lessen (intr. and trans.) = OFris. *wonia*, OS. *wanon*, OHG. *wanōn*, *wanēn*, ON. *vana* diminish, *vanask* grow less, Goth. **wanan* (cf. *wanains* loss) :– CGerm. **wanōjan*, **wanæjan*, f. **wano-* lacking (whence OE. *wan*, ON. *vanr*, Goth. *wans*), f. IE. **wā̆*, repr. also by L. *vānus* VAIN. Cf. WANT. So **wane** sb. †want, lack OE.; amount by which a plank falls short of the squared shape XVII. OE. *wana*; cf. Du. *wan* shrinkage, Goth. *wan* lack; f. **wan-* adj. Hence **waney** wei·ni (of timber). XVII; see -Y[1].

wangle wæ·ŋgl accomplish or obtain by irregular or insidious means. XIX. First recorded as printers' sl., 'arrange or fake to one's own satisfaction' (Jacobi 'Printers' Vocabulary', 1888); perh. based on *waggle* and dial. *wankle* unsteady, unconstant, precarious (OE. *wancol*) under the infl. of a vague sense of phonetic symbolism. Hence sb.

wangun wæ·ŋgən (U.S.) boat or chest for provisions and outfit. XIX. Shortened – Montagnais Indian *atawangan*, f. *atawan* buy or sell.

wanion wɔ·njən (arch.) phr. *with (in) a w.* with a vengeance. XVI (revived by Scott). alt. of †*waniand* (XIV) in phr. †*in the w.*, prob. with ellipsis of *mone* moon, repr. OE. *on waniġendum mōnan* at the time of the waning moon, i.e. in an unlucky hour; see WANE.

want wɔnt condition or fact of being deficient XIII (Cursor M.); lack of the necessaries of life XIV; requirement XVI. Earlier (as in 'Ormulum') used as predic. adj. 'lacking', 'wanting' – ON. **want*, *vant*, n. of *vanr* lacking, missing, which was used quasi-sb. in such expressions as *var þeim vættugis vant* they were in want of nothing, *var vant kýr* a cow was missing, in which the construction is impers. So **want** vb. is lacking; be without XII. – ON. **wanta*, *vanta*, impers. vb. with accus. of person and thing, prob. :– **wanatōn*, f. **wan-* (see WANE). ¶ For similar adoptions of Scand. neuters in *-t* cf. SCANT, THWART[1], WIGHT[2].

wanton wɔ·ntən †undisciplined XIII (Cursor M.); lascivious, lewd XIV (Ch., PPl., Gower); †sportive, capricious XIV; †insolent; (poet.) luxurious XVI; reckless of justice or pity XVI. ME. *wantowen*, *wantoun*, f. *wan-*, prefix equiv. to UN-[1], MIS-[1], OE. *wan-* = OFris., OS., OHG. *wan-*, *wana-* (Du. *wan-*, G. *wahn-*, in *wahnsinn*, *wahnwitz* insanity), ON. *van-*, orig. identical with adj. †*wane* (see WANE) + *towen*, *toȝen*, OE. *togen*, pp. of *tēon* discipline, train :– **teohan* (see TIE). ¶ The prefix is repr. also in ME. *wanhope* despair (XIII), corr. to MLG., MDu. *wanhope*, and is prolific in Sc. and north. dialects, e.g. *wanchancy* unlucky (XVIII), *wanfortune* (XV), *wanhap*, *wanrest* (XVI), *wanruly* unruly (XVIII), *wansonsy* mischievous (XIX).

wapentake wɔ·pənteik subdivision of some shires (in which the Danish element of the population was large), corr. to a hundred. Late OE. *wǣpen(ġe)tæc* – ON. *vápnatak*, f. *vápna*, g. pl. of *vápn* WEAPON + *tak* act of taking, f. *taka* TAKE. The evolution of the Eng. sense from that of the ON. word, 'vote or consent expressed by waving or brandishing weapons', can only be conjectured.

wapiti wɔ·piti N. Amer. stag or elk, Cervus canadensis. XIX. – Shawnee *wapiti* 'white deer' (*wap* white), so named to distinguish it from the moose.

wappato(o) wɔ·pətou, -tū tubers of Sagittaria variabilis. XIX. – Chinook jargon *wappatoo*, – Cree *wapatowa* 'white mushroom'.

wappens(c)haw, -s(c)hawing wɔ·pənʃɔ̄, -iŋ (Sc.) muster or review of men under arms. XVI (revived by Scott). f. north. Eng. *wapen* (– ON. *vápn* WEAPON) + *schaw*, *schawing* SHOW.

war wɔ̄ɹ hostile contention of armed forces. XII (Peterborough Chron.). Late ME. *war(r)*, *warre* (XV), earlier *werre* (XIII–XV; e.g. PPl., Ch., Wyclif), *wyrre* (XII), *weorre* (XIII) – AN., ONF. *werre*, var. of (O)F. *guerre* = Pr., Sp., Pg., It. *guerra*, of Germ. origin, f. base repr. by OHG. *werra* confusion, discord, strife, OS., OHG. *werran* bring into confusion (G. *wirren* confuse, perplex); cf. WORSE. Hence **war** vb., partly after AN. *werreier* (in F. *guerroyer*) XII. comp. **wa·r**FARE[1]. XV. ¶ The formal coincidence of L. *bellu-s* (cf. BEAU) and *bellu-m* war (cf. BELLICOSE) led to the disappearance of the latter from Rom. In OE. there were several words for 'war', 'warfare', 'hostility', none of which survived; one of these, OE. *orleġe*, corr. to OFris. *orlog*, OS. *orlag*, *-log*, MDu. *orloghe* (Du. *oorlog*), OHG. *urliugi*,

ON. *ørlygi*. G. *krieg* war is a spec. use of its basic sense 'strife', 'contention'; ON. *úfriðr* is lit. 'no-peace'; synon. L. *bellum* and Gr. *pólemos* are of unkn. origin.

warble wɔ̄·ɹbl †tune, melody XIV, later (infl. by the vb.) act of warbling. Late ME. *werble* XIV – ONF. *werble*, var. of OF. **guerble* – OFrank. *hwirbilōn* whirl, trill; cf. OHG. *wirbil* whirlwind (MHG. *werbel*, *wirbel*, G. *wirbel* whirlpool, whirlwind, spinning-top, etc.), rel. to (M)Du. *wervel* harp, ON. *hvirfill* circle, ring, crown of the head; see WHIRL. So **warble** vb. sing with trills and quavers (XVI; ME. exx. of XIV are of doubtful meaning); in ONF. *werbler*, OF. *guerbler*, *-oier*.

ward[1] wɔ̄ɹd A. watching, guarding, custody OE.; charge of a prisoner XIII; B. administrative division of a city, etc. XIV (in AL. *warda* XIII); C. separate room or division of a prison, hospital, etc. XVI; D. pl. notches or projections in a key or lock to prevent opening XV. OE. *weard* = MLG. *warde*, OHG. *warta* watch (G. *warte* watch-tower) :- WGerm. **warðo* (whence ONF. *warde*, with the repr. of which the native word coalesced = (O)F. *garde* GUARD, Pr., Sp., Pg. *guarda*), f. **warð-*, extension of **war-* be on guard, watch (see WARE[2]).

ward[2] wɔ̄ɹd guard, defend OE.; parry, fend off XVI. OE. *weardian* = OFris. *wardia*, OS. *wardon*, OHG. *wartēn* (G. *warten* nurse, look after), ON. *varða* :- CGerm. (exc. Gothic) **warðōjan*, **warðǣjan*, f. **warðō* WARD[1]; reinforced in ME. by ONF. *warder*, var. of (O)F. *garder* GUARD vb.

-ward wəɹd suffix denoting direction, orig. (and so only in OE.) appended to local advs. (e.g. *hāmweard* homeward); a second stage is repr. by *to heavenward*, etc., which was followed by forms lacking the prep. (e.g. *earthward*, *Godward*). OE. *-weard* = OFris., OS. *-ward*, OHG. *-wart*, f. Germ. **-warð*, var. of **werþ-* :- **wert-* turn (L. *vertere*); in the suffix the primary sense is preserved, but in the related vb. *werþan* it has the derived sense of 'become' (see WORTH[3]).

warden wɔ̄·ɹdn †guardian; in various designations of office involving control or governorship. XIII. – AN., ONF. *wardein*, var. of OF. *g(u)arden* GUARDIAN.

warder[1] wɔ̄·ɹdəɹ soldier set to guard an entrance XIV; gaoler XIX. – AN. *wardere*, *wardour*, f. OF. *warder*; see WARD[2], -ER[2].

warder[2] wɔ̄·ɹdəɹ (arch.) staff, truncheon XV. Reduced form of †*warderer* (XIV), perh. orig. joc. use of †*warderere* look out behind (Ch.). – AN. **ware derere*, i.e. *ware* var. of (O)F. *gare* (– Germ. **war-* WARE[2]) + *derere* (modF. *derrière*) behind :- Rom. **dē rētrō*, i.e. L. *dē* from, *rētrō* behind (cf. REAR[2]).

Wardour Street wɔ̄·ɹdəɹ strīt name of a street in London mainly occupied by dealers in antique and pseudo-antique furniture applied to a pseudo-archaic style of English affected by writers esp. of historical novels. XIX.

wardrobe wɔ̄·ɹdroub †room in which wearing apparel was kept XIV (movable closed cupboard for this XVIII); department of a great household charged with the keeping of this; person's stock of this XV. – ONF. *warderobe*, var. of (O)F. *garderobe*, f. *garder* keep, GUARD, WARD[2] + *robe* garment, ROBE.

-wards wəɹdz OE. *-weardes*, corr. to OS., MLG. *-wardes*, Du *-waarts*, OHG. *-wartes*, f. Germ. **warða-*, with parallel **werþa-*, repr. by Goth. *-wairþs*, OHG. *-wertes* (G. *-wärts*, earlier *-werts*); g. sg. n. formations gen. identical in sense with -WARD though differing in details of usage.

ware[1] wɛəɹ articles of merchandise or manufacture (in comps. *earthenware*, *hardware*), OE. *waru* = OFris. *ware*, *were*, MLG. (whence MHG., G.), MDu. *ware* (Du. *waar*), ON. *vara* :- Germ. **warō*, perh. orig. 'object of care' and f. **war-* (see next). Comp. **wa·re**HOUSE XIV; cf. Du. *waarenhuis*, G. *warenhaus*; hence vb. XVIII.

ware[2] wɛəɹ (arch.) †aware; careful in avoiding (surviving in BEWARE). OE. *wær*, also *ġewær* = OS. *war*, also (and OHG.) *giwor*, Goth. **wars* (in pl. *warai*) :- Germ. **(ga)waraz*, f. **war-* **wer-* observe, take care (poss. cogn. with L. *verērī* fear).

ware[3] wɛəɹ †intr. take care; trans. beware of OE. (imper. in hunting use sometimes wɔ̄ɹ, continuing ME. *war*). OE. *warian* (imper. *wara* 'cave') = OFris. *waria*, OS. *waron*, OHG. *bi|warōn* beware, ON. *vara*; in ME. coalescing with ONF. *warer* (mod. *garer*), of Germ. origin (cf. prec.).

warison wɔ·risən †wealth, possessions; †reward XIII; (misused by Scott for) note of assault, prob. by misinterpretation of 'Mynstrells, playe vp for your waryson' (Battle of Otterbourne). – ONF. *warison*, var. of OF. *garison* (see GARRISON).

warlock wɔ̄·ɹlək †traitor, scoundrel; †the Devil; savage or monstrous creature OE.; sorcerer, wizard XIV. OE. *wǣrloga* = OS. *wārlogo* perh. deceiver (pl. applied to the Pharisees); f. OE. *wǣr* covenant = OHG. *wāra* truth, ON. *várar* pl., solemn promise, vow (cf. *Vǽringi* confederate, VARANGIAN), rel. to OS., OHG. *wār* true (see VERY) + **log*, wk. base of *lēoġan* LIE[2], appearing also in OE. *āþloga*, *trēowloga*, *wedloga* oath- or pledge-breaker. ME. *warlow(e)* (repr. OE. *wǣrloga*) was superseded by the Sc. var. *warlo(c)k* (XVI), which was familiarized through Burns and Scott.

warm wɔ̄ɹm moderately hot OE.; †comfortable, securely established XIV (Ch.); ardent, eager XIV (Gower); comfortably off; cordial, tender XV; lively, heated, excited XVI. OE. *wearm* = OFris., OS. *warm*, OHG. *war(a)m* (Du., G. *warm*), ON. *varmr*

:- CGerm. **warmaz* (cf. Goth. *warmjan* warm, cherish), with var. **werm-*, repr. by OHG. *wirma*, ON. *vermi* warmth; prob. to be referred to IE. **ghworm- *ghwerm-*, repr. by Skr. *gharmás* heat, Av. *garᵊmō-* hot, Gr. *thermós* hot, L. *formus* warm, and forms in OPruss., Alb., and Arm. So **warm** vb. (i) OE. **wierman, werman, wirman* trans. = OS. *wermian* (Du. *warmen*), OHG. *wermen* (G. *wärmen*), ON. *verma*, Goth. *warmjan* :- CGerm. **warmjan*; (ii) OE. *wearmian* intr. = OHG. *war(a)mēn* (early modG. *warmen*) :- **warmǣjan*.

warmTH[1] wɔːmþ XII. OE. **wiermþu, *wærmþu* = MLG. *wermede* (Du. *warmte*), MHG. *wermede* (G. †*wärmte*) :- WGerm. **warmiþō*.

warn wɔːɹn put on one's guard, give a caution to OE.; inform, notify XIII. OE. *war(e)nian, wearnian* = MLG. *warnen*, OHG. *warnōn, warnēn* (G. *warnen*, whence Sw. *varna*, Da. *varne*) :- WGerm. **waranōjan, -ǣjan*, f. **war-* be cautious (see WARE[2]).

warp wɔːɹp A. †cast, throw OE.; (after ON. *orðum verpa*) †utter XIII; B. (after ON. *orpinn* pp. warped) trans. and intr. bend, twist aside XIV (fig. distort XVI); C. weave, twine XIII; D. tow XVI. OE. *weorpan*, pt. *wearp, wurpon*, pp. *worpen* (the ordinary vb. for 'cast', 'throw') = OS. *werpan*, OHG. *werfan* (Du. *werpen*, G. *werfen*), ON. *verpa*, Goth. *wairpan*; CGerm. str. vb. (becoming wk. in Eng. XIV), having no certain cogns. So **warp** sb. threads extended lengthwise in the loom OE.)(*weft*; rope, hawser XIII. OE. *wearp*, with Continental equivs.; some later senses are from the vb.

warrant wɔ·rənt A. † protector, defence; authoritative witness; authorization XIII; B. document conveying authority or security XV; justifying reason XVI. – ONF. *warant*, var. of OF. *guarant, -and* (mod. *garant*), whence Pr. *garens*, Sp. *garante*, It. *guarento*, cf. medL. *warens, warandus* – OFrank. *werēnd* (= OHG. *werēnt*, f. *gi|werēn* (G. *gewähren*) = OFris. *wera* be surety for, guarantee). So **warrant** vb. †keep safe XIII; guarantee the security of XVI. (Also *war(r)and*) – OF. *warantir, warandir*, vars. of *g(u)arantir, -andir*. **wa·rrant**Y[3] legal covenant. XIV (R. Mannyng) – AN. *warantie*, var. of *garantie* GUARANTEE.

warren wɔ·rən piece of land preserved for breeding game, esp. for the breeding of rabbits XIV; fig. XVII. – AN., ONF. *warenne*, var. of (O)F. *garenne* game-park, now esp. rabbit warren, Pr. *garena* – Gaulish **varrenna* area marked off by palisading, f. **varros* post (cf. Ir. *farr* pillar, post), evidenced in Gaulish place-names. So **wa·rren**ER[2] officer having charge of a warren (survives as surname) XIV. – AN. *warener*, ONF. *warrennier*, (O)F. *garennier*.

warrigal wɔ·rigəl dingo; wild Australian aboriginal XIX. Native Australian word, recorded as *warregal, wor-re-gal, worrikul*, etc.

warrior wɔ·riəɹ fighting man. XIII. ME. *werre(y)our* – ONF. *werreieor, werrieur*, var. of OF. *guerreieor* (mod. *guerroyeur*), f. *werreier, guerreier* (whence ME. †*warray*), corr. to Pr. *guerreiar*, Sp., Pg. *guerrear*, It. *guerreggiare*, Rom. deriv. of **werra* WAR; see -OR[1].

wart wɔːɹt round dry tough excrescence on the skin. OE. *wearte* = OFris. *warte, worte*, OS. *warta*, OHG. *warza* (Du. *wrat*, G. *warze*), ON. *varta* :- CGerm. (exc. Goth.) **wartōn*.

wary wɛə·ri marked by caution. XVI. Extension of WARE[2] by the addition of -Y[1] to impart a more adjectival appearance; cf. *chilly, slippery*.

was wɔz, wəz see BE.

wash wɔʃ cleanse with or as with water OE. (also refl. and intr. XII); of the sea, etc., flow over or past; remove with or as with water XV. OE. *wæsćan, wasćan, waxan*, pt. *wōsć, wēosć, wēox*, pl. *wōxon, wēosćon*, pp. *-wæsćen* = OS. *wascan* (Du. *wasschen, wiesch, gewasschen*), OHG. *wascan, wuosc, giwascan* (G. *waschen, wusch, gewaschen*), ON. *vaska* (conjugated wk.) :- CGerm. (exc. Goth.) orig. str. vb. **waskan* :- **watskan*, f. **wat-* WATER. Traces of wk. conjugation appear XIV, but str. forms prevailed till XVI, after which they are mostly only dial. (pt. *weesh, wush*, pp. *washen, weshen*). Hence **wash** sb. (not continuous with OE. *wasć* 'ablutio', *ġewæsć* 'alluvium'); in many unconnected applications, some of which are of obscure origin; tract of land alternately covered and exposed by the sea XIV (in AL. *whasshum maris* XIV); liquid refuse XV; watery infusion or mixture XVI. comp. **wa·sh-leather** XVII; earlier †*washen leather* (*wesshyn leddyr* XV), † *washed leather* (XVII) suggest that the orig. ref. was to the washing which was a part of the manufacture.

washer[1] wɔ·ʃəɹ one who washes XV; comp. **wa·sher**WOːMAN XVII, earlier (now U.S.) *washwoman* XVI; see -ER[1].

washer[2] wɔ·ʃəɹ perforated annular disc to prevent friction or looseness of parts. XIV (*whasher*). Of unkn. origin.

wasp wɔsp insect of the genus Vespa. OE. *wæsp, wæps, wæfs*, corr. to OS. *wepsia, wespa, wasp*, OHG. *wafsa, wefsa* (G. *wespe*, dial. *webes*), MLG. *wepse, wespe, wispe* :- WGerm. **waƀis-, *waps-* :- IE. **wobhes-, *wops-*, whence OSl., Russ. *osa*, OPruss. *wobse* wasp, Lith. *vapsá* gadfly, OBret. *guohi*, Cornish *guhien*, L. *vespa* (:- **wopsā*), usu. taken to be f. **webh- wobh-* WEAVE[1], with ref. to the weblike construction of the insect's nest. Hence **wa·sp**ISH[1]. XVI (Drant, Sh.).

wassail wɔ·sl, wɔ·seil salutation used when presenting drink to a guest or drinking his health XIII (*wæs hæil*, *wassayl*, *-ail*, Laȝ.; after XIV only hist. and dial.); liquor for drinking healths XIII; carousal XVII (Sh.). ME. *wæs hæil*, *wassayl* – ON. *ves heill* 'be in good health' (see HALE[1]); recorded earlier (XII) in Geoffrey of Monmouth's 'Historia Brittonum' VI xii (*wes heil*), Wace's 'Brut' (*weshel*, *waisseil*) and 'Roman de Rou', and Nigellus de Wireker's 'Speculum Stultorum' (*wessail*). In the orig. use coupled with *drinkhail*, the response of the guest.

wast wɔst, wəst see BE.

waste weist A. desert land XII; B. action of wasting XIII; C. waste matter XV. – ONF. *wast(e)*, var. of OF. *guast(e)*, *gast(e)*, partly repr. L. *vāstum*, n. of *vāstus* waste, desert, partly f. *waster* vb. So **waste** adj. uncultivated, barren XIII; superfluous, refuse XV. – ONF. *wast*, var. of *g(u)ast* = Pr. *gast*, Pg. *gasto*, It. *guasto* :– Rom. **wasto*, repr. (with infl. from rel. and synon. OFrank. *wōsti*) L. *vāstus*; superseded OE., ME. *wēste* :– **wōstiz*. **waste** vb. devastate, consume by loss, decay, etc. XIII; consume or expend uselessly XIV. – ONF. *waster*, var. of *g(u)aster* = Pr. *g(u)astar*, Sp. *gastar*, It. *guastare* :– CRom. **wastāre*, for L. *vāstare*, f. *vāstus*. Hence **wa·steFUL**[1] causing devastation XIV; extravagant XV. **wa·stER**[1]. XIV.

wastel wɔ·stəl (hist.) bread or loaf made of the finest flour. XIII (Havelok). – north-eastern var. *wastel* of OF. *guastel* (mod. *gâteau* cake), prob. of Germ. origin.

wastrel wei·strəl (in Cornwall) tract of waste land XVI; article rejected as unserviceable XVIII; unhealthy animal; good-for-nothing person, waster XIX. f. WASTE vb. + -REL.

watch wɔtʃ †be awake OE.; be on the alert or look-out XIII; keep in view XIV. OE. **wæċċan* (in Nhb. *wæċċa*, WS. prp. *wæċċende*), doublet of *wacian* WAKE[3]. So **watch** sb. A. †vigil; action of watching XIV; (naut.) period of watching; one set to watch XVI; B. †alarm-clock XV; small spring-driven time-piece for the pocket XVI; OE. *wæċċe*, f. stem of **wæċċan*; in some later uses directly f. the vb. Hence **wa·tchFUL**[1] XVI. comp. **wa·tchMAN** XIV, **wa·tchWORD** XIV.

water wɔ̄·təɹ transparent liquid (chemically compounded of two parts hydrogen and one part oxygen) forming the material of seas, lakes, and rivers; (prob. after Arab. *mā'* water, lustre, splendour) transparency and lustre of a gem XVII (Sh.), whence in popular phr. *of the first w.* (equivalent uses are common to Germ. and Rom. langs.). OE. *wæter* = OFris. *weter*, OS. *watar*, OHG. *wazzar* (Du. *water*, G. *wasser*) :– WGerm. **watar* (ON. *vatn*, Goth. *wato*, g. *watins*, show a var. with *n*-formative), f. CGerm. **wat* :– IE. **wod-*, repr. by OSl., Russ. *voda* (cf. VODKA); the var. **wĕd-* is repr. by WET, the var. **ud-* (sometimes with nasal infix) by L. *unda* (cf. UNDULATE), Umbrian *utur* wave, Gr. *húdōr*, g. *húdatos* (:– *udn̥tos*), *hudro-* HYDRO-, Lith. *vanduõ*, OPruss. *unds*, Skr. *udán*. See also OTTER, WHISKY[1]. So **wa·ter** vb. trans. OE.; intr. XIV. OE. (*ġe*)*wæterian*, corr. to MLG. *wateren*, *weteren* (Du. *wateren*), MHG. *wezzern* (G. *wässern*). **wa·terY**[1]. OE. *wæteriġ* = MLG. *waterich*, etc. comps. **wa·terFALL** XIV (OE. had *wætergefeall*; cf. G. *wasserfall*, ON. *vatnfall*). **watershed** wɔ̄·təɹʃed line separating waters flowing into different river basins XIX; after G. *wasserscheide*, which became common in scientific use *c.*1800; see SHED[2].

waterlog wɔ̄·təɹlɔg render unmanageable by flooding with water. XVIII. perh. orig. with sense 'make like a LOG[1]'.

Waterloo wɔ̄təɹlū· name given to the battle fought outside Waterloo, near Brussels, in which Napoleon Bonaparte was finally defeated (18 June 1815); used allusively for: a decisive and final contest, a 'settler'. XIX (Byron calls the Armenian 'a W. of an Alphabet').

water-souchy wɔ̄·təɹ sū·tʃi, sū·ʃi fish boiled and served in its liquor. XVIII. – Du. *waterzootje*, f. *water* WATER + *zootje*, *zoodje* boiling (of fish), f. *zode* boiling, rel. to *zieden* SEETHE.

watt wɔt (physics) unit of activity or power. XIX (Siemens, 1882). f. name of James *Watt* (1736–1819), inventor of the modern steam engine and a pioneer in the science of energy.

wattle[1] wɔ·tl (pl. and coll. sg.) stakes intertwined with twigs or branches used as fencing, etc. OE. *watul*, perh. rel. to *wætla* bandage for a wound and poss. :– **waðlaz* (for the treatment of *ð* cf. *bottle*, *bottom*), f. IE. **wodh-* weave; see WEED[2], -LE[1]. Hence vb. XIV (PPl.).

wattle[2] wɔ·tl fleshy lobe pendent from the head or neck of poultry, etc. XVI. Of unkn. origin; the occurrence of *watel* for 'bag' or 'basket' in some MSS. (others *walet*) in PPl. C. XI 269 and the casual use of *wallets of flesh* in Sh. 'Tempest' III iii 46 do not afford sufficient evidence that *wattle* is a metathetic var. of *wallet*.

wave[1] weiv move to and fro, shake or sway as with the wind. The word in the above senses as at present used is not clearly evident before XVI. Though of similar meaning, it is not certainly continuous with OE. *wafian* (recorded twice) make a movement to and fro with the hands, corr. to MHG. *waben* wave, undulate, f. Germ. **wab-*, repr. also by ON. *vafi* doubt, uncertainty, *vafl*, *vafla* wavering and WAVER. The grade-var. **wǣb-* is repr. by ON. *váfa* swing, vibrate.

wave[2] weiv movement in an extent of water by which a portion of it rises above the general level. XVI (Tindale, 1526). alt., by assoc. with WAVE[1], of ME. †*wawe*, earlier *waȝe*, rel. to OE. *wagian*, ME. *wawe*, sway to and fro, wave (cf. WAG[1]). Hence **wa·vy**[1]. XVI.

waver wei·vəɹ †wander, rove; fluctuate, vacillate; †sway. XIV. orig. north. and eastern; – ON. *vafra* move unsteadily, flicker (Norw. *vavra* go to and fro, stagger) = MHG. *waberen* (G. *wabern*) move about, frequent. f. Germ. **waƀ-*; cf. WAVE[1], -ER[4].

wavey wei·vi Amer. goose of the genus Chen. XVIII. var. of **wawa** wei·wə – Cree *wehwew*, Ojibwa *wēwe* goose.

wax[1] wæks substance produced by bees to make the honeycomb; beeswax melted down, etc.; as used for sealing, superseded by a compound of lac, etc. OE. *wæx*, *weax* = OFris. *wax*, OS., OHG. *wahs* (Da. *was*, G. *wachs*), ON. *vax* :– CGerm. (exc. Goth.) **waχsam*, cogn. with OSl. *voskŭ* (Russ. *vosk*), Czech *vosk*, to be referred ult. to IE. **weg-* weave, whence OIr. *figim* I weave, L. *vēlum* VEIL (for the sense connexion cf. OHG. *wabe* honeycomb, f. **webh-* WEAVE[1]). Hence **wax** vb. XIV, **wa·xen**[3]. XIV; repl. OE. *wexen*, **wiexen*. **wa·xwork** modelling in wax. XVII.

wax[2] wæks grow OE.; become XII (Orm). OE. *weaxan*, pt. *wēox*, Nhb. *wōx*, pp. *weaxen* = OFris. *waxa*, OS., OHG. *wahsan* (Du. *wassen*, G. *wachsen*), ON. *vaxa*, Goth. *wahsjan* (with *-ja-* in pres. stem) :– CGerm. str. vb. f. **waχs-* :– IE. **woks-*, **aweks-*, **auks-*, **uks-* repr. by Gr. *aéxein*, *aúxein*, *auxánein* increase, Skr. *ukš* grow (pt. *vakša*), L. *augēre* (see AUCTION), Lith. *áugu* I grow; cf. EKE[2]. The str. conjugation was retained in Nhb. OE.; pt. *wex* became rare after XIV; pp. *waxed* occurs 4 times in A.V., *waxen* 8 times. The survival of the vb. has depended partly upon its association with *wane* in reference to the moon.

wax[3] wæks (sl.) fit of anger. XIX. perh. evolved from a usage such as *wax wroth* (WAX[2]).

way wei road, path; course of travel, life, or action, distance travelled. OE. *weġ* = OFris. *wei*, *wī*, OS., OHG. *weg* (Du., G. *weg*), ON. *vegr*, Goth. *wigs* :– CGerm. **wegaz*, f. **weg-* move, journey, carry (see WEIGH, WAIN) :– IE. **wegh-*, repr. also by L. *vehere* carry (cf. VEHICLE). ¶ The sense development has been influenced by L. *via* and F. *voie*, of which the Eng. word has been the normal rendering; many senses are of biblical origin; Heb. *dérek* and Gr. *hodós* (rendered in Vulg. by *via*) have a wide range; phr. *under way* (naut.) having begun to move through the water. XVIII. – Du. *onderweg*; also sp. *weigh*; whence perh. sense 'rate of progress, velocity' XVIII.

-way wei terminal el. orig. joined in a phr. with an adj. surviving in a few comps., as *anyway*, *crossway*, *edgeway*, *everyway*, *half-way*, *midway*, *noway*, *someway*, *straightway*, the earliest being *alway* (OE. accus. *ealne weġ*); most of these have parallel and synon. forms in -WAYS.

waybread wei·bred plantain. OE. *weġbrǣde*, corr. to OS. *wegabreda*, OHG. *wegabreita* (G. *wegbreit* m., *wegebreite* f.), WGerm. comp. of WAY and **braiðjōn*, f. **braið-* BROAD, the etymol. sense being 'broad-leaved plant of the roadside(s)'.

wayfare wei·fɛəɹ (arch.) travelling. XIV. f. WAY + FARE, after *wayfaring*, OE. *weġfarende* = Icel. *vegfarandi*, varying in OE. and ME. with †*wayfering*. Hence **way·farer**[1] traveller by road XV; **wayfaring** (*man's*) **tree** Viburnus Lantana, growing wild in hedges XVI (Gerarde).

waylay weilei· lie in wait for. XVI. f. WAY + LAY[1], after MLG., MDu. *wegelāgen*, f. Germ. **wega laga* besetting of ways, i.e. *wega*, g. pl. of *weg* WAY + *lāga* besetting, ambush, f. *lag-* LAY[1]. Hence **way·layer**[1] XVII; earlier †*weiligger* (Lydg.), i.e. 'way-lier'.

wayleave wei·līv permission to convey supplies, apparatus, etc. over land, etc. XV. f. WAY + LEAVE[1].

-ways weiz (in *always* wiz), repr. *weġes*, g. sg. of OE. *weġ* WAY, as in *ōþres weġes* (XII), dial. *otherways* by another route, *alles weis* ALWAYS, *nanes weis* (XIII) NO[2]WAYS.

way·side side of a road or path. XIV.

wayward wei·wəɹd disposed to be self-willed XIV (Wyclif); capriciously wilful XVI. Aphetic of *awayward* (XIV), f. AWAY + -WARD; the sense development was prob. infl. by the notion of the word being f. WAY, as if 'bent on going one's own way'; cf. FROWARD.

waywiser wei·waizəɹ instrument for measuring distance travelled by road. XVII. – G. *wegweiser*, f. *weg* WAY + *weiser* indicator, f. *weisen* show, indicate, f. *weise* WISE[2]; see -ER[1].

waywode wei·woud see VOIVODE.

wayzgoose wei·zgūs entertainment given to printers orig. at Bartholomew-tide (24 August), when working by candle-light began; later, annual feast held in summer. Earlier *waygoose* (XVII, Moxon), the present form being recorded first by Bailey (1731) and explained as 'stubble goose', f. alleged var. *wayz* of *wase* bundle of straw, of which there is no confirmation.

wazir waziə·ɹ see VIZIER. XVIII.

we wī, wi you, he, she, or they, and I. OE. *wē̆*, corr. to OFris. *wī̆*, OS. *wi*, *wē*, OHG. *wir* (Du. *wij*, G. *wir*), ON. *vér*, *vær*, Goth. *weis*. These forms repr. more than one Germ. type; Goth. *weis* repr. Germ. **wīz* :– **weis*, extension (with pl. *-s*) of **wei*, repr. also by Skr. *vayám*, Av. *vaēm*; other forms may repr. **wī̆z*, of doubtful origin; Tokh. has *was*;

dual OE. *wit* = OS. *wit*, ON. *vit*, Goth. *wit*, has a parallel in Lith. *vèdu*. For the obl. cases see OUR, US.

weak wīk not strong, feeble XIII; †pliant, flexible XIV. ME. *wayke* – ON. *veikr* (**weikr*) = OE. *wāc* weak, slothful, pliant, insignificant, mean (ME. *wōke*), OS. *wēk*, OHG. *weih* (Du. *week*, G. *weich* soft) :– Germ. **waikwaz*, f. **waikw*- **wikw*- yield, give way (cf. WEEK). Hence **wea·k**EN[5]. XIV. **wea·k**LING[1]. XVI (first used by Tindale after G. *weichling* (Luther)). **wea·k**LY[1]. XVI, -LY[2] XIV, -NESS XIII (Cursor M.).

weal[1] wīl †wealth, riches; welfare OE.; the public good XV. OE. *wela* = OS. *welo*, (cf. OHG. *wela*, *wola* adv.) :– WGerm. **welon*, f. **wel*-; see WELL[3]. In the sense of *w. public* (XV) rendering L. *bonum publicum*, F. *le bien publique*, COMMONWEAL (L. *rēs commūnis* or *publica*, F. *le bien commun*).

weal[2] wīl var. of WALE infl. by WHEAL.

weald wīld the tract of country, formerly wooded, lying between the North and the South Downs. OE., WS. var. of *wald* WOLD; normally repr. by ME. *weld*, the present *weald* being a reversion to the OE. *weald*, due to Lambarde. Hence **Wealden** wī·ldən (pert. to) a formation of cretaceous deposits extensively developed in the Weald. XIX; the use of the suffix -EN[3] is arbitrary.

wealth welþ A. †well-being XIII; welfare of a community (cf. COMMONWEALTH) XIV; B. worldly goods, riches XIII. ME. *welþe* ('Genesis & Exodus', Cursor M.), f. WELL[0] or WEAL[1], after *health*; cf. (M)Du. *weelde*, OHG. *welida*. Hence **wealth**Y[1] we·lþi XIV; superseded †*wealy*, f. WEAL[1].

wean wīn accustom to the loss of its mother's milk. OE. *wenian* accustom, (rare) wean (usu. *āwenian*, sometimes *ġewenian*; cf. G. *entwöhnen*), OFris. *wenna*, OS. *wennian* (Du. *wennen*), OHG. *gi|wennen* (G. *-wöhnen*), ON. *venja* :– CGerm. (exc. Gothic) **wanjan*, f. **wanaz* accustomed (ON. *vanr*, rel. to *vani* custom, habit, f. **wan*- **wun*- (see WONT).

weapon we·pn instrument used for warfare or combat. OE. *wǣpn* = OFris. *wēpen*, OS. *wāpan* (Du. *wapen*), OHG. *wāf(f)an* (G. *waffe*; *wappen* armorial bearings is – MLG. *wāp(p)en*), ON. *vápn*, Goth **wēpn* (in pl. *wēpna*) :– CGerm. **wǣpnam*, of unkn. origin.

wear[1] wɛəɹ pt. **wore** wɔəɹ, pp. **worn** wɔ̄ɹn A. 'to carry appendant to the body' (J.) OE.; B. waste, decay XIII; C. last out in use XVI. OE. *werian*, pt. *werede*, pp. *wered* = OS. *werian*, OHG. *werien*, ON. *verja*, Goth. *wasjan* clothe :– CGerm. wk. vb. **wazjan*, f. **was*- (as in Goth. *wasti* garment, MHG. *wester* christening-robe), CGerm. and IE. **wes*-, repr. also by ON. *vest* cloak, L. *vestis* clothing (cf. VEST[1]), Gr. *hennúnai* (:– **wesnu*-) clothe, *ϝesthḗs* raiment, Skr. *vas* clothe. The change of conjugation from wk. to str., due to assoc. with *bear*, *swear*, *tear*, is shown in XIV but is hardly established before XVI; there is an early anticipation of it in late OE. *forworen* (beside *forwered*) worn away, wasted. Hence sb. action of wearing XV; what is worn XVI (now current esp. in comps., *footwear*, *headwear*, *knitwear*).

wear[2] wɛəɹ pt., pp. **wore** wɔəɹ (naut.) come round on the other tack by turning stern to windward. XVII. Early forms *weare*, *wayer*, *warre*, *werr*; of unkn. origin; not identical with VEER[2], with which it is partly synon.

weary wiə·ri having the feeling of loss of strength. OE. *wēriġ*, *wǣriġ*, corr. to OS. *sīð|wōrig* weary (with journey), OHG. *wuarag* drunk :– WGerm. **wōriga*, *-*aga*, f. **wōr*-, repr. also by OE. *wōrian* wander, go astray, ON. *órar*, pl. fits of madness (*hǫfuðórar* delirium), *œrr* mad, insane (:– **wōrja*); cf. Gr. *hōrākiân* faint. Hence vb. OE. *wer(i)ġian*, *ġewerġian*.

weasand wī·zənd, wi·zən (dial.) gullet OE.; windpipe XIV; throat XV. OE. *wāsend*, corr. to OFris. *wāsanda*, *-enda*, OS. *wāsend(i)*, OHG. *weisant*, *-ont*, *-unt* (MHG. *weisen*, early modG. *waise(n)*, dial. *wäs*); a WGerm. word having the appearance of a prp. formation (cf. ON. *vélendi* gullet). OE. *wāsend* is repr. directly by w. midl. ME. *wōsen* (XIV), dial. *wozen*, *(h)oosen*; but the more gen. current *weasand*, *weason*, *wizen* point to an OE. var. **wǣsend*.

weasel wī·zəl ferocious carnivore, Putorius nivalis. OE. *wesule*, *wesle*, *weosule* = MLG. *wesel*, *wezel*, OHG. *wisula* (G. *wiesel*) :– WGerm. **wisulōn* (Scand. forms are from G. dial.), of unkn. origin.

weather we·ðəɹ condition of the atmosphere with respect to heat or cold, calm or storm, etc. XII; (with adverse implication) XII; direction of wind (perh. – ON.) XIV. OE. *weder* = OFris. *wedar*, OS. *wedar*, OHG. *wetar* (Du. *weer*, G. *wetter*), ON. *veðr* :– CGerm. (exc. Goth.) **weðram* :– either **wedhrom* (whence OSl. *vedro*, Russ. *vëdro* good weather, Lith. *vidrus*, *vydra* storm) or **wetróm* (Lith. *vétra* storm, OSl. *větrŭ* wind); prob. f. **wē̆* WIND[1]. The change from d to ð (shown XV) is paralleled in FATHER. comp. **w. cock** vane in the form of a cock (cf. Du. *weerhaan*). XIII: preserves the connexion with wind as the attrib. or adj. uses do of the side turned towards the wind (perh. after ON. *veðr*). Hence vb. trans. and intr. in various uses concerning exposure to wind and weather XV (*wether*); earlier in **weather**ING (early ME. *widerung*; cf. OE. *widerian* be good weather, corr. to MHG. *witeren*, ON. *viðra* be stormy).

weave[1] wīv pt. **wove** wouv, pp. **woven** wou·vn fabricate by interlacing yarns. OE. *wefan*, pt. *wæf*, *wǣfon*, pp. *wefen* =

OFris. *weva* (WFris. *weve*, etc.), (M)LG., (M)Du. *weven*, OHG. *weban* (G. *weben*), ON. *vefa* :- CGerm. (exc. Goth.) **weƀan*, f. Germ. **weƀ-* **waƀ-* :- IE. **webh-* **wobh-* **ubh-*, repr. also by Gr. *huphḗ*, *húphos* web, *huphaínein* weave, Skr. *ūrṇa|vā́bhis* spider, lit. 'wool-weaver'; cf. WASP, WEB, WEFT, WOOF[1].

weave[2] wīv move repeatedly from side to side, pursue a devious course XVI; (pugilism) creep close into one's opponent XIX. prob. continuation of ME. †*weve* (XIII) move from place to place, wave, brandish, var. of †*waive* – ON. *veifa*, corr. to (M)Du. *weiven*, OHG. *-weiben* :- Germ. **weiƀjan*, rel. ult. to L. *vibrāre* VIBRATE.

web web woven fabric OE.; cobweb; tissue, membrane XIII. OE. *web(b)*, corr. to OFris. *webb*, OS. *webbi* (MDu. *webbe*, Du. *web*), OHG. *wappi*, *weppi*, ON. *vefr* (g. *vefjar*) :- CGerm. (exc. Goth.) **waƀjam*, *-az*, f. **waƀ-*; see WEAVE[1]. Hence **we·bSTER** female weaver OE. (*webbestre*); male weaver XIV; survives as a surname, as do also OE. *webba* m., *webbe* fem. (ME. *webbe*) as *Webb*, *Webbe*.

weber vei·bəɹ, wī·bəɹ old name for the coulomb and the ampère. XIX. f. name of Wilhelm *Weber* (1804–91), German physicist.

wed wed marry, trans. OE., pass. XII, intr. XIII. OE. *weddian* covenant, marry, bind in wedlock = OFris. *weddia*, MLG. *wedden*, OHG. *wettōn* (G. *wetten*) pledge, wager, ON. *veðja* pledge, Goth. *ga|wadjōn* espouse :- CGerm. **waðjōjan*, f. **waðjam* pledge (OE. *wedd*, in mod. dial. *wed*, OFris. *wedd*, OS. *weddi*, Du. *wedde*, OHG. *wetti*, G. *wette*, ON. *veð*, Goth. *wadi*), rel. to L. *vad-*, nom. *vas* surety, Lith. *wadúoti* redeem a pledge. Hence **weddING**[1] we·diŋ late OE. *weddung*. ¶ For reprs. in Rom. see GAGE[1], WAGE.

wedge wedʒ piece of wood, etc. thick at one end and tapering to a thin edge at the other; †ingot OE.; other special senses from XVI. OE. *weċġ* = OS. *weggi* (Du. *wegge* wedge-shaped cake), OHG. *weggi*, *wecki* (G. dial. *wecken*, *weck*), ON. *veggr* :- CGerm. (exc. Fris. and Goth.) **wagjaz* (whence Finnish *vaaja* wedge), prob. rel. to Lith. *vágis* pin, plug.

Wedgwood we·dʒwud designating a kind of pottery; name of inventor, Josiah *Wedgwood* (1730–95), and his successors at Etruria, Staffordshire. XVIII.

wedlock we·dlɔk †marriage vow OE.; union of man and woman as husband and wife. XIII. Late OE. *wedlāc*, f. *wed* pledge, WED + *-lāc* -LOCK.

Wednesday we·nzdi fourth day of the week. ME. *wednesdei* (XIII), corr. to OFris. *wēnsdei*, which, together with the place-names *Wednesbury* and *Wednesfield* in Staffordshire, and *Wensley* in Derbyshire, appear to repr. a form with mutation due to suffix-variation (**wōðinaz*), and repl. OE. *wōdnesdæġ* = OFris. *wōnsdei*, MLG. *wōdensdach* (Du. *woensdag*), ON. *óðinsdagr* 'day of Odin', tr. late L. *Mercurii diēs* 'day of the planet Mercury' (whence F. *mercredi*, Sp. *miercoles*, It. *mercoledì*). The local and individual pronunc. with -dn- repr. the sp. while the established -nz- goes back to ME. *wendesdei* (XIII). The identification of Woden, the highest god of the Germ. pantheon, with Mercury is shown in Tacitus' 'Germania' ix (Deorum maxime Mercurium colunt). OE. *Wōden* = OS. *Wōden*, OHG. *Wuotan*, ON. *Óðin* is referred to the base **wōð-* be excited or inspired (whence OE. *wōd*, dial. *wood* mad) :- IE. **wāt-*, repr. by L. *vātēs* seer, poet (cf. VATICINATE), (O)Ir. *fáith* poet, W. *gwawd* song, poetry. ¶ In HG. the name of W. appears to have been always 'midweek' (G. *Mittwoch*); for the apprehension of planetary names as those of deities cf. FRIDAY, etc.

wee wī sb. orig. chiefly in *a little wee*, †a small thing or quantity; a short time XIII; adj. extremely small, tiny XV. north. ME. *wei*, *we*, repr. Anglian *wēġ*, *wēġe* (WS. *wǣġ*, *-e*) weight, rel. to *weġan* WEIGH; the use appears to have originated in such a phr. as *a little wee thing* 'a small amount of a thing', similar to *a bit thing* 'a bit of a thing', hence 'a little thing'. The adj. use has been current in southern Eng. since *c.*1600. Cf. WEENY.

weed[1] wīd small plant, esp. one that cumbers the ground. OE. *wēod* = OS. *wiod*, rel. to OHG. *wiota* fern; of unkn. origin. Hence vb. clear of weeds. OE. *wēodian* = OS. *wiodon*, (M)LG. *weden*, (M)Du. *wieden*. Hence **wee·dY**[1]. XV.

weed[2] wīd garment OE.; now chiefly pl. deep mourning apparel, spec. of widows XVI, ME. *wēde*, repr. two OE. formations: (i) *wǣd* = OFris. *wēd*, OS. *wād* (in Du. *lijnwaad*), OHG. *wāt*, ON. *váð*, *vóð* :- Germ. **wǣðiz*; (ii) OE. *wǣde*, *ġewǣde* = OFris. *wēde*, OS. *wādi*, *giwādi* (Du. *gewaad*), OHG. *giwāti* :- Germ. **gawǣðjam*, of disputed origin.

week wīk period of seven days. OE. *wice*, *wicu* = OFris. *wike*, OS. *-wika*, in *crūcewika* Holy Week (Du. *week*), OHG. *wehha*, *wohha* (G. *woche*), ON. *vika*, Goth. *wikō* (once, rendering τάξις 'order' in Luke i 8) :- CGerm. **wikōn* (whence Finnish *wijkko* week), prob. orig. 'succession, series', usu. referred to **wīk-* 'bend', 'turn', 'change', repr. also by OE. *wice*, OS., OHG. *wehsal* (G. *wechsel*), ON. *-vixl* change. Cf. VICE[4]. OE. *wice* and *wucu* are repr. by the ME. types *wike*, *wēke*, and *wuke*, *wōke*, whence mod. *week*, dial. *wick*, *ook*, Sc. *ouk*.

weel wīl ME. var. of WELL[3]; mod. Sc. established in Eng. colloq. use in *ne'er-do-weel*.

ween wīn (arch.) think, suppose, expect. OE. *wēnan* = OFris. *wēna*, OS. *wānian* (Du. *wanen* fancy, imagine), OHG. *wan-(n)ēn* (G. *wähnen* suppose wrongly), ON. *vǽna*, Goth. *wēnjan* hope :- CGerm. **wǣnjan*, f. **wǣniz* opinion, expectation, hope (OE., OFris. *wēn*, OS., OHG. *wān*, G. *wahn* delusion, ON. *ván*, Goth. *wēns* hope), based on var. of CGerm. (IE.) **wen-* (cf. WINSOME, WISH).

weeny wī·ni (colloq., dial.) very small. XVIII (Grose). f. WEE + *-ny*; cf. TINY, TEENY.

weep wīp pt., pp. **wept** shed tears. OE. *wēpan* (*wǣpan*), pt. *wēop*, pp. *wōpen*, corr. to OFris. *wēpa* (pp. *wēpen*) cry aloud, OS. *wōpian* bewail (pt. *weop*), OHG. *wuofan* (pt. *wiof*), also *wuoffen* (pt. *wuofta*), ON. *ǿpa* (pt. *ǿpta*) scream, shout, Goth. *wōpjan*; f. Germ. **wōp-* (repr. also by OE. *wōp* weeping, OS. *wōp*, OHG. *wuof* lamentation, ON. *óp* cry); without cogns., prob. of imit. origin. Weak inflexions appeared XIII and became prevalent XIV. Hence **wee·per**[1] mourner XIV; badge of mourning XVIII; **wee·ping**[2]. OE. *wǣpende*; in names of trees with drooping branches XVII (so F. *pleureur*).

weet wīt (arch.) know. XVI. repr. ME. *wēte(n)*, var. of *wite(n)* WIT[2].

weever wī·vəɹ fish of the genus Trachinus, having venomous spines. XVII. perh. orig. *wiver* – transf. use of OF. (NE.) *wivre* serpent, dragon, var. of *guivre* :- L. *vīpera* VIPER.

weevil wī·vil beetle the larva of which is destructive to grain, etc. XV. Late ME. *wevyl* or *malte boode*, i.e. 'malt bug' (Promp. Parv.), prob. – MLG. *wevel* = OE. *wifel* beetle (cf. *tordwifel* dung-beetle), OS. *gold|wivil* glowworm, OHG. *wibil*, *wipil* beetle, chafer, ON. **vifill* (in *tordýfill* dung-beetle) :- Germ. **webilaz*, f. **web-* move briskly (see WEAVE[2], or **web-* WEAVE[1]); cf. OE. *wibba* beetle, glowworm :- **webjon*. Continuity with OE. *wifel* is not shown, and the word may be due to commercial relations with the Low Countries.

weft weft threads that extend from side to side of a web)(*warp*. OE. *wefta*, *weft*, corr. to ON. *veptr*, *vipta*, weft, MHG. *wift* fine thread :- Germ. **wefton* **weftaz* **weftiz*, f. **web* WEAVE[1].

wegotism wī·gətizm obtrusive use of first person pl. XVIII. joc. f. WE and EGOTISM.

weigh wei A. bear, carry, lift (spec. raise an anchor XIV); B. balance in the scales; C. have heaviness or weight. OE. *weġan*, pt. *wæġ*, *wǣġon*, pp. *weġen* = OFris. *wega*, *weia* move, weigh, OS. *wegan* (Du. *wegen*) weigh, OHG. *wegan* move, shake, weigh (in G. *bewegen* move), ON. *vega* lift, weigh, Goth. **wigan* in pp. *gawigans* shaken :- CGerm. **wegan*, f. **weg-*, **wag-* **wǣg-* :- IE. **wegh-* **wogh-* **wēgh-* (see WAG[1], WAIN, WAY, WEY). So **weight** weit measurement or amount determined by weighing. The OE. form was *wiht*, more usu. *ġewiht*, corr. to OFris. *wicht*, MDu. *wicht*, *ghewichte*, MHG. *gewichte* (Du. *wicht*, *gewicht*, G. *gewicht*), ON. *vétt*, *vǽtt* :- Germ. *-weχtiz* and **gaweχtjam*, f. **weg-*, see -T[1]. This form was directly repr. by ME. *wiht*, *wiȝt*, *wight*, which was superseded by *weȝt*, *weght*, *weiht*, *weight*, appearing first in northerly texts (Ormulum, Cursor M). – ON. **weht*, *vétt*; the prevalence of this form was assisted by the phonology of WEIGH. Hence **wei·ghty**[1]. XV.

weir wiəɹ river-dam; enclosure for taking fish. OE. *wer*, corr. to OS *werr*, MLG., MHG. *wer*, *were* (LG. *wēr*, *wēre*, G. *wehr*), f. OE. *werian* defend = OFris. *wera*, OS. *werian*, OHG. *werian* (G. *wehren*), ON. *verja*, Goth. *warjan*. The present form derives from OE. obl. cases *were*, etc.; the pronunc. follows that of *shear*, *smear*, *spear*, and *mere*, but the spellings †*wier*, *weir* are aberrant; another development is repr. by dial. *wair*, *ware* (cf. *bear*, *mare*, *tear*, etc.).

weird wiəɹd (arch.) fate, lot, destiny, as in phr. *dree one's w.*, suffer one's fate. OE. *wyrd* = OS. *wurd*, OHG. *wurt*, ON. *urðr*, f. wk. grade of **werþ-* **warþ-* *wurþ-* become (see WORTH[3]). So adj. controlling the destinies of men XIV (*werde sister*); unaccountably mysterious, uncanny, odd XIX (Shelley, Keats). First in *w. sister*, one of (i) the Fates, (ii) the witches in Shakespeare's 'Macbeth', the later currency and adj. use being derived from its occurrence in the story of Macbeth. ¶ The normal development is repr. by ME. *wird*, which would have produced mod. wəːɹd; the present form depends on Nhb. ME. and MSc. vars. *wirid*, *werid*, *wērd*, *weird* (the *i* denoting length).

Welch var. of WELSH.

welcome we·lkəm used as voc. to express pleasure at a person's coming; hence in predicative and later (XVI) attrib. use. ME. *welcume* (XII), f. WELL[3] and *come* pp. as a rendering of (O)F. *bienvenu* (f. *bien* well, *venu* come) or ON. *velkominn* (i.e. 'well-come'), and in part repl. OE. *wilcuma* (corr. to MLG. *willekome*, OHG. *willicumo*), comp. of WILL[1] and *cuma* comer, agent-noun of *cuman* COME. So vb. greet with 'welcome', late OE. *wellcumian*, early ME. *welcume(n)*, repl. OE. *wilcumian*.

weld[1] weld plant yielding yellow dye, Reseda luteola; the dye itself. XIV (Ch.). Late ME. *welde*, also *wolde* (Promp. Parv.), repr. OE. **wealde*, **walde* = (M)LG. †*walde*, †*wolde*, *waude*, MDu. *woude* (Du. *wouw*, whence G. *wau*, †*waube*, Sw., Da. *vau*), poss. rel. to *weald*, *wald*, WOLD. ¶ The Germ. word is the source of F. *gaude*, Sp. *gualda*, Pg. *gualde*.

weld[2] weld intr. be joined by heating and hammering XVI; trans. join in this way XVII. var. of WELL[2], from XV in this sense, prob.

after Sw. *välle*; the *-d* appears to have come from the pt. and pp., as in *woold* (see O.E.D.).

welfare we·lfɛəɹ good fortune, well-being. XIV (RMannyng). f. phr. ME. *wel fare* (see WELL[3], FARE[1]), prob. after ON. *velferð*; cf. G. *wohlfahrt* (XVI), f. MHG. phr. *wol varn* live happily.

weli, wely we·li Mohammedan saint, tomb of a weli. XIX. – Arab. *welī*, var. of *walī* friend (of God), saint.

welk welk (dial.) wilt, wither. XIII. prob. of LDu. origin (cf. (M)LG., (M)Du. *welken*). ¶ Used by Trevisa, Gower, Spenser, and Milton.

welkin we·lkin †cloud OE.; (arch.) sky, firmament XII. OE. *weolcen*, *wolc(e)n*, corr. to OFris. *wolken*, *wulken*, OS. *wolkan*, OHG. *wolkan* (Du. *wolk*, G. *wolke*) :– CWGerm. word conn. by some with Balto-Sl. words (IE. **wolg-* **welg-* **wlg-*) meaning 'moist, damp'.

well[1] wel spring of water, pit dug to obtain a supply of spring water OE.; various transf. senses from XVII. OE. (Anglian) *wella*, *wælla*, **welle*, **well* (WS. **wiella*, late *willa*, *wylla*, *wylle*, *will*, *wyll*), corr. to OHG. *wella* (G. *welle*) wave, ON. *vella* boiling heat, ebullition, f. Germ. **wall-*; see WELL[2].

well[2] wel †boil, melt OE.; (dial.) weld XV; rise *up* to the eyes XIV (Ch.). OE. redupl. str. vb. *weallan*, pt. *wēoll*, pp. *ġeweallen* (mod. dial. *wall*) = OFris. *walla*, OS. *wallan*, OHG. *wallan* (G. *wallen* boil, swarm) :– WGerm. **wallan*, a parallel syn. of which, **wellan*, is repr. by ON. *vella*, MHG. *wellen*, cf. WELL[1].

well[3] wel in a good manner, to a good extent, fully (from the earliest times one of the commonest advs. of commendation, with derivative colloq. uses of modified force). OE. *wel(l)* = OFris., OS. (Du.) *wel*, ON. *vel*; also with advb. suffix (and vowel-variation) OS. *wela*, *wala*, *wola*, OHG. *wela*, *wola* (G. *wohl*), Goth. *waila*; prob. f. IE. *wel-* *wol-* WILL[2]. Cf. WEAL[1]. As adj. †happy, fortunate XIII; prosperous (now only in *well to do*, *well off*, formerly †*well to live*) XIV (Ch.); in sound health XVI; orig. developed from the adv. in impers. uses, e.g. *wel is þe* (cf. L. *bene est tibi*, and similar features of *woe*). comp. **well-wi·sh**ER[1] XVI, repl. earlier *well-willer* (XV), modelled on *well-willing* (OE. *welwillende*, cf. Du. *welwillend*), †*well-willy* (XIV, Ch.), †*well-willed* (Trevisa), after L. *benevolus*, *benevolēns* BENEVOLENT.

welladay weladei· excl. of lamentation. XVI. alt., by substitution of *day* or *aday* as used in *wo worth the day* and *lackaday*, of **wellaway** welawei·, ME. *weleaway*, earlier *welawei*, *wailawai*, OE. *weġ lā weġ*, var. of *wā lā wā*, whence ME. *walawa*, *wolowo*, *welawo*, f. WOE and LO, infl. by ON. *vei* WOE and WELL[3].

Wellington we·liŋtən short for *W. boot*, *coat*, etc., named after Arthur, first duke of *Wellington* (1769–1852). XIX. So **Welling-ton**IA[1] weliŋtou·niə large coniferous tree, Sequoia (W.) gigantea, native of California, so named by Lindley.

well off wel ɔ̀f favourably or fortunately situated. XVIII. f. phr. *come* (etc.) *well off* be prosperously circumstanced in the event; see WELL[3], OFF.

welsh welʃ swindle out of money laid as a bet. XIX. Hence **we·lsh**ER[1]. XIX. Of unkn. origin.

Welsh welʃ pert. to the native British population as opp. to the Anglo-Saxons, (hence) pert. to Wales. OE. (Anglian, Kentish) *Wēlisċ*, *Wǣlisċ*, (WS.) *Wīlisċ*, *Wȳlisċ*, **Wīelisċ*, corr. to OHG. *wal(a)hisc*, *walesc* (G. *wälsch*, *welsch*), Roman, Italian, French, Du. *waalsch* WALLOON, ON. *valskr* Gaulish, French; f. OE. *Walh*, *Wealh*, corr. to OHG. *Wal(a)h*, ON. **Valr*, pl. *Valir* :– Germ. **walχaz* foreign (Celtic or Roman), pl. *-ōs* – L. *Volcæ* name of a Celtic people, of unkn. origin. Cf. WALACH, VLACH. The two Anglian and Kentish OE. forms co-existed till XVI, after which *Welsh* became the only form in gen. use, *Walsh* surviving as a surname; the pl. of *wealh*, *Wēalas*, is repr. by *Wales* and *Cornwall*; the var. *Welch* is retained in the titles of regiments. ¶ AN. var. *waleis* remains as the personal name *Wallace*.

Welsh rabbit welʃ ræ·bit dish of toasted cheese. XVIII. ¶ Perverted without justification to *Welsh rarebit* (XVIII; Grose 1785).

welt welt in shoemaking, strip of leather placed between the edge of the sole and the upper XV; border, hem; ridge, raised stripe XVI. The co-existence of forms *walt* and *welt* suggests OE. **wealt*, with Anglian var. **wælt*, but the ult. origin is unknown.

welter we·ltəɹ roll about (in various ways). XIII = MLG., MDu. *welteren* = MHG. *welzern*, frequent. f. **welt-* **walt-* roll, be unsteady, repr. also by OE. **wealt* (in *un|wealt* steady), *-wæltan*, **wieltan*, *wyltan*, OHG. *walzan*, *welzen* (G. *wälzen*, WALTZ), ON. **welta* intr. str. and trans. wk. (Icel. *velta*, also *välta*, Da. *vælte*), Goth. *waltjan*; cf. ME. *walten* (XIII), dial. *walt* and see -EN[5]. Hence **we·lter** sb. turmoil XVI, rolling of the sea; heavy-weight horseman or pugilist XIX (whence *w. weight*).

wen wen morbid lump on the body; (in mod. use) sebaceous tumour under the skin. OE. *wen(n)*, *wæn(n)* = Du. *wen*, WFlem. *wan*, prob. rel. to MLG. *wene*, LG. *wehne*, *wähne* tumour, wart; of unkn. origin.

wench wentʃ young woman, girl XIII; (arch.) wanton woman; maidservant XIV. ME. *wenche*, clipped form of *wenchel*, OE. *wenċel* :– **waŋkil-*, perh. rel. to *wancol* (dial.

wankle) unsteady, inconstant, f. **waŋk-* waver, falter, repr. by OHG. *wankōn* (G. †*wanken*). ¶ For the loss of final syll. cf. EVE, GAME[1], MUCH.

wend wend turn (trans. and intr. in many senses), go. OE. *wendan* = OFris. *wenda*, OS. *wendian*, OHG. *wentan* (MDu., Du., MHG., G. *wenden*), ON. *venda*, Goth. (and CGerm.) *wandjan*, causative of **windan* WIND[2]. Cf. WANDER. From *c.*1500 the new formation *wended* has prevailed for pt. and pp. in the trans. senses, and *went*, regularly evolved from OE. *wende*, *ġewend*, has repl. the older pts. belonging to GO.

Wend wend member of a Slavonic race formerly extending over N. Germany. XVIII. – G. *Wende*, pl. *Wenden* (= OE. *Winedas*, *Weonod|land*, OHG. *Winida*, ON. *Vindr*), of unkn. origin. So **We·nd**ISH[1]. XVII.

Wensleydale we·nzlideil name of a district of the North Riding of Yorkshire designating a long-woolled breed of sheep and a variety of blue-mould cheese.

went pt. of WEND functioning since *c.*1500 as pt. of GO.

wept pt. of WEEP.

were wɛəɹ, wə̄ɹ, wə see BE.

werewolf wiə·ɹwulf, **werwolf** wə̄·ɹwulf person transformed or capable of transforming himself into a wolf. Late OE. *werewulf* (once) = LG. *werwulf*, (M)Du. *weerwolf*, MHG. *werwolf* (G. *wer-*, *wehrwolf*); cf. WFris. *waerūl*, *warūle*, Norw., Da. *varulv*, Sw. *varulf*, the latter perh. repr. ON. **varulfr*, whence ONF. *garwall* (Marie de France), later *garoul* (in modF. *loup-garou*). The first el. is doubtful, but it has been identified with OE. *wer* (= L. *vir*) man. After the ME. period chiefly Sc. until its revival through folklore studies (XIX).

werf werf homestead or space surrounding a S. African farm. XIX. Older and dial. Du. *werf* = LG. *warf* orig. raised plot on which a house is built (identical with WHARF).

wergeld, -gild wə̄·ɹgeld, -gild (hist.) price set upon a man according to rank. OE. *werġeld*, WS. *-ġild*, in early Sc. *weregeheld* (XIII), *wargeld*, *weregylt* (XV), in AL. *weregildum*, *-us* (XII–XIV); f. *wer* man, of CGerm. range and = L. *vir*, OIr. *fer*, W. *gŵr*+*ġield* YIELD. ¶ The OE. forms were taken up by antiquaries in XVII.

werowance we·rowàns (hist.) chief of the Indians of Virginia and Maryland. XVI. Algonquian.

wert arch. or obs. 2nd pers. sg. pt. of BE.

Wesleyan we·sliən, we·z-, wezlī·ən XVIII. pert. to John *Wesley* (1703–1791), originator of METHODISM; see -AN.

west west in or to the quarter of the horizon where the sun sets. OE. *west* = OFris., OS., OHG. (Du., G.) *west*, ON. *vestr* :- CGerm. (exc. Gothic) **westaz*, f. IE. **wes-*, repr. also in Gr. *hésperos*, L. *vesper* :- **wesperos*, with poss. connexions in Celtic, Balto-Sl. and Arm. Hence **west** sb. XII, adj. XIV (anticipated by OE. comps. such as *westdǣl* west part, *westwind*). Cf. ON. *vestri* more westerly, *vestastr* most westerly. Cf. dial. *wester*.

we·sterly adj. XVI; adv. XVII; see -LY[1], -LY[2]; cf. ON. *vestarliga* towards the west.

we·stern late OE. *westerne*; cf. OS., OHG. *westrōni*, ON. *vestrœnn*.

we·stWARD XIII, -WARDS XVI. OE. *westweard*, *-weardes*. Cf. MLG. *westwart*, Du. *westwaards*, G. *westwärts*.

wet wet containing moisture, made moist or damp. From XIV repr. pp. of the vb. *wet*, repl. *wēt* (mod. dial. *weet*) in standard Eng., from OE. *wǣt*, *wēt* = OFris. *wēt*, ON. *vátr* (repr. by ME. *wate*, *wote*), a word of the Anglo-Frisian and Scand. groups, based on the lengthened stem of WATER. So sb. and vb., with shortening of vowel of OE. *wǣt*, *wǣtan*, ME. *weet(e)*.

wether we·ðəɹ male sheep, ram. OE. *weþer* = OFris. **wether* (so NFris.), OS. *withar* (Du. *weer*), OHG. *widar* (G. *widder*), ON. *veðr* ram, Goth. *wiþrus* lamb :- CGerm. **weþruz*, of disputed origin (perh. basically 'yearling', rel. to Gr. ϝέτος year).

wey wei standard of dry-goods weight. OE. *wǣġ*, *wǣġe* balance, weight = OS., OHG. *wāga* (Du. *waag*, G. *wage*), ON. *vág* :- CGerm. (exc. Goth.) **wǣgō -ōn*, f. **wǣg-* **weg-* WEIGH.

Weymouth wei·məþ *W. pine*, American white pine, Pinus Strobus, extensively planted in England 1705 by the first Lord Weymouth. XVIII.

wh- repr. primarily OE. *hw-*, which was succeeded partly by *w* (sporadically at least until mod. times) and partly by *wh* (†Sc. *quh-*), which was used systematically in the 'Ormulum'. Pronunciation as an unvoiced w varying with a voiced w, acc. to local or individual custom, e.g. in the considerable series of interrog.-relative words *what*, etc., is denoted in this dictionary by ʍ. OE. *hw-* corr. to OFris. *(h)w-*, (M)LG., (M)Du. *w-*, OHG. *(h)w-* (G. *w-*), ON. *hv-*, Goth. *hw-* :- CGerm. **χw-*. Assoc. with whistling or rushing noise has led to the prevalence of *wh-* in such words as *whip* and *whisk*; repr. orig. *h* it is standardized in *whole* and *whore*, and is an alternative in *whoop/hoop*.

whack ʍæk vigorous resounding blow. XVIII. First recorded in Sc.; perh. alt. of THWACK. Also Sc. as vb. Cf. Sc. *whang*, var. of *thwang* THONG.

whale ʍeil large fish-like marine animal of the order Cetacea. OE. *hwæl* = OHG. *wal* (in modG. *walfisch*), ON. *hvalr*, rel. to OHG. *walira*, MHG., G. *wels* (:– **χwalis*) sheath-fish; cf. OPruss. *kalis*. The present form reflects obl. cases of OE. *hwæl*, which is itself repr. by †*whall* (XIV–XVII), and is parallel to *all*, *awl*, *small*. comp. **wha·le**-BONE elastic bony substance of the upper jaw of whales XVII; †*whalës bone* ivory from the walrus or a similar animal confused with the whale XIII.

whangee ʍæŋgī· cane made from bamboo-like plants. XIX. f. Chinese *huang* bamboo sprouts too old for eating.

wharf ʍɔ̄ɹf structure of timber, etc. built along the water's edge. Late OE. *hwearf*, *w*(*e*)*arf* (earlier in poet. comp. *merewhearf* seashore), corr. to MLG. *warf*, *werf* mole, dam, wharf (whence Du. *werf* shipyard, G. *werft* wharf, shipyard); f. Germ. **χwerƀ*-, **χwarƀ*- repr. also by a series of vbs. having the meanings turn, change, wander, be active, proceed, go.

wharfinger ʍɔ̄·ɹfindʒəɹ owner or keeper of a wharf. XVI. alt. (cf. HARBINGER) of **wharfag*ER[1], f. **wha·rf**AGE provision of, charge for use of, a wharf. XV (in AL. *wharfagium* XIII–XIV).

what ʍɔt n. of interrog. pron. OE.; interrog. adj. XII (from OE. use of *hwæt* with partitive g.; as excl. OE.; as relative XII; as indefinite (*somewhat*) XIII. OE. *hwæt* = OFris. *hwet*, OS. *huat* (Du. *wat*), OHG. *hwaz*, *waz* (G. *was*), ON. *hvat*, Goth. *hwa* :– CGerm. **χwat* :– IE. **q*ʷ*od* (cf. L. *quod*), n. of **q*ʷ*os* WHO. In phrasal comps. **what d'ye call it**. ʍɔ(t)djəkōlit, wɔ·(t)dʒ- XVI (*whatchicalt*), also **her, him, 'm. what not** anything whatever XVI; article of furniture for holding odds and ends XIX; **what's-his-name** XVII (Dryden). Hence **what**E·VER XIV. **wha·tso** (arch.) XII (Orm), **what**SOE·VER. XIII = (dial.) **whatsome·ver** XIII.

wheal ʍīl var. of WALE due to assoc. with †*wheal* suppurate, OE. *hwelian*, rel. to **hwele*, ME. *whele* pustule, and OE. *hwylca*, arch. or dial. *whelk*.

wheat ʍīt (grain of) the cereal so named, esp. Triticum vulgare. OE. *hwǣte* = OS. *hwēti* (Du. *weit*), OHG. *weizi* (also *weizzi*, whence G. *weizen*), ON. *hveiti*, Goth. *hwaiteis* :– CGerm. **χvaitjaz*, f. var. of **χwīt*- WHITE. Hence **whea·t**EN[4]. OE. *hwǣten*.

wheatear ʍī·tiəɹ small passerine bird, Saxicola œnanthe. XVI. Lack of earlier evidence leaves the origin in doubt, but the dial. syns. *whiteass*, *white rump*, *white-tail* (†*whittaile* Cotgr. 1611 glossing F. *cul-blanc*, dial. *wittol*), Du. *witstaart*, G. *weiss-schwanz*, F. *culblanc* 'white tail', 'white rump', suggest that †*wheatears* (XVII) is for **whiteeres* 'white ARSE'; the present form being inferred as a sg. of *wheatears*, in which the first syll. had been assim. to WHEAT.

wheedle ʍī·dl entice or persuade by cajolery XVII. 'A late word of fancy' (Blount 'Glossographia' 1661), by which is prob. meant a canting term; perh. – G. *wedeln* fawn (upon), cringe or crouch (to), f. *wedel* tail, fan (OHG. *wedil*), f. **wa*-, **wē*- blow, wave (cf. WIND[1]) + **þla*- suffix of instrument.

wheel ʍīl circular frame, often spoked, revolving on an axis. OE. *hwēol*, *hweogol*, *hweowol* = (M)LG. *wēl*, (M)Du. *wiel*, ON. *hjól*, *hvél* :– Germ. (exc. Gothic) **χwe*(*g*)*ula*, **χweχula* :– IE. **q*ʷ*eq*ʷ*lo*-, repr. by Skr. *ca-krá*- circle, wheel (cf. *chukka*, *chukker* (Polo)), Gr. *kúklos* CYCLE: redupl. of **q*ʷ*elo*-, **q*ʷ*olo*- move around, (hence) be occupied with, repr. by Gr. *pólos* axis, POLE[2], L. *colus* distaff, *colere* cultivate, inhabit, *in|cola* inhabitant, *in|quil|inus* sojourner, *agri|cola* farmer (cf. COLONY, CULTURE), Gr. *pélesthai* be in motion, Skr. *cárati* moves, Tokh. *kokale* wheel. Hence **wheel** vb. intr. XIII (AncrR.), trans. XIV (Ch.). **whee·l**ER[1] wheelwright XV, **whee·l**-WRIGHT XIII.

wheeze ʍīz breathe hard with a whistling sound. XV. prob. – ON. *hvæsa* hiss; or imit.

whelk ʍelk mollusc of the genus Buccinum. OE. *weoloc*, *wioloc*; cf. WFlem. *willok*, *wullok*, OF. *willo*. The sp. with *wh*- (XV) is perh. due to assoc. with *whelk* pustule, pimple: see WHEAL.

whelm ʍelm †capsize XIII; (dial.) turn upside down XIV; (arch.) engulf, OVERWHELM XV. repr. OE. **hwielman*, **hwelman*, parallel to OE. *hwylfan*, **hwielfan*, (dial.) *whelve* = OS. *bi|hwelƀian* cover over, OHG. *welben* (G. *wölben*) vault, ON. *hvelfa*, f. **χwalƀ*-, whence also OE. *hwealf* sb. arch, adj. vaulted, OHG. *walbe* curved object, ON. *hvalf* concavity, related further to Goth. *hwilftrjom* (dat. pl.) coffin, Gr. *kólpos* bosom. A metathetic form *whemmel* (XVI) is Sc. and north. dial.

whelp ʍelp young of the dog and other animals. OE. *hwelp* = OS. *hwelp* (Du. *welp*), OHG. *hwelf*, (also mod.) *welf*, ON. *hvelpr*; a CGerm. word (exc. in Gothic) of which no cogns. are known. Hence **whelp** vb. bring forth young. XII (Orm).

when ʍen at what time (?). OE. *hwenne*, *hwænne*, beside *hwanne*, *hwonne* when (interrog. and relative), corr. to OFris. *hwanne*, *hwenne* until, if, OS. *hwan*(*na*) when, at some time, when, MDu. *wen*, *wan* surviving in Du. *wanneer* = OS. *hwan ēr* as soon as, OHG. *wenne*, *wanne* (G. *wenn* if, *wann* when), Goth. *hwan* when, how :– CGerm. (exc. in Scand.), advb. deriv. of the interrog. base **χwa*- WHO, WHAT; as THEN, THAN of the demons. **þa*- THE, THAT; cf. Av. *kəm* how, L. *quom*, *cum* when, OIr. *can*, W. *pan* when. Monosyll. forms appear XIII; the var. *whon* survives till XV, *whan* till XVI. So **whence** ʍens from what place. XIII. ME. *whannes*, *whennes*, f. *whanne*, *whenne*, OE. *hwanon*(*e*), = OS. *hwanan*(*a*), OHG. (*h*)*wanana*, (*h*)*wanān*; cf. HENCE, THENCE. **whe·n**SO XII, **whenso**E·VER XIV.

where ʍɛəɹ in what place (?). OE. *hwǣr*, beside *hwăr* and *hwăra*, corr. to OFris. *hwēr*, OS. *hwār* (Du. *waar*), OHG. (*h*)*wār*, *wā* (G. *wo*; *wār*, surviving in *warum* why), ON. *hvar*, Goth. *hwar*; CGerm. derivs. (monosyll. or disyll., with long or short stem vowel) of **χwa-* WHO, WHAT, as HERE is of **χi-* HE[1] and THERE of **þa-* THE[1]; cf. L. *cūr* why, W. *pyr* why. The earliest comps. with preps. are **where**A·T, **where**BY·, **where**I·N, †**wheremid**, **where**O·F, **where**THROU·GH, **where**UPO·N, **where**WI·TH; later are **where**U·NTO, **where**WITHA·L (XVI).

wherefor ʍɛə·ɹfōɹ for what purpose or cause XII; for which XII; (now **-fore**) on what account XIII; sb. cause, reason XVI (Sh.).

wherry ʍe·ri light rowing-boat for transport XV; barge XVI. Of unkn. origin.

whet ʍet sharpen (also fig.). OE. *hwettan* = (M)LG., (M)Du. *wetten*, OHG. *wezzan* (G. *wetzen*), ON. *hvetja* :- Germ. **χwatjan*, f. **χwattaz* sharp (OE. *hwæt* quick, active, brave, OS. *hwat* keen, bold, OHG. (*h*)*waz* sharp, rough, severe, ON. *hvatr* bold, vigorous), f. a base assumed to be cogn. with L. *tri|quetrus* triangular. comp. **whe·t**STONE OE. *hwetstān* = (M)Du. *wetsteen*, OHG. *wez*(*z*)*estein* (G. *wetzstein*).

whether ʍe·ðəɹ pron. and adj. which of the two; conj. introducing a question expressing choice between alternatives. OE. *hweþer*, beside *hwæþer*, corr. to OFris. *hwed*(*d*)*er*, OS. *hweðar*, OHG. (*h*)*wedar* (surviving in G. *weder* neither), ON. *hvaðarr*, Goth. *hwaþar* :- CGerm. **χwa-*, **χweþaraz*, f. **χwa-*, **χwe-* WHO + compar. suffix as in OTHER; cf. Skr. *katarás*, Gr. *póteros*, Lith. *katràs*, which of the two.

whew ʍjū excl. of astonishment, dismay, etc. XVI (Sh.), prob. intended to repr. a whistling sound. The earlier *quhewe* (XV, Wyntoun) may be a separate word rel. immed. to north. *quhew*, *qwe*, *whewe* (XIV) pipe, whistling sound, *whewe* vb. (XV) pipe.

whey ʍei watery part of milk remaining after the curd is separated. OE. *hwæġ*, *hweġ* = OFris. **wei* (WFris. *waei*, etc.), MDu. *wey* (Du. *wei*) :- Anglo-Frisian and LG. **χwaja-*, rel. by gradation to MLG. *huy*, *hoie*, Du. *hui* :- **χwuja-*.

which ʍitʃ †of what kind?; †what?; what one? OE.; as rel. adj. pron. XII. OE. *hwilċ* = OS. (*h*)*wilik*, MLG., MDu. *wilk*, ON. *hvílikr*, corr. with a different grade to OE. *hwelċ* = OFris. *hwel*(*i*)*k*, MDu. *wel*(*i*)*c*, *walc*, OHG. *hwelīh*, Goth. *hvileiks*; CGerm. formation on **χwa-* **χwe-* (see WHO) and **lika-* body, form; see LICH and cf. EACH, SUCH. Hence **which**E·VER XIV (Wycl. Bible). **which**SOE·VER. XV.

whidah, whydah ʍi·da name of a town in Dahomey, W. Africa, applied spec. to animals found in this locality; *w. bird* (XVIII), alt. of *widow-bird*, which is based on L. generic name *Vidua* 'widow' = F. *veuve* (Brisson, 1760), Pg. *viuva*, the bird being so called from the prevailingly black plumage and long train of tail feathers of the male.

whiff ʍif A. slight puff or gust; inhalation of tobacco-smoke XVI; wave or waft of odour XVII; puffing or whistling sound XVIII; B. flag hoisted as a signal XVII; C. light outrigger XIX. Late XVI, of imit. formation. Hence vb. XVI.

whiffler ʍi·fləɹ attendant armed with a weapon to keep the way clear for a procession, etc. XVI. f. *wifle* javelin, battle-axe, OE. *wifel*, f. Germ. **wiƀ* (cf. ON. *vifr* sword) :- IE. **wip-* wave, swing; see -ER[1].

whig ʍig †yokel; adherent of the Presbyterian cause in Scotland (esp. one of the rebellious covenanters who marched on Edinburgh in 1648); exclusioner (opposing succession of James, duke of York) XVII; from 1689, one of the two great political parties in England)(*Tory*. prob. shortening of Sc. *whiggamaire*, *-mer*, *wiggomer* (used in the second sense, the expedition being called 'the whiggamore raid'), f. *whig* drive + *mere* MARE[1].

while ʍail time (now chiefly in phr. *a good*, *great* (etc.) *while*, *a while* for a certain or some time, cf. MEANWHILE, *between whiles* at intervals of time); as conj. (XII), shortening of ME. *þe while þat*, in OE. *þā hwīle þe* during the time that = OHG. *dia wīla sō* so long as (G. *dieweil* whilst, whereas; cf. Du. *dewijl*, G. *weil* because), based on accus. of OE. *hwīl* = OFris. *hwīle*, OS. *hwīl*(*a*) time, OHG. (*h*)*wīla* point or period of time (G. *weile*, Du. *wijl*), ON. *hvíla* bed, Goth. *hweila* time :- CGerm. **χwīlō*. The base is IE. **qwi-*, repr. also by L. *quiēt-* QUIET, *tranquillus* (:- *-*quilnos*) TRANQUIL (for the sense cf. ON. *hvíla*, *hvíld* rest, repose). Cf. EREWHILE, ERSTWHILE. So **whilom** ʍai·ləm †at times OE.; (arch.) at some time past XII. OE. *hwīlum* (d. pl. of *hwīl*) = OS. *hwīlon* (MLG., MDu. *wīlem* formerly; Du. *wijlen* late, deceased), OHG. *hwīlōm*, *wīlōn* (cf. G. *weiland* of old). **whilst** ʍailst alt., with parasitic *t* (as in *amidst*, *amongst*), of †*whiles*, formed with advb. -s on the sb. and used finally (XIII) as conj. like *while*.

whim ʍim A. †pun, play on words; †fanciful creation; odd fancy XVII; machine for raising ore, etc. from a mine XVIII. Synonyms are (1) **whims(e)y** ʍi·mzi XVII (B. Jonson), whence **whi·msical** XVII, and (2) **whim-wham** ʍi·mʍæm XVI (Skelton) redupl. formation with vowel-variation resembling that in *flim-flam*, *jim-jam*, *trim-tram*; the origin is unkn.

whimbrel ʍi·mbrəl curlew. XVI (*whympernell*). f. (dial.) *whimp* (XVI) or WHIMPER, on account of the bird's cry; for the ending cf. *dotterel* (plover).

whimper ʍi·mpəɹ utter a feeble broken cry. XVI (Douglas, More). Extension of (dial.) *whimp* (XVI), of echoic origin; see -ER[4].

whin ʍin furze, gorse. XI. prob. of Scand. origin; cf. Sw. *hven*, ODa. *hvine*, *hvinegræs*, *-strå*, Norw. *hvine*, applied to certain grasses. First recorded in place-names of Scandinavianized areas: *Wineberga* (Domesday Book), *Quyneberge* Whinburgh in Norfolk, *Wynfel*, *Quynfel* Whinfell in Cumberland. Hence **whi·nchat** bird allied to the stonechat, also called *furze-chat*, *gorse-chat* XVII.

whine ʍain utter a low somewhat shrill protracted sound. OE. *hwīnan* (once of the droning flight of an arrow); ME. *hwyne*, *whyne* of persons, complain querulously XVI. An immed. cogn. is ON. *hvína* whiz, whistle in the air; a wk. grade of the imit. base is repr. by ON. *hvinr* whizzing, late OE. *hwinsian* (whence dial. *whinge* whine) = OHG. *win(i)sōn* (whence G. *winseln*) :- Germ. **χwinisōjan*.

whinny ʍi·ni neigh. XVI. Of imit. origin (cf. L. *hinnīre*); syns. were *whine* (XIV) and *whrinny* (XV).

whinyard ʍi·njəɹd short sword, hanger. XV. Early forms are *whyneherd*, *whyn(e)ard*, of obscure formation; for the ending cf. *daggard* (DAGGER), *poniard*. The Sc. form is **whinger** ʍi·ŋ(g)əɹ XVI; hence Gaelic *cuinnsear*.

whip ʍip move briskly XIII; strike with a whip XIV; overlay with cord, thread, etc. XV. ME. *(h)wippen*, prob. - (M)LG., (M)Du. *wippen* swing, vacillate, leap (= MHG. *wipfen* dance), f. Germ. **wip-* move quickly, repr. also in (M)LG. *wipgalge*, Du. *wipgalg* strappado, Du. *wipbrug* drawbridge, *wipplank* see-saw, *wipstaart* wagtail, OHG. *wipfil* (G. *wipfel*) tree-top, and in Goth. *wipja* crown, which appears to exemplify a sense 'wind or bind round', more extensively shown by the var. **waip-* **weip-*, as in Goth. *waips* wreath, crown, *weipan* (vb.) crown, ON. *veipr* head-dress, OHG. *weif* bandage (see also WIPE). So **whip** sb. instrument of flagellation XIV; †brisk movement XVI; cf. (M)LG. *wippe*, *wip* quick movement, moment of time, lift for hoisting, lever = Du. *wip* see-saw, strappado, OHG. *wipf* quick movement. Chronological relations and sense-developments are obscure; the form with *wh* was presumably finally adopted as being symbolically appropriate as in WHISK.

whipper-snapper ʍi·pəɹsnæpəɹ sprightly insignificant but young person. XVII. orig. a canting term for a 'rough'; prob. based on *whipster* (XVI) 'cracker of whips', lively, violent, or mischievous person, also insignificant fellow, and *snipper-snapper* (XVI).

whippet ʍi·pit †lively young woman XVI; small breed of dog XVII. prob. f. †*whippet* vb. move briskly (XVI 'skyp or whyppyt about', Palsgr.), i.e. *whip it*, intr. use with *it* of WHIP vb. move nimbly.

whip-poor-will ʍi·puəɹwi·l species of goatsucker noted for its persistent call. XVIII. imit. of the bird's note; cf. *bobolink*, *katydid*, *mopoke*, *whip-tom-kelly*, *willet*, *wishtonwish*.

whirl ʍə̄ɹl move in a circle XIII; revolve or cause to revolve; move or cause to move swiftly XIV; hurl XV - ON. *hvirfla* turn about, rel. to *hvirfill* circle, ring, summit = (M)LG., (M)Du. *wervel* †whirlpool, †spindle, vertebra, OHG. *wirbil* whirlwind (G. *wirbel*) :- Germ. **χwerƀilaz*, f. **χwerƀ-* **χwarƀ-*.

whirlpool ʍə̄·ɹpūl circular eddy in a river, etc. XV. f. WHIRL + POOL; cf. OE. *hwyrfepōl*, *wirfelmere*.

whirlwind ʍə̄·ɹlwind rotating wind. XIV (Rolle). prob. - ON. *hvirfilvindr* (see WHIRL, WIND[1]), whence Du. *wervelwind*, G. *wirbelwind*.

whir(r) ʍə̄ɹ †fling, hurl; move swiftly with a vibratory sound XIV. prob. first of Scand. origin (cf. Da. *hvirre*, Norw. *kvirra*, Sw. dial. *hvirra*, which are perh. assim. forms of ON. **hvirfa*, repr. the base of *hvirfill*, *hvirfla* WHIRL); reinforced later by echoism.

whish[1] ʍiʃ int., vb. XVI. imit. of the sound made by something rushing through air or over water; hence sb. XIX.

whish[2] ʍiʃ synon. with WHIST[1]. XVI.

whisk ʍisk sb. (XIV Barbour) and vb. (XV, Henryson) denoting light rapid sweeping motion. orig. *wisk*, *wysk* (but *quhisk* as early as XV) and first in Sc. texts; - Scand. stem repr. by ON. *visk* wisp, Sw. *viska* besom, wisp, swab, *viska* whisk (off), sponge, Norw. *visk* wisp, cluster, pull, tug, Da. *viske* wipe, rub, sponge, corr. to (M)Du. *wisch* wisp, LG. *wisk* quick movement, OHG. *wisc* (G. *wisch*) wisp of hay, dishcloth, *wisken* (*wischen*) wipe, †move briskly, f. symbolic Germ. base **wisk-*, with development of initial *wh-* as in WHIP. Hence **whisk**ER[1] ʍi·skəɹ †fan, †switch, (dial.) feather brush XV; hair on the face, †moustache XVI; cf. Sw. *viskare* sponge, LG. *wisker* duster, G. *wischer* rubber, clout.

whisky[1], **whiskey** ʍi·ski spirituous liquor distilled from malted barley, etc. (*Scotch whisky*, *Irish whiskey*). XVIII. Shortening of *whiskybae*, var. of USQUEBAUGH (Gael. *uisgebeatha*).

whisky[2] ʍi·ski light carriage. XVIII. f. WHISK + -Y[1], so named from its swift motion.

whiskyjohn ʍi·skidʒən grey jay of Canada. XVIII. alt., with assim. to JOHN, of N. Amer. Indian name (Cree *wiskatjan*, Montagnais *wishkutshan*). Hence, by substitution of JACK, **whi·skyjack**. XVIII.

whisper ʍi·spəɹ speak softly under one's breath. OE. *hwisprian* = early Flem. *wisperen*, G. *wispern* (of LG. origin), f. Germ. imit. base **χwis-*, whence also synon. MLG., MDu. *wispelen*, OHG. *(h)wispalōn*

(G. *wispeln*), ON. *hvískra, hvísla*; cf. dial. *whister* (XIV), OE. *hwǣstrian*.

whist[1] ʌist excl. to call for silence. XIV (Wycl. Bible). Varying from XVI with *whisht*; cf. HIST, ST. Hence as adj. silent, hushed XV, as vb. become or †make silent XVI (Surrey, Wyatt).

whist[2] ʌist card-game. XVII. alt. of earlier XVII name *whisk*, perh. f. WHISK vb. from the action of whisking away the tricks; but, acc. to Cotton's 'The Complete Gamester', 1680, 'called Whist from the silence that is to be observed in the play', and so assoc. with prec.

whistle ʌi·sl sb. tubular wind instrument OE.; throat XIV (Ch.); act of whistling XV. OE. *hwistle, wistle* (also in *wuduhwistle* hemlock). So vb. OE. *hwistlian, wistlian*, corr. to ON. *hvísla* whisper, MSw. *hvisla*, Sw. *vissla* whistle, Da. *hvisle* hiss, of echoic origin.

whit[1] ʌit (arch.) very small or the least portion or amount. XV. Early mod. *whyt, wyt, whit(t)*, prob. modification of form of WIGHT[1], as in *any wight, no wight* (cf. AUGHT, NAUGHT); but the sp. *wh-* is unexpl. Now always in neg. context or in *every whit* (e.g. 1 Sam. iii. 18).

whit[2] ʌit int., sb., vb. imit. of a shrill abrupt sound. XIX. Cf. TU WHIT TU WHOO.

white ʌait the colour of fresh snow or common salt. OE. *hwīt* = OFris., OS. *hwīt*, OHG. *(h)wīz* (G. *weiss*), ON. *hvítr*, Goth. *hweits* :– Germ. **χwītaz*, of which a var. with short vowel in repr. by OFris. *hwit(t)*, (M)Du., (M)LG. *wit* :– **χwittaz* :– IE. **kwitnos, *kwidnos*, the base of which is found also in Skr. and Balto-Sl. words denoting brightness or light. phr. and comp. **whi·te**BAIT small fry of fish XVIII; **white friar** Carmelite XV; **whi·te-livered** cowardly (having, acc. to popular belief, a liver lacking bile or choler) XVI; **whi·te**SMITH worker in metal XIV; **whi·te**THORN hawthorn XIII; tr. L. *alba spina* (whence F. *aubépine*); **whi·te**THROAT warbler XVII (Grew); **whi·te**WASH, plaster with a white composition XVI; hence sb. XVII. Hence **white** vb. †become or make white OE.; whitewash XII. **whi·te**N[5] XIII; cf. ON. *hvítna*; superseding OE. *hwītian* = OHG. *wīzen*, Goth. *ga|hweitjan*. ¶ Shortening of the vowel is seen in the comps. *whitleather, whitlow, Whitsunday*, and many place-names.

whither ʌi·ðəɹ to what or which place. OE. *hwider*, f. Germ. **χwi-* (see WHICH); synon. Goth. *hwadrē* is f. **χwa-* (see WHO); for the suffix cf. HITHER, THITHER. Hence †**whi·ther**SO OE., **whi:ther**SOE·VER XIII.

whiting[1] ʌai·tiŋ fish of genus Merlangus. XV. – (M)Du. *wijting*; see WHITE, -ING[3], and cf. ON. *hvítingr* white whale, late OE. *hwītling* (perh.) whiting.

whiting[2] ʌai·tiŋ †whitewashing; finely powdered chalk as used for this XV. f. WHITE vb.+-ING[1].

whitleather ʌi·tle:ðəɹ whiteleather (XV) dressed with alum instead of being tanned. XIV. f. WHITE (with normal shortening).

whitlow ʌi·tlou inflammatory sore on finger or thumb. XIV. orig. *whitflaw, -flow*, i.e. WHITE+FLAW[1] breach, fissure; but the similarity of the first syll. to Du. *fijt*, †*vijt*, LG. *fit*, suggests a poss. alien origin; the alt. to *whitlow* (XV) and †*whitblow* (XVI) is not accounted for.

whitster ʌi·tstəɹ bleacher. XV (Promp. Parv.). f. WHITE+-STER.

Whit Sunday, Whitsunday ʌi·tsʌ·ndi, ʌi·tsəndei seventh Sunday after Easter Day, Pentecost. Late OE. *Hwīta Sunnandæġ* (extant only in obl. case *Hwītan S.*) 'White Sunday', so named prob. from the ancient custom of wearing white robes by the newly baptized at the Feast of Pentecost (cf. *Dominica in albis* 'Sunday in whites'; name of the First Sunday after Easter, so given for the same reason; MLG. *witsondach*, MDu. *wittensondagh* are also so applied). The normal shortening of the vowel of the first syll., by obscuring the composition of the word, led to various apprehensions of it, so that it has been differently divided, whence *Whitsun eve* and *week* (XIII) beside *Whit Monday* (XVI), etc. **Whi·tsun**TIDE ʌi·tsəntaid Whitsunday and the days immediately following. XIII. ¶ As the name of a Sc. term-day (15 May) *W.* has been long dissociated from the church festival.

whittle ʌi·tl cut thin slices from XVI; fig. XVIII. f. (dial.) *whittle* large knife (XV), var. of *thwi·ttle*, f. *thwite* (OE. *þwītan* shave off, cogn. with *ġeþwit* chip, ON. *þveita* small axe, *þveit(i)* cut-off piece).

Whitworth ʌi·twəɹþ name of a rifle invented by Sir Joseph *Whitworth* of Manchester (1854).

whiz(z) ʌiz make, or move with, a sound as of a body rushing through the air. XVI (Surrey). imit.

who hū what or which person?; used as relative pron. from XIII. ME. *hwo* (XII–XIII), *who* (from XIII), *hoo* (XIII–XV), repr. OE. *hwā̆*, corr. to OFris. *hwā̆*, OS. *hwē*, *hwie*, OHG. *(h)wer* (Du. *wie*, G. *wer*), OSw. *ho*, ODa. *hwa* (Da. *hvo*), Goth. *hwas* :– Germ. **χwaz *χwez* :– IE. **qwos *ques* (cf. Lith. *kàs*, Skr. *kás*), parallel to **qwi-* (cf. L. *quis*, OSl. *čĭto*, Ir. *čia*, W. *pwy*). Hence **who**·SO XII, **who**SOE·VER XIII, **who**SOME·VER XV. For the base types as repr. in derivs. see WHAT, WHEN, WHERE, WHETHER, WHICH, WHOM, WHOSE. ¶ For the pronunc. cf. TWO.

whoa wou call to a horse to stop. XIX. var. of *who* (XV), var. of HO; preceded by †*whoa ho* call from a distance XVII.

whole houl in good or sound condition; not divided into parts OE.; sb. *the* complete amount XIV; a combination of parts XVII. OE. *hāl* (and *ġehāl*) = OFris., OS. *hēl* (Du. *heel* and *geheel*), (O)HG. *heil*, ON. *heill*, Goth. *hails*, *gahails* (also *unhails* sick) :- CGerm. **(ga)χailaz* :- IE. **qoilos* (repr. also in Balto-Sl.). For other connexions see HAIL[2], HALE[1], HEAL. **who·le**SALE first in phr. *by w.*, †*by the w.*)(*by retail.* XV **who·le**SOME[1] conducive to well-being XII. prob. OE. **hālsum*, with Germ. parallels. **whol**LY[2] hou·lli, hou·li to the full or complete extent, in full. OE. **hālliċe*, the normal descendant of which was *holliche* (whence dial. *holly*), in which *ō* was substituted by influence of the adj., whence the standard pronunc.; the simplification of *ll* is shown in sp. XIV; cf. †*fouly*, †*soly*. ¶ The sp. with *wh-*, corr. to a widespread dial. pronunc. with w, appeared in XVI.

whom hūm accusative-dative of WHO. OE. *hwām*, late var. of *hwǣm*, d. of *hwā* WHO, *hwæt* WHAT; in its later uses *whom* combined the functions of OE. *hwone*, *hwane*, accus. sg. of *hwā* and of the dative OE. *hwǣm* = OFris. *hwām*, OS. *hwem(u)*, OHG. *hwemu*. Hence (synon.) **whom**E·VER XIV, **who·m**SO XII, **whom**SOE·VER XV.

whoop hūp shout, hollo XIV. imit.; so sb. XVI. Hence **whoo·p**ER[1] whistling swan, Cygnus musicus XVII. **whoo·ping-cough,** cough accompanied by a sound like 'whoop' XVIII.

whoopee hūpī·, ʍu·pi excl. accompanying riotous enjoyment; orig. U.S. XIX.

whoosh ʍūʃ imit. of a sibilant sound as of something rushing through the air. XIX (Dickens).

whop ʍɔp cast or pull violently XIV; strike heavily XVI. var. of *wap* (XIV), of echoic origin. **who·pp**ING[2] that is a whopper XVII. Hence **who·pp**ER[1] uncommonly large one XVIII (Grose).

whore hōəɹ prostitute. Late OE. *hōre*, corr. to (M)LG. *hore*, MDu. *hoere* (Du. *hoer*), OHG. *huora* (G. *hure*), ON. *hóra* :- Germ. **χōrōn*, f. base repr. also by ON. *hórr*, Goth. *hors* adulterer; the IE. base **qār-* appears in L. *cārus*, OIr. *cara* friend, *caraim* I love. Hence **who·re**DOM. XII. prob. – ON. *hórdómr* = OFris. *hōrdōm*. comp. **who·re**MASTER. XVI (Dunbar). **who·re**MONGER. XVI (Tindale), *-monging* (Coverdale), **who·re**SON bastard, term of abuse XIII. Hence vb. XVI. For *wh-* cf. WHOLE. The normally developed pronunc. huəɹ remains in local use.

whorl ʍɔ̄ɹl, ʍə̄ɹl small fly-wheel or pulley in a spinning machine XV; ring of leaves, etc. round a stem XVI. Earliest forms *wharwyl*, *whorwhil*, of E. Anglian or north. provenance; prob. vars. of *wherwille*, WHIRL, infl. by †*wharve* turn (cf. WHARF) and Du. †*worvel*, var. of *wervel*.

whortleberry ʍə̄·ɹtlberi (fruit of) shrub Vaccinium Myrtillus. XVI (Lyte, a Somerset man). s.w. dial. var. of *hurtleberry*, as (dial.) *whort* (Lyte) is of *hurt*, which is of unkn. origin; for the sp. with *wh-* cf. (dial.) *whoam* home, WHOLE, WHORE.

whose hūz g. of *who* and *what*. Early ME. *hwās*, *hwōs* (XII–XIII), alt., by assim. to *hwā*, *hwō* WHO, of *hwas*, *hwes*, OE. *hwæs* g. of m. *hwă* and *hwæt* WHAT, in interrog. use only :- **χwasa*, beside which are monosyll. OS. *hwes*, OHG. *(h)wes* (Du., G. *wes*), ON. *hves(s)*, Goth. *hwis* :- **χwesa* :- IE. *qʷheso*, repr. also by Gr. *téo* (:- **téso*), OSl. *česo*. Hence **whose**SOE·VER XVII (A.V.). Cf. WHOM.

why ʍai for what reason or purpose (?); int. as a note of surprise or calling attention XVI. OE. *hwī*, *hwȳ*, instr. case of *hwæt* WHAT, governed by *tō* or *for* (whence †*forwhy* why, because), or simply as adv., corr. to OS. *hwī*, ON. *hví* :- Germ. **χwī* :- IE. **qʷei*, loc. of **qwo-* WHO, WHAT (cf. Doric Gr. *peî* where).

wick[1] wik bundle of fibre by which a flame is kept supplied with fat. OE. *wēoc* (in *candelwēoc*), *wēoce*, corr. to MDu. *wiecke* (Du. *wiek*), MLG. *wēke*, OHG. *wiohha* (G. *wieche*), of unkn. origin. ¶ For the vocalism cf. SICK.

wick[2] wik †dwelling; (dial.) town, hamlet OE.; farm XI. OE. *wīc* = OFris. *wik*, OS. *wīc* (Du. *wijk* quarter, district, ward), OHG. *wīh* (G. in *weichbild* municipal area), Goth. *weihs*. prob. Germ. – L. *vīcus* row of houses, quarter of a town, street, village, cogn. with Gr. *oîkos* house. ¶ Survives locally in place-names (the distribution of *-wich* and *-wick* presents difficulties) and in BAILIWICK.

wicked wi·kid morally or otherwise bad. XIII (Laȝ., Cursor M.). f. (dial.) *wick*, adj. use of OE. *wicca* wizard, the fem. of which is *wiċċe* WITCH. ¶ For the unusual formation cf. WRETCHED; there was also a rare syn. *wicci* (Peterborough Chron.).

wicker wi·kəɹ pliant twig or rod. XIV (Trevisa). Of E. Scand. origin (cf. Sw. *viker*, Da. *viger* willow), f. base of Sw. *vika* bend (cf. OE. *wīcan* give way, collapse, and WEAK).

wicket wi·kit small door or gate XIII; (in cricket) set of three stumps and two bails (formerly of two stumps and one bail) XVIII. – AN., ONF. *wiket* = (O)F. *guichet*, usu. referred to the Germ. base appearing in ON. *vikja* move, turn (Sw. *vika*, Da. *vige*).

widdershins var. of WITHERSHINS.

wide waid of great extent (esp. horizontally), (in limited use) from side to side. OE. *wīd* = OFris., OS. *wīd*, OHG. *wīt* (Du. *wijd*, G. *weit*), ON. *víðr* :- CGerm. (exc. Goth.) **wīdaz*, of unkn. origin; perh. f. IE. **wi-* apart, whence Skr. *vitarám* further. So **wide** adv. OE. *wīde*, with corr. Germ.

cogns. Hence **wi·de**N[5]. XVII (Sh.). comp. **wi·de**AWA·KE fully awake with eyes open XIX; said to be applied joc. to a kind of soft felt hat because of its having no 'nap'. **wi·de**SPREAD XVIII. See also WIDTH.

widgeon, wigeon wi·dʒən wild duck of genus Mareca. XVI. perh. f. echoic base **wi-*, after PIGEON[1]; parallel formations of later date are F. *vigeon, vingeon, gingeon, digeon.*

widow wi·dou wife bereaved of her husband. OE. *widewe, wuduwe* = OFris. *widwe*, OS. *widowa*, OHG. *wituwa* (Du. *weduwe, weeuw*, G. *witwe*), Goth. *widuwō*, adj. formation (not Scand.) of IE. range, **widhewo*, repr. by Skr. *vidhawā*, widow, Gr. *ē(ϝ)íthe(ϝ)os* unmarried man, L. *viduus* bereft, void, widowed (fem. *vidua* widow, whence F. *veuve*, etc.), OSl. *vŭdova* (Russ. *vdová*), OIr. *fedb*, W. *gweddw* widow, perh. f. **widh* as in Skr. *vidh* be destitute, lack, L. *dī|videre* DIVIDE. So **widow**ER[1] wi·dŏuəɹ man whose wife is dead. XIV (PPl.), in late ME. substituted as an unequivocal form for †*widow* (OE. masc. *widewa*). Hence **wi·dow** vb. XV, **wi·dow**ED[1] XVI (Sh.), **wi·dow**HEAD XIII, **wi·dow**HOOD (OE. *widewanhād*).

width widþ, witþ extent across. XVII (1627 *wydth* 'opening', Drayton; Moxon, Dryden; called by J. 'a low word'). f. first syll. of *wīdness* (the normal form from OE. *wīdnes* wideness, f. *wīd* WIDE + *-nes* -NESS) + -TH[1], an analogy being provided by *bredth* BREADTH.

wield wīld †rule, direct, command; handle with skill or effect. ME. *wēlde(n)*, repr. (1) redupl. str. vb. OE. *wealdan*, pt. *wēold*, pp. *(ġe)wealden* = OS. *waldan*, OHG. *waltan* (G. *walten*), ON. *valda*, Goth. *waldan*, and (2) wk. vb. OE. *wieldan*, f. mutated form of **walð-*, cogn. with Balto-Sl. forms denoting rule and power, and prob. ult. with **wal-* of L. *valēre* be strong (cf. VALID, VALOUR, VALUE). Hence **wield**Y[1] wī·ldi †capable of easy movement XIV (Ch.); (now chiefly as back-formation from UNWIELDY) manageable, handy XVI.

wife waif woman (surviving in *fishwife, old wives' tale*); woman joined to a man by marriage OE.; mistress of a household (surviving in *goodwife, housewife*) XIV (Ch.). OE. *wīf* = OFris., OS. *wīf* (Du. *wijf*), OHG. *wīp* (G. *weib* woman), ON. *víf*; of unkn. origin; not extant in Goth., which has *qinō* 'mulier', QUEAN, and *qēns* 'uxor' QUEEN. See also WIVE, WOMAN.

wig wig artificial covering of hair for the head. XVII. Shortening of PERIWIG, as WINKLE of *periwinkle.*

wiggle wi·gl move to and fro irregularly. XIII (AncrR.). – (M)Du., (M)LG. *wiggelen*, frequent. (see -LE[3]) of **wig-*, repr. by LG. *wiggen*; cf. *wag, waggle.*

wight[1] wait †living creature OE.; (arch.) being XII. OE. *wiht*, corr. (with variation of gender and meaning) to OS. *wiht* thing, (pl.) demons (MLG. *wicht* thing, creature, demon, LG. *wicht* girl, (M)Du. *wicht* little child), OHG., MHG. *wiht* creature, being, thing, esp. of elves and dwarfs (G. *wicht* being, infant), ON. *vættr, véttr, vítr*, living creature, thing (also in idiomatic uses, e.g. *ekki vætta, vættki* not a whit, not, *vættugi* nothing), Goth. *waiht* n. (in *ni . . . waiht* or *waihtais* nothing); ult. connexions uncertain. See also AUGHT, NAUGHT, NOUGHT, WHIT[1].

wight[2] wait (arch., dial.) valiant, doughty; strong, stalwart XIII; active, brisk XIV. – ON. *vígt*, n. of *vígr* of fighting age, skilled in arms, cogn. with OE. *wīġ* battle, conflict, *wiġa* warrior, based on IE. **wik-*, **wīk-*, repr. by L. *vincere* conquer, perf. *vīci* (cf. VICTOR). ¶ For similar adoptions of ON. neuters in *-t* see SCANT, THWART[1], WANT.

wigwam wi·gwɔm, -wæm N. Amer. Indian cabin, tent, or hut. XVII. – Ojibwa *wigwaum, wigiwam*, var. of *wikiwam, weekuwom* (Delaware *wiquoam*) lit. 'their house' (cf. *neek* my house, *keek* thy house, *week* his house).

wild waild living in a state of nature; uninhabited, waste; uncontrolled. OE. *wilde* = OFris. *wilde*, OS., OHG. *wildi* (Du., G. *wild*), ON. *villr*, Goth. *wilþeis* :– CGerm. **wilþijaz*, prob. – IE. **ghweltijos*, the base of which is repr. by W. *gwyllt*, Ir. *geilt* wild.

wildebeest wi·ldəbēst gnu. XIX. Afrikaans (now *wildebees*, pl. *wildebeeste*), f. Du. *wild* WILD + *beest* BEAST.

wilder wi·ldəɹ lead astray; go astray. XVII. Of unkn. origin; perh. extracted from WILDERNESS but cf. MDu. *verwilderen*, G. *(ver)wildern*, and BEWILDER, which is, however, of later appearance.

wilderness wi·ldəɹnės uncultivated tract of land. OE. *wild(d)ēornes* (Lye, Sweet), f. *wild(d)ēor* wild beast (cf. (M)Du., G. *wildernis*). ¶ For the concr. use of the suffix cf. OE. *hēanes* summit, *smēþnes* level place.

wile wail crafty or deceitful trick. XII (Peterborough Chron.). Early ME. *wīl*, evidenced first from Scandinavianized areas and therefore poss. – ON. **wīhl-* (*vél*) craft, artifice, rel. to *véla* defraud. Hence **wil**Y[1] wai·li XIII (Cursor M.).

will[1] wil desire, act or power of willing OE.; testamentary document XIV (Trevisa). OE. *willa* = OFris. *willa*, OS. *willio*, OHG. *willo, willio* (Du. *wil*, G. *wille*), ON. *vili, vilja-*, Goth. *wilja* :– CGerm. **wiljon* :– **weljon*; also OE. *(ġe)wil(l)* = ON. *vil*; f. **wel-* be pleasing (see WELL[3]). Hence **wi·l**FUL[1] self-willed XII; †willing, wishful XIV; earlier in adv. (late OE. *wilfullīċe*).

will[2] wil expressing various phases of desire, wish, intention, or determination; in combination with SHALL forming a future tense. OE. **willan, wyllan* (1st and 3rd pers. pres. ind. *wile, wyle*; from XIV *will*; 2nd pers. *wilt*), pt. **would** wud (1st and

3rd pers. *wolde*, 2nd pers. *woldest*, from XVI *wouldest*, *wouldst*) = OFris. *willa*, *wilde*, OS. *willian*, *wolda* (Du. *willen*, *wilde*), ON. *vilja*, *vilda*, Goth. *wiljan*, *wilda* :- Germ. **wel(l)jan*, parallel with Germ. **wal(l)jan*, repr. by OFris. *wella*, OHG. *wellen* (G. *wollen*, *wollte*, *gewollt*), ON. *velja*, *valði*, Goth. *waljan*; based on IE. **wol-* **wel-* (cf. L. *velle*, *volo*, *velim*, *volui*, and see WILL[1], WELL[3]).

will[3] wil pt., pp. **willed** wild; pres. ind. 2nd sg. *willest*, 3rd sg. *wills*, *willeth* wish or desire (to); determine by the will OE. OE. *willian* (pt. *willode*) = OHG. *willōn* (G. *willen*, pp. *gewillt*); f. WILL[1]. ¶ A synon. vb. having the same base with *n*-formative, OE. *wilnian*, continued through ME. *wilne* to XVI.

willemite wi·ləmait (min.) native silicate of iron. XIX. – Du. *willemit* (A. Levy, 1829), f. *Willem* William I of the Netherlands; see -ITE.

willet wi·lėt N. Amer. bird of the snipe family whose cry is expressed by *pill-will-willet*. XIX. Cf. WHIP-POOR-WILL, etc.

William wi·ljəm as plant-name now only in SWEET WILLIAM.

Williamite wi·ljəmait †A. member of the order of Augustinian hermits, Guillemin XVII. B. supporters of William of Orange (King William III) XVII; see -ITE.

Williams (pear) wi·ljəmz very juicy variety of the bon chrétien pear, so called from its first distributor in England XIX.

willies wi·liz (orig. U.S.) *the w.* spell of nervousness. XIX. Of unkn. origin.

willing wi·liŋ vbl. sb. desire, inclination (chiefly in conjunction with *nilling*) OE.; voluntary choice XIV. OE. *willung*. So **will**ING[2] ppl. adj. XIII.

will o' the wisp wi·ləðəwi·sp ignis fatuus. XVII. The earliest form is *Will with the* or *a wisp*, i.e. *Will* (pet form of *William*) and WISP in the sense 'bundle of hay, etc., for use as a torch'; for the use of proper name cf. *Jack-a-lantern*, and, for the second el., G. *irrwisch* lit. 'wander-wisp'.

willow wi·lou plant of genus Salix. OE. *welig* = OS. *wilgia*, (M)LG. *wilge*, Du. *wilg*; the form history is obscure, the change of vowel may be due to assoc. with *willy*, OE. *wilige* wicker basket.

willy-nilly wilini·li whether one likes it or not. XVII. Later sp. of *wil I nil I* (XVI) 'I am willing, I am unwilling'; based on WILL[2] and its neg. (OE. *nyllan*, f. *ne* NE+*willan*) with a variety of prons. (*we*, *ye*, *I*); earlier †*willing nilling*.

wilt[1] wilt become limp. XVII (Ray). Of dial. origin, in early XIX largely U.S.; perh. alt. of *wilk*, WELK.

wilt[2] 2nd pers. sg. pres. ind. of WILL[2].

Wilton wi·ltən kind of Brussels carpet made at *Wilton* in Wiltshire. XVIII.

wimble wi·mbl (dial., techn.) gimlet XIII; auger XIV; boring instrument XVII; – AN. **wimble*, var. of **guimble*, whence ME. *gymble* and GIMLET.

wimple wi·mpl woman's garment enveloping head, chin, sides of the face and neck (now worn by nuns). XIII. Late OE. *wimpel* = OFris., (M)LG., (M)Du. *wimpel*, OHG. *wimpal* veil, bonnet (G. *wimpel* streamer, pennon), ON. *vimpill*; the Germ. word was adopted as OF. *guimple* (mod. *guimpe*), of which the var. *wimple* coincided with the native word.

win win pt., pp. **won** wʌn †work; †vanquish OE.; be victorious (also trans.); gain XII. OE. *winnan* (also freq. *ġewinnan*), pt. *wann*, *wonn* = OFris. *winna* obtain, OS. *winnan* suffer, win, MLG., MDu. *winnen* till, obtain, acquire, OHG. *winnan* rage, contend, *gewinnan* gain by labour (G. *gewinnen* earn, gain, produce), ON. *vinna* labour, gain, Goth. *(ga)winnan* suffer; CGerm. str. vb. the senses of which are largely parallel to those of *gain* and *get*, but of uncertain relations. So **win** sb. †A. conflict, strife OE.; †gain, wealth XII; B. victory; gains XIX. In A OE. *win(n)*, more freq. *ġewin(n)*, ME. *(i)win*; in B f. the vb.

wince wins (dial.) kick restlessly XIII (S. Eng. Leg.); make an involuntary shrinking movement XVIII. – AN. **wencir*, var. of OF. *guenchir* turn aside, avoid (whence *winch* XIII, surviving dial.) – Germ. **weŋkjan* (OHG. *wenken*, OS. *wenkian*) :- **waŋkjan*.

wincey, winsey wi·nsi durable cloth having a linen warp and a woollen weft. XIX. orig. Sc., app. alt. of *woolsey* in LINSEY-WOOLSEY, through assim. **linsey-winsey*.

winch wintʃ reel, roller OE.; hoisting or hauling apparatus XVI. Late OE. *winċe* :- Germ. **wiŋkjo-* :- **weŋkjo-*, f. IE. **weŋg-* WINK.

Winchester wi·ntʃėstəɹ A. name of a city in Hampshire, used as a designation of certain measures XVI; B. name of Oliver F. *Winchester* (1810–80), an American manufacturer, designating a type of breech-loading rifle XIX.

wind[1] wind (arch. and dial. waind) air in motion. OE. *wind* = OFris., OS. *wind*, OHG. *wint* (Du., G. *wind*), ON. *vindr*, Goth. *winds* :- CGerm. **windaz*, based on IE. prp. **went-* (whence L. *ventus* wind, W. *gwynt*), with parallel forms on **we-* in Lith. *vėjas* wind, OSl. *vějati* blow, OIr. *feth* air, Gr. *áēsi* (:- **awēsi*) blows, *aḗtēs* wind, Skr. *vā́ti* blows, *vā́tas* wind (cf. NIRVANA). comp. **wi·nd**FALL[1] something blown down by the wind XV; unexpected acquisition XVI; cf. (M)HG. *wintval*, G. *windfall*.

wind[2], waind pt., pp. **wound** waund †move in a certain direction OE.; move in a circular path XIII; pass (a thing) round something else XIV; set (a mechanism) in order XVII. OE. *windan*, pt. *wand*, *wundon*, pp. *wunden* = OFris. *winda*, OS. *windan*, OHG. *wintan* (Du., G. *winden*), ON. *vinda*, Goth. **windan*, in *biwindan*, *uswindan* :- CGerm. **windan*, rel. to **wand*- in WANDER, WEND.

wind[3] (with pronunc. wind) A. get the wind of XV; deprive of breath XIX; B. (with pronunc. waind) sound a horn, etc. by blowing into it XVI. f. WIND[1].

windlass wi·ndləs machine for hauling or hoisting. XIV. Presumably obscure alt. of †*windas* – AN. *windas* (AL. *windasium*) = OF. *guindas* – ON. *vindáss* (whence also MLG., MDu., Du. *windas*), f. *vinda* WIND[2] + *áss* pole (= Goth. *ans* beam).

windlestraw wi·ndlstrɔ̄ (dial.) withered stalk. OE. *windelstrēaw*, f. *windel* basket, (dial.) measure of corn XIII, f. *windan* WIND[2] (see -LE[1]) + *strēaw* STRAW[1].

window wi·ndou opening in a wall or side of a structure to admit light and air. XIII (AncrR.). ME. *windoȝe* – ON. *vindauga*, f. *vindr* WIND[1] + *auga* EYE; superseded OE. *ēaġþyrel*, *ēaġduru* 'eye-hole, -door', but *fenester* (of F. origin) was in concurrent use till late XVI; the alt. forms *wind(d)-ore*, *-door* (XVI) had some currency.

Windsor wi·nzəɹ town in Berkshire, place of residence of British Royal Family (*W. Castle*), designation of the family (*House of W.*); used attrib. in *W. chair* (XVIII), *soap*, *uniform* (XIX) (worn by the Royal Family).

wine wain fermented juice of the grape. OE. *wīn* = OFris., OS., OHG. *wīn* (Du. *wijn*, G. *wein*), ON. *vín*, Goth. *wein* :- CGerm. **wīnam* – L. *vīnum*, **wīnom* (whence also OSl. *vino*, Lith. *vỹnas*, W. *gwin*, Ir. *fín*), primitively rel. to Gr. (ϝ)οἶνος wine, *oínē* vine, wine, Alb. *vēne*, Arm. *gini*, perh. all derived from a common Mediterranean source, but referred by some to pre-Arm. **woinijo*; cf. also Arab. *wain*, Heb. *yayin*, Ass. *inn*, the relation with which, if any, is not clear. Comp. **wi·nebi:bb**ER[1] XVI (Coverdale; cf. Luther's *weinsäufer*). **wi·ne**PRESS[1], **wi·ne**VAT. XVI (Tindale).

wing wiŋ organ of flight XII; lateral part or appendage XIII (RGlouc.). protection, care XIII; division (right or left) of a force XIV; side scene in a theatre XVIII. First in pl. *wenge(n)*, *-es* – ON. *vængir*, accus. *vængi*, pl. of *vængr* wing of a bird, aisle (Sw., Da. *vinge*, Norw. *veng*), repl. OE. *feþra* wings, pl. of *feþer* FEATHER, and *fiþere*. Hence **wing** vb. use the wings XVII (Sh.); wound in the wing XIX: **wing**ED[2] wi·ŋid, wiŋd. XIV (Ch.); phr. *w. words* (XVII, Chapman), after Homeric ἔπεα πτερόεντα.

wink wiŋk †close the eyes; †give a significant glance OE.; blink XIII; 'shut the eyes' to (const. *at*) XV; close one eye momentarily in a flippant manner XIX. OE. *wincian* = OS. *wincan* (MLG., MDu. *winken*), rel. to OHG. *winchan* (G. *winken*) move sideways, stagger, nod, f. Germ. **wiŋk*- (**weŋk*-) **waŋk*- :- IE. **weŋg*- **woŋg*- move sideways or from side to side, whence also WINCE, WINCH.

winkle wi·ŋkl XVI. Shortening of PERIWINKLE[2], as *wig* of *periwig*.

winnow wi·nou free (grain) from chaff, separate (chaff) from grain. OE. *windwian*, f. *wind* WIND[1], rel. immed. to *windwiġċeaf* chaff, *windwiġsife* winnowing-sieve, and remotely to OHG. *wintōn*, ON. *vinza* (:- **windisōjan*) winnow, Goth. *dis|winþjan* scatter like chaff, *winþiskaurō* winnowing-fan; cf. synon. L. *ventilāre* VENTILATE, Lith. *vétyti*.

winsey wi·nsi var. of WINCEY.

winsome wi·nsəm †pleasant OE. to XIII; of attractive appearance or disposition XVII. OE. *wynsum* (= OS. *wunsam*, OHG. *wunnisam*), f. *wyn(n)* joy, pleasure = OS. *wunnia*, OHG. *wunnia*, *wunna* (G. *wonne*), f. Germ. **wun*-, repr. also in WISH, WONT[1]; see -SOME[1]. ¶ The current sense came into the literary lang. from the north, where it must have survived with a specialized meaning.

winter wi·ntəɹ fourth season of the year; used typically for *year* (as in general Germ. use). OE. *winter* = OFris. *winter*, OS., OHG. *wintar* (Du., G. *winter*), ON. *vetr*, earlier *vettr*, *vittr*, Goth. *wintrus* :- CGerm. **wentrus*, prob. f. nasalized var. of IE. base **wed*- **wod*- be wet (see WATER, WET). Hence **wi·nter** vb. spend the winter. XIV (Wycl. Bible); after L. *hiemāre*, *hibernāre* HIBERNATE; cf. MLG., etc. *winteren*, ON. *vetra*. **wi·nter**LY[1], **wi·ntr**Y[1]. OE. *winterlić*, *wintriġ*, with cogns. in OHG., etc.; present currency is due to new formations in XVI.

wipe waip rub gently with a cloth, etc. OE.; fig. uses from XIII. OE. *wīpian*, corr. formally to OHG. *wīfan* wind round, Goth. *weipan* crown, and rel. further to OHG. *waif* bandage, ON. *veipr* head-covering, Goth. *waips* wreath, and the forms given s.v. WHIP. Hence sb. slashing blow or remark XVI; (sl.) handkerchief XVIII (superseding earlier *wiper*).

wire waiəɹ (piece or length of) metal in the form of a slender rod OE.; network of this XVI. OE. *wīr*, corr. to MLG. *wīre* (LG. *wīr*), ON. **vírr* in *víra virki* filigree work, rel. to OHG. *wiara* (ornament of) finest gold; prob. f. base **wi*- of L. *viēre* plait, weave (cf. WITHE). Hence **wi·re**LESS (of telegraphy and telephony) operated without the use of conducting wires XIX; **wi·re-pu:ller** (orig. U.S.) one who exerts underhand influence XIX; **wi·re**WORM larva of click-beetles XVIII. **wir**Y[1] waiə·ri. XVI.

wis wis (pseudo-arch.) know. XVII. See IWIS.

wisdom wi·zdəm quality of being wise; †knowledge, learning. OE. *wīsdōm* = OFris., OS. *wīsdōm*, OHG. *wīstuom* (G. *weistum* legal sentence, precedent), ON. *vísdómr*; CGerm., exc. Goth.; see WISE², -DOM. *Wisdom tooth* (XIX), usu. pl., earlier *teeth of wisdom* (XVII), tr. modL. *dentes sapientiæ*, tr. Arab. *aḍrāsu 'lḥikmi* (*ḍirs* tooth, *ḥikm* wisdom), after Gr. σωφρονιστῆρες (Hippocrates). ¶ Short i is shown by Orm's *wissdom*.

wise¹ waiz (arch.) manner, fashion. OE. *wīse* (rarely *wīs*) mode, condition, thing, cause, occas. song, corr. to OFris. *wīs*, OS. *wīsa* (Du. *wijze*), OHG. *wīsa*, *wīs* manner, custom, tune (G. *weise*), ON. *vísa* stanza, **vís* in *ǫðruvís* otherwise :- CGerm. (exc. Goth.) **wīsōn*, **wīsō*, f. **wit-* WIT²; for the sense-development cf. rel. Gr. *eîdos* form, shape, kind, state of things, course of action. See -WISE.

wise² waiz having sound judgement; †learned OE.; informed XII. OE. *wīs* = OFris., OS., OHG. *wīs(i)* (Du. *wijs*, G. *weise*), ON. *víss*, Goth. *-weis* :- CGerm. **wīsaz* :- **wittos*, f. IE. **weid-* WIT²+ppl. suffix **-tos*. The pronunc. with z is due to old inflected forms; s survives in some north. dials.

-wise waiz terminal el. (suffix) descending from OE. *wīse* WISE¹ as used (like cogn. forms in other Germ. langs.) in various advb. expressions meaning 'in such-and-such a manner, way, or respect' and containing an adj. or an attrib. sb. with or without a governing prep., e.g. OE. (*on*) *ōþre wīsan* in another fashion, OTHERWISE, *on sċipwīsan* after the manner of a ship, like a ship. Several of these have become permanent, as *anywise*, *likewise*, *nowise*. Sense-contact with -WAYS, denoting direction, appears in late ME., and *lengthways*, *longways*, *sideways* are contemp. in XVI with *lengthwise*, *longwise*, *sidewise*.

wiseacre wai·zeikəɹ pretender to wisdom. XVI. – (with unexpl. assim. to *acre*) MDu. *wijsseggher* wai·szegəɹ soothsayer, prob. – (with assim. to *segghen* say) OHG. *wīssago*, alt., by assoc. with *wīs* WISE²+ *sagen* SAY¹, of *wīzago* = OE. *wītega* prophet, f. **wit-* WIT.

wish wiʃ have a desire (for). OE. *wȳsċan* = MLG. *wünschen*, MDu. *wonscen*, *wunscen*, OHG. *wunsken* (G. *wünschen*), ON. *œ́skja* :- CGerm. (exc. Goth.) **wunskjan*, f. **wunska-*, *-ō* (OE. *wūsċ*, MDu. *wunsc*, *wonsc*, OHG. *wunsc* (G. *wunsch*), ON. *ósk* wish), f. **wun-* **wen-* **wan-* (see WEEN, WONT¹); cf. Skr. *vāñchā* (:- **vānskā*), *vāñch* wish. Hence sb. XIV. **wi·sh**FUL¹ †desirable, †longing XVI; desirous XVIII; coloured by what one desires for the future XX.

wishtonwish wi·ʃtənwiʃ prairie dog of N. America. XIX. imit. of the animal's cry.

wishy-washy wi·ʃiwɔːʃi weak and insipid. XVIII. redupl. formation on *washy* (XVII), with vowel alternation; so **wish-wash** washy drink or talk XVIII, and cf. *swish-swash* wishy-washy drink (XVI) and *swash* pig-wash, wet refuse (XVI).

wisp wisp handful, bunch, twisted band (of hay, etc.). XIV. corr. forms are only in WFris., but cf. synon. vars. s.v. WHISK.

wist wist Sussex land measure of area XVII. – AL. *wista*, *wysta* (XII), perh. a use of OE. *wist* provision, sustenance.

wistaria, -eria wistɛə·riə -iə·riə mauve-flowered climbing plant. XIX. – modL., f. name of Caspar *Wistar* or *Wister* (1761–1818), American anatomist; see -IA¹.

wistful wi·stfəl †closely attentive; yearningly eager, mournfully expectant. XVII. perh. f. †*wistly* intently (XV), var. of †*whishtly* silently (cf. WHIST¹)+-FUL¹, and assoc. with WISHFUL and (dial.) *wishly* steadfastly (XVI).

wistiti wi·stiti S. Amer. monkey. XVIII (Goldsmith). – F. *ouistiti*, named by Buffon from the animal's cry.

wit¹ wit A. †mind, understanding, sense OE.; B. right mind, good judgement, (pl.) senses XII; C. (power of) giving pleasure by combining or contrasting ideas XVI. D. †wise man XVI; witty man XVII. OE. *wit(t)*, more freq. *ġewit(t)*, corr. to OFris., OS. *wit*, OHG. *wizzi* (Du. *weet*, G. *witz*), ON. *vit*, Goth. *un|witi* ignorance, f. **wit-* (see next).

wit² wit know; surviving in phr. *to wit* that is to say, namely, viz., short for *that is to wit*, tr. AN. *cestasavoir*, lit. that is to know, SCILICET. OE. *witan*, 1st and 3rd pres. ind. sg. *wāt*, 2nd pres. *wāst*, pl. *witon*, pt. *wisse*, *wiste*, pp. *ġewiten* = OFris. *wita*, *wēt*, *witon*, *wiste*, OS. *witan*, *wēt*, *wissa*, OHG. *wizzan*, *weiz*, *wissa*, *wista* (Du. *weten*, G. *wissen*, *weiss*, *wusste*, *gewusst*), ON. *vita*, *veit*, *vissa*, *vitaðr*, Goth. *witan*, *wait*, *witum*, *wissa*, f. CGerm. **wait-*, **wit* :- IE. **woid-* **weid-* **wid-*, whence Skr. *véda* (cf. VEDA), *véttha*, *vidmá*, Gr. *oîda*, *oîstha*, *oîde*, *ídmen* (cf. IDEA), L. *vidēre* see (cf. VISION), OSl. *viděti* see, *věděti* know, and, with nasal infix, Skr. *vindáti* finds, OIr. *finnaim* I find out. See also WIS, IWIS, WISE¹, WOT, and prec.

witan wi·tən (hist.) national council of Anglo-Saxon times. OE. *witan*, pl. of *wita* wise man, councillor, f. base of *witan* know, WIT². So **witenagemot** wi·tənəjəmouːt OE., f. g. pl. of *wita*+*ġemōt* meeting, assembly (see MOOT).

witch witʃ female magician or wizard. OE. *wiċċe*, fem. corr. to *wiċċa* male magician, sorcerer, wizard (whence dial. *witch*), rel. to *wiċċian* practise magic arts, corr. to (M)LG. *wikken*, *wicken*, agent-noun *wikker*, and noun of action *wikkerie*, the source of which is unkn.; later senses of the vb. are those of BEWITCH, of which in mod. use it is mainly an aphetic deriv., surviving esp. in echoes of *the verie witching time of night* (Sh.). Hence **wi·tch**CRAFT. OE. *wiććecræft*.

witch elm, hazel see WYCH-ELM, WYCH HAZEL.

with wið, wiþ †A. denoting opposition. OE. B. denoting accompaniment or addition (esp. repl. OE., ME. *mid*). C. denoting instrumentality, causation, agency XII. OE. *wiþ* = OFris. *with*, OS. *wið*, prob. shortening of Germ. prep. repr. by OE. *wiþer* = OFris. *wither*, OS. *withar*, OHG. *widar* (Du. *weder*, *weer*, G. *wieder* adv. again, *wider* prep. against), ON. *viðr*, Goth. *wiþra*; f. IE. **wi-*, denoting separation or division + compar. suffix *-*tero-* (cf. Skr. *vitarám* further).

with- wið, wiþ repr. OE. *wiþ-*, prep. WITH used as a prefix to vbs. (and derived sbs.) in the senses (1) away, back, (2) against, as in WITHDRAW, WITHHOLD, WITHSTAND.

withal wiðɔ̄·l adv. (arch.) along with the rest, as well XII (Orm); with it or them XIII; prep. with XIII. f. WITH + ALL sb.; ult. superseding earlier *mid alle* (cf. MID); cf. *therewithal*, *wherewithal*.

withdraw wið-, wiþdrɔ̄· take back or away XIII (AncrR.); cf. RETIRE, RETRACT; *withdrawing*-ROOM room to withdraw into XVI; repl. *withdrawing-chamber* (XIV); see -ING[1] and DRAWING-ROOM. **withdraw·**AL[2] XIX; repl. *withdrawment* (XVII), which superseded *withdraught* (XIV), *withdraw* (XV).

withe, with[2] waið, wið, wiþ (dial.) bond, shackle OE.; †halter XIII; metal band or hoop XVII. OE. *wiþþe* = OFris. *withthe*, MDu. *wisse* (Du. *wis*), OHG. *wit*, *withi*, *wid*, *widi*, cf. *khuna|widi*, *chun|widi*, Goth. *kunawida* bonds, ON. *við*, *viðja* :- CGerm. **wiþōn*, **wiþi*; cf. WITHY; f. base **weit-* **wit-*, of IE. range (cf. Av. *vaēti-*, Gr. *ītéā* (:- *ϝeiteϝā*) willow), ult. L. **wi-* as in L. *viēre* plait, WIRE.

wither wi·ðəɹ become dried up and shrivelled XIV; trans. XVI. The earliest forms are *wydder*, *widder*, the present sp. dating from XVI. gen. assumed to be a use of WEATHER vb. ult. differentiated for certain senses; G. *verwittern* weather, disintegrate.

withers wi·ðəɹz (sb. pl.) highest part of a horse's back. XVI. Shortening of †*wider-somes*, *-sones*, f. *wider-*, *wither-* (see WITH)+ (perh.) var. of SINEW; the force of the first el. is obscure (? 'opposing the strain') but it is paralleled in synon. G. *widerrist* (*rist* WRIST instep, withers).

withershins wi·ðəɹʃinz A. (Sc.) the wrong way; B. in a direction contrary to the apparent course of the sun. XVI. – MLG. *weddersin(ne)s* – MHG. *widersinnes*, f. *wider-* against = OE. *wiþer* (see WITH) + g. of *sin*, *sind*, *sint* = OE. *sīþ* journey, course (cf. SEND[1]); in sense B (f. vars. *-sones*, *-sonnis*, by assoc. with SUN).

withhold wiðhou·ld hold or keep back. XII. f. WITH- + HOLD[1].

within wiði·n adv. on the inner side OE.; prep. in the interior of, in the limits of XII. Late OE. *wiþinnan* (f. *wiþ* WITH + *innan*, ME. *inne* forming with *wiþæftan* behind, *wiþforan* before, *wiþġeondan* beyond, *wiþhindan* behind, *wiþneoþan* beneath, *wiþufan*, *-uppan* above, *wiþūtan* WITHOUT, a group peculiar to Eng. presumably modelled on formations with *be-* (cf. BEHIND).

without wiðau·t adv. outside; prep. on the outside of OE.; not accompanied by, not having XII. Late OE. *wiþūtan*, f. *wiþ* WITH + *ūtan* ME. *ute(n)* OUT; see prec.

withstand wiðstæ·nd pt., pp. **withstoo·d** stand or maintain one's position against. OE. *wiþstandan* = OFris. *withstonda*, ON. *viðstanda*; see WITH-, STAND.

withy wi·ði willow. OE. *wīþiġ* (cf. OHG. *wīda* (G. *weide*), ON. *víðir* willow), for the connexions of which see WITHE. ¶ In Sc. and north. dial. *widdy* (XV).

witness wi·tnis †knowledge, wisdom; attestation of a fact, etc., testimony. OE. *witnes*, more freq. *ġewitnes* (ME. *iwitnesse*), f. WIT[1] + -NESS; cf. OHG. *giwiʒnessi*, MDu. *wetenisse*, ON. *vitni*, *vitnis-*. The passage from abstr. to concr. meaning is paralleled in F. *témoin* (:- L. *testimonium* TESTIMONY). Hence vb. bear w. to XIII (Cursor M.); be a w. of XVI.

witney wi·tni woollen material manufactured and made into blankets at *Witney*, a town in Oxfordshire. XVIII.

witticism wi·tisizm witty saying or remark. XVII ('A mighty Wittycism, (if you will pardon a new word!) but there is some difference between a Laugher and a Critique', Dryden, 1677). f. WITTY, irreg. after CRITICISM.

wittingly wi·tiŋli knowingly, designedly. XIV (*witandly*, R. Rolle). f. *witting*, prp. of WIT[2] + -LY[2]; cf. (O)F. *sciemment*, L. *scienter*.

wittol wi·təl (arch.) acquiescent cuckold. XV. Late ME. *wetewold*, perh. formed on *cokewold* CUCKOLD by substituting *wete* WIT[2] for the first syll.

witty wi·ti †wise OE.; †clever, ingenious XIV; cleverly amusing XVI (Sh.). OE. *(ġe)wittiġ* = OS. *wittig*, OHG. *wizzīg*, ON. *vitugr*; cf. WIT[1] + -Y[1].

wive waiv take a wife OE.; take as a wife. OE. *(ġe)wīfian* = MLG., MDu. *wīven*; f. WIFE. **wi·**VING[1]. OE. *wīfung* marrying.

wivern see WYVERN.

wizard wi·zəɹd †philosopher, sage XV (Promp. Parv.); man skilled in occult arts XVI. Earliest forms *wis(e)ard*, *wissard*; f. ME. *wīs* WISE[2] + -ARD; the pronunc. with ĭ and z follows *wisdom*. Hence **wi·zard**RY. XVI (Golding).

wizened wi·znd shrivelled, shrunken. XVI (G. Douglas), rarely evidenced before XVIII

(Ramsay, Burns). In early use Sc. and prob. brought into gen. use by Scott; pp. of *wizen*, repr. OE. *wisnian* dry up, wither, corr. to OHG. *wesanēn*, ON. *visna*, f. Germ. **wis-* with widespread IE. cogns., as L. *viēscere*, Lith. *vysti*, W. *gwyw*, OIr. *feugud*.

wo wou int. (in *wo ho ho*, etc.) falconer's call to his hawk XVI; early form of WHOA XVIII.

woad woud blue dye-stuff obtained from the plant Isatis tinctoria. OE. *wād* = OFris. *wēd*, MLG., MDu. *wēt*, *weede*, OHG. *weit* (Du. *weede*, G. *waid*) :- WGerm. **waida-* (whence OF. *waide*, *gaide*, It. *guado*), by-form of **waisda-* (whence medL. *waisdo*, AN. *waisde*, OF. *guesde*, F. *guède*), with a var. repr. by Gothic **wizdila* (latinized as *ouisdelem*, Oribasius), Gr. *isátis* (:- **ϝitsatis*).

wobble, wabble wɔ·bl move erratically from side to side. XVII. corr. to Upper, Middle, and Low G. *wab(b)eln*, prob. f. base of WAVER; see -LE[3]. ¶ 'A low barbarous word' (J.). Hence **wo·bbly**[1]; cf. LG. *wabbelig*. XIX.

wodge wɔdʒ (sl.) lumpy protuberant object. XX. Expressive alt. of WEDGE.

woe wou A. int. and adv. as excl. of distress or grief (const. dative) OE.; B. sb. (arch.) misery, misfortune XII; C. adj. grieved, wretched XII. OE. *wā* (also *wǣ*), corr. to OFris., OS., MLG. *wē*, (M)Du. *wee*, OHG. *wē* (G. *weh*), ON. *vei*, *væ*, Goth. *wai* (from Germ. are F. *ouais*, Sp., Pg., It. *guai*); of CIE. range (Gr. *oâ*, later *ouá*, *ouaí*, L. *væ*, Lett. *wai*, W. *gwae*). ¶ The development of the adj. was through the apprehension of the d. as a nom. in such constr. as *wo is mi soule*. Hence **woe·**FUL[1]. XIII (Cursor M.).

woe-begone wou·bigɔn †oppressed with misfortune or grief XIV; (of looks, etc.) revealing a state of distress or sorrow XIX. Evolved from constr. such as ME. *me is wo begon* woe has beset or surrounded me (†*bego* beset as an affecting influence), which gives place to *I am wo begon*, and as *me is wo* to *I am wo* (see prec.). The second sense was due to archaistic revival, perh. derived from such contexts as that of 'So dull, so dead in look, so woe-begone' (Sh. '2 Hen. IV' I i 71).

wold would †forest, wooded upland OE.; hill, down; piece of open country, (later) upland, moorland XIII. OE. (Anglian) *wald*, (WS.) *weald* (see WEALD) = OFris., OS., OHG. *wald* (Du. *woud*, G. *wald*) forest, ON. *vǫllr* untilled field, plain:- CGerm. (exc. Goth.) **walþus*, perh. cogn. with WILD. ¶ After *c.*1500 it fell out of gen. use and was restricted to names of particular areas (e.g. Yorkshire wolds), prob. once thickly wooded, whence it was generalized in literary use after *c.*1600.

wolf wulf pl. **wolves** wulvz canine animal, Canis lupus. OE. *wulf* = OFris. *wolf*, OS. *wulf*, (O)HG. *wolf* (Du., G. *wolf*), ON. *ulfr*, Goth. *wulfs* :- CGerm. **wulfaz* :- IE. **wl̥qʷos*, repr. also by L. *lupus* (of dial. origin), Gr. *lúkos*, OSl. *vlŭkŭ*, OPruss. *wilkis*, Lith. *vil̃kas*, Alb. *ul'k*, Arm. *gail*, Av. *vəhrkō*, Skr. *vṛ́kas*. ¶ A corr. fem. **wl̥qwī-* is repr. by OE. *wylf*, OHG. *wulpa* (G. *wülpe*), ON. *ylgr*, Lith. *vìlkė*, Russ. *volčica*. **wo·lf**ISH[1] XVI, †*wolvish* (XV Lydg.; Sidney, Sh., Coleridge).

wolfram wu·lfræm, vɔ·lfrəm (min.) tungstate of iron and manganese. XVIII. – G. *wolfram*, gen. assumed to be an old miner's term, f. *wolf* WOLF + *rahm* cream (= OE. *rēam*, etc.) or MHG. *rām* soot, and to be the source of modL. *lupi spuma* (Agricola 1546), which corr., however, prop. to G. *wolfsschaum*; the vars. of the G. word, *wolffram(m)*, *wolfert*, *wolfrath*, suggest assoc. with a proper name. ¶ Presumably orig. a pejorative term ('a kind of mock tin', 1757) with ref. to its inferiority compared with the tin which it accompanies; cf. *cobalt*, *nickel*.

wolverine wulvərī·n glutton Gulo luscus. XVI. Also *-ene*, in earliest use *-ing*; obscurely f. *wolv-*, inflexional stem of WOLF.

woman wu·mən pl. **women** wi·min adult female human being; female servant. OE. *wīfman(n)* m., later fem., f. *wīf* woman + *man(n)* MAN; a formation peculiar to Eng. not in the oldest OE. records, the primitive words being *wīf* WIFE and *cwene* QUEAN; assim. of *-fm-* to *-mm-* is evident in late OE. sp. (cf. LEMAN) and rounding of *wim-* to *wum-*, *wom-* in XIII. **wo·man**ISH[1]. XIV (Ch., Gower). **wo·man**KIND. XIV. **wo·man**LY[1]. XIII (AncrR.). **wo·man**IZE emasculate XVI; consort XIX.

womb wūm †belly; uterus. OE. *wamb*, *womb* = OFris., MLG., MDu. *wamme* (Du. *wam*), OHG. *wamba*, *wampa* (G. *wamme*, dial. *wampe*), ON. *vǫmb*, Goth. *wamba*; CGerm., of unkn. origin.

wombat wɔ·mbæt burrowing marsupial Phascolomys. XVIII. Native Australian name; *womat*, *womback*, *wo(o)mback* are recorded vars.

wonder wʌ·ndəɹ astonishing or marvellous thing OE.; perplexed astonishment XIII. OE. *wundor* = OFris. *wunder*, OS. *wundar*, OHG. *wuntar* (Du. *wonder*, G. *wunder*), ON. *undr*; of unkn. origin. So vb. OE. *wundrian* = OFris. *ur|wunderia*, OS. *wundrōn*, etc.

wont[1] wount, (now chiefly U.S.) wʌnt. accustomed, used. OE. *ġewunod*, pp. of *wunian* dwell, continue (chiefly *ġewunian*), be accustomed or used = OFris. *wunia*, *wonia*, OS. *wunon*, *wonon*, OHG. *wonēn* (Du. *wonen*, G. *wohnen*) be accustomed, remain, dwell, ON. *una* be content in a place, enjoy, Goth. **wunan*, in prp. *unwunands* troubled :- CGerm. **wunōjan*, **wunǣjan*, f. **wun-* **wen-* **wan-* (see WEAN, WEEN, WINSOME, WISH).

wont² wount, (now chiefly U.S.) wʌnt. custom, habit. XIV (rare before XVI). Of doubtful origin; perh. due to a conflation of *it is my wone* (OE. *ġewuna* custom) and *I am wont* (see prec.).

won't wount (colloq.) will not. XVII. contr. of *wonnot*, assim. of *wol not* (see WILL²); for *-nn-* cf. Sc. *winna* will not.

wonted wou·ntėd, (chiefly U.S.) wʌ·ntėd accustomed, customary. XV. Of doubtful origin; f. either WONT¹ or WONT²+-ED¹ or -ED².

woo wū sue in love (intr.) XI; (trans., also fig.) XIII. Late OE. *wōgian* (also, trans., *āwōgian*), whence *wōgere* **woo**·ER¹; of unkn. origin.

wood wud †A. tree. B. collection of trees growing together; substance of which trees consist. OE. *wudu*, later form of *widu*, *wiodu* = OHG. *witu*, ON. *viðr* :- Germ. **widuz*, rel. to OIr. *fid* tree, wood, Gael. *fiodh*, W. *gwŷdd* trees. Comp. **woo·d-bine -bind** -bain(d) any of various climbing plants, e.g. honeysuckle, ivy, convolvulus. OE. *wudubinde*, f. base of *bindan* BIND; for loss of *d* cf. *line*, *rine*, for *lind*, *rind*. **woodchuck** wu·dtʃʌk N. Amer. marmot. XVII. alt., by assoc. with *wood*, of the Algonquian name (e.g. Cree *wuchak*, *otchock*); the var. *wejack* has been used. **woo·d**COCK¹ migratory bird Scolopax rusticula. OE. *wuducocc* (whence OF. *witecos*, *huitecox*). **woo·d**EN³. XVI. **woo·dpecker** -peːkəɹ bird of a genus such as Picus, which habitually pecks the wood of trees. XVI; cf. Gr. *druokoláptēs*, *-kólaps*, *-kópos* 'tree-striker'; **woodruff** wu·drʌf OE. *wudurofe* (the second el. is of unkn. origin), low-growing shrub Asperula odorata. **woods**Y wu·dzi (U.S.) sylvan. XIX. f. pl. *woods* of WOOD. **woo·d**Y¹ †wooded XIV; ligneous XVI. **woo·d**WARD keeper of a wood. OE. *wuduweard* (survives as a surname, with var. *Woodard*).

woof¹ wūf threads crossing the web at right angles to the warp OE.; woven fabric XVII. OE. *ōwef*, alt. of *ōwebb* (see WEB) after *wefan* WEAVE; ME. *oof* became *woof* partly by assoc. in the phr. *warp and (w)oof*.

woof² wuf dog's low gruff bark XIX. So **wough, wuff** wʌf, a variety of this XIX. imit.

wool wul fine hair of fleece. OE. *wull* = OFris. *wolle*, *ulle*, MLG., MDu., *wulle*, *wolle*, OHG. *wolla* (Du. *wol*, G. *wolle*), ON. *ull*, Goth. *wulla* :- GCerm. **wullō* :- IE. **wl̥nā́*, whence Skr. *ū́rnā*, OSl. *vlŭna*, L. *lāna*, beside *vellus* (:- **welnos*) fleece; of doubtful ult. origin.

Woolwich wu·lidʒ name of a town in Kent used attrib. (XVIII) to designate products of its old dockyard and the Royal Arsenal.

woorali see CURARE.

woozy wū·zi (sl.) fuddled; muzzy XIX. perh. alt. of *oozy*, f. OOZE².

Wop wɔp mid- or south-European (esp. Italian) immigrant in the U.S.A. XX. Alleged to be – It. *guappo*, a local greeting.

word wɜ̄ɹd (coll. pl. and sg.) things or something said; report, tidings; divine communication; vocable. OE. *word* = OFris., OS. *word* (Du. *woord*), (O)HG. *wort*, ON. *orð*, Goth. *waurd* :- CGerm. **wordam* :- **wr̥dho-* **werdh-*, which is held to be based on **wer-*, repr. by Gr. *ϝeréō* I shall say, L. *verbum* word (cf. VERB), Skr. *vrátam* command, law, vow, OPruss. *wirds* word, Lith. *var̃das* name. Hence **wo·rd**-BOOK lexicon, dictionary. XVI (Florio); cf. G. *wörterbuch* (1631 in Kluge), Du. *woordenboek* (†*woord-*), Icel. *orðabók*, Sw. *ordbok*, Da. *ordbog*. **wo·rd**Y¹. OE. *wordiġ*. ¶ For parallel IE. phonetics cf. BEARD, RED.

work wɜ̄ɹk something done, what one does; manufactured article (esp. with qualification, as *fire-*, *frame-*, *wax-*). OE. *weorc*, *werc*, *worc*, *wurc* = OFris., OS. *werk*, OHG. *werah*, *werc* (Du., G. *werk*), ON. *verk* :- CGerm. (exc. Goth.; cf. the vb.) **werkam* :- IE. **wergon*, whence also Gr. (*ϝ*)*érgon* (cf. ENERGY), with poss. cogns. in Av., Arm., Celtic, Tokh. So **work** vb. OE. *wyrćan*, pt. *worhte*, pp. *ġeworht* (see WROUGHT), repr. directly by ME. *wirch(e)*, *wyrch(e)*, but infl. at an early date by the sb. and the various ON. vbs. (*virkja*, *verkja*, *yrkja*, *verka*), *-k-* prevailing in XV. For parallel forms cf. OFris. *werkia*, OS. *wirkian*, OHG. *wirchen* (G. *wirken*), ON. *verkja*, *virkja* feel pain (cf. Goth. *waurkjan*), and for IE. cogns. see ENERGY, ERG, LITURGY, ORGAN, ORGY, THEURGY, ZYMURGY. comp. **wo·rkaday** ME. *werkedai* (trisyll.) XI, of uncertain origin, perh. after *sunnedei* SUNDAY, the later *workyday* being after *holiday*, with *workaday* quite late. **wo·rk**DAY XV. **wo·rk**-HOUSE †workshop OE.; poor-law institution XVII. **wo·rk**MAN OE. *weorcman(n)*, with corr. forms in Du., OHG., ON. ¶ In dial. *wark*, *warch* there are survivals of the OE. *wærc* sb., *wærcan* vb., a parallel formation on Germ. **wark-*.

world wɜ̄ɹld human existence or a period of it; *the* earth, *the* universe; *the* human race, human society. OE. *weorold*, *worold*, *world* = OFris. *wrald*, *warld*, OS. *werold* (Du. *wereld*), OHG. *weralt* (MHG. *werlt*, G. *welt*), ON. *verǫld*; a formation peculiar to Germ. (not in Goth.) f. **weraz* man (OE., OS., OHG. *wer*, cogn. with L. *vir* and forms in OIr., Lith., and Skr.)+**alđ-* age (cf. OLD), the etymol. meaning being, therefore, 'age' or 'life of man'. Hence **wo·rld**LING¹ (XVI; cf. G. *weltling*). **wo·rld**-LY¹. OE. *woruldliċ*.

worm wɜ̄ɹm (arch.) serpent, dragon; †reptile; creeping limbless member of the genus Lumbricus; endoparasitic helminth; larva of insect, maggot OE.; earthworm XIII; vermiform ligament; spiral tool, etc. XVI. OE. *wyrm*, later *wurm*, corr. to OFris. *wirm*, OS., (O)HG. *wurm* (Du. *worm*),

ON. *ormr* serpent, Goth. *waurms* :- Germ. **wurmiz* and **wurmaz*, rel. to L. *vermis* worm, Gr. *rhómos*, *rhómox* woodworm, Lith. *var̃mas* insect, midge. Hence vb. hunt worms; get rid of, make one's way, etc. by subtle means XVI; **wo·rm-eaten** XIV (Trevisa). **wo·rm-**HOLE. XVI (Sh.). ¶ For the vocalism cf. *worse*, and *wort*.

wormwood wɔ̄·ɹmwud plant Artemisia Absinthium, proverbial for its bitter taste. XV. alt., by assim. of the second syll. to WOOD, of late ME. *wormod*, OE. *wormōd*, corr. to MLG. *wormōde*, OHG. *wormuota*, alt. by assim. to WORM of OE. *wermōd* = OS. *wer(i)moda*, OHG. *wer(i)muota* (G. †*wermuth*; cf. VERMOUTH); of unkn. origin; the assim. is due to the use of Artemisia as a remedy for worms in the body.

worrit wʌ·rit worry. XIX (Lamb). dial. var. of WORRY; cf. *werret*, *wherret* XVIII.

worry wʌ·ri †strangle OE.; †choke XIII; seize by the throat with the teeth XIV; harass, assail XVI; afflict mentally; intr. for refl. XIX. OE. *wyrgan* = OFris. *wergia* kill, MLG., MDu. *worgen*, OHG. *wurgan* (Du. *wurgen*, G. *würgen*) :- WGerm. **wurgjan*; ME. *werry*, *wirry*, surviving dial., are normal developments of the OE. form, which contains a var. of IE. **wergh-* as seen in MHG. *erwergen* throttle.

worse wɔ̄ɹs compar. of *bad*, *evil*, *ill*. OE. adj. *wiersa*, *wyrsa* = OFris. *werra*, *wirra*, OS. *wirsa*, OHG. *wirsiro*, ON. *verri*, (:- **wersi*), Goth. *wairsiza* :- CGerm. **wersizon*, f. **wers-*, found also in OS., OHG. *werran* (G. *ver|wirren* entangle, confound; cf. WAR); see -ER[3]. So adv. OE. *wiers* = OS., OHG. *wirs*, ON. *verr*, Goth. *wairs*. Also WORST. Hence **wo·rs**EN[5] wɔ̄·ɹsn make worse XIII; become worse XVIII. Erratic in currency till XVIII, when it was taken up by such writers as Wordsworth, De Quincey, and Southey as less formal than *deteriorate*, etc. **wo·rs**ER[3]. XV; double compar. like *lesser*, in XVII–XVIII in full use as an alternative to *worse*, and surviving later in some phrs. like *worser part*, and in dial. and vulgar use. ¶ ON. *verri* was adopted as ME. *werre*, which was succeeded by *warre*, *war*, this giving *waur* in Sc. (XVIII), a form familiarized by Burns and Scott, and generalized in Sc. use.

worship wɔ̄·ɹʃip (arch.) good name, credit, dignity, importance; respect shown OE.; veneration of a power held divine XIII. OE. *weorþsċipe*, *wurþ-*, *wyrþ-*, f. *weorþ* WORTH[2] + *-sċipe* -SHIP. Hence vb. XII. ME. *worþshipie*. **wo·rship**FUL[1]. XIII; as an honorific title XIV. ¶ Formations peculiarly Eng.

worst wɔ̄ɹst adj. and adv.; superl. of *bad*, *evil*, *ill*. OE. *wierresta*, *wyrresta* = OFris. *wersta*, OS. *wirsista*, OHG. *-isto*, ON. *verstr*; see -EST. Hence vb. †impair, damage; overcome, defeat. XVII.

worsted wu·stid (woollen fabric made of) closely twisted yarn. XIII (*wrstede*). f. name of a parish in Norfolk, OE. *Wurþestede*, later *Worthstede*, now *Worstead*; in AL. *pannus*, in AN. *drap*, *de Wurthstede*.

wort[1] wɔ̄ɹt herb, vegetable OE.; cabbage (surviving in COLEWORT) XIV. OE. *wyrt* root, plant = OS. *wurt*, (O)HG. *wurz*, ON. *urt*, Goth. *waurts*; cf. ROOT[1].

wort[2] wɔ̄ɹt infusion of grain for the making of beer. OE. *wyrt* = OS. *wurtja* spicery, (M)HG. *würze*.

worth[1] wɔ̄ɹþ money value (e.g. *pennyworth*) OE.; relative value in character XIV; (high) personal merit XVI. OE. *worþ*, *weorþ*, *wurþ* = OFris. *werth*, OS. *werð*, OHG. *werd* (G. *wert*), ON. *verð*, Goth. *wairþ*; sb. use of next. Hence **wo·rth**LESS. XVI (Sh.).

worth[2] wɔ̄ɹþ of the value of a specified amount OE.; having a value of (so much) XII; possessed of XV. OE. *worþ*, *weorþ*, *wurþ* = OFris. *werth*, OS. *werð*, MDu. *waert*, *wert*, OHG. *werd* (Du. *waard*, G. *wert*), ON. *verðr*, Goth. *wairþs*; CGerm. adj. of doubtful etym.

worth[3] wɔ̄ɹþ (arch.) come to be, become. OE. *weorþan*, *wurþan*, pt. *wearþ*, *wurdon*, pp. *ġewordan* = OFris. *wertha*, OS. *werðan*, OHG. *werdan* (Du. *worden*, G. *werden*), ON. *verða*, Goth. *wairþan* :- CGerm. **werþan*, f. IE. **wert*, whence L. *vertere*, earlier *vortere* turn (with many comps.), OSl. *vrĭtěti* turn, Skr. *vártatē* turns, passes on, takes place. Cf. VERSE, VERTEBRA, VERTIGO, -WARD.

worth[4] wɔ̄ɹþ (hist.) enclosed place. XVI. Used mainly as extracted from place-names containing it as final el., e.g. *Kenilworth*. OE. *worþ* = OS. *wurð* soil, MLG. *wurt*, *wort* homestead; of unkn. origin (but see A. H. Smith, *Eng. Place-Name Elements*).

worthy wɔ̄·ɹði (arch.) having worth or value; of sufficient worth XIII; sb. XIV. ME. *wurþi*, *worþi*, f. WORTH[1] + -Y[1]; superseding OE. *wurþe*, *weorþe*, *wierþe* and *weorþ* WORTH[2].

-worthy wɔ̄·ɹði the adj. WORTHY used from XIII (e.g. in *deathworthy*) as a second el. of comps., repl. *-wurthe*, repr. OE. *-wyrþe*, *-wierþe*, f. *weorþ* WORTH[2]. Only a few are now in regular use, as *blame-* (Trevisa), *note-*, *praise-* (XVI), *seaworthy* XIX; (so *airworthy*).

wot wɔt (arch.) know. XIII. Arising from the carrying over of the perfect-present stem 1st and 3rd sg. *wōt* (OE. *wāt*) into other parts of WIT[2]; the substitution appears first in the 2nd pers. sg. (*wāt*, *wōt* for *wāst*, *wōst*) and the pl. (for *witen*) of the present tense; it was established throughout by XVI.

would, would(e)st see WILL[2].

wound wūnd bodily hurt, external injury; also fig. OE. *wund* = OFris. *wunde*, *wund*, OS. *wunda*, OHG. *wunta* (Du. *wond*,

G. *wunde*), ON. *und*: CGerm. (exc. Goth., which has adj. *wunds* = OHG., G., OE. *wund*), abstr. formation in *-*tō*; the base is of uncertain origin. So vb. OE. *wundian* = OFris. *wundia*, etc. ¶ The normally developed pronunc. waund, recorded in some dicts. of XVIII, survived dial., in the adj. **wou·nd**Y[1] and adv. **wou·ndi**LY[2], and the ints. *wounds* (for *Christ's wounds*, etc.) and ZOUNDS. comp. **wou·nd**WORT[1] pop. name of various plants reputed to heal wounds. XVI (Turner, Gerarde, tr. Du. *wondkruid*).

wourali see CURARE.

wove wouv var. of *woven*, pp. of WEAVE XVIII; from early XIX in techn. use of paper.

wow wau excl. of aversion, surprise, or admiration. XVI (Douglas). In earliest and main use Sc. Hence sb. (U.S. sl.) something sensational. XX.

wow-wow wau·wau silver gibbon of Java. XIX. – Malay *wauwau*, Javanese *wawa* (whence Du. *wouwouw*, *wawwaw*); imit. of its cry.

wr- r cons.-combination occurring initially in many words implying twisting or distortion, the earlier of which often have cogns. in other Germ. langs. Difficulty in pronouncing the combination is shown by ONhb. sps. with *wur-*, as by later *wer-* (XIV–XV). Loss of the *w* is shown by reduction to *r* in writing and by the converse use of *wr-* for *r-*, which appeared in XV and became frequent in XVI. Retention of *w* has remained locally where in standard Eng. it has been lost.

wrack[1] ræk (arch.) retributive punishment, vengeance OE.; damage XV. OE. *wræc*, f. var. of base of *wrecan* WREAK.

wrack[2] ræk (dial.) wreck, wreckage XIV; marine vegetation XVI. – MDu. *wrak*, corr. to OE. *wræc* WRACK[1]. Cf. VAREC(H).

Wraf ræf *W*omen's *R*oyal *A*ir *F*orce.

wraith reiþ phantom, ghost. XVI (G. Douglas). Sc., of unkn. origin; familiarized through Scott's use.

wrangle ræ·ŋgl dispute angrily or noisily. XIV (PPl.; not common before XVI). prob. of LDu. origin; cf. LG., G. dial. *wrangeln*. Cf. WRING. See -LE[3]. Hence **wra·ngl**ER[1] disputant XVI, spec. one placed in the first class in the mathematical tripos at Cambridge university XVIII.

wrap ræp cover or enfold in clothing or the like XIV (R. Mannyng); in various transf. and fig. uses from late XIV. Of unkn. origin; similar in form and sense are NFris. *wrappe* stop up, Da. dial. *vrappe* stuff; and cf. ME. *bewrappe*, beside *wlappe* (XIV), LAP[3].

wrasse ræs fish of various species of Labrus or Labridæ. XVII (Willughby). – Corn. *wrach*, var. of *gwrach* = W. *gwrach* wrasse, old woman (cf. *old wife* as a name for the wrasse).

wrath rɔ̄þ, U.S. rāþ anger (esp. intense or violent). OE. *wrǣþþu* (whence ME. *wraþþe*, *wreþþe*; *wrath* from XIV), f. *wrāþ* WROTH + -**iþō* -TH[1].

wreak rīk †drive away, expel, give vent to (anger, etc.); avenge, revenge OE.; take (vengeance) *on* XV. OE. *wrecan*, pt. *wræc*, *wrǣcon*, pp. *wrecen* = OFris. *wreka*, OS. *wrekan*, OHG. *rehhan* (Du. *wreken*, G. *rächen*), ON. *reka*, Goth. *wrikan* persecute :- *CGerm. **wrekan*, f. **wrek-* (cf. **wrak-* s.v. WRETCH) :- IE. **wreg-*, prob. cogn. with L. *urgēre* subject to pressure, drive, URGE, Gr. *eirgein* shut up.

wreath rīþ pl. *wreaths* rīðz A. twisted band or coil OE.; bank or drift of snow XVIII; B. chaplet or garland of flowers, leaves, etc. XVI. OE. *wriþa*, f. reduced var. of the base of WRITHE. So **wreathe** rīð twist, coil. XVI. perh. back-formation f. *wreathen* (XIV) arranged in coils or curves, ME. *wrēthen*, var. of *writhen*, OE. *wriþen*, pp. of *wrīþan* WRITHE.

wreck rek what is cast ashore by the sea; ruined or disabled ship XIII; disabling of a vessel XV. – AN. *wrec* – ON. **wrek*, f. **wrekan* drive (see WREAK, WRACK[2]); hence **wreck** vb. make a wreck of. XV (but cf. AL. *wrecāre* XII). **wre·ck**AGE wrecking; remains of a wrecked vessel. XIX.

wren ren small dentirostral passerine bird of the genus Troglodites. OE. *wrenna*, with var. *wrænna* (surviving in dial. *wran*), obscurely cogn. with synon. OHG. *wrendo*, *wrendilo*, Icel. *rindill*.

Wren ren woman of the *W*omen's *R*oyal *N*aval *S*ervice (*Wrens*). XX.

wrench rentʃ turn, twist (intr. OE.; trans. XIII). Late OE. *wrenćan* = OHG. *renchen* (G. *renken*), of unkn. origin.

wrest rest turn, twist OE.; pull or pluck away XIII; strain the meaning of, deflect the course of XVI. OE. *wrǣstan* = ON. **wreista* (ONorw., Icel. *reista*, MDa. *vreste*, Da. *vriste*) :- **wraistjan*; cf. WRIST.

wrestle re·sl strive to overcome another by grappling with his body. OE. **wrǣstlian* (implied in late OE. *wrǣstlung* 'palestram'), corr. to LDu. repr. by NFris. *wrassele*, MLG. *worstelen*, *wrostelen*, (M)Du. *worstelen*, OE. *wraxlian*, OFris. *wrāxlia*, perh. f. **wrasc-*, dial. *wrasle*.

wretch retʃ †exile (of doubtful survival after OE.); miserable being; despicable person OE.; †niggard, miser XIV (RMannyng). OE. *wrećća* = OS. *wrekkio* (applied to the Magi), OHG. (*w*)*recch*(*e*)*o* exile, adventurer, knight errant (MHG., G. *recke* warrior, hero, dial. giant) :- WGerm. **wrakjo*, f. **wrak-* (see WREAK), whence popL. *waraciō*(*n-*), the source of F. GARÇON).

wretched re·tʃid marked by distress or misery XII; contemptible XIII. f. WRETCH + -ED[2]; for the unusual formation cf. WICKED.

wriggle ri·gl twist the body about with short sinuous movements. XV. – (M)LG. (= Du.) *wriggelen*, frequent. of *wriggen* (Du. *wriggen*); see -LE[3], and cf. WIGGLE.

wright rait artificer, handicraftsman (esp. one who works in wood), surviving mainly in *cartwright, playwright, shipwright, wainwright, wheelwright*, of which the first and fourth, together with the simplex, are common surnames. OE. *wryhta* metathetic var. of *wyrhta* = OFris. *wrichta*, OS. *wurhtio*, OHG. *wurhto* :– WGerm. **wurhtjo*, f. **wurk-* WORK.

wring riŋ pt., pp. **wrung** rʌŋ squeeze, twist, wrench, wrest (lit. and fig.). OE. *wringan*, pt. *wrang*, *wrungon*, pp. *wrungen* = OS. *-wringan* (MLG., Du. *wringen*); WGerm. str. vb. f. base *wreŋg-*, rel. to **wraŋg-* WRONG. Cf. WRANGLE.

wrinkle ri·ŋkl †winding; fold XV. OE. *ġewrinclod* winding (of a ditch), ppl. formation with no recorded infin. The earliest members of the group are *wrinkling, wrinklingly* (XIV, Trevisa), and *wrinkled* (XV, Lydg.). So **wri·nkle** vb. undergo contraction into small folds. XVI. prob. orig. of local status and consequently rarely evidenced in early use.

wrist rist joint uniting the hand to the forearm OE.; (dial.) ankle, instep XVI. OE. *wrist*, corr. to OFris. *wrist, wirst*, (M)LG. *wrist*, (M)HG. *rist* wrist, instep, withers, ON. *rist* instep :– CGerm. (exc. Goth.) **wristiz*, prob. f. **wrið-*, f. wk. grade of the stem of WRITHE. Comp. **wri·st**BAND[2] part of a sleeve that covers the wrist. XVI. **wristlet**. XIX.

writ rit writing, spec. legal document. OE. *writ* = OHG. *riz* stroke, written character (G. *riss*, as in *umriss* outline), ON. *rit* writing, writ, letter, Goth. *writs* pen-stroke, f. **writ-* **wrīt-* WRITE.

write rait pt. **wrote** rout, pp. **written** ri·tn form or delineate with an implement; inscribe (letters). OE. *wrītan*, pt. *wrāt*, *writon*, pp. (*ġe*)*writen*, engrave, draw, depict, write = OFris. *wrīta* score, write, OS. *wrītan* cut, write, OHG. *rīzan* tear, draw (G. *reissen* †sketch, tear, pull, drag), ON. *ríta* score, write (Norw. *rita*, dial. *vrita*) :– CGerm. (exc. Gothic; cf. WRIT) **wrītan*, of unkn. origin. ¶ The sense-development is due to the earliest forms of inscribed symbols being made on stone and wood with sharp tools.

writhe raið twist, e.g. the body (trans. and intr.). OE. *wrīþan*, pt. *wrāþ*, *wriþon*, pp. *ġewriþen* = OHG. *rīdan*, ON. *ríða* (OSw. *vrīþa*), rel. to WREATH.

wrong rɔŋ (perh.) †crooked, twisted OE. (*on wrangan hylle* XIII copy of 944 document); deviating from equity or the right XIII; incorrect, erroneous XIV. Late OE. *wrang*, *wrong* – ON. **wrangr*, *rangr* awry, unjust (MSw. *vranger*, Sw. *vrång*, MDa., Da. *vrang*) = MLG. *wrangh* sour, tart, MDu. *wrangh* bitter, hostile, Du. *wrang* acid, rel. to WRING. Hence adv. XIII, sb. that which is wrong, unjust, or immoral XI (Wulfstan); vb. XIV. **wro·ng**FUL[1]. XIV, **wro·ng**LY[2]. XIV (all R. Mannyng).

wroth rouþ, rɔþ (arch.) angered, wrathful. OE. *wrāþ* = OFris. *wrēth*, OS. *wrēð* (Du. *wreed* cruel), OHG. *reid*, ON. *reiðr*, f. Germ. **wraiþ-* **wrīþ-* WRITHE. Rare *c.*1530–1850 exc. in or after biblical use, and said by J. to be 'out of use', its revival being begun by early-XIX poets.

wrought rɔ̄t fashioned or formed, esp. by labour or art XIV; manufactured; decorated, elaborated XV; (of metals) shaped by hammering, etc. XVI. ME. *wroȝt*, metathetic var. of *worȝt*, *worht*, pp. of WORK.

wry rai twisted, distorted (lit. and fig.) XVI. f. (dial.) *wry* vb., OE. *wrīgian* strive, go forward, tend, in ME. deviate, swerve, contort = OFris. *wrīgia* bend, stoop; cf. AWRY, WRIGGLE. comp. **wry·**NECK bird of the genus Iynx, distinguished by a habit of writhing head and neck XVI.

Wyandot(te) wai·əndɔt breed of domestic fowl. XIX. f. name of an Iroquoian tribe of N. Amer. Indians.

wych-elm, witch-elm wi·tʃelm witch hazel, Ulmus montana. XVII (*weech elm*, Bacon). Earlier *witchen elm* (XVI); f. *wych*, *witch*, OE. *wiće*, *wić*, prob. f. Germ. **wik-* bend (see WEAK) + ELM.

wych hazel, witch hazel applied to various trees with pliant branches XVI. See prec., HAZEL.

Wyclif(f)ian wikli·fiən follower of John *Wycliffe* or *Wyclif*, *Wiclif(fe)*, English theologian and reformer (*c.* 1320–84). XVI. Also **Wy·clif(f)**IST XV (Pecock, Capgrave), **Wy·clif(f)**ITE (XVI). – medL.

Wykehamical wikæ·mikəl pert. to Winchester College, or pupils or the staff of this. XVIII. f. modL. *Wiccamicus*, f. name of William of *Wykeham* bishop of Winchester and founder of the college (1382); see -ICAL.

wyn(n) win runic character ƿ. OE. 'joy', corr. to OS. *wunnia*, OHG. *wunnja*, *wunnia*, *wunna* (G. *wonne*); WGerm. (cf. WINSOME, WISH).

wyvern, †wivern wai·vəɹn (her.) winged two-footed dragon. XVII. alt. of †*wyver* (XIII) – OF. *wivre*, (also mod.) *guivre* :– L. *vīpera* VIPER; for excrescent *n* cf. BITTERN.

X

x eks (math.) as the symbol of an unknown quantity XVII; (transf.) undetermined number or quantity XIX. Derived ult. from Arab. *shei* a thing, something, written by Sp. convention *xei*, translated by It. *cosa*, of which the abbreviation *co* was read as *x*; prob. taken directly from the *Géométrie* (1637) of Descartes, who used z, y, x for three unknowns.

xanth(o)- zæ·nþ(ou), comb. form of Gr. *xanthós* yellow, used in many techn. terms. XIX.

xebec zī·bek small three-masted vessel of the Mediterranean. XVIII. alt., after Sp. †*xabeque*, now *jabeque*, of *chebec* – F. *chebec* – It. *sciabecco* – Arab. *shabbāk*.

xeno- ze·nou repr. comb. form of Gr. *xénos* guest, stranger, foreign, strange (cf. GUEST), used in techn. terms. XIX. **xeno**PHO·BIA morbid dislike or dread of foreigners.

xenon ze·nən (chem.) heavy inert gaseous element present in the atmosphere (X, Xe). 1898 (Sir Wm. Ramsay). – Gr. n. of *xénos* (see prec.).

Xeres *sack, wine* XVII; see SHERRY.

xero- ziə·rou, ziərə· comb. form of Gr. *xērós* dry, used in techn. terms XIX. An early ex. is **xero**PHAGY ziərə·fədʒi eating of dry food (as a form of fasting) XVII. – Gr. *xērophagiā*.

xiphias zi·fiæs swordfish, esp. X. gladius, having the upper jaw prolonged into a sword-like weapon. XVI (*Ziffius*, Spenser). – L. – Gr. *xiphías*, f. *xíphos* sword.

xiphoid zi·foid sword-shaped, ensiform. XVIII. – modL. *xiphoidēs* – Gr. *xiphoeidḗs*, f. *xíphos* sword; see -OID.

X-rays eksrei·z form of radiation discovered by W. C. Röntgen of Würzburg in 1895, also called *Röntgen rays*. – G. *x-strahlen*.

xylo- zai·lou, zai·lə· comb. form of Gr. *xúlon* wood, used in techn. terms XIX. **xy·lon**ITE celluloid. XIX; earlier form *xyloinite*, irreg. f. *xyloidin* afterwards assim. to Gr. *xúlon*. **xy·lo**PHONE musical instrument consisting of flat wooden bars XIX.

xystus, pl. **-i** zi·stəs, -ai portico, colonnade. XVII (Evelyn). – L. – Gr. *xustós, xustón*.

Y

y- i prefix repr. OE. *ġe-* = OFris. *gi-*, *ge-*, *ie-*, *e-*, OS. *gi-*, *ge-*, *i-*, MLG., MDu. *ge-*, *ghe-* (LG., Du. *ge-*), OHG. *ga-*, *ka-*, *gi-*, *ki-* (G. *ge-*, dial. *je-*), Goth. *ga-* :- Germ. **ga-*; in Scand. the prefix had disappeared as a living element in prehistoric times but relics survive in ON. *glíkr* LIKE[1], *gnógr* ENOUGH. The parallelism of form and meaning shown by such words as L. *commūnis* and Goth. *gamains*, OE. *ġemǣne* COMMON, L. *convenīre* CONVENE and Goth. *gaqiman* assemble, has suggested the possibility of the identity of Germ. **ga-* and L. COM-. This prefix is disguised in form or its force is obliterated in AFFORD, ALIKE, AMONG, AWARE, EACH, EITHER, NEITHER, ENOUGH, EVERYWHERE, HANDICRAFT, HANDIWORK. From mid-XVI archaizing poets created new formations, e.g. *ychain'd*, *ydrop*, *yglaunst*, *yshrilled*, occas. with prp., as *ycausing* (Sackville), *star-ypointing* (Milton). The orig. physical meaning 'with', 'together', yielded the notion of associations, and hence of appropriateness, suitability, and collectivity, the final stage being the notion of completeness and perfectivity, a special application being the use of the prefix in pps., regular in OE. and continuing in southern ME. till XV, and repr. by *a-* in mod. dial. use. The OE. form *ġe-* was succeeded in ME. by *ȝe-*, *ie-*, *i-*, *y-*, the last of which is regular in Spenser and his imitators, as in YCLAD clothed, YCLEPT called, *yfet* fetched, *ywrit* written.

-y[1] i suffix of adjs. denoting 'having the character of . .', 'inclined to . .', 'full or consisting of . .'; OE. *-iġ*, earlier *-eġ*, *-ǣġ*, in early ME. *-i*, later *-ie*, *-ye*, finally *-y*, with variant *-ey* in certain positions, as *bluey*, *gluey*, *nosey* (beside *nosy*). Some adjs. of OE. date have long ceased to show their etymol. relations, as *empty*, *dizzy*, *giddy*, *merry*, as distinguished from others such as *bloody*, *mighty*, *speedy*. The sp. of *fiery* (f. *fire*) is notable. For the addition of *-y* to produce a more adjectival appearance see *chilly*, *haughty*, *murky*, *slippery*, *wary*, and compare *hugy*, †*paly*. An exceptional etym. is *handy*. To be noted is the ð in *swarthy* and *worthy*; the coexistence of *leafy* and *leavy*, the double cons. in *baggy*, *catty*, *chummy*, *leggy*, *soppy*, etc.; the *ck* in *panicky* and the like. In the foll. the origin is different, but the suffix is assoc. with this: *faulty, hardy, jolly, risky, sturdy, tardy*. Recent derivs. (since *c.*1800) have been very numerous, and have tended to be joc., undignified, or trivial, as *balmy, batty, boosy, bossy, cushy, doggy, dotty, hammy, hors(e)y, mousy, oniony, sexy, shirty, squiffy*. The suffix is added less frequently to verbs with the meaning 'inclined to, liable to', as in *choky, drowsy, slippy, sticky* (XVI), later *blowy, clingy, quavery, rollicky, runny* (e.g. of eggs).

-y[2] i suffix orig. of weak vbs. of the second class, of OE. inf. *-ian*, (with pt. in *-ode*, pp. in *-od*) = OFris. *-ia*, OS. *-ōian, -ōn*, OHG. *-ōn* (Du., G. *-en*), Goth. *-ōn* :– Germ. **-ōjan*. By XIII it was restricted to southern and western areas and remains in mod. dial. (Somerset, Devon, and Dorset) in intr. inf. use.

-y[3] i suffix repr. ultimately, partly through (O)F. *-ie*, CRom. *-ía*, L. *-ĭa* -IA[1]. It is the vocalic el. of -CY, -RY, and the final el. of many disyll. suffixes, viz. -ACY, -ANCY, -CRACY, -ENCY, -ERY, -GRAPHY, -LATRY, -LOGY, -MANCY, -PATHY, -PHILY, -TOMY. It is exemplified in names of countries such as *Brittany, Italy*; contrast *Arabia* (†*Araby*), *Britannia, Syria* (†*Syrie*).

-y[4] i repr., partly through AN. *-ie*, L. *-ium* as appended to verbal bases, as in *augury, colloquy, perjury, obloquy, remedy, subsidy*; not a productive el. in Eng., but perh. supplying the analogy for *expiry* and *inquiry*, and a basis for *entreaty*, f. *entreat* vb. after *treat, treaty*. The *y* of *effigy, mercy, navy, pigmy*, is different.

-y[5] i suffix repr. AN., OF. *-e, -ee* (mod.F. *-é, -ée*) :– L. *-atu-, -ata* (see -ATE[1], -ATE[2]; in sbs. = -ATE[1] as in (1) *county, duchy, pasty, patty, treaty*, (2) *army, delivery, entry, livery*; in adjs. = -ATE[2], as in *easy, privy, puny, tawny*; there are few gen. adjs. of this class, but the number of heraldic descriptive terms is considerable, as *bendy, gyronny, lozengy, sarcelly*, the earliest of which have the forms *-e, -ee, -i*; *wavy* as a syn. of *undy* is isolated as a formation on a native word.

-y[6] i also *-ie*, (in some special cases) *-ey*, as *Charley* (beside *Charlie*), *jockey, sawney, slavey*; originating in hypocoristic Sc. formations, several of which have been the basis of surnames, as *Christie, Christison, Jamieson, Mathieson, Robison*, and forming pet names and familiar diminutives, as well as transf. uses such as applications to implements; for miscellaneous exx. see *babby, Betty, bobby, cuddy*[2], *daddy, dandy*[1], *dicky*[1], *jemmy, jockey, joey*[2], *johnny, kiddy, namby-pamby, nanny, paddy*[2], *Sally Lunn, teddy, Tommy*. Addition to a curtailed form of a disyllable or polysyllable is exemplified by *baccy, cabby, hubby, middy, nighty, toady, tummy, tweeny*; exx. of proper names are *Bozzy* (f. *Boswell*), *Dizzy* (f. *Disraeli*). Isolated formations are *comfy* (for *comfortable*), *conchy* (for *conscientious objector*), *gutty* (for *guttapercha*), *hanky* (formerly *handky*, for *handkerchief*), *navvy* (for *navigator*). (For applications of the pl. see -IES.) Cf. -SY.

yabber jæ·bəɹ language of Australian aborigines. XIX. Native *yabba*.

yacht jɔt light fast-sailing ship. XVI. – early modDu. *jaght(e)*, now *jacht*, short for *jaghtschip* (ship for chasing), f. *jaght* hunting, chase, f. *jagen* hunt, chase (see -T[2]); from Du. are also G. *jacht*, Sw. *jakt*, Da. *jagt*, F. *jacht* jak, Sp. *yacte, yate, yac*, Pg. *hiate*, Russ. *jakhta*. Owing mainly to the presence in the Du. word of the sound χ the Eng. sp. has been various and erratic; the present pronunc. is shown by *yott* in XVII; a former pronunc. jɔtʃ or jætʃ is shown by the sp. *yatch* (XVII–XIX). Hence **yacht**ING[1] jɔ·tiŋ, **ya·cht**SMAN, superseding *yachtman*. XIX.

yaffingale jæ·fiŋgeil (dial.) green woodpecker. XVII. imit. of the bird's laughing cry. Also **yaffil, yaffle** jæ·fl XVIII, **ya·ffl**ER[1] XIX.

yager jei·gəɹ anglicized sp. of JÄGER. XIX (Byron, Campbell).

yah[1] jā excl. of disgust or defiance. XIX.

yah[2] jā repeated *yah! yah!* denoting perperverted pronunc. of *hear! hear!* used as a form of applause. XIX.

yahoo jahū· name invented by Swift (Gulliver's Travels, 1726) for a brute in human form. Cf. HOUYHNHNM.

Yahvist see JAHVIST.

yak jæk bovine animal Poephagus grunniens. XIX. – Tibetan *γyag*.

yale lock jeil lɔk form of lock invented by Linus *Yale* (1821–68), a locksmith of New England. XIX.

yam jæm (tuberous root of) species of Dioscorea. XVII (earlier in Eng. writings in various alien forms, e.g. *inany, nname, igname*) – Pg. *inhame* or Sp. †*igñame* (mod. *ñame*), whence F. *igname*; ult. source unkn.

yamen, -un jā·mən office of a Chinese mandarin. XIX. Chinese, f. *ya* general's tent or pavilion, official residence + *mun* gate.

yank jæŋk (dial., U.S.) pull suddenly and vigorously; also sb. XIX. Of unkn. origin.

Yank jæŋk short for YANKEE. XVIII.

Yankee jæ·ŋki native of New England, (hence of the U.S.A.). XVIII. None of the proposed etyms. is convincing; most plausibly on formal grounds, spec. application of *Yankee, Yank(e)y* (XVII–XVIII) as a surname or nickname, and may be based on Du. *Jan* John and intended as a dim. form (= *Jantje*). ¶ *Yanky* was formerly the name of a craft of Du. build.

yaourt ja·uɹt semi-solid curd-like food prepared from milk. XIX. — Turk. *yoghurt* (with quiescent *gh*).

yap bark sharply. XVII. imit. Cf. YAWP.

yapock jæ·pɔk S. Amer. water opossum. XIX. f. name of a river between French Guiana and Brazil.

yapp book-binding with projecting limp leather cover. XIX. Name of a London bookseller to whose order the binding was first made.

yarak jæ·ræk *in y.* (of a hawk) in condition for hunting. XIX. perh. – Pers. *yārakī* strength.

yarborough jā·ɹbərə hand containing no card above a nine. XIX. Said to be named after an earl of *Yarborough* who bet 1000 to 1 against its occurrence.

yard[1] yāɹd enclosed space attached to a building OE.; enclosure in which animals are kept or some work is done XIII (Cursor M., Havelok). OE. *ġeard* fence, enclosure, courtyard, dwelling, region (as in *middan|ġeard*, ME. *middenerd* the earth, *ort|ġeard* ORCHARD). Corr., with variation of declension, to OFris. *garda*, OS. *gardō*, OHG. *gart*, *garto* (Du. *gaard*, G. *garten* garden), ON. *garðr* GARTH, Goth. *gards* house, *garda* enclosure, stall :– CGerm. **gardaz* **gardon*, rel. to OSl. *gradŭ* city, garden, Russ. *górod* town (cf. the place-names Petro*grad*, Bel*grade*, Nov*gorod*), Lith. *gar̃das* enclosure. Cf. GARDEN.

yard[2] jāɹd †rod, staff; (naut.) spar to which a square sail is bent; †measuring-rod; †rood (of land) OE.; measure of 3 feet XIV. OE. *ġerd*, (WS.) **ġierd*, *ġird*, *ġyrd* = OFris. *jerde*, OS. *gerdia* switch, *segal|gerd* sail-yard (Du. *gard* twig, rod), OHG. *gart(e)a*, *gerta* (G. *gerte*) :– WGerm. **gazdjō*, f. Germ. **gazdaz* GAD[1].

yare jɛəɹ ready OE.; (of a ship) easily manageable XIV (Gower). OE. *ġearu* = OS. *garu*, *-o* (Du. *gaar* done, dressed, clever), OHG. *garo* (G. *gar* ready, prepared, adv. quite), ON. *gǫrr*, *gǫrv-* ready-made, prompt, skilled :– Germ. **garwu-* (cf. GAR).

yarn jāɹn spun fibre of cotton, silk, etc. OE. *ġearn* = MDu. *gaern* (Du. *garen*), OHG., G., ON. *garn*, prob. f. base repr. also by **garnō* in ON. *gǫrn*, pl. *garnar* guts, and **garnjo-* in OE. *micġern*, OS. *midgarni*, OHG. *mittigarni* entrail fat, suet, and rel. outside Germ. to Lith. *žárna* intestine, L. *haru|spex* one who divines from inspection of entrails, Gr. *khordḗ* intestine, guts, tripe, string of gut, of a lyre, CHORD[2], Skr. *hirā* vein. The sense 'story, tale' is from naut. sl. phr. *spin a yarn.*

yarrow jæ·rou plant Achillea Millefolium. OE. *ġearwe*, corr. to MDu. *garwe*, *gherwe* (Du. *gerwe*), OHG. *gar(a)wa* (G. *schaf|garbe*); WGerm., of unkn. origin.

yashmak jæ·ʃmæk Moslem woman's veil. XIX. – Arab. *yashmaq*.

yataghan jæ·təgən sword of Moslem countries. XIX. – Turk. *yātāghan*, adopted in many Eur. langs. Cf. *ataghan* (Byron).

yaw jɔ̄ (orig. naut.) deviate in the course. XVI. Of unkn. origin.

yawl[1] jɔ̄l cry out loudly. XIV (*ȝaule*). Parallel to YOWL with vowel-variation; cf. LG. *jaulen* (of cats).

yawl[2] jɔ̄l ship's boat; small sailing-boat or fishing-boat. XVII (*yale*, *yall*, *yaule*). – (M)LG. *jolle* or Du. *jol*, whence also F. *yole*, It. *jolo*, Sw. *julle*, G., Da. *jolle*, Russ. *jal*; ult. origin unkn. Cf. JOLLY-BOAT.

yawn jɔ̄n open the mouth wide (now only from fatigue, etc.); lie wide open. XVI. spec. symbolic alt. of ME. *ȝone*, which with *ȝene* repr. OE. *ġeonian*, var. of *ġinian* = OHG. *ginōn*, *-ēn*, MDu. *ghēnen*, rel. to synon. OE. *gānian*, OHG. *geinōn* and OE. *gīnan*, OS. *gīnan*, ON. *gína*; all *n*-formations on Germ. **gai-*, **gĭ-*; a parallel with *w* appears in OHG. *giwēn*, MDu. *ghēwen*, the simple base being shown by OHG. *gīēn* gape, ON. *gjá* cleft. Outside Germ. (**ghoi-*) **ghei-* **ghi-* is repr. by L. *hiāre*, *hīscere* gape, yawn (cf. HIATUS, DEHISCENT), OSl. *zijati*, Lith. *žióti*; cf. Gr. *kháskein*, *khaínein* gape, and CHASM.

yawp, yaup jɔ̄p (chiefly dial.) perh. identical with late ME. *ȝolpe* cry or shout harshly; in XVI–XVII *yalp*, also of a dog = YAP; imit. of loud or strident utterance.

yaws jɔ̄z contagious disease affecting Negroes. XVI. So *jas* in Du. Guiana; identity with synon. *pians* pl. (F. *pian*, Sp., Pg. *epian*, *pian* – Guarani *piá*) has been suggested, through Negro jargon.

yclad iklæ·d clothed; arch. as in Spenser, Sh., Thomson, Byron; see Y-, CLAD.

yclept ikle·pt arch. called (so-and-so). OE. *ġecleopod*, pp. of *cleopian*, *clipian* call; see Y-, -T[3].

ye jī, ji (arch. and joc., dial.) nom. pl. of 2nd pers. pron. OE. *ġĕ* = OFris. *jī*, OS. *gi*, *ge* (Du. *gij*), OHG. *ir* (G. *ihr*), ON. *ér* (:– **jēr*), analogically modified forms (after the 1st pers. pron., e.g. OE. *ġe* after *we*, OHG. *ir* after *wir*, ON. *ér* after *vér*) of CGerm. **juz*, accented **jūs*, repr. by Goth. *jūs*, f. **ju-* (with pl. ending); see YOU, YOUR.

ye jī late writing of *þ*ᵉ THE[1].

yea jei affirmative adv. (now dial. and arch.) OE. *ġē*, (WS.) *ġēa*, corr. to OFris. *gē*, *jē*, OS., OHG. *jā* (Du., G. *ja*), ON. *já*, Goth. *ja*, *jai*; ult. CGerm. **ja*, **je*, which was variously modified through stress or emotional emphasis. The standard sp. *yea* and pronunc. jei show retarded development, perh. partly due to assoc. with *nay* (but the normal development jī is current locally). ¶ For the former spec. distinction of usage cf. YES.

yean jīn (arch., dial.) of a ewe, bring forth. XIV (Trevisa). repr. OE. **ġeēanian* (rel. to *ġeēan* 'feta'), f. *ġe-* Y- + *ēanian* = WFris. *eandje*, Du. dial. *oonen* :- Germ. **aunōjan*, f. **aun-* :- IE. **agwn-*, whence also L. *agnus*, Gr. *amnós*, OSl. *agnę*, OIr. *úan*, W. *oen* lamb. Cf. **ea·n**LING[1] young lamb (Sh.), f. dial. *ean*, OE. *ēanian*.

year jiəɹ period of the earth's revolution round the sun; 12 months; pl. age OE.; pl. period, times XIII. OE. (Anglian) *ġēr*, (WS.) *ġēar* = OFris. *jār*, *jēr*, OS. *jār*, *gēr* (Du. *jaar*), OHG. *jār* (G. *jahr*), ON. *ár*, Goth. *jēr* :- CGerm. **jǣram*, f. IE. base **jēr-* **jōr-*, repr. also by Av. *yāre* year, Gr. *hṓrā* season (whence L. *hōra* HOUR), time of year, time of day, *hôros* year, pl. annals, OSl. *jara* spring (Russ. *yarovói*, Pol. *jary*, Serb. *jari* (of crops) spring-sown), and L. *hornus* of this year :- **hōjōrinus*, f. **hō jōrō* (cf. G. *heuer* this year, OHG. *hiuru* :- **hiu jāru*). comp. **year**MIND jiə·ɹmaind yearly obit. OE. *ġearġemynd*, superseded by *year's mind* from XV.

yearn jəɹn have a strong desire. OE. *ġiernan* = OS. *ġernean*, *ġirnean*, ON. *girna*, Goth. *gairnjan* :- Germ. (not in HG.) **gernjan*, f. **gernaz* (whence Finn. *kernas* desirous), repr. by OE. *ġeorn* eager, OS., OHG. *gern* (G. *gern* willingly), ON. *gjarn*, Goth. *seina|gairns* selfish, f. **ger-*, repr. also by OHG. *gerōn* (G. *begehren*) desire, ON. *gerr* greedy, with prob. cogns. in Skr. and Av., Gr. *kháris* favour, grace, *khaírein* rejoice, L. *horīrī*, *hortarī* EXHORT.

yeast jīst frothy substance produced by fermentation of malt, etc. OE. (Anglian) **ġest*, WS. **giest* (late *ġist*), corr. to MLG. *gest* dregs, dirt, MDu. *ghist*, *ghest* (Du. *gist*, *gest* yeast), MHG. *jist*, *jest*, *gist*, *gest* (G. *gischt*, earlier *gäscht*), yeast, froth, ON. *jǫstr*, rel. to OHG. *jesan*, *gesan*; IE. **jes-* is repr. also by Skr. *yás(y)ati* seethe, boil, Gr. *zeîn* boil, *zestós* boiled, W. *iās* seething.

yelk see YOLK[1].

yell jel utter a loud strident cry. OE. (Anglian) *ġellan*, (WS.) *ġiellan*, pt. *ġeal*, *gullon* = MLG., MDu. *ghellen*, OHG. *gellan* (Du. *gillen*, G. *gellen*), ON. *gjalla*, f. Germ. **gel-* **gal-*, whence also OE., OHG. *galan*, ON. *gala* sing, cry out, OE. *nihte|gale* NIGHTINGALE, ON. *hana|gal* cockcrow, OS., OHG. *galm* outcry. Weak inflexions began XIV.

yellow je·lou of the colour of gold, yolk of egg, buttercups OE. †jealous XVII; in phr. *y. press* sensational XIX. OE. *ġeolu*, *-o* = OS. *gelo*, (M)LG. *geel*, MDu. *gel(e)u*, *geel*, OHG. *gelo* (Du. *gel*, G. *gelb*) :- WGerm. **gelwa* :- IE. **ghelwo-*, rel. to L. *helvus*. Gr. *khlóos*, *khlóē*, Lith. *želvas*. Cf. GALL[1], GOLD. sb. XIV.

yellow hammer, ammer je·lou (h)æ·məɹ species of bunting Emberiza citrinella, having bright yellow plumage. XVI (*yelambre*, *yellowhamer*). The source of *(h)ammer* may be OE. *amore* 'scorellus' (unidentified), with poss. conflation with *hama* covering, feathers, there being a syn. in dial. *yellowham* (XVI); there are numerous Continental names of birds which contain el. meaning 'yellow' or 'gold'.

yelp jelp A. †boast; †cry aloud XV; B. utter a cry characteristic of dogs, etc. XVI (the corr. sense of the sb. is earlier in Sc., as used by Dunbar and Douglas). OE. *ġielpan*, *ġelpan*, *ġilpan* (pt. *ġealp*, *gulpon*, pp. *golpen*) = MHG. *gelfen*, *gelpfen*, f. echoic base otherwise repr. in OS. *galpon* (LG. *galpen*), ME. *ȝolpe*, dial. *yawp*.

yen jen gold or silver coin, the monetary unit. XIX. Jap. – Chin. *yüan* round, round thing, circle, dollar.

yeoman jou·mən, pl. **yeomen** attendant below the rank of 'sergeant' XIV; freeholder below the rank of a gentleman, (hence) man of good standing XV. ME. *ȝoman*, *ȝuman*, *ȝeman*, *ȝiman*, prob. reduced forms of *ȝong-*, *ȝung-*, *ȝeng-*, *ȝingman*, i.e. *youngman*, which was similarly used in ME. ¶ The phonetic development of *ngm* to *m(m)* may be paralleled in dial. *yeomath*, *yemmath*, etc. from **young math* late mowing. Swift in 1706 rhymes *ye'man* with *Philemon*.

yes jes word expressing an affirmative reply (peculiar to Eng.). OE. *ġēse*, *ġīse*, *ġȳse*, prob. for **ġīese*, f. **ġīa sīe* 'yea, may it be (so)'; formerly used spec. in response to a neg. question)(YEA.

yester- je·stəɹ of or pert. to the day before today. OE. *ġeostran*, *ġiestran* = OHG. *gestaron*, *gesterēn*, MHG. *gester(n)*, G. *gestern*, MLG. *ghist(e)ren*, Du. *gisteren*; in comps. **yester**DAY je·stəɹdi, -dei. OE. *ġeostran*, *ġystran dæġ* (also, with metathesis *gierstan dæġ*, Nhb. *ġiosterdoeġ*), having one Germ. parallel in Gothic (once) *gistradagis* tomorrow, the other langs. having only the simplex, as above; **yester**E·VE XVII, -E·VEN XV, -MO·RN XVIII, -MO·RNING XVII; †**yesterneve** OE.–XIV; **yester**NI·GHT (arch.), OE. *ġystran niht*; **yester**YEA·R last year. XIX (D. G. Rossetti, rendering Villon's *antan*). **yes-tr**EE·N yesterday evening (chiefly Sc. and poet.). XIV.

Of IE. extent (exc. Balto-Sl.), the Germ. forms showing the addition of compar. *-ter-* (cf. L. *hesternus* of yesterday) to the stem of Gr. *khthés*, *ekhthés*, Skr. *hyás*, L. *herī* yesterday. ¶ The basic sense is 'another day reckoning from yesterday'; the double meaning is seen in OHG. *ēgestern* and ON. *í gær*; there is an isolated ex. of the meaning of 'tomorrow' for *yesterday* in Sir Thomas More's works.

yet jet (arch.) in addition, further, moreover, still; till now. OE. *ġīet*, *ġīeta* = OFris. *iēta*, *ēta*, *īta*, of unkn. origin, like the synon. OE. *ġēn*, *ġēna*. ¶ The meanings of *yet* are expressed in Germ. langs. outside the

Anglo-Frisian group by *noh, OS., OHG. *noh* (Du. *nog*, G. *noch*), Goth. *nauh* (:- IE. **nuqe* 'and now').

yeti jei·ti XX. Native Sherpa (Tibetan) name of the Abominable Snowman, a sub-human animal supposed to leave tracks in the snow of the Himalayas.

yew jū tree of the genus Taxus. OE. *īw, ēow*, corr. with cons.-alternation and variation in gender to OE. *ī(o)h, ēoh*, OS. *īh*, MLG., MDu. *īwe, īewe, uwe*, OHG. *īwu, īwi, īwa, īhu, īga* (G. *eibe*), ON. *ýr* (chiefly 'bow') :- CGerm. (exc. Goth.) **īχwaz, īgwaz, īχwō, īgwō*, with parallel forms in Celtic and Balto-Sl.; F. *if* and Sp. *iva* are from Germ., and (M)Du. *ijf* from F. *if*. ¶ Often planted in churchyards and regarded as symbolical of grief; the wood was formerly much used for bows.

yex jeks, **yesk** jesk (dial.) †sob; hiccups. OE. *ġesca, ġeocsa*, rel. to vb. *ġiscian, ġeocsian*, corr. to OHG. *geskōn, geskizōn*; of echoic origin.

Yggdrasil i·gdrəsil (Norse myth.) the great yew tree whose branches and roots extend through the universe. XVIII. ON., also *askr yg(g)drasils* 'ash-tree of Y.'; perh. f. *Yggr* name of Odin + *drasill* horse.

Yiddish ji·diʃ language of Jews in Europe and America, consisting mainly of German (printed in Heb. characters). XIX. – G. *jüdisch* jü·diʃ Jewish, f. *Jude* JEW (the full G. name is *jüdisch-deutsch* Jewish-German) + *-isch* -ISH[1].

yield jīld pay, repay (mainly obs.) OE.; give forth, produce XI; give way, surrender XIII. OE. (non-WS.) *ġeldan*, (WS.) *-ġieldan*, pt. *ġeald*, pp. *ġolden* = OFris. *gelda, ielda*, OS. *geldan*, OHG. *geltan* (Du. *gelden*, G. *gelten*), ON. *gjalda*, Goth. *-gildan* (as in *fragildan, usgildan* compensate) :- CGerm. **gelðan* pay, requite, further cogns. of which are doubtful. ¶ The sense-development of the Eng. word is largely due to its rendering of L. *reddere* and F. *rendre* with their comps. On the Continent the only gen. surviving senses are 'be worth or valid', 'concern', 'apply to'.

-yl il (formerly occas. *-ule*) terminal el. of chemical terms – F. *-yle*, (†*-ule*) – Gr. *húlē* wood, matter, substance, used for 'chemical principle', 'radical', introduced by Wöhler and Liebig 1832 and first used by them in *benzoyle*.

ylang-ylang ī·læŋ ī·læŋ anonaceous tree Canangium odoratum, of Malaysia, etc. XIX. Tagalog.

yo jou excl. of incitement or warning. XV (*ȝo, io*). Also (naut.) **yo**|HO· **yo**HO· XVIII, **yo**-HEAVE-HO XIX.

yod jɔd 10th (and smallest) letter of the Heb. alphabet XVIII; (philol.) front voiced open consonant denoted by j. Cf. IOTA, JOT.

yode joud (arch., as used, e.g. by Spenser, Thomson, and Scott) went. ME. *ȝ(e)ode*, var. of *ȝede, ede* (OE. *ēode, ġeēode*), functioning as pt. of *gān* GO and parallel to Goth. *iddja*, pt. of *gaggan*; of disputed origin but presumably ult. cogn. with Gr. *eîmi* I shall go, L. *eō* I go (inf. *īre*). Cf. †*yede*, used pseudo-arch. as inf. XVI–XVIII.

yodel jou·dəl sing with mixture of falsetto like Swiss and Tyrolese mountain-dwellers. XIX. – G. *jodeln* (prop.) utter the syll. *jo*.

yoga jou·ga union with the Supreme Spirit. XIX. Hind.; Skr. *yoga* union (see YOKE). So **yo·gi** Indian ascetic who practises this XVII. Hind. :- Skr. *yogin*.

yog(h)urt jou·guəɹt var. of YAOURT. XIX.

yoicks joiks fox-hunting cry. XVIII. Contemp. with ***yoaks*** and ***hoicks*** (also ***hoick, hoik*** XVII), which appears to be a var. of earlier *hike*, as in ***hike hallow, hike a Bewmont*** (Turberville XVI).

yoke jouk contrivance for coupling draught animals by the neck; pair of animals so coupled (often with uninflected pl.); fig. subjection, suppression. OE. *ġeoc* = OS. *juc*, OHG. *joh* (Du. *juk*, G. *joch*), ON. *ok*, Goth. *juk* :- CGerm. **jukam* (whence Finn. *juko*) :- IE. **jugom*, corr. to L. *jugum*, Gr. *zugón*, W. *iau*, OSl. *igo*, Skr. *yugám*, f. **jug-* **jeug-* **joug-*, repr. also by L. *jungere* JOIN, Gr. *zeugnúnai* (cf. ZEUGMA), Lith. *jùngiu* harness, Skr. YOGA, Hitt. *jugan*. So **yoke** vb. OE. *ġeocian*. ¶ The standard form *yoke* descends from the obl. OE. forms, the nom. being normally repr. by dial. *yock*.

yokel jou·kl illiterate rustic, country bumpkin. XIX. First recorded from flash or sporting language; identical in form with dial. *yokel* green woodpecker, yellow-hammer, of which it may be a fig. application.

yolk[1] jouk yellow of an egg. OE. *ġeolca, ġeoloca*, f. *ġeolu* YELLOW. ¶ The parallel development repr. by **yelk** (XIV), with corr. pronunc. jelk, survived dial. and the sp. was common till late XIX, esp. in techn. use.

yolk[2] jouk greasy substance of sheep's skin glands. XVII. repr. OE. **eowoca*, in the adj. *eowociġ* (local *yolky*); see -Y[1]; cf. Flem. *ieke*, whence Sc. *eik*.

yon jɔn (arch., dial.) yonder. adj. (OE., once), pron. (XIII, Cursor M.). OE. *ġeon*, corr., with variation of vowels, to OFris. *jen(a), -e*, MLG. *gene*, MDu. *ghens*; OHG. *jenēr* (G. *jener* that one), Goth. *jains* that; there is a parallel series of forms without cons. initial, viz. OHG. *enēr*, ON. *enn, inn* (definite article), cogn. with Gr. *énē* day after tomorrow, *énioi* some, Lith. *anàs*, OSl. *onŭ* that, Skr. *āna-* this one. So **yond** jɔnd (dial.) yonder (adv. used adj.). OE. *ġeond* (*iand*), which enters into some 35 comps., corr. to MLG. *gent, genten, jint*, LG. *gunt, gunten*, early Flem. *ghins*, Du. *ginds*, Goth.

jaind thither; cf. BEYOND, ME. (dial.) *ayond*. **yonder** jɔ·ndəɹ (now literary, arch., or dial.) over there. XIII; adj. XIV. ME. *ȝonder* (beside *ȝender*), corr. to OS. *gendra* (adj.), WFris. *ginder* (adj.), on this side, MDu. *ghinder*, *gunder* (Du. *ginder*), Goth. *jaindre*. **yon**SIDE jɔ·nsaid (on) *the* further side (of) XVI (Coverdale); also adv. XVII; cf. LG. *gunsiet*, G. *jenseits*.

yore jɔəɹ (arch.) †a long time ago, †formerly, †for a long time past; *of y.*, formerly, of old XIV. OE. *ġeāra*, *ġeāre*, *ġeāro*, advb. formations of obscure origin, perh. f. *ġe-* Y-+*ār* ERE, on the model of *ġefyrn*, f. *ġe-* Y-+*fyrn* long ago.

yorker jɔ̄·ɹkəɹ (in cricket) ball that pitches inside the crease. XIX. prob. f. *York*, capital of Yorkshire, as being introduced by Yorkshire players; see -ER[1].

Yorkshire jɔ̄·ɹkʃəɹ name of the largest of the Eng. counties often used with reference to the alleged boorishness, cunning, or trickery of Y. people XVII; *Y. pudding*, batter pudding baked under meat XVIII.

you jū, ju, jə orig. accusative and dative pl. of the 2nd pers. pron. (see THOU); began to be used XV for nom. YE and somewhat earlier (XIV) as a substitute for *thee* and *thou* in respectful address to a superior; also from late XVI as an indef. pron., 'one', 'anyone'. OE. *īow*, *ēow* (also *ēowic*, Nhb. *iuih*) = OFris. *ju*, OS. *iu* (Du. *u*), OHG. (MHG.) dat. *iu*, *eu*, accus. *īuwih*, *iuch* (G. *euch*) :- WGerm. **iwwiz*, paralleled by **izwiz* in ON. *yðr*, Goth. *izwis*. The primary stem **jū̆* is repr. by Skr. *yūyám*, Gr. *úmme* (:- *(j)usme*), Lith. *jū̃s* you, *jùdu* you two (cf. OE. *ġit*). Fully str. OE. *ēow* would be repr. by **jau*; actual jū arose from re-stressing an unstressed var. (cf. I). ¶ The obl. case *you*, together with its adj. YOUR and corr. absolute YOURS, have displaced in gen. use nom. pl. YE and the orig. sgs. THOU, THEE, THY, THINE.

young jʌŋ that has lived a short time (also transf.). OE. *ġ(e)ong*, *ġung*, later *iung* = OFris., OS. *jung*, OHG. *junc* (Du. *jong*, G. *jung*), ON. *ungr*, Goth. *juggs* :- CGerm. **juŋgaz*, contr. of **juwuŋgaz* :- IE. **juwŋkós*, repr. by Skr. *juvaçás* youthful, L. *juvencus* young bull, W. *ieuanc*, OIr. *ōac*, *ōc* young, extension of **juwen-*, **jū̆n-*, repr. directly by Skr. *yúvan-*, L. *juvenis* young, compar. *jūnior* JUNIOR, Lith *jáunas*, OSl. *junŭ*, and (with abstr. suffix) L. *juventa*, *juventus*, OIr. *ōitiu* YOUTH. Hence **you·ng**LING[1] young person OE. *ġeongling* = OFris. *jongeling*, OS. *jungling*, OHG. *jungaling*, ON. *ynglingr*. **you·ng**STER young person. XVI (Greene, Nashe).

your juəɹ, jūɹ, jəɹ of or belonging to you. (i) OE. *ēower*, usu. in partitive sense, g. of *ġē* YE, corr. to OFris. *iuwer*, OS. *iuwar*, OHG. *iuwēr* (G. *euer*); cf. ON. *yðr*, Goth. *izwara*; (ii) OE. *ēower* m. and n., *ēowru* fem., poss. adj. corr. to OHG. *iuwar* (G. *euer*); cf. ON. *yð(v)arr*, Goth. *izwar*. Hence **yours** juəɹz poss. pron. (repl. †*your*) with *-s* as in HERS, OURS, THEIRS. XIII (Cursor M., Havelok). **your**SE·LF XIV, *-se·lves* XVI.

yourt juəɹt semi-subterranean dwelling of certain natives of Asia. XVIII. – Russ. *jurta*, through F. *yourte* or G. *jurte*.

youth jūþ fact or state of being young; young people OE.; young person XIII. OE. *ġeoguþ*, (late) *iuguþ* = OFris. *jogethe*, OS. *juguð* (Du. *jeugd*), OHG. *jugund* (G. *jugend*) :- WGerm. **jugunþ-*, alt. of **juwunþ-* (cf. L. *juventa*, *-tus*, Goth. *junda*), f. **guwuŋ-* YOUNG; see -TH[1]. Hence **you·th**FUL[1]. XVI; **you·th**HOOD OE. – XIII; re-formed XVII.

yowl jaul (dial.) cry loudly with pain; caterwaul, howl. XIII. Echoic; cf. dial. *yawl*, ME. *ȝaule* YAWL[1], and dial. *gawl* (ON. *gaula*), G. *johlen*.

yo-yo jou·jou toy resembling the bandalore. XX. Introduced from Canada, of unkn. origin.

yperite ai·pərait mustard gas. XX. – F. f. *Ypres*, a town of Belgium. See -ITE.

yttrium i·triəm (chem.) rare metal of the cerium group (symbol Y). XIX. – modL., f. *yttria* (1797), f. name of *Ytterby*, Sweden, whence also **ytterbium** itɔ̄·ɹbiəm (min.) element occurring in gadolinite; **y·tterb**ITE, syn. of *gadolinite*.

yucca jʌ·kə, **yuca** jū·kə in Western and Central America, cassava XVI (Eden), plant of N. Amer. genus Yucca XVII (Evelyn). Of Carib origin.

Yugoslav see JUGOSLAV.

Yule jūl Christmas. OE. *ġēol*, earlier *ġeo(h)ol*, *ġeh(h)ol*, also *ġēola* Christmas Day, (pl.) Christmastide (and in phr. *se ǣrra ġēola* December, *se æfterra ġēola* January, i.e. the former, the latter 'Yule', attrib. in OE. *ǣresta ġeohheldæġ*, 'first Yuleday', Christmas Day), corr. to ON. *jól* pl. heathen feast lasting twelve days, (later) Christmas; rel. to OE. (Anglian) *ġiuli* December and January (Bede) = ON. *ýlir* month beginning on the second day of the week falling within November 10–17, Goth. *jiuleis* in *fruma jiuleis* November; ult. origin unkn.

ywis see IWIS.

Z

zabra zā·brə small coastal vessel in the Bay of Biscay. XVI. – Sp. *zabra.*

zaffre zæ·fəɹ impure oxide of cobalt. XVII. – It. *zaffera* (Neri) or its source (O)F. *safre* – Arab. *sofr.*

zag zæg second el. of ZIGZAG used to denote a direction at an angle to that expressed by *zig.* XVIII (*zig here, zag there,* Burns).

zamorin zæ·mərin title of the Hindu sovereign of Calicut. XVI. – Pg. *samorin, çamorin* – Malayalam *sāmūri.*

zany zei·ni comic performer attending on a clown, etc. and imitating him XVI (Sh.); †attendant, hanger-on XVII (Jonson); †mimic, buffoon XVII; simpleton, idiot XVIII (J.). – F. *zani,* or its source It. *zani, zanni* servant acting as clown in the commedia dell' arte, orig. Venetian and Lombardic form of *Gianni = Giovanni* John (cf. *Zanipolo* title of the Church of St. John and St. Paul in Venice) used as an appellation for a porter, etc. from the mountain country of Bergamo who had taken service in a seaside town.

zaptieh zæ·ptiei Turkish policeman. XIX. – Turk. *ḍabtiyeh,* f. Arab. *ḍabt* administration, regulation.

Zarathustrian see ZOROASTRIAN.

zariba zərī·bə fenced camp in the Sudan, etc. XIX. – Arab. *zarībah* enclosure for cattle, f. *zarb* sheepfold.

zayat zā·jət public hall for worship, shelter, etc. XIX. Burmese.

zeal zīl (in biblical language) fervour, 'jealousy' XIV (Wycl. Bible); †ardent love, fervent longing XV; intense ardour in a pursuit XVI. Late ME. *zele* – late L. *zēlus* (whence OF. *zel,* modF. *zèle,* Sp. *celo,* It. *zelo*) – Gr. *zêlos.* So **zealot** ze·lət member of an ancient Jewish sect XVI; zealous person XVII. – late L. *zēlōtēs* – Gr. *zēlōtḗs* (fr. Aram. *qamania* f. Heb. *qana* be jealous), f. *zēloûn* be zealous, f. *zêlos.* **zeal**ous ze·ləs XVI (Tindale, Coverdale). – medL. *zēlōsus*; cf. JEALOUS.

zebra ze·brə, zī·brə S. African equine quadruped, Equus or Hippotigris zebra. XVI. – It. or Pg. *zebra,* of Congolese origin. Other forms have been used reflecting F. *zèbre* or Sp. *cebra.*

zebu zī·bju humped species of ox. XVIII (Goldsmith). – F. *zébu* (Buffon, who states that it was shown under this name at a fair in Paris in 1752); of unkn. origin.

zecchin ze·kin gold coin, CHEQUEEN, SEQUIN. XVIII. – It. *zecchino,* f. *zecca* the mint at Venice = Sp. *seca* – Arab. *sekkah* coin.

zed zed name of the letter Z, z. XV. – (O)F. *zède* (= Sp., It. *zeta*) – late L. *zēta* – Gr. *zêta*; vars. are dial. *zad* (XVII), occas. †*zard* (XVII), IZZARD (XVIII), ZEE.

zedoary ze·dəəri (root of) species of Curcuma. XV. – medL. *zedoārium* – Arab. *zedwār,* which is repr. in many other Eur. langs.

zee zī name (now spec. U.S.) of the letter z. XVII.

Zeitgeist tsai·tgaist spirit of the age. XIX. G., f. *zeit* time + *geist* spirit; see TIDE, GHOST.

zelotic zīlɔ·tik (earlier *zealotic*) pert. to a ZEALOT. XVII. – Gr. *zēlōtikós,* f. *zēlōtḗs*; see -IC.

zeme, zemi zī·mi idol, or spirit represented thereby, worshipped by W. Indian natives. XVII (Purchas). Carib *cemi.*

zemindar zĕmī·ndāɹ collector of revenue from land held by a number of cultivators. XVII. Early forms *gem-, jem-, sam-*; Hind. – Pers. *zamīndār,* f. *zamī(n)* earth + *dār* holder.

zemstvo ze·mstvou provincial council in Russia. XIX. Russ., f. *zemlyá* land, rel. to Gr. *khamaí* on the ground, L. *humus* earth (see HUMUS).

zenana zīnā·nə E. Indian harem. XVIII. – Hind. (– Pers.) *zenāna,* f. *zan* woman, rel. to Gr. *gunḗ* woman (see QUEAN).

Zend zend language of the Zend-Avesta, Avestic. XVIII. – F. *zend* (used as the name of the language by Anquetil du Perron, 1771), abstracted from *Avesta-va-Zend,* i.e. Avesta with interpretation, in Pers. *zand(a) vastā, zandastā,* whence **Zend-Avesta** zendəve·stə, in which *Zend* was erron. taken for an attrib. el. denoting the language of the books.

zenith ze·niþ, zī·niþ point of the sky directly overhead (Trevisa), †point of the horizon at which a heavenly body rises (Ch.); highest point or state XVII (Sh.). Late ME. *cenyth, senith, cinit* – OF. *cenit* (mod. *zénith*) or medL. *cenit* (cf. Sp. *cenit,* It. *zenit,* etc.), obscurely – Arab. *samt* in *samt arrās* 'path over the head' (*samt* way, *al* the, AL-, *rās* head); cf. AZIMUTH.

zeolite zī·əlait (min.) generic name of a group of minerals consisting of hydrous silicates, characterized by swelling up and fusing under the blowpipe. XVIII. – Sw., G., etc. *zeolit,* f. Gr. *zeîn* boil + *líthos* -LITE.

zephyr ze·fəɹ west wind XVI (earlier in L. form); mild gentle wind XVII (Sh.); light article of clothing XVIII. – F. *zéphyr* (Marot) or L. *zephyrus* (whence also Sp. *cefiro,* It. *zefiro,* etc.) – Gr. *zéphuros.*

zeppelin ze·pəlin rigid dirigible airship invented by the German Count Ferdinand von *Zeppelin.* 1900.

zero ziə·rou (pl. *zeroes* -ouz) cipher, o XVII; point marked o on a scale, temperature denoted by this XVIII; nought, nothing XIX. – F. *zéro* or its source It. *zero* – OSp. *zero* (mod. *cero*) – Arab. *çifr* CIPHER.

zerumbet zīrʌ·mbet E. India plant or its root (Curcuma). XVI. – Pg. – Hind., Pers. *zerunbād.*

zest zest †orange or lemon peel used for flavouring XVII; something that imparts a relish; keen relish, gusto XVIII. – F. *zeste*, †*zest*, *zec* 'the thicke skin .. whereby the kernell of a wall-nut is diuided' (Cotgr.), orange or lemon peel, of unkn. origin.

zeta zī·tə sixth letter of the Gr. alphabet, zed (*Z*, *ζ*). Gr. *zêta*, alt. of Heb. *zayin*, after *ἦτα*, *θῆτα*. Hence **ze·ta**ISM; cf. *etacism*, *lambdacism*, *rhotacism*.

zetetic zīte·tik pert. to, adherent of, the ancient Greek sceptic school of philosophy; investigator, investigation. XVII. – Gr. *zētētikós*, f. *zēteîn* seek; see -IC.

zeugma zjū·gmə (rhet.) figure by which a single word or phrase is made improperly to apply to two or more words or phrases XIX, earlier in wider use XVI. – L. – Gr. *zeûgma* yoking, f. *zeugnúnai* vb. rel. to *zugón* YOKE.

zeuxite zjū·ksait (min.) variety of tourmaline. XIX. f. Gr. *zeûxis* yoking, joining, f. **zeug-* **zug-* YOKE.

zho ʒou hybrid between a yak and a common cow. XIX. – Tibetan *mdso*.

zibeline zi·bəlin, -lain sable, Mustela zibellina. XVI. – F. *zibeline* (also †*zabelline*, †*zebeline*, OF. *sebelin*), with It. *zibellino*, Sp. *s-*, *cebellina*, Pg. *zebelina*), repr. Rom. deriv. of Sl. original of SABLE[1].

zibet zi·bet var. of CIVET – medL. *zibethum*, whence It. *zibetto*, etc.

zig see ZAG.

zigzag zi·gzæg (object) having the form ʌʌʌʌ. XVIII. Earliest forms *ziczac*; *zig-zac* – F. *zigzag*, †*ziczac* – G. *zickzack*, of symbolic formation suggesting alternation of direction, applied first to fortifications. Hence **zi·gzag** vb. (Burns), **zi·gzagged** (Goldsmith), **zi·gzagg**ERY (Sterne).

zinc zink hard bluish-white metal. XVII. – G. *zink*, †*zinken* (of unkn. origin), whence also F. *zinc*, †*zin*, Sp. *zinc*, It. *zinco*, etc., modL. *zincum*. Comb. form **zi·nco-**, **zinco-·**, as in **zinco**·GRAPHY. ¶ Conjecturally supposed to be so called from its setting in the furnace in the form of spikes (*Zinken*).

zingaro zi·ŋgărou gipsy. XVI. It., alt. of †*zingano* = Gr. *Athígganoi*, an oriental people.

zinnia zi·niə plant of genus so named of Amer. plants. XVIII. modL. (Linnæus 1763), f. name of J. G. *Zinn*, German botanist; see -IA[1].

Zion, Sion zai·ən one of the hills of Jerusalem on which the city of David was built; (hence) house of God, the Christian Church, place of worship (cf. BETHEL, EBENEZER). – eccl.L. *Siōn*, Gr. *Seṓn*, *Seiṓn*, tr. Heb. *tsīyōn*.

zip zip (slight sharp sound accompanying) a movement or contact. XIX. imit.

zircon zɜ̄·ɹkɔn (min.) native silicate of the metallic element zirconium. XVIII. – G. *zirkon*.

zither zi·þəɹ XIX. – G. *zither* (OHG. *cithara*, *zitera*) CITHER. Also **zi·thern** XIX; after CITHERN.

zizyphus zi·zifəs (plant of) genus so named of the buckthorn family. XV (*zizifus*). – L. – Gr. *zízuphon*. So †**zi·zypha** fruit of this. XVI. modL. pl.

zodiac zou·diæk belt of the celestial sphere within which the apparent motions of celestial bodies take place, divided into 12 'signs' named after the 12 constellations. XIV (Gower). – (O)F. *zodiaque* (= Pr. *zodiac*, Sp., It. *zodiaco*) – L. *zōdiacus* (Cicero) – Gr. *zōidiakós* (sc. *kúklos* the circle of the figures or signs, ὁ τῶν ζῳδίων κύκλος), f. *zṓidion* sculptured figure (of an animal), sign of the zodiac, dim. of *zôion* animal, f. *zōós* living (:– **gwjō*; cf. QUICK); see -AC. So **zodiac**AL -ai·əkəl. XVI. – F. *zodiacal*.

zoea zouī·ə larva of some crustaceans. XIX. – modL., extension with -A[1] of earlier form †*zoe* – Gr. *zōḗ* life, rel. to *zōós* living (cf. ZODIAC, ZOO-).

zoetrope zou·itroup scientific toy converting a series of pictures of successive attitudes into the semblance of continuous motion. XIX. irreg. f. Gr. *zōḗ* life, rel. to *zōós* living (cf. prec.) + -*tropos* turning (cf. TROPE, TROPIC).

zoic zou·ik showing traces of life, containing organic remains. XIX (Dana). – Gr. *zōïkós*, f. *zôion* animal; see -IC. ¶ Taken as if f. Gr. *zōḗ* life.

Zoilus zou·iləs (also anglicized *Zoil*(*e*) XVI–XVII, after F. *Zoïle*) cynic philosopher, of Amphipolis (IV B.C.), notorious for bitter attacks on Homer, Isocrates, and Plato. Hence **Zo·il**ISM XVII, **Zo·il**IST XVI.

zollverein tsɔ·lfərain union of states of the German Empire for the maintenance of uniform custom dues XIX. G., f. *zoll* tax, TOLL[1] + *verein* union, f. (*sich*) *vereinen* unite, f. *ver-* FOR-[1] + *ein* ONE.

zone zoun each of the 5 belts into which the earth's surface is divided XV; climatic region; girdle, ring XVI; stripe of colour, etc. XVIII. – (O)F. *zone* or L. *zōna* girdle (whence also Sp., It. *zona*) – Gr. *zṓnē* :– **jōsmnā*, f. base repr. also by Lith. *júostas*, Skr. *yāstas* girt.

zoo zū collection of live animals made and maintained for public exhibition. XIX (*the Clifton Zoo*, Macaulay); first three letters of *Zoological Gardens* (Regent's Park, London) taken as one syll. (cf. next).

zoo- zou·o(u), zouə·, before a vowel prop. **zo-**, repr. Gr. *zōio-*, comb. form of *zôion* animal (see ZODIAC).

zooid zou·oid animal-like creature. XIX (Huxley). f. Gr. *zôion*.

zoology zouɔ·lədʒi science which treats of animals. XVII. First applied to that part of medical science which treats of remedies obtainable from animals; the first sense recorded in Eng. dicts. (from Bailey, 1726) is 'a treatise concerning living creatures'. – modL. *zōologia* (Sperling), modGr. *zōiología* (Schröder), f. Gr. *zôion* animal; see ZODIAC, -LOGY. Hence **zoolo·gICAL**. XIX; sb. *the Z.* = ZOO. **zoo·logER**[1], **-logIST**. XVII (both used by Boyle).

zoom zūm make a continuous low-pitched hum; (of aircraft) rise abruptly from level flight. XIX. imit.

zoophyte zou·ŏfait †plant (such as the sensitive plant having some qualities of animals); gen. term (now disused) for organisms regarded as intermediate between animals and plants. XVII. – F. *zoophyte* (Rabelais, 1546) – modL. *zōophyton* – Gr. *zōióphuton* (Aristotle), f. *zôion* animal (see ZOO-)+*phúesthai* grow (cf. BE).

zorilla zŏri·lə animal of an African genus allied to the skunks. XVIII (Goldsmith). – Sp. *zorrilla*, *-illo*, dim. of *zorro* fox; cf. F. *zorille*.

Zoroastrian zɔro(u)æ·striən, **Zarathustrian** zærəþu·striən pert. to (adherent of the religious system of) *Zoroaster*, *Zarathustra* (Zend *Zarathustra*, Pers. *Zardusht*) contained in the Zendavesta; see -IAN.

zouave zwāv one of a body of light infantry in the French army. XIX. – F. *zouave* – *Zouaoua* name of an Algerian Kabyle tribe, from which the force was first recruited.

zounds zau·ndz (arch.) euph. abbrev. of (*by*) *God's wounds*. XVI (*zownes*, *zoones*); for the pronunc. see WOUND. ¶ 'Zoons is only us'd by the disbanded Officers and Bullies; but Zauns is the Beaux pronunciation', Farquhar 1699.

zucchetto tsuke·tou ecclesiastic's skull-cap. XIX. Incorrect but usual form for It. *zucchetta* small gourd, cap, dim. of *zucca* gourd, head (cf. late L. *cucutia*, gourd, *cucutium* kind of hood).

zwieback tsvī·bæk rusk. XIX. G. tr. of It. *biscotto* 'twice-baked' (see BISCUIT); cf. TWO, BAKE.

Zwinglian zwi·ŋgliən, tsvi·ŋgliæn pert. to (a follower of) Ulrich *Zwingli* (1484–1531), Swiss religious reformer. XVI (More). See -IAN.

zygo- zai·gou, zi·gou repr. comb. form of Gr. *zugón* YOKE.

zygoma zaigou·mə (anat.) bony arch on each side of the skull. XVII. – modL. – Gr. *zúgōma*, f. *zugón* YOKE.

zymo- zai·mou (before a vowel **zym-**) comb. form of Gr. *zū́mē* leaven, in techn. terms (gen.) fermentation XIX. So **zymosis** zaimou·sis. XIX. – modL. – Gr. *zū́mōsis*. **zymotIC** zaimɔ·tik. XIX. – Gr. *zūmōtikós* causing fermentation, f. *zūmoûn* leaven, (pass.) ferment, f. *zū́mē*, cogn. with L. *jūs* (see JUICE).

zymurgy zai·mɔ̄ɹdʒi act of fermentation. XIX. f. Gr. *zū́mē* (see prec.)+*-urgy* as in *metallurgy*. Cf. Gr. *zūmourgós* maker of leaven.

ADDENDA

common weal, commonweal kɔ·mənwī·l the body politic, state, community XIV; the general good, public welfare XV. orig. and properly two words, rendering L. *rēs commūnis*, F. *le bien commun*; cf. *weal public* (XV) repr. L. *bonum publicum*, F. *le bien publique*. See WEAL[1]. ¶ In the sense of 'state' in XVI more esp. Sc., and now archaic or rhetorical.

commonwealth kɔ·mənwelþ, earlier, and still occas., kɔ·mənwe·lþ †public welfare XV; the body politic, state, community; in spec. fig. and transf. uses, e.g. *c. of Christendom, of learning, of nations* XVI; republic, or democratic state; spec. (hist.) the republican government established under Oliver Cromwell XVII. See WEALTH. ¶ Both *common weal* and *common wealth* were at first used indiscriminately in the senses 'public welfare' and 'body politic', but in XVI *commonwealth* became the ordinary Eng. term for the latter sense, whence the later sense 'republic' was developed.

feldspar fe·ldspāɹ, **felspar** fe·lspāɹ any of a group of crystalline white or flesh-red minerals. XVIII. alt. of G. *feldspat(h)*, f. *feld* field+*spat(h)* spar. Cf. SPAR[3]. Hence **feldspa·thic** adj. ¶ The common sp. *fels* is due to false deriv. f. G. *fels* rock. The current G. form is *feldspat*.

fen fen low marshy land. OE. *fen(n)* = OFris. *fen(n)e*, OS. *fen(n)i* (Du. *veen*), OHG. *fenna, fenni* (G. *fenn*), ON. *fen*, Goth. *fani* :–CGmc. **fanjam, -jaz, -jō* :– IE. **pano-*, rel. to Skr. *pañka* mud, OPruss. *pannean* bog, fen, marsh.

fetid, fœtid fe·tid, fī·- stinking XVI. – L. *fētidus, foet-*, f. *fētēre, foet-* stink. Hence **fe·tid**NESS XVIII.

wage weidʒ †a pledge or security; †a challenge or engagement to fight; payment for service rendered; fig., reward, recompense XIV; †payment for use or possession of property XV. ME. *wage* – AF., ONF. *wage* (AL. *vagium, wagium*) = OF. *guage*, (also mod.) *gage* – Gmc. **waðjam*; see GAGE[1], and for the Gmc. collateral forms, WED. So **wage** vb. A. †deposit or give as a pledge or security, esp. for the fulfilment of (something promised) XIV; †agree to forfeit in some contingency XV; †(exc. hist.) pledge oneself to judicial combat XVI; B. †engage or employ for wages, hire; †pay wages to XIV; C. carry on (war, a contest) XV. ME. *wage(n)* – AF., ONF. *wagier, waigier* = OF. *guagier* (mod. *gager*), f. *gage* (see the sb.).